РУССКО ▸ АНГЛИЙСКИЙ
АНГЛО ▸ РУССКИЙ
СЛОВАРЬ

RUSSIAN ▸ ENGLISH
ENGLISH ▸ RUSSIAN
DICTIONARY

COLLINS

РУССКО ▸ АНГЛИЙСКИЙ
АНГЛО ▸ РУССКИЙ
СЛОВАРЬ

HarperCollins*Publishers*

COLLINS

RUSSIAN ▶ ENGLISH
ENGLISH ▶ RUSSIAN
DICTIONARY

HarperCollins*Publishers*

First published in this edition 1994

© Copyright 1994 HarperCollins Publishers

latest reprint 1996

HarperCollins Publishers
P.O. Box, Glasgow G4 ONB, Great Britain

ISBN 0 00 433388-8

10 East 53rd Street, New York, NY 10022

ISBN 0–06–276528–0 (paperback)

First HarperCollins edition published 1995

Library of Congress Cataloging-in-Publication Data

Ozieva, Albina.
    Collins Russian English English Russian dictionary / Albina
Ozieva, Olga Stott, Marina Hepburn.
      p. cm.
    ISBN 0-06-276528-0 :
     1. Russian language-Dictionaries-English. 2. English language-
Dictionaries-Russian. I. Stott, Olga. II. Hepburn, Marina.
III. Title.
PG2640.098 1994
491.73'21–dc20   94-13824
                                        CIP

96 97 98 99 00 CIBM 10 9 8 7 6 5 4 3 2

Typeset by / Набор текста произведён
Tradespools Ltd, Somerset, Great Britain

Printed and bound in Great Britain by
Caledonian International Book Manufacturing Ltd, Glasgow, G64

АВТОРСКИЙ КОЛЛЕКТИВ/MAIN CONTRIBUTORS

Albina Ozieva • Olga Stott • Marina Hepburn • Katya Butler
Maria Marquise • Elena Cook • Irina Moore • Dr Lara Ryazanova
Dr Natasha Vasilyeva McGrath • Tanya Herries • Fatima Eloyeva
Daniel Brennan • Rose France • Rebecca Brown
Michael Cowan-Young • Sheila Bentley
Professor D. Ward

РЕДАКТОР СЕРИИ/SERIES EDITOR

Lorna Sinclair Knight

ЗАВЕДУЮЩИЙ РЕДАКЦИЕЙ/EDITORIAL MANAGEMENT

Jeremy Butterfield

ВЕДУЩИЙ РЕДАКТОР/EDITOR

Maree Airlie

РЕДАКТОРЫ/EDITORIAL STAFF

Judith Turtle • Andrew Knox • Isobel Gordon
Sandra Harper • Elspeth Anderson
Mary Steele • Merle Read

КОМПЬЮТЕРНОЕ ОБСЛУЖИВАНИЕ/COMPUTING

André Gautier • Colette Clenaghan

Содержание

Contents

ТОВАРНЫЕ ЗНАКИ ®

TRADEMARKS ®

Мы рады, что Вы выбрали словарь, подготовленный издательством Коллинз. Мы надеемся, что он окажется Вам полезен, где бы Вы им ни пользовались – дома, на отдыхе или на работе.

В настоящем введении излагаются некоторые советы по эффективному использованию данного издания: его обширного словника и сведений, содержащихся в каждой словарной статье. Правильное и максимально полное использование приводимой информации поможет Вам не только читать и понимать современный английский, но также овладеть устной речью.

В начале словаря Коллинз помещён список условных сокращений, используемых в корпусе словаря. Далее следуют произносительные таблицы для русского и английского языков. Между двумя частями словаря помещён раздел, посвящённый русской грамматике. В конце англо-русской части даётся список английских неправильных глаголов а также таблицы русских неправильных форм. Некоторые словарные статьи отсылают читателя к данным таблицам для получения нужной грамматической информации. Числительные и фразы, обозначающие даты и время находятся в самом конце словаря.

We are delighted that you have decided to use the Collins Russian Dictionary and hope that you will enjoy it and benefit from using it at home, on holiday or at work.

This introduction gives you a few tips on how to get the most out of your dictionary – not simply from its comprehensive wordlist but also from the information provided in each entry. This will help you to read and understand modern Russian, as well as communicate and express yourself in the language.

The Collins Russian Dictionary begins by listing the abbreviations used in the text, followed by a guide to Russian and English pronunciation. Between the two sides of the dictionary you will find a section on Russian grammar, and at the end of the English-Russian text are listed English irregular verbs, plus the tables of irregular Russian forms to which entries in the text are referred. Numbers and expressions using time and date are situated at the very back of the dictionary.

О Пользовании Словарём

Заглавные слова

Заглавными называются слова, начинающие словарную статью. Они напечатаны жирным шрифтом и расположены в строго алфавитном порядке. При многих из них приводятся словосочетания и сращения, частью которых выступает данное заглавное слово. Они напечатаны жирным шрифтом меньшего размера. Два заглавных слова в верхней части страницы указывают на первое и последнее слово, отрезка словника, представленного на данной странице.

Перевод

Перевод заглавных слов напечатан обычным шрифтом. Как правило, варианты перевода рассматриваемого слова разделяются запятой, если они синонимичны и взаимозаменяемы в значении, обозначенном пометой. Различные значения многозначного слова разделены точкой с запятой. Более подробно о пометах см. ниже.

Переводы для различных значений многозначных производных слов часто разделены только точкой с запятой и перед ними даётся одна помета типа (*см прил*). Это означает, что последовательное разделение значений рассматриваемого слова и их переводов даётся при слове, от которого данное производное слово образовано. Например, **annul/annulment**.

В некоторых случаях точный эквивалент перевода невозможен, например, когда английское слово обозначает явление или учреждение, не существующие в России, или же существующие в несколько иной форме. Если возможен приблизительный эквивалент перевода, то он обозначается знаком (≈). Если же культурный эквивалент в языке перевода отсутствует, то вместо него приводится толкование.

Пометы

Пометы, служат для разделения значений многозначного слова. Они приводятся на языке-источнике. Их цель – помочь читателю выбрать перевод, наиболее подходящий в том или ином контексте. Пометы являют собой либо синоним, либо слово, указывающее на характерную для данного значения слова лексическую сочетаемость. Пометы также обозначают переносные значения. Пометы напечатаны курсивом и заключены в круглые скобки.

При многих заглавных словах даны необходимые стилистические пометы, обозначающие разговорное или просторечное использование этих слов. Эмоционально – стилистическая окраска перевода обычно совпадает с окраской переводимого слова. Нецензурные или грубые слова помечены восклицательным знаком (!).

Произношение

В англо-русской части словаря все заглавные слова снабжены фонетической транскрипцией, которая заключена в квадратные скобки. В тех случаях, где в роли заглавного слова выступает словосочетание, состоящее из двух или более слов, которые, в свою очередь, приводятся в словаре по отдельности, их произношение указывается только там, где они даны как одиночные слова в алфавитном порядке. Список фонетических знаков приводится на страницах xxix–xxx.

В русско-английской части словаря все русские слова снабжены знаком ударения, поскольку их произношение большей частью достаточно ясно, если указано место ударения. В тех словах, где возможно двоякое ударение, обычно указывается только одно, наиболее часто употребляющееся. Омографы (слова, имеющие одинаковое написание, но различное ударение и значение) приводятся как самостоятельные заглавные слова в том порядке, в котором в них проставлено ударение, например, первым даётся слово **за́мок**, затем - **замо́к**. Более подробную информацию о принципах русского произношения читатель может найти в разделе на страницах xxiv-xxviii.

Служебные слова

В словаре уделяется особое внимание тем русским и английским словам, которые обладают сложной грамматической или семантической структурой. Таковыми являются в первую очередь служебные слова, вспомогательные глаголы, местоимения, частицы итп. Они обозначены пометой KEYWORD.

Английские фразовые глаголы

Фразовыми глаголами называются устойчивые сочетания глагола с элементами **in**, **out**, **up** итп, типа **blow up**, **cut down** итп. Они приводятся в словарной статье базовых глаголов, таких как **blow**, **cut**, и сгруппированы в алфавитном порядке.

Аббревиатуры и собственные имена существительные

Аббревиатуры, сложносокращённые слова и собственные имена существительные включены в общий словник словаря в алфавитном порядке.

Употребление "Вы/ты" при переводе "You"

При переводе на русский язык английских фраз, содержащих местоимения "you/your", даются две формы местоимения:одна в ед. числе, а другая во мн. числе --» "ты/твой", "Вы/Ваш". Если в состав фразы входит глагол в форме повелительного наклонения, то он также переводится двумя формами: 2-го лица ед. числа / 2-го лица мн. числа. В тех случаях, где эмоционально-стилистическая окраска фразы является явно неформальной, для местоимения даётся только форма "ты/твой", а для глаголов в повелительном наклонении форма 2-го лица ед. числа, например, "get lost!" переводится как "отстань!"

Употребление or/или, косой черты и скобок

В англо-русской части словаря между взаимозаменяемыми вариантами перевода, а также частями фразы на языке-источнике употребляется союз "*or*". В русско-английской части словаря ему соответствует союз "*или*". Косая черта (/) означает, что приведённые варианты перевода или фразы в языке-источнике не являются взаимозаменяемыми. В круглые скобки заключаются необязательные но возможные в данном выражении слова, как в переводе, так и во фразе на языке-источнике.

Употребление тильды (~)

Тильда в англо-русской части заменяет заглавное слово в словосочетаниях. Например, если в качестве заглавного выступает слово "**order**", то фраза "**out of order**" будет представлена следующим образом: **out of** ~. В русско-английской части тильда заменяет: 1) целое заглавное слово: например, в статье "**до́брый**" фраза "**до́брый день**" показана следующим образом: ~ **день**. 2) тильда заменяет часть заглавного слова, предшествующую вертикальной черте: например, в статье "**до́б|рый**" фраза "**до́брое у́тро**" показана следующим образом: ~**ое у́тро**.

Употребление звёздочки (*)

При переводе звёздочкой (*) отмечаются те существительные, в склонении которых наблюдаются те или иные отклонения от нормы. В русско-английской части даётся дополнительная информация относительно отклонений от правил склонения и спряжения.

USING THE DICTIONARY

Headwords

The **headword** is the word you look up in a dictionary. Headwords are listed in alphabetical order, and printed in bold type so that they stand out on the page. Each headword may contain other references such as **phrases** and **compounds**, which are in smaller bold type. The two headwords appearing at the top of each page indicate the first and last word dealt with on the page in question.

Translations

The translations of the headword are printed in ordinary roman type. As a rule, translations separated by a comma can be regarded as interchangeable for the meaning indicated. Translations separated by a semi-colon are not interchangeable, though the different meaning splits are generally marked by an indicator (see below). Where a semi-colon separates translations and the indicator refers to a different part of speech eg. (*see adj*), the translations mirror the splits shown at the other part of speech eg. **annul/annulment**.

It is not always possible to give an exact translation equivalent, for instance when the English word denotes an object or institution which does not exist or exists in a different form in Russia or in the Republics. If an approximate equivalent exists, it is given preceded by ≈. If there is no cultural equivalent, a *gloss* is given to explain the source item.

Indicators

An *indicator* is a piece of information in the source language about the usage of the headword to guide you to the most appropriate translation. Indicators give some idea of the contexts in which the headword might appear, or they provide synonyms for the headword. They are printed in italic type and shown in brackets.

Colloquial and informal language in the dictionary is marked at the headword. You should assume that the translations will match the source language in register, and rude or offensive translations are also marked with (!).

Pronunciation

On the English-Russian side of the dictionary you will find the phonetic spelling of the word in square brackets after the headword. Where the entry is composed of two or more unhyphenated words, each of which is given elsewhere in this dictionary, you will find the pronunication of each word in its alphabetical position. A list of the symbols used is given on pages xxix-xxx.

For Russian-English, stress is given on all Russian words as a guide to pronunciation. Where stress can be placed over either of two vowels, the most common or correct stress position is shown for the purpose of this dictionary. Words which are spelt in the same way, but have different stress positions are treated as separate entries, the order following the order of the stress eg. **за́мок** comes before **замо́к**. The section on pages xxiv-xxviii explains Russian pronunciation in more detail.

Keywords

In this dictionary we have given special status to "key" Russian and English words. As these words can be grammatically complex and often have many different usages, they have been given special attention in the dictionary, and are labelled with KEYWORD.

Abbreviations and proper names

Abbreviations, acronyms and proper names have been included in the word list in alphabetical order.

"You" in phrases

In translations of English phrases containing "you/your" or the imperative, "Вы/Ваш" and the formal form is given, unless the phrase is very colloquial eg. "get lost!" where it would be more natural to give the familiar form of the imperative.

Use of or/или, oblique and brackets

The words "*or*" on the English-Russian side, and "*или*" on the Russian-English side are used between interchangeable parts of a translation or source phrase. The oblique (/) is used between non-interchangeable alternatives in the translation or source phrase. Round brackets are used to show optional parts of the translation or source phrase.

Use of the swung dash (~)

The swung dash (~) is used on the English-Russian side of the dictionary to stand for the headword in phrases eg. at "order" the phrase "**out of order**" is shown as "**out of ~**". On the Russian-English side of the dictionary the swung dash can either stand for the full headword eg. at "**добрый**" the phrase "**добрый день**" is shown as "**~ день**", or it can stand for the part of the word before the hairline eg. at "**добрый**" the phrase "**доброе утро**" appears as "**~ое утро**".

Use of the superior asterisk (*)

The asterisk (*) is used to mark translations which are in some way irregular in their declension. The Russian-English side of the dictionary contains further information on irregularities.

American variants

American spelling variants are generally shown at the British headword eg. **colour/color** and also as a separate entry if they are not alphabetically adjacent to the British form. Variant forms are generally shown as headwords in their own right eg. **trousers/pants**, unless the British and American forms are alphabetically adjacent, in which case the American form is only shown separately if phonetics are required eg. **jump leads/jumper cables**.

Russian reflexive verbs

Russian reflexive verbs eg. **мыться**, **краситься** are listed under the basic verb eg. **мыть, красить**.

STYLE AND LAYOUT OF THE DICTIONARY

RUSSIAN-ENGLISH

Inflectional and grammatical information

Inflectional information is shown in the dictionary in brackets immediately after the headword and before the part of speech eg. **стол (-á)** *м*.

Grammatical information is shown after the part of speech and refers to the whole entry eg. **завйд|овать (-ую**; *perf* **позавйдовать)** *несов неперех* (+*dat*).

Where grammatical information eg. *no perf* is given in the middle of the entry, it then governs all the following senses.

Use of hairline (|)

The hairline is used in headwords to show where the inflection adds on eg. **кнйг|а (-и)**. It is also used for swung dash relacement where the swung dash stands for the part of the word before the hairline in phrases.

Stress

Stress changes are shown where they occur, the last form given being indicative of the rest of the pattern eg. **игр|á (-ы**; *nom pl* **-ы)**. In this example the stress is on the last syllable for the singular declension, moves to the first syllable for the plural and remains there for the rest of the plural declension.

Tables

Some headwords which have particularly irregular inflections are declined in full in tables at the back of the dictionary. Shown in these tables are a small group of nouns, verbs, all cardinal and collective numerals, and personal, interrogative and negative pronouns.

Nouns

In order to help you determine the declension and stress pattern of nouns, we have shown the genitive singular for all singular nouns, and the genitive plural for all plural nouns. This is given as the first piece of information after the headword and is not labelled eg. **стол (-á)**.

Where the noun has further irregularities in declension such as irregular plural forms, partitive genitive, locative singular in "у/ю" or change in stress throughout the declension these are shown at the headword and labelled eg. **яблок|о (-а**; *nom pl* **-и)**.

Adjectives

As the declension of a large number of adjectives in the long form is governed by regular rules, we have not shown the long form endings for these adjectives.

Long form endings have been shown for adjectives which may cause problems in declension in the long form such as adjectives ending in **-ий**, where you might be unsure whether the adjective is "soft" or not, and adjectives ending in **-ин** and **-ов**.

Short form endings have been shown for all adjectives where they exist.

Numerals and pronouns

The genitive has been shown for all numerals and pronouns.

Verbs

Where to look:

The majority of verbs are dealt with in aspectual pairs, and we have chosen to show the translation of the verb at the base form of the pair.

Where the perfective is formed by adding a prefix to the imperfective, the imperfective is considered to be the base form and the translation is shown there. The corresponding perfective aspect can also be found in the dictionary in its alphabetical position, cross-referred to the imperfective aspect.

Where the aspect to be cross-referred is alphabetically adjacent to the aspect to which it will be referred, it is not shown separately unless there is some irregularity in its declension. With the pair **завинчивать/завинтить, завинчивать** is not shown separately.

Where the imperfective is formed by adding a suffix to the perfective, the perfective is considered to be the base form and the translation is shown there. The corresponding imperfective aspect can also be found in the dictionary in its alphabetical position, cross-referred to the perfective aspect.

Verbs which do not occur in aspectual pairs are dealt with at their individual headwords.

In phrases both aspects are shown if both work in the context.

To help you see how a verb conjugates, inflections are shown immediately after the verb headword for all verbs according to the following rules:

– for regular 1st conjugation verbs the 1st person singular only is shown eg. **работа|ть (-ю)**

– for 1st conjugation verbs which contain vowel/consonant mutation the 1st and 2nd person singular are shown eg. **жд|ать (-у, -ёшь)**
пи|са́ть (-шу́, -шешь)

– for regular 2nd conjugation verbs the 1st and 2nd person singular are shown eg. **говор|и́ть (-ю́, -и́шь)**

– for 2nd conjugation verbs which contain vowel/consonant mutation, insert "л", or where the stress changes throughout the declension the 1st and 2nd person singular are shown eg. **люб|и́ть (-лю́, -ишь)**

– for verbs where the verb form changes more than once throughout the conjugation, the 1st, 2nd person singular and 3rd person plural are shown. *umn* is inserted after the 2nd person singular to show that the pattern continues until the next form shown eg. **тол|о́чь (-ку́, -чёшь** *umn*, **-ку́т)**

– for verbs which are not used in the 1st person singular, the inflections are shown for their usual usage eg. **темне|ть** (*3sg* **-ет**) Where the restriction applies to one of the senses, the inflections are shown at the sense itself only if they are irregular.

The imperative mood is shown at the headword where it is irregularly formed.

The past tense is shown at the headword where it is irregularly formed or contains a change in stress.

Inflections given as separate entries

Irregular inflected forms are also shown at their alphabetical position and cross-referred to the base headword. In places an inflected form appears as a separate entry and is followed by *umn*, meaning that there are other inflected forms of the same headword which follow the same pattern eg. **отца́** *umn* means that the other inflections of **оте́ц** follow the same pattern by dropping a vowel in oblique cases.

Spelling rules

Russian has the following spelling rules which we have not taken as irregular when showing inflection information:

- after ж,ч,ш,щ,г,к and x, ы is replaced by и, я by a and ю by у.
- after ж,ч,ш,щ and ц, е replaces an unstressed o.
- the letter и is replaced by ы following a prefix ending in a consonant.

ENGLISH-RUSSIAN

Gender

The gender of Russian nouns given as translations is not shown for:

- masculine nouns which end in a hard consonant eg. труд, in -й eg. музе́й or in a hard or soft sibilant eg. нож, плащ
- feminine nouns which end in -a eg. страна́ or in -я eg. земля́
- neuter nouns which end in -o eg. окно́, in -e eg. мо́ре or in -ё eg. ружьё.

Nouns for which the gender is shown are:

- those ending in -ь which can be either masculine or feminine eg. дождь
- neuter nouns ending in -я
- masculine nouns ending in -a eg. па́па or -я eg. дя́дя

Nouns which have a common gender eg. сирота́ are labelled *m/f*.

Indeclinable nouns are labelled with gender followed by the abbreviation *ind* eg. кино́ *nt ind*.

Adjectives used as nouns are labelled with gender followed by the abbreviation *adj* eg. столо́вая *f adj*.

Where the feminine form of a masculine noun is also given as a translation, and the gender of the masculine noun is shown according to the guidelines given above, the gender of the feminine is shown as follows: учи́тель(ница) *m(f)*.

Plural noun translations are always labelled with the abbreviation *pl*, eg. кани́кулы *pl*, and the gender is shown if a singular form exists.

Noun translations are only marked with *sg* where a plural noun headword has a singular translation.

The label *no pl* is used for nouns which do not have a plural form and are only used in the singular eg. лу́ковица, unless the English is also not used in the plural.

Feminine forms

The following conventions are used in this dictionary to show feminine forms of masculine nouns.

- If the feminine ending adds on to the masculine form, the feminine ending is bracketed eg. учи́тель(ница).

- If the feminine ending substitutes part of the masculine form, the last common letter of the masculine and feminine form is shown before the feminine ending, preceded by a dash and enclosed in brackets eg. актёр(-три́са). Where an adjective is used as a noun and has a feminine form, the last common letter does not have to be given eg. безрабо́тный(- ая).

- If the feminine form is given in full, it is bracketed and separated from the masculine form by a character space eg. чех (чёшка).

Adjectives

Russian translations of adjectives are always given in the masculine, unless the adjective relates only to a feminine noun eg. бере́менная.

The masculine short form (or feminine if the adjective only applies to a feminine noun) is also given where it is appropriate.

Verbs

In translation of the headword, imperfective and perfective aspects are shown in full where they both apply eg. **to do** де́лать (сде́лать *perf*). If only one aspect is shown, it means that only one aspect works for this sense.

In infinitve phrases, if the two aspects apply they are shown and labelled eg. **to buy sth** покупа́ть (купи́ть *perf*) что-н.

Where the English phrase contains the construction "to do" standing for any verb, it has been replaced by +*infin*/+*impf infin*/+*perf infin* in the Russian translation, depending on which aspects of the Russian verb work in the given context.

Where the English phrase contains the past tense of a verb in the 1st person singular, the Russian translation gives only the masculine form eg. **I was glad** я был рад

Where both the present tense and the past tense of the verb "to be" are given in a phrase, eg. **he is/was** ..., it means that the Russian translation will govern the nominative case in either tense. If, however, only the present tense is shown, it can be assumed that the past tense of the Russian translation will govern the instrumental case.

Prepositions

Unless they are bracketed, prepositions and cases which follow verbs, adjectives etc are obligatory as part of the translation eg. **to inundate with** зава́ливать (завали́ть *perf*) +*instr*

Where they are separated by *or* they are interchangeable.

An oblique (/) is used to separate prepositions when the preposition depends on the following noun rather than on the preceding verb eg. идти в/на.

Условные Сокращения в Англо-Русской Части

сокращение	*abbr*	abbreviation
винительный падеж	*acc*	accusative
прилагательное	*adj*	adjective
администрация	*ADMIN*	administration
наречие	*adv*	adverb
сельское хозяйство	*AGR*	agriculture
анатомия	*ANAT*	anatomy
архитектура	*ARCHIT*	architecture
автомобильное дело	*AUT*	automobiles
вспомогательный глагол	*aux vb*	auxiliary verb
авиация	*AVIAT*	aviation
биология	*BIO*	biology
ботаника	*BOT*	botany
британский английский	*BRIT*	British English
химия	*CHEM*	chemistry
коммерция	*COMM*	commerce
компьютер	*COMPUT*	computing
союз	*conj*	conjunction
строительство	*CONSTR*	construction
сращение	*cpd*	compound
кулинария	*CULIN*	culinary
дательный падеж	*dat*	dative
склоняется	*decl*	declines
определённый артикль	*def art*	definite article
уменьшительное	*dimin*	diminutive
экономика	*ECON*	economics
электроника	*ELEC*	electricity
особенно	*esp*	especially
и тому подобное	*etc*	et cetera
междометие	*excl*	exclamation
женский род	*f*	feminine
в переносном значении	*fig*	figurative
родительный падеж	*gen*	genitive
география	*GEO*	geography
геометрия	*GEOM*	geometry
безличный	*impers*	impersonal
несовершенный вид	*impf*	imperfective verb
несклоняемое	*ind*	indeclinable
неопределённый артикль	*indef art*	indefinite article
разговорное	*inf*	informal
грубо	*inf!*	offensive
инфинитив	*infin*	infinitive
творительный падеж	*instr*	instrumental
неизменяемое	*inv*	invariable
неправильный	*irreg*	irregular
лингвистика	*LING*	linguistics

Условные Сокращения в Англо-Русской Части

местный падеж	*loc*	locative
мужской род	*m*	masculine
субстантивированное прилагательное	*m/f/nt adj*	adjectival noun
математика	**MATH**	mathematics
медицина	**MED**	medicine
военный термин	**MIL**	military
музыка	**MUS**	music
имя существительное	*n*	noun
морской термин	**NAUT**	nautical
именительный падеж	*nom*	nominative
существительное во множественном числе	*npl*	plural noun
средний род	*nt*	neuter
числительное	*num*	numeral
себя	*o.s.*	oneself
разделительный	*part*	partitive
пренебрежительное	*pej*	pejorative
совершенный вид	*perf*	perfective verb
фотография	**PHOT**	photography
физика	**PHYS**	physics
физиология	**PHYSIOL**	physiology
множественное число	*pl*	plural
политика	**POL**	politics
страдательное причастие	*pp*	past participle
предлог	*prep*	preposition
местоимение	*pron*	pronoun
предложный падеж	*prp*	prepositional
психология	**PSYCH**	psychiatry
прошедшее время	*pt*	past tense
железнодорожный термин	**RAIL**	railways
религия	**REL**	religion
кто-нибудь	*sb*	somebody
просвещение	**SCOL**	school
единственное число	*sg*	singular
что-нибудь	*sth*	something
подлежащее	*subj*	subject
превосходная степень	*superl*	superlative
техника	**TECH**	technology
теле(связь)	**TEL**	telecommunications
театр	**THEAT**	theatre
телевидение	**TV**	television
типографский термин	**TYP**	printing

Условные Сокращения в Англо-Русской Части

американский английский	US	American English
обычно	usu	usually
глагол	vb	verb
непереходный глагол	vi	intransitive verb
звательный падеж	voc	vocative
фразовый глагол	vt fus	inseparable verb
переходный глагол	vt	transitive verb
зоология	ZOOL	zoology
зарегистрированный товарный знак	®	registered trademark
вводит культурный эквивалент	≈	introduces a cultural equivalent

Abbreviations Used in Russian-English

aviation	**АВИА**	авиация
automobiles	**АВТ**	автомобильное дело
administration	**АДМИН**	администрация
anatomy	**АНАТ**	анатомия
architecture	**АРХИТ**	архитектура
impersonal	**безл**	безличный
biology	**БИО**	биология
botany	**БОТ**	ботаника
parenthesis	**вводн сл**	вводное слово
military	**ВОЕН**	военный термин
reflexive	**возв**	возвратный глагол
geography	**ГЕО**	география
geometry	**ГЕОМ**	геометрия
verb	**глаг**	глагол
offensive	**груб**!	грубо
singular	**ед**	единственное число
feminine	**ж**	женский род
zoology	**ЗООЛ**	зоология
history	**ИСТ**	история
et cetera	**итп**	и тому подобное
predicate	**как сказ**	как сказуемое
commercial	**КОММ**	коммерция
computing	**КОМП**	компьютер
somebody	**кто-н**	кто-нибудь
culinary	**КУЛИН**	кулинария
linguistics	**ЛИНГ**	лингвистика
masculine	**м**	мужской род
mathematics	**МАТ**	математика
medicine	**МЕД**	медицина
exclamation	**межд**	междометие
pronoun	**мест**	местоимение
plural	**мн**	множественное число
nautical	**МОР**	морской термин
music	**МУЗ**	музыка
adverb	**нареч**	наречие
invariable	**неизм**	неизменяемое
intransitive	**неперех**	непереходный глагол
indeclinable	**нескл**	несклоняемое
imperfective	**несов**	несовершенный вид
attributive	**опред**	определение
figurative	**перен**	в переносном значении
transitive	**перех**	переходный
subject	**подлеж**	подлежащее
politics	**ПОЛИТ**	политика
superlative	**превос**	превосходная степень
preposition	**предл**	предлог

ABBREVIATIONS USED IN RUSSIAN-ENGLISH

pejorative	*пренебр*	пренебрежительное
adjective	*прил*	имя прилагательное
possessive	*притяж*	притяжательный
school	*ПРОСВЕЩ*	просвещение
psychology	*ПСИХОЛ*	психология
informal	*разг*	разговорное
religion	*РЕЛ*	религия
see	*см*	смотри
collective	*собир*	собирательное
perfective	*сов*	совершенный вид
abbreviation	*сокр*	сокращение
neuter	*ср*	средний род
comparative	*сравн*	сравнительная степень
construction	*СТРОИТ*	строительство
noun	*сущ*	имя существительное
agriculture	*С.-Х.*	сельское хозяйство
television	*ТЕЛ*	телевидение
technology	*ТЕХ*	техника
printing	*ТИПОГ*	типографский термин
diminutive	*уменьш*	уменьшительное
physics	*ФИЗ*	физика
photography	*ФОТО*	фотография
chemistry	*ХИМ*	химия
particle	*част*	частица
somebody's	*чей-н*	чей-нибудь
numeral	*чис*	числительное
something	*что-н*	что-нибудь
economics	*ЭКОН*	экономика
eletricity	*ЭЛЕК*	электроника
law	*ЮР*	юридический термин
registered trademark	®	зарегистрированный товарный знак
introduces a cultural equivalent	≈	вводит культурный эквивалент

Vowels

1. Russian vowels are inherently short, whereas in English some vowels are inherently long (eg. **beat**) while others are inherently short (eg. **bit**). Russian stressed vowels, however, tend to be slightly longer than unstressed vowels. In unstressed positions all vowels are "reduced" ie. their individual characteristics are not as definite as those of their stressed counterparts.

2. In unstressed positions the letter **o** has the same value as the letter **a** eg. **города́** [gərʌ'da]. Some loanwords and acronyms are exceptions eg. **ра́дио** ['raɖio], **госба́нк** [goz'bank].

3. In unstressed positions the letter **e** is pronounced like **bit** eg. **село́** [şi'lo]. The same is true of **я** before stressed syllables eg. **пяти́** [pi'ţi], and of **a** when it follows **ч** or **щ** eg. **щади́ть** [ɕi'ɖiţ]. After **ж, ц** and **ш** unstressed **e** is pronounced as [+] eg. **жена́** [ʒ+'na].

4. All Russian diphthongs end in [j], which in diphthongs is pronounced as [i] (eg. **sheet**) with the tongue very close to the roof of the mouth.

N.B. The letter **ё**, always stressed, is not an independent letter of the alphabet, being used only in grammar books, dictionaries etc. to avoid ambiguity eg. **не́бо** and **нёбо**.

Consonants

1. The consonants **п, б, м, ф, в, т, д, н, с, з, л, р, к, г, х** have "soft" or "palatalised" consonants, which are indicated by a "softening" vowel letter **e, ё, и, ю, я** or the soft sign **ь** following the consonant letter: **те** [ţɛ], **ни́ва** ['ɳvə], **ся́ду** ['şadu], **мать** [maţ]. Consonants preceding a "soft" consonant may also be pronounced soft, usually if they are pronounced in the same place in the mouth (ie. are "homorganic") eg. **стих** [şţix], though this is not always the case eg. **свет** [şɣɛt].

2. The "soft" consonants **п, б, м, ф, в, г** are pronounced like their "hard" counterparts with simultaneous [j] (as in **yet**).

3. In pronouncing "soft" **т, д, н** the tip of the tongue is drawn back slightly from the position for **т, д, н** and in these "soft" consonants, togther with "soft" **с, з**, the front of the tongue is arched up towards the [j] position.

4. "Soft" **л** is very different from **л**. The front of the tongue is raised to the [j] position, while the back of the tongue must not be raised at all, cf. **лот** [lot] and **лёт** [ḷot], **по́лка** ['polkə] and **по́лька** ['poḷkə].

5. In "soft" **к, г, х** the back of the tongue is raised somewhat further forward in the mouth than in **к, г, х** and a good portion of the middle of the tongue touches or approaches the roof of the mouth eg. **руки́** [ru'ķi], **ноги́** [nʌ'gi].

6. The consonants **т, д, н** eg. **ток** [tok], **дом** [dom], **нас** [nas] are pronounced with the tongue-tip slightly further forward in the mouth than in the English counterparts.

7. The consonants **п, т, к** eg. **пасть** [paşţ], **ток** [tok] and **кот** [tok] are pronounced without the slight puff of air which follows them in English before stressed vowels.

8. **л** eg. **ло́дка** ['lotkə] is pronounced with the tongue-tip in the same position as in English [l], but the back of the tongue is raised as if one were pronouncing [u], while the middle of the

tongue is depressed. The result is an **л** which is even "darker" than that at the end of English **wall**.

9. There are pairs of voiced and voiceless consonants –

Voiced: **б, в, д, з, г** and their "soft" counterparts
Voiceless: **п, ф, т, с, к** and their "soft" counterparts

a) At the end of a word a voiced consonant is replaced by the corresponding voiceless consonant eg. **го́род** [ˈgorət] (cf. **го́рода** [ˈgorədə]).

b) When a voiced consonant occurs before a voiceless consonant in the same word or at the close juncture of two words it is replaced by the corresponding voiceless consonant eg. **городка́** [gərʌtˈka], **из того́** [is tʌˈvo] (cf. **из э́того** [lˈzɛtəvə]).

c) When a voiceless consonant occurs before one of the voiced members of the pairs (except **в** and its "soft" counterpart), the converse happens, and the voiceless consonant is replaced by a voiced consonant eg. **сдава́ть** [zdˈvaṭ] (cf. **сойти́** [śʌjˈṭi]), but **свой** [svoj], **свет** [şɣɛt].

N.B. The spelling does not reflect these consonant changes except that the prefixes **воз-/вз-**, **из-**, **(с)низ-** and **раз-/роз-** change to **вос-/вс-**, **ис-**, **(с)нис-** and **рас-/рос-** respectively in the appropriate circumstances eg. **изойти́** [ɪzʌjˈṭi] to **исходи́ть** [isxʌˈḍiṭ].

RUSSIAN PRONUNCIATION

Vowels and Diphthongs

Symbol	Russian Example	English Example/Explanation
[ɑ]	д**а**ть	pronounced like the beginning of diphthong in "eye"
[æ]	ч**а**сть	c**a**t
[ʌ]	д**а**ва́л, **а**двока́т	c**u**p
[ə]	сту́л**а**	**a**long
[ı]	ч**а**сы́, щ**а**ди́ть	b**i**t
[ɛ]	с**е**л	g**e**t
[e]	с**е́**ли	pronounced like the beginning of diphthong in "eight"
[jɛ]	**е**л	**y**et
[je]	**е**сть	only before "soft" consonants
[ı]	с**е**ло́	b**i**t
[ji]	**е**го́	**yi**p
[ɨ]	ж**е**на́	*see note 3 under Vowels*
[o]	дёсны, ч**ё**рный	**aw**e
[jo]	**ё**лка, мо**ё**	**yaw**n
[i]	**у**х, ни́в**а**	sh**ee**t
[ı]	**и**гра́	b**i**t
[ɨ]	ж**и**ть	after "ж, ц, ш"
[j]	**й**од, мо**й**	**y**ield
[o]	к**о**т	**aw**e
[ʌ]	**но**га́, **о**ткрыва́ть	c**u**p
[ə]	к**о**лбаса́, я́бл**око**	**a**long
[u]	**у**м	sh**oo**t
[ɨ]	с**ы**н	pronounced like "ee", but with the tongue arched further back in the mouth
[ɛ]	**э́**то	g**e**t
[e]	**э́**ти	pronounced like the beginning of diphthong in "eight"
[ɨ]	с**э**коно́мить	not after "soft" consonants
[u]	ут**ю́**г	n**oo**n
[ju]	**ю**г, обо**ю**дный	**you**, **you**th
[a]	т**я́**жкий	pronounced like the beginning of diphthong in "eye"

xxvi

[ja]	я́сно	initially and after vowels
[æ]	ся́дь	c*a*t
[jæ]	я́сень	*ya*k
[ɪ]	пя́ти́	b*i*t
[jɪ]	я́зы́к, поя́cá	*yi*p
[ə]	ды́ня́	*a*long
[jə]	сча́стья́	"y" + *a*long

Consonants

Symbol	*Russian Example*	*English Example/Explanation*
[b]	*б*анк	*b*ut
[b̦]	о*б*е́д	*see note 2 under Consonants*
[p]	зу*б*, ю́*б*ка	*p*ut
[p̦]	го́лу*бь*	*see note 2 under Consonants*
[v]	*в*от	*v*at
[ɣ]	*в*е́тка	*see note 2 under Consonants*
[f]	ле*в*	*f*at
[f̦]	бро*вь*	*see note 2 under Consonants*
[g]	*г*од	*g*ot
[g̦]	но*г*и́	*see note 5 under Consonants*
[k]	но*г*, но́*г*ти	*c*at
[d]	*д*ом	*d*og
[d̦]	*д*е́вушка	*see note 3 under Consonants*
[t]	ca*д*	*t*op
[ț]	ло́ша*дь*	*see note 3 under Consonants*
[ʒ]	*ж*ена́	mea*s*ure
[ʃ]	ёж, ло́*ж*ка	*sh*oot
[z]	*з*а́втра	do*z*e
[z̦]	га*з*е́та	*see note 3 under Consonants*
[s]	га*з*	ga*s*
[ș]	гря*зь*	at end of word or before voiceless consonant
[ʒ]	и*з*жо́га	mea*s*ure
[k]	*к*от	*c*ot
[k̦]	ру*к*и́	*see note 5 under Consonants*

[ʃ]	из шёлка	*sh*oot
[ɹ]	из чего́	*sh*eet
[l]	ло́дка	wa*ll*
[ļ]	лес	*see note 4 under Consonants*
[m]	мать	*m*at
[ɱ]	мять	*see note 2 under Consonants*
[n]	нас	*n*o
[ņ]	нет	*see note 3 under Consonants*
[p]	пасть	*p*ut
[p̧]	петь	*see note 2 under Consonants*
[b]	осле́н	*b*ut
[r]	рот	pronounced like rolled Scots "r"
[ɹ]	ряд	*see note 2 under Consonants*
[s]	сад	*s*at
[ş]	сел	*see note 3 under Consonants*
[z]	сдава́ть	do*z*e
[ʐ]	сде́лать	before some voiced consonants
[ɹ]	сшить	*sh*oot
[ʒ]	сжать	mea*s*ure
[ɹ]	счи́стить	*sh*eet
[t]	ток	*t*op
[ḍ]	ме	*see note 3 under Consonants*
[d]	отговори́ть	*d*og
[ţ]	отде́лать	before "soft" "д"
[f]	фо́рма	*f*at
[f̧]	буфе́т	*see note 2 under Consonants*
[v]	афга́нец	*v*at
[x]	ход	pronounced like Scots "ch" in "loch"
[ҳ]	хи́мик	*see note 5 under Consonants*
[ts]	цель	bi*ts*
[dz]	оте́ц бы	a*dz*e
[tʃ]	ча́сто	*ch*ip
[dʒ]	дочь бы	*j*ig
[ʃ]	шу́тка	*sh*oot
[ɕ]	щит	fre*sh sh*eets

Английское Произношение

Гласные и дифтонги

Знак	Английский Пример	Русское Соответствие/Описание
[ɑ:]	father	ма́ма
[ʌ]	but, come	алья́нс
[æ]	man, cat	э́тот
[ə]	father, ago	ра́на, парохо́д
[ə:]	bird, heard	фёдор
[ɛ]	get, bed	жест
[ɪ]	it, big	кит
[i:]	tea, sea	и́ва
[ɔ]	hot, wash	ход
[ɔ:]	saw, all	о́чень
[u]	put, book	бук
[u:]	too, you	у́лица
[aɪ]	fly, high	лай
[au]	how, house	аут
[ɛə]	there, bear	произно́сится как сочета́ние зву́ков "э" и кра́ткого "а"
[eɪ]	day, obey	эй
[ɪə]	here, hear	произно́сится как сочета́ние зву́ков "и" и кра́ткого "а"
[əu]	go, note	о́у
[ɔɪ]	boy, oil	бой
[uə]	poor, sure	произно́сится как сочета́ние зву́ков "у" и кра́ткого "а"
[juə]	pure	произно́сится как сочета́ние зву́ков "ю" и кра́ткого "а"

Согласные

Знак	Английский Пример	Русское Соответствие/Описание
[b]	**b**ut	**б**ал
[d]	men**ded**	аре́н**д**а
[g]	**g**o, **g**et, bi**g**	**г**ол, ми**г**
[dʒ]	**g**in, ju**dg**e	**дж**и́нсы, и́ми**дж**
[ŋ]	si**ng**	произно́сится как ру́сский "н", но не ко́нчиком языка́, а за́дней ча́стью его́ спи́нки
[h]	**h**ouse, **h**e	**х**а́ос, **х**и́мия
[j]	**y**oung, **y**es	**й**од, **й**емен
[k]	**c**ome, mo**ck**	**к**а́мень, ро**к**
[r]	**r**ed, t**r**ead	**р**от, т**р**ава́
[s]	**s**and, ye**s**	**с**ад, ри**с**
[z]	ro**s**e, **z**ebra	ро́**з**а, **з**е́бра
[ʃ]	**sh**e, ma**ch**ine	**ш**и́на, ма**ш**и́на
[tʃ]	**ch**in, ri**ch**	**ч**ин, кули́**ч**
[v]	**v**alley	**в**альс
[w]	**w**ater, **wh**ich	**у**о́тергейт, **у**ик-э́нд
[ʒ]	vi**s**ion	ва́**ж**ный
[θ]	**th**ink, my**th**	произно́сится как ру́сский "с", но ко́нчик языка́ нахо́дится ме́жду зуба́ми
[ð]	**th**is, **th**e	произно́сится как ру́сский "з", но ко́нчик языка́ нахо́дится ме́жду зуба́ми
[f]	**f**ace	**ф**акт
[l]	**l**ake, **l**ick	**л**ай, **л**ом
[m]	**m**ust	**м**ат
[n]	**n**ut	**н**ет
[p]	**p**at, **p**ond	**п**арохо́д
[t]	**t**ake, ha**t**	э́**т**от, не**т**
[x]	lo**ch**	**х**од

[ɑʒ]	**А,** а
[be]	**Б,** б
[ve]	**В,** в
[ge]	**Г,** г
[de]	**Д,** д
[je]	**Е,** е
[jɔ]	**Ё,** ё
[ʒe]	**Ж,** ж
[ze]	**З,** з
[i]	**И,** и
[i'kratkɔje]	**Й,** й
[ka]	**К,** к
[ɛl]	**Л,** л
[ɛm]	**М,** м
[ɛn]	**Н,** н
[ɔ]	**О,** о
[pe]	**П,** п
[ɛr]	**Р,** р
[ɛs]	**С,** с
[te]	**Т,** т
[u]	**У,** у
[ɛf]	**Ф,** ф
[xa]	**Х,** х
[tse]	**Ц,** ц
[tʃe]	**Ч,** ч
[ʃa]	**Ш,** ш
[ʃta]	**Щ,** щ
['tʋɔrd+ znak]	**Ъ,** ъ
[+]	**Ы,** ы
['m̩akk+ znak]	**Ь,** ь
[ɛ]	**Э,** э
[ju]	**Ю,** ю
[ja]	**Я,** я

A, a [eɪ]
B, b [biː]
C, c [siː]
D, d [diː]
E, e [iː]
F, f [ɛf]
G, g [dʒiː]
H, h [eɪtʃ]
I, i [aɪ]
J, j [dʒeɪ]
K, k [keɪ]
L, l [ɛl]
M, m [ɛm]
N, n [ɛn]
O, o [əu]
P, p [piː]
Q, q [kjuː]
R, r [ɑː*]
S, s [ɛs]
T, t [tiː]
U, u [juː]
V, v [viː]
W, w ['dʌblju]
X, x [ɛks]
Y, y [waɪ]
Z, z [zɛd, (*US*) ziː]

~ A, a ~

A, а *сущ нескл* (*буква*) the 1st letter of the Russian alphabet; **от ~ до я** from A to Z.

> **KEYWORD**
>
> **а** *союз* **1** (*выражает противопоставление*) but; **он согласи́лся, а я отказа́лся** he agreed, but I refused; **я чита́л, а он рисова́л** I was reading and he was drawing
>
> **2** (*выражает присоединение*) and; **снача́ла говори́л он, а пото́м мы** first he spoke, and then we did
>
> **3** (*перед перечислением*) namely; (*перед уточнением*) to be exact *или* precise; **пришли́ дво́е, а и́менно: Ивано́в и Петро́в** two people came, namely Ivanov and Petrov; **я до́лжен встать ра́но, а и́менно в 6 утра́** I have to get up early, at 6 am to be exact *или* precise
>
> **4** (*во фразах*): **а (не) то** or (else); **спеши́, а (не) то опозда́ешь** hurry, or (else) you'll be late; **а и́менно** (*то есть*) that is; **а вот** but
>
> ♦ *част* **1** (*усиливает обращение*) hey; **Ма́ша, а Ма́ша!** hey, Masha!
>
> **2** (*обозначает отклик*): **иди́ сюда́! – а, что тако́е!** come here! – yes? what is it?; **а как же** (*разг*) of course; **ты обе́дал? а как же** have you had lunch? of course
>
> ♦ *межд* (*выражает припоминание, догадку*) ah; (*выражает ужас, боль*) oh; **а ну** (*разг*) go on; **а ну, беги́ в дом!** go on, run along in!; **а ну́ его́!** (*разг*) stuff him!

А- *сокр*: **~72, ~76** *different grades of petrol.*

абажу́р (-а) *м* lampshade.

абба́т (-а) *м* (*в монастыре*) abbot.

абба́ти́с|а (-ы) *ж* abbess.

абба́тств|о (-а) *ср* abbey.

аббревиату́р|а (-ы) *ж* abbreviation.

Аберди́н (-а) *м* Aberdeen.

абза́ц (-а) *м* paragraph.

абитурие́нт (-а) *м entrant to university, college etc.*

абитурие́нт|ка (-ки; *gen pl* **-ок)** *ж см* **абитурие́нт.**

абонеме́нт (-а) *м* season ticket.

абонеме́нтный *прил* (*концерт, лекция*) for season-ticket holders.

абоне́нт (-а) *м* subscriber.

абориге́н (-а) *м* aborigine.

або́рт (-а) *м* abortion; **де́лать (сде́лать** *perf*) **~** to have an abortion.

абрази́в (-а) *м* abrasive.

абракада́бр|а (-ы) *ж* gobbledegook.

абрико́с (-а) *м* (*плод*) apricot; (*дерево*) apricot tree.

абсолю́тен *прил см* **абсолю́тный.**

абсолюти́зм (-а) *м* absolutism.

абсолю́тно *нареч* absolutely.

абсолю́т|ный (-ен, -на, -но) *прил* absolute; **~ная монопо́лия** absolute monopoly; **абсолю́тный слух** perfect pitch.

абсорби́р|овать (-ую) (*не*)*сов перех* to absorb.

абстраги́р|оваться (-уюсь) (*не*)*сов возв*: **~ (от** +*gen*) to detach o.s. (from).

абстра́кт|ный (-ен, -на, -но) *прил* abstract; **абстра́ктное (и́мя) существи́тельное** abstract noun.

абстра́кци|я (-и) *ж* abstraction.

абсу́рд (-а) *м* absurdity; **доводи́ть (довести́** *perf*) **что-н до ~а** to take sth to the point of absurdity.

абсу́рд|ный (-ен, -на, -но) *прил* absurd.

абсце́сс (-а) *м* abscess.

аванга́рд (-а) *м* (*также* ВОЕН) vanguard; (*ИСКУССТВО*) avant-garde; **в ~е** (+*gen*) in the vanguard (of).

авангарди́зм (-а) *м* the avant-garde.

ава́нс (-а) *м* (*КОММ*) advance; **~ в счёт платеже́й** advance against payments.

аванси́р|овать (-ую) (*не*)*сов перех*: **~ что-н кому́-н** to advance sb sth; (*КОММ*) to make sb an advance payment of sth.

ава́нсом *нареч* in advance.

авансце́н|а (-ы) *ж* proscenium.

авантю́р|а (-ы) *ж* adventurism; **втя́гивать (втяну́ть** *perf*) **кого́-н в ~у** to involve sb in a risky undertaking.

авантюри́ст (-а) *м* adventurist.

авантюри́ст|ка (-ки; *gen pl* **-ок)** *ж см* **авантюри́ст.**

авари́йный *прил* (*служба, машина*) emergency *опред*; (*дом, состояние техники*) unsafe; **авари́йный сигна́л** alarm signal.

ава́ри|я (-и) *ж* accident; (*повреждение:*

механизма, аппаратуры) breakdown; **терпе́ть (потерпе́ть** *perf*) ~**ю** (*машина, самолёт итп*) to crash; **попа́сть** (*perf*) **в** ~**ю** to have an accident.

а́вгуст (-а) м August; *см также* **октя́брь**.

а́вгустовск|ий (-ая, -ое, -ие) *прил* August *опред*.

а́виа *нескл* (*авиапочта*) air mail.

авиали́ни|я (-и) ж flight path.

авиано́с|ец (-ца) м aircraft carrier.

авиацио́нный *прил* aviation *опред*.

авиа́ци|я (-и) ж aviation; **гражда́нская** ~ civil aviation.

ави́зо *ср нескл* (*КОММ*) advice note.

авитамино́з (-а) м vitamin deficiency, avitaminosis.

аво́сек *сущ см* **аво́ська**.

аво́сь *част* (*разг*) perhaps; **на** ~ (*разг*) on the off chance; (: *наугад*) by guesswork; **наде́яться** (*impf*) **на** ~ to trust to luck.

аво́сь|ка (-ьки; *gen pl* -ек) ж (*разг*) (string) bag.

авра́л (-а) м (*МОР*) emergency task; (*перен: разг*) rush job.

австрали́ек *сущ см* **австрали́йка**.

австрали́|ец (-йца) м Australian.

австрали́|йка (-йки; *gen pl* -ек) ж *см* **австрали́ец**.

австрали́йск|ий (-ая, -ое, -ие) *прил* Australian.

австрали́йца *итп сущ см* **австрали́ец**.

Австра́ли|я (-и) ж Australia.

австри́ек *сущ см* **австри́йка**.

австри́|ец (-йца) м Austrian.

австри́|йка (-йки; *gen pl* -ек) ж *см* **австри́ец**.

австри́йск|ий (-ая, -ое, -ие) *прил* Austrian.

австри́йца *итп сущ см* **австри́ец**.

А́встри|я (-и) ж Austria.

авт. *сокр* (= *автомоби́льный*) auto. (= *automobile*); = **автоно́мный**, **а́вторский**, **а́втор**.

авто- *часть сложных слов* (*со значением автоматический*) *indicating sth done automatically eg.* **автопило́т**; (*со значением автомобильный*) *indicating a connection with vehicles eg.* **автозаво́д**; (*со значением свой, само-*) *self- or auto-, indicating a connection with oneself eg.* **автобиогра́фия**.

автоба́з|а (-ы) ж depot (*where a company's vehicles are kept and maintained*).

автобиографи́ческ|ий (-ая, -ое, -ие) *прил* autobiographical.

автобиогра́фи|я (-и) ж autobiography.

авто́бус (-а) м bus; (*на дальние расстояния*) coach (*BRIT*), bus (*US*).

авто́бусный *прил* (*см сущ*) bus *опред*; coach *опред* (*BRIT*).

автовокза́л (-а) м bus *или* coach (*BRIT*) station.

авто́граф (-а) м autograph.

автодоро́жный *прил* (*происшествие*) road *опред*; (*инспекция*) traffic *опред*.

автозаво́д (-а) м car (*BRIT*) *или* automobile (*US*) plant.

автозапра́вочн|ая (-ой; *decl like adj*) ж (*также:* ~ **ста́нция**) filling station.

автока́р (-а) м fork-lift truck.

автола́в|ка (-ки; *gen pl* -ок) ж mobile shop.

автомагистра́л|ь (-и) ж motorway (*BRIT*), expressway (*US*).

автома́т (-а) м automatic machine; (*ВОЕН*) sub-machine-gun.

автоматиза́ци|я (-и) ж automation.

автоматизи́р|овать (-ую) (*не)сов перех* to automate.

автома́тик|а (-и) ж automatic equipment.

автомати́ческ|ий (-ая, -ое, -ие) *прил* automatic.

автомаши́н|а (-ы) ж (motor)car, automobile (*US*).

автомоби́л|ь (-я) м (motor)car, automobile (*US*); **легково́й** ~ (passenger) car.

автоно́мен *прил см* **автоно́мный**.

автоно́ми|я (-и) ж autonomy.

автоно́м|ный (-ен, -на, -но) *прил* autonomous; (*ТЕХ*) independent; (*КОМП*) off-line, stand-alone.

автоотве́тчик (-а) м answering machine.

автопило́т (-а) м automatic pilot.

автопортре́т (-а) м self-portrait.

а́втор (-а) м author.

авторефера́т (-а) м abstract (*of dissertation*).

авторизова́ть (-у́ю) (*не)сов перех* to authorize.

авторита́р|ный (-ен, -на, -но) *прил* authoritarian.

авторите́т (-а) м authority; **по́льзоваться** (*impf*) ~**ом** to enjoy authority; **завоёвывать** (**завоева́ть** *perf*) ~ to gain authority.

авторите́т|ный (-ен, -на, -но) *прил* authoritative.

а́вторск|ий (-ая, -ое, -ие) *прил* author's; **а́вторский ве́чер** (*поэта итп*) reading; (*композитора*) recital (*given by the composer*); **а́вторское пра́во** copyright; **а́вторское свиде́тельство** patent.

авторуч|ка (-ки; *gen pl* -ек) ж fountain pen.

автосто́п (-а) м (*способ путешествия*) hitchhiking.

автостра́д|а (-ы) ж motorway (*BRIT*), expressway (*US*).

автотра́нспорт (-а) м road transport.

ауа́р|ы (-ов) *мн* (*КОММ*) assets *мн*.

ага́ *межд* aha ♦ *част* (*разг: выражает согласие*) uh huh.

ага́т (-а) м agate.

аге́нт (-а) м agent.

аге́нтств|о (-а) *ср* agency; **телегра́фное** ~ news agency; **аге́нтство печа́ти** press agency.

агенту́р|а (-ы) ж intelligence service ♦ *собир* agents *мн*.

агита́тор (-а) м (political) campaigner; (*на выборах*) canvasser.

агитацио́нный *прил* (political) promotional.

агита́ци|я (-и) ж campaigning.

агити́р|овать (-ую) *несов неперех*: ~ (**за** +*acc*) to campaign (for).

аго́ни|я (-и) ж death throes *мн*.

агра́рный *прил* agrarian.
агрега́т (**-а**) *м* machine; (*узел*) unit (*of machine*).
агресси́в|ный (**-ен, -на, -но**) *прил* aggressive.
агре́сси|я (**-и**) *ж* aggression.
агроно́м (**-а**) *м* agronomist.
агрономи́ческ|ий (**-ая, -ое, -ие**) *прил* agronomic.
агроно́ми|я (**-и**) *ж* agronomy.
ад (**-а**) *м* hell.
ада́жио *ср нескл, нареч* adagio.
ада́мово *прил*: **А~ я́блоко** Adam's apple.
адапта́ци|я (**-и**) *ж* adaptation.
ада́птер (**-а**) *м* adaptor.
адапти́р|овать (**-ую**) (*не)сов перех* to adapt
▶ **адапти́роваться** (*не)сов возв* to adapt.
адвока́т (**-а**) *м* (*ЮР*) ≈ barrister (*BRIT*), ≈ attorney (*US*); (*консультант*) solicitor; **колле́гия ~ов** ≈ the Bar (*BRIT*).
адвокату́р|а (**-ы**) *ж собир* ≈ the Bar (*BRIT*).
АДД *м сокр* (= *авторефера́т диссерта́ции на соиска́ние учёной сте́пени до́ктора нау́к*) abstract of doctoral thesis.
Адди́с-Абе́б|а (**-ы**) *ж* Addis Ababa.
адеква́т|ный (**-ен, -на, -но**) *прил* adequate; (*совпадающий*) identical.
адено́ид|ы (**-ов**) *мн* (*МЕД*) adenoids *мн*.
адм. *сокр* (= **администра́ция**) admin (= *administration*).
администрати́вн|ый *прил* administrative; (*способности*) managerial, management *опред*; **в ~ом поря́дке** by authority; **~ тон** an official tone of voice.
администра́тор (**-а**) *м* administrator; (*в театре, гостинице, кино*) manager.
администра́ци|я (**-и**) *ж, собир* administration; (*гостиницы*) management.
администри́р|овать (**-ую**) *несов неперех* (+*instr*) to administrate.
адмира́л (**-а**) *м* admiral.
АДМП *ж сокр* = *Агра́рно-демократи́ческая па́ртия*.
а́дрес (**-а;** *nom pl* **-а́**) *м* address; **в ~ +***gen* (addressed) to; **Ва́ше обвине́ние не по ~у** (*разг*) you've got the wrong person; **по ~у кого́-н** concerning *или* about sb; **абсолю́тный/относи́тельный ~** (*КОМП*) absolute/relative address.
адре́сный *прил*: **~ стол** address bureau.
адрес|ова́ть (**-ую**) (*не)сов перех*: **~ что-н кому́-н** to address sth to sb; (*критику*) to direct sth at sb.
адриати́ческ|ий (**-ая, -ое, -ие**) *прил*: **А~ое мо́ре** the Adriatic (Sea).
а́дск|ий (**-ая, -ое, -ие**) *прил* (*РЕЛ*) infernal; (*разг: холод, условия*) diabolical; (: *терпение, выносливость*) fantastic; (*замысел*) cunning.
адъюта́нт (**-а**) *м* aide-de-camp.
аж *част, союз* (*разг*) even; **он ~ вскри́кнул от**

удивле́ния he even cried out in surprise.
ажиота́ж (**-а**) *м* (*перен*) commotion; (*КОММ*) stockjobbing.
ажу́р (**-а**) *м keeping of books up to date*; **в ~е** (*разг*) in cracking order.
ажу́рный *прил* lace; **ажу́рная рабо́та** fine *или* delicate work.
АЗС *ж сокр* (= *автозапра́вочная ста́нция*) filling station.
аз|ы́ (**-о́в**) *мн* (*перен*) basics *мн*; **начина́ть** (**нача́ть** *perf*) **с ~о́в** to start from scratch.
аза́ли|я (**-и**) *м* azalea.
аза́рт (**-а**) *м* ardour (*BRIT*), ardor (*US*); **с ~ом** with zest; **входи́ть** (**войти́** *perf*) **в ~** to get carried away.
аза́ртный (**-ен, -на, -но**) *прил* ardent; **аза́ртная игра́** game of chance.
а́збук|а (**-и**) *м* alphabet; (*буква́рь*) first reading book; (*перен: основны́е нача́ла*) rudiments *мн*; **но́тная ~** *the system of musical notation*; **а́збука Мо́рзе** Morse code.
а́збучный *прил* alphabetical; **а́збучная и́стина** truism.
Азербайджа́н (**-а**) *м* Azerbaijan.
азербайджа́н|ец (**-ца**) *м* Azerbaijani.
азербайджа́н|ка (**-ки;** *gen pl* **-ок**) *ж см* **азербайджа́нец**.
азербайджа́нск|ий (**-ая, -ое, -ие**) *прил* Azerbaijani.
азербайджа́нца *итп сущ см* **азербайджа́нец**.
азиа́т (**-а**) *м* Asian.
азиа́т|ка (**-ки;** *gen pl* **-ок**) *ж см* **азиа́т**.
азиа́тск|ий (**-ая, -ое, -ие**) *прил* Asian.
а́зимут (**-а**) *м* azimuth.
А́зи|я (**-и**) *ж* Asia.
азо́вск|ий (**-ая, -ое, -ие**) *прил*: **А~ое мо́ре** the Sea of Azov.
азо́рск|ий (**-ая, -ое, -ие**) *прил*: **А~ие острова́** the Azores.
азо́т (**-а**) *м* nitrogen.
азо́тный *прил* nitric.
а́ист (**-а**) *м* stork.
ай *межд* (*выражает боль*) ow, ouch; (*выражет испуг, страх*) oh; **~ да Мари́я!** good for Maria!
айв|а́ (**-ы́**) *м* (*плод*) quince; (*дерево*) quince tree.
айда́ *межд* (*разг*) let's go; **~ купа́ться!** let's go for a swim!
а́йсберг (**-а**) *м* iceberg.
акад. *сокр* = **акаде́мик**.
акаде́мик (**-а**) *м* academician.
академи́ческ|ий (**-ая, -ое, -ие**) *прил* (*также перен*) academic; **академи́ческий теа́тр** *honorary title given to theatres*.
акаде́ми|я (**-и**) *ж* academy; **акаде́мия нау́к** the Academy of Sciences; **акаде́мия худо́жеств** the Academy of Arts.
а́ка|ть (**-ю**) *несов неперех to pronounce unstressed "o" as "a" in Russian*.

ака́ци|я (**-и**) *ж* acacia.
аквала́нг (**-а**) *м* aqualung.
аквамари́н (**-а**) *м* aquamarine.
аквамари́новый *прил* aquamarine.
акваре́л|ь (**-и**) *ж* watercolours *мн* (*BRIT*),
watercolors *мн* (*US*); (*картина*) watercolo(u)r.
акваре́льный *прил* watercolour *опред* (*BRIT*),
watercolor *опред* (*US*).
аква́риум (**-а**) *м* aquarium, fish tank.
акватори|я (**-и**) *ж*: ~ **по́рта** area of water near
the port.
акведу́к (**-а**) *м* aqueduct.
АКД *м сокр* (= *авторефера́т диссерта́ции на
соиска́ние учёной сте́пени кандида́та нау́к*)
*abstract of dissertation for first level of
postgraduate degree.*
акклиматиза́ци|я (**-и**) *м* acclimatization,
acclimation (*US*).
акклиматизи́р|оваться (**-уюсь**) (*не*)*сов возв*
to acclimatize, acclimate (*US*).
аккомпанеме́нт (**-а**) *м* (*МУЗ, перен*)
accompaniment.
аккомпани́р|овать (**-ую**) *несов неперех* (+*dat*;
МУЗ) to accompany.
акко́рд (**-а**) *м* chord; **брать** (**взять** *perf*) ~ to play
a chord; **заключи́тельный** ~ (*перен*) climax.
аккордео́н (**-а**) *м* accordion.
акко́рдн|ый *прил*: ~**ая рабо́та** piecework; **он на**
~**ой опла́те** he is on piecework.
аккредити́в (**-а**) *м* letter of credit.
аккредити́вный *прил* credit *опред*.
аккредито́ванный *прил*: ~ **аге́нт** accredited
agent.
аккредит|ова́ть (**-у́ю**) (*не*)*сов перех* to accredit.
аккумули́р|овать (**-ую**) (*не*)*сов перех* (*ТЕХ,
перен*) to accumulate.
аккумуля́тор (**-а**) *м* accumulator.
аккура́тен *прил см* **аккура́тный**.
аккура́тно *нареч* (*регуля́рно*) regularly;
(*стара́тельно*) carefully; (*опря́тно*) neatly.
аккура́тност|ь (**-и**) *ж* (*см прил*) regularity;
meticulousness; accuracy; neatness.
аккура́т|ный (**-ен, -на, -но**) *прил* (*посеще́ние*)
regular; (*рабо́тник*) meticulous; (*рабо́та*)
accurate; (*костю́м*) neat.
акр (**-а**) *м* acre.
акри́л (**-а**) *м* acrylic.
акри́ловый *прил* acrylic.
акроба́т (**-а**) *м* acrobat.
акроба́тик|а (**-и**) *ж* acrobatics.
акселера́т (**-а**) *м* early developer (*physically*).
акселера́тор (**-а**) *м* accelerator.
акселера́ци|я (**-и**) *ж* early physical maturity.
аксессуа́р (**-а**) *м* (*оде́жды*) accessory; *см также*
аксессуа́ры.
аксессуа́р|ы (**-ов**) *мн* (*перен*: *в живописи
итп*) details *мн*; (: *в театре*) props *мн*
(= *properties*).
аксио́м|а (**-ы**) *ж* axiom.
акт (**-а**) *м* act; (*торже́ственное собра́ние*)
ceremony; **составля́ть** (**соста́вить** *perf*) ~ to

draw up a formal document; **а́кты
гражда́нского состоя́ния** register (*of births,
marriages, deaths*).
актёр (**-а**) *м* actor.
акти́в (**-а**) *м* activists *мн* (*in organization*);
(*КОММ*) assets *мн*; **запи́сывать** (**записа́ть** *perf*)
что-н в ~ to count sth as an asset;
заморо́женные ~**ы** (*КОММ*) frozen assets.
акти́вен *прил см* **акти́вный**.
активизи́р|овать (**-ую**) (*не*)*сов перех* to
enliven.
акти́вно *нареч* (*уча́ствовать*) actively;
(*рабо́тать*) energetically.
акти́в|ный (**-ен, -на, -но**) *прил* active; **акти́вный
бала́нс** balance of assets; **акти́вный слова́рь
или запа́с слов** active vocabulary.
актри́с|а (**-ы**) *ж* actress.
актуа́лен *прил см* **актуа́льный**.
актуа́льност|ь (**-и**) *ж* topicality.
актуа́льный (**-ен, -ьна, -ьно**) *прил* topical.
аку́л|а (**-ы**) *ж* shark.
акупункту́р|а (**-ы**) *ж* acupuncture.
аку́стик|а (**-и**) *ж* acoustics *ед*; (*в за́ле, в сту́дии*)
acoustics *мн*.
акусти́ческ|ий (**-ая, -ое, -ие**) *прил* acoustic(al);
~ **соедини́тель** (*КОМП*) acoustic coupler.
акуше́р (**-а**) *м* obstetrician.
акуше́р|ка (**-ки**; *gen pl* **-ок**) *ж* midwife.
акуше́рск|ий (**-ая, -ое, -ие**) *прил* obstetric(al).
акце́нт (**-а**) *м* accent; **де́лать** (**сде́лать** *perf*) ~ **на**
+*prp* (*перен*) to emphasize; **расставля́ть**
(**расста́вить** *perf*) **все** ~**ы** (*перен*) to draw
attention to the most important things.
акценти́р|овать (**-ую**) (*не*)*сов перех* (*перен*) to
accentuate.
акце́пт (**-а**) *м* (*КОММ, ЮР*) acceptance.
акце́птный *прил* (*КОММ*): ~ **банк** accepting
house.
акцепт|ова́ть (**-у́ю**) (*не*)*сов перех* (*КОММ*) to
accept.
акци́з (**-а**) *м* (*КОММ*) excise (tax).
акци́зный *прил* (*КОММ*) excise *опред*.
акционе́р (**-а**) *м* shareholder.
акционе́рный *прил* joint-stock *опред*;
акционе́рное о́бщество joint-stock company;
акционе́рный капита́л share capital.
акционе́рск|ий (**-ая, -ое, -ие**) *прил* (*права́,
до́ля*) shareholders'.
а́кци|я (**-и**) *ж* (*КОММ*) share; (*де́йствие*) action;
именна́я/обыкнове́нная ~ registered/ordinary
share; **паке́т** ~**й** block of shares; **по́лностью
опла́ченная** ~ fully-paid share; ~**и без пра́ва
го́лоса** non-voting shares; **дипломати́ческая** ~
diplomatic move.
алба́н|ец (**-ца**) *м* Albanian.
Алба́ни|я (**-и**) *ж* Albania.
алба́н|ка (**-ки**; *gen pl* **-ок**) *ж см* **алба́нец**.
алба́нск|ий (**-ая, -ое, -ие**) *прил* Albanian.
алба́нц|а *итп сущ см* **алба́нец**.
а́лгебр|а (**-ы**) *ж* algebra.
алгори́тм (**-а**) *м* algorithm.

алеба́стр (-а) *м* alabaster.
алеба́стровый *прил* alabaster *опред*.
александри́т (-а) *м* (*ГЕО*) alexandrite.
Александри́я (-и) *ж* Alexandria.
але́|ть (-ю) *несов неперех* (*флаг, мак*) to show scarlet; (*закат*) to glow scarlet; (*perf* **заале́ть**; *закат, небо*) to turn scarlet.
Алжи́р (-а) *м* Algeria.
алжи́р|ец (-ца) *м* Algerian.
алжи́р|ка (-ки; *gen pl* -ок) *ж см* **алжи́рец**.
алжи́рск|ий (-ая, -ое, -ие) *прил* Algerian.
алжи́рца *итп сущ см* **алжи́рец**.
а́либи *ср нескл* alibi.
алиме́нтщик (-а) *м* (*разг: пренебр*) *man paying alimony or maintenance*.
алиме́нт|ы (-ов) *мн* alimony *ед*, maintenance *ед*.
алка́ш (-á) *м* (*разг: пренебр*) alky.
алкоголи́зм (-а) *м* alcoholism.
алкого́лик (-а) *м* alcoholic.
алкоголи́ч|ка (-ки; *gen pl* -ек) *ж* (*разг*) *см* **алкого́лик**.
алкого́л|ь (-я) *м* alcohol.
Алла́х (-а) *м* Allah.
аллего́ри|я (-и) *ж* allegory.
алле́гро *ср нескл, нареч* allegro.
аллерге́н (-а) *м* allergen.
аллерги́ческ|ий (-ая, -ое, -ие) *прил* allergic.
аллерги́|я (-и) *ж* allergy.
алле́|я (-и) *ж* alley.
аллига́тор (-а) *м* alligator.
аллилу́йя *межд* hallelujah.
алло́ *межд* hello (*on answering phone*).
аллю́р (-а) *м* gait (*of horses*).
А́лма-Ат|á (-ы́) *ж* Alma-Ata.
алма́з (-а) *м* diamond.
алма́зный *прил* diamond *опред*; (*инструмент*) diamond-tipped.
алоэ *ср нескл* aloe.
алта́р|ь (-я́) *м* (*в церкви*) chancel; (*жертвенник*) altar; **возлага́ть** (**возложи́ть** *perf*) **что-н на ~ чего́-н** to sacrifice sth on the altar of sth.
алфави́т (-а) *м* alphabet; **по ~у** in alphabetical order.
а́лчен *прил см* **а́лчный**.
а́лчность (-и) *ж* greed.
а́лч|ный (-ен, -на, -но) *прил* greedy.
а́л|ый (-, -а, -о) *прил* scarlet.
алыч|а́ (-и́) *ж* cherry plum.
альбо́м (-а) *м* album; (*по искусству*) *book of art reproductions*.
альмана́х (-а) *м* anthology.
альпи́йск|ий (-ая, -ое, -ие) *прил* alpine; (*в Альпах*) Alpine.
альпини́зм (-а) *м* mountaineering.
А́льп|ы (-) *мн* the Alps.
альт (-á) *м* (*голос*) alto; (*инструмент*) viola.
альтернати́в|а (-ы) *ж* alternative.
альтернати́вный *прил* alternative.

альтруи́зм (-а) *м* altruism.
алья́нс (-а) *м* alliance.
Аля́ск|а (-и) *ж* Alaska.
алюми́ниевый *прил* aluminium *опред* (*BRIT*), aluminum *опред* (*US*).
алюми́ни|й (-я) *м* aluminium (*BRIT*), aluminum (*US*).
аляпова́т|ый (-, -а, -о) *прил* gaudy.
амазо́н|ка (-ки; *gen pl* -ок) *ж* (*всадница*) horsewoman (*мн* horsewomen); (*платье*) riding habit.
амальга́м|а (-ы) *ж* (*хим, перен*) amalgam.
амба́р (-а) *м* barn.
амбицио́з|ный (-ен, -на, -но) *прил* (*человек*) arrogant; (*планы*) presumptuous.
амби́ци|я (-и) *ж* (*самолюбие*) pride, arrogance; (*обычно мн: притязания*) ambition; **ударя́ться** (**уда́риться** *perf*) **в ~ю** (*разг*) to go into a huff.
амбулато́ри|я (-и) *ж* doctor's surgery (*BRIT*) *или* office (*US*).
амво́н (-а) *м* (*РЕЛ*) ≈ pulpit.
амёб|а (-ы) *ж* amoeba (*BRIT*), ameba (*US*).
Аме́рик|а (-и) *ж* America.
америка́н|ец (-ца) *м* American.
американиза́ци|я (-и) *ж* Americanization.
американизи́р|овать (-ую) (*не*)*сов перех* to Americanize.
америка́н|ка (-ки; *gen pl* -ок) *ж см* **америка́нец**.
америка́нск|ий (-ая, -ое, -ие) *прил* American.
америка́нца *итп сущ см* **америка́нец**.
амети́ст (-а) *м* amethyst.
аминокисло|та́ (-ты́; *nom pl* -ты) *ж* amino acid.
ами́нь *част* (*РЕЛ*) amen.
аммиа́к (-а) *м* ammonia.
АМН *ж сокр* (= Акаде́мия медици́нских нау́к) Academy of Medical Sciences.
амнисти́р|овать (-ую) (*не*)*сов перех* to grant (an) amnesty to.
амни́сти|я (-и) *ж* amnesty; **попада́ть** (**попа́сть** *perf*) **под ~ю** to be granted (an) amnesty.
амора́лен *прил см* **амора́льный**.
амора́льность (-и) *ж* (*см прил*) immorality; amorality.
амора́льный (-ен, -ьна, -ьно) *прил* (*поступок*) immoral; (*человек*) amoral.
амортиза́тор (-а) *м* (*ТЕХ*) shock absorber.
амортизацио́нный *прил* (*ТЕХ*) shock-absorbing; (*ЭКОН*) depreciation *опред*; **амортизацио́нные отчисле́ния** (*ЭКОН*) depreciation deductions *мн*; **амортизацио́нный срок** (*ЭКОН*) period of depreciation.
амортиза́ци|я (-и) *ж* (*ТЕХ*) shock absorption; (*ЭКОН*) depreciation; (*КОММ*) amortization.
амо́рф|ный (-ен, -на, -но) *прил* amorphous.
ампе́р (-а) *м* amp (= *ampère*).
амплиту́д|а (-ы) *ж* amplitude.
амплуа́ *ср нескл* (*актёра*) speciality; **э́то не**

моё ~ (*разг*) that's not (in) my line.
áмпул|а (-ы) ж ampoule (*BRIT*), ampule (*US*).
ампута́ци|я (-и) ж amputation.
ампути́р|овать (-ую) (*не*)*сов перех* to amputate.
АМТС ж *сокр* (= *автомати́ческая междугоро́дная телефо́нная связь*) ≈ STD (*BRIT*) (= *subscriber trunk dialling*).
амуни́ци|я (-и) ж *собир* ammunition.
Аму́р (-а) м Cupid; *см также* **аму́ры**.
аму́р|ы (-ов) мн (*разг: любовные дела*) intrigues мн, love affairs мн.
амфи́би|я (-и) ж amphibian.
амфитеа́тр (-а) м amphitheatre (*BRIT*), amphitheater (*US*).
АН ж *сокр* (= *Акаде́мия нау́к*) Academy of Sciences ♦ м *сокр* = *самолёт констру́кции О. К. Антоно́ва*.
Ан м *сокр* = **АН**.
ана́лиз (-а) м analysis; **сдава́ть (сдать** *perf*) **кровь/мочу́ на** ~ to give a blood/urine sample; **подверга́ть (подве́ргнуть** *perf*) ~**у** to analyse (*BRIT*), analyze (*US*); ~ **изде́ржек и при́были** (*КОММ*) cost-benefit analysis; ~ **эффекти́вности рабо́ты** time and motion study; **ана́лиз кро́ви** blood test.
анализи́р|овать (-ую; *perf* **проанализи́ровать**) *несов перех* to analyse (*BRIT*), analyze (*US*).
анали́тик (-а) м (*специалист*) analyst; **он хоро́ший** ~ (*склонный к анализу*) he has a very analytical mind.
ана́лог (-а) м analogue (*BRIT*), analog (*US*).
аналоги́ч|ный (-ен, -на, -но) *прил* analogous.
анало́ги|я (-и) ж analogy; **по** ~**и (с** +*instr*) in a similar way (to); **проводи́ть (провести́** *perf*) ~**ю ме́жду** +*instr* to draw an analogy between.
анало́й (-я) м lectern.
ана́мнез (-а) м (*МЕД*) case history.
анана́с (-а) м pineapple.
анархи́зм (-а) м anarchism.
анархи́стск|ий (-ая, -ое, -ие) *прил* anarchist опред.
ана́рхи|я (-и) ж anarchy.
анато́ми|я (-и) ж anatomy.
ана́фем|а (-ы) ж anathema; **предава́ть (преда́ть** *perf*) ~**е** to anathematize.
анахрони́зм (-а) м anachronism.
анахрони́ч|ный (-ен, -на, -но) *прил* anachronistic.
анга́р (-а) м hangar.
а́нгел (-а) м (*также разг*) angel.
а́нгельск|ий (-ая, -ое, -ие) *прил* angelic; **а́нгельское терпе́ние** the patience of a saint.
анги́н|а (-ы) ж tonsillitis, quinsy.
англи́йск|ий (-ая, -ое, -ие) *прил* English; (*британский*) British; ~ **язы́к** English; **англи́йская була́вка** safety pin; **англи́йский газо́н** lawn.
англика́нск|ий (-ая, -ое, -ие) *прил* Anglican; **англика́нская це́рковь** the Anglican church.

англича́н|ин (-ина; *nom pl* -е, *gen pl* -) м Englishman (мн Englishmen).
англича́н|ка (-ки; *gen pl* -ок) ж Englishwoman (мн Englishwomen).
А́нгли|я (-и) ж England.
Анго́л|а (-ы) ж Angola.
анго́л|ец (-ьца) м Angolan.
анго́л|ка (-ки; *gen pl* -ок) ж *см* **анго́лец**.
анго́льск|ий (-ая, -ое, -ие) *прил* Angolan.
анго́льца *итп сущ см* **анго́лец**.
анго́рск|ий (-ая, -ое, -ие) *прил* angora опред; **анго́рская шерсть** angora (wool).
А́нд|ы (-) мн the Andes.
анекдо́т (-а) м joke; **со мной случи́лся** ~ (*разг*) something funny happened to me.
анекдоти́ч|ный (-ен, -на, -но) *прил* (*смешной и странный*) funny.
анеми́ч|ный (-ен, -на, -но) *прил* anaemic (*BRIT*), anemic (*US*).
анеми́|я (-и) ж anaemia (*BRIT*), anemia (*US*).
анестезио́лог (-а) м anaesthetist (*BRIT*), anesthesiologist (*US*).
анестези́р|овать (-ую) (*не*)*сов перех* to anaesthetize (*BRIT*), anesthetize (*US*).
анестези́|я (-и) ж anaesthesia (*BRIT*), anesthesia (*US*); **ме́стная/о́бщая** ~ local/general ana(e)sthesia.
анили́н (-а) м aniline.
анили́новый *прил* aniline опред.
ани́совый *прил* aniseed опред; **ани́совая во́дка** aniseed vodka.
АНК м *сокр* (= *Африка́нский национа́льный конгре́сс*) ANC (= *African National Congress*).
Анкара́ (-ы́) ж Ankara.
анке́т|а (-ы) ж (*опросный лист*) questionnaire; (*бланк для сведений*) form; (*сбор сведений*) survey; **проводи́ть (провести́** *perf*) ~**у** to carry out a survey.
анке́тн|ый *прил*: ~**ые да́нные** personal details мн; **анке́тный лист** questionnaire.
анна́л|ы (-ов) мн annals мн; **в** ~**ах исто́рии** in the annals of history.
анне́кси|я (-и) ж annexation.
аннота́ци|я (-и) ж précis.
анноти́р|овать (-ую; *perf* **проанноти́ровать**) *несов перех* to summarize.
аннуите́т (-а) м (*КОММ*) annuity; **пожи́зненный** ~ life annuity.
аннули́рование| (-я) *ср* (*см глаг*) annulment; repeal; cancellation.
аннули́р|овать (-ую) (*не*)*сов перех* (*брак, договор*) to annul; (*закон*) to repeal; (*долг*) to cancel.
ано́д (-а) м anode.
анома́льный (-ен, -ьна, -ьно) *прил* anomalous.
анони́м (-а) м anonymous author.
анони́мен *прил см* **анони́мный**.
анони́м|ка (-ки; *gen pl* -ок) ж (*разг: пренебр*) poison-pen letter.
анони́м|ный (-ен, -на, -но) *прил* anonymous.
анони́мок *сущ см* **анони́мка**.
ано́нс (-а) м announcement.

анорéкси|я (-и) *ж* anorexia; **онá страдáет ~ей** she is anorexic.

ансáмбл|ь (-я) *м* ensemble; (*танцоров*) troupe; (*эстрадный*) group.

АНТ *м сокр* = самолёт констрýкции А. Н. Тýполева.

антагони́зм (-а) *м* antagonism.

Антаркти́д|а (-ы) *ж* Antarctica.

Антáркти|ка (-и) *ж* Antarctica, the Antarctic.

антаркти́ческ|ий (-ая, -ое, -ие) *прил* Antarctic.

Антвéрпен (-а) *ж* Antwerp.

антéнн|а (-ы) *ж* aerial (*BRIT*), antenna (*US*); **~ косми́ческой свя́зи** satellite dish.

антибио́тик (-а) *м* antibiotic.

антивоéнный *прил* antiwar.

антидемократи́ческ|ий (-ая, -ое, -ие) *прил* antidemocratic.

антиквáр (-а) *м* antiquary.

антиквариáт (-а) *м собир* antiques *мн*.

антиквáр|ный *прил* antique *опред*; **антиквáрный магази́н** antique shop.

антило́п|а (-ы) *ж* antelope.

антинаýчный (-ен, -на, -но) *прил* antiscientific.

антипати́чный (-ен, -на, -но) *прил* unlikable.

антипáти|я (-и) *ж* antipathy.

антипо́д (-а) *м* antithesis.

антирелиги́озный *прил* antireligious.

антисанитáрен *прил см* **антисанитáрный**.

антисанитари́|я (-и) *ж* unhygienic *или* insanitary conditions *мн*.

антисанитáр|ный (-ен, -на, -но) *прил* unhygienic, insanitary.

антисеми́т (-а) *м* anti-Semite.

антисемити́зм (-а) *м* anti-Semitism.

антисеми́т|ка (-ки; *gen pl* -ок) *ж см* **антисеми́т**.

антисеми́ток *сущ см* **антисеми́тка**.

антисеми́тск|ий (-ая, -ое, -ие) *прил* anti-Semitic.

антисéптик (-а) *м* antiseptic.

антисепти́ческ|ий (-ая, -ое, -ие) *прил* antiseptic.

антитéз|а (-ы) *ж* antithesis.

антитéл|о (-а; *nom pl* -á) *ср* (*обычно мн*) antibody.

антифаши́стск|ий (-ая, -ое, -ие) *прил* antifascist.

антифри́з (-а) *м* antifreeze.

анти́христ (-а) *м* Antichrist.

антициклóн (-а) *м* anticyclone.

анти́чность (-и) *ж* antiquity.

анти́чный *прил* classical; **анти́чный мир** the Ancient World.

антоло́ги|я (-и) *ж* anthology.

антóним (-а) *м* antonym.

антóнов|ка (-ки; *gen pl* -ок) *ж* antonovka (*apple*).

антрáкт (-а) *м* interval.

антраци́т (-а) *м* anthracite.

антрекóт (-а) *м* entrecôte.

антрепренёр (-а) *м* impresario.

антресóл|и (-ей) *мн* (*полуэтаж*) mezzanine *ед*; (*балкон*) gallery *ед*; (*под потолком*) cupboard *ед*.

антрополо́ги|я (-и) *ж* anthropology.

анфáс *нареч* full face.

анфилáд|а (-ы) *ж* suite (*of rooms*).

анчóус (-а) *м* anchovy.

аншлáг (-а) *м* (*объявление*) sellout; (*заголовок*) banner headline; **проходи́ть** (**пройти́** *perf*) **с ~ом** to be a sellout.

аню́тины *прил*: **~ глáзки** pansy *ед*.

АО *ж сокр* = автонóмная óбласть ♦ *м сокр* = автонóмный óкруг.

А/О *ср сокр* (= акционéрное óбщество) joint-stock company.

аóрт|а (-ы) *ж* aorta.

АП *м сокр* (= Ассóшиэйтед пресс) AP (= *Associated Press*).

апартéйд (-а) *м* apartheid.

апати́чный (-ен, -на, -но) *прил* apathetic.

апáти|я (-и) *ж* apathy.

апелли́р|овать (-ую) (*не*)*сов неперех* (*ЮР*) to appeal; **~** (*impf/perf*) **к** +*dat* to appeal to.

апелляцио́нный *прил* (*ЮР*) appeal *опред*; **апелляцио́нный суд** court of appeal.

апелля́ци|я (-и) *ж* (*ЮР*) appeal; **~ к** +*dat* appeal to.

апельси́н (-а) *м* orange.

апельси́нный *прил* = **апельси́новый**.

апельси́новый *прил* orange.

аперити́в (-а) *м* aperitif.

АПК *м сокр* = агрáрно-промы́шленный кóмплекс.

аплоди́р|овать (-ую) *несов неперех* (+*dat*) to applaud.

аплодисмéнт|ы (-ов) *мн* applause *ед*.

апло́мб (-а) *м* assurance; **с ~ом** with aplomb.

АПН *ср сокр* (= агéнтство печáти "Нóвости") "Novosti" Press Agency ♦ *ж сокр* (= Акадéмия педагоги́ческих наýк) Academy of Pedagogical Sciences.

апогé|й (-я) *м* (*также перен*) apogee; **он в ~е слáвы** he is at the height of his fame.

апокáлипсис (-а) *м* (*РЕЛ*) (the Book of) Revelation, the Apocalypse.

аполити́чный (-ен, -на, -но) *прил* apolitical.

апологéт (-а) *м* apologist.

апóстол (-а) *м* apostle; (*книга*) the Acts of the Apostles and the Epistles.

апóстольск|ий (-ая, -ое, -ие) *прил* apostolic.

апострóф (-а) *м* apostrophe.

апофеóз (-а) *м* (*восхваление*) apotheosis; (*ТЕАТР*) grand finale.

аппарáт (-а) *м* apparatus; (*ФИЗИОЛОГИЯ*) system; (*штат*) staff; **телефóнный ~** telephone; **госудáрственный ~** state apparatus.

аппарáтн|ая (-ой; *decl like adj*) *ж* equipment room.

аппаратýр|а (-ы) *ж собир* apparatus, equipment;

(*приборы*) instruments *мн*.

аппара́тчик (-а) *м* operative; (*разг: работник аппара́та*) apparatchik.

аппе́ндикс (-а) *м* appendix.

аппендици́т (-а) *м* appendicitis.

аппети́т (-а) *м* appetite; (*обычно мн: перен: разг*) craving; **прия́тного ~а!** bon appétit!; **перебива́ть (переби́ть** *perf*) ~ to spoil one's appetite; **во́лчий ~** a voracious appetite.

аппети́тный (-ен, -на, -но) *прил* appetizing.

апплика́ци|я (-и) *ж* appliqué.

апре́л|ь (-я) *м* April; *см также* **октя́брь**.

апроби́р|овать (-ую) (*не)сов перех* to approve.

апте́к|а (-и) *ж* dispensing chemist's (*BRIT*), pharmacy.

апте́карск|ий (-ая, -ое, -ие) *прил* (*товары*) pharmaceutical.

апте́кар|ь (-я) *м* chemist (*BRIT*), pharmacist.

апте́ч|ка (-ки; *gen pl* -ек) *ж* medicine chest; (*первой помощи*) first-aid kit.

апте́чный *прил* chemist's.

апчхи́ *межд*: ~! atishoo!

ара́б (-а) *м* Arab.

арабе́с|ка (-ки; *gen pl* -ок) *ж* arabesque (*ART*).

ара́б|ка (-ки; *gen pl* -ок) *ж см* **ара́б**.

ара́бск|ий (-ая, -ое, -ие) *прил* (*страны*) Arab; ~ **язы́к** Arabic; **ара́бские ци́фры** Arabic numerals.

арави́ек *сущ см* **арави́йка**.

арави́ец (-**йца**) *м* Arabian.

арави́й|ка (-ки; *gen pl* -ок) *ж см* **арави́ец**.

арави́йск|ий (-ая, -ое, -ие) *прил* Arabian *опред*.

арави́йца *итп сущ см* **арави́ец**.

Ара́ви|я (-и) *ж* Arabia.

ара́льск|ий (-ая, -ое, -ие) *прил*: **А~ое мо́ре** Aral Sea.

аранжи́р|овать (-ую) (*не)сов перех* to arrange.

аранжиро́в|ка (-ки; *gen pl* -ок) *ж* arrangement.

ара́хис (-а) *м* peanut.

ара́хисовый *прил* peanut *опред*.

АРБ *ж сокр* (= *Ассоциа́ция росси́йских ба́нков*) association of Russian banks.

арби́тр (-а) *м* (*в спорах*) arbitrator; (*в футболе*) referee; (*в бейсболе, теннисе*) umpire.

арбитра́ж (-а) *м* arbitration; (*орган*) arbitration service.

арбитра́жный *прил* arbitration *опред*.

арбу́з (-а) *м* watermelon.

Аргенти́н|а (-ы) *ж* Argentina.

аргенти́н|ец (-ца) *м* Argentinian.

аргенти́н|ка (-ки; *gen pl* -ок) *ж см* **аргенти́нец**.

аргенти́нск|ий (-ая, -ое, -ие) *прил* Argentinian.

аргенти́нца *итп сущ см* **аргенти́нец**.

арго́н (-а) *м* argon.

аргуме́нт (-а) *м* (*также МАТ*) argument.

аргумента́ци|я (-и) *ж* argument.

аргументи́р|овать (-ую) (*не)сов перех* to argue.

аре́н|а (-ы) *ж* (*в цирке*) ring; (*часть стадиона, перен*) arena.

аре́нд|а (-ы) *ж* (*наём*) lease; (*плата*) rent; **сдава́ть (сдать** *perf*) **в ~у** to lease.

аренда́тор (-а) *м* leaseholder.

аре́ндн|ый *прил* lease *опред*; **на ~ых нача́лах** on a rental basis; **аре́ндная пла́та** rent; **аре́ндный подря́д** rental agreement, lease.

аренд|ова́ть (-у́ю) (*не)сов перех* to lease.

аре́ст (-а) *м* (*преступника*) arrest; (*имущества*) sequestration; **брать (взять** *perf*) **кого́-н под ~** to place sb under arrest; **налага́ть (наложи́ть** *perf*) ~ **на** +*acc* to sequester; **находи́ться** (*impf*) **под ~ом** to be under arrest.

аресто́ванн|ая (-ой; *decl like adj*) *ж см* **аресто́ванный**.

аресто́ванн|ый (-ого; *decl like adj*) *м person held in custody*.

арест|ова́ть (-у́ю; *impf* **аресто́вывать**) *сов перех* (*преступника*) to arrest; (*имущество*) to sequestrate.

аристокра́т (-а) *м* aristocrat.

аристократи́ческ|ий (-ая, -ое, -ие) *прил* aristocratic.

аристокра́ти|я (-и) *ж* aristocracy.

аритми́|я (-и) *ж* arrhythmia (*irregular heartbeat*).

арифме́тик|а (-и) *ж* arithmetic.

арифмети́ческ|ий (-ая, -ое, -ие) *прил* arithmetic(al).

а́ри|я (-и) *ж* aria.

АРКА *м сокр* (= *Америка́но-Росси́йский комме́рческий алья́нс*) *American-Russian commercial alliance*.

а́р|ка (-ки; *gen pl* -ок) *ж* arch.

арка́д|а (-ы) *ж* (*АРХИТ*) arcade.

арка́н (-а) *м* lasso.

арка́н|ить (-ю, -ишь; *perf* **заарка́нить**) *несов перех* to lasso.

А́рктик|а (-и) *ж* the Arctic.

аркти́ческ|ий (-ая, -ое, -ие) *прил* Arctic.

арлеки́н (-а) *м* harlequin.

армату́р|а (-ы) *ж собир* (*СТРОИТ*) steel framework; (*вспомогательные устройства*) fittings *мн*.

арме́йск|ий (-ая, -ое, -ие) *прил* army *опред*.

Арме́ни|я (-и) *ж* Armenia.

а́рми|я (-и) *ж* army; (*перен*): ~ +*gen* (*помощников, читателей*) army of.

армяни́н (-а; *nom pl* **армя́не**, *gen pl* **армя́н**) *м* Armenian.

армя́н|ка (-ки; *gen pl* -ок) *ж см* **армяни́н**.

армя́нск|ий (-ая, -ое, -ие) *прил* Armenian *опред*; ~ **язы́к** Armenian.

а́рок *сущ см* **а́рка**.

арома́т (-а) *м* (*цветов*) fragrance; (*кофе итп*) aroma; (*перен: молодости*) spirit.

арома́тен *прил см* **арома́тный**.

аромати́ческ|ий (-ая, -ое, -ие) *прил* aromatic.

арома́тн|ый (-ен, -на, -но) *прил* fragrant.

арсена́л (-а) *м* (*склад*) arsenal; (*завод*) munitions factory; **в ~е** (*перен*) at one's disposal.

арта́ч|иться (-усь, -ишься) *несов возв* (*разг*) to be pig-headed.

артезиа́нск|ий (**-ая, -ое, -ие**) *прил* artesian.
арте́л|ь (**-и**) *ж worker's or peasant's cooperative.*
арте́льн|ый *прил* collective *опред*; **на ~ых нача́лах** on a collective basis.
артериа́льн|ый *прил*: **~ое давле́ние** blood pressure.
арте́ри|я (**-и**) *ж (также перен)* artery; **со́нная ~** carotid artery.
арти́кл|ь (**-я**) *м (линг)* article.
артиллери́йск|ий (**-ая, -ое, -ие**) *прил* artillery *опред.*
артиллери́ст (**-а**) *м* artilleryman (*мн* artillerymen), gunner (*вRIT*).
артилле́ри|я (**-и**) *ж* artillery.
арти́ст (**-а**) *м* artist(e); (*кино*) actor; **он ~ расска́зывать исто́рии** he's ace at telling stories.
артисти́ческ|ий (**-ая, -ое, -ие**) *прил* artistic; **~ая убо́рная** dressing room.
арти́ст|ка (**-ки**; *gen pl* **-ок**) *ж (см м)* artist(e); actress.
артишо́к (**-а**) *м* (globe) artichoke.
артри́т (**-а**) *м* arthritis.
а́рф|а (**-ы**) *ж* harp.
арфи́ст (**-а**) *м* harpist.
арфи́ст|ка (**-ки**; *gen pl* **-ок**) *ж см* **арфи́ст**.
арха́йзм (**-а**) *м* archaism.
арха́йчный (**-ен, -на, -но**) *прил* archaic.
арха́нгел (**-а**) *м* archangel.
Арха́нгельск (**-а**) *м* Archangel.
архео́лог (**-а**) *м* archaeologist (*вRIT*), archeologist.
археологи́ческ|ий (**-ая, -ое, -ие**) *прил* archaeological.
археоло́ги|я (**-и**) *ж* archaeology.
архи́в (**-а**) *м* (*учреждение, отдел*) archive; (*собрание рукописей итп*) archives *мн*; **сда́ть** (*perf*) **что-н в ~** (*перен*) to consign sth to history.
архива́риус (**-а**) *м* archivist.
архи́вный *прил* archival; **~ файл** (*комп*) archive file.
архиепи́скоп (**-а**) *м* archbishop.
архиере́й (**-я**) *м general term for upper orders of the church.*
архимандри́т (**-а**) *м* archimandrite.
архипела́г (**-а**) *м* archipelago.
архите́ктор (**-а**) *м* architect.
архитекту́р|а (**-ы**) *ж* architecture.
архитекту́рный *прил* architectural.
арши́н (**-а**; *gen pl* **-** *или* **-ов**) *м* (*устаревший*) arshin (*unit of measurement equal to 0.71 m*); **ме́рить** (*impf*) **кого́-н на свой ~** (*перен*) to judge sb by one's own standards.
арши́нный *прил* (*разг*) *very big, tall, high or long.*
ас (**-а**) *м* (*лётчик*) ace; (*перен*) expert.
асбе́ст (**-а**) *м* asbestos.
АСЕА́Н *ж сокр* ASEAN (= *Association of South-*

East Asian Nations).
асепти́ческ|ий (**-ая, -ое, -ие**) *прил* aseptic.
асимметри́ч|ный (**-ен, -на, -но**) *прил* asymmetric(al).
асимме́три|я (**-и**) *ж* asymmetry.
аске́т (**-а**) *м* ascetic.
аскети́зм (**-а**) *м* asceticism.
аскети́ческ|ий (**-ая, -ое, -ие**) *прил* ascetic *опред.*
аскорби́нов|ый *прил*: **~ая кислота́** ascorbic acid.
аспе́кт (**-а**) *м* aspect; **в ~е** + *gen* in (the) light of.
аспира́нт (**-а**) *м* postgraduate (*doing a PhD*).
аспиранту́р|а (**-ы**) *ж* postgraduate studies *мн* (*leading to a PhD*).
аспири́н (**-а**) *м* aspirin.
ассамбле́|я (**-и**) *ж* assembly; **Генера́льная А~ Организа́ции Объединённых На́ций** General Assembly of the United Nations.
ассе́мблер (**-а**) *м* (*комп*) assembler.
ассениза́ци|я (**-и**) *ж* sewage disposal system.
ассигнова́ни|е (**-я**) *ср* allocation.
ассигн|ова́ть (**-у́ю**) (*не*)*сов перех* to allocate.
ассимили́р|овать (**-ую**) (*не*)*сов перех* to assimilate
► **ассимили́роваться** (*не*)*сов возв* to become assimilated.
ассимиля́ци|я (**-и**) *ж* assimilation.
ассисте́нт (**-а**) *м* assistant; (*в вузе*) assistant lecturer.
ассисти́р|овать (**-ую**) *несов неперех* (+*dat*) to assist.
ассорти́ *ср нескл* assortment.
ассортиме́нт (**-а**) *м* assortment.
ассоциати́в|ный (**-ен, -на, -но**) *прил* based on association.
ассоциа́ци|я (**-и**) *ж* association.
ассоции́р|овать (**-ую**) (*не*)*сов перех*: **~ что-н с кем-н/чем-н** to associate sth with sb/sth
► **ассоции́роваться** (*не*)*сов возв*: **~ся с** +*instr* to be associated with.
АССР *ж сокр* (*ист*: = *автоно́мная сове́тская социалисти́ческая республика*) ASSR (= *Autonomous Soviet Socialist Republic*).
астеро́ид (**-а**) *м* asteroid.
астигмати́зм (**-а**) *м* astigmatism.
а́стм|а (**-ы**) *ж* asthma.
астма́тик (**-а**) *м* asthmatic.
астмати́ческ|ий (**-ая, -ое, -ие**) *прил* asthmatic.
а́стр|а (**-ы**) *ж* aster.
астро́лог (**-а**) *м* astrologer.
астроло́ги|я (**-и**) *ж* astrology.
астрона́вт (**-а**) *м* astronaut.
астрона́втик|а (**-и**) *ж* astronautics.
астроно́м (**-а**) *м* astronomer.
астрономи́ческ|ий (**-ая, -ое, -ие**) *прил* (*также перен*) astronomic(al).
астроно́ми|я (**-и**) *ж* astronomy.

АСУ ж сокр (= автоматизи́рованная систе́ма управле́ния) automatic control system.

асфа́льт (-а) м asphalt.

асфальти́р|овать (-ую; perf **заасфальти́ровать**) (не)сов перех to asphalt.

асфикси́|я (-и) ж asphyxia.

ата́к|а (-и) ж (также перен) attack; **идти́ (пойти́** perf) **в ~у** to launch an attack; **~ на кого́-н/что-н** an attack on sb/sth.

атак|ова́ть (-у́ю) (не)сов перех (также перен) to attack.

атама́н (-а) м ataman (Cossack leader); (перен: банды) leader.

атеи́зм (-а) м atheism.

атеи́ст (-а) м atheist.

атеи́ст|ка (-ки; gen pl **-ок**) ж см **атеи́ст**.

атеисти́ческ|ий (-ая, -ое, -ие) прил atheist опред.

атеи́сток сущ см **атеи́стка**.

ателье́ ср нескл (художника, фотографа) studio; (мод) tailor's shop; **телевизио́нное ~** television repair shop; **ателье́ прока́та** rental shop.

атланти́ческ|ий (-ая, -ое, -ие) прил: **А~ океа́н** Atlantic Ocean.

а́тлас (-а) м atlas.

атла́с (-а) м satin.

атла́сный прил satin; (шелкови́стый) satiny; **атла́сная ко́жа** (перен) skin like satin.

атле́т (-а) м athlete; (крепкий человек) muscleman.

атлети́зм (-а) м (телосложение) athletic build; (культуризм) body building.

атле́тик|а (-и) ж athletics; **лёгкая ~** track and field events; **тяжёлая ~** weightlifting.

атлети́ческ|ий (-ая, -ое, -ие) прил athletic.

АТМ ж сокр (= автомати́ческая ка́ссовая маши́на) ATM (= automated telling machine).

атмосфе́р|а (-ы) ж (также перен) atmosphere.

атмосфе́рный прил atmospheric.

а́том (-а) м atom.

а́томный прил atomic; **а́томный вес** atomic weight.

а́томщик (-а) м (разг) atomic scientist.

атрибу́т (-а) м attribute.

атрибути́вный прил (линг) attributive.

атрофи́рованный прил atrophied.

атрофи́р|оваться (3sg **-уется**, 3pl **-уются**) (не)сов возв to atrophy.

атрофи́|я (-и) ж atrophy.

АТС ж сокр (= автомати́ческая телефо́нная ста́нция) automatic telephone exchange.

атташе́ м нескл attaché.

аттеста́т (-а) м certificate; **аттеста́т зре́лости** certificate attained for passing school-leaving examinations.

аттеста́ци|я (-и) ж certification; (отзыв) recommendation.

аттест|ова́ть (-у́ю) (не)сов перех (давать характеристику) to recommend; (оценивать знания) to give a mark.

аттракцио́н (-а) м (цирковой номер) attraction; (качели, карусель итп) amusement.

ау́ межд hallo (cry for attention).

аудие́нци|я (-и) ж (приём) audience.

ауди́т (-а) м (КОММ) audit; **о́бщий ~** general audit.

аудито́ри|я (-и) ж (помещение) lecture hall ♦ собир (слушатели) audience.

аукцио́н (-а) м auction; **продава́ть (прода́ть** perf) **что-н с ~a** to sell sth by auction; **покупа́ть (купи́ть** perf) **что-н на ~е** to buy sth at an auction.

аукционе́р (-а) м person attending an auction.

аукциони́ст (-а) м auctioneer.

аул (-а) м aul (mountain village in the Caucasus and Middle Asia).

а́ут (-а) м (в теннисе) out; (в футболе): **мяч в а́уте** the ball is out of play; (в боксе): **~!** knockout!

аутенти́ч|ный (-ен, -на, -но) прил authentic.

аутоге́нн|ый прил: **~ая трениро́вка** autogenic training.

аутса́йдер (-а) м outsider.

афга́н|ец (-ца) м Afghan; (ветеран) Afghan war veteran.

Афганиста́н (-а) м Afghanistan.

афга́н|ка (-ки; gen pl **-ок**) ж см **афга́нец**.

афга́нца итп сущ см **афга́нец**.

афе́р|а (-ы) ж swindle.

афери́ст (-а) м swindler.

афери́ст|ка (-ки; gen pl **-ок**) ж см **афери́ст**.

Афи́н|ы (-) мн Athens.

афи́ш|а (-и) ж poster.

афиши́р|овать (-ую) (не)сов перех to parade.

афори́зм (-а) м aphorism.

А́фрик|а (-и) ж Africa.

африка́н|ец (-ца) м African.

африка́н|ка (-ки; gen pl **-ок**) ж см **африка́нец**.

африка́нск|ий (-ая, -ое, -ие) прил African.

африка́нца итп сущ см **африка́нец**.

аффе́кт (-а) м fit of passion.

ах межд: **~!** oh!, ah!; **~ да!** (разг) ah yes!; **не ~** (разг) not up to much.

а́ха|ть (-ю; perf **а́хнуть**) несов неперех (разг) to express surprise, regret etc.

ахиле́сова прил: **~ пята́** Achilles' heel.

ахине́|я (-и) ж (разг) rubbish; **нести́** (impf) **~ю** to talk rubbish.

а́хн|уть (-у, -ешь) сов от **а́хать** ♦ неперех (разг: орудие итп) to bang ♦ перех (разг: сломать) to smash; (: выпить) to knock back; **он и ~ не успе́л, как они́ убежа́ли** (разг) before he could get a word out, they ran away.

АХО м сокр (= администрати́вно-хозя́йственный отде́л) department concerned with property and maintenance.

ахти́ межд (разг): **не ~ как** not specially; **не ~ (како́й)** (разг) not specially good.

ацето́н (-а) м acetone.

Ашхаба́д (-а) м Ashkhabad.

аэро́бик|а (-и) ж aerobics.

аэро́бус (-а) м airbus.

аэровокза́л (-а) м air terminal (*BRIT*).
аэродина́мик|а (-и) ж aerodynamics.
аэродинами́ческ|ий (-ая, -ое, -ие) *прил*
  aerodynamic; **аэродинами́ческая труба́** wind
  tunnel.
аэродро́м (-а) м aerodrome.
аэрозо́л|ь (-я) м aerosol.
аэро́н (-а) м air-sickness tablets *мн*.

аэропла́н (-а) м aeroplane (*BRIT*), airplane (*US*).
аэропо́рт (-а; *loc sg* -у́) м airport.
аэроста́т (-а) м aerostat.
аэрофотосъём|ка (-ки; *gen pl* -ок) ж aerial
  photography.
АЭС ж *сокр* (= *а́томная электроста́нция*)
  atomic power station.
аятолл|а́ (-ы́) м ayatollah.

~ Б, б ~

Б, б *сущ нескл (буква)* the 2nd letter of the Russian alphabet.

б *част см* **бы**.

ба *межд* well, well!; ~! **кого́ я ви́жу!** gosh! look who it is!

ба́б|а (**-ы**) *ж (разг)* woman; (: *пренебр: мужчина*) old woman.

ба́б|а-яга́ (**-ы, -й**) *ж* Baba Yaga (*old witch in Russian folk-tales*); (*разг*) old witch (*fig*).

ба́б|ий (**-ья, -ье, -ьи**) *прил (разг: пренебр)* womanish; **ба́бье ле́то** Indian summer; **ба́бьи разгово́ры** women's talk; **ба́бьи ска́зки** old wives' tales.

ба́б|ка (**-ки**; *gen pl* **-ок**) *ж (бабушка)* grandmother; (*разг: старуха*) old woman.

ба́боч|ка (**-ки**; *gen pl* **-ек**) *ж* butterfly; (*галстук*) bow tie.

ба́буш|ка (**-ки**; *gen pl* **-ек**) *ж* grandma, granny; (*разг*) old woman; ~ **на́двое сказа́ла** we shall see (what we shall see).

Бава́ри|я (**-и**) *ж* Bavaria.

бава́рск|ий (**-ая, -ое, -ие**) *прил* Bavarian.

бага́ж (**-а́**) *м* luggage (*BRIT*), baggage (*US*); **сдава́ть (сдать** *perf*) **ве́щи в** ~ to check in one's luggage (*BRIT*) *или* bags (*US*); **отправля́ть (отпра́вить** *perf*) **багажо́м** to send as unaccompanied baggage; **бага́ж зна́ний** knowledge.

бага́жник (**-а**) *м (в автомобиле)* boot (*BRIT*), trunk (*US*); (*на крыше автомобиля*) roof rack; (*на велосипеде*) carrier.

бага́жный *прил (BRIT)*, baggage *опред (US)*.

бага́мск|ий (**-ая, -ое, -ие**) *прил:* **Б~ие острова́** Bahama Islands, Bahamas.

Багда́д (**-а**) *м* Baghdad.

багрове́|ть (**-ю**; *perf* **побагрове́ть**) *несов неперех* to turn crimson; (*no perf; цветы*) to show crimson.

багро́в|ый (**-, -а, -о**) *прил* crimson.

багря́н|ый (**-, -а, -о**) *прил* crimson.

бадминто́н (**-а**) *м* badminton.

бадминтони́ст (**-а**) *м* badminton player.

бадминтони́ст|ка (**-ки**; *gen pl* **-ок**) *ж см* **бадминтони́ст**.

ба́з|а (**-ы**) *ж* basis; (*ВОЕН, АРХИТ*) base; (*для туристов, спортсменов*) centre (*BRIT*), center (*US*); (*продовольствия, товаров*) warehouse; **на** ~**е** +*gen* on the basis of; **ба́за да́нных**

database.

база́льт (**-а**) *м* basalt.

база́р (**-а**) *м* market; (*новогодний, книжный итп*) fair; (*перен: разг*) racket; **пти́чий** ~ bird colony.

база́рный *прил* market *опред*; **база́рная ба́ба** (*разг*) fishwife.

базили́к|а (**-и**) *ж* basilica.

бази́р|овать (**-ую**) *несов перех:* ~ **что-н на** +*prp* to base sth on

▶ **бази́роваться** *несов возв* to be based; ~**ся** (*impf*) **на** +*prp (на фактах итп)* to be based on.

ба́зис (**-а**) *м* basis.

байда́р|ка (**-ки**; *gen pl* **-ок**) *ж* canoe.

ба́йк|а (**-и**) *ж* flannelette.

Байка́л (**-а**) *м* Lake Baikal.

ба́йковый *прил* flannelette.

байт (**-а**; *gen pl* -) *м* byte.

бак (**-а**) *м* tank; (*МОР*) forecastle, fo'c'sle.

бакале́йн|ый *прил:* ~ **магази́н** grocer's shop (*BRIT*), grocery store (*US*); ~**ые това́ры** groceries.

бакале́|я (**-и**) *ж (в магазине)* grocery section; (*товары*) groceries *мн*.

ба́кен (**-а**) *м* buoy.

бакенба́рд|ы (-) *мн* sideburns *мн*.

баклажа́н (**-а**; *gen pl* **-или -ов**) *м* aubergine (*BRIT*), eggplant (*US*).

баклу́ши *мн:* **бить** ~ (*разг*) to idle away one's time.

бактериологи́ческ|ий (**-ая, -ое, -ие**) *прил* bacteriological; **бактериологи́ческая война́** germ *или* bacteriological warfare.

бактеници́дный *прил* bactericidal, germicidal.

бакте́ри|я (**-и**) *ж* bacterium (*мн* bacteria).

Баку́ *м нескл* Baku.

бал (**-а**; *loc sg* **-у́**, *nom pl* **-ы́**) *м (вечер)* ball.

балага́н (**-а**) *м (перен: разг)* farce.

балала́йк|а (**-йки**; *gen pl* **-ек**) *ж* balalaika.

бала́нс (**-а**) *м (также КОММ)* balance; (*ведомость*) balance sheet; **расчётный** ~ balance of claims and liabilities; **бухга́лтерский** ~ balance sheet; **платёжный/торго́вый** ~ balance of payments/trade.

баланси́р|овать (**-ую**) *несов неперех:* ~ **(на** +*prp*) to balance (on) ◆ (*perf* **сбаланси́ровать**) *перех (КОММ)* to balance; ~ (*impf*) **на гра́ни чего́-н** (*перен*) to be poised on the verge *или* brink of sth.

бала́нсовый *прил* balance *опред*; **бала́нсовый**

отчёт balance sheet.

балахо́н (-а) м (*разг*) sack (*baggy, shapeless garment*).

балд|а́ (-ы́) м/ж chump.

балери́н|а (-ы) ж ballerina.

бале́т (-а) м ballet.

балетме́йстер (-а) м ballet master.

ба́л|ка (-ки; *gen pl* -ок) ж (*железобетонная, деревянная*) beam; (*металлическая*) girder; (*овраг*) gully.

Балка́н|ы (-) мн the Balkans.

балко́н (-а) м (*АРХИТ*) balcony; (*ТЕАТР*) circle (*BRIT*), balcony (*US*).

балл (-а) м (*на экзамене*) mark; (*на соревновании*) point; **проходно́й** ~ pass mark; **ве́тер си́лой в 5 ба́ллов** a force 5 wind.

балла́д|а (-ы) ж ballad.

балла́ст (-а) м ballast; (*перен*) dead weight.

балли́стик|а (-и) ж ballistics.

баллисти́ческ|ий (-ая, -ое, -ие) *прил* ballistic *опред*; **баллисти́ческая раке́та** ballistic missile.

балло́н (-а) м (*газовый*) cylinder; (*с жидкостью*) jar; (*с кислотой, щёлочью*) carboy; (*АВТ*) balloon tyre.

баллоти́р|овать (-ую) *несов перех* to vote for
▶ **баллоти́роваться** *несов возв*: ~**ся в** +*acc или* **на пост** +*gen* to stand (*BRIT*) *или* run (*US*) for.

баллотиро́вочный *прил*: ~ **бюллете́нь** ballot paper.

ба́л|овать (-ую; *perf* **избалова́ть**) *несов перех* to spoil
▶ **ба́ловаться** *несов возв* to fool around.

ба́лок *сущ см* **ба́лка**.

балти́йск|ий (-ая, -ое, -ие) *прил*: **Б**~**ое мо́ре** the Baltic (Sea).

бальза́м (-а) м balsam; (*перен*) balm.

бальзами́р|овать (-ую) (*не*)*сов перех* to embalm.

ба́льн|ый *прил*: ~**ое пла́тье** ball gown; **ба́льные та́нцы** ballroom dancing.

балюстра́д|а (-ы) ж balustrade.

БАМ (-а) м *сокр* (= Байка́ло-Аму́рская (*железнодоро́жная*) магистра́ль) Baikal-Amur Railway.

бамбу́к (-а) м bamboo.

ба́мпер (-а) м bumper.

БАН м *сокр* (= Библиоте́ка Акаде́мии нау́к) *library of the Academy of Sciences.*

бана́лен *прил см* **бана́льный**.

бана́льность (-и) ж banality, platitude.

бана́л|ьный (-ен, -ьна, -ьно) *прил* banal, trite.

бана́н (-а) м banana.

Бангладе́ш (-а) м Bangladesh.

бангладе́шск|ий (-ая, -ое, -ие) *прил* Bangladeshi.

ба́нд|а (-ы) ж gang.

банда́ж (-а́) м support bandage.

бандеро́л|ь (-и) ж package; **я посла́л кни́гу** ~**ю** I packaged the book and sent it.

банди́т (-а) м bandit.

банк (-а) м bank; **сберега́тельный** ~ savings bank; **акционе́рный** ~ joint-stock bank; **э́кспортно-и́мпортный** ~ export-import bank.

ба́н|ка (-ки; *gen pl* -ок) ж (*стеклянная*) jar; (*жестяная*) tin (*BRIT*), can (*US*); (*обычно мн*: *МЕД*) cupping glass.

банке́т (-а) м banquet.

банки́р (-а) м banker.

банкно́т (-а; *gen pl* -) м banknote.

ба́нковск|ий (-ая, -ое, -ие) *прил* bank *опред*.

банкро́т (-а) м bankrupt; **объявля́ть** (**объяви́ть** *perf*) **кого́-н** ~**ом** to declare sb bankrupt.

банкро́тств|о (-а) *ср* bankruptcy.

ба́нный *прил* bath *опред*.

ба́нок *сущ см* **ба́нка**.

бант (-а) м bow.

ба́н|я (-и; *gen pl* -ь) ж bathhouse; (*разг*: *мытьё*) bath; **фи́нская** ~ sauna; **ру́сская/туре́цкая** ~ Russian/Turkish baths; **задава́ть** (**зада́ть** *perf*) **кому́-н** ~**ю** (*разг*) to give sb what for.

бапти́зм (-а) м baptism.

бапти́ст (-а) м Baptist.

бар (-а) м bar; (*gen pl* -; *ФИЗ*) bar.

бараба́н (-а) м drum.

бараба́н|ить (-ю, -ишь) *несов неперех* to drum.

бараба́нн|ый *прил*: ~**ая перепо́нка** eardrum.

бара́к (-а) м barracks мн.

бара́н (-а) м sheep; **смотре́ть** (*impf*) **на кого́-н/что-н как** ~ **на но́вые воро́та** (*разг*) to gawk at sb/sth; **ста́д|о** ~**ов** (*также перен*: *пренебр*) flock of sheep.

бара́н|ий (-ья, -ье, -ьи) *прил* (*суп, котлета*) lamb; (*тулуп*) sheepskin.

бара́нин|а (-ы) ж mutton; (*молодая*) lamb.

бара́н|ка (-ки; *gen pl* -ок) ж small, hard bread ring; (*перен*: *разг*) wheel.

барахл|о́ (-а́) *ср собир* junk; (*разг*: человек, вещь) trash.

барахо́л|ка (-ки; *gen pl* -ок) ж flea market.

бара́хта|ться (-юсь) *несов возв* (*разг*) to flounder; (*играя*) to wallow.

бара́шек (-ка) м (*разг*) lamb; (*шкура*) lambskin; *см также* **бара́шки**.

бара́шк|и (-ов) мн (*облака*) fleecy clouds мн; (*волны*) white horses мн, whitecaps мн.

барбари́с (-а) м barberry.

бард (-а) м singer-songwriter.

барда́к (-а́) м (*груб!*: *беспорядок*) hell broke loose (*!*)

барелье́ф (-а) м bas-relief.

ба́ренцев (-а, -о, -ы) *прил*: **Б**~**о мо́ре** Barents Sea.

ба́рж|а (-и) ж barge.

ба́рин (-а; *nom pl* **господа́**, *gen pl* **госпо́д**) м (*ИСТ*) ≈ lord (*member of the landowning gentry*);

жить *(impf)* **как ~** to live like a king.
баритóн (-а) *м* baritone.
бáрмен (-а) *м* barman (*мн* barmen), bartender (*US*).
барокáмер|а (-ы) *ж* pressure chamber.
барóкко *ср нескл* baroque.
барóметр (-а) *м* barometer.
баррéл|ь (-я) *м* barrel (*unit of measurement*).
баррикáд|а (-ы) *ж* barricade; **быть** *(impf)* **по рáзные стóроны баррикáд** to be on opposite sides of the fence.
баррикади́р|овать (-ую; *perf* **забаррикади́ровать**) *несов перех* to barricade.
барс (-а) *м* snow leopard.
Барселóн|а (-ы) *ж* Barcelona.
бáрск|ий (-ая, -ое, -ие) *прил (перен)* lordly, haughty; **бáрская усáдьба** manor house.
барсýк (-á) *м* badger.
бáртер (-а) *м* barter; **по ~у** on a barter basis.
бáртерн|ый *прил*: **~ая торгóвля** goods *мн* for barter; **на ~ой оснóве** on a barter basis.
бáрхат (-а) *м* velvet.
бáрхатный *прил* velvet; (*перен: кожа, голос*) velvety; **бáрхатный сезóн** *warm autumn days by the sea.*
барьéр (-а) *м* (*в беге*) hurdle; (*на скачках*) fence; (*перен*) barrier; **тари́фный ~** tariff barrier.
бас (-а; *nom pl* -ы́) *м* bass.
бáсен *сущ см* **бáсня**.
баскетбóл (-а) *м* basketball.
баскетболи́ст (-а) *м* basketball player.
баскетболи́ст|ка (-ки; *gen pl* -ок) *ж см* **баскетболи́ст**.
баснослóв|ный (-ен, -на, -но) *прил* fabulous.
бáс|ня (-ни; *gen pl* -ен) *ж* fable; (*обычно мн: перен: разг*) fairy story.
басóвый *прил* bass *опред*.
бассéйн (-а) *м* (*swimming*) pool; (*реки, озера итп*) basin; **каменноугóльный ~** coalfield.
бастовáть (-ýю) *несов неперех* to be on strike.
батальóн (-а) *м* battalion.
батарéй|ка (-йки; *gen pl* -ек) *ж* (*ЭЛЕК*) battery.
батарé|я (-и) *ж* (*отопительная*) radiator; (*ВОЕН, ЭЛЕК*) battery.
бати́ст (-а) *м* cambric, lawn.
батóн (-а) *м* (white) loaf (*long or oval*).
батрáк (-á) *м* farm hand.
батрá́ч|ка (-ки; *gen pl* -ек) *ж см* **батрáк**.
баттерфля́|й (-я) *м* butterfly (stroke).
бáтюш|ка (-ки; *gen pl* -ек) *м* (*также РЕЛ*) father; *см также* **бáтюшки**.
бáтюшки *межд*: **~ (мой)!** good heavens!
бах *межд* bang.
бáхн|уть (-у, -ешь; *impf* **бáхать**) *сов (не)перех* to bang.
Бахрéйн (-а) *м* Bahrain.
бахром|á (-ы́) *ж* fringe.
бахч|á (-и́) *ж* melon or pumpkin patch.
бахчевы́е *прил*: **~ культýры** *melons or pumpkins.*
баци́лл|а (-ы) *ж* bacillus (*мн* bacilli).

бáшен *сущ см* **бáшня**.
башк|á (-и́) *ж* (*разг*) head.
башмáк (-á) *м* (*туфля*) shoe; (*ботинок*) boot; **деревя́нный ~** clog; **быть** *(impf)* **под башмакóм у когó-н** to be under sb's thumb.
бáш|ня (-ни; *gen pl* -ен) *ж* tower; (*ВОЕН*) gun turret; (*разг*) tower block.
баю-бáй *межд* refrain (*in lullaby*).
баю́ка|ть (-ю) *несов перех* to lull to sleep.
бáюшки-баю́ *межд см* **баю-бáй**.
бая́н (-а) *м* bayan (*kind of concertina*).
БВЛ *ж сокр* (= Библиотéка всеми́рной литерату́ры) series of books on world literature.
бди́тельн|ый (-ен, -ьна, -ьно) *прил* vigilant.
бег (-а) *м* running; (*СПОРТ*) race; **~ на дли́нные диста́нции** long-distance race; **~ на корóткие диста́нции** sprint; *см также* **бегá**.
бег|á (-óв) *мн* the races *мн*; **быть** *(impf)* **в ~х** (*разг*) to be on the run *или* go.
бéга|ть (-ю) *несов неперех* to run; (*челнок*) to fly to and fro; **~** *(impf)* **от** +*gen* (*разг*) to avoid; **~** *(impf)* **за кем-н** (*разг*) to chase *или* run after sb; **у негó глазá ~ли** he looked shifty.
бегемóт (-а) *м* hippopotamus.
беги́(те) *несов см* **бежáть**.
беглéц (-á) *м* fugitive.
бéгло *нареч* (*читать, говорить*) fluently; (*просмотреть, ознакомиться*) cursorily.
бéглый *прил* (*каторжник, преступник*) escaped; (*крепостной*) runaway *опред*; (*речь, чтение*) fluent; (*обзор*) cursory; **бéглые гла́сные** fleeting vowels; **бéглый огóнь** (*ВОЕН*) rapid fire.
бегля́н|ка (-ки; *gen pl* -ок) *ж см* **беглéц**.
беговóй *прил* (*лошадь*) race *опред*; (*лыжи*) racing; **~ая дорóжка** running track.
бегóм *нареч* quickly; (*перен: разг*) in a rush; **бежáть** *(impf)* **~** to race, fly.
бегóни|я (-и) *ж* begonia.
бéгств|о (-а) *ср* (*из плена*) escape; (*из дома*) flight; (*с поля боя*) rout; **обращáть (обрати́ть** *perf*) **в ~** to rout; **спасáться (спасти́сь** *perf*) **~м** to escape.
бегý *итп несов см* **бежáть**.
бегýн (-á) *м* runner.
бегýнь|я (-и) *ж см* **бегýн**.
бед|á (-ы́; *nom pl* -ы) *ж* tragedy; (*личная*) misfortune; **прóсто ~!** it's just awful!; **попадáть (попáсть** *perf*) **в ~ý** to get into trouble; **быть** *(impf)* **в ~é** to be in trouble; **~ в том, что** the trouble is (that) ...; **~ (мне)** с ним (*разг*) he's nothing but trouble (to me); **на ~ý** (*разг*) unfortunately; **не ~!** (*разг*) (it's) nothing!; **лихá ~ начáло** (*разг*) the first step is always the hardest.
бéден *прил см* **бéдный**.
бёдер *сущ см* **бедрó**.
беднé|ть (-ю; *perf* **обеднéть**) *несов неперех* to become poor.
бéдность (-и) *ж* (*также перен*) poverty.

бе́д|ный (**-ен, -на́, -но**) *прил* poor.
бедня́г|а (**-и**) *м/ж (разг)* poor thing.
бедня́к (**-а́**) *м* poor man.
бе́дренный *прил (см сущ)* thigh *опред*; hip *опред*.
бедр|о́ (**-а́**; *nom pl* **бёдра**, *gen pl* **бёдер**) *ср* (*верхняя часть ноги*) thigh; (*таз*) hip.
бе́дствен|ный (**-, -на, -но**) *прил* disastrous.
бе́дстви|е (**-я**) *ср* disaster.
бе́дств|овать (**-ую**) *несов неперех* to live in poverty.
бежа́ть (*см* Table 20) *несов неперех* to run; (*время*) to fly; (*облака*) to scud ♦ (*не)сов (из плена, из тюрьмы*) to escape.
бе́жевый *прил* beige.
бе́жен|ец (**-ца**) *м* refugee.
бе́жен|ка (**-ки**; *gen pl* **-ок**) *ж см* **бе́женец**.
бе́женца *итп сущ см* **бе́женец**.
бежи́шь *итп несов см* **бежа́ть**.
без *предл* (+*gen*) without; ~ **пяти́/десяти́ мину́т шесть** five to/ten to six; **не** ~ +*gen* (*труда, осложений*) not without; **и** ~ **того́** (*и так уже*) already; **не** ~ **того́** (*разг*) sort of; ~ **уста́ли** tirelessly; ~ **тебя́ пробле́м хвата́ет** there are enough problems without you adding to them *.
безава́рийный *прил* accident-free.
безала́бер|ный (**-ен, -на, -но**) *прил (разг)* sloppy.
безалкого́льный *прил* nonalcoholic, alcohol-free; **безалкого́льный напи́ток** soft drink.
безапелляцио́н|ный (**-ен, -на, -но**) *прил (тон, ответ*) peremptory; (*ЮР: решение*) final; ~**ый приговор** *a sentence without the right of appeal*.
безбе́д|ный (**-ен, -на, -но**) *прил* comfortable.
безбиле́тник (**-а**) *м (разг: пассажир)* fare dodger.
безбиле́тниц|а (**-ы**) *ж см* **безбиле́тник**.
безбо́жен *прил см* **безбо́жный**.
безбо́жник (**-а**) *м (разг)* heathen.
безбо́жно *нареч (разг)* shamelessly.
безбо́ж|ный (**-ен, -на, -но**) *прил (разг)* shameless.
безболе́знен|ный (**-, -на, -но**) *прил (также перен*) painless.
безбоя́знен|ный (**-, -на, -но**) *прил* fearless.
безбра́чи|е (**-я**) *ср* celibacy.
безбре́ж|ный (**-ен, -на, -но**) *прил (также перен*) boundless.
безве́ст|ный (**-ен, -на, -но**) *прил* unknown.
безве́трен|ный (**-, -на, -но**) *прил* calm.
безвку́сен *прил см* **безвку́сный**.
безвку́сиц|а (**-ы**) *ж* bad taste.
безвку́с|ный (**-ен, -на, -но**) *прил* tasteless.
безвла́сти|е (**-я**) *ср* anarchy.
безво́д|ный (**-ен, -на, -но**) *прил (среда, почва*) arid.
безвозвра́т|ный (**-ен, -на, -но**) *прил* irretrievable; **безвозвра́тная ссу́да**
nonrepayable subsidy.
безвозме́здно *нареч* for free.
безвозме́здный *прил* free.
безво́л|ьный (**-ен, -ьна, -ьно**) *прил* weak-willed.
безвре́д|ный (**-ен, -на, -но**) *прил* harmless.
безвре́мен|ный (**-ен, -на, -но**) *прил* untimely.
безвы́ездно *нареч* continuously.
безвы́ход|ный (**-ен, -на, -но**) *прил* hopeless.
безгла́с|ный *прил (перен*) silent.
безголо́в|ый (**-, -а, -о**) *прил (перен: разг)* brainless.
безголо́с|ый (**-, -а, -о**) *прил*: ~ **пе́вец** singer with a weak voice.
безгра́мот|ный (**-ен, -на, -но**) *прил* illiterate; (*работник*) incompetent.
безграни́ч|ный (**-ен, -на, -но**) *прил (также перен*) boundless.
безгре́ш|ный (**-ен, -на, -но**) *прил* sinless.
безда́р|ный (**-ен, -на, -но**) *прил (писатель, музыкант*) talentless; (*произведение, роман*) mediocre.
безда́р|ь (**-и**) *ж (разг)* nobody.
безде́йств|овать (**-ую**) *несов неперех (машина, предприятие*) to be out of action; (*человек*) to take no action.
безделу́ш|ка (**-ки**; *gen pl* **-ек**) *ж (разг)* trinket, knick-knack.
безде́ль|е (**-я**) *ср* idleness.
безде́льник (**-а**) *м (разг)* loafer.
безде́льниц|а (**-ы**) *ж см* **безде́льник**.
безде́льнича|ть (**-ю**) *несов неперех (разг)* to loaf *или* lounge about.
безде́нежный *прил (расчёт, перевод*) noncash; (*разг: человек*) hard up.
безде́т|ный (**-ен, -на, -но**) *прил* childless.
безде́ятель|ный (**-ен, -ьна, -ьно**) *прил* inactive.
бе́здн|а (**-ы**) *ж* abyss; **у меня́** ~ **дел** (*разг*) I've got heaps of things to do.
бездоказа́тель|ный (**-ен, -ьна, -ьно**) *прил* unsubstantiated.
бездо́м|ный (**-ен, -на, -но**) *прил (человек*) homeless; (*собака*) stray *опред*.
бездо́н|ный (**-ен, -на, -но**) *прил* bottomless; **бездо́нная бо́чка** (*разг*) bottomless pit; (: *человек*) (old) soak.
безду́м|ный (**-ен, -на, -но**) *прил* thoughtless.
безду́ш|ный (**-ен, -на, -но**) *прил (человек*) heartless; (*игра актёра*) soulless.
безе́ *ср нескл* meringue.
безжа́лост|ный (**-ен, -на, -но**) *прил* ruthless.
безжи́знен|ный (**-, -на, -но**) *прил* lifeless; (*взгляд, лицо*) expressionless.
беззабо́т|ный (**-ен, -на, -но**) *прил* carefree.
беззако́нен *прил см* **беззако́нный**.
беззако́ни|е (**-я**) *ср* lawlessness; (*поступок*) unlawful act.

беззако́н|ный (-ен, -на, -но) *прил* unlawful.
беззасте́нчив|ый (-, -а, -о) *прил* shameless; ~ лгун barefaced liar.
беззащи́т|ный (-ен, -на, -но) *прил* defenceless (*BRIT*), defenseless (*US*).
беззву́ч|ный (-ен, -на, -но) *прил* inaudible.
беззло́б|ный (-ен, -на, -но) *прил* good-natured.
беззу́б|ый (-, -а, -о) *прил* toothless; (*перен*) feeble.
безли́к|ий (-ая, -ое, -ие; -, -а, -о) *прил* nondescript.
безли́чный *прил* (*линг*) impersonal.
безлю́д|ный (-ен, -на, -но) *прил* (*улица, место*) deserted, empty; **безлю́дная техноло́гия** automated technology; **безлю́дный фонд** *funds for employees not on regular staff.*
безме́р|ный (-ен, -на, -но) *прил* (*счастье, любовь*) boundless; (*требования*) unlimited.
безмо́зглый *прил* (*разг*) brainless.
безмо́лв|ный (-ен, -на, -но) *прил* (*также перен*) silent; ~ное согла́сие tacit agreement.
безмяте́ж|ный (-ен, -на, -но) *прил* tranquil.
безнаде́ж|ный (-ен, -на, -но) *прил* hopeless; ~ больно́й hopeless case (*MED*).
безнака́зан|ный (-, -на, -но) *прил* unpunished.
безнали́чный *прил* noncash; **безнали́чный расчёт** clearing settlement.
безно́г|ий (-ая, -ое, -ие) *прил* one-legged; (*без двух ног*) legless.
безнра́вствен|ный (-, -на, -но) *прил* immoral.
безо *предл см* **без**.
безоби́д|ный (-ен, -на, -но) *прил* harmless; (*шутка, высказывание*) inoffensive, innocuous.
безо́блач|ный (-ен, -на, -но) *прил* cloudless; (*перен: жизнь, детство*) carefree; (: *счастье*) unclouded.
безобра́зен *прил см* **безобра́зный**.
безобра́зи|е (-я) *ср* (*физическое уродство*) ugliness; (*поступок*) outrage; ~! it's outrageous!, it's a disgrace!
безобра́зник (-а) *м* (*разг*) (little) horror.
безобра́зниц|а (-ы) *ж см* **безобра́зник**.
безобра́знича|ть (-ю; *perf* **набезобра́зничать**) *несов неперех* (*разг*) to carry on.
безобра́з|ный (-ен, -на, -но) *прил* ugly; (*поступок, действие*) outrageous, disgraceful.
безогово́роч|ный (-ен, -на, -но) *прил* unconditional.
безопа́сен *прил см* **безопа́сный**.
безопа́сност|ь (-и) *ж* safety; (*международная*) security; в ~и out of danger; **Сове́т Б~и** Security Council; **те́хника ~и** health and safety; **безопа́сность движе́ния** road safety.
безопа́с|ный (-ен, -на, -но) *прил* safe.
безору́ж|ный (-ен, -на, -но) *прил* unarmed; (*перен: в споре*) defenceless (*BRIT*), defenseless (*US*).
безостано́вочно *нареч* incessantly.
безотве́т|ный (-ен, -на, -но) *прил* (*любовь*) unrequited; (*существо*) meek.
безотве́тственност|ь (-и) *ж* irresponsibility.

безотве́тствен|ный (-, -на, -но) *прил* irresponsible.
безотка́з|ный (-ен, -на, -но) *прил* reliable.
безотлага́тел|ьный (-ен, -ьна, -ьно) *прил* urgent.
безотноси́тельно *нареч*: ~ к +*dat* irrespective of.
безотра́д|ный (-ен, -на, -но) *прил* (*жизнь*) dreary; (*положение*) bleak.
безотхо́д|ный (-ен, -на, -но) *прил*: ~ное произво́дство *production process which recycles waste.*
безотчёт|ный (-ен, -на, -но) *прил* (*чувство*) irrational; (*поведение*) unaccountable.
безоши́боч|ный (-ен, -на, -но) *прил* (*решение, догадка*) correct; (*судья, ценитель*) infallible.
безрабо́тиц|а (-ы) *ж* unemployment.
безрабо́тн|ая (-ой; *decl like adj*) *ж см* **безрабо́тный**.
безрабо́тный *прил* unemployed ♦ (-ого; *decl like adj*) *м* unemployed person; ~ые the unemployed.
безра́дост|ный (-ен, -на, -но) *прил* (*жизнь, детство*) cheerless, joyless; (*голос, взгляд*) dull.
безразде́л|ьный (-ен, -ьна, -ьно) *прил* (*господство, владение*) absolute; (*внимание*) undivided.
безразли́чен *прил см* **безразли́чный**.
безразли́чно *нареч* indifferently ♦ *как сказ*: мне ~ it doesn't matter to me, it makes no difference to me; ~, придёт он или нет it makes no difference whether he comes or not; ~ кто/что no matter who/what.
безразли́ч|ный (-ен, -на, -но) *прил* indifferent.
безразме́р|ный *прил*: ~ые носки́/чулки́ one-size socks/stockings.
безрассу́д|ный (-ен, -на, -но) *прил* (*поведение*) reckless; (*любовь*) impulsive.
безрезульта́т|ный (-ен, -на, -но) *прил* fruitless.
безро́пот|ный (-ен, -на, -но) *прил* uncomplaining.
безрука́в|ка (-ки; *gen pl* -ок) *ж* (*кофта*) sleeveless top; (*куртка*) sleeveless jacket.
безру́к|ий (-ая, -ое, -ие; -, -а, -о) *прил* one-armed; (*без двух рук*) with no arms; (*перен: разг*) ham-fisted.
безры́бь|е (-я) *ср*: на ~ и рак ры́ба something is better than nothing.
безубы́точ|ный (-ен, -на, -но) *прил*: ~ное предприя́тие *business which is not making a loss.*
безуда́р|ный (-ен, -на, -но) *прил* (*линг*) unstressed.
безукори́знен|ный (-, -на, -но) *прил* (*поведение, человек*) irreproachable; (*работа*) flawless.
безу́мен *прил см* **безу́мный**.
безу́м|ец (-ца) *м* madman (*мн* madmen).
безу́ми|е (-я) *ср* madness; **до ~я** madly.

безу́мно *нареч* (*любить*) madly; (*устать*) terribly.

безу́м|ный (**-ен, -на, -но**) *прил* (*план, намерение*) mad; (*счастье, ярость итп*) wild; **он зараба́тывает ~ные де́ньги** (*разг*) he earns crazy money; **~ная ро́скошь** unbelievable luxury.

безу́мца *итп сущ см* **безу́мец**.

безупре́ч|ный (**-ен, -на, -но**) *прил* (*поведение, человек*) irreproachable; (*работа*) flawless.

безусло́вен *прил см* **безусло́вный**.

безусло́вно *нареч* (*повиноваться, доверить*) unconditionally ♦ *част* (*несомненно*) without a doubt; **~, я бу́ду рад помо́чь Вам** naturally, I'll be happy to help you.

безусло́в|ный (**-ен, -на, -но**) *прил* (*повиновение, доверие*) unconditional, absolute; (*успех, превосходство*) indisputable.

безуспе́ш|ный (**-ен, -на, -но**) *прил* unsuccessful.

безуча́ст|ный (**-ен, -на, -но**) *прил* disinterested.

безъя́дерный *прил* nuclear-free.

безымя́н|ный (**-ен, -на, -но**) *прил* (*река, гора*) unnamed; (*герой, автор*) anonymous; **безымя́нный па́лец** ring finger.

безысхо́д|ный (**-ен, -на, -но**) *прил* hopeless.

бей(ся) *несов см* **би́ть(ся)**.

Бейру́т (**-а**) *м* Beirut.

бе́йте(сь) *несов см* **би́ть(ся)**.

беко́н (**-а**) *м* bacon.

БелА́З (**-а**) *м сокр* = *Белору́сский автомоби́льный заво́д*; (*автомобиль*) *vehicle manufactured at the Belorussian car factory*.

Беларýсь (**-и**) *ж* Belarus.

Белгра́д (**-а**) *м* Belgrade.

беле́ть (**-ю**; *perf* **побеле́ть**) *несов неперех* (*лицо*) to go *или* turn white; (*no perf*; *цветы*) to show white.

белиберд|а́ (**-ы́**) *ж* (*разг*) gobbledegook.

Бели́з (**-а**) *м* Belize.

бели́л|а (**-**) *мн* emulsion *ед*.

бели́ть (**-ю́, -ишь**; *perf* **побели́ть**) *несов перех* to whitewash.

бе́личий (**-ья, -ье, -ьи**) *прил* squirrel's; (*шуба*) squirrel (fur).

бе́лк|а (**-ки**; *gen pl* **-ок**) *ж* squirrel; **верте́ться** (*impf*) **как ~ в колесе́** to run round in circles.

белка́ *итп сущ см* **бело́к**.

белко́вый *прил* proteinous.

беллетри́стик|а (**-и**) *ж* fiction; (*лёгкое чтение*) light reading.

белови́к (**-а́**) *м* fair copy.

белогварде́|ец (**-йца**) *м* (*ИСТ*) White Guardsman (*мн* Guardsmen).

бело́к *сущ см* **бе́лка**.

бел|о́к (**-ка́**) *м* protein; (*яйца*) (egg) white; (*АНАТ*) white (of the eye).

белокро́ви|е (**-я**) *ср* (*МЕД*) leukaemia (*BRIT*), leukemia (*US*).

белоку́р|ый (**-, -а, -о**) *прил* (*человек*) fair(-haired); (*волосы*) fair.

белору́с (**-а**) *м* Belorussian.

белору́с|ка (**-ки**; *gen pl* **-ок**) *ж см* **белору́с**.

белору́сск|ий (**-ая, -ое, -ие**) *прил* Belorussian.

белору́ч|ка (**-ки**; *gen pl* **-ек**) *м/ж* (*разг*: *пренебр*) shirker.

белосне́ж|ный (**-ен, -на, -но**) *прил* snow-white.

белу́г|а (**-и**) *ж* beluga (*sturgeon*).

белу́ж|ий (**-ья, -ье, -ьи**) *прил* beluga *опред*.

Бе́лфаст (**-а**) *м* Belfast.

бе́л|ые (**-ых**; *decl like adj*) *мн* (*ШАХМАТЫ*) white *ед*.

бе́л|ый (**-, -а́, -о**) *прил* white; (*гриб*) сер ♦ (**-ого**; *decl like adj*) *м* (*человек*) white (person); **средь ~а дня** (*разг*) in broad daylight; **бе́лая воро́на** the odd one out; **бе́лая гва́рдия** (*ИСТ*) the White Guard; **бе́лая горя́чка** the DT's (= *delirium tremens*); **бе́лое духове́нство** secular clergy; **бе́лый медве́дь** polar bear; *см также* **бе́лые**.

бельги́ек *сущ см* **бельги́йка**.

бельги́|ец (**-йца**) *м* Belgian.

бельги́|йка (**-йки**; *gen pl* **-ек**) *ж см* **бельги́ец**.

бельги́йск|ий (**-ая, -ое, -ие**) *прил* Belgian.

бельги́йца *итп сущ см* **бельги́ец**.

Бе́льги|я (**-и**) *ж* Belgium.

бель|ё (**-я́**) *ср собир* linen; (*стиранное*) washing; **ни́жнее ~** underwear; **посте́льное ~** bedclothes, bed linen.

бельэта́ж (**-а**) *м* (*ТЕАТР*) dress circle; (*АРХИТ*) first floor, second floor (*US*).

беля́ш (**-а́**) *м* meat pie.

бемо́ль (**-я**) *м* (*МУЗ*) flat.

бенефи́с (**-а**) *м performance commemorating and featuring an actor.*

бензи́н (**-а**) *м* petrol (*BRIT*), gas (*US*).

бензи́новый *прил* petrol (*BRIT*), gas (*US*); **~ дви́гатель** petrol engine.

бензоба́к (**-а**) *м* petrol (*BRIT*) *или* gas (*US*) tank.

бензоколо́н|ка (**-ки**; *gen pl* **-ок**) *ж* petrol (*BRIT*) *или* gas (*US*) pump.

Бенилю́кс (**-а**) *м* Benelux.

бенуа́р (**-а**) *м* (*ТЕАТР*) boxes *мн*.

бе́рег (**-а**; *loc sg* **-ý**, *nom pl* **-а́**) *м* (*моря, озера*) shore; (*реки*) bank.

берёг(ся) *итп несов см* **бере́чь(ся)**.

берегов|о́й *прил* (*см сущ*) coastal; riverside; **берегова́я ли́ния** coastline; **берегова́я слу́жба** coastguard.

берегу́(сь) *итп несов см* **бере́чь(ся)**.

бе́режен *прил см* **бе́режный**.

бережёшь(ся) *итп несов см* **бере́чь(ся)**.

бережли́вость (**-и**) *ж* economy, thrift.

бережли́в|ый (**-, -а, -о**) *прил* economical, thrifty.

бе́режность (**-и**) *ж* care.

бе́реж|ный (**-ен, -на, -но**) *прил* (*заботливый*)

caring; (*осторожный*) careful.
берёз|а (**-ы**) ж birch (tree).
Берёз|ка (**-ки**; *gen pl* **-ок**) ж Beriozka (*hard-currency shop in the USSR*).
берёзовый *прил* birch.
Берёзок *сущ см* **Берёзка**.
берём *несов см* **брать**.
беремене|ть (**-ю**; *perf* **забере́менеть**) *сов неперех* to get pregnant.
бере́менн|ая (**-а**) *прил* pregnant ♦ (**-ой**; *decl like adj*) ж pregnant woman.
бере́менность (**-и**) ж pregnancy.
бере́т (**-а**) м beret.
берёт *итп несов см* **брать**.
бер|е́чь (**-егу́, -ежёшь** *итп*, **-егу́т**; *pt* **-ёг, -егла́, -егло́**) *несов перех* (*документы*) to keep; (*деньги*) to be careful with; (*время*) to make good use of; (*здоровье, детей*) to look after, take care of; ~ (*impf*) **как зени́цу о́ка** to guard with one's life
▸ **бере́чься** (*perf* **побере́чься**) *несов возв* (+*gen*) to watch out for; **~еги́тесь просту́ды** take care you don't catch a cold; **~еги́тесь!** watch out!
бе́рингов (**-а, -о, -ы**) *прил*: **Б~ проли́в** Bering Strait.
Берли́н (**-а**) м Berlin.
берму́дск|ий (**-ая, -ое, -ие**) *прил*: **Б~ие острова́** Bermuda, the Bermudas.
Берн (**-а**) м Berne.
беру́(сь) *итп несов см* **брать(ся)**.
берцо́в|ый *прил*: **~ая кость** shinbone.
бес (**-а**) м demon, devil; (*перен*) devil.
бесе́д|а (**-ы**) ж conversation; (*не официальная*) chat; (*популярный доклад*) discussion.
бесе́д|ка (**-ки**; *gen pl* **-ок**) ж pavilion.
бесе́д|овать (**-ую**) *несов неперех*: ~ (**с** +*instr*) to talk (to); (*не официально*) to chat (to).
бесе́док *сущ см* **бесе́дка**.
бе|си́ть (**-шу́, -сишь**; *perf* **взбеси́ть**) *несов перех* to infuriate
▸ **беси́ться** *несов возв* (*раз*) to run wild; (*perf* **взбеси́ться**; *раздражаться*) to become furious; **с жи́ру ~ся** (*impf*) (*разг*) to become spoilt and fussy.
бескла́ссовый *прил* classless.
бескомпроми́сс|ный (**-ен, -на, -но**) *прил* uncompromising.
бесконе́чен *прил см* **бесконе́чный**.
бесконе́чно *нареч* (*очень долго*) endlessly; (*чрезвычайно*) infinitely.
бесконе́чность (**-и**) ж infinity; **до ~и** (*очень долго*) endlessly; (*очень сильно*) infinitely.
бесконе́ч|ный (**-ен, -на, -но**) *прил* (*пространство, дорога*) endless; (*время, удовольствие*) endless, infinite; (*число*) infinite; (*вечер, песня*) interminable; (*любовь, ненависть*) undying.
бесконтро́л|ьный (**-ен, -ьна, -ьно**) *прил* uncontrolled.
бескоры́стен *прил см* **бескоры́стный**.

бескоры́сти|е (**-я**) *ср* unselfishness.
бескоры́ст|ный (**-ен, -на, -но**) *прил* unselfish.
бескро́в|ный (**-ен, -на, -но**) *прил* bloodless.
беспардо́н|ный (**-ен, -на, -но**) *прил* shameless, brazen.
беспереб́о́й|ный (**-ен, -йна, -йно**) *прил* uninterrupted.
бесперспекти́в|ный (**-ен, -на, -но**) *прил* (*работа*) without prospects; (*отношения*) with no future.
беспе́чен *прил см* **беспе́чный**.
беспе́чность (**-и**) ж carefreeness.
беспе́ч|ный (**-ен, -на, -но**) *прил* carefree.
беспла́т|ный (**-ен, -на, -но**) *прил* free.
беспло́ден *прил см* **беспло́дный**.
беспло́ди|е (**-я**) *ср* (*женщины*) infertility; (*земли*) barrenness, infertility.
беспло́д|ный (**-ен, -на, -но**) *прил* (*женщина*) infertile; (*брак*) childless; (*почва*) barren, infertile; (*попытки, дискуссии*) fruitless.
беспорово́т|ный (**-ен, -на, -но**) *прил* irrevocable.
бесподо́б|ный (**-ен, -на, -но**) *прил* (*разг*) fantastic.
беспоко́ен *прил см* **беспоко́йный**.
беспоко́|ить (**-ю, -ишь**) *несов перех* (*причинять боль*) to trouble; (*perf* **побеспоко́ить**; *мешать*) to disturb; (*perf* **обеспоко́ить**; *тревожить*) to bother, worry
▸ **беспоко́иться** *несов возв* (*утруждать себя*) to put o.s. out, trouble o.s.; (*тревожиться*): **~ся о** +*prp* или **за** +*acc* to worry about; **не ~йтесь, я сде́лаю всё сам** don't put yourself out, I'll do it myself.
беспоко́й|ный (**-ен, -йна, -йно**) *прил* (*человек*) anxious; (*взгляд*) uneasy, anxious; (*поездка*) uncomfortable; (*ребёнок*) fidgety, restless; (*море, сон, время*) troubled; **э́то о́чень ~йная рабо́та** it's a very stressful job.
беспоко́йств|о (**-а**) *ср* anxiety, unease; (*заботы, хлопоты*) trouble; **прости́те за ~!** sorry to trouble you!
беспол́ез|ный (**-ен, -на, -но**) *прил* useless.
беспо́мощен *прил см* **беспо́мощный**.
беспо́мощность (**-и**) ж (*см прил*) helplessness; weakness.
беспо́мощ|ный (**-ен, -на, -но**) *прил* helpless; (*перен*) weak.
беспоря́дк|и (**-ов**) *мн* disturbances *мн*.
беспоря́д|ок (**-ка**) м disorder; **в ~ке** (*комната, дела*) in a mess; *см также* **беспоря́дки**.
беспоря́доч|ный (**-ен, -на, -но**) *прил* (*груда бумаг*) disorderly, untidy; (*рассказ, записи*) confused.
беспоса́дочный *прил* nonstop.
беспо́чвен|ный (**-, -на, -но**) *прил* groundless.
беспо́шлинный *прил* duty-free.
беспоща́д|ный (**-ен, -на, -но**) *прил* (*наказание, удар*) merciless; (*критика, сатира*) ruthless; ~ **к** +*dat* ruthless или merciless towards.
беспра́вен *прил см* **беспра́вный**.

беспра́ви|е (-я) *ср* (*беззаконие*) lawlessness.
беспра́в|ный (-ен, -на, -но) *прил* without (civil) rights.
беспреде́л|ьный (-ен, -ьна, -ьно) *прил* (*пространство, море*) boundless; (*любовь, ненависть*) immeasurable.
беспрекосло́в|ный (-ен, -на, -но) *прил* unquestioning.
беспрепя́тственно *нареч* without difficulty.
беспрепя́тствен|ный (-, -на, -но) *прил* unimpeded.
беспрецеде́нт|ный (-ен, -на, -но) *прил* unprecedented.
бесприбы́л|ьный (-ен, -ьна, -ьно) *прил* unprofitable.
беспризо́рен *прил см* **беспризо́рный**.
беспризо́рник (-а) *м* (street) urchin.
беспризо́рниц|а (-ы) *ж см* **беспризо́рник**.
беспризо́р|ный (-ен, -на, -но) *прил* (*ребёнок*) homeless; (*дом, хозяйство*) neglected.
беспринци́п|ный (-ен, -на, -но) *прил* unscrupulous.
беспристра́ст|ный (-ен, -на, -но) *прил* unbias(s)ed.
беспричи́н|ный (-ен, -на, -но) *прил* irrational.
беспросве́т|ный (-ен, -на, -но) *прил* (*нужда*) desperate; (*грусть*) hopeless; (*ночь, мгла*) impenetrable.
беспроце́нтный *прил* interest-free.
Бессара́би|я (-и) *ж* Bessarabia.
бессвя́з|ный (-ен, -на, -но) *прил* disjointed.
бессерде́чен *прил см* **бессерде́чный**.
бессерде́чность (-и) *ж* heartlessness.
бессерде́ч|ный (-ен, -на, -но) *прил* heartless.
бесси́лен *прил см* **бесси́льный**.
бесси́ли|е (-я) *ср* (*больного, старика*) debility; (*чувства*) impotence.
бесси́л|ьный (-ен, -ьна, -ьно) *прил* (*больной, старик*) feeble, weak; (*гнев, ненависть*) impotent; **он/президе́нт ~ен (измени́ть ситуа́цию)** he/the president is powerless (to change the situation).
бессме́ртен *прил см* **бессме́ртный**.
бессме́рти|е (-я) *ср* immortality.
бессме́рт|ный (-ен, -на, -но) *прил* immortal.
бессмы́сленность (-и) *ж* (*слов*) meaninglessness; (*поступка*) senselessness, pointlessness.
бессмы́слен|ный (-, -на, -но) *прил* (*слова*) meaningless; (*поступок*) senseless, pointless; (*взгляд, улыбка*) inane.
бессо́вест|ный (-ен, -на, -но) *прил* (*нечестный*) unscrupulous; (*наглый*) shameless.
бессодержа́тел|ьный (-ен, -ьна, -ьно) *прил* (*слова*) empty; (*статья*) thin.
бессозна́тел|ьный (-ен, -ьна, -ьно) *прил* (*страх, действия*) instinctive; **быть** (*impf*) **в**

~**ьном состоя́нии** to be unconscious.
бессо́нниц|а (-ы) *ж* insomnia.
бессо́нный *прил* (*ночь*) sleepless; (*страж, сиделка*) wakeful.
бесспо́рен *прил см* **бесспо́рный**.
бесспо́рно *нареч* indisputably ♦ *част* (*несомненно*) absolutely; **он, ~, умён** he is indisputably clever.
бесспо́р|ный (-ен, -на, -но) *прил* indisputable.
бессро́ч|ный (-ен, -на, -но) *прил* indefinite.
бесстра́ш|ный (-ен, -на, -но) *прил* fearless.
бессты́д|ный (-ен, -на, -но) *прил* shameless, brazen; (*ложь*) barefaced.
беста́кт|ный (-ен, -на, -но) *прил* tactless.
бе́сти|я (-и) *м/ж* (*разг*) rogue.
бестолко́в|ый (-, -а, -о) *прил* (*глупый*) stupid; (*неразумительный*) incoherent.
бестсе́ллер (-а) *м* best seller.
бесхи́трост|ный (-ен, -на, -но) *прил* simple.
бесхо́зный *прил* ownerless.
бесхозя́йствен|ный (-, -на, -но) *прил* (*руководитель*) inefficient; (*политика*) uneconomic; ~**ная же́нщина** a bad housekeeper.
бесцве́т|ный (-ен, -на, -но) *прил* colourless (*BRIT*), colorless (*US*).
бесце́л|ьный (-ен, -ьна, -ьно) *прил* pointless, futile.
бесце́н|ный (-ен, -на, -но) *прил* (*коллекция, сокровища*) priceless; (*друг, жена*) invaluable.
бесце́нок *м*: **за ~** dirt cheap, for next to nothing.
бесцеремо́н|ный (-ен, -на, -но) *прил* unceremonious, familiar.
бесчелове́ч|ный (-ен, -на, -но) *прил* inhuman.
бесче́|стить (-щу, -стишь; *perf* **обесче́стить**) *несов перех* (*девушку*) to violate.
бесчи́слен|ный (-, -на, -но) *прил* numerous.
бесчу́вствен|ный (-, -на, -но) *прил* (*жестокий*) unfeeling; (*лишённый сознания*) senseless.
бето́н (-а; *part gen* -у) *м* concrete.
бетони́р|овать (-ую; *perf* **забетони́ровать**) *несов перех* to concrete.
бефстро́ганов *м нескл* boeuf *или* beef stroganoff.
бе́шенств|о (-а) *ср* (*перен*) rage; (*МЕД*) rabies; **приходи́ть** (**прийти́** *perf*) **в ~** to fly into a rage.
бе́шен|ый *прил* (*взгляд*) furious; (*характер, темперамент, ураган*) violent; (*МЕД*) rabid; (*разг: деньги, цены*) crazy; **э́то сто́ит ~ых де́нег** (*разг*) it costs a bomb.
бешу́(сь) *несов см* **беси́ть(ся)**.
биатло́н (-а) *м* biathlon.
биатлони́ст (-а) *м* biathlete.
биатлони́ст|ка (-ки; *gen pl* -ок) *ж см* **биатлони́ст**.
Би-би-си *ж сокр* (= *Брита́нская радиовеща́тельная корпора́ция*) BBC (=

British Broadcasting Corporation).
библе́йск|ий (-ая, -ое, -ие) *прил* biblical.
библиографи́ческ|ий (-ая, -ое, -ие) *прил*
bibliographical; **библиографи́ческая
ре́дкость** rare edition.
библиогра́фи|я (-и) *ж* bibliography.
библиоте́к|а (-и) *ж* library.
библиоте́кар|ь (-я) *м* librarian.
библиоте́чный *прил* library *опред.*
Би́бли|я (-и) *ж* the Bible.
бигуди́ *ср/мн нескл* curlers *мн;* **накру́чивать
(накрути́ть** *perf*) **во́лосы на ~** to put one's hair
in curlers.
бидо́н (-а) *м* (*для молока*) churn; (*маленький*)
can.
бижуте́ри|я (-и) *ж* costume jewellery.
би́знес (-а) *м* business; **де́лать (сде́лать** *perf*) **~
на** +*prp* to make a living from.
бизнесме́н (-а) *м* businessman (*мн*
businessmen).
бики́ни *ср нескл* bikini.
биле́т (-а) *м* ticket; (*члена организации*)
(membership) card; **обра́тный ~** return (*BRIT*)
или roundtrip (*US*) ticket; **казначе́йский ~**
banknote; **входно́й ~** ticket (*for standing
room*).
биллио́н (-а) *м* billion (*one thousand million*).
билья́рд (-а) *м* (*игра*) billiards; (*стол*) billiard
table.
бино́кл|ь (-я) *м* binoculars *мн.*
бинт (-á) *м* bandage; **накла́дывать (наложи́ть**
perf) **~ы на** +*acc* to put a bandage on.
бинт|ова́ть (-у́ю, *perf* **забинтова́ть**) *несов
перех* to bandage.
био́граф (-а) *м* biographer.
биогра́фи|я (-и) *ж* biography.
био́лог (-а) *м* biologist.
биоло́ги|я (-и) *ж* biology.
би́рж|а (-и) *ж* (*комм*) exchange; **валю́тная ~**
exchange market; **~ це́нных бума́г** securities
exchange; **това́рная ~** commodity exchange;
фо́ндовая ~ stock exchange *или* market;
игра́ть (*impf*) **на ~е** to play the stock exchange.
биржеви́к (-á) *м* stockbroker.
биржево́й *прил* (*сделка*) stock-exchange;
биржево́й бро́кер stockbroker.
би́р|ка (-ки; *gen pl* **-ок**) *ж* tag.
Бирминге́м (-а) *м* Birmingham.
би́рок *сущ см* **би́рка.**
бирюз|а́ (-ы́) *ж* (*ГЕО*) turquoise.
бис *межд*: **Б~!** encore!; **исполня́ть (испо́лнить**
perf) **что-н на ~** to do sth as an encore.
би́сер (-а; *part gen* **-у**) *м собир* glass beads *мн;*
мета́ть (*impf*) **~ пе́ред сви́ньями** to cast pearls
before swine.
бискви́т (-а) *м* sponge (cake).
бистро́ *ср нескл* bistro.
бит (-а) *м* (*КОМП*) bit.
би́тв|а (-ы) *ж* battle.
битко́м *нареч*: **~ (наби́т)** (*разг*) chock-a-block,
jam-packed.

би́тый *прил* broken; **би́тый час** (*разг*) a good
hour.
бить (бью, бьёшь; *imper* **бей(те),** *perf* **поби́ть)**
несов перех (*также перен*) to beat; (*стёкла*) to
break ◆ (*perf* **проби́ть**) *неперех* (*часы*) to strike;
~ (*impf*) **в** +*acc* (*в дверь*) to bang at; (*дождь,
ветер*) to beat against; (*орудие*) to hit; **~** (*impf*)
на +*acc* (*стремиться к*) to aim for; **~** (*impf*) **по
столу́** to bang on the table; **~** (*impf*) **в бараба́н**
to beat a drum; **свет бьёт мне в глаза́** the light
is blinding me; **~** (*impf*) **по чьим-н недоста́ткам**
to severely criticize sb's failings; **~** (*impf*) **по
карма́ну** to hit one's pocket; **э́то бьёт по мои́м
интере́сам** it conflicts with my interests; **его́
бьёт озно́б** he's got a fit of the shivers
▶ **би́ться** *несов возв* (*сердце, пульс*) to beat;
(*стекло, фарфор*) to be breakable;
(*сражаться*) to fight; **би́ться** (*impf*) **о** +*acc* to
bang against; **би́ться** (*impf*) **над** +*instr* (*над
задачей, над решением*) to struggle with; **хоть
голово́й об сте́ну бе́йся** you might as well
bang your head against a brick wall.
бифште́кс (-а) *м* steak.
бич (-á) *м* (*плеть*) whip; (*перен*) scourge.
Бишке́к (-а) *м* Bishkek.
б-ка *сокр* = **библиоте́ка.**
бла́г|а (-) *мн* rewards *мн;* **всех благ!** all the best!
бла́г|о (-а) *ср* benefit; **на ~** +*gen* for the benefit of;
см также **бла́га.**
благови́дный (-ен, -на, -но) *прил* (*предлог*)
plausible; (*стремления, поступки*) seemingly
well-intentioned.
благодар|и́ть (-ю́, -и́шь; *perf* **поблагодари́ть**)
несов перех to thank.
благода́рность (-и) *ж* gratitude, thanks;
приноси́ть (принести́ *perf*) **~ кому́-н** to express
one's gratitude to sb.
благодаря́ *предл* (+*dat*) thanks to ◆ *союз*: **~
тому́, что** owing to the fact that; **здоро́в, ~
тому́, что занима́юсь спо́ртом** I'm healthy
thanks to *или* owing to the fact that I play sport.
благоде́тел|ь (-я) *м* benefactor.
благоде́тельниц|а (-ы) *ж* benefactress.
благ|о́й *прил*: **~и́е наме́рения** good intentions
мн; **крича́ть** (*impf*) **~и́м ма́том** (*разг*) to shout at
the top of one's voice.
благонадёжный (-ен, -на, -но) *прил*
trustworthy.
благополу́чи|е (-я) *ср* (*в семье, в отношениях*)
wellbeing; (*материальная обеспеченность*)
prosperity; **жела́ю Вам вся́кого ~я** I wish you
all the very best.
благополу́ч|ный (-ен, -на, -но) *прил*
successful.
благоприя́т|ный (-ен, -на, -но) *прил* favourable
(*BRIT*), favorable (*US*).
благоприя́тствование (-я) *ср*:
усло́вия/поли́тика наибо́льшего ~я the most
favourable (*BRIT*) *или* favorable (*US*) conditions/
policy.
благоразу́ми|е (-я) *ср* prudence.

благоразу́м|ный (-ен, -на, -но) *прил* prudent.
благоро́д|ный (-ен, -на, -но) *прил* noble; **он ~ного происхожде́ния** he is of noble birth; **благоро́дные га́зы** the noble gases; **благоро́дные мета́ллы** precious metals.
благоро́дств|о (-а) *ср* nobility.
благослов|и́ть (-лю́, -и́шь; *impf* **благословля́ть**) *сов перех* to bless; **~** *(perf)* **кого́-н (на что-н)** to give sb one's blessing (for sth).
благосостоя́ни|е (-я) *ср* wellbeing.
благотвори́тел|ь (-я) *м* philanthropist.
благотвори́тельниц|а (-ы) *ж см* **благотвори́тель**.
благотвори́тельность (-и) *ж* charity.
благотвори́тельн|ый *прил* charitable; **~ая организа́ция** charity (organization); **~ конце́рт** charity concert.
благоустро́ен|ный (-, -на, -но) *прил* (*квартира, дом*) with all modern conveniences; **~ го́род** a city with every amenity; **~ная ку́хня** a well-equipped kitchen.
блаже́н|ный (-, -на, -но) *прил* blissful; (*no short form; РЕЛ*) Blessed.
блаже́нств|о (-а) *ср* bliss; **быть** (*impf*) **на верху́ ~a** to be in seventh heaven.
бланк (-а) *м* form.
блат (-а) *м* (*разг*) connections *мн*; **по бла́ту** (*разг*) through (one's) connections.
блатно́й *прил* criminal.
бле́ден *прил см* **бле́дный**.
бледне́|ть (-ю; *perf* **побледне́ть**) *несов неперех* to (grow) pale; (*перен*): **~ (пе́ред** +*instr*) to pale (beside).
бле́дность (-и) *ж* (*см прил*) pallor, paleness; dullness.
бле́д|ный (-ен, -на́, -но) *прил* pale; (*перен*) dull.
блёкн|уть (-у, -ешь; *perf* **поблёкнуть**) *несов неперех* to fade.
блеск (-а; *part gen* -у) *м* (*огней, молнии*) brilliance, brightness; (*металла*) shine; (*перен*) brilliance; **во всём бле́ске** in full splendour (*BRIT*) *или* splendor (*US*); **с блеском** brilliantly; **сдать** (*perf*) **экза́мен с бле́ском** to pass an exam with flying colours.
блесн|у́ть (-у́, -ёшь) *сов неперех* to flash; **у него́ ~у́ла мысль** a thought flashed through his mind; **~у́ла наде́жда** there was a ray of hope.
бле|сте́ть (-щу́, -сти́шь *или* -щешь) *несов неперех* (*звёзды, металл*) to shine; (*камни, глаза*) to sparkle; **она́ бле́щет красото́й** she is dazzling; **он бле́щет умо́м** he shines intellectually.
блестя́ще *нареч* brilliantly; **дела́ иду́т ~** everything's going brilliantly.
блестя́щ|ий (-ая, -ее, -ие; -, -а, -е) *прил* (*звезда*) bright; (*металл*) shining; (*глаза*) sparkling; (*перен*) brilliant.

блещу́ *итп несов см* **блесте́ть**.
бле́|ять (-ю) *несов неперех* to bleat.
ближа́йш|ий (-ая, -ее, -ие) *прил* (*город, дом*) the nearest; (*год*) the next; (*планы*) immediate; (*друга*) closest; **в ~ем бу́дущем** in the near future; **при ~ем уча́стии** +*gen* with the close cooperation of; **при ~ем рассмотре́нии** on closer inspection; **ближа́йший ро́дственник** next of kin.
бли́же *сравн прил от* **бли́зкий**.
бли́жн|ий (-яя, -ее, -ие) *прил* (*город, деревня*) neighbouring (*BRIT*), neighboring (*US*); **е́хать** (**пое́хать** *perf*) **~им путём** to take the shortest route; **Б~ Восто́к** Middle East.
бли́зк|ие (-их; *decl like adj*) *мн* (*родственники*) relatives *мн*.
бли́з|кий (-кая, -кое, -кие; -ок, -ка́, -ко) *прил* (*город*) nearby; (*конец*) imminent; (*друг, отношения*) close; **~** +*dat* (*интересы, тема*) similar *или* close to; **~ по** +*dat* (*по содержанию, по цели*) similar *или* close in; **они́ близки́ во мне́ниях** they think alike; **бли́зкий ро́дственник** close relative.
бли́зко *нареч* near *или* close by ◆ *как сказ* not far off; **~ от** +*gen* near, close to; **го́род ~** the town isn't far off; **~ узна́ть** (*perf*) **кого́-н** to get to know sb well; **принима́ть (приня́ть** *perf*) **что-н ~ к се́рдцу** to take sth to heart.
близне́ц (-а́) *м* (*обычно мн*) twin; **бра́тья/сёстры-близнецы́** twin brothers/sisters; *см также* **Близнецы́**.
Близнец|ы́ (-о́в) *мн* (*созвездие*) Gemini.
бли́зок *прил см* **бли́зкий**.
близору́к|ий (-ая, -ое, -ие; -, -а, -о) *прил* short-sighted (*BRIT*), nearsighted (*US*).
близору́кость (-и) *ж* (*см прил*) short-sightedness, nearsightedness.
бли́зост|ь (-и) *ж* proximity; (*интересов, мнений*) closeness; (*близкие отношения*) intimacy.
блин (-а́) *м* pancake.
бли́нчик (-а) *м уменьш от* **блин**.
блок (-а) *м* (*ПОЛИТ*) bloc; (*ТЕХ*) unit.
блока́д|а (-ы) *ж* (*ВОЕН*) siege; (*ЭКОН*) blockade; **устана́вливать (установи́ть** *perf*) / **снима́ть (снять** *perf*) **~у** to impose/lift a blockade.
блоки́р|овать (-ую) (*не*)*сов перех* to blockade; (*СПОРТ, КОМП*) to block.
блокно́т (-а) *м* notebook.
блонди́н (-а) *м*: **он ~** he is blond.
блонди́н|ка (-ки; *gen pl* -ок) *ж* blonde.
блох|а́ (-и́; *nom pl* -и) *ж* flea.
блужда́|ть (-ю) *несов неперех* to wander *или* roam (around); (*перен: мысли*) to wander; (*: взгляд*) to rove.
блу́з|ка (-ки; *gen pl* -ок) *ж* blouse.
блю́д|о (-а) *ср* dish.
блю|сти́ (-ду́, -дёшь; *pt* -л, -ла́-ло́, *perf*

соблюсти́) несов перех (интересы) to guard; (чистоту́) to maintain.

блядь (-и) ж (груб!: проститутка) whore (!) ◆ м/ж (груб!: женщина) bitch (!); (: мужчина) bastard (!)

бля́х|а (-и) ж (на форме) badge; (на ремне) buckle.

БМП ж сокр (= боева́я маши́на пехо́ты) armoured car for infantry.

БМР м сокр (= Банк междунаро́дных расчётов) BIS (= Bank for International Settlements).

боб (-á) м bean; **на ~áх оста́ться** (perf) to be left high and dry.

бобр (-á) м beaver.

Бог (-а; voc **Бо́же**) м God; **ве́рить** (impf) **в Бо́га** to believe in God; **~ зна́ет** или **весть что** God knows what; **благослови́ Вас ~!** God bless you!; **не дай ~!** God forbid!; **ра́ди Бо́га!** for God's sake!; **сла́ва Бо́гу** (к сча́стью) thank God.

богате́|ть (-ю; perf **разбогате́ть**) несов неперех to become rich.

бога́тств|а (-) мн resources мн.

бога́тств|о (-а) ср wealth, riches мн; (обстано́вки, оде́жды) richness; см также **бога́тства**.

бога́т|ый (-, -а, -о) прил rich; **~ урожа́й** bumper harvest; **~ +instr** (ископа́емыми, собы́тиями) rich in; **чем ~ы, тем и ра́ды** what's ours is yours.

богаты́р|ь (-я́) м warrior hero of Russian folk epics; (перен) Hercules.

бога́ч (-á) м rich man (мн men).

бога́че сравн прил от **бога́тый**.

боге́м|а (-ы) ж собир bohemians мн; (образ жи́зни) bohemian lifestyle.

боги́н|я (-и) ж goddess.

богоро́диц|а (-ы) ж the Virgin Mary.

богосло́ви|е (-я) ср theology.

богослуже́ни|е (-я) ср service; **соверша́ть** (**соверши́ть** perf) **~** to take a service.

боготвор|и́ть (-ю́, -и́шь) несов перех to worship, idolize.

богоуго́дный прил: **~ое заведе́ние** charitable institution.

богоху́льный прил blasphemous.

бод (-а) м (КОМП) baud.

бода́|ть (-ю; perf **забода́ть**) несов перех to butt.

бо́дрост|ь (-и) ж (см прил) energy, liveliness; cheerfulness.

бо́др|ый (-, -á, -о) прил (челове́к, похо́дка) energetic, lively; (настрое́ние, му́зыка) cheerful.

боеви́к (-á) м (солдат) fighter; (фильм) action movie.

боево́й прил military; (настрое́ние, дух) fighting опред.

боеголо́в|ка (-ки; gen pl -ок) ж warhead.

бо́ек прил см **бо́йкий**.

бо́ен сущ см **бо́йня**.

боеприпа́с|ы (-ов) мн ammunition ед.

бо|е́ц (-йца́) м (солдат) soldier; (участник боя) fighter.

Бо́же сущ см **Бог** ◆ межд: **~ (ты мой)!** good Lord или God!; **~!** кака́я красота́! God, it's beautiful!; **~ сохрани́** или **упаси́** или **изба́ви** (разг) God forbid.

бо́жеск|ий (-ая, -ое, -ие) прил (РЕЛ) divine; (разг: цены, усло́вия) half-decent; **приводи́ть** (**привести́** perf) **кого́-н/что-н в ~ вид** to make sb/sth look decent.

боже́ствен|ный (-ен, -на, -но) прил divine.

бо́ж|ий (-ья, -ье, -ьи) прил God's; **ка́ждый ~ день** every single day; **бо́жий дар** God-given talent; **бо́жья коро́вка** ladybird.

бо|й (-я; loc sg -ю́, nom pl -и́, gen pl -ёв) м battle; (боксёров, быко́в) fight; (бараба́нов) beating; (часо́в) striking.

бо́йк|ий (-ая, -ое, -ие; -ек, -á, -о) прил (распоряди́тель, продаве́ц) smart; (движе́ния) brisk; (речь, отве́т) quick; (no short form; ме́сто, база́р) busy.

бойко́т (-а) м boycott.

бойкоти́р|овать (-ую) (не)сов перех to boycott.

бо́йлер (-а) м boiler.

бо́йн|я (-йни; gen pl -ен) ж slaughterhouse, abattoir.

бойца́ итп сущ см **бое́ц**.

бо́йче сравн прил от **бо́йкий**.

бок (-а; part gen -у, loc sg -ý, nom pl -á) м side; **под бо́ком** (разг) right nearby; **~ ó ~** side by side.

бока́л (-а) м (wine)glass, goblet; **поднима́ть** (**подня́ть** perf) **~ за кого́-н/что-н** to raise one's glass to sb/sth.

бо́ком нареч (вы́йти, пройти́) sideways; **э́то ему́ ~ вы́шло** (разг) it was all screwed up for him.

бокс (-а) м (СПОРТ) boxing; (МЕД) cubicle.

боксёр (-а) м boxer.

болва́н (-а) м (разг) blockhead.

болга́р|ин (-ина; nom pl -ы, gen pl -) м Bulgarian.

Болга́ри|я (-и) ж Bulgaria.

болга́р|ки (-ки; gen pl -ок) ж см **болга́рин**.

болга́рск|ий (-ая, -ое, -ие) прил Bulgarian; **~ язы́к** Bulgarian.

бо́лее нареч more; **~ или ме́нее** more or less; **~ того́** what's more; **тем ~** all the more so; **~ чем** more than.

боле́знен|ный (-, -на, -но) прил sickly; (уко́л, перевя́зка) painful; (перен: подозри́тельность) unhealthy; **у него́ ~ное самолю́бие** he's ultra-sensitive.

боле́зн|ь (-и) ж illness; (зара́зная) disease; **~и ро́ста** growing pains.

боле́льщик (-а) м fan.

боле́льщиц|а (-ы) ж см **боле́льщик**.

бо́лен прил см **больно́й**.

бол|е́ть (-е́ю) несов неперех: **~ (+instr)** to be ill (with); (3sg -и́т, 3pl -я́т; подлеж: руки итп) to ache; **~** (impf) **за +acc** to be a fan of; **у меня́ душа́ ~ит за них** (перен) I'm very worried about them.

болеутоля́ющ|ий (-ая, -ее, -ие) *прил*: ~ее сре́дство painkiller.

боло́н|ка (-ки; *gen pl* -ок) *ж* lapdog.

боло́нь|я (-и) *ж* (*ткань*) *lightweight waterproof material.*

боло́т|о (-а) *ср* marsh, bog; (*перен*) backwater.

болт (-а́) *м* bolt.

болта́|ть (-ю) *несов перех* (*разг*) to talk ♦ *неперех* (*разговаривать*) to chat; (: *много*) to chatter; (*без толку*) to drivel; (*лишнее*) to blab; ~ (*impf*) **по-англи́йски** to chatter away in English; ~ (*impf*) **нога́ми** to dangle one's legs

▸ **болта́ться** *несов возв* (*разг*) to dangle; ~**ся** (*impf*) **без де́ла** to hang around with nothing to do.

болтовн|я́ (-и́) *ж* (*разг*) waffle.

болту́н (-а́) *м* chatterbox.

болту́ш|ка (-ки; *gen pl* -ек) *ж см* **болту́н**.

бол|ь (-и) *ж* pain, ache; **зубна́я** ~ toothache; **головна́я** ~ headache; ~ **в груди́/живо́те** chest/abdominal pain.

больни́ц|а (-ы) *ж* hospital; **ложи́ться** (**лечь** *perf*) **в** ~**у** to go into hospital; **выпи́сываться** (**вы́писаться** *perf*) **из** ~**ы** to be discharged from hospital.

больни́чный *прил* hospital *опред*; **больни́чный лист** medical certificate.

бо́льно *нареч* (*удариться, упасть*) badly, painfully; (*обидеть*) deeply; ~**!** that hurts!; **мне** ~ I am in pain; **де́лать** (**сде́лать** *perf*) ~ **кому́-н** to hurt sb; **мне** ~ **поду́мать об э́том** it hurts me to think about it.

бол|ьно́й *прил* (*рука итп*) sore; (*воображение*) unhealthy; (-ен, -ьна́, -ьно́; *нездоров*) ill, sick ♦ (-ьно́го; *decl like adj*) *м* (*тот, кто болеет*) sick person; (*пациент*) patient; **у неё** ~ **вид** she doesn't look very well; **де́ти** ~**ьны́** the children are ill *или* sick; **больно́е се́рдце** a bad heart; **больно́й вопро́с** a sore point.

бо́льше *сравн прил от* **большо́й** ♦ *сравн нареч от* **мно́го** ♦ *нареч*: ~ +*gen* (*часа, килограмма итп*) more than; ~ **не бу́ду** (*разг*) I won't do it again; ~ **так не де́лай** don't do that again; ~ **того́** what's more; ~ **всего́** most of all; **ни** ~ **ни ме́ньше** (**чем** *или* **как**) no more, no less (than); **она́ здесь** ~ **не живёт** she doesn't live here any more.

большеви́к (-а́) *м* Bolshevik.

большинств|о́ (-а́) *ср* majority; **в** ~**е́** (*слу́чаев*) in most cases; **подавля́ющее** ~ an overwhelming majority.

больш|о́й *прил* (*дом, река, дерево*) big, large; (*радость*) great; (*дети*) grown-up; **бо́льшей ча́стью, по бо́льшей ча́сти** for the most part; **я не** ~ **люби́тель бале́та** I'm not a great ballet fan; **я не** ~ **знато́к э́того де́ла** I'm no expert in this matter; **больша́я бу́ква** capital letter; **большо́й па́лец** (*руки*) thumb; (*ноги*) big toe.

боля́ч|ка (-ки; *gen pl* -ек) *ж* sore.

бо́мб|а (-ы) *ж* bomb.

бомб|и́ть (-лю́, -и́шь) *несов перех* to bomb.

бомбоубе́жищ|е (-а) *ср* bomb shelter.

бо́н|а (-ы) *ж* (*обычно мн*: *комм*) bond; (*временные деньги*) voucher.

бордо́вый *прил* dark red.

бордю́р (-а) *м* border; (*тротуара*) kerb (*BRIT*), curb (*US*).

боре́|ц (-ца́) *м* (*за свободу итп*) fighter; (*СПОРТ*) wrestler.

бормо|та́ть (-чу́, -чешь) *несов перех* to mutter.

бо́рн|ый *прил*: ~**ая кислота́** boric acid.

борови́к (-а́) *м* cep.

бор|ода́ (*acc sg* -оду, *gen sg* -оды́, *nom pl* -оды, *gen pl* -о́д, *dat pl* -ода́м) *ж* beard; **отпуска́ть** (**отпусти́ть** *perf*) **бо́роду** to grow a beard; **с** ~**одо́й** (*перен*: *разг*) ancient; **анекдо́т с** ~**одо́й** an old chestnut.

борода́в|ка (-ки; *gen pl* -ок) *ж* (*на пальцах итп*) wart.

борозд|и́ть (-жу́, -ди́шь) *perf* **избороди́ть**) *несов перех* to furrow; (*корабль*) to leave a wake.

бор|о́ться (-ю́сь, -ешься) *несов возв* (*СПОРТ*) to wrestle; ~ (*impf*) (**с** +*instr*) to fight (with *или* against); ~ (*impf*) **с** +*instr или* **про́тив** +*gen* (*конкуре́нтами*) to compete with *или* against; (*с предрассу́дками, с нарко́тиками*) to fight (against); ~ (*impf*) **за** +*acc* (*за мир*) to fight for.

борт (-а́; *acc sg* **за́ борт** *или* **за бо́рт**, *instr sg* **за бо́ртом** *или* **за бо́ртом**, *loc sg* -у́, *nom pl* -а́) *м* side; **на** ~**у́** *или* ~ on board, aboard; **челове́к за** ~**о́м!** man overboard!; **остава́ться** (**оста́ться** *perf*) **за** ~**о́м** (*перен*) to be left behind.

бортпроводни́к (-а́) *м* steward (*on plane*).

бортпроводни́ц|а (-ы) *ж* air hostess, stewardess (*on plane*).

борца́ *итп сущ см* **боре́ц**.

борщ (-а́) *м* borsch (*beetroot-based soup*).

борьб|а́ (-ы́) *ж* fight; (*СПОРТ*) wrestling.

босико́м *нареч* barefoot.

бос|о́й (-, -а́, -о) *прил* barefoot.

босоно́ж|ка (-и) *ж* (*обычно мн*) sandal; (: *закрытым носом*) slingback.

босс (-а) *м* boss.

Босфо́р (-а) *м* Bosphorus.

бося́к (-а́) *м* tramp.

бося́ч|ка (-ки; *gen pl* -ек) *ж см* **бося́к**.

бота́ник|а (-и) *ж* botany.

боти́н|ок (-ка) *м* (*обычно мн*) ankle boot.

бо́цман (-а) *м* boatswain, bosun.

бо́ч|ка (-ки; *gen pl* -ек) *ж* (*сосуд*) barrel.

бо|я́ться (-ю́сь, -и́шься) *несов возв*: ~ (+*gen*) to be afraid (of); ~ (*impf*) +*infin* to be afraid of doing *или* to do; **я** ~**ю́сь ходи́ть** (*impf*) **но́чью** I'm afraid of being out *или* to be out at night; ~**ю́сь сказа́ть** I wouldn't like to say.

бра́во *межд* bravo.
брази́л|ец (-ьца) *м* Brazilian.
Брази́ли|я (-и) *ж* Brazil.
брази́льск|ий (-ая, -ое, -ие) *прил* Brazilian.
брази́льца *итп сущ см* **брази́лец**.
бразилья́н|ка (-ки; *gen pl* **-ок)** *ж см* **брази́лец**.
бразды́ *мн*: ~ **правле́ния** the reins of power *или* government.
брак (-а) *м* (*супружество*) marriage; (*продукция*) rejects *мн*; (*деффект*) flaw; **вступа́ть (вступи́ть** *perf*) **в** ~ to get married; **расторга́ть (расто́ргнуть** *perf*) ~ to dissolve a marriage.
брако́ванн|ый *прил* reject *опред*.
брак|ова́ть (-у́ю; *perf* **забракова́ть)** *несов перех* to reject.
браконье́р (-а) *м* poacher.
браконье́рств|о (-а) *ср* poaching.
бракосочета́ни|е (-я) *ср* marriage ceremony.
брасле́т (-а) *м* bracelet; (*кольцо из металла, кости итп*) bangle.
брасс (-а) *м* breaststroke.
брат (-а; *nom pl* **-ья,** *gen pl* **-ьев)** *м* brother; **сво́дный** ~ stepbrother; **двою́родный** ~ cousin.
Братисла́в|а (-ы) *ж* Bratislava.
бра́ти|я (-и) *ср* brotherhood.
бра́тск|ий (-ая, -ое, -ие) *прил* brotherly, fraternal; **бра́тская моги́ла** communal grave.
бра́тств|о (-а) *ср* (*содружество*) brotherhood.
бра|ть (беру́, берёшь; *pt* **-л, -ла́, -ло,** *perf* **взять)** *несов перех* to take; (*билет*) to get; (*няню*) to take on; (*крепость, город*) to take, seize; (*высоту*) to conquer; (*барьер*) to clear; ~ (*impf*) **нало́г у кого́-н/за что-н** to tax sb/sth; ~ (**взять** *perf*) **что-н в расчёт** *или* **во внима́ние** to take sth into account *или* consideration
▶ **бра́ться** (*perf* **взя́ться)** *несов возв*: **бра́ться за** +*acc* (*дотронуться*) to touch; (*хватать рукой*) to take hold of; (*за чтение, за работу*) to get down to; (*за перо*) to take up; (*за книгу*) to begin; (*решение проблемы*) to take on, undertake; **отку́да у тебя́ вре́мя берётся?** where do you find the time?; **отку́да у него́ де́ньги беру́тся?** where does he get the money?; **бра́ться (взя́ться** *perf*) **за ум** to come to one's senses.
бра́тья *итп сущ см* **брат**.
бра́чный *прил* (*контракт*) marriage *опред*; (*союз*) conjugal.
бревн|о́ (-а́; *nom pl* **брёвна,** *gen pl* **брёвен)** *ср* log; (*СПОРТ*) the beam; (*перен*) oaf.
бред (-а; *loc pl* **-у́)** *м* delirium; (*перен*) nonsense; ~ **сумасше́дшего** the ravings of a madman.
бре́|дить (-жу, -дишь) *несов неперех* to be delirious; ~ (*impf*) **кем-н/чем-н** to be mad about sb/sth.
бредо́вый *прил* (*разг*) crazy.
бреду́ *итп несов см* **брести́**.
бре́жу *несов см* **бре́дить**.
бре́зга|ть (-ю) *несов* = **брезгова́ть**.

брезгли́в|ый (-, -а, -о) *прил* (*человек*) fastidious; (*взгляд*) disgusted.
брезг|овать (-ую; *perf* **побре́зговать)** *несов неперех* (+*instr*) to be fastidious about.
брезе́нт (-а; *part gen* **-у)** *м* tarpaulin.
брёл *итп несов см* **брести́**.
брём|я (-ени; *как* **вре́мя;** *см* **Table 4)** *ср* burden.
бр|ести́ (-еду́, -едёшь; *pt* **-ёл, -ела́, -ело́)** *несов неперех* (*человек*) to trudge; (*лошадь*) to plod.
брета́нск|ий (-ая, -ое, -ие) *прил* Breton.
Брета́ни|я (-и) *ж* Brittany.
брето́нск|ий (-ая, -ое, -ие) *прил* = **брета́нский**.
Брето́н|ь (-и) *ж* = **Брета́нь**.
брешь (-и) *ж* (*пролом*) breach.
бре́|ю(сь) *итп несов см* **брить(ся)**.
брига́д|а (-ы) *ж* (*ВОЕН*) brigade; (*в поезде*) crew; (*на производстве*) (work) team.
бригади́р (-а) *м* (*в поезде*) ≈ chief guard (*BRIT*), ≈ senior conductor (*US*); (*на производстве*) team leader.
бриз (-а) *м* sea breeze.
бриллиа́нт (-а) *м* (*cut*) diamond.
бриллиа́нтовый *прил* diamond *опред*.
брита́н|ец (-ца) *м* Briton; ~**цы** the British.
Брита́ни|я (-и) *ж* Britain.
брита́н|ка (-ки; *gen pl* **-ок)** *ж см* **брита́нец**.
брита́нск|ий (-ая, -ое, -ие) *прил* British.
брита́нца *итп сущ см* **брита́нец**.
бри́тв|а (-ы) *ж* razor; **безопа́сная** ~ safety razor.
бр|ить (-е́ю, -е́ешь; *perf* **побри́ть)** *несов перех* (*человека*) to shave; (*бороду*) to shave off
▶ **бри́ться** (*perf* **побри́ться)** *несов возв* to shave.
бри́финг (-а) *м* briefing.
бров|ь (-и; *gen pl* **-е́й)** *ж* eyebrow; **попа́сть** (*perf*) **не в** ~, **а в глаз** to hit the nail on the head; **он и бро́вью не повёл** he didn't bat an eyelid.
бро|ди́ть (-жу́, -дишь) *несов неперех* to wander; (*perf* **вы́бродить;** *вино, пиво*) to ferment.
бродя́г|а (-и) *м/ж* tramp; (*любящий странствовать*) drifter.
броже́ни|е (-я) *ср* fermentation; (*перен*) ferment.
брожу́ *несов см* **броди́ть**.
бро́йлер (-а) *м* broiler.
бро́кер (-а) *м* broker; **биржево́й** ~ stockbroker.
бро́керск|ий (-ая, -ое, -ие) *прил* broker's.
бром (-а) *м* bromine.
бронема́ши́н|а (-ы) *ж* armoured (*BRIT*) *или* armored (*US*) car.
бронетранспортёр (-а) *м* armoured (*BRIT*) *или* armored (*US*) personnel carrier.
бро́нз|а (-ы) *ж* bronze.
бро́нзовый *прил* bronze; **бро́нзовый век** the Bronze Age; **бро́нзовый призёр** bronze medallist (*BRIT*) *или* medalist (*US*).
брони́рова́ни|е (-я) *ср* reservation.
брони́р|овать (-ую; *perf* **заброни́ровать)** (*не*)*сов перех* to reserve.
бронх (-а) *м* (*обычно мн*) bronchial tube.
бронхи́т (-а) *м* bronchitis.
брон|ь (-и) *ж* (*разг*) reservation.

бро́н|я (-и) ж reservation.
брон|я́ (-и́) ж armour (*BRIT*) *или* armor (*US*)
  plating.
броса́|ть (-ю) *несов от* **бро́сить**
▶ **броса́ться** *несов от* **бро́ситься** ♦ *возв*: ~**ся**
  снежка́ми/камня́ми to throw snowballs/stones
  at each other; ~**ся** (*impf*) **деньга́ми** to throw
  one's money around; ~**ся** (*impf*) **друзья́ми** to
  abandon one's friends.
бро́|сить (-шу, -сишь; *impf* **броса́ть**) *сов перех*
  (*камень, мяч итп*) to throw; (*якорь*) to drop,
  cast; (*сети*) to cast; (*семью, друга*) to abandon;
  (*войска, отряд*) to dispatch; (*спорт*) to give up;
  броса́ть (~ *perf*) **замеча́ние** to pass comment;
  меня́ ~**сило в жар** I broke out in a (cold) sweat;
  броса́ть (~ *perf*) +*infin* to give up doing; ~**сьте!**
  stop it!
▶ **бро́ситься** (*impf* **броса́ться**) *сов возв*: ~**ся на**
  +*acc* (*на врага, на обидчика*) to throw o.s. at;
  броса́ться (~**ся** *perf*) **в дра́ку/ата́ку** to rush into
  the fray/to the attack; **броса́ться** (~**ся** *perf*)
  кому́-н на по́мощь to rush to sb's aid; ~**ся** (*perf*)
  по ле́стнице вниз to rush downstairs; ~**ся** (*perf*)
  кому́-н в объя́тия to fall into sb's arms; **кра́ска**
  ~**силась ему́ в лицо́** the colour rushed to his
  face.
бро́совый *прил* (*разг*) trashy; **бро́совая цена́**
  giveaway price; **бро́совый э́кспорт** (*КОММ*)
  dumping.
бро́ш|ка (-ки; *gen pl* -**ек**) ж brooch.
бро́шу(сь) *сов см* **бро́сить(ся)**.
брошь (-и) ж *см* **бро́шка**.
брошю́р|а (-ы) ж (*небольшая книжка*) pamphlet;
  (*рекламный буклет*) brochure.
брус (-а; *nom pl* -**ья**, *gen pl* -**ьев**) м beam; *см*
  также **бру́сья**.
бруска́ *итп сущ см* **брусо́к**.
брусни́к|а (-и) ж cowberry.
брусо́к (-ка́) м (*камень для точки*) whetstone;
  (*мыла*) bar.
бру́сь|я (-ев) *мн* parallel bars *мн*.
бру́тто *прил неизм* gross *опред*.
бры́зга|ть (-жу, -жешь) *несов неперех*
  (*фонтан, грязь*) to splash; (-гаю;
  опрыскивать): ~ **на** +*acc* to splash.
бры́зг|и (-) *мн* splashes *мн*; (*мелкие*) spray *ед*;
  (*стекла, камня*) fragments *мн*, splinters *мн*.
бры́зжу *итп несов см* **бры́згать**.
бры́нз|а (-ы) ж brynza (*sheep's milk cheese*).
брысь *межд* shoo.
брю́кв|а (-ы) ж swede.
брю́к|и (-) *мн* trousers *мн*, pants *мн* (*US*).
брюне́т (-а) м: **он** ~ he has dark hair.
брюне́т|ка (-ки; *gen pl* -**ок**) ж brunette.
Брюссе́л|ь (-я) м Brussels.
брю́х|о (-а) *ср* (*также разг*) belly; (*разг*:
  толстое) pot.
брюшно́й *прил* abdominal; **брюшно́й тиф**

typhoid fever.
БСЭ ж *сокр* = **Больша́я Сове́тская
  Энциклопе́дия**.
бубён *сущ см* **бу́бны**.
бу́блик (-а) м ≈ bagel.
бу́б|ны (-ён; *dat pl* -**нам**) *мн* (*КАРТЫ*) diamonds
  мн.
буго́р (-ра́) м mound; (*на коже*) lump.
Будапе́шт (-а) м Budapest.
будди́зм (-а) м Buddhism.
будди́ст (-а) м Buddhist.
будди́ст|ка (-ки; *gen pl* -**ок**) ж см **будди́ст**.
бу́дем *несов см* **быть**.
бу́дет *несов см* **быть** ♦ *част* that's enough;
  попла́кали и ~ that's enough crying; ~ **тебе́!**
  that's enough from you!
бу́дешь *итп несов см* **быть**.
буди́льник (-а) м alarm clock; **заводи́ть**
  (**завести́** *perf*) ~ **на** +*acc* to set the alarm (clock)
  for.
бу|ди́ть (-жу́, -дишь; *perf* **разбуди́ть**) *несов
  перех* to wake (up), awaken; (*perf* **пробуди́ть**;
  перен) to awaken.
бу́д|ка (-ки; *gen pl* -**ок**) ж (*сторожа*) hut; (*для
  собаки*) kennel; **часова́я** ~ sentry box;
  телефо́нная ~ telephone booth *или* box.
бу́дн|и (-ей) *мн* working *или* week days *мн*;
  (*перен*: *обыденная жизнь*) routine *ед*.
бу́док *сущ см* **бу́дка**.
будора́жить (-у, -ишь) *несов от*
  взбудора́жить.
бу́дто *союз* (*якобы*) apparently; (*словно*): (**как**) ~
  (**бы**) as if; **уверя́ет,** ~ **сам её ви́дел** he claims
  to have seen her himself; **он** ~ **бы до́лжен
  е́хать в Москву́** apparently he has to go to
  Moscow; **он улыба́лся,** ~ (**бы**) **был рад
  ви́деть нас** he smiled as if he were glad to see
  us.
бу́ду *итп несов см* **быть**.
бу́дущ|ее (-его; *decl like adj*) *ср* the future; **в** ~**ем**
  in the future; **на** ~ for the future; **не де́лайте
  э́того в** ~**ем** don't do it in future.
бу́дущ|ий (-ая, -ее, -ие) *прил* (*следующий*) next;
  (*предстоящий*) future; **бу́дущее вре́мя** future
  tense.
бу́дь(те) *несов см* **быть** ♦ *союз*: **будь то** to be it.
бу́ен *прил см* **бу́йный**.
буженин|а (-ы) ж *cold cooked and seasoned
  pork*.
бужу́ *несов см* **буди́ть**.
бу|й (-я; *nom pl* -**й**) м buoy.
бу́йвол (-а) м buffalo.
бу́йволиц|а (-ы) ж см **бу́йвол**.
бу́йный (-ен, -йна́, -йно) *прил* wild; (*обильный*:
  растительность) luxuriant, lush.
бук (-а) м beech.
бу́кв|а (-ы) ж letter; (*перен*): ~ +*gen* (*закона,
  документа*) the letter of; **прописна́я/строчна́я**

~ capital/small letter; ~ **в бу́кву** word for word.

буква́льно *нареч* literally.

буква́льный *прил* literal.

буква́рь (-я́) *м* first reading book.

буке́т (-а) *м* (*цветов, вина*) bouquet; (*перен: разг: болезней, недостатков*) range.

букини́ст (-а) *м* second-hand bookseller.

букинисти́ческий (-ая, -ое, -ие) *прил*: ~ **магази́н** second-hand bookshop.

букле́т (-а) *м* booklet.

букси́р (-а) *м* (*трос*) towrope; **тяну́ть** (*impf*) *или* **вести́** (*impf*) **на ~е** to give sb a tow.

була́в|ка (-ки; *gen pl* -ок) *ж* pin; **англи́йская ~** safety pin.

була́н|ый (-ого; *decl like adj*) *м* dun.

була́т (-а) *м* Damascus *или* damask steel.

бу́л|ка (-ки; *gen pl* -ок) *ж* roll; (*белый хлеб*) loaf.

бу́лоч|ка (-ки; *gen pl* -ек) *ж см* **бу́лка**.

бу́лочн|ая (-ой; *decl like adj*) *ж* baker, baker's (shop).

булы́жник (-а) *м* cobblestone.

булы́жн|ый *прил*: ~**ая мостова́я** cobbled street.

бульва́р (-а) *м* boulevard.

бульва́рный *прил* boulevard *опред*; ~ **рома́н** trashy novel; **бульва́рная пре́сса** gutter press.

бульдо́г (-а) *м* bulldog.

бульдо́зер (-а) *м* bulldozer.

бульо́н (-а; *part gen* -у) *м* stock.

бум (-а) *м* (*оживление*) boom.

бума́г|а (-и) *ж* paper; ~ **за по́дписью кого́-н** a document signed by sb; **це́нные ~и** securities; **ге́рбовая ~** headed paper; *см также* **бума́ги**.

бума́ги (-) *мн* papers *мн*.

бума́ж|ка (-ки; *gen pl* -ек) *ж* piece of paper.

бума́жник (-а) *м* wallet, pocketbook (*US*).

бума́жный *прил* paper; (*бюрократический*) bureaucratic; **бума́жная волоки́та** red tape.

бумера́нг (-а) *м* boomerang.

бу́нгало *ср нескл* bungalow.

бу́нкер (-а) *м* bunker.

бунт (-а) *м* (*мятеж*) riot; (: *на корабле*) mutiny.

бунт|ова́ть (-у́ю) *несов неперех* (*см сущ*) to riot; to mutiny.

бура́в|ить (-лю, -ишь; *perf* **пробура́вить**) *несов перех* to drill.

бура́к (-а́) *м* beetroot.

бура́н (-а) *м* blizzard, snowstorm.

бу́ргер (-а) *м* burger.

бургоми́стр (-а) *м* ≈ mayor.

бурд|а́ (-ы́) *ж* (*разг*): **э́тот чай про́сто ~** the tea is just like dishwater.

бу́рен *прил см* **бу́рный**.

буре́ни|е (-я) *ср* boring, drilling.

буржуази́|я (-и) *ж* bourgeoisie; **ме́лкая ~** petty bourgeoisie.

буржуа́зный *прил* bourgeois.

буржу́|й (-я) *м* (*разг*) bourgeois.

бур|и́ть (-ю́, -и́шь; *perf* **пробури́ть**) *несов перех* to bore, drill.

бу́ркнуть (-у, -ешь) *сов перех* (*разг*) to grunt.

бурл|и́ть (-ю́, -и́шь) *несов неперех* (*вода*) to boil; (*ручей*) to bubble; (*толпа*) to seethe (*with excitement*).

бу́р|ный (-ен, -на́, -но) *прил* (*погода, океан*) stormy, rough; (*река*) turbulent; (*чувство, порыв*) wild; (*спор*) heated; (*рост*) rapid.

бурови́к (-а́) *м* driller.

бурово́й *прил* boring, drilling; **бурова́я вы́шка** derrick; **бурова́я сква́жина** bore(hole).

бурч|а́ть (-у́, -и́шь; *perf* **пробурча́ть**) *несов неперех* (*разг: ворчать*) to mutter; ~ (**пробурча́ть** *perf*) **себе́ под нос** to mutter *или* grumble to o.s.

бу́р|ый (-, -а́, -о) *прил* brown; **бу́рый у́голь** (*ГЕО*) brown coal, lignite.

бу́р|я (-и) *ж* storm; (*перен*) burst; ~ **в стака́не воды́** storm in a teacup.

буря́т (-а; *gen pl* -) *м* Buryat.

Буря́ти|я (-и) *ж* Buryatia.

буря́т|ка (-ки; *gen pl* -ок) *ж см* **буря́т**.

бу́с|ы (-) *мн* beads *мн*.

бутафо́ри|я (-и) *ж* (*ТЕАТР*) props *мн* (= *properties*;) (*перен*) sham.

бутербро́д (-а) *м* sandwich.

буто́н (-а) *м* bud.

бу́тс|а (-ы) *ж* (*обычно мн*) football boot.

буты́л|ка (-ки; *gen pl* -ок) *ж* bottle.

буты́лочный *прил* bottle *опред*; (*цвет*) bottle-green.

бу́фер (-а; *nom pl* -а́) *м* (*также перен, КОМП*) buffer.

буфериза́ци|я (-и) *ж* (*КОМП*) buffering.

бу́ферный *прил* (*также перен*) buffer *опред*.

буфе́т (-а) *м* (*для продажи закусок*) snack bar; (*шкаф*) sideboard.

буфе́тчик (-а) *м* assistant (*in snack bar*).

буфе́тчиц|а (-ы) *ж см* **буфе́тчик**.

бух *межд*: ~! bang!; (*разг: упал*) whoops!

буха́н|ка (-ки; *gen pl* -ок) *ж* loaf.

Бухаре́ст (-а) *м* Bucharest.

бу́ха|ть (-ю) *несов от* **бу́хнуть**.

бухга́лтер (-а) *м* accountant, book-keeper; ~**-ревизо́р** auditor.

бухгалте́ри|я (-и) *ж* accountancy, book-keeping; (*отдел*) accounts office.

бухга́лтерский (-ая, -ое, -ие) *прил* book-keeping *опред*, accountancy *опред*; **бухга́лтерские кни́ги** books; **бухга́лтерский учёт** book-keeping, accountancy.

бу́хн|уть (-у, -ешь; *impf* **бу́хать**) *сов неперех* (*дверь*) to bang; (*пушка*) to thunder ♦ *несов неперех* to swell.

бу́хт|а (-ы) *ж* bay.

бу́хты-ба́рахты *нареч*: **с ~** just like that; (*внезапно*) out of the blue.

буш|ева́ть (-у́ю) *несов неперех* (*пожар, ураган*) to rage.

Буэ́нос-А́йрес (-а) *м* Buenos Aires.

БЦЖ *ж сокр* BCG (= *Bacillus Calmette-Guérin*).

KEYWORD

бы *част* **1** (*выражает предположительную возможность*): **купи́л бы, е́сли бы бы́ли де́ньги** I would buy it if I had the money; **я бы**

давнó ужé купи́л э́ту кни́гу, éсли бы у меня́ бы́ли дéньги I would have bought this book long ago if I had had the money

2 (*выражает пожелание*): **я бы хотéл поговори́ть с тобóй** I would like to speak to you; **я бы не хотéл об э́том говори́ть** I would rather not talk about it; **чáю бы** I could do with some tea

3 (*выражает совет*): **ты бы написáл ей** you should write to her

4 (*выражает опасение*): **не захвати́л бы нас дождь** I hope we don't get caught in the rain; **отдохну́ть/погуля́ть бы** it would be nice to have a rest/walk; **не опоздáть бы** better not to be late.

бывáло *част expresses a repeated action in the past*; **~ сиди́м и разговáриваем** we used to sit and talk.

бывáть (-ю) *несов неперех* (*приходи́ть, посещáть*) to be; (*случáться, происходи́ть*) to happen, take place; **он ~ет у нас чáсто** he often comes to see us; **~ют стрáнные слу́чаи** strange things happen; **как не ~ло** (*разг*) as if it had never been; **как ни в чём не ~ло** (*разг*) as if nothing had happened; **с кем не ~ет** it happens to the best of us.

бы́вш|ий (-ая, -ее, -ие) *прил* former; (*жена, муж*) ex-, former.

бык (-á) *м* bull; (*рабочий*) ox; **брать** (**взять** *perf*) **~á за рогá** to take the bull by the horns.

был *итп несов см* **быть**.

были́н|а (-ы) *ж* bylina (*Russian folk epic*).

бы́ло *част expresses non-fulfilment of an intended action*; **он нáчал ~ говори́ть, но останови́лся** he was about to say something, but stopped; **мы нáчали ~ уходи́ть, но пошёл дождь** we were about to leave, but it began to rain.

бы|ль (-и) *ж* (*рассказ*) true story.

бы́стро *нареч* quickly.

быстрот|á (-ы́) *ж* speed; (*умá, рук*) quickness.

быстрохóд|ный (-ен, -на, -но) *прил* fast.

бы́стр|ый (-, á, -о) *прил* fast; (*лóшадь*) swift, fast; (*провóрный, бéглый*) quick.

быт (-а; *loc sg* -ý) *м* life; (*повседнéвная жизнь*) everyday life; **э́то вошлó в ~** this has become a part of our everyday life; **слу́жба бы́та** consumer services *мн*.

бытовóй *прил* everyday *опред*; **бытовáя жи́вопись** genre painting; **бытовóе обслу́живание населéния** consumer services *мн*; **бытовóе явлéние** everyday occurrence.

KEYWORD

быть (*см* **Table 21**) *несов* **1** (*omitted in present tense*) to be; **кни́га на столé** the book is on the table; **зáвтра я бу́ду в шкóле** I will be at school tomorrow; **дом был на краю́ гóрода** the house stood on the edge of the town; **на ней краси́вое плáтье** she is wearing a beautiful dress; **вчерá был дождь** it rained yesterday

2 (*часть составнóго сказ*) to be; **я хочу́ быть учи́телем** I want to be a teacher; **я был рад ви́деть тебя́** I was happy to see you; **так и быть!** so be it!; **как быть?** what is to be done?; **э́того не мóжет быть** that's impossible; **кто/какóй бы то ни был** whoever/whatever it might be; **бу́дьте добры́!** excuse me, please!; **бу́дьте добры́ – позови́те егó!** would you be so good *или* kind as to call him?; **бу́дьте здорóвы!** take care!

3 (*образует будущее время*: +*impf vb*): **вéчером я бу́ду писáть пи́сьма** I'll be writing letters this evening; **я бу́ду люби́ть тебя́ всегдá** I'll love you forever.

бью(сь) *итп несов см* **бить(ся)**.

Бэ́йсик (-а) *м* (*комп*) BASIC.

бюджéт (-а) *м* budget; **дохóдный ~** income, revenue; **расхóдный ~** expenditure.

бюджéтный *прил* budgetary.

бюллетéн|ь (-я) *м* bulletin; (*листóк: для голосовáния*) ballot paper; (: *нетрудоспосóбности*) medical certificate; **быть** (*impf*) **на ~е** to be off sick (*from work*).

бюрó *ср нескл* office, agency; **спрáвочное ~** inquiry office; **бюрó (дóбрых) услу́г** domestic help agency; **бюрó нахóдок** lost property office; **бюрó по трудоустрóйству** employment agency.

бюрокрáт (-а) *м* bureaucrat.

бюрократи́зм (-а) *м* bureaucracy.

бюрократи́ческ|ий (-ая, -ое, -ие) *прил* bureaucratic.

бюрокрáти|я (-и) *ж* bureaucracy.

бюст (-а) *м* bust.

бюстгáльтер (-а) *м* bra (= *brassiere*).

бяз|ь (-и) *ж* calico.

~ В, в ~

В, в *сущ нескл (буква)* the 3rd letter of the Russian alphabet.

В *сокр* (= вольт) v. (= volt).

KEYWORD

в *предл* (+*acc*) **1** (*о месте направления*) in(to); **я положи́л кни́гу в портфе́ль** I put the book in(to) my briefcase; **я сел в маши́ну** I got in(to) the car

2 (*уехать, пойти*) to; **он уе́хал в Москву́** he went to Moscow; **идти́ (пойти́** *perf*) **в учителя́** to become a teacher; **выбира́ть (вы́брать** *perf*) **кого́-н в комите́т** to elect sb to a committee

3 (*об изменении состояния*): **погружа́ться в рабо́ту** to be absorbed in one's work; **погружа́ться** (*impf*) **в разду́мье** to be deep in thought

4 (*об объекте физического действия*): **он постуча́л в дверь** he knocked on the door; **он посмотре́л мне в глаза́/в лицо́** he looked me in the eyes/face; **мать поцелова́ла меня́ в щёку** mother kissed me on the cheek

5 (*обозначает форму, вид*): **брю́ки в кле́тку** checked trousers; **лека́рство в табле́тках** medicine in tablet form; **разрыва́ть (разорва́ть** *perf*) **что-н в кло́чья** to tear sth to shreds; **растира́ть (растере́ть** *perf*) **что-н в порошо́к** to grind sth to a powder

6 (*о размере, количестве*): **ве́сом в 3 то́нны** 3 tons *или* tonnes in weight; (: +*prp*): **дра́ма в трёх частя́х** a drama in three acts; **отря́д в де́сять челове́к** a detachment of ten men; **в пяти́ ме́трах от доро́ги** five metres (*BRIT*) *или* meters (*US*) from the road

7 (*о соотношении величин*): **в два ра́за бо́льше/длинне́е/то́лще** twice as big/long/thick; **во мно́го раз лу́чше/умне́е** much better/cleverer; **во мно́го раз поле́знее/краси́вее** much more useful/beautiful

8 (*о времени совершения чего-н*): **он пришёл в понеде́льник** he came on Monday; **я ви́дел его́ в про́шлом году́** I saw him last year; **я встре́тил его́ в два часа́** I met him at two o'clock; **э́то случи́лось в ма́рте/в двадца́том ве́ке** it happened in March/in the twentieth century

9 (+*prp*; *о месте*) in; **ко́шка сиди́т в корзи́не** the cat is sitting in the basket; **я живу́ в дере́вне** I live in the country; **сын у́чится в шко́ле/университе́те** my son is at school/university; **в отдале́нии/сосе́дстве** in the distance/the neighbourhood

10 (*о чём-н облегающем, покрывающем*): **ру́ки в кра́ске/са́же** hands covered in paint/soot; **това́р в упако́вке** packaged goods; **не́бо в ту́чах** the sky is overcast

11 (*об одежде*) in; **мужчи́на в очка́х/в ша́пке** a man *или* wearing glasses/a hat

12 (*о состоянии*): **быть в у́жасе/негодова́нии** to be terrified/indignant.

в. *сокр* (= век) c (= *century*); (= восто́к) E (= *East*); (= восто́чный) E (= *East*).

ва-ба́нк *нареч* (*также перен*): **идти́ ~** to stake everything.

ваго́н (-а) *м* (*пассажирский*) carriage (*BRIT*), coach (*BRIT*), car (*US*); (*товарный*) wagon (*BRIT*), truck; **спа́льный ~** couchette car; **мя́гкий ~** ≈ sleeping car; **ваго́н-рестора́н** dining (*BRIT*) *или* club (*US*) car.

вагоне́т|ка (-ки; *gen pl* **-ок)** *ж* trolley (*RAIL*).

ваго́нный *прил* carriage *опред* (*BRIT*), car *опред* (*US*); **ваго́нный парк** train depot.

вагоноремо́нтный *прил* (*завод*) coach (*BRIT*) *или* car (*US*) reparation *опред*.

вагонострои́тельный *прил* (*завод*) coach (*BRIT*) *или* car (*US*) building *опред*.

ва́жен *прил см* **ва́жный**.

ва́жнича|ть (-ю) *несов неперех* to act in a self-important manner.

ва́жность (-и) *ж* importance; (*надменность*) self-importance; **(не) велика́ ~** what does it matter.

ва́жный (-ен, -на́, -но) *прил* important; (*гордый*) pompous.

ВАЗ (-а) *м сокр* = **Во́лжский автомоби́льный заво́д**; (*автомобиль*) *vehicle manufactured at the Volga car factory*.

ва́з|а (-ы) *ж* vase.

вазели́н (-а; *part gen* **-у)** *м* Vaseline®.

вака́нси|я (-и) *ж* vacancy; **откры́лась ~ в бухгалте́рии** a vacancy has now arisen in accounts.

вака́нт|ный (-ен, -на, -но) *прил* vacant; **~ная до́лжность** vacancy.

ва́кс|а (-ы) *ж* black shoe polish.

ва́куум (-а) *м* (*также перен*) vacuum.

вакци́н|а (-ы) *ж* vaccine.

вакцини́р|овать (-ую) *(не)сов перех* to vaccinate.

вал (-а; *loc sg* -ý, *nom pl* -ы́) *м* (*насыпь*) bank; (: *крепости*) rampart; (*стержень*) shaft; (*волна*) breaker; (*экон*) gross product.

вале́жник (-а) *м собир* dead wood.

ва́лен|ок (-ка) *м* (*обычно мн*) felt boot.

валериа́н|а (-ы) *ж* valerian.

валериа́нк|а (-и) *ж* valerian drops *мн*.

валериа́нов|ый *прил*: ~ые ка́пли valerian drops.

валерья́н|а (-ы) *ж* = **валериа́на**.

вале́т (-а) *м* (*КАРТЫ*) jack.

валидо́л (-а) *м type of mild sedative*.

ва́лик (-а) *м* (*в механизме*) cylinder; (*для краски*) roller; (*подушка*) bolster.

вал|и́ть (-ю́, -ишь; *perf* **свали́ть** *или* **повали́ть**) *несов перех* (*заставить падать*) to knock over; (*рубить*) to fell; (*perf* **свали́ть**; *разг*: *бросать*) to dump ◆ *неперех* (*no perf*; *народ*) to flock; (*дым, пар*) to pour out; ~ **(свали́ть** *perf***) вину́ на** +*acc* (*разг*) to point the finger at; **ва́лит снег** it's snowing heavily; **толпа́ ~и́ла на конце́рт** the crowd flocked to the concert

▸ **вали́ться** (*perf* **свали́ться** *или* **повали́ться**) *несов возв* (*падать*) to fall; (*разг*: *опускаться*) to flake out; **все бе́ды ва́лятся на него́** he attracts misfortune; **у него́ всё ва́лится из рук** everything he does fails; ~**ся с ног** (*разг*) to be dead on one's feet.

валово́й *прил* (*доход*) gross *опред*; **валово́й вну́тренний проду́кт** gross domestic product; **валово́й национа́льный проду́кт** gross national product; **валова́я при́быль** gross profit; ~ **объём прода́жи** gross sales *мн*.

ва́лом *нареч*: ~ **вали́ть** (*разг*: *народ*) to flock.

валто́рн|а (-ы) *ж* French horn.

валу́н (-а́) *м* boulder.

вальс (-а) *м* waltz.

вальцева́ть (-у́ю) *несов перех* to roll.

вальц|ы́ (-о́в) *мн* (*станок*) rolling press *ед*.

валю́т|а (-ы) *ж* currency ◆ *собир* foreign currency; **твёрдая** ~ hard currency.

валю́тно-фина́нсовый *прил* monetary.

валю́тный *прил* currency *опред*; ~ **контро́ль** exchange control; **валю́тный курс** rate of exchange; **валю́тный фонд** currency reserves *мн*.

валю́тчик (-а) *м* (*разг*) *person illegally dealing in foreign currency*.

валю́тчиц|а (-ы) *ж см* **валю́тчик**.

валя́|ть (-ю) *несов перех* (*катать*) to roll; (*perf* **свалять**; *скатывать*) to shape

▸ **валя́ться** *несов возв* (*кататься*) to roll about; (*разг*: *человек, бумаги итп*) to lie about; (: *с гриппом итп*) to be laid up; **де́ньги на земле́** *или* **на доро́ге не** ~**ются** (*разг*) money doesn't grow on trees.

вам *мтп мест см* **вы**.

вампи́р (-а) *м* vampire.

ВАН *м сокр* (= **Ве́стник Акаде́мии нау́к Росси́и**) Bulletin of the Russian Academy of Science.

вандали́зм (-а) *м* vandalism.

ванили́н (-а; *part gen* -у) *м* vanillin.

вани́л|ь (-и) *ж* vanilla.

ва́нн|а (-ы) *ж* bath; **принима́ть** (**приня́ть** *perf*) ~**у** to take *или* have a bath.

ва́нн|ая (-ой; *decl like adj*) *ж* bathroom.

ва́рвар (-а) *м* barbarian.

ва́рварск|ий (-ая, -ое, -ие) *прил* barbaric.

ва́рварств|о (-а) *ср* (*бескульту́рие*) barbarism; (*жестокость*) barbarity.

ва́реж|ка (-ки; *gen pl* -ек) *ж* (*обычно мн*) mitten.

варе́ник (-а) *м* (*обычно мн*) sweet dumpling (*with curd or fruit filling*).

варёный *прил* boiled.

варе́нь|е (-я) *ср* jam.

вариа́нт (-а) *м* version; (*возможность*) option; (*разновидность*) variant.

вариа́ци|я (-и) *ж* variation.

вар|и́ть (-ю́, -ишь; *perf* **свари́ть**) *несов перех* (*обед*) to cook; (*суп, кофе*) to make; (*картофель, мясо*) to boil; (*ТЕХ*) to weld; (*сталь*) to found; **у него́ голова́** *или* **котело́к ва́рит** (*разг*) he has a good head on his shoulders

▸ **вари́ться** (*perf* **свари́ться**) *несов возв* (*приготовляться*) to be cooking; ~**ся** (*impf*) **в со́бственном соку́** (*перен*) to live in a world of one's own; **до́лго/бы́стро** ~**ся** (*impf*) to cook slowly/quickly.

Варша́в|а (-ы) *ж* Warsaw.

варьете́ *ср нескл* variety show.

варьи́р|овать (-ую) *несов* (*не)перех* to vary.

вас *мест см* **вы**.

василёк (-ька́) *м* cornflower.

ВАТА *ж сокр* (= **Всеми́рная ассоциа́ция тристи́ческих аге́нтств**) IATA (= *International Association of Travel Agencies*).

ва́т|а (-ы) *ж* cotton wool (*BRIT*), (absorbent) cotton (*US*).

вата́г|а (-и) *ж* (*ребят*) gang.

ватерли́ни|я (-и) *ж* water line.

ватерпа́с (-а) *м* spirit level.

ватерполи́ст (-а) *м* water-polo player.

ватерпо́ло *ср нескл* water polo.

вати́н (-а) *м* padding.

ва́тк|а (-и) *ж* cotton wool ball.

ва́тман (-а) *м heavy paper for drawing etc*.

ва́тник (-а) *м* quilted jacket.

ва́тный *прил* cotton-wool (*BRIT*), absorbent cotton *опред* (*US*); **ва́тное одея́ло** quilt.

ватру́ш|ка (-ки; *gen pl* -ек) *ж* curd tart.

ватт (-а) *м* watt.

ва́учер (-а) *м* voucher.

ва́фельный *прил*: ~ **торт** waffle.

ва́ф|ля (-ли; *gen pl* -ель) *ж* wafer.

ва́хт|а (-ы) *ж* watch; **стоя́ть** *(impf)* **на ~е** to keep watch.

ва́хтенный *прил (служба)* watch *опред*; **ва́хтенный журна́л** log(book).

вахтёр (-а) *м* caretaker, janitor.

Ваш *мест см* **ваш**.

ваш (-его; *f* **-а,** *nt* **-е,** *pl* **-и;** *как* **наш;** *см* **Table 9)** *притяж мест* your; **э́то ва́ше** this is yours; **наш дом бо́льше ва́шего** our house is bigger than yours; *см также* **ва́ши**.

ва́ш|и (-их; *decl like adj)* *мн* your nearest and dearest *мн*; **и на́шим и ~м** *(разг: пренебр)* all things to all people.

Вашингто́н (-а) *м* Washington.

вбежа́ть *(как* **бежа́ть;** *см* **Table 20;** *impf* **вбега́ть)** *сов неперех*: **~ (в** +*acc)* to run in(to).

вберу́ *итп сов см* **вобра́ть**.

вбива́|ть (-ю) *несов от* **вбить**.

вбира́|ть (-ю) *несов от* **вобра́ть**.

вбить (вобью, вобьёшь; *impf* **вбива́ть)** *сов перех*: **~ (в** +*acc)* to drive *или* hammer in(to); **я не могу́ ~ э́то ей в го́лову** *(разг)* I can't seem to get it into her thick skull.

вблизи́ *нареч* nearby ♦ *предл*: **~** +*gen или* **от** +*gen* near (to).

вбок *нареч* sideways.

вбра́сыва|ть (-ю) *несов от* **вбро́сить**.

вброд *нареч*: **переходи́ть (перейти́** *perf)* **~** to ford.

вбро́сить (-шу, -сишь; *impf* **вбра́сывать)** *сов перех* to throw in; **вбра́сывать (~** *perf)* **мяч** *(СПОРТ)* to take a throw-in.

ввали́|ться (-юсь, -ишься; *impf* **вва́ливаться)** *сов возв (разг)*: **~ (в** +*acc)* to burst in(to); **(щёки, глаза́)** to become sunken.

введе́ни|е (-я) *ср* introduction; *(войск)* sending in; *(данных)* input.

ввезти́ (-у́, -ёшь; *pt* **ввёз, -ла́, -ло́,** *impf* **ввози́ть)** *сов перех (в дом итп)* to take in; *(в страну́)* to import.

вве́ргн|уть (-у, -ешь; *impf* **вверга́ть)** *сов перех (перен)*: **~ в** +*acc* to reduce to; **он вверга́ет меня́ в тоску́** he depresses me.

вверну́ть (-у́, -ёшь; *impf* **вверты́вать)** *сов перех* to screw in; *(перен: разг: сло́во)* to put in.

вверх *нареч* up ♦ *предл*: **~ по** +*dat* up; **~ по тече́нию** upstream; **всё в до́ме/в ко́мнате ~ дном** *(разг)* everything in the house/room is topsy-turvy; **~ нога́ми** *(разг)* upside down.

вверху́ *нареч* up ♦ *предл* (+*gen)* at the top of.

вве|сти́ (-ду́, -дёшь; *pt* **-ёл, -ела́, -ело́,** *impf* **вводи́ть)** *сов перех* to take in; *(маши́ну: в гара́ж)* to put in; *(иглу́: в ве́ну итп)* to slip in; *(лека́рство, раство́р)* to inject; *(в компью́тер)* to enter; *(установи́ть: зако́н, по́шлины итп)* to introduce; *(сде́лать де́йствующим)*: **~ что-н в** +*acc* to put sth into; **вводи́ть (~** *perf)* **кого́-н в заблужде́ние/искуше́ние** to mislead/tempt sb; **вводи́ть (~** *perf)* **кого́-н в расхо́ды** to cause sb expense; **вводи́ть (~** *perf)* **что-н в мо́ду** to bring sth into fashion; **вводи́ть (~** *perf)* **кого́-н в курс собы́тий** to bring sb up-to-date with events.

ввиду́ *предл* (+*gen)* in view of ♦ *союз*: **~ того́, что** in view of the fact that; **~ плохо́й пого́ды рейс отло́жен** the flight has been delayed because of the bad weather.

ввин|ти́ть (-чу́, -ти́шь; *impf* **вви́нчивать)** *сов перех* to screw in.

ввод (-а) *м* bringing in; *(данных)* input, feeding in; *(электри́ческий, телефо́нный)* lead-in.

ввод|и́ть (-жу́, -дишь) *несов от* **ввести́**.

вво́дн|ый *прил (статья́)* introductory; *(устро́йство)* lead-in *опред*; **вво́дное отве́рстие** input; **вво́дное сло́во** parenthesis.

ввожу́ *несов см* **ввози́ть**.

ввоз (-а) *м (проце́сс)* importation; *(импорт)* imports *мн*; **беспо́шлинный ~** duty-free imports.

ввоз|и́ть (-жу́, -зишь) *несов от* **ввезти́**.

ввозн|о́й *прил* imported; **ввозны́е по́шлины** import duty *ед*.

вво́лю *нареч* to one's heart's content.

ввосьмеро́м *нареч* in a group of eight; **они́ живу́т там ~** there are eight of them living there.

ВВП *м сокр (= валово́й вну́тренний проду́кт)* GDP (= *gross domestic product)*.

ВВС *мн сокр (= вое́нно-возду́шные си́лы)* ≈ RAF (= *Royal Air Force* ед).

ВВФ *м сокр (= Вое́нно-возду́шный флот)* ≈ RAF (= *Royal Air Force)*.

ввысь *нареч* upwards.

ввяза́ться (-жу́сь, -жешься; *impf* **ввя́зываться)** *сов возв (разг)* to get involved.

вгиба́|ть (-ю) *несов от* **вогну́ть**.

вглубь *нареч* (down) into the depths ♦ *предл* (+*gen*; *вниз)* into the depths of; *(внутрь)* into the heart of.

вгляде́|ться (-жу́сь, -ди́шься; *impf* **вгля́дываться)** *сов возв*: **~ в** +*acc* to peer at.

вгоню́ *итп сов см* **вогна́ть**.

вгоня́|ть (-ю) *несов от* **вогна́ть**.

вда|ва́ться (-ю́сь) *несов от* **вда́ться**.

вдав|и́ть (-лю́, -ишь; *impf* **вда́вливать)** *сов перех*: **~ (в** +*acc)* to press in(to).

вдади́мся *итп сов см* **вда́ться**.

вдалеке́ *нареч* in the distance; **~ от** +*gen* a long way from.

вдали́ *нареч* = **вдалеке́**.

вдаль *нареч* into the distance.

вда́|ться (*как* **дать;** *см* **Table 14;** *impf* **вдава́ться)** *сов возв*: **~ в** +*acc* to jut out into; *(перен: в рассужде́ния)* to get caught up in; **вдава́ться** *(impf)* **в подро́бности** to go into details.

вдво́е *нареч (сложи́ть)* in two; **~ сильне́е/умне́е** twice as strong/clever.

вдвоём *нареч*: **они́ живу́т/рабо́тают ~** the two of them live/work together.

вдвойне́ *нареч (получи́ть, заплати́ть)* double (the amount).

вде́ла|ть (-ю; *impf* **вде́лывать)** *сов перех*: **~ в** +*acc (вста́вить)* to set into.

вде|ть (-ну, -нешь; *impf* **вдева́ть**) *сов перех* to put in; **вдева́ть** (~ *perf*) **ни́тку в иго́лку** to thread a needle.

ВДНХ *ж сокр* (= **Вы́ставка достиже́ний наро́дного хозя́йства СССР**) *exhibition of economic achievements of the USSR.*

вдоба́вок *нареч* (*разг*) in addition ◆ *предл*: ~ **к** +*dat* in addition to.

вдов|а́ (-ы́; *nom pl* -ы) *ж* widow.

вдове́ц (-ца́) *м* widower.

вдо́воль *нареч* to one's heart's content; **(в до́ме) всего́** ~ there is plenty of everything (in the house).

вдовца́ *итп сущ см* **вдове́ц**.

вдо́вый *прил* widowed.

вдого́нку *нареч* (*бежа́ть*) behind ◆ *предл*: ~ **за** +*instr* after.

вдоль *нареч* (*слома́ться, расколо́ться*) lengthways ◆ *предл* (+*gen*) along; ~ **и поперёк** here, there and everywhere; (*перен*) inside out.

вдох (-а) *м*: **де́лать** (**сде́лать** *perf*) ~ to breathe in.

вдохнове́ни|е (-я) *ср* inspiration.

вдохнове́н|ный (-ен, -на, -но) *прил* inspired.

вдохнов|и́ть (-лю́, -и́шь; *impf* **вдохновля́ть**) *сов перех* to inspire; ~ (*perf*) **кого́-н на что-н** to inspire sb to sth

▶ **вдохнови́ться** (*impf* **вдохновля́ться**) *сов возв* (+*instr*) to be inspired by.

вдохн|у́ть (-у́, -ёшь; *impf* **вдыха́ть**) *сов перех* (*во́здух*) to breathe in; (*дым, лека́рство*) to inhale; **вдыха́ть** (~ *perf*) **уве́ренность/ве́ру в кого́-н** to inspire confidence/faith in sb.

вдре́безги *нареч* to smithereens.

вдруг *нареч* suddenly; (*а е́сли*) what if; ~ **он не придёт** what if he doesn't come.

вду́ма|ться (-юсь; *impf* **вду́мываться**) *сов возв*: ~ **в** +*acc* to think over.

вду́мчив|ый (-, -а, -о) *прил* contemplative.

вду́мыва|ться (-юсь) *несов от* **вду́маться**.

вдыха́ни|е (-я) *ср* inhalation.

вдыха́|ть (-ю) *несов от* **вдохну́ть**.

вегетариа́н|ец (-ца) *м* vegetarian.

вегетариа́н|ка (-ки; *gen pl* -ок) *ж см* **вегетариа́нец**.

вегетариа́нск|ий (-ая, -ое, -ие) *прил* vegetarian.

вегетариа́нца *сущ см* **вегетариа́нец**.

вегета́ци|я (-и) *ж* vegetation.

ве́да|ть (-ю) *несов см* **вести́** ◆ *неперех*: ~ +*instr* (*управля́ть*) to be in charge of.

ведём *несов см* **вести́**.

ве́дени|е (-я) *ср* authority; **принима́ть** (**приня́ть** *perf*) **в своё** ~ to take charge of; **быть** (*impf*) **в** ~**и кого́-н** to be under sb's authority.

веде́ни|е (-я) *ср* (*уро́ка, сле́дствия*) conducting; (*войны́*) waging; ~ **хозя́йства** housekeeping.

ве́дер *сущ см* **ведро́**.

ведёт(ся) *итп несов см* **вести́(сь)**.

ве́домо *ср*: **с/без ве́дома кого́-н** (*согла́сие*) with/without sb's consent; (*уведомле́ние*) with/without sb's knowledge.

ве́домости (-ей) *мн* gazette *ед*.

ве́домост|ь (-и; *gen pl* -ей) *ж* register; **расчётная** *или* **платёжная** ~ payroll; *см также* **ве́домости**.

ве́домственный *прил* departmental; (*подхо́д*) narrow-minded.

ве́домств|о (-а) *ср* department.

ведр|о́ (-а́; *nom pl* **вёдра**, *gen pl* **вёдер**) *ср* bucket, pail; **(дождь) льёт, как из** ~**а** it's pouring *или* bucketing (with rain).

веду́(сь) *итп несов см* **вести́(сь)**.

веду́щ|ая (-ей; *decl like adj*) *ж см* **веду́щий**.

веду́щ|ий (-ая, -ее, -ие) *прил* leading ◆ (-его; *decl like adj*) *м* presenter.

ведь *нареч* (*в вопро́се*): ~ **ты хо́чешь пое́хать?** you do want to go, don't you?; (*в утвержде́нии*): ~ **она́ не спра́вится одна́!** she surely can't manage alone! ~ **соиз** (*ука́зывает на причи́ну*) seeing as; ~ **она́ ра́да?** she is glad, isn't she?; **пое́шь, ~ ты го́лоден** you should eat, seeing as you're hungry; ~ **я проси́л тебя́!** I asked YOU!

ве́дьм|а (-ы) *ж* (*та́кже перен*) witch; **охо́та за** ~**ми** *или* **на ведьм** witch-hunt.

ве́ер (-а; *nom pl* -а́) *м* fan.

ве́жливо *нареч* politely.

ве́жливост|ь (-и) *ж* politeness.

ве́жлив|ый (-, -а, -о) *прил* polite.

вёз *итп несов см* **везти́**.

везде́ *нареч* everywhere; ~ **и всю́ду** everywhere you go.

вездесу́щ|ий (-ая, -ее, -ие; -, -а, -е) *прил* (*Бог*) omnipresent; (*челове́к*) ubiquitous.

вездехо́д (-а) *м* ≈ Landrover®.

везе́ни|е (-я) *ср* luck.

вез|ти́ (-у́, -ёшь; *pt* вёз, -ла́, -ло́) *несов перех* to transport, carry; (*дви́гать: за собо́й*) to pull; (: *перед собо́й*) to push ◆ (*perf* **повезти́**) *безл* (+*dat*; *разг*) to be lucky; **ему́ (ча́сто)** ~**ёт** he is (often) lucky.

Везу́вий (-я) *м* Vesuvius.

везу́ч|ий (-ая, -ее, -ие; -, -а, -е) *прил* lucky.

вей(те) *несов см* **вить**.

век (-а; *loc sg* -у́, *nom pl* -а́) *м* century; (*истори́ческий пери́од*) age; (*чья-н жизнь*) lifetime; **це́лый** ~ **тебя́ не ви́дел** I haven't seen you for ages; **на** ~**а́** forever; **в ко́и-то ве́ки** (*разг*) for the first time in ages; **жить** (*impf*) **в** ~**а́х** to live on forever; **во ве́ки** ~**о́в** forever.

ве́к|о (-а) *ср* eyelid.

веково́й *прил* (*тради́ция, де́рево*) ancient.

ве́ксел|ь (-я; *nom pl* -я́) *м* promissory note; **переводно́й** ~ bill of exchange; **казначе́йский**

~ treasury bill; **плати́ть (заплати́ть** *perf***) по ~ю**
to settle an account.
вёл(ся) *итп несов см* **вести́(сь).**
велé|ть (-ю, -ишь) *(не)сов неперех* (+*dat*) to
order; **он ~ёл мне прийти́, он ~ёл что́бы я**
пришёл he ordered me to come.
велика́н (-а) *м* giant.
вели́к|ий (-ая, -ое, -ие; -, -á, -ó) *прил* great; (*no*
full form; *обувь, одежда*) too big; **сапоги́ велики́**
the boots are too big; **вели́кие держа́вы** the
Great Powers.
Великобрита́ни|я (-и) *ж* Great Britain.
великоду́ш|ный (-ен, -на, -но) *прил*
magnanimous, big-hearted.
великолéп|ный (-ен, -на, -но) *прил*
(*роскошный*) magnificent, splendid; (*разг*)
fantastic.
великому́ченик (-а) *м* holy martyr.
великоро́сс (-а) *м* (*ист: обычно мн*) Great
Russian (*old name for a Russian*).
вели́чественн|ый (-, -на, -но) *прил* majestic.
вели́честв|о (-а) *ср*: **Ва́ше** *итп* **~** Your *итп*
Majesty.
вели́чи|е (-я) *ср* grandeur.
величина́ (-ы́) *ж* size; (*МАТ*) quantity; (*КОМП*:
значение) value.
вело́(сь) *несов см* **вести́(сь).**
велого́н|ка (-ки; *gen pl* **-ок)** *ж* (*СПОРТ: обычно*
мн) cycle race.
велодро́м (-а) *м* velodrome.
велосипéд (-а) *м* bicycle; **го́ночный ~** racing
bicycle, racer.
велосипеди́ст (-а) *м* cyclist.
велосипеди́ст|ка (-ки; *gen pl* **-ок)** *ж см*
велосипеди́ст.
вельвéт (-а) *м* corduroy.
вельмо́ж|а (-и) *м* dignitary.
велю́р (-а) *м* velours.
Вéн|а (-ы) *ж* Vienna.
вéн|а (-ы) *ж* vein.
венгéр|ка (-ки; *gen pl* **-ок)** *ж см* **венгр.**
венгéрск|ий (-ая, -ое, -ие) *прил* Hungarian; **~**
язы́к Hungarian.
венгр (-а) *м* Hungarian.
Вéнгри|я (-и) *ж* Hungary.
Венéр|а (-ы) *ж* Venus.
венери́ческ|ий (-ая, -ое, -ие) *прил*: **~ая**
боле́знь venereal disease.
венероло́ги|я (-и) *ж* venereology.
Венесуэ́л|а (-ы) *ж* Venezuela.
венесуэ́л|ец (-ьца) *м* Venezuelan.
венесуэ́л|ка (-ки; *gen pl* **-ок)** *ж см* **венесуэ́лец.**
венесуэ́льск|ий (-ая, -ое, -ие) *прил*
Venezuelan.
венесуэ́льца *итп сущ см* **венесуэ́лец.**
вен|éц (-ца́) *м* crown; (*АСТРОНОМИЯ*) corona;
идти́ (пойти́ *perf***) под ~ с кем-н** to walk down
the aisle with sb.
венециа́нск|ий (-ая, -ое, -ие) *прил* Venetian.
Венéци|я (-и) *ж* Venice.
вéнзел|ь (-я; *nom pl* **-я)** *м* monogram.
вéник (-а) *м* broom, besom.

венка́ *итп сущ см* **вено́к.**
венó́зный *прил* venous.
венóк (-ка́) *м* wreath.
вентили́р|овать (-ую; *perf*
провентили́ровать) *несов перех* (*помещение*)
to ventilate.
вéнтил|ь (-я) *м* valve.
вентиля́тор (-а) *м* (ventilator) fan.
вентиля́ци|я (-и) *ж* ventilation.
венца́ *итп сущ см* **венéц.**
венча́ни|е (-я) *ср* (*коронование*) coronation;
(*бракосочетание*) church wedding.
венча́|ть (-ю; *perf* **обвенча́ть** *или* **повенча́ть)**
несов перех (*соединять браком*) to marry;
(*находиться наверху*) to crown; **~** (*impf*) **на**
ца́рство кого́-н to crown sb
► **венча́ться** (*perf* **обвенча́ться**) *несов возв* to
be married (*in church*).
вéнчик (-а) *м* (*БОТ*) corolla.
венчу́рн|ый *прил*: **~ое предприя́тие** venture;
~ капита́л venture capital.
вéр|а (-ы) *ж* faith; (*в бога*) belief; **~ в**
кого́-н/что-н faith in sb/sth; **~ой и пра́вдой**
служи́ть (*impf*) **кому́-н/чему́-н** to serve sb/sth
faithfully; **на ~у принима́ть (приня́ть** *perf***)**
что-н to take sth on trust.
вера́нд|а (-ы) *ж* verandah.
вéрб|а (-ы) *ж* pussy willow.
верба́льный *прил* verbal.
верблю́д (-а) *м* camel.
верблю́диц|а (-ы) *ж см* **верблю́д.**
вéрбн|ый *прил*: **~ое воскресéнье** ≈ Palm
Sunday.
верб|ова́ть (-у́ю; *perf* **завербова́ть)** *несов*
перех to recruit.
вербо́в|ка (-ки; *gen pl* **-ок)** *ж* recruitment.
верди́кт (-а) *м* verdict; **выноси́ть (вы́нести**
*perf***) обвини́тельный/оправда́тельный ~** to
pronounce a verdict of guilty/not guilty.
верёв|ка (-ки; *gen pl* **-ок)** *ж* (*толстая*) rope;
(*тонкая*) string; (*для белья*) line; **вить** (*impf*)
~ки из кого́-н to twist sb round one's little
finger.
вéрен *прил см* **вéрный.**
верени́ц|а (-ы) *ж* (*предметов*) line; (*людей*)
file; (*перен: мыслей итп*) series.
вéреск (-а) *м* heather.
верет|ено́ (-ена́; *nom pl* **-ёна)** *ср* spindle.
вереща́|ть (-у́, -и́шь) *несов неперех* (*женщина*)
to chatter.
верзи́л|а (-ы) *м/ж* (*разг*) beanpole.
вери́г|а (-и) *ж* (*обычно мн*) chain (*worn for*
religious reasons).
вери́тельн|ый *прил*: **~ая гра́мота** credentials
мн.
вéр|ить (-ю, -ишь; *perf* **повéрить)** *несов*
неперех (+*dat*) to believe; (*доверять*) to trust; **~**
(**повéрить** *perf***) в кого́-н/что-н** to believe *или*
have faith in sb/sth; **~** (*impf*) (**в Бо́га**) to believe
(in God); **~** (**повéрить** *perf***) на́ слово кому́-н** to
take sb at his *итп* word; **я не ~ю свои́м**

глаза́м/уша́м I don't believe my eyes/ears
▶ **ве́риться** *несов безл:* **не** ~**ится, что э́то пра́вда** it's hard to believe it's true.
вермише́л|ь (-и) *ж* vermicelli.
ве́рмут (-а) *м* vermouth.
верне́е *вводн сл* or rather; ~ **всего́** most likely.
верниса́ж (-а) *м* private view (*of art exhibition etc*).
ве́рно *нареч* (*пре́данно*) faithfully; (*пра́вильно*) correctly ◆ *как сказ* that's right ◆ *вводн сл* probably; **она́,** ~**, больна́** she must be *или* is probably ill.
верноподданн|ая (-ой; *decl like adj*) *ж см* **верноподданный**.
верноподданн|ый (-ого; *decl like adj*) *м* loyal subject.
ве́рност|ь (-и) *ж* (*пре́данность*) faithfulness, loyalty; (*пра́вильность*) correctness; **для** ~**и** just to make sure.
верну́ть (-у́, -ёшь) *сов перех* to return, give back; (*долг*) to pay back; (*здоро́вье, наде́жду итп*) to restore; ~ (*perf*) **кого́-н к де́йствительности** to bring sb back (down) to earth; ~ (*perf*) **кого́-н про́шлому** to take sb back
▶ **верну́ться** *сов возв:* ~**ся (к** +*dat*) to return (to).
ве́р|ный (-ен, -на́, -но) *прил* (*пре́данный*) faithful; (*надёжный*) sure; (*пра́вильный*) correct; (*no short form; неизбе́жный*) certain; ~ **сло́ву** true to one's word; **она́ верна́ само́й себе́** she acts true to form.
ве́рование (-я) *ср* (*обычно мн*) belief.
ве́р|овать (-ую) *несов неперех* to believe (in God).
вероиспове́дани|е (-я) *ср* faith.
вероло́м|ный (-ен, -на, -но) *прил* (*друг*) treacherous; (*нападе́ние*) deceitful.
вероотсту́пник (-а) *м* apostate.
веротерпи́мост|ь (-и) *ж* (*РЕЛ*) tolerance.
вероуче́ни|е (-я) *ср* teachings *мн*.
вероя́тен *прил см* **вероя́тный**.
вероя́тно *как сказ* it is likely *или* probable ◆ *вводн сл* probably.
вероя́тност|ь (-и) *ж* probability; **по всей** ~**и** in all probability.
вероя́т|ный (-ен, -на, -но) *прил* likely, probable; ~**нее всего́** most likely *или* probably.
ве́рси|я (-и) *ж* version.
верст|а́ (-ы́; *nom pl* **вёрсты)** *ж* verst (*former Russian unit of measurement equal to 1.06 km*); **ви́дно за** ~**у́** it is visible from a long way away.
верста́к (-а́) *м* (*ТЕХ*) (work)bench.
верста́|ть (-ю; *perf* **сверста́ть)** *несов перех* to set.
вёрстк|а (-и) *ж* (page)proof.
ве́ртел (-а; *nom pl* **-а́)** *м* spit (*for roasting*).
вер|те́ть (-чу́, -ишь) *несов перех* (*руль*) to turn; ~ (*impf*) +*instr* (*зо́нтиком, тро́стью*) to twirl;

как ни ~**ти́, а он прав** (*разг*) no matter which way you look at it, he's right; ~ (*impf*) **в рука́х что-н** to fiddle with sth
▶ **верте́ться** *несов возв* (*колесо́*) to spin; (*челове́к*) to fidget; (: *хлопота́ть*) to be kept busy; ~**ся** (*impf*) **в голове́** (*разг: мысль*) to go round and round in one's head; **его́ и́мя ве́ртится у меня́ на языке́** his name is on the tip of my tongue; ~**ся** (*impf*) **под нога́ми** (*разг*) to get *или* be under one's feet.
вертика́л|ьный (-ен, -ьна, -ьно) *прил* vertical.
вертихво́ст|ка (-ки; *gen pl* **-ок)** *ж* flirt.
вертолёт (-а) *м* helicopter.
вертолётчик (-а) *м* helicopter pilot.
верту́ш|ка (-ки; *gen pl* **-ек)** *ж* revolving object; (*разг: о челове́ке*) featherbrain; **дверь-**~ revolving door.
ве́рующ|ая (-ей; *decl like adj*) *ж см* **ве́рующий**.
ве́рующ|ий (-его; *decl like adj*) *м* believer.
верф|ь (-и) *ж* shipyard; (*вое́нная*) dockyard.
верх (-а; *loc sg* **-у́,** *nom pl* **-и́)** *м* (*до́ма, стола́*) top; (*экипа́жа, коля́ски*) hood; (*шу́бы*) outer layer; (*обу́ви*) upper; ~ **соверше́нства/глу́пости** the height of perfection/stupidity; **оде́рживать (одержа́ть** *perf*) *или* **брать (взять** *perf*) ~ **над кем-н** to get the upper hand over sb; *см также* **верхи́**.
верх|и́ (-о́в) *мн:* **в** ~**а́х** at the top; **встре́ча/ перегово́ры в** ~**а́х** summit meeting/talks.
ве́рхн|ий (-яя, -ее, -ие) *прил* top; **ве́рхняя оде́жда** outer clothing *или* garments *мн*.
верхо́вный *прил* (*гла́вный*) supreme; **Верхо́вный Сове́т** Supreme Soviet; **Верхо́вный Суд** High Court (*BRIT*), Supreme Court (*US*).
верхов|о́й *прил:* ~**а́я езда́** riding, horseback riding (*US*); ~**а́я ло́шадь** mount.
верхо́вь|е (-я) *ср* upper reaches *мн*.
верхола́з (-а) *м* steeplejack.
верхо́м *нареч* astride; ~ **на ло́шади** on horseback.
верху́ш|ка (-ки; *gen pl* **-ек)** *ж* (*де́рева, на́сыпи*) top; (*перен: пра́вящая*) elite.
верчу́(сь) *несов см* **верте́ть(ся)**.
верши́н|а (-ы) *ж* (*холма́, де́рева*) top; (*горы́*) summit, peak; **на** ~**е сла́вы** at the height of his *итп* fame; **на** ~**е сча́стья** in seventh heaven.
верш|и́ть (-у́, -и́шь) *несов перех* (*суд*) to conduct ◆ *непере́х:* ~ +*instr* (*су́дьбами*) to control.
вес (-а; *part gen* **-у,** *nom pl* **-а́)** *м* weight; (*перен: влия́ние*) authority; **ве́сом в 5 килогра́мм** weighing 5 kilogrammes; **закрепля́ть (закрепи́ть** *perf*) **что-н на** ~**у́** to suspend sth; **прибавля́ть (приба́вить** *perf*) **в ве́се** to put on weight; **боре́ц лёгкого/тяжёлого ве́са** light-/heavyweight wrestler; **цени́ться** (*impf*) *или* **быть** (*impf*) **на** ~ **зо́лота** to be worth one's weight in

gold.

ве́сел *прил см* **весёлый**.

вёсел *сущ см* **весло́**.

веселе́|ть (-ю; *perf* **повеселе́ть**) *несов неперех* to cheer up.

весел|и́ть (-ю́, -и́шь; *perf* **развесели́ть**) *несов перех* to amuse

▶ **весели́ться** *несов возв* to have fun.

ве́село *нареч* (*сказать*) cheerfully ♦ *как сказ*: **здесь** ~ it's fun here; **мне** ~ I'm having fun.

весёлый (-ел, -ла́, -ло) *прил* cheerful.

весе́ль|е (-я) *ср* (*настроение*) cheerfulness; (*времяпровождение*) merriment.

весе́нн|ий (-яя, -ее, -ие) *прил* spring *опред*.

ве́|сить (-шу, -сишь) *несов неперех* to weigh.

ве́ский (-кая, -кое, -кие; -ок, -ка, -ко) *прил*: ~ **аргуме́нт** an argument that carries a lot of weight.

весл|о́ (-а́; *nom pl* **вёсла**, *gen pl* **вёсел**) *ср* oar.

весн|а́ (-ы́; *nom pl* **вёсны**, *gen pl* **вёсен**) *ж* spring.

весно́й *нареч* in (the) spring.

весно́ю *нареч* = **весно́й**.

весну́ш|ка (-ки; *gen pl* -ек) *ж* (*обычно мн*) freckle.

весов|о́й *прил* (*хлеб, конфеты итп*) *sold or bought by weight*; **весова́я катего́рия** (weight) category (*in boxing etc*).

ве́сок *прил см* **ве́ский**.

весо́м|ый (-, -а, -о) *прил* (*перен*) substantial.

вест (-а) *м* (*МОР*) west; (*ветер*) west wind.

ве́стерн (-а) *м* western.

ве|сти́ (-ду́, -дёшь; *pt* **вёл**, -ла́, -ло́) *несов перех* to take; (*машину, поезд*) to drive; (*корабль*) to navigate; (*войско, отряд*) to lead; (*собрание, заседание*) to chair; (*работу, исследования*) to conduct; (*хозяйство*) to run; (*дневник, записи*) to keep ♦ (*perf* **привести́**) *неперех*: ~ **к** +*dat* to lead to; ~ (*impf*) **себя́** to behave; ~ (*impf*) **речь о** +*prp* to talk about; ~ (*impf*) **нача́ло от** +*gen* to originate from

▶ **вести́сь** *несов возв* (*расследование*) to be carried out; (*переговоры*) to go on.

вестибю́л|ь (-я) *м* (*в гостинице*) lobby; (*в метро*) entrance hall.

ве́стник (-а) *м* messenger; (*перен*) herald; (*издание*) bulletin.

вест|ь (-и) *ж* news; **пропада́ть** (**пропа́сть** *perf*) **без ~и** (*ВОЕН*) to go missing; **без ~и пропа́вший** (*ВОЕН*) missing feared dead; **Бог ~ кто/что** (*разг*) God knows who/what; **пье́са была́ не Бог ~ кака́я** (*разг*) the play wasn't up to much.

вес|ы́ (-о́в) *мн* scales *мн*; (*созвездие*): **В**~ Libra.

весь (*всего́*; *f* **вся**, *nt* **всё**, *pl* **все**) *мест* (*целый, полностью*) all; ~ **день** all day; **я стара́лась изо всех сил** I tried with all my might; **он появи́лся** ~ **мо́крый/гря́зный** he appeared all wet/dirty; **при всём жела́нии я не смогу́ тебе́ помо́чь** with the best will in the world, I can't help you; **всего́ хоро́шего** *или* **до́брого!** all the best!; **без всего́** with nothing;

по всему́ (*по всем призна́кам*) by all the signs.

весьма́ *нареч* quite; ~ **непло́хо** not bad.

ветв|ь (-и; *gen pl* -е́й) *ж* branch.

ве́т|ер (-ра) *м* wind; **каки́м ~ром его́ сюда́ занесло́?** (*разг*) what brought him here?; **у него́ ~ в голове́** (*разг*) he hasn't a serious thought in his head.

ветера́н (-а) *м* veteran.

ветерина́р (-а) *м* vet (*inf*)) (= *veterinary surgeon*,) veterinarian (*US*).

ве́т|ка (-ки; *gen pl* -ок) *ж* branch; **железнодоро́жная ве́тка** branch line.

ве́то *ср нескл* veto; **накла́дывать** (**наложи́ть** *perf*) ~ **на что-н** to veto sth.

ве́ток *сущ см* **ве́тка**.

ве́тра *сущ см* **ве́тер**.

ве́треный *прил* windy; (*девушка*) empty-headed.

ветро́вк|а (-и) *ж* windcheater.

ветрово́й *прил* wind *опред*; **ветрово́е стекло́** windscreen (*BRIT*), windshield (*US*).

ветря́н|ка (-ки) *ж* (*МЕД*) chickenpox.

ветрян|о́й *прил* (*двигатель*) wind-powered; ~**а́я ме́льница** windmill.

ветх|ий (-ая, -ое, -ие; -, -а́, -о) *прил* (*старик*) decrepit; (*дом*) dilapidated; (*одежда*) shabby; **Ве́тхий Заве́т** the Old Testament.

ветхозаве́тный *прил* Old Testament *опред*; (*перен*) antediluvian.

ветчин|а́ (-ины́; *nom pl* -и́ны) *ж* ham.

ве́х|а (-и) *ж* (*обычно мн*) landmark.

ве́ч|е (-а) *ср* (*ИСТ*) *town assembly in medieval Russia*.

ве́чен *прил см* **ве́чный**.

ве́ч|ер (-а; *nom pl* -а́) *м* evening; (*праздник*) party; **на ~е** at a party.

вечере́|ть (*3sg* -ет) *несов безл* to grow dark.

вечери́н|ка (-ки; *gen pl* -ок) *ж* party.

вече́рн|ий (-яя, -ее, -ие) *прил* evening *опред*; ~**ие ку́рсы** evening classes.

вече́рник (-а) *м* (*разг*) part-timer (*studying in the evening*).

ве́чером *нареч* in the evening.

ве́чно *нареч* eternally; (*разг: жаловаться*) perpetually.

вечнозелёный *прил* evergreen.

ве́чност|ь (-и) *ж* eternity; **не ви́дел тебя́ це́лую ~** (*разг*) I haven't seen you for ages.

ве́ч|ный (-ен, -на, -но) *прил* eternal, everlasting; (*бессрочный*) indefinite; (*разг: непрестанный*) perpetual; **ве́чная мерзлота́** permafrost; **ве́чные снега́** everlasting snows.

ве́шал|ка (-ки; *gen pl* -ок) *ж* (*планка*) rack; (*стойка*) hatstand; (*плечики*) coat hanger; (*гардероб*) cloakroom; (*петля*) loop.

ве́ша|ть (-ю; *perf* **пове́сить**) *несов перех* to hang; (*perf* **све́шать**; *товар*) to weigh; ~ (**пове́сить** *perf*) **го́лову** to look downcast

▶ **ве́шаться** (*perf* **пове́ситься**) *несов возв* to hang o.s.; ~**ся** (*impf*) **на ше́ю кому́-н** (*разг: пренебр*) to throw o.s. at sb.

ве́шу *несов см* **ве́сить**.

веща́|ть (*3sg* -ет, *3pl* -ют) *несов неперех* to broadcast; ~ (*impf*) **на Москву́** to broadcast to Moscow.

веще́ственный *прил* material; **веще́ственное доказа́тельство** material evidence.

вещество́ (-а́) *ср* substance.

ве́щ|ий (-ая, -ее, -ие) *прил* prophetic.

вещь (-и; *gen pl* -**е́й**) *ж* thing; (*кни́га, фильм*) piece; **она́ оста́вила ве́щи в маши́не** she left her things in the car; **называ́ть (назва́ть** *perf*) **ве́щи свои́ми имена́ми** to call a spade a spade.

ве́яни|е (-я) *ср* breath; (*перен: в иску́сстве*) trend.

ве́|ять (-ю, -ешь) *несов неперех* (*ве́тер*) to blow lightly; (*флаг, па́рус*) to flutter; **в во́здухе —ет весно́й** spring is in the air.

вжи́|ться (-ву́сь, -вёшься; *pt* -лся, -ла́сь, -ло́сь, *impf* **вжива́ться**) *сов возв*: ~ **в роль** to get into a role.

взад *нареч*: ~-**вперёд** (*разг*) back and forth; **он не дви́гался ни** ~ **ни вперёд** he didn't budge (an inch).

взаи́мен *прил см* **взаи́мный**.

взаи́мность (-и) *ж* mutual feeling; **любо́вь без** ~**и** unrequited love; **отвеча́ть** (*impf*) **кому́-н** ~**ю** to reciprocate sb's feelings; **по́льзоваться** (*impf*) ~**ю** to be loved in return.

взаи́м|ный (-ен, -на, -но) *прил* mutual.

взаимовы́руч|ка (-ки; *gen pl* -ек) *ж* team spirit.

взаимоде́йстви|е (-я) *ср* (*связь*) interaction; (*подде́ржка*) cooperation.

взаимообусло́вленность (-и) *ж* interdependence.

взаимоотноше́ни|е (-я) *ср* (*обы́чно мн*) (inter) relationship.

взаимопо́мощь (-и) *ж* mutual assistance *или* aid.

взаимопонима́ни|е (-я) *ср* mutual understanding; **достига́ть (дости́гнуть** *или* **дости́чь** *perf*) ~**я** to come to *или* reach a mutual understanding.

взаимосвя́з|ь (-и) *ж* interconnection.

взаймы́ *нареч*: **дава́ть/брать де́ньги** ~ to lend/borrow money.

взаме́н *нареч* in exchange ♦ *предл* (+*gen*; *вме́сто*) instead of; (*в обме́н*) in exchange for; **он ничего́ че про́сит** ~ he doesn't want anything in return.

взаперти́ *нареч* under lock and key; **сиде́ть** (*impf*) ~ (*перен*) to stay indoors.

взахлёб *нареч* (*разг*) eagerly; ~ **хвали́ть** (*impf*) **что-н** to gush over sth.

взбадри́ва|ть (-ю) *несов от* **взбодри́ть**.

взба́лмош|ный (-ен, -на, -но) *прил* (*разг*) hysterical.

взба́лтыва|ть (-ю) *несов перех от* **взболта́ть**.

взбе́й(те) *сов см* **взбить**.

взберу́сь *сов см* **взобра́ться**.

взбе|си́ть(ся) (-шу́(сь), -си́шь(ся)) *сов от* **беси́ть(ся)**.

взбива́|ть (-ю) *несов от* **взбить**.

взбира́|ться (-юсь) *несов от* **взобра́ться**.

взбить (взобью́, взобьёшь; *imper* **взбе́й(те)**) *сов перех* (*я́йца*) to beat; (*сли́вки*) to whip; (*во́лосы*) to fluff up; (*поду́шки*) to plump up.

взбодр|и́ть (-ю́, -и́шь; *impf* **взба́дривать**) *сов перех* (*эмоциона́льно*) to hearten, cheer; (*физи́чески*) to invigorate.

взболта́|ть (-ю; *impf* **взба́лтывать**) *сов перех* to shake.

взбре|сти́ (-ду́, -дёшь; *pt* **взбрёл**, -ла́, -ло́) *сов неперех*: ~ **на́ гору** to slog up a hill; **ему́** ~**ло́ в го́лову** +*infin* ... (*разг*) he took it into his head to ....

взбудора́ж|ить (-у, -ишь; *impf* **взбудора́живать** *или* **будора́жить**) *сов перех* to agitate.

взбунт|ова́ться (-у́ю(сь)) *сов возв* to rebel.

взбу́ч|ка (-ки; *gen pl* -ек) *ж* (*разг*) dressing-down.

взвал|и́ть (-ю́, -ишь; *impf* **взва́ливать**) *сов перех*: ~ **что-н на** +*acc* to haul sth up onto; **взва́ливать** (~ *perf*) **отве́тственность на кого́-н** (*перен: разг*) to burden sb with responsibility.

взведу́ *итп сов см* **взвести́**.

взвёл *сов см* **взвести́**.

взве́|сить (-шу, -сишь; *impf* **взве́шивать**) *сов перех* (*това́р*) to weigh; (*перен: фа́кты*) to weigh up, consider.

взве|сти́ (-ду́, -дёшь; *pt* **взвёл**, -ла́, -ло́, *impf* **взводи́ть**) *сов перех*: **взводи́ть куро́к** to cock a gun.

взве́шен|ный (-, -на, -но) *прил* (*обду́манный*) considered; **во** ~**ном состоя́нии** (*перен: разг*) in suspense.

взве́шива|ть (-ю) *несов от* **взве́сить**.

взве́шу *сов см* **взве́сить**.

взвива́|ться (-юсь) *несов от* **взви́ться**.

взви́згн|уть (-у, -ешь; *impf* **взви́згивать**) *сов неперех* to let out a squeal.

взвин|ти́ть (-чу́, -ти́шь; *impf* **взви́нчивать**) *сов перех* (*разг: це́ны*) to jack up.

взви́нчен|ный (-, -на, -но) *прил* (*состоя́ние*) agitated; **он взви́нчен** he is worked up.

взви́|ться (-овью́сь, -овьёшься; *impf* **взвива́ться**) *сов возв* to shoot up; (*перен*) to fly off the handle.

взвод (-а) *м* platoon; **на взво́де** (*куро́к*) cocked; (*разг: челове́к*) on edge.

взводи́|ть (-жу́, -дишь) *несов от* **взвести́**.

взволно́ван|ный (-, -на, -но) *прил* (*в трево́ге*) agitated; (*ра́достный*) excited.

взволн|ова́ть(ся) (-у́ю(сь)) *сов от* **волнова́ть(ся)**.

взв|ыть (-о́ю, -о́ешь) *сов неперех* (*живо́тное,*

человек) to howl; (сире́на) to wail; ~ (perf) **от бо́ли** to howl in или with pain.

взгляд (-а) м glance; (выраже́ние) look; (перен: мне́ние) view; **с пе́рвого взгля́да, на пе́рвый** ~ at first sight или glance; **обме́ниваться (обменя́ться** perf) **взгля́дами** to exchange glances; **на мой/твой** ~ in my/your view; **остана́вливать (останови́ть** perf) ~ **на** +acc to rest one's gaze on.

взгля́н|у́ть (-у́, -ешь; impf **взгля́дывать**) сов непере́х: ~ **на** +acc to look at; (кра́тко) to glance at; (no impf; обрати́ть внима́ние) to look at.

взгромоз|ди́ть (-жу́, -ди́шь; impf **взгромождать**) сов перех: ~ (**на** +prp) to haul up (onto).

взгрустн|у́ться (3sg -ётся) сов безл (+dat; разг) to feel sad.

вздёрн|уть (-у, -ешь; impf **вздёргивать**) сов перех to jerk up; (ру́ку) to throw up; ~ (perf) **кого́-н на ви́селицу** (разг) to string sb up.

вздор (-а) м (разг) rubbish; **нести́** (impf) или **моло́ть** (impf) ~ (разг) to talk rubbish.

вздо́рен прил см **вздо́рный**.

вздо́р|ить (-ю, -ишь; perf **повздо́рить**) несов непере́х to squabble.

вздо́рный (-ен, -на, -но) прил (неле́пый) absurd; (сварли́вый) crotchety.

вздорожа́|ть (-ю) сов от **дорожа́ть**.

вздох (-а) м (облегче́ния итп) sigh; (у́жаса) gasp.

вздохн|у́ть (-у́, -нёшь) сов непере́х to sigh; (разг: отдохну́ть) to have a breather; **мне** ~ **не́когда** I'm rushed off my feet.

вздра́гива|ть (-ю) несов от **вздро́гнуть**.

вздремн|у́ть (-у́, -ёшь) сов непере́х (разг) to have a nap или snooze.

вздро́гн|уть (-у, -ешь) сов непере́х to shudder.

вздуться (-юсь) несов от **взду́ться**.

взду́ма|ть (-ю) сов непере́х (разг): **он** ~**л заня́ться ру́сским языко́м** he took it into his head to learn Russian; **не** ~**йте лгать!** don't even think of lying!

взду|ть (-ю, -ешь) сов перех (разг: це́ны) to inflate; **у него́ вздуло живо́т** his stomach became bloated

► **взду́ться** (impf **вздува́ться**) сов возв (щека́, живо́т) to swell up; (разг: це́ны) to shoot up.

вздыма́|ться (3sg -ется, 3pl -ются) несов возв (грудь) to heave; (во́лны) to rise.

вздыха́|ть (-ю) несов непере́х to sigh; (тоскова́ть): ~ **о** +prp (о мо́лодости) to yearn for; ~ (impf) **по** +dat to pine for.

взима́ни|е (-я) ср collecting.

взима́|ть (-ю) несов перех to collect.

взла́мыва|ть (-ю) несов от **взлома́ть**.

взлёт (-а) м (самолёта) takeoff; (перен: мы́сли) flight.

взлете́|ть (-чу́, -ти́шь; impf **взлета́ть**) сов непере́х (пти́ца) to soar; (самолёт) to take off;

взлета́ть (~ perf) **на во́здух** to explode.

взлётно-поса́дочный прил: **взлётно-поса́дочная полоса́** runway.

взлётный прил: ~**ая полоса́** или **доро́жка** runway, airstrip.

взлечу́ сов см **взлете́ть**.

взлома́ть (-ю; impf **взла́мывать**) сов перех to break open, force.

взло́мщик (-а) м burglar.

взлохма́тить (-чу, -тишь) сов от **лохма́тить**.

взма́лива|ться (-юсь) несов от **взмоли́ться**.

взмахн|у́ть (-у́, -ёшь; impf **взма́хивать**) сов непере́х (+instr; руко́й) to wave; (крыло́м) to flap.

взметн|у́ться (-у́сь, -ёшься) сов возв (пыль, и́скры) to fly up; (пла́мя, конь) to leap up.

взмол|и́ться (-ю́сь, -ишься; impf **взма́ливаться**) сов возв to beg.

взмо́р|ье (-я) ср seashore.

взму|ти́ть (-чу́, -ти́шь) сов от **мути́ть**.

взм|ыть (-о́ю, -о́ешь; impf **взмыва́ть**) сов непере́х to soar.

взнос (-а) м (страхово́й) payment; (в фонд) contribution; (чле́нский, вступи́тельный) fee; **ежеме́сячный** ~ monthly instalment.

взобра́|ться (взберу́сь, взберёшься; pt -лся, -лась, -ло́сь, impf **взбира́ться**) сов возв: ~ **на** +acc to climb (up) onto; **взбира́ться** (~ perf) **на́ го́ру** to climb (up) a hill.

взобью́ итп сов см **взбить**.

взовью́сь итп сов см **взви́ться**.

взойти́ (как **идти́**; см **Table 18**; impf **всходи́ть** или **восходи́ть**) сов непере́х (со́лнце, луна́) to rise; (семена́) to come up; (на го́ру, на престо́л) to ascend.

взор (-а) м glance; (выраже́ние) look.

взорв|а́ть (-у́, -ёшь; pt -а́л, -ала́, -а́ло, impf **взрыва́ть**) сов перех (бо́мбу) to detonate; (дом, мост) to blow up

► **взорва́ться** (impf **взрыва́ться**) сов возв (грана́та, бо́мба) to explode; (мост, дом) to be blown up; (разг: не сдержа́ться) to blow up.

взошёл итп сов см **взойти́**.

взра|сти́ть (-щу́, -сти́шь; impf **взра́щивать**) сов перех to cultivate, grow; (перен) to nurture.

взреве́|ть (-у́, -ёшь) сов непере́х to roar.

взро́сл|ая (-ой; decl like adj) ж см **взро́слый**.

взросле́|ть (-ю; perf **повзросле́ть**) несов непере́х to grow up; (духо́вно) to mature.

взро́слый прил (челове́к) grown-up опред; (фильм, биле́т, живо́тное) adult опред ◆ (-ого; decl like adj) м adult.

взрыв (-а) м explosion; (до́ма) blowing up; (+gen; возмуще́ния) outburst of; **разда́лся** ~ there was an explosion; ~ **сме́ха** a burst of laughter.

взрыва́|ть(ся) (-ю(сь)) несов от **взорва́ть(ся)**.

взрывно́й прил: ~**ая волна́** blast.

взрывоопа́сный (-ен, -на, -но) прил (также перен) explosive.

взрывча́т|ка (-ки; gen pl -ок) ж explosive

(substance); **закла́дывать (заложи́ть** *perf*) **~ку** to plant an explosive.

взры́вчатый *прил* explosive.

взрыхли́ть (-ю, -и́шь) *сов от* **рыхли́ть** ◆ (*impf* **взрыхля́ть**) *перех* to break up.

взъеро́ш|**ить** (-ю, -ишь) *сов от* **еро́шить**.

взыва́ть (-ю; *perf* **воззва́ть**) *несов неперех*: ~ **к кому́-н о** +*prp* to appeal to sb for; ~ (**воззва́ть** *perf*) **к чему́-н милосе́рдию/ра́зуму** to appeal to sb's sense of compassion/reason.

взыска́ни|**е** (-я) *ср* (*долга*) recovery; (*штрафа*) exaction; (*выговор*) reprimand; **накла́дывать** (**наложи́ть** *perf*) ~ **на кого́-н** to reprimand sb.

взыска́тель|**ный** (-ен, -ьна, -ьно) *прил* (*публика*) demanding; (*нача́льник*) exacting; (*критика*) severe.

взы́с|**ка́ть** (-щу́, -ще́шь; *impf* **взы́скивать**) *сов перех* (*долга*) to recover; (*штраф*) to exact ◆ *неперех*: ~ **с кого́-н** to call sb to account; **не ~щи́те!** I'm sorry!

взя́ти|**е** (-я) *ср* (*власти, террито́рии*) seizure; (*города, кре́пости*) capture.

взя́т|**ка** (-ки; *gen pl* -**ок**) *ж* (*подкуп*) bribe; (*ка́рты*) trick; **дава́ть (дать** *perf*) **кому́-н ~ку** to bribe sb; **брать** (*impf*) **~ку** to take a bribe.

взя́точник (-а) *м* bribe-taker.

взя́точниц|**а** (-ы) *ж см* **взя́точник**.

взя|**ть** (-ьму́, -ьмёшь; *pt* -л, -ла́, -ло) *сов от* **брать** ◆ *перех* (*разг*) to nick; **возьму́ и** *или* **да и откажу́сь** (*разг*) I could refuse just like that; **~л да и пое́хал** (*разг*) he upped and left; **~ или возьми́те хотя́ бы тако́й приме́р** let's take this example; **с чего́** *или* **отку́да ты ~л** (*разг: пренебр*) whatever gave you that idea?

▶ **взя́ться** *сов от* **бра́ться** ◆ *возв*: **отку́да ни возьми́сь, появи́лась Ма́ша** Masha appeared from out of the blue *или* as if from nowhere.

вибри́р|**овать** (-ую) *несов неперех* to vibrate.

вивисе́кци|**я** (-и) *ж* vivisection.

вид (-а; *part sing* -**у**, *loc sg* -**ý**) *м* (*вне́шность*) appearance; (*состояние: предмета*) form; (*панорама*) view; (*разновидность: расте́ний, живо́тных*) species; (: *спо́рта*) type; (: *иску́сства*) form; (*линг*) aspect; (*состояние*): **у него́ больно́й/серди́тый ~** he looks ill/angry; **в ви́де** +*gen* in the form of; **на ~ý у** +*gen* in full view of; **под ви́дом** +*gen* in the guise of; ~ **на о́зеро/го́ры/пло́щадь** a view of the lake/hills/square; **в ви́де шу́тки** as a joke; **име́ть** (*impf*) **в ~ý** to mean; (*учи́тывать*) to bear in mind; **скрыва́ться (скры́ться** *perf*)**/исчеза́ть (исче́знуть** *perf*) **из ви́да** to hide/disappear from view; **де́лать (сде́лать** *perf*) ~ to pretend; **упуска́ть (упусти́ть** *perf*) **из ви́ду что-н** (*перен*) to lose sight of sth; **теря́ть** (*потеря́ть perf*) **кого́-н из ви́ду** to lose sight of sb; **вид на жи́тельство** residence permit; *см также* **ви́ды.**

вида́ть (-ю; *perf* **повида́ть**) *несов перех* to see;

(*испыта́ть*) to know ◆ *вводн сл* obviously; **где э́то ви́дано!** (*разг*) whatever next!

▶ **вида́ться** (*perf* **повида́ться**) *несов возв* (*разг*) to see each other.

ви́ден *прил см* **ви́дный**.

ви́дени|**е** (-я) *ср* vision.

виде́ни|**е** (-я) *ср* (*во сне*) vision; (*при́зрак*) apparition.

видеоза́пис|**ь** (-и) *ж* video (recording).

видеоигр|**а́** (-ы́; *nom pl* -ы) *ж* video game.

видеока́мер|**а** (-ы) *ж* camcorder, videocamera.

видеокассе́т|**а** (-ы) *ж* video cassette.

видеомагнитофо́н (-а) *м* video (recorder).

видеоплён|**ка** (-ки; *gen pl* -ок) *ж* (video) tape.

видеофи́льм (-а) *м* video (film).

ви́|**деть** (-жу, -дишь) *несов неперех* to see ◆ (*perf* **уви́деть**) *перех* to see; (*испыта́ть*) to know; **рад Вас ~** it's good to see you; **~дите ли** you see; (**там**) **уви́дим** (*разг*) we'll see

▶ **ви́деться** *несов от* **привиде́ться** ◆ (*perf* **уви́деться**) *возв* to see each other; **вы́ход ~дится в эконо́мии средств** economizing is viewed as the solution; **мы с ним ча́сто ~димся** we see a lot of each other.

ви́димо *вводн сл* it looks like; **он, ~, не придёт** it looks like he's not coming.

ви́димо-неви́димо *нареч* (*разг*): **наро́ду на пло́щади ~** there are masses of people in the square.

ви́димост|**ь** (-и) *ж* visibility; (*подо́бие*) outward appearance; **по всей ~и** seemingly; **для ~и** for the sake of appearances.

ви́дим|**ый** (-, -а, -о) *прил* visible; (*no short form*; *ка́жущийся*) superficial; ~ **э́кспорт/и́мпорт** visible exports/imports *мн*.

видне́|**ться** (*3sg* -ется, *3pl* -ются) *несов возв* to be visible.

ви́дно *как сказ* (*мо́жно ви́деть*) one can see; (*мо́жно поня́ть*) clearly ◆ *вводн сл* probably; **из окна́ ~ го́ры** you can see the hills from the window; **~, что он волну́ется** clearly he is worried; **~, он уста́л** he is probably tired; **тебе́ видне́е** you know best; **как ~** as it happens; **там ~ бу́дет** we'll see.

ви́д|**ный** (-ен, -на́, -но, -ны́) *прил* (*заме́тный*) visible; (*no short form*; *изве́стный*) prominent; (*привлека́тельный*): **он ~ мужчи́на** he's a fine figure of a man; **~ен успе́х** success is in sight.

видоизмени́ть (-ю́, -и́шь; *impf* **видоизменя́ть**) *сов перех* to modify

▶ **видоизмени́ться** (*impf* **видоизменя́ться**) *сов возв* to alter.

ви́д|**ы** (-ов) *мн* prospects *мн*; **име́ть** (*impf*) ~ **на что-н** to have one's sights set on sth.

ви́жу(сь) *несов см* **ви́деть(ся)**.

ви́з|**а** (-ы) *ж* visa; (*дире́ктора, реда́ктора*) official stamp.

византи́йск|**ий** (-ая, -ое, -ие) *ж* Byzantine.

Византи|я (-и) *ж* Byzantine Empire.
визг (-а) *м* (*собаки*) yelp; (*ребёнка, поросёнка*) squeal; (*человека*) shriek; (*металла, тормозов итп*) screech.
визжа́ть (-у́, -и́шь) *несов неперех* (*см сущ*) to yelp; to squeal; to shriek; to screech.
визи́р|овать (-ую; *perf* завизи́ровать) *несов перех* (*документ*) to stamp; **ему́ ~ова́ли па́спорт** he was issued with a visa.
визи́т (-а) *м* visit; **прибыва́ть** (**при́быть** *perf*) **с ~ом** to arrive on an official visit; **де́лать** (**сде́лать** *perf* *или* **наноси́ть** (**нанести́** *perf*) **~ кому́-н** to visit sb.
визи́тн|ый *прил*: **~ая ка́рточка** (business) card.
визуа́л|ьный (-ен, -ьна, -ьно) *прил* visual.
вика́рий (-я) *м* vicar.
виктори́н|а (-ы) *ж* quiz game.
ви́л|ка (-ки; *gen pl* -ок) *ж* fork; **штéпсельная ~** two-pin plug.
ви́лл|а (-ы) *ж* villa.
ви́лок *сущ см* **ви́лка**.
ви́л|ы (-) *мн* pitchfork *ед*; **~ами на водé пи́сано** (*разг*) it's pie in the sky.
вильну́ть (-у́, -ёшь) *сов неперех*: **~ +instr** (*хвостом*) to wag; (*бёдрами*) to wiggle; (*дорога, река итп*) to bend sharply.
Ви́льнюс (-а) *м* Vilnius.
виля́|ть (-ю) *несов неперех*: **~ +instr** (*хвостом*) to wag; (*бёдрами*) to wiggle; (*дорога, река итп*) to wind (along); (*перен: разг: человек*) to be shifty.
вин|а́ (-ы́; *nom pl* -ы) *ж* (*чувство*) guilt; (*ответственность*) blame; **возлага́ть** (**возложи́ть** *perf*) **~у́ на +acc** to place the blame on; **ава́рия произошла́ по егó ~é** the accident was his fault, he was to blame for the accident.
винегрéт (-а) *м* beetroot salad.
вини́тельный *прил*: **~ падéж** accusative (case).
вин|и́ть (-ю́, -и́шь) *несов перех* to blame sb for; (*упрекать*): **~ когó-н за +acc** to accuse sb of.
вин|ó (-а́; *nom pl* -а) *ср* wine.
винова́т|ый *прил* (*взгляд итп*) guilty; (-, -а, -о): **~ (в +prp)** (*в проигрыше, неудаче*) responsible (for), to blame (for); **~!** sorry!, excuse me!; **чу́вствовать** (*impf*) **себя́ ~ым** to feel guilty; **он винова́т пéред дру́гом** he has failed his friend; **он винова́т в том, что ...** it is his fault that ....
вино́вен *прил см* **вино́вный**.
вино́вн|ая (-ой; *decl like adj*) *ж см* **вино́вный**.
вино́вник (-а) *м* culprit; **он – ~ трагéдии** he is to blame for the tragedy.
вино́вниц|а (-ы) *ж см* **вино́вник**.
вино́вност|ь (-и) *ж* guilt; **устана́вливать** (**установи́ть** *perf*) **~** to establish guilt.
вино́вн|ый (-ен, -на, -но) *прил* guilty ◆ (-ного; *decl like adj*) *м* guilty party; **признава́ть** (**призна́ть** *perf*) **себя́ ~ым** to plead guilty.
виногра́д (-а) *м* (*растение*) (grape)vine; (*ягоды*) grapes *мн*.
виногра́дник (-а) *м* vineyard.

виноде́ли|е (-я) *ср* wine-making.
винт (-а́) *м* screw; (*самолёта*) propeller.
ви́нтик (-а) *м* screw.
винто́в|ка (-ки; *gen pl* -ок) *ж* rifle.
виньéт|ка (-ки; *gen pl* -ок) *ж* vignette.
вио́л|а (-ы) *ж* (*муз*) viol.
виолончели́ст (-а) *м* cellist.
виолончели́ст|ка (-ки; *gen pl* -ок) *ж см* **виолончели́ст**.
виолончéл|ь (-и) *ж* cello.
ви́ра *межд*: **~!** lift!
вира́ж (-а́) *м* (*поворот*) turn; (*СПОРТ*) bend.
виртуа́льный *прил* (*КОМП*) virtual.
виртуо́з (-а) *м* virtuoso.
виртуо́з|ный (-ен, -на, -но) *прил* masterly; **~ное исполнéние** a virtuoso performance.
ви́рус (-а) *м* virus.
вис *итп несов см* **ви́снуть**.
ви́селиц|а (-ы) *ж* gallows *ед*.
ви|сéть (-шу́, -си́шь) *несов неперех* to hang; (*угрожать*): **~ над +instr** to hang over; **~** (*impf*) **в во́здухе** (*перен*) to be up in the air; **у негó на шéе ~ся́т ро́дственники жены́** (*разг*) his wife's relatives are a burden to him; **~** (*impf*) **на телефóне** (*разг*) to spend ages on the phone.
виска́ *сущ см* **висóк**.
ви́ски *ср нескл* whisky (*BRIT*), whiskey (*US, IRELAND*).
виско́з|а (-ы) *ж* viscose.
Ви́сл|а (-ы) *ж* Vistula (*river*).
ви́с|нуть (-ну, -нешь; *pt* -, -ла, -ло, *perf* **пови́снуть**) *несов неперех* (*цветы*) to droop; (*волосы*) to hang limply; **~** (*impf*) **у когó-н на шéе** (*перен*) to cling to sb.
висó|к (-ка́) *м* (*АНАТ*) temple.
високóсный *прил*: **~ год** leap year.
вист (-а) *м* whist.
вися́ч|ий (-ая, -ее, -ие) *прил*: **~ мост** suspension bridge; **закрепля́ть** (**закрепи́ть** *perf*) **что-н в ~ем положéнии** to suspend sth.
витами́н (-а) *м* vitamin.
вита́|ть (-ю) *несов неперех* (*запах*) to hang in the air; **~** *perf* **над +instr** (*опасность, смерть*) to hang *или* hover over; **~** (*impf*) **в облака́х** (*перен*) to have one's head in the clouds.
витиева́т|ый (-, -а, -о) *прил* flowery.
витка́ *сущ см* **витóк**.
витóй *прил* twisted; (*лестница*) spiral.
вит|óк (-ка́) *м* (*спирали*) twist; (*перен: этап*) stage.
витра́ж (-а́) *м* stained-glass window.
витри́н|а (-ы) *ж* (*в магазине*) shop window; (*в музее*) display case.
витри́но-вы́ставочн|ый *прил*: **~ая рекла́ма** display advertising.
ви|ть (вью, вьёшь; *pt* -л, -ла́, -ло, *imper* **вéй(те)**, *perf* **свить**) *несов перех* (*венок, верёвку*) to weave; (*гнездо*) to build
  ▶ **ви́ться** *несов возв* (*растения*) to trail; (*волосы*) to curl; (*флаг, лента*) to flutter; (*дым*) to spiral up.
вихó|р (-ра́) *м* forelock.

вихр|ь (-я) *м* whirlwind; (*перен: революции*) maelstrom; (*: развлечений*) whirl.

ви́це-председа́тел|ь (-я) *м* vice-chairman.

ви́це-президе́нт (-а) *м* vice president.

ВИЧ *м сокр* (= *ви́рус иммунодефици́та челове́ка*) HIV (= *human immunodeficiency virus*); **~-инфици́рованный** HIV-positive.

ви́шен *сущ см* **ви́шня**.

вишнёвый *прил* cherry.

ви́шн|я (-ни; *gen pl* -ен) *ж* (*дерево*) cherry (tree); (*плод*) cherry.

вишу́ *несов см* **висе́ть**.

вишь *част* (*разг*) (just) look (*used sarcastically*); ~ **(ты), како́й он сме́лый** look how brave he is, what a hero.

вка́лыва|ть (-ю) *несов от* **вколо́ть ◆** *неперех* (*no perf; разг*) to slog.

вка́пыва|ть (-ю) *несов от* **вкопа́ть**.

вка|ти́ть (-чу́, -тишь; *impf* **вка́тывать**) *сов перех* (*тачку, коляску*) to wheel in; (*бочку*) to roll in; (*перен: разг*): ~ **кому́-н пощёчину/вы́говор** to give sb a slap across the face/a dressing-down.

вклад (-а) *м* (*действие*) investment; (*в банке*) deposit; (*в науку, в литературу*) contribution; **вноси́ть** (**внести́** *perf*) ~ **в** +*acc* to make a contribution to.

вкла́дчик (-а) *м* investor.

вкла́дчиц|а (-ы) *ж см* **вкла́дчик**.

вкла́дыва|ть (-ю) *несов от* **вложи́ть**.

вкла́дыш (-а) *м* (*в книге, в альбоме*) insert; (*в детали*) inlay.

включа́|ть (-ю) *несов от* **включи́ть ◆** *перех*: ~ **(в себя́)** to include

▶ **включа́ться** *несов от* **включи́ться**.

включа́я *предл* (+*acc*) including; **пришли́ все** ~ **дире́ктора** everybody came including the director.

включи́тельно *нареч* inclusive; **с 1-го по 5-ое ма́я** ~ from (the) 1st to (the) 5th of May inclusive.

включ|и́ть (-у́, -и́шь; *impf* **включа́ть**) *сов перех* to turn *или* switch on; **включа́ть** (~ *perf*) **кого́-н в что-то** to include sb in sth

▶ **включи́ться** (*impf* **включа́ться**) *сов возв* to come on; (*присоединиться*): **~ся в** +*acc* to join in.

вкол|о́ть (-ю́, -ешь; *impf* **вка́лывать**) *сов перех* to stick in.

вконе́ц *нареч* completely and utterly.

вкопа́|ть (-ю; *impf* **вка́пывать**) *сов перех*: ~ **что-н в** +*acc* to sink sth into.

вкось *нареч* at an angle; **смотре́ть** (**посмотре́ть** *perf*) ~ **на кого́-н** to look at sb out of the corner of one's eye.

вкраду́сь *итп сов см* **вкра́сться**.

вкра́дчив|ый (-, -а, -о) *прил* ingratiating.

вкра́дыва|ться (-юсь) *несов от* **вкра́сться**.

вкрапле́ни|е (-я) *ср* (*обычно мн: в горных*

породах) fragment; (*в тексте*) interspersion.

вкра́|сться (-ду́сь, -дёшься; *impf* **вкра́дываться**) *сов возв* to creep in; **вкра́дываться** (~ *perf*) **в дове́рие к кому́-н** to worm one's way into sb's confidence.

вкра́тце *нареч* briefly.

вкривь *нареч*: ~ **и вкось** (*разг*) squint.

вкругову́ю *нареч*: **ходи́ть** ~ to go the long way round.

вкру|ти́ть (-чу́, -тишь; *impf* **вкру́чивать**) *сов перех* to screw in.

вкруту́ю *нареч* hard-boiled; **вари́ть (свари́ть** *perf*) **яйцо́** ~ to hard-boil an egg.

вкру́чива|ть (-ю) *несов от* **вкрути́ть**.

вкручу́ *сов см* **вкрути́ть**.

вку́пе *нареч*: ~ **с** +*instr* together with.

вкус (-а; *part gen* -у) *м* taste; **про́бовать** (**попро́бовать** *perf*) **что-н на** ~ (*еду*) to taste sth; **на чей-н** ~, **в чьём-н вку́се** to sb's taste; **приходи́ться** (**прийти́сь** *perf*) **кому́-н по вку́су** to be to sb's taste *или* liking; **она́ оде́та со вку́сом** she is tastefully dressed; **входи́ть** (**войти́** *perf*) **во** ~ to start to enjoy o.s.; **о вку́сах не спо́рят** there is no accounting for taste.

вку́сен *прил см* **вку́сный**.

вку́сно *нареч* tastily ◆ *как сказ*: **о́чень** ~ it's delicious; **она́** ~ **гото́вит** she is a good cook; **здесь** ~ **ко́рмят** the food here is very good.

вку́с|ный (-ен, -на́, -но) *прил* tasty; **обе́д был о́чень** ~ the lunch was delicious.

вла́г|а (-и) *ж* moisture.

влага́лищ|е (-а) *ср* vagina.

владе́л|ец (-ьца) *м* (*магазина, завода*) owner, proprietor; (*книги, картины*) owner.

владе́лиц|а (-ы) *ж см* **владе́лец**.

владе́льца *сущ см* **владе́лец**.

владе́ни|е (-я) *ср* estate; (*заводом*) ownership; (*обычно мн: британские итп*) possession; **вступа́ть** (**вступи́ть** *perf*) **во** ~ **чем-н** to assume ownership *или* possession of sth.

владе́|ть (-ю) *несов неперех* (+*instr; обладать*) to own, possess; (*уметь пользоваться*): **хорошо́** ~ **шпа́гой** to be a proficient *или* skilful swordsman; ~ (*impf*) **собо́й** to control o.s.; ~ (*impf*) **рука́ми/нога́ми** to have the use of one's arms/legs; **она́ в соверше́нстве ~ет англи́йским** she has a perfect command of English.

Владивосто́к (-а) *м* Vladivostok.

Владикавка́з (-а) *м* Vladikavkaz.

вла́жность (-и) *ж* humidity.

вла́ж|ный (-ен, -на́, -но) *прил* (*земля, воздух*) damp; (*глаза, кожа*) moist.

вла́ств|овать (-ую) *несов неперех*: ~ **над** +*instr* to rule; (*перен*) to hold sway over.

вла́стен *прил см* **вла́стный**.

вла́ст|и (-е́й) *мн* authorities *мн*.

вла́ст|ный (-ен, -на, -но) *прил* (*человек,*

характер) imperious; **он не ~ен** +*infin* ... it's not within his power to ....

власт|ь (-и; *gen pl* **-éй**) *ж* (*политическая*) power; (*родительская*) authority; **быть** (*impf*) **у вла́сти** to be in power; **приходи́ть** (**прийти́** *perf*) **к вла́сти** to come to power; **теря́ть** (**потеря́ть** *perf*) ~ **над собо́й** to lose one's self-control; *см также* **вла́сти**.

вле́во *нареч* (to the) left; ~ **от доро́ги** to the left of the road.

влез|ть (-у, -ешь; *pt* -, -ла, -ло, *impf* **влеза́ть**) *сов непереx*: ~ **на** +*acc* (*на дерево*) to climb (up); (*на крышу, на стул итп*) to climb onto; **влеза́ть** (~ *perf*) **в** +*acc* (*забраться*) to climb into; (*разг: в трамвай, в автобус итп*) to get on; (*пренебр: в разговор*) to butt in on; (: *в дело*) to meddle in; **ешь ско́лько вле́зет** (*разг*) eat as much as you want *или* like.

вле́й(те) *сов см* **влить**.

влёк *итп несов см* **влечь**.

влеку́ *итп несов см* **влечь**.

влете́|ть (-чу́, -ти́шь; *impf* **влета́ть**) *сов непереx*: ~ **в** +*acc* to fly into ◆ *безл* (+*dat*; *разг*) to be told off; **вмести́ ~ло за учи́теля за опозда́ние** he was told off by his teacher for being late.

влече́ни|е (-я) *ср*: ~ (**к** +*dat*) (*к человеку*) attraction (to); (*к искусству итп*) liking (for); (*к науке, к политике*) interest (in).

влечу́ *сов см* **влете́ть**.

вле|чь (-ку́, -чёшь *итп*, -ку́т; *pt* **влёк, -кла́, -кло́,** *perf* **повле́чь**) *несов перех*: ~ **за собо́й** to lead to; (*no perf*): **его́ ~чёт нау́ка** he is drawn to science.

влива́ни|е (-я) *ср* injection.

влива́|ть (-ю) *несов от* **влить**.

вли́п|нуть (-ну, -нешь; *pt* -, -ла, -ло) *сов непереx* (*в мёд*) to get stuck; (*перен: разг*) to get into a mess.

вли|ть (**волью́, вольёшь;** *pt* **-л, -ла́, -ло,** *imper* **вле́й(те),** *impf* **влива́ть**) *сов перех* to pour in; (*перен: средства*) to inject

► **вли́ться** *сов возв*: **вли́ться в** +*acc* to flow into.

влия́ни|е (-я) *ср* influence; **ока́зывать** (**оказа́ть** *perf*) ~ **на** +*acc* to influence, have an influence on; **под ~м** +*gen* under the influence of.

влия́тел|ьный (-ен, -ьна, -ьно) *прил* influential.

влия́|ть (-ю) *несов непереx*: ~ **на** +*acc* (*на людей, на события*) to influence; (*на организм, на климат*) to affect; **хорошо́/пло́хо ~** (*impf*) **на** +*acc* to have a good/bad influence on.

ВЛКСМ *м сокр* (*ист*: = *Всесою́зный Ле́нинский Коммунисти́ческий Сою́з Молодёжи*) Leninist Communist Youth League.

вложе́ни|е (-я) *ср* (*обычно мн: экон*) investment.

вложи́|ть (-у́, -ишь; *impf* **вкла́дывать**) *сов перех* (*средства, деньги*) to invest; (*положить внутрь*) to insert.

влюби́|ться (-лю́сь, -ишься; *impf* **влюбля́ться**) *сов возв*: ~ **в** +*acc* to fall in love

with; **влюбля́ться** (~ *perf*) **в кого́-н с пе́рвого взгля́да** to fall in love with sb at first sight.

влюблён|ный (-, -á, -о) *прил* in love; (*no short form*; *взгляд, глаза*) loving ◆ (**-ного**; *decl like adj*) *м*: ~**ные** lovers; **смотре́ть** (*impf*) **на кого́-н ~ными глаза́ми** to look lovingly at sb.

влюблю́сь *сов см* **влюби́ться**.

влюбля́|ться (-юсь) *несов от* **влюби́ться**.

вмени́|ть (-ю, -йшь; *impf* **вменя́ть**) *несов перех*: ~ **что-н кому́-н в вину́** to lay the blame for sth on sb; **вменя́ть** (~ *perf*) **кому́-н в обя́занность** +*infin* to charge sb to do.

вменя́ем|ый (-, -а, -о) *прил* (*ЮР*) of sound mind.

вменя́|ть (-ю) *несов от* **вмени́ть**.

вме́сте *нареч* together; ~ **с** +*instr* together with; ~ **с тем** at the same time.

вмести́тел|ьный (-ен, -ьна, -ьно) *прил* (*помещение, автобус*) spacious; **э́тот чемода́н о́чень ~** this suitcase holds a lot.

вме|сти́ть (-щу́, -сти́шь; *impf* **вмеща́ть**) *сов перех* (*подлеж: зал*) to hold; (: *гостиница*) to accommodate; (*уместить*): ~ **что-н/кого́-н в** +*acc* to fit sth/sb into

► **вмести́ться** (*impf* **вмеща́ться**) *несов возв* to fit in.

вме́сто *предл* (+*gen*; *взамен*) instead of; (*замещая*) in place *или* instead of ◆ *союз*: ~ **того́ что́бы** instead of, rather than; **пошли́ в теа́тр ~ конце́рта** let's go to the theatre instead of the concert; **он рабо́тает ~ отца́** he's standing in for his father; ~ **того́ что́бы критикова́ть, постара́йтесь поня́ть** try and understand instead of just criticizing.

вмеша́тельств|о (-а) *ср* (*в разговор, в спор*) interference; (*ВОЕН, ЭКОН*) intervention.

вмеша́|ть (-ю; *impf* **вме́шивать**) *сов перех* (*добавить*) to mix in; (*перен*): ~ **кого́-н в** +*acc* to get sb mixed up in

► **вмеша́ться** (*impf* **вме́шиваться**) *сов возв* (*вторгнуться*) to interfere; (*присоединиться*: *в преговоры итп*) to intervene.

вмеща́|ть(ся) (-ю(сь)) *несов от* **вмести́ть(ся)**.

вмещу́(сь) *сов см* **вмести́ть(ся)**.

вмиг *нареч* instantly.

вмонти́р|овать (-ую) *сов перех*: ~ **что-н в** +*acc* to fix sth to.

вмя́тин|а (-ы) *ж* dent.

внаём *нареч*: **отдава́ть ~** to let, rent out; „**сдаётся ~**" (*объявление*) "to let (*BRIT*) *или* rent (*US*)".

внаймы́ *нареч* = **внаём**.

внакла́де *как сказ* (*разг*): **остава́ться ~** to come out worse off.

внача́ле *нареч* at first; ~ **она́ испуга́лась** at first she was scared.

вне *предл* (+*gen*) outside; (*чьих-н обязанностей*) outwith; (*сверх: плана*) over and above; ~ **о́череди** out of turn; **он был ~ себя́** he was beside himself; **э́то ~ вся́кого сомне́ния** that is beyond any doubt.

внебра́чный *прил* (*отношения*) extramarital;

(*ребёнок*) illegitimate.

внедре́ни|**е** (**-я**) *ср* introduction.

внедр|**и́ть** (**-ю́, -и́шь;** *impf* **внедря́ть**) *сов перех* (*ввести*) to introduce

▶ **внедри́ться** (*impf* **внедря́ться**) *сов возв* (*методы*) to become established; (*идеи, тради́ции*) to take root.

внеза́п|**ный** (**-ен, -на, -но**) *прил* sudden.

внекла́ссный *прил* extracurricular.

внема́точ|**ный** *прил*: **~ная бере́менность** ectopic pregnancy.

внеочередно́й *прил* unscheduled; (*заседание*) extraordinary.

внес|**ти́** (**-у́, -ёшь;** *pt* **внёс, -сла́, -сло́,** *impf* **вноси́ть**) *сов перех* (*вещи, мебель итп*) to carry *или* bring in; (*взнос, сумму*) to pay; (*законопроект*) to bring in; (*поправку, пара́граф*) to insert; (*раздор, путаницу*) to cause; **вноси́ть** (**~** *perf*) **предложе́ние/пла́ту** to make a proposal/payment; **он внёс оживле́ние в вечери́нку** he livened up the party; **вноси́ть** (**~** *perf*) **я́сность в де́ло** to shed light on the proceedings.

внешко́льный *прил* extracurricular.

вне́шне *нареч* outwardly.

внешнеполити́ческ|**ий** (**-ая, -ое, -ие**) *прил* foreign-policy.

внешнеторго́в|**ый** *прил* (*связи, оборот*) foreign-trade.

вне́шн|**ий** (**-яя, -ее, -ие**) *прил* (*стена*) exterior *орпед*; (*спокойствие*) outward; (*связи*) external; **~яя охра́на** outer guard; **~ мир** outside world; **~яя сторона́** +*gen* the outside of; **вне́шний вид** appearance; **вне́шняя поли́тика** foreign policy; **вне́шняя торго́вля** foreign trade.

вне́шность (**-и**) *ж* appearance; **у неё прия́тная ~** she is good-looking.

внешта́тный *прил* freelance.

Внешторгба́нк (**-а**) *м сокр* (= **Банк для** *вне́шней торго́вли*) foreign trade bank.

вниз *нареч*; **~** (**по** +*dat*) down; **~ по тече́нию** downstream.

внизу́ *нареч* below; (*в здании*) downstairs ♦ *предл* (+*gen*): **~ страни́цы** at the foot *или* bottom of the page; **доро́га прохо́дит ~** the road runs down below; **~ магази́н нахо́дится** there is a shop on the ground (*BRIT*) *или* first (*US*) floor.

вни́к|**нуть** (**-ну, -нешь;** *pt* **-, -ла, -ло,** *impf* **вника́ть**) *сов неперех*: **~ в** +*acc* to understand well.

внима́ни|**е** (**-я**) *ср* attention; **~ю покупа́телей/пассажи́ров!** attention all shoppers/passengers!; **привле́чь** (**привле́чь** *perf*) **~ к** +*dat* to draw attention to; **принима́ть** (**приня́ть** *perf*) **во ~ что-н** to take sth into account *или* consideration; **ока́зывать** (**оказа́ть** *perf*) **~**

кому́-н to pay attention to sb.

внима́тельность (**-и**) *ж* (*в работе*) care; (*заботливость*) attentiveness.

внима́тельный (**-ен, -ьна, -ьно**) *прил* (*сосредото́ченный*) attentive; (*тща́тельный*) careful; (*заботливый*): **~ к** +*dat* attentive to.

внима́ть (**-ю**) *несов от* **внять**.

вничью́ *нареч* (*СПОРТ*): **сыгра́ть ~** to draw.

вновь *нареч* again.

вно|**си́ть** (**-шу́, -сишь**) *несов от* **внести́**.

ВНП *м сокр* (= **валово́й национа́льный проду́кт**) GNP (= *gross national product*).

вну́|**к** (**-ка;** *nom pl* **-ки** *или* **-ча́та**) *м* grandson; *см также* **вну́ки**.

вну́к|**и** (**-ов**) *мн* grandchildren *мн*.

вну́тренне *нареч* inwardly.

вну́тренн|**ий** (**-яя, -ее, -ие**) *прил* (*поверхность, стенка*) interior; (*побужде́ние, голос*) inner; (*политика, рынок*) domestic; (*рана, кровотече́ние*) internal; **Министе́рство вну́тренних дел** ≈ the Home Office (*BRIT*), ≈ the Department of the Interior (*US*); **вну́тренние о́рганы** internal organs *мн*.

вну́тренност|**и** (**-ей**) *мн* (*АНАТ*) insides *мн*; (*кулин*) offal *ед*.

вну́тренность (**-и**) *ж*: **~** (+*gen*) interior (of); *см также* **вну́тренности**.

внутри́ *нареч* inside; (*в преде́лах, в ра́мках*) within ♦ *предл*: **~** +*gen* (*дома, я́щика*) inside; (*организа́ции*) within.

внутриве́нный *прил* intravenous.

внутриполити́ческ|**ий** (**-ая, -ое, -ие**) *прил* (*кризис*) internal political *опред*; **-ая борьба́** political infighting.

внутрь *нареч* inside ♦ *предл* (+*gen*) inside; **принима́ть** (*impf*) **лека́рство ~** to be taken internally.

внуча́та *сущ см* **внук**.

внуча́т(**н**)**ый** *прил*: **~ племя́нник** great-nephew.

вну́ч|**ка** (**-ки;** *gen pl* **-ек**) *ж* granddaughter.

внуша́ть (**-ю**) *несов от* **внуши́ть**.

внуши́тельный (**-ен, -ьна, -ьно**) *прил* (*внешность*) imposing; (*сумма, успех*) impressive.

внуш|**и́ть** (**-у́, -и́шь;** *impf* **внуша́ть**) *сов перех* (*вызвать*) to inspire; **внуша́ть** (**~** *perf*) **что-н кому́-н** to instil (*BRIT*) *или* instill (*US*) sth in sb.

вня́тный (**-ен, -на, -но**) *прил* (*отчётливый*) clear; (*вразумительный*) intelligible.

вня|**ть** (*pt* **-л, -ла́, -ло,** *impf* **внима́ть**) *сов неперех* (+*dat*; *просьбам*) to heed.

В.О. *м сокр* = **Васи́льевский о́стров** (*Петербург*).

ВО *м сокр* = **вое́нный о́круг**.

во *предл см* **в** ♦ *част* (*разг: вот*) there; (: *выража́ет согла́сие*) that's it; (: *выража́ет оце́нку*) great.

во́бл|**а** (**-ы**) *ж* Caspian roach.

вобра́|ть (вберу́, вберёшь; *pt* -л, -ла́, -ло, *impf* **вбира́ть**) *сов перех* (*воздух, воду*) to take in; **вбира́ть** (*~ perf*) **в себя́** to incorporate; **вбира́ть** (*~ perf*) **го́лову в пле́чи** to hunch one's shoulders.

вове́к(и) *нареч* (*навек*) forever; (*никогда*) never; **~ его́ не прощу́** I will never forgive him.

вовл|е́чь (-еку́, -ечёшь *итп* -еку́т; *pt* -ёк, -екла́, -екло́, *impf* **вовлека́ть**) *сов перех*: **~ кого́-н в** +*acc* (*в разговор, в спор*) to draw sb into; (*в работу*) to involve sb in.

во́время *нареч* on time.

во́все *нареч* (*разг*) completely; **~ нет** not at all; **она́ на тебя́ ~ не се́рдится** she's not angry with you at all.

вовсю́ *нареч* (*разг*): **бежа́ть/гнать (маши́ну) ~** to run/drive as fast as one can; **он стара́ется ~** he is giving it his all.

во-вторы́х *вводн сл* secondly, in the second place.

вогна́|ть (вгоню́, вго́нишь; *pt* -л, -ла́, -ло, *impf* **вгоня́ть**) *сов перех*: **~ (во что-н)** to drive in(to sth); **вгоня́ть** (*~ perf*) **кого́-н в отча́яние** to drive sb to despair; **вгоня́ть** (*~ perf*) **в кра́ску кого́-н** to make sb blush.

во́гнут|ый (-, -а, -о) *прил* concave.

вогн|у́ть (-у́, -ёшь; *impf* **вгиба́ть**) *сов перех* to bend *или* curve inwards.

вод|а́ (*acc sg* -у, *gen sg* -ы́, *nom pl* -ы) *ж* water; (*no pl*; *перен*: *в докладе*) padding; **что ты как ~ы в рот набра́л?** (*разг*) has the cat got your tongue?; **как в во́ду опу́щенный** (*разг*) down in the dumps; **похо́жи как две ка́пли ~ы** as like as two peas in a pod; **выходи́ть (вы́йти** *perf*) **сухи́м из ~ы** (*разг*) to get off scot-free; **выводи́ть (вы́вести** *perf*) **на чи́стую во́ду кого́-н** (*разг*) to force sb to come clean; *см также* **во́ды**.

водвор|и́ть (-ю́, -и́шь; *сов перех* (*поселить*) to settle; (*тишину*) to establish

▶ **водвори́ться** *возв* (*тишина*) to be established.

водеви́л|ь (-и) *ж* musical comedy.

води́тел|ь (-я) *м* driver.

води́тельск|ий (-ая, -ое, -ие) *прил*: **~ие права́** driving licence (*BRIT*), driver's license (*US*).

во|ди́ть (-жу́, -дишь) *несов перех* (*ребёнка, собаку*) to take; (*лошадь, войско*) to lead; (*машину, поезд*) to drive; (*самолёт*) to fly; (*корабль*) to sail; **~ (***impf***) дру́жбу/знако́мство с кем-н** to be friends/acquainted with sb; **~ (***impf***) за́ нос кого́-н** to lead sb on

▶ **води́ться** *несов возв* (*рыба итп*) to be (found); **~ся** (*impf*) **с** +*instr* (*разг*) to be pals with; **у него́ во́дятся де́ньги** (*разг*) he's got money; **как во́дится** (*разг*) as is usually the way.

во́дк|а (-и) *ж* vodka.

во́дн|ый *прил* water *опред*; **во́дные лы́жи** water-skiing; **во́дное по́ло** water polo; **во́дные процеду́ры** hydrotherapy.

водоворо́т (-а) *м* whirlpool; (*перен*) whirlpool, maelstrom.

водоём (-а) *м* reservoir.

водоизмеще́ни|е (-я) *ср* displacement; **су́дно ~м в 10 ты́сяч тонн** a vessel of 10 thousand tons displacement.

водока́ч|ка (-ки; *gen pl* -ек) *ж* (*ТЕХ*) waterworks.

водола́з (-а) *м* (*человек*) diver.

Водоле́|й (-я) *м* (*созвездие*) Aquarius.

водолече́бниц|а (-ы) *ж* hydrotherapy clinic.

водолюби́в|ый *прил* (*растение*) water-loving.

водонапо́рн|ый *прил*: **~ая ба́шня** water tower.

водонепроница́емый *прил* waterproof.

водоотта́лкивающ|ий (-ая, -ее, -ие) *прил* water-repellent.

водоочистно́й *прил* water-purifying.

водопа́д (-а) *м* waterfall.

водопо́|й (-я) *м* (*для животных*) (water) trough.

водопрово́д (-а) *м* water supply system; **у них в до́ме ~** their house has running water.

водопрово́дный *прил* (*труба, кран*) water *опред*; (*система*) plumbing *опред*.

водопрово́дчик (-а) *м* plumber.

водоразде́л (-а) *м* (*также перен*) watershed.

водоро́д (-а) *м* hydrogen.

водоро́дный *прил* hydrogen *опред*; **водоро́дная бо́мба** hydrogen bomb.

во́доросл|ь (-и) *ж* (*обычно мн*) algae *мн*; (*разг*: *в реке*) waterweed; (*в море*) seaweed.

водосбро́с (-а) *м* floodgate.

водосто́чн|ый *прил*: **~ая труба́** drainpipe; **~ая кана́ва** gutter.

водохрани́лищ|е (-а) *ср* reservoir.

водру|зи́ть (-жу́, -зи́шь; *impf* **водружа́ть**) *сов перех* to raise.

во́д|ы (-) *мн* (*государственные, нейтральные*) waters *мн*; (*минеральные источники*) spa *ед*.

водяни́стый *прил* watery.

водяно́й *прил* water *опред*; **водяно́й знак** watermark; **водяно́й пар** steam.

во|ева́ть (-ю́ю) *несов неперех* (*страна*) to be at war; (*человек*) to fight; **~ (***impf***) с бюрокра́тами** *или* **про́тив бюрокра́тов** (*перен*) to wage war on *или* against bureaucracy.

воеди́но *нареч* together.

военача́льник (-а) *м* (*military*) commander.

военизи́р|овать (-ую) (*не*)*сов перех* to militarize.

военкома́т (-а) *м сокр* (= **вое́нный комиссариа́т**) ministry for war.

вое́нно-возду́шн|ый *прил*: **вое́нно-возду́шные си́лы** (the) air force.

вое́нно-морско́й *прил*: **~ флот** (the) navy.

военнообя́занн|ый (-ого; *decl like adj*) *м person eligible for compulsory military service.*

военноплённ|ый (-ого; *decl like adj*) *м* prisoner of war.

вое́нно-полево́й *прил* (*госпиталь*) field *опред*; **вое́нно-полево́й суд** court martial.

вое́нно-промы́шленн|ый *прил*: **~ ко́мплекс** military-industrial complex.

военнослу́жащ|ий (-его; *decl like adj*) *м*

serviceman (*мн* servicemen).

вое́нн|ые (-ых; *decl like adj*) *мн собир* the military.

вое́нн|ый *прил* military; (*врач*) army *опред* ◆ (-ого; *decl like adj*) *м* serviceman (*мн* servicemen); **вое́нное положе́ние** martial law; **вое́нная промы́шленность** military-related industry; *см также* **вое́нные**.

вое́нщин|а (-ы) *ж собир* (*пренебр*) warmongers *мн*.

вожа́к (-а́) *м* leader.

вожа́тый (-ого; *decl like adj*) *м* (*в горах*) guide.

вожделе́ни|е (-я) *ср* (*к женщине*) lust; (*к власти, к пище*) craving.

вожде́ни|е (-я) *ср* (*машины, поезда*) driving; (*судна*) steering; (*яхты*) sailing; (*самолёта*) flying.

вождь (-я́) *м* (*племени*) chief, chieftain; (*движения, партии*) leader.

вожж|а́ (-и́; *nom pl* -и, *gen pl* -е́й) *ж* (*обычно мн*) rein.

вожу́(сь) *несов см* **води́ть(ся)**, **вози́ть(ся)**.

ВОЗ *м сокр* (= *Всеми́рная организа́ция здравоохране́ния*) WHO (= *World Health Organization*).

воз (-а; *loc sg* -у́, *nom pl* -ы́) *м* loaded cart; (*перен: разг*) loads *мн*, heaps *мн*.

возbraня́|ться (*3sg* -ется, *3pl* -ются) *несов возв* (*запрещается*) to be prohibited.

возбуди́м|ый (-, -а, -о) *прил* excitable.

возбуди́тел|ь (-я) *м* (*МЕД*) pathogen.

возб|уди́ть (-ужу́, -у́дишь; *impf* **возбужда́ть**) *сов перех* (*вызвать*) to arouse; (*взволновать*) to excite; **возбужда́ть** (~ *perf*) **де́ло** *или* **проце́сс про́тив** +*gen* to bring a case against; **возбужда́ть** (~ *perf*) **иск** to begin legal proceedings; **возбужда́ть** (~ *perf*) **хода́тайство о** +*prp* to submit a petition for; **возбужда́ть** (~ *perf*) **не́нависть** to incite hatred

▶ **возбуди́ться** *сов возв* (*возникнуть*) to be aroused; (*взволноваться*) to become excited.

возбужда́ющ|ий (-ая, -ее, -ие) *прил*: **~ее сре́дство** stimulant.

возбужде́ни|е (-я) *ср* (*волнение*) agitation; (: *радостное*) excitement.

возбужде́нный *прил* (*см сущ*) agitated; excited.

возбужу́(сь) *сов см* **возбуди́ть(ся)**.

возведе́ни|е (-я) *ср* (*здания, стены итп*) elevation.

возвели́ч|ить (-у, -ишь; *impf* **возвели́чивать**) *сов перех* to extol.

возве|сти́ (-ду́, -дёшь; *pt* **возвёл**, -ла́, -ло́, *impf* **возводи́ть**) *сов перех* to erect; **возводи́ть** (~ *perf*) **что-н в при́нцип** to adopt sth as a fundamental principle; **э́то бы́ло ~дено́ в зако́н** it was enshrined in law; **возводи́ть** (~

perf) **обвине́ние на кого́-н** to level an accusation against sb; **возводи́ть** (~ *perf*) **клевету́ на кого́-н** to slander sb; **возводи́ть** (~ *perf*) **что-н к** +*dat* to trace sth back to.

возве|сти́ть (-щу́, -сти́шь; *impf* **возвеща́ть**) *сов перех* to proclaim.

возво|ди́ть (-жу́, -дишь) *несов от* **возвести́**.

возвра́т (-а) *м* return; (*долга, займа*) repayment; **без ~а** irrevocably; **подлежа́щий ~у** returnable; **не подлежа́щий ~у** nonreturnable; **возвра́т нало́га** tax refund.

возвра|ти́ть (-щу́, -ти́шь; *impf* **возвраща́ть**) *сов перех* (*книгу, покупку*) to return; (*долг, ссуду*) to repay; (*свободу, здоровье, счастье*) to restore; **возвраща́ть** (~ *perf*) **кого́-н к жи́зни** (*больного*) to bring sb back from the brink of death

▶ **возврати́ться** (*impf* **возвраща́ться**) *сов возв*: **~ся (к** +*dat*) to return *или* come back (to).

возвра́тный *прил* (*КОММ*) repayable; (*ЛИНГ*) reflexive.

возвраща́|ть(ся) (-ю(сь)) *несов от* **возврати́ть(ся)**.

возвраще́ни|е (-я) *ср* return.

возвраща́|ю(сь) *сов см* **возврати́ть(ся)**.

возвы́|сить (-шу, -сишь; *impf* **возвыша́ть**) *сов перех* (*работника итп*) to elevate; **возвыша́ть** (~ *perf*) **кого́-н в чьих-н глаза́х** to raise sb in sb's estimation

▶ **возвы́ситься** (*impf* **возвыша́ться**) *сов возв* to be elevated.

возвыша́|ться (-юсь) *несов возв* to tower.

возвыше́ни|е (-я) *ср* elevation.

возвы́шен|ный (-, -на, -но) *прил* (*перен: идея, цель*) lofty; (*натура, музыка*) sublime; (*берег*) high.

возвы́шу(сь) *сов см* **возвы́сить(ся)**.

возгла́в|ить (-лю, -ишь; *impf* **возглавля́ть**) *сов перех* to head.

во́зглас (-а) *м* exclamation.

возда|ва́ть (-ю́) *несов от* **возда́ть**.

возда́ть (*как* **дать**; *см* **Table 14**; *impf* **воздава́ть**) *сов перех*: **~ хвалу́** *или* **по́чести кому́-н** to eulogize sb, pay homage to sb; **воздава́ть** (~ *perf*) **кому́-н по заслу́гам** (*в награду*) to reward sb for their services; (*в наказание*) to give sb what they deserve; **воздава́ть** (~ *perf*) **до́лжное кому́-н** to give sb their due.

воздви́г *итп сов см* **воздви́гнуть**.

воздвига́|ть (-ю; *perf* **воздви́гнуть**) *несов перех* to erect.

воздви́г|нуть (-ну, -нешь; *pt* -, -ла, -ло) *несов от* **воздвига́ть**.

возде́йстви|е (-я) *ср* effect; (*идеологическое, педагогическое*) influence; **ока́зывать** (**оказа́ть** *perf*) **~ на** +*acc* to influence; **под ~м** +*gen* under the influence of.

возде́йств|овать (-ую) (*не*)*сов неперех*: **~ на**

+acc ((по)влиять) to have an effect on; *(оказать действие)* to influence.

возде́ла|ть (-ю; *impf* **возде́лывать**) *сов перех (обрабатывать)* to cultivate; *(растить)* to grow.

воздержа́вш|аяся (-ейся; *decl like adj*) *ж см* **воздержа́вшийся**.

воздержа́вш|ийся (-егося; *decl like adj*) *м (полит)* abstainer.

воздержан|ный (-, -на, -но) *прил* frugal; *(в напитках, еде)* abstemious; **он возде́ржан в оце́нках/в сужде́ниях** he is cautious in his evaluations/judgements.

возде|ржа́ться (-ержу́сь, -е́ржишься; *impf* **возде́рживаться**) *сов возв*: ~ **от** *+gen (от комментариев, от курения)* to refrain from; *(от голосования)* to abstain from; **~ержа́лось 10 челове́к** there were 10 abstentions.

во́здух (-а) *м* air; *(перен)* atmosphere; **на (откры́том)** ~е outside, outdoors; **в ~е но́сится опа́сность** there is danger in the air.

возду́шн|ый *прил* air *опред*; *(десант)* airborne; **посыла́ть (посла́ть** *perf)* **кому́-н ~ поцелу́й** to blow sb a kiss; **возду́шная трево́га** air-raid warning; **возду́шная я́ма** air pocket; **возду́шный флот** air force.

воззва́ни|е (-я) *ср* appeal.

воззв|а́ть (-ову́, -вёшь) *сов от* **взыва́ть**.

воззре́ни|е (-я) *ср* view.

во|зи́ть (-жу́, -зишь) *несов перех* to take; **нас ~зи́ли по Ло́ндону на авто́бусе** we were taken round London on a bus; **ка́ждый день она́ во́зит дете́й в шко́лу на маши́не** every day she takes *или* drives the children to school; ~ *(impf)* **во́ду на ком-н** *(разг)* to work sb into the ground
▶ **вози́ться** *несов возв* to potter about; *(дети)* to romp around *или* about; **~ся** *(impf)* **с** *+instr (разг: с работой итп)* to make heavy weather of; *(с детьми итп)* to spend a lot of time with.

возлага́|ть (-ю) *несов от* **возложи́ть**.

во́зле *нареч* nearby ♦ *предл (+g n)* near; **де́ти игра́ли ~** the children were playing nearby; **дом был ~ реки́** the house stood near the river.

возлож|и́ть (-у́, -ишь; *impf* **возлага́ть**) *сов перех (положить)* to lay, place; *(поручить)* to entrust; **возлага́ть (~** *perf)* **вину́ на кого́-н** to lay the blame on sb; **возлага́ть (~** *perf)* **отве́тственность на кого́-н** to hold sb responsible; **возлага́ть (~** *perf)* **наде́жды на кого́-н** to pin one's hopes on sb.

возлю́бленн|ая (-ой) *ж см* **возлю́бленный**.

возлю́бленн|ый (-ого; *decl like adj*) *м* beloved.

возме́зди|е (-я) *ср* retribution.

возме|сти́ть (-щу́, -сти́шь; *impf* **возмеща́ть**) *сов перех (ущерб, убытки)* to compensate for; *(затраты)* to refund, reimburse.

возмеще́ни|е (-я) *ср*: ~ **убы́тков** compensation; ~ **затра́т** reimbursement; **изде́ржки ~я** replacement cost; **сто́имость страхово́го ~я** *(комм)* replacement value.

возмещу́ *сов см* **возмести́ть**.

возмо́жен *прил см* **возмо́жный**.

возмо́жно *как сказ* it is possible ♦ *вводн сл (может быть)* possibly ♦ *нареч*: ~ **лу́чше/ бы́стрее** as well/quickly as possible; ~ **ему́ помо́чь** it is possible to help him; ~, **он согласи́тся** he may possibly agree.

возмо́жност|и (-ей) *мн (творческие)* potential; **фина́нсовые** *или* **материа́льные ~** financial resources.

возмо́жност|ь (-и) *ж* opportunity; *(допустимость)* possibility; **по (ме́ре) ~и** as far as possible; **име́ть** *(impf)* ~ *+infin* to be able to do; **при пе́рвой ~и** at the first opportunity; *см также* **возмо́жности**.

возмо́жн|ый (-ен, -на, -но) *прил* possible.

возмужа́|ть (-ю) *сов от* **мужа́ть**.

возмути́тел|ьный (-ен, -ьна, -ьно) *прил* appalling.

возму|ти́ть (-щу́, -ти́шь; *impf* **возмуща́ть**) *сов перех* to appal *(BRIT)*, appall *(US)*
▶ **возмути́ться** *(impf* **возмуща́ться**) *сов возв* to be appalled.

возмуще́ни|е (-я) *ср* indignation.

возмущённо *нареч* indignantly.

возмущённый *прил* indignant.

возмущу́(сь) *сов см* **возмути́ть(ся)**.

вознагра|ди́ть (-жу́, -ди́шь; *impf* **вознагражда́ть**) *сов перех* to reward; *(комм)* to remunerate.

вознагражде́ни|е (-я) *ср* reward.

вознагражу́ *сов см* **вознагради́ть**.

возненави́де|ть (-жу, -дишь) *сов перех* to come to hate.

Вознесе́ни|е (-я) *ср* Ascension Day.

возне|сти́ (-у́, -ёшь; *pt* **вознёс**, **-ла́**, **-ло́**, *impf* **возноси́ть**) *сов перех (хвалить)* to exalt; **возноси́ть (~** *perf)* **чьи-н досто́инства** to extol *(BRIT)* или extoll *(US)* sb's virtues
▶ **вознести́сь** *(impf* **возноси́ться**) *сов возв* to rise (up).

возни́|к *итп сов см* **возни́кнуть**.

возника́|ть (-ю) *несов от* **возни́кнуть**.

возникнове́ни|е (-я) *ср* emergence.

возни́к|нуть (-ну, -нешь; *pt* -, -ла, -ло, *impf* **возника́ть**) *сов неперех* to arise.

возно|си́ть (-шу́, -сишь) *несов от* **вознести́**.

возн|я́ (-и́) *ж (при игре)* frolicking; *(перен: интриги)* intrigue; ~ **с** *+instr (хлопоты)* bother with; **мыши́ная ~** *(перен)* a lot of fuss about nothing.

возоблада́|ть (*3sg* -ет, *3pl* -ют) *сов неперех*: ~ **над** *+instr* to prevail over.

возобнов|и́ть (-лю́, -и́шь; *impf* **возобновля́ть**) *сов перех (начать снова)* to resume; **возобновля́ть (~** *perf)* **контра́кт** to renew a contract
▶ **возобнови́ться** *(impf* **возобновля́ться**) *сов возв* to resume.

возомн|и́ть (-ю́, -и́шь) *сов перех*: ~ **себя́ ге́нием/поэ́том** to consider o.s. a genius/poet.

возража́|ть (-ю) *несов от* **возрази́ть**.

возраже́ни|е (-я) *ср* objection; **предложе́ние встре́тило ~я** the proposal met with opposition.

возра|зи́ть (-жу́, -зи́шь; *impf* **возража́ть**) *сов неперех*: ~ (+*dat*) to object (to); **возража́ть** (~ *perf*) **на замеча́ние/обвине́ние** to object to a remark/an allegation.

во́зраст (-а) *м* age; **ребёнок в ~е десяти́ лет** a ten-year-old child; **он был уже́ в ~е** he was getting on in years; **вы́йти** (*perf*) **из ~а** to be over the age limit.

возр|асти́ (*3sg* -асте́т, *3pl* -асту́т, *pt* -о́с, -осла́, -осло́, *impf* **возраста́ть**) *сов неперех* to grow.

возрастно́й *прил* age *опред*.

возро|ди́ть (-жу́, -ди́шь; *impf* **возрожда́ть**) *сов перех* to revive.

▶ **возроди́ться** (*impf* **возрожда́ться**) *сов возв* to revive.

возрожде́ни|е (-я) *ср* (*хозяйства, традиции*) revival; (*нации, веры*) rebirth; (*территории, демократии*) regeneration; **В~** Renaissance.

возро́с *итп сов см* **возрасти́**.

возыме́|ть (-ю) *сов перех*: ~ **де́йствие** to take effect.

возьму́(сь) *итп сов см* **взя́ть(ся)**.

во́ин (-а) *м* warrior.

во́инск|ий (-ая, -ое, -ие) *прил* military; **во́инская пови́нность** conscription.

войнствен|ный (-ен, -на, -но) *прил* (*племена*) warlike; (*вид, тон, намерения*) belligerent; (*воинствующий*) militant.

во́истину *нареч* in truth.

во|й (-я) *м* howl.

войду́ *итп сов см* **войти́**.

во́йлок (-а) *м* felt.

войн|а́ (-ы; *nom pl* -ы) *ж* war; **вести́** (*impf*) ~**у́** to wage war; **идти́ (пойти́** *perf*) **на** ~**у́** to go to war.

во́йск|о (-а; *nom pl* -а́) *ср* (*обычно мн*) (the) forces *мн*.

войти́ (*как* **идти́**; *см* **Table 18**; *impf* **входи́ть**) *сов неперех*: ~ (**в** +*acc*) to enter, go in(to); (*включиться*) to become a member (of); (*уместиться*) to fit in(to); **в шкаф вхо́дит мно́го книг** the cupboard holds a lot of books; **э́та статья́ не вошла́ в сбо́рник** this article was not included in the collection; **входи́ть** (~ *perf*) **в спи́сок** to be added to the list; **входи́ть** (~ *perf*) **в систе́му** (*комп*) to log in.

вокали́ст (-а) *м* vocalist.

вока́льный *прил* vocal; (*конкурс*) singing *опред*; **она́ у́чится на ~ом отделе́нии** she is studying singing.

вокза́л (-а) *м* station.

вокру́г *нареч* around, round ◆ *предл*: ~ +*gen* (*кругом*) around, round; (*по поводу*) about, over; ~ **го́рода лес** the town is surrounded by a forest; ~ **рефо́рмы бы́ло мно́го спо́ров** there was a lot of controversy surrounding *или* over the reforms; **ходи́ть** (*impf*) ~ **да о́коло** (*разг*) to

beat about the bush.

вол (-а́) *м* ох (*мн* oxen), bullock.

вола́н (-а) *м* (*на одежде*) flounce; (*в бадминтоне*) shuttlecock.

Во́лг|а (-и) *ж* Volga.

Волгогра́д (-а) *м* Volgograd.

волды́р|ь (-я́) *м* blister.

волево́й *прил* (*человек, характер*) strong-willed; (*усилие, натура*) determined.

волейбо́л (-а) *м* volleyball.

волейболи́ст (-а) *м* volleyball player.

волейболи́ст|ка (-ки; *gen pl* -ок) *ж см* **волейболи́ст**.

во́лей-нево́лей *нареч* (*без желания*) like it or not; **ему́** ~ **пришло́сь э́то сде́лать** he had no choice but to do it.

во́лен *прил см* **во́льный**.

во́лжск|ий (-ая, -ое, -ие) *прил* Volga *опред*, of the Volga.

волк (-а; *gen pl* -о́в) *м* wolf (*мн* wolves); **во́лком смотре́ть** (*impf*) **на кого́-н** to look daggers at sb.

волкода́в (-а) *м* wolfhound.

волн|а́ (-ы́; *nom pl* **во́лны**) *ж* (*также перен*) wave; **на коро́тких/сре́дних/дли́нных во́лнах** on short/medium/long wave.

волне́ни|е (-я) *ср* (*на море*) choppiness; (*человека: радостное*) excitement; (: *нервное*) agitation; (*обычно мн: в массах*) disturbance, unrest *ед*.

волни́ст|ый (-, -а, -о) *прил* (*волосы*) wavy.

волн|ова́ть (-у́ю; *perf* **взволнова́ть**) *несов перех* (*общество, человека*) to be concerned about ; (*море*) to agitate

▶ **волнова́ться** (*perf* **взволнова́ться**) *несов возв* (*море*) to be rough *или* choppy; (*человек*) to worry.

волоки́т|а (-ы) *ж* red tape.

вол|окно́ (-окна́; *nom pl* -о́кна, *gen pl* -о́кон) *ср* fibre (*BRIT*), fiber (*US*).

во́лос (-а; *gen pl* **воло́с**, *dat pl* -а́м) *м* hair *только ед*; ~**ы рвать** (*impf*) **на себе́** (*перен*) to kick o.s.; **э́то притя́нуто за́ волосы** that's a bit far-fetched.

волоса́т|ый (-, -а, -о) *прил* (*грудь*) hairy.

волос|о́к (-ка́) *м* hair; (*лампочки*) filament; **быть** (*impf*) *или* **находи́ться** (*impf*) **на** ~ *или* **на волоске́ от** +*gen* to be within a hair's-breadth of; **висе́ть** (*impf*) *или* **держа́ться** (*impf*) **на** ~**ке́** to hang by a thread.

во́лост|ь (-и) *ж* volost (*administrative division*).

волосяно́й *прил* (*покров*) hair *опред*.

волоч|и́ть (-у́, -и́шь) *несов перех* to drag; **едва́** *или* **е́ле но́ги** ~ (*impf*) to drag o.s. along.

волча́та *итп сущ см* **волчо́нок**.

во́лч|ий (-ья, -ье, -ьи) *прил* wolf *опред*; ~ **зако́н** the law of the jungle; ~ **аппети́т** voracious appetite.

волчи́ц|а (-ы) *ж* she-wolf.

волчо́нок (-о́нка; *nom pl* -а́та, *gen pl* -а́т) *м* wolf cub.

волше́бник (-а) *м* wizard.

волше́бница (-ы) *ж* (good *или* white) witch.

волше́бный *прил* magic *опред*; (*перен: чарующий*) magical.

волшебство́ (-а́) *ср* (*также перен*) magic.

волы́н|ка (-ки; *gen pl* -ок) *ж* bagpipes *мн*; (*разг: канитель*) palaver.

вольго́т|ный (-ен, -на, -но) *прил* free and easy.

вольер (-а) *м* enclosure.

вольнича́|ть (-ю) *несов неперех* (*разг*) to take liberties.

во́льно *нареч* freely; ~! (*ВОЕН*) at ease!; ~ *или* нево́льно willing or not.

вольноду́м|ец (-ца) *м* freethinker.

вольнолюби́в|ый (-, -а, -о) *прил* freedom-loving.

вольнонаёмный *прил* (*рабочий, труд*) casual.

во́льность (-и) *ж* (*нескромность*) licence (*BRIT*), license (*US*).

во́льный (-ен, -ьна́, -ьно) *прил* (*свободный*) free; (*нескромный*) familiar ♦ *как сказ* (*no full form*): ~ен +*infin* he is free to do; во́льная борьба́ freestyle wrestling; во́льные упражне́ния free floor routine; во́льный перево́д free translation.

вольт (-а; *gen pl* -) *м* volt.

вольтме́тр (-а) *м* voltmeter.

вольй *итп сов см* влить.

во́л|я (-и) *ж* will; (*стремление*): ~ к побе́де/достиже́нию чего́-н the will to win/to achieve sth; дава́ть (дать *perf*) ~ю слеза́м/языку́ to cry/speak without restraint; дава́ть (дать *perf*) ~ю чу́вствам to give free rein to one's feelings; де́лать (сде́лать *perf*) что-н по свое́й ~е to do sth of one's own volition *или* free will; э́то не в мое́й ~е it's not in *или* within my power.

вон *нареч* (*разг: прочь*) out; (: *там*) (over) there ♦ *част*: ~ туда́ иди́те you need to go THAT way; ~ отсю́да! get lost!; вы́йди ~! get out!; ~ она́ идёт look, there she is; ~ (оно́) что so that's it!

вонз|и́ть (-жу́, -зи́шь; *impf* вонза́ть) *сов перех*: ~ (в +*acc*) (иголка, кинжал) to stick in(to); (зубы, когти) to sink in(to)

▶ **вонзи́ться** (*impf* вонза́ться) *сов возв* (иголка, кинжал) to stick out; (когти, зубы) to sink in.

вонь (-и) *ж* (*разг*) pong.

воню́чий (-ая, -ее, -ие; -, -а, -е) *прил* (*разг*) pongy.

воня́|ть (-ю) *несов неперех* (*разг*) to pong.

вообража́|ть (-ю) *несов от* вообрази́ть ♦ *неперех* (*разг: гордиться*) to think a lot of o.s.

вообраз|и́ть (-жу́, -зи́шь; *impf* вообража́ть) *сов перех* to imagine; он ~зи́л, что все про́тив него́ he imagined that everyone was against him; он ~зи́л себя́ ге́нием he fancied himself as a genius; ~зи́те! (just) imagine!

вообще́ *нареч* **1** (*в общем*) on the whole; она́ вообще́ до́брая on the whole she is kind **2** (*при любых обстоятельствах*) absolutely; ходи́ть в кино́ он вообще́ запрети́л he absolutely forbade us to go to the cinema; э́то нам вообще́ не подхо́дит that does not suit us at all **3** (+*noun*; *не касаясь частностей*) in general; мы говори́ли о поли́тике вообще́ we talked about politics in general; вообще́ говоря́ generally speaking.

воодушев|и́ть (-лю́, -и́шь; *impf* воодушевля́ть) *сов перех* to inspire; ~ (*perf*) кого́-н на то, что́бы +*infin* to inspire sb to do

▶ **воодушеви́ться** *сов возв* (+*instr*) to be inspired by.

воодушевле́ни|е (-я) *ср* enthusiasm.

воодушевлю́ *сов см* воодушеви́ть.

воодушевля́|ть (-ю) *несов от* воодушеви́ть.

вооружа́|ть(ся) (-ю(сь)) *сов см* вооружи́ть(ся).

вооруже́ни|е (-я) *ср* (*процесс*) arming; (*оружие*) arms *мн*; (*техника*) armament equipment; брать (взять *perf*) на ~ (*перен*) to make use of.

вооружённость (-и) *ж* (*оснащённость*) armed capability; техни́ческая ~ technical capability.

вооружённый *прил* armed; вооружённые си́лы (the) armed forces.

вооруж|и́ть (-у́, -и́шь; *impf* вооружа́ть) *сов перех* to arm; (*перен*) to equip

▶ **вооружи́ться** (*impf* вооружа́ться) *сов возв* (человек, полиция) to arm o.s.; (население) to take up arms; вооружа́ться (~ся *perf*) терпе́нием to arm o.s. with patience.

воо́чию *нареч* with one's own eyes.

во-пе́рвых *нареч* firstly, first of all.

вопи́|ть (-лю́, -и́шь) *несов неперех* (*разг: кричать*) to shriek; (*громко плакать*) to keen.

вопию́щий (-ая, -ее, -ие) *прил* (*ошибка, несправедливость*) glaring; (*безобразие, обман*) brazen ♦ (-его; *decl like adj*) *м*: глас ~его в пусты́не a voice in the wilderness.

воплоти́|ть (-щу́, -ти́шь; *impf* воплоща́ть) *сов перех* to embody; воплоща́ть (~ *perf*) в себе́ to be the embodiment of; воплоща́ть (~ *perf*) в жизнь to realize

▶ **воплоти́ться** (*impf* воплоща́ться) *сов возв*: ~ся в +*prp* to be embodied in; воплоща́ться (~ся *perf*) в жизнь to be realized.

воплоще́ни|е (-я) *ср* embodiment.

воплощу́ *сов см* воплоти́ть.

вопл|ь (-я) *м* scream.

воплю́ *несов см* вопи́ть.

вопреки́ *предл* (+*dat*; *ожиданию, прогнозу*) contrary to; (*желанию, приказу*) against.

вопро́с (-а) *м* question; (*проблема*) question, issue; задава́ть (зада́ть *perf*) ~ to ask a question; ста́вить (поста́вить *perf*) под ~ to call into question; быть (*impf*) *или* находи́ться

(*impf*) **под** ~**ом** to be in question; **поднима́ть**
(**подня́ть** *perf*) ~ to raise an issue; **э́то** ~ ~
де́нег/вре́мени it's a question of money/time;
~ **по поря́дку веде́ния** (*ЮР*) point of order.
вопроси́тельный *прил* (*взгляд, интона́ция*)
questioning; (*ЛИНГ*) interrogative;
вопроси́тельный знак question mark.
вопью́сь *итп сов см* **впи́ться.**
вор (-а; *gen pl* -о́в) *м* thief.
ворв|а́ться (-у́сь, -ёшься; *pt* -а́лся, -ала́сь,
-ало́сь, *impf* **врыва́ться**) *сов возв* to burst in;
(*звуки*) to flood in.
ворк|ова́ть (-у́ю) *несов непере́х* (*также пере́н*)
to coo.
воробе́й (-ья́) *м* sparrow.
воро́ванный *прил* stolen.
вор|ова́ть (-у́ю) *несов пере́х* to steal.
воро́в|ка (-ки; *gen pl* -ок) *ж см* **вор.**
воровств|о́ (-а́) *ср* theft.
во́рон (-а) *м* raven.
воро́н|а (-ы) *ж* crow; (*пере́н: разг*) scatterbrain.
воро́н|ить (-ю, -ишь; *perf* **проворо́нить**) *сов*
пере́х (*разг*) to miss.
воро́н|ка (-ки; *gen pl* -ок) *ж* (*для перелива́ния*)
funnel; (*после взры́ва*) crater.
воро́н|о́й *прил* black ♦ (-о́го; *decl like adj*) *м* black
horse.
воро́нок *сущ см* **воро́нка.**
во́рот (-а) *м* neck (*of clothes*).
воро́т|а (-) *мн* gates *мн*; (*вход*) gateway *ед*;
(*СПОРТ*) goal *ед*; **э́то ни в каки́е** ~ **не ле́зет**
(*разг*) this is daft.
вороти́л|а (-ы) *м* (*разг*) big shot.
воротни́к (-а́) *м* collar.
во́рох (-а; *nom pl* -а́) *м* heap.
воро́ча|ть (-ю) *несов пере́х* to shift ♦ *непере́х*
(+*instr*; *разг*) to have control of
▶ **воро́чаться** *несов возв* to toss and turn.
вороши́|ть (-у́, -ишь) *несов пере́х* (*листья́,
пе́пел*) to stir up; ~ (*impf*) **се́но** to toss hay; ~
(*impf*) **про́шлое** to stir up the past.
ворс (-а) *м* (*на тка́ни*) nap.
ворча́ни|е (-я) *ср* (*живо́тного*) growling;
(*челове́ка*) grumbling.
ворч|а́ть (-у́, -и́шь) *несов непере́х* (*см сущ*) to
growl; to grumble.
ворчли́в|ый (-, -а, -о) *прил* querulous.
ворчу́н (-а́) *м* (*разг*) whinger.
восемна́дцати *чис см* **восемна́дцать.**
восемна́дцат|ый (-ая, -ое, -ые) *чис* eighteenth;
см также **пя́тый.**
восемна́дцат|ь (-и; *как* **пять;** *см* **Table 27**) *чис*
eighteen; *см также* **пять.**
во́с|емь (-ьми́; *как* **пять;** *см* **Table 27**) *чис* eight;
см также **пять.**
во́с|емьдеся́т (-ьми́десяти; *как* **пятьдеся́т;** *см*
Table 29) *чис* eighty; *см также* **пятьдеся́т.**
во́с|емьсо́т (-ьмисо́т; *как* **пятьсо́т;** *см* **Table**

34) *чис* eight hundred; *см также* **сто.**
воск (-а; *part gen* -у) *м* wax.
воскли́кн|уть (-у, -ешь; *impf* **восклица́ть**) *сов*
непере́х to exclaim.
восклица́ни|е (-я) *ср* exclamation.
восклица́тельный *прил* (*интона́ция*)
exclamatory; **восклица́тельный знак**
exclamation mark (*BRIT*) *или* point (*US*).
восклица́|ть (-ю) *несов от* **восклинуть.**
восково́й *прил* wax; (*цвет*) waxen.
воскре́с *итп сов см* **воскре́снуть.**
воскреса́|ть (-ю) *несов от* **воскре́снуть.**
воскресе́ни|е (-я) *ср* (*РЕЛ*) resurrection; (*пере́н:*
обновле́ние) regeneration; (: *иде́и, движе́ния*)
revival.
воскресе́нь|е (-я) *ср* Sunday; **в** ~ on Sunday;
по ~**ям** on Sundays; **в сле́дующее/про́шлое** ~
next/last Sunday; **сего́дня** ~ **деся́тое ма́я** today
is Sunday (the) 10th (of) May.
воскре|си́ть (-шу́, -си́шь; *impf* **воскреша́ть**) *сов*
пере́х to resurrect, raise from the dead; (*пере́н*)
to revive.
воскре́с|нуть (-ну, -нешь; *pt* -, -ла, -ло, *impf*
воскреса́ть) *сов непере́х* to be resurrected, rise
from the dead; (*пере́н*) to be revived.
воскре́сный *прил* Sunday *опред.*
воскреша́|ть (-ю) *несов от* **воскреси́ть.**
воскреше́ни|е (-я) *ср* resurrection.
воскрешу́ *сов см* **воскреси́ть.**
воспале́ни|е (-я) *ср* inflammation; **воспале́ние**
лёгких pneumonia.
воспал|и́ться (-ю́сь, -и́шься; *impf*
воспаля́ться) *сов возв* to become inflamed.
восп|е́ть (-ою́, -оёшь; *impf* **воспева́ть**) *сов*
пере́х to extol (*BRIT*), extoll (*US*).
воспита́ни|е (-я) *ср* upbringing; (*шко́льников,*
гра́ждан) education; ~ **че́стности** instilling of
honesty; **брать** (**взять** *perf*) **на** ~ to adopt.
воспи́танник (-а) *м* (*учи́теля, тре́нера*) pupil;
(*ву́за*) student; (*приёмный ребёнок*) adopted
child.
воспи́танниц|а (-ы) *ж см* **воспи́танник.**
воспи́тан|ный (-, -на, -но) *прил* well-
brought-up.
воспита́тел|ь (-я) *м* teacher; (*в ла́гере, в*
коло́нии) instructor.
воспита́|ть (-ю; *impf* **воспи́тывать**) *сов пере́х*
(*ребёнка*) to bring up; (*трудолю́бие,*
че́стность итп) to foster, cultivate;
воспи́тывать (~ *perf*) **из кого́-н специали́ста/**
спортсме́на to make a specialist/sportsman of
sb.
воспламен|и́ться (-ю́сь, -и́шься; *impf*
воспламеня́ться) *сов возв* to ignite.
воспо́лн|ить (-ю, -ишь; *impf* **восполня́ть**) *сов*
пере́х (*недоста́тки*) to make up *или*
compensate for; (*пробе́лы*) to fill in.
воспо́льз|оваться (-уюсь) *сов от*

пóльзоваться.
воспоминáни|**е** (**-я**) *ср* memory, recollection; *см также* **воспоминáния.**
воспоминáни|**я** (**-й**) *мн* memoirs *мн*, reminiscences *мн*.
воспою́ *итп сов см* **воспéть.**
воспрепя́тств|**овать** (**-ую**) *сов от* **препя́тствовать.**
воспре|**ти́ть** (**-щу́, -ти́шь**; *impf* **воспреща́ть**) *сов перех* to forbid.
воспреща́|**ться** (*3sg* **-ется**, *3pl* **-ются**) *несов возв* to be forbidden; **посторóнним вход** ~**ется** no entry to unauthorized persons.
воспрещу́ *сов см* **воспрети́ть.**
восприи́мчив|**ый** (**-, -а, -о**) *прил* (*легко усваивающий*) receptive; (*подверженный*) susceptible.
воспр|**иня́ть** (**-иму́, -и́мешь**; *impf* **воспринима́ть**) *сов перех* to perceive; (*идею, смысл*) to comprehend.
восприя́ти|**е** (**-я**) *ср* perception.
воспроизведéни|**е** (**-я**) *ср* (*звука, мелодии*) reproduction; (*событий, пейзажа*) re-creation.
воспроизв|**ести́** (**-еду́, -едéшь**; *pt* **-ёл, -лá, -лó**, *impf* **воспроизводи́ть**) *сов перех* to reproduce; (*капитал*) to restore.
воспроизв|**оди́ть** (**-ожу́, -óдишь**) *несов от* **воспроизвести́.**
воспроти́в|**иться** (**-люсь, -ишься**) *сов от* **проти́виться.**
воспря́н|**уть** (**-у, -ешь**) *сов неперех*: ~ **ду́хом** to take heart.
воссозда|**вáть** (**-ю́**) *несов от* **воссоздáть.**
воссоздáть (*как* **дать**; *см* **Table 14**; *impf* **воссоздавáть**) *сов перех* (*образ, события*) to re-create.
восста|**вáть** (**-ю́, -ёшь**) *несов от* **восстáть.**
восстанá|**вливать(ся)** (**-ю(сь)**) *несов от* **восстанови́ть(ся).**
восстáни|**е** (**-я**) *ср* uprising.
восстанови́тельный *прил* (*работы*) restoration *опред*; ~ **перíод** period of restoration.
восстан|**ови́ть** (**-овлю́, -óвишь**; *impf* **восстанáвливать**) *сов перех* to restore; **восстанáвливать** (~ *perf*) **когó-н в дóлжности** to reinstate sb; **восстанáвливать** (~ *perf*) **когó-н в правáх** to restore sb's rights; **восстанáвливать** (~ *perf*) **когó-н прóтив когó-н/чегó-н** to turn *или* set sb against sb/sth
▶ **восстанови́ться** (*impf* **восстанáвливаться**) *сов возв* to be restored.
восстá|**ть** (**-ну, -нешь**; *impf* **восставáть**) *сов неперех*: ~ **прóтив** +*gen* to rise up (against); (*перен*) to take a stand (against).
востóк (**-а**) *м* east; **В**~ the East, the Orient; **éхать** (*impf*) **на** ~ to travel east; **лежáть** (*impf*)/**находи́ться** (*impf*) **к** ~**у от** +*gen* to lie/be situated to the east of.
востóрг (**-а**) *м* rapture; **быть** (*impf*) **в** ~**е от** +*gen* to be enraptured by; **приходи́ть** (**прийти́** *perf*) **в**

~ **от** +*gen* to be thrilled by.
восторгá|**ть** (**-ю**) *несов перех* to delight, enrapture
▶ **восторгáться** *несов возв* (+*instr*) to be delighted *или* enraptured by.
востóржен|**ный** (**-, -на, -но**) *прил* (*зритель, поклонник итп*) ecstatic; (*слова, похвала*) rapturous.
восторжеств|**овáть** (**-у́ю**) *сов неперех*: ~ (**над** +*instr*) to triumph (over).
востóчный *прил* eastern; ~ **вéтер** east wind.
вострéбование (**-я**) *ср* (*багажа, груза*) claim; **письмó до** ~**я** a letter sent poste restante (*BRIT*) *или* general delivery (*US*).
вострéб|**овать** (**-ую**) *сов перех* to claim.
вострó *нареч*: **держáть у́хо** ~ (*разг*) to keep an ear to the ground.
восхити́тел|**ьный** (**-ен, -на, -но**) *прил* (*музыка, стихи итп*) delightful; (*красавица*) ravishing.
восхи|**ти́ть** (**-щу́, -ти́шь**; *impf* **восхищáть**) *сов перех*: **меня́** ~**щáет он/егó хрáбость** I admire him/his courage
▶ **восхити́ться** (*impf* **восхищáться**) *сов возв* (+*instr*) to be delighted with.
восхищéни|**е** (**-я**) *ср* admiration; (*восторг*) delight; **приходи́ть** (**прийти́** *perf*) **в** ~ **от** +*gen* to be enraptured *или* delighted by; **приводи́ть** (**привести́** *perf*) **в** ~ **когó-н** to delight sb.
восхищу́(сь) *сов см* **восхити́ть(ся).**
восхóд (**-а**) *м*: ~ **сóлнца** sunrise; ~ **луны́** moonrise.
восх|**оди́ть** (**-ожу́, -óдишь**) *несов от* **взойти́** ♦ *неперех*: ~ **к** +*dat* (*к периоду времени*) to date back to; (*к традиции*) to be based on.
восходя́щий (**-ая, -ее, -и**) *прил* rising.
восхожу́ *несов см* **восходи́ть.**
восьм|**áя** (**-óй**; *decl like adj*) *ж*: **однá** ~ one eighth.
восьмёр|**ка** (**-ки**; *gen pl* **-ок**) *ж* (*разг*: *цифра*) eight; (*группа из восьми*) group of eight; (*разг*: *автобус, трамвай итп*) (number) eight (*bus, tram etc*); **лóдка-**~ eight (*ROWING*).
вóсьмер|**о** (**-ы́х**; *как* **чéтверо**; *см* **Table 36a**) *чис* eight; *см также* **двóе.**
восьми́ *чис см* **вóсемь.**
восьми́десяти *чис см* **вóсемьдесят.**
восьмидесятилéти|**е** (**-я**) *ср* (*срок*) eighty years *мн*; (*годовщина*) eightieth anniversary; (*день рождения*) eightieth birthday.
восьмидесятилéтн|**ий** (**-яя, -ее, -ие**) *прил* (*период*) eighty-year; (*старик*) eighty-year-old.
восьмидеся́т|**ый** (**-ая, -ое, -ые**) *чис* eightieth; *см также* **пятидеся́тый.**
восьмиднéвный *прил* eight-day.
восьмиклáссник (**-а**) *м pupil in eighth year at school (usually 14 years old)*.
восьмиклáссниц|**а** (**-ы**) *ж см* **восьмиклáссник.**
восьмикрáтный *прил*: ~ **чемпиóн** eight-times champion; **в** ~**ом размéре** eightfold.
восьмилéти|**е** (**-я**) *ср* (*срок*) eight years; (*годовщина*) eighth anniversary.

восьмиле́тн|ий (-яя, -ее, -ие) *прил* (*период*) eight-year; (*ребёнок*) eight-year-old.

восьмиме́сячный *прил* eight-month; (*ребёнок*) eight-month-old.

восьминеде́льный *прил* eight-week; (*ребёнок*) eight-week-old.

восьмисо́т *чис см* **восемьсо́т**.

восьмисотле́ти|е (-я) *ср* (*срок*) eight hundred years *мн*; (*годовщина*) eight-hundredth anniversary, octocentenary.

восьмисотле́тн|ий (-яя, -ее, -ие) *прил* (*период*) eight hundred-year; (*дерево*) eight hundred-year-old.

восьмисо́т|ый (-ая, -ое, -ые) *чис* eight-hundredth.

восьмиуго́льник (-а) *м* octagon.

восьмичасово́й *прил* (*рабочий день*) eight-hour; (*поезд*) eight-o'clock.

восьм|о́й (-а́я, -о́е, -ы́е) *чис* eighth; *см также* **пя́тый**.

KEYWORD

вот *част* **1** (*при указании*): **вот моя́ ма́ма** there is my mother; **вот мой де́ти** here are my children; **вот он идёт** here he comes
2 (*выражает указание*) this; **вот в чём де́ло** this is what it's about; **вот где ну́жно иска́ть** this is where we need to look
3 (*при эмфатике*): **вот посмотри́, како́е безобра́зие** just look at the mess; **вот ты и сде́лай э́то** YOU do this; **вот негодя́й!** what a rascal!
4 (*как часть сказ*): **но́вая кни́га – вот моя́ цель** a new book – that's my goal; **вот-во́т** (*разг: вот именно*) you've got it; **он вот-во́т ля́жет спать** he is just about to go to bed; **вот ещё!** (*разг*) not likely!; **вот (оно́) как или что!** is that so *или* right?; **вот тебе́ (и) погуля́ли!** (*разг*) so much for the walk!; **вот тебе́ и на** *или* **те раз!** (*разг*) well I never!

воткн|у́ть (-у́, -ёшь; *impf* **втыка́ть**) *сов перех* (*иголку, нож*) to stick in; **втыка́ть** (~ *perf*) **кол в зе́млю** to drive a stake into the ground.

вотру́(сь) *итп сов см* **втере́ть(ся)**.

во́тум (-а) *м*: ~ **дове́рия/недове́рия** vote of confidence/no confidence.

вошёл *итп сов см* **войти́**.

вошь (**вши**; *instr sg* **во́шью**, *nom pl* **вши**) *ж* louse (*мн* lice).

вошью́ *итп сов см* **вшить**.

вощёный *прил* waxed.

во́ю *итп несов см* **выть**.

впада́|ть (-ю) *несов от* **впасть** ♦ *неперех*: ~ **в** +*acc* to flow into.

впа́дин|а (-ы) *ж* (*в земле*) gully; (*на дне моря*) trench; **глазна́я** ~ eye socket.

впа|сть (-ду́, -дёшь; *impf* **впада́ть**) *сов неперех* (*щёки, глаза*) to become sunken; **впада́ть** (~

perf) **в отча́яние** to fall into despair; **впада́ть** (~ *perf*) **в исте́рику** to go into hysterics; **впада́ть** (~ *perf*) **в па́нику** to get into a panic; **впада́ть** (~ *perf*) **в оши́бку** to err; **впада́ть** (~ *perf*) **в кра́йность** to go to extremes; **впада́ть** (~ *perf*) **в заблужде́ние** to be deluded.

впервы́е *нареч* for the first time.

вперёд *нареч* (*идти, смотреть итп*) (straight) ahead, forward; (*заплатить, требовать*) in advance.

впереди́ *нареч* in front; (*в будущем*) ahead ♦ *предл* (+*gen*) in front of; **у Вас вся жизнь** ~ you have your whole life in front of you.

вереме́шку *нареч* higgledy-piggledy.

впечатле́ни|е (-я) *ср* impression; **находи́ться** (*impf*) **под** ~**м чего́-н** to be impressed by sth; **производи́ть** (**произвести́** *perf*) ~ **на** +*acc* to make an impression on; **тако́е** ~, **что** *или* **бу́дто** it looks as if.

впечатли́тельный (-ен, -ьна, -ьно) *прил* impressionable.

впечатля́|ть (-ю) *несов неперех* to be impressive.

впива́|ться (-юсь) *несов от* **впи́ться**.

впи|са́ть (-шу́, -шешь; *impf* **впи́сывать**) *сов перех* to insert, include

▶ **вписа́ться** (*impf* **впи́сываться**) *сов возв* (*перен*) to fit in well.

впита́|ть (-ю; *impf* **впи́тывать**) *сов перех* to absorb; (*перен*) to absorb, take in

▶ **впита́ться** *сов возв* to be absorbed.

впи́|ться (**вопью́сь, вопьёшься;** *impf* **впива́ться**) *сов возв*: ~ **в** +*acc* (*комар*) to bite; **впива́ться** (~ *perf*) **глаза́ми в** +*acc* to fix *или* fasten one's eyes on; **впива́ться** (~ *perf*) **когтя́ми/зуба́ми в** +*acc* to sink one's claws/teeth into.

впишу́(сь) *итп сов см* **вписа́ть(ся)**.

ВПК *сокр* (= **вое́нно-промы́шленный ко́мплекс**) ≈ military-industrial complex.

вплавь *нареч* by swimming.

вплотну́ю *нареч* (*близко*) close (by) ♦ *предл*: ~ **к** +*dat* (*близко: к городу*) right up close to; (: **к стене́**) right up against; **занима́ться** (**заня́ться** *perf*) **чем-н** *или* **бра́ться** (**взя́ться** *perf*) **за что-н** ~ to get down to sth in earnest.

вплоть *предл*: ~ **до** +*gen* (*вчера, зимы*) right up till; (*включая*) right up to; ~ **до того́, что** ... to the extent that ....

вполго́лоса *нареч* (*говорить, спросить*) in hushed tones; (*петь*) softly.

впо́ру *как сказ*: ~ +*infin* there is nothing for it but to do; **пла́тье/шля́па** ~ the dress/hat fits nicely.

впосле́дствии *нареч* subsequently.

впотьма́х *нареч* in the dark.

впп *ж сокр* (= **взлётно-поса́дочная полоса́**) landing strip.

впра́ве *как сказ*: ~ +*infin* to do rightly *или* justly;

он не ~ так поступа́ть he's got no right to behave like that.

впра́в|ить (-лю, -ишь; impf вправля́ть) сов перех to set.

впра́во нареч to the right; ~ от до́ма to the right of the house.

впредь нареч in future ◆ предл: ~ до +gen pending.

впритъ́к нареч (разг) right up close.

впро́голодь нареч: жить ~ to live from hand to mouth.

впрок нареч for future use ◆ как сказ: идти́ ~ кому́-н to do sb good.

впроса́к нареч: попа́сть(ся) ~ (разг) to get (o.s.) into a fix.

впро́чем союз however, though ◆ вводн сл but then again; пого́да здесь хоро́шая, ~ не всегда́ the weather's good here, though not always; ~, я не уве́рен but then again, I'm not sure.

впряг итп сов см впрячь.

впряга́|ть (-ю) несов от впрячь.

впрягу́ итп сов см впрячь.

впрямь част: и ~ (разг) really; он и ~ испуга́лся he really got a fright.

впря́чь (-гу́, -жёшь итп, -гут; pt -г, -гла́, -гло́, impf впряга́ть) сов перех to harness.

впу|сти́ть (-щу́, -стишь; impf впуска́ть) сов перех (в дом, в зал) to admit, let in.

впу́та|ть (-ю) сов от пу́тать ◆ (impf впу́тывать) перех (разг): ~ кого́-н (в +acc) to get sb mixed up (in)

▶ впу́таться сов от пу́таться ◆ (impf впу́тываться) возв to get involved.

впущу́ сов см впусти́ть.

впя́теро нареч (больше, меньше) five times; (увеличить) fivefold.

впятеро́м нареч in a group of five.

в-пя́тых вводн сл fifthly, in the fifth place.

враг (-а́) м enemy ◆ собир (воен) the enemy.

вражда́ (-ы́) ж enmity, hostility; пита́ть (impf) ~у́ к +dat to harbour enmity towards.

враждéб|ный (-ен, -на, -но) прил (отношение, тон) hostile; (лагерь, сторона) enemy опред.

враждова́|ть (-ую) несов неперех: ~ (с +instr) to be on hostile terms (with).

враз нареч (разг) at once.

вразбро́д нареч separately.

вразбро́с нареч (разг) scattered about.

вразва́лку нареч (разг): ходи́ть ~ to waddle.

вразнобо́й нареч (разг) in a muddled way.

вразно́с нареч: торгова́ть ~ to peddle.

вразре́з нареч: ~ с +instr in contravention of.

вразуми́тельный (-ен, -ьна, -ьно) прил comprehensible.

вразум|и́ть (-лю́, -и́шь; impf вразумля́ть) сов перех: ~ кого́-н to make sb understand.

вранью́ё (-я́) ср (разг) lies мн.

врасплóх нареч unawares.

врассыпну́ю нареч in all directions.

врата́р|ь (-я́) м goalkeeper.

вр|ать (-у́, -ёшь; pt -ал, -ла́, -ло, perf навра́ть или совра́ть) несов неперех (разг: человек) to fib; (: часы) to be wrong.

врач (-а́) м doctor.

враче́бный прил medical.

враща́|ть (-ю) несов перех (колесо) to turn

▶ враща́ться несов возв (колесо, планета) to revolve, rotate; ~ся (impf) в полити́ческих круга́х to move in political circles; разгово́р ~лся вокру́г теа́тра the conversation revolved around the theatre.

враще́ни|е (-я) ср revolution, rotation.

вред (-а́) м (делу, здоровью) damage; (человеку) harm, injury ◆ предл: во ~ +dat to the detriment of; его́ де́йствия бы́ли во ~ интере́сам фи́рмы his actions were against the company's interests; причиня́ть (причини́ть perf) или приноси́ть (принести́ perf) ~ кому́-н to harm sb, do sb harm; причиня́ть (причини́ть perf) или приноси́ть (принести́ perf) ~ чему́-н to damage или cause damage to sth.

вре́ден прил см вре́дный.

вреди́тел|ь (-я) м (насекомое) pest; (человек) saboteur.

вре|ди́ть (-жу́, -ди́шь; perf навреди́ть) несов неперех (+dat) to harm, hurt; (здоровью) to damage; (врагу́) to inflict damage on.

вре́дно нареч: ~ влия́ть на +acc to have a harmful effect on ◆ как сказ: кури́ть ~ smoking is bad for you; ему́ ~ есть жи́рное fatty foods are bad for him.

вре́д|ный (-ен, -на́, -но) прил harmful; (no short form; разг) nasty.

вре́|зать (-жу, -жешь) сов перех (замок) to fit ◆ неперех (разг: ударить): ~ кому́-н to bash sb.

врежу́ несов см вреди́ть.

вре́|заться (-жусь, -жешься; impf вреза́ться) сов возв: ~ в +acc (пила, верёвка) to cut into; (ворва́ться) to plough (BRIT) или plow (US) into; (в сердце, в память) to engrave itself on.

врем|ена́ (-ён; dat pl -ена́м) мн (эпоха) the time ед; ~ Петра́ Пе́рвого the time of Peter the First.

времена́ми нареч at times.

вре́мени итп сущ см вре́мя.

вре́мен|ный (-ен, -на, -но) прил temporary.

вре́м|я (-ени; см Table 4) ср time; (линг) tense ◆ предл: во ~ +gen during; в то ~ как или когда́ while; (а) в то же ~ (but) at the same time; во вре́мя during; ~ от вре́мени from time to time; в после́днее ~ recently; в своё ~ (когда́ необходимо) in due course; в своё ~ она́ была́ краса́вицей she was a real beauty in her day; на ~ for a while; со ~енем with или in time; тем ~енем meanwhile; ско́лько ~ени? what time is it?; в 8 часо́в по моско́вскому ~ени at 8 o'clock (by) Moscow time; ~ до́ступа (комп) access time; ~ реализа́ции зака́за (комм) lead time; лу́чшее эфи́рное ~ prime time; хорошо́ проводи́ть (провести́ perf) ~ to have a good time; вре́мя го́да season; см та́кже времена́.

времяисчислéни|е (-я) *ср* calendar.
времяпрепровождéни|е (-я) *ср* way of
spending time.
врéмя́н|ка (-ки; *gen pl* -ок) *ж* (*печка*) makeshift
stove; (*жилище*) makeshift hut (*next to new
rural dwelling*).
врóвень *нареч*: ~ с +*instr* level with.
врóде *предл* (+*gen*) like ♦ *част* it looks as if; **он
у меня** ~ **совéтника** he's like an advisor to me;
он ~ **уéхал** it looks as if he's gone.
врождённый *прил* (*способности*) innate;
(*уродство, болезнь*) congenital.
врозь *нареч* (*жить*) apart; (*работать, ехать*)
separately ♦ *предл*: ~ **с** +*instr или* **от** +*gen* (*разг*)
separate from.
врóю *итп сов см* **врыть**.
вру *несов см* **врать**.
врубѝть (-лю́, -ишь; *impf* **врубáть**) *сов перех*
(*разг*: *включить*) to turn on.
врун (-á) *м* (*разг*) fibber.
врýнь|я (-и) *ж см* **врун**.
вручѝть (-у́, -ишь; *impf* **вручáть**) *сов перех*: ~
что-н комý-н to hand sth (over) to sb; (*орден,
премию*) to present sb with sth.
вручнýю *нареч* (*разг*) by hand.
врывáться (-ю́сь) *несов от* **ворвáться**.
врыть (-óю, -óешь; *impf* **врывáть**) *сов перех*
(*столб*) to sink in; (*дерево*) to plant firmly.
вряд *част*: ~ **ли** hardly; ~ **ли он согласѝтся**
he's hardly likely to agree.
ВС *мн сокр* (= *Вооружённые Сѝлы*) armed forces
мн; (= *Верхóвный Совéт*) Supreme Soviet.
всадѝть (-жу́, -дишь; *impf* **всáживать**) *сов
перех*: ~ **в** +*acc* (*нож, стрелу*) to sink into;
всáживать (-*perf*) **пýлю в лоб комý-н** (*разг*)
to put a bullet in sb's head.
всáдник (-а) *м* rider, horseman (*мн* horsemen).
всáдниц|а (-ы) *ж* rider, horsewoman (*мн*
horsewomen).
всáжива|ть (-ю) *несов от* **всадѝть**.
всажý *сов см* **всадѝть**.
всáсыва|ть (-ю) *несов от* **всосáть**.
все *мест см* **весь**.

KEYWORD

всё (**всегó**) *мест см* **весь**
   ♦ *ср* (*как сущ*: *без исключения*) everything; **вот
и всё, э́то всё** that's all; **чáще всегó** most
often; **лýчше всегó написáть ей письмó** it
would be best to write to her; **меня́ э́то волнýет
мéньше всегó** that is the least of my worries;
мне всё равнó it's all the same to me; **Вы
хотѝте чай или кóфе? – всё равнó** do you
want tea or coffee? – I don't mind; **я всё равнó
пойдý тудá** I'll go there all the same
   ♦ *нареч* **1** (*разг*: *всё время*) all the time
2 (*разг*: *до сих пор*) still
3 (*только*) all; **э́то всё он виновáт** it's all his
fault

4 (*о нарастании признака*): **шум всё
усѝливается** the noise keeps getting louder
5 (*о постоянстве признака*): **всё так же** still
the same; **всё там же** still there; **всё же** all the
same; **всё ещё** still.

всевлáсти|е (-я) *ср* absolute power.
всевозмóжный (-ен, -на, -но) *прил* all sorts of.
всегдá *нареч* always.
всегó *мест см* **весь, всё** ♦ *нареч* in all ♦ *част*
only; ~ **лишь** (*разг*) only; ~-**нáвсего** (*разг*) all
in all.
вселéнн|ая (-ой; *decl like adj*) *ж* the whole world;
В~ universe.
вселѝть (-ю́, -ѝшь; *impf* **вселя́ть**) *сов перех*
(*жильцов*) to install; (*перен*) to instil (*BRIT*),
instill (*US*).
▶ **вселѝться** (*impf* **вселя́ться**) *сов возв*
(*жильцы*) to move in; (*перен*) to be instilled.
всем *мест см* **весь, всё, все**.
всемéрный *прил* (*помощь*) all possible.
всемерóм *нареч* in a group of seven.
всéми *мест см* **все**.
всемѝрный *прил* worldwide; (*конгресс*) world
опред.
всемогýщ|ий (-ая, -ее, -ие; -, -а, -е) *прил*
omnipotent, all-powerful.
всемý *мест см* **весь, всё**.
всенарóден *прил см* **всенарóдный**.
всенарóдно *нареч* publicly.
всенарóдный (-ен, -на, -но) *прил* national.
всéнощн|ая (-ой; *decl like adj*) *ж* (*РЕЛ*) vespers.
всеóбуч (-а) *м сокр* (= *всеóбщее обучéние*)
general education.
всеóбщ|ий (-ая, -ее, -ие; -, -а, -е) *прил* universal;
всеóбщая забастóвка/пéрепись general
strike/census.
всеобъéмлющ|ий (-ая, -ее, -ие; -, -а, -о) *прил*
comprehensive.
всеорýжи|е (-я) *ср*: **во** ~**и знáний** armed with
knowledge; **встречáть** (**встрéтить** *perf*) **врагá
во** ~**и** to be primed for battle.
всероссѝйск|ий (-ая, -ое, -ие) *прил* All-Russia.
всерьёз *нареч* in earnest; **ты э́то говорѝшь** ~?
are you serious?
всесѝл|ьный (-ен, -ьна, -ьно) *прил* all-
powerful.
всесторóн|ний (-няя, -нее, -ние; -ен, -ня, -не)
прил comprehensive.
всё-таки *част* still, all the same ♦ *союз*: **а** ~ all
the same, nevertheless; **мóжет,** ~ **поéдем?** can
we not still go?; **бы́ло скýчно, и** ~ **я не ушёл** I
was bored, but all the same I didn't leave.
всеуслы́шание *ср*: **во** ~ publicly.
всех *мест см* **все**.
всецéло *нареч* completely.
всея́дный *прил* omnivorous.
вскáкива|ть (-ю) *несов от* **вскочѝть**.
вскáпыва|ть (-ю) *несов от* **вскопáть**.

вскара́бка|ться (**-юсь**) *сов от* **кара́бкаться**.

вскачь *нареч* at a gallop; **пуска́ть** (**пусти́ть** *perf*) **коня́** ~ to break into a gallop.

вски́н|уть (**-у, -ешь;** *impf* **вски́дывать**) *сов перех* (*на плечи*) to shoulder; (*голову*) to jerk up; (*руки*) to throw up; **вски́дывать** (~ *perf*) **что-н на что-н** to throw sth on(to) sth; **вски́дывать** (~ *perf*) **глаза́ на кого́-н** to glance up at sb.

вскипе́ть (**-лю́, -и́шь;** *impf* **кипе́ть**) *сов неперех* to boil; (*перен*) to flare up; ~ (*perf*) **от гне́ва** to fly into a rage.

вскипяти́ть(ся) (**-чу́(сь), -ти́шь(ся)**) *сов от* **кипяти́ть(ся)**.

всклоко́ченный *прил* (*разг*) tousled.

всколыхн|у́ть (**-у́, -ёшь**) *сов перех* (*подлеж: ветер*) to stir; (*перен: массы*) to stir up

▶ **всколыхну́ться** *сов возв* (*перен*) to become stirred up.

вско́льзь *нареч* in passing.

вскопа́|ть (**-ю;** *impf* **вска́пывать**) *сов перех* to dig (over).

вско́ре *нареч* soon ♦ *предл*: ~ **по́сле** +*gen* soon *или* shortly after.

вскоч|и́ть (**-у́, -ишь;** *impf* **вска́кивать**) *сов неперех*: ~ **в/на** +*acc* (*на коня, в седло*) to leap up onto; **вска́кивать** (~ *perf*) (**на́ ноги**) to leap to one's feet.

вскри́кн|уть (**-у, -ешь;** *impf* **вскри́кивать**) *сов неперех* to cry out.

вскро́ю(сь) *итп сов см* **вскры́ть(ся)**.

вскру́ж|ить (**-у́, -ишь**) *сов перех*: ~ **го́лову кому́-н** to turn sb's head (*fig*).

вскрыва́|ть (**-ю**) *несов от* **вскрыть**.

вскры́ти|е (**-я**) *ср* (*трупа*) postmortem (examination); (*сейфа итп*) opening.

вскр|ы́ть (**-о́ю, -о́ешь;** *impf* **вскрыва́ть**) *сов перех* (*открыть*) to open; (: *с силой*) to force open; (*выявить*) to reveal; (*нарыв*) to lance; (*труп*) to carry out a postmortem on

▶ **вскры́ться** *сов возв* (*перен: выявиться*) to come to light, be revealed; **река́ ~ы́лась** the ice on the river cracked.

вслась *нареч* to one's heart's content.

вслед *нареч* (*бежать*) behind ♦ *предл*: ~ (**за** +*instr*) after; ~ +*dat* (*другу, поезду*) after.

всле́дствие *предл* (+*gen*) as a result of, because of ♦ *союз*: ~ **того́ что** because; ~ **чего́** as a result of which.

вслепу́ю *нареч* blindly; **печа́тать** (*impf*) **на маши́нке** ~ to touch-type.

вслух *нареч* aloud; **сказа́ть** (*perf*) **что-н** ~ to say sth out loud.

вслу́ша|ться (**-юсь;** *impf* **вслу́шиваться**) *сов возв*: ~ **в** +*acc* to listen carefully to.

ВСМ *м сокр* (= *Всеми́рный Сове́т Ми́ра*) World Peace Council.

всмотр|е́ться (**-ю́сь, -ишься;** *impf* **всма́триваться**) *сов возв*: ~ **в** +*acc* to peer at.

всмя́тку *нареч*: **яйцо́** ~ soft-boiled egg.

всо́выва|ть (**-ю**) *несов от* **всу́нуть**.

всоса́|ть (**-у́, -ёшь;** *impf* **вса́сывать**) *сов перех* (*втянуть*) to suck; (*впитать*) to absorb.

вспа́рхива|ть (**-ю**) *несов от* **вспорхну́ть**.

вспа|ха́ть (**-шу́, -шешь**) *сов от* **паха́ть**.

вспе́н|иться (**-юсь, -ишься**) *сов от* **пе́ниться**.

всплеск (**-а**) *м* (*волны*) splash.

всплесн|у́ть (**-у́, -ёшь;** *impf* **всплёскивать**) *сов неперех* (*рыба, пловец*) to splash; ~ (*perf*) **рука́ми** to throw up one's hands.

всплыва́|ть (**-ю**) *несов от* **всплыть**.

всплыву́ *итп сов см* **всплыть**.

всплы́ти|е (**-я**) *ср* surfacing.

всплы|ть (**-ву́, -вёшь;** *pt* **-л, -ла́, -ло,** *impf* **всплыва́ть**) *сов неперех* to surface, come to the surface; (*перен*) to come to light; **всплыва́ть** (~ *perf*) **в па́мяти** to pop into one's head; **всплыва́ть** (~ *perf*) **в созна́нии** to appear before one.

всполош|и́ть(ся) (**-у́(сь), -и́шь(ся)**) *сов от* **полоши́ть(ся)**.

вспо́мн|ить (**-ю, -ишь;** *impf* **вспомина́ть**) *сов перех* to remember ♦ *неперех*: ~ **о** +*prp* to remember about.

вспомога́тельный *прил* (*материал, литература*) supplementary; (*судно, отряд*) auxiliary; **вспомога́тельный глаго́л** auxiliary verb.

вспорхн|у́ть (**-у́, -ёшь;** *impf* **вспа́рхивать**) *сов неперех* to fly off.

вспоте́|ть (**-ю**) *сов от* **потеть**.

вспры́сн|уть (**-у, -ешь;** *impf* **вспры́скивать**) *сов перех* to spray.

вспугн|у́ть (**-у́, -ёшь;** *impf* **вспу́гивать**) *сов перех* to scare away *или* off.

вспу́хн|уть (**-у, -ешь**) *сов от* **пу́хнуть** ♦ (*impf* **вспуха́ть**) *сов неперех* to swell up.

вспу́ч|иться (*3sg* **-ится,** *3pl* **-атся**) *несов от* **пу́читься**.

вспыл|и́ть (**-ю́, -и́шь**) *сов неперех* to lose one's temper.

вспы́льчивость (**-и**) *ж* short-temperedness.

вспы́льчив|ый (**-, -а, -о**) *прил* short-tempered.

вспыхн|уть (**-у, -ешь;** *impf* **вспы́хивать**) *сов неперех* (*солома, бумага*) to burst into flames; (*спичка, конфликт, страсть*) to flare up; (*покраснеть: человек*) to blush; **в окне́ ~ул свет** the window lit up.

вспы́ш|ка (**-ки;** *gen pl* **-ек**) *ж* flash; (*энтузиазма*) burst; (*гнева*) outburst; (*болезни*) outbreak.

вспять *нареч* back.

ВСРФ *мн сокр* = **вооружённые си́лы росси́йской федера́ции.**

встава́|ть (**-ю;** *imper* **-ва́й(те)**) *несов от* **встать** ♦ *неперех*: **рабо́тать/писа́ть не ~ва́я** to work/write without a break.

вста́в|ить (**-лю, -ишь;** *impf* **вставля́ть**) *сов перех* to insert, put in; **вставля́ть** (~ *perf*) **зу́бы** to have a set of dentures *или* false teeth made; **вставля́ть** (~ *perf*) **ка́мень в опра́ву** to set a stone.

вста́в|ка (**-ки;** *gen pl* **-ок**) *ж* insertion; (*в одежде*)

inset.
вста́влю *сов см* **вста́вить.**
вставля́|ть (-ю) *несов от* **вста́вить.**
вставн|о́й *прил* (*рамы*) removable; ~ы́е зу́бы dentures, false teeth.
вста́вок *сущ см* **вста́вка.**
вста|ть (-ну, -нешь; *impf* **встава́ть**) *сов неперех* (*на ноги*) to stand up; (*с постели*) to get up; (*солнце*) to rise; (*трудности, вопрос*) to arise; (*no impf, разг: часы, мотор*) to stop; **пе́ред на́ми вста́ли но́вые тру́дности** we were faced with new difficulties.
встопо́рщ|ить(ся) (-ю(сь), -ишь(ся)) *сов от* **топо́рщить(ся).**
встрева́|ть (-ю) *несов неперех* (*разг: вмешиваться*) to stick one's oar in.
встрево́жен|ный (-, -а, -о) *прил* anxious.
встрево́ж|ить(ся) (-у(сь), -ишь(ся)) *несов от* **трево́жить(ся).**
встрепен|у́ться (-у́сь, -ёшься) *сов возв* to give a start.
встре́|тить (-чу, -тишь; *impf* **встреча́ть**) *сов перех* to meet; (*гостей, делегацию итп*) to meet, welcome; (*обнаружить: слово, цитату*) to come across; (*оппозицию, сопротивление*) to meet with, encounter; (*праздник итп*) to celebrate
▶ **встре́титься** (*impf* **встреча́ться**) *сов возв*: ~ся с +*instr* to meet; (*перен: с сопротивлением итп*) to meet with, encounter; **мне ~тились друзья́/интере́сные фа́кты** I came across some friends/interesting facts.
встре́ч|а (-и) *ж* meeting; (*поединок*) match.
встреча́|ть (-ю) *несов от* **встре́тить**
▶ **встреча́ться** *несов от* **встре́титься** ◆ *возв* (*регулярно видеться*) to meet; (*попадаться*) to be found.
встре́чн|ый *прил* (*машина, поезд итп*) oncoming; (*мера*) counter *опред* ◆ (-ого; *decl like adj*) *м* someone coming from the opposite direction; ~ **ве́тер** head wind; **пе́рвый** ~ (*разг*) anyone; **встре́чная ата́ка** counterattack; **встре́чный иск** counterclaim.
встре́чу(сь) *сов см* **встре́тить(ся).**
встря́с|ка (-ки; *gen pl* -ок) *ж* (*потрясение*) shock; (*системы*) upheaval.
встряхн|у́ть (-у́, -ёшь; *impf* **встря́хивать**) *сов перех* to shake (out); (*перен: общество*) to shake (up).
вступа́|ть(ся) (-ю(сь)) *несов от* **вступи́ть(ся).**
вступи́тельный *прил* (*речь, статья*) introductory; **вступи́тельный взнос** subscription fee; **вступи́тельный экза́мен** entrance exam.
вступ|и́ть (-лю́, -ишь; *impf* **вступа́ть**) *сов неперех*: ~ **в** +*acc* to enter; (*в партию, в общество*) to join; (*в спор, в переговоры*) to enter into; **вступа́ть** (~ *perf*) **на** +*acc* to mount;

вступа́ть (~ *perf*) **в бой** to join battle
▶ **вступи́ться** (*impf* **вступа́ться**) *сов возв*: ~ся за +*acc* to stand up for.
вступле́ни|е (-я) *ср* (*войск: в город*) entry; (*в партию*) joining; (*в стадию*) entering; (*в книге, в статье*) introduction; (*в беседе*) preamble.
вступлю́ *сов см* **вступи́ть.**
всу́н|уть (-у, -ешь; *impf* **всо́вывать**) *сов перех*: ~ **в** +*acc* to stick *или* put in(to).
всухомя́тку *нареч*: **пита́ться** ~ *to live off cold snacks*; **есть** (*impf*) **хлеб** ~ to eat dry bread.
всуч|и́ть (-у́, -ишь; *impf* **всу́чивать**) *сов перех* (*навязать*) to palm off.
всхли́п (-а) *м* sob.
всхли́пыва|ть (-ю) *несов неперех* to sob.
всхо|ди́ть (-жу́, -дишь) *несов от* **взойти́.**
всхо́д|ы (-ов) *мн* shoots *мн*.
всхожу́ *сов см* **всходи́ть.**
всы́п|ать (-лю, -лешь; *impf* **всыпа́ть**) *сов перех*: ~ **в** +*acc* to pour into ◆ *неперех*: ~ **кому́-н** (*разг: отчитать*) to give sb what for.
всю *мест см* **вся.**
всю́ду *нареч* everywhere.
вся (-ей) *мест см* **весь.**
вся́к|ий (-ая, -ое, -ие) *мест* (*каждый*) every; (*разнообразный*) all kinds of; (*любой*) any ◆ (-ого; *decl like adj*) *м* (*любой*) anyone; (*каждый*) everyone; **здесь продаю́т** ~**ие това́ры** all kinds of goods are sold here; **у меня́ пропа́ло** ~**ое жела́ние помо́чь** I have lost all desire to help; **без** ~**ого сомне́ния/интере́са/жела́ния** without the slightest doubt/interest/desire; **без** ~**ого** *или* ~**их согласи́ться** (*perf*)/**приня́ть** (*perf*) (*разг*) to agree/accept without a second thought.
вся́ко *нареч* (*разг*) all sorts of things.
вся́чески *нареч* in every possible way.
вся́ческ|ий (-ая, -ое, -ие) *мест* (*поддержка, сопротивление*) all possible; (*товары*) all kinds of.
вся́чин|а (-ы) *ж* (*разг*): **вся́кая** ~ all sorts of things.
Вт *сокр* (= *ватт*) W (= *watt*).
вта́йне *нареч* secretly, in secret.
вта́лкива|ть (-ю) *несов от* **втолкну́ть.**
вта́птыва|ть (-ю) *несов от* **втопта́ть.**
втащ|и́ть (-у́, -ишь; *impf* **вта́скивать**) *сов перех*: ~ (**в** +*acc*) to drag in(to).
втёк *итп сов см* **втечь.**
втека́|ть (*3sg* -ет, *3pl* -ют) *несов неперех* to flow into.
втеку́т *сов см* **втечь.**
втере́ть (вотру́, вотрёшь; *pt* втёр, втёрла, втёрло, *impf* **втира́ть**) *сов перех*: ~ (**в** +*acc*) to rub in(to)
▶ **втере́ться** (*impf* **втира́ться**) *сов возв* to be absorbed; (*разг: пренебр*) to worm one's way in; ~ся (*perf*) **в дове́рие кому́-н** to worm one's way into sb's confidence.

вте|чь (*3sg* -чёт, *3pl* -кут, *pt* втёк, -кла, -кло, *impf*
втека́ть) *сов неперех:* ~ **в** +*acc* to flow into.
втира́ть(ся) (-ю(сь)) *несов от* **втере́ть(ся).**
вти́сн|уть (-у, -ешь; *impf* **вти́скивать**) *сов*
перех: ~ **(в** +*acc*) to cram in(to)
► **вти́снуться** *сов возв* (*разг*) (*impf*
вти́скиваться): ~**ся (в** +*acc*) (*человек*) to
squeeze in(to).
втихомо́лку *нареч* (*разг*) on the quiet.
втолкн|у́ть (-у́, -ёшь; *impf* **вта́лкивать**) *сов*
перех: ~ **(в** +*acc*) to push in(to).
втолк|ова́ть (-у́ю; *impf* **втолко́вывать**) *сов*
перех (*разг*): ~ **что-н кому́-н** to get sth through
to sb.
втоп|та́ть (-чу́, -чешь; *impf* **вта́птывать**) *сов*
перех: ~ **(в** +*acc*) to trample in(to); **вта́птывать**
(~ *perf*) **кого́-н в грязь** (*перен*) to humiliate sb.
втор|а́я (-о́й; *decl like adj*) *ж:* **одна́** ~ one half.
вто́рг|нуться (-усь, -ешься; *impf* **вторга́ться**)
сов возв: ~ **в** +*acc* (*в страну*) to invade;
(*вмешаться*) to interfere with *или* in.
вто́р|ить (-ю, -ишь) *несов неперех* (+*dat; петь*)
to sing the second part to; (*разг: поддакивать*)
to parrot.
втори́чный *прил* (*повторный*) second;
(*второстепенный*) secondary; **втори́чное**
сырьё recyclable materials.
вто́рник (-а) *м* Tuesday; **в** ~ on Tuesday; **по**
~**ам** on Tuesdays; **в сле́дующий/про́шлый** ~
next/last Tuesday; **сего́дня** ~, **деся́тое ма́я**
today is Tuesday (the) 10th (of) May.
второго́дник (-а) *м pupil repeating a year at*
school.
второго́дниц|а (-ы) *ж см* **второго́дник.**
втор|о́е (-о́го; *decl like adj*) *ср* main course; **на** ~ –
бифште́кс the main course is steak.
втор|о́й (-а́я, -о́е, -ы́е) *прил* second; (*роль*)
secondary; **быть** (*impf*) **на** ~**о́м пла́не** to stay in
the background; **сейча́с** ~ **час** it's after one;
сейча́с полови́на ~**о́го** it's half past one;
второ́е дыха́ние second wind; **втора́я**
мо́лодость second wind; **второ́й сорт** second
class; *см также* **пя́тый.**
второкла́ссник (-а) *м pupil in second year at*
school (usually eight years old).
второкла́ссниц|а (-ы) *ж см* **второкла́ссник.**
второпя́х *нареч* in a hurry.
второсо́рт|ный (-ен, -на, -но) *прил* second-
class; (*посредственный*) second-rate.
второстепе́н|ный (-ен, -на, -но) *прил*
secondary.
в-тре́тьих *вводн сл* thirdly, in the third place.
втри́дорога *нареч* (*разг*): **плати́ть** ~ to pay a
mint *или* bomb.
втро́е *нареч* (*больше, меньше*) three times;
(*увеличить*) threefold.
втроём *нареч* in a group of three.
втройне́ *нареч* three times as much.
вту́л|ка (-ки; *gen pl* -ок) *ж* (*пробка*) plug; (*ТЕХ*)
bush.
втыка́|ть (-ю) *несов от* **воткну́ть.**

втян|у́ть (-у́, -ешь; *impf* **втя́гивать**) *сов перех*
(*втащить*) to pull in; (*вобрать*) to take in;
втя́гивать (~ *perf*) **кого́-н в** +*acc* (*перен: в дело*)
to involve sb in; (: *в конфликт итп*) to draw sb
into
► **втяну́ться** (*impf* **втя́гиваться**) *сов возв:* ~**ся**
в +*acc* to get involved in; (*привыкнуть*) to settle
into.
вуали́р|овать (-ую; *perf* **завуали́ровать**) *несов*
перех to veil.
вуа́л|ь (-и) *ж* veil.
вуз (-а) *м сокр* (= **вы́сшее уче́бное заведе́ние**)
institution of higher education.
ву́зовск|ий (-ая, -ое, -ие) *прил* university *опред*;
~**ая систе́ма** higher education system.
вулка́н (-а) *м* volcano; **де́йствующий/**
поту́хший ~ active/extinct volcano.
вульга́рен *прил см* **вульга́рный.**
вульга́рность (-и) *ж* vulgarity.
вульга́р|ный (-ен, -на, -но) *прил* (*человек,*
слова) vulgar.
вундерки́нд (-а) *м* child prodigy.
вход (-а) *м* (*движение*) entry; (*место*) entrance;
(*ТЕХ*) inlet; (*КОМП*) input.
вхо|ди́ть (-жу́, -дишь) *несов от* **войти́.**
входно́й *прил* (*дверь*) entrance *опред*; (*КОМП*)
input *опред*; **входно́й биле́т** entrance ticket.
входя́щ|ий (-ая, -ее, -ие) *прил* incoming.
вхожу́ *сов см* **входи́ть.**
вхолосту́ю *нареч:* **рабо́тать** ~ to idle.
вцеп|и́ться (-лю́сь, -ишься; *impf* **вцепля́ться**)
сов возв: ~ **в** +*acc* to seize.
ВЦСПС *м сокр* (= **Всеросси́йский Центра́льный**
Сове́т профессиона́льных сою́зов) *central*
trade-union council.
ВЧ *ж сокр* (= **высо́кая частота́**) HF (= *high*
frequency) ♦ *прил* (*высокочасто́тный*) HF (=
high-frequency).
вчера́ *нареч, м нескл* yesterday.
вчера́шн|ий (-яя, -ее, -ие) *прил* (*также перен*)
yesterday's; **жить** (*impf*) ~**им днём** to live in the
past.
вчерне́ *нареч* in rough.
вче́тверо *нареч* (*больше, меньше*) four times;
(*увеличить*) fourfold.
вчетверо́м *нареч* in a group of four.
в-четвёртых *нареч* fourthly, in the fourth place.
вчита́|ться (-юсь; *impf* **вчи́тываться**) *сов возв:*
~ **(в** +*acc*) to g... ...(of).
вшей(те) *сов с... ...ть.*
вше́стеро *нар... (бо...ше, меньше)* si... ...mes;
(*увеличить*) ...
вшестеро́м *нареч* in a group of six.
вши *итп сущ см* **вошь.**
вшива́|ть (-ю) *несов от* **вшить.**
вши́ве|ть (-ю; *perf* **завши́веть**) *несов неперех* to
become lice-ridden.
вши́вый *прил* lice-ridden.
вширь *нареч* in breadth; **раздава́ться**
(*разда́ться perf*) ~ to put on weight.
вшить (**вошью́, вошьёшь;** *imper* **вшей(те)**), *impf*

вшива́ть) *сов перех* to sew in.
въеда́|ться (-юсь) *несов от* въе́сться.
въе́дешь *итп сов см* въе́хать.
въе́длив|ый (-, -а, -о) *прил* meticulous.
въе́ду *итп сов см* въе́хать.
въедя́тся *сов см* въе́сться.
въезд (-а) *м* (*движение*) entry; (*место*) entrance.
въездно́й *прил* entry *опред*.
въезжа́|ть (-ю) *несов от* въе́хать.
въе́|сться (*3sg* -стся, *3pl* -дя́тся, *impf* въеда́ться) *сов возв*: ~ в +*acc* (*кислота́*, *ржа́вчина*) to eat into; (*кра́ска, грязь*) to become ingrained in.
въе́|хать (*как* е́хать; *см* **Table 19**; *impf* въезжа́ть) *сов неперех* to enter; (*в но́вый дом*) to move in; (*наве́рх: на маши́не*) to drive up; (: *на коне́, велосипе́де*) to ride up.
вы- *префикс* (*in verbs*; *об исче́рпанности де́йствия*) *indicating completion of action eg.* вы́яснить, вы́спаться; (*о движе́нии изнутри́*) *indicating movement outwards eg.* вы́бежать.
Вы (Вас; *см* **Table 5b**) *мест* you; быть (*impf*) на ~ с кем-н to be on formal terms with sb.
вы (вас; *см* **Table 5b**) *мест* you (*plural*).
вы́бе|жать (*как* бежа́ть; *см* **Table 20**; *impf* выбега́ть) *сов неперех* to run out.
вы́бей(те) *сов см* вы́бить.
вы́бел|ить (-ю, -ишь) *сов от* бели́ть.
вы́беру(сь) *итп сов см* вы́брать(ся).
выбива́ть(ся) (-ю(сь)) *несов от* вы́бить(ся).
выбира́|ть (-ю) *несов от* вы́брать ♦ *перех*: ~ слова́ to choose one's words
▸ выбира́ться *несов от* вы́браться.
вы́б|ить (-ью, -ешь; *imper* вы́бей(те), *impf* выбива́ть) *сов перех* to knock out; (*проти́вника*) to oust; (*ковёр*) to beat; (*на́дпись*) to carve; (*разг: де́ньги, контра́кт*) to manage to get; выбива́ть (~ *perf*) чек (*касси́р*) to ring up the total; выбива́ть (~ *perf*) чек в ка́ссе (*покупа́тель*) to get a ticket from the cashier (*to claim purchase*)
▸ вы́биться (*impf* выбива́ться) *сов возв*: ~ся из +*gen* (*освободи́ться*) to get out of; выбива́ться (~ся *perf*) из сил to wear o.s. out; выбива́ться (~ся *perf*) из гра́фика to fall behind schedule; ~ся (*perf*) в лю́ди to make one's way up in the world.
вы́боин|а (-ы) *ж* (*на доро́ге*) pothole; (*на мета́лле, в стене́*) dent.
вы́бор (-а) *м* choice; (*ассортиме́нт*) choice, selection; предлага́ть (предложи́ть *perf*) что-н на ~ to offer a selection of sth; по чьему́-н ~у of sb's choice.
вы́бор|ка (-ки; *gen pl* -ок) *ж* (*обы́чно мн: из те́кста*) extract; (*статисти́ческая*) sample.
вы́борный *прил* (*собра́ние, кампа́ния*) election

опре́д; (*бюллете́нь*) ballot *опред*; (*до́лжность, о́рган*) elective.
вы́борок *сущ см* вы́борка.
вы́бороч|ный (-ен, -на, -но) *прил* selective.
вы́борщик (-а) *м* (*полит*) ≈ elector (*US*), *elected representative taking part in elections on a higher level.*
вы́бор|ы (-ов) *мн* election *ед*.
выбра́ть(ся) (-ю(сь)) *несов от* вы́бросить(ся).
вы́б|рать (-еру, -ерешь; *impf* выбира́ть) *сов перех* to choose; (*отобра́ть*) to pick; (*голосова́нием*) to elect
▸ вы́браться (*impf* выбира́ться) *сов возв* to manage to get out; (*разг: в теа́тр*) to find time to go.
вы́бр|ить (-ею, -еешь; *impf* выбрива́ть) *сов перех* to shave.
вы́брод|ить (-жу, -дишь) *сов от* броди́ть.
вы́брос (-а) *м* (*га́за, радиа́ции*) emission; (*отхо́дов*) discharge; (*не́фти*) spillage; (*деса́нта*) landing.
вы́бро|сить (-шу, -сишь; *impf* выбра́сывать) *сов перех* to throw out; (*разг: с рабо́ты*) to sack; (*отхо́ды*) to discharge; (*га́зы*) to emit; (*деса́нт*) to land; выбра́сывать (~ *perf*) на ры́нок to bring onto the market
▸ вы́броситься (*impf* выбра́сываться) *сов возв* (*из окна́*) to throw o.s. out; выбра́сываться (~ся *perf*) с балко́на to throw o.s. off the balcony; выбра́сываться (~ся *perf*) с парашю́том to bale out.
вы́б|ыть (*как* быть; *см* **Table 21**; *impf* выбыва́ть) *сов неперех*: ~ из +*gen* to leave.
вы́бью *итп сов см* вы́бить.
вы́вал|ить (-ю, -ишь; *impf* выва́ливать) *сов перех*: ~ (из +*gen*) to empty (out of)
▸ вы́валиться (*impf* выва́ливаться) *сов возв* (*вы́пасть*) to fall out; (*разг: толпа́*) to pour out.
выведе́ни|е (-я) *ср* (*фо́рмулы*) deduction; (*цыпля́т, птенцо́в*) hatching; (*сорта́, поро́ды*) breeding; (*вреди́телей*) extermination.
вы́веду(сь) *итп сов см* вы́вести(сь).
вы́вез|ти (-у, -ешь; *impf* вывози́ть) *сов перех* to take; (*това́р: из страны́*) to take out.
вы́вер|ить (-ю, -ишь; *impf* выверя́ть) *сов перех* to check; (*часы́*) to set (*to the right time*).
вы́верн|уть (-у, -ешь; *impf* вывёртывать *или* вывора́чивать) *сов перех* (*винт, ла́мпу*) to unscrew; (*про́бку*) to pull out; (*карма́ны, рукава́*) to turn inside out
▸ вы́вернуться (*impf* вывёртываться *или* вывора́чиваться) *сов возв* (*винт, ла́мпа*) to come unscrewed; (*про́бка*) to come out; (*челове́к: из беды́*) to get out.
выверя́|ть (-ю) *несов от* вы́верить.
вы́ве|сить (-шу, -сишь; *impf* выве́шивать) *сов перех* (*флаг, ло́зунг*) to put up; (*бельё*) to hang

out; (*объявление*) to post (up).

вы́вес|ка (-ки; *gen pl* -ок) ж sign; (*перен*) front; **под ~кой чего́-н** under the guise of sth.

вы́ве|сти (-ду, -дешь; *impf* **выводи́ть**) *сов перех* to take out; (*войска: из города*) to pull out; (: *на парад*) to bring out; (*формулу*) to deduce; (*заключение*) to draw; (*птенцов*) to hatch; (*сорт, породу*) to breed; (*вредителей*) to exterminate; (*КОМП*) to output; (*изобразить*) to portray; (*исключить*): ~ **кого́-н из** +*gen* (*из партии, из комитета*) to expel sb from; (*из игры*) to take sb off; **выводи́ть** (~ *perf*) **кого́-н из шо́ка/из тра́нса** to bring sb out of a shock/trance; **выводи́ть** (~ *perf*) **кого́-н из терпе́ния** to exasperate sb; **выводи́ть** (~ *perf*) **кого́-н из равнове́сия** to disturb sb's equilibrium; **выводи́ть** (~ *perf*) **кого́-н в лю́ди** to help sb on in life; **выводи́ть** (~ *perf*) **кого́-н из себя́** to drive sb mad

▶ **вы́вестись** (*impf* **выводи́ться**) *сов возв* (*цыплята*) to hatch (out); (*исчезнуть*) to be eradicated.

вы́ветр|иться (*3sg* -ится, *3pl* -ятся, *impf* **выве́триваться**) *сов возв* (*запах, дым*) to disperse; (*берег, горные породы*) to weather.

выве́шива|ть (-ю) *несов от* **вы́весить**.

вы́вешу *сов см* **вы́весить**.

вы́вих (-а) *м* dislocation.

вы́вихн|уть (-у, -ешь; *impf* **выви́хивать**) *сов перех* to dislocate.

вы́вод (-а) *м* (*войск: из города*) withdrawal; (*формулы*) deduction; (*умозаключение*) conclusion; (*ЭЛЕК*) outlet; (*КОМП*) output; **приходи́ть** (**прийти́** *perf*) **к ~у** to come to a conclusion.

вы́вод|ок (-ка) *м* brood.

вывожу́(сь) *несов см* **выводи́ть(ся)**.

вы́воз (-а) *м* removal; (*детей: на дачу*) taking out; (*товаров*) export.

вывози́ть (-вожу́, -во́зишь) *несов от* **вы́везти**.

вывозно́й *прил* export *опред*.

вывора́чива|ть(ся) (-ю(сь)) *несов от* **вы́вернуть(ся)**.

вы́гада|ть (-ю; *impf* **выга́дывать**) *сов перех* (*получить преимущество*) to gain; (*сэкономить*) to save.

вы́гиб (-а) *м* curve.

выгиба́|ть (-ю) *несов от* **вы́гнуть**.

выгла́|дить (-жу, -дишь; *сов от* **гла́дить**.

вы́гля|деть (-жу, -дишь) *несов неперех* to look; **она хорошо́ ~дит сего́дня** she looks nice today; **он ~дит печа́льным** he looks sad.

выгля́дыва|ть (-ю) *несов от* **вы́глянуть**.

вы́гляжу *несов см* **вы́глядеть**.

вы́глян|уть (-у, -ешь; *impf* **выгля́дывать**) *сов неперех* to look out.

вы́гн|ать (-оню, -онишь; *impf* **выгоня́ть**) *сов*

перех to throw out; (*из страны*) to banish; (*разг: с работы*) to sack; (*стадо, табун*) to drive out.

вы́гн|уть (-у, -ешь; *impf* **выгиба́ть**) *сов перех* to bend; (*спину*) to arch.

выгова́рива|ть (-ю) *несов от* **вы́говорить**.

вы́говор (-а) *м* (*произношение*) accent; (*за провинность*) reprimand; **де́лать** (**сде́лать** *perf*) ~ **кому́-н за что-н** to tell sb off for sth; **выноси́ть** (**вы́нести** *perf*) ~ **кому́-н** to issue sb with a reprimand.

вы́говор|ить (-ю, -ишь; *impf* **выгова́ривать**) *сов перех* (*произнести*) to pronounce; (*сказать*) to say

▶ **вы́говориться** *сов возв* (*разг*) to say what's on one's mind.

вы́год|а (-ы) ж advantage, benefit; (*прибыль*) profit; **кака́я ему́ от э́того ~?** what does he hope to gain from this?

вы́годно *нареч* (*продать*) at a profit ◆ *как сказ* it is profitable; **мне э́то ~** this is to my advantage; (*финансово*) this is profitable for me.

вы́годный (-ен, -на, -но) *прил* (*сделка*) profitable; (*условия*) advantageous; (*впечатление*) favourable (*BRIT*), favorable (*US*); **выставля́ть** (**вы́ставить** *perf*) **или представля́ть** (**предста́вить** *perf*) **что-н в ~ном све́те** to show sth to (the) best advantage.

вы́гоню *итп сов см* **вы́гнать**.

выгоня́|ть (-ю) *несов от* **вы́гнать**.

вы́гор|еть (*3sg* -ит, *3pl* -ят, *impf* **выгора́ть**) *сов неперех* (*сгореть*) to burn down; (*высохнуть*) to be scorched; (*выцвести*) to fade; (*разг: удаваться*) to come off.

вы́город|ить (-жу, -дишь; *impf* **выгора́живать**) *сов перех* (*разг*) to fence off.

вы́гравир|овать (-ую) *несов от* **гравирова́ть**.

вы́гре|сти (-бу, -бешь; *pt* -б, -ла, -ло, *impf* **выгреба́ть**) *сов перех* to rake out.

вы́гру|зить (-жу, -зишь; *impf* **выгружа́ть**) *сов перех* to unload; (*КОМП*) to dump

▶ **вы́грузиться** (*impf* **выгружа́ться**) *сов возв* to unload; (*высадиться*) to disembark; (: *из поезда*) to get off.

выдава́|ть (-ю) *несов от* **вы́дать**

▶ **выдава́ться** *несов от* **вы́даться** ◆ *возв*: **~ся чем-н** to stand out by virtue of sth.

вы́дав|ить (-лю, -ишь; *impf* **выда́вливать**) *сов перех* (*лимон*) to squeeze; (*ягоды*) to press; (*дверь*) to break down; **выда́вливать** (~ *perf*) **что-н из чего́-н** to squeeze sth out of sth.

вы́да|ть (*как* **дать**; *см* **Table 14**; *impf* **выдава́ть**) *сов перех* to give out; (*свидетельство, патент итп*) to issue; (*продукцию*) to produce; (*тайну, сообщников*) to give away; **выдава́ть** (~ *perf*) **кого́-н/что-н за** +*acc* to pass sb/sth off as; **выдава́ть** (~ *perf*) **де́вушку за́муж** to marry a girl off

▶ **вы́даться** (*impf* **выдава́ться**) *сов возв* (*берег*) to jut out; **сего́дня ~лся хоро́ший день** (*разг*) it's turned out fine today.

вы́дач|а (-и) ж (*справки*) issue; (*зарплаты*) payment; (*продукции*) output; (*заложников*) release.

вы́дашь(ся) *сов см* **вы́дать(ся)**.

выдаю́щийся (-аяся, -ееся, -иеся) *прил* outstanding.

выдвига́|ть(ся) (-ю(сь)) *несов от* **вы́двинуть(ся)**.

выдвиже́ни|е (-я) *ср* (*кандидата*) nomination; (*предложения*) proposal.

выдвижно́й *прил* sliding.

вы́двин|уть (-у, -ешь; *impf* **выдвига́ть**) *сов перех* to pull out; (*предложение, гипотезу, человека*) to put forward; (*обвинение*) to level

▶ **вы́двинуться** (*impf* **выдвига́ться**) *сов возв* to slide out; (*работник*) to get ahead, advance; **выдвига́ться** (~*ся perf*) **на руководя́щую рабо́ту** to be promoted to a management position.

вы́двор|ить (-ю, -ишь; *impf* **выдворя́ть**) *сов перех* (*разг*) to kick out.

вы́дела|ть (-ю; *impf* **выде́лывать**) *сов перех* to treat.

выделе́ни|е (-я) *ср* (*средств*) allocation; (*физиология*) secretion; (*обычно мн: в гинекологии*) discharge.

вы́дел|ить (-ю, -ишь; *impf* **выделя́ть**) *сов перех* to assign, allocate; (*время*) to allot; (*отличить: ученика, цитату*) to pick out; (*пот*) to secrete; (*газы, вредные вещества*) to emit

▶ **вы́делиться** (*impf* **выделя́ться**) *сов возв* (*в отдельное предприятие*) to split off; (*пот*) to be secreted; (*газ, вредные вещества*) to be emitted; **выделя́ться** (~*ся perf*) **чем-н** to stand out by virtue of sth.

вы́делк|а (-и) ж treatment.

выде́лыва|ть (-ю) *несов от* **вы́делать** ◆ *перех* (*разг: вытворять*) to get up to; **что э́то он там** ~**ет?** what is he up to?

выделя́|ть(ся) (-ю(сь)) *несов от* **вы́делить(ся)**.

выдёргива|ть (-ю) *несов от* **вы́дернуть**.

вы́держанный (-, -на, -но) *прил* (*человек*) self-possessed; (*no short form*) изложение, *теория*) consistent; (*вино, сыр*) mature; (*древесина*) seasoned.

вы́держ|ать (-у, -ишь; *impf* **выде́рживать**) *сов перех* (*давление, тяжесть*) to withstand; (*боль*) to bear; (*экзамен, испытание*) to get through; (*график, параметры*) to keep to; (*вино, сыр*) to let mature; (*древесину*) to season ◆ *неперех*: **он не** ~**ал и рассмея́лся** he couldn't contain his laughter; **кни́га** ~**ала мно́го изда́ний** the book has been published in several editions; **выде́рживать** (~ *perf*) **хара́ктер** to hold one's ground.

вы́держек *сущ см* **вы́держка**.

выде́ржива|ть (-ю) *несов от* **вы́держать**.

вы́держ|ка (-ки; *gen pl* -ек) ж (*самообладание*) self-control; (*из текста*) excerpt; (*вина*) maturing; (*древесины*) seasoning; (*ФОТО*) exposure.

вы́дерн|уть (-у, -ешь; *impf* **выдёргивать**) *сов перех* to pull out.

вы́деру *итп сов см* **вы́драть**.

выдира́|ть (-ю) *несов от* **вы́драть**.

вы́долб|ить (-лю, -ишь) *сов от* **долби́ть**.

вы́дох (-а) *м* exhalation; **де́лать (сде́лать** *perf*) ~ to breathe out.

вы́дохн|уть (-у, -ешь; *impf* **выдыха́ть**) *сов перех* to exhale, breathe out

▶ **вы́дохнуться** (*impf* **выдыха́ться**) *сов возв* (*вино, духи*) to lose all smell; (*разг*) to be washed out.

вы́др|а (-ы) ж otter.

вы́дра|ить (-ю, -ишь) *сов от* **дра́ить**.

вы́др|ать (-еру, -ерешь) *сов от* **драть** ◆ (*impf* **выдира́ть**) *перех* (*разг: вырвать*) to tear out.

вы́дрессир|овать (-ую) *сов от* **дрессирова́ть**.

вы́дуб|ить (-лю, -ишь) *несов от* **дуби́ть**.

выдува́|ть (-ю) *несов от* **вы́дуть**.

вы́думанный *прил* made-up.

вы́дума|ть (-ю; *impf* **выду́мывать**) *сов перех* (*историю*) to make up, invent; (*игру*) to invent.

вы́дум|ка (-ки; *gen pl* -ок) ж invention.

выду́мыва|ть (-ю) *несов от* **вы́думать**.

вы́д|уть (-ю; *impf* **выдува́ть**) *сов перех* to blow out; (*разг: водку итп*) to knock back; (*impf* **выдува́ть** *или* **дуть**, *тех*) to blow.

выдыха́ни|е (-я) *ср* exhalation.

выдыха́|ть(ся) (-ю(сь)) *несов от* **вы́дохнуть(ся)**.

выеда́|ть (-ю) *несов от* **вы́есть**.

вы́еду *итп сов см* **вы́ехать**.

вы́езд (-а) *м* (*отъезд*) departure; (*место*) way out.

вы́езд|ить (-жу, -дишь; *impf* **выезжа́ть**) *сов перех* (*лошадь*) to break in.

вы́ездк|а (-и) ж (*СПОРТ*) dressage.

выездно́й *прил* (*виза, документ*) exit *опред*; (*сессия суда*) in temporary premises; (*спектакль*) travelling (*BRIT*), traveling (*US*); ~ **матч** away match.

выезжа́|ть (-ю) *несов от* **вы́ехать**.

вы́езжу *сов см* **вы́ездить**.

вы́ем|ка (-ки; *gen pl* -ок) ж (*писем*) collection; (*грунта*) excavation; (*углубление*) hollow.

вы́есть (*как есть*; *см* **Table 15**; *impf* **выеда́ть**) *сов перех* (*съесть*) to eat; (*испортить*) to eat through.

вы́ехать (*как ехать*; *см* **Table 19**; *impf* **выезжа́ть**) *сов неперех* (*уехать*) to leave; (*машина, танк*) to drive out; (*всадник*) to ride out; **выезжа́ть** (~ *perf*) **на ком-н/чём-н** (*перен: разг*) to use sb/sth.

вы́жа|ть (**-му, -мешь;** *impf* **выжима́ть**) *сов перех* (*лимон*) to squeeze; (*ягоды*) to press; (*бельё*) to wring (out); **выжима́ть** (**~** *perf*) **что-н из чего́-н** to squeeze sth out of sth; **выжима́ть** (**~** *perf*) **что-н из кого́-н** (*перен*) to wring sth out of sb.

вы́жгу *итп сов см* **вы́жечь**.

вы́жда|ть (**-у, -ёшь;** *impf* **выжида́ть**) *сов перех*: **~ подходя́щий моме́нт** to pick one's moment.

вы́ж|ечь (**-гу, -жешь** *итп* **-гут;** *pt* **-ег, -гла, -гло,** *impf* **выжига́ть**) *сов перех* to burn; (*подлеж: солнце*) to scorch; **выжига́ть** (**~** *perf*) **клеймо́** to brand; **выжига́ть** (*impf*) **по де́реву** to do pokerwork.

выжива́ни|е (**-я**) *ср* survival.

выжива́|ть (**-ю**) *несов от* **вы́жить**.

вы́живу *итп сов см* **вы́жить**.

выжига́|ть (**-ю**) *несов от* **вы́жечь**.

выжида́тельный (**-ен, -ьна, -ьно**) *прил* (*тактика, политика*) delaying; **занима́ть** (**заня́ть** *perf*) **~ьную пози́цию** to play a waiting game.

выжида́|ть (**-ю**) *несов от* **вы́ждать**.

выжима́|ть (**-ю**) *несов от* **вы́жать**.

вы́жи|ть (**-ву, -вешь;** *impf* **выжива́ть**) *сов неперех* to survive ♦ *перех* (*разг*) to drive out; **~** (*perf*) **из ума́** to become senile.

вы́жму *итп сов см* **вы́жать**.

вы́з|вать (**-ову, -овешь;** *impf* **вызыва́ть**) *сов перех* to call; (*гнев, критику*) to provoke; (*восторг*) to arouse; (*пожар*) to cause; **вызыва́ть** (**~** *perf*) **кого́-н на что́-н** to challenge sb to sth; **вызыва́ть** (**~** *perf*) **что-н к жи́зни** to give rise to sth; **вызыва́ть** (**~** *perf*) **врача́ на́ дом** to call out a doctor

▶ **вы́зваться** (*impf* **вызыва́ться**) *сов возв*: **~ся** +*infin* to volunteer to do.

вы́зво́л|ить (**-ю, -ишь;** *impf* **вызволя́ть**) *сов перех* (*разг*) to bale out.

вы́здоров|еть (**-лю, -ишь;** *impf* **выздора́вливать**) *сов неперех* to recover.

вы́зов (**-а**) *м* call; (*в суд, к директору*) summons; **~** +*dat* (*обществу, родителям итп*) challenge to; **броса́ть** (**бро́сить** *perf*) **~ кому́-н/чему́-н** to challenge sb/sth.

вы́зову(сь) *сов см* **вы́звать(ся)**.

вы́зубр|ить (**-ю, -ишь**) *сов от* **зубри́ть**.

вызыва́|ть(ся) (**-ю(сь)**) *несов от* **вы́звать(ся)**.

вызыва́ющий (**-ая, -ее, -ие**) *прил* provocative.

вы́игра|ть (**-ю;** *impf* **выи́грывать**) *сов перех* to win ♦ *неперех* (*получить выгоду*) to gain, benefit.

вы́игрыш (**-а**) *м* (*матча*) winning; (*крупный, денежный*) winnings *мн*; (*выгода*) advantage; **~ пал на но́мер 10** number 10 wins.

вы́игрыш|ный (**-ен, -на, -но**) *прил* (*выгодный*) advantageous; **~ вклад** ≈ premium bonds.

вы́|йти (*как* **идти́;** *см* **Table 18;** *impf* **выходи́ть**) *сов неперех* to leave; (*из игры*) to drop out; (*сойти*) to get off; (*появиться*) to come out; (*случиться*) to ensue; (*КОМП*) to exit; (*иссякнуть*) to run out; (*оказаться*): **~** +*instr* to

come out; **выходи́ть** (**~** *perf*) **из** +*gen* (*из затрудне́ния*) to get out of; (*из употребления, из моды*) to go out of; (*из крестьян*) to be descended from; (*из графика, из расписания*) to fall behind; **выходи́ть** (**~** *perf*) **на** +*acc* to get in with; **выходи́ть** (**~** *perf*) **за́муж за** +*acc* to marry (*of woman*), get married to; **выходи́ть** (**~** *perf*) **из больни́цы** to leave hospital; **выходи́ть** (**~** *perf*) **из себя́** to lose one's temper; **выходи́ть** (**~** *perf*) **из систе́мы** (*КОМП*) to log off; **из него́ ~шел хоро́ший врач** he has turned out to be a good doctor; **из э́того ничего́ не ~шло** nothing came of it.

выка́лыва|ть (**-ю**) *несов от* **вы́колоть**.

выка́пыва|ть (**-ю**) *несов от* **вы́копать**.

вы́карабка|ться (**-юсь;** *impf* **выкара́бкиваться**) *сов возв*: **~ (из** +*gen*) to clamber out (of); (*разг: из трудностей*) to get o.s. out (of); (: *из болезни*) to pull through.

выка́рмлива|ть (**-ю**) *несов от* **вы́кормить**.

вы́кат|ить (**-чу, -тишь;** *impf* **выка́тывать**) *сов перех* (*что-н круглое*) to roll out; (*что-н на колесах*) to wheel out; **выка́тывать** (**~** *perf*) **глаза́** (*разг*) to open one's eyes wide.

вы́кача|ть (**-ю;** *impf* **выка́чивать**) *сов перех* to pump out; (*перен: разг: деньги*) to squeeze *или* wring out.

вы́качу *сов см* **вы́катить**.

выка́шива|ть (**-ю**) *несов от* **вы́косить**.

выки́дыва|ть (**-ю**) *несов от* **вы́кинуть**.

вы́кидыш (**-а**) *м* miscarriage.

вы́кин|уть (**-у, -ешь;** *impf* **выки́дывать**) *сов перех* (*мусор*) to throw out; (*пропустить*) to omit; (*разг: товар*) to put on sale; **выки́дывать** (**~** *perf*) **шу́тку** *или* **фо́кус** (*разг*) to play a trick.

вы́кип|еть (*3sg* **-ит,** *3pl* **-ят,** *impf* **выкипа́ть**) *сов неперех* to boil away.

вы́клад|ка (**-ки;** *gen pl* **-ок**) *ж* (*облицовка*) facing; (*обычно мн: расчёты*) calculation.

выкла́дыва|ть(ся) (**-ю(сь)**) *несов от* **вы́ложить(ся)**.

выключа́тел|ь (**-я**) *м* switch.

вы́ключ|ить (**-у, -ишь;** *impf* **выключа́ть**) *сов перех* to turn off; (*исключить*) to expel

▶ **вы́ключиться** (*impf* **выключа́ться**) *сов возв* (*мотор, телевизор итп*) to go off; (*свет*) to go out; (*перен*) to switch off.

вы́клянч|ить (**-у, -ишь**) *сов от* **кля́нчить**.

вы́к|овать (**-ую;** *impf* **выко́вывать**) *сов перех* (*металл*) to forge.

выко́лачива|ть (**-ю**) *несов от* **вы́колотить**.

вы́коло|тить (**-чу, -тишь;** *impf* **выкола́чивать**) *сов перех* (*ковёр*) to beat; (*налоги*) to wring out.

вы́кол|оть (**-ю, -ешь;** *impf* **выка́лывать**) *сов перех* to poke out.

вы́колочу *сов см* **вы́колотить**.

вы́копа|ть (**-ю;** *impf* **выка́пывать** *или* **копа́ть**) *сов перех* (*яму*) to dig; (*колодец*) to sink; (*овощи*) to dig up.

вы́корм|ить (**-лю, -ишь;** *impf* **выка́рмливать**) *сов перех* to rear.

вы́корче|вать (-ую; *impf* **выкорчёвывать** *или* **корчева́ть**) *сов перех* to uproot; *(перен)* to root out.

вы́ко|сить (-шу, -сишь; *impf* **выка́шивать**) *сов перех* to mow.

выкра́дыва|ть (-ю) *несов от* **вы́красть**.

выкра́ива|ть (-ю) *несов перех* to cut out.

вы́кра|сить(ся) (-шу(сь), -сишь(ся)) *сов от* **кра́сить(ся)**.

вы́кра|сть (-ду, -дёшь; *impf* **выкра́дывать**) *сов перех* to steal.

вы́крик (-а) *м* shout.

вы́крикн|уть (-у, -ешь; *impf* **выкри́кивать**) *сов перех* to shout *или* cry out.

вы́кристаллиз|ова́ться (*3sg* -уется, *3pl* -уются) *сов от* **кристаллизова́ться**.

вы́кроек *сущ см* **вы́кройка**.

вы́кро|ить (-ю, -ишь) *сов от* **кро́ить** ♦ (*impf* **выкра́ивать**) *перех (перен)*: ~ **вре́мя на** +*acc* to find time for; ~ (*perf*) **де́ньги на** +*acc* to scrape together money for.

вы́кро|йка (-йки; *gen pl* -ек) *ж* pattern.

выкрута́с|ы (-ов) *мн (разг: в танце)* fancy footwork *ед*; *(перен: в речи)* fancy turns *мн* of phrase; (: *в поведении*) foibles *мн*.

вы́кру|тить (-чу, -тишь; *impf* **выкру́чивать**) *сов перех* to unscrew; **выкру́чивать** (~ *perf*) **ру́ки кому́-н** *(также перен)* to twist sb's arm

▶ **вы́крутиться** *сов возв* to come unscrewed; *(перен)* to get o.s. out.

вы́куп (-а) *м (действие: заложника)* ransoming; (: *вещей*) redemption; *(плата)* ransom.

выкупа́|ть(ся) (-ю(сь)) *несов от* **купа́ть(ся)**.

вы́куп|ить (-лю, -ишь; *impf* **выкупа́ть**) *сов перех (заложника)* to ransom; *(вещи)* to redeem.

вы́кур|ить (-ю, -ишь; *impf* **выку́ривать**) *сов перех (трубку)* to smoke; *(зверя)* to smoke out.

выла́влива|ть (-ю) *несов от* **вы́ловить**.

выла́з|ка (-ки; *gen pl* -ок) *ж (ВОЕН)* sortie.

выла́мыва|ть (-ю) *несов от* **вы́ломать**.

вылеза́|ть (-ю) *несов от* **вы́лезти**.

вы́лез|ти (-у, -ешь; *pt* -, -ла, -ло, *impf* **вылеза́ть**) *сов неперех (волосы, шерсть)* to fall out; **вылеза́ть** (~ *perf*) (**из** +*gen*) to climb out (of); *(разг: из долгов)* to get o.s. out (of); (: *из болезней*) to pull through; (: *рубашка*) to hang out.

вы́леп|ить (-лю, -ишь) *сов от* **лепи́ть**.

вы́лет (-а) *м* departure.

вы́ле|теть (-чу, -тишь; *impf* **вылета́ть**) *сов неперех* to fly out; *(машина)* to hurtle out; **его́ и́мя ~тело у меня́ из головы́** his name has slipped my mind.

вы́леч|ить (-у, -ишь; *impf* **вылечивать** *или* **лечи́ть**) *сов перех* to cure

▶ **вы́лечиться** (*impf* **вылечиваться** *или* **лечи́ться**) *несов возв* to be cured.

вы́лечу *сов см* **вы́лететь**.

вылива́|ть(ся) (-ю(сь)) *несов от* **вы́лить(ся)**.

вы́ли|зать (-жу, -жешь; *impf* **вылизывать**) *сов перех (тарелку)* to lick clean; *(разг: дом)* to spring-clean.

вы́л|ить (-ью, -ешь; *impf* **вылива́ть**) *сов перех* to pour out; (*impf* **лить**; *деталь, статую*) to cast

▶ **вы́литься** (*impf* **вылива́ться**) *сов возв (также перен)* to pour out; **вылива́ться** (~*ся perf*) **в** +*acc* to turn into.

вы́лов|ить (-лю, -ишь; *impf* **выла́вливать**) *сов перех* to catch.

вы́лож|ить (-у, -ишь; *impf* **выкла́дывать**) *сов перех* to lay out; *(перен: правду)* to lay bare; **выкла́дывать** (~ *perf*) **что-н чем-н** *(кирпичом, плиткой)* to face sth with sth

▶ **вы́ложиться** (*impf* **выкла́дываться**) *сов возв* to apply o.s.

вы́лома|ть (-ю; *impf* **выла́мывать**) *сов перех* to break open.

вы́луп|иться (*3sg* -ится, *3pl* -ятся, *impf* **вылу́пливаться**) *сов возв (птенцы)* to hatch (out).

вы́лью(сь) *итп сов см* **вы́лить(ся)**.

вы́ма|зать (-жу, -жешь) *сов от* **ма́зать** ♦ (*impf* **выма́зывать**) *перех (покрыть)* to coat; *(разг: запачкать)* to smear

▶ **вы́мазаться** *сов от* **ма́заться**.

выма́лива|ть (-ю) *несов от* **вы́молить**.

вы́ман|ить (-ю, -ишь; *impf* **выма́нивать**) *сов перех (зверя)* to lure out; **выма́нивать** (~ *perf*) **что-н у кого́-н** to cheat sb out of sth.

вы́мара|ть(ся) (-ю(сь)) *сов от* **мара́ть(ся)**.

выма́чива|ть (-ю) *несов от* **вы́мочить**.

вы́мени *итп сущ см* **вы́мя**.

вы́м|ереть (*3sg* -рет, *3pl* -рут, *impf* **вымира́ть**) *сов неперех (динозавры)* to die out, become extinct; *(город, селение)* to be dead.

вы́ме|сти (-ту, -тешь; *pt* -л, -ла, -ло, *impf* **вымета́ть**) *сов перех* to sweep out.

вы́ме|стить (-щу, -стишь; *impf* **вымеща́ть**) *сов перех*: ~ **что-н на ком-н** to take sth out on sb.

вымета́|ть (-ю) *несов от* **вы́мести**.

вы́мету *итп сов см* **вы́мести**.

вымеща́|ть (-ю) *несов от* **вы́местить**.

вы́мещу *сов см* **вы́местить**.

вымира́|ть (*3sg* -ет, *3pl* -ют) *несов от* **вы́мереть**.

вымога́тель (-я) *м* extortionist.

вымога́тельств|о (-а) *ср* extortion.

вымога́|ть (-ю) *несов перех* to extort.

вы́мок|нуть (-ну, -нешь; *pt* -, -ла, -ло) *сов неперех* to get soaked through.

вы́молв|ить (-лю, -ишь) *сов перех* to utter.

вы́мол|ить (-ю, -ишь; *impf* **выма́ливать**) *сов перех* to successfully plead for.

вы́мо|стить (-щу, -стишь) *сов от* **мости́ть**.

вы́моч|ить (-у, -ишь; *impf* **выма́чивать**) *сов*

The spelling rules for Russian are shown on page xvii.

перех to soak.
вы́мощу *сов см* **вы́мостить.**
вы́мою *итп сов см* **вы́мыть.**
вы́мпел (-а) *м* (*на мачте корабля*) pennant; (*награда*) award (*in the form of a pennant*).
вы́мрет *итп сов см* **вы́мереть.**
вы́муштр|овать (-ую) *сов от* **муштрова́ть.**
вымыва́|ть (-ю) *несов от* **вы́мыть.**
вы́мыс|ел (-ла) *м* fantasy; (*ложь*) fabrication.
вы́м|ыть (-ою, -оешь; *impf* **мыть**) *сов перех* to wash; (*impf* **вымыва́ть**; *яму*) to hollow out; (*русло*) to channel out.
вы́мышлен|ный (-, -на, -но) *прил* fictitious.
вы́м|я (-ени; *как* **вре́мя**; *см* **Table 4**) *ср* udder.
вына́шива|ть (-ю) *несов от* **вы́носить.**
вы́нес|ти (-у, -ешь; *pt* -, -ла, -ло, *impf* **выноси́ть**) *сов перех* to carry *или* take out; (*приговор, вердикт*) to pass, pronounce; (*впечатления, знания*) to gain; (*боль, оскорбление*) to bear; **выноси́ть** (*~ perf*) **кому́-н благода́рность** to officially thank sb; **выноси́ть** (*~ perf*) **кому́-н вы́говор** to issue sb with a reprimand
▸ **вы́нестись** (*impf* **выноси́ться**) *сов возв* to fly *или* rush out.
вынима́|ть (-ю) *несов от* **вы́нуть.**
вы́нос (-а) *м* (*тела*) bearing out (*of coffin*); **продава́ть** (*impf*) **на ~** to do take-aways.
выно|си́ть (-шу, -сишь; *impf* **вына́шивать**) *сов перех* (*перен*) to nurture; (*младенца*) to carry to term.
выно|си́ть (-ошу, -о́сишь) *несов от* **вы́нести** ◆ *перех*: **я его́ не ~ошу́** I can't bear *или* stand him
▸ **выноси́ться** *несов от* **вы́нестись.**
выно́слив|ый (-, -а, -о) *прил* hardy.
вы́ношу *сов см* **вы́носить.**
выношу́(сь) *несов см* **выноси́ть(ся).**
вы́ну|дить (-жу, -дишь; *impf* **вынужда́ть**) *сов перех*: **~ кого́-н/что-н к чему́-н** to force sb/sth into sth; **вынужда́ть** (*~ perf*) **кого́-н/что-н** +*infin* to force sb/sth into doing.
вы́нужденный *прил* forced; **вы́нужденная поса́дка** emergency landing.
вы́нужу *сов см* **вы́нудить.**
вы́н|уть (-у, -ешь; *impf* **вынима́ть**) *сов перех* to take out.
вы́нырн|уть (-у, -ешь; *impf* **выны́ривать**) *сов неперех* (*из воды*) to surface; (*разг: из-за угла*) to pop up.
вы́пад (-а) *м* (*враждебное действие*) attack; (*СПОРТ*) lunge (*in fencing*).
выпада́|ть (-ю) *несов от* **вы́пасть.**
выпаде́ни|е (-я) *ср* (*осадков*) fall; (*зубов, волос*) falling out.
вы́паду *итп сов см* **вы́пасть.**
вы́пал|ить (-ю, -ишь) *сов от* **пали́ть** ◆ (*impf* **выпа́ливать**) *перех* (*перен: разг*) to blurt out.
вы́пар|иться (*3sg* -ится, *3pl* -ятся, *impf* **выпа́риваться**) *сов возв* to evaporate.
вы́па|сть (-ду, -дешь; *impf* **выпада́ть**) *сов неперех* to fall out; (*осадки*) to fall; (+*dat*;

задание, задача итп) to fall to; **мне ~л слу́чай/сча́стье встре́тить его́** I chanced to/ had the luck to meet him.
вы́пачка|ть(ся) (-ю(сь)) *сов от* **па́чкать(ся).**
вы́пей(те) *сов см* **вы́пить.**
выпека|ть (-ю) *несов от* **вы́печь.**
вы́пеку *итп сов см* **вы́печь.**
вы́п|ереть (-ру, -решь; *pt* -ер, -ерла, -ерло, *impf* **выпира́ть**) *сов перех* (*разг*) to chuck out.
вы́пест|овать (-ую) *сов от* **пе́стовать.**
вы́печк|а (-и) *ж* baking.
выпечн|о́й *прил*: **~ые изде́лия** bakery products *мн*.
вы́пе|чь (-ку, -чешь *итп*, -кут; *impf* **выпека́ть**) *сов перех* to bake.
вы́пивк|а (-и) *ж* (*разг: попойка*) boozing ◆ *собир* (*спиртное*) booze.
выпира́|ть (-ю) *несов от* **вы́переть** ◆ *неперех* (*разг: выпячиваться*) to stick out.
вы́пи|сать (-шу, -шешь; *impf* **выпи́сывать**) *сов перех* (*цитату, данные*) to copy *или* write out; (*пропуск, счёт, рецепт*) to make out; (*газету, журнал*) to subscribe to; (*пациента*) to discharge; (*с местопроживания*) to change sb's residence permit
▸ **вы́писаться** (*impf* **выпи́сываться**) *несов возв* (*из больницы*) to be discharged; (*с местопроживания*) to change one's residence permit.
вы́пис|ка (-ки; *gen pl* -ок) *ж* (*действие*) copying *или* writing out; (*цитата*) extract; **~ с ба́нковского счёта** bank statement.
выпи́сыва|ть(ся) (-ю(сь)) *несов от* **вы́писать(ся).**
вы́п|ить (-ью, -ьешь; *imper* -ей(те)) *сов от* **пить.**
вы́пишу(сь) *итп сов см* **вы́писать(ся).**
вы́плав|ить (-лю, -ишь; *impf* **выплавля́ть**) *сов перех* to smelt.
вы́плав|ка (-ки; *gen pl* -ок) *ж* (*действие*) smelting; (*продукция*) smelted metal.
вы́плавлю *сов см* **вы́плавить.**
выплавля́|ть (-ю) *несов от* **вы́плавить.**
вы́плавок *сущ см* **вы́плавка.**
вы́плат|а (-ы) *ж* payment.
вы́пла|тить (-чу, -тишь; *impf* **выпла́чивать**) *сов перех* to pay; (*долг*) to pay off.
выплёскива|ть (-ю) *несов от* **вы́плеснуть.**
вы́плесн|уть (-у, -ешь; *impf* **выплёскивать**) *сов перех* to pour out.
вы́плы|ть (-ву, -вешь; *impf* **выплыва́ть**) *сов неперех* to swim out; (*всплыть*) to surface; (*перен*) to emerge, come to light.
вы́плюн|уть (-у, -ешь; *impf* **выплёвывать**) *сов перех* to spit out.
вы́полз|ти (-у, -ешь; *pt* -, -ла, -ло, *impf* **выполза́ть**) *сов неперех* to crawl out.
выполни́м|ый (-, -а, -о) *прил* practicable, feasible.
вы́полн|ить (-ю, -ишь; *impf* **выполня́ть**) *сов перех* (*задание, заказ*) to carry out; (*план, условие*) to fulfil (*BRIT*), fulfill (*US*); (*рисунок,*

чертёж) to execute; (*КОМП*) to run.

вы́полоска|ть (-ю) *сов от* полоска́ть.

вы́пол|оть (-ю, -ешь) *сов от* поло́ть.

вы́пор|оть (-ю, -ешь) *сов от* поро́ть.

вы́порхн|уть (-у, -ешь) *сов неперех* to dart out.

вы́потрош|ить (-у, -ишь) *сов от* потроши́ть.

вы́прав|ить (-лю, -ишь; *impf* выправля́ть) *сов перех* (*расспрямить*) to straighten (up); (*текст, чертёж*) to correct; (*положение, ситуацию*) to rectify, put right

▶ **вы́правиться** (*impf* выправля́ться) *несов возв* (*что-н кривое*) to straighten (out); (*положение, ситуация*) to be rectified.

вы́прав|ка (-ки; *gen pl* -ок) *ж* bearing.

вы́правлю(сь) *сов см* вы́править(ся).

выправля́|ть(ся) (-ю(сь)) *несов от* вы́править(ся).

вы́правок *сущ см* вы́правка.

выпра́шива|ть (-ю) *несов перех* to beg for.

вы́про|сить (-шу, -сишь) *сов перех*: **он ~сил у отца́ маши́ну** he persuaded his father to give him the car.

вы́пру *итп сов см* вы́переть.

вы́прыгн|уть (-у, -ешь; *impf* выпры́гивать) *сов неперех* to jump out.

вы́прям|ить (-лю, -ишь; *impf* выпрямля́ть) *сов перех* to straighten (out)

▶ **вы́прямиться** (*impf* выпрямля́ться) *несов возв* to straighten (up).

выпрямля́|ть(ся) (-ю(сь)) *несов от* вы́прямить(ся).

вы́пуклый *прил* (*лоб, глаза итп*) bulging; (*стекло, линза*) convex; (*буква*) embossed.

вы́пуск (-а) *м* (*продукции*) output; (*газа, воздуха*) emission, release; (*книги*) instalment (*BRIT*), installment (*US*); (*денег, марок, акций*) issue; (*учащиеся*) school leavers *мн* (*BRIT*), graduates *мн* (*US*).

выпуска́|ть (-ю) *несов от* вы́пустить.

выпускни́к (-а́) *м* final-year student; (*окончивший вуз*) graduate.

выпускни́ц|а (-ы) *ж см* выпускни́к.

выпускн|о́й *прил* (*класс*) final-year; (*ТЕХ*): ~ **кла́пан** exhaust valve; ~**о́е отве́рстие** outlet; **выпускно́й ве́чер** graduation; **выпускно́й экза́мен** final exam, finals *мн*.

вы́пу|стить (-щу, -стишь; *impf* выпуска́ть) *сов перех* to let out; (*дым*) to exhale; (*заключённого, заложника*) to release; (*специалистов*) to turn out; (*продукцию*) to produce; (*книгу, газету итп*) to publish; (*заём, марки*) to issue; (*деньги*) to put into circulation; (*исключить: часть текста, параграф*) to omit; **выпуска́ть** (~ *perf*) (**из рук**) to let go of; **выпуска́ть** (~ *perf*) **в свет** (*книгу, журнал*) to publish; **выпуска́ть** (~ *perf*) **из рук возмо́жность/шанс** to miss an opportunity/a chance; **выпуска́ть** (~ *perf*) **кого́-н/что-н из**

ви́ду to let sb/sth out of sight.

вы́пута|ться (-юсь; *impf* выпу́тываться) *сов возв* (*также перен*) to extricate o.s.

выпу́тыва|ться (-юсь) *несов от* вы́путаться.

вы́пущу *сов см* вы́пустить.

вы́пью *итп сов см* вы́пить.

вы́пя|тить (-чу, -тишь; *impf* выпя́чивать) *перех* (*разг: грудь*) to stick out; **выпя́чивать** (~ *perf*) **губу́** to pout.

вы́работа|ть (-ю; *impf* выраба́тывать) *сов перех* to produce; (*план*) to work out; (*характер, стиль, привычку*) to develop.

вы́работ|ка (-ки; *gen pl* -ок) *ж* (*действие*) production; (*годовая, промышленная*) output, production; (*продукты*) yield.

выра́внива|ть(ся) (-ю(сь)) *несов от* вы́ровнять(ся).

выража́|ть (-ю) *несов от* вы́разить

▶ **выража́ться** *несов от* вы́разиться ◆ *возв* (*разг*) to swear.

выраже́ни|е (-я) *ср* expression.

вы́ражу(сь) *сов см* вы́разить(ся).

вырази́тельно *нареч* (*читать*) expressively.

вырази́тел|ьный (-ен, -ьна, -ьно) *прил* expressive.

вы́ра|зить (-жу, -зишь; *impf* выража́ть) *сов перех* to express

▶ **вы́разиться** (*impf* выража́ться) *сов возв* (*чувство, состояние*) to manifest *или* express itself; (*человек*) to express o.s.

выраста́|ть (-ю) *несов от* вы́расти.

вы́рас|ти (-ту, -астешь; *pt* -ос, -осла, -осли) *сов от* расти́ ◆ (*impf* выраста́ть) *неперех* (*горы, башня*) to rise up; **выраста́ть** (~ *perf*) **в** +*acc* to become; **выраста́ть** (~ *perf*) **из оде́жды** to grow out of one's clothes.

вы́рас|тить (-у, -ишь; *impf* выра́щивать) *сов перех* (*детей*) to raise; (*растение*) to grow; (*животных*) to rear.

выра́щивани|е (-я) *ср* (*растений*) cultivation; (*животных*) rearing.

выра́щива|ть (-ю) *несов от* вы́растить.

вы́ращу *сов см* вы́растить.

вы́рв|ать (-у, -ешь; *impf* вырыва́ть) *сов перех* to pull out; (*отнять*): ~ **что-н у кого́-н** to snatch sth from sb; (*перен*) to wring sth from sb ◆ (*impf* **рвать**) *безл* (*разг*): **её ~ало** she threw up; **ему́ ~али зуб** he had his tooth taken out

▶ **вы́рваться** (*impf* вырыва́ться) *сов возв* (*из объя́тий*) to free o.s.; (*из рук, из пут*) to break free, escape; (*из тюрьми*) to make a break; (*перен: в театр, на концерт*) to manage to get away; (*пламя*) to shoot out; (*дым*) to pour out.

вы́режу *итп сов см* вы́резать.

вы́рез (-а) *м*: **пла́тье с больши́м ~ом** a low-cut dress.

вы́ре|зать (-жу, -жешь; *impf* выреза́ть) *сов перех* (*фотогра́фию итп*) to cut out; (*опухоль,* гно́йник) to remove; (*из де́рева, из ко́сти итп*) to carve; (*на ка́мне, на мета́лле итп*) to engrave; (*населе́ние, живо́тных*) to slaughter.

вы́рез|ка (**-ки**; *gen pl* **-ок**) *ж* (*газе́тная*) cutting, clipping; (*мясна́я*) fillet.

вы́рисо́ваться (*3sg* **-уется**, *3pl* **-уются**, *impf* **вырисо́вываться**) *сов возв* (*стать ви́дным*) to stand out; (*стать я́вным*) to appear; (*перен: ситуа́ция*) to emerge.

вы́ровня́ть (**-ю**) *сов от* **ровня́ть** ♦ (*impf* **выра́внивать**) *перех* to level

▶ **вы́ровня́ться** (*impf* **выра́внивать**) *сов возв* (*отря́д*) to form ranks; (*перен: хара́ктер*) to improve.

вы́род|иться (*3sg* **-ится**, *3pl* **-ятся**, *impf* **вырожда́ться**) *сов возв* (*та́кже перен*) to degenerate.

вы́род|ок (**-ка**) *м* (*разг*) degenerate.

вырожда́ться (**-юсь**) *несов от* **вы́родиться**.

вырожде́ни|е (**-я**) *ср* degeneration.

вы́рон|ить (**-ю**, **-ишь**) *сов перех* to drop.

вы́рос итп *сов см* **вы́расти**.

вы́рост (**-а**) *м*: **шить/покупа́ть оде́жду на ~** (*разг*) *to make/buy clothes with room for growth.*

вы́рою итп *сов см* **вы́рыть**.

выруба́|ть (**-ю**) *несов от* **вы́рубить**.

вы́руб|ить (**-лю**, **-ишь**; *impf* **выруба́ть**) *сов перех* (*лес, дере́вья*) to cut down; (*я́му, углубле́ние*) to hew out; (*свет, сигнализа́цию*) to cut off.

вы́руга́|ть(ся) (**-ю(сь)**) *сов от* **руга́ть(ся)**.

вы́руч|ить (**-у**, **-ишь**; *impf* **выруча́ть**) *сов перех* to rescue, help out; (*де́ньги*) to make; **выруча́ть** (**~** *perf*) **кого́-н из беды́** to help sb out of trouble.

вы́руч|ка (**-и**) *ж* rescue; (*де́ньги*) takings *мн*; **приходи́ть** (**прийти́** *perf*) **на ~у кому́-н** to come to sb's rescue.

вырыва́|ть(ся) (**-ю(сь)**) *несов от* **вы́рвать(ся)**, **вы́рыть**.

вы́р|ыть (**-ою**, **-оешь**) *сов от* **рыть** ♦ (*impf* **вырыва́ть**) *перех* (*карто́фель, ка́мень итп*) to dig up.

вы́сад|ить (**-жу**, **-дишь**; *impf* **выса́живать**) *сов перех* (*расте́ние*) to plant out; (*пассажи́ра: дать вы́йти*) to drop off; (: *заста́вить вы́йти*) to throw out; (*войска́, отря́д*) to land; **~** (*perf*) **деса́нт** to make a landing

▶ **вы́садиться** (*impf* **выса́живаться**) *сов возв*: **~ся (из** +*gen*) to get off.

выса́сыва|ть (**-ю**) *несов от* **вы́сосать**.

высве́чивани|е (**-я**) *ср* (*комп*) highlighting.

вы́свобо|дить (**-жу**, **-дишь**; *impf* **высвобожда́ть**) *сов перех* (*но́гу, ру́ку*) to free; (*рабо́чую си́лу, сре́дства*) to release; (*вре́мя*) to set aside.

вы́сек итп *сов см* **вы́сечь**.

высека́|ть (**-ю**) *несов от* **вы́сечь**.

вы́сек итп *сов см* **вы́сечь**.

вы́сел|ить (**-ю**, **-ишь**; *impf* **выселя́ть**) *сов перех* to evict.

вы́се|чь (**-ку**, **-чешь** итп, **-кут**; *pt* **-к**, **-кла**, **-кло**) *сов от* **сечь** ♦ (*impf* **высека́ть**) *перех* (*фигу́ру*) to carve, sculpt; (*на́дпись*) to engrave.

вы́сид|еть (**-жу**, **-дишь**; *impf* **выси́живать**) *сов перех* to hatch; (*перен: ле́кцию*) to sit out.

вы́с|иться (*3sg* **-ится**, *3pl* **-ятся**) *несов возв* to tower.

выска́блива|ть (**-ю**) *несов от* **вы́скоблить**.

выска́за|ть (**-жу**, **-жешь**; *impf* **выска́зывать**) *сов перех* to express; **я ему́ всё ~зал** I told him exactly what I thought

▶ **вы́сказаться** (*impf* **выска́зываться**) *сов возв* to speak one's mind; **выска́зываться** (**~ся** *perf*) **про́тив** +*gen*/**за** +*acc* to speak out against/in favour of.

выска́зывани|е (**-я**) *ср* (*мне́ния*) expression; (*сужде́ние*) statement.

выска́зыва|ть(ся) (**-ю(сь)**) *несов от* **вы́сказать(ся)**.

выска́кива|ть (**-ю**) *несов от* **вы́скочить**.

выска́льзыва|ть (**-ю**) *несов от* **выскользну́ть**.

вы́скобл|ить (**-ю**, **-ишь**; *impf* **выска́бливать**) *сов перех* (*очи́стить*) to scrape; (*удали́ть скобле́нием*) to remove.

выскользну́|ть (**-у**, **-ешь**; *impf* **выска́льзывать**) *сов неперех* (*та́кже перен*) to slip out.

вы́скоч|ить (**-у**, **-ишь**; *impf* **выска́кивать**) *сов неперех* to jump out; **его́ и́мя ~ило у меня́ из головы́** (*разг*) his name has slipped my mind.

вы́скоч|ка (**-ки**; *gen pl* **-ек**) *м/ж* (*разг: пренебр*) upstart.

вы́сла|ть (**-шлю**, **-шлешь**; *impf* **высыла́ть**) *сов перех* (*посы́лку, де́ньги*) to send off; (*поли́т*) to exile; (*шпио́на*) to deport.

вы́сле|дить (**-жу**, **-дишь**; *impf* **выслеживать**) *сов перех* to track down.

вы́слуг|а (**-и**) *ж*: **за ~у лет** for long service.

вы́служ|ить (**-у**, **-ишь**; *impf* **выслу́живать**) *сов перех* (*пе́нсию, повыше́ние*) to qualify for; (*о́рден, награ́ду*) to earn

▶ **вы́служиться** *сов возв* to work one's way up.

вы́слуша|ть (**-ю**; *impf* **выслу́шивать**) *сов перех* to hear out.

вы́сме|ять (**-ю**; *impf* **высме́ивать**) *сов перех* to ridicule.

вы́сморка|ть (**-ю**) *сов от* **сморка́ть** ♦ *перех*: **~ нос** to blow one's nose.

▶ **вы́сморкаться** *сов от* **сморка́ться**.

вы́сов|ывать(ся) (**-ю(сь)**) *несов от* **вы́сунуть(ся)**.

высо́к|ий (**-ая**, **-ое**, **-ие**; **-**, **-а́**, **-о́**) *прил* high; (*челове́к*) tall; (*честь, отве́тственность*) great; (*гость*) distinguished; **быть** (*impf*) **~ого мне́ния о** +*prp* to have a high opinion of; **высо́кая вода́** high tide.

высоко́ *нареч* high (up) ♦ *как сказ* it's high (up), it's a long way up; **до верши́ны ~** it is a long way to the top.

высокого́рный *прил* alpine.

высокока́чественный *прил* high-quality.

высококвалифици́рованный *прил* (*учитель, юрист*) highly qualified; (*слесарь, токарь*) highly skilled.

высокоме́рен *прил см* **высокоме́рный**.

высокоме́ри|е (-я) *ср* haughtiness, arrogance.

высокоме́р|ный (-ен, -на, -но) *прил* haughty, arrogant.

высокоопла́чиваемый *прил* highly paid.

высокопа́р|ный (-ен, -на, -но) *прил* (*речь*) high-flown, pompous.

высокопоста́вленный *прил* high-ranking.

высокопроизводи́тельный (-ен, -ьна, -ьно) *прил* highly productive.

вы́сос|ать (-у, -ешь; *impf* **выса́сывать**) *сов перех* to suck out; (*насосом*) to pump out.

высота́ (-оты́; *nom pl* -о́ты) *ж* height; (*ГЕО*) altitude; (*звука*) pitch; (*давления, температуры*) level; **набира́ть** (**набра́ть** *perf*) ~оту́ to climb, gain height; **на большо́й** ~оте́ at a high altitude *или* great height; **быть** (*impf*) *или* **оказа́ться** (*perf*) **на** ~оте́ (**положе́ния**) to be equal to the occasion.

высо́тный *прил* (*полёт*) high-altitude; (*здание*) high-rise.

вы́сох|нуть (-ну, -нешь; *pt* -, -ла, -ло) *сов от* **со́хнуть** ♦ (*impf* **высыха́ть**) *неперех* (*бельё, дрова*) to dry out; (*лужа, река*) to dry up.

высо́честв|о (-а) *ср*: **Ва́ше** *итп* **В~** Your *итп* Highness.

вы́сп|аться (-люсь, -ишься; *impf* **высыпа́ться**) *сов возв* to sleep well.

вы́став|ить (-лю, -ишь; *impf* **выставля́ть**) *сов перех* (*поставить наружу*) to put out; (*грудь*) to stick out; (*кандидатуру*) to put forward; (*требования*) to lay down; (*картину*) to exhibit; (*товар*) to display; (*часовых, охрану*) to post; (*разг: выгнать*) to chuck out; **выставля́ть** (~ *perf*) **кого́-н в дурно́м све́те** to show sb in an unfavourable light

▶ **вы́ставиться** (*impf* **выставля́ться**) *сов возв* (*на выставке*) to exhibit.

вы́став|ка (-ки; *gen pl* -ок) *ж* exhibition, show; ~-прода́жа кни́г book fair.

вы́ставлю(сь) *сов см* **вы́ставить(ся)**.

выставля́|ть(ся) (-ю(сь)) *несов от* **вы́ставить(ся)**.

вы́ставок *сущ см* **вы́ставка**.

выста́ива|ть (-ю) *несов от* **вы́стоять**.

выстега|ть (-ю) *сов от* **стега́ть**.

вы́стл|ать (-елю, -елешь; *impf* **выстила́ть**) *сов перех*: ~ **что-н чем-н** to line sth with sth.

вы́сто|ять (-ю, -ишь; *impf* **выста́ивать**) *сов неперех* (*долго простоять*) to stand; (*удержаться*) to remain standing; (*не сдаться*) to stand one's ground.

вы́страда|ть (-ю) *сов перех* to suffer; (*счастье, свободу*) *to achieve through much suffering*.

выстра́ива|ть(ся) (-ю(сь)) *несов* = **стро́ить(ся)**.

вы́стрел (-а) *м* shot; **разда́лся** ~ a shot rang out.

вы́стрел|ить (-ю, -ишь) *сов неперех* to fire; ~ (*perf*) **из ружья́/из пу́шки** to fire a gun/cannon.

вы́строга|ть (-ю) *сов от* **строга́ть**.

вы́стро|ить(ся) (-ю(сь), -ишь(ся)) *сов от* **стро́ить(ся)**.

вы́ступ (-а) *м* ledge.

выступа́|ть (-ю) *несов от* **вы́ступить** ♦ *неперех* (*берег*) to jut out; (*скулы*) to protrude.

вы́ступ|ить (-лю, -ишь; *impf* **выступа́ть**) *сов неперех* (*против закона, в защиту друга*) to come out; (*из толпы, из рядов*) to step out; (*оркестр, актёр*) to perform; (*пот, сыпь*) to break out; (*в поход, на поиски*) to set off *или* out; **выступа́ть** (~ *perf*) **с ре́чью** to make a speech.

выступле́ни|е (-я) *ср* (*МУЗ*) performance; (*в поход*) departure; (*в печати*) article; (*речь*) speech.

вы́ступлю *сов см* **вы́ступить**.

вы́сун|уть (-у, -ешь; *impf* **высо́вывать**) *сов перех* to stick out; **бежа́ть** (*impf*), ~ув язы́к (*перен: разг*) to run flat out

▶ **вы́сунуться** (*impf* **высо́вываться**) *сов возв* to lean out; (*рука, нога*) to stick out; (*перен: разг*): ~ся **с** +*instr* to come out with.

вы́суш|ить(ся) (-у(сь), -ишь(ся)) *сов от* **суши́ть(ся)**.

вы́счита|ть (-ю; *impf* **высчи́тывать**) *сов перех* to calculate.

вы́сш|ий (-ая, -ее, -ие) *прил* (*орган власти, нача́льство*) highest, supreme; **в** ~**ей сте́пени** extremely; **това́ры** ~**его со́рта** goods of the highest quality; **вы́сшая ме́ра наказа́ния** capital punishment; **вы́сшая шко́ла** university; **вы́сшее образова́ние** higher education; **вы́сшее уче́бное заведе́ние** higher education establishment.

высыла́|ть (-ю) *несов от* **вы́слать**.

вы́сыл|ка (-ки; *gen pl* -ок) *ж* (*посылки, денег*) sending; (*осуждённого*) exile; (*шпиона*) deportation.

вы́сып|ать (-лю, -лешь; *impf* **высыпа́ть**) *сов перех* to pour out ♦ *неперех* (*сыпь, прыщи*) to break out; (*разг: толпа, народ итп*) to pour out

▶ **вы́сыпаться** (*impf* **высыпа́ться**) *сов возв* to pour out.

высыха́|ть (-ю) *несов от* **вы́сохнуть**.

высь (-и) *ж* height.

выта́лкива|ть (-ю) *несов от* **вы́толкнуть**.

выта́птыва|ть (-ю) *несов от* **вы́топтать**.

вы́тараш|ить(ся) (-у(сь), -ишь(ся)) *сов от* **тара́щить(ся)**.

выта́скива|ть (-ю) *несов см* **вы́тащить**.

вы́тащ|ить (-у, -ишь) *сов от* **тащи́ть** ♦ (*impf* **выта́скивать**) *перех* (*мебель*) to drag out.

вы́твер|дить (-жу, -дишь) *сов от* **тверди́ть**.

вытворя́|ть (-ю) *сов перех (разг)* to get up to.

вы́тек *итп сов см* **вы́течь**.

вытека́|ть (*3sg* -ет, *3pl* -ют) *несов от* **вы́течь** ♦ *неперех (вывод)* to follow; *(река)* to flow out.

вы́тер|еть (-ру, -решь; *pt* -ер, -ерла, -ерло, *impf* **вытира́ть**) *сов перех (грязь, лужу)* to wipe up; *(посуду)* to dry (up); *(руки, глаза)* to wipe; **вытира́ть** (~ *perf*) **пыль** to dust

▸ **вы́тереться** (*impf* **вытира́ться**) *сов возв (человек)* to dry o.s.

вы́терп|еть (-лю, -ишь) *сов перех* to bear, endure.

вы́тесн|ить (-ю, -ишь; *impf* **вытесня́ть**) *сов перех (удалить)* to oust; *(заменить собой)* to supplant.

вы́те|чь (*3sg* -чет, *3pl* -кут, *pt* -к, -кла, -кло, *impf* **вытека́ть**) *сов неперех* to flow out.

вытира́|ть(ся) (-ю(сь)) *несов от* **вы́тереть(ся)**.

вы́тк|ать (-у, -ешь) *сов перех* to weave.

вы́толкн|уть (-у, -ешь; *impf* **выта́лкивать**) *сов перех* to push out.

вы́топ|тать (-чу, -чешь; *impf* **выта́птывать**) *сов перех* to trample down.

вы́точ|ить (-у, -ишь) *сов от* **точи́ть**.

вы́трав|ить (-лю, -ишь; *impf* **вытра́вливать**) *сов перех (пятно)* to remove; *(крыс, тараканов)* to exterminate; *(рисунок)* to etch.

вытрезви́тел|ь (-я) *м overnight police cell for drunks.*

вы́тру(сь) *итп сов см* **вы́тереть(ся)**.

вы́тряс|ти (-у, -ешь; *pt* -, -ла, -ло) *сов от* **трясти́**.

вы́тряхн|уть (-у, -ешь; *impf* **вытря́хивать**) *сов перех* to shake out.

выть (во́ю, во́ешь) *несов неперех (зверь, ветер, вьюга)* to howl; *(сирена)* to wail; *(разг: плакать)* to howl, wail.

вытя́гива|ть(ся) (-ю(сь)) *несов от* **вы́тянуть(ся)**.

вы́тяж|ка (-ки; *gen pl* -ек) *ж (действие: дыма, вредных частиц)* extraction; *(экстракт)* extract.

вы́тян|уть (-у, -ешь; *impf* **вытя́гивать**) *сов перех* to pull out; *(дым, вредные вещества)* to extract; *(руки, ноги, ткань)* to stretch ♦ *неперех (разг: выдержать)* to last out; ~ (~ *perf*) **(всю) ду́шу из кого́-н** *(разг)* to wear sb out; **из него́ сло́ва не ~ешь** *(разг)* you won't get a word out of him

▸ **вы́тянуться** (*impf* **вытя́гиваться**) *сов возв (дым, газ)* to escape; *(одежда)* to stretch; *(на диване, вдоль берега)* to stretch out; *(разг: вырасти)* to shoot up; *(встать смирно)* to stand at attention; **у него́ ~улось лицо́** *(перен)* his face fell.

вы́у|дить (-жу, -дишь; *impf* **выу́живать**) *сов перех (рыбу)* to catch; *(перен: разг: сведения)* to wheedle out.

вы́утюж|ить (-у, -ишь) *сов от* **утю́жить**.

выучива́|ть (-ю) *несов* to learn.

вы́уч|ить(ся) (-у(сь), -ишь(сь)) *сов от* **учи́ть(ся)**.

выха́жива|ть (-ю) *несов от* **вы́ходить**.

вы́хва|тить (-чу, -тишь; *impf* **выхва́тывать**) *сов перех (вырвать)* to snatch; *(пистолет)* to draw.

выхлопно́й *прил* exhaust *опред*; **выхлопны́е га́зы** exhaust fumes.

вы́ход (-а) *м (войск)* withdrawal; *(из партии, из комиссии)* departure; *(из кризиса)* way out; *(на сцену)* appearance; *(в море)* sailing; *(книги)* publication; *(на экран)* showing; *(место, КОМП)* exit; **дава́ть (дать** *perf*) ~ **чему́-н** to give vent to sth.

вы́ходец (-ца) *м*: **он ~ из Росси́и** he is of Russian origin *или* is Russian by birth.

вы́ходит *вводн сл (разг)* it turns out.

вы́ходить (-жу, -дишь; *impf* **выха́живать**) *сов перех (больного)* to nurse (back to health).

выхо|ди́ть (-ожу́, -о́дишь) *несов от* **вы́йти** ♦ *неперех*: ~ **на** *+acc (юг, север)* to face; **окно́ ~о́дит в парк** the window looks out onto the park; **дверь ~о́дит в коридо́р** the door opens onto the corridor.

выхо́д|ка (-ки) *ж* prank.

выходн|о́й *прил* exit *опред*; *(платье, костюм)* best ♦ (-о́го; *decl like adj*) *м (также*: ~ **день**) day off (work); ~**о́е отве́рстие** outlet; **сего́дня** ~ *(разг)* today is a holiday; **я сего́дня** ~ *(разг)* I have a day off today; ~**ы́е** weekend *ед*; **выходна́я дверь** exit; **выходно́е посо́бие** redundancy payment; **выходны́е да́нные** imprint.

вы́ходца *итп сущ см* **вы́ходец**.

вы́хожу *сов см* **вы́ходить**.

выхожу́ *несов см* **выходи́ть**.

вы́царапа|ть (-ю; *impf* **выцара́пывать**) *сов перех* to scratch out; *(перен: деньги, путёвку)* to wring out.

вы́цве|сти (*3sg* -тет, *3pl* -тут, *impf* **выцвета́ть**) *сов неперех* to fade.

вы́черкн|уть (-у, -ешь; *impf* **вычёркивать**) *сов перех* to cross *или* score out.

вы́черпа|ть (-ю; *impf* **вычёрпывать**) *сов перех (извлечь)* to scoop out; *(опорожнить)* to drain; **вычёрпывать** (~ *perf*) **во́ду из ло́дки** to bail out a boat.

вы́ч|есть (-ту, -тешь; *impf* **вычита́ть**) *сов перех (МАТ)* to subtract; *(долг, налог)* to deduct.

вы́чет (-а) *м* deduction ♦ *предл*: **за** ~**ом** *+gen* minus; **до** ~**а нало́гов** pre-tax.

вычисле́ни|е (-я) *ср* calculation.

вычисли́тельный *прил (операция, функция)* computing; **вычисли́тельная маши́на** computer; **вычисли́тельная те́хника** computers *мн*; **вычисли́тельный центр** computer centre (*BRIT*) *или* center (*US*).

вычисл|ить (-ю, -ишь; *impf* **вычисля́ть**) *сов перех* to calculate.

вы́чи|стить (-щу, -стишь) *сов от* **чи́стить**.

вычита́ни|е (-я) *ср* subtraction.
вы́чита|ть (-ю; *impf* **вычи́тывать**) *сов перех* (*разг*: *узнать*) to find out (*by reading*).
вычита́|ть (-ю) *несов от* **вы́честь**.
вы́чту *сов см* **вы́честь**.
вычи́тыва|ть (-ю) *несов от* **вы́читать**.
вы́чур|ный (-ен, -на, -но) *прил* elaborate.
вы́швырн|уть (-у, -ешь; *impf* **вышвы́ривать**) *сов перех* (*также перен*: *разг*) to chuck out.
вы́ше *сравн прил от* **высо́кий** ◆ *нареч* higher; (*в тексте*) above ◆ *предл* (+*gen*) above; **мы подня́ли́сь** ~ we went further up, we climbed higher; ~ **мы привели́ но́вые да́нные** we have cited new data above; **самолёт лете́л** ~ **облако́в** the plane was flying above the clouds; **э́то** ~ **моего́ понима́ния** it is beyond me *или* my comprehension.
вы́шек *сущ см* **вы́шка**.
вы́шел *сов см* **вы́йти**.
вышестоя́щ|ий (-ая, -ее, -ие) *прил* higher; ~**ее лицо́** superior.
вы́шиб|ить (-у, -ешь; *pt* -, -ла, -ло, *impf* **вышиба́ть**) *сов перех* (*выбить*) to knock out; (*разг*: *прогнать*) to chuck out.
вышива́ни|е (-я) *ср* needlework.
вышива́|ть (-ю) *несов от* **вы́шить**.
вы́шив|ка (-ки; *gen pl* -ок) *ж* embroidery.
вышин|а́ (-ы́) *ж* (*высота*) height.
вы́ш|ить (-ью, -ешь; *impf* **вышива́ть**) *сов перех* to embroider.
вы́ш|ка (-ки; *gen pl* -ек) *ж* (*высокое строение*) tower; (*разг*: *преступнику*) death penalty; (*СПОРТ*) diving board; **бурова́я** *или* **нефтяна́я** ~ derrick; **прыжки́ в во́ду с** ~**ки** high diving.
вы́школ|ить (-ю, -ишь) *сов перех* to train.
вы́шла *итп сов см* **вы́йти**.
вы́шлю *итп сов см* **вы́слать**.
вы́шью *итп сов см* **вы́шить**.
выщипа́|ть (-ю; *impf* **выщи́пывать**) *сов перех* to pluck.
вы́яв|ить (-лю, -ишь; *impf* **выявля́ть**) *сов перех* (*талант*) to discover; (*недостатки*) to expose

▶ **вы́яв|иться** (*impf* **выявля́ться**) *сов возв* to come to light, be revealed.
вы́ясн|ить (-ю, -ишь; *impf* **выясня́ть**) *сов перех* (*обнаружить*) to find out; (*сделать ясным*) to clarify; **нам ну́жно** ~ **отноше́ния** we have to sort things out between us
▶ **вы́ясн|иться** (*impf* **выясня́ться**) *сов возв* to become clear.
Вьетна́м (-а) *м* Vietnam.
вьетна́м|ец (-ца) *м* Vietnamese.
вьетна́м|ка (-ки; *gen pl* -ок) *ж см* **вьетна́мец**.
вьетна́мск|ий (-ая, -ое, -ие) *прил* Vietnamese.
вьетна́мца *итп сущ см* **вьетна́мец**.
вью́г|а (-и) *ж* snowstorm, blizzard.
вью́чный *прил*: ~**ое живо́тное** beast of burden.
вяжу́ *сов см* **вяза́ть**.
вя́жущ|ий (-ая, -ее, -ие) *прил* (*вкус*) acerbic; (*материал*, *состав*) binding, cementing.
вяз *итп несов см* **вя́знуть** ◆ (-а) *м* elm.
вяза́ни|е (-я) *ср* (*снопов*) tying, binding; (*рукоделие*) knitting.
вя́заный *прил* knitted.
вяза́|ть (-жу́, -жешь; *perf* **связа́ть**) *несов перех* to tie up, bind; (*кофту*, *носки*) to knit ◆ *безл* (*no perf*): **э́то лека́рство вя́жет во рту** this medicine burns the inside of your mouth.
вя́з|кий (-кая, -кое, -кие; -ок, -ка́, -ко) *прил* (*тягучий*) viscous; (*топкий*) boggy.
вя́з|нуть (-ну, -нешь; *pt* -, -ла, -ло, *perf* **завя́знуть** *или* **увя́знуть**) *несов неперех*: ~ (**в** +*prp*) to get stuck (in).
вя́зок *итп сов см* **вя́зкий**.
вя́леный *прил* dried.
вя́л|ить (-ю, -ишь) *несов перех* to dry.
вя́ло *нареч* (*говорить*) dully.
вя́лост|ь (-и) *ж* sluggishness.
вя́л|ый (-, -а, -о) *прил* (*листья*, *цветы*) wilted, withered; (*человек*, *речь*) sluggish.
вя́|нуть (-ну, -нешь; *perf* **завя́нуть** *или* **увя́нуть**) *несов неперех* (*цветы*) to wilt, wither; (*перен*: *красота*) to fade; **его́ слу́шать – у́ши** ~**нут** (*разг*) it makes you sick to listen to him.

~ Г, г ~

Г, г *сущ нескл* (*буква*) the 4th letter of the Russian alphabet.

г *сокр* (= **грамм**) g, gm (= *gram*).

г. *сокр* = **год**, **го́род**.

га *м сокр* (= **гекта́р**) ha (= *hectare*).

Гаа́г|а (**-и**) *ж* The Hague.

габари́т (**-а**) *м* (*обычно мн: ТЕХ*) dimension; *см также* **габари́ты**.

габари́т|ы (**-ов**) *мн* (*разг: человека*) size *ед*.

ГАБТ (**-а**) *м сокр* (= **Госуда́рственный академи́ческий Большо́й теа́тр**) (State Academic) Bolshoi Theatre (*BRIT*) *или* Theater (*US*).

Гава́йи *м нескл* Hawaii.

Гава́н|а (**-ы**) *ж* Havana.

га́вань (**-и**) *ж* harbour (*BRIT*), harbor (*US*).

га́вка|ть (**-ю**) *несов неперех* (*разг: также перен*) to yap.

гага́р|а (**-ы**) *ж* diver (*BRIT*), loon (*US*).

гага́т (**-а**) *м* (*ГЕО*) jet.

гад (**-а**) *м* (*разг*) rat.

гада́л|ка (**-ки**; *gen pl* **-ок**) *ж* fortune-teller.

гада́|ть (**-ю**) *несов неперех* (*строить предположения*) to guess; (*perf* **погада́ть**): ~ **кому́-н** to tell sb's fortune; ~ (**погада́ть** *perf*) **на ка́ртах** to read the cards; ~ (*impf*) **на кофе́йной гу́ще** ≈ to read the tea leaves.

га́ди|на (**-ы**) *ж* (*разг*) rat.

га́дить (**-жу, -дишь**; *perf* **нага́дить**) *несов неперех* (*разг: животное*) to defecate; ~ (**нага́дить** *perf*) +*dat* (*разг*) to do the dirty on.

га́д|кий (**-кая, -кое, -кие**; **-ок, -ка́, -ко**) *прил* loathsome.

га́дко *нареч* (*поступить*) terribly ♦ *как сказ*: **э́то** ~ it's disgusting.

га́дость (**-и**) *ж* (*поступка, слов*) nastiness; (*разг*) filth; **де́лать** (**сде́лать** *perf*)/**говори́ть** (**сказа́ть** *perf*) ~**и** to do/say nasty things; **э́то** ~ it's disgusting.

гадю́к|а (**-и**) *ж* viper.

га́ек *сущ см* **га́йка**.

га́ечный *прил*: ~ **ключ** spanner.

га́же *сравн прил от* **га́дкий** ♦ *сравн нареч от* **га́дко**.

га́жу *несов см* **га́дить**.

ГАЗ (**-а**) *м сокр* (*автомобиль*) *vehicle manufactured at the Gorky car factory*.

газ (**-а**; *part gen* **-у**) *м* gas; **гото́вить** (**пригото́вить** *perf*) **на га́зе** to cook with gas; **дава́ть** (**дать** *perf*)

~ (*разг*) to put one's foot down (*BRIT*), step on the gas (*US*); *см также* **га́зы**.

газе́т|а (**-ы**) *ж* newspaper.

газе́тный *прил* newspaper *опред*.

газе́тчик (**-а**) *м* (*разг: сотрудник*) journalist; (*продавец*) newspaper vendor.

га́зик (**-а**) *м* (*разг*) *car manufactured at the Gorky car plant*.

газиро́ванн|ый *прил*: ~**ая вода́** carbonated water.

газиро́в|ка (**-ки**; *gen pl* **-ок**) *ж* (*разг*) soda.

газовщи́к (**-а́**) *м* (*разг*) gasman (*мн* gasmen).

га́зов|ый *прил* gas; **га́зовая ка́мера** gas chamber.

газо́н (**-а**) *м* lawn.

газопрово́д (**-а**) *м* gas pipeline.

га́з|ы (**-ов**) *мн* (*МЕД*) wind *ед*.

ГАИ *ж сокр* (= **Госуда́рственная автомоби́льная инспе́кция**) *state motor vehicle inspectorate*.

Гаи́ти *м нескл* Haiti.

гаитя́нск|ий (**-ая, -ое, -ие**) *прил* Haitian.

гаи́шник (**-а**) *м* (*разг*) ≈ traffic cop.

га́йк|а (**-йки**; *gen pl* **-ек**) *ж* nut; **закру́чивать** (**закрути́ть** *perf*) ~**йки** (*разг*) to put the screws on.

гаймори́т (**-а**) *м* sinusitis.

гала́ *прил неизм* gala *опред*.

гала́ктик|а (**-и**) *ж* galaxy; **На́ша Г**~ the Galaxy.

гала́нтен *прил см* **гала́нтный**.

галантере́|я (**-и**) *ж* haberdashery (*BRIT*), notions store (*US*).

гала́нтн|ый (**-ен, -на, -но**) *прил* gallant.

галере́|я (**-и**) *ж* gallery.

гале́т|а (**-ы**) *ж sort of biscuit*.

галиматья́ (**-и́**) *ж* (*разг*) gobbledygook.

галифе́ *мн/ср нескл* riding breeches *мн* ♦ *прил неизм*: **брю́ки** ~ jodphurs.

га́л|ка (**-ки**; *gen pl* **-ок**) *ж* jackdaw.

галло́н (**-а**) *м* gallon.

галлюцина́ция (**-и**) *ж* hallucination.

га́лок *сущ см* **га́лка**.

гало́п (**-а**) *м* (*бег лошади*) gallop; (*танец*) galop.

гало́пом *нареч* at a gallop; **я прочита́л кни́гу** ~ (*разг*) I raced through the book.

га́лочк|а (**-ки**; *gen pl* **-ек**) *ж* (*в тексте*) tick, check (*US*).

гало́ш|а (**-и**) *ж* (*обычно мн: обувь*) galosh; **сажа́ть** (**посади́ть** *perf*) **кого́-н в** ~**у** (*разг*) to put sb on the spot; **садúться (сесть** _perf_**)** в ~у (_разг_) to get into a jam.

гáлстук (-а) _м_ tie, necktie (_US_); **завязывать (завязáть** _perf_**)** ~ to tie a tie.

гальванизáци|я (-и) _ж_ galvanization.

гальванизúр|овать (-ую) (_не)сов перех_ to galvanize.

гáльк|а (-и) _ж_, _собир_ pebble.

гам (-а) _м_ uproar.

гамáк (-á) _м_ hammock.

гамáш|а (-и) _ж_ (_обычно мн_) gaiter.

Гáмбург (-а) _м_ Hamburg.

гáмбургер (-а) _м_ hamburger.

гáмм|а (-ы) _ж_ (_муз_) scale; (_чувств, красок_) range.

гáмма-глобулú́н (-а) _м_ gamma globulin.

гáмма-излучéни|е (-я) _ср_ gamma radiation.

Гáн|а (-ы) _ж_ Ghana.

гангрéн|а (-ы) _ж_ gangrene.

гáнгстер (-а) _м_ gangster.

гандбóл (-а) _м_ handball.

гандболúст (-а) _м_ handball player.

гандболúст|ка (-ки; _gen pl_ **-ок)** _ж см_ **гандболúст.**

гантéл|ь (-и) _ж_ dumbbell.

гарáж (-á) _м_ garage.

гарáнт (-а) _м_ guarantor.

гарантúйный _прил_ guarantee _опред_, warranty _опред_; **гарантúйное письмó** letter of guarantee.

гарантú́р|овать (-ую) (_не)сов перех_ to guarantee; ~ (_impf/perf_) **когó-н от** +_gen_ to protect sb against.

гарáнти|я (-и) _ж_ guarantee; ~ **от убытков** guarantee against damage; **товáр с ~ей** item under guarantee; **бáнковская** ~ bank's letter of guarantee; **авáрийная** ~ warranty; ~ **зáнятости** job security.

гардерóб (-а) _м_ wardrobe; (_в общественном здании_) cloakroom.

гардерóбщик (-а) _м_ cloakroom attendant.

гардерóбщиц|а (-ы) _ж см_ **гардерóбщик.**

гардú́н|а (-ы) _ж_ curtain.

гáрев|ый _прил_: ~**ая дорóжка** cinder track.

гарéм (-а) _м_ harem.

гармóник|а (-и) _ж_ concertina; **губнáя** ~ mouth organ.

гармонú́р|овать (-ую) _несов неперех_: ~ **с** +_instr_ (_со средóй_) to be in harmony with; (_одежда_) to go with.

гармонúст (-а) _м_ concertina player.

гармонú́чный (-ен, -на, -но) _прил_ harmonious.

гармóни|я (-и) _ж_ harmony.

гармóш|ка (-ки; _gen pl_ **-ек)** _ж_ (_разг_) ≈ squeeze-box; (_одежда_) **в ~ку** creased; **при удáре машú́на смялась в ~ку** the car concertinaed on impact.

гарнизóн (-а) _м_ garrison.

гарнú́р (-а) _м_ side dish.

гарнитú́р (-а) _м_ (_одежды_) outfit; (_украшения_) set; (_мебели_) suite.

гарпун (-á) _м_ harpoon.

гар|ь (-и) _ж_ (_угля_) cinders _мн_; **пáхнет гáрью** there's a smell of burning.

гас _итп несов см_ **гáснуть.**

га|сú́ть (-шу́, -сишь; _perf_ **погасú́ть)** _несов перех_ (_лампу, свет_) to put out; (_пожар_) to extinguish, put out; (_скорость_) to reduce; (_звук_) to deaden; (_марку_) to frank; (_no perf; перен: инициативу_) to stifle, suppress; ~ **(погасú́ть** _perf_**) задóлженность** to settle one's debts; ~ **(погасú́ть** _perf_**) известь** to slake lime.

гá|снуть (-ну, -нешь; _pt_ **-или -нул, -ла, -ло,** _perf_ **погáснуть или угáснуть)** _несов неперех_ (_огни_) to go out; (_звезды, чувства, надежда_) to fade.

гастрú́т (-а) _м_ gastritis.

гастрóл|и (-ей) _мн performances of a touring company_; **éздить/éхать (поéхать** _perf_**) на** ~ to go on tour.

гастролú́р|овать (-ую) _несов неперех_ to be on tour.

гастронóм (-а) _м_ food store.

гастрономú́ческ|ий (-ая, -ое, ие) _прил_: ~ **магазú́н** = **гастронóм.**

гастронóми|я (-и) _ж_ delicatessen.

ГАТТ _м сокр_ (= _Генерáльное соглашéние о тарú́фах и торгóвле_) GATT (= _General Agreement on Tariffs and Trade_)

гауптвáхт|а (-ы) _ж_ (_воен_) guardroom (_as a place of detention_); **сажáть (посадú́ть** _perf_**) когó-н на** ~у to confine sb to the guardroom.

гашёный _прил_ (_марка_) franked; ~**ая известь** slaked lime.

гашú́ш (-а) _м_ hashish.

гашу́ _несов см_ **гасú́ть.**

ГБ _ж сокр_ = **госбезопáсность.**

гвалт (-а) _м_ (_разг_) row.

гвардé|ец (-йца) _м_ (_воен_) guardsman (_мн_ guardsmen).

гвáрди|я (-и) _ж_ (_воен_) Guards _мн_; **Крáсная/Бéлая** ~ (_ист_) the Red/White Guard.

Гватемáл|а (-ы) _ж_ Guatemala.

Гвинé|я (-и) _ж_ Guinea.

гвоздú́к|а (-и) _ж_ (_цветок_) carnation; (_пряность_) cloves _мн_.

гвозд|ь (-я; _nom pl_ **-и,** _gen pl_ **-éй)** _м_ nail; ~ **прогрáммы** the highlight of the show; **и никакú́х ~éй!** (_разг_) and that's that!

гг _сокр_ = **гóды;** (= **господá**) Messrs (= _messieurs_).

ГД _ж сокр_ = **Госудáрственная Дýма.**

Гдáньск (-а) _м_ Gdansk.

где _нареч_ where; (_разг: где-нибудь_) somewhere, anywhere ♦ _союз_ where; ~ **Вы живёте?** where do you live?; **подýмайте, не забыли ли** ~ try and think whether you left it anywhere _или_ somewhere; **гóрод,** ~ **я жил** the town where I lived; **ты скóро бýдешь богáтым** – ~ **уж там!**

(*разг*) you'll soon be rich – hardly!

гдé-либо *нареч* = **где́-нибудь**.

где́-нибудь *нареч* somewhere; (*в вопросе*) anywhere.

где́-то *нареч* somewhere.

ГДР *ж сокр* (*ист*: = *Герма́нская Демократи́ческая Респу́блика*) GDR (= *German Democratic Republic*).

гегемони́зм (-а) *м* hegemony.

ге́йзер (-а) *м* geyser.

гейм (-а) *м* (*СПОРТ*) game.

гекта́р (-а) *м* hectare.

гель (-я) *м* gel (*for hair*).

гемоглоби́н (-а) *м* haemoglobin (*BRIT*), hemoglobin (*US*).

геморро́й (-я) *м* haemorrhoids *мн* (*BRIT*), hemorrhoids *мн* (*US*), piles *мн*.

гемофили́|я (-и) *ж* haemophilia (*BRIT*), hemophilia (*US*).

ген (-а) *м* gene.

генеалоги́ческ|ий (-ая, -ое, -ие) *прил*: ~ое де́рево genealogical chart; (*семьи*) family tree.

генеало́ги|я (-и) *ж* genealogy.

ге́незис (-а) *м* genesis.

генера́л (-а) *м* (*ВОЕН*) general; **генера́л а́рмии** general (*BRIT*), General of the Army (*US*).

генера́льный *прил* general; (*главный*) main; ~ая убо́рка spring-clean; **генера́льная репети́ция** dress rehearsal; **генера́льное сраже́ние** decisive battle; **генера́льный штаб** chief headquarters.

генера́тор (-а) *м* generator.

гене́тик (-а) *м* geneticist.

гене́тик|а (-и) *ж* genetics.

генети́ческий (-ая, -ое, -ие) *прил* genetic.

генина́льно *нареч* (*написанный*) superbly ♦ *как сказ* it's great.

гениа́л|ьный (-ен, -ьна, -ьно) *прил* great.

ге́ни|й (-я) *м* genius.

геноци́д (-а) *м* genocide.

генсе́к (-а) *м сокр* = *генера́льный секрета́рь*; (*полит*) General Secretary (*of the Communist Party*).

Ге́ну|я (-и) *ж* Genoa.

гео́граф (-а) *м* geographer.

геогра́фи|я (-и) *ж* geography.

геоде́зи|я (-и) *ж* geodesy.

гео́лог (-а) *м* geologist.

геоло́ги|я (-и) *ж* geology.

геоме́три|я (-и) *ж* geometry.

геополи́тик|а (-и) *ж* geopolitics.

георги́н (-а) *м* dahlia.

георги́н|а (-ы) *ж* = **георги́н**.

гепа́рд (-а) *м* cheetah.

гепати́т (-а) *м* hepatitis.

гера́льдик|а (-и) *ж* heraldry.

гера́н|ь (-и) *ж* geranium.

герб (-á) *м* coat of arms; **госуда́рственный** ~ national emblem.

герба́ри|й (-я) *м* herbarium.

гербици́д (-а) *м* herbicide.

ге́рбов|ый *прил* heraldic; (*с гербом*) bearing a

coat of arms; **ге́рбовая бума́га** headed paper; **ге́рбовая ма́рка** official stamp (*relating to stamp duty*); **ге́рбовый сбор** stamp duty.

геркуле́с (-а) *м* (*человек*) Hercules; (*кулин*) porridge oats *мн*.

герма́н|ец (-ца) *м* (*обычно мн*: *ист*) Teuton.

Герма́ни|я (-и) *ж* Germany.

герма́нский (-ая, -ое, -ие) *прил* German.

герма́нца *итп сущ см* **герма́нец**.

герметизи́р|овать (-ую; *perf* **загерметизи́ровать**) *несов неперех* to make airtight.

гермети́ч|ный (-ен, -на, -но) *прил* hermetic.

геро́изм (-а) *м* heroism.

геро́ин (-а) *м* heroin.

геро́ин|я (-и) *ж* heroine.

герои́ческ|ий (-ая, -ое, -ие) *прил* heroic; **герои́ческий эпос** heroic epic.

геро́й (-я) *м* hero.

герц (-а) *м* hertz.

ге́рцог (-а) *м* duke.

герцоги́н|я (-и) *ж* duchess.

геста́по *ср нескл* the Gestapo.

геста́пов|ец (-ца) *м* member of the Gestapo.

гетероге́нный *прил* heterogeneous.

ге́тр|а (-ы) *ж* (*обычно мн*) legwarmer.

ге́тто *ср нескл* ghetto.

г-жа *м сокр* = **госпожа́**.

гжел|ь (-и) *ж type of ceramic made in Gzhel*.

гиаци́нт (-а) *м* hyacinth.

гиб *итп несов см* **ги́бнуть**.

ги́белен *прил см* **ги́бельный**.

ги́бел|ь (-и) *ж* (*человека*) death; (*армии*) destruction; (*самолета*, *надежды*, *ценностей*) loss; (*карьеры*) ruin; **они́ бы́ли обречены́ на** ~ they were doomed; **на краю́** ~и (*дело*) on the brink of disaster; (*человек*) on the verge of death.

ги́бел|ьный (-ен, -ьна, -ьно) *прил* disastrous.

ги́бкий (-кая, -кое, -кие; -ок, -ка́, -ко) *прил* flexible; **ги́бкий диск** (*КОМП*) floppy disk; **ги́бкое произво́дство** (*ТЕХ*) flexible production methods.

ги́бкост|ь (-и) *ж* flexibility.

ги́б|нуть (-ну, -нешь; *pt* ~, ла, -ло, *perf* **поги́бнуть**) *несов неперех* to perish; (*растения*) to die; (*перен*) to come to nothing; ~ (**поги́бнуть** *perf*) **от** +*gen* to die of.

ги́бок *прил см* **ги́бкий**.

Гибралта́р (-а) *м* Gibraltar.

гибри́д (-а) *м* hybrid.

ги́бче *сравн прил от* **ги́бкий**.

гига́нт (-а) *м* giant; **пласти́нка-**~, **диск-**~ twelve-inch record.

гига́нтск|ий (-ая, -ое, -ие) *прил* gigantic.

гигие́н|а (-ы) *ж* hygiene.

гигиени́ческ|ий (-ая, -ое, -ие) *прил* sanitary; **гигиени́ческий тампо́н** tampon.

гигиени́ч|ный (-ен, -на, -но) *прил* hygienic.

гигроскопи́чный *прил* absorbent.

гид (-а) *м* guide.

гидравли́ческий (-ая, -ое, -ие) *прил*

hydraulic.

гидрокостю́м (-а) *м* diving suit.

гидрометце́нтр (-а) *м сокр* = *Гидрометеорологи́ческий центр.*

гидроста́нци|я (-и) *ж см* **гидроэлектроста́нция.**

гидроэлектроста́нци|я (-и) *ж* hydroelectric power station.

гие́н|а (-ы) *ж* hyena.

ги́льди|я (-и) *ж* guild.

ги́льз|а (-ы) *ж* cartridge case.

гильоти́н|а (-ы) *ж* guillotine.

Гимала́|и (-ев) *мн* the Himalayas.

гимн (-а) *м (госуда́рственный)* anthem; *(хвале́бная пе́сня)* hymn.

гимнази́ст (-а) *м* ≈ grammar school student.

гимнази́ст|ка (-ки; *gen pl* **-ок)** *ж см* **гимнази́ст.**

гимна́зи|я (-и) *ж* ≈ grammar school.

гимна́ст (-а) *м* gymnast.

гимнастёр|ка (-ки; *gen pl* **-ок)** *ж* soldier's blouse.

гимна́стик|а (-и) *ж* exercises *мн*; **(спорти́вная)** ~ gymnastics *мн*; **худо́жественная** ~ modern rhythmic gymnastics; **де́лать (сде́лать** *perf)* **~у** to do one's exercises.

гимна́ст|ка (-ки; *gen pl* **-ок)** *ж см* **гимна́ст.**

гинеко́лог (-а) *м* gynaecologist (*BRIT*), gynecologist (*US*).

гинеколо́ги|я (-и) *ж* gynaecology (*BRIT*), gynecology (*US*).

гипе́рбол|а (-ы) *ж* hyperbole.

гиперто́ник (-а) *м person suffering from high blood pressure.*

гипертони|я (-и) *ж* high blood pressure.

гипертрофи́рованный *прил (МЕД)* hypertrophied; *(перен)* excessive.

гипно́з (-а) *м* hypnosis.

гипнотизи́р|овать (-ую; *perf* **загипнотизи́ровать)** *несов перех* to hypnotize.

гипо́тез|а (-ы) *ж* hypothesis; **выдвига́ть (вы́двинуть** *perf)* **~у** to put forward a hypothesis.

гипотети́ческ|ий (-ая, -ое, -ие) *прил* hypothetical.

гипото́ник (-а) *м person suffering from low blood pressure.*

гипотони|я (-и) *ж* low blood pressure.

гиппопота́м (-а) *м* hippopotamus.

гипс (-а) *м (ГЕО)* gypsum; *(ИСКУССТВО)* plaster of Paris; *(МЕД)* plaster; **накла́дывать (наложи́ть** *perf)* ~ **на что-н** to put sth in plaster.

гипю́р (-а) *м (guipure)* lace.

гирля́нд|а (-ы) *ж* garland.

ги́р|я (-и) *ж (весо́в)* weight; *(СПОРТ)* dumbbell.

гита́р|а (-ы) *ж* guitar.

гитари́ст (-а) *м* guitarist.

гитари́ст|ка (-ки; *gen pl* **-ок)** *ж см* **гитари́ст.**

ГК *м сокр* (= *Гражда́нский Ко́декс*) civil code.

гл. *сокр* (= *глава́*) ch. (= *chapter*).

глав|а́ (-ы́; *nom pl* **-ы)** *ж (делега́ции, семьи́)* head; *(це́ркви)* dome; *(кни́ги, статьи́)* chapter; **во** ~**е́ с** +*instr* headed by; **во** ~**е́** +*gen* at the head of; **во** ~**у́ угла́ ста́вить (поста́вить** *perf)* **что-н** to give top priority to sth.

глава́р|ь (-я́) *м (ба́нды)* leader.

главе́нств|о (-а) *ср* leading role.

главе́нств|овать (-ую) *несов неперех:* ~ **над** +*instr* to hold sway over.

главк (-а) *м сокр* (= *гла́вный комите́т*) *chief administrative body within a ministry.*

гла́вное *вводн сл* the main thing; **он,** ~, **все отрица́ет** the main thing is, he denies everything.

главнокома́ндующ|ий (-его; *decl like adj)* *м* commander in chief.

гла́вн|ый *прил* main; *(ста́рший по положе́нию)* senior, head *опред;* ~**ым о́бразом** chiefly, mainly; **гла́вная кни́га** *(КОММ)* general ledger.

глаго́л (-а) *м* verb.

глади́л|ьный (-ен, -ьна, -ьно) *прил:* ~**ьная доска́** ironing board.

гладио́лус (-а) *м* gladiolus.

гла́|дить (-жу, -дишь; *perf* **погла́дить)** *несов перех* to iron; *(во́лосы)* to stroke; **они́ тебя́ не погла́дят по голо́вке за э́то** they won't be best pleased with you for this.

гла́д|кий (-кая, -кое, -кие; -ок, -ка́, -ко) *прил (ро́вный)* smooth; *(одноцве́тный)* plain, unpatterned; *(пла́вный)* flowing; *(прямо́й)* straight.

гла́дко *нареч (ро́вно)* smoothly; *(причёсанный)* tightly; ~ **вы́бритый** clean-shaven.

гла́же *сравн прил от* **гла́дкий** ♦ *сравн нареч от* **гла́дко.**

гла́жу *несов см* **гла́дить.**

глаз (-а; *loc sg* **-у́,** *nom pl* **-а́,** *gen pl* **-)** *м (также перен)* eye; *(зре́ние)* eyesight; **в** ~**а́х** +*gen* in the eyes of; **на** ~**а́х у кого́-н** before sb's eyes; **с гла́зу на** ~ tête à tête; **на** ~ roughly; **она́ всегда́ говори́т о нём за** ~**а́** *(разг)* she is always talking about him behind his back; **за ним ну́жен** ~ **да** ~ you need to keep your eye on him; **куда́** ~**а́ глядя́т идти́ (пойти́** *perf) (разг)* to go where one's fancy takes one; **де́лать (сде́лать** *perf)* **больши́е** ~**а́** to look amazed.

глаза́стый *прил (разг)* with big eyes; *(зо́ркий)* sharp-eyed.

Гла́зго *м нескл* Glasgow.

глазе́|ть (-ю) *несов неперех:* ~ **на** +*acc* to stare at.

глазир|ова́ть (-у́ю) *(не)сов перех (также ТЕХ)* to glaze; *(торт)* to ice, frost (*US*).

глазка́ *сущ см* **глазо́к.**

глазни́к (-а́) *м (разг)* eye doctor.

глазни́ц|а (-ы) *ж* eyeball.

глазно́й *прил* eye *опред.*

глаз|о́к (-ка́) *м* peephole.

The spelling rules for Russian are shown on page xvii.

глазоме́р (-а) *м*: у него́ хоро́ший ~ he has a good eye.

глазу́нь|**я** (-и) *ж* fried egg.

глазу́р|**ь** (-и) *ж* (*на кера́мике итп*) glaze; (*на то́рте*) icing, frosting (*US*).

гла́нд|**а** (-ы) *ж* (*обы́чно мн*) tonsil.

гласи́ть (*3sg* -и́т, *3pl* -я́т) *несов перех* to state; зако́н/пра́вило ~и́т, что ... the law/rule states that ...; уста́в ~и́т, что the regulations stipulate that.

гла́сность (-и) *ж* openness; (*ист*) glasnost; предава́ть (преда́ть *perf*) ~и to make public.

гла́сн|**ый** *прил* (*суд, проце́сс*) public; (*линг*) voiced ♦ (-ого; *decl like adj*) *м* vowel.

глауко́м|**а** (-ы) *ж* glaucoma.

гли́н|**а** (-ы) *ж* clay.

глинтве́йн (-а; *part gen* -у) *м* mulled wine.

гли́няный *прил* clay.

глист (-а́) *м* (*обы́чно мн*) (intestinal) worm.

глицери́н (-а) *м* glycerin(e).

глици́ни|**я** (-и) *ж* wisteria.

глоба́льный (-ен, -ьна, -ьно) *прил* (*перен*) thorough; (*no short form; кли́мат, поли́тика*) global.

гло́бус (-а) *м* globe.

глода́ть (-ю) *несов перех* to gnaw at.

глота́ть (-ю; *perf* **проглоти́ть**) *несов перех* to swallow; (*разг: обе́д*) to scoff; (*перен: кни́гу*) to devour; ~ (**проглоти́ть** *perf*) слёзы to choke back one's tears.

гло́тк|**а** (-и; *gen pl* -ок) *ж* gullet.

глото́к (-ка́) *м* gulp, swallow; (*воды́, ча́я*) drop.

гло́х|**нуть** (-ну, -нешь; *pt* -, -ла, -ло, *perf* **огло́хнуть**) *несов непере́х* to grow deaf; (*perf* **загло́хнуть**; *шум*) to die away; (*мото́р*) to stall.

глу́бже *сравн прил от* **глубо́кий** ♦ *сравн нареч от* **глубоко́**.

глуби́на́ (-ины́; *nom pl* -и́ны) *ж* depth; (*дно*) depths *мн*; (*ле́са*) heart; (*за́ла, са́да*) middle; (*перен*) ~ +*gen* (*иде́и итп*) profundity of; на ~ине́ 10 ме́тров at a depth of 10 metres (*BRIT*) *или* meters (*US*); в ~ине́ души́ in one's heart of hearts; до ~ины́ души́ тро́нут deeply moved; до ~ины́ души́ удивлён astounded; до ~ины́ души́ огорчён cut to the quick.

глубо́к|**ий** (-ая, -ое, -ие; -, -а́, -о́) *прил* deep; (*прови́нция*) remote; (*мысль, интере́с*) profound; (*зима́, о́сень*) late; ~ая ста́рость ripe old age; ~ая ночь the dead of night; ~ снег deep snow; ~ покло́н deep bow; ~ая та́йна deep secret.

глубоко́ *нареч* deeply ♦ *как сказ*: здесь ~ it's deep here.

глубоково́дный (-ен, -на, -но) *прил* deep; (*no short form; иссле́дования*) deep-sea.

глубокомы́слен|**ный** (-, -на, -но) *прил* (*речь, замеча́ние*) profound; (*взгляд, вид*) thoughtful.

глубокоуважа́емый *прил* dear.

глуб|**ь** (-и́) *ж* (*ле́са*) heart; (*океа́на*) depths *мн*.

глуми́ться (-лю́сь, -и́шься) *несов возв*: ~ над +*instr* to mock.

глупе́ть (-ю; *perf* **поглупе́ть**) *несов непере́х* to grow stupid.

глупи́ть (-лю́, -и́шь; *perf* **сглупи́ть**) *несов непере́х* to be silly *или* stupid.

глу́по *нареч* stupidly ♦ *как сказ* it's stupid *или* silly.

глу́пость (-и) *ж* stupidity, silliness; (*посту́пок*) stupid *или* silly thing; (*слова́*) nonsense; де́лать (*impf*) ~и to do silly things; написа́ть ей письмо́ бы́ло ~о it was foolish *или* stupid to write to her; име́ть (*impf*) ~ +*infin* to be foolish enough to do; ~и! никуда́ не пойдёшь nonsense! you're not going anywhere.

глу́пый (-, -а́, -о) *прил* stupid, silly.

глуха́р|**ь** (-я́) *м* (*зоол*) capercaillie.

глухо́й (-, -а́, -о) *прил* deaf; (*волне́ние, недово́льство*) suppressed, pent-up; (*звук*) muffled; (*no short form; пора́*) dead; ~ лес dense forest; ~а́я стена́ blank wall; он глух к про́сьбам/жа́лобам he is deaf to requests/complaints.

глухонем|**о́й** *прил* deaf-and-dumb ♦ (-о́го; *decl like adj*) *м* deaf-mute; а́збука для ~ы́х deaf-and-dumb alphabet.

глухот|**а́** (-ы́) *ж* deafness.

глуши́тел|**ь** (-я) *м* (*тех*) silencer; (*авт*) silencer (*BRIT*), muffler (*US*); (*перен*) suppressor.

глуш|**и́ть** (-у́, -и́шь; *perf* **заглуши́ть**) *несов перех* (*зву́ки, шум итп*) to muffle; (*мото́р*) to turn off; (*перен: инициати́ву*) to stifle, suppress; (*perf* **оглуши́ть**; *ры́бу*) to stun; ~ (*impf*) во́дку/вино́ to hit the vodka/wine.

глуш|**ь** (-и́; *instr sg* -ью, *loc sg* -и́) *ж* wilderness; (*ле́са*) deepest part; (*перен*) backwoods *мн*.

глы́б|**а** (-ы) *ж* (*ледяна́я*) block; ка́менная ~ boulder.

глюко́з|**а** (-ы) *ж* glucose.

гля|**де́ть** (-жу́, -ди́шь; *perf* **погляде́ть**) *несов непере́х* to look; (*забо́титься*): ~ за +*instr* to look after; (*оце́нивать*): ~ на +*acc* to look at; на́ ночь гля́дя (so) late at night; на́ зиму гля́дя just before winter; я захоте́л есть, гля́дя на тебя́ seeing you eat has made me hungry; того́ и ~ди́ дождь пойдёт (*разг*) it looks like it could rain any minute; того́ и ~ди́ де́ньги зако́нчатся the money might run out at any time; там погля́ди́м (*разг*) we'll see

▶ **гляде́ться** *несов возв*: ~ся в +*acc* to look at o.s. in.

гля́н|**ец** (-ца) *м* lustre (*BRIT*), luster (*US*), sheen; наводи́ть (навести́ *perf*) ~ на что-н (*перен*) to add the finishing touches to sth.

гля́нцевый *прил* glossy.

гм *межд* h'm.

гна|**ть** (гоню́, го́нишь; *pt* -л, -ла́, -ло́) *несов перех* (*ста́до*) to drive; (*зве́ря*) to chase; (*удаля́ть: челове́ка*) to throw out; (*ло́шадь*) to drive *или* urge on; (*маши́ну*) to drive fast; (*во́дку итп*) to distil (*BRIT*), distill (*US*); (*разг: проду́кцию*) to churn out; ~ (*impf*) от себя́ to drive off *или* away; ~ (*impf*) кого́-н с +*instr* to rush sb with; **гони́те де́ньги/еду́!** (*разг*) give us your money/some food!

▶ **гна́ться** *несов возв*: **гна́ться за** +*instr* (*преследовать*) to pursue; (*добиваться*) to strive after.

гнев (-а) *м* wrath; **быть** (*impf*) **в гне́ве** to be in a rage.

гне́ва|ться (-юсь) *несов возв* to be angry.

гне́вен *прил см* **гне́вный**.

гневи́ть (-лю́, -йшь) *несов перех* to anger; **не ~й Бо́га!** ≈ you should count your blessings!

гне́в|ный (-ен, -на́, -но) *прил* wrathful.

гнедо́й *прил* (*масть лошади*) bay.

гнезди́ться (*3sg* -и́тся, *3pl* -я́тся) *несов возв* (*птицы*) to nest; (*мысль, чувство*) to take root.

гнезд|о́ (-а́; *nom pl* гнёзда, *gen pl* гнёзд) *ср* (*у птиц*) nest; (*для патронов*) socket, pocket; (*для посуды*) compartment; (*линг*) word family; **вить** (**свить** *perf*) ~ to build a nest.

гнездо́вье (-я) *ср* nesting.

гне|сти́ (-ту́, -тёшь) *несов перех* to gnaw.

гнёт (-а) *м* (*бедности итп*) yoke; **под ~ом** under the yoke.

гнету́щий (-ая, -ее, -ие) *прил* depressing.

гни́д|а (-ы) *ж* nit; (*разг: пренебр*) louse.

гнил|о́й (-, -á, -о) *прил* (*продукты, ткань итп*) rotten; (*климат*) unhealthy; (*перен: настроения, теория*) decadent.

гниль (-и) *ж* rotten stuff.

гни|ть (-ю́, -ёшь; *perf* **сгнить**) *несов неперех* to rot.

гно|и́ть (-ю́, -и́шь; *perf* **сгнои́ть**) *несов перех* to let rot.

▶ **гнои́ться** *несов возв* (*рана*) to discharge.

гной (-я) *м* pus.

гнойни́к (-á) *м* boil.

гном (-а) *м* gnome.

гнуса́в|ить (-лю, -ишь) *несов неперех* to talk through one's nose.

гнуса́в|ый (-, -а, -о) *прил* (*голос, тон*) affected and nasal.

гну́сен *прил см* **гну́сный**.

гну́снос|ть (-и) *ж* (*клеветы, поведения*) vileness; (*поступок*) vile thing.

гну́с|ный (-ен, -на́, -но) *прил* vile.

гн|у́ть (-у, -ёшь; *perf* **согну́ть**) *несов перех* to bend; ~ (*impf*) **свою́ ли́нию** (*разг*) to have things one's own way; **куда́** *или* **к чему́ он ~ёт?** (*разг*) what's he driving at?; ~ (*impf*) **спи́ну на кого́-н** to slave away for sb

▶ **гну́ться** *несов возв* (*ветка, полка*) to bend.

гнуша́|ться (-юсь; *perf* **погнуша́ться**) *несов возв* (+*gen*) to abhor; **ниче́м не** ~ (*impf*) to have no scruples whatsoever.

гобеле́н (-а) *м* tapestry.

гобо́|й (-я) *м* oboe.

гове́|ть (-ю) *несов неперех to fast and attend church in preparation for confession and*

Communion.

говн|о́ (-á) *ср* (*груб!*) shit (*!*)

го́вор (-а) *м* (*линг*) dialect; (*звуки разговора*) voices *мн*.

говор|и́ть (-ю́, -и́шь; *perf* **сказа́ть**) *несов перех* to say; (*правду*) to tell ♦ *неперех* to speak, talk; (*обсуждать*): ~ **о** +*prp* to discuss, talk about; (*общаться*): ~ **с** +*instr* to talk to *или* with; **~я́т** it's said, they say; ~ (*impf*) **по-ру́сски** to speak Russian; **что вы ~и́те?** you don't say!, really?; **не ~я́ (уже́) о** +*prp* not to mention; **что и ~!** (*разг*) what else is there to say?; **что ни ~и́!** (*разг*) say what you like!; **коро́че** *или* **коро́тко ~я́** in short; **стро́го ~я́** strictly speaking; **открове́нно ~я́** to be frank; **по пра́вде ~я́** to tell (you) the truth; **ина́че ~я́** in other words

▶ **говори́ться** *несов возв* (*произноситься*) to be said; **как ~и́тся** as they say.

говорли́в|ый (-, -а, -о) *прил* talkative.

говя́дин|а (-ы) *ж* beef.

го́гот (-а) *м* (*гусей*) honking; (*разг: пренебр*) guffaw.

гого|та́ть (-чу́, -чешь; *perf* **прогогота́ть**) *несов неперех* (*см сущ*) to honk; to guffaw.

год (-а; *part gen* -у, *loc sg* -ý, *nom pl* -ы, *gen pl* -о́в/ лет) *м* year; **прошло́ 3 го́да/5 лет** 3/5 years passed; **из го́да в** ~ year in year out; **кру́глый** ~ all year round; **с ~а́ми** with the years; **от го́да** from year to year; *см также* **го́ды**.

года́ми *нареч* for years.

го́ден *прил см* **го́дный**.

год|и́ться (-жу́сь, -ди́шься) *несов возв* (+*dat*) to suit; ~ (*impf*) **в** +*nom pl* to be (well) suited to be; ~ (*impf*) **для** +*gen* to be suitable for; **куда́ э́то ~ди́тся?** (*разг*) what good is this?; ~ (*impf*) **в отцы́/в ма́тери кому́-н** to be old enough to be sb's father/mother; ~ (*impf*) **в сыновья́ кому́-н** to be young enough to be sb's son.

го́дность (-и) *ж* suitability; (*билета*) validity; **срок ~и** shelf life.

го́д|ный (-ен, -на́, -но) *прил*: ~ **к** +*dat или* **для** +*gen* fit *или* suitable for; **биле́т ~ен до ...** the ticket is valid until ....

годовщи́н|а (-ы) *ж* anniversary; ~ **со дня́ сме́рти кого́-н** the anniversary of sb's death.

го́ды (-о́в) *мн*: **де́тские/вое́нные** ~ childhood/ war years; **он уже́ в года́х** he's getting on (in years) now; **пятидеся́тые** ~ the Fifties *или* 1950s.

гожу́сь *несов см* **годи́ться**.

Гозна́к (-а) *м сокр* = *Гла́вное управле́ние произво́дством госуда́рственных зна́ков, моне́т и ордено́в*.

гол (-а; *nom pl* -ы́) *м* goal; **забива́ть (заби́ть** *perf*) ~ to score a goal.

голеносто́пный *прил*: ~ **суста́в** ankle.

го́лен|ь (-и) *ж* shin; (*у животного*) shank.

голки́пер (-а) *м* goalkeeper.

голла́нд|ец (-ца) *м* Dutchman (*мн* Dutchmen).
Голла́нди|я (-и) *ж* Holland.
голла́нд|ка (-ки; *gen pl* -ок) *ж* Dutchwoman (*мн* Dutchwomen).
голла́ндск|ий (-ая, -ое, -ие) *прил* Dutch; ~ язы́к Dutch; „Г~ аукцио́н" (*комм*) Dutch auction.
голла́ндца *итп сущ см* **голла́ндец**.
Голливу́д (-а) *м* Hollywood.
гол|ова́ (-овы́; *acc sg* -ову, *dat sg* -ове́, *nom pl* -овы, *gen pl* -о́в, *dat pl* -ова́м) *ж* head; **с ~овы́ до ног** from head to foot; **его́ имя́ вы́летало у меня́ из ~овы́** his name slipped my mind; **на ~ову вы́ше кого́-н** head and shoulders above sb; **де́лать (сде́лать** *perf*) **что-н на свою́/чью-н го́лову** (*разг*) to make matters worse for o.s./sb; **они́ де́йствовали че́рез мою́/его́ го́лову** they acted over my/his head.
голове́ш|ка (-ки; *gen pl* -ок) *ж* smouldering (*BRIT*) *или* smoldering (*US*) log.
голо́в|ка (-ки; *gen pl* -ок) *ж* (*гвоздя́*) head; (*чеснока́*) bulb; ~ **лу́ка** onion.
головно́й *прил* (*плато́к итп*) head *опред*; (*отря́д*) front *опред*; (*предприя́тие*) main; **головно́й мозг** brain.
голо́вок *сущ см* **голо́вка**.
головокруже́ни|е (-я) *ср* giddiness.
головокружи́тельный *прил* (*высота́*) dizzy; (*карье́ра*) breath-taking.
головоло́м|ка (-ки; *gen pl* -ок) *ж* (*та́кже перен*) puzzle; **задава́ть (зада́ть** *perf*) **(кому́-н) ~ку** (*перен*) to pose a problem (to sb).
головомо́йк|а (-и) *ж* (*разг*) telling off.
головоре́з (-а) *м* (*банди́т*) cutthroat.
го́лод (-а) *м* hunger; (*дли́тельное недоеда́ние*) starvation; (*ма́ссовое бе́дствие*) famine; (*перен*): **кни́жный/бума́жный ~** severe shortage of books/paper; **умира́ть (умере́ть** *perf*) **с ~у** *или* **от ~а** to die of hunger.
голода́ни|е (-я) *ср* starvation; (*воздержа́ние*) fasting; **кислоро́дное ~** oxygen deficiency.
голода́|ть (-ю) *несов неперех* to starve; (*возде́рживаться от пи́щи*) to fast.
голо́дный (-оден, -одна́, -одно) *прил* hungry; (*год, вре́мя*) hunger-stricken; (*край*) barren; **~дные бо́ли** hunger pangs; **~одная смерть** death from starvation.
голодо́в|ка (-ки; *gen pl* -ок) *ж* hunger strike; (*разг*) famine; **объявля́ть (объяви́ть** *perf*) **~ку** to go on hunger strike.
гололёд (-а) *м* (*на доро́гах*) black ice.
гололе́диц|а (-ы) *ж* (*на дере́вьях*) ice; (*на доро́гах*) black ice.
го́лос (-а; *part sg* -у, *nom pl* -а́) *м* voice; (*в хо́ре*) part; (*кро́ви*) the call; (*полит*) vote; **~ рассу́дка/со́вести** the voice of reason/conscience; **подава́ть (пода́ть** *perf*) **~** to vote; **пра́во ~а** the right to vote; **в оди́н ~** with one voice; **во весь ~** at the top of one's voice; *см та́кже* **голоса́**.
голос|а́ (-о́в) *мн foreign-controlled radio*

stations *broadcasting to the Soviet Union*.
голоси́ст|ый (-, -а, -о) *прил* loud.
голосло́в|ный (-ен, -на, -но) *прил* unsubstantiated.
голосова́ни|е (-я) *ср* ballot, vote; **откры́тое/та́йное ~** open/secret ballot; **манда́тное** *или* **представи́тельское ~** card *или* block vote.
голос|ова́ть (-у́ю; *perf* **проголосова́ть**) *несов неперех* to vote; (*разг*) to hitch (a lift); **~ (проголосова́ть** *perf*) **за** +*acc*/**про́тив** +*gen* to vote for/against.
голосов|о́й *прил* vocal; **~ы́е свя́зки** vocal chords.
голубе́|ть (-ю) *несов неперех* to show blue; (*perf* **поголубе́ть**) to turn blue.
голуб|е́ц (-ца́) *м* (*обы́чно мн*) stuffed cabbage leaf.
голуби́к|а (-и) *ж* great bilberry.
голу́бк|а (-и) *ж* (*обраще́ние*) pet.
голуб|о́й *прил* light blue ◆ (-о́го; *decl like adj*) *м* (*разг: гомосексуали́ст*) gay; **голуба́я мечта́** pipe dream; **голубо́й экра́н** small screen.
голу́бушк|а (-и) *ж см* **голу́бчик**.
голубца́ *итп сущ см* **голубе́ц**.
голу́бчик (-а) *м* (*разг*) (my) dear.
го́луб|ь (-я; *gen pl* -е́й) *м* pigeon; dove; ~ **ми́ра** dove of peace.
голубя́т|ня (-ни; *gen pl* -ен) *ж* pigeon loft; dovecot.
го́л|ый (-, -а́, -о) *прил* (*челове́к*) naked; (*че́реп*) bald; (*де́рево, сте́ны*) bare; (*no short form*; *пра́вда*) naked; (*ци́фры, фа́кты*) bare; **~ыми рука́ми** with one's bare hands; **его́ ~ыми рука́ми не возьмёшь** (*перен*) he's a slippery character; **го́лый про́вод** bare wire.
голышо́м *нареч* starkers.
гол|ь (-и) *ж собир* rabble; ~ **на вы́думки хитра́** ≈ necessity is the mother of invention.
гольф (-а) *м* golf; (*обы́чно мн: чулки́*) knee sock; *см та́кже* **го́льфы**.
го́льф|ы (-ов) *мн* (*брю́ки*) plus-fours *мн*.
гомеопа́т (-а) *м* homoeopath (*BRIT*), homeopath (*US*).
гомеопати́ческ|ий (-ая, -ое, -ие) *прил* homoeopathic (*BRIT*), homeopathic (*US*); **~ая до́за** (*перен*) tiny amount.
гомеопа́ти|я (-и) *ж* homoeopathy (*BRIT*), homeopathy (*US*).
гомери́ческ|ий (-ая, -ое, -ие) *прил*: ~ **смех** *или* **хо́хот** roar of laughter.
гомоге́нный *прил* homogenous.
го́мон (-а) *м* (*толпы́*) hubbub; **пти́чий ~** chorus of birdsong; **поднима́ть (подня́ть** *perf*) **~** to make a din.
гомосексуали́зм (-а) *м* homosexuality.
гомосексуали́ст (-а) *м* homosexual.
гонг (-а) *м* gong; **уда́рить** (*perf*) **в ~** to beat a gong.
гондо́л|а (-ы) *ж* gondola; (*дирижа́бля*) car (*of airship*).

Гондура́с (-а) *м* Honduras.
гоне́ни|е (-я) *ср* persecution; **подверга́ться**
(**подве́ргнуться** *perf*) **~ям** to be persecuted; **~я**
на кого́-н/что-н persecution of sb/sth.
гоне́|ц (-ца́) *м* messenger.
го́н|ка (-ки; *gen pl* -ок) *ж* (*разг*: спешка) rush;
(*обычно мн*: соревнования) racing; **го́нка**
вооруже́ний arms race.
Гонко́нг (-а) *м* Hong Kong.
го́нок *итп сущ см* **го́нка**.
го́нор (-а) *м* arrogance.
гонора́р (-а) *м* fee; **а́вторский ~** royalty.
гоноре́|я (-и) *ж* gonorrhoea (*BRIT*), gonorrhea
(*US*).
го́ночный *прил* racing *опред*; **го́ночный**
велосипе́д racer.
гонт (-а) *м* (*СТРОИТ*) shingles *мн*.
гонца́ *итп сущ см* **гоне́ц**.
гонча́р (-а́) *м* potter.
го́нч|ая (-ей; *decl like adj*) *ж* hound.
го́нщик (-а) *м* (*автомобиля*) racing (*BRIT*) *или*
race car (*US*) driver; (*велосипеда*) racing cyclist.
гоню́(сь) *итп несов см* **гнать(ся)**.
гоня́|ть (-ю, -ешь) *несов перех* (*стадо*) to drive;
(*птиц, поклонников*) to chase off *или* away;
(*разг*: курьера) to keep on the go; (: мяч) to
knock about; (: ученика) to grill ◆ *неперех* to
race; **~** (*impf*) **голубе́й** (*СПОРТ*) to race pigeons;
(*перен*: *разг*) to loaf around; **~** (*impf*) **чай** (*разг*)
to lounge around drinking tea
▶ **гоня́ться** *несов возв*: **~ся за** +*instr*
(*преследовать*) to chase (after); (*перен*) to
pursue.
гоп-компа́ни|я (-и) *ж* (*разг*) rowdy bunch.
гор. *сокр* = **го́род, городско́й**.
гор|а́ (*acc sg* -у, *gen sg* -ы́, *nom pl* -ы, *dat pl* -а́м) *ж*
mountain; (*небольшая*) hill; (*перен*: *разг*) heap;
идти́ (**пойти́** *perf*) **в го́ру** to go uphill; (*перен*:
разг: улучшаться) to be looking up; (: делать
карьеру) to go up in the world; **идти́** (**пойти́**
perf) **под ~у** (*также перен*: *разг*) to go
downhill; **у меня́ ~ с плеч свали́лась** (*разг*)
that's a weight off my mind; **обеща́ть** (*impf*)
золоты́е го́ры to promise the earth; **стоя́ть**
(*impf*) **~ой за кого́-н** (*разг*) to stand up for sb;
пир ~ой (*разг*) celebratory blowout; *см также*
го́ры.
гора́зд (-а, -о) *как сказ* (*разг*): **~ на что-н**/+*infin*
very good at sth/at doing; **кто во что ~** (*разг*:
пренебр) everyone doing his own thing.
гора́здо *нареч* much.
горб (-а́; *loc sg* -у́) *м* hump; **тащи́ть** (*impf*) **всё на**
~у́ (*перен*: *разг*) to take everything upon o.s.;
испы́тывать (**испыта́ть** *perf*) **что-н на своём**
~у́ (*разг*) to learn sth the hard way; **он**
зарабо́тал всё свои́м ~о́м (*разг*) he earned
everything through his own hard graft.
горба́т|ый (-, -а, -о) *прил* (*человек*)

hunchbacked; (*нос*) hooked; **~ого моги́ла**
испра́вит he *итп* will never change, ≈ a leopard
can't change his spots.
горби́н|ка (-ки; *gen pl* -ок) *ж*: **нос с ~кой** Roman
nose.
го́рб|ить (-лю, -ишь; *perf* **сго́рбить**) *несов*
перех: **~ спи́ну** to stoop.
▶ **го́рбиться** (*perf* **сго́рбиться**) *несов возв* to
stoop; (*от старости*) to develop a stoop.
горбоно́с|ый (-, -а, -о) *прил* hooknosed.
горбу́н (-а́) *м* hunchback.
горбу́нь|я (-и) *ж см* **горбу́н**.
горбу́ш|а (-и) *ж* (hunchback) salmon.
горбу́ш|ка (-ки; *gen pl* -ек) *ж* crust.
горделѝв|ый (-, -а, -о) *прил* proud.
горд|и́ться (-жу́сь, -ди́шься) *несов возв* (+*instr*)
to be proud of.
го́рдост|ь (-и) *ж* pride; (+*instr*; *победой*,
успехами) pride in; **он ~ на́шей семьи́** he's
the pride and joy of the family.
го́рд|ый (-, -а́, -о, -ы́) *прил* proud; (+*instr*;
победой, успехами) proud of.
го́р|е (-я) *ср* (*скорбь*) grief, sorrow; (*несчастье*)
misfortune; **хлебну́ть** (*perf*) **~я** (*разг*) to suffer
one's share of misfortune; **помога́ть** (**помо́чь**
perf) **~ю** to help out in times of trouble; **с ~я**
with *или* from grief; **в ~** in (one's) grief; **как на**
~ (*разг*) as ill luck would have it; **~ ты моё!**
you'll be the death of me!; **ему́ и ~я ма́ло**
(*разг*) he couldn't care less.
горева́ть (-ю́ю) *несов неперех* to grieve; **~**
(*impf*) **о** +*prp* to grieve for; **не ~ю́й!** cheer up!
го́рек *прил см* **го́рький**.
горе́л|ка (-ки; *gen pl* -ок) *ж* burner; **пая́льная ~**
blowtorch.
горе́лый *прил* burnt.
горелье́ф (-а) *м* high relief.
горемы́|ка (-и) *м/ж* (*разг*) poor soul.
го́рест|ный (-ен, -на, -но) *прил* sorrowful.
го́рест|ь (-и) *ж* grief, sorrow; (*обычно мн*:
несчастье) trouble.
горе́|ть (-ю, -ишь; *perf* **сгоре́ть**) *несов неперех*
to burn; (*no perf*; *дом, лес*) to be on fire;
(*больной, лоб*) to be burning hot; (*рана*) to
smart; (*глаза*) to shine; (+*instr*; *ненавистью*,
нетерпением) to burn with; **зака́т ~е́л** there
was a blazing sunset; **~** (*impf*) **от стыда́/**
любопы́тства to burn with shame/curiosity; **он**
~и́т на рабо́те he puts everything into his work;
план/спекта́кль ~и́т! the plan/play is in danger
of being a complete failure!; **~и́ всё си́ним**
огнём *или* **пла́менем!** (*разг*) to hell with it!; **не**
~и́т! there's no hurry; **у меня́ душа́ ~и́т**
I'm bursting with enthusiasm.
го́р|ец (-ца) *м* mountain dweller.
го́реч|ь (-и) *ж* bitter taste; (*потери*) bitterness.
горже́т|ка (-ки; *gen pl* -ок) *ж* boa.
горжу́сь *несов см* **горди́ться**.

горизо́нт (-а) м horizon; **появля́ться (появи́ться** perf**) на чьём-н ~е** to come into sb's life.

горизонта́лен прил см **горизонта́льный**.

горизонта́л|ь (-и) ж horizontal; (на карте) contour; (на шахматной доске) rank.

горизонта́льный (-ен, -ьна, -ьно) прил horizontal.

гори́лл|а (-ы) ж gorilla.

горисполко́м (-а) м сокр (ИСТ: = городско́й исполни́тельный комите́т) town или city executive complex.

гори́стый прил mountainous.

го́р|ка (-ки; gen pl -ок) ж hill; (склон) slope; (шкаф) cabinet; (кучка) small pile; (АВИА) steep climb.

го́ркн|уть (3sg -ет, perf **прого́ркнуть**) несов неперех (масло) to go rancid.

горко́м (-а) м сокр (ИСТ: = городско́й комите́т) town или city committee.

горла́н|ить (-ю, -ишь) несов неперех (разг) to bawl.

горла́стый (-, -а, -о) прил (разг) noisy.

горли́ц|а (-ы) ж turtledove.

го́рл|о (-а) ср throat; (у сосуда) neck; **стать** (perf) **поперёк ~а кому́-н** (перен: разг) to stick in sb's throat; **во всё ~** (разг) at the top of one's voice; **пристава́ть (приста́ть** perf**) к кому́-н с ножо́м к ~у** (разг: пренебр) to pester the life out of sb; **у меня́ рабо́ты по ~** (разг) I'm up to my ears in work; **я сыт по ~** (разг) I'm stuffed; (: перен: обеща́ниями, упрёками) I've had it up to here.

го́рлыш|ко (-ка; nom pl -ки, gen pl -ек) ср (бутылки, сосуда) neck.

гормо́н (-а) м hormone.

гормона́льный прил hormonal.

горн (-а) м (для переплавки) furnace; (для обжига) kiln; (МУЗ) bugle.

горни́ст (-а) м bugler.

го́рничн|ая (-ой; decl like adj) ж chambermaid.

горно-бурово́й прил mining опред, mine-excavation опред.

горнодобыва́ющий (-ая, -ее, -ие) прил mining опред.

горнозаво́дск|ий (-ая, -ое, -ие) прил mining опред.

горнолы́жный прил ski опред.

горнопромы́шленный прил = **горнозаво́дский**.

горнопрохо́дческ|ий (-ая, -ое, -ие) прил: **~ие рабо́ты** tunnelling work ед.

горнорабо́ч|ий (-его; decl like adj) м miner.

горноспаса́тельный прил mountain-rescue опред.

горноста́|й (-я) м stoat; (мех) ermine.

го́рн|ый прил mountain опред; (лыжи) downhill опред; (страна) mountainous; (богатства) mineral опред; (промышленность) mining опред; **~ые поро́ды** rocks; **~ хруста́ль** rock crystal; **го́рная боле́знь** altitude sickness;

го́рный хребе́т mountain range.

горня́к (-а́) м (рабочий) miner; (инженер) mining engineer.

го́род (-а; nom pl -а́) м (большой) city; (небольшой) town; **е́хать (пое́хать** perf**) за́ город** to go out of town; **жить** (impf) **за́ городом** to live out of town.

горо|ди́ть (-жу́, -ди́шь) несов перех: **~ ерунду́** или **вздор** или **чушь** (разг: пренебр) to talk rubbish.

горо|до́к (-ка́) м small town; **спорти́вный ~** sports complex; **вое́нный ~** military settlement; **университе́тский ~** (university) campus; **де́тский ~** playground.

городско́й прил urban; (сад) municipal; **~ жи́тель** town dweller; (большого города) city dweller.

горожа́н|ин (-ина, nom pl -е, gen pl -) м city dweller.

горожа́н|ка (-ки; gen pl -ок) ж см **горожа́нин**.

горожу́ несов см **городи́ть**.

го́рок сущ см **го́рка**.

гороско́п (-а) м horoscope.

горо́х (-а; part gen -у) м собир peas мн; (на платье итп) polka dots мн; **как об сте́ну ~** like talking to a brick wall.

горо́ховый прил (суп) pea; **шут ~** (разг: пренебр) buffoon.

горо́ш|ек (-ка) м собир peas мн; (на платье итп) polka dots мн; **ткань в ~** spotted material; **зелёный ~** garden peas мн; **души́стый ~** sweet pea.

горо́шин|а (-ы) ж pea.

горо́шка итп сущ см **горо́шек**.

горсове́т (-а) м сокр (= городско́й сове́т) ≈ town или city council.

го́рст|ка (-ки; gen pl -ок) ж (также перен) handful.

горст|ь (-и; gen pl -е́й) ж (руки) cupped hand; (также перен) handful.

горта́нный прил guttural.

горта́н|ь (-и) ж larynx.

горте́нзи|я (-и) ж hydrangea.

го́рца итп сущ см **го́рец**.

го́рче сравн прил от **го́рький** ♦ сравн нареч от **го́рько**.

горч|и́ть (3sg -и́т, 3pl -а́т) несов неперех to taste bitter.

горчи́ц|а (-ы) ж mustard.

горчи́чник (-а) м mustard plaster.

горчи́чный прил mustard.

го́рше сравн прил от **го́рький** ♦ сравн нареч от **го́рько**.

горшо́к (-ка́) м pot; (также: ночно́й ~) chamber pot; **цвето́чный ~** flowerpot.

го́р|ы (-; dat pl -а́м) мн mountains мн.

го́р|ький (-ькая, -ькое, -ькие; -ек, -ька́, -ько) прил (вкус, разочарова́ние) bitter; (обида, событие) painful; **го́рькая и́стина** the painful truth; **го́рький пья́ница** (разг) a hopeless drunkard; **го́рькие слёзы** bitter tears; **го́рький**

смех bitter laughter.
го́рько нареч (плакать) bitterly ♦ как сказ: **во рту** ~ I have a bitter taste in my mouth; **мне** ~, **что меня́ не понима́ют** I feel bitter that nobody understands me.
горю́ч|ее (-его; decl like adj) ср fuel.
горю́ч|ий (-ая, -ее, -ие) прил flammable; ~**ие слёзы** bitter tears.
горя́чек сущ см **горя́чка**.
горя́ч|ий (-ая, -ее, -ие; -, -а́, -о́) прил hot; (перен: любовь) passionate; (: спор) heated; (: желание) burning; (: человек) hot-tempered; (день итп) hectic; ~ **хара́ктер** hot temper; **де́лать (сде́лать** perf) **что-н по** ~**им следа́м** to do sth without delay; **я попа́л ему́ под** ~**ую ру́ку** I caught him while he was in a bad mood; **горя́чая то́чка** trouble spot.
горя́ч|и́ться (-у́сь, -и́шься; perf **разгорячи́ться**) несов возв to get worked up.
горя́ч|ка (-ки; gen pl -ек) ж (разг) frenzy; **поро́ть** (impf) ~**ку** to rush.
горя́чность (-и) ж irascibility.
горячо́ нареч (спорить, любить) passionately ♦ как сказ it's hot.
Госба́нк (-а) м сокр (= госуда́рственный банк) state bank.
госбезопа́сность (-и) ж сокр (ИСТ: = госуда́рственная безопа́сность) national security.
госбюдже́т (-а) м сокр (= госуда́рственный бюдже́т) state budget.
госдепарта́мент (-а) м сокр (= госуда́рственный департа́мент) State Department.
Госкомизда́т м сокр = Госуда́рственный комите́т Сове́та Мини́стров по дела́м изда́тельства полигра́фии и кни́жной торго́вли.
госкомите́т (-а) м сокр (= госуда́рственный комите́т) state committee.
госкреди́т (-а) м сокр (= госуда́рственный креди́т) state credit.
госпитализи́р|овать (-ую) (не)сов перех to hospitalize.
го́спиталь (-я) м army hospital.
Госпла́н м сокр (ИСТ: = Госуда́рственная пла́новая коми́ссия) state planning committee.
господа́ итп сущ см **господи́н**.
го́споди межд: **Г**~! good Lord!
госпо́д|ин (-одина; nom pl -одá, gen pl -óд) м gentleman (мн gentlemen); (хозяин) master; (при обращении) sir; (при фамилии, звании) Mr (= Mister).
госпо́дств|о (-а) ср supremacy; (над страной) dominion; (идей) predominance.
госпо́дств|овать (-ую) несов неперех to rule; (мнение) to prevail; ~ (impf) **на мо́ре** to rule the seas; ~ (impf) **над** +instr (местностью) to tower

above, dominate.
госпо́дствующ|ий (-ая, -ее, -ие) прил (партия, класс) ruling; (взгляды) prevailing; (гора, башня итп) imposing.
Госпо́дь (Го́спода; voc Го́споди) м (также: ~ **Бог**) the Lord; **не дай Го́споди!** God forbid!; **сла́ва тебе́ Го́споди!** Glory be to God!; (разг) thank God!
госпож|а́ (-и́) ж lady; (хозяйка) mistress; (при обращении, звании) Madam; (при фамилии: замужняя) Mrs; (: незамужняя) Miss; (: замужняя или незамужняя) Ms.
Госстра́х (-а) м сокр (= Гла́вное управле́ние госуда́рственного страхова́ния Министе́рства фина́нсов России) department dealing with national insurance.
госстра́х (-а) м сокр (= госуда́рственное страхова́ние) ≈ national insurance.
ГОСТ (-а) м сокр (= госуда́рственный общесою́зный станда́рт) standard manufacturing specifications under the Soviet system.
гост (-а) м сокр = **ГОСТ**.
гостеприи́м|ный (-ен, -на, -но) прил hospitable.
гости́н|ая (-ой; decl like adj) ж living или sitting room, lounge (BRIT); (мебель) living-room suite.
гости́ниц|а (-ы) ж hotel.
го|сти́ть (-щу́, -сти́шь) несов неперех to stay.
гост|ь (-я; gen pl -е́й) м guest; **идти́ (пойти́** perf) **в го́сти к кому́-н** to go to see sb; **быть** (impf) **в** ~**я́х у кого́-н** to be at sb's house; **в** ~**я́х хорошо́, а до́ма лу́чше** there's no place like home.
го́сть|я (-и; gen pl -ий) ж см **гость**.
госуда́рственн|ый прил state опред; ~ **язы́к** official language; ~ **строй** government system; **госуда́рственное пра́во** public law; **госуда́рственный экза́мен** Finals мн.
госэкза́мен (-а) м сокр (= госуда́рственный экза́мен) ≈ finals мн.
госуда́рств|о (-а) ср state.
госуда́рын|я (-и; gen pl -ь) ж sovereign; (при обращении) Your Majesty; **ми́лостивая** ~ Madam.
госуда́р|ь (-я) м sovereign; (при обращении) Your Majesty; **ми́лостивый** ~ Sir.
го́тик|а (-и) ж Gothic.
готи́ческ|ий (-ая, -ое, -ие) прил Gothic.
готова́льн|я (-ьни; gen pl -ен) ж (архитектора) drawing instruments мн; (школьника) geometry set.
гото́в|ить (-лю, -ишь; perf **пригото́вить**) несов перех to get ready; (уроки, обед) to prepare; **make**; (perf **подгото́вить**) (специалиста) to train; (ученика) to coach ♦ неперех to cook; **она́ хорошо́** ~**ит** she's a good cook

▶ **готóвиться** (*perf* **приготóвиться**) *несов возв*: **~ся к** +*dat* (*к отъезду*) to get ready for; **~ся** (**подготóвиться** *perf*) **к** +*dat* (*к экзамену*) to prepare for; **~ятся больши́е собы́тия/ измене́ния** great events/changes are in the offing.

готóвность (**-и**) *ж* readiness; **~** +*infin* readiness *или* willingness to do; **в боево́й ~и** ready for action.

готóво *как сказ* that's it.

готóв|**ый** (**-**, **-а**, **-о**) *прил* (*обед*) ready; (*no short form*; *изделие*) ready-made; **~ к** +*dat*/+*infin* prepared for/to do; **~ на перегово́ры** prepared *или* willing to negotiate; **~ на всё** ready for anything; **она́ живёт на всём ~ом** her every need is catered for; **гото́вое пла́тье** off-the-peg (*BRIT*) *или* off-the -rack (*US*) dress.

гофриро́ванный *прил* (*юбка*) pleated; (*жесть*) corrugated.

гофрир|**ова́ть** (**-у́ю**) *несов перех* (*см прил*) to pleat; to corrugate.

гощу́ *несов см* **гости́ть**.

ГПТУ *ср сокр* (= **городско́е профессиона́льно-техни́ческое учи́лище**) ≈ CTC (= city technology college).

гр. *сокр* (= **гра́дус**) d. (= *degree*); (= **граждани́н**) Mr (= *Mister*); (= **гражда́нка**) Mrs; = **гру́ппа**.

граб (**-а**) *м* hornbeam.

граб|**ёж** (**-ежа́**) *м* (*также перен*) robbery; (*дома*) burglary; **~ среди́ бе́ла дня** (*разг*) daylight robbery.

гра́бель *сущ см* **гра́бли**.

граби́тел|**ь** (**-я**) *м* (*см сущ*) robber; burglar.

граби́тельск|**ий** (**-ая**, **-ое**, **-ие**) *прил* (*цены*) extortionate; **~ое нападе́ние** (*на дом*) burglary; (*на банк*) robbery; (*на страну*) pillage.

граб|**ить** (**-лю**, **-ишь**; *perf* **огра́бить**) *несов перех* (*также перен*: *человека*) to rob; (*дом*) to burgle; (*город*) to pillage.

гра́б|**ли** (**-ель** *или* **-лей**) *мн* rake *ед*.

гра́блю *несов см* **гра́бить**.

граве́р (**-а**) *м* engraver.

гра́ви|**й** (**-я**) *м* gravel.

гравир|**ова́ть** (**-у́ю**; *perf* **вы́гравировать**) *несов перех* to engrave ♦ *неперех* to etch.

гравита́ци|**я** (**-и**) *ж* gravitation.

гравю́р|**а** (**-ы**) *ж* (*оттиск*) engraving; (*офорт*) etching.

град (**-а**) *м* (*также перен*) hail; (*перен*): **~** +*gen* (*пуль*) hail of; (*упрёков*) stream of.

града́ци|**я** (**-и**) *ж* gradation.

гра́дин|**а** (**-ы**) *ж* hailstone.

гради́р|**ня** (**-ни**; *gen pl* **-ен**) *ж* cooling tower.

гра́дом *нареч* thick and fast; **кати́ться** (*impf*) **~** (*слёзы*) to stream down.

градострои́тел|**ь** (**-я**) *м* town (*BRIT*) *или* city (*US*) planner.

градострои́тельств|**о** (**-а**) *ср* town (*BRIT*) *или* city (*US*) planning.

гра́дус (**-а**) *м* degree; **под ~ом** (*разг*) tiddly.

гра́дусник (**-а**) *м* thermometer.

граждани́н (**-а**; *nom pl* **гра́ждане**, *gen pl* **гра́ждан**) *м* citizen.

гражда́н|**ка** (**-ки**; *gen pl* **-ок**) *ж см* **граждани́н**.

гражда́нск|**ий** (**-ая**, **-ое**, **-ие**) *прил* civil; (*долг*) civic; (*платье*) civilian; **гражда́нская война́** civil war; **гражда́нская панихи́да** civil funeral service; **гражда́нский ко́декс** civil code.

гражда́нств|**о** (**-а**) *ср* citizenship; **получа́ть** (**получи́ть** *perf*) **~** *или* **права́ гражда́нства** to be granted citizenship.

грамза́пис|**ь** (**-и**) *ж* recording; **о́пера в ~и** recording of an opera.

грамм (**-а**; *gen pl* **-** *или* **-ов**) *м* gramme (*BRIT*), gram (*US*); **у него́ (нет) ни гра́мма со́вести** (*разг*) he doesn't have an ounce of conscience.

грамма́тик|**а** (**-и**) *ж* grammar.

граммати́ческ|**ий** (**-ая**, **-ое**, **-ие**) *прил* (*ошибка*) grammatical; (*упражнение*) grammar *опред*.

гра́мот|**а** (**-ы**) *ж* reading and writing; (*документ*) certificate; **для меня́ э́то кита́йская ~** (*разг*) it's Greek *или* double Dutch (*BRIT*) to me; **почётная ~** certificate of merit.

гра́мот|**ный** (**-ен**, **-на**, **-но**) *прил* (*человек*) literate; (*текст*) properly *или* correctly written; (*специалист*, *план*) competent.

граммпласти́нк|**а** (**-и**) *ж* gramophone (*BRIT*) *или* phonograph (*US*) record.

грана́т (**-а**) *м* (*плод*) pomegranate; (*дерево*) pomegranate (tree); (*минерал*) garnet.

грана́т|**а** (**-ы**) *ж* grenade.

грана́товый *прил* (*сок*) pomegranate *опред*; (*браслет*) garnet *опред*; (*цвет*) deep red.

гранатомёт (**-а**) *м* grenade launcher.

грандио́з|**ный** (**-ен**, **-на**, **-но**) *прил* (*сооружение*) grand; (*масштабы*, *планы*) grandiose.

гранёный *прил* (*стакан*) cut-glass *опред*; (*алмаз*) cut *опред*.

грани́т (**-а**) *м* granite.

грани́тный *прил* (*плита*) granite.

гран|**и́ть** (**-ю́**, **-и́шь**) *несов перех* to cut.

грани́ц|**а** (**-ы**) *ж* (*государства*) border; (*участка*) boundary; (*обычно мн*: *перен*) limit; **е́хать** (**пое́хать** *perf*) **за ~у** to go abroad; **жить** (*impf*) **за ~ей** to live abroad; **из-за ~ы** from abroad; **в ~х прили́чия/зако́на** within the bounds of decency/the law; **его́ поведе́ние перехо́дит все ~ы!** he's gone too far!

грани́ч|**ить** (**-у**, **-ишь**) *несов неперех*: **~ с** +*instr* to border on; (*перен*) to verge on.

гра́н|**ка** (**-ки**; *gen pl* **-ок**) *ж* (*типог*) proof.

гра́нул|**а** (**-ы**) *ж* granule.

гра́н|**ь** (**-и**) *ж* (*ГЕОМ*) face; (*алмаза*) facet; (*перен*) bounds *мн*; **переступа́ть** (**переступи́ть** *perf*) **~** to overstep the mark; **на гра́ни** +*gen* on the brink *или* verge of.

граф (**-а**) *м* count, earl (*BRIT*).

графа́ (**-ы́**) *ж* column.

гра́фик (**-а**) *м* (*МАТ*) graph; (*план*) schedule,

timetable; (*худо́жник*) graphic artist; **рабо́тать**
(*impf*) по ~у to work to schedule; **по́езд идёт по**
~у the train is running to time; ~ **расчёта то́чки**
„нулево́й" при́были (*комм*) break-even chart.
гра́фик|а (**-и**) ж graphic art; (*бу́квы*) script ♦
собир (*рису́нки*) graphics мн.
графи́н (**-а**) м (*для воды́*) water jug; (*для вина́*)
decanter; (: *откры́тый*) carafe.
графи́н|я (**-и**) ж countess.
графи́т (**-а**) м (*минера́л*) graphite; (*грифель*)
(pencil) lead.
графи́|ть (**-лю́, -йшь**; *perf* **разграфи́ть**) несов
перех to rule (*lines*).
графи́ческий (**-ая, -ое, -ие**) прил graphic.
графлю́ несов см **графи́ть**.
гра́фств|о (**-а**) ср county.
грацио́зный (**-ен, -на, -но**) прил graceful.
гра́ци|я (**-и**) ж grace; (*корсе́т*) corset.
грач (**-а́**) м rook.
грёб итп несов см **грести́**.
гребён|ка (**-ки**; *gen pl* **-ок**) ж (*также тех*) comb;
стричь (*impf*) **всех под одну́** ~ку to lump
everyone together.
греб|ень (**-ня**) м comb; (*во́лны, го́ры*) crest.
греб|е́ц (**-ца́**) м oarsman (*мн* oarsmen), rower.
гребешо́|к (**-ка́**) м comb; (*также:* **морско́й** ~)
scallop.
гре́бл|я (**-и**) ж rowing.
гребно́й прил: ~ **спорт** rowing.
гре́бня итп сущ см **гре́бень**.
гребо́|к (**-ка**) м stroke.
гребу́ итп несов см **грести́**.
гребца́ итп сущ см **гребе́ц**.
гре́жу(сь) несов см **гре́зить(ся)**.
грё́з|а (**-ы**) ж (*обычно мн*) daydream.
гре́|зить (**-жу, -зишь**) несов неперех to (day)
dream, fantasize
▶ **гре́зиться** (*perf* **пригре́зиться**) несов возв:
ему́ ~зится... he dreams of ....
гре́йдер (**-а**) м grader; (*разг: доро́га*) dirt road.
гре́йпфрут (**-а**) м grapefruit.
грек (**-а**) м Greek (man) (*мн* men).
гре́л|ка (**-ки**; *gen pl* **-ок**) ж hot-water bottle;
электри́ческая ~ electric blanket.
греме́|ть (**-лю́, -йшь**; *perf* **прогреме́ть**) несов
неперех (*по́езд*) to thunder by; (*вы́стрелы*) to
thunder out; (*гром*) to rumble; (*перен*) to
resound; ~ (**прогреме́ть** *perf*) +*instr* (*ведро́м,*
кастрю́лями) to clatter; (*ключа́ми*) to jangle.
грему́чий (**-ая, -ее, -ие**) прил: ~ая **змея́**
rattlesnake; ~ **газ** firedamp.
Грена́д|а (**-ы**) ж Grenada.
гренадёр (**-а**; *gen pl* **-** *или* **-ов**) м (*солда́т*)
grenadier; **он настоя́щий** ~ (*разг*) he's a real
hulk.
гренка́ итп сущ см **грено́к**.
Гренла́нди|я (**-и**) ж Greenland.
гренла́ндск|ий (**-ая, -ое, -ие**) прил Greenlandic.

грен|о́к (**-ка́**; *nom pl* **-ки́**) м (*обы́чно мн*) crouton.
гре|сти́ (**-бу́, -бёшь**; *pt* **грёб, -бла́, -бло́**) несов
неперех to row; (*весло́м, рука́ми*) to paddle ♦
перех to rake.
гре|ть (**-ю**) несов перех (*подлеж: со́лнце, печь*)
to heat, warm; (: *шу́ба*) to keep warm; (*во́ду*) to
heat (up); (*ру́ки*) to warm; ~ (*impf*) **ру́ки на**
чём-н (*разг*) to line one's pockets with sth
▶ **гре́ться** несов возв (*челове́к*) to warm o.s.;
(*вода́*) to warm *или* heat up.
грех (**-а́**) м sin ♦ *как сказ*: ~ +*infin* (*разг*) it's a sin
to do; **как на** ~ (*разг*) as ill luck would have it;
от ~**а́ пода́льше** just to be on the safe side;
уйди́ от ~**а́ пода́льше!** go away and stay out of
trouble!; **с** ~**о́м попола́м** (*разг*) by a hair('s
breadth).
грехо́вный (**-ен, -на, -но**) прил sinful.
грехопаде́ни|е (**-я**) ж the Fall.
Гре́ци|я (**-и**) ж Greece.
гре́цк|ий (**-ая, -ое, -ие**) прил: ~ **оре́х** walnut.
греча́н|ка (**-ки**; *gen pl* **-ок**) ж Greek (woman) (*мн*
women).
гре́ческ|ий (**-ая, -ое, -ие**) прил Greek;
(*культу́ра*) (Ancient) Greek; ~ **язы́к** Greek.
гречи́х|а (**-и**) ж buckwheat.
гре́чк|а (**-и**) ж buckwheat.
гре́чневый прил buckwheat.
гре́шен прил см **гре́шный**.
греши́|ть (**-у́, -йшь**; *perf* **согреши́ть**) несов
неперех to sin; (*perf* **погреши́ть**;
противоре́чить): ~ **про́тив** +*gen* to sin against.
гре́шник (**-а**) м sinner.
гре́шниц|а (**-ы**) ж см **гре́шник**.
гре́шный (**-ен, -на, -но**) прил sinful.
гриб (**-а́**) м fungus (*мн* fungi); (*съедо́бный*)
(edible) mushroom; **несъедо́бный** ~ toadstool.
грибка́ итп сущ см **грибо́к**.
грибни́к (**-а́**) м mushroom picker.
грибни́ц|а (**-ы**) ж mushroom spore.
грибно́й прил (*суп*) mushroom; ~**о́е ме́сто** a
good place for mushrooms; **грибно́й дождь**
rain during sunshine.
грибо́|к (**-ка́**) м (*на ко́же*) fungal infection; (*на*
де́реве) fungus; (*на хле́бе итп*) mould;
(*укры́тие*) *mushroom-shaped shelter in a*
playground, on the beach etc.
гри́в|а (**-ы**) ж mane.
гри́венник (**-а**) м (*разг*) ten-kopeck piece.
грим (**-а**) м stage make-up, greasepaint.
грима́с|а (**-ы**) ж grimace; **стро́ить** (**состро́ить**
perf) *или* **ко́рчить** (**ско́рчить** *perf*) ~**ы** to make
или pull faces.
грима́снича|ть (**-ю**) несов неперех to make *или*
pull faces.
гримёр (**-а**) м make-up artist.
гримёрн|ая (**-ой**; *decl like adj*) ж dressing room.
гримиров|а́ть (**-у́ю**; *perf* **загримирова́ть**) несов
перех: ~ **кого́-н** to make sb up

▶ **гримирова́ться** (*perf* **загримирова́ться** *или* **нагримирова́ться**) *несов возв* to put on one's make-up.

грипп (**-а**) *м* flu.

гриппо́зный *прил* flu *опред*; **у больно́го ~ое состоя́ние** the patient has influenza.

гриф (**-а**) *м* (*ЗООЛ*) vulture; (*МИФОЛОГИЯ*) griffin; (*МУЗ*) fingerboard; (*штемпель*) stamp.

гри́фел|ь (**-я**) *м* (pencil)lead.

гроб (**-а**; *loc sg* **-у́**, *nom pl* **-ы́**) *м* coffin; **вгоня́ть** (**вогна́ть** *perf*) **кого́-н в ~** (*разг*) to drive sb to their grave; **в ~у́ я э́то ви́дел!** (*разг*) I don't give a damn about it!

гро́б|ить (**-лю, -ишь**; *perf* **угро́бить**) *несов перех* (*разг*) to screw up.

гробни́ц|а (**-ы**) *ж* tomb.

гробов|о́й *прил*: **~ го́лос** sepulchral tones *мн*; **гробово́е молча́ние** deathly silence; **гробова́я тишина́** deathly hush.

грог (**-а**; *part gen* **-у**) *м* grog.

грожу́(сь) *несов см* **грози́ть(ся)**.

гр|оза́ (**-озы́**; *nom pl* **-о́зы**) *ж* thunderstorm; (*перен*): **~ +gen** (*садов, звере́й*) threat to.

гроздь (**-и**; *gen pl* **-е́й**) *ж* (*виногра́да*) bunch; (*сире́ни*) cluster.

гро́зен *прил см* **гро́зный**.

гро|зи́ть (**-жу́, -зи́шь**) *несов неперех* (*no perf*; *опа́сность*) to loom; (*+instr*; *катастро́фой*) to be threatened by; (*perf* **погрози́ть**): **~ кому́-н чем-н** to threaten sb with sth; **~ (пригрози́ть** *perf*) **кому́-н разво́дом** to threaten sb with divorce; **он пригрози́л нача́льнику уйти́** he threatened the boss that he would resign

▶ **грози́ться** (*perf* **пригрози́ться**) *несов возв* to threaten.

гро́з|ный (**-ен, -на́, -но**) *прил* (*взгляд, письмо́*) threatening; (*проти́вник, ору́жие*) formidable; (*царь*) severe, harsh; (*учи́тель*) strict.

грозов|о́й *прил*: **~а́я ту́ча** storm cloud.

гром (**-а**; *gen pl* **-о́в**) *м* thunder; (*перен*) din; **пока́ ~ не гря́нет** (*разг*) until it's too late; **мета́ть** (*impf*) **гро́мы и мо́лнии** (*перен: разг*) to rant and rave.

грома́д|а (**-ы**) *ж* bulk.

грома́ден *прил см* **грома́дный**.

грома́дин|а (**-ы**) *ж* (*разг*) whopper, monster.

грома́дный *прил* enormous, huge.

гром|и́ть (**-лю́, -и́шь**) *несов перех* to destroy; (*перен: разг*) to slag (off).

гро́м|кий (**-кая, -кое, -кие; -ок, -ка, -ко**) *прил* (*голос*) loud; (*no short form*; *сканда́л*) big; (*имя, де́ло*) famous; (*слова́*) high-flown.

гро́мко *нареч* loudly.

громкоговори́тел|ь (**-я**) *м* (loud)speaker.

громлю́ *несов см* **громи́ть**.

громов|о́й *прил* (*го́лос*) thunderous; **~ы́е раска́ты** thunderclaps *мн*.

громогла́с|ный (**-ен, -на, -но**) *прил* very loud; **~ное заявле́ние** public announcement.

громозди́ть (**-жу́, -ди́шь**; *perf* **нагромозди́ть**) *несов перех* to pile up

▶ **громозди́ться** (*perf* **нагромозди́ться**) *несов возв* (*ска́лы*) to loom; **~ся** (**взгромозди́ться** *perf*) **на +acc** (*разг*) to clamber up onto.

громо́здкий (**-кая, -кое, -кие; -ок, -ка, -ко**) *прил* cumbersome; (*перен*) clumsy.

громозжу́(сь) *несов см* **громозди́ть(ся)**.

гро́мок *прил см* **гро́мкий**.

громоотво́д (**-а**) *м* lightning conductor.

гро́мче *сравн прил от* **гро́мкий** ◆ *сравн нареч от* **гро́мко**.

громыха́|ть (**-ю**; *perf* **прогромыха́ть**) *несов неперех* (*разг: гром*) to rumble; (*колёса*) to rattle; **~ (прогромыха́ть** *perf*) **+instr** (*кастрю́лями, ведро́м*) to clatter.

гроссме́йстер (**-а**) *м* grandmaster.

грот (**-а**) *м* (*пеще́ра*) grotto; (*па́рус*) mainsail.

гроте́ск (**-а**) *м* grotesque.

гро́х|нуть (**-у, -ешь**) *сов неперех* (*разг: вы́стрел*) to ring out; (: *рассмея́ться*) to go into stitches ◆ *перех* (*разг: ва́зу итп*) to smash; (: *мешо́к*) to bang down

▶ **гро́хнуться** (*impf* **гро́хаться**) *сов возв* (*разг*) to come crashing down.

гро́хот (**-а**) *м* racket.

грох|ота́ть (**-очу́, -о́чешь**; *perf* **прогрохота́ть**) *несов неперех* to rumble.

грош (**-а́**) *м* half-kopeck coin; **э́то сто́ит ~й** it costs next to nothing; **у меня́ нет ни ~а́** (*разг*) I'm stony broke; **~а́ ло́маного не сто́ит** (*разг*) it's not worth a brass farthing (*BRIT*) *или* a plugged nickel (*US*).

грошо́вый *прил* (*разг: вещь*) dirt-cheap; (*су́мма*) paltry; (*расчёты*) petty.

грубе́|ть (**-ю**; *perf* **огрубе́ть**) *несов неперех* (*челове́к*) to grow rude; (*душа́*) to grow hard; (*perf* **загрубе́ть**; *ко́жа*) to become rough; (*perf* **погрубе́ть**; *черты́*) to harden.

груб|и́ть (**-лю́, -и́шь**; *perf* **нагруби́ть**) *несов неперех* (**+dat**) to be rude to.

грубия́н (**-а**) *м* rude person (*мн* people).

грубия́н|ка (**-ки**; *gen pl* **-ок**) *ж см* **грубия́н**.

грублю́ *несов см* **груби́ть**.

гру́бо *нареч* (*отвеча́ть*) rudely; (*разгова́ривать*) crudely; (*обточи́ть, подсчита́ть*) roughly; **~ говоря́** roughly speaking.

гру́бост|ь (**-и**) *ж* (*выраже́ние*) crudeness, coarseness; (*посту́пок*) rudeness.

гру́б|ый (**-, -а́, -о**) *прил* (*челове́к, поведе́ние*) rude; (*ткань, пи́ща*) coarse; (*ко́жа, подсчёт*) rough; (*го́лос*) gruff; (*оши́бка, шу́тка*) crude; (*наруше́ние пра́вил*) gross.

гру́д|а (**-ы**) *ж* pile, heap.

груди́н|ка (**-и**) *ж* (*говя́дина*) brisket; (*копчёная свини́на*) bacon; **бара́нья ~** breast of lamb; **свина́я ~** pork fillet.

грудни́ц|а (**-ы**) *ж* mastitis.

грудн|о́й *прил* (*молоко́*) breast *опред*; (*ка́шель*) chest *опред*; (*младе́нец*): **~ ребёнок** baby; **грудно́й го́лос** chest voice; **грудны́е же́лезы** mammary glands *мн*; **грудна́я кле́тка** thorax;

груднóе кормлéние breast-feeding.
гр|удь (-удú; *instr sg* -ýдью, *nom pl* -ýди) ж (*АНАТ*) chest; (: *женщины*) breasts *мн*; ~ рубáшки shirt front; вставáть (встать *perf*) ~ýдью на защúту когó-н/чегó-н to stake one's life in defence (*BRIT*) *или* defense (*US*) of sb/sth; кормúть (*impf*) ~ýдью to breast-feed.
гружёный *прил* loaded.
гружý(сь) *несов см* грузúть(ся).
груз (-а) м (*тяжесть*) weight; (*товар*) cargo, freight.
груздь (-я) м milk agaric.
грýзен *прил см* грýзный.
грузúл|о (-а) *ср* sinker, weight.
грузúн (-а) м Georgian.
грузúн|ка (-ки; *gen pl* -ок) ж *см* грузúн.
грузúнск|ий (-ая, -ое, -ие) *прил* Georgian.
гр|узúть (-ужý, -ýзишь; *perf* загрузúть *или* нагрузúть) *несов перех* (*корабль итп*) to load (up); ~ (погрузúть *perf*) (в/на +*acc*) (*товар*) to load (onto)
► грузúться (*perf* погрузúться) *несов возв* (*люди*) to board; (*судно*) to take on cargo; (*машина*) to be loaded up.
Грýзи|я (-и) ж Georgia.
грýз|ный (-ен, -нá, -но) *прил* (*человек*) hefty; (*походка*) lumbering.
грузовúк (-á) м lorry (*BRIT*), truck (*US*).
грузов|óй *прил* (*судно, самолёт*) cargo *опред*; грузовáя машúна goods vehicle; грузовóе таксú removal (*BRIT*) *или* moving (*US*) van.
грузооборóт (-а) м turnover of goods.
грузоотправúтел|ь (-я) м consignor of goods.
грузоподъёмност|ь (и) ж freight *или* cargo capacity.
грузополучáтел|ь (-я) м consignee.
грýзчик (-а) м (*на складе*) warehouse porter; (*в магазине*) stockroom worker; (*в порту*) docker (*BRIT*), stevedore (*US*); (*на вокзале*) porter.
грунт (-а) м soil, earth; (*дно водоёма*) bottom; (*краска*) primer.
грунт|овáть (-ýю; *perf* загрунтовáть) *несов перех* to prime.
грунтóвк|а (-и) ж undercoat.
грунтов|óй *прил*: ~áя дорóга dirt road; ~áя крáска primer.
грýпп|а (-ы) ж group; грýппа крóви blood group.
группир|овáть (-ýю; *perf* сгруппировáть) *несов перех* (*людей*) to group; (*отдел*) to establish, set up; (*данные, цифры*) to group, classify
► группировáться (*perf* сгруппировáться) *несов возв* (*объединяться*) to form groups; (*классифицироваться*) to be grouped *или* classified.
группирóв|ка (-ки; *gen pl* -ок) ж grouping; (*религиозная*) group.
группов|óй *прил* group *опред*.

грýстен *прил см* грýстный.
гру|стúть (-щý, -стúшь) *несов неперех* to be melancholy, feel very sad; ~ (*impf*) по +*dat или* о +*prp* (*семье, дому*) to pine for.
грýстно *нареч* sadly ♦ *как сказ* (+*dat*): мне ~ I feel sad.
грýст|ный (-ен, -нá, -но) *прил* (*настроение*) sad, melancholy; (*no short form; конец*) sad.
грýст|ь (-и) ж sadness, melancholy.
грýш|а (-и) ж (*плод*) pear; (*дерево*) pear (tree).
грущý *несов см* грустúть.
грыж|а (-и) ж hernia.
грыз *итп несов см* грызть.
грызн|я́ (-и́) ж (*разг: собак итп*) scrap; (*перен: пренебр*) squabble.
гры|зть (-у́, -ёшь; *pt* -, -ла, -ло) *несов перех* (*печенье, яблоки*) to nibble (at); (*perf* разгры́зть; *кость*) to gnaw (on); (*орехи*) to nibble; (*перен: разг: человека*) to get at; ~ (*impf*) нóгти to bite one's nails; меня́ гры́зло раскáяние/сомнéние I was consumed by remorse/doubt
► гры́зться *несов возв* (*собаки итп*) to fight; (*перен: разг*) to squabble.
грызýн (-á) м rodent.
гряд|á (-ы́; *nom pl* -ы) ж row (*of flowers, vegetables*); (*гор*) range; (*волн*) series; ~ облакóв bank of cloud.
грядёт *итп несов см* грясти́.
гря́д|ка (-ки; *gen pl* -ок) ж row.
грядýще|е (-его; *decl like adj*) *ср* the future.
грядýщ|ий (-ая, -ее, -ие) *прил* (*год*) coming; на сон ~ before going to bed.
грязелечéни|е (-я) *ср* mud cure.
гря́зен *прил см* гря́зный.
гря́з|и (-ей) *мн* mud cure; (*место*) mud baths *мн*.
грязн|и́ть (-ю́, -и́шь; *perf* загрязни́ть) *несов перех* (*платье*) to get dirty; (*пол*) to make dirty; (*перен: репутацию*) to tarnish ♦ *perf* нагрязни́ть *неперех* (*в доме*) to make a mess; (*на улице*) to drop litter
► грязни́ться (*perf* загрязни́ться) *несов возв* to become dirty.
гря́зно *как сказ безл*: дóма/на ýлице ~ the street/house is filthy.
грязнýл|я (-и) м/ж (*разг*) pig; (: *ребёнок*) mucky kid.
гря́з|ный (-ен, -нá, -но) *прил* dirty; (*ребёнок, платье*) dirty, grubby; (*перен: анекдот, личность*) sordid; (*цвет*) murky; ~ное дéло dirty business; ~ная войнá dirty war.
гряз|ь (-и; *loc sg* -й) ж dirt; (*на дороге*) mud; (*перен*) filth; обливáть (обли́ть *perf*) когó-н гря́зью, мешáть (смешáть *perf*) когó-н с гря́зью (*перен*) to sling mud at sb; *см также* гря́зи.
гря́|нуть (-у, -ешь) *сов перех* (*марш*) to strike up ♦ *неперех* (*выстрел*) to ring out; (*война*) to

break out; ~ *(perf)* **пе́сню** to burst into song; ~**ул гром** there was a clap of thunder.

грясти́ *(3sg* -дёт, *3pl* -ду́т) *несов неперех* to draw near.

гуа́ш|ь (-и) *ж* gouache.

губ|а́ (-ы́; *nom pl* -ы, *dat pl* -а́м) *ж* lip; *(обычно мн: тисков)* jaw *(of pliers etc)*; *(залив)* bay *(in North Russia)*; **дуть (наду́ть** *perf)* **гу́бы** *(перен: разг)* to be in a huff; **у него́ ~ не ду́ра** *(разг)* he knows what's good for him.

губе́рни|я (-и) *ж* gubernia *(administrative region)*.

губерна́тор (-а) *м* governor.

губи́тель|ный (-ен, -ьна, -ьно) *прил (климат)* unhealthy; *(влияние)* pernicious; *(последствия)* ruinous; *(привычка)* harmful; *(мороз)*: ~ **(для** +*gen)* disastrous (for).

губи́|ть (-лю́, -ишь; *perf* **погуби́ть)** *несов перех* to kill; *(урожай, здоровье)* to ruin; **он её погу́бит** he'll be the ruin of her.

гу́б|ка (-ки; *gen pl* -ок) *ж* sponge.

гублю́ *несов см* **губи́ть.**

губн|о́й *прил*: ~**а́я пома́да** lipstick; ~**а́я гармо́шка** harmonica.

гу́бок *сущ см* **гу́бка.**

гуверна́нт|ка (-ки; *gen pl* -ок) *ж* governess.

гуверне́р (-а) *м* (private) tutor.

гугу́ *как сказ*: **она́ ни ~** *(разг)* she doesn't say a word; **ни ~!** *(разг)* not a word!

гуде́ни|е (-я) *ср (жуков)* drone; *(проводов)* hum; *(ветра)* moan.

гу|де́ть (-жу́, -ди́шь) *несов неперех (шмель, провода)* to hum; *(ветер)* to moan; *(толпа)* to murmur; *(машина)* to hoot; *(разг: ноги итп)* to throb.

гуд|о́к (-ка́) *м (устройство: автомобиля)* horn; (: *парохода, завода)* siren; *(звук)* hoot.

гудро́н (-а) *м* tar.

гужу́ *несов см* **гуде́ть.**

гул (-а) *м (машин, голосов)* drone; *(море)* murmur.

гу́л|кий (-кая, -кое, -кие; -ок, -ка́, -ко) *прил (удар, шаги)* resounding; *(свод)* echoing.

гу́лькин *прил*: **с ~ нос** *(разг)* next to nothing.

гуля́нь|е (-ья; *nom pl* -ий) *ср*: **наро́дное ~** outdoor merrymaking on a public holiday.

гуля́|ть (-ю; *perf* **погуля́ть)** *несов неперех (прогуливаться)* to stroll; *(быть на улице)* to be out; *(на свадьбе)* to have a good time, enjoy o.s.; **идти́ (пойти́** *perf)* ~ to go for a walk; **я сего́дня ~ю** *(разг)* I am taking the day off

today.

гуля́ш (-а́) *м* goulash.

ГУМ (-а) *м сокр* (= Госуда́рственный универса́льный магази́н) *state department store.*

гуманита́рн|ый *прил (помощь)* humanitarian; *(образование, факультет)* arts *опред*; **гуманита́рные нау́ки** the humanities *или* arts.

гума́нность (-и) *ж* humaneness, humanity.

гума́н|ный (-ен, -на, -но) *прил* humane.

гумн|о́ (-а́) *ср (сарай)* barn; *(площадка)* threshing floor.

гурма́н (-а) *м* gourmet.

гурт (-а́) *м (коров)* herd.

гурто́м *нареч (разг: отправиться)* en masse; (: *продать, купить)* in bulk.

гурьб|а́ (-ы́) *ж* crowd; **ходи́ть** *(impf)* **или гуля́ть** *(impf)* ~**о́й** to go about in a gang.

гуса́к (-а́) *м* gander.

гу́сениц|а (-ы) *ж* caterpillar; *(трактора)* caterpillar track.

гусёнок (-ёнка; *nom pl* -я́та, *gen pl* -я́т) *м* gosling.

гуси́н|ый *прил (яйцо)* goose; ~**ое ста́до** gaggle of geese; ~**ая ко́жа** goose flesh, goose pimples *(BRIT) или* bumps *(US)*.

густе́|ть *(3sg* -ет, *3pl* -ют, *perf* **погусте́ть)** *несов неперех (туман)* to grow *или* become denser; *(perf* **загусте́ть,** *каша)* to thicken.

густ|о́й (-, -а́, -о) *прил (лес, облака)* dense; *(брови)* bushy; *(суп, волосы)* thick; *(цвет, бас)* deep, rich.

густонаселённый *прил* densely-populated.

густот|а́ (-ы́) *ж (волос, каши)* thickness; *(зарослей, дыма)* density; *(голоса, цвета)* richness, deepness.

гусы́н|я (-и) *ж* goose *(female)*.

гус|ь (-я; *gen pl* -е́й) *м* goose; **как с гу́ся вода́** *(разг)* like water off a duck's back; **хоро́ш ~!** *(разг: пренебр)* a fine one!

гусько́м *нареч* in single file.

гуся́та *итп сущ см* **гусёнок.**

гуся́тниц|а (-ы) *ж* casserole (dish).

гутали́н (-а) *м* shoe polish.

гу́щ|а (-и) *ж (кофейная)* grounds *мн*; *(пивная)* lees *мн*, dregs *мн*; *(супа)* solids *(in soup etc)*; *(леса)* thicket; **в ~е собы́тий/толпы́** in the thick of things/the crowd.

гу́ще *сравн прил от* **густо́й.**

Гц *сокр* (= герц) Hz (= *hertz).*

ГЭС *ж сокр* (= гидроэлектроста́нция) hydroelectric power station.

~ Д, д ~

Д, д *сущ нескл (буква)* the 5th letter of the Russian alphabet.

д. *сокр* = **дере́вня, дом.**

KEYWORD

да *част* **1** (*выражает утвержде́ние, согла́сие*) yes

2 (*не так ли*): **ты придёшь, да?** you're coming, aren't you?; **ты меня́ лю́бишь, да?** you love me, don't you?; **я получи́л письмо́ от ма́мы – да?** I got a letter from my mum – really?

3 (*при воспомина́нии, размышле́нии*) oh, yes

4 (*пусть: в лозунгах, призы́вах*): **да – ми́ру!** yes to peace!; **да здра́вствует демокра́тия!** long live democracy!; **вот э́то да!** (*разг*) cool!; **ну да!** (*разг*) sure!; (*выражает недове́рие*) I'll bet!; **да ну́!** (*разг*) no way!

◆ *союз* (*и*) and; (*но, одна́ко*) but; **помога́ет ма́ло, да и то неохо́тно** he doesn't help much, and then only unwillingly; **у неё то́лько одно́ пла́тье, да и то ста́рое** she only has one dress and even that's old; **пла́чет, да и то́лько** he does nothing but cry.

да́бы *союз*: ~ +*infin* in order to do; **он спря́тал де́ньги, ~ никто́ не нашёл** he hid the money in order that it wouldn't be found.

дава́й(те) *несов см* **дава́ть** ◆ *част* let's; ~ **пить чай** let's have some tea; ~ **помоги́(те) мне!** come on, give me a hand!; **дава́й-дава́й!** (*разг*) come on!, get on with it!

дава́ть (-ю́; *imper* **дава́й(те)**) *несов от* **дать** ◆ *перех* (*no perf*; *разг*: **продава́ть**) to sell; **вот (во) ~ёт!** (*разг*) that's incredible!; **в магази́не ~ю́т мя́со** (*разг*) they sell meat in the shop

▶ **дава́ться** *несов от* **да́ться** ◆ *возв* (*име́ть ме́сто*) to take place.

дави́ть (-лю́, -ишь) *несов перех* (*подлеж: о́бувь*) to pinch; (*perf* **задави́ть**; **кале́чить**) to crush, trample; (*подлеж: маши́на*) to run over; (*perf* **раздави́ть**; **насеко́мых**) to squash; (*подлеж: чу́вства*) to oppress; ~ (*impf*) **на** +*acc* (*налега́ть тя́жестью*) to press *или* weigh down on; ~ (*impf*) **кого́-н свои́м авторите́том** (*разг*) to intimidate sb; **воротни́к да́вит** the collar feels tight

▶ **дави́ться** *несов возв* (*разг: в авто́бусе, в*

тесной ко́мнате) to be crushed *или* squashed; ~**ся** (**подави́ться** *perf*) +*instr* (ко́стью, слова́ми) to choke on.

да́вка (-ки; *gen pl* -ок) ж crush.

давле́ние (-я) *ср* (*га́за, жи́дкости, во́здуха*) pressure; **кровяно́е** ~ blood pressure; **атмосфе́рное** ~ atmospheric pressure; **под ~м** +*gen* under the pressure of; **ока́зывать** (**оказа́ть** *perf*) ~ **на** +*acc* to put pressure on.

давлю́(сь) *несов см* **дави́ть(ся)**.

да́вний (-яя, -ее, -ие) *прил*: **в ~ие времена́** a long time ago; **с ~их пор** for a long time; **э́то ~ слу́чай** it happened a long time ago.

давно́ *нареч* (*случи́ться, встре́титься*) a long time ago; (*ждать*) for a long time; ~ **бы так!** about time too!

да́вность (-и) *ж* (*ЮР: срок*) prescription; (*дли́тельное существова́ние*): **дру́жба/ вражда́ име́ет большу́ю** ~ the friendship/feud is of long standing; **за ~ю лет** due to the number of years which have elapsed.

давны́м-давно́ *нареч* (*разг*) ages ago.

да́вок *сущ см* **да́вка**.

дади́м(ся) *итп сов см* **дать(ся)**.

да́же *част* even; **так испуга́лся, ~ вскри́кнул** I was so frightened, I even screamed; ~ **я согласи́лся** even I agreed.

да́йджест (-а) *м* newspaper rubric.

да́й(те) *сов см* **дать** ◆ *част* (*разг*): ~ **я поду́маю** let me think.

дактилоскопи́я (-и) *ж* fingerprinting.

дал *итп сов см* **дать**.

да́лее *нареч* further; **и так** ~ and so on; **не** ~ **как** *или* **чем вчера́** only yesterday.

далёкий (-ая, -ое, -ие; -, -а́, -о́) *прил* (*страна́, зву́ки*) distant; (*про́шлое, бу́дущее*) distant; (*путь, путеше́ствие*) long; **в ~ие го́ды** in the distant past; **они́ далеки́ друг от дру́га** they have nothing in common; ~ **от реа́льности** far removed from reality; **она́ – челове́к ~ от нау́ки** she's far from being an expert when it comes to science.

далеко́ *нареч* (*о расстоя́нии*) far (away); (*о вре́мени*) a long way off ◆ *как сказ* (*распол- ага́ться*) it's a long way away; **до го́рода ещё** ~ the town is still a long way off; **до ле́та** ~

summer is a long way off; ~ **от** +*gen* far (away) from; ~ **за** +*acc* long after; **ему́** ~ **за 50** he's well over 50; ~ **не** far from, by no means; ~ **пойти́** *(perf)* *(перен)* to go far; **мне** ~ **до него́** I'm no match for him.

да́ло *итп сов см* **дать**.

даль (**-и**; *loc sg* **-и́**) *ж* faraway place; **э́то така́я** ~ *(разг)* it's such a long way (away).

дальне́йш|ий (**-ая, -ее, -ие**) *прил* further; **в** ~**ем** in the future.

да́льн|ий (**-яя, -ее, -ие**) *прил* distant; **Д~ Восто́к** the Far East; **раке́та** ~**его де́йствия** long-range missile; **по́езд/авто́бус** ~**его сле́дования** long-distance train/bus.

дальнобо́йный *прил* *(воен)* long-range.

дальнови́д|ный (**-ен, -на, -но**) *прил* far-sighted.

дальнозо́р|кий (**-кая, -кое, -кие; -ок, -ка, -ко**) *прил* long-sighted (*brit*), far-sighted (*us*); *(дальновидный)* far-sighted.

да́льше *сравн прил от* **далёкий ♦** *сравн нареч от* **далеко́ ♦** *нареч* next; **так пло́хо,** ~ **не́куда** *(разг)* things couldn't be any worse; **не** ~ **как** *или* **чем вчера́/у́тром** only yesterday/this morning.

дам(ся) *сов см* **дать(ся)**.

да́м|а (**-ы**) *ж* lady; *(карты)* queen.

Дама́ск (**-а**) *м* Damascus.

дама́сск|ий (**-ая, -ое, -ие**) *прил:* ~**ая сталь** Damascus steel, damask.

да́мб|а (**-ы**) *ж* dam.

да́м|ка (**-ки**; *gen pl* **-ок**) *ж* king (*in draughts or checkers*).

да́мский (**-ая, -ое, -ие**) *прил* ladylike; *(одежда, парикмахер)* ladies'.

Да́ни|я (**-и**) *ж* Denmark.

да́нность (**-и**) *ж* actuality.

да́нн|ые (**-ых**; *decl like adj*) *мн* *(сведения)* data *ед*, information *ед*; *(способности)* talent *ед*.

да́нн|ый *прил* this, the given; **в** ~**ом слу́чае** in this case; **в** ~ **моме́нт** at present.

дан|ь (**-и**) *ж* tribute; *(перен: моде, традиции)* concession; **отдава́ть** (**отда́ть** *perf*) ~ **кому́-н/чему́-н** to pay tribute to sb/sth.

дар (**-а**; *nom pl* **-ы́**) *м* *(также перен)* gift; **получа́ть** (**получи́ть** *perf*) **что-н в** ~ to be given sth as a present.

дар|и́ть (**-ю́, -ишь**; *perf* **подари́ть**) *несов перех* to give; ~ *(impf)* **что-н кому́-н** to give sb sth as a present.

дармов|о́й (**-а́я, -о́е, -ы́е**) *прил* *(разг)* free.

дармое́д (**-а**) *м* *(разг)* sponger.

дарова́ни|е (**-я**) *ср* gift.

дарови́т|ый (**-, -а, -о**) *прил* gifted.

да́ром *нареч* *(бесплатно)* free, for nothing; *(бесполезно)* in vain; **теря́ть** (**потеря́ть** *perf*) **вре́мя** ~ to waste time; **э́то ему́** ~ **не пройдёт** he'll pay for this; ~ **пропада́ть** (**пропа́сть** *perf*) to be wasted, go to waste.

да́рственн|ый *прил:* ~**ая на́дпись** dedication.

даст(ся) *сов см* **дать(ся)**.

да́т|а (**-ы**) *ж* date; **кру́глая** ~ *anniversary which is a multiple of ten years*; ~ **вступле́ния в си́лу** effective date.

да́тельный *прил:* ~ **паде́ж** dative case.

дати́р|овать (**-ую**) *(не)сов перех* to date.

да́тск|ий (**-ая, -ое, -ие**) *прил* Danish; ~ **язы́к** Danish.

датча́н|ин (**-ина**; *nom pl* **-е**, *gen pl* **-**) *м* Dane.

датча́н|ка (**-ки**; *gen pl* **-ок**) *ж см* **датча́нин**.

да́тчик (**-а**) *м* sensor.

дать (*см* **Table 14**; *impf* **дава́ть**) *сов* to give; *(разг: ударить)* to clout; *(устроить: концерт, спектакль)* to put on; *(позволить):* ~ **кому́-н** +*infin* to allow sb to do, let sb do; **дава́ть** (~ *perf*) **кому́-н что-н** to give sb sth, give sth to sb; **дава́ть** (~ *perf*) **себя́ знать** to make itself felt; **зима́ даёт себя́ знать** winter is making its presence felt; **ни** ~ **ни взять** *(разг)* no more, no less; **я тебе́ дам!** *(угроза)* I'll get you!; ~ (**дава́ть** *impf*) **кому́-н знать о чём-н** *(сообщить)* to let sb know about sth

▶ **да́ться** (*impf* **дава́ться**) *сов возв* *(разг):* **я не да́мся им в ру́ки** I won't let them catch me; **ей легко́ даю́тся языки́** languages come easily to her; **дала́сь тебе́ э́та те́ма!** *(разг)* you're obsessed with the subject!

да́ч|а (**-и**) *ж* *(дом)* dacha (*holiday cottage in the country*); *(корма)* portion; *(показаний, консульта́ций)* provision; **они́ всё ле́то живу́т на** ~**е** they are spending the whole of the summer at their dacha.

да́чник (**-а**) *м person who spends time at his or her dacha*.

да́чниц|а (**-ы**) *ж см* **да́чник**.

дашь(ся) *сов см* **дать(ся)**.

ДВ *сокр* (= **дли́нные во́лны**) LW= *long wave ед ♦ прил сокр* (= **длинноволново́й**) LW (= *long-wave*).

дв|а (**-ух**; *см* **Table 23**; *f* **две**, *nt* **два**) *м чис* two **♦** *м нескл* *(просвещ)* ≈ poor *(school mark)*; **ей** ~ **го́да** she is two (years old); **они́ живу́т в до́ме но́мер** ~ they live at number two; **о́коло** ~**ух** about two; **кни́га сто́ит** ~ **рубля́** the book costs two roubles; ~ **с полови́ной часа́** two and a half hours; ~**е с полови́ной мину́ты** two and a half minutes; **сейча́с** ~ **часа́** it's two o'clock; **я́блоки продаю́тся по** ~**е шту́ки** the apples are sold in twos; **дели́ть** (**раздели́ть** *perf*) **что-н на** ~ to divide sth into two; **в** ~**ух шага́х** (**от** +*gen*) within a stone's throw (of *или* from); **в** ~**ух слова́х** in a few words; **в** ~ **счёта** *(разг)* in a jiffy.

двадцати́ *чис см* **два́дцать**.

двадцатиле́ти|е (**-я**) *ср* *(срок)* twenty years; *(годовщина)* twentieth anniversary.

двадцатиле́тн|ий (**-яя, -ее, -ие**) *прил* *(период)* twenty-year; *(человек)* twenty-year-old.

двадцатипятиле́ти|е (**-я**) *ср* *(срок)* twenty-five years; *(годовщина)* twenty-fifth anniversary.

двадца́т|ый (**-ая, -ое, -ые**) *чис* twentieth; *см также* **пятидеся́тый**.

двáдцат|ь (**-и**; *как* **пять**; *см* **Table 27**) *чис* twenty; *см также* **пятьдеся́т**.

двáжды *нареч* twice; **он приходи́л сюда́** ~ he has come here twice; ~ **три – шесть** two times three is six; **я́сно как** ~ **два** (*разг*) as plain as day.

две *ж чис см* **два**.

двена́дцати *чис см* **двена́дцать**.

двенадцатипе́рстн|ый *прил*: ~**ая кишка́** duodenum.

двенадцатичасово́й *прил* (*рабочий день*) twelve-hour; (*отправление*) twelve-o'clock.

двена́дцат|ый (**-ая, -ое, -ые**) *чис* twelfth; *см также* **пя́тый**.

двена́дцат|ь (**-и**; *как* **пять**; *см* **Table 27**) *чис* twelve; *см также* **пять**.

две́р|ца (**-цы**; *gen pl* **-ец**) *ж* door.

двер|ь (**-и**; *loc sg* **-и́**, *gen pl* **-éй**) *ж* door; **при закры́тых** ~**я́х** behind closed doors; **стоя́ть** (*impf*) **в** ~**я́х** to stand in the doorway; **показа́ть** (*perf*) **на** ~ **кому́-н** (*перен*) to show sb the door; **день откры́тых** ~**éй** open day.

две́сти (**-ухсо́т**; *см* **Table 31**) *чис* two hundred; *см также* **сто**.

дви́гател|ь (**-я**) *м* engine, motor; (*перен*) driving force; ~ **вну́треннего сгора́ния** internal-combustion engine.

дви́гать (**-аю**; *perf* **дви́нуть**) *несов перех* to move; (*3sg* **-жет**, *3pl* **-жут**; *перен*) to further; (*no perf*; *механизм*) to drive; **им** ~**жет за́висть/любо́вь** he is motivated by envy/love; ~ (**дви́нуть** *perf*) **па́льцами/руко́й** to move one's fingers/hand

▶ **дви́гаться** (*perf* **дви́нуться**) *несов возв* to move; (*отправляться*): ~**ся в/на** +*acc* to set off *или* start out for; ~**ся** (**дви́нуться** *perf*) **в путь** to set off on a journey; **де́ло не** ~**гается** we are making no progress.

движе́ни|е (**-я**) *ср* movement; (*дорожное*) traffic; (*перен*) impulse; **приводи́ть** (**привести́** *perf*) **что-н в** ~ to set sth in motion; **пра́вила доро́жного** *или* **у́личного** ~**я** ≈ the Highway Code; ~ **в защи́ту ми́ра** the peace movement.

дви́жимост|ь (**-и**) *ж* movables *мн*.

дви́жим|ый (**-, -а, -о**) *прил*: ~ +*instr* motivated by; **дви́жимое иму́щество** movables.

движо́к (**-ка́**) *м* (*ТЕХ*) *sliding part of a mechanism*.

дви́нуть(ся) (**-у(сь), -ешь(ся)**) *сов от* **дви́гать(ся)**.

дво|е (**-и́х**; *см* **Table 36а**) *м чис* two; ~ **часо́в/сане́й** two watches/sledges; ~ **брюк/но́жниц** two pairs of trousers/scissors; **их бы́ло** ~ there were two of them; **он не спал** ~ **су́ток** he didn't sleep for forty-eight hours; **есть** (*impf*) **за двои́х** to eat enough for two; **на свои́х двои́х** (*разг*) on foot.

двоебо́р|ье (**-я**) *ср* biathlon.

двоебра́чи|е (**-я**) *ср* bigamy.

двоевла́сти|е (**-я**) *ср* dual power, diarchy.

дво́ек *сущ см* **дво́йка**.

дво́ен *сущ см* **дво́йня**.

двоето́чи|е (**-я**) *ср* (*линг*) colon.

дво́ечник (**-а**) *м* (*разг*) dimwit.

дво́ечни|ца (**-ы**) *ж см* **дво́ечник**.

двои́м *итп см* **дво́е**.

дво|и́ться (*3sg* **-и́тся**) *несов возв*: **у него́ в глаза́х** ~**и́тся** he is seeing double.

двои́х *чис см* **дво́е**.

дво́ичный *прил* binary.

дво́|йка (**-йки**; *gen pl* **-ек**) *ж* (*цифра, карта*) two; (*ПРОСВЕЩ*) ≈ D (*school mark*); (*разг*: *автобус, трамвай итп*) (number) two (*bus, tram etc*).

двойн|о́й (**-а́я, -о́е, -ы́е**) *прил* double; **двойна́я игра́** double-dealing.

дво́|йня (**-йни**; *gen pl* **-ен**) *ж* twins *мн*.

дво́йственн|ый (**-, -на, -но**) *прил* ambiguous.

двор (**-а́**) *м* (*между домами*) courtyard, yard; (*при отдельном доме*) yard; (*крестьянское хозяйство*) homestead; (*королевский*) court; **моне́тный** ~ mint; **при** ~**é** at court; **на** ~**é темно́** (*разг*) it's dark outside; **не ко** ~**у́ оказа́ться** (*perf*) *или* **прийти́сь** (*perf*) (*разг*) to be like a fish out of water.

двор|е́ц (**-ца́**) *м* palace; **дворе́ц бракосочета́ния** wedding palace (*venue for wedding ceremonies*), ≈ registry office (*BRIT*); **дворе́ц спо́рта** sports centre (*BRIT*) *или* center (*US*).

дво́рник (**-а**) *м* (*работник*) road sweeper; (*АВТ*) windscreen (*BRIT*) *или* windshield (*US*) wiper.

дворня́г|а (**-и**) *м* mongrel.

дворня́|жка (**-ки**; *gen pl* **-ек**) *ж* = **дворня́га**.

дворца́ *сущ см* **дворе́ц**.

дворцо́вый *прил* palace *опред*.

дворяни́н (**-яни́на**; *nom pl* **-я́не**, *gen pl* **-я́н**) *м* nobleman (*мн* noblemen).

дворя́н|ка (**-ки**; *gen pl* **-ок**) *ж* noblewoman (*мн* noblewomen).

дворя́нств|о (**-а**) *ср* nobility.

двою́родн|ый *прил*: ~ **брат** (first) cousin (*male*); ~**ая сестра́** (first) cousin (*female*).

двоя́к|ий (**-ая, -ое, -ие**; ~**, -ка, -ко**) *прил* dual.

двубо́ртный *прил* double-breasted.

двузна́чный *прил* (*число*) two-digit; (*слово, выражение*) ambiguous.

двукра́тн|ый *прил*: ~ **чемпио́н** two-times champion; **в** ~**ом разме́ре** twofold.

двули́ч|ный (**-ен, -на, -но**) *прил* two-faced.

двум *итп см* **два**, **две**.

двумста́м *итп чис см* **две́сти**.

двунапра́вленный *прил* (*КОМП*) bidirectional.

двуно́г|ий (**-ая, -ое, -ие**) *прил* two-legged.

двусло́жный *прил* two-syllable.

двусмы́слен|ный (**-, -на, -но**) *прил* ambiguous; ~**ная шу́тка** double entendre.

двуспа́льн|ый *прил*: ~**ая крова́ть** double bed;

двуспáльная палáтка two-person tent.

двуствóльный *прил*: ~ое ружьё double-barrelled (*BRIT*) *или* double-barreled (*US*) shotgun.

двусторóн|ний (-няя, -нее, -ние; -ен, -ня, -не) *прил* (*движение*) two-way; (*соглашение*, *переговоры*) bilateral; ~нее воспалéние лёгких double pneumonia.

двух *чис см* два.

двухгодúчный *прил* two-year.

двухднéвный *прил* two-day.

двухкопéеч|ный *прил*: ~ная монéта two-kopeck coin.

двухлéти|е (-я) *ср* (*срок*) two years; (*годовщина*) second anniversary.

двухлéт|ний (-яя, -ее, -ие) *прил* (*период*) two-year; (*ребёнок*) two-year-old; (*БОТ*) biennial.

двухмéстный *прил* (*номер*) double; (*купе*, *каюта*) two-berth.

двухмéсячный *прил* two-month; (*ребёнок*) two-month-old; (*издание*) bimonthly.

двухнедéльный *прил* two-week; (*ребёнок*) two-week-old; (*издание*) fortnightly.

двухпалáтный *прил* (*ПОЛИТ*) two-chamber.

двухсмéн|ка (-ки; *gen pl* -ок) *ж* (*разг*) *two shift working pattern*.

двухсóт *чис см* двéсти.

двухсотлéтие (-я) *ср* (*срок*) two hundred years; (*годовщина*) bicentenary (*BRIT*), bicentennial (*US*).

двухсотлéт|ний (-яя, -ее, -ие) *прил* (*период*) two-hundred-year; (*дерево*) two-hundred-year-old.

двухсóт|ый (-ая, -ое, -ые) *чис* two hundredth.

двухстáх *чис см* двéсти.

двухтóмник (-а) *м* two-volume edition.

двухцвéтный *прил* two-coloured (*BRIT*), two-colored (*US*).

двухчасов|óй (-áя, -óе, -ы́е) *прил* (*фильм*) two-hour; (*отправление*) two-o'clock.

двухэтáжный *прил* two-storey (*BRIT*), two-story (*US*).

двуш|ка (-ки; *gen pl* -ек) *ж* (*разг*) two-kopeck coin.

двуязы́чный (-ен, -на, -но) *прил* bilingual.

дебаркáдер (-а) *м* landing stage.

дебатú|ровать (-ую) *несов перех* to debate.

дебáт|ы (-ов) *мн* debate *ед*.

дéбет (-а) *м* debit; заносúть (занестú *perf*) что-н в ~ to debit sth.

дебетовáни|е (-я) *ср*: прямóе ~ direct debit.

дебет|овáть (-у́ю) (*не*)*сов перех* to debit.

дебетóвый *прил*: ~ остáток debit balance; дебетóвое авúзо debit note.

дебúл (-а) *м* (*разг*: *пренебр*) moron.

дебитóр (-а) *м* debtor.

дéбр|и (-ей) *мн* (*в лесу*) thicket *ед*; (*перен*): ~ +*gen* (*науки*, *техники*) maze of.

·дебю́т (-а) *м* debut; (*в шахматах*) opening.

дебютáнт (-а) *м person making his debut*.

дебютáнт|ка (-ки; *gen pl* -ок) *ж см* дебютáнт.

дéв|а (-ы) *ж*: стáрая ~ spinster; (*созвездие*): Д~ Virgo.

девальвáци|я (-и) *ж* devaluation.

девальвú|ровать (-ую) (*не*)*сов перех* to devalue.

девá|ть (-ю) *несов от* деть ♦ *сов перех* (*разг*) to put; мне нéкуда ~ дéньги/врéмя I've got more money/time than I know what to do with

▸ девá|ться *несов от* дéться ♦ *сов возв* (*разг*): кудá онá ~лась? where has she got to?; кудá ~ся it can't be helped.

дéверь (-я) *м* brother-in-law (*wife's brother*).

девúз (-а) *м* motto.

дéвиц|а (-ы) *ж* (*ФОЛЬКЛОР*) maiden.

девúц|а (-ы) *ж* (*девушка*) girl.

девúчеств|о (-а) *ср* (*до замужества*) girlhood; в ~е Петрóва née Petrova.

дéвич|ий (-ья, -ье, -ьи) *прил*: ~ья фамúлия maiden name.

дéв|ка (-ки; *gen pl* -ок) *ж* (*разг*: *девушка*) girl.

дéвоч|ка (-ки; *gen pl* -ек) *ж* (*ребёнок*) little girl; (*разг*: *девушка*) girl.

дéвуш|ка (-ки; *gen pl* -ек) *ж* girl; (*разг*: *обращение*) miss.

девчóн|ка (-ки; *gen pl* -ок) *ж* (*разг*: *девочка*) little girl, kid.

девянóст|о (-а; *как* сто; *см* Table 30) *чис* ninety; *см также* пятьдесят.

девяностолéти|е (-я) *ср* (*срок*) ninety years; (*годовщина*) ninetieth anniversary.

девяностолéт|ний (-яя, -ее, -ие) *прил* (*период*) ninety-year; (*человек*) ninety-year-old.

девянóст|ый (-ая, -ое, -ые) *чис* ninetieth; *см также* пятидесятый.

девя́т|ая (-ой; *decl like adj*) *ж*: однá ~ one ninth.

дéвятер|о (-ы́х; *как* чéтверо; *см* Table 36a) *чис* nine; (*ботинок, перчаток*) nine pairs; *см также* двóе.

девятú *чис см* дéвять.

девятиднéвный *прил* nine-day.

девятиклáссник (-а) *м pupil in ninth year at school (usually 15 years old)*.

девятиклáссниц|а (-ы) *ж см* девятиклáссник.

девятикрáтный *прил*: ~ чемпиóн nine-times champion; в ~ом размéре ninefold.

девятилéти|е (-я) *ср* (*срок*) nine years; (*годовщина*) ninth anniversary.

девятилéт|ний (-яя, -ее, -ие) *прил* (*период*) nine-year; (*ребёнок*) nine-year-old.

девятимéсячный *прил* nine-month; (*ребёнок*) nine-month-old.

девятинедéльный *прил* nine-week; (*ребёнок*) nine-week-old.

девятисóт *чис см* девятьсóт.

девятисотлéти|е (-я) *ср* (*срок*) nine hundred years *мн*; (*годовщина*) nine-hundredth anniversary.

девятисотлéт|ний (-яя, -ее, -ие) *прил* (*период*) nine hundred-year; (*дерево*) nine hundred-year-old.

девятисóт|ый (-ая, -ое, -ые) *чис* nine-hundredth.

девятистám *итп чис см* **девятьсóт**.

девятичасов|óй (**-áя, -óе, -ы́е**) *прил* (*операция*) nine-hour; (*отправление*) nine o'clock.

девя́т|ка (**-ки**; *gen pl* **-ок**) *ж* (*цифра, карта*) nine; (*группа из девяти́*) group of nine; (*разг: автобус, трамвай итп*) (number) nine (*bus, tram etc*).

девятнáдцати *чис см* **девятнáдцать**.

девятнáдцатый (**-ая, -ое, -ые**) *чис* nineteenth; *см также* **пя́тый**.

девятнáдцат|ь (**-и**; *как* **пять**; *см* **Table 27**) *чис* nineteen; *см также* **пять**.

девя́ток *сущ см* **девя́тка**.

девя́тый (**-ая, -ое, -ые**) *чис* ninth; *см также* **пя́тый**.

дéвят|ь (**-и**; *как* **пять**; *см* **Table 27**) *чис* nine; *см также* **пять**.

девятьсóт (**-исóт**; *как* **пятьсóт**; *см* **Table 34**) *чис* nine hundred; *см также* **сто**.

девятью́ *чис см* **дéвять** ♦ *нареч* nine times; ~ **пять – сóрок** пять nine times five is forty-five.

девятью́стáми *чис см* **девятьсóт**.

дегенерати́в|ный (**-ен, -на, -но**) *прил* degenerate.

дегенерáци|я (**-и**) *ж* degeneration.

дёг|оть (**-тя**) *м* tar.

деградúр|овать (**-ую**) (*не*)*сов неперех* to degenerate.

дёгтя *сущ см* **дёготь**.

дегустúр|овать (**-ую**) (*не*)*сов перех* to taste, sample.

дед (**-а**) *м* grandfather; (*разг*) old man; **Дед Морóз** ≈ Father Christmas; *см также* **деды́**.

дéдовск|ий (**-ая, -ое, -ие**) *прил* grandfather's; (*перен*) old-fashioned.

дедовщúн|а (**-ы**) *ж the abuse of new conscripts by older soldiers*.

деду́кци|я (**-и**) *ж* deduction.

деды́ (**-óв**) *мн* (*разг*) *final-year conscripts*.

деепричáсти|е (**-я**) *ср* gerund.

дееспосóб|ный (**-ен, -на, -но**) *прил* (*войска*) functional; (*ЮР*) responsible.

дежу́р|ить (**-ю, -ишь**) *несов неперех* (*в порядке очереди*) to be on duty; ~ (*impf*) **у чегó-н** to guard sth; ~ (*impf*) **у постéли больнóго** to sit at a patient's bedside.

дежу́рн|ая (**-ой**; *decl like adj*) *ж см* **дежу́рный**.

дежу́рн|ый *прил* (*пренебр: цитаты, остроты*) hackneyed; ~ **врач/милиционéр** doctor/(police) officer on duty ♦ (**-ого**; *decl like adj*) *м* person on duty; (*по станции*) assistant station master; **дежу́рный магазúн** late-night shop; **дежу́рное блю́до** dish of the day.

дезертúр (**-а**) *м* deserter.

дезертúр|овать (**-ую**) (*не*)*сов неперех* to desert.

дезинсéкци|я (**-и**) *ж* pest control (*of insects*).

дезинфéкци|я (**-и**) *ж* disinfection.

дезинфицúр|овать (**-ую**) (*не*)*сов перех* to disinfect.

дезинформáци|я (**-и**) *ж* misinformation.

дезинформúр|овать (**-ую**) (*не*)*сов перех* to misinform.

дезодорáнт (**-а**) *м* antiperspirant.

дезорганизáци|я (**-и**) *ж* disorganization.

дезорганиз|овáть (**-у́ю**) (*не*)*сов перех* to disorganize.

дезориентúр|овать (**-ую**) (*не*)*сов перех* to disorientate.

дéйствен|ный (**-, -на, -но**) *прил* effective.

дéйстви|е (**-я**) *ср* (*механизма, закона*) functioning; (*романа итп*) action; (*часть пьесы*) act; (*лекарства, предупреждения*) effect; **вводúть** (**ввести́** *perf*) **в** ~ (*фабрику*) to open; (*турбину*) to activate; (*закон*) to introduce; **приводúть** (**привести́** *perf*) **в** ~ to carry out, implement; **под** ~**м** +*gen* under the influence of; *см также* **дéйствия**.

дéйствителен *прил см* **дéйствительный**.

дéйствительно *нареч, вводн сл* really; **онá** ~ **красúва** she is really beautiful; ~, **ужé порá идти́** it really is time to go.

дéйствительност|ь (**-и**) *ж* reality; **в** ~**и** in reality.

дéйствительный *прил* (*факт, польза*) real, actual; (**-ен, -ьна, -ьно**; *пропуск, удостоверéние*) valid; **дéйствительный залóг** active voice; **дéйствительная** (**воéнная**) **слу́жба** active service (*BRIT*) *или* duty (*esp US*).

дéйстви|я (**-й**) *мн* (*поступки*) actions *мн*; (*ВОЕН*) operations *мн*.

дéйств|овать (**-ую**) *несов неперех* (*человек*) to act; (*механизмы, закон*) to operate, work; (*perf* **подéйствовать**; *влиять*): ~ **на** +*acc* (*лекарство, уговóры*) to have an effect on.

дéйствующий (**-ая, -ее, -ее**) *прил*: ~**ие лúца** (*персонажи*) characters *мн*; (*участники событий*) protagonists *мн*; **дéйствующая áрмия** standing army; **дéйствующий вулкáн** active volcano.

декабрúст (**-а**) *м* (*ИСТ*) Decembrist.

декáбр|ь (**-я́**) *м* December; *см также* **октя́брь**.

декáд|а (**-ы**) *ж* ten-day period; ~ **францу́зского кинó** ten-day festival of French cinema.

декадéнт (**-а**) *м* decadent.

декадéнтск|ий (**-ая, -ое, -ие**) *прил* decadent.

декадéнтств|о (**-а**) *ср* decadence.

декáн (**-а**) *м* dean.

деканáт (**-а**) *м* faculty office.

декламúр|овать (**-ую**; *perf* **продеклами́ровать**) *несов перех* to recite.

декларáци|я (**-и**) *ж* declaration; **тамóженная** ~ customs declaration; ~ **судовóго гру́за** ship's manifest.

деклари́р|овать (-ую) *(не)сов перех* to declare.

декласси́рованн|ый *прил*: ~ые элеме́нты social outcasts.

деко́дер (-а) *м* (КОМП) decoder.

декоди́р|овать (-ую) *(не)сов перех* to decode.

декольте́ *ср нескл, прил неизм* décolleté.

декорати́вный *прил* (*растения*) ornamental; (*искусство*) decorative.

декора́ци|я (-и) *ж* (ТЕАТР) set.

декре́т (-а) *м* (*постановление*) decree; (*разг: отпуск*) maternity leave; **издава́ть (изда́ть** *perf*) ~ **о** +*prp* to issue a decree on; **уходи́ть (уйти́** *perf*) **в** ~ (*разг*) to take maternity leave.

декре́тный *прил*: ~ **о́тпуск** maternity leave.

де́ланный *прил* (*смех*) false.

де́ла|ть (-ю; *perf* **сде́лать**) *сов перех* to make; (*упражнения, опыты, подлость итп*) to do; ~ **(сде́лать** *perf*) **уро́ки** to do one's homework; ~ **(сде́лать** *perf*) **прыжо́к** to jump; ~ **(сде́лать** *perf*) **из кого́-н что-н** to make sth out of sb; ~ (*impf*) **не́чего** ~ there is nothing to be done; **от не́чего** ~ for want of something better to do; **что** ~? what can be done?

▶ **де́латься** (*perf* **сде́латься**) *несов возв* (*происходить*) to happen; ~**ся (сде́латься** *perf*) +*instr* to become.

делега́т (-а) *м* delegate.

делега́т|ка (-ки; *gen pl* -**ок**) *ж см* **делега́т**.

делега́ци|я (-и) *ж* delegation.

де́лен *прил см* **де́льный**.

деле́ни|е (-я) *ср* division; (*на линейке, в термо́метре*) point.

деле́ц (-**ьца**) *м* dealer.

Де́ли *м нескл* Delhi.

деликате́с (-а) *м* delicacy.

делика́тно *нареч* tactfully.

делика́тный *прил* delicate.

дели́ть (-ю́, -ишь; *perf* **подели́ть** *или* **раздели́ть**) *несов перех* (*также* МАТ) to divide; ~ **(раздели́ть** *perf*) **что-н на** +*acc* to divide sth by; ~ **(раздели́ть** *perf*) **что-н с** +*instr* to share sth with; ~ **(раздели́ть** *perf*) **ра́дость/го́ре (с кем-н)** to share one's joy/grief (with sb)

▶ **дели́ться** (*perf* **раздели́ться**) *несов возв*: ~**ся (на** +*acc*) (*отряд*) to divide *или* split up (into); ~**ся** (*impf*) **на** +*acc* (*книга, статья*) to be divided into; (МАТ) to be divisible by; ~**ся (подели́ться** *perf*) **чем-н с кем-н** to share sth with sb.

де́л|о (-а) *ср* matter; (*надобность, также* КОММ) business; (*положение*) situation; (*поступок*) act; (ЮР) case; (АДМИН) file; **э́то моё** ~ that's my business; **э́то не твоё** ~ it's none of your business; **я пришёл по** ~**у** I've come on business; **у меня́ к Вам** ~ I have something to discuss with you; **как дела́?** how are things?; **в чём** ~? what's wrong?; ~ **в том, что** ... the thing is that ...; **не в э́том** ~ this isn't the issue; **на (са́мом)** ~**е** in (actual) fact; **на** ~**е** in practise; **пе́рвым** ~**м** in the first case *или* instance; **за** ~ fairly; **ме́жду** ~**м** in between times; **то и** ~ every now and then.

делови́тость (-и) *ж* businesslike manner.

делови́тый (-, -а, -о) *прил* businesslike.

делово́й (-а́я, -о́е, -ы́е) *прил* (*встреча, круги*) business *опред*; (*человек*) efficient; (*вид, тон*) businesslike.

делопроизводи́тел|ь (-я) *м* clerk.

делопроизво́дств|о (-а) *ср* clerical work.

де́льный (-ен, -ьна, -ьно) *прил* (*человек*) businesslike, efficient; (*совет, предложение*) practical.

де́льт|а (-ы) *ж* delta.

дельтапла́н (-а) *м* hang-glider.

дельфи́н (-а) *м* dolphin.

дельца́ *итп сущ см* **деле́ц**.

деля́|га (-и) *м* (*разг: пренебр*) wheeler-dealer.

демаго́г (-а) *м* demagogue.

демаго́ги|я (-и) *ж* demagogy; **разводи́ть (развести́** *perf*) ~**ю** (*разг*) to talk a lot of hot air.

демаркацио́нн|ый *прил*: ~**ая ли́ния** demarcation line.

демилитариза́ци|я (-и) *ж* demilitarization.

демисезо́нн|ый *прил*: ~**ое пальто́** *coat for spring and autumn wear*.

демобилиза́ци|я (-и) *ж* demobilization.

демобилиз|ова́ться (-у́юсь) *(не)сов возв* to be demobilized.

демографи́ческ|ий (-ая, -ое, -ие) *прил* (*исследование*) population *опред*, demographic; **демографи́ческий взрыв** population explosion.

демогра́фи|я (-и) *ж* demography.

демокра́т (-а) *м* democrat.

демократи́зм (-а) *м* democracy.

демократи́ческ|ий (-ая, -ое, -ие) *прил* democratic.

демокра́ти|я (-и) *ж* democracy.

де́мон (-а) *м* demon.

демонстра́нт (-а) *м* demonstrator.

демонстра́нт|ка (-ки; *gen pl* -**ок**) *ж см* **демонстра́нт**.

демонстрати́в|ный (-ен, -на, -но) *прил* (*поведение, уход*) theatrical.

демонстра́ци|я (-и) *ж* demonstration; (*показ: фильма*) showing; (: *экспонатов*) show.

демонстри́р|овать (-ую) *(не)сов неперех* (*полит*) to demonstrate ◆ *несов перех* to show.

демонти́р|овать (-ую) *(не)сов перех* to dismantle.

деморализа́ци|я (-и) *ж* demoralization.

де́мпинг (-а) *м* (КОММ) dumping.

де́мпингов|ый *прил*: ~**ые це́ны** artificially lowered prices.

денатура́т (-а) *м* meths.

денационализа́ци|я (-и) *ж* denationalization.

денационализи́р|овать (-ую) *(не)сов перех* to denationalize.

дендра́рий (-я) *м* arboretum.

де́нег *сущ см* **де́ньги**.

де́нежный *прил* (*реформа*) monetary; (*рынок*) money *опред*; (*разг*) well-off; **де́нежный знак**

banknote; **де́нежный штраф** fine.
деномина́ци|я (-и) ж (ЭКОН) denomination.
де́ну(сь) итп сов см **де́ть(ся)**.
день (дня) м day; **Д~ Побе́ды** ≈ V-E Day,
Victory Day (*the anniversary of the USSR's
victory over Germany in World War 2*);
светово́й ~ daylight; **~ ото дня** day by day;
изо дня в ~ day in, day out; **че́рез ~** every
other day; **со дня на́ ~** (*постепенно*) from one
day to the next; (*скоро*) in the next few days; **на
друго́й ~** the next day; **на днях** (*скоро*) in the
next few days; (*недавно*) the other day; **день
рожде́ния** birthday.
де́нь|ги (-ег; *dat pl* -ьга́м) *мн* money *ед*; **броса́ть**
(*impf*) *или* **швыря́ть** (*impf*) **~ на ве́тер** to throw
money down the drain; **бума́жные ~** paper
money, banknotes; **нали́чные ~** (ready) cash.
департа́мент (-а) м department.
депе́ш|а (-и) ж dispatch.
депо́ *ср нескл* depot.
депози́т (-а) м deposit.
депози́тный *прил* deposit *опред*.
депози́тор (-а) м depositor.
депоне́нт (-а) м = **депози́тор**.
депони́р|овать (-ую) (*не*)*сов перех* to deposit.
депорта́ци|я (-и) ж deportation.
депорти́р|овать (-ую) (*не*)*сов перех* to deport.
депре́сси|я (-и) ж depression.
депута́т (-а) м deputy (*POL*).
депута́тск|ий (-ая, -ое, -ие) *прил* deputies'.
дёрга|ть (-ю) *несов перех* to tug *или* pull (at);
(*перен: разг*) to hassle ♦ *неперех* (*+instr*;
плечом, головой) to jerk
▶ **дёргаться** *несов возв* (*машина, лошадь*) to
jerk; (*лицо, губы*) to twitch; (*перен: разг*) to
(make a) fuss.
деревене́|ть (-ю) *perf* **одеревене́ть**) *несов
неперех* to grow *или* go numb.
дереве́нск|ий (-ая, -ое, -ие) *прил* (*дом,
житель*) country *опред*; (*тишина, пейзаж*)
rural; (*площадь, колодец*) village *опред*.
дере́в|ня (-ни; *gen pl* -е́нь, *dat* -ня́м) ж (*селение*)
village; (*местность*) the country;
олимпи́йская ~ Olympic Village.
де́р|ево (-ева; *nom pl* -е́вья, *gen pl* -е́вьев) *ср*
tree; (*древесина*) wood; **родосло́вное ~** family
tree; **кра́сное ~** mahogany.
деревообрабо́т|ка (-ки; *gen pl* -ок) ж timber
processing.
дере́вья итп *сущ см* **де́рево**.
деревя́нный *прил* (*также перен*) wooden.
держа́в|а (-ы) ж (*государство*) power;
(*эмблема*) orb; **вели́кие ~ы** The Great (World)
Powers.
держа́тель (-я) м holder.
держа́|ть (-у́, -ишь) *сов перех* to keep; (*в руках,
во рту, в зубах*) to hold; (*не отпускать*) to
keep hold of; (*поддерживать*) to hold up;

(*нанимать*) to take on; **~** (*impf*) **речь** to make a
speech; **~** (*impf*) **экза́мен** to sit an exam; **~** (*impf*)
отве́т to be responsible; **~** (*impf*) **сло́во** to keep
one's word; **~** (*impf*) **себя́ про́сто/
высокоме́рно** to behave simply/haughtily; **~**
(*impf*) **себя́ в рука́х** to keep one's head
▶ **держа́ться** *несов возв* to stay; (*на колоннах,
на сваях*) to be supported; (*иметь осанку*) to
stand; (*вести себя*) to behave; **~ся** (*impf*) *+gen*
(*берега, стены итп*) to keep to; (*перен*) to
adhere to; **~ся** (*impf*) **за** *+acc* (*за сумку, за
стену*) to hold onto; **~ся** (*impf*) **за го́лову** to
hold one's head.
дерз|и́ть (*2sg* -и́шь, *3sg* -и́т) *несов неперех*: **~
кому́-н** to be rude to sb.
де́рз|кий (-кая, -кое, -кие; -ок, -ка́, -ко) *прил*
(*грубый*) impertinent; (*смелый*) audacious.
де́рзост|ь (-и) ж (*см прил*) impertinence;
audacity; **говори́ть** (**сказа́ть** *perf*) **~и** to be
impertinent; **име́ть** (*impf*) **~** *+infin* to have the
cheek to do.
дерива́т (-а) м (*ЛИНГ*) derivative.
дермати́н (-а) м leatherette.
дерматоло́ги|я (-и) ж dermatology.
дёрн (-а) м turf.
дёрн|уть (-у, -ешь) *несов перех* to tug (at) ♦
неперех (*+instr*; *плечом, головой*) to jerk; **~уло
меня́** *или* **чёрт ~ул меня́ сде́лать э́то** (*разг*) I
don't know what possessed me to do it
▶ **дёрнуться** *несов возв* (*машина*) to start with a
jerk; (*лошадь*) to shy; (*лицо, губы*) to twitch.
деру́(сь) *несов перех см* **дра́ть(ся)**.
дерьм|о́ (-а́) *ср* (*груб!: также перен*) shit (*!*),
crap (*!*)
деса́нт (-а) м landing troops *мн*; (*высадка войск*)
landing; **выса́живать** (**вы́садить** *perf*) **~** to
make a landing.
деса́нтник (-а) м (*ВОЕН*) paratrooper.
десён *сущ см* **десна́**.
десе́рт (-а) м dessert.
де́скать *част*: **она́, ~, ничего́ не зна́ет** she
claims she doesn't know anything.
десн|а́ (-ы́; *nom pl* **дёсны**, *gen pl* **дёсен**) ж (*АНАТ*)
gum.
деспоти́ческ|ий (-ая, -ое, -ие) *прил* despotic.
деся́т|ая (-ой; *decl like adj*) ж: **одна́ ~** one tenth.
де́стер|о (-ы́х; *как* **че́тверо**; *см* **Table 36a**) *чис*
ten; (*десять пар*) ten pairs; *см также* **дво́е**.
десяти́ *сущ см* **де́сять**.
десятибо́р|ец (-ца) м decathlete.
десятибо́рь|е (-я) *ср* decathlon.
десятидне́вный *прил* ten-day.
десятикла́ссник (-а) м pupil in tenth year at
school (*usually 17 years old*).
десятикла́ссниц|а (-ы) ж *см* **десятикла́ссник**.
десятикопе́ечный *прил*: **~ая моне́та** ten-
kopeck coin.
десятикра́тн|ый *прил*: **~ чемпио́н** ten-times

The spelling rules for Russian are shown on page xvii.

champion; **в ~ом разме́ре** tenfold.

десятиле́ти|е (-я) *ср (срок)* decade; *(годовщина)* tenth anniversary.

десятиле́т|ка (-ки; *gen pl* **-ок) ж** *(разг)* ≈ secondary school *(BRIT),* ≈ high school *(US).*

десятиле́тн|ий (-яя, -ее, -ие) *прил (период)* ten-year; *(ребёнок)* ten-year-old.

десятиле́ток *сущ см* **десятиле́тка.**

десятиме́сячный *прил* ten-month; *(ребёнок)* ten-month-old.

десятин|а (-ы) ж *old unit of measurement approximately equal to 2.7 acres.*

десятинеде́льный *прил* ten-week; *(ребёнок)* ten-week-old.

десятирублёв|ка (-ки; *gen pl* **-ок) ж** *(разг)* ten-rouble note.

десятичасов|о́й (-а́я, -о́е, -ы́е) *прил (операция)* ten-hour; *(отправление)* ten o'clock *опред.*

десяти́чный *прил* decimal.

деся́т|ка (-ки; *gen pl* **-ок) ж** *(цифра)* ten; *(группа из десяти)* group of ten; *(разг: денежный знак)* tenner; (*: автобус, трамвай итп*) (number) ten *(bus, tram etc).*

деся́тк|и (-ов) мн: ~ люде́й/книг scores of people/books.

деся́т|ок (-ка) м ten; **он не ро́бкого ~ка** he's not afraid of anything; **ему́ пошёл шесто́й ~** he has turned fifty; *см также* **деся́тки.**

деся́т|ый (-ая, -ое, -ые) *прил* tenth; *см также* **пя́тый.**

де́сять (-й; *как* **пять;** *см* **Table 27)** *чис* ten; *см также* **пять.**

дета́лен *прил см* **дета́льный.**

детализи́р|овать (-ую) *(не)сов перех* to work out in detail.

дета́л|ь (-и) ж detail; *(механизма, прибора)* component, part.

дета́льно *нареч (обсудить)* in detail.

дета́льный (-ен, -ьна, -ьно) *прил* detailed.

детвор|а́ (-ы́) ж *собир* little children *мн.*

детдо́м (-а; *nom pl* **-а́) м** *сокр* (= **де́тский дом**) children's home.

детдо́мов|ец (-ца) м *child in care.*

детдо́мов|ка (-ки; *gen pl* **-ок) ж** *см* **детдо́мовец.**

детдо́мовца *сущ см* **детдо́мовец.**

детекти́в (-а) м *(следователь)* detective; *(фильм)* detective film; *(книга)* detective novel.

детекти́вный *прил* detective *опред.*

дете́ктор (-а) м detector.

детёныш (-а) м cub.

де́т|и (-е́й; *dat pl* **-ям,** *instr pl* **-ьми́,** *prp pl* **-ях,** *nom sg* **ребёнок) мн** children *мн.*

дети́н|а (-ы) м *(разг)* hulk.

дети́ще (-а) ср creation.

де́тка (-и) ж *(в обращении)* sweetheart.

детона́тор (-а) м detonator.

детса́д (-а; *nom pl* **-ы́) м** *сокр* (= **де́тский сад**) kindergarten.

де́тск|ая (-ой; *decl like adj)* **ж** nursery.

де́тск|ий (-ая, -ое, -ие) *прил (годы, болезнь)* childhood; *(книга, игра)* children's; *(рассуждение, затея)* childish; **де́тская площа́дка** playground; **де́тский дом** children's home; **де́тский сад** kindergarten.

де́тств|о (-а) ср childhood; **впада́ть (впасть** *perf)* **в ~** to go senile.

де|ть (-ну, -нешь; *impf* **дева́ть) сов перех** *(разг)* to put; *(время, деньги)* to do with; **куда́ же я ~л э́ту кни́гу?** what on earth have I done with that book?; **э́того никуда́ не де́нешь** there's no arguing with that

▶ **де́ться (***impf* **дева́ться) сов возв** *(разг)* to get to; **куда́ она́/кни́га де́лась?** where has she/the book got to?; **не́куда ~ва́ться** *(impf) (разг)* there's nothing else for it.

де-фа́кто *нареч* de facto.

дефе́кт (-а) м defect.

дефекти́в|ный (-ен, -на, -но) *прил (умственно)* mentally defective; *(физически)* physically handicapped.

дефе́ктный *прил* defective.

дефектоскопи́|я (-и) ж *(ТЕХ)* detection of flaws.

дефи́с (-а) м hyphen.

дефици́т (-а) м *(ЭКОН)* deficit; *(нехватка):* **~ +***gen* или **в +***prp* shortage of; **~ платёжного бала́нса** *(ЭКОН)* balance of payments deficit.

дефици́тный *прил (предприятие, производство)* unprofitable; *(товар, сырьё)* scarce, in short supply.

дефля́ци|я (-и) ж *(ЭКОН)* deflation.

деформа́ци|я (-и) ж deformation.

деформи́р|овать (-ую) *(не)сов перех* to deform

▶ **деформи́роваться** *(не)сов возв* to be deformed.

децентрализа́ци|я (-и) ж decentralization.

децентрализ|ова́ть (-у́ю) *(не)сов перех* to decentralize.

дециб́ел (-а) м decibel.

дециме́тр (-а) м decimetre *(BRIT),* decimeter *(US).*

дешеве́|ть (*3sg* **-ет,** *3pl* **-ют,** *perf* **подешеве́ть) несов неперех** to go down in price.

дешёв|ка (-ки; *gen pl* **-ок) ж** *(перен: пренебр):* **э́та карти́на ~** this picture is tacky; **купи́ть** *(perf)*/**прода́ть** *(perf)* **что-н по ~ке** to buy/sell sth dirt-cheap.

деше́вле *сравн прил от* **дешёвый** ♦ *сравн нареч от* **дёшево.**

дёшево *нареч (купить)* cheaply.

дешёвое *сущ см* **дешёвка.**

дешёвый (дёшев, дешева́, дёшево) *прил (также раза)* cheap.

дешифр|ова́ть (-у́ю) *(не)сов перех* to decipher.

де-ю́ре *нареч* de jure.

де́ятелен *прил см* **де́ятельный.**

де́ятел|ь (-я) м: госуда́рственный ~ statesman; **полити́ческий ~** politician; **~ культу́ры** *person involved in the arts.*

де́ятельност|ь (-и) ж *(научная, педагогическая)* work, activity; *(сердца, мозга)*

activity.
де́ятел|ьный (-ен, -ьна, -ьно) *прил* active, energetic.
джаз (-а) *м* jazz.
джем (-а) *м* jam.
дже́мпер (-а) *м* jumper.
джентльме́н (-а) *м* gentleman (*мн* gentlemen).
джин (-а) *м* gin.
джи́нсов|ый *прил* denim; **джи́нсовая ткань** denim.
джи́нс|ы (-ов) *мн* jeans *мн*.
джо́йстик (-а) *м* (*КОМП*) joystick.
джо́кер (-а) *м* (*КАРТЫ*) joker.
джу́нгл|и (-ей) *мн* jungle *ед*.
джут (-а) *м* jute.
дзюдо́ *ср нескл* judo.
дзюдои́ст (-а) *м* judoist.
диабе́т (-а) *м*: **са́харный** ~ diabetes.
диабе́тик (-а) *м* diabetic.
диа́гноз (-а) *м* diagnosis; **ста́вить (поста́вить** *perf*) ~ to make a diagnosis.
диагности́р|овать (-ую) (*не*)*сов перех* (*МЕД*) to diagnose; (*ТЕХ*) to check.
диагона́ль (-и) *ж* diagonal.
диагра́мм|а (-ы) *ж* diagram.
диакрити́ческ|ий (-ая, -ое, -ие) *прил*: ~ **знак** diacritical mark.
диале́кт (-а) *м* dialect.
диале́ктик|а (-и) *ж* dialectics; (*событий, процесса*) dialectic.
диало́г (-а) *м* dialogue.
диало́говый *прил* (*КОМП*) conversational.
диа́метр (-а) *м* diameter.
диапазо́н (-а) *м* range; (*частот*) waveband; (*голоса, звука*) range, diapason.
диапозити́в (-а) *м* (*ФОТО*) slide.
диате́з (-а) *м* diathesis.
диафи́льм (-а) *м* (*ФОТО*) slide film.
диафра́гм|а (-ы) *ж* diaphragm.
дива́н (-а) *м* sofa.
дива́н-крова́ть (-и) *ж* sofa bed.
ди́вен *прил см* **ди́вный**.
диверса́нт (-а) *м* saboteur.
диверсифика́ци|я (-и) *ж* diversification.
диве́рси|я (-и) *ж* sabotage; **соверша́ть (соверши́ть** *perf*) ~**ю** to commit sabotage.
дивертисме́нт (-а) *м* divertissement.
дивиде́нд (-а) *м* dividend; **приноси́ть (принести́** *perf*) ~**ы** to pay dividends.
дивизио́н (-а) *м* unit; (*военных кораблей*) division.
диви́зи|я (-и) *ж* division.
ди́в|ный (-ен, -на, -но) *прил* marvellous.
дидакти́ческ|ий (-ая, -ое, -ие) *прил* didactic.
дие́з (-а) *м* (*МУЗ*) sharp.
дие́т|а (-ы) *ж* diet; **быть** (*impf*) **на** ~**е** to be on a diet; **соблюда́ть** (*impf*) ~**у** to keep to a diet.
диети́ческ|ий (-ая, -ое, -ие) *прил* dietetic.
диза́йн (-а) *м* design.

диза́йнер (-а) *м* designer.
ди́зел|ь (-я) *м* diesel engine.
дизентери́|я (-и) *ж* dysentery.
дика́р|ка (-ки; *gen pl* -ок) *ж* savage; (*перен*) *shy, unsociable woman or girl.*
дика́р|ь (-я́) *м* savage; (*перен*) *shy, unsociable man or boy*; (: *разг*) independent holidaymaker; **е́хать (пое́хать** *perf*) **дикарём на юг/на мо́ре** to go off on spec to the South/the seaside.
ди́к|ий (-ая, -ое, -ие; -, -а́, -о) *прил* wild; (*человек*) savage; (*ребёнок*) shy and unsociable; (*голод, холод*) terrible.
дикобра́з (-а) *м* porcupine.
дико́вин|а (-ы) *ж* (*разг*) marvel; **э́то мне в** ~**у** this is all too new.
дико́вин|ка (-ки; *gen pl* -ок) *ж* = **дико́вина**.
дикорасту́щ|ий (-ая, -ее, -ие) *прил* wild.
ди́кост|ь (-и) *ж* wildness; (*поступка, мысли*) absurdity.
дикта́нт (-а) *м* dictation.
дикта́тор (-а) *м* dictator.
диктату́р|а (-ы) *ж* dictatorship.
дикт|ова́ть (-у́ю; *perf* **продиктова́ть**) *несов перех* to dictate.
дикто́в|ка (-ки; *gen pl* -ок) *ж* dictation; **под чью-н** ~**ку** (*записывать*) from sb's dictation; (*действовать*) at sb's bidding.
ди́ктор (-а) *м* announcer; (*читающий новости*) newsreader.
диктофо́н (-а) *м* Dictaphone®.
ди́кци|я (-и) *ж* diction.
диле́мм|а (-ы) *ж* dilemma.
ди́лер (-а) *м*: ~ (**по** +*prp*) dealer (in).
дина́мик (-а) *м* (loud)speaker.
дина́мик|а (-и) *ж* (*ФИЗ*) dynamics; (*развития, процесса*) dynamics *мн*.
динами́т (-а) *м* dynamite.
динами́ч|ный (-ен, -на, -но) *прил* dynamic.
дина́сти|я (-и) *ж* dynasty.
диноза́вр (-а) *м* dinosaur.
дио́д (-а) *м* diode.
диоптри́|я (-и) *ж* dioptre (*BRIT*), diopter (*US*).
дипко́рпус (-а) *м сокр* (= *дипломати́ческий ко́рпус*) CD (= *Corps Diplomatique*).
дипло́м (-а) *м* (*ПРОСВЕЩ: свидетельство*) degree certificate; (: *на конкурсе*) certificate, diploma; (*научная работа*) dissertation (*for undergraduate degree*); **защища́ть (защити́ть** *perf*) ~ to have a viva (*for undergraduate degree*).
диплома́нт (-а) *м* award winner.
диплома́т (-а) *м* diplomat; (*разг: портфель*) briefcase.
дипломати́ческ|ий (-ая, -ое, -ие) *прил* diplomatic.
диплома́ти|я (-и) *ж* diplomacy.
диплломи́рованный *прил* qualified.
дир. *сокр* (= **дире́ктор**) dir. (= *director*).

The spelling rules for Russian are shown on page xvii.

директи́в|а (**-ы**) *ж* directive.
дире́ктор (**-а**; *nom pl* **-á**) *м* director; ~ **шкóлы** headmaster; ~**распоряди́тель** managing director; **глáвный исполни́тельный** ~ chief executive.
дире́кци|я (**-и**) *ж* (*завода, фáбрики*) management; (*шкóлы*) ≈ board (of governors); (*фи́рмы*) board (of directors).
дирижáбл|ь (**-я**) *м* airship, dirigible.
дирижёр (**-а**) *м* (*МУЗ*) conductor.
дирижёрск|ий (**-ая, -ое, -ие**) *прил*: ~**ая пáлочка** (conductor's) baton.
дирижи́р|овать (**-ую**) *несов неперех* (+*instr*) to conduct.
дисгармóни|я (**-и**) *ж* discord.
диск (**-а**) *м* (*тáкже КОМП*) disk; (*СПОРТ*) discus; (*МУЗ*) record; **ги́бкий/жёсткий** ~ floppy/hard disk; ~ **с удвóенной плóтностью** double-density floppy disk.
дисквалифици́р|овать (**-ую**) (*не*)*сов перех* (*врачá, юри́ста*) to strike off; (*спортсме́на*) to disqualify.
диске́т (**-а**) *м* diskette.
диске́т|а (**-ы**) *ж* = **диске́т**.
диск-жоке́|й (**-я**) *м* disc jockey.
ди́ско *ср нескл* disco.
дискóнт (**-а**) *м* (*КОММ*) discount.
дискоте́к|а (**-и**) *ж* (*собрáние пласти́нок*) record collection; (*тáнцы*) discotheque.
дискредити́р|овать (**-ую**) (*не*)*сов перех* to discredit.
дискримина́ци|я (**-и**) *ж* discrimination.
дискримини́р|овать (**-ую**) (*не*)*сов перех* to discriminate against.
дискуссиóнный *прил* (*спóрный*) debat(e)able.
диску́сси|я (**-и**) *ж* discussion.
дискути́р|овать (**-ую**) *несов перех* to discuss.
дислокáци|я (**-и**) *ж* (*ВОЕН*) deployment; (*МЕД*) dislocation.
дислоци́р|овать (**-ую**) (*не*)*сов перех* (*ВОЕН*) to deploy.
диспансе́р (**-а**) *м* dispensary.
диспе́тчер (**-а**) *м* controller; **авиациóнный** ~ air-traffic controller.
диспе́тчерск|ая (**-ой**; *decl like adj*) *ж* controller's office; (*АВИА*) control tower.
диспе́тчерск|ий (**-ая, -ое, -ие**) *прил*: ~**ая слу́жба** control section; ~**ая вы́шка** control tower.
дисплé|й (**-я**) *м* (*КОМП*) display.
диспропóрци|я (**-и**) *ж* disproportion.
ди́спут (**-а**) *м* debate.
диссертáнт (**-а**) *м* (*post-graduate*) *student defending a PhD thesis*.
диссертáци|я (**-и**) *ж* ≈ PhD thesis; **защищáть** (*impf*) ~**ю** to be examined on one's thesis; **защити́ть** (*perf*) ~**ю** to pass a viva.
диссиде́нт (**-а**) *м* dissident.
диссонáнс (**-а**) *м* (*МУЗ*) dissonance; (*перен*) discord; **вноси́ть** (**внести́** *perf*) ~ **во что-н** (*перен*) to bring a note of discord into sth.

дистанциóнн|ый *прил*: ~**ое управле́ние** remote control.
дистáнци|я (**-и**) *ж* distance; **сохраня́ть** (**сохрани́ть** *perf*) ~**ю** (*перен*) to keep one's distance; **он сошёл с** ~**и** (*СПОРТ*) he didn't last the distance.
дистилли́р|овать (**-ую**) (*не*)*сов перех* to distil (*BRIT*), distill (*US*).
дистрибью́тор (**-а**) *м* distributor.
дистрофи́|я (**-и**) *ж* dystrophy.
дисципли́н|а (**-ы**) *ж* discipline.
дисциплини́рован|ный (**-, -на, -но**) *прил* disciplined.
дит|я́ (**-и́**; *nom pl* **дéти**) *ср* child; *см тáкже* **дéти**.
дифтери́т (**-а**) *м* diphtheria.
дифтóнг (**-а**) *м* diphthong.
дифференциáльный *прил* (*ЭКОН*) differential *опред*.
дифференци́рованн|ый *прил*: ~**ая зарплáта** differential.
дифференци́р|овать (**-ую**) (*не*)*сов перех* to differentiate.
дича́|ть (**-ю**; *perf* **одича́ть**) *несов неперех* to grow wild.
дичь (**-и**) *ж собир* game; (*разг*) rubbish.
диэле́ктрик (**-а**) *м* dielectric.
ДК *м сокр* (= **Дворе́ц культу́ры, Дом культу́ры**) *centre for social and cultural activities*.
длин|á (**-ы́**) *ж* length; **в** ~**у́** lengthways; ~**óй 10 ме́тров** 10 metres (*BRIT*) *или* meters (*US*) long; ~ **ткáни – 10 метрóв** the cloth is 10 metres long.
дли́нен *прил см* **дли́нный**.
длинноволновóй *прил* long-wave.
длинноволóсый *прил* long-haired.
длиннонóг|ий (**-ая, -ое, -ие**) *прил* long-legged.
длинноýк|ий (**-ая, -ое, -ие**) *прил* with long arms.
дли́нно *нареч* (*рассуждáть*) at length ♦ *как сказ*: **плáтье мне** ~ the dress is too long for me.
дли́н|ный (**-ен, -á, -но**) *прил* long; (*разг*: *человéк*) tall; **у негó** ~ **язы́к** (*разг*) he's got a big mouth; **дли́нный рубль** (*разг*) easy money.
дли́тельность (**-и**) *ж* length.
дли́тельный *прил* lengthy.
дли́|ться (*3sg* **-и́тся**, *3pl* **-я́тся**, *perf* **продли́ться**) *несов возв* (*урóк, бесéда*) to last.

KEYWORD

для *предл* (+*gen*) **1** for; **для óбщего блáга** for the general good; **мéсто для пóдписи** space for a signature; **крем для лицá** face cream; **альбóм для рисовáния** sketch pad
2 (*в отношéнии когó-н/чегó-н*): **для меня́ э́то имéет большóе значéние** this is very important to me; **для тогó чтóбы** in order to; **для негó э́то прóсто рабóта** this is just work to him; **э́то полéзно для здорóвья** this is good for one's health; **для своегó вóзраста он óчень развитóй** he is very advanced for his age.

дм *сокр* (= **дециме́тр**) dm= *decimetre* (*BRIT*) *или decimeter* (*US*).
дн|евáть (**-ю́ю, -ю́ешь**) *несов неперех*: ~ **и**

ночева́ть где́-нибудь (*разг*) to be somewhere day and night.

дневни́к (**-а́**) *м* diary; (*ПРОСВЕЩ*) register; **вести́** (*impf*) ~ to keep a diary.

дневн|о́й *прил* (*выработка, заработок*) daily; **~а́я фо́рма обуче́ния** full-time education; ~ **свет** daylight; **~о́е вре́мя** daytime; **дневно́й спекта́кль** matinee.

днём *сущ см* **день** ♦ *нареч*: ~ in the daytime; (*после обеда*) in the afternoon; **его́ ~ с огнём не найти́** he is absolutely nowhere to be found.

Днепр (**-а**) *м* Dnieper.

Днестр (**-а**) *м* Dniester.

дни *итп сущ см* **день**.

дни́ще (**-а**) *ср* bottom.

ДНК *ж сокр* (= дезоксирибонуклеи́новая кислота́) DNA (= *deoxyribonucleic acid*).

дн|о (**-а**) *ср* (*моря, реки*) bottom, bed; (*ямы, овра́га*) bottom; (*nom pl* **до́нья**, *gen pl* **до́ньев**; *бочки, ящика*) bottom; **идти́** (**пойти́** *perf*) **ко ~у** to sink to the bottom; (*перен: предприятие*) to go under; (: *человек*) to sink.

дня *итп сущ см* **день**.

KEYWORD

до *предл* (+*gen*) **1** (*о пределе движения*) as far as, to; **мы дое́хали до реки́** we went as far as *или* to the river; **я проводи́л его́ до ста́нции** I saw him off at the station

2 (*о расстоянии*) to; **до го́рода 3 киломе́тра** it is 3 kilometres (*BRIT*) *или* kilometers (*US*) to the town

3 (*о временно́м пределе*) till, until; **я отложи́л заседа́ние до утра́** I postponed the meeting till *или* until morning; **я рабо́таю с восьми́ до пяти́** I work from eight to five; **до свида́ния!** goodbye!

4 (*перед*) before; **мы зако́нчили до переры́ва** we finished before the break

5 (*о пределе состояния*): **мне бы́ло оби́дно до слёз** I was so hurt I cried; **он крича́л до хрипоты́** he shouted himself hoarse; **на́до нагре́ть во́ду до кипе́ния** the water must be heated until it boils

6 (*полностью*): **я отда́л ей всё до копе́йки** I gave her everything down to my last kopeck; **он вы́пил буты́лку до дна** he drank the bottle dry

7 (*направление действия*): **ребёнок дотро́нулся до игру́шки** the child touched the toy; **мне до него́ нет никако́го де́ла** (*разг*) I have no truck with him

♦ *ср нескл* (*МУЗ*) doh.

до- *префикс* (*in verbs*; *доведеине действия до конца*) indicating completion of action eg. **добежа́ть**; (*о достижении какого-нибудь результата*) indicating achievement of a certain goal eg. **дозвони́ться**; (*in adverbs*;

доведение качества до какого-нибудь предела) indicating attainment of a quality to a certain degree eg. **докрасна́**; (*о дополнительном действии*) indicating supplement to an action eg. **дода́ть**; (*in adjectives*; **бывший прежде чего-н**) pre-.

доба́в|ить (**-лю, -ишь**; *impf* **добавля́ть**) *сов перех* to add.

доба́в|ка (**-ки**; *gen pl* **-ок**) *ж* (*к обеду*) additional helping; (*пищевая, бетонная*) additive.

добавле́ни|е (**-я**) *ср* addition; **де́лать** (**сде́лать** *perf*) **~я к** +*dat* to make an addition to; **в ~ к** +*dat* in addition to.

доба́влю *сов см* **доба́вить**.

добавля́|ть (**-ю**) *несов от* **доба́вить**.

доба́вок *сущ см* **доба́вка**.

доба́вочн|ый *прил* additional ♦ (**-ого**; *decl like adj*) *м* (*также*: **~ телефо́н**) extension number.

добе|жа́ть (*как* **бежа́ть**; *см* Table 20; *impf* **добега́ть**) *сов неперех*: ~ **до** +*gen* to run to *или* as far as; (*звуки, волны*) to reach.

добела́ *нареч*: **отмы́ть что-н** ~ to wash sth clean; **раскали́ть** (*perf*) **что-н** ~ to heat sth until it's white-hot.

доберу́сь *итп сов см* **добра́ться**.

добива́|ть(ся) (**-ю(сь)**) *несов от* **доби́ть(ся)**.

добира́|ться (**-юсь**) *несов от* **добра́ться**.

доб|и́ть (**-ью, -ьёшь**; *impf* **добива́ть**) *сов перех* (*убить*) to finish off; (*разбить*) to break

► **доби́ться** (*impf* **добива́ться**) *сов возв* (+*gen*) to achieve; **добива́ться** (**~ся** *perf*) **своего́** to get what one wants.

до́блестн|ый (**-ен, -на, -но**) *прил* valiant.

до́блест|ь (**-и**) *ж* valour (*BRIT*), valor (*US*).

доб|ра́ться (**-еру́сь, -ерёшься**; *impf* **добира́ться**) *сов возв*: ~ **до** +*gen* to get to, reach; (*решения*) to reach; **добира́ться** (**~** *perf*) **до су́ти** (**де́ла**) to get to the heart of the matter; **я до тебя́ ~еру́сь!** (*разг*) I'll get you!

добр|е́ть (**-ю**; *perf* **подобре́ть**) *несов неперех* to become kinder; (*perf* **раздобре́ть**; *разг*) to fill out.

добр|о́ (**-а́**) *ср* good; (*разг: имущество*) things *мн* ♦ *част* (*разг: ладно*) fine; **жела́ть** (**пожела́ть** *perf*) **кому́-н ~а́** to wish sb well; ~ **пожа́ловать** (**в Москву́**)! welcome to Moscow)!; **дава́ть** (**дать** *perf*) **кому́-н ~ на что-н** to give sb the go-ahead for sth; **получа́ть** (**получи́ть** *perf*) ~ (**на что-н**) to get the go-ahead (for sth).

доброво́л|ец (**-ьца**) *м* volunteer; **идти́** (**пойти́** *perf*) **~ьцем** to volunteer.

доброво́л|ьный (**-ен, -ьна, -ьно**) *прил* voluntary; **на ~ьных нача́лах** on a voluntary basis.

доброво́льца *итп сущ см* **доброво́лец**.

доброде́тел|ь (**-и**) *ж* virtue.

доброде́тельный *прил* virtuous.

добродуш|ный (-ен, -на, -но) *прил* good-natured.

доброжела́тельность (-и) *ж* benevolence.

доброжела́тельный *прил* benevolent.

доброка́чествен|ный (-, -на, -но) *прил* (*продукт, изделие*) quality *опред*; (*no short form*; *опухоль*) benign.

добропоря́доч|ный (-ен, -на, -но) *прил* respectable.

добросерде́ч|ный (-ен, -на, -но) *прил* (*человек*) kind-hearted; (*слова*) kind.

добросо́вест|ный (-ен, -на, -но) *прил* conscientious.

добрососе́дств|о (-а) *ср* neighbourliness (*BRIT*), neighborliness (*US*).

доброт|а́ (-ы́) *ж* kindness.

добро́т|ный (-ен, -на, -но) *прил* good-quality.

до́бр|ый (-, -а́, -о, -ы) *прил* kind; (*совет, имя*) good; (*милый*: *друг итп*) dear; **бу́дьте добры́!** excuse me!; **бу́дьте добры́, позвони́те нам за́втра!** would you be so good as to phone us tomorrow?; **всего́ ~ого!** all the best!; **~ого здоро́вья!** take care!; **~ день/ве́чер!** good afternoon/evening!; **~ое у́тро!** good morning!; **по ~ой во́ле** of one's own free will; **чего́ ~ого** (*разг*) it's not impossible.

добу́ду *итп сов см* **добы́ть**.

добыва́|ть (-ю) *несов от* **добы́ть**.

добыва́ющий (-ая, -ее, -ие) *прил*: **~ая промы́шленность** *mining, gas and oil industries.*

добы́тчик (-а) *м* (*золота*) miner; (*нефти*) oil worker.

добы́ть (*как быть; см* **Table 21**; *impf* **добыва́ть**) *сов перех* (*денга, машину*) to get; (*нефть*) to extract; (*руду, золото*) to mine.

добы́ч|а (-и) *ж* (*процесс: нефти*) extraction; (: *руды*) mining, extraction; (*то, что добыто*) output; (: *на охоте, ловле*) catch.

добью́(сь) *итп сов см* **доби́ть(ся)**.

доведу́(сь) *итп сов см* **довести́(сь)**.

довез|ти́ (-у́; *pt* довёз, -ла́, -ло́, *impf* **довози́ть**) *сов перех*: **~ кого́-н до** +*gen* to take sb to *или* as far as.

довёл(ся) *итп сов см* **довести́(сь)**.

дове́ренность (-и) *ж* power of attorney; **де́йствовать** (*impf*) **по ~и** to act by proxy.

дове́ренн|ый (-ого; *decl like adj*) *м* (*также*: **~ое лицо́**) proxy.

дове́ри|е (-я) *ср* confidence, trust; **по́льзоваться** (*impf*) **чьим-н ~м** to enjoy sb's confidence; **входи́ть** (**войти́** *perf*) **в чьё-н ~** to gain sb's confidence; **выходи́ть** (**вы́йти** *perf*) **из чьего́-н ~я** to lose sb's confidence.

довери́телен *прил см* **довери́тельный**.

довери́тел|ь (-я) *м person who empowers another to act on his or her behalf.*

довери́тел|ьный (-ен, -ьна, -ьно) *прил* trusting.

дове́р|ить (-ю, -ишь; *impf* **доверя́ть**) *сов перех*: **~ что-н кому́-н** to entrust sb with sth

▸ **дове́риться** (*impf* **доверя́ться**) *сов возв*: **~ся** +*dat* to confide in; (*положи́ться*) to trust.

до́верху *нареч* (up) to the top; **напо́лненный ~** full to the brim.

дове́рчивость (-и) *ж* trustingness.

дове́рчив|ый (-, -а, -о) *прил* trusting.

доверша́|ть (-ю) *несов от* **доверши́ть**.

доверше́ни|е (-я) *ср* completion; **в ~ или к доверше́нию всего́** on top of everything else.

доверш|и́ть (-у́, -и́шь; *impf* **доверша́ть**) *сов перех* to complete.

доверя́|ть (-ю) *несов от* **дове́рить** ◆ *неперех*: **~** +*dat* to trust.

дове|сти́ (-ду́, -дёшь; *pt* довёл, -ла́, -ло́, *impf* **доводи́ть**) *сов перех*: **~ кого́-н/что-н до** +*gen* to take sb/sth to *или* as far as; **доводи́ть** (**~** *perf*) **что-н до конца́** to see sth through to the end; **доводи́ть** (**~** *perf*) **кого́-н до слёз** to reduce sb to tears; **доводи́ть** (**~** *perf*) **кого́-н до отча́яния** to drive sb to despair; **доводи́ть** (**~** *perf*) **что-н до соверше́нства** to perfect sth; **доводи́ть** (**~** *perf*) **ско́рость до преде́ла** to reach the speed limit; **доводи́ть** (**~** *perf*) **что-н до све́дения кого́-н** to inform sb of sth

▸ **довести́сь** *сов безл*: **мне не ~дётся верну́ться туда́** I won't get the opportunity *или* chance to go back there; **переда́йте приве́т, е́сли Вам ~дётся встре́тить её** say hello if you happen to see her.

до́вод (-а) *м* argument; **приводи́ть** (**привести́** *perf*) **~** to put forward an argument.

довод|и́ть (-жу́, -дишь) *несов от* **довести́**

▸ **доводи́ться** *несов от* **довести́сь** ◆ *возв*: **он дово́дится ей бра́том/вну́ком** (*разг*) he is her brother/grandson.

дово́енный *прил* prewar.

довожу́(сь) *несов см* **доводи́ть(ся)**.

дово|зи́ть (-жу́, -зишь) *несов от* **довезти́**.

довол|ен *прил см* **дово́льный**.

дово́льно *нареч* (*известный, сильный*) quite; (*улыбаться, сказать*) with satisfaction ◆ *как сказ* it's enough; **~ спо́ров** *или* **спо́рить!** that's enough arguing!

дово́л|ьный (-ен, -ьна, -ьно) *прил* satisfied, contented; **он ~ен рабо́той/жи́знью** he's satisfied *или* happy with his work/life.

дово́льств|оваться (-уюсь) *несов возв*: **~** +*instr* to be happy *или* content with; **он ~уется ма́лым** *или* **немно́гим** it doesn't take much to make him happy.

довооруж|и́ть (-у́, -и́шь; *impf* **довооружа́ть**) *сов перех* (*оконча́тельно*) to arm; (*дополни́тельно*) to provide with additional arms.

довы́бор|ы (-ов) *мн* ≈ by-election *ед*.

дог (-а) *м* (*ЗООЛ*) Great Dane.

догада́|ться (-юсь; *impf* **дога́дываться**) *сов возв* to guess.

дога́дк|а (-ки; *gen pl* -ок) *ж* guess; **стро́ить** (*impf*) **~ки о** +*prp* to speculate about; **теря́ться** (*impf*) **в ~х** to be baffled *или* at a loss.

догáдлив|ый (-, -а, -о) *прил* quick-witted.
догáдок *сущ см* **догáдка**.
догáдыва|ться (-юсь) *несов от* **догадáться**.
дóгм|а (-ы) *ж* dogma.
догмáт (-а) *м* (*РЕЛ*) dogma.
догмати́ческий (-ая, -ое, -ие) *прил* dogmatic.
дог|нáть (-оню́, -о́нишь; *impf* **догоня́ть**) *сов перех* to catch up with; ~ (*perf*) **кого́-н/что-н до** +*gen* to drive sb/sth to.
догова́рива|ться (-юсь) *несов от* **договори́ться**.
догово́р (-а) *м* (*ПОЛИТ*) treaty; (*КОММ*) agreement; ~ **о** +*prp*/**на** +*acc* agreement on *или* about; **заключа́ть (заключи́ть** *perf*)/**расторга́ть (расто́ргнуть** *perf*) ~ to sign/annul a treaty.
договорённост|ь (-и) *ж* agreement; **достигáть (дости́гнуть** *perf*) ~**и в чём-н** to reach an agreement on *или* about sth; **по ~и** by agreement.
договорено́ *как сказ*: ~ **о** +*prp* ... there's been an agreement on ....
договор|и́ться (-ю́сь, -и́шься; *impf* **догова́риваться**) *сов возв*: ~ **с кем-н о чём-н** (*о встрече*) to arrange sth with sb; (*о цене*) to agree sth with sb; **мы ~и́лись до глу́постей/гру́бостей** we ended up talking nonsense/insulting each other; **мы ~и́лись встре́титься** we agreed to meet.
догово́рник (-а) *м* (*разг*) contract worker.
догово́рный *прил* (*цена*) agreed; (*обязательство*) contractual; **на ~ых начáлах** on a contractual basis.
догола́ *нареч*: **раздéться** ~ to strip bare; **постри́чься** (*perf*) ~ to have all one's hair cut off.
догоню́ *итп сов см* **догнáть**.
догоня́|ть (-ю) *несов от* **догнáть**.
догор|éть (-ю́, -и́шь; *impf* **догорáть**) *сов неперех* to burn out.
догру|зи́ть (-жу́, -зишь) *сов перех* to finish loading.
дода́|ть (*как* **дать**; *см* **Table 14**; *impf* **додавáть**) *сов перех*: ~ **кому́-н 10 рублéй** to give sb an extra 10 roubles.
додéла|ть (-ю; *impf* **додéлывать**) *сов перех* to finish.
доду́ма|ться (-юсь; *impf* **доду́мываться**) *сов возв*: ~ **до** +*gen* to hit on; **как ты мог до такóго ~?** what on earth gave you that idea?
доеда́|ть (-ю) *несов от* **доéсть**.
доéдешь *итп сов см* **доéхать**.
доеди́м *итп сов см* **доéсть**.
доéду *итп сов см* **доéхать**.
доезжáй(те) *сов см* **доéхать**.
доезжá|ть (-ю) *несов от* **доéхать**.
доéсть (*как* **есть**; *см* **Table 15**; *impf* **доедáть**) *сов перех* to finish off, eat up.

доéхать (*как* **éхать**; *см* **Table 19**; *impf* **доезжáть**) *сов неперех*: ~ **до** +*gen* to reach.
доéшь *сов см* **доéсть**.
дожд|áться (-у́сь, -ёшься; *pt* -áлся, -алáсь, -алóсь, *imper* -и́(те)сь) *сов неперех*: ~ **когó-н/чегó-н** to wait until sb/sth comes; ~ (*perf*) **пóезда** to wait until the train arrives; **он ~ётся вы́говора** (*разг*) he'll end up getting told off; **ты у меня́ ~ёшься!** (*разг*) just you wait!; **он ждёт не ~ётся** (*разг*) he can't wait.
дождли́в|ый (-, -а, -о) *прил* rainy.
дожд|ь (-я́) *м* rain; (*перен*) cascade; **идти́ гуля́ть** (*impf*) **в** ~ to go for a walk in the rain; ~ **идёт** it's raining; ~ **пошёл** it has started to rain; **попадáть (попáсть** *perf*) **под** ~ to get caught in the rain; ~ **льёт как из ведрá** it's bucketing (with rain).
дожива́|ть (-ю) *несов от* **дожи́ть** ♦ *неперех* (*жизнь, годы*) to live out.
дожидá|ться (-юсь) *несов возв* (+*gen*) to wait for.
дожи́|ть (-ву́, -вёшь; *impf* **дожива́ть**) *сов неперех*: ~ **до** +*gen* (*до старости*) to live to; (*до конца года*) to live until.
дóз|а (-ы) *ж* dose; ~ **облучéния** dose of radiation.
дозвáнива|ться (-юсь) *несов от* **дозвони́ться**.
дозвóленный *прил* permitted.
дозвон|и́ться (-ю́сь, -и́шься; *impf* **дозвáниваться**) *сов возв* to get through.
дози́метр (-а) *м* dosimetre (*BRIT*), dosimeter (*US*).
дози́р|овать (-ую) (*не*)*сов перех* to measure out.
дозóр (-а) *м* patrol; **быть** (*impf*) **в** ~**е** to be on patrol.
доигрá|ть (-ю; *impf* **доигрывать**) *сов перех* to finish (playing).
доигрывани|е (-я) *ср* (*СПОРТ*) playing to a finish.
доигрыва|ть (-ю) *несов от* **доигрáть**.
доистори́ческий (-ая, -ое, -ие) *прил* prehistoric.
до|и́ть (-ю́, -ишь; *perf* **подои́ть**) *несов перех* to milk.
дóйн|ый *прил*: ~**ая корóва** dairy cow.
доймý *итп сов см* **доня́ть**.
дойти́ (*как* **идти́**; *см* **Table 18**; *impf* **доходи́ть**) *сов неперех*: ~ **до** +*gen* to reach; (*традиции, предания*) to be passed down to; (*слова, смысл*) to get through to; **доходи́ть** (~ *perf*) **до отчáяния/истощéния** to reach the point of desperation/exhaustion; **до моего́ свéдения дошлó, что** ... it has been brought to my attention that ....
док (-а) *м* dock.
докажý *итп сов см* **доказáть**.

доказа́тельств|о (-а) *ср* (*правоты, дружбы*) proof, evidence; (*теории*) demonstration; **служи́ть** (**послужи́ть** *perf*) **~м** +*gen* to be evidence of.

доказа́ть (-жу́, -жешь; *impf* **дока́зывать**) *сов перех* (*правду, виновность*) to prove; (*теорему*) to demonstrate.

дока́нчива|ть (-ю) *несов от* **доко́нчить**.

дока́нывать (-ю) *несов от* **докона́ть**.

дока́пыва|ться (-юсь) *несов от* **докопа́ться**.

докати́ться (-чу́сь, -тишься; *impf* **дока́тываться**) *сов возв* (*звуки, шум*) to reach; **дока́тываться** (~ *perf*) **до** +*gen* (*мяч, волны*) to roll in to; **дока́тываться** (~ *perf*) **до преступле́ния** to stoop to crime.

до́кер (-а) *м* docker.

докла́д (-а) *м* (*на съезде итп*) paper; (*директору итп*) report.

докладн|а́я (-о́й; *decl like adj*) *ж* (*также:* ~ **запи́ска**) memo.

докла́дчик (-а) *м* speaker.

докла́дчиц|а (-ы) *ж см* **докла́дчик**.

докла́дыва|ть (-ю) *несов от* **доложи́ть**.

докона́|ть (-ю; *impf* **дока́нывать**) *сов перех* (*разг*) ~ **кого́-н** to do sb in.

доко́нчить (-у, -ишь; *impf* **дока́нчивать**) *сов перех* to finish off.

докопа́|ться (-юсь; *impf* **дока́пываться**) *возв*: ~ **до** +*gen* (*перен: разг: до фактов, истины*) to dig up; (*до клада, воды*) to dig down to.

до́ктор (-а; *nom pl* -á) *м* doctor; ~ **нау́к** Doctor of Sciences (*postdoctoral research degree in Russia*).

до́кторск|ий (-ая, -ое, -ие) *прил* (*МЕД*) doctor's; (*ПРОСВЕЩ*) postdoctoral.

доктри́н|а (-ы) *ж* doctrine.

докуме́нт (-а) *м* document.

докуча́|ть (-ю) *несов неперех*: ~ **кому́-н чем-н** to pester sb with sth.

документа́л|ьный (-ен, -ьна, -ьно) *прил* documentary; **документа́льный фильм** documentary.

документа́ци|я (-и) *ж собир* documentation.

документи́р|овать (-ую) (*не)сов перех* to document.

долби́ть (-лю́, -и́шь; *perf* **продолби́ть**) *несов перех* to hollow out; (*no perf; разг: зубрить*) to learn by rote; ~ (*impf*) **в дверь** (*разг*) to hammer on the door.

долг (-а; *loc sg* -у́, *nom pl* -и́) *м* debt; **вне́шний/госуда́рственный** ~ (*ЭКОН*) foreign/national debt; **дава́ть** (**дать** *perf*)/**брать** (**взять** *perf*) **что-н в** ~ to lend/borrow sth; **входи́ть** (**войти́** *perf*)/**залеза́ть** (**зале́зть** *perf*) **в** ~ to get/fall into debt; **быть** (*impf*) **в** ~ý **пе́ред кем-н** *или* **у кого́-н** to be indebted to sb; **по до́лгу слу́жбы** in the course of duty; **пе́рвым до́лгом** (*разг*) first of all.

до́лг|ий (-гая, -гое, -гие; -ог, -гá, -го) *прил* long; **в** ~ **я́щик откла́дывать** (**отложи́ть** *perf*) **что-н**

to put sth off, postpone sth; **до́лгий гла́сный** long vowel.

до́лго *нареч* for a long time; **как** ~ **продли́тся фильм?** how long will the film last?

долгове́чный (-ен, -на, -но) *прил* (*материал*) durable, long-lasting; (*дружба*) lasting.

долгов|о́й *прил*: ~**а́я распи́ска** IOU; ~**о́е обяза́тельство** promissory note.

долговре́менный *прил* prolonged.

долгожда́нный *прил* long-awaited.

долгожи́тел|ь (-я) *м* long-lived person.

долгожи́тельниц|а (-ы) *ж см* **долгожи́тель**.

долгоигра́ющий (-ая, -ее, -ие) *прил*: ~**ая пласти́нка** L.P. (= *long-playing record*).

долголе́тн|ий (-яя, -ее, -ие) *прил*: ~**ее сотру́дничество** long-standing cooperation.

долгосро́чный *прил* long-term.

долгот|á (-ы́) *ж* length; (*ГЕО*) longitude.

до́лее *сравн прил от* **до́лгий** ♦ *сравн нареч от* **до́лго**.

до́лек *сущ см* **до́лька**.

доле|те́ть (-чу́, -ти́шь; *impf* **долета́ть**) *сов неперех*: ~ **до** +*gen* to fly to, reach; (*звук, слухи*) to reach.

┌─────────────┐
│ **KEYWORD** │
└─────────────┘

до́лж|ен (-нá, -нó, -ны́) *часть сказуемого* (+*infin*) **1** (*обязан*): **я до́лжен уйти́** I must go; **я до́лжен бу́ду уйти́** I will have to go; **она́ должна́ была́ уйти́** she had to go

2 (*выражает предположение*): **он до́лжен ско́ро прийти́** he should arrive soon

3 (+*dat; о долге*): **ты до́лжен мне 5 рубле́й** you owe me 5 roubles

4: **должно́ быть** (*вероятно*) probably; **кто́-то, должно́ быть сто́рож, закры́л дверь** somebody, probably the night watchman, closed the door; **должно́ быть, она́ о́чень уста́ла** she must have been very tired.

должни́|к (-á) *м* debtor.

должни́ц|а (-ы) *ж см* **должни́к**.

до́лжн|ое (-ого; *decl like adj*) *ср* due; **отдава́ть** (**отда́ть** *perf*) *или* **воздава́ть** (**возда́ть** *perf*) ~ **кому́-н** to give sb his *итп* due.

должностн|о́й *прил* official; ~**о́е преступле́ние** malfeasance; **должностно́е лицо́** official.

до́лжност|ь (-и; *gen pl* -éй) *ж* (*пост*) post; (*обязанность*) duties *мн*; **вступа́ть** (**вступи́ть** *perf*) **в** ~ **кого́-н** to assume sb's post; **по** ~**и** ex officio.

до́лжн|ый *прил* (*уровень*) required; (*внимание*) sufficient.

доли́н|а (-ы) *ж* valley.

до́ллар (-а) *м* dollar.

до́лларов|ый *прил* dollar *опред*; ~ **счёт** dollar account.

доложи́ть (-ý, -ишь; *impf* **докла́дывать**) *сов перех* to report ♦ *неперех*: ~ **о** +*prp* to give a report on; ~ (*perf*) **о прихо́де кого́-н** to announce sb.

доло́й *нареч* away with; ~ **апарте́йд!** down

with apartheid!

доло|то́ (-ота́; *nom pl* **-о́та**) *ср* chisel; (*для бурения*) drill.

до́льше *сравн прил от* **до́лгий** ♦ *сравн нареч от* **до́лго**.

до́ль|ка (-ки; *gen pl* **-ек**) *ж* (*апельсина*) segment.

до́л|я (-и; *gen pl* **-ей**) *ж* share; (*пирога*) portion; (*судьба*) lot, fate; ~ **секу́нды/сантиме́тра** a fraction of a second/centimetre (*BRIT*) *или* centimeter (*US*); **входи́ть** (**войти́** *perf*) **в ~ю с кем-н** to go shares with sb; **выпада́ть** (**вы́пасть** *perf*) **на чью-н ~ю** to fall to sb's lot.

дом (-а; *nom pl* **-а́**) *м* house; (*многоэтажный*) block of flats (*BRIT*), apartment building (*US*); (*свое жильё*) home; (*семья*) household; ~ **Рома́новых** the house of Romanov; ~ **культу́ры** *centre for social and cultural activities*; **рабо́тать** (*impf*) **на ~у́** to work from home; **рабо́тать** (*impf*) **по до́му** to do the housework; **дом моде́лей** fashion house; **дом о́тдыха** ≈ holiday centre (*BRIT*) *или* center (*US*).

до́ма *нареч* at home; **быть** (*impf*) *или* **чу́вствовать** (*impf*) **себя́ как** ~ to feel at home; **его́ нет** ~ he's out *или* not at home; **сиде́ть** (*impf*) ~ to stay in *или* at home; **у него́ не все** ~ (*разг*) he's not all there.

дома́шн|ий (-яя, -ее, -ие) *прил* (*адрес, телефон*) home *опред*; (*еда*) home-made; (*животное*) domestic; **~ие ту́фли** (carpet) slippers; **~ее пла́тье** housecoat; **дома́шняя хозя́йка** housewife; **дома́шняя рабо́тница** domestic help (*BRIT*), maid (*US*); **дома́шнее зада́ние** homework.

до́менн|ый *прил* (*цех*) smelting *опред*; **~ая печь** blast furnace.

доминика́нск|ий (-ая, -ое, -ие) *прил*: **Д~ая Респу́блика** Dominican Republic.

доминио́н (-а) *м* dominion.

домини́р|овать (-ую) *несов неперех* (*идея, мелодия*) to predominate; ~ (*impf*) **над** +*instr* to dominate.

домино́ *ср нескл* (*игра*) dominoes *ед*; (*фишка, костюм*) domino.

домко́м (-а) *м сокр* (= **домово́й комите́т**) ≈ residents' association.

домкра́т (-а) *м* (*ТЕХ*) jack.

домовладе́л|ец (-ьца) *м* home owner.

домовладе́ни|е (-я) *ср* (*дом с участком*) *house with grounds attached*; (*владение домом*) home ownership.

домово́дств|о (-а) *ср* home economics.

домов|о́й (-о́го; *decl like adj*) *м* (*ФОЛЬКЛОР*) house spirit.

домо́в|ый *прил* (*ворота*) house *опред*; **домо́вая кни́га** property register.

домога́|ться (-юсь) *несов возв*: ~ +*gen* (*власти*) to strive for; ~ (*impf*) **чьей-н руки́** to court *или* woo sb.

домо́й *нареч* home; **мне пора́** ~ it's time for me to go home.

доморо́щенный *прил* (*разг: пренебр*) homespun.

домосе́д (-а) *м* stay-at-home.

домоуправле́ни|е (-я) *ср* ≈ housing department.

домофо́н (-а) *м* intercom.

домохозя́|йка (-йки; *gen pl* **-ек**) *ж* (= **дома́шняя хозя́йка**) housewife.

домоча́д|ец (-ца) *м* (*обычно мн*) member of the household.

домрабо́тниц|а (-ы) *ж* (= **дома́шняя рабо́тница**) domestic help (*BRIT*), maid (*US*).

домч|а́ться (-у́сь, -и́шься) *сов возв*: ~ (**до** +*gen*) to rush (to).

до́мысел (-ла) *м* conjecture.

донага́ *нареч*: **разде́ть кого́-н** ~ to strip sb naked.

дона́шива|ть (-ю) *несов от* **доноси́ть**.

доне́льзя *нареч* (*разг*) terribly.

донёс *итп сов см* **донести́**.

донесе́ни|е (-я) *ср* report.

донес|ти́ (-у́, -ёшь; *pt* **донёс, -ла́, -ло́**, *impf* **доноси́ть**) *сов перех* to carry ♦ *неперех*: ~ **на** +*acc* to inform on; ~ (*perf*) **о** +*prp* to report on

▸ **донести́сь** (*impf* **доноси́ться**) *сов возв*: **~сь до** +*gen* to reach.

до́низу *нареч* to the bottom; **све́рху** ~ from top to bottom.

донима́|ть (-ю) *несов от* **доня́ть**.

до́нор (-а) *м* donor.

до́норск|ий (-ая, -ое, -ие) *прил* donor *опред*.

доно́с (-а) *м*: ~ (**на** +*acc*) denunciation (of); **де́лать** (**сде́лать** *perf*) ~ **на кого́-н** to inform on sb.

доно|си́ть (-шу́, -сишь) *несов от* **донести́** ♦ (*impf* **дона́шивать**) *сов перех* (*одежду*) to wear out; (*ребёнка*) to carry to term; **дона́шивать** (~ *perf*) **ве́щи за кем-н** to wear sb's hand-me-downs

▸ **доноси́ться** *несов от* **донести́сь**.

доно́счик (-а) *м* informer.

доно́счиц|а (-ы) *ж см* **доно́счик**.

доношу́(сь) *сов см* **доноси́ть(ся)**.

до́нь|я *итп сущ см* **дно**.

до|ня́ть (-йму́, -ймёшь; *impf* **донима́ть**) *сов перех* (*разг*) to exasperate.

доп. *сокр* = **дополни́тельный**.

допе́й(те) *сов см* **допи́ть**.

допива́|ть (-ю) *несов от* **допи́ть**.

до́пинг (-а) *м* drugs *мн*.

допи|са́ть (-шу́, -шешь; *impf* **допи́сывать**) *сов перех* (*письмо*) to finish (writing); (*картину*) to finish (painting); (*написать дополнительно*) to add.

допи́ть (**допью́, допьёшь**; *pt* **-, -ла́, -ло**, *imper* **допе́й(те)**, *impf* **допива́ть**) *сов перех* to drink up.

допишу́ *итп сов см* **дописа́ть**.

допла́т|**а** (-ы) *ж* additional payment; ~ **за бага́ж** excess baggage (charge).

доплы́|**ть** (-ву́, -вёшь; *pt* -л, -ла́, -ло, *impf* **доплыва́ть**) *сов неперех:* ~ **до** +*gen* (*на корабле́*) to sail to; (*вплавь*) to swim to.

допо́длинно *нареч:* ~ **изве́стно** for certain.

допоздна́ *нареч* (*разг*) till late.

дополне́ни|**е** (-я) *ср* supplement; (*линг*) object; **в** ~ (**к** +*dat*) in addition (to); **прямо́е/ко́свенное** ~ direct/indirect object.

дополни́тельно *нареч* in addition.

дополни́тельный *прил* additional.

допо́лн|**ить** (-ю, -ишь; *impf* **дополня́ть**) *сов перех* to supplement; **дополня́ть** (~ *perf*) **кого́-н** to add to what sb has said; **дополня́ть** (*impf*) **друг дру́га** to complement one another.

допото́пный *прил* (*разг*) ancient.

допра́шива|**ть** (-ю) *несов см* **допроси́ть**.

допро́с (-а) *м* interrogation; **подверга́ть** (**подве́ргнуть** *perf*) **кого́-н** ~**у** to subject sb to an interrogation.

допро|**си́ть** (-шу́, -сишь; *impf* **допра́шивать**) *сов перех* to interrogate, question.

до́пуск (-а) *м* (*к зда́нию*) admittance; (*к докуме́нтам*) access; (*TEX*) tolerance.

допуска́|**ть** (-ю; *perf* **допусти́ть**) *несов перех* to admit, allow in; (*предположи́ть*) to assume; ~ (**допусти́ть** *perf*) **оши́бку** (*де́лать*) to make a mistake; (*позволя́ть*) to allow for a mistake; ~ (**допусти́ть** *perf*) **кого́-н до уча́стия/ соревнова́ния** to allow sb to participate/ compete.

допу́стим *вводн сл* let us assume.

допусти́м|**ый** (-, -а, -о) *прил* permissible, acceptable; (*мысль*) feasible.

допу|**сти́ть** (-щу́, -стишь) *несов от* **допуска́ть**.

допуще́ни|**е** (-я) *ср* (*см глаг*) admittance; assumption.

допущу́ *сов см* **допусти́ть**.

допью́ *итп сов см* **допи́ть**.

дорабо́та|**ть** (-ю; *impf* **дораба́тывать**) *сов неперех:* ~ **до** +*gen* to work until ◆ *перех* to finish.

дораст|**и́** (-у́, -ёшь; *pt* **доро́с, доросла́, доросло́,** *impf* **дораста́ть**) *сов неперех:* ~ **до** +*gen* (*до потолка́*) to grow to; (*до како́го-н во́зраста*) to reach; **он доро́с до дире́ктора** he rose to become a director.

дорв|**а́ться** (-у́сь, -ёшься; *pt* -а́лся, -ала́сь, -ало́сь, *impf* **дорыва́ться**) *сов неперех:* ~ **до** +*gen* (*разг: до вла́сти*) to grab; (: *до еды́*) to fall (up)on.

дореволюцио́нный *прил* pre-revolutionary.

доро́г|**а** (-и) *ж* way; (*путь сообще́ния*) road; **по** ~**е** on the way; **мне с тобо́й** *или* **нам по** ~**е** we're going the same way; **сбива́ться (сби́ться** *perf*) **с** ~**и** (*та́кже перен*) to lose one's way; **желе́зная** ~ railway (*BRIT*), railroad (*US*).

до́рого *нареч* (*купи́ть, прода́ть*) at a high price

◆ *как сказ* it's expensive; **заплати́ть** (*perf*) ~ **за что-н** (*перен*) to pay dearly for sth; ~ **бы дал** *или* **заплати́л** **I** *итп* would give anything; **э́то** ~ **сто́ит** it's expensive.

дороговизн|**а** (-ы) *ж* high prices *мн*.

доро́гой *нареч* on the way.

дор|**о́гой** (-ог, -ога́, -ого) *прил* (*кни́га, дом*) expensive; (*цена́*) high; (*no short form*; *друг, мать*) dear; (*no full form*; *воспомина́ния, пода́рок*) cherished ◆ (-о́гого; *decl like adj*) *м* dear, darling; ~ **цено́й плати́ть (заплати́ть** *perf*) **за что-н** (*перен*) to pay dearly for sth.

дорож|**а́ть** (*3sg* -ет, *3pl* -ют, *perf* **вздорожа́ть** *или* **подорожа́ть**) *несов неперех* to rise *или* go up in price.

доро́же *сравн прил от* **дорого́й** ◆ *сравн нареч от* **до́рого**.

доро́жек *сущ см* **доро́жка**.

дорож|**и́ть** (-у́, -и́шь) *несов неперех:* ~ +*instr* to value.

доро́ж|**ка** (-ки; *gen pl* -ек) *ж* pathway; (*для пла́вания*) lane; (*для бе́га, на магнитофо́не*) track; (*ковёр*) runner; (*в аэропорту́*) runway.

доро́жный *прил* (*знак, строи́тельство*) road *опред*; (*костю́м, расхо́ды*) travelling (*BRIT*), traveling (*US*); (*су́мка*) travel; **доро́жный чек** traveller's cheque (*BRIT*), traveler's check (*US*).

доро́с *итп сов см* **дорасти́**.

дорыва́|**ться** (-юсь) *несов от* **дорва́ться**.

ДОС *ж сокр* (= **ди́сковая операцио́нная систе́ма**) DOS (= *disk operating system*).

ДОСА́АФ *м сокр* = **Доброво́льное о́бщество соде́йствия а́рмии, авиа́ции и фло́ту**.

Досаа́ф *м сокр* = **ДОСА́АФ**.

доса́д|**а** (-ы) *ж* annoyance; ~ ~**ы** out of annoyance; ~ **берёт меня́ I** am annoyed.

доса́дный (-ен, -на, -но) *прил* annoying.

доск|**а́** (-ки́; *nom pl* -ки, *gen pl* -ок) *ж* board; (*мра́морная*) slab; (*чугу́нная*) plate; **их нельзя́ ста́вить на одну́ до́ску** they're not in the same league; **доска́ объявле́ний** notice (*BRIT*) *или* bulletin (*US*) board.

доска|**за́ть** (-жу́, -жешь; *impf* **доска́зывать**) *сов перех* to finish (telling).

доскона́л|**ьный** (-ен, -ьна, -ьно) *прил* thorough.

досле́довани|**е** (-я) *ср* (*ЮР*) further examination *или* inquiry.

досло́вно *нареч* verbatim, word for word.

досло́вный *прил* literal, word-for-word.

дослуж|**и́ться** (-у́сь, -ишься; *impf* **дослу́живаться**) *сов возв:* ~ **до** +*gen* to rise to the rank of.

дослу́ша|**ть** (-ю; *impf* **дослу́шивать**) *сов перех* to listen to.

досма́трива|**ть** (-ю) *несов от* **досмотре́ть**.

досмо́тр (-а) *м:* **тамо́женный** ~ customs examination.

досмотре́ть (-ю́, -ишь; *impf* **досма́тривать**) *сов перех* to watch the end of; (*бага́ж*) to check; ~ (*perf*) **до** +*gen* to watch until.

досо́к *сущ см* **доска́**.

доспе́х|и (-ов) *мн* (*рыцаря*) armour *ед* (*BRIT*), armor *ед* (*US*); (*перен: разг*) gear *ед*.

досро́чно *нареч* early, ahead of time.

досро́чный *прил* early.

доста|ва́ть(ся) (-ю́(сь)) *несов от* **доста́ть(ся)**.

доста́в|ить (-лю, -ишь; *impf* **доставля́ть**) *сов перех* (*груз*) to deliver; (*пассажиров*) to carry, transport; (*удовольствие, возможность*) to give; (*трудности*) to cause.

доста́в|ка (-ки; *gen pl* -ок) *ж* delivery; **с ~кой на дом** ≈ recorded delivery (*BRIT*), ≈ certified mail (*US*).

доста́влю *сов см* **доста́вить**.

доставля́|ть (-ю) *несов от* **доста́вить**.

доста́вок *сущ см* **доста́вка**.

доста́ну(сь) *итп сов см* **доста́ть(ся)**.

доста́нь(те) *сов см* **доста́ть**.

доста́т|ок (-ка) *м:* **жить в ~ке** to be well provided for.

доста́точно *нареч:* ~ **хорошо́/подро́бно** good/detailed enough ♦ *как сказ* that's enough; ~ **де́нег/хле́ба** enough money/bread; ~ **шепта́ться/болта́ть!** that's enough whispering/chattering!; ~ **уви́деть, что́бы поня́ть** one only has to see to understand; ~ **сказа́ть, что** ... suffice it to say, that ....

доста́|ть (-ну, -нешь; *imper* **доста́нь(те)**, *impf* **достава́ть**) *сов перех* to take; (*раздобыть*) to get ♦ *неперех:* ~ **до** +*gen* to reach

▶ **доста́ться** (*impf* **достава́ться**) *сов возв* (+*dat; при разделе*): **мне ~лся дом** I got the house; **мно́го забо́т ему́ ~лось** he was burdened down with a lot of worries; **мне ~лось** (*разг*) I got it in the neck.

дости́г *итп сов см* **дости́чь**.

достига́|ть (-ю) *несов от* **дости́гнуть**, **дости́чь**.

дости́гну *итп сов см* **дости́чь**.

дости́гн|уть (-у, -ешь) *сов см* **дости́чь**.

достиже́ни|е (-я) *ср* achievement; (*предела, возраста*) reaching.

достижи́м|ый (-, -а, -о) *прил* achievable, attainable.

дости́|чь (-гну, -гнешь; *pt* -г, -гла, -гло, *impf* **достига́ть**) *сов неперех* (+*gen*) to reach; (*результата, цели*) to achieve; (*положения*) to attain.

достове́р|ный (-ен, -на, -но) *прил* reliable; **из ~ных исто́чников** from reliable sources.

досто́ен *прил см* **досто́йный**.

досто́инств|о (-а) *ср* (*книги, плана*) merit; (*моральные качества*) virtue; (*уважение к себе*) dignity; (*комм*) value; **чу́вство со́бственного ~а** self-respect; **счита́ть (посчита́ть** *perf*) **что-н ни́же своего́ ~а** to consider sth beneath one's dignity; **ба́нковский биле́т ~м в 100 рубле́й** a banknote to the value of 100 roubles; **оце́нивать (оцени́ть** *perf*) **по ~у кого́-н/что-н** to judge sb/sth on his/its merits.

досто́йно *нареч* with dignity.

досто́й|ный *прил* (*награда, кара*) fitting; (*человек*) worthy; (-ен, -йна, -йно; +*gen*): ~ **любви́/уваже́ния** worthy of love/respect.

достопримеча́тельност|ь (-и) *ж* sight; (*музея*) interesting exhibit; **осма́тривать (осмотре́ть** *perf*) ~**и** to go sightseeing.

достопримеча́тел|ьный (-ен, -ьна, -ьно) *прил* noteworthy.

достоя́ни|е (-я) *ср* property; **стать** (*perf*) *или* **сде́латься** (*perf*) ~**м наро́да** to become public property.

до́ступ (-а) *м* admittance; (*к документам итп*) access; **открыва́ть (откры́ть** *perf*) ~ **кому́-н куда́-нибудь** to give sb access to somewhere; **нет ~а во́здуха/кислоро́да** there is no way for air/oxygen to get in.

досту́п|ный (-ен, -на, -но) *прил* (*место*) accessible; (*цены*) affordable; (*объяснение, изложение*) comprehensible; (*человек*) approachable.

досу́г (-а) *м* leisure (time); **на ~е** in one's spare *или* free time.

до́суха *нареч:* **вы́тереть ~** to dry.

до́сыта *нареч:* **их накорми́ли ~** they were fed until they could eat no more.

досье́ *ср нескл* dossier, file; **заводи́ть (завести́** *perf*) ~ **на кого́-н** to open a file on sb.

досяга́емост|ь (-и) *ж:* **вне ~и** unattainable; **в преде́лах ~и** attainable.

досяга́ем|ый (-, -а, -о) *прил* (*задача, цель*) attainable; (*место*) accessible.

дота́скива|ть(ся) (-ю(сь)) *несов от* **дотащи́ть(ся)**.

дота́ци|я (-и) *ж* subsidy.

дотащ|и́ть (-у́, -ишь; *impf* **дота́скивать**) *сов перех* to lug; **е́ле дота́скивать (~** *perf*) **но́ги** to drag one's feet

▶ **дотащи́ться** (*impf* **дота́скиваться**) *сов возв* (*разг*): **~ся до** +*gen* to drag o.s. to.

дотемна́ *нареч* until dark.

дотла́ *нареч:* **сгоре́ть ~** to burn down (to the ground).

дото́ш|ный (-ен, -на, -но) *прил* (*разг*) meticulous.

дотро́н|уться (-усь, -ешься; *impf* **дотра́гиваться**) *сов возв:* ~ **до** +*gen* to touch.

дотян|у́ть (-у́, -ешь; *impf* **дотя́гивать**) *сов перех:* ~ **что-н до** +*gen* to extend sth as far as; **он ~у́л рабо́ту до ве́чера** he dragged the work out until the evening

▶ **дотяну́ться** (*impf* **дотя́гиваться**) *сов возв:* ~**ся до** +*gen* to reach.

доучи́|ться (-у́сь, -ишься; *impf* **доу́чиваться**) *сов возв* to complete one's education; ~ (*perf*) **до конца́ го́да/пя́того кла́сса** to study up until the end of the year/of fifth form.

до́хл|ый *прил* dead; (*разг: слабосильный*) wimpish.

до́х|нуть (**-ну, -нешь;** *pt* **-, -ла, -ло,** *perf* **подо́хнуть**) *несов неперех* (*животное*) to die; (*разг: человек*) to snuff it.

дохн|у́ть (**-у́, -ёшь**) *сов неперех* (*разг: человек*) to breathe; **мне ~ не́когда** (*разг*) I don't get a moment's rest.

дохо́д (**-а**) *м* (*предприятия*) income, revenue; (*человека*) income; **национа́льный ~** the national income; **дава́ть** (**дать** *perf*) *или* **приноси́ть** (**принести́** *perf*) **~** to generate income; **извлека́ть** (**извле́чь** *perf*) **~ из чего́-н** to make a profit from sth.

дохо́ден *прил см* **дохо́дный.**

доходи́ть *несов от* **дойти́.**

дохо́д|ный (**-ен, -на, -но**) *прил* profitable.

дохо́дчив|ый (**-, -а, -о**) *прил* clear, easy to understand.

доце́нт (**-а**) *м* ≈ reader (*BRIT*), ≈ associate professor (*US*).

до́чек *сущ см* **до́чка.**

до́чери *итп сущ см* **дочь.**

доче́рн|ий (**-яя, -ее, -ие**) *прил* daughter's; **~яя компа́ния/фи́рма** subsidiary company/firm.

до́чиста *нареч* clean.

дочита́|ть (**-ю;** *impf* **дочи́тывать**) *сов перех* to finish (reading); **~** (*perf*) **до** +*gen* to read until.

до́ч|ка (**-ки;** *gen pl* **-ек**) *ж* daughter.

дочь (**-ери;** *см* **Table 2**) *ж* daughter.

дошёл *сов см* **дойти́.**

дошко́льник (**-а**) *м* preschool child.

дошко́льниц|а (**-ы**) *ж см* **дошко́льник.**

дошко́льный *прил* preschool.

дошла́ *сов см* **дойти́.**

доща́тый *прил* made of boards.

доя́р|ка (**-ки;** *gen pl* **-ок**) *ж* milkmaid.

ДПР *ж сокр* = **Демократи́ческая па́ртия Росси́и.**

др. *сокр* = **друго́й, други́е.**

драгоце́нност|ь (**-и**) *ж* jewel; (*перен*) gem, treasure.

драгоце́нный *прил* (*камень, металл*) precious; (*время, сведения, мех*) valuable.

драже́ *ср нескл* dragée.

дразн|и́ть (**-ю́, -ишь**) *несов перех* to tease; (*аппетит, воображение*) to stimulate.

дра́|ить (**-ю, -ишь;** *perf* **надра́ить**) *несов перех* to scrub.

дра́к|а (**-и**) *ж* fight; (*битва*) battle; **лезть (поле́зть** *perf*) *или* **вввя́зываться (ввяза́ться** *perf*) **в ~у** to get into a fight.

драко́н (**-а**) *м* dragon; (*зоол*) draco *или* flying lizard.

драко́новск|ий (**-ая, -ое, -ие**) *прил:* **~ие ме́ры** Draconian measures.

дра́м|а (**-ы**) *ж* drama; (*событие*) crisis; **пережива́ть (пережи́ть** *perf*) **тяжёлую ~у** to go through a crisis.

драматизи́р|овать (**-ую**) (*не*)*сов перех* to

dramatize.

драмати́ческ|ий (**-ая, -ое, -ие**) *прил* dramatic; (*актёр*) stage *опред*; **драмати́ческий кружо́к** drama group; **драмати́ческий теа́тр** theatre, theater (*US*).

драмату́рг (**-а**) *м* playwright.

драматурги́|я (**-и**) *ж* drama ♦ *собир* plays.

драмкружо́к (**-ка́**) *м сокр* (= **драмати́ческий кружо́к**) drama group.

дра́ный *прил* (*разг*) ragged.

драп (**-а**) *м* *thick woollen cloth.*

драпир|ова́ть (**-у́ю;** *perf* **задрапирова́ть**) *несов перех:* **~ (чем-н)** to drape (with sth).

драпиро́в|ка (**-ки;** *gen pl* **-ок**) *ж* drapery.

драть (**деру́, дерёшь;** *perf* **разодра́ть**) *несов перех* (*бумагу, одежду*) to tear *или* rip up; (*perf* **задра́ть;** *подлеж: волк, лиса*) to tear to pieces; (*perf* **вы́драть;** *разг: побить*) to thrash; (*perf* **содра́ть;** *кору, обои*) to strip; **~ (содра́ть** *perf*) **шку́ру с живо́тного** to skin an animal; **~ (содра́ть** *perf*) **де́ньги с кого́-н** (*разг*) to rip sb off; **он с меня́ шку́ру сдерёт** (*разг*) he'll have my guts for garters; **~** (*impf*) **го́рло** (*разг*) to bawl

▶ **дра́ться** *несов возв:* **дра́ться (с** +*instr*) to fight (with); (*perf* **подра́ться;** *дети*) to fight.

дребеде́н|ь (**-и**) *ж* (*разг*) rubbish.

дре́безг (**-а**) *м:* **разби́ться с ~ом** to shatter; **разбива́ть (разби́ть** *perf*) **в ме́лкие ~и** to smash to smithereens.

дребезж|а́ть (*3sg* **-и́т,** *3pl* **-а́т**) *несов неперех* to jingle.

древеси́н|а (**-ы**) *ж собир* wood.

древе́сный *прил* wood; **древе́сные поро́ды** species of tree; **древе́сный у́голь** charcoal.

дре́вк|о (**-а**) *ср* (*копья*) shaft; **~ фла́га** flagpole.

дре́вн|ий (**-яя, -ее, -ие**) *прил* ancient; **дре́вняя исто́рия** ancient history.

дре́вност|ь (**-и**) *ж* antiquity.

дрези́н|а (**-ы**) *ж* trolley (*BRIT*), handcar (*US*).

дрейф (**-а**) *м* drift; **снима́ться (сня́ться** *perf*) **с дре́йфа** to regain course; **лежа́ть** (*impf*) **в дре́йфе** to heave to.

дрейф|ова́ть (**-у́ю**) *несов неперех* to drift.

дрель (**-и**) *ж* drill.

дрем|а́ть (**-лю́, -лешь**) *несов неперех* to doze; **враг не дре́млет** (*перен*) the enemy never sleeps.

дремот|а́ (**-ы́**) *ж* drowsiness.

дрему́ч|ий (**-ая, -ее, -ие; -, -а, -е**) *прил* dense; (*перен: невежда*) absolute.

дрена́ж (**-а́**) *м* (*почвы*) drainage; (*раны*) draining.

дрессир|ова́ть (**-у́ю;** *perf* **вы́дрессировать**) *несов перех* to train.

дро́бен *прил см* **дро́бный.**

дроб|и́ть (**-лю́, -и́шь;** *perf* **раздроби́ть**) *несов перех* (*камень, кость*) to crush; (*силы, отряд*) to divide.

дроблёный *прил* (*орехи*) crushed.

дро́б|ный (**-ен, -на, -но**) *прил* (*перечень,*

спúсок) itemized; (*стук, шаг*) staccato; (*no short form*; мат) fractional.

дроб|ь (-и; *gen pl* **-éй**) ж fraction; (*дождя, шагов*) patter; (*барабана*) beat.

дров|á (-; *dat pl* **-áм**) мн firewood *ед*; **он наломáл ~!** (*перен: разг*) he made a hash of it!; **кто в лес, кто по ~** at sixes and sevens.

дро́гн|уть (**-у, -ешь**) *сов неперех* (*стёкла, руки, голос*) to shake, tremble; (*лицо*) to quiver; (*свет, огонь*) to flicker; (*человек*) to waver; **у меня́ рукá не ~ет** +*infin* ... I won't hesitate to ....

дрожáни|е (**-я**) *ср* (*стёкол*) vibration; (*колен, голоса*) trembling; (*лица*) quivering; (*света, огня*) flickering.

дрожá|ть (**-ý, -ишь**) *несов неперех* (*стёкла*) to vibrate; (*руки, голос*) to shake, tremble; (*лицо*) to quiver; (*свет, огонь*) to flicker; **~** (*impf*) **за** +*acc или* **над** +*instr* (*разг*) to fuss over; **~** (*impf*) **над (кáждой) копéйкой** to grudge every penny; **~** (*impf*) **пéред кем-н** to tremble before sb.

дро́жж|и (**-éй**) *мн* yeast *ед*.

дрож|ь (**-и**) *ж* (*от холода*) shiver; (*от страха*) shudder; (*от*) **бросáет в ~** he is shuddering.

дрозд (**-á**) *м* thrush; **чёрный ~** blackbird.

дру́г (**-га**; *nom pl* **-зья́**, *gen pl* **-зéй**) *м* friend; (*разг: обращéние*) mate; **~ дрýга** one another, each other; **~ дрýгу** (*говори́ть*) to one another *или* each other; **~ за дрýгом** one after another; **~ о дрýге** (*говори́ть*) about one another *или* each other.

другúе (**-úх**; *decl like adj*) *мн* others *мн*.

друго́й *прил* (*иной*) another; (*второй*) the other; (*не такой, как этот*) different ♦ (**-óго**; *decl like adj*) *м* (*кто-то иной*) another (person); (*второй*) the other (one); **~óе мнéние** different opinion; **в ~ раз** another time; **и тот и ~** both; **чтó-то ~óе** something else; **~úми словáми** in other words; **на ~ день** the next day; **э́то ~óе дéло** that's a different matter; *см также* **другúе**.

дрýжб|а (**-ы**) *ж* friendship.

дружелю́би|е (**-я**) *ср* friendliness.

дружелю́б|ный (**-ен, -на, -но**) *прил* friendly, amicable.

дрýжен *прил см* **дрýжный**.

дрýжески *нареч* in a friendly manner, amicably.

дрýжеск|ий (**-ая, -ое, -ие**) *прил* friendly.

дрýжественн|ый (**-ен, -на, -но**) *прил* friendly.

дружúн|а (**-ы**) *ж* (ист, воен) host.

дружú|ть (**-ý, -ишь**) *несов неперех*: **~ с** +*instr* to be friends with

▶ **дружúться** (*perf* **подружúться**) *несов возв*: **~ся с** +*instr* to make friends with.

дружúщ|е (**-а**) *м* (*разг*) mate.

дрýж|ный (**-ен, -нá, -но, -ны**) *прил* (*семья, коллектив*) close-knit; (*апплодисменты, смех*) general; (*усилия*) concerted.

друж|óк (**-кá**) *м* (*друг*) friend; (*разг: пренебр*) crony; (*обращéние*) love.

друзья́ *итп сущ см* **друг**.

дры́га|ть (**-ю**) *несов неперех*: **~ ногáми** to kick.

дры́хн|уть (**-у, -ешь**) *несов неперех* (*разг*) to kip, sleep.

дря́бл|ый (**-, -á, -о**) *прил* (*кожа*) sagging; (*человек, тело*) flabby.

дря́зг|и (**-**) *мн* (*разг*) squabbles *мн*.

дря́нн|óй *прил* (*разг: товар, работа*) trashy; (: *характер*) rotten.

дря́н|ь (**-и**) *ж* (*разг*) rubbish (BRIT), trash (US).

дряхлé|ть (**-ю**; *perf* **одряхлéть**) *несов неперех* to become infirm.

дря́хл|ый (**-, -á, -о**) *прил* (*человек*) infirm; (*здание*) dilapidated, decrepit.

ДСО *ср сокр* (= *доброво́льное спорти́вное о́бщество*) amateur sports association.

дуб (**-а**; *loc sg* **-ý**, *nom pl* **-ы́**) *м* (БОТ) oak (tree); (*древеси́на*) oak; (*перен: разг*) blockhead.

дуби́н|а (**-ы**) *ж* club ♦ *м/ж* (*разг*) blockhead.

дуби́н|ка (**-ки**; *gen pl* **-ок**) *ж* cudgel; **рези́новая ~** truncheon.

дуб|и́ть (**-лю́, -ишь**; *perf* **вы́дубить**) *несов перех* to tan.

дублён|ка (**-ки**; *gen pl* **-ок**) *ж* sheepskin coat.

дублёный *прил* (*мех*) tanned.

дублёр (**-а**) *м* backup; (ТЕАТР) understudy; (КИНО) double.

дубликáт (**-а**) *м* duplicate.

Дýблин (**-а**) *м* Dublin.

дубли́р|овать (**-ую**) *несов перех* (*дéятельность*) to duplicate; (ТЕАТР) to understudy; (КИНО) to dub; (КОМП) to back up.

дубл|ь (**-я**) *м* (КИНО) take.

дублю́ *несов см* **дубли́ть**.

дубóв|ый *прил* oak; (*перен: стиль, язык*) ponderous.

Дувр (**-а**) *м* Dover.

дуг|á (**-и́**; *nom pl* **-и**) *ж* (ГЕОМ) arc.

дуд|éть (*2sg* **-и́шь**, *3sg* **-и́т**) *несов неперех* to play the pipe.

дý|дка (**-ки**; *gen pl* **-ок**) *ж* (МУЗ) pipe; **пляса́ть** (*impf*) **под чью-н ~ку** (*перен*) to dance to sb's tune.

дýж|ка (**-ки**; *gen pl* **-ек**) *ж* (*серёг*) hoop; (*ведра*) handle.

дýл|о (**-а**) *ср* (*отвéрстие ствола́*) muzzle; (*сам ствол*) barrel.

дýм|а (**-ы**) *ж* (*размышлéние*) meditation, thought; **Д~** (ПОЛИТ) the Duma (*lower house of the Russian parliament*); **Госудáрственная Д~** the State Duma.

дýма|ть (**-ю**) *несов неперех*: **~ (о чём-н)** to think (about sth); **~** (*impf*) **над чем-н** to think sth over; **он ~ет купи́ть маши́ну** he is thinking of buying a car; **я ~ю, что да/нет** I think/don't think so; **и не ~йте!** (*разг*) don't even think of it!

▶ **дýматься** (*perf* **подýматься**) *несов безл* (+*dat*) to seem; **мне ~ется, он прав** I think he's right.

Дуна́й (-я) м Danube.

дунове́ни|е (-я) ср breath.

ду́н|уть (-у, -ешь) сов неперех to blow.

дупл|о́ (-а́; nom pl **-а́,** gen pl **-ел)** ср (дерева)
hollow; (зуба) cavity.

ду́р|а (-ы) ж (разг) fool, idiot.

дура́к (-а́) м (разг) fool, idiot; **игра́ть** (impf) **в
дурака́** to play "durak" (Russian card game); **он
не ~ вы́пить/пое́сть** (разг) he loves his drink/
food; **дурака́ валя́ть** (impf) (разг: дура́читься)
to clown about, play the fool; (: безде́льничать)
to lounge about; **оста́ваться (оста́ться** perf) **в
дурака́х** (перен: разг) to be made a fool of.

дура́цк|ий (-ая, -ое, -ие) прил (разг) stupid,
idiotic.

дура́честв|о (-а) ср stupidity, idiocy.

дура́ч|ить (-у, -ишь; perf **одура́чить)** несов
перех (разг) to con

▸ **дура́читься** несов возв (разг) to play the fool.

дурачь|ё (-я́) ср собир (разг) bunch of idiots.

дурён сущ см **дурно́й.**

ду́р|ень (-ня) м (разг) dimwit, fool.

дуре́|ть (-ю; perf **одуре́ть)** несов неперех (разг):
~ от +gen to grow stupid from.

ду́р|ий (-ья, -ье, -ьи) прил: **~ья голова́** или
башка́ (разг) dope, fool.

дур|и́ть (-ю́, -и́шь) несов неперех (разг:
человек) to fool around; (животное) to be
stubborn; **~ (задури́ть** perf) **го́лову кому́-н**
(разг) to mix sb up.

дурма́н (-а) м thorn apple, jimson weed (US);
(опьяня́юще сре́дство) intoxicant; (: перен)
drug.

дурма́н|ить (-ю, -ишь; perf **одурма́нить)** несов
перех to intoxicate.

дурне́|ть (-ю; perf **подурне́ть)** несов неперех to
lose one's looks.

ду́рно нареч (пахнуть, выглядеть) bad; (вести
себя) badly ♦ как сказ: **мне ~** I don't feel well;
ему́ сде́лалось ~ he felt faint.

дур|но́й (-ён, -на́, -но) прил nasty; (питание)
bad; **она́ ~на́ собо́й** she is very plain; **дурно́й
при́знак** bad omen.

дурнот|а́ (-ы́) ж faintness.

ду́рня итп сущ см **ду́рень.**

ду́рочк|а (-ки; gen pl **-ек)** ж (разг) silly girl.

дуршла́г (-а) м colander.

дур|ь (-и) ж (разг) rubbish, nonsense; **вы́брось
э́ту ~ из головы́!** (разг) get that foolish idea
out of your head!; **ду́рью ма́яться** (impf) или
му́читься (impf) (разг) to muck around.

ду́тый прил hollow; (перен) exaggerated,
inflated.

ду|ть (-ю, -ешь) несов неперех to blow ♦ (perf
вы́дуть) перех to blow; **здесь ду́ет** it's
draughty (BRIT) или drafty (US) in here.

дух (-а; part gen **-у)** м spirit; (разг): **перевести́ ~**
to get one's breath back; **в ду́хе** +gen in the spirit
of; **па́дать** (impf) **ду́хом** to lose heart; **быть**
(impf) **в ду́хе/не в ду́хе** to be in high/low spirits;

сохраня́ть (сохрани́ть perf**) прису́тствие ду́ха**
to retain one's presence of mind; **у меня́ не
хва́тит ду́ху на э́то** (разг) I don't have the heart
to do this; **во весь ~** (разг) at full или top
speed; **чтоб ду́ху твоего́ здесь не́ было!**
(разг) get out of my sight!

дух|и́ (-о́в) мн perfume ед, scent ед.

духове́нств|о (-а) ср собир clergy;
(правосла́вное, католи́ческое) priesthood.

духо́вк|а (-и) ж oven.

духо́вник (-а) м confessor.

духо́вность (-и) ж spirituality.

духо́вный прил (интересы, запросы) spiritual;
(сила, мир, жизнь) inner; (музыка) sacred,
church опред; **духо́вная акаде́мия** seminary;
духо́вное зва́ние ecclesiastical rank; **духо́вное
лицо́** ecclesiastic, cleric; **духо́вный сан** holy
orders мн.

духово́й прил (муз) wind опред.

духот|а́ (-ы́) ж stuffiness; (жара) closeness.

душ (-а) м shower; **принима́ть (приня́ть** perf**) ~**
to have или take a shower.

душ|а́ (-и́; nom pl **-и)** ж soul; (ист: крестьянин)
serf; **до́брая ~** kind heart; **ни́зкая/по́длая ~**
mean/ignoble spirit; **~ моя́** my dear; **рабо́тать**
(impf) **с ~о́й** to put one's heart into one's work; **в
~е́** at heart; **на ду́шу (населе́ния)** per head (of
the population); **он в ней ~и́ не ча́ет** she's the
apple of his eye; **быть** (impf) **~о́й** +gen
(общества, дела) to be the life and soul of; **не
име́ть** (impf) **гроша́ за ~о́й** to be without a
penny to one's name; **говори́ть** (impf)/
бесе́довать (impf) **по ~м** to have a heart-to-
heart talk/chat; **отводи́ть (отвести́** perf**) ду́шу** to
pour out one's heart; **как Бог на́ ~у поло́жит**
(разг) any old way; **у меня́ ~ в пя́тки ушла́**
(разг) I was scared to death; **от всей ~й** from
the bottom of one's heart; **в глубине́ ~й** in
one's heart of hearts.

Душанбе́ м нескл Dushanbe.

душевнобольн|а́я (-о́й; decl like adj**)** ж см
душевнобольно́й.

душевнобольн|о́й (-о́го; decl like adj**)** м
mentally-ill person.

душе́вный прил (силы, подъём) inner;
(разговор) sincere, heartfelt; (человек) kindly;
~ое потрясе́ние shock.

душегре́йк|а (-и; разг**)** ж body warmer.

душегу́б (-а) ж (разг) butcher.

душегу́бк|а (-ки; gen pl **-ок)** ж см душегу́б;
(автомаши́на) mobile gas chamber.

ду́шен сущ см **ду́шный.**

душераздира́ющий (-ая, -ее, -ие; -, -а, -е)
прил (крик) bloodcurdling; (плач) heart-rending.

души́стый прил (цветок) fragrant; (мыло)
perfumed.

души́тел|ь (-я) м (перен) suppressor.

душ|и́ть (-у́, -ишь; perf **задуши́ть** или **удуши́ть)**
несов перех to strangle; (свободу, прогресс) to
stifle, suppress; (perf **надуши́ть;** платок) to
scent; **его́ ду́шит смех** he is choking with

laughter; ~ (*impf*) **в объятиях кого-н** to smother sb in one's embrace.

душиц|а (-ы) ж marjoram.

душно *как сказ* it's stuffy *или* close; **в комнате** ~ the room is very stuffy; **мне ~, откройте окно** I find it very stuffy *или* close, open the window.

душ|ный (-ен, -на, -но) *прил* stuffy; (*жаркий*) sultry.

дуэл|ь (-и) ж duel; **вызывать (вызвать** *perf***) кого-н на ~** to challenge sb to a duel.

дуэт (-а) м (*произведение*) duet, duo; (*исполнители*) duo.

дыбом *нареч*: **вставать ~** (*волосы, шерсть*) to stand on end.

дыб|ы (-ов) *мн*: **на ~ становиться** (*лошадь*) to rear up; (*перен*: *разг*) to kick up a fuss.

дым (-а; *part gen* -у, *loc sg* -у, *nom pl* -ы) м smoke; **поругаться** (*perf*) **в ~** to fall out completely.

дым|ить (-лю, -ишь; *perf* **надымить**) *несов неперех* (*печь, дрова*) to smoulder (*BRIT*), smolder (*US*); (*разг*): ~ *+instr* to puff on

▸ **дымиться** *несов возв* (*труба*) to be smoking.

дымк|а (-и) ж haze.

дымно *как сказ*: (*здесь*) ~ it's smoky (in here).

дымный *прил* (*дрова, головешка*) smouldering (*BRIT*), smoldering (*US*); (*комната, помещение*) smoky, smoke-filled.

дымоход (-а) м flue.

дымчатый *прил* (*кот*) smoky; **дымчатые очки** tinted glasses.

дын|я (-и) ж melon.

дыр|а (-ы; *nom pl* -ы) ж hole; **в дырах** full of holes.

дыр|ка (-ки; *gen pl* -ок) ж hole.

дырокол (-а) м punch.

дыряв|ый (-, -а, -о) *прил* (*разг*) holey; **у него ~ая голова** (*разг*) he has a head like a sieve.

дыхани|е (-я) *ср* breathing, respiration; ~ **весны** a breath of spring; **с затаённым ~м** with bated breath; **второе ~** second wind; **искусственное** ~ artificial respiration.

дыхательный *прил* (*упражнения*) breathing *опред*; (*процесс*) respiratory; **дыхательное горло** windpipe; **дыхательные пути** respiratory tract *ед*.

дыш|ать (-у, -ишь) *несов неперех* to breathe; ~ (*impf*) *+instr* (*ненавистью*) to exude; (*любовью*) to radiate

▸ **дышаться** *несов возв* (+*dat*): **мне здесь легче дышится** I can breathe more easily here.

дьявол (-а) м devil; **за каким ~ом я должен идти туда!** (*разг*) why the devil should I go there!; **какого ~а ...!** what the devil ...!

дьявольск|ий (-ая, -ое, -ие) *прил* diabolic(al); (*разг*: *холод*) devilish; **~ое терпение** ≈ the patience of Job.

дьякон (-а) м deacon.

дюжин|а (-ы) ж dozen; **чёртова ~** baker's dozen.

дюйм (-а) м inch.

дюн|а (-ы; *gen pl* -) ж (*обычно мн*) dune.

дюралюмини|й (-я) м Duralumin®.

дюшес (-а) м (*БОТ*) Duchess pear.

дягил|ь (-я) м angelica.

дядь|ка (-ьки; *gen pl* -ек) м uncle; (*разг*) guy.

дяд|я (-и) м uncle; (*разг*) man; (: *обращение*) mister.

дят|ел (-ла) м woodpecker.

~ E, e ~

Е, е *сущ нескл* (*буква*) the 6th letter of the Russian alphabet.

ЕАСТ *ж сокр* (= Европейская ассоциация свободной торговли) EFTA (= *European Free Trade Association*).

ЕБРР *м сокр* (= Европейский банк реконструкции и развития) EBRD (= *European Bank for Reconstruction and Development*).

ева́нгели|е (-я) *ср* the Gospels *мн*; (*одна из книг*) gospel.

евангели́ст (-а) *м* evangelist.

евангели́ческ|ий (-ая, -ое, -ие) *прил* evangelical.

ева́нгельск|ий (-ая, -ое, -ие) *прил*: ~ **текст** gospel.

е́внух (-а) *м* eunuch.

Евра́зи|я (-и) *ж* Eurasia.

евре́ек *сущ см* **евре́йка**.

евре́|й (-я) *м* Jew.

евре́йк|а (-йки; *gen pl* -ек) *ж* Jewess.

евре́йск|ий (-ая, -ое, -ие) *прил* (*народ, обычаи*) Jewish; ~ **язы́к** Hebrew.

евроазиа́тск|ий (-ая, -ое, -ие) *прил* Eurasian.

Еврови́дени|е (-я) *ср* Eurovision.

Евро́п|а (-ы) *ж* Europe.

европе́|ец (-йца) *м* European.

европе́йк|а (-и) *ж см* **европе́ец**.

европе́йск|ий (-ая, -ое, -ие) *прил* European; **европе́йский сове́т** Council of Europe; **европе́йский суд** European Court of Justice; **европе́йское соо́бщество** European Community.

европе́йца *итп сущ см* **европе́ец**.

ЕВС *ж сокр* (= Европейская валютная система) EMS (= *European Monetary System*).

ЕВФ *м сокр* (= Европейский валютный фонд) (= *European monetary fund*).

е́гер|ь (-я) *м* (*на охоте*) huntsman (*мн* huntsmen).

Еги́п|ет (-та) *м* Egypt.

еги́петск|ий (-ая, -ое, -ие) *прил* Egyptian.

Еги́пта *итп сущ см* **Еги́пет**.

египтя́н|ин (-ина; *nom pl* -е, *gen pl* -) *м* Egyptian.

египтя́нк|а (-ки; *gen pl* -ок) *ж см* **египтя́нин**.

его́ *мест см* **он, оно́** ◆ *притяж мест* (*относительно мужчины итп*) his; (*относительно предмета итп*) its.

егожу́ *несов см* **егози́ть**.

егоз|а́ (-ы́) *м/ж* (*разг*) fidget.

егози́ть (-жу́, -зи́шь) *несов неперех* (*разг*) to fidget; ~ (*impf*) **пе́ред** +*instr* (*перен*) to fawn on.

ед|а́ (-ы́) *ж* (*пища*) food; (*процесс*): **за ~о́й, во вре́мя ~ы́** at mealtimes; **мо́йте ру́ки пе́ред ~о́й** wash your hands before eating.

KEYWORD

едва́ *нареч* **1** (*с трудом*: *нашёл, достал, доехал итп*) only just

2 (*только, немного*) barely, hardly; **больно́й едва́ ды́шит** the patient is barely *или* hardly breathing; **едва́ созре́вший плод** a barely ripe fruit

3 (*только что*) just; **ему́ едва́ испо́лнилось 20 лет** he has just turned 20

◆ *союз* (*как только*) as soon as; **едва́ он пришёл, на́чал рабо́тать** as soon as he arrived, he set to work; **едва́ ли** hardly; **уже́ по́здно, едва́ ли он придёт** it's late, he's hardly likely to come now; **едва́ ли не** almost; **он едва́ ли не са́мый лу́чший учени́к** he is almost the best pupil.

е́дем *итп сов см* **е́хать**.

еди́м *несов см* **есть**.

едине́ни|е (-я) *ср* unity.

едини́ц|а (-ы) *ж* (*цифра*) one; (*изображение*) the figure 1; (*ПРОСВЕЩ*) ≈ very poor (*school mark*); (*измерения, часть целого*) unit; **де́нежная ~** monetary unit; **шта́тная ~** member of staff; *см также* **едини́цы**.

едини́ц|ы (-) *мн* a few; **оста́лись в живы́х ~** only a few people survived.

едини́ч|ный (-ен, -на, -но) *прил* (*редкий*: *экземпляр*) single; (*случай*) isolated.

единобо́рств|о (-а) *ср* single combat; **вступа́ть** (**вступи́ть** *perf*) **в ~ с** +*instr* to enter into combat with.

единобра́чи|е (-я) *ср* monogamy.

единовла́стен *прил см* **единовла́стный**.

единовла́сти|е (-я) *ср* autocracy.

единовла́ст|ный (-ен, -на, -но) *прил* autocratic.

единовре́мен|ный (-ен, -на, -но) *прил* one-off; **~ное посо́бие** one-off benefit payment.

единогла́сен *прил см* **единогла́сный**.

единогла́си|е (-я) *ср* unanimity.

единогла́сно *нареч* unanimously; **при́нято ~** carried unanimously.

единогла́с|ный (-ен, -на, -но) *прил* unanimous.
единоду́ши|е (-я) *ср* unanimity.
единоду́шно *нареч* unanimously.
единоду́шный *прил* unanimous.
единокро́вный *прил*: ~ **брат** half-brother (*with the same father*).
единоли́чник (-а) *м* (*ИСТ*) peasant smallholder; (*пренебр*) maverick.
единоли́чный *прил* (*индивидуальный: власть, решение*) individual.
единомы́сли|е (-я) *ср* like-mindedness.
единомы́шленник (-а) *м* like-minded person; (*сообщник*) confederate.
единонача́ли|е (-я) *ср* one-man rule.
единообра́з|ный (-ен, -на, -но) *прил* unified.
единоро́г (-а) *м* unicorn.
единоутро́бный *прил*: ~ **брат** half-brother (*with the same mother*).
еди́нственен *прил см* **еди́нственный**.
еди́нственно *част* (*только*) only ♦ *нареч*: ~ **пра́вильный/возмо́жный путь** the only correct/possible way; ~, **о чём я прошу́** the only thing I ask.
еди́нствен|ный (-ен, -на, -но) *прил* (the) only; ~ **в своём ро́де** one of a kind; ~**ная наде́жда** the only hope; **он** – ~ **ребёнок** he is an only child; **еди́нственное число́** (*линг*) singular.
еди́нств|о (-а) *ср* unity.
еди́н|ый *прил* (*цельный*) united; (*общий*) common; (*только один*) one, single; ~**ое це́лое** a unified whole; **все до** ~**ого** to a man; **еди́ный** (**проездно́й**) **биле́т** travel pass (*for use on all forms of transport*).
еди́те *несов см* **есть**.
е́дкий (-кая, -кое, -кие; -ок, -ка́, -ко) *прил* (*также перен*) caustic; (*запах, дым*) acrid.
е́дкост|ь (-и) *ж* (*хим*) causticity; (*перен*) acerbity.
едо́к *прил см* **е́дкий**.
едо́к (-а́) *м*: **у него́ в семье́ пять едоко́в** he has five mouths to feed.
е́ду *итп несов см* **е́хать**.
еди́т *несов см* **есть**.
её *мест от* **она́** ♦ *притяж мест* (*относительно женщины итп*) her; (*относительно предмета итп*) its.
ёж (-а́) *м* hedgehog; **морско́й** ~ sea urchin; **ежу́ поня́тно** (*разг*) it's as plain as the nose on your face.
ежеви́к|а (-и) *ж* (*растение*) bramble; (*ягода*) blackberry; (*собир*) blackberries *мн*, brambles *мн*.
ежеви́чный *прил* (*варенье, куст*) blackberry *опред*, bramble *опред*.
ежего́дник (-а) *м* annual (publication).
ежего́дно *нареч* annually.
ежего́дный *прил* annual *опред*.
ежедне́вен *прил см* **ежедне́вный**.

ежедне́вник (-а) *м* (*блокнот-дневник*) diary.
ежедне́вно *нареч* daily, every day.
ежедне́в|ный (-ен, -на, -но) *прил* daily; (*повседневный*) everyday.
ежеме́сячник (-а) *м* (*периодическое издание*) monthly.
ежеме́сячно *нареч* monthly.
ежеме́сячный *прил* monthly *опред*.
ежемину́тен *прил см* **ежемину́тный**.
ежемину́тно *нареч* every minute; (*постоянно*) constantly.
ежемину́т|ный (-ен, -на, -но) *прил*: ~**ная прове́рка** checks at one-minute intervals; (*очень частый*) constant.
еженеде́льник (-а) *м* weekly.
еженеде́льно *нареч* weekly.
еженеде́льный *прил* weekly *опред*.
ежесеку́нд|ный (-ен, -на, -но) *прил* occurring every second; (*чрезвычайно частый*) incessant.
ёжик (-а) *м* hedgehog; (*причёска*) crew cut; **стри́чься** (**постри́чься** *perf*) ~**ом** to have a crew cut.
ёж|иться (-усь, -ишься; *perf* **съёжиться**) *несов возв*: ~ **от** +*gen* (*от холода*) to huddle up from; (*от страха, от стыда*) to cringe with.
ежо́вый *прил*: **держа́ть кого́-н в ежо́вых рукави́цах** to rule sb with a rod of iron.
езд|а́ (-ы́) *ж* (*перемещение: на велосипеде, верхом*) riding; (: *на машине*) driving; (*мера: на машине*) drive; **в двадцати́ мину́тах** ~**ы́ от** +*gen* a twenty-minute drive from.
е́зд|ить (-жу, -дишь) *несов неперех* to go; ~ (*impf*) **на** +*prp* (*на лошади, на велосипеде*) to ride; (*на поезде, на автобусе итп*) to travel *или* go by; (*разг: эксплуатировать*) to make use of.
ездово́й *прил*: **ездова́я соба́ка** sled dog; **ездова́я ло́шадь** draught horse.
ездо́к (-а́) *м* rider; **туда́ я бо́льше не** ~ I'm not going there again.
е́зжу *несов см* **е́здить**.
ей *мест см* **она́**.
ей-бо́гу *межд* (*разг*) really, truly.
ЕКА́ *ср сокр* (= *Европе́йское косми́ческое аге́нство*) ESA (= *European Space Agency*).
Екатеринбу́рг (-а) *м* Ekaterinburg.
ёка|ть (*3sg* -ет, *3pl* -ют, *perf* **ёкнуть**) *несов неперех* (*сердце*) to miss a beat.
ёкн|уть (*3sg* -ет, *3pl* -ут) *сов от* **ёкать**.
ел *итп несов см* **есть**.
е́ле *нареч* (*с трудом*) only just; (*едва*) barely, hardly.
е́ле-е́ле *нареч*: **он** ~ **спа́сся** he had a narrow escape; **ло́шадь** ~ **плетётся** the horse is on its last legs.
еле́й|ный (-ен, -йна, -йно) *прил* (*перен: слащавый*) unctuous.
ёл|ка (-ки; *gen pl* -ок) *ж* fir (tree); (*БОТ*) spruce; (*праздник*) New Year party for children;

(**рождéственская** *или* **новогóдняя**) ~ ≈ Christmas tree.
елóвый *прил* fir; (*БОТ*) spruce.
ёлок *сущ см* **ёлка**.
ёлочный *прил*: ~**ые украшéния** *или* **игрýшки** Christmas-tree decorations *мн*.
ел|ь (**-и**) *ж* fir (tree); (*БОТ*) spruce.
éльник (**-а**) *м* (*лес*) fir grove; (*плантация*) fir plantation; (*ветки*) fir branches *мн*.
ем *несов см* **есть**.
ём|кий (**-кая, -кое, -кие; -ок, -ка, -ко**) *прил* (*вместительный*) capacious; (*перен: содержательный*) meaningful.
ёмкост|ь (**-и**) *ж* (*вместимость*) capacity; (*вместилище*) container; **мéры** ~**и** units of volume.
ёмок *прил см* **ёмкий**.
емý *мест см* **он, онó**.
енóт (**-а**) *м* raccoon.
енóтовый *прил* raccoon.
епáрхи|я (**-и**) *ж* diocese; (*в православной церкви*) eparchy.
епúскоп (**-а**) *м* bishop.
ералáш (**-а**) *м* (*разг: беспорядок*) mess.
Еревáн (**-а**) *м* Yerevan.
éрес|ь (**-и**) *ж* heresy; (*перен*) nonsense.
еретúк (**-á**) *м* heretic.
еретúческ|ий (**-ая, -ое, -ие**) *прил* heretical.
ёрза|ть (**-ю**) *несов неперех* (*разг: беспокойно сидеть*) to fidget.
ерóш|ить (**-у, -ишь;** *perf* **взъерóшить**) *несов перех* (*разг: волосы*) to ruffle.
ерунд|á (**-ы́**) *ж* (*разг: чепуха*) rubbish, nonsense; **э́то** ~ (*пустяк*) it's a mere trifle, it's nothing.
ёрш (**-á**) *м* (*рыба*) ruff(e); (*щётка*) brush.
ерш|úться (**-у́сь, -и́шься**) *несов возв* (*о волосах*) to stick up; (*разг: горячиться*) to fly off the handle.
ЕС *ср сокр* (= *Европéйское соóбщество*) EC (= *European Community*) ♦ *м сокр* (= *Европéйский совéт*) Council of Europe.
есаýл (**-а**) *м* esaul (*rank equivalent to captain in Cossack army*).

KEYWORD

éсли *союз* **1** (*в том случае когда*) if; **éсли онá придёт, дай ей э́то письмó** if she comes, give her this letter; **éсли ..., то ...** (*éсли*) if ..., then ...; **éсли он опоздáет, то идú одúн** if he is late, (then) go alone
2 (*об условном действии*): **éсли бы, (то/ тогдá)** if; **éсли бы я мог, (то) помóг бы тебé** if I could, I would help you
3 (*выражает сильное желание*): (**ах** *или* **о**) **éсли бы** if only; **ах éсли бы он позвонúл!** oh, if only he would phone (*BRIT*) *или* call (*US*)!
4 (*выражает противопоставление*) if; **éсли с мáмой я чáсто спóрю, то с отцóм мне легкó** if I argue with Mum, I get on all the better with Dad; **éсли не ..., то ...** if not ..., then ...; **éсли не кáждый день, то чáсто** often, if not every day; **éсли уж на то пошлó** if it comes to it; **éсли**

хотúте *или* **угóдно** (*возможно*) perhaps; **что éсли...?** (*а вдруг*) what if...?

ест *несов см* **есть**.
естéственен *прил см* **естéственный**.
естéственно *нареч* naturally ♦ *вводн сл* (*конéчно*) of course.
естéственност|ь (**-и**) *ж* (*нормальность*) naturalness; (*непринуждённость*) spontaneity.
естéствен|ный (**-ен, -на, -но**) *прил* natural; ~**ные наýки** natural sciences; ~**ная смерть** death from natural causes.
естествознáни|е (**-я**) *ср* natural sciences *мн*.
естествоиспытáтел|ь (**-я**) *м* (natural) scientist.
есть (*см* **Table 15;** *perf* **поéсть** *или* **съесть**) *несов перех* (*питаться*) to eat; (*perf* **съесть;** *разрушать химически: металл*) to corrode; (*no perf; раздражать*) to sting, irritate; **мне хóчется** ~ I'm hungry; ~ (*impf*) **когó-н глазáми** (*разг*) to gaze at sb.
есть *несов* (*один предмет*) there is; (*много предметов*) there are ♦ *межд*: ~! (*ВОЕН*) yes, sir!; ~ **мнóго возмóжностей** there are many possibilities; **на столé** ~ **я́блоки** there are apples on the table; **у меня** ~ **друг** I have a friend.
ЕФР *м сокр* (= *Европéйский фонд развúтия*) EDF (= *European Development Fund*).
ефрéйтор (**-а**) *м* (*ВОЕН*) lance corporal.
éхать (*см* **Table 19**) *несов неперех* to go; (*поезд, автомобиль: приближаться*) to come; (: *двигаться*) to go, travel; (*разг: скользить*) to slide; ~ (*impf*) **на** +*prp* (*на лошади, на велосипеде*) to ride; ~ (*impf*) +*instr* *или* **на** +*prp* (*на поезде, на автобусе*) to travel *или* go by.
ехúден *прил см* **ехúдный**.
ехúдн|а (**-ы**) *ж* echidna, spiny anteater.
ехúдничa|ть (**-ю;** *perf* **съехúдничать**) *несов неперех* (*разг: язвить*) to make spiteful remarks.
ехúд|ный (**-ен, -на, -но**) *прил* malicious, spiteful.
ехúдств|о (**-а**) *ср* (*язвительность*) spite.
ешь *несов см* **есть**.

KEYWORD

ещё *нареч* **1** (*дополнительно*) more; **хочý ещё кóфе** I want more coffee; **купú ещё 3 кнúги** buy 3 more books; **нáдо ещё поработáть** we must do some more work
2 (*опять: приеду, позвоню итп*) again; **позвоню ещё зáвтра** I'll phone again tomorrow
3 (*до сих пор*) still; **ты ещё не знáешь, что случúлось?** do you still not know what happened?; **нет ещё** not yet
4 (*уже*): **он закóнчил рабóту ещё вчерá** he had already finished the work the day before; **онá уéхала ещё три гóда назáд** she left as long as three years ago; **ещё студéнтом он сдéлал вáжное открытие** while still a student he made an important discovery

5 (*о наличии возможности*) still; **ещё успéю на самолёт** I can still catch the plane
6 (+*comparative*; *лучше, красивее итп*) even; **в результáте он стал ёще богáче** as a result he became even richer
♦ *част* (*усиливает выразительность*): **ещё как рассердúлся/испугáлся** boy, did he get angry/frightened; **дай мне кнúгу! какýю ещё кнúгу!** give me the book! what book for goodness sake!; **всё ещё** still; **онú всё ещё не помирúлись** they still haven't made up; **ещё бы!** (*разг*) you bet!; **вот ещё!** (*разг*) not likely!; **ещё чегó!** (*разг*) not likely!

ЕЭС *ср сокр* (= *Европéйское экономúческое сообщество*) EEC (= *European Economic Community*).
ёю *мест см* **онá**.

～ Ж, ж ～

Ж, ж *сущ нескл* (*буква*) the 7th letter of the Russian alphabet.

ж *союз, част см* **же.**

жа́б|а (-ы) *ж* (*ЗООЛ*) toad.

жабо́ *ср нескл* jabot.

жа́бр|а (-ы) *ж* (*ЗООЛ: обычно мн*) gill; **брать** (**взять** *perf*) **за** ~**ы** кого-н (*разг*) to twist sb's arm.

жа́ворон|ок (-ка) *м* (*ЗООЛ*) lark.

жа́ден *прил см* **жа́дный.**

жа́дин|а (-ы) *м/ж* (*разг: пренебр*) meanie.

жа́дничать (-ю; *perf* **пожа́дничать**) *несов неперех* (*разг*) to be mingy.

жа́дность (-и) *ж*: ~ (**к** +*dat*) (*к вещам, к деньгам*) greed (for); (*к жизни*) lust (for); (*к развлечениям*) desire (for); ~ **к еде́** greed; **с** ~**ю** (*есть*) greedily; (*слушать, смотреть*) avidly.

жа́дный (-ен, -на́, -но) *прил* greedy; (*на работу*) eager.

жа́жд|а (-ы) *ж* thirst; ~ **зна́ний** (*перен*) thirst for knowledge; ~ +*infin* eagerness to do; **утоля́ть** (**утоли́ть** *perf*) ~**у** to quench one's thirst.

жа́жд|ать (-у, -ешь) *несов неперех*: ~ +*gen* (*перен: мира*) to long for; ~ (*impf*) +*infin* (*познавать*) to long to do.

жакéт (-а) *м* (woman's) jacket.

жал(ся) *итп несов см* **жать(ся).**

жалéть (-ю; *perf* **пожалéть**) *несов перех* to feel sorry for; (*скупиться*) to grudge ♦ *неперех*: ~ **о** +*prp* to regret; **не** ~**я сил** sparing no effort; ~ (**пожалéть** *perf*), **что** ... to regret that ....

жа́л|ить (-ю, -ишь; *perf* **ужа́лить**) *несов перех* (*подлеж: оса*) to sting; (: *змея*) to bite.

жа́лкий (-кая, -кое, -кие; -ок, -ка, -ко) *прил* (*вид*) pitiful, pathetic; (*одежда*) shabby; (*трус*) abject.

жа́лко *как сказ* = **жаль.**

жа́л|о (-а) *ср* (*пчелы*) sting; (*змеи*) forked tongue.

жа́лоб|а (-ы) *ж* complaint; **подава́ть** (**пода́ть** *perf*) ~**у на** кого-н to lodge a complaint against sb.

жа́лоб|ный (-ен, -на, -но) *прил* (*голос, песня*) plaintive; (*лицо*) sorrowful; **жа́лобная кни́га** complaints book (*in shop, post office etc*).

жалова́нь|е (-я) *ср* salary.

жа́л|овать (-ую) *несов перех* (*разг*): **колле́ги его́ не** ~**уют** he is not very popular with his colleagues

▶ **жа́ловаться** (*perf* **пожа́ловаться**) *несов возв*: ~**ся на** +*acc* to complain about; (*разг:*

я́бедничать) to tell on.

жа́лок *прил см* **жа́лкий.**

жа́лостен *прил см* **жа́лостный.**

жа́лостлив|ый (-, -а, -о) *прил* sympathetic.

жа́лост|ный (-ен, -на, -но) *прил* mournful; ~ **фильм** tear-jerker.

жа́лость (-и) *ж*: ~ **к** +*dat* sympathy for; **кака́я** ~ what a shame; **де́лать** (**сде́лать** *perf*) **что-н из** ~**и** to do sth out of pity.

жаль *как сказ* **1** (+*acc*; *о сострадании*): (**мне**) **жаль дру́га** I am sorry for my friend **2** (+*acc или* +*gen*; *о сожалении, о досаде*): (**мне**) **жаль вре́мени/де́нег** I grudge the time/money **3** (+*infin*): **жаль уезжа́ть так бы́стро** it's a pity *или* shame to leave so soon; **жаль, что ты меня́ не понима́ешь** it's a pity *или* shame you don't understand me

♦ *вводн сл* (*к сожалению*) unfortunately; **хоте́л пое́хать в Ло́ндон, да, жаль, нет вре́мени** I wanted to go to London, but unfortunately I didn't have time.

жанр (-а) *м* (*лирический*) genre; (*перен*) style.

жар (-а; *part gen* -у, *loc sg* -у́) *м* (*тепло*) heat; (*перен*) fervour (*BRIT*), fervor (*US*); (*МЕД*) fever; **его́ бро́сило в** ~ (*перен*) he broke out in a sweat.

жар|а́ (-ы́) *ж* heat.

жарго́н (-а) *м* slang; (*профессиональный*) jargon.

жа́реный *прил* (*на сковороде*) fried; (*в духовке*) roast.

жа́р|ить (-ю, -ишь; *perf* **зажа́рить**) *несов перех* (*на сковороде*) to fry; (*в духовке*) to roast

▶ **жа́риться** (*perf* **зажа́риться**) *несов возв* to fry; ~**ся** (*impf*) **на со́лнце** (*разг*) to bask in the sun.

жа́рк|а (-и) *ж* frying.

жа́ркий (-кая, -кое, -кие; -ок, -ка́, -ко) *прил* hot; (*перен*) heated; **жа́ркие стра́ны** tropical countries.

жа́рко *нареч* (*спорить*) heatedly; (*целовать*) passionately ♦ *как сказ* it's hot; **мне** ~ I'm hot; **ему́ ни хо́лодно ни** ~ (*разг*) it's all the same to him.

жарко́е (-о́го; *decl like adj*) *ср* meat (*fried*).

жа́рок *прил см* **жа́ркий.**

жаропонижа́ющий (-ая, -ее, -ие) *прил* febrifugal.

жаропро́ч|ный (-ен, -на, -но) *прил* (*материал*) heat-resistant; (*посуда*) ovenproof.

жар-пти́ц|а (-ы) *ж* Firebird.

жа́рче *сравн прил от* **жа́ркий**.

жасми́н (-а) *м* jasmine.

жа́тв|а (-ы) *ж* harvest.

жать (**жму, жмёшь**) *несов перех* (*руку*) to shake; (*лимон, сок*) to squeeze; (**жну, жнёшь**; *perf* **сжать**; to harvest; **сапоги́ мне жмут**; my boots are pinching (my feet); **э́то пла́тье жмёт в та́лии**; this dress is too tight at the waist;

▶ **жа́ться**; жмусь, жмёшься ◆ *несов возв* (*от холода*) to huddle up; (*разг: колебаться*) to dither; (: *скупиться*) to be stingy.

жва́ч|ка (-ки; *gen pl* -ек) *ж* cud; (*разг: жевательная резинка*) chewing gum.

жгу(сь) *итп несов см* **жечь(ся)**.

жгут (-а́) *м* (*из соломы*) rope; (*МЕД*) tourniquet.

жгу́ч|ий (-ая, -ее, -ие; -, -а, -е) *прил* (*также перен*) burning; (*мороз*) biting; **жгу́чий брюне́т** man with jet-black hair.

ж.д. *сокр* (= **желе́зная доро́га**) R., r. (= *railway*), RR (*US*) (= *railroad*).

ж/д *сокр* = **ж.д.**

ж.-д. *сокр* = **ж.д.**

жд|ать (-у, -ёшь; *pt* -ал, -ала́, -а́ло) *несов перех* (*also* +*gen*; *письмо, дождя, гостей*) to expect; (*друга, поезда*) to wait for; (*надеяться: награды, пощады*) to hope for; **что нас ~ёт?** what's in store for us?; **~а́ли, что он извини́тся** they hoped that he would apologize; **вре́мя не ~ёт** there's no time to lose; **я ~у не дожду́сь кани́кул** (*разг*) I can't wait for the holidays.

┌─────────────┐
│ **KEYWORD** │
└─────────────┘

же *союз* **1** (*при противопоставлении*) but; **я не люблю́ матема́тику, литерату́ру же обожа́ю** I don't like mathematics, but I love literature
2 (*вводит дополнительные сведения*) and; **успе́х зави́сит от нали́чия ресу́рсов, ресу́рсов же ма́ло** success depends on the presence of resources, and the resources are insufficient

◆ *част* **1** (*ведь*): **вы́пей ещё ча́ю, хо́чешь же!** have more tea, you want some, don't you?
2 (*именно*): **приду́ сейча́с же** I'll come right now; **когда́ же ты уйдёшь?** when will you go then?
3 (*выражает сходство*): **тако́й же** the same; **тако́й же дом** the same (kind of) house; **в э́том же году́** this very year; **те же лю́ди** the same (kind of) people.

жев|а́ть (-у́ю) *несов перех* to chew.

жёг(ся) *итп несов см* **жечь(ся)**.

жезл (-а) *м* baton.

жела́нен *прил см* **жела́нный**.

жела́ни|е (-я) *ср* (*просьба*) request; **~** +*gen*/+*infin* desire for/to do; **горе́ть** (*impf*) **~м** +*infin* to be eager to do.

жела́н|ный (-ен, -на, -но) *прил* (*гость, весть*) welcome.

жела́телен *прил см* **жела́тельный**.

жела́тельно *как сказ*: **~** +*infin* it is desirable to do; **~, что́бы Вы пришли́** it would be preferable if you could come.

жела́тель|ный (-ен, -ьна, -ьно) *прил* desirable.

жела́|ть (-ю; *perf* **пожела́ть**) *несов непер ех* (+*gen*) to desire; **~** (**пожела́ть** *perf*) +*infin* to wish *или* want to do; **~** (**пожела́ть** *perf*) **кому́-н сча́стья/всего́ хоро́шего** to wish sb happiness/all the best; **Ва́ша рабо́та оставля́ет ~ лу́чшего** your work leaves much to be desired.

жела́ющ|ий (-его; *decl like adj*) *м* (*обычно мн*): **~ие пое́хать/порабо́тать** those interested in going/working; **~ие есть?** is anybody interested?

желва́к (-а́) *м* (*разг*) lump.

желе́ *ср нескл* jelly.

железа́ (-езы́; *nom pl* -езы, *gen pl* -ёз, *dat pl* -еза́м) *ж* gland.

железнодоро́жник (-а) *м* rail(way) (*BRIT*) *или* railroad (*US*) worker.

железнодоро́жный *прил* (*вокзал*) railway *опред* (*BRIT*), railroad *опред* (*US*); (*транспорт*) rail *опред*.

желе́зн|ый *прил* (*также перен*) iron; (: *логика*) cast-iron; **~ые не́рвы** nerves of steel; **желе́зная доро́га** railway (*BRIT*), railroad (*US*).

желе́з|о (-а) *ср* iron.

железобето́н (-а) *м* reinforced concrete.

жёлоб (-а; *nom pl* -а́) *м* (*водосточный*) gutter.

желте́|ть (-ю; *perf* **пожелте́ть**) *несов непер ех* to turn yellow; (*no perf*; *виднеться*) to show yellow.

желто́к (-а́) *м* yolk.

желторо́т|ый (-, -а, -о) *прил* yellow-beaked (*of young birds*); (*разг: пренебр*) **он ещё ~ юне́ц** he's still wet behind the ears.

желту́х|а (-и) *ж* jaundice.

жёлт|ый (-, -а́, -о) *прил* yellow; **жёлтая пре́сса** the gutter press.

желу́д|ок (-ка) *м* (*АНАТ*) stomach; **расстро́йство ~ка** stomach upset.

желу́дочный *прил* (*боль*) stomach *опред*; (*сок*) gastric.

жёлуд|ь (-я) *м* acorn.

жёлч|ный *прил*: **~ пузы́рь** gall bladder; (-ен, -на, -но; *перен*) bilious.

жёлч|ь (-и) *ж* (*также перен*) bile.

жема́н|ный (-ен, -на, -но) *прил* affected.

жемчуг (-а; *nom pl* -а́) *м* pearls *мн*; **бу́сы из ~а** pearl necklace.

жемчу́жин|а (-ы) *ж* pearl; (*перен*) treasure.

жемчу́жный *прил* pearl; (*перен: зубы*) pearly.

жен|а́ (-ы́; *nom pl* **жёны**, *gen pl* **жён**) *ж* wife.

жена́т|ый (-, -ы) *прил* married (*of man*); **он**

жена́т на +*prp* he is married to; **они́ ~ы** they are married.

Жене́в|а (-ы) *ж* Geneva.

жен|и́ть (-ю́, -ишь) *(не)сов перех* (сына, внука): **~ (на** +*prp*) to marry (off) (to); (*perf* **пожени́ть**; *разг*) to marry

▶ **жени́ться** *(не)сов возв*: **~ся на** +*prp* to marry (*of man*); (*perf* **пожени́ться**; *разг*) to get hitched.

жени́х (-а́) *м* (*до свадьбы*) fiancé; (*на свадьбе*) (bride)groom.

женонена́ви́стник (-а) *м* misogynist, woman-hater.

женоподо́б|ный (-ен) *прил* effeminate.

же́нск|ий (-ая, -ое, -ие) *прил* (*одежда, раздевалка*) women's; (*логика, органы*) female; **же́нская консульта́ция** ≈ gynaecological and antenatal (*BRIT*) *или* gynecological and prenatal (*US*) clinic; **же́нский пол** the female sex; **же́нский род** feminine gender.

же́нственный *прил* feminine.

же́нщин|а (-ы) *ж* woman.

женьше́н|ь (-я) *м* ginseng.

жерд|ь (-и; *gen pl* **-е́й**) *ж* pole.

жеребёнок (-ёнка; *nom pl* **-я́та**, *gen pl* **-я́т**) *м* foal.

жереб|е́ц (-ца́) *м* stallion.

жереб|и́ться (*3sg* **-и́тся**, *3pl* **-я́тся**, *perf* **ожереби́ться**) *несов возв* to foal.

жеребца́ *итп сущ см* **жеребе́ц**.

жеребёв|ка (-ки; *gen pl* **-ок**) *ж* casting *или* drawing of lots.

жеребя́та *итп сущ см* **жеребёнок**.

жерл|о́ (-а́; *nom pl* **-а**) *ср* (*пушки, вулкана*) mouth.

жёрнов (-а; *nom pl* **-а́**) *м* millstone.

же́ртв|а (-ы) *ж* victim; (*РЕЛ*) sacrifice; **приноси́ть** (**принести́** *perf*) **кого́-н/что́-н в ~у кому́-н/чему́-н** to sacrifice sb/sth for sb/sth; **челове́ческие ~ы** casualties; **пасть** (*perf*) **~ой чего́-н** to fall victim to sth.

же́ртв|овать (-ую; *perf* **поже́ртвовать**) *несов непepex* (+*instr*) to sacrifice ◆ *перех* to donate.

жертвоприноше́ни|е (-я) *ср* (*РЕЛ*) sacrifice; **соверша́ть** (**соверши́ть** *perf*) **~** to offer up a sacrifice.

жест (-а) *м* gesture; **язы́к же́стов** sign language.

жестикули́р|овать (-ую) *несов непepex* to gesticulate.

жёст|кий (-кая, -кое, -кие; -ок, -ка́, -ко) *прил* (*кровать, человек*) hard; (*мясо*) tough; (*волосы*) coarse; (*условия*) strict; **жёсткий ваго́н** *railway carriage with hard seats*; **жёсткая вода́** hard water; **жёсткий диск** hard disk.

жесто́к|ий (-ая, -ое, -ие; -, -а́, -о) *прил* cruel; (*перен*) severe; **~ая необходи́мость** cruel necessity.

жесто́ко *нареч* (*расправиться*) cruelly.

жесто́кост|ь (-и) *ж* cruelty.

жёстче *сравн прил от* **жёсткий**.

жест|ь (-и) *ж* tin-plated sheet metal.

жестя́н|ка (-ки; *gen pl* **-ок**) *ж* tin box.

жето́н (-а) *м* tag; (*в метро*) token.

жечь (**жгу, жжёшь** *итп*, **жгут**; *pt* **жёг, жгла, жгло**, *perf* **сжечь**) *несов перех* to burn

▶ **же́чься** *несов возв* (*утюг*) to be very hot; (*крапива*) to sting; (*perf* **обже́чься**; *разг*) to burn o.s.

жже́ни|е (-я) *ср* burning sensation.

жжёшь(ся) *итп несов см* **жечь(ся)**.

живи́тел|ьный (-ен, -ьна, -ьно) *прил* (*воздух*) invigorating.

жи́во *нареч* (*представить себе*) vividly; (*откликнуться*) animatedly.

жив|о́й (-, -а́, -о) *прил* alive; (*no short form*; *организм*) living; (*животное*) live; (*человек: энергичный*) lively; (*выразительный*) vivid; **~ приме́р** a living example; **он ~ наде́ждой/воспомина́ниями** he lives in hope/for his memories; **он ещё ~?** is he still alive?; **жив – здоро́в** (*разг*) alive and well; **в нём ещё ~а́ оби́да** the insult still rankles with him; **ни жив ни мёртв** (*разг*) petrified; **задева́ть** (**заде́ть** *perf*) **кого́-н за ~о́е** to cut sb to the quick; **оста́ться** (*perf*) **в ~ых** to survive; **жива́я и́згородь** hedge; **живо́й уголо́к** *area in school where pets are kept for pupils to look after*; **живо́й язы́к** living language; **живы́е цветы́** fresh flowers.

живопи́сен *прил см* **живопи́сный**.

живопи́с|ец (-ца) *м* painter.

живопи́с|ный (-ен, -на, -но) *прил* picturesque.

живопи́сца *итп сущ см* **живопи́сец**.

жи́вопис|ь (-и) *ж* (*искусство*) painting.

живо́т (-а́) *м* stomach, abdomen; (*разг*) belly, tummy.

животново́д (-а) *м farmer specializing in animal husbandry.*

животново́дств|о (-а) *ср* animal husbandry.

живо́тн|ое (-ого; *decl like adj*) *ср* (*также перен*) animal.

живо́тный *прил* animal *опред*; (*перен*) bestial.

животрепе́щущий (-ая, -ее, -ие) *прил* topical.

живу́ *итп несов см* **жить**.

живу́ч|ий (-ая, -ее, -ие; -, -а, -е) *прил* hardy; (*обычай, представление*) enduring; (*предрассудки*) deep-rooted; **он ~ как ко́шка** he has nine lives.

живьём *нареч* alive.

жи́д|кий (-кая, -кое, -кие) *прил* liquid; (-ок, -ка́, -ко) *молоко, суп*) watery; (*состояние, мускулы, голос*) weak; (*волосы*) sparse, thin; **жи́дкое то́пливо** liquid fuel.

жи́дкост|ь (-и) *ж* liquid.

жи́док *прил см* **жи́дкий**.

жи́ж|а (-и) *ж* slurry.

жи́же *сравн прил от* **жи́дкий**.

жизнеде́ятельност|ь (-и) *ж* (*организма, клетки*) (vital) activity.

жи́знен|ный (-, -на, -но) *прил* (*вопрос, интересы*) vital; (*необходимость*) basic; **~ у́ровень** standard of living; **~ о́пыт** experience;

~ **путь** journey through life.
жизнера́дост|ный (-ен, -на, -но) *прил* cheerful.
жизнеспосо́б|ный (-ен, -на, -но) *прил (также перен)* viable.
жизн|ь (-и) *ж* life; **о́браз жи́зни** way of life; **у́ровень жи́зни** standard of living; **как ~?** *(разг)* how's life?
жи́л|а (-ы) *ж (также ГЕО)* vein; *(сухожилие)* tendon, sinew; **золота́я ~** *(перен: разг)* gold mine.
жиле́т (-а) *м* waistcoat *(BRIT)*, vest *(US)*; **спаса́тельный ~** life jacket.
жиле́|ц (-ьца́) *м (квартиросъёмщик)* tenant; *(квартирант)* lodger; **он не ~** *(разг)* he's not long for this world.
жи́листый (-, -а, -о) *прил (мясо)* stringy; *(старик)* sinewy; *(рука)* veiny.
жили́щ|е (-а) *ср (дом)* dwelling.
жили́щный *прил* housing *опред.*
жи́л|ка (-ки; *gen pl* -ок) *ж* vein; *(перен: склонность)* streak.
жило́й *прил (дом, здание)* residential; *(комната, помещение)* inhabited; **жила́я пло́щадь** accommodation.
жи́лок *сущ см* **жи́лка.**
жилпло́щад|ь (-и) *ж сокр* = **жила́я пло́щадь.**
жиль|ё (-я́) *ср (человеческое)* habitation; *(жилище)* accommodation *(BRIT)*, lodgings *мн.*
жильца́ *итп сущ см* **жиле́ц.**
жи́молост|ь (-и) *ж* honeysuckle.
жир (-а; *part gen* -у, *loc sg* -у́, *nom pl* -ы́) *м (животный)* fat; *(растительный)* oil; **с жи́ру беси́ться** *(impf) (разг)* to become spoilt; **ры́бий ~** *(МЕД)* cod-liver oil.
жира́ф (-а) *м* giraffe.
жи́рен *прил см* **жи́рный.**
жире́|ть (-ю; *perf* **разжире́ть** *или* **ожире́ть)** *несов неперех* to grow fat.
жи́рный (-ен, -на́, -но) *прил (пища)* fatty; *(человек)* fat; *(no short form; волосы)* greasy; *(чернозём, известь)* rich; **жи́рный шрифт** bold type.
жирови́к (-а́) *м* lipoma.
жирорасчёт (-а) *м* Giro.
жите́йск|ий (-ая, -ое, -ие) *прил (мудрость)* worldly; *(проблемы)* everyday; **де́ло ~ое!** *(разг)* that's nothing unusual!
жи́тел|ь (-я) *м* resident; **городско́й ~** city dweller.
жи́тельниц|а (-ы) *ж см* **жи́тель.**
жи́тельств|о (-а) *ср* residence; **ме́сто постоя́нного ~а** permanent place of residence.
жи́тниц|а (-ы) *ж (перен)* breadbasket.
жи|ть (-ву́, -вёшь; *pt* -л, -ла́, -ло) *несов неперех* to live; *(также перен):* ~ **в** +*prp* to live in; ~ *(impf)* +*instr* (детьми, наукой) to live for; ~ *(impf)* **на** +*acc/***с** +*instr* to live on/with; ~ *(impf)* **на свои́ сре́дства** to support o.s.; **~л-был** there once

was, once upon a time there was
▶ **жи́ться** *несов возв (разг):* **ему́ ве́село/ то́скливо ~вётся** he's having a good/miserable time; **как Вам ~вётся?** how's life?
жмот (-а) *м (разг)* skinflint.
жму(сь) *итп несов см* **жа́ть(ся).**
жму́р|ить (-ю, -ишь; *perf* **зажму́рить)** *несов неперех:* ~ **глаза́** to screw up one's eyes
▶ **жму́риться** *(perf* **зажму́риться)** *несов возв* to squint; **~ся (зажму́риться** *perf)* **от све́та** to squint in the light.
жму́р|ки (-ок) *мн* blind man's buff *ед;* **игра́ть** *(impf)* **в ~** to play blind man's buff.
жнец (-а́) *м* reaper.
жни́ц|а (-ы) *ж см* **жнец.**
жну *итп несов см* **жать.**
жоке́|й (-я) *м* jockey.
жонглёр (-а) *м* juggler.
жонгли́р|овать (-ую) *несов неперех:* ~ +*instr* to juggle (with).
жо́п|а (-ы) *ж (груб!)* arse *(BRIT)* (!), ass *(US)* (!)
жр|ать (-у, -ёшь; *pt* -ал, -ала́, -а́ло, *perf* **сожра́ть)** *несов перех (разг)* to scoff.
жре́би|й (-я) *м:* **броса́ть ~** to cast lots.
жрец (-а́) *м (РЕЛ)* (pagan) priest; *(перен)* devotee.
жри́ц|а (-ы) *ж (РЕЛ)* (pagan) priestess.
ЖСК *м сокр* (= **жили́щно-строи́тельный кооперати́в)** *housing cooperative.*
жу́желиц|а (-ы) *ж* ground beetle.
жужж|а́ть (-у́, -и́шь) *несов неперех* to buzz.
жук (-а́) *м* beetle.
жу́лик (-а) *м* swindler; *(в игре)* cheat.
жу́льнича|ть (-ю; *perf* **сжу́льничать)** *несов неперех (разг)* to cheat.
жу́льничеств|о (-а) *ср* underhandedness; *(в игре)* cheating.
жура́вл|ь (-я́) *м* crane.
жур|и́ть (-ю́, -и́шь) *несов перех (разг)* to chide.
журна́л (-а) *м* magazine; *(судово́й)* journal; *(классный)* register; *(кино́)* short; ~ **протоко́лов** minute book.
журнали́ст (-а) *м* journalist.
журнали́ст|ка (-ки; *gen pl* -ок) *ж см* **журнали́ст.**
журнали́стик|а (-и) *ж* journalism.
журнали́сток *сущ см* **журнали́стка.**
журч|а́ть (-у́, -и́шь) *несов неперех (ручей итп)* to babble, murmur.
жу́тк|ий (-кая, -кое, -кие; -ок, -ка́, -ко) *прил* terrible.
жу́тко *нареч (неприятный)* terribly ◆ *как сказ:* **здесь ~** it's terrifying here; **мне ~** I am terrified.
жу́ток *прил см* **жу́ткий.**
жут|ь (-и) *ж (разг)* terror ◆ *как сказ* it's terrible; **кака́я ~!** *(разг)* how terrible!
жу́хлый *прил* faded.
ЖЭК (-а) *м сокр* (= **жили́щно-эксплуатацио́нная конто́ра)** ≈ housing office.
жюри́ *ср нескл* panel of judges.

~ З, з ~

З, з *сущ нескл (буква)* the 8th letter of the Russian alphabet.

з. *сокр* (= запад) W (= West); (= западный) W (= West).

KEYWORD

за *предл (+acc)* **1** out (of); **выйти** *(perf)* **за дверь** to go out (of) the door

2 *(позади)* behind; **спрятаться** *(perf)* **за дерево** to hide behind a tree

3 *(около: сесть, встать)* at; **сесть** *(perf)* **за стол** to sit down at the table

4 *(свыше какого-н предела)* over; **ему за сорок** he is over forty; **мороз за двадцать градусов** over twenty degrees of frost

5 *(при указании на расстояние, на время)*: **за пять километров отсюда** five kilometres (*BRIT*) *или* kilometers (*US*) from here; **за три часа до начала спектакля** three hours before the beginning of the show; **за эти десять лет он постарел** he has aged over the last ten years

6 *(при указании объекта действия)*: **держаться за** +acc to hold onto; **ухватиться** *(perf)* **за** +acc to take hold of; **взять** *(perf)* **кого-н за руку** to take sb by the hand; **взяться** *(perf)* **за работу** to start work

7 *(об объекте чувств)* for; **радоваться** *(impf)* **за сына** to be happy for one's son; **отвечать** *(impf)* **за успех предприятия** to be responsible for the success of an enterprise; **беспокоиться** *(impf)* **за мужа** to worry about one's husband

8 *(о цели)* for; **сражаться** *(impf)* **за победу** to fight for victory

9 *(в пользу)* for, in favour (*BRIT*) *или* favor (*US*) of; **голосовать** *(impf)* **за предложение** to vote for *или* in favour (*BRIT*) *или* favor (*US*) of a proposal

10 *(по причине, в обмен)* for; **благодарю Вас за помощь** thank you for your help; **платить** (**заплатить** *perf*) **за что-н** to pay for sth; **быть** *(impf)* **наказанным за воровство** to be punished for stealing; **я сделал это за деньги** I did it for money

11 *(вместо кого-н)* for; **работать** *(impf)* **за друга** to fill in for a friend

◆ *предл (+instr)* **1** *(по другую сторону)* on the other side of; **жить** *(impf)* **за рекой** to live on the other side of the river

2 *(вне)* outside; **жить** *(impf)* **за городом** to live outside the town; **за границей** abroad

3 *(позади)* behind; **стоять** *(impf)* **за дверью** to stand behind the door; **я шёл за ним** I walked behind him; **бежать** *(impf/perf)* **за преступником** to run after a criminal

4 *(около: стоять, сидеть)* at; **сидеть** *(impf)* **за столом** to sit at the table

5 *(о смене событий)* after; **год за годом** year after year; **за зимой идёт весна** spring comes after winter

6 *(во время чего-н)* over; **поговорить** *(perf)* **за завтраком** to talk over breakfast

7 *(о объекте внимания)*: **смотреть** *или* **ухаживать за** +instr to look after; **моя сестра замужем за врачом** my sister is married to a doctor

8 *(с целью получить, достать что-н)* for; **я послал его за газетой** I sent him out for a paper; **он пошёл за врачом** he went to fetch the doctor

9 *(по причине)* owing to; **за отсутствием доказательств** in the absence of proof

◆ *как сказ (согласен)* in favour (*BRIT*) *или* favor (*US*); **кто за?** who is in favour (*BRIT*) *или* favor (*US*)?

◆ *ср нескл* pro; **взвесить** *(perf)* **все за и против** to weigh up all the pros and cons.

за- *префикс (in verbs; о начале действия) indicating beginning of an action eg.* **зааплодировать**; *(о доведении действия до крайней степени) indicating taking sth to an extreme degree eg.* **завраться**; *(образует совершенный вид) used in the formation of some perfective aspects eg.* **заасфальтировать**; *(in nouns and adjectives; находящийся по ту сторону чего-н)* trans-.

заале|ть *(3sg -ет, 3pl -ют) сов неперех* to turn scarlet.

заарка́н|ить (**-ю, -ишь;** *impf* **заарканивать**) *сов неперех* to lasso.

заарта́ч|иться (**-усь, -ишься**) *сов возв (разг)* to become obstinate.

заасфальти́р|овать (**-ую**) *сов от* **асфальтировать**.

заба́в|а (**-ы**) *ж* amusement.

заба́вен *прил см* **забавный**.

забавля́|ть (**-ю**) *несов перех* to amuse

▶ **забавля́ться** *несов возв* to amuse o.s.

заба́вно *нареч (рассказывать)* in an amusing way ♦ **как сказ** it's funny.

заба́в|ный (-ен, -на, -но) *прил* amusing.

забаллоти́р|овать (-ую) *сов перех* to reject.

забальзами́р|овать (-ую) *сов от* **бальзами́ровать.**

забарахл|и́ть *(3sg -и́т, 3pl -я́т) сов неперех (разг: мотор, компьютер итп)* to go on the blink.

забаррикади́р|овать (-ую) *сов от* **баррикади́ровать.**

забасто|ва́ть (-ую) *сов неперех* to go on strike.

забасто́в|ка (-ки, *gen pl* **-ок)** *ж* strike; **всео́бщая ~** general strike; **сидя́чая ~** sit-in.

забасто́вочный *прил* strike *опред*.

забасто́вщик (-а) *м* striker.

забасто́вщи|ца (-ы) *ж см* **забасто́вщик.**

забве́ни|е (-я) *ср (забытьё)* oblivion; **предава́ть (преда́ть** *perf)* **что-н ~ю** to consign sth to oblivion.

забе́г (-а) *м (СПОРТ)* race; **предвари́тельный ~** preliminary heat; **~ на сто ме́тров** the hundred metres.

забе́га|ть (-ю) *сов неперех (люди)* to start running; *(глаза)* to roam about.

забе|жа́ть (*как* **бежа́ть;** *см* **Table 20;** *impf* **забега́ть)** *сов неперех:* **~ (в** *+acc) (в дом, в деревню)* to run in(to); *(разг: в музей)* to drop in(to); **забега́ть (~** *perf)* **к знако́мым** *(разг)* to drop in on one's friends; **забега́ть (~** *perf)* **со стороны́** *(разг)* to come up from the side; **забега́ть (~** *perf)* **вперёд** to run ahead; *(перен)* to race ahead.

забере́мене|ть (-ю) *сов от* **бере́менеть.**

забер|у́(сь) *итп сов см* **забра́ть(ся).**

забеспоко́|иться (-юсь, -ишься) *сов возв* to start to worry.

забетони́р|овать (-ую) *сов от* **бетони́ровать.**

забива́|ть(ся) (-ю(сь)) *несов от* **заби́ть(ся).**

забинт|ова́ть (-у́ю) *impf* **бинтова́ть** *или* **забинто́вывать)** *сов перех* to bandage.

забира́|ть(ся) (-ю(сь)) *несов от* **забра́ть(ся).**

заби́т|ый (-, -а, -о) *прил* cowed.

заб|и́ть (-ью́, -ьёшь) *сов неперех (часы)* to begin to strike; *(орудие, пушка)* to start firing; *(озноб, лихора́дка)* to begin to spread; *(вода)* to begin to flow; *(фонтан)* to start up ♦ *(impf* **забива́ть)** *перех (гвоздь, сваю)* to drive in; *(СПОРТ: гол)* to score; *(: мяч, шар)* to drive home; *(окно, дом)* to board up; *(наполнить: склад, холоди́льник)* to overfill; *(засорить: трубу, сток)* to clog (up); *(скот, зверя)* to slaughter; *(перен: человека)* to knock flat; **~** *(perf)* **в бараба́н/ко́локол** to start drumming/ ringing a bell; **забива́ть (~** *perf)* **го́лову чем-н** to fill one's head with sth

▸ **заби́ться** *сов возв (сердце, пульс)* to start beating; *(impf* **забива́ться;** *спрятаться)* to hide

(away); *(засориться: труба, сток)* to clog up; **~ся** *(perf)* **в су́дорогах** to have a fit; **~ся** *(perf)* **в исте́рике** to have a fit of hysterics.

забия́к|а (-и) *м/ж (разг)* bully.

заблаговре́менно *нареч* in good time.

заблагорассу́д|иться *(3sg -ится) сов безл (вздуматься):* **поступа́йте, как Вам ~ится** act as you see fit.

забле|сте́ть (-щу́, -сти́шь) *сов неперех (река, слёзы)* to glisten; *(глаза)* to light up; *(металл)* to gleam.

заблуд|и́ться (-ужу́сь, -у́дишься) *сов возв* to get lost.

заблу́дш|ий (-ая, -ее, -ие) *прил:* **~ челове́к** *person who has lost his or her way;* **заблу́дшая овца́** *(перен)* a lost sheep.

заблужда́|ться (-юсь) *несов возв* to be mistaken.

заблужде́ни|е (-я) *ср* error, delusion; **вводи́ть (ввести́** *perf)* **кого́-н в ~** to delude sb; **выводи́ть (вы́вести** *perf)* **кого́-н из ~я** to open sb's eyes.

заблужу́сь *сов см* **заблуди́ться.**

забода́|ть *(3sg -ет, 3pl -ю́т) сов от* **бода́ть.**

забо́|й (-я) *м (ГЕО)* (working) face; *(действие: скота)* slaughtering.

забо́йщик (-а) *м* face worker.

заболева́емост|ь (-и) *ж (по стране́)* incidence *(of illness)*.

заболева́ни|е (-я) *ср* illness.

заболе́|ть (-ю; *impf* **заболева́ть)** *сов неперех:* **~** *+instr (ветря́нкой, гриппом)* to fall ill with; *(разг: компьютерами, теа́тром итп)* to get hooked on; *(нога, горло)* to begin to hurt.

заболо́ченн|ый (-, -а, -о) *прил* marshy, boggy.

забо́р (-а) *м* fence.

забо́т|а (-ы) *ж (беспоко́йство)* worry; *(уход)* concern; *(обычно мн: хло́поты)* trouble.

забо́|тить (-чу, -тишь) *несов перех* to worry, trouble

▸ **забо́титься** *(perf* **позабо́титься)** *несов возв:* **~ся о** *+prp* to take care of.

забо́тлив|ый (-, -а, -о) *прил (человек)* caring, thoughtful.

забо́чу(сь) *несов см* **забо́тить(ся).**

забрак|ова́ть (-у́ю; *impf* **бракова́ть** *или* **забрако́вывать)** *сов перех* to reject.

забра́л|о (-а) *ср (у шлема)* visor; *(ТЕХ)* screen.

забра́сыва|ть (-ю) *несов от* **заброса́ть, забро́сить.**

заб|ра́ть (-еру́, -ерёшь; *pt* **-ра́л, -рала́, -ра́ло,** *impf* **забира́ть)** *сов перех* to take; *(разг: захвати́ть)* to nick; *(перен: подлеж: страх, тоска́)* to grip; **забира́ть (~** *perf)* **впра́во/ вле́во** to veer off to the right/left

▸ **забра́ться** *(impf* **забира́ться)** *сов возв (спря́таться)* to hide (o.s.) away; *(разг: уехать)* to go off; **забира́ться (~ся** *perf)* **в/на**

+*асс* (*в шкаф, в дом*) to get inside *или* into; (*на дереве*) to climb up; (*в скважину*) to go down; **забира́ться** (**~ся** *perf*) **под одея́ло** to crawl under the blanket; **забира́ться** (**~ся** *perf*) **внутрь/наве́рх** to get inside/to the top.

забреда́ть (-ю) *несов от* **забрести́**.

забреду́ *итп сов см* **забрести́**.

забре́зж|ить (*3sg* -ит) *сов неперех* (*огонь*) to flicker; (*рассвет, утро*) to break.

забр|ести́ (-еду́, -еде́шь; *pt* -ёл, -ела́, -ело́, *impf* **забреда́ть**) *сов неперех* (*разг: в лес*) to saunter off; (: *в гости*) to drop in.

заброни́р|овать (-ую) *сов от* **брони́ровать**.

заброса́|ть (-ю; *impf* **забра́сывать**) *сов перех*: **~ что-н чем-н** (*канаву, яму*) to fill with; (*камнями*) to pelt with; (*цветами*) to shower with; (*перен: фактами, вопросами*) to bombard with.

забро́|сить (-шу, -сишь; *impf* **забра́сывать**) *сов перех* (*мяч, камень*) to fling; (*десант*) to drop; (*шпиона*) to plant; (*разг: доста́вить*) to drop off; (*не занима́ться*) to neglect.

забро́шен|ный (-, -а, -о) *прил* (*дом*) derelict; (*ша́хта*) disused; (*вид, сад, ребёнок*) neglected.

забро́шу *сов см* **забро́сить**.

забры́зга|ть (-ю; *impf* **забры́згивать**) *сов перех* to splash.

забу́ду(сь) *итп сов см* **забы́ть(ся)**.

забыва́|ть(ся) (-ю(сь)) *несов от* **забы́ть(ся)**.

забы́вчив|ый (-, -а, -о) *прил* forgetful.

забы́|ть (*как* **быть**; *см* **Table 21**; *impf* **забыва́ть**) *сов перех* to forget; **~у́дь туда́/сюда́ доро́гу!** don't go there/come here any more!; **себя́ не забыва́ть** (**~** *perf*) to look out for o.s.

▸ **забы́|ться** (*impf* **забыва́ться**) *сов возв* (*задрема́ть*) to doze off; (*в мечта́х*) to lose o.s.; (*сорва́ться*) to forget o.s.; (*собы́тия, фа́кты*) to be forgotten.

забы́ть|е́ (-я́) *ср* (*беспа́мятство*) oblivion; (*полусо́н*) drowsiness; (*заду́мчивость*) pensiveness; **впа́дать** (**впасть** *perf*) **в ~** to lose consciousness; (*усну́ть*) to doze off.

забью́(сь) *итп сов см* **забы́ть(ся)**.

зав (-а) *м сокр* (*разг*: = **заве́дующий**) boss.

зав. *сокр* = **заве́дующий**.

зава́л (-а) *м* obstruction; (*иску́сственный*) barrier; **у нас сейча́с ~ с рабо́той** we have a backlog of work.

зава|ли́ть (-алю́, -а́лишь; *impf* **зава́ливать**) *сов перех* (*вход, дверь*) to block off; (*дом, сте́ну*) to knock down; (*разг: экза́мен, мероприя́тие*) to mess up; **зава́ливать** (**~** *perf*) +*instr* (*доро́гу: сне́гом*) to cover with; (*я́му: землёй*) to fill with; (*разг: магази́ны: това́рами*) to cram with; (*перен: разг: поруче́ниями*) to saddle with.

▸ **завали́|ться** (*impf* **зава́ливаться**) *сов возв* (*упа́сть*) to fall; (*стена́, забо́р*) to collapse; (*разг: де́ло*) to go to the wall; (: *на экза́мене*) to come a cropper; **зава́ливаться** (**~ся** *perf*) **в го́сти к кому́-н** (*разг*) to turn up on sb's doorstep; (**хоть**) **~али́сь!** (*разг: очень мно́го*)

you can't move for them!

заваля́|ться (*3sg* -ется, *3pl* -ются) *сов возв* (*разг*) to be kicking about.

зав|ари́ть (-арю́, -а́ришь; *impf* **зава́ривать**) *сов перех* (*чай, кофе*) to brew; (*ТЕХ*) to weld; **зава́ривать** (**~** *perf*) **ка́шу** (*разг*) to stir up trouble

▸ **завари́ться** (*impf* **зава́риваться**) *сов возв* (*чай, кофе*) to brew; (*разг: де́ло, кутерьма́*) to start.

зава́рк|а (-и) *ж* (*де́йствие: ча́я, кофе*) brewing; (*разг: сухо́й чай*) char; (*заваренный чай*) brew.

заварн|о́й *прил* (*КУЛИН*): **~о́е те́сто** choux pastry; **~ крем** custard filling.

заведе́ни|е (-я) *ср* (*учрежде́ние*) establishment; **уче́бное ~** educational establishment.

заве́д|овать (-ую) *несов неперех* (+*instr*) to be in charge of.

заве́домый *прил* (*обма́нщик, лжец*) notorious; (*обма́н, ложь*) blatant.

заведу́(сь) *итп сов см* **завести́(сь)**.

заве́дующа|я (-ей) *ж см* **заве́дующий**.

заве́дующ|ий (-его; *decl like adj*) *м* (*скла́дом, реда́кцией*) manager; (*лаборато́рией, ка́федрой*) head.

зав|езти́ (-езу́, -езёшь; *pt* -ёз, -езла́, -езло́, *impf* **завози́ть**) *сов перех* to drop off; (*увезти́*) to take.

заверб|ова́ть (-у́ю) *сов от* **вербова́ть**.

заве́рени|е (-я) *ср* assurance.

заве́ренный *прил* (*ко́пия, по́дпись*) authenticated, certified.

завери́тел|ь (-я) *м* (*докуме́нта, ко́пии*) witness, attestant.

заве́р|ить (-ю, -ишь; *impf* **заверя́ть**) *сов перех* (*ко́пию, по́дпись*) to witness; **заверя́ть** (**~** *perf*) **кого́-н в чём-н** to assure sb of sth.

заверн|у́ть (-у́, -ёшь; *impf* **завёртывать** *или* **завора́чивать**) *сов перех* (*рука́в*) to roll up; (*кран*) to turn up; (*га́йку*) to tighten up; (*нале́во, напра́во, за́ угол*) to turn; (*разг: в го́сти, к дру́гу*) to drop by *или* round; **завёртывать** *или* **завора́чивать** (**~** *perf*) (**в** +*acc*) (*посы́лку, кни́гу, ребёнка*) to wrap (in).

▸ **заверну́|ться** (*impf* **завёртываться** *или* **завора́чиваться**) *сов возв* (*рука́в*) to roll up; **завёртываться** *или* **завора́чиваться** (**~ся** *perf*) **в** +*acc* (*в полоте́нце, в плед*) to wrap o.s. up in.

заверт|е́ть (-ерчу́, -е́ртишь) *сов неперех* (+*instr*; *верёвкой*) to twirl; (*глаза́ми*) to roll

▸ **заверте́ться** *сов возв* (*колесо́, кару́сель*) to start turning; (*разг: захлопота́ться*) to be run off one's feet.

завёртыва|ть(ся) (-ю(сь)) *несов см* **заверну́ть(ся)**.

заверчу́(сь) *сов см* **заверте́ть(ся)**.

заверша́|ть(ся) (-ю(сь)) *несов от* **заверши́ть(ся)**.

заверша́ющ|ий (-ая, -ее, -ие) *прил* final.

заверше́ни|е (-я) *ср* (*рабо́ты*) completion;

(*разговора, лекции*) conclusion; **в ~** +*gen* at the conclusion of.

заверш|и́ть (**-у́, -и́шь**; *impf* **заверша́ть**) *сов перех* to complete; (*разговор*) to end

▶ **заверши́ться** (*impf* **заверша́ться**) *сов возв* to be completed; (*разговор*) to end.

заверя́|ть (**-ю**) *несов от* **заве́рить**.

заве́с|а (**-ы**) *ж* (*перен*) veil; **дымова́я ~** (*перен*) smoke screen.

заве́|сить (**-шу, -сишь**; *impf* **заве́шивать**) *сов перех* (*окно*) to curtain; (*картину, лампу*) to cover.

зав|ести́ (**-еду́, -едёшь**; *pt* **-ёл, -ела́, -ело́**, *impf* **заводи́ть**) *сов перех* to take; (*увести далеко*) to lead; (*приобрести*) to get; (*установить*) to introduce; (*переписку, разговор*) to initiate; (*часы*) to wind up; (*машину*) to start; (*разг: разозлить*): **~ кого́-н** to wind sb up

▶ **завести́сь** (*impf* **заводи́ться**) *сов возв* (*появиться*) to appear; (*мотор, часы*) to start working; (*разг: разозлиться*) to get (all) wound up.

заве́т (**-а**) *м* (*наставление*) precept; (*РЕЛ*): **Ве́тхий/Но́вый ~** the Old/New Testament.

заве́тный (**-ен, -на, -но**) *прил* treasured.

заве́ша|ть (**-ю**; *impf* **заве́шивать**) *сов перех* to hang; **заве́шивать** (**~** *perf*) **сте́ны карти́нами** to hang pictures on the walls.

заве́шива|ть (**-ю**) *несов от* **заве́сить**, **заве́шать**.

заве́шу *сов см* **заве́сить**.

завеща́ни|е (**-я**) *ср* (*документ*) will; (*наставление*) precept.

завеща́|ть (**-ю**) (*не*)*сов перех*: **~ что-н кому́-н** (*наследство*) to bequeath sth to sb; **~** (*impf/perf*) **кому́-н** +*infin* to call upon sb to do.

завзя́тый *прил* (*разг: курильщик*) inveterate; **он ~ футболи́ст/охо́тник** he is a football/hunting fanatic.

завива́|ть(ся) (**-ю(сь)**) *несов от* **зави́ть(ся)**.

зави́вк|а (**-и**) *ж* (*волос*) curling; (*причёска*) curly hair.

зави́ден *прил см* **зави́дный**.

зави́дно *нареч*: **он ~ краси́в/умён** he has enviable good looks/intelligence ♦ *как сказ*: **~ как она́ говори́т по-англи́йски** her English is enviable; **ему́ ~** he feels envious.

зави́дный (**-ен, -на, -но**) *прил* enviable.

зави́д|овать (**-ую**; *perf* **позави́довать**) *несов неперех* (+*dat*) to envy, be jealous of.

завизжа́|ть (**-у́, -и́шь**) *сов неперех* to begin to yelp.

завизи́р|овать (**-ую**) *сов от* **визи́ровать**.

завин|ти́ть (**-чу́, -ти́шь**; *impf* **зави́нчивать**) *сов перех* to tighten (up).

завира́|ться (**-юсь**) *несов от* **завра́ться**.

зави́|сеть (**-шу, -сишь**) *несов неперех*: **~ от** +*gen* to depend on.

зави́симост|ь (**-и**) *ж* (*отношение*) correlation; **~** (**от** +*gen*) dependence (on); **в ~и от** +*gen* depending on.

зави́сим|ый (**-, -а, -о**) *прил* (*человек, страна*) dependent; **~ от** +*gen* (*погоды, обстоятельств*) dependent on.

зави́стлив|ый (**-, -а, -о**) *прил* envious.

за́вист|ь (**-и**) *ж* envy, jealousy; **она́ вы́глядит на ~ хорошо́** (*разг*) it makes you sick how well she looks.

завитка́ *сущ см* **завито́к**.

завито́й *прил* (*волосы*) curly; (*девушка*) curly-haired; (*проволока, шнур*) coiled.

завит|о́к (**-ка́**) *м* (*локон*) curl; (*спирали*) twist; (*орнамента*) flourish, whorl.

зав|и́ть (**-ью, -ьёшь**; *pt* **-и́л, -ила́, -ило́**, *impf* **завива́ть**) *сов перех* (*волосы, усы*) to curl; (*проволоку, шнур*) to twist

▶ **зави́ться** (*impf* **завива́ться**) *сов возв* (*волосы, усы*) to curl; (*проволока, шнур*) to get twisted; (*сделать завивку*) to curl one's hair.

завихре́ни|е (**-я**) *ср* whirl; (*перен*) peculiarity.

завью́ *несов см* **зави́сеть**.

завладе́|ть (**-ю**; *impf* **завладева́ть**) *сов неперех* (+*instr*; *имуществом*) to take possession of; (*ВОЕН, вниманием*) to capture.

завле́|чь (**-еку́, -ечёшь** *итп*, **-еку́т**; *pt* **-ёк, -екла́, -екло́**, *impf* **завлека́ть**) *сов перех* (*зверя, врага*) to lure; (*перен*) to captivate.

заво́д (**-а**) *м* factory; (*в часах, у игрушки*) clockwork; (*действие*) winding up; **ко́нный ~** stud farm.

зав|оди́ть(ся) (**-ожу́(сь), -о́дишь(ся)**) *несов от* **завести́(сь)**.

заводно́й *прил* (*механизм, игрушка*) clockwork *опред*; (*ключ, ручка*) winding *опред*; (*разг: человек*) easily excitable.

заводско́й *прил* factory *опред*.

за́вод|ь (**-и**) *ж* backwater.

завоева́ни|е (**-я**) *ср* (*земель, страны*) conquest; (*обычно мн: достижения*) achievement.

завоева́тел|ь (**-я**) *м* conqueror.

завоева́тельн|ый *прил* (*политика*) aggressive; (*набеги*) offensive; **~ые во́йны** wars of conquest.

заво|ева́ть (**-ю́ю**; *impf* **завоёвывать**) *сов перех* to conquer; (*перен: доверие*) to win.

завожу́ *несов см* **заводи́ть**, **завози́ть**.

завожу́сь *несов см* **заводи́ться**.

заво́з (**-а**) *м* delivery.

зав|ози́ть (**-ожу́, -о́зишь**) *несов от* **завезти́**.

заволн|ова́ться (**-у́юсь**) *сов возв* to become agitated.

завора́чива|ть(ся) (**-ю(сь)**) *несов от* **заверну́ть(ся)**.

за́ворот (**-а**) *м*: **~ кишо́к** (*МЕД*) acute intestinal illness.

заворо́т (**-а**) *м* (*реки, дороги*) bend; (*движение*) turn.

заворча́ть (-у́, -йшь) *сов непepex* to start grumbling.

заво́ю *итп сов см* **завы́ть**.

завр|а́ться (-у́сь, -ёшься; *pt* -а́лся, -ала́сь, -а́лось, *impf* завира́ться) *сов возв* (*разг*) to get tied (up) in knots (*by lying*).

завсегда́та|й (-я) *м* (*разг*) regular.

за́втра *нареч, ср нескл* tomorrow; **до ~**! see you tomorrow!; **откла́дывать** (**отложи́ть** *perf*) **что-н на** *или* **до ~** to put sth off until tomorrow.

за́втрак (-а) *м* breakfast.

за́втрака|ть (-ю; *impf* **поза́втракать**) *несов непepex* to have breakfast.

за́втрашн|ий (-яя, -ее, -ие) *прил* tomorrow's; **за́втрашний день** tomorrow.

завуали́р|овать (-ую) *сов от* вуали́ровать.

за́вуч (-а) *м сокр* = заве́дующий уче́бной ча́стью; (*в школе, в училище*) ≈ deputy head.

завхо́з (-а) *м сокр* = заве́дующий хозя́йством; (*в школе, в институте*) bursar; (*на заводе*) *person in charge of supplies*.

завши́ве|ть (-ю) *сов от* вши́веть.

завыва́ни|е (-я) *ср* (*собак, метели*) howling; (*сирены*) wail; (*самолёта*) shriek.

завыва́|ть (-ю) *несов непepex* (*собака, метель*) to howl; (*сирена*) to wail; (*самолёт*) to shriek.

завы́|сить (-шу, -сишь; *impf* **завыша́ть**) *сов перех* (*нормы, цены*) to increase excessively; **~** (*perf*) **план** to set unreasonable targets.

завы́|ть (-о́ю, -о́ешь) *сов непepex* (*собака*) to begin to howl; (*сирена*) to start to wail.

завыша́|ть (-ю) *несов от* завы́сить.

завыше́ни|е (-я) *ср* excessive increase.

завы́шен|ный (-, -а, -о) *прил* excessively increased.

завы́шу *сов см* завы́сить.

завью́(сь) *итп сов см* завй́ть(ся).

зав|яза́ть (-яза́ю, -яза́ешь) *несов от* завя́знуть ♦ (-яжу́, -я́жешь; *impf* **завя́зывать**) *сов перех* (*верёвку, ленту*) to tie; (*руку, посылку*) to bind; (*разговор*) to start (up); (*дружбу*) to form; (*отношение*) to establish; (*разг: пить, воровать*) to quit; **завя́зывать** (**~** *perf*) **глаза́ кому́-н** to blindfold sb

▶ **завяза́ться** (*impf* **завя́зываться**) *сов возв* (*шнурки, бант*) to be tied; (*разговор*) to start (up); (*дружба*) to form; (*отношения*) to become established; (*бот*) to set.

завя́з|ка (-ки; *gen pl* -ок) *ж* (*тесьма*) band; (*лента*) ribbon; (*разговора, событий*) beginning; (*боя*) onset; (*романа, рассказа*) opening.

завя́з|нуть (-у, -ешь; *impf* **завяза́ть** *или* **вя́знуть**) *сов непepex* (*в снегу, в грязи*) to get stuck; (*перен: разг*): **~ в** +*prp* (*в трудностях, в долгах*) to be up to one's neck in.

завя́зок *сущ см* завя́зка.

завя́зыва|ть(ся) (-ю(сь)) *несов от* завяза́ть(ся).

завя́н|уть (-у, -ешь) *сов от* вя́нуть.

загада́|ть (-ю; *impf* **зага́дывать**) *сов перех* (*зага́дку*) to set; (*шараду*) to act out; (*число, слово*) to think of; (*желание*) to make ♦ *непepex* (*разг*) to guess.

зага́|дить (-жу, -дишь) *сов перех* (*разг*) to mess up.

зага́д|ка (-ки; *gen pl* -ок) *ж* riddle; (*перен*) puzzle, mystery.

зага́доч|ный (-ен, -на, -но) *прил* (*явление, событие*) puzzling, mysterious; (*выражение лица, слова*) enigmatic.

зага́дыва|ть (-ю) *несов от* загада́ть.

зага́жу *сов см* зага́дить.

загазо́ван|ный (-, -а, -о) *прил* (*атмосфера*) polluted.

зага́р (-а) *м* (sun)tan.

загво́здк|а (-и) *ж* (*разг*) obstacle; **в э́том вся ~** (*разг*) that's the whole problem.

загерметизи́р|овать (-ую) *сов от* герметизи́ровать.

заги́б (-а) *м* (*на бума́ге*) crease; (*перен: разг*) twist.

загиба́|ть(ся) (-ю(сь)) *несов от* загну́ть(ся).

загипнотизи́р|овать (-ую) *сов от* гипнотизи́ровать.

загла́ви|е (-я) *ср* title.

загла́в|ный *прил*: **~ая бу́ква** capital letter; **загла́вная роль** title role.

загла́|дить (-жу, -дишь; *impf* **загла́живать**) *сов перех* (*складки*) to iron; (*лист*) to fold; (*сгиб*) to make; (*перен: ошибки*) to put right; (: *обиду*) to make up for; **загла́живать** (**~** *perf*) **вину́** to make amends.

загло́хн|уть (-у, -ешь) *сов от* гло́хнуть ♦ *непepex* (*сад, тропинка*) to become overgrown; (*перен: раз: стройка, дело*) to die a death.

загло́хш|ий (-ая, -ее, -ие) *прил* overgrown.

заглуша́|ть (-ю; *perf* **заглуши́ть**) *несов перех* = глуши́ть.

заглуш|и́ть (-у́, -у́шишь) *сов от* глуши́ть, заглуша́ть.

загляде́нь|е (-я) *ср* (*разг*) feast for the eyes.

загля|де́ться (-жу́сь, -ди́шься; *impf* **загля́дываться**) *сов возв* to gaze.

загля|ну́ть (-яну́, -я́нешь; *impf* **загля́дывать**) *сов непepex* (*в окно, в спальню*) to peep; (*в книгу, в словарь*) to glance; (*разг: к соседу, к друзьям*) to pop in; **загля́дывать** (**~** *perf*) **вперёд** to take a brief look ahead.

загна́ива|ться (-юсь) *несов от* загнои́ться.

заг|на́ть (-оню́, -о́нишь; *pt* -на́л, -нала́, -на́ло, *impf* **загоня́ть**) *сов перех* (*коров, детей*) to drive; (*разг: гвоздь, нож*) to ram in; (: *продать*) to flog (*BRIT*), sell; (*изнурить: лошадь*) to ride too hard; (: *рабочих*) to drive into the ground.

загн|и́ть (-ию́, -иёшь; *pt* -и́л, -ила́, *impf* **загнива́ть**) *сов непepex* to begin to rot.

загно|и́ться (-ю́сь, -и́шься; *impf* **загна́иваться**) *сов возв* (*рана*) to fester; (*глаз*) to become inflamed.

за́гнут|ый (-, -а, -о) *прил* bent.

загн|у́ть (-у́, -ёшь; *impf* **загиба́ть**) *сов перех*
(*гвоздь*) to bend; (*край*) to fold; (*страницу*) to
dog-ear; (*разг: сказать*) to spout; **загиба́ть** (~
perf) **рука́в вверх/вниз** to pull a sleeve up/down
▶ **загну́ться** (*impf* **загиба́ться**) *сов возв* (*гвоздь*)
to bend; (*край*) to fold; (*страница*) to become
dog-eared; (*воротник*) to twist; (*разг: умереть*)
to kick the bucket.
загова́рива|ть (-ю) *несов от* **заговори́ть** ◆
неперех: **зу́бы** ~ **кому́-н** (*разг*) to steer sb off a
subject
▶ **загова́риваться** *несов возв* (*говорить
бессвязно*) to rave.
за́говень|е (-я) *ср* (*РЕЛ*) eve of fast, ≈ Shrove
Tuesday.
за́говор (-а) *м* conspiracy; (*от болезни*) spell.
заговор|и́ть (-ю́, -и́шь) *сов неперех* (*начать
говорить*) to begin to speak; (*по-английски,
по-русски*) to be able to speak; (*перен: совесть,
гордость итп*) to stir ◆ (*impf* **загова́ривать**)
перех (*болезнь, боль*) to magic away;
загова́ривать (~ *perf*) **кого́-н** to wear sb out
through constant talk; **в нём** ~**и́ла со́весть** his
conscience stirred in him.
загово́рщик (-а) *м* conspirator.
загово́рщиц|а (-ы) *ж см* **загово́рщик**.
заголо́в|ок (-ка) *м* headline.
заго́н (-а) *м* (*скота, овец*) driving in; (*для
скота*) enclosure; (*для овец*) pen; **быть** (*impf*) **в**
~**е** (*разг*) to be pushed to one side.
загоню́ *итп сов см* **загна́ть**.
загоня́|ть (-ю) *несов от* **загна́ть**.
загора́жива|ть(ся) (-ю(сь)) *несов от*
загороди́ть(ся).
загора́|ть(ся) (-ю(сь)) *несов от* **загоре́ть(ся)**.
загоре́л|ый (-, -а, -о) *прил* tanned.
загор|е́ть (-ю́, -и́шь; *impf* **загора́ть**) *сов неперех*
to go brown, get a tan
▶ **загоре́ться** (*impf* **загора́ться**) *сов возв*
(*дрова, костёр*) to light; (*здание итп*) to catch
fire; (*лампочка, глаза*) to light up; **загора́ться**
(~**ся** *perf*) **жела́нием** +*infin* to have a burning
desire to do; **он** ~**е́лся э́той иде́ей** the idea fired
his imagination.
за́город (-а) *м* (*разг*) the country.
загор|оди́ть (-ожу́, -о́дишь; *impf*
загора́живать) *сов перех* (*улицу, вход*) to block
off; (*свет*) to block out; **загора́живать** (~ *perf*)
кого́-н собо́й to shield sb; **загора́живать** (~
perf) **кому́-н доро́гу** (*перен*) to stand on sb's
way
▶ **загороди́ться** (*impf* **загора́живаться**) *сов
возв*: ~**ся** (**от** +*gen*) (*от солнца, от удара*) to
shield o.s. (from).
загоро́д|ка (-ки; *gen pl* -**ок**) *ж* barrier; (*в
комнате*) partition.
за́городн|ый *прил* (*экскурсия*) out-of-town;
(*дом*) country *опред*; ~**ая пое́здка** a trip out of

town *или* into the country.
загоро́док *сущ см* **загоро́дка**.
загорожу́(сь) *сов см* **загороди́ть(ся)**.
загота́влива|ть (-ю) *несов от* **загото́вить**.
заготови́тел|ь (-я) *м person responsible for
state procurements of timber, grain etc.*
заготови́тельн|ый *прил*: ~ **пункт** collection
point; **заготови́тельная цена́** state procurement
price.
загото́в|ить (-лю, -ишь; *impf* **загота́вливать**
или **заготовля́ть**) *сов перех* (*сено, корм итп*)
to lay in; (*билеты, документы итп*) to prepare.
загото́в|ка (-ки; *gen pl* -**ок**) *ж* (*действие: кормов,
леса итп*) laying in; (*закупка государством*)
procurement; (*полуфабрикат*) component;
(: *для туфель*) upper.
загото́влю *сов см* **загото́вить**.
заготовля́|ть (-ю) *несов от* **загото́вить**.
загото́вок *сущ см* **загото́вка**.
загради́тельн|ый *прил*: ~**ое сооруже́ние**
barrier; **загради́тельный ого́нь** (*ВОЕН*)
defensive fire; **загради́тельный патру́ль**
roadblock.
загра|ди́ть (-жу́, -ди́шь; *impf* **загражда́ть**) *сов
перех* to obstruct.
загражде́ни|е (-я) *ср* barrier.
загражу́ *сов см* **загради́ть**.
заграни́ц|а (-ы) *ж* (*разг*) foreign countries *мн*.
заграни́чный *прил* foreign; **заграни́чный
па́спорт** passport (*issued specifically for travel
abroad*).
За́греб (-а) *м* Zagreb.
загреб|у́ *итп сов см* **загрести́**.
загреба́|ть (-ю) *несов от* **загрести́** ◆ *неперех*
(*вёслами*) to row; (*руками, лапами*) to paddle ◆
перех: ~ **де́ньги** (*разг*) to rake in the money.
загребу́ *итп сов см* **загрести́**.
загрем|е́ть (-лю́, -и́шь) *сов неперех* (*гром*) to
crash out; (*голос*) to thunder; (*тарелки итп*) to
start to rattle.
загр|ести́ (-ебу́, -ебёшь; *pt* -ёб, -ебла́, -ебло́,
impf **загреба́ть**) *сов перех* (*мусор, листья итп*)
to rake up.
загри́в|ок (-ка) *м* (*у лошади*) withers *мн*; **взять**
(*perf*) **кого́-н за** ~ (*разг*) to grab sb by the scruff
of the neck.
загримир|ова́ть (-у́ю; *impf* **загримиро́вывать**
или **гримирова́ть**) *сов перех* to make up
▶ **загримирова́ться** (*impf*
загримиро́вываться *или* **гримирова́ться**) *сов
возв* to make o.s. up.
загро́бный *прил*: ~ **мир** the next world; (*перен:
голос*) gloomy; **загро́бная жизнь** the afterlife.
загромозд|и́ть (-жу́, -ди́шь; *impf*
загроможда́ть) *сов перех* to clutter (up).
загрубе́л|ый (-, -а, -о) *прил* (*кожа, руки*)
calloused, rough; (*лицо*) coarse; (*голос*) gruff;
(*перен: человек, душа*) hardened.

загрубе́|ть (-ю) *сов от* **грубе́ть**.

загру́зи́ть (-ужу́, -у́зишь) *сов от* **грузи́ть ♦** (*impf* **загружа́ть**) *перех* (*машину, судно*) to load up; (*комп*) to boot, load up; (*перен: сотрудников, учеников*) to load with work; (: *день*) to fill up; (: *печь, домну*) to load.

загру́зк|а (-и) *ж* (*машины, судна*) loading; (*предприятия, станка*) capacity.

загрунт|ова́ть (-у́ю) *impf* **загрунто́вывать** *или* **грунтова́ть**) *сов перех* to prime.

загру́|сти́ть (-щу́, -сти́шь) *сов неперех* to become sad; ~ (*perf*) **по до́му** to start to feel homesick.

загры́|зть (-зу́, -зёшь; *impf* **загрыза́ть**) *сов перех* (*овцу, петуха*) to kill; (*no impf; перен: разг: замучить*) to nag to death; **её ~́зла со́весть** she was tormented by her conscience.

загрязне́ни|е (-я) *ср* pollution; **загрязне́ние окружа́ющей среды́** (environmental) pollution.

загрязнённый (-ён, -ена́, -ено́) *прил* polluted.

загрязни́|ть (-ю́, -и́шь) *сов от* **грязни́ть ♦** (*impf* **загрязня́ть**) *перех* (*воздух, водоём*) to pollute; **загрязня́ть** (~ *perf*) **что-н** (*сапоги, платье итп*) to get sth dirty

▶ **загрязни́|ться** *сов от* **грязни́ться ♦** (*impf* **загрязня́ться**) *возв* (*см перех*) to become polluted; to get dirty.

ЗАГС (-а) *м сокр* (= за́пись а́ктов гражда́нского состоя́ния) ≈ registry office.

загу|би́ть (-ублю́, -у́бишь) *сов от* **губи́ть ♦** *перех* (*человека*) to destroy; (*растение*) to kill; (*жизнь, вечер*) to ruin; (*разг: деньги, средства*) to waste.

загу|де́ть (-жу́, -ди́шь) *сов неперех* (*машина*) to honk; (*гудок*) to sound.

загу́л (-а) *м* (*разг*) drinking session; **уда́риться** (*perf*) **в** ~ to go on a bender.

загуля́|ть (-ю; *impf* **загу́ливать**) *сов неперех* (*разг: кутить*) to booze.

загусте́|ть (*3sg* -ет, *3pl* -ют) *сов от* **густе́ть**.

зад (-а; *part gen* -у, *loc sg* -у́, *nom pl* -ы́, *gen pl* -о́в) *м* (*человека*) behind, rear; (*животного*) rump; (*машины, дома*) rear.

задабрива|ть (-ю) *несов от* **задо́брить**.

задава́|ть (-ю́, -ёшь) *несов от* **зада́ть**

▶ **задава́|ться** *несов от* **зада́ться ♦** *возв* (*разг: важничать*) to be cocky.

зада|ви́ть (-авлю́, -а́вишь) *сов от* **дави́ть ♦** *перех* to crush; **её ~ави́ло де́ревом** she was crushed under a tree; **его́ ~ави́ла маши́на** he was run over by a car.

зада́|м(ся) *итп сов см* **зада́ть(ся)**.

зада́ни|е (-я) *ср* (*поручение*) task; (*упражнение*) exercise; (*воен*) mission; **дома́шнее** ~ homework.

задари́|ть (-арю́, -а́ришь; *impf* **зада́ривать**) *сов перех*: ~ **кого́-н пода́рками** to shower sb with presents.

зада́ром *нареч* (*разг: дёшево*) for next to nothing; (: *зря*) for nothing.

зада́ст(ся) *сов см* **зада́ть(ся)**.

зада́тка *сущ см* **зада́ток**.

зада́тк|и (-ов) *мн* (*о способностях*) ability *ед*.

зада́т|ок (-ка) *м* deposit; **дава́ть** (**дать** *perf*) ~ to put down a deposit; *см также* **зада́тки**.

зада́ть (*как* **дать**; *см* Table 14; *impf* **задава́ть**) *сов перех* to set; **задава́ть** (~ *perf*) **кому́-н вопро́с** to ask sb a question; **задава́ть** (~ *perf*) **пир** (*разг*) to lay on a spread; **я тебе́ ~а́м!** (*разг*) just you wait!

▶ **зада́ться** (*impf* **задава́ться**) *сов возв*: ~**ся це́лью** +*infin* (*сделать, написать итп*) to set o.s. the task of doing; ~**ся** (*perf*) **вопро́сом** to ask o.s.

зада́ч|а (-и) *ж* task; (*мат*) problem; **ста́вить** (**поста́вить** *perf*) **пе́ред собо́й** ~у to set o.s. a task; **реша́ть** (**реши́ть** *perf*) ~у to solve a problem.

зада́чник (-а) *м* book of problems.

зада́шь(ся) *сов см* **зада́ть(ся)**.

задви́га|ть (-ю) *сов неперех* (+*instr*) to begin to move

▶ **задви́гаться** *сов возв* to begin to move.

задвига́|ть(ся) (-ю(сь)) *несов от* **задви́нуть(ся)**.

задви́жк|а (-и) *ж* bolt; **закрыва́ть** (**закры́ть** *perf*) **дверь на** ~у to bolt the door.

задвижн|о́й *прил*: ~**а́я дверь** sliding door.

задви́|нуть (-у, -ешь; *impf* **задвига́ть**) *сов перех* to push; (*ящик, занавески*) to close

▶ **задви́нуться** (*impf* **задвига́ться**) *сов возв* to close.

задво́рк|и (-ок) *мн* backyard *ед*; **на** ~**ках о́бщества** (*перен*) on the margins of society; **на** ~**ках исто́рии** (*перен*) in the footnotes of history.

задева́|ть (-ю) *несов от* **заде́ть ♦** *сов перех* (*разг: положить*) to put; **куда́ ты** ~**л мою́ су́мку?** where have you put my bag?

▶ **задева́ться** *сов возв* (*разг*) to go missing; **куда́** ~**лась моя́ ру́чка?** what's happened to my pen?

заде́йств|овать (-ую) *сов перех* (*оборудование*) to render operational; (*полк, диви́зию*) to mobilize **♦** *неперех* (*взяться за дело*) to get busy.

заде́л (-а) *м* groundwork; **создава́ть** (**созда́ть** *perf*) ~ **на бу́дущее** to create foundations for the future.

заде́ла|ть (-ю; *impf* **заде́лывать**) *сов перех* to seal up.

заде́ну *итп сов см* **заде́ть**.

задёрга|ть (-ю) *сов неперех* (+*instr*; **ного́й, во́жжами**) to jerk **♦** *перех* (*разг: измучить*) to wear out

▶ **задёргаться** *сов возв* (*тело, глаз, гу́бы*) to twitch; (*начать нервничать*) to become twitchy; (*разг: измучиться*) to reach the end of one's tether.

задёргива|ть (-ю) *несов от* **задёрнуть**.

задеревене́|ть (-ю) *сов неперех* to go stiff.

задержа́ни|е (-я) *ср* (*юр*) detention.

зад|ержа́ть (-ержу́, -е́ржишь; *impf*
заде́рживать) *сов перех* (самолёт, поезд итп)
to delay, hold up; (зарплату, уплату долгов) to
withhold; (преступника) to detain;
(школьников) to keep back; **я не хочу́ Вас**
~е́рживать I don't want to hold you back;
заде́рживать (~ *perf*) **дыха́ние** to hold one's
breath; **заде́рживать** (~ *perf*) **взгляд на** +*prp* to
stare at; **заде́рживать** (~ *perf*) **шаг** to slow up
▸ **задержа́ться** (*impf* **заде́рживаться**) *сов возв*
to be delayed *или* held up; (у две́ри, перед
до́мом итп) to pause; **заде́рживаться** (~ся
perf) **с отве́том/рабо́той** to be late in
answering/finishing the work.

заде́рж|ка (-ки; *gen pl* -ек) *ж* delay, hold-up; **без**
~ек without further delay.

задёрн|уть (-у, -ешь; *impf* **задёргивать**) *сов*
перех (шторы) to pull shut; **задёргивать** (~
perf) **окно́ занаве́ской/што́рой** to shut the
curtains/blind.

задеру́(сь) *итп сов см* **задра́ть(ся)**.

заде́|ть (-ну, -нешь; *impf* **задева́ть**) *сов перех:* ~
(за +*acc*) (стол итп) to brush against; (кость,
лёгкое) to graze; (перен: самолю́бие, человека)
to wound; **его́ тон меня́ ~л** I found his tone
offensive; ~ (*perf*) **кого́-н за живо́е** to cut sb to
the quick.

задир|а (-ы) *м/ж* (разг) troublemaker.

задира́|ть(ся) (-ю(сь)) *несов от* **задра́ть(ся)**.

задири́ст|ый (-, -а, -о) *прил* quarrelsome.

за́дн|ий (-яя, -ее, -ие) *прил* back *опред*;
помеча́ть (**поме́тить** *perf*) **~им число́м** to
backdate; **опла́чивать** (**оплати́ть** *perf*) **~им**
число́м to make a back payment; **она́ ~им**
умо́м крепка́ she's simply being wise after the
event; **он был без ~их ног** (разг) he was dead
on his feet; **~яя мысль** ulterior motive; **~ие**
но́ги hind legs; **за́дний прохо́д** (АНАТ) rectum;
за́дний ход back entrance.

за́дник (-а) *м* (боти́нка) back; (ТЕА́ТР) backdrop.

за́дниц|а (-ы) *ж* (разг) backside.

задо́бр|ить (-ю, -ишь; *impf* **зада́бривать**) *сов*
перех to soften up.

за́дом *нареч* backwards; ~ **до** +*gen* long before.

задолжа́|ть (-ю) *сов перех* to owe.

задо́лженност|ь (-и) *ж* debts *мн*; (по рабо́те,в
учёбе) work outstanding.

за́дом *нареч* backwards; **повора́чиваться** (**поверну́ться** *perf*) ~ **к**
кому́-н to turn one's back to sb; **стоя́ть** (*impf*) ~
к кому́-н to stand with one's back to sb.

задо́р (-а) *м* enthusiasm.

задо́р|ный (-ен, -на, -но) *прил* lively.

задохну́ться (-у́сь, -ёшься; *impf* **задыха́ться**)
сов возв (в дыму́) to suffocate; (от бе́га, при
ходьбе́) to be out of breath; (от зло́сти, от
сме́ха) to choke.

задра́|ить (-ю, -ишь; *impf* **задра́ивать**) *сов*

перех (МОР) to batten down.

задрапиро́ва́|ть (-у́ю) *сов от* **драпирова́ть**.

задр|а́ть (-еру́, -ерёшь; *pt* -ра́л, -рала́, -ра́ло,
impf **драть** *или* **задира́ть**) *сов перех* (пла́тье,
ю́бка) to hitch *или* hike up; (растерза́ть) to
savage; **задира́ть** (~ *perf*) **го́лову** to tip one's
head back; **задира́ть** (~ *perf*) **нос** (разг) to be
stuck-up.

▸ **задра́ться** (*impf* **задира́ться**) *сов возв* (разг:
пла́тье, руба́шка) to hitch itself up; (рука́в) to
ruck.

задрема́|ть (-емлю́, -е́млешь) *сов неперех* to
doze off.

задрож|а́ть (-у́, -и́шь) *сов неперех* (челове́к,
го́лос) to begin to tremble; (зда́ние, стекло́) to
begin to shake.

задува́|ть (-ю) *несов от* **заду́ть**.

зад|у́мать (-у́маю; *impf* **заду́мывать**) *сов перех*
(по́весть, план) to think up; (ка́рту, число́) to
think of; (+*infin*: уе́хать итп) to think of doing

▸ **заду́маться** (*impf* **заду́мываться**) *сов возв*
(погрузи́ться в разду́мье) to be deep in
thought; **заду́мываться** (~ся *perf*) **над** +*instr*/**о**
+*prp* (над зада́чей, над жи́знью) to ponder; **о**
чём Вы ~лись? what are you thinking about?;
он отве́тил, не заду́мываясь he answered
without hesitation; **она́ на мину́ту ~лась** she
reflected for a moment.

заду́мчивост|ь (-и) *ж* pensiveness; **быть** (*impf*)
в глубо́кой ~и to be deep in thought.

заду́мчив|ый (-, -а, -о) *прил* pensive,
thoughtful.

заду́ма|ть(ся) (-ю(сь)) *несов от*
заду́мать(ся).

зад|у́ть (-у́ю, -у́ешь; *impf* **задува́ть**) *сов перех*
(ого́нь, свечу́ итп) to blow out ♦ *неперех*
(ве́тер) to get up; **ве́тром ~ло песо́к в**
ко́мнату the wind blew sand into the room.

задуше́в|ный (-ен, -на, -но) *прил* (мы́сли,
та́йна, разгово́р) intimate; (пе́сня, расска́з)
soulful; (друг, челове́к) genial.

зад|уши́ть (-ушу́, -у́шишь) *сов от* **души́ть**.

задым|и́ть (-лю́, -и́шь) *сов неперех* to begin to
smoulder (BRIT) *или* smolder (US)

▸ **задыми́ться** *сов возв* to begin to give off
smoke.

задыха́|ться (-юсь) *несов от* **задохну́ться**.

заеда́|ть (-ю) *несов от* **зае́сть**.

зае́дешь *итп сов см* **зае́хать**.

заеди́м *итп сов см* **зае́сть**.

зае́ду *итп сов см* **зае́хать**.

заедя́т *итп сов см* **зае́сть**.

зае́зд (-а) *м* (СПОРТ) race (*in horse-racing,
motor-racing*), (: отбо́рочный) heat;
(тури́стов, отдыха́ющих) arrival; **с ~ом/без**
зае́зда в Москву́ with/without a stopoff in
Moscow.

зае́з|дить (-жу, -дишь) *сов перех* (перен: разг):

~ кого́-н to drive sb too hard.

заезжа́|ть (-ю) *несов от* **зае́хать.**

зае́зжу *сов см* **зае́здить.**

зае́л *итп сов см* **зае́сть.**

зае́м *итп сов см* **зае́сть.**

заём (**за́йма**) *м* loan.

заёмщик (-а) *м* borrower.

зае́сть (*как* **есть**; *см* **Table 15**; *impf* **заеда́ть**) *сов перех* (*подлеж*: *комары*) to eat; (*разг*: *подлеж*: *жена, начальник, среда́*) to get to ◆ *безл* (*разг*: *ружьё*) to jam; **пласти́нку зае́ло** (*разг*) the record is stuck; **заеда́ть** (~ *perf*) **лека́рство/во́дку чем-н** to eat sth to take away the taste of the medicine/vodka.

зае́хать (*как* **е́хать**; *см* **Table 19**; *impf* **заезжа́ть**) *сов неперех*: ~ **за кем-н** to go to fetch sb; **заезжа́ть** (~ *perf*) **в** +*acc* (*в канаву, во двор*) to drive into; (*в Москву, в магазин итп*) to stop off at; ~ (*perf*) **к друзья́м** to stop off at friends; ~ (*perf*) **кому́-н в лицо́** (*разг*) to smash sb in the face; ~ (*perf*) **кому́-н в у́хо** (*разг*) to box sb's ears.

зажа́р|ить (-ю, -ишь) *сов от* **жа́рить** ◆ (*impf* **зажа́ривать**) *перех* (*на сковоро́дке*) to fry; (*в духо́вке*) to roast.

▶ **зажа́риться** *сов от* **жа́риться** ◆ (*impf* **зажа́риваться**) *возв* (*см перех*) to fry; to roast.

зажа́ть (-му́, -мёшь; *impf* **зажима́ть**) *сов перех* (*рот, у́ши*) to squeeze; (*перен*: *инициати́ву, прое́кт*) to stifle, suppress; (*разг*: *де́ньги*) to pocket; **зажима́ть** (~ *perf*) **нос** to hold one's nose; **зажима́ть** (~ *perf*) **рот кому́-н** (*перен*) to silence sb.

зажгу́(сь) *итп сов см* **заже́чь(ся).**

зажда́|ться (-у́сь, -ёшься) *сов возв* (+*gen*; *разг*) to be sick of waiting for.

заже́чь (-гу́, -жёшь *итп*, -гу́т; *pt* -ёг, -гла́, -гло́, *impf* **зажига́ть**) *сов перех* (*свечу́, спи́чку итп*) to light; (*свет*) to turn on; (*перен*: *аудито́рию*) to inflame; (: *интере́с, любо́вь*) to spark (off)

▶ **заже́чься** (*impf* **зажига́ться**) *сов возв* (*свеча́, спи́чка итп*) to light; (*свет*) to go on; (*перен*: *интере́с, любо́вь*) to be sparked off.

зажива́|ть (-ю) *несов от* **зажи́ть.**

заживу́ *итп сов см* **зажи́ть.**

зажига́л|ка (-и) *ж* (cigarette) lighter; (*разг*: *бо́мба*) firebomb.

зажига́ни|е (-я) *ср* (*де́йствие*) lighting; (*АВТ*) ignition; **включа́ть** (**включи́ть** *perf*) ~ to turn on the ignition.

зажига́тельный (-ен, -ьна, -ьно) *прил* (*также перен*) inflammatory; (*снаря́д*) incendiary; **зажига́тельный шнур** fuse wire.

зажига́|ть(ся) (-ю(сь)) *несов от* **заже́чь(ся).**

зажи́м (-а) *м* (*ТЕХ*) clamp; (*ЭЛЕК*) terminal; (*перен*: *инициати́вы, кри́тики*) stifling, suppression.

зажима́|ть (-ю) *несов от* **зажа́ть.**

зажи́точ|ный (-ен, -на, -но) *прил* prosperous.

зажи́ть (-иву́, -ивёшь; *pt* -ил, -ила́, -ило, *impf* **зажива́ть**) *сов неперех* (*ра́на*) to heal (up); (*no*

impf; *нача́ть жить*) to start to live; ~ (*perf*) **по-но́вому** to change one's lifestyle.

зажму́ *итп сов см* **зажа́ть.**

зажму́р|ить (-ю, -ишь) *сов от* **жму́рить** ◆ (*impf* **зажму́ривать**) *перех*: ~ **глаза́** to screw up one's eyes

▶ **зажму́риться** *сов от* **жму́риться** ◆ (*impf* **зажму́риваться**) *возв* to screw up one's eyes.

зажужж|а́ть (-у́, -и́шь) *сов неперех* to start buzzing.

зазва́ть (-ову́, -овёшь; *pt* -ва́л, -вала́, -ва́ло, *impf* **зазыва́ть**) *сов перех* (*разг*): ~ **кого́-н в го́сти** to invite sb over.

зазвен|е́ть (-ю́, -и́шь) *сов неперех* to start ringing; **у меня́ ~е́ло в уша́х** my ears started ringing.

зазвон|и́ть (-ю́, -и́шь) *сов неперех* to start ringing.

зазвуч|а́ть (*3sg* -и́т, *3pl* -а́т) *сов неперех* to be heard.

заздра́вный *прил* congratulatory.

зазелене́ть (*3sg* -ет) *сов неперех* to turn green.

заземле́ни|е (-я) *ср* (*ЭЛЕК*: *де́йствие*) earthing (*BRIT*), grounding (*US*); (: *устро́йство*) earth (*BRIT*), ground (*US*).

заземл|и́ть (-ю́, -и́шь; *impf* **заземля́ть**) *сов перех* to earth (*BRIT*), ground (*US*).

зазн|ава́ться (-аю́сь) *несов от* **зазна́ться.**

зазна́|йка (-йки; *gen pl* -ек) *м/ж* (*разг*) bighead.

зазна́|ться (-ю́сь; *impf* **зазнава́ться**) *сов возв* (*разг*) to think a lot of o.s.

зазову́ *итп сов см* **зазва́ть.**

зазо́р (-а) *м* gap.

зазре́ни|е (-я) *ср*: **без ~я со́вести** without a twinge of conscience.

зазу́брен|ный (-, -а, -о) *прил* serrated, jagged.

зазу́брива|ть (-ю) *несов от* **зазубри́ть.**

зазу́брин|а (-ы) *ж* serration.

зазубр|и́ть (-ю́, -и́шь; *impf* **зазу́бривать**) *сов перех* (*разг*): ~ **что-н** to learn sth parrot-fashion.

зазыва́|ть (-ю) *несов от* **зазва́ть.**

заигра́|ть (-ю) *сов* (*не*)*перех* (*музыка́нт, орке́стр*) to begin to play ◆ *неперех* (*му́зыка*) to begin ◆ (*impf* **заи́грывать**) *перех* (*пласти́нку, коло́ду карт*) to wear out

▶ **заигра́ться** (*impf* **заи́грываться**) *сов возв* to be absorbed in one's games.

заи́грыва|ть (-ю) *несов от* **заигра́ть** ◆ *неперех*: ~ **с** +*instr* (*разг*: *любе́зничать*) to flirt with; (: *заи́скивать*) to suck up to

▶ **заи́грываться** *несов от* **заигра́ться.**

заи́к|а (-и) *м/ж* stutterer.

заика́ни|е (-я) *ср* (*де́йствие*) stuttering; (*поро́к ре́чи*) stutter.

заика́|ться (-юсь) *несов возв* to have a stutter; (*разг*: *от испу́га, от волне́ния*) to stammer; (*perf* **заикну́ться**): ~ **о** +*prp* (*пое́здке, приглаше́нии*) to drop hints about.

займообра́зно *нареч* on loan.

займствова́ни|е (-я) *ср* borrowing.

займств|овать (-ую; *impf* **позаймствовать**)

(не)сов перех (слова, сюжет) to borrow; *(опыт)* to benefit from.

заиндеве́вш|ий (-ая, -ое, -ие) *прил* frost-covered.

за́йндеве|ть (-ю) *сов от* и́ндеветь.

заинтересо́ван|ный (-, -а, -о) *прил* interested; **я заинтересо́ван в э́том де́ле** I have an interest in the matter; **заинтересо́ванная сторона́** interested party.

заинтерес|ова́ть (-у́ю; *impf* заинтерес-о́вывать) *сов перех* to interest

▸ **заинтересова́ться** (*impf* заинтерес-о́вываться) *сов возв* (+*instr*) to become interested in.

заинтриг|ова́ть (-у́ю; *impf* заинтриго́вывать) *сов перех* to intrigue.

Заи́р (-а) *м* Zaire.

заи́рск|ий (-ая, -ое, -ие) *прил* Zairean.

заи́скива|ть (-ю) *несов неперех:* ~ **пе́ред** +*instr* to ingratiate o.s. with.

заи́скивающ|ий (-ая, -ее, -ие) *прил* ingratiating.

зайду́ *итп сов см* зайти́.

за́йма *сущ см* заём.

за́ймов|ый *прил:* ~**ая опера́ция** loan transaction; ~ **проце́нт** interest (*on loan*).

займу́(сь) *итп сов см* заня́ть(ся).

зайти́ (*как* идти́; *см* **Table 18**; *impf* заходи́ть) *сов неперех (солнце, луна)* to go down; *(спор, разговор)* to start up; *(посетить):* ~ **(в/на** +*acc*/**к** +*dat*) to call in (at); *(попасть):* ~ **в/на** +*acc* to stray into; **заходи́ть** (~ *perf*) **за кем-н** to go to fetch sb; **заходи́ть** (~ *perf*) **за хле́бом/молоко́м** to pop in for bread/milk; **заходи́ть** (~ *perf*) **на рабо́ту/к дру́гу** to call in at work/a friend's; **заходи́ть** (~ *perf*) **спра́ва/сле́ва** to come in from the right/left; **мы зашли́ в незнако́мую часть го́рода** we strayed into an unfamiliar part of town; **заходи́ть** (~ *perf*) **в тупи́к** *(перен)* to reach a dead end; **де́ло зашло́ сли́шком далеко́** things have gone too far.

за́йца *сущ см* за́яц.

зайча́та *итп сущ см* зайчо́нок.

за́йчик (-а) *м уменьш от* за́яц; *(разг: также:* **со́лнечный** ~) reflection of the sun.

зайчи́х|а (-и) *ж* doe, female hare.

зайч|о́нок (-о́нка; *nom pl* -а́та, *gen pl* -а́т) *м* leveret.

закабал|и́ть (-ю́, -и́шь; *impf* закабаля́ть) *перех* to enslave.

закавка́зск|ий (-ая, -ое, -ие) *прил* Transcaucasian.

закады́чный *прил:* ~ **друг** bosom friend.

закажу́ *итп сов от* заказа́ть.

зака́з (-а) *м (действие: платья, обеда итп)* ordering; *(: телефонного разговора)* booking; *(: портрета)* commissioning; *(заказанный предмет)* order; **де́лать (сде́лать** *perf*) **что-н**

на ~ to make sth to order; **по** ~**у** *(также перен)* to order.

зак|аза́ть (-ажу́, -а́жешь; *impf* зака́зывать) *сов перех (см сущ)* to order; to book; to commission.

заказн|о́й *прил:* ~**о́е письмо́** registered letter.

зака́зчик (-а) *м* customer.

зака́зчица (-ы) *ж см* зака́зчик.

зака́зыва|ть (-ю) *несов от* заказа́ть.

закалённый (-ён, -ена́, -ено́) *прил (физически)* resistant; *(нравственно)* resilient.

зака́ливани|е (-я) *ср (ребёнка, организма)* toughening up.

закал|и́ть (-ю́, -и́шь; *impf* зака́ливать или закаля́ть) *сов перех (сталь)* to harden, temper; *(ребёнка, организм)* to toughen up; *(волю, характер)* to toughen

▸ **закали́ться** (*impf* зака́ливаться или закаля́ться) *сов возв (сталь)* to be hardened или tempered; *(ребёнок, организм)* to build up one's resistance; *(воля, характер)* to toughen.

зака́лк|а (-и) *ж (см глаг)* hardening, tempering; toughening up; toughening; *(стойкость)* toughness.

зака́лыва|ть (-ю) *несов от* заколо́ть.

закаля́|ть(ся) (-ю(сь)) *несов от* закали́ть(ся).

закамуфли́р|овать (-ую) *сов от* камуфли́ровать.

зака́нчива|ть(ся) (-ю(сь)) *несов от* зако́нчить(ся).

зака́па|ть (-ю; *impf* зака́пывать) *сов перех (платье, тетрадь итп)* to splatter; *(лекарство, капли)* to apply ◆ *неперех (no impf):* **дождь** ~**л** it started spitting (with rain).

зака́пыва|ть (-ю) *несов от* зака́пать, закопа́ть

▸ **зака́пываться** *несов от* закопа́ться.

зака́т (-а) *м:* ~ **(со́лнца)** sunset; *(перен: жизни, карьеры)* twilight; **на** ~**е дней** in the twilight of one's years.

закат|а́ть (-ю; *impf* зака́тывать) *сов перех* to roll up.

зака|ти́ть (-чу́, -а́тишь; *impf* зака́тывать) *сов перех* to roll; **зака́тывать** (~ *perf*) **сканда́л** *(разг)* to create a scandal; **зака́тывать** (~ *perf*) **исте́рику** *(разг)* to get hysterical; **зака́тывать** (~ *perf*) **глаза́** to roll one's eyes

▸ **закати́ться** (*impf* зака́тываться) *сов возв* to roll; *(солнце)* to set.

закача́|ться (-юсь) *сов возв* to begin to sway.

закачу́(сь) *сов см* закати́ть(ся).

закашля́|ть (-ю) *сов неперех* to start coughing

▸ **зака́шляться** *сов возв* to have a coughing fit.

закваси|ть (-шу, -сишь; *impf* заква́шивать) *сов перех (капусту)* to pickle; *(молоко)* to sour

▸ **закваси́ться** (*impf* заква́шиваться) *сов возв* to be pickled; to be soured.

заква́ск|а (-и) *ж (для теста)* leaven; *(для кефира)* culture.

заква́шива|ть(ся) (-ю(сь)) *несов от* **заква́сить(ся)**.

заква́шу(сь) *сов см* **заква́сить(ся)**.

закида́ть (-ю; *impf* **заки́дывать**) *сов перех* = **заброса́ть**.

заки́н|уть (-у, -ешь; *impf* **заки́дывать**) *сов перех* to throw; **судьба́ ~ула меня́ в Шотла́ндию** fate has brought me to Scotland; **заки́дывать (~** *perf*) **у́дочку** to cast a line; (*перен: разг*) to put out feelers.

закип|е́ть (*3sg* -и́т, *3pl* -я́т, *impf* **закипа́ть**) *сов неперех* to start to boil; (*перен: работа*) to increase.

заки́с|нуть (-ну, -нешь; *pt* -, -ла, -ло, *impf* **закиса́ть**) *сов неперех* (*тесто, квас*) to turn sour; (*перен*) to stagnate.

за́кис|ь (-и) *ж* oxide.

закла́д (-а) *м*: **в ~е** in pawn; **би́ться** (*impf*) **об ~** (*разг*) to bet.

закла́дк|а (-и) *ж* (*сада, фундамента*) laying; (*в кни́ге*) bookmark.

закладн|а́я (-о́й; *decl like adj*) *ж* mortgage deed.

закла́дыва|ть (-ю) *несов от* **заложи́ть**.

закл|ева́ть (-юю́, -юёшь; *impf* **заклёвывать**) *сов перех* to peek at; (*перен: разг*) to harass.

закле́|ить (-ю, -ишь; *impf* **закле́ивать**) *сов перех* to seal (up)

▶ **закле́|иться** (*impf* **закле́иваться**) *сов возв* to seal.

заклейм|и́ть (-лю́, -и́шь) *сов от* **клейми́ть**.

заклепа́|ть (-ю; *impf* **заклёпывать**) *сов перех* to rivet.

заклёпк|а (-и) *ж* (*стержень*) rivet.

заклёпыва|ть (-ю) *несов от* **заклепа́ть**.

заклина́ни|е (-я) *ср* (*маги́ческие слова́*) incantation; (*перен: мольба́*) plea.

заклина́|ть (-ю) *несов перех* (*духов, змея́*) to charm; (*перен: умоля́ть*) to plead with.

закли́н|ить (-ю, -ишь; *impf* **закли́нивать**) *сов перех* (*дверь итп*) to jam; **руль ~ило** the wheel has jammed.

заключа́|ть (-ю) *несов от* **заключи́ть**.

заключа́|ться (*3sg* -ется, *3pl* -ются) *несов возв*: **~ в** +*prp* (*состоя́ть в*) to lie in; (*содержа́ться в*) to be contained in; (*зака́нчиваться*): **~** +*instr* to conclude with; **дело́/пробле́ма ~ется в том, что** ... the point/problem is that ...; **на́ша цель ~ется в том, что́бы привле́чь инвести́ции в го́род** our aim is to attract investment into the city.

заключе́ни|е (-я) *ср* conclusion; (*в тюрьме́*) imprisonment, confinement; **в ~** in conclusion; **тюре́мное ~** imprisonment; **находи́ться** (*impf*) **в ~и** to be held in confinement.

заключённ|ая (-ой; *decl like adj*) *ж см* **заключённый**.

заключённ|ый (-ого; *decl like adj*) *м* prisoner.

заключи́тельный *прил* concluding, final.

заключ|и́ть (-у́, -и́шь; *impf* **заключа́ть**) *сов перех* (*соглаше́ние, догово́р, сде́лку*) to conclude, seal; **заключа́ть (~** *perf*) **в себе́** to comprise; **заключа́ть (~** *perf*) **контра́кт** to conclude a contract; **заключа́ть (~** *perf*) **кого́-н в тюрьму́** to put sb in prison; **заключа́ть (~** *perf*) **кого́-н под стра́жу** to take sb into custody; **заключа́ть (~** *perf*) **кого́-н в объя́тия** to embrace sb.

закля́тый *прил*: **~ враг** sworn enemy.

заков|а́ть (-ую́; *impf* **закова́ть**) *сов перех* to chain up; (*подлеж: лёд*) to cover.

закоди́р|овать (-ую) *сов от* **коди́ровать**.

закола́чива|ть (-ю) *несов от* **заколоти́ть**.

заколдо́ван|ный (-, -а, -о) *прил* enchanted; **заколдо́ванный круг** vicious circle.

заколд|ова́ть (-у́ю; *impf* **заколдо́вывать**) *сов перех* to bewitch.

зако́лк|а (-и) *ж* (*для воло́с*) hairpin, hairclip.

заколо|ти́ть (-очу́, -о́тишь; *impf* **закола́чивать**) *сов перех* (*окна, дом*) to board up; (*ящик*) to nail up.

заколо́ть (-олю́, -о́лешь) *сов от* **коло́ть** ♦ (*impf* **зака́лывать**) *сов перех* (*свинью, индейку*) to slaughter; (*волосы*) to pin up; (*галстук, воротник*) to pin back; **у меня́ ~оло́ло в боку́** I've got a stitch.

заколочу́ *сов см* **заколоти́ть**.

закомпости́р|овать (-ую) *сов от* **компости́ровать**.

зако́н (-а) *м* law; **вне ~а** outside the law; **объявля́ть (объяви́ть** *perf*) **кого́-н вне ~а** to outlaw sb; **Зако́н Бо́жий** religious education.

зако́нен *прил см* **зако́нный**.

зако́нност|ь (-и) *ж* (*докуме́нта, завеща́ния*) legality; (*в стране́*) law and order.

зако́н|ный (-ен, -на, -но) *прил* legitimate, lawful; (*право, приём*) legal; (*докуме́нт*) valid; **на ~ном основа́нии** on a legal basis; **~ным о́бразом** legally, lawfully; **зако́нный брак/муж** lawful wedlock/wedded husband.

законода́тел|ь (-я) *м* legislator; (*перен: вку́сов, мне́ний*) arbiter; **~ мод** trendsetter.

законода́тельниц|а (-ы) *ж см* **законода́тель**.

законода́тельный *прил* legislative.

законода́тельств|о (-а) *ср* legislation.

закономе́р|ный (-ен, -на, -но) *прил* (*результа́т, явле́ние*) predictable; (*поня́тный*) legitimate.

законопа́|тить (-чу, -тишь; *impf* **законопа́чивать**) *сов перех* to patch up.

законоположе́ни|е (-я) *ср* statute.

законопрое́кт (-а) *м* (*полит*) bill.

законсерви́р|овать (-ую) *сов от* **консерви́ровать**.

законспекти́р|овать (-ую) *сов от* **конспекти́ровать**.

законтракт|ова́ть (-у́ю; *impf* **законтракто́вывать**) *сов перех* to sign a contract for.

зако́нчен|ный (-, -на, -но) *прил* (*мысль, расска́з*) complete; (*него́дяй, мерза́вец*) utter.

зако́нч|ить (-у, -ишь; *impf* **зака́нчивать**) *сов перех* to finish, end

▶ **зако́нчиться** (*impf* зака́нчиваться) *сов возв* to finish, end.

закопа́|ть (-ю; *impf* зака́пывать) *сов перех* (*деньги, золото итп*) to bury; (*канаву, яму*) to fill in

▶ **закопа́ться** (*impf* зака́пываться) *сов возв* (*в землю итп*) to bury o.s.

закопти́ть (-чу́, -ти́шь) *сов от* копти́ть

▶ **закопти́ться** *сов возв* to be covered in smoke.

закопчённый *прил* (*чайник итп*) charred; (*потолок*) smoke-stained.

закопчу́(сь) *сов см* закопти́ть(ся).

закорене́лый *прил* (*традиции, предрассудки итп*) deep-rooted; (*дурак, кокетка итп*) incorrigible; ~ **престу́пник** hardened criminal.

закорене́|ть (-ю) *сов неперех*: ~ **в** +*prp* (*мнении, предрассудках*) to be entrenched in.

зако́р|ки (-ок) *мн* (*разг*): **посади́ть кого́-н на** ~ to lift sb onto one's back; **нести́** (*impf*) **кого́-н на** ~**ках** to give sb a piggyback.

закорю́ч|ка (-ки; *gen pl* -ек) *ж* squiggle.

закоснё|ть (-ю) *сов от* коснéть.

закостенéлый *прил* stiff.

закостенé|ть (-ю) *сов от* костенéть.

закоу́л|ок (-ка) *м* (*города*) back street *или* alley; (*дома, замка, двора*) nook; **обы́скивать** (**обыска́ть** *perf*) **все** ~**ки** to look in all the nooks and crannies.

закоченéлый *прил* numb.

закоченé|ть (-ю) *сов неперех* to go numb.

закрадётся *итп сов см* закра́сться.

закра́дыва|ться (*3sg* -ется, *3pl* -ются) *несов от* закра́сться.

закра́|сить (-шу, -сишь; *impf* закра́шивать) *сов перех* to paint over.

закра́|сться (*3sg* -адётся, *3pl* -аду́тся, *pt* -а́лся, -а́лась, -а́лось, *impf* закра́дываться) *сов возв* to creep in.

закра́шива|ть (-ю) *несов от* закра́сить.

закра́шу *сов см* закра́сить.

закрепи́тель (-я) *м* (*ФОТО*) fixative.

закреп|и́ть (-лю́, -и́шь; *impf* закрепля́ть) *сов перех* (*деталь, грунт*) to fasten; (*победу, позицию*) to consolidate; (*ФОТО*) to fix; **закрепля́ть** (~ *perf*) **что-н за кем-н** to secure sth for sb; **закрепля́ть** (~ *perf*) **кого́-н за кем-н** to assign sb to sb

▶ **закрепи́ться** (*impf* закрепля́ться) *сов возв* (*деталь, грунт*) to be fastened; (*победа, успехи*) to be consolidated; (*слово, привычка*) to become established; (*ВОЕН*): ~**ся на** +*acc* (*на высоте*) to consolidate one's position on.

закрéп|ка (-и) *ж* fastener.

закрепля́ю(сь) *сов см* закрепи́ть(ся).

закрепля́|ть(ся) (-ю(сь)) *несов от* закрепи́ть(ся).

закрепо|сти́ть (-щу́, -сти́шь; *impf* закрепоща́ть) *сов перех* to enslave.

закрепощéни|е (-я) *ср* enslavement.

закрепощу́ *сов см* закрепости́ть.

закрич|а́ть (-у́, -и́шь) *сов неперех* to start shouting.

закро́йщик (-а) *м* cutter (*DRESSMAKING*).

закро́йщиц|а (-ы) *ж см* закро́йщик.

за́кром (-а; *nom pl* -а́) *м* (*в амбаре*) grain store; *см также* закрома́.

закром|а́ (-о́в) *мн* (*перен*) breadbasket *ед* (*esp US*), granary *ед*.

закро́ю(сь) *итп сов см* закры́ть(ся).

закруглéни|е (-я) *ср* curve.

закруглён|ный (-, -на, -но) *прил* curved, rounded.

закругл|и́ть (-ю́, -и́шь; *impf* закругля́ть) *сов перех* (*край*) to round off; (*поверхность*) to make round

▶ **закругли́ться** (*impf* закругля́ться) *сов возв* to become rounded; (*перен: разг: закончить*) to round off.

закр|ужи́ть (-ужу́, -у́жишь) *сов перех*: ~ **кого́-н** (*начать кружить*) (to start) to spin sb round; (*довести до головокружения*) to make sb dizzy

▶ **закружи́ться** *сов возв* (*начать кружиться*) to start spinning; (*ослабеть*) to start to feel dizzy; (*перен: разг: захлопотаться*) to get o.s. into a tizzy; **у меня́ ~ужи́лась голова́** my head has started spinning.

закр|ути́ть (-учу́, -у́тишь; *impf* закру́чивать) *сов перех* (*волосы, усы*) to twist; (*верёвку, ленту*) to wind; (*кран*) to turn off; (*гайку*) to screw in

▶ **закрути́ться** (*impf* закру́чиваться) *сов возв* (*верёвка, лента*) to wind up; (*перен: разг: захлопотаться*) to get o.s. into a flap.

закрыва́|ть(ся) (-ю(сь)) *несов от* закры́ть(ся).

закры́ти|е (-я) *ср* (*магазина итп*) closing (time); (*сезона, конкурса*) close.

закры́т|ый (-, -а, -о) *прил* shut, closed; (*no short form*) enclosed; (*стадион, бассейн*) indoor; (*собрание, заседание*) closed, private; (*перелом, рана*) internal; **в** ~**ом помещéнии** indoors; **при** ~**ых дверя́х** behind closed doors; **вопро́с закры́т** the matter is closed; **закры́тое голосова́ние** secret vote *или* ballot; **закры́тое мо́ре** inland sea; **закры́тое пла́тье** dress with a high neck; **закры́тый ко́нкурс** closed competition.

закр|ы́ть (-о́ю, -о́ешь; *impf* закрыва́ть) *сов перех* to close, shut; (*заслонить, накрыть*) to cover (up); (*проход, проезд, границу*) to close (off); (*воду, газ итп*) to shut off; **закрыва́ть** (~ *perf*) **кого́-н в ко́мнате** to shut sb in a room; **закрыва́ть** (~ *perf*) **счёт** to close an account; **закрыва́ть** (~ *perf*) **глаза́ на что-н** to close one's eyes to sth

▶ **закры́ться** (*impf* закрыва́ться) *сов возв* to close, shut; (*магазин, предприятие*) to close *или* shut down; (*накрыться*) to cover o.s. up; (*запереться: в доме итп*) to shut o.s. up; (*рана*) to close up.

закули́сн|ый *прил* backstage *опред*; (*перен: интриги, борьба*) behind-the-scenes; **~ая жизнь** off-stage life.

заку́п|и́ть (-уплю́, -у́пишь; *impf* **закупа́ть**) *сов перех* (*купить оптом*) to buy up; (*запастись*) to stock up with.

заку́пк|а (-и) *ж* purchase.

закуплю́ *сов см* **закупи́ть**.

заку́пор|ить (-ю, -ишь; *impf* **заку́поривать**) *сов перех* (*бутылку*) to cork (up); (*бочку*) to seal up.

заку́порк|а (-и) *ж* (*см перех*) corking; sealing; (*МЕД: кишечника, сосудов*) blockage; **заку́порка вен** (*МЕД*) embolism.

заку́почн|ый *прил*: **~ая цена́** purchase price.

заку́пщик (-а) *м* buyer.

заку́р|и́ть (-урю́, -у́ришь; *impf* **заку́ривать**) *сов перех* to light (up) ◆ *неперех* to start smoking.

закуса́|ть (-ю) *сов перех* (*разг*) to bite; **меня ~ли комары́** I've been bitten to death by mosquitoes.

заку́с|и́ть (-ушу́, -у́сишь; *impf* **заку́сывать**) *сов неперех* (*поесть*) to have a bite to eat ◆ *перех*: **~ во́дку/лека́рство** *итп* to have sth to eat with the vodka/medicine; **заку́сывать (~** *perf*) **губу́** to bite one's lip; **заку́сывать (~** *perf*) **удила́** (*перен*) to take the bit between one's teeth.

заку́ск|а (-и) *ж* snack; (*обычно мн: для водки*) zakuska (*мн* zakuski), nibbles *мн*; (*в начале обеда*) hors d'oeuvre; **на ~у** (*перен: разг*) for the finale.

заку́сочн|ая (-ой; *decl like adj*) *ж* snack bar.

заку́сыва|ть (-ю) *несов от* **закуси́ть**.

заку́та|ть (-ю) *сов от* **ку́тать** ◆ (*impf* **заку́тывать**) *перех* (*ребёнка*) to wrap up; (*ноги итп*) to cover

▶ **заку́таться** *сов от* **ку́таться** ◆ (*impf* **заку́тываться**) *возв* to wrap (o.s.) up.

закут|о́к (-ка́) *м* (*разг*) dark corner.

заку́тыва|ть(ся) (-ю(сь)) *несов от* **заку́тать(ся)**.

закушу́ *сов см* **закуси́ть**.

зал (-а) *м* hall; (*в музее, в библиотеке*) room; **зал ожида́ния** waiting room.

зала́|дить (-жу, -дишь) *сов (не)перех* (*разг*) to harp on (about); (*+infin*) to take to doing.

зала́мыва|ть (-ю) *несов от* **заломи́ть**.

залата́|ть (-ю) *сов от* **лата́ть**.

зала́|ять (-ю) *сов неперех* to start barking, start to bark.

залёг *итп сов см* **зале́чь**.

залега́|ть (-ю) *несов от* **зале́чь**.

заледене́лый *прил* covered in ice; (*пальцы, руки*) icy.

заледене́|ть (-ю) *сов неперех* (*дорога*) to ice over; (*перен: пальцы, руки*) to freeze.

залежа́л|ый (-, -а, -о) *прил* (*разг*) old.

залежа́|ться (-у́сь, -и́шься; *impf* **зале́живаться**) *сов возв*: **~ в магази́не/в**

посте́ли to lie in the shop/in bed for too long.

за́леж|ь (-и) *ж* (*угля, золота*) seam; (*с.-х.*) fallow land.

зале́з|ть (-у, -ешь; *impf* **залеза́ть**) *сов неперех*: **~ на** +*acc* (*на крышу*) to climb onto; (*на дерево, на лестницу*) to climb (up); (*разг*): **~ в** +*acc* (*в квартиру, в магазин*) to break into; **залеза́ть (~** *perf*) **кому́-н в карма́н** to pick sb's pockets; **залеза́ть (~** *perf*) **в долги́** to get into debt.

зале|пи́ть (-еплю́, -е́пишь; *impf* **залепля́ть**) *сов перех* (*дыру, трещину*) to plaster up; (*подлеж: снег, грязь*) to plaster; **~** (*perf*) **кому́-н пощёчину** (*разг*) to give sb a slap round the face.

зале|те́ть (-чу́, -ти́шь; *impf* **залета́ть**) *сов неперех*: **~ (в** +*acc*) to fly in(to); **залета́ть (~** *perf*) **за** +*acc* (*за море, за облака итп*) to fly over; **залета́ть (~** *perf*) **далеко́** to fly a long way; (*перен*) to go far; **самолёт ~те́л в Москву́ за горю́чим** the plane stopped off in Moscow for refuelling.

зале|чи́ть (-чу́, -чишь; *impf* **зале́чивать**) *сов перех* (*язву, рану*) to heal; **~** (*perf*) **кого́-н** (*разг*) to make sb feel worse (*by excessive medication*)

▶ **зале́читься** (*impf* **зале́чиваться**) *сов возв* to heal (up).

залечу́ *сов см* **залете́ть**.

зале́|чь (-я́гу, -я́жешь *итп*, -я́гут; *pt* -ёг, -егла́, -егло́, *impf* **залега́ть**) *сов неперех* (*в постель*) to lie down; (*в нору*) to retreat; (*укрыться*) to lie low; (*ГЕО: уголь, золото*) to be deposited; **залега́ть (~** *perf*) **в заса́де** to lie in wait.

зали́в (-а) *м* (*длинный*) gulf.

залива́|ть(ся) (-ю(сь)) *несов от* **зали́ть(ся)**.

заливн|о́е (-о́го; *decl like adj*) *ср* (*КУЛИН*) fish or meat in aspic.

заливно́й *прил* (*рыба, мясо*) jellied; **заливно́й луг** water meadow.

зали́|ть (-ью, -ьёшь; *pt* -и́л, -ила́, -и́ло, *impf* **залива́ть**) *сов перех* to flood; (*костёр, огонь*) to extinguish; **залива́ть (~** *perf*) **руба́шку пи́вом** to spill beer on one's shirt; **залива́ть (~** *perf*) **бензи́н в маши́ну** to fill a car with petrol; **залива́ть (~** *perf*) **доро́гу асфа́льтом** to cover a road with asphalt; **залива́ть (~** *perf*) **го́ре** to drown one's sorrows; **слёзы ~и́ли его́ лицо́** the tears poured down her face

▶ **зали́ться** (*impf* **залива́ться**) *сов возв* (*луг, пол*) to be flooded; (*вода*) to seep; **залива́ться . (~ся** *perf*) **слеза́ми/сме́хом** to burst into tears/out laughing; **её лицо́ ~и́лось румя́нцем** the colour flooded into her cheeks.

зало́г (-а) *м* (*действие: вещей*) pawning; (: *квартиры*) mortgaging; (*заложенная вещь*) security; (*ЛИНГ: активный, пассивный*) voice; (*перен: знак*) token.

зал|ожи́ть (-ожу́, -о́жишь; *impf* **закла́дывать**) *сов перех* (*покрыть*) to clutter up; (*отметить*) to mark; (*отдать в залог: кольцо, шубу*) to pawn; (: *дом*) to mortgage; (*заполнить: трубу, дыру*) to block up; **закла́дывать (~** *perf*) **что-н**

за что-н to put sth behind sth; **закладывать (~** *perf*) **го́род** to lay the foundations of a city; **у меня́ ~ожи́ло нос/го́рло** (*разг*) my nose/throat is all bunged up.

зало́жник (-а) *м* hostage.

зало́жниц|а (-ы) *ж см* **зало́жник.**

зало|ми́ть (-омлю́, -о́мишь; *impf* **зала́мывать)** *сов перех* to tear off; **зала́мывать (~** *perf*) **ру́ки** to throw up one's hands; **зала́мывать (~** *perf*) **высо́кую це́ну** to ask too high a price.

залп (-а) *м* salvo (*мн* salvoes), volley.

за́лпом *нареч* (*раза: проглоти́ть, проговори́ть*) all in one go; **вы́стрелить** (*perf*) ~ to fire a volley *или* salvo of bullets.

залы́син|а (-ы) *ж* bald patch.

залью́(сь) *итп сов см* **зали́ть(ся).**

залюб|ова́ться (-у́юсь) *сов возв* (+*instr*; *картиной, девушкой*) to be transfixed by.

заля́гу *итп сов см* **зале́чь.**

заля́жешь *итп сов см* **зале́чь.**

заля́па|ть (-ю; *impf* **заля́пывать)** *сов перех* (*разг*) to mess up.

зам (-а) *м сокр* (*разг:* = *замести́тель*) number two.

зам. *м сокр* (= **замести́тель**) dep. (= *deputy*).

зам- *префикс* deputy.

зама́за|ть (-жу, -жешь; *impf* **зама́зывать)** *сов перех* (*пятно, рисунок*) to paint over; (*окна, щели*) to fill with putty; (*запа́чкать*) to smear.

▶ **зама́заться (**impf **зама́зываться)** *сов возв*: ~**ся** (+*instr*) to become smeared (with).

зама́зк|а (-и) *ж* putty.

зама́зыва|ть(ся) (-ю(сь)) *несов от* **зама́зать(ся).**

зама́чива|ть (-ю) *несов от* **замолча́ть.**

зам|ани́ть (-аню́, -а́нишь; *impf* **зама́нивать)** *сов перех* to lure, entice.

зама́нчив|ый (-, -а, -о) *прил* tempting.

замара́|ть(ся) (-ю(сь)) *несов от* **мара́ть(ся).**

замарин|ова́ть (-у́ю) *сов от* **маринова́ть.**

замаскиро́ван|ный (-, -а, -о) *прил* disguised; (*намёк, угроза*) veiled.

замаскир|ова́ть (-у́ю; *impf* **замаскиро́вывать** *или* **маскирова́ть)** *сов перех* to disguise; (*самолёт, танк*) to camouflage.

▶ **замаскирова́ться (**impf **замаскиро́вываться** *или* **маскирова́ться)** *сов возв* to disguise o.s.; (*солдаты*) to camouflage o.s.

зама́тыва|ть(ся) (-ю(сь)) *несов от* **замота́ть(ся).**

зам|аха́ть (-ашу́, -а́шешь) *сов неперех* (+*instr*; *палкой, газе́той итп*) to brandish; ~ (*perf*) **руко́й** to start waving.

замахн|у́ться (-у́сь, -ёшься; *impf* **зама́хиваться)** *сов возв*: ~ **на** +*acc* (*на собаку, на ребёнка*) to raise one's hand to; (*перен*) to set one's sights on; **он ~у́лся на бо́льшее** he has

set his sights on bigger and better things.

зама́чива|ть (-ю) *несов от* **замочи́ть.**

зама́шк|и (-ек) *мн* manners *мн*.

замби́йск|ий (-ая, -ое, -ие) *прил* Zambian.

За́мби|я (-и) *ж* Zambia.

замедле́ни|е (-я) *ср* slowing down; **без ~я** without delay.

заме́дленный *прил* retarded; ~ **ход** reduced speed.

заме́дл|ить (-ю, -ишь; *impf* **замедля́ть)** *сов перех* to slow down; (*no impf*; *задержа́ться*): ~ **с** +*instr* to be slow with; **не** ~ (*perf*) +*infin* to be quick to do

▶ **заме́длиться (**impf **замедля́ться)** *сов возв* to slow down.

заме́л *итп сов см* **замести́.**

заме́н|а (-ы) *ж* replacement; (*СПОРТ*) substitution.

замени́м|ый (-, -а, -о) *прил* replaceable.

замени́тел|ь (-я) *м* (*суррога́т*) substitute.

зам|ени́ть (-еню́, -е́нишь; *impf* **заменя́ть)** *сов перех* to replace; **она́ ~ени́ла им мать** she was like a mother to them.

зам|ере́ть (-ру́, -рёшь; *pt* **-ер, -ерла́, -ерло,** *impf* **замира́ть)** *сов неперех* (*человек, живо́тное*) to stop dead; (*перен: душа́, се́рдце*) to stand still; (: *работа, страна́*) to come to a standstill; (*звук*) to die away; (*шум, стрельба́*) to die down; ~ (*perf*) **на ме́сте** to stop dead in one's tracks.

замерза́ни|е (-я) *ср* freezing; **то́чка ~я** freezing point.

замёрз|нуть (-ну, -нешь; *pt* **-, -ла, -ло,** *impf* **замерза́ть)** *сов неперех* to freeze; (*река́*) to freeze (up); (*окно́*) to ice up; **я совсе́м замёрз** I'm completely frozen.

заме́р|ить (-ю, -ишь; *impf* **замеря́ть)** *сов перех* to measure.

за́мертво *нареч*: **упа́сть** *или* **ру́хнуть** ~ to collapse in a heap.

замеря́|ть (-ю) *несов от* **заме́рить.**

зам|еси́ть (-ешу́, -е́сишь; *impf* **заме́шивать)** *сов перех* (*бето́н, гли́ну*) to mix up; (*те́сто*) to knead.

зам|ести́ (-ету́, -етёшь; *pt* **-ёл, -ела́, -ело́,** *impf* **замета́ть)** *сов перех* (*му́сор, листья*) to sweep up; (*подлеж: мете́ль: доро́гу итп*) to cover; **замета́ть (~** *perf*) **следы́** (*также перен*) to cover one's tracks.

замести́тел|ь (-я) *м* replacement; (*до́лжность*) deputy; ~ **дире́ктора/премье́р-мини́стра** deputy director/prime minister.

замести́тельниц|а (-ы) *ж см* **замести́тель.**

заме|сти́ть (-щу́, -сти́шь) *сов от* **замеща́ть.**

замета́|ть (-ю) *несов от* **замести́.**

замета́|ться (-чусь, -чешься) *сов возв* (*в крова́ти, в бреду́*) to start tossing and turning; (*в отча́янии*) to get into a state; **он ~та́лся по**

ко́мнате he began to rush about the room.
заме́тен *прил см* **заме́тный**.
заме́|тить (-чу, -тишь; *impf* **замеча́ть**) *сов перех*
to notice; (*запомнить*) to take note of;
(*сказать*) to remark.
заме́т|ка (-ки; *gen pl* **-ок**) *ж* (*на дереве итп*)
mark, notch; (*в записной книжке итп*) note; (*в
газете итп*) short piece *или* article; **брать**
(**взять** *perf*) что-н на ~ку to make a (mental)
note of sth; **он на** ~ке у мили́ции (*разг*) the
police have got their eye on him.
заме́тно *нареч* noticeably ♦ *как сказ* (*видно*) it is
obvious.
заме́т|ный (-ен, -на, -но) *прил* noticeable;
(*личность, человек*) prominent.
замету́ *итп сов см* **замести́**.
замеча́ни|е (-я) *ср* comment, remark; (*выговор*)
reprimand.
замеча́телен *прил см* **замеча́тельный**.
замеча́тельно *нареч* (*красив, умён*) extremely;
(*писать*) wonderfully, brilliantly ♦ *как сказ*: ~!
that's brilliant *или* wonderful!
замеча́тел|ьный (-ен, -ьна, -ьно) *прил* (*очень
хороший*) wonderful, brilliant;
(*необыкновенный*) remarkable; (*выдающийся*)
outstanding.
замеча́|ть (-ю) *несов от* **заме́тить**.
замечта́|ться (-юсь) *сов возв* to start
daydreaming.
заме́чу *сов см* **заме́тить**.
замечу́сь *итп сов см* **замета́ться**.
замеша́тельств|о (-а) *ср* confusion;
приводи́ть (**привести́** *perf*) **кого-н в** ~ to throw
sb into confusion; **приходи́ть** (**прийти́** *perf*) **в** ~
to become confused.
замеша́|ть (-ю; *impf* **заме́шивать**) *сов перех*: ~
кого-н во что-н to get sb mixed up in sth
▸ **замеша́ться** (*impf* **заме́шиваться**) *сов возв*:
~ся в +*acc* (*в историю, в преступление*) to get
mixed up in; (*скрыться: в толпе*) to mingle
with.
заме́шива|ть (-ю) *несов от* **замеси́ть**,
замеша́ть
▸ **заме́шиваться** *несов от* **замеша́ться**.
заме́шка|ть (-ю) *сов от* **ме́шкать**
▸ **заме́шкаться** *сов возв* (*разг: с работой, с
ответом*) to drag one's heels; (: *пробыть
дольше*) to faff about.
замешу́ *сов см* **замеси́ть**.
замеща́|ть (-ю) *несов перех* (*начальника итп*)
to stand in *или* deputize for; (*perf* **замести́ть**;
заменять: работника итп) to replace; (:
игрока) to substitute; (*вакантную должность*)
to fill.
замеще́ни|е (-я) *ср* (*работника, директора*)
replacement; (*игрока*) substitution; ~
вака́нтной до́лжности filling of a vacancy.
замещу́ *сов см* **замести́ть**.
замина́|ть(ся) (-ю(сь)) *несов от* **замя́ть(ся)**.
замини́р|овать (-ую) *сов от* **мини́ровать**.
зами́нк|а (-и) *ж* (*в работе*) hitch; (*в речи*)

stumble.
замира́|ть (-ю) *несов от* **замере́ть**.
за́мка *сущ см* **за́мок**.
замка́ *сущ см* **замо́к**.
за́мкнут|ый (-, -а, -о) *прил* (*среда, жизнь*)
cloistered; (*человек, характер*) reclusive;
за́мкнутая цепь (*ЭЛЕК*) closed circuit;
за́мкнутый круг vicious circle.
замкн|у́ть (-у́, -ёшь; *impf* **замыка́ть**) *сов перех*
to close
▸ **замкну́ться** (*impf* **замыка́ться**) *сов возв* to
close; (*перен: обособиться*) to shut o.s. off;
замыка́ться (~**ся** *perf*) **в себе́** to withdraw into
o.s.
замну́(сь) *итп сов см* **замя́ть(ся)**.
замоги́льный *прил*: ~ **го́лос** ghostly voice.
за́м|ок (-ка) *м* castle.
замо́|к (-ка) *м* lock; (*также: вися́чий* ~) padlock;
(*браслета, цепочки*) clasp; **на** ~ке́ locked; **под**
~ко́м under lock and key; **храни́ть** (*impf*) **что-н
за семью́** ~ка́ми to keep sth very closely
guarded.
замо́к|нуть (*3sg* **-нет**, *pt* **-**, **-ла**, **-ло**, *impf*
замока́ть) *сов неперех* to get soaked.
замо́лв|ить (-лю, -ишь) *сов перех*: ~ **сло́во за
кого́-н** (**пе́ред кем-н**) (*разг*) to put in a word for
sb (with sb).
замо́лк|нуть (-ну, -нешь; *pt* **-**, **-ла**, **-ло**, *impf*
замолка́ть) *сов неперех* to fall silent; (*звук,
песня, спор итп*) to stop.
замолча́|ть (-у́, -и́шь) *сов неперех* (*человек*) to
go quiet; (*перестать писать*): **он** ~**л ещё
два го́да наза́д** I haven't heard from him for
two years ♦ (*impf* **зама́лчивать**) *перех* (*разг:
факты, происшествие*) to hush up; ~**й!** be
quiet!, shut up!
заморажива́ни|е (-я) *ср* (*продуктов, овощей*)
refrigeration; **замора́живание цен/
за́работной пла́ты** price/wage freeze.
замора́жива|ть (-ю) *несов от* **заморо́зить**.
замор|и́ть (-ю́, -и́шь) *сов от* **мори́ть**.
заморо́|зить (-жу, -зишь; *impf* **замора́живать**)
сов перех (*продукты, овощи*) to freeze; (*десну,
палец*) to freeze, numb; (*перен:
строительство*) to put on hold;
замора́живать (~ *perf*) **це́ны/зарпла́ту/счёт** to
freeze prices/wages/an account.
заморо́зк|и (-ов) *мн* frosts мн.
заморо́ч|ить (-у, -ишь) *сов от* **моро́чить**.
замо́рск|ий (-ая, -ое, -ие) *прил* (*разг*) foreign.
замо́рыш (-а) *м* (*разг*) weed, wimp.
замо́|сти́ть (-щу́, -сти́шь) *сов от* **мости́ть**.
замо́тан|ный (-, -а, -о) *прил* (*разг*) knackered,
whacked.
замота́|ть (-ю; *impf* **зама́тывать**) *сов перех*
(*разг: утомить*) to knacker out; (*верёвку,
канат*): ~ **что-н во что-н** to wind sth around sth
▸ **замота́ться** (*impf* **зама́тываться**) *сов возв* (*в
платок, шарфом*) to bundle o.s. up; (*разг:
утомиться*) to be knackered (out).
замощу́ *сов см* **замости́ть**.

зам|очи́ть (-очу́, -о́чишь; *impf* **зама́чивать**) *сов перех*: ~ **кого́-н/что-н** to get sb/sth wet; (*бельё, кожу*) to soak.

замру́ *итп сов см* **замере́ть**.

за́муж *нареч*: **выходи́ть** ~ (**за** +*acc*) to get married (to), marry; **выдава́ть** (**вы́дать** *perf*) **кого́-н** ~ (**за** +*acc*) to marry sb off (to).

за́мужем *нареч* married; **быть** (*impf*) ~ **за кем-н** to be married to sb.

заму́жеств|о (-а) *ср* marriage.

заму́жн|яя *прил* married ◆ (-**ей**; *decl like adj*) *ж* married woman (*мн* women).

замур|ова́ть (-у́ю; *impf* **замуро́вывать**) *сов перех* (*отверстие, окно*) to brick up; (*человека, ценности*) to brick in.

заму|ти́ть(ся) (-чу́(сь), -ти́шь(ся)) *сов от* **мути́ть(ся)**.

заму́ч|ить (-у, -ишь) *сов от* **му́чить** ◆ *перех* (*заставить страдать*) to torment; (*утомить*) to exhaust; (*до смерти*) to torture to death

▶ **заму́читься** *сов от* **му́читься** ◆ *возв* (*утомиться*) to exhaust o.s.

замучу́(сь) *сов см* **замути́ть(ся)**.

за́мш|а (-и) *ж* suede.

за́мшевый *прил* suede.

замше́лый *прил* mossy, moss-covered.

замыва́|ть (-ю) *несов от* **замы́ть**.

замыка́ни|е (-я) *ср* (*также*: **коро́ткое** ~) short circuit.

замыка́|ть (-ю) *несов от* **замкну́ть** ◆ *перех* (*колонну, шествие*) to bring up the rear of

▶ **замыка́ться** *несов от* **замкну́ться**.

за́мыс|ел (-ла) *м* (*человека, правительства*) scheme; (*картины, произведения*) idea.

замы́сл|ить (-ю, -ишь; *impf* **замышля́ть**) *сов перех* (*план, побег*) to think up; (+*infin*) to think about doing; **он** ~**ил купи́ть себе́ дом** he is thinking about buying a house.

замыслова́т|ый (-, -а, -о) *прил* intricate.

зам|ы́ть (-о́ю, -о́ешь; *impf* **замыва́ть**) *сов перех* to wash out.

замышля́|ть (-ю) *несов от* **замы́слить**.

замя́|ть (-ну́, -нёшь; *impf* **замина́ть**) *сов перех* (*разг*: *сделать незаметным*: *вопрос*) to hush up; (: *приостановить*: *разговор*) to put an end *или* a stop to

▶ **замя́ться** (*impf* **замина́ться**) *сов возв* to clam up; (*разг*: *замолчать*) to stop short.

за́навес (-а) *м* (ТЕАТР) curtain; **желе́зный** ~ (ИСТ) the Iron Curtain.

занаве́|сить (-шу, -сишь; *impf* **занаве́шивать**) *сов перех* to hang a curtain over.

занаве́с|ка (-ки; *gen pl* -ок) *ж* curtain.

занаве́шива|ть (-ю) *несов от* **занаве́сить**.

занаве́шу *сов см* **занаве́сить**.

зана́шива|ть (-ю) *несов от* **заноси́ть**.

зан|ести́ (-есу́, -есёшь; *pt* -ёс, -есла́, -есло́, *impf* **заноси́ть**) *сов перех* (*принести*) to bring;

(*поднять*: *ногу, руку*) to lift; (*записать*) to take down; (*доставить*): ~ **что-н кому́-н** to drop sth off to sb; (*отнести*): ~ **за** +*acc* to take behind; **доро́гу** ~**есло́ сне́гом** the road is covered over with snow; **судьба́** ~**есла́ меня́ сюда́ мно́го лет наза́д** fate brought me here many years ago.

зани́|зить (-жу, -зишь; *impf* **занижа́ть**) *сов перех* to lower; **занижа́ть** (**занизи́ть** *perf*) **отме́тки кому́-н** to undermark sb.

занима́тел|ьный (-ен, -ьна, -ьно) *прил* engaging.

занима́|ть (-ю) *несов от* **заня́ть**

▶ **занима́ться** *несов возв*: ~**ся** (+*instr*) (*учиться*) to study; (*работать*) to work (in); (*на рояле итп*) to practise (BRIT), practice (US); ~**ся** (*impf*) **англи́йским (языко́м)** to study English; ~**ся** (*impf*) **спо́ртом/му́зыкой** to play sports/music; **чем** ~**ется Ваш оте́ц?** what does your father do (for a living)?; **он** ~**ется би́знесом/поли́тикой** he's a businessman/ politician; **чем ты сейча́с** ~**ешься?** what are you doing at the moment?

за́ново *нареч* again.

заножу́ *сов см* **занози́ть**.

зано́з|а (-ы) *ж* splinter.

зано|зи́ть (-жу́, -зи́шь) *сов перех* to get a splinter in.

зано́с (-а) *м* (*обычно мн*) drift; **сне́жные** ~**ы** snowdrift.

зан|оси́ть (-ошу́, -о́сишь) *несов от* **занести́** ◆ (*impf* **зана́шивать**) *сов перех* (*платье, пальто итп*) to wear out.

зано́счив|ый (-, -а, -о) *прил* arrogant.

заноче́ва́|ть (-у́ю) *сов непepex* to spend the night.

заношу́ (*не*)*сов см* **заноси́ть**.

зану́д|а (-ы) *м/ж* bore.

зану́д|ный (-ен, -на, -но) *прил* tiresome, tedious.

зан|ы́ть (-о́ю, -о́ешь) *сов непepex* (*ребёнок*) to start whinging; (*сердце, зуб*) to begin to ache.

за́нят (-, -а́, -о) *прил* busy; **он был о́чень** ~ he was very busy; **телефо́н** ~ the phone *или* line is engaged.

за́нятен *прил см* **заня́тный**.

заня́ти|е (-я) *ср* occupation; (*обычно мн*: *в школе, в институте*) lesson, class; (*времяпрепровождение*) pastime, pursuit; **нача́ло шко́льных** ~**й** (*начало учебного года*) the beginning of the school year; (*утром*) the beginning of the school day.

заня́т|ный (-ен, -на, -но) *прил* entertaining.

занят|о́й *прил* busy; **он** -~ **челове́к** he is a busy man.

за́нятост|ь (-и) *ж* (ЭКОН) employment; **по́лная** ~ full employment.

зан|я́ть (**займу́, займёшь**; *pt* -я́л, -яла́, -я́ло, *impf* **занима́ть**) *сов перех* (*квартиру, город*) to occupy; (*должность, позицию*) to take up;

(*деньги*) to borrow; (*время*) to take; (*развлечь*) to occupy; ~ (*perf*) **ме́сто кому́-н** to keep a place for sb; **все ~я́ли свои́ места́** everyone took their places; ~ (*perf*) **пе́рвое/второ́е ме́сто** to take first/second place; **э́та рабо́та ~я́ла (у меня́) два часа́** the work took (me) two hours; **э́то займёт всего́ одну́ мину́тку** it will only take a minute

▸ **заня́ться** *сов возв*: ~**ся** +*instr* (*языком, предметом, спортом*) to take up; (*бизнесом, поли́тикой*) to go into; (*помочь*): ~**ся с кем-н (чем-н)** to assist sb with sth; ~**ся** (*perf*) **собо́й/детьми́** to devote time to o.s./one's children; ~**ся** (*perf*) **убо́ркой** to do the cleaning; **ему́ пора́ ~ся де́лом** it's time that he did something serious with his life.

заобла́чный *прил* lofty.

заодно́ *нареч* (*вместе*) as one; (*попутно*) at the same time; **де́йствовать** (*impf*) ~ to act as one *или* with one accord; **мы с ни́ми ~** we are in total accord.

заостри́ть (-ю́, -и́шь; *impf* **заостря́ть**) *сов перех* (*копьё, каранда́ш*) to sharpen; (*перен: мысль, вопро́с*) to define; **заостри́ть** (~ *perf*) **внима́ние на чём-н** to focus one's attention on sth

▸ **заостри́ться** (*impf* **заостря́ться**) *сов возв* (*черты́ лица́*) to become more pointed.

зао́чник (-а) *м* part-time student (*studying by correspondence*).

зао́чница (-ы) *ж см* **зао́чник**.

зао́чно *нареч* **учи́ться** ~ to study part-time (*by correspondence*); **обсужда́ть** (*impf*) **кого́-н** ~ to discuss sb in his *итп* absence.

зао́чный *прил* part-time; **зао́чное обуче́ние** distance learning; **зао́чный институ́т** correspondence school.

за́пад (-а) *м* west; **З~** (*ПОЛИТ*) the West.

запада́ть (3sg -ет, 3pl -ют) *несов от* **запа́сть**.

западе́т *итп см* **запа́сть**.

за́падник (-а) *м* westernizer.

западноевропе́йский (-ая, -ое, -ие) *прил* West European.

за́падный *прил* western; (*ветер*) westerly.

западня́ (-и́) *ж* snare; (*перен*) trap.

запа́ивать (-ю) *несов от* **запая́ть**.

запакова́ть (-ю) *сов от* **пакова́ть** ♦ (*impf* **запако́вывать**) *перех* to wrap up.

запа́костить (-щу, -стишь) *сов от* **па́костить**.

запа́л (-а) *м* (*заряда*) fuse; (*разг: пыл*) fire (*fig*).

запа́льчивый (-, -а, -о) *прил* (*челове́к, хара́ктер*) quick-tempered; (*отве́т, тон*) impatient.

запанибра́та *нареч* (*разг*): **обраща́ться ~ с кем-н** to be overly familiar with sb.

запаникова́ть (-ю) *сов непе́рех* (*разг*) to panic.

запа́рка (-и) *ж* (*разг*) mad rush.

запа́рывать (-ю) *несов от* **запоро́ть**.

запа́с (-а) *м* (*проду́ктов, то́плива итп*) store, supply; (*руды́, поле́зных ископа́емых*) deposit;

(*перен: зна́ний*) store; (*на брю́ках, на пла́тье*) hem; (*ВОЕН*) the reserves *мн*; **у меня́ два часа́ в ~е** I've got two hours to spare; **оставля́ть (оста́вить** *perf*) **себе́ что-н про ~** to put sth by; **золото́й ~** gold reserves *мн*; **запа́с слов** vocabulary.

запаса́ть(ся) (-ю(сь)) *несов от* **запасти́(сь)**.

запа́сливый (-, -а, -о) *прил* thrifty.

запа́сник (-а) *м* (*в музе́е*) storage room; (*разг: ВОЕН*) reserve.

запасно́й *прил* spare ♦ (-о́го; *decl like adj*) *м* (*СПОРТ: также:* ~ **игро́к**) substitute; (*ВОЕН*) reservist; **запасно́й вы́ход** emergency exit; **запасно́й путь** siding; **запасно́й соста́в** (*ВОЕН*) the reserves.

запа́сный *прил* = **запасно́й**.

запа|сти́ (-су́, -сёшь; *pt* -с, -сла́, -сло́, *impf* **запаса́ть**) *сов перех* (*дрова́, то́пливо*) to lay in

▸ **запасти́сь** (*impf* **запаса́ться**) *сов возв*: ~**сь** (+*instr*) (*хле́бом, молоко́м*) to stock up (on); **запаса́ться** (~**сь** *perf*) **терпе́нием** to arm o.s. with patience.

запа́|сть (3sg -дёт, 3pl -ду́т, *pt* -л, -ла, -ло, *impf* **запада́ть**) *сов непере́х* (*глаза́, щёки*) to become sunken; (*перен: фра́за, слова́*) to be imprinted; **его́ слова́ ~ли мне в па́мять** his words remain imprinted on my memory.

запатент|ова́ть (-у́ю) *сов от* **патентова́ть** ♦ (*impf* **запатенто́вывать**) *перех* to patent.

за́пах (-а; *part gen* -у) *м* smell.

запа́х (-а) *м* (*хала́та, пальто́*) fold.

запа́хивать (-ю) *несов от* **запахну́ть**.

запа́х|нуть (-ну, -нешь; *pt* -, -ла, -ло) *сов непере́х*: ~ (+*instr*) to start to smell (of).

запахну́ть (-у́, -ёшь; *impf* **запа́хивать**) *сов перех* to wrap round.

запа́чка|ть (-ю) *сов от* **па́чкать** ♦ *перех* to soil, dirty; (*перен: со́весть, и́мя*) to tarnish, sully

▸ **запа́чкаться** *сов от* **па́чкаться** ♦ *возв* to get dirty.

запая́ть (-ю; *impf* **запа́ивать**) *сов перех* to solder.

запева́ла (-ы) *м/ж* (*МУЗ*) leader (*of a song*).

запева́|ть (-ю) *несов непере́х* to lead off ♦ *перех*: ~ **пе́сню** to start up a song.

запе́й(те) *сов см* **запи́ть**.

запе́к *итп см* **запе́чь(ся)**.

запека́н|ка (-и) *ж* (*карто́фельная итп*) bake; (*сла́дкая*) baked pudding.

запека́ть(ся) (-ю(сь)) *несов от* **запе́чь(ся)**.

запеку́ (сь) *итп см* **запе́чь(ся)**.

запелена́|ть (-ю) *сов от* **пелена́ть**.

запеленг|ова́ть (-у́ю) *сов от* **пеленгова́ть**.

запе|ре́ть (-ру́, -рёшь; *pt* -ер, -ерла́, -ерло, *impf* **запира́ть**) *сов перех* (*дверь, шкаф, замо́к*) to lock; (*дом, челове́ка, де́ньги*) to lock up

▸ **запере́ться** (*impf* **запира́ться**) *сов возв* (*дверь, шкаф, замо́к*) to lock; (*челове́к*) to lock o.s. up; (*разг: не призна́ться*) to clam up.

запе́ть (-ою́, -оёшь) *сов перех*: ~ **пе́сню** to start singing a song.

запеча́та|ть (-ю; *impf* **запеча́тывать**) *сов перех* to seal up.

запечатле́|ть (-ю; *impf* **запечатлева́ть**) *сов перех* (*на картине, в повести итп*) to capture; (*в памяти*) to impress

▸ **запечатле́ться** (*impf* **запечатлева́ться**) *сов возв*: ~**ся в па́мяти** to be imprinted on one's memory.

запеча́тыва|ть (-ю) *несов от* **запеча́тать**.

запе́|чь (-еку́, -ечёшь итп, -еку́т; *pt* -ёк, -екла́, -екло́, *impf* **запека́ть**) *сов перех* to bake;

▸ **запе́чься** (*impf* **запека́ться**) *сов возв* to bake; (*кровь*) to congeal; (*губы, рот*) to become parched.

запива́|ть (-ю) *несов от* **запи́ть**.

запина́|ться (-юсь) *несов от* **запну́ться**.

запи́н|ка (-ки; *gen pl* -ок) *ж* hesitation; **без** ~**ки** smoothly.

запира́тельств|о (-а) *ср* obstinacy.

запира́|ть(ся) (-ю(сь)) *несов от* **запере́ть(ся)**.

запис|а́ть (-ишу́, -и́шешь; *impf* **запи́сывать**) *сов перех* (*адрес, имя итп*) to write down; (*концерт, пластинку*) to record; (*в кружок, на курсы*) to enrol; **записывать** (~ *perf*) **ле́кцию** to take notes (*in a lecture*); ~ (*perf*) **кого́-н (на приём) к врачу́** to make a doctor's appointment for sb

▸ **записа́ться** (*impf* **запи́сываться**) *сов возв* (*в кружок, на курсы*) to enrol (o.s.); (*музыкант: на плёнку*) to make a recording; ~**ся** (*perf*) (**на приём) к врачу́** to make a doctor's appointment.

за́пис|и (-ей) *мн* (*лекции итп*) notes *мн*.

запи́ск|а (-и) *ж* note; (*служебная*) memo; *см также* **записки**.

запи́ск|и (-ок) *мн* (*короткие записи*) jottings *мн*; (*ЛИТЕРАТУРА*) notes *мн*, sketches *мн*.

записн|о́й *прил*: ~**а́я кни́жка** notebook.

запи́сок *сущ см* **записки**.

запи́сыва|ть(ся) (-ю(сь)) *несов от* **записа́ть(ся)**.

за́пис|ь (-и) *ж* (*событий, КОМП*) record; (*в дневнике*) entry; (*МУЗ*) recording; (*в кружок, на курсы*) enrolment (*BRIT*), enrollment (*US*); (*на приём к врачу*) registration; *см также* **записи**.

зап|и́ть (-ью, -ьёшь; *pt* -и́л, -ила́, -и́ло, *imper* -е́й(те), *impf* **запива́ть**) *сов перех* (*лекарство, обед*): ~ **что-н (чем-н)** to wash sth down (with sth) ♦ (*pt* -и́л, -ила́, -ило) *непéрех* (*начать пить*) to take to drink.

запиха́|ть (-ю; *impf* **запи́хивать**) *сов перех*: ~ **что-н в** +*acc* (*разг*) to stuff sth into.

запихн|у́ть (-у́, -ёшь) *сов* = **запиха́ть**.

запишу́(сь) итп *сов см* **записа́ть(ся)**.

запла́кан|ный (-, -а, -о) *прил* tearful; (*глаза*) puffy.

запла́|кать (-чу, -чешь) *сов непéрех* to start crying *или* to cry.

заплани́р|овать (-ую) *сов перех* to plan.

запла́т|а (-ы) *ж* patch.

заплат|и́ть (-ачу́, -а́тишь) *сов от* **плати́ть**.

запла́т|ка (-ки; *gen pl* -ок) *ж* = **запла́та**.

заплачу́ итп *сов см* **запла́кать**.

заплачу́ *сов см* **заплати́ть**.

заплёв|а́ть (-ю́ю; *impf* **заплёвывать**) *сов перех* (*пол итп*) to spit on; (*человека*) to spit at.

заплёл итп *сов см* **заплести́**.

заплесневе́лый *прил* mouldy (*BRIT*), moldy (*US*).

заплёсневе|ть (*3sg* -ет, *3pl* -ют) *сов от* **плёсневеть**.

запл|ести́ (-ету́, -етёшь; *pt* -ёл, -ела́, -ело́, *impf* **заплета́ть**) *сов перех* (*волосы, косу*) to plait.

заплета́|ться (*3sg* -ется, *3pl* -ются) *несов возв*: **у него́ но́ги** ~**ются** he keeps tripping over his feet; **у неё язы́к** ~**ется** she is muddling her words.

заплету́ итп *сов см* **заплести́**.

запломбир|ова́ть (-у́ю) *сов от* **пломбирова́ть**.

заплы́в (-а) *м* (*СПОРТ*) race (*in swimming*); (: *отборочный*) heat.

запл|ы́ть (-ыву́, -ывёшь; *impf* **заплыва́ть**) *сов непéрех* (*человек*) to swim off; (*корабль*) to sail off; (*бревно*) to float off; (*глаза*) to become swollen.

запн|у́ться (-у́сь, -ёшься; *impf* **запина́ться**) *сов возв* to falter, stumble.

запове́дник (-а) *м* (*природный*) nature reserve; **пти́чий** ~ bird reserve.

запове́дный *прил* (*лес, территория*) protected.

за́повед|ь (-и) *ж* (*РЕЛ*) commandment; (*перен*) cardinal rule; **де́сять** ~**ей** the Ten Commandments.

заподо́зр|ить (-ю, -ишь) *сов перех* to suspect; ~ (*perf*) **кого́-н в** +*acc* to suspect sb of.

запо́ем *нареч*: **пить** ~ to drink heavily; **он чита́ет** ~ (*разг*) he's an avid reader.

запозда́лый *прил* (*помощь, тревога итп*) belated; (*гость, весна*) late.

запо́|й (-я) *м* binge.

заполз|ти́ (-у́, -ёшь; *impf* **заполза́ть**) *сов непéрех* to crawl.

заполне́ни|е (-я) *ср* (*бака, резервуара*) filling; (*анкеты, бланка*) completion.

запо́лн|ить (-ю, -ишь; *impf* **заполня́ть**) *сов перех* (*бак, комнату*) to fill (up); (*анкету, бланк*) to fill in *или* out

▸ **запо́лниться** (*impf* **заполня́ться**) *сов возв* to fill up.

заполя́рный *прил* polar.

запомина́|ть (-ю) *несов от* **запо́мнить**

▸ **запомина́ться** *несов от* **запо́мниться**: **легко́/тру́дно** ~**ся** (*impf*) to be easy/difficult to remember.

запомина́ющ|ий (-ая, -ее, -ие) *прил* (*КОМП*):

~ее устро́йство memory; ~ее устро́йство с произво́льной вы́боркой random access memory.

запо́мн|ить (-ю, -ишь; *impf* **запомина́ть**) *сов перех* to remember

▸ **запо́мниться** (*impf* **запомина́ться**) *сов возв*: мне ~ились его́ слова́ I remembered his words.

за́понк|а (-и) *ж* cuff link.

запо́р (-а) *м* (*МЕД*) constipation; (*замок*) lock; **быть** (*impf*) **на** ~**е** to be locked.

запоро́ть (-орю́, -о́решь; *impf* **запа́рывать**) *сов перех* (*разг: испо́ртить*) to botch up.

запоро́ш|ить (*3sg* -ит) *сов перех безл* to sprinkle; **доро́гу** ~**и́ло сне́гом** a sprinkling of snow covered the road.

запотева́|ть (-ю) *несов от* **запоте́ть**.

запоте́вш|ий (-ая, -ее, -ие) *прил* misty.

запоте́|ть (-ю; *impf* **запотева́ть**) *сов неперех* to steam up.

запою́ *итп сов см* **запе́ть**.

запра́в|ить (-лю, -ишь; *impf* **заправля́ть**) *сов перех* (*руба́шку*) to tuck in; (*ла́мпу*) to fill; (*сала́т*) to dress; **заправля́ть** (~ *perf*) **маши́ну** to fill up the engine

▸ **запра́виться** (*impf* **заправля́ться**) *сов возв* (*разг: горю́чим*) to tank up; (: *пое́сть*) to fuel up.

запра́в|ка (-ки; *gen pl* -ок) *ж* (*маши́ны, самолёта итп*) refuelling; (*КУЛИН*) dressing; (*разг: также:* ~**очная ста́нция**) filling station.

заправлю́(сь) *сов см* **запра́вить(ся)**.

заправля́|ть (-ю) *несов от* **запра́вить** ♦ *неперех*: ~ (+*instr*) (*разг: дела́ми итп*) to be in charge (of)

▸ **заправля́ться** *несов возв от* **запра́виться**.

запра́вок *сущ см* **запра́вка**.

запра́вск|ий (-ая, -ое, -ие) *прил* true, real.

запра́шива|ть (-ю) *несов от* **запроси́ть**.

запре́т (-а) *м*: ~ (**на** +*acc, +infin*) ban (on/on doing); **быть** (*impf*) **под** ~**ом** to be banned.

запре́тен *прил см* **запре́тный**.

запре|ти́ть (-щу́, -ти́шь; *impf* **запреща́ть**) *сов перех* to ban.

запре́т|ный (-ен, -на, -но) *прил* forbidden; ~**ная те́ма** taboo subject; **запре́тная зо́на** restricted area *или* zone; **запре́тный плод** forbidden fruit.

запреща́|ть (-ю) *несов от* **запрети́ть**.

▸ **запреща́ться** *несов возв* to be forbidden *или* prohibited.

запреще́ни|е (-я) *ср* banning.

запрещ|ённый (-, -а, -о) *прил* banned; **запрещённый приём** (*СПОРТ*) foul; (*перен*) underhand tactic.

запрещу́ *сов см* **запрети́ть**.

запрограмми́р|овать (-ую) *сов от* **программи́ровать**.

запроекти́р|овать (-ую) *сов от* **проекти́ровать**.

запроки́н|уть (-у, -ешь; *impf* **запроки́дывать**) *сов перех*: ~ **го́лову** to throw one's head back

▸ **запроки́нуться** (*impf* **запроки́дываться**) *сов возв* to jerk backwards.

запропа|сти́ться (-щу́сь, -сти́шься) *сов неперех* (*разг*) to disappear.

запро́с (-а) *м* inquiry; (*обычно мн: тре́бования*) need, requirement; (*стремле́ния*) expectation.

запро|си́ть (-ошу́, -о́сишь; *impf* **запра́шивать**) *сов перех* (*мне́ние, отве́т итп*) to request; (*це́ну*) to ask.

за́просто *нареч* (*разг: без уси́лий*) easily; (*без церемо́ний*) without making a fuss; **он обы́чно захо́дит к нам** ~ he usually just drops in.

запротесто́ва|ть (-ю) *сов неперех* to start protesting.

запротоколи́р|овать (-ую) *сов от* **протоколи́ровать**.

запрошу́ *сов см* **запроси́ть**.

запру́(сь) *итп сов см* **запере́ть(ся)**.

запру́д|а (-ы) *ж* (*плоти́на*) weir; (*водоём*) millpond.

запру|ди́ть (-жу́, -у́дишь; *impf* **запру́живать** *или* **пруди́ть**) *сов перех* (*ре́ку, руче́й*) to dam; (*impf* **запру́живать**; *перен: пло́щадь итп*) to pack.

запры́га|ть (-ю) *сов неперех* to start jumping.

запря́чь (-ягу́, -яжёшь итп, -ягу́т; *pt* -я́г, -ягла́, -ягло́, *impf* **запряга́ть**) *сов перех* (*ло́шадь*) to harness, hitch up; (*разг: нагрузи́ть рабо́той*) to weigh down.

запу́ган|ный (-, -на, -но) *прил* frightened, scared.

запуга́|ть (-ю; *impf* **запу́гивать**) *сов перех* to frighten, scare.

за́пуск (-а) *м* (*мото́ра, станка́*) starting; (*раке́ты, спу́тника*) launch.

запуска́|ть (-ю) *несов от* **запусти́ть**.

запусте́ни|е (-я) *ср* neglect.

запу|сти́ть (-щу́, -у́стишь; *impf* **запуска́ть**) *сов перех* (*бро́сить*) to hurl; (*мото́р, стано́к*) to start (up); (*раке́ту, спу́тник*) to launch; (*хозя́йство, рабо́ту, боле́знь*) to neglect; (*разг: ру́ку, ко́гти*) to plunge; (: *впусти́ть*) to let in ♦ *неперех*: ~ **чем-н в кого́-н** to hurl sth at sb; **запуска́ть** (~ *perf*) **что-н в произво́дство** to launch production of sth.

запу́тан|ный (-, -на, -но) *прил* (*ни́тки, во́лосы*) tangled, entangled; (*де́ло, вопро́с*) confused; (*фра́за*) muddled.

запу́та|ть (-ю) *сов от* **пу́тать** ♦ (*impf* **запу́тывать**) *перех* (*ни́тки, во́лосы*) to tangle; (*вопро́с, челове́ка*) to confuse

▸ **запу́таться** *сов от* **пу́таться** ♦ (*impf* **запу́тываться**) *возв* (*ни́тки, во́лосы*) to become tangled (up); (*челове́к: в верёвках*) to get tangled *или* caught up; (*де́ло, вопро́с*) to become confused; (*разг: сби́ться с то́лку*) to get o.s. in a tangle; (: *сби́ться с пути́*) to get lost; **запу́тываться** (~**ся** *perf*) **в долга́х** to become trapped in debt; **запу́тываться** (~**ся** *perf*) **в отве́те** to get muddled up.

запу́щен|ный (-, -на, -но) *прил* neglected.

запущу́ *сов см* **запусти́ть.**

запча́ст|ь (**-и**) *ж сокр* = *запасна́я часть*; (*обычно мн*) spare (part).

запыла́ть (**-ю**) *сов неперех* (*костёр, камин*) to flare up; (*щёки, человек*) to flush.

запыл|и́ть(ся) (**-ю́(сь)**, **-и́шь(ся)**) *сов от* **пыли́ть(ся).**

запыха́ться (**-юсь**) *сов возв* to be out of breath.

запью́ *итп сов см* **запи́ть.**

запя́ст|ье (**-ья**; *gen pl* **-ий**) *ср* wrist.

запя́т|ая (**-ой**; *decl like adj*) *ж* comma.

запятна́ть (**-ю**) *сов от* **пятна́ть.**

зарабо́та|ть (**-ю**; *impf* **зараба́тывать**) *сов перех* to earn ◆ *неперех* (*no impf*; *начать работать*) to start up

▶ **зарабо́таться** (*impf* **зараба́тываться**) *сов возв* (*разг*) to work o.s. into the ground.

за́работка *сущ см* **за́работок.**

за́работн|ый *прил*: **~ая пла́та** pay, wages *мн.*

за́работ|ок (**-ка**) *м* earnings *мн.*

зара́внива|ть (**-ю**) *несов от* **заровня́ть.**

заража́ть(ся) (**-ю(сь)**) *несов от* **зарази́ть(ся).**

зараже́ни|е (**-я**) *ср* (*организма, крови итп*) infection; (*местности, водоёма итп*) contamination.

заражён|ный (**-**, **-а**, **-о**) *прил* (*см сущ*) infected; contaminated.

заражу́(сь) *сов см* **зарази́ть(ся).**

зара́з|а (**-ы**) *ж* infection ◆ *м/ж* (*разг: мерзавец*) pain, pest.

зара́зен *прил см* **зара́зный.**

зарази́тельный (**-ен**, **-ьна**, **-ьно**) *прил* (*перен*) infectious.

зара|зи́ть (**-жу́**, **-зи́шь**; *impf* **заража́ть**) *сов перех* (*человека: также перен*) to infect; (*воду, местность*) to contaminate

▶ **зарази́ться** (*impf* **заража́ться**) *сов возв* (*+instr; гриппом, корью итп*) to catch; (*перен: страхом, весельем*) to be infected by.

зара́з|ный (**-ен**, **-на**, **-но**) *прил* infectious.

зара́нее *нареч* in advance.

зар|асти́ (**-асту́**, **-астёшь**; *pt* **-о́с**, **-осла́**, **-осло́**, *impf* **зараста́ть**) *сов неперех* (*зажить: рана, порез*) to close up; **зараста́ть** (**~** *perf*) (*+instr*) (*травой итп*) to be overgrown (with); **он ~о́с** **щети́ной** he has let his beard grow.

зарв|а́ться (**-у́сь**, **-ёшься**; *impf* **зарыва́ться**) *сов неперех* (*разг*) to go too far; **зарыва́ться** (**~** *perf*) **в тре́бованиях** to demand too much.

зарёван|ный (**-**, **-а**, **-о**) *прил* (*разг*) = **запла́канный.**

зареве́ть (**-у́**, **-ёшь**) *сов неперех* (*медведь, лев*) to start roaring; (*бык*) to start bellowing; (*разг: заплакать*) to start bawling.

за́рев|о (**-а**) *ср* glow.

зарегистри́рованный *прил* registered; **~ торго́вый знак** registered trademark.

зарегистри́р|овать (**-ую**) *сов от* регистри́ровать.

заре́жу(сь) *итп сов см* **заре́зать(ся).**

заре́з (**-а**) *м*: **по ~**, **до ~у** (*разг*) badly; **мне по ~ нужна́ твоя́ по́мощь** I badly need your help.

заре́|зать (**-жу**, **-жешь**) *сов от* **ре́зать** ◆ *перех* (*человека*) to knife; (*impf* **ре́зать**; *козу, поросёнка*) to slaughter; (*разг: книгу, проект*) to axe (*BRIT*), ax (*US*)

▶ **заре́заться** *сов возв* (*разг*) to knife o.s.

зарека́|ться (**-юсь**) *несов от* **заре́чься.**

зарекоменд|ова́ть (**-у́ю**; *impf* **зарекоменд-о́вывать**) *сов перех*: **~ себя́** +*instr* to prove *или* show o.s. to be; **он хорошо́ себя́ ~ова́л** he proved to be good.

зар|е́чься (**-еку́сь**, **-ечёшься** *итп*, **-еку́тся**; *pt* **-ёкся**, **-екла́сь**, **-екло́сь**, *impf* **зарека́ться**) *сов возв* (+*infin*) to swear *или* vow never to do; **она́ ~екла́сь ходи́ть туда́** she vowed never to go there.

заржа́ве|ть (**3sg** **-ет**) *сов от* **ржа́веть.**

заржа́влен|ный (**-**, **-а**, **-о**) *прил* rusty.

заржа́ть (**-у́**, **-ёшь**) *сов неперех* (*лошадь*) to neigh; (*разг: человек*) to roar with laughter.

зарис|ова́ть (**-у́ю**; *impf* **зарисо́вывать**) *сов перех* (*дом, лодку*) to sketch; **они́ ~ова́ли всю сте́ну** (*разг*) they drew all over the wall.

зарисо́в|ка (**-ки**; *gen pl* **-ок**) *ж* (*действие*) sketching; (*обычно мн: рисунок*) sketch.

зарисо́выва|ть (**-ю**) *несов от* **зарисова́ть.**

зарни́ц|а (**-ы**) *ж* sheet lightning.

заровня́ть (**-ю**; *impf* **зара́внивать**) *сов перех* (*поверхность*) to level; (*яму, канаву*) to fill up.

зарод|и́ться (**3sg** **-и́тся**, **3pl** **-я́тся**, *impf* **зарожда́ться**) *сов возв* (*явление*) to emerge; (*перен: идея*) to be born; (: *чувство, сомнения*) to arise.

заро́дыш (**-а**) *м* (*био*) embryo (*растения, также перен*) germ; **в ~е** (*перен*) in embryo; **подавля́ть (подави́ть** *perf*) **что-н в ~е** to nip sth in the bud.

зарожда́|ться (**3sg** **-ется**, **3pl** **-ются**) *несов от* **зароди́ться.**

зарожде́ни|е (**-я**) *ср* (*жизни*) emergence; (*идеи, чувства*) conception.

заро́к (**-а**) *м* pledge, vow.

заро́с *итп сов см* **зарасти́.**

за́росл|ь (**-и**; *обычно мн*) *ж* thicket.

зарпла́т|а (**-ы**) *ж* pay.

заруба́|ть (**-ю**) *несов от* **заруби́ть.**

зарубе́жный *прил* foreign.

зарубе́жь|е (**-я**) *ср* overseas; **стра́ны бли́жнего ~я** "near abroad" (*the republics of the former USSR*).

зар|уби́ть (**-ублю́**, **-у́бишь**; *impf* **заруба́ть**) *сов перех* to hack down; **~уби́ себе́ на носу́** *или* **лбу** (*разг*) mark my words.

зару́б|ка (**-и**) *ж* notch.

зарублю́ *сов см* **заруби́ть.**

зарубц|ева́ться (*3sg* -у́ется, *3pl* -у́ются) *сов от* **рубцева́ться ♦** (*impf* **зарубцо́вываться**) *возв* to cicatrize.

зарумя́н|иться (-юсь, -ишься; *impf* **зарумя́ниваться**) *сов возв* (*лицо, щёки*) to colour (*BRIT*), color (*US*); (*пирог, мясо*) to brown.

заруч|и́ться (-у́сь, -и́шься; *impf* **заруча́ться**) *сов возв* (+*instr*; *помощью, согласием*) to secure.

зарыва́|ть (-ю) *несов от* **зары́ть**
▶ **зарыва́ться** *несов от* **зары́ться, зарва́ться.**

зарыда́|ть (-ю) *сов неперех* to begin to weep.

зар|ы́ть (-о́ю, -о́ешь; *impf* **зарыва́ть**) *сов перех* to bury; (*яму, канаву*) to fill
▶ **зары́ться** (*impf* **зарыва́ться**) *сов возв*: ~ся в +*acc* (*в землю, в песок*) to bury o.s. in; **зарыва́ться** (~ся *perf*) **в рабо́ту/учёбу** to bury o.s. in one's work/books; **она́ ~ы́лась голово́й в поду́шку** she buried her head in the pillow.

зар|я́ (-и́; *nom pl* **зо́ри**, *gen pl* **зорь**, *dat pl* **зо́рям**) *ж* (*утренняя, также перен*) dawn; (*вечерняя*) sundown; (*ВОЕН*) reveille; **ни свет ни ~** at the crack of dawn; **от ~и́ до ~и́** from dawn to dusk.

заря́д (-а) *м* (*ВОЕН, ЭЛЕК*) charge; (*перен*: *бодрости, энергии*) charge, boost.

заряди́ть (-жу́, -ди́шь; *impf* **заряжа́ть**) *сов перех* (*пистолет, пушку, фотоаппарат*) to load; (*батарейку, аккумулятор*) to charge; **он ~ди́л одно́ и то же** (*разг*) he keeps going on about it; **дождь ~ди́л** (*разг*) it started pouring
▶ **заряди́ться** (*impf* **заряжа́ться**) *сов возв* (*батарейка, аккумулятор*) to recharge; **заряжа́ться** (~ся *perf*) **эне́ргией** (*перен*) to recharge one's batteries.

заря́д|ка (-и) *ж* (*упражнения*) exercises *мн*.

заряжа́|ть(ся) (-ю(сь)) *несов от* **заряди́ть(ся).**

заряжу́(сь) *сов см* **заряди́ть(ся).**

заса́д|а (-ы) *ж* ambush; (*отряд*) ambush party; **устра́ивать** (**устро́ить** *perf*) **~у** to set up an ambush; **сиде́ть** (*impf*) **в ~е** to lie in ambush.

зас|ади́ть (-ажу́, -а́дишь; *impf* **заса́живать**) *сов перех* (*грядку, клумбу*): ~ (+*instr*) to plant (with); (*разг*: *нож, топор*): ~ **в** +*acc* to sink into; ~ (*perf*) **кого́-н за решётку** (*разг*) to stick sb behind bars; **заса́живать** (~ *perf*) **кого́-н за рабо́ту** to set sb to work.

заса́ленный *прил* greasy.

заса́лива|ть (-ю) *несов от* **засоли́ть, заса́лить**
▶ **заса́ливаться** *несов от* **заса́литься.**

заса́л|ить (-ю, -ишь; *impf* **заса́ливать**) *сов перех* to soil
▶ **заса́литься** (*impf* **заса́ливаться**) *сов возв* to get greasy.

заса́сыва|ть (*3sg* -ет, *3pl* -ют) *несов от* **засоса́ть.**

заса́харенн|ый *прил*: ~ые фру́кты crystallized fruits *мн*.

заса́хар|ить (-ю, -ишь; *impf* **заса́харивать**) *сов перех* to crystallize
▶ **заса́хариться** (*impf* **заса́хариваться**) *сов*

возв (*мёд, варенье*) to crystallize.

засверка́|ть (-ю) *сов неперех* (*молния, глаза*) to flash.

засв|ети́ть (-ечу́, -е́тишь; *impf* **засве́чивать**) *сов перех* (*ФОТО*) to expose
▶ **засвети́ться** (*impf* **засве́чиваться**) *сов возв* to be exposed.

за́светло *нареч* before nightfall *или* dark.

засве́чива|ть(ся) (-ю(сь)) *несов от* **засвети́ть(ся).**

засвечу́(сь) *сов см* **засвети́ть(ся).**

засвиде́тельств|овать (-ую) *сов перех* (*факт*) to testify to; (*документ, копию*) to certify.

засева́|ть (-ю) *несов от* **засе́ять.**

заседа́ни|е (-я) *ср* (*собрание*) meeting; (*парламента, суда*) session, sitting.

заседа́тел|ь (-я) *м*: **прися́жный ~** member of the jury.

заседа́|ть (-ю) *несов неперех* (*на совещании*) to meet; (*в парламенте, в суде*) to sit; (*парламент, суд*) to be in session.

засе́ива|ть (-ю) *несов от* **засе́ять.**

засёк *итп сов см* **засе́чь.**

засека́|ть (-ю) *несов от* **засе́чь.**

засекре́|тить (-чу, -тишь; *impf* **засекре́чивать**) *сов перех* (*сведения, документы*) to restrict access to.

засекре́ченный *прил* (*сведения, документы*) classified; (*завод итп*) secret.

засекре́чива|ть (-ю) *несов от* **засекре́тить.**

засекре́чу *сов см* **засекре́тить.**

засеку́ *итп сов см* **засе́чь.**

засе́л *итп сов см* **засе́сть.**

заселе́ни|е (-я) *ср* (*земель*) settlement; (*дома*) occupation.

заселённый (-ён, -ена́, -ено́) *прил* (*область, район*) settled; (*дом, квартира*) occupied.

засел|и́ть (-ю́, -и́шь; *impf* **заселя́ть**) *сов перех* (*земли*) to settle; (*дом*) to take up occupancy of.

зас|е́сть (-я́ду, -я́дешь; *pt* -е́л, -е́ла, -е́ло) *сов неперех* (*надолго остаться*: *дома*) to ensconce o.s.; (*спрятаться*) to sit tight; (*застрять*) to lodge; ~ (*perf*) **за что-н**/+*infin* to get down to sth/down to doing.

засе́ч|ка (-ки; *gen pl* -ек) *ж* notch.

засе́|чь (-еку́, -ечёшь итп, -еку́т; *pt* -ёк, -екла́, -екло́, *impf* **засека́ть**) *сов перех* (*место*) to locate; (*разг*: *заметить*) to nail down; (*выпороть*) to flog; **засека́ть** (~ *perf*) **вре́мя** to record the time.

засе́|ять (-ю; *impf* **засева́ть** *или* **засе́ивать**) *сов перех* to sow.

засиде́ться (-жу́сь, -ди́шься; *impf* **заси́живаться**) *сов неперех* to stay for a long time; **мы вчера́ ~де́лись в гостя́х** we stayed late at friends yesterday.

заси́ль|е (-я) *ср* dominance.

засия́|ть (-ю) *сов неперех* to begin to shine.

заско́к (-а) *м* (*разг*: *в мыслях*) peculiarity.

заскору́зл|ый (-, -а, -о) *прил* (*кожа, руки*)

calloused.

заск|очи́ть (-очу́, -о́чишь) *сов неперех* (*разг: в гости*) to drop in.

заскреж|ета́ть (-ещу́, -е́щешь) *сов неперех*: ~ **зуба́ми** to grind one's teeth.

заскуча́|ть (-ю) *сов неперех* to get bored; ~ (*perf*) **по кому́-н/чему́-н** to start to miss sb/sth.

за|сла́ть (-шлю́, -шлёшь; *impf* **засыла́ть**) *сов перех* to send out.

засло́н (-а) *м* screen, shield.

заслон|и́ть (-ю́, -и́шь; *impf* **заслоня́ть**) *сов перех* to block out; (*от ветра, от пули*) to shield, screen.

засло́н|ка (-ки; *gen pl* -ок) *ж* (*печи*) vent; (*шлюза*) gate.

заслоня́|ть (-ю) *несов от* **заслони́ть**.

заслу́г|а (-и) *ж* (*обычно мн*) service; ~**и пе́ред страно́й** services to one's country; **награди́ть** (*perf*) **кого́-н по ~м** to fully reward sb; **его́ наказа́ли по ~м** he got what he deserved.

заслу́женный *прил* well-deserved, well-merited; (*врач, учёный итп*) renowned; **Заслу́женный арти́ст Росси́и/ма́стер спо́рта** *title awarded by the state in honour of cultural/sporting achievement*.

заслу́жива|ть (-ю) *несов от* **заслужи́ть** ♦ *перех* (*дове́рия, внима́ния итп*) to deserve.

заслу́ж|ить (-ужу́, -у́жишь; *impf* **заслу́живать**) *сов перех* to earn.

заслу́ша|ть (-ю; *impf* **заслу́шивать**) *сов перех* to listen to.

▸ **заслу́шаться** (*impf* **заслу́шиваться**) *сов возв*: ~**ся** (+*instr*) (*му́зыкой, расска́зом*) to be captivated (by).

засма́трива|ться (-юсь) *несов от* **засмотре́ться**.

засме|я́ть (-ю́, -ёшь; *impf* **засме́ивать**) *сов перех* to taunt.

▸ **засмея́ться** *сов возв* to start laughing.

засм|отре́ться (-отрю́сь, -о́тришься; *impf* **засма́триваться**) *сов неперех*: ~ **на** +*acc* to be transfixed by.

заснё́жен|ный (-, -а, -о) *прил* snow-covered.

засн|у́ть (-у́, -ёшь; *impf* **засыпа́ть**) *сов неперех* to go to sleep, fall asleep.

засо́в (-а) *м* bolt.

засо́выва|ть (-ю) *несов от* **засу́нуть**.

засо́л (-а) *м* (*рыбы*) salting.

зас|оли́ть (-олю́, -о́лишь; *impf* **заса́ливать**) *сов перех* to salt.

засоре́ни|е (-я) *ср* (*рек*) pollution; (*ра́ковины, туале́та*) blockage; **засоре́ние желу́дка** stomach upset.

засор|и́ть (-ю́, -и́шь; *impf* **засоря́ть**) *сов перех* (*комнату, поля́ну*) to litter; (*ра́ковину, туале́т*) to block *или* clog up; (*перен: мысли, речь*) to contaminate; ~ (*perf*) **глаза́** to get grit in one's eyes; ~ (*perf*) **желу́док** to get a stomach upset

▸ **засори́ться** (*impf* **засоря́ться**) *сов возв* (*ра́ковина, туале́т*) to become clogged up.

засос|а́ть (-у́, -ёшь; *impf* **заса́сывать**) *сов перех* to suck in ♦ *неперех* (*no impf*; *подлеж*: *младе́нец*) to start feeding.

засо́хн|уть (-у, -ешь) *сов от* **со́хнуть** ♦ (*impf* **засыха́ть**) *неперех* (*грязь*) to dry up; (*расте́ние*) to wither.

за́спан|ный (-, -на, -но) *прил* sleepy.

заспо́р|ить (-ю, -ишь) *сов неперех* to start arguing.

заста́в|а (-ы) *ж* (*также*: **пограни́чная ~**) frontier post; (*ВОЕН: отря́д*) party, detachment.

застава́|ть (-ю́, -ёшь) *несов от* **заста́ть**.

заста́в|ить (-лю, -ишь; *impf* **заставля́ть**) *сов перех* (*заня́ть*) to clutter up; (*закры́ть*) to block off; **заставля́ть** (~ *perf*) **кого́-н** +*infin* to force sb to do, make sb do; **он ~л меня́ помо́чь ему́** he made me help him.

заста́ива|ться (*3sg* -ется, *3pl* -ются) *несов от* **засто́яться**.

заста́ну *итп сов см* **заста́ть**.

застаре́лый *прил* old.

заста́|ть (-ну, -нешь; *impf* **застава́ть**) *сов перех* to catch, find; **я его́ не ~л до́ма** I didn't manage to catch him at home; **я ~л её за рабо́той** I found her at work.

застегн|у́ть (-у́, -ёшь; *impf* **застёгивать**) *сов перех* to do up

▸ **застегну́ться** (*impf* **застёгиваться**) *сов возв* (*челове́к: на пу́говицы*) to button o.s. up; (: *на мо́лнию*) to zip o.s. up; (*пу́говицы, мо́лния*) to do up.

застё́ж|ка (-ки; *gen pl* -ек) *ж* fastener.

застекл|и́ть (-ю́, -и́шь; *impf* **застекля́ть**) *сов перех* to glaze.

застел|и́ть (-ю́, -ишь; *impf* **застила́ть**) *сов перех* (*крова́ть*) to make up; (*стол, пол*) to cover.

застелю́ *итп сов см* **застла́ть**.

засте́нка *сущ см* **засте́нок**.

засте́н|ок (-ка; *nom pl* -ки) *м* torture chamber.

засте́нчив|ый (-, -а, -о) *прил* shy.

застесня́|ться (-юсь) *сов возв* (*разг*) to go all shy.

засти́г *итп сов см* **засти́чь**.

застига́|ть (-ю) *несов от* **засти́гнуть, засти́чь**.

засти́гну *итп сов см* **засти́чь**.

засти́гн|уть (-ну, -нешь; *pt* - *или* -нул, -ла, -ло, *impf* **застига́ть**) *сов* = **засти́чь**.

застила́|ть (-ю) *несов от* **застели́ть, застла́ть**.

застира́|ть (-ю; *impf* **засти́рывать**) *сов перех* (*бельё, оде́жду*) to overwash; (*пятно́*) to wash off *или* out.

засти́|чь (-гну, -гнешь; *pt* -г, -гла, -гло, *impf* **застига́ть**) *сов перех* to catch.

застл|а́ть (-елю́, -е́лешь; *impf* **застила́ть**) *сов перех* (*подлеж: облака, туман*) to cover; (: *слёзы, дым*) to blur.

засто́|й (-я) *м* (*в делах, в работе*) standstill; (*в жизни, в мыслях*) stagnation.

засто́йный *прил* (*также перен*) stagnant.

засто́льн|ый *прил*: **~ые разгово́ры** table talk; **~ая пе́сня** drinking song.

застон|а́ть (-ону́, -о́нешь) *сов неперех* to groan.

засто́пор|ить (-ю, -ишь) *сов от* **сто́порить**

► **засто́пориться** *сов возв* (*машина, станок*) to come to a halt; (*дело, работа*) to be held up.

засто|я́ться (*3sg* -и́тся, *3pl* -я́ться, *impf* **заста́иваться**) *сов перех* (*вода*) to go stagnant.

застра́ива|ть (-ю) *несов от* **застро́ить**.

застрахо́ван|ный (-, -а, -о) *прил* insured.

застрах|ова́ть (-у́ю; *impf* **застрахо́вывать**) *сов перех*: **~** (**от** +*gen*) (*также перен*) to insure (against)

► **застрахова́ться** (*impf* **застрахо́вываться**) *сов возв*: **~ся** (**от** +*gen*) to insure o.s. (against).

застра́чива|ть (-ю) *несов от* **застрочи́ть**.

застрева́|ть (-ю) *несов от* **застря́ть**.

застрел|и́ть (-елю́, -е́лишь; *impf* **застре́ливать**) *сов перех* to shoot

► **застрели́ться** (*impf* **застре́ливаться**) *сов возв* to shoot o.s.

застро́енный *прил* built-up.

застро́|ить (-ю, -ишь; *impf* **застра́ивать**) *перех* to build on, develop.

застро́йк|а (-и) *ж* development.

застроч|и́ть (-у́, -и́шь; *impf* **застра́чивать**) *сов перех* (*выточки, складки*) to stitch ♦ *неперех* (*no impf; пулемёт*) to spray bullets; (*начать писать*) to start scribbling away.

застр|я́ть (-ну, -нешь; *impf* **застрева́ть**) *сов неперех* to get stuck.

застуд|и́ть (-ужу́, -у́дишь; *impf* **засту́живать**) *сов перех* (*разг*): **~ го́рло/у́ши** to get a sore throat/sore ears.

заступ|и́ться (-уплю́сь, -у́пишься; *impf* **заступа́ться**) *сов возв*: **~ за** +*acc* to stand up for.

засту́пник (-а) *м* defender.

засту́пниц|а (-ы) *ж см* **засту́пник**.

застыва́|ть (-ю) *несов от* **засты́ть**.

засты́вш|ий (-ая, -ее, -ие) *прил* (*также перен*) frozen; (*лава*) solidified; (*цемент, желе*) set.

засты́|ть (-ну, -нешь; *impf* **застыва́ть**) *сов неперех* to freeze; (*лава*) to solidify; (*цемент*) to set; **застыва́ть (~** *perf*) **на ме́сте** to freeze, stop dead; **~** (*perf*) **от стра́ха** to be paralysed with fear.

засуе|ти́ться (-чу́сь, -ти́шься) *сов возв* to start bustling about.

засу́н|уть (-у, -ешь; *impf* **засо́вывать**) *сов перех*: **~ что-н в** +*acc* to thrust sth into.

за́сух|а (-и) *ж* drought.

засухоусто́йчив|ый (-, -а, -о) *прил* drought-resistant.

засуч|и́ть (-учу́, -у́чишь; *impf* **засу́чивать**) *сов*

перех (*штанину, рукав*) to roll up; **~учи́в рукава́** (*перен*) in earnest.

засуш|и́ть (-ушу́, -у́шишь; *impf* **засу́шивать**) *сов перех* to dry up.

засу́шлив|ый (-, -а, -о) *прил* dry.

засчита́|ть (-ю; *impf* **засчи́тывать**) *сов перех* to take into account; (*гол, результат*) to allow (to stand).

засыла́|ть (-ю) *несов от* **засла́ть**.

засы́п|ать (-лю, -лешь; *impf* **засыпа́ть**) *сов перех* (*яму, канаву*) to fill (up); (*покрыть*) to cover; (*разг: студента*) to flunk; (*муку, крупу итп*) to pour; **засыпа́ть (~** *perf*) **кого́-н вопро́сами/пода́рками** to bombard sb with questions/gifts; **его́ ~ало песко́м** he was buried under the sand

► **засы́паться** (*impf* **засыпа́ться**) *сов возв*: **~ся** +*instr* (*песком, землёй*) to be covered with; (*разг: попасться*) to cock up; (: *на экзамене*) to flunk; **засыпа́ться (~ся** *perf*) **в** +*acc*/**за** +*acc* to get into/behind.

засыпа́|ть (-ю) *несов от* **засну́ть**, **засы́пать**.

► **засыпа́ться** *несов от* **засы́паться**.

засы́плю(сь) *итп сов см* **засы́пать(ся)**.

засыха́|ть (-ю) *несов от* **засо́хнуть**.

зася́ду *итп сов см* **засе́сть**.

зата|и́ть (-ю́, -и́шь; *impf* **зата́ивать**) *сов перех* (*неприязнь, мечту*) to harbour (*BRIT*), harbor (*US*); **зата́ивать (~** *perf*) **оби́ду** to harbour a grudge; **зата́ивать (~** *perf*) **дыха́ние** to hold one's breath

► **зата́иться** *сов возв* to hide.

зата́лкива|ть (-ю) *несов от* **затолка́ть**, **затолкну́ть**.

зата́плива|ть (-ю) *несов от* **затопи́ть**.

зата́птыва|ть (-ю) *несов от* **затопта́ть**.

зата́скан|ный (-, -на, -но) *прил* worn-out.

затаска́|ть (-ю; *impf* **зата́скивать**) *сов перех* (*разг: одежду, шутку*) to wear out; **зата́скивать (~** *perf*) **кого́-н по магази́нам** (*разг*) to drag sb round the shops; **~** (*perf*) **кого́-н по суда́м** (*разг*) to drag sb through the courts.

зата́скива|ть (-ю) *несов от* **затаска́ть**, **затащи́ть**.

зата́чива|ть (-ю) *несов от* **заточи́ть**.

затащ|и́ть (-ащу́, -а́щишь; *impf* **зата́скивать**) *сов перех* to drag; **~** (*perf*) **кого́-н в кино́** (*разг*) to drag sb off to the cinema.

затвердева́|ть (*3sg* -ет, *3pl* -ют) *несов от* **затверде́ть**.

затверде́лый *прил* hardened.

затверде́ни|е (-я) *ср* (*МЕД*) callus.

затверде́|ть (*3sg* -ет, *3pl* -ют, *impf* **затвердева́ть**) *сов неперех* (*земля, цемент*) to harden; (*жидкость*) to solidify.

затверд|и́ть (-жу́, -ди́шь) *сов от* **тверди́ть** ♦ (*impf* **затве́рживать**) *перех* to learn by rote.

затво́р (-а) *м* (*плотины*) floodgate; (*фотоаппарата*) shutter; (*винтовки*) breech.

затво́рник *м* (*РЕЛ*) hermit; (*перен*) hermit, recluse.

затво́рниц|**а** (-ы) *ж см* **затво́рник**.
затева́ть (-ю) *несов от* **зате́ять**.
зате́йлив|**ый** (-, -а, -о) *прил* intricate.
зате́йник (-а) *м* entertainer.
затёк *итп сов см* **зате́чь**.
затека́ть (-ю) *несов от* **зате́чь**.
затеку́т *сов см* **зате́чь**.
зате́м *нареч* (*потом*) then; (*для того*) for that reason; ~ **что́бы** in order to.
затемне́ни|**е** (-я) *ср* (*перен: рассудка*) obscuring; (*ВОЕН*) blackout.
затемнённый *прил* (*очки, стекло*) tinted.
затемн|**и́ть** (-ю́, -и́шь; *impf* **затемня́ть**) *сов перех* to darken; (*перен: рассудок*) to obscure; (*город, окна*) to black out.
за́темно *нареч* (*разг: до рассвета*) before light; (: *когда стемнело*) after dark.
затемня́|**ть** (-ю) *несов от* **затемни́ть**.
затен|**и́ть** (-ю́, -и́шь; *impf* **затеня́ть**) *сов перех* to shade; (*комнату*) to darken.
затеп|**ли́ться** (*3sg* -ится, *3pl* -ятся) *сов неперех* (*огонёк*) to begin to flicker; (*надежда*) to appear.
зат|**ере́ть** (-ру́, -рёшь; *pt* -ёр, -ёрла, -ёрло, *impf* **затира́ть**) *сов перех* (*пятно, надпись*) to rub out; (*перен: разг: работника*) to shackle; **её** ~**ёрли в толпе́** she got caught up in the crowd; **кора́бль** ~**ёрло льда́ми** the ship was icebound.
зате́рянный *прил* (*человек*) forgotten; (*место, дом*) forsaken.
затеря́|**ться** (-юсь) *сов от* **теря́ться** ♦ *возв* (*разг*) to go missing, disappear; (*в дали, в толпе*) to disappear.
зате́чь (*3sg* -ечёт, *3pl* -еку́т, *pt* -ёк, -екла́, -екло́, *impf* **затека́ть**) *сов неперех* (*опухнуть*) to swell up; (*онеметь*) to go numb; (*вода*) ~ **за** +*acc*/**в** +*acc* to seep behind/into.
затещу́сь *итп сов см* **затеса́ться**.
зате́|**я** (-и) *ж* (*замысел*) idea, scheme; (*забава*) escapade; **без** ~**й** without frills.
зате́|**ять** (-ю; *impf* **затева́ть**) *сов перех* (*разговор, игру*) to start (up); **он, ка́жется, что́-то затева́ет** (*разг*) he's got something up his sleeve.
затира́|**ть** (-ю) *несов от* **затере́ть**.
зати́х|**нуть** (-ну, -нешь; *pt* -, -ла, -ло, *impf* **затиха́ть**) *сов неперех* (*люди, место*) to quieten (*BRIT*) *или* quiet (*US*) down; (*шум, ветер, буря*) to die down.
зати́шь|**е** (-я) *ср* lull.
заткн|**у́ть** (-у́, -ёшь; *impf* **затыка́ть**) *сов перех* to stop up, plug; ~ (*perf*) **что-н за** +*acc*/**в** +*acc* to stuff sth behind/into; **затыка́ть** (~ *perf*) **кого́-н** *или* **рот кому́-н** (*разг*) to shut sb up; **затыка́ть** (~ *perf*) **кого́-н за по́яс** (*перен: разг*) to outdo sb
▶ **заткну́ться** (*impf* **затыка́ться**) *сов возв* (*разг: замолчать*) to shut up; ~**йсь!** (*разг: пренебр*) shut it!
затмева́|**ть** (-ю) *несов от* **затми́ть**.

затме́ни|**е** (-я) *ср* (*солнца, луны*) eclipse; (*разг: ума*) blackout; **на меня́ нашло́** ~ my mind went blank.
затм|**и́ть** (-и́шь; *impf* **затмева́ть**) *сов перех* (*также перен*) to eclipse.
зато́ *союз* (*также: но* ~: *однако*) but then (again); (*поэтому*) but (to make up for it); **кварти́ра ма́ленькая, (но)** ~ **в хоро́шем райо́не** the flat is small, but then again it's in a nice district.
затова́риванил|**е** (-я) *ср* (*КОММ: скопление товаров*) stockpiling; (*склада, магазина*) overstocking.
затова́р|**ить** (-ю, -ишь; *impf* **затова́ривать**) *сов перех* (*см сущ*) to stockpile; to overstock.
затолка́|**ть** (-ю; *impf* **зата́лкивать**) *сов перех* (*разг*) to shove; (*в автобусе, в толпе*) to squash.
затолкн|**у́ть** (-у́, -ёшь; *impf* **зата́лкивать**) *сов перех* to shove.
зато́н|**уть** (-ону́, -о́нешь) *сов неперех* to sink.
затоп|**и́ть** (-оплю́, -о́пишь; *impf* **зата́пливать**) *сов перех* (*печь, камин*) to light; (*impf* **затопля́ть**: *остров, деревню*) to flood; (*судно*) to sink.
затоп|**та́ть** (-опчу́, -о́пчешь; *impf* **зата́птывать**) *сов перех* (*цветы, газон*) to trample on; (*огонь, следы*) to stamp out; (*убить*) to trample to death.
зато́р (-а) *м* congestion; (*на улице*) traffic jam; (*на реке*) log jam.
затормоз|**и́ть(ся)** (-жу́, -зи́шь) *сов от* **тормози́ть(ся)**.
затороп|**и́ться** (-оплю́сь, -о́пишься) *сов возв* to hasten.
затоск|**ова́ть** (-у́ю) *сов неперех* to begin to feel melancholic; ~ (*perf*) **по** +*dat* to start to miss.
заточа́|**ть** (-ю) *несов от* **заточи́ть**.
заточе́ни|**е** (-я) *ср* incarceration.
зато́ч|**ить** (-очу́, -о́чишь; *impf* **зата́чивать**) *сов перех* to sharpen; (*impf* **заточа́ть**: *в тюрьму*) to incarcerate.
затошн|**и́ть** (*3sg* -и́т) *сов безл*: **меня́** ~**и́ло** I began to feel sick.
затра́в|**ить** (-влю́, -а́вишь) *сов от* **трави́ть** ♦ (*impf* **затра́вливать**) *перех* (*зайца, утку*) to hunt; (*перен: человека*) to harass.
затра́гива|**ть** (-ю) *несов от* **затро́нуть**.
затрапе́з|**ный** (-ен, -на, -но) *прил* (*разг*) shabby.
затра́т|**а** (-ы) *ж* expenditure.
затра́т|**ить** (-чу, -тишь; *impf* **затра́чивать**) *сов перех* to expend.
затре́б|**овать** (-ую) *сов перех* to request.
затреп|**ета́ть** (-ещу́, -е́щешь) *сов неперех* to begin to tremble.
затреща́|**ть** (-у́, -и́шь) *сов неперех* (*стул, дерево*) to start to split.

затре́щин|а (-ы) *ж* whack.

затро́н|уть (-у, -ешь; *impf* **затра́гивать**) *сов перех* (*подлеж: пуля*) to graze; (*перен: вопрос, тему*) to touch on; (: *душу, человека*) to affect; **затра́гивать** (~ *perf*) **чьё-н самолю́бие** to dent sb's ego.

затру́ *итп сов см* **затере́ть**.

затрудне́ни|е (-я) *ср* difficulty.

затрудне́нный (-ён, -ена́, -ено́) *прил* laboured (*BRIT*), labored (*US*).

затрудни́тел|ьный (-ен, -ьна, -ьно) *прил* difficult, awkward.

затрудн|и́ть (-ю́, -и́шь; *impf* **затрудня́ть**) *сов перех*: ~ **что-н** to make sth difficult; **е́сли Вас не** ~**и́т** if it isn't too much trouble

▶ **затрудни́ться** (*impf* **затрудня́ться**) *сов возв*: ~**ся с** +*instr* / +*infin* to have difficulty with/doing; **я** ~**я́юсь** (**Вам**) **сказа́ть** that is difficult to say.

затр|ясти́сь (-ясу́сь, -ясёшься; *pt* -я́сся, -ясла́сь, -ясло́сь) *сов возв* (to start) to shake.

затума́н|ить (-ю, -ишь) *сов от* **тума́нить**

▶ **затума́ниться** *сов от* **тума́ниться** ♦ (*impf* **затума́ниваться**) *возв* (*небо*) to cloud over; (*глаза*) to mist over; (*перен: сознание*) to become blurred.

зат|упи́ть (-уплю́, -у́пишь) *сов от* **тупи́ть** ♦ (*impf* **затупля́ть**) *перех* to blunt

▶ **затупи́ться** *сов от* **тупи́ться** ♦ (*impf* **затупля́ться**) *возв* to become blunt.

затух|нуть (*3sg* -нет, *3pl* -нут, *pt* -, -ла, -ло, *impf* **затуха́ть**) *сов неперех* (*огонь*) to die out; (*сигнал*) to die away; (*колебания*) to die down.

зату|шева́ть (-ю́ю; *impf* **затушёвывать**) *перех* to shade (in); (*перен: сгладить*) to brush over.

зат|уши́ть (-ушу́, -у́шишь) *сов от* **туши́ть**.

за́тхл|ый (-, -а, -о) *прил* stale; (*запах*) musty.

затыка́ть(ся) (-ю(сь)) *несов от* **заткну́ть(ся)**.

заты́л|ок (-ка) *м* the back of the head.

заты́ч|ка (-ки; *gen pl* -ек) *ж* (*разг*) stopper.

затю́ка|ть (-ю) *сов перех* (*разг*) to bug.

затя́гива|ть(ся) (-ю(сь)) *несов от* **затяну́ть(ся)**.

затя́ж|ка (-ки; *gen pl* -ек) *ж* (*промедление*) delay; (*при курении*) drag, puff.

затяжно́й *прил* protracted, prolonged; **затяжны́е дожди́** long periods of rain; **затяжно́й прыжо́к** delayed drop.

зат|яну́ть (-яну́, -я́нешь) *сов перех* (*шнурки, гайку*) to tighten; (*замедлить*) to drag out; (*вовлечь*): ~ **кого́-н в** +*acc* to drag sb into; **она́** ~**яну́ла та́лию по́ясом** she pulled the belt tight around her waist; **не́бо** ~**яну́ло ту́чами** storm clouds gathered in the sky; **затя́гивать** (~ *perf*) **пе́сню** to strike up a song

▶ **затяну́ться** (*impf* **затя́гиваться**) *сов возв* (*петля, узел*) to tighten; (*рана*) to close up; (*дело, переговоры итп*) to drag on; (*при курении*) to inhale; **затя́гиваться** (~**ся** *perf*) +*instr* (*поясом, корсетом*) to tighten.

зау́мный (-ен, -на, -но) *прил* unintelligible.

зауны́в|ный (-ен, -на, -но) *прил* mournful.

заупоко́й|ный *прил*: ~**ая моли́тва** prayer for the dead; **заупоко́йная слу́жба** funeral service.

заупря́м|иться (-люсь, -ишься) *сов возв* to become stubborn.

заурядный (-ен, -на, -но) *прил* unexceptional, mediocre.

заусе́н|ец (-ца; *nom pl* -цы) *м* (*на металле*) burr; (*у ногтя*) hangnail.

зау́трен|я (-и) *ж* (*РЕЛ*) dawn mass, ≈ matins.

зау́чен|ный (-, -на, -но) *прил* (*ответ, жест*) (pre)rehearsed.

за|учи́ть (-учу́, -у́чишь; *impf* **зау́чивать**) *сов перех* to memorize, learn

▶ **заучи́ться** (*impf* **зау́чиваться**) *сов возв* (*разг*) to study too hard.

зафарши́р|ова́ть (-у́ю) *сов от* **фарширова́ть**.

зафикси́р|овать (-ую) *сов от* **фикси́ровать**.

зафрахт|ова́ть (-у́ю; *impf* **зафрахто́вывать** *или* **фрахтова́ть**) *сов перех* to charter.

захва́л|ить (-ю, -ишь; *impf* **захва́ливать**) *сов перех* to overpraise.

захва́т (-а) *м* seizure, capture; (*СПОРТ*) hold; (*ТЕХ*) clamp.

захва|ти́ть (-чу́, -тишь; *impf* **захва́тывать**) *сов перех* to seize, capture; (*взять с собой*) to take; (*подлеж: музыка, работа*) to captivate; (*болезнь, пожар*) to catch (in time); **дух** ~**а́тывает** it takes your breath away; **у меня́ дух** ~**ати́ло от волне́ния** I was breathless with excitement.

захва́тническ|ий (-ая, -ое, -ие) *прил* (*намерения, политика*) aggressive; ~**ая война́** war of aggression.

захва́тчик (-а) *м* invader.

захва́тывающ|ий (-ая, -ее, -ие) *прил* (*книга, занятие*) gripping, absorbing; (*вид*) breathtaking.

захва́тыва|ть (-ю) *несов от* **захвати́ть**.

захвачу́ *итп сов см* **захвати́ть**.

захвора́|ть (-ю) *сов неперех* (*разг*) to be taken ill.

захире́|ть (-ю) *сов от* **хире́ть**.

захлам|и́ть (-лю́, -и́шь; *impf* **захламля́ть**) *сов перех* to clutter up.

захламлённый (-ён, -ена́, -ено́) *прил* cluttered.

захламлю́ *сов см* **захлами́ть**.

захламля́|ть (-ю) *несов от* **захлами́ть**.

захлебн|у́ться (-у́сь, -ёшься; *impf* **захлёбываться**) *сов возв* to choke; (*перен: атака, наступление*) to be stopped in its tracks; (: *мотор*) to fail to start; **захлёбываться** (~ *perf*) **от сме́ха/слёз** to choke with laughter/on one's tears; **захлёбываться** (~ *perf*) **от сча́стья/восто́рга** to gasp in joy/elation.

захлестн|у́ть (-у́, -ёшь; *impf* **захлёстывать**) *сов перех* (*подлеж: волна*) to swallow; (*перен: подлеж: чувство*) to overwhelm ♦ *неперех* (*вода*) to wash over.

захло́па|ть (-ю) *сов неперех* (*двери*) to slam;

(*выстрелы*) to crash out; (*слушатели, зрители*): ~ **(в ладо́ши)** to start clapping.

захло́пн|уть (**-у, -ешь**; *impf* **захло́пывать**) *сов перех*: ~ **что-н** to slam sth shut

▸ **захло́пнуться** (*impf* **захло́пываться**) *сов возв* to slam shut.

захо́д (**-а**) *м* (*также*: ~ **со́лнца**) sundown; (*в порт*) call; (*попытка*) go; **с пе́рвого/второ́го** ~**а** at the first/second attempt; **с** ~**ом/без захо́да в** +*acc* stopping off/without stopping off at.

захо|ди́ть (**-ожу́, -о́дишь**) *несов от* **зайти́** ♦ *сов непере́х* to start pacing.

захолу́сть|е (**-я**) *ср* provincial backwater.

захороне́ни|е (**-я**) *ср* (*действие*) burial; (*могила, могильник*) burial ground.

захор|они́ть (**-оню́, -о́нишь**) *сов перех* to bury.

зах|оте́ть (*как* **хоте́ть**; *см* **Table 16**) *сов (не)перех* to want

▸ **захоте́ться** *сов безл* (+*dat*): **мне** ~**оте́лось есть/пить** I started to feel hungry/thirsty.

захуда́лый *прил* wretched.

зацв|ести́ (*3sg* **-ете́т**, *3pl* **-ету́т**, *pt* **-ёл, -ела́, -ело́**, *impf* **зацвета́ть**) *сов непере́х* (*цветы*) to blossom, bloom; (*разг: сыр, хлеб*) to go mouldy (*BRIT*) *или* moldy (*US*).

зацел|ова́ть (**-у́ю**) *сов перех*: ~ **кого́-н** to smother sb with kisses.

зацементи́р|овать (**-ую**) *сов от* **цементи́ровать**.

зац|епи́ть (**-еплю́, -е́пишь**; *impf* **зацепля́ть**) *сов перех* (*поддеть*) to hook up; (*разг: случайно задеть*) to catch against

▸ **зацепи́ться** (*impf* **зацепля́ться**) *сов возв*: ~**ся за** +*acc* (*задеть за*) to catch *или* get caught on; (*ухвати́ться за*) to grab hold of; **я** ~**епи́лся рука́вом за гвоздь** I caught my sleeve on a nail.

заце́п|ка (**-ки**; *gen pl* **-ок**) *ж* (*перен*) pretext.

зацеплю́(сь) *сов см* **зацепи́ть(ся)**.

зацепля́ть(ся) (**-ю(сь)**) *несов от* **зацепи́ть(ся)**.

заци́кл|иться (**-юсь, -ишься**; *impf* **заци́кливаться**) *сов возв*: ~ **на** +*acc* (*разг*) to be crazy about.

зачар|ова́ть (**-у́ю**; *impf* **зачаро́вывать**) *сов перех* to enthral (*BRIT*), enthrall (*US*).

зача|сти́ть (**-щу́, -сти́шь**) *сов непере́х* to come more often; **дождь** ~**сти́л** the rain got heavier.

зачасту́ю *нареч* often.

зача́ти|е (**-я**) *ср* conception.

зача́т|ок (**-ка**; *nom pl* **-ки**) *м* (*обычно мн: любви, идеи итп*) beginning, germ *только ед*; **в** ~**ке** (*перен*) in embryo.

зача́точный (**-ен, -на, -но**) *прил* (*также перен*) embryonic; **в** ~**ном состоя́нии** in an embryonic state.

зач|а́ть (**-ну́, -нёшь**; *pt* **-а́л, -ала́, -а́ло**, *impf* **зачина́ть**) *сов (не)перех* to conceive.

зача́х|нуть (**-ну, -нешь**; *pt* **-**, **-ла, -ло**) *сов от* **ча́хнуть**.

зачащу́ *сов см* **зачасти́ть**.

заче́м *нареч* why; ~ **он э́то сде́лал?** why did he do it?; **ей ста́ло поня́тно,** ~ **он э́то сде́лал** it became clear to her why he had done it.

заче́м-нибудь *нареч* for any reason.

заче́м-то *нареч* for some reason.

зачеркн|у́ть (**-у́, -ёшь**; *impf* **зачёркивать**) *сов перех* to cross out; (*перен: прошлое*) to blot out.

зачерпн|у́ть (**-у́, -ёшь**; *impf* **заче́рпывать**) *сов перех* to scoop up.

зачерстве́|ть (**-ю**) *сов от* **черстве́ть**.

зач|еса́ть (**-ешу́, -е́шешь**; *impf* **зачёсывать**) *сов перех* to comb.

зач|е́сть (**-ту́, -тёшь**; *pt* **-ёл, -ла́, -ло́**, *impf* **зачи́тывать**) *сов перех* (*одобрить*) to pass; (*засчитать: диплом, опыт*) to take into account; **ему́** ~**ли отрабо́танные дни в счёт о́тпуска** he was given time off in lieu

▸ **заче́сться** (*impf* **зачи́тываться**) *сов возв* to be taken into account.

зачёсыва|ть (**-ю**) *несов от* **зачеса́ть**.

зачёт (**-а**) *м* (*ПРОСВЕЩ*) test; **сдава́ть** (*impf*)/ **сдать** (*perf*) ~ **по фи́зике** to sit (*BRIT*) *или* take/ pass a physics test.

зачётный *прил*: **зачётная рабо́та** assessed essay (*BRIT*), term paper (*US*); **зачётная кни́жка** assessment record book.

зачешу́ *итп сов см* **зачеса́ть**.

зачина́тель (**-я**) *м* originator.

зачина́|ть (**-ю**) *несов от* **зача́ть**.

зачи́нщик (**-а**) *м* instigator.

зачи́сл|ить (**-ю, -ишь**; *impf* **зачисля́ть**) *сов перех* (*в институт*) to enrol; (*на работу*) to take on; (*на счёт*) to enter; **зачисля́ть** (~ *perf*) **расхо́ды** to keep a record of expenditure

▸ **зачи́слиться** (*impf* **зачисля́ться**) *сов возв* (*в институт*) to enrol; (*на работу*) to be taken on.

зачита́|ть (**-ю**; *impf* **зачи́тывать**) *сов перех* (*прочесть вслух*) to read out; ~ (*perf*) **у кого́-н кни́гу** to borrow a book from sb and not give it back

▸ **зачита́ться** (*impf* **зачи́тываться**) *сов возв*: ~**ся** +*instr* (*книгой*) to be engrossed in; **я** ~**лся до утра́** I read until morning.

зачи́тыва|ть(ся) (**-ю(сь)**) *несов от* **заче́сть(ся)**, **зачита́ть(ся)**.

зачну́ *итп сов см* **зача́ть**.

зачту́(сь) *итп сов см* **заче́сть(ся)**.

зашага́|ть (**-ю**) *сов непере́х* to start walking.

зашата́|ться (**-юсь**) *сов возв* (*здание*) to start to shake; (*дерево, пьяница*) to begin to sway.

зашвырн|у́ть (**-у́, -нёшь**; *impf* **зашвы́ривать**) *сов перех* to hurl.

зашвыря́|ть (**-ю**) *сов перех*: ~ **кого́-н чем-н** to pelt sb with sth.

The spelling rules for Russian are shown on page xvii.

зашевел|и́ть (-ю́, -и́шь) *сов неперех* (+*instr*) to move

► **зашевели́ться** *сов возв* to move.

зашёл *сов см* **зайти́.**

заш|и́ть (-ью, -ьёшь) *impf* **зашива́ть**) *сов перех* (*дырку, носки*) to mend; (*шов, рану*) to stitch.

зашифр|ова́ть (-у́ю) *сов перех* (*impf* **зашифро́вывать**) *сов перех* to encode, put into code.

зашла́ *итп сов см* **зайти́.**

зашлю́ *итп сов см* **засла́ть.**

зашнур|ова́ть (-у́ю; *impf* **зашнуро́вывать**) *сов перех* to lace up.

зашпакл|ева́ть (-ю́ю) *сов от* **шпаклева́ть.**

зашто́па|ть (-ю; *impf* **што́пать**) *сов перех* to darn.

заштрих|ова́ть (-у́ю; *impf* **заштрихо́вывать**) *сов перех* to shade (in).

зашум|е́ть (-лю́, -и́шь) *сов неперех* (*люди, толпа*) to become noisy; **внизу́ ~е́ли голоса́** from downstairs came the sound of voices.

зашью́ *итп сов см* **заши́ть.**

защёлк|а (-и) *ж* (*на двери*) latch; (*на шкатулке, у замка*) catch.

защёлкн|уть (-у, -ешь; *impf* **защёлкивать**) *сов перех* to shut

► **защёлкнуться** (*impf* **защёлкиваться**) *сов возв* to click shut.

защем|и́ть (-лю́, -и́шь; *impf* **защемля́ть**) *сов перех* to clamp.

защи́т|а (-ы) *ж* (*также* ЮР, СПОРТ) defence (*BRIT*), defense (*US*); (*от комаров, пыли*) protection; (*диплома, диссертации*) viva (*open to the public*); **брать** (**взять** *perf*) **под ~у** to defend

защит|и́ть (-щу́, -ти́шь; *impf* **защища́ть**) *сов перех* to defend; (*от солнца, от комаров итп*) to protect; **защища́ть** (~ *perf*) **диссерта́цию** to defend one's thesis (*at public viva*)

► **защити́ться** (*impf* **защища́ться**) *сов возв* to defend o.s.; (*диссертант, студент*) to defend one's thesis.

защи́тник (-а) *м* (*также* СПОРТ) defender; (*ЮР*) defence counsel (*BRIT*), defense attorney (*US*); **ле́вый/пра́вый ~** (*футбол*) left/right back.

защи́тный *прил* protective; **защи́тный цвет** khaki.

защища́|ть (-ю) *несов от* **защити́ть** ◆ *перех* (*подсудимого, преступника*) to defend

► **защища́ться** *несов от* **защити́ться.**

защищу́(сь) *сов см* **защити́ть(ся).**

за|яви́ть (-явлю́, -я́вишь; *impf* **заявля́ть**) *сов перех* (*претензию, протест*) to declare ◆ *неперех*: ~ **о** +*prp* to announce; **заявля́ть** (~ *perf*) **о свои́х права́х** (**на** +*acc*) to claim one's rights (to); **заявля́ть** (~ *perf*) **на кого́-н в мили́цию** to report sb to the police

► **заяви́ться** (*impf* **заявля́ться**) *сов возв* (*разг*) to turn up.

зая́в|ка (-ки; *gen pl* -ок) *ж*: ~ (**на** +*acc*) application (for); (*на билеты*) order (for); ~ **на изобре́тение** patent application; **присыла́йте**

ва́ши ~ки по а́дресу ... please apply to the following address ....

заявле́ни|е (-я) *ср* (*правительства*) statement; (*просьба*): ~ (**о** +*prp*) application (for); **де́лать** (**сде́лать** *perf*) ~ to make a statement; **подава́ть** (**пода́ть** *perf*) ~ **на рабо́ту/об о́тпуске** to apply for a job/leave.

заявлю́(сь) *сов см* **заяви́ть(ся).**

заявля́|ть(ся) (-ю(сь)) *несов от* **заяви́ть(ся).**

зая́длый *прил* (*разг: курильщик*) inveterate; **он ~ футболи́ст/охо́тник** he is a football/hunting fanatic.

за́|яц (-йца) *м* (ЗООЛ) hare; (*разг: безбиле́тник*) fare dodger.

за́ячий (-ья, -ье, -ьи) *прил* (*мех, хвост*) hare's; **за́ячья губа́** harelip.

зва́ни|е (-я) *ср* (*воинское*) rank; (*учёное, почётное*) title; **присва́ивать** (**присво́ить** *perf*) **кому́** ~ to award sb a title.

зва́ный *прил*: ~ **гость** welcome guest; **зва́ный обе́д** dinner party.

зв|ать (зову́, зовёшь; *pt* -ал, -ала́, -а́ло, *perf* **позва́ть**) *несов перех* to call; (*приглашать*) to ask; (*no perf*; +*instr*; *называть*): ~ **кого́-н кем-н** to call sb sth; **как Вас зову́т?** what is your name?; **меня́/его́ зову́т Алекса́ндр** my/his name is Alexander; ~ (**позва́ть** *perf*) **кого́-н в го́сти/в кино́** to ask sb over/to the cinema

► **зва́ться** *несов возв* (+*instr*) to be called.

звезда́ (-ы́; *nom pl* **звёзды**) *ж* (*также перен*) star; **морска́я** ~ starfish.

звёздный *прил* (*ночь, небо*) starry, starlit; **э́то был его́ ~ час** that was his finest hour; **звёздные во́йны** Star Wars; **Звёздный городо́к** Star City (*training centre for Russian cosmonauts*).

звёздо́ч|ка (-ки; *gen pl* -ек) *ж уменьш от* **звезда́**; (*типог*) asterisk.

звен|е́ть (-ю́, -и́шь) *несов неперех* (*звонок*) to ring; (*колокольчик*) to jingle; (*голос*) to chime; (*стаканы*) to clink; (*монеты*) to jangle.

звен|о́ (-а́; *nom pl* -ья, *gen pl* -ьев) *ср* (*цепи, также перен*) link; (*конструкции*) section; (*ВОЕН: самолётов*) flight; (*в школе*) group; (*на работе*) team.

звер|е́ть (-ю; *perf* **озвере́ть**) *несов неперех* to go wild.

звери́н|ец (-ца) *м* menagerie.

звери́ный *прил* (*вой, тропа, шкура*) (wild) animal *опред*; (*перен: законы*) bestial; (: *страх, инстинкт*) animal *опред*.

зверово́дств|о (-а) *ср breeding of animals for their fur*.

звероло́в (-а) *м* trapper.

зве́рск|ий (-ая, -ое, -ие) *прил* (*убийство, поступок*) brutal, savage; (*разг: жара, аппетит*) wicked; (: *скука*) severe.

зве́рств|о (-а) *ср* (*жестокость*) brutality; (*обычно мн: ужас*) atrocity.

зве́рств|овать (-ую) *несов неперех* to commit atrocities.

зверь (-я; *gen pl* **-éй**) *м* beast, wild animal; (*перен*) beast, animal.

звон (-а) *м* clinking; (*колокола*) peal, chime.

звонáрь (-я) *м* bell-ringer.

звонить (-ю, -йшь; *perf* **позвонить**) *несов неперех* to ring; (*по телефону*): ~ **комý** to ring *или* phone *или* call (*US*) sb; ~ (*impf*) **в звонóк** to ring the bell.

звонка *сущ см* **звонóк**.

звóнкий (-óнок, -онкá, -óнко) *прил* (*голос, песня*) sonorous; (*дно, свод*) resonant; **звóнкий соглáсный** (*линг*) voiced consonant.

звонóк (-кá; *nom pl* **-ки**) *м* (*на двери, на велосипеде*) bell; (*звук*) ring; (*по телефону*) (telephone) call; **отсидéть** (*perf*) **от** ~**кá до** ~**кá** ≈ to work from nine to five.

звóнче *сравн прил от* **звóнкий**.

звук (-а) *м* sound; **он не произнёс ни звýка** he didn't utter a sound; **без звýка** (*сделать, согласиться*) without so much as a word.

звуковóй *прил* sound *опред*, audio; **звуковáя волнá** sound wave; **звуковáя дорóжка** track (*on audio tape*); **звуковáя аппаратýра** hi-fi equipment.

звукозáпис|ь (-и) *ж* sound recording; **стýдия** ~**и** recording studio.

звукоизоляци|я (-и) *ж* soundproofing.

звуконепроницáем|ый (-, -а, -о) *прил* soundproof.

звукооперáтор (-а) *м* sound technician.

звукоподражáни|е (-я) *ср* onomatopoeia.

звукоподражáтельн|ый *прил*: ~**ое слóво** onomatopoeic word.

звукопровóдност|ь (-и) *ж* conductivity (*of sound*).

звукопроводя́щ|ий (-яя, -ее, -ие) *прил* conductive (*of sound*).

звукорежиссёр (-а) *м* sound engineer.

звукоснимáтел|ь (-я) *м* pick-up.

звучáни|е (-я) *ср* sound; (*перен: политическое итп*) resonance.

звуч|áть (*3sg* **-ит**, *3pl* **-áт**) *несов неперех* (*издавать звуки*) to sound; (*раздаваться*) to be heard; ~**ит убедительно** it sounds convincing; **в её гóлосе** ~**áла обида** she sounded hurt.

звýчн|ый (-ýчен, -учнá, -ýчно) *прил* (*смех, голос*) deep, resounding; (*инструмент*) rich-sounding.

звя́кн|уть (-у, -ешь; *impf* **звя́кать**) *сов неперех* (*звонок*) to ring; (*стакан*) to clink; (*стекло*) to tinkle; (+*instr*; *стаканами*) to clink; (*ключами*) to jangle.

зги: **ни** ~ **не видно** it's pitch-black.

з-д *сокр* = **завóд**.

здáни|е (-я) *ср* building.

здесь *нареч* here; **есть ли** ~ **ктó-нибудь?** is (there) anyone here?; ~ **нет ничегó смешнóго** there's nothing funny about it.

здéшн|ий (-яя, -ее, -ие) *прил* (*разг*) local.

здорóва|ться (-юсь; *perf* **поздорóваться**) *несов возв*: ~ **с** +*instr* to say hello to; ~ (**поздорóваться** *perf*) **друг с дрýгом** to greet each other; ~ (**поздорóваться** *perf*) **зá руку** to shake hands.

здóрово *нареч* (*разг: отлично*) really well; (: *очень сильно*) terribly ♦ *как сказ* (*разг*) it's great.

здорóв|ый (-ó́в, -ó́ва, -ó́во) *прил* healthy; (*питание*) wholesome; (*перен: идея*) sound; (-ó́в, -овá, -овó; *разг: большой*) hefty; **бýдьте** ~**ó́вы!** (*при прощании*) take care!; (*при чихании*) bless you!

здорóв|ье (-я) *ср* health; **как Вáше** ~? how are you keeping?; **за Вáше** ~! (to) your good health!; **на** ~! enjoy it!

здрáвниц|а (-ы) *ж* convalescent home.

здрáво *нареч* sensibly.

здравомы́слящ|ий (-ая, -ее, -ие) *прил* sensible.

здравоохранéни|е (-я) *ср* health care; **систéма** ~**я** ≈ the Health Service (*BRIT*), ≈ Medicaid (*US*); **министéрство** ~**я** ≈ Department of Health.

здравоохранительный *прил* health-care.

здрáвств|овать (-ую) *несов неперех* to thrive; ~**уйте** hello; **да** ~**ует...!** long live ...!

здрáв|ый (-, -а, -о) *прил* (*политика, мысль*) sound.

зéбр|а (-ы) *ж* zebra; (*пешеходный переход*) zebra crossing (*BRIT*).

зев (-а) *м* pharynx.

зевá|ка (-и) *м/ж* (*разг*) idler.

зевá|ть (-ю) *несов неперех* to yawn; (*разг: глазеть*) to gawp; (*perf* **прозевáть**; *разг*) to miss out; **не** ~**й!** (*разг*) keep your wits about you!

зевкá *итп сущ см* **зевóк**.

зевн|ýть (-ý, -ёшь) *сов неперех* to yawn.

зевóк (-кá; *nom pl* **-ки**) *м* yawn.

зевóт|а (-ы) *ж* yawning.

зеленé|ть (-ю; *perf* **позеленéть**) *несов неперех* to go *или* turn green; **на горизóнте** ~**л лес** the green of the forest could be seen on the horizon.

зелён|ый (зéлен, зеленá, зéлено) *прил* (*также перен*) green; „**З**~**ые**" (*полит*) the Greens; **дать** (*perf*) **чемý-н** ~**ую ýлицу** to give sth the green light; **зелёные насаждéния** trees and shrubs; **зелёный лук** spring onion.

зéлен|ь (-и) *ж* (*цвет*) green ♦ *собир* (*растительность*) greenery; (*овощи и травы*) greens *мн*.

земéль *сущ см* **земля́**.

земéльн|ый *прил* land *опред*; ~ **надéл** *или* **учáсток** plot of land.

землевладéл|ец (-ьца) *м* landowner.

землевладéни|е (-я) *ср* landownership.

земледе́л|ец (-ьца) *м* arable farmer.
земледе́ли|е (-я) *ср* (*возделывание земли*) arable farming.
земледе́льца *сущ см* **земледе́лец**.
земледе́льческ|ий (-ая, -ое, -ие) *прил* (*район*) agricultural; (*машины*) farming *опред*.
землеме́рный *прил* surveying *опред*.
землепо́льзовани|е (-я) *ср* land tenure.
землеро́йн|ый *прил*: ~ые рабо́ты dredging; ~ая маши́на dredger.
землетрясе́ни|е (-я) *ср* earthquake.
землечерпа́лк|а (-и) *ж* dredger.
земли́ст|ый (-, -а, -о) *прил* (*цвет лица*) sallow; (*песок, торф*) earthy.
земл|я́ (-и́; *acc sg* -лю́, *nom pl* -ли, *gen pl* -е́ль) *ж* land; (*планета*) earth; (*поверхность*) ground; (*почва*) earth, soil.
земля́к (-а́) *м* compatriot.
земля́н|е (-) *мн* earth dwellers *мн*.
земляни́к|а (-и) *ж* (*растение*) wild strawberry; (*собир: ягоды*) wild stawberries *мн*.
земля́н|ка (-ки; *gen pl* -ок) *ж* dugout (*shelter*).
земляно́й *прил* (*вал, пол*) earthen; ~ые рабо́ты excavations; **земляно́й червь** earthworm.
земля́ч|ка (-ки; *gen pl* -ек) *ж см* **земля́к**.
земново́дн|ые (-ых; *decl like adj*) *мн* amphibians *мн*.
земново́дный *прил* amphibious.
земно́й *прил* (*поверхность, кора*) earth's; (*перен: блага, желания*) earthly; **земно́й шар** the globe.
зени́т (-а) *м* (*также перен*) zenith.
зени́т|ка (-ки; *gen pl* -ок) *ж* anti-aircraft gun.
зени́тный *прил* (*АСТРОНОМИЯ*) zenithal; (*ВОЕН*) anti-aircraft.
зёрен *сущ см* **зерно́**.
зерка́лен *прил см* **зерка́льный**.
зе́рк|ало (-ала; *nom pl* -ала́, *gen pl* -а́л, *dat pl* -ала́м) *ср* mirror; (*перен: воды, залива*) glassy surface.
зерка́льный (-ен, -ьна, -ьно) *прил* (*производство*) mirror *опред*; (*поверхность*) glassy; **его́ пье́са – э́то ~ное отображе́ние действи́тельности** his play is a true reflection of real life; ~ шкаф mirror wardrobe; **зерка́льный карп** mirror carp.
зерни́ст|ый (-, -а, -о) *прил* (*масса, снег*) granular; (*поверхность*) grainy; **зерни́стая икра́** unpressed caviar.
зерно́ (зерна́; *nom pl* зёрна, *gen pl* зёрен) *ср* (*пшеницы*) grain; (*кофе*) bean; (*мака*) seed; (*пороха*) granule ♦ *собир* (*семенное, на хлеб*) grain; ~ и́стины a grain of truth; **жемчу́жное ~** pearl.
зернов|о́й *прил* (*торговля, запас*) grain *опред*; **зерновы́е культу́ры** cereals *мн*.
зернов|ы́е (-ы́х; *decl like adj*) *мн* cereals *мн*.
зерносуши́л|ка (-и) *ж* grain drier.
зерноубо́рочный *прил* harvesting *опред*; ~ **комба́йн** combine harvester.

зернохрани́лище (-а) *ср* granary.
зефи́р (-а) *м* ≈ marshmallow.
зигза́г (-а) *м* zigzag.
зи́жд|иться (*3sg* -ится, *3pl* -утся) *несов возв*: ~ **на** +*prp* to be based on.
ЗИЛ *м сокр* = Моско́вский автомоби́льный заво́д и́мени И.А. Лихачёва; (*автомобиль*) *vehicle manufactured at the Moscow car factory*.
зим|а́ (-ы́; *acc sg* -у, *dat sg* -е́, *nom pl* -ы) *ж* winter.
Зимба́бве *ср нескл* Zimbabwe.
зимбабви́йск|ий (-ая, -ое, -ие) *прил* Zimbabwean.
зи́мн|ий (-яя, -ее, -ие) *прил* (*день*) winter's; (*погода*) wintry; (*лес, одежда*) winter *опред*.
зим|ова́ть (-у́ю; *perf* **прозимова́ть**) *несов неперех* (*человек*) to spend the winter; (*птицы*) to winter.
зимо́в|ка (-ки; *gen pl* -ок) *ж* wintering place; (*для птиц*) wintering ground; **остава́ться (оста́ться** *perf*) **на ~ку** to spend the winter.
зимо́вь|е (-я) *ср* (*для людей*) winter hut; (*зверей, птиц*) wintering ground.
зимо́й *нареч* in the winter.
зия́|ть (*3sg* -ет, *3pl* -ют) *несов неперех* to gape.
злак (-а) *м* grass; **зернов|о́й** ~ cereal.
зла́чн|ый *прил*: ~ое ме́сто (*разг*) den of iniquity.
зле́йш|ий (-ая, -ее, -ие) *превос прил*: ~ **враг** worst enemy.
зл|ить (-ю, -ишь; *perf* **разозли́ть**) *несов перех* to annoy.
▶ **зли́ться** (*perf* **разозли́ться**) *несов возв* to get angry.
зло (зла; *gen pl* зол) *ср* evil; (*неприятность*) harm ♦ *нареч* (*посмотреть, сказать*) spitefully; **со зла** out of spite; **причиня́ть (причини́ть** *perf*) **кому́-н** ~ to cause sb harm; **меня́** ~ **берёт** (*разг*) it makes me angry; **у меня́ на неё зла не хвата́ет** (*разг*) she annoys me no end; **из двух зол выбира́ть (вы́брать** *perf*) **ме́ньшее** to choose the lesser of two evils.
зло́б|а (-ы) *ж* malice; **статья́ на ~у дня** an article tackling the burning issue of the moment.
зло́бн|ый (-ен, -на, -но) *прил* (*характер, человек*) mean; (*улыбка*) hateful, wicked; (*тон, голос*) nasty.
злободне́вный (-ен, -на, -но) *прил* topical.
зло́бств|овать (-ую) *несов неперех* to rage.
злове́щ|ий (-ая, -ее, -ие; -, -а, -е) *прил* (*улыбка, вид, слухи*) sinister; (*тишина*) ominous.
зловно́нен *прил см* **злово́нный**.
злово́ни|е (-я) *ср* noxious odour (*BRIT*) или odor (*US*).
злово́нный (-ен, -на, -но) *прил* rank, fetid.
зловре́дный (-ен, -на, -но) *прил* mean, horrid.
злоде́|й (-я) *м* villain.
злоде́й|ка (-и) *ж см* **злоде́й**.
злоде́йский (-ая, -ое, -ие) *прил* wicked.
злоде́йств|о (-а) *ср* act of evil.
злодея́ни|е (-я) *ср* evil deed, crime.
злой (зол, зла, зло) *прил* (*человек, жена*) mean,

bad-tempered; (*соба́ка*) vicious; (*глаза́, лицо́*) mean; (*мы́сли*) evil; (*карикату́ра, замеча́ние*) scathing; (*перен: разг: моро́з*) cruel; (: *пе́рец, горчи́ца*) lethal; **я зол на тебя́** I'm angry with you; **без зло́го у́мысла** no harm meant; **зла́я судьба́** cruel fate; **злы́е языки́** malicious talk.

злока́чествен|ный (-, -на, -но) *прил* malignant.

злоключе́ни|е (-я) *ср* misadventure.

злонаме́рен|ный (-, -на, -но) *прил* ill-intentioned.

злопа́мят|ный (-ен, -на, -но) *прил* (*челове́к*) unforgiving.

злополу́ч|ный (-ен, -на, -но) *прил* (*охо́тник*) ill-fated; (*день, час*) fateful.

злопыха́тел|ь (-я) *м* malevolent person (*мн* people).

злопы́ха|ть (-ю) *несов непере*х to rant.

злора́д|ный (-ен, -на, -но) *прил* gloating.

злора́дств|о (-а) *ср* malicious pleasure.

злора́дств|овать (-ую) *несов непере*х to gloat.

злосло́ви|е (-я) *ср* abuse, ridicule.

злосло́в|ить (-лю, -ишь) *несов непере*х to indulge in ridicule.

зло́ст|ный (-ен, -на, -но) *прил* (*наме́рение*) malicious; (*правонаруши́тель*) persistent.

злост|ь (-и) *ж* malice; **сказа́ть** (*perf*) **что-н со зло́стью** to say sth angrily.

злосча́ст|ный (-ен, -на, -но) *прил* ill-fated.

злоумы́шленник (-а) *м* conspirator.

злоумы́шленный *прил* (*посту́пок*) malicious.

злоупотреб|и́ть (-лю́, -и́шь; *impf* **злоупотребля́ть**) *сов непере*х (+*instr*) to abuse; (*дове́рием*) to breach; (*сла́дким*) to indulge in.

злоупотребле́ни|е (-я) *ср* (+*instr*) abuse of; (*обы́чно мн: незако́нные де́йствия*) malpractise; ~ **дове́рием** breach of confidence.

злоупотреблю́ *сов см* **злоупотреби́ть**.

злоупотребля́|ть (-ю) *несов от* **злоупотреби́ть**.

злю́к|а (-и) *м/ж* crosspatch.

змееви́к (-а́) *м* coil.

змеёныш (-а) *м* (*перен*) little sneak.

змеи́ный *прил* (*ко́жа*) snake *опред*; (*нора́, пито́мник*) snake's; (*перен: улы́бка, усме́шка*) venomous; ~ **яд** venom.

зме́|й (-я; *gen pl* -ев) *м* serpent; (*та́кже:* **возду́шный** ~) kite; **змей-горы́ныч** many-headed dragon.

зме|я́ (-и́; *nom pl* -и́, *gen pl* -е́й) *ж* (*та́кже перен*) snake; **змея́ подколо́дная** (*разг*) snake in the grass.

знак (-а) *м* sign; (*мат, муз, типог*) symbol; (*комп*) character; **в** ~ +*gen* as a sign of; **под зна́ком** +*gen* in an atmosphere of; **знак ра́венства** equals sign; **зна́ки препина́ния** punctuation marks; **зна́ки разли́чия** (*воен*) stripes; **зна́ки отли́чия** decorations; **зна́ки зодиа́ка** signs of the Zodiac.

знако́м|ая (-ой; *decl like adj*) *ж см* **знако́мый**.

знако́м|ить (-лю, -ишь; *perf* **познако́мить**) *несов перех*: ~ **кого́-н с** +*instr* to introduce sb to; (*perf* **ознако́мить**; *с прика́зом, с докуме́нтом*) to acquaint sb with

▶ **знако́миться** (*perf* **познако́миться**) *несов возв*: ~**ся с** +*instr* (*с челове́ком*) to meet; (*perf* **ознако́миться**; *с прика́зом, с докуме́нтом*) to acquaint o.s. with.

знако́мств|о (-а) *ср* (*отноше́ния*) acquaintance; ~**а** (*круг знако́мых*) acquaintances; ~ **с** +*instr* acquaintance with; **пе́рвое** ~ **с** +*instr* first introduction to; **завя́зывать** (**завяза́ть** *perf*) ~ **с кем-н** to make sb's acquaintance.

знако́м|ый (-, -а, -о) *прил*: ~ (**с** +*instr*) familiar (with) ♦ (**-ого**; *decl like adj*) *м* acquaintance.

знамена́телен *прил см* **знамена́тельный**.

знамена́тел|ь (-я) *м* denominator; **приводи́ть** (**привести́** *perf*) **к о́бщему** ~**ю** to reduce to a common denominator.

знамена́тель|ный (-ен, -ьна, -ьно) *прил* momentous.

зна́мени *итп сущ см* **зна́мя**.

знаме́ни|е (-я) *ср* (*предзнаменова́ние*) omen; **знаме́ние вре́мени** sign of the times.

знамени́тост|ь (-и) *ж* celebrity.

знамени́т|ый (-, -а, -о) *прил* famous.

знамен|ова́ть (-у́ю) *несов перех* to mark.

знамено́с|ец (-ца) *м* standard-bearer.

зна́м|я (-ени; *как вре́мя; см* **Table 4**) *ср* banner; (*перен: руководя́щая иде́я*) flag; **под** ~**енем** +*gen* (*перен*) under the banner of.

зна́ни|е (-я) *ср* knowledge *то́лько ед*; **со** ~**м де́ла** knowledgeably.

зна́|тный (-́тен, -тна́, -́тно) *прил* (*род, челове́к*) noble; (*учёный*) prominent.

знато́к (-а́) *м* (*литерату́ры*) expert; (*вина́*) connoisseur.

зна|ть (-ти) *ж* nobility; ♦ (-ю) *несов перех* to know; **она́ не зна́ет ме́ры** she doesn't know when to stop; ~ (*impf*) **своё ме́сто** to know one's place; **кто (его́) зна́ет?** (*разг*) who knows?; **так и** ~**й** (*разг*) mark my words; ~ (*impf*) **це́ну** +*dat* to appreciate; **дава́ть** (**дать** *perf*) **себя́** ~ to make itself known; **как** ~ maybe; **как зна́ешь** as you wish; **он не** ~**л пораже́ний** he had never known defeat; **он не зна́ет уста́лости** he never tires; **я не зна́ю поко́я** I don't have a moment's peace

▶ **зна́ться** *несов возв*: **зна́ться с** +*instr* (*разг*) to associate with.

значе́ни|е (-я) *ср* (*сло́ва, взгля́да*) meaning; (*реше́ния, побе́ды*) importance; **э́то не име́ет** ~**я** it's not important; **придава́ть** (**прида́ть** *perf*) **осо́бое/большо́е** ~ **чему́-н** to attach special/ great importance to sth.

зна́чимост|ь (-и) *ж* (*ва́жность*) significance; (*нали́чие смы́сла*) meaningfulness.

зна́чим|ый (-, -а, -о) *прил* important; ~**ая часть**

сло́ва unit of meaning.

зна́чит вводн сл (разг) so ♦ союз (следовательно) that means; ~, ты не зна́ешь so, you don't know then; идёт снег, ~, сего́дня бу́дет хо́лодно it's snowing, that means it's going to be cold today.

значи́тел|ьный (-ен, -ьна, -ьно) прил significant; (вид, взгляд) meaningful; в ~ьной сте́пени to a significant degree.

зна́ч|ить (-у, -ишь) несов (не)перех to mean; что э́то ~ит? what does it mean?; э́то ничего́ не ~ит it doesn't mean anything

▶ зна́читься несов возв (состоять) to appear; (числиться): ~ся больны́м to be considered ill; его́ и́мя ~ится в спи́ске his name appears on the list.

знач|о́к (-ка́) м badge; (пометка) mark.

зна́юш|ий (-ая, -ее, -ие; -, -а, -е) прил competent.

зноб|и́ть (3sg -и́т) несов безл: его́ ~и́т he's shivery.

зно́ен прил см зно́йный.

зно|й (-я) м intense heat.

зно́|йный (-ен, -йна, -йно) прил (день, лето) scorching; (перен: взгляд) intense; (: чувство) burning.

зоб (-а; loc sg -у́, nom pl -ы́) м (у птицы) crop; (МЕД) goitre (BRIT), goiter (US).

зов (-а) м (о помощи, громкий) call; приходи́ть (прийти́ perf) по пе́рвому зо́ву to come at the first call.

зову́ итп несов см звать.

зодиа́к (-а) м zodiac.

зо́дчеств|о (-а) ср architecture.

зо́дч|ий (-его; decl like adj) м architect.

зол сущ см зло ♦ прил см злой.

зол|а́ (-ы́) ж cinders мн.

золо́в|ка (-ки; gen pl -ок) ж sister-in-law, husband's sister.

золоти́ст|ый (-, -а, -о) прил golden.

золот|и́ть (-чу́, -ти́шь; perf позолоти́ть) несов перех to gild; со́лнце позолоти́ло верху́шки дере́вьев the sun cast a golden light over the tree tops.

золотни́к (-а) м slide valve.

зо́лот|о (-а) ср gold; (золотые нити) gold thread; она́ про́сто ~ (перен) she's a real gem.

золотоиска́тел|ь (-я) м gold-digger.

золот|о́й прил gold; (рубль, локоны, лучи солнца итп) golden; (перен: человек, время) wonderful; (: работник) priceless ♦ (-о́го; decl like adj) м gold coin; (дорогой) precious; золота́я сва́дьба golden wedding или anniversary; золота́я середи́на the golden mean; золото́е дно gold mine; золото́е се́рдце heart of gold; золото́е пра́вило golden rule; золото́й век golden age; золото́й фонд gold reserves.

золотоно́с|ный (-ен, -на, -но) прил: ~ райо́н goldfield.

золотопромы́шленност|ь (-и) ж gold-

mining.

золочёный прил gilt.

золочу́ несов см золоти́ть.

Зо́лушк|а (-и) ж Cinderella.

зо́н|а (-ы) ж zone; (лесная) area; (для заключённых) prison; при́городная ~ suburb; ~ о́тдыха holiday area; ~ обстре́ла field of fire.

зона́л|ьный (-ен, -ьна, -ьно) прил (граница, деление) zone опред; (особенности, соревнование) regional.

зонд (-а) м (МЕД, ТЕХ) probe.

зонди́р|овать (-ую; perf прозонди́ровать) несов перех to probe; ~ (прозонди́ровать perf) по́чву или обстано́вку (перен) to test the water.

зонт (-а́) м (от дождя) umbrella; (от солнца) parasol; (над дверью, над ветриной) awning.

зо́нтик (-а) м (от дождя) umbrella; (от солнца) parasol.

зоо́лог (-а) м zoologist.

зоологи́ческ|ий (-ая, -ое, -ие) прил zoological.

зооло́ги|я (-и) ж zoology.

зоомагази́н (-а) м pet shop.

зоопа́рк (-а) м zoo.

зоотéхник (-а) м animal geneticist.

зо́ри итп сущ см заря́.

зо́р|кий (-кая, -кое, -кие; -ок, -ка, -ко) прил (человек) sharp-eyed; (глаза, ум) sharp; (перен: наблюдатель) observant.

зрач|о́к (-ка́) м (АНАТ) pupil.

зре́лищ|е (-а) ср (предмет обозрения) sight, spectacle; (представление) show.

зре́лищный прил: ~ые предприя́тия entertainment venues мн.

зре́лост|ь (-и) ж (плода, яблока) ripeness; (организма, человека) maturity.

зре́л|ый (-, -а, -о) прил mature; (плод, зерно) ripe.

зре́ни|е (-я) ср (eye)sight.

зре|ть (-ю; perf созре́ть) несов неперех to mature; (плод, яблоко) to ripen; (решение, мысль) to develop; (обида) to grow.

зри́тел|ь (-я) м (в театре, в кино) member of the audience; (на стадионе) spectator; (наблюдатель) onlooker.

зри́тельный прил (память, восприятие) visual; зри́тельный зал auditorium; зри́тельный нерв optic nerve.

зря нареч (разг: без пользы) for nothing, in vain; ~ тра́тить (impf) де́ньги/вре́мя to waste money/time; ~ ты ему́ э́то сказа́л you shouldn't have told him about it; ты ~ купи́л э́ту кни́гу there was no need to buy this book.

зря́ч|ий (-ая, -ее, -ие) прил sighted.

зуб (-а; nom pl -ы, gen pl -о́в) м tooth (мн teeth); (nom pl -ья, gen pl -ьев: пилы, шестерни) tooth (мн teeth); (грабель, вилки) prong; у неё ~ на́ ~ не попада́ет her teeth are chattering; говори́ть (impf) сквозь зу́бы (разг) to talk through one's teeth; э́то мне не по ~а́м (перен) it's too much for me; он вооружён до ~о́в he's armed to the teeth; **она́ на него́** ~ **име́ет** (*разг*) she bears a grudge against him; **ни в** ~ **ного́й** (*разг*) he *итп* doesn't have a clue; **зуб му́дрости** wisdom tooth.

зуба́ст|ый (-, -а, -о) *прил* (*разг*: *щука, собака*) with big sharp teeth; (*перен*: *разг*) sharp-tongued.

зуб|е́ц (-ца́; *nom pl* -цы́) *м* (*пилы, шестерни*) tooth (*мн* teeth); (*грабель, вилки*) prong.

зуби́л|о (-а) *ср* chisel.

зубка́ *итп сущ см* **зубо́к**.

зубно́й *прил* dental; **зубна́я боль** toothache; **зубна́я па́ста** toothpaste; **зубна́я щётка** toothbrush; **зубно́й врач** dentist; **зубно́й проте́з** dentures.

зубоврачéбный *прил*: ~ **кабинéт** dental surgery (*BRIT*), dentist's office (*US*).

зубоска́л (-а) *м* (*разг*) scoffer.

зубоска́л|ить (-ю, -ишь) *несов неперех* (*разг*) to scoff.

зубочи́ст|ка (-ки; *gen pl* -ок) *ж* toothpick.

зубр (-а) *м* bison; (*перен*: *ретроград*) die-hard; (*разг*: *опытный специалист*) boffin.

зубри́л|а (-ы) *м/ж* (*разг*) swot (*BRIT*), grind (*US*).

зубр|и́ть (-ю́, -йшь; *impf* **вы́зубрить**) *несов перех* (*разг*) to swot (*BRIT*), grind (*US*).

зубца́ *итп сущ см* **зубе́ц**.

зубча́т|ый *прил* (*стена, башня*) castellated; ~**ое колесо́** cog(wheel); ~**ая переда́ча** toothed

gear; ~ **край** serrated edge.

зуд (-а) *м* (*также перен*) itch.

зу|де́ть (*3sg* -ди́т, *3pl* -дя́т) *несов неперех* (*разг*: *чеса́ться*) to itch; (-жу́, -ди́шь; *комар, пчела́*) to buzz; (*перен*: *нуди́ться*) to nag.

ЗУПВ *сокр* (= *запомина́ющее устро́йство с произво́льной вы́боркой*) RAM (= *random access memory*).

зы́б|кий (-кая, -кое, -кие; -ок, -ка, -ко) *прил* (*поверхность озера*) ripply; (*грунт, болото*) swampy; (*основание*) shaky; (*перен*: *положение*) unstable.

зыбу́ч|ий (-ая, -ее, -ие; -, -а, -е) *прил*: ~**ие пески́** quicksands *мн*.

зы́б|ь (-и) *ж* ripple.

зы́ч|ный (-ен, -на, -но) *прил* (*голос*) booming; (*хохот*) thunderous.

зя́бко *как сказ* (*разг*: *холодно*): **мне** ~ I feel chilly.

зя́блик (-а) *м* chaffinch.

зя́бн|уть (-у, -ешь; *perf* **озя́бнуть**) *несов неперех* to be cold.

зяб|ь (-и) *ж field ploughed in autumn ready for sowing in the spring.*

зять (-я) *м* (*муж дочери*) son-in-law; (*муж сестры*) brother-in-law, sister's husband; (*муж золовки*) brother-in-law (*husband's sister's husband*).

~ И, и ~

И, и *сущ нескл (буква)* the 9th letter of the Russian alphabet.

KEYWORD

и *союз* **1** and; **я и мой друг** my friend and I; **и вот показа́лся лес** and then a forest appeared

2 *(тоже)*: **и он пошёл в теа́тр** he went to the theatre too; **и он не пришёл** he didn't come either

3 *(даже)* even; **и сам не рад** even he himself is not pleased

4 *(именно)*: **о том и речь!** that's just it!

5 *(во фразах)*: **ну и нагле́ц же ты!** what a cheek you have!; **туда́ и сюда́** here and there; **и ... и ...** both ... and ....

и́бо *союз (так как)* for, because.

и́в|а (-ы) *ж* willow.

ива́н-ча́|й (-я) *м (no pl)* rosebay willowherb.

и́вовый *прил* willow.

и́вол|га (-ги; *gen pl* -) *ж* oriole.

игл|а́ (-ы́; *nom pl* -ы) *ж* needle; *(у ежа)* spine; *(проигрывателя)* needle, stylus.

иглодержа́тел|ь (-я) *м (МЕД)* needleholder; *(проигрывателя)* cartridge.

иглоука́лывани|е (-я) *ср* acupuncture.

игнори́р|овать (-ую; *perf* **игнори́ровать** *или* **проигнори́ровать**) *несов перех* to ignore.

и́г|о (-а) *ср (рабства итп)* yoke.

иго́л|ка (-ки; *gen pl* -ок) *ж* = **игла́**; **сиде́ть** *(impf)* **как на ~х** to be on tenterhooks.

иго́льн|ый *прил*: **~ое у́шко** eye of a needle.

иго́льчатый *прил (мех)* spiky; *(подшипник)* needle *опред*.

иго́рный *прил*: **~ дом** gaming club.

игр|а́ (-ы́; *nom pl* -ы) *ж* game; *(на скрипке итп)* playing; *(актёра)* performance; **~ воображе́ния** fantasy; **~ слов** play on words.

игра́льный *прил*: **~ые ка́рты** playing cards *мн*.

игра́|ть (-ю) *несов неперех* to play ◆ *(perf* **сыгра́ть)** *перех* to play; *(пьесу)* to perform; **~** *(***сыгра́ть** *perf)* **в** +*acc (СПОРТ)* to play; **~** *(impf)* **в пря́тки** to play hide-and-seek *(BRIT)* или hide-and-go-seek *(US)*; **~** *(impf)* **людьми́/в демокра́тию** *(перен)* to play with people/at democracy; **~** *(impf)* **на** +*prp (МУЗ)* to play; **~** *(***сыгра́ть** *perf)* **конём/королём** to play one's knight/king; **~** *(***сыгра́ть** *perf)* **на чьих-н сла́бостях** to play on sb's weaknesses; **~** *(impf)* **на чьих-н не́рвах** to irritate sb; *(***сыгра́ть** *perf)*

сва́дьбу to celebrate a wedding; **вино́ ~ло в бока́ле** the wine sparkled in the glass.

игра́ючи *нареч (разг: легко)* with one's eyes closed.

игри́вый (-, -а, -о) *прил* playful.

игри́стый *прил* sparkling.

игров|о́й *прил*: **~а́я ко́мната** playroom; **~ы́е ви́ды спо́рта** team sports; **игрово́й автома́т** fruit machine.

игро́к (-а́) *м* player; *(в азартные игры)* gambler.

игроте́к|а (-и) *ж (собрание игр)* compendium *(BRIT)*; *(комната)* games room.

игру́шечный *прил см* **игру́шка**.

игру́шечный *прил* toy *опред*; *(перен)* tiny.

игру́ш|ка (-ки; *gen pl* -ек) *ж* toy; *(перен)* puppet; **ёлочные ~ки** Christmas tree decorations.

идеа́л (-а) *м* ideal; **~** democratic ideal; **он – мой ~** he's someone I look up to.

идеа́лен *прил см* **идеа́льный**.

идеализи́р|овать (-ую) *(не)сов перех* to idealize.

идеали́зм (-а) *м* idealism.

идеали́ст (-а) *м* idealist.

идеалисти́ческ|ий (-ая, -ое, -ие) *прил* idealistic.

идеалисти́чный *прил* idealistic.

идеа́льн|ый (-ен, -ьна, -ьно) *прил* ideal.

иде́йн|ый (-ен, -йна, -йно) *прил (идеологический)* ideological; *(прогрессивный)* radical; **~йная осно́ва рома́на** the main theme of the novel.

идём *несов см* **идти́**.

идентифици́р|овать (-ую) *(не)сов перех* to identify.

иденти́ч|ный (-ен, -на, -но) *прил* identical.

идео́лог (-а) *м* ideologist.

идеологи́ческ|ий (-ая, -ое, -ие) *прил* ideological.

идеоло́ги|я (-и) *ж* ideology.

идёшь *итп несов см* **идти́**.

иде́|я (-и) *ж* idea; **по ~е** *(разг)* supposedly; **по ~** +*gen* in accordance with; **подава́ть (пода́ть** *perf)* **кому́-н ~ю** to give sb an idea.

идилли́ческ|ий (-ая, -ое, -ие) *прил* idyllic.

иди́лли|я (-и) *ж* idyll.

идио́м|а (-ы) *ж* idiom.

идио́т (-а) *м (также МЕД)* idiot.

идиоти́зм (-а) *м (МЕД)* mental retardation; *(разг: глупость)* idiocy.

идио́тск|ий (-ая, -ое, -ие) *прил* idiotic.
йдол (-а) *м* idol.

идти́ (*см* **Table 18)** *несов неперех* to go;
(*пешком*) to walk; (*дни, годы*) to go by; (*фильм,
спектакль итп*) to be on; (*часы*) to work;
(*товар*) to sell; (*подходить: одежда*): ~ **к** +*dat*
to go with; ~ **(пойти́** *perf*) **(в/на** +*acc*) to go (to);
~ **(пойти́** *perf*) +*instr* (*конём, тузом итп*) to
play; **я шёл 3 часа́** I walked for 3 hours; **иди́
сюда́!** come here!; **иду́!** (I'm) coming!; **идёт
по́езд/авто́бус** the train/bus is coming; **по́езд
идёт до Москвы́** the train goes as far as
Moscow; **маши́на идёт со ско́ростью 100км в
час** the car is going at *или* doing 100km per
hour; **идёт дождь/снег** it's raining/snowing;
идёт зима́ winter is coming; **идёт гроза́** there is
a storm coming; **дела́ иду́т хорошо́/пло́хо**
things are going well/badly; **сейча́с иду́т
перегово́ры/экза́мены** the talks/exams are in
progress; **что сейча́с идёт в кино́?** what's on at
the cinema just now?; **спекта́кль идёт 2 часа́**
the play goes on for 2 hours; **мои́ часы́ иду́т
ме́дленно/бы́стро** my watch is slow/fast; **Вам
идёт э́та шля́па** the hat suits you; **из трубы́
идёт дым** there is smoke coming from the
chimney; **у меня́ идёт кровь из но́са** my nose
is bleeding; **ему́ идёт пя́тый год** he was four on
his last birthday; ~ **(пойти́** *perf*) **пешко́м** to walk,
go on foot; ~ **(пойти́** *perf*) **на рабо́ту/в теа́тр** to
go to work/the theatre; ~ **(пойти́** *perf*) **на
э́кспорт/прода́жу** to be for export/sale; **э́ти
я́блоки пойду́т на варе́нье** these apples will do
for making jam; ~ **(пойти́** *perf*) **на у́быль** to
decrease; ~ **(пойти́** *perf*) **на сниже́ние** to
descend; ~ **(пойти́** *perf*) **на риск** to take a risk; ~
(пойти́ *perf*) **на компроми́сс** to go for a
compromise; ~ **(пойти́** *perf*) **на хи́трость/
обма́н** to resort to cunning/deception; **идёт!**
(*разг*) fine!

иезуи́т (-а) *м* Jesuit.
ие́н|а (-ы) *ж* yen.
иера́рхи|я (-и) *ж* hierarchy.
иеро́глиф (-а) *м* (*китайский, японский*)
character; (*египетский*) hieroglyph (*мн*
hieroglyphics).
Иерусали́м (-а) *м* Jerusalem.
ИЖ *м сокр* = Иже́вский мотоцикле́тный заво́д;
(*мотоцикл*) *motorcycle manufactured at the
Izhevsk motorcycle factory.*
иждиве́н|ец (-ца) *м* (*ребёнок, престарелые*)
dependant; (*бездельник*) sponger.
иждиве́ни|е (-я) *ср* maintenance; **состоя́ть**
(*impf*) *или* **быть** (*impf*) **на ~и у** +*gen* to be
dependent on.
иждиве́нца *итп сущ см* **иждиве́нец.**
иждиве́нчеств|о (-а) *ср* dependence.

из *предл* (+*gen*) **1** (*о направлении действия
откуда-нибудь*) out of; **он вы́шел из ко́мнаты**
he went out of the room; **она́ доста́ла из
карма́на плато́к** she took a handkerchief out of
her pocket
2 (*при обозначении происхождения,
источника*) from; **све́дения из кни́ги**
information from a book; **из достове́рных
исто́чников** from reliable sources; **я из Москвы́**
I am from Moscow
3 (*при выделении части из целого*) of; **вот
оди́н из приме́ров** here is one of the examples
4 (*при обозначении компонентов целого*)
made of; **э́тот стол сде́лан из сосны́** this table
is made of pine; **ва́за из стекла́** a glass vase;
варе́нье из я́блок apple jam; **блу́за из
нейло́на** nylon blouse
5 (*при указании причины*) out of; **из
осторо́жности/за́висти** out of wariness/envy;
из эконо́мии in order to save money
6 (*во фразах*): **из го́да в год** year in, year out; **я
бежа́л изо всех сил** I ran at top speed.

изб|а́ (-ы́; *nom pl* **-ы)** *ж* hut.
избави́тел|ь (-я) *м* saviour.
избави́тельниц|а (-ы) *ж см* **избави́тель.**
изба́в|ить (-лю, -ишь; *impf* **избавля́ть)** *сов
перех*: ~ **кого́-н от** +*gen* (*от проблем, от
забот*) to relieve sb of; (*от врагов*) to deliver
sb from
▸ **изба́виться (***impf* **избавля́ться)** *сов возв*:
~**ся от** +*gen* (*от проблем, от посетителей*) to
get rid of; (*от страха, от предрассудков*) to
get over.
избало́ван|ный (-, -на, -но) *прил* spoilt.
избало́в|ать (-ую) *сов от* **баловать.**
избало́в|аться (-уюсь; *impf* **избало́вываться)**
сов возв (*разг*) to become spoilt.
избега́|ть (-ю) *сов перех* (*разг*) to run around.
избега́|ть (-ю) *несов от* **избежа́ть, избе́гнуть** ◆
неперех: ~ **чего́-н/** +*infin* to avoid sth/doing.
избе́гнуть (-ну, -нешь; *pt* **-, -ла, -ло,** *impf*
избега́ть) *сов неперех* = **избежа́ть.**
избегу́ *итп сов см* **избежа́ть.**
избежа́ни|е (-я) *ср*: **во ~** +*gen* (in order) to
avoid.
избежа́ть (*как* **бежа́ть;** *см* **Table 20;** *impf*
избега́ть) *сов неперех*: ~ +*gen* to avoid.
избер|у́ *итп сов см* **избра́ть.**
избива́|ть (-ю) *несов от* **изби́ть.**
избие́ни|е (-я) *ср* beating; (*массовое убийство*)
massacre.
избира́телен *прил см* **избира́тельный.**
избира́тел|ь (-я) *м* voter.
избира́тельниц|а (-ы) *ж см* **избира́тель.**
избира́тельный *прил* (*система*) electoral;
(**-ен, -ьна, -ьно;** *эффект*) selective; **~ьная
кампа́ния** election campaign; **избира́тельный**

The spelling rules for Russian are shown on page xvii.

уча́сток polling station; **избира́тельный бюллете́нь** ballot paper.

избира́ть (-ю) *несов от* **избра́ть** ♦ *перех* to elect.

изби́т|ый (-, -а, -о) *прил* clichéd, hackneyed.

изби́ть (-обью́, -обьёшь; *impf* **избива́ть**) *сов перех* (*человека*) to beat; (*обувь*) to wear out.

изборозди́ть (-жу́, -ди́шь) *сов от* **борозди́ть**.

избра́ни|е (-я) *ср* election.

избра́нник (-а) *м* chosen one; ~ **судьбы́** fate's darling; **наро́дные** ~**и** deputies.

избра́нниц|а (-ы) *ж см* **избра́нник**.

и́збранн|ые (-ых; *decl like adj*) *мн* select *или* chosen few *мн*.

и́збранный *прил* (*рассказы, стихи*) selected; (*люди, круг*) select; *см также* **и́збранные**.

избра́ть (-еру́, -ерёшь; *pt* -ра́л, -рала́, -ра́ло, *impf* **избира́ть**) *сов перех* (*профессию*) to choose; (*президента*) to elect; **избира́ть** (~ *perf*) **кого́-н в парла́мент** to elect sb to parliament.

избы́т|ок (-ка) *м* (*излишек*) surplus; (*обилие*) excess; **име́ть** (*impf*) **что-н в** ~**ке** to have plenty of sth; **э́того хва́тит с** ~**ком** it is more than enough; **она́ запла́кала от** ~**ка чувств** overwhelmed by emotion, she burst into tears.

избы́точ|ный (-ен, -на, -но) *прил* (*вес, влага*) excess *или* (*информация*) abundant; ~**ное предложе́ние** (*экон*) excess supply.

изва́ни|е (-я) *ср* effigy.

изве́да|ть (-ю; *impf* **изве́дывать**) *сов перех* to come to know.

изведу́(сь) *итп сов см* **извести́(сь)**.

изве́дыва|ть (-ю) *несов от* **изве́дать**.

и́зверг (-а) *м* monster (*fig*).

изве́ргн|уть (-у, -ешь; *impf* **изверга́ть**) *сов перех* to spew (out).

изверже́ни|е (-я) *ср* eruption.

изве́р|иться (-юсь, -ишься) *сов возв* ~ **в** +*prp* to lose faith in.

изверну́ться (-у́сь, -ёшься; *impf* **извёртываться** *или* **изворачиваться**) *сов возв* to twist around; (*перен*) to pull through.

изве́стен *прил см* **изве́стный**.

изв|ести́ (-еду́, -едёшь; *pt* -ёл, -ела́, -ело́, *impf* **изводи́ть**) *сов перех* (*разг: истратить*) to fritter away; (: *измучить*) to exasperate; (*истребить*) to exterminate.

▶ **извести́сь** (*impf* **изводи́ться**) *сов возв* to torment o.s.

изве́сти|е (-я) *ср* news; *см также* **изве́стия**.

изве|сти́ть (-щу́, -сти́шь; *impf* **извеща́ть**) *сов перех*: ~ **кого́-н о** +*prp* to inform sb of.

изве́сти|я (-й) *мн* (*издание*) bulletin *ед*.

изве́стк|а (-и) *ж* slaked lime.

изве́стно *как сказ*: ~, **что** ... it is well known that ...; **мне э́то** ~ I know about it; **наско́лько мне** ~ as far as I know; **как** ~ as is well known.

изве́стност|ь (-и) *ж* fame; **по́льзоваться** (*impf*) ~**ю** to be well known; **ста́вить** (**поста́вить** *perf*) **кого́-н в** ~ to inform sb.

изве́ст|ный (-ен, -на, -но) *прил* famous, well-known; (*no short form*; *разг:* **лентя́й, ба́бник**) notorious; (*условия*) certain; ~ +*instr* famous *или* well-known for; **он** ~**ен как тала́нтливый руководи́тель** he is known to be a talented leader; ~**ное де́ло!** (*разг*) that's no surprise!

известня́к (-á) *м* limestone.

и́звест|ь (-и) *ж* lime.

изве́ч|ный (-ен, -на, -но) *прил* (*проблема, спор*) perpetual.

извеща́|ть (-ю) *несов от* **извести́ть**.

извеще́ни|е (-я) *ср* notification; (*комм*) advice note; **почто́вое** ~ signed receipt of delivery.

извещу́ *сов см* **извести́ть**.

извива́|ться (-юсь) *несов возв* (*змея*) to slither; (*человек*) to writhe; (*дорога, река*) to wind.

изви́лин|а (-ы) *ж* bend; ~ **мо́зга** convolution.

изви́лист|ый (-, -а, -о) *прил* winding, twisting.

извине́ни|е (-я) *ср* apology; (*оправдание*) excuse; **проси́ть** (**попроси́ть** *perf*) ~**я** (**у кого́-н**) to apologize (to sb).

извини́тельный *прил* (*тон, улыбка*) apologetic; (-ен, -ьна, -ьно; *ошибка, слабость*) excusable, forgivable.

извин|и́ть (-ю́, -и́шь; *impf* **извиня́ть**) *сов перех* (*простить*): ~ **что-н** (**кому́-н**) to excuse (sb for) sth; ~**и́те!** excuse me!; ~**и́те, Вы не ска́жете где вокза́л?** excuse me, could you tell me where the station is?; **в э́том,** ~**и́те, я с Ва́ми не согла́сен** sorry, but I cannot agree with you on that

▶ **извини́ться** (*impf* **извиня́ться**) *сов возв*: ~**ся** (**за** +*acc*) to apologize (for); **он** ~**и́лся, что не позвони́л** he apologized for not phoning (*BRIT*) *или* calling (*US*).

извиня́ющ|ийся (-аяся, -ееся, -иеся) *прил* apologetic.

извлёк *итп сов см* **извле́чь**.

извлека́|ть (-ю) *несов от* **извле́чь**.

извлеку́ *итп сов см* **извле́чь**.

извлече́ни|е (-я) *ср* (*золота, пользы итп*) extraction; (*из документа*) extract, excerpt.

извл|е́чь (-еку́, -ечёшь *итп*, -еку́т; *pt* -ёк, -екла́, -екло́, *impf* **извлека́ть**) *сов перех* (*занозу, осколок*) to remove, take out; (*золото*) to extract; (*перен: пользу, выгоду итп*) to derive; **извлека́ть** (~ *perf*) **уро́к** to learn a lesson; **извлека́ть** (~ *perf*) **ко́рень** (*мат*) to find the root.

извне́ *нареч* from outside.

изв|оди́ть(ся) (-ожу́(сь), -о́дишь(ся)) *несов от* **извести́(сь)**.

изво́зчик (-а) *м* (*кучер*) coachman (*мн* coachmen); (*экипаж*) cab (*coach*).

изво́л|ить (-ю, -ишь) *несов неперех*: ~ +*infin* to condescend to do; ~**ьте не крича́ть** would you mind not shouting.

изворачива|ться (-юсь) *несов от* **изверну́ться**.

изворо́тлив|ый (-, -а, -о) *прил* (*человек*) wily; (*ум, делец*) shrewd.

изврати́ть (-щу́, -ти́шь; *impf* **извраща́ть**) *сов перех* to distort.

извраще́ни|е (-я) *ср* distortion; **полово́е ~** sexual perversion.

извращё|нный (-, -на, -но) *прил* perverted.

извращу́ *сов см* **изврати́ть**.

изга́|дить (-жу, -дишь) *сов перех* (*разг*) to mess up.

изги́б (-а) *м* bend.

изгиба́|ть(ся) (-ю(сь)) *несов от* **изогну́ть(ся)**.

изгла́|дить (-жу, -дишь) *impf* **изгла́живать** *сов перех*: **~ что-н из па́мяти** to blot sth out of one's memory

▶ **изгла́диться** (*impf* **изгла́живаться**) *сов возв* to be blotted out.

изгна́ни|е (-я) *ср* (*ссылка*) exile; (*врага*) expulsion; (*злых духов*) exorcism.

изгна́нник (-а) *м* exile.

изгна́нниц|а (-ы) *ж см* **изгна́нник**.

изгн|а́ть (-оню́, -о́нишь; *pt* -на́л, -нала́, -на́ло, *impf* **изгоня́ть**) *сов перех* to drive out; (*сослать*) to exile.

изго́|й (-я) *м* outcast.

изголо́вь|е (-я) *ср*: **у ~я** at the head of the bed.

изголода́|ться (-юсь) *сов возв* to be starving; (*перен*): **~ по** +*dat* (*по книгам*) to long *или* yearn for; **~** (*perf*) **по ла́ске** to crave affection.

изгоню́ *итп сов см* **изгна́ть**.

изгоня́|ть (-ю) *несов от* **изгна́ть**.

и́згород|ь (-и) *ж* fence; **живая ~** hedge.

изгото́в|ить (-лю, -ишь) *impf* **изготовля́ть** *сов перех* to manufacture.

изготовле́ни|е (-я) *ср* manufacture.

изгото́влю *сов см* **изгото́вить**.

изготовля́|ть (-ю) *несов от* **изгото́вить**.

изгры́з|ть (-у́, -ёшь; *pt* -, -ла, -ло) *сов перех* to gnaw (away) at.

изд. *сокр* (= **изда́ние**) ed. (= *edition*).

изда|ва́ть (-ю́, -ёшь) *несов от* **изда́ть**.

и́здавна *нареч* for a long time.

издади́м *итп сов см* **изда́ть**.

издалека́ *нареч* from a long way off *или* away; **начина́ть** (**нача́ть** *perf*) **разгово́р ~** (*перен*) to start a conversation in a roundabout way.

и́здали *нареч* = **издалека́**.

изда́м *итп сов см* **изда́ть**.

изда́ни|е (-я) *ср* (*действие*) publication; (*изданная вещь*) edition.

изда́ст *сов см* **изда́ть**.

изда́тель (-я) *м* publisher.

изда́тельск|ий (-ая, -ое, -ие) *прил* publishing *опред*.

изда́тельств|о (-а) *ср* publisher, publishing house.

изда́ть (*как* **дать**; *см* **Table 14**; *impf* **издава́ть**) *сов перех* (*книгу*) to publish; (*закон, постановление*) to issue; (*крик, стон*) to let out; (*запах*) to give off.

изд-во *сокр* (= **изда́тельство**) pub(l). (= *publisher*).

издева́тельск|ий (-ая, -ое, -ие) *прил* (*насмешливый*) mocking, scoffing; (*оскорбительный*) abusive.

издева́тельств|о (-а) *ср* mockery; (*наглое*) jibe; (*жестокое*) abuse.

издева́|ться (-юсь) *несов возв*: **~ над** +*instr* (*над подчинёнными*) to make a mockery of; (*над книгой*) to pour scorn on; (*над чьей-н одеждой*) to mock, ridicule.

издёв|ка (-ки; *gen pl* -ок) *ж* (*разг*) jibe.

изде́ли|е (-я) *ср* (*товар*) article; **ювели́рные ~я** jewellery (*BRIT*), jewelery (*US*); **стекля́нные ~я** glassware; **игру́шка куста́рного ~я** handmade toy.

издёрга|нный (-, -на, -но) *прил* (*разг*) edgy.

издёрга|ть (-ю) *сов перех* (*разг*) to put on edge.

▶ **издёргаться** *сов возв* (*разг*) to become edgy.

издерж|а́ть (-ержу́, -е́ржишь; *impf* **изде́рживать**) *сов перех* (*деньги*) to use up; (*ресурсы*) to exhaust.

изде́рж|ки (-ек) *мн* (*производственные*) expenses *мн*; **суде́бные ~** legal costs; **э́то всё – ~ плохо́го воспита́ния** it's all the result of bad upbringing.

издеру́ *итп сов см* **изодра́ть**.

издыха́ни|е (-я) *ср*: **при после́днем ~и** on one's deathbed.

изжи́|ть (-ву́, -вёшь; *pt* -л, -ла́, -ло, *impf* **изжива́ть**) *сов перех* (*плохую привычку*) to overcome; (*преступность*) to eliminate; **изжива́ть** (**~** *perf*) **себя** to outlive its usefulness.

изжо́г|а (-и) *ж* heartburn.

из-за *предл*: **~** +*gen* (*занавески*) from behind; (*угла*) from around; (*по вине*) because of; **встава́ть** (**встать** *perf*) **~ стола́** to get up from the table; **~ того́ что** because; **~ тебя́ мы пропусти́ли по́езд** we missed the train because of you.

иззя́б|нуть (-ну, -нешь; *pt* -, -ла, -ло) *сов неперех* (*разг*) to be frozen stiff.

излага́|ть (-ю) *несов от* **изложи́ть**.

изла́мыва|ть (-ю) *несов от* **изломать**.

излече́ни|е (-я) *ср* (*лечение*) treatment; (*выздоровление*) recovery; **быть** (*impf*) **на ~и** to undergo treatment.

изле́чива|ть (-ю) *несов от* **излечи́ть**.

▶ **изле́чиваться** *несов от* **излечи́ться** ♦ *возв* (*болезнь*) to be curable.

излечи́м|ый (-, -а, -о) *прил* curable.

изл|ечи́ть (-ечу́, -е́чишь; *impf* **изле́чивать**) *сов перех*: **~ кого́-н** (**от** +*gen*) to cure sb (of)

▶ **излечи́ться** *сов возв*: **~ся от** +*gen* (*от болезни*) to recover from; (*от наркомании, от алкоголизма*) to be cured of.

изли́|ть (**изолью́, изольёшь**; *pt* -л, -ла́, -ло, *impf* **излива́ть**) *сов перех* (*перен: тоску*) to pour out; **изливáть** (~ *perf*) **дýшу** to pour one's heart out; **изливáть** (~ *perf*) **гнев** to vent one's anger

▶ **изли́ться** (*impf* **изливáться**) *сов возв* to pour one's heart out; **изливáться** (*impf*) **в благодáрностях** to express one's great appreciation.

изли́ш|ек (**-ка**) *м* (*остаток*) remainder; ~ **+gen** (*влаги, веса*) excess of.

изли́шеств|о (**-а**) *ср* overindulgence.

изли́шка *итп сущ см* **изли́шек**.

изли́ш|ний (**-няя, -нее, -ние; -ен, -ня, -не**) *прил* unnecessary; **комментáрии ~ни** there is nothing to add.

излия́ни|е (**-я**) *ср* (*чувств*) gush; (*обычно мн: дружеские, любовные*) outburst.

изловчи́ться (**-ýсь, -и́шься**) *сов возв* (*приспособиться*) to manage.

изложéни|е (**-я**) *ср* presentation.

изл|ожи́ть (**-ожý, -óжишь**; *impf* **излагáть**) *сов перех* (*события*) to recount; (*просьбу, решение итп*) to state.

изло́ман|ный (**-, -на, -но**) *прил* (*судьба, жизнь*) ruined; (*характер*) unbalanced.

изломáть (**-ю**; *impf* **излáмывать**) *сов перех* (*забор, игрушку*) to smash; (*перен: жизнь*) to ruin; (: *характер*) to unbalance.

излучáть (**-ю**) *несов перех* (*также перен*) to radiate

▶ **излучáться** *несов возв* to radiate.

излучéни|е (**-я**) *ср* radiation.

излýчин|а (**-ы**) *ж* bend.

излюбленный *прил* favourite (*BRIT*), favorite (*US*).

измá|зать(ся) (**-жу(сь), -жешь(ся)**) *сов от* **мáзать(ся)**.

измарá|ть(ся) (**-ю(сь)**) *сов от* **марáть(ся)**.

измáтыва|ть(ся) (**-ю(сь)**) *несов от* **измотáть(ся)**.

измельчáть (**-ю**) *сов от* **мельчáть**.

измельчи́ть (**-ý, -и́шь**) *сов перех* **мельчи́ть**

▶ **измельчи́ться** *сов возв* to crumble.

измéн|а (**-ы**) *ж* (*родине*) treason; (*другу*) betrayal; **госудáрственная ~** high treason; **супрýжеская ~** adultery.

изменéни|е (**-я**) *ср* change; (*поправка*) alteration.

изм|ени́ть (**-еню́, -éнишь**; *impf* **изменя́ть**) *сов перех* to change ♦ *неперех*: ~ **+dat** (*родине, другу*) to betray; (*супругу*) to be unfaithful to; (*память*) to fail; **си́лы емý ~ени́ли** his strength failed him

▶ **измени́ться** (*impf* **изменя́ться**) *сов возв* to change.

измéнник (**-а**) *м* (*родине*) traitor.

измéнниц|а (**-ы**) *ж см* **измéнник**.

измéнчивый (**-, -а, -о**) *прил* changeable.

изменя́ем|ый (**-, -а, -о**) *прил* (*линг*): **~ое окончáние** variable ending.

изменя́|ть(ся) (**-ю(сь)**) *несов от* **измени́ть(ся)**.

измерéни|е (**-я**) *ср* (*действие: площади*) measurement; (*величина*) dimension.

измери́тельный *прил* measuring *опред*.

изм|éрить (**-ю, -ишь**; *impf* **измеря́ть**) *сов перех* to measure; **измеря́ть** (~ *perf*) **температýру комý-н** to take sb's temperature; ~ (*perf*) **когó-н взгля́дом** to look sb up and down.

измеря́|ться (*3sg* **-ется**, *3pl* **-ются**) *несов возв* (**+instr**): ~ **килогрáммами/мéтрами** to be measured in kilogrammes/metres (*BRIT*) *или* meters (*US*).

измождéни|е (**-я**) *ср* exhaustion.

измождённый (**-, -á, -ó**) *прил* (*человек*) worn out; (**-, -на, -но**; *вид, лицо*) haggard.

измóк|нуть (**-ну, -нешь**; *pt* **-, -ла, -ло**) *сов неперех* to get soaked.

измóр (**-а**) *м*: **взять когó-н/чтó-н ~ом** (*гóрод*) to wage a war of attrition against sb/sth; (*перен: разг*) to wear down.

и́змороз|ь (**-и**) *ж* hoarfrost.

и́зморос|ь (**-и**) *ж* drizzle.

измотá|ть (**-ю**; *impf* **измáтывать**) *сов перех* to wear out

▶ **измотáться** (*impf* **измáтываться**) *сов возв* (*разг*) to be worn out.

измýчен|ный (**-, -а, -о**) *прил* (*человек*) worn out; (**-, -на, -но**; *лицо*) haggard.

измýч|ить (**-у, -ишь**) *сов от* **мýчить**.

измывá|ться (**-юсь**) *несов возв*: ~ **над +instr** (*разг*) to taunt.

измышлéни|е (**-я**) *ср* fabrication.

из|мя́ть(ся) (**-омнý(сь), -омнёшь(ся)**) *сов от* **мя́ть(ся)**.

изнáнк|а (**-и**) *ж* (*одежды*) inside; (*ткани*) wrong side; (*перен: жизни, событий*) dark side.

изнаси́л|овать (**-ую**) *сов от* **наси́ловать**.

изначáльный (**-ен, -ьна, -ьно**) *прил* initial.

изнáшива|ть(ся) (**-ю(сь)**) *несов от* **износи́ть(ся)**.

изнéжен|ный (**-, -а, -о**) *прил* pampered.

изнéж|ить (**-у, -ишь**) *сов перех* to pamper

▶ **изнéжиться** *сов возв* to be pampered.

изнемóг *итп сов см* **изнемóчь**.

изнемогá|ть (**-ю**) *несов от* **изнемóчь**.

изнемогý *итп сов см* **изнемóчь**.

изнеможéни|е (**-я**) *ср* exhaustion; **до ~я** to the point of exhaustion.

изнеможённый (**-, -á, -ó**) *прил* (*человек*) worn out; (**-, -на, -но**; *вид, лицо*) haggard.

изнемó|чь (**-гý, -жешь** *итп*, **-гýт**; *pt* **-г, -глá, -глó**, *impf* **изнемогáть**) *сов неперех* to be exhausted.

изнóс (**-а**) *м* (*механизмов*) wear; (*перен: организма*) ageing; **рабóтать** (*impf*) **на ~** (*перен*) to work o.s. into the ground.

изн|оси́ть (**-ошý, -óсишь**; *impf* **изнáшивать**) *сов перех* to wear out

▶ **износи́ться** (*impf* **изнáшиваться**) *сов возв* to wear out.

изнóшен|ный (**-, -а, -о**) *прил* worn-out.

изношý(сь) *сов см* **износи́ть(ся)**.

изнурён|ный (**-, -á, -ó**) *прил* (*человек*) exhausted; (**-, -на, -но**; *лицо, вид*) haggard.

изнури́тел|ьный (**-ен, -ьна, -ьно**) *прил*

exhausting.

изнур|и́ть (-ю́, -и́шь; *impf* **изнуря́ть**) *сов перех* to exhaust.

изнутри́ *нареч* from inside.

изныва́|ть (-ю) *несов неперех* to languish.

изо *предл* = **из**.

изоби́ли|е (-я) *ср* abundance; **в ~и** in abundance.

изоби́л|овать (*3sg* -ует, *3pl* -уют) *несов неперех* (+*instr*) to abound in.

изоби́льный (-ен, -ьна, -ьно) *прил* abundant.

изоблича́|ть (-ю) *несов от* **изоличи́ть ◆** *перех* (обнаружить): **~ кого́-н в** +*prp* (подлеж: одежда, акцент итп) to give sb away as.

изоличи́|ть (-у́, -и́шь; *impf* **изоблича́ть**) *сов перех* (шпиона, взяточника итп) to expose; **изоблича́ть** (~ *perf*) **кого́-н во лжи/в моше́нничестве** to expose sb's lies/deception.

изобража́|ть(ся) (-ю(сь)) *несов от* **изобрази́ть(ся)**.

изображе́ни|е (-я) *ср* image; (действие: событий) depiction, representation.

изобраку́(сь) *сов см* **изобрази́ть(ся)**.

изобрази́тельный (-ен, -ьна, -ьно) *прил* descriptive; **изобрази́тельное иску́сство** fine art.

изобра|зи́ть (-жу́, -зи́шь; *impf* **изобража́ть**) *сов перех* (на картине, в романе итп) to depict, portray; (подлеж: лицо) to show; (копировать) to impersonate; **изобража́ть** (~ *perf*) **из себя́ наи́вного/знатока́** to make o.s. out to be naive/an expert

▶ **изобрази́ться** (*impf* **изобража́ться**) *сов возв* to show; **на его́ лице́ ~зи́лся у́жас** a look of horror came over his face.

изобр|ести́ (-ету́, -ете́шь; *pt* -ёл, -ела́, -ело́, *impf* **изобрета́ть**) *сов перех* to invent.

изобрета́тел|ь (-я) *м* inventor.

изобрета́тельниц|а (-ы) *ж см* **изобрета́тель**.

изобрета́тельност|ь (-и) *ж* inventiveness.

изобрета́тельств|о (-а) *ср* innovation.

изобрета́|ть (-ю) *несов от* **изобрести́**.

изобрете́ни|е (-я) *ср* invention.

изобью́(сь) *итп сов см* **избить**.

изогн|у́ть (-у́, -ёшь; *impf* **изгиба́ть**) *сов перех* to bend.

▶ **изогну́ться** (*impf* **изгиба́ться**) *сов возв* to bend.

изо|дра́ть (-деру́, -дерёшь; *pt* -одра́л, -одрала́, -одра́ло) *сов перех* (разг) to rip to shreds.

изо|йти́ (как идти́; *см* **Table 18**; *impf* **исходи́ть**) *сов неперех*: **~ слеза́ми** to cry one's eyes out; **она́ ~шла́ го́рем** she was completely grief-stricken.

изоли́рованный *прил* (случай, явление итп) isolated; (комната, провод) insulated.

изоли́р|овать (-ую) *(не)сов перех* (больного, преступника) to isolate; (вход) to cut off; (ТЕХ,

ЭЛЕК) to insulate

▶ **изоли́роваться** (*не)сов возв* (человек) to isolate o.s.

изолью́(сь) *итп сов см* **изли́ть(ся)**.

изоля́тор (-а) *м* (ТЕХ, ЭЛЕК) insulator; (в больни́це) isolation unit; (в тюрьме́) solitary confinement.

изоляцио́нн|ый *прил*: **~ая ле́нта** insulating tape.

изоля́ци|я (-и) *ж* (см глаг) isolation; insulation; **жить** (*impf*) **в ~и** to live in isolation.

изомну́(сь) *итп сов см* **измя́ть(ся)**.

изопью́ *итп сов см* **испи́ть**.

изорв|а́ть (-у́, -ёшь; *pt* -а́л, -ала́, -а́ло) *сов перех* to rip up; **~** (*perf*) **в кло́чья** to tear to shreds.

изото́п (-а) *м* isotope.

изотрётся *итп сов см* **истере́ться**.

изошёл *итп сов см* **изойти́**.

изощрённый (-, -на, -но) *прил* sophisticated.

изощр|и́ться (-ю́сь, -и́шься; *impf* **изощря́ться**) *сов возв* (отличиться) to surpass o.s.; (вкус, ум) to become sophisticated.

изощря́|ться (-юсь) *несов от* **изощри́ться ◆** *неперех*: **~ в** +*prp* to excel in.

из-под *предл* (+*gen*) from under(neath); (около) from outside; **~ стола́ вы́ползла ко́шка** a cat crawled from under the table; **он прие́хал ~ Ки́ева** he comes from outside Kiev; **выходи́ть** (**вы́йти** *perf*) **~ чьего́-н влия́ния** to free o.s. from sb's influence; **бежа́ть** (*impf*) **~ стра́жи** to escape from custody; **ба́нка ~ варе́нья** jam jar; **буты́лка ~ во́дки** vodka bottle.

изразе́ц (-ца́) *м* tile.

изразцо́вый *прил* tiled.

Изра́ил|ь (-я) *м* Israel.

изра́ильск|ий (-ая, -ое, -ие) *прил* Israeli.

израильтя́н|ин (-ина; *nom pl* -е, *gen pl* -) *м* Israeli.

израильтя́н|ка (-ки; *gen pl* -ок) *ж см* **израильтя́нин**.

изра́н|ить (-ю, -ишь) *сов перех* to injure badly.

израсхо́д|овать (-ую) *сов от* **расхо́довать**.

изре́дка *нареч* now and then and then или again.

изре́|зать (-жу, -жешь; *impf* **изреза́ть**) *сов перех* to cut up; (подлеж: дороги, каналы) to crisscross.

изрёк *итп сов см* **изре́чь**.

изрека́|ть (-ю) *несов от* **изре́чь**.

изреку́ *итп сов см* **изре́чь**.

изрече́ни|е (-я) *ср* utterance.

изре́|чь (-ку́, -чёшь итп, -ку́т; *pt* -ёк, -екла́, -екло́, *impf* **изрека́ть**) *сов перех* to utter.

изреше|ти́ть (-чу́, -ти́шь) *сов перех*: **~ кого́-н пу́лями** to pepper sb with bullets.

изруб|и́ть (-ублю́, -у́бишь; *impf* **изруба́ть** *сов перех* (убить) to hack to pieces.

изрыга́|ть (-ю) *несов перех* (лаву) to spew (out); (перен: проклятия) to let out a torrent of.

изры́т|ый (-, -а, -о) *прил* (*поверхность*) pitted;
~ **о́спой** pockmarked.

изры́ть (-о́ю, -о́ешь) *сов перех* to riddle.

изря́дный (-ен, -на, -но) *прил* (*сумма, доход*)
fair; (*разг: мошенник, пьяница итп*) real.

изуве́р (-а) *м* monster.

изуве́рский (-ая, -ое, -ие) *прил* monstrous.

изуве́рство (-а) *ср* monstrosity.

изуве́ч|ить (-у, -ишь; *impf* **изуве́чивать**) *сов
перех* to maim

▶ **изуве́читься** (*impf* **изуве́чиваться**) *сов возв*
to be maimed.

изукра́|сить (-шу, -сишь; *impf* **изукра́шивать**)
сов перех to adorn; (*разг: избить*) to beat black
and blue.

изуми́тельный (-ен, -ьна, -ьно) *прил*
marvellous (*BRIT*), marvelous (*US*), wonderful.

изум|и́ть (-лю́, -и́шь; *impf* **изумля́ть**) *сов перех*
to amaze, astound

▶ **изуми́ться** (*impf* **изумля́ться**) *сов возв* to be
amazed.

изумле́ни|е (-я) *ср* amazement; **приходи́ть**
(**прийти́** *perf*) **в** ~ to be amazed; **с** ~**м** (*слушать,
рассма́тривать*) in amazement; **с** ~**м**
обнару́жил, что ... to my great amazement I
discovered that ....

изумлю́(сь) *сов см* **изуми́ть(ся)**.

изумля́ть(ся) (-ю(сь)) *несов от* **изуми́ть(ся)**.

изумру́д (-а) *м* emerald.

изумру́дный *прил* (*кольцо́ итп*) emerald;
(*цвет*) emerald-green.

изуро́довать (-ую) *сов от* **уро́довать**.

изуча́|ть (-ю) *несов от* **изучи́ть** ♦ *перех* (*о
процессе*) to study.

изуче́ни|е (-я) *ср* study.

изуч|и́ть (-учу́, -у́чишь; *impf* **изуча́ть**) *сов перех*
(*язык, предмет*) to learn; (*поня́ть*) to get to
know; (*иссле́довать*) to study.

изъеда́|ть (*3sg* -ет, *3pl* -ют) *несов от* **изъе́сть**.

изъе́ден|ный (-, -а, -о) *прил*: ~ **мо́лью** moth-
eaten; ~ **кислото́й** eaten away by acid.

изъеди́м *итп сов см* **изъе́сть**.

изъе́з|дить (-жу, -дишь) *сов перех* to travel
(round).

изъе́сть (*как* **есть**; *см* **Table 15**; *impf* **изъеда́ть**)
сов перех (*мех, ткань*) to eat away; (*металл*) to
corrode.

изъяви́тельный *прил* (*линг*): ~**ое
наклоне́ние** the indicative mood.

изъяв|и́ть (-явлю́, -я́вишь; *impf* **изъявля́ть**)
сов перех to indicate.

изъя́н (-а) *м* flaw.

изъясн|и́ть (-ю́, -и́шь; *impf* **изъясня́ть**) *сов
перех* to clarify.

изъя́ти|е (-я) *ср* (*см глаг*) withdrawal; removal.

изъя́ть (**изыму́, изы́мешь**; *impf* **изыма́ть**) *сов
перех* (*из обраще́ния, из прода́жи*) to withdraw;
(*отобра́ть*) to remove.

изыска́ни|е (-я) *ср* investigation;
(*геологи́ческие*) exploration.

изы́сканност|ь (-и) *ж* refinement.

изы́скан|ный (-, -на, -но) *прил* refined.

изыска́тел|ь (-я) *м* surveyor.

изыска́тельск|ий (-ая, -ое, -ие) *прил*
exploratory.

изыска́ть (-ыщу́, -ы́щешь; *impf* **изы́скивать**)
сов перех to find.

изы́скива|ть (-ю) *несов от* **изыска́ть** ♦ *перех*
(*иска́ть*) to seek out.

изыщу́ *итп сов см* **изыска́ть**.

изю́м (-а) *м собир* raisins *мн*.

изю́мин|а (-ы) *ж* raisin.

изю́мин|ка (-ки; *gen pl* -ок) *ж уменьш от*
изю́мина; (*перен*) highlight; **без** ~**ки** lacklustre.

изя́щен *прил см* **изя́щный**.

изя́щество (-а) *ср* elegance.

изя́щ|ный (-ен, -на, -но) *прил* elegant.

ика́|ть (-ю) *несов неперех* to hiccup.

икн|у́ть (-у́, -ёшь) *сов неперех* to hiccup.

ико́н|а (-ы) *ж* (*РЕЛ*) icon.

иконопи́с|ец (-ца) *м* icon painter.

и́конопис|ь (-и) *ж* icon painting.

иконоста́с (-а) *м* iconostasis.

ико́т|а (-ы) *ж* hiccups *мн*.

икр|а́ (-ы́) *ж* (*рыбы*) roe; (*чёрная, красная*)
caviar; (*кабачко́вая, баклажа́нная*) pâté; (*nom pl*
-ы; *АНАТ*) calf (*мн* calves).

икри́н|ка (-ки; *gen pl* -ок) *ж* grain of caviar.

икс (-а) *м* (*МАТ*) X; **ми́стер И́**~ Mr X.

ИЛ (-а) *м сокр* = **самолёт констру́кции С.В.
Илью́шина**.

ил (-а) *м* silt.

и́ли *союз* or; **чай** ~ **ко́фе** tea or coffee; ~ ... ~ ...
either ... or ...; ~ **ты не понима́ешь?** (*разг*)
don't you understand or something?

и́листый (-, -а, -о) *прил* silt *опред*.

иллюзиони́ст (-а) *м* conjurer.

иллю́зи|я (-и) *ж* (*та́кже перен*) illusion.

иллюзо́р|ный (-ен, -на, -но) *прил* illusory.

иллюмина́тор (-а) *м* (*корабля́*) porthole;
(*самолёта*) window.

иллюмина́ци|я (-и) *ж* illuminations *мн*.

иллюстра́тор (-а) *м* illustrator.

иллюстра́ци|я (-и) *ж* illustration.

иллюстри́р|овать (-ую; *perf* **иллюстри́ровать**
или **проиллюстри́ровать**) *несов перех* to
illustrate.

ильм (-а) *м* elm.

им *мест см* **он, оно́, они́**.

им. *сокр* = **и́мени**.

имби́р|ь (-я́) *м* ginger.

и́мени *итп сущ см* **и́мя**.

име́ни|е (-я) *ср* estate.

имени́нник (-а) *м person who is celebrating his
name day or birthday*.

имени́нниц|а (-ы) *ж см* **имени́нник**.

имени́н|ы (-) *мн* (*РЕЛ*) name day *ед*.

имени́тельный *прил* (*линг*): ~ **паде́ж** the
nominative case.

имени́т|ый (-, -а, -о) *прил* renowned.

и́менно *част* exactly, precisely ♦ *союз* (*перед
перечисле́нием*): **а** ~ namely; **э́то на́до
сде́лать** ~ **сего́дня** it has to be done today; ~ **в**

э́том до́ме я роди́лся it was in this house that I was born; ~ так я и поступи́л that is exactly what I did; вот ~! exactly!, precisely!; на собра́нии прису́тствовало 6 челове́к а ~: Ивано́в, Петро́в ... there were 6 people present at the meeting, namely Ivanov, Petrov ....

именно́й *прил* (*оружие, часы*) personalized; (*акции, чек*) nontransferable; **именно́й про́пуск** pass (*issued in somebody's name*); **именно́й спи́сок** nominal roll.

имен|ова́ть (-у́ю; *perf* **наименова́ть**) *несов перех* to name.

име́|ть (-ю) *несов перех* to have; ~ *(impf)* **ме́сто** (*совершаться*) to take place; ~ *(impf)* **де́ло с** +*instr* to deal with; **я не хочу́ ~ с ним де́ло** I don't want anything to do with him; ~ *(impf)* **в виду́** (*подразумевать*) to mean; **я ~ю зада́чу/цель** *или* **зада́чей/це́лью** +*infin* my task/aim is to do; ~ *(impf)* **что́-нибудь про́тив** +*gen* to have something against; **ничего́ не** ~ *(impf)* **про́тив** +*gen* to have nothing against

▸ **име́ться** *несов возв* (*сведения, средства*) to be available; **у нас ~ются ну́жные сре́дства** we have the necessary resources available.

и́ми *мест см* **они́**.

и́мидж (-а) *м* image.

имита́ци|я (-и) *ж* imitation.

имити́р|овать (-ую; *perf* **сымити́ровать**) *несов перех* to imitate.

иммигра́нт (-а) *м* immigrant.

иммигра́нт|ка (-ки; *gen pl* -ок) *ж см* **иммигра́нт**.

иммиграцио́нный *прил* immigration.

иммигра́ци|я (-и) *ж* immigration ♦ *собир* immigrants *мн*.

иммигри́р|овать (-ую) *(не)сов неперех* to immigrate.

иммуните́т (-а) *м* (*МЕД, перен*): ~ (**к** +*dat*) immunity (to); **выраба́тывать** (**вы́работать** *perf*) ~ **к** +*dat* to develop an immunity to; **у меня́ ~ к шу́му/кри́тике** I'm immune to noise/criticism; **дипломати́ческий** ~ diplomatic immunity.

имму́нн|ый *прил* (*МЕД*): ~**ая систе́ма** immune system.

иммуноло́ги|я (-и) *ж* immunology.

императи́в (-а) *м* (*также линг*) imperative.

импера́тор (-а) *м* emperor.

импера́торск|ий (-ая, -ое, -ие) *прил* imperial.

императри́ц|а (-ы) *ж* empress.

империали́зм (-а) *м* imperialism.

империали́ст (-а) *м* imperialist.

империалисти́ческ|ий (-ая, -ое, -ие) *прил* imperialistic.

импе́ри|я (-и) *ж* empire.

импе́рск|ий (-ая, -ое, -ие) *прил* imperial.

импи́чмент (-а) *м* (*ПОЛИТ*) impeachment.

имплантáт (-а) *м* (*МЕД*) implant.

имплантáци|я (-и) *ж* implantation.

имплантти́р|овать (-ую) *(не)сов перех* to implant.

импони́р|овать (-ую) *несов неперех* (+*dat*) to appeal to.

и́мпорт (-а) *м* (*ввоз*) importation ♦ *собир* (*товары*) imports *мн*; (*разг: о заграничных товарах*) foreign goods *мн*; **по́шлины/нало́г на** ~ import duty/tax; **и́мпорт капита́ла** capital investment from abroad.

импортёр (-а) *м* importer.

импорти́р|овать (-ую) *(не)сов перех* to import.

и́мпортный *прил* imported; **и́мпортная кво́та** import quota.

импоте́нт (-а) *м* impotent male.

импоте́нт|ный (-ен, -на, -но) *прил* (*МЕД*) impotent.

импоте́нци|я (-и) *ж* (*МЕД*) impotence.

импреса́рио *м нескл* (*музыканта*) agent; (*устроитель концертов итп*) impresario.

импрессиони́зм (-а) *м* impressionism.

импрессионисти́ческ|ий (-ая, -ое, -ие) *прил* impressionist.

импровиза́тор (-а) *м* improviser.

импровиза́ци|я (-и) *ж* improvisation.

импровизи́р|овать (-ую; *perf* **импровизи́ровать** *или* **сымпровизи́ровать**) *(не)сов перех* to improvise.

и́мпульс (-а) *м* (*ФИЗ, БИО*) impulse; (*перен*): ~ (**к** +*dat*) (**к рабо́те, к рефо́рмам** итп) impetus (for).

импульси́в|ный (-ен, -на, -но) *прил* impulsive.

иму́щественный *прил* property *опред*.

иму́ществ|о (-а) *ср* property; (*принадлежности*) belongings *мн*; **дви́жимое** ~ (*ЮР*) movables; **недви́жимое** ~ (*ЮР*) property.

иму́щ|ий (-ая, -ее, -ие) *прил* (*классы*) propertied; **власть ~ие** the powers that be.

и́м|я (-ени; *как* **вре́мя**; *см* **Table 4**) *ср* (*также перен*) name; (*также:* **ли́чное** ~) first *или* Christian name; (*знаменитый человек*) famous name; **во** ~ +*gen* (*ради*) in the name of; **на** ~ +*gen* (*письмо*) addressed to; **биле́ты оста́влены на Ва́ше** ~ the tickets have been left under your name; **от** ~**ени** +*gen* on behalf of; **моё** ~ — **Мари́я** my name is Maria; **Теа́тр** ~**ени Че́хова** the Chekhov Theatre; ~**енем зако́на** in the name of the law; **называ́ть** *(impf)* **ве́щи свои́ми имена́ми** to call a spade a spade; **и́мя прилага́тельное** adjective; **и́мя существи́тельное** noun.

инакомы́слящ|ий (-его; *decl like adj*) *м* dissident.

ина́че *нареч* (*по-другому*) differently ♦ *союз* otherwise, or else; **вы́глядеть** *(impf)* ~ to look different; **так и́ли** ~ one way or another; **а как же** ~? how else?

инвали́д (-а) *м* disabled person (*мн* people).

инвали́дн|ый *прил*: ~**ая коля́ска** wheelchair; **инвали́дный дом** home for the disabled.
инвали́дность (-и) *ж* disability; **пе́нсия по ~и** disablement benefit; **получа́ть (получи́ть** *perf***)** ~ to be registered as disabled.
инвалю́т|а (-ы) *ж сокр* (= *иностра́нная валю́та*) foreign currency.
инвалю́тный *прил* (*поступле́ния, счёт*) foreign-currency.
инвентариза́ци|я (-и) *ж* stocktaking.
инвента́р|ь (-я́) *м* (*предме́ты*) equipment; (*о́пись*) inventory.
инве́рси|я (-и) *ж* (*линг*) inversion.
инвести́р|овать (-ую) (*не*)*сов* (*не*)*перех* (*эко́н*) to invest.
инвестицио́нный *прил* investment *опред*; **инвестицио́нный банк** investment bank.
инвести́ци|я (-и) *ж* (*обы́чно мн*) investment; **иностра́нные ~и** foreign investment; **дохо́д от ~й** investment income.
инве́стор (-а) *м* investor.
ингаля́тор (-а) *м* (*мед*) inhaler.
ингаля́ци|я (-и) *ж* inhalation.
ингредие́нт (-а) *м* ingredient.
ингу́ш (-а́) *м* Ingush.
Ингуше́ти|я (-и) *ж* Ingushetia.
ингу́ш|ка (-ки; *gen pl* -**ек**) *ж см* **ингу́ш**.
йндеве́ть (-ю; *perf* **зайндеве́ть**) *несов неперех* to become covered in frost.
инде́ек *сущ см* **инде́йка**.
инде́|ец (-йца) *м* Native American, North American Indian.
инде́|йка (-йки; *gen pl* -**ек**) *ж* turkey.
инде́йца *итп сущ см* **инде́ец**.
йндекс (-а) *м* (*цен, книг*) index (*мн* indexes); (*также*: **почто́вый ~**) post (*BRIT*) *или* zip (*US*) code; **фо́ндовый ~** share index; **йндекс (ро́зничных/потреби́тельных) цен** (retail/consumer) price index.
индекса́ци|я (-и) *ж* (*эко́н*) index-linking (*BRIT*), indexing (*US*).
индекси́р|овать (-ую) *несов перех* (*эко́н: зарпла́ту*) to index, index-link (*BRIT*).
индиа́н|ка (-ки; *gen pl* -**ок**) *ж см* **инди́ец, инде́ец**.
индиви́д (-а) *м* individual.
индивидуа́лен *прил см* **индивидуа́льный**.
индивидуали́зм (-а) *м* individualism.
индивидуали́ст (-а) *м* individualist.
индивидуа́льность (-и) *ж* (*совоку́пность черт*) individuality; (*ли́чность*) individual.
индивидуа́льный (-ен, -ьна, -ьно) *прил* individual.
индиви́дуум (-а) *м* individual.
инди́го *ср нескл* indigo.
инди́|ец (-йца) *м* Indian.
инди́йский (-ая, -ое, -ие) *прил* Indian; **Инди́йский океа́н** the Indian Ocean.
инди́йца *итп сущ см* **инди́ец**.
Йнди|я (-и) *ж* India.
индонези́ек *сущ см* **индонези́йка**.
индонези́|ец (-йца) *м* Indonesian.
индонези́|йка (-йки; *gen pl* -**ек**) *ж см*

индонези́ец.
индонези́йск|ий (-ая, -ое, -ие) *прил* Indonesian.
индонези́йца *итп сущ см* **индонези́ец**.
Индоне́зи|я (-и) *ж* Indonesia.
индосса́нт (-а) *м* (*комм*) endorser.
индосса́т (-а) *м* (*комм*) endorsee.
индуи́зм (-а) *м* Hinduism.
инду́кци|я (-и) *ж* (*физ*) induction.
инду́с (-а) *м* Hindu.
индустриализа́ци|я (-и) *ж* industrialization.
индустриализи́р|овать (-ую) (*не*)*сов перех* to industrialize.
индустриа́льный *прил* industrial.
индустри́|я (-и) *ж* industry; ~ **мо́ды/кино́/тури́зма** the fashion/film/tourist industry.
индю́к (-а́) *м* turkey cock.
индю́ш|ка (-ки; *gen pl* -**ек**) *ж* (*разг*) = **инде́йка**.
йне|й (-я) *м* hoarfrost.
ине́рт|ный (-ен, -на, -но) *прил* (*физ, хим*) inert; (*перен*) inactive.
ине́рци|я (-и) *ж* (*физ, перен*) inertia; **дви́гаться** (*impf*) **по ~и** (*физ*) to move by inertia; **де́лать** (*impf*) **что-н по ~и** to do sth out of habit; **я по ~и дал ему́ ста́рый телефо́н** I gave him my old telephone number automatically.
инжене́р (-а) *м* engineer; ~ **по те́хнике безопа́сности** health and safety officer; **инжене́р-меха́ник/-констру́ктор/-строи́тель** mechanical/design/construction engineer.
инжене́рн|ый *прил*: ~**ая нау́ка** engineering (*science*); ~**ое де́ло** engineering (*profession*).
инжи́р (-а) *м* (*де́рево*) fig ♦ *собир* (*плоды́*) figs *мн*.
ИНИО́Н (-а) *м сокр* = *Институ́т нау́чной информа́ции по обще́ственным нау́кам*.
инициализи́р|овать (-ую) (*не*)*сов перех* (*комп*) to initialize.
инициа́л|ы (-ов) *мн* initials *мн*.
инициати́в|а (-ы) *ж* initiative; **по со́бственной ~е** on one's own initiative.
инициати́в|ный (-ен, -на, -но) *прил* enterprising; **он о́чень ~ челове́к** he has a lot of initiative; **инициати́вная гру́ппа** action group.
инициа́тор (-а) *м* initiator.
инкасса́тор (-а) *м* security guard (*employed to collect and deliver money*).
инкасси́р|овать (-ую) (*не*)*сов перех* (*комм*) to encash.
инка́ссо *ср нескл* (*комм*) encashment.
инквизи́тор (-а) *м* (*перен*) inquisitor.
инквизи́ци|я (-и) *ж* (*перен*) inquisition.
инко́гнито *нареч, м/ж нескл* incognito.
Инкомба́нк (-а) *м сокр* (= *Иностра́нный комме́рческий банк*) foreign commercial bank.
инкримини́р|овать (-ую) (*не*)*сов перех*: ~ **что-н кому́-н** to charge sb with sth.
инкруста́ци|я (-и) *ж* inlay.
инкрусти́р|овать (-ую) (*не*)*сов перех* to inlay.
инкуба́тор (-а) *м* incubator.

инкубацио́нный *прил*: ~ пери́од (*БИО, МЕД*) incubation period.
инкуба́ци|я (-и) *ж* incubation.
иногда́ *нареч* sometimes.
иногоро́дн|ий (-яя, -ее, -ие) *прил* from another town ♦ (-его; *decl like adj*) *м person from another town*.
иноземный *прил* foreign.
ин|о́й *прил* different ♦ *мест* (*некоторый*) some (people); ~ раз at times; ~ыми слова́ми in other words; не что ~о́е, как ..., не кто ~, как ... none other than ...; ~ые счита́ют, что ... some (people) think (that) ....
йнок (-а) *м* monk (*in the Orthodox Church*).
инопланетя́н|ин (-ина; *nom pl* -е, *gen pl* -) *м* alien.
иноро́д|ный (-ен, -на, -но) *прил* alien; иноро́дное те́ло (*МЕД*) foreign body.
иносказа́ни|е (-я) *ср* allegory.
иносказа́тел|ьный (-ен, -ьна, -ьно) *прил* allegorical.
иностра́н|ец (-ца) *м* foreigner.
иностра́н|ка (-ки; *gen pl* -ок) *ж см* иностра́нец.
иностра́нный *прил* foreign; Министе́рство ~ых дел Ministry of Foreign Affairs, ≈ Foreign Office (*BRIT*), ≈ State Department (*US*).
иностра́нок *сущ см* иностра́нка.
иностра́нца *итп сущ см* иностра́нец.
иноязы́чн|ый *прил* (*слово*) foreign; ~ое населе́ние foreign-language-speaking population.
инсинуа́ци|я (-и) *ж* insinuation.
инспекти́р|овать (-ую; *perf* проинспекти́ровать) *несов перех* to inspect.
инспе́ктор (-а) *м* inspector.
инспе́кци|я (-и) *ж* inspection; (*организация*) inspectorate.
инста́нци|я (-и) *ж* (*ПОЛИТ*) body, authority.
инсти́нкт (-а) *м* instinct.
инстинкти́в|ный (-ен, -на, -но) *прил* instinctive.
институ́т (-а) *м* institute; (*семьи, брака*) institution.
институ́тск|ий (-ая, -ое, -ие) *прил* institute опред.
инструкти́р|овать (-ую; *perf* проинструкти́ровать) *(не)сов перех* to instruct.
инстру́ктор (-а) *м* instructor; ~ по пла́ванию/лы́жам swimming/ski instructor.
инстру́кци|я (-и) *ж* instructions *мн*; (*также:* ~ по эксплуата́ции) instructions (for use).
инструме́нт (-а) *м* (*МУЗ, ТЕХ, перен*) instrument ♦ *собир* instruments *мн*.
инструмента́льный *прил* (*МУЗ*) instrumental; инструмента́льная му́зыка instrumental music; инструмента́льный анса́мбль instrumental ensemble; инструмента́льный

цех tool workshop.
инсули́н (-а) *м* insulin.
инсу́льт (-а) *м* (*МЕД*) stroke.
инсцени́р|овать (-ую) *(не)сов перех* (*перен: обморок, ограбление*) to stage; (*роман*) to adapt.
инсцениро́вк|а (-и) *ж* adaptation.
ин-т *сокр* = институ́т.
интегра́л (-а) *м* (*МАТ*) integral.
интегра́ль|ный *прил*: ~ое исчисле́ние integral calculus.
интегри́р|овать (-ую) *(не)сов перех* (*также МАТ*) to integrate.
интегра́ци|я (-и) *ж* (*также МАТ*) integration.
интелле́кт (-а) *м* intellect.
интеллектуа́л (-а) *м* intellectual.
интеллектуа́л|ьный (-ен, -ьна, -ьно) *прил* intellectual; интеллектуа́льная со́бственность intellectual property.
интеллиге́нт (-а) *м* member of the intelligentsia.
интеллиге́нт|ный (-ен, -на, -но) *прил* cultured and educated.
интеллиге́нци|я (-и) *ж собир* the intelligentsia; техни́ческая/тво́рческая ~ the science/arts community.
интенда́нт (-а) *м* (*ВОЕН*) quartermaster.
интенси́в|ный (-ен, -на, -но) *прил* intensive; (*окраска*) intense.
интенсифика́ци|я (-и) *ж* intensification.
интенсифици́р|овать (-ую) *(не)сов перех* to intensify.
интеракти́вный *прил* (*КОМП*) interactive.
интерва́л (-а) *м* interval; (*ТИПОГ*) spacing; с ~ом в 10 мину́т with a 10 minute interval.
интерве́нт (-а) *м* interventionist.
интерве́нци|я (-и) *ж* intervention.
интервью́ *ср нескл* interview; брать (взять *perf*)/дава́ть (дать *perf*) ~ to do/give an interview.
интервьюи́р|овать (-ую; *perf* проинтервьюи́ровать) *(не)сов перех* to interview.
интере́с (-а) *м*: ~ (к +*dat*) interest (in); представля́ть (предста́вить *perf*) ~ (для +*gen*) to be of interest (to); *см также* интере́сы.
интере́сен *прил см* интере́сный.
интере́сно *нареч*: он о́чень ~ расска́зывает he is very interesting to listen to ♦ *как сказ*: ~(, что ...) it's interesting (that ...); мне э́то о́чень ~ I find it very interesting; э́то никому́ не ~ that is of no interest to anyone; ~, где он э́то нашёл I wonder where he found that; ~ знать, где он был I'd be interested to know where he was; как ~! that's really interesting!; ~! (*разг: выражает недовольство, возражение*) so!; она́ ~ мы́слит she has an interesting way of thinking.

интере́с|ный (-ен, -на, -но) *прил* interesting; (*внешность, женщина*) attractive.

интересова́ть (-у́ю) *несов перех* to interest

► **интересова́ться** *несов возв* (+*instr*) to be interested in; (*осведомляться*) to inquire after; **он ~ова́лся, когда́ ты приезжа́ешь/где ты бу́дешь жить** he was asking when you would be arriving/where you would be living.

интере́с|ы (-ов) *мн* (*госуда́рства, фи́рмы итп*) interests *мн*; (*духо́вные*) concerns *мн*; **в ~ах** +*gen* in the interests of; **затра́гивать** (**затро́нуть** *perf*) *или* **задева́ть** (**заде́ть** *perf*) **чьи-н ~** to touch on sb's interests.

интерлю́ди|я (-и) *ж* (*муз*) interlude.

интерме́ди|я (-и) *ж* (*ТЕАТР*) interlude.

интéрн (-а) *м* (*МЕД*) ≈ houseman (*BRIT*) (*мн* housemen), ≈ intern (*US*).

интерна́т (-а) *м* boarding school.

Интернациона́л (-а) *м* (*ИСТ*) the International.

интернационализа́ци|я (-и) *ж* internationalization.

интернационали́зм (-а) *м* internationalism.

интернационали́ст (-а) *м* internationalist.

интернациона́льный *прил* international.

ИНТЕРПО́Л (-а) *м сокр* (= *Междунаро́дная организа́ция уголо́вной поли́ции*) Interpol (= *International Criminal Police Organization*).

интерпрета́тор (-а) *м* interpreter.

интерпрета́ци|я (-и) *ж* interpretation.

интерпрети́р|овать (-ую) (*не*)*сов перех* to interpret.

интерфе́йс (-а) *м* (*КОМП*) interface.

интерье́р (-а) *м* (*зда́ния*) interior.

инти́м|ный (-ен, -на, -но) *прил* intimate.

интоксика́ци|я (-и) *ж* intoxication.

интона́ци|я (-и) *ж* (*линг, муз*) intonation; (*недово́льная, трево́жная итп*) note.

интри́г|а (-и) *ж* (*полити́ческая*) intrigue; (*любо́вная*) affair; (*рома́на*) plot.

интрига́н (-а) *м* intriguer.

интрига́н|ка (-ки; *gen pl* -ок) *ж см* **интрига́н**.

интриг|ова́ть (-у́ю; *perf* **заинтригова́ть**) *несов перех* to intrigue ◆ *несов непepex* (*no perf*): ~ **про́тив** +*gen* to intrigue against.

интрове́рт (-а) *м* introvert.

интуити́в|ный (-ен, -на, -но) *прил* intuitive.

интуи́ци|я (-и) *ж* intuition.

Интури́ст (-а) *м сокр* (= *Гла́вное управле́ние по иностра́нному тури́зму*) *Russian tourist agency dealing with foreign tourism.*

инфа́ркт (-а) *м* (*также:* ~ **миока́рда**) heart attack; **обши́рный ~** (**миока́рда**) massive heart attack.

инфекцио́нный *прил* infectious; **инфекцио́нная больни́ца** hospital for infectious diseases.

инфе́кци|я (-и) *ж* infection.

инфинити́в (-а) *м* infinitive.

инфици́рован|ный (-, -на, -но) *прил* infected.

инфля́ци|я (-и) *ж* (*ЭКОН*) inflation.

инфляцио́нный *прил* inflationary.

информати́в|ный (-ен, -на, -но) *прил* informative.

информа́ти|ка (-и) *ж* information technology.

информа́тор (-а) *м* informant.

информацио́нный *прил* information *опред*; **информацио́нная програ́мма** news programme (*BRIT*) *или* program (*US*).

информа́ци|я (-и) *ж* information.

информи́рованный *прил* well-informed.

информи́р|овать (-ую; *perf* **информи́ровать** *или* **проинформи́ровать**) *несов перех* to inform.

инфракра́сный *прил* infrared.

инфраструкту́р|а (-ы) *ж* infrastructure.

инциде́нт (-а) *м* incident.

инъе́кци|я (-и) *ж* injection.

инъя́з (-а) *м сокр* = *институ́т иностра́нных языко́в; факульте́т иностра́нных языко́в.*

и.о. *сокр* (= *исполня́ющий обя́занности*) acting.

ио́н (-а) *м* ion.

иорда́н|ец (-ца) *м* Jordanian.

Иорда́ни|я (-и) *ж* Jordan.

иорда́н|ка (-ки; *gen pl* -ок) *ж см* **иорда́нец**.

иорда́нский (-ая, -ое, -ие) *прил* Jordanian.

иорда́нца *сущ см* **иорда́нец**.

ипоста́с|ь (-и) *ж* (*РЕЛ*) hypostasis; **в ~и** +*gen* (*перен*) in the role of.

ипоте́|ка (-и) *ж* (*КОММ*) mortgage.

ипоте́ч|ный *прил* mortgage; ~**ая ссу́да** mortgage; ~ **банк** ≈ building society.

ипохо́ндрик (-а) *м* hypochondriac.

ипохо́ндри|я (-и) *ж* hypochondria.

ипподро́м (-а) *м* racecourse (*BRIT*), racetrack (*US*).

ипри́т (-а) *м* mustard gas.

Ира́к (-а) *м* Iraq.

ира́к|ец (-ца) *м* Iraqi.

ира́кский (-ая, -ое, -ие) *прил* Iraqi.

ира́кца *итп сущ см* **ира́кец**.

Ира́н (-а) *м* Iran.

ира́н|ец (-ца) *м* Iranian.

ира́н|ка (-ки; *gen pl* -ок) *ж см* **ира́нец**.

ира́нский (-ая, -ое, -ие) *прил* Iranian.

ира́нца *итп сущ см* **ира́нец**.

и́рис (-а) *м* (*БОТ*) iris; (*ни́тки*) thread (*for embroidery etc*).

ири́с (-а) *м* (*конфе́та*) toffee.

ири́с|ка (-ки; *gen pl* -ок) *ж* (*разг*) toffee.

ирла́нд|ец (-ца) *м* Irishman (*мн* Irishmen).

Ирла́нди|я (-и) *ж* Ireland.

ирла́нд|ка (-ки; *gen pl* -ок) *ж* Irishwoman (*мн* Irishwomen).

ирла́ндский (-ая, -ое, -ие) *прил* Irish.

ирла́ндца *итп сущ см* **ирла́ндец**.

ИРЛИ *м сокр* = *Институ́т ру́сской литерату́ры.*

ирони́зи́р|овать (-ую) *несов непepex*: ~ **(над** +*instr*) to be ironic (about).

ирони́ч|ный (-ен, -на, -но) *прил* ironic.

иро́ни|я (-и) *ж* irony; ~ **судьбы́** the irony of fate.

иррациона́л|ьный (-ен, -ьна, -ьно) *прил* irrational.

иррегуля́рн|ый *прил*: ~ые войска́ irregular forces *мн*, irregulars *мн*.

иррига́ци|я (-и) *ж* irrigation.

иск (-а) *м* lawsuit; встре́чный ~ counterclaim; де́нежный ~ damages; предъявля́ть (предъяви́ть *perf*) кому́-н ~ to take legal action against sb.

искажа́ть(ся) (-ю(сь)) *несов от* исказить(ся).

искаже́ни|е (-я) *ср* (*фактов*) distortion; (*в тексте*) error.

иска|зи́ть (-жу́, -зи́шь; *impf* искажа́ть) *сов перех* (*факты, смысл*) to distort; (*лицо*) to contort; (*КОМП*) to corrupt; зло́ба ~зи́ла его́ лицо́ his face contorted with malice

▸ искази́ться (*impf* искажа́ться) *сов возв* (*изображение, смысл*) to be distorted; (*выражение лица, голос*) to contort.

искале́ч|ить (-у, -ишь) *сов от* кале́чить.

иска́ни|е (-я) *ср* (*обычно мн: творческие, научные*) quest.

иска́тель (-я) *м* (*золота*) prospector; (*стремящийся к новому*) explorer; ~ приключе́ний adventure seeker.

иска́тельниц|а (-ы) *ж см* иска́тель.

иска́ть (ищу́, и́щешь) *несов перех* to look *или* search for.

исключа́ть (-ю) *несов от* исключи́ть.

исключа́|я *предл* (+*acc*) excluding; не ~ +*gen* including.

исключе́ни|е (-я) *ср* (*из списка, из очереди*) exclusion; (*из института*) expulsion; (*отклонение от нормы*) exception; ~ из пра́вила exception to the rule; за ~м +*gen* with the exception of; де́лать (сде́лать *perf*) что-н в ви́де ~я to make an exception of sth.

исключи́телен *прил см* исключи́тельный.

исключи́тельно *нареч* (*особенно*) exceptionally; (*только*) exclusively.

исключи́тельный (-ен, -ьна, -ьно) *прил* exceptional; (*no short form*; *право*) exclusive.

исключ|и́ть (-у́, -и́шь; *impf* исключа́ть) *сов перех* (*удалить: из списка*) to exclude; (: *из института*) to expel; (*ошибку, случайность*) to exclude the possibility of; э́то ~ено́ that is out of the question; компроми́сс ~ён a compromise is out of the question.

исковерка́ть (-ю) *сов от* кове́ркать.

исколе|си́ть (-шу́, -си́шь) *сов перех* (*разг*) to travel; он ~си́л весь мир he's been all over the world.

иско́мка|ть (-ю) *сов от* ко́мкать.

иско́м|ый *прил* (*МАТ*): ~ая величина́ unknown value ♦ (-ого; *decl like adj*) *ср* (*МАТ*) unknown.

иско́нный (-ен, -на, -но) *прил* (*население*) original; (*право*) intrinsic; ~ язы́к the vernacular.

ископа́ем|ое (-ого; *decl like adj*) *ср* fossil; (*также*: поле́зное ~: *обычно мн*) mineral.

ископа́емый *прил* (*животное, растение*) fossilized.

искорёж|ить (-у, -ишь) *сов от* корёжить.

искорен|и́ть (-ю́, -и́шь; *impf* искореня́ть) *сов перех* to eradicate.

и́скоса *нареч* (*взглянуть, смотреть*) sideways; смотре́ть (*impf*) ~ на кого́-н (*перен*) to look askance at sb.

и́скр|а (-ы) *ж* (*огня, также перен*) spark; (*снега, бриллианта*) glint, glistening; у меня́ ~ы из глаз посы́пались I began to see stars; зарони́ть (*perf*) в ком-н ~у наде́жды to give sb a glimmer of hope.

и́скренне *нареч* sincerely; ~ Ваш Yours sincerely.

и́скрен|ний (-няя, -нее, -ние; -ен, -на, -но *или* -не) *прил* sincere.

и́скренност|ь (-и) *ж* sincerity.

искрив|и́ть (-лю́, -и́шь; *impf* искривля́ть) *сов перех* to bend.

искривле́ни|е (-я) *ср* bend; искривле́ние позвоно́чника (*МЕД*) curvature of the spine.

искривлю́ *сов см* искриви́ть.

искривля́|ть (-ю) *несов от* искриви́ть.

искри́ст|ый (-, -а, -о) *прил* glistening, sparkling.

искри́ться (-ю́сь, -и́шься) *несов возв* to glisten, sparkle.

искроме́тный (-ен, -на, -но) *прил* (*перен: взгляд*) fiery; (: *остроумие*) sparkling.

искромса́ть (-ю) *сов от* кромса́ть.

искрош|и́ть (-у́, -и́шь) *сов от* кроши́ть.

искупа́ть(ся) (-ю(сь)) *сов от* купа́ть(ся).

иск|упи́ть (-уплю́, -у́пишь; *impf* искупа́ть) *сов перех* (*перен: вину, проступок*) to atone for, expiate; (*возмещать, также РЕЛ*) to redeem.

искупле́ни|е (-я) *ср* (*вины, проступка*) atonement, expiation; (*РЕЛ*) redemption.

искуплю́ *сов см* искупи́ть.

искуса́|ть (-ю; *impf* искусывать) *сов перех* (*подлеж: комары*) to bite all over; (: *пчёлы*) to sting all over.

иску́сен *прил см* иску́сный.

искуси́тель (-я) *м* tempter.

иску́сник (-а) *м* master.

иску́сниц|а (-ы) *ж см* иску́сник.

иску́с|ный (-ен, -на, -но) *прил* (*работник*) skilful (*BRIT*), skillful (*US*); (*работа*) fine.

иску́сственник (-а) *м* bottle-fed baby.

иску́сственниц|а (-ы) *ж см* иску́сственник.

иску́сствен|ный *прил* artificial; (*волокно, ткань, камин*) synthetic; (*мех*) fake; (-, -на, -но; *притворный: смех*) faked; иску́сственное дыха́ние artificial respiration; иску́сственный интелле́кт artificial intelligence; иску́сственный спу́тник Земли́ artificial satellite.

иску́сств|о (-а) *ср* art; де́лать (*impf*) что-н из любви́ к ~у (*разг*) to do sth for its own sake.

The spelling rules for Russian are shown on page xvii.

искусствовéд (**-а**) *м* art historian.
искусствовéдени|е (**-я**) *ср* art history.
искýсыва|ть (**-ю**) *несов от* **искусáть**.
искуша|ть (**-ю**) *несов перех* to tempt; ~ (*impf*) **судьбý** to tempt fate.
искушéни|е (**-я**) *ср* temptation; **поддавáться** (**поддáться** *perf*) ~**ю** to give in to temptation.
искушён|ный (**-**, **-á**, **-ó**) *прил* (*зритель, публика*) sophisticated; (*политик*) seasoned; (*женщина*) worldly; **он искушён в такúх делáх** he is well versed in such matters.
ислáм (**-а**) *м* Islam.
ислáмский (**-ая**, **-ое**, **-ие**) *прил* Islamic.
ислáнд|ец (**-ца**) *м* Icelander.
Ислáнди|я (**-и**) *ж* Iceland.
ислáнд|ка (**-ки**; *gen pl* **-ок**) *ж см* **ислáндец**.
ислáндский (**-ая**, **-ое**, **-ие**) *прил* Icelandic; ~ **язы́к** Icelandic.
ислáндца *итп сущ см* **ислáндец**.
испáко|стить (**-щу**, **-стишь**) *сов от* **пáкостить**.
испáн|ец (**-ца**) *м* Spaniard.
Испáни|я (**-и**) *ж* Spain.
испáн|ка (**-ки**; *gen pl* **-ок**) *ж см* **испáнец**.
испáнский (**-ая**, **-ое**, **-ие**) *прил* Spanish; ~ **язы́к** Spanish.
испáнца *итп сущ см* **испáнец**.
испарéни|е (**-я**) *ср* (*действие: воды*) evaporation; (*обычно мн: продукт*) vapour (*BRIT*), vapor (*US*).
испáрин|а (**-ы**) *ж* perspiration.
испар|и́ть (**-ю**, **-и́шь**; *impf* **испаря́ть**) *сов перех* to evaporate
▶ **испари́ться** (*impf* **испаря́ться**) *сов возв* (*также перен*) to evaporate.
испáчка|ть(ся) (**-ю(сь)**) *сов от* **пáчкать(ся)**.
испеку́(сь) *итп сов см* **испéчь(ся)**.
испепел|и́ть (**-ю́**, **-и́шь**; *impf* **испепеля́ть**) *сов перех* to reduce to ashes; **испепеля́ть** (~ *perf*) **кого́-н взгля́дом** to give sb a withering look.
испéч|ь(ся) (**-ку́(сь)**, **-чёшь(ся)** *итп*, **-ку́т(ся)**) *сов от* **пéчь(ся)**.
испещр|и́ть (**-ю́**, **-и́шь**; *impf* **испещря́ть**) *сов перех* to speckle.
испис|áть (**-ишу́**, **-и́шешь**; *impf* **испи́сывать**) *сов перех* (*тетрадь, дневник*) to fill up; (*карандаш, ручку*) to wear out; (*бумагу*) to use up
▶ **исписáться** (*impf* **испи́сываться**) *несов возв* (*карандаш*) to wear out; (*ручка*) to run out; (*разг: писатель*) to lose one's touch.
испи|ть (**изопью́**, **изопьёшь**; *pt* **-л**, **-лá**, **-ло**) *сов неперех* (+*gen*; *перен: горя, разочарований*) to suffer; (*воды*) to sup.
испишý(сь) *итп сов см* **исписáть(ся)**.
исповедáль|ня (**-ьни**; *gen pl* **-ен**) *ж* (*РЕЛ*) confessional.
исповéдани|е (**-я**) *ср* denomination.
исповéда|ть(ся) (**-ю(сь)**) (*не*)*сов* = **исповéдовать(ся)**.
исповéдник (**-а**) *м* (*РЕЛ*) confessor.
исповéд|овать (**-ую**) *несов перех* (*религию,*

мораль, идею) to profess ◆ (*не*)*сов перех* (*РЕЛ*): ~ **кого́-н** to hear sb's confession
▶ **исповéдоваться** (*не*)*сов возв*: ~**ся кому́-н** *или* **у кого́-н** to confess to sb.
и́споведь (**-и**) *ж* (*РЕЛ, перен*) confession.
и́сподволь *нареч* unbeknown to all.
исподло́бья *нареч*: **гляде́ть на кого́-н** ~ to look at sb with mistrust.
исподтишка́ *нареч* (*разг: действовать*) on the sly *или* quiet.
испоко́н *предл*: ~ **веко́в** from time immemorial.
исполи́н (**-а**) *м* giant.
исполи́нский (**-ая**, **-ое**, **-ие**) *прил* gargantuan.
исполко́м (**-а**) *м сокр* (= **исполни́тельный комите́т**) executive committee.
исполнéни|е (**-я**) *ср* (*приказа, указа*) execution; (*обещания, желания*) fulfilment (*BRIT*), fulfillment (*US*) (*симфонии, роли итп*) performance; **в** ~**и** +*gen* performed by; **приводи́ть** (**привести́** *perf*) **что-н в** ~ to carry sth out; **э́кспортное** ~ (*КОММ*) export version.
испо́лнен|ный (**-**, **-а**, **-о**) *прил* (+*gen*) full of, filled with.
исполни́м|ый (**-**, **-а**, **-о**) *прил* (*просьба, желание*) realizable.
исполни́телен *прил см* **исполни́тельный**.
исполни́тел|ь (**-я**) *м* (*пьесы, роли*) performer; (*приказа, политики*) executive; **судéбный** ~ bailiff.
исполни́тельниц|а (**-ы**) *ж см* **исполни́тель**.
исполни́тельный *прил* (*комитет, власть*) executive; (**-ен**, **-ьна**, **-ьно**; *старательный*) efficient; **исполни́тельный дирéктор** executive director; **исполни́тельный лист** (*ЮР*) court order.
испо́лн|ить (**-ю**, **-ишь**; *impf* **исполня́ть**) *сов перех* (*приказ*) to carry out; (*обещание, долг, желание*) to fulfil (*BRIT*), fulfill (*US*); (*танец, симфонию, роль итп*) to perform; ~ (*perf*) **кого́-н надéждой/рáдостью** *итп* to fill sb with hope/joy *итп*
▶ **испо́лниться** (*impf* **исполня́ться**) *сов возв* (*желание*) to be fulfilled; (+*instr*; *надеждой, радостью*) to be filled with; **ему́** ~**илось 10 лет** he is 10.
испо́льзовани|е (**-я**) *ср* use.
испо́льз|овать (**-ую**) (*не*)*сов перех* to use.
испо́рт|ить(ся) (**-чу(сь)**, **-тишь(ся)**) *сов от* **по́ртить(ся)**.
испо́рченный *прил* (*замок*) broken; (*настроение*) bad; (*ребёнок*) spoilt; (*КОМП*) corrupt.
испрáвен *прил см* **испрáвный**.
исправи́м|ый (**-**, **-а**, **-о**) *прил* correctable.
исправи́тельный *прил* (*меры*) corrective; **исправи́тельные рабо́ты** (*ЮР*) corrective labour.
исправи́тельно-трудово́й *прил*: **исправи́тельно-трудовáя коло́ния** labour (*BRIT*) *или* labor (*US*) colony.
испрáв|ить (**-лю**, **-ишь**; *impf* **исправля́ть**) *сов*

перех (повреждение, телефон) to repair;
(ошибку) to correct; *(характер, дисциплину)* to
improve

▶ **испра́виться** *(impf* **исправля́ться)** *сов возв*
(характер, человек) to change (for the better).

исправле́ни|е *(-я)* *ср (повреждения)* repairing;
(: характера) reforming; *(текста,*
преступника) correction; **вноси́ть (внести́** *perf)*
~я в +*acc* to make corrections to.

испра́влю(сь) *сов см* **испра́вить(ся)**.

исправля́ть(ся) *(-ю(сь))* *несов от*
испра́вить(ся).

испра́вность *(-и)* *ж:* **в (по́лной) ~и** in (full)
working order; **всё в ~и** everything's in order.

испра́вный *(-ен, -на, -но)* *прил (механизм)* in
good working order; *(работник)* diligent.

испражне́ни|е *(-я)* *ср* faeces *мн*.

испражня́ться *(-юсь)* *несов возв* to defecate.

испро́б|овать *(-ую)* *сов от* **про́бовать**.

испу́г *(-а; part gen* **-у)** *м* fright; **в ~е, с ~у** in *или*
with fright.

испу́ган|ный *(-, -а, -о)* *прил (человек)*
frightened; *(-, -на, -но; вид, взгляд)* frightened.

испуга́|ть(ся) *(-ю(сь))* *сов от* **пуга́ть(ся)**.

испу|сти́ть *(-ущу́, -у́стишь; impf* **испуска́ть)** *сов*
перех (крик, стон) to let out; *(свет)* to give off,
emit.

испыта́ни|е *(-я)* *ср (машины, прибора итп)*
testing; *(нового работника)* trial; *(обычно мн:*
экзамен) test; *(несчастье)* ordeal.

испы́тан|ный *(-, -на, -но)* *прил (приём)* tried
and tested; *(друг)* proven.

испыта́тел|ь *(-я)* *м* tester; **лётчик-испыта́тель**
test pilot.

испыта́тельный *прил:* **~ срок** trial period,
probation; **испыта́тельная тра́сса** test circuit;
испыта́тельный полёт test flight.

испыта́|ть *(-ю; impf* **испы́тывать)** *сов перех*
(механизм) to test; *(работника)* to try out;
(нужду, трудности, радость итп) to
experience.

испыту́ющий *(-ая, -ее, -ие; -, -а, -е)* *прил:* **~**
взгляд searching look.

испы́тыва|ть *(-ю)* *несов от* **испыта́ть**.

иссе́|чь *(-еку́, -ечёшь итп, -еку́т; pt* **-ёк, -екла́,**
-екло́) *сов перех (кнутом)* to flog.

и́ссиня- *префикс:* **~чёрный** blue-black.

иссле́довани|е *(-я)* *ср (см глаг)* research;
examination; *(научный труд)* study;
занима́ться *(impf)* **~ями в о́бласти** +*gen* to
conduct research into.

иссле́довател|ь *(-я)* *м* researcher.

иссле́довательск|ий *(-ая, -ое, -ие)* *прил:* **~ая**
рабо́та research; **~ институ́т** research institute.

иссле́д|овать *(-ую)* *(не)сов перех* to research;
(больного) to examine.

иссо́х|нуть *(-ну, -нешь; pt* **-, -ла, -ло,** *impf*
иссыха́ть) *сов непepex (водоём)* to dry up;

(трава) to dry out; *(исхудать)* to wither away.

и́сстари *нареч* since days of old.

исстрада́|ться *(-юсь)* *сов возв* to suffer a great
deal.

исстреля́|ть *(-ю; impf* **исстре́ливать)** *сов перех*
(патроны) to use up.

исступле́ни|е *(-я)* *ср* frenzy; **приходи́ть**
(прийти́ *perf)* **в ~** to go into a frenzy.

исступлён|ный *(-, -на, -но)* *прил* frenzied.

иссыха́|ть *(-ю)* *несов от* **иссо́хнуть**.

иссяк|нуть *(3sg* **-нет,** *3pl* **-нут,** *pt* **-, -ла, -ло,** *impf*
иссяка́ть) *сов непepex (источник, запасы)* to
run dry; *(перен: терпение, силы)* to run out.

иста́плива|ть *(-ю)* *несов от* **истопи́ть**.

иста́птыва|ть *(-ю)* *несов от* **истопта́ть**.

иста́скан|ный *(-, -на, -но)* *прил (разг: вид)*
bedraggled.

истаска́|ть *(-ю; impf* **иста́скивать)** *сов перех*
(разг) to wear out.

▶ **истаска́ться** *(impf* **иста́скиваться)** *сов возв*
(разг) to wear out.

исте́блишмент *(-а)* *м* the Establishment.

истёк *итп сов см* **исте́чь**.

истека́|ть *(-ю)* *несов от* **исте́чь**.

истеку́т *итп сов см* **исте́чь**.

исте́кш|ий *(-ая, -ее, -ие)* *прил* past, previous.

ист|ере́ться *(3sg* **изотрётся,** *3pl* **изотру́тся,** *pt*
-ёрся, -ёрлась, -ёрлось, *impf* **истира́ться)** *сов*
возв (подошвы, канат) to wear down.

исте́рзан|ный *(-, -на, -но)* *прил (душа, вид)*
tortured.

истерза́|ть *(-ю)* *несов от* **терза́ть**.

исте́рик *(-а)* *м* hysterical man *(мн* men).

исте́рик|а *(-и)* *ж* hysterics *мн;* **устра́ивать**
(устро́ить *perf) или* **зака́тывать (закати́ть** *perf)*
~у to become hysterical.

истери́чек *сущ см* **истери́чка**.

истери́чен *прил см* **истери́чный**.

истери́ческ|ий *(-ая, -ое, -ие)* *прил (больной,*
смех, плач) hysterical; **~ припа́док** a fit of
hysterics.

истери́чк|а *(-ка; gen pl* **-ек)** *ж* hysterical woman
(мн women).

истери́ч|ный *(-ен, -на, -но)* *прил* hysterical.

истери́|я *(-и)* *ж (мед, перен)* hysteria.

исте́ц *(-ца́)* *м* plaintiff.

истече́ни|е *(-я)* *ср:* **по ~и** +*gen (года, месяца*
итп) after a period of; **по ~и э́того сро́ка** once
this period has elapsed; **за ~м сро́ка Ва́шего**
па́спорта due to expiry of your passport.

исте́|чь *(3sg* **-чёт,** *3pl* **-ку́т,** *pt* **-ёк, -екла́, -екло́,**
impf **истека́ть)** *сов непepex (срок)* to run out;
(время) to run out; **истека́ть (~** *perf)* **кро́вью** to
bleed.

исти́н|а *(-ы)* *ж* truth.

и́стинен *прил см* **и́стинный**.

и́стинност|ь *(-и)* *ж* truthfulness.

и́стин|ный *(-ен, -на, -но)* *прил* true.

истира́ться (*3sg* -ется, *3pl* -ются) *несов от* истере́ться.

истле́ть (-ю; *impf* истлева́ть) *сов неперех* (*сгнить*) to decompose; (*сгореть*) to turn to ash.

исто́к (-а) *м* (*обычно мн: реки*) source *только ед*; (: *перен*) source.

истолкова́ть (-у́ю; *impf* истолко́вывать) *сов перех* to interpret.

истоло́чь (-ку́, -чёшь *итп*, -ку́т; *pt* -о́к, -кла́, -кло́) *сов от* толо́чь.

исто́м|**а** (-ы) *ж* languor.

истоми́ть(ся) (-лю́(сь), -и́шь(ся)) *сов от* томи́ть(ся).

истопи́ть (-оплю́, -о́пишь; *impf* иста́пливать) *сов перех* to heat up.

истопта́ть (-опчу́, -о́пчешь; *impf* иста́птывать) *сов перех* to trample all over; (*разг: обувь*) to wear out.

исто́рик (-а) *м* historian.

истори́ческ|**ий** (-ая, -ое, -ие) *прил* historical; (*важный: событие, решение итп*) historic.

исто́ри|**я** (-и) *ж* (*наука, предмет*) history; (*рассказ, происшествие*) story; **попада́ть** (**попа́сть** *perf*) **в ~ю** (*разг*) to get into a tricky situation; **со мной произошла́ стра́нная/ заба́вная ~** a strange/funny thing happened to me; **ве́чная ~!** (*разг*) it's the same old story!; **исто́рия боле́зни** (*МЕД*) case history.

истоскова́ться (-у́юсь) *сов возв*: **~ по** +*dat* to yearn for.

источа́ть (-ю) *несов перех* (*аромат, свет, тепло*) to emit; (*ненависть, доброту итп*) to exude.

исто́чник (-а) *м* (*водный*) source, spring.

исто́ш|**ный** (-ен, -на, -но) *прил* (*крик*) desperate.

истоща́ть(ся) (-ю(сь)) *несов от* истощи́ть(ся).

истоще́ни|**е** (-я) *ср* (*организма*) depletion; (*средств, запасов*) exhaustion; **~ не́рвной систе́мы** nervous exhaustion; **доводи́ть** (**довести́** *perf*) **себя́ до по́лного ~я** to run o.s. into the ground.

истощённый (-ён, -ена́, -ено́) *прил* (*человек*) malnourished; (-ён, -ённа, -ённо; *вид, лицо*) drained.

истощи́ть (-у́, -и́шь; *impf* истоща́ть) *сов перех* (*организм*) to run down; (*почву, ресурсы*) to deplete.

▶ **истощи́ться** (*impf* истоща́ться) *сов возв* (*силы, организм, почва*) to become depleted; (*запасы, терпение*) to run out.

истра́тить(ся) (-чу(сь), -тишь(ся)) *сов от* тра́тить(ся).

истреби́тел|**ь** (-я) *м* (*ВОЕН: самолёт*) fighter (plane); (: *лётчик*) fighter pilot; (*тараканов, мышей итп*) exterminator.

истреби́тельный *прил* (*огонь*) destructive; **~ая война́** war of destruction; **~ая авиа́ция** fighter planes.

истреби́ть (-лю́, -и́шь; *impf* истребля́ть) *сов* перех (*лес, посевы итп*) to destroy; (*крыс, тараканов*) to exterminate.

истребле́ни|**е** (-я) *ср* (*см глаг*) destruction; extermination.

истребля́ю *сов см* истреби́ть.

истребля́|**ть** (-ю) *несов от* истреби́ть.

истрепа́ть(ся) (-еплю́(сь), -е́плешь(ся)) *сов от* трепа́ть(ся).

истре́ска|**ться** (*3sg* -ется, *3pl* -ются, *impf* истре́скиваться) *сов возв* to crack.

истука́н (-а) *м* idol.

истца́ *итп сущ см* исте́ц.

и́стый *прил* genuine.

истяза́ни|**е** (-я) *ср* torture.

истяза́|**ть** (-ю) *несов перех* to torture.

исхл|**еста́ть** (-ещу́, -е́щешь; *impf* исхлёстывать) *сов перех* to whip.

исхо́д (-а) *м* outcome; **у меня́ де́ньги/терпе́ние на ~е** my money/patience is running out; **на ~е дня** at the end of the day; **с лета́льным ~ом** resulting in death.

исхо|**ди́ть** (-ожу́, -о́дишь) *несов от* изойти́ ♦ *сов перех* (*обойти*) to walk all over ♦ *несов неперех*: **~ из** +*gen* (*сведения, слухи*) to emanate from; (*основываться: из данных*) to be derived from; **~одя́ из/от** +*gen* on the basis of; **я ~ожу́ из того́, что...** I am working on the premise that ....

исхо́дный *прил* (*идея, данные*) primary; **~ те́зис** premise; **исхо́дное положе́ние** (*СПОРТ*) starting position; **исхо́дный пункт** starting point.

исходя́щий (-ая, -ее, -ие) *прил* (*корреспонденция*) outgoing; **исходя́щий но́мер** (*АДМИН*) reference number.

исхожу́ (*не*)*сов см* исходи́ть.

исхуда́лый *прил* emaciated.

исхуда́ть (-ю) *сов неперех* to become emaciated.

исцара́пать (-ю; *impf* исцара́пывать) *сов перех* to scratch all over.

исцеле́ни|**е** (-я) *ср* healing.

исцел|**и́ть** (-ю́, -и́шь; *impf* исцеля́ть) *сов перех* to heal.

▶ **исцели́ться** (*impf* исцеля́ться) *сов возв* to recover.

исча́ди|**е** (-я) *ср*: **~ а́да** the devil incarnate.

исчеза́|**ть** (-ю) *несов от* исче́знуть.

исчезнове́ние (-я) *ср* disappearance.

исче́з|**нуть** (-ну, -нешь; *pt* -, -ла, -ло, *impf* исчеза́ть) *сов неперех* to disappear.

исчёрка|**ть** (-ю; *impf* исчёркивать) *сов перех* to scribble over.

исче́рпа|**ть** (-ю; *impf* исче́рпывать) *сов перех* to exhaust; **инциде́нт ~н** the matter is closed

▶ **исчерпа́ться** (*impf* исче́рпываться) *несов возв* (*запасы, терпение*) to be exhausted.

исче́рпыва|**ться** (*3sg* -ется, *3pl* -ются) *несов от* исчерпа́ться ♦ *возв* (*разрешаться*) to end; **э́тим де́ло не ~ется** the matter does not end here.

исчёрпывающ|ий (-ая, -ее, -ие; -, -а, -е) *прил* exhaustive.

исчислёни|е (-я) *ср* (*расходов, стоимости итп*) calculation; (*МАТ*) calculus.

исчйсл|ить (-ю, -ишь; *impf* **исчислять**) *сов перех* to calculate.

исчисля|ться (*3pl* -ются) *несов возв* (+*instr*; *тысячами*) to amount to.

итáк *союз* thus, hence; ~, **мóжно заключйть, что** ... thus it can be concluded that ....

Итáли|я (-и) *ж* Italy.

итальян|ец (-ца) *м* Italian.

итальян|ка (-ки; *gen pl* -ок) *ж см* **итальянец**.

итальянск|ий (-ая, -ое, -ие) *прил* Italian; ~ **язык** Italian.

итальянца *итп сущ см* **итальянец**.

ИТАР *м сокр* (= *Информациóнное телеграфное агéнтство Россúи*) *Russian telegraph agency*.

и т.д. *сокр* (= **и так дáлее**) etc. (= *et cetera*).

ИТК *м сокр* (= *исправúтельно-трудовáя колóния*) labour (*BRIT*) *или* labor (*US*) colony.

итóг (-а) *м* (*работы, переговоров итп*) result; (*общая сумма*) total; **в** ~**е** (*при подсчёте*) in total; **в** (**конéчном**) ~**е** in the end; **подводúть** (**подвестú** *perf*) ~**и** to sum up.

итогó *нареч* in total, altogether; ~, **мы заработали 100 рублéй** in total *или* altogether we made 100 roubles.

итóговый *прил* (*сумма, цифры*) total; (*результат*) final; **итóговый отчёт** (*КОММ*) financial report.

и т.п. *сокр* (= **и тому подóбное**) etc. (= *et cetera*).

иудайзм (-а) *м* Judaism.

их *мест см* **онú** ♦ *притяж мест* their; ~ **дом бóльше нáшего** their house is bigger than ours; **чья эта машúна? –** ~ whose car is this? – it's theirs.

йхн|ий (-яя, -ее, -ие) *притяж мест* (*разг*) = **их**.

ишáк (-á) *м* (*ЗООЛ*) donkey; (*перен: работяга*) dogsbody.

ишáч|ить (-у, -ишь) *несов неперех* (*разг*) to slog away.

ишь *част* (*разг*): ~ **чего захотéл!** you're asking a lot, aren't you?; ~ **какóй он нáглый!** how cheeky can he get!

ищé|йка (-йки; *gen pl* -ек) *ж* bloodhound; **полицéйская** ~ sniffer dog.

ищу *итп несов см* **искáть**.

июл|ь (-я) *м* July; *см также* **октябрь**.

июльск|ий (-ая, -ое, -ие) *прил* July *опред*.

июн|ь (-я) *м* June; *см также* **октябрь**.

июньск|ий (-ая, -ое, -ие) *прил* June *опред*.

~ *Й, й* ~

Й, й *сущ нескл (буква) the 10th letter of the Russian alphabet.*

Йе́мен (-а) *м* Yemen.

йе́мен|ец (-ца) *м* Yemeni.

йе́мен|ка (-ки; *gen pl* -ок) *ж см* **йе́менец**.

йе́менск|ий (-ая, -ое, -ие) *прил* Yemeni.

йог (-и) *ж* yogi.

йо́г|а (-и) *ж* yoga; **занима́ться** *(impf)* ~**ой** to do yoga.

йо́гурт (-а) *м* yoghurt.

йод (-а) *м* iodine.

йо́дистый *прил* = **йо́дный**.

йо́дный *прил* iodine *опред*.

Йорк (-а) *м* York.

йо́т|а (-ы) *ж*: **ни на** ~**у** not one iota.

йота́ци|я (-и) *ж* vowel softening.

Йоха́ннесбург (-а) *м* Johannesburg.

~ К, к ~

К, к сущ нескл (буква) the 11th letter of the Russian alphabet.

KEYWORD

к предл (+dat) **1** (обозначает направление) towards; **я пошёл к дóму/вокзáлу** I went towards the house/station; **звать (позвáть** perf) **когó-н к телефóну** to call sb to the phone; **мы поéхали к друзья́м** we went to see friends; **постáвь лéстницу к стенé** put the ladder against the wall
2 (обозначает добавление, включение) to; **к ужé существу́ющим проблéмам прибáвились нóвые осложнéния** new complications were added to the existing problems; **эта бáбочка отнóсится к óчень рéдкому ви́ду** this butterfly belongs to a very rare species
3 (обозначает отношение) of; **любóвь к му́зыке/поря́дку** love of music/order; **он привы́к к хорóшей едé** he is used to good food; **к моему́ удивлéнию** to my surprise
4 (обозначает назначение) with; **Вы хоти́те печéнья к чáю?** would you like biscuits (BRIT) или cookies (US) with your tea?; **припрáвы к мя́су** seasonings for meat.

к. сокр = **копéйка.**

-ка част (разг) used to moderate imperative or indicate indecision; **иди́-ка сюдá** could you come here; **пойду́-ка я домóй** I think I'll maybe be off home.

кабáк (-á) м tavern; (разг) pub.

кабалá (-ы́) ж (перен) slavery; **быть** (impf) **в ~é у когó-н** to be at sb's mercy.

кабáль|ный прил: ~ **труд** slave labour (BRIT) или labor (US); ~**ая зави́симость** slavery (fig).

кабáн (-á) м boar; (дикий) wild boar.

кабарé ср нескл cabaret.

кабач|óк (-кá) м уменьш от **кабáк**; (БОТ, КУЛИН) marrow (BRIT), squash (US).

кáбел|ь (-я) м cable.

кáбельный прил cable опред; **кáбельное телеви́дение** cable television.

каби́н|а (-ы) ж (телефóнная) booth; (грузовика) cab; (самолёта) cabin; (лифта) cage; (для голосования) voting booth; **пля́жная ~** beach

hut.

кабинéт (-а) м (в доме) study; (на работе) office; (ПРОСВЕЩ) classroom; (врача) surgery (BRIT), office (US); (ПОЛИТ: также: ~ **мини́стров**) cabinet.

каблогрáмм|а (-ы) ж cablegram.

каблу́к (-á) м heel; **быть** (impf) **под каблукóм у когó-н** (разг) to be under sb's thumb.

каботáж (-а) м coastal shipping.

Кабу́л (-а) м Kabul.

кавалéр (-а) м (в танце) partner; (поклонник) suitor; (награждённый орденом): ~ +gen knight of; **Геóргиевский** ~ knight of St George.

кавалери́й|ский (-ая, -ое, -ие) прил cavalry опред.

кавалери́ст (-а) м cavalryman (мн cavalrymen).

кавалéри|я (-и) ж cavalry.

кавалькáд|а (-ы) ж cavalcade.

кавардáк (-á) м (разг) mess.

кáверз|а (-ы) ж dirty trick; **подстрóить** (perf) **кому́-н** ~у to play a dirty trick on sb.

кáверз|ный (-ен, -на, -но) прил tricky.

Кавкáз (-а) м Caucasus.

кавкáз|ский (-ая, -ое, -ие) прил Caucasian.

кавы́ч|ки (-ек; dat pl -кам) мн inverted commas мн, quotation marks мн; **открывáть (откры́ть** perf)/**закрывáть (закры́ть** perf) ~ to open/close inverted commas; **в ~ках** (также перен) in inverted commas.

кагóр (-а) м red dessert wine.

кадéнци|я (-и) ж cadence.

кадéт (-а) м (ВОЕН) cadet; (ИСТ: = конституциóнный демокрáт) Cadet (Constitutional Democrat).

кадéт|ский (-ая, -ое, -ие) прил (форма) cadet's; **кадéтский кóрпус** officer training corps.

кади́л|о (-а) ср (РЕЛ) censer.

кади́|ть (-жу́, -ди́шь) несов неперех (РЕЛ) to burn incense.

кáд|ка (-ки; gen pl -ок) ж vat.

кáдми|й (-я) м cadmium.

кáдок сущ см **кáдка.**

кáдочный прил (огурцы, капуста итп) preserved in vats.

кадр (-а) м (ФОТО, КИНО) shot; (разг: работник) worker; см также **кáдры.**

ка́дров|ый *прил* (*офицер, войска*) regular опред; (*АДМИН*): **~ая поли́тика** staffing policy.

ка́др|ы (**-ов**) *мн* (*работники*) personnel *ед*, staff *ед*; (*ВОЕН*) regular army personnel *ед*; (*партийные*) cadres *мн*; **отде́л ~ов** personnel department.

кады́к (**-á**) *м* Adam's apple.

каём *сущ см* **кайма́**.

каём|ка (**-ки**; *gen pl* **-ок**) *ж* = **кайма́**.

каждодне́вный *прил* daily.

ка́ждый *прил* each, every.

кажу́ *несов см* **кади́ть**.

кажу́сь *итп несов см* **каза́ться**.

каза́к (**-á**; *nom pl* **каза́ки**) *м* Cossack.

каза́н (**-á**) *м large round copper cooking vessel.*

Каза́н|ь (**-и**) *ж* Kazan.

каза́рм|а (**-ы**) *ж* barracks *мн*.

каза́рменный *прил*: **~ поря́док** barracks regime; **каза́рменное положе́ние** confinement to barracks.

каза́|ться (**-жу́сь, -жешься**; *perf* **показа́ться**) *несов возв* (+*instr*) to look; (**мне**) **ка́жется/ каза́лось, что ...** it seems/seemed (to me) that ...; **он ~за́лся ста́рше свои́х лет** he looked older than his years.

каза́х (**-а**) *м* Kazakh.

каза́хск|ий (**-ая, -ое, -ие**) *прил* Kazakh.

Казахста́н (**-а**) *м* Kazakhstan.

каза́цк|ий (**-ая, -ое, -ие**) *прил* = **каза́чий**.

каза́чек *сущ см* **каза́чка**.

каза́честв|о (**-а**) *ср собир* the Cossacks *мн*.

каза́ч|ий (**-ья, -ье, -ьи**) *прил* Cossack.

каза́ч|ка (**-ки**; *gen pl* **-ек**) *ж см* **каза́к**.

каземáт (**-а**) *м* cell.

казённый *прил* public; (*отношение, язык*) officious; **на ~ счёт** at public expense; **казённая кварти́ра** tied accommodation; **казённое иму́щество** government property.

казино́ *ср нескл* casino.

казн|á (**-ы́**) *ж* treasury.

казначе́|й (**-я**) *м* treasurer.

казни́ть (**-ю́, -ишь**) *несов перех* to execute; (*перен*) to punish

▶ **казни́ться** *несов возв* (*разг*) to torture o.s.

казн|ь (**-и**) *ж* execution; **смéртная ~** the death penalty; **приговори́ть** (*perf*) **кого́-н к сме́ртной ка́зни** to sentence sb to death.

Каи́р (**-а**) *м* Cairo.

кайм|á (**-ы́мы**; *nom pl* **-ы́мы́**, *gen pl* **-ём**) *ж* hem.

кайф (**-а**) *м* (*разг*) high, kick.

кайф|ова́ть (**-у́ю**) *несов неперех* (*разг*: **на пляже, в отпуске итп**) to chill out; (: *от наркотиков, от вина*) to get high.

как *местоимённое нареч* **1** (*вопросительное*) how; **как Вы себя́ чу́вствуете?** how do you feel?; **как дела́/де́ти?** how are things/the children?; **как тебя́ зову́т?** what's your name?

2 (*относительное*): **я сде́лал, как ты проси́ла** I did as you asked; **я не зна́ю, как э́то могло́ случи́ться** I don't know how that could have happened

3 (*насколько*): **как бы́стро/то́чно/давно́** how quickly/accurately/long ago

4 (*до какой степени*): **как краси́во/по́дло!** how beautiful/mean!; **как жаль!** what a pity *или* shame!

5 (*выражает возмущение*) what; **как! он опя́ть напи́лся!** what! he's drunk again!

6 (*о внезапном действии*): **она́ как закричи́т/заплáчет** she suddenly cried out/ burst into tears

◆ *союз* **1** (*подобно*) as; **мя́гкий, как ва́та** as soft as cotton wool; **как мо́жно скоре́е/гро́мче** as soon/loud as possible; **он оде́т, как бродя́га** he is dressed like a tramp

2 (*в качестве*) as; **как консульта́нт он о́чень поле́зен** as a consultant he is very useful

3 (*о временны́х отношениях*: *о будущем, об одновременности*) when; (: *о прошлом*) since; **как зако́нчишь, позвони́ мне** phone (*BRIT*) *или* call (*US*) me when you finish; **как вспо́мню об э́том, хо́чется пла́кать** when I remember it I feel like crying; **прошло́ два го́да, как она́ исче́зла** two years have passed since she disappeared

4: **как бу́дто, как бы** as if; **он согласи́лся как бы не́хотя** he agreed as if unwillingly; **как же** of course; **как говоря́т** *или* **говори́тся** as it were; **как ни** however; **как ника́к** after all; **как раз во́время/то, что на́до** just in time/what we need; **э́то пла́тье/пальто́ мне как раз** this dress/coat is just my size; **как ..., так и ...** both ... and ...; **как то́лько** as soon as.

какаду́ *м нескл* cockatoo.

кака́о *ср нескл* cocoa.

ка́ка|ть (**-ю**; *perf* **пока́кать**) *несов неперех* (*разг*) to do a pooh.

как-ли́бо *нареч* = **как-нибудь**.

как-нибудь *нареч* (*так или иначе*) somehow; (*когда-нибудь*) sometime; (*кое-как*) anyhow; **уговори́те его́ ~** try to convince him somehow; **зайди́ ~** pop in sometime; **ты всё де́лаешь ~** you're doing everything just anyhow.

како́в (**-á, -ó, -ы́**) *мест* what; **~ нагле́ц!** what a cheek!; **~ он собо́й?** what does he look like?

как|о́й (**-áя, -óе, -и́е**) *мест* **1** (*вопросительное*) what; **како́й тебе́ нра́вится цвет?** what colour do you like?; **кака́я сего́дня пого́да?** what's the weather like today?; **в како́м году́ э́то бы́ло?** in what year was that?

2 (*относительное*) which; **скажи́, кака́я кни́га интере́снее** tell me which book is more interesting; **скажи́, в како́м го́роде нахо́дится Колизе́й** tell me in which city the Coliseum is

3 (*выражает оценку*) what; **како́й подле́ц!** what a rascal!; **кака́я неожи́данность!** what a surprise!

4 (*в риторических вопросах*: *совсем не*) what kind of; **како́й он дире́ктор?** what kind of director is he?

5 (*раз*: *неопределённое*) any; **нет ли каки́х вопро́сов?** are there any questions?; **како́й ни на есть** any you like; **ни в каку́ю** not for anything; **каки́м о́бразом** in what way; **како́е там!** no way!

как|о́й-либо (**-а́я, -о́е, -и́е**) *мест* = **како́й-нибудь**.

как|о́й-нибудь (**-а́я, -о́е, -и́е**) *мест* (*тот или иной*) any; (*приблизительно*) some; **он и́щет ~ рабо́ты** he's looking for any kind of work; **~и́х-нибудь два-три ме́сяца** in some two or three months.

как|о́й-то (**-а́я, -о́е, -и́е**) *мест*: **Вам ~о́е-то письмо́** there's a letter for you; (*напоминающий*): **она́ ~а́я-то стра́нная сего́дня** she's acting a bit oddly today; **э́то не ко́мната, а свина́рник ~** it's more like a pigsty than a room.

какофони́ческ|ий (**-ая, -ое, -ие**) *прил* cacophonous.

какофони|я (**-и**) *ж* cacophony.

ка́к-то *мест* (*каким-то образом*) somehow; (*в некоторой степени*) somewhat; (*раз*): **~ (раз)** once; **мне бы́ло ~ не по себе́** I was feeling somewhat *или* a little out of sorts; **я ~ встре́тил его́ на у́лице** I bumped into him once in the street.

ка́ктус (**-а**) *м* cactus (*мн* cacti).

кал (**-а**) *м* excrement.

каламбу́р (**-а**) *м* pun.

каламбу́р|ить (**-ю, -ишь**; *perf* **скаламбу́рить**) *несов неперех* to pun, make puns.

каланч|а́ (**-и́**; *gen pl* **-е́й**) *ж* watchtower; (*раз*: *человек*) beanpole.

кала́ч (**-а́**) *м* ≈ cottage loaf; **его́ калачо́м не зама́нишь** nothing will persuade him.

кала́чиком *нареч*: **сверну́ться ~** to curl up in a ball.

калейдоско́п (**-а**) *м* (*также перен*) kaleidoscope.

ка́лек *сущ см* **ка́лька**.

кале́к|а (**-и**) *м/ж* cripple.

календа́рный *прил*: **~ ме́сяц/год** calendar month/year.

календа́р|ь (**-я́**) *м* calendar.

кале́ни|е (**-я**) *ср* incandescence; **довести́** (*perf*) **кого́-н до бе́лого ~я** to send sb into a blind rage.

кале́ный *прил* red-hot; **выжига́ть** (**вы́жечь** *perf*) **~ым желе́зом** to brand.

кале́ч|ить (**-у, -ишь**; *perf* **покале́чить** *или* **искале́чить**) *несов перех* to cripple.

кали́бр (**-а**) *м* (*воен, перен*) calibre (*BRIT*), caliber (*US*); (*тех*) gauge.

калибр|ова́ть (**-у́ю**) (*не*)*сов перех* to calibrate.

калибро́вк|а (**-и**) *ж* calibration.

ка́ли|й (**-я**) *м* potassium.

кали́н|а (**-ы**) *ж* guelder-rose.

кали́т|ка (**-ки**; *gen pl* **-ок**) *ж* gate.

Калифо́рни|я (**-и**) *ж* California.

каллиграфи́ческ|ий (**-ая, -ое, -ие**) *прил*: **~ по́черк** beautiful handwriting.

каллигра́фи|я (**-и**) *ж* calligraphy.

калмы́|к (**-а**) *м* Kalmyk.

Калмы́ки|я (**-и**) *ж* Kalmykia.

калмы́ч|ка (**-ки**; *gen pl* **-ек**) *ж см* **калмы́к**.

калори́йност|ь (**-и**) *ж* (*пищи*) calorie content; (*физ*) calorific value.

кало́ри|я (**-и**) *ж* calorie.

ка́льк|а (**-ьки**; *gen pl* **-ек**) *ж* (*бумага*) tracing paper; (*копия*) traced copy; (*линг*) calque.

кальки́р|овать (**-ую**; *perf* **скалькировать**) *несов перех* (*чертёж*) to trace.

калькуля́тор (**-а**) *м* calculator.

кальма́р (**-а**) *м* squid.

кальсо́н|ы (**-**) *мн* long johns *мн*.

ка́льци|й (**-я**) *м* calcium.

КамА́З (**-а**) *м сокр* = **Ка́мский автомоби́льный заво́д**; (*автомобиль*) *vehicle manufactured at the Kamskiy car factory*.

ка́мбал|а (**-ы**) *ж* flatfish.

Камбо́дж|а (**-и**) *ж* Cambodia.

камбоджи́йский (**-ая, -ое, -ие**) *прил* Cambodian.

ка́мбуз (**-а**) *м* galley.

каме́ли|я (**-и**) *ж* camelia.

камене́|ть (**-ю**) *несов от* **окамене́ть**.

камени́ст|ый (**-, -а, -о**) *прил* (*почва*) stony.

каменноу́гольный *прил* coal *опред*; **~ бассе́йн** coalfield.

ка́менн|ый *прил* stone; (*перен*) stony; **у неё ~ое се́рдце** she has a heart of stone; **ка́менный век** the Stone Age.

каменоло́мн|я (**-ни**; *gen pl* **-ен**) *ж* quarry.

каменотёс (**-а**) *м* stonemason.

ка́менщик (**-а**) *м* bricklayer; **во́льный ~** Freemason.

ка́м|ень (**-ня**; *gen pl* **-не́й**) *м* stone; **драгоце́нный ~** precious stone; **краеуго́льный ~** (*перен*) cornerstone; **~ в по́чках** kidney stone; **~ преткнове́ния** stumbling block; **у него́ ~ на се́рдце лежи́т** there's a weight lying heavy on his heart; **у меня́ ~ с души́ свали́лся** it was a great weight off my mind; **держа́ть** (*impf*) **~ за па́зухой** to bear a grudge.

ка́мер|а (**-ы**) *ж* (*тюремная*) cell; (*авт*) inner tube; (*также*: **телека́мера, кинока́мера**) camera; (*тех, анат*) chamber; **снима́ть** (**снять** *perf*) **что-н скры́той ~ой** to film sth secretly; **ка́мера хране́ния** (*на вокзале*) left-luggage office (*BRIT*), checkroom (*US*); (*в музее*) cloakroom.

камерди́нер (**-а**) *м* (*ист*) valet.

ка́мерный *прил* (*обстановка*) cosy; **ка́мерная му́зыка** chamber music; **ка́мерный орке́стр** chamber orchestra.

камертóн (-а) *м* tuning fork.
кáмеш|ек (-ка; *nom pl* -ки, *gen pl* -ков) *м* stone.
камé|я (-и) *ж* cameo (*in jewellery*).
камзóл (-а) *м* frock coat.
камúн (-а) *м* fireplace.
камнепáд (-а) *м* avalanche (*of rocks, stones*).
кáмня *итп сущ см* **кáмень**.
камóрк|а (-и) *ж* (*разг*) cubbyhole.
кампáни|я (-и) *ж* campaign.
кампучúйск|ий (-ая, -ое, -ие) *прил*
  Kampuchean.
Кампучú|я (-и) *ж* Kampuchea.
камуфлú|ровать (-ую; *perf*
  закамуфлúровать) *несов перех* to camouflage.
камуфля́ж (-а) *м* camouflage.
кáмфор|а (-ы) *ж* camphor.
камфóрк|а (-и) *ж* ring (*on stove*).
кáмфорн|ый *прил:* ~ое мáсло camphorated oil.
камы́ш (-á) *м* rushes *мн*.
кана́в|а (-ы) *ж* ditch; **стóчная** ~ gutter.
Кана́д|а (-ы) *ж* Canada.
кана́д|ец (-ца) *м* Canadian.
кана́дк|а (-и; *gen pl* -ок) *ж см* **кана́дец**.
кана́дск|ий (-ая, -ое, -ие) *прил* Canadian.
кана́дца *итп сущ см* **кана́дец**.
кана́л (-а) *м* (*также АНАТ*) canal; (*связь, тел,
  перен*) channel; **я бýду дéйствовать по своúм
  ~ам** I shall use the means available to me.
канализацио́нн|ый *прил:* ~ая трубá sewer
  pipe; **канализацио́нная сеть** the sewers.
канализа́ци|я (-и) *ж* sewerage.
кана́л|ья (-ьи; *gen pl* -ий) *м/ж* rogue.
канаре́|йка (-йки; *gen pl* -ек) *ж* canary.
кана́рск|ий (-ая, -ое, -ие) *прил:* **К~ие островá**
  the Canary Islands, the Canaries.
кана́т (-а) *м* cable.
кана́тн|ый *прил:* ~ая доро́га cable car.
канатохо́д|ец (-ца) *м* tightrope walker.
канв|á (-ы́) *ж* (*в вышивании*) sampler; (*перен:
  рассказа*) outline.
кандалы́ (-óв) *мн* shackles *мн*.
канделя́бр (-а) *м* candelabra (*мн* candelabra).
кандида́т (-а) *м* candidate; (*ПРОСВЕЩ*): ~ **наýк** ≈
  Doctor.
кандида́тск|ий (-ая, -ое, -ие) *прил* candidate's;
  кандида́тская диссерта́ция ≈ doctoral thesis;
  кандида́тский экза́мен *entrance exam for
  postgraduate study*.
кандидату́р|а (-ы) *ж* candidacy; **выставля́ть
  (вы́ставить** *perf*) **чью-н** ~у to nominate sb.
кани́кул|ы (-) *мн* holidays *мн* (*BRIT*), vacation *ед*
  (*US*); **парла́ментские** ~ parliamentary recess.
каникуля́рный *прил* holiday *опред* (*BRIT*),
  vacation *опред* (*US*).
кани́стр|а (-ы) *ж* jerry can.
канителú|ться (-юсь, -ишься) *несов возв*
  (*разг*): ~ (**с** +*instr*) to waste one's time (over).
канитéл|ь (-и) *ж* (*золотáя итп*) thread; (*перен*)
  bore, drag; **тянýть** (*impf*) ~ (*перен: разг*) to drag
  things out.
канифóл|ь (-и) *ж* (*ХИМ*) resin; (*МУЗ*) rosin.
канка́н (-а) *м* cancan.

канниба́л (-а) *м* cannibal.
каннибалú|зм (-а) *м* cannibalism.
кано́ист (-а) *м* canoeist.
кано́н (-а) *м* canon.
канона́д|а (-ы) *ж* cannonade.
канониза́ци|я (-и) *ж* (*также перен*)
  canonization.
канонизú|ровать (-ую) (*не*)*сов перех* (*также
  перен*) to canonize.
кано́ник (-а) *м* canon (*REL*).
канонúческ|ий (-ая, -ое, -ие) *прил* (*РЕЛ*)
  canonical; (*перен: правила, образец*) definitive;
  ~**ое пра́во** canon law.
кано́э *ср нескл* canoe.
канта́т|а (-ы) *ж* cantata.
кант|ова́ть (-ýю; *perf* **оканто́вать**) *несов перех*
  (*окаймлять*) to mount; (*no perf;
  переворачивать*) to tilt; *„не* ~!" "keep
  upright!"
кану́н (-а) *м* eve; **в** ~ +*gen* on the eve of; ~
  Но́вого го́да New Year's Eve.
ка́н|уть (-у, -ешь) *сов неперех* (*исчезнуть*) to
  vanish; ~ (*perf*) **в Ле́ту** *или* **ве́чность** to fade
  into obscurity; **он сло́вно в во́ду** ~ул he
  vanished into thin air.
канцеляри́|зм (-а) *м* official jargon.
канцеля́ри|я (-и) *ж* office.
канцеля́рск|ий (-ая, -ое, -ие) *прил* office
  опред; ~ **слог** *или* **язы́к** officialese.
канцеля́рщин|а (-ы) *ж* (*формализм*) red tape.
ка́нцлер (-а) *м* (*глава государства*) chancellor.
каньо́н (-а) *м* canyon.
каню́к (-á) *м* buzzard.
каню́ч|ить (-у, -ишь) *несов неперех* (*разг*) to
  whinge.
каоли́н (-а) *м* kaolin.
ка́па|ть (-ю) *несов неперех* (*вода*) to drip ♦ (*perf
  нака́пать) *перех* (*микстуру*) to pour out drop
  by drop; **дождь** ~**ет** it's spotting with rain.
ка́пелек *сущ см* **ка́пелька**.
капéлл|а (-ы) *ж* (*МУЗ*) choir; (*РЕЛ*) chapel.
капелла́н (-а) *м* chaplain.
ка́пель *сущ см* **ка́пля**.
капéл|ь (-и) *ж* thaw.
ка́пельк|а (-и; *gen pl* -ек) *ж* droplet; ~ +*gen*
  (*молока итп*) a drop of; (*счастья, правды*) a
  grain of; **всё до после́дней** ~**ки** every last
  little bit.
ка́пельку *нареч* (*разг*) a tad *или* touch; **ну ещё**
  ~ a little bit more; **почита́й хоть** ~ read for just
  a little while at least.
капельме́йстер (-а) *м* bandmaster.
капéльниц|а (-ы) *ж* (*МЕД*) drip(-feed); **ста́вить
  (поста́вить** *perf*) **кому́-н** ~**у** to put sb on a drip.
ка́персы (-ов) *мн* (*КУЛИН*) capers *мн*.
капилля́р (-а) *м* capillary.
капита́л (-а) *м* (*КОММ*) capital; (*перен:
  политический*) power; **вы́пущенный
  акционе́рный** ~ (*КОММ*) issued capital.
капита́лен *прил см* **капита́льный**.
капитализа́ци|я (-и) *ж* capitalization.
капитализú|ровать (-ую) (*не*)*сов перех*

(КОММ) to capitalize.

капитали́зм (-а) *м* capitalism.

капитали́ст (-а) *м* capitalist.

капиталисти́ческ|ий (-ая, -ое, -ие) *прил* capitalist.

капиталовложе́ни|я (-й) *мн* capital investment *ед*.

капита́л|ьный *прил* (ЭКОН, КОММ) capital *опред*; (-ен, -ьна, -ьно; *сооруже́ние, труд*) main; (*вопрос, покупка*) major; **капита́льная стена́** supporting wall; **капита́льное строи́тельство** major construction work; **капита́льные расхо́ды** capital expenditure; **капита́льный ремо́нт** major repairs; **капита́льные това́ры** capital goods.

капита́н (-а) *м* captain.

капита́нск|ий (-ая, -ое, -ие) *прил* captain's; **капита́нский мо́стик** (МОР) bridge.

капите́ль (-и) *ж* (АРХИТ) capital.

капитули́р|овать (-ую) (*не*)*сов неперех* to capitulate.

капитуля́ци|я (-и) *ж* capitulation.

капка́н (-а) *м* trap.

ка́п|ли (-ель) *мн* (МЕД) drops *мн*.

ка́п|ля (-ли; *gen pl* -ель) *ж* (*также перен*) drop; **ни ~ли** not a bit; **вы́пить** (*perf*) **всё до ~ли** to drink every last drop; **подожди́те хоть ~лю** (*разг*) wait just one second; **они́ похо́жи как две ~ли воды́** they're like two peas in a pod; **~ в мо́ре** a drop in the ocean; *см также* **ка́пли**.

капо́т (-а) *м* (АВТ) bonnet (*BRIT*), hood (*US*); (*халат*) housecoat.

капра́л (-а) *м* corporal.

капри́з (-а) *ж* caprice, whim.

капри́зен *прил см* **капри́зный**.

капри́знича|ть (-ю; *perf* **покапри́зничать**) *несов неперех* to behave capriciously.

капри́з|ный (-ен, -на, -но) *прил* (*человек, характер*) capricious; (*мода, погода итп*) fickle.

капро́н (-а) *м* synthetic thread.

ка́псул|а (-ы) *ж* (МЕД, ТЕХ) capsule.

капу́ст|а (-ы) *ж* cabbage; **брюссе́льская ~** Brussels sprouts *мн*; **цветна́я ~** cauliflower.

капу́стник (-а) *м* amateur revue.

капу́стный *прил* cabbage.

капу́т *м нескл*: **магнитофо́ну ~** (*разг*) the tape recorder's kaput; **ему́ ~** he's finished.

капюшо́н (-а) *м* hood.

ка́р|а (-ы) *ж* retribution.

караби́н (-а) *м* (ВОЕН) carbine; (ТЕХ) karabiner.

кара́бка|ться (-юсь; *perf* **вскара́бкаться**) *несов возв*: **~ на** +*acc* (*человек*) to clamber up; (*растение*) to creep up.

карава́|й (-я) *м* cob (*loaf*).

карава́н (-а) *м* (*судов*) convoy; (*верблюдов*) caravan.

карава́н-сара́|й (-я) *м* caravanserai.

карака́тиц|а (-ы) *ж* (ЗООЛ) cuttlefish; (*перен: разг*) clodhopper.

кара́кулевый *прил* astrakhan.

кара́кул|и (-ей) *мн* (*разг*) scrawl *ед*.

кара́кул|ь (-я) *м* astrakhan; *см также* **кара́кули**.

караме́л|ь (-и) *ж собир* (*леденцы*) caramels *мн*; (*жжёный сахар*) caramel.

каранда́ш (-а́; *gen pl* **-е́й**) *м* pencil.

каранти́н (-а) *м* quarantine.

карапу́з (-а) *м* (*разг*) fatty.

кара́с|ь (-я́) *м* crucian (*type of carp*).

кара́т (-а) *м* carat (*BRIT*), karat (*US*).

кара́тельный *прил* punitive; **~ отря́д** death squad.

кара́|ть (-ю; *perf* **покара́ть**) *несов перех* to punish.

карате́ *ср нескл* karate.

карау́л (-а) *м* guard; **выставля́ть (вы́ставить** *perf*) **~** to post a guard; **стоя́ть** (*impf*) **в ~е** to stand guard; **~! help!**

карау́л|ить (-ю, -ишь) *несов перех* to guard; (*разг: ожидать*) to lie in wait for.

карбо́ван|ец (-ца) *м* karbovanets (*Ukrainian currency unit*).

карбо́ловый *прил*: **~ая кислота́** carbolic acid.

карбу́нкул (-а) *м* (ГЕО, МЕД) carbuncle.

карбюра́тор (-а) *м* carburettor (*BRIT*), carburetor (*US*).

карг|а́ (-и́) *ж* (*разг*) hag.

кардамо́н (-а; *no pl*) *м* cardamom.

кардина́л (-а) *м* (РЕЛ) cardinal.

кардина́льно *нареч* (*изменить*) drastically.

кардина́л|ьный (-ен, -ьна, -ьно) *прил* cardinal *опред*; of cardinal importance.

кардио́лог (-а) *м* cardiologist, heart specialist.

кардиологи́ческ|ий (-ая, -ое, -ие) *прил* (*отделе́ние*) cardiac.

кардиоло́ги|я (-и) *ж* cardiology.

каре́ *ср нескл* (ВОЕН) square formation; (КАРТЫ) four of a kind.

каре́т|а (-ы) *ж* carriage.

каре́т|ка (-ки; *gen pl* **-ок**) *ж* carriage.

ка́р|ий (-яя, -ее, -ие) *прил* (*глаза*) hazel; (*масть*) chestnut.

карикату́р|а (-ы) *ж* caricature.

карикату́рен *прил см* **карикату́рный**.

карикатури́ст (-а) *м* caricaturist.

карикату́р|ный (-ен, -на, -но) *прил* caricatured.

карка́с (-а) *м* shell (*of a building*).

ка́рка|ть (-ю) *несов неперех* (*ворона*) to caw; (*perf* **нака́ркать**; *перен: разг*) to predict the worst.

ка́рлик (-а) *м* dwarf.

ка́рликовый *прил* (*племена*) pygmy *опред*; (*растения*) dwarf *опред*.

ка́рлиц|а (-ы) *ж см* **ка́рлик**.

карма́н (-а) *м* pocket; **набива́ть (наби́ть** *perf*) **~** (*пренебр*) to line one's pockets; **э́то мне не по ~у** I can't afford it; **нало́ги уда́рили по ~у** the taxes have hit the population hard; **держи́ ~ ши́ре!** fat chance!; **он не полéзет за сло́вом в ~** he's never short of something to say.

карма́нн|ый *прил*: **~ые де́ньги/часы́** pocket money/watch; **карма́нный вор** pickpocket; **карма́нный нож** pocketknife; **карма́нные расхо́ды** petty expenses.

карма́ш|ек (-ка) *м уменьш от* **карма́н**; (*мешочек*) pouch.

карнава́л (-а) *м* carnival.

карнава́льный *прил* carnival *опред*.

карни́з (-а) *м* (*под крышей здания*) cornice; (*над дверью*) lintel.

карп (-а) *м* carp.

Карпа́т|ы (-) *мн* Carpathians, Carpathian Mountains.

карт (-а) *м* go-cart.

ка́рт|а (-ы) *ж* (*ГЕО*) map; (*также: игра́льная ~*) (playing) card; **ста́вить (поста́вить** *perf*) **на ~у что-н** (*перен*) to put sth at stake; *см также* **ка́рты**.

карта́в|ый (-, -а, -о) *прил*: **он ~** he can't pronounce the letter "r" properly.

картёжник (-а) *м* card player.

картёжниц|а (-ы) *ж см* **картёжник**.

карте́л|ь (-и) *ж* (*ЭКОН*) cartel.

карти́н|а (-ы) *ж* (*также КИНО, перен*) picture; (*ТЕАТР*) scene; (*обычно мн: прошлого, природы*) image.

карти́н|ка (-ки; *gen pl* **-ок)** *ж уменьш от* **карти́на**; (*иллюстрация*) picture (*in book etc*); **кни́га с ~ми** picture book; **пря́мо как ~!** it's beautiful!

карти́н|ный *прил* picture *опред*; (**-ен, -на, -но;** *красивый*) picturesque.

карто́граф (-а) *м* cartographer.

картографи́р|овать (-ую) (*не)сов перех* to map.

картографи́ческ|ий (-ая, -ое, -ие) *прил* cartographic.

картогра́фи|я (-и) *ж* cartography.

карто́н (-а) *м* cardboard.

карто́нный *прил* cardboard.

картоте́к|а (-и) *ж* card index.

картофелин|а (-ы) *ж* potato (*мн* potatoes).

карто́фел|ь (-я) *м* (*растение*) potato plant; (*плод*) potatoes *мн*; **~ в мунди́ре** baked *или* jacket potatoes.

карто́фельный *прил* potato; **карто́фельное пюре́** mashed potato.

ка́рточ|ка (-ки; *gen pl* **-ек)** *ж* card; (*также: фотока́рточка*) photo; **хле́бная/визи́тная ~** ration/business card.

ка́рточн|ый *прил*: **~ая игра́** card game; **~ая систе́ма** rationing; **~ долг** gambling debt; **~ до́мик** (*также перен*) house of cards.

карто́ш|ка (-и) *ж собир* potatoes *мн*; **нос ~ой** bulbous nose.

ка́ртридж (-а) *м* cartridge.

карту́з (-а́) *м* peaked cap.

ка́рт|ы (-) *мн* cards *мн*; **игра́ть** (*impf*) **в ~** to play

cards; **раскрыва́ть (раскры́ть** *perf*) **свои́ ~** (*перен*) to show one's hand.

карусе́л|ь (-и) *ж* merry-go-round (*BRIT*), carousel (*US*).

ка́рцер (-а) *м* isolation cell.

карье́р (-а) *м* (*ТЕХ*) quarry; (*галоп*) full gallop; **пуска́ться (пусти́ться** *perf*) **с ме́ста в ~** (*перен*) to rush straight in.

карье́р|а (-ы) *ж* career; **де́лать (сде́лать** *perf*) **~у** to build a career for o.s.

карьери́зм (-а) *м* careerism.

карьери́ст (-а) *м* careerist.

карьери́стск|ий (-ая, -ое, -ие) *прил* careerist *опред*.

каса́ни|е (-я) *ср* contact.

каса́|ться (-юсь; *perf* **косну́ться)** *несов возв*: **~ +gen** (*дотрагиваться*) to touch; (*затрагивать*) to touch on; **э́то тебя́ не ~ется** it doesn't concern you; **что ~ется Вас, то ...** as far as you are concerned ....

ка́с|ка (-ки; *gen pl* **-ок)** *ж* helmet.

каска́д (-а) *м* cascade; (*трюк*) stunt; (*перен*) flood.

каскадёр (-а) *м* stunt man (*мн* men).

ка́сок *сущ см* **ка́ска**.

каспи́йск|ий (-ая, -ое, -ие) *прил*: **К~ое мо́ре** Caspian Sea.

ка́сс|а (-ы) *ж* (*ТЕАТР, КИНО*) box office; (*железнодорожная*) ticket office; (*в магазине*) cash desk; (*аппарат*) cash register; (*ящик*) cash box; (*деньги*) cash; (*ТИПОГ*) case.

кассацио́нный *прил*: **~ суд** court of appeal.

кассаци|я (-и) *ж* (*ЮР*) cassation, annulment; **подава́ть (пода́ть** *perf*) **на ~ю** to lodge an appeal.

кассе́т|а (-ы) *ж* (*магнитофонная*) cassette; (*ФОТО*) cartridge.

касси́р (-а) *м* cashier.

ка́ст|а (-ы) *ж* caste.

кастеля́нш|а (-и) *ж* laundrywoman (*мн* laundrywomen).

касте́т (-а) *м* knuckle-duster.

касто́р|ка (-и) *ж* (*разг*) = **касто́ровое ма́сло**.

касто́ров|ый *прил*: **~ое ма́сло** castor oil.

кастри́р|овать (-ую) (*не)сов перех* to castrate.

кастрю́л|я (-и) *ж* saucepan.

катава́си|я (-и) *ж* (*разг*) mayhem.

катакли́зм (-а) *м* cataclysm.

катако́мб|ы (-) *мн* catacombs *мн*.

катализа́тор (-а) *м* catalyst.

катало́г (-а) *м* catalogue (*BRIT*), catalog (*US*).

каталогизи́р|овать (-ую) (*не)сов перех* (*книги*) to catalogue (*BRIT*), catalog (*US*).

ката́ни|е (-я) *ср*: **~ на маши́не** driving; **~ на велосипе́де** cycling; **~ на конька́х** skating; **~ на ло́шади** horse (*BRIT*) *или* horseback (*US*) riding; **~ на лы́жах** skiing.

катапу́льт|а (-ы) *ж* (*ТЕХ*) catapult.

катапульти́р|оваться (-уюсь) (*не)сов возв* to eject.

ката́р (-а) *м* catarrh.

катара́кт|а (-ы) ж (*МЕД*) cataract.
катастро́ф|а (-ы) ж (*авиационная, железнодорожная*) disaster; (*перен*) catastrophe.
катастрофи́ческий (-ая, -ое, -ие) *прил* catastrophic, disastrous.
ката́|ть (-ю) *несов перех* (*что-н круглое*) to roll; (*что-н на колёсах*) to wheel; ~ (*impf*) **кого́-н на маши́не** to take sb for a drive
▶ **ката́ться** *несов возв*: ~**ся на маши́не/ велосипе́де** to go for a drive/cycle; ~**ся** (*impf*) **на конька́х/ло́шади** to go skating/horse (*BRIT*) *или* horseback (*US*) riding; ~**ся** (*impf*) **от бо́ли** to roll about in pain; ~**ся** (*impf*) **со́ смеху** to fall about laughing; **как сыр в ма́сле** ~**ся** (*impf*) to be in clover.
катафа́лк (-а) м hearse.
категори́чен *прил см* **категори́чный**.
категори́ческий (-ая, -ое, -ие) *прил* categoric.
категори́ч|ный (-ен, -на, -но) *прил* categorical.
катего́ри|я (-и) ж category.
ка́тер (-а) м boat; **сторожево́й/торпе́дный** ~ patrol/torpedo boat.
катехи́зис (-а) м catechism.
ка|ти́ть (-чу́, -тишь) *несов перех* (*что-н круглое*) to roll; (*что-н на колёсах*) to wheel ♦ *неперех* (*разг*: *в автомобиле*) to bomb along; ~ (*impf*) **бо́чки на кого́-н** (*перен*) to snipe at sb.
катка́ *сущ см* **като́к**.
като́д (-а) м cathode.
като́к (-ка́) м ice *или* skating rink; (*ТЕХ*: *также:* **асфа́льтовый** ~) steamroller.
като́лик (-а) м Catholic.
католици́зм (-а) м Catholicism.
католи́чек *сущ см* **като́личка**.
католи́ческий (-ая, -ое, -ие) *прил* Catholic.
католи́ч|ка (-ки; *gen pl* -ек) ж см **като́лик**.
ка́торг|а (-и) ж hard labour (*BRIT*) *или* labor (*US*).
каторжа́н|ин (-ина; *nom pl* -е, *gen pl* -) м convict (*in a labour camp*).
каторжа́нк|а (-и) ж см **каторжа́нин**.
ка́торжник (-а) м см **каторжа́нин**.
кату́ш|ка (-ки; *gen pl* -ек) ж spool.
каучу́к (-а) м rubber.
каучу́ковый *прил* rubber.
КАФ *м сокр* CAF (= *cost and freight*).
кафе́ *ср нескл* café.
ка́федр|а (-ы) ж (*ПРОСВЕЩ*) department; (*РЕЛ*) pulpit; (*лекторская*) rostrum; **заве́дующий** ~**ой** chair; **он получи́л** ~**у** he obtained a chair.
кафедра́льный *прил*: ~ **собо́р** cathedral.
ка́фел|ь (-я) м собир tiles *мн*.
ка́фельный *прил* tiled.
кафете́ри|й (-я) м cafeteria.
кафта́н (-а) м caftan.
кача́л|ка (-ки; *gen pl* -ок) ж rocking chair.
кача́ни|е (-я) ср (*на качелях*) swinging; (*на волнах*) rocking, roll.

кача́|ть (-ю) *несов перех* (*колыбель*) to rock; (*подбрасывать*) to throw into the air; (*нефть*) to pump; ~ (*impf*) **голово́й** to shake one's head; **кора́бль си́льно** ~**ло** the ship was rocking violently
▶ **кача́ться** *несов возв* to swing; (*на волнах*) to rock, roll; (*от усталости*) to sway.
каче́л|и (-ей) мн swing *ед*.
ка́чественно *нареч* (*другой*) essentially; (*делать, работать*) to a high standard.
ка́чествен|ный *прил* qualitative; (-, -на, -но; *товар, изделие*) high-quality; **ка́чественное прилага́тельное** qualitative adjective.
ка́честв|о (-а) ср quality ♦ *предл*: **в** ~**е** +*gen* as; **в** ~**е приме́ра** by way of example; **я рабо́таю в** ~**е меха́ника** I work as a mechanic.
ка́ч|ка (-и) ж: **бортова́я** ~ rolling; **килева́я** ~ pitching.
качну́|ть (-у́, -ёшь) *сов перех* to swing
▶ **качну́ться** *сов возв* to swing.
ка́ш|а (-и) ж ≈ porridge; **у него́ в голове́** ~ he's totally mixed up.
кашало́т (-а) м sperm whale.
ка́шел|ь (-ля) м cough.
кашеми́р (-а) м cashmere.
ка́шля *сущ см* **ка́шель**.
ка́шля|нуть (-у, -ешь) *сов неперех* to cough.
ка́шля|ть (-ю) *несов неперех* to cough.
Кашми́р (-а) м Kashmir.
кашне́ *ср нескл narrow scarf, usually worn under a coat*.
кашта́н (-а) м (*дерево*) chestnut (tree); (*плод*) chestnut; (: *несъедобный*) conker; **таска́ть** (*impf*) ~**ы из огня́** to do the dirty work; **ко́нский** ~ horse chestnut.
кашта́новый *прил* (*аллея, волосы*) chestnut.
каю́к (-а) м *как сказ* (*разг*): **ему́** ~ he's finished.
каю́т|а (-ы) ж (*МОР*) cabin.
каю́т-компа́ни|я (-и) ж *naval officers' lounge*.
ка́|яться (-юсь; *perf* **пока́яться)** *несов возв*: ~ (**в чём-н пе́ред кем-н**) to confess (sth to sb); **я хочу́ тебе́ пока́яться в чём-то** I must tell you something; **до́лжен пока́яться, я никогда́ не люби́л её** I must confess, I never loved her.
кБт *сокр* (= **килоба́йт**) KB, kbyte (= *kilobyte*); = **килоби́т**.
КВ *мн сокр* (= **коро́ткие во́лны**) SW = *short wave ед*.
кв. *сокр* (= **квадра́тный**) sq. (= *square*); (= **кварти́ра**) Apt. (= *apartment*).
квадра́т (-а) м square; **возводи́ть (возвести́** *perf*) **что-н в** ~ to square sth.
квадра́т|ный (-ен, -на, -но) *прил* square; ~ **ко́рень** square root; **квадра́тные ско́бки** square brackets.
ква́кань|е (-я) ср croaking.
ква́кн|уть (*3sg* -ет, *3pl* -ут) *сов неперех* to croak.
квалификацио́нный *прил*: ~ **экза́мен**

professional exam.

квалифика́ци|я (-и) ж qualification; (*профессия*) profession.

квалифици́рованно *нареч* competently.

квалифици́рован|ный (-, -на, -но) *прил* (*рабо́тник*) qualified; (*труд*) skilled.

квалифици́р|овать (-ую) *(не)сов перех* (*спортсме́на*) to rank; (*преступле́ние, поведе́ние*) to categorize.

квант (-а) м quantum.

ква́нтов|ый *прил*: ~ая меха́ника/фи́зика quantum mechanics/physics.

кварта́л (-а) м quarter.

кварта́льный *прил* (*отчёт, план*) quarterly.

кварте́т (-а) м quartet.

кварти́р|а (-ы) ж flat (*BRIT*), apartment (*US*); (*снима́емое жильё*) lodgings мн; жить (*impf*) на ~е to rent a flat *или* apartment; съезжа́ть (съе́хать *perf*) с ~ы to move out of lodgings.

квартира́нт (-а) м lodger.

квартира́нт|ка (-ки; gen pl -ок) ж см **квартира́нт**.

квартир|ова́ть (-у́ю) *несов неперех* (*разг: снима́ть жильё*) to rent a flat (*BRIT*) *или* apartment (*US*).

квартиросъёмщик (-а) м leaseholder.

квартпла́т|а (-ы) ж сокр (= кварти́рная пла́та) rent (*for a flat*).

кварц (-а) м quartz.

ква́рцев|ый *прил* (*поро́да, руда́*) quartz; ~ая ла́мпа quartz lamp.

квас (-а; nom pl -ы́) м kvass (*mildly alcoholic drink made from fermented rye bread, yeast or berries*).

ква́|сить (-шу, -сишь; perf заква́сить) *несов перех* to pickle; (*молоко́*) to sour.

ква́шен|ый *прил* (*молоко́*) sour; ~ая капу́ста sauerkraut, pickled cabbage.

квашн|я́ (-и́; gen pl -е́й) ж (*кадушка*) fermenting bucket (*for dough*); (*разг: челове́к*) clodhopper.

ква́шу *несов см* **ква́сить**.

Квебе́к (-а) м Quebec.

квинте́т (-а) м quintet.

квинтэссе́нци|я (-и) ж quintessence.

квита́нци|я (-и) ж receipt.

кви́ты *как сказ* (*разг*): мы ~ we're quits.

КВН м сокр (= клуб весёлых и нахо́дчивых) contest in which teams compete in various activities.

кво́рум (-а) м quorum.

кво́т|а (-ы) ж quota; и́мпортная ~ import quota.

кВт *сокр* (= килова́тт) kW (= *kilowatt*).

кг *сокр* (= килогра́мм) kg (= *kilogram(me)*).

КГБ м сокр (*ист*: = Комите́т госуда́рственной безопа́сности) KGB.

ке́гл|и (-ей) мн skittles мн; (*игра́*) skittles ед.

кедр (-а) м cedar (tree).

ке́ды (-) мн pumps мн.

Кейпта́ун (-а) м Cape Town.

кейф (-а) м = **кайф**.

кейф|ова́ть (-у́ю) *несов* = **кайфова́ть**.

кекс (-а) м (fruit)cake.

келе́ен *прил см* **келе́йный**.

келе́йно *нареч* secretly.

келе́йный *прил* (*жизнь*) reclusive; (*тишина́*) sublime; (-ен, -йна, -йно; *перен: перегово́ры, совеща́ния*) secret.

Кёльн (-а) м Cologne.

кельт (-а) м Celt.

ке́льтск|ий (-ая, -ое, -ие) *прил* Celtic.

ке́л|ья (-ьи; gen pl -ий) ж (*мона́шеская*) cell.

кем *мест см* **кто**.

Ке́мбридж (-а) м Cambridge.

ке́мпинг (-а) м camping site, campsite.

кенгуру́ *ср нескл* kangaroo.

кени́йск|ий (-ая, -ое, -ие) *прил* Kenyan.

Ке́ни|я (-и) ж Kenya.

ке́пи *ср нескл* peaked cap.

ке́п|ка (-ки; gen pl -ок) ж cap.

кера́мик|а (-и) ж *собир* ceramics мн.

керами́ческ|ий (-ая, -ое, -ие) *прил* ceramic.

кероси́н (-а) м paraffin, kerosene (*US*).

кероси́н|ка (-ки; gen pl -ок) ж paraffin stove.

ке́сарев *прил*: ~о сече́ние Caesarean (*BRIT*) *или* Cesarean (*US*) section.

кессо́нн|ый *прил*: ~ая боле́знь decompression sickness, the bends мн.

ке́т|а (-ы) ж Keta salmon.

кефа́л|ь (-и) ж grey mullet.

кефи́р (-а) м kefir (*yoghurt drink*).

киберне́тик (-а) м specialist in cybernetics.

киберне́тик|а (-и) ж cybernetics.

киберне́тическ|ий (-ая, -ое, -ие) *прил* cybernetic.

киби́т|ка (-и) ж carriage.

кив|а́ть (-ю) *несов неперех* (+*dat*) to nod; ~ (*impf*) на кого́-н (*разг*) to pin the blame on sb.

кивка́ *сущ см* **киво́к**.

кивн|у́ть (-у́, -ёшь) *сов неперех* to nod.

киво́к (-ка́) м nod.

кида́|ть (-ю) *несов от* **ки́нуть**

▶ **кида́ться** *несов от* **ки́нуться** ♦ *возв*: ~ся камня́ми to throw stones at each other; ~ся (*impf*) деньга́ми to throw money around.

Ки́ев (-а) м Kiev.

кизи́л (-а) м cornel.

кизи́ловый *прил* cornel *опред*.

ки|й (-я; nom pl -й, gen pl -ёв) м (*СПОРТ*) cue.

кики́мор|а (-ы) ж *female goblin in Russian mythology*; (*пренебр: челове́к*) fright.

килоба́йт (-а) м kilobyte.

килова́тт (-а) м kilowatt.

килогра́мм (-а) м kilogram(me).

килогра́ммов|ый *прил* of one kilogram(me).

киломе́тр (-а) м kilometre (*BRIT*), kilometer (*US*).

километро́в|ый *прил* (*расстоя́ние*) of one kilometre (*BRIT*) *или* kilometer (*US*); (*го́нка*) one-kilometre.

кил|ь (-я) м keel.

кильва́тер (-а) м wake.

ки́лlь|ка (-и) ж sprat.

кимоно́ *ср нескл* kimono.

кинематóграф (-а) м (киноиндустрия) cinematography; (кинотеáтр) cinema.

кинематографи́ст (-а) м cinematographer.

кинематографи́ческ|ий (-ая, -ое, -ие) прил cinematographic.

кинематогрáфи|я (-и) ж cinematography.

кинéтик|а (-и) ж kinetics.

кинети́ческ|ий (-ая, -ое, -ие) прил kinetic.

кинжáл (-а) м dagger.

кинó ср нескл cinema; (разг: фильм) film, movie (US); **идти́ (пойти́** perf) **в ~** (разг) to go to the pictures (BRIT) или movies (US); **э́то прóсто ~** (разг) it's an absolute joke.

киноактёр (-а) м (film) actor.

киноактри́с|а (-ы) ж (film) actress.

киноарти́ст (-а) м = **киноактёр.**

киноарти́ст|ка (-ки; gen pl -ок) ж = **киноактри́са.**

кинокарти́н|а (-ы) ж film.

кинооперáтор (-а) м cameraman (мн cameramen).

кинорежиссёр (-а) м (film) director.

киностýди|я (-и) ж film studio.

киносъёмк|а (-и) ж filming, shooting.

кинотеáтр (-а) м cinema.

кинофи́льм (-а) м film.

ки́н|уть (-у, -ешь; impf кидáть) сов перех (дрова, кáмень) to throw; (взгляд) to cast; (друзéй) to desert; (си́лы, ресýрсы) to channel

▸ **ки́нуться** (impf кидáться) сов возв: **~ся на** +acc (на врагá) to attack; (на еду) to fall upon; **кидáться** (**~ся** perf) **комý-н на шéю** to fall on sb; **кидáться** (**~ся** perf) **к комý-н** to throw o.s. at sb; **кидáться** (**~ся** perf) **со скáлы** to throw o.s. off a cliff.

кирпáр (неразб)

кио́ск (-а) м kiosk.

кио́т (-а) м icon case.

ки́п|а (-ы) ж bundle.

кипари́с (-а) м cypress.

кипари́совый прил cypress опред.

кипéни|е (-я) ср boiling; **температýра** или **тóчка ~я** boiling point.

кип|éть (-лю́, -и́шь; perf вскипéть) несов неперех (водá, чáйник) to boil; **рабóта ~и́т** work is in full swing; **жизнь ~и́т** life is busy; **~** (**вскипéть** perf) **негодовáнием/злóбой** to seethe with indignation/anger.

Кипр (-а) м Cyprus.

киприóт (-а) м Cypriot.

киприóт|ка (-ки; gen pl -ок) ж см **киприóт.**

кипýч|ий (-ая, -ее, -ие) -, -а, -о) прил bubbling; (перен) busy.

кипяти́льник (-а) м element (for heating water).

кипя|ти́ть (-чý, -ти́шь; perf вскипяти́ть) несов перех to boil

▸ **кипяти́ться** несов возв (овощи) to boil; (шприцы, бельё) to be boiled; (перен: разг: горячи́ться) to get shirty.

кипятóк (-кá) м boiling water.

кипячёный прил boiled.

кипячý(сь) несов см **кипяти́ть(ся).**

кирги́з (-а) м Kirghiz.

Кирги́зи|я (-и) ж Kirghizia.

кирги́з|ка (-ки; gen pl -ок) ж см **кирги́з.**

кирги́зск|ий (-ая, -ое, -ие) прил Kirghiz.

кири́ллиц|а (-ы) ж the Cyrillic alphabet.

кирк|á (-и́) ж pick(axe).

кирпи́ч (-á) м (СТРОИТ) brick.

кирпи́чный прил brick; **кирпи́чный завóд** brickworks.

кисéйный прил muslin; **~ая бáрышня** prim young miss.

ки́сел прил см **ки́слый.**

кисéл|ь (-я́) м fruit jelly; **седьмáя водá на киселé** distant relative.

кисéт (-а) м tobacco pouch.

кисе|я (-и́) ж muslin.

кисли́нк|а (-и) ж sour taste.

кислорóд (-а) м oxygen.

ки́сло-слáд|кий (-кая, -кое, -кие; -ок, -ка, -ко) прил (хлеб) sweet with a bitter aftertaste; (ягоды) bittersweet.

кислот|á (-оты́; nom pl -óты) ж acid.

кислóтность (-и) ж acidity.

кислóтный прил acid; **~ дождь** acid rain.

ки́сл|ый (-ел, -лá, -ло) прил (также перен) sour; **ки́слая капýста** sauerkraut; **ки́слое молокó** soured milk.

ки́с|нуть (-ну, -нешь; pt -, -ла, -ло, perf проки́снуть или ски́снуть) несов неперех to go off; (no perf; перен: разг) to mope (about).

кист|á (-ы́) ж cyst.

ки́сточ|ка (-ки; gen pl -ек) ж (paint)brush; (виногрáда) bunch; (на берéте, на скáтерти итп) tassel.

кист|ь (-и) ж (АНАТ) hand; (гроздь: ряби́ны) cluster; (: виногрáда) bunch; (на скáтерти, на одéжде итп) tassel; (худóжника, маляра) (paint) brush; **он хорошó владéет ки́стью** he's a good painter; **полотнó ки́сти Мати́сса** painting by Matisse.

кит (-á) м whale.

кита́|ец (-йца) м Chinese.

Китá|й (-я) м China.

китáйск|ий (-ая, -ое, -ие) прил Chinese; **~ язы́к** Chinese; **~ая грáмота** double Dutch.

китáй|ка (итп сущ см **китáец.**

китая́н|ка (-ки; gen pl -ок) ж см **китáец.**

ки́тел|ь (-я; nom pl -и, gen pl -ей) м military jacket.

китобóйный прил whaling опред.

кито́вый прил whale опред.

кич|и́ться (-ýсь, -и́шься) несов возв: **~ +instr** to preen o.s. on.

кичли́вый прил (-, -а, -о) прил conceited.

киш|éть (3sg -и́т, 3pl -áт) несов неперех (мошкара, чéрви) to swarm; **~** (impf) **+instr** (людьми, рыбой) to teem with.

кише́чник (-а) *м* intestines *мн*.
кише́чный *прил* intestinal.
Кишинёв (-а) *м* Kishinev.
киш|ка́ (-ки́; *gen pl* -о́к, *dat pl* -ка́м) *ж* gut, intestine; **прямая ~** rectum; **то́лстая ~** large intestine.
кишла́к (-а́) *м village in Central Asia.*
кишми́ш (-а) *м собир* seedless grapes *мн*; *(изюм)* currants *мн*.
кишмя́ *нареч (разг)*: **~ кише́ть** to swarm.
кишо́к *сущ см* **кишка́**.
кл. *сокр* = **класс.**
клавеси́н (-а) *м* harpsichord.
клавиату́р|а (-ы) *ж* keyboard; **(ма́лая) ~** *(комп)* keypad.
кла́виш|а (-и) *ж* key; **~ «возвра́т каре́тки"/вы́хода** *(комп)* return/escape key.
кла́вишный *прил*: **~ инструме́нт** keyboard instrument.
клад (-а) *м* treasure.
кла́дбищ|е (-а) *ср* cemetery; *(возле церкви)* graveyard.
кладби́щенск|ий (-ая, -ое, -ие) *прил (см сущ)* cemetery *опред*; graveyard *опред*; **~ сто́рож** sexton.
кла́дезь (-я) *м (перен)*: **~ зна́ний** *или* **прему́дрости** mine of information.
кла́дк|а (-и) *ж (действие)* laying; **кирпи́чная ~** brickwork; **ка́менная ~** masonry.
кладова́|я (-ой; *decl like adj*) *ж* store.
кладо́в|ка (-ки; *gen pl* -ок) *ж (разг)* cubby-hole.
кладовщи́|к (-а́) *м* storeman *(мн* storemen).
кладовщи́ц|а (-ы) *ж* storewoman *(мн* storewomen).
кладу́ *итп несов см* **класть.**
кладь (-и) *ж* load; **ручна́я ~** hand luggage.
кла́ксон (-а) *м* horn.
клан (-а) *м* clan.
кла́ня|ться (-юсь; *perf* **поклони́ться**) *несов возв* to bow; *(свидетельствовать уважение)* to send one's regards; *(перен: униженно просить)* to beg.
кла́пан (-а) *м* valve.
кларне́т (-а) *м* clarinet.
кларнети́ст (-а) *м* clarinetist.
класс (-а) *м* class; *(комната)* classroom ♦ **как сказ** *(выражает восхищение)* it's great; **он вёл ~ фортепья́но в консервато́рии** he taught the piano at the conservatory; **специали́ст высо́кого кла́сса** highly-qualified specialist; **пока́зывать (показа́ть** *perf)* **~** *(разг)* to show one's class.
кла́ссен *прил см* **кла́ссный.**
кла́ссик (-а) *м (литературы, музыки)* classic; *(учёный)* classical scholar.
кла́ссик|а (-и) *ж* classics *мн*.
классификацио́нный *прил (экзамен)* assessment *опред*; *(таблица)* classification *опред*.
классифика́ци|я (-и) *ж* classification.
классифици́р|овать (-ую) *(не)сов перех* to classify.
классици́зм (-а) *м* classicism.
класси́ческ|ий (-ая, -ое, -ие) *прил (пример, работа)* classic; *(музыка, литература)* classical; *(разг: жулик, политикан итп)* typical; **~ая гимна́зия** grammar school specializing in Latin and Ancient Greek; **~ое образова́ние** classical education.
кла́сс|ный *прил (сочинение, собрание)* class *опред*; (-ен, -на, -но; *разг: водитель, обед)* great; **кла́ссный руководи́тель** form teacher.
кла́ссовый *прил* class *опред*.
кла|сть (-ду́, -дёшь; *pt* -л, -ла, -ло, *perf* **положи́ть)** *несов перех* to put; *(perf* **сложи́ть**; *фундамент)* to lay; **~ (положи́ть** *perf)* **основа́ние** to lay down the foundations; **~ (положи́ть** *perf)* **жизнь за кого́-н/что-н** to lay down one's life for sb/sth; **~ (положи́ть** *perf)* **что-н на му́зыку** to put sth to music; **~** *(impf)* **я́йца** to lay eggs.
кла́цань|е (-я) *ср (разг)* chattering.
кла́ца|ть (-ю) *несов неперех (разг)* to chatter.
клёв (-а) *м* bite; **сего́дня хоро́ший ~** the fish are biting today.
кл|ева́ть (-юю) *несов перех (подлеж: птица)* to peck ♦ *неперех (рыба)* to bite; **~** *(impf)* **но́сом** to nod; **у меня́ ~юёт** I've got a bite
▶ **клева́ться** *несов возв* to peck.
кле́вер (-а) *м* clover.
клевет|а́ (-ы́) *ж (устная)* slander; *(письменная)* libel.
клевет|а́ть (-ещу́, -е́щешь; *perf* **наклевета́ть)** *несов неперех*: **~ на** +*acc (см сущ)* to slander; to libel.
клеветни́|к (-а́) *м* slanderer.
клеветни́ческ|ий (-ая, -ое, -ие) *прил (см сущ)* slanderous; libellous.
клевещу́ *итп несов см* **клевета́ть.**
клее́к *прил см* **кле́йкий.**
клеён|ка (-ки; *gen pl* -ок) *ж* oilcloth.
клеёнчатый *прил* oilskin *опред*.
кле́|ить (-ю, -ишь; *perf* **скле́ить)** *несов перех* to glue
▶ **кле́иться** *несов возв* to stick; *(перен: работа)* to come together; *(: разговор)* to go smoothly.
кле|й (-я) *м* glue.
кле́йк|ий (-ая, -ое, -ие; -ек, -йка, -йко) *прил* sticky; **кле́йкая ле́нта** sticky tape.
клеймёный *прил (товар)* stamped; *(скот)* branded.
клейм|и́ть (-лю́, -и́шь; *perf* **заклейми́ть)** *несов перех (товар, груз)* to stamp; *(скот, преступника)* to brand; *(перен: человека, поведение)* to stigmatize; **~ (заклейми́ть** *perf)* **кого́-н позо́ром** to hold sb up to shame; **его́ заклейми́ли преда́телем** he was branded a traitor.
клейм|о́ (-а́; *nom pl* -а, *gen pl* -) *ср* stamp; *(на теле скота, осуждённого)* brand; **~ позо́ра** stigma.
кле́йстер (-а; *part gen* -у) *м* paste.

клéмм|а (-ы) ж *(ЭЛЕК)* terminal.
клён (-а) м maple.
кленóвый *прил* maple.
клеп|áть (-áю; *perf* **склепáть**) *несов перех* to rivet; ♦ (-лю́, -лешь; *perf* **наклепáть**) *неперех* *(разг)*: ~ **на** +*acc* to snitch on.
клептомáн (-а) м kleptomaniac.
клептомáни|я (-и) ж kleptomania.
клептомáн|ка (-ки; *gen pl* -ок) ж *см* **клептомáн**.
клерк (-а) м clerk.
клéт|ка (-ки; *gen pl* -ок) ж *(для птиц, животных)* cage; *(на ткани)* check; *(на бумаге)* square; *(БИО)* cell; **бумáга в** ~**ку** squared paper; **ткань в** ~**ку** checked material; **груднáя** ~ chest; **лéстничная** ~ landing.
клéточный *прил (БИО)* cell *опред*.
клетчáт|ка (-и) ж *(no pl; БОТ)* cellulose; *(АНАТ)* cell tissue.
клéтчатый *прил (ткань, шарф итп)* chequered, checked.
клёц|ка (-ки; *gen pl* -ек) ж *(обычно мн)* dumpling.
клёш (-а) м flare ♦ *прил неизм*: **брю́ки** ~ flares; **ю́бка** ~ flared skirt.
клешн|я́ (-и́; *gen pl* -éй) ж claw, pincer.
клещ (-á) м *(ЗООЛ)* tick.
клéщ|и (-éй) *мн* tongs *мн*.
клиéнт (-а) м client.
клиéнт|ка (-ки; *gen pl* -ок) ж *см* **клиéнт**.
клиенту́р|а (-ы) ж *собир* clientèle.
кли́зм|а (-ы) ж enema.
клик (-а) м *(человека)* cry; *(птицы)* call.
кли́к|а (-и) ж clique.
клику́ш|а (-и) ж hysterical woman *(мн* women) ♦ м/ж panicmonger.
кли́макс (-а) м *(БИО)* menopause.
климактери́ческий (-ая, -ое, -ие) *прил* menopausal; **климактери́ческий пери́од** menopause.
кли́мат (-а) м *(также перен)* climate.
климати́ческий (-ая, -ое, -ие) *прил* climactic.
клин (-а; *nom pl* -ья *или* -ы́, *gen pl* -ьев *или* -óв) м wedge; *(солдат, журавлей)* V-formation; **бородá кли́ном** goatee; ~ **кли́ном вышибáть** *(impf)* to fight fire with fire.
кли́ник|а (-и) ж clinic.
клини́ческий (-ая, -ое, -ие) *прил* clinical; **клини́ческая больни́ца** training hospital; **клини́ческая смерть** *(МЕД)* clinical death.
клин|óк (-ка́) м blade.
кли́пс|ы (-ов) *мн* clip-on earrings *мн*.
клир (-а) м *собир (РЕЛ)* the clergy.
кли́рик (-а) м clergyman *(мн* clergymen).
кли́ринг (-а) м *(КОММ)* clearing.
кли́рос (-а) м choir *(part of church)*.
клич (-а) м cry; **боевóй** ~ battle cry.
кли́ч|ка (-ки; *gen pl* -ек) ж *(собаки, кошки итп)* name; *(человека)* nickname.
клишé *ср нескл (перен)* cliché; *(ТИПОГ)* plate.
клоáк|а (-и) ж *(перен: загрязнённое место)*

cesspit; *(: безнравственная среда)* cesspool.
клобу́к (-á) м *(РЕЛ)* cowl.
кло|к (-ка́; *nom pl* -чья, *gen pl* -чьев) м *(волос)* tuft; *(ваты)* wad.
клокотáни|е (-я) ср *(воды)* gurgling.
клок|отáть (-очу́, -óчешь) *несов неперех (вода, поток)* to gurgle; *(перен: негодовать)* to seethe.
клон|и́ть (-ю́, -ишь) *несов перех* to bow, bend ♦ *неперех*: ~ **к** +*dat* to drive at; **егó** ~**и́ло ко сну** he was drifting off (to sleep); **лóдку клóнит нá бок** the boat is tilting; **к чему́ ты клóнишь?** what are you getting *или* driving at?
▸ **клони́ться** *несов возв (пригибаться)* to bend; *(близиться)*: ~**ся к** +*dat* to approach; **день** ~**и́лся к вéчеру** evening was drawing near.
клоп (-á) м bedbug.
клóун (-а) м clown.
клóунский (-ая, -ое, -ие) *прил* clown's; *(перен)* clownish.
клоч|óк (-ка́) м *уменьш от* **клок**; *(земли)* plot; *(бумаги)* scrap.
клóчья *итп сущ см* **клок**.
клуб (-а) м *(общество, здание)* club; *(обычно мн: дыма, пыли)* cloud.
клу́б|ень (-ня) м *(картофеля)* tuber.
клуб|и́ться *(3sg* -и́тся, *3pl* -я́тся) *несов возв* to swirl.
клубкá *сущ см* **клубóк**.
клубни́к|а (-и) ж strawberry ♦ *собир* strawberries *мн*.
клубни́чный *прил* strawberry.
клуб|óк (-ка́) м *(ниток, шерсти)* ball; *(перен: противоречий)* tangle, knot; **сверну́ться** *(perf)* ~**кóм** to curl up in a ball.
клу́мб|а (-ы) ж flowerbed.
клу́ш|а (-и) ж *(разг: пренебр)* clumsy woman.
клык (-á) м *(человека)* canine (tooth); *(животного)* fang.
клюв (-а) м beak.
клюк|á (-и́) ж walking stick.
клю́кв|а (-ы) ж cranberry ♦ *собир* cranberries *мн*; **развéсистая** ~ tall story.
клю́квенный *прил*: ~ **морс/кисéль** cranberry juice/jelly.
клю́н|уть (-у, -ешь) *сов перех* to peck.
ключ (-á) м *(также перен)* key; *(родник)* spring; *(МУЗ)*: **скрипи́чный/басóвый** ~ treble/bass clef; **гáечный** ~ spanner; ~ **от входнóй двéри** front-door key; **бить** *(impf)* *или* **кипéть** *(impf)* ~**óм** *(вода)* to jet, spout; **жизнь бьёт** *или* **кипи́т** ~**óм** life is really buzzing; **в прéжнем** ~**é** *(перен)* as before; **сдавáть (сдать** *perf)* **что-н под** ~ *(здание)* to offer sth ready for immediate entry; **ключ зажигáния** ignition key.
ключевóй *прил (позиция, проблемы итп)* key *опред*; **ключевáя водá** spring water.
ключи́ц|а (-ы) ж collarbone.

клю́ш|ка (-ки; *gen pl* -ек) ж (ХОККЕЙ) hockey stick; (ГОЛЬФ) club.

кля́кс|а (-ы) ж smudge.

кляну́(сь) *итп несов см* **кля́сть(ся)**.

кля́нч|ить (-у, -ишь; *perf* **вы́клянчить**) *несов перех* (*разг*): ~ что-н у кого́-н to pester sb for sth.

кляп (-а) *м* gag; **засу́нуть** (*perf*) кому́-н ~ в рот to gag sb.

кля́|сть (-ну́, -нёшь; *pt* -л, -ла́, -ло) *несов перех* to curse

▸ **кля́сться** (*perf* **покля́сться**) *несов возв* to swear; **кля́сться** (**покля́сться** *perf*) в ве́чной любви́ to swear eternal love; **кля́сться** (**покля́сться** *perf*) жи́знью/Бо́гу to swear on one's life/to God.

кля́тв|а (-ы) ж oath; **дава́ть** (**дать** *perf*)/ **сде́рживать** (**сдержа́ть** *perf*) ~у to take *или* swear/keep an oath; **наруша́ть** (**нару́шить** *perf*) ~у to break one's oath.

кля́уз|а (-ы) ж backbiting.

кля́узен *прил см* **кля́узный**.

кля́узник (-а) *м* (*пренебр*) scandalmonger.

кля́узнича|ть (-ю; *perf* **накля́узничать**) *несов непepex*: ~ (на +*acc*) to spread gossip (about).

кля́уз|ный (-ен, -на, -но) *прил*: ~ное письмо́ slanderous letter.

кля́ч|а (-и) ж (*разг*: *пренебр*: *лошадь*) old nag.

км. *сокр* (= киломе́тр) km (= kilometre (*BRIT*) *или* kilometer (*US*)).

км/ч *сокр* (= киломе́тров в час) km/h (= kilometres per hour).

КНДР ж *сокр* (= Коре́йская Наро́дно-Демократи́ческая Респу́блика) DPRK (= *Democratic People's Republic of Korea*).

кне́л|и (-ей) *мн* quenelles *мн*.

кни́г|а (-и) ж book; **ка́ссовая** ~ cash-book; **телефо́нная** ~ telephone book *или* directory; ~ **зака́зов** order book; ~ **уче́та** day book; **кни́га жа́лоб и предложе́ний** suggestions book.

книголю́б (-а) *м* book-lover.

книгопеча́тани|е (-я) *ср* book printing.

кни́ж|ка (-ки; *gen pl* -ек) ж book; **записна́я** ~ notebook; **зачётная** ~ (ПРОСВЕЩ) register; **трудова́я** ~ employment record book; **че́ковая** ~ chequebook (*BRIT*), checkbook (*US*).

кни́жник (-а) *м* (*знаток книг*) bibliophile.

кни́жный *прил* (*перен: знания, стиль*) bookish; **кни́жный магази́н** bookshop; **кни́жный шкаф** bookcase; **кни́жный червь** bookworm.

кни́зу *нареч* downwards.

кно́п|ка (-ки; *gen pl* -ок) ж (*звонка, лифта*) button; (*канцеля́рская*) drawing pin (*BRIT*), thumbtack (*US*); (*застёжка*) press stud, popper (*BRIT*).

КНР ж *сокр* (= Кита́йская Наро́дная Респу́блика) PRC (= *People's Republic of China*).

кнут (-а́) *м* whip; **поли́тика** ~а́ и пря́ника the carrot and the stick policy.

княги́н|я (-и) ж princess (*wife of a prince*).

княж|и́ть (-у, -и́шь) *несов непepex* to reign.

княжн|а́ (-ны́; *gen pl* -о́н) ж princess (*daughter of a prince*).

княз|ь (-я; *nom pl* -ья́, *gen pl* -е́й) *м* prince (*in Russia*); **вели́кий** ~ (ИСТ) grand prince (*son or brother of the tsar*).

ко *предл см* **к.**

коагули́р|овать (*3sg* -ует, *3pl* -уют) *несов перех* to coagulate.

коагуля́ци|я (-и) ж coagulation.

коа́л|а (-ы) ж koala (bear).

коалицио́нн|ый *прил*: ~ое прави́тельство coalition government; ~ догово́р coalition pact.

коали́ци|я (-и) ж coalition.

ко́бальт (-а) *м* cobalt.

кобе́л|ь (-я́) *м* dog (*male*).

ко́бр|а (-ы) ж cobra.

кобур|а́ (-ы́) ж holster.

кобы́л|а (-ы) ж mare; (*перен: разг*) strapping lass.

ко́ван|ый (-, -а, -о) *прил* (*меч, решётка итп*) forged; (*обитый железом*) metal-bound.

кова́рен *прил см* **кова́рный**.

кова́рность (-и) ж treachery.

кова́рн|ый (-ен, -на, -но) *прил* devious.

кова́рств|о (-а) *ср* deviousness.

ков|а́ть (**кую́, куёшь**; *imper* **куй(те)**, *perf* **скова́ть**) *несов перех* to forge; **куй желе́зо пока́ горячо́** strike while the iron's hot.

ковбо́й (-я) *м* cowboy.

ковёр (-ра́) *м* carpet; **вызыва́ть** (**вы́звать** *perf*) на ~ кого́-н to call sb to account.

кове́ркань|е (-я) *ср* mangling.

кове́рка|ть (-ю; *perf* **искове́ркать**) *несов перех* (*произношение, слова*) to mangle; (*язык*) to butcher; (*душу*) to twist; **коверка́ть** (**исковерка́ть** *perf*) чью-н мысль/чьи-н слова́ to twist sb's ideas/words.

ко́вк|а (-и) ж forging.

ковра́ *итп сущ см* **ковёр**.

коври́г|а (-и) ж loaf (*мн* loaves).

коври́ж|ка (-ки; *gen pl* -ек) ж ≈ gingerbread.

ко́врик (-а) *м* rug; (*дверно́й*) mat.

ковро́в|ый *прил*: ~ая доро́жка runner.

ковроде́ли|е (-я) *ср* carpet weaving.

ковче́г (-а) *м*: Но́ев ~ Noah's Ark.

ковш (-а́) *м* ladle; (*экскава́тора*) shovel.

ковы́л|ь (-я́) *м* (БОТ) feather grass.

ковыля́|ть (-ю) *несов непepex* to hobble.

ковыря́|ть (-ю) *несов перех* to dig up; ~ в зуба́х/носу́ to pick one's teeth/nose

▸ **ковыря́ться** *несов возв* (*медлить*) to faff about; ~ся (*impf*) (в +*prp*) (*копаться: в земле*) to root *или* poke about (in).

когда́ *нареч* when; (*иногда*) sometimes; ~ ты зако́нчишь? when will you finish?; мы не зна́ем, ~ э́то произошло́ we don't know when it happened; ~ пью ко́фе, ~ чай sometimes I drink coffee, sometimes tea.

когда́-либо *нареч* = **когда́-нибудь**.

когда́-нибудь *нареч* (*в вопроси́тельных предложе́ниях*) ever; (*в утверди́тельных* *предложениях*) some *или* one day; **Вы ~ там бы́ли?** have you ever been there?; **я ~ туда́ пое́ду** I'll go there some *или* one day.

когда́-то *нареч* once; **он был ~ бога́т** he was once a rich man; **~ ещё я туда́ пое́ду** just when will I have another chance to go there?

кого́ *мест от* **кто**.

когóрт|а (-ы) *ж* (*перен*) cohort.

кóг|оть (-тя; *gen pl* -те́й) *м* (*кошки, льва итп*) claw; (*орла*) talon; **пока́зывать** (**показа́ть** *perf*) **~ти** (*перен*) to bare one's teeth.

код (-а) *м* code; **передава́ть** (**переда́ть** *perf*) **сообще́ние по кóду** to send a message in code; **~ си́мвола** (*КОМП*) character code.

кодеи́н (-а) *м* codeine.

кóдекс (-а) *м* code; **гражда́нский/уголóвный ~** (*ЮР*) civil/criminal code.

коди́р|овать (-ую; *perf* **закоди́ровать**) *несов перех* to encode, code.

кодирóвк|а (-и) *ж* coding.

кодирóвщик (-а) *м* coder.

коди́рующий (-ая, -ее, -ие) *прил*: **~ее устрóйство** (*КОМП*) encoder.

кодифика́ци|я (-и) *ж* (*ЮР*) codification.

кодифици́р|овать (-ую) (*не*)*сов перех* (*ЮР*) to codify.

кóдов|ый *прил*: **~ые зна́ки** code symbols *мн*; **кóдовое назва́ние** codename.

кóе-где́ *нареч* here and there.

кóек *сущ см* **кóйка**.

кóе-ка́к *нареч* (*небрежно*) any old how; (*с трудóм*) somehow.

кóе-какóй (**кóе-какóго**) *мест* some; **нам нужна́ кóе-кака́я пóмощь** we need some sort of help.

кóе-когда́ *нареч* now and then, now and again.

кóе-ктó (**кóе-когó**) *мест* (*некоторые*) some (people).

кóе-куда́ *нареч* (*разг*) this place and that.

кóе-чегó *мест* (*нечто*) something; (*немногого*) a little.

кóж|а (-и) *ж* skin; (*материал*) leather; (*апельсина, яблока*) peel; **гуси́ная ~** goose bumps *мн или* pimples *мн*; **~ да кóсти** (*разг*) all skin and bone; **из ~и вон лезть** (*impf*) to sweat blood.

кóжаный *прил* leather.

кóже́венный *прил* leather; **коже́венный заво́д** tannery.

кóжник (-а) *м* (*МЕД*) dermatologist.

кóжн|ый *прил*: **~ые болéзни** skin diseases; **кóжный врач** dermatologist; **кóжный покрóв** skin.

кожур|á (-ы́) *ж* (*апельсина*) peel; (*орéха*) skin.

коз|á (-ы́; *nom pl* -ы) *ж* (nanny) goat.

козёл *сущ см* **кóзлы**.

козёл (-ла́; *nom pl* -лы) *м* (billy) goat; (*в гимнастике*) horse; (*разг: игра*) dominoes; **от негó как от ~ла́ молока́** (*разг*) he's worse than

useless; **забива́ть** (*impf*) **~ла́** to play dominoes; **козёл отпуще́ния** scapegoat.

Козерóг (-а) *м* (*созвездие*) Capricorn.

кóз|ий (-ья, -ье, -ьи) *прил* goat *опред*; **~ье молокó** goat's milk.

козла́ *итп сущ см* **козёл**.

козлёнок (-ёнка; *nom pl* -я́та, *gen pl* -я́т) *м* (*ЗООЛ*) kid.

козли́н|ый *прил* (*голос*) reedy; **~ая борóдка** goatee.

кóзл|ы (-ел) *мн* (*сиденье*) coach box *ед*; (*опора*) trestle *ед*.

козля́та *итп сущ см* **козлёнок**.

кóзн|и (-ей) *мн* intrigues *мн*; **стрóить** (*impf*) **~** to scheme.

козыр|ёк (-ька́) *м* (*картуза, фуражки*) peak; (*навес*) lintel; **брать** (**взять** *perf*) **под ~** to salute.

козырн|óй *прил*: **~а́я ка́рта** trump.

козырн|у́ть (-у́, -нёшь) *сов от* **козыря́ть**.

кóзыр|ь (-я) *м* (*КАРТЫ*) trump; (*перен*) trump card.

козырька́ *сущ см* **козырёк**.

козыря́|ть (-ю; *perf* **козырну́ть**) *несов неперех* (*разг: в картах*) to play a trump; (*хвастаться*): **~ +instr** to show off about; (: *отдавать честь*): **~ть +dat** to salute.

козя́вк|а (-ки; *gen pl* -ок) *ж* (*разг: букашка*) bug; (: *пренебр: человек*) small fry *только ед*.

кó|йка (-йки; *gen pl* -ек) *ж* (*на судне*) berth; (*в казарме*) bunk; (*в больнице, общежитии*) bed.

кок (-а) *м* (*повар*) ship's cook; (*вихор*) quiff.

кокаи́н (-а) *м* cocaine.

кокаини́ст (-а) *м* cocaine addict.

кокаини́ст|ка (-ки; *gen pl* -ок) *ж см* **кокаини́ст**.

кока́рд|а (-ы) *ж* cockade.

коке́т|ка (-ки; *gen pl* -ок) *ж* flirt, coquette.

коке́тливость (-и) *ж* flirtatiousness.

коке́тлив|ый (-, -а, -о) *прил* (*девушка, взгляд, смех*) flirtatious; (*шапочка, платье итп*) pretty.

коке́тнича|ть (-ю) *несов неперех* to flirt.

коке́ток *сущ см* **коке́тка**.

коке́тств|о (-а) *ср* flirting.

коклю́ш (-а) *м* whooping cough.

КОКÓМ *сокр* СОСОМ.

кóкон (-а) *м* cocoon.

кокóс (-а) *м* coconut.

кокóсов|ый *прил*: **~ая па́льма** coconut palm; **кокóсовое молокó** coconut milk; **кокóсовый орéх** coconut.

кокс (-а) *м* coke.

кокс|ова́ть (-у́ю) *несов перех* (*ТЕХ*) to coke.

кокте́йл|ь (-я) *м* cocktail.

кол (-á; *loc sg* -у́, *nom pl* -ья, *gen pl* -ьев) *м* stake; (*nom pl* -ы; *разг*: ПРОСВЕЩ) ≈ E (*school mark*); **у меня́ нет ни ~á ни двора́** I don't have a thing to my name; (**ему́** *итп*) **хоть ~ на головé чеши́** it's like talking to a brick wall.

ко́лб|а (-ы) ж (*хим*) flask.
колбас|а́ (-ы) ж sausage.
кол-во *сокр* (= *коли́чество*) amt (= *amount*).
колго́т|ки (-ок) *мн* tights *мн* (*BRIT*), panty hose *мн* (*US*).
колдо́бин|а (-ы) ж (*на доро́ге*) pothole.
колд|ова́ть (-у́ю) *несов неперех* to practise (*BRIT*) *или* practice (*US*) witchcraft; (*перен*): ~ **над** +*instr* (*над карти́ной, над у́жином итп*) to conjure up.
колдовско́й *прил* magical; (*перен*) bewitching.
колдовств|о́ (-а́) *ср* sorcery, witchcraft.
колду́н (-а́) *м* wizard, sorcerer.
колду́нь|я (-ьи; *gen pl* **-ий**, *dat pl* **-ьям**) ж sorceress.
колеба́ни|е (-я) *ср* (*физ*) oscillation; (*ма́ятника*) swing; (*по́чвы, зда́ния*) vibration; (*перен*: *цен, температу́ры*) fluctuation; (: *обы́чно мн*: *нереши́тельность*) wavering, vacillation.
колеба́тельный *прил* (*физ*) oscillatory.
кол|еба́ть (-е́блю, -е́блешь) *несов перех* to rock, swing; (*perf* **поколеба́ть**; *авторите́т*) to shake
► **колеба́ться** (*perf* **поколеба́ться**) *несов возв* (*физ*) to oscillate; (*ли́стья, пла́мя итп*) to flicker; (*це́ны, пого́да*) to fluctuate; (*сомнева́ться*) to waver, vacillate.
колеблю́щийся (-аяся, -ееся, -иеся) *прил* (*свет, те́ни*) flickering; (*челове́к*) vacillating.
коленко́р (-а) *м* calico.
коленко́ровый *прил* calico.
коле́нн|ый *прил*: ~**ая ча́шка** kneecap.
коле́н|о (-а; *nom pl* **-и**, *gen pl* **-ей**) *ср* knee; (*nom pl* **-а**; *трубы́*) joint; (*разг*: *муз*) phrase; (*поколе́ние*) generation; **встава́ть (встать** *perf*) **на** ~**и** to kneel (down); **стоя́ть** (*impf*) **на** ~**ях** to be kneeling (down); **опуска́ться (опусти́ться** *perf*) **на** ~**и** to go down on one's knees; **сиде́ть** (*impf*) **у кого́-н на** ~**ях** to sit on sb's knee *или* lap; **поста́вить** (*perf*) **кого́-н на** ~**и** (*перен*) to bring sb to his *итп* knees; **ей мо́ре по** ~ everything washes straight over her.
коленопреклонённый *прил* kneeling.
коле́нчатый *прил*: ~ **вал** crankshaft.
ко́лер (-а) *м* colour (*BRIT*), color (*US*).
колёсик|о (-а) *ср уменьш от* **колесо́**; (*часово́е*) wheel.
коле|си́ть (-шу́, -си́шь) *несов неперех* to get around; **я** ~**си́л по всему́ го́роду** I've been all over town.
колесни́ц|а (-ы) ж chariot.
кол|есо́ (-еса́; *nom pl* **-ёса**) *ср* wheel; **пя́тое** ~ (*перен*) fifth wheel (*fig*); **жизнь на** ~**ёсах** life on the road; **жить** (*impf*) **на** ~**ёсах** to live out of a suitcase.
коле́ц *сущ см* **кольцо́**.
колешу́ *несов см* **колеси́ть**.
коле́|я (-й) ж (*на доро́ге*) rut; (*для поездо́в*) track; (*перен*) routine; **выбива́ть (вы́бить** *perf*) **из** ~**й** to get out of a rut.

ко́лик|и (-) *мн* colic *ед*.
коли́чественный *прил* quantitative.
коли́честв|о (-а) *ср* quantity.
ко́лк|а (-и) ж (*дров*) chopping; (*льда*) breaking up.
ко́лкий (-кая, -кое, -кие; -ок, -ка́, -ко) *прил* (*хво́я, трава́*) prickly; (*перен*: *шу́тка, замеча́ния*) biting.
ко́лкость (-и) ж (*нра́ва, замеча́ний*) abrasiveness; (*насме́шка*) biting remark.
коллаборациони́зм (-а) *м* collaborationism.
коллаборациони́ст (-а) *м* collaborator.
колла́ж (-а) *м* collage.
колле́г|а (-и) *м/ж* colleague.
коллегиа́лен *прил см* **коллегиа́льный**.
коллегиа́льность (-и) ж: **при́нцип** ~**и** collective responsibility.
коллегиа́льный (-ен, -ьна, -ьно) *прил* collective.
колле́ги|я (-и) ж (*поли́т*) collegium (*executive body in charge of government ministry*); **адвока́тская** ~ ≈ the Bar; **редакцио́нная** ~ editorial board.
ко́лледж (-а) *м* college.
коллекти́в (-а) *м* collective; **а́вторский** ~ (team of) contributors.
коллекти́вен *прил см* **коллекти́вный**.
коллективиза́ци|я (-и) ж (*ист*) collectivization (*creation of collective farms in the late 1920's and 1930's*).
коллекти́вный (-ен, -на, -но) *прил* collective.
колле́ктор (-а) *м* (*библиоте́чный*) book depository; (*канализацио́нный*) manifold; (*элек*) collector.
коллекционе́р (-а) *м* collector.
коллекциони́ровани|е (-я) *ср* collecting.
коллекциони́р|овать (-ую) *несов перех* to collect.
коллекцио́нный *прил* collectable.
колле́кци|я (-и) ж collection.
ко́лли ж *нескл* collie.
колли́зи|я (-и) ж clash.
колло́квиум (-а) *м* (*просвещ*) seminar; (*совеща́ние специали́стов*) colloquium.
коловоро́т (-а) *м* (*водоворо́т*) eddy; (*тех*) ice drill; (*перен*: *столпотворе́ние*) hurly-burly; ~ **собы́тий** the vortex of events.
коло́д|а (-ы) ж (*бревно́*) block; (*карт*) pack, deck; **че́рез пень** ~**у** half-heartedly.
коло́дезн|ый *прил*: ~**ая вода́** water from the well.
коло́д|ец (-ца) *м* well; (*в ша́хте*) shaft.
коло́д|ка (-ки; *gen pl* **-ок**) ж (*обувна́я*) shoetree; (*орде́нская*) strip.
коло́дца *итп сущ см* **коло́дец**.
ко́лок *прил см* **ко́лкий**.
ко́локол (-а; *nom pl* **-а́**) *м* bell; **звони́ть** (*impf*) **в** ~ to ring a bell.
колоко́льн|я (-ьни; *gen pl* **-ен**) ж bell tower; **смотре́ть** (*impf*) **со свое́й** ~**ни на что-н** to take a narrow view of sth.
колоко́льчик (-а) *м* bell; (*бот*) bluebell.

колониали́зм (-а) *м* colonialism.
колониа́льный *прил* colonial.
колониза́тор (-а) *м* colonizer.
колонизи́р|овать (-ую) *(не)сов перех* to colonize.
колониз|ова́ть (-у́ю) *(не)сов* = колонизи́ровать.
колони́ст (-а) *м* colonist.
колони́ст|ка (-ки; *gen pl* -ок) *ж см* колони́ст.
коло́ни|я (-и) *ж* colony; исправи́тельно-трудова́я ~ penal colony; ~ для малоле́тних престу́пников *или* несовершенноле́тних young offenders' institution.
коло́н|ка (-ки; *gen pl* -ок) *ж* column; *(газовая)* geyser *(BRIT)*, water heater; *(для воды, для бензина)* pump.
колонка́ *сущ см* коло́нок.
колонко́вый *прил* polecat *опред*.
коло́нн|а (-ы) *ж (АРХИТ)* column; *(ряд)*: ~ солда́т/демонстра́нтов column of soldiers/ demonstrators.
колонна́д|а (-ы) *ж* colonnade.
коло́нок *сущ см* коло́нка.
колон|о́к (-ка́) *м* polecat.
колорату́рн|ый *прил*: ~ое сопра́но coloratura *(soprano)*.
колори́т (-а) *м (перен: эпохи, страны итп)* colour *(BRIT)*, color *(US)*; *(ИСКУССТВО)* use of colour; ме́стный ~ local colour.
колори́тный (-ен, -на, -но) *прил* colourful *(BRIT)*, colorful *(US)*.
ко́л|ос (-оса; *nom pl* -о́сья, *gen pl* -о́сьев) *м* ear *(of corn, wheat)*.
ко́лос (-а) *м (также перен)* colossus; ~ на гли́няных нога́х a giant with feet of clay.
колосса́льный (-ен, -ьна, -ьно) *прил* colossal; ~ьно! that's fantastic!
кол|оти́ть (-очу́, -о́тишь) *несов неперех (по столу, в дверь)* to thump ♦ *перех (разг: бить)* to whack; меня́ ~о́тит (дрожь) I'm shaking all over
▶ **колоти́ться** *несов возв (сердце)* to thump; ~ся *(impf)* в дверь to thump on the door.
ко́лот|ый *прил*: ~ са́хар lump sugar; ~ая ра́на stab wound.
кол|о́ть (-ю́, -ешь; *perf* расколо́ть) *несов перех (дрова)* to chop (up); *(орехи)* to crack; *(perf* заколо́ть; *штыком итп)* to spear; *(perf* уколо́ть; *иголкой)* to prick; *(разг: делать укол)*: ~ кого́-н to give sb an injection; ~ *(impf)* кому́-н что-н *(разг)* to inject sb with sth; у меня́ ко́лет в боку́ I've got a stitch; пра́вда глаза́ ко́лет the truth is hard to swallow
▶ **коло́ться** *несов возв (ёж, шиповник)* to be prickly; *(орех)* to crack; *(наркоман)* to be on drugs.
колочу́(сь) *несов см* колоти́ть(ся).

колпа́к (-а́) *м (шутовской, поварской)* hat; *(лампы)* lampshade.
колпач|о́к (-ка́) *м уменьш от* колпа́к; *(контрацептив)* (Dutch) cap.
колумби́йск|ий (-ая, -ое, -ие) *прил* Columbian.
Колу́мби|я (-и) *ж* Columbia.
колупа́|ть (-ю) *несов перех (разг)* to scratch.
колхо́з (-а) *м* kolkhoz, collective farm.
колхо́зник (-а) *м* kolkhoznik, collective farmer.
колхо́зный *прил* kolkhoz *опред*, collective farm *опред*.
колча́н (-а) *м* quiver.
колчеда́н (-а) *м* pyrite.
колыбе́л|ь (-и) *ж (также перен)* cradle; с ~и *(перен)* from the cradle.
колыбе́льн|ая (-ой; *decl like adj) ж (также:* ~ пе́сня) lullaby.
колыма́г|а (-и) *ж (разг: машина)* old banger.
колыха́ни|е (-я) *ср* rocking, swaying.
колых|а́ть (-ы́шу, -ы́шешь) *несов перех* to rock
▶ **колыха́ться** *несов возв (море, грудь)* to heave; *(трава, дерево)* to sway.
ко́лыш|ек (-ка) *м уменьш от* кол; *(для палатки)* (tent) peg.
колы́шу(сь) *итп несов см* колыха́ть(ся).
колье́ *ср нескл* necklace.
кольн|у́ть (-у́, -ёшь) *сов перех (иголкой)* to prick; *(перен: обидным намёком)* to sting; у меня́ ~у́ло в спине́ a pain shot up my back.
кольра́би *ж нескл* kohlrabi.
кольт (-а) *м* automatic (revolver).
кольц|ева́ть (-у́ю) *несов перех* to ring.
кольцево́й *прил* round, circular; кольцева́я доро́га ring road; кольцева́я ли́ния circle line.
кольц|о́ (-а́; *nom pl* -ьца, *gen pl* -е́ц) *ср* ring; *(в маршруте автобуса итп)* circle.
кольчу́г|а (-и) *ж (ИСТ)* chain-mail shirt.
ко́лья *сущ см* кол.
колю́чек *сущ см* колю́чка.
колю́ч|ий (-ая, -ее, -ие; -, -а, -е) *прил (куст, усы, мороз)* prickly; *(перен: насмешка, замечание, юмор)* barbed; колю́чая про́волока barbed wire.
колю́ч|ка (-ки; *gen pl* -ек) *ж (чертополоха, розы)* thorn; *(проволоки)* barb.
коля́д|ка (-ки; *gen pl* -ок) *ж* ≈ Christmas carol *(sung in rural Russia)*.
коляд|ова́ть (-у́ю) *несов неперех* ≈ to go carol singing.
коля́док *сущ см* коля́дка.
коля́с|ка (-ки; *gen pl* -ок) *ж (экипаж)* carriage; *(детская)* pram *(BRIT)*, baby carriage *(US)*; *(инвалидная)* wheelchair.
ком *мест см* кто ♦ (-а; *nom pl* -ья, *gen pl* -ьев) *м* lump; у меня́ ~ к го́рлу подкати́л I felt a lump in my throat; пе́рвый блин ко́мом ... *(перен)* ≈ if at first you don't succeed ....
ко́м|а (-ы) *ж* coma.

кома́нд|а (-ы) ж command; (*судна*) crew; (*СПОРТ*) team; **пожа́рная** ~ fire brigade; ~ **президе́нта** presidential team; **быть** (*impf*) **под ~ой кого́-н** to be under sb.

команди́р (-а) м commander, commanding officer.

командиро́ванн|ый (-ого; *decl like adj*) м = командиро́вочный.

командир|ова́ть (-у́ю) (*не*)*сов перех* to post; **его́ ~ова́ли в Москву́** he has been posted to Moscow.

командиро́в|ка (-ки; *gen pl* -ок) ж (*коро́ткая*) business trip; (*дли́тельная*) secondment (*BRIT*), posting; **е́хать (пое́хать** *perf*) **в ~ку** to go away on business; **получа́ть (получи́ть** *perf*) **~ку** to be seconded (*BRIT*) *или* posted.

командиро́вочные (-ых; *decl like adj*) мн (*де́ньги*) subsistence allowance *ед*.

командиро́вочный *прил:* ~**ое удостовере́ние** *permit issued to employee travelling on official business* ♦ (-ого; *decl like adj*) м person on business.

кома́ндн|ый *прил* command *опред*; (*до́лжность*) managerial; (*СПОРТ*): ~**ое состяза́ние** team event; ~**ые высо́ты** (*ВОЕН, перен*) key positions; **кома́ндный соста́в** (*ВОЕН*) command personnel.

кома́ндовани|е (-я) *ср:* ~ (+*instr*) (*судном, войском*) command (of) ♦ *собир* (*ВОЕН*) command.

кома́нд|овать (-ую; *perf* **скома́ндовать**) *несов неперех* to give orders; (*no perf*; +*instr*; *армией*) to command; (*мужем*) to order around.

кома́ндующ|ий (-его; *decl like adj*) м commanding officer, commander.

кома́р (-а́) м mosquito (*мн* mosquitoes); ~ **но́са не подто́чит** you can't fault it.

комато́зный *прил* comatose.

комба́йн (-а) м (*С.-Х.*) combine (harvester); **кухо́нный** ~ food processor.

комбайнёр (-а) м combine operator.

комбико́рм (-а) м *сокр* (= **комбини́рованный корм**) mixed fodder.

комбина́т (-а) м plant; **моло́чный/пищево́й** ~ dairy-/food-processing plant.

комбина́ци|я (-и) ж combination; (*разг: план*) scheme; (*ШАХМАТЫ*) position; (*же́нское бельё*) slip.

комбинезо́н (-а) м overalls *мн*; (*де́тский*) dungarees *мн*.

комбини́рованный *прил* (*ме́тод, подхо́д*) integrated.

комбини́р|овать (-ую; *perf* **скомбини́ровать**) *несов перех* (*блю́да*) to combine; (*оде́жду*) to match up ♦ *неперех* (*разг*) to scheme.

комедиа́нт (-а) м (*также перен*) comedian.

комедиа́нт|ка (-ки; *gen pl* -ок) ж comedienne.

коме́дийный (-ен, -йна, -йно) *прил* comic; (*актёр*) comedy *опред*.

коме́ди|я (-и) ж comedy; (*перен: смешно́е собы́тие*) farce; **лома́ть** (*impf*) ~**ю** to play-act.

коменда́нт (-а) м (*общежи́тия, тюрьмы́*) warden; (*ВОЕН*) commandant.

коменда́нтск|ий (-ая, -ое, -ие) *прил:* ~ **час** curfew.

комендату́р|а (-ы) ж (*ВОЕН*) commandant's office.

коме́т|а (-ы) ж comet.

коми́зм (-а) м comedy; ~ **ситуа́ции** the funny side of the situation.

ко́мик (-а) м (*актёр*) comedian, comic; (*разг: смешно́й челове́к*) comedian.

Коминте́рн (-а) м *сокр* (*ИСТ:* = **Коммунисти́ческий Интернациона́л**) Comintern.

комисса́р (-а) м (*ИСТ: также:* **Наро́дный К~**) People's Commissar; (*мили́ции ООН*) commissioner.

комиссионе́р (-а) м agent.

комиссио́н|ка (-ки; *gen pl* -ок) ж (*разг*) *second-hand shop which sells goods on a commission basis.*

комиссио́нн|ые (-ых; *decl like adj*) мн commission.

комиссио́нный *прил:* ~ **магази́н** = комиссио́нка.

комиссио́нок *сущ см* комиссио́нка.

коми́сси|я (-и) ж (*ПОЛИТ, КОММ*) commission; **брать (взять** *perf*) **что-н на ~ю** to take sth on commission; **постоя́нная** ~ standing committee.

комите́т (-а) м committee; **Комите́т Госуда́рственной Безопа́сности** (*ИСТ*) the KGB.

коми́чен *прил см* коми́чный.

коми́ческ|ий (-ая, -ое, -ие) *прил* comic; ~ **актёр** comic actor.

коми́чный (-ен, -на, -но) *прил* comical.

комка́ *сущ см* комо́к.

ко́мк|ать (-ю; *perf* **скомкать**) *несов перех* (*письмо́, бельё итп*) to crumple; (*перен: лекцию итп*) to make a mess of.

коммента́ри|й (-я) м (*поясне́ние, репорта́ж*) commentary; **дава́ть (дать** *perf*) ~ **к чему́-н** to provide a commentary on sth; **~и изли́шни** it speaks for itself.

коммента́тор (-а) м commentator.

комменти́р|овать (-ую) (*не*)*сов перех* (*текст*) to comment on; (*собы́тия, матч*) to commentate on.

коммерса́нт (-а) м businessman (*мн* businessmen).

комме́рческ|ий (-ая, -ое, -ие) *прил* commercial; **комме́рческий банк** commercial bank; **комме́рческий дире́ктор** sales and finance director; **комме́рческий магази́н** privately-run shop.

коммивояжёр (-а) м travelling (*BRIT*) *или* traveling (*US*) salesman (*мн* salesmen).

комму́н|а (-ы) ж commune.

коммуна́л|ка (-ки; *gen pl* -ек) ж (*разг*) communal flat (*BRIT*) *или* apartment (*US*).

коммунáльный *прил* communal;
  коммунáльная квартúра communal flat (*BRIT*)
  или apartment (*US*); **коммунáльные платежú**
  bills; **коммунáльные услýги** utilities.
коммунáр (-а) *м* (*ИСТ*) member of a commune.
коммунúзм (-а) *м* communism.
коммуникáбел|ьный (-ен, -ьна, -ьно) *прил*
  sociable.
коммуникатúвный *прил* (*мéтоды*)
  communicative.
коммуникацио́нн|ый *прил*: ~**ая лúния** line of
  communication.
коммуникáци|я (-и) *ж* communication.
коммунúст (-а) *м* communist.
коммунистúческ|ий (-ая, -ое, -ие) *прил*
  communist.
коммунúст|ка (-ки; *gen pl* -ок) *ж см* **коммунúст**.
коммутáтор (-а) *м* (*ТЕЛ*) switchboard; (*ЭЛЕК*)
  commutator.
коммутацио́нн|ый *прил*: ~**ая доскá**
  switchboard.
коммутáци|я (-и) *ж*: ~ **пакéтов/сообщéний**
  (*КОМП*) packet/message switching.
коммюникé *ср нескл* communiqué.
кóмнат|а (-ы) *ж* room; **кóмната мáтери и**
  ребёнка *room for mothers with young children*.
кóмнатный *прил* indoor *опред*; **кóмнатная**
  температýра room temperature; **кóмнатное**
  растéние house plant.
комóд (-а) *м* chest of drawers.
ком|óк (-кá) *м уменьш от* **ком**; (*ваты*) wad; ~
  бумáги crumpled-up piece of paper; **он –** ~
  нéрвов he's a bag *или* bundle of nerves.
компáкт-диск (-а) *м* compact disc.
компáкт|ный (-ен, -на, -но) *прил* compact;
  (*изложéние, доклáд*) concise.
компанéйск|ий (-ая, -ое, -ие) *прил* (*разг*): **он** ~
  пáрень he's good company.
компáни|я (-и) *ж* (*друзья*) group of friends;
  (*КОММ*) company; **вы́пей со мной за** ~**ю** have a
  drink, to keep me company; **он тебé не** ~ he's
  not the right company for you.
компаньóн (-а) *м* companion; (*КОММ*) partner.
компаньóн|ка (-ки; *gen pl* -ок) *ж* (*старой дáмы*)
  companion.
компáрти|я (-и) *ж* Communist party.
кóмпас (-а) *м* compass.
компенсацио́нный *прил* compensatory.
компенсáци|я (-и) *ж* compensation.
компенсúр|овать (-ую) (*не*)*сов перех* to
  compensate.
компетéнтен *прил см* **компетéнтный**.
компетéнтност|ь (-и) *ж* competence.
компетéнт|ный (-ен, -на, -но) *прил* competent;
  (*соотвéтствующий*) appropriate.
компетéнци|я (-и) *ж* jurisdiction; **э́то не вхóдит**
  в нáшу ~**ю** that is outside our jurisdiction.
компилúр|овать (-ую; *perf* **скомпилúровать**)

несов перех (*пренебр*) to cobble together.
компилятúв|ный (-ен, -на, -но) *прил*: ~ **труд**
  compilation.
компилятор (-а) *м* hack (writer).
компиляци|я (-и) *ж* rehash.
кóмплекс (-а) *м* (*упражнéний, мер, знáний итп*)
  range; **спортúвный** ~ sports complex;
  кóмплекс неполноцéнности inferiority
  complex.
кóмплексный *прил* integrated; (*соединéние,*
  числó) complex.
комплéкт (-а) *м* set.
комплектáци|я (-и) *ж* assembly; **отдéл** ~**и** (*в*
  библиотéке) acquisitions (department).
комплект|овáть (-ýю; *perf* **укомплектовáть**)
  несов перех to build up.
комплéкци|я (-и) *ж* build (*of person*).
комплимéнт (-а) *м* compliment; **дéлать**
  (**сдéлать** *perf*) **комý-н** ~ to pay sb a compliment;
  говорúть (*impf*) ~**ы** (**комý-н**) to pay (sb)
  compliments.
композúтор (-а) *м* composer.
композицио́нный *прил* compositional.
композúци|я (-и) *ж* composition.
компонéнт (-а) *м* component.
компон|овáть (-ýю; *perf* **скомпоновáть**) *несов*
  перех to arrange, set out.
компонóвк|а (-и) *ж* (*материáлов*) arranging.
компóст (-а) *м* compost.
компóстер (-а) *м* ticket punch.
компостúр|овать (-ую; *perf*
  закомпостúровать) *сов перех* to punch *или*
  clip (*ticket*).
компóст|ный *прил*: ~**ая я́ма** compost pit.
компóт (-а) *м* compote.
компрéсс (-а) *м* (*МЕД*) compress.
компрéссор (-а) *м* (*ТЕХ*) compressor.
компрометúр|овать (-ую; *perf*
  скомпрометúровать) *несов перех* to
  compromise.
компрометúрующ|ий (-ая, -ое, -ие) *прил*
  (*постýпок, словá*) damaging.
компромú|сс (-а) *м* (*соглашéние*) compromise;
  идтú (**пойтú** *perf*) **на** ~ to (make a) compromise;
  приходúть (**прийтú** *perf*) **к** ~**у** to come to a
  compromise.
компромúссный *прил* compromise *опред*.
компью́тер (-а) *м* computer.
компью́терный *прил* computer *опред*.
комсомóл (-а) *м* Komsomol (*communist youth*
  organization).
комсомóл|ец (-ьца) *м* komsomol member.
комсомóл|ка (-ки; *gen pl* -ок) *ж см*
  комсомóлец.
комсомóльск|ий (-ая, -ое, -ие) *прил* komsomol
  опред.
комсомóльца *сущ см* **комсомóлец**.
комý *мест см* **кто**.

комфóрт (-а) м comfort.
комфортáбел|ьный (-ен, -ьна, -ьно) прил comfortable.
комьéв итп сущ см ком.
кон (-á; nom pl -ы́, gen pl -óв) м (партия) round; (для ставки) kitty; (место: в городках) wicket.
конвéйер (-а) м conveyor (belt); **постáвить** (perf) **что-н на** ~ to mass-produce sth; (перен) to churn sth out.
конвéйерн|ый прил: ~ая лéнта conveyor belt.
конвéнци|я (-и) ж convention.
конвергéнци|я (-и) ж convergence.
конвéрси|я (-и) ж conversion.
конвéрт (-а) м (почтовый) envelope; (для младенца) baby nest.
конверти́р|овать (-ую) (не)сов перех to convert.
конверти́руемый прил convertible.
конвóй|р (-а) м escort.
конвóйр|овать (-ую) несов перех to escort.
конвóй (-я) м escort; **под** ~**ем** under escort.
конвóйн|ый прил escort опред ♦ (-ого; decl like adj) м escort.
конвýльси|я (-и) ж convulsion.
конгломерáт (-а) м conglomerate.
Кóнго ср нескл Congo (river and state).
конголéзск|ий (-ая, -ое, -ие) прил Congolese.
конгрéсс (-а) м (съезд) congress; (в США) Congress.
конгрессмéн (-а) м Congressman (мн Congressmen).
конденсáтор (-а) м condenser.
конденсáци|я (-и) ж condensation.
конденси́р|оваться (3sg -уется, 3pl -уются) (не)сов возв to condense.
конди́тер (-а) м confectioner.
конди́терск|ая (-ой; decl like adj) ж confectioner's.
конди́терск|ий (-ая, -ое, -ие) прил confectionery опред; **конди́терский магази́н** confectioner's.
кондиционéр (-а) м air conditioner.
кондицио́нный прил (условия поставки) conditional; (продукт, овощи итп) up to standard.
кондици|я (-и) ж standard; **я сейчáс не в** ~**и** (разг) I'm not in good shape at the moment; **доводи́ть** (довести́ perf) **что-н до** ~**и** to bring sth up to scratch.
кондóвый прил diehard опред.
кондрáшк|а (-и) ж: **его́ хвати́ла** ~ (разг) he had a fit.
кондýктор (-а) м (автобуса) conductor; (поезда) guard.
коневóд (-а) м horse-breeder.
коневóдств|о (-а) ср horse-breeding.
кон|ёк (-ькá) м уменьш от конь; (обычно мн: спорт) skate; (перен: любимая тема) hobbyhorse; **катáться** (impf) **на** ~**ькáх** to skate; **сади́ться** (impf) **на своегó** ~**ькá** to get on(to) one's hobbyhorse; **морско́й** ~ sea horse; см

также **конькú**.
кон|éц (-цá) м end; **без** ~**цá** endlessly; **из концá в** ~ from end to end; **и дéло с** ~**цóм** (разг) and that's the end of it; **в** ~**цé концóв** in the end; **билéт в оди́н** ~ single (BRIT) или one-way ticket; **мне** ~ (разг) I'm done for; **своди́ть** (impf) ~**цы́ с** ~**цáми** to make ends meet; **на худóй** ~ (разг) if the worst comes to the worst; **под** ~ towards the end; **отдáть** (perf) ~**цы́** (разг) to kick the bucket.
конéчно вводн сл of course, certainly; **мне мóжно закури́ть?** – ~ may I smoke? – of course.
конéчность (-и) ж (обычно мн) limb.
конéч|ный (-ен, -на, -но) прил (цель, итог) final; (станция, остановка) last; **в** ~**ном счёте** или **ито́ге** in the final analysis; **конéчный пóльзователь** (комп) end user.
кони́н|а (-ы) ж horse meat.
кони́ческ|ий (-ая, -ое, -ие) прил conical.
конкрéтен прил см конкрéтный.
конкретизи́р|овать (-ую) (не)сов перех: ~ **что-н** to make sth more concrete.
конкрéтно нареч (говорить) specifically.
конкрéт|ный (-ен, -на, -но) прил (реальный) concrete; (факт) actual.
конкурéнт (-а) м competitor.
конкурéнтк|а (-и) ж см конкурéнт.
конкурéнтный прил: ~**ая борьбá** competition.
конкурентоспосóб|ный (-ен, -на, -но) прил competitive.
конкурéнци|я (-и) ж competition; **наш товáр вне** ~**и** our product is in a class of its own.
конкури́р|овать (-ую) несов непéрех: ~ **с** +instr to compete with.
кóнкурс (-а) м competition; **проходи́ть** (пройти́ perf) **вне** ~**а** to be admitted to university etc under special provisions; **проходи́ть** (пройти́ perf) **по** ~**у** to attain the pass mark.
кóнкурсный прил competition опред; ~**ая коми́ссия** (в университете) examining committee; (в состязании) judging panel; **кóнкурсный экзáмен** entrance examination.
кóнниц|а (-ы) ж cavalry.
конногвардé|ец (-йца) м cavalryman (мн cavalrymen).
коннозаво́дчик (-а) м stud-farm owner.
кóнный прил (двор, сбруя) horse опред; **кóнная áрмия** cavalry; **кóнный завóд** stud farm; **кóнная мили́ция** mounted police.
конопá|тить (-чу, -тишь; перф законопáтить) несов перех (сруб, лодку, пол итп) to patch up.
конопá|тый (-, -а, -о) прил (разг: веснушчатый) freckled.
конопá|чу несов см конопáтить.
конопл|я́ (-и́) ж hemp.
конопля́ный прил hemp.
коносáмент (-а) м bill of lading.
консервати́вность (-и) ж conservatism.
консервати́в|ный (-ен, -на, -но) прил conservative.

консерва́тор (-а) м conservative; (*полит*) Conservative.

консервато́ри|я (-и) ж (*муз*) conservatoire (*BRIT*), conservatory (*US*).

консерва́ци|я (-и) ж (*стройки*) suspension; (*продуктов, здания*) preservation.

консерви́ровани|е (-я) ср (*в жестяных банках*) canning; (*в стеклянных банках*) bottling.

консерви́рованный прил (*см сущ*) canned; bottled.

консерви́р|овать (-ую) (*не)сов перех* to preserve; (*в жестяных банках*) to can; (*в стеклянных банках*) to bottle; (*стройку*) to suspend.

консе́рвный прил: ~ **заво́д** canned-food factory; **консе́рвная ба́нка** can.

консе́рв|ы (-ов) мн canned food *ед*.

конси́лиум (-а) м *consultation between doctors about a patient*.

консисте́нци|я (-и) ж consistency.

ко́нск|ий (-ая, -ое, -ие) прил horse's.

консолида́ци|я (-и) ж consolidation.

консолиди́р|овать (-ую) (*не)сов перех* to consolidate.

консо́л|ь (-и) ж cantilever.

консо́рциум (-а) м consortium.

конспе́кт (-а) м notes мн.

конспекти́в|ный (-ен, -на, -но) прил: **в ~ной фо́рме** in note form.

конспекти́р|овать (-ую; *perf* **законспекти́ровать**) *несов перех* to take notes on.

конспирати́вный прил conspiratorial; **конспирати́вная кварти́ра** safe house.

конспира́тор (-а) м conspirator.

конспира́ци|я (-и) ж conspiracy.

констата́ци|я (-и) ж: ~ **фа́ктов** stating of the facts.

констати́р|овать (-ую) (*не)сов перех* to certify; (*факты*) to state.

конституцио́нный прил constitutional.

конститу́ци|я (-и) ж constitution.

констру́и́р|овать (-ую; *perf* **сконструи́ровать**) *несов перех* to construct.

констру́кти́вен прил см **констру́кти́вный**.

констру́кти́вност|ь (-и) ж constructiveness.

констру́кти́в|ный прил construction *опред*; (-ен, -на, -но; *замысл, идея*) constructive.

констру́ктор (-а) м designer; (*детская игра*) construction set; **инжене́р-~** mechanical engineer.

констру́кторск|ий (-ая, -ое, -ие) прил: ~**ое бюро́** design studio.

констру́кци|я (-и) ж construction.

ко́нсул (-а) м consul.

ко́нсульск|ий (-ая, -ое, -ие) прил consular.

ко́нсульств|о (-а) ср consulate.

консульта́нт (-а) м consultant.

консультацио́нный прил consultative.

консульта́ци|я (-и) ж (*у врача, у юриста*) consultation; (*учреждение*) consultancy; **же́нская ~** ≈ gynaecological and antenatal (*BRIT*) *или* gynecological and prenatal (*US*) clinic; **дава́ть** (**дать** *perf*) ~**ю кому́-н** to give professional advice to sb.

консульти́р|овать (-ую; *perf* **проконсульти́ровать**) *несов перех* to give professional advice to

▶ **консульти́роваться** (*impf* **проконсульти́роваться**) *несов возв*: ~**ся с кем-н** to consult sb.

конта́кт (-а) м contact.

конта́ктный (-ен, -на, -но) прил (*человек*) approachable; **конта́ктные ли́нзы** contact lenses; **конта́ктный телефо́н** contact number.

конте́йнер (-а) м container.

конте́кст (-а) м context; **в ~е** +gen in the context of.

континге́нт (-а) м contingent.

контине́нт (-а) м continent.

континента́льный прил continental.

конто́р|а (-ы) ж office.

конто́рск|ий (-ая, -ое, -ие) прил office *опред*; **конто́рская кни́га** account book.

ко́нтр|а (-ы) ж (*разг*): **быть в ~х с кем-н** to be at odds with sb.

контраба́нд|а (-ы) ж smuggling; (*товары*) contraband.

контрабанди́ст (-а) м smuggler.

контрабанди́ст|ка (-ки; *gen pl* -ок) ж см **контрабанди́ст**.

контраба́ндный прил contraband.

контраба́с (-а) м double bass.

контрабаси́ст (-а) м double-bass player.

контрадмира́л (-а) м rear admiral.

контра́кт (-а) м contract; **фо́рвардный ~** (*комм*) forward contract.

контра́льто ср нескл contralto.

контрама́р|ка (-ки; *gen pl* -ок) ж ≈ complimentary ticket.

контрапу́нкт (-а) м counterpoint.

контра́ст (-а) м contrast.

контра́стен прил см **контра́стный**.

контрасти́р|овать (-ую) *несов неперех*: ~ **с** +instr to contrast with.

контра́стный (-ен, -на, -но) прил contrasting.

контрата́к|а (-и) ж counterattack.

контрацепти́в (-а) м contraceptive.

контрацепти́вный прил contraceptive *опред*.

контрибу́ци|я (-и) ж reparations мн; **налага́ть** (**наложи́ть** *perf*) ~**ю** to exact reparations.

контрнаступле́ни|е (-я) ср counteroffensive.

контролёр (-а) м (*железнодорожный*) (ticket) inspector; (*театральный*) ≈ usher; (*сберкассы*) cashier.

контроли́р|овать (-ую) *несов перех* to control.
контро́л|ь (-я) *м* (*наблюдение*) monitoring; (*проверка*) testing, checking; (*в транспорте*) ticket inspection; (*в магазине*) checkout ♦ *собир* (*проверяющие*) inspectors *мн*; **па́спортный ~** passport control; **~ за це́нами** price control; **~ ка́чества** quality control.
контро́льн|ая (-ой; *decl like adj*) *ж* (*также:~* **рабо́та**) class test.
контро́льн|ый *прил*: **~ая коми́ссия** inspection team; **~ая рабо́та по** +*prp* class test in; **контро́льные ци́фры** control figures.
контрразве́дк|а (-и) *ж* counterespionage.
контрреволюционе́р (-а) *м* counter-revolutionary.
контрреволю́ци|я (-и) *ж* counter-revolution.
контрфо́рс (-а) *м* buttress.
конту́|зить (-жу, -зишь) *сов безл*: **его́ ~зило** he was contused.
конту́зи|я (-и) *ж* (*МЕД*) contusion.
конту́р (-а) *м* contour.
ко́нтурный *прил* contour *опред*; **ко́нтурная ка́рта** contour map.
конур|а́ (-ы́) *ж* (*собачья*) kennel; (*перен*: *комната*) shoe box.
ко́нус (-а) *м* cone.
конусообра́зный (-ен, -на, -но) *прил* conical.
конферансье́ *ср нескл* compère.
конфере́нц-за́л (-а) *м* conference room.
конфере́нци|я (-и) *ж* conference.
конфе́т|а (-ы) *ж* sweet.
конфетти́ *ср нескл* confetti.
конфигура́ци|я (-и) *ж* configuration.
конфиденциа́льный (-ен, -ьна, -ьно) *прил* confidential.
конфиска́ци|я (-и) *ж* confiscation.
конфиск|ова́ть (-у́ю) (*не*)*сов перех* to confiscate.
конфли́кт (-а) *м* (*военный*) conflict; (*в семье, на рабо́те*) tension.
конфли́ктный *прил* (*ситуация*) conflict *опред*.
конфликт|ова́ть (-у́ю) *несов неперех*: **~ с** +*instr* (*разг*) to be at loggerheads with.
конфо́р|ка (-ки; *gen pl* -ок) *ж* ring (*on cooker*).
конфронта́ци|я (-и) *ж* confrontation.
конфу́жу(сь) *несов см* **конфу́зить(ся)**.
конфу́з (-а) *м* embarrassment.
конфу́|зить (-жу, -зишь; *perf* **сконфу́зить**) *несов перех* to embarrass
▶ **конфу́зиться** (*perf* **сконфу́зиться**) *несов возв* to get embarrassed.
конц|а́ *итп сущ см* **коне́ц**.
концентра́т (-а) *м* (*о корме*) concentrate; (*о руде*) concentration.
концентрацио́нный *прил*: **~ ла́герь** concentration camp.
концентра́ци|я (-и) *ж* concentration.
концентри́рованный *прил* concentrated.
концентри́р|овать (-ую; *perf* **сконцентри́ровать**) *несов перех* to concentrate
▶ **концентри́роваться** (*perf* **сконцентри́роваться**) *несов возв* (*капитал*) to

be concentrated; (*ученик*) to concentrate.
концентри́ческ|ий (-ая, -ое, -ие) *прил* concentric.
конце́пци|я (-и) *ж* concept.
конце́рн (-а) *м* (*ЭКОН*) concern.
конце́рт (-а) *м* concert; **дава́ть (дать** *perf*) **~** to give a concert; **~ для фортепья́но с орке́стром** piano concerto.
концерти́р|овать (-ую) *несов неперех* to give concerts.
концертме́йстер (-а) *м* (*МУЗ*) leader, concertmaster (*US*); (*аккомпаниатор*) accompanist.
конце́ртный *прил* concert *опред*.
конце́сси|я (-и) *ж* concession; **отдава́ть (отда́ть** *perf*) **что-н на ~ю** to grant sth as a concession.
концла́гер|ь (-я; *nom pl* -**я́**) *м сокр* concentration camp.
концо́в|ка (-ки; *gen pl* -ок) *ж* ending.
конча́|ть (-ю) *несов от* **ко́нчить**
▶ **конча́ться** *несов от* **ко́нчиться** ♦ *возв*: **~ся на** +*acc* to end in; **всё хорошо́, что хорошо́ ~ется** all's well that ends well.
конча́я *предл* (+*instr*) to; **начина́я с кого́-н/ чего́-н и ~ кем-н/чем-н** from sb/sth to sb/sth; **яви́лись все, ~ са́мыми да́льними ро́дственниками** everyone turned up, including the most distant relatives.
ко́нченый *прил*: **он ~ челове́к** he's a lost cause.
ко́нчик (-а) *м* tip.
кончи́н|а (-ы) *ж* end.
ко́нч|ить (-у, -ишь; *impf* **конча́ть**) *сов перех* (*жизнь, представление, отношения*) to end; (*университет, игру, книгу, работу*) to finish; **конча́ть (~** *perf*) +*instr* to end up as; (*пьесой, словами*) to finish with; **конча́ть (~** *perf*) **рабо́ту** *или* **рабо́тать** to finish work; **он пло́хо ~ил** he ended up in a bad way
▶ **ко́нчиться** (*impf* **конча́ться**) *сов возв* (*разговор, книга, игра*) to end, finish; (*запасы, деньги*) to run out; (*пустыня, лес итп*) to end.
конъюнктиви́т (-а) *м* conjunctivitis.
конъюнкту́р|а (-ы) *ж* climate; **~ ры́нка** state of the market; **понижа́тельная ры́ночная ~** (*КОММ*) falling market; **пониже́ние/ повыше́ние ~ы** downturn/upturn of the market; **он хорошо́ чу́вствует ~у** he is good at gauging the climate.
конъюнкту́рн|ый *прил* (*соображения*) tactical; **~ые це́ны** market prices *мн*.
конъюнкту́рщик (-а) *м* opportunist.
кон|ь (-я́; *nom pl* -и, *gen pl* -**е́й**) *м* (*лошадь*) horse; (*ШАХМАТЫ*) knight; **быть** (*impf*) **на ~е́** to be on the ball.
конька́ *итп сущ см* **конёк**.
конь|ки́ (-о́в) *мн* skates *мн*; (*разг*: *вид спорта*) skating *ед*.
конькобе́ж|ец (-ца) *м* speed skater.
конькобе́жный *прил* speed-skating; **конькобе́жный спорт** speed skating.

конькобе́жца *итп сущ см* **конькобе́жец.**
конья́к (**-а́**) *м* brandy, cognac.
ко́нюх (**-а**) *м* groom (*at stable*).
коню́шня (**-ни;** *gen pl* **-ен**) *ж* stable.
кооперати́в (**-а**) *м* cooperative; (*разг:* *кварти́ра*) flat in housing cooperative; **жили́щный** ~ *form of house or flat ownership*.
кооперати́вный *прил* cooperative; ~ **магази́н** *или* **ларёк** co-op; ~ **дом** cooperative (*form of house or flat ownership*).
коопера́тор (**-а**) *м member of a private enterprise.*
коопера́ци|я (**-и**) *ж* cooperative enterprise; (*труда́*) co-operation; **потреби́тельская** ~ cooperative (*society*).
коопери́р|овать (**-ую**) (*не*)*сов перех* (*труд,* *сре́дства*) to organize through a cooperative.
коопти́р|овать (**-ую**) (*не*)*сов перех* to coopt.
координа́т|а (**-ы**) *ж* (*ГЕОМ:* *обычно мн*) coordinate; (*разг: местонахожде́ние*) number (and address).
координа́ци|я (**-и**) *ж* (*уси́лий*) coordination.
координи́р|овать (**-ую**) (*не*)*сов перех* (*де́йствия, уси́лия, движе́ния*) to coordinate; ~ (*impf/perf*) **произво́дство с тре́бованиями ры́нка** to adjust production to meet the demands of the market.
коп. *сокр* = **копе́йка.**
копа́|ть (**-ю**) *несов от* **вы́копать** ◆ *перех* to dig; (*выка́пывать*) to dig up; ~ (*impf*) **под** +*acc* (*разг*) to cook up a scheme against
▶ **копа́ться** *несов возв* (*в огоро́де*) to potter about; (*в чужи́х веща́х*) to snoop about; (*разг: в душе́*) to search; (*: до́лго вози́ться*) to dawdle.
копе́ек *сущ см* **копе́йка.**
копе́ечк|а (**-и**) *ж:* **э́то тебе́ вста́нет в ~у** it'll cost you a pretty penny.
копе́йк|а (**-йки;** *gen pl* **-ек**) *ж* kopeck; **остава́ться** (**оста́ться** *perf*) **без ~йки** to be left without a penny.
Копенга́ген (**-а**) *м* Copenhagen.
копи́л|ка (**-ки;** *gen pl* **-ок**) *ж* piggy bank.
копира́йт (**-а**) *м* copyright.
копи́рк|а (**-и**) *ж* (*разг*) carbon paper; **писа́ть** (*impf*) **под ~у** to make a carbon copy of.
копирова́льно-мно́жительный *прил* copying *опред.*
копирова́льн|ый *прил:* ~**ая маши́на** photocopying machine, photocopier; **копирова́льная бума́га** carbon paper.
копи́р|овать (**-ую;** *perf* **скопи́ровать**) *несов перех* to copy.
копи́|ть (**-лю́, -ишь;** *perf* **накопи́ть** *или* **скопи́ть**) *несов перех* to save; (*перен: оби́ды*) to harbour (*BRIT*), harbor (*US*)
▶ **копи́ться** (*perf* **накопи́ться** *или* **скопи́ться**) *несов возв* to accumulate.
ко́пи|я (**-и**) *ж* copy; (*перен*) spitting image; **он ~ ~**

своего́ отца́! he's the spitting image of his father; **снима́ть** (**снять** *perf*) **~ю с чего́-н** to make a copy of sth.
коплю́(сь) *несов см* **копи́ть(ся).**
копн|а́ (**-ы́;** *nom pl* **-ы**) *ж* (*се́на*) stack; (*воло́с*) thatch.
копн|у́ть (**-у́, -ёшь**) *несов перех* to dig; (*перен*): **е́сли ~ поглу́бже ...** if you dig deeper ....
ко́пот|ь (**-и**) *ж* layer of soot.
копош|и́ться (**-у́сь, -и́шься**) *несов возв* (*мышь*) to busy itself; (*перен: подозре́ния*) to stir; (*вози́ться*) to dawdle.
копт|е́ть (**-чу́, -ти́шь**) *несов неперех* to give off black smoke; (*корпе́ть*): ~ **над** +*instr* to pore over.
копт|и́ть (**-чу́, -ти́шь**) *несов неперех* (*ла́мпа*) to give off soot ◆ (*perf* **закопти́ть**) *перех* (*мя́со, ры́бу*) to smoke; ~ (*impf*) **не́бо** to fritter one's life away.
копу́ш|а (**-и**) *м/ж* (*разг*) slowcoach (*BRIT*), slowpoke (*US*).
копче́ни|е (**-я**) *ср* (*ветчины́*) smoking; **ры́ба горя́чего/холо́дного ~я** *fish smoked at a high/ low temperature;* см также **копче́нья.**
копчёност|и (**-ей**) *мн* smoked food *ед.*
копчёный *прил* smoked.
копче́нь|я (**-ий**) *мн* = **копчёности.**
ко́пчик (**-а**) *м* coccyx (*мн* coccyxes).
копы́т|о (**-а**) *ср* hoof (*мн* hooves).
копь|ё (**-ья́;** *nom pl* **-ья,** *gen pl* **-ий**) *ср* spear; (*СПОРТ*) javelin; **мета́ние ~ья́** javelin.
кор. *сокр* (= **корреспонде́нт**) corr. (= *correspondent*).
кор|а́ (**-ы́**) *ж* (*де́рева*) bark; (*АНАТ*) cortex; **земна́я ~** the earth's crust; ~ **головно́го мо́зга** cerebral cortex.
корабе́льный *прил* ship's.
кораблестрое́ни|е (**-я**) *ср* shipbuilding.
кораблестрои́тел|ь (**-я**) *м* shipbuilder.
кораблестрои́тельный *прил* shipbuilding *опред.*
кора́бл|ь (**-я́**) *м* ship; **сжига́ть** (**сжечь** *perf*) **свои́ корабли́** to burn one's boats.
кора́лл (**-а**) *м* coral.
кора́лловый *прил* (*также цвет*) coral; **кора́лловый риф** coral reef.
Кора́н (**-а**) *м* the Koran.
кордебале́т (**-а**) *м* corps de ballet.
кордо́н (**-а**) *м* cordon; **за ~ом** (*разг*) abroad.
коре́|ец (**-йца**) *м* Korean.
корёж|ить (**-у, -ишь;** *perf* **искорёжить** *или* **покорёжить**) *несов перех* (*разг*) to twist; (*no perf; перен*): **его́ поведе́ние меня́ ~ит** his behaviour makes me cringe.
коре́йк|а (**-и**) *ж* smoked brisket of pork.
коре́йск|ий (**-ая, -ое, -ие**) *прил* Korean.
корена́ст|ый (**-, -а, -о**) *прил* stocky.
корен|и́ться (*3sg* **-и́тся,** *3pl* **-я́тся**) *несов возв:* ~

в +*prp* to be rooted in.
коренн|о́й *прил* (*население, традиции*)
indigenous; (*вопрос, преобразования*)
fundamental; **~ым о́бразом** fundamentally;
коренно́й зуб molar.
ко́р|ень (-ня; *nom pl* -ни, *gen pl* -не́й) *м* root; **в**
~не fundamentally; **пресека́ть** (**пресе́чь** *perf*)
что-н в ~не to nip sth in the bud; **пуска́ть**
(**пусти́ть** *perf*) ~ни to put down roots;
подруба́ть (**подруби́ть** *perf*) **под** ~ to uproot;
смотре́ть (*impf*) **в** ~ **вопро́са/де́ла** to examine
the root of the problem/matter.
коре́нь|я (-ев) *мн* (*БОТ*) roots *мн*.
ко́реш (-а) *м* (*разг*) mate, pal.
кореш|о́к (-ка́) *м уменьш от* **ко́рень**; (*чековой
книжки*) counterfoil; (*переплёта*) spine.
коре́йца *итп сущ см* **коре́ец**.
Коре́|я (-и) *ж* Korea.
корея́н|ка (-ки; *gen pl* -ок) *ж см* **коре́ец**.
корж (-а́) *м* layer (*of a cake*).
ко́ржик (-а) *м уменьш от* **корж**; (*пряник*) ≈
shortbread.
корзи́н|а (-ы) *ж* basket; **валю́тная** ~ (*ЭКОН*)
basket of currencies.
корзи́н|ка (-ки; *gen pl* -ок) *ж* (small) basket.
корзи́ноч|ка (-ки; *gen pl* -ек) *ж* (*КУЛИН*) tart.
корзи́нщик (-а) *м* basket weaver.
кориа́ндр (-а) *м* coriander.
коридо́р (-а) *м* corridor.
коридо́рн|ая (-ой; *decl like adj*) *ж* chambermaid.
коридо́рн|ый (-ого; *decl like adj*) *м* room
attendant (*in hotel*).
кор|и́ть (-ю́, -и́шь) *несов перех* to chastise.
корифе́|й (-я) *м* luminary.
кори́ц|а (-ы) *ж* cinnamon.
кори́чневый *прил* brown.
ко́р|ка (-ки; *gen pl* -ок) *ж уменьш от* **кора́**;
(*апельсинная*) peel; (*на коже*) scab; **прочита́ть**
(*perf*) **что-н от** ~ки **до** ~ки to read sth from
cover to cover.
корм (-а; *nom pl* -а́) *м* (*для скота*) fodder, feed;
(*диких животных*) food.
корм|а́ (-ы́) *ж* stern.
кормёж|ка (-и) *ж* (*разг: скота*) feeding; (: *еда*)
grub.
корми́л|ец (-ьца) *м* breadwinner.
корми́л|ица (-ы) *ж* breadwinner; (*грудного
ребёнка*) wet nurse.
корми́л|о (-а) *ср*: **стоя́ть** *или* **быть у** ~а вла́сти
to be at the helm.
корми́льца *сущ см* **корми́лец**.
корм|и́ть (-лю́, -ишь) *несов перех* to feed; (*perf
прокорми́ть*; *содержать*) to feed, keep; (*perf
накорми́ть*): ~ **кого́-н (чем-н)** to feed sb (sth);
~ (*impf*) **гру́дью** to breast-feed; **его́ хле́бом не**
~**й**, **то́лько дай в футбо́л поигра́ть** he's never
happier than when he's playing football
▶ **корм|и́ться** (*perf* **прокорми́ться**) *несов возв*
(*животное*) to feed; (+*instr*; *человек*) to live on.
кормле́ни|е (-я) *ср* feeding.
кормлю́(сь) *несов см* **корми́ть(ся)**.

кормов|о́й *прил* (*с.-х.*): ~**ые сорта́** fodder crops;
кормова́я свёкла beet; **кормово́е весло́**
rudder.
корму́ш|ка (-и) *ж* (*для скота*) trough; (*для
птиц*) bird table; (*перен: разг*) slush fund.
корневи́щ|е (-а) *ср* rhizome.
корнепло́д (-а) *м* root vegetable.
корнепло́дн|ый *прил*: ~**ое расте́ние** root
plant.
корне́т (-а) *м* cornet.
ко́рня *итп сущ см* **ко́рень**.
ко́роб (-а) *м* rectangular basket; **с три** ~**а**
наговори́ть (*perf*) to talk through one's hat; **с**
три ~**а наобеща́ть** (*perf*) **кому́-н** to promise sb
the earth.
коро́б|ить (-лю, -ишь; *perf* **покоро́бить**) *несов
перех* to warp; **меня́** ~**ит от его́ шу́ток** his jokes
make me cringe
▶ **коро́б|иться** (*perf* **покоро́биться**) *несов возв*
to warp.
коро́б|ка (-ки; *gen pl* -ок) *ж* box; (*остов дома*)
frame; **коро́бка скоросте́й** gearbox.
коробка́ *сущ см* **коробо́к**.
короблю́(сь) *несов см* **коро́бить(ся)**.
коро́бок *сущ см* **коро́бка**.
коробо́к (-ка́) *м*: ~ **спи́чек** box of matches.
коро́боч|ка (-ки; *gen pl* -ек) *ж уменьш от*
коро́бка; (*БОТ*) boll.
коро́в|а (-ы) *ж* cow; (*разг: пренебр*) silly cow;
до́йная ~ dairy cow.
коро́в|ий (-ья, -ье, -ьи) *прил*: ~**ье молоко́**
cow's milk.
коро́вник (-а) *м* cowshed.
коро́вниц|а (-ы) *ж* milkmaid.
ко́рок *сущ см* **ко́рка**.
короле́в|а (-ы) *ж* (*также ШАХМАТЫ, перен*)
queen; **короле́ва красоты́** beauty queen.
короле́вский (-ая, -ое, -ие) *прил* royal.
короле́вств|о (-а) *ср* kingdom.
короле́к (-ька́) *м* (*апельсин*) blood orange;
(*хурма*) sharon fruit; (*ЗООЛ*) goldcrest.
коро́л|ь (-я) *м* (*также ШАХМАТЫ, КАРТЫ*) king.
королька́ *сущ см* **короле́к**.
коро́н|а (-ы) *ж* crown.
корона́рный *прил* coronary *опред*.
корона́ци|я (-и) *ж* coronation.
коро́нный *прил* (*разг*) best, favourite; ~ **но́мер**
party piece.
коронова́ни|е (-я) *ср* crowning.
корон|ова́ть (-у́ю) (*не*)*сов перех* to crown.
коро́ст|а (-ы) *ж* scab.
коросте́л|ь (-я) *м* corncrake.
корота́|ть (-ю; *perf* **скорота́ть**) *несов перех*
(*вечер, время итп*) to while away; (*свои дни,
жизнь*) to live out.
коро́тк|ий (-ая, -ое, -ие; **ко́роток, коротка́,
ко́ротко, коротки**) *прил* short; (*отношения*)
close; **у него́** ~**ая па́мять** he has a short
memory; **у него́ ру́ки ко́ротки** he's not up to it;
мы с ним на ~**ой ноге́** we're on good terms;
коро́ткие во́лны short wave; **коро́ткое**

замыка́ние short circuit.

ко́ротко *нареч* briefly; *(стри́чься)* short; *(узна́ть)* intimately ♦ *как сказ:* **э́то пла́тье мне ~** this dress is too short for me.

коротково́лновый *прил* short-wave *опред.*

короткометра́жный *прил:* **~ фильм** short (film).

коротконо́г|ий (-**ая**, -**ое**, -**ие**) *прил* short-legged.

ко́роток *прил см* **коро́ткий.**

короты́ш (-**á**) *м (разг)* shorty.

коро́че *сравн прил от* **коро́ткий** ♦ *сравн нареч от* **ко́ротко**; **~ говоря́** to put it briefly.

ко́рочк|а (-**и**) *ж уменьш от* **ко́рка;** *(на пироге итп)* crust.

корп|е́ть (-**лю́**, -**и́шь**) *несов неперех:* **~ над** +*instr* to slave away at.

корпорати́вный *прил* corporate.

корпора́ци|я (-**и**) *ж* corporation.

ко́рпус (-**а**; *nom pl* -**ы**) *м* body; *(самолёта)* fuselage; (*nom pl* -**á**; *остов: су́дна, зда́ния*) frame; *(зда́ние)* block; *(ист: уче́бное заведе́ние)* academy; *(дипломати́ческий, офице́рский)* corps.

корре́ктен *прил см* **корре́ктный.**

корректи́в (-**а**) *м (попра́вка: обычно мн)* amendment; **вноси́ть (внести́** *perf*) **~ы в план** to amend a plan.

корректи́р|овать (-**ую**; *perf* **скорректи́ровать**) *несов перех (оши́бку)* to correct; (*perf* **откорректи́ровать;** *ру́копись, статью́*) to proofread.

корректиро́в|ка (-**ки;** *gen pl* -**ок**) *ж (комп: обновле́ние)* update.

корре́кт|ный (-**ен**, -**на**, -**но**) *прил* correct.

корре́ктор (-**а**) *м* proofreader.

корректу́р|а (-**ы**) *ж (исправле́ние оши́бок)* proofreading; *(о́ттиск с набо́ра)* proofs *мн.*

корре́кци|я (-**и**) *ж* correction.

корреля́ци|я (-**и**) *ж* correlation.

корреспонде́нт (-**а**) *м* correspondent.

корреспонде́нт|ка (-**ки;** *gen pl* -**ок**) *ж см* **корреспонде́нт.**

корреспонде́нци|я (-**и**) *ж* correspondence.

корри́д|а (-**ы**) *ж* bullfight.

корроди́р|овать (*3sg* -**ует**, *3pl* -**уют**) *(не)сов неперех* to corrode.

коррози́йный *прил* corrosive.

корро́зи|я (-**и**) *ж* corrosion.

коррумпи́рован|ный (-, -**а**, -**о**) *прил* corrupt.

корру́пци|я (-**и**) *ж* corruption.

корса́ж (-**а**) *м* bodice.

корсе́т (-**а**) *м* corset.

корт (-**а**) *м* (tennis) court.

корте́ж (-**а**) *м (тра́урный)* cortege; *(сва́дебный)* procession.

ко́ртик (-**а**) *м* dagger, knife (*мн* knives).

ко́рточ|ки (-**ек**) *мн:* **присе́сть на ~** to squat down; **сиде́ть** (*impf*) **на ~ках** to squat.

корчева́ть (-**у́ю**) *несов от* **вы́корчевать** ♦ *перех* to uproot.

ко́рч|ить (-**у**, -**ишь;** *perf* **ско́рчить**) *несов перех* to contort ♦ *безл:* **его́ всего́ ~ило от бо́ли** he was doubled up in pain; **~** (**ско́рчить** *perf*) **ро́жу** to pull a face; **~** (*impf*) **из себя́ дурака́/свято́го** *(разг)* to act the fool/saint

▸ **ко́рчиться** (*perf* **ско́рчиться**) *несов возв (от бо́ли, от сме́ха)* to writhe about.

ко́ршун (-**а**) *м (зоол)* kite.

коры́ст|ный (-**ен**, -**на**, -**но**) *прил (интере́с, цель)* mercenary; *(любо́вь)* selfish.

корыстолюби́в|ый (-, -**а**, -**о**) *прил* mercenary.

корыстолю́би|е (-**я**) *ср* greed.

коры́ст|ь (-**и**) *ж (вы́года)* gain; *(корыстолю́бие)* greed.

коры́т|о (-**а**) *ср* tub; **оста́ться** (*perf*) **у разби́того ~а** to end up with nothing.

кор|ь (-**и**) *ж* measles *мн.*

ко́рюш|ка (-**ки;** *gen pl* -**ек**) *ж* smelt (*fish*).

коря́в|ый (-, -**а**, -**о**) *прил (де́рево, па́льцы)* gnarled; *(по́черк)* squiggly; *(перен: фра́зы, стиль)* clumsy.

коря́г|а (-**и**) *ж* dead branch (*мн* branches).

кос|а́ (-**ы́;** *acc sg* -**у**, *dat sg* -**é**, *nom pl* -**ы**) *м* plait; *(ору́дие)* scythe; **заплета́ть** (*perf*) **ко́сы кому́-н** to plait sb's hair; **носи́ть** (*impf*) **ко́сы** to wear one's hair in plaits; **нашла́ ~ на ка́мень** they are an equal match for each other.

коса́р|ь (-**я́**) *м* mower (*person*).

коса́т|ка (-**и**) *ж* killer whale.

ко́свенный *прил* indirect; *(дополне́ние, паде́ж)* oblique; **ко́свенная речь** indirect speech.

ко́сен *прил см* **ко́сный.**

коси́л|ка (-**ки;** *gen pl* -**ок**) *ж* mower (*machine*).

ко́синус (-**а**) *м* cosine.

ко|си́ть (-**шу́**, -**сишь;** *perf* **скоси́ть**) *несов перех (газо́н, се́но)* to mow; *(перен: подлеж: эпиде́мия, боле́знь)* to wipe out; *(рот, глаза́)* to twist; *(глаза́)* to slant; **у него́ ~я́т глаза́** he has a slight squint

▸ **коси́ться** (*perf* **скоси́ться**) *несов возв (зда́ние)* to lean to one side; **~ся** (*impf*) **на кого́-н** *(смотре́ть и́скоса)* to give sb a sidelong glance; *(перен)* to look askance at sb.

коси́ч|ка (-**ки;** *gen pl* -**ек**) *ж* pigtail.

косма́т|ый (-, -**а**, -**о**) *прил* shaggy.

косме́тик|а (-**и**) *ж* make-up ♦ *собир* cosmetics *мн.*

космети́чек *сущ см* **космети́чка.**

космети́ческий (-**ая**, -**ое**, -**ие**) *прил* cosmetic; **~ ремо́нт** decorating; **космети́ческий кабине́т** beauty salon.

космети́ч|ка (-**ки;** *gen pl* -**ек**) *ж (челове́к)* beautician; *(су́мочка)* make-up bag.

космето́лог (-**а**) *м (та́кже:* **врач-~**) cosmetic surgeon.

космето́логи|я (-**и**) *ж* cosmetic surgery.

косми́ческ|ий (-ая, -ое, -ие) *прил* (*полёт,* *ракета*) space *опред*; (*теория*) cosmic; ~**ая** **ско́рость** (*перен*) terrific speed; **косми́ческий** **кора́бль** spaceship; **косми́ческое** **простра́нство** (outer) space.

космодро́м (-а) *м* spaceport.

космоло́ги|я (-и) *ж* cosmology.

космона́вт (-а) *м* cosmonaut; (*в США итп*) astronaut.

космона́втик|а (-и) *ж* space technology and exploration.

космополи́т (-а) *м* cosmopolitan.

космополити́зм (-а) *м* cosmopolitanism.

ко́смос (-а) *м* the cosmos.

ко́см|ы (-) *мн* (*разг*) tousled locks *мн*.

косне́|ть (-ю; *perf* **закосне́ть**) *несов неперех*: ~ (**в** +*prp*) to stagnate (in).

ко́сность (-и) *ж* intransigence.

косну́ться (-у́сь, -ёшься) *сов от* **каса́ться**.

ко́с|ный (-ен, -на, -но) *прил* (*ум, человек*) inflexible; (*среда, общество*) stagnant.

ко́со *нареч* (*расположить*) squint; ~ **смотре́ть** (*impf*) **на** +*acc* (*перен*) to look askance at.

кособо́к|ий (-ая, -ое, -ие; -, -а, -о) *прил* lopsided.

косоворо́т|ка (-ки; *gen pl* -ок) *ж* traditional Russian shirt with a collar fastening at the side.

косогла́зи|е (-я) *ср* squint.

косогла́з|ый (-, -а, -о) *прил* cross-eyed.

косого́р (-а) *м* hillside.

кос|о́й (-, -а́, -о) *прил* (*глаза*) squinty; (*дождь,* *лучи*) slanting; **броса́ть** (*impf*) ~**ые взгля́ды (на** +*acc*) to look askance (at); **у него́** ~**а́я са́жень в** **плеча́х** (*разг*) he's built like an ox.

косола́п|ый (-, -а, -о) *прил* (*человек*) pigeon-toed.

костене́|ть (-ю; *perf* **закостене́ть**) *несов* *неперех* to go stiff.

костёр (-ра́) *м* campfire.

кости́ст|ый (-, -а, -о) *прил* bony.

костля́в|ый (-, -а, -о) *прил* bony.

ко́стный *прил* (*АНАТ*): ~ **мозг** (bone) marrow.

ко́сточ|ка (-ки; *gen pl* -ек) *ж уменьш от* **кость**; (*абрикосовая, вишнёвая*) stone; (*винограда*) seed; (*лимона*) pip; **перемыва́ть** (*impf*) ~**ки** **кому́-н** (*разг*) to bitch about sb.

костра́ *сущ см* **костёр**.

костыл|ь (-я́) *м* (*инвалида*) crutch (*мн* crutches); (*гвоздь*) spike.

кост|ь (-и; *prp sg* -и́, *gen pl* -е́й) *ж* bone; (*игральная*) dice (*мн* die); **лечь** (*perf*) ~**ми́** (*погибнуть*) to lay down one's life; (*перен*) to do everything possible; **промока́ть** (**промо́кнуть** *perf*) **до** ~**е́й** to get soaked to the skin.

костю́м (-а) *м* outfit; (*маскарадный, на сцене*) costume; (*пиджак и брюки/юбка*) suit; **брю́чный** ~ trouser (*BRIT*) *или* pant (*US*) suit.

костюме́р (-а) *м* wardrobe assistant.

костюми́рованный *прил*: ~ **бал** costume ball.

костя́к (-а́) *м* skeleton; (*перен*) backbone.

костян|о́й *прил* (*нож, украшение*) bone; ~**а́я**

му́ка bone meal.

костя́ш|ка (-ки; *gen pl* -ек) *ж* (*пальцев*) knuckle; (*на счётах*) bead; (*домино*) domino.

косу́л|я (-и) *ж* (*ЗООЛ*) roe deer.

косы́н|ка (-ки; *gen pl* -ок) *ж* (triangular) scarf.

кося́к (-а́) *м* (*двери*) jamb; (*рыб*) school, shoal; (*птиц*) flock.

кот (-а́) *м* tomcat; **там хле́ба** ~ **напла́кал** (*разг*) there's hardly any bread left; **вся рабо́та пошла́** **ко́ту под хвост** (*разг*) all the work has gone down the plughole; ~ **в мешке́** a pig in a poke.

кот|ёл (-ла́) *м* (*сосуд*) pot; (*паровой*) boiler; **о́бщий** ~ kitty; **вари́ться** (*impf*) **в одно́м** ~**ле́** to live in each other's pockets.

котел|о́к (-ка́) *м уменьш от* **котёл**; (*походная* *кастрюля*) billycan; (*шляпа*) bowler (hat) (*BRIT*), derby (*US*).

коте́льн|ая (-ой; *decl like adj*) *ж* boilerhouse.

котён|ок (-ёнка; *nom pl* -я́та, *gen pl* -я́т) *м* kitten.

ко́тик (-а) *м уменьш от* **кот**; (*тюлень*) fur seal; (*мех*) sealskin.

ко́тиковый *прил* sealskin.

коти́р|овать (-ую) (*не*)*сов перех* (*КОММ*) to quote

▶ **коти́роваться** *несов возв* (*КОММ*): ~**ся (в** +*acc*) to be quoted (at); (*также перен*) to have a high value.

котиро́в|ка (-и) *ж* (*КОММ*) quotation.

коти́ться (*3sg* -и́тся, *perf* **окоти́ться**) *несов возв* (*кошка*) to have kittens; (*зайцы, кролики итп*) to give birth.

котла́ *сущ см* **котёл**.

котле́т|а (-ы) *ж* rissole; (*также:* **отбивна́я** ~) chop.

котлова́н (-а) *м* pit.

котлови́н|а (-ы) *ж* (*ГЕО*) basin.

кото́м|ка (-ки; *gen pl* -ок) *ж* knapsack; (*разг*) bag.

KEYWORD

кото́р|ый (-ая, -ое, -ые) *мест* **1** (*вопросительное*) which; **в кото́рый день он** **пришёл?** which day did he come?; **кото́рый** **час?** what time is it?

2 (*относительное: о предмете*) which; (: *о* *человеке*) who; **собы́тие, кото́рое нас** **потрясло́** an event which shook us; **ребёнок, у** **кото́рого моро́женое** the child who has the ice-cream; **челове́к, с кото́рым я говори́л** the person with whom I was speaking; **же́нщина,** **сы́на кото́рой я зна́ю** the woman whose son I know; **же́нщина, кото́рую я люблю́** the woman I love

3 (*не первый*): **кото́рый день/год мы не** **ви́делись** we haven't seen each other for many days/years.

котте́дж (-а) *м* cottage.

котя́та *итп сущ см* **котёнок**.

ко́фе *м нескл* coffee; ~ **в зёрнах** coffee beans.

кофева́р|ка (-ки; *gen pl* -ок) *ж* percolator.

кофе́ен *сущ см* **кофе́йня**.

кофеи́н (-а) *м* caffeine.

кофе́йник (-а) *м* coffeepot.

кофе́йн|ый *прил* coffee *мн*; **~ого цве́та** coffee-coloured; **кофе́йный серви́з** coffee service.

кофе́йня (*-йни*; *gen pl* **-ен**) *ж* coffee shop.

кофемо́л|ка (*-ки*; *gen pl* **-ок**) *ж* coffee grinder.

ко́фт|а (*-ы*) *ж* blouse; (*шерстяная*) cardigan.

коча́н (*-а́*) *м*: **~ капу́сты** cabbage.

коч|ева́ть (*-у́ю*) *несов неперех* (*также перен*) to lead a nomadic life; (*животные*) to roam.

коче́вник (*-а*) *м* nomad.

кочево́й *прил* nomadic.

коче́в|ье (*-ья*; *gen pl* **-ий**) *ср* nomad camp.

кочега́р (*-а*) *м* stoker.

кочега́р|ка (*-ки*; *gen pl* **-ок**) *ж* furnace room.

ко́чек *сущ см* **ко́чка**.

кочен|е́ть (*-ю*; *perf* **окочене́ть**) *несов неперех* (*руки, труп*) to go stiff; (*человек*) to get stiff.

кочер|га́ (*-ги́*; *gen pl* **-ёг**) *ж* poker.

кочеры́ж|ка (*-ки*; *gen pl* **-ек**) *ж* heart (*of cabbage*).

ко́ч|ка (*-ки*; *gen pl* **-ек**) *ж* tussock.

коша́р|а (*-ы*) *ж* sheepfold.

коша́тник (*-а*) *м* cat-lover.

коша́тниц|а (*-ы*) *ж см* **коша́тник**.

коша́чий (*-ья, -ье, -ьи*) *прил* (*также перен*) feline; (*мех, лапа*) cat's.

ко́шек *сущ см* **ко́шка**.

кошел|ёк (*-ька́*) *м* purse.

кошёл|ка (*-ки*; *gen pl* **-ок**) *ж* basket.

кошелька́ *сущ см* **кошелёк**.

ко́ш|ка (*-ки*; *gen pl* **-ек**) *ж* cat; (*скалолаза: обычно мн*) crampon; **~ки-мы́шки** (*игра*) tag; **игра́ть** (*impf*) **в ~ки-мы́шки с кем-н** (*перен*) to play cat and mouse with sb.

кошма́р (*-а*) *м* (*также перен*) nightmare.

кошма́р|ный (*-ен, -на, -но*) *прил* (*сон*) nightmarish; (*перен*) dreadful, nightmarish.

кошу́(сь) *несов см* **коси́ть(ся)**.

кощ|е́й (*-я*) *м*: **~ бессме́ртный** *evil spirit in Russian fairytales*.

кощу́нствен|ный (*-, -на, -но*) *прил* blasphemous.

кощу́нств|о (*-а*) *ср* blasphemy.

кощу́нств|овать (*-ую*) *несов неперех* to blaspheme.

коэффицие́нт (*-а*) *м* coefficient; **коэффицие́нт поле́зного де́йствия** efficiency.

КПСС *ж сокр* (*ист*: = *Коммунисти́ческая па́ртия Сове́тского Сою́за*) CPSU (= *Communist Party of the Soviet Union*).

краб (*-а*) *м* crab.

кра́деный *прил* stolen.

краду́(сь) *итп несов см* **кра́сть(ся)**.

кра́дучись *нареч* stealthily.

краеве́д (*-а*) *м* local historian.

краеве́дени|е (*-я*) *ср* local studies *мн*.

краеве́дческ|ий (*-ая, -ое, -ие*) *прил*: **~ музе́й** local-history museum.

краево́й *прил* regional.

краеуго́льный *прил* fundamental;

краеуго́льный ка́мень cornerstone.

кра́ж|а (*-и*) *ж* theft; **~ со взло́мом** burglary.

кра|й (*-я*; *loc sg* **-ю́**, *nom pl* **-я́**, *gen pl* **-ёв**) *м* edge; (*чашки, коробки*) rim; (*местность*) region; (*полит*) krai (*regional administrative unit*); **непоча́тый ~ рабо́ты** an endless amount of work; **на ~ све́та** to the ends of the earth; **на ~ю́ све́та** at the ends of the earth; **да́льние/тёплые ~я́** far-off/warm climes; **родно́й ~** native country; **находи́ться** (*impf*) **на ~ю́ ги́бели** to be on the verge of disaster; **кра́ем у́ха слу́шать** (*impf*) to half listen; **кра́ем у́ха слы́шать** (*impf*) to overhear; **хвати́ть** (*perf*) **че́рез ~** to go too far; **бить** (*impf*) **че́рез ~** to overflow.

кра́йне *нареч* extremely.

кра́йн|ий (*-яя, -ее, -ие*) *прил* extreme; (*дом*) end опред; (*пункт, маршрута*) last, final; **в ~ем слу́чае** as a last resort; **по ~ей ме́ре** at least; **кра́йний напада́ющий** winger; **Кра́йний Се́вер** the Arctic; **кра́йний срок** (final) deadline.

кра́йность (*-и*) *ж* (*крайняя степень*) extremity; (*противоположное*) extreme; **броса́ться** (*impf*) **в ~и** to go from one extreme to the other; **твоё поведе́ние надое́ло мне до ~и** I find your behaviour tedious in the extreme.

кра́л|я (*-и*) *ж* (*разг: подруга*) chick; (: *красотка*) queen bee.

крамо́л|а (*-ы*) *ж* subversion; **говори́ть** (*impf*)/ **писа́ть** (*impf*) **~у** to say/write subversive things.

крамо́льный *прил* subversive.

кран (*-а*) *м* tap, faucet (*US*); (*строит*) crane.

крановщи́к (*-а́*) *м* crane operator.

крановщи́ц|а (*-ы*) *ж см* **крановщи́к**.

крапи́в|а (*-ы*) *ж* nettle.

крапи́вниц|а (*-ы*) *ж* (*мед*) nettle rash.

крапи́вный *прил*: **~ щи** nettle soup.

кра́пин|а (*-ы*) *ж* = **кра́пинка**.

кра́пин|ка (*-ки*; *gen pl* **-ок**) *ж* fleck, speck.

краплёный *прил* (*карты*) marked.

кра́пчатый (*-, -а, -о*) *прил* speckled.

крас|а́ (*-ы́*) *ж* beauty; (*перен*): **~ +gen** (*школы итп*) the pride of.

краса́в|ец (*-ца*) *м* handsome *или* good-looking man (*мн* men).

краса́виц|а (*-ы*) *ж* beautiful woman (*мн* women).

краса́в|ка (*-и*) *ж* deadly nightshade.

краса́вца *итп сущ см* **краса́вец**.

кра́сен *прил см* **кра́сный**.

краси́вость (*-и*) *ж* superficial beauty.

краси́в|ый (*-, -а, -о*) *прил* beautiful; (*мужчина*) handsome; (*решение, фраза, слова*) fine.

краси́льный *прил* dye опред; **краси́льные вещества́** dyestuffs.

краси́тель (*-я*) *м* dye.

кра|́сить (*-шу, -сишь*; *perf* **покра́сить**) *несов перех* to paint; (*волосы*) to dye; (*perf* **накра́сить**; *щёки, губы итп*) to paint; (*no perf*;

перен: *украшать*) to adorn; **тако́е поведе́ние тебя́ не ~сит** such behaviour does not become you

▶ **кра́ситься** (*perf* **покра́ситься**) *несов возв* to be covered in paint; (*разг: пачкать*) to run; (*perf* **накра́ситься**) to wear make-up.

кра́с|ка (-ки; *gen pl* -ок) *ж* paint; (*обычно мн: нежные, весенние итп*) colour (*BRIT*), color (*US*); (*стыда*) blush; **опи́сывать** (**описа́ть** *perf*) **что-н чёрными ~ми** to paint a gloomy picture of sth.

красне́|ть (-ю; *perf* **покрасне́ть**) *несов неперех* to turn red; (*от стыда*) to blush, flush; (*от гнева*) to go red; (*перен*): ~ **пе́ред кем-н за кого́-н** to be ashamed of sb in front of sb; ~ (*impf*) **до корне́й воло́с** to blush to the roots of one's hair.

красноарме́|ец (-йца) *м* (*ИСТ*) Red-Army soldier.

красноба́|й (-я) *м* (*разг*) waffler.

красногварде́|ец (-йца) *м* (*ИСТ*) Red Guardsman (*мн* Guardsmen).

краснодере́вщик (-а) *м* cabinet-maker.

красноречи́в|ый (-, -а, -о) *прил* (*оратор, письмо*) eloquent; (*взгляд, жест*) expressive; (*цифры, факты*) revealing.

красноре́чи|е (-я) *ср* eloquence.

краснот|а́ (-ы́) *ж* (*лица*) redness; (*в горле*) inflammation.

краснощёк|ий (-ая, -ое, -ие) *прил* rosy-cheeked.

красну́х|а (-и) *ж* German measles.

кра́сн|ый (-ен, -на́, -но) *прил* red; **проходи́ть** (*impf*) ~**ной ни́тью** *или* **ли́нией** to run through; **кра́сная а́рмия** Red Army; **кра́сная ры́ба** salmon; **кра́сная строка́** new paragraph; **кра́сное вино́** red wine; **кра́сное де́рево** mahogany; **кра́сный пе́рец** paprika.

крас|ова́ться (-у́юсь) *несов возв* (*перед зеркалом, людьми*) to parade.

кра́сок *сущ см* **кра́ска**.

крас|ота́ (-оты́; *nom pl* -о́ты) *ж* beauty; ~**!** wonderful!; *см также* **красо́ты**.

красо́т|ка (-и) *ж* pretty girl.

красо́т|ы (-) *мн* (*природы*) beautiful scenery *ед*.

кра́соч|ный (-ен, -на, -но) *прил* (*язык, расцветка*) colourful (*BRIT*), colorful (*US*).

кра|сть (-ду́, -дёшь; *perf* **укра́сть**) *несов перех* to steal

▶ **кра́сться** *несов возв* (*человек*) to creep, steal.

кра́сящ|ий (-ая, -ее, -ие) *прил*: ~**ее вещество́** dye.

крат *нареч*: **во́ сто** ~ a hundred times.

кра́тер (-а) *м* crater.

кра́т|кий (-кая, -кое, -кие; -ок, -ка́, -ко) *прил* short; (*беседа*) brief, (*словарь, отчёт*) concise; ~**кое прилага́тельное** short-form adjective; **„и" ~кое** the 10th letter of the *Russian alphabet*.

кратковре́мен|ный (-ен, -на, -но) *прил* short.

краткосро́ч|ный (-ен, -на, -но) *прил* (*отпуск,*

командировка) short; (*заём, ссуда*) short-term.

кра́ткост|ь (-и) *ж* brevity.

кра́тный *прил* divisible.

кра́ток *прил см* **кра́ткий**.

кра́тче *сравн прил см* **кра́ткий**.

крах (-а) *м* collapse; (*перен*) destruction.

крахма́л (-а) *м* starch.

крахма́л|ить (-ю, -ишь; *perf* **накрахма́лить**) *несов перех* to starch.

крахма́льный *прил* starched.

кра́ше *сравн прил от* **краси́вый**.

краше́ни|е (-я) *ср* dyeing.

кра́шен|ый *прил* (*мех, ткань*) dyed; (*стол, дверь*) painted; ~**ая блонди́нка** (*разг*) peroxide blonde.

крашу́(сь) *несов см* **кра́сить(ся)**.

краю́х|а (-и) *ж* (*разг: хлеба*) doorstep.

креве́т|ка (-и) *ж* shrimp.

креди́т (-а) *м* credit; (*политический*) credibility; **в** ~ on credit; **превыша́ть** (**превы́сить** *perf*) ~ to overdraw; **брать** (**взять** *perf*) ~ **в ба́нке** to arrange an overdraft.

креди́тный *прил* credit *опред*; ~ **оста́ток на счёте** credit balance; **креди́тная ка́рточка** credit card; **креди́тный счёт** credit account.

кредит|ова́ть (-у́ю) (*не*)*сов перех* to grant credit to.

кредито́р (-а) *м* creditor; **незастрахо́ванный** ~ unsecured creditor.

кредито́рск|ий (-ая, -ое, -ие) *прил* creditor's.

кредитоспосо́бност|ь (-и) *ж* solvency.

кредитоспосо́бный *прил* solvent.

кре́до *ср нескл* credo.

кре́йсер (-а) *м* (*ВОЕН*) battleship, cruiser.

крейси́р|овать (-ую) *несов непepex* to sail (*along a specific route*); (*ВОЕН*) to patrol.

кре́кинг (-а) *м* (*нефти*) cracking.

крем (-а) *м* cream; **сапо́жный** ~ shoe polish.

кремато́ри|й (-я) *м* crematorium.

крема́ци|я (-и) *ж* cremation.

креме́нь (-ня́) *м* flint.

креми́р|овать (-ую) (*не*)*сов перех* to cremate.

кремль (-я́) *м* citadel; **К**~ the Kremlin.

кремнёвый *прил* flint.

кре́мни|й (-я) *м* silicon.

кремня́ *итп сущ см* **креме́нь**.

кре́мовый *прил* cream.

крен (-а) *м* (*судна*) list; (*самолёта*) bank; ~ **в сто́рону чего́-н** (*перен*) a move towards sth.

кре́ндел|ь (-я; *nom pl* -я́) *м* krendel (*sweet pastry*).

крен|и́ть (-ю́, -и́шь; *perf* **накрени́ть**) *несов перех* (*судно*) to list; (*самолёт*) to bank

▶ **крени́ться** (*perf* **накрени́ться**) *несов возв* (*судно*) to list; (*самолёт*) to bank.

креозо́т (-а) *м* creosote.

креп (-а) *м* crêpe.

крепдеши́н (-а) *м* crêpe de chine.

крепёжный *прил* reinforcing *опред*.

крепи́тельн|ый *прил* (*ТЕХ*) reinforcing *опред*; ~**ое сре́дство** anti-diarrhoea tablets.

креп|и́ть (-лю́, -и́шь) *несов перех* to fix;

(*делать прочным*) to reinforce; **меня́ ~ит** I'm constipated.

кре́п|кий (-кая, -кое, -кие; -ок, -ка́, -ко) *прил* strong; (*мороз, удар*) hard; ~ **оре́шек** (*перен*) tough nut; **кре́пкие напи́тки** spirits.

кре́пко *нареч* strongly; (*спать, любить*) deeply; (*завязать*) tightly.

кре́пко-на́крепко *нареч* (*связать, закрыть*) as tightly as possible.

крепле́ни|е (-я) *ср* (*свай*) reinforcement; (*обычно мн: лыжные*) binding.

креплён|ый *прил*: ~**ое вино́** fortified wine.

креплю́ *несов см* **крепи́ть**.

креп|нуть (-ну, -нешь; *pt* -, -ла, -ло, *perf* **окре́пнуть**) *несов неперех* to get stronger; (*уверенность*) to grow.

кре́пок *прил см* **кре́пкий**.

крепостни́к (-а́) *м* (*ИСТ*) serf owner.

крепостни́честв|о (-а) *ср* (*ИСТ*) serfdom.

крепостн|о́й *прил* (*ИСТ: отношения*) serf *опред*; (*башня, сооружение*) fortress *опред* ♦ (-о́го; *decl like adj*) *м* (*ИСТ: также:* ~ **крестья́нин**) serf; **крепостно́е пра́во** (*ИСТ*) serfdom.

кре́пост|ь (-и) *ж* strength; (*ВОЕН*) fortress.

крепча́|ть (*3sg* -ет, *3pl* -ют) *несов неперех* (*мороз*) to harden; (*ветер*) to get stronger.

кре́пче *сравн прил от* **кре́пкий** ♦ *сравн нареч от* **кре́пко**.

крепы́ш (-а́) *м* (*разг: ребёнок*) chubby chops.

кре́сл|о (-ла; *gen pl* -ел) *ср* armchair; (*в театре*) seat.

кре́сло-крова́т|ь (-а, -и) *ж* ≈ sofa bed.

крест (-а́) *м* cross; **поста́вить** (*perf*) ~ **на ком-н/чём-н** to give sb/sth up for lost.

крест|е́ц (-ца́) *м* sacrum.

кре́ст|и (-) *мн* (*разг: карты*) clubs *мн*.

кре|сти́ть (-щу́, -сти́шь; *perf* **окрести́ть**) *несов перех* to christen, baptize; ~ (**перекрести́ть** *perf*) **кого́-н** to make the sign of the cross over sb; ~ (**окрести́ть** *perf*) **кого́-н кем-н** to christen sb sth

► **крести́ться** (*не*)*сов возв* to be christened *или* baptized; (*perf* **перекрести́ться**; *крестить себя*) to cross o.s.

крест-на́крест *нареч* crosswise.

кре́стник (-а) *м* godson.

кре́стниц|а (-ы) *ж* goddaughter.

кре́стн|ый *прил*: ~**ое зна́мение** sign of the cross; ~ **ход** religious procession.

кре́стн|ый *прил*: ~**ая мать** godmother; ~ **оте́ц** godfather.

кресто́в|ый *прил*: ~ **похо́д** crusade; ~**ая да́ма/деся́тка** (*разг*) the queen/ten of clubs.

крестоно́с|ец (-ца) *м* crusader.

крестца́ *итп сущ см* **крестец**.

крестья́н|ин (-ина; *nom pl* -е, *gen pl* -) *м* peasant.

крестья́н|ка (-ки; *gen pl* -ок) *ж см* **крестья́нин**.

крестья́нск|ий (-ая, -ое, -ие) *прил* peasant *опред*.

крестья́нств|о (-а) *ср* peasantry.

крети́н (-а) *м* imbecile.

кре́чет (-а) *м* gerfalcon.

креще́ндо *нареч, ср нескл* crescendo.

креще́ни|е (-я) *ср* (*обряд*) christening, baptism; (*праздник*) ≈ the Epiphany; **он получи́л боево́е** ~ (*перен*) he fought his first battle.

креще́нск|ий (-ая, -ое, -ие) *прил*: ~ **пра́здник** the Epiphany; ~**ие моро́зы** *coldest time of the year, traditionally following the Epiphany*.

крещу́(сь) (*не*)*сов см* **крести́ть(ся)**.

крив|а́я (-о́й; *decl like adj*) *ж* (*МАТ*) curve.

криве́|ть (-ю; *perf* **окриве́ть**) *несов неперех* to become cockeyed.

кривизн|а́ (-ы́) *ж* (*пола, потолка*) unevenness; (*линии, позвоночника*) curvature.

крив|и́ть (-лю́, -и́шь; *perf* **скриви́ть** *или* **покриви́ть**) *несов перех* to curve; (*лицо, губы*) to twist; ~ (**покриви́ть** *perf*) **душо́й** to be insincere

► **криви́ться** (*perf* **скриви́ться**) *несов возв* (*забор, стена итп*) to lean; (*лицо, губы*) to twist; (*человек*) to slouch.

кривля́|ться (-юсь) *несов возв* (*гримасничать*) to squirm; (*манерничать*) to show off.

крив|о́й (-, -а́, -о) *прил* (*линия, палка, улыбка*) crooked; (*ноги*) bandy; (*разг: человек*) cockeyed; ~**о́е зе́ркало** (*перен*) distorting mirror.

криволине́йный *прил* (*движение*) curvilinear.

кривоно́г|ий (-ая, -ое, -ие) *прил* bow-legged.

кривото́лк|и (-ов) *мн* gossip *ед*.

кри́зис (-а) *м* crisis; (*болезни*) critical point, crisis.

кри́зисный *прил* crisis *опред*.

крик (-а; *part gen* -у) *м* cry; (*человека*) shout, cry; (*птиц*) call, cry; **после́дний ~ мо́ды** (*разг*) the last word in fashion.

кри́кет (-а) *м* (*СПОРТ*) cricket.

крикли́в|ый (-, -а, -о) *прил* (*женщина, платье*) loud; (*голос*) yapping.

крикн|уть (-у, -ешь) *сов неперех* to shout.

крику́н (-а́) *м* (*разг*) bawler.

крику́нь|я (-ьи; *gen pl* -ий) *ж см* **крику́н**.

кримина́л (-а) *м* (*разг*) criminal case; **я не ви́жу здесь ~а** I don't see anything criminal in it.

криминали́ст (-а) *м* specialist in crime detection.

криминали́стик|а (-и) *ж* crime detection.

кримина́льный *прил* (*случай*) criminal; (*история, хроника*) crime *опред*.

криминоло́г (-а) *м* criminologist.

криминоло́ги|я (-и) *ж* criminology.

кри́н|ка (-ки; *gen pl* -ок) *ж ceramic container for milk*.

криста́лен *прил см* **криста́льный**.
криста́лл (-а) *м* crystal.
кристаллиза́ци|я (-и) *ж* crystallization.
кристаллиз|ова́ться (*3sg* -у́ется, *3pl* -у́ются, *perf* **вы́кристаллизоваться**) (не)*сов возв* to crystallize.
криста́льный (-ен, -ьна, -ьно) *прил* (*светлый*) crystal-clear; (*безупречный*) pure.
Крит (-а) *м* Crete.
крите́рий (-я) *м* criterion (*мн* criteria).
кри́тик (-а) *м* critic.
кри́тик|а (-и) *ж* criticism; **литерату́рная** ~ literary criticism; **э́то не выде́рживает никако́й** ~**и** it doesn't stand up to criticism; **подверга́ть** (**подве́ргнуть** *perf*) **кого́-н/что-н** ~**е** to subject sb/sth to criticism.
критика́н (-а) *м* (*разг: пренебр*) nit-picker.
критик|ова́ть (-у́ю) *несов перех* to criticize.
критици́зм (-а) *м* criticism.
крити́чен *прил см* **крити́чный**.
крити́ческ|ий (-ая, -ое, -ие) *прил* critical; ~ **отде́л** review section; ~**ая статья́** critique.
крити́чный (-ен, -на, -но) *прил* critical.
крич|а́ть (-у́, -и́шь) *несов неперех* (*птица*) to cry; (*человек: от боли, от гнева*) to cry (out); (: *говорить громко*) to shout; ~ (*impf*) **на** +*acc* (*бранить*) to shout at.
крича́щий (-ая, -ее, -ие) *прил* (*перен: наряды*) loud; (: *реклама*) eye-catching.
кров (-а) *м* shelter; **оста́ться** (**оста́ться** *perf*) **без кро́ва** to have no roof over one's head.
крова́в|ый *прил* (*руки, одежда*) bloodied; (*нож*) bloodstained; (*рана, битва*) bloody; (*диктатура*) ruthless; ~**ая ба́ня** blood bath; ~ **бифште́кс** rare steak.
крова́т|ка (-ки; *gen pl* -ок) *ж* cot (*BRIT*), crib (*US*).
крова́т|ь (-и) *ж* bed.
кро́вель *сущ см* **кро́вля**.
кро́вельный *прил* roofing *опред*.
кро́вельщик (-а) *м* roofer.
кровено́сный *прил* blood *опред*.
кро́в|ля (-ли; *gen pl* -ель) *ж* roof; **жить** (*impf*) **под одно́й** ~**лей** to live under one roof.
кро́вн|ый *прил* (*родство*) blood *опред*; (*обида*) grave; ~**ые интере́сы** vested interests; ~ **враг** deadly enemy; ~**ые де́ньги** blood money; **кро́вная месть** blood feud.
кровожа́ден *прил см* **кровожа́дный**.
кровожа́дност|ь (-и) *ж* bloodthirstiness.
кровожа́дный (-ен, -на, -но) *прил* bloodthirsty.
кровоизлия́ни|е (-я) *ср* haemorrhage (*BRIT*), hemorrhage (*US*).
кровообраще́ни|е (-я) *ср* (*МЕД*) circulation.
кровооста́навливающий (-ая, -ее, -ие) *прил* (*средства*) clotting *опред*.
кровопи́йц|а (-ы) *м/ж* bloodsucker.
кровоподте́к (-а) *м* blood blister.
кровопроли́тен *прил см* **кровопроли́тный**.
кровопроли́ти|е (-я) *ср* bloodshed.
кровопроли́тный (-ен, -на, -но) *прил* bloody.
кровопуска́ни|е (-я) *ср* (*также МЕД*) blood-letting.

кровосмеше́ни|е (-я) *ср* incest.
кровотече́ни|е (-я) *ср* bleeding.
кровоточ|и́ть (*3sg* -и́т, *3pl* -а́т) *несов неперех* to bleed.
кров|ь (-и; *loc sg* -и́) *ж* blood; **го́лос кро́ви** call of the blood; **по́ртить** (*impf*) ~ **кому́-н** (*разг*) to make sb's blood boil; **пролива́ть** (**проли́ть** *perf*) (**свою́**) ~ **за кого́-н/что-н** to sacrifice o.s. for sb/sth; **пролива́ть** (**проли́ть** *perf*) **чью-н** ~ to spill sb's blood; **пить** (*impf*) **чью-н** ~ to suck the lifeblood out of sb; ~ **с молоко́м** *about a healthy, ruddy-faced person*; **плоть и** ~ (**чья**) (sb's) flesh and blood; **у меня́ се́рдце кро́вью облива́ется** my heart bleeds.
кровян|о́й *прил* blood *опред*; **кровяна́я колбаса́** black pudding; **кровяно́е давле́ние** blood pressure.
кро|и́ть (-ю́, -и́шь) *несов перех* to cut out.
крокоди́л (-а) *м* crocodile.
крокоди́лов (-а, -о, -ы) *прил*: ~**ы слёзы** crocodile tears *мн*.
крокоди́ловый *прил* crocodile *опред*.
кро́лик (-а) *м* rabbit; (*мех*) rabbit fur; **ша́пка из** ~**а** rabbit-fur hat.
кро́личий (-ья, -ье, -ьи) *прил* rabbit *опред*.
крольча́тник (-а) *м* rabbit hutch.
крольчи́х|а (-и) *ж* doe (*rabbit*).
кро́ме *предл*: ~ +*gen* (*за исключением*) except; (*сверх чего-н*) as well as; ~ **того́** besides; ~ **него́ я никого́ не ви́дел** I haven't seen anyone except for *или* apart from him; ~ **соба́ки у них есть ещё и ко́шка** as well as a dog, they also have a cat; ~ **шу́ток** (*разг*) joking apart; **ему́ ничего́ остало́сь** ~ **как уйти́** (*разг*) he had no choice but to leave; ~ **как от тебя́, ни от кого́ не́ было пи́сем** I didn't get a letter from anyone except (for) you; ~ **того́, мне на́до идти́ на собра́ние** apart from that *или* besides I have to go to a meeting.
кроме́шн|ый *прил*: **ад** ~ hell on earth; **здесь тьма** ~**ая** it's pitch-black in here.
кро́м|ка (-и) *ж* (*ткани*) trim; (*льда, поля*) edge.
кромса́|ть (-ю; *perf* **искромса́ть**) *несов перех* (*хлеб, материал*) to hack off; (*перен: рукопись, пьесу*) to chop.
кро́н|а (-ы) *ж* (*дерева*) crown; (*деньги*) krona.
кронште́йн (-а) *м* (*балкона*) support; (*лампы, полки*) bracket.
кропа́|ть (-ю; *perf* **накропа́ть**) *несов перех* (*разг*) to scribble.
кроп|и́ть (-лю́, -и́шь; *perf* **окропи́ть**) *несов перех* (*РЕЛ*) to sprinkle (*with holy water*).
кропотли́в|ый (-, -а, -о) *прил* (*работа*) painstaking; (*человек*) fastidious.
кросс (-а) *м* (*бег*) cross-country; (*гонки*) cross-country race.
кроссво́рд (-а) *м* crossword.
кроссо́в|ка (-ки; *gen pl* -ок) *ж* (*обычно мн*) trainer.
крот (-а́) *м* mole.
кро́т|кий (-кая, -кое, -кие; -ок, -ка́, -ко) *прил*

meek.
крото́вый *прил* moleskin.
кро́ток *прил см* **кро́ткий**.
кро́тост|ь (-и) *ж* meekness.
кро́х|а (-и) *ж* (*обычно мн*) scrap ♦ *м/ж* (*ребёнок*) little one.
крохобо́р (-а) *м* miser.
крохобо́рств|о (-а) *ср* (*пренебр*) stinginess.
кро́хотный (-ен, -на, -но) *прил* tiny.
кро́шек *сущ см* **кро́шка**.
кро́шечный (-ен, -на, -но) *прил* (*разг*) teeny-weeny, tiny.
крош|и́ть (-у́, -ишь) *несов перех* (*хлеб*) to crumble; (*кулин*) to dice ♦ *неперех* (*сорить*) to drop crumbs
▸ **кроши́ться** *несов возв* (*хлеб, мел*) to crumble.
кро́ш|ка (-ки; *gen pl* -ек) *ж* (*кусочек*) crumb; (*малютка*) little one.
кро́ю(сь) *итп несов см* **крыть(ся)**.
круг (-а; *nom pl* -и́) *м* circle; (*спорт*) lap; (*сыра, хлеба*) round; (*loc sg* -у́; *перен: знакомых*) circle; (: *обязанностей, интересов, вопросов*) range; **у меня́ голова́ кру́гом идёт** my head is spinning; **ходи́ть** (*impf*) **по кру́гу** to go round and round; **беговой** ~ racing track; **поля́рный** ~ polar circle; *см также* **круги́**.
круги́ (-о́в) *мн* (*литературные, политические*) circles мн.
кругле́|ть (-ю; *perf* **округле́ть**) *несов неперех* (*полнеть*) to fill out; (*становиться круглым*) to become round.
круглогоди́чный *прил* all-year-round.
круглоли́цый (-, -а, -о) *прил* round-faced.
круглосу́точный *прил* (*работа*) round-the-clock; (*детский сад*) twenty-four-hour.
кру́гл|ый (-, -а́, -о) *прил* round; (*no short form*; *идиот, дурак*) complete, total; (*цифра*) round; **год** all year (round); **~ые су́тки** twenty-four hours; **~ая су́мма** hefty sum.
круговой *прил* circular; **кругова́я пору́ка** mutual dependence; (*у преступников*) mutual cover-up.
кругооборо́т (-а) *м* cycle; (*событий*) turmoil.
кругозо́р (-а) *м*: **он челове́к широ́кого ~а** he is knowledgeable.
круго́м *нареч* around; (*разг: совершенно*) entirely; **идти́** (**пойти́** *perf*) ~ to make a detour; **~!** about turn! (*BRIT*), about face! (*US*).
кругооборо́т (-а) *м* (*комм*) turnover.
кругосве́тный *прил* round-the-world.
кружевни́ц|а (-ы) *ж* lace-maker.
кружевной *прил* lace.
кру́жев|о (-а; *nom pl* -а́, *gen pl* -) *ср* lace.
кру́жек *сущ см* **кру́жка**.
круж|и́ть (-у́, -ишь) *несов перех* to spin ♦ *неперех* (*птица*) to circle; (*по лесу итп*) to go round in circles
▸ **кружи́ться** *несов возв* (*в хороводе*) to move

in a circle; (*в танце*) to spin (around); **у меня́ голова́ кру́жится** my head's spinning.
кру́ж|ка (-ки; *gen pl* -ек) *ж* (*жестяная, глиняная*) mug; (*для пожертвований*) collection box.
кружка *сущ см* **кружо́к**.
кружко́в|ый *прил*: **~ые заня́тия** extracurricular activities.
кружо́к (-ка́) *м* circle; (*организация*) club.
круи́з (-а) *м* cruise.
круп (-а) *м* (*лошади*) crupper; (*мед*) croup.
круп|а́ (-ы́; *nom pl* -ы) *ж* grain.
кру́пен *прил см* **кру́пный**.
крупи́н|ка (-ки; *gen pl* -ок) *ж* (*разг*) grain.
крупи́ц|а (-ы) *ж* (*таланта, здравого смысла*) ounce; (*истины*) grain.
крупне́|ть (-ю; *perf* **покрупне́ть**) *несов неперех* to grow larger.
кру́пно *нареч* (*нарезать*) coarsely; **писа́ть** (**написа́ть** *perf*) ~ to write in big letters; ~ **поссо́риться** (*perf*) **с кем-н** to have a big row with sb.
крупномасшта́бный *прил* large-scale.
кру́п|ный (-ен, -на́, -но) *прил* (*песок, соль*) coarse; (*размеры, ребёнок, фирма*) large; (*талант*) great; (*учёный, дело, фабрикант*) prominent; (*ссора, событие, успех*) major; **у меня́ бу́дут ~ые неприя́тности** I'll be in serious trouble; ~ **разгово́р** (*разг*) serious talk; **кру́пный го́род** major city; **кру́пный план** close-up; **кру́пный рога́тый скот** (*с.-х.*) cattle.
крупо́зн|ый *прил*: **~ое воспале́ние лёгких** pneumonia with croup.
крутизн|а́ (-ы́) *ж* steepness.
кру|ти́ть (-чу́, -тишь) *несов перех* (*руль*) to turn; (*perf* **скрути́ть**; *руки*) to twist; (*верёвку*) to splice; (*папиросу*) to roll; ~ (*impf*) **кем-н** (*разг*) to manipulate sb; ~ (*impf*) **рома́н с кем-н** (*разг*) to have an affair with sb; **как ни ~ти́, нам придётся ..** (*разг*) we've no choice but to ...
▸ **крути́ться** *несов возв* (*вертеться*) to turn around; (: *колесо*) to spin; (: *дети*) to fidget; (*перен: хлопотать*) to be kept busy.
кру́то *нареч* (*подниматься*) steeply; (*поворачивать*) sharply; ~ **обходи́ться** (**обойти́сь** *perf*) **с кем-н** to give sb a hard time.
крут|о́й (-, -а́, -о) *прил* (*берег, подъём*) steep; (*поворот, перемены*) sharp; (*нрав, меры*) harsh; (*no short form*; *место*) stiff; (*каша*) thick; ~ **кипято́к** fiercely boiling water; ~ **па́рень** (*разг*) cool guy; **круто́е яйцо́** hard-boiled egg.
кру́ч|а (-и) *ж* ~ steep slope.
кру́че *сравн прил от* **круто́й** ♦ *сравн нареч от* **кру́то**.
кручён|ый *прил* (*нитки*) twisted; **кручёный уда́р** (*в теннисе*) spin shot.
кручу́(сь) *несов см* **крути́ть(ся)**.
круше́ни|е (-я) *ср* (*поезда*) crash; (*перен: надежд, планов*) shattering; **терпе́ть**

(потерпе́ть *perf)* ~ **(кора́бль)** to be wrecked; *(по́езд)* to crash.

круши́н|а (-ы) *ж* buckthorn *(used as a laxative).*

круши́ть (-у́, -и́шь) *несов перех (враго́в)* to crush; *(дере́вья, дома́)* to wreck.

крыжо́вник (-а) *м (куста́рник)* gooseberry (bush); *(я́года)* gooseberry.

крыла́тый *прил (насеко́мые)* winged; **~ые слова́** proverbial expressions; **крыла́тая раке́та** *(ВОЕН)* cruise missile.

крыл|о́ (-а́; *nom pl* **-ья,** *gen pl* **-ьев)** *ср* wing; *(ветряно́й ме́льницы)* sail; **подреза́ть (подре́зать** *perf)* **кры́лья кому́-н** *(перен)* to clip sb's wings; **расправля́ть (распра́вить** *perf)* **кры́лья** *(перен)* to spread one's wings.

крыли́шк|о (-а) *ср* wing; **под ~м у кого́-н** under sb's wing.

крыльц|о́ (-а́) *ср* porch.

Крым (-а) *м* Crimea.

кры́мский (-ая, -ое, -ие) *прил* Crimean.

кры́н|ка (-ки; *gen pl* **-ок)** *ж* = **кри́нка.**

кры́с|а (-ы) *ж* rat.

крыси́ный *прил (нора́, хвост)* rat's; **~ яд** rat poison.

кры́тый *прил* covered.

кры́ть (-о́ю, -о́ешь; *perf* **покры́ть)** *несов перех* to cover; *(ка́рту)* to trump; **~** *(impf)* **ма́том** *(разг)* to turn the air blue *(with bad language)*

▶ **кры́ться** *несов возв:* **~ы́ться в** *+prp (причи́на)* to lie; **в расчётах ~ы́лась оши́бка** the calculations contained a mistake; **причи́на э́того явле́ния ~о́ется в том, что ...** the reason for this lies in the fact that ....

кры́ш|а (-и) *ж* roof.

кры́ш|ка (-ки; *gen pl* **-ек)** *ж (я́щика, ча́йника)* lid; **тут ему́ и ~** *(разг)* that was the end of him.

крэк (-а) *м* crack *(drug).*

крю́|к (-ка́; *nom pl* **-чья,** *gen pl* **-чьев)** *м (в стене́)* hook; *(разг: ли́шнее расстоя́ние)* detour.

крю́ч|ить (3sg **-ит,** *perf* **скрю́чить)** *несов безл:* **его́ ~ит от бо́ли** he is bent double in pain

▶ **крю́читься** *(perf* **скрю́читься)** *несов возв* to be bent double.

крючка́ *итп сущ см* **крючо́к.**

крючкова́т|ый (-, -а, -о) *прил* hooked.

крюч|о́к (-ка́) *м* hook; **~ для вяза́ния** crochet hook.

крю́чья *итп сущ см* **крюк.**

крюшо́н (-а) *м (кули́н)* punch.

кря́ду *нареч:* **дождь шёл пять дней ~** it rained for five whole days.

кряж (-а) *м (го́рный)* ridge.

кря́жист|ый (-, -а, -о) *прил (также́ перен)* stumpy.

кря́кань|е (-я) *ср* quacking.

кря́ка|ть (-ю) *несов от* **кря́кнуть.**

кря́кну|ть (-у, -ешь) *сов неперех (у́тка)* to quack; *(перен: челове́к)* to grunt.

кряхте́ть (-чу́, -ти́шь) *несов неперех* to groan.

ксерокопи́|я (-и) *ж* photocopy, Xerox®.

ксе́рок|с (-а) *м (автома́т)* photocopier; *(ко́пия)*
photocopy, Xerox®.

ксилофо́н (-а) *м* xylophone.

ксилогра́фи|я (-и) *ж (образе́ц рабо́ты)* woodcut; *(проце́сс)* wood engraving.

кста́ти *вводн сл (ме́жду про́чим)* incidentally, by the way; *(случа́йно)* by any chance ♦ *нареч (к ме́сту)* relevant; **~, ты слы́шал, что ...?** by the way, did you hear that ...?; **Вы, ~, не зна́ете, что случи́лось?** you don't, by any chance, know what happened?; **де́ньги пришли́сь как нельзя́ ~** the money came just at the right time.

┌─────────────┐
KEYWORD
└─────────────┘

кто (кого́; *см* **Table 6)** *мест* **1** *(вопроси́тельное, относи́тельное)* who; **кто там?** who is there?; **на́до узна́ть, кто приходи́л** we must find out who has come

2 *(разг: кто-нибудь)* anyone; **е́сли кто позвони́т, позови́ меня́** if anyone phones, please call me

3: ма́ло ли кто many (people); **ма́ло кто** few (people); **ма́ло кто пошёл в кино́** only a few of us went to the cinema; **кто-кто, а он всегда́ пра́вду говори́т** I don't know about anyone else, but he always tells the truth; **кто из вас ...** which of you ...; **кто (его́) зна́ет!** who knows!

кто́-либо (кого́-либо; *как* **кто;** *см* **Table 6)** *мест* = **кто́-нибудь.**

кто́-нибудь (кого́-нибудь; *как* **кто;** *см* **Table 6)** *мест (в вопроси́тельных предложе́ниях)* anybody, anyone; *(в утверди́тельных предложе́ниях)* somebody, someone; **мне ~ звони́л?** did anybody *или* anyone phone for me?; **~ до́лжен ему́ помо́чь** somebody *или* someone should help him.

кто́-то (кого́-то; *как* **кто;** *см* **Table 6)** *мест* somebody, someone; **~ Вам звони́л** somebody *или* someone phoned for you.

куб (-а) *м (ГЕОМ, МАТ)* cube; **3 в ку́бе** 3 cubed.

куб. *сокр (= куби́ческий)* cu. *(= cubic).*

Ку́б|а (-ы) *ж* Cuba.

ку́барем *нареч (разг)* headfirst.

куби́зм (-а) *м* cubism.

ку́бик (-а) *м (игру́шка)* building brick *или* block.

куби́н|ец (-ца) *м* Cuban.

куби́н|ка (-ки; *gen pl* **-ок)** *ж см* **куби́нец.**

куби́нский (-ая, -ое, -ие) *прил* Cuban.

куби́нца *итп сущ см* **куби́нец.**

куби́ст (-а) *м* cubist.

куби́ческий (-ая, -ое, -ие) *прил* cubic; **куби́ческий ко́рень** cube root.

ку́б|ок (-ка) *м* goblet; *(СПОРТ)* cup.

кубоме́тр (-а) *м* cubic metre *(BRIT) или* meter *(US).*

ку́брик (-а) *м* crew's quarters *мн.*

кува́лд|а (-ы) *ж* sledgehammer.

Куве́йт (-а) *м* Kuwait.

кувши́н (-а) *м* jug *(BRIT)*, pitcher *(US).*

кувши́н|ка (-и) *ж* water lily.

кувырка́|ться (-юсь) *несов возв* to somersault.

кувыркну́ться (-у́сь, -ёшься) *сов возв* to turn a somersault.

кувырко́м *нареч* head over heels; **жизнь у меня́ пошла́ ~** my life has been turned on its head.
кувыр|о́к (**-ка́**) *м* somersault.

KEYWORD

куда́ *нареч* **1** (*вопросительное, относительное*) where; **куда́ ты положи́л мою́ ру́чку?** where did you put my pen?; **скажи́, куда́ ты идёшь** tell me where you are going **2** (*разг: для чего*) why; **куда́ мне сто́лько де́нег?** why would I want so much money?
3 (*+dat; разг: о невозможности чего-н*): **куда́ мне с ни́ми состяза́ться?** how can I compare with them?
4 (*+comparative; разг: гораздо*) much; **мой дом куда́ бо́льше** my house is much bigger.

куда́-либо *нареч* = **куда́-нибудь**.
куда́-нибудь *нареч* (*в вопросительных предложениях*) anywhere; (*в утвердительных предложениях*) somewhere; **Вы ~ съе́здили ле́том?** did you go anywhere in the summer?; **дава́й ~ пойдём** let's go somewhere.
куда́-то *нареч* somewhere; **он ~ ушёл** he has gone off somewhere.
куда́хтань|е (**-я**) *ср* clucking.
куда́х|тать (**-чу, -чешь**) *несов неперех* to cluck.
куде́сник (**-а**) *м* sorcerer.
ку́др|и (**-е́й**) *мн* curls *мн*.
кудря́в|ый (**-, -а, -о**) *прил* (*волосы*) curly; (*человек*) curly-haired; (*дерево*) bushy; (*перен: слог*) flowery.
кузне́ц (**-а́**) *м* blacksmith.
кузне́чик (**-а**) *м* grasshopper.
кузне́чный *прил* blacksmith's; **кузне́чные меха́** bellows *мн*.
ку́зниц|а (**-ы**) *ж* smithy, forge.
ку́зов (**-а**; *nom pl* **-а́**) *м* (*АВТ*) back (*of a van, lorry etc*).
куй(те) *несов см* **кова́ть**.
кукаре́к|ать (**-ю**) *несов неперех* to crow.
кукареку́ *межд* (*крик петуха*) cock-a-doodle-doo.
ку́киш (**-а**) *м* fig; **он показа́л мне ~** (*перен: разг*) ≈ he told me to get lost.
ку́кл|а (**-ы**; *gen pl* **-ол**) *ж* (*также перен*) doll; (*в театре*) puppet; **теа́тр ~ол** puppet theatre (*BRIT*) *или* theater (*US*).
кук|ова́ть (**-у́ю**) *несов неперех* to cuckoo; (*перен: разг*) to twiddle one's thumbs.
ку́кол *сущ см* **ку́кла**.
ку́кол|ка (**-ки**; *gen pl* **-ок**) *ж* уменьш от **ку́кла**; (*ЗООЛ*) pupa (*мн* pupae).
ку́кольный *прил* (*игрушечный*): **~ до́мик** doll's house; **ку́кольный теа́тр** puppet theatre (*BRIT*) *или* theater (*US*).
ку́к|ситься (**-шусь, -сишься**) *несов возв* (*разг*) to sulk.
кукуру́з|а (**-ы**) *ж* (*БОТ*) maize; (*КУЛИН*) (sweet) corn.

кукуру́зный *прил* (*см сущ*) maize; corn.
куку́шк|а (**-и**) *ж* cuckoo.
ку́кшусь *несов см* **ку́кситься**.
кула́к (**-а́**) *м* fist; (*ИСТ*) kulak (*member of the land-owning peasant class, eradicated during collectivization*).
кула́чный *прил*: **~ бой** fist fight.
кулебя́к|а (**-и**) *ж* pie made with meat, fish or rice.
кул|ёк (**-ька́**) *м* paper bag.
кули́к (**-а́**) *м* (*ЗООЛ*) wader.
кулина́р (**-а**) *м* master chef.
кулина́ри|я (**-и**) *ж* (*приготовление пищи*) cookery; (*магазин*) ≈ delicatessen ♦ *собир* (*продукты*) cooked foods and groceries.
кулина́рный *прил* (*искусство*) culinary.
кули́с|а (**-ы**) *ж* (*обычно мн: ТЕАТР*) wing; **за ~ми** (*также перен*) backstage, behind the scenes.
кули́ч (**-а́**) *м* kulich (*Easter cake*).
кули́чки *нареч* (*разг*): **у чёрта на кули́чках** in the middle of nowhere; **к чёрту на ~** to the back of beyond.
куло́н (**-а**) *м* (*украшение*) pendant; (*физ*) coulomb.
кулуа́рный *прил* (*встречи, сделки*) backstage.
кулуа́р|ы (**-ов**) *мн* (*полит*) lobby *ед*; **в ~ах бесе́ды иду́т** behind-the-scene talks are currently in progress.
кул|ь (**-я́**) *м* sack.
кулька́ *итп сущ см* **кулёк**.
кульминацио́нный *прил* climactic.
кульмина́ци|я (**-и**) *ж* (*АСТРОНОМИЯ*) culmination; (*перен*) high point, climax.
культ (**-а**) *м* (*служение божеству*) cult; (*совокупность обрядов: православный*) religion; (*перен: красоты, денег*) cult worship; **служи́тели ку́льта** church officials; **культ ли́чности** personality cult.
культиви́ровани|е (**-я**) *ср* cultivation.
культиви́р|овать (**-ую**) *несов перех* to cultivate.
ку́льтовый *прил* religious.
культу́р|а (**-ы**) *ж* (*также с.-х., БИО*) culture; (*разведение: льна итп*) cultivation, culture; (*быта*) high quality; **~ труда́** work ethic.
культу́рен *прил см* **культу́рный**.
культури́зм (**-а**) *м* body building.
культури́ст (**-а**) *м* body builder.
культу́р|ный (**-ен, -на, -но**) *прил* cultural; (*no short form; растение*) cultivated.
кум (**-а**; *nom pl* **-овья́**, *gen pl* **-овьёв**) *м* godfather.
кум|а́ (**-ы́**) *ж* godmother.
кума́чо́вый *прил* calico.
куми́р (**-а**) *м* (*также перен*) idol.
кумовство́ (**-а**) *ср* nepotism.
кумовь|я́ (**-ёв**) *мн от* **кум**.
кумы́с (**-а**) *м* fermented horse's milk.
куни́ц|а (**-ы**) *ж* marten.
купа́льник (**-а**) *м* swimming *или* bathing costume (*BRIT*), bathing suit (*US*).

купáльный *прил*: ~ **костю́м** swimming *или* bathing costume (*BRIT*), bathing suit (*US*); ~ **сезóн** swimming season.

купáны|е (**-я**) *ср* bathing; (*плáвание*) swimming.

купá|ть (**-ю**; *perf* **вы́купать** *или* **искупáть**) *несов перех* to bath

► **купáться** (*perf* **вы́купаться** *или* **искупáться**) *несов возв* to bathe; (*плáвать*) to swim; (*в вáнне*) to have a bath; ~**ся** (*impf*) **в зóлоте** to be rolling in money.

купé *ср нескл* compartment (*in railway carriage*).

купéйный *прил*: ~ **вагóн** Pullman (car).

купéл|ь (**-и**) *ж* (*РЕЛ*) font.

куп|éц (**-цá**) *м* merchant.

купéческ|ий (**-ая, -ое, -ие**) *прил* (*сослóвие*) merchant *опред*; (*перен: нрáвы*) vulgar.

купéчеств|о (**-а**) *ср собир* the merchants *мн*.

купи́рованный *прил* = **купéйный**.

куп|и́ть (**-лю́, -ишь**; *impf* **покупáть**) *сов перех* to buy.

куплéт (**-а**) *м* couplet; *см также* **куплéты**.

куплéт|ы (**-ов**) *мн satirical song in couplet form.*

куплю́ *сов см* **купи́ть**.

ку́пл|я (**-и**) *ж* purchase; ~**-продáжа** buying and selling.

ку́пол (**-а**; *nom pl* **-á**) *м* cupola.

купóн (**-а**) *м* (*цéнных бумáг*) ticket; (*денéжный знак*) coupon (*used as the Ukrainian currency*); **стричь** (*impf*) ~**ы** to make easy money; **подáрочный** ~ gift voucher.

купцá *итп сущ см* **купéц**.

ку́пч|ий (**-ая, -ее, -ие**) *прил* (*также:* ~**ая крéпость**: *ЮР*) deed of purchase.

купчи́х|а (**-и**) *ж см* **купéц**.

купю́р|а (**-ы**) *ж* (*сокращéние*) cut; (*ЭКОН*) denomination; **статья́ печáтается без купю́р** the article is printed in full.

ку́р|а (**-ы**) *ж* (*разг*) chicken.

курагá (**-и́**) *ж собир* dried apricots *мн*.

кура́ж|иться (**-усь, -ишься**) *несов возв*: ~ **над кем-н** to bully sb.

кура́нт|ы (**-ов**) *мн* chiming clock *ед*.

кура́тор (**-а**) *м* supervisor.

кургáн (**-а**) *м* (*моги́льник*) (burial) mound.

ку́рев|о (**-а**) *ср* (*разг*) smokes *мн*, fags *мн*.

курéни|е (**-я**) *ср* smoking.

кури́л|ка (**-ки**; *gen pl* **-ок**) *ж* (*разг*) smoking room.

кури́льщик (**-а**) *м* smoker.

кури́льщиц|а (**-ы**) *ж см* **кури́льщик**.

кури́ный *прил* (*яйцо́*) hen's; (*бульóн, пéрья*) chicken; **кури́ная слепотá** (*МЕД*) night blindness.

кури́тельный *прил*: ~ **табáк** rolling tobacco; **кури́тельная кóмната** smoking room.

кур|и́ть (**-ю́, -ишь**) *несов (пе)рех* to smoke; «~ **запрещáется**», «**не ~**» "no smoking"; «**у нас не ку́рят**» "kindly refrain from smoking"

► **кури́ться** *несов возв* (*вулкáн*) to smoke; (*вершины гор*) to be shrouded in mist.

ку́р|ица (**-ицы**; *nom pl* **ку́ры**) *ж* hen, chicken; (*мя́со*) chicken; ~**ам на смех** (*разг*) it's a complete joke; **дéнег у неё** ~**ы не клюю́т** (*разг*) she's absolutely loaded.

куркá *сущ см* **курóк**.

курнóс|ый (**-, -а, -о**) *прил* snub-nosed.

кур|óк (**-кá**) *м* hammer (*on gun*); **взводи́ть** (**взвести́** *perf*) ~ to cock a gun.

куроле́|сить (**-шу, -сишь**) *несов непéрех* to play up.

куропáт|ка (**-ки**; *gen pl* **-ок**) *ж* grouse.

курóрт (**-а**) *м* (holiday) resort.

курóртный *прил* (*зóна, гóрод*) resort *опред*; **курóртный сезóн** the holiday season.

курс (**-а**) *м* course; (*ПОЛИТ*) policy; (*КОММ*) exchange rate; (*ПРОСВЕЩ*) year (*of university studies*); **брать** (**взять** *perf*) ~ **на** +*acc* to set a course for; **идти́** (*impf*) **по ку́рсу** to be on the (right) course; **переходи́ть** (**перейти́** *perf*) **на четвёртый** ~ to go into the fourth year (*of university*); **быть** (*impf*) **в ку́рсе дéла** to be up on what's going on; **входи́ть** (**войти́** *perf*) **в** ~ **чегó-н** to put o.s. in the picture about sth; **вводи́ть** (**ввести́** *perf*) **когó-н в** ~ (**чегó-н**) to put sb in the picture (about sth).

курсáнт (**-а**) *м* (*ВОЕН*) cadet.

курси́в (**-а**) *м* italics *мн*; «~ **мой**» "the italics are mine".

курси́р|овать (**-ую**) *несов непéрех*: ~ **мéжду** +*instr* ... **и** +*instr* ... (*самолёт, автóбус*) to shuttle between ... and ...; (*суднó*) to sail between ... and ...

курсов|óй *прил*: ~**áя рабóта** project; ~**óе собрáние** student's year meeting; ~**áя рáзница** (*КОММ*) difference in exchange rates.

ку́рсор (**-а**) *м* cursor.

ку́рт|ка (**-ки**; *gen pl* **-ок**) *ж* jacket.

курчáв|ый (**-, -а, -о**) *прил* (*вóлосы*) curly; (*человéк, живóтное*) curly-haired.

ку́р|ы (**-**) *мн от* **ку́рица**.

курьёз (**-а**) *м* curious thing.

курьёз|ный (**-ен, -на, -но**) *прил* curious.

курьéр (**-а**) *м* messenger; (*дипломати́ческий*) courier.

курьéрск|ий (**-ая, -ое, -ие**) *прил*: ~ **отдéл** dispatch department; **курьéрский пóезд** express train.

куря́тин|а (**-ы**) *ж* chicken (*meat*).

куря́тник (**-а**) *м* chicken coop.

куса́|ть (**-ю**) *несов перех* to bite; (*сáхар, конфéты*) to crunch

► **куса́ться** *несов возв* (*живóтное*) to bite; (*растéние*) to sting; (*разг: цéны, налóги*) to hurt.

куса́ч|ки (**-ек**) *мн* wire cutters *мн*.

кускá *итп сущ см* **кусóк**.

кусковóй *прил*: ~ **сáхар** lump sugar.

кус|óк (**-кá**) *м* piece; ~ **сáхара** sugar lump; ~ **мы́ла** bar of soap; ~ **хлéба** (*перен*) daily bread.

куст (**-á**) *м* (*БОТ*) bush; **пря́таться** (**спря́таться** *perf*) **в** ~**ы́** (*перен*) to run for cover.

кустáрник (**-а**) *м* shrubbery ♦ *собир* bushes *мн*.

куста́рный *прил* handicraft *опред*; (*перен:
методы, оборудование*) crude, primitive; ~
труд craftwork; **куста́рные изде́лия**
handicrafts.

куста́р|ь (**-я́**) *м* craftsman (*мн* craftsmen).

кусти́стый (**-, -а, -о**) *прил* bushy.

ку́та|ть (**-ю**; *perf* **заку́тать**) *несов перех* (*плечи,
ноги итп*) to cover up; (*ребёнка*) to bundle up

▶ **ку́таться** (*perf* **заку́таться**) *несов возв*: ~**ся в**
+*acc* to wrap o.s. up in.

куте́ж (**-á**) *м* drinking spree.

кутерьм|а́ (**-ы́**) *ж* (*разг*) mayhem, chaos.

кути́ть (**-чу́, -тишь**) *несов неперех* to go on a
drinking spree.

куту́з|ка (**-ки**; *gen pl* **-ок**) *ж* (*разг*) the slammer, the
clink (*BRIT*).

куха́р|ка (**-ки**; *gen pl* **-ок**) *ж* cook.

ку́х|ня (**-ни**; *gen pl* **-онь**) *ж* (*помещение*) kitchen;
(*еда*) cooking; **ру́сская** ~ Russian cuisine.

кухо́нный *прил* kitchen *опред*.

ку́хонь *сущ см* **ку́хня**.

ку́цый (**-, -а, -о**) *прил* (*собака*) with no tail;
(*перен: программа, права*) limited.

ку́ч|а (**-и**) *ж* (*песка, листьев*) pile, heap; (+*gen*;
разг: денег, проблем) heaps *или* loads of;
вали́ть (*impf*) **всё в одну́** ~**y** to lump everything
together.

кучев|о́й *прил*: ~**ые облака́** cumulus (clouds
мн).

ку́чер (**-а**; *nom pl* **-á**) *м* coachman (*мн* coachmen).

кучу́ *несов см* **кути́ть**.

куш (**-а**) *м* jackpot; **срыва́ть** (**сорва́ть** *perf*) ~ to
hit the jackpot.

куша́к (**-á**) *м* sash.

куша́нь|е (**-ья**; *gen pl* **-ий**) *ср* food.

ку́ша|ть (**-ю**; *perf* **поку́шать** *или* **ску́шать**) *несов
перех* to eat; ~**йте, пожа́луйста** have something
to eat.

куше́т|ка (**-ки**; *gen pl* **-ок**) *ж* couch.

кюве́т (**-а**) *м* gutter.

~ Л, л ~

Л, **л** *сущ нескл* (*буква*) the 12th letter of the Russian alphabet.

л. *сокр* (= **лист**) f. (= *folio*).

лабири́нт (**-а**) *м* maze; (*перен*) labyrinth.

лабора́нт (**-а**) *м* (*в лаборатории*) lab technician; (*на кафедре*) secretary.

лабора́нт|ка (**-ки**; *gen pl* **-ок**) *ж см* **лабора́нт**.

лаборато́ри|я (**-и**) *ж* laboratory.

ла́в|а (**-ы**) *ж* lava; (*забой*) drift.

лава́нд|а (**-ы**) *ж* lavender.

лава́ш (**-а**) *м* lavash (*Caucasian flat bread*).

лави́н|а (**-ы**) *ж* (*также перен*) avalanche.

лави́р|овать (**-ую**; *perf* **слави́ровать**) *несов непepex* (*МОР*) to tack; (*перен*) to manoeuvre (*BRIT*), maneuver (*US*).

ла́в|ка (**-ки**; *gen pl* **-ок**) *ж* (*скамья*) bench; (*магазин*) shop.

ла́воч|ка (**-ки**; *gen pl* **-ек**) *ж уменьш от* **ла́вка**; (*перен*: *разг*) shady business.

ла́вочник (**-а**) *м* shopkeeper.

лавр (**-а**) *м* laurel; *см также* **ла́вры**.

ла́вр|а (**-ы**) *ж* monastery.

лавро́вый *прил* laurel; **лавро́вый лист** bay leaf.

ла́вр|ы (**-ов**) *мн* (*венок*) laurels *мн*; **пожина́ть** (*impf*) ~ to be crowned with laurels; **почи́ть** (*perf*) **на** ~**ах** to rest on one's laurels.

лавса́н (**-а**) *м* lavsan (*synthetic polyester fibre or fabric*).

ЛАГ *м сокр* (= **Ли́га ара́бских госуда́рств**) Arab League.

ла́герный *прил* camp *опред*.

ла́гер|ь (**-я**; *nom pl* **-я́**) *м* camp; (*nom pl* **-и**; *перен*) camp.

лагу́н|а (**-ы**) *ж* lagoon.

лад (**-а**; *loc sg* **-у́**, *nom pl* **-ы́**) *м* (*разг*: *гармония*) harmony; (*МУЗ*: *обычно мн*: *деление на грифе*) fret; (: *клавиша*) key; (: *строй*) mode; **быть** (*impf*) **не в** ~**áx с** +*instr* to be at odds with; **на свой** ~ in one's own way; **на все** ~**ы́** in all sorts of ways, every which way (*US*); **руга́ть** (*impf*) **кого́-н на все** ~**ы́** to call sb every name under the sun; **де́ло идёт на** ~ things are getting better.

ла́дан (**-а**) *м* incense; **дыша́ть** (*impf*) **на** ~ (*разг*) to be on one's last legs.

ла́ден *прил см* **ла́дный**.

ла́дить (**-жу, -дишь**; *perf* **пола́дить**) *несов непepex*: ~ **с** +*instr* to get on (well) with

► **ла́диться** *несов возв* to go well.

ла́дно *част* (*разг*) O.K., all right; **пойдём в кино –** ~ let's go to the cinema – O.K. *или* all right; ~ **тебе́!** (*разг*: *не стоит, не надо*) don't be silly!; ~ **тебе́ жа́ловаться/крича́ть** that's enough of your complaining/shouting; **да** ~! you don't say!

ла́д|ный (**-ен, -на́, -но**) *прил* (*разг*: *хорошо сложенный*) well-built; **у него́** ~**ная фигу́ра** he's a fine figure of a man.

ла́дожск|ий (**-ая, -ое, -ие**) *прил*: **Л**~**ое о́зеро** Lake Ladoga.

ладо́н|ь (**-и**) *ж* (*АНАТ*) palm; **отсю́да Москва́ видна́ как на** ~**и** from here you can see Moscow clearly.

ладо́ш|и (**-**) *мн*: **бить в** ~ to clap one's hands; **хло́пать** (*impf*) **в** ~ to clap.

ладь|я́ (**-и́**; *gen pl* **-е́й**) *ж* (*ШАХМАТЫ*) rook, castle.

ЛАЗ (**-а**) *м сокр* = **Льво́вский авто́бусный заво́д**; (*автобус*) *bus manufactured at the Lvov bus factory*.

лаз (**-а**) *м* gap.

лазаре́т (**-а**) *м* (*ВОЕН*) field hospital.

ла́за|ть (**-ю**) *несов* = **ла́зить**.

лазе́|йка (**-йки**; *gen pl* **-ек**) *ж* gap; (*перен*: *в правилах*) loophole.

ла́зер (**-а**) *м* laser.

ла́зерный *прил* laser *опред*; **ла́зерный при́нтер** laser printer.

ла́з|ить (**-жу, -зишь**) *несов непepex* to climb; (*под стол, под кровать итп*) to crawl.

лазури́т (**-а**) *м* lapis lazuli.

лазу́рный *прил* azure, sky-blue.

лазу́р|ь (**-и**) *ж* azure.

ла|й (**-я**) *м* barking.

ла́й|ка (**-и**) *ж* husky; (*кожа*) kid.

ла́йковый *прил* kid *опред*.

ла́йнер (**-а**) *м* liner.

лак (**-а**) *м* (*для ногтей, для пола*) varnish; (*для волос*) lacquer; **покрыва́ть** (**покры́ть** *perf*) **что-н ла́ком** to varnish sth.

лака́|ть (**-ю**) *несов перех* to lap up.

лаке́|й (**-я**) *м* (*слуга*) footman (*мн* footmen); (*подхалим*) lackey.

лакиро́ванный *прил* (*шкатулка*) lacquered; (*туфли*) patent-leather.

лакир|ова́ть (**-у́ю**; *perf* **отлакирова́ть**) *несов перех* (*изделие*) to lacquer; (*кожу*) to patent.

лакиро́в|ка (**-и**) *ж* (*изделия*) lacquer.

ла́кмусов|ый *прил*: ~**ая бума́га** litmus paper.
ла́ковый *прил* (*изделия*) lacquered; (*раствор, краски*) lacquer *опред*; **ла́ковая ко́жа** patent leather.
ла́ком|иться (-**люсь, -ишься**; *perf* **пола́комиться**) *несов неперех* (+*instr*) to feast on.
ла́ком|ка (-**ки**; *gen pl* -**ок**) *м/ж* (*любящий вкусное*) gourmet; **она́ настоя́щая ~** (*сладкоежка*) she has a sweet tooth.
ла́комлюсь *несов см* **ла́комиться**.
ла́комок *сущ см* **ла́комка**.
ла́комый *прил* delicious; **ла́комый кусо́к** titbit (*BRIT*), tidbit (*US*).
лакони́зм (-**а**) *м* succinctness.
лакони́чно *нареч* laconically, succinctly.
лакони́чный *прил* (*речь*) laconic, succinct; (*формы здания, рисунок*) spare, austere.
лакто́з|а (-**ы**) *ж* lactose.
ла́м|а (-**ы**) *ж* (*ЗООЛ*) llama ♦ *м* (*РЕЛ*) lama.
Ла-Ма́нш (-**а**) *м* the (English) Channel.
ла́мп|а (-**ы**) *ж* (*осветительная, керосиновая*) lamp; (*ТЕХ*) tube; **ла́мпа дневно́го све́та** fluorescent light.
лампа́д|а (-**ы**) *ж* icon lamp.
лампа́с (-**а**) *м* (*обычно мн*) stripe (*down trouser leg*).
ла́мпоч|ка (-**ки**; *gen pl* -**ек**) *ж* lamp; (*для освещения*) light bulb; **ему́ всё до ~ки** (*разг*) he couldn't care less.
ланге́т (-**а**) *м* fillet steak.
ландша́фт (-**а**) *м* landscape.
ла́ндыш (-**а**) *м* lily of the valley.
ланоли́н (-**а**) *м* lanolin.
ланце́т (-**а**) *м* (*МЕД*) lancet.
лан|ь (-**и**) *ж* fallow deer.
Лао́с (-**а**) *м* Laos.
лао́сск|ий (-**ая, -ое, -ие**) *прил* Laotian.
ла́п|а (-**ы**) *ж* (*зверя*) paw; (*птицы*) foot; (*сосны, ёлки*) bough; (*якоря*) fluke; **попада́ть** (**попа́сть** *perf*) **кому́-н в ~ы** (*разг*) to fall into sb's clutches; **дава́ть** (**дать** *perf*) **кому́-н у** (*разг*) to give sb a backhander; **ходи́ть** (*impf*) **на за́дних ~х пе́ред кем-н** (*перен: разг*) to dance attendance on sb.
ла́п|оть (-**тя**; *nom pl* -**ти**, *gen pl* -**те́й**) *м* (*обычно мн*) bast shoe.
ла́поч|ка (-**ки**; *gen pl* -**ек**) *м/ж* (*разг*) dear, darling.
лапт|а́ (-**ы́**) *ж* lapta (*traditional Russian ball game*).
ла́птя *итп сущ см* **ла́поть**.
ла́пушк|а (-**и**) *ж* dear, darling.
лапш|а́ (-**и́**) *ж* noodles *мн*; (*суп*) noodle soup.
ларёк (-**ька́**) *м* stall.
ларе́ц (-**ца́**) *м* (*шкатулка*) casket.
ларинги́т (-**а**) *м* laryngitis.
лариноло́ги|я (-**и**) *ж* laryngology.
ларца́ *итп сущ см* **ларе́ц**.

лар|ь (-**я́**) *м* bin.
ларька́ *итп сущ см* **ларёк**.
ла́с|ка (-**ки**) *ж* tenderness; (*gen pl* -**ок**; *ЗООЛ*) weasel.
ласка́тельный *прил*: ~ **су́ффикс** (*ЛИНГ*) diminutive suffix (*denoting affection*).
ласка́ть (-**ю**) *несов перех* (*ребёнка, девушку*) to caress; (*собаку*) to pet; ~ (*impf*) **слух/взор** to be pleasing to the ear/eye
▶ **ласка́ться** (*perf* **приласка́ться**) *несов возв*: ~**ся к** +*dat* (*ребёнок*) to snuggle up to; (*кошка*) to rub up against; (*собака*) to fawn on.
ла́сков|ый (-, -**а, -о**) *прил* affectionate; (*перен: ветер, солнце итп*) gentle.
ла́сок *сущ см* **ла́ска**.
ласт (-**а**) *м* (*ЗООЛ, СПОРТ: обычно мн*) flipper.
ла́стик (-**а**) *м* (*разг*) rubber (*BRIT*), eraser.
ла́сточ|ка (-**ки**; *gen pl* -**ек**) *ж* swallow; **городска́я/берегова́я ~** house/sand martin.
лат (-**а**) *м* lat (*Latvian currency unit*).
лата́|ть (-**ю**; *perf* **залата́ть**) *несов перех* to patch.
латви́йск|ий (-**ая, -ое, -ие**) *прил* Latvian.
Ла́тви|я (-**и**) *ж* Latvia.
лати́нск|ий (-**ая, -ое, -ие**) *прил* Latin; ~ **язы́к** Latin.
ла́т|ка (-**ки**; *gen pl* -**ок**) *ж* (*разг*) patch.
лату́н|ь (-**и**) *ж* brass.
ла́т|ы (-) *мн* armour *ед* (*BRIT*), armor *ед* (*US*).
латы́н|ь (-**и**) *ж* Latin.
латы́ш (-**á**) *м* Latvian.
латы́ш|ка (-**ки**; *gen pl* -**ек**) *ж см* **латы́ш**.
латы́шск|ий (-**ая, -ое, -ие**) *прил* Latvian; ~ **язы́к** Latvian.
лауреа́т (-**а**) *м* winner (*of an award*).
лафа́ *как сказ* (*разг*): **нам здесь ~** we've got it easy here.
ла́цкан (-**а**) *м* lapel.
лачу́г|а (-**и**) *ж* hovel.
ла́ять (-**ю**; *perf* **пройа́ть**) *несов неперех* to bark.
лба *итп сущ см* **лоб**.
ЛГ *ж сокр* (= „Литерату́рная газе́та") "Literary Gazette".
лгать (**лгу, лжёшь** *etc* **лгут**; *perf* **солга́ть** *или* **налга́ть**) *несов неперех* to lie.
лгун (-**á**) *м* liar.
лгу́н|ья (-**ьи**; *gen pl* -**ий**) *ж см* **лгун**.
ЛДПР *ж сокр* = Либера́льно-демократи́ческая па́ртия Росси́и.
лебед|а́ (-**ы́**) *ж* (*БОТ*) orache.
лебедёнок (-**ёнка**; *nom pl* -**я́та**, *gen pl* -**я́т**) *м* cygnet.
лебеди́н|ый *прил* swan *опред*; (*перен: шея*) swanlike; (: *поступь*) graceful; ~**ая ста́я** flock of swans; **лебеди́ная пе́сня** swan song.
лебёд|ка (-**ки**; *gen pl* -**ок**) *ж* winch.
ле́бед|ь (-**я**; *gen pl* -**ей**) *м* swan.
лебедя́та *итп сущ см* **лебедёнок**.
лебези́ть (-**жу́, -зи́шь**) *несов неперех*: ~ (**пе́ред**

+*instr*) (*разг*) to fawn (on).
лебя́ж|**ий** (-ья, -ье, -ьи) *прил*: ~ **пух** swan's-down.
лев (**льва**) *м* lion; (*созвездие*): **Л~** Leo.
левко́й (-я) *м* (*бот*) stock.
левосторо́нн|**ий** (-яя, -ее, -ие) *прил* on the left; **в Великобрита́нии ~ее движе́ние** in Britain they drive on the left.
левш|**а́** (-и́; *gen pl* -е́й) *м/ж* left-handed person; **он/она́** ~ he/she is left-handed.
ле́в|**ый** *прил* left, left-hand; (*партия, взгляды*) left-wing; **~ая рабо́та** (*разг*) moonlighting.
лёг *итп сов см* **лечь**.
лега́в|**ый** (-ого; *decl like adj*) *м type of gun dog.*
лега́лен *прил см* **лега́льный**.
легализи́р|**овать** (-ую) (*не*)*сов перех* to legalize.
лега́ль|**ный** (-ен, -ьна, -ьно) *прил* legal.
леге́нд|**а** (-ы) *ж* legend; (*перен*) fairy story.
легенда́р|**ный** (-ен, -на, -но) *прил* legendary.
легио́н (-а) *м* legion.
леги́рованн|**ый** *прил*: **~ая сталь** steel alloy.
лёг|**кий** (-кая, -кое, -кие; -ок, -ка́, -ко́) *прил* (*нетяжёлый*) light; (*нетру́дный, несерьёзный*) easy; (*боль, насморк*) slight; (*фигура*) graceful; (*характер, человек*) easy-going; **у него́ сли́шком ~кое отноше́ние к жи́зни** he doesn't take life seriously enough; **у него́ ~кая рука́** he brings good luck; **он нашёл рабо́ту с мое́й ~кой руки́** he found work thanks to me; **он ~ок на подъём** (*разг*) he doesn't take much persuading; **~ок на поми́не!** talk of the devil!; **лёгкая атле́тика** athletics (*BRIT*), track-and-field (*US*); **лёгкая промы́шленность** light industry.
легко́ *нареч* easily; ~ **сказа́ть** (*разг*) easier said than done; **мне здесь** ~ I feel at ease here; **э́то** ~ it's easy.
легкоатле́т (-а) *м* athlete (*in track and field events*).
легкоатле́т|**ка** (-ки; *gen pl* -ок) *ж см* **легкоатле́т**.
легкове́р|**ный** (-ен, -на, -но) *прил* gullible, credulous.
легкове́с|**ный** (-ен, -на, -но) *прил* superficial.
легков|**о́й** *прил*: **~а́я маши́на**, **~ автомоби́ль** car, automobile (*US*).
легку́ш|**ка** (-ки; *gen pl* -ек) *ж* (*разг*) motor (*BRIT*), auto (*US*).
лёгк|**ое** (-ого; *decl like adj*) *ср* (*обычно мн*) lung.
легкомы́слен|**ный** (-, -на, -но) *прил* (*человек*) frivolous; (*поступок*) thoughtless; (*отношение*) frivolous, flippant.
легкомы́сли|**е** (-я) *ср* (*человека*) frivolity; (*поступка*) thoughtlessness.
легкопла́в|**кий** (-кая, -кое, -кие; -ок, -ка, -ко) *прил* fusible.
лёгкост|**ь** (-и) *ж* (*походки, веса*) lightness; (*задания*) simplicity, easiness; (*характера*) easy-going nature; **у него́ мно́го друзе́й благодаря́ ~и его́ хара́ктера** he has many friends thanks to his easy-going nature.

лёгок *прил см* **лёгкий**.
лёгочный *прил* pulmonary, lung *опред*; ~ **больно́й** patient with a pulmonary *или* lung condition.
ле́гче *сравн прил от* **лёгкий** ♦ *сравн нареч от* **легко́** ♦ *как сказ*: **больно́му сего́дня** ~ the patient is feeling better today.
лёд (**льда**; *loc sg* **льду**) *м* ice; ~ **тро́нулся** (*перен*) things are moving now.
леден|**е́ть** (-ю; *perf* **заледене́ть** *или* **оледене́ть**) *несов неперех* to freeze; (*человек, руки*) to be freezing; **он оледене́л от стра́ха** fear made his blood run cold.
ледене́ц (-ца́) *м* fruit drop.
леден|**и́ть** (*3sg* -и́т, *3pl* -я́т) *несов перех* to freeze; **у́жас ~и́т (его́) кровь** terror makes his blood run cold.
леденца́ *итп сущ см* **ледене́ц**.
леденя́щ|**ий** (-ая, -ее, -ие) *прил* (*ветер, вода*) icy; (*перен: ужас, страх*) chilling.
ле́ди *ж нескл* lady.
ледни́к (-а́) *м* glacier.
леднико́вый *прил* glacial.
ледо́вый *прил* ice *опред*.
ледоко́л (-а) *м* icebreaker.
ледору́б (-а) *м* ice axe.
ледохо́д (-а) *м breaking up and drifting of ice on rivers in spring.*
ледяно́й *прил* (*глыба, покров*) ice *опред*; (*ветер, вода, взгляд*) icy.
ле́ек *сущ см* **ле́йка**.
лежа́к (-а́) *м* lounger.
лежа́лый *прил* (*хлеб*) stale; (*товар*) old.
леж|**а́ть** (-у́, -и́шь) *несов неперех* (*человек, животное*) to lie; (*предмет, вещи: на столе́, на по́лке*) to be (lying); (: *в я́щике, в шкафу́ итп*) to be; ~ (*impf*) **в больни́це** to be in hospital; **на нём ~а́т забо́ты о семье́** he is responsible for looking after his family; (**у меня́**) **душа́ не ~и́т к э́той рабо́те** my heart's not in this work; (**у меня́**) **душа́ не ~и́т к нему́** I don't feel very well disposed towards him.
лежа́ч|**ий** (-ая, -ее, -ие) *прил* lying; ~ **больно́й** bedridden patient; **рабо́та – не бей ~его** (*разг*) it's a cushy job.
ле́жбищ|**е** (-а) *ср* rookery (*of seals etc*).
лежебо́к|**а** (-и) *м/ж* (*разг*) couch potato.
лез *итп несов см* **лезть**.
ле́зви|**е** (-я) *ср* blade.
лез|**ть** (-у, -ешь; *pt* -, -ла, -ло) *несов неперех* (*выпадать: волосы, шерсть*) to fall out; (*проникать куда-н*): ~ **в** +*acc* to climb in(to); ~ (*impf*) **на** +*acc* to climb (up); ~ (*impf*) **в карма́н** (*разг*) to reach into one's pocket; ~ (*impf*) **в чужи́е дела́** (*разг*) to poke one's nose into other people's business; ~ (*impf*) **в разгово́р** (*разг*) to butt into a conversation; ~ (*impf*) **кому́-н на глаза́** (*разг*) to hang around sb.
лей *несов см* **лить** ♦ (**ле́я**) *м* lay (*Moldavian currency unit*).
лейбори́ст (-а) *м* Labour party member.

лейбори́стск|ий (**-ая, -ое, -ие**) *прил* Labour.
ле́йк|а (**-йки**; *gen pl* **-ек**) *ж* watering can.
лейко́з (**-а**) *м* leukaemia (*BRIT*), leukemia (*US*).
лейкопла́стыр|ь (**-я**) *м* sticking plaster (*BRIT*), adhesive tape (*US*).
лейкоци́т (**-а**) *м* (*обычно мн*) leucocyte.
Ле́йпциг (**-а**) *м* Leipzig.
ле́йте *несов см* **лить**.
лейтена́нт (**-а**) *м* lieutenant.
лейтмоти́в (**-а**) *м* (*также перен*) leitmotif.
лека́л|о (**-а**) *ср* French curve.
лека́рственный *прил* medicinal; **лека́рственная фо́рма** medicine.
лека́рств|о (**-а**) *ср* medicine; **~ от** +*gen* medicine for; **~ от ка́шля** cough medicine; **принима́ть** (**приня́ть** *perf*)**/пропи́сывать** (**прописа́ть** *perf*) **~** to take/prescribe medicine.
ле́ксик|а (**-и**) *ж* vocabulary.
лексико́граф (**-а**) *м* lexicographer.
лексикографи́ческ|ий (**-ая, -ое, -ие**) *прил* lexicographical.
лексикогра́фи|я (**-и**) *ж* lexicography.
лексиколо́ги|я (**-и**) *ж* lexicology.
лексико́н (**-а**) *м* vocabulary.
ле́ктор (**-а**) *м* lecturer.
лекцио́нный *прил* lecture *опред*; **~ курс** course of lectures.
ле́кци|я (**-и**) *ж* lecture.
леле́|ять (**-ю**; *perf* **взлеле́ять**) *несов перех* (*также перен*) to cherish.
ле́мех (**-а**) *м* ploughshare (*BRIT*), plowshare (*US*).
лему́р (**-а**) *м* lemur.
лён (**льна**) *м* (*БОТ*) flax; (*ткань*) linen.
лени́в|ый (**-, -а, -о**) *прил* lazy.
Ленингра́д (**-а**) *м* Leningrad.
ленини́зм (**-а**) *м* Leninism.
лен|и́ться (**-ю́сь, -ишься**; *perf* **полени́ться**) *несов возв* to be lazy; **~** (**полени́ться** *perf*) +*infin* to be too lazy to do.
ле́нт|а (**-ы**) *ж* (*в косе, на шляпе*) ribbon; (*изоляционная, магнитная*) tape; (*фильм*) film.
ле́нточный *прил*: **~ червь** tapeworm; **~ транспортёр** conveyor belt.
лентя́ек *сущ см* **лентя́йка**.
лентя́|й (**-я**) *м* lazybones.
лентя́йк|а (**-йки**; *gen pl* **-ек**) *ж см* **лентя́й**.
лентя́йнича|ть (**-ю**) *несов неперех* (*разг*) to lounge about.
лен|ь (**-и**) *ж* laziness ◆ *как сказ*: **ему́ ~ учи́ться/рабо́тать** he can't be bothered studying/working; (**все**) **кому́ не ~** (*разг*) anyone who feels like it.
леопа́рд (**-а**) *м* leopard.
лепест|о́к (**-ка́**) *м* petal.
ле́пет (**-а**) *м* babble; **де́тский ~** (*перен*) drivel.
лепёшк|а (**-ки**; *gen pl* **-ек**) *ж* flat bread.
леп|и́ть (**-лю́, -ишь**; *perf* **вы́лепить**) *несов перех* (*из глины, из пластилина*) to model; (*perf* **слепи́ть**; *соты, гнёзда*) to build

леп|и́ться *несов возв* (*на деревьях, на склонах*) to cling.
ле́пк|а (**-и**) *ж* modelling (*BRIT*), modeling (*US*).
леплю́(сь) *несов см* **лепи́ть(ся)**.
лепно́й *прил* modelled (*BRIT*), modeled (*US*); (*потолок*) moulded (*BRIT*), molded (*US*).
ле́пт|а (**-ы**) *ж* contribution; **вноси́ть** (**внести́** *perf*) **свою́ ~у** (**во что-н**) to do one's bit (for sth); (*внести деньги*) to make a contribution (to sth).
лес (**-а**; *loc sg* **-у́**, *nom pl* **-а́**) *м* (*большой*) forest; (*небольшой*) wood ◆ *собир* (*материал*) timber (*BRIT*), lumber (*US*); **кто в ~, кто по дрова́** at sixes and sevens; *см также* **леса́**.
лес|а́ (**-о́в**) *мн* (*СТРОИТ*) scaffolding *ед*.
лесбия́н|ка (**-ки**; *gen pl* **-ок**) *ж* lesbian.
леси́ст|ый (**-, -а, -о**) *прил* wooded.
ле́ск|а (**-и**) *ж* fishing line.
лесни́к (**-а́**) *м* forester.
лесни́честв|о (**-а**) *ср* (*участок леса*) area of forest; (*учреждение*) ≈ forestry commission.
лесни́ч|ий (**-его**; *decl like adj*) *м* forest ranger.
лесно́й *прил* (*см сущ*) forest *опред*; woodland *опред*.
лесово́дств|о (**-а**) *ср* forestry.
лесозагото́в|ка (**-ки**; *gen pl* **-ок**) *ж* (*обычно мн*) logging *ед*.
лесозащи́тн|ый *прил*: **~ая зо́на** shelter belt (*of trees*).
лесоматериа́л (**-а**) *м* (*обычно мн*) timber *только ед* (*BRIT*), lumber *только ед* (*US*).
лесонасажде́ни|е (**-я**) *ср* (*искусственный лес*) plantation; (*разведение леса*) afforestation.
лесопа́рк (**-а**) *м* woodland park.
лесопи́л|ка (**-и**) *ж* (*разг*) sawmill.
лесопромы́шленност|ь (**-и**) *ж сокр* (= **лесна́я промы́шленность**) timber (*BRIT*) *или* lumber (*US*) industry.
лесопромы́шленный *прил* timber-industry *опред* (*BRIT*), lumber-industry *опред* (*US*).
лесоразрабо́т|ки (**-ок**) *мн* timber (*BRIT*) *или* lumber (*US*) processing.
лесору́б (**-а**) *м* lumberjack.
лесосе́к|а (**-и**) *ж* felling area.
лесоспла́в (**-а**) *м* timber rafting.
лесосте́п|ь (**-и**) *ж* forest-steppe (*area in which forest and steppe are mixed*).
ле́стен *прил см* **ле́стный**.
ле́стниц|а (**-ы**) *ж* (*лестничная клетка*) staircase; (*ступени*) stairs *мн*; (*переносная*) ladder; (*стремянка*) stepladder; **служе́бная ~** career ladder.
ле́стничн|ый *прил*: **~ая площа́дка** landing; **~ пролёт** stairway; **~ая кле́тка** stairwell.
ле́стн|ый (**-ен, -на, -но**) *прил* flattering.
лест|ь (**-и**) *ж* flattery.
лёт (**-а**) *м*: **на лету́** in flight; (*перен: понимать, усваивать*) very quickly; **он по́нял всё с ~у** (*разг*) he understood everything in a flash.

летá (лет) *мн см* **год**; (*возраст*): **скóлько Вам лет?** how old are you?; **емý 16 лет** he is 16 (years old); **он в ~х** he is getting on; **он однѝх лет со мнóй** he is the same age as me.

летáл|ьный (-ен, -ьна, -ьно) *прил* fatal; ~**ьная дóза** lethal dose.

летаргѝческий (-ая, -ое, -ие) *прил* lethargic.

летáтельный *прил* flying *опред*.

летá|ть (-ю) *несов неперех* to fly.

лет|éть (-чý, -тѝшь) *несов неперех* to fly; (*перен: мчаться*) to fly, rush; (*perf* **полетéть**; *разг*): ~ **с** +*gen* (*со стула*) to fall off; (*с лестницы*) to fall down; **врéмя ~тѝт** time flies; **все нáши плáны полетéли** (*разг*) all our plans were dashed.

лéтн|ий (-яя, -ее, -ие) *прил* summer *опред*.

лётн|ый *прил*: ~**ая погóда** good weather for flying; **лётное пóле** airfield; **лётная шкóла** flying school.

лéт|о (-а) *ср* summer; **скóлько лет, скóлько зим!** it's been ages!

летопѝс|ец (-ца) *м* chronicler.

лéтопис|ь (-и) *ж* chronicle.

летосчислéни|е (-я) *ср* calendar.

летýчек *сущ см* **летýчка**.

летýч|ий (-ая, -ее, -ие) *прил* (*газ, масло*) volatile; (*семена*) winged; (*песок*) shifting; (*перен: собрание, разговор*) brief; **летýчая мышь** bat.

летýчк|а (-ки; *gen pl* -ек) *ж* (*разг: собрание*) brief meeting; (: *листок*) leaflet.

лётчик (-а) *м* pilot; ~**-испытáтель** test pilot; ~**-истребѝтель** fighter pilot.

лётчиц|а (-ы) *ж см* **лётчик**.

лéчащ|ий (-ая, -ее, -ие) *прил*: ~ **врач** ≈ consultant-in-charge (*BRIT*), ≈ attending physician (*US*).

лечéбниц|а (-ы) *ж* clinic.

лечéбный *прил* (*учреждение*) medical; (*свойства, трава*) medicinal; (*ванна*) medicated; **у негó богáтая ~ая прáктика** he has extensive clinical experience; ~**ая гимнáстика** therapeutic exercise; **лечéбное срéдство** medication.

лечéни|е (-я) *ср* (*раненных, детей*) treatment; (*от простуды, от туберкулёза итп*) cure.

леч|ѝть (-ý, -ишь) *несов* от **вы́лечить** ♦ *перех* to treat; (*больного*): ~ **когó-н от** +*gen* to treat sb for

▶ **лечѝться** *несов* от **вы́лечиться** ♦ *возв* to undergo treatment.

лечý *несов см* **летéть**.

лечь (ля́гу, ля́жешь *итп*, ля́гут; *pt* лёг, леглá, леглó, *imper* ля́г(те), *impf* **ложѝться**) *сов неперех* (*на землю, на диван итп*) to lie down; (*пойти спать*) to go to bed; (*снег*) to fall; (*перен*): ~ **на** +*acc* (*ответственность, заботы*) to fall on; **ложѝться** (~ *perf*) **в больнѝцу** to be in hospital; **ложѝться** (~ *perf*) **в дрейф** to drift.

лéш|ий (-его; *decl like adj*) *м* wood goblin.

лещ (-á) *м* bream.

лженаýк|а (-и) *ж* pseudoscience.

лжесвидéтель (-я) *м* perjurer.

лжесвидéтельниц|а (-ы) *ж см* **лжесвидéтель**.

лжесвидéтельств|о (-а) *ср* perjury.

лжесвидéтельств|овать (-ую) *несов неперех* to commit perjury.

лжец (-á) *м* liar.

лжи *итп сущ см* **ложь**.

лжѝвост|ь (-и) *ж* falseness.

лжѝв|ый (-, -а, -о) *прил* (*человек*) deceitful; (*улыбка, заверения*) false.

ли *част* (*в вопросе*): **знáешь ~ ты, что ...** do you know that ...; (*в косвенном вопросе*): **спросѝ, смóжет ~ он нам помóчь** ask if he can help us ♦ *союз*: **придёт ~, не придёт, не вáжно** it's not important if he comes or not; **онá красѝва, не так ~?** she's beautiful, isn't she?; **онѝ бы́ли прáвы, не так ~?** they were right, weren't they?

лиáн|а (-ы) *ж* (*БОТ: растение*) liana.

либерáл (-а) *м* Liberal; (*о терпимом человеке*) liberal.

либерáлен *прил см* **либерáльный**.

либерализáци|я (-и) *ж* liberalization.

либералѝзм (-а) *м* liberalism; (*с бездельниками, с подчинёнными итп*) tolerance.

либерáльнича|ть (-ю) *несов неперех*: ~ **с** +*instr* (*с подчинёнными*) to fraternize with; (*с бездельниками*) to connive at.

либерáльный (-ен, -ьна, -ьно) *прил* liberal; (*no short form*; *партия*) Liberal.

лѝбо *союз* (*или*) or; ~ **я**, ~ **он** it's either me or him.

либреттѝст (-а) *м* librettist.

либрéтто *ср нескл* libretto.

Ливáн (-а) *м* (the) Lebanon.

ливáнск|ий (-ая, -ое, -ие) *прил* Lebanese.

лѝв|ень (-ня) *м* (*дождь*) downpour; (*перен: огня, свинца*) shower.

лѝвер (-а) *м* offal.

лѝверн|ый *прил*: ~**ая колбасá** *sausage made with offal*.

Ливерпýл|ь (-я) *м* Liverpool.

лѝвнев|ый *прил*: ~ **дождь** downpour; ~**ые вóды** rainwater.

лѝвня *итп сущ см* **лѝвень**.

ливрé|я (-и) *ж* livery.

лѝг|а (-и) *ж* (*ПОЛИТ, СПОРТ*) league.

лигатýр|а (-ы) *ж* (*МЕД, ЛИНГ*) ligature.

лѝдер (-а) *м* leader.

лѝдерств|о (-а) *ср* leadership.

лидѝр|овать (-ую) *несов неперех* to be in the lead, lead.

лиз|áть (-жý, -жешь) *несов перех* (*тарелку, мороженое*) to lick; (*подлеж: пламя, волны*) to lap.

лѝзинг (-а) *м* leasing.

лизн|ýть (-ý, -ёшь) *сов перех* to lick.

лик (-а) *м* countenance.

ликбéз (-а) *м сокр* (*ИСТ*: = **ликвидáция**

безгра́мотности) campaign against illiteracy; (*перен: обучение элементарному*) basic teaching.

ликвида́тор (**-а**) *м* (*пожара, последствий аварии*) relief worker; (*комм*) liquidator.

ликвида́ци|я (**-и**) *ж* (*также экон*) liquidation; (*оружия*) destruction; **доброво́льная ~** (*ЭКОН*) voluntary liquidation.

ликвиди́р|овать (**-ую**) (*не*)*сов перех* (*оружие*) to destroy; (*фирму, дела*) to liquidate

▸ **ликвиди́роваться** (*не*)*сов возв* (*ЭКОН: фирма, трест итп*) to be liquidated.

ликви́дност|ь (**-и**) *ж* liquidity.

ликви́дн|ый *прил*: **~ые акти́вы** *или* **сре́дства** liquid assets.

ликви́ды (**-ов**) *мн* liquid assets *мн*.

ликёр (**-а**) *м* liqueur.

ликёро-во́дочный *прил*: **~ заво́д** distillery.

ликова́ни|е (**-я**) *ср* rejoicing.

лик|ова́ть (**-ую**) *несов неперех* to be elated.

лилипу́т (**-а**) *м* midget.

лилипу́т|ка (**-ки**; *gen pl* **-ок**) *ж см* **лилипу́т**.

ли́ли|я (**-и**) *ж* lily.

лило́вый *прил* purple.

лима́н (**-а**) *м* mud flats *мн*.

лими́т (**-а**) *м* (*на электроэнергию, на бензин*) quota; (*цен*) limit.

лимити́р|овать (**-ую**) (*не*)*сов перех* (*потребление, импорт*) to limit; (*цены*) to cap.

лими́тчик (**-а**) *м* (*разг*) *person who holds a temporary residence permit issued in connection with work.*

лимо́н (**-а**) *м* (*дерево*) lemon tree; (*плод*) lemon; **он как вы́жатый ~** he's completely washed out.

лимона́д (**-а**) *м* lemonade; (*разг: любой газированный напиток*) fizzy drink.

лимо́нный *прил* lemon; **лимо́нная кислота́** citric acid.

лимузи́н (**-а**) *м* limousine.

лимфати́ческ|ий (**-ая, -ое, -ие**) *прил* lymphatic.

лингафо́нный *прил*: **~ кабине́т** language laboratory.

лингви́ст (**-а**) *м* linguist.

лингви́стик|а (**-и**) *ж* linguistics.

лингвисти́ческ|ий (**-ая, -ое, -ие**) *прил* linguistic.

лине́й|ка (**-йки**; *gen pl* **-ек**) *ж* (*линия*) line; (*инструмент*) ruler; (*шеренга*) ≈ assembly; **тетра́дь в ~йку** lined notebook.

лине́йн|ый *прил* (*расположение, построение*) linear; **~ солда́т** soldier of the line; **~ые ме́ры** linear measures; **лине́йные войска́** regular forces; **лине́йный кре́йсер** battle cruiser.

ли́нз|а (**-ы**) *ж* lens.

ли́ни|я (**-и**) *ж* line; (*перен: партийная, профсоюзная*) policy, line; **по ~и** +*gen* in the line of; **вести́** (*impf*) *или* **проводи́ть** (*impf*) **~ю**

на +*acc* to pursue a policy of; **проводи́ть** (**провести́** *perf*) **~ю** to draw a line; **вести́** (*impf*) *или* **гнуть** (*impf*) **свою́ ~ю** (*разг*) to have one's own way; **желе́знодоро́жная ~** railway (*BRIT*) *или* railroad (*US*) track; **возду́шная ~** airway; **морска́я ~** sea route; **трамва́йная ~** tramway; **ли́ния фро́нта** (*ВОЕН*) front line; **ли́ния воро́т** goal line.

линко́р (**-а**) *м сокр* (= *лине́йный кора́бль*) destroyer.

лино́ванный *прил* lined, ruled.

лин|ова́ть (**-у́ю**; *perf* **разлинова́ть**) *несов перех* to rule.

лино́леум (**-а**) *м* linoleum.

линч|ева́ть (**-у́ю**) (*не*)*сов перех* to lynch.

линя́лый *прил* discoloured (*BRIT*), discolored (*US*).

линя́|ть (*3sg* **-ет**, *3pl* **-ют**, *perf* **полиня́ть**) *несов неперех* to run (*colour*); (*perf* **облиня́ть**; *животные*) to moult (*BRIT*), molt (*US*).

Лио́н (**-а**) *м* Lyon.

ли́п|а (**-ы**) *ж* (*дерево*) lime (tree); (*разг: фальшивка*) fake.

ли́п|кий (**-кая, -кое, -кие; -ок, -ка́, -ко**) *прил* sticky.

ли́п|нуть (**-ну, -нешь**; *pt* **-, -ла, -ло**, *perf* **прили́пнуть**) *несов неперех* (*грязь, тесто*) to stick; (*перен: человек*) to cling.

ли́повый *прил* (*цвет, лист*) lime; (*из липы*) lime-blossom *опред*; (*разг: фальшивый*) forged.

ли́пок *прил см* **ли́пкий**.

липу́ч|ка (**-ки**; *gen pl* **-ек**) *ж* (*разг: липкая лента*) sticky tape; (: *застёжка*) Velcro® fastening.

ли́р|а (**-ы**) *ж* (*муз*) lyre; (*денежная единица*) lira.

лири́зм (**-а**) *м* lyricism.

ли́рик (**-а**) *м* lyric poet.

ли́рик|а (**-и**) *ж* lyric poetry.

лири́чен *прил см* **лири́чный**.

лири́ческ|ий (**-ая, -ое, -ие**) *прил* lyrical.

лири́чн|ый (**-ен, -на, -но**) *прил* lyrical.

лис (**-а**) *м* (male) fox, dog fox.

лис|а́ (**-ы́**; *nom pl* **-ы**) *ж* fox; (*перен: хитрый человек*) sly fox.

лисёнок (**-ёнка**; *nom pl* **-я́та**, *gen pl* **-я́т**) *м* fox cub.

ли́с|ий (**-ья, -ье, -ьи**) *прил* (*след, нора*) fox's; (*шуба, воротник, горжетка*) fox-fur.

лиси́ц|а (**-ы**) *ж* vixen.

лиси́ч|ка (**-ки**; *gen pl* **-ек**) *ж уменьш от* **лиса́**; (*гриб*) chanterelle.

лист (**-а́**; *nom pl* **-ья**) *м* (*растения, дерева*) leaf; (*nom pl* **-ы́**; *бумаги, железа*) sheet; **исполни́тельный ~** writ of execution; **опро́сный ~** questionnaire.

листа́|ть (**-ю**) *несов перех* (*страницы*) to turn; **~** (*impf*) **кни́гу** to leaf through a book.

листв|а́ (**-ы́**) *ж собир* foliage, leaves *мн*.

ли́ственниц|а (-ы) ж larch.
ли́ственный прил deciduous.
листка́ итп сущ см **листо́к**.
листо́в|ка (-ки; gen pl -ок) ж leaflet.
листово́й прил (сталь, железо) sheet опред; (табак) leaf опред.
листо́вок сущ см **листо́вка**.
лист|о́к (-ка́) м (бумаги) sheet; (бланк: контрольный, техосмотра) certificate; **листо́к нетрудоспосо́бности** disability certificate.
листопа́д (-а) м fall of leaves.
ли́стья итп сущ см **лист**.
лися́та итп сущ см **лисёнок**.
лит (-а) м lit (Lithuanian currency unit).
лита́вр|ы (-) мн kettledrum ед; **бить** (impf) **в ~** (перен: торжествовать) to sound the trumpets.
Литв|а́ (-ы́) ж Lithuania.
лите́йный прил: **~ цех** foundry.
лите́йщик (-а) м foundry worker.
ли́тер|а (-ы) ж (типог) type.
литера́тор (-а) м literary man.
литерату́р|а (-ы) ж literature; (также: худо́жественная **~**) fiction.
литерату́рный прил literary; **литерату́рный язы́к** literary language.
литературове́д (-а) м literary critic.
литературове́дени|е (-я) ср literary criticism.
литературове́дческ|ий (-ая, -ое, -ие) прил literary.
ли́терный прил (с цифрой) lettered; **~ набо́р** typesetting.
ли́ти|й (-я) м lithium.
лито́в|ец (-ца) м Lithuanian.
лито́в|ка (-ки; gen pl -ок) ж см **лито́вец**.
лито́вск|ий (-ая, -ое, -ие) прил Lithuanian; **~ язы́к** Lithuanian.
лито́вца итп сущ см **лито́вец**.
литографи́ческ|ий (-ая, -ое, -ие) прил lithographic.
литогра́фи|я (-и) ж (искусство) lithograph; (типог) lithography.
лито́й прил (ТЕХ) moulded (BRIT), molded (US), cast; **лито́е изде́лие** cast.
литр (-а) м litre (BRIT), liter (US).
литро́вый прил (бутылка, фляга итп) (one-)litre (BRIT), (one-)liter (US).
литурги́|я (-и) ж liturgy.
лить (лью, льёшь; pt лил, лила́, ли́ло) несов перех (воду) to pour; (слёзы) to shed; (ТЕХ: детали, изделия) to cast, mould (BRIT), mold (US) ♦ неперех (вода, дождь) to pour; **дождь льёт как из ведра́** it's pouring (down)
► **ли́ться** несов возв (вода) to pour; (перен: звуки) to float; (: свет) to flood.
лить|ё (-я́) ср (действие: деталей) casting, moulding (BRIT), molding (US) ♦ собир (литые изделия) casts мн.
лиф (-а) м bodice.
лифт (-а) м lift.
лифтёр (-а) м lift operator.
лифтёрш|а (-и) ж см **лифтёр**.

ли́фчик (-а) м bra.
лиха́ч (-а́) м (разг) reckless driver.
лиха́честв|о (-а) ср (при вождении) reckless driving; (в поведении) recklessness.
лихв|а́ (-ы́) ж: **он отплати́л мне с ~о́й за мою́ доброту́** he more than repaid me for my kindness; **тебе́ вре́мени/де́нег хва́тит с ~о́й** you've got more than enough time/money.
ли́х|о (-а) ср: **не помина́й(те) ~м** (разг) remember me kindly.
лих|о́й (-, -а́, -о) прил (наездник) dashing; (скакун) swift; (пора, враг) evil; **~а́ беда́ нача́ло** the first step is the hardest.
лихора́дить (3sg -ит) несов безл: **меня́ ~ит** I feel feverish; **эконо́мику ~ит** the economy is ailing.
лихора́д|ка (-и) ж (МЕД, также перен) fever; (: на губах) cold sore; **золота́я ~** gold fever.
лихора́доч|ный (-ен, -на, -но) прил (также перен) feverish.
Лихтенште́йн (-а) м Liechtenstein.
лицев|о́й прил (нерв) facial; **~а́я сторона́ мате́рии** the right side of the material; **лицево́й счёт** personal account.
лицезре́|ть (-ю, -ишь) несов перех to behold.
лице́йст (-а) м lycée pupil, ≈ secondary school pupil.
лиц|е́й (-я) м lycée, ≈ secondary school.
лицеме́р (-а) м hypocrite.
лицеме́рен прил см **лицеме́рный**.
лицеме́ри|е (-я) ср hypocrisy.
лицеме́р|ить (-ю, -ишь) несов неперех to be hypocritical или a hypocrite.
лицеме́р|ный (-ен, -на, -но) прил hypocritical.
лицензи́ровани|е (-я) ср licensing.
лице́нзи|я (-и) ж licence (BRIT), license (US).
лиц|о́ (-а́; nom pl -а) ср face; (перен: индивидуальность) image; (ткани итп) right side; (ЛИНГ) person; **от ~а́** +gen in the name of, on behalf of; **пе́ред ~м** +gen in the face of; **э́та блу́за тебе́ к ~у́** that blouse suits you; **тебе́ не к ~у́ безде́льничать** shame on you for being so lazy; **знать** (impf) **кого́-н в ~** to know sb's face; **на ней ~ца́ нет** she looks dreadful; **они́ уда́рили в грязь ~м** they didn't disgrace themselves; **стира́ть** (**стере́ть** perf) **с ~ца́ земли́** to wipe from или off the face of the earth; **пе́рвое/тре́тье ~** (ЛИНГ) first/third person; **показа́ть** (perf) **това́р ~м** to show sth to advantage; **~м к лицу́** face to face; **официа́льное ~** official; **физи́ческое ~** (ЮР) natural person, individual.
личи́н|а (-ы) ж mask; **под ~ой** +gen under the guise of.
личи́н|ка (-ки; gen pl -ок) ж maggot.
ли́чно нареч (знать) personally; (встретить) in person; **~ я ...** (разг) as for me ...; **~ мне всё равно́** (разг) personally, I don't care; **он всё проверя́ет ~** he checks everything personally или himself.
ли́чност|ь (-и) ж (выдающаяся, загадочная)

individual; (*обычно мн: обидные замечания*)
personal remark; **устана́вливать (установи́ть**
perf) **чью-н ~** to establish sb's identity.
ли́чный *прил* (*персона́льный*) personal;
(*частный*) private; **ли́чная ссу́да** (*КОММ*)
personal loan; **ли́чное де́ло** personal records;
ли́чный соста́в staff.
лиша́й (**-я́**) *м* herpes.
лиша́йник (**-а**) *м* lichen.
лиша́ть (**-ю**) *несов от* **лиши́ть**.
лишён (**-á, -ó, -ы́**) *как сказ*: **он ~ та́кта/чу́вства
ю́мора** he is devoid of tact/a sense of humour;
э́то не лишено́ основа́ния/смы́сла this is not
totally lacking in reason/sense.
лише́ние (**-я**) *ср* (*прав, привилегий*)
deprivation; (*большое, горькое*) loss; (*обычно
мн: нужда*) privation; **~ свобо́ды**
imprisonment; **терпе́ть** (*impf*) **~я** to suffer
privation; **~ пра́ва со́бственности** (*ЮР*)
foreclosure.
лиши́ть (**-у́, -и́шь;** *impf* **лиша́ть**) *сов перех*: **~
кого́-н/что-н** +*gen* (*отнять: прав, привилегий*)
to deprive sb/sth of; (*покоя, счастья*) to rob
sb/sth of; **лиша́ть** (**~** *perf*) **кого́-н насле́дства** to
disinherit sb; **лиша́ть** (**~** *perf*) **жи́зни кого́-н** to
take sb's life; **лиша́ть** (**~** *perf*) **кого́-н сло́ва** to
deny sb the right to speak.
ли́шний (**-яя, -ее, -ие**) *прил* (*вес*) extra; (*деньги,
билет*) spare; (*расходы, вещи*) unnecessary; **~
раз** once again *или* more; **не ~ее** *или* **~е** +*infin*
... it would not be a bad idea to ...; **сказа́ть** (*perf*)
~ее to say the wrong thing; **три килогра́мма с
~им** over three kilogrammes; **тре́тий ~** three's
a crowd.
лишь *част* (*только*) only ◆ *союз* (*как только*)
as soon as; **~ бы она́ согласи́лась!** if only she
would agree!; **ему́ не ва́жно что де́лать, ~ бы
не рабо́тать** he doesn't care what he does, as
long as he doesn't have to work; **ему́ ~ бы уйти́**
he just wants to leave.
лоб (**лба;** *loc sg* **лбу**) *м* forehead; **сказа́ть** (*perf*)
кому́-н в ~ (*перен*) to tell sb straight; **у него́ на
лбу напи́сано, что он врёт** (*разг*) it's written
all over his face that he's lying.
ло́бби *ср нескл* lobby.
лобби́ст (**-а**) *м* lobbyist.
ло́бзик (**-а**) *м* fret saw.
ло́бный *прил* (*АНАТ*) frontal.
лобово́й *прил* frontal; **лобово́е стекло́**
windscreen (*BRIT*), windshield (*US*).
лоботря́с (**-а**) *м* (*разг*) lazybones.
лов (**-а**) *м* catching.
лове́ц (**-ца́**) *м* catcher; **~ же́мчуга** pearl diver.
лови́ть (**-лю́, -ишь;** *perf* **пойма́ть**) *несов перех*
to catch; (*случай, момент*) to seize; **~** (*impf*)
ры́бу to fish; **~** (*impf*) **кого́-н на лжи** to catch sb
out; **пойма́ть** (*perf*) **кого́-н на сло́ве** to take sb at
their word; **~** (**пойма́ть** *perf*) **на себе́ чей-н**

взгляд to catch sb's eye; **~** (**пойма́ть** *perf*) **себя́
на мы́сли, что ...** to catch o.s. thinking that ....
ловка́ч (**-а́**) *м* (*разг*) dodgy character.
ло́вкий (**-кая, -кое, -кие; -ок, -ка́, -ко**) *прил*
(*человек*) agile; (*прыжок, движение*) nimble;
(*удар*) swift; (*разг: торговец*) sharp.
ло́вко *нареч* (*прыгнуть*) nimbly; (*придумать*)
smartly; (*придумано, сделано*) smartly ◆ *как
сказ* that's smart.
ловлю́ *несов см* **лови́ть**.
ло́вля (**-и**) *ж* (*действие*) catching; **ры́бная ~**
fishing.
ло́вок *прил см* **ло́вкий**.
лову́шка (**-ки;** *gen pl* **-ек**) *ж* (*также перен*) trap.
ловца́ *итп сущ см* **лове́ц**.
логари́фм (**-а**) *м* logarithm.
логарифми́ческий (**-ая, -ое, -ие**) *прил*: **~ая
лине́йка** slide rule.
ло́гика (**-и**) *ж* logic.
логи́чен *прил см* **логи́чный**.
логи́ческий (**-ая, -ое, -ие**) *прил* logical.
логи́чный (**-ен, -на, -но**) *прил* logical.
ло́говище (**-а**) *ср* (*также перен*) den, lair.
ло́гово (**-а**) *ср* = **ло́говище**.
ло́джия (**-и**) *ж* recess balcony.
ло́дка (**-ки;** *gen pl* **-ок**) *ж* boat; **подво́дная ~**
submarine.
ло́дочка (**-ки;** *gen pl* **-ек**) *ж уменьш от* **ло́дка**;
(*обычно мн: открытые туфли*) court shoe.
ло́дочный *прил* (*вёсла*) boat's; **ло́дочная
ста́нция** boat-hire place.
лоды́жка (**-ки;** *gen pl* **-ек**) *ж* ankle.
ло́дырничать (**-ю**) *несов неперех* (*разг*) to
idle.
ло́дырь (**-я**) *м* (*разг*) idler.
ло́жа (**-и**) *ж* (*в театре, в зале*) box;
(*массонская*) lodge; **ло́жа пре́ссы** press gallery.
ложби́на (**-ы**) *ж* dip (*in the ground*).
ло́же (**-а**) *ср* bed.
ло́жек *сущ см* **ло́жка**.
ло́жен *прил см* **ло́жный**.
ложи́ться (**-у́сь, -и́шься**) *несов от* **лечь**.
ло́жка (**-ки;** *gen pl* **-ек**) *ж* spoon.
ло́жный (**-ен, -на, -но**) *прил* false; (*вывод*)
wrong; **представля́ть** (**предста́вить** *perf*) **что-н
в ~ом све́те** to show sth in a false light;
ло́жные показа́ния false evidence; **ло́жная
трево́га** false alarm.
ложь (**лжи;** *instr sg* **ло́жью**) *ж* lie.
лоза́ (**-ы́;** *nom pl* **-ы**) *ж* (*ивы итп*) cane;
(*винограда*) vine.
ло́зунг (**-а**) *м* (*призыв*) slogan; (*плакат*) banner.
лока́лен *прил см* **лока́льный**.
локализа́ция (**-и**) *ж* localization.
локализова́ть (**-у́ю**) (*не*)*сов перех* to localize.
лока́льный (**-ен, -ьна, -ьно**) *прил* local.
лока́тор (**-а**) *м*: **опти́ческий ~** radar; **звуково́й
~** sonar.

локомоти́в (**-а**) *м* locomotive.
ло́кон (**-а**) *м* singlet.
ло́к|оть (**-тя**; *gen pl* **-те́й**, *dat pl* **-тя́м**) *м* elbow; **куса́ть** (*impf*) **~ти** (*разг*) to kick o.s.; **чу́вство ~тя** team spirit.
ло́ктя *итп сущ см* **ло́коть**.
лом (**-а**) *м* crowbar ◆ *собир* (*для перерабо́тки*) scrap; **металли́ческий ~** scrap metal.
ло́ма|ный *прил* broken; **~ая ли́ния** zigzag.
лома́ть (**-ю**; *perf* **слома́ть** *или* **разлома́ть**) *несов перех* (*разделя́ть на куски́*) to break; (*perf* **слома́ть** *или* **полома́ть**; *приводи́ть в него́дность*) to break; (*perf* **полома́ть**; *устои, тради́ции*) to challenge; (*пла́ны*) to frustrate; **~** (*impf*) **го́лову над чем-то** to rack one's brains over sth; **~** (*impf*) **привы́чки** to force o.s. to change one's habits; **жизнь слома́ла его́** life dealt him a cruel blow
▸ **лома́ться** (*perf* **полома́ться** *или* **слома́ться**) *несов возв* to break; (*no perf*; *перен: обы́чаи, усто́и*) to be challenged; (: *челове́к*) to show off; (: *заставля́ть себя́ проси́ть*) to be fussy.
ломба́рд (**-а**) *м* pawnshop; **закла́дывать** (**заложи́ть** *perf*) **что-н в ~** to pawn sth.
ломба́рдный *прил* pawn *опред*.
лом|и́ть (**-лю́**, **-ишь**) *несов безл*: **у меня́ ло́мит ко́сти** my bones are aching; **наро́д ло́мит туда́** (*разг*) the people are flocking there
▸ **ломи́ться** *несов возв* (*ве́тви, дере́вья*) to groan; (*разг: идти́ наси́льно*) to pour in; **стол ~и́лся от еды́** (*перен*) the table groaned under the food.
ло́мк|а (**-и**) *ж* breaking.
ло́мкий (**-кая**, **-кое**, **-кие**; **-ок**, **-ка́**, **-ко**) *прил* (*хру́пкий: стекло́*) fragile; (: *лёд*) brittle.
ломлю́(сь) *несов см* **ломи́ть(ся)**.
ломово́й *прил*: **~а́я ло́шадь** carthorse; (*перен: разг*) dogsbody.
ло́мок *прил см* **ло́мкий**.
ломо́т|а (**-ы**) *ж* ache.
ломо́ть (**-тя**) *м* slice.
ло́мтик (**-а**) *м* = **ломо́ть**.
ломтя́ *итп сущ см* **ломо́ть**.
Ло́ндон (**-а**) *м* London.
ло́ндон|ец (**-ца**) *м* Londoner.
ло́ндон|ка (**-ки**; *gen pl* **-ок**) *ж см* **ло́ндонец**.
ло́ндонца *итп сущ см* **ло́ндонец**.
ло́н|о (**-а**) *ср* (*же́нщины*) bosom; (*перен*): **на ~е приро́ды** in the open air.
ло́пасть (**-и**; *gen pl* **-е́й**) *ж* (*также* тех) blade.
лопа́т|а (**-ы**) *ж* spade.
лопа́т|ка (**-ки**; *gen pl* **-ок**) *ж уменьш от* **лопа́та**; (АНАТ) shoulder blade; **класть** (**положи́ть** *perf*) **кого́-н на о́бе ~ки** (*перен*) to beat sb hands down.
ло́па|ть (**-ю**; *perf* **сло́пать**) *несов перех* (*разг*) to gobble (up).
ло́па|ться (**-юсь**) *сов от* **ло́пнуть**.
ло́пну|ть (**-ну**, **-нешь**; *perf* **ло́пать**) *сов неперех* (*разрыва́ться: шар*) to burst; (*стекло́*) to shatter; (*верёвка, струна́*) to snap; (*разг:*

банк, предприя́тие*) to go bust; **у меня́ терпе́ние ~уло (*разг*) I've run out of patience.
лопу́х (**-а́**) *м* burdock; (*перен: разг: проста́к*) simpleton.
ЛОР (**-а**) *м сокр* (= *оторинолари́нго́логия*) ORL (= *otorhinolaryngology*), ENT (= *ear-nose-throat*).
лорд (**-а**) *м* lord.
лорне́т (**-а**) *ж* lorgnette.
Лос-А́нджелес (**-а**) *м* Los Angeles.
лоси́н|а (**-ы**) *ж* (*ко́жа ло́ся*) elkskin; (*мя́со ло́ся*) elk (meat); *см та́кже* **лоси́ны**.
лоси́ны (**-**) *мн* leggings *мн*.
лоси́х|а (**-и**) *ж* female elk *или* moose (*мн* moose).
лоск (**-а**) *м* (*гля́нец*) shine; (*перен: в до́ме*) spotlessness; (: *в оде́жде*) flair; **наводи́ть** (**навести́** *perf*) **~ на что-н** to give sth a polish.
лоску́т (**-а́**) *м* (*мате́рии, ко́жи*) scrap.
лоску́тный *прил*: **~ое одея́ло** patchwork quilt.
лосн|и́ться (**-ю́сь**, **-и́шься**) *несов возв* (*от жи́ра, от кре́ма*) to shine.
лососёвый *прил* salmon.
лососи́н|а (**-ы**) *ж* salmon (*meat*).
лосо́с|ь (**-я**) *м* salmon.
лос|ь (**-я**; *gen pl* **-е́й**) *м* elk, moose (*мн* moose).
лосьо́н (**-а**) *м* lotion.
лот (**-а**) *м* (*мор*) lead line; (*комм: на аукцио́не, на торга́х*) lot.
лотере́йный *прил* lottery *опред*.
лотере́|я (**-и**) *ж* lottery.
лотка́ *итп сущ см* **лото́к**.
лото́ (**-**) *ср нескл* lotto.
лот|о́к (**-ка́**) *м* (*прила́вок*) stall; (*я́щик для торго́вли*) trader's tray; (*жёлоб*) trough.
ло́тос (**-а**) *м* lotus.
лото́чник (**-а**) *м* stallholder.
лохма́|тить (**-чу**, **-тишь**; *perf* **взлохма́тить**) *несов перех* to fluff up.
лохма́т|ый (**-**, **-а**, **-о**) *прил* (*живо́тное*) shaggy; (*во́лосы*) straggly; (*челове́к*) dishevelled.
лохма́чу *сов см* **лохма́тить**.
лохмо́ть|я (**-ев**) *мн* rags *мн*.
ло́цман (**-а**) *м* pilot (*on ship*).
лошади́ный *прил* (*седло́, упря́жь*) horse's; (*лицо́*) equine; **лошади́ная си́ла** horsepower.
лоша́дник (**-а**) *м* (*разг: люби́тель лошаде́й*) horse-lover; (*торго́вец лошадьми́*) horse-trader.
ло́шад|ь (**-и**; *gen pl* **-е́й**) *ж* horse.
лощёный *прил* (*бума́га*) glossy; (*перен: челове́к, вне́шность*) polished.
лощи́н|а (**-ы**) *ж* dell.
лоя́льный (**-ен**, **-ьна**, **-ьно**) *прил* loyal (*to the state*).
л.с. *сокр* (= *лошади́ная си́ла*) h.p. (= *horsepower*).
ЛСД *м сокр* LSD (= *lysergic acid diethylamide*).
Луа́р|а (**-ы**) *ж* the Loire.
лубо́к (**-ка́**) *м* (*кора́*) bast; (*повя́зка*) splint; **ру́сский ~** (ФОЛЬКЛОР) lubok (*popular colour print*).

лубрика́тор (-а) *м* lubricant.
луг (-а; *loc sg* -ý, *nom pl* -á) *м* meadow.
лу|ди́ть (-жý, -ди́шь) *несов перех* to tin.
луж|а́ (-и) *ж* (*на у́лице, на доро́ге*) puddle; (*на полу́, на столе́*) pool; **сади́ться (сесть** *perf*) **в ~у** (*перен: разг*) to get o.s. into a mess.
лужа́|йка (-йки; *gen pl* -ек) *ж* (*поля́нка*) glade; (*газо́н*) lawn.
лужён|ый *прил* (*самова́р, ча́йник итп*) tin-plated; **у него́ ~ая гло́тка** (*перен: разг*) he has iron lungs.
лужý *несов см* **луди́ть**.
лу́з|а (-ы) *ж* pocket (*on a billiard table*).
лук (-а) *м собир* onions *мн* ♦ *м* (*ору́жие*) bow; **зелёный ~** spring onion (*BRIT*), scallion; **ре́пчатый ~** onion bulbs.
лука́в|ить (-лю, -ишь; *perf* **слука́вить**) *несов непе́рех* to be deceitful; **ты, ка́жется, ~ишь** you're being a bit vague.
лука́в|ый (-, -а, -о) *прил* (*челове́к, посту́пок*) crafty; (*взгляд, улы́бка*) sly; (*де́вушка*) coquettish.
лу́кови|ца (-ы) *ж* bulb; (*во́лоса*) follicle.
луко́ш|ко (-ка; *gen pl* -ек) *ср* basket.
лун|á (-ы́) *ж* moon; **ты что, с ~ы́ свали́лся?** where've you been all this time?
лу́на-па́рк (-а) *м* funfair (*BRIT*), amusement park (*US*).
луна́тик (-а) *м* sleepwalker.
лу́н|ка (-ки; *gen pl* -ок) *ж* hole.
лу́нн|ый *прил*: **~ые фа́зы** phases of the moon; **лу́нный свет** moonlight.
лу́нок *сущ см* **лу́нка**.
луноход (-а) *м* lunar research module.
лун|ь (-я́) *м* harrier.
лу́п|а (-ы) *ж* magnifying glass.
луп|и́ть (-лю́, -ишь; *perf* **облупи́ть**) *несов перех* (*яйцо́*) to shell; (*perf* **отлупи́ть**; *разг: бить*) to thrash; (*no perf*; *разг: сильно ударя́ть*) to hammer on
▶ **лупи́ться** (*perf* **облупи́ться**) *несов возв* (*шелуши́ться*) to peel (off).
луч (-а) *м* ray; (*проже́ктора, фонаря́*) beam; **рентге́новские ~й** X-ray; **~ наде́жды** a ray of hope; **ла́зерный ~** laser beam.
лучев|о́й *прил* (*физ: эне́ргия*) beamed; **~а́я кость** radius (*bone*); **лучева́я боле́знь** radiation sickness.
лучеза́р|ный (-ен, -на, -но) *прил* (*бу́дущее*) glorious; (*улы́бка*) radiant.
лучи́н|а (-ы) *ж* (*ще́пка*) splinter ♦ *собир* (*ще́пки*) kindling wood *собир*.
лучи́ст|ый (-, -а, -о) *прил* (*улы́бка, лицо́*) beaming; (*глаза́*) shining.
лу́чник (-а) *м* archer.
лу́чни|ца (-ы) *ж см* **лу́чник**.
лу́чше *сравн прил от* **хоро́ший** ♦ *сравн нареч от* **хорошо́** ♦ *как сказ*: **больно́му ~** the patient is feeling better ♦ *част*: **~ не опра́вдывайся** don't try and justify yourself ♦ *вводн сл*: **~ (всего́) е́сли ты позвони́шь ве́чером** it would be better if you phone in the evening; **от э́того никому́ не ~** it doesn't do anyone any good; **нам ~ чем им** we're better off than them; **будь осторо́жен и́ли, ~, вообще́ не ходи́ туда́** take care, or better still, don't go there at all; **~ возьми́ маши́ну** you'd better take the car; **как нельзя́ ~** couldn't be better; **~ не спра́шивай** don't ask.
лу́чш|ий (-ая, -ее, -ие) *прил* (*са́мый хоро́ший*) best; **э́то ~ая рабо́та в кла́ссе** it's the best work in the class; **в ~ем слу́чае нам уда́стся зако́нчить рабо́ту за́втра** if we're lucky we'll finish the work tomorrow; **за неиме́нием ~его** for want of something better; **э́то (всё) к ~ему** it's (all) for the best.
лущ|и́ть (-ý, -ишь; *perf* **облущи́ть**) *несов перех* (*се́мечки, оре́хи*) to crack (open); (*горо́х*) to shell.
лы́ж|а (-и) *ж* (*обы́чно мн*) ski; *см та́кже* **лы́жи**.
лы́ж|и (-) *мн* (*вид спо́рта*) skiing; **во́дные ~** (*са́ми лы́жи*) water-skis; (*вид спо́рта*) water-skiing; **го́рные ~** downhill skis; **ходи́ть** (*impf*) **на ~ах** to go cross-country skiing.
лы́жник (-а) *м* skier.
лы́жни|ца (-ы) *ж см* **лы́жник**.
лы́жный *прил* (*крепле́ния, мазь итп*) ski *опред*; (*соревнова́ния*) skiing *опред*; **лы́жный костю́м** ski suit; **лы́жные па́лки** ski poles.
лыжн|я́ (-и́) *ж* ski track.
лы́к|о (-а) *ср* (*ли́пы, и́вы*) bast; **он ~а не вя́жет** (*разг*) he's roaring drunk; **он не ~м шит** (*разг*) he's someone to be reckoned with.
лысе́|ть (-ю; *perf* **облысе́ть** *или* **полысе́ть**) *несов непе́рех* to go bald.
лыси́н|а (-ы) *ж* bald patch.
лы́с|ый (-, -а, -о) *прил* (*голова́, челове́к*) bald; (*гора́, холм*) bare.
ль *част* = **ли**.
львёнок (-ёнка; *nom pl* -я́та, *gen pl* -я́т) *м* lion cub.
льви́н|ый *прил* (*шку́ра, гри́ва итп*) lion's; **~ая ста́я** pride of lions; **~ая до́ля** the lion's share; **льви́ный зев** (*БОТ*) snapdragon.
льви́|ца (-ы) *ж* lioness.
Львов (-а) *м* Lvov.
львя́та *итп сущ см* **львёнок**.
льго́т|а (-ы) *ж* (*инвали́дам, бере́менным итп*) benefit; (*обы́чно мн: предприя́тиям, экспортёрам*) special term; (*эли́те, ветера́нам*) privilege; **нало́говые ~ы** tax relief.
льго́тный *прил* (*тари́ф*) concessionary; (*усло́вия*) privileged; (*заём*) special-rate; **льго́тный биле́т** concessionary ticket.
льда *итп сущ см* **лёд**.
льди́н|а (-ы) *ж* ice floe.

льди́н|ка (-ки; *gen pl* -ок) *ж* piece of ice.

льна *итп сущ см* **лён**.

льново́дств|о (-а) *ср* flax-growing.

льн|у́ть (-у́, -ёшь; *perf* **прильну́ть**) *несов непepex:* ~ **к** +*dat* (*к ма́тери*) to cling to; (*перен: к богача́м, к влия́тельным лю́дям*) to try to get in with.

льняно́й *прил* (*полоте́нце, пла́тье*) linen; (*цвет*) flaxen; **~ое полотно́** linen; **льняно́е ма́сло** linseed oil.

льстец (-а́) *м* flatterer.

льсти́в|ый (-, -а, -о) *прил* (*челове́к*) smarmy; (*улы́бка*) unctuous; (*завере́ния, речь*) flattering.

ль|сти́ть (-щу, -стишь; *perf* **польсти́ть**) *несов непepex* (+*dat*; *хвали́ть из коры́сти*) to flatter; (*доставля́ть удовлетворе́ние*) to gratify; ~ (*impf*) **себя́ наде́ждой** to live in hope.

лью(сь) *итп несов см* **лить(ся)**.

любвеоби́л|ьный (-ен, -ьна, -ьно) *прил* loving.

любви́ *итп сущ см* **любо́вь**.

любе́зен *прил см* **любе́зный**.

любе́знича|ть (-ю) *несов непepex:* ~ **с** +*instr* (*разг*) to pay compliments to.

любе́зность (-и) *ж* (*одолже́ние*) favour (*BRIT*), favor (*US*); (*комплиме́нт*) compliment; (*в поведе́нии*) courtesy; **ока́зывать (оказа́ть** *perf*) ~ **кому́-н** to do sb a favour; **не откажи́те в** ~**и?** would you do me a favour?

любе́з|ный (-ен, -на, -но) *прил* polite; **бу́дьте ~ны!** excuse me, please!; **бу́дьте ~ны, принеси́те нам ко́фе?** could you be so kind as to bring us some coffee?

люби́м|ая (-ой; *decl like adj*) *ж* beloved.

люби́м|ец (-ца) *м* (*челове́к, живо́тное*) favourite (*BRIT*), favorite (*US*).

люби́миц|а (-ы) *ж см* **люби́мец**.

люби́мца *итп сущ см* **люби́мец**.

люби́мчик (-а) *м* (*разг*) pet; **быть** (*impf*) **в ~ах у кого́-н** to be sb's pet.

люби́м|ый (-, -а, -о) *прил* (*же́нщина, брат*) beloved; (*писа́тель, заня́тие итп*) favourite (*BRIT*), favorite (*US*) ◆ (-ого; *decl like adj*) *м* beloved.

люби́тель (-я) *м* (*непрофессиона́л*) amateur; ~ **му́зыки/спо́рта** music-/sports-lover.

люби́тельниц|а (-ы) *ж:* ~ **му́зыки/чте́ния** music-/book-lover.

люби́тельск|ий (-ая, -ое, -ие) *прил* (*спорт, теа́тр итп*) amateur; **люби́тельские права́** driving licence (*BRIT*) *или* driver's license (*US*).

люб|и́ть (-лю́, -ишь) *несов перех* (*ро́дину, мать, му́жа итп*) to love; (*му́зыку, спорт итп*) to like; **я ~лю́ его́ всем се́рдцем** I love him with all my heart; **цветы́ лю́бят тепло́** plants like the warmth; **я ~лю́, когда́ мне говоря́т комплиме́нты** I like it when people pay me compliments; **я ~лю́, когда́ лю́ди прихо́дят во́время** I like it when people come on time.

люб|ова́ться (-у́юсь; *perf* **полюбова́ться**) *несов возв* (+*instr*) to admire; **полюбу́йтесь на**

него́! take a look at him!

любо́вник (-а) *м* lover.

любо́вниц|а (-ы) *ж см* **любо́вник**.

любо́вный *прил* (*дела́, похожде́ния*) lover's; (*пе́сня, письмо́*) love *опред*; (*отноше́ние, подхо́д*) loving.

любо́в|ь (-ви́) *ж* love; (*привя́занность*) ~ **к** +*dat* (*к ро́дине, к ма́тери итп*) love for; (*к чте́нию, к иску́сству итп*) love of; **занима́ться** (*impf*) ~**ю** to make love.

любозна́телен *прил см* **любозна́тельный**.

любозна́тельность (-и) *ж* inquisitiveness.

любозна́тел|ьный (-ен, -ьна, -ьно) *прил* inquisitive.

люб|о́й *мест* (*вся́кий*) any ◆ (-о́го; *decl like adj*) *м* (*любо́й челове́к*) anyone; **в ~ое вре́мя** at any time; ~ **цено́й** at any price.

любопы́тен *прил см* **любопы́тный**.

любопы́тно *нареч* curiously ◆ *как сказ:* ~! that's interesting!; (*мне*) ~ **узна́ть** I'm intrigued *или* curious to know.

любопы́т|ный (-ен, -на, -но) *прил* (*приме́р, кни́га итп*) interesting; (*челове́к, толпа́*) curious.

любопы́тств|о (-а) *ср* curiosity; **из ~а** out of curiosity.

лю́бящ|ий (-ая, -ее, -ие) *прил* loving.

люд (-а) *м собир* (*разг*) folk.

лю́ден *прил см* **лю́дный**.

лю́д|и (-е́й; *dat pl* -ям, *instr pl* -ьми́, *prp pl* -ях) *мн* people *мн*; (*солда́ты и офице́ры*) men *мн*; (*ка́дры*) staff *ед*; **выходи́ть (вы́йти** *perf*) **в** ~ to get on in life; **на ~ях** (*разг*) in public; **молоды́е** ~ young men; (*молодёжь*) young people; *см также* **челове́к**.

лю́д|ный (-ен, -на, -но) *прил* (*у́лица итп*) busy; (*го́род*) lively; (*сбо́рище*) crowded.

людое́д (-а) *м* (*челове́к*) cannibal; (*живо́тное*) man-eater; (*в ска́зке*) ogre.

людое́дств|о (-а) *ср* cannibalism.

людско́й *прил* human; **род** ~ humankind.

люк (-а) *м* (*та́нка, самолёта*) hatch; (*на доро́ге*) manhole; (*на сце́не*) trap door.

люкс (-а) *м* (*о ваго́не*) first-class carriage; (*о каю́те*) first-class cabin ◆ *прил неизм* (*вы́сшего кла́сса*) first-class; **мы живём в лю́ксе** we've got a luxury suite.

Люксембу́рг (-а) *м* Luxemburg.

лю́л|ька (-ьки; *gen pl* -ек) *ж* (*также* **стро́ит**) cradle; (*мотоци́кла*) sidecar.

лю́мпен (-а) *м* member of the lumpen proletariat.

люпи́н (-а) *м* lupin.

лю́рекс (-а) *м* lurex.

лю́стр|а (-ы) *ж* chandelier.

лю́тен *сущ см* **лю́тня**.

лютера́н|ин (-ина; *nom pl* -е, *gen pl* -) *м* Lutheran.

лютера́н|ка (-ки; *gen pl* -ок) *ж см* **лютера́нин**.

лютера́нск|ий (-ая, -ое, -ие) *прил* Lutheran.

лю́тик (-а) *м* buttercup.

лю́т|ня (-ни; *gen pl* -ен) *ж* lute.

лю́т|ый (-, -а́, -о) *прил* (*враг, зверь*) fierce;

(ненависть, горе) intense; (мороз) severe.
люце́рн|а (-ы) ж lucerne.
ля ср нескл (муз) lah.
ляга́|ть (-ю) несов перех (подлеж: лошадь, корова) to kick
► **ляга́ться** несов возв (лошадь, корова) to kick.
лягну́ть (-у́, -ёшь) сов перех to kick.
ля́г(те) сов см лечь.
ля́гу итп сов см лечь.
лягуша́та итп сущ см лягушо́нок.
лягуша́тник (-а) м (разг) shallow end.
лягу́ш|ка (-ки; gen pl -ек) ж frog.
лягуш|о́нок (-о́нка; nom pl -а́та, gen pl -а́т) м young frog.
ля́жек сущ см ля́жка.
ля́жешь итп сов см лечь.

ля́ж|ка (-ки; gen pl -ек) ж thigh.
лязг (-а) м (звук: цепей, оружия) clanging; (: зубов) gnash; (: подков) clatter.
ля́зга|ть (-ю) несов неперех (засов, цепь) to clang; (+instr; зубами) to gnash; (ключами) to rattle.
ля́м|ка (-ки; gen pl -ок) ж strap; **тяну́ть** (impf) ~**ку** (разг) to toil away.
ля́па|ть (-ю) несов от **ля́пнуть** ♦ (perf **сля́пать**) перех (разг: делать наспех) to slap together ♦ (perf **наля́пать**) перех to make a mess of ♦ неперех to make a mess.
ля́пн|уть (-у, -ешь; impf **ля́пать**) сов перех: ~ **глу́пость** to make a blunder.
ля́псус (-а) м blunder.

~ М, м ~

М, м *сущ нескл (буква)* the 13th letter of the Russian alphabet.

М *сокр* = **метро́**; (= *мегаба́йт*) MB (= *megabyte*).

м *сокр* (= **метр**) m= *metre* (*BRIT*) *или* meter (*US*); (= **мину́та**) m (= *minute*).

мавзоле́й (-**я**) *м* mausoleum.

маг (-**а**) *м* magician, wizard; (*разг*) tape recorder.

магази́н (-**а**) *м* shop; (*ружья*) magazine.

МАГАТЭ *ср сокр* (= *Междунаро́дное аге́нтство по а́томной эне́ргии*) IAEA (= *International Atomic Energy Agency*).

маги́стр (-**а**) *м* (*учёная степень*) master's degree; ~ **гуманита́рных нау́к** Master of Arts.

магистра́л|**ь** (-**и**) *ж* (*железнодорожная*) main line; (*дорожная*) arterial road; **во́дная** ~ main waterway.

магистра́льный *прил* main.

маги́ческ|**ий** (-**ая, -ое, -ие**) *прил* (*перен*) magic *опред*.

ма́ги|**я** (-**и**) *ж* magic.

магна́т (-**а**) *м* magnate.

магне́зи|**я** (-**и**) *ж* magnesia.

магнети́зм (-**а**) *м* magnetism.

ма́гни|**й** (-**я**) *м* magnesium.

магни́т (-**а**) *м* magnet.

магни́тный *прил* magnetic; ~ **диск** (*КОМП*) magnetic disk.

магнито́л|**а** (-**ы**) *ж* radio cassette player.

магнитофо́н (-**а**) *м* tape recorder; (*кассетный*) tape *или* cassette recorder.

магнитофо́нный *прил*: ~**ая за́пись** tape recording; ~**ая кассе́та** (audio)cassette.

магно́ли|**я** (-**и**) *ж* magnolia.

Мадагаска́р (-**а**) *м* Madagascar.

мада́м *ж нескл* madame.

мадемуазе́ль (-**и**) *ж* mademoiselle.

мадо́нн|**а** (-**ы**) *ж* madonna.

Мадри́д (-**а**) *м* Madrid.

ма́ек *сущ см* **ма́йка**.

мает|**а́** (-**ы́**) *ж* (*разг*) bother.

мажо́р (-**а**) *м* (*МУЗ*) major key.

мажорита́рный *прил*: ~**ая систе́ма** (*ПОЛИТ*) system of majority rule.

мажо́рный *прил* (*МУЗ*) major; (*перен: настроение*) cheerful.

МАЗ (-**а**) *м сокр* = *Ми́нский автомоби́льный заво́д*; (*автомобиль*) *vehicle manufactured at the Minsk car factory*.

ма́з|**ать** (-**жу, -жешь**; *perf* **нама́зать** *или*

пома́зать) *несов перех* to spread; (*perf* **изма́зать**; *разг: пачкать*) to get dirty; (: *рисовать*) to daub ♦ (*perf* **прома́зать**) *неперех* (*разг*) to miss; ~ (**нама́зать** *perf*) **что-н** to spread sth with sth; ~ (**нама́зать** *perf*) **гу́бы пома́дой** to put on lipstick

▶ **ма́заться** (*perf* **нама́заться**) *несов возв* (*разг: делать макияж*) to put on make-up; (*perf* **вы́мазаться** *или* **изма́заться**; *разг: пачкаться*) to get dirty; ~**ся** (**нама́заться** *perf*) **кре́мом/ма́зью** to apply cream/ointment.

мазк|**а́** *сущ см* **мазо́к**.

мазн|**я́** (-**и́**) *ж* (*разг: о рисовании*) daub; (: *о письме*) scribble.

мазо́к (-**ка́**) *м* (*кисти*) stroke; (*МЕД*) smear.

мазу́рк|**а** (-**и**) *ж* mazurka.

мазу́т (-**а**) *м* fuel oil.

маз|**ь** (-**и**) *ж* (*МЕД*) ointment; (*лыжная*) wax; (*колёсная*) grease; **де́ло на** ~**й** (*разг*) things are going smoothly.

маи́с (-**а**) *м* maize (*BRIT*), corn (*US*).

маи́совый *прил* maize (*BRIT*), corn (*US*).

ма|**й** (-**я**) *м* May; *см также* **октя́брь**.

ма́йк|**а** (-**йки**; *gen pl* -**ек**) *ж* vest (*BRIT*), sleeveless undershirt (*US*).

майо́лик|**а** (-**и**) *ж собир* majolica.

майоне́з (-**а**) *м* mayonnaise.

майо́р (-**а**) *м* (*ВОЕН*) major.

ма́йск|**ий** (-**ая, -ое, -ие**) *прил* May *опред*; **ма́йский жук** May beetle, cockchafer.

мак (-**а**) *м* (*поппи*) poppy; (*кулин*) poppy seeds *мн*.

мака́к|**а** (-**и**) *ж* macaque.

макаро́нник (-**а**) *м* pasta bake.

макаро́н|**ы** (-) *мн* pasta *ед*.

макаро́нный *прил* (*кулин*) pasta *опред*; **макаро́нные изде́лия** pasta.

мака́ть (-**ю**) *несов перех* to dip.

македо́н|**ец** (-**ца**) *м* Macedonian.

Македо́ни|**я** (-**и**) *ж* Macedonia.

македо́н|**ка** (-**ки**; *gen pl* -**ок**) *ж см* **македо́нец**.

македо́нск|**ий** (-**ая, -ое, -ие**) *прил* Macedonian.

македо́нца *сущ см* **македо́нец**.

маке́т (-**а**) *м* (*модель*) model; (*КОМП*) breadboard.

макинто́ш (-**а**) *м* mackintosh.

ма́клер (-**а**) *м* (*КОММ*) broker.

макн|**у́ть** (-**у́, -ёшь**) *сов перех* (*перо, кисть*) to dip.

ма́ковк|**а** (-**и**) *ж* poppyhead; (*разг: купол церкви*) (onion) dome.

ма́ков|ый (-, -а, -о) *прил* poppy-seed *опред*; **с ~о зёрнышко** as small as a pinhead; **у него́ с утра́ во рту́ ~ой роси́нки не бы́ло** he hasn't had a bite to eat since morning.

макраме́ *ср нескл* macramé.

макре́л|ь (-и) *ж* mackerel.

макроэконо́мик|а (-и) *ж* macroeconomics *мн*.

ма́кси *ср нескл* maxi ♦ *прил неизм* maxi *опред*.

макс(им). *сокр* (= максима́льный) max. (= *maximum*).

максима́лен *прил см* **максима́льный**.

максима́лист (-а) *м* maximalist.

максима́л|ьный (-ен, -ьна, -ьно) *прил* maximum *опред*.

ма́ксимум (-а) *м* maximum ♦ *нареч* at most, maximum.

макулату́р|а (-ы) *ж собир* wastepaper (*for recycling*); (*перен: пренебр*) pulp literature.

маку́шк|а (-ки; *gen pl* -ек) *ж* (*разг: дерева, горы*) top; (*головы*) crown; **у него́ у́шки на ~ке** he's keeping his ear to the ground.

Мала́ви *ср нескл* Malawi.

мала́г|а (-и) *ж* (*вино*) Malaga (wine).

мала́|ец (-йца) *м* Malay.

Мала́йзи|я (-и) *ж* Malaysia.

мала́йк|а (-йки; *gen pl* -ек) *ж см* **мала́ец**.

мала́йск|ий (-ая, -ое, -ие) *прил* Malaysian.

мала́йца *сущ см* **мала́ец**.

малахи́т (-а) *м* malachite.

мал|ева́ть (-ю́ю, -ю́ешь; *perf* **намалева́ть**) *несов перех* (*разг*) to daub.

мале́йш|ий (-ая, -ее, -ие) *прил* (*ошибка, промах*) the slightest; **не име́ть** (*impf*) **ни ~его представле́ния о чём-н** to not have the slightest idea about sth.

малёк (-ька́) *м* young (fish), fry.

ма́леньк|ий (-ая, -ое, -ие) *прил* small, little; (*незначительный*) slight; (*малолетний*) little ♦ (-ого; *decl like adj*) *м* little one; **моё де́ло ~ое** (*разг*) it's none of my business; **ма́ленькая бу́ква** small letter.

Мали́ *ср нескл* Mali.

мали́н|а (-ы) *ж* (*кустарник*) raspberry cane *или* bush; (*ягода*) raspberries *мн*; **не жизнь, а ~!** (*разг*) it's a cushy life!

мали́нник (-а) *м собир* raspberry canes *мн*.

мали́новк|а (-и) *ж* robin (redbreast).

мали́новый *прил* (*варенье, куст*) raspberry; (*цвет*) crimson.

KEYWORD

ма́ло *чис* (+*gen*; *друзей, книг*) only a few; (*работы, денег*) not much; **нам да́ли ма́ло книг** they only gave us a few books; **я ви́дел ма́ло друзе́й** I only saw a few friends; **у меня́ ма́ло де́нег** I don't have much money; **ма́ло ра́дости** little joy

♦ *нареч* not much; **она́ ма́ло измени́лась** she hasn't changed much; **они́ ма́ло рабо́тают** they

don't work much

♦ *как сказ*: **критикова́ть ма́ло, на́до помо́чь** it's not enough to criticize, you have to help; **мне э́того ма́ло** this is not enough for me; **ему́ всё ма́ло** it is impossible to satisfy him; **ма́ло ли что** so what?; **ма́ло ли кто/где/когда́** it doesn't matter who/where/when; **ма́ло того́** (and) what's more; **ма́ло того́, она́ ещё груби́ла** (and) what's more, she was rude; **ма́ло того́ что** not only; **ма́ло того́ что бы́ло хо́лодно, нам ещё не да́ли у́жин** not only was it cold, but they didn't give us any supper.

малова́ж|ный (-ен, -на, -но) *прил* of little importance.

малова́т *как сказ* (*разг: о размере*) on the small side.

малова́то *нареч* (*разг*) not quite enough.

малове́р (-а) *м* sceptic.

малове́роя́т|ный (-ен, -на, -но) *прил* improbable.

малово́дь|е (-ья; *gen pl* -ий) *ср* low water level; (*недостаток воды*) drought.

малов|ы́год|ный (-ен, -на, -но) *прил* unprofitable.

малогабари́т|ный (-ен, -на, -но) *прил* small.

малоговоря́щ|ий (-ая, -ее, -ие) *прил* unimpressive.

малогра́мот|ный (-ен, -на, -но) *прил* semiliterate; (*руководитель*) incompetent.

малодосту́п|ный (-ен, -на, -но) *прил* (*место*) inaccessible.

малоду́шен *прил см* **малоду́шный**.

малоду́шнича|ть (-ю; *perf* **смалоду́шничать**) *несов неперех* (*разг*) to be yellow (*fig*).

малоду́ш|ный (-ен, -на, -но) *прил* cowardly.

малозаме́т|ный (-ен, -на, -но) *прил* (*пятно, окраска*) hardly noticeable; (*человек, событие*) insignificant.

малознако́м|ый (-, -а, -о) *прил* unfamiliar.

малокали́берный *прил* small-bore, small-calibre (*BRIT*), small-caliber (*US*).

малокро́ви|е (-я) *ср* (sickle-cell) anaemia (*BRIT*) *или* anemia (*US*).

малоле́тк|а (-и) *м/ж* (*разг*) kid.

малоле́т|ний (-яя, -ее, -ие) *прил* young.

малолитра́ж|ка (-ки; *gen pl* -ек) *ж* (*разг*) small car (*with small cylinder capacity*).

малолитра́жный *прил*: ~ **автомоби́ль** small car (*with small cylinder capacity*).

малолю́д|ный (-ен, -на, -но) *прил* (*улица*) unfrequented; (*район, село*) sparsely populated.

ма́ло-ма́льски *нареч* (*разг*) quite.

малома́льск|ий (-ая, -ое, ие) *прил* (*разг*) the slightest.

маломо́щ|ный (-ен, -на, -но) *прил* weak.

малонаселён|ный *прил* sparsely populated.

малообеспе́ченный *прил* disadvantaged.

малообла́ч|ный (-ен, -на, -но) *прил* (*небо*,

пого́да) slightly cloudy.

малообразо́ван|ный (-, -на, -но) *прил* undereducated.

малоподви́ж|ный (-ен, -на, -но) *прил* (*о́браз жи́зни*) sedentary.

ма́ло-пома́лу *нареч* (*разг*) little by little.

малора́звит|ый (-, -а, -о) *прил* underdeveloped.

малоро́слый *прил* undersized.

малосеме́й|ный (-ен, -йна, -йно) *прил* with a small family.

малоси́л|ьный (-ен, -ьна, -ьно) *прил* (*дви́гатель*) low-powered; (*ло́шадь*) weak.

малосо́л|ьный (-ен, -ьна, -ьно) *прил* pickled (*in weak brine*).

ма́лост|ь (-и) *ж* (*разг*) trifle ◆ *нареч* (*разг*) a bit.

малотира́жный *прил* (*газе́та, журна́л*) with a low circulation; (*кни́га*) *published in a small edition.*

малочи́слен|ный (-, -на, -но) *прил* small; (*поселе́ния*) scarce.

ма́л|ый (-, -а́, -о́) *прил* small, little; (*дохо́д, ско́рость*) low ◆ (-**ого**; *decl like adj*) *м* (*разг*) chap; (*молодо́й челове́к*) lad ◆ *как сказ* (*no full form*): **пла́тье/пальто́ мало́** the dress/coat is too small; **дово́льствоваться** (*impf*) ~**ым** to have modest needs; **с** ~**ых лет** from childhood; **у него́ семья́ мал мала́ ме́ньше** he has a very large family of small children; **он мал да уда́л** (*разг*) he's a smart little guy; **без** ~**ого два часа́** (*разг*) just before two o'clock; **са́мое** ~**ое** at the very least; **Ма́лая А́зия** Asia Minor.

малы́ш (-а́) *м* little boy.

малы́ш|ка (-ки; *gen pl* -ек) *ж* little girl.

малышня́ (-й) *ж собир* (*разг*) little kids *мн*.

ма́льв|а (-ы) *ж* mallow.

мальди́вский (-ая, -ое, -ие) *прил*: **М**~**ие острова́** Maldives, Maldive Islands.

малька́ *сущ см* **малёк**.

Ма́льт|а (-ы) *ж* Malta.

мальти́|ец (-йца) *м* Maltese.

мальти́|йка (-йки; *gen pl* -ек) *ж см* **мальти́ец**.

мальти́йский (-ая, -ое, -ие) *прил* Maltese.

мальти́йца *сущ см* **мальти́ец**.

ма́льчик (-а) *м* boy.

мальчи́шек *сущ см* **мальчи́шка**.

мальчи́шеский (-ая, -ое, -ие) *прил* (*задо́р, вид*) boyish; (*несерьёзный*) childish, puerile.

мальчи́шеств|о (-а) *ср* childishness.

мальчи́ш|ка (-ки; *gen pl* -ек) *м* (*разг*) boy; (*нео́пытный мужчи́на*) child.

мальчи́шник (-а) *м* stag night *или* party (*BRIT*), stag (*US*).

малю́сеньк|ий (-ая, -ое, -ие) *прил* (*разг*) tiny, wee (*esp SCOTTISH*).

малю́т|ка (-ки; *gen pl* -ок) *м/ж* baby; **кни́жка/фотоаппара́т-**~ miniature book/camera.

маля́в|ка (-ки; *gen pl* -ок) *ж* small fish ◆ *м/ж* (*разг*: *пренебр*) shrimp.

маля́р (-а́) *м* painter (and decorator).

маляри́йный *прил* malarial.

маляри́|я (-и) *ж* malaria.

маля́рный *прил* painter's; ~**ая кисть** paintbrush.

ма́м|а (-ы) *ж* mummy (*BRIT*), mommy (*US*).

мама́лыг|а (-и) *ж* polenta, maize porridge.

мама́ш|а (-и) *ж* (*разг*: *мать*) mummy (*BRIT*), mommy (*US*); (: *обраще́ние к пожило́й же́нщине*) missus.

ма́меньк|ин (-а, -о, -ы) *прил*: ~ **сыно́к** (*разг*: *пренебр*) mummy's boy; ~**а до́чка** (*разг*) mummy's girl.

ма́монт (-а) *м* mammoth.

мана́т|ки (-ок) *мн* (*разг*) stuff *ед*.

ма́нго *ср нескл* mango.

мангу́ст|а (-ы) *ж* mongoose.

мандари́н (-а) *м* tangerine.

мандари́новый *прил* tangerine.

манда́т (-а) *м* mandate.

мандоли́н|а (-ы) *ж* mandoline.

манёвр (-а) *м* (*также перен*) manoevre (*BRIT*), maneuver (*US*); *см также* **манёвры**.

маневри́р|овать (-ую; *perf* **сманеври́ровать**) *несов неперех* (*войска́, диплома́т итп*): to manoeuvre (*BRIT*), maneuver (*US*); (*перен*): ~ +*instr* (*ресу́рсами, фина́нсами*) to make full use of.

манёвр|ы (-ов) *мн* manoeuvres *мн* (*BRIT*), maneuvers *мн* (*US*); (*на желе́зной доро́ге*) shunting *ед*.

мане́ж (-а) *м* (*для верхово́й езды́*) manège; (*ци́рка*) ring; (*для младе́нцев*) playpen; (*также*: **легкоатлети́ческий** ~) indoor stadium (*мн* stadia).

манеке́н (-а) *м* (*портно́го*) dummy; (*в витри́не*) dummy, mannequin.

манеке́нщик (-а) *м* model.

манеке́нщиц|а (-ы) *ж см* **манеке́нщик**.

мане́р (-а) *м* (*разг*): таки́м ~**ом** like this ◆ *предл*: **на** ~ +*gen* like.

мане́р|а (-ы) *ж* manner; (*худо́жника, поэ́та*) style; *см также* **мане́ры**.

мане́рен *прил см* **мане́рный**.

мане́рнича|ть (-ю) *несов неперех* to put on airs.

мане́рный (-ен, -на, -но) *прил* affected.

мане́р|ы (-) *мн* manners *мн*.

манже́т|а (-ы) *ж* cuff.

маниака́льный *прил* maniacal.

маникю́р (-а) *м* manicure.

маникю́рный *прил* manicure *опред*.

маникю́рш|а (-и) *ж* manicurist.

Мани́л|а (-ы) *ж* Manila.

манипули́р|овать (-ую) *несов неперех* (+*instr*; *также перен*) to manipulate.

манипуля́ци|я (-и) *ж* (*также перен*) manipulation.

ман|и́ть (-ю́, -ишь; *perf* **помани́ть**) *несов перех* to beckon; (*no perf*; *перен*: *привлека́ть*) to attract.

манифе́ст (-а) *м* manifesto.

манифеста́ци|я (-и) *ж* demonstration.

мани́ш|ка (-ки; *gen pl* -ек) *ж* (*часть руба́шки*) shirt front; (*нагру́дник*) dicky.

мА́ни|я (-и) ж mania.

мА́нк|а (-и) ж (разг) semolina.

мА́нн|а (-ы) ж manna; ждать (impf) как ~ы небе́сной to await impatiently.

мА́нн|ый прил: ~ая кА́ша, ~ая крупА́ semolina.

манО́метр (-а) м manometer.

мансА́рд|а (-ы) ж garret.

мА́нти|я (-и) ж robe.

мантО́ ср нескл (ladies') fur coat.

мануфактУ́р|а (-ы) ж (ист: фабрика) (textile) mill.

Манче́стер (-а) м Manchester.

МаньчжУ́ри|я (-и) ж Manchuria.

маньЯ́к (-а) м maniac.

марА́зм (-а) м (мед) dementia; (перен: разг) idiocy; стА́рческий ~ senility, senile dementia.

марА́л (-а) м Siberian deer.

марА́ть (-ю; perf вЫ́марать или измарА́ть) несов перех (разг: пачкать) to get dirty; (perf замарА́ть; перен: разг) to drag through the dirt; (perf намарА́ть; разг: рисовать, писать) to scribble; ~ (impf) рУ́ки (перен: разг) to get one's hands dirty

▶ марА́ться (perf вЫ́мараться или измарА́ться) несов возв (разг: пачкаться) to get dirty; (perf замарА́ться; разг: портить репутацию) to ruin one's reputation.

марафе́т (-а) м (разг): навести́ ~ to tidy up; (: прихорашиваться) to smarten (o.s.) up.

марафО́н (-а) м marathon.

марафО́н|ец (-ца) м marathon runner.

мА́рган|ец (-ца) м manganese.

марганцО́вк|а (-и) ж (разг) potassium permanganate.

маргари́н (-а) м margarine.

маргари́т|ка (-ки; gen pl -ок) ж daisy.

маргинА́льный прил marginal.

мА́рж|а (-и) ж (комм) margin.

маринА́д (-а) м (соус) marinade; (обычно мн: маринованные овощи) pickle.

марин|овА́ть (-У́ю; perf замаринова́ть) несов перех (грибы, овощи) to pickle; (мясо, рыбу) to marinate, marinade; (no perf; разг: дело) to put off.

марионе́т|ка (-ки; gen pl -ок) ж (также перен) puppet.

марионе́точный прил (также перен) puppet опред.

МариУ́пол|ь (-я) м Mariupol.

мА́р|ка (-ки; gen pl -ок) ж (почтовая) stamp; (торговая) trademark; (сорт) brand; (качество) grade; (модель) make; (денежная единица) mark; держА́ть (impf) ~ку to keep up one's reputation; держи́те ~ку шкО́лы/фи́рмы don't let your school/the firm down.

мА́ркетинг (-а) м marketing.

мА́ркий (-кая, -кое, -кие; -ок, -ка, -ко) прил: это пальтО́ О́чень ~кое this coat shows the dirt easily.

маркир|овА́ть (-У́ю) несов перех (продукцию) to trademark.

маркси́зм (-а) м Marxism.

маркси́ст (-а) м Marxist.

мА́рлевый прил gauze.

мА́рл|я (-и) ж gauze.

мармелА́д (-а; part gen -у) м fruit jellies мн.

мародёр (-а) м looter; (разг: спекулянт) profiteer.

мародёрств|о (-а) ср looting.

мА́рок сущ см мА́рка ♦ прил см мА́ркий.

МарО́кко ср нескл Morocco.

мА́рочный прил (изделие) branded; (вино) vintage.

Марс (-а) м Mars.

Марсе́л|ь (-я) м Marseilles.

март (-а) м March; см также октЯ́брь.

мартЫ́шк|а (-и) ж marmoset ♦ м/ж (перен: разг) monkey.

марципА́н (-а) м marzipan.

марш (-а) м (также перен) march ♦ межд (воен): ~! forward march!; ле́стничный ~ flight of stairs; ~ домО́й! (разг) off you go home!

мА́ршал (-а) м marshal.

марш|ировА́ть (-У́ю; perf промарширова́ть) несов неперех to march.

маршрУ́т (-а) м route.

маршрУ́т|ка (-ки; gen pl -ок) ж (разг) fixed-route taxi.

маршрУ́т|ный прил: ~ое такси́ fixed-route taxi.

маршрУ́ток сущ см маршрУ́тка.

мА́сел сущ см мА́сло.

мА́с|ка (-ки; gen pl -ок) ж (также перен) mask; (косметическая) face pack.

маскарА́д (-а) м masked ball; (перен) masquerade.

маскир|овА́ть (-У́ю; perf замаскирова́ть) несов перех (также перен) to camouflage

▶ маскировА́ться (perf замаскирова́ться) несов возв to camouflage o.s.

маскирО́в|ка (-и) ж (воен) camouflage; (перен) disguise.

маскирО́вочный прил camouflage опред.

мА́сленица (-ы) ж ≈ Shrovetide.

маслён|ка (-ки; gen pl -ок) ж butter dish; (тех) oilcan.

маслёнок (-ёнка; nom pl -Я́та, gen pl -Я́т) м annulated или yellow boletus (edible mushroom).

мА́сленый прил (в масле) buttery; (запачканный маслом) oily; (перен: разг: льсти́вый) slick; (: сластолюби́вый) voluptuous; мА́сленая неде́ля ≈ Shrovetide.

масли́н|а (-ы) ж (дерево) olive (tree); (плод) olive.

мА́сл|ить (-ю, -ишь; perf намА́слить или

помáслить) *несов перех* to butter.
мáсличный *прил* oil-yielding.
мáсло (-ла; *nom pl* -лá, *gen pl* -ел) *ср* (*сливочное*) butter; (*растительное, смазочное*) oil; (*искусство*) oils *мн*; **дéло идёт как по ~лу** (*разг*) things are going smoothly; **подливáть (подли́ть** *perf*) **~ла в огóнь** to add fuel to the fire; **~ мáсляное** (*разг*) tautology.
маслобóйня (-йни; *gen pl* -ен) *ж* creamery.
маслозавóд (-а) *м* creamery.
масляни́ст|ый (-, -а, -о) *прил* oily.
мáсляный *прил* (*краска, фильтр*) oil *опред*; (*пятно*) oily.
масля́та *итп сущ см* **маслёнок**.
мáсок *прил см* **мáска**.
масóн (-а) *м* Freemason, Mason.
масóнск|ий (-ая, -ое, -ие) *прил* Masonic.
мáсс|а (-ы) *ж* (*также физ*) mass; (*керамическая*) paste; (*древесная*) pulp; (*no pl*; *много*) loads *мн*; **дéнежная ~** money supply; *см также* **мáссы**.
массáж (-а) *м* massage; **~ сéрдца** cardiac massage.
массажи́ст (-а) *м* masseur.
массажи́ст|ка (-ки; *gen pl* -ок) *ж* masseuse.
масси́в (-а) *м* (*водный*) expanse; (*земельный, лесной*) tract; (*КОМП*) array; **гóрный ~** massif; **жилóй** *или* **жили́щный ~** housing estate (*BRIT*) *или* project (*US*).
масси́в|ный (-ен, -на, -но) *прил* massive.
масси́рованный *прил* (*атака*) all-out.
масси́р|овать (-ую) *несов перех* to massage.
массови́к (-á) *м organizer of group activities.*
массóв|ка (-ки; *gen pl* -ок) *ж* (*КИНО, ТЕАТР*: *массовая сцена*) crowd scene; (: *статисты*) extras *мн*; (*разг*) group outing.
мáссов|ый *прил* mass *опред*; (*поставка*) bulk *опред*; **товáры ~ого спрóса** mass-market goods; **мáссовое произвóдство** (*ЭКОН*) mass production.
мáсс|ы (-) *мн* (*народ*) the masses *мн*.
мастáк (-á) *м* (*разг*): **~ на** +*acc*/**в** +*prp* a dab hand at.
мáстер (-а; *nom pl* -á) *м* master; (*на производстве*) foreman (*мн* foremen); (*ремесленник*) craftsman (*мн* craftsmen); **часовóй ~** watchmaker; **~ на** +*acc* expert at; **~ на все рýки** handyman (*мн* handymen); **мáстер спóрта** master sportsman (*title awarded to sportsmen*).
мастер|и́ть (-ю́, -и́шь; *perf* **смастери́ть**) *несов перех* to make (by hand).
мастерóк (-кá) *м* trowel.
мастерск|áя (-óй; *decl like adj*) *ж* (*часовая, столярная*) workshop; (*художника, скульптора*) studio; (*на заводе*) shop.
мастерств|ó (-á) *ср* (*квалификация*) skill; (*ремесло*) trade.
масти́к|а (-и) *ж* mastic; (*для натирания полов*) floor polish.
масти́т (-а) *м* mastitis.
масти́т|ый (-, -а, -о) *прил* eminent.

маст|ь (-и; *gen pl* -éй) *ж* (*лошади*) colour (*BRIT*), color (*US*); (*карты*) suit.
масштáб (-а) *м* scale.
масштáб|ный *прил* scale *опред*; (-ен, -на, -но; *произведение, стройка*) large-scale; **масштáбная лине́йка** scale.
мат (-а) *м* (*ШАХМАТЫ*) checkmate; (*половик, также СПОРТ*) mat; (*ругательства*) bad language; **ругáться** (*impf*) **мáтом** (*разг*) to use bad language.
матадóр (-а) *м* matador.
матемáтик (-а) *м* mathematician.
матемáтик|а (-и) *ж* mathematics.
математи́ческ|ий (-ая, -ое, -ие) *прил* mathematical; (*факультет*) mathematics *опред*.
мáтери *итп сущ см* **мать**.
материáл (-а) *м* material; (*обычно мн*: *служебные, следствия*) document.
материáлен *прил см* **материáльный**.
материали́зм (-а) *м* materialism.
материали́ст (-а) *м* materialist.
материáл|ьный (-ен, -ьна, -ьно) *прил* material *опред*; (*no short form*; *финансовый*) financial, material *опред*; **~ ущéрб** material damage; **материáльная пóмощь** financial assistance.
матери́к (-á) *м* continent; (*суша*) mainland.
материкóвый *прил* mainland *опред*.
матери́нск|ий (-ая, -ое, -ие) *прил* maternal; (*БИО, БОТ*) parent *опред*.
матери́нств|о (-а) *ср* maternity, motherhood; (*чувство*) motherliness.
матер|и́ться (-ю́сь, -и́шься) *несов возв* (*разг*) to swear.
матéри|я (-и) *ж* matter; (*разг*: *ткань*) cloth; **говори́ть** (*impf*) **о высóких ~х** to speak about elevated matters.
мáтерный *прил* (*разг*) obscene.
матéрчатый *прил* cloth.
матёрый *прил* (*волк, медведь*) mature, full-grown; (*перен*: *преступник*) hardened.
мáтер|ь (-и) *ж*: **М~ Бóжья** Mother of God.
мáтерью *итп сущ см* **мать**.
мáт|ка (-ки; *gen pl* -ок) *ж* uterus, womb; (*ЗООЛ*: *также*: **пчели́ная ~**) queen bee.
мáтов|ый (-, -а, -о) *прил* (*без блеска*) mat(t); **мáтовое стеклó** frosted glass.
мáток *сущ см* **мáтка**.
матрáс (-а) *м* mattress.
матрáц (-а) *м* = **матрáс**.
матрёш|ка (-ки; *gen pl* -ек) *ж* Russian doll.
матриархáт (-а) *м* (*ИСТ*) matriarchy.
мáтричный *прил*: **~ при́нтер** (*КОМП*) dot-matrix printer.
матрóс (-а) *м* sailor.
матрóс|ка (-и) *ж* sailor top *или* shirt.
матрóсск|ий (-ая, -ое, -ие) *прил* sailor's.
мáтуш|ка (-ки; *gen pl* -ек) *ж* (*мать*) mother; (*РЕЛ*) priest's wife.
матч (-а) *м* (*СПОРТ*) match.
мать (-ери; *см* **Table 1**) *ж* mother; (*разг*: *как обращение*) missus; **в чём ~ роди́ла** (*разг*) in

one's birthday suit; **мать-одино́чка** single mother.

мать-и-ма́чех|а (-и) ж coltsfoot.

мафио́зи м нескл mafioso.

мафио́зный прил mafia опред.

ма́фи|я (-и) ж the Mafia; (перен) Mafia.

мах (-а; part gen -у) м (крыла) flap; (колеса) turn; (ного́й) swing; (руко́й) swing, stroke; **дать** (perf) **ма́ху** (разг: ошиби́ться) to boob.

ма|ха́ть (-шу́, -шешь) несов непер (+instr) to wave; (кры́льями) to flap; ~ (impf) **кому́-н руко́й** to wave to sb.

махи́н|а (-ы) ж (разг) monster (fig).

махина́тор (-а) м machinator, schemer.

махина́ци|я (-и) ж machination, scheme.

махн|у́ть (-у́, -ёшь) сов непер to give a wave; (разг: пое́хать) to go; (через забо́р) to jump; ~ (perf) **на кого́-н/что-н руко́й** to give sb/sth up as a bad job

► **махну́ться** сов возв (разг: +instr) to swap.

махо́рк|а (-и) ж ≈ shag, coarse tobacco.

махро́в|ый прил (хала́т) towelling; (цвето́к) double; (перен: отъя́вленный) out-and-out; ~ая ткань terry towelling.

ма́чех|а (-и) ж stepmother.

ма́чт|а (-ы) ж mast.

машбюро́ ср нескл сокр (= маши́нопи́сное бюро́) typing pool.

маши́н|а (-ы) ж (также перен) machine; (автомоби́ль) car.

машина́лен прил см машина́льный.

машина́льно нареч mechanically.

машина́льный (-ен, -ьна, -ьно) прил mechanical.

машини́ст (-а) м (комба́йна, экскава́тора) driver, operator; ~ **локомоти́ва** engine driver (esp BRIT), engineer (US).

машини́ст|ка (-ки; gen pl -ок) ж typist.

маши́н|ка (-ки; gen pl -ок) ж machine; **пи́шущая** ~ typewriter.

маши́нный прил (произво́дство, ча́сти, ма́сло) machine опред; (счёт, обрабо́тка) mechanical; **маши́нное отделе́ние** engine room; **маши́нный код/язы́к** (КОМП) machine code/language.

маши́нок сущ см маши́нка.

машинопи́сный прил (текст) typewritten; **машинопи́сное бюро́** typing pool.

машинопи́сь (-и) ж (печа́тание) typing; (текст) typescript.

машинострое́ни|е (-я) ср mechanical engineering.

машу́ итп несов см маха́ть.

мая́к (-а́) м lighthouse.

ма́ятник (-а) м (часо́в) pendulum.

ма́|яться (-юсь; perf ума́яться) несов возв (разг: томи́ться) to suffer.

мая́ч|ить (-у, -ишь) несов непер (разг: видне́ться) to be visible; (: надое́дливо

возника́ть) to hang around.

МБ м сокр (= Министе́рство безопа́сности) ministry for security.

МБР м сокр (= Министе́рство безопа́сности Росси́и) Russian Ministry for security; (= межконтинента́льная баллисти́ческая раке́та) ICBM (= intercontinental ballistic missile).

МБРР м сокр (= Междунаро́дный банк реконстру́кции и разви́тия) IBRD (= International Bank for Reconstruction and Development).

МВД ср сокр (= Министе́рство вну́тренних дел) ≈ the Home Office (BRIT), ≈ the Department of the Interior (US).

МВК м сокр (= механи́зм валю́тных ку́рсов) ERM (= Exchange Rate Mechanism).

МВФ м сокр (= Междунаро́дный валю́тный фонд) IMF (= International Monetary Fund).

МВЭС ср сокр (= Министе́рство внешнеэкономи́ческих свя́зей) ministry of foreign economic links.

мг. сокр (= миллигра́мм) mg = milligram(me)).

мгл|а (-ы) ж haze; (вече́рняя) gloom.

мгнове́нен прил см мгнове́нный.

мгнове́ни|е (-я) ср moment; **в одно́** ~ right away.

мгнове́нный (-ен, -на, -но) прил (реше́ние, реа́кция, фотогра́фия) instant; (смерть) instantaneous; (злость, раздраже́ние) momentary; (вспы́шка) lightning опред.

МГУ м сокр (= Моско́вский госуда́рственный университе́т) Moscow State University.

МГц сокр (= мегаге́рц) MHz (= megahertz).

ме́бел|ь (-и) ж собир furniture; **мя́гкая** ~ three-piece suite.

ме́бельный прил furniture опред.

ме́бельщик (-а) м furniture-maker.

мегаба́йт (-а) м megabyte.

мегава́тт (-а) м megawatt.

мегафо́н (-а) м megaphone.

меге́р|а (-ы) ж (разг) dragon.

мёд (-а; part gen -у, loc sg -у́, nom pl -ы́) м honey.

медали́ст (-а) м (челове́к) medallist (BRIT), medalist (US).

медали́ст|ка (-ки; gen pl -ок) ж medallist (BRIT), medalist (US).

меда́л|ь (-и) ж medal; **оборо́тная сторона́** ~**и** (перен) the other side of the coin.

медальо́н (-а) м medallion.

медбра́т (-а) м сокр (= медици́нский брат) nurse (male).

медве́диц|а (-ы) ж she-bear; **Больша́я М**~ the Great Bear.

медве́д|ь (-я) м (также перен) bear.

медвежа́та итп сущ см медвежо́нок.

медве́жий (-ья, -ье, -ьи) прил bear опред; **медве́жья услу́га** ≈ more of a hindrance than a help.

медвежо́нок (-о́нка; *nom pl* -а́та, *gen pl* -а́т) *м* bear cub.

ме́дик (-а) *м* medic.

медикаме́нт (-а) *м* (*обычно мн*) medicine.

медици́н|а (-ы) *ж* medicine.

медици́нск|ий (-ая, -ое, -ие) *прил* medical.

ме́дленно *нареч* slowly.

ме́дленный *прил* slow.

ме́дл|ить (-ю, -ишь) *несов неперех* to delay; ~ (*impf*) **с реше́нием/отве́том** to be slow in deciding/answering.

ме́дный *прил* copper; (*муз*) brass.

медо́вый *прил* honey *опред*; ~ **вкус/арома́т** taste/smell of honey; **медо́вый ме́сяц** honeymoon.

медпу́нкт (-а) *м сокр* (= **медици́нский пункт**) ≈ first-aid post.

медсестр|а́ (-ы́) *ж сокр* (= **медици́нская сестра́**) nurse.

меду́з|а (-ы) *ж* jellyfish.

медь (-и) *ж* copper ♦ *собир* coppers *мн*.

медя́к (-а́) *м* (*разг*) copper (*coin*).

меж|а́ (-и́; *nom pl* -и) *ж* boundary.

междоме́ти|е (-я) *ср* interjection.

KEYWORD

ме́жду *предл* (+*instr*) **1** between; **ме́жду дома́ми/города́ми** between the houses/towns; **ме́жду заседа́ниями/ле́кциями** between the meetings/lectures; **доро́га ме́жду Москво́й и Петербу́ргом** the road between Moscow and St. Petersburg

2: **они́ договори́лись ме́жду собо́й** they agreed among themselves; **ме́жду на́ми (говоря́)** between ourselves

3 (+*gen*; *в окружении*) amongst; **ме́жду домо́в росло́ большо́е де́рево** a big tree grew in amongst the houses

4: **ме́жду про́чим** (*попутно*) in passing; (*кстати*) by the way; **ме́жду про́чим, мы ви́дели Ма́шу** by the way, we saw Masha; **ме́жду тем** meanwhile; **ме́жду тем как** while.

междуве́домственный *прил* interdepartmental.

междугоро́дный *прил* intercity.

междунаро́дный *прил* international.

мезони́н (-а) *м* attic.

Ме́кк|а (-и) *ж* Mecca.

Ме́ксик|а (-и) *ж* Mexico.

мексика́н|ец (-ца) *м* Mexican.

мексика́н|ка (-ки; *gen pl* -ок) *ж см* **мексика́нец**.

мексика́нск|ий (-ая, -ое, -ие) *прил* Mexican.

мексика́нца *сущ см* **мексика́нец**.

мел (-а; *part gen* -у, *loc sg* -у́) *м* chalk.

меланхо́лик (-а) *м* melancholic.

меланхоли́чный *прил* melancholic *опред*.

меланхо́ли|я (-и) *ж* melancholy.

меле́|ть (*3sg* -ет, *3pl* -ют, *perf* **обмеле́ть**) *несов неперех* to become shallower.

мелиора́ци|я (-и) *ж* soil improvement.

мелка́ *сущ см* **мело́к**.

ме́л|кий (-кая, -кое, -кие; -лок, -лка́, -лко) *прил* (*почерк*) small; (*песок, дождь*) fine; (*неглубокий*) shallow; (*малозначительный*) petty; (*no short form; собственник*) small; (*несущественный*) minor; ~**кие де́ньги** (*мелочь*) small change; **ме́лкая буржуази́я** petty bourgeoisie.

ме́лко *нареч* (*резать, дробить*) finely; (*писать*) small ♦ *как сказ* (*у берега итп*) it's shallow.

мелкобуржуа́з|ный (-ен, -на, -но) *прил* petty-bourgeois.

мелково́д|ный (-ен, -на, -но) *прил* shallow.

мелкокали́берный *прил* small-bore, small-calibre (*BRIT*), small-caliber (*US*).

мелоди́|ный (-ен, -на, -но) *прил* melodious.

мело́ди|я (-и) *ж* tune, melody.

мелодра́м|а (-ы) *ж* (*также перен*) melodrama.

мело́к *прил см* **ме́лкий**.

мел|о́к (-ка́) *м* piece of chalk.

мелома́н (-а) *м* music-lover.

ме́лочен *прил см* **ме́лочный**.

мело́ч|иться (-у́сь, -и́шься) *несов возв* (*разг*) to be petty.

ме́лоч|ный (-ен, -на, -но) *прил* petty; (*человек*) small-minded, petty.

ме́лочь (-и; *gen pl* -е́й) *ж* (*пустяк*) triviality; (*подробность*) detail ♦ *ж собир* little things *мн*; (*мелкие монеты*) small change; „**Ты́сяча мелоче́й**" *name of shops selling household goods*; **разме́ниваться** (*impf*) **по мелоча́м** to waste one's talents.

мел|ь (-и; *loc sg* -и́) *ж* shallows *мн*, shoal; **сади́ться** (**сесть** *perf*) **на** ~ (*мор*) to run aground; **быть** (*impf*) **на мели́** (*перен: разг*) to be (stony (*BRIT*) *или* stone (*US*)) broke.

Ме́льбурн (-а) *м* Melbourne.

мелька́|ть (-ю) *несов неперех* (*появиться и исчезнуть*) to flash past; (*мерцать*) to twinkle; ~ (*impf*) **в уме́** *или* **голове́** to flash through one's mind.

мелькн|у́ть (-у́, -ёшь) *сов неперех* to flash.

ме́льком *нареч* in passing.

ме́льник (-а) *м* miller.

ме́льниц|а (-ы) *ж* mill.

ме́льничный *прил* mill *опред*.

мельхио́р (-а) *м* nickel silver.

мельча́|ть (-ю; *perf* **измельча́ть**) *несов неперех* (*река, залив*) to get shallower; (*интересы, люди*) to become petty; (*хозяйство итп*) to become smaller.

ме́льче *сравн прил от* **ме́лкий** ♦ *сравн нареч от* **ме́лко**.

мельч|и́ть (-у́, -и́шь; *perf* **измельчи́ть** *или* **размельчи́ть**) *несов перех* (*ножом*) to cut up small; (*в ступке*) to crush.

мелю́ *итп несов см* **моло́ть**.

мелюзга́ (-и́) *ж собир* (*разг: пренебр*) small fry.

мембра́н|а (-ы) *ж* (*тех*) diaphragm.

мемора́ндум (-а) *м* memorandum.

мемориа́л (-а) м memorial.
мемориа́льный прил memorial опред.
мемуа́р|ы (-ов) мн memoirs мн.
ме́неджер (-а) м manager; ~ по ма́ркетингу marketing manager.
менеджме́нт (-а) м management.
ме́нее сравн нареч от ма́ло ♦ нареч less; **тем не** ~ nevertheless; ~ **всего́** least of all; ~ **всего́ удо́бный** least convenient of all.
мензу́р|ка (-ки; gen pl -ок) ж measuring glass.
менинги́т (-а) м meningitis.
менструа́ци|я (-и) ж menstruation.
менто́л (-а) м menthol.
ме́ньше сравн прил от ма́лый, ма́ленький ♦ сравн нареч от ма́ло ♦ нареч less than; ~ **всего́** least of all.
ме́ньш|ий (-ая, -ее, -ие) сравн прил от ма́лый, ма́ленький ♦ прил (младший) younger; **по ~ей ме́ре** at least; **са́мое ~ее** no less than.
меньшинств|о́ (-а́) ср собир minority; **национа́льное** ~ ethnic minority.
меню́ ср нескл menu.
меня́ мест см я.
меня́|ть (-ю; perf поменя́ть) несов перех to change; ~ **(поменя́ть** perf**) что-н на** +acc to exchange sth for
▶ **меня́ться** (perf поменя́ться) несов возв to change; (жилплощадью) to swap; (perf измени́ться; погода, вкусы) to change; **~ся (поменя́ться** perf**) чем-н с кем-н** to exchange sth with sb.
ме́р|а (-ы) ж measure; (предел) limit; **без ~ы** extremely; **сверх ~ы** excessively; **в по́лной ~е** fully; **по ~е** +gen with; **по ~е того́ как** as; **по ~е сил** as much as one can; **по ~е возмо́жности** as far as possible; **принима́ть (приня́ть** perf**) ~ы по** +prp to take measures as regards; **вы́сшая ~а наказа́ния** capital punishment.
ме́рен прил см ме́рный.
мер|е́ть (3sg мрёт, 3pl мрут, pt мёр, -ла, -ло) несов неперех (разг: умирать) to snuff it.
мере́щиться (-усь, -ишься; perf помере́щиться) несов возв (+dat) to appear; **ему́ ~ился о́браз** he thought he saw a figure.
мёрз итп несов см мёрзнуть.
мерза́вец (-ца) м (разг) nasty piece of work.
мерза́в|ка (-ки; gen pl -ок) ж см мерза́вец.
мерза́вца сущ см мерза́вец.
ме́рз|кий (-кая, -кое, -кие; -ок, -ка́, -ко) прил (слова, личность, поступок) disgusting; (погода, настроение) foul.
мерзлот|а́ (-ы́) ж: **ве́чная ~** permafrost.
мёрзлый прил (земля) frozen; (овощи) frost-damaged.
мёрз|нуть (-ну, -нешь; pt -, -ла, -ло, perf замё рзнуть) несов неперех to freeze.
мёрзок прил см ме́рзкий.
ме́рзост|ь (-и) ж disgusting thing; (поступка)

baseness; **кака́я ~!** how disgusting!
меридиа́н (-а) м meridian.
мери́л|о (-а) ср criterion (мн criteria).
ме́рин (-а) м gelding.
ме́р|ить (-ю, -ишь; perf сме́рить или изме́рить) несов перех to measure; (perf поме́рить; примерять) to try on; ~ **(сме́рить** perf**) взгля́дом кого́-н** (перен) to look sb up and down
▶ **ме́риться** (perf поме́риться) несов возв (+instr): **~ся зна́ниями/си́лами с кем-н** to measure one's knowledge/strengths against sb.
мерк итп несов см ме́ркнуть.
ме́р|ка (-ки; gen pl -ок) ж measurements мн; (перен: критерий) standard; (мерило) measure; **снима́ть (снять** perf**) ~ку с кого́-н** to take sb's measurements.
ме́рк|нуть (3sg -нет, 3pl -нут, pt -, -ла, -ло, perf поме́ркнуть) несов неперех (также перен) to fade.
Мерку́ри|й (-я) м Mercury.
ме́рный (-ен, -на, -но) прил (размеренный) measured; (no short form; ТЕХ) measuring.
ме́рок сущ см ме́рка.
мероприя́ти|е (-я) ср measure; **культу́рное ~** cultural event.
мертве́|ть (-ю; perf омертве́ть) несов неперех (от холода) to go numb; (perf помертве́ть; от страха, от горя) to be numb.
мертве́ц (-а́) м dead person (мн people).
мёртв|ый (-, -а́, -о) прил dead; (взгляд, улица) lifeless; **спать** (impf) **~ым сном** to sleep the sleep of the dead; **лежа́ть** (impf) **~ым гру́зом** to lie unused; **мёртвый сезо́н** dead season; **мёртвая хва́тка** mortal grip; **мёртвый язы́к** dead language.
мертвя́щ|ий (ая, -ое, -ие) прил (обстановка) lifeless.
мерца́|ть (3sg -ет, 3pl -ют) несов неперех to glimmer, flicker; (звёзды) to twinkle.
ме́сив|о (-а) ср mush; (на дороге) slush.
мес|и́ть (-шу́, -сишь; perf смеси́ть) несов перех (тесто, глину) to knead; ~ (impf) **грязь** (перен) to wade through the mud.
ме́сс|а (-ы) ж (РЕЛ) Mass.
мест|а́ (-) мн provinces мн.
места́ми нареч in places.
мес|ти́ (-ту́, -тёшь; pt мёл, -ла́, -ло́, perf подмести́) несов перех (пол, комнату итп) to sweep; (мусор, листья итп) to sweep up; (подлеж: метель) to whirl; **на дворе́ ~тёт** it's a blizzard outside.
местко́м (-а) м сокр (= ме́стный комите́т) local trade-union committee.
ме́стност|ь (-и) ж (холмистая, ровная) terrain; (сельская, дачная) area, district.
ме́стный прил local ♦ (-ого; decl like adj) м local (inhabitant); **ме́стные вла́сти** local authorities

мн; **ме́стный нарко́з** (МЕД) local anaesthetic (BRIT) или anesthetic (US).

ме́ст|о (-а; nom pl -а́) ср place; (для постройки) site; (действия, происшествия) scene; (работа) job; (: вакантное) post; (в театре, поезде итп) seat; (багажа, груза) item; (в книге, в пьесе) part; **сла́бое ~** weak spot; **здесь не ~ говори́ть о деньга́х** this is not the place to talk about money; **реши́ть** (perf) **на ~е** to decide on the spot; **~а себе́ не находи́ть** (impf) to worry; **к ~у** to the point; **спа́льное ~** berth; **на Ва́шем ~е я бы ...** in your place или if I were you, I would ...; **ни с ~а!** don't move!; **у меня́ душа́** или **се́рдце не на ~е** I'm worried; см также **места́**.

местожи́тельств|о (-а) ср place of residence.

местоиме́ни|е (-я) ср pronoun.

местонахожде́ни|е (-я) ср location.

местопребыва́ни|е (-я) ср residence.

месторожде́ни|е (-я) ср (скопление) deposit; (угля, нефти, золота) field.

мест|ь (-и) ж vengeance, revenge.

ме́сяц (-а; nom pl -ы) м month; (часть луны) crescent moon; (диск луны) moon.

ме́сячн|ые (-ых; decl like adj) мн (разг) (menstrual) period ед.

ме́сячный прил monthly.

мета́лл (-а) м metal.

металли́ческ|ий (-ая, -ое, -ие) прил metal; (блеск, скрежет) metallic.

металлоло́м (-а) м scrap metal.

металлу́рги|я (-и) ж metallurgy.

метаморфо́з|а (-ы) ж metamorphosis.

мета́тель (-я) м thrower; **~ ди́ска** discus thrower.

мета́ть (-чу́, -чешь) несов перех (гранату, диск итп) to throw; (perf **намета́ть**; шов) to tack, baste; (perf **промета́ть** или **смета́ть**; для примерки) to tack; **~** (impf) **жре́бий** to draw lots; **~** (смета́ть perf) **стог се́на** to stack hay; **~** (вы́метать perf) **икру́** to spawn; **рвать** (impf) **и ~** (impf) (разг) to storm and rage

▶ **мета́ться** несов возв (в постели, в бреду) to toss and turn; (по комнате) to rush about.

мета́фор|а (-ы) ж metaphor.

мётел сущ см **метла́**.

мете́ль (-и) ж snowstorm, blizzard.

метео́р (-а) м meteor.

метеори́т (-а) м meteorite.

метеоро́лог (-а) м meteorologist.

метеороло́ги|я (-и) ж meteorology.

метеосво́д|ка (-ки; gen pl -ок) ж сокр (= метеорологи́ческая сво́дка) weather forecast или report.

метеоста́нци|я (-и) ж сокр (= метеорологи́ческая ста́нция) weather station.

ме́тить (-чу, -тишь; perf **поме́тить**) несов перех to mark ◆ неперех: **~ в** +acc (в противника, в цель) to aim at; **он ~тил в профессора́/ нача́льники** his ambition was to become a professor/manager

▶ **ме́титься** (perf **наме́титься**) несов возв: **~ся в** +acc to aim at.

ме́т|ка (-ки; gen pl -ок) ж mark.

ме́тк|ий (-ая, -ое, -ие; -ок, -ка́, -ко) прил (точный) accurate; (перен) apt; **име́ть** (impf) **~ глаз** to have a good aim.

метл|а́ (-ы́; nom pl мётлы, gen pl мётел) ж broom; **но́вая ~** (разг) new broom (fig).

метн|у́ть (-у́, -ёшь) сов перех (диск, камень) to throw

▶ **метну́ться** сов возв (разг: устреми́ться) to rush.

ме́тод (-а) м method.

мето́дик|а (-и) ж (преподавания) teaching methodology; (исследований, работы) methods мн.

методи́ческ|ий (-ая, -ое, -ие) прил systematic.

ме́ток прил см **ме́ткий**.

метр (-а) м metre (BRIT), meter (US); (линейка) measure.

метра́ж (-а́) м (квартиры, помещения) (metric) area; (ткани) length.

метрдоте́л|ь (-я) м head waiter.

метрик|а (-и) ж birth certificate.

метри́ческ|ий (-ая, -ое, -ие) прил metric; **~ая систе́ма мер** metric system; **~ая то́нна** metric ton.

метро́ ср нескл metro, tube (BRIT).

мету́ итп несов см **мести́**.

мех (-а; loc sg -у́, nom pl -а́) м fur; см также **меха́**.

мех|а́ (-о́в) мн (кузнечный, аккордеона) bellows мн.

механиза́тор (-а) м (С.-Х.) machine operator.

механизи́р|овать (-ую) (не)сов перех to mechanize.

механи́зм (-а) м mechanism; (перен: бюрократический) machinery.

меха́ник (-а) м mechanic.

меха́ник|а (-и) ж mechanics.

механи́ческ|ий (-ая, -ое, -ие) прил mechanical; (цех) machine опред.

Ме́хико (нескл) м Mexico City.

мехово́й прил fur; **~ магази́н** furrier's.

меч (-а́) м sword.

ме́ченый прил marked.

мече́т|ь (-и) ж mosque.

мечт|а́ (-ы́; gen pl -а́ний) ж dream; **не о́тдых, а ~!** (разг) it's a dream holiday!

мечта́ни|е (-я) ср (обычно мн) daydream; **преде́л ~й** ultimate dream.

мечта́тельный прил dreamy.

мечта́тель (-я) м dreamer.

мечта́тельниц|а (-ы) ж см **мечта́тель**.

мечта́|ть (-ю) несов неперех: **~ (о** +prp) to dream (of); **~** (impf) **стать врачо́м/учи́ться** to dream of becoming a doctor/studying.

ме́чу(сь) сов см **ме́тить(ся)**.

мечу́(сь) итп несов см **мета́ть(ся)**.

мешани́н|а (-ы) ж (разг) jumble.

меша́ть (-ю; perf **помеша́ть**) несов перех (суп, чай) to stir; (perf **смеша́ть**; напитки, краски) to mix ♦ *неперех* (+*dat*; *быть помехой*) to disturb, bother; (*создавать затруднения*) to hinder; **не ~ло бы поéсть** (*разг*) it wouldn't hurt to eat; **~ (помешáть** *perf*) **комý-н** +*infin* (*препятствовать*) to make it difficult for sb to do

▶ **мешáться** *несов возв* (*разг: ребёнок, вещи*) to be a pain; (*perf* **смешáться**; *путаться*) to get mixed up; **~ся** (*impf*) **в** +*acc* (*вмешиваться*) to meddle *или* interfere in.

мешкá *сущ см* **мешóк**.

мéшка|ть (**-ю**; *perf* **замéшкать**) *несов неперех* (*разг*) to dawdle; **~ (замéшкать** *perf*) **с отвéтом/ отъéздом** to be slow in answering/leaving.

мешковá|тый (**-**, **-а**, **-о**) *прил* (*пальто, платье*) baggy; (*фигура*) clumsy.

мешкови́н|а (**-ы**) *ж* sacking.

мешó|к (**-ка́**) *м* sack; (*спальный, вещевой*) bag; (*разг: человек*) lump; **~** +*gen* sack(ful) of; **дéнежный ~** moneybags; **у негó ~ки́ под глазáми** he has bags under his eyes; **костю́м сиди́т на нём ~ком** his suit hangs like a sack on him.

мешó|чек (**-ка**) *м*: **в ~** (*яйцо*) soft-boiled.

мешý *несов см* **меси́ть**.

мещани́н (**-ани́на**; *nom pl* **-áне**, *gen pl* **-áн**) *м* petty bourgeois.

мещáн|ка (**-и**) *ж см* **мещани́н**.

мещáнск|ий (**-ая**, **-ое**, **-ие**) *прил* (*взгляды*) petty-bourgeois; (*вкусы*) philistine.

мещáнств|о (**-а**) *ср* petty-bourgeois mentality; (*вкусы*) vulgarity; (*сословие*) petty bourgeoisie.

ми *ср нескл* (*муз*) mi.

МИГ (**-а**) *м сокр* = **самолёт констрýкции А.И. Микоя́на и М.И. Гурéвича**.

миг (**-а**) *м* moment.

мига́|ть (**-ю**) *несов неперех* to wink; (*перен*) to twinkle.

мигнý|ть (**-ý**, **-ёшь**) *сов неперех* to wink.

ми́гом *нареч* (*разг*) as quick as a flash; **придý ~!** I'll be there in a jiffy!

мигрáци|я (**-и**) *ж* migration.

мигрéн|ь (**-и**) *ж* migraine.

МИД (**-а**) *м сокр* (= **Министéрство инострáнных дел**) ≈ the Foreign Office (*BRIT*), ≈ the State Department (*US*).

ми́ди *ср нескл* midi ♦ *прил неизм* midi *опред*.

ми́ди|я (**-и**) *ж* mussel.

ми́зер|ный (**-ен**, **-на**, **-но**) *прил* meagre (*BRIT*), meager (*US*).

мизи́н|ец (**-ца**) *м* (*на руке*) little finger; (*на ноге*) little toe.

микроавтóбус (**-а**) *м* minibus.

микрóб (**-а**) *м* microbe.

микробиóлог (**-а**) *м* microbiologist.

микробиолóги|я (**-и**) *ж* microbiology.

микрокли́мат (**-а**) *м* microclimate; (*перен*)

atmosphere.

микрóн (**-а**) *м* micron.

микроорганúзм (**-а**) *м* microorganism.

микропроцéссор (**-а**) *м* microprocessor.

микрорайóн (**-а**) *м* ≈ catchment area (*administrative subdivision of urban region in Russia*).

микроскóп (**-а**) *м* microscope.

микроскопи́ческ|ий (**-ая**, **-ое**, **-ие**) *прил* (*также перен*) microscopic.

микросхéм|а (**-ы**) *ж* (micro)chip.

микрофи́льм (**-а**) *м* microfilm.

микрофи́ш|а (**-и**) *ж* microfiche.

микрофóн (**-а**) *м* microphone.

микрохирурги́|я (**-и**) *ж* microsurgery.

микроэконóмик|а (**-и**) *ж* microeconomics *мн*.

ми́ксер (**-а**) *м* mixer.

микстýр|а (**-ы**) *ж* mixture; **~ от кáшля** cough mixture *или* linctus.

Милáн (**-а**) *м* Milan.

ми́леньк|ий (**-ая**, **-ое**, **-ие**) *прил* (*хорошенький*) pretty *или* sweet little; (: *любимый*) darling; **он сдéлает éто как ~** he'll do it or else.

милитари́зм (**-а**) *м* militarism.

милитаризовá|ть (**-ю**) (*не*)*сов перех* to militarize.

милитари́ст (**-а**) *м* militarist.

милиционéр (**-а**) *м* policeman (*in Russia*) (*мн* policemen).

мили́ци|я (**-и**) *ж*, *собир* police (*in Russia*); (*разг: участок*) police station.

миллиáрд (**-а**) *м* billion.

миллиардéр (**-а**) *м* billionaire.

миллигрáмм (**-а**) *м* milligram(me).

миллимéтр (**-а**) *м* millimetre (*BRIT*), millimeter (*US*).

миллиметрóвк|а (**-и**) *ж* (*разг*) graph paper.

миллиóн (**-а**) *м* million.

миллионéр (**-а**) *м* millionaire.

миллиóнн|ый (**-ая**, **-ое**, **-ые**) *чис* (*посетитель, автомобиль итп*) millionth; (*исчисляемый миллионами*) million-strong; **у негó ~ое состоя́ние** he is worth millions.

ми́ло *нареч* (*улыбнуться*) sweetly ♦ *как сказ*: **как ~!** how sweet!

ми́л|овать (**-ую**; *perf* **поми́ловать**) *несов перех* to have mercy on.

милови́д|ный (**-ен**, **-на**, **-но**) *прил* pleasing; **онá ~на** she has a pleasing appearance.

милосéрден *прил см* **милосéрдный**.

милосéрди|е (**-я**) *ср* compassion; **сестрá ~я** nurse.

милосéрд|ный (**-ен**, **-на**, **-но**) *прил* compassionate.

ми́лостын|я (**-и**) *ж* alms.

ми́лост|ь (**-и**) *ж* (*доброта*) kind-heartedness; **дéлать (сдéлать** *perf*) **что-н из ~и** to do sth out of the kindness of one's heart; **~и прóсим!**

welcome!; **по твое́й ~и опозда́ли** thanks to you we are late; **скажи́те на ~** you don't say.

ми́лочк|а (-и) ж (*разг: обращение*) dearest.

ми́лый (-, -á, -о) прил (*симпатичный*) pleasant, nice; (*дорогой*) dear ♦ (-ого; *decl like adj*) м (*возлюбленный*) darling.

ми́л|я (-и) ж mile; **морска́я ~** nautical mile.

мим (-а) м mime (artist).

ми́мик|а (-и) ж expression.

ми́мо нареч past ♦ предл (+gen) past.

мимо́з|а (-ы) ж (*БОТ*) mimosa.

мимолёт|ный (-ен, -на, -но) прил fleeting.

мимохо́дом нареч on the way; (*перен: упомянуть*) in passing.

мин. сокр (= **мину́та**) min. (= *minute*); (= **минима́льный**) min. (= *minimum*).

ми́н|а (-ы) ж (*ВОЕН*) mine; (*выражение лица*) expression.

минаре́т (-а) м minaret.

миндалеви́дный прил almond-shaped; **у него́ миндалеви́дные глаза́** he is almond-eyed.

минда́лин|а (-ы) ж (*МЕД: обычно мн*) tonsil.

минда́л|ь (-я) м almond.

минда́льный прил almond.

минёр (-а) м (*ВОЕН*) *person who lays mines*.

минера́л (-а) м mineral.

минера́лк|а (-и) ж (*разг*) mineral water.

минера́льный прил mineral.

минздра́в (-а) м сокр (= **министе́рство здравоохране́ния**) Ministry of Health.

ми́ни ср нескл mini; **~ ю́бка** miniskirt; **~ пла́тье** minidress.

миниатю́р|а (-ы) ж (*ИСКУССТВО*) miniature; (*ТЕАТР*) short play; **в ~е** in miniature.

миниатю́р|ный (-ен, -на, -но) прил (*статуэтка*) miniature опред; (*перен: женщина*) dainty.

минима́л|ьный (-ен, -ьна, -ьно) прил minimum опред.

ми́нимум (-а) м minimum ♦ нареч minimum; **прожи́точный ми́нимум** minimum living wage.

мини́р|овать (-ую; *perf* **замини́ровать**) (не)сов перех (*ВОЕН*) to mine.

минисериа́л (-а) м mini-series.

министе́рск|ий (-ая, -ое, -ие) прил ministerial.

министе́рств|о (-а) ср ministry.

мини́стр (-а) м (*ПОЛИТ*) minister.

мин|ова́ть (-у́ю) (не)сов перех to pass; (*no impf*; +gen; *избежать*) to escape, avoid ♦ неперех to pass, be over.

мино́г|а (-и) ж lamprey.

миноиска́тел|ь (-я) м mine detector.

миномёт (-а) м mortar.

миноно́с|ец (-ца) м destroyer.

мино́р (-а) м minor key.

мино́рный прил (*МУЗ*) minor; (*перен*) subdued.

Минск (-а) м Minsk.

мину́вш|ее (-его; *decl like adj*) ср the past.

мину́вший (-ая, -ее, -ие) прил past.

ми́нус (-а) м (*также МАТ*) minus; (*перен: недостаток*) drawback ♦ м нескл minus; **пять ~ два – три** five minus two equals three.

ми́нусовый прил (*температура*) subzero.

мину́т|а (-ы) ж minute; **(одну́) ~у!** (*просьба подожда́ть*) just a minute!; **~ в мину́ту** to the minute; **он без пяти́ мину́т врач/юри́ст** (*разг*) he's a step away from qualifying as a doctor/lawyer; **она́ придёт с ~ы на ~у** she will be here any minute.

мину́тный прил (*стрелка*) minute опред; (*дело, разговор*) brief; (*порыв, увлечение*) momentary.

ми́н|уть (*3sg* -ет, *3pl* -ут) сов неперех (+dat; *исполниться*): **ей ~уло 16 лет** she has turned 16.

мин|у́ть (-у́, -ёшь) сов (не)перех to pass.

мир (-а; *nom pl* -ы́) м world; (*Вселенная*) universe; (*loc sg* -ý; *РЕЛ*) (secular) world; (*состояние без войны*) peace; **~ те́сен** it's a small world; **он не от ми́ра сего́** he has his head in the clouds; **заключа́ть (заключи́ть** *perf*) **~** to make peace; **чемпио́н ми́ра** world champion.

мира́ж (-á) м (*также перен*) mirage.

ми́рен прил см **ми́рный**.

мир|и́ть (-ю́, -и́шь; *perf* **помири́ть** или **примири́ть**) несов перех to reconcile

▶ **мири́ться** (*perf* **помири́ться**) несов возв: **~ся с** +instr to make up или be reconciled with; (*perf* **примири́ться**; **с недоста́тками, с положе́нием**) to come to terms with, reconcile o.s to.

ми́р|ный (-ен, -на, -но) прил peaceful; **ми́рное вре́мя** peacetime; **ми́рное населе́ние** civilian population; **ми́рные перегово́ры** peace talks или negotiations.

мировоззре́ни|е (-я) ср (*писателя, общества*) philosophy of life.

мирово́й прил world опред; (*перен: разг: хороший*) fantastic.

мирозда́ни|е (-я) ср universe.

миролюби́в|ый (-, -а, -о) прил peaceable.

миропонима́ни|е (-я) ср conception of the world.

миротво́р|ец (-ца) м peacemaker.

миротво́рческ|ий (-ая, -ое, -ие) прил peacemaking; **миротво́рческие войска́** peacekeeping force ед.

мирско́й прил (*РЕЛ*) worldly.

ми́с|ка (-ки; *gen pl* -ок) ж bowl.

мисс ж нескл Miss.

миссионе́р (-а) м missionary.

ми́ссис ж нескл Mrs.

Миссиси́пи ср нескл Mississippi.

ми́сси|я (-и) ж mission.

ми́стер (-а) м Mr.

ми́стик|а (-и) ж mysticism; (*разг: о чём-н загадочном*) mystery.

мистифика́ци|я (-и) ж hoax.

мисти́ческ|ий (-ая, -ое, -ие) прил mystical.

ми́тинг (-а) м mass meeting, rally.

митингова́ть (-у́ю) несов неперех to hold a mass meeting или rally.

митрополи́т (-а) м (*РЕЛ*) metropolitan.

миф (-а) *м* (*также перен*) myth.
мифи́ческий (-ая, -ое, -ие) *прил* mythical.
мифоло́ги|я (-и) *ж* mythology.
мише́н|ь (-и) *ж* (*также перен*) target.
ми́шк|а (-и) *м* (*разг*) bear; (*игрушка*) teddy (bear).
мишур|а́ (-ы́) *м* tinsel.
МКК *м сокр* (= *Междунаро́дный Кра́сный Крест*) IRC (= *International Red Cross*).
мл. *сокр* (= *мла́дший*) Junr (= *junior*).
младе́н|ец (-ца) *м* infant, baby.
младе́нческий (-ая, -ое, -ие) *прил*: ~ие го́ды infancy.
младе́нчеств|о (-а) *ср* infancy, babyhood.
мла́дше *сравн прил от* **молодо́й**.
мла́дший (-ая, -ее, -ие) *прил* younger; (*самый младший*) (the) youngest; (*сотрудник, класс*) junior; ~ **лейтена́нт** second lieutenant.
млекопита́ющее (-его; *decl like adj*) *ср* mammal.
мле|ть (-ю) *несов неперех*: ~ (**от** +*gen*) (*от счастья, от любви*) to be overcome (with).
мле́чный *прил* milky; **М~ Путь** the Milky Way; **мле́чный сок** latex.
млн. *сокр* = **миллио́н**.
мм *сокр* (= *миллиме́тр*) mm= millimetre (*BRIT*) *или* millimeter (*US*).
мне *мест см* **я**.
мне́ни|е (-я) *ср* opinion.
мни́мый *прил* (*кажущийся*) imaginary; (*ложный*) fake.
мни́телен *прил см* **мни́тельный**.
мни́тельност|ь (-и) *ж* suspiciousness.
мни́тельный (-ен, -ьна, -ьно) *прил* suspicious.
мно́гие *прил* many ♦ (-их; *decl like adj*) мн (*много людей*) many (people).

┌─────────────────────────────┐
│ **KEYWORD** │
└─────────────────────────────┘

мно́го *чис* (+*gen*) a lot of; **они́ созда́ли нам мно́го пробле́м** they created a lot of problems for us; **мно́го книг тебе́ да́ли?** did they give you many *или* a lot of books?; **мно́го рабо́ты тебе́ да́ли?** did they give you much *или* a lot of work?
♦ *нареч* **1** (*разговаривать, пить итп*) a lot; **он мно́го рабо́тает** he works a lot
2 (+*comparative*; *гораздо*) much
♦ *как сказ*: **у него́ мно́го враго́в** he has a lot of enemies; **у него́ мно́го друзе́й?** does he have many friends?; **по мно́гу** +*gen* many; **они́ приходи́ли по мно́гу раз** they came many times.

многобо́р|ец (-ца) *м competitor in multi-event competition*.
многобо́рь|е (-я) *ср multi-event competition*.
многогра́нен *прил см* **многогра́нный**.
многогра́нник (-а) *м* polyhedron.
многогра́н|ный (-ен, -на, -но) *прил* (*талант,

камень, личность) multifaceted; (*фигура*) polyhedral.
многоде́т|ный (-ен, -на, -но) *прил* with many children.
мно́г|ое (-ого; *decl like adj*) *ср* a great deal.
многожёнств|о (-а) *ср* polygamy.
многозна́чен *прил см* **многозна́чный**.
многозначи́тел|ьный (-ен, -ьна, -ьно) *прил* significant.
многозна́ч|ный (-ен, -на, -но) *прил* (*число, номер*) multi-digit; (*слово, глагол*) polysemantic.
многокра́т|ный (-ен, -на, -но) *прил* (*визиты*) repeated; (*виза*) multiple(-entry); ~ **чемпио́н/призёр** many-times champion/prizewinner.
многоле́т|ний (-яя, -ее, -ие) *прил* (*планы*) long-term; (*труд, усилия*) of many years; (*растения*) perennial.
многолю́д|ный (-ен, -на, -но) *прил* (*улица*) crowded; (*митинг*) well-attended.
многонациона́л|ьный (-ен, -ьна, -ьно) *прил* multinational.
многопо́льзовательск|ий (-ая, -ое, -ие) *прил* (*КОМП*) multiaccess.
многообеща́ющий (-ая, -ее, -ие) *прил* promising.
многообра́зен *прил см* **многообра́зный**.
многообра́зи|е (-я) *ср* (*жизни*) variety; (*растений, животных*) diversity.
многообра́з|ный (-ен, -на, -но) *прил* diverse, varied.
многосеме́й|ный (-ен, -йна, -йно) *прил* with a large family.
многосло́в|ный (-ен, -на, -но) *прил* verbose, long-winded.
многосло́жный *прил* polysyllabic.
многосторо́н|ний (-няя, -нее, -ние) *прил* (*ГЕОМ*) polygonal; (*переговоры, встреча*) multilateral; (*вопрос, личность*) many-sided; (-ен, -ня, -не; *интересы*) diverse.
многотира́жк|а (-и) *ж* (*разг*) factory news sheet.
многотира́жный *прил* with a large circulation.
многото́чи|е (-я) *ср* (*линг*) ellipsis.
многоуважа́емый *прил* esteemed; (*в письме*) Dear.
многоуго́льник (-а) *м* polygon.
многочи́слен|ный (-, -на, -но) *прил* numerous.
многочле́н (-а) *м* (*МАТ*) multinomial.
многоэта́жный *прил* multistorey (*BRIT*), multistory (*US*).
мно́жествен|ный *прил*: ~ое число́ (*линг*) the plural (number).
мно́жеств|о (-а) *ср* (*МАТ*) set; ~ +*gen* a great number of.
мно́жител|ьный *прил*: ~ая те́хника photocopying equipment.
мно́ж|ить (-у, -ишь; *perf* умно́жить) *несов перех* (*увеличивать*) to multiply; (*perf* помно́жить;

МАТ): ~ (**на** +*acc*) to multiply (by)
▶ **мно́житься** (*perf* **умно́житься**) *несов возв* to multiply.
мной *мест см* **я**.
мнс *м сокр* (= *мла́дший нау́чный сотру́дник*) junior researcher.
мну (**сь**) *итп несов см* **мя́ть(ся)**.
моби́лен *прил см* **моби́льный**.
мобилиза́ци|я (**-и**) *ж* mobilization.
мобилиз|ова́ть (**-у́ю**) (**не**)*сов перех* to mobilize; ~ (*impf/perf*) **кого́-н на что-н** to mobilize sb for sth.
моби́льный (**-ен, -ьна, -ьно**) *прил* (*войска, дом*) mobile; (*ум, руководство*) active.
мог *несов см* **мочь**.
моги́л|а (**-ы**) *ж* grave; **стоя́ть** (*impf*) **одно́й ного́й в** ~**е** (*разг*) to have one foot in the grave.
моги́льник (**-а**) *м* burial ground; (*для радиоактивных отходов*) dumping ground.
моги́льный *прил* (*плита*) grave *опред*; (*холм, участок*) burial *опред*.
моги́льщик (**-а**) *м* grave digger.
могла́ *итп несов см* **мочь**.
могу́ *итп несов см* **мочь**.
могу́ч|ий (**-ая, -ее, -ие; -, -а, -е**) *прил* mighty; (*талант, ум*) great.
могу́ществен|ный (**-, -на, -но**) *прил* mighty, powerful.
могу́ществ|о (**-а**) *ср* might, power.
мо́д|а (**-ы**) *ж* fashion; (*разг: манера поведения*) habit; **по** ~**е** fashionably; **быть в** ~**е** to be in fashion; **входи́ть** (**войти́** *perf*) **в** ~**у** to come into fashion; **выходи́ть** (**вы́йти** *perf*) **из** ~**ы** to go out of fashion; *см также* **мо́ды**.
модели́р|овать (**-ую**) (**не**)*сов перех* (*одежду*) to design; (*perf* **смодели́ровать**; *процесс, поведение*) to simulate.
моде́л|ь (**-и**) *ж* model.
модельер (**-а**) *м* fashion designer.
моде́льный *прил* (*обувь, одежда*) high-fashion.
моде́м (**-а**) *м* (*КОМП*) modem.
мо́ден *прил см* **мо́дный**.
модерниза́ци|я (**-и**) *ж* modernization.
модерн (**-а**) *м* (*ИСКУССТВО*) art nouveau.
модернизи́р|овать (**-ую**) (**не**)*сов перех* to modernize.
модифика́ци|я (**-и**) *ж* modification.
мо́дник (**-а**) *м* (*разг*) snappy dresser.
мо́дниц|а (**-ы**) *ж см* **мо́дник**.
мо́днича|ть (**-ю**) *несов неперех* (*разг*) to be a snappy dresser.
мо́дно *нареч* (*одеваться, стричься*) fashionably ◆ *как сказ*: ~ **носи́ть ми́ни** miniskirts are in fashion.
мо́д|ный (**-ен, -на, -но**) *прил* fashionable; (*no short form*; *журнал*) fashion *опред*.
мо́д|ы (**-**) *мн* fashions *мн*; **журна́л мод** fashion magazine.
мо|ё (**-его́**) *притяж мест см* **мой**.
мо́жет *несов см* **мочь** ◆ *вводн сл* (*разг*) maybe, perhaps.

мо́жешь *итп несов см* **мочь**.
можжеве́льник (**-а**) *м* juniper.
мо́жно *как сказ* (*возможно*): ~ +*infin* it is possible to do; ~ **кури́ть** smoking is allowed *или* permitted; ~ (**войти́**)**?** may I (come in)?; **как** ~ (*разг: выражает осуждение*) how could he *итп*; **как** ~ **лу́чше/быстре́е** as well/quickly as possible.
моза́ик|а (**-и**) *ж* (*узор*) mosaic; (*искусство*) mosaic work.
моза́ич|ный (**-ен, -на, -но**) *прил* mosaic.
Мозамби́к (**-а**) *м* Mozambique.
мозг (**-а**; *loc sg* **-у́**, *nom sg* **-й**) *м* brain; (*перен: центр*) nerve centre (*BRIT*) *или* center (*US*); **спинно́й** ~ spinal cord; **ко́стный** ~ (bone) marrow; **до мо́зга косте́й** through and through; **шевели́ть** (**пошевели́ть** *perf*) ~**а́ми** (*разг*) to use one's head; *см также* **мозги́**.
мозг|и́ (**-о́в**) *мн* (*КУЛИН*) brains *мн*.
мозг|ова́ть (**-у́ю**) *несов неперех* (*разг*) to think.
мозгови́тый *прил* (*разг*) brainy.
мозгово́й *прил* cerebral; (*интеллектуальный*) intellectual; ~ **центр** nerve centre (*BRIT*) *или* center (*US*).
мозо́лист|ый (**-, -а, -о**) *прил* calloused.
мозо́л|ить (**-ю, -ишь**) *несов перех*: ~ **глаза́ кому́-н** (*разг*) to bug sb by one's very presence.
мозо́л|ь (**-и**) *ж* corn, callus.
мозо́льный *прил*: ~ **пла́стырь** corn plaster.
мой (**моего́**; *см* **Table 8**; *f* **моя́**, *nt* **моё**, *pl* **мои́**) *притяж мест* my; **по-мо́ему** my way; (*по моему мнению*) in my opinion.
мо́йк|а (**-и**) *ж* (*мытьё*) washing; (*раковина*) sink.
МОК (**-а**) *м сокр* (= *Междунаро́дный олимпи́йский комите́т*) IOC (= *International Olympic Committee*).
мо́к|нуть (**-ну, -нешь**; *pt* **-, -ла, -ло**) *несов неперех* to get wet; (*лежать в воде*) to be soaking.
мо́кро *как сказ* it's wet.
мокро́т|а (**-ы**) *ж* phlegm.
мокрота́ (**-ы́**) *ж* (*разг*) dampness.
мо́кр|ый (**-, -а́, -о**) *прил* wet.
мол (**-а**; *loc sg* **-у́**) *м* breakwater, mole ◆ *част* (*разг*): **он, ~, ничего́ не зна́ет** he says he knows nothing.
молв|а́ (**-ы́**) *ж* rumour (*BRIT*), rumor (*US*).
молда́вск|ий (**-ая, -ое, -ие**) *прил* Moldavian.
Молдо́в|а (**-ы**) *ж* Moldova.
молдава́н|ин (**-ина**; *nom pl* **-е**) *м* Moldavian.
молдава́н|ка (**-ки**; *gen pl* **-ок**) *ж см* **молдава́нин**.
моле́б|ен (**-на**) *м* (*РЕЛ*) service.
молеку́л|а (**-ы**) *ж* molecule.
молекуля́рный *прил* molecular.
моле́ни|е (**-я**) *ср* praying; (*мольба*) entreaty.
моли́тв|а (**-ы**) *ж* prayer.
моли́твенник (**-а**) *м* prayer book.
моли́|ться (**-ю́сь, -ишься**; *perf* **помоли́ться**) *несов возв*: ~ +*dat* to pray to; (*no perf*; *перен*): ~ **на** +*acc* to idolize.

моллю́ск (-а) *м* mollusc.

молниено́с|ный (-ен, -на, -но) *прил* lightning *опред*.

мо́лни|я (-и) *ж* lightning; (*застёжка*) zip (fastener); (*BRIT*), zipper (*US*); **телегра́мма-~** express telegram.

молодёжный *прил* (*клуб, театр*) youth *опред*; (*мода, газета*) for young people.

молодёж|ь (-и) *ж собир* young people *мн*.

молоде́|ть (-ю; *perf* **помолоде́ть**) *несов неперех* (*выглядеть моложе*) to look younger; (*чувствовать себя моложе*) to feel younger; (*население*) to become younger.

мо́лод|ец (-ца) *м* (*ФОЛЬКЛОР*) brave lad, fine young man.

молоде́|ц (-ца́) *м* strong fellow; ~! (*разг*) well done!; **она́/он** ~! (*разг*) she/he has done well!; **держа́ться** (*impf*) ~цо́м to put up a good show.

молоде́цк|ий (-ая, -ое, -ие) *прил* (*вид*) dashing; (*поступок*) valiant.

молоди́ть (-жу́, -ди́шь) *несов перех*: ~ **кого́-н** to make sb look younger

▶ **молоди́ться** *несов возв* to try to look younger.

молодня́|к (-а́) *м собир* (*ЗООЛ*) young (*of animals*); (*БОТ*) saplings *мн*.

молодожён (-а) *м* (*обычно мн*) newlywed.

молодо́й (**мо́лод, молода́, мо́лодо**) *прил* young; (*картофель, листва*) new; (*задор, отвага*) youthful; (*no short form*; *вино, пиво*) young; (*no short form*) unripe.

мо́лодост|ь (-и) *ж* youth; **он не пе́рвой** ~**и** he's getting on in years.

мо́лодца *итп сущ см* **мо́лодец**.

молодца́ *итп сущ см* **молодец**.

молодцева́тый *прил* sprightly.

моло́дчик (-а) *м* thug.

моложа́в|ый (-, -а, -о) *прил* (*человек*) young-looking; (*вид, лицо*) youthful.

моло́же *сравн прил от* **молодо́й**.

моложу́(сь) *несов см* **молоди́ть(ся)**.

молоко́ (-а́) *ср* milk.

молокосо́с (-а) *м* (*разг: пренебр*) greenhorn.

мо́лот (-а) *м* hammer.

молоти́л|ка (-ки; *gen pl* -ок) *ж* threshing machine.

мол|оти́ть (-очу́, -о́тишь) *несов перех* (*пшеницу*) to thresh; (*разг: колотить*) to hammer.

молот|о́к (-ка́) *м* hammer; **продава́ть** (**прода́ть** *perf*) **что-н с ~ка́** to sell sth by auction, auction sth.

мо́лотый *прил* (*кофе, перец*) ground.

мол|о́ть (**мелю́, ме́лешь**; *perf* **смоло́ть** *или* **помоло́ть**) *несов перех* (*зерно, кофе*) to grind; ~ (*impf*) **вздор** *или* **чепуху́** (*разг*) to talk rubbish.

молоч|ко́ (-а́) *ср* (*жидкий крем*) lotion.

моло́чник (-а) *м* (*посуда*) milk jug; (*разносчик молока*) milkman (*мн* milkmen).

моло́чниц|а (-ы) *ж* milklady.

моло́чный *прил* (*продукты, скот*) dairy *опред*; (*каша, коктейль*) milk *опред*; (*поросёнок, телёнок*) sucking; (*железа*) mammary; (*хим*) lactic; **моло́чная ку́хня** *place where baby food is prepared*; **моло́чная сестра́** foster sister; **моло́чный брат** foster brother; **моло́чный зуб** milk tooth.

молочу́ *несов см* **молоти́ть**.

мо́лча *нареч* (*кивнуть, уйти*) silently; (*согласиться*) tacitly.

молчали́в|ый (-, -а, -о) *прил* silent; (*no short form*; *согласие, одобрение*) tacit; ~ **мужчи́на** a man of few words.

молча́ни|е (-я) *ср* (*безмолвие*) silence; ~ – **знак согла́сия** silence can be taken to mean approval.

молч|а́ть (-у́, -и́шь) *несов неперех* to be silent; ~ (*impf*) **о** +*prp* to keep silent *или* quiet about.

мол|ь (-и) *ж* moth.

мольб|а́ (-ы́) *ж* entreaty.

мольбе́рт (-а) *м* easel.

моме́нт (-а) *м* moment; (*в фильме*) episode; (*доклада, исследования*) point; **теку́щий** ~ the current situation.

момента́лен *прил см* **момента́льный**.

момента́льно *нареч* instantly.

момента́л|ьный (-ен, -ьна, -ьно) *прил* instant.

мона́рх (-а) *м* monarch.

мона́рхи|я (-и) *ж* monarchy.

монасты́р|ь (-я́) *м* (*мужской*) monastery; (*женский*) convent.

мона́х (-а) *м* monk.

мона́хин|я (-и; *gen pl* -ь) *ж* nun.

мона́шеск|ий (-ая, -ое, -ие) *прил* (*также перен*) monastic.

мона́шеств|о (-а) *ср* monastic life.

Монбла́н (-а) *м* Mont Blanc.

монго́л (-а) *м* Mongol, Mongolian.

монго́л|ка (-ки; *gen pl* -ок) *ж см* **монго́л**.

монго́льск|ий (-ая, -ое, -ие) *прил* Mongolian.

Монго́ли|я (-и) *ж* Mongolia.

моне́т|а (-ы) *ж* coin; **плати́ть** (**отплати́ть** *perf*) **кому́-н той же** ~**ой** (*отомстить*) to pay sb back in kind; **принима́ть** (**приня́ть** *perf*) **что-н за чи́стую** ~**у** to take sth at face value.

монетари́ст (-а) *м* monetarist.

монета́рный *прил* monetary.

моне́тный *прил*: ~ **двор** mint.

монито́р (-а) *м* monitor.

моногра́мм|а (-ы) *ж* monogram.

моногра́фи|я (-и) *ж* monograph.

моноли́т (-а) *м* monolith.

моноли́т|ный (-ен, -на, -но) *прил* (*глыба, колонна*) monolithic; (*перен*) united.

моноло́г (-а) *м* monologue.

монополиза́ци|я (-и) *ж* monopolization.

монополизи́р|овать (-ую) (*не*)*сов перех* to

monopolize.

монополист (-а) *м* monopolist.

монополия (-и) *ж* monopoly.

монопольный *прил* monopoly *опред*.

монотонный (-ен, -на, -но) *прил* (*также перен*) monotonous.

монохромный *прил* (*комп*) monochrome.

Монреаль (-я) *м* Montreal.

монтаж (-á) *ж* (*сооружения*) erection; (*оборудования*) mounting, assembly; (*кадров, фильма*) editing.

монтажник (-а) *м* (*на стройке*) rigger; (*на фабрике*) fitter.

монтажница (-ы) *ж см* **монтажник**.

монтёр (-а) *м* fitter; (*электромонтёр*) electrician.

монтировать (-ую; *perf* **смонтировать**) *несов перех* (*оборудование, схему*) to assemble; (*фильм, передачу*) to edit.

монумент (-а) *м* monument.

монументальный (-ен, -ьна, -ьно) *прил* monumental.

мопед (-а) *м* moped (*with movable pedals*).

мор (-а) *м* pestilence, plague.

морален *прил см* **моральный**.

морализировать (-ую) *несов неперех* to moralize.

мораль (-и) *ж* (*этика поведения*) morals *мн*, ethics *мн*; (*басни, сказки*) moral; (*разг: нравоучение*) moralizing.

моральный (-ен, -ьна, -ьно) *прил* moral; (*no short form*; *кодекс, нормы*) moral, ethical; **моральный износ, моральное устаревание** obsolescence.

мораторий (-я) *м* moratorium.

морг (-а) *м* morgue.

моргать (-ю) *несов неперех* to blink; (*подмигивать*): ~ (+*dat*) to wink (at).

моргнуть (-ý, -ёшь) *сов неперех* to blink; (*подмигнуть*): ~ (+*dat*) to wink (at); **не ~ýв глазом** (*разг*) without batting an eyelid.

морда (-ы) *ж* (*животного*) muzzle; (*разг: лицо*) mug.

мордвин (-а) *м* Mordvin.

мордвинка (-ки; *gen pl* -ок) *ж см* **мордвин**.

Мордвия (-и) *ж* Mordvia.

море (-я; *nom pl* -я, *gen pl* -éй) *ср* (*также перен*) sea; **открытое** ~ open sea; **емý ~ по колено** (*разг*) he's afraid of nothing.

мореплавание (-я) *ср* (*плавание*) seafaring; (*вождение судов*) navigation.

мореплаватель (-я) *м* seafarer.

мореходка (-и) *ж* (*разг*) naval college.

мореходный *прил* (*училище, испытания*) naval; (*инструменты*) navigational.

морж (-á) *м* walrus; (*перен*) *wintertime open-air bather*.

моржиха (-и) *ж см* **морж**.

моржовый *прил* walrus *опред*.

морилка (-и) *ж* (*разг: краска*) stain; (*от насекомых*) insecticide.

морить (-ю, -ишь; *perf* **поморить**) *несов перех* (*насекомых*) to exterminate; (*дерево*) to stain; (*дуб*) to fume; (*perf* **разморить**; *подлеж: сон, жара*) to exhaust, drain; ~ (*заморить perf*) **голодом кого-н** to starve sb; ~ (**уморить** *perf*) **шутками кого-н** (*разг*) to have sb in stitches with one's jokes.

морковка (-ки; *gen pl* -ок) *ж* (*разг: одна штука*) carrot; (*морковь*) carrots *мн*.

морковный *прил* carrot *опред*.

морковь (-и) *ж* carrots *мн*.

мороженица (-ы) *ж* (*аппарат*) ice-cream maker; (*кафе*) ice-cream parlour (*BRIT*) *или* parlor (*US*).

мороженое (-ого; *decl like adj*) *ср* ice cream.

мороженый *прил* frozen; (*испорченный морозом*) frost-damaged.

морожу *несов см* **морозить**.

мороз (-а) *м* frost; **у нас стоят ~ы** we're having a spell of freezing (cold) weather; **Дед М~** ≈ Father Christmas.

морозен *прил см* **морозный**.

морозильник (-а) *м* freezer.

морозильный *прил* freezing; **морозильная камера** deepfreeze.

морозить (-жу, -зишь) *несов перех* to freeze ♦ *безл*; **на улице ~зит** it's freezing outside.

морозный (-ен, -на, -но) *прил* frosty.

морозостойкий (-йкая, -йкое, -йкие; -ек, -йка, -йко) *прил* frost-resistant.

моросить (*3sg* -ит, *3pl* -ят) *несов неперех* to drizzle.

морочить (-у, -ишь; *perf* **заморочить**) *несов перех* (*разг*) to fool; ~ (**заморочить** *perf*) **голову комý-н** (*разг*) to pull sb's leg.

морошка (-и) *ж* cloudberry.

морс (-а; *part gen* -у) *м* (fruit) drink.

морской (-ая, -ое, -ие) *прил* sea *опред*; (*био, воен*) marine; (*курорт, лечебница*) seaside *опред*; ~**ое страхование** marine insurance; ~**ое право** maritime law; **морская болезнь** seasickness; **морской волк** sea dog; **морская свинка** guinea pig.

морфий (-я) *м* morphine, morphia.

морфология (-и) *ж* morphology.

морщина (-ы) *ж* (*на лице*) wrinkle; (*на ткани*) crease.

морщинистый (-, -а, -о) *прил* (*лицо*) wrinkled.

морщить (-у, -ишь; *perf* **наморщить**) *несов перех* (*брови*) to knit; (*perf* **сморщить**; *нос, лоб*) to wrinkle; (*лицо*) to screw up

▶ **морщиться** (*perf* **наморщиться**) *несов возв* to screw up one's face; (*одежда, ткань*) to crease; ~**ся** (**сморщиться** *perf*) **от** +*gen* (*от старости, от солнца*) to become wrinkled from; (*от боли*) to wince in.

морщить (*3sg* -ит, *3pl* -ят) *несов неперех* (*разг*) to be wrinkled.

моряк (-á) *м* sailor.

Москва (-ы́) *ж* Moscow.

москвич (-á) *м* Muscovite.

москви́ч|ка (-ки; *gen pl* -ек) ж см **москви́ч**.

мост (-á; *loc sg* -ý) м bridge; (*телевизионный, космический*) link; (*АВТ*) axle.

мо́стик (-a) м bridge; **капита́нский** ~ bridge (*NAUT*).

мо|сти́ть (-щý, -сти́шь; *perf* **вы́мостить**) *несов перех* (*площадь, улицу*) to pave; (*perf* **намости́ть**; *пол*) to lay.

мостк|и́ (-óв) *мн* (*через лужу*) duckboard *ед*; (*у реки, у пруда*) wooden platform *ед*.

мостов|а́я (-óй; *decl like adj*) ж road.

МОТ ж *сокр* (= *международная организация труда*) ILO (= *International Labour Organization*).

мота́|ть (-ю; *perf* **намота́ть**) *несов перех* (*нитки*) to wind ◆ (*perf* **умота́ть**) *неперех* (*разг: уехать*) to go off; (*perf* **помота́ть**): ~ +*instr* (*головой*) to shake; ~**й отсю́да!** get lost!; ~ (*impf*) **кому́-н не́рвы** (*разг*) to get on sb's nerves.

► **мота́|ться** *несов возв* to swing; (*разг: хлопотать*) to rush about.

моте́л|ь (-я) м motel.

моти́в (-a) м (*преступления*) motive; (*для развода*) grounds *мн*; (*мелодия*) motif.

мотиви́р|овать (-ую) (*не*)*сов перех* to justify.

мотка́ *сущ см* **мото́к**.

мотого́н|ка (-ки; *gen pl* -ок) ж (*обычно мн*) motorcycle race.

мотого́нщик (-a) м motorcycle racer.

мото́к (-ка́) м skein.

мото́р (-a) м motor; (*автомобиля, лодки*) engine.

мотори́ст (-a) м motor mechanic.

мото́рный *прил* motor *опред*; **мото́рная ло́дка** motorboat.

моторо́ллер (-a) м (motor) scooter.

мотоци́кл (-a) м motorcycle.

моты́г|а (-и) ж hoe.

мотыл|ёк (-ька́) м moth.

м|ох (мха; *loc sg* мху, *nom pl* мхи) м moss.

мохе́р (-a) м mohair.

мохе́ровый *прил* mohair.

мохна́тый (-, -a, -о) *прил* (*животное*) shaggy; (*ель, сосна*) bushy; (*no short form*; плед, шапка) fluffy.

мохови́к (-á) м (*БОТ*) variegated boletus.

моцио́н (-a) м (*прогулка*) constitutional.

моча́ (-и́) ж urine.

моча́л|ка (-ки; *gen pl* -ок) ж sponge.

мочево́й *прил*: ~ **пузы́рь** bladder.

мочего́нный *прил* diuretic.

мо́чек *сущ см* **мо́чка**.

мочёный *прил* (*яблоко, брусника*) preserved (*in sugar solution*).

моч|и́ть (-ý, -ишь; *perf* **намочи́ть**) *несов перех* (*ноги, волосы, одежду*) to wet; (*perf* **замочи́ть**; бельё) to soak; (*яблоки*) to preserve

► **мочи́ться** (*perf* **помочи́ться**) *несов возв* to

urinate.

мо́ч|ка (-ки; *gen pl* -ек) ж ear lobe.

мо́чь (-гý, -жешь *итп*, -гут; *pt* -г, -гла́, -гло́, *perf* **смочь**) *несов неперех*: ~ +*infin* to be able to do ◆ (-чи) ж: **и́зо всей мо́чи** with all one's might; **я** ~**гý игра́ть на гита́ре/говори́ть по-англи́йски** I can play the guitar/talk English; **он мо́жет прийти́** he can come *или* is able to come; **она́ не** ~**гла́ купи́ть дом** she couldn't buy *или* wasn't able to buy the house; **я сде́лаю всё, что** ~**гý** I will do all I can; **за́втра мо́жешь не приходи́ть** you don't have to come tomorrow; **он мо́жет оби́деться** he may well be offended; **не** ~**гý поня́ть э́того** I can't understand this; **мо́жешь бо́льше не извиня́ться** don't bother apologising any more; **мо́жет быть** maybe; **не мо́жет быть!** (*выражение сомнения*) it's impossible!

мо́шек *сущ см* **мо́шка**.

моше́нник (-a) м swindler, crook.

моше́нничаю|ть (-ю; *perf* **смоше́нничать**) *несов неперех* to swindle.

моше́нническ|ий (-ая, -ое, -ие) *прил* devious.

моше́нничеств|о (-a) *ср* deviousness.

мо́ш|ка (-ки; *gen pl* -ек) ж midge.

мошкар|а́ (-ы́) ж *собир* midges *мн*.

мо́щен *сущ см* **мо́щный**.

мощёный *прил* paved.

мо́щности|и (-ей) *мн* facilities *мн*.

мо́щност|ь (-и) ж power; (*воздействие*) force; **неиспо́льзуемая произво́дственная** ~ idle capacity; *см также* **мо́щности**.

мо́щ|ный (-ен, -на́, -но) *прил* (*взрыв, выступление*) powerful; (*организм, дуб*) mighty; (*рост, подъём*) vigorous; (*массивный*) massive; (*no short form*; двигатель, агрегат) powerful.

мощý *несов см* **мости́ть**.

мощ|ь (-и) ж power, might.

мо́ю(сь) *итп несов см* **мы́ть(ся)**.

мо́|я (-е́й) *притяж мест см* **мой**.

м.п. *сокр* = *место печа́ти*.

МП м *сокр* (= *маши́нный перево́д*) MT (= *machine translation*).

мрак (-a) м (*темнота*) darkness; (*перен*) gloom.

мракобе́с (-a) м obscurantist.

мра́мор (-a) м marble.

мра́морный *прил* (*также перен*) marble; (*узор, линолеум*) marbled; **Мра́морное мо́ре** Sea of Marmara.

мра́чен *прил см* **мра́чный**.

мрачне́|ть (-ю; *perf* **помрачне́ть**) *несов неперех* (*небо, горизонт*) to grow dark; (*взгляд, лицо*) to darken.

мра́ч|ный (-ен, -на́, -но) *прил* (*небо, мысли, взгляд*) gloomy; (*времена, годы, период*) dark.

мсти́тел|ь (-я) м avenger.

мсти́тельниц|а (-ы) ж см **мсти́тель**.

мсти́тел|ьный (-ен, -ьна, -ьно) *прил* vindictive.

мстить (мщу, мсти́шь; *perf* **отомсти́ть**) *несов неперех*: ~ **кому́-н** to take revenge on sb.

МТП *ж сокр* (= *междунаро́дная торго́вая пала́та*) ICC (= *International Chamber of Commerce*).

МТС *ж сокр* (= *междугоро́дная телефо́нная ста́нция*) ≈ intercity telephone exchange.

мудр|ёный (-ён, -ена́, -ено́) *прил* (*непоня́тный*) strange; (*сло́жный*) tricky, complicated; **не ~ено́, что** ... it's no wonder that ....

мудре́ц (-а́) *м* wise man (*мн* men).

мудр|и́ть (-ю́, -и́шь; *perf* **намудри́ть**) *несов неперех* to try to be clever.

му́дрост|ь (-и) *ж* wisdom; **зуб ~и** wisdom tooth.

му́др|ый (-, -а́, -о) *прил* wise.

муж (-а; *nom pl* -ья́, *gen pl* -е́й) *м* husband; (*nom pl* -й): **госуда́рственный ~** elder statesman (*мн* statesmen); **учёный ~** man of science.

муж|а́ть (-ю) *perf* **возмужа́ть**) *несов неперех* to mature

▶ **муж|а́ться** *несов возв* to take heart, have courage.

мужеподо́б|ный (-ен, -на, -но) *прил* masculine.

му́жествен|ный (-, -на, -но) *прил* (*лицо́, нату́ра*) strong; (*посту́пок, шаг*) courageous.

му́жеств|о (-а) *ср* courage.

мужи́к (-а́) *м* (*разг: мужчи́на*) man (*мн* men); (*крестья́нин*) muzhik.

мужикова́тый *прил* boorish.

мужск|о́й (-а́я, -о́е, -и́е) *прил* (*боти́нки, туале́т, парикма́хер*) men's; (*хара́ктер, рукопожа́тие*) masculine; (*о́рганы, кле́тка*) male; **мужско́й пол** male sex; **мужско́й род** masculine gender.

мужчи́н|а (-ы) *м* man (*мн* men).

мужья́ *сущ см* **муж**.

му́з|а (-ы) *ж* muse.

музе́й (-я) *м* museum.

музе́йный *прил* museum *опред*.

му́зык|а (-и) *ж* (*та́кже перен*) music.

музыка́л|ьный (-ен, -ьна, -ьно) *прил* musical; **музыка́льная шко́ла** music school.

музыка́нт (-а) *м* musician.

му́к|а (-и) *ж* torment.

мук|а́ (-и́) *ж* flour; (*гру́бого помо́ла*) meal; **ко́стная ~** bone meal; **карто́фельная ~** (*крахма́л*) potato starch.

мул (-а) *м* mule.

мулл|а́ (-ы́) *м* mullah.

му́льтик (-а) *м* (*разг*) cartoon.

мультиплика́тор (-а) *м* animator.

мультипликацио́нный *прил*: ~ **фильм** cartoon.

мультиплика́ци|я (-и) *ж* cartoon.

мультфи́льм (-а) *м сокр* (= *мультипликацио́нный фильм*) cartoon, animation film.

му́ми|я (-и) *ж* mummy.

мунди́р (-а) *м* uniform; **карто́фель в ~е** jacket potatoes.

мундшту́к (-а́) *м* cigarette holder; (*муз*) mouthpiece.

муниципалите́т (-а) *м* municipality, city council.

муниципа́льный *прил* municipal.

МУР (-а) *м сокр* (= *Моско́вский уголо́вный ро́зыск*) Moscow Criminal Investigation Department.

мур|а́ (-ы́) *ж* (*разг*) rubbish.

мураве́й (-ья́) *м* ant.

мураве́йник (-а) *м* ant hill.

муравья́ *итп сущ см* **мураве́й**.

мура́шк|и (-ек) *мн*: **у меня́ ~ по спине́ бе́гают** shivers are running down my spine; **покрыва́ться (покры́ться** *perf*) **~ками** to come out in goose pimples (*BRIT*) *или* goose bumps (*US*).

мурлы́|кать (-чу, -чешь) *несов неперех* to purr ◆ (*perf* **промурлы́кать**) *перех* to hum.

муска́т (-а) *м* (*оре́х*) nutmeg; (*сорт виногра́да*) muscat; (*сорт вина́*) muscat(el).

му́скул (-а) *м* muscle.

мускулату́р|а (-ы) *ж* собир musculature.

мускули́ст|ый (-, -а, -о) *прил* muscular.

му́сор (-а) *м* rubbish (*BRIT*), garbage (*US*).

му́сор|ить (-ю, -ишь; *perf* **наму́сорить**) *несов неперех* to make a mess.

му́сорный *прил* rubbish *опред* (*BRIT*), garbage *опред* (*US*); **му́сорное ведро́** dustbin.

мусоропрово́д (-а) *м* refuse *или* garbage (*US*) chute.

мусс (-а) *м* (*кули́н*) mousse.

мусульма́нин (-а) *м* Muslim.

мусульма́н|ка (-ки; *gen pl* -ок) *ж см* **мусульма́нин**.

мусульма́нский (-ая, -ое, -ие) *прил* Muslim.

мусульма́нств|о (-а) *ср* Islam.

му́тен *прил см* **му́тный**.

му|ти́ть (-чу́, -ти́шь; *perf* **взмути́ть** *или* **замути́ть**) *несов перех* (*жи́дкость*) to muddy; (*perf* **помути́ть**; *перен: рассу́док*) to cloud; (*no perf; разг: наро́д, толпу́*) to work up ◆ *несов безл* (*разг*): **меня́ му́тит** I feel sick

▶ **мути́ться** (*perf* **замути́ться**) *несов возв* (*вода́, раство́р*) to become cloudy; (*perf* **помути́ться**; *перен: рассу́док*) to become clouded ◆ *безл* (*разг*): **у меня́ в глаза́х** *или* **в голове́ помути́лось** I felt giddy.

мутне́|ть (*3sg* -ет, *3pl* -ют, *perf* **помутне́ть**) *несов неперех* (*жи́дкость*) to become cloudy; (*взор, глаза́*) to grow dull; **он так уста́л, что у него́ созна́ние ~ет** he is so tired, he can't think straight.

му́т|ный (-ен, -на́, -но) *прил* (*жи́дкость*) cloudy; (*стекло́, взор, глаза́*) dull; (*взор, глаза́*) glazed; (*перен: голова́, рассу́док*) confused.

мут|ь (-и) *ж* sediment; (*разг: фильм, кни́га итп*) rubbish; (*перен: на душе́*) ache.

му́фт|а (-ы) *ж* (*ТЕХ*) sleeve; (*же́нская оде́жда*) muff.

му́х|а (-и) *ж* fly; **де́лать (сде́лать** *perf*) **из ~и**

слона́ ≈ to make a mountain out of a molehill;
   под ~ой (*разг*) legless.
мухомо́р (-а) *м* (*БОТ*) fly agaric.
муче́ни|е (-я) *ср* torment, torture.
му́ченик (-а) *м* martyr.
му́чениц|а (-ы) *ж см* **му́ченик**.
мучи́телен *прил см* **мучи́тельный**.
мучи́тел|ь (-я) *м* tormentor.
мучи́тельниц|а (-ы) *ж см* **мучи́тель**.
мучи́тельный (-ен, -ьна, -ьно) *прил* agonizing.
му́ч|ить (-у, -ишь; *perf* **заму́чить** *или* **изму́чить**)
   несов перех to torment
▶ **му́читься** (*perf* **заму́читься**) *несов возв:* ~ся
   +*instr* (*сомне́ниями, угрызе́ниями со́вести*) to
   be tormented by; ~ся (**заму́читься** *perf*) **от** +*gen*
   (*от боле́й, от при́ступов*) to suffer from; ~ся
   (**заму́читься** *perf*) **с** +*instr* (*разг*) to have a lot of
   hassle with; ~ся (*impf*) **над** +*instr* to agonize
   over.
мучн|о́е (-о́го; *decl like adj*) *ср* starchy foods *мн*.
му́шк|а (-и; *gen pl* -**ек**) *ж* (*для прице́ла*) sight; (*на
   лице́*) beauty spot; **брать** (**взять** *perf*) **кого́-н/
   что-н на** ~**ку** (*прице́литься*) to take aim at
   sb/sth; (*перен*) to keep a close eye on sb/sth.
муштр|ова́ть (-у́ю; *perf* **вы́муштровать**) *несов
   перех* (*солда́т*) to drill.
мха *итп сущ см* **мох**.
МХАТ (-а) *м сокр* (= Моско́вский
   Худо́жественный академи́ческий теа́тр)
   Moscow Arts Theatre (*BRIT*) *или* Theater (*US*).
мч|а́ть (-у, -ишь) *несов неперех* (*по́езд,
   автомоби́ль*) to speed along; (*ло́шадь*) to race
   along ◆ *перех* to rush
▶ **мча́ться** *несов возв* (*по́езд, автомоби́ль*) to
   speed along; (*ло́шадь*) to race along; (*перен:
   го́ды, вре́мя*) to fly past.
мще́ни|е (-я) *ср* revenge, vengeance.
мщу *несов см* **мстить**.
мы (нас; *см* **Table 5b**) *мест* we; ~ **с тобо́й/
   жено́й** you/my wife and I; **кто зако́нчил
   рабо́ту?** – ~ who finished the job? – we did; **кто
   винова́т?** – ~ who is to blame? – we are.
мы́л|ить (-ю, -ишь; *perf* **намы́лить**) *несов перех*
   to soap
▶ **мы́литься** (*perf* **намы́литься**) *несов возв* to
   soap o.s.; (*мы́ло, шампу́нь*) to lather.
мы́л|о (-а) *ср* soap; **он весь в** ~**е** (*перен: разг: в
   поту́*) he's in a lather.
мы́льниц|а (-ы) *ж* soap dish.
мы́льный *прил* soap *опред*.
мыс (-а; *loc sg* -**ý**, *nom pl* -**ы**) *м* cape, promontory.
мы́сленно *нареч* mentally.
мы́сленный *прил* mental.
мысли́тел|ь (-я) *м* thinker.
мысли́тельный *прил* (*проце́сс*) thought *опред*;
   (*спосо́бности, у́ровень*) intellectual.
мы́сл|ить (-ю, -ишь) *несов неперех* to think,
   reason ◆ *перех* to imagine; **я не** ~**ю жи́зни без**

рабо́ты I can't imagine life without work.
мысл|ь (-и) *ж* thought; (*иде́я*) idea; **за́дняя** ~
   ulterior motive; **о́браз мы́слей** way of thinking;
   собира́ться (**собра́ться** *perf*) **с мы́слями** to
   collect one's thoughts; **э́то** ~! that's a thought!
мы́слящий (-ая, -ее, -ие) *прил* thinking *опред*.
мыть (**мо́ю, мо́ешь**; *perf* **вы́мыть** *или* **помы́ть**)
   несов перех to wash; **рука́ ру́ку мо́ет** *partners
   in crime will always cover for each other*
▶ **мы́ться** (*perf* **вы́мыться** *или* **помы́ться**)
   несов возв to wash o.s.
мыч|а́ть (-у́, -и́шь; *perf* **промыча́ть**) *несов
   неперех* (*коро́ва*) to moo; (*бык*) to bellow;
   (*разг: челове́к*) to mumble.
мы́шек *сущ см* **мы́шка**.
мышело́вк|а (-и; *gen pl* -**ок**) *ж* mousetrap.
мы́шечный *прил* muscular.
мыши́н|ый *прил* (*цвет*) grey (*BRIT*), gray (*US*);
   ~**ая нора́** mouse hole; **мыши́ная возня́** (*перен*)
   intrigue.
мы́шк|а (-и; *gen pl* -**ек**) *ж уменьш от* **мышь**;
   под ~**кой** under one's arm.
мышле́ни|е (-я) *ср* thought, thinking.
мы́шц|а (-ы) *ж* muscle.
мыш|ь (-и) *ж* (*ЗООЛ, КОМП*) mouse.
мышья́к (-а́; *part gen* -**ý**) *м* arsenic.
мэр (-а) *м* mayor.
мэ́ри|я (-и) *ж* city hall.
мя́гкий (-кая, -кое, -кие; -ок, -ка́, -ко) *прил* soft;
   (*движе́ния, похо́дка*) smooth; (*хара́ктер,
   челове́к*) mild, gentle; (*пригово́р, вы́говор,
   наказа́ние*) lenient; (*кли́мат, зима́, пого́да*)
   mild; **мя́гкий ваго́н** *railway carriage with soft
   seats*; **мя́гкий знак** soft sign (*Russian letter*).
мя́гко *нареч* gently; (*отруга́ть*) mildly; ~
   выража́ясь to put it mildly.
мягкосерде́чный (-ен, -на, -но) *прил* kind-
   hearted.
мя́гок *прил см* **мя́гкий**.
мя́гче *сравн прил от* **мя́гкий** ◆ *сравн нареч от*
   мя́гко.
мя́киш (-а) *м* crumb.
мя́кот|ь (-и) *ж* flesh; (*мя́со без косте́й*) meat off
   the bone.
мя́мл|ить (-ю, -ишь; *perf* **промя́млить**) *несов
   перех* (*разг*) to mumble.
мяси́стый (-, -а, -о) *прил* meaty; (*пле́чи, лицо́,
   плод*) fleshy.
мясни́к (-а́) *м* butcher.
мясно́й *прил* (*из мя́са*) meat; (*коро́ва, скот*)
   beef; (*отде́л, магази́н*) butcher's; ~**ы́е
   консе́рвы** tinned meat.
мя́с|о (-а) *ср* meat; (*разг: говя́дина*) beef.
мясору́бк|а (-и; *gen pl* -**ок**) *ж* mincer (*BRIT*),
   grinder (*US*).
мя́т|а (-ы) *ж* mint.
мяте́ж (-а́) *м* revolt.
мяте́жный *прил* rebellious; (*душа́, хара́ктер*)

restless.

МЯ́ТНЫЙ *прил* mint.

МЯ́ТЫЙ *прил* (*одежда*) creased; (*бумага*) crumpled.

МЯТЬ (**мну, мнёшь**; *perf* **размя́ть**) *несов перех* (*глину*) to knead; (*кожу*) to work; (*perf* **измя́ть** *или* **смять**; *одежду*) to crease; (*бумагу*) to rumple; (*волосы*) to ruffle

▶ **МЯ́ТЬСЯ** *несов возв* (*разг: человек*) to shilly-shally; (*perf* **измя́ться** *или* **помя́ться** *или* **смя́ться**; *одежда*) to get creased; (*бумага*) to get rumpled.

МЯУ́КАТЬ (**-ю**; *perf* **промяу́кать**) *несов неперех* to miaow, mew.

МЯЧ (**-á**) *м* ball; **ручно́й** ~ (*СПОРТ*) handball; **футбо́льный** ~ football.

~ Н, н ~

Н, н *сущ нескл* (*буква*) the 14th letter of the Russian alphabet.

на *предл* (+*acc*) **1** (*направление на поверхность*) on; **положи таре́лку на стол** put the plate on the table; **я пове́сил карти́ну на сте́ну** I hung the picture on the wall; **на́до накле́ить ма́рку на конве́рт** you need to stick the stamp on the envelope

2 (*направление в какое-н место*) to; **на Юг/Украи́ну** to the South/Ukraine; **е́здить** (*impf*) **на мо́ре/рабо́ту/конфере́нции** to go to the seaside/to work/to a conference; **сесть** (*perf*) **на по́езд** to get on(to) the train

3 (*об объекте воздействия*): **обрати́ внима́ние на э́того челове́ка** pay attention to this man; **нажми́ на педа́ль/кно́пку** press the pedal/button; **я люблю́ смотре́ть на дете́й/на звёзды** I love watching the children/the stars

4 (*о времени, сроке*) for; **назнача́ть** (**назна́чить** *perf*) **на за́втра/на 5 часо́в** to arrange sth for tomorrow/for 5 o'clock; **он уе́хал на час/ме́сяц** he has gone away for an hour/a month

5 (*о цели, о назначении*) for; **де́ньги на кни́ги** money for books; **ткань на пла́тье** material for a dress; **на написа́ние докла́да ушло́ мно́го вре́мени** much time was spent writing the report; **прове́рка на сообрази́тельность** intelligence test

6 (*о мере*) into; **дели́ть** (*impf*) **что-н на ча́сти/пара́графы** to divide sth into parts/paragraphs

7 (*при сравнении*): **я получа́ю на сто рубле́й ме́ньше** I get one hundred roubles less

8 (*об изменении состояния*) into; **на́до перевести́ текст на англи́йский** the text must be translated into English; **мы перешли́ на ру́сский язы́к** we switched (in)to Russian; **я обменя́л маши́ну на я́хту** I exchanged the car for a yacht ◆ *предл* (+*prp*) **1** (*нахождение на поверхности*) on; **кни́га на по́лке** the book is on the shelf; **я сижу́ на дива́не** I am sitting on the sofa; **на де́вочке ша́пка/шу́ба** the girl has a hat/fur coat on

2 (*о пребывании где-н*) in; **на Украи́не/Кавка́зе** in the Ukraine/Caucasus; **на у́лице** in the street;

быть (*impf*) **на рабо́те/заседа́нии** to be at work/at a meeting

3 (*о времени осуществления чего-н*): **встре́тимся на сле́дующей неде́ле** let's meet next week; **на пе́рвых пора́х** at first; **на ходу́** (*сказа́ть, бро́сить итп*) in passing; (*пойма́ть*) without stopping

4 (*об объекте воздействия*) on; **сосредото́читься** (*perf*)**/останови́ться** (*perf*) **на чём-н** to concentrate/dwell on sth; **сойти́** (*perf*) **с ума́ на чём-н** to go mad about sth

5 (*о средстве осуществления чего-н*): **е́здить на по́езде/велосипе́де** to travel by train/bicycle; **игра́ть** (*impf*) **на роя́ле/скри́пке** to play the piano/violin; **ката́ться** (*impf*) **на лы́жах/конька́х** to go skiing/skating; **говори́ть** (*impf*) **на ру́сском/англи́йском языке́** to speak (in) English/Russian

6 (*о составной части предмета*): **раство́р на йо́де** iodine solution; **ка́ша на воде́** porridge made with water

7 (*разг: о большом коли́честве чего-н*): **оши́бка на оши́бке** mistake upon mistake.

на (**на́те**) *част* (*разг*) here (you are).
наб. *сокр* = **на́бережная**.
наба́в|ить (**-лю, -ишь**; *impf* **набавля́ть**) *сов перех* to increase.
балда́шник (**-а**) *м* knob (*of walking stick*).
наба́лтыва|ть (**-ю**) *несов от* **наболта́ть**.
наба́т (**-а**) *м* alarm bell; **бить** (*impf*) **в ~** (*перен*) to sound the alarm.
набе́г (**-а**) *м* raid.
набе́га|ть (**-ю**) *сов перех* (*киломе́тра итп*) to run; **~** (*perf*) **инфа́ркт** (*разг*) to give o.s. a heart attack (*by running*).
набе́га|ть (**-ю**) *несов от* **набежа́ть**.
набе́га|ться (**-юсь**) *сов возв* to wear o.s. out running.
набегу́ *итп сов см* **набежа́ть**.
набе́дренн|ый *прил*: **~ая повя́зка** loincloth.
набежа́ть (*как* **бежа́ть**; *см* **Table 20**; *impf* **набега́ть**) *сов непе́рех* (*разг: ту́чи*) to gather; (: *толпа́, бука́шки*) to come running; (: *вода́*) to well up; (*проце́нты, вы́ходные итп*) to mount up; (*наскочи́ть*): **~ на** +*acc* to run into; (*во́лны: на бе́рег*) to lap against.

The spelling rules for Russian are shown on page xvii.

набезобра́знича|ть (-ю) *сов от* **безобра́зничать**.

набекре́нь *нареч* (*шапка*) tilted to one side; **у него́ мозги́ ~** (*разг*) he's not with it.

на́бело *нареч*: **переписа́ть что-н ~** to write sth out in neat.

на́бережн|ая (-ой; *decl like adj*) ж embankment.

наберу́(сь) *итп сов см* **набра́ть(ся)**.

набива́|ть(ся) (-ю(сь)) *несов от* **наби́ть(ся)**.

наби́вк|а (-и) ж stuffing.

набивно́й *прил* (*матрас, подушка*) stuffed; (*ткань*) printed.

набира́|ть(ся) (-ю(сь)) *несов от* **набра́ть(ся)**.

наби|ть (-ью, -ьёшь; *impf* **набива́ть**) *сов перех* (*прикрепить гвоздями*) to nail; (*полотно, ситец*) to print; (*разг: тарелок, чашек*) to smash; (: *настрелять*) to bag; **набива́ть (~** *perf*) **(**+*instr*) (*матрас, чемодан итп*) to stuff (with); **~** (*perf*) **ши́шку/синя́к** (*разг*) to get a bump/bruise; **~** (*perf*) **оско́мину** (*перен*) to reach saturation point; **~** (*perf*) **ру́ку (на** +*prp*) (*разг*) to get the knack (of); **набива́ть (~** *perf*) **це́ну** (*разг*) to talk up the price

► **наби́ться** (*impf* **набива́ться**) *сов возв* (*разг*): **~ся в** +*acc* (*в комнату, в автобус*) to pack; **она́ всё вре́мя ~ива́ется к нам в го́сти** she's always inviting herself round.

наблюда́телен *прил см* **наблюда́тельный**.

наблюда́тел|ь (-я) м observer.

наблюда́тел|ьный (-ен, -ьна, -ьно) *прил* (*человек*) observant; **~ пункт** observation point.

наблюда́|ть (-ю) *несов перех* to observe; (*пациента*) to treat ◆ *неперех*: **~ за** +*instr* to monitor; (*за порядком, за детьми*) to watch over

► **наблюда́ться** *несов возв* (*случаться*) to be; **~ся** (*impf*) **у** +*gen* (*лечиться*) to be treated by; **в стране́ ~ется рост престу́пности** there has been an increase in crime across the country.

на́бож|ный (-ен, -на, -но) *прил* devout.

набо́йк|а (-йки; *gen pl* -ек) ж (*ткани, узора*) printing; (*ткань*) printed fabric; (*на каблуке*) heel.

на́бок *нареч* to one side.

наболева́|ть (*3sg* -ет) *несов от* **наболе́ть**.

наболе́вш|ий (-ая, -ее, -ие) *прил* (*перен: проблема, тема*) sensitive; **~ вопро́с** sore point.

наболе́|ть (*3sg* -ет, *impf* **наболева́ть**) *сов неперех* to become sore; (*проблема*) to become acute; **у неё ~ло на душе́** she has suffered a great deal.

наболта́|ть (-ю; *impf* **набо́лтывать**) *сов перех* (*разг*): **~ глу́постей** to talk a lot of rubbish ◆ *неперех*: **~ кому́-н про кого́-н** to tell sb stories about sb.

набо́р (-а) м (*совокупность*) set; (*студентов*) selection; (*армии, штата*) recruitment; (*типог*) typesetting; **~ слов** (*перен*) gibberish.

набо́рный *прил* (*типог*): **~ цех** typesetter's; **набо́рный стано́к** galley.

набо́рщик (-а) м (*типог*) typesetter.

набо́рщиц|а (-ы) ж см **набо́рщик**.

набра́сыва|ть (-ю) *несов от* **набро́са́ть**, **набро́сить**.

► **набра́сываться** *несов от* **набро́ситься**.

наб|ра́ть (-еру́, -ерёшь; *pt* -ра́л, -рала́, -ра́ло, *impf* **набира́ть**) *сов (не)перех* (+*acc или* +*gen*; *грибов, цветов*) to pick; (*воды*) to fetch; (*работы, студентов, работников*) to take on; (*армию, труппу*) to assemble; (*скорость, высоту, баллы*) to gain; (*код, номер телефона*) to dial; (*статью, текст*) to typeset; **набира́ть (~** *perf*) **о́пыт** to gain experience

► **набра́ться** (*impf* **набира́ться**) *сов возв* (+*gen*; *много наро́ду*) to gather; (*сумма де́нег*) to accumulate; (*разг: напиться*) to get sloshed; **~ся** (*perf*) +*gen* (*предрассу́дков итп*) to acquire; **набира́ться (~ся** *perf*) **сил** to build up one's strength; **набира́ться (~ся** *perf*) **хра́брости** to muster up courage; **набира́ться (~ся** *perf*) **терпе́ния** to arm o.s. with patience.

набр|ести́ (-еду́, -едёшь; *pt* -ёл, -ела́, -ело́, *impf* **набреда́ть**) *сов неперех* (*разг*): **~ на** +*acc* (*перен*) to come across; **~** (*perf*) **на мысль** (*перен*) to hit upon an idea.

наброса́|ть (-ю; *impf* **набра́сывать**) *сов перех* (*план, текст*) to sketch out ◆ (*не)перех* (+*acc или* +*gen*; *вещей, окурков*) to throw about.

набро́|сить (-шу, -сишь; *impf* **набра́сывать**) *сов перех* (*пальто, плато́к*) to throw on; (*покрыва́ло*) to throw over

► **набро́ситься** (*impf* **набра́сываться**) *сов возв*: **~ся на** +*acc* (*на добы́чу, на же́ртву*) to fall upon; (*разг: на еду, на работу*) to get stuck into; **~ся** (*perf*) **на кого́-н** (*разг: с упрёками*) to lay into sb.

набро́с|ок (-ка) м (*плана*) sketch; (*статьи, письма*) draft.

набро́шу(сь) *сов см* **набро́сить(ся)**.

набры́зга|ть (-ю) *сов (не)перех*: **~** +*acc или* +*gen или* +*instr* to splash.

набу́х|нуть (*3sg* -нет, *3pl* -нут, *pt* -, -ла, -ло, *impf* **набуха́ть**) *сов неперех* to swell up.

набью́(сь) *итп сов см* **наби́ть(ся)**.

нава́г|а (-и) ж (*зоол*) type of cod.

наважде́ни|е (-я) *ср* apparition.

навал|и́ть (-аю́, -а́лишь; *impf* **нава́ливать**) *сов (не)перех* (+*acc или* +*gen*; *мусору, кирпиче́й итп*) to pile up ◆ *неперех* (*no impf; толпа*) to flock; **нава́ливать (~** *perf*) **(на** +*acc*) to pile on(to); **нава́ливать (~** *perf*) **на кого́-н рабо́ту/обя́занности** to load sb with work/responsibilities; **в э́том году́ ~и́ло мно́го сне́гу** there was a lot of snow this year

► **навали́ться** (*impf* **нава́ливаться**) *сов возв*: **~ся на** +*acc* (*на дверь итп*) to lean into; (*насыпаться: земля́*) to pile up on; (*разг: набро́ситься: на еду*) to get stuck into; **на меня́ ~али́лось мно́го рабо́ты** (*разг*) I'm swamped with work.

нава́лом нареч: **грузи́ть** ~ to pile up ◆ как сказ: ~ +gen (разг: фру́ктов, де́нег итп) there's loads of.

нава́р (-а) м (бульон) broth; (жир) fat; (разг: прибыль) take-in.

нава́рива|ть (-ю) несов от **навари́ть**.

нава́ристый (-, -а, -о) прил rich.

нава|ри́ть (-арю́, -а́ришь; impf **нава́ривать**) сов перех (тех: стали) to weld on ◆ (не)перех (+acc или +gen; супа, варе́нья) to make a lot of.

навева́|ть (-ю) несов от **наве́ять**.

наве́да|ться (-юсь; impf **наве́дываться**) сов возв (разг): ~ к +dat to call in on.

наведе́ни|е (-я) ср (поря́дка) establishment; (справок) making; (орудия) aiming.

наведу́ итп сов см **навести́**.

наве́дыва|ться (-юсь) несов от **наве́даться**.

наве|зти́ (-зу́, -зёшь; pt -ёз, -езла́, -езло́, impf **навози́ть**) сов перех to bring a lot of.

наве́к нареч (навсегда́) for good, forever.

наве́ки нареч = **наве́к**.

навёл итп сов см **навести́**.

наве́рно вводн сл probably ◆ нареч (точно) for sure.

наве́рное нареч = **наве́рно**.

наверн|у́ть (-у́, -ёшь; impf **навёртывать**) сов перех: ~ **(на** +acc) (навинти́ть) to screw on(to); (намота́ть) to wrap (around)

▸ **наверну́ться** (impf **навёртываться**) сов возв (слёзы) to well up.

наверняка́ вводн сл (конечно) certainly ◆ нареч (несомненно) definitely, for sure; **он де́йствует** ~ he doesn't take any chances.

наверста́|ть (-ю; impf **навёрстывать**) сов перех (типог) to typeset; **навёрстывать** (~ perf) **упу́щенное** или **поте́рянное вре́мя** to make up for lost time.

наве|рте́ть (-рчу́, -ртишь; impf **навёртывать**) сов перех: ~ **(на** +acc) to twist (around)

навёртыва|ть (-ю) несов от **наверну́ть**, **наверте́ть**

▸ **навёртываться** несов от **наверну́ться**.

наве́рх нареч up; (на ве́рхний эта́ж) upstairs; (на пове́рхность) to the top; **посмотре́ть** (perf) ~ to look up; **обраща́ться (обрати́ться** perf) ~ (перен: разг) to go to the top.

наверху́ нареч (та́кже перен) at the top; (в ве́рхнем этаже́) upstairs; (на пове́рхности) on (the) top ◆ предл (+gen) at the top of.

наверчу́ сов см **наверте́ть**.

наве́с (-а) м (над прила́вком, у подъе́зда) canopy; (скалы́, бе́рега) overhang.

навеселе́ нареч (разг): **быть** ~ to be merry или tipsy.

наве́|сить (-шу, -сишь; impf **наве́шивать**) сов перех (дверь, замок) to hang; (разг: картин,

плака́тов) to hang up; (спорт) to lob.

наве|сти́ (-еду́, -едёшь; pt ёл, -ела́, -ело́, impf **наводи́ть**) сов перех (вы́звать: ужас, грусть итп) to cause; (бинокль, объекти́в) to focus; (ору́дие) to aim; (мост) to lay; (лак, кра́ску) to apply; (разг: гостей, прия́телей, друзей) to bring; (поря́док) to establish; **наводи́ть** (~ perf) **кого́-н на** +acc (на ме́сто, на след) to lead sb to; **наводи́ть** (~ perf) **спра́вки** to make inquiries; **наводи́ть** (~ perf) **чистоту́** to clean up; **наводи́ть** (~ perf) **красоту́** (разг) to tart o.s. up; **э́та му́зыка ~о́дит на меня́ тоску́** this music makes me sad; **наводи́ть** (~ perf) **кого́-н на мысль** to give sb an idea; **его́ расска́з ~ёл меня́ на размышле́ния** his story started me thinking.

наве|сти́ть (-щу́, -сти́шь; impf **навеща́ть**) сов перех to visit.

наве́чно нареч for evermore.

наве́ша|ть (-ю; impf **наве́шивать**) сов (не)перех (+acc или +gen; белья́, карти́н, украше́ния) to hang up; (муки́, пече́ний) to weigh out.

наве́шива|ть (-ю) несов от **наве́сить**, **наве́шать**.

наве́шу сов см **наве́сить**.

наве́ша|ть (-ю) несов от **навести́ть**.

навещу́ сов см **навести́ть**.

наве́|ять (-ю, -ешь; impf **навева́ть**) сов перех (перен: тоску́ итп) to evoke.

на́взничь нареч on one's back.

навзры́д нареч: **пла́кать** ~ to sob loudly.

навига́тор (-а) м navigator.

навига́ци|я (-и) ж navigation.

навин|ти́ть (-чу́, -ти́шь; impf **нави́нчивать**) сов перех (га́йку, про́бку) to screw in; (кры́шку) to screw on.

нави́с|нуть (-ну, -нешь; pt -, -ла, -ло, impf **нависа́ть**) сов непере: ~ **на** +acc (во́лосы: на лоб) to hang down over; **нависа́ть** (~ perf) **на** +prp (сосу́льки: на ве́тках) to hang from; **нависа́ть** (~ perf) **над** +instr (ска́лы) to overhang; (ту́чи, опа́сность) to loom over.

нави́сш|ий (-ая, -ее, -ие) прил (бе́рег, скала́) overhanging.

навле́|чь (-ку́, -чёшь итп, -ку́т; pt -ёк, -екла́, -екло́, impf **навлека́ть**) сов перех (подозре́ния, несча́стье) to attract; **навлека́ть** (~ perf) **на кого́-н беду́** to bring sb bad luck; **навлека́ть** (~ perf) **на себя́ чей-н гнев** to incur sb's wrath.

наво|ди́ть (-ожу́, -о́дишь) несов от **навести́**.

наво́дк|а (-и) ж (объекти́ва) focusing; (ору́жия) aiming.

наводне́ни|е (-я) ср flood; (ры́нков това́ром) flooding.

наводн|и́ть (-ю́, -и́шь; impf **наводня́ть**) сов перех: ~ **что-н** +instr (това́рами, проду́ктами) to flood sth with.

наво́дчик (-а) м (сообщник) informant who tips

thieves off.

наводя́щий (-ая, -ее, -ие) *прил*: ~ **вопро́с** pointer, hint.

наво́жу *несов см* **наво́зить**.

наво́жу *несов см* **наводи́ть**, **навози́ть**.

наво́з (-а) *м* manure.

наво́зить (-жу, -зишь; *perf* **унаво́зить**) *несов перех* to fertilize.

навози́ть (-ожу́, -о́зишь) *несов от* **навезти́**.

на́волоч|ка (-ки; *gen pl* **-ек**) *ж* pillowcase.

навостр|и́ть (-ю́, -и́шь) *сов перех* (*разг*): ~ **у́ши** to prick up one's ears; ~ (*perf*) **лы́жи** (*разг*) to be ready to shoot off.

навр|а́ть (-у́, -ёшь, *pt* **-а́л**, **-ала́**, **-а́ло**) *сов от* **врать**.

навре|ди́ть (-жу́, -ди́шь) *сов от* **вреди́ть**.

навсегда́ *нареч* forever; **раз и** ~ once and for all.

навстре́чу *предл* (+*dat*) towards ◆ *нареч*: **бежа́ть** ~ **кому́-н** to run towards sb; **она́ вы́шла** ~ **гостя́м** she came out to meet the guests; **идти́** (**пойти́** *perf*) ~ **кому́-н** (*перен*) to give sb a hand.

навы́ворот *нареч* (*разг*: *наизнанку*) inside out; (*перен*: *наоборот*) the wrong way round.

на́вык (-а) *м* skill.

навы́кат(е) *нареч*: **глаза́** ~ bulging eyes.

навы́лет *нареч* right through; **его́ ра́нило пуле́й** ~ the bullet went right through him.

навы́нос *нареч* to take away (*BRIT*), to go (*US*); **мы не продаём** ~ we don't do takeaways (*BRIT*) *или* takeouts (*US*).

навы́пуск *нареч* outside, over; **он но́сит руба́шку** ~ he wears his shirt outside his trousers.

навы́тяжку *нареч*: **стоя́ть** ~ to stand to attention.

навью́ч|ить (-у, -ишь; *impf* **навью́чивать**) *сов перех* to load.

навяз|а́ть (-яжу́, -я́жешь; *impf* **навя́зывать**) *сов перех*: ~ (**на** +*acc*) (*на шею, на удочку*) to tie on(to); **навя́зывать** (~ *perf*) +*gen* (*связать*) to knit a lot of; (*снопов, веников*) to tie a lot of; (*венков*) to weave a lot of; **навя́зывать** (~ *perf*) **что-н кому́-н** (*перен*) to impose sth on sb

▶ **навяз|а́ться** (*impf* **навя́зываться**) *сов возв* (*разг*): ~**ся кому́-н в друзья́** to impose o.s. on sb; ~**ся** (*perf*) **в го́сти** to invite o.s. round.

навя́зчив|ый (-, -а, -о) *прил* (*мысль*) persistent; (*человек*) bothersome; **она́ ужа́сно** ~**ая** she's a real pest.

навя́зыва|ть(ся) (-ю(сь)) *несов от* **навяза́ть(ся)**.

нагад|а́ть (-ю; *impf* **нага́дывать**) *сов перех* (*разг*) to predict.

нага́|дить (-жу, -дишь) *сов от* **га́дить**.

нага́дыва|ть (-ю) *несов от* **нагада́ть**.

нага́жу *сов см* **нага́дить**.

нага́й|ка (-йки; *gen pl* **-ек**) *ж* whip.

нага́н (-а) *м* revolver.

нага́р (-а) *м* snuff (*of candle*).

нагиба́|ть(ся) (-ю(сь)) *несов от* **нагну́ть(ся)**.

нагишо́м *нареч* (*разг*) stark-naked.

нагла́|дить (-жу, -дишь; *impf* **нагла́живать**) *сов перех* to iron.

нагле́|ть (-ю; *perf* **обнагле́ть**) *несов неперех* to get impudent.

нагле́ц (-а́) *м* impudent upstart.

на́гло *нареч* impudently.

на́глость (-и) *ж* impudence, impertinence.

наглота́|ться (-юсь) *сов возв* (+*gen*) to swallow.

на́глухо *нареч* tight, securely; **застёгиваться** (**застегну́ться** *perf*) ~ to do one's coat right up.

на́гл|ый (-, -а́, -о) *прил* insolent, impudent; ~**ая ложь** brazen lie.

нагля́ден *прил см* **нагля́дный**.

нагля|де́ться (-жу́сь, -ди́шься) *сов возв*: ~ **на** +*acc* to tire of looking at; **дай мне на тебя́** ~ let me take a good look at you.

нагля́д|ный (-ен, -на, -но) *прил* (*пример, случай*) clear; (*no short form*; *метод обучения*) visual; **нагля́дные посо́бия** visual aids.

нагляжу́сь *сов см* **нагляде́ться**.

наг|на́ть (-оню́, -о́нишь; *pt* **-на́л**, **-нала́**, **-на́ло**, *impf* **нагоня́ть**) *сов перех* (*беглеца*) to catch up with; (*упущенное, пройденное*) to make up for; (*подлеж: ветер: грозу, тучи*) to blow; (*спирта, самогона*) to distil (*BRIT*), distill (*US*); **нагоня́ть** (~ *perf*) **страх на кого́-н** to strike fear into sb; **нагоня́ть** (~ *perf*) **тоску́ на кого́-н** to fill sb with sadness.

нагне|сти́ (-ту́, -тёшь; *impf* **нагнета́ть**) *сов перех* to pump.

нагнета́|ть (-ю) *несов от* **нагнести́** ◆ *перех* (*перен: напряжение*) to heighten.

нагное́ни|е (-я) *ср* festering.

нагно|и́ться (*3sg* **-и́тся**, *3pl* **-я́тся**) *сов возв* to fester.

нагн|у́ть (-у́, -ёшь; *impf* **нагиба́ть**) *сов перех* (*ветку, человека*) to pull down; (*шею, голову*) to bend

▶ **нагну́ться** (*impf* **нагиба́ться**) *сов возв* to bend down.

нагова́рива|ть(ся) (-ю(сь)) *несов от* **наговори́ть(ся)**.

нагово́р (-а) *м* (*разг: клевета*) slander; (*колдовской*) spell.

наговор|и́ть (-ю́, -и́шь; *impf* **нагова́ривать**) *сов перех* (*текст: на плёнку*) to record ◆ *неперех* (*разг: наклеветать*): ~ **на** +*acc* to slander; ~ (*perf*) **чепухи́** to talk a lot of nonsense; ~ (*perf*) **кому́-н комплиме́нтов** to shower sb with compliments

▶ **наговори́ться** (*impf* **нагова́риваться**) *сов возв* to talk one's fill.

наг|о́й (-, -а́, -о) *прил* (*человек*) naked, nude; (*руки, ноги, лес*) bare.

на́голо *нареч*: **остри́чься** ~ to shave one's head; **обри́ть** (*perf*) **кого́-н** ~ to shave sb's head.

наголо́ *нареч*: **ша́шки** ~ drawn swords.

на́голову *нареч*: **разби́ть** *или* **разгроми́ть** ~ to rout.

нагоню *итп сов см* **нагнать**.

нагоня|й (-я) *м* (*разг*): **получить** ~ **(от кого-н)** to get a ticking off (from sb).

нагоня|ть (-ю) *несов от* **нагнать**.

нагоре́ть (*3sg* -ит, *impf* **нагора́ть**) *сов безл* (+*gen*; *израсходоваться*) to be used up.

наго́рный *прил* (*пастбище, растительность*) alpine, mountain *опред*; (*гористый*) hilly.

нагор|оди́ть (-ожу́, -о́дишь) *сов* (*не*)*перех* (+*acc или* +*gen*; *разг*: *построек*) to put up; **он ~оди́л ерунды́** (*разг*) he came out with a load of nonsense.

наго́рь|е (-я) *ср* plateau.

нагота́ (-ы́) *ж* nudity, nakedness.

нагота́влива|ть (-ю) *несов от* **наготовить**.

нагото́ве *нареч* at the ready.

нагото́в|ить (-лю, -ишь; *impf* **нагота́вливать**) *сов перех* (*запасти*) to stock up with; (*сварить*) to cook.

награ́б|ить (-лю, -ишь) *сов перех* to plunder.

награ́д|а (-ы) *ж* reward; (*за учёбу, за работу*) prize; (*ВОЕН*) decoration; **дать** (*perf*) **что-н кому́-н в** ~**у** to give sb sth as a reward.

награ|ди́ть (-жу́, -ди́шь; *impf* **награжда́ть**) *сов перех*: ~ **кого́-н чем-н** (*орденом*) to award sb sth, award sth to sb; (*перен: способностями*) to endow sb with sth; (: *поцелуем, улыбкой*) to reward sb with sth.

награжде́ни|е (-я) *ср* awards ceremony.

награжу́ *сов см* **награди́ть**.

нагреба́|ть (-ю) *несов от* **нагрести́**.

нагребу́ *итп сов см* **нагрести́**.

нагрева́ни|е (-я) *ср* heating.

нагрева́тельный *прил*: ~ **прибо́р** heating appliance.

нагрева́|ть(ся) (-ю(сь)) *несов от* **нагре́ть(ся)**.

нагр|ести́ (-ебу́, -ебёшь; *pt* -ёб, -ебла́, -ебло́, *impf* **нагреба́ть**) *сов перех* to rake together.

нагре́|ть (-ю; *impf* **нагрева́ть**) *сов перех* to heat, warm; ~ (*perf*) **ру́ки** (**на** +*prp*) (*перен*) to line one's pockets (with)

▶ **нагре́ться** (*impf* **нагрева́ться**) *сов возв* to warm up.

нагримир|ова́ться (-у́юсь) *сов от* **гримирова́ться**.

нагромозд|а́ть (-ю) *несов от* **громозди́ть**.

нагроможде́ни|е (-я) *ср* (*предметов*) pile; (*фактов*) mound.

нагромозд|и́ть (-жу́, -ди́шь) *сов от* **громозди́ть**.

нагруб|и́ть (-лю, -и́шь) *сов от* **груби́ть**.

нагру́дник (-а) *м* bib; (*рыцарский*) breastplate.

нагру́дный *прил*: ~ **карма́н** breast pocket.

нагру|зи́ть (-ужу́, -у́зишь) *сов от* **грузи́ть** ◆ (*impf* **нагружа́ть**) *перех* to load up; **нагружа́ть** (~ *perf*) **кого́-н рабо́той** to load sb with work.

нагру́зк|а (-и) *ж* (*действие*) loading; (*груз, также ЭЛЕК, ТЕХ*) load; (*занятость*) workload;

(*общественная*) responsibilities *мн*.

нагрязн|и́ть (-ю́, -и́шь) *сов от* **грязни́ть**.

нагря́н|уть (-у, -ешь) *сов неперех* (*гости, полиция*) to descend on; (*холода*) to set in; ~**ула беда́** tragedy struck.

нагуля́|ть (-ю; *impf* **нагу́ливать**) *сов перех* (*разг*): ~ **аппети́т** to work up an appetite; **нагу́ливать** (~ *perf*) **румя́нец** to get some colour in one's cheeks

▶ **нагуля́ться** *сов возв* to have a good walk.

над *предл* (+*instr*) above; **рабо́тать** (*impf*) ~ **прое́ктом** to work on a project; **ду́мать** (*impf*) ~ **зада́чей** to think about a problem; **смея́ться** (*impf*) ~ **ребёнком** to laugh at a child; **сиде́ть** (*impf*) ~ **кни́гой** to sit over a book.

над- *префикс* (*in verbs*; *об увеличении чего-н*) *indicating an increase in sth eg*. **надстро́ить**; (*о неполном действии*) *indicating an incomplete action eg*. **надкуси́ть**; (*in nouns and adjectives*; *поверх чего-н*) *indicating position above sth eg*. **надзе́мный**.

нада|ва́ть (-ю́, -ёшь) *сов перех* (*разг*): ~ **кому́-н чего́-н** (*подарков, советов, обещаний*) to give sb lots of sth ◆ *неперех*: ~ **кому́-н** (*разг*) to thrash sb.

нада|ви́ть (-авлю́, -а́вишь; *impf* **нада́вливать**) *сов* (*не*)*перех* (+*acc или* +*gen*; *соку*) to squeeze; (*разг*: *тараканов итп*) to squash ◆ *неперех*: ~ **на** +*acc* (*на дверь итп*) to lean against; (*на кнопку*) to press.

нада|ива́ть (-ю) *несов от* **надои́ть**.

надар|и́ть (-ю́, -ишь; *impf* **нада́ривать**) *сов перех* (*разг*): ~ **кому́-н пода́рков** to give sb lots of presents.

надба́в|ить (-лю, -ишь; *impf* **надбавля́ть**) *сов перех* (*разг*) = **наба́вить**.

надба́вк|а (-и) *ж* (*к зарплате*) rise; (*к пенсии*) supplement; (*к цене*) surcharge; **надба́вка за вре́дность** danger money (*BRIT*), hazard pay (*US*).

надба́влю *сов см* **надба́вить**.

надбавля́|ть (-ю) *несов от* **надба́вить**.

надви́н|уть (-у, -ешь; *impf* **надвига́ть**) *сов перех*: ~ **что-н** (**на** +*acc*) to pull sth down (over)

▶ **надви́нуться** (*impf* **надвига́ться**) *сов возв* (*гроза, опасность, старость*) to approach; **надвига́ться** (~**ся** *perf*) (**на** +*acc*) (*на лоб, на уши*) to slide down (over).

надво́дный *прил* above water; (*корабль*) surface *опред*.

на́двое *нареч* in(to) two.

надво́рный *прил*: ~**ые постро́йки** outbuildings *мн*.

надвя|за́ть (-жу́, -я́жешь; *impf* **надвя́зывать**) *сов перех* (*свитер, рукава*) to lengthen (*knitted garment*); (*верёвку, нитку*) to tie on.

надгро́би|е (-я) *ср* gravestone, tombstone.

надгро́бный *прил* (*речь*) at the graveside;

(*надпись*) gravestone *опред*; **надгро́бный ка́мень** headstone; **надгро́бный па́мятник** memorial.

надёванный *прил* (*разг*) worn.

надева́|ть (-ю) *несов от* **наде́ть**.

наде́жд|а (-ы) *ж* hope; **в ~е на** +*acc* in the hope of; **пита́ть** (*impf*) **~у на что-н** to hope for sth; **подава́ть** (*impf*) **~ы** to show promise.

наде́жен *прил см* **надёжный**.

надёжно *нареч* securely.

надёжност|ь (-и) *ж* reliability.

надёж|ный (-ен, -на, -но) *прил* reliable; (*дверь, механизм*) secure; (*средство, путь*) safe.

наде́ла|ть (-ю) *сов* (*не*)*перех* (+*acc или* +*gen*; *ошибок, салатов*) to make lots of; (*неприятностей, вреда*) to cause a lot of; **не ~й глу́постей** don't do anything stupid; **что ты ~л?** what have you done?

надел|и́ть (-ю́, -и́шь; *impf* **наделя́ть**) *сов перех*: **~ кого́-н чем-н** (*землёй, участком*) to grant sb sth; (*перен: талантом, умом*) to endow sb with sth.

наде́ну *итп сов см* **наде́ть**.

надёрга|ть (-ю; *impf* **надёргивать**) *сов* (*не*)*перех* (+*acc или* +*gen*; *перьев, сорняков*) to pull out; (*разг: цитат, примеров*) to choose carefully.

надёрн|уть (-у, -ешь; *impf* **надёргивать**) *сов перех* to pull over.

наде́|ть (-ну, -нешь; *impf* **надева́ть**) *сов перех* to put on.

надея́|ться (-юсь) *несов возв*: **~** +*infin* (*отдохнуть, успеть итп*) to hope to do; (*perf* **понаде́яться**): **~ на** +*acc* (*на друга, на семью*) to rely on; (*на улучшение*) to hope for; **я наде́юсь, что ...** I hope that ....

надзе́мный *прил* (*сооружение*) overground; (*часть растения*) above ground.

надзира́тел|ь (-я) *м* guard.

надзо́р (-а) *м* control.

надира́|ться (-юсь) *несов см* **надра́ться**.

надку|си́ть (-шу́, -́сишь; *impf* **надку́сывать**) *сов перех* to take a bite of.

надла́мыва|ть(ся) (-ю(сь)) *несов от* **надломи́ть(ся)**.

надлежа́щий (-ая, -ее, -ие) *прил* appropriate, suitable; **~им о́бразом** in the appropriate manner.

надлежи́т (*pt* -́ало) *несов безл*: **ему́ ~ яви́ться в 9 часо́в** he is required to make an appearance at 9 o'clock.

надло́м (-а) *м* (*на ветке*) crack; (*угнетение*) breakdown.

надло|ми́ть (-омлю́, -́омишь; *impf* **надла́мывать**) *сов перех* (*также перен*) to break; (*здоровье, психику*) to damage

▶ **надломи́ться** (*impf* **надла́мываться**) *сов возв* to break; (*перен: здоровье*) to suffer; (: *человек*) to damage one's health.

надмéн|ный (-ен, -на, -но) *прил* haughty.

KEYWORD

на́до *как сказ* **1** (*о долженствовании*): **на́до ему́ помо́чь** it is necessary to help him; **на́до, что́бы он пришёл во́время** he must come on time; **на́до всегда́ говори́ть пра́вду** one must always speak the truth; **мне/ему́ на́до зако́нчить рабо́ту** I/he must finish the job; **помо́чь тебе́? – не на́до!** can I help you? – there's no need!; **не на́до!** (*не делай этого*) don't!

2 (*о потребности*): **на́до мно́го лет** it takes many years; **на варе́нье на́до мно́го са́хара** you need a lot of sugar to make jam; **им на́до 5 рубле́й** they need 5 roubles; **мне на́до спать** I need to sleep; **что тебе́ на́до?** what do you want?; **так ему́/ей на́до** (*разг*) it serves him/her right; **на́до же!** (*разг*) of all things!; **на́до ду́мать** (*вероятно*) probably; (*конечно*) of course; **что на́до** (*разг*) excellent; **фильм что на́до!** it's an excellent film!

на́до *предл см* **над**.

на́добност|ь (-и) *ж* necessity.

надоеда́|ть (-ю) *несов от* **надое́сть**.

надоеди́м *итп сов см* **надое́сть**.

надое́дливый (-, -а, -о) *прил* tedious, tiresome.

надое́|сть (*как есть; см* Table 15; *impf* **надоеда́ть**) *сов неперех*: **~ кому́-н** (+*instr*) (*разговорами, упрёками*) to bore sb (with); **мне ~ло ждать** I'm tired of waiting; **он мне ~л** I've had enough of him; **переста́нь мне надоеда́ть!** stop bothering me!

надо́|ить (-ю́, -́ишь; *impf* **нада́ивать**) *сов* (*не*)*перех* (+*acc или* +*gen*; *молока*) to get.

надо́лго *нареч* for a long time; **Вы здесь ~?** are you here for long?

надо́мник (-а) *м* homeworker.

надо́мниц|а (-ы) *ж см* **надо́мник**.

надорв|а́ть (-у́, -ёшь; *impf* **надрыва́ть**) *сов перех* (*лист, материю*) to make a tear in; (*пакет*) to start to tear open; (*перен: голос*) to strain; (: *силы, здоровье*) to tax

▶ **надорва́ться** (*impf* **надрыва́ться**) *сов возв* (*конверт, воротник*) to tear slightly; (*перенапря́чься*) to do o.s. an injury; (*перен*) to overexhaust o.s.

надоу́м|ить (-лю, -ишь) *сов перех*: **~ кого́-н** +*infin* (*разг*) to advise sb to do; **э́то он меня́ ~ил** he was the one who gave me the idea.

надпи|са́ть (-ишу́, -́ишешь; *impf* **надпи́сывать**) *сов перех* (*книгу, фотографию*) to inscribe; (*посылку, конверт*) to address; **надпи́сывать** (**~** *perf*) **а́дрес на** +*acc* to address.

на́дпис|ь (-и) *ж* inscription.

надпишу́ *итп сов см* **надписа́ть**.

надра́|ить (-ю, -ишь) *сов от* **дра́ить**.

надра́ться (-еру́сь, -ерёшься; *impf* **надира́ться**) *сов возв* (*разг*) to get sozzled.

надре́жу *итп сов см* **надре́зать**.

надре́з (-а) *м* cut.

надре́|зать (-́жу, -́жешь; *impf* **надреза́ть**) *сов перех* to cut into.

надруга́тельств|о (-а) *ср*: ~ (**над** +*instr*) (*над па́мятью, над че́стью*) violation (of); (*над челове́ком*) abuse (of).

надруга́|ться (-юсь) (*не*)*сов возв*: ~ **над** +*instr* to abuse.

надры́в (-а) *м* (*надо́рванное ме́сто*) tear, rip; (*перен: физический*) strain; (: *в пе́нии итп*) hysterical streak; **с ~ом в го́лосе** with a trembling voice.

надрыва́|ть (-ю) *несов от* **надорва́ть**

▶ **надрыва́ться** *несов от* **надорва́ться** ♦ *возв* (*крича́ть*) to scream away; (*разг*): ~**ся** (**над** +*instr*) to break one's back (over) (*fig*); **у меня́ се́рдце** *или* **душа́ ~ется** my heart bleeds.

надры́в|ный (-ен, -на, -но) *прил* hysterical.

надсмо́трщик (-а) *м* (*тюре́мный*) warden; (*на планта́ции*) overseer.

надсмо́трщиц|а (-ы) *ж см* **надсмо́трщик**.

надста́в|ить (-лю, -ишь; *impf* **надставля́ть**) *сов перех* to lengthen (*by adding extra material*).

надстра́ива|ть (-ю) *несов от* **надстро́ить**.

надстро́ек *сущ см* **надстро́йка**.

надстро́|ить (-ю, -ишь; *impf* **надстра́ивать**) *сов перех* (*сте́ну, дом*) to build onto; (*эта́ж*) to add.

надстро́йк|а (-йки; *gen pl* -ек) *ж* (*зда́ния*) additional floor; (*ФИЛОСОФИЯ*) superstructure.

надува́тельств|о (-а) *ср* (*разг*) con.

надува́|ть(ся) (-ю(сь)) *несов от* **наду́ть(ся)**.

надувно́й *прил* inflatable.

наду́манный *прил* contrived.

наду́ма|ть (-ю; *impf* **наду́мывать**) *сов неперех* (+*infin*; *разг*) to take it into one's head to do.

наду́т|ый (-, -а, -о) *прил* (*по́чки, ве́на*) swollen; (*разг: высокоме́рный*) puffed-up; (: *оби́женный*) sulky.

наду́|ть (-ю, -ешь; *impf* **надува́ть**) *сов перех* (*мяч, колесо́*) to inflate, blow up; (*разг: обману́ть*) to con ♦ *безл* (+*gen*; *пыли, хо́лоду итп*) to blow; (*в у́хо, в ше́ю итп*) to catch a chill; **мне ~ло в грудь** I've caught a chill (on my chest)

▶ **наду́ться** (*impf* **надува́ться**) *сов возв* (*матра́с, мяч*) to inflate; (*па́рус*) to billow; (*по́чка, ве́на, река́*) to swell; (*перен: от ва́жности*) to swell up; (: *разг: оби́деться*) to sulk; ~ (*perf*) **гу́бы** (*разг*) to go into a sulk.

надым|и́ть (-лю́, -и́шь) *сов от* **дыми́ть**.

надыша́|ть (-у́, -ишь) *сов неперех* (*в ко́мнате, в купе́*) to get warm (*from body heat*); ~ (*perf*) **на** +*acc* (*на стекло́, на очки́*) to breathe on

▶ **надыша́ться** *сов возв* (+*instr*; *ды́мом, га́зом*) to breathe in; ~**ся** (*perf*) **во́здухом** to get plenty of fresh air; **пе́ред сме́ртью не нады́шишься** it's too late to do anything about it now.

наеда́|ться (-юсь) *несов от* **нае́сться**.

нае́дешь *итп сов см* **нае́хать**.

наеди́мся *сов см* **нае́сться**.

наедине́ *нареч*: ~ (**с** +*instr*) alone (with); **они́**

оста́лись ~ they were left on their own; **я до́лжен оста́ться ~ с собо́й** I need time to be by myself.

наеди́те(сь) *сов см* **нае́сть(ся)**.

нае́ду *сов см* **нае́хать**.

наедя́тся *сов см* **нае́сться**.

нае́зд (-а) *м* (*визи́т*) visit.

нае́зд|ить (-зжу, -здишь; *impf* **наезжа́ть**) *сов перех* (*сто киломе́тров*) to clock up; (*доро́гу*) to flatten; (*ло́шадь*) to break in

▶ **нае́здиться** *сов возв* to travel a lot; **я ~здился в командиро́вки** I'm tired of going away on business.

нае́здник (-а) *м* rider.

нае́здниц|а (-ы) *ж см* **нае́здник**.

наезжа́|ть (-ю) *несов от* **нае́здить**, **нае́хать** ♦ *неперех*: ~ (**в го́сти**) **к кому́-н** to pay sb visits.

нае́зженный *прил* well-used.

нае́зжу(сь) *сов см* **нае́здить(ся)**.

нае́лся *итп сов см* **нае́сться**.

нае́мся *сов см* **нае́сться**.

наём (-йма) *м* hiring; (*кварти́ры*) renting.

наёмник (-а) *м* (*ВОЕН, также перен*) mercenary; (*наёмный рабо́тник*) casual worker.

наёмный *прил* (*труд, рабо́тник*) hired; (*помеще́ние*) rented, leased; (*земля́*) leased; ~ **уби́йца** hitman.

нае́|сться (*как* **есть**; *см* **Table 15**; *impf* **наеда́ться**) *сов возв* (+*gen*; *сла́дкого, овоще́й*) to eat a lot of; (+*instr*; *су́пом*) to fill o.s. up on; **я нае́лся** I'm full.

нае́|хать (*как* **е́хать**; *см* **Table 19**; *impf* **наезжа́ть**) *сов неперех* (*разг: тури́сты, го́сти*) to arrive in droves; **наезжа́ть** (~ *perf*) **на** +*acc* to drive into.

нае́шься *сов см* **нае́сться**.

нажа́л|оваться (-уюсь) *сов возв* (*разг*): ~ (**кому́-н на** +*acc*) to complain (to sb about).

нажа́р|ить (-ю, -ишь; *impf* **нажа́ривать**) *сов перех* to fry.

нажа́|ть (-му́, -мёшь; *impf* **нажима́ть**) *сов* (*не*)*перех* (+*acc* или +*gen*; *со́ку*) to squeeze; (*снопо́в, хле́ба*) to reap ♦ *перех* (*перен*): ~ **на** +*acc* (*на рабо́тников, на руково́дство*) to put pressure on; (*разг: на рабо́ту, на учёбу*) to get moving with; **нажима́ть** (~ *perf*) **на** +*acc* (*на кно́пку*) to press; (*на рыча́г*) to press (down).

нажгу́ *итп сов см* **нажжечь**.

наждак (-а́) *м* emery.

наждач|ный *прил*: ~**ая бума́га** emery paper.

нажжечь (-гу́, -жёшь *итп*, -гу́т; *pt* -ёг, -гла́, -гло́, *impf* **нажига́ть**) *сов* (*не*)*перех* (+*acc* или +*gen*; *дров, у́гля, кероси́на*) to burn a lot of; (*разг: лицо́, спи́ну итп*) to burn.

нажи́в|а (-ы) *ж* gain.

нажива́|ть(ся) (-ю(сь)) *несов от* **нажи́ть(ся)**.

нажив|и́ть (-лю́, -и́шь; *impf* **наживля́ть**) *сов перех* to bait.

нажи́вк|а (**-и**) *ж* bait.
наживлю́ *сов см* **наживи́ть**.
наживля́|ть (**-ю**) *несов от* **наживи́ть**.
наживн|о́й *прил*: **де́ньги – де́ло** ~**о́е** money will start to roll in given time.
нажи́ву(сь) *итп сов см* **нажи́ть**.
нажига́|ть (**-ю**) *несов от* **нажа́чь**.
нажи́м (**-а**) *м* (*также перен*) pressure; **сде́лать** (*perf*) **что-н под** ~**ом** to do sth under pressure.
нажима́|ть (**-ю**) *несов от* **нажа́ть**.
нажира́|ться (**-юсь**) *несов от* **нажра́ться**.
нажи́|ть (**-ву́**, **-вёшь**; *impf* **нажива́ть**) *сов перех* (*состоя́ние, миллио́ны*) to acquire; ~ (*perf*) (**себе́**) **враго́в** to make enemies; ~ (*perf*) (**себе́**) **неприя́тность** to get o.s. into trouble; **наживёшь себе́ радикули́т** you'll end up with backache
▶ **нажи́ться** (*impf* **нажива́ться**) *сов возв*: ~**ся** (**на** +*prp*) (*на войне́, на спекуля́ции*) to gain (from).
нажму́ *итп сов см* **нажа́ть**.
нажр|а́ться (**-у́сь**, **-ёшься**; *impf* **нажира́ться**) *сов возв* (*живо́тное*) to eat its fill; (*разг*: *челове́к*) to stuff o.s.; (: *напи́ться*) to get plastered.
наза́втра *нареч* (*разг*) next day.
наза́д *нареч* back; (*нагну́ться, кати́ться итп*) backwards; (**тому́**) ~ ago; **де́сять лет/неде́лю** (**тому́**) ~ ten years/one week ago.
назва́нива|ть (**-ю**) *несов неперех* (*разг*) to keep ringing.
назва́ни|е (**-я**) *ср* name; (*отде́льное изда́ние*) title; **под** ~**м** +*gen* named, called; **э́то не велосипе́д, а одно́** ~ you can hardly call it a proper bicycle; **торго́вое** ~ trade name.
назв|а́ть (**-ову́**, **-овёшь**; *pt* **-ва́л**, **-вала́**, **-ва́ло**, *impf* **называ́ть**) *сов перех* to call; (*ребёнка, соба́ку*) to name, call; (*назна́чить: кандида́тов, день, це́ну*) to name; **называ́ть** (~ *perf*) **ве́щи свои́ми имена́ми** to call a spade a spade
▶ **назва́ться** (*impf* **называ́ться**) *сов возв* (+*instr*; *предста́виться*) to call o.s.
назе́мный *прил* surface *опред*; **назе́мные войска́** ground troops.
на́земь *нареч* (*упа́сть, бро́сить*) to the ground.
назида́ни|е (**-я**) *ср* edification.
назида́те|льный (**-ен**, **-ьна**, **-ьно**) *прил* edifying.
назло́ *нареч* out of spite; ~ **кому́-н** to spite sb; **как** ~ to make things worse.
назнача́|ть (**-ю**) *несов от* **назна́чить**.
назначе́ни|е (**-я**) *ср* (*вре́мени, це́ны итп*) setting; (*на рабо́ту*) appointment; (*лека́рства*) prescription; (*фу́нкция*) function; **пункт** *или* **ме́сто** ~**я** destination.
назна́ч|ить (**-у**, **-ишь**; *impf* **назнача́ть**) *сов перех* (*нача́льником*) to appoint; (*вре́мя, це́ну*) to set; (*встре́чу*) to arrange; (*лека́рство, курс лече́ния*) to prescribe; **он** ~**ил ей свида́ние** he asked her to meet him.
назову́(сь) *итп сов см* **назва́ть(ся)**.

назо́йлив|ый (**-**, **-а**, **-о**) *прил* (*челове́к*) tiresome; (*вопро́с, мысль*) persistent.
назре́|ть (*3sg* **-ет**, *3pl* **-ют**, *impf* **назрева́ть**) *сов неперех* to come to a head; (*перен: вопро́с, разгово́р*) to become unavoidable.
назубо́к *нареч* (*разг*): **вы́учить/знать** ~ to learn/know off by heart.
называ́емый *прил*: **так** ~ so-called.
называ́|ть (**-ю**) *несов от* **назва́ть**
▶ **называ́ться** *несов от* **назва́ться** ♦ *возв* (*носи́ть назва́ние*) to be called; **как** ~**ется э́то ме́сто?** what is this place called?; **ситуа́ция, что** ~**ется, крити́ческая** the situation is what you might call critical.
наибо́лее *нареч*: ~ **интере́сный/краси́вый** the most interesting/beautiful.
наибо́льш|ий (**-ая**, **-ее**, **-ие**) *прил* the greatest.
наи́вн|ый (**-ен**, **-на**, **-но**) *прил* naive.
наивы́сш|ий (**-ая**, **-ее**, **-ие**) *прил* the highest.
наи́гранный *прил* artificial, false.
наигра́|ть (**-ю**; *impf* **наи́грывать**) *сов перех* (*мело́дию*) to play; (*для за́писи*) to record
▶ **наигра́ться** *сов возв* to play for a long time.
наи́грыва|ть (**-ю**) *несов от* **наигра́ть** ♦ *неперех*: ~ **на** +*prp* (*на фле́йте*) to play quietly on.
на́игрыш (**-а**) *м* tune.
наизна́нку *нареч* inside out.
наизу́сть *нареч*: **знать/вы́учить** ~ to know/learn by heart.
наилу́чш|ий (**-ая**, **-ее**, **-ие**) *прил* the best.
наиме́нее *нареч*: ~ **уда́чный/спосо́бный** the least successful/capable.
наименова́ни|е (**-я**) *ср* name; (*прое́кта, кни́ги*) title, name.
наименова́|ть (**-ую**) *сов от* **именова́ть**.
наиме́ньш|ий (**-ая**, **-ее**, **-ие**) *прил* (*длина́, высота́ итп*) the smallest; (*уси́лие*) the least.
наискосо́к *нареч* (*разг: разре́зать*) crosswise; (: *идти́*) diagonally.
на́искось *нареч* diagonally.
наиху́дш|ий (**-ая**, **-ее**, **-ие**) *прил* the worst.
найдёныш (**-а**) *м* foundling.
найду́(сь) *итп сов см* **найти́(сь)**.
на́йма *итп сущ см* **наём**.
найми́т (**-а**) *м* hireling.
найму́(сь) *итп сов см* **наня́ть(ся)**.
най|ти́ (**-ду́**, **-дёшь**; *pt* **-шёл**, **-шла́**, **-шло́**, *impf* **находи́ть**) *сов перех* to find ♦ *неперех* (*толпа́, го́сти, ту́чи*) to gather; (*натолкну́ться*): ~ **на** +*acc* to stumble into; **на него́** ~**шла́ тоска́** he was overcome with sadness; **на меня́** ~**шёл смех** I couldn't help laughing; ~**шёл чем горди́ться!** (*разг*) is that all you've got to be proud of?; **находи́ть** (~ *perf*) **о́бщий язы́к** to find a common language; ~ (*perf*) **себя́** to find o.s.
▶ **найти́сь** (*impf* **находи́ться**) *сов возв* (*ключи́, ребёнок итп*) to turn up; (*доброво́льцы, жела́ющие*) to come forward; (*не растеря́ться*) to come up with an answer.

накажу́ *итп сов см* **наказа́ть**.

нака́з (-а) *м* (*полит*) mandate (*to govern*); (*наставление*) wish.

наказа́ни|е (-я) *ср* punishment; (*перен: разг*) pain, hassle.

нак|аза́ть (-ажу́, -а́жешь; *impf* нака́зывать) *сов перех* (*за проступок итп*) to punish; (*приказать*) to order.

нака́л (-а) *м* (*борьбы*) heat.

накал|и́ть (-ю́, -и́шь; *impf* нака́ливать *или* накаля́ть) *сов перех* to heat up; (*перен: обстановку*) to hot up

▶ накали́ться (*impf* нака́ливаться *или* накаля́ться) *сов возв* to heat; (*перен: обстановка*) to become heated; (: *страсти*) to become inflamed; ~ся (*perf*) **докрасна́/добела́** to become red-/white-hot.

нака́лыва|ть(ся) (-ю(сь)) *несов от* **наколо́ть(ся)**.

накаля́|ть(ся) (-ю(сь)) *несов от* **накали́ть(ся)**.

накану́не *нареч* the day before, the previous day ◆ *предл* (+*gen*) on the eve of.

нака́па|ть (-ю) *сов от* **ка́пать**.

нака́плива|ть(ся) (-ю(сь)) *несов от* **накопи́ть(ся)**.

нака́пыва|ть (-ю) *несов от* **накопа́ть**.

нака́рка|ть (-ю) *сов от* **ка́ркать** ◆ *перех* (*разг*): ~ кому́-н беду́ to bring sb bad luck.

наката́|ть (-ю; *impf* нака́тывать) *сов перех* to roll; (*дорогу, колею*) to flatten out; (*разг: написать*) to rattle off

▶ наката́ться *сов возв* (*на коньках*) to have a good time skating; (*на лыжах*) to have a good time skiing.

нак|ати́ть (-ачу́, -а́тишь; *impf* нака́тывать) *сов непepeх* (*разг: толпа, гости*) to surge forward; (*тоска*) to be overwhelming ◆ *перех*: ~ что-н на +*acc* to roll sth onto; нака́тывать (~ *perf*) (на +*acc*) (*волна*) to roll up (onto)

▶ накати́ться (*impf* нака́тываться) *сов возв*: ~ся на +*acc* (*волна, лавина*) to roll up onto.

нака́тыва|ть (-ю) *несов от* **наката́ть, накати́ть**.

▶ нака́тываться *несов от* **накати́ться**.

накача́|ть (-ю; *impf* нака́чивать) *сов (не)перех* (+*acc или* +*gen*; *воды, воздуха*) to pump; (*камеру, шину*) to pump up.

накида́|ть (-ю; *impf* наки́дывать) *сов перех* to throw.

наки́д|ка (-ки; *gen pl* -ок) *ж* (*одежда*) wrap; (*покрывало*) bedspread, thrower.

наки́дыва|ть (-ю) *несов от* **накида́ть, наки́нуть**.

▶ наки́дываться *несов от* **наки́нуться**.

наки́н|уть (-у, -ешь; *impf* наки́дывать) *сов перех* (*платок*) to throw on; (*разг: набавить*) to add on

▶ наки́нуться (*impf* наки́дываться) *сов возв*: ~ся на +*acc* (*на человека*) to hurl o.s. at; (*разг:*

на еду́, на кни́гу) to get stuck into; наки́дываться (~ся *perf*) на кого́-н с вопро́сами/жа́лобами (*разг*) to bombard sb with questions/complaints.

накип|е́ть (*3sg* -и́т, *impf* накипа́ть) *сов неперех* (*накипь, пена*) to form ◆ *безл* (*перен: злоба, обида*) to build up

на́кип|ь (-и) *ж* (*на бульо́не*) scum; (*в ча́йнике*) fur (*BRIT*), scale (*US*).

накла́д|ка (-ки; *gen pl* -ок) *ж* (*шиньон*) hairpiece; (*разг: недоразумение*) mix-up.

накладн|а́я (-о́й; *decl like adj*) *ж* (*комм*) bill of lading (*BRIT*), waybill (*US*); **грузова́я ~** consignment note.

накладн|о́й *прил* (*волосы, борода*) false; (*карман*) sewn-on; **накладно́е зо́лото** rolled gold; **накладны́е расхо́ды** (*экон*) overheads *мн* (*BRIT*), overhead (*US*).

накла́док *сущ см* **накла́дка**.

накла́дыва|ть (-ю) *несов от* **наложи́ть**.

наклеве|та́ть (-щу́, -щешь) *сов от* **клевета́ть**.

наклёвыва|ться (*3sg* -ется, *3pl* -ются) *несов от* **наклюну́ться**.

накле́ек *сущ см* **накле́йка**.

накле́|ить (-ю, -ишь; *impf* накле́ивать) *сов перех* (*афишу, ма́рку итп*) to stick on; (*фона́риков, украше́ний итп*) to make (*with glue and paper*).

накле́|йка (-йка; *gen pl* -ек) *ж* label.

наклепа́|ть (-ю) *сов от* **клепа́ть** ◆ (*impf* наклёпывать) *перех* to rivet on.

наклёп|ка (-и) *ж* stud.

наклёпыва|ть (-ю) *несов от* **наклепа́ть**.

накли́ка|ть (-чу, -чешь; *impf* наклика́ть) *сов перех*: ~ кому́-н несча́стье to bring misfortune on sb.

накло́н (-а) *м* incline, slope; (*головы*) tilt; (*по́черка*) slope.

наклоне́ни|е (-я) *ср* (*линг*) mood.

накл|они́ть (-оню́, -о́нишь; *impf* наклоня́ть) *сов перех* to tilt

▶ наклони́ться (*impf* наклоня́ться) *сов возв* to bend down.

накло́нност|ь (-и) *ж*: ~ к +*dat* (*к му́зыке итп*) aptitude for; (*к мела́нхолии итп*) tendency toward; **дурны́е/хоро́шие накло́нности** bad/ good habits.

накло́нный *прил* slanting.

наклоня́|ть(ся) (-ю(сь)) *несов от* **наклони́ть(ся)**.

наклюн|у́ться (*3sg* -ется, *3pl* -утся, *impf* наклё вываться) *сов возв* (*цыплёнок*) to peck its way out of the shell; (*перен: по́чки, росто́к*) to form; (: *вы́годное де́ло*) to turn up.

накля́узнича|ть (-ю) *сов от* **кля́узничать**.

накова́льн|я (-ьни; *gen pl* -ен) *ж* anvil.

накóжный *прил* skin *опред*.

наколе́нник (-а) *м (СПОРТ)* kneepad.

нако́лк|а (-и) *ж (разг: татуировка)* tattoo.

наколо́ть (-олю́, -о́лешь; *impf* **нака́лывать**) *сов перех (руку, палец)* to prick; *(татуировку)* to apply; *(прикрепить)*: ~ **(на** +*acc) (на шляпу, на дверь)* to pin on(to) ♦ *(не)перех* (+*acc или* +*gen*; *дров)* to chop; *(сахару)* to break up

▸ **наколо́ться** (*impf* **нака́лываться**) *сов возв*: ~**ся (на** +*acc)* to prick o.s. (on).

наконе́ц *нареч* at last, finally ♦ *вводн сл* after all; ~**-то**! at long last!; **он** ~ **по́нял** he finally understood; **ты мог бы,** ~**, позвони́ть** if nothing else, you could have phoned; **ну, иди́ же** ~! come on, it really is time for you to go!

наконе́чник (-а) *м* tip, end.

накопа́ть (-ю; *impf* **нака́пывать**) *сов перех* to dig up.

накопи́тельств|о (-а) *ср* acquisitiveness.

накопи́ть (-лю́, -ишь) *сов от* **копи́ть** ♦ (*impf* **нака́пливать**) *перех (силы, информацию)* to store up; *(средства)* to accumulate

▸ **накопи́ться** *сов от* **копи́ться** ♦ (*impf* **нака́пливаться**) *возв (силы, толпа)* to build up; *(средства)* to accumulate; *(раздражение)* to mount.

накопле́ни|е (-я) *ср (действие)* accumulation; ~ **да́нных** *(КОМП)* data storage; *см также* **накопле́ния**.

накопле́ни|я (-й) *мн (сбережения)* savings *мн*.

накоплю́(сь) *сов см* **накопи́ть(ся)**.

накопти́ть (-чу́, -ти́шь) *сов от* **копти́ть** ♦ *перех (рыбы, колбасы)* to smoke.

накорм|и́ть (-лю́, -ишь) *сов от* **корми́ть**.

накра́пыва|ть (*3sg* -ет) *несов неперех* to drizzle.

накра́|сить (-шу, -сишь) *сов от* **кра́сить** ♦ (*impf* **накра́шивать**) *перех* to paint

▸ **накра́ситься** *сов от* **кра́ситься** ♦ (*impf* **накра́шиваться**) *возв* to put on make-up.

накрахма́л|ить (-ю, -ишь) *сов от* **крахма́лить**.

накра́шива|ть(ся) (-ю(сь)) *несов от* **накра́сить(ся)**.

накра́шу(сь) *сов см* **накра́сить(ся)**.

накрен|и́ть(ся) (-ю́(сь), -и́шь(ся)) *сов от* **крени́ть(ся)**.

на́крепко *нареч (запереть, забить)* tight; *(также: кре́пко-~: запретить, наказать)* strictly; **запо́мни** ~ be sure to remember.

на́крест *нареч (также: крест-~)* crosswise.

накрич|а́ть (-у́, -и́шь) *сов неперех*: ~ **на** +*acc (на ребёнка, на подчинённого)* to shout at

▸ **накрича́ться** *сов возв (разг)* to shout a lot; **ну что,** ~**а́лся?** are you through shouting?

накропа́ть (-ю) *сов от* **кропа́ть**.

накрош|и́ть (-у́, -ишь) *сов от* **кроши́ть**.

накро́ю(сь) *итп сов см* **накры́ть(ся)**.

накрут|и́ть (-учу́, -у́тишь; *impf* **накру́чивать**) *сов перех (веревок, пряжи)* to twist; *(разг: ерунды, небылиц)* to spin; **накру́чивать** (~ *perf*) **(на** +*acc) (гайку: на болт)* to screw on(to); *(канат: на столб)* to wind (round)

▸ **накрути́ться** (*impf* **накру́чиваться**) *сов возв (разг: завить)* to put one's hair in rollers; **накру́чиваться** (~**ся** *perf*) **на** +*acc* to wind around.

накры́ть (-о́ю, -о́ешь; *impf* **накрыва́ть**) *сов перех* to cover; *(разг: преступника, вора)* to nail, nab; **накрыва́ть** (~ *perf*) **(на) стол** to lay the table

▸ **накры́ться** (*impf* **накрыва́ться**) *сов возв (разг: мероприятие, прогулка)* to fall through; **накрыва́ться** (~**ся** *perf*) (+*instr*) *(пледом, одеялом)* to cover o.s. up (with).

накуп|и́ть (-лю́, -ишь; *impf* **накупа́ть**) *сов перех* to buy lots of.

накур|и́ть (-урю́, -у́ришь; *impf* **наку́ривать**) *сов неперех*: ~ **в ко́мнате** to fill a room with smoke

▸ **накури́ться** (*impf* **наку́риваться**) *сов возв* to smoke too much.

налага́|ть (-ю) *несов от* **наложи́ть**.

нала́|дить (-жу, -дишь; *impf* **нала́живать**) *сов перех (мотор, станок)* to repair, fix; *(сотрудничество)* to initiate; *(хозяйство)* to sort out; *(порядок)* to establish; *(разг: гитару, рояль)* to tune

▸ **нала́диться** (*impf* **нала́живаться**) *сов возв (работа)* to go well; *(отношения, здоровье)* to improve.

нала́мыва|ть (-ю) *несов от* **наломи́ть**.

нал|га́ть (-гу́, -жёшь) *сов от* **лгать**.

нале́во *нареч (повернуть, посмотреть)* (to the) left; *(разг: продать, сбыть)* on the side.

налёг *итп сов см* **нале́чь**.

налега́|ть (-ю) *несов от* **нале́чь**.

налегке́ *нареч (ехать)* without luggage; *(в лёгкой одежде)* lightly-clad; **путеше́ствовать** (*impf*) ~ to travel light.

нале́з|ть (-у, -ешь; *impf* **налеза́ть**) *сов неперех (разг: насекомые, дети)* to accumulate; *(надеться)* to fit; *(шапка)*: ~ **на** +*acc (на глаза)* to slide over.

налеп|и́ть (-лю́, -ишь) *сов от* **лепи́ть** ♦ *(не)перех* (+*acc или* +*gen*; *фигурок, птиц)* to model.

налёт (-а) *м (птиц, авиации)* flying in, approach; *(на врага, на город)* raid; *(на банк, на квартиру)* robbery; *(пыли, плесени)* thin coating *или* layer; *(МЕД)* spot, patch; **с** ~**а(-у)** *(на полном ходу)* at full pelt; *(перен: сразу)* in a flash.

налете́ть (-чу́, -ти́шь; *impf* **налета́ть**) *сов неперех*: ~ **на** +*acc (натолкнуться)* to fly against; *(перен: разг: на приятеля, на столб)* to run into; *(напасть)* to swoop down on; *(перен: разг: с бранью, с упрёками)* to lay into; *(буря, ветер)* to spring up; *(саранча, стая)* to fly in; *(пыль, листва)* to drift in.

налётчик (-а) *м* burglar.

налечу́ *сов см* **налете́ть**.

нал|е́чь (-я́гу, -я́жешь *итп*, -я́гут; *pt* -ёг, -егла́, -егло́, *impf* **налега́ть**) *сов неперех*: ~ **на** +*acc* (*на стол*) to lean on; (*плечом: на дверь*) to press against; (*перен: на работников*) to exert pressure on; (: *на учёбу, на работу*) to apply o.s. to; (*роса, снег*) to settle on; **налегать** (~*perf*) **на вёсла** to ply one's oars.

налива|ть(ся) (-ю(сь)) *несов от* **налить(ся)**.

нали́в|ка (-ки; *gen pl* -ок) *ж* fruit liquor.

наливн|о́й *прил:* ~о́е су́дно tanker; (*яблоко, хлеба*) ripe.

нали́вок *сущ см* **нали́вка**.

нали́м (-а) *м* (ЗООЛ) burbot, eelpout.

налип|ну́ть (*3sg* -ет, *3pl* -ут, *impf* **налипа́ть**) *сов неперех:* ~ **на** +*acc* to stick to.

налит|о́й *прил* (*колос, яблоко*) ripe; (*мускулы, щёки итп*) fleshy.

нал|и́ть (-ью, -ьёшь; *impf* **налива́ть**) *сов перех* to pour (out); **налива́ть** (~ *perf*) **стака́н вина́** to pour a glass of wine

▸ **нали́ться** (*impf* **налива́ться**) *сов возв* (*натечь во что-н*): ~**ся в** +*acc* to pour into; (*наполниться*): ~**ся** +*instr* to fill with; (*рожь, плоды*) to ripen; (*перен: злобой*) to brim over; ~**ся** (*perf*) **кро́вью** to turn red.

налицо́ *как сказ:* **фа́кты** ~ the facts are obvious; **доказа́тельство** ~ there is proof; **свиде́тели** ~ there are witnesses on hand.

нали́чи|е (-я) *ср* presence.

нали́чник (-а) *м* casing, jambs and lintel (*of door or window*).

нали́чность| (-и) *ж* cash.

нали́чн|ые (-ых; *decl like adj*) *мн* cash *ед*; **платёж** ~**ыми при доста́вке гру́за** cash on delivery.

нали́чн|ый *прил:* ~**ые де́ньги** cash; ~ **расчёт** cash payment; ~ **счёт** cash account.

наловч|и́ться (-у́сь, -и́шься) *сов возв* (*разг:* +*infin*) to get the hang of doing.

нало́г (-а) *м* (ЭКОН) tax; **подохо́дный** ~ income tax; **поиму́щественный** ~ property tax; ~ **на ввоз** +*gen* import duty on; ~ **на при́быль** profits tax; ~ **на предме́ты ро́скоши** luxury tax; ~ **на перево́д капита́ла** capital transfer tax; **ко́свенный** ~ hidden tax.

нало́говый *прил зав опред*.

налогоплате́льщик (-а) *м* taxpayer.

налогоплате́льщиц|а (-ы) *ж см* **налогоплате́льщик**.

нало́женн|ый *прил:* ~**ым платежо́м** cash on delivery.

нал|ожи́ть (-ожу́, -о́жишь; *impf* **накла́дывать**) *сов перех* to put *или* place on; (*кальку*) to superimpose; (*МЕД: шину*) to fasten; (: *компресс, бинт*) to apply; (*лак, позолоту*) to apply; (*печать*) to affix; (*резолюцию*) to append; (*кашу итп*) to dish up; (*дров: в печку*) to put on; (*impf* **налага́ть**) (*штраф*) to impose; (*запрет*) to place.

налома́|ть (-ю; *impf* **нала́мывать**) *сов перех* (+*gen*) to break; ~ (*perf*) **дров** (*разг*) to do

something stupid.

налью́(сь) *итп сов см* **налить(ся)**.

налюб|ова́ться (-у́юсь) *сов возв* to gaze one's fill; **не могу́** ~ **са́дом** I am lost in admiration for the garden.

наля́гу *итп сов см* **нале́чь**.

наля́па|ть (-ю) *сов от* **ля́пать**.

нам *мест см* **мы**.

нама́жу(сь) *итп сов см* **нама́зать(ся)**.

нама́з (-а) *м* (РЕЛ) (*Mohammedan*) *prayer*.

нама́|зать(ся) (-жу(сь), -жешь(ся)) *сов от* **ма́зать(ся)**.

намалева́|ть (-ю) *сов от* **малева́ть**.

нама́лыва|ть (-ю) *несов от* **намоло́ть**.

намара́|ть (-ю) *сов от* **мара́ть**.

нама́сл|ить (-ю, -ишь) *сов от* **ма́слить**.

нама́тыва|ть(ся) (-ю(сь)) *несов от* **намота́ть(ся)**.

намёк (-а) *м* (*также перен*) hint.

намека́|ть (-ю; *perf* **намекну́ть**) *несов неперех:* ~ **на** +*acc* to hint at.

намелю́ *итп сов см* **намоло́ть**.

наменя́|ть (-ю) *сов* (*не)перех* (+*acc или* +*gen;* *денег, марок, значков*) to get *или* obtain by exchange.

намерева́|ться (-юсь) *несов возв:* ~ +*infin* to intend to do.

наме́рен (-а, -о) *как сказ:* **он** ~ **уе́хать** he intends to leave.

наме́рени|е (-я) *ср* intention.

наме́рен|ный (-, -на, -но) *прил* intentional, deliberate.

на́мертво *нареч* (*разг*) tightly, fast.

намётанный *прил:* ~ **глаз** trained eye; **у него́ глаз намётан** he has a good eye.

намета́|ть (-ю) *сов от* **мета́ть**.

наме́|тить (-чу, -тишь) *сов от* **ме́тить** ◆ (*impf* **намеча́ть**) *перех* to plan; (*план*) to project; (*контуры*) to outline

▸ **наме́титься** *сов от* **ме́титься** ◆ (*impf* **намеча́ться**) *возв* (*маршрут*) to take shape; (*разногласия, усы*) to begin to show.

намётк|а (-и) *ж* (*юбки, платья*) tacking (BRIT), basting; (*нитка*) tacking (BRIT) *или* basting thread; (*плана*) rough draft; (*маршрута*) preliminary outline.

намеча́|ть(ся) (-ю(сь)) *несов от* **наме́тить(ся)**.

наме́чу(сь) *сов см* **наме́тить(ся)**.

на́ми *мест см* **мы**.

намина́|ть (-ю) *несов от* **намя́ть**.

намно́го *нареч* much, far; ~ **ху́же/интере́снее** much worse/more interesting.

намну́ *итп сов см* **намя́ть**.

намо́к|нуть (-у, -ешь; *impf* **намока́ть**) *сов неперех* to get wet.

намо|ло́ть (-елю́, -е́лешь; *impf* **нама́лывать**) *сов перех* to grind, mill.

намо́рдник (-а) *м* muzzle.

намо́рщить(ся) (-у(сь), -ишь(ся)) *сов от*
мо́рщить(ся).
намо|сти́ть (-щу́, -сти́шь) *сов от* **мости́ть**.
намота́ть (-ю) *сов от* **мота́ть** ♦ (*impf*
нама́тывать) *перех* to wind.
► **намота́ться** (*impf* **нама́тываться**) *сов возв*
(*нитка на шпу́льку*) to be wound; (*разг:*
устать) to run o.s. ragged.
нам|очи́ть (-очу́, -о́чишь) *сов от* **мочи́ть**.
намощу́ *сов см* **намости́ть**.
намо́ю *итп сов см* **намы́ть**.
намудри́ть (-ю́, -и́шь) *сов от* **мудри́ть**.
намусо́рить (-ю, -ишь) *сов от* **му́сорить**.
наму́ч|иться (-усь, -ишься) *сов возв* (*разг*) to
wear o.s. out.
намы́лива|ть (-ю; *perf* **намы́лить**) *несов перех*
= **мы́лить**.
намы́л|ить(ся) (-ю(сь), -ишь(ся)) *сов от*
мы́лить(ся).
намы́|ть (-о́ю, -о́ешь) *сов перех* to wash;
(*плотину*) to deposit; (*золота*) to pan out.
намя́|ть (-ну́, -нёшь; *impf* **намина́ть**) *сов*
(*не*)*перех* (+*acc или* +*gen*; *льна, кож, глины*) to
mash; (*траву, солому*) to trample.
нан|ести́ (-есу́, -есёшь; *pt* -ёс, -есла́, -есло́, *impf*
наноси́ть) *сов* (*не*)*перех* (+*acc или* +*gen*;
подарков, продуктов) to bring; (*снегу, песку*) to
heap, pile up ♦ *перех* (*лак, мазь, краску*) to
apply; (*узор, рисунок, резьбу*) to draw; (*на*
карту, на схему) to plot; (*удар*) to deliver;
(*урон*) to inflict; **наноси́ть** (~ *perf*) **кому́-н**
оскорбле́ние to insult; **наноси́ть** (~ *perf*)
кому́-н пораже́ние to defeat sb; ~ (*perf*) **кому́-н**
визи́т to pay sb a visit.
нани́зыва|ть (-ю) *несов перех* (*жемчуг,*
бусинки) to string, thread; (*перен: слова,*
фразы) to string.
нанима́тел|ь (-я) *м* tenant; (*рабочей силы*)
employer.
нанима́тельниц|а (-ы) *ж см* **нанима́тель**.
нанима́|ть(ся) (-ю(сь)) *несов от* **наня́ть(ся)**.
нано́с (-а) *м* (*речной*) alluvium; (*ледниковый,*
снежный) drift.
нан|оси́ть (-ошу́, -о́сишь) *сов от* **нанести́** ♦
перех (*воды, песку, камней*) to bring.
нано́сный *прил* (*ил*) alluvial; (*перен:*
увлечения) alien.
на|ня́ть (-йму́, -ймёшь; *pt* -нял, -няла́, -няло,
impf **нанима́ть**) *сов перех* (*работника*) to hire;
(*лодку, машину*) to hire, rent
► **наня́ться** (*impf* **нанима́ться**) *сов возв* to get a
job; **нанима́ться** (~ся *perf*) **секретарём/**
реда́ктором to get a job as a secretary/editor.
наоборо́т *нареч* (*прочитать слово*)
backwards; (*поступать, делать*) the wrong
way (round) ♦ *вводн сл, част* (*при*
противопоставлении) on the contrary.
наобу́м *нареч* (*разг: делать, отвечать*)
without thinking; (*стрелять*) at random.
на́отмашь *нареч* with a bold swipe.
наотре́з *нареч* flatly, point-blank.

напада́|ть (-ю) *несов от* **напа́сть**.
напада́|ющий (-его; *decl like adj*) *м* (*СПОРТ*)
forward.
нападе́ни|е (-я) *ср* attack; (*СПОРТ*) forwards *мн*.
напа́д|ки (-ок) *мн* attacks *мн*.
нападу́ *итп сов см* **напа́сть**.
напа́ко|стить (-щу, -стишь) *сов от* **па́костить**.
напа́лм (-а) *м* napalm.
напа́рник (-а) *м* fellow worker.
напа́рниц|а (-ы) *ж см* **напа́рник**.
напа́рыва|ться (-юсь) *несов от* **напоро́ться**.
напас|ти́сь (-у́сь, -ёшься) *сов возв:* **на тебя́**
са́хара не ~ёшься you haven't got in enough
sugar.
напа́|сть (-а́сти) *ж* (*разг: беда*) calamity; ♦
(-аду́, -адёшь; *pt* -а́л, -а́ла, -а́ло, *impf*
напада́ть) *сов неперех:* ~ **на** +*acc* to attack; (*на*
золоту́ю жи́лу) to come across, stumble (up)on;
(*перен: на иде́ю*) to have; (*тоска, грусть,*
страх) to grip, seize.
напе́в (-а) *м* tune, melody.
напева́|ть (-ю) *несов от* **напе́ть** ♦ *перех*
(*песенку*) to hum.
напе́в|ный (-ен, -на, -но) *прил* melodious.
напёк *итп сов см* **напе́чь**.
напека́|ть (-ю) *несов от* **напе́чь**.
напеку́ *итп сов см* **напе́чь**.
наперебо́й *нареч* vying with each other.
наперове́с *нареч:* **держа́ть ружьё ~** to hold
one's gun at the ready.
наперего́нки *нареч* (*разг*) racing each other.
наперёд *нареч* (*знать, угада́ть*) in advance;
за́дом ~ back to front.
наперекор *нареч* (*говорить, поступать,*
идти́) defiantly ♦ *предл* (+*dat*; *судьбе, врагу,*
здравому смыслу) in defiance of.
наперере́з *нареч* (*бежать, идти́, плыть итп*)
in order to intercept.
напер|е́ть (-ру́, -рёшь; *pt* -ёр, -ёрла, -ёрло, *impf*
напира́ть) *сов неперех:* ~ **на** +*acc* (*разг: на*
дверь) to push against.
наперечёт *нареч* (*знать, помнить*) without
exception.
наперсто|к (-ка) *м* thimble.
наперч|и́ть (-у́, -и́шь) *сов от* **перчи́ть**.
напе́|ть (-ою, -оёшь; *impf* **напева́ть**) *сов перех*
(*мотив, песню, мелодию*) to sing; **напева́ть** (~
perf) **пласти́нку** to make a recording of one's
singing.
напеча́та|ть(ся) (-ю(сь)) *сов от* **печа́тать(ся)**.
нап|е́чь (-еку́, -ечёшь *итп*, -еку́т; *pt* -ёк, -екла́,
-екло́, *impf* **напека́ть**) *сов перех* (*блинов,*
пирогов) to bake ♦ *безл* (*разг: голову, плечи*) to
burn.
напива́|ться (-юсь) *несов от* **напи́ться**.
напи́льник (-а) *м* file.
напира́|ть (-ю) *несов от* **напере́ть** ♦ *неперех:*
~ **на** +*acc* (*теснить*) to push against; (*перен*) to
stress.
написа́ни|е (-я) *ср* writing; (*буквы*) spelling.
напи|са́ть (-шу́, -шешь) *сов от* **писа́ть**.

напи́т|ок (**-ка**) *м* drink.

напи́ться (**-ью́сь, -ьёшься;** *impf* **напива́ться**) *сов возв* (*воды, сока, чаю*) to have a drink; (*квасом, лимонадом*) to quench one's thirst; (*разг: опьянеть*) to get drunk.

напиха́|ть (**-ю;** *impf* **напи́хивать**) *сов перех* (*разг*): **~ в** +*acc* to stuff into.

напи́чка|ть (**-ю**) *сов от* **пи́чкать**.

напишу́ *итп сов см* **написа́ть**.

напла́кать *сов перех*: **кот напла́кал** (*разг*) very little; **у нас де́нег – кот напла́кал** we have very little money

▶ **напла́|каться** ♦ (**-чусь, -чешься**) *сов возв* (*ребёнок*) to cry one's eyes out; **напла́чешься ты с ней** (*перен*) you'll have nothing but problems with her.

наплева́тельск|ий (**-ая, -ое, -ие**) *прил* (*разг: отношение*) harum-scarum.

наплев|а́ть (**-ю́ю**) *сов от* **плева́ть** ♦ *неперех* to spit; **~!** (*разг*) to hell with it!

наплы́в (**-а**) *м* (*перен: туристов*) influx; (: *заявлений, чувств*) flood.

наплы́|ть (**-ву́, -вёшь;** *impf* **наплыва́ть**) *сов неперех*: **~ на** +*acc* (*на мель, на камень*) to run against; (*облако, туча*) to drift over *или* in front of; (*мина, водоросли*) to be washed up; (*перен: воспоминания*) to come flooding back.

напова́л *нареч* outright.

наподо́бие *предл* (+*gen*) like, resembling.

нап|ои́ть (**-ою́, -о́ишь**) *сов от* **пои́ть**.

напока́з *нареч* for show.

наполз|ти́ (**-у́, -ёшь;** *impf* **наполза́ть**) *сов неперех*: **~ на** +*acc* (*на преграду*) to crawl onto; (*туча*) to creep up; (*муравьи*) to crawl in.

напо́лн|ить (**-ю, -ишь;** *impf* **наполня́ть**) *сов перех*: **~** +*instr* to fill with

▶ **напо́лниться** (*impf* **наполня́ться**) *сов возв*: **~ся** +*instr* to fill with.

наполови́ну *нареч* (*уменьшить, увеличить*) by half; (*наполнить, налить*) half.

напо́льн|ый *прил* floor *опред*; **~ые часы́** grandfather clock.

напомина́ни|е (**-я**) *ср* reminder.

напомина́|ть (**-ю**) *несов от* **напо́мнить** ♦ *перех* (*иметь сходство*) to resemble; **он ~ет мне моего́ отца́** he resembles my father.

напо́мн|ить (**-ю, -ишь;** *impf* **напомина́ть**) *сов перех*: **~** +*acc* *или* **о** +*prp* to remind of.

напо́р (**-а**) *м* (*воды, воздуха*) pressure; (*ветра*) force; (*войск*) onslaught; (*разг: настойчивость*) push, go.

напо́рист|ый (**-, -а, -о**) *прил* forceful.

напор|о́ть (**-ю́, -ешь**) *сов от* **поро́ть** ♦ *перех* (*разг: руку, ногу*) to cut

▶ **напоро́ться** (*impf* **напа́рываться**) *сов возв*: **~ся на** +*acc* (*разг: на гвоздь, на сучок*) to cut o.s. on; (: *на беду, на скандал*) to run up against.

напо́р|тить (**-чу, -тишь**) *сов (не)перех* (+*acc или*

+*gen*; *бумаги, материала*) to spoil ♦ *неперех* (+*dat*; *разг: делу*) to wreck; (: *другу*) to harm.

напосле́док *нареч* (*разг*) in the end, finally.

напою́ *итп сов см* **напе́ть**.

напра́в|ить (**-лю, -ишь;** *impf* **направля́ть**) *сов перех* (*взгляд, внимание, разговор*) to direct; (*в госпиталь, к врачу*) to refer; (*на завод*) to assign; (*телеграмму, послание*) to send; **направля́ть** (**~** *perf*) **свой путь куда́-нибудь** to make one's way somewhere

▶ **напра́виться** (*impf* **направля́ться**) *сов возв*: **~ся в** +*acc*/**к** +*dat* (*в город, к острову*) to make for.

направле́ни|е (**-я**) *ср* direction; (*специалистов*) sending; (*деятельности, также ВОЕН*) line; (*политики*) orientation; (*течение*) school; (*документ: в больницу*) referral; (: *на работу, на учёбу*) directive; **по ~ю к** +*dat* towards.

напра́вленность (**-и**) *ж* focus.

напра́влю(сь) *сов см* **напра́вить(ся)**.

направля́|ть(ся) (**-ю(сь)**) *несов от* **напра́вить(ся)**.

напра́во *нареч* (*идти, повернуть*) (to the) right; (*от дороги, от дома*) to the right.

напра́сен *прил см* **напра́сный**.

напра́сно *нареч* in vain.

напра́сн|ый (**-ен, -на, -но**) *прил* (*труд, усилия*) vain; (*тревога, страх*) unfounded.

напра́шива|ться (**-юсь**) *несов от* **напроси́ться**.

наприме́р *вводн сл* for example *или* instance.

напрока́знича|ть (**-ю**) *сов от* **прока́зничать**.

напрока́т *нареч*: **взять ~** to hire; **отдава́ть** (**отда́ть** *perf*) **~** to hire out.

напролёт *нареч* without a break.

напроло́м *нареч* stopping at nothing.

напроро́чить (**-у, -ишь**) *сов от* **проро́чить**.

напро|си́ться (**-шу́сь, -о́сишься;** *impf* **напра́шиваться**) *сов возв* (*разг: в гости, на должность*) to force o.s.; **напра́шиваться** (**~** *perf*) **на** +*acc* (*на комплимент, на оскорбление*) to invite.

напро́тив *нареч* opposite ♦ *вводн сл* on the contrary ♦ *предл* (+*gen*) opposite.

на́прочь *нареч* (*разг*) completely.

напрошу́сь *сов см* **напроси́ться**.

напря́г(ся) *итп сов см* **напря́чь(ся)**.

напряга́|ть(ся) (**-ю(сь)**) *несов от* **напря́чь(ся)**.

напрягу́(сь) *итп сов см* **напря́чь(ся)**.

напряже́ни|е (**-я**) *ср* tension; (*внимания, с ресурсами*) strain; (*физ: механическое*) strain, stress; (: *электрическое*) voltage.

напряжённ|ый (**-, -на, -но**) *прил* tense; (*отношения, голос, встреча*) strained.

напрями́к *нареч* (*идти, ехать*) straight; (*перен: сказать*) straight out.

напря́чь (**-ягу́, -яжёшь** *итп*, **-ягу́т;** *pt* **-я́г, -ягла́,**

-ягло́, *impf* **напряга́ть**) *сов перех* to strain

► **напря́чься** (*impf* **напряга́ться**) *сов возв* (*мускулы, леска*) to become tense; (*внутренне*) to strain o.s.

напуга́ть(ся) (-ю(сь)) *сов от* пуга́ть(ся).

напу́др|ить(ся) (-ю(сь), -ишь(ся)) *сов от* пу́дрить(ся).

напуска́ть(ся) (-ю(сь)) *несов от* напусти́ть(ся).

напускно́й *прил* (*грубость*) affected; (*спокойствие*) feigned.

напусти́ть (-ущу́, -у́стишь; *impf* **напуска́ть**) *сов перех*: ~ +*gen* (*дыму, воды, рыбы*) to fill with; (*разг*): ~ на +*acc* to put on; (*раза: собак*) to set on; **напуска́ть (**~ *perf*) **на себя́ что-н** to assume sth

► **напусти́ться** (*impf* **напуска́ться**) *сов возв* (*разг*): ~ся на +*acc* to attack.

напута|ть (-ю; *impf* **напу́тывать**) *сов (не)перех* (+*acc или* +*gen*; *ниток, пряжи*) to tangle; **напу́тывать (**~ *perf*) **в** +*prp* (*в делах итп*) to make a mess of.

напу́тственный *прил* (*речь*) farewell *опред*; ~**ое сло́во** parting words *мн*.

напу́тстви|е (-я) *ср* parting words *мн или* wishes *мн*, farewell speech.

напу́тыва|ть (-ю) *несов от* напу́тать.

напущу́(сь) *сов см* напусти́ть(ся).

напы́ж|иться (-усь, -ишься) *сов от* пы́житься.

напыл|и́ть (-ю́, -и́шь) *сов от* пыли́ть.

напы́щен|ный (-, -на, -но) *прил* (*вид, человек*) pompous; (*речь, рассказ*) high-flown, bombastic.

напью́сь *итп сов см* напи́ться.

наравне́ *нареч*: ~ **с** +*instr* (*по одной линии*) on a level with; (*на равных правах*) on an equal footing with.

нара́д|оваться (-уюсь) *сов возв*: ~ **на** +*acc* to fully enjoy.

нараспа́шку *нареч* (*разг: одежда*) unbuttoned; **душа́** ~ **у неё** she is very open.

нараспе́в *нареч* drawlingly.

нараст|и́ (*3sg* -тёт, *3pl* -ту́т, *impf* **нараста́ть**) *сов неперех* (*много грибов, трава*) to spring up; (*долги, проценты*) to accumulate; (*волнение, сопротивление*) to grow; **нараста́ть (**~ *perf*) **на** +*prp* (*мох*) to grow on; (*плесень*) to form on; (*водоросли*) to build up on.

нара|сти́ть (-щу́, -сти́шь; *impf* **нара́щивать**) *сов перех* (*мускулы*) to develop; (*канат, трубу*) to lengthen.

нарасхва́т *нареч* (*продаваться, покупаться*) like hot cakes; **таки́е специали́сты сейча́с** ~ such specialists are in great demand nowadays.

нара́щива|ть (-ю) *несов от* нарасти́ть ♦ *перех* (*темпы, объём итп*) to increase.

наращу́ *сов см* нарасти́ть.

нарв|а́ть (-у́, -ёшь; *impf* **нарыва́ть**) *сов (не)перех* (+*acc или* +*gen*; *травы, цветов, земляники*) to pick; (*бумаги*) to tear

► **нарва́ться** (*impf* **нарыва́ться**) *сов возв*

(*разг*): ~ся на +*acc* (*на хулигана, грубияна*) to run up against; (*на оскорбление*) to have to take *или* swallow; **нарыва́ться (**~ся *perf*) **на неприя́тность** to run into some trouble.

наре́|зать (-жу, -жешь; *impf* **нареза́ть**) *сов (не)перех* (+*acc или* +*gen*; *колбасы, хлеба, сыр*) to slice, cut; (*веток, цветов*) to cut; (*земли, участки*) to allot (*ТЕХ*) to thread.

наре́зк|а (-и) *ж* (*винта*) thread.

нарека́ни|е (-я) *ср* reprimand, censure.

наре́чи|е (-я) *ср* (*линг: говоры*) dialect; (: *часть речи*) adverb.

нарза́н (-а) *м* Narzan (*kind of mineral water*).

нарис|ова́ть (-у́ю) *сов от* рисова́ть.

нарица́тельный *прил*: **и́мя** ~**ое** (*линг*) common noun; ~**ая сто́имость** (*ЭКОН*) nominal cost.

нарко́з (-а) *м* (*МЕД*) narcosis, anaesthesia (*BRIT*), anesthesia (*US*).

нарко́лог (-а) *м* (*МЕД*) expert in narcotics.

наркологи́ческ|ий (-ая, -ое, -ие) *прил*: ~ **диспансе́р** drug-abuse clinic.

наркома́н (-а) *м* drug addict *или* abuser.

наркома́ни|я (-и) *ж* (*МЕД*) drug addiction *или* abuse.

наркома́н|ка (-ки; *gen pl* -ок) *ж см* наркома́н.

нарко́тик (-а) *м* narcotic, drug.

наро́д (-а; *part gen* -у) *м* people *мн*; **ру́сский** ~ the Russian people; **мно́го** ~у many people.

наро́ден *прил см* наро́дный.

наро́дность (-и) *ж* nation; (*литературы*) national character.

наро́дный (-ен, -на, -но) *прил* national; (*фронт*) popular; (*искусство*) folk *опред*; ~ **поэ́т** national poet *или* bard; ~ **худо́жник/ арти́ст** artist/actor who has received an official honour from the state.

народонаселе́ни|е (-я) *ср* population.

нарож|а́ть (-а́ю) *сов перех* (*разг*) to give birth to.

наро́ст (-а) *м* (*наслоение*) covering; (*утолщение: на дереве*) outgrowth; (: *на суставах*) growth.

нарочи́т|ый (-, -а, -о) *прил* deliberate, intentional.

наро́чно *нареч* (*опоздать, отверну́ться*) purposely, on purpose; (*разг: сказать, заплакать*) for fun; **как** ~ (*разг*) to make things worse; ~ **не приду́маешь!** (*разг*) this is quite something!

на́рочный (-ого; *decl like adj*) *м* courier.

на́рт|а (-ы) *ж* sledge (*BRIT*) *или* sled (*US*) (*drawn by reindeer or dogs*).

наруб|и́ть (-лю́, -ишь; *impf* **наруба́ть**) *сов (не)перех* (+*acc или* +*gen*; *дров, капусты*) to chop.

нару́жен *прил см* нару́жный.

нару́жность (-и) *ж* exterior; (*строения, города*) outward appearance.

нару́ж|ный (-ен, -на, -но) *прил* (*дверь, стена*) exterior; (*лекарство*) for external application; (*спокойствие, сдержанность*) outward.

нару́жу *нареч* out.

нарумя́н|ить(ся) (**-ю(сь)**, **-ишь(ся)**) *сов от* **румя́нить(ся)**.

нару́чник (**-а**) *м* (*обычно мн*) handcuff.

нару́чн|ый *прил*: ~**ые часы́** wristwatch.

наруша́|ть(ся) (**-ю(сь)**) *несов от* **нару́шить(ся)**.

наруши́тель (**-я**) *м* (*закона*) transgressor, infringer; (*границы*) trespasser; (*ЮР: порядка*) offender; ~ **дисципли́ны** troublemaker.

наруши́тельниц|а (**-ы**) *ж см* **наруши́тель**.

нару́ш|ить (**-у**, **-ишь**; *impf* **наруша́ть**) *сов перех* (*покой, тишину*) to break, disturb; (*связь*) to break; (*правила, договор*) to break, violate; (*дисциплину*) to breach; **наруша́ть** (~ *perf*) **грани́цу** to illegally cross a border

► **нару́шиться** (*impf* **наруша́ться**) *сов возв* to be broken *или* disturbed.

нарци́сс (**-а**) *м* daffodil, narcissus.

на́р|ы (**-**) *мн* plank bed *ед*.

нары́в (**-а**) *м* (*МЕД*) abscess, boil.

нарыва́|ть (**-ю**) *несов от* **нарва́ть** ♦ *наперех* (*рана*) to fester; **у меня́ па́лец** ~**ет** I have a boil on my finger

► **нарыва́ться** *несов от* **нарва́ться**.

наря́д (**-а**) *м* (*одежда*) outfit; (*красивая одежда*) attire; (*распоряжение*) directive; (*КОММ*) order; (*ВОЕН: подразделение*) division; (: *задание*) assignment.

наря́ден *прил см* **наря́дный**.

наря́д|ить (**-яжу́**, **-я́дишь**; *impf* **наряжа́ть**) *сов перех* (*невесту итп*) to dress; (*в караул, на кухню итп*) to assign; **наряжа́ть** (~ *perf*) **ёлку** ≈ to decorate (*BRIT*) *или* trim (*US*) the Christmas tree; **наря́жать** (~ *perf*) **кого́-н** +*instr*/**в** +*acc* to dress sb as/in

► **наряди́ться** (*impf* **наряжа́ться**) *сов возв*: ~**ся** (**в** +*acc*) to dress o.s. (in).

наря́д|ный (**-ен**, **-на**, **-но**) *прил* (*человек*) well-dressed; (*комната, улица*) well-decorated; (*шляпа, платье*) fancy.

наряду́ *нареч*: ~ **с** +*instr* at the same time as; (*наравне*) on an equal footing with.

наряжа́|ть(ся) (**-ю(сь)**) *несов от* **наряди́ть(ся)**.

наряжу́(сь) *сов см* **наряди́ть(ся)**.

нас *мест см* **мы**.

НАСА *ср сокр* NASA (= *National Aeronautics and Space Administration*).

насад|и́ть (**-ажу́**, **-а́дишь**; *impf* **наса́живать**) *сов перех* (*садить*) to put.

наса́д|ка (**-ки**; *gen pl* **-ок**) *ж* (*для рыбы*) bait; (*ТЕХ*) nozzle.

насажде́ни|е (**-я**) *ср* (*БОТ*) plantation.

наса́жива|ть (**-ю**) *несов от* **насади́ть**.

насажу́ *сов см* **насади́ть**.

насви́стыва|ть (**-ю**) *несов перех*: ~ **мело́дию** to whistle a tune under one's breath.

наседа́|ть (**-ю**) *несов от* **насе́сть** ♦ *неперех* (*разг: толпа*) to press forward.

насе́д|ка (**-ки**; *gen pl* **-ок**) *ж* broody hen.

насеко́м|ое (**-ого**; *decl like adj*) *ср* insect.

населе́ни|е (**-я**) *ср* population.

населённый *прил* (*район, область*) populated, inhabited; (*квартира*) inhabited; ~ **пункт** locality.

насел|и́ть (**-ю́**, **-и́шь**; *impf* **населя́ть**) *сов перех* (*край*) to settle; (*дом*) to move into.

населя́|ть (**-ю**) *несов от* **насели́ть** ♦ *перех* (*лес, страну*) to inhabit.

насе́ст (**-а**) *м* (*для кур итп*) roost.

насе́|сть (**-я́ду**, **-я́дешь**; *impf* **наседа́ть**) *сов неперех* (*пыль, копоть*) to settle; **наседа́ть** (~ *perf*) **на** +*acc* (*перен: разг: с просьбами, в вопросами*) to pester; (*на противника*) to fall upon.

насе́ч|ка (**-ки**; *gen pl* **-ек**) *ж* notch.

наси́женн|ый *прил*: ~**ое ме́сто** (*разг*) familiar surroundings *мн*.

наси́ли|е (**-я**) *ср* (*физическое*) violence; (*над личностью*) suppression.

наси́л|овать (**-ую**; *perf* **изнаси́ловать**) *несов перех* (*женщину, девушку*) to rape; (*no perf*; *личность*) to suppress.

наси́лу *нареч* (*разг: успеть, догнать*) only just.

наси́льник (**-а**) *м person who commits an act of violence*; (*над женщиной*) rapist.

наси́льно *нареч* forcibly; ~ **заста́вить** (*perf*) **кого́-н** +*infin* to force sb to do.

наси́льственный *прил* (*меры*) violent; **наси́льственная смерть** violent death.

наска́кива|ть (**-ю**) *несов от* **наскочи́ть**.

наскво́зь *нареч* through; **ви́деть** (*impf*) ~ **кого́-н** to see (right) through sb.

наско́к (**-а**) *м* (*разг*) slagging; **с** ~**а** (*разг*) impromptu.

наско́лько *нареч* so much.

на́скоро *нареч* (*разг*) on the double.

наскоч|и́ть (**-очу́**, **-о́чишь**; *impf* **наска́кивать**) *сов неперех*: ~ **на** +*acc* to run into; (*перен: разг: на обидчика, на оппонента*) to attack; (: *на неприятность*) to get into.

наскре|сти́ (**-бу́**, **-бёшь**; *pt* **-ёб**, **-ебла́**, **-ебло́**, *impf* **наскреба́ть**) *сов перех* (*крошек, муки*) to collect; (*перен: мелочи, денег*) to scrape together.

наску́ч|ить (**-у**, **-ишь**) *сов неперех*: ~ **кому́-н** to bore sb.

наслад|и́ться (**-жу́сь**, **-ди́шься**; *impf* **наслажда́ться**) *сов возв*: ~ +*instr* to enjoy.

наслажде́ни|е (**-я**) *ср* enjoyment.

наслажу́сь *сов см* **наслади́ться**.

насла́ива|ться (*3sg* **-ется**, *3pl* **-ются**) *несов от* **наслои́ться**.

насле́ди|е (**-я**) *ср* (*культурное*) heritage; (*идеологическое*) legacy.

насле́д|ить (**-жу́**, **-ди́шь**) *сов см* **следи́ть**.

наслéдник (**-а**) *м* (*престола, состояния*) heir; (*перен: преемник*) inheritor.

наслéдниц|**а** (**-ы**) *ж* (*см м*) heiress; inheritor.

наслéдный *прил*: ~ **принц** prince next in line (to the throne).

наслéдовани|**е** (**-я**) *ср* inheritance; (*престола*) succession.

наслéд|**овать** (**-ую**) (*не*)*сов перех* to inherit; (*престол*) to succeed.

наслéдственный *прил* inherited; (*черты, болезнь*) hereditary.

наслéдств|**о** (**-а**) *ср* (*имущество*) inheritance; (*культурное*) heritage; (*идеологическое*) legacy; **получáть** (**получи́ть** *perf*) **что-н в** ~ to inherit sth.

наслежу́ *сов см* **наследи́ть**.

наслоéни|**е** (**-я**) *ср* (*ГЕО*) stratification.

насло|**и́ться** (*3sg* **-и́тся**, *3pl* **-я́тся**, *impf* **насла́иваться**) *сов возв*: ~ **на** +*acc* to settle on; (*перен*) to add to.

наслу́ша|**ться** (**-юсь**) *сов возв*: ~ +*gen* to hear a lot of; (*вдоволь послушать*) to hear enough of.

наслы́шан *как сказ*: **я** ~ **об э́том/о нём** I have heard a lot about it/him.

наслы́ш|**аться** (**-усь, -ишься**) *сов возв* (*разг*): ~ **о** +*prp* to hear a lot about.

насма́рку *нареч* (*разг*): **идти́** ~ to be wasted.

на́смерть *нареч* (*сражаться*) to the death; (*разбиться, ранить*) fatally; (*перен: разг: перепугаться*) to death; (: *поругаться*) strongly.

насмеха́|**ться** (**-юсь**) *несов возв*: ~ **над** +*instr* to mock.

насмéшек *сущ см* **насмéшка**.

насмеш|**и́ть** (**-у́, -и́шь**) *сов от* **смеши́ть**.

насмéш|**ка** (**-ки**; *gen pl* **-ек**) *ж* (*обидная шутка*) jibe; **сказáть** (*perf*) **что-н в** ~**ку** to say sth mockingly.

насмéшлив|**ый** (**-, -а, -о**) *прил* mocking.

насмея́|**ться** (**-юсь**) *сов возв*: ~ **над** +*instr* to offend.

на́сморк (**-а**) *м* runny nose.

насм|**отрéться** (**-отрю́сь, -о́тришься**) *сов возв*: ~ (**на** +*acc*) to see enough (of); (+*gen*; *чудес, людéй*) to see a lot of.

насовсéм *нареч* (*разг*) for good.

насол|**и́ть** (**-ю́, -ишь**) *сов перех* to preserve (*in brine*) ♦ *неперех* (+*dat*; *перен: разг: сделать неприятность*) to be nasty to.

насор|**и́ть** (**-ю́, -и́шь**) *сов от* **сори́ть**.

насо́с (**-а**) *м* pump.

на́спех *нареч* hurriedly.

настав|**а́ть** (*3sg* **-ёт**, *3pl* **-ю́т**) *несов от* **наста́ть**.

настави́тел|**ьный** (**-ен, -ьна, -ьно**) *прил* (*тон*) preaching.

наста́в|**ить** (**-лю, -ишь**) *сов неперех* (+*gen*; *поставить*) to put; (*синяков, шишек*) to cause ♦ (*impf* **наставля́ть**) *перех* (*платье, рукав*) to lengthen; (*револьвер, ружьё*) to aim; **наставля́ть** (~ *perf*) **кого-н на путь и́стинный** to set sb on the right path.

наставлéни|**е** (**-я**) *ср* (*поучение*) lecture; (*руководство*) instructions *мн*.

наста́влю *сов см* **наста́вить**.

наставля́|**ть** (**-ю**) *несов от* **наста́вить** ♦ *перех* (*учеников*) to teach.

наста́вник (**-а**) *м* mentor.

наста́ива|**ть**(**ся**) (**-ю**(**сь**)) *несов от* **настоя́ть**(**ся**).

наста́|**ть** (*3sg* **-нет**, *3pl* **-нут**, *impf* **наставáть**) *сов неперех* (*лето*) to begin; (*молчание, ночь*) to fall; (*день отъезда*) to come.

на́стежь *нареч* (*открыть*) wide; (*окно, дверь итп*) wide open; **распахну́ть** (*perf*) ~ to fling wide open.

насте|**ли́ть** (**-лю́, -éлишь**) *сов от* **стели́ть**.

настéнный *прил* wall *опред*.

настига́|**ть** (**-ю**) *несов от* **насти́чь**.

насти́гн|**уть** (**-у, -ешь**) *impf* **настига́ть**) *сов перех* = **насти́чь**.

насти́л (**-а**) *м* (*из сена*) bedding; (*деревянный*) boarding.

насти́чь (**-гну, -гнешь**; *pt* **-г, -гла, -гло**, *impf* **настига́ть**) *сов перех* to catch up with.

настóек *сущ см* **настóйка**.

настó|**й** (**-я**) *м* infusion.

настóй|**ка** (**-йки**; *gen pl* **-ек**) *ж* (*экстракт*) tincture; (*алкоголь*) liqueur.

настóйчив|**ый** (**-, -а, -о**) *прил* (*человек, характер*) persistent; (*просьба, взгляд итп*) insistent.

настóлько *нареч* so.

настóл|**ьный** *прил* (*лампа, часы*) table *опред*; (*календарь*) desk *опред*; (~**ая кни́га** (*перен*) bible; **настóльный тéннис** table tennis.

настора́жива|**ть**(**ся**) (**-ю**(**сь**)) *несов от* **насторожи́ть**(**ся**).

насторожé *нареч* on the alert ♦ *как сказ*: **он всегдá** ~ he is always on the alert.

насторóженно *нареч* intently.

насторóжен|**ный** (**-, -на, -но**) *прил* alert.

насторожён|**ный** (**-, -на, -но**) *прил* = **насторóженный**.

насторож|**и́ть** (**-у́, -и́шь**; *impf* **настора́живать**) *сов перех* to alert

▶ **насторожи́ться** (*impf* **настора́живаться**) *сов возв* to become more alert.

настоя́ни|**е** (**-я**) *ср*: **по**~**ю кого-н** on sb's insistence.

настоя́тел|**ьный** (**-ен, -ьна, -ьно**) *прил* (*просьба*) persistent; (*задача*) urgent.

настоя́|**ть** (**-ю́, -и́шь**; *impf* **наста́ивать**) *сов неперех*: ~ **на** +*prp* to insist on ♦ *перех* (*ромашку*) to infuse; **наста́ивать** (~ *perf*) **на своём** to insist on having one's own way

▶ **настоя́ться** (*impf* **наста́иваться**) *сов возв* (*чай, ромашка*) to infuse.

настоя́щ|**ее** (**-его**; *decl like adj*) *ср* the present.

настоя́щий (**-ая, -ее, -ие**) *прил* real; (*момент, время*) present; (*данный: статья*) this; **по-**~**ему** (*как надо*) properly; (*преданный*) really; **настоя́щее врéмя** (*линг*) the present

настрадá|ться (-юсь) *сов возв* to suffer a lot.
настрáива|ть(ся) (-ю(сь)) *несов от* **настрóить(ся)**.
нáстрого *нареч* (*разг*) strictly.
настроéни|е (-я) *ср* mood; (*антивоенное*) feeling; **не в ~и** in a bad mood; **общéственное ~** the mood in society.
настрó|ить (-ю, -ишь; *impf* **настрáивать**) *сов* (*не*)*перех* (+*acc или* +*gen*; *домов, мостов, больниц*) to build ◆ *перех* (*гитару, пианино итп*) to tune; (*приёмник*) to tune in; (*механизм*) to adjust; **настрáивать** (~ *perf*) **когó-н на** +*acc* to put sb in the right frame of mind for; **настрáивать** (~ *perf*) **когó-н прóтив** +*gen* to incite sb against
▶ **настрóиться** (*impf* **настрáиваться**) *сов возв* (*приёмник*) to be tuned in; (*дружелюбно, враждебно*) to be disposed; **~ся** (*perf*) +*infin* to be disposed to do.
настрó|й (-я) *м* mood.
настрóйщик (-а) *м*: ~ **роя́ля** piano tuner.
наступáтельный (-ен, -ьна, -ьно) *прил* (*бой, дéйствие*) offensive.
наступá|ть (-ю) *несов от* **наступи́ть** ◆ *неперех* (*ВОЕН*) to go on the offensive.
наступ|и́ть (-уплю́, -у́пишь; *impf* **наступáть**) *сов неперех*: ~ **на** +*acc* (*на камень, на ногу итп*) to step on; (*ночь, тишина*) to fall; (*утро, лето*) to begin; (*день отъéзда*) to come.
наступлéни|е (-я) *ср* (*ВОЕН*) offensive; (*весны, стáрости*) beginning; (*темноты́*) fall; **с ~м зимы́** at the beginning of winter; **с ~м темноты́** at nightfall.
наступлю́ *сов см* **наступи́ть**.
настýрци|я (-и) *ж* nasturtium.
насты́р|ный (ен, -на, -но) *прил* (*разг*) persistent.
насýп|иться (-люсь, -ишься) *сов возв* (*разг*) to frown.
нáсухо *нареч*: **вы́тереть что-н ~** to dry sth thoroughly.
насýщ|ный (-ен, -на, -но) *прил* vital.
насчёт *предл* (+*gen*) regarding.
насчитá|ть (-ю; *impf* **насчи́тывать**) *сов перех* to count.
насчи́тыва|ть (-ю) *несов от* **насчитáть** ◆ *неперех* to have; **дерéвня ~ет ты́сячу жи́телей** the village has a thousand inhabitants
▶ **насчи́тываться** *несов возв безл* to have.
насы́п|ать (-лю, -лешь; *impf* **насыпáть**) *сов перех* to pour; (*набросáть*) to strew.
нáсып|ь (-и) *ж* embankment.
насы́|тить (-щу, -тишь; *impf* **насыщáть**) *сов перех* (*голóдного, ребёнка*) to satiate; (*запáхом, водóй, рáдостью*) to fill; (*раствóр, ры́нок*) to saturate
▶ **насы́титься** (*impf* **насыщáться**) *сов возв*

(*наéсться*) to eat one's fill; (*земля*) to be saturated.
насы́щенный *прил* (*хим*) saturated; (*перен: жизнь*) rich.
насы́щу(сь) *сов см* **насы́тить(ся)**.
нася́ду *итп сов см* **насéсть**.
натáлкива|ть(ся) (-ю(сь)) *несов от* **натолкнýть(ся)**.
натаскá|ть (-ю; *impf* **натáскивать**) *сов* (*не*)*перех* (+*acc или* +*gen*; *дров, сучьев итп*) to bring; (*разг: перен: цитáт, отры́вков*) to fish out; (: *студéнта, ученикá*) to coach (*for examination*).
натащ|и́ть (-ý, -ишь) *сов* (*не*)*перех* (+*acc или* +*gen*; *разг: камнéй, сучьев, гря́зи*) to bring in.
натвор|и́ть (-ю́, -и́шь) *сов* (*не*)*перех* (+*acc или* +*gen*; *разг*) to get up to.
нат|ерéть (-рý, -рёшь; *pt* -ёр, -ёрла, -ёрло, *impf* **натирáть**) *сов перех* (*ботинки, полы́*) to polish; (*рýку, шéю итп*) to chafe; (*морковь, сыр итп*) to grate; **натирáть** (~ *perf*) **что-н чем-н** (*руки итп: мáзью, крéмом*) to rub sth into sth; **натирáть** (~ *perf*) **себé мозóли** to get a callus
▶ **натерéться** (*impf* **натирáться**) *сов возв*: **~ся** (+*instr*; *мáзью, крéмом*) to rub o.s. (with).
натерп|éться (-лю́сь, -ишься) *сов возв*: ~ +*gen* (*разг: гóря, беды́*) to experience a lot of.
натирá|ть(ся) (-ю(сь)) *несов от* **натерéть(ся)**.
нáтиск (-а) *м* pressure.
наткн|ýться (-ýсь, -ёшься; *impf* **натыкáться**) *сов возв*: **~уться на** +*acc* (*разг: на пень, на прегрáду*) to bump into; (*перен: на непонимáние, на сопротивлéние*) to come up against.
НÁТО *ср сокр* NATO (= *North Atlantic Treaty Organization*).
натолкн|ýть (-ý, -ёшь; *impf* **натáлкивать**) *сов перех*: ~ **когó-н на** +*acc* (*разг: на идéю*) to lead sb to; **натáлкивать** (~ *perf*) **когó-н на мысль** to put a thought into sb's head
▶ **натолкнýться** (*impf* **натáлкиваться**) *сов возв*: **~ся на** +*acc* (*тáкже перен*) to bump into.
натоп|и́ть (-лю́, -ишь) *сов перех* (*избу, печь*) to heat; (*жир, воск*) to melt.
натоп|тáть (-чý, -чешь) *сов перех* (*разг*) to make dirty footmarks across.
нат|очи́ть (-очý, -óчишь) *сов от* **точи́ть**.
натоща́к *нареч* on an empty stomach.
натрав|и́ть (-лю́, -ишь; *impf* **натрáвливать**) *сов перех*: ~ **когó-н на** +*acc* to set sb on; (*перен*) to incite sb against.
натренирóван|ный (-, -а, -о) *прил* trained.
натренир|овáть(ся) (-ýю(сь)) *сов от* **тренировáть(ся)**.
нáтри|й (-я) *м* sodium.
нáтрое *нареч* in(to) three.
натрý(сь) *итп сов см* **натерéть(ся)**.
натруд|и́ться (-ужýсь, -ýдишься) *сов возв* (*разг*) to work hard.

нату́г|а (-и) ж (разг) effort.
на́туго нареч (разг) tightly.
нату́житься (-усь, -ишься; impf
  нату́живаться) сов возв (разг) to strain.
нату́р|а (-ы) ж (характер); (натурщик)
  model (ART); **увиде́ть** (perf) **что-н/кого-н ~е** to
  see sth/sb in real life; **рисова́ть** (impf) **с ~ы** to
  paint from nature; **~ой, в ~е** (ЭКОН) in kind.
натура́лен прил см **натура́льный**.
натурализа́ци|я (-и) ж naturalization.
натурали́зм (-а) м naturalism.
натурали́ст (-а) м naturalist.
натура́льный (-ен, -ьна, -ьно) прил natural;
  (мех, кожа, слёзы) real; (обмен, доходы, налог)
  in kind; **~ьная величина́** life-sized.
нату́рщик (-а) м model (ART).
нату́рщиц|а (-ы) ж см **нату́рщик**.
натыка́|ться (-юсь) несов от **наткну́ться**.
натюрмо́рт (-а) м still life.
натя́гива|ть(ся) (-ю(сь)) несов от
  натяну́ть(ся).
натя́ж|ка (-ки; gen pl -ек) ж (в аргументах)
  distortion; **с ~кой** at a pinch.
натя́ну|тый (-, -а, -о) прил strained.
натяну́ть (-у́, -ешь; impf **натя́гивать**) сов перех
  (струны, вожжи, холст) to pull tight; (разг:
  сапоги, перчатки) to pull on; (: одеяло) to pull
  over; **он ~у́л ему́ пятёрку** (разг) he stretched
  his mark to an A
▶ **натяну́ться** (impf **натя́гиваться**) сов возв to
  tighten.
науга́д нареч (идти, взять) at random;
  отвеча́ть (impf) **~** to guess.
нау́к|а (-и) ж science; (разг: урок) lesson;
  есте́ственные ~и science; **гуманита́рные ~и**
  arts.
наутёк нареч (разг: пуститься, броситься) at
  full tilt.
нау́тро нареч next morning.
нау́чен прил см **нау́чный**.
на́учи́ть(ся) (-учу́(сь), -у́чишь(ся)) сов от
  учи́ть(ся).
нау́чно-популя́рный прил (программа)
  science опред; (литература) scientific.
нау́чно-техни́ческий (-ая, -ое, -ие) прил
  scientific.
нау́чный (-ен, -на, -но) прил scientific; **нау́чная
  фанта́стика** science fiction.
нау́шник (-а) м (обычно мн: на шапке) earflap;
  магнитофо́нные ~и headphones.
нафтали́н (-а; part gen -у) м naphthalene.
наха́л (-а) м (разг) cheeky beggar.
наха́лен прил см **наха́льный**.
наха́лк|а (-и) ж см **наха́л**.
наха́льный (-ен, -ьна, -ьно) прил cheeky.
наха́льств|о (-а) ср cheek.
нахам|и́ть (-лю́, -и́шь) сов от **хами́ть**.
нахвата́|ть (-ю) сов неперех (+gen; разг:
  товаров, знаний) to pick up
▶ **нахвата́ться** сов возв (+gen; разг: знаний,
  привычек) to pick up; (: воды) to gulp.

нахле́бник (-а) м (разг) sponger.
нахлобу́ч|ить (-у, -ишь; impf **нахлобу́чивать**)
  сов перех (разг) to pull down.
нахлы́н|уть (3sg -ет, 3pl -ут) сов неперех
  (поток) to surge; (перен: толпа) to surge
  forward; (: мысли) to surge up; **~ули
  воспомина́ния** memories came flooding back.
нахму́р|ить(ся) (-ю(сь), -ишь(ся)) несов от
  хму́рить(ся).
нах|оди́ть (-ожу́, -о́дишь) несов от **найти́**
▶ **находи́ться** несов от **найти́сь** ◆ возв (дом,
  город) to be situated; (человек) to be.
нахо́д|ка (-ки; gen pl -ок) ж (потерянного)
  discovery; (приём: писателя, актёра)
  innovation; **он ~ для нас** he is a real find for
  us; **Бюро́ ~ок** lost property office (BRIT), lost
  and found (US).
нахо́дчив|ый (-, -а, -о) прил (человек)
  resourceful; (ответ) apt.
нахожде́ни|е (-я) ср (преступника)
  whereabouts.
нахо́жен|ный (-, -а, -о) прил (тропа) well-
  trodden.
нахожу́(сь) несов см **находи́ть(ся)**.
нахох|ота́ться (-очу́сь, -о́чешься) сов возв to
  have a good laugh.
нахра́пист|ый (-, -а, -о) прил (разг: продавец,
  посетитель) pushy.
нахра́пом нареч (разг): **де́йствовать ~** to be
  pushy.
нахулига́н|ить (-ю, -ишь) сов от **хулига́нить**.
нацара́па|ть (-ю) сов от **цара́пать**.
наце|ди́ть (-жу́, -́дишь; impf **наце́живать**) сов
  перех to strain.
наце́лен|ный (-, -а, -о) прил: **~ на** +acc (на
  победу) aiming for.
наце́л|ить (-ю, -ишь) сов от **це́лить** ◆ (impf
  наце́ливать) перех: **~ кого́-н на** +acc to push
  sb towards
▶ **наце́литься** сов от **це́литься**.
наце́н|ка (-ки; gen pl -ок) ж (на товар) surcharge;
  (ресторанная) cover charge.
нацеп|и́ть (-лю́, -ишь; impf **нацепля́ть**) сов
  перех (повесить) to hang on; (разг: украшения,
  шляпу) to doll o.s. up in.
наци́зм (-а) м Nazism.
национализа́ци|я (-и) ж nationalization.
национализи́р|овать (-ую) (не)сов перех to
  nationalize.
национали́зм (-а) м nationalism.
национали́ст (-а) м nationalist.
национали́ст|ка (-ки; gen pl -ок) ж см
  национали́ст.
националисти́ческ|ий (-ая, -ое, -ие) прил
  (политика, лозунг) nationalistic.
национа́льность (-и) ж (нация) nation;
  (принадлежность к нации) nationality.
национа́льный прил national; **национа́льный
  о́круг** administrative division of minor
  nationalities.
наци́ст (-а) м Nazi.

наци́стск|ий (**-ая, -ое, -ие**) *прил* Nazi.
на́ци|я (**-и**) *ж* nation; **Организа́ция Объединённых Н~й** United Nations Organization.
нацме́н (**-а**) *м сокр* = *представи́тель национа́льного меньшинства́*.
нач. *сокр* = **нача́льник**.
начад|и́ть (**-жу́, -ди́шь**) *сов от* **чади́ть**.
нача́л|а (**-**) *мн* (*мето́ды*) basis *ед*; (*при́нципы*) fundamentals *мн*; **на коллекти́вных/комме́рческих ~х** on a collective/commercial basis.
нача́л|о (**-а**) *ср* beginning, start; (*осно́ва: организу́ющее, сде́рживающее*) foundation; (*: волево́е, поэти́ческое*) nature; **быть** (*impf*) **под ~м кого́-н** *или* **у кого́-н** to be under sb; **брать** (*impf*) **~** to start; **вести́** (*impf*) **своё ~ от** +*gen* to have its origins in; **положи́ть** (*perf*) *или* **дать** (*perf*) **~ чему́-н** to make a start on sth; *см также* **нача́ла**.
нача́льник (**-а**) *м* (*це́ха*) floor manager; (*управле́ния*) head; (*экспеди́ции*) leader.
нача́льническ|ий (**-ая, -ое, -ие**) *прил* (*тон*) authoritative.
нача́льный *прил* (*пери́од, эта́п*) initial; (*глава́ кни́ги*) first; (*первонача́льный: све́дения, уро́ки*) very first; **нача́льная шко́ла** (*ПРОСВЕЩ*) primary *или* elementary (*US*) school; **нача́льное образова́ние** (*ПРОСВЕЩ*) primary (*BRIT*) *или* elementary (*US*) education; **нача́льные кла́ссы** (*ПРОСВЕЩ*) *the first three classes of primary school.*
нача́льственный *прил* superior.
нача́льств|о (**-а**) *ср* (*власть*) authority ◆ *собир* (*руководи́тели*) management; **под ~м кого́-н** (*служи́ть, находи́ться*) under sb.
нача́льствующ|ий (**-ая, -ее, -ие**) *прил* managing *опред*.
нача́тк|и (**-ов**) *мн* fundamentals *мн*.
нача́|ть (**-ну́, -нёшь**; *pt* **-ал, -ала́, -ало**, *impf* **начина́ть**) *сов перех* to begin, start; (*нача́ть испо́льзовать*) to start; **начина́ть** (**~** *perf*) +*infin* to start doing
▶ **нача́ться** (*impf* **начина́ться**) *сов возв* to begin, start.
начеку́ *нареч*: **быть ~** to be on one's guard.
начерка́|ть (**-ю**) *сов от* **черка́ть** ◆ *перех* (*разг: ли́нии, штрихи́ итп*) to draw (*randomly*); (*запи́ску*) to scribble.
начерн|и́ть (**-ю́, -и́шь**) *сов от* **черни́ть**.
на́черно *нареч* (*написа́ть, подгото́вить*) roughly.
начерта́ни|е (**-я**) *ср* (*букв*) outline.
начер|ти́ть (**-чу́, -ртишь**) *сов от* **черти́ть**.
начёс (**-а**) *м* (*на ше́рсти, на тка́ни*) nap; (*вид причёски*) bouffant.
начёт (**-а**) *м* (*де́нежное взыска́ние*) penalty.
начина́ни|е (**-я**) *ср* initiative.

начина́тел|ь (**-я**) *м* initiator.
начина́|ть(ся) (**-ю(сь)**) *несов от* **нача́ть(ся)**.
начина́|ющая (**-ей**; *decl like adj*) *ж см* **начина́ющий**.
начина́|ющий (**-ая, -ее, -ие**) *прил* (*писа́тель, учи́тель*) novice *опред* ◆ (**-его**; *decl like adj*) *м* beginner.
начина́|я *предл* (+*instr*) including; **~ с** +*gen* from; **~ от** +*gen* или **с** +*gen* (*включа́я*) including.
начин|и́ть (**-ю́, -и́шь**; *impf* **начиня́ть**) *сов перех* (*пиро́г*) to fill.
начи́н|ка (**-ки**; *gen pl* **-ок**) *ж* filling.
начиня́|ть (**-ю**) *несов от* **начини́ть**.
начисле́ни|е (**-я**) *ср* (*де́йствие*) addition; (*начи́сленная су́мма*) surcharge.
начи́сл|ить (**-ю, -ишь**; *impf* **начисля́ть**) *сов перех* (*проце́нты*) to add on.
начи́|стить (**-щу, -стишь**; *impf* **начища́ть**) *сов перех* (*ту́фли*) to clean ◆ *непе́рех* (+*gen*; *карто́шки*) to peel.
на́чисто *нареч* (*на́бело*) cleanly; (*разг: соверше́нно*) absolutely.
начистоту́ *нареч* (*разг*) straight.
начи́танный (**-, -на, -но**) *прил* well-read.
начита́|ть (**-ю**; *impf* **начи́тывать**) *сов перех* to read
▶ **начита́ться** *сов возв* (+*gen*) to read a lot of.
начи́тыва|ть (**-ю**) *несов от* **начита́ть**.
начиха́|ть (**-ю**) *сов непе́рех* (*перен: разг*): **ему́ ~ на сове́ты** he doesn't give a toss about taking people's advice.
начища́|ть (**-ю**) *несов от* **начи́стить**.
начи́щу *сов см* **начи́стить**.
начме́д (**-а**) *м сокр* SG (= *Surgeon General*).
начну́(сь) *итп сов см* **нача́ть(ся)**.
наш (**-его**; *см* **Table 9**; *f* **-а**, *nt* **-е**, *pl* **-и**) *притяж мест* our; **~ го́род о́чень ста́рый** our city is very old; **чей э́то дом? –** whose is this house? – ours; **чьи э́то кни́ги? – на́ши** whose are these books? – ours; **по-на́шему** our way; (*по на́шему мне́нию*) in our opinion; **на́ша взяла́!** (*разг*) we won!; *см также* **на́ши**.
нашаты́рный *прил*: **~ спирт** (*МЕД*) liquid ammonia.
нашаты́р|ь (**-я́**) *м* (*хим*) ammonium chloride; (*разг: нашаты́рный спирт*) liquid ammonia.
на́ше (**-го**) *притяж мест см* **наш**.
наше́стви|е (**-я**) *ср* invasion.
на́ш|и (**-их**) *притяж мест см* **наш**; ◆ *decl like adj* *мн* (*о чле́нах семьи́*) relatives *мн*; (*о соотече́ственниках*) compatriots *мн*; **и ~м и ва́шим** (*разг*) all things to all people; **~ вы́играли** we won.
нашива́|ть (**-ю**) *несов от* **наши́ть**.
наши́в|ка (**-ки**; *gen pl* **-ок**) *ж* (*на пого́нах*) stripe (*showing rank*).
на́шим *притяж мест см* **наш, на́ше, на́ши**.
на́шими *притяж мест см* **на́ши**.

нашинк|ова́ть (-у́ю) *сов от* **шинкова́ть**.

наш|и́ть (-ью́, -ьёшь; *impf* **нашива́ть**) *сов перех* (тесьму, эмблему) to sew on ◆ *неперех* (*no perf*): ~ +*gen* (нарядов) to sew.

на́ших *притяж мест см* **наш**.

нашлёпа|ть (-ю) *сов перех* (*разг*) to smack.

нашпиг|ова́ть (-у́ю) *сов от* **шпигова́ть**.

нашум|е́ть (-лю́, -и́шь) *сов неперех* to make a lot of noise; (фильм, книга) to cause a stir.

нашью́ *итп сов см* **наши́ть**.

нащу́па|ть (-ю; *impf* **нащу́пывать**) *сов перех* (также перен) to find.

наэлектриз|ова́ть (-у́ю) *сов от* **электризова́ть**.

ная́бедничать (-ю) *сов от* **я́бедничать**.

ная́ву *нареч* in reality; **как** ~ distinctly.

НДС *м сокр* (= нало́г на доба́вленную сто́имость) VAT (= *value-added tax*).

не *част* not; ~ **я написа́л э́то письмо́** I didn't write this letter; **я** ~ **рабо́таю** I don't work; ~ **пла́чьте/опозда́йте** don't cry/be late; ~ **могу́** ~ **согласи́ться/не возрази́ть** I can't help agreeing/objecting; ~ **мне на́до помо́чь, а ему́** I am not the one who needs help, he is; **слу́шаю** ~ **без удово́льствия/удивле́ния** I listen not without pleasure/surprise; ~ **до** +*gen* no time for; **мне** ~ **до тебя́** I have no time for you; ~ **без того́** (*разг: в положительных ответах*) that's about it; ~ **то** (*разг: в противном случае*) or else; **откро́й дверь,** ~ **то я её слома́ю** open the door or else I'll break it down.

неадеква́т|ный (-ен, -на, -но) *прил* inadequate.

неаккура́т|ный (-ен, -на, -но) *прил* (человек) untidy; (подсчёт) inaccurate; (работа) sloppy.

неактуа́л|ьный (-ен, -ьна, -ьно) *прил* irrelevant.

неаполита́нск|ий (-ая, -ое, -ие) *прил* Neapolitan.

Неа́пол|ь (-я) *м* Naples.

небезопа́с|ный (-ен, -на, -но) *прил* somewhat dangerous.

небезоснова́тел|ьный (-ен, -ьна, -ьно) *прил* not unreasonable.

небезызве́ст|ный (-ен, -на, -но) *прил* (факты) reasonably well-known; (сплетник, интриган) notorious.

небезынтере́с|ный (-ен, -на, -но) *прил* reasonably interesting.

небеса́ *итп сущ см* **не́бо**.

небе́сный *прил* (небосвод, сфера) celestial; (*перен*) heavenly; **небе́сные тела́** heavenly bodies; **небе́сные си́лы** (*РЕЛ*) the heavenly host; **небе́сный цвет** sky blue.

небеспол́ез|ный (-ен, -на, -но) *прил* reasonably useful.

неблагови́д|ный (-ен, -на, -но) *прил* unseemly.

неблагода́рен *прил см* **неблагода́рный**.

неблагода́рност|ь (-и) *ж* ingratitude.

неблагода́р|ный (-ен, -на, -но) *прил* (человек) ungrateful; (занятие, работа) thankless.

неблагозву́ч|ный (-ен, -на, -но) *прил* dissonant.

неблагополу́ч|ный (-ен, -на, -но) *прил* unsuccessful.

не́б|о (-а; *nom pl* **небеса́**, *gen pl* **небе́с**) *ср* sky; (*РЕЛ*) Heaven; **на седьмо́м** ~ in seventh heaven; **под откры́тым** ~**м** out in the open; **с** ~**а свали́ться** (*perf*) (*разг: неожиданно появиться*) to appear out of nowhere; **я был ме́жду** ~**м и землёй** I didn't know whether I was coming or going; **превозноси́ть** (*impf*) **кого́-н до небе́с** to praise sb to the skies.

нёб|о (-а) *ср* (*АНАТ*) palate.

небога́т|ый (-, -а, -о) *прил* (страна) not wealthy; (выбор, улов) fairly poor; **он челове́к** ~ he has a modest income.

небольш|о́й *прил* small; (расстояние, промежуток времени) short; (должность, звание) minor; (польза, авторитет) limited; **на** ~ **глуби́не/высоте́** not very deep/high; **ей три́дцать (лет) с** ~**им** she is a little over thirty.

небосво́д (-а) *м* the heavens *мн*.

небоскрёб (-а) *м* skyscraper.

небо́сь *вводн сл* (*разг*) I dare say.

небре́жен *прил см* **небре́жный**.

небре́жност|ь (-и) *ж* (в работе, подсчётов) carelessness; (родителей, работников) negligence; (тона, в обращении) offhandedness.

небре́ж|ный (-ен, -на, -но) *прил* (человек, работа, подсчёт) careless; (причёска, почерк) untidy; (тон, отношение) offhand(ed).

небыва́л|ый (-, -а, -о) *прил* (чувство, ощущение) unknown; (случай) unprecedented.

небыли́ц|а (-ы) *ж* tall story.

небыти|е́ (-я́) *ср* nonexistence.

Нев|а́ (-ы́) *ж* the Neva.

нева́жен *прил см* **нева́жный**.

нева́жно *нареч* (работать, делать что-н) not very well ◆ *как сказ* it's not important; **я чу́вствую себя́** ~ I'm not feeling too good; **он** ~ **у́чится в шко́ле** he isn't doing very well at school.

нева́ж|ный (-ен, -на, -но) *прил* unimportant; (не очень хороший) poor; **обе́д был нава́жный** dinner wasn't great; **у неё** ~**ное здоро́вье** her health isn't very good.

невдалеке́ *нареч* (слышаться, видеться) not far off; ~ **от** +*gen* not far from.

невдомёк *как сказ* (+*dat*): **ей** ~, **что** ... (*разг*) she doesn't realize that ....

неве́ден|ие (-я) *ср* ignorance; **сде́лать** (*perf*)/ **сказа́ть** (*perf*) **что-н по** ~**ю** to do/say sth out of ignorance; **он пребыва́ет в по́лном** ~**и** he doesn't know anything about it).

неве́домо *нареч*: ~ **кто/что/как** *итп* (*разг*) God knows who/what/how *итп*.

неве́дом|ый (-, -а, -о) *прил* unknown.

неве́ж|а (-и) *м/ж* boor.

неве́жд|а (-ы) *м/ж* ignoramus.

неве́жествен|ный (-, -на, -но) *прил* ignorant.

неве́жеств|о (-а) *ср* ignorance.

неве́жлив|ый (-, -а, -о) *прил* impolite.
невезе́ни|е (-я) *ср* (*разг*) bad luck.
невели́к|ий (-ая, -ое, -ие; -, -á, -ó) *прил* (*по размеру*) small; (*по длине*) short; (*убытки, ущерб*) minor; **он ро́стом невели́к** he's not very tall; **невелика́ беда́!** (*разг*) it's no big deal!
неве́рен *прил см* **неве́рный.**
неве́ри|е (-я) *ср* lack of faith.
неве́рно *нареч* incorrectly ♦ *как сказ:* (**э́то**) ~ that's not right.
неве́рност|ь (-и) *ж* (*рассужде́ний, поня́тия*) incorrectness; (*друга, сою́зника*) disloyalty; (*жены, мужа*) infidelity.
неве́рн|ый (-ен, -на, -но) *прил* (*см сущ*) incorrect; disloyal; unfaithful; (*шаги, движения*) unsteady; (*голос, звук*) faltering; (*нота*) false.
невероя́тен *прил см* **невероя́тный.**
невероя́тно *нареч* incredibly ♦ *как сказ* it's incredible.
невероя́тност|ь (-и) *ж* (*сообщения, результатов*) improbability; **до ~и** incredibly.
невероя́т|ный (-ен, -на, -но) *прил* (*неправдоподобный*) improbable; (*чрезвычайный*) incredible.
неве́рующий (-ая, -ее, -ие) *прил* (*РЕЛ*) faithless ♦ **(-его;** *decl like adj*) *м* unbeliever.
невесёлый (-е́сел, -есела́, -е́село) *прил* gloomy.
невесо́мост|ь (-и) *ж* (*ФИЗ*) weightlessness.
невесо́м|ый (-, -а, -о) *прил* weightless; (*перен: преимущество, превосходство*) negligible.
неве́ст|а (-ы) *ж* (*после помолвки*) fiancée; (*на свадьбе*) bride.
неве́ст|ка (-ки; *gen pl* **-ок)** *ж* (*жена сына*) daughter-in-law; (*жена брата*) sister-in-law.
неве́сть *нареч:* ~ **кто/что/куда́** *итп* (*разг*) goodness knows who/what/where *итп*.
невзго́д|а (-ы) *ж* (*обычно мн*) adversity.
невзира́|я *предл:* ~ **на** +*acc* in spite of.
невзлюби́ть (-юблю́, -ю́бишь) *сов перех* to take a dislike to.
невзнача́й *нареч* (*разг*) by accident.
невзра́ч|ный (-ен, -на, -но) *прил* ordinary-looking.
невзыска́тел|ьный (-ен, -ьна, -ьно) *прил* undemanding.
не́видал|ь (-и) *ж* (*разг*) oddity; ~ **кака́я!** now there's a surprise!
неви́дан|ный (-, -на, -но) *прил* unprecedented.
неви́ди́м|ка (-ки; *gen pl* **-ок)** *м/ж* (*человек*) invisible being ♦ *ж* (*шпилька*) hairpin.
неви́дим|ый (-, -а, -о) *прил* invisible.
неви́дящий (-ая, -ее, -ие) *прил* unseeing.
неви́нен *прил см* **неви́нный.**
неви́нност|ь (-и) *ж* innocence.
неви́н|ный (-ен, -на, -но) *прил* innocent.
невино́вен *прил см* **невино́вный.**

невино́вност|ь (-и) *ж* innocence.
невино́в|ный (-ен, -на, -но) *прил* innocent.
невку́сен *прил см* **невку́сный.**
невку́сно *нареч:* **она́ ~ гото́вит** she is a bad cook; **здесь ~ ко́рмят** the food here is not very nice.
невку́с|ный (-ен, -на́, -но) *прил* (*суп, салат, пища*) tasteless.
невменя́емост|ь (-и) *ж* derangement; **в состоя́нии ~и** (*ЮР*) non compos mentis.
невменя́ем|ый (-, -а, -о) *прил* deranged.
невмеша́тельств|о (-а) *ср* non interference; (*ЭКОН*) laissez faire.
невнима́ни|е (-я) *ср* (*невнимательность*) lack of attention; (*равнодушие*) lack of concern.
невнима́телен *прил см* **невнима́тельный.**
невнима́тельност|ь (-и) *ж* (*см прил*) inattention; lack of consideration; carelessness.
невнима́тел|ьный (-ен, -ьна, -ьно) *прил* (*ученик, слушатель*) inattentive; (*незаботливый: сын, дочь*) inconsiderate; (: *отношение, обращение*) careless.
невня́т|ный (-ен, -на, -но) *прил* muffled.
не́вод (-а) *м* fishing net.
невозвра́тен *прил см* **невозвра́тный.**
невозврати́м|ый (-, -а, -о) *прил* irretrievable.
невозвра́т|ный (-ен, на, -но) *прил =* **невозврати́мый.**
невозвраще́н|ец (-ца) *м* defector.
невозвраще́н|ка (-ки; *gen pl* **-ок)** *ж см* **невозвраще́нец.**
невозвраще́нца *итп сущ см* **невозвраще́нец.**
невозде́ржан|ный (-, -на, -но) *прил* highly strung (*BRIT*), high-strung (*US*).
невозмо́жен *прил см* **невозмо́жный.**
невозмо́жно *как сказ:* ~ **+**infin (*сде́лать, найти́* *итп*) it is impossible to do ♦ *нареч* (*большой, трудный*) impossibly; (*э́то*) ~ that's impossible.
невозмо́жност|ь (-и) *ж:* **до ~и** exceedingly.
невозмо́ж|ный (-ен, -на, -но) *прил* impossible; (*боль, жара*) unbearable; (*тон, поведение, вид*) insufferable.
невозмути́м|ый (-, -а, -о) *прил* (*человек*) unflappable; (*тон, ответ*) unruffled; (*тишина, спокойствие*) undisturbed.
нево́лен *прил см* **нево́льный.**
нево́л|ить (-ю, -ишь) *несов перех* (*разг*): ~ **кого́-н** +infin (*согласиться, отказаться* *итп*) to force sb to do.
нево́льник (-а) *м* slave.
нево́льниц|а (-ы) *ж см* **нево́льник.**
нево́л|ьный (-ен, -ьна, -ьно) *прил* (*ложь, вина*) unintentional; (*движение, улыбка, свидетель*) involuntary.
нево́л|я (-и) *ж* captivity; **в ~е** in captivity.
невообрази́м|ый (-, -а, -о) *прил* unimaginable.
невооружён|ный *прил* unarmed; **~ым гла́зом**

(*без оптических приборов*) with the naked eye; э́то ви́дно ~ым глазо́м (*перен*) it's plain for all to see.

невоспи́тан|ный (-, -на, -но) *прил* ill-bred.

невосприи́мчивый (-, -а, -о) *прил*: ~ (к +*dat*) (*к знаниям*) unreceptive (to); (*к болезням*) immune (to).

невостре́бованный *прил* unclaimed.

невпопа́д *нареч* (*разг*) out of turn.

невразуми́тельный (-ен, -ьна, -ьно) *прил* unintelligible.

невралги́ческ|ий (-ая, -ое, -ие) *прил* neuralgic.

невралги́|я (-и) *ж* neuralgia.

неврасте́ник (-а) *м* neurotic.

неврастени́ч|ный (-ен, -на, -но) *прил* neurotic.

неврастени́|я (-и) *ж* (*МЕД*) nervous tension.

невреди́м|ый (-, -а, -о) *прил* (*лодка, машина*) undamaged; (*человек*) unharmed.

невро́з (-а) *м* neurosis (*мн* neuroses).

невропато́лог (-а) *м* neurologist.

невтерпёж *как сказ* (+*dat*): ей ~ пойти́/узна́ть she can't wait to go/find out; ему́ всё ~ he is always in a hurry.

невы́год|ный (-ен, -на, -но) *прил* unprofitable; (*условия, ситуация, впечатление*) unfavourable (*BRIT*), unfavorable (*US*); (*внешность*) unattractive.

невы́держан|ный (-, -на, -но) *прил* (*человек, поведение*) uncontrolled; (*стиль*) erratic.

невыноси́м|ый (-, -а, -о) *прил* unbearable, intolerable.

невыполне́ни|е (-я) *ср* (*обязательства, плана*) failure to carry out; (*обещания*) failure to keep.

невыполни́м|ый (-, -а, -о) *прил* not feasible.

невырази́м|ый (-, -а, -о) *прил* inexpressible.

невырази́тельный (-ен, -ьна, -ьно) *прил* (*лицо, глаза*) expressionless; (*рассказ, исполнение*) bland.

невысо́к|ий (-ая, -ое, -ие; -, -á, -о) *прил* low; (*человек*) short.

нéг|а (-и) *ж* bliss.

негати́в (-а) *м* (*ФОТО*) negative.

негати́в|ный (-ен, -на, -но) *прил* negative.

негашёный *прил*: негашёная ма́рка unused stamp; негашёная и́звесть quicklime.

нéгде *как сказ* (+*infin*) there is nowhere to do; мне ~ жить I don't have anywhere to live; здесь ~ купи́ть еды́ there is nowhere to buy food around here.

неги́б|кий (-кая, -кое, -кие; -ок, -кá, -ко) *прил* (*также перен*) inflexible.

негла́с|ный (-ен, -на, -но) *прил* secret.

неглубо́к|ий (-ая, -ое, -ие; -, -á, -о) *прил* (*яма, река*) shallow; (*знания, человек, чувство*) superficial; (*сон*) light.

неглу́п|ый (-, -á, -о) *прил* fairly clever; он о́чень неглу́п he's by no means stupid.

негó *мест от* он, онó.

негóден *прил см* негóдный.

негóдност|ь (-и) *ж* worthlessness; приходи́ть

(прийти́ *perf*) в ~ (*оборудование*) to become defunct; (*одежда*) to be worn out.

негóд|ный (-ен, -на, -но) *прил* (*непригодный*) unusable; (*скверный*) good-for-nothing.

негодова́ни|е (-я) *ср* indignation.

негод|ова́ть (-у́ю) *несов неперех* to be indignant.

негоду́ющ|ий (-ая, -ее, -ие) *прил* indignant.

негодя́|й (-я) *м* scoundrel.

негр (-а) *м* black man (*мн* men).

негра́мот|ный (-ен, -на, -но) *прил* (*человек, ученик*) illiterate; (*содержащий ошибки: речь*) ungrammatical; (*специалист, работа*) incompetent.

негритёнок (-ёнка; *nom pl* -я́та, *gen pl* -я́т) *м* black child (*мн* children).

негритя́н|ка (-ки; *gen pl* -ок) *ж* black woman (*мн* women).

негритя́нск|ий (-ая, -ое, -ие) *прил* black.

негритя́нц|а *итп сущ см* негритёнок.

негрóм|кий (-кая, -кое, -кие; -ок, -кá, -ко) *прил* quiet.

нéгр|ы (-ов) *мн* black people *мн*.

неда́вн|ий (-яя, -ее, -ие) *прил* recent; до ~его вре́мени until recently.

неда́вно *нареч* recently.

недалёк|ий (-ая, -ое, -ие; -, -á, -о) *прил* (*место*) nearby; (*расстояние, путь*) short; (*недавний*) near; (-, -а, -о; *перен: человек, ум*) limited; в ~ом бу́дущем in the near future; она́ недалекá от и́стины she is not far from the truth.

недалекó *нареч* (*жить, находиться*) nearby; (*идти, ехать*) not far ◆ *как сказ*: ~ (до +*gen*) it isn't far (to); ~ от +*gen* not far from; до утра́ ~ it will soon be morning.

недальнови́д|ный (-ен, -на, -но) *прил* short-sighted.

неда́ром *нареч* (*не напрасно*) not in vain; (*не без цели*) for a reason; я ~ сто́лько учи́лся all of that studying has paid off; я ~ прие́хал сего́дня I do have a reason for coming today.

недви́жимост|ь (-и) *ж* property.

недви́жимый *прил*: недви́жимое иму́щество = недви́жимость.

недвижи́м|ый (-, -а, -о) *прил* (*неподвижный*) motionless; (*не способный двигаться: больной*) immobile.

недвусмы́слен|ный (-, -на, -но) *прил* unambiguous.

недееспосо́б|ный (-ен, -на, -но) *прил* (*ЮР: человек*) incapacitated; (: *организация, структура*) impotent, ineffective.

недействи́тел|ьный (-ен, -ьна, -ьно) *прил* invalid.

неделика́т|ный (-ен, -на, -но) *прил* (*человек*) tactless; (*замечание, вопрос*) indelicate, tactless.

недели́м|ый (-, -а, -о) *прил* indivisible; недели́мое число́ prime number.

недéль|ный *прил* (*срок, отпуск*) one-week; (*запас, заработок итп*) *а или* one week's.

неде́л|я (-и) ж week; **че́рез ~ю** in a week; **на про́шлой/э́той/сле́дующей ~е** last/this/next week.

недобо́р (-а) м shortage.

недоброжела́тел|ьный (-ен, -ьна, -ьно) прил hostile.

недоброка́чествен|ный (-, -на, -но) прил poor-quality.

недобросо́вест|ный (-ен, -на, -но) прил (небрежный) unconscientious; (нечестный) unscrupulous.

недо́бр|ый (-, -а́, -о) прил unkind; (чувства, намерения) ill; (время, сон, предчувствие) bad; **~ые ве́сти** ill tidings.

недова́р|ить (-арю́, -а́ришь; impf **недова́ривать**) сов перех to undercook.

недове́ри|е (-я) ср mistrust, distrust; **относи́ться (отнести́сь** perf**) к кому́-н/чему́-н с ~м** to be mistrustful или distrustful of sb/sth.

недове́рчивост|ь (-и) ж mistrust, distrust.

недове́рчив|ый (-, -а, -о) прил mistrustful, distrustful.

недове́с (-а) м shortfall (in weight).

недове́|сить (-шу, -сишь; impf **недове́шивать**) сов перех: **~ кому́-н чего́-н** to give sb too little of sth.

недово́л|ьный (-ен, -ьна, -ьно) прил discontented, dissatisfied; **она́ всем ~ьна** she is never satisfied.

недово́льств|о (-а) ср: **~** (+instr) dissatisfaction (with).

недога́длив|ый (-, -а, -о) прил inscrutable.

недогля|де́ть (-жу́, -ди́шь) сов перех (ошибки, опечатки) to overlook ◆ неперех: **~ за** +acc to fail to keep an eye on.

недоговор|и́ть (-ю́, -и́шь; impf **недогова́ривать**) сов перех to leave unsaid; **он что́-то недогова́ривает** there is something that he's not saying.

недоде́лан|ный (-, -на, -но) прил unfinished.

недоде́л|ка (-ки; gen pl -ок) ж loose end.

недоеда́|ть несов неперех to eat badly; **они́ постоя́нно ~ют** they never eat enough.

недозре́лый прил unripe.

недойм|ка (-ки; gen pl -ок) ж arrears мн.

недока́зан|ный (-, -на, -но) прил unproven.

недо́л|гий (-гая, -гое, -гие; -ог, -га́, -го) прил short.

недо́лго нареч for a short time, not for long ◆ как сказ (разг): **мне ~ э́то сде́лать** it won't take me long (to do); **~ по́сле** +gen not long after; **я там бу́ду ~** I won't be there for long; **ему́ оста́лось ~ (жить)** he hasn't got long (to live).

недолгове́ч|ный (-ен, -на, -но) прил short-lived.

недо́лог прил см **недо́лгий**.

недолю́блива|ть (-ю) несов перех to dislike.

недомога́ни|е (-я) ср queasiness; **чу́вствовать** (impf) **~** to feel queasy.

недомога́|ть (-ю) несов неперех to feel unwell.

недомо́лв|ка (-ки; gen pl -ок) ж indirect reference; **говори́ть** (impf) **о чём-н ~ми** to refer to sth indirectly.

недомы́сли|е (-я) ср: **по ~ю** without thinking.

недоно́шен|ный (-, -а, -о) прил: **~ ребёнок** premature baby.

недооце|ни́ть (-ню́, -нишь; impf **недооце́нивать**) сов перех to underestimate.

недооце́н|ка (-и) ж underestimation.

недопусти́м|ый (-, -а, -о) прил not permissible.

недорабо́т|ка (-и) ж = **недоде́лка**.

недоразви́т|ый (-, -а, -о) прил underdeveloped; (разг) dumb.

недоразуме́ни|е (-я) ср misunderstanding.

недо́рого нареч cheaply.

недорог|о́й (-, -а́, -о) прил inexpensive.

недосо́лива|ть (-ю) несов от **недосоли́ть**.

недосмо́тр (-а) м oversight; **по ~у** through lack of attention.

недосмо́тр|еть (-ю́, -ишь) сов неперех = **недогляде́ть**.

недосо|ли́ть (-лю́, -лишь; impf **недоса́ливать**) сов перех: **ты ~оли́л суп** you haven't put enough salt in the soup.

недосп|а́ть (-лю́, -и́шь; impf **недосыпа́ть**) сов неперех to not get enough sleep.

недоста|ва́ть (3sg -ёт) несов безл (+gen; не хвата́ть; (быть нужным) to lack; **ей ~ёт терпе́ния** she lacks patience; **нам о́чень тебя́ ~ва́ло** we really needed you; **э́того ещё ~ва́ло!** as if that were not enough!

недоста́т|ок (-ка; nom pl -ки) м shortage, lack; (в характере, в работе) shortcoming.

недоста́точен прил см **недоста́точный**.

недоста́точно нареч insufficiently ◆ как сказ (+gen): **у нас ~ еды́/де́нег** we don't have enough food/money; **я ~ зна́ю об э́том** I don't know enough about it; **~ критикова́ть, на́до помо́чь** it's not enough to criticize, you need to help.

недоста́точност|ь (-и) ж inadequacy; **серде́чная ~** heart failure.

недоста́точ|ный (-ен, -на, -но) прил insufficient.

недоста́ч|а (-и) ж (разг: материалов, оборудования) lack; (денег: при проверке) shortfall; **у нас в ка́ссе ~** the till is short.

недостаю́щий (-ая, -ое, -ие) прил missing.

недостижи́м|ый (-, -а, -о) прил (высота, уровень) unreachable; (мечта, идеал) unattainable.

недостове́р|ный (-ен, -на, -но) прил unreliable.

недосто́й|ный (-ен, -йна, -йно) прил: **~** (+gen) unworthy (of).

недосту́п|ный (-ен, -на, -но) *прил (также перен)* inaccessible; (*цена*) unaffordable; (*человек*) unapproachable; **э́то ~но моему́ понима́нию** it is beyond my understanding.

недосу́г *как сказ:* **ему́ ~** (+*infin* ...) (*разг*) he can never find the time (to ...).

недосчита́|ться (-юсь; *impf* **недосчи́тываться**) *сов возв* (+*gen*) to be short; **я ~лся пяти́ до́лларов** I'm five dollars short; **мы ~лись двух челове́к** we are missing two people.

недосыпа́|ть (-ю) *несов от* **недоспа́ть**.

недосяга́ем|ый (-, -а, -о) *прил* unattainable.

недотро́г|а (-и) *м/ж* (*разг*): **он тако́й ~** he's very touchy.

недоумева́|ть (-ю) *несов неперех* to be perplexed *или* bewildered.

недоумева́ющий (-ая, -ее, -ие) *прил* perplexed, bewildered.

недоуме́ни|е (-я) *ср* perplexity, bewilderment.

недоуме́нный *прил* perplexed, bewildered.

недоу́ч|ка (-ки; *gen pl* -ек) *м/ж* (*разг*): **он/она́ ~** he/she is badly educated.

недочёт (-а) *м* (*в подсчётах*) shortfall; (*обычно мн: в работе*) deficiency.

не́др|а (-) *мн* depths *мн*; **в ~х земли́** in the bowels of the earth; **в ~х души́** in the depths of one's soul; **в ~х о́бщества** at the heart of society.

недре́млющий (-ая, -ее, -ие) *прил* vigilant.

не́друг (-а) *м* foe.

недружелю́б|ный (-ен, -на, -но) *прил* unfriendly.

неду́г (-а) *м* ailment.

неду́рно *нареч* not badly.

недур|но́й (-ён, -на́, -но) *прил* not bad; **он ~ён собо́й** he's not bad-looking.

неё *мест см* **она́**.

неесте́ственный (-, -на, -но) *прил* unnatural.

нежда́н|ный (-ен, -на, -но) *прил* unexpected.

нежела́ни|е (-я) *ср* unwillingness.

нежела́тель|ный (-ен, -ьна, -ьно) *прил* undesirable.

не́жен *прил см* **не́жный**.

нежена́т|ый *прил* unmarried.

не́жен|ка (-ки; *gen pl* -ок) *м/ж* (*разг*) softy.

неживо́й *прил* dead; (*природа, мир*) inorganic; (*перен: взгляд, голос*) lifeless.

нежизнеспосо́б|ный (-ен, -на, -но) *прил* (*организм, растение*) incapable of surviving; (*перен: теория*) impractical.

нежило́й *прил* nonresidential.

не́ж|иться (-усь, -ишься) *несов возв* to laze about; ~ (*impf*) **на со́лнце** to bask in the sun.

не́жнича|ть (-ю) *несов неперех* (*разг*): ~ **с** +*instr* to make a fuss of.

не́жност|ь (-и) *ж* tenderness; **шепта́ть** (*impf*) ~**и кому́-н на́ ухо** to whisper sweet nothings in sb's ear.

не́жно *нареч* gently.

не́ж|ный (-ен, -на́, -но) *прил* tender, gentle; (*кожа, пух*) soft; (*запах*) subtle; (*сложение, здоровье*) fragile.

незабве́н|ный (-ен, -на, -но) *прил* beloved.

незабу́д|ка (-ки; *gen pl* -ок) *ж* forget-me-not.

незабыва́ем|ый (-, -а, -о) *прил* unforgettable.

незави́д|ный (-ен, -на, -но) *прил* unenviable.

незави́симо *нареч* independently; ~ **от** +*gen* (*условий, времени*) regardless of.

незави́симост|ь (-и) *ж* independence.

незави́сим|ый (-, -а, -о) *прил* independent.

незави́сящий (-ая, -ее, -ие) *прил:* **по ~им от нас обстоя́тельствам** due to circumstances beyond our control.

незада́ч|а (-и) *ж* (*разг*) pain.

незада́члив|ый (-, -а, -о) *прил* (*разг*) unlucky.

незадо́лго *нареч:* ~ **до** +*gen или* **пе́ред** +*instr* shortly before.

незаинтересо́ван|ный (-, -на, -но) *прил* (*ученик, слушатели итп*) indifferent; (*лицо, сторона*) disinterested.

незако́нность (-и) *ж* illegality.

незако́н|ный (-ен, -на, -но) *прил* illegal; (*ребёнок*) illegitimate.

незако́нчен|ный (-, -на, -но) *прил* unfinished, incomplete.

незамедли́тель|ный (-ен, -ьна, -ьно) *прил* immediate.

незамени́м|ый (-, -а, -о) *прил* irreplaceable.

незаме́тен *прил см* **незаме́тный**.

незаме́тно *нареч* (*изменяться*) imperceptibly ◆ *как сказ* it isn't noticeable; **он ~ подошёл/ушёл** he approached/left unnoticed; ~, **что ты всю ночь не спал** you may not have slept all night, but it doesn't show.

незаме́т|ный (-ен, -на, -но) *прил* not noticeable; (*перемены, изменения*) imperceptible; (*перен: человек, внешность*) unremarkable.

незаме́чен|ный (-, -на, -но) *прил* unnoticed.

незаму́жняя *прил* unmarried.

незамыслова́т|ый (-, -а, -о) *прил* uncomplicated.

незаня́т|ый *прил* (*дом, помещение*) unoccupied; (*человек, работник*) not occupied; (*вечер, утро*) free; ~**ая часть населе́ния** the non-working population.

незапа́мятный *прил:* **с ~ых времён** from time immemorial; **в ~ые времена́** in the days of yore.

незара́з|ный (-ен, -на, -но) *прил* noncontagious.

незаслу́жен|ный (-, -на, -но) *прил* undeserved.

незауря́д|ный (-ен, -на, -но) *прил* exceptional.

не́зачем *как сказ* (*разг*): ~ **ходи́ть/э́то де́лать** there's no reason to go/do it.

незва́н|ый *прил* unwanted.

нездоро́в|иться (3*sg* -ится) *несов безл:* **мне ~ится** I feel unwell, I don't feel well.

нездоро́в|ый (-, -а, -о) *прил* unhealthy; **он нездоро́в** he isn't well; **у него́ ~ цвет лица́** his face is an unhealthy colour; **у неё ~ вид** she doesn't look well.

неземно́й *прил* (*тело, объект итп*) alien;

(*силы, красота*) unearthly.

незнако́м|ец (**-ца**) *м* stranger.

незнако́м|ка (**-ки**; *gen pl* **-ок**) *ж см* **незнако́мец**.

незнако́мца *итп сущ см* **незнако́мец**.

незнако́м|ый (**-**, **-а**, **-о**) *прил* unfamiliar; **я незнако́м с ним** I am not acquainted with him; **я незнако́м с э́тими фа́ктами** I am not familiar with these facts.

незна́ни|е (**-я**) *ср* ignorance.

незнача́щ|ий (**-ая**, **-ее**, **-ие**) *прил* meaningless.

незначи́тел|ьный (**-ен**, **-ьна**, **-ьно**) *прил* (*небольшой*) insignificant; (*несущественный*) trivial.

незре́л|ый (**-**, **-а**, **-о**) *прил* (*яблоко итп*) unripe; (*человек, книга*) immature; (*мысль*) half-formed.

незри́м|ый (**-**, **-а**, **-о**) *прил* anonymous; (*бой*) hidden.

незы́блем|ый (**-**, **-а**, **-о**) *прил* unshakable.

неизбе́жен *прил см* **неизбе́жный**.

неизбе́жно *как сказ*: **э́то ~** it's inevitable.

неизбе́ж|ный (**-ен**, **-на**, **-но**) *прил* inescapable, inevitable.

неизве́дан|ный (**-**, **-на**, **-но**) *прил* (*путь, пространство*) unexplored; (*счастье, чувство*) new.

неизве́стен *прил см* **неизве́стный**.

неизве́стно *как сказ* it's not known; **никому́ ~** nobody knows; **~ кто/что/почему́** Heaven (only) knows who/what/why.

неизве́стн|ое (**-ого**; *decl like adj*) *ср* (*МАТ*) unknown.

неизве́стность (**-и**) *ж* uncertainty; (*незаметное существование*) obscurity.

неизве́ст|ный (**-ен**, **-на**, **-но**) *прил* unknown ◆ (**-ного**; *decl like adj*) *м* stranger.

неизглади́м|ый (**-**, **-а**, **-о**) *прил* indelible.

неизлечи́м|ый (**-**, **-а**, **-о**) *прил* (*болезнь*) incurable; (*больной*) terminally ill.

неизме́н|ный (**-ен**, **-на**, **-но**) *прил* (*постоянный*) unchanging; (*верный*) steadfast.

неизменя́ем|ый (**-**, **-а**, **-о**) *прил* invariable.

неизмери́мо *нареч* immeasurably.

неизмери́м|ый (**-**, **-а**, **-о**) *прил* immeasurable.

неизу́ченный *прил* (*вопрос, проблема*) unexplored.

неиме́ни|е (**-я**) *ср*: **за ~м** +*gen* for want of; **за ~м лу́чшего** for want of something better.

неимове́р|ный (**-ен**, **-на**, **-но**) *прил* extreme.

неиму́щий (**-ая**, **-ее**, **-ие**) *прил* deprived.

неинтере́с|ный (**-ен**, **-на**, **-но**) *прил* boring, uninteresting; (*некрасивый*) plain.

неискорени́м|ый (**-**, **-а**, **-о**) *прил* deep-rooted.

неискрен|ний (**-няя**, **-нее**, **-ние**; **-ен**, **-на**, **-но** *или* **не**) *прил* insincere.

неискушённый *прил* unsophisticated.

неисполне́ни|е (**-я**) *ср* failure to carry out.

неисполни́м|ый (**-**, **-а**, **-о**) *прил* unrealizable.

неиспо́льзованный *прил* unused.

неиспо́рченный *прил* (*человек*) innocent.

неиспра́вен *прил см* **неиспра́вный**.

неисправи́м|ый (**-**, **-а**, **-о**) *прил* (*ошибка*) irreversible; (*пьяница*) incorrigible.

неиспра́вность (**-и**) *ж* (*механизма, станка*) fault.

неиспра́в|ный (**-ен**, **-на**, **-но**) *прил* (*механизм, станок*) faulty; (*плательщик, поставщик*) unreliable.

неиспы́танный *прил* (*самолёт, машина*) untested; (*чувство, счастье*) unexperienced.

неиссле́дованный *прил* (*вопрос, район*) unexplored.

неиссяка́ем|ый (**-**, **-а**, **-о**) *прил* inexhaustible.

нейстовство (**-а**) *ср* (*исступление*) frenzy; (*жестокость*) atrocity; **приходи́ть** (**прийти́** *perf*) **в ~** to go into a frenzy.

нейстовств|овать (**-ую**) *несов неперех* to be in a frenzy; (*перен*: *буря, метель*) to rage; (: *каратели*) to commit atrocities.

нейстов|ый (**-**, **-а**, **-о**) *прил* (*ужас, радость*) intense; (*крики*) frenzied; (*аплодисменты, буря*) wild; (*грохот*) crashing.

неистощи́м|ый (**-**, **-а**, **-о**) *прил* inexhaustible.

неисчерпа́ем|ый (**-**, **-а**, **-о**) *прил* inexhaustible.

неисчисли́м|ый (**-**, **-а**, **-о**) *прил* (*силы*) countless; (*неприятности*) innumerable.

ней *мест см* **она́**.

нейло́н (**-а**) *м* nylon.

нейло́новый *прил* nylon *опред*.

нейрохиру́рг (**-а**) *м* neurosurgeon.

нейрохирурги́|я (**-и**) *ж* neurosurgery.

нейтра́лен *прил см* **нейтра́льный**.

нейтрализа́ци|я (**-и**) *ж* neutrality.

нейтрализ|ова́ть (**-у́ю**) (*не*)*сов перех* to neutralize.

нейтралите́т (**-а**) *м* neutrality.

нейтра́л|ьный (**-ен**, **-ьна**, **-ьно**) *прил* neutral.

нейтро́н (**-а**) *м* neutron.

неказ́ист|ый (**-**, **-а**, **-о**) *прил* unsightly.

нека́чественно *нареч*: **~ сде́ланный** badly made.

нека́чествен|ный (**-ен**, **-на**, **-но**) *прил* poor-quality.

неквалифици́рован|ный (**-**, **-на**, **-но**) *прил* (*работник*) unqualified, unskilled; (*работа*) unskilled.

не́кем *мест см* **не́кого**.

не́к|ий (**-ого**; *f* **-ая**, *nt* **-ое**, *pl* **-ие**) *мест* a certain; (*момент, время*) some.

не́когда *как сказ* (*читать, гулять*) there is no time; **ей ~** she is busy; **ей ~** +*infin* ... she has no time to ....

не́к|ого (*как* **кто**; *см* **Table 6**) *мест*: **~ спроси́ть/позва́ть** there is nobody to ask/call.

некомпете́нт|ный (**-ен**, **-на**, **-но**) *прил* (*человек*) incompetent; (*суждение*)

The spelling rules for Russian are shown on page xvii.

inappropriate.

не́кому *мест см* **не́кого**.

не́котор|ые (-ых) *мест* (*отдельные*) several.

не́котор|ый (-ого; *f* -ая, *nt* -ое, *pl* -ые) *мест* some; **с ~ых пор** for some time; **в ~ой сте́пени** to a certain degree; **в ~ом ро́де** somewhat; **~ым о́бразом** somehow; *см также* **не́которые**.

некраси́в|ый (-, -а, -о) *прил* (*человек, лицо*) unattractive, ugly; (*поступок, поведение*) ugly.

некроло́г (-а) *м* obituary.

некста́ти *нареч* (*сказать, явиться итп*) at the wrong time ♦ *как сказ*: **э́то ~** this is untimely.

некта́р (-а) *м* nectar.

не́кто *мест* a certain person (*мн* certain people).

не́куда *как сказ* (*идти, поехать*) there is nowhere; **да́льше** *или* **хуже́/лу́чше ~** (*разг*) it can't get any worse/better.

некульту́р|ный (-ен, -на, -но) *прил* (*растение*) uncultivated; (*человек, поведение*) uncivilized.

некуря́щий (-его; *decl like adj*) *м* non-smoker; ♦ (-ая, -ее, -ие) *прил*: **~ мужчи́на, некуря́щая же́нщина** non-smoker.

нела́дно *как сказ* (*в семье, на душе*) there's unease.

нела́д|ы (-ов) *мн* (*разг: в семье, в коллективе*) tension *ед*; (: *с учёбой, с работой*) problems *мн*.

нелега́л|ьный (-ен, -ьна, -ьно) *прил* (*газета, въезд*) illegal.

нелегити́м|ный (-ен, -на, -но) *прил* illegitimate.

нелёг|кий (-кая, -кое, -кие; -ок, -ка́, -ко́) *прил* (*ноша, груз*) heavy; (*задание, работа*) difficult.

нелегко́ *как сказ* it's not easy; **мне нелегко́ согласи́ться на э́то** it's not easy for me to agree to this.

неле́пост|ь (-и) *ж* stupidity; **говори́ть** (*impf*)/**де́лать** (*impf*) **~и** to say/do stupid things.

неле́п|ый (-, -а, -о) *прил* stupid.

неле́ст|ный (-ен, -на, -но) *прил* (*высказывание, характеристика*) unflattering.

нелётн|ый *прил*: **~ая пого́да** poor weather for flying; **~ое вре́мя** not a good time to fly.

нело́в|кий (-кая, -кое, -кие; -ок, -ка́, -ко) *прил* awkward; **нело́вкое положе́ние** awkward situation.

нело́вко *нареч* awkwardly ♦ *как сказ* (*говорить, просить*) it's awkward; **мне ~ (перед ней)** I feel awkward (with her).

нело́вкост|ь (-и) *ж* awkwardness; **чу́вствовать** (*почу́вствовать* *perf*) **~** to feel awkward.

нело́вок *прил см* **нело́вкий**.

нелоги́ч|ный (-ен, -на, -но) *прил* (*довод, доказательство*) illogical.

нельзя́ *как сказ* (*невозможно*) it is impossible; (*не разрешается*) it is forbidden; **~ ли?** would it be possible?; **~ сказа́ть, что она́ умна́** she can hardly be described as clever; **как ~ лу́чше** as well as could be expected.

нелюби́м|ый (-, -а, -о) *прил* unloved.

нелюди́м|ый (-, -а, -о) *прил* (*человек, сосед*)

unsociable.

нём *мест см* **он, оно́**.

нема́ло *нареч* (+*gen*; *денег*) a good deal of; (*идей, людей, книг*) a good few.

немаловаж|ный (-ен, -на, -но) *прил* significant.

нема́л|ый *прил* (*доход*) reasonable; (*труд*) much; (*успех*) considerable; (*чин, должность*) important; **~ые де́ньги** a sizeable sum of money.

неме́дленен *прил см* **неме́дленный**.

неме́дленно *нареч* immediately.

неме́дленн|ый (-ен, -на, -но) *прил* immediate.

неме́ркнущ|ий (-ая, -ее, -ие) *прил* (*также перен*) unfading.

немета́лл (-а) *м* (*хим*) nonmetal.

неме́|ть (-ю; *perf* **онеме́ть**) *несов неперех* (*от ужаса, от восторга*) to be struck dumb; (*нога, руки*) to go numb.

не́м|ец (-ца) *м* German.

неме́цк|ий (-ая, -ое, -ие) *прил* German; **~ язы́к** German.

неми́лост|ь (-и) *ж* disfavour; **впада́ть (впасть** *perf*) **в ~** to fall out of favour (*BRIT*) *или* favor (*US*).

неминуе́м|ый (-, -а, -о) *прил* (*беда, события*) unavoidable.

не́м|ка (-ки; *gen pl* -ок) *ж см* **не́мец**.

немно́г|ие (-их; *decl like adj*) *мн* few.

немно́г|ий (-ая, -ое, -ие) *прил* (*части, слова, люди*) a few; **~им хуже/лу́чше/бо́льше/ме́ньше** a little worse/better/more/less; **за ~им исключе́нием** with few exceptions.

немно́го *нареч* (*отдохнуть, старше*) a little, a bit; (*друзей, слов*) a few.

немно́г|ое (-ого; *decl like adj*) *ср* (*можно сказать, увидеть*) little.

немногосло́в|ный (-ен, -на, -но) *прил* (*отзыв, изложение*) brief; (*человек*) laconic.

немногочи́слен|ный (-ен, -на, -но) *прил* (*ошибки*) few; **на дипломати́ческом приёме бы́ло ~ное о́бщество** there weren't many (people present) at the diplomatic reception.

немно́жко *нареч* (*разг*) = **немно́го**.

немну́щийся (-аяся, -ееся, -иеся) *прил* (*брюки, материя, юбка*) crease-resistant.

нем|о́й (-, -а́, -о) *прил* (*человек*) dumb; (*перен: ночь, лес, глубина*) silent; (: *вопрос, упрёк*) implied ♦ (-о́го; *decl like adj*) *м* mute; **нема́я сце́на** *situation in which somebody freezes in surprise, shock etc*; **немо́й фильм** silent film.

немолод|о́й (-о́лод, -олода́, -о́лодо) *прил* old.

немот|а́ (-ы́) *ж* (*ребёнка, мужчины*) dumbness.

не́мощ|ный (-ен, -на, -но) *прил* (*старик, человек*) sick, ailing.

нему́ *мест от* **он, оно́**.

немудрён|ый (-, -а, -о) *прил* (*разг*) simple.

не́мца *итп сущ см* **не́мец**.

немысли́м|ый (-, -а, -о) *прил* unthinkable.

ненави́деть (-жу, -дишь) *несов перех* to hate.

ненави́ст|ный (-ен, -на, -но) *прил* (*человек, работа*) hateful.

не́навист|ь (-и) ж hatred.
ненагля́дный прил (разг) beloved.
ненадёж|ный (-ен, -на, -но) прил (человек, сведения) unreliable; (механизм) unsafe.
ненадобност|ь (-и) ж: вы́бросить что-н за ~ю to throw sth out или away because it is not needed.
ненадо́лго нареч for a short while.
ненападе́ни|е (-я) ср nonaggression.
ненаро́ком нареч (разг: случайно) without meaning to.
нена́ст|ный (-ен, -на, -но) прил (день, осень) wet and dismal.
ненастоя́щий (-ая, -ее, -ие) прил (мех, золото) artificial; (дружба, любовь) contrived.
нена́сть|е (-я) ср awful weather.
ненасы́т|ный (-ен, -на, -но) прил (также перен) insatiable.
ненатура́л|ьный (-ен, -ьна, -ьно) прил (мех, свет) artificial; (смех) forced; (поведение) affected.
ненорма́лен прил см **ненорма́льный**.
ненорма́льность (-и) ж abnormality.
ненорма́л|ьный (-ен, -ьна, -ьно) прил abnormal; (разг: сумасшедший) mad ♦ (-ьного; decl like adj) м (разг) crackpot.
нену́ж|ный (-ен, -на́, -но) прил (осторожность) unnecessary; (человек) dispensable; (инструмент) inessential.
необду́манно нареч (поступить) rashly.
необду́ман|ный (-, -на, -но) прил ill-considered.
необеспе́ченный прил poor.
необита́ем|ый (-, -а, -о) прил (место) uninhabited; ~ о́стров desert island.
необозри́м|ый (-, -а, -о) прил (просторы, дали) vast.
необосно́ван|ный (-, -на, -но) прил unfounded.
необрабо́танный прил (земля) uncultivated; (деталь) unfinished; (металл, дерево) untreated.
необразо́ван|ный (-, -на, -но) прил uneducated.
необу́здан|ный (-, -на, -но) прил (страсть) unbridled; (человек, характер) ungovernable.
необходи́мо как сказ it is necessary; мне ~ с Ва́ми поговори́ть I really need to talk to you.
необходи́мость (-и) ж (увидеть, сделать) need, necessity; ~ в +prp need for; по ме́ре ~и as (far as is) necessary; по ~и out of necessity; предме́ты пе́рвой ~и bare essentials.
необходи́м|ый (-, -а, -о) прил necessary.
необщи́тел|ьный (-ен, -ьна, -ьно) прил unsociable.
необъекти́в|ный (-ен, -на, -но) прил (отношение, критика) not objective, bias(s)ed.
необъясни́м|ый (-, -а, -о) прил inexplicable.

необъя́т|ный (-ен, -на, -но) прил (просторы, дали, познания) vast.
необыкнове́н|ный (-ен, -на, -но) прил exceptional.
необыча́й|ный (-ен, -йна, -йно) прил = **необыкнове́нный**.
необы́ч|ный (-ен, -на, -но) прил (человек, явления) unusual.
необяза́тел|ьный (-ен, -ьна, -ьно) прил (предмет, лекция) optional; (факты) nonessential; (человек) unreliable.
неограни́чен|ный (-, -на, -но) прил unlimited; неограни́ченная мона́рхия absolute monarchy.
неодина́ков|ый (-, -а, -о) прил (размер) different.
неоднокра́тен прил см **неоднокра́тный**.
неоднокра́тно нареч (говорить) repeatedly; (повторять) time after time.
неоднокра́т|ный (-ен, -на, -но) прил repeated.
неоднор́дный (-ен, -на, -но) прил (масса) heterogeneous; (тесто) mixed; (явления) dissimilar.
неодобре́ни|е (-я) ср disapproval.
неодобри́тел|ьный (-ен, -ьна, -ьно) прил disapproving.
неодоли́м|ый (-, -а, -о) прил (упорство, страх) insurmountable; (сила) invincible.
неодушевлённый прил inanimate.
неожи́данно нареч unexpectedly.
неожи́данност|ь (-и) ж (атаки) unexpectedness; (приятная, большая) surprise; вздра́гивать (вздро́гнуть perf) от ~и to start in surprise.
неожи́дан|ный (-, -на, -но) прил unexpected.
неоконча́тел|ьный (-ен, -ьна, -ьно) прил (вариант, решение) not final.
неоко́нченный прил unfinished.
неоли́т (-а) м Neolithic.
неологи́зм (-а) м neologism.
нео́н (-а) м (хим) neon.
неонаци́зм (-а) м Neo-Nazism.
нео́новый прил neon опред.
неопа́сен прил см **неопа́сный**.
неопа́сно нареч safely ♦ как сказ it's safe, it's not dangerous.
неопа́с|ный (-ен, -на, -но) прил (путешествие, место) safe; (противник, заболевание) harmless.
неописуе́м|ый (-, -а, -о) прил indescribable.
неоплат́ный (-ен, -на, -но) прил: ~ долг debt that cannot be repaid; я твой ~ должни́к I'm greatly indebted to you.
неопла́ченный прил unpaid.
неопо́знан|ный (-, -на, -но) прил unidentified.
неопра́вданный прил (вывод, обвинение) unjustified; (траты, потери) unwarranted.
неопределённость (-и) ж uncertainty.

неопределён|ный (-, -на, -но) *прил* (*время, срок*) indefinite; (*путь*) undecided; (*ответ, выражение, жест*) vague; (*звук*) indistinct.
неопроверж́им|ый (-, -а, -о) *прил* irrefutable.
неопря́т|ный (-ен, -на, -но) *прил* untidy.
неопублико́ванный *прил* unpublished.
нео́пытен *прил см* **нео́пытный**.
нео́пытност|ь (-и) *ж* inexperience.
нео́пыт|ный (-ен, -на, -но) *прил* inexperienced.
неорганизо́ванный *прил* disorganized; (*массы*) unorganized.
неоргани́ческ|ий (-ая, -ое, -ие) *прил* inorganic.
неосведомлённый *прил* ill-informed.
неосла́б|ный (-ен, -на, -но) *прил* (*надзор*) constant; (*контроль*) unrelenting.
неосмотр́ител|ный (-ен, -ьна, -ьно) *прил* (*человек*) careless; (*поступок*) imprudent.
неоспор́им|ый (-, -а, -о) *прил* (*преимущество*) unquestionable; (*доказательство*) incontrovertible.
неосторо́жен *прил см* **неосторо́жный**.
неосторо́жност|ь (-и) *ж* carelessness.
неосторо́ж|ный (-ен, -на, -но) *прил* (*поступок*) careless; (*поведение, высказывание*) imprudent.
неосуществ́им|ый (-, -а, -о) *прил* unrealizable, unattainable.
неотврат́им|ый (-, -а, -о) *прил* inevitable.
неотдел́им|ый (-, -а, -о) *прил*: ~ **(от** +*gen*) inseparable (from).
неотёсан|ный (-, -а, -о) *прил* unpolished; (*перен: разг*) crude.
не́откуда *как сказ*: **мне** *итп* **де́нег взять** ~ I *итп* can't get money from anywhere.
неотло́жен *прил см* **неотло́жный**.
неотло́жк|а (-и) *ж* (*разг: учреждение*) ambulance service; (: *машина*) emergency medical care.
неотло́ж|ный (-ен, -на, -но) *прил* urgent; **неотло́жная медици́нская по́мощь** emergency medical service.
неотраз́им|ый (-, -а, -о) *прил* (*атака, красота*) irresistible; (*перен: довод*) compelling; (*удар, впечатление*) powerful.
неотсту́п|ный (-ен, -на, -но) *прил* (*мечта, мысль*) constant; (*преследование*) relentless.
неотъе́млем|ый (-, -а, -о) *прил* (*право*) inalienable; (*часть*) integral.
неофаши́зм (-а) *м* Neo-fascism.
неофаши́ст (-а) *м* Neo-fascist.
неофаши́стск|ий (-ая, -ое, -ие) *прил* Neo-fascist.
неофициа́льный (-ен, -ьна, -ьно) *прил* unofficial.
неохо́т|а (-ы) *ж* (*разг: нежелание*) reluctance ◆ *как сказ*: **мне** ~ **спо́рить** I don't feel like arguing.
неохо́тно *нареч* reluctantly.
неохо́тный *прил* reluctant.
неоцен́им|ый (-, -а, -о) *прил* invaluable.
неощут́им|ый (-, -а, -о) *прил* (*незаметный*) imperceptible.
Непа́л (-а) *м* Nepal.
непа́льск|ий (-ая, -ое, -ие) *прил* Nepalese.
непа́рный *прил* (*перчатки, ботинки*) odd.
непереводи́м|ый (-, -а, -о) *прил* untranslatable.
непередава́ем|ый (-, -а, -о) *прил* (*страх, впечатление*) inexpressible.
непереходный *прил*: ~ **глаго́л** (*линг*) intransitive verb.
непеча́тный *прил* (*разг*) unprintable.
непи́саный *прил* unwritten.
неплатёж (-ежа́) *м* nonpayment.
неплатёжеспосо́б|ный (-ен, -на, -но) *прил* (*человек*) unable to pay; (*предприятие*) insolvent.
неплате́льщик (-а) *м* (*налогов, алиментов*) defaulter.
неплате́льщиц|а (-ы) *ж см* **неплате́льщик**.
неплодоро́д|ный (-ен, -на, -но) *прил* infertile, barren.
непло́тно *нареч* not tightly *или* firmly.
непло́хо *нареч* not badly, quite well ◆ *как сказ* it's not bad.
непл|охо́й (-о́х, -оха́, -о́хо) *прил* not bad, quite good.
непобеди́м|ый (-, -а, -о) *прил* invincible.
неповинове́ни|е (-я) *ср* disobedience, insubordination.
неповоро́тлив|ый (-, -а, -о) *прил* (*неуклюжий*) clumsy; (*медлительный*) slow.
неповтори́м|ый (-, -а, -о) *прил* unique.
непого́д|а (-ы) *ж* bad weather.
непогреши́м|ый (-, -а, -о) *прил* infallible.
неподалёку *нареч* (*разг*) not far off ◆ *предл*: ~ **от** +*gen* not far from.
неподви́жен *прил см* **неподви́жный**.
неподви́жно *нареч* without moving.
неподви́ж|ный (-ен, -на, -но) *прил* (*больной, рука, туман*) motionless; (*взгляд*) fixed; (*лицо*) rigid; (*медлительный*) slow.
неподда́ю́щийся (-аяся, -ееся, -иеся) *прил* (*разг: перевоспитанию, лечению*) resistant, unresponsive.
неподде́л|ьный (-ен, -ьна, -ьно) *прил* (*также перен*) genuine.
неподку́п|ный (-ен, -на, -но) *прил* (*человек, ревизор*) incorruptible; (*совесть, принципы*) honourable (*BRIT*), honorable (*US*).
неподража́ем|ый (-, -а, -о) *прил* inimitable.
неподходя́щий (-ая, -ее, -ие) *прил* (*место*) unsuitable; (*время*) inappropriate.
неподчине́ни|е (-я) *ср* (*закону, властям*) insubordination.
неподъём|ный (-ен, -на, -но) *прил* (*разг*) very heavy.
непозволи́тел|ьный (-ен, -ьна, -ьно) *прил* inadmissible.
непоколеби́м|ый (-, -а, -о) *прил* unshakable.
непоко́р|ный (-ен, -на, -но) *прил* (*конь, слуга*) recalcitrant; (*характер, нрав*) rebellious.
непокры́тый *прил*: **с ~ой голово́й**

bareheaded.

неполадки (-ок) *мн* fault *ед*, defect *ед*; (*разг: в семье*) quarrel *ед*.

неполноправный (-ен, -на, -но) *прил* not possessing full rights.

неполнота (-ы) *ж* incompleteness.

неполноценность (-и) *ж* lack; **комплекс ~и** inferiority complex.

неполноцен|ный (-ен, -на, -но) *прил* insufficient.

неполный (-он, -на, -но) *прил* (*чашка, мешок*) not full; (*список, перечень, данные*) incomplete.

непомер|ный (-ен, -на, -но) *прил* excessive.

непонима́ние (-я) *ср* (*задачи, происходящего*) incomprehension; (*равнодушие*) indifference.

непоня́тен *прил см* **непоня́тный**.

непоня́тлив|ый (-, -а, -о) *прил* (*ученик, студент*) slow on the uptake, dull.

непоня́тно *нареч* incomprehensibly ◆ *как сказ* it is incomprehensible; **мне ~, что происхо́дит** I cannot understand what is going on.

непоня́т|ный (-ен, -на, -но) *прил* incomprehensible.

непоправи́м|ый (-, -а, -о) *прил* (*ошибка*) irreparable; (*шаг, несчастье*) irreversible.

непоро́ч|ный (-ен, -на, -но) *прил* pure, chaste.

непоря́д|ок (-ка; *nom pl* -ки) *м* disorder.

непоря́доч|ный (-ен, -на, -но) *прил* (*человек, поведение*) dishonourable (*BRIT*), dishonorable (*US*).

непосе́д|а (-ы) *м/ж* (*разг*) fidget.

непосе́длив|ый (-, -а, -о) *прил* restless.

непоси́льный (-ен, -ьна, -ьно) *прил* (*труд, задача*) beyond one's strength.

непосле́довательность (-и) *ж* inconsistency.

непосле́довательный (-ен, -ьна, -ьно) *прил* inconsistent.

непослуша́ние (-я) *ср* (*детей, подчинённых*) disobedience.

непослу́ш|ный (-ен, -на, -но) *прил* (*ребёнок, собака*) disobedient; (*перен: волосы, кудри*) unmanageable.

непосре́дственность (-и) *ж* spontaneity.

непосре́дствен|ный *прил* (*начальник*) immediate; (*результат, свидетель, участник*) direct; (-ен, -на, -но; *натура, тон*) spontaneous.

непостижи́м|ый (-, -а, -о) *прил* (*загадка, сила*) incomprehensible; **уму́ ~о** it's incomprehensible.

непостоя́н|ный (-ен, -на, -но) *прил* changeable.

непостоя́нств|о (-а) *ж* inconstancy, changeability.

непотре́б|ный (-ен, -на, -но) *прил* (*разг*) indecent.

непохо́ж|ий (-ая, -ее, -ие; -, -а, -е) *прил* dissimilar.

непоча́т|ый (-, -а, -о) *прил* (*бутылка, пачка*) unopened; (*чашка кофе*) full, untouched; (*перен: силы*) unused; (: *запас, энергии*)

untapped; **непоча́тый край** no end, a great deal.

непочте́ни|е (-я) *ср* disrespect.

непочти́тельно *нареч* disrespectfully.

непра́в (-á, -о, -ы) *как сказ:* **ты ~** you are wrong.

непра́вд|а (-ы) *ж* lie, untruth ◆ *как сказ* it's not true; **э́то ~!** it's *или* this is a lie!

неправдоподо́б|ный (-ен, -на, -но) *прил* (*история, рассказ*) improbable, implausible.

непра́вилен *прил см* **непра́вильный**.

непра́вильно *нареч* (*решить*) incorrectly, wrongly ◆ *как сказ:* **э́то ~** it's wrong; **~ ду́мать, что** ... it's wrong to think that ...; **~ понима́ть** (**поня́ть** *perf*) to misunderstand; **~ написа́ть** (*perf*) to misspell.

непра́вильный (-ен, -ьна, -ьно) *прил* (*решение, произношение, идея*) wrong; (*черты лица, форма*) irregular; **непра́вильная дробь** (*МАТ*) improper fraction.

неправоме́р|ный (-ен, -на, -но) *прил* unjustifiable.

неправомо́ч|ный (-ен, -на, -но) *прил* (*неправомо́чная организа́ция*) organization without legal authority.

непревзойдён|ный (-, -на, -но) *прил* (*рекорд, мастерство*) unsurpassed; (*тупость, жестокость*) unprecedented.

непредви́денный *прил* unforeseen.

непреднаме́рен|ный (-, -на, -но) *прил* unpremeditated.

непредсказу́ем|ый (-, -а, -о) *прил* unpredictable.

непредубеждённый *прил* unbias(s)ed.

непредусмо́тренный *прил* unforeseen, unanticipated.

непредусмотри́тел|ьный (-ен, -ьна, -ьно) *прил* short-sighted.

непрекло́н|ный (-ен, -на, -но) *прил* (*человек*) unbending; (*противник*) uncompromising; (*воля*) unshakable; (*характер*) strong, firm; (*решение*) firm.

непрекраща́ющийся (-аяся, -ееся, -иеся) *прил* (*дождь*) persistent; (*ссора*) endless; (*стрельба*) continuous.

непрело́ж|ный (-ен, -на, -но) *прил* (*правило, закон*) immutable; **непрело́жная и́стина** unquestionable truth.

непреме́нен *прил см* **непреме́нный**.

непреме́нно *нареч* (*обязательно*) by all means.

непреме́н|ный (-ен, -на, -но) *прил* (*условие*) necessary; (*следствие*) unavoidable; (*деталь, черта*) indispensable.

непреодоли́м|ый (-, -а, -о) *прил* (*препятствие*) insurmountable; (*желание, смущение*) overwhelming.

непререка́ем|ый (-, -а, -о) *прил* (*авторитет*) unquestionable; (*интонация*) peremptory.

непреры́вен *прил см* **непреры́вный**.

непреры́вно *нареч (спрашивать, меняться)* uninterruptedly, continuously.

непреры́в|ный (-ен, -на, -но) *прил* uninterrupted, continuous.

неприве́тлив|ый (-, -а, -о) *прил (человек, тон)* unfriendly; *(перен: лес, место)* bleak.

непривлека́тел|ьный (-ен, -ьна, -ьно) *прил* unattractive.

непривы́чен *прил см* **непривы́чный**.

непривы́чк|а (-и) *ж*: **с ~и к физи́ческому труду́ он бы́стро уста́л** *(разг)* not being used to physical work, he got tired quickly.

непривы́чно *как сказ*: **мне ~** +*infin* I'm not used to doing.

непривы́ч|ный (-ен, -на, -но) *прил (мысль)* unusual; *(обстановка)* not the usual; *(человек)* unaccustomed.

непригля́д|ный (-ен, -на, -но) *прил (вид, внешность)* unsightly, unattractive; *(поступок, поведение)* unseemly.

непригод|ный (-ен, -на, -но) *прил* unsuitable.

неприе́млем|ый (-, -а, -о) *прил* unacceptable.

непри́знанный *прил (писатель, художник)* unrecognized, unacknowledged.

неприка́ян|ный (-, -на, -но) *прил (разг)* restless and drifting.

неприкоснове́нност|ь (-и) *ж* inviolability; **дипломати́ческая ~** diplomatic immunity.

неприкоснове́н|ный (-ен, -на, -но) *прил (фонд)* reserve *опред*; *(ценность)* inviolable; *(лицо, личность)* protected by law; **неприкоснове́нный запа́с** emergency ration.

неприкра́шенный *прил (действительность)* plain, unvarnished; *(вид)* plain.

неприкры́т|ый (-, -а, -о) *прил (дверь)* open; *(отряд, батальон)* open, exposed; *(перен: правда)* plain; *(: ложь)* barefaced, blatant; *(: грубость)* undisguised.

неприли́чен *прил см* **неприли́чный**.

неприли́чи|е (-я) *ср*: **до ~я** extremely.

неприли́чно *нареч* indecently, improperly.

неприли́ч|ный (-ен, -на, -но) *прил (вид, анекдот, рисунок)* indecent; *(платье)* outrageous.

неприме́т|ный (-ен, -на, -но) *прил (незаметный)* imperceptible; *(непримечательный)* unremarkable.

непримири́м|ый (-, -а, -о) *прил (спорщики, противоречия)* irreconcilable; *(характер)* uncompromising.

непринуждённост|ь (-и) *ж (беседы)* informality; *(движений)* freeness, casualness.

непринуждён|ный (-, -на, -но) *прил* informal, relaxed.

неприсоедине́ни|е (-я) *ср (полит)* nonalignment.

непристо́ен *прил см* **непристо́йный**.

непристо́йност|ь (-и) *ж* obscenity.

непристо́й|ный (-ен, -йна, -йно) *прил* obscene.

непристу́п|ный (-ен, -на, -но) *прил (крепость)* impregnable; *(высота)* inaccessible; *(человек)*

unapproachable; *(характер, вид)* unfriendly.

непритво́р|ный (-ен, -на, -но) *прил* unfeigned.

непритяза́тел|ьный (-ен, -ьна, -ьно) *прил (читатель, зритель, вкус)* undiscriminating; *(острота, стихи)* unsubtle.

неприхотли́в|ый (-, -а, -о) *прил (человек, студент)* unpretentious; *(вкус, требования)* modest; *(растение, цветок)* undemanding; *(простой: пища)* frugal; *(: рисунок)* simple.

неприя́знен|ный (-ен, -на, -но) *прил* hostile.

неприя́зн|ь (-и) *ж* hostility.

неприя́тел|ь (-я) *м собир* the enemy.

неприя́тен *прил см* **неприя́тный**.

неприя́ти|е (-я) *ср* rejection.

неприя́тно *как сказ*: **~** +*infin (думать, слушать)* it's unpleasant *или* disagreeable to do; **мне ~ говори́ть об э́том** I don't enjoy talking about it.

неприя́тност|ь (-и) *ж (обычно мн: на работе, в семье)* trouble.

неприя́т|ный (-ен, -на, -но) *прил* unpleasant, disagreeable.

непробива́ем|ый (-, -а, -о) *прил (броня, борт)* impregnable; *(перен: спокойствие)* imperturbable; *(: разг: дурак)* utter.

непробу́д|ный (-ен, -на, -но) *прил (пьяница)* inveterate; **~ сон** deep sleep; **~ное пья́нство** drunken stupor.

непроводни́к (-а́) *м (физ)* nonconductor, dielectric.

непрогля́д|ный (-ен, -на, -но) *прил (ночь)* pitch-dark; *(тьма)* impenetrable.

непродолжи́тел|ьный (-ен, -ьна, -ьно) *прил* short.

непродукти́в|ный (-ен, -на, -но) *прил* unproductive.

непроду́манный *прил* ill-considered.

непрое́зж|ий (-ая, -ее, -ие) *прил* impassable.

непрозра́ч|ный (-ен, -на, -но) *прил* opaque.

непроизводи́тел|ьный (-ен, -ьна, -ьно) *прил (труд)* unproductive; *(расходы)* wasteful.

непроизво́л|ьный (-ен, -ьна, -ьно) *прил* involuntary.

непрола́з|ный (-ен, -на, -но) *прил (разг)* impassable.

непромока́ем|ый (-, -а, -о) *прил (куртка, сапоги)* waterproof.

непроница́ем|ый (-, -а, -о) *прил (мрак, туман)* impenetrable; *(перен: вид, лицо)* inscrutable; **~ для** +*gen* impervious to.

непропорциона́л|ьный (-ен, -ьна, -ьно) *прил* disproportionate.

непрости́тел|ьный (-ен, -ьна, -ьно) *прил* unforgivable, inexcusable.

непроходи́мост|ь (-и) *ж (мед)* blockage.

непроходи́м|ый (-, -а, -о) *прил (чаща, болото)* impassable; *(no short form; перен: разг: дурак)* utter.

непро́ч|ный (-ен, -на́, -но) *прил (дом)* unstable; *(материал)* flimsy; *(перен: чувства)* questionable; *(: привязанность)* precarious.

непро́шеный *прил* (*разг*) uninvited.

непрямо́й *прил* (*путь*) indirect; (*ответ*) evasive.

Непту́н (**-а**) *м* Neptune.

непью́щий (**-ая, -ее, -ие**) *прил* (*человек*) teetotal.

неработоспосо́б|**ный** (**-ен, -на, -но**) *прил* unable to work.

нерабо́чий (**-ая, -ее, -ие**) *прил*: ~**ее вре́мя** time off; ~**ая обстано́вка** atmosphere which is not conducive to work.

нера́вен *прил см* **нера́вный**.

нера́венств|**о** (**-а**) *ср* inequality; **знак** ~**а** (*МАТ*) inequality sign.

неравноду́ш|**ный** (**-ен, -на, -но**) *прил*: ~ (**к** +*dat*) not indifferent (to); **он к ней** ~**ен** he finds her attractive.

неравноме́р|**ный** (**-ен, -на, -но**) *прил* (*развитие, глубина*) uneven; (*движения*) irregular.

неравнопра́вен *прил см* **неравнопра́вный**.

неравнопра́ви|**е** (**-я**) *ср* inequality (of rights).

неравнопра́в|**ный** (**-ен, -на, -но**) *прил* unequal.

нера́в|**ный** (**-ен, -на́, -но**) *прил* unequal.

неради́в|**ый** (**-, -а, -о**) *прил* careless, negligent.

неразбери́х|**а** (**-и**) *ж* (*разг*) muddle.

неразбо́рчив|**ый** (**-, -а, -о**) *прил* (*буквы, по́черк*) illegible; (*читатель, вкус*) undiscriminating; ~ **в сре́дствах** unscrupulous.

неразви́т|**о́й** (**-, -а, -о**) *прил* undeveloped.

неразга́данный *прил* unsolved.

неразгово́рчив|**ый** (**-, -а, -о**) *прил* taciturn.

неразде́льный (**-ен, -ьна, -ьно**) *прил* inseparable, indivisible.

неразличи́м|**ый** (**-, -а, -о**) *прил* (*схожий*) indistinguishable; (*издали, в темноте*) indiscernible.

неразлу́чный (**-ен, -на, -но**) *прил* inseparable.

неразрешённый *прил* (*запрещённый*) prohibited; (*оставшийся неясным*) unsolved.

неразреши́мый (**-, -а, -о**) *прил* insoluble.

неразры́в|**ный** (**-ен, -на, -но**) *прил* indissoluble.

неразу́м|**ный** (**-ен, -на, -но**) *прил* (*поведение, поступок*) foolish; (*разг: малыш, ребёнок*) silly.

нераспростране́ни|**е** (**-я**) *ср* nonproliferation; ~ **я́дерного ору́жия** nonproliferation of nuclear weapons.

нерассуди́тельный (**-ен, -ьна, -ьно**) *прил* lacking (in) common sense.

нерасторжи́м|**ый** (**-, -а, -о**) *прил* indissoluble.

нерасторо́п|**ный** (**-ен, -на, -но**) *прил* slow, sluggish.

нерасчётлив|**ый** (**-, -а, -о**) *прил* wasteful.

нерв (**-а**) *м* (*АНАТ*) nerve; **больны́е не́рвы** nervous disorder; **он всем де́йствует на не́рвы** he gets on everyone's nerves; **переста́нь трепа́ть мне не́рвы!** (*разг*) stop getting on my nerves!

нерви́р|**овать** (**-ую**) *несов перех* to make nervous.

не́рвнича|**ть** (**-ю**) *несов неперех* to fret.

не́рвно *нареч* nervously.

нервнобольн|**о́й** (**-о́го**; *decl like adj*) *м* person *suffering from a nervous disorder*.

не́рвный *прил* nervous; (*работа, занятие*) nerve-racking; (*окончания, клетки*) nerve *опред*; **не́рвная систе́ма** the nervous system.

нерво́зен *прил см* **нерво́зный**.

нерво́зность (**-и**) *ж* nervousness.

нерво́з|**ный** (**-ен, -на, -но**) *прил* (*человек*) nervous, highly (*BRIT*) *или* high (*US*) strung; (*тон, характер*) nervous; (*обстановка*) nerve-racking.

нервотрёпк|**а** (**-и**) *ж* (*разг*) hassle.

нереа́лен *прил см* **нереа́льный**.

нереа́льность (**-и**) *ж* (*событий, обстановки*) unreality; (*неосуществимость*) impracticality.

нереа́л|**ьный** (**-ен, -ьна, -ьно**) *прил* (*мир, события*) unreal; (*неосуществимый*) impractical.

нерегуля́р|**ный** (**-ен, -на, -но**) *прил* irregular.

нере́дко *нареч* (*часто*) not infrequently, quite often.

нерента́белен *прил см* **нерента́бельный**.

нерента́бельность (**-и**) *ж* unprofitability.

нерента́бель|**ный** (**-ен, -на, -но**) *прил* unprofitable.

не́рест (**-а**) *м* spawning.

нереши́мость (**-и**) *ж* indecision.

нереши́телен *прил см* **нереши́тельный**.

нереши́тельно *нареч* indecisively.

нереши́тельность (**-и**) *ж* indecision, indecisiveness; **быть** (*impf*) **в** ~**и** to be undecided.

нереши́тель|**ный** (**-ен, -ьна, -ьно**) *прил* indecisive.

нержаве́йк|**а** (**-йки**; *gen pl* **-ек**) *ж* (*разг*) stainless steel.

нержаве́ющий (**-ая, -ее, -ие**) *прил* (*крыша, бочка*) rustproof; **нержаве́ющая ста́ль** stainless steel.

неро́вно *нареч* (*порезать*) unevenly.

неро́вный *прил* (*поверхность, край*) uneven; (*местность*) rough, rugged; (*линия*) crooked; (*пульс*) irregular; (*характер, поведение*) unbalanced.

не́рп|**а** (**-ы**) *ж* (*ЗООЛ*) seal.

неруши́мый *прил* (*союз*) indestructible.

неря́х|**а** (**-и**) *м/ж* (*разг*) scruff.

неря́шлив|**ый** (**-, -а, -о**) *прил* (*человек, одежда*) scruffy; (*работа*) careless.

несамостоя́тельный (**-ен, -ьна, -ьно**) *прил* dependent; **Ва́ша рабо́та** ~**ьна** this is not all your own work.

несбы́точ|**ный** (**-ен, -на, -но**) *прил* unrealizable;

~ные ме́чты pipe dreams.
несваре́ни|е (-я) *ср:* ~ желу́дка indigestion.
несве́дущ|ий (-ая, -ее, -ие; -, -а, -е, -и) *прил*
ignorant.
несве́ж|ий (-ая, -ее, -ие; -, -а́, -о) *прил*
(*руба́шка*) dirty; **о́вощи** ~**ие** the vegetables are
not very fresh; **у тебя́** ~ **вид** you look weary.
несвоевре́мен|ный (-ен, -на, -но) *прил*
untimely.
несвя́зный *прил* disjointed.
несгиба́емый *прил* staunch.
несгово́рчив|ый (-, -а, -о) *прил* pig-headed.
несгора́емый *прил* fireproof.
несде́ржанность (-и) *ж* fieriness.
несде́ржан|ный (-, -на, -но) *прил* (*хара́ктер,
челове́к*) fiery; (*тон, поведе́ние*) passionate.
несдоброва́ть *как сказ:* **ему́** ~ (*разг*) he's in
trouble.
несе́ни|е (-я) *ср* (*охра́ны, слу́жбы*) carrying out;
(*наказа́ния*) taking.
несери́йный *прил* (*изде́лие*) custom-made.
несерьёз|ный (-ен, -на, -но) *прил* (*челове́к*)
frivolous; (*предложе́ние*) flippant; (*боле́знь*)
mild; ~**ная ра́на** flesh wound.
несимметри́чный (-ен, -на, -но) *прил*
asymmetrical.
несказа́н|ный (-ен, -на, -но) *прил* inexpressive.
нескла́д|ный (-ен, -на, -но) *прил* (*расска́з,
жизнь*) disjointed; (*челове́к, фигу́ра*) ungainly.
несклоня́емый *прил* (*линг*) indeclinable.
не́сколько|о (-их) *чис* (+*gen*) a few ◆ *нареч*
(*немно́го: оби́деться*) somewhat; **в** ~**их**
слова́х in a few words, briefly.
несконча́ем|ый (-, -а, -о) *прил* unending.
нескро́м|ный (-ен, -на, -но) *прил* (*челове́к,
поведе́ние*) immodest; (*вопро́с*) indelicate;
(*жест, предложе́ние*) brazen.
нескрыва́ем|ый (-, -а, -о) *прил* undisguised.
несло́ж|ный (-ен, -на, -но) *прил* simple.
неслы́хан|ный (-, -на, -но) *прил* unheard of.
неслы́шно *нареч* (*сказа́ть, прое́хать*) quietly
◆ *как сказ:* **мне** ~ I can't hear.
неслы́ш|ный (-ен, -на, -но) *прил* inaudible.
несме́т|ный (-ен, -на, -но) *прил* infinite.
несмолка́ем|ый (-, -а, -о) *прил* unceasing.
несмотря́ *предл:* ~ **на** +*acc* (*тру́дности,
уста́лость*) in spite of, despite; ~ **на то что** ...
in spite of *или* despite the fact that ...; ~ **ни на
что** no matter what.
несмыва́емый *прил* (*пятно́*) indelible; (*позо́р*)
ineradicable.
несмышлённый *прил* (*ребёнок*) innocent.
несно́с|ный (-ен, -на, -но) *прил* (*челове́к,
поведе́ние итп*) insufferable; (*жара́, хо́лод*)
unbearable.
несоблюде́ни|е (-я) *ср* nonobservance.
несоверше́нен *прил см* **несоверше́нный**.
несовершенноле́тн|ий (-его; *decl like adj*) *м*
minor; ◆ (-яя, -ее, -ее) *прил*: ~ **ребёнок** minor.
несовершенноле́тн|яя (-ей; *decl like adj*) *ж см*
несовершенноле́тний.

несоверше́н|ный (-ен, -на, -но) *прил* flawed;
несоверше́нный вид (*линг*) imperfective
(aspect).
несоверше́нств|о (-а) *ср* (*о́бщества,
систе́мы*) imperfect nature.
несовмести́мость (-и) *ж* incompatibility;
несовмести́мость тка́ней (*мед*) antagonism.
несовмести́м|ый (-, -а, -о) *прил* incompatible.
несогла́си|е (-я) *ср* (*отка́з*) refusal; (*в семье́*)
disagreement.
несогласо́ванность (-и) *ж* lack of
coordination.
несогласо́ван|ный (-, -на, -но) *прил*
(*де́йствия*) uncoordinated.
несозна́телен *прил см* **несозна́тельный**.
несозна́тельность (-и) *ж* irresponsibility.
несозна́тельн|ый (-ен, -ьна, -ьно) *прил*
irresponsible.
несоизмери́м|ый (-, -а, -о) *прил* (*поня́тия*)
disproportionate.
несокруши́м|ый (-, -а, -о) *прил* indestructible.
несомне́нен *прил см* **несомне́нный**.
несомне́нно *нареч* (*пра́вильный, хоро́ший
итп*) indisputably ◆ *вводн сл* without a doubt ◆
как сказ: **э́то** ~ this is indisputable; ~, **что он
придёт** there is no doubt that he will come.
несомне́нность (-и) *ж* indisputability.
несомне́н|ный (-ен, -на, -но) *прил* (*факт,
успе́х*) indisputable.
несообра́зен *прил см* **несообра́зный**.
несообрази́тельн|ый (-ен, -ьна, -ьно) *прил*
(*челове́к*) slow, thick.
несообра́зность (-и) *ж* (*поведе́ния*)
foolishness; **говори́ть** (*impf*)/**де́лать** (*impf*) ~**и**
to say/do foolish things.
несообра́з|ный (-ен, -на, -но) *прил*
(*поведе́ние*) foolish; ~ **с** +*instr* (*с
возмо́жностями, с обстоя́тельствами*) out of
line with.
несоотве́тстви|е (-я) *ср:* ~ +*dat* (*пра́вилам,
зако́ну*) nonconformity with; (*возмо́жностям,
обстоя́тельствам*) discrepancy with.
несоразме́р|ный (-ен, -на, -но) *прил*
unbalanced.
несостоя́телен *прил см* **несостоя́тельный**.
несостоя́тельность (-и) *ж* (*до́вода*) lack of
substantiation; (*комм*) insolvency;
обнару́живать (**обнару́жить** *perf*) **свою́** ~ to
prove to be worthless.
несостоя́тел|ьный (-ен, -ьна, -но) *прил* (*до́вод*)
unsubstantiated; (*комм: компа́ния, должни́к*)
insolvent; (*руководи́тель*) incompetent.
неспе́ш|ный (-ен, -на, -но) *прил* unhurried.
несподру́чно *как сказ* (*разг*) it is inconvenient;
мне ~ **де́лать э́то** it's inconvenient for me to do
this.
несподру́чный *прил* (*разг*) inconvenient.
неспоко́ен *прил см* **неспоко́йный**.
неспоко́йно *как сказ* (*в до́ме, в стране́*) there's
unease; **у меня́ на душе́** ~ I feel uneasy.
неспоко́й|ный (-ен, -йна, -йно) *прил* (*сон*)

uneasy; (*жизнь*) troubled.

неспосо́бен *прил см* **неспосо́бный**.

неспосо́бност|**ь** (-и) *ж* inability; ~ **на** +*acc* (*на жертвы, на уступки итп*) inability to make.

неспосо́б|**ный** (-ен, -на, -но) *прил*: ~ **к** +*dat* incapable of; ~ **к языка́м/матема́тике** incapable of learning languages/doing maths; ~ **на** +*acc* (*на жертвы, на уступки*) incapable of making.

несправедли́во *нареч* unfairly, unjustly ♦ *как сказ*: **э́то** ~ this is unfair *или* unjust.

несправедли́вост|**ь** (-и) *ж* injustice.

несправедли́в|**ый** (-, -а, -о) *прил* (*человек, суд, упрёк*) unfair, unjust; (*сообщение*) unfounded.

неспроста́ *нареч* (*разг*) for a reason.

неспряга́емый *прил* (*линг*) inconjugable.

несрабо́танност|**ь** (-и) *ж* lack of harmony at work.

несравне́нен *прил см* **несравне́нный**.

несравне́нно *нареч* (*лучшее, красивее итп*) incomparably.

несравне́н|**ный** (-ен, -на, -но) *прил* incomparable.

несравни́м|**ый** (-, -а, -о) *прил* incomparable.

нестанда́рт|**ный** (-ен, -на, -но) *прил* (*подход*) original; (*товар*) substandard.

нестерпи́м|**ый** (-, -а, -о) *прил* intolerable.

нес|**ти́** (-у́, -ёшь; *pt* нёс, -ла́, -ло́) *несов от* носи́ть ♦ *перех* to carry; (*влечь: хаос, разруху, неприятности*) to bring; (*разг: чепуху, вздор*) to spout; (*perf* **понести́**; *службу, охрану*) to carry out; (*perf* **снести́**; *яйцо*) to lay ♦ *безл*: ~**ёт бензи́ном/во́дкой** there's a smell of petrol (*BRIT*) *или* gas (*US*)/of vodka; **с мо́ря** ~**ёт прохла́дой** coolness wafted in from the sea; ~ (**понести́** *perf*) **наказа́ние** to take punishment; ~ (**понести́** *perf*) **поте́ри** to suffer losses; ~ (**понести́** *perf*) **уще́рб** to be damaged; **куда́ тебя** ~**ёт?** (*разг*) where on earth are you going?; **кого́ э́то** ~**ёт?** (*разг*) who on earth is that?

► **нести́сь** *несов возв* (*человек, машина*) to race; (*перен: сплетни*) to spread; (: *музыка*) to carry; (*perf* **снести́сь**; *курица*) to lay eggs.

несто́ящий (-ая, -ее, -ие) *прил* (*человек*) worthless; (*дело*) valueless.

нестро́йный (-ен, -йна, -йно) *прил* shapeless; (*ряды*) ragged.

несудохо́дный *прил* not navigable.

несура́зен *прил см* **несура́зный**.

несура́зност|**ь** (-и) *ж* silliness; **говори́ть** (*impf*)/ **де́лать** (*impf*) ~**и** to say/do silly things.

несура́з|**ный** (-ен, -на, -но) *прил* silly; (*характер*) idiotic.

несуще́ственный *прил* inconsequential.

несхо́дный (-ен, -на, -но) *прил* dissimilar.

несча́стен *прил см* **несча́стный**.

несчастли́вый (несча́стлив, несча́стлива,

несча́стливо) *прил* (*человек*) unhappy; (*попытка*) unfortunate.

несча́ст|**ный** (-ен, -на, -но) *прил* (*человек, лицо*) unhappy; (*день*) sad; (*no short form; разг: жалкий*) wretched; **у него́ о́чень** ~ **вид** he looks very unhappy; **несча́стная любо́вь** unrequited love; **несча́стный слу́чай** accident.

несча́сть|**е** (-я) *ср* (*беда*) misfortune; **к** ~**ю** unfortunately.

несчётный *прил* incalculable.

несъедо́б|**ный** (-ен, -на, -но) *прил* inedible.

KEYWORD

нет *част* **1** (*при отрицании, несогласии*) no; **ты согла́сен? – нет** do you agree? – no; **нет, э́то не то** no, that's not right; **тебе́ не нра́вится мой суп? – нет, нра́вится** don't you like my soup? – yes, I do

2 (*для привлечения внимания*): **нет, ты то́лько посмотри́ на него́!** would you just look at him!

3 (*выражает недоверие*): **нет, ты действи́тельно не се́рдишься?** so you are really not angry?

♦ *как сказ* (+*gen*; *не име́ется: об одно́м предме́те*) there is no; (: *о нескольких предме́тах*) there are no; **нет вре́мени** there is no time; **нет биле́тов** *или* **биле́тов нет** there are no tickets; **у меня́ нет де́нег** I have no money; **его́ нет в го́роде** he is not in town

♦ *союз*: **1**: (**так**) **нет** (**же**) (*разг: однако*) but; **я помога́л ему́ три дня, (так) нет (же) ему́ всё ма́ло** I helped him for three days, but it still wasn't enough; **своди́ть (свести́** *perf*) **что-н на нет** to bring sth to nothing; **сойти́** (*perf*) **на нет** to come to nothing

2 (*во фразах*): **нет – так нет** it can't be helped; **нет-нет да и зайдёт/ска́жет** every now and then he called in/said; **чего́ то́лько нет?** what don't they have?; **нет чтобы извини́ться/ сказа́ть пра́вду** (*разг*) instead of saying sorry/ telling the truth.

нетакти́чен *прил см* **нетакти́чный**.

нетакти́чност|**ь** (-и) *ж* tactlessness.

нетакти́ч|**ный** (-ен, -на, -но) *прил* tactless.

нетвёрдый *прил* (*походка*) unsteady; (*решение*) shaky.

нетерпели́во *нареч* impatiently.

нетерпели́в|**ый** (-, -а, -о) *прил* impatient.

нетерпе́ни|**е** (-я) *ср* impatience; **с** ~**м ждать** (*impf*)/**слу́шать** (*impf*) to wait/listen impatiently.

нетерпи́мост|**ь** (-и) *ж* intolerance.

нетерпи́м|**ый** (-, -а, -о) *прил* (*недопустимый*) intolerant; (*непримиримый*): ~ **к** +*dat* (*ко лжи*) intolerant of.

нетороп-ли́во *нареч* unhurriedly.

нетороп-ли́в|**ый** (-, -а, -о) *прил* unhurried.

нето́чност|**ь** (-и) *ж* (*данных, описания*) inexactness; (*в работе, в описании*) inexactitude.

нето́ч|ный (-ен, -но, -на) *прил* inexact.

нетре́бовател|ьный (-ен, -ьна, -ьно) *прил* (*начальник*) undemanding; (*вкус, публика*) unsophisticated; (*человек*) unassuming.

нетре́звый *прил* drunk; **в нетре́звом состоя́нии** drunk.

нетро́нут|ый (-, -а, -о) *прил* (*снег*) virgin; (*обед*) untouched.

нетру́ден *прил см* **нетру́дный**.

нетру́дно *как сказ*: **э́то ~** it's easy *или* not difficult; **~ поня́ть** it's easy *или* not difficult to understand.

нетру́д|ный (-ен, -но, -на) *прил* easy.

нетрудово́й *прил*: **~ дохо́д** unearned income.

нетрудоспосо́бен *прил см* **нетрудоспосо́бный**.

нетрудоспосо́бност|ь (-и) *ж* disability; **посо́бие по ~и** disability living allowance.

нетрудоспосо́б|ный (-ен, -на, -но) *прил* *unable to work through disability*.

не́тто *прил неизм* (*о весе*) net *опред*; **вес ~** net weight; **~-акти́вы** (*КОММ*) net assets.

неубеди́тел|ьный (-ен, -ьна, -ьно) *прил* unconvincing.

неу́бранный *прил* (*урожай*) ungathered; (*поля*) unharvested; (*постель*) unmade; (*комната*) untidy.

неуваже́ни|е (-я) *ср* disrespect.

неуве́ренно *нареч* uncertainly.

неуве́ренный *прил* (*человек*) unsure; (*тон*) uncertain; **~ в себе́** unsure of o.s.

неувяда́ем|ый (-, -а, -о) *прил* (*талант, слава*) enduring; (*красота*) unfading.

неувя́з|ка (-ки; *gen pl* -ок) *ж* (*разг: в описании, в аргументации*) discrepancy; (*недоразумение*) misunderstanding.

неугаси́м|ый (-, -а, -о) *прил* inextinguishable.

неугомо́н|ный (-ен, -на, -но) *прил* unruly.

неуда́ч|а (-и) *ж* (*в делах*) failure; **терпе́ть** (**потерпе́ть** *perf*) **~у** to meet with failure.

неуда́чен *прил см* **неуда́чный**.

неуда́члив|ый (-, -а, -о) *прил* (*человек*) unlucky.

неуда́чно *нареч* unsuccessfully; **её жизнь сложи́лась ~** her life was a failure.

неуда́ч|ный (-ен, -на, -но) *прил* (*попытка*) unsuccessful; (*фильм, стихи*) bad.

неудержи́м|ый (-, -а, -о) *прил* (*поток, бег*) uncontrollable; (*слёзы, радость*) unrestrained.

неудиви́тельно *как сказ* it's not surprising.

неудо́бен *прил см* **неудо́бный**.

неудо́бно *нареч* (*расположенный, сидеть*) uncomfortably ♦ *как сказ* it's uncomfortable; (*неприлично*) it's awkward; **мне ~** I am uncomfortable; **~ задава́ть лю́дям таки́е вопро́сы** it's awkward to ask people such questions; (**мне**) **~ сказа́ть ему́ об э́том** I feel uncomfortable telling him that.

неудо́б|ный (-ен, -на, -но) *прил* uncomfortable.

неудобовари́м|ый (-, -а, -о) *прил* (*также*

перен) indigestible.

неудо́бств|о (-а) *ср* (*неловкость*) discomfort; (*в поезде итп*) lack of comfort.

неудовлетворённост|ь (-и) *ж*: **~ +instr** (*работой, жизнью*) dissatisfaction with.

неудовлетворённый *прил* (*любопытство*) unsatisfied; (*читатель, зритель*) dissatisfied.

неудовлетвори́телен *прил см* **неудовлетвори́тельный**.

неудовлетвори́тельно *нареч* (*сделать*) unsatisfactorily ♦ *ср нескл* (*ПРОСВЕЩ*) ≈ D (*school mark*).

неудовлетвори́тел|ьный (-ен, -ьна, -ьно) *прил* unsatisfactory.

неудово́льстви|е (-я) *ср* dissatisfaction.

неуём|ный (-ен, -на, -но) *прил* (*энергия*) irrepressible; (*тоска*) unrestrained.

неуже́ли *част* really; **~ она́ так ду́мает?** does she really think that?

неужи́вчив|ый (-, -а, -о) *прил* unaccommodating.

неузнава́емост|ь (-и) *ж*: **до ~и** beyond (all) recognition.

неузнава́ем|ый (-, -а, -о) *прил* unrecognizable.

неукло́нно *нареч* steadily.

неукло́н|ный (-ен, -на, -но) *прил* steady.

неуклю́ж|ий (-ая, -ее, -ие; -, -а, -е) *прил* clumsy.

неукосни́телен *прил см* **неукосни́тельный**.

неукосни́тельно *нареч* strictly.

неукосни́тел|ьный (-ен, -ьна, -ьно) *прил* strict.

неукроти́м|ый (-, -а, -о) *прил* (*гнев*) unrestrained; (*энергия*) irrepressible.

неулови́м|ый (-, -а, -о) *прил* imperceptible; (*человек*) elusive.

неуме́л|ый *прил* inept.

неуме́ни|е (-я) *ср* incapability.

неуме́рен|ный (-, -на, -но) *прил* (*восторг*) boundless; (*потребности*) unlimited.

неуме́ст|ный (-ен, -на, -но) *прил* inappropriate; **шу́тка была́ соверше́нно ~на** the joke was completely out of place.

неу́мный *прил* (*политика*) unintelligent.

неумоли́м|ый (-, -а, -о) *прил* (*мститель*) relentless; (*закон*) stringent.

неумо́лч|ный (-ен, -на, -но) *прил* unremitting.

неумы́шленный *прил* (*поступок*) unintentional; (*убийство*) unpremeditated.

неупла́т|а (-ы) *ж* nonpayment.

неупоря́доченный *прил* disorderly.

неупотреби́тел|ьный (-ен, -ьна, -ьно) *прил*: **э́то сло́во сейча́с ~но** this word is not in use any more.

неуправля́ем|ый (-, -а, -о) *прил* (*недисциплинированный*) unruly.

неуравнове́шенност|ь (-и) *ж* irascibility.

неуравнове́шен|ный (-, -на, -но) *прил* unbalanced.

неурожа́|й (-я) *м* poor harvest.

неурожа́йный *прил*: **~ год** year with a poor harvest.

неуро́чный *прил* (*время, час*) unearthly.

неуря́диц|а (-ы) ж (*разг: обычно мн: в семье, на работе*) squabble.
неуспева́емость (-и) ж poor performance.
неуспева́ющий (-ая, -ее, -ие) *прил* (*ученик*) poor.
неуста́нен *прил см* **неуста́нный**.
неуста́нно *нареч* indefatigably.
неуста́н|ный (-ен, -на, -но) *прил* indefatigable.
неусто́йка (-йки; *gen pl* -ек) ж (*КОММ*) penalty; (*разг: неудача*) flop.
неусто́йчивость (-и) ж (*цен*) instability.
неусто́йчив|ый (-, -а, -о) *прил* (*стул, цены*) unstable; (*погода*) unsettled.
неустрани́м|ый (-, -а, -о) *прил* insurmountable.
неустраши́м|ый (-, -а, -о) *прил* fearless.
неустро́ен|ный (-, -на, -но) *прил* (*жизнь, быт*) uncomfortable.
неусы́п|ный (-ен, -на, -но) *прил* vigilant.
неуте́шен *прил см* **неуте́шный**.
неутеши́тель|ный (-ен, -ьна, -ьно) *прил* upsetting.
неуте́ш|ный (-ен, -на, -но) *прил* inconsolable.
неутоли́м|ый (-, -а, -о) *прил* (*жажда*) unquenchable; (*голод, также перен*) insatiable.
неутоми́м|ый (-, -а, -о) *прил* untiring.
нéуч (-а) м (*разг*) dunce.
неучти́вость (-и) ж lack of civility; **говори́ть** (*impf*) ~**и** to be uncivil.
неучти́в|ый (-, -а, -о) *прил* uncivil.
неую́тно *нареч* (*сидеть*) uncomfortably ◆ *как сказ* it's uncomfortable; **мне** ~ **с чужи́ми людьми́** I don't feel at ease with strangers.
неуязви́м|ый (-, -а, -о) *прил* (*противник, позиция*) impregnable; (*аргумент*) unassailable.
неформа́л (-а) м (*разг*) *member of a nonconformist organization*.
неформа́льный *прил* (*отношение*) relaxed; (*организация*) nonconformist.
нефри́т (-а) м (*МЕД*) nephritis; (*ГЕО*) jade.
нефтедобыва́ющий (-ая, -ее, -ие) *прил* (*промышленность*) oil *опред*.
нефтедобы́ч|а (-и) ж drilling for oil.
нефтедо́ллар|ы (-ов) мн petrodollars мн.
нефтено́сный *прил*: ~ **пласт** oilfield.
нефтеперерабо́тк|а (-и) ж oil-processing plant.
нефтепрово́д (-а) м oil pipeline.
нефтепроду́кт (-а) м (*обычно мн*) oil product.
нефтехрани́лищ|е (-а) ср oil storage tank.
нефт|ь (-и) ж oil, petroleum.
нефтяни́к (-а) м *worker in the oil industry*.
нефтян|о́й *прил*: ~**а́я платфо́рма** oil rig; **нефтяна́я вы́шка** (oil) derrick.
нехва́тк|а (-и) ж: ~ +*gen* (*разг*) shortage of.
нехи́трый *прил* (*простой*) simple.
нехо́жен|ый (-, -а, -о) *прил* little-used.
нехоро́ш|ий (-ая, -ее, -ие) *прил* bad.
нехорошо́ *нареч* (*поступить*) badly ◆ *как сказ*

it's bad; **мне** ~ I'm not well; ~ **на душе́** I feel uneasy; **он нехоро́ш собо́й** he isn't good-looking.
нéхотя *нареч* unwillingly.
нецензу́р|ный (-ен, -на, -но) *прил* unprintable; ~**ное сло́во** swearword.
неча́янно *нареч* unintentionally.
неча́ян|ный (-на, -но) *прил* (*неумышленный*) unintentional; (*неожиданный*) chance *опред*.
нéчего *как сказ*: ~ **рассказа́ть** there is nothing to tell; (*разг: не следует*) there's no need to do; **нé для чего стара́ться** there is nothing to try for; **нé к чему придра́ться** there is nothing to find fault with; **мне нé с чем идти́** I have nothing to take; **нé о чем говори́ть** there is nothing to talk about; **нéчему серди́ться** there is nothing to be angry about; **нé за что!** (*в ответ на благодарность*) not at all!, you're welcome! (*US*); ~ (**и**) **говори́ть** (*разг: конечно*) no buts about it; ~ **сказа́ть!** (*разг*) would you credit it!; **от** ~ **де́лать** (*разг*) for want of something better to do; **де́лать** ~ there's nothing else to be done.
нечелове́ческ|ий (-ая, -ое, -ие) *прил* inhuman; (*колоссальный: усилия*) superhuman.
нечёсаный *прил* unkempt.
нече́стен *прил см* **нече́стный**.
нече́стно *нареч* dishonestly ◆ *как сказ*: **э́то** ~ this is dishonest.
нече́стность (-и) ж dishonesty.
нече́ст|ный (-ен, -на, -но) *прил* dishonest.
нечётный *прил* (*число*) odd.
нечи́сто *как сказ*: **в ко́мнате** ~ the room is untidy; **здесь что́-то** ~ (*разг*) there's something fishy here.
нечистопло́т|ный (-ен, -на, -но) *прил* (*неопрятный*) untidy; (*неразборчивый*) unscrupulous.
нечисто́т|ы (-) мн sewage *ед*; (*отбросы*) waste *ед*.
нечи́ст|ый (-, -а, -о) *прил* (*одежда, комната*) dirty; (*произношение*) indistinct; (*приёмы, игра*) unscrupulous; **у негó** ~**ая со́весть** he has a guilty conscience; **он нечи́ст на́ руку** (*нечестен*) he is dishonest; (*ворует*) he is light-fingered; **нечи́стая си́ла** evil spirit.
нечи́ст|ь (-и) ж собир (*нечистая сила*) evil spirit; (*перен: преступная, нацистская*) scum.
нечленоразде́ль|ный (-ен, -ьна, -ьно) *прил* inarticulate.
нéчто мест something.
нечувстви́телен *прил см* **нечувстви́тельный**.
нечувстви́тельность (-и) ж insensitivity.
нечувстви́тель|ный (-ен, -ьна, -ьно) *прил* insensitive.
нечу́тк|ий (-ая, -ое, -ие) *прил* (*человек*) unsympathetic.
нешу́точ|ный (-ен, -на, -но) *прил* (*серьёзный*)

serious; (*значительный*) large; это ~ное дело it's no laughing matter.

нещаден *прил см* **нещадный**.

нещадно *нареч* unmercifully.

нещадн|ый (-ен, -на, -но) *прил* (*критика, наказание*) merciless; (*перен: жара*) relentless.

неэкономичен *прил см* **неэкономичный**.

неэкономичность (-и) *ж* (*методов, технологии*) inefficiency.

неэкономич|ный (-ен, -на, -но) *прил* (*технология, отрасль*) inefficient; (*мотор*) uneconomical.

неэтичный *прил* (*поведение*) unethical.

неэффективн|ый (-ен, -на, -но) *прил* ineffective.

нея́в|ка (-ки; *gen pl* -ок) *ж* (*на работу*) absence; (*на суд*) failure to appear; **за ~кой, по ~ке** by default.

неясен *прил см* **неясный**.

неясно *нареч*: **он ~ объяснил положение** he didn't explain the situation clearly ♦ *как сказ* it's not clear; **мне ~, почему он отказался** I'm not clear *или* it's not clear to me why he refused.

неясност|ь (-и) *ж* vagueness; (*в тексте*) ambiguity.

нея́сн|ый (-ен, -на, -но) *прил* (*очертания, звук*) indistinct; (*мысль, вопрос*) vague.

НЗ *м сокр* = **неприкосновенный запас**.

KEYWORD

ни *част* **1** (*усиливает отрицание*) not a; **ни один** not one, not a single; **она не произнесла ни слова** she didn't say a word; **она ни разу не пришла** she didn't come once; **у меня не осталось ни рубля** I don't have a single rouble left;

2: **кто/что/как ни** who/what/however; **сколько ни** however much; **что ни говори, а ей приходится трудно** whatever you say, it is hard for her; **как ни старайся, не убедишь его** however hard you try, you will not convince him; **куда ни посмотри, везде бедность** wherever you look, there is poverty

♦ *союз* (*in negative sentences*; *при перечислении*): **ни ..., ни ...** neither ... nor ...; **ни денег, ни еды у неё нет** she has neither money nor food; **ни за что** no way; **ни за какие деньги** not for any money; **ни-ни!** (*разг*) no way!

нив|а (-ы) *ж* field (*of crops*).

нивелир|овать (-ую) (*не*)*сов перех* (*перен*) to even out.

нигде *нареч* nowhere; **его ~ не было** he was nowhere to be found; **~ нет моей книги** I can't find my book anywhere, my book is nowhere to be found; **~ не мог поесть** I couldn't find anywhere to get something to eat.

нигерийск|ий (-ая, -ое, -ие) *ж* Nigerian.

Нигери|я (-и) *ж* Nigeria.

нигилизм (-а) *м* nihilism.

нигилист (-а) *м* nihilist.

нидерландск|ий (-ая, -ое, -ие) *прил* Dutch.

Нидерланд|ы (-ов) *мн* the Netherlands.

ниже *сравн прил от* **низкий** ♦ *сравн нареч от* **низко** ♦ *нареч* (*далее*) later on ♦ *предл* (+*gen*) below; **~ речь пойдёт о** +*prp* ... later (on) we will deal with ...; **он выступил ~ своих возможностей** he performed below his capabilities.

нижеизложенн|ый *прил*: **~ые данные/аргументы** the facts/arguments given below.

нижеподписавш|ийся (-аяся, -ееся, -иеся) *прил* undersigned.

нижесказанн|ое (-ого; *decl like adj*) *ср* what has been said below.

нижестоя|щий (-ая, -ее, -ие) *прил* lower.

нижеуказанный *прил* undermentioned.

нижеупомянутый *прил* = **нижеуказанный**.

нижн|ий (-яя, -ее, -ие) *прил* (*ступенька, ящик*) bottom; (*течение реки*) lower reaches *мн*; (*регистр*) low; **~ этаж** ground (*BRIT*) *или* first (*US*) floor; **Н~ Новгород** Nizhni Novgorod; **нижнее бельё** underwear; **нижняя юбка** underskirt.

низ (-а; *loc sg* -у, *nom pl* -ы) *м* (*стола, ящика итп*) bottom; (*дома*) ground (*BRIT*) *или* first (*US*) floor; **по́ ~у** along the bottom; *см также* **низы́**.

низвергн|уть (-у, -ешь; *impf* **низвергать**) *сов перех* to overthrow

▶ **низвергнуться** *сов возв* to hurtle down.

низин|а (-ы) *ж* low-lying land.

низ|кий (-кая, -кое, -кие; -ок, -ка, -ко) *прил* low; (*no short form*; *происхождение*) low; **этот стол мне ~ок** this table is too low for me; **~ лоб** narrow forehead; **~кое место** (*низменность*) low-lying area; **~ поклон** low bow; (*перен*) forelock tugging.

низко *нареч* low.

низкооплачиваемый *прил* low-paid.

низкопоклонник (-а) *м* sycophant.

низкопоклонств|о (-а) *ср* sycophancy.

низкопробн|ый (-ен, -на, -но) *прил* (*золото, серебро*) low-grade; (*книга, газета*) trashy; (*делец*) amoral.

низкорослый *прил* (*человек*) small; (*дерево, кустарник*) stunted.

низкосортн|ый (-ен, -на, -но) *прил* low-quality.

низкокачественный *прил* low-quality.

низл|ожить (-ожу, -ожишь; *impf* **низлагать**) *сов перех* to depose.

низменност|ь (-и) *ж* (*ГЕО*) low-lying area; (*интересов*) baseness.

низмен|ный *прил* (*местность, болота*) low-lying; (-, -на, -но; *интересы, мысли*) base; (*инстинкты*) basic.

низовой *прил* (*организация*) grass-roots; **низовые работники** the grass roots.

низовь|е (-ья; *gen pl* -ьев) *ср* lower reaches *мн*.

низок *прил см* **низкий**.

низом *нареч* along the bottom.

низост|ь (-и) *ж* baseness; **говорить** (*impf*) ~**и** to say base things; **делать** (*impf*) ~**и** to behave basely.

ни́зш|ий (**-ая, -ее, -ие**) *сравн прил от* **ни́зкий**; (*звание*) junior; **~ие чины́** the lowest ranks.

низ|ы́ (**-о́в**) *мн* (*низший классы*) lowest classes *мн*; (*широкие массы*) masses *мн*; **он вы́шел из ~о́в** he came from the lowest classes of society; **опира́ться** (*impf*) **на ~** to rely for support on the masses.

ника́к *нареч* (*никаким образом*) no way; **~ не могу́ запо́мнить э́то сло́во** I can't remember this word at all; **дверь ~ не открыва́лась** the door just wouldn't open; **ему́ ~ не удава́лось её встре́тить** there's no way he could have managed to meet her; **~ нельзя́** +*infin* ... one can't do ....

никако́й (**-а́я, -о́е, -и́е**) *мест:* **~и́е де́ньги не помогли́** no amount of money would have helped; (*разг*): **~ он не врач** he's not a doctor at all; (: *плохой*): **писа́тель он ~** he can't be called a writer; **ни у како́го челове́ка не бу́дет сомне́ния** nobody will have any doubt about it; **ни к како́му де́лу он не спосо́бен** he is not capable of anything; **он не соглаша́лся ни с каки́м аргуме́нтном** he didn't agree with any of the arguments; **нет ~о́го сомне́ния** there is absolutely no doubt (at all); **у меня́ нет ~о́го сомне́ния** I have absolutely no doubts; **и ~и́х!** and that's that!

Никара́гуа *ж нескл* Nicaragua.

никарагуа́нск|ий (**-ая, -ое, -ие**) *прил* Nicaraguan.

никелир|ова́ть (**-у́ю**; *perf* **отникелирова́ть**) *несов перех* to nickel.

никелиро́вк|а (**-и**) *ж* (*действие*) nickelling (*BRIT*), nickeling (*US*); (*покрытие*) nickel plate.

ни́кел|ь (**-я**) *м* (*ХИМ*) nickel.

ни́кн|уть (**-у, -ешь**) *несов от* **пони́кнуть** ♦ *неперех* (*трава, цветы*) to droop.

никогда́ *нареч* never; **как ~** as never before.

никого́ *мест см* **никто́**.

нико́й *нареч:* **нико́им образом** not at all; **ни в ко́ем слу́чае** under no circumstances.

ни|кто́ (**-кого́;** *как кто; см* **Table 6**) *мест* nobody ♦ *м:* **она́ мне ~** (*разг: не родственник*) she's not a relative of mine; (*не друг*) she's nothing to me; **ни у кого́ нет сомне́ний** nobody has any doubts; **ни к кому́ не подходи́л** I didn't approach anyone; **ни с кем не говори́л** I didn't speak to anyone; **ни о ком не зна́ю** I don't know anything about anyone.

никуда́ *местоимённое нареч* nowhere ♦ *как сказ* (*разг*): **обслу́живание здесь – ~** the service here is terrible; **я ~ не пое́ду** I'm not going anywhere; **~ я не пое́ду** I'm going nowhere; **э́то ~ не годи́тся** that just won't do.

никуды́шный (**-ен, -на, -но**) *прил* (*разг*) good-for-nothing.

никчёмный (**-ен, -на, -но**) *прил* no good for anything.

Нил (**-а**) *м* the Nile.

НИИ *м сокр* (= *научно-иссле́довательский институ́т*) scientific research institute.

ни́мб (**-а**) *м* nimbus.

ниотку́да *местоимённое нареч* from nowhere; **~ нет по́мощи** I get no help from anywhere.

нипочём *как сказ:* **бе́дность ему́ ~** (*разг*) being poor doesn't bother him; **ему́ всё ~** (*разг*) nothing hassles him.

ни́ппел|ь (**-я**) *м* (*ТЕХ*) nipple.

ниско́лько *местоимённое нареч* not at all; (*не лучше, не полезнее*) no; (*не рад, не удивлён*) at all; **ты рад? – ~** are you pleased? – not at all *или* in the slightest.

ниспада́|ть (*3sg* **-ет,** *3pl* **-ют**) *несов неперех* to fall.

ниспрове́рг|нуть (**-ну, -нешь;** *pt* **-, -ла, -ло,** *impf* **ниспроверга́ть**) *сов перех* to overthrow.

нисходя́щий (**-ая, -ее, -ие**) *прил* (*линия*) descending; (*интонация*) falling.

нитеви́дный (**-ен, -на, -но**) *прил* long and thin.

ни́т|ка (**-ки;** *gen pl* **-ок**) *ж* (*обычно мн: для шитья*) thread *ед*; (*для вязания*) yarn; **~ же́мчуга** string of pearls; **~ газопрово́да** gas pipeline; **промо́кнуть** (*perf*) **до ~ки** to get soaked right through; **вдева́ть** (**вдеть** *perf*) **~ку в иго́лку** to thread a needle.

нитра́т (**-а**) *м* nitrate.

нит|ь (**-и**) *ж* thread; (*для вязания*) yarn; (+*gen*; *повествования, воспоминаний*) thread of; **ни́ти за́говора** strands of a plot; **ни́ти дру́жбы** threads of friendship.

них *мест см* **они́**.

ниц *м:* **па́дать ~** to prostrate o.s.

Ни́цц|а (**-ы**) *ж* Nice.

ничего́ *мест см* **ничто́** ♦ *нареч* fairly well; (**э́то**) **~, что** ... it's all right that ...; **извини́те, я Вас побеспоко́ю – ~!** sorry to disturb you – it's all right!; **как живёшь? – ~** how are you? – all right; **~ себе́** (*сносно*) fairly well; **~ себе́!** (*выражает удивление*) well, I never!

ниче́й (**-ьего́;** *f* **-ья́,** *nt* **-ьё,** *pl* **-ьи;** *как чей; см* **Table 7**) *мест* nobody's; **он не слу́шает ~ьих сове́тов** he doesn't follow anybody's advice; **ни к чьему́ сове́ту не прислу́шивается** he doesn't listen to anybody's advice; **ни с чьим мне́нием не счита́ется** he doesn't consider anyone's views; **ни о чьём благополу́чии не беспоко́ится** he doesn't worry about anyone's wellbeing.

ниче́йный *прил* (*полоса, зона*) no man's; **~ая земля́** no-man's-land; **~ результа́т, ниче́йная па́рти|я** draw.

ничко́м *нареч* face down.

нич|то́ (**-его́;** *как что; см* **Table 6**) *мест, ср* nothing; **ни для чего́ не приго́дный** not suitable for anything; **ни с чем не согла́сен** I don't agree with anything; **ни о чём не прошу́** I don't ask for anything; **~ мне не интере́сно** nothing interests me; **~его́ с ним не случи́тся** nothing will happen to him; **~его́ подобного не ви́дел** I've never seen anything like it; **~его́ подобного!** (*разг: совсем не так*) nothing like it!; **всего́ ~его́** (*разг*) next to nothing; **ни за что!** (*ни в коем случае*) no way!; **ни за что не соглаша́йся** whatever you do, don't agree; **ни за что ни про что** for nothing; **я здесь ни при чём** it has nothing to do with me; **~его́ не поде́лаешь** there's nothing to be done.

ничто́жен *прил см* **ничто́жный**.

ничто́жеств|о (-а) *ср* nonentity.

ничто́ж|ный (-ен, -на, -но) *прил* paltry.

ничу́ть *местоимённое нареч* (*нисколько*) not at all; (*не лучше, не больше*) no; (*не испугался, не огорчился*) at all; **~ не быва́ло** not at all.

ничь|я́ (-ей) *ж* (*СПОРТ*) draw; **сыгра́ть** (*perf*) **в ~ю́** to draw (*BRIT*), tie (*US*).

ни́ш|а (-и) *ж* niche.

нища́|ть (-ю; *perf* **обнища́ть**) *несов неперех* to become impoverished.

ни́щая (-ей; *decl like adj*) *ж* beggar.

ни́щен|ка (-ки; *gen pl* **-ок**) *ж* = **ни́щая**.

ни́щенск|ий (-ая, -ое, -ие) *прил* (*ничтожный*) beggarly; **~ая жизнь** life of begging.

нищет|а́ (-ы́) *ж* poverty.

ни́щ|ий (-ая, -ее, -ие) *прил* poverty-stricken ♦ (-его; *decl like adj*) *м* beggar.

НЛО *м сокр* (= *неопо́знанный лета́ющий объе́кт*) UFO (= *unidentified flying object*).

но *союз* but ♦ *ср нескл* (*препятствие*) setback ♦ *межд* gee up; **я предложи́л ему́ по́мощь, ~ он отказа́лся** I offered to help him, but he refused; **~ вдруг** then suddenly; **~ то́лько** only; **~-но, осторо́жнее!** now then, be more careful!

нова́тор (-а) *м* innovator.

нова́торств|о (-а) *ср* innovation.

нова́ци|я (-и) *ж* innovation.

нове́лл|а (-ы) *ж* novella.

новелли́ст (-а) *м* writer of novellas.

новелли́ст|ка (-ки; *gen pl* **-ок**) *ж см* **новелли́ст**.

но́веньк|ая (-ой; *decl like adj*) *ж* newcomer; (*в классе*) new pupil.

но́веньк|ий (-ая, -ое, -ие) *прил* (*разг*) new ♦ (-ого; *decl like adj*) *м* newcomer; (*в классе*) new pupil; **что ~ого?** what's new?

новизн|а́ (-ы́) *ж* (*идей, подхода*) novelty.

нови́н|ка (-ки; *gen pl* **-ок**) *ж* new product; **~ мо́ды** new fashion item; **кни́жная ~** new book; **мне э́то в ~ку** it's new to me.

новичо́к (-ка́) *м* newcomer; (*в классе*) new pupil; **я ~ в** +*prp* I am a newcomer to.

но́во *как сказ*: **здесь мне всё ~** it's all new to me here.

новобра́н|ец (-ца) *м* new recruit.

новобра́чн|ая (-ой; *decl like adj*) *ж см* **новобра́чный**.

новобра́чн|ый (-ого; *decl like adj*) *м* newlywed.

нововведе́ни|е (-я) *ср* innovation.

нового́дн|ий (-яя, -ее, -ие) *прил* New Year

опред; **нового́дняя ёлка** ≈ Christmas tree.

новозела́ндск|ий (-ая, -ое, -ие) *прил* New Zealand *опред*.

новокаи́н (-а) *м* (*МЕД*) Novocaine ®.

новолу́ни|е (-я) *ср* new moon.

новорождён|ная (-ой; *decl like adj*) *ж* newborn girl.

новорождён|ный *прил* newborn ♦ (-ого; *decl like adj*) *м* newborn boy.

новосёл (-а) *м* (*дома*) new owner.

новосе́л|ье (-ья; *gen pl* **-ий**) *ср* house-warming.

Новосиби́рск (-а) *м* Novosibirsk.

новостро́|йка (-йки; *gen pl* **-ек**) *ж* (*строительство*) construction of new buildings; (*новое здание*) new building; **больни́ца-~** newly-built hospital.

но́вост|ь (-и; *gen pl* **-е́й**) *ж* (*известие*) news; (*медицины, техники*) innovation.

новоя́вленный *прил* new.

но́вшеств|о (-а) *ср* (*в жизни, в обществе*) novelty; (*техническое*) innovation.

но́в|ый (-, -а́, -о) *прил* new; **но́вая исто́рия** modern history; **Но́вый Заве́т** the New Testament; **Но́вая Зела́ндия** New Zealand; **Но́вая Земля́** Novaya Zemlya.

нов|ь (-и) *ж* new era.

ног|а́ (-и́; *acc sg* **-у**, *nom pl* **-и**, *gen pl* **-**, *dat pl* **-а́м**) *ж* (*ступня*) foot; (*выше ступни*) leg; **переступа́ть** (*impf*) или **перемина́ться** (*impf*) **с ~й на́ ~у** to shift from one foot to the other; **идти́** (*impf*) **в но́гу со вре́менем** (*перен*) to move with the times; **он бежа́л со всех ног** he ran as fast as his legs would carry him; **сби́ться** (*perf*) **с ног** to be run off one's feet; **поста́вить** (*perf*) **кого́-н на́ ~и** (*перен: больного*) to get sb back on his *итп* feet; (*детей*) to make sb stand on his *итп* own two feet; **с ног на́ голову переворо́чивать** (**переверну́ть** *perf*) или **ста́вить** (**поста́вить** *perf*) to turn *или* put sth on its head; **е́ле но́ги унести́** (*perf*) to escape by the skin of one's teeth; **~й моей́ там не бу́дет** (*разг*) I won't step foot there again; **в ~х** (*постели*) at the foot of the bed; **вверх ~ми** upside down; **в до́ме все вверх ~ми** the house is completely topsy turvy; **жить** (*impf*) **на широ́кую но́гу** to live lavishly; **на коро́ткой** *или* **дру́жеской ~é с** +*instr* on friendly terms with.

ноготк|и́ (-о́в) *мн* marigold.

но́гот|ь (-тя; *gen pl* **-те́й**) *м* nail; **до ко́нчиков ногте́й** (*перен: совершенно*) from top to toe.

нож (-а́) *м* knife; **быть** (*impf*) **с кем-н на ~а́х** (*враждовать*) to be at daggers drawn with sb; **твой посту́пок мне ~ о́стрый** (*перен: разг*) your behaviour gives me a lot of grief.

ножево́й *прил* (*рана*) knife *опред*.

но́жек *сущ см* **но́жка**.

но́жен *сущ см* **но́жны**.

но́ж|ик (-а) *м*: **перочи́нный ~** penknife; **складно́й ~** flick knife (*BRIT*), switchblade (*US*).

но́ж|ка (-ки; *gen pl* -ек) *ж уменьш от* **нога́**; (*стула, стола итп*) leg; (*циркуля*) arm; **подставля́ть** (**подста́вить** *perf*) ~ку кому́-н (*также перен*) to trip sb up.

но́жниц|ы (-) *мн* (*инструмент*) scissors *мн*, pair *ед* of scissors (*мн* pairs of scissors); (*расхождение*) disproportion.

ножно́й *прил* foot *опред*.

но́ж|ны (-ен) *мн* (*для кинжала*) sheath *ед*; (*для шпаги, сабли итп*) scabbard *ед*.

ножо́в|ка (-ки; *gen pl* -ок) *ж* hacksaw.

ноздрева́т|ый (-, -а, -о) *прил* (*сыр*) holey.

ноздр|я́ (-и́; *nom pl* -и, *gen pl* -е́й) *ж* (*обычно мн*) nostril.

нока́ут (-а) *м* knockout.

нокаути́р|овать (-ую) (*не*)*сов перех* to knock out.

нокда́ун (-а) *м* knockdown.

нол|ь (-я́) *м* (*МАТ*) zero, nought; (*при исчислении температуры*) zero; (*перен: человека*) nothing; ~ це́лых пять деся́тых, 0.5 zero *или* nought point five, 0.5; встре́титься (*perf*) в де́сять ~ноль to meet at exactly ten o'clock.

номенклату́р|а (-ы) *ж* (*товаров, услуг*) list ♦ *собир* (*номенклатурные работники*) nomenklatura.

номенклату́рный *прил* (*единица*) listed; **номенклату́рный рабо́тник** nomenklatura.

но́мер (-а; *nom pl* -а́) *м* number; (*журнала, газеты*) issue; (*перчаток*) size; (*в гостинице*) room; (*концерта*) number, turn; **но́мер маши́ны** registration (number).

номерка́ *сущ см* **номеро́к**.

номерно́й *прил* (*завод*) *identified only by a number*; **номерно́й знак** (*автомоби́ля*) (car) number (*BRIT*) *или* license (*US*) plate; **номерно́й счёт** (**в ба́нке**) numbered account.

номер|о́к (-ка́) *ж* (*для пальто*) ≈ ticket.

номина́л (-а) *м* (*КОММ*) face value.

номина́л|ьный (-ен, -ьна, -ьно) *прил* (*зарплата*) nominal; ~ьная цена́ face value.

но́нсенс (-а) *м* nonsense.

нор|а́ (-ы́; *nom pl* -ы) *ж* (*зайца*) burrow; (*лисы*) den; (*барсука*) set; (*перен*) hole.

Норве́ги|я (-и) *ж* Norway.

норве́ж|ец (-ца) *м* Norwegian.

норве́ж|ка (-ки; *gen pl* -ек) *ж см* **норве́жец**.

норве́жск|ий (-ая, -ое, -ие) *прил* Norwegian; ~ язы́к Norwegian.

норве́жца *итп сущ см* **норве́жец**.

но́р|ка (-ки; *gen pl* -ок) *ж* mink.

но́рковый *прил* mink *опред*.

но́рм|а (-ы) *ж* standard; (*выработки, прибыли*) rate; (*поведе́ния*) behavioural norm; **войти́** (*perf*) *или* **прийти́** (*perf*) **в** ~**у** (*в обычное состояние*) to return to normal; **он сего́дня в** ~**е** (*разг*) he's fine today.

норма́лен *прил см* **норма́льный**.

нормализа́ци|я (-и) *ж* normalization.

нормализ|ова́ть (-у́ю) (*не*)*сов перех* (*обстановку, отношения*) to normalize
▸ **нормализова́ться** (*не*)*сов возв* to stabilize.

норма́льно *нареч* normally ♦ *как сказ:* э́то вполне́ ~ this is quite normal; **как дела́? –** ~ how are things? – not bad; **у нас всё** ~ everything's fine with us.

норма́льность (-и) *ж* normality.

норма́льный (-ен, -ьна, -ьно) *прил* normal; (*психически*) of sound mind.

Норма́нди|я (-и) *ж* Normandy.

норма́тив (-а) *м* norm.

нормати́вный *прил* normative.

норми́ровани|е (-я) *ср* (*цен*) standardization; (*мяса*) rationing.

норми́р|овать (-ую) (*не*)*сов перех* to standardize.

норов|и́ть (-лю́, -и́шь) *несов неперех* (*разг*): ~ +*infin* to take pains to do.

но́рок *сущ см* **но́рка**.

нос (-а; *part gen* -у, *loc sg* -у́, *nom pl* -ы́) *м* nose; (*корабля*) bow; (*птицы*) beak, bill; (*ботинка*) toe; **из-под но́са** у +*gen* from under the nose of; **отъе́зд/экза́мен на** ~**у́** (*разг*) the departure/ exam is imminent; **под но́сом** (*разг: близко*) under one's (very) nose; **с но́сом оста́ться** (*perf*) (*разг*) to be left with nothing; **води́ть** (*impf*) **кого́-н за** ~ to lead sb by the nose; **он не ви́дит да́льше со́бственного но́са** (*разг*) he can't see further than his own nose; **сова́ть** (*impf*) ~ **в** +*acc* (*разг*) to poke *или* stick one's nose into.

носа́т|ый (-, -а, -о) *прил* with a big nose.

но́сик (-а) *м* (*человека*) small nose; (*чайника*) spout.

носи́л|ки (-ок) *мн* (*для раненых*) stretcher.

носи́льщик (-а) *м* porter.

носи́тел|ь (-я) *м* (*идей, прогресса*) bearer; (*инфекции*) carrier; (*данных, информации*) transmitter; **носи́тель языка́** native speaker.

носи́тельниц|а (-ы) *ж* (*идей, прогресса*) bearer.

нос|и́ть (-шу́, -сишь) *несов перех* (*вещи, камни*) to carry; (*платье, очки*) to wear; (*усы, бороду, причёску*) to sport; (*фамилию мужа*) to use; (*отличаться: подлеж: предложение, спор.*) to be characterized by; **на́ши отноше́ния но́сят делово́й хара́ктер** our relations are of a business nature; ~ (*impf*) **на рука́х** to carry; (*перен: любить*) to adore
▸ **носи́ться** *несов возв* (*человек*) to rush; (*слухи*) to spread; (*одежда*) to wear; (*разг: увлекаться*): ~**ся с** +*instr* (*с иде́ей*) to be preoccupied with; (*с челове́ком*) to make a fuss of; ~**ся** (*impf*) **в во́здухе** (*настроения*) to be in the air; (*идея*) to be widespread.

но́ск|а (-и) *ж* (*одежды, обуви*) wearing; **удо́бный в** ~**е** comfortable (to wear).

носка́ итп сущ см **носо́к**.
но́с|**кий** (-кая, -кое, -кие; -ок, -ка́, -ко) прил (туфли, ткань) hard-wearing.
носов|**о́й** прил (звук) nasal; ~**а́я часть** bow; **носово́й плато́к** handkerchief.
но́сок прил см **но́ский**.
носо́к (-ка́; gen pl -о́к) м (обычно мн: чулок) sock; (gen pl -ко́в; ботинка, чулка, ноги) toe; **встава́ть** (**встать** perf) **на** ~**ки́** to stand on tiptoe.
носоро́г (-а) м rhinoceros, rhino (inf).
ностальги́ческий (-ая, -ое, -ие) прил nostalgic.
ностальги́|**я** (-и) ж (по дому) homesickness, nostalgia; (по утраченному) nostalgia.
но́т|**а** (-ы) ж note; см также **но́ты**.
нотариа́льный прил (услуги) notarial; **нотариа́льная конто́ра** notarial office.
нота́риус (-а) м notary (public).
нота́ци|**я** (-и) ж (выговор) lecture.
но́тный прил: ~**ое письмо́** musical notation.
но́т|**ы** (-) мн (муз) sheet music; **как по** ~**ам** (перен) smoothly.
но́у-ха́у ср нескл know-how.
ноч|**ева́ть** (-у́ю; perf **переночева́ть**) несов неперех to spend the night.
ночёв|**ка** (-ки; gen pl -ок) ж: **останови́ться на** ~**ку** to spend the night; **они́ прие́хали с** ~**кой** they came and stayed the night.
ночле́г (-а) м (место) somewhere to spend the night; **останови́ться** (perf) **на** ~ to spend the night.
ночле́жный прил: ~ **дом** hostel.
ночни́к (-а́) м night-light.
ночн|**о́й** прил (час, холод) night опред; **ночна́я руба́шка** nightshirt; **ночна́я сме́на** night shift.
ноч|**ь** (-и; loc sg -и́, nom pl -и, gen pl -е́й) ж night; **с утра́ до** ~**и** from dawn to dusk; **на́** ~ before bed; **споко́йной но́чи!** good night!
но́чью нареч at night; **и днём и** ~ day and night.
но́ш|**а** (-и) ж burden.
ноше́ни|**е** (-я) ср (действие) wearing; ~ **ору́жия** (юр) carrying of offensive weapons.
но́шеный прил (одежда, туфли) second-hand.
ношу́(сь) несов см **носи́ть(ся)**.
но́ю итп несов см **ныть**.
ноя́бр|**ь** (-я́) м November; см также **октя́брь**.
ноя́брьский (-ая, -ое, -ие) прил November опред.
нрав (-а) м (человека) temperament; **э́то мне по нра́ву** this is to my liking; см также **нра́вы**.
нра́в|**иться** (-люсь, -ишься; perf **понра́виться**) несов возв (+dat): **мне** ~**ится э́тот фильм** I like this film; **мне** ~**ится чита́ть/гуля́ть** I like to read/go for a walk.
нравоуче́ни|**е** (-я) ср lecture on morals; (в басне) moral; **чита́ть** (impf) **кому́-н** ~**я** to give sb a lecture on morals.
нравоучи́тельный (-ен, -ьна, -ьно) прил (рассказ, история) with a moral; (тон) moralizing.

нра́вственность (-и) ж morals мн.
нра́вствен|**ный** (-, -на, -но) прил moral.
нра́в|**ы** (-ов) мн (обычаи) customs мн.
н.с. сокр (= но́вого сти́ля) NS (New Style).
НТР ж сокр = **нау́чно-техни́ческая револю́ция**.

ну межд **1** (выражает побуждение) come on; **ну, начина́й!** come on, get started!
2 (выражает восхищение) what; **ну и си́ла!** what strength!
3 (выражает иронию) well (well); **ну и у́мник же ты!** well (well), what a clever fellow you are!
♦ част **1** (неужели): **(да) ну?!** not really?!; **я женю́сь – да ну?!** I'm getting married – not really?!
2 (усиливает выразительность): **ну коне́чно** why of course!; **ну, я тебе́ покажу́!** why, I'll show you!
3 (допустим): **ты говори́шь по-англи́йски?- ну, говорю́** do you speak English? – what if I do
4 (во фразах): **ну и ну!** (разг) well well!; **ну-ка!** (разг) come on!; **ну тебя́/его́!** (разг) to hell with you/him!

нувори́ш (-а) м nouveau riche.
нуг|**а́** (-и́) ж nougat.
ну́ден прил см **ну́дный**.
нуди́ст (-а) м nudist.
нуди́ст|**ка** (-и) ж см **нуди́ст**.
ну́дно нареч tediously.
ну́д|**ный** (-ен, -на́, -но) прил tedious.
нужд|**а́** (-ы́; nom pl -ы) ж (no pl; бедность) poverty; (потребность): ~ (**в** +prp) need (for); **ну́жды населе́ния** the needs of the population; **в э́том нет** ~**ы́** there is no need for it.
нужда́|**ться** (-юсь) несов возв (бедствовать) to be needy; ~ (impf) **в** +prp to need, be in need of.
ну́жен прил см **ну́жный**.
ну́жно как сказ (необходимо): ~ **им помо́чь** или ~, **что́бы им помогли́** it is necessary to help them; ~ **хоро́шего специали́ста** a good specialist is needed; **мне** ~ **идти́** I have to go, I must go; **мне** ~ **10 рубле́й** I need 10 roubles; **о́чень** ~! (разг) my foot!
ну́жный (-ен, -на́, -но, -ны́) прил necessary.
нулев|**о́й** прил: ~**а́я температу́ра** temperature of zero; ~**а́я отме́тка** (mark of) zero; ~ **результа́т** no result.
нул|**ь** (-я́) м (мат) zero, nought; (при исчислении температуры) zero; (перен: человек) nothing; **начина́ть** (**нача́ть** perf) **с** ~**я́** to start from scratch; **своди́ться** (**свести́сь** perf) **к** ~**ю́** to come to nothing.
нумера́ци|**я** (-и) ж numbering.
нумер|**ова́ть** (-у́ю; perf **пронумерова́ть**) несов перех to number.
нумизма́т (-а) м numismatist.
нумизма́ти|**ка** (-и) ж numismatics.
ну́три|**я** (-и) ж (зоол) coypu.
нутр|**о́** (-а́) ср (разг: интуиция) instincts мн; **э́то**

мне не по ~у́ I'm not too keen on this.
НФ м сокр (= национа́льный фронт) NF (= *National Front*;) (= нау́чная фанта́стика) sci-fi, SF (= *science fiction*).
НХЛ ж сокр (= Национа́льная хокке́йная ли́га) NHL (= *National Hockey League*).
НЧ сокр (= ни́зкая частота́) LF (= *low frequency*) ◆ прил (низкочасто́тный) LF (= *low-frequency*).
ны́не нареч today.
ны́нешн|ий (-яя, -ее, -ие) прил (собы́тия, прави́тельство) the present; (молодёжь) today's; ~ее ле́то this summer.
ны́нче нареч (разг: сего́дня) today; (: тепе́рь) nowadays.
нырн|у́ть (-у́, -ёшь) сов неперех (также перен) to dive.
ныря́льщик (-а) м diver.
ныря́льщиц|а (-ы) ж см ныря́льщик.
ныря́|ть (-ю) несов неперех (также перен) to dive.
ныть (но́ю, но́ешь) несов неперех (ра́на, зуб) to ache; (жа́ловаться) to moan.

Нью-Йо́рк (-а) м New York.
н.э. сокр (= на́шей э́ры) AD (= *anno Domini*).
НЭП м сокр (ист: = но́вая экономи́ческая поли́тика) NEP (= *New Economic Policy*).
нюа́нс (-а) м nuance.
Ню́рнберг (-а) м Nuremberg.
нюх (-а) м (соба́ки) nose; (перен: разг): ~ на +acc nose for.
нюха́|ть (-ю; perf поню́хать) несов перех (цветы́, во́здух) to smell; (спирт) to sniff; ~ (impf) таба́к to take snuff.
ня́нек сущ см ня́нька.
ня́неч|ка (-ки; gen pl -ек) ж (разг) = ня́ня.
ня́нч|ить (-у, -ишь) несов перех to mind
► **ня́нчиться** несов возв: ~ся с +instr (с младе́нцем) to mind; (разг: с лентя́ем, с му́жем) to fuss over.
ня́н|ька (-ьки; gen pl -ек) ж (разг: ребёнка) nanny.
ня́н|я (-и; gen pl -ь) ж nanny; (рабо́тающая на дому́) child minder; (в больни́це) auxiliary nurse; (в де́тском саду́) cleaner; приходя́щая ~ babysitter.

~ O, o ~

O, o *сущ нескл* (*буква*) the 15th letter of the Russian alphabet.

o *предл* (+*prp*) about; (+*acc*; *опереться, удариться*) against; (*споткнуться*) over ◆ *межд* oh; **кни́га ~ Росси́и** a book on *или* about Russia; **мы́сли ~ до́ме** thoughts of home; **во́лны бью́тся ~ ска́лы** the waves are beating against the cliffs; **~ да/нет!** oh yes/no!; **~, е́сли бы ты знал!** oh, if only you knew!

o. *сокр* (= **о́стров**) I (= *island*); (= **о́зеро**) L (= *lake*).

о- *префикс* (*in verbs*; *сделать каким-нибудь*) *indicating change of state eg.* округли́ть; (*снабдить чем-н*) *indicating suppy of sth eg.* озагла́вить; (*распространить действие на всю поверхность*) *indicating covering of a surface with sth eg.* охвати́ть; (*распространить действие на многих*) *indicating action involving many people eg.* одари́ть.

оа́зис (-а) *м* (*также перен*) oasis.

ОАЕ *ж сокр* (= **Организа́ция африка́нского еди́нства**) OAU (= *Organization of African Unity*).

ОАПЕК *ж сокр* (= **Организа́ция ара́бских стран-экспортёров не́фти**) OAPEC (= *Organization of Arab Petroleum-Exporting Countries*).

об *предл* = **о**.

об- *префикс см* **о-**.

о́б|а (-**о́их**; *см* **Table 26**; *f* **о́бе**, *nt* **о́ба**) *м чис* both; **смотре́ть** (*impf*) **в ~** (*разг: быть осторожным*) to watch out; (*: быть внимательным*) to keep one's eyes peeled.

обалде́ть (-ю; *impf* **обалдева́ть**) *сов неперех* (*разг*) to go crazy.

обанкро́титься (-чусь, -тишься) *сов возв* to go bankrupt; (*перен: идея, политика*) to prove (to be) bankrupt.

обая́ни|е (-я) *ср* charm.

обая́тельный (-ен, -ьна, -ьно) *прил* charming.

обва́л (-а) *м* (*в шахте, в штольне*) rock fall; (*снежный*) avalanche; (*здания*) collapse.

обва́лива|ть (-ю) *несов от* **обваля́ть**.

обвал|и́ться (*3sg* -ится, *3pl* -ятся, *impf* **обва́ливаться**) *сов возв* to collapse; (*потолок, крыша*) to cave in.

обваля́|ть (-ю; *impf* **обва́ливать**) *сов перех*: **~ кого́-н/что-н в** +*prp* to roll sb/sth in.

обвар|и́ть (-ю́, -áришь; *impf* **обва́ривать**) *сов перех* to pour boiling water over; (*кулин*) to blanch; (*обжечь*) to scald

▶ **обвари́ться** (*impf* **обва́риваться**) *сов возв* (*обжечься*) to scald o.s.

обведу́ *итп сов см* **обвести́**.

обвенча́|ть (-ю; *impf* **венча́ть**) *сов перех* to marry

▶ **обвенча́ться** (*impf* **венча́ться**) *сов возв* to get married, marry.

обв|ести́ (-еду́, -едёшь; *pt* -ёл, -ела́, -ело́, *impf* **обводи́ть**) *сов перех* (*букву, чертёж*) to go over (*drawing, outline etc*); (*окаймить: заголовок, рисунок*) to edge; (*футболиста*) to pass (*while keeping possession of the ball/puck etc*); **обводи́ть** (**~** *perf*) **вокру́г** +*gen* (*стола, дома*) to lead *или* take round; **обводи́ть** (**~** *perf*) **что-н/кого́-н глаза́ми** to run one's eye over sth/sb; **~** (*perf*) **кого́-н вокру́г па́льца** (*разг*) to twist sb round one's little finger.

обве́тренный *прил* weather-beaten.

обве́тр|иться (-юсь, -ишься; *impf* **обве́триваться**) *сов возв* to become weather-beaten.

обветша́лый *прил* dilapidated.

обвива́|ть(ся) (-ю(сь)) *несов от* **обви́ть(ся)**.

обвине́ни|е (-я) *ср*: **~ (в** +*prp*) accusation (of); (*юр*) charge (of) ◆ *собир* (*обвиняющая сторона*) the prosecution; **свиде́тели ~я** witnesses for the prosecution.

обвини́тель (-я) *м* accuser; (*юр*) prosecutor.

обвини́тельный *прил* (*речь, выступление*) accusatory; **~ пригово́р** (*юр*) verdict of guilty; **~ акт** (*юр*) indictment.

обвин|и́ть (-ю́, -и́шь; *impf* **обвиня́ть**) *сов перех*: **~ кого́-н (в** +*prp*) to accuse sb (of); (*юр*) to charge sb (with).

обвиня́ем|ая (-ой; *decl like adj*) *ж см* **обвиня́емый**.

обвиня́ем|ый (-ого; *decl like adj*) *м* the accused *или* defendant.

обвиня́|ть (-ю) *несов от* **обвини́ть** ◆ *перех* (*юр*) to prosecute.

обвиса́|ть (*3sg* -ет, *3pl* -ют, *perf* **обви́снуть**) *несов неперех* to droop.

обви́слый *прил* (*раза: кожа*) sagging; (*: усы*) drooping; (*: тело*) flabby.

обви́с|нуть (*3sg* -нет, *3pl* -нут, *pt* -, -ла, -ло) *сов от* **обвиса́ть**.

обви́ть (-овью́, -овьёшь; *impf* **обвива́ть**) *сов перех* (*подлеж: плющ, вьюн*) to twine around; **обвива́ть** (~ *perf*) **кого́-н/что-н чем-н** to wind sth round sb/sth; **обвива́ть** (~ *perf*) **чью-н ше́ю рука́ми** to wrap one's arms around sb's neck
▶ **обви́ться** (*impf* **обвива́ться**) *сов возв*: ~**ся вокру́г** +*gen* to twine around.

обво|ди́ть (-ожу́, -о́дишь) *несов от* **обвести́**.

обводн|и́ть (-ю́, -и́шь; *impf* **обводня́ть**) *сов перех* to irrigate.

обво́дный *прил*: ~ **кана́л** *canal encircling a town*.

обводня́|ть (-ю) *несов от* **обводни́ть**.

обвожу́ *несов см* **обводи́ть**.

обвора́жива|ть (-ю) *несов от* **обворожи́ть**.

обвор|ова́ть (-у́ю; *impf* **обворо́вывать**) *сов перех* (*разг: квартиру*) to do over; (: *соседа*) to rob.

обворожи́тель|ный (-ен, -ьна, -ьно) *прил* captivating.

обворож|и́ть (-у́, -и́шь; *impf* **обвора́живать**) *сов перех* to captivate.

обвя|за́ть (-жу́, -жешь; *impf* **обвя́зывать**) *сов перех*: ~ **кого́-н/что-н чем-н** (*верёвкой, платком*) to tie sth round sb/sth; ~ (*perf*) **что-н спи́цами/крючко́м** to knit/crochet a border on sth
▶ **обвяза́ться** (*impf* **обвя́зываться**) *сов возв*: ~**ся чем-н** to tie sth round o.s.

обгл|ода́ть (-ожу́, -о́жешь; *impf* **обгла́дывать**) *сов перех* to pick clean.

обговор|и́ть (-ю́, -и́шь; *impf* **обгова́ривать**) *сов перех* (*разг*) to discuss.

обго́н (-а) *м* overtaking.

обгоню́ *итп сов см* **обогна́ть**.

обгоня́|ть (-ю) *несов от* **обогна́ть**.

обгора́|ть (-ю) *несов от* **обгоре́ть**.

обгоре́лый *прил* (*дом, дерево*) burnt; (*разг: спина, плечи*) sunburnt.

обгор|е́ть (-ю́, -и́шь; *impf* **обгора́ть**) *сов неперех* (*дом*) to be burnt; (*разг: на пожаре*) to get burnt; (: *на солнце*) to get sunburnt.

обгры́з|ть (-у́, -ёшь; *impf* **обгрыза́ть**) *сов перех* (*яблоко, кость*) to gnaw; **обгрыза́ть** (~ *perf*) **но́гти** to bite one's nails right down.

обдел|и́ть (-елю́, -е́лишь; *impf* **обделя́ть**) *сов перех*: **он** ~**ели́л её деньга́ми** he didn't give her the money; **приро́да** ~**ели́ла его́ умо́м/си́лой** he is not blessed with intelligence/strength; **всем да́ли пода́рки, а его́** ~**ели́ли** everybody got a present but he was left out.

обдеру́ *итп сов см* **ободра́ть**.

обдира́|ть (-ю) *несов от* **ободра́ть**.

обду́ман|ный (-, -на, -но) *прил* considered.

обду́ма|ть (-ю; *impf* **обду́мывать**) *сов перех* to consider, think over.

обдур|и́ть (-ю́, -и́шь; *impf* **обдуря́ть**) *сов перех*: ~ **кого́-н** (*разг: обмануть*) to pull the wool over

sb's eyes; (: *смошенничать*) to rip sb off.

об|е (-е́их) *ж чис см* **о́ба**.

обе́га|ть (-ю; *impf* **обега́ть**) *сов перех* (*разг*) to rush round.

обега́|ть (-ю) *несов от* **обе́гать**, **обежа́ть**.

обегу́ *итп сов см* **обежа́ть**.

обе́д (-а) *м* lunch, dinner; (*время*) lunch *или* dinner time; (*разг: перерыв*) lunch break; **за** ~**ом** at lunch *или* dinner; **по́сле** ~**а** after lunch *или* dinner; (*после 12 часов дня*) in the afternoon; **закры́т на** ~ closed for lunch.

обе́да|ть (-ю; *perf* **пообе́дать**) *несов неперех* to have lunch *или* dinner; (*разг: уходить на перерыв*) to take a lunch break.

обе́ден *сущ см* **обе́дня**.

обе́денный *прил* (*стол, сервиз*) dinner *опред*; (*часы, время*) lunch *опред*, dinner *опред*.

обедне́вш|ий (-ая, -ее, -ие) *прил* impoverished.

обедне́|ть (-ю) *сов от* **бедне́ть**.

обе́дн|я (-ни; *gen pl* -ен) *ж* (*РЕЛ*) Mass; **идти́** (**пойти́** *perf*) **к** ~**не** to go to Mass; **служи́ть** (*impf*) ~**ню** to hear Mass.

обежа́ть (*как* **бежа́ть**; *см* **Table 20**; *impf* **обега́ть**) *сов перех* (*разг: магазины*) to rush round ♦ *неперех*: ~ **вокру́г** +*gen* to run round.

обезбо́ливани|е (-я) *ж* anaesthetization (*BRIT*), anesthetization (*US*).

обезбо́лива|ть (-ю) *несов от* **обезбо́лить**.

обезбо́ливающ|ее (-его; *decl like adj*) *ср* (*разг*) painkiller.

обезбо́ливающ|ий (-ая, -ее, -ие) *прил* anaesthetic *опред* (*BRIT*), anesthetic *опред* (*US*).

обезбо́л|ить (-ю, -ишь; *impf* **обезбо́ливать**) *сов перех* to anaesthetize (*BRIT*), anesthetize (*US*); **обезбо́ливать** (~ *perf*) **кому́-н ро́ды** to give sb an anaesthetic (*BRIT*) *или* anesthetic (*US*) during childbirth.

обезво́|дить (-жу, -дишь; *impf* **обезво́живать**) *сов перех* (*землю*) to drain; (*организм*) to dehydrate.

обезво́жу *сов см* **обезво́дить**.

обезвре́|дить (-жу, -дишь; *impf* **обезвре́живать**) *сов перех* (*бомбу*) to defuse; (*воду*) to purify; (*преступника*) to make powerless.

обезгла́в|ить (-лю, -ишь; *impf* **обезгла́вливать**) *сов перех* to behead; (*перен: восстание*) to leave without a leader.

обездо́лен|ный (-, -на, -но) *прил* deprived.

обездо́л|ить (-ю, -ишь) *сов перех* to deprive.

обезжи́ренный *прил* fat-free.

обезжи́р|ить (-ю, -ишь; *impf* **обезжи́ривать**) *сов перех* (*молоко, творог*) to skim; (*шерсть*) to remove fat from.

обезли́ч|ить (-у, -ишь; *impf* **обезли́чивать**) *сов перех* to depersonalize; (*работу, руководство*) to remove individual responsibility from.

обезобра́|зить (-жу, -зишь; *impf*

обезобра́|живать) *сов перех* to disfigure.

обезопа́|сить (-шу, -сишь) *сов перех (себя, друга)* to protect

▸ **обезопа́ситься** *сов возв* to protect o.s.

обезору́ж|ить (-у, -ишь) *impf* **обезору́живать)** *сов перех (также перен)* to disarm.

обезу́ме|ть (-ю) *сов неперех:* ~ **от** +*gen (страха, горя итп)* to go out of one's mind with.

обезья́н|а (-ы) *ж (с хвостом)* monkey; *(без хвоста)* ape; *(перен: разг)* copycat.

обезья́н|ий (-ья, -ье, -ьи) *прил (хвост)* monkey's; *(повадки)* apelike.

обезья́нничать *impf* **собезья́нничать)** *несов неперех (разг)* to be a copycat.

обе́их *чис см* **о́бе.**

обе́й(те) *сов см* **оби́ть.**

обели́ск (-а) *м* obelisk.

обел|и́ть (-ю́, -и́шь; *impf* **обеля́ть)** *сов перех* to whitewash.

оберега́|ть (-ю) *несов перех (человека)* to protect; *(имущество)* to guard.

оберн|у́ть (-у́, -ёшь; *impf* **обёртывать** *или* **обора́чивать)** *сов перех (книгу, посылку)* to wrap (up); *(impf* **обора́чивать;** *капитал)* to turn over; **обёртывать** *или* **обора́чивать (~** *perf)* **что-н вокру́г** +*gen (талии, головы)* to wrap sth round; **обора́чивать (~** *perf)* **де́ло в свою́ по́льзу** *(перен)* to turn things to one's own advantage

▸ **оберн|у́ться (** *impf* **обора́чиваться)** *сов возв (повернуться назад)* to turn (round); *(капитал, деньги)* to be recovered; **обора́чиваться (~ся** *perf)* +*instr (неприятностями, сюрпризом)* to turn out to be; *(лебедем, волком)* to turn into.

обёрт|ка (-ки; *gen pl* **-ок)** *ж (книжная, конфетная)* wrapper; *(на посылке)* wrapping.

обёрточн|ый *прил:* ~**ая бума́га** wrapping paper.

обёртыва|ть (-ю) *несов от* **оберну́ть.**

оберу́(сь) *итп сов см* **обобра́ть(ся).**

обескро́в|ить (-лю, -ишь) *сов перех (перен)* to sap the strength of.

обескура́жен|ный (-, -на, -но) *прил* baffled.

обескура́ж|ить (-у, -ишь; *impf* **обескура́живать)** *сов перех (озадачить)* to baffle.

обеспе́чени|е (-я) *ср (мира, безопасности, договора)* guarantee; ~ +*instr (сырьём, продуктами)* provision of; **материа́льное** ~ financial security.

обеспе́ченност|ь (-и) *ж* (material) comfort; *(школ, завода итп)* provision; **фина́нсовая** ~ financial security.

обеспе́чен|ный (-, -на, -но) *прил* well-off, well-to-do.

обеспе́ч|ить (-у, -ишь; *impf* **обеспе́чивать)** *сов перех (семью)* to provide for; *(мир, успех)* to guarantee, ensure; **обеспе́чивать (~** *perf)* **кого-н/что-н чем-н** to provide *или* supply sb/sth with sth, provide *или* supply sth for sb/sth.

обеспоко́|ить (-ю, -ишь) *сов от* **беспоко́ить.**

обесси́ле|ть (-ю; *impf* **обесси́левать)** *сов неперех* to become *или* grow weak.

обесси́л|ить (-ю, -ишь; *impf* **обесси́ливать)** *сов перех* to weaken.

обессла́в|ить (-лю, -ишь) *сов перех* to besmirch.

обессме́рт|ить (-чу, -тишь) *сов перех* to immortalize.

обесто́ч|ить (-у, -ишь; *impf* **обесто́чивать)** *сов перех (ТЕХ)* to cut off the power to.

обесцве́|тить (-чу, -тишь; *impf* **обесцве́чивать)** *несов перех* to bleach; *(перен: рассказ)* to tone down

▸ **обесцве́|титься (** *impf* **обесцве́чиваться)** *сов возв* to be bleached; *(ткань: от времени)* to fade; *(перен: рассказ)* to become flat.

обесце́нивани|е (-я) *ср (валюты)* depreciation; *(: намеренное)* devaluation.

обесце́н|ить (-ю, -ишь; *impf* **обесце́нивать)** *сов перех (также перен)* to devalue

▸ **обесце́н|иться (** *impf* **обесце́ниваться)** *сов возв* to be devalued; *(вещь)* to depreciate.

обесче́|стить (-щу, -стишь) *сов от* **бесче́стить.**

обе́т (-а) *м* vow.

обетова́нн|ый *прил:* ~**ая земля́** the Promised Land.

обеща́ни|е (-я) *ср* promise.

обеща́|ть (-ю; *perf* **обеща́ть** *или* **пообеща́ть)** *несов (не)перех* to promise.

обжа́ловани|е (-я) *ср* appeal.

обжа́л|овать (-ую) *сов перех* to appeal against.

обжа́р|ить (-ю, -ишь; *impf* **обжа́ривать)** *сов перех* to brown.

обж|е́чь (-огу́, -ожжёшь *итп,* **-огу́т;** *pt* **-жёг, -огла́, -огло́)** *сов от* **жечь** ♦ *(impf* **обжига́ть)** *перех* to burn; *(кирпич итп)* to fire; *(дерево итп)* to scorch; *(подлеж: крапива)* to sting

▸ **обж|е́чься** *сов от* **же́чься** ♦ *(impf* **обжига́ться)** *возв* to burn o.s.; *(перен: потерпеть неудачу)* to get one's fingers burnt.

обжира́|ться (-юсь) *несов от* **обожра́ться.**

обжит|о́й *прил (дом)* lived-in.

обжо́р|а (-ы) *м/ж (разг)* pig, greedy guts.

обжо́рств|о (-а) *ср (разг)* greediness.

обжу́л|ить (-ю, -ишь; *impf* **обжу́ливать)** *сов перех (разг)* to con.

обзаве|сти́сь (-ду́сь, -дёшься; *impf* **обзаводи́ться)** *сов возв (+instr; разг)* to get o.s.

обзвон|и́ть (-ю́, -и́шь; *impf* **обзва́нивать)** *сов перех (разг)* to phone round.

обзову́ *итп сов см* **обозва́ть.**

обзо́р (-а) *м* view; *(статьи, новостей)* review.

обзо́рн|ый *прил* general; ~**ая статья́** review.

обзыва́|ть (-ю) *несов от* **обозва́ть**

▸ **обзыва́|ться** *несов возв (разг)* to call people names.

обива́|ть (-ю) *несов от* **оби́ть.**

оби́в|ка (-и) *ж* upholstery.

оби́д|а (-ы) *ж (несправедливость)* insult;

(*горечь*) grievance; **какáя ~!** what a pity!; **наносúть (нанестú** *perf*) **~у комý-н** to hurt *или* offend sb; **не давáть (дать** *perf*) **когó-н в ~у** (*раза*) to stand *или* stick up for sb; **быть** (*impf*) **в ~е на когó-н** to be in a huff with sb.

обйден *прил см* **обйдный**.

обйд|еть (-жу, -дишь; *impf* **обижáть**) *сов перех* to hurt, offend; **он ~жен умóм/красотóй** (*разг*) he's not too smart/good-looking

▸ **обйдеться** (*impf* **обижáться**) *сов возв*: **~ся (на** +*acc*) to be hurt *или* offended (by).

обйдно *как сказ* (*см прил*) it's offensive; it's annoying; **мне ~ слышать э́то** it hurts me to hear this; **~, что мы не встрéтились** it's annoying that we didn't meet.

обйдный (-ен, -на, -но) *прил* (*оскорбительный*) offensive; (*разг: досадный*) annoying.

обйдчивый (-, -а, -о) *прил* touchy.

обижáть(ся) (-ю(сь)) *несов от* **обйдеть(ся)**.

обйженный (-, -на, -но) *прил* aggrieved.

обйжу(сь) *сов см* **обйдеть(ся)**.

обйлен *прил см* **обйльный**.

обйли|е (-я) *ср* abundance.

обйльный (-ен, -ьна, -ьно) *прил* abundant; (+*instr*; *рыбой, талантами*) rich in; **~ьная едá** food in abundance.

обинякъ (-á) *м*: **без обинякóв** plainly.

обирáть (-ю) *несов от* **обобрáть**.

обитáемый (-, -а, -о) *прил* inhabited.

обитáтел|ь (-я) *м* inhabitant.

обитáть (-ю) *несов неперех* to live.

об|йть (-обью, -обьёшь; *imper* **обéй(те)**, *impf* **обивáть**) *сов перех*: **~** (+*instr*) to cover (with); **обивáть (~** *perf*) **порóги у когó-н** to camp on sb's doorstep.

обихóд (-а) *м*: **быть в ~е** to be in use; **входúть (войтú** *perf*) **в ~** to come into use; **выходúть (выйти** *perf*) **из ~а** to go out of use.

обихóдный (-ен, -на, -но) *прил* everyday.

обкатá|ть (-ю; *impf* **обкáтывать**) *сов перех* (*поверхность, дорогу*) to flatten (out); (*машину*) to run in; (*станок итп*) to test (out).

обкáт|ка (-и) *ж* (*дороги*) flattening; (*машины, станка*) testing.

обкáтыва|ть (-ю) *несов от* **обкатáть**.

обклáдыва|ть(ся) (-ю(сь)) *несов от* **обложúть(ся)**.

обклé|ить (-ю, -ишь; *impf* **обклéивать**) *сов перех* (*плакатами, бумагой*) to cover; (*обоями*) to (wall)paper.

обкóм (-а) *м сокр* = *областнóй комитéт*; (*профсоюза, партии*) ≈ regional committee.

обкрадý *итп сов см* **обокрáсть**.

обкрáдыва|ть (-ю) *несов от* **обокрáсть**.

обкур|úть (-урю, -ýришь; *impf* **обкýривать**) *сов перех* (*раза: комнату*) to fill with smoke; **ты меня совсéм ~урúл** your smoke is suffocating

me.

обкусá|ть (-ю; *impf* **обкýсывать**) *сов перех* to nibble; **обкýсывать (~** *perf*) **нóгти** to bite one's nails.

обл. *сокр* = **óбласть**.

обла́в|а (-ы) *ж* (*на преступников*) roundup; **устрóить** (*perf*) **~у на** +*acc* (*на зверя*) to close in on.

облагá|ть (-ю) *несов от* **обложúть**.

облагодéтельств|овать (-ую) *сов перех*: **~ когó-н** to do sb a great favour (*BRIT*) *или* favor (*US*).

облáдáтел|ь (-я) *м* possessor.

облáдá|ть (-ю) *несов неперех* (+*instr*) to possess; (*женщиной*) to have; **~** (*impf*) **здорóвьем** to enjoy good health; **~** (*impf*) **красотóй** to be beautiful.

облá|зить (-жу, -зишь) *сов перех* (*разг*) to go round.

облáива|ть (-ю) *несов от* **облáять**.

óблак|о (-а; *nom pl* **-á**, *gen pl* **-óв**) *ср* (*также перен*) cloud; **витáть** (*impf*) **в облакáх** to have one's head in the clouds.

облáмыва|ть(ся) (-ю(сь)) *несов от* **обломáть(ся)**.

обласкá|ть (-ю) *сов перех* to be kind to.

областнóй *прил* (*центр, театр*) ≈ regional, oblast *опред*; (*выражение, слово*) regional.

óбласт|ь (-и; *gen pl* **-éй**) *ж* region; (*АДМИН*) ≈ region, oblast; (*науки, искусства*) field; **в ~и** +*gen* (*в сфере*) in the field of.

óблачен *прил см* **óблачный**.

óблачность (-и) *ж* cloud.

óблач|ный (-ен, -на, -но) *прил* cloudy.

облá|ять (-ю; *impf* **облáивать**) *сов перех* to bark at; (*перен: разг*) to swear at.

облёг *итп сов см* **облéчь**.

облегá|ть (-ю) *несов от* **облéчь** ♦ *перех* to fit.

облегáющ|ий (-ая, -ее, -ие) *прил* close-fitting.

облегчá|ть (-ю) *несов от* **облегчúть**.

облегчéни|е (-я) *ср* (*условий труда, жизни*) improvement; (*успокоение*) relief.

облегчённо *нареч* with relief.

облегчённый *прил* (*ткань, инструмент*) light; (*труд, экзамен*) easier; (*ответ, улыбка*) relieved.

облегч|úть (-ý, -úшь; *impf* **облегчáть**) *сов перех* (*вес*) to lighten; (*экзамен, жизнь*) to make easier; (*боль, страдание*) to relieve; **облегчáть (~** *perf*) **дýшу** to ease one's mind.

обледенéлый *прил* (*ступени, горка*) icy; (*борода*) frozen.

обледенé|ть (-ю) *сов неперех* (*см прил*) to become icy; to freeze.

облезá|ть (-ю) *несов от* **облéзть**.

облéзлый *прил* (*разг: собака, птица*) mangy; (*вид, внешность*) scruffy; (*стены*) peeling.

облéз|ть (-у, -ешь; *impf* **облезáть**) *сов неперех*

(*разг*) to grow mangy; (*краска, обои*) to peel (off); (*стены*) to peel.

облёк *итп сов см* **облёчь.**

облека́|ть (-ю) *несов от* **облёчь.**

облеку́ *сов см* **облёчь.**

обл|ени́ться (-ено́сь, -е́нишься) *сов возв* to grow lazy.

обл|епи́ть (-еплю́, -е́пишь; *impf* **облепля́ть**) *сов перех* (*подлеж: грязь, глина*) to stick to; (*перен: подлеж: люди, мухи*) to surround; (*разг: покрыть*): ~ **что-н чем-н** to plaster sth with sth.

обле|те́ть (-чу́, -ти́шь; *impf* **облета́ть**) *сов перех* to fly round; (*новость*) to spread ♦ *неперех* (*листья*) to fall off.

облё|чь (-еку́, -ечёшь *итп*, -еку́т; *pt* -ёк, -екла́, -екло́, *impf* **облека́ть**) *сов перех*: ~ **кого-н/что-н чем-н** (*властью, доверием*) to vest sb/sth with sth; (*тайной*) to shroud sb/sth in sth; (*impf* **облега́ть**, *3sg* -**я́жет**, *3pl* -**я́гут**, *pt* -**ёг**, -**егла́**, -**егло́**) to envelop; **облека́ть** (~ *perf*) **что-н в** +*acc* to express sth in.

облива́|ть (-ю) *несов от* **обли́ть**

▶ **облива́ться** *несов от* **обли́ться** ♦ *возв*: ~**ся слеза́ми** to be in floods of tears; **у меня́ се́рдце кро́вью** ~**ется** my heart bleeds.

облига́ци|я (-и) *ж* (*комм*) debenture (bond); **премиа́льные** ~**и** premium bond; **прави́тельственные** ~**и** government stock.

обл|иза́ть (-ижу́, -и́жешь; *impf* **обли́зывать**) *сов перех* (*губы, ложку*) to lick; **пиро́г – па́льчики** ~**и́жешь** (*разг*) the pie is scrumptious

▶ **облиза́ться** (*impf* **обли́зываться**) *сов возв* (*человек*) to lick one's lips; (*собака, кошка*) to lick itself.

о́блик (-а) *м* (*внешний вид*) appearance; (*характер, также перен*) character.

облиня́|ть (-ю) *сов от* **линя́ть.**

обл|и́ть (-олью́, -ольёшь; *impf* **облива́ть**) *сов перех*: ~ **кого-н/что-н чем-н** (*намеренно*) to pour sth over sb/sth; (*случайно*) to spill sth over sb/sth; **облива́ть** (~ *perf*) **кого-н гря́зью** (*перен*) to throw mud at sb; **облива́ть** (~ *perf*) **кого-н презре́нием** to pour scorn on sb; **облива́ть** (~ *perf*) **что-н слеза́ми** to shed tears over sth

▶ **обли́ться** (*impf* **облива́ться**) *сов возв*: ~**ся** +*instr* (*водой*) to sluice o.s. with; (*соком*) to spill over o.s.; **облива́ться** (~**ся** *perf*) **по́том** to be bathed in sweat.

облицева́|ть (-ую; *impf* **облицо́вывать**) *сов перех*: ~ **что-н чем-н** to face sth with sth.

облицо́вк|а (-и) *ж* facing.

облицо́выва|ть (-ю) *несов от* **облицева́ть.**

облича́|ть (-ю) *несов от* **обличи́ть.**

обличи́тельный (-ен, -ьна, -ьно) *прил* damning.

облич|и́ть (-у́, -и́шь; *impf* **облича́ть**) *сов перех* to expose.

обло́жек *сущ см* **обло́жка.**

обложе́ни|е (-я) *ср* (*действие: налогом итп*) imposition; (*сбор*) levy.

обл|ожи́ть (-ожу́, -о́жишь; *impf* **облага́ть**) *сов перех*: ~**нало́гом** to tax; (*impf* **обкла́дывать**) to surround; (*печь*) to face; (*подлеж: тучи, облака*) to cover; (*разг: обругать*) to swear at; **го́рло** ~**ожи́ло** my throat is furred

▶ **обложи́ться** (*impf* **обкла́дываться**) *сов возв*: ~**ся** +*instr* to surround o.s. with.

обло́жк|а (-ки; *gen pl* -ек) *ж* (*книги, тетради*) cover; (*для паспорта итп*) holder.

облок|оти́ться (-очу́сь, -о́тишься; *impf* **облока́чиваться**) *сов возв*: ~ **на** +*acc* to lean on (*with elbows*).

облома́|ть (-ю; *impf* **обла́мывать**) *сов перех* (*ветки, ногти итп*) to break off; (*перен: разг*): ~ **кого-н** to talk sb round

▶ **облома́ться** (*impf* **обла́мываться**) *сов возв* (*ветка, ногти итп*) to break off.

обло́м|ок (-ка) *м* fragment.

обл|упи́ть (-уплю́, -у́пишь) *сов от* **лупи́ть** ♦ (*impf* **облу́пливать**) *перех* to peel

▶ **облупи́ться** *сов от* **лупи́ться** ♦ (*impf* **облу́пливаться**) *возв* (*разг*) to peel.

облу́пленн|ый *прил* (*разг*) peeling; **знать** (*impf*) **кого-н как** ~**ого** (*разг*) to know sb inside out.

облу́плива|ть(ся) (-ю(сь)) *несов от* **облупи́ть(ся).**

облуплю́(сь) *сов см* **облупи́ть(ся).**

облуча́|ть(ся) (-ю(сь)) *несов от* **облучи́ть(ся).**

облуче́ни|е (-я) *ср* irradiation.

облуч|и́ть (-у́, -и́шь; *impf* **облуча́ть**) *сов перех* to irradiate

▶ **облучи́ться** (*impf* **облуча́ться**) *сов возв* to be irradiated.

облущ|и́ть (-у́, -и́шь) *сов от* **лущи́ть.**

облысе́|ть (-ю) *сов от* **лысе́ть.**

облюб|ова́ть (-у́ю; *impf* **облюбо́вывать**) *сов перех* to choose.

обля́жет *итп сов см* **облёчь.**

обма́|зать (-жу, -жешь; *impf* **обма́зывать**) *сов перех*: ~ **кого-н/что-н чем-н** to coat sb/sth with sth; (*разг: испачкать*) to get sb/sth covered in sth.

обмакну́|ть (-у́, -ёшь; *impf* **обма́кивать**) *сов перех*: ~ **что-н в** +*acc* to dip sth into.

обма́н (-а) *м* deception; ~ **зре́ния** optical illusion.

обма́нный *прил* fraudulent; **обма́нным путём** fraudulently.

обм|ану́ть (-ану́, -а́нешь; *impf* **обма́нывать**) *сов перех* to deceive; (*поступить нечестно*) to cheat; (*не выполнить обещание*) to fail

▶ **обману́ться** (*impf* **обма́нываться**) *сов возв*: ~**ся в** +*prp* to be disappointed in.

обма́нчив|ый (-, -а, -о) *прил* deceptive.

обма́нщик (-а) *м* cheat.

обма́нщиц|а (-ы) *ж см* **обма́нщик.**

обма́нываіть(ся) (-ю(сь)) *несов от* **обману́ть(ся).**

обма́тыва|ть(ся) (-ю(сь)) *несов от* **обмота́ть(ся).**

обмахну́ть (-у́, -ёшь; *impf* **обма́хивать**) *сов*
перех (*пыль*) to brush off; (*стол*) to wipe down;
обма́хивать (~ *perf*) **лицо́ ве́ером** to fan one's
face *или* o.s.

▶ **обмахну́ться** (*impf* **обма́хиваться**) *сов возв*:
~**ся ве́ером** to fan o.s.

обмеле́ть (-ю) *сов от* **меле́ть**.

обме́н (-а) *м* (*также экон*) exchange;
(*докуме́нтов*) renewal; (*также:* ~ **веще́ств**:
био) metabolism; (*также:* ~ **жилпло́щадью**)
exchange (*of flats etc*); **в** ~ **на** +*acc* in exchange
for.

обменя́ть (-ю) *impf* **обме́нивать**) *сов перех*
(*ве́щи, биле́ты*) to change

▶ **обменя́ться** (*impf* **обме́ниваться**) *сов возв*:
~**ся** +*instr* to exchange.

обме́рить (-ю, -ишь; *impf* **обме́ривать**) *сов*
перех (*участок итп*) to measure.

обмести́ (-ту́, -тёшь; *impf* **обмета́ть**) *сов перех*
(*песок, паутину*) to brush away.

обм|ета́ть (-ечу́, -е́тишь; *impf* **обмётывать**) *сов*
перех to oversew ♦ *безл* (*разг*): **гу́бы** ~**ета́ло**
my lips are chapped.

обмету́ *итп сов см* **обмести́**.

обмётыва|ть (-ю) *несов от* **обмета́ть**.

обмечу́ *сов см* **обмета́ть**.

обмола́чива|ть (-ю) *несов от* **обмолоти́ть**.

обмо́лв|иться (-люсь, -ишься) *сов возв* (*разг*:
сказать невзначай) to slip in; (: *оговориться*)
to slip up; **сло́вом не** ~ (*perf*) (*разг*) to keep
mum.

обмоло́т (-а) *м* (*действие*) threshing;
(*количество*) yield (*from threshing*).

обмол|оти́ть (-очу́, -о́тишь; *impf*
обмола́чивать) *сов перех* to thresh.

обморо́зить (-жу, -зишь; *impf* **обмора́живать**)
сов перех: ~ **но́гу/ру́ку** to get frostbite in one's
foot/hand

▶ **обморо́зиться** (*impf* **обмора́живаться**) *сов*
возв to suffer from frostbite.

о́бморок (-а) *м* faint; **па́дать** (**упа́сть** *perf*) **в** ~
to faint.

обмота́|ть (-ю; *impf* **обма́тывать**) *сов перех*: ~
кого́-н/что-н чем-н to wrap sth round sb/sth;
(*обвить*): ~ **что-н вокру́г** +*gen* (*пальца,*
столба) to wind sth round

▶ **обмота́ться** (*impf* **обма́тываться**) *сов возв*:
~**ся вокру́г** +*gen* to be wound round;
обма́тываться (~**ся** *perf*) +*instr* (*разг*: *шарфом,*
одеялом) to wrap o.s. in.

обмо́тк|а (-и) *ж* (*элек*) winding.

обмо́ю *итп сов см* **обмы́ть**.

обмундирова́ни|е (-я) *ср* (*воен*: *действие*)
fitting out; (*комплект одежды*) uniform.

обмундир|ова́ть (-у́ю; *impf*
обмундиро́вывать) *сов перех* to fit out.

обм|ы́ть (-о́ю, -о́ешь; *impf* **обмыва́ть**) *сов*
перех (*рану*) to bathe; (*разг: событие, премию*)

to celebrate (*by drinking*).

обнагле́|ть (-ю) *сов от* **нагле́ть**.

обнадёж|ить (-у, -ишь; *impf* **обнадёживать**)
сов перех to reassure; (*обещать*) to assure.

обнажа́|ть(ся) (-ю(сь)) *несов от*
обнажи́ть(ся).

обнажённый (-ён, -ена́, -ено́) *прил* bare;
(*корни*) exposed.

обнаж|и́ть (-у́, -и́шь; *impf* **обнажа́ть**) *сов перех*
to expose; (*руки, ноги*) to bare; (*ветки*) to strip
bare; (*шпагу, меч*) to draw

▶ **обнажи́ться** (*impf* **обнажа́ться**) *сов возв* to be
exposed; (*человек*) to strip; (*рука, нога итп*) to
be bared; (*лес, дерево*) to become bare.

обнаро́дование (-я) *ср* (*см глаг*) publication;
promulgation.

обнаро́д|овать (-ую) *сов перех* (*факты,*
статью) to make public; (*закон, указ*) to
promulgate.

обнару́ж|ить (-у, -ишь; *impf* **обнару́живать**)
сов перех (*найти*) to find; (*проявить*) to show;
(*раскрыть*) to reveal

▶ **обнару́житься** (*impf* **обнару́живаться**) *сов*
возв (*найтись*) to be found; (*проявиться*) to
show; (*стать явным*) to become evident.

обна́шива|ться (-юсь) *несов от* **обноси́ться**.

обн|ести́ (-есу́, -есёшь; *pt* -ёс, -есла́, -есло́, *impf*
обноси́ть) *сов перех*: ~ **что-н/кого́-н вокру́г**
+*gen* to carry sth/sb round; (*огородить*): ~
что-н чем-н to surround sth with sth; **обноси́ть**
(~ *perf*) **кого́-н чем-н** (*вином*) to serve sb with
sth.

обнима́|ть(ся) (-ю(сь)) *несов от* **обня́ть(ся)**.

обни́мк|а *ж*: **в** ~**у** (*разг*) with their arms around
each other.

обниму́(сь) *итп сов см* **обня́ть(ся)**.

обнища́|ть (-ю) *сов от* **нища́ть**.

обнов|и́ть (-лю́, -и́шь; *impf* **обновля́ть**) *сов*
перех (*оборудование, гардероб*) to replenish;
(*репертуар, знания*) to refresh; (*памятник,*
дом) to renovate; (*жизнь, искусство*) to
revitalize; (*разг: платье*) to christen

▶ **обнови́ться** (*impf* **обновля́ться**) *сов возв*
(*оборудование, гардероб*) to be replenished;
(*репертуар*) to be refreshed; (*организм,*
природа) to be regenerated; (*жизнь, искусство*)
to be revitalized.

обновле́ние (-я) *ср* (*см возв*) replenishment;
refreshment; regeneration; revitalization.

обновлю́(сь) *сов см* **обнови́ть(ся)**.

обновля́|ть(ся) (-ю(сь)) *несов от*
обнови́ть(ся).

обн|оси́ть (-ошу́, -о́сишь) *несов от* **обнести́**.

обн|оси́ться (-ошу́сь, -о́сишься; *impf*
обна́шиваться) *сов возв* (*разг: старик,*
ребёнок) to wear out one's clothes; (: *одежда*) to
become worn to bits.

обно́ск|и (-ов) *мн* old clothes *мн*.

обношу́(сь) *несов см* **обноси́ть(ся).**
обню́ха|ть (-ю; *impf* **обню́хивать**) *сов перех* to sniff.
обня́ть (-иму́, -и́мешь; *pt* -ял, -яла́, -яло, *impf* **обнима́ть**) *сов перех* to embrace
▶ **обня́ться** (*impf* **обнима́ться**) *сов возв* to embrace (each other).
обо *предл см* **о.**
об|обра́ть (-еру́, -ерёшь; *impf* **обира́ть**) *сов перех* (*смородину, черешню*) to pick; (*разг: прохожего, клиента*) to fleece
▶ **обобра́ться** *сов возв*: **забо́т не ~ерёшься** (*разг*) no end of worries.
обобща́ть (-ю) *несов от* **обобщи́ть.**
обобще́ни|е (-я) *ср* generalization.
обобщённ|ый (-, -на́, -но) *прил* general.
обобществ|и́ть (-лю́, -и́шь; *impf* **обобществля́ть**) *сов перех* (*производство, хозяйство*) to socialize; (*землю, труд*) to collectivize.
обобществле́ни|е (-я) *ср* socialization.
обобществлю́ *сов см* **обобществи́ть.**
обобществля́|ть (-ю) *несов от* **обобществи́ть.**
обобщ|и́ть (-у́, -и́шь; *impf* **обобща́ть**) *сов перех* (*результаты, факты*) to generalize from; (*статью, выступление*) to summarize.
обобью́ *итп сов см* **обви́ть.**
обовью́(сь) *итп сов см* **обви́ть(ся).**
обога|ти́ть (-щу́, -ти́шь; *impf* **обогаща́ть**) *сов перех* to enrich; (*руду*) to concentrate
▶ **обогати́ться** (*impf* **обогаща́ться**) *сов возв* (*человек, страна*) to be enriched; (*почва, руда*) to be concentrated.
об|огна́ть (-гоню́, -го́нишь; *impf* **обгоня́ть**) *сов перех* to overtake; (*перен*) to outstrip.
обогн|у́ть (-у́, -ёшь; *impf* **огиба́ть**) *сов перех* (*стол, дом*) to go round.
обогре́в (-а) *м* heating.
обогре́|ть (-ю; *impf* **обогрева́ть**) *сов перех* (*помещение*) to heat; (*замёрзших*) to warm; (*перен: приласкать*) to be kind to
▶ **обогре́ться** (*impf* **обогрева́ться**) *сов возв* (*согреться: человек*) to warm o.s.; (*помещение*) to heat up; (*душа*) to be warmed.
о́бод (-ода; *nom pl* -о́дья, *gen pl* -о́дьев) *м* rim; (*ракетки*) frame.
ободо́к (-ка́) *м уменьш от* **о́бод**; (*на рисунке, платье*) border.
обо́дран|ный (-, -а, -о) *прил* (*стена*) stripped; (*дом, одежда*) shabby; (*руки*) scratched; (*колени*) skinned.
об|одра́ть (-деру́, -дерёшь; *impf* **обдира́ть**) *сов перех* (*кору, шкуру*) to strip; (*руки*) to scratch; (*колени*) to skin; (*перен: разг: покупателя, клиента*) to fleece.
ободре́ни|е (-я) *ср* encouragement.
ободри́тельный (-ен, -ьна, -ьно) *прил* encouraging.
ободр|и́ть (-ю́, -и́шь; *impf* **ободря́ть**) *сов перех* to encourage.

обожа́|ть (-ю) *несов перех* to adore; ~ (*impf*) **что-н/+***infin* (*разг*) to adore sth/doing.
обожгу́(сь) *итп сов см* **обже́чь(ся).**
обожеств|и́ть (-лю́, -и́шь; *impf* **обожествля́ть**) *сов перех* to worship.
обожествле́ни|е (-я) *ср* worship.
обожествлю́ *сов см* **обожестви́ть.**
обожествля́|ть (-ю) *несов от* **обожестви́ть.**
обожжёшь(ся) *итп сов см* **обже́чь(ся).**
обожр|а́ться (-у́сь, -ёшься; *pt* -а́лся, -ала́сь, -ало́сь, *impf* **обжира́ться**) *сов возв* (*разг*) to stuff o.s.
обо́з (-а) *м* convoy.
об|озва́ть (-зову́, -зовёшь; *impf* **обзыва́ть**) *сов перех*: ~ **кого́-н кем-н** (*разг*) to call sb sth.
обозл|и́ть(ся) (-ю́(сь), -и́шь(ся)) *сов от* **злить(ся).**
обозна́|ться (-юсь) *сов возв* (*разг*) to be mistaken.
обознача́|ть (-ю) *несов от* **обозна́чить** ◆ *перех* (*о знаках*) to signify
▶ **обознача́ться** *несов от* **обозна́читься.**
обозначе́ни|е (-я) *ср* (*границы, направления*) marking; (*на карте, в тексте итп*) symbol.
обозна́ч|ить (-у, -ишь; *impf* **обознача́ть**) *сов перех* (*границу, направление*) to mark; (*no impf*): ~ **что-н** (*нос, черты лица*) to make sth stand out
▶ **обозна́читься** (*impf* **обознача́ться**) *сов возв* to appear; (*становиться ощутимым*) to become noticeable.
обозрева́тель (-я) *м* (*событий*) observer; (*на радио и телевидении*) editor; **междунаро́дный/полити́ческий** ~ international/political editor.
обозре́ни|е (-я) *ср* review; (*представление*) revue.
обозри́м|ый (-, -а, -о) *прил* (*пространство*) visible; (*события*) observable; **~ое бу́дущее** the foreseeable future.
обо́|и (-ев) *мн* wallpaper *ед*.
обо́их *чис см* **о́ба.**
обойду́(сь) *итп сов см* **обойти́(сь).**
обо́йм|а (-ы) *ж* (*воен*) (cartridge) clip; (*тех*) ring, hoop; (*перен: вопросов, аргументов*) round.
обо|йти́ (*как* **идти́**; *см* **Table 18**; *impf* **обходи́ть**) *сов перех* to go round; (*пройти стороной: лужу, канаву*) to skirt, go round; (*перен: вопрос, тему*) to skirt; (: *закон, указ*) to get round; (*обогнать*) to pass; (*перен: обмануть*) to take in; **обходи́ть** (~ *perf*) **что-н молча́нием** to ignore
▶ **обойти́сь** (*impf* **обходи́ться**) *сов возв* (*уладиться*) to turn out; (*стоить*): **~сь в** +*acc* to cost; **обходи́ться** (**~сь** *perf*) **с кем-н/чем-н** to treat sb/sth; **обходи́ться** (**~сь** *perf*) +*instr* (*разг*) to get by with; **обходи́ться** (**~сь** *perf*) **без** +*gen* (*разг*) to get by without; (*без скандала*) to be settled without.
об|окра́сть (-краду́, -крадёшь; *impf*

обкра́дывать) *сов перех* to rob.
оболг|а́ть (-гу́, -жёшь; *pt* -га́л, -гала́, -га́ло) *сов перех* (*разг: человека*) to slander.
оболо́ч|ка (-ки; *gen pl* -ек) *ж* (*плода*) pericarp; (*зерна*) testa, (seed) coat; (*Земли*) crust; (*перен: человека*) shell; (: *вопроса*) surface; (*аэростата*) hull; **сли́зистая** ~ mucous membrane.
обо́лтус (-а) *м* (*разг*) waster.
оболь|сти́ть (-щу́, -сти́шь; *impf* **обольща́ть**) *сов перех* (*соблазнить*) to seduce; (*увлечь*) to captivate.
обольща́|ться (-юсь) *несов возв* to be under a delusion.
обольщу́ *сов см* **обольсти́ть**.
обольью́(сь) *итп сов см* **обли́ть(ся)**.
обомле́|ть (-ю) *сов неперех* (*разг*) to freeze.
обоня́ни|е (-я) *ср* sense of smell.
обопру́сь *итп сов см* **опере́ться**.
обора́чиваемост|ь (-и) *ж* (*КОММ*) turnover.
обора́чива|ть(ся) (-ю(сь)) *несов от* **оберну́ть(ся)**.
обора́н|ец (-ца) *м* (*разг*) scruff.
обо́рван|ный (-, -а, -о) *прил* (*разг: одежда*) tattered; (: *рассказ, мысли*) fragmented.
оборва́нца *итп сущ см* **оборва́нец**.
оборв|а́ть (-у́, -ёшь; *pt* -а́л, -ала́, -а́ло, *impf* **обрыва́ть**) *сов перех* (*верёвку, нитку*) to break, snap; (*ягоды, цветы*) to pick; (*перен: разговор, дружбу*) to break off; (: *разг: говорящего*) to cut short
▸ **оборва́ться** (*impf* **обрыва́ться**) *сов возв* (*верёвка, нитка*) to break, snap; (*со скалы*) to fall; (*перен: жизнь, разговор, дружба*) to be cut short suddenly.
обо́р|ка (-ки; *gen pl* -ок) *ж* frill.
оборо́н|а (-ы) *ж* defence (*BRIT*), defense (*US*); (*линия сооружений*) defences *мн* (*BRIT*), defenses *мн* (*US*); **занима́ть (заня́ть** *perf*) ~у to take up a defensive position; **держа́ть** (*impf*) ~у to hold the defence.
оборо́нный *прил* (*промышленность*) defence *опред*, defense *опред* (*US*).
обороноспосо́бност|ь (-и) *ж* defence (*BRIT*) *или* defense (*US*) capacity.
обороня́|ть (-ю) *несов перех* to defend
▸ **обороня́ться** *несов возв* (*защищаться*) to defend o.s.
оборо́т (-а) *м* (*полный круг*) revolution; (*КОММ*) turnover; (*обратная сторона*) back; (*перен: поворот событий*) turn; (*судов, вагонов*) turnaround; (*словесное выражение*) turn of phrase; **в** ~е in use; **входи́ть (войти́** *perf*) **в** ~ to come into use; **пуска́ть (пусти́ть** *perf*) **в** ~ (*деньги*) to put into circulation; (*средства, сбережения*) to invest; **брать (взять** *perf*) **кого́-н в** ~ (*разг*) to take sb in hand.
оборо́тлив|ый (-, -а, -о) *прил* resourceful.

оборо́тный *прил* (*КОММ*) working *опред*.
обору́дование (-я) *ср* (*действие: завода*) equipping; (*предметы*) equipment; (*КОМП*) hardware.
обору́д|овать (-ую) (*не)сов перех* to equip.
обоснова́ни|е (-я) *ср* (*действие: теории*) substantiation; (*довод*) basis.
обосно́ван|ный (-, -на, -но) *прил* substantiated; ~ **изно́с** (*КОММ*) fair wear and tear.
обосн|ова́ть (-у́ю; *impf* **обосно́вывать**) *сов перех* (*теорию, вывод*) to substantiate
▸ **обоснова́ться** (*impf* **обосно́вываться**) *сов возв* (*расположиться*) to be (situated); (*разг: прочно устроиться*) to settle.
обосо́б|ить (-лю, -ишь; *impf* **обособля́ть**) *сов перех* to set apart; (*предложение*) to detach
▸ **обосо́биться** (*impf* **обособля́ться**) *сов возв* (*от коллектива, от семьи*) to alienate o.s.
обосо́блен|ный (-, -на, -но) *прил* (*дом, также линг*) detached; (*комната*) separate; (*жизнь*) solitary.
обосо́блю(сь) *сов см* **обосо́бить(ся)**.
обособля́|ть(ся) (-ю(сь)) *несов от* **обосо́бить(ся)**.
обостре́ни|е (-я) *ср* (*см глаг*) sharpening; intensification; aggravation; straining.
обостр|и́ть (-ю́, -и́шь; *impf* **обостря́ть**) *сов перех* to sharpen; (*желания, конфликт*) to intensify; (*боль, какое-нибудь чувство*) to aggravate; (*отношения*) to strain
▸ **обостри́ться** (*impf* **обостря́ться**) *сов возв* to sharpen; (*желание, разногласия*) to intensify; (*боль, какое-нибудь чувство*) to become more acute; (*отношения*) to become strained.
оботру́(сь) *итп сов см* **обтере́ть(ся)**.
обо́чин|а (-ы) *ж* verge.
обошёл(ся) *итп сов см* **обойти́(сь)**.
обошью́ *итп сов см* **обши́ть**.
обою́д|ный (-ен, -на, -но) *прил* mutual.
обрабо́та|ть (-ю; *impf* **обраба́тывать**) *сов перех* (*камень*) to cut; (*кожу*) to cure; (*деталь: на станке*) to turn; (*статью, песню*) to polish up; (*землю, поле*) to till; (*перен: разг: человека*) to work on.
обрабо́т|ка (-ки; *gen pl* -ок) *ж* (*см глаг*) cutting; curing; turning; polishing up; tilling; (*перен: человека*) influencing; ~ **да́нных** (*КОМП*) computing; **пла́та за** ~**ку** (*КОММ*) handling charge.
обра́д|овать(ся) (-ую(сь)) *сов от* **ра́довать(ся)**.
о́браз (-а) *м* image; (*человека, зверя*) appearance; (*ЛИТЕРАТУРА*) figure; (*жизни, мыслей*) way; (*икона*) icon; **каки́м** ~**ом?** in what way?; **таки́м** ~**ом** in this way; (*следовательно*) consequently; **гла́вным** ~**ом** mainly; **ра́вным** ~**ом** similarly; **не́которым** ~**ом** to some extent.

о́бразен *прил см* **о́бразный**.

образ|е́ц (-ца́) *м* (*ткани, изделий, оружия*) sample; (*скромности, мужества, также TEX*) model.

образ|ный (-ен, -на, -но) *прил* vivid; **о́бразное выраже́ние** (*ЛИНГ*) figure of speech.

образова́ни|е (-я) *ср* formation; (*получение знаний*) education.

образо́ван|ный (-, -на, -но) *прил* educated.

образ|ова́ть (-у́ю) *impf* **образова́ть** *или* **образо́вывать**) *сов перех* to form

▶ **образова́ться** (*impf* **образова́ться** *или* **образо́вываться**) *сов возв* (*трещина, опухоль*) to form; (*группа, комиссия*) to be formed; (*разг: уладиться*) to turn out all right.

образу́м|ить (-лю, -ишь) *сов перех*: ~ **кого́-н** to make sb see sense

▶ **образу́миться** *сов возв* (*стать благоразумным*) to come to one's senses.

образца́ *итп сущ см* **образе́ц**.

образцо́в|ый (-, -а, -о) *прил* exemplary.

обраст|и́ (-у́, -ёшь; *pt* **обро́с, обросла́, обросло́**, *impf* **обраста́ть**) *сов неперех*: ~ +*instr* (*травой, деревьями*) to become overgrown with; (*разг: волосами, грязью*) to be covered in; (: *хозяйством, барахлом*) to surround o.s. with.

обрати́м|ый (-, -а, -о) *прил* reversible.

обра|ти́ть (-щу́, -ти́шь; *impf* **обраща́ть**) *сов перех* (*взгляд, мысли*) to turn; **обраща́ть** (~ *perf*) **кого́-н/что-н в** +*acc* to turn sb/sth into; **обраща́ть** (~ *perf*) **внима́ние на** +*acc* to pay attention to; **обраща́ть** (~ *perf*) **кого́-н в бе́гство** to force sb to take flight; **обраща́ть** (~ *perf*) **кого́-н в свою́ ве́ру** to convert sb to one's own faith

▶ **обрати́ться** (*impf* **обраща́ться**) *сов возв* (*подлеж: взгляд*) to turn; (*с вопросом*) to inquire; (*превратиться*): ~**ся в** +*acc* to turn into; **обраща́ться** (~**ся** *perf*) **к** +*dat* (*к врачу итп*) to consult; (*к зрителям*) to address; **обраща́ться** (~**ся** *perf*) **в суд** to go to court; **обраща́ться** (~**ся** *perf*) **в бе́гство** to take flight.

обра́тно *нареч* back; **туда́ и** ~ there and back; **биле́т туда́ и** ~ return ticket (*BRIT*), round-trip ticket (*US*).

обра́тн|ое (-ого; *decl like adj*) *ср* the opposite; **убежда́ть** (**убеди́ть** *perf*) **кого́-н в** ~**ом** to convince sb of the opposite.

обра́тн|ый *прил* (*порядок, движение, мысль*) reverse; (*дорога, путь*) return **опред; на** ~**ом пути́** on the way back; **в** ~**ую сто́рону** in the opposite direction; **в** ~**ом направле́нии** the other way; **обра́тная сторона́** reverse (side); **обра́тный а́дрес** return address; **обра́тный биле́т** return (*BRIT*) *или* round-trip (*US*) ticket.

обраща́|ть (-ю) *несов от* **обрати́ть**

▶ **обраща́ться** *несов от* **обрати́ться** ♦ *возв* (*деньги, товар*) to circulate; ~**ся** (*impf*) **с** +*instr* (*применять*) to use; (*уметь справляться*) to handle; (*с человеком*) to treat.

обраще́ни|е (-я) *ср* address; (*ЭКОН*) circulation;

~ **к** +*dat* (*к народу итп*) address to; ~ **с** +*instr* (*с прибором, с огнём*) handling of; (*с животными, с больным*) treatment of; **находи́ться** (*impf*) **в** ~**и** to be in circulation.

обращу́(сь) *сов см* **обрати́ть(ся)**.

обре́жу *итп сов см* **обре́зать**.

обре́з (-а) *м* (*книги, альбома*) edge; (*оружие*) sawn-off (*BRIT*) *или* sawed-off (*US*) shotgun; **вре́мени/де́нег в** ~ (*разг*) there's just enough time/money.

обре́|зать (-жу, -жешь; *impf* **обреза́ть**) *сов перех* to trim; (*разг: прервать*) to cut short; (*РЕЛ*) to circumcise.

обре́з|ок (-ка) *м* scrap.

обрёк *итп сов см* **обре́чь**.

обрека́|ть (-ю) *несов от* **обре́чь**.

обреку́ *итп сов см* **обре́чь**.

обремени́тел|ьный (-ен, -ьна, -ьно) *прил* onerous.

обремен|и́ть (-ю́, -и́шь; *impf* **обременя́ть**) *сов перех*: ~ **кого́-н чем-н** to load sb down with sth.

обр|ести́ (-ету́, -етёшь; *pt* -ёл, -ела́, -ело́, *impf* **обрета́ть**) *сов перех* to find.

обречён|ный (-ён, -ена́, -ено́) *прил* doomed.

обр|е́чь (-еку́, -ечёшь *итп*, -еку́т; *pt* -ёк, -екла́, -екло́, *impf* **обрека́ть**) *сов перех*: ~ **кого́-н на что-н** to condemn sb to sth.

обрис|ова́ть (-у́ю; *impf* **обрисо́вывать**) *сов перех* (*перен*) to describe.

обр|они́ть (-оню́, -о́нишь) *сов перех* to drop; (*замечание, фразу*) to let drop.

обро́с *итп сов см* **обрасти́**.

обр|уби́ть (-ублю́, -у́бишь; *impf* **обруба́ть**) *сов перех* to lop off.

обру́б|ок (-ка) *м* (*пень, хвоста*) stump; (*дерева*) chunk.

обруга́|ть (-ю) *сов перех* (*выбранить*) to curse; (*обозвать*) to swear at; (*разг: раскритиковать*) to pan, slate (*BRIT*).

о́бруч (-а) *м* hoop; (*для волос*) (Alice) band.

обруча́льн|ый *прил*: ~**ое кольцо́** wedding ring.

обруча́|ть(ся) (-ю(сь)) *несов от* **обручи́ть(ся)**.

обруче́ни|е (-я) *ср* betrothal.

обруч|и́ть (-у́, -и́шь; *impf* **обруча́ть**) *сов перех* to betroth

▶ **обручи́ться** (*impf* **обруча́ться**) *сов возв* to get betrothed.

обру́ш|ить (-у, -ишь; *impf* **обру́шивать**) *сов перех* (*стену, крышу*) to bring down; **обру́шивать** (~ *perf*) **что-н на** +*acc* to bring sth down onto; ~ (*perf*) **обвине́ния/угро́зы на кого́-н** to bombard sb with accusations/threats

▶ **обру́шиться** (*impf* **обру́шиваться**) *сов возв* (*крыша, здание*) to collapse; **обру́шиваться** (~**ся** *perf*) **на** +*acc* (*на голову*) to crash down onto; (*на врага*) to fall upon; (*на человека: с упрёками*) to come down on; **на него́** ~**илась беда́** he was struck down by misfortune.

обры́в (-а) *м* (*ГЕО*) precipice; (*на линии*) break.

обрыва́|ть(ся) (-ю(сь)) *несов от*

оборва́ть(ся).

обры́вист|ый (-, -а, -о) *прил* (*склон, берег*) steep; (*мысли, фразы*) fragmentary.

обры́в|ок (-ка) *м* (*верёвки*) piece; (*бумаги*) scrap; (*обычно мн: мыслей, воспоминаний*) fragment; (: *разговора*) snatch.

обры́воч|ный (-ен, -на, -но) *прил* fragmentary.

обры́зга|ть (-ю; *impf* **обры́згивать**) *сов перех*: ~ кого́-н/что-н +*instr* (*водой*) to splash sb/sth with; (*грязью, краской*) to splatter sb/sth with

▶ **обры́згаться** (*impf* **обры́згиваться**) *сов возв*: ~ся +*instr* (*см перех*) to get splashed with; to get splattered with.

обря́д (-а) *м* ritual.

обря́довый *прил* (*песни*) ceremonial; (*действия*) ritual.

обса́сыва|ть (-ю) *несов от* **обсоса́ть**.

обсервато́ри|я (-и) *ж* observatory.

обсле́довани|е (-я) *ср* (*см глаг*) inspection; examination.

обсле́д|овать (-ую) (*не*)*сов перех* to inspect; (*больного*) to examine.

обслу́живани|е (-я) *ср* service; **медици́нское** ~ health care; **сфе́ра** ~**я** service industry.

обслу́жива|ть (-ю) *несов от* **обслужи́ть** ♦ *перех* (*подлеж: магазин*) to supply; (: *поликлиника*) to see to.

обслу́живающ|ий (-ая, -ее, -ие) *прил*: ~ **персона́л** ancilliary staff.

обслужи́ть (-ужу́, -у́жишь; *impf* **обслу́живать**) *сов перех* (*покупателей*) to serve; (*клиентов*) to attend to; (*подлеж: поликлиника, магазин*) to see to; (*станки*) to operate.

обсоса́ть (-у́, -ёшь; *impf* **обса́сывать**) *сов перех* to suck.

обста́в|ить (-лю, -ишь; *impf* **обставля́ть**) *сов перех* (*квартиру, кабинет*) to furnish; **обставля́ть** (~ *perf*) **стол сту́льями** to put chairs around the table.

обстано́в|ка (-ки; *gen pl* -ок) *ж* (*квартиры, кабинета*) furnishings *мн*; (*в мире, в семье*) situation; **междунаро́дная** ~ the international situation.

обстоя́тельно *нареч* in detail.

обстоя́тель|ный (-ен, -ьна, -ьно) *прил* detailed; (*разг: человек*) solid.

обстоя́тельств|о (-а) *ср* circumstance; (*линг*) adverbial modifier; **ни при каки́х** ~**ах** under no circumstances; **стече́ние обстоя́тельств** coincidence; **смотря́ по** ~**ам** depending on the circumstances; (*как ответ на вопрос*) it depends.

обсто|я́ть (*3sg* -и́т, *3pl* -я́т) *несов неперех* (*дела, работа, учёба*) to be; **как** ~**я́т дела?** how are things going?; **всё** ~**и́т хорошо́** everything is going well.

обстра́гива|ть (-ю) *несов от* **обстрога́ть**.

обстре́л (-а) *м* fire; **артиллери́йский** ~ artillery fire.

обстреля́|ть (-ю; *impf* **обстре́ливать**) *сов перех* to fire at.

обстри́|чь (-гу́, -жёшь *итп*, -гу́т) *сов от* **стричь**.

обстрога́|ть (-ю; *impf* **обстра́гивать**) *сов перех* to plane.

обстру́кци|я (-и) *ж* obstruction.

обсту́п|ить (*3sg* -у́пит, *3pl* -у́пят, *impf* **обступа́ть**) *сов перех* to surround.

обсуди́ть (-ужу́, -у́дишь; *impf* **обсужда́ть**) *сов перех* to discuss.

обсужде́ни|е (-я) *ср* discussion; **предложи́ть** (**предлага́ть** *impf*) **что-н на** ~ to bring sth up for discussion.

обсужу́ *сов см* **обсуди́ть**.

обсчита́|ть (-ю; *impf* **обсчи́тывать**) *сов перех* to overcharge; (*результат, параметры*) to calculate

▶ **обсчита́ться** (*impf* **обсчи́тываться**) *сов возв* (*разг*) to miscalculate.

обсы́п|ать (-лю, -лешь; *impf* **обсыпа́ть**) *сов перех*: ~ **что-н чем-н** to sprinkle sth with sth

▶ **обсы́паться** (*impf* **обсыпа́ться**) *сов возв*: ~**ся** +*instr* to get covered in.

обта́чива|ть (-ю) *несов от* **обточи́ть**.

обтека́ем|ый (-, -а, -о) *прил* (*поверхность, форма*) streamlined; (*разг: ответ, объяснение*) ambiguous.

обт|ере́ть (-ру́, -рёшь; *impf* **обтира́ть**) *сов перех* to wipe

▶ **обтере́ться** (*impf* **обтира́ться**) *сов возв* to sponge o.s. down.

обт|еса́ть (-ешу́, -е́шешь; *impf* **обтёсывать**) *сов перех* (*бревно*) to trim; (*разг: манеры, человека*) to bring up to scratch.

обтира́|ть(ся) (-ю(сь)) *несов от* **обтере́ть(ся)**.

обточи́ть (-очу́, -о́чишь; *impf* **обта́чивать**) *сов перех* (*на станке*) to turn; (*на точильном камне*) to sharpen.

обто́ч|ка (-и) *ж* (*см глаг*) turning; sharpening.

обтрёпан|ный (-, -на, -но) *прил* shabby.

обтр|епа́ть (-еплю́, -е́плешь) *сов перех* to wear out

▶ **обтрепа́ться** *сов возв* (*износиться*) to wear out.

обтя́гива|ть (-ю) *несов от* **обтяну́ть**.

обтя́ж|ка (-и) *ж*: **в** ~**у** skintight.

обтяну́ть (-яну́, -я́нешь; *impf* **обтя́гивать**) *сов перех* (*кресло, диван*) to cover; (*фигуру*) to fit tightly.

обува́|ть(ся) (-ю(сь)) *несов от* **обу́ть(ся)**.

обувно́й *прил* shoe *опред*.

о́був|ь (-и) *ж* footwear.

обу́гл|иться (*3sg* -ится, *3pl* -ятся, *impf* **обу́гливаться**) *сов возв* to become charred.

обу́жива|ть (-ю) *несов от* **обу́зить**.

обу́жу *сов см* **обу́зить**.

обу́з|а (-ы) *ж* burden; **быть** (*impf*) ~**ой для**

кого́-н (*разг*) to be a burden to sb.

обу́|зить (-жу, -зишь; *impf* обу́живать) *сов перех* to make too tight.

обусло́в|ить (-лю, -ишь; *impf* обусла́вливать) *сов перех* (*явиться причиной*) to lead to; обусла́вливать (~ *perf*) что-н чем-н to make sth conditional on sth.

обу́|тый (-, -а, -о) *прил*: ~ в ту́фли/сапоги́ wearing shoes/boots; (*no full form*; *обеспеченный обувью*) provided with shoes or boots.

обу́|ть (-ю; *impf* обува́ть) *сов перех* (*туфли, сапоги*) to put on; (*разг: снабдить обувью*) *to provide with shoes or boots*; (*ребёнка*) to put shoes on

▶ обу́ться (*impf* обува́ться) *сов возв* to put on one's shoes or boots; (*разг: обеспечить себя обувью*) *to provide o.s. with shoes or boots.*

о́бух (-а) *м* (*топора*) blunt end; как ~ом по голове́ like a bolt from the blue.

обуча́|ть(ся) (-ю(сь)) *несов от* обучи́ть(ся).

обуче́ни|е (-я) *ср*: ~ +*dat* (*преподавание*) teaching of, instruction in; (*изучение*) education in.

обу́ч|ить (-учу́, -у́чишь; *impf* обуча́ть) *сов перех*: ~ кого́-н чему́-н/+*infin* to teach sb sth/to do

▶ обучи́ться (*impf* обуча́ться) *сов возв*: ~ся чему́-н/+*infin* to learn sth/to do.

обуя́|ть (*3sg* -ет, *3pl* -ют) *сов перех* to overcome.

обхам|и́ть (-лю́, -йшь) *сов перех* (*разг*) to be rude to.

обхва́т (-а) *м* circumference (*measured by putting arms around object*); в ~е in circumference.

обхва|ти́ть (-чу́, -́тишь; *impf* обхва́тывать) *сов перех*: ~ что-н (рука́ми) to put one's arms round sth.

обхо́д (-а) *м* (*путь*) way round; (*в больнице, на предприятии*) round; (*воен*) turning movement; в ~ +*gen* (*озера, закона*) bypassing; идти́ (*impf*) в ~ чего́-н to go round sth; (*закона, правил*) to evade sth.

обходи́тел|ьный (-ен, -ьна, -ьно) *прил* courteous.

обх|оди́ть(ся) (-ожу́(сь), -о́дишь(ся)) *несов от* обойти́(сь).

обходно́й *прил* (*путь*) detour *опред*; (*маневр, движение*) turning; обходно́й лист *a certificate which must be signed on leaving job to prove that all property has been returned.*

обхожде́ни|е (-я) *ср* manners *мн*.

обхожу́(сь) *несов см* обходи́ть(ся).

обхох|ота́ться (-очу́сь, -о́чешься) *сов возв* (*разг*) to kill o.s. laughing.

обчи́|стить (-щу, -стишь) *сов от* чи́стить.

обша́р|ить (-ю, -ишь; *impf* обша́ривать) *сов перех* (*разг*) to ransack.

обшива́|ть (-ю) *несов от* обши́ть.

обши́в|ка (-ки; *gen pl* -ок) *ж* (*платья, пальто*) trim; (*корабля*) plating; (*дома*) cladding.

обши́р|ный (-ен, -на, -но) *прил* extensive;

(*комната*) spacious.

обши́|тый (-, -а, -о) *прил*: ~ +*instr* (*бахромой, мехом*) trimmed with; (*досками*) faced with; (*металлом*) plated with.

об|ши́ть (-ошью, -ошьёшь; *impf* обшива́ть) *сов перех* (*разг: семью итп*) to make clothes for; обшива́ть (~ *perf*) (+*instr*) (*мехом, бахромой*) to trim (with); (*деревом*) to face (with); (*металлом*) to plate *или* cover (with).

обшла́г (-ага́; *nom pl* -ага́) *м* cuff.

обща́|ться (-юсь) *несов возв*: ~ с +*instr* (*с друзьями, с родственниками*) to spend time with; (*с политиками, с преступниками итп*) to associate with; я бо́льше с ним не ~юсь I don't see him any more.

общевойсково́й *прил* military.

общегородско́й *прил* town *опред*, city *опред*.

общегосуда́рственный *прил* state *опред*.

общедосту́пный *прил* (*средства, способ*) available to everyone; (*цены*) affordable; (*изложение, лекция*) accessible.

о́бщ|ее (-его; *decl like adj*) *ср* similarity; в ~ем (*разг*) on the whole; в ~ем и це́лом by and large; у них мно́го/нет ничего́ ~его they have a lot/nothing in common.

общежи́ти|е (-я) *ср* (*рабочее*) hostel; (*студенческое*) hall of residence (*brit*), dormitory *или* hall (*us*); (*сосуществование*) communal living.

общеизве́ст|ный (-ен, -на, -но) *прил* well-known.

общенаро́дный *прил* national *опред*.

общенациона́льный *прил* national *опред*.

обще́ни|е (-я) *ср* (*деловые, дружеские*) relations *мн*; (*с природой, с друзьями*) communication.

общеобразова́тельный *прил* comprehensive.

общепи́т (-а) *м сокр* (= обще́ственное пита́ние) public catering.

общепри́знанный *прил* universally recognized.

общепри́ня|тый *прил* generally accepted; в ~ом смы́сле сло́ва in the accepted sense of the word.

общераспространённый *прил* widespread.

обще́ственност|ь (-и) *ж собир* community.

обще́ствен|ный *прил* social; (*признание, собственность, жизнь*) public; (*организация*) civic; обще́ственное мне́ние public opinion; обще́ственные нау́ки social sciences.

о́бществ|о (-а) *ср* society; (*компания*) company; в ~е +*gen* in the company of.

обществове́дени|е (-я) *ср* social science.

общеупотреби́тел|ьный (-ен, -ьна, -ьно) *прил* commonly-used.

общечелове́ческ|ий (-ая, -ое, -ие) *прил* universal.

о́бщ|ий (-ая, -ее, -ие) *прил* general; (*труд*) communal; (*дом, книги*) shared; (*друзья*) mutual; (*интересы, увлечения, ненависть*) common; (*стоимость, количество*) total; (-, -á,

-ó; (*картина, описание*) general; **~ими
уси́лиями** together; **в ~ей сло́жности**
altogether; **на ~их основа́ниях** on equal terms;
в ~их черта́х in general terms; **находи́ть
(найти́** *perf*) **~ язы́к** to find a common language;
~ие слова́ waffle; **о́бщее образова́ние**
general education.

общи́н|а (-ы) ж community.

общипа́ть (-иплю́, -и́плешь; *impf*
общи́пывать) *сов перех* to pluck.

общи́телен *прил см* **общи́тельный**.

общи́тельность (-и) ж sociability.

общи́тел|ьный (-ен, -ьна, -ьно) *прил* sociable.

о́бщность (-и) ж (*взглядов, целей*) similarity;
(*историческая, социальная: community*).

объеда́|ть(ся) (-ю(сь)) *несов см* **объе́сть(ся)**.

объе́дешь *итп сов см* **объе́хать**.

объеди́м(ся) *сов см* **объе́сть(ся)**.

объедине́ни|е (-я) *ср* (*сил, усилий, талантов*)
concentration; (*литераторов,
производственное*) association; (*воен*) unit.

объединённ|ый *прил* (*заседание, собрание*)
joint; (*усилия, ресурсы*) joint, united; **О~ые
Ара́бские Эмира́ты** United Arab Emirates.

объедин|и́ть (-ю́, -и́шь; *impf* **объединя́ть**) *сов
перех* to join, unite; (*ресурсы*) to pool;
(*компании*) to amalgamate.

▸ **объедини́ться** (*impf* **объединя́ться**) *сов
возв* (*люди*) to unite; (*компании*) to amalgamate.

объеди́те(сь) *сов см* **объе́сть(ся)**.

объе́дк|и (-ов) *мн* (*разг*) leftovers *мн*.

объе́ду *итп сов см* **объе́хать**.

объедя́т(ся) *сов см* **объе́сть(ся)**.

объе́зд (-а) *м* detour; (*с целью осмотра*) tour;
е́хать (пое́хать *perf*) **в ~** to make a detour.

объе́з|дить (-жу, -дишь; *impf* **объезжа́ть**) *сов
перех* (*место*) to travel round; (*лошадь*) to
break in; (*друзей*) to visit.

объезжа́|ть (-ю) *несов от* **объе́здить**,
объе́хать.

объе́зжу *сов см* **объе́здить**.

объе́кт (-а) *м* (*изучения, наблюдения*) subject;
(*строит, воен*) site.

объекти́в (-а) *м* lens.

объекти́вен *прил см* **объекти́вный**.

объекти́вность (-и) ж objectivity.

объекти́в|ный (-ен, -на, -но) *прил* objective.

объе́л(ся) *итп сов см* **объе́сть(ся)**.

объе́м(ся) *сов см* **объе́сть(ся)**.

объём (-а) *м* (*геом*) volume; (*ведра, чашки*)
capacity; (*работы, знаний*) amount.

объёмен *прил см* **объёмный**.

объёмист|ый (-, -а, -о) *прил* bulky.

объём|ный (-ен, -на, -но) *прил* (*геом*)
volumetric; (*изображение, кино*) three-
dimensional; (*книга, папка*) bulky.

объе́сть (*как* **есть**; *см* **Table 15**; *impf*
объеда́ть) *сов перех* (*кость, яблоко*) to nibble

(at); **~** (*perf*) **кого́-н** (*разг*) to eat sb out of house
and home

▸ **объе́сться** (*impf* **объеда́ться**) *сов возв* to
overeat.

объе́хать (*как* **е́хать**; *см* **Table 19**; *impf*
объезжа́ть) *сов перех* (*камень, яму*) to go или
drive round; (*с целью осмотра*) to travel round;
(*друзей, страны*) to visit.

объе́шь(ся) *сов см* **объе́сть(ся)**.

объяв|и́ть (-явлю́, -я́вишь; *impf* **объявля́ть**)
сов перех to announce; (*войну*) to declare ♦
неперех: **~ о** +*prp* (*о решении, о случившемся*)
to announce; **объявля́ть** (**~** *perf*) **собра́ние
закры́тым/кого́-н победи́телем** to declare the
meeting closed/sb the winner

▸ **объяви́ться** (*impf* **объявля́ться**) *сов возв*
(*разг*) to turn up.

объявле́ни|е (-я) *ср* announcement; (*войны*)
declaration; (*рекламное сообщение*)
advertisement; (*извещение*) notice.

объявлю́(сь) *сов см* **объяви́ть(ся)**.

объявля́|ть(ся) (-ю(сь)) *несов от*
объяви́ть(ся).

объясне́ни|е (-я) *ср* explanation; **~ в любви́**
declaration of love.

объясни́м|ый (-, -а, -о) *прил* explicable.

объясн|и́ть (-ю́, -и́шь; *impf* **объясня́ть**) *сов
перех* to explain

▸ **объясни́ться** (*impf* **объясня́ться**) *сов возв*:
~ся (с +*instr*) to clear things up (with); **всё
~и́лось** everything became clear; **объясня́ться**
(**~ся** *perf*) (**кому́-н**) **в любви́** to declare one's
love (to sb).

объясня́|ться (-юсь) *несов от* **объясни́ться** ♦
возв (*жестами, на английском языке*) to
communicate; **~** (*impf*) +*instr* (*трудностями,
усталостью*) to be explained by.

объя́ти|е (-я) *ср* embrace; **встреча́ть
(встре́тить** *perf*) **кого́-н с распростёртыми
~ями** to welcome sb with open arms.

обыва́тел|ь (-я) *м* (*пренебр*) philistine; (*ист*)
resident.

обыва́тельск|ий (-ая, -ое, -ие) *прил* philistine.

обыгра́|ть (-ю; *impf* **обы́грывать**) *сов перех*
(*команду, соперника*) to beat; (*разг: ошибку,
оговорку*) to turn to one's advantage.

обы́ден|ный (-, -на, -но) *прил* mundane.

обыкнове́ни|е (-я) *ср* habit; **име́ть** (*impf*) **~**
+*infin* to be in the habit of doing; **по ~ю** as usual;
про́тив ~я against the norm; **по своему́ ~ю** as
is his *итп* wont.

обыкнове́нно *нареч* usually.

обыкнове́н|ный (-ен, -на, -но) *прил*
(*заурядный: человек, явление*) ordinary;
(*частый*) common.

о́быск (-а) *м* search; **производи́ть (произвести́**
perf) **~** to carry out a search.

обы́ск|а́ть (-ыщу́, -ы́щешь; *impf* **обы́скивать**)

сов перех to search.

обы́ча|**й** (**-я**) *м* custom.

обы́чен *прил см* **обы́чный**.

обы́чно *нареч* usually.

обы́ч|**ный** (**-ен, -на, -но**) *прил* usual; (*заурядный*) ordinary.

обыщу́ *итп сов см* **обыска́ть**.

обяжу́(сь) *итп сов см* **обяза́ть(ся)**.

обя́занност|**и** (**-ей**) *мн* (*директора итп*) duties *мн*, responsibilities *мн*; **исполня́ть** (*impf*) ~ +*gen* to act as; **он исполня́ет** ~ **дире́ктора** he is the acting director.

обя́занност|**ь** (**-и**) *ж* duty; *см также* **обя́занности**.

обя́зан|**ный** (**-, -а, -о**) *прил*: ~ +*infin* (*помочь, сделать итп*) obliged to do; ~ +*dat* obliged *или* indebted to; **я Вам о́чень обя́зан** I am greatly obliged to you.

обяза́телен *прил см* **обяза́тельный**.

обяза́тельно *нареч* definitely, without fail; **не** ~ not necessarily.

обяза́тельный (**-ен, -ьна, -ьно**) *прил* (*правило, условие*) binding; (*исполнение, обучение*) compulsory, obligatory; (*человек, работник*) reliable; **в ~ьном поря́дке** as a compulsory measure.

обяза́тельств|**о** (**-а**) *ср* commitment, obligation; (*обычно мн: комм*) liability; **долгово́е** ~ (*комм*) promissory note; **брать** (**взять** *perf*) **на себя́** ~ to take on some commitment.

обяза́ть (**-яжу́, -я́жешь;** *impf* **обя́зывать**) *сов перех*: ~ **кого́-н** +*infin* to oblige sb to do; **Вы меня́** ~**я́жите, е́сли сде́лаете э́то** I would be very much obliged if you would do this; **он** ~**яза́л меня́ свое́й добро́той** I am obliged to him for his kindness

▶ **обяза́ться** (*impf* **обя́зываться**) *сов возв* to pledge.

обя́зыва|**ть** (**-ю**) *несов от* **обяза́ть** ♦ *перех* (*подлеж: правила, закон, факты*) to oblige; **положе́ние** ~**ет** his *итп* position demands it

▶ **обя́зываться** *несов от* **обяза́ться**.

ова́л (**-а**) *м* oval; **у неё краси́вый** ~ **лица́** her face is a lovely shape.

ова́льный (**-ен, -ьна, -ьно**) *прил* oval.

ова́ци|**я** (**-и**) *ж* ovation.

ОВД *м сокр* = **отде́л вну́тренних дел**.

овдове́|**ть** (**-ю**) *сов неперех* (*женщина*) to become a widow, be widowed; (*мужчина*) to become a widower, be widowed.

Ов|**е́н** (**-на́**) *м* (*созвездие*) Aries.

ове́с (**-са́**) *м собир* oats *мн*.

ове́ц *сущ см* **овца́**.

ове́ч|**ий** (**-ья, -ье, -ьи**) *прил* (*шерсть, сыр*) sheep's; (*молоко*) ewe's.

ОВИР *м сокр* = **Отде́л виз и регистра́ции иностра́нных гра́ждан**.

овладе́|**ть** (**-ю, -ешь;** *impf* **овладева́ть**) *сов неперех*: ~ +*instr* (*городом, высотой*) to capture, seize; (*перен: разговором*) to take

control of; (: *вниманием*) to capture; (: *языком, профессией*) to master; **им** ~**ла ра́дость** he was overcome with joy.

Овна́ *сущ см* **Ове́н**.

о́вод (**-а**) *м* gadfly.

о́вощ (**-а**) *м* vegetable; *см также* **о́вощи**.

о́вощ|**и** (**-ей**) *мн* vegetables *мн*.

овощно́й *прил* (*суп, блюдо*) vegetable *опред*; **овощно́й магази́н** greengrocer's (*BRIT*), fruit and vegetable shop.

овра́г (**-а**) *м* ravine.

овса́ *итп сущ см* **ове́с**.

овся́нк|**а** (**-и**) *ж собир* (*разг: крупа*) oats *мн*; (*каша*) porridge (*BRIT*), oatmeal (*US*).

овся́ный *прил* oat *опред*.

овуля́ци|**я** (**-и**) *ж* ovulation.

овц|**а́** (**-ы́;** *nom pl* **-цы,** *gen pl* **-е́ц**) *ж* sheep (*мн* sheep); (*самка*) ewe.

овцево́дств|**о** (**-а**) *ср* sheep-farming.

ОВЧ *сокр* (= **о́чень высо́кая частота́**) VHF (= *very high frequency*).

овча́р|**ка** (**-ки;** *gen pl* **-ок**) *ж* sheepdog.

овча́р|**ня** (**-и**) *ж* sheepfold.

овчи́н|**а** (**-ы**) *ж* sheepskin.

ога́р|**ок** (**-ка**) *м* candle end.

огиба́|**ть** (**-ю**) *несов от* **обогну́ть**.

оглавле́ни|**е** (**-я**) *ср* (table of) contents.

огласи́ть (**-шу́, -си́шь;** *impf* **оглаша́ть**) *сов перех* (*решение, проект*) to announce; (*приказ, закон*) to proclaim; (*телеграмму*) to read out; (*perf*) **что-н чем-н** to fill sth with sth

▶ **огласи́ться** (*impf* **оглаша́ться**) *сов возв*: ~**ся** +*instr* to resound with.

огла́ск|**а** (**-и**) *ж* publicity; **предава́ть** (**преда́ть** *perf*) **что-н** ~**е** to make sth public.

оглаша́|**ть(ся)** (**-ю(сь)**) *несов от* **огласи́ть(ся)**.

оглашу́(сь) *сов см* **огласи́ть(ся)**.

огло́б|**ля** (**-ли;** *gen pl* **-ель**) *ж* shaft (*on cart*).

огло́хн|**уть** (**-у, -ешь**) *сов от* **гло́хнуть**.

оглуша́|**ть** (**-ю**) *несов от* **оглуши́ть**.

оглуши́тельный (**-ен, -ьна, -ьно**) *прил* deafening.

оглуши́ть (**-ушу́, -у́шишь;** *impf* **оглуша́ть**) *сов перех*: ~ **кого́-н чем-н** (*звуками, криками*) to deafen sb with sth; (*ударом*) to stun sb with sth.

огля|**де́ть** (**-жу́, -ди́шь;** *impf* **огля́дывать**) *сов перех* to look round

▶ **огляде́ться** (*impf* **огля́дываться**) *сов возв* to look around.

огля́д|**ка** (**-и**) *ж*: **с** ~**ой** with caution; **де́лать** (**сде́лать** *perf*) **что-н без** ~**и** to do sth resolutely; **он бежа́л без** ~**и** (*разг*) he ran as fast as his legs would carry him.

огля́дыва|**ть** (**-ю**) *несов от* **огляде́ть**

▶ **огля́дываться** *несов от* **огляде́ться**, **огляну́ться**.

огляжу́(сь) *сов см* **огляде́ть(ся)**.

огляну́ться (**-яну́сь, -я́нешься;** *impf* **огля́дываться**) *сов возв* to look back; (**я**) **не успе́л** ~, **как** ... before I knew it ....

огнево́й *прил* (*характер, взгляд*) fiery; **огнева́я**

заве́са (*ВОЕН*) curtain of fire; **огнева́я пози́ция** firing position; **огнева́я то́чка** (*ВОЕН*) emplacement.

огнеды́шащ|ий (**-ая, -ее, -ие**) *прил* (*дракон*) fire-breathing; (*вулкан*) erupting.

огнемёт (**-а**) *м* flame-thrower.

о́гненный *прил* (*цвет, глаза, характер*) fiery; (*поцелуй*) passionate; **~ столб** burst of flames.

огнеопа́с|ный (**-ен, -на, -но**) *прил* (in)flammable.

огнесто́йкий (**-йкая, -йкое, -йкие; -ек, -йка, -йко**) *прил* fireproof.

огнестре́льн|ый *прил*: **~ое ору́жие** firearms *мн*; **огнестре́льная ра́на** bullet wound.

огнетуши́тел|ь (**-я**) *м* fire-extinguisher.

огнеупо́р|ный (**-ен, -на, -но**) *прил* (*материал*) fire-proof; **огнеупо́рная гли́на** fire clay; **огнеупо́рный кирпи́ч** firebrick.

огня́ *итп сущ см* **ого́нь.**

ого́ *межд*: **~!** well!; **~, каки́м ты стал взро́слым!** my, how you've grown!

оговор|и́ть (**-ю́, -и́шь;** *impf* **огова́ривать**) *сов перех* to slander; (*условия, срок*) to agree (on); (*подлеж: правила*) to stipulate

▸ **оговори́ться** (*impf* **огова́риваться**) *сов возв*: **я ~и́лся** it was a slip of the tongue.

огово́р|ка (**-ки;** *gen pl* **-ок**) *ж* (*обмолвка*) slip of the tongue; (*условие*) proviso; **я могу́ сказа́ть без ~ок, что ...** I can say without reservation that ....

оголённый (**-ён, -ена́, -ено́**) *прил* bare.

огол|и́ть (**-ю́, -и́шь;** *impf* **оголя́ть**) *сов перех* to bare, expose; (*деревья, провод, землю*) to strip; (*меч, кинжал*) to draw; (*фронт, участок*) to expose

▸ **оголи́ться** (*impf* **оголя́ться**) *сов возв* (*шея, плечо итп*) to become uncovered; (*деревья, земля*) to become bare; (*провод*) to be exposed; (*фронт, участок*) to become exposed.

оголте́л|ый (**-, -а, -о**) *прил* mad.

оголя́|ть(ся) (**-ю(сь)**) *несов перех от* **оголи́ть(ся).**

огон|ёк (**-ька́**) *м уменьш от* **ого́нь;** (*блеск глаз*) twinkle; **рабо́тать** (*impf*) **с ~ько́м** to work enthusiastically *или* with enthusiasm; **заходи́ть** (**зайти́** *perf*) **на ~** to drop in.

ог|о́нь (**-ня́**) *м* fire; (*фонарей, в окне*) light; (*перен: любви, негодования*) flame; **разводи́ть** (**развести́** *perf*) **~** to light a fire; **зажига́ть** (**заже́чь** *perf*) **~** to turn on the light; **открыва́ть** (**откры́ть** *perf*) **~** to open fire; **в ~не́ сраже́ния** in the heat of battle; **боя́ться** (*impf*) **чего́-н/кого́-н как ~ня́** to be terrified by sb/sth; **игра́ть** (*impf*) **с ~нём** (*перен*) to play with fire; **ме́жду двух ~не́й** between two fires.

огонька́ *итп сущ см* **огонёк.**

огора́жива|ть (**-ю**) *несов от* **огороди́ть.**

огоро́д (**-а**) *м* vegetable *или* kitchen garden.

огор|оди́ть (**-ожу́, -о́дишь;** *impf* **огора́живать**) *сов перех*: **~ что-н (чем-н)** to fence sth in (with sth).

огоро́ш|ить (**-у, -ишь;** *impf* **огоро́шивать**) *сов перех* (*разг*) to astound.

огорча́|ть(ся) (**-ю(сь)**) *несов от* **огорчи́ть(ся).**

огорче́ни|е (**-я**) *ср* distress; **к моему́ ~ю** to my dismay.

огорчённ|ый (**-ён, -ена́, -ено́**) *прил* distressed; **у него́ был ~ вид** he looked upset.

огорчи́тельный (**-ен, -ьна, -ьно**) *прил* distressing.

огорч|и́ть (**-у́, -и́шь;** *impf* **огорча́ть**) *сов перех* to distress

▸ **огорчи́ться** (*impf* **огорча́ться**) *сов возв* to be upset *или* distressed.

огра́б|ить (**-лю, -ишь**) *сов от* **гра́бить.**

ограбле́ни|е (**-я**) *ср* robbery.

огра́блю *сов см* **огра́бить.**

огра́|да (**-ы**) *ж* (*стена*) wall; (*забор*) fence; (*решётка*) railings *мн*.

огра|ди́ть (**-жу́, -ди́шь;** *impf* **огражда́ть**) *сов перех* (*перен*) to defend, protect.

огражде́ни|е (**-я**) *ср* barrier.

ограж|у́ *сов см* **огради́ть.**

огран|и́ть (**-ю́, -и́шь;** *impf* **огра́нивать**) *сов перех* to cut.

ограниче́ни|е (**-я**) *ср* restriction, limitation; (*правило*) restriction.

ограни́чен|ный (**-, -на, -но**) *прил* limited; (*человек*) narrow-minded.

ограни́чива|ть(ся) (**-ю(сь)**) *несов от* **ограни́чить(ся).**

ограничи́тельный (**-ен, -ьна, -ьно**) *прил*: **~ьные ме́ры** restrictive measures *мн*.

ограни́ч|ить (**-у, -ишь;** *impf* **ограни́чивать**) *сов перех* to limit, restrict

▸ **ограни́читься** (*impf* **ограни́чиваться**) *сов возв*: **~ся** +*instr* (*удовлетвориться*) to content o.s with; (*свестись*) to become limited to.

огре́|ть (**-ю**) *сов перех* (*разг*) to whack.

огро́м|ный (**-ен, -на, -но**) *прил* enormous.

огрубе́л|ый *прил* (*руки, кожа*) coarse; (*сердце, душа*) hardened.

огрубе́|ть (**-ю**) *сов от* **грубе́ть.**

огрыза́|ться (**-юсь**) *несов возв* to snap.

огрызну́|ться (**-усь, -ёшься**) *сов возв* to snap.

огры́з|ок (**-ка**) *м* (*огурца, яблока*) half-eaten bit; (*карандаша, ластика*) stub; (*бумажки*) scrap.

огу́л|ьный (**-ен, -ьна, -ьно**) *прил* unfounded.

огур|е́ц (**-ца́**) *м* cucumber; (*маринованный*) gherkin.

о́д|а (**-ы**) *ж* ode.

ода́лжива|ть (**-ю**) *несов от* **одолжи́ть.**

одарённый (**-, -на, -но**) *прил* gifted.

одар|и́ть (**-ю́, -и́шь;** *impf* **ода́ривать** *или* **одаря́ть**) *сов перех*: **~ кого́-н чем-н** to give sb sth; **приро́да ~и́ла её красото́й** she is blessed with good looks.

одева́ть (-ю) *несов от* **оде́ть**

▶ **одева́ться** *несов от* **оде́ться ◆ возв** (*носить одежду*) to dress.

оде́жд|а (-ы) *ж* clothes *мн*.

одеколо́н (-а) *м* eau de Cologne.

одел|и́ть (-ю́, -и́шь; *impf* **оделя́ть**) *сов перех*: ~ **кого́-н чем-н** to give sth out to sb.

оде́ну(сь) *итп сов см* **оде́ть(ся)**

одёргива|ть (-ю) *несов от* **одёрнуть**.

одеревене́лый *прил* (*руки, пальцы*) numb; (*человек*) paralysed (*BRIT*), paralyzed (*US*).

одеревене́|ть (-ю) *сов от* **деревене́ть**.

одерж|а́ть (-ержу́, -е́ржишь; *impf* **оде́рживать**) *сов перех*: ~ **побе́ду** to be victorious; **оде́рживать** (~ *perf*) **верх на соревнова́нии/в спо́ре** to win a competition/argument.

одержи́мый (-, -а, -о) *прил*: ~ +*instr* (*эмоциями*) possessed by; (*мыслью*) obsessed by.

одёрн|уть (-у, -ешь; *impf* **одёргивать**) *сов перех* (*одежду*) to straighten; (*разг: человека*) to check.

Оде́сс|а (-ы) *ж* Odessa.

оде́т|ый (-, -а, -о) *прил* dressed; (*разг: обеспеченный одеждой*) clothed; (*покрытый*): ~ +*instr* (*снегом итп*) covered with.

оде́|ть (-ну, -нешь; *impf* **одева́ть**) *сов перех* to dress; (*разг: снабдить одеждой*) to clothe; (*перен: снегом*) to cover

▶ **оде́ться** (*impf* **одева́ться**) *сов возв* to get dressed; (*также разг: тепло, легко, приобретать одежду*) to dress; (*покрываться*): ~**ся** +*instr* to be covered with.

одея́л|о (-а) *ср* (*шерстяное*) blanket; (*стёганое*) quilt; (*пуховое*) eiderdown.

KEYWORD

оди́н (-ного; *см* **Table 22**; *f* **одна́**, *nt* **одно́**, *pl* **одни́**) *м чис* one; **одна́ кни́га** one book; **одни́ брю́ки** one pair of trousers; **ей оди́н год** she is one (year old); **они́ живу́т в до́ме но́мер оди́н** they live at number one; **кни́га сто́ит оди́н рубль** the book costs one rouble; **я́блоки продаю́тся по одно́й шту́ке** the apples are sold singly

◆ *прил* alone; (*единственный, единый*) one; (*одинаковый, тот же самый*) the same; **он идёт в кино́ оди́н** he goes to the cinema alone; **есть то́лько оди́н вы́ход** there is only one way out; **у них одни́ взгля́ды** they hold similar views; **я оди́н** (*без супруги*) I am single

◆ *мест* **1** (*какой-то*): **оди́н мой знако́мый** a friend; **одни́ неприя́тности** nothing but problems

2 (*во фразах*): **оди́н из** +*gen pl* one of; **оди́н и тот же** the one and the same thing; **оди́н раз** once; **оди́н на оди́н** one to one; **все до одного́** all to a man; **ни оди́н** not one; **оди́н за други́м** one after the other; **по одному́** one by one; **одно́ к одному́** (*разг*) one thing after another; **оди́н к одному́** one as good as another;

одно́ из двух one of two things; **одно́ вре́мя** for some time; **в оди́н го́лос** with one voice; **оди́н-еди́нственный** only one; **оди́н-одинёшенек** (*разг*) all alone.

одина́ково *нареч* in the same way.

одина́ков|ый (-, -а, -о) *прил* similar.

одина́рный *прил* single.

одиннадцатичасово́й *прил* eleven-hour; (*отправление*) eleven-o'clock.

оди́ннадцат|ый (-ая, -ое, -ые) *чис* eleventh; *см также* **пя́тый**.

оди́ннадцат|ь (-и; *как* **пять**; *см* **Table 27**) *чис* eleven; *см также* **пять**.

одино́к|ий (-ая, -ое, -ие; -, -а, -о) *прил* (*дом, дерево*) solitary; (*жизнь, человек*) lonely; (*без семьи: женщина, мужчина*) single.

одино́чек *сущ см* **одино́чка**.

одино́честв|о (-а) *ср* loneliness.

одино́чк|а (-ки; *gen pl* -ек) *ж* (*человек*): **жить ~кой** to live alone; **байда́рка-~** one-man canoe; **в ~ку** on one's own; **сиде́ть** (*impf*) **в ~ке** (*разг*) to be in solitary confinement.

одино́чн|ый *прил* (*стук, выстрел*) single, lone; (*прохожие, дома*) solitary; ~ **полёт** solo flight; ~**ое заключе́ние** solitary confinement; **одино́чное ката́ние** (**на конька́х**) (*СПОРТ*) singles figure skating.

одио́зный (-ен, -на, -но) *прил* odious.

одича́лый *прил* wild.

одича́|ть (-ю) *сов от* **дича́ть**.

одн|а́ (-о́й) *ж чис см* **оди́н**.

одна́жды *нареч* once.

одна́ко *союз, вводн сл* however; **его́ повы́сили** – ~ –! he's been promoted – no, really!; ~ **же** even so.

одни́ (-х) *мн чис см* **оди́н**.

одно́ (-го́) *ср чис см* **оди́н**.

одноа́ктный *прил* one-act, in one act.

однобо́ртный *прил* single-breasted.

одновреме́нно *нареч*: ~ (**с** +*instr*) at the same time (as).

одновреме́нный *прил* simultaneous.

одного́ *итп чис см* **оди́н, одно́**.

одного́д|ок (-ка) *м* (*разг*): **он мой** ~ he was born in the same year as me.

однодне́вн|ый *прил* (*зарплата, работа*) one day's; ~**ая пое́здка** day trip.

однозву́чный (-ен, -на, -но) *прил* monotonous.

однозна́чный (-ен, -на, -но) *прил* (*тождественный*) synonymous; (*с одним значением: слово*) monosemantic; (: *выражение, ответ*) unambiguous; (*МАТ*) single-figure; **однозна́чное число́** single-digit number.

одноимённый *прил* of the same name.

однокла́ссник (-а) *м* classmate.

однокла́ссниц|а (-ы) *ж см* **однокла́ссник**.

однокле́точный *прил* single-cell.

одноколе́йный *прил* single-lane.

однокра́тный *прил* single.

одноле́тн|ий (-яя, -ее, -ие) *прил* annual.

одноме́стный *прил* (*купе, номер*) single; (*каюта*) single-berth.

однообра́зи|е (*-я*) *ср* monotony.

однообра́зный *прил* monotonous.

однопо́лый *прил* unisexual.

однора́зовый *прил* disposable; ~ **про́пуск** temporary pass (*valid only once*).

одноро́д|ный (*-ен, -на, -но*) *прил* (*явления, понятия*) similar; (*жидкость, масса*) homogenous.

односло́ж|ный (*-ен, -на, -но*) *прил* (*также перен*) monosyllabic.

односторо́н|ний (*-няя, -нее, -ние*) *прил* (*ткань*) one-sided; (*разоружение*) unilateral; (*движение, связь*) one-way; (*-ен, -ня, -не; перен: взгляд, развитие*) narrow; (: *мышление*) parochial; **у него́ ~ парали́ч** he is paralysed (*BRIT*) *или* paralyzed (*US*) down one side.

одноти́п|ный (*-ен, -на, -но*) *прил* of the same type *или* kind.

однотóмный *прил* one-volume.

однофами́л|ец (*-ьца*) *м* namesake (*with same surname*).

однофами́лица (*-ы*) *ж см* **однофами́лец**.

однофами́льца *итп сущ см* **однофами́лец**.

одноцве́т|ный (*-ен, -на, -но*) *прил* plain.

одночле́н (*-а*) *м* monomial.

одноэта́жный *прил* single-storey (*BRIT*), single-story (*US*), one-storey (*BRIT*), one-story (*US*).

одобре́ни|е (*-я*) *ср* approval.

одобри́телен *прил см* **одобри́тельный**.

одобри́тельно *нареч* favourably.

одобри́тель|ный (*-ен, -ьна, -ьно*) *прил* (*отзыв, реакция*) favourable (*BRIT*), favorable (*US*); (*восклицание, взгляд*) of approval; (*статья*) positive.

одо́бр|ить (*-ю, -ишь; impf* **одобря́ть**) *сов перех* to approve.

одоле́|ть (*-ю; impf* **одолева́ть**) *сов перех* (*врага*) to overpower; (*смущение, неприязнь*) to overcome; (*разг: книгу, задачу*) to get through; (: *подлеж: жара, комары*) to bug; (*науку*) to master; **его́ ~ла грусть/лень** he was overwhelmed by sadness/a feeling of laziness.

одолже́ни|е (*-я*) *ср* favour (*BRIT*), favor (*US*); **сде́лайте ~** would you do me a favour?; (*ответ*) be my guest.

одолж|и́ть (*-у́, -и́шь; impf* **ода́лживать**) *сов перех*: ~ **что-н кому́-н** to lend sth to sb; **ода́лживать** (~ *perf*) **что-н у кого́-н** (*разг*) to borrow sth from sb.

одряхле́|ть (*-ю*) *сов от* **дряхле́ть**.

одува́нчик (*-а*) *м* dandelion.

оду́ма|ться (*-юсь; impf* **оду́мываться**) *сов возв* to think again.

одура́ч|ить (*-у, -ишь*) *сов от* **дура́чить**.

одуре́лый *прил* (*разг*) befuddled.

одуре́|ть (*-ю*) *сов от* **дуре́ть**.

одурма́н|ить (*-ю, -ишь*) *сов от* **дурма́нить**.

о́дур|ь (*-и*) *ж*: **напи́ться до ~и** (*разг*) to drink o.s. silly; **набе́гаться** (*perf*) **до ~и** (*разг*) to run until one is ready to drop; **я насмотре́лся детекти́вов до ~и** (*разг*) I've watched thrillers until I'm sick of them.

одутлова́т|ый (*-, -а, -о*) *прил* puffed up, puffy.

одухотворён|ный (*-, -на, -но*) *прил* (*вид, лицо*) spiritual; (*речь*) inspired.

одухотвор|и́ть (*-ю́, -и́шь; impf* **одухотворя́ть**) *сов перех* to inspire.

оды́шк|а (*-и*) *ж*: **у него́ ~** he is short of breath; **страда́ть** (*impf*) **~ой** to be short-winded.

ОЕЭС *ж сокр* (= *Организа́ция европе́йского экономи́ческого сотру́дничества*) OEEC (= *Organization for European Economic Cooperation*).

ожереб|и́ться (*3sg -и́тся, 3pl -я́тся*) *сов от* **жереби́ться**.

ожере́лье (*-я*) *ср* necklace.

ожесточа́|ть(ся) (*-ю(сь)*) *несов от* **ожесточи́ть(ся)**.

ожесточе́ни|е (*-я*) *ср* bitterness; **с ~м** furiously.

ожесточён|ный (*-, -на, -но*) *прил* (*человек*) hardened, embittered; (*спор, сражение*) fierce.

ожесточ|и́ть (*-у́, -и́шь; impf* **ожесточа́ть**) *сов перех* (*человека*) to harden, embitter

▸ **ожесточи́ться** (*impf* **ожесточа́ться**) *сов возв* to become hardened *или* embittered

ожива́|ть (*-ю*) *несов от* **ожи́ть**.

ожив|и́ть (*-лю́, -и́шь; impf* **оживля́ть**) *сов перех* to revive; (*глаза, лицо*) to light up; (*улицу, долину*) to bring to life; (*торговлю, работу*) to revitalize

▸ **оживи́ться** (*impf* **оживля́ться**) *сов возв* to liven up; (*лицо*) to brighten; (*улица, школа*) to come to life.

оживле́ни|е (*-я*) *ср* (*на улице, в доме*) bustle; (*организма, растения*) revival.

оживлён|ный (*-, -на, -но*) *прил* (*беседа, спор*) animated; (*улица, место, деятельность*) lively; (*торговля*) brisk; (*-, -á, -ó; человек*) lively.

оживлю́(сь) *сов см* **оживи́ть(ся)**.

оживля́|ть(ся) (*-ю(сь)*) *несов от* **оживи́ть(ся)**.

оживу́ *итп сов см* **ожи́ть**.

ожида́ни|е (*-я*) *ср* anticipation; (*обычно мн: надежды*) expectation; **в ~и чего́-н** in anticipation of sth; **обма́нывать** (**обману́ть** *perf*) **чьи-н ~я** to fail to come up to sb's expectations.

ожида́|ть (*-ю*) *несов перех* (*ждать*) to expect; (+*gen; надеяться*) to expect; **его́ ~ет блестя́щая карье́ра** he has a brilliant career ahead of him; **э́того мо́жно бы́ло ~** that was to be expected

▸ **ожида́ться** *несов возв* to be expected.

ожире́ни|е (-я) *ср* obesity.

ожире́|ть (-ю) *сов от* жире́ть.

ож|и́ть (-иву́, -иве́шь; *impf* оживáть) *сов неперех* to come to life; (*перен: чувства, человек*) to revive.

ожо́г (-а) *м* burn.

озабо́т|ить (-чу, -тишь) *сов перех* to worry, trouble.

озабо́чен|ный (-, -на, -но) *прил* worried.

озабо́чу *сов см* озабо́тить.

озагла́в|ить (-лю, -ишь; *impf* озагла́вливать) *сов перех* to entitle.

озада́чен|ный (-, -на, -но) *прил* puzzled.

озада́ч|ить (-у, -ишь; *impf* озада́чивать) *сов перех* to puzzle, perplex.

озар|и́ть (-ю́, -и́шь; *impf* озаря́ть) *сов перех* (*подлеж: солнце, улыбка*) to light up; (: *идея, догадка*) to dawn on

▶ **озари́ться** (*impf* озаря́ться) *сов возв*: ~ся +*instr* (*также перен*) to be lit up by.

озвере́|ть (-ю) *сов от* звере́ть ◆ *неперех* to become violent.

озву́ч|ить (-у, -ишь; *impf* озву́чивать) *сов перех*: ~ фильм to record the soundtrack for a film.

оздорови́тельн|ый *прил*: ~ые мероприя́тия health-improving measures; **оздорови́тельный ко́мплекс** ≈ health farm.

оздоро́в|ить (-лю, -ишь; *impf* оздоровля́ть) *сов перех* (*перен: коллектив, обстановку*) to clean up; **оздоровля́ть** (~ *perf*) **органи́зм** to improve one's health; ~ (*perf*) **ме́стность** to improve the ecology of an area.

озелен|и́ть (-ю́, -и́шь; *impf* озеленя́ть) *несов перех* to green.

о́з|еро (-ера; *nom pl* -ёра) *ср* lake.

ози́м|ые (-ых; *decl like adj*) *мн* winter crops *мн*.

ози́м|ый *прил*: ~ая пшени́ца/рожь winter wheat/rye; *см также* ози́мые.

озира́|ться (-юсь) *несов возв*: ~ (по сторона́м) to glance about *или* around.

озло́б|ить (-лю, -ишь; *impf* озлобля́ть) *сов перех* to anger

▶ **озло́биться** (*impf* озлобля́ться) *сов возв* to become angry.

озлобле́ни|е (-я) *ср* anger.

озло́блен|ный (-, -на, -но) *прил* angry.

озло́блю(сь) *сов см* озло́бить(ся).

озлобля́|ть(ся) (-ю(сь)) *несов от* озло́бить(ся).

озна́ком|ить (-лю, -ишь) *сов от* знако́мить ◆ (*impf* ознакомля́ть) *перех*: ~ кого́-н с +*instr* to familiarize sb with

▶ **ознако́миться** *сов от* знако́миться ◆ (*impf* ознакомля́ться) *возв*: ~ся с +*instr* to familiarize o.s. with.

ознаменова́ни|е (-я) *ср*: в ~ +*gen* (*в память*) in commemoration of.

ознамен|ова́ть (-у́ю; *impf* ознамено́вывать) *сов перех* to commemorate, mark; **его́ побе́да ~ова́ла э́тот год** his victory made this a memorable year

▶ **ознаменова́ться** (*impf* ознамено́вываться) *сов возв* (+*instr*) to be remembered for.

означа́|ть (-ю) *несов перех* to mean.

озно́б (-а) *м* shivering.

ОЗО *ср сокр* (= отделе́ние зао́чного обуче́ния) *extra-mural department*.

озо́н (-а) *м* ozone.

озо́нов|ый *прил*: ~ **слой** ozone layer; **озо́новая дыра́** hole in the ozone layer.

озорни́|к (-а́) *м* (*разг*) scallywag.

озорно́й *прил* mischievous.

озорств|о́ (-а́) *ср* mischief.

озя́бн|уть (-у, -ешь) *сов от* зя́бнуть.

ой *межд*: ~! (*выражает испуг*) argh!; (*выражает удивление, восхищение*) oh!; (*выражает боль*) ouch!, ow!; **им жило́сь ~ как тру́дно** their life was ever so difficult.

ОК *м сокр* (= отде́л ка́дров) personnel department.

ок|аза́ть (-ажу́, -а́жешь; *impf* ока́зывать) *сов перех*: ~ **по́мощь/соде́йствие кому́-н** to provide help/assistance for sb; **ока́зывать** (~ *perf*) **влия́ние на** +*acc* to exercise influence over *или* on; **ока́зывать** (~ *perf*) **давле́ние на** +*acc* to put pressure on *или* upon; **ока́зывать** (~ *perf*) **внима́ние кому́-н** to pay attention to sb; **ока́зывать** (~ *perf*) **предпочте́ние кому́-н** to give preference to sb; **ока́зывать** (~ *perf*) **сопротивле́ние (кому́-н)** to offer resistance (to sb); **ока́зывать** (~ *perf*) **услу́гу кому́-н** to do sb a service

▶ **оказа́ться** (*impf* ока́зываться) *сов возв* (*найтись: на столе итп*) to appear; (*очути́ться: на острове итп*) to find o.s.; **ока́зываться** (~ся *perf*) +*instr* (*вором, шпионом*) to turn out to be; ~**а́зывается, она́ была́ права́** it turns out that she was right; **у него́ не ~аза́лось де́нег** it turned out that he didn't have any money.

ока́зи|я (-и) *ж* opportunity; **посыла́ть (посла́ть** *perf*) **что-н ~ей** to send sth with somebody.

ока́зыва|ть(ся) (-ю(сь)) *несов от* оказа́ть(ся).

окайм|и́ть (-лю́, -и́шь; *impf* окаймля́ть) *сов перех* (*рисунок*) to frame; (*платок*) to border.

окамени́ва|ть (-ю) *сов от* камене́ть.

окамене́л|ый *прил* (*дерево, растение*) fossilized; (*хлеб, сыр*) rock-hard; (*перен: человек, взгляд, лицо*) motionless.

окамене́|ть (-ю; *impf* окаменева́ть *или* камене́ть) *сов неперех* (*дерево, растение*) to fossilize; (*хлеб, сыр*) to go stale; (*перен: лицо, взгляд*) to freeze; (: *душа, сердце*) to turn to stone; ~ (*perf*) **от стра́ха** to turn rigid with fear; ~ (*perf*) **от го́ря** to be numb with grief.

окант|ова́ть (-у́ю; *impf* оканто́вывать) *сов перех* (*картину, фотогра́фию*) to frame; (*воротник, платок*) to border.

ока́нчива|ть (-ю) *несов от* око́нчить.

▶ **ока́нчиваться** *несов от* око́нчиться ◆ *возв*: ~ся **на гла́сную/согла́сную** to end in a vowel/

consonant; **э́та у́лица ~ется тупико́м** this (street) is a dead end.

ока́пыва|ть(ся) (-ю(сь)) *несов от* **окопа́ть(ся)**.

ока|ти́ть (-чу́, -́тишь; *impf* **ока́чивать**) *сов перех*: ~ **кого́-н/что-н чем-н** to pour sth over sb/sth.

океа́н (-а) *м* (*также перен*) ocean.

Океа́ни|я (-и) *ж* Oceania.

океаноло́ги|я (-и) *ж* oceanography.

оки́|нуть (-у, -ешь; *impf* **оки́дывать**) *сов перех*: ~ **кого́-н/что-н взгля́дом** to glance over at sb/sth.

о́кис|ел (-ла) *м* oxide.

окисле́ни|е (-я) *ср* oxidation.

окисл|и́ть (*3sg* -и́т, *3pl* -я́т, *impf* **окисля́ть**) *сов перех* to oxidize.

▶ **окисли́ться** (*impf* **окисля́ться**) *сов возв* to oxidize.

о́кис|ь (-и) *ж* oxide.

оккупа́нт (-а) *м* (*захватчик*) occupier.

оккупацио́нный *прил* occupation *опред*.

оккупа́ци|я (-и) *ж* occupation.

оккупи́р|овать (-ую) (*не*)*сов перех* to occupy.

окла́д (-а) *м* (*зарплата*) salary; (*на иконе*) overlay.

оклевета́ть (-ещу́, -е́щешь) *сов перех* to slander.

окле́|ить (-ю, -ишь; *impf* **окле́ивать**) *сов перех*: ~ **что-н чем-н** to cover sth with sth; **окле́ивать** (~ *perf*) **сте́ны обо́ями** to paper the walls.

оклик|нуть (-у, -ешь; *impf* **оклика́ть**) *сов перех* to call out to.

ок|но́ (-на́; *nom pl* -на, *gen pl* -он) *ср* window; (*подоконник*) windowsill; (*разг: между уроками*) gap.

око́в|ы (-) *мн* (*также перен*) fetters *мн*.

окола́чива|ться (-юсь) *несов возв* (*разг*) to hang about.

околд|ова́ть (-у́ю; *impf* **околдо́вывать**) *сов перех* (*также перен*) to bewitch.

околева́|ть (-ю) *несов от* **околе́ть**.

околе́сиц|а (-ы) *ж* (*разг*) claptrap, tripe; **нести́** (*impf*) ~**у** to talk tripe.

околе́|ть (-ю; *impf* **околева́ть**) *сов неперех* (*животное*) to die.

о́коло *нареч* nearby ♦ *предл* (+*gen*; *рядом с*) near; (*приблизительно*) about.

околозе́мн|ый *прил* around the earth; ~**ая орби́та** the earth's orbit.

око́льн|ый *прил* roundabout *опред*; (*перен: метод*) devious; **мы пошли́** ~**ым путём** we took a roundabout route.

окольцева́ть (-у́ю) *сов от* **кольцева́ть**.

о́кон *сущ см* **окно́**.

оконе́чност|ь (-и) *ж* tip.

око́нн|ый *прил*: ~**ая ра́ма** window frame; ~**ое стекло́** windowpane.

оконча́ни|е (-я) *ср* end; (*линг*) ending.

оконча́телен *прил см* **оконча́тельный**.

оконча́тельно *нареч* (*решить, ответить*) definitely; (*разбить, победить, влюби́ться*) completely; (*отредакти́ровать, прове́рить*) finally.

оконча́тельн|ый (-ен, -ьна, -ьно) *прил* (*вывод, реда́кция, ответ*) final; (*победа, сверже́ние*) complete.

око́нч|ить (-у, -ишь; *impf* **ока́нчивать**) *сов перех* to finish; (*вуз*) to graduate from

▶ **око́нчиться** (*impf* **ока́нчиваться**) *сов возв* to finish; ~**ся** (*perf*) +*instr* (*сканда́лом, сва́дьбой*) to result in.

око́п (-а) *м* trench.

окопа́|ть (-ю; *impf* **ока́пывать**) *сов перех*: ~ **расте́ние** to loosen the soil around a plant

▶ **окопа́ться** (*impf* **ока́пываться**) *сов возв* (*воен*) to dig (o.s.) in; (*разг: в библиоте́ке, в кабине́те*) to bury o.s.

о́корок (-а; *nom pl* -á) *м* gammon.

окосе́|ть (-ю) *сов неперех* (*разг: коси́ть*) to squint; (: *ослепну́ть*) to lose an eye; (: *опьяне́ть*) to get drunk.

окостенева́|ть (-ю) *несов от* **окостене́ть**.

окостене́лый *прил* ossified; (*руки, ноги*) stiff; (*ум, жизнь*) fossilized.

окостене́|ть (-ю; *impf* **окостенева́ть**) *сов неперех* to ossify; (*руки, ноги*) to stiffen; (*ум*) to fossilize.

око́т (-а) *м* (*кошки*) birth of kittens; (*овцы*) lambing.

око|ти́ться (*3sg* -и́тся, *3pl* -я́тся) *сов от* **коти́ться**.

окочене́лый *прил* stiff with cold.

окочене́|ть (-ю) *сов от* **кочене́ть**.

окра́ин|а (-ы) *ж* (*поля, леса*) edge; (*города*) outskirts *мн*; (*страны*) remote parts *мн*.

окра́|сить (-шу, -сишь; *impf* **окра́шивать**) *сов перех* (*ткань, волосы*) to dye; (*рассказ, жизнь*) to colour (*BRIT*), color (*US*)

▶ **окра́ситься** (*impf* **окра́шиваться**) *сов возв*: ~**ся в чёрный/кра́сный цвет** to come out black/red; **облака́** ~**сились в ро́зовый цвет** the clouds were tinged with pink.

окра́с|ка (-ки; *gen pl* -ок) *ж* (*ткани, волос*) dyeing; (*животного, выраже́ния*) colouring (*BRIT*), coloring (*US*); **принима́ть** (**приня́ть** *perf*) **совсе́м другу́ю** ~**ку** (*перен*) to take on a different complexion.

окра́шива|ть(ся) (-ю(сь)) *несов от* **окра́сить(ся)**.

окра́шу(сь) *сов см* **окра́сить(ся)**.

окре́п|нуть (-у, -ешь) *сов см* **кре́пнуть**.

окре|сти́ть (-щу́, -́стишь) *сов от* **крести́ть** ♦ *сов перех*: ~ **кого́-н/что-н чем-н** (*разг*) to nickname sb/sth sth

▶ **окрести́ться** *сов от* **крести́ться**.

окре́стност|ь (-и) *ж* (*города, дере́вни*) environs

мн; **в ~и** +gen in the vicinity of.
окре́стн|ый прил (города́, дере́вни)
neighbouring (BRIT), neighboring (US); **~ое
населе́ние** the population of the surrounding
area.
окрещу́(сь) сов см **окрести́ть(ся)**.
окриве́|ть (-ю) сов от **криве́ть**.
о́крик (-а) м shout.
окри́кн|уть (-у, -ешь; impf **окри́кивать**) сов
перех: **~ кого́-н** to shout to sb.
окрова́влен|ный (-, -а, -о) прил bloodstained.
окропи́|ть (-лю́, -йшь) сов от **кропи́ть**.
окро́шк|а (-и) ж okroshka (cold kvass soup with
vegetables and cooked meat).
о́круг (-а) м (администрати́вный, вое́нный)
district; (избира́тельный) ward;
(национа́льный) territory; (города́) area.
окру́г|а (-и) ж (разг) neighbourhood (BRIT),
neighborhood (US).
округле́|ть (-ю) сов от **кругле́ть**.
округли́|ть (-ю, -йшь; impf **округля́ть**) сов
перех (фо́рму, загото́вку) to round off; (ци́фру,
результа́т) to round up или down; (разг:
су́мму, капита́л) to increase; **округля́ть (~** perf)
глаза́ (от удивле́ния, от стра́ха) to open one's
eyes wide
▸ **округли́ться** (impf **округля́ться**) сов возв
(фигу́ра, лицо́) to fill out; (перен: разг:
капита́л, су́мма) to increase; **у неё́ ~йлись
глаза́** her eyes widened.
окру́глый прил rounded; (лицо́) round.
округля́|ть(ся) (-ю(сь)) несов от
округли́ть(ся).
окружа́|ть (-ю) несов от **окружи́ть** ♦ перех to
surround.
окружа́ющее (-его; decl like adj) ср
environment.
окружа́ющие (-их; decl like adj) мн (та́кже: ~
лю́ди) the people around one; **ничего́ нельзя́
скрыть от ~их** you can't hide anything from
(other) people.
окружа́ющий (-ая, -ее, -ие) прил surrounding;
окружа́ющая среда́ environment.
окруже́ни|е (-я) ср (среда́) environment;
(компа́ния) company; (ВОЕН) encirclement; **в
~и** +gen (в сопровожде́ние) in the company of;
(среди́) surrounded by.
окруж|и́ть (-у́, -и́шь; impf **окружа́ть**) сов перех
to surround; **окружа́ть (~** perf) **что-н** +instr to
surround sth by; **окружа́ть (~** perf) **кого́-н** +instr
to surround sb with.
окружно́й прил (центр, конфере́нция) regional;
окружна́я доро́га bypass; **окружна́я
избира́тельная коми́ссия** constituency
electoral committee.
окру́жность (-и) ж circle; **на три киломе́тра в
~и** three kilometres (BRIT) или kilometers (US)
in circumference.
О́ксфорд (-а) м Oxford.
окта́в|а (-ы) ж octave.
октя́бр|ь (-я́) м October; **прие́ду пе́рвого**

октября́ I shall arrive on the first of October; **в
про́шлом/бу́дущем октябре́** last/next October;
в конце́/нача́ле/середи́не октября́ at the end
of/beginning of/in the middle of October.
октя́брьск|ий (-ая, -ое, -ие) прил October
опред.
окули́ст (-а) м ophthalmologist.
окун|у́ть (-у́, -ёшь; impf **окуна́ть**) сов перех to
dip
▸ **окуну́ться** (impf **окуна́ться**) сов возв to
plunge.
о́кун|ь (-я) м (ЗООЛ) perch.
окупа́емость (-и) ж viability.
ок|упи́ть (-уплю́, -у́пишь; impf **окупа́ть**) сов
перех (расхо́ды) to cover; (пое́здку, прое́кт) to
cover the cost of
▸ **окупи́ться** (impf **окупа́ться**) сов возв to pay
for itself; (перен: уси́лия, рабо́та) to be
rewarded.
оку́р|ок (-ка; nom pl -ки) м stub, butt.
оку́та|ть (-ю; impf **оку́тывать**) сов перех
(подлеж: тума́н, дым) to envelop; **оку́тывать
(~** perf) **что-н/кого́-н чем-н** to wrap sth/sb (up)
in sth
▸ **оку́таться** (impf **оку́тываться**) сов возв: **~ся
**+instr to wrap up in; (перен: земля́ итп) to be
enveloped in.
оку́ч|ить (-у, -ишь; impf **оку́чивать**) сов перех to
earth up.
ола́дь|я (-и; gen pl -ий) ж ≈ drop scone, ≈
(Scotch) pancake.
оледене́ни|е (-я) ср freezing.
оледене́|ть (-ю) сов от **ледене́ть**.
олен|ёнок (-ёнка; nom pl -я́та, gen pl -я́т) м fawn.
оле́н|ий (-ья, -ье, -ьи) прил deer's; **~ьи рога́**
antlers.
олени́н|а (-ы) ж venison.
оле́н|ь (-я) м deer (мн deer).
оленя́та итп сущ см **оленёнок**.
оли́вк|а (-и) ж olive.
оли́вковый прил olive опред; (цвет) olive-
green.
олимпиа́д|а (-ы) ж (СПОРТ) the Olympics мн;
(по фи́зике итп) Olympiad; **Бе́лая/Ле́тняя О~**
the Winter/Summer Olympics.
олимпи́йск|ий (-ая, -ое, -ие) прил Olympic
опред; **~ое споко́йствие** superhuman calm;
олимпи́йские и́гры the Olympic Games.
оли́ф|а (-ы) ж drying oil.
олицетвор|и́ть (-ю́, -и́шь; impf **олицетворя́ть**)
сов перех to personify.
о́лов|о (-а) ср (ХИМ) tin.
оловя́нный прил tin.
о́лух (-а) м (разг) oaf.
О́льстер (-а) м Ulster.
ольх|а́ (-и́) ж alder.
ом (-а) м ohm.
Ома́н (-а) м Oman.
ома́р (-а) м lobster.
оме́г|а (-и) ж omega.
омерзе́ни|е (-я) ср disgust.

омерзи́тельн|ый (-ен, -ьна, -ьно) *прил* disgusting.

омертве́лый *прил* dead.

омертве́|ть (-ю) *сов от* **мертве́ть**.

омле́т (-а) *м* omelette.

омоло|ди́ть (-жу́, -ди́шь; *impf* **омола́живать**) *сов перех* to rejuvenate

▶ **омолоди́ться** (*impf* **омола́живаться**) *сов возв* to be rejuvenated.

ОМО́Н *м сокр* (= отря́д мили́ции осо́бого назначе́ния) *special police force*.

омо́ним (-а) *м* homonym.

омоно́в|ец (-ца) *м member of ОМОН*.

омо́ю *итп сов см* **омы́ть**.

омрач|и́ть (-у́, -и́шь; *impf* **омрача́ть**) *сов перех* (настрое́ние, ра́дость, лицо́) to cloud; (пра́здник, встре́чу) to cast a cloud over

▶ **омрачи́ться** (*impf* **омрача́ться**) *сов возв* (взгляд, лицо́, настрое́ние) to darken.

о́мут (-а) *м* (водоворо́т) whirlpool.

омыва́|ть (-ю) *несов от* **омы́ть** ♦ *перех* (подлеж: мо́ре, океа́н) to wash.

омы́|ть (-о́ю, -о́ешь; *impf* **омыва́ть**) *сов перех* to wash.

он (его́; *см* Table 5a) *мест* (челове́к) he; (живо́тное, предме́т) it.

она́ (её; *см* Table 5a) *мест* (челове́к) she; (живо́тное, предме́т) it.

онани́зм (-а) *м* masturbation.

онда́тр|а (-ы) *ж* musquash, muskrat.

онеме́лый *прил* numb.

онеме́|ть (-ю) *сов от* **неме́ть**.

они́ (их; *см* Table 5b) *мест* they.

онко́лог (-а) *м* oncologist.

онкологи́ческ|ий (-ая, -ое, -ие) *прил* oncological; **~ая кли́ника** cancer clinic.

оно́ (его́; *см* Table 5a) *мест* it; **~ и ви́дно!** (*разг*) sure! (*used ironically*); **я хоте́л помо́чь Вам – ~ и ви́дно** I was only trying to help you – sure you were; **вот ~ что** или **как!** (*разг*) so that's what it is!

ОНЧ *сокр* (= о́чень ни́зкая частота́) VLF (= *very low frequency*).

ООН *ж сокр* (= Организа́ция Объединённых На́ций) UNO (= *United Nations Organization*).

ООП *ж сокр* (= Организа́ция освобожде́ния Палести́ны) PLO (= *Palestine Liberation Organization*).

опада́|ть (*3sg* -ет, *3pl* -ют) *несов от* **опа́сть**.

опаду́т *итп сов см* **опа́сть**.

опа́здыва|ть (-ю) *несов от* **опозда́ть**.

опа́л (-а) *м* opal.

опа́л|а (-ы) *ж* (перен) disfavour (*BRIT*), disfavor (*US*); **быть** (*impf*) **в ~е** (**у** +*gen*) to be out of favour (with).

опал|и́ть (-ю́, -и́шь; *impf* **опа́ливать** или **опаля́ть**) *сов перех* (во́лосы, кры́лья, де́рево итп) to singe; (ко́жу, лицо́) to burn; (*impf*

опа́ливать; ку́рицу, у́тку) to singe.

опа́р|а (-ы) *ж* leaven.

опаса́|ться (-юсь) *несов возв*: **~** +*gen* (неприя́теля, реце́нзента) to be afraid of; (сквозняка́, просту́ды) to avoid; **~** (*impf*) **за** +*acc* to be worried about.

опа́сен *прил см* **опа́сный**.

опасе́ни|е (-я) *ср* apprehension.

опа́ск|а (-и) *ж*: **с ~ой** cautiously; **без ~и** fearlessly.

опа́сно *нареч* dangerously ♦ *как сказ* it's dangerous; **э́то ~ для жи́зни** it's life-threatening.

опа́сность (-и) *ж* danger; **в ~и** in danger; **с ~ю для жи́зни** endangering one's life.

опа́с|ный (-ен, -на, -но) *прил* dangerous.

опа́|сть (*3sg* -дёт, *3pl* -ду́т, *impf* **опада́ть**) *сов неперех* (цветы́, ли́стья) to fall; (о́пухоль, ши́шка) to go down; (*разг*: щёки, бока́) to get thinner.

ОПЕК *м/ж сокр* (= Организа́ция стран-экспортёров не́фти) OPEC (= *Organization of Petroleum-Exporting Countries*).

опе́к|а (-и) *ж* (попечи́тельство: госуда́рства) guardianship; (: ма́тери, отца́) custody; (забо́та) care ♦ *собир* guardians *мн*; **брать** (**взять** *perf*) **кого́-н под ~у** to take sb into one's care; **она́ рабо́тает под мое́й ~ой** she works under my supervision.

опека́|ть (-ю) *несов перех* to take care of; (сироту́) to be guardian to.

опеку́н (-а́) *м* (сироты́) guardian; (насле́дника, насле́дства) trustee.

опеку́нш|а (-и) *ж* (сироты́) guardian.

опёнок (-ёнка; *nom pl* -я́та, *gen pl* -я́т) *м* (БОТ) honey agaric.

о́пер|а (-ы) *ж* opera.

операти́вен *прил см* **операти́вный**.

операти́вность (-и) *ж* efficiency.

операти́в|ный (-ен, -на, -но) *прил* (рабо́та, гру́ппа, штаб) executive *опред*; (ме́ры, де́йствия, руково́дство) efficient; (хирурги́ческий) surgical; **операти́вное вмеша́тельство** surgical intervention.

опера́тор (-а) *м* operator.

операцио́нн|ая (-ой; *decl like adj*) *ж* (МЕД) operating theatre (*BRIT*) или room (*US*).

операцио́нный *прил* (инструме́нты, отделе́ние) surgical; **операцио́нный стол** operating table.

опера́ци|я (-и) *ж* operation.

опере|ди́ть (-жу́, -ди́шь; *impf* **опережа́ть**) *сов перех* (в бе́ге, в учёбе, в разви́тии) to outstrip; **~** (*perf*) **кого́-н** (в разгово́ре) to beat sb to it.

опере́ни|е (-я) *ср* (ЗООЛ) plumage; (АВИА): **хвостово́е ~** tail.

опере́тт|а (-ы) *ж* operetta.

опере́ться (обопру́сь, обопрёшься; *pt*
опёрся, оперла́сь, оперло́сь, *impf* опира́ться)
сов неперех: ~ на +*acc* (*дерево, трость*) to
lean on; (*перен: на това́рища, на коллекти́в*)
to rely on; (*перен: на фа́кты, на тео́рию*) to be
supported *или* backed up by.
опери́р|овать (-ую; *perf* опери́ровать *или*
проопери́ровать) *несов перех* (*больно́го*) to
operate on ♦ *неперех* (*no perf; ВОЕН*) to operate;
~ (*impf*) +*instr* (*а́кциями, це́нными бума́гами*) to
deal in; (*перен: ци́фрами, фа́ктами*) to use.
опери́ться (*3sg* -и́тся, *3pl* -я́тся, *impf*
оперя́ться) *сов возв* to become fully fledged.
о́перный *прил* (*а́рия, партиту́ра*) operatic;
(*певец*) opera *опред*; ~ теа́тр opera house.
оперя́|ться (*3sg* -ется, *3pl* -ются) *несов от*
опери́ться.
опеча́л|иться (-юсь) *сов от* печа́литься.
опеча́та|ть (-ю; *impf* опеча́тывать) *сов перех* to
seal.
опеча́т|ка (-ки; *gen pl* -ок) *ж* misprint; спи́сок
~ок errata.
опеча́тыва|ть (-ю) *несов от* опеча́тать.
опе́ш|ить (-у, -ишь) *сов неперех* (*разг*) to be
taken aback.
опи́л|ки (-ок) *мн* (*древе́сные*) sawdust *ед*;
(*металли́ческие*) filings *мн*.
опира́|ться (-юсь) *несов от* опере́ться.
описа́ни|е (-я) *ср* description.
описа́тел|ьный (-ен, -ьна, -ьно) *прил*
descriptive.
опи|са́ть (-ишу́, -и́шешь; *impf* опи́сывать) *сов*
перех to describe; (*соста́вить пере́чень*) to
make a list *или* an inventory of; (*наложи́ть*
аре́ст) to distrain.
опи|са́ться (-шу́сь) *сов возв* (*разг*) to wet o.s.
опи́сыва|ть (-ю) *несов от* описа́ть.
о́пис|ь (-и) *ж* (*спи́сок*) list, inventory; (*аре́ст*)
distraint.
о́пиум (-а) *м* opium.
опишу́ *итп сов см* описа́ть.
опла́к|ать (-чу, -чешь; *impf* опла́кивать) *сов*
перех to mourn.
опла́т|а (-ы) *ж* payment.
опла|ти́ть (-чу́, -а́тишь; *impf* опла́чивать) *сов*
перех (*рабо́ту, труд*) to pay for; (*счёт*) to pay.
оплачу́ *итп сов см* оплати́ть.
опла́чу *сов см* опла́кать.
оплеу́х|а (-и) *ж* (*разг*) clout; (*перен:*
оскорбле́ние) slap in the face.
оплодотворе́ни|е (-я) *ср* fertilization.
оплодотвор|и́ть (-ю́, -и́шь; *impf*
оплодотворя́ть) *сов перех* to fertilize.
опломбир|ова́ть (-у́ю) *сов от* пломбирова́ть.
опло́т (-а) *м* stronghold, bastion.
опло|ша́ть (-ю) *сов неперех* (*разг*) to boob.
опло́шност|ь (-и) *ж* mistake; допуска́ть
(допусти́ть *perf*) ~ to make a mistake.
опове|сти́ть (-щу́, -сти́шь; *impf* оповеща́ть)
сов перех to notify.
оповеще́ни|е (-я) *ср* notification.

оповещу́ *сов см* оповести́ть.
опога́н|ить (-ю) *сов от* пога́нить.
опозда́|вший (-его; *decl like adj*) *м* latecomer.
опозда́ни|е (-я) *ср* lateness; (*по́езда, самолёта*)
late arrival; приходи́ть (прийти́ *perf*) с ~м/без
опозда́ния to arrive late/on time.
опозда́|ть (-ю; *impf* опа́здывать) *сов неперех*:
опа́здывать (в/на +*acc*) (*в шко́лу, на рабо́ту*
итп) to be late (for); опа́здывать (~ *perf*) с
чем-н to be late with sth; ~ (*perf*) на
по́езд/самолёт to miss the train/plane.
опознава́тельный *прил* (*знак*) identifying;
(*огни́*) distinguishing.
опозна|ва́ть (-ю́) *несов от* опозна́ть.
опозна́ни|е (-я) *ср* identification.
опозна́|ть (-ю; *impf* опознава́ть) *сов перех* to
identify.
опозо́р|ить(ся) (-ю(сь)) *сов от* позо́рить(ся).
ополо́скива|ть (-ю) *несов от* ополосну́ть.
о́ползен|ь (-ня) *м* landslide.
ополосн|у́ть (-у́, -ёшь; *impf* ополо́скивать) *сов*
перех (*посу́ду*) to rinse; (*лицо́, ру́ки*) to wash.
ополоу́ме|ть (-ю) *сов неперех* (*разг*) to go
wild.
ополча́|ться (-юсь) *несов от* ополчи́ться.
ополче́н|ец (-ца) *м* member of the home guard.
ополче́ни|е (-я) *ср* home guard.
ополче́нца *итп сущ см* ополче́нец.
ополч|и́ться (-у́сь, -и́шься; *impf* ополча́ться)
сов возв: ~ на +*acc или* про́тив +*gen* (*челове́ка*)
to turn against; (*тео́рию, недоста́тки*) to
attack.
опо́мн|иться (-юсь, -ишься) *сов возв* (*прийти́*
в созна́ние) to come round; (*оду́маться*) to
come to one's senses; ~ись, что ты де́лаешь!
think what you're doing!
опо́р (-а) *м*: во весь ~ at top speed.
опо́р|а (-ы) *ж* (*та́кже перен*) support; (*стро́ит*)
pile; то́чка ~ы fulcrum; опо́ра
электропереда́ч (*обы́чно мн*) electricity pylon.
опо́рный *прил* supporting *опред*; опо́рный
прыжо́к vault; опо́рный пункт base; (*ВОЕН*)
strongpoint.
опорожн|и́ть (-ю́, -и́шь; *impf* опорожня́ть) *сов*
перех to drain, empty.
опоро́с (-а) *м* farrowing.
опоро́ч|ить (-у, -ишь) *сов от* поро́чить.
опохмел|и́ться (-ю́сь, -и́шься; *impf*
опохмеля́ться) *сов возв* (*разг*) to take the hair
of the dog (*to cure a hangover*).
опо́шл|ить (-ю, -ишь; *impf* опошля́ть) *сов*
перех (*мысль, челове́ка, и́мя*) to debase,
demean; (*сло́во, пе́сню*) to vulgarize.
опоэтизи́р|овать (-ую) *сов от*
поэтизи́ровать.
оппозицио́н|ный (-ен, -на, -но) *прил* (*па́ртия,*
блок) opposition; ~ные настрое́ния mood of
opposition.
оппози́ци|я (-и) *ж* opposition; быть (*impf*) в ~и
(*полит*) to be in opposition; быть (*impf*) в ~и к
+*dat* to oppose.

оппонéнт (-а) *м* external examiner (*for doctoral thesis*); (*в споре*) opponent.

опрáв|**а** (-ы) *ж* frame.

оправдáни|**е** (-я) *ср* justification; (*ЮР*) acquittal; (*извинение*) excuse; **говорить** (**сказáть** *perf*) **что-н в своё ~** to say sth in one's defence (*BRIT*) *или* defense (*US*).

опрáвдан|**ный** (-, -на, -но) *прил* justified.

оправдá|**ть** (-ю; *impf* **опрáвдывать**) *сов перех* to justify; (*ЮР*) to acquit, find not guilty

▶ **оправдáться** (*impf* **опрáвдываться**) *сов возв* to justify o.s.; (*надежды, опасения, расходы*) to be justified.

опрáв|**ить** (-лю, -ишь; *impf* **оправлять**) *сов перех* (*платье, постель*) to straighten; (*драгоценный камень, зеркало*) to mount; (*линзы*) to frame

▶ **опрáвиться** (*impf* **оправляться**) *сов возв*: **~ся от** +*gen* to recover from.

опрáшива|**ть** (-ю) *несов от* **опросить**.

определéни|**е** (-я) *ср* determination; (*понятия, значения*) definition; (*линг*) attribute; (*ЮР*) ruling.

определён|**ный** (-ен, -на, -но) *прил* (*установленный*) definite; (*некоторый*) certain; (*явный: успех, способности*) unqualified; **при ~ных обстоятельствах** under certain circumstances.

определ|**ить** (-ю, -ишь; *impf* **определять**) *сов перех* to determine; (*явление, понятие*) to define

▶ **определиться** (*impf* **определяться**) *сов возв* (*болезнь*) to be diagnosed; (*задачи*) to become clear; (*разг: характер*) to take shape; (*пилот*) to get one's bearings.

опрéлост|**ь** (-и) *ж* rash; (*у младенца*) nappy (*BRIT*) *или* diaper (*US*) rash.

опресн|**ить** (-ю, -ишь; *impf* **опреснять**) *сов перех* to desalinate.

оприхóд|**овать** (-ую) *сов от* **прихóдовать**.

опрóб|**овать** (-ую) (*не)сов перех* to test.

опровéргн|**уть** (-у, -ешь; *impf* **опровергáть**) *сов перех* to refute.

опровержéни|**е** (-я) *ср* refutation.

опрокин|**уть** (-у, -ешь; *impf* **опрокидывать**) *сов перех* (*стакан, стул*) to knock over; (*лодку*) to capsize, overturn; (*прохожего, ребёнка*) to knock down *или* over; (*перен: войска, наступление*) to repel; (: *взгляды, представления*) to demolish

▶ **опрокинуться** (*impf* **опрокидываться**) *сов возв* (*стакан, стул, человек*) to fall over; (*лодка*) to capsize.

опромéтчив|**ый** (-, -а, -о) *прил* precipitate, hasty.

óпрометью *нареч* headlong.

опрóс (-а) *м* (*свидетелей*) questioning; (*населения*) survey; **опрóс общéственного**

мнéния opinion poll.

опр|**осить** (-ошу, -óсишь; *impf* **опрáшивать**) *сов перех* (*свидетелей*) to question; (*население*) to survey.

опрóсный *прил*: **~ лист** questionnaire.

опротест|**овáть** (-ую; *impf* **опротестóвывать**) *сов перех* (*ЮР*) to appeal against; (*вексель*) to protest.

опротив|**е**|**ть** (-ю) *сов неперех*: **мне э́то ~ло** I am sick of it.

опрошу́ *сов см* **опросить**.

опры́ск|**ать** (-ю; *impf* **опры́скивать**) *сов перех* to spray.

опры́скиватель (-я) *м* sprayer; (*садовый*) sprinkler.

опры́скива|**ть** (-ю) *несов от* **опры́скать**.

опря́тный (-ен, -на, -но) *прил* neat, tidy.

óптик|**а** (-и) *ж* (*раздел физики*) optics ◆ *собир* optical instruments *мн*.

оптимáль|**ный** (-ен, -ьна, -ьно) *прил* optimum.

оптимизм (-а) *м* optimism.

оптимист (-а) *м* optimist.

оптимисти́ч|**ный** (-ен, -на, -но) *прил* optimistic.

опти́ческ|**ий** (-ая, -ое, -ие) *прил* optical.

оптови́к (-á) *м* wholesaler.

оптóв|**ый** *прил* wholesale; **~ые закýпки** (*КОММ*) bulk buying.

óптом *нареч*: **купи́ть/прода́ть ~** to buy/sell wholesale.

опубликóвани|**е** (-я) *ср* (*статьи, книги*) publication; (*закона*) promulgation.

опублик|**овáть** (-ýю; *impf* **опубликóвывать** *или* **публиковáть**) *сов перех* (*статью, книгу*) to publish; (*закон*) to promulgate.

опускá|**ть(ся)** (-ю(сь)) *несов от* **опустить(ся)**.

опустéлый *прил* (*дом, сад*) empty; (*улица*) deserted.

опустé|**ть** (*3sg* -ет, *3pl* -ют) *сов от* **пустéть**.

оп|**устить** (-ущý, -ýстишь; *impf* **опускáть**) *сов перех* to lower; (*голову*) to bow; (*воротник*) to turn down; (*слово, параграф*) to miss out; **опускáть** (**~** *perf*) **в** +*acc* (*в стакан, в ящик*) to drop *или* put in(to); (*человека: в яму*) to lower into; **опускáть** (**~** *perf*) **рýки** (*перен*) to give up

▶ **опуститься** (*impf* **опускáться**) *сов возв* (*человек: на диван, на землю*) to sit (down); (*солнце*) to sink; (*мост, шлагбаум*) to be lowered; (*перен: человек*) to let o.s. go.

опустошá|**ть** (-ю) *несов от* **опустошить**.

опустошён|**ный** (-, -а, -о) *прил* (*человек, душа*) empty.

опустоши́тель|**ный** (-ен, -ьна, -ьно) *прил* devastating.

опустош|**и́ть** (-ý, -и́шь; *impf* **опустошáть**) *сов перех* (*страну, поле*) to devastate; (*разг: бутылку, ящик*) to empty; (*перен: жизнь, человека*) to ruin.

опу́та|**ть** (-ю; *impf* **опу́тывать**) *сов перех* (*подлеж: ветки, плющ*) to entangle; **опу́тывать** (~ *perf*) **чем-н** (*верёвками, интригами*) to enmesh in sth.

опу́хн|**уть** (-у, -ешь) *сов от* **пу́хнуть** ♦ (*impf* **опуха́ть**) *неперех* to swell (up).

о́пухол|**ь** (-и) *ж* (*на руке, на ноге*) swelling; (*внутренняя*) tumour (*BRIT*), tumor (*US*).

опу́хш|**ий** (-ая, -ее, -ие) *прил* swollen.

опу́шк|**а** (-и) *ж* (*леса*) edge; (*шапки, воротника*) trim(ming).

опуще́ни|**е** (-я) *ср* (*деталей, слов*) omission; (*желудка, матки*) prolapse.

опущу́(сь) *сов см* **опусти́ть(ся)**.

опыле́ни|**е** (-я) *ср* pollination.

опыл|**и́ть** (-ю́, -и́шь; *impf* **опыля́ть**) *сов перех* to pollinate; (*от вредителей*) to spray (*with insecticide*).

о́пыт (-а) *м* (*знания*) experience; (*эксперимент*) experiment; (*попытка*) attempt; **на со́бственном ~е** from (one's own) experience.

о́пыт|**ный** (-ен, -на, -но) *прил* (*врач, рабочий*) experienced; (*лаборатория, отдел*) experimental; (*экземпляр*) sample *опред*; (*полёт*) test *опред*; **~ экземпля́р** (test) sample; **дока́зывать** (**доказа́ть** *perf*) **что-н ~ным путём** to prove sth by experiment; **~ный образе́ц** sample.

опьяне́ни|**е** (-я) *ср* intoxication.

опьяне́ть (-ю) *сов от* **пьяне́ть**.

опьян|**и́ть** (-ю́, -и́шь; *impf* **опьяня́ть** *или* **пьяни́ть**) *сов перех* (*также перен*) to intoxicate.

опя́та *итп сущ см* **опёнок**.

опя́ть *нареч* again; **~ же** (*разг*) yet again; **~ два́дцать пять!** (*разг*) not again!

ора́в|**а** (-ы) *ж* (*разг*) gang.

орангута́н(г) (-а) *м* orang-utan.

ора́нжевый *прил* orange.

оранжере́йный *прил* hothouse *опред*.

оранжере́|**я** (-и) *ж* hothouse.

ора́тор (-а) *м* orator; (*выступающий*) speaker.

орато́ри|**я** (-и) *ж* oratorio.

ора́торск|**ий** (-ая, -ое, -ие) *прил* oratorical.

ор|**а́ть** (-у́, -ёшь) *несов неперех* (*разг*) to yell; (: *ребёнок*) to bawl, howl; **~** (*impf*) **во всё го́рло** (*разг*) to yell at the top of one's voice.

орби́т|**а** (-ы) *ж* orbit.

орбита́льный *прил* orbital.

о́рган (-а) *м* (*также АНАТ*) organ; (*здравоохранения*) body; (*орудие*): **~ +gen** (*пропаганды*) vehicle for; **ме́стные ~ы вла́сти** local authorities (*BRIT*) *или* government (*US*); **половы́е ~ы** genitals; *см также* **о́рганы**.

орга́н (-а) *м* (*МУЗ*) organ.

организа́тор (-а) *м* organizer.

организа́торск|**ий** (-ая, -ое, -ие) *прил* organizational.

организацио́нный *прил* organizational.

организа́ци|**я** (-и) *ж* organization; (*устройство*) system; **Организа́ция Объединённых На́ций** United Nations Organization.

органи́зм (-а) *м* organism.

организо́ван|**ный** (-, -на, -но) *прил* organized; **организо́ванная престу́пность** organized crime.

организ|**ова́ть** (-у́ю) (*не*)*сов перех* (*создать*) to organize

▸ **организова́ться** (*не*)*сов возв* to be organized; (*в отряд, в ансамбль*) to organize o.s.; (*разг: жизнь*) to sort o.s. out.

органи́ст (-а) *м* organist.

органи́ческ|**ий** (-ая, -ое, -ие) *прил* organic; (*перен: неприязнь, отвращение*) natural; **~ поро́к се́рдца** heart defect.

о́рган|**ы** (-ов) *мн* (*разг*) *the Ministry of Internal Affairs and the KGB*.

о́рги|**я** (-и) *ж* orgy.

оргкомите́т (-а) *м сокр* (= *организацио́нный комите́т*) organizational committee.

орграбо́т|**а** (-ы) *ж сокр* (= *организацио́нная рабо́та*) organizational work.

оргте́хник|**а** (-и) *ж* office automation equipment.

орд|**а́** (-ы́; *nom pl* **о́рды**) *ж* horde.

о́рден (-а; *nom pl* **-а́**) *м* order; (*nom pl* **-ы**; *рыцарский, масонский*) order.

орденоно́сный *прил* (*батальон, театр*) order-bearing.

орденоно́сца *итп сущ см* **орденоно́сец**.

о́рдер (-а) *м* (*на арест, на обыск*) warrant; (*на кварти́ру*) authorization.

ордина́р|**ный** (-ен, -на, -но) *прил* ordinary.

ордина́тор (-а) *м* (*МЕД*) ≈ registrar (*BRIT*), ≈ resident (*US*).

ординату́р|**а** (-ы) *ж two-year period in which junior doctor specializes in particular field*.

ор|**ёл** (орла́; *nom pl* **орлы́**) *м* eagle; (*перен: человек*) hero; **~ или ре́шка?** (*разг*) heads or tails?

Оренбу́рг (-а) *м* Orenburg.

оре́л (-а) *м* halo; (*перен: славы, таинственности*) aura.

оре́х (-а) *м* nut; (*древесина*) walnut; **мне доста́лось на ~и** (*разг*) I got it in the neck.

оре́ховый *прил* nut; (*мебель*) walnut.

оре́шник (-а) *м* (*кустарник*) hazel; (*собир: заросль*) hazel grove.

ОРЗ *ср сокр* (= *о́строе респирато́рное заболева́ние*) ARD (= *acute respiratory disease*).

оригина́л (-а) *м* original; (*разг: чудак*) eccentric.

оригина́льный (-ен, -ьна, -ьно) *прил* original.

ориента́ци|**я** (-и) *ж* orientation; **име́ть** (*impf*) **хоро́шую ~ю в чём-н** to have a good grasp of sth.

ориенти́р (-а) *м* landmark.

ориенти́р|**овать** (-ую) (*не*)*сов перех* to orient, orientate; (*перен*): **~ кого́-н на +acc** to orient *или* orientate sb towards

▸ **ориенти́роваться** (*perf* **ориенти́роваться**

или **сориенти́роваться**) *несов возв* to find *или* get one's bearings; (*перен: в ситуа́ции*) to find one's feet; (*разбира́ться*) to be versed; **~ся** (*impf/perf*) **на** +*acc* (*перен*) to be oriented *или* orientated towards; (*на мая́к, на со́лнце*) to find one's bearings by.

ориентиро́воч|ный (-ен, -на, -но) *прил* provisional; **~ пункт** landmark.

орке́стр (-а) *м* orchestra.

оркестра́нт (-а) *м* member of an orchestra.

оркестро́в|ка (-ки; *gen pl* -ок) *ж* orchestration.

оркне́йск|ий (-ая, -ое, -ие) *прил*: **О~ие острова́** Orkney Islands, Orkneys.

орла́ *итп сущ см* **орёл**.

орли́ный *прил* (*клюв, гнездо́*) eagle's; **~ взгляд** proud look.

орна́мент (-а) *м* (decorative) pattern.

орнито́лог (-а) *м* ornithologist.

орнитоло́ги|я (-и) *ж* ornithology.

оробе́|ть (-ю) *сов от* **робе́ть**.

ороси́тельный *прил* irrigation *опред*.

оро|си́ть (-шу́, -си́шь; *impf* **ороша́ть**) *сов перех* to irrigate; (*подлеж: дождь*) to water.

ороше́ни|е (-я) *ср* irrigation.

орошу́ *сов см* **ороси́ть**.

ортодокса́л|ьный (-ен, -ьна, -ьно) *прил* orthodox.

ортопе́д (-а) *м* orthopaedic (*BRIT*) *или* orthopedic (*US*) surgeon.

ортопеди́ческ|ий (-ая, -ое, -ие) *прил* orthopaedic (*BRIT*), orthopedic (*US*).

ору́ди|е (-я) *ср* (*также перен*) tool; (*ВОЕН*) gun (*used of artillery*).

ору́д|овать (-ую) *несов неперех* (+*instr*; *разг*: *вёслами, лопа́той*) to work away with; (: *вор, браконье́р*) to be at work.

оруже́йный *прил*: **~ заво́д** arsenal; **~ ма́стер** armourer (*BRIT*), armorer (*US*); **Оруже́йная пала́та** The Armoury Palace.

ору́жи|е (-я) *ж* (*также перен*) weapon; (*собир*) arms *мн*.

орфографи́ческ|ий (-ая, -ое, -ие) *прил* orthographical.

орфогра́фи|я (-и) *ж* (*правописа́ние*) spelling; (*правила*) orthography.

орхиде́|я (-и) *ж* orchid.

ос|а́ (-ы́; *nom pl* **о́сы**) *ж* wasp.

оса́д|а (-ы) *ж* siege; **снима́ть** (**снять** *perf*) **~у** to lift a siege.

оса|ди́ть (-жу́, -ди́шь; *impf* **осажда́ть**) *сов перех* to besiege; (*хим*) to precipitate; (*impf* **оса́живать**; *коня́, ло́шадь*) to rein in; **осажда́ть** (**~** *perf*) **кого́-н чем-н** (*перен*) to besiege sb with sth; **~** (*perf*) **кого́-н** (*разг*) to put sb in his *итп* place.

оса́дка *сущ см* **оса́док**.

оса́дк|и (-ов) *мн* precipitation *ед*.

оса́дн|ый *прил*: **~ое положе́ние** state of siege.

оса́д|ок (-ка) *м* sediment; **у меня́ оста́лся неприя́тный ~ от э́той встре́чи** the meeting left me with an unpleasant aftertaste.

оса́дочный *прил* sedimentary.

осажда́|ть (-ю) *несов от* **осади́ть**.

▶ **осажда́|ться** *несов возв* to precipitate.

оса́жива|ть (-ю) *несов от* **осади́ть**.

осажу́ *сов см* **осади́ть**.

оса́нист|ый (-, -а, -о) *прил* imposing.

оса́нк|а (-и) *ж* posture.

осатанева́|ть (-ю) *несов от* **осатане́ть**.

осатане́лый *прил* (*разг*) frenzied; (: *челове́к*) furious.

осатане́|ть (-ю; *impf* **осатанева́ть**) *сов неперех* (*разг*) to go wild; (: *надоеда́ть*): **~ кому́-н** to drive sb mad.

ОСВ *сокр = ограниче́ние стратеги́ческих наступа́тельных вооруже́ний*: **перегово́ры/догово́р ~** SALT (= *Strategic Arms Limitation Talks/Treaty*).

освА́ива|ть(ся) (-ю(сь)) *несов от* **осво́ить(ся)**.

осведоми́тел|ь (-я) *м* informer.

осведоми́тельниц|а (-ы) *ж см* **осведоми́тель**.

осведо́м|ить (-лю, -ишь; *impf* **осведомля́ть**) *сов перех* to inform

▶ **осведо́миться** (*impf* **осведомля́ться**) *сов возв*: **~ся о** +*prp* to inquire about; **осведомля́ться** (**~ся** *perf*) **о чьём-н здоро́вье** to inquire after sb's health.

осведомлён|ный (-, -на, -но) *прил* knowledgeable.

осведомлю́(сь) *сов см* **осве́домить(ся)**.

осведомля́|ть(ся) (-ю(сь)) *несов от* **осве́домить(ся)**.

освеж|и́ть (-у́, -и́шь; *impf* **освежа́ть**) *сов перех* (*во́здух*) to freshen; (*ко́мнату, пла́тье*) to freshen up; (*кра́ски*) to liven up; (*воспомина́ния, зна́ния*) to refresh; **о́тдых ~и́л меня́** I feel refreshed after my rest

▶ **освежи́ться** (*impf* **освежа́ться**) *сов возв* (*во́здух*) to freshen; (*челове́к: под ду́шем итп*) to freshen up; (*кра́ски*) to brighten up; (*воспомина́ния, зна́ния*) to be refreshed.

освети́тел|ь (-я) *м* (*ТЕА́ТР*) lighting technician.

освети́тельный *прил*: **~ прибо́р** light; **освети́тельная раке́та** flare.

осве|ти́ть (-щу́, -ти́шь; *impf* **освеща́ть**) *сов перех* (*также перен*) to light up; (*вопро́с, пробле́му, де́ло*) to highlight

▶ **освети́ться** (*impf* **освеща́ться**) *сов возв* (*также перен*) to be lit up; (*лицо́*) to light up.

освеще́ни|е (-я) *ср* lighting; (*вопро́са, пробле́мы, де́ла*) coverage.

освещу́(сь) *сов см* **освети́ть(ся)**.

осв|иста́ть (-ищу́, -и́щешь; *impf* **освистывать**) *сов перех* to boo.

освободи́тел|ь (-я) *м* liberator.

освободи́тельниц|**а** (-ы) *ж см* **освободи́тель**.

освободи́тельн|**ый** *прил* liberation *опред*; ~**ая война́** war of liberation.

освобод|**и́ть** (-жу́, -ди́шь; *impf* **освобожда́ть**) *сов перех* to release; (*из капкана*) to free; (*город, деревню*) to liberate; (*полку, комнату*) to clear; (*дом, квартиру*) to vacate; (*время, день*) to leave free; ~ *кого-н от* **хлопо́т/наказа́ния** to spare sb the trouble/from punishment; ~ (*perf*) **кого́-н от эксплуата́ции** to liberate sb from exploitation; ~ (*perf*) **кого́-н от до́лжности** to dismiss sb

▶ **освободи́ться** (*impf* **освобожда́ться**) *сов возв* (*из тюрьмы́*) to be released; (*из капкана: зверь*) to free itself; (: *человек*) to free o.s.; (*квартира, дом*) to be vacated; (*место, полка*) to be cleared; ~**ся** (*perf*) **от наказа́ния** to escape punishment; ~**ся** (*perf*) **от рабо́ты** to finish work.

освобожде́ни|**е** (-я) *ср* release, freeing; (*города, деревни*) liberation; ~ **от до́лжности** dismissal; ~ **от нало́гов** tax exemption.

освобожу́(сь) *сов см* **освободи́ть(ся)**.

ОСВОД *м сокр* = **Всеросси́йское о́бщество спасе́ния на во́дах**.

освое́ни|**е** (-я) *ср* (*см глаг*) mastering; cultivation.

осво́|**ить** (-ю, -ишь; *impf* **осва́ивать**) *сов перех* (*технику, язык*) to master; (*земли, пустыню*) to cultivate

▶ **осво́иться** (*impf* **осва́иваться**) *сов возв* (*на новой рабо́те*) to find one's feet.

освя|**ти́ть** (-щу́, -ти́шь; *impf* **освяща́ть** или **святи́ть**) *сов перех* (*РЕЛ*) to bless.

оседа́ть (-ю) *несов от* **осе́сть**.

оседла́ть (-ю) *сов от* **седла́ть** ♦ (*impf* **осёдлывать**) *несов перех* (*разг: стул, бревно́*) to straddle; (: *родственников, знакомых*) to take advantage of.

осе́длый *прил* settled.

осека́ться (-юсь) *несов от* **осе́чься**.

осе́кся *итп сов см* **осе́чься**.

осеку́сь *итп сов см* **осе́чься**.

ос|**ёл** (-ла́) *м* donkey; (*перен: разг*) ass.

осен|**и́ть** (3sg -и́т, 3pl -я́т, *impf* **осеня́ть**) *сов перех* (*подлеж: мысль*) to strike; **меня́ ~и́ло, что ...** it struck me that ...; **осеня́ть** (~ *perf*) **кресто́м** to bless.

осе́нн|**ий** (-яя, -ее, -ие) *прил* autumn *опред*, fall *опред* (*US*); (*похожий на осень: погода, день*) autumnal, fall.

о́сен|**ь** (-и) *ж* autumn, fall (*US*).

о́сенью *нареч* in autumn, in the fall (*US*).

осеня́ть (-ю) *несов от* **осени́ть**.

ос|**е́сть** (-я́ду, -я́дешь; *impf* **оседа́ть**) *сов неперех* (*пол, дом*) to subside; (*пыль, осадок*) to settle; **они́ ~е́ли в го́роде** they settled in the city.

осети́н (-а; *gen pl* -) *м* Ossetian.

осети́н|**ка** (-ки; *gen pl* -ок) *ж см* **осети́н**.

Осе́ти|**я** (-и) *ж*: **Се́верная/Южная ~** North/South Ossetia.

ос|**ётр** (-етра́) *м* sturgeon (*ZOOL*).

осетри́н|**а** (-ы) *ж* sturgeon (*CULIN*).

осе́ч|**ка** (-ки; *gen pl* -ек) *ж* (*перен: разг*) cockup (*BRIT*), mess (*US*); **дава́ть** (**дать** *perf*) ~**ку** to misfire.

ос|**е́чься** (-еку́сь, -ечёшься *итп*, -еку́тся; *pt* **ёкся, -ёклась, -ёклось**, *impf* **осека́ться**) *сов неперех* to stop short.

оси́л|**ить** (-ю, -ишь; *impf* **оси́ливать**) *сов перех* (*противника*) to overpower; (*разг: книгу*) to get through; (: *физику, упражне́ние*) to get to grips with.

оси́н|**а** (-ы) *ж* aspen.

оси́новый *прил* aspen *опред*.

оси́ный *прил*: ~**ое гнездо́** wasp's nest; (*перен*) hornet's nest.

оси́пн|**уть** (-у, -ешь) *сов от* **си́пнуть**.

осироте́вш|**ий** (-ая, -ее, -ие) *прил* (*ребёнок*) orphaned; (*перен: дом, сад*) abandoned.

осироте́лый *прил* = **осироте́вший**.

осироте́ть (-ю) *сов от* **сироте́ть**.

оска́л|**ить** (-ю, -ишь; *impf* **оска́ливать** или **ска́лить**) *сов перех*: ~ **зу́бы** (*также перен*) to bare one's teeth

▶ **оска́литься** (*impf* **оска́ливаться** или **ска́литься**) *сов возв* (*также перен*) to bare one's teeth; (*разг: осклабиться*) to smirk.

осканда́л|**иться** (-юсь, -ишься) *сов возв* (*разг*) to show o.s. up.

оскверн|**и́ть** (-ю́, -и́шь; *impf* **оскверня́ть**) *сов перех* to defile; (*чувства, иде́и*) to debase.

оскла́б|**иться** (-люсь, -ишся) *сов неперех* to grin.

оско́л|**ок** (-ка) *м* (*стекла, чашки*) piece; (: *мелкий*) sliver; (*бомбы, снаряда*) shrapnel *только ед*; (*перен: прошлого*) fragment.

оско́лочный *прил* (*рана, бомба*) shrapnel *опред*.

оско́мин|**а** (-ы) *ж* acidic taste; **наби́ть** (*perf*) **кому́-н** ~**у** (*перен*) to bore sb stupid.

оскоп|**и́ть** (-лю́, -и́шь; *impf* **оскопля́ть**) *сов перех* to castrate.

оскорби́тел|**ьный** (-ен, -ьна, -ьно) *прил* offensive.

оскорб|**и́ть** (-лю́, -и́шь; *impf* **оскорбля́ть**) *сов перех* to insult, offend; **оскорбля́ть** (~ *perf*) **кого́-н в лу́чших чу́вствах** to offend sb's finer feelings; **оскорбля́ть** (~ *perf*) **слух** to offend the ear

▶ **оскорби́ться** (*impf* **оскорбля́ться**) *сов возв* to be offended, take offence *или* offense (*US*).

оскорбле́ни|**е** (-я) *ср* insult.

оскорблю́(сь) *сов см* **оскорби́ть(ся)**.

оскорбля́ть(ся) (-ю(сь)) *несов от* **оскорби́ть(ся)**.

оскуде́ть (-ю; *impf* **оскудева́ть** или **скуде́ть**) *сов неперех* (*страна*) to become impoverished; (*запасы итп*) to become depleted.

осла́ *итп сущ см* **осёл**.

ослабе|ть (-ю; *impf* **ослабева́ть** *или* **слабе́ть**) *сов неперех* to weaken; (*давление, ветер*) to drop; (*внимание*) to wander; (*дождь*) to slacken *или* ease off; (*шум*) to die down; (*ремень*) to loosen; (*дисциплина*) to slacken.

осла́б|ить (-лю, -ишь; *impf* **ослабля́ть**) *сов перех* to weaken; (*внимание*) to let wander; (*ремень*) to loosen; (*дисциплину*) to relax.

ослабле́ни|е (-я) *ср* weakening; (*давления, шума*) reduction; (*внимания*) slackening; (*дисциплины*) decline; **за́втра ожида́ется ~ ве́тра/дождя́** the wind/rain should ease off by tomorrow.

ослабля́ю *сов см* **осла́бить**.

ослабля́|ть (-ю) *несов от* **осла́бить**.

осла́бн|уть (-у, -ешь) *сов от* **сла́бнуть**.

осла́в|ить (-лю, -ишь) *сов перех* (*разг*) to smear

▶ **осла́виться** *сов возв* (*разг*) to get o.s. a bad name.

осл|ёнок (-ёнка; *nom pl* **-я́та**, *gen pl* **-я́т**) *м* foal (*of donkey*).

ослепи́тельный (-ен, -ьна, -ьно) *прил* dazzling.

ослеп|и́ть (-лю́, -и́шь; *impf* **ослепля́ть**) *сов перех* (*также перен*) to blind; (*подлеж: солнце, красота*) to dazzle.

ослепле́ни|е (-я) *ср* (*перен*) blindness.

ослеплю́ *сов см* **ослепи́ть**.

ослепля́|ть (-ю) *несов от* **ослепи́ть**.

осле́п|нуть (-ну, -нешь; *pt* -, -ла, -ло) *сов от* **сле́пнуть** ♦ *неперех* (*перен*): **~ от не́нависти/любви́** to be blinded by hatred/love.

осли́|ный *прил* donkey's; **~ое упря́мство** pig-headedness.

осли́ц|а (-ы) *ж* female donkey.

О́сло *м нескл* Oslo.

осложне́ни|е (-я) *ср* complication.

осложн|и́ть (-ю́, -и́шь; *impf* **осложня́ть**) *сов перех* to complicate

▶ **осложни́ться** (*impf* **осложня́ться**) *сов возв* to become complicated; (*болезнь*) to develop complications.

ослы́ш|аться (-усь, -ишься) *сов возв* to mishear.

осля́та *итп сущ см* **ослёнок**.

осма́трива|ть(ся) (-ю(сь)) *несов от* **осмотре́ть(ся)**.

осме́ива|ть (-ю) *несов от* **осмея́ть**.

осмеле́|ть (-ю) *несов от* **смеле́ть**.

осме́л|иться (-юсь, -ишься) *сов возв* to dare.

осме|я́ть (-ю́; *impf* **осме́ивать**) *сов перех* (*поведение, человека*) to mock; (*теорию*) to ridicule.

осмо́тр (-а) *м* inspection; (*больного*) examination; (*выставки, музея*) visit.

осмо|тре́ть (-отрю́, -о́тришь; *impf* **осма́тривать**) *сов перех* (*см сущ*) to inspect; to examine; to visit

▶ **осмотре́ться** (*impf* **осма́триваться**) *сов возв* (*по сторонам*) to look around; (*перен: на новом месте*) to settle in.

осмотри́тельность (-и) *ж* circumspection.

осмотри́тельный *прил* prudent, cautious.

осмысле́ни|е (-я) *ср* comprehension.

осмы́слен|ный (-, -на, -но) *прил* (*взгляд*) intelligent; (*поступок, поведение*) premeditated.

осмы́сл|ить (-ю, -ишь; *impf* **осмы́сливать** *или* **осмысля́ть**) *сов перех* to comprehend.

осна|сти́ть (-щу́, -сти́шь; *impf* **оснаща́ть**) *сов перех* (*предприятие, лабораторию*) to equip; (*судно*) to rig.

оснаще́ни|е (-я) *ср* (*предприятия, лаборатории, армии*) equipment; (*судна*) rigging.

оснащённость (-и) *ж* equipping.

оснащу́ *сов см* **оснасти́ть**.

осно́в|а (-ы) *ж* (*сооружения*) foundation; (*общества, развития*) basis; (*ткани, материи*) warp; (*линг*) stem; **на ~е** +*gen* on the basis of; **класть (положи́ть** *perf*) **в ~у чего́-н** to use as a basis for sth; **быть** (*impf*) *или* **лежа́ть** (*impf*) **в ~е чего́-н** to be the basis of sth; *см также* **осно́вы**.

основа́ни|е (-я) *ср* (*также мат, хим*) base; (*города, общества*) founding; (*теории, науки*) basis; (*опоздания, поступка*) grounds *мн*; (*здания*) foundation; **без вся́ких ~й** without any reason; **до ~я** completely; **на ~и** on the grounds of; **на како́м ~и?** on what grounds?; **на о́бщем ~и** on an equal basis; **с по́лным ~м** with good reason.

основа́телен *прил см* **основа́тельный**.

основа́тел|ь (-я) *м* founder.

основа́тельниц|а (-ы) *ж см* **основа́тель**.

основа́тельный (-ен, -ьна, -ьно) *прил* (*причины, довод*) good; (*сооружение, человек*) solid; (*разг: вес, сумма*) fair; (*проверка, осмотр*) thorough.

основ|а́ть (*pt* -л, -ла, -ло, *impf* **осно́вывать**) *сов перех* to found; **осно́вывать** (**~** *perf*) **что-н на** +*prp* to base sth on *или* upon

▶ **основа́ться** (*impf* **осно́вываться**) *сов возв* (*общество, компания*) to be founded; (*разг: в Москве, на новом месте*) to settle down.

основн|о́й *прил* (*цель, задача*) main; (*закон, принцип*) fundamental, basic; **в ~о́м** on the whole.

основополо́жник (-а) *м* founder.

осно́выва|ть (-ю) *несов от* **основа́ть**

▶ **осно́вываться** *несов от* **основа́ться** ♦ *возв*: **~ся на** +*prp* to be based on.

осно́в|ы (-) *мн* (*физики итп*) basics *мн*, rudiments *мн*.

осо́б|а (-ы) *ж* individual.

осо́бенен *прил см* **осо́бенный**.

осо́бенно *нареч* particularly; (*смотреть, вести себя*) in an unusual way; (*приятно, хорошо*) especially, particularly; **не ~** (*разг*) not particularly.

осо́бенность (-и) *ж* (*не обыкновенность*) uniqueness; (*свойство*) peculiarity; **в ~и** in particular.

осо́бен|ный (-ен, -на, -но) *прил* special; **ничего ~ного** (*разг*) nothing special.

особня́к (-á) *м* mansion.

особняко́м *нареч* by oneself.

осо́б|ый *прил* (*вид, случай*) special, particular; (*вход, помещение*) separate; **у него́ ~ое мне́ние на э́тот счёт** he has his own opinion about this.

о́соб|ь (-и) *ж* individual.

осовреме́н|ить (-ю, -ишь; *impf* **осовреме́нивать**) *сов перех* to update.

осозна|ва́ть (-ю́, -ёшь) *несов от* **осозна́ть**.

осо́знанный *прил* (*риск, поступок*) calculated; (*необходимость*) acknowledged.

осозна́|ть (-ю; *impf* **осознава́ть**) *сов перех* to realize.

осо́к|а (-и) *ж* sedge.

осолове́|ть (-ю) *сов от* **солове́ть**.

о́сп|а (-ы) *ж* smallpox; (*разг: шрам*) pockmarks *мн*.

оспа́рива|ть (-ю) *несов от* **оспо́рить** ♦ *перех* (*первенство*) to contend *или* compete for.

о́спин|а (-ы) *ж* pockmark.

оспо́р|ить (-ю, -ишь; *impf* **оспа́ривать**) *сов перех* (*мнение, решение*) to question.

осрам|и́ть(ся) (-лю́(сь), -и́шь(ся)) *сов от* **срами́ть(ся)**.

оста|ва́ться (-ю́сь, -ёшься) *несов от* **оста́ться** ♦ *возв*: **счастли́во ~!** good luck!, all the best!

оста́в|ить (-лю, -ишь; *impf* **оставля́ть**) *сов перех* to leave; (*сохранить*) to keep; (*задержать: после уроков*) to keep in; (*работу, занятие, разговор*) to stop; (*перен: мысли, мечты, надежды*) to give up; **~ь!** stop it!; **оставля́ть** (~ *perf*) **кого́-н позади́** (*перен*) to leave sb standing; **оставля́ть** (~ *perf*) **кого́-н/что-н в поко́е** to leave sb/sth in peace *или* alone; **оставля́ть** (~ *perf*) **кого́-н на второ́й год** (*ПРОСВЕЩ*) to make sb repeat a year; **оставля́ть** (~ *perf*) **кого́-н в дурака́х** to make a fool of sb; **мы ~или госте́й ночева́ть** we asked our guests to stay overnight; **созна́ние ~ило его́** he lost consciousness.

остальн|о́е (-о́го; *decl like adj*) *ср* the rest; **в ~о́м** in other respects.

остальн|о́й *прил* (*часть*) the remaining; **~ые де́ньги/де́ти** the rest of the money/children; **~о́е вре́мя** the rest of the time.

остальн|ы́е (-ы́х; *decl like adj*) *мн* the others; **все ~** all the others; (*вещи*) all the rest.

остана́влива|ть(ся) (-ю(сь)) *несов от* **останови́ть(ся)**.

оста́нк|и (-ов) *мн* remains *мн*.

остан|ови́ть (-овлю́, -о́вишь; *impf*

остана́влива|ть (-ю) *сов перех* to stop;

остана́влива|ть (~ *perf*) **взгляд/внима́ние на чём-н** to let one's gaze/attention rest on sth;

остана́влива|ть (~ *perf*) **свой вы́бор на** +*acc* to choose

▶ **останов|и́ться** (*impf* **остана́вливаться**) *сов возв* to stop; (*в гостинице, у друзей*) to stay; **~ся** (*perf*) **на** +*prp* (*на вопросе, на описании*) to dwell on; (*на решении, на заключении*) to come to; (*взгляд*) to rest on; **не остана́вливаться** (~*ся perf*) **ни пе́ред чем** to stop at nothing.

остано́вк|а (-и) *ж* (*мотора, часов, эксперимента*) stopping; (*в речи, в работе*) pause; (*автобусная, поезда, в пути*) stop; **за кем/чем ~?** (*разг*) who/what is holding us up?

остановлю́(сь) *сов см* **останови́ть(ся)**.

оста́нусь *итп сов см* **оста́ться**.

оста́т|ок (-ка) *м* (*пищи, дня*) the remainder, the rest; (*материи*) remnant; (*МАТ*) remainder; **~ки** (*дома, стены*) remains *мн*; (*еды*) leftovers *мн*; (*красоты, чувства*) traces *мн*; **всё без ~ка** absolutely everything.

оста́|ться (-нусь, -нешься; *impf* **остава́ться**) *сов непер* to stay; (*сохраниться: дом, чувство*) to remain; (*оказаться*) to be left; (*разг: проиграть*) to lose; **остава́ться** (~ *perf*) **сиде́ть/стоя́ть** to remain sitting/standing; **мне ~лось дочита́ть 2 страни́цы** I have 2 pages left to read; **остава́ться** (~ *perf*) **на второ́й год** (*ПРОСВЕЩ*) to repeat a year; **остава́ться** (~ *perf*) **при своём мне́нии** to stick to one's opinion; **остава́ться** (~ *perf*) **ни с чем** to end up with nothing; **остава́ться** (~ *perf*) **ни при чём** to be left out; **остава́ться** (~ *perf*) **в живы́х** to survive; **не остаётся ничего́ друго́го как ...** there is nothing for it but ....

остеклене́|ть (-ю) *сов от* **стеклене́ть**.

остепен|и́ться (-ю́сь, -и́шься; *impf* **остепеня́ться**) *сов неперех* to settle down.

остервене́лый *прил* frenzied, furious.

остервене́|ть (-ю) *сов от* **стервене́ть**.

остерега́|ть (-ю; *perf* **остере́чь**) *несов перех* to warn

▶ **остерега́|ться** (*perf* **остере́чься**) *несов возв*: **~ся** +*gen* to be wary of; **~йтесь просту́ды!** mind you don't catch cold!

о́стов (-а) *м* (*здания, корабля*) frame; (*зверя*) skeleton; (*словаря, романа*) framework.

остолбене́|ть (-ю) *сов от* **столбене́ть**.

остоло́п (-а) *м* (*разг*) dimwit.

осторо́жен *прил см* **осторо́жный**.

осторо́жно *нареч* (*взять, подня́ть*) carefully; (*ходить, выступать, говорить*) cautiously; **~!** look out!

осторо́жность (-и) *ж* (*обращения, ухода*) care; (*поступка, поведения*) caution; **забыва́ть** (**забы́ть** *perf*) **о вся́кой ~и** to throw caution to the winds.

осторо́ж|ный (-ен, -на, -но) *прил* careful; (*осмотрительный*) cautious.

осточерте́|ть (-ю; *impf* **осточертева́ть**) *сов*

неперех (+*dat*; *разг*) to bore rigid.
остёр *прил см* **óстрый**.
остригý(сь) *сов см* **остри́чь(ся)**.
остри|ё (**-я́**) *ср* (*пера, иглы, шпиля*) point; (*ножа, меча, бритвы*) edge; (*критики, сатиры*) cutting edge.
остр|и́ть (**-ю́, -и́шь**) *несов перех* (*нож, меч*) to sharpen ♦ (*perf* **состри́ть**) *неперех* (*шутить*) to make witty remarks.
остри́|чь(ся) (**-игу́(сь), -ижёшь(ся)** *итп*, **-игу́т(ся)**) *сов от* **стри́чь(ся)**.
óстров (**-а**; *nom pl* **-á**) *м* (*также перен*) island.
остров|о́к (**-ка́**) *м* island; **островóк безопáсности** traffic island.
остроконéч|ный (**-ен, -на, -но**) *прил* pointed.
остронóс|ый (**-, -а, -о**) *прил* (*человек*) sharp-nosed; (*туфли*) pointed.
острослó|вить (**-лю, -ишь**) *несов неперех* to be witty.
остросоврем́н|ный (**-ен, -на, -но**) *прил* (*пьеса*) extremely topical.
остросюжéт|ный (**-ен, -на, -но**) *прил* (*фильм, пьеса*) gripping; **~ фильм**, **~ ромáн** thriller.
остро́т|а (**-ы**) *ж* witticism.
острот|á (**-ы́**) *ж* (*ножа*) sharpness; (*зрения, слуха*) sharpness, keenness; (*шутки, слова*) wit; (*запаха, вкуса*) pungency; (*пищи*) spiciness; (*желания, радости*) poignancy; (*положения, ситуации*) acuteness; (*игры*) tension.
остроугó|льный (**-ен, -ьна, -ьно**) *прил* acute-angled.
остроýмен *прил см* **остроýмный**.
остроýми|е (**-я**) *ср* wit; (*рассказа*) wittiness.
остроýм|ный (**-ен, -на, -но**) *прил* witty.
óстр|ый (**-р** *или* **-ёр, -рá, -рó** *или* **-ро**) *прил* (*нож, память, вкус*) sharp; (*борода, нос, носок*) pointed; (*зрение, слух*) keen; (*шутка, слово*) witty; (*запах*) pungent; (*блюдо, еда*) spicy; (*сыр*) strong; (*желание*) burning; (*боль*) acute; (*ситуация*) critical; (*игра*) tense; (*no short form*; *аппендицит, воспаление лёгких*) acute; **óстрый ýгол** acute angle; **óстрый язы́к** sharp tongue.
остря́к (**-á**) *м* (*разг*) wit.
остря́|чка (**-ки**; *gen pl* **-ек**) *ж* (*разг*) *см* **остря́к**.
остуж|áть (**-у́, -у́дишь**; *impf* **остужáть** *или* **студи́ть**) *сов перех* (*молоко, чай, суп*) to cool; (*перен: желания*) to curb; (*: чувства*) to restrain.
оступи́|ться (**-уплю́сь, -у́пишься**; *impf* **оступáться**) *сов возв* to trip, stumble; (*разг*: *совершить ошибку*) to trip up.
осты́|ть (**-ну, -нешь**; *impf* **остывáть**) *сов неперех* (*также перен*) to cool down; (*чувства, желание*) to cool; (*суп*) to get cold; **остывáть** (**~** *perf*) **к** +*dat* (*перен*) to lose interest in.
осу|ди́ть (**-жу́, -́дишь**; *impf* **осуждáть**) *сов перех* to condemn; (*приговорить*) to convict.

осуждéни|е (**-я**) *ср* (*см глаг*) condemnation; conviction.
осуждённ|ая (**-ой**; *decl like adj*) *ж см* **осуждённый**.
осуждённ|ый (**-ого**; *decl like adj*) *м* convict.
осужý *сов см* **осуди́ть**.
осýн|уться (**-усь, -ешься**) *сов возв* to look drawn.
осуш|áть (**-ю**) *несов от* **осуши́ть**.
осушéни|е (**-я**) *ср* drainage.
осуши́тельный *прил* drainage *опред*.
осу|ши́ть (**-шý, -́шишь**; *impf* **осушáть**) *сов перех* to drain.
осуществи́м|ый (**-, -а, -о**) *прил* (*мечты, желания*) realizable.
осуществлéни|е (**-я**) *ср* (*мечты, идеи, намерения*) realization; (*плана, реорганизации*) implementation.
осуществ|и́ть (**-лю́, -и́шь**; *impf* **осуществля́ть**) *сов перех* (*мечту, намерение*) to realize; (*идею*) to put into practice; (*план, реорганизацию*) to implement
► **осуществи́ться** (*impf* **осуществля́ться**) *сов возв* (*мечты*) to come true; (*идея*) to materialize; (*надежды*) to be fulfilled.
осчастли́в|ить (**-лю, -ишь**) *сов перех* to make happy.
осып|áть (**-лю, -лешь**; *impf* **осыпáть**) *сов перех* (*кучу песка, землю*) to knock down; **осыпáть** (**~** *perf*) **когó-н/чтó-н чем-н** to scatter sth over sb/sth; (*перен: подарками, поцелуями*) to shower sb/sth with sth; (*оскорблéниями*) to heap sth on sb/sth
► **осыпаться** (*impf* **осыпáться**) *сов возв* (*земля, насыпь, песок*) to subside; (*штукатурка, потолок*) to crumble; (*листья, цветы*) to fall.
ос|ь (**-и**; *loc sg* **-и́**) *ж* (*колеса, механизма*) axle; (*ГЕОМ*) axis (*мн* axes); (*перен: событий, происходящего*) centre (*BRIT*), center (*US*), hub.
осьминó|г (**-а**) *м* octopus (*мн* octopuses).
осяду *итп сов см* **осéсть**.
осязáем|ый (**-, -а, -о**) *прил* (*перен: результат*) tangible.
осязáни|е (**-я**) *ср* touch.
осязáтельный *прил* (*нервные окончания, органы*) tactile; (*перен: результат, разница, успех*) tangible.

KEYWORD

от *предл* (+*gen*) **1** from; **он отошёл от столá** he moved away from the table; **недалекó от меня́** not far from me; **он узнáл об э́том от дрýга** he found out about it from a friend; **у негó есть сын от пéрвого брáка** he has a son from his first marriage; **от чáса до двух** from one (o'clock) to two (o'clock); **он ушёл от семьи́** he left his family
2 (*указывает на причину*): **бумáга размóкла**

The spelling rules for Russian are shown on page xvii.

от дождя the paper got wet with rain; **от злости** with anger; **от радости** for *или* in joy; **от удивления** in surprise; **от разочарования/страха** out of disappointment/fear

3 (*о подлежащем устранению*): **отмой лицо от грязи** wash the dirt off your face

4 (*указывает на что-н, против чего направлено действие*) for; **лекарство от кашля** medicine for a cough, cough medicine

5 (*о части целого*): **ручка/ключ от двери** door handle/key; **я потерял пуговицу от пальто** I lost the button off my coat

6 (*при противопоставлении*) from; **они не могут отличить добро от зла** they can't tell right from wrong

7 (*в датах*): **письмо от первого февраля** a letter *или* dated the first of February

8 (*о временной последовательности*): **год от года** from year to year; **время от времени** from time to time.

от- *префикс* (*in verbs*; *прекращение действия*) indicating cessation of action eg. **отзвучать**; (*удаление от чего-н*) indicating removal from sth eg. **отклеить**; (*об уклонении от чего-н*) indicating avoidance of sth eg. **отшутиться**.

отапливать (**-ю**) *несов перех* to heat
► **отапливаться** *несов возв* to be heated.

отара (**-ы**) *ж* flock (*of sheep*).

отбавить (**-лю, -ишь**; *impf* **отбавлять**) *сов перех* (*сахар, порцию*) to take away; (*молоко, воду*) to pour off; **хоть отбавляй** (*разг*) more than enough.

отбарабанить (**-ю, -ишь**; *impf* **отбарабанивать**) *сов перех* (*мелодию*) to tap out; (*разг: ответ, вопрос*) to rattle off.

отбежать (*как* **бежать**; *см* **Table 20**; *impf* **отбегать**) *сов неперех* to run off.

отбеливатель (**-я**) *м* bleach.

отбелить (**-елю, -елишь**; *impf* **отбеливать**) *сов перех* to bleach.

отберу *итп сов см* **отобрать**.

отбивать(ся) (**-ю**) *несов от* **отбить(ся)**.

отбивная (**-ой**; *decl like adj*) *ж* tenderized steak; (*также:* **~ котлета**) chop.

отбирать (**-ю**) *несов от* **отобрать**.

отбить (**-обью, -обьёшь**; *impf* **отбивать**) *сов перех* (*отколоть*) to break off; (*мяч, удар*) to parry; (*атаку, нападение*) to repulse; (*город, пленных*) to recapture; (*разг: жениха, невесту*) to pinch; (*такт, мелодию*) to beat out; (*мясо*) to tenderize; **запах ~бил у меня желание есть** the smell put me off my food; **я ~бил себе ноги** my feet are sore

► **отбиться** (*impf* **отбиваться**) *сов возв* (*отколоться*) to break off; **~ся** (*perf*) (**от** +*gen*) (*от нападающих, от собак*) to defend o.s. (against); (*от компании, от стада*) to fall behind; **~ся** (*perf*) **от рук** to get out of hand.

отблагодарить (**-ю, -ишь**) *сов перех* to show one's gratitude to.

отблеск (**-а**) *м* reflection.

отбой (**-я**) *м* (*ВОЕН: ко сну*) the last post; (: *после воздушной тревоги*) all-clear (signal); (: *к отступлению*) retreat; **у неё ~ю нет от поклонников** (*разг*) she has an endless stream of admirers.

отбойный *прил*: **~ молоток** pickaxe (*BRIT*), pickax (*US*).

отбор (**-а**) *м* selection.

отборный *прил* (*картофель, семена*) selected; (*ругань, выражения*) well-chosen; **~ые войска** crack troops.

отборочный *прил* (*СПОРТ*) qualifying; **~ая комиссия** selection committee.

отбросить (**-шу, -сишь**; *impf* **отбрасывать**) *сов перех* to throw aside; (*противника, войска*) to repel; (*перен: сомнения, тревоги итп*) to cast aside; (*тень, свет*) to cast.

отбросы (**-ов**) *мн* (*производства*) waste *ед*; (*пищевые*) scraps *мн*.

отброшу *сов см* **отбросить**.

отбыть (*как* **быть**; *см* **Table 21**; *impf* **отбывать**) *сов неперех*: **~ (из** +*gen*/**в** +*acc*) to depart (from/for) ♦ (*pt* **-ыл, -ыла, -ыло**) *перех*: **~ наказание** to serve a sentence.

отвага (**-и**) *ж* bravery.

отвадить (**-жу, -дишь**; *impf* **отваживать**) *сов перех* (*разг*): **~ кого-н от чего-н** (*от вредных привычек*) to wean sb off sth; (*от дома*) to drive sb away from sth.

отважен *прил см* **отважный**.

отваживать (**-ю**) *несов от* **отвадить**.

отважиться (**-усь, -ишься**; *impf* **отваживаться**) *сов возв*: **~** +*infin* (*пойти, сказать итп*) to find the courage to do; **~** (*perf*) **на** +*acc* to venture on.

отважный (**-ен, -на, -но**) *прил* brave.

отважу *сов см* **отвадить**.

отважусь *сов см* **отважиться**.

отвал (**-а**) *м* (*породы, земли*) heap; **наесться** (*perf*) **до ~а** (*разг*) to eat one's fill; **накормить** (*perf*) **кого-н до ~а** to stuff sb with food.

отвалить (**-алю, -алишь**; *impf* **отваливать**) *сов перех* (*камень, бревно*) to push aside; (*разг: кучу денег*) to fork out

► **отвалиться** (*impf* **отваливаться**) *сов возв* (*обои, штукатурка*) to fall off; (*разг: откинуться назад*) to slump.

отвар (**-а**; *part gen* **-у**) *м* (*из трав*) decoction; **мясной ~** meat broth.

отварить (**-арю, -аришь**; *impf* **отваривать**) *сов перех* to boil

► **отвариться** (*impf* **отвариваться**) *сов возв* to boil.

отварной *прил* boiled.

отведу *итп сов см* **отвести**.

отвезти (**-езу, -езёшь**; *pt* **-ёз, -езла, -езло**, *impf* **отвозить**) *сов перех* (*увезти*) to take away; **отвозить** (**~** *perf*) **кого-н/что-н в город/на дачу** to take sb/sth off to town/the dacha.

отвергнуть (**-у, -ешь**; *impf* **отвергать**) *сов*

перех (*решение, помощь*) to reject; (*жениха*) to spurn.

отверде́|ть (*3sg* -ет, *3pl* -ют, *impf* **отвердева́ть**) *сов неперех* to harden.

отве́рженн|ая (-ой; *decl like adj*) *ж см* **отве́рженный**.

отве́рженн|ый *прил* outcast *опред* ♦ (-ого; *decl like adj*) *м* outcast.

отверн|у́ть (-у́, -ёшь; *impf* **отвёртывать**) *сов перех* (*гайку, пробку*) to unscrew; (*кран*) to be turned on; (*пола, рукав*) to turn back; (*impf* **отвора́чивать**; *лицо, голову*) to turn aside; (*разг: отломать: ручку*) to twist off

▸ **отверну́ться** (*impf* **отвёртываться**) *сов возв* (*гайка, пробка*) to come unscrewed; (*кран*) to be turned on; (*поля, рукав*) to be turned back; (*impf* **отвора́чиваться**; *человек*) to turn away; **~ся** (*perf*) **от кого́-н** to ostracize sb.

отве́рсти|е (-я) *ср* opening.

отвёрт|ка (-ки; *gen pl* -ок) *ж* screwdriver.

отвёртывать(ся) (-ю(сь)) *несов от* **отверну́ть(ся)**.

отве́с (-а) *м* (*груз*) plumb; **~ скалы́** cliff face.

отве́сен *прил см* **отве́сный**.

отве́|сить (-шу, -сишь; *impf* **отве́шивать**) *сов перех* to weigh out; **~** (*perf*) **кому́-н пощёчину** (*разг*) to give sb a slap in the face.

отве́сный (-ен, -на, -но) *прил* (*склон, берег, стена*) vertical.

отве|сти́ (-еду́, -едёшь; *pt* -ёл, -ела́, -ело́, *impf* **отводи́ть**) *сов перех* (*человека: домой, к врачу*) to take (off); (: *от окна*) to lead away; (*войска, полк*) to relocate, move; (*воду, реку*) to divert; (*ветки*) to push aside; (*глаза, взгляд*) to avert, turn away; (*перен: беду, удар*) to avert; (*заявление, кандидатуру*) to reject; (*участок, сад*) to allot; (*средства*) to allocate; **отводи́ть** (**~** *perf*) **кого́-н в сто́рону** to take *или* lead sb aside; **отводи́ть** (**~** *perf*) **вре́мя на что-н** (*себе*) to set aside time for sth; (*другим*) to allocate time for sth; **отводи́ть** (**~** *perf*) **ду́шу** to unburden one's soul.

отве́т (-а) *м* (*на вопрос*) answer; (*реакция*) response; (*на письмо, на приглашение*) reply; **в ~** (**на** +*acc*) in response (to); **быть** (*impf*) **в ~е за** +*acc* to be answerable for; **призыва́ть** (**призва́ть** *perf*) **к ~у** to call to account.

ответв|и́ться (*3sg* -и́тся, *3pl* -я́тся, *impf* **ответвля́ться**) *сов возв* to branch.

ответвле́ни|е (-я) *ср* (*дерева, дороги*) branch; (*перен: движения, религии*) branch, offshoot.

ответвля́|ться (*3sg* -ется, *3pl* -ются) *несов от* **ответви́ться**.

отве́|тить (-чу, -тишь; *impf* **отвеча́ть**) *сов неперех*: **~** (**на** +*acc*) to answer, reply (to); (*на увольнение, на грубость*) to retaliate (against); **~** (*perf*) **за** +*acc* (*за преступление, за поступок*) to answer for; **отвеча́ть** (**~** *perf*) **любо́вью на**

(**чью-н**) **любо́вь** to return sb's love.

отве́тственност|ь (-и) *ж* (*задания, заказа*) importance; (*за поступки, за действия*) responsibility; **нести́** (**понести́** *perf*) **~ за** +*acc* to be responsible for; **привлека́ть** (**привле́чь** *perf*) **кого́-н к ~и** to call sb to account.

отве́тственный (-, -на, -но) *прил* responsible; (*работа, поручение, момент*) important; **отве́тственный квартиросъёмщик** responsible tenant; **отве́тственный рабо́тник** executive.

отве́тчик (-а) *м* (*ЮР*) defendant.

отве́тчиц|а (-ы) *ж см* **отве́тчик**.

отвеча́|ть (-ю) *несов от* **отве́тить** ♦ *неперех*: **~** +*dat* (*требованиям*) to meet; (*описанию*) to answer; (*интересам итп*) to suit; **~** (*impf*) **за кого́-н/что-н** to be responsible for sb/sth.

отве́чу *сов см* **отве́тить**.

отве́шива|ть (-ю) *несов от* **отве́сить**.

отве́шу *сов см* **отве́сить**.

отви́лива|ть (-ю; *perf* **отвильну́ть**) *несов неперех*: **~ от** +*gen* (*разг: от работы итп*) to dodge.

отвин|ти́ть (-чу́, -ти́шь; *impf* **отви́нчивать**) *сов перех* to unscrew

▸ **отвинти́ться** (*impf* **отви́нчиваться**) *сов возв* to come unscrewed.

отвиса́|ть (*3sg* -ет, *3pl* -ют) *несов от* **отви́снуть**.

отви́слый *прил* (*щёки*) sagging; (*уши*) droopy.

отви́с|нуть (*3sg* -ет, *3pl* -ут, *impf* **отвиса́ть**) *сов неперех* to sag.

отвлёк(ся) *сов см* **отвле́чь(ся)**.

отвлека́|ть(ся) (-ю(сь)) *несов от* **отвле́чь(ся)**.

отвлеку́(сь) *итп сов см* **отвле́чь(ся)**.

отвлече́ни|е (-я) *ср* (*внимания, интереса*) distraction; (*абстракция*) abstraction.

отвлечённый (-, -на, -но) *прил* abstract.

отвл|е́чь (-еку́, -ечёшь итп, -еку́т; *pt* -ёк, -екла́, -екло́, *impf* **отвлека́ть**) *сов перех*: **~** (**от** +*gen*) (*противника*) to divert (from); (*от дел*) to distract (from); **отвлека́ть** (**~** *perf*) **чьё-н внима́ние** to distract sb's attention

▸ **отвле́чься** (*impf* **отвлека́ться**) *сов возв*: **~ся** (**от** +*gen*) to be distracted (from); (*от темы*) to digress (from); (*абстрагироваться*) to abstract o.s. (from).

отво́д (-а) *м* (*воды, газа*) diversion; (*войск*) relocation; (*кандидатуры, судьи*) rejection; **для ~а глаз** (*разг*) as a distraction.

отво|ди́ть (-ожу́, -о́дишь) *несов от* **отвести́**.

отводно́й *прил* drainage *опред*.

отво|ева́ть (-юю; *impf* **отвоёвывать**) *сов перех* (*также перен*) to win back ♦ *неперех* (*разг: кончить воевать*) to finish fighting

▸ **отвоева́ться** *сов возв* (*разг: солдат, полк*) to finish fighting.

отвожу́ *несов см* **отводи́ть**.

отв|озить (-ожу́, -о́зишь) *несов от* **отвезти́**.

отвора́чива|ть(ся) (-ю(сь)) *несов от* **отверну́ть(ся)**.

отвор|и́ть (-ю́, -и́шь; *impf* **отворя́ть**) *сов перех* to open.

отвра́тен *прил см* **отвра́тный**.

отврати́телен *прил см* **орврати́тельный**.

отврати́тельно *нареч* (*пахнуть*) disgusting; (*поступить*) abominably ♦ *как сказ* it's disgusting.

отврати́тельный (-ен, -ьна, -ьно) *прил* disgusting.

отвра|ти́ть (-щу́, -ти́шь; *impf* **отвраща́ть**) *сов перех* to avert.

отвра́тный (-ен, -на, -но) *прил* (*разг*) revolting.

отвраща́|ть (-ю) *несов от* **отврати́ть**.

отвраще́ни|е (-я) *ср* disgust, repulsion.

отвращу́ *сов см* **отврати́ть**.

отвы́к|нуть (-ну, -нешь; *pt* -, -ла, -ло, *impf* **отвыка́ть**) *сов неперех*: ~ **от** +*gen* (*от наркотиков*) to give up; (*от людей, от дома, от работы*) to become unaccustomed to; **отвыка́ть** (~ *perf*) **от куре́ния** to give up smoking; **он отвы́к от до́ма/рабо́ты** he is not used to living at home/working any more.

отв|яза́ть (-яжу́, -я́жешь; *impf* **отвя́зывать**) *сов перех* (*верёвку*) to untie; (*собаку, коня*) to untie, untether

▶ **отвяза́ться** (*impf* **отвя́зываться**) *сов возв* (*верёвка*) to come undone; (*собака, конь*) to break loose; (*разг*): ~**ся от** +*gen* (*от человека*) to leave in peace; (*отделаться*) to get rid of; ~**я́жись (от меня́)!** (*разг*) get lost!

отгада́|ть (-ю; *impf* **отга́дывать**) *сов перех* to guess.

отга́д|ка (-ки; *gen pl* -ок) *ж* answer (*to riddle*).

отга́дыва|ть (-ю) *несов от* **отгада́ть**.

отгиба́|ть(ся) (-ю(сь)) *несов от* **отогну́ть(ся)**.

отглаго́льный *прил* verbal.

отгла́|дить (-жу, -дишь; *impf* **отгла́живать**) *сов перех* to iron

▶ **отгла́диться** (*impf* **отгла́живаться**) *сов возв* to be ironed.

отговор|и́ть (-ю́, -и́шь; *impf* **отгова́ривать**) *сов перех*: ~ **кого́-н от чего́-н**/+*infin* to dissuade sb from sth/from doing

▶ **отговори́ться** (*impf* **отгова́риваться**) *сов возв* (+*instr*; *разг*: *незнанием, болезнью*) to plead; ~ (*perf*) **незна́нием** to plead ignorance; **он ~и́лся боле́знью** he gave the excuse that he was ill.

отгово́р|ка (-ки; *gen pl* -ок) *ж* excuse.

отголо́с|ок (-ка; *nom pl* -ки) *м* (*также перен*) echo.

отгоню́ *итп сов см* **отогна́ть**.

отгоня́|ть (-ю) *несов от* **отогна́ть**.

отгор|оди́ть (-ожу́, -о́дишь; *impf* **отгора́живать**) *сов перех* (*дом, участок*) to fence off; (*часть комнаты*) to partition off; (*от жизни*) to isolate; (*от забот*) to shelter

▶ **отгороди́ться** (*impf* **отгора́живаться**) *сов*

возв (*забором*) to fence o.s. off; (*ширмой*) to screen o.s. off; (*от жизни, от забот*) to cut o.s. off.

отгрёб *итп сов см* **отгрести́**.

отгреба́|ть (-ю) *несов от* **отгрести́**.

отгребу́ *итп сов см* **отгрести́**.

отгрем|е́ть (*3sg* -и́т, *3pl* -я́т) *сов неперех* (*гром, аплодисменты*) to stop; **его́ сла́ва ~е́ла** he is no longer famous; **бой ~е́л** the battle is over.

отгр|ести́ (-ебу́, -ебёшь; *pt* -ёб, -ебла́, -ебло́, *impf* **отгреба́ть**) *сов перех* (*листья, снег*) to rake away ♦ *неперех* (*от берега*) to row away.

отгр|узи́ть (-ужу́, -у́зишь; *impf* **отгружа́ть**) *сов перех* (*отправить*) to ship.

отгру́з|ка (-и) *ж* shipment.

отгр|ы́зть (-у́, -ёшь; *pt* -, -ла, -ло, *impf* **отгрыза́ть**) *сов перех* to bite off.

отгу́л (-а) *м* day off.

отгуля́|ть (-ю; *impf* **отгу́ливать**) *сов перех* (*разг*: *отпуск, праздники*) to finish (*one's holidays etc*); (: *за дежу́рство, за сверхуро́чные*) to have time off; **мы ~ли о́тпуск** our holidays are over.

отда|ва́ть (-ю́, -ёшь) *несов от* **отда́ть** ♦ *неперех*: ~ +*instr* (*разг*: *пахнуть*) to reek of

▶ **отдава́ться** *несов от* **отда́ться**.

отд|ави́ть (-авлю́, -а́вишь; *impf* **отда́вливать**) *сов перех* to crush.

отдади́м(ся) *итп сов см* **отда́ть(ся)**.

отдай(ся) *сов см* **отда́ть(ся)**.

отда́йте(сь) *сов см* **отда́ть(ся)**.

отдале́ни|е (-и) *ср*: **в ~и, на ~и** in the distance; **в ~и от** +*gen* some way away from.

отдалённый (-, -на, -но) *прил* distant; (*место, сходство*) remote.

отдал|и́ть (-ю́, -и́шь; *impf* **отдаля́ть**) *сов перех* (*смерть, разлу́ку*) to postpone; (*сына, друзей*) to alienate

▶ **отдали́ться** (*impf* **отдаля́ться**) *сов возв*: ~**ся от** +*gen* (*от бе́рега, от го́рода*) to move away from; (*от темы, от дел*) to digress from; (*от друзей, от семьи*) to become alienated from.

отда́|ть (*как* **дать**; *см* **Table 14**; *impf* **отдава́ть**) *сов перех* (*возвратить*) to return; (*дать*) to give; (*сдать: город, крепость*) to surrender; (*ребёнка*: *в школу, в де́тский сад*) to send; (*разг*: *заплатить*) to pay; (*подлеж: ружьё*) to kick; (: *боль*) to spread; **он ~л жизнь нау́ке** he devoted his life to science; **отдава́ть** (~ *perf*) **ту́фли в ремо́нт** to put one's shoes in for repair; **отдава́ть** (~ *perf*) **что-н за бесце́нок** to give sth away; **отдава́ть** (~ *perf*) **дочь за́муж** to give one's daughter away (*in marriage*); **отдава́ть** (~ *perf*) **кому́-н) распоряже́ние/прика́з** (sb) instructions/an order; **отдава́ть** (~ *perf*) **кому́-н/чему́-н предпочте́ние** to give preference to sb/sth; **отдава́ть** (~ *perf*) **кого́-н под суд** to prosecute sb; **отдава́ть** (~ *perf*) **кому́-н честь** to salute sb; **отдава́ть** (~ *perf*) **себе́ отчёт** to realize; **отдава́ть** (~ *perf*) **до́лжное** *или* **справедли́вость кому́-н** to give sb his *итп* due; **отдава́ть (~** *perf*) **кому́-н после́дний долг** to pay one's last respects to sb; **отдава́ть (~** *perf*) **концы́** (*разг: умере́ть*) to kick the bucket

▶ **отда́ться** (*impf* **отдава́ться**) *сов возв* (*голос, эхо*) to resound, reverberate; **отдава́ться (~ся** *perf*) +*dat* to give o.s. up *или* surrender to; (*воспомина́ниям*) to lose o.s. in; (*иску́сству*) to devote o.s. to; (*любо́внику*) to give o.s. to; **боль отдава́лась в спине́** the pain spread to his back.

отда́ч|а (**-и**) *ж* (*при вы́стреле*) recoil; (*СПОРТ*) return; **рабо́тать** (*impf*) **с по́лной ~ей** to put a lot into one's work.

отда́шь(ся) *сов см* **отда́ть(ся)**.

отде́л (**-а**) *м* (*учрежде́ния, универма́га*) department; (*кни́ги, газе́ты*) section; (*исто́рии, нау́ки*) branch; **отде́л здравоохране́ния** health department; **отде́л ка́дров** personnel department; **отде́л отпра́вки** dispatch department.

отде́ла|ть (**-ю**; *impf* **отде́лывать**) *сов перех* (*кварти́ру*) to do up; (*разг: поколоти́ть*) to do over; **отде́лывать (~** *perf*) **что-н чем-н** (*пальто́: ме́хом*) to trim sth with sth; (*ко́мнату: де́ревом*) to do sth out with sth

▶ **отде́латься** (*impf* **отде́лываться**) *сов возв*: **~ся от** +*gen* (*разг: от рабо́ты, от дел*) to get away from; (: *от челове́ка*) to get rid of; **~ся** (*perf*) +*instr* (*разг: лёгким уши́бом*) to get away with; **легко́ ~ся** (*perf*) to get off lightly; **он ~лся обеща́ниями** he did no more than make a few promises; **он ~лся испу́гом** more than anything he got a fright.

отделе́ни|е (**-я**) *ср* (*де́йствие: от семьи́ итп*) separation; (*пена́ла, стола́*) section; (*су́мки*) compartment; (*уче́бного заведе́ния, больни́цы*) department; (*ба́нка*) branch; (*конце́рта*) part; (*ВОЕН*) section; **отделе́ние свя́зи** post office; **отделе́ние мили́ции** police station.

отдели́ть (**-елю́, -е́лишь**; *impf* **отделя́ть**) *сов перех*: **~** (**от** +*gen*) to separate (from); (*уча́сток, часть ко́мнаты*) to separate *или* divide off (from)

▶ **отдели́ться** (*impf* **отделя́ться**) *сов возв*: **~ся** (**от** +*gen*) to separate (from); **~ся** (*perf*) **от роди́телей** to alienate o.s. from one's parents.

отде́л|ка (**-ки**; *gen pl* **-ок**) *ж* decoration; (*в кварти́ре*) decor; (*на пла́тье*) trimmings *мн*.

отде́лочный *прил* (*материа́лы, тесьма́, пу́говицы*) decorative; **отде́лочные рабо́ты** decorating.

отде́лыва|ть(ся) (**-ю(сь)**) *несов от* **отде́лать(ся)**.

отде́льно *нареч* separately.

отде́льност|ь (**-и**) *ж*: **в ~и** separately.

отде́льный *прил* separate; (*едини́чный: приме́ры, возраже́ния*) isolated.

отделя́|ть(ся) (**-ю(сь)**) *несов от* **отдели́ть(ся)**.

отдёрн|уть (**-у, -ешь**; *impf* **отдёргивать**) *сов перех* to pull back.

отдеру́(сь) *итп сов см* **отодра́ть(ся)**.

отдира́|ть (**-ю**) *несов от* **отодра́ть**.

отдохн|у́ть (**-у́, -ёшь**; *impf* **отдыха́ть**) *сов неперех* to (have a) rest; (*на мо́ре*) to have a holiday; **я хорошо́ ~у́л** I had a good rest.

отдува́|ться (**-юсь**) *несов неперех* (*разг*) to pant; (: *за оши́бки, за други́х*) to carry the can.

отду́шин|а (**-ы**) *ж* vent; (*перен*) escape.

о́тдых (**-а**) *м* rest; (*о́тпуск*) holiday; **на ~е** (*в о́тпуске*) on holiday; **он на заслу́женном ~е** (*на пе́нсии*) he is having a well-earned rest; **дом ~а** holiday centre; **без ~а** without a moment's rest.

отдыха́|ть (**-ю**) *несов от* **отдохну́ть**.

отдыха́ющ|ая (**-ей**; *decl like adj*) *ж см* **отдыха́ющий**.

отдыха́ющ|ий (**-его**; *decl like adj*) *м* holidaymaker (*BRIT*).

отды|ша́ться (**-шу́сь, -́шишься**) *сов возв* to get one's breath back.

отёк (**-а**) *м* swelling; **отёк лёгких** (*МЕД*) emphysema.

отёк *итп сов см* **оте́чь**.

отека́|ть (**-ю**) *несов от* **оте́чь**.

отеку́ *итп сов см* **оте́чь**.

отёл (**-а**) *м* calving.

оте|ли́ться (*3sg* **-́лится**, *3pl* **-́лятся**) *сов от* **тели́ться**.

оте́л|ь (**-я**) *м* hotel.

оте́|ц (**-ца́**) *м* (*та́кже РЕЛ, перен*) father.

оте́ческий (**-ая, -ое, -ие**) *прил* fatherly, paternal.

оте́чественн|ый *прил* (*не иностра́нный: промы́шленность*) domestic; **това́р ~ого произво́дства** home-produced goods; **Вели́кая О~ая Война́** Great Patriotic War (*World War II*); **Оте́чественная Война́** patriotic war (*fought in defence of one's country*).

оте́честв|о (**-а**) *ср* fatherland.

оте́чный *прил* swollen.

оте́|чь (**-ку́, -чёшь** *итп*, **-ку́т**; *pt* **отёк, -екла́, -екло́**, *impf* **отека́ть**) *сов неперех* to swell up.

отжа́|ть (**-ожму́, -ожмёшь**; *impf* **отжима́ть**) *сов перех* (*рука́ми*) to wring out; (*в стира́льной маши́не*) to spin dry.

отзвен|е́ть (*3sg* **-и́т**, *3pl* **-я́т**) *сов неперех* to stop ringing.

отзвон|и́ть (**-ю́, -и́шь**) *сов перех* (*подлеж: ко́локол*) to ring out; **часы́ ~и́ли по́лночь** the clock struck midnight.

о́тзвук (**-а**) *м* (*та́кже перен*) echo.

отзвуч|а́ть (*3sg* **-и́т**, *3pl* **-а́т**) *сов неперех* to come to an end (*of music, speeches etc*).

отзову́(сь) *итп сов см* **отозва́ть(ся)**.

о́тзыв (**-а**) *м* (*мне́ние*) impression; (*реце́нзия*) review; (*перен: в душе́*) echo; (*ВОЕН*) reply (*to a password*).

The spelling rules for Russian are shown on page xvii.

отзы́в (-а) *м* (*представителя, посла*) recall.

отзыва́|ть(ся) (-ю(сь)) *несов от* **отозва́ть(ся)**.

отзы́вчив|ый (-, -а, -о) *прил* ready to help.

оти́т (-а) *м* (*МЕД*) otitis (*ear infection*).

ОТК *м сокр = отде́л техни́ческого контро́ля*.

откажу́(сь) *итп сов см* **отказа́ть(ся)**.

отка́з (-а) *м* refusal; (*на заявление, от решения*) rejection; (*механизма*) failure; **закру́чивать** (**закрути́ть** *perf*) до ~а to turn full on; **рабо́тать** (*impf*) **без** ~а to operate smoothly; **набива́ть** (**наби́ть** *perf*) до ~а to cram.

отк|аза́ть (-ажу́, -а́жешь; *impf* **отка́зывать**) *сов неперех*: ~ кому́-н в чём-н to refuse sb sth; (*лишить кого-н чего-н*) to deny sb sth; (*мотор, нервы*) to fail; **ему́ не** ~а́жешь **в тала́нте** you can't deny that he's talented

▶ **отказа́ться** (*impf* **отка́зываться**) *сов возв*: ~ся (от +*gen*) to refuse; **отка́зываться** (~ся *perf*) **от свои́х слов** to retract one's words; **отка́зываться** (~ся *perf*) **от мы́сли** to give up on an idea; **не** ~ажу́сь I wouldn't say no.

отка́пыва|ть(ся) (-ю(сь)) *несов от* **отколо́ть(ся)**.

отка́пыва|ть (-ю) *несов от* **откопа́ть**.

отка́рмлива|ть (-ю) *несов от* **откорми́ть**.

отка|ти́ть (-ачу́, -а́тишь; *impf* **отка́тывать**) *сов перех* (*что-н круглое*) to roll away; (*что-н на колёсах*) to wheel away ◆ *неперех* (*разг: быстро отъехать*) to speed off

▶ **откати́ться** (*impf* **отка́тываться**) *сов возв* to roll away.

отка|ча́ть (-ю; *impf* **отка́чивать**) *сов перех* (*жидкость, газ*) to pump (out); (*привести в чувство*) to resuscitate.

откачу́(сь) *сов см* **откати́ть(ся)**.

отка́шлива|ться (-юсь) *несов от* **отка́шляться**.

отка́шлян|уть (-у, -ешь; *impf* **отка́шливать**) *сов перех* to cough up.

отка́шля|ться (-юсь; *impf* **отка́шливаться**) *сов возв* to clear one's throat.

откидно́й *прил* foldaway.

отки́н|уть (-у, -ешь; *impf* **отки́дывать**) *сов перех* to throw; (*перен: тревоги, сомнения*) to cast aside; (*верх, сиденье*) to open; (*руку*) to throw back; (*волосы, голову*) to toss back; (*в дуршлаг: макароны, рис*) to tip out; (*разг: войска, противника*) to push back

▶ **отки́нуться** (*impf* **отки́дываться**) *сов возв*: ~ся на +*acc* to lean back against; **отки́дываться** (~ся *perf*) наза́д to lean backwards.

откла́дыва|ть (-ю) *несов от* **отложи́ть**.

откле́|ить (-ю, -ишь; *impf* **откле́ивать**) *сов перех* to peel off

▶ **откле́иться** (*impf* **откле́иваться**) *сов возв* to come off.

о́тклик (-а) *м* response; (*перен*) echo; (*обычно мн: в печати*) comment.

откли́кн|уться (-усь, -ешься; *impf* **откликаться**) *сов возв*: ~ (на +*acc*) to answer;

(*на события, на просьбу*) to respond (to).

отклоне́ни|е (-я) *ср* deflection; (*перен: просьбы*) rejection; (*от курса*) deviation; (*МЕД*) abnormality; ~ **от те́мы** digression.

откл|они́ть (-оню́, -о́нишь; *impf* **отклоня́ть**) *сов перех* (*стрелку*) to deflect; (*перен: предложение, просьбу*) to reject

▶ **отклони́ться** (*impf* **отклоня́ться**) *сов возв* (*стрелка*) to deflect; (*перен: в сторону, от удара*) to dodge; (*от курса, на север*) to be deflected; **отклоня́ться** (~ся *perf*) **от те́мы** to digress.

отключ|и́ть (-у́, -и́шь; *impf* **отключа́ть**) *сов перех* to switch off; (*телефон*) to cut off

▶ **отключи́ться** (*impf* **отключа́ться**) *сов возв* (*также перен*) to switch off.

отковыр|я́ть (-ю; *impf* **отковы́ривать**) *сов перех* to pick off.

откозыр|я́ть (-ю) *сов от* **козыря́ть**.

откол|оти́ть (-очу́, -о́тишь) *сов перех* (*разг*): ~ кого́-н to give sb a thrashing.

отк|оло́ть (-олю́, -о́лешь; *impf* **отка́лывать**) *сов перех* (*кусок*) to break off; (*бант, булавку*) to unpin; ~ (*perf*) **но́мер** (*разг*) to pull a fast one

▶ **отколо́ться** (*impf* **отка́лываться**) *сов возв* (*также перен*) to break off; (*бант, булавка*) to come unpinned.

отколочу́ *сов см* **отколоти́ть**.

откомандир|ова́ть (-у́ю; *impf* **откомандиро́вывать**) *сов перех* to post, second.

отко|па́ть (-ю; *impf* **отка́пывать**) *сов перех* to dig up; (*перен: книгу, сведения*) to unearth.

отк|орми́ть (-ормлю́, -о́рмишь; *impf* **отка́рмливать**) *сов перех* to fatten (up).

откорректи́р|овать (-ую) *сов от* **корректи́ровать**.

отко́с (-а) *м* (*горы, берега*) slope; (*железной дороги*) embankment; **пуска́ть** (**пусти́ть** *perf*) **по́езд под** ~ to derail a train.

открепи́ть (-лю́, -и́шь; *impf* **открепля́ть**) *сов перех* (*значок, вывеску*) to unfasten; (*снять с учёта*) to take off the register

▶ **открепи́ться** (*impf* **открепля́ться**) *сов возв* (*вывеска*) to come unfastened; (*сняться с учёта*) to sign o.s. off the register.

открове́нен *прил см* **открове́нный**.

открове́ни|е (-я) *ср* revelation.

открове́ннича|ть (-ю) *несов неперех*: ~ (**с** +*instr*) to bare one's soul (to).

открове́нно *нареч* frankly; ~ **говоря́** frankly speaking.

открове́нност|ь (-и) *ж* frankness.

открове́нн|ый (-ен, -на, -но) *прил* frank; (*хамство, обман*) blatant; (*разг: платье, туалет*) revealing.

откро́ю(сь) *итп сов см* **откры́ть(ся)**.

открут|и́ть (-учу́, -у́тишь; *impf* **откру́чивать**) *сов перех* to unscrew.

открыва́лка (-ки; *gen pl* -ок) *ж* (*для консервов*) tin-opener; (*для бутылок*) bottle-opener.

открыва́|ть(ся) (-ю(сь)) *несов от* **откры́ть(ся)**.

откры́ти|е (-я) *ср* (*также перен*) discovery; (*сезона, выставки, клуба*) opening.

откры́т|ка (-ки; *gen pl* -ок) *ж* postcard.

откры́тый (-, -а, -о) *прил* open; (*голова, шея*) bare; (*лицо, взгляд, человек*) frank; **в ~ую** openly; **на ~ом во́здухе** outside, outdoors; **музе́й под ~ым не́бом** open-air museum; **~ая маши́на** open-top car; **~ое пла́тье** low-cut dress; **откры́тая ра́на** open wound; **откры́тое голосова́ние/письмо́** open vote/letter; **откры́тый вопро́с** open question.

откры́|ть (-ою, -о́ешь; *impf* **открыва́ть**) *сов перех* to open; (*лицо итп*) to uncover; (*намерения, правду итп*) to reveal; (*воду, кран*) to turn on; (*возможность, путь, позицию*) to open up; (*явление, закон*) to discover; **открыва́ть** (~ *perf*) **торго́влю чем-н** to start selling sth; **открыва́ть** (~ *perf*) **Аме́рику** (*перен*) to reinvent the wheel; **открыва́ть** (~ *perf*) **счёт** (*КОММ*) to open an account; (*СПОРТ*) to open the scoring; **открыва́ть** (~ *perf*) **ого́нь** to open fire

► **откры́ться** (*impf* **открыва́ться**) *сов возв* to open; (*возможность, путь, позиция*) to open up; (*тайна*) to be revealed; (*пейзаж, река*) to open out; ~ (*perf*) **кому́-н** to open up to sb; **у него́ глаза́ ~ылись** (*перен*) he has begun to see things clearly.

отку́да *нареч* where from ♦ *союз* whence, from where; **Вы ~ ?** where are you from?; ~ **Вы прие́хали?** where have you come from?; ~ **ты э́то зна́ешь?** how do you know about that?; **он не мог поня́ть, ~ слы́шался звук** he couldn't work out where the sound was coming from; ~ **сле́дует...** hence ...; ~ **ни возьми́сь** out of nowhere; ~ **я зна́ю?** (*разг*) how do I know?

отку́да-нибудь *нареч* from somewhere (or other).

отку́да-то *нареч* from somewhere.

откуп|и́ться (-лю́сь, -ишься; *impf* **откупа́ться**) *сов возв*: ~ **от** +*gen* to buy one's way out of.

отку́пор|ить (-ю, -ишь; *impf* **отку́поривать**) *сов перех* to unseal.

откус|и́ть (-ушу́, -у́сишь; *impf* **откусывать**) *сов перех* (*зубами*) to bite off; (*кусачками*) to snip off.

отл. *сокр* (= **отли́чно**) ≈ O (*US*) (= *outstanding*), ≈ A (*BRIT*).

отлага́тельств|о (-а) *ср* delay.

отла́д|ка (-и) *ж* (*КОМП*) debugging.

отлакиров́а́ть (-у́ю) *сов от* **лакирова́ть**.

отла́мыва|ть(ся) (-ю) *несов от* **отлома́ть(ся)**, **отломи́ть(ся)**.

отлеж|а́ть (-у́, -и́шь) *сов перех*: **я ~а́л но́гу/ру́ку** my leg/arm has gone dead

► **отлежа́ться** (*impf* **отлёживаться**) *сов возв*

(*разг*) to rest up.

отлеп|и́ть (-еплю́, -е́пишь; *impf* **отлепля́ть**) *сов перех* to peel off

► **отлепи́ться** (*impf* **отлепля́ться**) *сов возв* to peel off.

отлёт (-а) *м* (*птиц*) flight; (*самолёта*) departure; **на ~е** (*жить*) on the outskirts; (*держать*) in one's outstretched hand.

отле|те́ть (-чу́, -ти́шь; *impf* **отлета́ть**) *сов непер* to fly off; (*мяч*) to fly back; (*человек: от удара*) to be sent flying back.

отл|е́чь (*3sg* -я́жет, *3pl* -я́гут, *pt* -ёг, -егла́, -егло́) *сов безл*: **у меня́ ~егло́ от се́рдца** a weight has been lifted from my mind.

отли́в (-а) *м* (*в море*) ebb; (*оттенок*) sheen.

отлива́|ть (-ю) *несов от* **отли́ть** ♦ *неперех* (+*instr*; *серебром, лиловым*) to be tinted with.

отли́в|ка (-и) *ж* (*деталей, форм*) casting.

отл|и́ть (-олью́, -олье́шь; *pt* -и́л, -ила́, -и́ло, *impf* **отлива́ть**) *сов перех* (*воду, вино*) to pour off; (*ТЕХ: деталь, форму*) to cast; **у него́ кровь ~ила́ от лица́** the blood drained from his face.

отлича́|ть (-ю) *несов от* **отличи́ть** ♦ *перех* (*подлеж: красота, новизна*) to be a feature of

► **отлича́ться** *несов от* **отличи́ться** ♦ *возв* (*не походить*): ~**ся** (**от** +*gen*) to be different (from); ~**ся** (*impf*) +*instr* (*оригина́льностью, красото́й итп*) to be distinguished by; **она́ ~ется умо́м** she has a distinguished mind.

отли́чен *прил см* **отли́чный**.

отли́чи|е (-я) *ср* distinction; **зна́ки ~я** decorations; **дипло́м с ~м** ≈ first-class degree with distinction; **в ~ от** +*gen* unlike.

отличи́тельный *прил* distinguishing.

отлич|и́ть (-у́, -и́шь; *impf* **отлича́ть**) *сов перех*: ~ **кого́-н/что-н от** +*gen* to tell sb/sth from; (*награди́ть*) to honour (*BRIT*), honor (*US*); **отлича́ть** (~ *perf*) **плохо́е от хоро́шего** to tell the difference between good and bad; **я не могу́ ~ их (друг от дру́га)** I can't tell them apart

► **отличи́ться** (*impf* **отлича́ться**) *сов возв* to distinguish o.s.; (*разг: сде́лать что-н необы́чное*) to outdo o.s.

отли́чник (-а) *м* 'A'grade pupil.

отли́чниц|а (-ы) *ж см* **отли́чник**.

отли́чно *нареч* extremely well ♦ *как сказ* it's great ♦ *ср нескл* (*ПРОСВЕЩ*) excellent или outstanding (*school mark*); **он ~ зна́ет, что он винова́т** he knows perfectly well that he's wrong; **здесь ~** it's great here; **учи́ться** (*impf*) **на ~** to get top marks; ~! (that's) excellent!

отли́ч|ный (-ен, -на, -но) *прил* excellent; (*иной*): ~ **от** +*gen* distinct from.

отло́г|ий (-ая, -ое, -ие; -, -а, -о) *прил* sloping.

отложе́ни|е (-я) *ср* (*ГЕО, МЕД*) deposit.

отл|ожи́ть (-ожу́, -о́жишь; *impf* **откла́дывать**) *сов перех* to put aside; (*отсро́чить*) to postpone; (*яйцо*) to lay.

отложно́й *прил* (*воротник, манжеты*)
turndown.

отлома́ть (-ю; *impf* **отла́мывать**) *сов перех* to
break off.

▶ **отлома́ться** (*impf* **отла́мываться**) *сов возв* to
break off.

отл|оми́ть (-омлю́, -о́мишь; *impf* **отла́мывать**)
сов перех to break off

▶ **отломи́ться** (*impf* **отла́мываться**) *сов возв*
to break off.

отлупи́ть (-уплю́, -у́пишь) *сов от* **лупи́ть**.

отлуч|и́ть (-у́, -и́шь; *impf* **отлуча́ть**) *сов перех*:
~ **кого́-н от** +*gen* (*от дома, от семьи*) to take sb
from; **отлуча́ть** (~ *perf*) **кого́-н от це́ркви** to
excommunicate sb

▶ **отлучи́ться** (*impf* **отлуча́ться**) *сов возв*; **я
до́лжен** ~**ся на полчаса́** I'll have to go out for
half an hour.

отлы́нива|ть (-ю) *несов неперех*: ~ **от** +*gen* to
try to get out of.

отма́лчива|ться (-юсь) *несов от*
отмолча́ться.

отма́тыва|ть (-ю) *несов от* **отмота́ть**.

отмахн|у́ться (-у́сь, -ёшься; *impf*
отма́хиваться) *сов возв*: ~ **от** +*gen* (*от мухи*)
to brush away; (*от человека, от предложения*)
to brush *или* wave aside.

отма́чива|ть (-ю) *несов от* **отмочи́ть**.

отмеж|ева́ться (-у́юсь; *impf*
отмежёвываться) *сов возв*: ~ **от** +*gen* (*перен*)
to distance o.s. from.

о́тмел|ь (-и) *ж*: **песча́ная** ~ sandbank.

отме́н|а (-ы) *ж* (*см глаг*) repeal; reversal;
abolition; cancellation.

отмен|и́ть (-ю́, -ёнишь; *impf* **отменя́ть**) *сов
перех* (*закон*) to repeal; (*решение, приговор*) to
reverse; (*налога*) to abolish; (*лекцию*) to cancel.

от|мере́ть (*3sg* -омрёт, *3pl* -омру́т, *pt* -мер,
-мерла́, -мерло, *impf* **отмира́ть**) *сов неперех*
(*ткань, ветка*) to die; (*перен: обычаи,
привычки*) to die (out).

отмёрз|нуть (*3sg* -нет, *3pl* -нут, *pt* -, -ла, -ло,
impf **отмерза́ть**) *сов неперех* (*ветки, побеги*) to
freeze; (*разг: руки, ноги*) to be frozen.

отме́р|ить (-ю, -ишь; *impf* **отмеря́ть**) *сов перех*
to measure out.

отм|ести́ (-ету́, -етёшь; *pt* -ёл, -ела́, -ело́, *impf*
отмета́ть) *сов перех* (*мусор, снег*) to sweep
away; (*перен: доводы, возражения*) to sweep
aside.

отмёстк|а (-и) *ж*: **в** ~**у за** +*acc* in revenge for.

отмета́|ть (-ю) *несов от* **отмести́**.

отме́тин|а (-ы) *ж* mark.

отме́|тить (-чу, -тишь; *impf* **отмеча́ть**) *сов перех*
(*на карте, в книге*) to mark; (*затраты,
расходы*) to record; (*присутствующих,
отсутствующих*) to take a note of;
(*достоинства, недостатки, успехи*) to
recognise; (*юбилей, день рождения*) to
celebrate; **ну́жно** ~, **что** ... it should be noted
that ...

▶ **отме́титься** (*impf* **отмеча́ться**) *сов возв* to
register.

отме́т|ка (-ки; *gen pl* -ок) *ж* mark; (*в документе,
в паспорте*) note.

отмету́ *итп сов см* **отмести́**.

отмеча́|ть (-ю) *несов от* **отме́тить**

▶ **отмеча́ться** *несов от* **отме́титься** ◆ *возв*
(*успехи, талант*) to be apparent.

отме́чу(сь) *сов см* **отме́тить(ся)**.

отмира́|ть (*3sg* -ет, *3pl* -ют) *несов от* **отмере́ть**.

отмо́к|нуть (*3sg* -нет, *3pl* -нут, *pt* -, -ла, -ло, *impf*
отмока́ть) *сов неперех* to get damp; (*бельё*) to
soak; (*отклеиться*) to come off (*as a result of
soaking*).

отмолч|а́ться (-у́сь, -и́шься; *impf*
отма́лчиваться) *сов неперех* to keep silent.

отморо́|зить (-жу, -зишь; *impf* **отмора́живать**)
сов перех: ~ **ру́ки/но́ги** to get frostbite in one's
hands/feet.

отмота́|ть (-ю; *impf* **отма́тывать**) *сов перех* to
unwind.

отм|очи́ть (-очу́, -о́чишь; *impf* **отма́чивать**) *сов
перех* (*наклейку, бинт*) to soak off; (*разг:
глупость*) to come out with.

отмо́ю(сь) *итп сов см* **отмы́ть(ся)**.

отму́ч|иться (-усь, -ишься) *сов возв*: **он
наконе́ц** ~**ился** his suffering has finally come to
an end.

отм|ы́ть (-о́ю, -о́ешь; *impf* **отмыва́ть**) *сов
перех*: ~ **что-н** to get sth clean; (*грязь, пятно*)
to wash out

▶ **отмы́ться** (*impf* **отмыва́ться**) *сов возв* (*см
перех*) to wash; to wash out; **у меня́ ру́ки не
** ~**ыва́ются** I can't get my hands clean.

отмы́ч|ка (-и) *ж* skeleton key.

отнёкива|ться (-юсь) *несов неперех* (*разг:
отказываться*) to keep saying no; (*не
признаваться*) to refuse to own up.

отн|ести́ (-есу́, -есёшь; *pt* -ёс, -есла́, -есло́, *impf*
относи́ть) *сов перех* to take (off); (*подлеж:
течение, ветер*) to carry off; (*причислить к*):
~ **что-н к** +*dat* (*к периоду, к году*) to date sth
back to; (*к разряду, к категории*) to classify sth
as; **относи́ть** (~ *perf*) **что-н за** *или* **на счёт** +*gen*
to put sth down to, attribute sth to

▶ **отнести́сь** (*impf* **относи́ться**) *сов возв*: ~**сь к**
+*dat* (*к человеку*) to treat; (*к предложению, к
событию*) to take; **как он** ~**ёсся к Ва́шему
предложе́нию?** what did he think of your
suggestion?

отникелир|ова́ть (-у́ю) *сов от* **никелирова́ть**.

отнима́|ть(ся) (-ю(сь)) *несов от* **отня́ть(ся)**.

отниму́(сь) *итп сов см* **отня́ть(ся)**.

относи́телен *прил см* **относи́тельный**.

относи́тельно *нареч* relatively ◆ *предл* (+*gen*;
в отношении) regarding, with regard to.

относи́тел|ьный (-ен, -ьна, -ьно) *прил*
relative; **относи́тельное местоиме́ние/
прилага́тельное** (*линг*) relative pronoun/
adjective.

отн|оси́ть (-ошу́, -о́сишь) *несов от* **отнести́**

▶ **ОТНОСИ́ТЬСЯ** *несов от* **отнести́сь** ♦ *возв:* ~**ся к** +*dat* to relate to; (*к классу, к категории*) to belong to; (*к году, к эпохе*) to date from; **он к ней хорошо́** ~**о́сится** he likes her; **как ты** ~**о́сишься к нему́?** what do you think about him?; **э́то к нам не** ~**о́сится** it has nothing to do with us.

ОТНОШÉНИ|Е (-я) *ср:* ~ **к** +*dat* attitude (to); (*связь*) relation (to); (*МАТ*) ratio; (*документ*) letter; **в** ~**и** +*gen* with regard to; **по** ~**ю к** +*dat* towards; **в э́том** ~**и** in this respect *или* regard; **в не́котором** ~**и** in certain respects *или* regards; **во всех** ~**ях** in all respects *или* regards; **име́ть** (*impf*) ~ **к** +*dat* to be connected with; **не име́ть** (*impf*) ~**я к** +*dat* to have nothing to do with; *см также* **отноше́ния**.

ОТНОШÉНИ|Я (-й) *мн* (*политические, семейные итп*) relations *мн*.

ОТНОШУ́(СЬ) *сов см* **относи́ть(ся)**.

ОТНЫ́НЕ *нареч* henceforth.

ОТНЮ́ДЬ *нареч:* ~ **не** by no means, far from; ~ **нет** absolutely not.

ОТНЯ́ТЬ (-иму́, -и́мешь; *pt* -я́л, -яла́, -я́ло, *impf* **отнима́ть**) *сов перех* to take away; (*силы, время*) to take up; (*ногу, руку*) to take off; **отнима́ть** (~ *perf*) **от груди́** to wean; **э́того у него́ не** ~**и́мешь** (*перен*) you can't take that away from him

▶ **ОТНЯ́ТЬСЯ** (*impf* **отнима́ться**) *сов возв:* **у него́** ~**яли́сь но́ги/ру́ки** he has lost the use of his legs/arms; **у меня́ язы́к** ~**я́лся** (*перен: разг*) I was left speechless.

ОТО *предл см* **от**.

ОТОБРАЖА́|ТЬ (-ю) *несов от* **отобрази́ть**.

ОТОБРАЖÉНИ|Е (-я) *ср* representation.

ОТОБРАЗ|И́ТЬ (-жу́, -зи́шь; *impf* **отобража́ть**) *сов перех* to represent.

ОТ|ОБРА́ТЬ (-беру́, -берёшь; *pt* -обра́л, -обрала́, -обра́ло, *impf* **отбира́ть**) *сов перех* (*отнять*) to take away; (*выбрать*) to select.

ОТОБЬЮ́(СЬ) *итп сов см* **отби́ть(ся)**.

ОТОВСЮ́ДУ *нареч* from all around.

ОТ|ОГНА́ТЬ (-гоню́, -го́нишь; *impf* **отгоня́ть**) *сов перех* to chase away; (*перен: мысли, сомнения*) to drive out.

ОТОГН|У́ТЬ (-у́, -ёшь; *impf* **отгиба́ть**) *сов перех* (*металл*) to bend back; (*скатерть, страницу*) to fold back

▶ **ОТОГНУ́ТЬСЯ** (*impf* **отгиба́ться**) *сов возв* to bend back.

ОТОГРÉ|ТЬ (-ю; *impf* **отогрева́ть**) *сов перех* to warm

▶ **ОТОГРÉТЬСЯ** (*impf* **отогрева́ться**) *сов возв* to get warm.

ОТОДВИ́Н|УТЬ (-у, -ешь; *impf* **отодвига́ть**) *сов перех* (*шкаф*) to move; (*щеколду, засов*) to slide back; (*срок, экзамен*) to put back

▶ **ОТОДВИ́НУТЬСЯ** (*impf* **отодвига́ться**) *сов возв*

(*человек*) to move; (*срок, экзамен*) to be put back.

ОТ|ОДРА́ТЬ (-деру́, -дерёшь; *impf* **отдира́ть**) *сов перех* (*разг: оторвать*) to rip off; (: *высечь*) to thrash

▶ **ОТОДРА́ТЬСЯ** *сов возв* (*разг*) to come off.

ОТОЖДЕСТВ|И́ТЬ (-лю́, -и́шь; *impf* **отождествля́ть**) *сов перех* to equate.

ОТОЖДЕСТВЛÉНИ|Е (-я) *ср* equating.

ОТОЖДЕСТВЛЮ́ *сов см* **отождестви́ть**.

ОТОЖДЕСТВЛЯ́|ТЬ (-ю) *несов от* **отождестви́ть**.

ОТОЖМУ́ *итп сов см* **отжа́ть**.

ОТ|ОЗВА́ТЬ (-зову́, -зовёшь; *impf* **отзыва́ть**) *сов перех* to call back; (*посла, представителя, документы*) to recall; **отзыва́ть** (~ *perf*) **кого́-н в сто́рону** to take sb aside; **отзыва́ть** (~ *perf*) **иск** (*ЮР*) to drop a case

▶ **ОТОЗВА́ТЬСЯ** (*impf* **отзыва́ться**) *сов возв:* ~**ся (на** +*acc*) to respond (to); **хорошо́/пло́хо** ~**ся** (*perf*) **о** +*prp* to speak well/badly of; ~**ся** (*perf*) **о** +*prp* (*о книге*) to voice one's opinion about.

ОТО|ЙТИ́ (*как* **идти́**; *см* Table 18; *impf* **отходи́ть**) *сов непepex:* ~ **от** +*gen* to move away from; (*перен: от друзей, от взглядов*) to distance o.s. from; (*от темы, от оригинала*) to depart from; (*поезд, автобус*) to leave; (*войска, полк*) to withdraw; (*обои, краска*) to come off; (*пятно, грязь*) to come out; (*отлучиться*) to go off; (*оттаять*) to thaw; (*перестать сердиться*) to calm down; **я** ~**йду́ на 5 мину́т** I'll be back in 5 minutes.

ОТОЛЬЮ́ *итп сов см* **отли́ть**.

ОТОЛАРИНГÓЛОГ (-а) *м* ear, nose and throat specialist.

ОТОМРЁТ *итп сов см* **отмере́ть**.

ОТОМ|СТИ́ТЬ (-щу́, -сти́шь) *сов от* **мстить**.

ОТОПИ́ТЕЛЬНЫЙ *прил* (*прибор*) heating *опред;* ~ **сезо́н** the cold season.

ОТОПЛÉНИ|Е (-я) *ср* heating.

ОТОПРУ́(СЬ) *итп сов см* **отпере́ть(ся)**.

ОТОПЬЮ́ *итп сов см* **отпи́ть**.

ОТО́РВАН|НЫЙ (-, -а, -о) *прил:* ~ **от** +*gen* (*от жизни, от друзей*) cut off from; (*воротник, пуговица*) torn-off.

ОТОРВ|А́ТЬ (-у́, -ёшь; *impf* **отрыва́ть**) *сов перех:* ~ (**от** +*gen*) to tear away (from); (*воротник, пуговицу*) to tear off; **ему́** ~**а́ло но́гу** his leg was blown off; **отрыва́ть** (~ *perf*) **что-н от себя́** to sacrifice sth

▶ **ОТОРВА́ТЬСЯ** (*impf* **отрыва́ться**) *сов возв:* ~**ся (от** +*gen*) (*от работы*) to tear o.s. away (from); (*от отряда, от бегунов, от преследователей*) to break away (from); (*от семьи, от друзей, от жизни*) to lose touch (with); (*воротник, штанина*) to tear; (*пуговица*) to come off; **отрыва́ться** (~**ся** *perf*) **от земли́** to take off.

ОТОРОПÉЛЫЙ *прил* (*разг*) dumbstruck.

оторопе́ть (-ю) *сов неперех* (*разг*) to be dumbstruck.

ото|сла́ть (-шлю́, -шлёшь; *impf* **отсыла́ть**) *сов перех*: ~ **кого́-н к** +*dat* to refer sb to; (*письмо, посылку*) to send (off); (*человека, машину*) to send back.

отосп|а́ться (-лю́сь, -и́шься; *impf* **отсыпа́ться**) *сов перех* (*разг*) to have a good sleep.

ототру́ *итп сов см* **оттере́ть**.

от|очи́ть (-очу́, -о́чишь) *сов перех* to sharpen.

отошёл *итп сов см* **отойти́**.

отошлю́ *итп сов см* **отосла́ть**.

отоща́|ть (-ю) *сов от* **тоща́ть**.

отпада́ет *итп сов см* **отпа́сть**.

отпада́|ть (-ю) *несов от* **отпа́сть**.

отпа́ива|ть (-ю) *несов от* **отпая́ть, отпои́ть**.

отпа́рива|ть (-ю) *несов от* **отпа́рить**.

отпари́р|овать (-ую) *сов от* **пари́ровать**.

отпа́р|ить (-ю, -ишь; *impf* **отпа́ривать**) *сов перех* (*брюки, юбку*) to steam press.

отпа́рыва|ть(ся) (-ю(сь)) *несов от* **отпоро́ть(ся)**.

отпа́|сть (*3sg* -дёт, *3pl* -ду́т, *impf* **отпада́ть**) *сов неперех* (*обои, штукатурка*) to come off; (*желание, необходимость*) to pass; **у меня́ ~ла охо́та идти́ туда́** I don't feel like going there any more.

отпая́|ть (-ю; *impf* **отпа́ивать**) *сов перех* to melt off.

отпева́ни|е (-я) *ср* funeral service.

отпева́|ть (-ю) *несов от* **отпе́ть**.

от|пере́ть (-опру́, -опрёшь; *pt* -пер, -перла́, -перло, *impf* **отпира́ть**) *сов перех* to unlock

▸ **отпере́ться** (*impf* **отпира́ться**) *сов возв* (*дверь, ворота, шкаф*) to open.

отпе́тый *прил* (*разг*) out-and-out.

отп|е́ть (-ою́, -оёшь; *impf* **отпева́ть**) *сов перех* (*РЕЛ*) to read a service for.

отпеча́та|ть (-ю; *impf* **отпеча́тывать**) *сов перех* (*также* ФОТО) to print; (*на компьютере*) to finish typing; (*следы*) to leave; (*помещение*) to open up

▸ **отпеча́таться** (*impf* **отпеча́тываться**) *сов возв* (*на земле, на песке*) to leave a print; (*перен: в памяти, в сознании*) to imprint itself.

отпеча́т|ок (-ка; *также перен*) imprint; **отпеча́тки па́льцев** fingerprints.

отпеча́тыва|ть(ся) (-ю(сь)) *несов от* **отпеча́тать(ся)**.

отпива́|ть (-ю) *несов от* **отпи́ть**.

отп|или́ть (-илю́, -и́лишь; *impf* **отпи́ливать**) *сов перех* to saw off.

отпира́тельств|о (-а) *ср* denial.

отпира́|ть (-ю) *несов от* **отпере́ть**

▸ **отпира́ться** *несов от* **отпере́ться** ♦ *возв*: ~**ся (от** +*gen*) (*от слов итп*) to deny.

отпи|са́ться (-шу́сь, -шешься; *impf* **отпи́сываться**) *сов неперех* (*разг*) to send a formal reply.

отпи́с|ка (-ки; *gen pl* -ок) *ж* formal reply.

отпи́сыва|ться (-юсь) *несов от* **отписа́ться**.

от|пи́ть (-опью́, -опьёшь; *impf* **отпива́ть**) *сов*

перех (*полстакана итп*) to drink; ~ (*perf*) **глото́к** to take a sip.

отпихн|у́ть (-у́, -ёшь; *impf* **отпи́хивать**) *сов перех* (*разг*) to shove

▸ **отпихну́ться** (*impf* **отпи́хиваться**) *сов возв* (*разг*): ~**ся (от** +*gen*) (*от берега*) to push off (from).

отпишу́сь *итп сов см* **отписа́ться**.

отпла́т|а (-ы) *ж* repayment (*fig*); **в** ~**у за** +*acc* in repayment *или* as a reward for.

отпл|ати́ть (-ачу́, -а́тишь; *impf* **отпла́чивать**) *сов неперех* (+*dat*; *наградить*) to repay; (*отомстить*) to pay back.

отплыва́|ть (-ю) *несов от* **отплы́ть**.

отплыву́ *итп сов см* **отплы́ть**.

отплы́ти|е (-я) *ср* (*отправление*) departure.

отплы́|ть (-ву́, -вёшь; *impf* **отплыва́ть**) *сов неперех* (*человек*) to swim off; (*корабль*) to set sail.

о́тповед|ь (-и) *ж* rebuke.

отпо|и́ть (-ю́, -и́шь; *impf* **отпа́ивать**) *сов перех*: ~ **кого́-н чем-н** (*разг*) to give sb sth (to drink).

отполз|ти́ (-у́, -ёшь; *impf* **отполза́ть**) *сов неперех* to crawl away.

отполир|ова́ть (-у́ю) *сов от* **полирова́ть**.

отпо́р (-а) *м*: **дать** ~ +*dat* (*врагу*) to repel, repulse; (*идее*) to rebuff; **получа́ть (получи́ть** *perf*) **реши́тельный** ~ to be rebuffed.

отп|оро́ть (-орю́, -о́решь; *impf* **отпа́рывать**) *сов перех* (*рукав, пу́говицу*) to unstitch

▸ **отпоро́ться** (*impf* **отпа́рываться**) *сов возв* (*рукав*) to come unstitched; (*пуговица*) to come off.

отпою́ *итп сов см* **отпо́йть**.

отправи́тел|ь (-я) *м* sender.

отпра́в|ить (-лю, -ишь; *impf* **отправля́ть**) *сов перех* to send; **отправля́ть** (~ *perf*) **кого́-н на тот свет** to do away with sb

▸ **отпра́виться** (*impf* **отправля́ться**) *сов возв* (*человек*) to set off; (*поезд, теплоход*) to depart.

отпра́в|ка (-ки; *gen pl* -ок) *ж* (*письма, посылки*) posting; (*груза*) dispatch; (*поезда, теплохода*) departure.

отправле́ни|е (-я) *ср* (*письма, посылки*) dispatch; (*поезда, теплохода*) departure; (*обязанностей, правосудия*) administration; (*заказное, почтовое*) item; **отправле́ния органи́зма** bodily function.

отпра́влю(сь) *сов см* **отпра́вить(ся)**.

отправля́|ть (-ю) *несов от* **отпра́вить** ♦ *перех* (*обязанности*) to exercise; (*правосудие*) to adminster

▸ **отправля́ться** *несов от* **отпра́виться**.

отправн|о́й *прил*: ~ **пункт** point of departure; ~**а́я цена́** (*КОММ*) reserve price (*BRIT*), upset price (*US*); **отправна́я то́чка** (*перен*) starting point.

отпра́здн|овать (-ую) *сов от* **пра́здновать**.

отпра́шива|ться (-юсь) *несов от* **отпроси́ться**.

отпресс|ова́ть (-у́ю) *сов от* прессова́ть.
отпр|оси́ться (-ошу́сь, -о́сишься; *impf* **отпра́шиваться**) *сов возв* to ask to be let off; **он ~оси́лся домо́й** he asked to be allowed to go home.
отпры́гн|уть (-у, -ешь; *impf* **отпры́гивать**) *сов неперех* to jump.
о́тпрыск (-а) *м* shoot; (*перен*) offspring.
отпря́г *итп сов см* отпря́чь.
отпряга́|ть (-ю) *несов от* отпря́чь.
отпрягу́ *итп сов см* отпря́чь.
отпря́н|уть (-у, -ешь) *сов неперех* to recoil.
отпря́|чь (-гу́, -жёшь *итп*, -гу́т; *pt* -г, -гла́, -гло́, *impf* **отпряга́ть**) *сов перех* to unharness.
о́тпуск (-а) *м* leave, holiday (*BRIT*), vacation (*US*); (*ВОЕН*) leave; (*това́ров*) sale; **ежего́дный ~** annual leave; **быть** (*impf*) **в ~е** to be on holiday; **идти́** (**пойти́** *perf*) **в ~** to go on holiday; **брать** (**взять** *perf*) **~** to take leave.
отпуска́|ть (-ю) *несов от* отпусти́ть.
отпускни́к (-а́) *м* holiday-maker; (*ВОЕН*) soldier on leave.
отпускни́|ца (-ы) *ж* (*разг*) *см* отпускни́к.
отпускны́|е (-х; *decl like adj*) *мн* (*также: ~* **де́ньги**) holiday pay *ед*.
отпу|сти́ть (-щу́, -у́стишь; *impf* **отпуска́ть**) *сов перех* to let out; (*из рук*) to let go of; (*това́р, проду́кты*) to sell; (*де́ньги, сре́дства*) to release; (*бо́роду, во́лосы*) to grow ♦ *безл* (*разг: боль*) to ease off; **отпуска́ть** (~ *perf*) **кому́-н грехи́** (*РЕЛ*) to absolve sb of his sins; **отпуска́ть** (~ *perf*) **комплиме́нт** (*разг*) to compliment sb; **отпуска́ть** (~ *perf*) **шу́тку** (*разг*) to crack a joke.
отраба́тыва|ть (-ю) *несов от* отрабо́тать.
отрабо́танный *прил* (*поро́да*) worked out; (*газ*) waste *опред*.
отрабо́та|ть (-ю; *impf* **отраба́тывать**) *сов перех* (*долги*) to work off; (*како́е-то вре́мя*) to work; (*осво́ить*) to work on, polish ♦ *неперех* (*ко́нчить рабо́тать*) to finish work.
отра́в|а (-ы) *ж* poison.
отрави́тель (-я) *м* poisoner.
отрави́тельни|ца (-ы) *ж см* отрави́тель.
отр|ави́ть (-авлю́, -а́вишь; *impf* **отравля́ть**) *сов перех* to poison; (*перен: удово́льствие, пра́здник итп*) to spoil.
▶ **отрави́ться** *сов от* трави́ться ♦ (*impf* **отравля́ться**) *возв* to poison o.s.; (*едо́й*) to get food-poisoning; (*га́зом итп*) to be poisoned.
отравле́ни|е (-я) *ср* poisoning.
отравлю́(сь) *сов см* отрави́ть(ся).
отравля́|ть(ся) (-ю(сь)) *несов от* отрави́ть(ся).
отравля́ющий (-ая, -ее, -ие) *прил* poisonous, toxic.
отра́д|а (-ы) *ж* joy.

отра́д|ный (-ен, -на, -но) *прил* satisfying.
отража́тель (-я) *м* reflector.
отража́|ть(ся) (-ю(сь)) *несов от* отрази́ть(ся).
отраже́ни|е (-я) *ср* (*см глаг*) reflection; deflection.
отра|зи́ть (-жу́, -зи́шь; *impf* **отража́ть**) *сов перех* (*также перен*) to reflect; (*нападе́ние, уда́р*) to deflect
▶ **отрази́ться** (*impf* **отража́ться**) *сов возв* (*также перен*) to be reflected; **отража́ться** (**~ся** *perf*) **на** +*prp* (*на здоро́вье, на успе́хах итп*) to have an effect on.
отрапорт|ова́ть (-у́ю) *сов от* рапортова́ть.
отраслево́й *прил related to a particular branch of industry.*
о́трасл|ь (-и) *ж* branch (*of research, industry*).
отр|асти́ (*3sg* -астёт, *3pl* -асту́т, *pt* -о́с, -осла́, -осло́, *impf* **отраста́ть**) *сов неперех* to grow.
отра|сти́ть (-щу́, -сти́шь; *impf* **отра́щивать**) *сов перех* to grow.
отреаги́р|овать (-ую) *сов от* реаги́ровать.
отре́бь|е (-я) *ср собир* (*пренебр*) scum.
отрегули́р|овать (-ую) *сов от* регули́ровать.
отредакти́р|овать (-ую) *сов от* редакти́ровать.
отре́жу *итп сов см* отре́зать.
отре́з (-а) *м* piece of fabric; **ли́ния ~а** dotted line.
отре́|зать (-жу, -жешь; *impf* **отреза́ть**) *сов перех* to cut off ♦ *несов перех* (*разг: ре́зко отве́тить*) to cut short.
отрезве́|ть (-ю) *сов от* трезве́ть.
отрезв|и́ть (-лю́, -и́шь; *impf* **отрезвля́ть**) *сов перех* (*также перен*) to sober up.
отре́зка *итп сущ см* отре́зок.
отрезно́й *прил* (*тало́н*) tear-off; (*рука́в*) detachable.
отре́з|ок (-ка) *м* (*тка́ни*) piece; (*пути́*) section; (*вре́мени*) period; (*ГЕОМ*) segment.
отрека́|ться (-юсь) *несов от* отре́чься.
отрекоменд|ова́ть (-у́ю) *сов от* рекомендова́ть.
отрёкся *итп сов см* отре́чься.
отреку́сь *итп сов от* отре́чься.
отремонти́р|овать (-ую) *сов от* ремонти́ровать.
отрепети́р|овать (-ую) *сов от* репети́ровать.
отреставри́р|овать (-ую) *сов от* реставри́ровать.
отрецензи́р|овать (-ую) *сов от* рецензи́ровать.
отрече́ни|е (-я) *ср*: **~ от** +*gen* renunciation of; **отрече́ние от престо́ла** abdication.
отре́|чься (-ку́сь, -чёшься *итп*, -ку́тся; *pt* -ёкся, -екла́сь, -екло́сь, *impf* **отрека́ться**) *сов возв*: **~ от** +*gen* to renounce; **отрека́ться** (~ *perf*) **от престо́ла** to abdicate.
отреша́|ться (-юсь) *несов от* отреши́ться.

отрешён|ный (-, -а, -о) *прил* resolute.
отреши́|ться (-у́сь, -и́шься; *impf* **отреша́ться**) *сов возв*: ~ **от** +*gen* to reject.
отрица́ни|е (-я) *ср* denial; (*линг*) negation.
отрица́тел|ьный (-ен, -ьна, -ьно) *прил* (*также* МАТ, ЭЛЕК) negative.
отрица́|ть (-ю) *несов перех* to deny; (*литературу, моду итп*) to reject.
отро́г (-а) *м* (*ГЕО*) spur.
о́троду *нареч*: ~ **не** +*pt* (*разг*) never; **я ~ тако́го не ви́дел** I've never ever seen anything like it.
отро́дь|е (-я) *ср* (*разг: пренебр*) scum.
отро́с *итп сов см* **отрасти́**.
отро́ст|ок (-ка) *м* (*побег*) shoot; (*ответвление*) branch; ~ **слепо́й кишки́** appendix.
о́трочеств|о (-а) *ср* adolescence.
отро́ю *итп сов см* **отры́ть**.
отруба́|ть (-ю) *несов от* **отруби́ть**.
о́труб|и (-ей) *мн* bran *ед*.
отруби́|ть (-ублю́, -у́бишь; *impf* **отруба́ть**) *сов перех* (*ветку, голову*) to chop off ♦ *неперех* (*разг: резко ответить*) to cut short.
отруга́|ть (-ю) *сов от* **руга́ть**.
отры́в (-а) *м*: ~ **от** +*gen* (*отряда, семьи*) separation from; **ли́ния ~а** a perforated line; **учи́ться** (*impf*) **без ~а от произво́дства** *to study without giving up work*; **быть** (*impf*) **в ~е от** +*gen* to be cut off from.
отрыва́|ть (-ю) *несов от* **оторва́ть**, **отры́ть**
▶ **отрыва́ться** *несов от* **оторва́ться**.
отры́вист|ый (-, -а, -о) *прил* (*смех*) spasmodic; (*сигнал*) interrupted; (*речь, замечания*) disjointed.
отры́вка *итп сущ см* **отры́вок**.
отрывно́й *прил* (*блокнот, талоны*) tear-off.
отры́в|ок (-ка) *м* excerpt.
отры́воч|ный (-ен, -на, -но) *прил* fragmented, disjointed.
отрыгн|у́ть (-у́, -ёшь; *impf* **отры́гивать**) *сов* (*не)перех* to burp (*inf*).
отры́жк|а (-и) *ж* burp (*inf*).
отр|ы́ть (-о́ю, -о́ешь; *impf* **отрыва́ть**) *сов перех* (*также перен*) to dig up.
отря́д (-а) *м* party, group; (*ВОЕН*) detachment; (*ЗООЛ*) order; **поиско́вый ~** search party.
отряхн|у́ть (-у́, -ёшь; *impf* **отря́хивать**) *сов перех* (*снег, пыль*) to shake off; (*пальто, сапоги*) to shake down
▶ **отряхну́ться** (*impf* **отря́хиваться**) *сов возв* to shake o.s. down.
отсади́|ть (-ажу́, -а́дишь; *impf* **отса́живать**) *сов перех* (*ученика, болтуна*) to move; (*растение, цветок*) to add new soil to.
отса́жива|ть (-юсь) *несов от* **отсе́сть**.
отсажу́ *сов см* **отсади́ть**.
отсалют|ова́ть (-у́ю) *сов от* **салютова́ть**.
отса́сыва|ть (-ю) *несов от* **отсоса́ть**.
о́тсвет (-а) *м* reflection.
отсве́чива|ть (*3sg* -ет, *3pl* -ют) *несов неперех* to reflect the light.
отсебя́тин|а (-ы) *ж* (*разг: пренебр*): **нести́ ~у** to say whatever comes into one's head; **занима́ться** (*impf*) **~ой** to do whatever comes into one's head.
отсе́в (-а) *м* (*действие: шелухи*) separation; (*то, что отсеяно*) siftings *мн*; (*кандидатов*) elimination; (*студентов*) expulsion.
отсе́ива|ть(ся) (-ю(сь)) *несов от* **отсе́ять(ся)**.
отсе́к (-а) *м* (*судна, помещения*) compartment; (*ракеты*) module.
отсёк *итп сов см* **отсе́чь**.
отсека́|ть (-ю) *несов от* **отсе́чь**.
отсеку́ *итп сов см* **отсе́чь**.
отс|е́сть (-я́ду, -я́дешь; *impf* **отса́живаться**) *сов неперех*: ~ (**от** +*gen*) to move away (from); ~ (*impf*) **пода́льше** to sit further away.
отсе́|чь (-еку́, -ечёшь *итп*, -ку́т; *pt* -ёк, -екла́, -екло́, *impf* **отсека́ть**) *сов перех* to cut off.
отсе́|ять (-ю; *impf* **отсе́ивать**) *сов перех* (*семена, шелуху*) to sift out; (*перен: кандидатов*) to eliminate; (: *учеников*) to expel
▶ **отсе́яться** (*impf* **отсе́иваться**) *сов возв* (*см перех*) to be separated; to be eliminated; to drop out.
отсиде́|ть (-жу́, -ди́шь; *impf* **отси́живать**) *сов неперех* (*просидеть*) to wait; (*лекцию*) to sit through; (*разг: в тюрьме*) to do time ♦ *перех*: **я ~де́л но́гу** my leg has gone dead; **я ~де́л там два часа́** I sat (and waited) there for two hours
▶ **отсиде́ться** (*impf* **отси́живаться**) *сов возв* (*разг*) to sit tight.
отска́блива|ть (-ю) *несов от* **отскобли́ть**.
отска́кива|ть (-ю) *несов от* **отскочи́ть**.
отскобл|и́ть (-ю́, -и́шь; *impf* **отска́бливать**) *сов перех* to scrub off.
отск|очи́ть (-очу́, -о́чишь; *impf* **отска́кивать**) *сов неперех*: ~ **от** +*gen* (*мяч*) to bounce off; (*человек*) to jump off; (*в сторону, назад*) to jump; (*разг: пуговица, кнопка*) to come off; **отска́кивать** (~ *perf*) **в сто́рону/наза́д** to jump to the side/back.
отскре|сти́ (-бу́, -бёшь; *impf* **отскреба́ть**) *сов перех* to scratch off.
отсло|и́ть (-ю́, -и́шь; *impf* **отсла́ивать**) *сов перех* to strip away.
отслуж|и́ть (-ужу́, -у́жишь) *сов неперех* (*какое-то время*) to serve ♦ *перех* (*военную службу*) to serve out; (*панихиду, молебен*) to conduct.
отсн|я́ть (-иму́, -и́мешь) *сов перех* (*плёнку*) to finish off, use up; (*фильм, серию*) to finish shooting.
отсове́т|овать (-ую) *сов неперех*: ~ **кому́-н** +*infin* (*делать, ездить итп*) to advise sb not to do или against doing.
отсоедин|и́ть (-ю́, -и́шь; *impf* **отсоединя́ть**) *сов перех* to disconnect.
отсо́с (-а) *м* (*действие*) suction; (*устройство*) suction pump.
отсос|а́ть (-у́, -ёшь; *impf* **отса́сывать**) *сов перех* to draw off.
отсо́хн|уть (-у, -ешь; *impf* **отсыха́ть**) *сов*

неперех to wither.
отсро́ч|ить (**-у, -ишь;** *impf* **отсро́чивать**) *сов перех* to defer.
отсро́чк|а (**-и**) *ж* deferral.
отстава́ни|е (**-я**) *ср* (*в работе, в учёбе*) falling behind; (*в развитии*) retardation.
отста|ва́ть (**-ю́, -ёшь**) *несов от* **отста́ть.**
отста́в|ить (**-лю, -ишь;** *impf* **отставля́ть**) *сов перех* to move aside; **~!** (*ВОЕН*) as you were!
отста́в|ка (**-ки;** *gen pl* **-ок**) *ж* (*ВОЕН*) retirement; (*с государственной службы*) resignation; **подава́ть** (**пода́ть** *perf*) **в ~ку** to offer one's resignation; **уходи́ть** (**уйти́** *perf*) **в ~ку** to resign one's commission; **офице́р в ~ке** retired officer; **~ прави́тельства/кабине́та** resignation of the government/cabinet.
отста́влю *сов см* **отста́вить.**
отставля́|ть (**-ю**) *несов от* **отста́вить.**
отста́вок *сущ см* **отста́вка.**
отста́|ива|ть(ся) (**-ю**) *несов от* **отстоя́ть(ся).**
отста́лост|ь (**-и**) *ж* backwardness.
отста́лый *прил* backward.
отста́|ть (**-ну, -нешь;** *impf* **отстава́ть**) *сов неперех*: **~** (**от** +*gen*) (*от группы, от друзей*) to fall behind; (*от поезда, от автобуса*) to be left behind; (*перен: в учёбе, в работе, в развитии*) to fall behind; (*обои, пластырь*) to come off; (*часы*) to be slow; **~нь от меня́!** stop pestering me!; **часы́ отстаю́т на 5 мину́т** the clock is 5 minutes slow; **отстава́ть** (**~** *perf*) **от вре́мени** (*перен*) to be behind the times; **отстава́ть** (**~** *perf*) **от жи́зни** to be out of touch.
отстега́|ть (**-ю**) *сов от* **стега́ть.**
отстегн|у́ть (**-у́, -ёшь;** *impf* **отстёгивать**) *сов перех* (*крючок*) to unfasten; (*капюшон, рукава*) to detach
▶ **отстегну́ться** (*impf* **отстёгиваться**) *сов возв* (*крючок*) to come unfastened.
отстира́|ть (**-ю;** *impf* **отсти́рывать**) *сов перех* (*пятно, грязь*) to wash out; (*рубашку, юбку*) to wash clean
▶ **отстира́ться** (*impf* **отсти́рываться**) *сов возв* (*см перех*) to wash out; to wash clean.
отсто́й (**-я**) *м* sediment.
отсто́йник (**-а**) *м* (*ТЕХ*) settling tank.
отсто|я́ть (**-ю́, -и́шь;** *impf* **отста́ивать**) *сов перех* (*город, своё мнение*) to defend; (*воду, раствор*) to allow to stand; (*службу, концерт*) to stand through; (*два часа итп*) to wait; **мы ~я́ли всю слу́жбу** we stood through the whole service; **я ~я́л два часа́ в о́череди** I stood (and waited) for two hours in the queue ♦ *несов неперех* (*no perf*): **~ от** +*gen* to be situated away from; **их дом ~и́т на 3 киломе́тра от го́рода** their house is situated 3 kilometres from the town
▶ **отстоя́ться** (*impf* **отста́иваться**) *сов возв* to settle.
отстра́ива|ть (**-ю**) *несов от* **отстро́ить.**

отстран|и́ть (**-ю́, -и́шь;** *impf* **отстраня́ть**) *сов перех* (*уволить*): **~ от** +*gen* (*от должности*) to relieve of; (*отодвинуть*) to push away
▶ **отстрани́ться** (*impf* **отстраня́ться**) *сов возв*: **~ся от** +*gen* (*от должности*) to relinquish; (*отодвинуться*) to draw back.
отстреля́|ться (**-юсь;** *impf* **отстре́ливаться**) *сов возв*: **~ от** +*gen* to drive back (*with gunfire*); (*разг: кончить дела*) to do one's bit.
отстри́|чь (**-гу́, -жёшь** *итп*, **-гу́т;** *impf* **отстрига́ть**) *сов перех* to cut off.
отстро́|ить (**-ю, -ишь;** *impf* **отстра́ивать**) *сов перех* to finish building.
о́тступ (**-а**) *м* (*в нача́ле строки́*) indentation.
отступ|и́ть (**-уплю́, -у́пишь;** *impf* **отступа́ть**) *сов неперех* to step back; (*ВОЕН*) to retreat; (*перен: перед трудностями, перед опасностью*) to give up; (*морозы, холода*) to abate; **отступа́ть** (**~** *perf*) **наза́д** to step back; **он ~упи́л на 2 ша́га** he took 2 steps back; **отступа́ть** (**~** *perf*) **от свои́х взгля́дов** to retreat from one's beliefs; **отступа́ть** (**~** *perf*) **от те́мы** to digress
▶ **отступи́ться** (*impf* **отступа́ться**) *сов возв*: **~ся от** +*gen* (*от взглядов, от требований итп*) to abandon.
отступле́ни|е (**-я**) *ср* (*также ВОЕН*) retreat; (*от темы*) digression.
отступлю́(сь) *сов см* **отступи́ть(ся).**
отсту́пник (**-а**) *м* apostate.
отсту́пниц|а (**-ы**) *ж см* **отсту́пник.**
отсту́пничеств|о (**-а**) *ср* apostasy.
отступя́ *нареч* away, off; **немно́го от** +*gen* away from.
отсу́тстви|е (**-я**) *ср* (*человека*) absence; (*денег, вкуса*) lack; **в ~** +*gen* in the absence of.
отсу́тств|овать (**-ую**) *несов неперех* (*в классе итп*) to be absent; (*желание, аппетит*) to be lacking.
отсу́тствующ|ий (**-ая, -ее, -ие**) *прил* (*взгляд, вид*) absent ♦ (**-его;** *decl like adj*) *м* absentee.
отсчёт (**-а**) *м* (*шагов, минут*) calculation; **~ вре́мени** time-keeping.
отсчита́|ть (**-ю;** *impf* **отсчи́тывать**) *сов перех* (*шаги, минуты*) to count; (*де́ньги*) to count out.
отсыла́|ть (**-ю**) *несов от* **отосла́ть.**
отсы́лк|а (**-и**) *ж* cross-reference.
отсы́п|ать (**-лю, -лешь;** *impf* **отсыпа́ть**) *сов перех* (+*gen*) to pour off; **отсыпа́ть** (**~** *perf*) **кому́-н чего́-н** to give sb sth.
отсыпа́|ться (**-юсь**) *несов от* **отоспа́ться.**
отсы́плю *сов см* **отсы́пать.**
отсыре́|ть (**-ю;** *impf* **отсырева́ть**) *сов неперех* to get damp.
отсыха́|ть (*3sg* **-ет,** *3pl* **-ют**) *несов от* **отсо́хнуть.**
отсю́да *нареч* from here; **~ мо́жно заключи́ть, что ...** from this we can conclude that ....

отся́ду *итп сов см* **отсе́сть**.

Отта́в|а (-ы) *ж* Ottawa.

отта́ива|ть (-ю) *несов от* **отта́ять**.

отта́лкива|ть(ся) (-ю(сь)) *несов от* **оттолкну́ть(ся)**.

отта́лкивающ|ий (-ая, -ее, -ие) *прил* repellent.

отт|ащи́ть (-ащу́, -а́щишь; *impf* **отта́скивать**) *сов перех*: ~ **(от** +*gen*) *(от огня, от окна)* to drag away (from); *(в сторону, назад)* to drag.

отта́|ять (-ю; *impf* **отта́ивать**) *сов неперех* *(земля)* to thaw; *(мясо, рыба)* to thaw out; *(перен: человек)* to soften ♦ *перех* *(разморозить)* to defrost.

оттен|и́ть (-ю́, -и́шь; *impf* **оттеня́ть**) *сов перех* *(рисунок, контур)* to shade in; *(перен: главное, подробности)* to highlight.

отте́н|ок (-ка) *м* *(также перен)* shade.

оттеня́|ть (-ю) *несов от* **оттени́ть**.

о́ттепел|ь (-и) *ж* thaw; *(полит)* the Thaw *(the period of political liberalization)*.

от|тере́ть (-отру́, -отрёшь; *pt* -тёр, -тёрла, -тёрло, *impf* **оттира́ть**) *сов перех* *(грязь, пятно)* to rub out; *(щёки, руки)* to rub.

оттесн|и́ть (-ю́, -и́шь; *impf* **оттесня́ть**) *сов перех* to drive back.

оттира́|ть (-ю) *несов от* **оттере́ть**.

о́ттиск (-а) *м* *(ступни, ладони)* impression; *(рисунка, гравюры)* print; *(также: корректу́рный* ~) proof; *(статьи)* offprint.

оттого́ *нареч* that is why; ~ **что** because.

оттолкн|у́ть (-у́, -ёшь; *impf* **отта́лкивать**) *сов перех* to push away; *(перен: друзей)* to shun

▶ **оттолкн|у́ться** (*impf* **отта́лкиваться**) *сов возв*: ~**ся от** +*gen* *(от берега)* to push o.s. away *или* back from; *(перен: от какого-н положения, от данных)* to take as one's starting point.

оттопы́ренный *прил* *(карманы)* bulging; *(губа)* pouting; *(уши)* protruding.

оттопы́р|иться (*3sg* -ится, *3pl* -ятся, *impf* **оттопы́риваться**) *сов возв* to stick out; *(карман)* to bulge.

отто́рг|нуть (-у, -ешь; *impf* **оттopга́ть**) *сов перех* *(МЕД: орган, ткань)* to reject; *(земли, имущество)* to seize.

отторже́ни|е (-я) *ср* *(см глаг)* rejection; seizure.

отту́да *нареч* from there.

оття́гива|ть (-ю) *несов от* **оттяну́ть**.

оття́ж|ка (-ки; *gen pl* -ок) *ж* delay.

отт|яну́ть (-яну́, -я́нешь; *impf* **оття́гивать**) *сов перех* to pull back; *(разг: человека)* to pull away; *(карман)* to stretch; *(разг: выполнение, решение)* to delay; **оття́гивать** (~ *impf*) **вре́мя** to play for time.

отупе́лый *прил* glazed, dazed.

отупе́ни|е (-я) *ср* stupor.

отупе́|ть (-ю) *сов от* **тупе́ть**.

отутю́ж|ить (-у, -ишь) *сов от* **утю́жить**.

от|учи́ть (-учу́, -у́чишь; *impf* **отуча́ть**) *сов перех*: ~ **от** +*gen* *(от куре́ния, от буты́лки)* to wean sb off; *(+infin: воровать, врать)* to teach sb not to do

▶ **отучи́ться** (*impf* **отуча́ться**) *сов возв* (+*infin*) to get out of the habit of doing; **отуча́ться** (~**ся** *perf*) **от плохи́х привы́чек** to get out of bad habits.

отфильтр|ова́ть (-ую; *impf* **отфильтро́вывать**) *сов перех* to filter off.

отфутбо́л|ить (-ю, -ишь; *impf* **отфутбо́ливать**) *сов перех (разг)*: ~ **кого́-н** to send sb packing.

отха́ркивающ|ий (-ая, -ее, -ие) *прил (МЕД)*: ~**ее сре́дство** expectorant.

отхва|ти́ть (-чу́, -а́тишь; *impf* **охва́тывать**) *сов перех (разг: отрубить)* to cut off; *(: достать)* to get.

отхлебн|у́ть (-у́, -ёшь; *impf* **отхлёбывать**) *сов перех (разг)* to take a swig of.

отхлеста́|ть (-ю; *impf* **отхлёстывать**) *сов перех (разг)*: ~ **кого́-н** to give sb a hiding.

отхлы́н|уть (*3sg* -ет, *3pl* -ут) *сов неперех* *(волны)* to roll back; *(кровь от лица)* to drain; *(перен: толпа)* to draw back.

отхо́д (-а) *м* departure; *(ВОЕН)* withdrawal; ~ **от тради́ций/действи́тельности** departure from tradition/reality; *см также* **отхо́ды**.

отхо|ди́ть (-ожу́, -о́дишь) *несов от* **отойти́**.

отхо́дн|ая (-ой; *decl like adj*) *ж (РЕЛ)* prayer for the dying.

отхо́дчив|ый (-, -а, -о) *прил*: **он** ~ he doesn't stay angry for long.

отхо́д|ы (-ов) *мн (промышленности итп)* waste *мн*.

отхожу́ *несов см* **отходи́ть**.

отца́ *итп сущ см* **оте́ц**.

отцве|сти́ (-ту́, -тёшь; *impf* **отцвета́ть**) *неперех* to finish blossoming.

отце|ди́ть (-жу́, -дишь; *impf* **отце́живать**) *сов перех* to strain off.

отцеп|и́ть (-еплю́, -е́пишь; *impf* **отцепля́ть**) *сов перех (вагон, паровоз)* to uncouple; *(колючку)* to unsnag

▶ **отцеп|и́ться** (*impf* **отцепля́ться**) *сов возв (вагон, паровоз)* to come uncoupled; ~**епи́сь от меня́!** *(разг)* leave me alone!

отцо́вск|ий (-ая, -ое, -ие) *прил* father's; *(перен)* paternal, fatherly.

отцо́вств|о (-а) *ср* fatherhood.

отча́ива|ться (-юсь) *несов от* **отча́яться**.

отча́л|ить (-ю, -ишь; *impf* **отча́ливать**) *сов неперех* to set sail.

отча́сти *нареч* partially.

отча́яни|е (-я) *ср* despair.

отча́янно *нареч (пытаться)* desperately; *(кричать)* in despair; *(спорить)* terribly.

отча́янн|ый (-, -на, -но) *прил* desperate; *(смелый)* daring; *(разг: врун, болтун итп)* terrible.

отча́|яться (-юсь; *impf* **отча́иваться**) *сов возв*: ~ (+*infin*) to despair (of doing).

отчего́ *нареч (почему)* why ♦ *союз (вследствие чего)* which is why; ~ **же?** *(разг)* what for?

отчего́-либо *нареч* = **отчего́-нибудь**.

отчего́-нибудь *нареч* for any reason.

отчего́-то *нареч* for some reason.

отчека́н|ить (-ю, -ишь; *impf* **отчека́нивать**) *сов перех* (*монету*) to mint; (*изделие*) to emboss; (*перен: слово*) to pronounce distinctly; **отчека́нивать** (~ *perf*) **отве́т** to answer distinctly.

о́тчеств|о (-а) *ср* patronymic.

отчёт (-а) *м* account; **фина́нсовый** ~ financial report; **годово́й** ~ annual report; **отдава́ть** (**отда́ть** *perf*) **себе́** ~ **в чём-н** to realize sth.

отчётлив|ый (-, -а, -о) *прил* (*звук, отпечаток*) distinct; (*объяснение, повествование*) clear.

отчётност|ь (-и) *ж* accountability ◆ *собир* (*финансовая, административная*) records *мн*.

отчётный *прил* (*собрание*) review *опред*; (*год*) current; ~ **докла́д** report; **отчётный пери́од** accounting period.

отчи́зн|а (-ы) *ж* mother country.

о́тч|ий (-ая, -ее, -ие) *прил* (*ласка, совет*) fatherly; ~ **дом** one's father's house.

о́тчим (-а) *м* stepfather.

отчисле́ни|е (-я) *ср* (*работника*) dismissal; (*студента*) expulsion; (*обычно мн: на строительство*) allocation *ед*; (: *денежные: удержание*) deduction; (: *выделение*) assignment.

отчи́сл|ить (-ю, -ишь; *impf* **отчисля́ть**) *сов перех* (*работника*) to dismiss; (*студента*) to expel; (*деньги: удержать*) to deduct; (: *выделить*) to assign
▶ **отчи́слиться** (*impf* **отчисля́ться**) *сов возв*: ~**ся** (**из** +*gen*) to leave.

отчи́|стить (-щу, -стишь; *impf* **отчища́ть**) *сов перех* (*грязь*) to clean off; (*пятно*) to remove; (*пальто, туфли*) to clean
▶ **отчи́ститься** (*impf* **отчища́ться**) *сов возв* (*грязь*) to come off; (*пятно*) to come out; (*пальто, туфли*) to come clean.

отчита́|ть (-ю; *impf* **отчи́тывать**) *сов перех* (*ребёнка*) to tell off
▶ **отчита́ться** (*impf* **отчи́тываться**) *сов возв* to report; **отчи́тываться** (~**ся** *perf*) **пе́ред** +*instr*/**о** +*prp* to report to/on.

отчища́|ть(ся) (-ю(сь)) *несов от* **отчи́стить(ся)**.

отчи́щу(сь) *сов см* **отчи́стить(ся)**.

отчуд|и́ть (-и́шь) *сов перех* (*разг*): **он сего́дня тако́е** ~**и́л!** he did something really weird today!

отчужда́|ть (-ю) *несов перех* (*также ЮР*) to alienate.

отчужде́ни|е (-я) *ср* (*прекращение отношений*) estrangement; (*ЮР*) alienation.

отчуждённост|ь (-и) *ж* alienation.

отчуждённый (-, -на, -но) *прил* (*взгляд, вид*) indifferent.

отшатн|у́ться (-у́сь, -ёшься; *impf* **отша́тываться**) *сов возв* (*от удара*) to recoil;

(*назад, в сторону*) to move; **отша́тываться** (~ *perf*) **от** +*gen* (*разг: от друзей итп*) to ditch.

отшвырн|у́ть (-у́, -ёшь; *impf* **отшвы́ривать**) *сов перех* (*разг: предмет*) to toss away; (: *человека*) to shove aside.

отше́льник (-а) *м* (*также перен*) hermit.

отше́льниц|а (-ы) *ж см* **отше́льник**.

отши́б (-а) *м*: **на** ~**е** (*разг: жить*) alone, on one's tod (*BRIT*); (*стоять: дом итп*) on its own.

отшиб|и́ть (-у́, -ёшь; *impf* **отшиба́ть**) *сов перех* (*разг: руку, ногу*) to hurt; **у меня́ па́мять отши́бло** (*разг*) my memory's gone.

отшлёпа|ть (-ю; *impf* **отшлёпывать**) *сов перех* (*разг*): ~ **кого́-н** (*ребёнка*) to give sb a walloping.

отшлиф|ова́ть (-у́ю; *impf* **отшлифо́вывать**) *сов перех* (*деталь, поверхность*) to grind; (*рассказ, пьесу*) to put the finishing touches to.

отштамп|ова́ть (-у́ю) *сов от* **штампова́ть**.

отштукату́р|ить (-ю, -ишь) *сов от* **штукату́рить**.

отшут|и́ться (-учу́сь, -у́тишься; *impf* **отшу́чиваться**) *сов возв* to reply with a joke.

отщеп|и́ть (-лю́, -ишь; *impf* **отщепля́ть**) *сов перех* (*кусочек дерева итп*) to chip off
▶ **отщепи́ться** (*impf* **отщепля́ться**) *сов возв* (*кусочек дерева итп*) to split off.

отъеда́|ться (-юсь) *несов от* **отъе́сться**.

отъе́дешь *итп сов см* **отъе́хать**.

отъеди́мся *итп сов см* **отъе́сться**.

отъе́ду *итп сов см* **отъе́хать**.

отъедя́тся *сов см* **отъе́сться**.

отъе́зд (-а) *м* departure; **быть** (*impf*) **в** ~**е** to be away.

отъезжа́|ть (-ю) *несов от* **отъе́хать**.

отъе́сться (*как* **есть**; *см* **Table 15**; *impf* **отъеда́ться**) *сов возв* (*после голода*) to eat one's fill; (*потолстеть*) to grow fat.

отъе́хать (*как* **е́хать**; *см* **Table 19**; *impf* **отъезжа́ть**) *сов неперех* to travel; (~ *perf*) **от** +*gen* to move away from.

отъе́шься *сов см* **отъе́сться**.

отъя́вленный *прил* (*мошенник итп*) absolute.

отыгра́|ть (-ю; *impf* **оты́грывать**) *сов перех* to win back
▶ **отыгра́ться** (*impf* **оты́грываться**) *сов возв* (*в карты, в шахматы*) to win again; (*перен*) to get one's own back.

отыск|а́ть (-ищу́, -и́щешь; *impf* **оты́скивать**) *сов перех* to hunt out; (*КОМП*) to retrieve
▶ **отыска́ться** (*impf* **оты́скиваться**) *сов возв* to turn up.

отяго|ти́ть (-щу́, -ти́шь; *impf* **отягоща́ть**) *сов перех*: ~ **кого́-н чем-н** to burden sb with sth.

отягча́ющ|ий (-ая, -ее, -ие) *прил*: ~**ие обстоя́тельства** (*ЮР*) aggravating circumstances.

отягч|и́ть (-у́, -и́шь; *impf* **отягча́ть**) *сов перех* (*вину, положение*) to aggravate.

отяжеле́|ть (**-ю**) *сов от* **тяжеле́ть.**

о́фис (**-а**) *м* office.

офице́р (**-а**) *м* (*ВОЕН*) officer; (*разг: ШАХМАТЫ*) bishop.

офице́рск|ий (**-ая, -ое, -ие**) *прил* (*звание, форма*) officer's; (*комната, столовая*) officers'.

офице́рств|о (**-а**) *ср собир* officers *мн.*

официа́л|ьный (**-ен, -ьна, -ьно**) *прил* official; **официа́льное лицо́** official.

официа́нт (**-а**) *м* waiter.

официа́нт|ка (**-ки**; *gen pl* **-ок**) *ж* waitress.

официо́з|ный (**-ен, -на, -но**) *прил*: ~**ная газе́та** *newspaper which supports the government.*

оформи́тел|ь (**-я**) *м*: ~ **интерье́ра/спекта́кля** interior/set designer; ~ **витри́ны** window-dresser.

оформи́тельниц|а (**-ы**) *ж см* **оформи́тель.**

офо́рм|ить (**-лю, -ишь**; *impf* **оформля́ть**) *сов перех* (*книгу*) to design the layout of; (*витрину*) to dress; (*спектакль*) to design the sets for; (*документы, договор*) to draw up; **оформля́ть** (~ *perf*) **кого́-н на рабо́ту** (+*instr*) to take sb on (as)

▶ **офо́рмиться** (*impf* **оформля́ться**) *сов возв* (*мнение, взгляды*) to form; **оформля́ться** (~**ся** *perf*) **на рабо́ту** (+*instr*) to be taken on (as).

оформле́ни|е (**-я**) *ср* design; (*документов, договора*) drawing up; (*на работу*) taking on; **музыка́льное** ~ music.

оформлю́(сь) *сов см* **офо́рмить(ся).**

оформля́|ть(ся) (**-ю(сь)**) *несов от* **офо́рмить(ся).**

офо́рт (**-а**) *м* etching.

офсе́т (**-а**) *м* offset (process).

офтальмо́лог (**-а**) *м* ophthalmologist.

ох *межд* oh.

оха́ива|ть (**-ю**) *несов от* **оха́ять.**

охаме́|ть (**-ю**) *сов от* **хаме́ть.**

оха́п|ка (**-ки**; *gen pl* **-ок**) *ж* armful; **схвати́ть** (*perf*) **что-н в** ~**ку** to grab sth in one's arms.

охарактериз|ова́ть (**-у́ю**) *сов от* **характеризова́ть.**

о́ха|ть (**-ю**) *несов неперех* (*от боли*) to groan; (*от сожаления, печали*) to sigh.

оха́|ять (**-ю**; *impf* **оха́ивать**) *сов перех* (*разг*) to slate (*BRIT*), to slag (off).

охва|ти́ть (**-чу́, -а́тишь**; *impf* **охва́тывать**) *сов перех* (*подлеж: пламя, чувства, темнота*) to engulf; (*подписчиков, население*) to cover; (*ВОЕН*) to envelop; **охва́тывать** (~ *perf*) **что-н чем-н** (*руками, лентой*) to put sth round sth; **охва́тывать** (~ *perf*) **взгля́дом** to take in; **охва́тывать** (~ *perf*) **умо́м** to grasp.

охладе́|ть (**-ю**; *impf* **охладева́ть**) *сов неперех* (*отношения*) to cool; **охладева́ть** (~ *perf*) **к** +*dat* (*к мужу, к невесте*) to grow cool towards; (*к футболу, к сладкому*) to go off.

охлади́|ть (**-жу́, -ди́шь**; *impf* **охлажда́ть**) *сов перех* (*воду, чувства*) to cool; (*забияку*) to cool down

▶ **охлади́ться** (*impf* **охлажда́ться**) *сов возв* (*печка, вода*) to cool down; (*человек: водой*) to cool off.

охлажде́ни|е (**-я**) *ср* (*также перен*) cooling.

охлажу́(сь) *сов см* **охлади́ть(ся).**

охламо́н (**-а**) *м* (*разг: пренебр*) loafer.

охмур|и́ть (**-ю́, -и́шь**; *impf* **охмуря́ть**) *сов перех* (*разг*) to lead on.

о́хн|уть (**-у, -ешь**) *сов неперех* to gasp.

охо́т|а (**-ы**) *ж* hunt; (*желание*): ~ **к чему́-н**/+*infin* desire for sth/to do; ~ **на лис** fox hunting (*to kill*); ~ **за лисо́й** fox hunting (*to catch*); **ходи́ть/идти́** (**пойти́** *perf*) **на** ~**у** to go hunting; ~ **за престу́пником/уби́йцей** the hunt for a criminal/murderer; **мне** ~ **посмотре́ть э́ту переда́чу** (*разг*) I fancy watching this programme; **что Вам за** ~ **спо́рить с ней?** (*разг*) what do you get out of arguing with her?; ~ **тебе́ спо́рить!** (*разг*) do you really have to argue?

охо́|титься (**-чусь, -тишься**) *несов возв*: ~ **на** +*acc* to hunt (*to kill*); ~ (*impf*) **за** +*instr* to hunt (*to catch*); (*перен: разг*) to hunt for.

охо́тник (**-а**) *м* hunter; ~ +*infin* volunteer to do; **быть** (*impf*) **больши́м** ~**ом до** +*gen* (*разг: до женщин, сладкого*) to be crazy about.

охо́тничий (**-ья, -ье, -ьи**) *прил* hunting *опред.*

охо́тно *нареч* gladly.

охо́чусь *несов см* **охо́титься.**

о́хр|а (**-ы**) *ж* ochre, ocher (*US*).

охра́н|а (**-ы**) *ж* (*защита: помещения, президента*) security; (*группа людей: президента*) bodyguard; (: *помещения*) guard; (*здоровья, растений, животных*) protection; **под** ~**ой зако́на** protected by law; **охра́на поря́дка** maintenance of law and order; **охра́на приро́ды** nature conservation; **охра́на труда́** health and safety regulations *мн.*

охране́ни|е (**-я**) *ср* (*также ВОЕН*) protection.

охра́нник (**-а**) *м* guard.

охра́нниц|а (**-ы**) *ж см* **охра́нник.**

охра́нн|ый *прил* (*зона, территория*) guarded; ~**ая ро́та** security company.

охран|я́ть (**-ю**) *несов перех* (*помещение, президента*) to guard; (*здоровье*) to look after; (*природу*) to protect.

охри́плый *прил* (*разг: голос, крик*) hoarse.

охри́п|нуть (**-у, -ешь**) *сов от* **хри́пнуть.**

охри́пший (**-ая, -ее, -ие**) *прил* hoarse.

охроме́|ть (**-ю**) *сов неперех* to go lame.

оцара́па|ть(ся) (**-ю(сь)**) *сов от* **цара́пать(ся).**

оцен|и́ть (**-ю́, -е́нишь**; *impf* **оце́нивать**) *сов перех* (*определить цену*) to value; (*определить уровень*) to assess; (*признать достоинства*) to appreciate; **оце́нивать** (~ *perf*) **что-н по досто́инству** to appreciate the true value of sth.

оце́н|ка (**-ки**; *gen pl* **-ок**) *ж* (*вещи*) valuation; (*работника, поступка*) assessment; (*отметка*) mark.

оце́нщик (-а) *м* valuer.

оцепене́лый *прил* (*взгляд, человек*) stunned; **оцепене́лое состоя́ние** stupor.

оцепене́ни|е (-я) *ср* numbness; (*БИО*) dormancy.

оцепене́|ть (-ю) *сов от* цепене́ть.

оцепи́ть (-еплю́, -е́пишь; *impf* оцепля́ть) *сов перех* to cordon off.

оцепле́ни|е (-я) *ср* (*действие*) cordoning off; (*группа*) cordon.

оцеплю́ *сов см* оцепи́ть.

оцепля́|ть (-ю) *несов от* оцепи́ть.

оцинк|ова́ть (-у́ю; *impf* оцинко́вывать) *сов перех* (*ТЕХ*) to galvanize.

оча́г (-а́) *м* hearth; (*перен: заболевания*) source; (: *культуры*) heart; ~ **войны́** flash point; **дома́шний** ~ hearth and home.

очарова́ни|е (-я) *ср* charm.

очарова́тел|ьный (-ен, -ьна, -ьно) *прил* charming.

очар|ова́ть (-у́ю; *impf* очаро́вывать) *сов перех* to charm.

очеви́ден *прил см* очеви́дный.

очеви́д|ец (-ца) *м* eyewitness.

очеви́дно *нареч, част* obviously ◆ *как сказ:* ~, **что он винова́т** it's obvious that he is guilty ◆ *вводн сл:* ~, **он не придёт** apparently he's not coming; **э́то соверше́нно ~!** it is perfectly obvious!; **он винова́т? – ~!** is he guilty? – obviously!

очеви́д|ный (-ен, -но, -на) *прил* (*факт, истина*) plain; (*желание, намерение*) obvious.

очеви́дца *итп сущ см* очеви́дец.

о́чень *нареч* (+*adv*, +*adj*) very; (+*vb*) very much; ~ **удо́бный/удо́бно** very comfortable/comfortably; **мы** ~ **хоти́м, что́бы она́ пришла́** we would very much like her to come.

очередно́й *прил* next; (*ближайший: задача*) immediate; (: *номер газеты*) latest; (*следующий по порядку: собрание, отпуск*) regular; (*повторяющийся: ссора, глупость*) usual.

о́черед|ь (-и) *ж* (*порядок*) order; (*место в порядке*) turn; (*группа людей*) queue (*BRIT*), line (*US*); (*туннеля, завода итп*) section; **в пе́рвую** ~ in the first instance; **в поря́дке** ~**и** when one's turn comes; **в свою́** ~ in turn; ~ **за ни́ми** it is their turn; **по** ~**и** in turn; **стоя́ть** (*impf*) **на** ~**и на** +*acc* (*на кварти́ру итп*) to be on the waiting list for; **пулемётная** ~ (*ВОЕН*) burst of automatic rifle fire; **на** ~**и стои́т вопро́с/зада́ча** this is the next question/task.

о́черк (-а) *м* (*литературный*) essay; (*газетный*) sketch.

очерн|и́ть (-ю́, -и́шь) *сов от* черни́ть.

очерстве́|ть (-ю) *сов от* черстве́ть.

очерта́ни|е (-я) *ср* (*обычно мн*) outline *ед*.

очер|ти́ть (-чу́, -́тишь; *impf* оче́рчивать) *сов перех* to outline.

оче́чник (-а) *м* spectacle case.

очин|и́ть (-ю́, -́ишь; *impf* очиня́ть) *сов перех* to sharpen.

очисти́тельный *прил* purifying, purification *опред*.

очи́|стить (-щу, -стишь; *impf* очища́ть) *перех* to clean; (*газ, воду*) to purify; (*совесть, город, квартиру*) to clear; (*душу*) to cleanse; (*раза: обокрасть: дом итп*) to clean out; (*impf* очища́ть *или* чи́стить; *яблоко, картошку*) to peel; (*рыбу*) to clean

▸ **очи́ститься** (*impf* очища́ться) *сов возв* (*газ, вода*) to be purified; (*перен: совесть*) to be cleared; (: *душа*) to be cleansed; **не́бо** ~**стилось от туч** the sky cleared.

очи́стк|а (-и) *ж* purification; **для** ~**и со́вести** to ease one's conscience; *см также* очи́стки.

очи́стк|и (-ов) *мн* peelings *мн*.

очистн|о́й *прил:* ~**ые сооруже́ния** purification plant *ед*.

очища́|ть(ся) (-ю(сь)) *несов от* очи́стить(ся).

очи́щенный *прил* (*ХИМ*) purified; (*яблоко, картошка*) peeled; (*рыба*) cleaned.

очи́щу(сь) *сов см* очи́стить(ся).

очк|и́ (-о́в) *мн* (*для чтения*) glasses *мн*, spectacles *мн*; (*для плавания*) goggles *мн*; **со́лнечные** ~ sunglasses; **защи́тные** ~ safety specs.

очк|о́ (-а) *ср* (*СПОРТ*) point; (*КАРТЫ*) pip; **дать** (*perf*) **сто** ~**в вперёд** to be miles better.

очковтира́тел|ь (-я) *м* deceiver.

очковтира́тельств|о (-а) *ср* deception.

очко́вый *прил:* ~**ая змея́** cobra.

очн|у́ться (-у́сь, -ёшься) *сов возв* (*после сна*) to wake up; (*после обморока*) to come to; (*после испуга*) to steady o.s.

о́чный *прил* (*обучение, институт итп*) with direct contact between students and teachers; **о́чная ста́вка** (*ЮР*) confrontation.

очуме́|ть (-ю) *сов неперех* (*разг*) to go off one's head.

оч|ути́ться (2*sg* -у́тишься, 3*sg* -у́тится) *сов возв* to find o.s.

ошара́ш|ить (-у, -ишь; *impf* ошара́шивать) *сов перех* (*раза: вопросом, поведением*) to dumbfound.

оше́йник (-а) *м* collar.

ошеломи́тел|ьный (-ен, -ьна, -ьно) *прил* stunning.

ошелом|и́ть (-лю́, -и́шь; *impf* ошеломля́ть) *сов перех* to stun.

ошеломля́ющий (-ая, -ее, -ие; -, -а, -е) *прил* = ошеломи́тельный.

ошиб|и́ться (-у́сь, -ёшься; *pt* -́бся, -́блась, -́блось, *impf* ошиба́ться) *сов возв* to make a mistake; **ошиба́ться** (~ *perf*) **в ком-н** to misjudge sb.

оши́б|ка (-ки; *gen pl* -ок) *ж* mistake, error; (*КОМП*) bug; **по ~ке** by mistake.

оши́боч|ный (-ен, -на, -но) *прил (мнение, представление)* mistaken, erroneous; *(суждение, вывод)* wrong.

ошива́|ться (-юсь) *несов возв (разг: пренебр)* to hang about.

ошпа́р|ить (-ю, -ишь; *impf* **ошпа́ривать**) *сов перех (разг: ногу, палец, помидор)* to scald

▸ **ошпа́риться** (*impf* **ошпа́риваться**) *сов возв (разг)* to scald o.s.

оштраф|ова́ть (-у́ю) *сов от* **штрафова́ть**.

оштукату́р|ить (-ю, -ишь) *сов от* штукату́рить.

ощен|и́ться (*3sg* -и́тся, *3pl* -я́тся) *сов от* щени́ться.

ощети́нива|ться (*3sg* -ется, *3pl* -ются) *несов* = щети́ниться.

ощети́н|иться (*3sg* -ится, *3pl* -ятся) *сов от* щети́ниться.

ощип|а́ть (-иплю́, -и́плешь) *сов от* щипа́ть.

ощи́пыва|ть (-ю) *несов перех* = щипа́ть.

ощу́па|ть (-ю; *impf* **ощу́пывать**) *сов перех (стол)* to feel for; *(лицо)* to feel.

о́щуп|ь (-и) *ж:* **на ~** by touch; **пробира́ться** (*impf*) **на ~** to grope one's way through.

о́щупью *нареч* by touch; *(перен)* blindly; **пробира́ться** (*impf*) **~** to grope one's way through.

ощути́м|ый (-, -а, -о) *прил (потепление, запах)* noticeable; *(успех, расходы)* appreciable.

ощути́|тель|ный (-ен, -ьна, -ьно) *прил* = ощути́мый.

ощу|ти́ть (-щу́, -ти́шь; *impf* **ощуща́ть**) *сов перех (запах)* to notice; *(радость, желание, боль)* to feel.

ощуща́|ть (-ю) *несов от* ощути́ть.

ощуще́ни|е (-я) *ср (прикосновения, запаха)* sense; *(радости, боли)* feeling.

ощущу́ *сов см* ощути́ть.

ОЭСР *ж сокр* (= Организа́ция экономи́ческого сотру́дничества и разви́тия) OECD (= *Organization for Economic Cooperation and Development*).

оягн|и́ться (*3sg* -и́тся, *3pl* -я́тся) *сов от* ягни́ться.

~ П, п ~

П, п *сущ нескл* (*буква*) the 16th letter of the Russian alphabet.

п. *сокр* (= **пара́граф**) par. (= *paragraph*); = **посёлок**.

па *ср нескл* (dance) step.

п.а. *сокр* (= **почто́вый а́дрес**) postal address.

павиа́н (-а) *м* baboon.

павильо́н (-а) *м* pavilion; (*кино*) studio.

павли́н (-а) *м* peacock.

па́водо|к (-ка) *м* flood.

па́губ|ный (-ен, -на, -но) *прил* (*последствия*) ruinous; (*влияние, привычка*) pernicious.

па́дал|ь (-и) *ж собир* carrion.

па́да|ть (-ю; *perf* **упа́сть** *или* **пасть**) *несов непереx* to fall; (*настроение*) to sink; (*дисциплина, нравы*) to decline; (*умирать: животное*) to die; (*no perf; снег*) to fall; ~ (**упа́сть** *perf*) **на** +*acc* (*ложиться: тень*) to fall on; ~ (**пасть** *perf*) **на** +*acc* (*подозрение*) to fall on; (*ответственность*) to fall to *или* on; ~ (**упа́сть** *perf*) **ду́хом** to lose heart; **у неё упа́ло настрое́ние** her spirits sank; ~ (**упа́сть** *perf*) **в чьих-н глаза́х** to fall in sb's estimation; ~ (**упа́сть** *perf*) **в о́бморок** to faint.

паде́ж (-а́) *м* (*линг*) case.

паде́жный *прил* (*линг*) case *опред*.

Па-де-Кале́ *м нескл* Pas de Calais.

паде́ни|е (-я) *ср* (*также перен*) fall; (*нравов, дисциплины*) decline.

па́дк|ий (-кая, -кое, -кие; -ок, -ка, -ко) *прил*: ~ **на** +*acc* greedy for.

паду́ *итп сов см* **пасть**.

па́дчери|ца (-ы) *ж* stepdaughter.

па́дш|ий (-ая, -ее, -ие) *прил* fallen.

паев|о́й *прил* (*экон*) share *опред*; **на ~ы́х нача́лах** on a shareholder basis.

пае́к (-йка́) *м* ration; **сухо́й** ~ dry ration.

паж (-а́) *м* page(boy).

ПАЗ *м сокр* = **Па́вловский авто́бусный заво́д**; (*автобус*) vehicle manufactured at the Pavlovsk car factory.

паз (-а; *loc sg* -ý, *nom pl* -ы́) *м* (*ТЕХ*) groove.

па́зух|а (-и) *ж* bosom; **держа́ть** (*impf*) **ка́мень за ~ой на кого́-н** to bear a grudge against sb, bear sb a grudge; **жить** (*impf*) **как у Христа́ за ~ой** (*разг*) to be without a care in the world.

па|й (-я; *nom pl* -и́) *м* (*ЭКОН*) share; **на ~я́х** jointly.

пайка́ *итп сущ см* **пае́к**.

па́йщик (-а) *м* shareholder.

пакга́уз (-а) *м* warehouse.

паке́т (-а) *м* (*бумажный свёрток, комп*) package; (*мешок*) (paper *или* plastic) bag; (*конверт*) official envelope (*containing important or secret documents*); (*комм*): (**контро́льный**) ~ **а́кций** (controlling) shareholding; ~ **програ́мм** (*комп*) software package; ~ **прикладны́х програ́мм** (*комп*) applications package.

паке́т|ный *прил*: ~**ая обрабо́тка** (*комп*) batch processing.

Пакиста́н (-а) *м* Pakistan.

пакиста́не|ц (-ца) *м* Pakistani.

пакиста́н|ка (-ки; *gen pl* -ок) *ж см* **пакиста́нец**.

пакиста́нск|ий (-ая, -ое, -ие) *прил* Pakistani.

пакиста́нца *сущ см* **пакиста́нец**.

пак|ова́ть (-у́ю; *perf* **запакова́ть** *или* **упакова́ть**) *несов перех* to pack.

па́костен *прил см* **па́костный**.

па́ко|стить (-щу, -стишь; *perf* **запа́костить**) *несов перех* (*разг*) to soil, dirty ◆ (*perf* **напа́костить**) *непереx*: ~ (**кому́-н**) to play a dirty trick (on sb).

па́кост|ный (-ен, -на, -но) *прил* (*разг*) vile, nasty.

па́кощу *несов см* **па́костить**.

пакт (-а) *м* pact.

ПАЛ *сокр* PAL (= *phase alternation line*).

пала́с (-а) *м* double-sided woven rug.

пала́т|а (-ы) *ж* (*в больнице*) ward; (*полит*) chamber, house; **ве́рхняя/ни́жняя** ~ (*полит*) Upper/Lower Chamber; ~ **о́бщин/ло́рдов** House of Commons/Lords; **Кни́жная** ~ Book Chamber (*Bibliographical centre in Moscow*); **Торго́вая** ~ Chamber of Commerce.

пала́т|ка (-ки; *gen pl* -ок) *ж* (*туристическая*) tent; (*ларёк*) stall.

пала́ч (-а́) *м* executioner.

Палести́н|а (-ы) *ж* Palestine.

палести́нск|ий (-ая, -ое, -ие) *прил* Palestinian.

па́л|ец (-ьца) *м* (*руки*) finger; (*ноги*) toe; **безымя́нный** ~ fourth *или* ring finger; **большо́й** ~ (*руки*) thumb; (*ноги*) big toe;

сре́дний ~ middle finger; **указа́тельный** ~ index finger; **знать** (*impf*) **что-н как свои́ пять** **~ьцев** to know sth like the back of one's hand; **он ~ о ~ не уда́рил, он па́льцем не** **шевельну́л** he didn't lift a finger; **смотре́ть** (*impf*) **сквозь ~ьцы на что-н** to shut one's eyes to sth.

палиса́дник (-а) *м* (small) front garden (*BRIT*) *или* yard (*US*).

пали́тр|а (-ы) *ж* (*также перен*) palette.

пали́ть (-ю́, -и́шь; *perf* **опали́ть**) *несов перех* (*волосы*) to singe; (*perf* **спали́ть**; *подлеж*: *солнце*) to scorch; (*perf* **вы́палить**; *разг*: *стреля́ть*) to fire.

па́л|ка (-ки; *gen pl* -**ок**) *ж* stick; **лы́жные ~ки** ski poles; **де́лать** (**сде́лать** *perf*) **что-н из-под ~ки** (*разг*) to be bludgeoned into doing sth; **э́то ~ о** **двух конца́х** it cuts both ways; **~ки в колёса** **вставля́ть** (*impf*) **кому́-н** to put a spoke in sb's wheel.

пало́мник (-а) *м* pilgrim.

пало́мничеств|о (-а) *ср* pilgrimage.

па́лоч|ка (-ки; *gen pl* -**ек**) *ж уменьш от* **па́лка**; (*МЕД*) bacillus (*мн* bacilli); **дирижёрская ~** (conductor's) baton; **волше́бная ~** magic wand.

па́лочн|ый *прил*: **~ая дисципли́на** (*перен*) heavy-handed discipline.

па́луб|а (-ы) *ж* (*МОР*) deck.

па́льм|а (-ы) *ж* palm (tree).

пальто́ *ср нескл* overcoat.

па́льца *итп сущ см* **па́лец**.

памфле́т (-а) *м* lampoon.

па́мятен *прил см* **па́мятный**.

па́мят|ка (-ки; *gen pl* -**ок**) *ж* (*туриста,* *отдыха́ющих*) guidelines *мн*; (*на рабо́те*) memorandum (*мн* memoranda).

па́мятник (-а) *м* monument; (*на моги́ле*) tombstone; (*археологический*) relic; **~и** **старины́** ancient monuments; **па́мятники** **пи́сьменности** ancient manuscripts.

па́мятн|ый (-ен, -на, -но) *прил* (*незабыва́емый*) memorable; (*no short form*; *сде́ланный в па́мять*) commemorative.

па́мяток *сущ см* **па́мятка**.

па́мят|ь (-и) *ж* (*также КОМП*) memory; (*воспомина́ние*) memories *мн*; **в чью-н ~, в ~ о** **ком-н** in memory of sb; **на ~** (*чита́ть стихи*) from memory; (*подари́ть, взять*) as a memento; **быть** (*impf*) **без ~и** to be unconscious; **он люби́т её без ~и** (*разг*) he is crazy about her; **она́ без ~и от э́того актёра** (*разг*) she's mad about that actor.

Пана́м|а (-ы) *ж* Panama.

пана́м|а (-ы) *ж* Panama (hat).

пана́мск|ий (-ая, -ое, -ие) *прил*: **П~ кана́л** Panamanian Canal.

панаце́|я (-и) *ж* panacea.

па́нд|а (-ы) *ж* panda.

пандеми́|я (-и) *ж* pandemia.

пане́л|ь (-и) *ж* (*тротуа́р*) pavement (*BRIT*), sidewalk (*US*); (*СТРОИТ*) panel; (*ТЕХ*) control panel.

панибра́тств|о (-а) *ср* familiarity.

па́ник|а (-и) *ж* panic.

паник|ова́ть (-у́ю) *несов неперех* (*разг*) to panic.

панихи́д|а (-ы) *ж* (*РЕЛ*) funeral service; **гражда́нская ~** civil funeral.

пани́ческ|ий (-ая, -ое, -ие) *прил* (*состоя́ние,* *бе́гство итп*) panic-stricken; (*слу́хи*) alarming.

панно́ *ср нескл* decorative panel.

панора́м|а (-ы) *ж* panorama.

пансио́н (-а) *м* (*шко́ла*) boarding school; (*по́лное содержа́ние*) (full) board and lodging.

пансиона́т (-а) *м* boarding house.

пантео́н (-а) *м* pantheon.

панте́р|а (-ы) *ж* panther.

пантоми́м|а (-ы) *ж* mime.

па́нцир|ь (-я) *м* (*черепа́хи*) shell; (*ры́царя*) coat of armour (*BRIT*) *или* armor (*US*).

па́п|а (-ы) *м* dad; (*также*: **Ри́мский ~**) the Pope.

папа́х|а (-и) *ж* papakha (*tall fur cap*).

папа́ш|а (-и) *м* (*разг*: *па́па*) old man; (: *как* *обраще́ние*) grandad.

па́перт|ь (-и) *ж* church porch.

папиро́с|а (-ы) *ж type of cheap Russian cigarette* *with cardboard filter*.

папиро́сн|ый *прил*: **~ая бума́га** (*для куре́ния*) cigarette paper; (*то́нкая бума́га*) tissue paper.

папи́рус (-а) *м* papyrus.

па́п|ка (-ки; *gen pl* -**ок**) *ж* folder (*BRIT*), file (*US*).

па́поротник (-а) *м* fern.

папье́-маше́ *ср нескл* papier-mâché.

пар (-а; *loc sg* -**у́**, *nom pl* -**ы́**) *м* steam; (*С.-Х.*) fallow land; **на всех ~а́х** (*перен*) full steam ahead; *см* *также* **па́ры**.

па́р|а (-ы) *ж* (*ту́фель итп*) pair; (*супру́жеская*) couple; (*ПРОСВЕЩ*) ≈ poor (*school mark*); **~** **слов/мину́т** (*разг*) a couple of words/minutes; **рабо́тать** (*impf*)/**игра́ть** (*impf*) **в ~е с кем-н** to work/play with sb; **э́то ~ пустяко́в** (*разг*) it's child's play; **они́ два сапога́ ~** (*разг*) they are as bad as each other.

Парагва́|й (-я) *м* Paraguay.

пара́граф (-а) *м* paragraph.

пара́д (-а) *м* parade; **в по́лном** *или* **при всём ~е** (*разг*) dressed up to the nines.

пара́дн|ая (-ой; *decl like adj*) *ж* = **пара́дное**.

пара́дн|ое (-ого; *decl like adj*) *ср* entrance.

пара́дн|ый *прил* (*обе́д*) formal; (*стол*) festive; (*вид*) smart (*BRIT*), stylish (*US*); (*вход,* *ле́стница*) front *опред*, main; **пара́дный** **костю́м, пара́дная фо́рма** full dress.

парадо́кс (-а) *м* paradox.

парадокса́л|ьный (-ен, -ьна, -ьно) *прил* paradoxical.

парази́т (-а) *м* parasite.

парализ|ова́ть (-у́ю) (*не*)*сов перех* (*также* *перен*) to paralyze; **у́жас ~ова́л его́** he was paralyzed with fear.

парали́ч (-а́) *м* paralysis.

паралле́лен *прил см* **паралле́льный**.

параллель (-и) ж (также перен) parallel.
параллельный (-ен, -ьна, -ьно) прил parallel.
парамедик (-а) м paramedic.
параметр (-а) м (также перен) parameter; (КОМП) default option.
паранджа́ (-и́) ж yashmak.
паранойя (-и) ж paranoia.
парапет (-а) м parapet.
парапсихоло́гия (-и) ж parapsychology.
парафи́н (-а) м paraffin (wax).
парафи́новый прил paraffin опред.
парашю́т (-а) м parachute.
парашюти́ст (-а) м parachutist.
парашюти́стка (-ки; gen pl -ок) ж см парашюти́ст.
па́рень (-ня; gen pl -не́й) м (разг: юноша) lad, boy; (: мужчина) chap или fellow (BRIT), guy (US); **он свой ~** (разг) he's an easy-going guy.
пари́ ср нескл bet; **держа́ть** (impf) **~, что ...** to bet that ...; **заключа́ть (заключи́ть** perf) **~ с кем-н (на что-н)** to make a bet with sb (about sth).
Пари́ж (-а) м Paris.
парижа́нин (-ина; nom pl -е, gen pl -)) м Parisian.
парижа́нка (-ки; gen pl -ок) ж Parisienne.
пари́жский (-ая, -ое, -ие) прил Parisian.
пари́к (-а́) м wig.
парикма́хер (-а) м hairdresser.
парикма́херская (-ой; decl like adj) ж hairdresser's (BRIT), beauty salon (US).
пари́лка (-ки; gen pl -ок) ж steam room (in sauna).
пари́ровать (-ую; perf **пари́ровать** или **отпари́ровать**) несов перех (также перен) to parry.
парите́т (-а) м parity.
па́рить (-ю, -ишь) несов перех (овощи) to steam
► **па́риться** несов возв (овощи) to be steamed; (в бане) to have a sauna; (разг: в тёплой одежде) to sweat.
пари́ть (-ю, -ишь) несов неперех to glide; **~** (impf) **в облака́х** (перен) to have one's head in the clouds.
парк (-а) м park; (трамвайный) depot; **ваго́нный ~** rolling stock; **автомоби́льный ~** fleet of cars.
парке́т (-а) м parquet.
паркова́ть (-у́ю) несов перех to park.
парла́мент (-а) м parliament.
парламента́рий (-я) м parliamentarian.
парла́ментский (-ая, -ое, -ие) прил parliamentary.
парни́к (-а́) м (из стекла) greenhouse; (из полиэтилена) (poly)tunnel.
парнико́вый прил (растение) hothouse опред; **~ое хозя́йство** glasshouse nursery; **парнико́вый эффе́кт** greenhouse effect.
парно́й прил fresh.
па́рный прил: **~ боти́нок/носо́к** one of a pair of boots/socks; **~ое ката́нье (на конька́х)** pairs' ice-skating; **где ~ боти́нок?** where is the other boot?
па́рня итп сущ см **па́рень**.
парово́з (-а) м steam engine или locomotive.
парово́й прил steam опред.
пароди́ровать (-ую) (не)сов перех to parody.
паро́дия (-и) ж (также перен): **~ (на** +acc) parody (of).
паро́ль (-я) м password.
паро́м (-а) м ferry.
парохо́д (-а) м steamer, steamship.
парохо́дство (-а) ср shipping; (учреждения) ≈ port and navigation authority; (фирма) shipping company.
па́рта (-ы) ж desk.
партбиле́т (-а) м сокр (= парти́йный биле́т) (Party) membership card (of the Communist Party).
парте́р (-а) м the stalls мн.
партиза́н (-а; gen pl -) м partisan, guerrilla.
парти́йный прил (съезд) party опред ♦ (-ого; decl like adj) м Party member.
партиту́ра (-ы) ж score.
па́ртия (-и) ж (ПОЛИТ) party; (: в СССР) the (Communist) Party; (МУЗ) part; (груза) consignment; (изделий: в производстве) batch, lot; (группа): **по́исковая ~** search party; (СПОРТ): **~ в ша́хматы/волейбо́л** a game of chess/volleyball.
партко́м (-а) м сокр (= парти́йный комите́т) (Communist) Party committee.
партнёр (-а) м partner.
партнёрство (-а) ср (ЭКОН) partnership.
парторганиза́ция (-и) ж сокр (= парти́йная организа́ция) (Communist) Party organization.
па́рус (-а; nom pl -а́) м sail; **на всех паруса́х** (перен) at full speed.
паруси́на (-ы) ж canvas.
паруси́новый прил canvas опред.
па́русник (-а) м sailing vessel.
парфюме́рия (-и) ж собир perfume and cosmetic goods.
парча́ (-и́) ж brocade.
парши́вый (-, -а, -о) прил (разг) lousy, rotten.
па́ры (-о́в) мн vapour ед (BRIT), vapor ед (US).
пас (-а) м (СПОРТ) pass.
пас(ся) итп несов см пасти́(сь).
па́сека (-и) ж apiary.
па́сечник (-а) м bee keeper.
па́сквиль (-я) м send-up (inf).
паску́дный (-ен, -на, -но) прил (разг) nasty.
па́смурен прил см па́смурный.
па́смурно как сказ: **сего́дня ~** it is overcast today.
па́смурный (-ен, -на, -но) прил overcast, dull; (перен) gloomy.
пасова́ть (-у́ю) несов перех (мяч) to pass ♦

(*perf* **спасова́ть**) *неперех*: ~ **пе́ред** +*instr* to give in to.

па́спорт (-а; *nom pl* -**а́**) *м* passport; (*автомобиля, станка*) registration document; **заграни́чный** ~ passport (*for foreign travel*).

пасса́ж (-а) *м* arcade; (*МУЗ*) passage.

пассажи́р (-а) *м* passenger.

пассажи́р|ка (-ки; *gen pl* -**ок**) *ж см* **пассажи́р**.

пассажи́рский (-ая, -ое, -ие) *прил* passenger *опред*.

пасси́в (-а) *м* (*КОММ*) liabilities *мн*; (*ЛИНГ*) passive (voice).

пасси́вный (-ен, -на, -но) *прил* (*также ЛИНГ*) passive; (*no short form*; *КОММ*): ~ **бала́нс** unfavourable (*BRIT*) *или* unfavorable (*US*) balance; ~ **партнёр** (*КОММ*) silent partner.

па́ст|а (-ы) *ж* (*томатная*) purée; (*в ручке*) ink; **зубна́я** ~ toothpaste.

па́стбищ|е (-а) *ср* pasture.

пасте́л|ь (-и) *ж* pastel.

пасте́льный *прил* pastel *опред*.

пастеризо́ванный *прил* pasteurized.

пастериз|ова́ть (-**у́ю**) (*не*)*сов перех* to pasteurize.

пастерна́к (-а) *м* parsnip.

пас|ти́ (-**у́**, -**ёшь**; *pt* -, **ла́**, -**ло́**) *несов перех* (*скот*) to graze

▶ **пасти́сь** *несов возв* to graze.

пас|тила́ (-**илы́**; *nom pl* -**и́лы**) *ж* ≈ marshmallow.

па́стор (-а) *м* minister, pastor.

пасту́х (-**а́**) *м* (*коров*) herdsman (*мн* herdsmen); (*овец*) shepherd.

па́стыр|ь (-я) *м* pastor.

па|сть (-**ду́**, -**дёшь**; *pt* -л, -ла, -ло) *сов от* **па́дать**
◆ *неперех* (*no impf*; *крепость, правительство*) to fall ◆ (-**сти**) *ж* (*зверя*) mouth.

па́сх|а (-и) *ж* (*в иудаизме*) Passover; (*в христианстве*) ≈ Easter; (*кушанье*) paskha (*sweet dish made with cream cheese at Easter*).

па́сын|ок (-ка) *м* stepson.

пат (-а) *м* (*в шахматах*) stalemate.

пате́нт (-а) *м* (*на изобретение*) patent; (*торговый*) licence (*BRIT*), license (*US*).

пате́нтный *прил* patent *опред*; **пате́нтное бюро́/пра́во** patent office/rights.

патент|ова́ть (-**у́ю**; *perf* **запатентова́ть**) *несов перех* to patent.

патети́ческий (-ая, -ое, -ие) *прил* (*страстный*) passionate, emotional.

па́ток|а (-и) *ж* treacle.

патологи́ческий (-ая, -ое, -ие) *прил* (*также перен*) pathological.

патоло́ги|я (-и) *ж* pathology.

патриа́рх (-а) *м* patriarch.

патриарха́льный *прил* patriarchal.

патриа́рхи|я (-и) *ж* patriarchate.

патрио́т (-а) *м* patriot.

патриоти́зм (-а) *м* patriotism.

патрио́т|ка (-ки; *gen pl* -**ок**) *ж см* **патрио́т**.

патро́н (-а) *м* (*ВОЕН*) cartridge; (*дрели*) chuck; (*лампы*) socket; (*покровитель*) patron.

патрона́ж (-а) *м* (*МЕД*) home visiting by a district nurse for newborn babies or the chronically ill.

патрона́жный *прил*: ~**ая сестра́** (*МЕД*) ≈ district (*BRIT*) *или* visiting (*US*) nurse.

патру́б|ок (-ка) *м* branch pipe.

патрули́р|овать (-**ую**) *несов* (*не*)*перех* to patrol.

патру́л|ь (-**я́**) *м* patrol.

па́уз|а (-ы) *ж* (*также МУЗ*) pause.

пау́к (-**а́**) *м* spider.

паути́н|а (-ы) *ж* spider's web, spiderweb (*US*); (*в помещении*) cobweb; (*перен*) web.

па́фос (-а) *м* zeal, fervour (*BRIT*), fervor (*US*).

пах (-а; *loc sg* -**у́**) *м* groin.

пах *итп несов см* **па́хнуть**.

па́хар|ь (-я) *м* ploughman (*BRIT*), plowman (*US*) (*мн* ploughmen *или* plowmen).

пах|а́ть (-**шу́**, -**шешь**; *perf* **вспаха́ть**) *несов перех* to plough (*BRIT*), plow (*US*).

па́х|нуть (-ну, -нешь; *pt* -, -ла, -ло) *несов неперех*: ~ (+*instr*) to smell (of); (*разг*): ~ +*instr* (*скандалом*) to smack of; **от неё** ~**нет духа́ми** she smells of perfume.

пахн|у́ть (*3sg* -**ёт**, *3pl* -**у́т**) *сов неперех* (+*instr*): ~**у́ло ро́зам** the scent of roses wafted by.

па́хот|а (-ы) *ж* ploughing (*BRIT*), plowing (*US*).

паху́чий (-ая, -ее, -ие; -, -а, -е) *прил* strong-smelling.

паца́н (-**а́**) *м* (*разг*) boy, lad.

пацие́нт (-а) *м* patient.

пацие́нт|ка (-ки; *gen pl* -**ок**) *ж см* **пацие́нт**.

пацифи́ст (-а) *м* pacifist.

па́ч|ка (-ки; *gen pl* -**ек**) *ж* (*бумаг, денег итп*) bundle; (*чая, сигарет итп*) packet; (*балерины*) tutu.

па́чка|ть (-ю; *perf* **запа́чкать** *или* **испа́чкать**) *несов перех*: ~ **что-н** to get sth dirty; (*perf* **запа́чкать**; *перен: репутацию*) to sully, tarnish

▶ **па́чкаться** (*perf* **запа́чкаться** *или* **испа́чкаться**) *несов возв* to get dirty.

па́ш|ня (-ни; *gen pl* -**ен**) *ж* ploughed (*BRIT*) *или* plowed (*US*) field.

паште́т (-а) *м* pâté.

пашу́ *итп несов см* **паха́ть**.

па́юсн|ый *прил*: ~**ая икра́** pressed caviar(e).

пая́льник (-а) *м* soldering iron.

пая́сни|ча|ть (-ю) *несов неперех* (*разг*) to play the fool.

пая́|ть (-ю) *несов перех* to solder.

пая́ц (-а) *м* clown.

ПВО *ж сокр* (= **противовозду́шная оборо́на**) anti-aircraft defence (*BRIT*) *или* defense (*US*) system.

ПДВ *м сокр* (= **преде́льно допусти́мый вы́брос**) maximum permitted discharge.

пев|е́ц (-**ца́**) *м* singer.

пев|и́ца (-**ы**) *ж см* **певе́ц**.

певц|а́ *итп сущ см* **певе́ц**.

пе́вчий (-ая, -ее, -ие) *прил*: ~**ая пти́ца** songbird
◆ (-**его**; *decl like adj*) *м* chorister.

пе́гий (-ая, -ое, -ие) *прил* piebald *опред*.

педаго́г (**-а**) *м* (*учитель*) teacher.

педаго́гик|а (**-и**) *ж* education science.

педагоги́ческ|ий (**-ая, -ое, -ие**) *прил* (*коллектив*) teaching *опред*; ~ **институ́т** teacher-training (*BRIT*) *или* teachers' (*US*) college; **у неё ~ тала́нт** she has a talent for teaching; **у него́ ~ое образова́ние** he trained as a teacher.

педа́л|ь (**-и**) *ж* pedal.

педа́нт (**-а**) *м* pedant.

педиа́тр (**-а**) *м* paediatrician (*BRIT*), pediatrician (*US*).

педиатри́|я (**-и**) *ж* paediatrics (*BRIT*), pediatrics (*US*).

педикю́р (**-а**) *м* pedicure.

пединститу́т (**-а**) *м сокр* (= *педагоги́ческий институ́т*) teacher-training college.

педсове́т (**-а**) *м сокр* (= *педагоги́ческий сове́т*) staff meeting.

педучи́лищ|е (**-а**) *ср сокр* (= *педагоги́ческое учи́лище*) teacher-training college (*for nursery and primary level*).

пей *несов см* **пить**.

пейза́ж (**-а**) *м* (*также ИСКУССТВО*) landscape; **морско́й ~** (*ИСКУССТВО*) seascape.

пейзажи́ст (**-а**) *м* landscape painter.

пе́йте *несов см* **пить**.

пёк(ся) *итп несов см* **печь(ся)**.

пека́р|ня (**-ни**; *gen pl* **-ен**) *ж* bakery.

пе́кар|ь (**-я**) *м* baker.

Пеки́н (**-а**) *м* Beijing, Peking.

пекл|о́ (**-а**) *ср* (*зной*) scorching heat; (*перен: ад*) hell.

пеку́(сь) *итп несов см* **печь(ся)**.

пелен|а́ (**-ы́**) *ж* (*тумана, облаков*) veil, shroud; **у него́ сло́вно ~ с глаз упа́ла** the scales fell from his eyes.

пелена́|ть (**-ю**; *perf* **запелена́ть**) *несов перех* to swaddle.

пеленгова́|ть (**-ю́**; *perf* **запеленгова́ть**) *несов перех* (*TEX*) to take the bearings of.

пелён|ка (**-ки**; *gen pl* **-ок**) *ж* swaddling clothes *мн*; **с ~ок** (*перен*) from a very early age.

пелика́н (**-а**) *м* pelican.

пельме́н|ь (**-я**; *nom pl* **-и**) *м* (*обычно мн*) ≈ ravioli *только ед*.

пе́мз|а (**-ы**) *ж* pumice (stone).

пе́н|а (**-ы**) *ж* (*мыльная*) suds *мн*; (*морская*) foam; (*бульонная*) froth; **говори́ть** (*impf*) **с ~ой у рта́** to foam at the mouth.

пена́л (**-а**) *м* pencil case.

пена́льти *ср нескл* penalty.

Пенджа́б (**-а**) *м* Punjab.

пенджа́бск|ий (**-ая, -ое, -ие**) *прил* Punjabi.

пе́ней *сущ см* **пе́ня**.

пе́н|и (**-ей**) *мн* = **пе́ня**.

пе́ни|е (**-я**) *ср* singing.

пе́нистый *прил* frothy.

пе́н|иться (*3sg* **-ится**, *3pl* **-ятся**, *perf* **вспе́ниться**) *несов возв* to foam, froth.

пеницилли́н (**-а**) *м* penicillin.

пе́нк|а (**-и**) *ж* (*на молоке*) skin; **снима́ть** (*impf*) **~и** (*перен*) to cream off the best for o.s.

пе́нни *ср нескл* penny.

пенопла́ст (**-а**) *м* foam plastic.

пенс (**-а**) *м* pence *мн*.

пенсионе́р (**-а**) *м* pensioner.

пенсионе́р|ка (**-ки**; *gen pl* **-ок**) *ж см* **пенсионе́р**.

пенсио́нный *прил* (*фонд*) pension *опред*; **пенсио́нный во́зраст** pension age.

пе́нси|я (**-и**) *ж* pension; **~ по инвали́дности** ≈ invalidity benefit; **выходи́ть** (**вы́йти** *perf*) **на ~ю** to retire.

пенсне́ *ср нескл* pince-nez.

пень (**пня**) *м* (tree) stump; (*разг: пренебр: о человеке*) dolt, blockhead.

пеньк|а́ (**-и́**) *ж* hemp (*fibre*).

пенью́а́р (**-а**) *м* negligee.

пе́н|я (**-и**; *gen pl* **-ей**) *ж* fine.

пеня́|ть (**-ю**) *несов неперех*: **~ на себя́** (*разг*) to blame *или* reproach o.s.; **пусть он ~ет на себя́** he has only himself to blame.

пе́пел (**-ла**) *м* ash; (*хлопья*) ashes *мн*.

пепели́щ|е (**-а**) *ср* site of a fire.

пе́пельниц|а (**-ы**) *ж* ashtray.

пе́пла *итп сущ см* **пе́пел**.

пер. *сокр* = **переу́лок**.

пёр *итп несов см* **пере́ть**.

перве́йш|ий (**-ая, -ее, -ие**) *прил* primary.

пе́рвен|ец (**-ца**) *м* first-born.

пе́рвенств|о (**-а**) *ср* (*положение*) first place; (*соревнование*) championship.

пе́рвенств|овать (**-ую**) *несов неперех* to take first place, come first.

пе́рвенца *итп сущ см* **пе́рвенец**.

перви́чный *прил* (*самый ранний*) initial *опред*, primary; (*низовой*) grass root.

перв|о́е (**-ого**; *decl like adj*) *ср* first course.

первозда́нный *прил* primordial.

первоисто́чник (**-а**) *м* primary source.

первокла́ссник (**-а**) *м pupil in first year at school* (*usually seven years old*).

первокла́ссниц|а (**-ы**) *ж см* **первокла́ссник**.

первокла́ссн|ый *прил*: **~ые инвести́ции** (*КОММ*) blue-chip investment.

пе́рво-на́перво *нареч* (*разг*) first of all.

первонача́льный (**-ен, -ьна, -ьно**) *прил* (*исходный*) original, initial *опред*.

первообра́з (**-а**) *м* prototype.

первооткрыва́тел|ь (**-я**) *м* discoverer.

первоочередно́й *прил* (*неотложный*) immediate.

первоочерёдный *прил* = **первоочередно́й**.

первопрохо́д|ец (**-ца**) *м* (*поселенец*) pioneer; (*исследователь*) explorer.

перворазря́дный *прил* first-class, top-class.
первосо́рт|ный (**-ен, -на, -но**) *прил* top-quality, top-grade, first-rate.
первостепе́н|ный (**-ен, -на, -но**) *прил* (*задача, значение*) paramount.
первоцве́т (**-а**) *м* primrose.
пе́рв|ый (**-ая, -ое, -ые**) *чис* first; (*по времени*) first, earliest; ~ **эта́ж** ground (*BRIT*) *или* first (*US*) floor; ~**ое вре́мя** at first; **в** ~**ую о́чередь** in the first place *или* instance; ~ **час дня/но́чи** after midday/midnight; **из** ~**ых рук** first-hand; **он** ~ **учени́к** he is top of the class; ~**ым де́лом** *или* **до́лгом** first of all; **това́р** ~**ого со́рта** top grade product (*on a scale of 1-3*); **пе́рвая по́мощь** first aid; *см также* **пя́тый**.
перга́мент (**-а**) *м* parchment.
пере- *префикс* (*in verbs*; *о направлении действия через что-н*) *indicating movement over or across sth eg.* **переходи́ть**; (*о направлении действия из одного места в другое*) *indicating movement from one place to another eg.* **передви́нуть**; (*разделение что-н на две части*) *indicating division of sth into two parts eg.* **перепили́ть**; (*изменение направленности действия*) *indicating redirection of sth eg.* **передове́рить**; (*повторение действия*) *indicating repetition of sth eg.* **переде́лать**; (*обозначает превосходство в чём-н*) *indicating superiority in sth eg.* **переспо́рить**; (*чрезмерность действия*) *indicating excessive action eg.* **перепи́ть**; (*прекращение действия после длительного проявления*) *indicating cessation of action after certain length of time eg.* **переволнова́ться**; (*распространение действия на много лиц или предметов*) *indicating action involving of many people or objects eg.* **перечита́ть**; (*обозначает взаимность действия*) *indicating reciprocal nature of action eg.* **переписыва́ться**; (*in nouns*; *обозначает промежуточность*) *indicating intermediate stage of sth eg.* **переми́рие**.
переадрес|ова́ть (**-у́ю**; *impf* **переадресо́вывать**) *сов перех* to readdress.
перебази́р|овать (**-ую**) *сов перех* to relocate.
переба́рщива|ть (**-ю**) *несов от* **переборщи́ть**.
перебежа́ть (*как* **бежа́ть**; *см* **Table 20**; *impf* **перебега́ть**) *сов неперех*: ~ (**че́рез** +*acc*) to run across; **перебега́ть** (~ *perf*) **к** +*dat* (*разг*: *к противнику итп*) to go over to.
перебе́й(те) *сов см* **переби́ть**.
переберу́(сь) *итп сов см* **перебра́ть(ся)**.
перебе́|ситься (**-шусь, -сишься**) *сов возв* to run riot; (*разг*) to sow one's wild oats.
перебива́|ть(ся) (**-ю(сь)**) *несов от* **переби́ть(ся)**.
перебира́|ть (**-ю**) *несов от* **перебра́ть** ♦ *перех*: ~ **кла́виши** to run one's fingers over the keys
▸ **перебира́ться** *несов от* **перебра́ться**.
перебь|ть (**-ю́, -ьёшь**; *impf* **перебива́ть**) *сов*

перех to interrupt; (*убить*) to kill; (*разбить*) to break; (*обить*) to reupholster; **перебива́ть** (~ *perf*) **аппети́т** to spoil *или* ruin one's appetite; **перебива́ть** (~ *perf*) **мысль** to interrupt one's train of thought; **перебива́ть** (~ *perf*) **за́пах чего-н** to conceal the smell of sth
▸ **переби́ться** (*impf* **перебива́ться**) *сов возв* to make ends meet, get by; (*no impf*; *обойти́сь*): ~**ся** (**без** +*gen*) (*разг*) to go without; **они́ с трудо́м** ~**и́лись до зарпла́ты** they managed to get by till payday; **он** ~**ьётся!** he'll survive *или* manage!
перебо́|й (**-я**) *м* (*сердца*) irregularity; (*двигателя*) misfire; (*задержка*) interruption, break.
переболе́|ть (**-ю**) *сов неперех*: ~ +*instr* to recover from; (*дети, люди*: *корью, гриппом*) to come down with; **у него́ душа́** ~**ла** he is over the heartache.
перебо́р (**-а**) *м* (*МУЗ*) strumming; (*излишнее*): **э́то уже́** ~ that's too much.
перебор|о́ть (**-ю́, -о́решь**) *сов перех* to overcome.
переборщ|и́ть (**-у́, -и́шь**; *impf* **переба́рщивать**) *сов неперех*: ~ **в** +*prp* (*разг*) to go over the top with.
перебра́сыва|ть(ся) (**-ю(сь)**) *несов от* **переброси́ть(ся)**.
перебр|а́ть (**-еру́, -ерёшь**; *impf* **перебира́ть**) *сов перех* (*пересмотреть*: *бумаги*) to sort out; (: *крупу, ягоды*) to sort; (*мысленно воспроизвести*) to go over *или* through (in one's mind); (*взять слишком много*) to take too much; (*выпить лишнее*) to drink too much; (*струны*) to pluck (*BRIT*), pick (*US*)
▸ **перебра́ться** (*impf* **перебира́ться**) *сов возв* (*разг*: *через реку*) to manage to get across; (*на новую кварти́ру*) to move.
перебро́|сить (**-шу, -сишь**; *impf* **переба́сывать**) *сов перех* (*мяч, мешок*) to throw over; (*войска*) to transfer, move
▸ **перебро́ситься** (*impf* **переба́сываться**) *сов возв* (*войска*) to be transferred; **переба́сываться** (~**ся** *perf*) +*instr* (*мячом*) to throw to each other); (*словами*) to exchange (with one another).
перебыва́|ть (**-ю**) *сов неперех* (*у многих людей*) to call on; (*во многих местах*): **он везде́** ~**л** he has been all over the world.
перебью́(сь) *итп сов см* **переби́ть(ся)**.
перева́л (**-а**) *м* (*в горах*) pass.
перева́л|ить (**-ю́, -алишь**; *impf* **перева́ливать**) *сов неперех*: ~ (**че́рез** +*acc*) to cross; **перева́ливать** (~ *perf*) **за** +*acc* (*разг*) to top.
перева́лочный *прил*: ~ **пункт/ла́герь** transit area/camp.
перева́р|ить (**-ю́, -аришь**; *impf* **перева́ривать**) *сов перех* to overcook (*by boiling*); (*пищу, информацию*) to digest
▸ **перевари́ться** (*impf* **перева́риваться**) *сов*

возе to be overdone *или* overcooked; (*пища*) to be digested.

переведу́(сь) *итп сов см* **перевести́(сь)**.

перев|езти́ (-езу́, -езёшь; *pt* -ёз, -езла́, -езло́, *impf* **перевози́ть**) *сов перех* (*переместить*) to take *или* transport across; (*доставить*) to transport, take.

переверн|у́ть (-у́, -ёшь; *impf* **перевёртывать** *или* **перевора́чивать**) *сов перех* to turn over; (*изменить*) to change (completely); (*no impf*; *комнату*) to turn upside down

▶ **переверну́ться** (*impf* **перевёртываться** *или* **перевора́чиваться**) *сов возв* (*человек*) to turn over; (*лодка, машина*) to overturn.

переве́с (-а) *м* (*преимущество*) advantage.

переве́|сить (-шу, -сишь; *impf* **переве́шивать**) *сов перех* (*товар*) to reweigh; (*подлеж*: *аргумент*) to outweigh.

перев|ести́ (-еду́, -едёшь; *pt* -ёл, -ела́, -ело́, *impf* **переводи́ть**) *сов перех* (*помочь перейти*) to take across; (*часы*) to reset; (*учреждение, сотрудника*) to transfer, move; (*текст*) to translate; (: *устно*) to interpret; (*переслать*: *деньги*) to send, transfer; (*доллары, метры итп*) to convert; (*разг: израсходовать*) to waste; **переводи́ть** (~ *perf*) **разгово́р** to change the subject; **переводи́ть** (~ *perf*) **текст с ру́сского языка́ на англи́йский** to translate a text from Russian into English; **переводи́ть** (~ *perf*) **дух** *или* **дыха́ние** to take a (deep) breath

▶ **перевести́сь** (*impf* **переводи́ться**) *сов возв* to move; (*разг: исчезнуть*) to die out.

переве́шива|ть (-ю) *несов от* **переве́сить**.

переве́шу *сов см* **переве́сить**.

перевида́|ть (-ю) *сов перех* to see.

перевира́|ть (-ю) *несов от* **переврать**.

перево́д (-а) *м* (*на другую должность*) transfer; (*стрелки часов*) resetting; (*текст*) translation; (*деньги*) remittance; ~ **строки́** (*КОМП*) line feed; **креди́тный** ~ (*КОММ*) credit transfer, bank giro.

перев|оди́ть(ся) (-ожу́(сь), -о́дишь(ся)) *несов от* **перевести́(сь)**.

перево́дный *прил* in translation.

перево́дчик (-а) *м* translator; (*устный*) interpreter.

перево́дчиц|а (-ы) *ж см* **перево́дчик**.

перевожу́ *несов см* **перевози́ть**.

перевожу́(сь) *несов см* **переводи́ть(ся)**.

перево́з (-а) *м* (*груза*) transportation.

перев|ози́ть (-ожу́, -о́зишь) *несов от* **перевезти́**.

перево́з|ка (-ки; *gen pl* -ок) *ж* transportation, conveyance.

переволн|ова́ться (-у́юсь) *сов возв* to be worried sick.

перевоору́ж|ить (-у́, -и́шь; *impf* **перевооружа́ть**) *сов перех* (*армию*) to rearm; (*промышленность*) to re-equip.

перевопло|ти́ться (-щу́сь, -ти́шься; *impf* **перевоплоща́ться**) *сов возв* (*актёр*) to be transformed.

перевора́чива|ть(ся) (-ю(сь)) *несов от* **переверну́ться(ся)**.

переворо́т (-а) *м* (*ПОЛИТ*) coup (d'état); (*в судьбе*) upheaval.

перевоспита́|ть (-ю; *impf* **перевоспи́тывать**) *сов перех* to re-educate.

перевр|а́ть (-у́, -ёшь; *impf* **перевира́ть**) *сов перех* (*разг: содержание*) to muddle.

перевы́бор|ы (-ов) *мн* election *ед* (*occurring at regular intervals*).

перевы́полн|ить (-ю, -ишь; *impf* **перевыполня́ть**) *сов перех* (*задание, план*) to overfulfil; (*норму*) to exceed.

перевяз|а́ть (-яжу́, -я́жешь; *impf* **перевя́зывать**) *сов перех* (*руку, раненого*) to bandage; (*рану*) to dress, bandage; (*коробку*) to tie up; (*чулки, свитер*) to reknit.

перевя́з|ка (-ки; *gen pl* -ок) *ж* (*раны, раненых*) bandaging.

перевя́зочный *прил*: ~ **материа́л** bandage.

перевя́зыва|ть (-ю) *несов от* **перевяза́ть**.

пе́ревяз|ь (-и) *ж* shoulder-belt; (*для руки*) sling.

перега́р (-а) *м smell or taste of (stale) alcohol*; **от него́ несёт** ~**ом** he reeks of alcohol.

переги́б (-а) *м* (*страницы, ткани*) fold; (*перен*: *крайность*) excesses *мн*.

перегиба́|ть (-ю) *несов от* **перегну́ть**.

перегля|ну́ться (-ну́сь, -я́нешься; *impf* **перегля́дываться**) *сов возв*: ~ (**с** +*instr*) to exchange glances (with).

перегн|а́ть (-оню́, -о́нишь; *pt* -на́л,-нала́,-на́ло, *impf* **перегоня́ть**) *сов перех* (*переместить*: *скот, машину*) to drive; (*обогнать*: *бегуна, конкурента*) to overtake; (*нефть*) to refine; (*спирт*) to distil (*BRIT*), distill (*US*).

перегно́|й (-я) *м* humus.

перегн|у́ть (-у́, -ёшь; *impf* **перегиба́ть**) *сов перех* (*бумагу*) to fold (over) ♦ *неперех* (*с критикой*) to go too far; **перегиба́ть** (~ *perf*) **па́лку** (*перен*) to go too far.

перегова́рива|ться (-юсь) *несов возв*: ~ (**с** +*instr*) to exchange remarks (with).

переговор|и́ть (-ю́, -и́шь) *сов неперех*: ~ **с** +*instr* (*обсудить*) to have a talk with ♦ *перех* (*разг*) to outtalk.

переговор́ный *прил*: ~ **пункт** telephone office (*for long-distance calls*).

переговор|ы (-ов) *мн* negotiations *мн*, talks *мн*; (*по телефону*) call *ед*; **зака́зывать** (**заказа́ть** *perf*) ~ **с** +*instr* to book a call to.

перего́н (-а) *м* (*на железной дороге*) stage (*between two railway stations*).

перего́н|ка (-ки; *gen pl* -ок) *ж* (*нефти*) refining; (*спирта*) distillation.

перегоню́ *итп сов см* **перегна́ть**.

перегоня́|ть (-ю) *несов от* **перегна́ть**.
перегора́жива|ть (-ю) *несов от*
перегороди́ть.
перегор|е́ть (*3sg* -и́т, *3pl* -я́т, *impf* **перегора́ть**)
сов неперех (*лампочка*) to fuse; (*двигатель*) to
burn out.
перегоро|ди́ть (-жу́, -ди́шь; *impf*
перегора́живать) *сов перех* (*комнату*) to
partition (off); (*дорогу*) to block.
перегоро́д|ка (-ки; *gen pl* -ок) ж partition.
перегорожу́ *сов см* **перегороди́ть**.
перегре́|ть (-ю; *impf* **перегрева́ть**) *сов перех* to
overheat
▶ **перегре́ться** (*impf* **перегрева́ться**) *сов возв*
to overheat; **он ~лся на со́лнце** he got a touch
of sunstroke.
перегру|зи́ть (-ужу́, -у́зишь; *impf* **перегружа́ть**)
сов перех to overload.
перегру́з|ка (-ки; *gen pl* -ок) ж overload; (*обычно*
мн: нервные) strain.
перегры́з|ть (-у́, -ёшь; *impf* **перегрыза́ть**) *сов*
перех to gnaw through
▶ **перегры́зться** (*impf* **перегрыза́ться**) *сов*
возв to fight.

KEYWORD

пе́ред *предл* (+*instr*) **1** (*о положении, в*
присутствии): in front of); **пе́ред до́мом/**
зе́ркалом in front of the house/mirror; **он**
робе́л пе́ред де́вушками he was shy in front of
girls; **моли́ться** (*impf*) **пе́ред ико́ной** to pray
before an icon
2 (*раньше чего-н: ужином, войной, концом*
итп) before; **я говори́л с ним пе́ред уро́ком** I
spoke to him before the lesson
3 (*об объекте воздействия*): **устоя́ть пе́ред**
тру́дностями to stand one's ground in the face
of difficulties; **извиня́ться** (**извини́ться** *perf*)
пе́ред кем-н to apologize to sb; **я винова́т**
пе́ред тобо́й I am guilty in your eyes;
отчи́тываться (**отчита́ться** *perf*) **пе́ред** +*instr*
to report to
4 (*по сравнению*) compared to; **пе́ред ним ты**
челове́к ничто́жный compared to him, you are
a nonentity
5 (*как союз*): **пе́ред тем как** before; **пе́ред тем**
как уйти́/зако́нчить before leaving/finishing.

перёд (**пе́реда**) *м* front.
переда|ва́ть(ся) (-ю́(сь); *imper* **передава́й(те)**)
несов от **переда́ть(ся)**.
переда́м(ся) *итп сов см* **переда́ть(ся)**.
переда́тчик (-а) *м* (*ТЕХ*) transmitter.
переда́|ть (*как* **дать**; *см* **Table 14**; *impf*
передава́ть) *сов перех*: ~ **что-н** (**кому́-н**)
(*письмо, подарок*) to pass *или* hand sth (over)
(to sb); (*известие, любовь, интерес*) to pass sth
on (to sb); (*идеи, эмоции*) to convey sth *или* get
sth across (to sb); ~**йте ей, что я не приду́** tell
her I am not coming; **передава́ть** (~ *perf*) **что-н**
по телеви́дению/ра́дио to televise/broadcast

sth; **передава́ть** (~ *perf*) **де́ло в суд** to take a
case to court
▶ **переда́ться** (*impf* **передава́ться**) *сов возв*
(+*dat*; *эмоция*): **его́ страх ~лся други́м** his fear
communicated itself to the others; **ему́ ~лся**
тала́нт отца́ he has inherited his father's talent.
переда́ч|а (-и) ж (*известия*) passing on;
(*концерта, новостей*) transmission; (*ТЕЛ,*
РАДИО: интересная) programme (*BRIT*),
program (*US*); (*больному, заключённому*)
parcel; **програ́мма переда́ч** television and
radio guide.
переда́шь(ся) *сов см* **переда́ть(ся)**.
передвига́|ть (-ю) *несов от* **передви́нуть**
▶ **передвига́ться** *несов от* **передви́нуться** ♦
возв (*на машине, на танке итп*) to move.
передвиже́ни|е (-я) *ср* (*предмета, войск*)
movement; (*срока*) alteration, change; **сре́дства**
~**я** means of transport.
передвижно́й *прил* (*выставка, цирк*) travelling
(*BRIT*), traveling (*US*); (*лаборатория,*
библиотека) mobile.
передви́|нуть (-у, -ешь; *impf* **передвига́ть**) *сов*
перех to move
▶ **передви́нуться** (*impf* **передвига́ться**) *сов*
возв to move.
переде́ла|ть (-ю; *impf* **переде́лывать**) *сов*
перех (*работу*) to redo; (*характер*) to change;
(*рассказ*) to rewrite; ~ (*perf*) **все дела́** to get
everything done.
переде́л|ка (-ки; *gen pl* -ок) ж (*одежды*)
alteration; (*характера*) change; **попада́ть**
(**попа́сть** *perf*) **в ~ку** (*разг*) to get into a fix;
побыва́ть (*perf*) **в ~х** (*разг*) to be in a fix.
переде́лыва|ть (-ю) *несов от* **переде́лать**.
передёргива|ть (-ю) *несов от* **передёрнуть**.
переде́р|жа́ть (-ержу́, -е́ржишь; *impf*
переде́рживать) *сов перех*: **он ~ержа́л мя́со в**
духо́вке he left the meat in the oven for too
long.
передёрн|уть (-у, -ешь; *impf* **передёргивать**)
сов перех (*разг: факты, цифры*) to massage ♦
безл (+*acc*): **его́ ~уло от хо́лода** he convulsed
from the cold; **его́ ~уло от отвраще́ния** he
shuddered in disgust.
пере́дн|ий (-яя, -ее, -ие) *прил* front; **П~яя А́зия**
the Middle East; ~ **план** (*КОМП*) foreground;
пере́дний край (*ВОЕН, перен*) front line.
пере́дник (-а) *м* apron.
пере́дн|яя (-ей; *decl like adj*) ж (*entrance*) hall.
пе́редо *предл*: ~ **мно́й** in front of me; = **пе́ред**.
передов|а́я (-о́й; *decl like adj*) ж (*также:* ~
статья́) editorial; (*также:* ~ **пози́ция**: *ВОЕН*)
vanguard.
передово́й *прил* (*отряд*) advance, forward;
(*машина*) front *опред*; (*технология*) advanced;
(*писатель, взгляды*) progressive.
передохн|у́ть (-у́, -ёшь) *сов неперех* (*разг*) to
take a breather (*BRIT*) *или* break (*US*).
передра|зни́ть (-азню́, -а́знишь; *impf*
передра́знивать) *сов перех* to mimic.

переду́ма|ть (-ю; *impf* **переду́мывать**) *сов неперех* to change one's mind.

переды́ш|ка (-ки; *gen pl* -ек) *ж* rest; (*перерыв*) (short) break.

перее́ду *итп сов см* **перее́хать**.

перее́зд (-а) *м* (*в новый дом*) move; (*на железной дороге*) level crossing.

перее́|хать (*как* **е́хать**; *см* Table 19; *impf* **переезжа́ть**) *сов неперех* (*переселиться*) to move; **переезжа́ть** (~ *perf*) (**че́рез** +*acc*) to cross.

пережгу́ *итп сов см* **переже́чь**.

пережда́ть (-у́, -ёшь; *impf* **пережида́ть**) *сов перех*: ~ **дождь** to wait for the rain to pass.

переже́|чь (-гу́, -жёшь *итп*, -гу́т; *pt* -ёг, -гла́, -гло́, *impf* **пережига́ть**) *сов перех* (*зерна кофе*) to burn; (*глину*) to overfire.

пережива́ни|е (-я) *ср* (*обычно мн*) feeling.

пережива́|ть (-ю) *несов от* **пережи́ть** ♦ *неперех*: ~ (**за** +*acc*) (*разг*) to worry (about).

переживу́ *итп сов см* **пережи́ть**.

пережига́|ть (-ю) *несов от* **переже́чь**.

пережида́|ть (-ю) *несов от* **пережда́ть**.

пережи́т|ок (-ка) *м* relic.

пережи́|ть (-ву́, -вёшь; *impf* **пережива́ть**) *сов перех* (*прожить дольше*) to outlive; (*выжить*) to survive; (*испытать*) to experience; (*вытерпеть*) to suffer.

перезаря|ди́ть (-жу́, -ди́шь; *impf* **перезаряжа́ть**) *сов перех* (*аккумулятор*) to recharge; (*ружьё*) to reload.

перезвон|и́ть (-ю́, -и́шь; *impf* **перезва́нивать**) *сов неперех* to phone (*BRIT*) *или* call (*US*) back.

перезим|ова́ть (-у́ю) *сов от* **зимова́ть**.

перезре́|ть (-ю; *impf* **перезрева́ть**) *сов неперех* to become overripe.

переигра́|ть (-ю; *impf* **переи́грывать**) *сов перех* (*играть снова*) to replay ♦ *неперех* (*разг*) to overact; **э́то де́ло на́до** ~ (*разг*) this will have to be looked at again.

переизб|ра́ть (-еру́, -ерёшь; *pt* -ра́л, -рала́, -ра́ло, *impf* **переизбира́ть**) *сов перех* to re-elect.

переизда|ва́ть (-ю́; *imper* **переизда́й(те)**) *несов от* **переизда́ть**.

переизда́м *итп сов см* **переизда́ть**.

переизда́ни|е (-я) *ср* (*действие*) republication; (*исправленное, дополненное*) new edition.

переизда́|ть (*как* **дать**; *см* Table 14; *impf* **переиздава́ть**) *сов перех* to republish.

переимен|ова́ть (-у́ю; *impf* **переимено́вывать**) *сов перех* to rename.

перейду́ *итп сов см* **перейти́**.

перейму́ *итп сов см* **переня́ть**.

пере|йти́ (*как* **идти́**; *см* Table 18; *impf* **переходи́ть**) *сов перех*: ~ (**че́рез** +*acc*) to cross ♦ *неперех*: ~ **в/на** +*acc* (*поменять место*) to go to; (*на другую работу*) to move to;

переходи́ть (~ *perf*) **к** +*dat* (*к сыну итп*) to pass to; (*к делу, к обсуждению*) to turn to; **переходи́ть** (~ *perf*) **в ата́ку** to launch an attack; **переходи́ть** (~ *perf*) **на** +*acc* to switch to; **переходи́ть** (~ *perf*) **грани́цу** to cross the frontier *или* border; (*перен*) to overstep the bounds *или* mark; **переходи́ть** (~ *perf*) **из рук в ру́ки** to change hands; **переходи́ть** (~ *perf*) **на гру́бости** to resort to bad language; **дру́жба** ~**шла́ в любо́вь** friendship turned *или* developed into love.

перека́пыва|ть (-ю) *несов от* **перекопа́ть**.

перека́рмлива|ть (-ю) *несов от* **перекорми́ть**.

перек|ати́ть (-ачу́, -а́тишь; *impf* **перека́тывать**) *сов перех* (*что-н круглое*) to roll; (*что-н на колёсах*) to wheel.

перека́шива|ть(ся) (-ю(сь)) *несов от* **перекоси́ть(ся)**.

переквалифици́р|оваться (-уюсь) *сов возв* to retrain.

перекидно́й *прил*: ~ **мост** gangplank; ~ **календа́рь** desk calendar.

переки́н|уть (-у, -ешь; *impf* **переки́дывать**) *сов перех* to throw over

▶ **переки́нуться** (*impf* **переки́дываться**) *сов возв*: ~+*instr* (*мячом*) to throw to each other.

перекла́дин|а (-ы) *ж* crossbeam; (*СПОРТ*) (horizontal *или* high) bar.

перекладн|ы́е (-ы́х; *decl like adj*) *мн* stagecoach *ед*.

перекла́дыва|ть (-ю) *несов от* **переложи́ть**.

перекли́ка́|ться (-юсь) *несов возв* (*люди, животные*) to call to each other; ~ (*impf*) (**с** +*instr*) (*перен: образы, идеи*) to have something in common (with).

перекли́ч|ка (-ки; *gen pl* -ек) *ж* roll call.

переключа́тел|ь (-я) *м* switch.

переключа́|ть(ся) (-ю(сь)) *несов от* **переключи́ть(ся)**.

переключе́ни|е (-я) *ср* switching; (*скорости*) changing (*BRIT*), shifting (*US*).

переключ|и́ть (-у́, -и́шь; *impf* **переключа́ть**) *сов перех* to switch; **переключа́ть** (~ *perf*) **ско́рость** to change (*BRIT*) *или* shift (*US*) gear; **переключа́ть** (~ *perf*) **разгово́р** to change the subject

▶ **переключи́ться** (*impf* **переключа́ться**) *сов возв*: ~**ся** (**на** +*acc*) (*внимание*) to shift (to).

перек|ова́ть (-у́ю; *impf* **перекóвывать**) *сов перех* (*коня*) to reshoe; (*изделие, деталь*) to reforge.

перекопа́|ть (-ю; *impf* **перека́пывать**) *сов перех* (*огород*) to dig up; (*разг: чемодан, шкаф*) to rummage through.

перекорм|и́ть (-лю́, -ишь; *impf* **перека́рмливать**) *сов перех* to overfeed.

перекоси́ть (-шу́, -си́шь; *impf* **перека́шивать**)

сов перех (рисуя) to draw crooked; *(вырезая)* to cut crooked

▶ **перекоси́ться** *(impf* **перека́шиваться)** *сов возв (деталь, рисунок)* to come out crooked; *(лицо, тело)* to become distorted.

перекоч|ева́ть (**-у́ю;** *impf* **перекочёвывать)** *сов неперех (стадо, табор)* to move on.

перекошу́(сь) *сов см* **перекоси́ть(ся)**.

перекра́ива|ть (**-ю**) *несов от* **перекро́ить**.

▶ **перекрести́ть** (**-ещу́, -е́стишь)** *сов от* **крести́ть**

▶ **перекрести́ться** *сов от* **крести́ться** ♦ *(impf* **перекре́щиваться)** *возв (также перен)* to cross.

перекрёстка *сущ см* **перекрёсток**.

перекрёстный *прил* intersecting; **перекрёстный допро́с** cross-examination; **перекрёстный ого́нь** crossfire.

перекрёст|ок (**-ка**) *м* crossroads.

перекре́щива|ться (**-юсь**) *несов от* **перекрести́ться**.

перекрещу́(сь) *сов см* **перекрести́ть(ся)**.

перекрича́|ть (**-у́, -и́шь;** *impf* **перекри́кивать)** *сов перех (в споре)* to shout down; *(шум, музыку)* to shout above.

перекро́|ить (**-ю́, -и́шь;** *impf* **перекра́ивать)** *сов перех (платье)* to cut differently; *(карту)* to redraw.

перекро́ю *итп сов см* **перекры́ть**.

перекру|ти́ть (**-чу́, -у́тишь;** *impf* **перекру́чивать)** *сов перех (гайку, кран)* to overtighten

▶ **перекрути́ться** *(impf* **перекру́чиваться)** *сов возв* to get tangled up.

перекрыва́|ть (**-ю**) *несов от* **перекры́ть**.

перекры́ти|е (**-я**) *ср* ceiling; *(реки)* damming.

перекры́|ть (**-о́ю, -о́ешь;** *impf* **перекрыва́ть)** *сов перех (покрыть заново)* to re-cover; *(реку)* to dam; *(дорогу, улицу)* to close off; *(воду, газ)* to cut off; *(разг: план)* to exceed.

перекуп|и́ть (**-уплю́, -у́пишь;** *impf* **перекупа́ть)** *сов перех* to buy.

перекупщик (**-а**) *м* dealer.

перекур (**-а**) *м (разг: перерыв)* cigarette break.

перекур|и́ть (**-урю́, -у́ришь;** *impf* **перекур́ивать)** *сов перех (разг)* to break for a cigarette; *(: сделать перерыв)* to take a break.

перекус|и́ть (**-ушу́, -у́сишь;** *impf* **переку́сывать)** *сов перех* to bite through ♦ *неперех (разг)* to have a snack.

перела́влива|ть (**-ю**) *несов от* **перелови́ть**.

перелага́|ть (**-ю**) *несов от* **переложи́ть**.

перела́мыва|ть (**-ю**) *несов от* **переломи́ть**.

перелез|ть (**-у, -ешь;** *pt* **-, -ла, -ло,** *impf* **перелеза́ть)** *сов (не)перех:* **~ (че́рез** *+acc)* *(забор, канаву)* to climb (over); **перелеза́ть (~** *perf)* **в/на** *+acc* to get *или* climb into.

перелес|ок (**-ка**) *м (небольшой лес)* copse, coppice; *(редкий лес)* sparsely wooded area.

перелёт (**-а**) *м* flight; *(птиц)* migration.

перелете́ть (**-чу́, -ти́шь;** *impf* **перелета́ть)** *сов (не)перех:* **~ (че́рез** *+acc)* to fly over.

перелётный *прил (птицы)* migratory.

перелечу́ *сов см* **перелете́ть**.

перели́в (**-а**) *м (красок, звуков)* (subtle) gradation; *(голоса)* modulation.

перелива́ни|е (**-я**) *ср:* **~ кро́ви** blood transfusion.

перелива́|ть (**-ю**) *несов от* **перели́ть** ♦ *неперех (блестеть):* **~** *+instr* to shimmer with; **~** *(impf)* **все́ми цвета́ми ра́дуги** to be iridescent.

перелиста́|ть (**-ю;** *impf* **перели́стывать)** *сов перех (просмотреть)* to leaf through; *(быстро перебрать)* to flick through.

перел|и́ть (**-ью, -ьёшь;** *impf* **перелива́ть)** *сов перех* to pour *(from one container to another)*; **перелива́ть (~** *perf)* **кровь кому́-н** to give sb a blood transfusion.

перел|ови́ть (**-овлю́, -о́вишь;** *impf* **перела́вливать)** *сов перех* to catch.

переложе́ни|е (**-я**) *ср (пьесы, повести)* adaptation; *(музыкального произведения)* arrangement.

перел|ожи́ть (**-ожу́, -о́жишь;** *impf* **перекла́дывать)** *сов перех* to move, shift; *(impf* **перекла́дывать** *или* **перелага́ть;** *повесть, пьесу)* to adapt; **перекла́дывать (~** *perf)* **что-н на кого́-н** *(ответственность, работу итп)* to pass sth onto sb; **~** *(perf)* **со́ли в суп** to put too much salt in the soup.

перело́м (**-а**) *м (МЕД)* fracture; *(перен)* turning point.

перелома́|ть (**-ю**) *сов перех* to break.

перел|оми́ть (**-омлю́, -о́мишь;** *impf* **перела́мывать)** *сов перех (палку)* to break in two; *(перен: ход событий)* to change dramatically.

перело́мный *прил* critical.

перелью́ *итп сов см* **перели́ть**.

перема́|зать (**-жу, -жешь;** *impf* **перема́зывать)** *сов перех* to cover.

перема́лыва|ть (**-ю**) *несов от* **перемоло́ть**.

перема́н|ить (**-ю́, -а́нишь;** *impf* **перема́нивать)** *сов перех (разг)* to entice.

перема́тыва|ть (**-ю**) *несов от* **перемота́ть**.

перемежа́|ть (**-ю**) *несов перех:* **~ что-н с чем-н** to alternate sth with sth

▶ **перемежа́ться** *несов возв:* **~ся с** *+instr* to alternate with.

перемелю́ *итп сов см* **перемоло́ть**.

переме́н|а (**-ы**) *ж* change; *(в школе)* break *(BRIT)*, recess *(US)*.

перемен|и́ть (**-ю́, -е́нишь)** *сов перех* to change

▶ **перемени́ться** *сов возв (жизнь, погода)* to change; **он ~е́нился в лице́** *(от волнения итп)* his expression changed.

переме́нный *прил (погода)* changeable; *(успех, ветер)* variable; **переме́нный ток** alternating current.

переме́р|ить (**-ю, -ишь;** *impf* **переме́ривать)**

сов перех (измерить снова) to remeasure; *(примерить)* to try on.

переме|сти́ть (**-щу́, -сти́шь;** *impf* **перемеща́ть**) *сов перех (предмет)* to move, shift; *(людей)* to transfer

▶ **перемести́ться** (*impf* **перемеща́ться**) *сов возв* to move.

переметн|у́ть (**-у́, -ёшь**) *сов (не)перех:* ~ **(че́рез** +*acc*) to throw over

▶ **переметну́ться** *сов возв (на сторону противника итп)* to go over; ~**ся** (*perf*) **че́рез** +*acc* to leap over.

перемеша́ть (**-ю**; *impf* **переме́шивать**) *сов перех (кашу)* to stir; *(угли, дрова)* to poke; *(вещи, бумаги)* to mix up

▶ **перемеша́ться** (*impf* **переме́шиваться**) *сов возв* to get mixed up.

перемеща́|ть(ся) (**-ю(сь)**) *несов от* **перемести́ть(ся)**.

перемеще́ни|е (**-я**) *ср* reshuffle (*in government, of jobs*); *(передвижение)* transfer.

перемещённ|ый *прил:* ~**ое лицо́** *(обычно мн)* displaced person (*мн* people).

перемещу́(сь) *сов см* **перемести́ть(ся)**.

перемигн|у́ться (**-у́сь, -ёшься;** *impf* **переми́гиваться**) *сов возв (раза)* to wink at each other; **он** ~**у́лся с де́вушкой** he winked at the girl and she winked back.

перемина́|ться (**-юсь**) *несов возв:* ~ **с ноги́ на́ ногу** to shift from one foot to the other.

переми́ри|е (**-я**) *ср* truce.

перемно́ж|ить (**-у, -ишь;** *impf* **перемножа́ть**) *сов перех (числа)* to multiply.

перемо́лв|иться (**-люсь, -ишься**) *сов возв:* ~ **(сло́вом) с кем-н** *(разг)* to pass the time of day with sb.

перемо|ло́ть (**-елю́, -е́лешь;** *impf* **перема́лывать**) *сов перех* to grind.

перемота́|ть (**-ю**; *impf* **перема́тывать**) *сов перех (нитку, шерсть)* to wind; *(магнитофо́нную плёнку)* to rewind.

перемы́|ть (**-о́ю, -о́ешь**; *impf* **перемыва́ть**) *сов перех* to wash; *(вымыть заново)* to wash again, rewash; **перемыва́ть** (~ *perf*) **ко́сточки кому́-н** *(раза)* to gossip about sb.

перемы́ч|ка (**-ки;** *gen pl* **-ек**) *ж (соединение)* crosspiece; *(перекрытие: окна, двери)* lintel.

перенапря́г *итп сов см* **перенапря́чь**.

перенапряга́|ть (**-ю**) *несов от* **перенапря́чь**.

перенапрягу́ *итп сов см* **перенапря́чь**.

перенапряже́ни|е (**-я**) *ср (физическое, умственное)* overexertion.

перенапря́|чь (**-гу́, -жёшь** *итп*, **-гу́т;** *pt* **-г, -гла́, -гло́**) *(impf* **перенапряга́ть**) *сов перех* to overstrain, overexert.

перенаселён|ный (**-, -á, -ó**) *прил* overpopulated.

перенасы́|тить (**-щу, -тишь;** *impf*

перенасыща́ть) *сов перех* to oversaturate; **он** ~**тил свою́ речь цита́тами** his speech was riddled with quotations.

перен|ести́ (**-есу́, -есёшь;** *pt* **-ёс, -есла́, -есло́,** *impf* **переноси́ть**) *сов перех:* ~ **что-н че́рез** +*acc* to carry sth over *или* across; *(поменять место)* to move; *(встречу, заседание)* to reschedule; *(болезнь)* to suffer from; *(несчастье, голод, холод итп)* to endure; **переноси́ть** (~ *perf*) **сло́во на другу́ю стро́ку** to carry a word over to the next line

▶ **перенести́сь** (*impf* **переноси́ться**) *сов возв (также перен)* to be transported.

перенима́|ть (**-ю**) *несов от* **переня́ть**.

перено́с (**-а**) *м (вещей, предметов)* transfer; *(заседания)* rescheduling; *(линг)* hyphen.

перен|оси́ть (**-ошу́, -о́сишь**) *несов от* **перенести́** ♦ *перех:* **не** ~ **антибио́тиков/ самолёта** to react badly to antibiotics/flying; **он хорошо́** ~**ёс доро́гу** he coped well with the journey; **она́ не** ~**о́сит его́** she can't stand him

▶ **переноси́ться** *несов от* **перенести́сь**.

перено́сиц|а (**-ы**) *ж* bridge of the nose.

перено́сной *прил* portable.

перено́сный *прил (значение)* figurative.

перено́счик (**-а**) *м (МЕД)* carrier.

переноч|ева́ть (**-у́ю**) *сов от* **ночева́ть**.

переношу́(сь) *несов см* **переноси́ть(ся)**.

пере|ня́ть (**-йму́, -ймёшь;** *pt* **-ня́л, -няла́, -ня́ло,** *impf* **перенима́ть**) *сов перех (опыт, идеи)* to assimilate; *(обычаи, привычки)* to adopt.

переобору́д|овать (**-ую**) *сов перех* to re-equip.

переобу́|ть (**-ю, -ешь;** *impf* **переобува́ть**) *сов перех (туфли)* to change (out of); **переобува́ть** (~ *perf*) **кого́-н** to change sb's shoes.

переоде́|ть (**-ну, -нешь;** *impf* **переодева́ть**) *сов перех (одежду)* to change (out of); **переодева́ть** (~ *perf*) **кого́-н** to change sb's clothes

▶ **переоде́ться** (*impf* **переодева́ться**) *сов возв* to change, get changed.

переосмы́сл|ить (**-ю, -ишь;** *impf* **переосмы́сливать**) *сов перех (осмыслить заново)* to reassess.

переоце|ни́ть (**-ню́, -нишь;** *impf* **переоце́нивать**) *сов перех (дать новую цену)* to re-evaluate, revalue; *(оценить слишком высоко)* to overestimate.

переоце́н|ка (**-ки;** *gen pl* **-ок**) *ж (см глаг)* re-evaluation, revaluation; overestimation; ~ **це́нностей** *(перен)* reappraisal *или* reassessment of values.

перепа́д (**-а**) *м:* ~ +*gen* drop in.

перепада́|ть (*3sg* **-ет,** *3pl* **-ют**) *несов от* **перепа́сть**.

перепадёт *итп сов см* **перепа́сть**.

перепа́л|ка (**-ки;** *gen pl* **-ок**) *ж (разг)* row.

перепа́|сть (*3sg* -дёт, *3pl* -ду́т, *impf* **перепада́ть**) *сов неперех* (+*dat*; *достаться*) to come one's way; **мне ~ла ко́е-кака́я ме́бель** some furniture has come my way.

перепа́чка|ть (-ю) *сов перех* (*разг*) to get filthy.

перепева́|ть (-ю) *несов перех* (*перен*) to rehash.

пе́репел (-а; *nom pl* -а́) *м* quail.

перепёл|ка (-ки; *gen pl* -ок) *ж см* **пе́репел**.

перепеча́та|ть (-ю) *сов перех* (*статью*) to reprint; (*рукопись*) to type.

перепи|ли́ть (-илю́, -и́лишь; *impf* **перепи́ливать**) *сов перех* (*много дров*) to saw; (*доску*) to saw in two.

перепи|са́ть (-ишу́, -и́шешь; *impf* **перепи́сывать**) *сов перех* (*написать заново*) to rewrite; (*скопировать*) to copy; (*сделать список*) to list, make a list of; (*комп*) to overwrite.

перепи́с|ка (-ки; *gen pl* -ок) *ж* (*см глаг*) rewriting; copying; listing; (*деловая*) correspondence ♦ *собир* (*письма*) letters *мн*; **быть** (*impf*) **в ~ке с** +*instr* to be in correspondence with.

перепи́сыва|ть (-ю) *несов от* **переписа́ть**

► **перепи́сываться** *несов возв*: ~**ся (с** +*instr*) to correspond (with).

пе́репис|ь (-и) *ж* (*населения*) census; (*имущества*) inventory.

перепишу́ *итп сов см* **переписа́ть**.

перепла|ти́ть (-чу́, -́тишь; *impf* **перепла́чивать**) *сов неперех* to pay too much.

переплес|ти́ (-ту́, -тёшь; *pt* -ёл, -ела́, -ело́, *impf* **переплета́ть**) *сов перех* (*книгу, диссертацию*) to bind; (*верёвки, пальцы*) to interlace

► **переплести́сь** (*impf* **переплета́ться**) *сов возв* to intertwine; (*перен: события*) to become interwoven.

переплёт (-а; *обложка*) binding; **попа́сть** (**попа́сть** *perf*) **в ~** (*перен: разг*) to get into a fix; **отдава́ть** (**отда́ть** *perf*) **кни́гу/диссерта́цию в ~** to have a book/thesis bound; **око́нный ~** window sash.

переплета́|ть(ся) (-ю(сь)) *несов от* **переплести́(сь)**.

переплётн|ая (-ой; *decl like adj*) *ж* (*book*) bindery.

переплету́(сь) *итп сов см* **переплести́(сь)**.

переплы́|ть (-ву́, -вёшь; *pt* -л, -ла́, -ло, *impf* **переплыва́ть**) *сов (не)перех*: ~ (**че́рез** +*acc*) (*вплавь*) to swim (across); (*на лодке, на корабле*) to sail (across).

переплю́н|уть (-у, -ешь) *сов перех* (*перен: разг*) to go one up on.

переподгото́в|ка (-ки; *gen pl* -ок) *ж* retraining.

переполз|ти́ (-у́, -ёшь; *pt* -, -ла́, -ло́, *impf* **переполза́ть**) *сов (не)перех* to crawl; **переполза́ть** (~ *perf*) (**че́рез** +*acc*) (*дорогу, поле итп*) to crawl across.

перепо́лн|ить (-ю, -ишь; *impf* **переполня́ть**) *сов перех* (*сосуд, контейнер*) to overfill;

(*вагон, автобус итп*) to overcrowd; **моё се́рдце ~ено любо́вью** my heart is overflowing with love

► **перепо́лниться** (*impf* **переполня́ться**) *сов возв* (*сосуд*) to be overfilled; (*душа, сердце*) to overflow.

переполо́х (-а) *м* hullabaloo.

переполоши́|ть (-у́, -и́шь) *сов перех* (*разг*) to alarm

► **переполоши́ться** *сов возв* (*разг*) to become alarmed.

перепо́н|ка (-ки; *gen pl* -ок) *ж* membrane; **бараба́нная ~** eardrum.

перепра́в|а (-ы) *ж* crossing.

перепра́в|ить (-лю, -ишь; *impf* **переправля́ть**) *сов перех* (*через реку, границу*) to take across; (*посылку, письмо*) to forward; (*ошибку, фразу*) to correct

► **перепра́виться** (*impf* **переправля́ться**) *сов возв* (*через реку, горы итп*) to cross.

перепро́б|овать (-ую) *сов перех* (*еду*) to taste; (*способы*) to try (out).

перепрода|ва́ть (-ю́; *imper* **перепродава́й(те)**) *несов от* **перепрода́ть**.

перепрода́ть (*как* **дать**; *см* **Table 14**; *impf* **перепродава́ть**) *сов перех* to resell.

перепроизво́дств|о (-а) *ср* overproduction.

перепры́гн|уть (-у, -ешь; *impf* **перепры́гивать**) *сов (не)перех*: ~ (**че́рез** +*acc*) to jump (over).

перепу́г (-а) *м* (*разг*): **с ~у** in fright.

перепуга́|ть (-ю) *сов перех*: ~ **кого́-н** to scare the life out of sb.

перепу́та|ть (-ю; *impf* **перепу́тывать** *или* **пу́тать**) *сов перех* (*нитки, провода*) to tangle (up); (*факты*) to confuse; (*имена, адреса*) to mix up

► **перепу́таться** (*impf* **перепу́тываться** *или* **пу́таться**) *сов возв* (*нитки, провода*) to get tangled up; (*перен: мысли, воспоминания*) to get confused.

перепу́ть|е (-я) *ср* crossroads; **на ~** (*перен*) at a crossroads.

перерабо́та|ть (-ю; *impf* **перераба́тывать**) *сов перех* (*сырьё, нефть*) to process; (*идеи, статью, теорию*) to rework ♦ *неперех* (*переутомиться*) to be overworked.

перераспредел|и́ть (-ю́, -и́шь; *impf* **перераспределя́ть**) *сов перех* to redistribute.

перер|асти́ (-асту́, -асте́шь; *pt* -о́с, -осла́, -осло́, *impf* **перераста́ть**) *сов перех* (*также перен*) to outgrow; **перераста́ть** (~ *perf*) **в** +*acc* (*превратиться*) to escalate into.

перерасхо́д (-а) *м* (*энергии, денег*) overexpenditure; (*комм*) overdraft.

перерасхо́д|овать (-ую) *сов перех*: ~ **эне́ргию/де́ньги** to expend too much energy/money.

перерасчёт (-а) *м* (*счёт заново*) recalculation; (*комм: в другие единицы*) conversion.

перере́за|ть (-жу, -жешь; *impf* **перереза́ть**) *сов перех* (*провод*) to cut in two; (*перен:*

преградить) to cut off.

перерис|ова́ть (-у́ю; *impf* **перерисо́вывать**) *сов перех* to copy.

перо|ди́ться (-жу́сь, -ди́шься; *impf* **перерожда́ться**) *сов возв* (*природа, общество*) to be regenerated; (*человек*) to be transformed.

перерожде́ни|е (-я) *ср* (*см глаг*) regeneration; transformation.

перерожу́сь *сов см* **перероди́ться**.

перерос *итп сов см* **перерасти́**.

переро́ю *итп сов см* **переры́ть**.

переруга́|ться (-юсь) *сов возв* to quarrel.

переры́в (-а) *м* break; **обе́денный** ~ lunch break; **де́лать** (**сде́лать** *perf*) ~ to take a break.

переры́|ть (-о́ю, -о́ешь) *сов перех* (*перекопать*) to dig up; (*разг: вещи, книги*) to rummage through.

перес|ади́ть (-ажу́, -а́дишь; *impf* **переса́живать**) *сов перех* to move; (*на другой поезд, самолёт итп*) to transfer; (*дерево, цветок, сердце*) to transplant; (*кость, кожу*) to graft; **переса́живать** (~ *perf*) **кого́-н на друго́е ме́сто** to move sb to another seat.

переса́д|ка (-ки; *gen pl* -ок) *ж* (*растения*) transplantation; (*на поезд итп*) change; (*МЕД: сердца*) transplant; (: *кожи*) graft; **де́лать** (**сде́лать** *perf*) **~ку в Москве́** to change in Moscow.

переса́жива|ть (-ю) *несов от* **пересади́ть**.

переса́жива|ться (-юсь) *несов от* **пересе́сть**.

пересажу́ *сов см* **пересади́ть**.

переса́лива|ть (-ю) *несов от* **пересоли́ть**.

пересдава́|ть (-ю́; *imper* **пересдава́й(те)**) *несов перех* to resit.

пересда́ть (*как* **дать**; *см* **Table 14**) *сов перех* (*экзамен, зачёт*) to pass (*after resit*).

пересёк(ся) *итп сов см* **пересе́чь(ся)**.

пересека́|ть(ся) (-ю(сь)) *несов от* **пересе́чь(ся)**.

пересеку́(сь) *итп сов см* **пересе́чь(ся)**.

переселе́н|ец (-ца) *м* (*на новую территорию*) settler; (*временно переселяемый*) *person having to move to temporary accommodation*.

переселе́н|ка (-ки; *gen pl* -ок) *ж см* **переселе́нец**.

переселе́нца *итп сущ см* **переселе́нец**.

пересел|и́ть (-ю́, -и́шь; *impf* **переселя́ть**) *сов перех* (*на новые земли*) to settle; (*в новую квартиру*) to move

▶ **пересели́ться** (*impf* **переселя́ться**) *сов возв* (*в другую страну*) to emigrate; (*в новый дом*) to move.

перес|е́сть (-я́ду, -я́дешь; *impf* **переса́живаться**) *сов неперех* (*на другое место*) to move; **переса́живаться** (~ *perf*) **на друго́е ме́сто** to move to another seat; **переса́живаться** (~ *perf*) **на друго́й по́езд/**

самолёт to change trains/planes.

пересече́ни|е (-я) *ср* (*действие*) crossing; (*место*) intersection.

пересечённый *прил* (*ГЕО: местность итп*) broken.

перес|е́чь (-еку́, -ечёшь *итп*, -еку́т; *pt* -ёк, -екла́, -екло́, *impf* **пересека́ть**) *сов перех* to cross

▶ **пересе́чься** (*impf* **пересека́ться**) *сов возв* to intersect; (*интересы*) to cross.

пересил|ить (-ю, -ишь; *impf* **переси́ливать**) *сов перех* (*человека*) to overpower; (*чувство*) to overcome.

перескажу́ *итп сов см* **пересказа́ть**.

переска́з (-а) *м* (*содержания фильма*) retelling; (*изложение*) exposition.

переск|аза́ть (-ажу́, -а́жешь; *impf* **переска́зывать**) *сов перех* to tell.

переск|очи́ть (-очу́, -о́чишь; *impf* **переска́кивать**) *сов* (*не*)*перех*: ~ (**че́рез** *+acc*) to jump (over); (*перен*): ~ **на** *+acc* (*на другую тему*) to jump to.

пересла|сти́ть (-щу́, -сти́шь; *impf* **пересла́щивать**) *сов перех*: ~ **что-н** to put too much sugar in sth.

пере|сла́ть (-шлю́, -шлёшь; *impf* **пересыла́ть**) *сов перех* (*отослать*) to send; (*по другому адресу*) to forward.

пересла́щива|ть (-ю) *несов от* **пересласти́ть**.

переслащу́ *сов см* **пересласти́ть**.

пересма́трива|ть (-ю) *несов от* **пересмотре́ть**.

пересме́ива|ться (-юсь) *несов возв* to smile at each other.

пересме́н|а (-ы) *ж* (*на заводе, на вахте*) change of shift.

пересме́шник (-а) *м* mockingbird.

пересм|отре́ть (-отрю́, -о́тришь; *impf* **пересма́тривать**) *сов перех* (*книги, вещи*) to look through; (*решение, вопрос, позицию*) to reconsider.

пересн|я́ть (-иму́, -и́мешь; *pt* -я́л,-яла́,-я́ло, *impf* **переснима́ть**) *сов перех* (*документ*) to make a copy of; (*сцену в фильме*) to reshoot; (*фотографию*) to take again.

перес|оли́ть (-олю́, -о́лишь; *impf* **переса́ливать**) *сов перех*: ~ **что-н** to put too much salt in sth.

пересо́х|нуть (*3sg* -нет, *3pl* -нут, *pt* -, -ла, -ло, *impf* **пересыха́ть**) *сов неперех* (*почва, бельё*) to dry out; (*река, ручей*) to dry up.

пересп|а́ть (-лю́, -и́шь; *impf* **пересыпа́ть**) *сов неперех* (*спать слишком долго*) to oversleep; ~ (*perf*) **с кем-н** (*разг*) to sleep with sb.

переспе́лый *прил* overripe.

переспе́|ть (*3sg* -ет, *3pl* -ют) *сов неперех* to become overripe.

пересплю́ *сов см* **переспа́ть**.

переспо́р|ить (-ю, -ишь) *сов перех:* ~ **кого́-н** to defeat sb in an argument.

переспро́с|и́ть (-ошу́, -о́сишь; *impf* **переспра́шивать**) *сов перех* to ask again.

перессо́р|иться (-юсь, -ишься) *сов возв:* ~ **(c** +*instr*) to quarrel *или* fall out (with).

переста|ва́ть (-ю́; *imper* **переставай́(те)**) *несов от* **переста́ть**.

переста́в|ить (-лю, -ишь; *impf* **переставля́ть**) *сов перех* to move; (*изменить порядок*) to rearrange.

переста́ну *итп сов см* **переста́ть**.

перестара́|ться (-юсь) *сов возв* to overdo it.

переста́ть (-ну, -нешь; *impf* **переставать**) *сов непepex* to stop; **переставать** (~ *perf*) +*infin* to stop doing; ~**ньте!** stop it!

перестира́|ть (-ю; *impf* **перести́рывать**) *сов перех* (*все вещи*) to wash; (*постирать заново*) to wash again, rewash.

пересто|я́ть (*3sg* -и́т, *3pl* -я́т) *сов непepex* (*квас, суп*) to stand too long; (*молоко*) to go off.

перестрада́|ть (-ю) *сов (не)перех* to suffer.

перестра́ива|ть(ся) (-ю(сь)) *несов от* **перестро́ить(ся)**.

перестрах|ова́ться (-у́юсь; *impf* **перестрахо́вываться**) *сов возв* (*КОММ*) to reinsure; (*перен*) to play safe.

перестрахо́в|ка (-ки; *gen pl* -ок) *ж* (*см глаг*) reinsurance; playing safe.

перестрахо́выва|ться (-юсь) *несов от* **перестрахова́ться**.

перестре́л|ка (-ки; *gen pl* -ок) *ж* exchange of fire.

перестро́ек *сущ см* **перестро́йка**.

перестро́ечный *прил* (*процессы, явления*) perestroika *опред*.

перестро́|ить (-ю, -ишь; *impf* **перестра́ивать**) *сов перех* (*дом, мост*) to rebuild, reconstruct; (*программу, экономику*) to reorganize; (*ряды, колонны*) to re-form; (*музыкальный инструмент*) to retune

▶ **перестро́иться** (*impf* **перестра́иваться**) *сов возв* (*человек*) to reorganize o.s.; (*фабрика, коллектив*) to restructure; (*солдаты, шеренги*) to re-form.

перестро́|йка (-йки; *gen pl* -ек) *ж* (*дома*) rebuilding, reconstruction; (*расписания, экономики*) reorganization; (*МУЗ*) retuning; (*ИСТ*) perestroika.

переступ|и́ть (-уплю́, -у́пишь; *impf* **переступа́ть**) *сов (не)перех* (*перен*) to overstep; **переступа́ть** (~ *perf*) (**че́рез** +*acc*) (*порог, предмет*) to step over.

пересу́|ды (-ов) *мн* (*разг*) gossip *ед*.

пересчёт (-а) *м* count; (*повторный*) re-count; **ско́лько э́то в** ~**е на рубли́?** how much is it when converted into roubles?

пересчита́|ть (-ю; *impf* **пересчи́тывать**) *сов перех* to count; (*повторно*) to re-count, count again; (*в других единицах*) to convert.

пересыла́|ть (-ю) *несов от* **пересла́ть**.

пересы́л|ка (-ки; *gen pl* -ок) *ж* sending;

(*тюрьма*) transit prison (*where prisoners stay temporarily*).

пересы́п|ать (-лю, -лешь; *impf* **пересыпа́ть**) *сов перех* (*насыпать*) to pour; (*перен: речь, рассказ*) to intersperse.

пересыпа́|ть (-ю) *несов от* **переспа́ть**.

пересы́плю *итп сов см* **пересы́пать**.

пересыха́|ть (*3sg* -ет, *3pl* -ют) *несов от* **пересо́хнуть**.

переся́ду *итп сов см* **пересе́сть**.

перета́скива|ть (-ю) *несов от* **перетащи́ть**.

перетас|ова́ть (-у́ю; *impf* **перетасо́вывать**) *сов перех* (*карты*) to shuffle; (*перен: министров*) to reshuffle.

перет|ащи́ть (-ащу́, -а́щишь; *impf* **перета́скивать**) *сов перех* (*мешок*) to drag over.

перетр|уди́ться (-ужу́сь, -у́дишься; *impf* **перетружда́ться**) *сов возв* (*разг*) to be burnt out.

перетру́|сить (-шу, -сишь) *сов непepex* (*разг*) to be scared out of one's wits.

перетряс|ти́ (-у́, -ёшь; *pt* -, -ла́, -ло́) *сов перех* to shake out.

пере́|ть (пру, прёшь; *pt* пёр, пёрла, пёрло) *несов непepex* (*разг: идти*) to trudge; (*ломиться*) to barge through; (*perf* **спере́ть**; *красть*) to pinch

▶ **пере́ться** *несов возв* (*разг: идти*) to trudge.

перет|яну́ть (-яну́, -я́нешь; *impf* **перетя́гивать**) *сов перех* (*передвинуть*) to pull, tow; (*быть более тяжёлым*) to outweigh; (*стянуть*): ~ **что-н чем-н** to tie sth tightly round sth.

переубе|ди́ть (-жу́, -ди́шь; *impf* **переубежда́ть**) *сов перех:* ~ **кого́-н** to make sb change his mind.

переу́л|ок (-ка) *м* lane, alley.

переустро́йств|о (-а) *ср* reconstruction.

переутом|и́ться (-лю́сь, -и́шься; *impf* **переутомля́ться**) *сов возв* to tire o.s. out.

переутомле́ни|е (-я) *ср* exhaustion.

переутомлю́сь *сов см* **переутоми́ться**.

переутомля́|ться (-юсь) *несов от* **переутоми́ться**.

переучёт (-а) *м* stocktaking.

переуч|и́ть (-учу́, -у́чишь; *impf* **переу́чивать**) *сов перех* to retrain

▶ **переучи́ться** (*impf* **переу́чиваться**) *сов возв* to undergo retraining.

переформати́р|овать (-ую) (*не)сов перех* (*КОМП*) to reformat.

перефрази́р|овать (-ую) (*не)сов перех* to paraphrase.

перехв|ати́ть (-ачу́, -а́тишь; *impf* **перехва́тывать**) *сов перех* (*захватить на пути*) to intercept; (*разг: переборщить*) to go too far; (*обвязать*): ~ **что-н чем-н** to tie sth round sth; **у него́** ~**ати́ло дыха́ние** he caught his breath; **перехва́тывать** (~ *perf*) **бутербро́д** (*разг*) to grab a sandwich; **перехва́тывать** (~ *perf*) **чей-н взгляд** (*перен*) to catch sb's eye.

перехитри́|ть (-ю, -и́шь) *сов перех* to outwit.
перехо́д (-а) *м* crossing; (*к другой системе*) transition; (*в здании, между зданиями*) passage.
перехо́д|и́ть (-ожу́, -о́дишь) *несов от* **перейти́**.
перехо́дный *прил* (*промежуточный*) transitional; **перехо́дный глаго́л** transitive verb.
переходя́щий (-ая, -ее, -ие) *прил*: ~ **ку́бок** (*СПОРТ*) challenge cup.
перехожу́ *несов см* **переходи́ть**.
пе́р|ец (-ца) *м* pepper; (*зёрнышко*) peppercorn; **жгу́чий** ~ chilli pepper; **болга́рский** ~ capsicum.
пе́реч|ень (-ня) *м* list; ~ **служе́бных обя́занностей** job specification.
перечеркн|у́ть (-у́, -ёшь; *impf* **перечёркивать**) *сов перех* to cross out; (*перен: надежды*) to shatter.
переч|ерти́ть (-ерчу́, -е́ртишь; *impf* **перече́рчивать**) *сов перех* (*начертить снова*) to draw again; (*скопировать*) to copy.
переч|е́сть (-ту́, -тёшь; *pt* -ёл, -ла́, -ло́) *сов перех* (*пересчитать*) to re-count, count again; (*перечитать*) to reread, read again.
перечисле́ни|е (-я) *ср* transfer; **плати́ть** (*заплати́ть perf*) **по** ~**ю** to pay by transfer.
перечи́сл|ить (-ю, -ишь; *impf* **перечисля́ть**) *сов перех* (*упомянуть*) to list; (*КОММ*) to transfer.
перечита́|ть (-ю; *impf* **перечи́тывать**) *сов перех* to read; (*читать заново*) to reread, read again.
пе́речну *итп сущ см* **пе́речень**.
перечту́ *итп сов см* **перече́сть**.
перешагн|у́ть (-у́, -ёшь; *impf* **переша́гивать**) *сов* (*не*)*перех*: ~ (**че́рез** +*acc*) to step over.
переше́|ек (-йка) *м* isthmus.
перешёл *итп сов см* **перейти́**.
перешёптыва|ться (-юсь) *несов возв* to whisper to each other.
переш|и́ть (-ью, -ьёшь; *impf* **перешива́ть**) *сов перех* (*платье, костюм*) to alter; (*пуговицу, крючок*) to move (*by sewing on somewhere else*).
перешлю́ *сов см* **пересла́ть**.
перещеголя́|ть (-ю) *сов перех* (*разг*) to outshine.
переэкзамено́в|ка (-ки; *gen pl* -ок) *ж* resit.
перил|а (-) *мн* railing *ед*; (*лестницы*) banisters *мн*.
пери́метр (-а) *м* perimeter.
пери́н|а (-ы) *ж* feather bed.
пери́од (-а) *м* period; **пе́рвый/второ́й** ~ **игры́** (*СПОРТ*) first/second half (of the game).
периоди́к|а (-и) *ж собир* periodicals *мн*.
периоди́чески *нареч* periodically.
периоди́чес|кий (-ая, -ое, -ие) *прил* periodical

опред; **периоди́ческая печа́ть** the periodical press.
периоди́чност|ь (-и) *ж* regularity.
перипети́|я (-и) *ж* (*обычно мн*) upheaval.
перитони́т (-а) *м* peritonitis.
перифери́йный *прил* peripheral.
перифери́|я (-и) *ж* the provinces *мн* ♦ *собир* (*КОМП*) peripherals *мн*, peripheral devices *мн*.
перифрази́р|овать (-ую) (*не*)*сов перех* to paraphrase.
перл (-а) *м* (*также перен*) pearl.
перламу́тр (-а) *м* mother-of-pearl.
перламу́тровый *прил* mother-of-pearl *опред*; (*цвет*) pearly.
перло́в|ка (-ки; *gen pl* -ок) *ж* (*разг*) pearl barley.
перло́в|ый *прил* (*суп, каша*) barley *опред*; ~**ая крупа́** pearl barley.
перлюстри́р|овать (-ую) *сов перех* to censor.
пермане́нт (-а) *м* perm (= *permanent wave*).
пермане́нт|ный (-ен, -на, -но) *прил* permanent.
перна́т|ый (-ого; *decl like adj*) *м* (*обычно мн*) bird.
пёрн|уть (-у, -ешь) *сов неперех* (*груб!*) to fart (*!*).
пер|о́ (-а́; *nom pl* -ья, *gen pl* -ьев) *ср* (*птицы*) feather; (*для письма*: *гусиное*) quill; (: *стальное, золотое*) nib.
перочи́нный *прил*: ~ **нож** penknife (*мн* penknives).
перпендикуля́р|ный (-ен, -на, -но) *прил* perpendicular.
перро́н (-а) *м* platform (*RAIL*).
перс (-а) *м* Persian.
перси́д|ский (-ая, -ое, -ие) *прил* Persian; **Перси́дский зали́в** Persian Gulf.
перси́к (-а) *м* (*дерево*) peach tree; (*плод*) peach.
Пе́рси|я (-и) *ж* Persia.
персия́н|ка (-ки; *gen pl* -ок) *ж см* **перс**.
персо́н|а (-ы) *ж* person; **со́бственной** ~**ой** in person.
персона́ж (-а) *м* character.
персона́л (-а) *м* (*АДМИН*) personnel, staff.
персона́льный *прил* personal; **персона́льная вы́ставка** one-man exhibition; **персона́льный компью́тер** PC (= *personal computer*).
перспекти́в|а (-ы) *ж* (*ГЕОМ*) perspective; (*вид*) view; ~**ы** (*планы*) prospects *мн*; **в** ~**е** (*в будущем*) in store.
перспекти́вный *прил* (*изображение*) in perspective; (*планирование*) long-term; (*многообещающий*) promising; ~ **план** plan of future developments.
пе́рст|ень (-ня) *м* ring.
Перу́ *ж нескл* Peru.
перуа́н|ский (-ая, -ое, -ие) *прил* Peruvian.
перфока́рт|а (-ы) *ж сокр* (= *перфорацио́нная ка́рта*) punched *или* punch (*BRIT*) card.
перфоле́нт|а (-ы) *ж сокр* (= *перфорацио́нная ле́нта*) punched tape.

пе́рхот|ь (-и) *ж собир* dandruff.
пе́рца *итп сущ см* **пе́рец**.
перча́т|ка (-ки; *gen pl* -ок) *ж* glove; (*боксёра*) (boxing) glove; **пе́рвая ~** (*СПОРТ*) champion boxer.
пе́рч|ить (-у, -ишь; *perf* **наперчи́ть** *или* **поперчи́ть**) *сов перех* to pepper.
перш|и́ть (*3sg* -и́т) *несов безл* (*разг*): **у меня́ ~и́т в го́рле** I've got a frog in my throat.
пе́рья *итп сущ см* **перо́**.
пёс (пса) *м* dog.
пе́сен *сущ см* **пе́сня**.
пе́сенник (-а) *м* songbook; (*композитор*) songwriter.
пес|е́ц (-ца́) *м* arctic fox.
песка́ *итп сущ см* **песо́к**.
песка́р|ь (-я́) *м* gudgeon.
пе3ск|и́ (-о́в) *мн* sands *мн*.
песн|ь (-и; *gen pl* -ей) *ж* (*в поэме*) canto.
пе́с|ня (-ни; *gen pl* -ен) *ж* song; **ста́рая ~** (*разг*) the same old story.
пес|о́к (-ка́; *part gen* -ку́) *м* sand; **са́харный ~** granulated sugar; **см также пески́**.
песо́чница (-ы) *ж* sandpit (*BRIT*), sandbox (*US*).
песо́чный *прил* (*цвет*) sandy; (*тесто, печенье*) short; **песо́чные часы́** hourglass.
пессими́ст (-а) *м* pessimist.
пессимисти́ч|ный (-ен, -на, -но) *прил* pessimistic.
пестици́|д (-а) *м* pesticide.
пе́ст|овать (-ую; *perf* **вы́пестовать**) *несов перех* (*перен*) to nurture.
пестре́|ть (*3sg* -ет, *3pl* -ют) *несов неперех* (*виднеться*) to be colourful (*BRIT*) *или* colorful (*US*); (*3pl* -я́т; *мелькать*) to make a colo(u)rful display; **в саду́/на лугу́ ~ют цветы́** the garden/meadow is bright with flowers.
пестр|и́ть (*3sg* -и́т, *3pl* -я́т) *несов неперех*: **~ +instr** to be full of.
пёстр|ый (-, -а́, -о) *прил* (*ткань, ковёр*) multi-coloured (*BRIT*), multi-colored (*US*); (*перен: разнородный*) mixed.
песца́ *итп сущ см* **песе́ц**.
песча́ник (-а) *м* sandstone.
песча́н|ый *прил* (*берег, дно реки*) sandy; **песча́ная бу́ря** sandstorm.
пе́тель *сущ см* **пе́тля**.
Петербу́рг *сущ* = **Санкт-Петербу́рг**.
пети́ция (-и) *ж* petition.
петли́|ца (-ы) *ж* (*петля*) buttonhole; (*нашивка*) tab (*on uniform*).
пе́т|ля (-ли; *gen pl* -ель) *ж* loop; (*в вязании*) stitch; (*двери, крышки*) hinge; (*в одежде: для пуговицы*) buttonhole; (: *для крючка*) eye.
петля́|ть (-ю) *несов неперех* to meander.
петру́шка (-и) *ж* parsley.
пету́н|ья (-и) *ж* petunia.
пету́х (-а́) *м* cock, rooster (*US*).
петуши́н|ый *прил* (*пение*) cocks'; **~ бой** cockfight; **~ го́лос** a squeaky voice.
пе|ть (пою́, поёшь; *pt* -л, -ла, -ло, *imper* **пой(те)**, *perf* **спеть**) *несов перех* to sing.

пехо́т|а (-ы) *ж* infantry.
пехоти́н|ец (-ца) *м* infantryman (*мн* infantrymen).
пехо́тный *прил* infantry *опред*.
печа́лен *прил см* **печа́льный**.
печа́л|иться (-юсь, -ишься; *perf* **опеча́литься**) *несов возв* to be sad.
печа́л|ь (-и) *ж* (*грусть*) sadness, sorrow; **не́ было ~и!** (*разг*) what a nuisance!
печа́льно *нареч* (*петь, вы́глядеть*) sadly ◆ *как сказ* it's sad; **~, что мы не встре́тились** it's sad that we didn't meet; **~ изве́стный** notorious.
печа́л|ьный (-ен, -ьна, -ьно) *прил* sad; (*ошибка, судьба, память*) unhappy; **~ьная изве́стность** *или* **сла́ва** ill repute.
печа́та|ть (-ю; *perf* **напеча́тать**) *несов перех* (*также* ФОТО) to print; (*публиковать*) to publish; (*на пишущей машинке*) to type
▶ **печа́таться** (*perf* **напеча́таться**) *несов возв* to have one's work published.
печа́тающий (-ая, -ее, -ие) *прил*: **~ая голо́вка** (*КОМП*) printhead; **~ее колесо́** (*КОМП*) printwheel.
печа́т|ка (-ки; *gen pl* -ок) *ж* signet.
печа́тник (-а) *м* (*работник*) printer.
печа́т|ный *прил* (*станок*) printing *опред*; (*цех*) print *опред*; (*интервью итп*) published; **писа́ть** (*написа́ть perf*) **~ыми бу́квами** to print; **печа́тные бу́квы** block letters; **печа́тный лист** (*единица измерения*) printer's sheet.
печа́ток *сущ см* **печа́тка**.
печа́т|ь (-и) *ж* stamp, seal; (*на дверях, на сейфе*) seal; (*издательское дело*) printing; (*след: страданий*) mark ◆ *собир* (*пресса*) press; **выходи́ть** (**вы́йти** *perf*) **из ~и** to come out, be published.
пе́чек *сущ см* **пе́чка**.
печён|ка (-ки; *gen pl* -ок) *ж* liver; **в ~х сиде́ть** (*impf*) **у кого́-н** (*разг*) to get on sb's nerves.
печёный *прил* baked.
пе́чен|ь (-и) *ж* (*АНАТ*) liver.
пече́нье (-я) *ср* biscuit (*BRIT*), cookie (*US*).
пе́ч|ка (-ки; *gen pl* -ек) *ж* stove.
пе|чь (-чи; *loc sg* -чи́, *gen pl* -е́й) *ж* stove; (*ТЕХ*) furnace; (: *обжиговая*) kiln; ◆ (-ку́, -чёшь *итп*, -ку́т; *pt* пёк, -кла́, -кло́, *perf* **испе́чь**) *несов перех* to bake; **микроволно́вая ~** microwave oven
▶ **пе́чься** (*perf* **испе́чься**) *несов возв* to bake; (*заботиться*) о **+prp** to look after (*BRIT*), take care of (*US*).
пе́шек *сущ см* **пе́шка**.
пешехо́|д (-а) *м* pedestrian.
пешехо́дный *прил* pedestrian *опред*; (*совершаемый пешком*) on foot; **пешехо́дный мост** footbridge.
пе́ш|ий (-ая, -ее, -ие) *прил* (*солдат*) foot *опред*; (*движение*) pedestrian *опред*; (*совершаемый пешком*) on foot; **~им хо́дом** on foot.
пе́ш|ка (-ки; *gen pl* -ек) *ж* (*также перен*) pawn.
пешко́м *нареч* on foot.

пеще́р|а (-ы) ж cave.
пеще́рный прил (живопись) cave опред;
   пеще́рный челове́к caveman (мн cavemen).
ПЗУ ср сокр (= постоя́нное запомина́ющее
   устро́йство) ROM (= read-only memory).
пиал|а́ (-ы́) ж handleless cup used in Central
   Asia.
пиани́но ср нескл (upright) piano.
пиани́ст (-а) м pianist.
пиани́ст|ка (-ки; gen pl -ок) ж см **пиани́ст**.
пивн|а́я (-ой; decl like adj) ж ≈ bar, ≈ pub (BRIT).
пивно́й прил (бар, бочка) beer опред; (дрожжи)
   brewer's.
пи́в|о (-а) ср beer.
пи́галиц|а (-ы) ж (перен: пренебр) pipsqueak.
пигме́й (-я) м pygmy.
пигме́нт (-а) м pigment.
пигмента́ци|я (-и) ж pigmentation.
пиджа́к (-а́) м jacket.
пижа́м|а (-ы) ж pyjamas мн.
пи́жм|а (-ы) ж (трава) feverfew; (дерево) wild
   rowan.
пижо́н (-а) м (разг: пренебр) pose(u)r.
пик (-а) м (также перен) peak ♦ прил неизм
   (часы, период, время) peak опред; **часы́** ~ (в
   работе транспорта) rush hour;
   (электростанции, телефона итп) peak
   period.
пи́к|а (-и) ж (рыцаря) lance; (солдата) pike; **в**
   ~**у кому́-н** to get at sb.
пика́нт|ный (-ен, -на, -но) прил (вкус) piquant;
   (случай, слухи) spicy; (женщина, внешность)
   alluring.
пике́т (-а) м picket.
пикети́р|овать (-ую) несов перех to picket.
пи́к|и (-) мн (в картах) spades мн.
пики́р|овать (-ую) (не)сов неперех (АВИА) to
   dive.
пикиро́вщик (-а) м (АВИА) dive-bomber.
пикни́к (-а́) м picnic.
пи́кн|уть (-у, -ешь) сов неперех (разг:
   животное) to let out a squeak; (: птица) to let
   out a squawk; **он при ней не сме́л и** ~ he
   wouldn't dare speak out in her presence.
пи́ков|ый прил (наивысший) peak опред; (в
   картах) of spades; ~**ое положе́ние** (разг)
   mess.
пи́ксел|ь (-я) м (КОМП) pixel.
пил итп несов см **пить**.
пил|а́ (-ы́; nom pl -ы) ж saw.
пилигри́м (-а) м pilgrim.
пили́ка|ть (-ю) несов неперех (разг): ~ **на** +prp
   (на скрипке) to scrape away on.
пил|и́ть (-ю́, -ишь) несов перех to saw; (перен:
   разг) to nag.
пи́л|ка (-ки; gen pl -ок) ж nail file.
пиломатериа́л|ы (-ов) мн sawn timber ед.
пило́т (-а) м pilot; (СПОРТ) driver.
пилоти́р|овать (-ую) несов перех to pilot.

пило́т|ка (-ки; gen pl -ок) ж cloth cap worn as
   part of uniform.
пилю́л|я (-и) ж pill; **проглоти́ть** (perf) ~**ю**
   (перен) to swallow a bitter pill.
пиля́стр|а (-ы) ж pilaster.
пина́|ть (-ю) несов перех to kick.
пингви́н (-а) м penguin.
пинг-по́нг (-а) м table tennis, ping-pong.
пине́т|ка (-ки; gen pl -ок) ж (обычно мн) bootee.
пино́к (-ка́) м kick.
пинце́т (-а) м (МЕД) tweezers мн; (ТЕХ) pincers
   мн.
пио́н (-а) м peony.
пионе́р (-а) м pioneer; (в СССР) member of
   Communist Youth organisation.
пипе́т|ка (-ки; gen pl -ок) ж pipette.
пир (-а; loc sg -у́, nom pl -ы́) м feast.
пирами́д|а (-ы) ж pyramid.
пира́т (-а) м pirate.
пира́тск|ий (-ая, -ое, -ие) прил pirate опред.
Пирене́|и (-ев) мн Pyrenees.
пир|ова́ть (-у́ю) несов неперех to feast.
пиро́г (-а́) м pie.
пирожка́ итп сущ см **пирожо́к**.
пирожко́в|ая (-ой; decl like adj) ж (тип
   закусочной) snack-bar.
пиро́жн|ое (-ого; decl like adj) ср cake, sweet
   pastry.
пирож|о́к (-ка́) м (с мясом) pasty, pie; (с
   вареньем) turnover, tart.
пирс (-а) м pier.
пируэ́т (-а) м pirouette.
пи́ршеств|о (-а) ср feast.
писа́к|а (-и) м/ж (разг: пренебр) scribbler.
писа́ни|е (-я) ср (действие) writing;
   Свяще́нное П~ Holy Scripture.
писани́н|а (-ы) ж (разг: пренебр) scribblings мн.
пи́саный прил (разг): **она́** ~**ая краса́вица** she
   is a picture of beauty ♦ (-ого; decl like adj) м:
   говори́ть как по ~**ому** to speak fluently.
пи́сар|ь (-я) м clerk.
писа́тель (-я) м writer.
писа́тельниц|а (-ы) ж см **писа́тель**.
пи́с|а́ть (-шу́, -шешь; perf написа́ть) несов
   перех to write; (картину, пейзаж) to paint ♦
   неперех (no perf; ребёнок, ученик) to be able to
   write; (ручка) to write; **он написа́л, как**
   дое́хал/где устро́ился he wrote to say he had
   arrived safely/where he was staying; ~**ши́**
   пропа́ло (разг) it is as good as lost
   ► **писа́ться** несов возв (слово) to be spelt или
   spelled; **как пи́шется э́то сло́во?** how do you
   spell this word?; **мне сего́дня не пи́шется** I
   don't feel like writing today.
пи́сем сущ см **письмо́**.
пис|е́ц (-ца́) м (ИСТ) scribe.
писк (-а) м (ребёнка) squeak; (птицы) cheep.
пискли́вый прил (голос) squeaky.
пискля́вый прил = **пискли́вый**.

The spelling rules for Russian are shown on page xvii.

пи́скн|уть (**-у, -ешь**) *сов непepex* (*ребёнок, животное*) to give a squeak; (*птица*) to give a cheep.

пистоле́т (**-а**) *м* pistol.

писто́н (**-а**) *м* (*в патроне*) percussion cap.

писца́ *итп сущ см* **писе́ц**.

писчебума́жный *прил*: ~ **магази́н** stationer's.

пи́сч|ий (**-ая, -ее, -ие**) *прил* writing *опред*.

пи́сьменно *нареч* in writing.

пи́сьменност|ь (**-и**) *ж* written language; (*памятники*) literary texts *мн*.

пи́сьменн|ый *прил* (*просьба, экзамен*) written; (*стол, прибор*) writing; **в ~ой фо́рме** in writing.

письмо́ (**-ьма́**; *nom pl* **-ьма**, *gen pl* **-ем**) *ср* letter; (*no pl*; *иероглифическое, алфавитное*) script; (*искусство: манера*) style.

пита́ни|е (**-я**) *ср* (*больного, ребёнка*) feeding; (*ТЕХ*) supply; (*вегетарианское, плохое*) diet; **обще́ственное ~** public catering.

пита́те|льный *прил* (*соли, вещества*) nutritious; (*крем, лосьон итп*) nourishing; (*клапан, станция, насос*) supply *опред*; (**-ен, -ьна, -ьно**; *каша, бульон*) filling; **пита́тельная среда́** (*БИО: перен*) breeding ground.

пита́|ть (**-ю**) *несов перех* (*кормить*) to feed; (*снабжать*) to supply; (*перен: испытывать*) to feel

► **пита́ться** *несов возв*: ~**ся** *+instr* (*человек, растение*) to live on; (*животное*) to feed on; (*ТЕХ*) to run on, use.

пито́м|ец (**-ца**) *м* (*воспитанник*) pupil.

пито́мник (**-а**) *м* (*БОТ*) nursery.

пито́н (**-а**) *м* python.

пи|ть (**пью, пьёшь**; *pt* **-л, -ла́, -ло**, *imper* **пе́й(те)**, *perf* **вы́пить**) *несов перех* to drink ♦ *неперех*: ~ **за кого́-н/что́-н** to drink to sb/sth; **как ~ дать** (*разг*) for sure.

питьев|о́й *прил*: ~**а́я вода́** drinking water.

пиха́|ть (**-ю**) *несов перех* (*разг: толкать*) to shove; (*разг: засовывать*) to cram

► **пиха́ться** *несов возв* to push and shove (each other).

пихн|у́ть (**-у́, -ёшь**) *сов перех* to give a shove; (*сунуть*) to push.

пи́хт|а (**-ы**) *ж* fir (tree).

пи́цц|а (**-ы**) *ж* pizza.

пиццери́|я (**-и**) *ж* pizzeria.

пи́чка|ть (**-ю**; *perf* **напи́чкать**) *несов перех* (*разг*): ~ **кого́-н чем-н** (*конфетами итп*) to stuff sb with sth; (*лекарствами*) to pour sth down sb's neck.

пишу́(сь) *итп несов см* **писа́ть(ся)**.

пи́шущ|ий (**-ая, -ее, -ие**) *прил*: ~**ая маши́нка** typewriter.

пи́щ|а (**-и**) *ж* food; ~ **для размышле́ний** *или* **ума́** food for thought; ~ **для воображе́ния** fuel to the imagination.

пища́|ть (**-у́, -и́шь**) *несов неперех* (*птицы*) to cheep; (*животные*) to squeak; (*ребёнок*) to cry.

пищебло́к (**-а**) *м* kitchen (*for catering*).

пищеваре́ни|е (**-я**) *ср* digestion.

пищев|о́й *прил* food *опред*; (*соль*) edible; **пищева́я со́да** baking soda.

пия́в|ка (**-ки**; *gen pl* **-ок**) *ж* leech.

ПК *м сокр* (= **персона́льный компью́тер**) PC (= *personal computer*).

пл. *сокр* (= **пло́щадь**) Sq. (= *Square*).

плав (**-а**) *м*: **на ~у́** afloat.

пла́вани|е (**-я**) *ср* swimming; (*на судне*) sailing; (*рейс*) voyage; **занима́ться** (*impf*) ~**м** to train as a swimmer.

пла́вательный *прил* swimming *опред*; **пла́вательный бассе́йн** swimming pool.

пла́ва|ть (**-ю**) *несов неперех* (*человек, животное*) to swim; (*корабль*) to sail; (*лист, облако*) to float; (*перен: на экзамене итп*) to be out of one's depth; (*служить на судне*): ~ *+instr* to work (at sea) as.

пла́вен *прил см* **пла́вный**.

пла́в|ить (**-лю, -ишь**; *perf* **распла́вить**) *несов перех* to smelt

► **пла́виться** (*perf* **распла́виться**) *несов возв* to smelt; (*стекло, пластмасса*) to melt.

пла́в|ка (**-ки**; *gen pl* **-ок**) *ж* (*действие*) smelting; (*продукт*) smelted metal.

пла́в|ки (**-ок**) *мн* swimming trunks *мн*.

плавле́ни|е (**-я**) *ср*: **температу́ра** *или* **то́чка ~я** melting point.

пла́вленый *прил*: ~ **сыр** processed cheese.

пла́влю(сь) *несов см* **пла́вить(ся)**.

плавни́к (**-а́**) *м* (*у рыб*) fin; (*у водных животных*) flipper.

пла́в|ный (**-ен, -на, -но**) *прил* smooth.

пла́вок *сущ см* **пла́вка, пла́вки**.

плаву́ч|ий (**-ая, -ее, -ие**) *прил* floating; **плаву́чая ба́за** (*в рыболовстве*) *floating unit for storing and processing fish*.

плагиа́т (**-а**) *м* plagiarism.

плагиа́тор (**-а**) *м* plagiarist.

пла́зм|а (**-ы**) *ж* plasma.

плака́т (**-а**) *м* poster.

пла́|кать (**-чу, -чешь**) *несов неперех* to cry, weep; ~ (*impf*) **от** *+gen* (*от боли итп*) to cry from; (*от радости*) to cry with; (*от горя*) to cry in; ~**кал мой выходно́й** (*разг*) so much for my day off; ~**кали мои́ де́ньги** (*разг*) that's my money up the spout; **па́лка по нему́ ~чет** (*разг*) he's asking for a beating

► **пла́каться** *несов возв* (*разг*): ~**ся** (**на** *+acc*) (*на судьбу, на участь*) to moan (about).

плаки́р|ова́ть (**-у́ю**) (*не)сов перех* (*ТЕХ*) to plate.

пла́кс|а (**-ы**) *м/ж* crybaby.

плаку́ч|ий (**-ая, -ее, -ие**) *прил*: ~**ая и́ва** weeping willow.

пла́мени *итп сущ см* **пла́мя**.

пла́менный *прил* (*цвета пламени*) flame-coloured (*BRIT*), flame-colored (*US*); (*горячий*) burning; (*перен: страстный*) ardent.

пла́м|я (**-ени**; *как* **вре́мя**; *см* Table 4) *ср* flame.

план (**-а**) *м* plan; (*чертёж*) plan, map; **кру́пный**

~ (*кино, фото*) close-up; **пла́ны на бу́дущее** future plans; **пере́дний** ~ foreground; **за́дний** ~ background; **на пе́рвом пла́не у неё учёба** her priority is studying; **в теорети́ческом пла́не** in theory; **отходи́ть (отойти́** *perf*) *или* **отступа́ть (отступи́ть** *perf*) **на второ́й** ~ to become less important.

планёр (-а) *м* glider.

планери́зм (-а) *м* gliding.

плане́т|а (-ы) *ж* planet.

планета́ри|й (-я) *м* planetarium.

плани́ровани|е (-я) *ср* planning.

плани́р|овать (-ую) *несов перех* to plan ♦ *неперех* (*perf* **заплани́ровать**; *намереваться*) to plan; (*АВИА*) to glide.

плани́р|ова́ть (-ую; *perf* **распланирова́ть**) *несов перех* to lay out.

плани́ро́вк|а (-и) *ж* (*участка, квартиры*) layout.

плани́ро́вщик (-а) *м* planner.

пла́н|ка (-ки; *gen pl* -ок) *ж* (*деревянная*) strip of wood; (*металлическая*) strip of metal.

планкто́н (-а) *м* plankton.

планови́к (-а́) *м* planner.

пла́новый *прил* (*задание, продукция*) planned; (*отдел, комиссия*) planning.

пла́нок *сущ см* **пла́нка**.

планоме́р|ный (-ен, -на, -но) *прил* systematic.

планта́ци|я (-и) *ж* plantation.

планше́т (-а) *м* mapcase.

пласт (-а́) *м* (*также перен*) stratum (*мн* strata).

пла́стик (-а) *м* = **пластма́сса**.

пла́стик|а (-и) *ж* (*скульптура*) the plastic arts *мн*; (*гармония*) grace; (*балетная*) eurhythmics; (*МЕД*) plastic surgery.

пластили́н (-а) *м* plasticine.

пласти́н|а (-ы) *ж* (*ГЕО*) plate.

пласти́н|ка (-ки; *gen pl* -ок) *ж* (*уменьш от* **пласти́на**; (*МУЗ*) record; **долгоигра́ющая** ~ album, L.P. (= *long-playing record*).

пласти́чен *прил см* **пласти́чный**.

пласти́ческ|ий (-ая, -ое, -ие) *прил* plastic *опред*; **пласти́ческая ма́сса** plastic; **пласти́ческая опера́ция** (*МЕД*) plastic surgery.

пласти́ч|ный (-ен, -на, -но) *прил* (*жесты, движения*) graceful; (*материалы, вещества*) plastic *опред*.

пластма́сс|а (-ы) *ж сокр* (= **пласти́ческая ма́сса**) plastic.

пласту́нск|ий (-ая, -ое, -ие) *прил*: **ползти́ по-~и** to crawl on one's belly.

пла́стыр|ь (-я) *ж* (*МЕД*) plaster.

пла́т|а (-ы) *ж* (*за труд, за услуги*) pay, salary; (*за квартиру*) payment; (*за проезд*) fee; (*перен: награда, кара*) reward; **зарабо́тная** ~ wages *мн*.

плата́н (-а) *м* plane (tree).

плат|ёж (-ежа́) *м* payment; **нало́женным ~ежо́м**

cash on delivery.

платёжеспосо́бен *прил см* **платёжеспосо́бный**.

платёжеспосо́бност|ь (-и) *ж* solvency.

платёжеспосо́б|ный (-ен, -на, -нс) *прил* (*КОММ*) solvent.

платёжн|ый *прил* (*КОММ*): ~ **бланк** payslip; ~**ая ве́домость** payroll; ~**ое поруче́ние** *или* **тре́бование** payment order.

пла́тин|а (-ы) *ж* platinum.

пла|ти́ть (-чу́, -тишь; *perf* **заплати́ть** *или* **уплати́ть**) *несов перех* to pay ♦ *неперех* (*перен*): ~ **чем-н за что-н** to repay sth with sth; ~ (**заплати́ть** *или* **уплати́ть** *perf*) **нали́чными/ нату́рой** to pay in cash/in kind

► **плати́ться** (*perf* **поплати́ться**) *несов возв*: ~**ся чем-н за что-н** to pay for sth with sth.

платка́ *итп сущ см* **плато́к**.

пла́тный *прил* (*вход, стоянка*) chargeable; (*школа*) fee-paying; (*больница*) private.

плато́ *ср нескл* plateau.

плат|о́к (-ка́) *м* (*головной*) headscarf (*мн* headscarves); (*наплечный*) shawl; (*также: носово́й* ~) handkerchief.

платфо́рм|а (-ы) *ж* platform; (*маленькая станция*) halt; (*открытый вагон*) open goods truck; (*основание*) foundation.

пла́ть|е (-я; *gen pl* -ев) *ср* dress ♦ *собир* (*одежда*) clothing, clothes *мн*.

плафо́н (-а) *м* decorated ceiling; (*абажур*) shade (*for ceiling light*).

пла́х|а (-и) *ж* (*ИСТ*) (executioner's) block.

плац (-а; *loc sg* -у́) *м* (*ВОЕН*) parade ground.

плацда́рм (-а) *м* (*ВОЕН*) bridgehead.

плаце́нт|а (-ы) *ж* placenta.

плацка́ртный *прил*: ~ **ваго́н** *railway car with open berths instead of compartments.*

плач (-а) *м* crying.

плаче́в|ный (-ен, -на, -но) *прил* (*бедственный*) lamentable; (*жалкий*) pitiful.

пла́чу(сь) *итп несов см* **пла́кать(ся)**.

плачу́(сь) *несов см* **плати́ть(ся)**.

плашмя́ *нареч* flat.

плащ (-а́) *м* cloak; (*пальто*) raincoat.

плащани́ц|а (-ы) *ж* (*РЕЛ*) the shroud of Christ.

плащ-пала́т|ка (-ки; *gen pl* -ок) *ж* (*ВОЕН*) waterproof cape.

плебе́|й (-я) *м* plebeian.

плебе́йск|ий (-ая, -ое, -ие) *прил* plebeian *опред*.

пл|ева́ть (-юю) *несов неперех* to spit; (*perf* **наплева́ть**; *перен*): ~ **на** +*acc* (*разг: на правила, на мнение других*) to not give a damn about; ~ (*impf*) **в потоло́к** (*разг*) to loaf (about)

► **плева́ться** *несов возв* to spit.

плев|о́к (-ка́) *м* spit, spittle.

плеври́т (-а) *м* pleurisy.

плёвый *прил* (*это*): ~**ое де́ло** (*разг*) it's a piece of cake.

плед (-а) *м* (tartan) rug.

пле́йер (-а) *м* Walkman®.

плёл *итп несов см* **плести́**.

пле́мени *итп сущ см* **пле́мя**.

племенн́ой *прил* (*язык, территория*) tribal; (*с.-х.: скот*) purebred; (*хозяйство, животноводство*) (pure-strain) stockbreeding *опред*; **племенн́ой бык** pedigree bull; **племенна́я ло́шадь** thoroughbred (horse).

плем|я (-ени; *как* вре́мя; *см* **Table 4**) *ср* (*также перен*) tribe; **молодо́е** ~ the younger generation.

племя́нник (-а) *м* nephew.

племя́нниц|а (-ы) *ж* niece.

плен (-а; *loc sg* -у́) *м* captivity; **брать (взять** *perf*) **кого́-н в** ~ to take sb prisoner; **попада́ть (попа́сть** *perf*) **в** ~ to be taken prisoner.

плена́рный *прил* plenary.

плени́тел|ьный (-ен, -ьна, -ьно) *прил* captivating, charming.

плен|и́ть (-ю́, -и́шь; *impf* **пленя́ть**; *сов перех* (*очаровывать*) to captivate, charm.

плён|ка (-ки; *gen pl* -ок) *ж* (*также* ФОТО) film; (*кожица*) film, membrane; (*магнитофонная*) tape; **запи́сывать (записа́ть** *perf*) **что-н на** ~**ку** to record sth (on tape).

плённ|ая (-ой; *decl like adj*) *ж см* **пле́нный**.

пле́нник (-а) *м* (*пленный*) prisoner, captive.

пле́нниц|а (-ы) *ж см* **пле́нник**.

пле́нн|ый *прил* captive *опред* ♦ (-ого; *decl like adj*) *м* prisoner, captive.

плёнок *сущ см* **плёнка**.

пле́нум (-а) *м* plenum.

пленя́|ть (-ю) *несов от* **плени́ть**.

пле́сень (-и) *ж* mould (*BRIT*), mold (*US*).

плеск (-а) *м* splash.

пле|ска́ть (-щу́, -щешь) *несов неперех* to splash; (*слегка*) to lap

► **плеска́ться** *несов возв* to splash; (*волны*: *слегка*) to lap.

пле́снев|еть (3sg -ет, 3pl -ют, *perf* **запле́сневеть**) *несов неперех* to go mouldy (*BRIT*) *или* moldy (*US*).

пл|ести́ (-ету́, -етёшь; *pt* -ёл, -ела́, -ело́, *perf* **сплести́**) *несов перех* (*сети*) to weave; (*венок, волосы*) to plait; (*глупости*) to spout; ~ (*impf*) **интри́ги** *или* **ко́зни** to weave a web of intrigue; ~ (*impf*) **небыли́цы** (*разг*) to spin yarns

► **плести́сь** *несов возв* (*разг: человек: медленно идти*) to trudge, plod.

плетёный *прил* (*корзина, мебель*) wicker; (*сандалии*) woven.

плет|ёнь (-ня́) *м* wattle fence.

плёт|ка (-ки; *gen pl* -ок) *ж* whip.

плетня́ *итп сущ см* **плете́нь**.

плёток *сущ см* **плётка**.

плету́(сь) *итп несов см* **плести́(сь)**.

плеть (-и; *gen pl* -ей) *ж* whip.

пле́чик|и (-ов) *мн* (*вешалка*) coat hangers *мн*; (*подкладки*) shoulder pads *мн*.

плечи́ст|ый (-, -а, -о) *прил* broad-shouldered.

плеч|о́ (-á; *nom pl* -и) *ср* shoulder; ~**м к** ~**у́** shoulder to shoulder; **э́то мне не по** ~**у́** I am not up to it; **за** ~**а́ми у него́ 5 лет учёбы** he has 5 years of study behind him *или* under his belt; **с чужо́го** ~**á** (*одежда*) second-hand; **выноси́ть (вы́нести** *perf*) **что-н на свои́х** ~**áх** to carry sth on one's shoulders.

плеши́в|ый (-, -а, -о) *прил* bald.

плешь (-и) *ж* bald patch.

пле́щет(ся) *итп несов см* **плеска́ть(ся)**.

плещу́сь *итп несов см* **плеска́ться**.

плея́д|а (-ы) *ж* (*учёных, музыкантов итп*) galaxy.

Пли́мут (-а) *м* Plymouth.

пли́нтус (-а) *м* skirting board (*BRIT*), baseboard (*US*).

плиссе́ *ср нескл* pleats *мн* ♦ *прил неизм*: **ю́бка/ пла́тье** ~ pleated skirt/dress.

плит|а́ (-ы́; *nom pl* -ы) *ж* (*каменная*) slab; (*металлическая*) plate; (*печь*) cooker, stove.

пли́т|ка (-ки; *gen pl* -ок) *ж* (*керамическая, кафельная*) tile; (*шоколада*) bar; (*электрическая*) hot plate; (*газовая*) camping stove.

плов (-а) *м* pilaff.

плов|е́ц (-ца́) *м* swimmer.

пловчи́х|а (-и) *ж см* **пловец**.

плод (-á) *м* (БОТ) fruit; (БИО) foetus (*BRIT*), fetus (*US*); ~ +gen (*перен*) fruits of.

плод|и́ться (3sg -и́тся, 3pl -я́тся, *perf* **расплоди́ться**) *несов возв* (*также перен*) to multiply.

плодови́т|ый (-, -а, -о) *прил* fertile; (*перен*) prolific.

плодово́дств|о (-а) *ср* fruit-growing.

плодоро́дный (-ен, -на, -но) *прил* fertile.

плодотво́рный (-ен, -на, -но) *прил* fruitful.

пло́мб|а (-ы) *ж* (*в зубе*) filling; (*на дверях, на сейфе*) seal.

пломби́р (-а) *м* rich creamy ice-cream.

пломбир|ова́ть (-у́ю; *perf* **запломбирова́ть**) *несов перех* (*зуб*) to fill; (*perf* **опломбирова́ть**) *дверь, сейф*) to seal.

пло́ск|ий (-ая, -ое, -ие; -ок, -ка́, -ко) *прил* flat; (*перен: неоригинальный*) feeble.

плоскогу́бц|ы (-ев) *мн* pliers *мн*.

пло́скост|ь (-и; *gen pl* -ей) *ж* (*также перен*) plane.

пло́сок *прил см* **пло́ский**.

плот (-á; *loc sg* -ý) *м* raft.

пло́тен *прил см* **пло́тный**.

плоти́н|а (-ы) *ж* dam.

пло́тник (-а) *м* carpenter.

пло́тно *нареч* (*закрыть дверь*) tightly; (*пообедать*) well.

пло́тност|ь (-и) *ж* density.

пло́тн|ый (-ен, -на́, -но) *прил* (*дым, туман*) dense, thick; (*население, толпа, лес*) dense; (*бумага, кожа*) thick; (*тело, человек*) thick-set; (*завтрак, обед*) substantial.

плотоя́д|ный (-ен, -на, -но) *прил* carnivorous; (*перен*) lustful.

пло́тск|ий (-ая, -ое, -ие) *прил* (*желания*) carnal.

пло́ттер (-а) *м* (*КОМП*) plotter.

плот|ь (-и) *ж* flesh; ~ **и кровь** flesh and blood; **а́нгел/дья́вол во ~й** angel/devil incarnate.

пло́хо *нареч* (*учиться, работать*) badly ◆ *как сказ* it's bad ◆ *ср нескл* (*ПРОСВЕЩ*) ≈ poor (*school mark*); **без друзе́й** ~ it's bad not to have friends; **мне** ~ I feel bad; **в го́роде** ~ **с хле́бом** there's a shortage of bread in the town; **у меня́** ~ **с деньга́ми** I am short of money.

плох|о́й (-а́я, -о́е, -и́е; -, -а́, -о) *прил* bad; **мать ста́ла** ~а́ mother is in a bad way.

площа́д|ка (-ки; *gen pl* -ок) *ж* (*детская*) playground; (*спортивная*) ground; (*строительная*) site; (*часть вагона*) corridor; **ле́стничная** ~ landing; **поса́дочная** ~ landing pad.

пло́щад|ь (-и; *gen pl* -е́й) *ж* (*место*) square; (*пространство, также МАТ*) area; (*разг: также: жила́я* ~) living space.

пло́ще *сравн прил от* **пло́ский**.

плуг (-а; *nom pl* -и́) *м* plough (*BRIT*), plow (*US*).

плут (-а́) *м* (*мошенник*) cheat; (*хитрец*) rogue.

плута́|ть (-ю) *несов неперех* (*разг*) to wander.

плут|ова́ть (-у́ю; *perf* **сплутова́ть**) *несов неперех* to cheat.

Плуто́н (-а) *м* Pluto.

плуто́ни|й (-я) *м* plutonium.

плы|ть (-ву́, -вёшь; *pt* -л, -ла́, -ло) *несов неперех* (*человек, животное*) to swim; (*судно*) to sail; (*лист, облако*) to float.

плюга́в|ый (-, -а, -о) *прил* (*разг: пренебр*) wimpish.

плю́|нуть (-у, -ешь) *сов неперех* to spit; ~ (*perf*) **на что-н** (*разг*) to stop bothering about sth; **плюнь!** (*разг*) forget it!; **э́то мне раз** ~ (*разг*) it's a doddle (for me).

плюрали́зм (-а) *м* pluralism.

плюралисти́ческ|ий (-ая, -ое, -ие) *прил* pluralist(ic).

плюс *м нескл, союз* plus ◆ (-а) *м* (*разг: преимущество*) plus (*мн* plusses); **два** ~ **два — четы́ре** two plus two is four; ~~-ми́нус 2см plus or minus *или* give or take 2cm.

плю́хн|уться (-усь, -ешься; *impf* **плю́хаться**) *сов возв* (*человек*) to flop down.

плюш (-а) *м* plush.

плю́ш|ка (-ки; *gen pl* -ек) *ж* bun.

плющ (-а́) *м* ivy.

плю́щ|ить (-у, -ишь; *perf* **сплю́щить**) *несов перех* to flatten.

пляж (-а) *м* beach.

пля|са́ть (-шу́, -шешь; *perf* **спляса́ть**) *несов перех* to dance.

пля́с|ка (-ки; *gen pl* -ок) *ж* dance.

пляшу́ *итп несов см* **пляса́ть**.

пневмати́ческ|ий (-ая, -ое, -ие) *прил* pneumatic.

пневмони́|я (-и) *ж* pneumonia.

Пномпе́н|ь (-я) *м* Pnomh Penh.

пн|у́ть (-у, -ёшь) *сов перех* (*разг*) to boot.

пня *итп сущ см* **пень**.

ПО *ср сокр* = **произво́дственное объедине́ние**.

KEYWORD

по *предл* (+*dat*) **1** (*о месте действия, вдоль*) along; **де́вочка идёт по у́лице** the little girl is walking along the street; **по берега́м расту́т кусты́** bushes grow along the banks; **ло́дка плывёт по реке́** the boat is sailing on the river; **спуска́ться** (**спусти́ться** *perf*) **по ле́стнице** to go down the stairs

2 (*при глаголах движения*) round; **ходи́ть** (*impf*) **по ко́мнате/са́ду** to walk round the room/ garden; **путеше́ствовать** (*impf*) **по стране́** to travel round the country; **плыть** (*impf*) **по тече́нию** to go downstream; (*перен*) to swim with the tide; **идти́** (*impf*) **по ве́тру** to sail with the wind

3 (*об объекте воздействия*) on; **уда́рить** (*impf*) **кого́-н по плечу́/лицу́** to hit on the shoulder/ face; **уда́рить** (*impf*) **по врагу́/по контрабанди́стам** to deal a blow to the enemy/to the smugglers

4 (*в соответствии с*): **де́йствовать по зако́ну/пра́вилам** to act in accordance with the law/the rules; **по расписа́нию/пла́ну** according to schedule/plan; **он ушёл по со́бственному жела́нию** he left voluntarily; **получа́ть** (**получи́ть** *perf*) **де́ньги по счёту** to receive payment of a bill

5 (*об основании*): **суди́ть по вне́шности** to judge by appearances; **жени́ться** (*impf/perf*) **по любви́** to marry for love

6 (*вследствие*) due to; **отсу́тствовать** (*impf*) **по боле́зни** to be absent due to illness; **по невнима́тельности** due to carelessness; **по необходи́мости** out of necessity

7 (*посредством*): **говори́ть по телефо́ну** to speak on the phone; **отправля́ть** (**отпра́вить** *perf*) **что-н по по́чте** to send sth by post; **передава́ть** (**переда́ть** *perf*) **что-н по ра́дио/по телеви́дению** to broadcast sth on radio/television

8 (*с целью, для*): **рабо́та по повыше́нию эффекти́вности** work towards increased efficiency; **о́рганы по борьбе́ с престу́пностью** organizations in the fight against crime; **опера́ция по захва́ту моста́** an operation to seize the bridge; **я позва́л тебя́ по де́лу** I called on you on business

9 (*о какой-н характеристике объекта*) in; **по интере́сам/до́лжности** in interests/position; **по профе́ссии** by profession; **дед по ма́тери** maternal grandfather; **това́рищ по шко́ле**

school friend

10 (*о сфере деятельности*) in; **занятия по литературе** studies in literature; **исследование по химии** research in chemistry

11 (*о мере времени*): **по вечерам/утрам** in the evenings/mornings; **по воскресеньям/ пятницам** on Sundays/Fridays; **я работаю по целым дням** I work all day long; **работа рассчитана по минутам** the work is planned by the minute

12 (*о единичности предметов*): **мама дала всем по яблоку** Mum gave them each an apple; **мы купили по одной книге** we bought a book each

♦ *предл* (+*acc*) **1** (*вплоть до*) up to; **стоять** (*impf*) **по пояс в воде** to stand up to the waist in water; **по настоящее время** up to the present time; **с первой по пятую главу** from the first to (*BRIT*) *или* through (*US*) the fifth chapter; **я занят по горло** (*разг: перен*) I am up to my eyes in work; **он по уши в неё влюблён** he is head over heels in love with her

2 (*при обозначении цены*): **по два/три рубля за штуку** two/three roubles each

3 (*при обозначении количества*): **по два/три человека** in twos/threes

♦ *предл* (+*prp*; *после*) on; **по окончании работы** on finishing work; **по приезде** on arrival.

по- *префикс* (*in verbs*; *о начале действия*) *indicating the beginning of an action eg.* побежать; (*об ограниченном действии*) *indicating limitation of an action eg.* поговорить; (*о прерывистом действии*) *indicating action carried out at intervals eg.* поглядывать; (*о действии, совершаемом многими*) *indicating action undertaken by many people eg.* повскакать; (*in adjectives and adverbs*; *о неинтенсивном качестве*) *indicating non-intensive quality of sth eg.* помягче; (*подобно чем-н*) *indicating comparison with sth eg.* по-новому.

п/о *сокр* = почтовое отделение; производственное объединение.

по-английски *нареч* in English; **как ~ это слово?** what is this word in English?

побагроветь (-ю) *сов от* **багроветь**.

побаива|ться (-юсь) *несов возв*: **~ +gen** to be a bit frightened of.

побалива|ть (*3sg* -ет, *3pl* -ют) *несов неперех* (*разг: иногда*) to ache now and again; (: *слегка*) to hurt a bit.

побег (-а) *м* (*из тюрьмы*) escape; (*БОТ*) shoot, sprout.

побегу *итп сов см* **побежать**.

побегушк|и (-*разг*): **быть на ~ах у кого-н** to run errands for sb; (*перен*) to be at sb's beck and call.

побед|а (-ы) *ж* victory; **одерживать (одержать** *perf*) **~у над кем-н/чем-н** to win a victory over

sb/sth.

победи́тель (-я) *м* (*в войне*) victor; (*в состязании*) winner.

победи́тельниц|а (-ы) *ж см* **победитель**.

побед|и́ть (*2sg* -ишь, *3sg* -ит, *impf* **побежда́ть**) *сов перех* to defeat ♦ *неперех* to win.

побе́дный *прил* victorious, triumphant; (*марш, салют*) victory *опред*.

победоно́с|ный (-ен, -на, -но) *прил* (*армия, атака*) victorious; (*перен: вид, слова*) triumphant.

побежа́ть (*как* **бежа́ть**; *см* **Table 20**) *сов неперех* (*человек, животное*) to start running; (*дни, годы*) to start to fly by; (*ручьи, слёзы*) to begin to flow.

побежда́ть (-ю) *несов от* **победи́ть**.

побежи́шь *итп сов см* **побежа́ть**.

побеле́ть (-ю) *сов от* **беле́ть**.

побел|и́ть (-ю́, -ишь) *сов от* **бели́ть**.

побе́лк|а (-и) *ж* whitewash; (*действие*) whitewashing.

поберёг(ся) *итп сов см* **побере́чь(ся)**.

поберегу́(сь) *итп сов см* **побере́чь(ся)**.

побере́жь|е (-я) *ср* coast.

побере́|чь (-гу́, -жёшь *итп*, -гу́т; *pt* -ёг, -гла́, -гло́) *сов перех* (*деньги, время*) to save; (*здоровье, мать*) to take care of, look after

▶ **побере́чься** *сов возв* to take care of o.s.

побесе́д|овать (-ую) *сов неперех* to have a chat.

побеспоко́|ить (-ю, -ишь) *сов перех* to disturb, bother; **позво́льте Вас ~** may I trouble you?; **~** (*perf*) **кого́-н прие́здом** to inconvenience sb by one's arrival

▶ **побеспоко́иться** *сов возв* (*проявить заботу*) to concern o.s.

поб|и́ть (-ью́, -ьёшь) *сов от* **бить** ♦ *перех* (*повредить*) to destroy; (*перебить*) to kill; (*разбить*) to break; (*impf* **побива́ть**; *СПОРТ*) to beat; **побива́ть** (**~** *perf*) **реко́рд** to break a record.

поблагодар|и́ть (-ю́, -ишь) *сов от* **благодари́ть**.

побла́жк|а (-ки; *gen pl* -ек) *ж* (*разг*) indulgence.

побледне́ть (-ю) *сов от* **бледне́ть**.

поблёк|нуть (-ну, -нешь; *pt* -, -ла, -ло) *сов от* **блёкнуть**.

побли́зости *нареч* nearby ♦ *предл*: **~ от** +*gen* near (to), close to.

побо́|и (-ев) *мн* beating *ед*.

побо́рник (-а) *м* champion (*of cause*).

побо́рниц|а (-ы) *ж см* **побо́рник**.

побор|о́ть (-ю́, -орешь) *сов перех* (*также перен*) to overcome.

побо́р|ы (-ов) *мн* (*ИСТ*) taxes *мн*, levies *мн*.

побо́ч|ный (-ен, -на, -но) *прил* (*продукт, реакция*) secondary; **~ эффе́кт** side effect.

побо|я́ться (-ю́сь, -и́шься) *сов от* **боя́ться** ♦ *возв*: **побо́йся Бо́га!** (*разг*) have a heart!

побрати́м (-а) *м*: **города́-~ы** twin towns *или* cities.

побреду́ *итп сов см* **побрести́**.

побрёзга|ть (-ю) *сов от* **брёзгать**.

побрёзг|овать (-ую) *сов от* **брёзговать**.

побр|ести́ (-еду́, -едёшь; *pt* -ёл, -ела́, -ело́) *сов неперех* to trudge.

побри́ть(ся) (-ёю(сь), -ёешь(ся)) *сов от* **бри́ть(ся)**.

поброса́|ть (-ю) *сов перех* (*вещи*) to throw about.

побряку́ш|ка (-ки; *gen pl* -ек) *ж* (*обычно мн*) trinket.

побу|ди́ть (-ужу́, -у́дишь; *impf* **побужда́ть**) *сов перех*: ~ кого́-н к чему́-н/+*infin* to prompt sb (in)to sth/to do.

побуду́ *итп сов см* **побы́ть**.

побужда́|ть (-ю) *несов от* **побуди́ть**.

побужде́ни|е (-я) *ср* (*действие*) prompting; (*стремление*) motive.

побужу́ *сов см* **побуди́ть**.

побыва́|ть (-ю) *сов неперех*: ~ в Áфрике/у роди́телей to visit Africa/one's parents.

поб|ы́ть (*как* **быть**; *см* **Table 21**) *сов неперех* to stay.

побью́ *итп сов см* **поби́ть**.

пова́|диться (-жусь, -дишься) *сов неперех*: ~ +*infin* to get into the way of doing.

пова́д|ка (-ки; *gen pl* -ок) *ж* (*разг*) way.

пова́жусь *сов см* **пова́диться**.

пова́лен *прил см* **пова́льный**.

пова|ли́ть (-алю́, -а́лишь) *сов от* **вали́ть** ♦ *неперех* (*снег, град*) to begin to fall; (*толпа*) to come pouring in.

► **повали́ться** *сов от* **вали́ться**.

пова́льн|ый (-ен, -ьна, -ьно) *прил* mass.

по́вар (-а; *nom pl* -á) *м* cook.

пова́ренн|ый *прил*: ~ая кни́га cookery (*BRIT*) *или* cook (*US*) book; ~ая соль table salt.

повари́х|а (-и) *ж см* **по́вар**.

пове́да|ть (-ю) *сов* (*не*)*перех*: ~ что-н *или* о чём-н кому́-н to tell sb sth.

поведе́ни|е (-я) *ср* behaviour (*BRIT*), behavior (*US*).

поведу́(сь) *итп сов см* **повести́(сь)**.

повез|ти́ (-у́, -ёшь; *pt* -ёз, -езла́, -езло́) *сов от* **везти́** ♦ *перех* to take.

повели́тельн|ый (-ен, -ьна, -ьно) *прил* imperious; **повели́тельное наклоне́ние** (*линг*) imperative mood.

повенча́|ть (-ю) *сов от* **венча́ть**.

поверг|ну́ть (-у, -ешь; *impf* **поверга́ть**) *сов перех* (*перен: врага*) to conquer; **поверга́ть** (~ *perf*) кого́-н в +*acc* (*в отчаяние, в уныние итп*) to plunge sb into.

пове́ренн|ый (-ого; *decl like adj*) *м*: ~ в дела́х chargé d'affaires; **прися́жный** ~ (*ист*) barrister (*in tsarist Russia*).

пове́р|ить (-ю, -ишь) *сов от* **ве́рить** ♦ (*impf* **поверя́ть**) *перех*: ~ что-н кому́-н to confide sth

to sb

► **пове́риться** *сов от* **ве́риться**.

пове́р|ка (-и) *ж* (*перекличка*) rollcall; на ~у in fact.

поверн|у́ть (-у́, -ёшь; *impf* **повора́чивать**) *сов* (*не*)*перех* to turn

► **поверну́ться** (*impf* **повора́чиваться**) *сов возв* to turn; **де́ло** ~у́лось к лу́чшему/ху́дшему things took a turn for the better/worse; **у меня́ язы́к не** ~ётся сказа́ть это (*разг*) I wouldn't have the guts to say that; ~ся не́где there isn't even room to turn round.

пове́рх *предл* (+*gen*) over.

пове́рхностн|ый *прил* surface *опред*; (-ен, -на, -но; *перен*) superficial.

пове́рхност|ь (-и) *ж* surface; лежа́ть (*impf*) на ~и to be perfectly obvious.

пове́рь|е (-ья; *gen pl* -ий) *ср* (popular) belief.

поверя́|ть (-ю) *несов от* **пове́рить**.

повеселе́|ть (-ю) *сов от* **веселе́ть**.

пове́|сить(ся) (-шу(сь), -сишь(ся)) *сов от* **ве́шать(ся)**.

повествова́ни|е (-я) *ср* narrative.

повеств|ова́ть (-у́ю) *несов неперех*: ~ о +*prp* (*роман итп*) to tell (the story) of.

пов|ести́ (-еду́, -едёшь; *pt* -ёл, -ла́, -ло́) *сов перех* (*начать вести: человека*) to take; (: *войска*) to lead; (*машину, поезд*) to drive; (*войну, следствие итп*) to begin ♦ (*impf* **поводи́ть**) *неперех*: ~ +*instr* (*бровью*) to raise; (*плечом*) to shrug; ~ (*perf*) себя́ наха́льно to start to behave impudently; **он и бро́вью не** ~ёл (*разг*) he didn't bat an eyelid

► **повести́сь** *сов возв* (*войти в обыкнове́ние*) to become the custom; ~сь (*perf*) с кем-н to become friends with sb.

пове́ст|ка (-ки; *gen pl* -ок) *ж* summons (*мн* summonses); (*также:* ~ дня) agenda.

по́вест|ь (-и) *ж* story.

пове́три|е (-я) *ср* tendency.

пове́шени|е (-я) *ср* hanging; **сме́ртная казнь че́рез** ~ sentence of death by hanging.

пове́шу(сь) *сов см* **пове́сить(ся)**.

пове́|ять (*3sg* -ет, *3pl* -ют) *сов безл* (+*instr*): ~яло прохла́дой/све́жестью there was a breath of cool/fresh air; ~яло свобо́дой/сча́стьем there was a feeling of freedom/happiness in the air.

повздо́р|ить (-ю, -ишь) *сов от* **вздо́рить**.

повзросле́|ть (-ю) *сов от* **взросле́ть**.

повида́|ть(ся) (-ю(сь)) *сов от* **вида́ть(ся)**.

по-ви́димому *вводн сл* apparently.

пови́дл|о (-а) *ср* jam (*BRIT*), jelly (*US*).

пови́нн|ая (-ой; *decl like adj*) *ж* confession; яви́ться (*perf*) *или* прийти́ (*perf*) с ~ой to give o.s. up.

пови́нност|ь (-и) *ж* duty; **во́инская** ~ conscription.

пови́н|ный (-ен, -на, -но) *прил* guilty.

повин|ова́ться (-у́юсь) *сов возв* (+*dat*) to obey.

повинове́ни|е (-я) *ср* obedience.

пови́с|нуть (-ну, -нешь; *pt* -, -ла, -ло, *impf* повиса́ть) *сов неперех* to hang; (*тучи*) to hang motionless; (*птица, вертолёт*) to hover.

повл|е́чь (-еку́, -ечёшь *итп*, -еку́т; *pt* -ёк, -екла́, -екло́) *сов от* влечь.

по́в|од (-ода; *loc sg* -оду́, *nom pl* -о́дья, *gen pl* -ьев) *м* (*лошади*) rein; (*nom pl* -оды; *причина*) reason ♦ *предл*: по ~у +*gen* regarding, concerning; дава́ть (дать *perf*) кому́-н ~ для чего́-н to give sb cause for sth; идти́ (*impf*) или быть (*impf*) на поводу́ у кого́-н to be under sb's thumb.

пов|оди́ть (-ожу́, -о́дишь) *несов от* повести́ ♦ *перех* (*водить недолго*) to walk.

повод|о́к (-ка́) *м* lead, leash.

пово́дья *итп сущ см* по́вод.

повожу́ *сов см* повади́ть.

пово́з|ка (-ки; *gen pl* -ок) *ж* cart.

поволо́к|а (-и) *ж* shroud, haze.

повора́чива|ть (-ю) *несов от* поверну́ть

▶ повора́чиваться *несов от* поверну́ться ♦ *возв* (*разг: быстро действовать*) to get a move on.

поворо́т (-а) *м* (*действие*) turning; (*место*) bend, turn; (*перен*) turning point.

поворо́тлив|ый (-, -а, -о) *прил* (*человек*) agile, nimble.

поворо́тный *прил* (*тех*) revolving; ~ пункт *или* моме́нт (*перен*) turning point; ~ день crucial day; поворо́тный круг turntable.

повре|ди́ть (-жу́, -ди́шь) *сов от* вреди́ть ♦ (*impf* поврежда́ть) *перех* (*поранить*) to injure; (*поломать*) to damage.

поврежде́ни|е (-я) *ср* (*см глаг*) injury; damage.

поврежу́ *сов см* повреди́ть.

повремен|и́ть (-ю́, -и́шь) *сов неперех*: ~ с чем-н to delay sth a little; ~ (*perf*) с отве́том to wait a little before answering.

повре́менный *прил*: повре́менная опла́та payment by the hour.

повседне́вен *прил см* повседне́вный.

повседне́вность (-и) *ж* everyday routine.

повседне́в|ный (-ен, -на, -но) *прил* everyday; (*занятия, встречи*) daily.

повсеме́ст|ный (-ен, -на, -но) *прил* widespread.

повск|ака́ть (*3sg* -а́чет, *3pl* -а́чут) *сов неперех* (*разг*) to jump up.

повстреча́|ть (-ю) *сов перех* (*разг*) to bump into

▶ повстреча́ться *сов возв* (*разг*): ~ся с кем-н to bump into sb.

повсю́ду *нареч* everywhere.

по-вся́кому *нареч* in different ways.

повто́рен *прил см* повто́рный.

повторе́ни|е (-я) *ср* repetition.

повтор|и́ть (-ю́, -и́шь; *impf* повторя́ть) *сов перех* to repeat

▶ повтори́ться (*impf* повторя́ться) *сов возв* (*ситуация*) to repeat itself; (*болезнь*) to recur.

повто́р|ный (-ен, -на, -но) *прил* repeated.

повторя́|ть(ся) (-ю(сь)) *несов от* повтори́ть(ся).

повы́|сить (-шу, -сишь; *impf* повыша́ть) *сов перех* to increase; (*интерес*) to heighten; (*качество, культуру*) to improve; (*работника*) to promote; повыша́ть (~ *perf*) кого́-н в обще́ственном мне́нии to raise sb in the opinion of the public; повыша́ть (~ *perf*) го́лос to raise one's voice

▶ повы́ситься (*impf* повыша́ться) *сов возв* to increase; (*интерес*) to heighten; (*качество, культура*) to improve.

повы́шенный *прил* (*спрос*) increased; (*интерес, чувствительность*) heightened; (*качество*) improved; повы́шенное давле́ние high blood pressure.

повы́шу(сь) *сов см* повы́сить(ся).

повяз|а́ть (-яжу́, -я́жешь; *impf* повя́зывать) *сов перех* to tie.

повя́з|ка (-ки; *gen pl* -ок) *ж* bandage; (*стерильная*) dressing; ги́псовая ~ plaster.

повя́зыва|ть (-ю) *несов от* повяза́ть.

погада́|ть (-ю) *сов от* гада́ть.

пога́н|ить (-ю, -ишь; *perf* опога́нить) *несов перех* (*разг*) to mess up.

пога́н|ка (-ки; *gen pl* -ок) *ж* toadstool.

пога́ный *прил* (*разг: отвратительный*) lousy; ~ гриб toadstool.

пога́с *итп сов см* пога́снуть.

погас|и́ть (-ашу́, -а́сишь) *сов от* гаси́ть ♦ (*impf* погаша́ть) *перех* (*задолженность, вексель,*) to pay (off).

пога́с|нуть (-ну, -нешь; *pt* -, -ла, -ло) *сов от* га́снуть.

погаша́|ть (-ю) *несов от* погаси́ть.

погаше́ни|е (-я) *ср*: срок ~я (*комм*) maturity date.

погашу́ *сов см* погаси́ть.

поги́б *итп сов см* поги́бнуть.

погиба́|ть (-ю) *несов от* поги́бнуть.

поги́бел|ь (-и) *ж*: согну́ться в три ~и (*разг*) to bend double.

поги́б|нуть (-ну, -нешь; *pt* -, -ла, -ло) *сов от* ги́бнуть.

поги́бш|ий (-его; *decl like adj*) *м* dead person; ~ие the dead.

погла́|дить (-жу, -дишь) *сов от* гла́дить.

поглот|и́ть (-ощу́, -о́тишь; *impf* поглоща́ть) *сов перех* to absorb; (*средства, время*) to take up; (: *усилия*) to demand.

поглоще́ни|е (-я) *ср*: попы́тка ~я (*комм*) takeover bid.

поглощу́ *сов см* поглоти́ть.

поглупе́|ть (-ю) *сов от* глупе́ть.

погля|де́ть (-жу́, -ди́шь) *сов от* гляде́ть.

погля́дыва|ть (-ю) *несов неперех* (*разг*) to have *или* take a squint.

погляжу́ *сов см* погляде́ть.

погн|а́ть (-оню́, -о́нишь) *сов перех* (*стадо,
лошадь*) to drive; (*машину, поезд*) to drive fast
► **погна́ться** *сов возв*: ~ся за кем-н/чем-н
(*также перен*) to set off in pursuit of sb/sth.
погнуша́|ться (-юсь) *несов от* гнуша́ться.
погова́рива|ть (-ю) *несов неперех*: ~ о +*prp* to
talk about; ~ют, что ... they say that ....
погово́р|ка (-ки; *gen pl* -ок) *ж* saying.
пого́д|а (-ы) *ж* weather; э́то не де́лает ~у it
doesn't make a lot of difference.
погод|и́ть (-жу́, -ди́шь) *сов неперех*: ~ с +*instr*
(*разг: подождать*) to take one's time with;
немно́го ~дя́ after a while; ~ди́! (*угроза*) just
you wait!
пого́дный *прил* weather *опред*.
пого́ж|ий (-ая, -ее, -ие; -, -а, -е) *прил* fine.
погожу́ *сов см* погоди́ть.
погол|о́вный *прил* (*всеобщий*) general.
погол|о́вье (-я) *ср* (*скота, лошадей*) total
number.
поголубе́|ть (-ю) *сов от* голубе́ть.
пого́н (-а) *м* (*обычно мн*) (shoulder) stripe.
пого́нщик (-а) *м* (cattle) driver.
погоню(сь) *итп сов см* погна́ть(ся).
пого́н|я (-и) *ж*: ~ за +*instr* (*также перен*) pursuit
of ◆ *собир* (*преследователи*) pursuers *мн*; в ~е
за +*instr* in pursuit of.
погоня́|ть (-ю) *несов перех* (*лошадь, скот*) to
drive; (*перен: разг*): ~ кого́-н to hurry sb up.
погор|е́ть (-ю́, -и́шь; *impf* погора́ть) *сов
неперех* to lose everything (*in a fire*); **погора́ть**
(~ *perf*) **на взя́тках/кра́же** (*разг*) to be caught
taking bribes/stealing.
погорячи́|ться (-у́сь, -и́шься) *сов возв* to get
worked up.
погранзаста́в|а (-ы) *ж сокр* (= пограни́чная
заста́ва) frontier post.
пограни́чник (-а) *м* frontier *или* border guard.
пограни́чный *прил* (*город, район*) frontier
опред, border *опред*; (*конфликт, знак*) border
опред.
по́греб (-а; *nom pl* -а́) *м* cellar; **ви́нный** ~ wine
cellar.
погреба́льный *прил* funeral *опред*.
погребе́ни|е (-я) *ср* (*похороны*) burial,
interment; (*могила*) grave.
погрему́ш|ка (-ки; *gen pl* -ек) *ж* rattle.
погре́|ть (-ю; *impf* погрева́ть) *сов перех* to warm
up
► **погре́ться** *сов возв* to warm up.
погреш|и́ть (-у́, -и́шь) *сов от* греши́ть.
погре́шность (-и) *ж* error, mistake.
погро|зи́ть (-жу́, -зи́шь) *сов от* грози́ть.
погро́м (-а) *м* pogrom; (*разг: беспорядок*)
chaos.
погрубе́|ть (-ю) *сов от* грубе́ть.
погр|узи́ть (-ужу́, -у́зишь) *сов перех от*
грузи́ть ◆ *перех*: (-ужу́, -у́зишь) *impf*

погружа́|ть; ~ что-н в +*acc*) to immerse sth in
► **погрузи́ться** *сов от* грузи́ться ◆ (*impf*
погружа́ться) *возв* (*человек*) to immerse o.s.;
(*предмет*) to sink; **погружа́ться** (~ся *perf*) в
+*acc* (*в сон, в апатию*) to sink into;
погружа́ться (~ся *perf*) **в размышле́ния** to be
deep in thought.
погру́з|ка (-ки; *gen pl* -ок) *ж* loading.
погру́зочный *прил* (*машина*) loading *опред*;
~ые рабо́ты loading.
погры́з|ться (-у́сь, -ёшься) *несов от*
грызться.
погря́зн|уть (-у, -ешь; *impf* погряза́ть) *сов
неперех*: ~ в +*prp* (*в грязи*) to get stuck in; (*в
долгах, во лжи*) to sink into; (*в разврате*) to
wallow in.
погу|би́ть (-блю́, -у́бишь) *сов от* губи́ть.
погуля́|ть (-ю) *сов от* гуля́ть.
погусте́|ть (-ю) *сов от* густе́ть.

KEYWORD

под *предл* (+*acc*) **1** (*в направлении ниже*) under;
я положи́л су́мку под стол I put the bag under
the table; **идти́** (*impf*) **под го́ру** to go downhill
2 (*поддерживая снизу*) by; **брать** (**взять** *perf*)
кого́-н под́ руку to take sb by the arm
3 (*указывает на положение, состояние*) under;
под контро́ль/наблюде́ние under control/
observation; **отдава́ть** (**отда́ть** *perf*) **кого́-н под
суд** to prosecute sb; **попада́ть** (**попа́сть** *perf*)
под дождь to be caught in the rain
4 (*близко к*): **под у́тро/ве́чер** towards morning/
evening; **под пра́здники** coming up to the
holidays; **под ста́рость** approaching old age
5 (*указывает на функцию*) as; **мы
приспосо́били помеще́ние под магази́н** we
fitted out the premises as a shop
6 (*в виде чего-н*): **ва́за под хруста́ль** an
imitation crystal vase; **сте́ны под мра́мор**
marble-effect walls
7 (*в обмен на*) on; **брать** (**взять** *perf*) **что-н под
зало́г/че́стное сло́во** to take sth on security/
trust
8 (*в сопровождении*): **под роя́ль/скри́пку** to
the piano/violin; **мне э́то не под си́лу** that is
beyond my powers
◆ *предл* (+*instr*) **1** (*ниже чего-н: о
расположении*) under; **чемода́н под столо́м**
the suitcase is under the table
2 (*около*) near; **под Петербу́ргом** near St.
Petersburg; **под бо́ком у кого́-н** very near to sb;
под но́сом у кого́-н under sb's nose; **под руко́й**
to hand, at hand
3 (*об условиях существования объекта*)
under; **быть** (*impf*) **под наблюде́нием/аре́стом**
to be under observation/arrest; **под назва́нием,
под и́менем** under the name of
4 (*вследствие*) under; **под влия́нием/
тя́жестью чего-н** under the influence/weight of

sth; **понима́ть** (*impf*)/**подразумева́ть** (*impf*) **под чем-н** to understand/imply by sth.

под- *префикс* (*in verbs*; *о движении снизу вверх*) *indicating movement upwards eg.* подбро́сить; (*о действии, содершающемся внизу*) *indicating movement below sth eg.* подби́ть; (*приближение*) *indicating movement towards eg.* подбежа́ть; (*добавление*) *indicating addition to sth eg.* подли́ть; (*ослабленная степень действия*) *indicating non-intensive quality of sth eg.* подкра́сить; (*тайное действие*) *indicating undercover nature of sth eg.* подслу́шать; (*in adjectives*; *расположенный ниже какой-нибудь поверхности*) under-; (*находящийся в ведении*) *indicating supervision of sth eg.* поднадзо́рный; (*in nouns*; *часть чего-н*) sub-; (*ниже по званию*) *indicating lower position or rank eg.* подмасте́рье.

пода́ва|ть(ся) (-ю(сь)) *несов от* **пода́ть(ся)**.

пода|ви́ть (-авлю́, -а́вишь; *impf* **подавля́ть**) *сов перех* to suppress; **подавля́ть** (~ *perf*) **кого́-н чем-н** to intimidate sb with sth

▶ **подави́ться** *сов от* **дави́ться**.

подавле́ни|е (-я) *ср* (*восстания*) suppression.

пода́вленност|ь (-и) *ж* depression.

пода́вленный *прил* (*настроение, состояние, человек*) depressed; (*смех, стон*) suppressed.

подавлю́(сь) *сов см* **подави́ть(ся)**.

подавля́|ть (-ю) *несов от* **подави́ть**.

подавля́ющий (-ая, -ее, -ие) *прил* overwhelming.

пода́вно *нареч*: **он бога́т, а она́ и** ~ (*разг*) he is rich and she is even more so; **е́сли я не могу́ э́то сде́лать, то ты и** ~ (*разг*) if I can't do this, then you certainly can't.

пода́м(ся) *итп см* **пода́ть(ся)**.

подар|и́ть (-арю́, -а́ришь) *сов от* **дари́ть**.

пода́р|ок (-ка) *м* gift, present.

пода́рочный *прил* (*магазин итп*) gift *опред*.

пода́ст(ся) *сов см* **пода́ть(ся)**.

пода́тлив|ый (-, -а, -о) *прил* pliable; (*тело*) supple.

по́дат|ь (-и) *ж* (*ИСТ*) tax.

пода́|ть (*как* **дать**; *см* **Table 14**; *impf* **подава́ть**) *сов перех* to give; (*еду*) to serve up; (*поезд, такси итп*) to bring; (*заявление, жалобу итп*) to submit; (*СПОРТ: в теннисе*) to serve; (: *в футболе*) to pass; **подава́ть** (~ *perf*) **что-н кому́-н** to give sth to sb, give sb sth; (*еду*) to serve sb up with sth; **подава́ть** (~ *perf*) **го́лос за** +*acc* to cast a vote for; **подава́ть** (~ *perf*) **иде́ю** to put forward an idea; **подава́ть** (~ *perf*) **ре́плику** to make a comment; **подава́ть** (~ *perf*) **в отста́вку** to hand in *или* submit one's resignation; **подава́ть** (~ *perf*) **на кого́-н в суд** to take sb to court; **подава́ть** (~ *perf*) **кому́-н ру́ку** (*при встрече*) to give sb one's hand; (*в трудной ситуации*) to give sb a hand; **подава́ть** (~ *perf*) **кому́-н пальто́** to help sb into

their coat

▶ **пода́ться** (*impf* **подава́ться**) *сов возв* (*сдвинуться*) to give way; (*разг: уехать*) to make tracks.

пода́ч|а (-и) *ж* (*действие: заявления, прошения*) submission; (: *обеда*) serving up; (*СПОРТ: в теннисе*) serve; (: *в футболе*) pass.

пода́ч|ка (-ки; *gen pl* -ек) *ж* (*собаке*) scraps *мн*; (*человеку*) hand-out.

пода́шь(ся) *сов см* **пода́ть(ся)**.

подая́ни|е (-я) *ср* alms *мн*.

подба́в|ить (-лю, -ишь; *impf* **подбавля́ть**) *сов перех* to add.

подба́дрива|ть (-ю) *несов от* **подбодри́ть**.

подбежа́ть (*как* **бежа́ть**; *см* **Table 20**; *impf* **подбега́ть**) *сов неперех* to run up.

подберёзовик (-а) *м* (*БОТ*) shaggy boletus.

подберу́(сь) *итп сов см* **подобра́ть(ся)**.

подбива́|ть (-ю) *несов от* **подби́ть**.

подбира́|ть(ся) (-ю(сь)) *несов от* **подобра́ть(ся)**.

под|би́ть (-обью́, -обьёшь; *impf* **подбива́ть**) *сов перех* (*птицу, самолёт*) to shoot down; (*глаз, крыло*) to injure; **подбива́ть** (~ *perf*) **каблуки́ на** +*prp* to reheel.

подбодр|и́ть (-ю́, -и́шь; *impf* **подба́дривать**) *сов перех* to cheer up.

подбо́р (-а) *м* selection; (*собрание*) collection; **как на** ~ all alike and all the very best.

подбо́рк|а (-и) *ж* (*журнальная*) *collection of articles on one general theme*.

подборо́д|ок (-ка) *м* chin.

подбро́|сить (-шу, -сишь; *impf* **подбра́сывать**) *сов перех* (*мяч, шар, камень итп*) to toss; (+*acc или* +*gen*; *добавить*) to put; (*тайно подложить: анонимку*) to leave; (: *ворованный товар, наркотик*) to plant; (*разг: подвезти*) to give a lift.

подва́л (-а) *м* cellar; (*для жилья*) basement.

подва́льный *прил* (*помещение*) basement *опред*; **подва́льный эта́ж** basement.

подведе́ни|е (-я) *ср* (*линии электропередачи*) connecting; **подведе́ние ито́гов** summing-up.

подведу́ *итп сов см* **подвести́**.

подв|езти́ (-езу́, -езёшь; *pt* -ёз, -езла́, -езло́, *impf* **подвози́ть**) *сов перех* (*машину, товар*) to take up; (*человека*) to give a lift.

подве́рг|нуть (-ну, -нешь; *pt* -, -ла, -ло, *impf* **подверга́ть**) *сов перех*: ~ **кого́-н/что-н чему́-н** to subject sb/sth to sth; **подверга́ть** (~ *perf*) **кого́-н ри́ску/опа́сности** to put sb at risk/in danger

▶ **подве́ргнуться** (*impf* **подверга́ться**) *сов возв*: ~**ся** +*dat* to be subjected to.

подве́ржен|ный (-, -а, -о) *прил*: ~ +*dat* (*дурному влиянию*) subject to; (*простуде*) susceptible to.

подверн|у́ть (-у́, -ёшь; *impf* **подвора́чивать**) *сов перех* (*сделать короче*) to turn up; **подвора́чивать** (~ *perf*) **но́гу** to turn *или* twist one's ankle

▶ **подверну́ться** (*impf* **подвора́чиваться**) *сов возв* (*разг: попасться*) to turn up; **мне ~у́лась по́д руку интере́сная кни́га** I came across an interesting book; **у меня́ нога́ ~у́лась** I've twisted my ankle.

подве́|сить (-шу, -сишь; *impf* **подве́шивать**) *сов перех* to hang up.

подве́с|ка (-ки; *gen pl* -ок) *ж* pendant.

подвесно́й *прил* (*в висячем положении*) hanging *опред*; **подвесно́й мост** suspension bridge.

подве́сок *сущ см* **подве́ска**.

подве|сти́ (-еду́, -еде́шь; *pt* -ёл, -ела́, -ело́, *impf* **подводи́ть**) *сов перех:* **~ к** +*dat* (*человека*) to bring up to; (*машину*) to drive up to; (*поезд*) to bring into; (*корабль*) to sail up to; (*электричество*) to bring to; (*дорогу*) to link to; (*разочаровать*) to let down; **подводи́ть (~** *perf*) **глаза́/гу́бы** to put eyeliner/lipstick on; **подводи́ть** (**~** *perf*) **ито́ги** to sum up.

подве́шива|ть (-ю) *несов от* **подве́сить**.

подве́шу *сов см* **подве́сить**.

по́двиг (-а) *м* exploit.

подвига|ть(ся) (-ю(сь)) *несов от* **подви́нуть(ся)**.

подви́жен *прил см* **подви́жный**.

подви́жник (-а) *м* devotee.

подвижно́й *прил:* **~ соста́в** (*на железной дороге*) rolling stock.

подви́жный (-ен, -на, -но) *прил* (*человек, животное*) agile; (*no short form; войска, контакт*) mobile.

подви́|нуть (-у, -ешь; *impf* **подвига́ть**) *сов перех* (*передвинуть: человека, предмет*) to move; (*перен: работу, дело*) to push ahead with

▶ **подви́нуться** (*impf* **подвига́ться**) *сов возв* (*человек*) to move.

подвла́ст|ный (-ен, -на, -но) *прил:* **~** +*dat* (*закону*) subject to; (*президенту*) under the control of.

подво́д|а (-ы) *ж* cart.

подво|ди́ть (-ожу́, -о́дишь) *несов от* **подвести́**.

подво́дник (-а) *м* (*моряк*) submariner; (*водолаз*) diver.

подво́дный *прил* (*растение, работы*) underwater *опред*; **подво́дная ло́дка** submarine; **подво́дное тече́ние** undercurrent.

подвожу́ *сов см* **подводи́ть**.

подво́|зить (-ожу́, -о́зишь) *несов от* **подвезти́**.

подвора́чива|ть (-ю) *несов от* **подверну́ть**.

подворо́т|ня (-ни; *gen pl* -ен) *ж* passage(way).

подво́х (-а) *м* (*разг: ловушка*) catch.

подвя|за́ть (-жу́, -жешь; *impf* **подвя́зывать**) *сов перех* to tie.

подгиба́|ть(ся) (-ю(сь)) *несов от* **подогну́ть(ся)**.

подгля|де́ть (-жу́, -ди́шь; *impf* **подгля́дывать**)

сов перех to peep through.

подговор|и́ть (-ю́, -и́шь; *impf* **подгова́ривать**) *сов перех:* **~ кого́-н на что-н**/+*infin* to put sb up to sth/to doing.

подгоню́ *итп сов см* **подогна́ть**.

подгоня́|ть (-ю) *несов от* **подогна́ть**.

подгор|е́ть (*3sg* -и́т, *3pl* -я́т, *impf* **подгора́ть**) *сов неперех* (*мясо, пирог*) to burn slightly.

подгота́влива|ть(ся) (-ю(сь)) *несов от* **подгото́вить(ся)**.

подготови́тельный *прил* (*предварительный*) preparatory; **подготови́тельный класс** (*в начальной школе*) reception.

подгото́в|ить (-лю, -ишь; *impf* **подгота́вливать**) *сов перех* to prepare

▶ **подгото́виться** (*impf* **подгота́вливаться**) *сов возв* to prepare (o.s.).

подгото́в|ка (-и) *ж* (*к экзамену, к отъезду*) preparation; (*запас знаний, умений*) training.

подготовлю́(сь) *сов см* **подгото́вить(ся)**.

подгу́зник (-а) *м* nappy (*BRIT*), diaper (*US*).

подда|ва́ться (-ю́сь) *несов от* **подда́ться** ♦ *возв:* **не ~ сравне́нию/описа́нию** to be beyond comparison/words.

поддади́мся *итп сов см* **подда́ться**.

подда́кива|ть (-ю) *несов неперех:* **~** +*dat* (*разг*) to agree with.

подда́мся *сов см* **подда́ться**.

по́дданн|ая (-ой; *decl like adj*) *ж см* **по́дданный**.

по́дданн|ый (-ого; *decl like adj*) *м* subject, citizen.

по́дданств|о (-а) *ср* nationality, citizenship.

подда́ться (*как* **дать**; *см* Table 14; *impf* **поддава́ться**) *сов возв* (*дверь итп*) to give way; **поддава́ться** (**~** *perf*) +*dat* (*панике*) to give way to; (*влиянию, соблазну*) to give in to; **поддава́ться** (**~** *perf*) +*dat или* **на** +*acc* (*на просьбы*) to give in to.

поддева́|ть (-ю) *несов от* **подде́ть**.

подде́ла|ть (-ю; *impf* **подде́лывать**) *сов перех* to forge

▶ **подде́латься** (*impf* **подде́лываться**) *сов возв:* **~ся под** +*acc* to imitate.

подде́л|ка (-ки; *gen pl* -ок) *ж* forgery.

подде́лыва|ть(ся) (-ю(сь)) *несов от* **подде́лать(ся)**.

подде́льный *прил* (*документ*) forged; (*радость, гостеприимство*) feigned.

подде́ну *итп сов см* **подде́ть**.

подд|ержа́ть (-ержу́, -е́ржишь; *impf* **подде́рживать**) *сов перех* to support; (*падающего*) to hold on to; (*выступление, предложение итп*) to second; (*беседу*) to keep up.

подде́ржива|ть (-ю) *несов от* **поддержа́ть** ♦ *перех* to support; (*переписку*) to keep up; (*порядок, отношения*) to maintain.

подде́рж|ка (-и) *ж* support.

поддéть (-ну, -нешь; *impf* **поддевáть**) *сов перех* (*приподнять*) to prise (*BRIT*) *или* prize (*US*) off; (*перен: разг*) to gibe at; **поддевáть** (**~** *perf*) **свúтер под кýртку** to put on a sweater under(neath) one's jacket; **поддевáть** (**~** *perf*) **крючкóм** to hook.

поддóн (-а) *м* (*для грузов*) pallet; (*для жидкости*) tray.

поддувáл|о (-а) *ср* damper.

подевáть(ся) (-ю(сь)) *сов от* **девáть(ся)**.

подéйствовать (-ую) *сов от* **дéйствовать**.

подéла|ть (-ю) *сов перех* (*разг*) to do; **ничегó не ~ешь, ничегó нельзя ~** (*разг*) it can't be helped.

подели́ть(ся) (-елю́(сь), -éлишь(ся)) *сов от* **дели́ть(ся)**.

подéл|ка (-ки; *gen pl* -ок) *ж any kind of handmade craft*.

поделóм *нареч*: **~ емý** it serves him right.

подёргива|ться (-юсь) *несов от* **подёрнуться** ◆ *возв* (*лицо*) to twitch.

подéржанный *прил* (*одежда, мебель итп*) second-hand.

подёрн|уться (*3sg* -ется, *3pl* -утся, *impf* **подёргиваться**) *сов возв*: **~ +instr** (*покрыться*) to be covered with; **у негó вóлосы ~улись сединóй** he had a lot of grey hair.

подерýсь *итп сов см* **подрáться**.

подешевé|ть (-ю) *сов от* **дешевéть**.

поджáрист|ый (-, -а, -о) *прил* (*мясо*) well-done; (*картошка, пирожок*) crisp.

поджáр|ый (-, -а, -о) *прил* lean.

поджá|ть (-ожмý, -ожмёшь; *impf* **поджимáть**) *сов перех* (*губы*) to purse; (*живот*) to pull in; **поджимáть** (**~** *perf*) **нóги под себя** to tuck one's legs under o.s.; **поджимáть** (**~** *perf*) **колéни** to pull one's knees up.

поджелýдочн|ый *прил*: **~ая железá** pancreas.

поджéчь (-ожгý, -ожжёшь итп, -ожгýт; *impf* **поджигáть**) *сов перех* to set fire to.

поджигáтел|ь (-я) *м* arsonist.

поджига|ть (-ю) *несов от* **поджéчь**.

поджида|ть (-ю) *несов перех* to wait for.

поджимá|ть (-ю) *несов от* **поджáть** ◆ *перех* (*разг*): **нас~ют срóки** we are working to a tight deadline.

поджóг (-а) *м* arson.

подзаголóв|ок (-ка) *м* subheading.

подзаты́льник (-а) *м* (*разг*) clip round the ear.

подзащи́тн|ая (-ой; *decl like adj*) *ж* (*ЮР*) *см* **подзащи́тный**.

подзащи́тн|ый (-ого; *decl like adj*) *м* (*ЮР*) client.

подземéл|ье (-ья; *gen pl* -ий) *ср* (*комната*) vault; (*проход*) underground passage; (*ряд помещений*) catacombs *мн*.

подзéмный *прил* underground.

подзовý *итп сов см* **подозвáть**.

подзóрн|ый *прил*: **~ая трубá** telescope.

подзывá|ть (-ю) *несов от* **подозвáть**.

поди́ *сов* (*разг*) go ◆ *вводн сл* (*наверное*) probably.

подира́|ть (*3sg* -ет) *несов безл*: **у меня́ морóз по кóже ~ет от э́того** (*разг*) it makes my skin crawl *или* my flesh creep.

подкá́лыва|ть (-ю) *несов от* **подколóть**.

подкáпыва|ться (-юсь) *несов от* **подкопáться**.

подкарау́л|ить (-ю, -ишь; *impf* **подкарау́ливать**) *сов перех* (*разг*) to lie in wait for.

подкáрмлива|ть (-ю) *несов от* **подкорми́ть**.

подкати́ть (-ачý, -áтишь; *impf* **подкáтывать**) *сов перех* (*что-н круглое*) to roll; (*что-н на колёсах*) to wheel ◆ *неперех* (*машина, экипаж*) to race up.

подкача́|ть (-ю) *сов* (*не)перех* (*разг*) to fail.

подкачý *сов см* **подкати́ть**.

подкáшива|ть(ся) (-ю(сь)) *несов от* **подкоси́ть(ся)**.

подки́дыва|ть (-ю) *несов от* **подки́нуть**.

подки́дыш (-а) *м* abandoned baby.

подки́н|уть (-у, -ешь; *impf* **подки́дывать**) *сов перех* (*кинуть вверх*) to toss; (+*acc или* +*gen*; *добавить*) to put; (*тайно подложить*: *анонимку*) to leave; (: *ворованный товар, наркотик*) to plant; **подки́дывать** (**~** *perf*) **комý-н дéнег** (*разг*) to give sb a sub; **подки́дывать** (**~** *perf*) **когó-н** (*разг*) to give sb a lift.

подклáд|ка (-ки; *gen pl* -ок) *ж* lining.

подклáдыва|ть (-ю) *несов от* **подложи́ть**.

подклé|ить (-ю, -ишь; *impf* **подклéивать**) *сов перех* to stick on.

подключ|и́ть (-ý, -и́шь; *impf* **подключáть**) *сов перех* (*телефон*) to connect; (*лампу*) to plug in; (*специалистов*) to involve; **подключáть** (**~** *perf*) **к систéме/центрáльной сети** (*КОМП*) to network, hook up to the main network

▸ **подключи́ться** (*impf* **подключáться**) *сов возв* to get involved.

подкóв|а (-ы) *ж* (*лошади итп*) shoe.

подков|áть (-ý́ю) *сов от* **ковáть** ◆ (*impf* **подкóвывать**) *перех* (*лошадь итп*) to shoe.

подкол|óть (-олю́, -óлешь; *impf* **подкáлывать**) *сов перех* (*скрепить*) to pin up; (*разг: уязвить*) to taunt; **подкáлывать** (**~** *perf*) **докумéнт к дéлу** to file a document.

подкóп (-а) *м* (*ход*) secret underground passage.

подкопá|ться (-юсь; *impf* **подкáпываться**) *сов возв*: **~ под +acc** (*под здание*) to tunnel under; (*разг: под начальника итп*) to undermine.

подкорм|и́ть (-ормлю́, -óрмишь; *impf* **подкáрмливать**) *сов перех* (*животных*) to fatten up; (*ребёнка, больного*) to feed up.

подкос|и́ть (-ошý, -óсишь; *impf* **подкáшивать**) *сов перех* (*подлеж: удар, пуля*) to fell; (*несчастье*) to devastate; (*усталость*) to overcome

▸ **подкоси́ться** (*impf* **подкáшиваться**) *сов возв*: **у негó нóги/колéни ~оси́лись** his legs/knees gave way.

подкрá|сться (-дýсь, -дёшься; *impf*

подкра́дываться) *сов возв* to sneak *или* steal up.

подкреп|и́ть (-лю́, -и́шь; *impf* **подкрепля́ть**) *сов перех* (*стену, крышу*) to support; (*мысли, утверждение*) to support, back up

▶ **подкрепи́ться** (*impf* **подкрепля́ться**) *несов возв* to fortify o.s.

подкрепле́ни|е (-я) *ср* (*ВОЕН*) reinforcement.

подкреплю́(сь) *сов см* **подкрепи́ть(ся)**.

подкрепля́|ть(ся) (-ю(сь)) *несов от* **подкрепи́ть(ся)**.

по́дкуп (-а) *м* bribery.

подк|упи́ть (-уплю́, -у́пишь; *impf* **подкупа́ть**) *сов перех* to bribe; (*перен: добротой*) to win over.

подла́мыва|ться (*3sg* -ется, *3pl* -ются) *несов от* **подломи́ться**.

по́дле *нареч* (*рядом*) nearby ◆ *предл* (*+gen*) beside, next to.

подлеж|а́ть (*3sg* -и́т, *3pl* -а́т) *несов неперех*: ~ *+dat* (*проверке, обложению налогом*) to be subject to; **приговóр не** ~**и́т обжа́лованию** (*ЮР*) the sentence is not open to appeal; **э́то не** ~**и́т сомне́нию** there can be no doubt about that.

подлежа́щ|ее (-его; *decl like adj*) *ср* (*ЛИНГ*) subject.

подле|те́ть (-чу́, -ти́шь; *impf* **подлета́ть**) *сов неперех* (*самолёт*) to fly in; (*птица*) to fly up; (*разг: человек*) to race up.

подле́ц (-а́) *м* scoundrel.

подле|чи́ть (-ечу́, -е́чишь; *impf* **подле́чивать**) *сов перех* to treat

▶ **подлечи́ться** (*impf* **подле́чиваться**) *сов возв* to undergo a short course of treatment.

подлечу́ *сов см* **подлете́ть**.

подлива́|ть (-ю) *несов от* **подли́ть**.

подли́в|ка (-ки; *gen pl* -ок) *ж* (*КУЛИН*) sauce.

подли́з|а (-ы) *м/ж* crawler.

подли́зыва|ться (-юсь; *perf* **подлиза́ться**) *несов возв*: ~ **к** *+dat* (*разг*) to crawl to.

по́длинен *прил см* **по́длинный**.

по́длинник (-а) *м* original.

по́длин|ный (-ен, -на, -но) *прил* original; (*документ*) authentic; (*no short form*; *герой, друг*) true.

под|ли́ть (-олью́, -ольёшь; *pt* -ли́л, -лила́, -ли́ло, *impf* **подлива́ть**) *сов перех* to add; **подлива́ть** (~ *perf*) **вина́ в стака́н** to top up a glass with wine; **подлива́ть** (~ *perf*) **ма́сла в огóнь** to add fuel to the fire *или* flames.

по́дло *нареч* (*поступить*) meanly ◆ *как сказ* it's mean.

подлóг (-а) *м* forgery.

подлóжен *прил см* **подлóжный**.

подл|ожи́ть (-ожу́, -óжишь; *impf* **подкла́дывать**) *сов перех* (*анонимку*) to leave; (*ворованный товар*) to plant; (*+acc или +gen*;

добавить) to put; (*дров, сахара*) to add; **подкла́дывать** (~ *perf*) **что-н под что-н** to put sth under sth.

подлóж|ный (-ен, -на, -но) *прил* forged.

подлокóтник (-а) *м* arm(rest).

подл|оми́ться (*3sg* -óмится, *3pl* -óмятся, *impf* **подла́мываться**) *сов возв*: ~ **под тя́жестью чего́-н** to give way under the weight of sth.

пóдлост|ь (-и) *ж* (*качество*) baseness; **кака́я** ~**!** what a base thing to do!

пóдл|ый (-, -а́, -о) *прил* base.

подмасте́рь|е (-я) *м* apprentice.

подма́чива|ть (-ю) *несов от* **подмочи́ть**.

подм|ени́ть (-еню́, -е́нишь; *impf* **подме́нивать**) *сов перех* (*заменить*) to substitute; **подме́нивать** (~ *perf*) **когó-н** (*разг*) to stand in for sb.

подм|ести́ (-ету́, -етёшь; *pt* -ёл, -ела́, -елó) *сов от* **мести́** ◆ (*impf* **подмета́ть**) *перех* (*пол*) to sweep; (*мусор*) to sweep up.

подме́|тить (-чу, -тишь; *impf* **подмеча́ть**) *сов перех* to notice.

подмёт|ка (-и) *ж* (*подошва*) sole; **он в** ~**и ей не годи́тся** (*разг*) he's not worth her little finger.

подмету́ *итп сов см* **подмести́**.

подмеча́|ть (-ю) *несов от* **подме́тить**.

подмечу́ *сов см* **подме́тить**.

подмигн|у́ть (-у́, -ёшь; *impf* **подми́гивать**) *сов неперех*: ~ **кому́-н** to wink at sb.

подмина́|ть (-ю) *несов от* **подмя́ть**.

подмóг|а (-и) *ж* (*разг*) help.

подмóстк|и (-ов) *мн* (*ТЕАТР*) stage *ед*.

подм|очи́ть (-очу́, -óчишь; *impf* **подма́чивать**) *сов перех* to dampen, moisten; (*разг: репута́цию*) to blacken.

подмóю *итп сов см* **подмы́ть**.

подмыва́|ть (-ю) *несов от* **подмы́ть** ◆ *безл* (*разг*): **его́** ~**ло** *+infin* ... he felt an urge to ....

подм|ы́ть (-óю, -óешь; *impf* **подмыва́ть**) *сов перех* (*ребёнка, больнóго*) to wash; (*берег, мост*) to undermine.

подмы́ш|ка (-ки; *gen pl* -ек) *ж* armpit.

подм|я́ть (-омну́, -омнёшь; *impf* **подмина́ть**) *сов перех* to crush.

подневóль|ный (-ен, -ьна, -ьно) *прил* (*человек*) subordinate; (*труд*) forced.

поднес|ти́ (-у́, -ёшь; *impf* **подноси́ть**) *сов перех*: ~ **к** *+dat* to bring up to; (*подарить*): ~ **что-н кому́-н** to present sth to sb.

поднима́|ть(ся) (-ю(сь)) *несов от* **подня́ть(ся)**.

подниму́(сь) *итп сов см* **подня́ть(ся)**.

поднов|и́ть (-лю́, -и́шь; *impf* **подновля́ть**) *сов перех* (*здание*) to refurbish; (*краску*) to touch up.

подногóтн|ая (-ой; *decl like adj*) *ж*: (*вся*) ~ the true nature.

поднóжек *сущ см* **поднóжка**.

поднóжи|е (-я) *ср (горы, памятника)* foot.
поднóж|ка (-ки; *gen pl* **-ек) ж** *(трамвая, автобуса итп)* step; **дать** *(perf)* или **постáвить** *(perf)* **~ку комý-н** to trip sb up.
поднóжн|ый *прил:* **быть на ~ом кормý** *(с.-х.)* to be out at pasture.
поднóс (-а) м tray.
подн|осить (-ошý, -óсишь) *несов от* **поднести**.
подн|ять (-имý, -имешь; *impf* **поднимáть)** *сов перех* to raise; *(что-н лёгкое)* to pick up; *(что-н тяжёлое)* to lift (up); *(флаг)* to hoist; *(спящего человека)* to rouse; *(панику, восстание)* to start; *(экономику, дисциплину)* to improve; *(архивные материалы, документацию итп)* to unearth; **поднимáть** *perf)* **крик** или **шум** to make a fuss; **поднимáть** *(~ perf)* **чьё-н настроéние** или **чей-н дух** to raise sb's spirits; **поднимáть** *(~ perf)* **когó-н нá смех** to make a laughing stock of sb
► **подн|яться (** *impf* **поднимáться)** *сов возв* to rise; *(на другой этаж, на сцену)* to go up; *(с постéли, со стýла)* to get up; *(паника, метель, драка)* to break out; **поднимáться** *(~ся perf)* **нá гóру** to climb a hill; **~ялся крик** there was an uproar; **~ялся вéтер** the wind got up.
подо *предл см* **под**.
подоб|ать (*3sg* **-ет,** *3pl* **-ют)** *несов неперех:* **~** *+dat* to befit; **Вам не ~ет откáзываться** it does not befit you to refuse.
подобáющий (-ая, -ее, -ие) *прил* appropriate.
подóбен *прил см* **подóбный**.
подóбно *предл:* **~** *+dat* like, similar to ◆ *союз:* **~ томý как** in the same way as, just as.
подóбн|ый (-ен, -на, -но) *прил:* **~** *+dat (сходный с)* like, similar to; **~ные лю́ди – рéдкость** there are very few people like this или of this type; **и томý ~ное** et cetera, and so on; **ничегó ~ного** *(раза)* nothing of the sort.
подобострáстн|ый (-ен, -на, -но) *прил* obsequious, servile.
под|обрáть (-берý, -берёшь; *impf* **подбирáть)** *сов перех* to pick up; *(приподнять вверх)* to gather (up); *(выбрать подходящее)* to select, pick
► **подобрáться (** *impf* **подбирáться)** *сов возв (коллектив)* to get together; *(библиотека, коллекция)* to be built up; *(подкрасться)* to steal up.
подобрéть (-ю) *сов от* **добрéть**.
подобрý-поздорóву *нареч (разг):* **убирáйся ~!** get out while the going's good!
подобью *итп сов см* **подбить**.
под|огнáть (-гоню, -гóнишь; *impf* **подгонять)** *сов перех:* **~ к** *+dat (стадо, машину)* to drive up to; *(лодку)* to take in to; **подгонять** *(~ perf)* **под** *+acc* to fit.
подогн|ýть (-ý, -ёшь; *impf* **подгибáть)** *сов перех (рукава, штанину)* to turn up
► **подогнýться (** *impf* **подгибáться)** *сов возв* to curl under; **у негó нóги/колéни ~ýлись** his

legs/knees gave way.
подогрéть (-ю; *impf* **подогревáть)** *сов перех* to warm up; *(перен: любопытство)* to heighten.
пододви́н|уть (-у, -ешь; *impf* **пододвигáть)** *сов перех* to move closer.
пододеяльник (-а) м ≈ duvet cover.
подожд|áть (-ý, -ёшь; *pt* **-áл, -алá, -áло)** *сов перех* to wait for; **~** *(perf)* **с чем-н** to put sth off; **~** *(perf)* *+infin* to put off doing; **~и́те!** wait a minute!; **~и́те, мóжет всё не так плóхо** wait a bit, maybe it won't be all that bad; **~и́те, я ведь знал Вáшего отцá** wait a minute, I think I knew your father.
подожгý *итп сов см* **поджéчь**.
подожмý *итп сов см* **поджáть**.
под|озвáть (-зовý, -зовёшь; *pt* **-озвáл, -озвалá, -озвáло,** *impf* **подзывáть)** *сов перех* to call over.
подозрев|áть (-ю) *несов перех* to suspect; **~** *(impf)* **когó-н в чём-н** to suspect sb of sth; **~** *(impf)* **(о чём-н)** to have an idea (about sth).
подозрéни|е (-я) *ср* suspicion; **~ на** *+acc (предположение)* suspicion of; **быть** *(impf)* **под ~м** или **на ~и** to be under suspicion; **он был задéржан/арестóван по ~ю в уби́йстве** he was held/arrested on suspicion of murder.
подозри́тельн|ый (-ен, -ьна, -ьно) *прил* suspicious.
подой|ти́ (-ý, -ишь) *сов от* **дойти́**.
подой|ти́ (*как* **идти́;** *см* **Table 18;** *impf* **подходи́ть)** *сов неперех:* **~ к** *+dat (также перен)* to approach; *(соответствовать):* **~ти́ к** *+dat (юбка)* to go (well) with; **подходи́ть** *(~ perf)* **на дóлжность** to be suited to a position; **э́то мне подхóдит** this suits me; **подходи́ть** *(~ perf)* **к концý** to come to an end.
подокóнник (-а) м windowsill.
подóл (-а) м hem.
подóлгу *нареч* for a long time.
подолью *итп сов см* **подли́ть**.
подомнý *итп сов см* **подмя́ть**.
подóн|ок (-ка) м scum.
подопéчн|ый (-ого; *decl like adj)* **м** ward ◆ *прил:* **~ ребёнок** ward; **подопéчная террито́рия** *(под опéкой ООН)* trust territory, trusteeship.
подоплёк|а (-и) ж underlying reason.
подопрý *итп сов см* **подпере́ть**.
подóпытн|ый *прил:* **~ое живóтное** animal used in experiments; **~ крóлик** *(перен)* guinea pig.
подорв|áть (-ý, -ёшь; *pt* **-áл, -алá, -áло,** *impf* **подрывáть)** *сов перех* to blow up; *(перен: авторитéт, дове́рие)* to undermine; *(: здоро́вье)* to destroy
► **подорвáться (** *impf* **подрывáться)** *сов возв* to be blown up; *(перен: авторитéт)* to be undermined; *(: здоро́вье)* to be destroyed.
подорожáть (-ю) *сов от* **дорожáть**.
подорóжник (-а) м plantain.
подо|слáть (-шлю, -шлёшь; *impf* **подсылáть)** *сов перех* to send *(secretly)*.

подоспе́|**ть** (-ю; *impf* **подоспева́ть**) *сов неперех* to arrive in time.

подотру́ *итп сов см* **подтере́ть**.

подотчё́т|**ный** (-ен, -на, -но) *прил* (*организация, работник итп*) accountable; счё́т ~ных сумм expense account; подотчё́тные де́ньги expenses.

подо́хн|**уть** (-у, -ешь) *сов см* **до́хнуть**.

подохо́дный *прил*: ~ нало́г income tax.

подо́шв|**а** (-ы) ж (*обуви*) sole.

подошё́л *итп сов см* **подойти́**.

подошлю́ *итп сов см* **подосла́ть**.

подошью́ *итп сов см* **подши́ть**.

подпа́|**сть** (-ду́, -дёшь) *сов неперех*: ~ под +*acc* to fall under.

подпева́|**ть** (-ю; *perf* **подпе́ть**) *несов неперех* (+*dat*) to join in with; (*перен: разг: пренебр*) to echo.

подпере́ть (-опру́, -опрёшь; *pt* -пё́р, -пё́рла, -пё́рло, *impf* **подпира́ть**) *сов перех*: ~ что-н чем-н to prop up; **подпира́ть** (~ *perf*) щё́ку кулако́м to rest one's head in one's hands.

подп|**е́ть** (-ою́, -оё́шь) *сов см* **подпева́ть**.

подпира́|**ть** (-ю) *несов от* **подпере́ть**.

подписа́ни|**е** (-я) *ср* signing.

подп|**иса́ть** (-ишу́, -и́шешь; *impf* **подпи́сывать**) *сов перех* to sign.

▶ **подписа́ться** (*impf* **подпи́сываться**) *сов возв*: ~ся под +*instr* to sign; **подпи́сываться** (~ся *perf*) на +*acc* (*на газету, на журнал*) to subscribe to.

подпи́с|**ка** (-ки; *gen pl* -ок) ж subscription; (*о невыезде, о неразглашении*) signed statement.

подписно́й *прил* subscription *опред*; акционе́рный капита́л (*КОММ*) subscribed capital; **подписно́й лист** list of subscribers.

подпи́сок *сущ см* **подпи́ска**.

подпи́счик (-а) *м* subscriber.

подпи́сыва|**ть(ся)** (-ю(сь)) *несов от* **подписа́ть(ся)**.

по́дпис|**ь** (-и) ж (*фамилия*) signature; (*под картиной*) title, caption; (*под стихами*) title.

подпишу́(сь) *итп сов см* **подписа́ть(ся)**.

подплы́|**ть** (-ву́, -вё́шь; *pt* -л, -ла́, -ло, *impf* **подплыва́ть**) *сов неперех* (*лодка*) to sail (up); (*пловец, рыба*) to swim (up).

подполко́вник (-а) *м* lieutenant colonel.

подпо́ль|**е** (-я) *ср* (*подвал*) cellar; (*конспирация*) underground activities *мн*; уходи́ть (уйти́ *perf*) в ~ to go underground.

подпо́льный *прил* underground *опред*.

подпо́р|**ка** (-ки; *gen pl* -ок) ж prop, support.

подпою́ *итп сов см* **подпе́ть**.

подпоя́|**сать** (-шу, -шешь; *impf* **подпоя́сывать**) *сов перех* to belt.

подпра́в|**ить** (-лю, -ишь; *impf* **подправля́ть**) *сов перех* to make minor corrections to.

подпрогра́мм|**а** (-ы) ж (*КОМП*) subroutine.

подпру́г|**а** (-и) ж girth.

подпры́гн|**уть** (-у, -ешь; *impf* **подпры́гивать**) *сов неперех* to jump.

подпуска́|**ть** (-ю) *несов от* **подпусти́ть** ♦ *перех*: ~ к +*dat* to allow access to.

подп|**усти́ть** (-ущу́, -у́стишь; *impf* **подпуска́ть**) *сов перех* (*человека, зверя*) to allow to approach.

подрабо́та|**ть** (-ю; *impf* **подраба́тывать**) *сов перех* (*статью*) to polish up ♦ (*не)перех* (+*acc или* +*gen*) to earn extra.

подра́внива|**ть** (-ю) *несов от* **подровня́ть**.

подра́гива|**ть** (-ю) *сов неперех* to tremble; (*ресницы*) to flutter.

подража́ни|**е** (-я) *ср* imitation.

подража́|**ть** (-ю) *несов неперех* (+*dat*) to imitate.

подразделе́ни|**е** (-я) *ср* (*воинское*) subunit; (*производственное*) subdivision.

подраздел|**и́ть** (-ю́, -и́шь; *impf* **подразделя́ть**) *сов перех* to subdivide.

подразделя́|**ться** (*3sg* -е́тся, *3pl* -ю́тся) *несов возв* to be subdivided.

подразумева́|**ть** (-ю) *несов перех* to mean.

▶ **подразумева́ться** *несов возв* to be implied.

подра́мник (-а) *м* stretcher.

подр|**асти́** (-асту́, -астё́шь; *pt* -о́с, -осла́, -осло́, *impf* **подраста́ть**) *сов неперех* to grow (a little).

подра́|**ться** (-еру́сь, -ерё́шься) *сов от* **дра́ться**.

подре́|**зать** (-жу, -жешь; *impf* **подреза́ть**) *сов перех* (*платье*) to shorten; (*волосы*) to cut; ~ (*perf*) кры́лья кому́-н (*перен*) to clip sb's wings.

подро́бен *прил см* **подро́бный**.

подро́бность (-и) ж detail; вдава́ться (*impf*) в ~и to go into detail.

подро́бный (-ен, -на, -но) *прил* detailed.

подровня́|**ть** (-ю; *impf* **подра́внивать**) *сов перех* to trim.

подро́с *итп сов см* **подрасти́**.

подро́стка *сущ см* **подро́сток**.

подростко́вый *прил* (*одежда итп*) teenage *опред*; (*проблемы*) adolescent *опред*; **подростко́вый во́зраст** teens *мн*.

подро́ст|**ок** (-ка) *м* teenager, adolescent.

подру́г|**а** (-и) ж (girl)friend; **подру́га жи́зни** wife.

по-друго́му *нареч* (*иначе*) differently.

подр|**ужи́ть** (-ужу́, -у́жишь) *сов от* **дружи́ть**.

▶ **подружи́ться** *сов от* **дружи́ться** ♦ *возв*: ~ся с +*instr* to make friends with; они́ бы́стро ~ужи́лись they quickly became friends.

подрул|**и́ть** (-ю́, -и́шь; *impf* **подру́ливать**) *сов неперех* (*самолёт*) to taxi; (*автомобиль*) to drive (up).

подрумя́н|**иться** (-юсь, -ишься) *сов от* **румя́ниться** ♦ (*impf* **подрумя́ниваться**) *возв* (*женщина*) to put on blusher; (*пирожки,* *булочки*) to brown.

подру́чн|ый *прил*: ~ **материа́л/инструме́нт** the material/instrument to hand ♦ (**-ого**; *decl like adj*) *м* assistant.

подрыва́|ть(ся) (-ю(сь)) *несов от* **подорва́ть(ся)**.

подрывно́й *прил* subversive.

подря́д *нареч* in succession ♦ (**-а**) *м* (*рабочий договор*) contract; **рабо́тали 5 дней** ~ they worked 5 days in a row *или* in succession; **все/всё** ~ everyone/everything without exception.

подря́дный *прил* contract *опред*.

подря́дчик (-а) *м* contractor.

подряхле́|ть (-ю) *сов от* **дряхле́ть**.

подса́д|и́ть (-ажу́, -а́дишь; *impf* **подса́живать)** *сов перех* (*на коня*) to help to mount; (*на высокий стул*) to help up; (*посадить рядом*) to place nearby.

подса́жива|ться (-юсь) *несов от* **подсе́сть**.

подсажу́ *сов см* **подсади́ть**.

подсве́чник (-а) *м* candlestick.

подсе́к *итп сов см* **подсе́чь**.

подсека́|ть (-ю) *несов от* **подсе́чь**.

подсеку́ *итп сов см* **подсе́чь**.

подсе́|сть (-я́ду, -я́дешь; *impf* **подса́живаться)** *сов неперех*: ~ **к** +*dat* to sit down beside.

подсе́|чь (-еку́, -ечёшь итп, -еку́т; *pt* **-ёк, -екла́, -екло́,** *impf* **подсека́ть)** *сов перех* to cut down; (*перен: подлеж: несчастье, болезнь*) to lay low.

подсин|и́ть (-ю́, -и́шь) *сов от* **сини́ть**.

подск|аза́ть (-ажу́, -а́жешь; *impf* **подска́зывать)** *сов перех* (*перен: идею, решение*) to suggest; (*разг: адрес, телефон*) to tell; **подска́зывать (**~ *perf*) **что-н кому́-н** to prompt sb with sth; **не** ~**а́жите, где у́лица Пу́шкина?** can you please tell me where Pushkin Street is?

подска́з|ка (-ки; *gen pl* **-ок)** *ж* prompt; **де́йствовать** (*impf*) **по чьей-н** ~**ке** (*перен*) to do as sb says.

подска́зыва|ть (-ю) *несов от* **подсказа́ть**.

подск|очи́ть (-очу́, -о́чишь; *impf* **подска́кивать)** *сов неперех* (*также перен*) to jump; (*подбежать*) to run up; **подска́кивать (**~ *perf*) **от испу́га/неожи́данности** to start (in fright/surprise).

подсла|сти́ть (-щу́, -сти́шь; *impf* **подсла́щивать)** *сов перех* to sweeten.

подсле́дственн|ая (-ой; *decl like adj*) *ж см* **подсле́дственный**.

подсле́дственн|ый (-ого; *decl like adj*) *м* the accused, the defendant; ~**ые** the accused.

подслу́ша|ть (-ю; *impf* **подслу́шивать)** *сов перех* to eavesdrop on.

подсма́трива|ть (-ю) *несов от* **подсмотре́ть**.

подсме́ива|ться (-юсь) *сов возв*: ~ **над** +*instr* to poke gentle fun at.

подсм|отре́ть (-отрю́, -о́тришь; *impf* **подсма́тривать)** *сов перех* (*увидеть*) to spy

on; ~ (*perf*), **что ...** to notice that ...; **я** ~**отре́л, как он брал конфе́ты** I saw him take the sweets.

подсне́жник (-а) *м* snowdrop.

подсо́бный *прил* (*помещение, хозяйство*) subsidiary; **подсо́бный рабо́чий** auxiliary.

подсо́выва|ть (-ю) *несов от* **подсу́нуть**.

подсозна́ни|е (-я) *ср* the subconscious.

подсозна́тельный (-ен, -ьна, -ьно) *прил* subconscious.

подсо́лнечник (-а) *м* sunflower.

подсо́лнечн|ый *прил*: ~**ое ма́сло** sunflower oil.

подсо́лнух (-а) *м* (*разг*) sunflower.

подсо́х|нуть (-ну, -нешь; *pt* **-, -ла, -ло,** *impf* **подсыха́ть)** *сов неперех* to dry out a little.

подспо́р|ье (-я) *ср* help.

подспу́дный (-ен, -на, -но) *прил* hidden.

подста́в|ить (-лю, -ишь; *impf* **подставля́ть)** *сов перех*: ~ **под** +*acc* to put under; **подставля́ть** (~ *perf*) **кого́-н под уда́р** (*перен*) to lay sb open to attack.

подста́в|ка (-ки; *gen pl* **-ок)** *ж* stand.

подста́влю *сов см* **подста́вить**.

подставля́|ть (-ю) *несов от* **подста́вить**.

подставно́й *прил* (*ложный*) false.

подста́вок *сущ см* **подста́вка**.

подстака́нник (-а) *м* glassholder.

подста́нци|я (-и) *ж* substation.

подстегн|у́ть (-у́, -ёшь; *impf* **подстёгивать)** *сов перех* to urge on; (*перен: разг*): ~ **кого́-н** to get sb moving.

подстел|и́ть (-ю́, -ишь; *impf* **подстила́ть)** *сов перех* (*плед, простыню*) to spread out.

подстерега́|ть (-ю) *несов от* **подстере́чь** ♦ *перех* (*ожидать*) to await.

подстере́|чь (-гу́, -жёшь итп, -гу́т; *impf* **подстерега́ть)** *сов перех* to lie in wait for.

подстила́|ть (-ю) *несов от* **подстели́ть**.

подсти́л|ка (-ки; *gen pl* **-ок)** *ж* covering.

подстра́ива|ть (-ю) *несов от* **подстро́ить**.

подстрах|ова́ть (-у́ю; *impf* **подстрахо́вывать)** *сов перех* (*гимнаста*) to be on hand for; (*в рискованном деле*) to insure.

подстрека́тель (-я) *м* instigator.

подстрека́|ть (-ю) *несов перех*: ~ **кого́-н к** +*dat* to drive sb to.

подстрел|и́ть (-ю́, -ишь; *impf* **подстре́ливать)** *сов перех* to wing.

подстри́|чь (-гу́, -жёшь итп, -гу́т; *pt* **-г, -ла, -ло,** *impf* **подстрига́ть)** *сов перех* to trim; (*для укорачивания*) to cut

▶ **подстри́чься** (*impf* **подстрига́ться**) *сов возв* to have one's hair cut.

подстро́|ить (-ю, -ишь; *impf* **подстра́ивать)** *сов перех* to fix.

подстро́чн|ый *прил*: ~**ое примеча́ние** footnote; ~ **перево́д** word-for-word translation.

по́дступ (-а) *м* (*обычно мн*) approach.

подступ|и́ть (-уплю́, -у́пишь; *impf* **подступа́ть)** *сов неперех* (*слёзы*) to well up; (*рыдания*) to

rise; **подступа́ть** (**~** *perf*) **к** +*dat* to approach
▶ **подступи́ться** (*impf* **подступа́ться**) *сов возв*: **~ся к** +*dat* to approach.
подсу́ден *прил см* **подсу́дный**.
подсуди́м|ая (**-ой**; *decl like adj*) *ж см* **подсуди́мый**.
подсуди́м|ый (**-ого**; *decl like adj*) *м* (*ЮР*) the accused, the defendant; **~ые** the accused.
подсу́дный (**-ен, -на, -но**) *прил* (*ЮР*) sub judice; **~ое де́ло** (*подлежащий суду*) *case due to come before court*; (*преступление*) crime.
подсу́н|уть (**-у, -ешь**; *impf* **подсо́вывать**) *сов перех* to shove; (*разг: что-н ненужное, плохое*) to get rid of.
подсуши́ть (**-ушу́, -у́шишь**; *impf* **подсу́шивать**) *сов перех* to dry slightly.
подсчёт (**-а**) *м* counting; (*обычно мн: итог*) calculation.
подсчита́|ть (**-ю**; *impf* **подсчи́тывать**) *сов перех* to count (up).
подсыла́|ть (**-ю**) *несов см* **подосла́ть**.
подсыха́|ть (**-ю**) *несов см* **подсо́хнуть**.
подся́ду *итп сов см* **подсе́сть**.
подта́лкива|ть (**-ю**) *несов от* **подтолкну́ть**.
подтас|ова́ть (**-у́ю**; *impf* **подтасо́вывать**) *сов перех* to juggle (with).
подта́чива|ть (**-ю**) *несов от* **подточи́ть**.
подтверд|и́ть (**-жу́, -ди́шь**; *impf* **подтвержда́ть**) *сов перех* to confirm; (*фактами, цифрами*) to back up
▶ **подтверди́ться** (*impf* **подтвержда́ться**) *сов возв* to be confirmed.
подтвержде́ни|е (**-я**) *ср* confirmation.
подтвержу́(сь) *сов см* **подтверди́ть(ся)**.
подтёк (**-а**) *м* bruise.
подте́кст (**-а**) *м* hidden meaning.
подтер|е́ть (**-отру́, -отрёшь**; *impf* **подтира́ть**) *сов перех* to mop up.
подтолкн|у́ть (**-у́, -ёшь**; *impf* **подта́лкивать**) *сов перех* to nudge; (*перен*) to urge on.
подт|очи́ть (**-очу́, -о́чишь**; *impf* **подта́чивать**) *сов перех* to sharpen (a little); (*перен: силы*) to weaken; (: *здоровье*) to destroy.
подтя́гива|ть(ся) (**-ю(сь)**) *несов от* **подтяну́ть(ся)**.
подтя́ж|ка (**-ки**; *gen pl* **-ек**) *ж* (*обычно мн*) braces *мн* (*BRIT*), suspenders *мн* (*US*).
подтя́нут|ый (**-, -а, -о**) *прил* smart.
подтян|у́ть (**-яну́, -я́нешь**; *impf* **подтя́гивать**) *сов перех* (*тяжёлый предмет*) to haul up; (*гайку, болт*) to tighten; (*войска*) to bring up
▶ **подтяну́ться** (*impf* **подтя́гиваться**) *сов возв* (*на брусьях, на перекладине*) to pull o.s. up; (*войска*) to move up; (*перен*) to get one's act together.
поду́ма|ть (**-ю**) *сов от* **ду́мать** ♦ *неперех*: **~** (*о* +*prp*) to think (about); **~** (*perf*) **над** +*instr или* **о** +*prp* to think about; **~, что...** to think that ...; **он**

и не ~л извини́ться he didn't even think of apologizing *или* to apologize; **~ешь! купи́л но́вую маши́ну** so what if he's bought a new car!; **~ то́лько!** (*разг*) just think!; **кто бы мог ~!** who would have thought it!; **и не ~ю!** (*разг*) I won't hear of it!
▶ **поду́маться** *сов от* **ду́маться**.
поду́мыва|ть (**-ю**) *несов неперех* (*разг*): **~ о** +*prp*/+*infin* to think about/of doing.
подурне́|ть (**-ю**) *сов от* **дурне́ть**.
поду́|ть (**-ю**) *сов неперех* to blow; (*ветер*) to begin to blow.
подуч|и́ть (**-учу́, -у́чишь**; *impf* **поду́чивать**) *сов перех* (*разг: выучить*) to learn; (*научить*) to teach.
поду́шек *сущ см* **поду́шка**.
подуш|и́ть (**-ушу́, -у́шишь**) *сов перех* to spray lightly with perfume.
поду́ш|ка (**-ки**; *gen pl* **-ек**) *ж* (*для сидения*) cushion; (*под голову*) pillow.
поду́шный *прил*: **~ нало́г** poll tax.
подхали́м (**-а**) *м* toady.
подхали́м|ка (**-ки**; *gen pl* **-ок**) *ж см* **подхали́м**.
подхва́т (**-а**) *м*: **быть на ~е** (*разг*) to be at hand.
подхв|ати́ть (**-ачу́, -а́тишь**; *impf* **подхва́тывать**) *сов перех* (*падающее*) to catch; (*подлеж: течение, толпа*) to carry away; (*слова, идею, болезнь*) to pick up; (*песню, мелодию*) to join in.
подхлестн|у́ть (**-у́, -ёшь**; *impf* **подхлёстывать**) *сов перех* to whip on.
подхо́д (**-а**) *м* approach; **экза́мены на ~е** the exams are approaching.
подх|оди́ть (**-ожу́, -о́дишь**) *несов от* **подойти́**.
подходя́щ|ий (**-ая, -ее, -ие**) *прил* (*дом*) suitable; (*момент, слова*) appropriate.
подхожу́ *несов см* **подходи́ть**.
подцеп|и́ть (**-еплю́, -е́пишь**) *сов перех* to attach; (*разг: болезнь, девушку, жениха*) to pick up.
подча́с *нареч* at times.
подчеркн|у́ть (**-у́, -ёшь**; *impf* **подчёркивать**) *сов перех* (*в тексте*) to underline; (*в речи*) to emphasize.
подчине́ни|е (**-я**) *ср* obedience.
подчинённ|ый *прил* subordinate *опред* ♦ (**-ого**; *decl like adj*) *м* subordinate.
подчин|и́ть (**-ю́, -и́шь**; *impf* **подчиня́ть**) *сов перех* (*народ, страну*) to subjugate; **подчиня́ть** (**~** *perf*) **что-н кому́-н** to place sth under the control of sb
▶ **подчини́ться** (*impf* **подчиня́ться**) *сов возв* (+*dat*) to obey.
подчи́|стить (**-щу, -стишь**; *impf* **подчища́ть**) *сов перех* (*пол итп*) to clean; (*написанное*) to erase.
подшей(те) *сов см* **подши́ть**.
подше́фный *прил*: **~ де́тский дом** children's

home under patronage.

подшива́|ть (**-ю**) *несов от* **подши́ть.**

подши́в|ка (**-ки**; *gen pl* **-ок**) *ж* (*газет, документов*) bundle.

подши́|пник (**-а**) *м* (*ТЕХ*) bearing.

под|ши́ть (**-ошью́, -ошьёшь**; *imper* **-ше́й(те)**, *impf* **подшива́ть**) *сов перех* (*рукав*) to hem; (*подол*) to take up; (*документ*) to file; (*пачку газет*) to bundle up.

подшу|ти́ть (**-учу́, -у́тишь**; *impf* **подшу́чивать**) *сов неперех*: ~ **над** +*instr* to make fun of.

подъ- *преф см* **под-.**

подъе́ду *итп сов см* **подъе́хать.**

подъе́зд (**-а**) *м* (*к городу, к дому*) approach; (*в здании*) entrance.

подъе́зжа́й(те) *сов см* **подъе́хать.**

подъезжа́|ть (**-ю**) *несов от* **подъе́хать.**

подъём (**-а**) *м* (*груза*) lifting; (*флага*) raising; (*на гору*) ascent; (*промышленный, культурный итп*) revival; (*в речи, в действиях*) enthusiasm; (*сигнал: к пробуждению*) reveille.

подъёмник (**-а**) *м* lift (*BRIT*), elevator (*US*).

подъёмн|ые (**-ых**; *decl like adj*) *мн* (*также:* ~ **де́ньги**) relocation costs *мн.*

подъёмный *прил* lifting *опред*; **подъёмный кран** crane.

подъ|е́хать (*как* **е́хать**; *см* **Table 19**; *impf* **подъезжа́ть**) *сов неперех* (*на автомобиле*) to drive up; (*на коне*) to ride up; (*разг*) to call in.

подыгра́|ть (**-ю**; *impf* **подыгрывать**) *сов неперех* +*dat*; *разг*) to accompany.

подыска́|ть (**-щу́, -щешь**; *impf* **подыскивать**) *сов перех* to find.

подыто́ж|ить (**-у, -ишь**) *сов перех* (*расходы, доходы*) to add up; (*сделанное, сказанное*) to sum up.

подыха́|ть (**-ю**) *несов неперех* (*животные*) to be dying; (*разг*): ~ **от** +*gen* (*от голода, от скуки итп*) to be dying of.

подыша́|ть (**-ышу́, -ы́шешь**) *сов неперех* to breathe.

подыщу́ *итп сов см* **подыска́ть.**

поеда́|ть (**-ю**) *несов от* **пое́сть.**

пое́дешь *итп сов см* **пое́хать.**

поеди́м *итп сов см* **пое́сть.**

поеди́н|ок (**-ка**) *м* duel.

поеди́те *сов см* **пое́сть.**

пое́ду *итп сов см* **пое́хать.**

поедя́т *сов см* **пое́сть.**

пое́ж|иться (**-усь, -ишься**; *impf* **поёживаться**) *сов возв* to shiver slightly.

по́езд (**-а**; *nom pl* **-а́**) *м* train; **ско́рый** ~ express train; ~ **да́льнего сле́дования** long-distance train; **е́хать** (*impf*) ~**ом** *или* **на** ~**е** to travel by train; **е́хать** (*impf*) **в** ~**е метро́** to travel by tube (*BRIT*) *или* subway (*US*).

пое́зд|ка (**-ки**; *gen pl* **-ок**) *ж* trip.

поезжа́й(те) *сов см* **пое́хать.**

пое́сть (*как* **есть**; *см* **Table 15**) *сов от* **есть** ◆ (*impf* **поеда́ть**) *перех*: ~ **чего́-н** to eat a little bit of sth; (*съесть всё*) to eat sth up; (*подлеж*:

моль) to eat sth away.

пое́хать (*как* **е́хать**; *см* **Table 19**) *сов неперех* (*автомобиль, поезд итп*) to set off.

пое́шь *сов см* **пое́сть.**

пожа́днича|ть (**-ю**) *сов от* **жа́дничать.**

пожале́|ть (**-ю**) *сов от* **жале́ть.**

пожа́л|овать (**-ую**) *сов от* **жа́ловать** ◆ *неперех*: ~ **к** +*dat* (*посетить*) to visit; **добро́** ~ welcome.

пожа́луй *вводн сл* (*возможно*) perhaps; (*выражает предпочтение*) likely; **он,** ~**, не придёт** he may not come; **я,** ~**, пойду́** I'd better go.

пожа́луйста *част* please; (*в ответ на благодарность*) don't mention it, you're welcome; ~**, помоги́те мне** please help me; **скажи́те** ~**!** you don't say!; **зако́нчил шко́лу и,** ~**, жени́лся** he left school and then, would you believe it, he got married.

пожа́р (**-а**) *м* fire; (+*gen*; *перен*: *войны́, револю́ции*) the inferno.

пожа́рищ|е (**-а**) *ср* site of fire.

пожа́рник (**-а**) *м* (*разг*) fireman (*мн* firemen).

пожа́рн|ый (**-ого**; *decl like adj*) *м* fireman (*мн* firemen) ◆ *прил*: ~**ая кома́нда** fire brigade (*BRIT*) *или* department (*US*); ~**ая маши́на** fire engine; **на вся́кий** ~ (**слу́чай**) (*разг*) in case of emergency.

пожа́ти|е (**-я**) *ср*: ~ (**руки́**) handshake.

пожа́|ть (**-му́, -мёшь**; *impf* **пожима́ть**) *сов перех* to squeeze; **он** ~**л мне ру́ку** he shook my hand; **пожима́ть** (~ *perf*) **плеча́ми** to shrug one's shoulders.

пожела́ни|е (**-я**) *ср* wish; **прими́те мои́ наилу́чшие** ~**я** please accept my best wishes.

пожела́|ть (**-ю**) *сов от* **жела́ть.**

пожелте́|ть (**-ю**) *сов от* **желте́ть.**

пожен|и́ть (**-ню́, -нишь**) *сов* ◆ *перех* (*разг*) to marry

▶ **пожени́ться** *сов от* **жени́ться** ◆ *возв* to marry, get married.

поже́ртвовани|е (**-я**) *ср* donation.

поже́ртв|овать (**-ую**) *несов от* **же́ртвовать.**

пожива́|ть (**-ю**) *несов неперех* (*разг*): **как ты** ~**ешь?** how are you?

пожи|ви́ться (**-лю́сь, -йшься**) *сов возв* (+*instr*; *разг*) to live off.

поживу́ *итп сов см* **пожи́ть.**

пожи́зненный *прил* lifelong, life *опред*; **пожи́зненное заключе́ние** life imprisonment.

пожило́й *прил* elderly.

пожима́|ть (**-ю**) *несов от* **пожа́ть.**

пожира́|ть (**-ю**) *несов от* **пожра́ть** ◆ *перех* (*книги*) to devour; **любопы́тство/честолю́бие** ~**ло его́** he was devoured by curiosity/ambition; ~ (*impf*) **кого́-н глаза́ми** to devour sb with one's eyes.

пожи́тк|и (**-ов**) *мн* (*разг*) belongings *мн.*

пожи́ть (**-иву́, -ивёшь**; *pt* **-и́л, -ила́, -и́ло**) *сов неперех* (*пробыть где-нибудь*) to stay for a while; ~**ивём – уви́дим** we shall see.

пожму́ *итп сов см* **пожа́ть**.

пожра́|ть (-у́, -ёшь; *impf* **пожира́ть**) *сов перех* (*подлеж: животное*) to devour; (*no impf; разг: подлеж: человек*) to gobble up.

по́з|а (-ы) *ж* posture; (*перен: поведение*) pose.

позабо́|титься (-чусь, -тишься) *сов от* **забо́титься**.

позави́д|овать (-ую) *сов от* **зави́довать**.

поза́втрака|ть (-ю) *несов от* **за́втракать**.

позавчера́ *нареч* the day before yesterday.

позади́ *нареч* (*сзади*) behind; (*в прошлом*) in the past ♦ *предл* (+*gen*) behind.

позаи́мств|овать (-ую) *сов от* **заи́мствовать**.

позапро́шл|ый *прил* before last; **~ая неде́ля** the week before last.

позаре́з *нареч* (*разг*) terribly.

поз|ва́ть (-ову́, -овёшь) *сов от* **звать**.

позволе́ни|е (-я) *ср* permission; **с Ва́шего ~я** with your permission.

позво́л|ить (-ю, -ишь; *impf* **позволя́ть**) *сов неперех* (*погода, обстоятельства*) to permit ♦ *перех*: **~ что-н кому́-н** to allow sb sth; **позволя́ть** (**~** *perf*) **кому́-н** +*infin* to allow sb to do; **~ьте!** excuse me!; **~ьте мне предста́вить моего́ колле́гу** allow me to introduce my colleague; **~ьте пройти́** excuse me please; **позволя́ть** (*impf*) **себе́ что-н** to afford sth.

позвон|и́ть (-ю́, -и́шь) *сов от* **звони́ть**.

позвоно́чник (-ка) *м* vertebra (*мн* vertebrae).

позвоно́чник (-а) *м* spine, spinal column.

поздне́е *сравн нареч от* **по́здно** ♦ *нареч* later ♦ *предл* (+*gen*) after; (**не**) **~** +*gen* (no) later than.

по́здн|ий (-яя, -ее, -ие) *прил* late; **са́мое ~ее** (*разг*) at the latest.

по́здно *нареч* late ♦ *как сказ* it's late.

поздоро́ва|ться (-юсь) *сов от* **здоро́ваться**.

поздоро́в|иться (*3sg* -ится) *сов возв*: **ему́ не ~ится** (*разг*) he's in trouble.

поздрави́тельный *прил* greetings *опред*.

поздра́в|ить (-лю, -ишь; *impf* **поздравля́ть**) *сов перех*: **~ кого́-н с** +*instr* to congratulate sb on; **поздравля́ть** (**~** *perf*) **кого́-н с днём рожде́ния** to wish sb a happy birthday.

поздравле́ни|е (-я) *ср* congratulation; (*с днём рождения*) greeting.

поздра́влю *итп сов см* **поздра́вить**.

поздравля́|ть (-ю) *несов от* **поздра́вить**.

позелене́|ть (-ю) *сов от* **зелене́ть**.

по́зже *нареч* = **поздне́е**.

пози́р|овать (-ую) *сов неперех* (+*dat*) to pose for.

позити́в (-а) *м* (*ФОТО*) positive.

позити́в|ный (-ен, -на, -но) *прил* positive.

пози́ци|я (-и) *ж* position; (*контракта, проекта*) item.

познава́тельный (-ен, -ьна, -ьно) *прил* educational.

позна|ва́ть (-ю́) *несов от* **позна́ть**

▶ **познава́ться** *несов возв* to become known.

познако́м|ить(ся) (-лю(сь), -ишь(ся)) *сов от* **знако́мить(ся)**.

позна́ни|е (-я) *ср* familiarization; (*приобретение знаний*) cognition; *см также* **позна́ния**.

позна́ни|я (-й) *мн* knowledge *ед*.

позна́|ть (-ю; *impf* **познава́ть**) *сов перех* (*любовь, бедность итп*) to experience.

позову́ *итп сов см* **позва́ть**.

позоло́т|а (-ы) *ж* gilding, gilt.

позоло́|тить (-чу, -тишь) *сов от* **золоти́ть**.

позо́р (-а) *м* disgrace; **выставля́ть (вы́ставить** *perf*) **кого́-н на ~** to bring disgrace on sb.

позо́рен *прил см* **позо́рный**.

позо́р|ить (-ю, -ишь; *perf* **опозо́рить**) *несов перех* to disgrace

▶ **позо́риться** (*perf* **опозо́риться**) *несов возв* to disgrace o.s.

позо́р|ный (-ен, -на, -но) *прил* disgraceful.

позывн|ы́е (-ы́х; *decl like adj*) *мн* call sign *ед*.

поимённый *прил*: **~ спи́сок** list of names.

пои́м|ка (-ки; *gen pl* -ок) *ж* capture.

по-ино́му *нареч* differently.

поинтерес|ова́ться (-у́юсь) *сов возв* (+*instr*) to take an interest in.

по́иск (-а) *м* (*научный, творческий итп*) quest; (*КОМП*) search; **"~ и заме́на"** "search and replace"; *см также* **по́иски**.

поиск|а́ть (-ищу́, -и́щешь) *сов перех* to have a look for.

по́иск|и (-ов) *мн*: **~** (+*gen*) search *ед* (for); **в ~ах** +*gen* in search of.

пои́стине *нареч* truly.

по|и́ть (-ю́, -ишь; *imper* **пои́(те)**, *perf* **напои́ть**) *несов перех*: **~ кого́-н чем-н** to give sb sth to drink; **его́ напои́ли во́дкой** he was plied with vodka.

поищу́ *итп сов см* **поиска́ть**.

пойду́ *итп сов см* **пойти́**.

по́йм|а (-ы) *ж* flood plain.

пойма́|ть (-ю) *сов перех* to catch.

пойму́ *итп сов см* **поня́ть**.

по́йнтер (-а) *м* pointer (*dog*).

пой|(те) *несов см* **петь**.

пойти́ (*как* **идти́**; *см* **Table 18**) *сов неперех* to set off; (*no пути рефрм*) to start off; (*о механизмах, к цели*) to start working; (*дождь, снег*) to begin to fall; (*дым, пар*) to begin to rise; (*кровь*) to start flowing; (*фильм итп*) to start showing; (*подойти*): **~** +*dat или* **к** +*dat* (*шляпа, поведение*) to suit; **~** (*perf*) **в кого́-н** (*в мать, в де́да итп*) to look like sb; **е́сли на то пошло́** if it comes to that; **так не пойдёт** that won't work.

┌─ **KEYWORD** ─────────┐

пока́ *нареч* **1** (*некоторое время*) for a while; **я пока́ подожду́** I'll wait for a while **2** (*тем временем*) in the meantime; **я ушёл, а**

она́ пока́ остава́лась в до́ме I left, and in the meantime she stayed at home
♦ *союз* **1** (*в то время как*) while; **пока́ он чита́л, я вы́шел на балко́н** while he was reading, I went out onto the balcony
2 (*до того времени как*): **пока́ не** until; **ребёнок бу́дет крича́ть, пока́ не полу́чит конфе́ту** the child will go on shouting until he gets a sweet; **пока́!** so long!; **пока́ что** for the moment.

покажу́(сь) *итп сов см* **показа́ть(ся)**.
пока́з (-а) *м* (*фильма*) showing; (*опыта*) demonstration; (*изменений, тенденций итп*) portrayal, depiction.
показа́ни|**е** (-я) *ср* (ЮР: *обычно мн*) evidence *ед*; (*на счётчике итп*) reading.
показа́телен *прил см* **показа́тельный**.
показа́тел|**ь** (-я) *м* indicator; (МАТ, ЭКОН) index (*мн* indices).
показа́тел|**ьный** (-ен, -ьна, -ьно) *прил* (*явление, пример итп*) revealing; (*no short form*): ~ьное выступле́ние гимна́стов gymnastics display; ~ **о́пыт** demonstration (*of an experiment*).
пока|**за́ть** (-жу́, -жешь; *impf* **пока́зывать**) *сов перех* to show; (*подлеж: часы, счётчик итп*) to say; (*на суде*) to testify; **пока́зывать** (~ *perf*) **что-н/кого́-н кому́-н** to show sth/sb to sb; **пока́зывать** (~ *perf*) **на что-н/кого́-н** to point to sth/sb; **пока́зывать** (~ *perf*) **приме́р** to set an example; **пока́зывать** (~ *perf*) **себя́** to prove o.s.; **он ~за́л себя́ не в лу́чшем све́те** he didn't show himself in a very good light; **я тебе́ ~жу́!** (*разг*) I'll show you!
▶ **показа́ться** *сов от* **каза́ться** ♦ (*impf* **пока́зываться**) *возв* to appear; ~**ся** (*perf*) **врачу́** to see a doctor.
показно́й *прил* (*энтузиазм, радость итп*) affected; (*роскошь*) ostentatious.
пока́зыва|**ть(ся)** (-ю(сь)) *несов от* **показа́ть(ся)**.
пока́ка|**ть** (-ю) *сов от* **ка́кать**.
покале́ч|**ить** (-у, -ишь) *сов от* **кале́чить**.
пока́лыва|**ть** (*3sg* -ет) *несов неперех*: **у меня́** ~**ет се́рдце/желу́док** I keep getting stabbing pains in my chest/stomach.
пока́мест *нареч* (*разг*) in the meantime ♦ *союз* (*разг*) while.
покапри́знича|**ть** (-ю) *сов от* **капри́зничать**.
покара́|**ть** (-ю) *сов от* **кара́ть**.
поката́|**ть** (-ю) *сов перех*: ~ **кого́-н на маши́не** to take sb for a drive; ~ (*perf*) **ребёнка на саня́х** to take a child sledging
▶ **поката́ться** *сов возв* to go for a ride.
пока|**ти́ть** (-чу́, -тишь) *сов перех* (*что-н кру́глое*) to roll; (*что-н на колёсах*) to wheel ♦ *неперех* (*машина*) to shoot off
▶ **покати́ться** *сов возв* to start rolling, start to roll; ~**ся** (*perf*) **со́ смеху** (*разг*) to burst out laughing.

пока́тыва|**ться** (-юсь) *несов возв*: ~ **со́ смеху** (*разг*) to roll about with laughter *или* laughing.
пока́тый (-, -а, -о) *прил* sloping.
покача́|**ть** (-ю) *сов перех* to rock; ~ (*perf*) **голово́й** to shake one's head
▶ **покача́ться** *сов возв* (*на качелях*) to swing.
пока́чива|**ться** (-юсь) *несов возв* to rock.
покачу́(сь) *сов см* **покати́ть(ся)**.
покая́ни|**е** (-я) *ср* repentance.
пока́|**яться** (-юсь) *несов от* **ка́яться**.
по́кер (-а) *м* poker (CARDS).
поки́|**нуть** (-у, -ешь; *impf* **покида́ть**) *сов перех* to abandon.
поклада́|**ть** (-ю) *несов перех*: **не** ~**я рук** tirelessly.
покла́дистый (-, -а, -о) *прил* flexible.
покло́н (-а) *м* (*жест*) bow; (*приветствие*) greeting; **посыла́ть (посла́ть** *perf*) *или* **передава́ть (переда́ть** *perf*) **кому́-н** ~ to send sb one's regards.
покл|**они́ться** (-оню́сь, -о́нишься) *сов от* **кла́няться** ♦ (*impf* **поклоня́ться**) *возв*: ~ (+*dat*) (*святым места́м*) to pay homage (at).
покло́нник (-а) *м* admirer.
поклоня́|**ться** (-юсь) *несов от* **поклони́ться** ♦ *возв* (+*dat*) to worship.
покля́|**сться** (-ну́сь, -нёшься) *сов от* **кля́сться**.
поко́|**иться** (-юсь, -ишься) *несов возв* (*быть похороненным*) to be at rest; (*основываться*): ~ **на** +*prp* to rest on.
поко́|**й** (-я) *м* peace; **оставля́ть (оста́вить** *perf*) **кого́-н в** ~**е** to leave sb in peace; **он не даёт мне** ~**я** he doesn't give me any peace.
поко́йн|**ая** (-ой; *decl like adj*) *ж см* **поко́йный**.
поко́йник (-а) *м* the deceased.
поко́йниц|**а** (-ы) *ж см* **поко́йник**.
поко́йн|**ый** *прил* the late ♦ (-ого; *decl like adj*) *м* the deceased.
поколеба́|**ть** (-ю) *сов от* **колеба́ть**
▶ **поколеба́ться** *сов от* **колеба́ться** ♦ *возв* to waver.
поколе́ни|**е** (-я) *ср* generation.
поко́нч|**ить** (-у, -ишь) *сов неперех*: ~ **с** +*instr* (*с дела́ми, с ремо́нтом итп*) to be finished with; (*с бе́дностью, с пробле́мой итп*) to put an end to; ~ (*perf*) **с собо́й** to kill o.s., commit suicide.
покорёж|**ить** (-у, -ишь) *несов от* **корёжить**.
поко́рен *прил см* **поко́рный**.
покори́тел|**ь** (-я) *м* conqueror.
покор|**и́ть** (-ю́, -и́шь; *impf* **покоря́ть**) *сов перех* (*страну, народ*) to conquer; (*подлеж: женщина, стихи*) to conquer the heart of; ~ (*perf*) **чьё-н се́рдце** to win sb's heart
▶ **покори́ться** (*impf* **покоря́ться**) *сов возв*: ~**ся** (+*dat*) to submit (to).
покорм|**и́ть** (-ормлю́, -о́рмишь) *сов от* **корми́ть**.
поко́р|**ный** (-ен, -на, -но) *прил* submissive.
покороб|**ить(ся)** (-лю(сь), -ишь(ся)) *сов от* **коро́бить(ся)**.

покоря́|ть(ся) (-ю(сь)) *несов от* **покори́ть(ся)**.

поко́с (-а) *м* (*трав*) mowing; (*время покоса*) haymaking.

поко|си́ть(ся) (-шу́(сь), -сишь(ся))) *сов от* **коси́ть(ся)**.

покра́|сить(ся) (-шу(сь), -сишь(ся))) *сов от* **кра́сить(ся)**.

покрасне́|ть (-ю) *сов от* **красне́ть**.

покрас|ова́ться (-у́юсь) *сов от* **красова́ться**.

покра́шу(сь) *сов см* **покра́сить(ся)**.

покри|ви́ть(ся) (-лю́(сь), -йшь(ся))) *несов от* **криви́ть(ся)**.

покри́кива|ть (-ю) *несов неперех* (*разг*): ~ **(на** +*acc*) to yell (at).

покро́в (-а) *м* (*верхний слой*) layer; (*рел*) shroud; **снéжный** ~ a blanket of snow; **под** ~**ом но́чи** under cover of darkness.

покрови́тель (-я) *м* protector.

покрови́тельни|ца (-ы) *ж см* **покрови́тель**.

покрови́тельствен|ный (-ен, -на, -но) *прил* patronizing.

покрови́тельств|о (-а) *ср* protection.

покро́|й (-я) *ср* cut (*of clothing*).

покро́ю(сь) *итп сов см* **покры́ть(ся)**.

покрупне́|ть (-ю) *сов от* **крупне́ть**.

покрыва́л|о (-а) *ср* bedspread.

покрыва́|ть(ся) (-ю(сь)) *несов от* **покры́ть(ся)**.

покры́ти|е (-я) *ср* covering; ~ **дивиде́нда** (*комм*) dividend cover.

покры́|ть (-о́ю, -о́ешь) *сов от* **крыть** ♦ (*impf* **покрыва́ть**) *перех* (*звуки, шум*) to cover up; (*расходы, убытки, расстояние*) to cover; **покры́ть** (~ *perf*) (**что-н/кого́-н чем-н**) to cover (sth/sb with sth)

► **покры́ться** (*impf* **покрыва́ться**) *сов возв* (+*instr*; *одеялом*) to cover o.s. with; (*румянцем, снéгом итп*) to be covered in.

покры́ш|ка (-ки; *gen pl* -ек) *ж* (*АВТ*) tyre (*BRIT*), tire (*US*).

покупа́тель (-я) *м* (*в магазине*) customer; (*товара, дома итп*) buyer, purchaser.

покупа́тельни|ца (-ы) *ж см* **покупа́тель**.

покупа́тельный *прил*: ~**ая спосо́бность** purchasing power.

покупа́тельск|ий (-ая, -ое, -ие) *прил* (*спрос, интересы*) consumer *опред*.

покупа́|ть (-ю) *несов от* **купи́ть**.

поку́п|ка (-ки; *gen pl* -ок) *ж* purchase; **де́лать** (**сде́лать** *perf*) ~**ки** to go shopping.

покупно́й *прил* (*торт*) bought.

поку́почн|ый *прил*: ~**ая цена́** purchase price.

поку́ша|ть (-ю) *сов от* **ку́шать** ♦ (*не)перех*: ~ **чего́-н** to have sth to eat.

покуша́|ться (-юсь) *несов возв*: ~ **на** +*acc* to attempt to take.

покуше́ни|е (-я) *ср*: ~ **(на** +*acc*) (*на свободу, на права*) infringement (of); (*на жизнь*) attempt

(on); **соверша́ть** (**соверши́ть** *perf*) ~ **на кого́-н** to make an attempt on sb's life.

пол (-а; *loc sg* -ý, *nom pl* -ы́) *м* floor; (*nom pl* -ы́, *gen pl* -о́в, *dat pl* -а́м) sex, gender.

пол|а́ (-ы́; *nom pl* -ы) *ж* (*обычно мн: пальто, пиджака итп*) side; **продава́ть** (**прода́ть** *perf*) **из-под** ~**ы́** to sell under the counter.

полага́|ть (-ю) *несов неперех* (*думать*) to suppose; **на́до** ~ supposedly; ~ (*impf*) **нача́ло чему́-н** to make a start on sth; ~ (*impf*) **коне́ц чему́-н** to put an end to sth.

полага́|ться (-юсь) *несов возв* на **положи́ться** ♦ *возв* (*быть до́лжным*) to be expected; ~**ется приходи́ть во́ время** one is expected to be punctual.

пола́|дить (-жу, -дишь) *сов от* **ла́дить**.

пола́ком|иться (-люсь, -ишься) *сов от* **ла́комиться**.

полбеды́ *ж нескл*: **э́то ещё** ~ (*разг*) it could be worse.

пол|ве́ка (-увека) *м* half a century.

пол|го́да (-угода) *м* half a year.

по́лдень (**полу́дня** *или* **по́лдня**) *м* midday, noon; **2 часа́ по́сле полу́дня** 2 p.m.

по́лдник (-а) *м* (afternoon) tea.

по́лдня *сущ см* **по́лдень**.

полдоро́г|и (-и) *ж*: **на** ~**е** halfway; **остана́вливаться** (**останови́ться** *perf*) **на** ~**е** (*также перен*) to stop halfway.

по́л|е (-я; *nom pl* -я́, *gen pl* -е́й) *ср* field; ~ **де́ятельности** sphere of activity; ~ **зре́ния** field of vision; *см также* **поля́**.

полево́дств|о (-а) *ср* crop cultivation.

полево́й *прил* field *опред*; ~**ые рабо́ты** work in the fields; **полево́й госпита́ль** field hospital.

полёг *итп сов см* **поле́чь**.

полежа́|ть (-ý, -йшь) *сов неперех* (*человек*) to have a lie down; (*книга на полке, продукты в ящике итп*) to lie.

полеза́й(те) *сов см* **лезть**.

поле́з|ный (-ен, -на, -но) *прил* useful; (*пища*) healthy; **чем могу́ быть** ~**ен?** how can I be of help?; ~**ная нагру́зка** (*комм*) payload; **поле́зные ископа́емые** minerals; **поле́зная жила́я пло́щадь** living space.

поле́з|ть (-у, -ешь) *сов неперех* (*начать лезть*) to start climbing, start to climb; (*в дра́ку, в спор*) to get involved.

поле́ми|ка (-и) *ж* polemic.

полеми́ческ|ий (-ая, -ое, -ие) *прил* polemical.

полен|и́ться (-ю́сь, -ишься) *сов от* **лени́ться**.

поле́н|о (-а; *nom pl* -ья, *gen pl* -ьев) *ср* log.

полёт (-а) *м* flight; ~ **фанта́зии** *или* **мы́сли** flight of fancy.

поле|те́ть (-чу́, -ти́шь) *сов от* **лете́ть** ♦ *неперех* (*птица, самолёт*) to fly off; (*годы, дни*) to start to fly by; (*слу́хи, но́вости*) to start to fly.

поле́|чь (-я́гу, -я́жешь *итп*, -я́гут; *pt* -ёг, -егла́, -егло́) *сов неперех* (*травы*) to be flattened; (*перен: погибнуть*) to fall, perish.

по́лза|ть (-ю) *несов неперех* to crawl; ~ (*impf*) в нога́х у кого́-н to come crawling to sb.

ползко́м *нареч:* **продвига́ться** ~ to crawl along on one's stomach.

ползз|ти́ (-у́, -ёшь; *pt* -, -ла́, -ло́) *несов неперех* to crawl; (*разг: медленно двигаться*) to crawl (along).

ползунк|и́ (-о́в) *мн* (*одежда*) rompers *мн*.

ползу́чий (-ая, -ее, -ие) *прил* (*животные*) crawling *опред*; (*растения*) creeping *опред*.

полива́ть (-ю) *несов от* **поли́ть**.

поливитами́н|ы (-ов) *мн* multivitamins *мн*.

полига́ми|я (-и) *ж* polygamy.

полиго́н (-а) *м* (*для учений*) shooting range; (*для испытания оружия*) test(ing) site.

полиграфи́ст (-а) *м* printer.

полигра́фи|я (-и) *ж* printing.

поликли́ник|а (-и) *ж* clinic.

полиня́ть (*3sg* -ет, *3pl* -ют) *сов от* **линя́ть**.

полиомиели́т (-а) *м* polio(myelitis).

полир|ова́ть (-у́ю; *perf* **отполирова́ть**) *несов перех* to polish.

по́лис (-а) *м:* **страхово́й** ~ insurance policy.

полисеми́|я (-и) *ж* polysemy.

политбюро́ *ср нескл* the Politburo.

полите́хникум (-а) *м* technical college.

политехни́ческ|ий (-ая, -ое, -ие) *прил:* ~ **институ́т** polytechnic.

поли́тик (-а) *м* politician.

поли́тик|а (-и) *ж* (*курс*) policy; (*события, наука*) politics.

политика́н (-а) *м* (*пренебр*) politico.

полити́ческ|ий (-ая, -ое, -ие) *прил* political; **полити́ческая эконо́мия** political economy; **полити́ческий обозрева́тель** political observer.

полито́лог (-а) *м* political scientist.

поли́|ть (-ью, -ьёшь; *pt* -йл, -ила́, -йло, *impf* **полива́ть**) *сов неперех* (*дождь*) to start pouring, start to pour ♦ *перех:* ~ **что-н чем-н** to pour sth on sth; **полива́ть** (~ *perf*) **цветы́** to water the flowers

► **поли́ться** *сов возв* to pour out.

политэконо́ми|я (-и) *ж сокр* (= **полити́ческая эконо́мия**) Pol. Econ. (= *political economy*).

полице́йск|ий (-ая, -ое, -ие) *прил* police *опред* ♦ (-ого; *decl like adj*) *м* policeman (*мн* policemen); **полице́йский уча́сток** police station.

поли́ци|я (-и) *ж* the police; **вызыва́ть** (**вы́звать** (*perf*))~**ю** to call the police.

поли́чн|ое (-ого; *decl like adj*) *ср:* **пойма́ть кого́-н с**~**ым** to catch sb at the scene of a crime; (*перен*) to catch sb red-handed *или* in the act.

полиэтиле́н (-а) *м* polythene.

полиэтиле́новый *прил* polythene *опред*.

полк (-а́; *loc sg* -у́) *м* regiment.

по́лк|а (-ки; *gen pl* -ок) *ж* shelf; (*в поезде: для*

багажа) luggage rack; (: *для лежания*) berth.

полко́вник (-а) *м* colonel.

полково́д|ец (-ца) *м* commander.

пол-ли́тра (**полули́тра**) *м* half a litre (*BRIT*) *или* liter (*US*).

полне́|ть (-ю; *perf* **пополне́ть**) *несов неперех* to put on weight.

по́лно *как сказ* that's enough; ~ **серди́ться/ расстра́иваться** stop getting so angry/upset.

полно́ *как сказ* (+*gen*; *разг*): **в до́ме** ~ **книг** the house is stacked full of books; **наро́ду** ~ there are a lot of people.

полнове́с|ный (-ен, -на, -но) *прил* (*аргумент, статья*) weighty; (*описание*) full-bodied.

полновла́ст|ный (-ен, -на, -но) *прил* fully empowered.

полново́д|ный (-ен, -на, -но) *прил* deep.

полнокро́в|ный (-ен, -на, -но) *прил* (*жизнь*) full-blooded.

полнолу́ни|е (-я) *ср* full moon.

полнометра́жный *прил:* ~ **фильм** full-length film.

полномо́чен *прил см* **полномо́чный**.

полномо́чи|е (-я) *ср* authority; (*обычно мн: право*) power; **облека́ть** (**обле́чь** (*perf*)) **кого́-н** ~**ями** +*infin* to authorize sb to do; **слага́ть** (**сложи́ть** (*perf*)) **с себя́** ~**я** to relinquish one's authority; **э́то не вхо́дит в мой** ~**я** it is not within my jurisdiction.

полномо́ч|ный (-ен, -на, -но) *прил* fully authorized.

полнопра́в|ный (-ен, -на, -но) *прил* (*гражданин*) fully-fledged; (*наследник*) rightful; **он** ~ **владе́лец** he has full ownership rights.

полностью *нареч* fully, completely.

полнот|а́ (-ы́) *ж* (*целостность*) completeness; (*тучность*) stoutness; **облада́ть** (*impf*) **всей** ~**ой вла́сти/прав** to enjoy full power/rights; **опи́сывать** (**описа́ть** *perf*) **что-н во всей** ~**е́** to describe sth in its entirety; **от** ~**ы́ чувств** *или* **души́** overcome by emotion.

полноце́н|ный (-ен, -на, -но) *прил* (*отдых, пища*) proper; (*работа, исследование*) valuable; (*деньги, валюта*) valued.

по́л|ночь (-у́ночи) *ж* midnight.

по́л|ный (-он, -на́, -но́ *или* -но) *прил* full; (*no short form: победа, власть, счастье итп*) complete, total; (*толстый*) stout; ~ +*gen или* +*instr* full of; (*тревоги, любви итп*) filled with; **ведро́,** ~**ное воды́** a bucket, full of water; **ко́мната была́ полна́ людьми́** the room was full of people; **она́ была́ полна́ трево́ги** she was filled with anxiety; ~**ным хо́дом** at full speed; **в** ~**ную си́лу** at full strength; **по́лным-полно́** (+*gen*) (*разг*) loads and loads (of); **по́лное собра́ние сочине́ний** complete works.

по́ло *ср нескл:* (**во́дное**) ~ (water) polo.

полови́к (-а́) *м* mat.

полови́н|а (-ы) *ж* half; **на** ~**е доро́ги** halfway; **сейча́с** ~ **пе́рвого/второ́го** it's (now) half past twelve/one; **приходи́те в** ~**е двена́дцатого** come at half past eleven; **встре́ча назна́чена на** ~**у деся́того** the meeting has been set for half past nine.

полови́нчат|ый (-, -а, -о) *прил* (*меры, решение*) half-baked.

поло́вник (-а) *м* ladle.

полово́дь|е (-я) *ср* high water.

полово́й *прил* (*тряпка, мастика*) floor *опред*; (*БИО*) sexual; **полова́я жизнь** sex life; **полова́я зре́лость** puberty; **полово́й о́рган** reproductive organ; **половы́е о́рганы** genitals.

поло́г|ий (-ая, -ое, -ие; -, -а, -о) *прил* (*склон*) gentle; (*гора, берег*) gently sloping.

положе́ни|е (-я) *ср* situation; (*географическое*) location, position; (*тела, головы итп*) position; (*социальное, семейное итп*) status; (*правила*) regulations *мн*; (*обычно мн: тезис*) point; **быть** (*impf*) **на высоте́** ~**я** to be on top of the situation; **входи́ть** (**войти́** *perf*) **в чьё-н** ~ to put o.s. in sb's position; **выходи́ть** (**вы́йти** *perf*) **из тру́дного/неприя́тного** ~**я** to get o.s. out of a difficult/unpleasant situation; **она́ в** ~**и** (*разг*) she's expecting; **положе́ние дел** the state of affairs.

поло́женный *прил* due.

положи́тель|ный (-ен, -ьна, -ьно) *прил* positive.

пол|ожи́ть (-ожу́, -о́жишь) *сов от* **класть** ♦ (*не*)*перех:* ~**о́жим, ты прав/я́ так** let us assume that you're right/this is the case; **положи́ть ру́ку на́ сердце** (*перен*) with hand on heart

▶ **положи́ться** (*impf* **полага́ться**) *сов возв:* ~**ся на** +*acc* to count on.

по́л|оз (-оза; *nom pl* -о́зья) *м* (*обычно мн*) runner (*on sledge*).

по́лок *сущ см* **по́лка**.

полома́ть(ся) (-ю(сь)) *сов от* **лома́ть(ся)**.

поло́м|ка (-ки; *gen pl* -ок) *ж* (*действие*) breakdown; (*поврежденное место*) damage.

по́лон *прил см* **по́лный**.

полос|а́ (-ы́; *nom pl* **по́лосы**, *gen pl* **поло́с**, *dat pl* **по́лосам**) *ж* (*ткани, металла итп*) strip; (*на ткани, на рисунке итп*) stripe; (*тумана, леса итп*) belt; (*неудач, плохой погоды*) spell; (*в газете*) column.

полоса́т|ый (-, -а, -о) *прил* striped, stripy.

поло́с|ка (-ки; *gen pl* -ок) *ж* (*ткани, бумаги, металла*) (thin) strip; (*на одежде, на ткани*) (thin) stripe; **в** ~**ку** striped.

пол|оска́ть (-ощу́, -о́щешь; *perf* **прополоска́ть**) *несов перех* (*бельё, посуду*) to rinse; (*рот*) to rinse out; ~ (**прополоска́ть** *perf*) **го́рло** to gargle.

поло́сок *сущ см* **поло́ска**.

по́лост|ь (-и; *gen pl* -е́й) *ж* (*АНАТ*) cavity.

поло́тен *сущ см* **полотно́**.

полоте́н|це (-ца; *gen pl* -ец) *ср* towel.

поло́тнищ|е (-а) *ср:* ~ **фла́га** flag.

пол|отно́ (-отна́; *nom pl* -о́тна, *gen pl* -о́тен) *ср* (*ткань*) sheet; (*картина*) canvas; **бле́дный как** ~ white as a sheet.

пол|о́ть (-ю, -ешь; *perf* **прополо́ть**) *несов перех* to weed.

полоу́мный *прил* (*разг: идея, речь*) crackpot *опред*.

полощу́ *итп несов см* **полоска́ть**.

полпре́д (-а) *м* (= **полномо́чный представи́тель**) plenipotentiary.

полпути́ *м нескл* half (*of journey*); **на** ~ halfway; (*перен: остановиться, бросить дело итп*) halfway through; **верну́ться** (*perf*) **с** ~ to turn back halfway.

полсло́ва (- *или* **полусло́ва**) *ср* half of the word; **мо́жно Вас на** ~? could I have a quick word?; **прерыва́ть** (**прерва́ть** *perf*) **кого́-н на пол(у)сло́ве** to cut sb short; **понима́ть** (**поня́ть** *perf*) **с пол(у)сло́ва** to understand in an instant.

полти́нник (-а) *м* (*сумма*) 50 kopecks; (*монета*) 50-kopeck piece.

пол|тора́ (-у́тора; *f* **полторы́**) *м/ср чис* one and a half; **ей** ~ **го́да** she is one and a half; **ей о́коло** ~**у́тора лет** she is about one and a half; **кни́га сто́ит** ~ **рубля́/полторы́ ма́рки** the book costs one and a half roubles/one and a half marks.

пол|тора́ста (-у́тораста) *чис* one hundred and fifty.

полуботи́н|ок (-ка) *м* (*обычно мн*) ankle *или* desert boot.

полуве́ка *сущ см* **полве́ка**.

полуго́да *сущ см* **полго́да**.

полуго́ди|е (-я) *ср* (*ПРОСВЕЩ*) semester; (*ЭКОН*) half (*of the year*).

полугоди́чный *прил* six-month.

полугодово́й *прил* six-monthly, half-yearly.

полу́дня *сущ см* **по́лдень**.

полузащи́т|а (-ы) *ж* midfield.

полузащи́тник (-а) *м* midfielder.

полукру́г (-а) *м* semicircle.

полукру́глый *прил* semicircular.

полуме́р|а (-ы) *ж* half-measure (*fig*).

полуме́сяц (-а) *м* half-moon.

полумра́к (-а) *м* semidarkness.

полу́ночи *сущ см* **по́лночи**.

полуо́стров (-а) *м* peninsular.

полупальто́ *ср нескл* jacket, short coat.

полупроводни́к (-а́) *м* (*ЭЛЕК*) semiconductor.

полусапо́ж|ек (-ка; *gen pl* -ек) *м* (*обычно мн*) half-boot.

полусло́ва *сущ см* **полсло́ва**.

полуто́н (-а) *м* (*МУЗ*) semitone, half step (*US*).

полу́тора *чис см* **полтора́**.

полуфабрика́т (-а) *м* (*КУЛИН*) *any products such as frozen foods and cake mixes which require partial preparation*; (*ТЕХ*) semifinished article.

The spelling rules for Russian are shown on page xvii.

полуфина́л (-а) *м* semifinal.
получа́са *сущ см* полчаса́.
получа́тел|ь (-я) *м* recipient.
получа́ть(ся) (-ю(сь)) *несов от* получи́ть(ся).
получек *сущ см* получка.
получе́ни|е (-я) *ср* receipt; (*урожая, результата*) obtaining.
полу|чи́ть (-чу́, -́чишь; *impf* получа́ть) *сов перех* to receive, get; (*урожай, результат, насморк, удовольствие*) to get; (*известность, распространение, применение итп*) to gain ♦ *неперех* (*разг: быть наказанным*) to get it in the neck
▶ **получи́ться** (*impf* получа́ться) *сов возв* to turn out; (*удаться*) to work; (*фотография*) to come out; **из него́ ~учится хоро́ший учи́тель** he'll make a good teacher; **пиро́г хорошо́ ~учи́лся** the pie turned out well; **у меня́ э́то не ~уча́ется** I can't do it; **из э́того ничего́ не ~учится** it won't come to anything.
полу́ч|ка (-ки; *gen pl* -ек) *ж* (*разг*) pay.
полуша́ри|е (-я) *ср* hemisphere.
полушу́б|ок (-ка) *м* (*из овчины*) sheepskin jacket; (*из меха*) short fur coat.
полцены́ *ж нескл* (*разг*): **за ~** for next to nothing.
пол|часа́ (-уча́са) *м* half an hour; **ка́ждые ~** every half hour; **прошло́ или прошли́ ~** half an hour went by.
по́лчищ|е (-а) *ср* (*обычно мн: врагов*) horde; (: *насекомых, крыс*) swarm.
по́л|ый (-, -а, -о) *прил* hollow.
полы́н|ь (-и) *ж* wormwood.
полыха́|ть (-ю) *несов неперех* to blaze.
полыс́е́|ть (-ю) *сов от* лысе́ть.
по́льз|а (-ы) *ж* benefit; **в ~у** +*gen* in favour (*BRIT*) *или* favor (*US*) of; **идти́ (пойти́** *perf*) **на ~у кому́-н** to be of benefit to sb.
по́льзовани|е (-я) *ср*: **~** (+*instr*) use (of).
по́льзовател|ь (-я) *м* (*также КОМП*) user.
по́льз|оваться (-уюсь; *perf* воспо́льзоваться) *несов возв* (+*instr*) to use; (*no perf; авторите́том, успе́хом итп*) to enjoy.
по́ль|ка (-ьки; *gen pl* -ек) *ж см* поля́к; (*танец*) polka.
по́льск|ий (-ая, -ое, -ие) *прил* Polish; **~ язы́к** Polish.
польсти́ть (-щу́, -сти́шь) *сов от* льсти́ть.
По́льш|а (-и) *ж* Poland.
польщён|ный (-, -а́, -о́) *прил*: **~** (+*instr*) flattered (by).
польщу́ *сов см* польсти́ть.
полью́(сь) *итп сов см* поли́ть(ся).
полюб|и́ть (-ю́блю́, -ю́бишь) *сов перех* (*человека*) to come to love; **~** (*perf*) **что-н** /+*infin* to develop a love for sth/doing.
полюб|ова́ться (-у́юсь) *сов от* любова́ться ♦ *возв* (*разг*): **~у́йтесь на него́/э́то!** take a look at him/that!
по́люс (-а; *nom pl* -а́) *м* (*ГЕО, ЭЛЕК*) pole.
пол|я́ (-е́й) *мн* (*шляпы*) brim *ед*; (*на странице*)

margin *ед*.
поля́гу *итп сов см* поле́чь.
поля́к (-а) *м* Pole.
поля́н|а (-ы) *ж* glade.
поля́рный *прил* (*ГЕО*) polar *опред*; (*интересы, точки зрения итп*) diametrically opposed; **поля́рная звезда́** the Pole Star; **поля́рная ночь** Arctic night; **поля́рный день** Arctic day.
пома́д|а (-ы) *ж* (*также:* **губна́я ~**) lipstick.
пома́|зать (-жу, -жешь) *сов от* ма́зать.
помале́ньку *нареч* (*разг*) bit by bit; **живём ~** we're getting by.
пома́лкива|ть (-ю) *несов неперех* (*разг*) to keep quiet.
пом|ани́ть (-аню́, -а́нишь) *несов от* мани́ть.
пома́р|ка (-ки; *gen pl* -ок) *ж* crossing out (*мн* crossings out).
пома́сл|ить (-ю, -ишь) *сов от* ма́слить.
помаха́|ть (-ашу́, -а́шешь) *сов неперех* (+*instr*) to wave.
поме́дл|ить (-ю, -ишь) *сов неперех*: **~ с** +*instr/* +*infin* to linger over sth/over doing.
помелю́ *итп сов см* помоло́ть.
поменя́ть(ся) (-ю(сь)) *сов от* меня́ть(ся).
помере́|щиться (*3sg* -ится, *3pl* -атся) *сов от* мере́щиться.
помер|ить(ся) (-ю(сь), -ишь(ся)) *сов от* ме́рить(ся).
поме́ркн|уть (-у, -ешь) *сов от* ме́ркнуть.
помертве́|ть (-ю) *сов от* мертве́ть.
пом|ести́ть (-ещу́, -ести́шь; *impf* помеща́ть) *сов перех* to put; (*поставить*) to place, put; (*поселить*) to put up; (*устроить*) to settle
▶ **помести́ться** (*impf* помеща́ться) *сов возв* (*уместиться*) to fit.
поме́сть|е (-ья; *gen pl* -ий) *ср* estate.
помёт (-а) *м* dung.
помёт|а (-ы) *ж* (*в словаре*) explanatory note.
поме́|тить (-чу, -тишь) *сов от* ме́тить ♦ (*impf* помеча́ть) *перех* to note.
поме́т|ка (-ки; *gen pl* -ок) *ж* note.
поме́х|а (-и) *ж* hindrance; (*связь: обычно мн*) interference *ед*.
помеча́|ть (-ю) *несов от* поме́тить.
помечу́ *сов см* поме́тить.
поме́шан|ный (-, -а, -о) *прил* mad; (*разг*): **~ на** +*prp* (*перен*) crazy about.
помеша́тельств|о (-а) *ср* madness.
помеша́|ть (-ю) *сов от* меша́ть
▶ **помеша́ться** *сов возв* to go mad; (*разг*): **~ся на** +*prp* to become crazy about.
помеща́|ть (-ю) *несов от* помести́ть
▶ **помеща́ться** *несов от* помести́ться ♦ *возв* (*находиться*) to be situated.
помеще́ни|е (-я) *ср* room; (*под офис*) premises *мн*; **жило́е ~** living space.
поме́щик (-а) *м* landowner.
поме́щиц|а (-ы) *ж см* поме́щик.
помещу́(сь) *сов см* помести́ть(ся).
помидо́р (-а) *м* tomato (*мн* tomatoes).
поми́лование (-я) *ср* (*преступника*) pardon.

поми́л|овать (-ую) *сов от* **ми́ловать** ♦ *неперех:* ~**уйте!** (*разг*) you can't be serious!

поми́мо *предл* (+*gen*) besides; (*без участия*) bypassing; ~ **де́нег нам нужна́ маши́на** besides money we need a car; ~ **того́/всего́ про́чего** apart from that/everything else.

поми́н (-а) *м*: **э́того и в** ~**е нет** it's nowhere to be found; **его́ у нас и в** ~**е не́ было** we haven't seen hide nor hair of him; **лёгок на** ~**е** (*разг*) speak of the devil.

помина́льный *прил* (*РЕЛ*) funeral *опред*.

помина́|ть (-ю) *несов от* **помяну́ть** ♦ *неперех:* ~**й как зва́ли** (*разг*) just like that.

поми́н|ки (-ок) *мн* wake *ед*; **справля́ть** (**спра́вить** *perf*) ~ **по кому́-н** to give a wake for sb.

помину́т|ный (-ен, -на, -но) *прил* at intervals of one minute; (*очень частый*) constant; (*оплата*) by the minute.

помири́|ть(ся) (-ю(сь), -и́шь(ся)) *сов от* **мири́ть(ся)**.

по́мн|ить (-ю, -ишь) *несов (не)перех:* ~ (**о** +*prp*/ **про** +*acc*) to remember; **я** ~**ю Ва́шу про́сьбу** *или* **о Ва́шей про́сьбе** I remember your request; **я** ~**ю, что Вы проси́ли об э́том** I remember that you asked about that

▶ **по́мниться** *несов возв* to be remembered; **мне** ~**ится на́ша встре́ча** I remember our meeting; ~**ится, мы об э́том говори́ли** I remember that we spoke about that.

помножа́|ть (-ю) *несов перех* = **мно́жить**.

помно́ж|ить (-у, -ишь) *сов от* **мно́жить**.

помну́(сь) *итп сов см* **помя́ть(ся)**.

помо́г *итп сов см* **помо́чь**.

помога́|ть (-ю) *несов от* **помо́чь**.

помогу́ *итп сов см* **помо́чь**.

помо́ек *сущ см* **помо́йка**.

по-мо́ему *нареч* my way ♦ *вводн сл* in my opinion.

помо́жешь *итп сов см* **помо́чь**.

помо́|и (-ев) *мн* dishwater; (*отходы*) slops *мн*.

помо́йка (-йки; *gen pl* -ек) *ж* (*помойная яма*) cesspit; (*для мусора*) rubbish (*BRIT*) *или* garbage (*US*) heap.

помо́л (-а) *м*: **мука́/ко́фе ме́лкого/кру́пного** ~**а** fine/coarse-ground flour/coffee.

помо́лв|ить (-лю, -ишь) *сов перех:* **они́** ~**лены** they are engaged; **она́** ~**лена с ним** she is engaged to him.

помоли́|ться (-олю́сь, -о́лишься) *сов от* **моли́ться**.

помолоде́|ть (-ю) *сов от* **молоде́ть**.

помоло́|ть (-елю́, -е́лешь) *несов от* **моло́ть**.

помолча́|ть (-у́, -и́шь) *сов неперех* to pause.

помор|и́ть (-ю́, -и́шь) *сов от* **мори́ть**.

помо́рщ|иться (-усь, -ишься) *сов возв* to screw up one's face.

помо́ст (-а) *м* (*для обозрения*) platform; (*для выступлений*) rostrum; (*для казни*) scaffold.

помота́|ть (-ю) *сов от* **мота́ть**.

помо́ч|иться (-очу́сь, -о́чишься) *сов от* **мочи́ться**.

помо́|чь (-огу́, -о́жешь *итп*, -о́гут; *pt* -о́г, -огла́, -огло́, *impf* **помога́ть**) *сов неперех* (+*dat*) to help; (*в работе*) to help, assist; (*другой стране*) to aid.

помо́щник (-а) *м* helper; (*должностное лицо*) assistant; ~ **капита́на** mate.

помо́щница (-ы) *ж* helper.

по́мощ|ь (-и) *ж* help, assistance; **с** ~**ю, при по́мощи** with; **звать** (**позва́ть** *perf*) **на** ~ to call for help; **ока́зывать** (**оказа́ть** *perf*) **кому́-н** ~ to help *или* assist sb; **проси́ть** (**попроси́ть** *perf*) **о** ~**и** to ask for help.

помо́ю(сь) *итп сов см* **помы́ть(ся)**.

помпо́н (-а) *м* pompom.

помрачне́|ть (-ю) *сов от* **мрачне́ть**.

помути́|ть(ся) (*3sg* -и́т(ся), *3pl* -я́т(ся)) *сов от* **мути́ть(ся)**.

помутне́|ть (-ю) *сов от* **мутне́ть**.

помуч|и́ть (-у, -ишь) *сов перех* to torment

▶ **помучи́ться** *сов возв* to suffer.

по́мысел (-ла) *м* intention.

помы́сл|ить (-ю, -ишь; *impf* **помышля́ть**) *сов неперех:* ~ **о чём-н** to have sth in mind.

помы́|ть(ся) (-о́ю(сь), -о́ешь(ся)) *сов от* **мы́ть(ся)**.

помышля́|ть (-ю) *несов от* **помы́слить**.

помян|у́ть (-яну́, -я́нешь; *impf* **помина́ть**) *сов перех* (*упомянуть*) to mention; (*устроить поминки*) to give a wake for; ~**яни́те моё сло́во** mark my words.

помя́тый (-, -а, -о) *прил* (*разг: одежда, внешность*) rumpled; (*бок машины*) dented.

помя́|ть(ся) (-ну́(сь), -нёшь(ся)) *сов от* **мя́ть(ся)**.

понаде́|яться (-юсь) *сов от* **наде́яться**.

пона́доб|иться (-люсь, -ишься) *сов возв* to be needed *или* required.

понаслы́шке *нареч:* **знать** ~ **о ком-н/чём-н** to hear a rumour (*BRIT*) *или* rumor (*US*) about sb/ sth.

по-настоя́щему *нареч* properly.

понача́лу *нареч* (*разг*) at first.

по-на́шему *нареч* our way ♦ *вводн сл* in our opinion.

понево́ле *нареч* against one's will.

понеде́льник (-а) *м* Monday; *см также* **вто́рник**.

понемно́гу *нареч* a little; (*постепенно*) little by little; **как пожива́ете?** – ~ how's life? – not too bad.

понес|ти́ (-у́, -ёшь; *pt* -ёс, -есла́, -есло́) *сов от* **нести́** ♦ *перех* (*начать нести*) to take

▶ **понести́сь** *сов возв* (*человек*) to tear off; (*лошадь*) to charge off; (*машина*) to speed off.

по́ни *м нескл* pony.

понижа́|ть(ся) (-ю(сь)) *несов от* **пони́зить(ся)**.

пониже́ни|е (-я) *ср* reduction; (*в должности*) demotion.

пони́|зить (-жу, -зишь; *impf* **понижа́ть**) *сов перех* to reduce; (*в должности*) to demote; (*голос*) to lower

▸ **пони́зиться** (*impf* **понижа́ться**) *сов возв* to be reduced.

по́низу *нареч* (*близко к земле*) low.

пони́кнуть (-у, -ешь) *сов от* **ни́кнуть**.

понима́ни|е (-я) *ср* (*способность ума*) understanding; (*толкование*) interpretation; **относи́ться** (**отнести́сь** *perf*) **к чему́-н с ~м** to be understanding about sth; **э́то вы́ше моего́ ~я** this is beyond me.

понима́|ть (-ю) *несов от* **поня́ть** ◆ *перех* to understand ◆ *непepex*: **~ в** +*prp* to know about; **~ете** you see; **вот э́то я ~ю!** (*разг*) that's great!

понома́р|ь (-я́) *м* (*РЕЛ*) ≈ acolyte.

поно́с (-а) *м* diarrhoea (*BRIT*), diarrhea (*US*).

поно|си́ть (-шу́, -сишь) *сов перех* to carry for a while; (*одежду*) to wear ◆ *несов перех* (*ругать*) to curse.

поно́шен|ный (-, -на, -но) *прил* (*одежда*) worn.

поношу́ (*не*)*сов см* **поноси́ть**.

понра́виться (-люсь, -ишься) *сов от* **нра́виться**.

понто́н (-а) *м* pontoon bridge.

понука́|ть (-ю) *несов перех* (*также перен*) to urge on.

пону́р|ить (-ю, -ишь) *сов перех*: **~ го́лову** to hang one's head.

пону́рый *прил* downcast.

по́нчик (-а) *м* doughnut (*BRIT*), donut (*US*).

поны́не *нареч* to this day.

поню́ха|ть (-ю) *сов от* **ню́хать**.

поня́тен *прил см* **поня́тный**.

поня́ти|е (-я) *ср* (*времени, пространства итп*) conception; (*о политике, о литературе*) idea; **~я не име́ю** (*разг*) I've no idea.

поня́тливый (-, -а, -о) *прил* quick.

поня́тно *нареч* intelligibly ◆ *как сказ*: **мне ~** I understand; **~!** I see!

поня́т|ный (-ен, -на, -но) *прил* intelligible; (*ясный*) clear; (*оправданный*) understandable.

поня́т|о́й (-о́го; *decl like adj*) *м* (*ЮР*) witness (*during official search*).

по|ня́ть (-йму́, -ймёшь; *pt* -нял, -няла́, -няло, *impf* **понима́ть**) *сов перех* to understand; **дава́ть** (**дать** *perf*) **~ кому́-н** to give sb to understand.

пообе́да|ть (-ю) *сов от* **обе́дать**.

пообеща́|ть (-ю) *сов от* **обеща́ть**.

пода́ль *нареч* a little way away ◆ *предл*: **~ от** +*gen* a little way from.

поодино́чке *нареч* one at a time.

поочерёдный *прил* (*дежурство, обслуживание*) alternating.

поощре́ни|е (-я) *ср* (*действие*) encouragement; (*то, чем поощряют*) incentive.

поощри́тельн|ый *прил*: **~ая пла́та** (*КОММ*) incentive bonus.

поощр|и́ть (-ю́, -и́шь; *impf* **поощря́ть**) *сов перех* to encourage.

поп (-а́) *м* (*разг*) priest.

по́п|а (-ы) *ж* (*разг*) bottom, bum.

попада́ни|е (-я) *ср* hit.

попада́|ть(ся) (-ю(сь)) *несов от* **попа́сть(ся)**.

попаду́(сь) *итп сов см* **попа́сть(ся)**.

попа́рно *нареч* in pairs.

попа́|сть (-ду́, -дёшь; *impf* **попада́ть**) *сов непepex*: **~ в** +*acc* (*в цель*) to hit; (*в ворота*) to end up in; (*в чужой город*) to find o.s. in; (*в беду*) to land in; **мы́ло ~ло в глаза́** the soap got in my eyes; **он ~л мячо́м в корзи́ну** he put the ball in the basket; **~** (*perf*) **в университе́т/на ку́рсы** to get into university/onto a course; **попада́ть** (**~** *perf*) **в ава́рию** to have an accident; **~** (*perf*) **в плен** to be taken prisoner; **попада́ть** (**~** *perf*) **под дождь** to be caught in the rain; **ему́ ~ло** (*разг*) he got a hiding; (**Вы**) **не туда́ ~ли** you've got the wrong number; **где ~ло** (*разг*) anywhere; **как ~ло** (*разг*) anyhow; **что ~ло** (*разг*) anything

▸ **попа́сться** (*impf* **попада́ться**) *сов возв* (*быть пойманным*) to be caught; **~ся** (*perf*) **на взя́тках/воровстве́** to be caught taking bribes/ stealing; **мне ~лась интере́сная кни́га** I came across an interesting book; **попа́сться** (**~ся** *perf*) **кому́-н на глаза́** to catch sb's eye.

попе́й(те) *сов см* **попи́ть**.

попёрек *нареч* crossways ◆ *предл* (+*gen*) across.

попеременно *нареч* in turns.

попере́чный *прил* horizontal.

поперхн|у́ться (-у́сь, -ёшься) *сов возв* to choke.

попе́рч|ить (-у, -ишь) *сов от* **перчи́ть**.

попече́ни|е (-я) *ср* (*о детях*) care; (*о делах, о доме*) charge; **оставля́ть** (**оста́вить** *perf*) **кого́-н/что-н на чьё-н ~** to leave sb/sth in sb's care.

попечи́тель (-я) *м* guardian; (*КОММ*) trustee.

попира́|ть (-ю) *несов от* **попра́ть**.

попи|са́ть (-шу́, -шешь) *сов* (*не*)*перех* to write; **ничего́ не ~шешь** (*разг*) there's nothing you can do.

поп|и́ть (-ью́, -ьёшь; *pt* -и́л, -ила́, -и́ло, *imper* -е́й(те)) *сов перех* to have a drink of.

попишу́ *итп сов см* **пописа́ть**.

по́пкорн (-а) *м* popcorn.

поплав|о́к (-ка́) *м* (*на удочке*) float.

попла|ти́ться (-чу́сь, -тишься) *сов от* **плати́ться**.

попли́н (-а) *м* poplin.

попл|ы́ть (-ву́, -вёшь; *pt* -л, -ла́, -ло) *сов непepex* (*человек, животное*) to start swimming; (*судно*) to set sail.

попола́м *нареч* in half; **~ с** +*instr* mixed with.

пополне́ни|е (-я) *ср* (*запасов*) replenishment; (*коллекции*) expansion; (*то, чем пополняется*) reinforcement.

пополне́|ть (-ю) *сов от* **полне́ть**.

попо́лн|ить (-ю, -ишь; *impf* **пополня́ть**) *сов перех*: ~ что-н +*instr* (*запасы*) to replenish sth with; (*коллекцию*) to expand sth with; (*коллектив*) to reinforce sth with; (*образование*) to supplement sth with

▶ **попо́лниться** (*impf* **пополня́ться**) *сов возв* (*запасы*) to be replenished; (*коллекция*) to be expanded.

поправи́м|ый (-, -а, -о) *прил* (*дело, ошибка*) rectifiable.

попра́в|ить (-лю, -ишь; *impf* **поправля́ть**) *сов перех* to correct; (*галстук, платье итп*) to straighten; (*причёску*) to tidy; (*здоровье, дела*) to improve

▶ **попра́виться** (*impf* **поправля́ться**) *сов возв* to improve; (*пополнеть*) to put on weight.

попра́в|ка (-ки; *gen pl* -ок) *ж* (*в решение, в закон*) amendment; **вноси́ть** (**внести́** *perf*) ~ку **в зако́н** to make an amendment to a law; **де́ло идёт на ~ку** things are looking up.

поправлю́(сь) *сов см* **попра́вить(ся)**.

поправля́|ть(ся) (-ю(сь)) *несов от* **попра́вить(ся)**.

попра́вок *сущ см* **попра́вка**.

попра́|ть (*pt* -л, -ла, -ло, *impf* **попира́ть**) *сов перех* (*права*) to disregard; (*гордость*) to offend; (*закон*) to flout.

по-пре́жнему *нареч* as before.

попрека́|ть (-ю) *несов перех* to reproach.

попрекн|у́ть (-у́, -ёшь) *сов перех* to reproach.

попривётств|овать (-ую) *сов от* **привётствовать**.

по́прищ|е (-а) *ср* (*науки итп*) field.

попро́б|овать (-ую) *сов от* **про́бовать** ◆ *неперех*: ~уйте! (*разг*) just you try!

попр|оси́ть(ся) (-ошу́(сь), -о́сишь(ся)) *сов от* **проси́ть(ся)**.

по́просту *част* simply; **он** ~ **уста́л** he's just *или* simply tired.

попрошу́(сь) *сов см* **попроси́ть(ся)**.

попроща́|ться (-юсь) *сов возв*: ~ **с** +*instr* to say goodbye to.

попуга́й (-я) *м* parrot.

популя́рен *прил см* **популя́рный**.

популяризи́р|овать (-ую) (*не*)*сов перех* to popularize.

популяриз|ова́ть (-у́ю) (*не*)*сов* = **популяризи́ровать**.

популя́рн|ость (-и) *ж* popularity.

популя́р|ный (-ен, -на, -но) *прил* popular; (*изложение*) accessible.

популя́ци|я (-и) *ж* population (*of plants or animals*).

попурри́ *ср нескл* (*муз*) medley.

попусти́тельств|овать (-ую) *несов неперех* (+*dat*) to tolerate.

по́пусту *нареч* (*разг*) in vain.

попу́тн|ый *прил* (*замечание, исправление*) accompanying; (*машина*) passing; (*ветер*) favourable (*BRIT*), favorable (*US*); (: *МОР*) fair.

попу́тчик (-а) *м* travelling (*BRIT*) *или* traveling (*US*) companion.

попыта́|ть (-ю) *сов перех*: ~ **сча́стья** to try one's luck

▶ **попыта́ться** *сов от* **пыта́ться**.

попы́т|ка (-ки; *gen pl* -ок) *ж* attempt; ~ **к бе́гству** attempted escape; **со второ́й/с тре́тьей ~ки** on *или* at the second/third attempt.

попью́ *итп см* **попи́ть**.

попя́|титься (-чусь, -тишься) *сов возв* to take a few steps backward.

попя́тн|ый *прил*: **идти́** *или* **пойти́ на** ~ *или* **на ~ую** to go back on one's word.

попя́чусь *сов см* **попя́титься**.

по́р|а (-ы) *ж* pore.

по́р|а (-ы́; *acc sg* -у, *dat sg* -е́, *nom pl* -ы) *ж* time ◆ **как сказ** it's time; **до каки́х** ~**р?** until when?; **до** ~**ры́ до вре́мени** for the time being; **до сих пор** (*раньше*) up till now; (*всё ещё*) still; **до тех пор** until then; **до тех пор, пока́** until; **на пе́рвых** ~**х** at first; **с каки́х пор?** since when?; (**мне**) ~ it's time (for me) to go; (**мне**) ~ **спать/рабо́тать** it's time (for me) to go to bed/ to work.

порабо́|тить (-щу́, -ти́шь; *impf* **порабоща́ть**) *сов перех* to enslave.

порабоще́ни|е (-я) *ср* enslavement.

порабощу́ *сов см* **порабо́тить**.

поравня́|ться (-юсь) *сов возв*: ~ **с** +*instr* (*человек*) to draw level with; (*машина*) to come alongside.

пора́д|овать(ся) (-ую(сь)) *сов от* **ра́довать(ся)**.

поража́|ть(ся) (-ю(сь)) *несов от* **порази́ть(ся)**.

пораже́ни|е (-я) *ср* (*цели*) hitting; (*МЕД: лёгких*) damage; (*в войне, в состязании итп*) defeat; **наноси́ть** (**нанести́** *perf*) **кому́-н** ~ to defeat sb; **терпе́ть** (**потерпе́ть** *perf*) ~ to be defeated.

поражу́(сь) *сов см* **порази́ть(ся)**.

порази́тель|ный (-ен, -ьна, -ьно) *прил* (*красота, талант*) striking; (*жестокость*) astonishing.

пора|зи́ть (-жу́, -зи́шь; *impf* **поража́ть**) *сов перех* (*цель*) to hit; (*подлеж: болезнь*) to affect; (*изумить*) to astonish

▶ **порази́ться** (*impf* **поража́ться**) *сов возв* to be astonished.

пора́н|ить (-ю, -ишь) *сов перех* to hurt.

пор|асти́ (*3sg* -астёт, *3pl* -асту́т, *pt* -о́с, -осла́, -осло́, *impf* **пораста́ть**) *сов неперех*: ~ +*instr* to become overgrown with.

порв|а́ть (-у́, -ёшь) *сов от* **рвать** ◆ *перех* to tear ◆ (*impf* **порыва́ть**) *неперех*: ~ **с** +*instr* (*с женой, с друзьями*) to break up with; **порыва́ть** (~ *perf*) **что-н с кем-н** to break off sth with sb

▶ порва́|ться *сов от* **рва́ться ◆ возв** (*нить*) to break; (*платье*) to tear.

пореде́|ть (*3sg* -ет, *3pl* -ют) *несов от* **редеть**.

поре́жу(сь) *итп сов см* **поре́зать(ся)**.

поре́з (-а) *м* cut.

поре́|зать (-жу, -жешь) *сов перех* to cut

▶ поре́заться *сов возв* to cut o.s.

поре́|й (-я) *м* leek.

порекоменд|ова́ть (-у́ю) *сов от* **рекомендова́ть**.

по́рист|ый (-, -а, -о) *прил* porous.

порица́ни|е (-я) *ср* reprimand.

порица́|ть (-ю) *несов перех* to reprimand.

порнографи́ческ|ий (-ая, -ое, -ие) *прил* pornographic.

порногра́фи|я (-и) *ж* pornography.

по́ровну *нареч* equally.

поро́г (-а) *м* (*также перен*) threshold; (*на реке*) rapids *мн*; **переступа́ть** (**переступи́ть** *perf*) ~ to cross the threshold; **я его́ на ~ не пущу́** he won't darken my door again.

поро́д|а (-ы) *ж* (*животных*) breed; (*древесная*) species; (*горная*) rock; (*перен: людей*) type.

поро́дист|ый (-, -а, -о) *прил* pedigree *опред*; (*лицо*) aristocratic.

поро|ди́ть (-жу́, -ди́шь; *impf* **порожда́ть**) *сов перех* (*стать причиной*) to give rise to.

породн|и́ться (-ю́сь, -и́шься) *сов от* **родни́ться**.

порожда́|ть (-ю) *несов от* **породи́ть**.

поро́жн|ий (-яя, -ее, -ие) *прил* empty; **перелива́ть** (*impf*) **из пусто́го в ~ее** to rabbit on.

порожня́|к (-а́) *м* empty vehicle.

порожн|ко́м *нареч* without a load.

порожу́ *сов см* **породи́ть**.

по́рознь *нареч* apart.

порозове́|ть (-ю) *сов от* **розове́ть**.

поро́й *нареч* from time to time.

поро́к (-а) *м* vice; **поро́к се́рдца** heart disease.

пороло́н (-а) *м* foam rubber.

поро́с *итп сов см* **порасти́**.

порос|ёнок (-ёнка; *nom pl* -я́та, *gen pl* -я́т) *м* piglet.

по́росл|ь (-и) *ж* (*побеги*) shoots *мн*; (*перен*) generation.

поро́сята *итп сущ см* **порося́тенок**.

пор|о́ть (-ю́, -ешь; *perf* **распоро́ть**) *несов перех* (*швы*) to unpick; (*perf* **вы́пороть**; *бить*) to belt; ~ (**напоро́ть** *perf*) **чушь** *или* **ерунду́** *или* **чепуху́** to talk nonsense; ~ (*impf*) **горя́чку** (*разг*) to get a move on.

по́рох (-а; *part gen* -у) *м* gunpowder.

поро́чен *прил см* **поро́чный**.

поро́ч|ить (-у, -ишь; *perf* **опоро́чить**) *несов перех* to bring shame on; (*чернить: человека*) to defame; (: *работу*) to bring into disrepute.

поро́ч|ный (-ен, -на, -но) *прил* (*безнравственный*) depraved; (*неправильный*) flawed.

порош|о́к (-ка́) *м* powder.

поро́|ю *нареч* = **поро́й**.

порт (-а; *loc sg* -у́, *nom pl* -ы, *gen pl* -о́в) *м* port; **возду́шный ~** airport.

порта́л (-а) *м* (*АРХИТ*) portal.

портати́вный *прил* portable.

портве́йн (-а) *м* port (*wine*).

по́рт|ить (-чу, -тишь; *perf* **испо́ртить**) *несов перех* (*механизм, здоровье, карьеру*) to damage; (*настроение, праздник, ребёнка*) to spoil; ~ (*impf*) **себе́ не́рвы** to worry

▶ по́ртиться (*perf* **испо́ртиться**) *сов возв* (*механизм*) to be damaged; (*здоровье, погода*) to deteriorate; (*настроение*) to be spoiled; (*молоко*) to go off; (*мясо, овощи*) to go bad.

портни́х|а (-и) *ж* dressmaker.

портн|о́й (-о́го; *decl like adj*) *м* tailor.

порто́вый *прил* port *опред*.

портре́т (-а) *м* portrait.

портсига́р (-а) *м* cigarette case.

По́ртсму́т (-а) *м* Portsmouth.

Португа́ли|я (-и) *ж* Portugal.

португа́льск|ий (-ая, -ое, -ие) *прил* Portuguese; ~ **язы́к** Portuguese.

портфе́л|ь (-я) *м* briefcase; (*ПОЛИТ, КОММ*) portfolio; ~ **це́нных бума́г** (*КОММ*) investment portfolio.

портье́ *м нескл* (*в гостинице*) porter.

портье́р|а (-ы) *ж* curtain.

портя́н|ка (-ки; *gen pl* -ок) *ж* (*обычно мн*) puttee.

поруга́ни|е (-я) *ср* desecration.

поруга́|ть (-ю) *сов перех* (*разг*) to scold

▶ поруга́ться *сов от* **руга́ться ◆ возв** (*разг*): ~**ся** (**с** +*instr*) to fall out (with).

пору́к|а (-и) *ж*: **брать кого́-н на ~и** to take sb on probation; (*ЮР*) to stand bail for sb; **кругова́я ~** mutual dependence; (*у преступников*) mutual cover-up; **отпуска́ть** (**отпусти́ть** *perf*) **кого́-н на ~и** to release sb on bail.

по-ру́сски *нареч* (*разговаривать, написать*) in Russian; **говори́ть** (*impf*)/**понима́ть** (*impf*) ~ to speak/understand Russian; **как ~ „book"?** what is the Russian for "book"?

поруча́|ть (-ю) *несов от* **поручи́ть**.

поруче́ни|е (-я) *ср* (*задание*) errand; (: *важное*) mission; **по ~ю** +*gen* on behalf of.

по́руч|ень (-ня) *м* handrail.

пору́чик (-а) *м* (*ИСТ*) first lieutenant.

поручи́тел|ь (-я) *м* (*КОММ*) guarantor.

поручи́тельств|о (-а) *ср* guarantee.

пор|учи́ть (-учу́, -у́чишь; *impf* **поруча́ть**) *сов неперех*: ~ **кому́-н что-н** to entrust sb with sth; **поруча́ть** (~ *perf*) **кому́-н** +*infin* to instruct sb to do; **поруча́ть** (~ *perf*) **кому́-н кого́-н/что-н** (*отдать на попечение*) to leave sb/sth in sb's care.

пор|учи́ться (-учу́сь, -у́чишься) *сов от* **руча́ться**.

по́ручня *итп сущ см* **по́ручень**.

порха́|ть (-ю) *несов неперех* (*бабочка*) to flutter about; (*птица*) to flit about.

по́рци|я (-и) *ж* portion; **принеси́те нам две ~и**

жа́реной говя́дины bring us two steaks.

по́рч|**а** (-и) ж damage.

по́рчу(сь) сов см **по́ртить(ся)**.

по́рш|**ень** (-ня) м (в двигателе) piston; (в насосе) plunger.

поры́в (-а) м (ветра) gust; (негодования, восторга итп) surge.

порыва́|**ть** (-ю) несов от **порва́ть**
▶ **порыва́ться** несов возв: ~**ся** +infin (стреми́ться) to strive to do.

поры́вист|**ый** (-, -а, -о) прил (ветер) gusty; (движения) jerky; (характер, человек) impetuous.

поря́дка итп сущ см **поря́док**.

поря́дковый прил (номер) ordinal; **поря́дковое числи́тельное** ordinal number.

поря́дком нареч (разг) pretty; **я** ~ **уста́л** I'm pretty tired.

поря́д|**ок** (-ка) м order; (правила) procedure; **в** ~**ке** +gen (в ка́честве) as; ~**ка** +gen about; **в рабо́чем** ~**ке** in the course of the proceedings; **э́то в** ~**ке веще́й** (это норма́льно) that's nothing out of the ordinary; **в** ~**ке** in order; **всё в** ~**ке** everything's OK; **поря́док дня** agenda; **поря́док слов** (линг) word order.

поря́дочно нареч decently; (устал) pretty; (хорошо́) quite well.

поря́доч|**ный** (-ен, -на, -но) прил (честный) decent; (значительный) fair.

пос. сокр = **посёлок**.

поса́|**дить** (-ажу́, -а́дишь) сов см **сажа́ть**.

поса́д|**ка** (-ки; gen pl -ок) ж (овощей, деревьев) planting; (пассажиров) boarding; (самолёта итп) landing; **произво́дится** ~ **на самолёт** ... the flight ... is boarding.

поса́дочный прил (трап, талон) boarding опред; (площадка, огни) landing опред.

посажу́ сов см **посади́ть**.

посва́та|**ть(ся)** (-ю(сь)) сов от **сва́таться**.

посвеже́|**ть** (-ю) сов от **свеже́ть**.

посвети́ть (-чу́, -тишь) сов от **свети́ть**.

посветле́|**ть** (-ю) сов от **светле́ть**.

посвечу́ сов см **посвети́ть**.

по-сво́ему нареч his итп way.

посвя|**ти́ть** (-щу́, -ти́шь; impf **посвяща́ть**) сов перех: ~ **что-н** +dat to devote sth to; (книгу, стихи) to dedicate sth to; **посвяща́ть** (~ perf) **кого́-н в** +acc (в тайну) to let sb into.

посвяща́|**ть** (-ю) несов от **посвяти́ть**.

посвяще́ни|**е** (-я) ср (в книге) dedication.

посвящу́ сов см **посвяти́ть**.

посе́в (-а) м sowing; см также **посе́вы**.

посевн|**о́й** прил: ~**ы́е рабо́ты** sowing; **посевны́е пло́щади** (с.-х.) area sown with crops.

посе́в|**ы** (-ов) мн crops мн.

поседе́|**ть** (-ю) сов от **седе́ть**.

поселе́н|**ец** (-ца) м settler; (высланный) deportee.

поселе́ни|**е** (-я) ср (селение) settlement; (как наказание) deportation.

поселе́нца итп сущ см **поселе́нец**.

посе|**ли́ть(ся)** (-елю́(сь), -е́лишь(ся)) сов от **сели́ть(ся)**.

посёл|**ок** (-ка) м village; **да́чный** ~ village made up of dachas.

поселя́|**ть(ся)** (-ю(сь)) несов = **сели́ть(ся)**.

посеребр|**и́ть** (-ю́, -и́шь) сов от **серебри́ть**.

посереди́не нареч in the middle ◆ предл (+gen) in the middle of.

посере́|**ть** (-ю) сов от **сере́ть**.

посети́тель (-я) м visitor.

посети́тельниц|**а** (-ы) ж см **посети́тель**.

посе|**ти́ть** (-щу́, -ти́шь; impf **посеща́ть**) сов перех to visit.

посе́т|**овать** (-ую) сов от **се́товать**.

посеща́емост|**ь** (-и) ж attendance.

посеща́|**ть** (-ю) несов от **посети́ть**.

посеще́ни|**е** (-я) ср visit.

посещу́ сов см **посети́ть**.

посе́|**ять** (-ю) сов от **се́ять** ◆ перех (разг: потерять) to lose.

поси|**де́ть** (-жу́, -ди́шь) сов неперех to sit for a while.

посил|**ьный** (-ен, -ьна, -ьно) прил feasible.

посине́|**ть** (-ю) сов от **сине́ть**.

посин|**и́ть** (-ю́, -и́шь) сов от **сини́ть**.

поска|**ка́ть** (-чу́, -чешь) сов от **скака́ть**.

посканда́л|**ить** (-ю, -ишь) сов от **сканда́лить**.

поскачу́ итп сов см **поскака́ть**.

поскользн|**у́ться** (-у́сь, -ёшься) сов возв to slip.

поско́льку союз as.

поскуп|**и́ться** (-лю́сь, -и́шься) сов от **скупи́ться**.

посла́ итп сущ см **посо́л**.

послабле́ни|**е** (-я) ср leniency.

посла́н|**ец** (-ца) м envoy.

посла́ни|**е** (-я) ср (официальное) dispatch; (дружеское, любовное) message.

посла́нник (-а) м (дипломатический) diplomat.

посла́нца итп сущ см **посла́нец**.

по|**сла́ть** (-шлю́, -шлёшь; impf **посыла́ть**) сов перех to send; **посыла́ть** (~ perf) **кого́-н к чёрту** (разг) to tell sb to go to hell.

по́сле нареч (потом) afterwards ◆ предл (+gen) after ◆ союз: ~ **того́ как** after.

послевое́нный прил postwar.

после́д (-а) м placenta.

после́дне|**е** (-его; decl like adj) ср the last; **до** ~**его** to the utmost.

после́дн|**ий** (-яя, -ее, -ие) прил last; (новости, мода) latest; (разг) ~ **негодя́й** utter rascal; **за** или **в** ~**ее вре́мя** recently; **руга́ться** (impf) ~**ими слова́ми** to use foul language.

после́дователь (-я) м follower.

после́довательност|**ь** (**-и**) ж sequence; (*политики*) consistency.

после́довательный *прил* (*этапы, движения*) consecutive; (*вывод, ход мысли*) consistent.

после́д|овать (**-ую**) *сов от* **сле́довать**.

после́дстви|е (**-я**) *ср* consequence.

после́дующий (**-ая, -ее, -ие**) *прил* subsequent.

послеза́втра *нареч* the day after tomorrow.

послеродово́й *прил* postnatal.

послесло́ви|е (**-я**) *ср* (*в книге*) epilogue.

посло́виц|а (**-ы**) ж proverb, saying; **войти́** (*perf*) **в** **~у** to become proverbial.

послуж|и́ть (**-у́, -у́жишь**) *сов от* **служи́ть**.

послужно́й *прил*: **~ спи́сок** (*военного*) service record; (*работника*) work record.

послуша́ни|е (**-я**) *ср* (*покорность*) obedience.

послу́ша|ть (**-ю**) *сов от* **слу́шать** ♦ *перех*: **~ что-н** to listen to sth for a while; **~йте!** listen!

▸ **послу́шаться** *сов от* **слу́шаться**.

послу́шен *прил см* **послу́шный**.

послу́шник (**-а**) *м* (*РЕЛ*) novice.

послу́шниц|а (**-ы**) ж *см* **послу́шник**.

послу́ш|ный (**-ен, -на, -но**) *прил* (*ребёнок, ученик*) obedient; (*механизм*) user-friendly.

послы́ш|аться (*3sg* **-ется,** *3pl* **-атся**) *сов от* **слы́шаться**.

послюня́в|ить (**-лю, -ишь**) *сов от* **слюня́вить**.

посма́трива|ть (**-ю**) *несов неперех* to glance occasionally.

посме́ива|ться (**-юсь**) *несов возв* (*смеяться*) to chuckle; **~** (*impf*) (**над** +*instr*) (*насмехаться*) to laugh at.

посме́нный *прил* shift *опред*.

посме́ртный *прил* posthumous.

посме́|ть (**-ю**) *сов от* **сметь**.

посме́шищ|е (**-а**) *ср* laughing stock; **выставля́ть** (*impf*) **кого́-н на ~** to make a laughing stock of sb.

посме́|яться (**-ю́сь, -ёшься**) *сов от* **смея́ться**.

посм|отре́ть (**-отрю́, -о́тришь**) *сов от* **смотре́ть** ♦ *неперех*: **~о́трим** (*разг*) we'll see; **там ~о́трим** (*разг*) we'll see later

▸ **посмотре́ться** *сов см* **смотре́ться**.

посо́би|е (**-я**) *ср* (*помощь*) benefit; (*ПРОСВЕЩ*: *учебное*) handout; (: *наглядное*) visual aids *мн*; **посо́бие по безрабо́тице** unemployment benefit; **посо́бие по инвали́дности** disability living allowance.

посо́бник (**-а**) *м* accomplice.

посове́т|овать(ся) (**-ую(сь)**) *сов от* **сове́товать(ся)**.

посоде́йств|овать (**-ую**) *сов от* **соде́йствовать**.

посо́л (**-ла́**) *м* ambassador; (**-о́ла**; *засол*) salting.

посо́л|и́ть (**-ю́, -о́лишь**) *сов от* **соли́ть**.

посо́льств|о (**-а**) *ср* embassy.

поспе́|ть (**-ю**) *сов от* **спеть** ♦ (*impf* **поспева́ть**) *неперех* (*успеть*) to make it.

поспе́шен *прил см* **поспе́шный**.

поспеш|и́ть (**-у́, -и́шь**) *сов от* **спеши́ть**.

поспе́ш|ный (**-ен, -на, -но**) *прил* rushed.

поспо́р|ить (**-ю, -ишь**) *сов от* **спо́рить** ♦ *неперех* to argue.

поспосо́бств|овать (**-ую**) *сов от* **спосо́бствовать**.

посрам|и́ть (**-лю́, -и́шь**; *impf* **посрамля́ть**) *сов перех* to disgrace.

посреди́ *нареч* in the middle ♦ *предл* (+*gen*) in the middle of; **~ толпы́** in the midst of the crowd.

посреди́не *нареч* in the middle ♦ *предл* (+*gen*) in the middle of.

посре́дник (**-а**) *м* intermediary; (*при конфликте*) mediator; **торго́вый ~** middleman (*мн* middlemen).

посре́днически|й (**-ая, -ое, -ие**) *прил* (*КОММ*) intermediary *опред*.

посре́дничеств|о (**-а**) *ср* mediation.

посре́дственно *нареч* (*учиться, писать, сочинять*) averagely ♦ *ср нескл* (*ПРОСВЕЩ*) ≈ satisfactory (*school mark*).

посре́дствен|ный (**-, -на, -но**) *прил* mediocre.

посре́дств|о (**-а**) *ср*: **при ~е** или **че́рез ~** +*gen* by means of.

посре́дством *предл* (+*gen*) by means of.

поссо́р|ить(ся) (**-ю(сь), -ишь(ся)**) *сов от* **ссо́рить(ся)**.

пост (**-а́**; *loc sg* **-у́**) *м* (*люди*) guard; (*место*) lookout post; (*должность*) position, post; (*РЕЛ*) fast; **~ автоинспе́кции** (traffic) police checkpoint.

поста́в|ить (**-лю, -ишь**) *сов от* **ста́вить** ♦ (*impf* **поставля́ть**) *перех* (*товар*) to supply.

поста́в|ка (**-ки**; *gen pl* **-ок**) ж (*снабжение*) supply.

поста́влю *сов см* **поста́вить**.

поставля́|ть (**-ю**) *несов от* **поста́вить**.

поста́вок *сущ см* **поста́вка**.

поставщи́|к (**-а́**) *м* supplier; **судово́й ~** ship chandler.

постаме́нт (**-а**) *м* pedestal.

постан|ови́ть (**-овлю́, -о́вишь**; *impf* **постановля́ть**) *сов неперех*: **~** +*infin* to resolve to do.

постано́в|ка (**-ки**; *gen pl* **-ок**) ж (*памятника*) erection; (*учебного процесса*) organization; (*ТЕАТР*) production; **у неё хоро́шая ~ головы́** she holds her head well; **~ вопро́са/пробле́мы** the formulation of the question/problem.

постановле́ни|е (**-я**) *ср* (*решение*) resolution; (*распоряжение*) decree.

постановлю́ *сов см* **постанови́ть**.

постановля́|ть (**-ю**) *несов от* **постанови́ть**.

постано́вок *сущ см* **постано́вка**.

постано́вщик (**-а**) *м* producer.

постара́|ться (**-юсь**) *сов от* **стара́ться**.

постаре́|ть (**-ю**) *сов от* **старе́ть**.

постел|и́ть(ся) (**-елю́(сь), -е́лишь(ся)**) *сов от* **стели́ть(ся)**.

посте́л|ь (**-и**) ж bed.

посте́л|ьный *прил*: **~ое бельё** bedclothes *мн*; **он на ~ом режи́ме** he is confined to bed.

постелю́ *итп сов см* **постла́ть**.

постепе́нно *нареч* gradually.
постепе́н|ный (-ен, -на, -но) *прил* gradual.
постесня́|ться (-юсь) *сов от* **стесня́ться**.
пости́г *итп сов см* **пости́чь**.
постига́|ть (-ю) *несов от* **пости́чь**.
пости́гну *итп сов см* **пости́чь**.
пости́г|нуть (-ну, -нешь; *pt* -, -ла, -ло) *сов* = **пости́чь**.
постила́|ть (-ю) *несов* = **стели́ть**.
постира́|ть (-ю) *сов от* **стира́ть**.
по|сти́ться (-щу́сь, -сти́шься) *несов возв* (РЕЛ) to fast.
пости́|чь (-гну, -гнешь; *pt* -г, -гла, -гло, *impf* **постига́ть**) *сов перех* (*смысл, значе́ние*) to grasp; (*подлеж: несча́стье*) to befall; **я не могу́ ~, как он мог э́то сде́лать** I can't comprehend how he could do something like that; **его́ ~гло разочарова́ние** he was disappointed.
пост|ла́ть (-елю́, -е́лешь) *сов от* **стлать**.
по́стный *прил* (*суп, обе́д*) vegetarian; (*мя́со*) lean; (*разг: хму́рый*) cheesed off; **по́стное ма́сло** vegetable oil.
постов|о́й *прил* (*слу́жба, бу́дка*) sentry *опред* ♦ (-о́го; *decl like adj*) *м* militiaman on duty.
посто́льку *союз*: ~ ... поско́льку in so far as ....
постор|они́ться (-оню́сь, -о́нишься) *сов от* **сторони́ться**.
посторо́нн|ий (-яя, -ее, -ие) *прил* (*чужо́й*) strange; (*по́мощь, влия́ние*) outside; (*вопро́с*) irrelevant ♦ (-его; *decl like adj*) *м* stranger, outsider; **~им вход воспрещён** authorized entry only.
постоя́н|ный (-ен, -на, -но) *прил* (*рабо́та, а́дрес*) permanent; (*шум, разгово́ры*) constant; (*вкус, взгля́ды*) consistent; **постоя́нная а́рмия** regular army; **постоя́нный ток** direct current.
посто|я́ть (-ю́, -и́шь) *сов от* **стоя́ть** ♦ *непере́х* (*стоя́ть недо́лго*) to stand for a while; **посто́йте!** (*подожди́те*) hang on!; **он за цено́й не ~и́т** (*разг*) money is no object to him.
пострада́|ть (-ю) *сов от* **страда́ть**.
постри́|г(ся) *итп сов см* **постри́чь(ся)**.
постригу́(сь) *итп сов см* **постри́чь(ся)**.
постриже́ни|е (-я) *ср* (*мужчи́ны*) taking the habit; (*же́нщины*) taking the veil.
постри́|чь (-гу́, -жёшь *итп*, -гу́т; *pt* -г, -гла, -гло) *сов перех*: ~ кого́-н to cut sb's hair; ~ (*perf*) кого́-н в монасты́рь to initiate sb into a monastery.
► **постри́чься** *сов возв* to have a haircut; **~ся** (*perf*) **в монасты́рь** to be initiated into a monastery.
постро́ек *сущ см* **постро́йка**.
постро́ени|е (-я) *ср* (*предложе́ния, фра́зы*) construction.
постро́|ить(ся) (-ю(сь), -ишь(ся)) *сов от* **стро́ить(ся)**.
постро́|йка (-йки; *gen pl* -ек) *ж* construction.

поступа́тельн|ый *прил* (*движе́ние*) forward *опред*; **~ое разви́тие** progress.
посту|пи́ть (-плю́, -́пишь; *impf* **поступа́ть**) *сов непере́х* (*благоро́дно, разу́мно*) to act; (*това́р, изве́стия*) to come in; (*жа́лоба: в суд*) to be received; **поступа́ть** (~ *perf*) **в** +acc (*в университе́т*) to enter; **поступа́ть** (~ *perf*) **на** +acc (*на рабо́ту, на ку́рсы*) to start
► **поступи́ться** (*impf* **поступа́ться**) *сов возв*: **~ся** +instr to give up.
посту́пка *сущ см* **посту́пок**.
поступле́ни|е (-я) *ср* (*де́йствие: в университе́т*) entrance; (*: на рабо́ту*) starting; (*: жа́лобы: в суд*) receipt; (*то, что поступи́ло: бюдже́тное*) revenue; (*: в библиоте́ке*) acquisition.
поступлю́(сь) *сов см* **поступи́ть(ся)**.
посту́п|ок (-ка) *м* (*благоро́дный, по́длый*) deed.
по́ступ|ь (-и) *ж* (*похо́дка*) gait.
постуч|а́ть(ся) (-у́(сь), -и́шь(ся)) *сов от* **стуча́ть(ся)**.
посты́ден *прил см* **посты́дный**.
постыд|и́ться (-жу́сь, -ди́шься) *сов от* **стыди́ться**.
посты́д|ный (-ен, -на, -но) *прил* shameful.
постыжу́сь *сов см* **постыди́ться**.
посу́д|а (-ы) *ж собир* crockery; **ку́хонная ~** kitchenware; **стекля́нная ~** glassware; **мыть** (**помы́ть** *perf*) **~у** to wash *или* do (*БРИТ*) the dishes.
посу́|ди́ть (-жу́, -дишь) *сов*: **~ди́те са́ми** judge for yourself.
посул|и́ть (-ю́, -и́шь) *сов от* **сули́ть**.
посчастли́в|иться (*3sg* -ится) *сов безл*: **мне ~илось** +infin ... I was lucky enough to ....
посчита́|ть(ся) (-ю(сь)) *сов от* **счита́ть(ся)**.
посыла́|ть (-ю) *несов от* **посла́ть**.
посы́л|ка (-ки; *gen pl* -ок) *ж* (*де́йствие: книг, де́нег*) sending; (*отправле́ние*) parcel; (*основа́ние*) premise.
посы́льн|ый (-ого; *decl like adj*) *м* messenger.
посы́п|ать (-лю, -лешь) *сов перех* to sprinkle.
посяга́тельств|о (-а) *ср*: ~ на что-н infringement on *или* of sth; ~ **на чью-н жизнь** an attempt on sb's life.
посяг|ну́ть (-у́, -ёшь; *impf* **посяга́ть**) *сов непере́х*: ~ **на** +acc to infringe; **посяга́ть** (~ *perf*) **на чью-н жизнь** to make an attempt on sb's life.
пот (-а; *part gen* -у, *loc sg* -у́, *nom pl* -ы́) *м* sweat; **в по́те лица́** hard; **пото́м и кро́вью добыва́ть** (**добы́ть** *perf*) **что-н** to sweat blood to get sth; **рабо́тать** (*impf*) **в по́те лица́** to sweat blood.
потайно́й *прил* secret *опред*.
потака́|ть (-ю) *несов непере́х*: ~ +dat (*агре́ссии*) to turn a blind eye to; (*агре́ссору*) to ignore.
потаску́х|а (-и) *ж* (*разг: пренебр*) hussy.
потасо́в|ка (-ки; *gen pl* -ок) *ж* (*разг*) punch-up.

по-твоёму *нареч* your way ◆ *вводн сл* in your opinion.

потворств|овать (-ую) *несов неперех*: ~ +*dat* (*агрессии*) to turn a blind eye to; (*агрессору*) to ignore.

потёк *итп сов см* **потёчь**.

потекут *сов см* **потёчь**.

потёмки (-ок) *мн* darkness *ед*.

потемне|ть (-ю) *сов от* **темнёть**.

потёмок *сущ см* **потёмки**.

потенциа́л (-а) *м* potential.

потенциа́льный (-ен, -ьна, -ьно) *прил* potential.

потепле́ни|е (-я) *ср* warmer spell.

потепле́|ть (*3sg* -ет, *3pl* -ют) *сов от* **теплёть**.

пот|ере́ть (-ру́, -рёшь; *pt* -ёр, -ёрла, -ёрло) *сов перех* (*ушиб*) to rub; (*морковь*) to grate

▶ **потере́ться** *сов от* **тере́ться**.

потерпе́вш|ая (-ей; *decl like adj*) *ж см* **потерпе́вший**.

потерпе́вш|ий (-его; *decl like adj*) *м* (*ЮР*) victim ◆ *прил*: (-ая, -ее, -ие) ~**ая сторона́** injured party.

пот|ерпе́ть (-ерплю́, -ерпишь) *сов от* **терпе́ть**.

потёртый *прил* (*одежда*) worn.

поте́р|я (-и) *ж* loss; **нести́ (понести́** *perf*) ~**и** (*в войне́*) to suffer losses.

поте́рянно *нареч* (*смотреть*) lost.

поте́рян|ный (-, -на, -но) *прил* (*растерянный*: *вид итп*) lost.

потеря́|ть(ся) (-ю(сь)) *сов от* **теря́ть(ся)**.

потесн|и́ть (-ю́, -и́шь) *сов от* **тесни́ть** ◆ *перех*: ~ **кого́-н** to make sb squeeze up

▶ **потесни́ться** *сов возв* to squeeze up.

поте́|ть (-ю; *impf* **вспоте́ть**) *несов неперех* to sweat.

поте́|чь (*3sg* -ечёт, *3pl* -екут, *pt* -ёк, -екла́, -екло́) *сов неперех* (*вода*) to start flowing; (*дни, жизнь*) to begin.

поте́ш|ить(ся) (-ю(сь)) *сов от* **те́шить(ся)**.

потихо́ньку *нареч* (*разг: медленно*) at a snail's pace; (: *тайно*) on the sly.

потни́ц|а (-ы) *ж* (*МЕД*) heat rash.

по́тный *прил* sweaty.

потого́н|ный *прил* (*перен*): ~**ая систе́ма** slave labour (*BRIT*) *или* labor (*US*).

пото́к (-а) *м* (*также ПРОСВЕЩ*) stream; **положи́тельный/отрица́тельный** ~ **нали́чности** (*КОММ*) positive/negative cash flow.

потол|о́к (-ка́) *м* (*также перен*) ceiling; **брать (взять** *perf*) **что-н с** ~**ка́** (*раза*) to pluck sth out of thin air.

потолсте́|ть (-ю) *сов от* **толсте́ть**.

пото́м *нареч* (*после: пойдём, закончим итп*) later ◆ *союз* (*после*) then; (*раза: кроме того*) anyhow; **на** ~ (*раза*) for later.

пото́мки (-ов) *мн* descendants *мн*.

пото́мственный *прил* (*имение, деньги*) inherited; **он** – ~ **музыка́нт** he is descended from a family of musicians.

пото́мств|о (-а) *ср собир* descendants *мн*; (*дети*) offspring *мн*.

потому́ *нареч*: ~ (**и**) that's why; **я не приду́**, ~ **что уста́л** I'm not coming because I'm tired; **потому́ что** because.

пот|ону́ть (-ону́, -о́нешь) *сов от* **тону́ть**.

пото́п (-а) *м* flood.

пот|опи́ть (-оплю́, -о́пишь) *сов от* **топи́ть**.

потоп|та́ть (-чу́, -чешь) *сов от* **топта́ть**.

потора́плива|ть (-ю) *несов перех*: ~ **кого́-н** to hurry sb up

▶ **потора́пливаться** *несов возв* to hurry.

поторо́п|ить(ся) (-лю́(сь), -ишь(ся)) *сов от* **торопи́ть(ся)**.

пото́чный *прил* (*производство*) mass *опред*; **пото́чная ли́ния** production line.

потрав|и́ть (-лю́, -ишь) *сов от* **трави́ть**.

потра́|тить(ся) (-чу(сь), -тишь(ся)) *сов от* **тра́тить(ся)**.

потреби́тель (-я) *м* consumer.

потреби́тельск|ий (-ая, -ое, -ие) *прил* (*спрос, товар*) consumer *опред*; **потреби́тельская коопера́ция** cooperative (society).

потреб|и́ть (-лю́, -и́шь) *сов от* **потребля́ть**.

потребле́ни|е (-я) *ср* (*действие*) consumption; **това́ры широ́кого** ~**я** consumer goods.

потреблю́ *сов см* **потреби́ть**.

потребля́|ть (-ю; *perf* **потреби́ть**) *несов перех* to consume.

потре́бность (-и) *ж* (*надобность*) requirement, demand; (*желание*) need.

потре́б|овать(ся) (-ую(сь)) *сов от* **тре́бовать(ся)**.

Потребсою́з (-а) *м сокр* = *Сою́з потреби́тельских коопера́ций*.

потрево́ж|ить(ся) (-у(сь), -ишь(ся)) *сов от* **трево́жить(ся)**.

потрёпан|ный (-, -на, -но) *прил* (*книга, одежда*) tattered, tatty; (*вид, лицо*) worn.

потреп|а́ть(ся) (-лю́(сь), -лешь(ся)) *сов от* **трепа́ть(ся)**.

потре́ска|ться (*3sg* -ется, *3pl* -ются) *сов от* **тре́скаться**.

потрох|а́ (-о́в) *мн* (*птицы*) giblets *мн*.

потрош|и́ть (-у́, -и́шь; *perf* **вы́потрошить**) *несов перех* (*курицу, рыбу*) to gut.

потру́(сь) *итп сов см* **потере́ть(ся)**.

потруди́ться (-жу́сь, -дишься) *сов возв* to work; ~ (*perf*) +*infin* to take the trouble to do; ~**ди́тесь переда́ть э́то письмо́** if you could be so kind as to pass on this letter.

потряса́|ть (-ю) *несов от* **потрясти́**.

потряса́ющ|ий (-ая, -ее, -ие) *прил* (*музыка, стихи*) fantastic; (*красота*) stunning.

потрясе́ни|е (-я) *ср* breakdown.

потряс|ти́ (-у́, -ёшь; *pt* -, -ла́, -ло́) *сов перех* to shake; (*impf* **потряса́ть**; *взволновать*) to stun ◆ *неперех*: ~ +*instr* to shake.

поту́г|а (-и) *ж* (*обычно мн*) contraction; (*перен: пренебр: усилия*) pathetic attempt.

поту́п|ить (-лю, -ишь; *impf* **потупля́ть**) *сов*

перех (голову, глаза) to lower
▸ **ПОТУ́ПИТЬСЯ** сов возв to lower one's eyes.
ПОТУСКНЕ́|ТЬ (-ю) сов от **ТУСКНЕ́ТЬ**.
ПОТУСТОРО́НН|ИЙ (-яя, -ее, -ие) прил (РЕЛ) on the other side.
ПОТУ́ХН|УТЬ (3sg -ет, 3pl -ут, impf **ПОТУХА́ТЬ**) сов неперех (лампа, свет) to go out; (жизнь, веселье) to end.
ПОТ|УШИ́ТЬ (-ушу́, -у́шишь) сов от **ТУШИ́ТЬ**.
ПОТЯГА́|ТЬСЯ (-юсь) сов от **ТЯГА́ТЬСЯ**.
ПОТЯ́ГИВА|ТЬ (-ю) несов перех (верёвку) to pull; (вино, чай) to sip
▸ **ПОТЯ́ГИВАТЬСЯ** несов от **ПОТЯНУ́ТЬСЯ**.
ПОТЯЖЕЛЕ́|ТЬ (-ю) сов от **ТЯЖЕЛЕ́ТЬ**.
ПОТ|ЯНУ́ТЬ (-яну́, -я́нешь) сов от **ТЯНУ́ТЬ**
▸ **ПОТЯНУ́ТЬСЯ** сов возв to start to drag; (impf **ПОТЯ́ГИВАТЬСЯ**; в постели, в кресле) to stretch out.
ПОУ́ЖИНА|ТЬ (-ю) сов от **У́ЖИНАТЬ**.
ПОУМНЕ́|ТЬ (-ю) сов от **УМНЕ́ТЬ**.
ПОУЧА́|ТЬ (-ю) несов перех to teach.
ПОУЧЕ́НИ|Е (-я) ср preaching.
ПОУЧИ́ТЕЛЬНЫЙ (-ен, -ьна, -ьно) прил (пример, история) instructive; (тон, голос) didactic; **его́ приме́р был для нас ~ен** we learnt from his example.
ПОХА́БНЫЙ (-ен, -на, -но) прил (непристойный) dirty.
ПОХА́ЖИВА|ТЬ (-ю) несов неперех (в парке итп) to stroll.
ПОХВАЛА́ (-ы́) ж praise; **отзыва́ться (отозва́ться** perf**) с ~о́й о ком-н** to praise sb.
ПОХВА́ЛЕН прил см **ПОХВА́ЛЬНЫЙ**.
ПОХВА|ЛИ́ТЬ(СЯ) (-алю́(сь), -а́лишь(ся)) сов от **ХВАЛИ́ТЬ(СЯ)**.
ПОХВА́ЛЬНЫЙ (-ен, -ьна, -ьно) прил praiseworthy; (отзыв) complimentary; **~ьное сло́во** word of praise; **похва́льная гра́мота** certificate of merit.
ПОХВА́СТА|ТЬ(СЯ) (-ю(сь)) сов от **ХВА́СТАТЬ(СЯ)**.
ПОХИТИ́ТЕЛ|Ь (-я) м (см глаг) thief; abductor; kidnapper.
ПОХИТИ́ТЕЛЬНИЦ|А (-ы) ж см **ПОХИТИ́ТЕЛЬ**.
ПОХИ́|ТИТЬ (-щу, -тишь; impf **ПОХИЩА́ТЬ**) сов перех (предмет) to steal; (человека) to abduct; (: для выкупа) to kidnap.
ПОХИЩЕ́НИ|Е (-я) ср (см глаг) theft; abduction; kidnap(ping).
ПОХИ́ЩУ сов см **ПОХИ́ТИТЬ**.
ПОХЛО́ПА|ТЬ (-ю) сов перех to pat ◆ неперех (человек: в ладоши) to clap; (птица) to flap.
ПОХЛОП|ОТА́ТЬ (-очу́, -о́чешь) сов от **ХЛОПОТА́ТЬ**.
ПОХМЕ́ЛЬ|Е (-я) ср hangover.
ПОХО́Д (-а) м (военный) campaign; (туристический) hike (walking and camping expedition).
ПОХОДА́ТАЙСТВ|ОВАТЬ (-ую) сов от

ходатайствовать.
ПОХ|ОДИ́ТЬ (-ожу́, -о́дишь) несов неперех: **~ на кого́-н/что-н** to resemble sb/sth ◆ сов неперех to walk.
ПОХО́ДК|А (-и) ж gait.
ПОХОЖДЕ́НИ|Е (-я) ср (обычно мн) adventure.
ПОХО́Ж|ИЙ (-ая, -ее, -ие) прил: **~ (на** +acc или **с** +instr) similar (to); **он похо́ж на бра́та, они́ с бра́том ~и** he looks like his brother; **они́ ~и** they look alike; **~е на то, что ...** it looks as if ...; **э́то на него́ не ~е** it's not like him.
ПОХОЖУ́ (не)сов см **ПОХОДИ́ТЬ**.
ПОХОЛОДА́НИ|Е (-я) ср cold spell.
ПОХОЛОДА́|ТЬ (3sg -ет) сов от **ХОЛОДА́ТЬ**.
ПОХОЛОДЕ́|ТЬ (-ю) сов от **ХОЛОДЕ́ТЬ**.
ПОХОР|ОНИ́ТЬ (-оню́, -о́нишь) сов от **ХОРОНИ́ТЬ**.
ПОХОРО́ННЫЙ прил funeral опред; **похоро́нное бюро́** undertaker's.
ПО́ХОР|ОНЫ (-о́н; dat pl -она́м) мн funeral ед.
ПОХОРОШЕ́|ТЬ (-ю) сов от **ХОРОШЕ́ТЬ**.
ПО́ХОТ|Ь (-и) ж lust.
ПОХУДЕ́|ТЬ (-ю) сов от **ХУДЕ́ТЬ**.
ПОЦАРА́ПА|ТЬ (-ю) сов от **ЦАРА́ПАТЬ**.
ПОЦЕЛ|ОВА́ТЬ(СЯ) (-у́ю(сь)) сов от **ЦЕЛОВА́ТЬ(СЯ)**.
ПОЦЕЛУ́|Й (-я) м kiss.
ПОЦЕРЕМО́Н|ИТЬСЯ (-юсь) сов от **ЦЕРЕМО́НИТЬСЯ**.
ПОЧАСОВИ́К (-а́) м part-time worker (paid by the hour).
ПОЧАСОВ|О́Й прил (оплата) hourly; **~а́я рабо́та** hourly-paid work.
ПОЧА́Т|ОК (-ка) м (кукурузы) cob.
ПО́ЧВ|А (-ы) ж soil; (перен) basis; **на ~е** +gen owing to; **он потеря́л ~у под нога́ми** he lost his confidence.
ПО́ЧЕК сущ см **ПО́ЧКА**.
ПОЧЁМ нареч (разг) how much; **~ я́блоки?** how much are the apples?
ПОЧЕМУ́ нареч why; **(и) вот ~** and that is why.
ПОЧЕМУ́-ЛИБО нареч for some reason.
ПОЧЕМУ́-НИБУДЬ нареч = **ПОЧЕМУ́-ЛИБО**.
ПОЧЕМУ́-ТО нареч for some reason.
ПО́ЧЕРК (-а) м handwriting; (перен: художника, грабителя) hallmark.
ПОЧЕРНЕ́|ТЬ (-ю) сов от **ЧЕРНЕ́ТЬ**.
ПОЧЕРПН|У́ТЬ (-у́, -ёшь) сов перех (сведения) to obtain; (идею) to draw.
ПОЧЕРСТВЕ́|ТЬ (-ю) сов от **ЧЕРСТВЕ́ТЬ**.
ПОЧЕ|СА́ТЬ(СЯ) (-шу́(сь), -шешь(ся)) сов от **ЧЕСА́ТЬ(СЯ)**.
ПО́ЧЕСТ|Ь (-и) ж (обычно мн) homage ед; **воздава́ть (возда́ть** perf**) ~и кому́-н** to pay homage to sb.
ПОЧ|Е́СТЬ (-ту́, -тёшь; pt -ёл, -ла́, -ло́, impf **ПОЧИТА́ТЬ**) сов неперех: **~ за долг/честь** +infin to consider it one's duty/an honour (BRIT) или honor (US) to do.

почёт (-а) *м* honour (*BRIT*), honor (*US*).
почётный *прил* (*гость*) honoured (*BRIT*), honored (*US*); (*член академии*) honorary; (*обязанность*) honourable (*BRIT*), honorable (*US*); **почётный караул** guard of honour (*BRIT*) *или* honor (*US*).
почечный *прил* kidney *опред*, renal; (*камни*) kidney *опред*.
почесу(сь) *итп сов см* **почесать(ся)**.
почин (-а) *м* initiative.
почин|ить (-иню, -инишь) *сов от* **чинить**.
почин|ка (-ки; *gen pl* -ок) *ж* (*обуви, телевизора*) repair.
почистить (-щу, -стишь) *сов от* **чистить**.
почитатель (-я) *м* admirer.
почитательница (-ы) *ж см* **почитатель**.
почита|ть (-ю) *несов от* **почесть** ♦ *перех* (*поклоняться*) to admire ♦ *сов перех* to read.
почищу *сов см* **почистить**.
поч|ка (-ки; *gen pl* -ек) *ж* (*БОТ*) bud; (*АНАТ*) kidney; ~**ки** (*КУЛИН*) kidneys.
почт|а (-ы) *ж* (*учреждение*) post office; (*корреспонденция*) mail, post; **отправлять** (*отправить perf*) **что-н** ~**ой** *или* **по** ~**е** to send sth by post.
почтальон (-а) *м* postman (*BRIT*) (*мн* postmen), mailman (*US*) (*мн* mailmen).
почтамт (-а) *м* main post office.
почтени|е (-я) *ср* esteem.
почтённый *прил* venerable; ~**ые годы** advanced years.
почти *нареч* almost, nearly; ~ **что** (*разг*) almost.
почтительный (-ен, -ьна, -ьно) *прил* respectful; **на** ~**ьном расстоянии** at a respectful distance.
почт|ить (*как* **чтить**; *см* **Table 17**) (-у, -йшь) *сов перех* (*память*) to pay homage to; ~ (*perf*) **кого-н своим присутствием** to honour (*BRIT*) *или* honor (*US*) sb with one's presence.
почтовый *прил* (*служба, связь*) postal; (*марка*) postage *опред*; **почтовая открытка** postcard; **почтовая бумага** writing paper; **почтовый индекс** postcode (*BRIT*), zip code (*US*); **почтовый перевод** (*деньги*) postal order; **почтовый ящик** postbox.
почту *итп сов см* **почесть**.
почувств|овать (-ую) *сов см* **чувствовать**.
почудиться (*3sg* -ится, *3pl* -ятся) *сов от* **чудиться**.
почу|ять (-ю) *сов от* **чуять**.
пошатн|уть (-у, -ёшь) *сов перех* (*веру*) to shake; (*здоровье*) to affect
▶ **пошатнуться** *сов возв* to sway; (*авторитет*) to be undermined; (*здоровье*) to suffer.
пошатыва|ться (-юсь) *несов возв* (*человек*) to sway slightly.
пошеве|ливаться (-юсь) *несов возв* to stir; (*разг*: *поторапливаться*) to get a move on.
пошевел|ить(ся) (-ю(сь), -йшь(ся)) *сов от* **шевелить(ся)**.

пошевельн|уться (-усь, -ёшься) *сов возв* to stir.
пошёл *сов см* **пойти**.
пошелохнуться (-усь, -ёшься) *сов* = **шелохнуться**.
пошиб (-а) *м* (*разг*: *пренебр*): **они люди одного** ~**а** they are cut from the same cloth; **низкий** *или* **невысокий** ~ second-rate.
пошив (-а) *м* (*действие*) sewing; **индивидуальный** ~ tailoring.
пошла *итп сов см* **пойти**.
пошлин|а (-ы) *ж* duty; **судебная** ~ legal costs *или* expenses; **облагать (обложить** *perf*) **что-н** ~**ой** to impose a duty on sth.
пошлинный *прил* customs *опред*.
пошло *сов см* **пойти**.
пошлость (-и) *ж* vulgarity; **говорить** (*impf*) ~**и** to make trite and vulgar comments.
пошл|ый (-, -а, -о) *прил* (*человек, поступок*) vulgar; (*анекдот*) corny; (*картинка*) kitsch; (*речи*) trite and vulgar.
пошлю *итп сов см* **послать**.
пошляк (-а) *м* (*разг*) vulgar person.
пошу|тить (-учу, -утишь) *сов от* **шутить**.
пощад|а (-ы) *ж* mercy.
пощад|ить (-жу, -дишь) *сов от* **щадить**.
пощек|отать (-очу, -очешь) *сов от* **щекотать**.
пощёчин|а (-ы) *ж* slap in the face.
пощупа|ть (-ю) *сов от* **щупать**.
пощусь *несов см* **поститься**.
поэзи|я (-и) *ж* (*также перен*) poetry.
поэм|а (-ы) *ж* poem.
поэт (-а) *м* poet.
поэтесс|а (-ы) *ж см* **поэт**.
поэтизир|овать (-ую; *perf* **опоэтизировать**) *несов перех* to wax poetic about.
поэтический (-ая, -ое, -ие) *прил* poetic.
поэтому *нареч* therefore.
пою *итп несов см* **петь**, **пойть**.
появ|иться (-явлюсь, -явишься; *impf* **появляться**) *сов возв* to appear; **у него** ~**явились идеи/сомнения** he has had an idea/ begun to have doubts; **появляться** (~ *perf*) **на свет** to come into the world.
появлени|е (-я) *ср* appearance.
появлюсь *сов см* **появиться**.
появля|ться (-юсь) *несов от* **появиться**.
пояс (-а; *nom pl* -а) *м* (*ремень*) belt; (*талия*) waist; (*ГЕО*) zone; **спасательный** ~ life belt; **тарифный** ~ (*ЭКОН*) tariff zone.
пояснени|е (-я) *ср* explanation.
поясн|ить (-ю, -йшь; *impf* **пояснять**) *сов перех* to explain.
поясниц|а (-ы) *ж* small of the back.
поясня|ть (-ю) *несов от* **пояснить**.
ППГ *м сокр* (= полевой подвижный госпиталь) field hospital, ≈ MASH (*US*) (= *mobile army surgical hospital*).
пр. *сокр* = **проезд, проспект, прочее, прочие**.
прабаб|ка (-ки; *gen pl* -ок) *ж* great-grandmother.
прабабуш|ка (-ки; *gen pl* -ек) *ж* = **прабабка**.

прав|а́ (-) *мн* (*также:* води́тельские ~) driving licence (*BRIT*), driver's license (*US*); права́ челове́ка human rights.

пра́вд|а (-ы) *ж* truth ♦ *нареч* really ♦ *вводн сл* true; он ~ измени́лся he really has changed; он, ~, сам созна́лся true, he did confess; ты винова́т в э́том ~ ~ you are to blame, it's true; ~у *или* по ~е говоря́ *или* сказа́ть to tell the truth; он уже́ уе́хал, не ~ ли? he's already gone, hasn't he?; хоро́шая пого́да, не ~ ли? the weather's good, isn't it?

правди́в|ый (-, -а, -о) *прил* truthful.

правдоподо́б|ный (-ен, -на, -но) *прил* plausible.

пра́веден *прил см* пра́ведный.

пра́ведник (-а) *ж* (*РЕЛ*) righteous man (*мн* men).

пра́ведный (-ен, -на, -но) *прил* (*человек*) righteous; (*суд*) just.

пра́вилен *прил см* пра́вильный.

пра́вил|о (-а) *ср* rule; э́то не в мои́х ~ах that's not my way; как ~ as a rule; по всем ~ам by the rules; пра́вила доро́жного движе́ния rules of the road; ≈ Highway Code.

пра́вильно *нареч* correctly ♦ *как сказ* that's correct.

пра́вильный (-ен, -ьна, -ьно) *прил* (*написание, произношение итп*) correct; (*вывод, ответ*) right; (*совет, суждение*) sound.

прави́тель (-я) *м* ruler.

прави́тельственный *прил* government *опред*.

прави́тельств|о (-а) *ср* government.

пра́в|ить (-лю, -ишь) *несов перех* (*исправлять*) to correct ♦ *неперех:* ~ +*instr* (*страной*) to rule, govern; (*машиной*) to drive.

пра́в|ка (-ки; *gen pl* -ок) *ж* proofreading.

правле́ни|е (-я) *ср* government; (*орган*) board.

пра́влю *несов см* пра́вить.

пра́внук (-а) *м* great-grandson.

пра́в|о (-а; *nom pl* -а́) *ср* (*нормы, наука*) law; (*свобода*) right ♦ *вводн сл* (*разг*) really; име́ть (*impf*) ~ на что-н/+*infin* to have the right *или* be entitled to sth/to do; быть (*impf*) в ~е +*infin* to be entitled *или* have the right to do; на права́х +*gen* as; по ~у (*законно*) by rights; (*с полным основанием*) rightly; на ра́вных права́х с +*instr* on equal terms with; *см также* права́.

правове́д (-а) *м* jurisprudent.

правове́дени|е (-я) *ср* jurisprudence.

правове́р|ный (-ен, -на, -но) *прил* orthodox.

правово́й *прил* (*нормы*) legal; правово́е госуда́рство lawful state.

правозащи́тник (-а) *м* human rights activist.

правозащи́тниц|а (-ы) *ж см* правозащи́тник.

правок *сущ см* пра́вка.

правоме́р|ный (-ен, -на, -но) *прил* (*вопрос*) valid; (*сомнения*) justifiable; (*действие, поступок*) lawful.

правомо́ч|ный (-ен, -на, -но) *прил* (*орган*) competent; (*лицо*) authorized.

правонаруше́ни|е (-я) *ср* offence.

правонаруши́тел|ь (-я) *м* offender.

правописа́ни|е (-я) *ср* spelling.

правопоря́д|ок (-ка) *м* law and order.

правосла́ви|е (-я) *ср* orthodoxy.

правосла́вн|ая (-ой; *decl like adj*) *ж см* правосла́вный.

правосла́вн|ый *прил* (*церковь, обряд*) orthodox ♦ (-ого; *decl like adj*) *м member of the Orthodox Church.*

правоспосо́б|ный (-ен, -на, -но) *прил* (*ЮР*) capable.

правосу́ди|е (-я) *ср* justice.

правот|а́ (-ы́) *ж* correctness; я не сомнева́юсь в Ва́шей ~е́ I don't doubt that you are right.

пра́в|ый *прил* right; (*ПОЛИТ*) right-wing; (-, -á, -о; *справедливый*) just; (*невиновный*) innocent; (*no full form*) он прав he is right; ~ суд fair trial.

пра́вящий (-ая, -ее, -ие) *прил* ruling *опред*.

Пра́г|а (-и) *ж* Prague.

прагмати́зм (-а) *м* pragmatism.

прагма́тик (-а) *м* pragmatist.

пра́дед (-а) *м* great-grandfather.

прадеду́ш|ка (-ки; *gen pl* -ек) *м* = пра́дед.

пра́зден *прил см* пра́здный.

пра́зднеств|о (-а) *ср* festival.

пра́здник (-а) *м* (*по случаю какого-н события*) public holiday; (*религиозный*) festival; (*нерабочий день*) holiday; (*радость, торжество*) celebration; с ~ом! best wishes!

пра́здни́ч|ный (-ен, -на, -но) *прил* (*салют, обед*) celebratory; (*одежда, настроение*) festive; ~ день, пра́здничная да́та holiday.

пра́здн|овать (-ую) *несов перех* to celebrate.

пра́здный (-ен, -на, -но) *прил* idle; ~ная жизнь life of idleness.

пра́ктик (-а) *м* (*о каком-н специалисте*) expert; (*практичный человек*) practical person (*мн* people); он хоро́ший ~, но плохо́й теоре́тик he's technically very good, but not so good at the theory.

пра́ктик|а (-и) *ж* practice; (*часть учёбы*) practical experience *или* work; на ~е in practice.

практика́нт (-а) *м* trainee (*on a placement*).

практика́нт|ка (-ки; *gen pl* -ок) *ж см* практика́нт.

практик|ова́ть (-у́ю) *несов перех* to practise (*BRIT*), practice (*US*)

► практикова́ться *несов возв* (*методы, приёмы*) to be used; (*обучаться*): ~ся в чем-н to practise sth.

практи́чен *прил см* практи́чный.

практи́чески *нареч* (*на практике*) in practice; (*по сути дела*) practically.

практи́ческ|ий (-ая, -ое, -ие) *прил* practical.

практи́ч|ный (-ен, -на, -но) *прил* practical.

пра́порщик (-а) *м* (*ВОЕН*) ≈ warrant officer.

прах (-а) *м* (*умершего*) ashes *мн;* **пойти́** (*perf*) пра́хом (*усилия, работа*) to be wasted.

пра́чек *сущ см* **пра́чка.**

пра́чечн|ая (-ой; *decl like adj*) *ж* laundry.

пра́чка (-ки; *gen pl* -ек) *ж* laundress.

преа́мбул|а (-ы) *ж* preamble.

пребыва́ни|е (-я) *ср* (*в каком-н месте*) stay; ~ у вла́сти term of office.

пребыва́|ть (-ю) *несов неперех* (*находиться*) to be.

превали́р|овать (-ую) *несов неперех:* ~ (над +*instr*) to prevail (over).

превенти́вный *прил* preventive; ~ уда́р preemptive strike.

превзойти́ (*как* идти́; *см* **Table 18**; *impf* **превосходи́ть**) *сов перех* (*соперника, врага*) to beat; (*прежние результаты, ожидания*) to surpass; (*доходы, скорость*) to exceed; ~ (*perf*) самого́ себя́ to surpass o.s.

превозм|о́чь (-огу́, -о́жешь *итп*, -о́гут; *pt* -о́г, -огла́, -огло́, *impf* **превозмога́ть**) *сов перех* to overcome.

превозн|ести́ (-есу́, -есёшь; *pt* -ёс, -есла́, -есло́) *сов перех* to extol.

превосхо́ден *прил см* **превосхо́дный.**

превосхо|ди́ть (-жу́, -дишь) *несов от* превзойти́.

превосхо́дно *нареч* excellently ◆ *как сказ* it's excellent.

превосхо́д|ный (-ен, -на, -но) *прил* superb; превосхо́дная сте́пень superlative degree.

превосхо́дств|о (-а) *ср* superiority.

превосхожу́ *несов см* **превосходи́ть.**

превра|ти́ть (-щу́, -ти́шь; *impf* **превраща́ть**) *сов перех:* ~ что-н в +*acc* to turn sth into; **превраща́ть** (~ *perf*) кого́-н в +*acc* to turn *или* transform sb into

▸ **преврати́ться** (*impf* **превраща́ться**) *сов возв* to turn.

превра́т|ный (-ен, -на, -но) *прил* wrong.

превраща́|ть(ся) (-ю(сь)) *несов от* преврати́ть(ся).

превраще́ни|е (-я) *ср* transformation.

превращу́(сь) *сов см* преврати́ть(ся).

превы́|сить (-шу, -сишь; *impf* **превыша́ть**) *сов перех* to exceed; (*рекорд*) to break.

прегра́д|а (-ы) *ж* barrier.

прегра|ди́ть (-жу́, -ди́шь; *impf* **прегражда́ть**) *сов перех:* ~ кому́-н доро́гу/вход to block *или* bar sb's way/entrance.

преда|ва́ть(ся) (-ю(сь)) *несов от* преда́ть(ся).

преда́м(ся) *итп сов см* преда́ть(ся).

преда́ни|е (-я) *ср* legend.

пре́дан|ный (-, -на, -но) *прил* devoted; **он пре́дан де́лу/жене́** he is devoted to the cause/ his wife.

преда́ст(ся) *сов см* преда́ть(ся).

преда́тел|ь (-я) *м* traitor.

преда́тельниц|а (-ы) *ж см* преда́тель.

преда́тельск|ий (-ая, -ое, -ие) *прил*

treacherous.

преда́тельств|о (-а) *ср* treachery.

преда́ть (*как* дать; *см* **Table 14**; *impf* **предава́ть**) *сов перех* to betray; **предава́ть** (~ *perf*) что-н гла́сности to make sth public; **преда́ть** (~ *perf*) кого́-н суду́ to prosecute sb; **предава́ть** (~ *perf*) забве́нию to consign to oblivion

▸ **преда́ться** (*impf* **предава́ться**) *сов возв:* ~ся +*dat* (*мечтам итп*) to give o.s. up to.

предвари́тельный (-ен, -ьна, -ьно) *прил* preliminary; (*продажа билетов*) advance опред; ~ счёт-факту́ра (*комм*) pro-forma invoice; **предвари́тельное заключе́ние** (*ЮР*) remand.

предвар|и́ть (-ю́, -и́шь; *impf* **предваря́ть**) *сов перех* (*события*) to anticipate.

предве́сти|е (-я) *ср* indication.

предвеща́|ть (-ю) *несов перех* (*будущее, успех*) to foretell; (*изменения, кризис*) to portend; (*плохую погоду*) to herald.

предвзя́т|ый (-, -а, -о) *прил* prejudiced.

предви́дени|е (-я) *ср* foresight; (*предположение*) prediction.

предви́|деть (-жу, -дишь) *сов перех* to foresee, predict

▸ **предви́деться** *сов неперех* to be expected.

предвкуша́|ть (-ю) *несов перех* to look forward to, anticipate.

предвкуше́ни|е (-я) *ср* anticipation.

предводи́тел|ь (-я) *м* leader.

предвосхи́|тить (-щу́, -ти́шь; *impf* **предвосхища́ть**) *сов перех* to anticipate.

предвы́борн|ый *прил* (*собрание*) pre-election опред; ~ая кампа́ния election campaign.

предго́рный *прил:* ~ райо́н foothills *мн.*

преддве́ри|е (-я) *ср:* в ~и чего́-н on the threshold of sth.

преде́л (-а) *м* (*обычно мн: города, страны*) boundary; (*перен: приличия*) bound; (: *терпения*) limit; (*изнеможения*) peak; (*совершенства, подлости*) height; (*мечтаний, желаний*) pinnacle; **на** ~ at breaking point; **дойти́** (*perf*) **до** ~**а** to reach the limit; **в** ~**ах** +*gen* (*закона, года*) within; (*приличия*) within the bounds of; **за** ~**ами** +*gen* (*страны, города*) outside.

преде́л|ьный (-ен, -ьна, -ьно) *прил* maximum; (*восторг, важность*) utmost; **преде́льный срок** deadline.

предзнаменова́ни|е (-я) *ср* omen.

предика́т (-а) *м* (*линг*) predicate.

предисло́ви|е (-я) *ср* foreword, preface.

пре́дк|а *сущ см* **пре́док.**

пре́дк|и (-ов) *мн* ancestors *мн.*

предлага́|ть (-ю) *несов от* предложи́ть.

предло́г (-а) *м* pretext; (*линг*) preposition; **под** ~**ом** +*gen* on the pretext of; **под** ~**ом того́, что,** **под тем** ~**ом что** on the pretext that.

предложе́ни|е (-я) *ср* (*конкретное, умное*) proposal, suggestion; (*замужества*) proposal;

(*комм*) offer; (*экон*) supply; (*линг*) sentence;
де́лать (сде́лать *perf*) ~ **кому́-н** (*де́вушке*) to
propose to sb; (*комм*) to make sb an offer;
вноси́ть (внести́ *perf*) ~ (*на собра́нии, на
съе́зде*) to propose a motion.

предлож|и́ть (-ожу́, -о́жишь; *impf* **предлага́ть)**
сов перех to offer; (*план, кандидату́ру*) to
propose ♦ *неперех* to suggest, propose;
(*попроси́ть*) to ask, invite; (*потре́бовать*) to
ask; **предлага́ть (~** *perf*) **что-н кому́-н** to offer
sth to sb, offer sb sth; **он ~ожи́л нам пойти́
туда́** he suggested that we went there.

предло́жный *прил* (*линг*) prepositional;
предло́жный паде́ж prepositional case.

предме́сть|е (-я) *ср* suburb.

предме́т (-а) *м* object; (*обсужде́ния, изуче́ния*)
subject; **на ~** +*gen* concerning; **предме́ты
дома́шнего обихо́да** household goods;
предме́ты пе́рвой необходи́мости
necessities.

предназнача́|ть (-ю) *несов от* **предназна́чить**
▸ **предназнача́|ться** *несов возв* (+*dat*) to be
destined for.

предназначе́ни|е (-я) *ср* role.

предназна́ч|ить (-у, -ишь; *impf*
предназнача́ть) *сов перех*: ~ **что-н/кого́-н**
+*dat* to intend sth/sb for.

преднаме́рен|ный (-, -на, -но) *прил*
(*преступле́ние*) premeditated; (*обма́н итп*)
deliberate.

пре́д|ок (-ка) *м* ancestor; *см та́кже* **пре́дки**.

предопредел|и́ть (-ю, -и́шь; *impf*
предопределя́ть) *сов перех* (*определи́ть*) to
predetermine; (*обусло́вить*) to bring about.

предоста́в|ить (-лю, -ишь) *сов перех*: ~ **что-н
кому́-н** to give sb sth ♦ *неперех*: ~ **кому́-н** +*infin*
(*выбира́ть, реша́ть*) to let sb do;
предоставля́ть (~ *perf*) **кого́-н самому́ себе́** to
leave sb to his own devices; **предоставля́ть (~**
perf) **кому́-н сло́во** to call upon sb to speak.

предостерёг *итп сов см* **предостере́чь**.

предостерега́|ть (-ю) *несов от*
предостере́чь.

предостерегу́ *итп сов см* **предостере́чь**.

предостереже́ни|е (-я) *ср* warning.

предостере́|чь (-гу́, -жёшь *итп*, **-гу́т;** *pt* **-ёг,
-егла́, -егло́,** *impf* **предостерега́ть)** *сов перех*:
~ **кого́-н (от** +*gen*) to warn sb (about).

предосторо́жност|ь (-и) *ж* caution; **ме́ры ~и**
precautionary measures, precautions.

предосуди́тел|ьный (-ен, -ьна, -ьно) *прил*
reprehensible.

предотвра|ти́ть (-щу́, -ти́шь; *impf*
предотвраща́ть) *сов перех* (*войну́, кри́зис*) to
avert; (*боле́знь, ава́рии*) to prevent.

предотвраще́ни|е (-я) *ср* (*см глаг*) averting;
prevention.

предотвращу́ *сов см* **предотврати́ть**.

предохрани́тел|ь (-я) *м* safety device;
(*электри́ческий*) fuse (*BRIT*), fuze (*US*);
(*руже́йный*) safety catch; (*замка́*) snib.

предохрани́тельный *прил* (*ТЕХ*) safety
опред.

предохран|и́ть (-ю́, -и́шь; *impf* **предохраня́ть)**
сов перех to protect.

предписа́ни|е (-я) *ср* (*распоряже́ние*)
instruction; (: *президе́нта, поли́ции*) order;
(: *врача́*) prescription.

предпи|са́ть (-шу́, -шешь; *impf*
предпи́сывать) *сов перех*: ~ **что-н кому́-н**
(*назна́чить*) to prescribe sth for sb ♦ *неперех*: ~
кому́-н +*infin* to order sb to do.

предполага́|ть (-ю) *несов от* **предположи́ть** ♦
перех to demand ♦ *неперех*: ~ +*infin*
(*намерева́ться*) to intend to do
▸ **предполага́|ться** *несов неперех*
(*намеча́ться*) to be planned.

предположе́ни|е (-я) *ср* (*дога́дка*) supposition;
(*наме́рение*) intention.

предположи́тел|ьный (-ен, -ьна, -ьно) *прил*
(*результа́т, вопро́с*) hypothetical; (*срок,
дохо́д*) anticipated.

предполож|и́ть (-ожу́, -о́жишь; *impf*
предполага́ть) *сов перех* (*допусти́ть
возмо́жность*) to allow for; **~о́жим** (*возмо́жно*)
suppose; **~о́жим, он опозда́ет** suppose he is
late.

предпо|сла́ть (-шлю́, -шлёшь; *impf*
предпосыла́ть) *сов перех*: ~ **что-н чему́-н** to
preface sth with sth.

предпосле́дн|ий (-яя, -ее, -ие) *прил* (*но́мер
журна́ла*) penultimate; (*в о́череди*) last but one.

предпосла́ть *сов см* **предпосла́ть**.

предпосы́л|ка (-ки; *gen pl* **-ок)** *ж* (*усло́вие*)
precondition, prerequisite; (*исхо́дное
положе́ние*) premise.

предпоч|е́сть (-ту́, -тёшь; *pt* **-ёл, -ла́, -ло́,** *impf*
предпочита́ть) *сов перех*: ~ **что-н/кого́-н** +*dat*
to prefer sth/sb to ♦ *неперех*: ~ +*infin* to prefer to
do.

предпочте́ни|е (-я) *ср* preference; **ока́зывать
(оказа́ть** *perf*) *или* **отдава́ть (отда́ть** *perf*) ~
кому́-н/чему́-н to show a preference for sb/sth.

предпочти́тел|ьный (-ен, -ьна, -ьно) *прил*
preferable.

предпочту́ *итп сов см* **предпоче́сть**.

предпошлю́ *итп сов см* **предпосла́ть**.

предприи́мчив|ый (-, -а, -о) *прил* enterprising.

предприму́ *итп сов см* **предприня́ть**.

предпринима́тел|ь (-я) *м* entrepreneur,
businessman (*мн* businessmen).

предпринима́тельск|ий (-ая, -ое, -ие) *прил*
enterprise *опред*, business *опред*.

предпринима́тельств|о (-а) *ср* enterprise.

предпри|ня́ть (-иму́, -и́мешь; *pt* **-и́нял, -иняла́,-
и́няло,** *impf* **предпринима́ть)** *сов перех* to

undertake; (*атаку, наступление итп*) to launch; (*меры*) to take.

предприя́ти|е (-я) *ср* enterprise, business.

предрасположе́ние (-я) *ср* predisposition.

предрасполо́женность (-и) *ж* = **предрасположе́ние**.

предрассу́д|ок (-ка) *м* prejudice.

предрека́ть (-ю) *несов перех* (*успех*) to foretell; (*плохую погоду*) to herald.

предреш|и́ть (-у́, -и́шь; *impf* **предреша́ть**) *сов перех* to predetermine.

председа́тел|ь (-я) *м* chairman (*мн* chairmen).

председа́тельств|о (-а) *ср* chairmanship; **под** ~**м** +*gen* under the chairmanship of.

председа́тельств|овать (-ую) *несов неперех* (*на заседании*) to be in the chair; (*работать председателем*) to be chairman; ~ (*impf*) **на собра́нии** to chair a meeting.

предскажу́ *итп сов см* **предсказа́ть**.

предсказа́ни|е (-я) *ср* (*действие*) predicting; (*то, что предсказано*) prediction.

предск|аза́ть (-ажу́, -а́жешь; *impf* **предска́зывать**) *сов перех* to predict; (*чью-н судьбу*) to foretell.

предсме́ртный *прил* (*агония*) death *опред*; (*вздох*) dying; (*воля*) last.

предста|ва́ть (-ю́) *несов от* **предста́ть**.

представи́тел|ь (-я) *м* representative; (*разряда животных итп*) specimen.

представи́тельниц|а (-ы) *ж* representative.

представи́тельный *прил* representative; (*видный*) imposing.

представи́тельств|о (-а) *ср* (*учреждение*) representatives *мн*; (*наличие представителей*) representation; **торго́вое** ~ trade mission; **дипломати́ческое** ~ diplomatic corps.

предста́в|ить (-лю, -ишь; *impf* **представля́ть**) *сов перех* to present; **представля́ть** (~ *perf*) **кого́-н кому́-н** (*познакомить*) to introduce sb to sb; **представля́ть** (**предста́вить** *perf*) **кого́-н к** +*dat* (*к награде, к премии итп*) to recommend sb for, put sb forward for; **представля́ть** (~ *perf*) **интере́с** to be of interest; **представля́ть** (~ *perf*) **себе́** to imagine; ~**ьте** (**себе́**)! (just) imagine!

▶ **предста́в|иться** (*impf* **представля́ться**) *несов возв* (*при знакомстве*) to introduce o.s.; (*появиться: возможность*) to present itself; **представля́ться** (~**ся** *perf*) **кому́-н** (*вид*) to appear before sb; (*интересная картина*) to meet sb's eyes; **ему́** ~**илась бу́дущая встре́ча** he pictured the future meeting; **ей** ~**илась возмо́жность пое́хать в Ло́ндон** an opportunity arose for her to go to London; **представля́ться** (~**ся** *perf*) **больны́м/спя́щим** to pretend to be ill/asleep.

представле́ни|е (-я) *ср* presentation; (*документ*) statement; (*ТЕАТР*) performance; (*знание*) idea; (*ПСИХОЛ*) representation; **не име́ть** (*impf*) (**никако́го**) ~**я о** +*prp* to have no idea about.

предста́влю(сь) *сов см* **предста́вить(ся)**.

представля́|ть (-ю) *несов от* **предста́вить** ◆ *перех* (*действовать от имени*) to represent; (*impf*) **собо́й** или **из себя́** (*являться*) to be; ~ (*impf*) **себе́ что-н** (*понимать*) to understand sth; (*осознавать*) to appreciate sth; **он ничего́ из себя́ не** ~**ет** he doesn't amount to much

▶ **представля́|ться** *несов от* **предста́виться** ◆ *возв*: **мне** ~**ется, (что) он прав** I think he's right; ~**ется, что ...** it appears that ....

предста́|ть (-ну, -нешь; *impf* **представа́ть**) *сов неперех*: ~ **пе́ред** +*instr* (*появиться*) to appear before; (*проявиться: человек*) to show o.s.; (: *характер*) to show itself.

предсто|я́ть (*3sg* -**и́т**, *3pl* -**я́т**) *несов неперех* to lie ahead; **нам** ~**и́т мно́го рабо́ты** there is a lot of work ahead of us.

предстоя́щий (-ая, -ее, -ие) *прил* (*сезон*) coming; (*трудности*) impending; (*работа, встреча*) forthcoming.

предубежде́ни|е (-я) *ср* prejudice.

предугада́|ть (-ю; *impf* **предуга́дывать**) *сов перех* to anticipate.

предупреди́тельный (-ен, -ьна, -ьно) *прил* (*предохраняющий*) preventive; (*любезный*) solicitous, attentive.

предупре|ди́ть (-жу́, -ди́шь; *impf* **предупрежда́ть**) *сов перех* to warn; (*предотвратить*) to prevent; (*опередить*) to anticipate; **предупрежда́ть** (~ *perf*) **кого́-н о** +*prp* to warn sb about.

предупрежде́ни|е (-я) *ср* warning; (*аварии, заболевания*) prevention; (*извещение*) notice.

предупрежу́ *сов см* **предупреди́ть**.

предусм|отре́ть (-отрю́, -о́тришь; *impf* **предусма́тривать**) *сов перех* (*учесть*) to foresee; (*принять меры*) to make provision for; (*подлеж: программа, закон*) to provide for.

предусмотри́тельный (-ен, -ьна, -ьно) *прил* prudent.

предчу́встви|е (-я) *ср* premonition.

предчу́вств|овать (-ую) *несов перех* to have a premonition of.

предше́ственник (-а) *м* predecessor.

предше́ствующий (-ая, -ее, -ие) *прил* previous; (*событие*) foregoing.

предъяви́тел|ь (-я) *м* bearer.

предъяви́тельниц|а (-ы) *ж см* **предъяви́тель**.

предъяв|и́ть (-явлю́, -я́вишь; *impf* **предъявля́ть**) *сов перех* (*паспорт, билет итп*) to show; (*доказательства*) to produce; (*требования, претензии*) to make; (*иск*) to bring; **предъявля́ть** (~ *perf*) **права́ на что-н** to lay claim to sth.

предъявле́ни|е (-я) *ср* (*паспорта, билета итп*) showing; (*претензий*) making; (*иска*) bringing; **по** ~**ю** (*КОММ*) at sight.

предъявлю́ *сов см* **предъяви́ть**.

предъявля́|ть (-ю) *несов от* **предъяви́ть**.

предыду́щий (-ая, -ее, -ие) *прил* previous.

предысто́ри|я (**-и**) *ж* background.
прее́мник (**-а**) *м* successor.
прее́мниц|а (**-ы**) *ж см* **прее́мник**.
прее́мственност|ь (**-и**) *ж* (*власти, традиций*) continuity.
прее́мственный *прил* successive.
пре́жде *нареч* (*в прошлом*) formerly; (*сначала*) first ♦ **предл** (*+gen*) before; **~ всего́** first of all; **~ чем** before; **~ она́ никогда́ об э́том не ду́мала** she never used to think about it.
преждевре́мен|ный (**-ен, -на, -но**) *прил* premature.
пре́жн|ий (**-яя, -ее, -ие**) *прил* former.
презента́ци|я (**-и**) *ж* presentation.
презервати́в (**-а**) *м* condom.
президе́нт (**-а**) *м* president.
прези́диум (**-а**) *м* presidium.
презира́ть (**-ю**) *несов перех* to hold in contempt.
презре́ни|е (**-я**) *ср* (*ко лжи, к предателю*) contempt; (*к опасности*) disregard; (*к богатству итп*) scorn.
презри́тел|ьный (**-ен, -ьна, -ьно**) *прил* contemptuous.
преиму́щественно *нареч* chiefly.
преиму́ществ|о (**-а**) *ср* advantage; (*ЮР*) privilege; **по ~у** (*главным образом*) chiefly; **име́ть** (*impf*) **~ пе́ред** *+instr* to have an advantage over.
преиспо́лн|иться (**-юсь**; *impf* **преисполня́ться**) *сов возв*: **~** *+instr* to be filled with.
прейскура́нт (**-а**) *м* price list.
преклоне́ни|е (**-я**) *ср*: **~** (**пе́ред** *+instr*) admiration (for).
прекло́нный *прил*: **~ во́зраст** old age.
преклоня́|ться (**-юсь**) *несов возв*: **~ пе́ред** *+instr* to admire.
прекра́сен *прил см* **прекра́сный**.
прекра́сн|ое (**-ого**; *decl like adj*) *ср* beauty.
прекра́сн|ый (**-ен, -на, -но**) *прил* (*красивый: женщина, природа*) beautiful; (*: город, вид, день*) fine, beautiful; (*отличный*) excellent; **в оди́н ~ день** (*однажды*) one fine day.
прекрати́ть (**-щу́, -ти́шь**; *impf* **прекраща́ть**) *сов перех* to stop; (*подачу энергии*) to cut off ♦ *неперех*: **~** *+infin* to stop doing; **прекраща́ть** (**~** *perf*) **отноше́ния с кем-н** to break off relations with sb
▶ **прекрати́ться** (*impf* **прекраща́ться**) *сов возв* (*дождь, занятия*) to stop; (*отношения, знакомство*) to end.
прекраще́ни|е (**-я**) *ср* (*работы*) stopping; (*поставок*) cutting off; (*отношений*) breaking off.
прекращу́(сь) *сов см* **прекрати́ть(ся)**.
преле́стн|ый (**-ен, -на, -но**) *прил* charming.
пре́лест|ь (**-и**) *ж* charm; **кака́я ~!** how

charming!
прел|оми́ться (*3sg* **-о́мится**, *3pl* **-о́мятся**, *impf* **преломля́ться**) *сов возв* (*ФИЗ*) to be refracted; (*перен*) to take on a different cast.
пре́лый *прил* rotten.
прель|сти́ть (**-щу́, -сти́шь**; *impf* **прельща́ть**) *сов перех* to attract; (*увлечь*): **~ кого́-н чем-н** to entice sb with sth
▶ **прельсти́ться** (*impf* **прельща́ться**) *сов возв*: **~ся** *+instr* (*возможностями*) to be attracted by; (*богатством*) to be enticed by.
прелю́ди|я (**-и**) *ж* prelude.
премиа́льн|ые (**-ых**; *decl like adj*) *мн* bonus *ед*.
премиа́льный *прил* bonus *опред*; *см также* **премиа́льные**.
премир|ова́ть (**-у́ю**) (*не*)*сов перех* (*работника*) to give a bonus to; (*победителя*) to award a prize to.
пре́ми|я (**-и**) *ж* (*работнику*) bonus; (*победителю*) prize; (*КОММ*) premium.
прему́дрост|ь (**-и**) *ж* (*разг: обычно мн*) ins *мн* and outs *мн*.
премье́р (**-а**) *м* (*также:* **~-мини́стр**) prime minister, premier.
премье́р|а (**-ы**) *ж* première.
премье́р-мини́стр (**-а**) *м* prime minister, premier.
пренебрёг *итп сов см* **пренебре́чь**.
пренебрега́|ть (**-ю**) *несов от* **пренебре́чь**.
пренебрегу́ *итп сов см* **пренебре́чь**.
пренебреже́ни|е (**-я**) *ср* (*законами итп*) disregard; (*: обязанностями*) neglect; (*высокомерие*) contempt.
пренебрежёшь *итп сов см* **пренебре́чь**.
пренебрежи́тел|ьный (**-ен, -ьна, -ьно**) *прил* contemptuous.
пренебр|е́чь (**-егу́, -ежёшь** *итп*, **-гу́т**; *pt* **-ёг, -егла́, -егло́**, *impf* **пренебрега́ть**) *сов неперех*: **~** *+instr* (*опасностью, последствиями*) to disregard; (*модной одеждой, правилами*) to scorn; (*советом, просьбой*) to ignore.
пре́ни|я (**-й**) *мн* debate *ед*.
преоблада́|ть (*3sg* **-ет**, *3pl* **-ют**) *несов неперех*: **~** (**над** *+instr*) to predominate (over).
преобра|зи́ть (**-жу́, -зи́шь**; *impf* **преображать**) *сов перех* to transform
▶ **преобрази́ться** (*impf* **преображаться**) *сов возв* to be transformed.
преобразова́ни|е (**-я**) *ср* (*общества, жизни*) transformation; (*тока, энергии*) conversion; (*революционное, социальное*) reform.
преобразова́тел|ь (**-я**) *м* (*тока, радиосигналов*) transformer; (*общества*) reformer.
преобраз|ова́ть (**-у́ю**; *impf* **преобразо́вывать**) *сов перех* to reorganize; **преобразо́вывать** (**~** *perf*) **что-н в** *+acc* (*превратить*) to convert sth into.

преодоле́|ть (-ю; *impf* **преодолева́ть**) *сов перех* to overcome; (*преграду*) to break down; (*трудный переход итп*) to get through.

препара́т (-а) *м* (*МЕД, ХИМ*) preparation.

препина́ни|е (-я) *ср*: **зна́ки ~я** punctuation marks *мн*.

препира́|ться (-юсь) *несов возв*: ~ **(с** +*instr*) to squabble *или* bicker (with).

преподава́ни|е (-я) *ср* teaching.

преподава́тел|ь (-я) *м* (*школы, курсов*) teacher; (*вуза*) lecturer.

преподава́тельниц|а (-ы) *ж см* **преподава́тель**.

препода|ва́ть (-ю́, -ёшь) *несов перех* to teach.

препода́ть (*как* **дать**; *см* **Table 14**) *сов перех* to teach; ~ (*perf*) **кому́-н уро́к терпе́ния** to teach sb patience.

преподн|ести́ (-есу́, -есёшь; *pt* -ёс, -есла́, -есло́, *impf* **преподноси́ть**) *сов перех*: ~ **что-н кому́-н** to present sb with sth; (*новость, сюрприз*) to give sb sth.

преподо́би|е (-я) *ср* (*РЕЛ*): **Ва́ше/Его́ ~** Your/His Eminence.

преподо́бный *прил* (*РЕЛ*) venerable.

препя́тстви|е (-я) *ср* obstacle.

препя́тств|овать (-ую; *perf* **воспрепя́тствовать**) *несов неперех* (+*dat*) to impede.

прерв|а́ть (-у́, -ёшь; *impf* **прерыва́ть**) *сов перех* (*разговор, работу итп*) to cut short; (*отношения, знакомство*) to break off; (*говорящего*) to interrupt; (*КОМП*) to abort

▶ **прерва́ться** (*impf* **прерыва́ться**) *сов возв* (*разговор, игра*) to be cut short; (*отношения, знакомство*) to be broken off.

пререка́|ться (-юсь) *несов возв* to squabble *или* bicker.

прерогати́в|а (-ы) *ж* prerogative.

прерыва́|ть(ся) (-ю(сь)) *несов от* **прерва́ть(ся)**.

прерыви́стый (-, -а, -о) *прил* (*звонок*) intermittent; (*линия*) broken.

пресёк *итп сов см* **пресе́чь**.

пресека́|ть (-ю) *несов от* **пресе́чь**.

пресеку́ *итп сов см* **пресе́чь**.

пре́сен *прил см* **пре́сный**.

пресече́ни|е (-я) *ср* suppression; **ме́ра ~я** (*ЮР*) injunction.

пресе́|чь (-еку́, -ечёшь *итп*, -еку́т; *pt* -ёк, -екла́, -екло́, *impf* **пресека́ть**) *сов перех* to suppress.

пресле́довани|е (-я) *ср* pursuit; (*инакомыслия*) persecution.

пресле́д|овать (-ую) *несов перех* to pursue; (*перен: женщину*) to chase; (*подлеж: мысли, чувства*) to haunt; (*правозащитника*) to persecute.

пресловутый *прил* notorious.

пресмыка́|ться (-юсь) *несов возв* (*пренебр*): ~ **пе́ред** +*instr* (*унижаться*) to crawl to.

пресмыка́ющееся (-егося; *nom pl* -иеся) *ср* reptile.

пресново́дный *прил* freshwater.

пре́сный (-ен, -на, -но) *прил* (*вода*) fresh; (*пища*) bland; (*перен: шутка*) feeble; (: *история, разговоры итп*) tedious.

пресс (-а) *м* (*ТЕХ*) press.

пре́сс|а (-ы) *ж собир* the press; **общенациона́льная ~** national press.

пресс-конфере́нци|я (-и) *ж* press conference.

пресс|ова́ть (-у́ю; *perf* **спрессова́ть**) *несов перех* (*детали*) to press; (*порошок, газ*) to compress.

пресс-це́нтр (-а) *м* press office.

престаре́л|ый *прил* aged; **дом (для) ~ых** old people's home.

прести́ж (-а) *м* prestige.

прести́ж|ный (-ен, -на, -но) *прил* prestigious.

престо́л (-а) *м* (*трон*) throne; **вступа́ть (вступи́ть** *perf*) *или* **восходи́ть (взойти́** *perf*) **на ~** to ascend the throne; **сверга́ть (све́ргнуть** *perf*) **кого́-н с ~а** to dethrone sb.

престу́пен *прил см* **престу́пный**.

преступи́ть (-уплю́, -у́пишь; *impf* **преступа́ть**) *сов перех* to breach.

преступле́ни|е (-я) *ср* crime.

преступлю́ *сов см* **преступи́ть**.

престу́пник (-а) *м* criminal.

престу́пниц|а (-ы) *ж см* **престу́пник**.

престу́пност|ь (-и) *ж* criminal nature; (*количество*) crime; **организо́ванная ~** organized crime.

престу́п|ный (-ен, -на, -но) *прил* criminal.

пресы́|титься (-щусь, -тишься; *impf* **пресыща́ться**) *сов возв* (+*instr*) to satiate o.s. with.

претвор|и́ть (-ю́, -и́шь; *impf* **претворя́ть**) *сов перех*: ~ **что-н в жизнь** *или* **в де́ло** *или* **в действи́тельность** (*планы, замыслы*) to put sth into practice; (*мечту*) to realize sth.

претенде́нт (-а) *м* (*на престол*) claimant; (*на должность*) candidate; (*на руку женщины*) suitor; (*СПОРТ*) contender; (*ШАХМАТЫ*) challenger.

претенд|ова́ть (-у́ю) *несов неперех*: ~ **на** +*acc* (*стремиться*) to aspire to; (*заявлять права*) to lay claim to.

прете́нзи|я (-и) *ж* (*обычно мн: на наследство, на престол*) claim *ед*; (: *на ум, на красоту итп*) pretension; (*жалоба*) complaint; **быть** (*impf*) **в ~и на** +*acc* to bear a grudge against.

претенцио́з|ный (-ен, -на, -но) *прил* pretentious.

претерп|е́ть (-ерплю́, , -е́рпишь; *impf* **претерпева́ть**) *сов перех* (*изменения*) to undergo; (*невзгоды*) to suffer.

прет|и́ть (*3sg* -и́т, *3pl* -я́т) *несов безл* (+*dat*): **ему́ ~и́т жа́дность** greed disgusts *или* sickens him.

преткнове́ни|е (-я) *ср*: **ка́мень ~я** stumbling block.

Прето́ри|я (-и) *ж* Pretoria.

пре|ть (-ю; *perf* **сопре́ть**) *несов неперех* (*листья*) to rot; (*пища*) to stew.

преувеличе́ни|**е** (-я) *ср* exaggeration.
преувели́ч|**ить** (-у, -ишь; *impf*
преувели́чивать) *сов перех* to exaggerate.
преуме́ньш|**ить** (-у, -ишь; *impf*
преуменьша́ть) *сов перех* (*недооценивать*) to
underestimate; (*показать в меньших размерах*)
to understate.
преуспева́|**ть** (-ю) *несов от* **преуспе́ть** ◆
неперех (*бизнесмен, писатель*) to be
successful.
преуспе́|**ть** (-ю; *impf* **преуспева́ть**) *сов неперех*
to be successful.
префе́кт (-а) *м head of administrative area of
Moscow.*
преходя́щий (-ая, -ее, -ие; -, -а, -е, -и) *прил*
(*временный*) transient.
прецеде́нт (-а) *м* precedent.

KEYWORD

при *предл* (+*prp*) **1** (*возле*) by, near; **при**
доро́ге/до́ме by *или* near the road/house;
сраже́ние при Ватерло́о the battle of Waterloo
2 (*указывает на прикреплённость*) at; **при**
институ́те есть столо́вая there is a canteen at
the institute; **я бу́ду при гостя́х** I will be with
the guests
3 (*в присутствии*) in front of; **при мне он не**
хо́чет говори́ть he doesn't want to speak in
front of me; **при свиде́телях** in front of *или* in
the presence of witnesses; **он всегда́ чита́ет**
при све́те ла́мпы he always reads by the light
of a lamp
4 (*о времени*) under; **при коммуни́стах/**
консерва́торах under the communists/
Conservatives; **при короле́ве Викто́рии** in the
time of Queen Victoria
5 (*о наличии чего-н у кого-н*) on; **он всегда́ при**
деньга́х he always has money on him; **я**
оста́влю э́то при себе́ I'll keep it on me; **при**
жела́нии мо́жно всё измени́ть if you wish
everything can be changed; **при слу́чае**
переда́й ему́ приве́т if the occasion arises, give
him my regards ; **он при́ смерти** he is close to
death; **я здесь ни при чём** it has nothing to do
with me.

при- *префикс* (*in verbs*; *о доведении движения до
конечной цели*) *indicating achievement of final
goal eg.* **прибежа́ть**; (*добавление*) *indicating
addition eg.* **пристро́ить**; (*скрепление*)
indicating fastening onto sth eg. **привинти́ть**;
(*сближение*) *indicating approach of sth eg.*
придви́нуться; (*о слабой мере действия*)
indicating slight action eg. **приоткры́ть**; (*о
сопутствующем действии*) *indicating
accompanying action eg.* **припева́ть**; (*in nouns
and adjectives*; *примыкающий*) *indicating
adjoining position eg.* **примо́рский**.

приба́в|**ить** (-лю, -ишь; *impf* **прибавля́ть**) *сов*

перех to add; (*увеличить*) to increase;
прибавля́ть (~ *perf*) **в ве́се** to put on weight
▶ **приба́виться** (*impf* **прибавля́ться**) *сов возв*
(*проблемы, работа итп*) to mount up ◆ *безл*
(*воды в реке*) to rise; (*народу в толпе*) to grow.
прибавле́ни|**е** (-я) *ср* addition; (*к зарплате,
воды в реке*) rise; ~ **семе́йства** new addition to
the family.
приба́влю(сь) *сов см* **приба́вить(ся)**.
прибавля́|**ть** (-ю) *несов от* **приба́вить**.
прибау́т|**ка** (-ки; *gen pl* -ок) *ж* catch phrase.
прибега́|**ть** (-ю) *несов от* **прибе́гнуть**,
прибежа́ть.
прибе́гн|**уть** (-у, -ешь; *impf* **прибега́ть**) *сов*
неперех: ~ **к** +*dat* to resort to.
прибегу́ *итп сов см* **прибежа́ть**.
прибедня́|**ться** (-юсь) *несов возв* (*разг*) to
pretend to be poor; (*преуменьшать свои
возможности*) to show false modesty.
прибежа́ть (*как* **бежа́ть**; *см* **Table 20**) *сов*
неперех to come running.
прибе́жищ|**е** (-а) *ср* refuge.
прибе́й(те) *сов см* **приби́ть**.
приберу́ *итп сов см* **прибра́ть**.
прибива́|**ть(ся)** (-ю(сь)) *несов от*
приби́ть(ся).
прибира́|**ть** (-ю) *несов от* **прибра́ть**.
приб|**и́ть** (-ью, -ьёшь; *imper* -е́й(те), *impf*
прибива́ть) *сов перех* (*прикрепить гвоздями*)
to nail; (*подлеж: вода, волна итп*) to wash up
▶ **приби́ться** (*impf* **прибива́ться**) *сов возв*
(*лодка к берегу*) to be washed up.
приближа́|**ть(ся)** (-ю(сь)) *несов от*
прибли́зить(ся).
приближе́ни|**е** (-я) *ср* (*дня, события*) approach.
прибли́жу(сь) *сов см* **прибли́зить(ся)**.
приблизи́тел|**ьный** (-ен, -ьна, -ьно) *прил*
approximate.
прибли́|**зить** (-жу, -зишь; *impf* **приближа́ть**)
сов перех (*придвинуть*) to move nearer;
(*ускорить*) to bring nearer
▶ **прибли́зиться** (*impf* **приближа́ться**) *сов*
возв (*человек к окну, машина к дому*) to
approach; (*развязка, победа итп*) to draw near.
прибо́|**й** (-я) *м* breakers *мн*.
прибо́р (-а) *м* (*измерительный*) device;
(*оптический*) instrument; (*нагревательный*)
appliance; (*бритвенный, чернильный*) set.
приб|**ра́ть** (-еру́, -ерёшь; *impf* **прибира́ть**) *сов*
перех to clear up; **прибира́ть** (~ *perf*) **что-н к**
рука́м to lay one's hands on sth; **прибира́ть** (~
perf) **кого́-н к рука́м** to take sb in hand.
прибре́жный *прил* (*у берега моря*) coastal; (*у
берега реки*) riverside *опред*.
прибу́ду *итп сов см* **прибы́ть**.
прибыва́|**ть** (-ю) *несов от* **прибы́ть**.
при́был|**ь** (-и) *ж* profit; **нереализо́ванная** ~
(*КОММ*) paper profit.

при́быль|ный (-ен, -ьна, -ьно) *прил* profitable.
прибы́ти|е (-я) *ср* arrival.
прибы́ть (*как* **быть**; *см* **Table 21**; *impf* **прибыва́ть**) *сов непepex* to arrive; (*вода в реке*) to rise.
прибью́(сь) *итп сов см* **прибы́ть(ся)**.
прива́л (-а) *м* (*в пути*) stop; (*место остановки*) stopping place.
прив|али́ть (-алю́, -а́лишь; *impf* **прива́ливать**) *сов перех* (*придвинуть что-н тяжёлое*) to heave ♦ *неперех* (*перен: разг*) to turn up.
приватиза́ци|я (-и) *ж* (*ЭКОН*) privatization.
приватизи́р|овать (-ую) (*не*)*сов перех* to privatize.
приведе́ни|е (-я) *ср* (*чего-н в порядок*) bringing; (*примеров*) introduction; **~ к прися́ге** swearing in; **~ пригово́ра в исполне́ние** (*ЮР*) carrying out of a sentence; **~ в движе́ние** setting in motion.
приведу́ *итп сов см* **привести́**.
прив|езти́ (-езу́, -езёшь; *pt* -ёз, -езла́, -езло́, *impf* **привози́ть**) *сов перех* to bring.
привере́длив|ый (-, -а, -о) *прил* fussy.
приве́ржен|ец (-ца) *м* (*идеи, традиции*) adherent.
приве́ржен|ный (-, -а, -о) *прил*: **~ (к** +*dat*) dedicated (to).
приве́рженца *итп сущ см* **приве́рженец**.
прив|ести́ (-еду́, -едёшь; *pt* -ёл, -ела́, -ело́, *impf* **приводи́ть**) *сов перех* (*ребёнка: домой*) to bring; (*подлеж: дорога: к дому*) to take; (*пример*) to give; (*чьи-н слова*) to quote; **~** (*perf*) **в у́жас** to horrify; **~** (*perf*) **в отча́яние** to bring to the point of despair; **~** (*perf*) **в восто́рг** to delight; **~** (*perf*) **в изумле́ние** to astonish; **~** (*perf*) **в исполне́ние** to put into effect; **~** (*perf*) **в гото́вность** to make ready; **~** (*perf*) **в поря́док** to put in order; **~** (*perf*) **в движе́ние** to set in motion.
приве́т (-а) *м* greetings *мн*, regards *мн*; (*разг: при встрече*) hi; (: *при расставании*) bye; **посыла́ть** (**посла́ть** *perf*) *или* **передава́ть** (**переда́ть** *perf*) **кому́-н ~** to send one's regards to sb; **~!** **рад тебя́ ви́деть** hi! it's nice to see you.
приве́тлив|ый (-, -а, -о) *прил* friendly.
приве́тстви|е (-я) *ср* (*при встрече*) greeting; (*съезду, делегации*) welcome.
приве́тств|овать (-ую; *perf* **поприве́тствовать**) *несов перех* (*также перен*) to welcome.
привива́|ть(ся) (-ю(сь)) *несов от* **приви́ть(ся)**.
приви́в|ка (-ки; *gen pl* -ок) *ж* (*МЕД*) vaccination.
привиде́ни|е (-я) *ср* ghost.
приви́д|еться (*3sg* -ится, *3pl* -ятся, *impf* **ви́деться**) *сов безл* (+*dat*) to appear to; **мне ~елся стра́шный сон** I had a terrifying dream.
привилегиро́ванный *прил* privileged.
привиле́ги|я (-и) *ж* privilege.
привин|ти́ть (-чу́, -ти́шь; *impf* **приви́нчивать**)

сов перех to screw on.
прив|и́ть (-ью́, -ьёшь; *impf* **привива́ть**) *сов перех* (*растение*) to graft; (*МЕД*): **~ кому́-н что-н** to inoculate *или* vaccinate sb against sth; (*перен*) to cultivate sth in sb
▶ **приви́ться** (*impf* **привива́ться**) *сов возв* (*прививка, черенок*) to take; (*новшество*) to catch on.
при́вкус (-а) *м* flavour (*BRIT*), flavor (*US*).
привлёк *итп сов см* **привле́чь**.
привлека́тельный (-ен, -ьна, -ьно) *прил* attractive.
привлека́|ть (-ю) *несов от* **привле́чь**.
привлеку́ *итп сов см* **привле́чь**.
привлече́ни|е (-я) *ср* (*покупателей, внимания*) attraction; (*ресурсов*) use; **~ к суду́** taking to court; **~ к отве́тственности** calling to account.
привл|е́чь (-еку́, -ечёшь *итп*, -еку́т; *pt* -ёк, -екла́, -екло́, *impf* **привлека́ть**) *сов перех* to attract; **привлека́ть** (**~** *perf*) **кого́-н к** +*dat* (*к рабо́те, к уча́стию*) to coax sb into; (*к суду́*) to take sb to; **привлека́ть** (**~** *perf*) **кого́-н к разгово́ру** to draw sb into a conversation; **привлека́ть** (**~** *perf*) **кого́-н к отве́тственности** to call sb to account.
привн|ести́ (-есу́, -есёшь; *pt* -ёс, -есла́, -есло́, *impf* **привноси́ть**) *сов перех*: **~ что-н в** +*acc* to inject sth into.
привн|оси́ть (-ошу́, -о́сишь) *несов от* **привнести́**.
при́вод (-а) *м* (*электрический*) drive; (*ручной*) gear.
приво́д (-а) *м* (*ЮР*) arrest.
прив|оди́ть (-ожу́, -о́дишь) *несов от* **привести́**.
привожу́ *несов см* **привози́ть**.
приво́з (-а) *м* (*товаров, сырья*) supply.
прив|ози́ть (-ожу́, -о́зишь) *несов от* **привезти́**.
привозно́й *прил* imported.
приво́лен *прил см* **приво́льный**.
приво́ль|е (-я) *ср* (*степное, полевое*) expanse.
приво́ль|ный (-ен, -ьна, -ьно) *прил* (*луга, поля итп*) expansive; (*жизнь*) free and easy.
привра́тник (-а) *м* doorman (*мн* doormen).
привста|ва́ть (-ю́) *несов от* **привста́ть**.
привста́|ть (-ну, -нешь; *impf* **привстава́ть**) *сов неперех* to half rise.
привы́к|нуть (-ну, -нешь, *pt* -, -ла, -ло, *impf* **привыка́ть**) *сов неперех*: **~** +*infin* (*гуля́ть, тра́тить де́ньги*) to get into the habit of doing; **привыка́ть** (**~** *perf*) **к** +*dat* (*к но́вым друзья́м, к шко́ле*) to get used to; **он ~, что́бы ему́ все помога́ли** he is used to everyone helping him.
привы́чек *сущ см* **привы́чка**.
привы́чен *прил см* **привы́чный**.
привы́ч|ка (-ки; *gen pl* -ек) *ж* habit; **по ~ке** out of habit.
привы́ч|ный (-ен, -на, -но) *прил* (*работа, звуки*) familiar.
привью́(сь) *итп сов см* **приви́ть(ся)**.
привяжу́(сь) *итп сов см* **привяза́ть(ся)**.

привя́занност|ь (**-и**) *ж* attachment.
привяза́ть (**-яжу́, -я́жешь;** *impf* **привя́зывать**) *сов перех:* ~ **что-н/кого́-н к** +*dat* to tie sth/sb to; **привя́зывать** (~ *perf*) **к себе́** +*acc* (*вызвать любо́вь*) to endear o.s. to
► **привяза́ться** (*impf* **привя́зываться**) *сов возв:* ~**ся к** +*dat* (*ремнём к сиде́нью*) to fasten o.s. to; (*полюби́ть*) to become attached to; (*разг: надоеда́ть*) to pester.
при́вяз|ь (**-и**) *ж* tie.
пригиба́|ть(ся) (**-ю(сь)**) *несов от* **пригну́ть(ся)**.
пригла́|дить (**-жу, -дишь;** *impf* **пригла́живать**) *сов перех* (*скла́дки на пла́тье*) to smooth out; (*во́лосы*) to smooth back.
пригласи́тельный *прил:* ~ **биле́т** invitation.
пригла|си́ть (**-шу́, -си́шь;** *impf* **приглаша́ть**) *сов перех* to invite; (*врача́*) to call; **приглаша́ть** (~ *perf*) **кого́-н в го́сти** to invite sb; **приглаша́ть** (~ *perf*) **кого́-н на та́нец** to ask sb to dance.
приглаше́ни|е (**-я**) *ср* invitation; (*КОМП*) prompt.
приглашу́ *сов см* **пригласи́ть**.
приглуш|и́ть (**-у́, -и́шь;** *impf* **приглуша́ть**) *сов перех* (*зву́ки*) to deaden; (*ра́дио*) to turn down; (*кра́ски*) to tone down; (*тона́*) to soften; (*перен: боль, тоску́*) to lessen.
пригля|де́ть (**-жу́, -ди́шь;** *impf* **пригля́дывать**) *сов неперех:* ~ **за** +*instr* to look after ♦ *перех* to search out, find
► **пригляде́ться** (*impf* **пригля́дываться**) *сов возв:* ~**ся (к** +*dat*) (*к карти́не, к незнако́мцу*) to look closely (at).
пригля|ну́ться (**-ну́сь, -нешься**) *сов возв:* ~ **кому́-н** to attract sb.
приг|на́ть (**-оню́, -о́нишь;** *impf* **пригоня́ть**) *сов перех* to drive; (*костю́м*) to adjust, alter.
пригн|у́ть (**-у́, -ёшь;** *impf* **пригиба́ть**) *сов перех* (*ве́тку, кусты́*) to bend
► **пригну́ться** (*impf* **пригиба́ться**) *сов возв* (*нагну́ться: челове́к*) to bend down; (*ве́тки, кусты́*) to bend.
пригова́рива|ть (**-ю**) *несов от* **приговори́ть** ♦ *неперех* (*сопровожда́ть слова́ми*) to talk at the same time (*as doing sth*).
пригово́р (**-а**) *м* (*ЮР*) sentence; (*перен*) condemnation; **выноси́ть** (**вы́нести** *perf*) ~ to pass sentence.
приговор|и́ть (**-ю́, -и́шь;** *impf* **пригова́ривать**) *сов перех:* ~ **кого́-н к** +*dat* to sentence sb to.
приго́ден *прил см* **приго́дный**.
приго|ди́ться (**-жу́сь, -ди́шься;** *impf* **пригожда́ться**) *сов возв* (+*dat*) to be useful to.
приго́дный (**-ен, -на, -но**) *прил* suitable.
пригожда́|ться (**-юсь**) *несов от* **пригоди́ться**.
пригожу́сь *сов см* **пригоди́ться**.
пригоню́ *итп сов см* **пригна́ть**.
пригоня́|ть (**-ю**) *несов от* **пригна́ть**.

пригора́|ть (*3sg* **-ет,** *3pl* **-ют**) *несов от* **пригоре́ть**.
пригоре́лый *прил* burnt.
пригор|е́ть (*3sg* **-и́т,** *3pl* **-я́т,** *impf* **пригора́ть**) *сов неперех* to burn.
приго́рка *сущ см* **приго́рок**.
при́город (**-а**) *м* suburb.
при́городный *прил* (*посёлок, жи́тель*) suburban; (*по́езд, авто́бус*) local.
приго́р|ок (**-ка**) *м* hillock.
при́горш|ня (**-ни;** *gen pl* **-ен**) *ж* handful.
пригото́в|ить (**-лю, -ишь;** *сов от* **гото́вить** ♦ (*impf* **пригота́вливать** *или* **приготовля́ть**) *перех* to prepare; (*посте́ль*) to make; (*ва́нну*) to run
► **пригото́виться** *сов от* **гото́виться** ♦ *возв:* ~**ся (к** +*dat*) (*к путеше́ствию*) to get ready (for); (*к уро́ку*) to prepare (o.s.) (for).
приготовле́ни|е (**-я**) *ср* preparation.
приготовлю́(сь) *сов см* **пригото́вить(ся)**.
приготовля́|ть (**-ю**) *несов от* **пригото́вить**.
пригрева́|ть (**-ю**) *несов от* **пригре́ть**.
пригре́|зиться (**-жусь, -зишься**) *сов от* **гре́зиться**.
пригре́|ть (**-ю;** *impf* **пригрева́ть**) *сов перех* (*подлеж: со́лнце: зе́млю*) to warm; (*перен: сироту́*) to take in.
пригрози́ть(ся) (**-жу́(сь), -зи́шь(ся)**) *сов от* **грози́ть(ся)**.
пригуб|и́ть (**-лю, -ишь;** *impf* **пригу́бливать**) *сов перех* to take a sip of.
прида|ва́ть (**-ю́, -ёшь**) *несов от* **прида́ть**.
придав|и́ть (**-авлю́, -а́вишь;** *impf* **прида́вливать**) *сов перех* to press, to squash.
прида́м *итп сов см* **прида́ть**.
прида́н|ое (**-ого;** *decl like adj* **ср** (*неве́сты*) dowry; (*новорождённого*) layette.
прида́ст *сов см* **прида́ть**.
прида́т|ок (**-ка**) *м* (*та́кже перен*) appendage.
прида́точный *прил:* **прида́точное предложе́ние** (*линг*) subordinate clause.
прида́|ть (*как* **дать;** *см* **Table 14;** *impf* **придава́ть**) *сов неперех:* ~ **чего́-н кому́-н** (*уве́ренности*) to instil sth in sb; **придава́ть** (~ *perf*) **что-н чему́-н** (*вид, фо́рму*) to give sth to sth; (*ва́жность*) to attach sth to sth; **придава́ть** (~ *perf*) **бо́дрости кому́-н** to hearten sb; **придава́ть** (~ *perf*) **сил кому́-н** to strengthen sb.
прида́ч|а (**-и**) *ж:* **в** ~**у** in addition.
прида́шь *сов см* **прида́ть**.
придви́н|уть (**-у, -ешь;** *impf* **придвига́ть**) *сов перех:* ~ (**к** +*dat*) to move over *или* up (to).
придво́рный *прил* court *опред* ♦ (**-ого;** *decl like adj*) *м* courtier.
приде́ла|ть (**-ю;** *impf* **приде́лывать**) *сов перех:* ~ **что-н к** +*dat* to attach *или* fix sth to.
придерж|а́ть (**-ержу́, -е́ржишь;** *impf* **приде́рживать**) *сов перех* (*дверь*) to hold

(steady); (*лошадь*) to restrain.

приде́ржива|ться (-юсь) *несов возв* (+*gen*; *каких-н взглядов*) to hold; (*за перила*): ~ **за** +*acc* to hold onto.

придеру́сь *итп сов см* **придра́ться**.

придира́|ться (-ю) *несов от* **придра́ться**.

приди́р|ка (-ки; *gen pl* -ок) *ж* quibble.

приди́рчив|ый (-, -а, -о) *прил* (*человек*) fussy; (*замечание, взгляд*) critical.

придра́|ться (-еру́сь, -ерёшься; *impf* **придира́ться**) *сов возв*: ~ **к** +*dat* to find fault with.

приду́(сь) *итп сов см* **прийти́(сь)**.

приду́ма|ть (-ю; *impf* **приду́мывать**) *сов перех* (*отговорку, причину*) to think of *или* up; (*новый прибор*) to devise; (*песню, стихотворение*) to make up; **он ~л, как спасти́ положе́ние** he thought of how to save the situation.

приду́рива|ться (-юсь) *несов возв* (*разг*) to pretend to be ignorant.

приду́сь *итп сов см* **прийти́сь**.

придыха́ни|е (-я) *ср* (*линг*) aspiration.

приеда́|ться (-юсь) *несов от* **прие́сться**.

прие́дим|ся *итп сов см* **прие́сться**.

прие́ду *итп сов см* **прие́хать**.

прие́дят|ся *сов см* **прие́сться**.

прие́зд (-а) *м* arrival.

приезжа́|ть (-ю) *несов от* **прие́хать**.

прие́зж|ий (-ая, -ее, -ие) *прил* visiting.

прие́м|ся *сов см* **прие́сться**.

прие́м (-а) *м* reception; (*у врача*) surgery (*BRIT*), office (*US*); (*борьбы, гимнастический*) technique; (*наказания, воздействия*) means; **за оди́н** ~ in one go; **в два/в три ~а** in two/three attempts; **устра́ивать** (**устро́ить** *perf*) ~ to organize a reception; **запи́сываться** (**записа́ться** *perf*) **на ~ к** +*dat* to make an appointment to see.

прие́м|ка (-и) *ж* (*товаров*) receipt.

прие́мн|ая (-ой; *decl like adj*) *ж* (*также:* ~ **ко́мната**) reception.

прие́мник (-а) *м* (*радиоприёмник*) radio; (*связь*) receiver.

прие́мный *прил* (*часы*) reception *опред*; (*день*) visiting *опред*; (*экзамены*) entrance *опред*; (*комиссия*) selection *опред*; (*родители, дети*) adoptive; **прие́мный поко́й** room where newly-arrived patients register and are given inital checkup before going to the ward.

прие́|сться (*как* **есть**; *см* Table 15; *impf* **приеда́ться**) *сов возв*: ~ **кому́-н** (*разг*) to bore sb stiff.

прие́|хать (*как* **е́хать**; *см* Table 19; *impf* **приезжа́ть**) *сов неперех* to arrive *или* come (*by transport*).

прие́шься *сов см* **прие́сться**.

прижа́|ть (-му́, -мёшь; *impf* **прижима́ть**) *сов перех* (*разг*: *притеснить*) to put the screws on; **прижима́ть** (~ *perf*) **что-н/кого́-н к** +*dat* to press sth/sb to *или* against

▸ **прижа́|ться** (*impf* **прижима́ться**) *сов возв*:

~**ся к** +*dat* to press o.s. against; (*ребёнок к груди*) to snuggle up to.

прижё́|чь (-гу́, -жёшь *итп*, -гу́т; *impf* **прижига́ть**) *сов перех* to cauterize.

прижива́|ться (-юсь) *несов от* **прижи́ться**.

приживу́сь *итп сов см* **прижи́ться**.

прижига́|ть (-ю) *несов от* **прижё́чь**.

прижи́зненн|ый *прил*: ~**ая сла́ва** fame during one's lifetime; **он ви́дел мно́го** ~**ых изда́ний свои́х поэ́м** many books of his poems were published during his lifetime.

прижима́|ть(ся) (-ю(сь)) *несов от* **прижа́ть(ся)**.

прижи́мист|ый (-, -а, -о) *прил* (*разг*) tightfisted.

прижи́|ться (-ву́сь, -вёшься; *pt* -лся, -ла́сь, -лось, *impf* **прижива́ться**) *сов возв* (*человек*) to settle in, get o.s. settled; (*животные*) to adapt, become acclimatized (*BRIT*) *или* acclimated (*US*); (*растения*) to take rest.

прижму́(сь) *сов см* **прижа́ть(ся)**.

приз (-а; *nom pl* -ы́) *м* prize.

призаду́ма|ться (-юсь; *impf* **призаду́мываться**) *сов возв*: ~ **над** +*instr* или **о** +*prp* to reflect upon.

призва́ни|е (-я) *ср* (*к искусству, к науке итп*) vocation; (*предназначение*) calling; ~ **теа́тра – воспи́тывать** the purpose of the theatre is to educate.

приз|ва́ть (-ову́, -овёшь; *pt* -ва́л, -вала́, -ва́ло, *impf* **призыва́ть**) *сов перех* (*на борьбу, к защите страны*) to call, summon; **призыва́ть** (~ *perf*) **к ми́ру/разоруже́нию** to call for peace/disarmament; **призыва́ть** (~ *perf*) **кого́-н к споко́йствию/повинове́нию** to appeal to sb to be calm/obedient; **призыва́ть** (~ *perf*) **кого́-н к поря́дку** to call sb to order; **призыва́ть** (~ *perf*) **в а́рмию** to call up (to join the army).

призе́мист|ый (-, -а, -о) *прил* (*человек*) squat.

приземл|и́ть (-ю́, -и́шь; *impf* **приземля́ть**) *сов перех* to land

▸ **приземл|и́ться** (*impf* **приземля́ться**) *сов возв* to land.

призё́р (-а) *м* prizewinner.

при́зм|а (-ы) *ж* prism; **сквозь** *или* **че́рез** ~**у** +*gen* (*перен*) in the light of.

призна|ва́ть(ся) (-ю́(сь), -ёшь(ся)) *несов от* **призна́ть(ся)**.

при́знак (-а) *м* (*кризиса, успеха*) sign; (*отравления*) symptom; **без** ~**ов жи́зни** not showing any sign of life.

призна́ни|е (-я) *ср* (*государства, писателя*) recognition; (*своего бессилия, чьих-н достижений*) acknowledgment, recognition; (*в любви*) declaration; (*в преступлении*) confession.

при́знан|ный (-, -а, -о) *прил* recognized.

призна́телен *прил см* **призна́тельный**.

призна́тельность (-и) *ж* gratitude.

призна́тел|ьный (-ен, -ьна, -ьно) *прил* grateful.

призна́|ть (-ю; *impf* **признава́ть**) *сов перех*

(*правительство, чьи-н права*) to recognize; (*положительно оценить: книгу, фильм*) to acclaim; (*счесть*): ~ **что-н/кого-н** +*instr* to recognize sth/sb as

▶ **призна|ться** (*impf* **признаваться**) *сов возв*: ~**ся кому-н в чём-н** (*в преступлении*) to confess sth to sb; **признаваться** (~**ся** *perf*) **кому-н в любви** to make a declaration of love to sb; ~**ся** *или* **признаюсь, я Вас не понимаю** I have to admit that I don't understand you.

призов|о́й *прил* (*деньги*) prize *опред*; ~**а́я меда́ль** prizewinner's medal; ~**о́е ме́сто** medal position.

призову́ *итп сов см* **призва́ть**.

призо́р (-**а**) *м*: **без** ~**а** (*разг*) unattended.

при́зрак (-**а**) *м* ghost.

при́зрачн|ый (-**ен**, -**на**, -**но**) *прил* (*успех, надежды*) illusory; (*опасность*) imagined.

призы́в (-**а**) *м* (*к восстанию, к защите*) call; (: *в армию*) conscription; (*лозунг*) slogan ◆ *собир* call-up.

призыва́|ть (-**ю**) *несов от* **призва́ть**.

призывни́к (-**а́**) *м* conscript.

призывн|о́й *прил* (*возраст*) call-up *опред*; (*пункт*) recruiting *опред*.

призы́вный *прил* summoning *опред*.

при́иск (-**а**) *м* mine.

прийти́ (*как* **идти́**; *см* **Table 18**; *impf* **приходи́ть**) *сов неперех* (*идя, достичь*) to come (*on foot*); (*письмо, телеграмма*) to arrive; (*весна, час свободы*) to come; (*достигнуть*): ~ **к** +*dat* (*к власти, к выводу*) to come to; (*к демократии*) to achieve; **приходи́ть** (~ *perf*) **в у́жас/недоуме́ние** to be horrified/bewildered; **приходи́ть** (~ *perf*) **в восто́рг** to go into raptures; **приходи́ть** (~ *perf*) **в него́дность** to become worthless; **приходи́ть** (~ *perf*) **в упа́док** to go into decline; **приходи́ть** (~ *perf*) **в запу́щенность** to fall into neglect; **приходи́ть** (~ *perf*) **кому-н в го́лову** *или* **на ум** to occur to sb; **приходи́ть** (~ *perf*) **в себя́** (*после обморока*) to come to *или* round; (*успокоиться*) to come to one's senses

▶ **прийти́сь** (*impf* **приходи́ться**) *сов возв*: ~**сь на** +*acc* to fall on; (*попасть*): ~**сь по** +*dat* to land on; (*подойти*): ~**сь по** +*dat*/**к** +*dat* (*одежда, ключ*) to fit; (*вещь: по вкусу*) to suit ◆ *безл* (+*infin*; *уступить, пойти на компромисс итп*) to have to do; (**нам**) **придётся согласи́ться** we'll have to agree; **нам пришло́сь тяжело́** we had a hard time; **как придётся** anyhow; **где придётся** anywhere; **что придётся** anything.

прикажу́ *итп сов см* **приказа́ть**.

прика́з (-**а**) *м* order; **отдава́ть** (**отда́ть** *perf*) ~ to give an order.

приказа́ни|е (-**я**) *ср* = **прика́з**.

прика|за́ть (-**ажу́**, -**а́жешь**; *impf* **прика́зывать**) *сов неперех*: ~ **кому-н** +*infin* to order sb to do;

как ~**а́жете** as you like.

приказн|о́й *прил* (*тон, жест*) commanding; **в приказно́м поря́дке** in the form of an order.

прика́зчик (-**а**) *м* (*в магазине*) sales assistant (*BRIT*) *или* clerk (*US*); (*в помещичьем хозяйстве*) *manager of estate or farm*.

прика́зыва|ть (-**ю**) *несов от* **приказа́ть**.

прика́лыва|ть (-**ю**) *несов от* **приколо́ть**.

прика́нчива|ть (-**ю**) *несов от* **прико́нчить**.

прикарма́н|ить (-**ю**, -**ишь**; *impf* **прикарма́нивать**) *сов перех* (*разг*) to pocket.

прика́рмлива|ть (-**ю**) *несов перех* (*младенца*) to supplement the diet of.

прикаса́ни|е (-**я**) *ср* (*рук*) touch.

прикаса́|ться (-**юсь**) *несов от* **прикосну́ться**.

прик|ати́ть (-**ачу́**, -**а́тишь**; *impf* **прика́тывать**) *сов перех* to roll up ◆ *неперех* (*разг: приехать*) to show up.

прики́|нуть (-**у**, -**ешь**; *impf* **прики́дывать**) *сов неперех* (*разг: посчитать*) to work out (roughly)

▶ **прики́нуться** (*impf* **прики́дываться**) *сов возв* (+*instr*; *разг*) to pretend to be.

прикла́д (-**а**) *м* (*ружья, автомата*) butt (*of gun etc*).

прикладн|о́й *прил* applied; **прикладна́я програ́мма** (*КОМП*) application program; **прикладно́е иску́сство** applied art.

прикла́дыва|ть(ся) (-**ю(сь)**) *несов от* **приложи́ть(ся)**.

прикле́|ить (-**ю**, -**ишь**; *impf* **прикле́ивать**) *сов перех* to glue, stick

▶ **прикле́иться** (*impf* **прикле́иваться**) *сов возв* to stick.

приключа́|ться (*3sg* -**ется**, *3pl* -**ются**) *несов от* **приключи́ться**.

приключе́ни|е (-**я**) *ср* adventure.

приключе́нческ|ий (-**ая**, -**ое**, -**ие**) *прил* adventure *опред*.

приключи́|ться (*3sg* -**йтся**, *3pl* -**а́тся**; *impf* **приключа́ться**) *сов возв* (*разг: произойти*) to happen.

прик|ова́ть (-**ую́**; *impf* **прико́вывать**) *сов перех* (*перен: внимание, взгляд*) to fix; **прико́вывать** (~ *perf*) **кого-н к** +*dat* to chain sb to; (*перен*) to confine sb to.

прико́л (-**а**) *м*: **стоя́ть на** ~**е** to be moored.

прик|оло́ть (-**олю́**, -**о́лешь**; *impf* **прика́лывать**) *сов перех* to fasten, fix.

прикомандир|ова́ть (-**у́ю**; *impf* **прикомандиро́вывать**) *сов перех* to second.

прико́нч|ить (-**у**, -**ишь**; *impf* **прика́нчивать**) *сов перех* (*умертвить*) to finish off.

прикорн|у́ть (-**у́**, -**ёшь**) *сов неперех* (*разг*) to curl up.

прикосн|у́ться (-**у́сь**, -**ёшься**; *impf* **прикаса́ться**) *сов возв*: ~ **к** +*dat* to touch lightly.

прикреп|и́ть (-лю́, -и́шь; *impf* **прикрепля́ть**) *сов перех*: ~ **что-н** +*dat* (*деталь, бант*) to fix sth to; **прикрепля́ть** (~ *perf*) **кого́-н/что-н** к +*dat* (*сове́тника к предприя́тию, институ́т к заво́ду*) to attach sb/sth to.

прикри́кн|уть (-у, -ешь; *impf* **прикри́кивать**) *сов неперех*: ~ **на** +*acc* to shout *или* yell at.

прикро́ю(сь) *итп сов см* **прикры́ть(ся)**.

прикрыва́|ть(ся) (-ю) *несов от* **прикры́ть(ся)**.

прикры́ти|е (-я) *ср* (*махина́ций*) cover-up; (*ты́ла, ВОЕН*) cover; **под** ~**м** +*gen* under the guise of.

прикр|ы́ть (-о́ю, -о́ешь; *impf* **прикрыва́ть**) *сов перех* to cover; (*закры́ть*) to close (over); (*разг: ликвиди́ровать*) to wind up; (*скрыва́ть*) to cover up

▶ **прикры́ться** (*impf* **прикрыва́ться**) *сов возв* (+*instr*; *одея́лом, плащо́м*) to cover o.s. with; (*отгово́рками, рито́рикой*) to hide behind; (*разг: ликвиди́роваться*) to close down.

прик|ури́ть (-урю́, -у́ришь; *impf* **прику́ривать**) *сов неперех* to get a light (*from lit cigarette*).

прик|уси́ть (-ушу́, -у́сишь; *impf* **прику́сывать**) *сов перех* (*гу́бу, язы́к*) to bite.

прила́в|ок (-ка) *м* (*в магази́не*) counter; (*на ры́нке*) stall.

прилага́тельн|ое (-ого; *decl like adj*) *ср* (*ЛИНГ: та́кже:* **и́мя** ~) adjective.

прилага́|ть (-ю) *несов от* **приложи́ть**.

прила́|дить (-жу, -дишь; *impf* **прила́живать**) *сов перех*: ~ **что-н** к +*dat* to fit sth on to.

приласка́|ть(ся) (-ю(сь)) *сов от* **ласка́ть(ся)**.

прилёг *итп сов см* **приле́чь**.

прилега́|ть (*3sg* -ет, *3pl* -ют) *несов неперех*: ~ **к** +*dat* (*каса́ться*) to fit tightly; (*находи́ться ря́дом*) to adjoin.

прилежа́ни|е (-я) *ср* diligence.

приле́ж|ный (-ен, -на, -но) *прил* diligent.

прилеп|и́ть (-лю́, -ишь; *impf* **прилепля́ть**) *сов перех* to stick.

приле|те́ть (-чу́, -ти́шь; *impf* **прилета́ть**) *сов неперех* to arrive (*by air*), fly in.

приле́|чь (-я́гу, -я́жешь *etc* -я́гут; *pt* -ёг, -егла́, -егло́) *сов неперех* to lie down for a while.

прили́в (-а) *м* (*в мо́ре, в океа́не*) tide; (*де́нег, тури́стов*) flood; (*негодова́ния, эне́ргии*) surge.

прилива́|ть (-ю) *несов от* **прили́ть**.

прилижу́ *итп сов см* **прилиза́ть**.

прили́занный *прил* (*разг: во́лосы*) slicked-down; (*вид*) fastidious; (*челове́к*) pernickety (*BRIT*), persnickety (*US*).

прил|иза́ть (-ижу́, -и́жешь; *impf* **прили́зывать**) *сов перех* (*разг: во́лосы*) to slick down.

прили́п|нуть (-ну, -нешь; *pt* -, -ла, -ло, *impf* **прилипа́ть** *или* **ли́пнуть**) *сов неперех*: ~ **к** +*dat* to stick to; (*разг: к де́вушке, к незнако́мцу*) to cling to.

прил|и́ть (*3sg* -ьёт, *3pl* -ью́т, *pt* -и́л, -ила́, -и́ло, *impf* **прилива́ть**) *сов неперех* (*вода́ в мо́ре*) to flow; (*кровь*) to rush.

прили́чен *прил см* **прили́чный**.

прили́чи|е (-я) *ср* decency; (*обы́чно мн*) manners *мн*.

прили́ч|ный (-ен, -на, -но) *прил* (*присто́йный: челове́к*) decent; (: *мане́ры*) proper; (*доста́точно хоро́ший, большо́й*) fair, decent.

приложе́ни|е (-я) *ср* (*си́лы, эне́ргии*) application; (*к журна́лу*) supplement; (*к докумета́ции*) addendum (*мн* addenda).

прил|ожи́ть (-ожу́, -о́жишь; *impf* **прилага́ть**) *сов перех* (*присоедини́ть*) to affix; (*си́лу, зна́ния итп*) to apply; (*прикла́дывать*): ~ **что-н** к +*dat* (*ру́ку ко лбу*) to put sth to; (*тру́бку к у́ху*) to hold sth to; **прилага́ть** (~ *perf*) **ру́ку** к +*dat* to put one's hand to; **ума́ не** ~**ожу́** (*разг*) I don't have a clue

▶ **приложи́ться** (*impf* **прикла́дываться**) *сов возв*: ~**ся у́хом/губа́ми** к +*dat* to press one's ear/lips against; **остально́е** ~**о́жится** the rest is a matter of course.

прильёт *итп сов см* **прили́ть**.

прильн|у́ть (-у́, -ёшь) *сов от* **льнуть** ♦ *неперех* (*прини́кнуть*): ~ **к** +*dat* (*к чьей-н груди́*) to cling to; (*к две́ри, к окну́*) to press o.s. against.

приля́гу *итп сов см* **приле́чь**.

при́м|а (-ы) *ж* (*МУЗ: веду́щий го́лос*) lead; (*разг: о балери́не*) prima ballerina.

при́м|а-балери́н|а (-ы, -ы) *ж* prima ballerina.

прим|ани́ть (-аню́, -а́нишь) *сов перех* (*разг*) to lure.

прима́н|ка (-ки; *gen pl* -ок) *ж* bait.

примелька́|ться (-юсь) *сов возв* to become familiar.

примене́ни|е (-я) *ср* (*ору́жия*) use; (*маши́н, лека́рств*) application; (*мер, ме́тода*) adoption; **в** ~**и к** +*dat* in application to.

примени́м|ый (-, -а, -о) *прил* applicable.

примени́тельно *предл*: ~ **к** +*dat* in conformity with.

прим|ени́ть (-еню́, -е́нишь; *impf* **применя́ть**) *сов перех* (*ме́ры*) to implement; (*си́лу*) to use; **применя́ть** (~ *perf*) **что-н** (к +*dat*) (*ме́тод, тео́рию*) to apply sth (to); **применя́ть** (~ *perf*) **са́нкции** к +*dat* to impose sanctions on.

применя́|ться (*3sg* -ется, *3pl* -ются) *несов неперех* (*испо́льзоваться*) to be used.

приме́р (-а) *м* example; **к** ~**у** for example; **не в** ~ +*dat* unlike; **по** ~**у** +*gen* (*схо́дно с*) after the example of; **ста́вить** (**поста́вить** *perf*) **кого́-н/что-н в** ~ to hold sb/sth up as an example; **брать** (**взять** *perf*) ~ **с** +*gen* to follow the example of.

приме́рен *прил см* **приме́рный**.

примёрз|нуть (-ну, -нешь; *pt* -, -ла, -ло, *impf* **примерза́ть**) *сов неперех*: ~ (**к** +*dat*) to freeze (to).

приме́р|ить (-ю, -ишь; *impf* **примеря́ть**) *сов перех* to try on.

приме́р|ка (-ки; *gen pl* -ок) *ж* trying on.

приме́рно *нареч* (*образцо́во*) in an exemplary fashion; (*приблизи́тельно*) approximately.

приме́р|ный (-ен, -на, -но) *прил* (*образцовый*) exemplary; (*приблизительный*) approximate.

приме́рок *сущ см* **приме́рка**.

примеря́|ть (-ю) *несов от* **приме́рить**.

при́мес|ь (-и) *ж* dash.

приме́т|а (-ы) *ж* (*признак*) sign; (*суеверная*) omen; **она́ у него́ на ~е** he has his eye on her.

примета́|ть (-ю; *impf* **примётывать**) *сов перех* to stitch on, tack on (*BRIT*).

приме́тен *прил см* **приме́тный**.

приме́|тить (-чу, -тишь; *impf* **примеча́ть**) *сов перех* (*разг*) to notice.

приме́т|ный (-ен, -на, -но) *прил* (*заметный*: *человек*) conspicuous; (: *событие*) prominent.

примётыва|ть (-ю) *несов от* **примета́ть**.

примеча́ни|е (-я) *ср* note, comment.

примеча́тельный (-ен, -ьна, -ьно) *прил* (*событие, внешность*) remarkable; (*изменение*) notable.

примеча́|ть (-ю) *несов от* **приме́тить**.

примечу́ *сов см* **приме́тить**.

примеша́|ть (-ю; *impf* **приме́шивать**) *сов перех* (*перен*) to bring; **приме́шива|ть** (~ *perf*) (**в** +*acc*) to add (to), mix in(to).

примина́|ть (-ю) *несов от* **примя́ть**.

примире́ни|е (-я) *ср* reconciliation.

примир|и́ть (-ю́, -и́шь; *impf* **примиря́ть** или **мири́ть**) *сов перех*: ~ **кого́-н с кем-н** to reconcile sb with sb; **примиря́ть** (~ *perf*) **кого́-н с чем-н** to help sb come to terms with sth

▶ **примир|и́ться** (*impf* **примиря́ться**) *сов возв*: ~**ся с** +*instr* (*с врагом, с мужем*) to be reconciled with; (*с действительностью*) to reconcile o.s. to.

примити́в|ный (-ен, -на, -но) *прил* primitive.

примкн|у́ть (-у́, -ёшь; *impf* **примыка́ть**) *сов неперех*: ~ **к** +*dat* (*к партии*) to join; (*к большинству*) to side with.

примну́ *итп сов см* **примя́ть**.

примо́лкн|уть (-у, -ешь) *сов неперех* (*разг*: *умолкнуть*) to shush.

примо́рский (-ая, -ое, -ие) *прил* seaside *опред*.

примо́рь|е (-я) *ср* seaside.

примо|сти́ться (-щу́сь, -сти́шься) *сов возв* (*разг*) to perch o.s.

примо́ч|ка (-ки; *gen pl* -ек) *ж* (*процедура*) bathing; (*лекарство*) lotion.

примощу́сь *сов см* **примости́ться**.

приму́(сь) *итп сов см* **приня́ть(ся)**.

при́мул|а (-ы) *ж* (*БОТ*) primrose.

при́мус (-а) *м* Primus (stove) ®.

примч|а́ться (-у́сь, -и́шься) *несов возв* to come tearing up.

примыка́|ть (-ю) *несов от* **примкну́ть** ♦ *неперех* (*прилегать*): ~ **к** +*dat* to adjoin.

прим|я́ть (-ну́, -нёшь; *impf* **примина́ть**) *сов перех* (*траву*) to trample on.

принадлеж|а́ть (-у́, -и́шь) *несов неперех*: ~

+*dat* to belong to; (*заслуга*) to go to; (*роль*) to be played by; ~ (*impf*) **к** +*dat* (*входить в состав*) to belong to, be a member of.

принадле́жност|ь (-и) *ж* characteristic; (*обычно мн*: *охотничьи, рыболовные*) tackle; (*письменные*) accessories *мн*; (*вхождение в состав*): ~ **к** +*dat* membership of.

принево́л|ить (-ю, -ишь) *сов от* **нево́лить**.

прин|ести́ (-есу́, -есёшь; *pt* -ёс, -есла́, -есло́, *impf* **приноси́ть**) *сов перех* (*стул, ребёнка, удачу итп*) to bring; (*подлеж: животные*) to bear; (: *растения*) to yield; (*доход, прибыль итп*) to bring in; (*извинения, благодарность*) to express; (*присягу*) to take; **приноси́ть** (~ *perf*) **по́льзу** to be of use; **приноси́ть** (~ *perf*) **вред**, **приноси́ть** (~ *perf*) **что-н в же́ртву** to sacrifice sth.

прини́|зить (-жу, -зишь; *impf* **принижа́ть**) *сов перех* (*унизить*) to humiliate; (*умалить*) to belittle.

прини́к|нуть (-ну, -нешь; *pt* -, -ла, -ло, *impf* **приника́ть**) *сов неперех*: ~ **к** +*dat* (*к земле*) to press o.s.; (*к подушке итп*) to nestle up against; (*к другу*) to snuggle up to; (*к двери, к окну*) to press o.s. against.

принима́|ть(ся) (-ю(сь)) *несов от* **приня́ть(ся)**.

приноров|и́ться (-лю́сь, -и́шься; *impf* **принора́вливаться**) *сов возв*: ~ **к** +*dat* (*к обстоятельствам*) to adapt o.s. to; (*к машине*) to get used to; (+*infin*) to get used to doing.

прино|си́ть (-шу́, -осишь) *несов перех* **принести́**.

при́нтер (-а) *м* (*КОМП*) printer.

принуди́тельный (-ен, -ьна, -ьно) *прил* (*труд, лечение итп*) forced; (*меры*) compulsory.

прину́|дить (-жу, -дишь; *impf* **принужда́ть**) *сов перех*: ~ **кого́-н/что-н к** +*dat*/+*infin* to force sb/sth into/to do.

принужде́ни|е (-я) *ср* compulsion; **по ~ю** under compulsion.

принуждённый (-ён, -на, -но) *прил* forced.

прину́жу *сов см* **прину́дить**.

принц (-а) *м* prince.

принце́сс|а (-ы) *ж* princess.

при́нцип (-а) *м* principle; **в ~е** (*в основном*) in principle; **из ~а** on principle; **по ~у** +*gen* on the principle of.

принципиа́льный (-ен, -ьна, -ьно) *прил* (*человек, политика*) of principle; (*согласие, договорённость*) in principle.

при́нят|ый (-, -а, -о) *прил* accepted.

прин|я́ть (-му́, -мешь; *pt* -ял, -яла́, -яло, *impf* **принима́ть**) *сов перех* to take; (*подарок, критику, условия*) to accept; (*какой-н пост*) to take up; (*гостей, делегацию, телеграмму*) to receive; (*закон, резолюцию, поправку*) to pass;

(*отноше́ние, вид*) to take on; (*христианство итп*) to adopt; **принима́ть** (~ *perf*) **в/на** +*acc* (*в университе́т, на рабо́ту*) to accept for; **принима́ть** (~ *perf*) **что-н/кого́-н за** +*acc* to mistake sth/sb for; (*счесть*) to take sth/sb as; **принима́ть** (~ *perf*) **ро́ды** to deliver a baby

▶ **приня́ться** (*impf* **принима́ться**) *сов воз* (*растение*) to take root; (+*infin*; *приступить*) to get down to doing; **принима́ться** (~**ся** *perf*) **за** +*acc* (*приступить*) to get down to; (*за лентя́ев, за престу́пников*) to take in hand; (*за десе́рт, за вино́*) to start using *или* get started on.

приободр|и́ть (-ю́, -и́шь; *impf* **приободря́ть**) *сов перех* to cheer up

▶ **приободри́ться** (*impf* **приободря́ться**) *несов воз* to cheer up.

приобр|ести́ (-ету́, -етёшь; *pt* -ёл, -ела́, -ело́, *impf* **приобрета́ть**) *сов перех* to acquire; (*друзей, врагов*) to make; (*опыт*) to gain.

приобре́тени|е (-я) *ср* acquisition; (*комм*) procurement.

приобрету́ *итп сов см* **приобрести́**.

приобщ|и́ть (-у́, -и́шь; *impf* **приобща́ть**) *сов перех* (*приложить*) to attach; (*познакомить*): ~ **кого́-н/что-н к** +*dat* to introduce sb/sth to; **приобща́ть** (~ *perf*) **к де́лу** to file

▶ **приобщи́ться** (*impf* **приобща́ться**) *сов воз*: ~ **к** +*dat* to become involved in.

приоде́|ть (-ну, -нешь) *сов перех* (*разг*) to dress up.

приорите́т (-а) *м* priority.

приорите́т|ный (-ен, -на, -но) *прил* main.

приостан|ови́ть (-овлю́, -о́вишь; *impf* **приостана́вливать**) *сов перех* to suspend.

приоткр|ы́ть (-о́ю, -о́ешь; *impf* **приоткрыва́ть**) *сов перех* (*дверь*) to open slightly; (*глаза*) to half open.

припада́|ть (-ю) *несов от* **припа́сть**.

припа́д|ок (-ка) *м* (*сердечный*) attack; (*гнева*) fit; (*веселья*) outburst; **истери́ческий** ~ fit of hysterics.

припаду́ *итп сов см* **припа́сть**.

припа́ива|ть (-ю) *несов от* **припая́ть**.

припа́р|ка (-ки; *gen pl* -ок) *ж* (*мед*) poultice.

прип|асти́ (-асу́, -асёшь; *pt* -а́с, -асла́, -асло́, *impf* **припаса́ть**) *сов перех* (*еду*) to store up; (*деньги*) to save up.

припа́|сть (-ду́, -дёшь; *impf* **припада́ть**) *сов неперех*: ~ **к** +*dat* to throw o.s. at.

припасу́ *итп сов см* **припасти́**.

припа́с|ы (-ов) *мн* (*еды, денежные*) supplies; (*воен*: *боевые, ружейные*) ammunition.

припая́|ть (-ю; *impf* **припа́ивать**) *сов перех* (*приделать паянием*) to solder on.

припе́в (-а) *м* (*песни*) chorus, refrain.

припева́|ючи *нареч* (*разг*): **жить** ~ to live the life of Riley.

припека́|ть (*3sg* -ет) *несов неперех* (*солнце*) to be burning hot.

прип|ере́ть (-ру́, -рёшь; *pt* -ёр, -ерла́, -ерло́, *impf* **припира́ть**) *сов перех* (*разг*): ~ **к** +*dat*

(*прижать*) to shove against; **припира́ть** (~ *perf*) **к сте́нке** (*перен*: *разг*) to put in a tight spot.

припи|са́ть (-шу́, -́шешь; *impf* **припи́сывать**) *сов перех* (*написать в дополнение*) to add; (*прикрепить*): ~ **кого́-н/что-н к** +*dat* to attach sb/sth to; (*счесть следствием*): ~ **что-н чему́-н** to put sth down to sth; (*счесть принадлежащим*): ~ **что-н кому́-н** to attribute sth to sb.

припи́с|ка (-ки; *gen pl* -ок) *ж* (*в письме*) postscript; (: *в документе*) addition; (*обычно мн: ложные данные: в отчёте, в докладе*) tampering with facts and figures.

припи́сыва|ть (-ю) *несов от* **приписа́ть**.

припишу́ *итп сов см* **приписа́ть**.

припл|ести́ (-ету́, -етёшь; *pt* -ёл, -ела́, -ело́, *impf* **приплета́ть**) *сов перех* (*вплетая, присоединить*) to plait in; (*перен*: *разг*: *имя*) to drag in; (: *событие, факт*) to drag up

▶ **приплести́сь** *сов воз* (*разг*) to drag o.s. along.

приплю́снут|ый (-, -а, -о) *прил* (*нос*) flat.

припля́сыва|ть (-ю) *несов неперех* to skip.

приподнима́|ть(ся) (-ю(сь)) *несов от* **приподня́ть(ся)**.

приподниму́(сь) *итп сов см* **приподня́ть(ся)**.

приподня́т|ый (-, -а, -о) *прил* (*оживлённый*) cheerful; (*торжественный*) elevated.

приподн|я́ть (-иму́, -и́мешь; *impf* **приподнима́ть**) *сов перех* (*чемодан*) to lift slightly; (*занавес*) to raise slightly

▶ **приподня́ться** (*impf* **приподнима́ться**) *сов воз* to raise o.s. a little.

припо́мн|ить (-ю, -ишь; *impf* **припомина́ть**) *сов перех* to remember; **припомина́ть** (~ *perf*) **что-н кому́-н** to make sb remember sth.

припра́в|а (-ы) *ж* seasoning.

припру́ *итп сов см* **припере́ть**.

припря́|тать (-чу, -чешь; *impf* **припря́тывать**) *сов перех* (*разг*) to stash (away).

припугн|у́ть (-у́, -ёшь; *impf* **припу́гивать**) *сов перех* (*разг*) to put the wind up.

припу́ск (-а) *м* allowance.

припу|сти́ть (-щу́, -́стишь; *impf* **припуска́ть**) *сов неперех* (*разг*: *побежать*) to speed up.

припу́хлый *прил* slightly swollen.

припущу́ *сов см* **припусти́ть**.

приравня́|ть (-ю; *impf* **прира́внивать**) *сов перех*: ~ **кого́-н/что-н к** +*dat* to equate sb/sth with.

прир|асти́ (-асту́, -астёшь; *pt* -о́с, -осла́, -осло́, *impf* **прираста́ть**) *сов неперех* (*прижиться*) to take; (*увеличиться*) to increase; (*перен*): ~ **к** +*dat* to become rooted to.

приро́д|а (-ы) *ж* nature; (*места вне города*) countryside; **от** ~**ы**, **по** ~**е** by nature; **жива́я** ~ natural world.

приро́дный *прил* natural; (*врождённый*) innate; **приро́дные бога́тства** natural resources; **приро́дный газ** natural gas.

природове́дени|е (-я) *ср* natural history.

природоохра́н|а (-ы) ж nature conservation.
прирождённый прил (чувство, грация)
inborn; (учитель, художник) born.
приро́с итп сов см **прирасти́**.
приро́ст (-а) м (населения) growth; (доходов,
урожая) increase.
приручи́|ть (-у́, -ишь; impf **прируча́ть**) сов
перех (животное) to tame; (перен: человека) to
bring to heel.
приса́жива|ться (-юсь) несов от **присе́сть**.
приса́сыва|ться (-юсь) несов от
присоса́ться.
присво́|ить (-ю, -ишь; impf **присва́ивать**) сов
перех to appropriate; (дать): ~ что-н кому́-н to
confer sth on sb.
приседа́ни|е (-я) ср squatting (physical
exercise).
приседа́|ть (-ю) несов от **присе́сть**.
присе́ст (-а) м (разг): в или за оди́н ~ at one
sitting или a single sitting.
прис|е́сть (-я́ду, -я́дешь; impf **приседа́ть**) сов
неперех to squat; (impf **приса́живаться**) to sit
down (for a short while).
приск|ака́ть (-ачу́, -а́чешь; impf **приска́кивать**)
сов неперех (лошадь, всадник) to gallop up,
come galloping up; (разг: быстро
прийти/приехать) to come tearing up.
приско́рбен прил см **приско́рбный**.
приско́рби|е (-я) ср: к мое́му глубо́кому ~ю to
my deepest regret; с глубо́ким ~м with deepest
regret.
приско́рб|ный (-ен, -на, -но) прил regrettable.
при|сла́ть (-шлю́, -шлёшь; impf **присыла́ть**)
сов перех to send.
прислон|и́ть (-ю́, -и́шь; impf **прислоня́ть**) сов
перех: ~ что-н к +dat to lean sth against
▶ **прислони́ться** (impf **прислоня́ться**) сов
возв: ~ся к + dat to lean against.
прислу́г|а (-и) ж собир servants мн.
прислу́жива|ть (-ю) несов неперех (+dat;
официант) to wait on
▶ **прислу́живаться** несов возв to ingratiate
o.s., grovel.
прислу́ша|ться (-юсь; impf **прислу́шиваться**)
сов возв: ~ к +dat (к звуку) to listen to; (к
совету) to take heed of.
присма́трива|ть (-ю) несов от **присмотре́ть**
◆ перех to look for
▶ **присма́триваться** несов от
присмотре́ться.
присмире́|ть (-ю) сов неперех to quieten (BRIT)
или quiet (US) down, calm down.
присмир|и́ть (-ю́, -и́шь; impf **присмиря́ть**) сов
перех to quieten (BRIT), quiet (US).
присмо́тр (-а) м care.
присм|отре́ть (-отрю́, -о́тришь) сов перех
(разг) to find ◆ (impf **присма́тривать**) неперех:
~ за +instr to look after

▶ **присмотре́ться** (impf **присма́триваться**)
сов возв: ~ся (к +dat) to take a good look (at).
присни́ться (3sg -и́тся, 3pl -я́тся) сов от
сни́ться.
присовокуп|и́ть (-лю́, -и́шь; impf
присовокупля́ть) сов перех (к делу) to file; (к
сказанному) to add.
присоедине́ни|е (-я) ср (см глаг) attachment;
connection; annexation; (к протесту итп)
joining; (к чьему-н мнению) supporting.
присоедин|и́ть (-ю́, -и́шь; impf **присоединя́ть**)
сов перех: ~ что-н к +dat to attach sth to;
(провод) to connect sth to; (территорию) to
annex sth to
▶ **присоедини́ться** (impf **присоединя́ться**)
сов возв: ~ся к +dat (к экскурсии, к протесту
итп) to join; (к чьему-н мнению) to support.
присос|а́ться (-у́сь, -ёшься; impf
приса́сываться) сов возв to attach itself by
suction.
приспе́шник (-а) м (пренебр) accomplice.
приспосо́б|ить (-лю, -ишь; impf
приспоса́бливать или **приспособля́ть**) сов
перех to adapt
▶ **приспосо́биться** (impf **приспоса́бливаться**
или **приспособля́ться**) сов возв (к условиям, к
климату) to adapt (o.s.); (делать что-н) to get
used to.
приспосо́блен прил см **приспосо́бленный**.
приспособле́ни|е (-я) ср (к условиям итп)
adaptation; (устройство, механизм итп)
appliance.
приспосо́блен|ный (-, -а, -о) прил: ~ к +dat
(пригодный) fit for, well-suited to.
приспосо́блю(сь) сов см **приспосо́бить(ся)**.
приспособля́|ть(ся) (-ю(сь)) несов от
приспосо́бить(ся).
пристава́ни|е (-я) ср pestering.
приста|ва́ть (-ю́, -ёшь) несов от **приста́ть**.
приста́в|ить (-лю, -ишь; impf **приставля́ть**) сов
перех: ~ что-н к +dat to put sth against;
(пистолет: к груди) to put sth to; **приставля́ть**
(~ perf) кого́-н к +dat to assign sb to look after.
приста́в|ка (-ки; gen pl -ок) ж fitting; (линг)
prefix.
приста́влю сов см **приста́вить**.
приставля́|ть (-ю) несов см **приста́вить**.
приста́вок сущ см **приста́вка**.
при́стал|ьный (-ен, -ьна, -ьно) прил (взгляд,
внимание) fixed; (интерес, наблюдение)
determined, resolute.
приста́нищ|е (-а) ср refuge.
приста́н|у итп сов см **приста́ть**.
при́стан|ь (-и) ж pier.
приста́|ть (-ну, -нешь; impf **пристава́ть**) сов
неперех: ~ к +dat (прилипнуть) to stick to;
(присоединиться) to join; (разг: с вопросами)
to pester; (причалить) to put into; **ему́ не ~ло**

так поступа́ть (*разг*) he shouldn't behave like that.

пристегн|у́ть (-у́, -ёшь; *impf* **пристёгивать**) *сов перех* to fasten

▸ **пристегну́ться** (*impf* **пристёгиваться**) *сов возв* (*в самолёте, в автомобиле*) to fasten one's seat belt.

присто́|йный (-ен, -йна, -йно) *прил* (*приличный*) decent.

пристра́ива|ть(ся) (-ю(сь)) *несов от* **пристро́ить(ся)**.

пристра́стен *прил см* **пристра́стный**.

пристра́сти|е (-я) *ср* (*склонность*) passion; (*предубеждение*) bias.

пристра|сти́ться (-щу́сь, -сти́шься) *сов возв*: ~ к +*dat* to develop a liking for.

пристра́ст|ный (-ен, -на, -но) *прил* bias(s)ed.

пристращу́сь *сов см* **пристрасти́ться**.

пристре|ли́ть (-елю́, -е́лишь; *impf* **пристре́ливать**) *сов перех* (*животное*) to put down; (*разг: человека*) to shoot.

пристро́ек *сущ см* **пристро́йка**.

пристро́|ить (-ю, -ишь; *impf* **пристра́ивать**) *сов перех* (*комнату*) to build onto; (*разг: устроить*) to fix up

▸ **пристро́иться** (*impf* **пристра́иваться**) *сов возв* (*на диване, в углу*) to settle o.s.; (*разг: на работу, на службу*) to get fixed up.

пристро́|йка (-йки; *gen pl* -ек) *ж* extension.

при́ступ (-а) *м* (*атака*) attack; (*смеха, гнева*) fit; (*кашля*) bout; (*припадок*): **серде́чный ~** heart attack; **~ уду́шья** asthma attack.

пристуг|и́ть (-уплю́, -у́пишь; *impf* **приступа́ть**) *сов неперех*: ~ к +*dat* (*начать*) to get down to.

пристыди́ть (-жу́, -ди́шь) *сов от* **стыди́ть**.

присуди́ть (-ужу́, -у́дишь; *impf* **присужда́ть**) *сов перех*: ~ **что-н кому́-н** (*приз, алименты итп*) to award sth to sb; (*учёную степень*) to confer sth on sb; (*приговорить*): ~ **кого́-н к** +*dat* to sentence sb to.

прису́тственный *прил* (*день, часы*) working опред.

прису́тстви|е (-я) *ср* presence; **в ~и** +*gen* in the presence of; **~ ду́ха** presence of mind.

прису́тств|овать (-ую) *несов неперех* to be present.

прису́тствующ|ие (-их; *decl like adj*) *мн* those present.

прису́щ|ий (-ая, -ее, -ие; -, -а, -о) *прил*: ~ +*dat* characteristic of.

присыла́|ть (-ю) *несов от* **присла́ть**.

присы́л|ка (-ки; *gen pl* -ок) *ж* (*письма*) sending.

присы́п|ка (-ки; *gen pl* -ок) *ж* powder.

прися́г|а (-и) *ж* oath; **под ~ой** under oath.

присяга́|ть (-ю; *perf* **присягну́ть**) *несов неперех* (+*dat*) to swear an oath to.

прися́ду *итп сов см* **присе́сть**.

прися́жн|ый (-ого; *decl like adj*) *м* (*ЮР: также*: ~ **заседа́тель**) juror; **суд ~ых** jury.

притаи́ться (-ю́сь, -и́шься; *impf* **прита́иваться**) *сов возв* to hide.

прита|щи́ть (-щу́, -́щишь; *impf* **прита́скивать**) *сов перех* (*что-н тяжёлое или громоздкое*) to drag; (*заставить пойти*) to drag along.

притво́рен *прил см* **притво́рный**.

притво|ри́ть (-рю́, -́ришь; *impf* **притворя́ть**) *сов перех* to shut (*not fully*).

притво|ри́ться (-ю́сь, -и́шься; *impf* **притворя́ться**) *сов возв* (+*instr*) to pretend to be.

притво́р|ный (-ен, -на, -но) *прил* feigned.

притво́рств|о (-а) *ср* pretence.

притворю́(сь) *сов см* **притвори́ть(ся)**.

притворя́|ть(ся) (-ю(сь)) *несов от* **притвори́ть(ся)**.

притесне́ни|е (-я) *ср* (*людей*) oppression; (*обычно мн: гонения*) persecution.

притесни́тел|ь (-я) *м* oppressor.

притесн|и́ть (-ю́, -и́шь; *impf* **притесня́ть**) *сов перех* to oppress.

прити́|хнуть (-ну, -нешь; *pt* -, -ла, -ло, *impf* **притиха́ть**) *сов неперех* to grow quiet.

приткн|у́ть (-у́, -ёшь; *impf* **притыка́ть**) *сов перех* to stick.

прито́к (-а) *м* (*река*) tributary; ~ +*gen* (*сил, энергии, средств*) supply of; (*населения*) influx of.

прито́м *союз* and what's more.

прито́н (-а) *м* den.

при́тор|ный (-ен, -на, -но) *прил* (*вкус, торт итп*) sickly sweet; (*перен: улыбка, выражение лица*) unctuous.

притро́|нуться (-усь, -ешься; *impf* **притра́гиваться**) *сов возв*: ~ **к** +*dat* to touch.

притуп|и́ться (*3sg* -у́пится, *3pl* -у́пятся, *impf* **притупля́ться**) *сов возв* (*нож, бритва, топор*) to go blunt; (*перен: внимание итп*) to diminish; (: *чувства*) to fade; (: *слух*) to fail.

при́тч|а (-и) *ж* parable.

притыка́|ть (-ю) *несов от* **приткну́ть**.

притяга́тел|ьный (-ен, -ьна, -ьно) *прил* attractive.

притя́гива|ть (-ю) *несов от* **притяну́ть**.

притяжа́тельный *прил* (*линг*) possessive.

притяза́ни|е (-я) *ср*: ~ **на** +*acc* (*на наследство, на территорию*) claim to; (*на остроумие, на красоту итп*) pretensions *мн* of.

притя|ну́ть (-ну́, -́нешь; *impf* **притя́гивать**) *сов перех* (*подтащить*) to drag up; (*привлечь*) to attract; **притя́гивать** (~ *perf*) **факт за́ уши** to come up with a far-fetched fact.

приукра́|сить (-шу, -сишь; *impf* **приукра́шивать**) *сов перех* (*события, чьи-н достоинства*) to exaggerate.

приумно́ж|ить (-у, -ишь; *impf* **приумножа́ть**) *сов перех* to increase.

приуны́|ть (-ю, -ешь; *impf* **приуныва́ть**) *сов неперех* to get depressed.

приуро́ч|ить (-у, -ишь; *impf* **приуро́чивать**) *сов перех*: ~ **что-н к** +*dat* to time sth to coincide with.

приуса́дебный *прил*: ~ уча́сток allotment.
приучи́ть (-учу́, -у́чишь; *impf* **приуча́ть**) *сов перех*: ~ кого́-н к +*dat*/+*infin* to train sb for/to do
▶ **приучи́ться** (*impf* **приуча́ться**) *сов возв*: ~ся к +*dat*/+*infin* to train for/to do.
прифронтово́й *прил* front(line) *опред*.
прихвастну́ть (-у́, -ёшь) *сов неперех* (*разг*) to blow one's own trumpet a bit.
прихвати́ть (-ачу́, -а́тишь; *impf* **прихва́тывать**) *сов перех* (*разг*: схвати́ть) to grab; (: взять с собо́й) to take ◆ *безл* (о боли) to grip.
прихлеба́тель (-я) *м* (*разг*: пренебр) sponger.
прихло́пнуть (-у, -ешь; *impf* **прихло́пывать**) *сов перех* (крышку) to slam shut; (*разг*: насекомое) to swat.
прихлы́нуть (*3sg* -ет, *3pl* -ут) *сов перех* (волна, толпа) to surge; (перен: воспомина́ния) to come flooding back.
прихо́д (-а) *м* (поезда, гостя, весны) arrival; (КОММ) receipts *мн*; (РЕЛ) parish; ~ и расхо́д (КОММ) credit and debit.
приходи́ть (-ожу́, -о́дишь) *несов от* **прийти́**
▶ **приходи́ться** *несов от* **прийти́сь** ◆ *возв*: ~ся кому́-н дя́дей/ро́дственником to be sb's uncle/relative; раз на раз не ~о́дится no two times are ever the same.
прихо́дный *прил* (КОММ): ~ая кни́га receipt book.
прихо́довать (-ую; *perf* **оприхо́довать**) *несов перех* (КОММ: сумму) to enter (*in receipt book*).
прихо́дский (-ая, -ое, ие) *прил* (РЕЛ) parish *опред*.
приходя́щий (-ая, -ее, -ие) *прил* nonresident; (медсестра) visiting *опред*; ~ая ня́ня babysitter; ~ больно́й outpatient.
прихожа́нин (-ина; *nom pl* -е) *м* (РЕЛ) parishioner.
прихожа́нка (-ки; *gen pl* -ок) *ж* (РЕЛ) см **прихожа́нин**.
прихо́жая (-ей; *decl like adj*) *ж* entrance hall.
прихожу́(сь) *несов см* **приходи́ть(ся)**.
прихора́шиваться (-юсь) *несов возв* (*разг*) to smarten o.s. up.
прихотли́вый (-, -а, -о) *прил* (человек) capricious, whimsical; (вкус) quirky; (узор) intricate.
при́хоть (-и) *ж* whim.
прихра́мывать (-ю) *сов неперех* to limp slightly.
прице́л (-а) *м* (ружья, пушки) sight(s); (прице́ливание) aiming; брать (взять *perf*) кого́-н/что-н на ~ to aim at sb/sth; (перен) to keep a close watch on sb/sth.
прице́литься (-юсь, -ишься; *impf* **прице́ливаться**) *сов возв* to take aim.
прицени́ться (-ею́сь, -е́нишься; *impf* **прице́ниваться**) *сов возв*: ~ к +*dat* to enquire about the price of.

прице́п (-а) *м* trailer.
прицепи́ть (-еплю́, -е́пишь; *impf* **прицепля́ть**) *сов перех* (вагон) to couple
▶ **прицепи́ться** (*impf* **прицепля́ться**) *сов возв* (перен: разг: пристать) to be a pain in the neck; **прицепля́ться** (~ся *perf*) к +*dat* to stick to; (перен: разг: к человеку) to nag; (: к слова́м) to find fault with.
прича́л (-а) *м* mooring; (пассажирский) quay; (грузовой, ремонтный) dock.
прича́лить (-ю, -ишь; *impf* **прича́ливать**) *сов* (не)перех to moor.
прича́стен *прил см* **прича́стный**.
прича́стие (-я) *ср* (ЛИНГ) participle; (РЕЛ) communion.
причасти́ть (-щу́, -сти́шь; *impf* **причаща́ть**) *сов перех* (РЕЛ) to give communion to
▶ **причасти́ться** (*impf* **причаща́ться**) *сов возв* (РЕЛ) to receive communion.
прича́стный *прил* (ЛИНГ) participial; (-ен, -на, -но; связанный): ~ к +*dat* connected with.
причаща́ть(ся) (-ю(сь)) *несов от* **причасти́ть(ся)**.
причаще́ние (-я) *ср* (РЕЛ) Eucharist.
причащу́(сь) *сов см* **причасти́ть(ся)**.
причём *союз* moreover.
причеса́ть (-ешу́, -е́шешь; *impf* **причёсывать**) *сов перех* (волосы) to comb, brush; **причёсывать** (~ *perf*) кого́-н to comb или brush sb's hair; **причёсывать** (~ *perf*) го́лову to do one's hair
▶ **причеса́ться** (*impf* **причёсываться**) *сов возв* to comb или brush one's hair.
причёска (-ки; *gen pl* -ок) *ж* hairstyle.
причёсывать(ся) (-ь(сь)) *несов от* **причеса́ть(ся)**.
причешу́(сь) *итп сов см* **причеса́ть(ся)**.
причи́на (-ы) *ж* cause, reason; по ~е +*gen* on account of.
причини́ть (-ю, -и́шь; *impf* **причиня́ть**) *сов перех* to cause.
причи́слить (-ю, -ишь; *impf* **причисля́ть**) *сов перех*: ~ кого́-н/что-н к +*dat* (отнести́ к) to number sb/sth among.
причита́ние (-я) *ср* lamentation; (похоронные) keening; сва́дебные ~я *old Russian wedding ritual where women wail and lament the bride*.
причита́ть (-ю) *несов неперех* (на похоронах) to wail
▶ **причита́ться** *несов возв*: мне ~ется 10 рубле́й I am owed 10 roubles; с Вас ~ется 10 рубле́й you owe 10 roubles.
причу́да (-ы) *ж* whim.
причу́дливый (-, -а, -о) *прил* (узор) intricate.
пришвартова́ть (-ую) *сов от* **швартова́ть**.
пришéй(те) *сов см* **приши́ть**.
пришёл(ся) *сов см* **прийти́(сь)**.
пришéлец (-ьца) *м* stranger.

пришéстви|е (-я) *ср* (*РЕЛ*) advent.

приши́бленный *прил* crestfallen.

приши́ть (-ью, -ьёшь; *imper* **-éй(те)**, *impf* **пришивáть**) *сов перех* to sew on; (*перен: разг*): ~ **комý-н что-н** to pin sth on sb.

пришлá *итп сов см* **прийти́**.

при́шлый *прил* (*человек*) strange; (*кошка*) stray.

пришлю́ *итп сов см* **присла́ть**.

пришпó|рить (-ю, -ишь; *impf* **пришпóривать**) *сов перех* to spur.

пришью́ *итп сов см* **приши́ть**.

прищеми́ть (-лю́, -и́шь; *impf* **прищемля́ть**) *сов перех* to catch.

прищéп|ка (-ки; *gen pl* **-ок**) *ж* clothes peg (*BRIT*), clothespin (*US*).

прищý́р|ить (-ю, -ишь; *impf* **прищýривать**) *сов перех* (*глаза*) to screw up

▸ **прищýриться** (*impf* **прищýриваться**) *сов возв* to screw up one's eyes.

прию́т (-a) *м* shelter; (*для сирот*) orphanage.

приюти́ть (-чý, -ти́шь) *сов перех* to shelter

▸ **приюти́ться** *сов возв* to take shelter.

прия́тел|ь (-я) *м* friend.

прия́тельниц|а (-ы) *ж см* **прия́тель**.

прия́тен *прил см* **прия́тный**.

прия́тно *нареч* (*удивлён, поражён*) pleasantly ♦ *как сказ* it is nice *или* pleasant; **мне ~ э́то слы́шать** I'm glad to hear that; **óчень ~** (*при знакомстве*) pleased to meet you.

прия́т|ный (-ен, -на, -но) *прил* (*встреча, поездка*) pleasant, enjoyable; (*разговор, вкус*) pleasant; (*человек, лицо, лицó*) nice, pleasant.

ПРО *ж сокр* (= *противоракéтная оборóна*) antimissile defence (*BRIT*) *или* defense (*US*) system.

про *предл* (+*acc*) about.

про- *префикс* (*in verbs*; *о действии, направленном сквозь что-н*) *indicating action through sth eg.* прострели́ть; (*о действии, распространяющемся на весь предмет*) *indicating action involving whole object eg.* прогрéть; (*о движении мимо чего-н*) *indicating movement past sth eg.* проéхать; (*об исчерпанности действия*) *indicating completion of action eg.* пронумеровáть; (*о звучании, осуществляемом в один приём*) *indicating single occurence of sound eg.* протруби́ть; (*о длительном действии*) *indicating prolonged action eg.* прорабóтать; (*in nouns and adjectives*; *сторонник чего-н*) pro-.

проанализи́р|овать (-ую) *сов от* **анализи́ровать**.

проанноти́р|овать (-ую) *сов от* **анноти́ровать**.

прóб|а (-ы) *ж* (*испытание*) test; (*образец*) sample; (*драгоценного металла*) standard (*of precious metals*); (*клеймо*) hallmark.

пробéг (-a) *м* (*СПОРТ*: *автомобильный, марафóнский*) race; (: *лыжный*) run; (*АВТ*) mileage.

пробéга|ть (-ю) *сов неперех* to run around.

пробежá|ть (*как* **бежáть**; *см* **Table 20**; *impf* **пробегáть**) *сов перех* (*бегло прочитать*) to skim; (*5 километров*) to cover ♦ *неперех* (*время, годы*) to pass; (*миновать бегом*): ~ **ми́мо** +*gen* to run past; (*появиться и исчезнуть*): ~ **по** +*dat* (*шум, дрожь*) to run through; (*по земле*) to run along; **пробегáть** (~ *perf*) **чéрез** +*acc* to run through

▸ **пробежáться** *сов возв* to run.

пробéж|ка (-ки; *gen pl* **-ек**) *ж* run.

пробéл (-a) *м* (*также перен*) gap.

проберý(сь) *итп сов см* **пробрáть(ся)**.

пробивá|ть(ся) (-ю(сь)) *несов от* **проби́ть(ся)**.

пробивнóй *прил* (*сила снаряда*) penetrating; (*перен: разг: человек*) pushy.

пробирá|ть(ся) (-ю(сь)) *несов от* **пробрáть(ся)**.

проби́р|ка (-ки; *gen pl* **-ок**) *ж* test-tube.

проби́|ть (-ью, -ьёшь) *сов от* **бить** ♦ (*impf* **пробивáть**) *перех* (*дыру, отверстие*) to knock; (*крышу, стену*) to make a hole in; (*разг: с трудом добиться*) to force through; **пробивáть** (~ *perf*) **себé дорóгу** (*перен*) to carve one's way

▸ **проби́ться** (*impf* **пробивáться**) *сов возв* (*прорвáться*) to fight one's way through; (*растения, ростки*) to push through *или* up; (*разг: прожить с трудом*) to struggle through.

прóб|ка (-ки; *gen pl* **-ок**) *ж* (*no pl*; *древесной коры*) cork; (*для закупоривания*) cork, stopper; (*перен: транспортная*) jam; (*ЭЛЕК*) fuse.

проблéм|а (-ы) *ж* problem.

проблемáтик|а (-и) *ж собир* problems *мн*.

проблемати́чен *прил см* **проблемати́чный**.

проблемати́ческ|ий (-ая, -ое, -ие) *прил* problematic(al).

проблемати́ч|ный (-ен, -на, -но) *прил* = **проблемати́ческий**.

прóблеск (-a) *м* (*блеск*) ray; (*таланта, понимания*) hint; ~ **надéжды** ray of hope.

прóбный *прил* (*образец, экземпляр*) trial *опред*; (*полёт*) test *опред*; ~ **кáмень** (*перен*) touchstone.

прóб|овать (-ую; *perf* **попрóбовать**) *несов перех* (*мотор*) to test; (*пирог, вино*) to taste; (+*infin*; *пытаться*) to try to do.

прободéни|е (-я) *ср* (*МЕД*) perforation.

пробóин|а (-ы) *ж* hole.

прóбок *сущ см* **прóбка**.

проболтá|ться (-юсь) *сов возв* (*разг: проговори́ться*) to blab; (: *пробездéльничать*) to loaf about.

пробóр (-a) *м* parting (*of hair*).

пробр|áть (-ерý, -ерёшь; *impf* **пробирáть**) *сов перех* (*страх*) to strike; (*дрожь*) to come over; (*мороз*) to chill

▸ **пробрáться** (*impf* **пробирáться**) *сов возв* (*с трудом пройти́*) to fight one's way through;

(тихо пройти) to steal past *или* through.

пробу́дешь *итп сов см* **пробы́ть**.

проб|уди́ть (-ужу́, -у́дишь; *impf* **пробужда́ть** *или* **буди́ть**) *сов перех (массы, людей)* to rouse, stir; *(перен: желания, чувства)* to arouse

► **пробуди́ться** (*impf* **пробужда́ться**) *сов возв (проснуться)* to awake, wake up; *(перен: появиться)* to appear.

пробу́ду *итп сов см* **пробы́ть**.

пробу́дь(те) *сов см* **пробы́ть**.

пробужда́|ть(ся) (-ю(сь)) *несов от* **пробуди́ть(ся)**.

пробужде́ни|е (-я) *ср (ото сна)* waking up; *(сознания, чувств)* awakening.

пробужу́(сь) *итп сов см* **пробуди́ть(ся)**.

пробура́в|ить (-лю, -ишь) *сов от* **бура́вить**.

пробур|и́ть (-ю́, -и́шь) *сов от* **бури́ть**.

пробурч|а́ть (-у́, -и́шь) *сов от* **бурча́ть**.

пробы́ть (*как быть; см* **Table 21**) *сов неперех (прожить)* to stay, remain; *(провести)* to go; **он пробы́л 10 лет учи́телем** he was a teacher for 10 years.

пробью́(сь) *итп сов см* **проби́ть(ся)**.

прова́л (-а) *м (в почве, в стене)* hole; *(перен: неудача)* flop; *(: памяти)* failure.

прова́л|ить (-алю́, -а́лишь; *impf* **прова́ливать**) *сов перех (крышу, пол)* to cause to collapse; *(разг: перен: дело, затею)* to make a mess of; *(: студента)* to fail

► **провали́ться** (*impf* **прова́ливаться**) *сов возв (упасть)* to fall; *(рухнуть)* to collapse; *(разг: перен: студент, попытка)* to fail; *(: исчезнуть)* to vanish; **как сквозь зе́млю ~али́лся** he disappeared into thin air.

прова́р|ить (-арю́, -а́ришь; *impf* **прова́ривать**) *сов перех* to boil *(for a long time)*.

прове́да|ть (-ю; *impf* **прове́дывать**) *сов перех (навестить)* to call on; *(разг: узнать)* to find out.

проведе́ни|е (-я) *ср (урока)* taking; *(репетиции, конкурса)* holding; *(границы)* drawing; *(линии передачи)* installation; *(машины)* driving; *(судна)* piloting.

проведу́ *итп сов см* **провести́**.

прове́да|ть(ся) (-ю) *несов от* **прове́дать**.

прове|зти́ (-зу́, -зёшь; *pt* -з, -зла́, -зло́, *impf* **провози́ть**) *сов перех (везя, доставить):* **~ по** +*dat*/**ми́мо** +*gen*/**че́рез** +*acc* to take along/ past/across; *(контрабанду, наркотики)* to smuggle.

провентили́р|овать (-ую) *сов от* **вентили́ровать**.

провер|ить (-ю, -ишь; *impf* **проверя́ть**) *сов перех* to check; *(выполнение правил)* to monitor; *(знание ученика, двигатель)* to test

► **прове́риться** (*impf* **проверя́ться**) *сов возв (у врача)* to get a check-up.

прове́р|ка (-ки; *gen pl* -ок) *ж (см глаг)* check;

monitoring; test.

проверн|у́ть (-у́, -ёшь; *impf* **провора́чивать**) *сов перех (кран, винт)* to crank; *(перен: разг: дело, обмен квартиры)* to rush through.

прове́рок *прил см* **прове́рка**.

проверя́ющ|ий (-его; *decl like adj*) *м* examiner.

проверя́|ть(ся) (-ю(сь)) *несов от* **прове́рить(ся)**.

прове|сти́ (-еду́, -едёшь; *pt* -ёл, -ела́, -ело́, *impf* **проводи́ть**) *сов перех (черту, границу)* to draw; *(дорогу, ход итп)* to build; *(линию передачи)* to install; *(план, реформу)* to implement; *(урок, репетицию)* to hold; *(операцию)* to carry out; *(детство, день)* to spend; *(обмануть)* to trick; **проводи́ть (~** *perf***) ми́мо** +*gen*/**че́рез** +*acc (людей, экскурсантов)* to take past/across; **проводи́ть (~** *perf***) что-н в жизнь** to put sth into effect.

прове́тр|ить (-ю, -ишь; *impf* **прове́тривать**) *сов перех* to air

► **прове́триться** (*impf* **прове́триваться**) *сов возв (комната, одежда)* to have an airing; *(человек: на свежем воздухе)* to take a breath of fresh air; *(перен: разг)* to have a change of scene.

прове́|ять (-ю) *сов от* **ве́ять**.

провиа́нт (-а) *м* provisions *мн*.

провиде́ни|е (-я) *ср* foresight.

провиде́ни|е (-я) *ср (РЕЛ)* Providence.

провин|и́ться (-ю́сь, -и́шься) *сов возв:* **~ (в** +*prp*) to be guilty (of).

прови́нность (-и) *ж* fault.

провинциа́л (-а) *м* provincial.

провинциа́л|ка (-ки; *gen pl* -ок) *ж см* **провинциа́л**.

провинциа́льный *прил* provincial.

прови́нци|я (-и) *ж* province; *(отдалённая местность)* provinces *мн*.

про́вод (-а; *nom pl* -а́) *м* cable.

проводи́мость (-и) *ж* conductivity.

провод|и́ть (-ожу́, -о́дишь) *несов от* **провести́**
◆ (*impf* **провожа́ть**) *сов перех* to see off; *(сына: в армию)* to send off; **провожа́ть (~** *perf***) глаза́ми/взгля́дом кого́-н** to follow sb with one's eyes/gaze.

прово́д|ка (-ки; *gen pl* -ок) *ж (ЭЛЕК)* wiring.

проводни́к (-а́) *м (в горах)* guide; *(в поезде)* steward *(BRIT)* *или* porter *(US)*; *(ЭЛЕК)* conductor; *(перен: идей, политики итп)* vehicle.

проводни́ца (-ы) *ж (в поезде)* stewardess *(BRIT)* *или* porter *(US)*.

проводо́к *сущ см* **прово́дка**.

про́вод|ы (-ов) *мн (прощание)* send-off *ед*.

провожа́тый (-ого; *decl like adj*) *м* escort.

провожа́|ть (-ю) *несов от* **проводи́ть**.

провожу́ *(не)сов см* **проводи́ть**.

провожу́(сь) *несов см* **провози́ть(ся)**.

провóз (-а) м (багажа) transport; (незаконный) smuggling.

провозгла|сить (-шý, -сишь; impf **провозглашáть**) сов перех to proclaim; **провозглашáть** (~ perf) когó-н/чтó-н +instr to hail sb/sth as.

провозглашéни|е (-я) ср proclamation.

провозглашý сов см **провозгласи́ть**.

пров|ози́ть (-ожý, -óзишь) несов от **провезти́**
▸ **провози́ться** сов возв (разг) to muck around или about; ~**ся** (perf) **с кем-н/чем-н** to spend time with sb/on sth.

провокáтор (-а) м agent provocateur.

провокацио́нный прил provocative.

провокáци|я (-и) ж provocation; **поддавáться** (**поддáться** perf) **на** ~**ю** to give in to provocation.

прóволок|а (-и) ж wire.

проволóч|ка (-ки; gen pl -ек) ж (разг) hold-up.

проворáчива|ть (-ю) несов от **провернýть**.

провóр|ный (-ен, -на, -но) прил agile.

провор|овáться (-ýюсь; impf **проворóвываться**) сов возв (разг) to be caught stealing.

проворóн|ить (-ю, -ишь) сов от **ворóнить**.

проворчáть (-ý, -и́шь) сов неперех (человек) to grumble ◆ перех to mutter.

провоци́р|овать (-ую; perf **спровоци́ровать**) несов перех to provoke; ~ (**спровоци́ровать** perf) **когó-н/чтó-н на чтó-н** to provoke sb/sth into sth.

провя́л|ить (-ю, -ишь) сов от **вя́лить**.

прогадá|ть (-ю; impf **прогáдывать**) сов неперех (разг) to miscalculate.

проги́б (-а) м (пола, балки) sagging; (место) sag.

прогибá|ть(ся) (-ю(сь)) несов от **прогнýть(ся)**.

прогл|оти́ть (-очý, -óтишь; impf **прогля́тывать** или **глотáть**) сов перех (также перен) to swallow; (перен: разг: книгу) to devour; **язы́к** ~**óтишь, так вкýсно** (разг) it's so tasty it makes your mouth water.

прогля|дéть (-жý, -ди́шь) сов перех (ошибку, изменения) to overlook.

прогля|нýть (3sg -́нет, 3pl -́нут) сов неперех (солнце) to peek out; **на егó лицé** ~**янýла улы́бка** there was a hint of a smile on his face.

прог|нáть (-оню́, -óнишь; pt -нáл, -налá, -нáло, impf **прогоня́ть**) сов перех (заставить двигаться) to drive; (заставить уйти) to turn out; (уволить) to dismiss; (избавиться) to drive away.

прогнев|и́ть (-лю́, -и́шь) сов от **гневи́ть**.

прогни́|ть (3sg -ёт, 3pl -ю́т, impf **прогнивáть**) сов неперех to rot through.

прогнóз (-а) м forecast.

прогнози́р|овать (-ую) (не)сов перех to forecast.

прогнýть (-ý, -ёшь; impf **прогибáть**) сов перех: ~ **чтó-н** to cause sth to sag

▸ **прогнýться** (impf **прогибáться**) сов возв to sag.

проговор|и́ть (-ю́, -и́шь; impf **проговáривать**) сов перех (произнести) to utter ◆ неперех (no impf; разговаривать) to chat

▸ **проговори́ться** (impf **проговáриваться**) сов возв to let out a secret; ~**ся** (perf) **о чём-н** to reveal sth.

прогого|тáть (-чý, -чешь) сов от **гоготáть**.

проголос|овáть (-ýю) сов от **голосовáть**.

прогоню́ итп сов см **прогнáть**.

прогоня́|ть (-ю) несов от **прогнáть**.

прогор|éть (-ю́, -и́шь; impf **прогорáть**) сов неперех (дрова) to burn through; (перен: разг: дело) to go bust.

прогóрклый прил (масло) rancid.

прогóркн|уть (3sg -ет, 3pl -ут) сов от **гóркнуть**.

прогрáмм|а (-ы) ж programme (BRIT), program (US); (ПОЛИТ) manifesto; (также: **вещáтельная** ~) channel; (ПРОСВЕЩ) curriculum; (КОМП) program.

программи́рование (-я) ср (КОМП) programming.

программи́р|овать (-ую; perf **запрограмми́ровать**) несов перех (КОМП) to program.

программи́ст (-а) м (КОМП) programmer.

прогрáмм|ка (-ки; gen pl -ок) ж (разг: в театре) programme (BRIT), program (US).

прогрáммный прил programmed (BRIT), programed (US); (экзамен, зачёт) set; (КОМП) programming (BRIT), programing (US); **прогрáммное обеспéчение** (КОМП) software; **прогрáммное управлéние** (КОМП) programmed (BRIT) или programed (US) control.

прогревá|ть(ся) (-ю(сь)) сов от **прогрéть(ся)**.

прогремéть (-лю́, -и́шь) сов от **гремéть**.

прогрéсс (-а) м progress.

прогресси́вный прил (писатель, идеи) progressive.

прогресси́р|овать (-ую) несов неперех to progress.

прогрé|ть (-ю; impf **прогревáть**) сов перех to warm up

▸ **прогрéться** (impf **прогревáться**) сов возв to warm up.

прогромыхá|ть (-ю) сов от **громыхáть**.

прогрохо|тáть (-чý, -чешь) сов от **грохотáть**.

прогры́з|ть (-ý, -ёшь; pt -, -ла, -ло, impf **прогрызáть**) сов перех to gnaw through.

прогу|дéть (-жý, -ди́шь) сов от **гудéть**.

прогýл (-а) м (на работе) absence; (в школе) truancy.

прогýлива|ть (-ю) несов от **прогуля́ть** ◆ перех (разг: собаку) to take

▸ **прогýливаться** несов от **прогуля́ться**.

прогýл|ка (-ки; gen pl -ок) ж walk; (недалекая поездка) trip.

прогýльщик (-а) м (работник) absentee; (ученик) truant.

прогýльщиц|а (-ы) ж см **прогýльщик**.

прогуля́|ть (-ю; *impf* **прогу́ливать**) *сов перех* (*работу*) to be absent from; (*уроки*) to miss ♦ *неперех* (*no impf*) to walk

▶ **прогуля́ться** (*impf* **прогу́ливаться**) *сов возв* to go for a walk.

прода|ва́ть(ся) (-ю́(сь)) *несов от* **прода́ть(ся)**.

продав|е́ц (-ца́) *м* seller; (*в магазине*) (shop-) assistant.

продав|и́ть (-авлю́, -а́вишь; *impf* **прода́вливать**) *сов перех* (*стекло*) to go through; **прода́вливать** (~ *perf*) **сиде́нье сту́ла** to make the seat of a chair sag.

продавца́ *итп сущ см* **продаве́ц**.

продавщи́ц|а (-ы) *ж см* **продаве́ц**.

продади́м(ся) *итп сов см* **прода́ть(ся)**.

прода́ж|а (-и) *ж* (*дома, товара*) sale; (*торговля*) trade; **быть** (*impf*) **в ~е, поступа́ть** (**поступи́ть** *perf*) **в ~у** to be on sale.

прода́ж|ный *прил* (*цена*) sale *опред*; (*вещь*) for sale; (-ен, -на, -но; *человек, пресса*) corrupt.

прода́лбливать (-ю) *несов от* **продолби́ть**.

прода́|ть (*как* **дать**; *см* **Table 14**; *impf* **продава́ть**) *сов перех* to sell; (*перен: друга*) to betray

▶ **прода́ться** (*impf* **продава́ться**) *сов возв* (*врагам*) to sell out.

продвига́|ть(ся) (-ю(сь)) *несов от* **продви́нуть(ся)**.

продвиже́ни|е (-я) *ср* (*по территории*) advance; (*по службе*) promotion.

продви́н|уть (-у, -ешь; *impf* **продвига́ть**) *сов перех* to move; (*перен: работника*) to promote

▶ **продви́нуться** (*impf* **продвига́ться**) *сов возв* to move; (*войска*) to advance; (*перен: работник*) to be promoted; (: *работа, строительство*) to progress.

продева́|ть (-ю) *несов от* **проде́ть**.

продезинфици́р|овать (-ую) *сов от* **дезинфици́ровать**.

продеклами́р|овать (-ую) *сов от* **деклами́ровать**.

проде́ла|ть (-ю; *impf* **проде́лывать**) *сов перех* (*отверстие*) to make; (*работу*) to do.

проде́л|ка (-ки; *gen pl* -ок) *ж* trick.

проде́лыва|ть (-ю) *несов от* **проде́лать**.

продемонстри́р|овать (-ую) *сов от* **демонстри́ровать**.

проде́ну *итп сов см* **проде́ть**.

продерж|а́ть (-жу́, -жишь) *сов перех* (*держать*) to hold; (: *библиотечную книгу, человека*) to keep

▶ **продержа́ться** *сов возв* (*держаться*) to hold out.

продеру́сь *итп сов см* **продра́ться**.

проде́|ть (-ну, -нешь; *impf* **продева́ть**) *сов перех* to thread; **продева́ть** (~ *perf*) **ни́тку в иго́лку** to thread a needle.

продикт|ова́ть (-у́ю) *сов от* **диктова́ть**.

продира́|ться (-юсь) *несов от* **продра́ться**.

продлева́|ть (-ю) *несов от* **продли́ть**.

продле́ни|е (-я) *ср* (*см глаг*) extension; prolongation.

продлённый *прил*: ~ **день** (*ПРОСВЕЩ*) extended school day (*for children whose parents work late*).

продл|и́ть (-ю́, -и́шь; *impf* **продлева́ть**) *сов перех* (*командировку, отпуск*) to extend; (*жизнь*) to prolong.

продли́ться (*3sg* -и́тся, *3pl* -я́тся) *сов от* **дли́ться**.

продма́г (-а) *м* (= **продово́льственный магази́н**) grocer's (shop) (*BRIT*), grocery (*US*).

продово́льственный *прил* food *опред*; **продово́льственный магази́н** grocer's (shop) (*BRIT*), grocery (*US*).

продово́льстви|е (-я) *ср* provisions *мн*.

продолб|и́ть (-лю́, -и́шь) *сов от* **долби́ть**.

продолгова́тый (-, -а, -о) *прил* elongated.

продолжа́тель (-я) *м* successor.

продолжа́|ть (-ю; *perf* **продо́лжить**) *несов перех* to continue, carry on; ~ (**продо́лжить** *perf*) +*impf infin* to continue *или* carry on doing

▶ **продолжа́ться** (*perf* **продо́лжиться**) *несов возв* to continue, carry on.

продолже́ни|е (-я) *ср* (*борьбы, лекции*) continuation; (*романа, рассказа*) sequel; **в ~** +*gen* for the duration of.

продолжи́телен *прил см* **продолжи́тельный**.

продолжи́тельност|ь (-и) *ж* duration; **сре́дняя ~ жи́зни** life expectancy; **продолжи́тельность жи́зни** lifespan.

продолжи́тельный (-ен, -ьна, -ьно) *прил* (*болезнь, разговор*) prolonged; (*урок*) extended.

продо́лж|ить(ся) (-у(сь), -ишь(ся)) *сов от* **продолжа́ть(ся)**.

продо́льный *прил* longitudinal.

продра́|ться (-еру́сь, -ерёшься; *impf* **продира́ться**) *сов возв*: ~ **сквозь** +*acc* to fight one's way through.

продро́гн|уть (-у, -ешь) *сов неперех* to be frozen to the bone.

продува́|ть (-ю) *несов от* **проду́ть** ♦ *перех*: **сквозня́к ~л ко́мнату** the draught blew through the room.

проду́кт (-а) *м* product; *см также* **проду́кты**.

продукти́вен *прил см* **продукти́вный**.

продукти́вност|ь (-и) *ж* productivity; (*КОМП*) throughput.

продукти́в|ный (-ен, -на, -но) *прил* productive.

продукто́вый *прил* food *опред*.

проду́кт|ы (-ов) *мн* (*также*: ~ **пита́ния**) foodstuffs *мн*.

проду́кци|я (-и) *ж* produce.

проду́ман|ный (-, -на, -но) *прил* well thought-out.

проду́ма|ть (-ю; *impf* **проду́мывать**) *сов перех*

(*действия, выступление*) to think out;
(*ответ*) to consider ♦ *неперех* to think.

проду́|ть (**-ю, -ешь;** *impf* **продува́ть**) *сов перех*
(*трубу*) to blow through; (*разг: проиграть*) to
lose ♦ *безл* (+*acc*): **меня́ ~ло** I've caught a chill.

продыря́в|ить (**-лю, -ишь**) *сов перех* to make a
hole in.

продю́сер (**-а**) *м* producer.

проеда́|ть (**-ю**) *несов от* **прое́сть.**

прое́дешь *итп сов см* **прое́хать.**

проеди́м *итп сов см* **прое́сть.**

прое́ду(сь) *итп сов см* **прое́хать(ся).**

проедя́т *сов см* **прое́сть.**

прое́зд (**-а**) *м* (*в транспорте*) journey; (*место*)
passage.

проездно́й *прил* (*документ*) travel *опред*;
проездно́й биле́т travel card.

прое́здом *нареч* en route.

проезжа́й(те) *сов см* **прое́хать.**

проезжа́|ть (**-ю**) *несов от* **прое́хать.**

прое́зж|ий (**-ая, -ее, -ие**) *прил* (*человек*) passing
♦ (**-его;** *decl like adj*) *м* traveller (*BRIT*), traveler
(*US*); **~ая часть** (**у́лицы**) road.

прое́кт (**-а**) *м* (*дома, памятника итп*) design;
(*закона, договора*) draft; (*замысел*) project.

проекти́р|овать (**-ую;** *perf* **спроекти́ровать**)
несов перех (*дом*) to design; (*perf*
запроекти́ровать; *наметить*) to plan.

проекти́ровщик (**-а**) *м* designer.

прое́ктор (**-а**) *м* (*ОПТИКА*) projector.

прое́кци|я (**-и**) *ж* (*также ГЕОМ*) projection.

проём (**-а**) *м* (*дверной, оконный*) aperture.

прое́сть (*как* **есть;** *см* **Table 15;** *impf* **проеда́ть**)
сов перех to eat through; (*разг: деньги*) to blow
on food.

прое́хать (*как* **е́хать;** *см* **Table 19**) *сов перех*
(*миновать*) to pass; (*остановку, поворот итп*)
to miss ♦ (*impf* **проезжа́ть**) *неперех:* **~ ми́мо**
+*gen*/**по** +*dat*/**че́рез** +*acc итп* to drive past/
along/across *итп*

▸ **прое́хаться** *сов возв* (*на велосипеде, на
санках*) to go for a ride; (*на машине*) to go for a
drive.

прое́шь *сов см* **прое́сть.**

прожа́р|ить (**-ю, -ишь;** *impf* **прожа́ривать**) *сов
перех* to fry

▸ **прожа́риться** (*impf* **прожа́риваться**) *сов
возв* to be well-fried.

прожгу́ *итп сов см* **прожё́чь.**

прожда́|ть (**-у́, -ёшь**) *сов перех* to wait a long
time for.

прожё́г *итп сов см* **прожё́чь.**

проже́ктор (**-а**) *м* floodlight.

прожё́|чь (**-гу́, -жёшь** *итп*, **-гу́т;** *pt* **-ё́г, -гла́, -гло́,**
impf **прожига́ть**) *сов перех* (*огнём, кислотой*)
to burn a hole in.

прожива́ни|е (**-я**) *ср* (*в гостинице*) stay.

прожива́|ть (**-ю**) *несов от* **прожи́ть** ♦ *неперех*
to live.

проживу́ *итп сов см* **прожи́ть.**

прожига́|ть (**-ю**) *несов от* **прожё́чь** ♦ *перех:* **~**

жизнь (*перен*) to live life in the fast lane.

прожи́л|ка (**-ки;** *gen pl* **-ок**) *ж* vein; (*дерева*)
grain.

прожи́ти|е (**-я**) *ср:* **на ~** to live on.

прожи́точный *прил:* **~ ми́нимум** minimum
living wage.

прожи́|ть (**-ву́, -вё́шь**) *сов неперех* (*пробыть
живым*) to live; (*жить*) to spend ♦ *перех*
(*деньги, состояние*) to squander.

прожо́рлив|ый (**-, -а, -о**) *прил* voracious.

про́з|а (**-ы**) *ж* prose; (*повседневность*) routine.

проза́ик (**-а**) *м* prosaist.

проза́ическ|ий (**-ая, -ое, -ие**) *прил*
(*произведение*) prose *опред*; (*жизнь*) prosaic.

прозва́ни|е (**-я**) *ср* nickname.

прозва́|ть (**-ову́, -овё́шь;** *impf* **прозыва́ть**) *сов
перех* to nickname.

прозвен|е́ть (*3sg* **-и́т,** *3pl* **-я́т**) *сов от* **звене́ть.**

про́звищ|е (**-а**) *ср* nickname.

прозвуч|а́ть (*3sg* **-и́т,** *3pl* **-а́т**) *сов неперех*
(*стать слышным*) to resound; (*проявиться*) to
come through.

прозева́|ть (**-ю**) *сов от* **зева́ть.**

прозим|ова́ть (**-у́ю**) *сов от* **зимова́ть.**

прозову́ *итп сов см* **прозва́ть.**

прозонди́р|овать (**-ую**) *сов от* **зонди́ровать.**

прозорли́в|ый (**-, -а, -о**) *прил* (*человек, ум*)
perceptive; (*политика*) farsighted.

прозра́чный (**-ен, -на, -но**) *прил* (*стекло,
намерение*) transparent; (*воздух, вода*) clear;
(*ткань, одежда*) see-through.

прозр|е́ть (**-ю́;** *impf* **прозрева́ть**) *сов неперех* to
gain one's sight; (*перен*) to see the light.

прозыва́|ть (**-ю**) *несов от* **прозва́ть.**

прозяба́|ть (**-ю**) *несов неперех* (*человек*) to
vegetate.

проигнори́р|овать (**-ую**) *сов от*
игнори́ровать.

проигра́|ть (**-ю;** *impf* **прои́грывать**) *сов перех*
to lose; (*играть*) to play ♦ *неперех* (*no impf*;
играть) to play.

прои́грыватель (**-я**) *м* record player.

прои́грыва|ть (**-ю**) *несов от* **проигра́ть.**

про́игрыш (**-а**) *м* loss.

произведе́ни|е (**-я**) *ср* (*литературы,
искусства*) work; (*МАТ*) product.

произв|ести́ (**-еду́, -едё́шь;** *pt* **-ё́л, -ела́, -ело́,**
impf **производи́ть**) *сов перех* (*обыск,
операцию*) to carry out; (*впечатление,
суматоху*) to create; **производи́ть** (**~** *perf*)
поса́дку to land; **производи́ть** (**~** *perf*) **кого́-н в
офице́ры/в генера́лы** to confer the rank of an
officer/a general on sb.

производи́телен *прил см*
производи́тельный.

производи́тел|ь (**-я**) *м* producer.

производи́тельност|ь (**-и**) *ж* productivity.

производи́тельный (**-ен, -ьна, -ьно**) *прил*
(*продуктивный*) productive;
производи́тельные си́лы (*ЭКОН*) labour (*BRIT*)
или labor (*US*) force.

произв|оди́ть (-ожу́, -о́дишь) *несов от* **произвести́** ♦ *перех* (*изготовлять*) to produce.

произво́дный *прил* derivative *опред*; **произво́дное сло́во** derivative.

произво́дственный *прил* (*процесс, план*) production *опред*; ~ **спрос** (*КОММ*) derived demand; ~ **несча́стный слу́чай** occupational accident; **произво́дственные отноше́ния** industrial relations.

произво́дств|о (-а) *ср* (*товаров*) production, manufacture; (*отрасль*) industry; (*завод, фабрика*) factory; (*опыта*) carrying out; **сельскохозя́йственное** ~ agricultural yield; (*отрасль*) agriculture; **промы́шленное** ~ industrial output; (*отрасль*) industry.

произвожу́ *несов см* **производи́ть**.

произво́л (-а) *м* (*самовластие*) arbitrary rule; **оставля́ть** (**оста́вить** *perf*) *или* **броса́ть** (**бро́сить** *perf*) **кого́-н на** ~ **судьбы́** to leave sb in the hands of fate.

произво́л|ьный (-ен, -ьна, -ьно) *прил* (*свободный*) free; (*no short form*; *СПОРТ*) freestyle *опред*; (*неосновательный*) arbitrary.

произн|ести́ (-есу́, -есёшь; *pt* -ёс, -есла́, -есло́, *impf* **произноси́ть**) *сов перех* (*выговорить*) to pronounce; (*сказать*) to say; **произноси́ть** (~ *perf*) **речь/тост** to make a speech/toast.

произн|оси́ть (-ошу́, -о́сишь) *несов от* **произнести́**.

произноше́ни|е (-я) *ср* pronunciation.

произношу́ *несов см* **произноси́ть**.

произойти́ (*как* **идти́**; *см* **Table 18**; *impf* **происходи́ть**) *сов неперех* (*случиться*) to occur; **происходи́ть** (~ *perf*) **из** +*gen* to come from.

проиллюстри́р|овать (-ую) *сов от* **иллюстри́ровать**.

проинспекти́р|овать (-ую) *сов от* **инспекти́ровать**.

проинструкти́р|овать (-ую) *сов от* **инструкти́ровать**.

проинтервью́и́р|овать (-ую) *сов от* **интервью́и́ровать**.

проинформи́р|овать (-ую) *сов от* **информи́ровать**.

про́иск|и (-ов) *мн* machinations *мн*.

проистека́|ть (*3sg* -ет, *3pl* -ют) *несов неперех*: ~ **из/от** +*gen* to result from.

происх|оди́ть (-ожу́, -о́дишь) *несов неперех* **произойти́** ♦ *неперех*: ~ **от/из** +*gen* to come from.

происхожде́ни|е (-я) *ср* origin; **по** ~**ю** by birth.

происхожу́ *несов см* **происходи́ть**.

происше́стви|е (-я) *ср* event; **доро́жное** ~ road accident.

пройдёшь(ся) *итп сов см* **пройти́(сь)**.

пройдо́х|а (-и) *м/ж* (*разг*) cad.

пройду́(сь) *итп сов см* **пройти́(сь)**.

пройму́ *итп сов см* **проня́ть**.

пройти́ (*как* **идти́**; *см* **Table 18**; *impf* **проходи́ть**) *сов неперех* to pass; (*расстояние*) to cover; (*слух, весть итп*) to spread; (*дорога, канал итп*) to stretch; (*дождь, снег*) to fall; (*состояться: операция, переговоры итп*) to go ♦ *перех* (*завершить: практику, службу итп*) to complete; (*изучить: тему итп*) to do; **проходи́ть** (~ *perf*) **в** +*acc* (*в институт итп*) to get into

▸ **пройти́сь** (*impf* **проха́живаться**) *сов возв* (*по комнате*) to pace; (*по парку*) to stroll; ~**сь** (*perf*) **на чей-н счёт** *или* **по чьему́-н а́дресу** (*разг*) to give sb a bad write-up.

прок (-а; *gen part* -у) *м* (*разг*) use.

прока́з|а (-ы) *ж* mischief; (*МЕД*) leprosy.

прока́зник (-а) *м* mischief-maker.

прока́знича|ть (-ю; *perf* **напрока́зничать**) *несов неперех* to get up to mischief.

прока́лыва|ть (-ю) *несов от* **проколо́ть**.

прока́пчива|ть (-ю) *несов от* **прокопти́ть**.

прока́лыва|ть (-ю) *несов от* **прокопа́ть**.

прока́т (-а) *м* (*телевизора, палатки итп*) hire; (*металл*) rolled iron; **брать** (**взять** *perf*) **что-н на** ~ to hire sth; **выпуска́ть** (**вы́пустить** *perf*) **фильм в** ~ to release a film.

прока|ти́ть (-чу́, -тишь; *impf* **прока́тывать**) *сов перех* (*разг: раскритиковать*) to pick holes in ♦ *неперех* (*разг*) to whizz past; **прока́тывать** (~ *perf*) **кого́-н** (*на маши́не итп*) to take sb for a ride

▸ **прокати́ться** (*impf* **прока́тываться**) *сов возв* (*также перен: гром*) to roll; (*на маши́не*) to go for a spin; (*перен: вы́стрел*) to ring out.

прока́тк|а (-и) *ж* (*ТЕХ*) rolling.

прока́тный *прил* (*производство, цех*) rolling; (*пункт, плата*) hire.

прока́тчик (-а) *м* (*в цеху*) worker (*in steel rolling mill*).

прока́тыва|ть(ся) (-ю(сь)) *несов от* **прокати́ть(ся)**.

прокачу́(сь) *сов см* **прокати́ть(ся)**.

прокипя|ти́ть (-чу́, -ти́шь) *сов перех* to boil.

проки́с|нуть (*3sg* -нет, *3pl* -нут, *pt* -, -ла, -ло) *сов от* **ки́снуть** ♦ (*impf* **прокиса́ть**) *неперех* to go off.

прокла́дк|а (-ки; *gen pl* -ок) *ж* (*действие: труб*) laying out; (: *линий передачи*) laying; (*защитная*) padding.

прокла́дыва|ть (-ю) *несов от* **проложи́ть**.

проклина́|ть (-ю) *несов от* **прокля́сть** ♦ *перех* to curse.

прокл|я́сть (-яну́, -янёшь; *pt* -ял, -яла́, -яло, *impf* **проклина́ть**) *сов перех* to curse.

прокля́ти|е (-я) *ср* curse.

прокля́тый *прил* damned; **рабо́тать** (*impf*) **как про́клятый** (*разг*) to work like a dog.

прокол (-а) *м* (*действие: шины*) puncturing; (: *нарыва*) lancing; (: *ушей*) piercing; (*отверстие: в шине*) puncture; (*в ушах*) hole; (*разг: неудача*) flop.

прокол|оть (-олю, -олешь; *impf* **прокалывать**) *сов перех* (*шину*) to puncture; (*уши*) to pierce; (*нарыв*) to lance.

прокомменти́р|овать (-ую) *сов от* **комменти́ровать**.

прокомпости́р|овать (-ую) *сов от* **компости́ровать**.

проконсульти́р|овать(ся) (-ую(сь)) *сов от* **консульти́ровать(ся)**.

прокопа́|ть (-ю; *impf* **прока́пывать**) *сов перех* (*канаву, ход*) to dig out.

прокоп|ти́ть (-чу́, -ти́шь) *сов от* **копти́ть** ♦ (*impf* **прока́пчивать**) *перех* (*копотью*) to cover with soot; (*дымом*) to fill with smoke.

прокорм (-а) *м* feeding.

прокорм|и́ть(ся) (-ормлю́(сь), -о́рмишь(ся)) *сов от* **корми́ть(ся)**.

прокорректи́р|овать (-ую) *сов от* **корректи́ровать**.

прокра́|сться (-аду́сь, -адёшься; *impf* **прокра́дываться**) *сов возв*: ~ **в** +*acc*/**ми́мо** +*gen*/**че́рез** +*acc итп* to creep (*BRIT*) *или* sneak (*US*) in(to)/past/through *итп*.

прокрича́|ть (-у́, -и́шь) *сов перех* (*выкрикнуть*) to shout out ♦ *неперех* (*ребёнок*) to cry.

прокру|ти́ть (-чу́, -́тишь; *impf* **прокру́чивать**) *сов перех* (*провернуть*) to turn; (*мясо*) to mince; (*КОМП*) to scroll; (*разг: фильм*) to roll; (: *пластинку, видеоплёнку*) to play.

прокру́чивани|е (-я) *ср* (*см глаг*) turning; mincing; rolling; playing.

прокру́чива|ть (-ю) *несов от* **прокрути́ть**.

прокручу́ *сов см* **прокрути́ть**.

прокурату́р|а (-ы) *ж* (*ЮР*) public prosecution office ♦ *собир* procurators *мн*.

прокур|и́ть (-ю́, -́уришь; *impf* **прокуривать**) *сов перех* to fill with smoke.

прокуро́р (-а) *м* (*района, города*) procurator; (*на суде*) counsel for the prosecution; **Генера́льный** ~ (*ЮР*) general procurator, attorney general (*US*).

прокуро́рск|ий (-ая, -ое, -ие) *прил*: ~ **надзо́р** (*ЮР*) procurator's powers *мн*.

прок|уси́ть (-ушу́, -́усишь; *impf* **прокусывать**) *сов перех* to bite through.

прокуру́|ть (-ю) *несов от* **проложи́ть**.

прола́мыва|ть (-ю) *несов от* **проломи́ть**.

прола́|ять (-ю) *сов от* **ла́ять**.

пролега́|ть (*3sg* -ет, *3pl* -ют) *несов от* **проле́чь**.

пролежа́|ть (-у́, -и́шь) *сов неперех* to lie.

проле́з|ть (-у, -ешь; *impf* **пролеза́ть**) *сов неперех* to get through; (*перен: разг: в руководство*) to worm one's way in.

пролёт (-а) *м* span; ~ **ле́стницы** a flight of stairs.

пролетариа́т (-а) *м* proletariat.

пролета́рск|ий (-ая, -ое, -ие) *прил* proletarian.

проле|те́ть (-чу́, -ти́шь; *impf* **пролета́ть**) *сов неперех* to fly; (*человек, поезд*) to fly past; (*лето, отпуск*) to fly by.

проле́|чь (*3sg* -́жет, *3pl* -́жгут, *impf* **пролега́ть**) *сов неперех* (*дорога, тропинка*) to stretch.

проли́в (-а) *м* strait(s) (*мн*).

пролива́|ть(ся) (-ю(сь)) *несов от* **проли́ть(ся)**.

проливно́й *прил*: ~ **дождь** pouring rain.

прол|и́ть (-ью́, -ьёшь; *pt* -и́л, -ила́, -и́ло, *impf* **пролива́ть**) *сов перех* to spill; **пролива́ть** (~ *perf*) **чью-н кровь** to spill sb's blood

▶ **проли́ться** (*impf* **пролива́ться**) *сов возв* to spill.

проло́г (-а) *м* prologue (*BRIT*), prolog (*US*).

прол|ожи́ть (-ожу́, -о́жишь; *impf* **прокла́дывать**) *сов перех* (*протянуть*) to lay; **прокла́дывать** (~ *perf*) **что-н чем-н** to interlay sth with sth; ~ (*perf*) **доро́гу** *или* **путь кому-н/чему-н** to pave the way for sb/sth.

проло́м (-а) *м* (*льда*) cracking; (*место*) crack.

пролома́|ть (-ю; *impf* **прола́мывать**) *сов перех* to break through.

пролом|и́ть (-омлю́, -о́мишь; *impf* **прола́мывать**) *сов перех* (*лёд*) to break; (*череп*) to fracture; **прола́мывать** (~ *perf*) **дыру́ в чём-н** to make a hole in sth.

проль|ю́(сь) *итп сов см* **проли́ть(ся)**.

проля́жет *итп сов см* **проле́чь**.

прома́|зать (-жу, -жешь) *сов от* **ма́зать**.

промаршир|ова́ть (-у́ю) *сов неперех* to march past.

прома́сл|ить (-ю, -ишь; *impf* **прома́сливать**) *сов перех* (*растительным маслом*) to oil; (*сливочным маслом*) to grease.

прома́тыва|ть (-ю) *несов от* **промота́ть**.

про́мах (-а) *м* miss; (*перен*) blunder; **дава́ть** (**дать** *perf*) ~ to miss the target; (*перен*) to make a blunder.

промахну́|ться (-у́сь, -ёшься; *impf* **прома́хиватся**) *сов возв* to miss; (*перен: разг*) to blunder.

прома́чива|ть (-ю) *несов от* **промочи́ть**.

прома́ш|ка (-ки; *gen pl* -ек) *ж* stroke of bad luck; (*упущение*) blunder.

промедле́ни|е (-я) *ср* delay.

промедл|ить (-ю, -ишь) *сов неперех*: ~ **с** +*instr* to delay.

промежу́т|ок (-ка) *м* (*пространство*) gap; (*перерыв*) break.

промежу́точный *прил* (*участок, период*) intervening; (*стадия, положение*) intermediate.

промелькн|у́ть (-у́, -ёшь) *сов неперех* to flash past; ~ (*perf*) **в** +*prp* (*в голове, в памяти*) to flash through.

променя́|ть (-ю; *impf* **проме́нивать**) *сов перех*: ~ **кого-н/что-н на** +*acc* to prefer sb/sth to.

промёрзн|уть (-у, -ешь; *impf* **промерза́ть**) *сов неперех* (*комната, дом*) to be chilled through; (*человек*) to freeze.

промета́|ть (-ю) *сов от* **мета́ть**.

промо́зглый *прил* cold and wet.

промока́тельн|ый *прил*: ~**ая бума́га** blotting paper.

промока́ть (-ю) *несов от* **промо́кнуть** ♦ *неперех* to let water through.

промока́шк|а (-ки; *gen pl* -ек) *ж* (*разг*) blotting paper.

промо́кнуть (-у, -ешь; *impf* **промока́ть**) *сов неперех* (*одежда, ноги*) to get soaked.

промокну́ть (-у́, -ёшь; *impf* **промока́ть**) *сов перех* to blot.

промо́лв|ить (-лю, -ишь) *сов перех* to utter.

промолча́ть (-у́, -и́шь) *сов неперех* to say nothing.

промота́ть (-ю; *impf* **прома́тывать**) *сов перех* (*раза*) to blow.

пром|оч́ить (-очу́, -о́чишь; *impf* **прома́чивать**) *сов перех* to get wet.

промо́ю *итп сов см* **промы́ть**.

промтова́рный *прил*: ~ **магази́н** *shop selling manufactured goods*.

промтова́р|ы (-ов) *мн* (= **промы́шленные това́ры**) manufactured goods *мн*.

промурлы́ка|ть (-ю) *сов от* **мурлы́кать**.

промча́ться (-у́сь, -и́шься) *сов возв* (*год, лето, жизнь*) to fly by; ~ (*perf*) **ми́мо** +*gen/* **че́рез** +*acc* (*поезд, человек*) to fly past/through.

промыва́ни|е (-я) *ср* (*желудка*) pumping; (*гла́за, раны*) bathing.

промыва́ть (-ю) *несов от* **промы́ть**.

про́мыс|ел (-ла) *м* (*ремесло́*) trade; **охо́тничий** ~ hunting; **пушно́й** ~ trapping; **ры́бный** ~ fishing; *см также* **про́мыслы**.

промысло́вый *прил* trading; (*рыба, зверь*) marketable.

про́мысл|ы (-ов) *мн* (*нефтяны́е*) fields *мн*; (*горные, соляны́е*) mines *мн*.

пром|ы́ть (-о́ю, -о́ешь; *impf* **промыва́ть**) *сов перех* (*желудок*) to pump; (*рану, глаз*) to bathe; (*золотой песок*) to pan out.

промыча́ть (-у́, -и́шь) *сов от* **мыча́ть**.

промы́шленник (-а) *м* industrialist.

промы́шленность (-и) *ж* industry; **лёгкая/тяжёлая** ~ light/heavy industry.

промы́шленный *прил* industrial.

промышля́|ть (-ю) *несов неперех*: ~ **охо́той** to hunt; ~ (*impf*) **ры́бой** to fish; ~ (*impf*) **перево́дами** (*разг*) to earn a living from translation.

промя́мл|ить (-ю, -ишь) *сов от* **мя́млить**.

промя́ука|ть (-ю) *сов от* **мя́укать**.

пронаблюда́|ть (-ю) *сов от* **наблюда́ть**.

прон|ести́ (-есу́, -есёшь; *pt* -ёс, -есла́, -есло́, *impf* **проноси́ть**) *сов перех* to carry; (*тайком*) to sneak in; (*сохранить*) to preserve ♦ *безл* (*перен*) to blow over

▸ **пронести́сь** (*impf* **проноси́ться**) *сов возв* (*машина, пуля, бегун*) to shoot by; (*лето, годы* итп) to fly by; (*буря, тайфун* итп) to whirl past.

пронж|у́ *сов см* **пронзи́ть**.

пронза́|ть (-ю) *несов от* **пронзи́ть**.

пронзи́тельн|ый (-ен, -ьна, -ьно) *прил* piercing; (*свет, цвет*) glaring.

прон|зи́ть (-жу́, -зи́шь; *impf* **пронза́ть**) *сов перех* (*также перен*) to pierce.

прон|иза́ть (-ижу́, -и́жешь; *impf* **прони́зывать**) *сов перех* to penetrate (into).

прони́к(ся) итп *сов см* **прони́кнуть(ся)**.

проника́|ть(ся) (-ю(сь)) *несов от* **прони́кнуть(ся)**.

проникнове́нн|ый (-ен, -на, -но) *прил* (*слова*) heartfelt; (*голос*) emotional.

прони́кнут|ый (-, -а, -о) *прил* (+*instr*) full of.

прони́к|нуть (-ну, -нешь; *pt* -, -ла, -ло, *impf* **проника́ть**) *сов перех*: ~ **в** +*acc* to penetrate (into); (*залеть*) to break into; (*распространи́ться*) to spread into; (*поня́ть*) to understand

▸ **прони́кнуться** (*impf* **проника́ться**) *сов возв* (+*instr*) to be filled with.

пронима́|ть (-ю) *несов от* **проня́ть**.

проница́тельный (-ен, -ьна, -ьно) *прил* (*человек, ум*) shrewd; (*взгляд*) penetrating.

проница́|ть (-ю) *сов неперех*: ~ **в** +*acc* (*свет*) to penetrate (into).

прон|оси́ть(ся) (-ошу́(сь), -о́сишь(ся)) *несов от* **пронести́(сь)**.

пронумер|ова́ть (-у́ю) *сов от* **нумерова́ть**.

проны́р|а (-ы) *ж* (*разг*) dodgy character.

проны́рлив|ый (-, -а, -о) *прил* (*раза*) dodgy.

прон|я́ть (-йму́, -ймёшь; *impf* **пронима́ть**) *сов перех* (*разг*: *подлеж: хо́лод*) to seize; (: *музыка*) to move.

прообраз (-а) *м* (*образец*) model; (*прототи́п*) prototype.

прооперир|ова́ть (-ую) *сов от* **опери́ровать**.

пропага́нд|а (-ы) *ж* propaganda; (*спорта*) promotion.

пропаганди́р|овать (-ую) *несов перех* (*полити́ческое уче́ние*) to spread propaganda about; (*знаний, спорт*) to promote.

пропаганди́ст (-а) *м* propagandist.

пропаганди́стск|ий (-ая, -ое, -ие) *прил* (*шуми́ха, кампа́ния*) propagandist *опред*.

пропада́|ть (-ю) *несов от* **пропа́сть** ♦ *неперех* (*разг*) to stay for a long time; **он вечера́ми ~ет на рабо́те** he spends all his evenings at work.

про́падом *нареч*: **пропади́** ~ (*разг*) to hell with it.

пропаду́ итп *сов см* **пропа́сть**.

пропа́ж|а (-и) *ж* (*денег, докуме́нтов*) loss; (*то, что пропа́ло*) lost object.

пропа́лыва|ть (-ю) *несов от* **прополо́ть**.

про́пасть (-и) *ж* precipice; (*перен: во взгля́дах*) abyss; (*no pl*; *разг*) masses *мн*.

проп|а́сть (-аду́, -адёшь; *impf* **пропада́ть**) *сов неперех* to disappear; (*деньги, письмо*) to go missing; (*аппетит, голос, слух*) to go; (*усилия, билет в театр*) to be wasted; (*погибнуть*) to die; **пропада́ть** (~ *perf*) **бе́з вести** (*человек*) to go missing.

проп|аха́ть (-ашу́, -а́шешь; *impf* **пропа́хивать**) *сов перех* to plough (*BRIT*), plow (*US*).

пропа́х|нуть (-ну, -нешь; *pt* -, -ла, -ло) *сов неперех* (+*instr*) to become filled with the smell of.

пропашу́ *итп сов см* **пропаха́ть**.

пропа́_____й (-яя, -ее, -ие) *прил* (*разг: безнадё жный*) hopeless; (*долго не приходивший*) long-lost; **э́ти де́ньги – ~ие** (*разг*) that money is lost for good.

пропе́й(те) *сов см* **пропи́ть**.

пропёк(ся) *итп сов см* **пропе́чь(ся)**.

пропека́|ть(ся) (-ю(сь)) *несов от* **пропе́чь(ся)**.

пропеку́(сь) *сов см* **пропе́чь(ся)**.

пропе́ллер (-а) *м* (*АВИА*) propeller.

проп|е́ть (-ою́, -оёшь) *сов от* **петь** ◆ *перех* (*петь*) to sing.

проп|е́чь (-еку́, -ечёшь *итп*, -еку́т; *pt* -ёк, -екла́, -екло́, *impf* **пропека́ть**) *сов перех* to bake

▶ **пропе́чься** (*impf* **пропека́ться**) *сов возв* to be well-baked.

пропива́|ть (-ю) *несов от* **пропи́ть**.

проп|или́ть (-илю́, -и́лишь; *impf* **пропи́ливать**) *сов перех* to saw through.

проп|иса́ть (-ишу́, -и́шешь; *impf* **пропи́сывать**) *сов перех* (*человека*) to register; (*лекарство*) to prescribe; (*статью, письмо*) to write

▶ **прописа́ться** *сов возв* to register.

пропи́|ска (-ки) *ж* (*в городе, в доме*) registration.

прописн|о́й *прил* (*общеизвестный*) commonplace; **~а́я и́стина** truism; **прописна́я бу́ква** capital letter.

пропи́сыва|ть (-ю) *несов от* **прописа́ть**.

про́пис|ь (-и) *ж* (*ПРОСВЕЩ*) writing samples *мн*.

про́писью *нареч* in full; **писа́ть** (**написа́ть** *perf*) **су́мму** ~ to write out a sum *или* amount in words.

пропита́ни|е (-я) *ср* food.

пропита́|ть (-ю; *impf* **пропи́тывать**) *сов перех* (*смочить*) to soak; (*насытить: бумагу*) to saturate; (: *комнату, воздух*) to fill

▶ **пропита́ться** (*impf* **пропи́тываться**) *сов возв*: ~**ся чем-н** (*водой*) to be soaked in sth; (*запахом: воздух*) to be filled with sth; (: *одежда*) to be saturated with sth.

пропи́т|ка (-ки; *gen pl* -ок) *ж* (*ткани, дерева*) soaking; (*водонепроницаемая*) impregnation; (*ромовая*) flavouring.

пропи́тыва|ть(ся) (-ю(сь)) *несов от* **пропита́ть(ся)**.

проп|и́ть (-ью́, -ьёшь; *pt* -и́л, -ила́, -и́ло, *imper* **пропе́й(те)**, *impf* **пропива́ть**) *сов перех* (*деньги, состояние*) to squander on drink; (*талант, карьеру*) to ruin (*through drinking*); (*по impf: пить*) to drink.

пропихн|у́ть (-у́, -ёшь) *сов перех* (*разг: в дверь итп*) to shove; (: *в университет итп*) to push.

пропишу́(сь) *итп сов см* **прописа́ть(ся)**.

пропла́ва|ть (-ю) *сов неперех* (*человек*) to swim; (*судно*) to sail.

пропла́|кать (-чу, -чешь) *сов неперех* to cry; ~ (*perf*) **все глаза́** to cry one's eyes out.

проплута́|ть (-ю) *сов неперех* to wander.

пропл|ы́ть (-ыву́, -ывёшь; *impf* **проплыва́ть**) *сов неперех* (*человек*) to swim; (: *миновать*) to swim past; (*судно*) to sail; (: *миновать*) to sail past; (*перен: птица, облака*) to sail by *или* past; (: *воспоминания, мысли итп*) to flash past.

пропове́дник (-а) *м* (*РЕЛ*) preacher; (*перен: убеждений, теории*) advocate.

пропове́дни|ца (-ы) *ж см* **пропове́дник**.

пропове́д|овать (-ую) *несов перех* (*РЕЛ*) to preach; (*идею*) to advocate.

про́повед|ь (-и) *ж* (*РЕЛ*) preaching; (*идей*) endorsement; (*речь*) sermon.

пропо́йц|а (-ы) *м* (*разг*) soak.

пропола́скива|ть (-ю) *несов от* **прополоска́ть**.

пропол|зти́ (-у́, -ёшь; *pt* -, -ла́, -ло́) *сов неперех*: ~ **по** +*dat*/**в** +*acc итп* (*насекомое, человек*) to crawl along/in(to) *итп*; (*змея*) to slither along/in (to) *итп*.

пропо́лис (-а) *м* propolis.

пропо́л|ка (-ки; *gen pl* -ок) *ж* weeding.

прополоска́|ть (-ю; *impf* **пропола́скивать** *или* **полоска́ть**) *сов перех* to rinse (out); **пропола́скивать** *или* **полоска́ть** (~ *perf*) **го́рло** to gargle.

пропол|о́ть (-олю́, -о́лешь; *impf* **пропа́лывать** *или* **поло́ть**) *сов перех* (*грядку итп*) to weed.

пропорциона́лен *прил см* **пропорциона́льный**.

пропорциона́льность (-и) *ж* proportion.

пропорциона́л|ьный (-ен, -ьна, -ьно) *прил* (*фигура, тело*) well-proportioned; (*развитие, распределение*) proportional; **пропорциона́льное представи́тельство** proportional representation.

пропо́рци|я (-и) *ж* proportion.

пропот|е́ть (-ю; *impf* **пропотева́ть**) *сов неперех* to sweat profusely; (*пропитаться потом*) to be soaked with sweat.

пропою́ *итп сов см* **пропе́ть**.

про́пуск (-а) *м* (*действие: в зал, через границу итп*) admission; (: *в школе*) non-attendance; (*в тексте, в изложении*) gap; (*неявка: на работу, в школу*) absence; (*nom pl* -а́; *документ*) pass.

пропуска́|ть (-ю) *несов от* **пропусти́ть** ◆ *перех* (*чернила, свет итп*) to let through; (*воду, холод*) to let in.

проп|усти́ть (-ущу́, -у́стишь; *impf* **пропуска́ть**) *сов перех* to miss; (*дать дорогу, обслужить*) to admit; (*разрешить*) to allow; (*заставить пройти*) to put through; (*выпустить*) to miss out; **пропуска́ть** (~ *perf*) **кого́-н че́рез грани́цу** to let sb across the border; **пропуска́ть** (~ *perf*)

когó-н вперёд to let sb go ahead.
пропылесóс|ить (-ю, -ишь) *сов от*
пылесóсить.
пропыл|и́ться (-ю́сь, -и́шься) *сов возв* to be
full of dust.
пропью́ *итп сов см* **пропи́ть**.
прораб (-а) *м* (= *производи́тель рабóт*)
foreman (*мн* foremen).
прорабóта|ть (-ю; *impf* **прораба́тывать**) *сов*
неперех to work ♦ *перех* (*учебник, статью́,*
урок) to study in detail; (*разг: критиковáть*) to
rip into.
прор|асти́ (*3sg* -аста́ет, *3pl* -асту́т, *pt* -óс, -осла́,
-осло́, *impf* **прораста́ть**) *сов неперех* (*семена́*)
to germinate; (*трава́*) to sprout.
прóрв|а (-ы) *ж* (*разг: очень много*) heaps *мн*,
masses *мн*; (: *о человéке*) pig.
прорв|а́ть (-у́, -ёшь; *pt* -а́л, -ала́, -а́ло, *impf*
прорыва́ть) *сов перех* (*одéжду, сýмку*) to tear;
(*плотину*) to burst; (*оборóну, фронт*) to break
through ♦ *безл* (+*acc*; *перен*) to explode;
наконéц егó ~а́ло (*перен*) he finally exploded
► **прорва́ться** (*impf* **прорыва́ться**) *сов возв*
(*карма́н, сýмка*) to tear; (*плоти́на, ша́рик*) to
burst; (*гнев, раздражéние*) to erupt; (*гóре*) to
break out; **прорыва́ться** (*~ся perf*) **в** +*acc* to
burst in(to).
прореаги́р|овать (-ую) *сов от* **реаги́ровать**.
прорéд|ить (-жу́, -ди́шь; *impf* **проре́живать**)
сов (*гря́дки, всхóды*) to thin out.
прорéз|ать (-жу, -жешь) *сов от* **рéзать** ♦ (*impf*
прорéзывать) *перех* to cut through; (*рéзать:*
мя́со, рыбу итп) to cut; (: *óвощи, фрýкты итп*)
to chop
► **прорéзаться** *сов от* **рéзаться** ♦ (*impf*
прорéзываться) *возв* (*появи́ться: зýбы*) to
come through; (: *ли́стья*) to come out.
прорези́н|ить (-ю, -ишь; *impf* **прорези́нивать**)
сов перех to cover with rubber.
прорезн|óй *прил*: **~ карма́н** slit pocket; **~а́я**
пéтля buttonhole.
прорéзыва|ть(ся) (-ю(сь)) *несов от*
прорéзать(ся).
прóрез|ь (-и) *ж* (*на тка́ни*) slit; (*на прицéле*
орýдия) aperture.
проре́ктор (-а) *м* vice-principal.
прорепети́р|овать (-ую) *сов от*
репети́ровать.
прорефери́р|овать (-ую) *сов от*
рефери́ровать.
прорéх|а (-и) *ж* (*дыра́*) tear; (*разг: недостáток*)
shortcoming.
прорецензи́р|овать (-ую) *сов от*
рецензи́ровать.
проржа́ве|ть (*3sg* -ет, *3pl* -ют) *сов неперех* to
rust through.
прорица́ни|е (-я) *ср* prophecy.
прорица́тел|ь (-я) *м* prophet.

прорица́тельниц|а (-ы) *ж см* **прорица́тель**.
прорица́|ть (-ю) *несов перех* to prophesy.
проро́к (-а) *м* (*РЕЛ, перен*) prophet.
прор|они́ть (-оню́, -óнишь) *сов перех*
(*сказáть*) to utter.
проро́с *итп сов см* **прорасти́**.
проро́ческ|ий (-ая, -ое, -ие) *прил* (*сон, словá,*
дар) prophetic.
проро́честв|о (-а) *ср* prophecy.
проро́ч|ить (-у, -ишь; *perf* **напроро́чить**) *несов*
перех to predict.
проро́ю *итп сов см* **проры́ть**.
прор|уби́ть (-ублю́, -у́бишь; *impf* **проруба́ть**)
сов перех (*стéну, лёд, гóру*) to make a hole in;
проруба́ть (*~ perf*) **про́секу в лесу́** to make a
clearing in a forest.
про́руб|ь (-и) *ж* ice-hole.
проры́в (-а) *м* (*фрóнта*) break-through;
(*плоти́ны*) bursting; (*прóрванное мéсто*)
breach.
прорыва́|ть(ся) (-ю(сь)) *несов от*
прорва́ть(ся).
прор|ы́ть (-óю, -óешь; *impf* **прорыва́ть**) *сов*
перех (*прокопáть*) to dig.
прос|ади́ть (-ажу́, -а́дишь; *impf* **проса́живать**)
сов перех (*разг: истрáтить*) to blow.
проса́лива|ть (-ю) *несов от* **просоли́ть**.
проса́чива|ться (*3sg* -ется, *3pl* -ются) *несов*
от **просочи́ться**.
просверл|и́ть (-ю́, -и́шь; *impf* **просверливать**
или **сверли́ть**) *сов перех* to bore, drill.
просвéт (-а) *м* (*в тýчах, в облакáх*) break; (*в*
забóре, в зана́весе) crack; (*перен: в тяжёлой*
ситуáции) light at the end of the tunnel.
просвети́тел|ь (-я) *м person who enlightens*
others about progressive ideas.
просвети́тельниц|а (-ы) *ж см* **просвети́тель**.
просвети́тельный *прил* enlightening.
просв|ети́ть (-ещу́, -ети́шь; *impf* **просвеща́ть**)
сов перех to enlighten; (-ечу́, -éтишь; *impf*
просвéчивать; *лёгкие*) to x-ray.
► **просвети́ться** ♦ (-щу́сь, -ти́шься; *impf*
просвеща́ться) *сов возв* to enlighten o.s.
просветлéни|е (-я) *ср* (*я́сность*) lucidity.
просветлённый *прил* lucid.
просветлé|ть (-ю) *сов от* **светлéть**.
просвéчива|ть (-ю) *несов от* **просвети́ть** ♦
неперех (*сóлнце*) to shine through; (*нéбо*) to be
visible through; (*ткань*) to let light through.
просвечу́ *сов см* **просвети́ть**.
просвеща́|ть(ся) (-ю(сь)) *несов от*
просвети́ть(ся).
просвещéни|е (-я) *ср* education;
Министéрство ~я ≈ Department of Education.
просвещённый *прил* educated.
просвещу́(сь) *сов см* **просвети́ть(ся)**.
просвир|а́ (-ы́) *ж* (*РЕЛ*) communion bread, Host.
просви|стéть (-щу́, -сти́шь) *сов см* **свистéть** ♦

(*impf* **просви́стывать**) *перех* (*мотив, песню*) to whistle (through) ♦ *неперех* (*пуля, снаряд*) to whistle past.

про́седь (-и) *ж* grey (*BRIT*) *или* gray (*US*) streak.

просе́ивание (-я) *ср* (*муки, песка*) sifting.

просе́ива|ть (-ю) *несов от* **просе́ять**.

про́сек|а (-и) *ж* (*в лесу*) clearing.

просёл|ок (-ка) *м* dirt-track.

просёлочный *прил*: ~**ая доро́га** dirt-track.

просе́|ять (-ю; *impf* **просе́ивать**) *сов перех* (*муку, песок*) to sift.

просигнализи́р|овать (-ую) *сов от* **сигнализи́ровать**.

просигна́л|ить (-ю, -ишь) *сов от* **сигна́лить**.

проси|де́ть (-жу́, -ди́шь; *impf* **проси́живать**) *сов перех* (*сидеть*) to sit; (*пробыть*) to stay.

проси́тельный *прил* pleading.

про|си́ть (-шу́, -сишь; *perf* **попроси́ть**) *несов перех* to ask; (*приглашать*) to invite; ~**шу́ Вас!** if you please!; ~ (**попроси́ть** *perf*) **кого́-н чём-н**/+*infin* to ask sb for sth/to do; ~ (**попроси́ть** *perf*) **кого́-н за кого́-н** to ask sb a favour (*BRIT*) *или* favor (*US*) on behalf of sb

▸ **проси́ться** (*perf* **попроси́ться**) *несов возв* (*просить разрешения*) to ask permission; **сло́во так и ~ся** (*impf*) **с языка́** to have a word on the tip of one's tongue; **её лицо́ про́сится на карти́ну** her face was crying out to be painted.

проси|я́ть (-ю) *сов неперех* (*солнце*) to begin to shine; (*радуга*) to appear; (*перен: человек*) to beam; (: *лицо*) to light up.

проск|ака́ть (-ачу́, -а́чешь) *сов неперех* (*человек*) to hop; ~ (*perf*) **че́рез/сквозь** +*acc* (*лошадь*) to gallop across/through; (*олень, заяц*) to bound across *или* by/through.

проска́кива|ть (-ю) *несов от* **проскочи́ть**.

проска́льзыва|ть (-ю) *несов от* **проскользну́ть**.

проскачу́ *итп сов см* **проскака́ть**.

прорскво|зи́ть (*3sg* -и́т, *3pl* -я́т) *сов безл* (+*acc*): **меня́ ~и́ло** I caught a chill.

проскло́ня́|ть (-ю) *сов от* **склоня́ть**.

проскользн|у́ть (-у́, -ёшь; *impf* **проска́льзывать**) *сов неперех* (*монета*) to slide in; (*человек*) to slip in; (*перен: сомнение, страх*) to creep in.

проск|очи́ть (-очу́, -о́чишь; *impf* **проска́кивать**) *сов неперех* (*проскользнуть*) to slide in; (*пройти, проехать*): ~ **в** +*acc*/**ми́мо** +*gen итп* to race in(to)/past *итп*; (*проникнуть*): ~ **в/че́рез** +*acc* to break in(to)/through.

проскуча́|ть (-ю) *сов неперех* to be bored.

просла́б|ить (*3sg* -ит, *3pl* -ят) *сов от* **сла́бить**.

просла́в|ить (-лю, -ишь; *impf* **прославля́ть**) *сов перех* (*сделать известным*) to make famous; (*impf* **прославля́ть** *или* **сла́вить**; *восхвалить*) to glorify

▸ **просла́виться** (*impf* **прославля́ться**) *сов возв* (*актёр, писатель*) to become famous; (*перен: разг: преступник*) to become notorious.

просла́вленный *прил* renowned.

просла́влю(сь) *сов см* **просла́вить(ся)**.

прославля́|ть(ся) (-ю(сь)) *несов от* **просла́вить(ся)**.

просле|ди́ть (-жу́, -ди́шь; *impf* **просле́живать**) *сов перех* (*следить глазами*) to follow; (*исследовать*) to trace ♦ *неперех*: ~ **за** +*instr* to follow; (*за выполнением приказа, за чьим-н поведением*) to monitor.

просле́д|овать (-ую) *сов неперех*: ~ (**ми́мо** +*gen*/**сквозь** +*acc*) to pass slowly (by/through).

просле́жива|ть (-ю) *несов от* **проследи́ть**.

прослежу́ *сов см* **проследи́ть**.

просле|зи́ться (-жу́сь, -зи́шься) *сов возв* to cry.

просло́|йка (-йки; *gen pl* -ек) *ж* (*слой*) layer; (*в горной породе*) stratum (*мн* strata).

прослу|жи́ть (-жу́, -ýжишь) *сов неперех* to serve; (*туфли, пальто итп*) to last.

прослу́ша|ть (-ю; *impf* **прослу́шивать**) *сов перех* to listen to; (*курс, лекции*) to attend; (*ответ, объяснение итп*) to miss; (*no impf; радио, музыку*) to listen to.

прослу́шива|ть (-ю) *несов от* **прослу́шать** ♦ *перех*: **их кварти́ру ~ют** their flat (*BRIT*) *или* apartment (*US*) is bugged.

просл|ы́ть (-ыву́, -ывёшь) *сов неперех* (+*instr*) to acquire a reputation as.

прослы́ш|ать (-у, -ишь) *сов неперех* (*разг*): ~ **о** +*prp* to hear about.

просма́лива|ть (-ю) *несов от* **просмоли́ть**.

просма́трива|ть (-ю) *несов от* **просмотре́ть**

▸ **просма́триваться** *несов возв* to be visible.

просмол|и́ть (-ю́, -и́шь; *impf* **просма́ливать**) *сов перех* to coat with tar.

просмо́тр (-а) *м* (*фильма, спектакля*) viewing; (*документов*) inspection; (*ошибка*) blunder.

просм|отре́ть (-отрю́, -о́тришь; *impf* **просма́тривать**) *сов перех* (*ознакомиться: читая*) to look through; (: *смотря*) to view; (*пропустить*) to overlook.

просн|у́ться (-у́сь, -ёшься; *impf* **просыпа́ться**) *сов возв* to wake up; (*перен: любовь, страх итп*) to be awakened.

про́с|о (-а) *ср* millet.

просо́выва|ть(ся) (-ю(сь)) *несов от* **просу́нуть(ся)**.

просо́ди|я (-и) *ж* prosody.

просол|и́ть (-олю́, -о́лишь; *impf* **проса́ливать**) *сов перех* to salt.

просо́х|нуть (-ну, -нешь; *pt* -, -ла, -ло, *impf* **просыха́ть**) *сов неперех* to dry out.

просоч|и́ться (*3sg* -и́тся, *3pl* -а́тся, *impf* **проса́чиваться**) *сов возв* (*также перен*) to filter through.

просп|а́ть (-лю́, -и́шь; *pt* -а́л, -ала́, -а́ло) *сов неперех* (*спать*) to sleep; (*impf* **просыпа́ть**; *встать поздно*) to oversleep ♦ *перех* (*разг: остановку*) to sleep through.

проспе́кт (-а) *м* avenue; (*план*) draft; (*издание*) brochure.

просплю́ *сов см* **проспа́ть**.

проспо́р|ить (-ю, -ишь; *impf* **проспо́ривать**) *сов перех* to lose in a bet ♦ *неперех* (*no impf*; *спорить*) to argue.

проспряга́|ть (-ю) *сов от* **спряга́ть**.

просро́чек *сущ см* **просро́чка**.

просро́ч|ить (-у, -ишь; *impf* **просро́чивать**) *сов перех* (*платёж*) to be late with; (*паспорт, билет*) to let expire.

просро́ч|ка (-ки; *gen pl* -ек) *ж* (*платежа*) expiry of time limit; (*паспорта, билета*) expiry.

проста́в|ить (-лю, -ишь; *impf* **проставля́ть**) *сов перех* to fill in.

проста́ива|ть (-ю) *несов от* **простоя́ть**.

проста́к (-а́) *м* simpleton.

простега́|ть (-ю) *сов от* **стега́ть**.

просте́н|ок (-ка) *м* section of wall between windows or doors.

прост|ере́ть(ся) (*pt* -ёр(ся), -ёрла(сь), -ёрло(сь)) *сов от* **простира́ть(ся)**.

простёц|кий (-ая, -ое, -ие) *прил* (*разг*) informal.

простира́|ть (-ю; *perf* **простере́ть**) *несов перех* (*планы, замыслы*) to raise; (*протягивать*): ~ **ру́ки** to hold out one's hands ♦ (*impf* **прости́рывать**) *сов перех* (*стирать тщательно*) to wash thoroughly ♦ *неперех* (*стирать*) to wash

► **простира́ться** (*perf* **простере́ться**) *несов возв* to extend.

простирн|у́ть (-у́, -ёшь) *сов перех* (*разг*): ~ **что-н** to give sth a quick wash.

прости́рыва|ть (-ю) *несов от* **простира́ть**.

прости́тель|ный (-ен, -на, -но) *прил* excusable, forgivable.

проститу́т|ка (-ки; *gen pl* -ок) *ж* prostitute.

проститу́ци|я (-и) *ж* prostitution.

прости́ть (прощу́, прости́шь; *impf* **проща́ть**) *сов перех* (*врага, ошибку итп*) to forgive; **проща́ть** (~ *perf*) **что-н кому́-н** to excuse или forgive sb (for) sth; **проща́ть** (~ *perf*) **долг кому́-н** to cancel sb's debt; **прости́те меня́, я был о́чень груб** forgive me, I was very rude; **прости́те, как пройти́ на ста́нцию?** excuse me, how do I get to the station?; **нет (уж) прости́те, я не согла́сен** I'm sorry, but I cannot agree

► **прости́ться** (*impf* **проща́ться**) *сов возв*: ~**ся с** +*instr* to say goodbye to; (*покинуть*) to leave.

про́сто *нареч* (*делать*) easily; (*интерпретировать*) simply ♦ *част* just; **я зашёл** ~ **повида́ться** I just popped in to see you; **всё э́то** ~ **недоразуме́ние** all this is simply a misunderstanding; ~ **(так)** for no particular reason; ~**на́просто** (*разг*) just.

простова́т|ый (-, -а, -о) *прил* simple-minded.

простоволо́сый *прил* (*разг*) bareheaded.

простоду́шен *прил см* **простоду́шный**.

простоду́ши|е (-я) *ср* ingenuousness.

простоду́ш|ный (-ен, -на, -но) *прил* ingenuous.

прост|о́й (-, -а́, -о) *прил* simple;

(*незамысловатый, грубый*) plain; (*не трудный*) easy, simple; (*прямой и нецеремонный*) unaffected; (*no short form*; *обыкновенный*) ordinary ♦ (-о́я) *м* downtime, idle time; (*рабочих*) stoppage; **маши́на на** ~**о́е** the machine is standing idle; **пла́та за** ~ **су́дна** demurrage; ~**ым гла́зом** with the naked eye; **про́ще** ~**о́го** (*разг*) as easy as pie; **просто́е письмо́** ordinary letter; **просто́й каранда́ш** lead pencil; **просты́е чулки́** cotton stockings.

простоква́ш|а (-и) *ж* soured milk (*type of yoghurt*).

простонаро́дный *прил* of the common people.

прост|она́ть (-ону́, -о́нешь) *сов (не)перех* to groan.

просто́р (-а) *м* expanse; (*свобода*) scope.

просто́рен *прил см* **просто́рный**.

проstoréчи|е (-я) *ср* common speech; **э́то** ~ it's a colloquial expression.

просторе́чный *прил* common.

просто́р|ный (-ен, -на, -но) *прил* roomy.

простосерде́ч|ный (-ен, -на, -но) *прил* open-hearted.

простот|а́ (-ы́) *ж* simplicity; (*задачи*) easiness, simplicity; (*одежды, рисунка*) plainness; (*характера*) unaffectedness; **по** ~**é душе́вной** или **серде́чной** in all innocence.

простофи́л|я (-и) *м/ж* dimwit.

просто|я́ть (-ю́, -и́шь; *impf* **проста́ивать**) *сов неперех* to stand; (*бездействуя*) to stand idle; (*no impf*; *просуществовать*) to stand.

простра́н|ный (-ен, -на, -но) *прил* (*подробный*) verbose.

простра́нственный *прил* spatial.

простра́нств|о (-а) *ср* (*также* АСТРОНОМИЯ) space; (*территория*) expanse.

простре́л (-а) *м* backache.

простре́лива|ть (-ю) *несов от* **прострели́ть** ♦ *перех* (*обстреливать*) to cover (*with artillery fire*).

простре́л|ить (-елю́, -е́лишь; *impf* **простре́ливать**) *сов перех* to shoot through.

простро́ч|ить (-очу́, -о́чишь) *сов от* **строчи́ть**.

просту́д|а (-ы) *ж* (МЕД) cold.

просту|ди́ть (-жу́, -́дишь; *impf* **простужа́ть**) *сов перех*: ~ **кого́-н** to give a cold to sb; **простужа́ть** (~ *perf*) **у́ши/го́рло** to get a cold in one's ears/throat

► **простуди́ться** (*impf* **простужа́ться**) *сов возв* to catch a cold.

просту́дный *прил* cold-related.

простужа́|ть(ся) (-ю(сь)) *несов от* **простуди́ть(ся)**.

просту́жен|ный (-, -а, -о) *прил*: **ребёнок просту́жен** the child has got a cold; **у Вас** ~ **го́лос** you sound as if you've got a cold.

простужу́(сь) *сов см* **простуди́ть(ся)**.

прост|упи́ть (*3sg* -у́пит, *3pl* -у́пят, *impf*

проступа́ть) *сов неперех (пот, пятна)* to come through; *(очертания)* to appear.

просту́п|ок (-ка) *м* misconduct; *(ЮР)* misdemeanour *(BRIT)*, misdemeanor *(US)*.

простыва́ть (-ю) *несов от* **просты́ть**.

просты́ну *итп сов см* **просты́ть**.

простын|я́ (-и́; *nom pl* про́стыни, *gen pl* про́стынь, *dat pl* -я́м) *ж* sheet.

просты́ть (-ну, -нешь; *impf* простыва́ть) *сов неперех (разг)* to catch a cold; **его́ и след ~л** *(разг)* he disappeared without a trace.

просу́н|уть (-у, -ешь; *impf* просо́вывать) *сов перех:* ~ **сквозь/в** +*acc итп* to push through/in (to) *итп*

► **просу́нуться** *(impf* **просо́вываться)** *сов возв (разг):* **в дверь/в окно́ ~улась голова́** a head came round the door/appeared at the window.

просуши́ть (-ушу́, -у́шишь; *impf* просу́шивать) *сов перех* to dry.

просуществова́ть (-у́ю) *сов неперех* to exist.

просфор|а́ (-ы́) *ж (РЕЛ)* communion bread, Host.

просчёт (-а) *м (счёт)* counting; *(ошибка: в подсчёте)* error; *(: в действиях)* miscalculation.

просчита́ть (-ю; *impf* просчи́тывать) *сов перех (считать)* to count; *(ошибиться)* to miscount

► **просчита́ться** *(impf* **просчи́тываться)** *сов возв (при счёте)* to miscount; *(в планах, в предположениях)* to miscalculate; **мы ~лись на сто рубле́й** we are out by one hundred roubles.

просы́п|ать (-лю, -лешь; *impf* просыпа́ть) *сов перех* to spill

► **просы́паться** *(impf* **просыпа́ться)** *сов возв* to spill.

просыпа́ть (-ю) *несов от* **проспа́ть**, **просы́пать**

► **просыпа́ться** *несов от* **просну́ться**, **просы́паться**.

просы́плю(сь) *итп сов см* **просы́пать(ся)**.

просыха́ть (-ю) *сов от* **просо́хнуть**.

про́сьб|а (-ы) *ж* request; **выполня́ть (вы́полнить *perf*) ~у** to fulfil a request; **обраща́ться (обрати́ться *perf*) к кому́-н с ~ой** to make a request to sb.

прота́лин|а (-ы) *ж* bare patch *(where snow has melted)*.

прота́лкива|ть(ся) (-ю(сь)) *несов от* **протолкну́ть(ся)**.

прота́плива|ть (-ю) *несов от* **протопи́ть**.

прота́птыва|ть (-ю) *несов от* **протопта́ть**.

протара́н|ить (-ю, -ишь) *сов от* **тара́нить**.

протаска́|ть (-ю) *сов перех (разг: сумку)* to carry round; *(: платье)* to wear.

прота́скива|ть (-ю) *несов от* **протащи́ть**.

прота́чива|ть (ю) *несов от* **проточи́ть**.

прот|ащи́ть (-ащу́, -а́щишь; *impf* прота́скивать) *сов перех (разг: перен: силой устроить)* to wangle; *(: критиковать)* to pan; **прота́скивать (~ *perf*) что-н по** +*dat*/**сквозь** +*acc* to drag sth along/through.

протеже́ *м/ж нескл* protégé(e).

проте́з (-а) *м* artificial *или* prosthetic limb; **зубно́й ~** denture.

проте́ин (-а) *м* protein.

протеи́новый *прил* protein *опред*.

протёк *сов см* **проте́чь**.

протека́ни|е (-я) *ср (болезни, явлений)* progression; *(в крыше)* leakage.

протека́|ть (*3sg* -ет, *3pl* -ют) *несов от* **проте́чь** ♦ *неперех (вода)* to flow, run; *(болезнь, явление)* to progress.

протеку́т *итп сов см* **проте́чь**.

протекциони́зм (-а) *м (ЭКОН)* protectionism.

проте́кци|я (-и) *ж* patronage; **ока́зывать (оказа́ть *perf*) ~ю кому́-н** to use one's influence on behalf of sb.

протелеграфи́р|овать (-ую) *сов от* **телеграфи́ровать**.

прот|ере́ть (-ру́, -рёшь; *pt* -ёр, -ёрла, -ёрло, *impf* протира́ть) *сов перех (сделать дыру)* to wear a hole in; *(очистить)* to wipe; **протира́ть (~ *perf*) что-н че́рез си́то** to rub sth through a sieve; **~ *(perf)* глаза́** to rub one's eyes

► **протере́ться** *(impf* **протира́ться)** *сов возв (одежда итп)* to wear through.

протёртый *прил* mashed.

проте́ст (-а) *м* protest; *(ЮР)* objection.

протеста́нт (-а) *м* Protestant.

протеста́нтск|ий (-ая, -ое, -ие) *прил* Protestant *опред*.

протест|ова́ть (-у́ю) *несов неперех:* ~ *(*про́тив +*gen*) to protest (against) ♦ *(perf* **опротестова́ть)** *перех (вексель, решение суда)* to object to.

протесту́ющий (-его; *decl like adj*) *м (обычно мн)* protestor.

проте́чек *сущ см* **проте́чка**.

проте́чет *итп сов см* **проте́чь**.

проте́ч|ка (-ки; *gen pl* -ек) *ж* leak.

проте́чь (*3sg* -ечёт, *3pl* -еку́т, *pt* -ёк, -екла́, -екло́, *impf* протека́ть) *сов неперех (вода)* to seep; *(крыша)* to leak; *(время, юность итп)* to pass by.

про́тив *предл* (+*gen*) against; *(прямо перед)* opposite ♦ *как сказ:* **я ~ да́нного предложе́ния** I am against the motion; **кто ~?** who is against?; **~ до́ма магази́н** opposite the house (there) is a shop; **~ и́мени/наименова́ния** against a name/designation; **~ ве́тра/тече́ния/со́лнца** against the wind/current/sun; **~ пра́вил/во́ли роди́телей** against the rules/one's parents wishes; **~ ожида́ния** contrary to expectation; **~ конкуре́нтов/врага́** against the competition/enemy; **лека́рство ~ ка́шля/головно́й бо́ли** medicine for a cough/headache.

проти́вен *прил см* **проти́вный**.

про́тив|ень (-ня) *м* baking tray.

прот|иви́ться (-люсь, -вишься; *perf* воспроти́виться) *несов возв* (+*dat*) to oppose.

проти́вник (-а) *м* opponent ♦ *собир (ВОЕН)* the enemy.

проти́вниц|а (-ы) ж opponent.

проти́вно нареч offensively ◆ как сказ безл it's disgusting; **мне ~ ви́деть э́то** it disgusts me to see this.

проти́вн|ое (-ого; decl like adj) ср the opposite.

проти́в|ный прил (точка зрения, мнение) opposite опред, contrary опред; (-ен, -на, -но; человек, работа) disgusting, revolting; **~** +dat (закону, разуму) contrary to; **в ~ном слу́чае** otherwise; **проти́вная сторона́** the opposing side.

про́тивня итп сущ см **про́тивень**.

противоа́томн|ый прил (защита) anti-nuclear; **~ое укры́тие** nuclear shelter.

противобо́рств|о (-а) ср struggle.

противобо́рств|овать (-ую) несов неперех (+dat) to fight.

противове́с (-а) м (тех, перен) counterbalance; **в ~ обще́ственному мне́нию** contrary to public opinion.

противовозду́шный прил anti-aircraft.

противога́з (-а) м gas mask.

противоде́йстви|е (-я) ср opposition; **встреча́ть (встре́тить** perf) **~ чему́-н** to meet with opposition over sth.

противоде́йств|овать (-ую) несов неперех (+dat) to oppose.

противоесте́ствен|ный (-, -на, -но) прил unnatural.

противозако́н|ный (-ен, -на, -но) прил unlawful.

противозача́точный прил contraceptive опред; **противозача́точное сре́дство** contraceptive.

противопожа́рный прил (меры) fire-prevention; (техника) fire-fighting.

противопоказа́ни|е (-я) ср contraindication.

противопока́зан|ный (-, -а, -о) прил: **ему́ ~о есть жи́рное** he's been advised not to eat fatty things.

противополо́жен прил см **противополо́жный**.

противополо́жност|ь (-и) ж (мнений, политики) contrast; (противоположное явление) opposite; **в ~** +dat in contrast to.

противополо́ж|ный (-ен, -на, -но) прил (берег, сторона итп) opposite; (мнение, политика итп) opposing.

противопоста́в|ить (-лю, -ишь; impf **противопоставля́ть**) сов перех: **~ кого́-н/что-н** +dat to contrast sb/sth with; (направить против) to oppose sb/sth with.

противопоставле́ни|е (-я) ср (мнений, взглядов) contrasting; (силы) opposing.

противопоста́влю сов см **противопоста́вить**.

противопоставля́|ть (-ю) несов от **противопоста́вить**.

противоречи́вост|ь (-и) ж paradox.

противоречи́в|ый (-, -а, -о) прил paradoxical.

противоре́чи|е (-я) ср contradiction; (классовое, политические) conflict; (возражение): **~** (+dat) (закону, старшим) defiance (of); **быть** (impf) **в ~и с** +instr to be in conflict with.

противоре́ч|ить (-у, -ишь) несов неперех: **~** +dat (человеку) to contradict; (логике, закону итп) to defy; **их показа́ния ~ат друг дру́гу** their evidence is contradictory.

противосто|я́ть (-ю́, -и́шь) несов неперех: **~** +dat (ветру, буре) to withstand; (уговорам, давлению) to resist; **~** (impf) **друг дру́гу** to confront each other.

противоя́ди|е (-я) ср (также перен) antidote.

протира́|ть(ся) (-ю(сь)) несов от **протере́ть(ся)**.

проти́сн|уть (-у, -ешь; impf **проти́скивать**) сов перех to squeeze through

▶ **проти́снуться** (impf **проти́скиваться**) сов возв: **~ в** +acc/**сквозь** +acc to squeeze in(to)/through; **~ся** (impf) **вперёд** to push forward.

проткн|у́ть (-у́, -ёшь; impf **протыка́ть**) сов перех to pierce.

протодья́кон (-а) м archdeacon.

протоиере́|й (-я) м high priest.

прото́к (-а) м (рукав реки) tributary; (соединяющая река) channel; (мед) duct.

протоко́л (-а) м (собрания) minutes мн; (допроса) transcript; (соглашение) protocol; **Дипломати́ческий ~** Diplomatic Protocol; **вести́** (impf) **~ собра́ния** to take the minutes of a meeting; **составля́ть (соста́вить** perf) **~ обы́ска** to record the details of a search; **журна́л ~ов** minute book.

протоколи́р|овать (-ую; perf **запротоколи́ровать**) несов перех (собрание, заседание) to minute; (осмотр, обыск) to record.

протоко́льный прил (стиль) condensed; **протоко́льная за́пись** record of proceedings; **~ журна́л** minutes book.

протолкн|у́ть (-у́, -ёшь; impf **прота́лкивать**) сов перех (также перен) to push through

▶ **протолкну́ться** (impf **прота́лкиваться**) сов возв to push one's way through.

прот|опи́ть (-оплю́, -о́пишь; impf **прота́пливать**) сов перех (комнату, дом) to warm through; (печь) to stoke up.

прот|опта́ть (-опчу́, -о́пчешь; impf **прота́птывать**) сов перех (тропинку, дорожку) to beat.

проторг|ова́ть (-у́ю; impf **проторго́вывать**) сов перех (потерять) to make a loss of; (no impf; торговать: товары) to sell; (жизнь) to fritter away.

проторён|ный прил (дорога, путь) well-trodden.

проторӣть (-ю, -ӣшь; *impf* **проторя́ть**) *сов перех* to beat.

прототи́п (-а) *м person upon which a character of a novel, play etc is based.*

прото́чи́ть (-очу́, -о́чишь; *impf* **прота́чивать**) *сов перех* (*прогры́зть отве́рстие*) to nibble through; (*тех*) to bore.

прото́чн|ый *прил* (*вода*) running; ~ое о́зеро lake with rivers flowing out of it; ~ая труба́ pipe.

протра́л|ить (-ю, -ишь) *сов от* **тра́лить**.

протрезве́|ть (-ю) *сов непepex* = **протрезви́ться**.

протрезви́|ть (-лю, -ӣшь; *impf* **протрезвля́ть**) *сов перех*: ~ кого́-н to sober sb up

▸ **протрезви́ться** (*impf* **протрезвля́ться**) *сов возв* to sober up.

протру́(сь) *итп сов см* **протере́ть(ся)**.

протру́б|ить (-лю, -ӣшь) *сов от* **труби́ть**.

проту́хн|уть (*3sg* -ет, *3pl* -ут, *impf* **протуха́ть** *или* **ту́хнуть**) *сов непepex* to go bad *или* off.

протыка́|ть (-ю) *несов см* **проткну́ть**.

протя́гива|ть(ся) (-ю(сь)) *несов от* **протяну́ть(ся)**.

протя́жен *прил см* **протя́жный**.

протяже́ни|е (-я) *ср*: на ~и двух неде́ль/ ме́сяцев over a period of two weeks/months; на всём ~и пути́ the whole way; на ~и всего́ на́шего визи́та for the whole duration of our visit.

протяжённость (-и) *ж* length.

протяжён|ный (-, -на, -но) *прил* prolonged.

протя́жн|ый (-ен, -на, -но) *прил* (*песня, крик итп*) long drawn-out.

протяну́ть (-яну́, -я́нешь; *impf* **протя́гивать**) *сов перех* (*верёвку*) to stretch; (*линию переда́чи*) to extend; (*руки, ноги*) to stretch (out); (*предмет*) to hold out; (*слово, ответ итп*) to say slowly; (*разг: критиковать*) to pan ◆ *непepex* (*разг: прожить*) to last; ~ (*perf*) но́ги (*разг*) to turn up one's toes; **протя́гивать** (~ *perf*) ру́ку по́мощи to lend a (helping) hand

▸ **протяну́ться** (*impf* **протя́гиваться**) *сов возв* (*дорога*) to stretch; (*линия переда́чи*) to extend; (*рука*) to stretch out.

проу́л|ок (-ка) *м* (*разг*) lane.

проучи́ть (-учу́, -у́чишь; *impf* **проу́чивать**) *сов перех* (*разг: наказать*) to teach a lesson; (*no impf*; *учить*) to study

▸ **проучи́ться** *сов возв* to study.

проф. *сокр* (= **профе́ссор**) Prof. (= *Professor*).

профа́н (-а) *м* ignoramus.

профана́ци|я (-и) *ж* (*непочтительное отношение*) profanity; (*обман*) sham.

профаши́ст (-а) *м* fascist sympathizer.

профаши́стск|ий (-ая, -ое, -ие) *прил* fascist опред.

профбюро́ *ср нескл сокр* (= **профсою́зное бюро́**) trade-union office.

профессиона́л (-а) *м* professional.

профессионали́зм (-а) *м* professionalism.

профессиона́льный *прил* professional опред; (*болезнь, привычка, обучение*) occupational; **профессиона́льный сою́з** trade (*BRIT*) *или* labor (*US*) union.

профе́сси|я (-и) *ж* profession; **по ~и он инжене́р** he is an engineer by profession; **получа́ть** (**получи́ть** *perf*) *или* **приобрета́ть** (**приобрести́** *perf*) ~**ю** to get professional qualifications.

профе́ссор (-а; *nom pl* -á) *м* professor.

профессу́р|а (-ы) *ж* professorship ◆ *собир* professors мн.

профила́кти|ка (-и) *ж* prevention.

профилакти́ческ|ий (-ая, -ое, -ие) *прил* (*меры*) prevent(at)ive; (*прививка*) prophylactic опред; ~ое сре́дство prophylactic.

про́фил|ь (-я) *м* profile; (*предмета, дороги*) cross section; (*учебного заведения*) type; (*работника*) field.

профильтр|ова́ть (-у́ю) *сов от* **фильтрова́ть**.

профко́м (-а) *м сокр* (= **профсою́зный комите́т**) trade-union committee.

профо́рг (-а) *м сокр* (= **профсою́зный организа́тор**) trade-union boss.

профо́рм|а (-ы) *ж* formality.

профсою́з (-а) *м сокр* (= **профессиона́льный сою́з**) trade (*BRIT*) *или* labor (*US*) union.

профсою́зный *прил* trade-union.

проха́жива|ться (-юсь) *несов от* **пройти́сь**.

прохва|ти́ть (*3sg* -а́тит, *3pl* -а́тят, *impf* **прохва́тывать**) *сов перех* (*подлеж: холод, мороз итп*) to chill to the bone.

прохво́ст (-а) *м* (*разг*) crook.

прохла́д|а (-ы) *ж* cool.

прохлади́тельный *прил*: ~ **напи́ток** cool soft drink.

прохла́дно *нареч* (*встретить*) coolly ◆ *как сказ* it's cool.

прохла́дный *прил* (*также перен*) cool.

прохла́дц|а (-ы) *ж*: **с ~ей** coolly.

прохлажда́|ться (-юсь) *несов возв* (*разг: бездельничать*) to doss about.

прохло́па|ть (-ю; *impf* **прохло́пывать**) *сов перех* (*разг*) to miss.

прохо́д (-а) *м* passage; **за́дний ~** (*АНАТ*) back passage, anus; ~**а нет от кого́-н/чего́-н** you can't get away from sb/sth; **не дава́ть** (*impf*) ~**а кому́-н** to pester sb.

проходи́м|ец (-ца) *м* swindler.

проходи́мость (-и) *ж* (*местности*) passability; (*АВТ*) off-road capability; (*МЕД*) permeability.

проходи́м|ый (-, -а, -о) *прил* passable.

прох|оди́ть (-ожу́, -о́дишь) *несов от* **пройти́** ◆ *сов возв перех* (*ходить*) to walk.

прохо́д|ка (-ки; *gen pl* -ок) *ж* sinking of shafts.

проходн|а́я (-о́й; *decl like adj*) *ж* checkpoint (*at entrance to factory etc*).

проходн|о́й *прил*: ~**ая ко́мната** hall;

проходно́й балл pass mark.
прохо́док *сущ см* **прохо́дка.**
прохо́дчик (-а) *м person who sinks shafts.*
прохо́ж|**ая** (-ей; *decl like adj*) *ж см* **прохо́жий.**
прохожде́ни|**е** (-я) *ср* (*по доро́ге*) passage; (*испыта́ний*) passing; (*слу́жбы*) term.
прохо́жий (-его; *decl like adj*) *м* passer-by.
прохожу́ (*не*)*сов см* **проходи́ть.**
прохуди́ться (*3sg* -**и́тся**, *3pl* -**я́тся**) *сов неперех* (*разг*) to wear thin.
процвета́ть (-ю) *несов неперех* (*фи́рма, бизнесме́н*) to prosper; (*теа́тр, нау́ка*) to flourish; (*ра́за: челове́к, семья́*) to thrive.
проце|**ди́ть** (-ежу́, -е́дишь; *impf* **проце́живать**) *сов перех* (*бульо́н, сок*) to strain; (*no impf: произнести́*): ~ (**сквозь зу́бы**) to say through one's teeth.
процеду́р|**а** (-ы) *ж* procedure; (*МЕД: обы́чно мн*) course of treatment.
процеду́рный *прил* procedural; (*МЕД*): ~**ая сестра́** nurse; ~ **кабине́т** treatment room.
проце́жива|**ть** (-ю) *несов от* **процеди́ть.**
процежу́ *сов см* **процеди́ть.**
проце́нт (-а) *м* percentage; **в разме́ре 5** ~**ов годовы́х** at a yearly rate of 5 percent; **на все сто** ~**ов** (*доверя́ть, подде́рживать*) one hundred percent; *см та́кже* **проце́нты.**
проце́нтный *прил* (*вы́раженный в проце́нтах*) percentage *опред;* **проце́нтная ста́вка** interest rate.
проце́нт|**ы** (-ов) *мн* (*КОММ*) interest *ед;* (: *вознагражде́ние*) commission; **просты́е/сло́жные/наро́сшие** ~ simple/compound/accrued interest.
проце́сс (-а) *м* process; (*ЮР: поря́док разбира́тельства*) proceedings *мн;* (: *та́кже:* **суде́бный** ~) trial; **воспали́тельный** ~ inflammation; **в** ~**е** +*gen* in the course of; **возбужда́ть** (**возбуди́ть** *perf*) ~ to institute proceedings.
проце́сси|**я** (-и) *ж* procession.
проце́ссор (-а) *м* word processor.
процессуа́льный *прил* (*ЮР*) procedural; **процессуа́льный ко́декс** procedural code.
процити́р|**овать** (-ую) *сов от* **цити́ровать.**
прочёл *сов см* **проче́сть.**
про́чен *прил см* **про́чный.**
про́черк (-а) *м* line.
проче|**рти́ть** (-рчу́, -ртишь; *impf* **проче́рчивать**) *сов перех:* ~ **ли́нию** to draw a line.
проче|**са́ть** (-шу́, -шешь; *impf* **прочёсывать**) *сов перех* (*та́кже перен*) to comb.
проче́сть (-ту́, -тёшь; *pt* -ёл, -ла́, -ло́) *сов от* **чита́ть.**
прочёсыва|**ть** (-ю) *несов от* **прочеса́ть.**
прочешу́ *итп сов см* **прочеса́ть.**
про́чий (-ая, -ее, -ие) *прил* other; **поми́мо**

всего́ ~**его** on top of everything else; **и про́чее** and so on.
прочи́|**стить** (-щу, -стишь; *impf* **прочища́ть**) *сов перех* to clean out; (*нос*) to clear.
прочита́ть (-ю) *сов от* **чита́ть.**
про́ч|**ить** (-у, -ишь) *несов перех:* ~ **что-н кому́-н** to predict sth for sb; **его́ роди́тели** ~**или его́ во врачи́** his parents intended him to be a doctor.
прочища́ть (-ю) *несов от* **прочи́стить.**
прочи́щу *сов см* **прочи́стить.**
прочла́ *итп сов см* **проче́сть.**
про́чно *нареч* (*закрепи́ть*) firmly; (*зау́чить*) well.
про́чность (-и) *ж* (*материа́ла итп*) durability; (*отноше́ний, семьи́*) stability; **запа́с** ~**и** reliability.
про́ч|**ный** (-ен, -на́, -но) *прил* (*материа́л итп*) durable; (*постро́йка*) solid, stable; (*зна́ния*) sound; (*отноше́ние, семья́*) stable; (*мир, сча́стье*) lasting.
прочте́ние (-я) *ср* reading.
прочту́ *итп сов см* **проче́сть.**
прочу́вствованный *прил* heartfelt.
прочу́вств|**овать** (-ую) *сов перех* to feel deeply; (*perf*) ~ **роль** to get inside a role.
прочь *нареч* (*в сто́рону*) away; **ру́ки** ~! hands off!; ~ **с доро́ги!** get out of the way!; **он не** ~ **вы́пить** he won't say no to a drink.
прошвыр|**ну́ться** (-у́сь, -ёшься) *сов возв* (*разг*) to stretch one's legs.
проше́дший (-ая, -ее, -ие) *прил* (*про́шлый*) past; **проше́дшее вре́мя** past tense.
проше́й(те) *сов см* **проши́ть.**
прошёл(ся) *сов см* **пройти́(сь).**
проше́ни|**е** (-я) *ср* plea; (*пи́сьменное хода́тайство*) petition; **подава́ть** (**пода́ть** *perf*) ~ **в** +*acc* to present a petition to.
прошепта́ть (-епчу́, -е́пчешь) *сов перех* to whisper.
проше́стви|**е** (-я) *ср:* **по** ~**и го́да/ме́сяца** after a year's/month's lapse.
прошиб|**и́ть** (-у́, -ёшь; *pt* -, -ла, -ло, *impf* **прошиба́ть**) *сов перех* (*разг: дверь, окно́ итп*) to smash through; **пот проши́б его́** he broke out in a sweat; **дрожь** ~**ла её** a shiver went down her spine.
прош|**и́ть** (-ью, -ьёшь; *imper* -е́й(те), *impf* **прошива́ть**) *сов перех* (*приши́ть*) to sew a seam on; (*перен: пу́лями стены́*) to pepper.
прошла́ *итп сов см* **пройти́.**
прошлого́дн|**ий** (-яя, -ее, -ие) *прил* last year's; ~**ие собы́тия** the events of last year.
про́шло|**е** (-го; *decl like adj*) *ср* the past; **отходи́ть** (**отойти́** *perf*) **в** ~ to become a thing of the past.
про́шл|**ый** *прил* last; (*пре́жний*) past; **в** ~ **раз** last time; **на** ~**ой неде́ле** last week; **в** ~**ом году́/ме́сяце** last year/month; **де́ло** ~**ое** it's in

the past.

прошмыгну́ть (-у́, -ёшь; *impf* **прошмы́гивать**) *сов неперех*: ~ ми́мо +*gen*/сквозь +*acc* *итп* (*разг*) to dart past/through *итп*.

проштампова́ть (-у́ю) *сов от* **штампова́ть**.

проштра́фиться (-люсь, -ишься) *сов возв* (*разг*) to lapse.

проштуди́ровать (-ую) *сов от* **штуди́ровать**.

прошу́(сь) *несов см* **проси́ть(ся)**.

прошью́ *итп сов см* **проши́ть**.

проща́йте *част* goodbye, farewell.

проща́льный *прил* parting *опред*; (*вечер, визит*) farewell *опред*.

проща́ние (-я) *ср* (*действие*) parting; **на ~** on parting.

проща́ть(ся) (-ю(сь)) *несов от* **прости́ть(ся)**.

про́ще *сравн нареч от* **про́сто** ♦ *сравн прил от* **просто́й**.

проще́ние (-я) *ср* (*ребёнка, друга итп*) forgiveness; (*преступника*) pardon; **проси́ть** (**попроси́ть** *perf*) **~я** to say sorry; **прошу́ ~я!** (I'm) sorry!

прощу́(сь) *сов см* **прости́ть(ся)**.

прощу́пать (-ю; *impf* **прощу́пывать**) *сов перех* to feel for; (*перен*) to check out; **прощу́пывать** (**~** *perf*) **по́чву** to see how the land lies.

проэкзамен|ова́ть (-у́ю) *сов от* **экзаменова́ть**.

проявй́тел|ь (-я) *м* (*ФОТО*) developer.

про|яви́ть (-явлю́, -я́вишь; *impf* **проявля́ть**) *сов перех* to display; (*ФОТО*) to develop; **проявля́ть** (**~** *perf*) **себя́ пло́хо/хорошо́** to show o.s. in a bad/good light

▸ **прояви́ться** (*impf* **проявля́ться**) *сов возв* (*талант, потенциал итп*) to reveal itself; (*решительность, сме́лость итп*) to show itself; (*ФОТО*) to be developed.

проявле́ние (-я) *ср* display; (*обычно мн: жизни*) manifestation.

проявлю́(сь) *сов см* **прояви́ть(ся)**.

проявля́ть(ся) (-ю(сь)) *несов от* **прояви́ть(ся)**.

проясне́ние (-я) *ср* (*погоды*) brightening *или* clearing up; (*ситуации*) clarification; **у меня́ наступи́ло ~ созна́ния** *или* **ума́** my mind cleared.

проясн|и́ть (-ю́, -и́шь; *impf* **проясня́ть**) *сов перех* (*обстано́вку*) to clarify; (*мысли*) to sort out; **проясня́ть** (**~** *perf*) **чьё-н созна́ние** to bring sb round

▸ **проясни́ться** (*impf* **проясня́ться**) *сов возв* (*погода, небо*) to brighten *или* clear up; (*обстано́вка*) to be clarified; (*мысли*) to be sorted out; **у него́ ~и́лось созна́ние** his mind cleared.

пру(сь) *итп несов см* **пере́ть(ся)**.

пруд (-а́; *loc sg* **-у́**) *м* (*есте́ственный*) pool, pond; (*иску́сственный*) pond.

пр|уди́ть (-ужу́, -у́дишь; *perf* **запруди́ть**) *несов перех* to dam; **де́нег у него́ хоть ~уд пруди́** (*разг*) he is rolling in cash.

пружи́н|а (-ы) *ж* (*ТЕХ*) spring; (*перен: движущая сила*) mainspring.

пружи́нист|ый (-, -а, -о) *прил* springy; **у него́ ~ шаг** he has a spring in his step.

пружу́ *сов см* **пруди́ть**.

прут (-а́; *nom pl* **-ья**) *м* (*БОТ*) twig; (*ТЕХ*) rod.

пры́гал|ка (-ки; *gen pl* **-ок**) *ж* skipping-rope (*BRIT*), skip rope (*US*).

пры́га|ть (-ю) *несов неперех* to jump; (*мяч*) to bounce.

пры́гн|уть (-у, -ешь) *сов неперех* to jump; (*мяч*) to bounce.

прыгу́н (-а́) *м* (*СПОРТ*) jumper; **~ в длину́** long jumper; **~ в высоту́** high jumper.

прыгу́нья (-ьи; *gen pl* **-ий**) *ж см* **прыгу́н**.

прыж|о́к (-ка́) *м* (*через лужу, с парашю́том*) jump; (*в воду*) dive; **~ки́ в высоту́/длину́** high/long jump; **~ки́ с шесто́м** pole vault; **опо́рный ~** (*СПОРТ*) vault.

прысн|уть (-у, -ешь; *impf* **пры́скать**) *сов неперех* (*кровь*) to spurt; (+*instr*; *водо́й*) to sprinkle with; (*духа́ми*) to spray with; **пры́скать** (**~** *perf*) **со́ сме́ху** (*разг*) to go into a fit of giggles.

пры́т|кий (-кая, -кое, -кие; -ок, -ка́, -ко) *прил* (*разг: подвижный*) bouncy.

прыт|ь (-и) *ж* (*разг: быстрота́*) bounce; **во всю ~** (*разг*) at full tilt.

прыщ (-а́) *м* spot.

прыща́в|ый (-, -а, -о) *прил* spotty.

пряди́льный *прил* spinning *опред*.

пряди́льщик (-а) *м* spinner.

пряди́льщиц|а (-ы) *ж см* **пряди́льщик**.

пряду́ *итп несов см* **прясть**.

прядь (-и) *ж* lock (*of hair*).

пря́ж|а (-и) *ж* yarn.

пря́ж|ка (-ки; *gen pl* **-ек**) *ж* (*на ремне́*) buckle; (*на ю́бке*) clasp.

пря́л|ка (-ки; *gen pl* **-ок**) *ж* spinning wheel.

пряма́|я (-о́й; *decl like adj*) *ж* straight line; **по ~о́й** in a straight line.

прямико́м *нареч*: **он прошёл ~ че́рез сад** (*разг*) he went straight across the garden.

пря́мо *нареч* (*в прямо́м направле́нии*) straight ahead; (*ро́вно*) upright; (*непосре́дственно*) straight; (*открове́нно*) directly ♦ *част* (*действи́тельно*) really; **приступа́ть** (**приступи́ть** *perf*) **~ к де́лу** to get straight down to business; **у меня́ ~ сил нет!** I really haven't (got) the strength!; **помоги́те ему́ – (ну) ~!** (*разг*) help him? no way!

прямоду́ш|ный (-ен, -на, -но) *прил* (*челове́к*) forthright; (*отве́т*) candid.

прям|о́й (-, -а́, -о) *прил* straight; (*путь, слова́, челове́к*) direct; (*отве́т, поли́тика*) open; (*вы́зов, обма́н*) obvious; (*улики*) solid; (*no short form*; *сообще́ние, рейс, обя́занность итп*) direct; (*вы́года, смысл, по́льза итп*) real; (*значе́ние сло́ва*) literal; **~ые изде́ржки** direct cost; **пряма́я кишка́** rectum; **пряма́я**

трансля́ци|я live broadcast; **прямо́е
дополне́ние** direct object; **прямо́е попада́ние**
direct hit; **прямо́й до́ступ** (*КОМП*) direct access;
прямо́й репорта́ж live coverage; **прямо́й у́гол**
right angle; **прямы́е вы́боры/нало́ги** direct
elections/taxes.

прямолине́|йный (-ен, -йна, -йно) *прил*
(*движение*) along a straight line; (*перен*) blunt.

пря́мо-таки *нареч* (*разг*) really.

прямоуго́льник (-а) *м* rectangle.

прямоуго́льный *прил* rectangular.

пря́ник (-а) *м* ≈ gingerbread.

пря́ность (-и) *ж* spice.

пря́н|ый (-, -а, -о) *прил* spicy.

пря|сть (-ду́, -дёшь; *perf* спрясть) *несов перех*
to spin.

пря́|тать (-чу, -чешь; *perf* спря́тать) *несов
перех* to hide; **он ~тал глаза́ от меня́** he didn't
look me straight in the eye

▶ пря́таться (*perf* спря́таться) *несов возв* to
hide; (*человек: от холода, ветра*) to shelter;
(*солнце*) to hide; **~ся (спря́таться** *perf*) **за
чужу́ю спи́ну** to redirect responsibility.

пря́т|ки (-ок; *dat pl* -кам) *мн* hide-and-seek *ед*;
игра́ть (*impf*) **в ~ с кем-н** to play hide-and-seek
with sb; (*перен*) to avoid sb.

пря́чу(сь) *итп несов см* **пря́тать(ся)**.

пса *итп сущ см* **пёс**.

псал|о́м (-ма́) *м* psalm.

псало́мщик (-а) *м* sexton.

псалты́р|ь (-и) *ж* Psalter.

пса́рн|я (-и) *ж* kennels *мн* (*for hunting dogs*).

псевдони́м (-а) *м* pseudonym.

псих (-а) *м* (*разг*) psycho.

психиа́тр (-а) *м* psychiatrist.

психиатри́ческ|ий (-ая, -ое, -ие) *прил*
psychiatric.

психиатри́|я (-и) *ж* psychiatry.

пси́хик|а (-и) *ж* psyche.

психи́ческ|ий (-ая, -ое, -ие) *прил* (*заболевание,
отклонение итп*) mental.

психоана́лиз (-а) *м* psychoanalysis.

псих|ова́ть (-у́ю) *несов неперех* (*разг*) to freak
out.

психо́з (-а) *м* (*МЕД*) psychosis; (*странность в
психике*) neurosis.

психо́лог (-а) *м* psychologist.

психологи́ческ|ий (-ая, -ое, -ие) *прил*
psychological.

психоло́ги|я (-и) *ж* psychology.

психопа́т (-а) *м* psychopath.

психопа́ти|я (-и) *ж* psychopathy.

психотерапе́вт (-а) *м* psychotherapist.

психотерапи́|я (-и) *ж* psychotherapy.

ПСС *м сокр* = по́лное собра́ние сочине́ний.

пта́х|а (-и) *ж* (*разг*) bird.

пта́ш|ка (-ки; *gen pl* -ек) *ж* bird.

птен|е́ц (-ца́) *м* chick.

пти́ц|а (-ы) *ж* bird ◆ *собир*: (**дома́шняя**) ~
poultry; **ва́жная** ~ (*разг*) big shot.

птицево́д (-а) *м* poulterer, poultry farmer.

птицево́дств|о (-а) *ср* poultry farming.

птицево́дческ|ий (-ая, -ое, -ие) *прил*: ~**ая
фе́рма** poultry farm.

птицефа́брик|а (-и) *ж* poultry farm.

пти́чек *сущ см* **пти́чка**.

пти́ч|ий (-ья, -ье, -ьи) *прил* (*корм, клетка*) bird
опред; **вид с высоты́ ~ьего полёта** bird's eye
view; **я сам здесь на ~ьих права́х** I don't have
any rights here myself; **пти́чий база́р** bird
colony.

пти́ч|ка (-ки; *gen pl* -ек) *ж уменьш от* **пти́ца**;
(*разг: в тексте*) tick (*BRIT*), check (*US*).

пти́чник (-а) *м* ≈ hen house.

ПТУ *ср сокр* (= профессиона́льно-техни́ческое
учи́лище) ≈ tech (= technical college).

пуа́нт (-а) *м* (*БАЛЕТ*) ballet shoe.

пу́блик|а (-и) *ж собир* audience; **широ́кая** ~ the
public; **игра́ть** (*impf*) **на ~у** to show off; **на ~у** in
company.

публика́ци|я (-и) *ж* publication.

публик|ова́ть (-у́ю; *perf* опубликова́ть) *несов
перех* to publish.

публици́ст (-а) *м* writer of sociopolitical
literature.

публици́стик|а (-и) *ж собир* sociopolitical
journalism.

публицисти́ческ|ий (-ая, -ое, -ие) *прил*
sociopolitical.

публи́ч|ный (-ен, -на, -но) *прил* public;
публи́чный дом brothel; **публи́чные торги́**,
публи́чная прода́жа (public) auction, public
sale.

пу́гал|о (-а) *ср* scarecrow; (*перен: некраси́вый
челове́к*) fright.

пуга́|ть (-ю; *perf* испуга́ть *или* напуга́ть) *несов
перех* to frighten, scare

▶ пуга́ться (*perf* испуга́ться *или* напуга́ться)
несов возв to be frightened *или* scared.

пугли́в|ый (-, -а, -о) *прил* timid.

пу́говиц|а (-ы) *ж* button; **застёгивать
(застегну́ть** *perf*) ~**у** to fasten a button.

пуд (-а; *nom pl* -ы́) *м* pood (*Russian measure of
weight equivalent to 16 kilogrammes*).

пу́дел|ь (-я) *м* poodle.

пу́динг (-а) *м* ≈ pudding.

пудо́в|ый *прил*: ~**ая ги́ря** a pood weight.

пу́др|а (-ы) *ж* powder; **са́харная** ~ icing sugar.

пу́дрениц|а (-ы) *ж* powder compact.

пу́др|ить (-ю, -ишь; *perf* напу́дрить) *несов
перех* to powder; ~ (*impf*) **мозги́ кому́-н** (*разг*)
to pull the wool over sb's eyes

▶ пу́дриться (*perf* напу́дриться) *несов возв* to
powder one's face.

пуза́т|ый (-, -а, -о) *прил* (*разг: человек*) tubby;
(*перен: чайник, комод*) rounded.

пýз|о (-а) *ср* (*разг: живот*) belly; (*брюхо*) paunch.

пузыр|ёк (-ька́) *м* (*уменьш*) *от* **пузы́рь**; (*для лекарства, черни́л*) vial.

пузыри́ться (*3sg* -и́тся, *3pl* -я́тся) *несов возв* (*жидкость*) to bubble; (*краска*) to blister; (*разг: одежда*) to blow up.

пузы́р|ь (-я́) *м* (*мыльный*) bubble; (*на коже*) blister; (*с водой*) water bottle; **жёлчный ~** gall bladder; **мочево́й ~** (urinary) bladder.

пузырька́ *итп сущ см* **пузырёк**.

пук (-а; *nom pl* -**и́**) *м* bundle.

пýка|ть (-ю; *perf* **пýкнуть**) *несов неперех* to fart.

пулево́й *прил* bullet *опред*.

пулемёт (-а) *м* machine gun.

пулемётчик (-а) *м* machine gunner.

пуленепробива́емый *прил* bullet-proof.

пуло́вер (-а) *м* pullover.

пульвериза́тор (-а) *м* atomizer.

пульс (-а) *м* (*МЕД, перен*) pulse.

пульси́р|овать (*3sg* -ует, *3pl* -уют) *несов неперех* (*артерии*) to pulsate; (*кровь*) to pulse; (*нарыв*) to throb.

пульт (-а) *м* panel; (*музыканта*) stand; **пульт управле́ния** control panel.

пýл|я (-и) *ж* bullet; **~ей вы́лететь** (*perf*) (*из* +*gen*) (*перен: разг*) to shoot out (from).

пýм|а (-ы) *ж* puma.

пункт (-а) *м* point; (*документа*) clause; (*медицинский*) centre (*BRIT*), center (*US*); (*наблюдательный, командный*) post; **населённый ~** inhabited area.

пункти́р (-а) *м* dotted line.

пунктуа́л|ьный (-ен, -ьна, -ьно) *прил* (*человек*) punctual.

пунктуа́ци|я (-и) *ж* punctuation.

пýнкци|я (-и) *ж* (*МЕД*) lumber puncture.

пунцо́вый *прил* scarlet *опред*.

пунш (-а) *м* (*КУЛИН*) punch.

пуп (-а́) *м* (*разг*) belly button; **~ земли́** (*разг*) the bee's knees.

пупка́ *сущ см* **пупо́к**.

пупови́н|а (-ы) *ж* umbilical cord.

пуп|о́к (-ка́) *м* (*АНАТ*) navel.

пупы́рыш|ек (-ка) *м* (*разг: на коже*) pimple.

пýрг|а (-и́) *ж* snowstorm.

пурге́н (-а) *м* phenol phthalene (*used as laxative*).

пурита́н|ин (-ина; *nom pl* -е, *gen pl* -) *м* puritan.

пурита́н|ка (-ки; *gen pl* -ок) *ж см* **пурита́нин**.

пурита́нск|ий (-ая, -ое, -ие) *прил* puritanical.

пýрпур (-а) *м* wine, Burgundy.

пурпýрный *прил* wine *опред*, Burgundy *опред*.

пуск (-а) *м* (*завода итп*) starting up; **~ в эксплуата́цию** commission.

пуска́й *част, союз* (*разг*) = **пусть**.

пуска́|ть(ся) (-ю(сь)) *несов от* **пусти́ть(ся)**.

пусково́й *прил* (*период*) initial *опред*; (*механизм, установка*) starting *опред*; (*платформа*) launching *опред*.

пусте́|ть (*3sg* -ет, *3pl* -ют, *perf* **опусте́ть**) *несов*

неперех to become empty.

пу|сти́ть (-щý, -стишь; *impf* **пуска́ть**) *сов перех* (*руку, человека*) to let go of; (*лошадь, санки итп*) to send off; (*завод, станок, электростанцию*) to start; (*в вагон, в зал*) to let in; (*пар, дым*) to give off; (*камень, снаряд*) to throw; (*сплетни*) to spread; (*корни*) to put out; **пуска́ть** (**~** *perf*) **что-н на** +*acc*/**под** +*acc* (*использовать*) to use sth as/for; **пуска́ть** (**~** *perf*) **кого́-н куда́-нибудь** to let sb go somewhere; **пуска́ть** (**~** *perf*) **това́р в прода́жу** to put goods onto the market; **пуска́ть** (**~** *perf*) **пузыри́** to blow bubbles; **пуска́ть** (**~** *perf*) **слю́ни** to dribble; **пуска́ть** (**~** *perf*) **во́ду/газ** to turn on the water/gas

► **пусти́ться** (*impf* **пуска́ться**) *сов возв*: **~ся в** +*acc* (*в объяснения*) to go into; **пуска́ться** (**~ся** *perf*) **в подро́бности** to go into detail; **пуска́ться** (**~ся** *perf*) **в пляс** *или* **пляса́ть** to start dancing; **пуска́ться** (**~ся** *perf*) **в путь** to set off.

пýсто *нареч* empty ♦ *как сказ* (*ничего нет*) there's nothing there; (*никого нет*) there's no-one there; **в го́роде/холоди́льнике ~** the town/fridge is empty.

пуст|ова́ть (*3sg* -у́ет, *3pl* -у́ют) *несов неперех* to be empty.

пуст|о́й (-, -а́, -о, -ы́) *прил* empty; (*взгляд*) vacant; (*предлог, причина, затея*) trifling; **он – ~о́е ме́сто** he's a real nobody; **с ~ы́ми рука́ми** empty-handed.

пустосло́ви|е (-я) *ср* idle talk.

пуст|ота́ (-оты́; *nom pl* -о́ты) *ж* emptiness; (*полое место*) cavity.

пýстошь (-и) *ж* wasteland.

пусты́н|ный *прил* desert *опред*; (-ен, -на, -но; *безлюдный*) deserted.

пусты́н|я (-и; *gen pl* -ь) *ж* desert; (*безлюдное место*) wilderness.

пусты́рник (-а) *м* motherwort.

пусты́р|ь (-я́) *м* wasteland.

пусты́ш|ка (-ки; *gen pl* -ек) *ж* (*разг: соска*) dummy (*BRIT*), pacifier (*US*); (*перен: о человеке*) airhead.

KEYWORD

пусть *част* (+*3sg/pl*) **1** (*выражает приказ, угрозу*): **пусть он придёт у́тром** let him come in the morning; **пусть она́ то́лько попро́бует отказа́ться** let her just try to refuse
2 (*выражает согласие*): **пусть бу́дет так** so be it; **пусть бу́дет по-тво́ему** have it your way
3 (*всё равно*) OK, all right; **она́ вини́т меня́, пусть!** OK *или* all right, so she blames me!
♦ *союз* (*допустим*) even if; **пусть он плохо́й дире́ктор, зато́ хоро́ший челове́к** even if he is a bad director, he is a good person; **на́до оправда́ть все, пусть да́же небольши́е, затра́ты** all expenses, even small ones, must be justified.

пустя́к (-а́) *м* trifle; (*неценный предмет*) trinket

♦ *как сказ*: э́то ~ it's nothing; **говори́ть** (*impf*) **пустяки́** to talk nonsense; **Вы огорчены́?** – **пустяки́!** are you upset? – it's nothing!

пустяко́вый *прил* (*разг: повод, жалоба*) trivial; **э́то пустяко́вая рабо́та** it's a piece of cake.

пустя́чный *прил* = **пустяко́вый**.

пута́н|а (**-ы**) *ж* *prostitute working for hard currency*.

пу́таница (**-ы**) *ж* (*в мыслях, в делах*) muddle; (*дорог, дверей*) maze.

пу́таный (**-, -а, -о**) *прил* (*объяснение, рассказ*) muddled.

пу́та|ть (**-ю**; *perf* **запу́тать** *или* **спу́тать**) *несов перех* (*нитки, волосы*) to tangle (up); (*разг: сбить с толку*) to bamboozle; (*perf* **спу́тать** *или* **перепу́тать**) *бумаги, факты итп*) to mix up; (*perf* **впу́тать**; *разг*): ~ **кого́-н в** +*acc* to get sb mixed up in; **я его́ с кем-то** ~**ю** I'm confusing him with somebody else; **он всегда́** ~**л на́ши имена́** he always got our names mixed up

► **пу́таться** (*perf* **запу́таться** *или* **спу́таться**) *несов возв* to get tangled (up); (*в рассказе, в объяснении*) to get mixed up; (*perf* **спу́таться**; *разг*): ~**ся с** +*instr* (*с мошенниками, с хулиганами итп*) to get mixed up with.

путёв|ка (**-ки**; *gen pl* **-ок**) *ж* holiday voucher (*given by employer*); (*водителя*) manifest (*of cargo drivers*).

путеводи́тель (**-я**) *м* guidebook.

путево́дный *прил* (*перен: идея, теория*) guiding; ~**ая нить** guiding light.

путево́й *прил* (*пост, сигнал*) railway *опред*; (*записки, дневник*) travel *опред*; **путево́й лист** (*водителя*) = **путёвка**.

путёвок *сущ см* **путёвка**.

путёвый *прил* (*разг*) = **пу́тный**.

путе́й *сущ см* **пути́**.

путём *сущ см* **путь** ♦ *предл* (+*gen*) by means of.

путеше́ственник (**-а**) *м* traveller (*BRIT*), traveler (*US*).

путеше́стви|е (**-я**) *ср* journey, trip; (*морской*) voyage.

путеше́ств|овать (**-ую**) *несов неперех* to travel.

пут|и́ *сущ см* **путь** ♦ (**-е́й**) *мн*: **дыха́тельные** ~ respiratory tract.

пу́тник (**-а**) *м* traveller (*BRIT*), traveler (*US*).

пу́тный *прил* (*человек*) decent; (*план, предложение*) practical.

путч (**-а**) *м* (*полит*) putsch.

пу́ты (**-**) *мн* (*также перен*) fetters *мн*.

пут|ь (**-и́**; *см* **Table 3**) *м* (*также перен*) way; (*платформа*) platform; (*рельсы*) track; (*путешествие*) journey; **запасно́й** ~ siding; **во́дные** ~**и** waterways; **возду́шные** ~**и** air lanes; **нам с Ва́ми не по** ~**и** we're not going the same way; (*перен*) we don't see eye to eye; **счастли́вого** ~**и́!** have a good trip!; **быть** (*impf*)

на ~**и́ к** +*dat* to be on the road *или* way to; **провожа́ть** (**проводи́ть** *perf*) **кого́-н в после́дний** ~ to lay sb to rest; **пути́ сообще́ния** transport network *ед*; *см также* **пути́**.

пуф (**-а**) *м* pouffe.

пух (**-а**; *loc sg* **-у́**) *м* (*у животных*) fluff; (*у птиц, у человека*) down; **в** ~ **и прах** (*разг*) totally and utterly; **ни пу́ха ни пера́!** good luck!

пух *итп несов см* **пу́хнуть**.

пу́хлый (**-, -а́, -о**) *прил* (*щёки, человек*) chubby; (*губы*) full; (*портфель, папка*) bulging.

пу́х|нуть (**-ну, -нешь**; *pt* ~, **-ла, -ло**, *perf* **вспу́хнуть** *или* **опу́хнуть**) *несов неперех* to swell (up); **у меня́ голова́** ~**нет** (*разг*) my head's buzzing.

пухо́вый *прил* (*подушка*) feather *опред*; (*платок*) angora *опред*; ~**ая ку́ртка** padded jacket.

пучегла́зый *прил* (*разг*) goggle-eyed, pop-eyed.

пучи́н|а (**-ы**) *ж* the deep.

пу́ч|ить (**-у, -ишь**; *perf* **вы́пучить**) *несов перех*: ~ **глаза́** to goggle; **он вы́пучил глаза́** his eyes popped out of his head; **меня́** ~**ит** I have flatulence

► **пу́читься** (*perf* **вспу́читься**) *несов возв* to swell (up).

пуч|о́к (**-ка́**) *м* bunch; (*света*) beam.

пу́шек *сущ см* **пу́шка**.

пуши́н|ка (**-ки**; *gen pl* **-ок**) *ж* piece of fluff; (*снега*) flake.

пуши́стый (**-, -а, -о**) *прил* (*мех, ковёр итп*) fluffy; (*волосы*) fuzzy; (*ткань*) fleecy; (*кот*) furry; (*цыплёнок*) downy.

пу́ш|ка (**-ки**; *gen pl* **-ек**) *ж* (*на танке*) artillery gun; (*ист*) cannon.

пушни́н|а (**-ы**) *ж собир* furs *мн*.

пушно́й *прил* furry; ~ **това́р** furs *мн*.

пуш|о́к (**-ка́**) *м уменьш от* **пух**; (*над губой*) fluff.

пу́щ|а (**-и**) *ж* dense forest.

пу́щий (**-ая, -ее, -ие**) *прил*: **для** ~**ей ва́жности** (*разг*) for more impact.

пущу́(сь) *сов см* **пусти́ть(ся)**.

пфе́нинг (**-а**) *м* pfennig.

Пхенья́н (**-а**) *м* Pyongyang.

пчел|а́ (**-ы́**; *nom pl* **пчёлы**) *ж* bee.

пчели́ный *прил* (*мёд*) bee's; ~ **воск** beeswax; ~ **рой** swarm of bees.

пчелово́д (**-а**) *м* bee-keeper.

пчелово́дств|о (**-а**) *ср* bee-keeping.

пшени́ц|а (**-ы**) *ж* wheat.

пшени́чный *прил* wheat *опред*.

пшён|ка (**-ки**) *ж* (*разг*) millet porridge.

пшённый *прил*: ~**ая ка́ша** millet porridge.

пшен|о́ (**-а́**) *ср* millet.

пы́ж|иться (**-усь, -ишься**; *perf* **напы́житься**) *несов возв* (*разг: напрягаться*) to puff and pant; (*держаться важно*) to puff up.

пыл (-а; *loc sg* -у́) м (*перен*) ardour (*BRIT*), ardor (*US*); в ~у́ спо́ра/сраже́ния in the heat of the argument/battle.

пыла́|ть (-ю) *несов неперех* (*костёр*) to blaze; (*перен: лицо*) to burn; (+*instr*; *перен: любовью, гневом итп*) to burn with.

пы́лен *прил см* **пы́льный**.

пылесо́с (-а) м vacuum cleaner, Hoover®.

пылесо́с|ить (-ишь; *perf* **пропылесо́сить**) *сов перех* to vacuum, hoover®.

пыли́н|ка (-ки; *gen pl* -ок) ж speck of dust.

пыл|и́ть (-ю́, -и́шь; *perf* **напыли́ть**) *несов неперех* to raise dust

▶ **пыли́ться** (*perf* **запыли́ться**) *несов возв* to get dusty.

пы́л|кий (-кая, -кое, -кие; -ок, -ка́, -ко) *прил* passionate.

пыл|ь (-и; *loc sg* -и́) ж dust; **вытира́ть (вы́тереть** *perf*) ~ to dust; **пуска́ть (пусти́ть** *perf*) ~ **в глаза́ кому́-н** to give sb the wrong idea.

пы́л|ьный (-ен, -ьна, -ьно) *прил* dusty.

пыльца́ (-ы́) ж pollen.

пырн|у́ть (-у́, -ёшь) *сов перех* (*разг*) to stab; ~ (*perf*) **ножо́м** to knife.

пыта́|ть (-ю) *несов перех* to torture; ~ (*impf*) **кого́-н о чём-н** to grill sb about sth

▶ **пыта́ться** (*perf* **попыта́ться**) *несов возв*: ~**ся** +*infin* to try to do.

пы́т|ка (-ки; *gen pl* -ок) ж torment.

пытли́в|ый (-, -а, -о) *прил* inquisitive.

пы́ток *сущ см* **пы́тка**.

пы|ха́ть (-шу, -шешь) *несов неперех*: ~ +*instr* to give off; ~ (*impf*) **зло́бой/за́вистью** to burn with anger/envy; **она́ ~шет здоро́вьем** she's bursting with health.

пых|те́ть (-чу́, -ти́шь) *несов неперех* (*тяжело дыша́ть*) to pant; (*самова́р*) to steam; (*парово́з*) to chug; ~ (*impf*) **над чем-н** (*разг*) to sweat over sth.

пы́шек *сущ см* **пы́шка**.

пы́шен *прил см* **пы́шный**.

пы́ш|ка (-ки; *gen pl* -ек) ж doughnut (*BRIT*), donut (*US*).

пышноволо́с|ый (-, -а, -о) *прил* fuzzy-haired.

пышногру́д|ый (-, -а, -о) *прил* busty.

пы́шност|ь (-и) ж (*волос*) luxuriance; (*хвоста итп*) bushiness; (*обстановки, приёма итп*) splendour (*BRIT*), splendor (*US*); **придава́ть (прида́ть** *perf*) ~ **волоса́м** to give body to one's hair.

пы́ш|ный (-ен, -на́, -но) *прил* (*волосы, хвост, усы итп*) bushy; (*полный*) voluptuous; (*роско́шный*) splendid.

пышу́ *итп несов см* **пыха́ть**.

пьедеста́л (-а) м (*основание*) pedestal; (*для победителей*) winners' rostrum.

пье́с|а (-ы) ж (*ЛИТЕРАТУРА*) play; (*МУЗ*) piece.

пью *итп несов см* **пить**.

пью́щий (-его; *decl like adj*) м heavy drinker.

пьяне́|ть (-ю; *perf* **опьяне́ть**) *несов неперех* to get drunk; (*перен*) to become intoxicated.

пьян|и́ть (-ю́, -и́шь; *perf* **опьяни́ть**) *несов перех* to get drunk; (*перен: подлеж: воздух, счастье итп*) to intoxicate.

пья́ниц|а (-ы) м/ж drunkard.

пья́н|ка (-ки; *gen pl* -ок) ж (*разг*) booze-up.

пья́нств|о (-а) ср heavy drinking; **борьба́ с ~м** anti-drinking campaign.

пья́нствова|ть (-ю) *несов неперех* to drink heavily.

пьянчу́г|а (-и) м/ж (*разг*) (old) soak.

пья́н|ый (-, -а́, -о) *прил* (*человек*) drunk; (*крики, песни итп*) drunken ♦ (-ого; *decl like adj*) м drunk; **под ~ую ру́ку** (*разг*) in a drunken rage.

пэр (-а) м peer.

пюпи́тр (-а) м lectern.

пюре́ ср нескл (*фрукто́вое*) purée; **карто́фельное** ~ mashed potato.

п/я *сокр* (= **почто́вый я́щик**) POB (= *Post Office Box*).

пяд|ь (-и) ж (*мера*) span; (*небольшо́е простра́нство*) stretch; **семи́ пя́дей во́ лбу** extraordinarily intelligent.

пя́лец *сущ см* **пя́льцы**.

пя́л|иться (-юсь, -ишься) *несов возв* (*разг*) to gawk.

пя́льц|ы (-ец; *dat pl* -ьцам) мн tambour *ед*.

пят|а́ (-ы́) ж: **до пят** (*очень дли́нный*) to the ground; **с головы́ до пят** from head to toe; **ходи́ть** (*impf*) или **гна́ться** (*impf*) **за кем-н по ~м** to follow hot on sb's heels.

пята́к (-а́) м (*разг*) five-kopeck piece.

пятачо́к (-ка́) м five-kopeck piece; (*небольша́я площа́дка*) spot; (*небольшо́е простра́нство*) stretch; (*свиньи*) snout.

пя́т|ая (-ой; *decl like adj*) ж: **одна́** ~ one fifth.

пя́тен *сущ см* **пятно́**.

пятёр|ка (-ки; *gen pl* -ок) ж (*цифра, карта*) five; (*разг: денежный знак*) fiver; (*ПРОСВЕЩ*) ≈ A (*school mark*); (*группа из пяти*) group of five; (*разг: автобус, трамвай итп*) (number) five (*bus, tram etc*).

пятерн|я́ (-и́) ж (*разг*) paw.

пя́тер|о (-ы́х; **как че́тверо**; *см* Table 36b) *чис* five; *см также* **дво́е**.

пятёрок *сущ см* **пятёрка**.

пяти́ *чис см* **пять**.

пятибо́рь|е (-я) ср pentathlon.

пятидеся́ти *чис см* **пятьдеся́т**.

пятидесятиле́ти|е (-я) ср fifty years *мн*; (*годовщина*) fiftieth anniversary.

пятидесятиле́тн|ий (-яя, -ее, -ие) *прил* (*период*) fifty-year; (*человек*) fifty-year-old.

пятидеся́т|ый (-ая, -ое, -ые) *чис* fiftieth; **я чита́ю ~ую страни́цу** I am on page fifty; **я живу́ в ~ой кварти́ре** I live in flat fifty; **я прие́хал в Петербу́рг в ~ом году́** I came to Petersburg in nineteen fifty; **~ые го́ды** the Fifties; **в ~ых года́х** in the Fifties.

пятидне́в|ка (-ки; *gen pl* -ок) ж (*разг*) five-day week.

пятидне́вный *прил* five-day.

пятикла́ссник (-а) *м pupil in fifth year at school (usually eleven years old).*

пятикла́ссниц|а (-ы) *ж см* **пятикла́ссник.**

пятикопе́ечный *прил* five-kopeck.

пятикра́тн|ый *прил*: ~ **чемпио́н** five-times champion; **в** ~**ом разме́ре** fivefold.

пятиле́ти|е (-я) *ср (срок)* five years; *(юбилей)* fifth anniversary.

пятиле́т|ка (-ки; *gen pl* -ок) *ж (ист, экон)* five-year plan.

пятиле́тн|ий (-яя, -ее, -ие) *прил (промежуток)* five-year; *(ребёнок)* five-year-old.

пятиле́ток *сущ см* **пятиле́тка.**

пятиме́сячный *прил* five-month; *(ребёнок)* five-month-old.

пятимину́т|ка (-ки; *gen pl* -ок) *ж (разг)* short meeting *(at work).*

пятинеде́льный *прил* five-week; *(ребёнок)* five-week-old.

пятисо́т *чис см* **пятьсо́т.**

пятисотле́ти|е (-я) *ср (срок)* five hundred years; *(годовщина)* quincentenary.

пятисотле́тн|ий (-яя, -ее, -ие) *прил (период)* five-hundred-year; *(дерево)* five hundred-year-old.

пятисо́т|ый (-ая, -ое, -ые) *чис* five-hundredth.

пя́|титься (-чусь, -тишься; *perf* **попя́титься**) *несов возв* to move backwards; **он попя́тился от меня́** he backed away from me.

пятиуго́льник (-а) *м* pentagon.

пятичасово́й *прил (рабочий день)* five-hour; *(поезд)* five-o'clock.

пятиэта́ж|ка (-ки; *gen pl* -ек) *ж (разг)* five-storey block of flats *(BRIT)*, five-story apartment block *(US).*

пятиэта́жный *прил* five-storey.

пя́т|ка (-ки; *gen pl* -ок) *ж* heel; **наступа́ть** *(impf)* **кому́-н на** ~**ки** *(перен)* to tread on sb's toes.

пятна́дцат|ый (-ая, -ое, -ые) *чис* fifteenth; *см также* **пя́тый.**

пятна́дцат|ь (-и; *как* пять; *см* **Table 27**) *чис* fifteen; *см также* **пять.**

пятна́|ть (-ю; *perf* **запятна́ть**) *несов перех* to tarnish.

пятни́ст|ый (-, -а, -о) *прил* spotted.

пя́тниц|а (-ы) *ж* Friday; **в** ~**у** on Friday; **по** ~**м** on Fridays; **в сле́дующую/про́шлую** ~**у** next/

last Friday; **сего́дняя** ~, **деся́тое ма́я** today is Friday (the) tenth (of) May.

пятно́ (-на́; *nom pl* **пя́тна**, *gen pl* -ен) *ср (также перен)* stain; *(выделяющееся по цвету)* spot.

пя́ток *сущ см* **пя́тка.**

пято́к (-ка́) *м (разг)* five *(when buying eggs etc).*

пя́т|ый (-ая, -ое, -ые) *чис* fifth; **сего́дня** ~**ое ию́ля** today is the fifth of July *или* July the fifth; **прие́ду** ~**ого ию́ля** I will arrive on the fifth of July; **встре́ча отло́жена до** ~**ого ию́ля** the meeting was postponed until the fifth of July; **сего́дня уже́** ~**ое (число́)** today is already the fifth; **сейча́с де́сять мину́т** ~**ого** it is ten minutes past four; **я прие́хал в Петербу́рг в ты́сяча девятьсо́т пятьдеся́ть** ~**ом году́** I came to Petersburg in nineteen fifty five; **ле́кция бу́дет в** ~**ой аудито́рии** the lecture will take place in room five; **я зако́нчил** ~**ым** I finished fifth; **я был** ~**ым ребёнком в семье́** I was child number five in the family; ~**ое – деся́тое** *(разг)* this and that; **переска́кивать** *(impf)* **с** ~**ого на деся́тое** *(разг)* to skip from one subject to another.

пят|ь (-и́; *см* **Table 27**) *чис* five; *(ПРОСВЕЩ)* ≈ A *(school mark)*; **ей** ~ **лет** she is five years old; **они́ живу́т в до́ме но́мер** ~ they live at number five; **о́коло** ~**и́** about five; **кни́га сто́ит** ~ **рубле́й** the book costs five roubles; ~ **с полови́ной часо́в** five and a half hours; **сейча́с** ~ **часо́в** it is five o'clock; **я́блоки продаю́тся по** ~ **штук** the apples are sold in fives; **дели́ть (раздели́ть** *perf***) что-н на** ~ to divide sth into five.

пят|ьдеся́т (-и́десяти; *см* **Table 29**) *чис* fifty; **здесь о́коло** ~**и́десяти челове́к** there are about fifty people here; **на сле́дующей неде́ле ему́ испо́лнится** ~ **(лет)** he will be fifty next week; **ему́ о́коло** ~**и́десят (лет)** he is about fifty (years old); **маши́на е́дет со ско́ростью** ~ **киломе́тров в час** the car is going at fifty kilometres *(BRIT) или* kilometers *(US)* per hour.

пят|ьсо́т (-исо́т; *см* **Table 34**) *чис* five hundred; *см также* **сто.**

пя́тью *нареч* five times; ~ **два – де́сять** five times two is ten.

пятью *чис см* **пять.**

пя́чусь *несов см* **пя́титься.**

~ P, p ~

P, p *сущ нескл* (*буква*) the 17th letter of the Russian alphabet.

p. *сокр* (= **река**) R., r. (= *river*); (= *родился*) b. (= *born*); (= **рубль**) R., r. (= *rouble*).

раб (**-а́**) *м* (*также перен*) slave; **~ любви́/мо́ды** *итп* a slave to love/fashion *итп*.

раба́ (**-ы́**; *no pl*) *ж см* **раб**.

рабовладе́л|ец (**-ьца**) *м* slave owner.

рабовладе́льческ|ий (**-ая, -ое, -ие**) *прил* slave-owning.

раболе́п|ный (**-ен, -на, -но**) *прил* servile.

раболе́пств|овать (**-ую**) *несов неперех*: **~ (пе́ред** +*instr*) to crawl (to).

рабо́т|а (**-ы**) *ж* (*труд, произведение*) work; (*источник заработка*) work, job; (*функционирование*) working; **поступа́ть (поступи́ть** *perf*) **на -у** to start a job; **постоя́нная/вре́менная/случа́йная ~** permanent/temporary/casual work *или* employment; **сде́льная ~** piecework; **сме́нная ~** shiftwork.

рабо́та|ть (**-ю**) *несов неперех* to work; (*магазин, библиотека итп*) to be open; **~** (*impf*) **на кого́-н/что́-н** to work for sb/sth; **~** (*impf*) **над чем-н** to work on sth; **кем Вы ~ете?** what do you do for a living?; **я ~ю инжене́ром** I'm an engineer

▶ **рабо́таться** *несов возв* (+*dat*): **сего́дня мне не ~ется** I can't get down to work today; **в библиоте́ке хорошо́ ~ется** the library is a good place to work.

рабо́тник (**-а**) *м* worker; (*учреждения*) employee; **руководя́щие ~и** management; **нау́чный ~** researcher.

рабо́тница (**-ы**) *ж* (female) worker.

работода́тель (**-я**) *м* employer.

работоспосо́бность (**-и**) *ж* (*человека*) ability to work hard; (*машины*) efficiency.

работоспосо́бный *прил* (*человек*) able to work hard; (*население*) working *опред*.

работя́г|а (**-и**) *м/ж* (*разг*) workhorse (*fig*).

работя́щий (**-ая, -ее, -ие**) *прил* (*разг*) hard-working.

рабо́ч|ая (**-ей**; *decl like adj*) *ж см* **рабо́чий**.

рабо́ч|ий (**-ая, -ее, -ие**) *прил* (*движение, посёлок, столовая*) worker's *опред*; (*человек, одежда, часть механизма, чертёж*) working *опред* ◆ (**-его**; *decl like adj*) *м* worker; **в ~ее вре́мя** during working hours; **у нас нехва́тка**

~их рук we are undermanned; **в ~ем поря́дке** in the course of the proceedings; **рабо́чая ло́шадь** workhorse; **рабо́чая си́ла** workforce; **рабо́чая ста́нция** (*КОМП*) work station; **рабо́чее ме́сто** (*помещение*) workplace; (*пост*) position; **рабо́чие ру́ки** workers; **рабо́чий визи́т** working visit; **рабо́чий день** working day (*BRIT*), workday (*US*); **рабо́чий класс** the working class.

ра́бск|ий (**-ая, -ое, -ие**) *прил* (*существование, условия*) slave-like; (*послушание, подражание*) slavish; **~ труд** slave labour (*BRIT*) *или* labor (*US*).

ра́бств|о (**-а**) *ср* slavery.

рабфа́к (**-а**) *м* (*ист*: = *рабочий факульте́т*) ≈ working man's college.

рабы́н|я (**-и**) *ж* slave.

равви́н (**-а**) *м* rabbi.

ра́вен *прил см* **ра́вный**.

ра́венств|о (**-а**) *ср* equality; (*чисел*) equal value; **знак ~а** (*МАТ*) equals sign; **ста́вить (поста́вить** *perf*) **знак ~а ме́жду чем-н и чем-н** to equate sth with sth.

равни́н|а (**-ы**) *ж* plain.

равно́ *нареч* equally ◆ *союз*: **~ (как) и** as well as ◆ *как сказ*: **э́то всё ~** it doesn't make any difference; **мне всё ~** it's all the same to me; **я всё ~ приду́** I'll come just the same; **два плюс пять ~ семи́** two plus five equals seven.

равнове́си|е (**-я**) *ср* (*также перен*) equilibrium; **теря́ть (потеря́ть** *perf*) **~** to lose one's balance; **~ сил** balance of power.

равноде́нстви|е (**-я**) *ср* equinox.

равноду́шен *прил см* **равноду́шный**.

равноду́ши|е (**-я**) *ср*: **~ (к** +*dat*) indifference (to).

равноду́шно *нареч* indifferently.

равноду́ш|ный (**-ен, -на, -но**) *прил*: **~ (к** +*dat*) indifferent (to).

равноме́р|ный (**-ен, -на, -но**) *прил* even.

равнопра́вен *прил см* **равнопра́вный**.

равнопра́ви|е (**-я**) *ср* equal rights *мн*.

равнопра́в|ный (**-ен, -на, -но**) *прил* equal.

равноси́л|ьный (**-ен, -ьна, -ьно**) *прил*: **~** +*dat* equivalent *или* equal to.

равноце́н|ный (**-ен, -на, -но**) *прил* of equal value *или* worth.

ра́в|ный (**-ен, -на́, -но**) *прил* equal; **~ным о́бразом** equally; **на ~ных** (*разг*) on an equal footing.

равня́|ть (-ю; *perf* **сравня́ть**) *несов перех*: ~ (**с** +*instr*) (*делать равным*) to make equal (with); (*одинаково оценивать*): ~ **кого́-н/что-н с** +*instr* to treat sb/sth the same as

▶ **равня́ться** (*perf* **сравня́ться**) *несов возв*: ~**ся по** +*dat* to draw level with; (*считать себя равным*): ~**ся с** +*instr* to compare o.s. with; (*быть равносильным*): ~**ся** +*dat* to be equal to; (*следовать примеру*): ~**ся на** +*acc* to emulate; **два плюс два ~ется четырём** two plus two equals four.

рагу́ *ср нескл* ragout.

рад (-а, -о, -ы) *как сказ*: ~ (+*dat*) glad (of); ~ +*infin* glad *или* pleased to do; ~ **познако́миться с Ва́ми** pleased to meet you; **я ~ за него́** I'm pleased *или* happy for him; **я всегда́ ~ помо́чь** I'm always glad to be of help; **я уже́ и не ра́да, что согласи́лась** I'm already regretting that I agreed.

ра́ди *предл*: ~ (+*gen*) for the sake of; **чего́ ~?** (*разг*) what for?; **шу́тки ~** (*разг*) for a joke; ~ **Бо́га!** (*разг*) for God's sake!

радиа́льный *прил* radial.

радиа́тор (-а) *м* radiator.

радиа́ци|я (-и) *ж* radiation.

ра́ди|й (-я) *м* radium.

радика́л (-а) *м* (*ПОЛИТ, МАТ*) radical.

радика́л|ьный (-ен, -ьна, -ьно) *прил* radical.

радикули́т (-а) *м* lower back pain.

ра́дио *ср нескл* radio; **по ~** on the radio; **слу́шать** (*impf*) ~ to listen to the radio.

радиоакти́вност|ь (-и) *ж* radioactivity.

радиоакти́вный *прил* radioactive.

радиовеща́ни|е (-я) *ср* (radio) broadcasting.

радиолока́тор (-а) *м* radar (*device*).

радиолока́ци|я (-и) *ж* radar (*system*).

радиолюби́тел|ь (-я) *м* radio ham.

радиопереда́ч|а (-и) *ж* radio programme (*BRIT*) *или* program (*US*).

радиоприёмник (-а) *м* radio (set).

радиосвя́з|ь (-и) *ж* radiocommunication.

радиослу́шател|ь (-я) *м* (radio) listener.

радиослу́шательни|ца (-ы) *ж см* **радиослу́шатель**.

радиоста́нци|я (-и) *ж* radio station.

радиотелефо́н (-а) *м* radiotelephone.

радиоте́хни|ка (-и) *ж* radio engineering.

радиоу́з|ел (-ла́) *м* public-address facilities *мн*.

радиоэлектро́ни|ка (-и) *ж* radio electronics.

ради́ст (-а) *м* radio operator.

ради́ст|ка (-ки; *gen pl* -ок) *ж см* **ради́ст**.

ра́диу|с (-а) *м* radius; (*перен: влияния, действия*) range.

ра́д|овать (-ую; *perf* **обра́довать**) *несов перех*: ~ **кого́-н** to make sb happy, please sb; ~ (*impf*) **глаз/слух** to be a joy to behold/hear

▶ **ра́доваться** *несов возв* (*перен: душа,*

сердце) to rejoice; (*perf* **обра́доваться**; +*dat*: солнцу, успехам) to take pleasure in; **я обра́довалась ему́** *или* **встре́че с ним** I was overjoyed to see him.

ра́достен *прил см* **ра́достный**.

ра́достно *нареч* joyfully; **они́ меня́ ~ встре́тили** they gave me a very warm welcome.

ра́дост|ный (-ен, -на, -но) *прил* joyful; (*день, новость*) joyous.

ра́дос|ть (-ти) *ж* joy; **от ~ти** (*плакать, смея́ться*) with joy; **пры́гать** (*impf*) **от ~ти** to jump for joy; **с ~ю** gladly; **на ~тях я его́ прости́л** (*разг*) I was so happy, I forgave him.

ра́дуг|а (-и) *ж* rainbow.

ра́дужный (-ен, -на, -но) *прил* (*перен: настроение, надежды*) bright; ~**ные цвета́** rainbow colours; **ра́дужная оболо́чка** (*АНАТ*) iris.

раду́шен *прил см* **раду́шный**.

раду́ши|е (-я) *ср* warmth.

раду́ш|ный (-ен, -на, -но) *прил* warm.

раз (-а; *nom pl* -ы́, *gen pl* -) *м* time ♦ *нескл* (*один*) one ♦ *нареч* (*разг: однажды*) once ♦ *союз* (*разг: если*) if; **в два/три/четы́ре ра́за бо́льше/ме́ньше** two/three/four times bigger/smaller; **в пять/шесть/семь** *итп* **бо́льше/ме́ньше** five/six/seven *итп* times bigger/smaller; **не ~** more than once; **в пе́рвый ~** (*впервы́е*) for the first time; (*в пе́рвом слу́чае*) on the first occasion; **в тот/про́шлый/сле́дующий ~** that/ last/next time; **на э́тот ~** this time; **ещё ~** (*once*) again; ~ **и навсегда́** once and for all; **ни ра́зу** not once; (*оди́н*) ~ **в день** once a day; **вот тебе́ и ~!** (*разг*) that's a turn up for the books!; **в са́мый ~** (*разг: о разме́ре*) just right; (*: о вре́мени*) at just the right time; ~**... то ...** (*разг*) if ... then ...; ~ **на ~ не прихо́дится** you can't win all the time; ~ **пришёл – сади́сь** now that you're here, have a seat.

раз- *префикс* (*in verbs; о разделе́нии на ча́сти*) *indicating division into parts eg.* **развяза́ть**; (*о распределе́нии по места́м, по пове́рхности*) *indicating positioning of sth somewhere eg.* **разложи́ть**; (*об интенси́вном де́йствии*) *indicating intensive action eg.* **разбушева́ться**; (*о направле́нии движе́ния в ра́зные сто́роны*) *indicating movement in different directions eg.* **разбежа́ться**; (*о прекраще́нии де́йствия*) *indicating cessation of action eg.* **разлюби́ть**; (*in adjectives; разг: о вы́сшей сте́пени ка́чества*) *indicating a great degree of a certain quality eg.* **развесёлый**.

разба́в|ить (-лю, -ишь; *impf* **разбавля́ть**) *сов перех* to dilute.

разбаза́р|ить (-ю, -ишь; *impf* **разбаза́ривать**) *сов перех* to squander.

разба́лива|ться (-юсь) *несов от* **разболе́ться**.

разба́лтыва|ть(ся) (-ю(сь)) несов от
разболта́ть(ся).
разбе́г (-а) м (машины) acceleration; (атлета)
run-up; **прыжо́к с ~а** или **~у** running jump.
разбежа́ть (как **бежа́ть**; см **Table 20**; impf
разбега́ться) сов возв to run off, scatter; (перед
прыжком) to take a run-up; (перен: мысли) to
wander; **у меня́ глаза́ разбега́ются** (разг) I'm
spoilt for choice.
разбе́й(те) сов см **разби́ть**.
разберу́(сь) сов см **разобра́ть(ся)**.
разбива́|ть(ся) (-ю(сь)) несов от **разби́ть(ся)**.
разби́в|ка (-ки; gen pl -ок) ж (данных, людей)
arranging; (сада, парка) layout.
разбира́тельств|о (-а) ср (ЮР) examination.
разбира́|ть (-ю) несов от **разобра́ть** ♦ перех
(разг: сотрудника, нарушителя итп) to take to
task
► **разбира́ться** несов от **разобра́ться** ♦ возв
(разг: понимать): **~ся в** +prp to understand.
разбитно́й прил carefree.
разби́|ть (-обью, -обьёшь; imper -бе́й(те), impf
разбива́ть) сов перех (стекло, тарелку,
голову) to break; (машину) to smash up; (врага,
армию) to crush; (на участки, на части) to
break up; (аллею, клумбу) to lay; (счастье,
мечты) to ruin; **разбива́ть** (~ perf) **ла́герь** to
set up camp
► **разби́ться** (impf **разбива́ться**) сов возв to
break, smash; (при падении, в аварии) to be
badly hurt; (на группы, на участки) to break up.
разбогате́|ть (-ю) сов от **богате́ть**.
разбо́й (-я) м robbery.
разбо́йник (-а) м robber; (разг: шалун)
troublemaker.
разбо́йниц|а (-ы) ж см **разбо́йник**.
разбо́йнича|ть (-ю) несов неперех to thieve;
(разг: шалить) to get up to mischief.
разбо́йный прил: **~ое нападе́ние** (ЮР) armed
assault.
разболе́|ться (-юсь; impf **разба́ливаться**) сов
возв (разг: человек) to be taken ill; (: рука,
живот итп) to hurt badly; **у меня́ голова́
~лась** I've got a splitting headache.
разбо́лтан|ный (-, -на, -но) прил (разг) slack;
~ная похо́дка swagger.
разболта́|ть (-ю; impf **разба́лтывать**) сов перех
(порошок, смесь итп) to mix in; (замок, гайку)
to weaken; (разг: секрет, новость) to blab; ~
(perf) **дисципли́ну** (разг) to let discipline slip; ~
(perf) **ребёнка** (разг) to lose control over a child
► **разболта́ться** (impf **разба́лтываться**) сов
возв (порошок, мука) to mix in; (дверь, запор)
to come loose; (дисциплина, поведение) to
slacken off; (no impf; болтать) to babble on.
разбомб|и́ть (-лю́, -и́шь) сов перех to bomb.
разбо́р (-а) м (статьи, вопроса итп) analysis;
(ЮР) examination; (линг) parsing; **без ~а**
without exception.
разбо́рный прил collapsible.
разбо́рчивост|ь (-и) ж (требовательность)

discernment; (почерка) legibility.
разбо́рчив|ый (-, -а, -о) прил (человек, вкус)
discerning; (почерк) legible.
разбра́сыва|ть (-ю) несов от **разброса́ть**
► **разбра́сываться** несов возв (разг) to try to
do too much (at once); (+instr; друзьями,
поклонниками итп) to underrate.
разбр|ести́сь (-еду́сь, -едёшься; pt -ёлся,
-ела́сь, -ело́сь, impf **разбреда́ться**) сов возв to
wander off (in different directions).
разброса́|ть (-ю; impf **разбра́сывать**) сов
перех to scatter.
разбуд|и́ть (-ужу́, -у́дишь) сов от **буди́ть**.
разбу́х|нуть (-ну, -нешь; pt -, -ла, -ло, impf
разбуха́ть) сов неперех to swell; (папка,
чемодан итп) to bulge; (лицо, рука итп) to
swell up.
разбуше́ва́|ться (-у́юсь) сов возв (море) to
rage; (разг) to rant.
разва́л (-а) м (в квартире, в делах) chaos;
(экономики) ruin; (системы) break-up; **у нас
до́ма по́лный ~** our home is in a state of chaos.
разва́лива|ть(ся) (-ю(сь)) несов от
развали́ть(ся).
разва́лин|а (-ы) ж (обычно мн) ruins мн;
(перен: человек) wreck.
развал|и́ть (-алю́, -а́лишь; impf **разва́ливать**)
сов перех (стену, дом) to knock down; (дело,
хозяйство) to ruin
► **развали́ться** (impf **разва́ливаться**) сов возв
to collapse; **он ~алился в кре́сле** he sat
slumped in the armchair.
разва́р|иться (3sg -ится, 3pl -ятся, impf
разва́риваться) сов возв to be overcooked;
бы́стро ~а́риваться (impf) to cook quickly.
ра́зве част really; ~ **он согласи́лся/не знал?**
did he really agree/not know?; ~ **то́лько** или
что except that.
развева́|ться (3sg -ется, 3pl -ются) несов возв
(флаг) to flutter; (волосы) to flow.
разве́да|ть (-ю; impf **разве́дывать**) сов перех
(ГЕО) to prospect; (ВОЕН) to reconnoitre (BRIT),
reconnoiter (US); ~ (perf)(о +prp) to find out
(about).
разведе́ни|е (-я) ср (животных) breeding;
(растений) cultivation; (костра) building;
(клея, краски) dilution; ~ **пчёл** beekeeping.
разведён|ный (-, -á, -ы) прил (в разводе)
divorced; (no short form; раствор, водка) diluted.
разве́д|ка (-ки; gen pl -ок) ж (ГЕО) prospecting;
(полит) intelligence; (ВОЕН) reconnaissance.
разведу́(сь) итп сов см **развести́(сь)**.
разве́дчик (-а) м (ГЕО) prospector; (полит)
intelligence agent; (ВОЕН) scout; (самолёт)
reconnaissance plane.
разве́дчиц|а (-ы) ж (ВОЕН) scout.
разве́дыва|ть (-ю) несов от **разве́дать**.
разве|зти́ (-зу́, -зёшь; pt -ёз, -зла́, -зло́, impf
развози́ть) сов перех to deliver ♦ безл: **меня́
~езло́ от жары́/во́дки** the heat/vodka knocked
me out; **доро́гу ~езло́** the road has become
impassable.

разве́ива|ть(ся) (-ю(сь)) *несов от* **разве́ять(ся)**.

разве́й(те) *сов см* **разви́ть**.

развенча́|ть (-ю; *impf* **развенчивать**) *сов перех* to discredit.

развёрну|тый (-, -а, -о) *прил* detailed; *(строительство)* extensive.

разверн|у́ть (-у́, -ёшь; *impf* **развёртывать** *или* **развора́чивать**) *сов перех (бумагу, карту)* to unfold; *(ковёр)* to unroll; *(парус, флаг)* to unfurl; *(проект, торговлю итп)* to launch; *(выставку, лагерь)* to set up; *(свои силы, талант)* to develop fully; *(корабль, машину, самолёт)* to turn around; *(батальон, полк итп)* to deploy; ~ *(perf)* **пле́чи** to pull one's shoulders back

▶ **разверн|у́ться** (*impf* **развёртываться** *или* **развора́чиваться**) *сов возв (борьба, кампания, работа)* to get under way; *(талант, человек)* to develop fully; *(автомобиль, судно)* to turn around; *(батальон)* to be deployed; *(вид, зрелище)* to open up.

развесел|и́ть (-ю́, -и́шь) *сов от* **весели́ть**.

развеси́ст|ый (-, -а, -о) *прил* spreading *опред*.

разве́|сить (-шу, -сишь; *impf* **разве́шивать**) *сов перех (ветви)* to spread; *(картины, вещи)* to hang; *(бельё)* to hang up *или* out; ~ *(perf)* **у́ши** *(разг)* to listen wide-eyed.

развесно́й *прил* sold by weight.

разв|ести́ (-еду́, -едёшь; *pt* -ёл, -ела́, -ело́, *impf* **разводи́ть**) *сов перех* to take; *(разъединить)* to divorce; *(порошок)* to dissolve; *(сок, краску)* to dilute; *(животных)* to breed; *(цветы, сад)* to grow; *(мост)* to raise; **разводи́ть** (~ *perf*) **дете́й по дома́м** to take the children home; **разводи́ть** (~ *perf*) **ого́нь** to get a fire going; **разводи́ть** (~ *perf*) **рука́ми** ≈ to shrug one's shoulders; **разводи́ть** (~ *perf*) **пусту́ю болтовню́** *(разг)* to talk hot air

▶ **разв|ести́сь** (*impf* **разводи́ться**) *сов возв (животные)* to breed; **разводи́ться** (~сь *perf*) (с +*instr*) to divorce, get divorced (from).

разветв|и́ть (-лю́, -и́шь; *impf* **разветвля́ть**) *сов перех* to expand

▶ **разветв|и́ться** (*impf* **разветвля́ться**) *сов возв (дерево, река, дорога)* to branch; *(компания, учреждение)* to branch out.

разветвле́ни|е (-я) *ср (действие: дорог, кроны деревьев)* branching; *(: компании)* expansion; *(место: железной дороги, канала)* fork.

разветвлё́нный (-ён, -ена́, -ено́) *прил* extensive.

разветвлю́(сь) *сов см* **разветви́ть(ся)**.

разветвля́|ть(ся) (-ю(сь)) *несов от* **разветви́ть(ся)**.

разве́ша|ть (-ю; *impf* **разве́шивать**) *сов перех (картины, фотографии)* to hang; *(бельё)* to hang up *или* out.

разве́шива|ть (-ю) *несов от* **разве́сить**, **разве́шать**.

разве́шу *сов см* **разве́сить**.

разве́|ять (-ю; *impf* **разве́ивать**) *сов перех (облака, туман)* to disperse; *(подозрения, сомнения, грусть)* to dispel; **разве́ивать** (~ *perf*) **миф** to shatter a myth

▶ **разве́|яться** (*impf* **разве́иваться**) *сов возв (облака)* to disperse; *(туман)* to lift; *(тоска, сомнения, мрачные мысли)* to be dispelled; *(человек)* to relax.

развива́|ть(ся) (-ю(сь)) *несов от* **разви́ть(ся)**.

развива́ющ|ийся (-аяся, -оеся, -иеся) *прил*: ~**аяся страна́** developing country.

развил|ка (-ки; *gen pl* -ок) *ж* fork *(in road)*.

разви́ти|е (-я) *ср* development; **высо́кое/ ни́зкое** ~ a high/low level of development.

ра́звит|ой (-, -а, -о) *прил* developed; *(духовно зрелый)* mature.

разв|и́ть (-овью́, -овьёшь; *pt* -и́л, -ила́, -и́ло, *imper* -ве́й(те), *impf* **развива́ть**) *сов перех* to develop; *(наступление, деятельность)* to step up; *(верёвку, плётку)* to unwind; *(волосы)* to straighten; **развива́ть** (~ *perf*) **ско́рость** to gather speed; **развива́ть** (~ *perf*) **ребёнка** to help a child to develop

▶ **разв|и́ться** (*impf* **развива́ться**) *сов возв* to develop; *(скорость)* to build up; *(верёвка, коса, плётка)* to come unwound; *(волосы)* to become straighter.

развлёк(ся) *итп сов см* **развлечь(ся)**.

развлека́тельный (-ен, -ьна, -ьно) *прил* entertaining.

развлека́|ть(ся) (-ю(сь)) *несов от* **развле́чь(ся)**.

развлеку́(сь) *итп сов см* **развле́чь(ся)**.

развлече́ни|е (-я) *ср (гостей, публики)* entertaining; *(спектакль итп)* entertainment.

развле́|чь (-ку́, -чёшь *итп*, -ку́т; *pt* -ёк, -екла́, -екло́, *impf* **развлека́ть**) *сов перех* to entertain

▶ **развле́|чься** (*impf* **развлека́ться**) *сов возв* to have fun.

разво́д (-а) *м (расторжение брака)* divorce; *(моста)* opening; **они́ в** ~**е** they are divorced; **подава́ть (пода́ть** *perf*) **на** ~ to apply for a divorce.

разво|ди́ть(ся) (-жу́(сь), -́дишь(ся)) *несов от* **развести́(сь)**.

разводно́й *прил*: ~ **ключ** monkey wrench; **разводно́й мост** drawbridge.

разво́д|ы (-ов) *мн (узор)* design *ед*; *(подтёки, пятна)* stains *мн*.

развожу́(сь) *несов см* **разводи́ть(ся)**.

разв|ози́ть (-ожу́, -о́зишь) *несов от* **развезти́**.

разволн|ова́ть (-у́ю) *сов перех* to alarm

▶ **разволн|ова́ться** *сов возв* to be alarmed.

развора́чива|ть(ся) (-ю(сь)) *несов от*

разверну́ть(ся).

разворо|ва́ть (-у́ю; *impf* разворо́вывать) *сов перех* to loot.

разворо́т (-а) *м* (*машины*) U-turn; (*в книге*) double page.

разворо|ти́ть (-чу́, -тишь) *сов перех* (*дорогу*) to dig up.

развра́т (-а) *м* promiscuity; (*духовный*) depravity.

развра́тен *прил см* развра́тный.

развра|ти́ть (-щу́, -ти́шь; *impf* развраща́ть) *сов перех* to pervert; (*деньгами*) to corrupt

► разврати́ться (*impf* развраща́ться) *сов возв* (*см перех*) to become promiscuous; to become corrupted.

развра́тник (-а) *м* promiscuous man (*мн* men).

развра́тни|ца (-ы) *ж* promiscuous woman (*мн* women).

развра́тнича|ть (-ю) *несов неперех* to lead a life of promiscuity.

развра́т|ный (-ен, -на, -но) *прил* promiscuous.

развраща́|ть(ся) (-ю(сь)) *несов от* разврати́ть(ся).

развращу́(сь) *несов см* разврати́ть(ся).

развя|за́ть (-жу́, -́жешь; *impf* развя́зывать) *сов перех* (*узел, шнурки, мешок*) to untie; (*перен: инициативу*) to unshackle; (: *войну, реакцию*) to unleash; развя́зывать (~ *perf*) кому́-н ру́ки (*перен*) to free sb's hands; развя́зывать (~ *perf*) кому́-н язы́к to loosen sb's tongue

► развяза́ться (*impf* развя́зываться) *сов возв* (*шнурки, бант итп*) to come untied: ~ся с +*instr* (*разг: с людьми, с экзаменами*) to be through with; (: *с долгами*) to get rid of.

развя́з|ка (-ки; *gen pl* -ок) *ж* (*конец*) ending; (*АВТ*) junction.

развя́з|ный (-ен, -на, -но) *прил* overly familiar.

развя́зок *сущ см* развя́зка.

развя́зыва|ть(ся) (-ю(сь)) *несов от* развяза́ть(ся).

разгада́|ть (-ю; *impf* разга́дывать) *сов перех* (*кроссворд, загадку*) to solve; (*замыслы, тайну*) to guess; (*сны*) to decipher; (*человека*) to fathom out.

разга́д|ка (-ки; *gen pl* -ок) *ж* (*снов, мыслей*) deciphering; (*тайны*) key; (*феномена*) explanation; (*решение загадки*) solution.

разга́дыва|ть (-ю) *несов от* разгада́ть.

разга́р (-а) *м*: в ~e +*gen* (*сезона*) at the height of; (*боя*) in the heart of; кани́кулы в (по́лном) ~e the holidays are in full swing.

разгиба́|ть(ся) (-ю(сь)) *несов от* разогну́ть(ся).

разгильдя́|й (-я) *м* (*разг*) layabout.

разгла́|дить (-жу, -дишь; *impf* разгла́живать) *сов перех* to smooth out.

разгла|си́ть (-шу́, -си́шь; *impf* разглаша́ть) *сов перех* to divulge, disclose.

разгляде́|ть (-жу́, -ди́шь; *impf* разгля́дывать) *сов перех* (*рассмотреть*) to scrutinize; (*no impf*; *понять*) to discern.

разгне́ван|ный (-, -а, -о) *прил*: ~ (+*instr*) angry (with).

разгова́рива|ть (-ю) *несов неперех*: ~ (с +*instr*) to talk (to); она́ бо́льше со мно́й не ~ет she doesn't talk to me any more.

разгово́р (-а) *м* conversation; э́то друго́й ~! (*разг*) that's another matter!; без ~ов without a word; *см также* разгово́ры.

разгово́рник (-а) *м* phrase book.

разгово́рный *прил* colloquial.

разгово́рчив|ый (-, -а, -о) *прил* talkative.

разгово́р|ы (-ов) *мн* (*толки*) gossip *ед*.

разго́н (-а) *м* (*демонстрации*) breaking up; (*самолёта, автомобиля*) acceleration; устра́ивать (устро́ить *perf*) кому́-н ~ (*разг*) to give sb a roasting.

разгоня́|ть(ся) (-ю(сь)) *несов от* разогна́ть(ся).

разгоре́|ться (*3sg* -и́тся, *3sg* -я́тся, *impf* разгора́ться) *сов возв* (*костёр, спор*) to flare up; (*закат*) to be ablaze; (*щёки, уши*) to burn; (*перен: страсти, любопытство*) to become inflamed.

разгорячён|ный (-, -а́, -о́) *прил*: ~ (+*instr*) (*человек*) inflamed (by); (-, на́, -но́; *лицо*) excited.

разгоряч|и́ться (-у́сь, -и́шься) *сов от* горячи́ться ♦ *возв* (*от волнения, от работы*) to get het up; (*от бега*) to be hot.

разграни́ч|ить (-у, -ишь; *impf* разграни́чивать) *сов перех* (*район, земли*) to demarcate; (*обязанности, понятия*) to delimit.

разграф|и́ть (-лю́, -и́шь) *сов от* графи́ть.

разгре|сти́ (-бу́, -бёшь; *pt* -ёб, -ебла́, -ебло́, *impf* разгреба́ть) *сов перех* to sweep aside.

разгро́м (-а) *м* rout; (*разг: беспорядок*) mayhem, havoc; (*статьи*) savaging.

разгром|и́ть (-лю́, -и́шь) *сов перех* (*врага, сопротивление*) to crush; (*город, страну*) to destroy; (*политику, статью, соперника*) to savage.

разгро́мный *прил* (*речь, критика*) savage.

разгру|зи́ть (-жу́, -́зишь; *impf* разгружа́ть) *сов перех* to unload; (*программу*) to ease; разгружа́ть (~ *perf*) кого́-н to lighten sb's load.

разгру́з|ка (-ки; *gen pl* -ок) *ж* (*вагонов, баржи*) unloading; (*перен: человека*) unburdening; (: *программы, плана*) easing up.

разгру́зоч|ный *прил*: ~ые рабо́ты unloading; разгру́зочный день *day during dieting programme on which diet is relaxed.*

разгры́з|ть (-у, -ёшь) *сов от* грызть ♦ (*impf* разгрыза́ть) *перех* (*редиску, кость*) to gnaw at; (*орех*) to crack open.

разгу́л (-а) *м* revelry; (+*gen*; *реакции, национализма итп*) outburst of.

разгу́лива|ть (-ю) *несов неперех* to have a wander

► разгу́ливаться *несов от* разгуля́ться.

разгуля́|ться (-юсь; *impf* разгу́ливаться) *сов*

возв (*дать себе волю*) to let o.s. go; (*перен: ветер, море*) to get up; (: *погода, день*) to clear up.
раздава́|ть(ся) (**-ю(сь), -ёшь(ся)**) *несов от* **разда́ть(ся).**
раздави́ть (**-авлю́, -а́вишь**) *сов от* **дави́ть ♦** (*impf* **раздавливать**) *перех* to squash.
разда́м(ся) *итп сов см* **разда́ть(ся).**
разда́точный *прил:* ~ **пункт** distribution centre (*BRIT*) *или* center (*US*).
разда́ть (*как дать; см* **Table 14**; *impf* **раздава́ть**) *сов перех* to give up, distribute
▶ **разда́ться** (*impf* **раздава́ться**) *сов возв* (*голос, шум итп*) to be heard; (*толпа*) to make way; (*обувь, сапоги*) to stretch; **раздава́ться** (**~ся** *perf*) **в бёдрах** (*разг*) to put weight on around the hips.
разда́ч|а (**-и**) *ж* distribution.
разда́шь(ся) *сов см* **разда́ть(ся).**
раздва́ива|ться (**-юсь**) *несов от* **раздво́иться.**
раздвига́|ть(ся) (**-ю**) *несов от* **раздви́нуть(ся).**
раздвижно́й *прил:* ~ **за́навес** curtain (*THEAT*); ~ **стол** extending table.
раздви́н|уть (**-у, -ешь**; *impf* **раздвига́ть**) *сов перех* to move apart; (*шторы*) to open; (*толпу*) to part; (*перен: рамки наблюдения, исследования*) to broaden
▶ **раздви́нуться** (*impf* **раздвига́ться**) *сов возв* (*шторы*) to open; (*толпа*) to part; (*перен: мир, возможности*) to open up.
раздво́ени|е (**-я**) *ср:* ~ **ли́чности** split personality.
раздво́|иться (**-ю́сь, -и́шься;** *impf* **раздва́иваться**) *сов возв* (*дорога, река*) to divide into two; (*перен: мнение*) to be divided.
раздева́л|ка (**-ки**; *gen pl* **-ок**) *ж* changing room.
раздева́|ть(ся) (**-ю(сь)**) *несов от* **разде́ть(ся).**
разде́л (**-а**) *м* (*действие: имущества*) division; (*часть, область*) section.
разде́ла|ть (**-ю;** *impf* **разде́лывать**) *сов перех* (*мясо, рыбу*) to dress; (*грядки*) to prepare; (*мебель*): ~ **что-н под дуб/мра́мор** to give sth an oak/a marble finish
▶ **разде́латься** (*impf* **разде́лываться**) *сов возв* (*разг*): **~ся с** +*instr* (*с делами, с долгами*) to settle; (*с соперником, с хулиганом*) to take care of.
разделе́ни|е (**-я**) *ср* division; ~ **труда́** division of labour (*BRIT*) *или* labor (*US*).
раздел|и́ть (**-елю́, -е́лишь**) *сов от* **дели́ть ♦** (*impf* **разделя́ть**) *перех* (*мнение, взгляды, энтузиазм*) to share
▶ **раздели́ться** *сов от* **дели́ться ♦** (*impf* **разделя́ться**) *возв* (*мнения, общество*) to become divided.
разде́лыва|ть(ся) (**-ю(сь)**) *несов от*

разде́лать(ся).
разделя́|ть(ся) (**-ю(сь)**) *несов от* **раздели́ть(ся).**
раздеру́ *итп сов см* **разодра́ть.**
разде́|ть (**-ну, -нешь;** *impf* **раздева́ть**) *сов перех* to undress; (*разг: ограбить*): ~ **кого́-н** to strip sb bare
▶ **разде́ться** (*impf* **раздева́ться**) *сов возв* to get undressed.
раздира́|ть (**-ю**) *несов от* **разодра́ть ♦** *перех* (*душу, человека, общество*) to tear apart.
раздобре́|ть (**-ю**) *сов от* **добре́ть.**
раздоб|ы́ть (*как* **быть;** *см* **Table 21**; *impf* **раздобыва́ть**) *сов перех* (*разг*) to get hold of, lay one's hands on.
раздо́лен *прил см* **раздо́льный.**
раздо́ль|е (**-я**) *ср* expanse; (*перен*) freedom; **мне здесь** ~ I feel free here.
раздо́л|ьный (**-ен, -ьна, -ьно**) *прил* vast; (*перен*) free.
раздо́р (**-а**) *м* (*обычно мн*) strife *ед*.
раздоса́д|овать (**-ую**) *сов перех* to upset.
раздража́|ть(ся) (**-ю(сь)**) *несов от* **раздражи́ть(ся).**
раздраже́ни|е (**-я**) *ср* irritation.
раздражённо *нареч* (*сказать*) irritably.
раздраж|ённый (**-ён, -ена́, -ено́**) *прил* (*человек, голос*) irritated; (**-ён, -енна́, -енно́**) *тон*) irritable; **у меня́ не́рвы ~ены́ до преде́ла** my nerves are on edge.
раздражи́тел|ьный (**-ен, -ьна, -ьно**) *прил* irritable.
раздраж|и́ть (**-у́, -и́шь;** *impf* **раздража́ть**) *сов перех* (*также МЕД*) to irritate; (*нервы*) to agitate; (*аппетит*) to stimulate
▶ **раздражи́ться** (*impf* **раздража́ться**) *сов возв* (*кожа, глаза*) to become irritated; (*человек*): **~ся** (+*instr*) to be irritated (by).
раздроб|и́ть (**-лю́, -и́шь**) *сов от* **дроби́ть ♦** (*impf* **раздробля́ть**) *перех* to shatter.
раздро́блен|ный (**-, -а, -о**) *прил* fragmented.
раздроблю́ *сов см* **раздроби́ть.**
раздробля́|ть (**-ю**) *несов от* **раздроби́ть.**
раздува́|ть(ся) (**-ю(сь)**) *несов от* **разду́ть(ся).**
разду́ма|ть (**-ю;** *impf* **разду́мывать**) *сов неперех:* ~ +*infin* (*пойти, жениться итп*) to decide not to do, decide against doing.
разду́мыва|ть (**-ю**) *несов от* **разду́мать ♦** *неперех:* ~ (**о** +*prp*) (*долго думать*) to contemplate.
разду́мь|е (**-я;** *gen pl* **-ий**) *ср* contemplation; (*обычно мн*) thought; **впада́ть (впасть** *perf*) **в** ~ to sink deep into thought; **по́сле до́лгих ~ий** *или* after lengthy consideration.
разду́|ть (**-ю;** *impf* **раздува́ть**) *сов перех* (*огонь, костёр*) to fan; (*пузырь*) to blow; (*разг: дело, скандал*) to blow up; (: *штаты*) to overstaff; **раздува́ть** (~ *perf*) **но́здри** to flare

one's nostrils; **у неё ~у́ло щёку/но́гу** her cheek/leg has swollen up

▶ **разду́ться** (*impf* **раздува́ться**) *сов возв* (*парус*) to swell; (*щека, губа, также перен*) to swell up; (*карманы, портфель*) to bulge.

разева́|ть (-ю) *несов от* **рази́нуть**.

разжа́лоб|ить (-лю, -ишь) *сов перех*: ~ **кого́-н** to evoke sympathy in sb.

разжа́л|овать (-ую) *сов перех* to demote; ~ (*perf*) **кого́-н в рядовы́е** to reduce sb to the ranks.

разж|а́ть (-ому́, -ожмёшь; *impf* **разжима́ть**) *сов перех* (*пальцы, губы*) to relax; (*пружину*) to uncoil.

▶ **разжа́ться** (*impf* **разжима́ться**) *сов возв* (*см перех*) to relax; to uncoil.

разж|ева́ть (-ую; *impf* **разжёвывать**) *сов перех* to chew; (*перен: разг: мысль*) to spell out in simple terms.

разж|е́чь (-огу́, -ожжёшь *итп*, -огу́т; *pt* -жёг, -огла́, -огло́, *impf* **разжига́ть**) *сов перех* (*также перен*) to kindle; (*войну, ненависть*) to incite.

разживу́сь *итп сов см* **разжи́ться**.

разжига́|ть (-ю) *несов от* **разже́чь**.

разжима́|ть(ся) (-ю(сь)) *несов от* **разжа́ть(ся)**.

разжире́|ть (-ю) *сов от* **жире́ть**.

разж|и́ться (-иву́сь, -ивёшься; *pt* -и́лся, -ила́сь, -ило́сь) *сов возв* (*разг: жить в достатке*) to do well for o.s.; ~ (*perf*) +*instr* (*деньгами*) to rake in.

раззадо́р|ить (-ю, -ишь; *impf* **раззадо́ривать**) *сов перех* to excite.

рази́н|уть (-у, -ешь; *impf* **разева́ть**) *сов перех* (*разг*): ~ **рот** to gape; **слу́шать** (*impf*) ~**ув рот** to listen open-mouthed.

рази́н|я (-и) *м/ж* (*разг*) scatterbrain.

рази́тельный (-ен, -ьна, -ьно) *прил* striking.

раз|и́ть (-жу́, -зи́шь) *сов перех* to strike; (*перен: пороки*) to strike out at ◆ *безл* (+*instr; разг*): **от неё ~зи́т духа́ми/чесноко́м** she reeks of perfume/garlic.

разлага́|ть(ся) (-ю(сь)) *несов от* **разложи́ть(ся)**.

разла́д (-а) *м* (*в делах, в работе*) disorder; (*с женой*) discord.

разла́мыва|ть (-ю) *несов от* **разлома́ть, разломи́ть**.

▶ **разла́мываться** *несов от* **разлома́ться, разломи́ться** ◆ *возв* (*разг*): **у меня́ ~ется спина́/голова́** my back/head is killing me.

разлёгся *итп сов см* **разле́чься**.

разле|те́ться (-чу́сь, -ти́шься; *impf* **разлета́ться**) *сов возв* (*птицы, перья*) to fly off (*in different directions*); (*перен: вы́росшие дети*) to fly the nest; (*разг: стекло, ваза итп*) to shatter; (: *новости*) to get around; (: *поезд*) to speed up.

разл|е́чься (-я́гусь, -я́жешься *итп*, -я́гутся; *pt* -ёгся, -егла́сь, -егло́сь) *сов возв* (*разг*) to stretch out.

разли́в (-а) *м* flooding; (*место, залитое водой*) flood plain; (*вина, воды*) bottling; (*металла*) casting.

разлива́|ть (-ю) *несов от* **разли́ть**.

▶ **разлива́ться** *несов от* **разли́ться** ◆ *возв* (*соловьи*) to sing; (*перен*): ~**ся соловьём** to wax lyrical.

разливн|о́й *прил*: ~**о́е пи́во** beer on tap.

разлин|ова́ть (-у́ю; *impf* **разлино́вывать**) *сов перех* to rule (*page*).

разл|и́ть (-олью́, -ольёшь; *pt* -и́л, -ила́, -и́ло, *impf* **разлива́ть**) *сов перех* to pour out; (*по бутылкам*) to bottle; (*пролить*) to spill; **их водо́й не ~ольёшь** they are never apart

▶ **разли́ться** (*impf* **разлива́ться**) *сов возв* (*пролиться*) to spill; (*река*) to overflow; **румя́нец ~ли́лся по его́ щека́м** the colour flooded into his cheeks; **по её лицу́ ~лила́сь улы́бка** a smile spread across her face.

различа́|ть (-ю) *несов от* **различи́ть**

▶ **различа́ться** *несов возв*: ~**ся по** +*dat* to differ in.

разли́чен *прил см* **разли́чный**.

разли́чи|е (-я) *ср* difference; **без ~я** indiscriminately.

различ|и́ть (-у́, -и́шь; *impf* **различа́ть**) *сов перех* (*увидеть, услышать*) to make out; (*отличить*): ~ (**по** +*dat*) to distinguish (by); **я их не ~а́ю** I can't tell them apart.

разли́чный (-ен, -на, -но) *прил* different.

разложе́ни|е (-я) *ср* (*ХИМ, БИО*) decomposition; (*общества, армии итп*) disintegration; (*МАТ*) expansion (*of equation*).

разлож|и́ть (-ожу́, -о́жишь; *impf* **раскла́дывать**) *сов перех* (*расположить*) to place, arrange; (*еду по тарелкам*) to dish out, serve; (*карту, диван, стол*) to open out; (*impf* **разлага́ть**; *ХИМ, БИО*) to decompose; (*МАТ*) to expand; (*перен: армию*) to demoralize; **раскла́дывать** (~ *perf*) **костёр** to build a fire

▶ **разложи́ться** (*impf* **раскла́дываться**) *сов возв* (*разг: разместить свои вещи*) to spread; (*impf* **разлага́ться**; *ХИМ, БИО*) to decompose; (*МАТ*) to expand; (*перен: армия, общество*) to fall apart.

разлома́|ть (-ю) *сов от* **лома́ть** ◆ (*impf* **разла́мывать**) *перех* to break up

▶ **разлома́ться** (*impf* **разла́мываться**) *сов возв* to break up; (*постройка*) to fall to pieces.

разл|оми́ть (-омлю́, -о́мишь; *impf* **разла́мывать**) *сов перех* (*на части: хлеб итп*) to break up

▶ **разломи́ться** (*impf* **разла́мываться**) *сов возв* to break up.

разлу́к|а (-и) *ж* separation; **жить** (*impf*) **в ~е с кем-н** to live apart from sb.

разлуч|и́ть (-у́, -и́шь; *impf* **разлуча́ть**) *сов перех*: ~ **кого́-н с** +*instr* to separate sb from

▶ **разлучи́ться** (*impf* **разлуча́ться**) *сов возв*: ~**ся (с** +*instr*) to be separated (from).

разл|юби́ть (-юблю́, -ю́бишь) *сов перех*: ~ +*infin* (*читать, гулять итп*) to lose one's enthusiasm for doing; **он меня́ ~юби́л** he doesn't love me any more.
разля́гусь *итп сов см* **разле́чься**.
разма́|зать (-жу, -жешь; *impf* **разма́зывать**) *сов перех* to smear
▶ **разма́заться** (*impf* **разма́зываться**) *сов возв* to be smeared.
размазн|я́ (-и́) *м/ж* dither.
разма́зыва|ть(ся) (-ю) *несов от* **разма́зать(ся)**.
разма́лыва|ть (-ю) *несов от* **размоло́ть**.
разма́рива|ть (*3sg* -ет, *3pl* -ют) *несов от* **разморить**
▶ **разма́риваться** *несов от* **размори́ться**.
разма́тыва|ть (-ю) *несов от* **размота́ть**.
разма́х (-а) *м* (*рук, крыльев*) span; (*маятника, колокола*) swing; (*перен: деятельности*) scope; (: *проекта*) scale; **уда́рить** (*perf*) **кого́-н с ~у** to take a swing at sb; **он челове́к с ~ом** he thinks on a large scale.
разма́хива|ть (-ю) *несов от* **размахну́ть** ◆ *неперех*: ~ +*instr* (*руками, флажком*) to wave; (*шашкой*) to brandish
▶ **разма́хиваться** *несов от* **размахну́ться**.
размахн|у́ть (-у́, -ёшь; *impf* **разма́хивать**) *сов перех* (*руки, крыля*) to spread ◆ *неперех*: ~ +*instr* (*кнутом, топором*) to swing
▶ **размахну́ться** (*impf* **разма́хиваться**) *сов возв* to swing one's arm back; (*перен: разг: со свадьбой, в делах итп*) to go to town.
разма́шист|ый (-, -а, -о) *прил* sweeping.
размельч|и́ть (-у́, -и́шь) *сов от* **мельчи́ть**.
размелю́ *итп сов см* **размоло́ть**.
разме́н (-а) *м* (*денег, пленных*) exchange; ~ **кварти́ры** flat swap (*in which one large flat is exchanged for two smaller ones*).
разме́нива|ть(ся) (-ю(сь)) *несов от* **разменя́ть(ся)**.
разме́нн|ый *прил*: ~ **автома́т** change machine; **~ая моне́та** (small) change.
разменя́|ть (-ю; *impf* **разме́нивать**) *сов перех* (*деньги*) to change; (*квартиру*) to exchange; (*перен: талант*) to waste; ~ (*perf*) **со́весть** to sell out (*fig*)
▶ **разменя́ться** (*impf* **разме́ниваться**) *сов возв* (*перен: разг: обменять жилплощадь*) to do a flat swap (*of one large flat for two smaller ones*); **разме́ниваться** (*impf*) **по мелоча́м или пустяка́м** (*разг*) to waste o.s.
разме́р (-а) *м* size; (*обычно мн: строительства: масштабы*) dimension; (*линг*) metre (*BRIT*), meter (*US*); **како́й у тебя́ ~?** what size do you take?
разме́рен|ный (-, -на, -но) *прил* (*звон, шаги*) measured; (*жизнь*) well-regulated.
разме|сти́ть (-щу́, -сти́шь; *impf* **размеща́ть**) *сов*

перех (*найти место для*) to place; (*расположить*) to arrange
▶ **размести́ться** (*impf* **размеща́ться**) *сов возв* to accommodate o.s.; **го́сти ~сти́лись за столо́м** the guests took their seats at the table.
разм|ета́ть (-ечу́, -е́чешь) *сов перех* (*листву, пепел итп*) to scatter; (*руки*) to fling open
▶ **размета́ться** *сов возв* (*волосы*) to fly everywhere; (*человек: во сне*) to sprawl out.
разме́|тить (-чу, -тишь; *impf* **размеча́ть**) *сов перех* to mark out.
размеча́|ться (-юсь) *сов возв* to start dreaming.
размечу́ *сов см* **разме́тить**.
размечу́(сь) *итп сов см* **размета́ть(ся)**.
размеша́|ть (-ю; *impf* **разме́шивать**) *сов перех* to stir.
размеща́|ть(ся) (-ю(сь)) *несов от* **размести́ть(ся)**.
размеще́ни|е (-я) *ср* (*вещей*) placing; (*расположение*) arrangement; (*людей: по комнатам*) accommodation.
размещу́(сь) *сов см* **размести́ть(ся)**.
размина́|ть(ся) (-ю(сь)) *несов от* **размя́ть(ся)**.
размини́р|овать (-ую) (*не*)*сов перех*: ~ **по́ле** to clear a field of mines.
разми́н|ка (-ки; *gen pl* -ок) *ж* (*ног, мускулов*) loosening up; (*спортсменов*) warm-up.
размин|у́ться (-у́сь, -ёшься) *сов возв* (*не встретиться*) to miss each other; (*дать пройти*) to pass; **мы с ним ~у́лись (на 5 мину́т)** we missed each other (by 5 minutes).
размножа́|ть (-ю) *несов от* **размно́жить**
▶ **размножа́ться** *несов от* **размно́житься** ◆ *возв* (*био*) to reproduce.
размноже́ни|е (-я) *ср* (*также* био) reproduction.
размно́ж|ить (-у, -ишь; *impf* **размножа́ть**) *сов перех* to make (multiple) copies of
▶ **размно́житься** (*perf* **размножа́ться**) *сов возв* (*био*) to reproduce.
размо́ю *итп сов см* **размы́ть**.
размозж|и́ть (-у́, -и́шь) *сов перех* to smash.
размо́к|нуть (-ну, -нешь; *pt* -, -ла, -ло, *impf* **размока́ть**) *сов неперех* (*хлеб, картон*) to go soggy; (*почва*) to become sodden.
размо́лв|ка (-ки; *gen pl* -ок) *ж* squabble.
размол|о́ть (-елю́, -е́лешь; *impf* **разма́лывать**) *сов перех* to grind.
размора́жива|ть(ся) (-ю(сь)) *несов от* **разморо́зить(ся)**.
размор|и́ть (*3sg* -и́т, *3pl* -я́т, *impf* **разма́ривать**) *сов перех* (*сон, усталость*) to come over; **меня́ ~и́ло от жары́/све́жего во́здуха** the heat/fresh air has made me drowsy
▶ **размори́ться** (*impf* **разма́риваться**) *сов возв* to become drowsy.
разморо́|зить (-жу, -зишь; *impf*

размора́живать) *сов перех* to defrost

► **разморо́зиться** (*impf* **размора́живаться**) *сов возв* to defrost.

размота́|ть (**-ю**; *impf* **разма́тывать**) *сов перех* to unwind.

размыва́|ть (*3sg* **-ет**, *3pl* **-ют**) *несов от* **размы́ть**.

размыка́|ть(ся) (**-ю**) *несов от* **разомкну́ть(ся)**.

размы́|тый (**-**, **-а**, **-о**) *прил* blurred.

размы́|ть (*3sg* **-о́ет**, *3sg* **-о́ют**, *impf* **размыва́ть**) *сов перех* to wash away.

размышле́ни|е (**-я**) *ср* reflection.

размышля́|ть (**-ю**) *несов неперех*: **~** (**о** +*prp*) to think (about), reflect (on).

размягч|и́ть (**у́**, **-и́шь**; *impf* **размягча́ть**) *сов перех* (*воск, кожу, душу*) to soften; (*перен: человека*) to soften up.

размя́к|нуть (**-ну**, **-нешь**; *pt* **-**, **-ла**, **-ло**, *impf* **размяка́ть**) *сов неперех* (*глина, почва*) to soften; (*перен: от спиртного, от духоты*) to (become) mellow; (: *от похвалы*) to soften up.

раз|мя́ть (**-омну́**, **-омнёшь**) *сов от* **мять** ♦ (*impf* **размина́ть**) *перех* to loosen up

► **размя́ться** (*impf* **размина́ться**) *сов возв* to warm up.

разнаря́д|ка (**-ки**; *gen pl* **-ок**) *ж* directive.

разна́шива|ть(ся) (**-ю**) *несов от* **разноси́ть(ся)**.

разн|ести́ (**-есу́**, **-есёшь**; *pt* **-ёс**, **-есла́**, **-есло́**, *impf* **разноси́ть**) *сов перех* (*письма, посылки*) to deliver; (*еду*) to serve (up); (*тарелки, чашки*) to put out; (*тучи, обрывки бумаги*) to disperse; (*заразу, слухи*) to spread; (*разг: разбить*) to smash up; (: *раскритиковать*) to slam, pan ♦ *безл* (*разг: опухнуть*) to puff up; (: *пополнеть*) to get fat; **разноси́ть** (**~** *perf*) **что-н в кло́чья** to smash sth to pieces

► **разнести́сь** (*impf* **разноси́ться**) *сов возв* (*весть, слух, запах*) to spread; (*звон, гудок, крик*) to resound.

разнима́|ть (**-ю**) *несов от* **разня́ть**.

разниму́ *итп сов см* **разня́ть**.

ра́зниц|а (**-ы**) *ж* difference; **кака́я ~?** what difference does it make?; **~ в ве́се/в во́зрасте** weight/age difference; **без ~ы** (*разг*) it makes no difference.

разнобо́|й (**-я**) *м* (*в работе, в де́йствиях*) lack of coordination; (*в правилах*) contradictions *мн*.

разнове́с (**-а**) *м* weights *мн* (*for set of scales*).

разнови́дность (**-и**) *ж* (*био*) variety; (*людей*) type, kind.

разногла́си|е (**-я**) *ср* disagreement.

разнообра́жу *сов см* **разнообра́зить**.

разнообра́зен *прил см* **разнообра́зный**.

разнообра́зи|е (**-я**) *ср* variety; **для ~я** for a change.

разнообра́|зить (**-жу**, **-зишь**) *несов перех* to vary.

разнообра́з|ный (**-ен**, **-на**, **-но**) *прил* (*вкусы, звуки, мнения*) various; **~ые лю́ди** different sorts of people; **~ная пу́блика** a diverse

audience.

разнорабо́ч|ий (**-его**; *decl like adj*) *м* labourer (*BRIT*), laborer (*US*).

разноречи́в|ый (**-**, **-а**, **-о**) *прил* conflicting.

разноро́д|ный (**-ен**, **-на**, **-но**) *прил* (*состав*) heterogeneous; (*вещества, предметы*) of various sorts; (*впечатления*) varied.

разно́с (**-а**) *м* delivery; (*разг: выговор*) pounding.

разн|оси́ть (**-ошу́**, **-о́сишь**) *несов от* **разнести́** ♦ (*impf* **разна́шивать**) *сов перех* (*туфли, сапоги*) to break in

► **разноси́ться** *несов от* **разнести́сь** ♦ (*impf* **разна́шиваться**) *сов возв* to wear loose.

разносторо́н|ний (**-няя**, **-нее**, **-нее**; **-ен**, **-ня**, **-не**) *прил* (*деятельность*) wide-ranging; (*соглашение, договор*) multilateral; (*ум, личность*) multifaceted; **он ~ челове́к** he has a wide range of interests; **~ее образова́ние** a broad education.

ра́зность (**-и**) *ж* (*также мат*) difference.

разно́счик (**-а**) *м* (*товара*) delivery man (*мн* men); (*телеграмм*) bearer; (*инфекции*) carrier.

разноцве́тный *прил* multicoloured (*BRIT*), multicolored (*US*).

разночи́н|ец (**-ца**) *м* (*ист*) raznochints (*educated person of nonaristocratic descent in 19th century Russia*).

разношёрстный *прил* (*перен*) motley.

разношу́(сь) (*не*)*сов см* **разноси́ть(ся)**.

разноязы́чный *прил* speaking different languages.

разну́здан|ный (**-**, **-на**, **-но**) *прил* (*человек, поведение*) unruly.

ра́зный *прил* different.

разн|я́ть (**-иму́**, **-и́мешь**; *pt* **-я́л**, **-яла́**, **-яло́**, *impf* **разнима́ть**) *сов перех* (*руки, зубы*) to unclench; (*драчуно́в, боксёров*) to separate, pull apart.

разоблач|и́ть (**-у́**, **-и́шь**; *impf* **разоблача́ть**) *сов перех* to expose.

раз|обра́ть (**-беру́**, **-берёшь**; *impf* **разбира́ть**) *сов перех* (*разг: раскупить, взять*) to snatch up; (*привести в порядок*) to sort out; (*подвергнуть анализу*) to analyse (*BRIT*), analyze (*US*); (*распознать: вкус, подпись итп*) to make out; **разбира́ть** (**~** *perf*) (**на ча́сти**) (*часы, механизм итп*) to take apart; **его́ ~бира́ет смех** (*разг*) he can hardly control his laughter

► **разобра́ться** (*impf* **разбира́ться**) *сов возв*: **~ся в** +*prp* (*в вопросе, в деле*) to form an understanding of.

разобщён|ный (**-**, **-на**, **-но**) *прил* isolated.

ра́зовый *прил*: **~ биле́т** single (*BRIT*) *или* one-way ticket.

разовью́(сь) *итп сов см* **разви́ть(ся)**.

раз|огна́ть (**-гоню́**, **-го́нишь**; *pt* **-огна́л**, **-огнала́**, **-огна́ло**, *impf* **разгоня́ть**) *сов перех* (*толпу, демонстра́цию*) to break up; (*разг: организа́цию*) to purge; (: *бездельников, тунея́дцев*) to come down on; (*тучи, тума́н*) to

disperse; (перен: сон, тоску, мысли) to drive away; (машину, самолёт) to increase the speed of
▶ **разогна́ться** (impf **разгоня́ться**) сов возв to build up speed.
разогну́ть (-ý, -ёшь; impf **разгиба́ть**) сов перех (спину) to straighten up; (проволоку, скрепку) to straighten out
▶ **разогну́ться** (impf **разгиба́ться**) сов возв to straighten up.
разогре́ть (-ю; impf **разгрева́ть**) сов перех (чайник, суп) to heat
▶ **разогре́ться** (impf **разгрева́ться**) сов возв (суп) to heat up; (человек, двигатель) to warm up.
разоде́тый (-, -a, -o) прил overdressed.
разоде́ться (-нусь, -нешься) сов возв (разг) to get dressed up.
раз|одра́ть (-деру́, -дерёшь; impf **раздира́ть**) сов перех to tear up.
разожгу́ итп сов см **разже́чь**.
разожму́(сь) итп сов см **разжа́ть(ся)**.
разозл|и́ть (-ю, -и́шь) сов от **злить** ♦ перех to anger
▶ **разозли́ться** сов от **зли́ться** ♦ возв to get angry.
разойти́сь (как **идти́**; см **Table 18**; impf **расходи́ться**) сов возв (гости) to leave; (облака, туман, толпа) to disperse; (запасы, деньги) to run out; (тираж) to sell out; (не встретиться) to miss each other; (дать дорогу) to pass each other; (супруги) to split up; (прекратить дружбу) to part company; (шов, крепления) to come apart; (перен: мнения, взгляды) to diverge; (: разг: дать волю себе) to get going; **на э́той доро́ге не** ~ the road is too narrow for passing.
разолью́(сь) итп сов см **разли́ть(ся)**.
ра́зом нареч (разг: все вместе) all at once; (: в один приём) all in one go.
разомкн|у́ть (-ý, -ёшь; impf **размыка́ть**) сов перех (цепь, крепление) to unfasten; (пальцы) to uncurl; ~ (perf) **ру́ки** to let go (of each other's hands)
▶ **разомкну́ться** (impf **размыка́ться**) сов возв (цепь, крепление) to come unfastened; (пальцы) to open.
разомну́(сь) итп сов см **размя́ть(ся)**.
разопью́ итп сов см **распи́ть**.
разорв|а́ть (-ý, -ёшь; pt -а́л, -ала́, -а́ло) сов от **рвать** ♦ (impf **разрыва́ть**) перех (письмо, бумагу) to tear или rip up; (конверт, обёртку) to tear или rip open; (одежду) to tear, rip; (перен: знакомство, связь) to break off; (: договор, контракт) to break ♦ безл (ногу, руку) to be blown off; (танк, стену) to be blown up
▶ **разорва́ться** сов от **рва́ться** ♦ (impf **разрыва́ться**) возв (одежда) to tear, rip;

(верёвка, цепь) to break; (связь, знакомство) to be severed; (снаряд, ракета) to explode.
разоре́ни|е (-я) ср (см глаг) plundering; impoverishment; ruin.
разори́тел|ьный (-ен, -ьна, -ьно) прил ruinous.
разор|и́ть (-ю́, -и́шь; impf **разоря́ть**) сов перех (деревню, гнездо) to plunder; (семью, население) to impoverish; (: компанию, страну) to ruin
▶ **разори́ться** (impf **разоря́ться**) сов возв to go to rack and ruin; (человек) to become impoverished; (разг): ~**ся на** +acc (потратить деньги) to splash out on.
разоружа́|ть(ся) (-ю(сь)) несов от **разоружи́ть(ся)**.
разоруже́ни|е (-я) ср (противника, пленных) disarming; (политический процесс) disarmament.
разоруж|и́ть (-ý, -и́шь; impf **разоружа́ть**) сов перех (также перен) to disarm
▶ **разоружи́ться** (impf **разоружа́ться**) сов возв to disarm.
разоря́|ть(ся) (-ю(сь)) несов от **разори́ть(ся)**.
разо|сла́ть (-шлю́, -шлёшь; impf **рассыла́ть**) сов перех to send out.
разостла́ть (**расстелю́, рассте́лешь**) несов = **расстели́ть**.
разотру́(сь) итп сов см **растере́ть(ся)**.
разочарова́ни|е (-я) ср disappointment; (потеря веры): ~ **в** +prp (в друге, в идеалах) disenchantment with.
разочаро́ван|ный (-, -на, -но) прил disappointed; (-, -a, -o): ~ **в** +prp disenchanted with.
разочар|ова́ть (-ýю; impf **разочаро́вывать**) сов перех to disappoint
▶ **разочарова́ться** (impf **разочаро́вываться**) сов возв: ~**ся в** +prp to become disenchanted with.
разошёлся итп сов см **разойти́сь**.
разошлю́ итп сов см **разосла́ть**.
разошью́ итп сов см **расши́ть**.
разрабо́та|ть (-ю; impf **разраба́тывать**) сов перех (план, технологию, теорию) to develop; (месторождение) to exploit.
разрабо́т|ка (-ки) ж (см глаг) development; exploitation; (gen pl -ок; обычно мн: научные) groundwork ед; см также **разрабо́тки**.
разрабо́т|ки (-ок) мн (ГЕО): **га́зовые** ~ gas fields мн; **нефтяны́е** ~ oilfields мн; **методи́ческие** ~ guidelines мн.
разра́внива|ть (-ю) несов от **разровня́ть**.
разраз|и́ться (-жу́сь, -зи́шься; impf **разража́ться**) сов возв (гроза, катастрофа) to break out; ~ (perf) **аплодисме́нтами/сме́хом** to break into applause/laughter.
разр|асти́сь (3sg -асте́тся, 3pl -асту́тся, pt -о́сся, -осла́сь, -осло́сь, impf **разраста́ться**)

сов воз (*лес, растение*) to spread; (*город, движение*) to grow.

разреве́|ться (-у́сь, -ёшься) *сов воз* (*разг*) to start bawling.

разрежё́нный (-, -а́, -о́) *прил* rarified.

разре́жу *сов см* **разре́зать**.

разре́з (-а) *м* (*на ю́бке*) slit; (*ГЕОМ*) section; **в ~е** +*gen* in the context of; ~ **глаз** the shape of one's eyes.

разре́|зать (-жу, -жешь) *сов от* **ре́зать**.

разреза́|ть (-ю) *несов перех* to cut up.

разрекла́ми́р|овать (-ую) *сов перех* to publicize.

разреша́|ть (-ю) *несов от* **разреши́ть**

▸ **разреша́ться** *несов от* **разреши́ться** ♦ *неперех* (*допуска́ться*) to be allowed *или* permitted; **здесь не ~ется кури́ть** smoking is not permitted here.

разреше́ни|е (-я) *ср* (*де́йствие*) authorization; (*позволе́ние, пра́во*) permission, authorization; (*докуме́нт*) permit; (*реше́ние*) resolution; **с Ва́шего ~я** with your permission.

разреш|и́ть (-у́, -и́шь; *impf* **разреша́ть**) *сов перех* (*реши́ть*) to resolve; (*позво́лить*) ~ **кому́-н** +*infin* to allow *или* permit sb to do; ~**и́те** +*infin* ... may I ...; ~? may I come in?; ~**и́те пройти́** let me through; **разреша́ть** (~ *perf*) **фильм/кни́гу** to pass a film for screening/book for publication

▸ **разреши́ться** (*impf* **разреша́ться**) *сов воз* to be resolved.

разрис|ова́ть (-у́ю; *impf* **разрисо́вывать**) *сов перех* (*карандашо́м*) to draw all over; (*кра́ской*) to paint all over.

разровня́|ть (-ю) *сов от* **ровня́ть** ♦ (*impf* **разра́внивать**) *перех* to level.

разро́знен|ный (-, -на, -но) *прил* (*де́йствия, си́лы*) uncoordinated; (*колле́кция, серви́з*) made up of odd parts; (*тома́*) odd.

разро́сся *итп сов см* **разрасти́сь**.

разр|уби́ть (-ублю́, -у́бишь; *impf* **разруба́ть**) *сов перех* to chop in two; **разруба́ть** (~ *perf*) **на куски́** to chop up.

разрумя́н|ить(ся) (-ю(сь)) *сов от* **румя́нить(ся)**.

разру́х|а (-и) *ж* ruin; **в стране́** ~ the country is in ruins.

разруша́|ть(ся) (-ю(сь)) *несов от* **разру́шить(ся)**.

разруши́тельный (-ен, -ьна, -ьно) *прил* destructive.

разру́ш|ить (-у, -ишь; *impf* **разруша́ть**) *сов перех* to destroy; (*пла́ны, жизнь*) to ruin

▸ **разру́шиться** (*impf* **разруша́ться**) *сов воз* (*см перех*) to be destroyed; to be ruined.

разры́в (-а) *м* (*дипломати́ческих отноше́ний, свя́зей*) severance; (*провода́, це́пи*) breaking; (*разо́рванная часть*) tear; (*снаря́да, грана́ты*) explosion; (*несоотве́тствие, промежу́ток вре́мени*) gap; **с ~ом в 10 лет** with a gap of 10 years; **разры́в се́рдца** (*МЕД*) heart attack.

разрыва́|ть(ся) (-ю(сь)) *несов от* **разорва́ть(ся)**.

разрыхл|и́ть (-ю́, -и́шь) *сов от* **рыхли́ть**.

разря́|д (-а) *м* (*люде́й, расте́ний*) class; (*спорти́вный*) grade; (*профессиона́льный*) status; (*ФИЗ*) discharge.

разря|ди́ть (-жу́, -ди́шь; *impf* **разряжа́ть**) *сов перех* (*ружьё, батаре́йку*) to discharge; **разряжа́ть** (~ *perf*) **обстано́вку** to diffuse the situation

▸ **разряди́ться** (*impf* **разряжа́ться**) *сов воз* (*перен*) to become less tense.

разря́|дка (-ки; *gen pl* -ок) *ж* release, outlet; (*в те́ксте*) spacing; ~ (**междунаро́дной**) **напряжённости** détente.

разряжа́|ть(ся) (-ю(сь)) *несов от* **разряди́ть(ся)**.

разряжу́(сь) *сов см* **разряди́ть(ся)**.

разубе|ди́ть (-жу́, -ди́шь; *impf* **разубежда́ть**) *сов перех*: ~ **кого́-н** (**в** +*prp*) to dissuade sb (from).

разува́|ть(ся) (-ю(сь)) *несов от* **разу́ть(ся)**.

разуве́р|иться (-юсь, -ишься; *impf* **разуверя́ться**) *сов воз*: ~ **в** +*prp* to lose faith in.

разузна́|ть (-ю; *impf* **разузнава́ть**) *сов перех* (*ра́зе*) to find out.

разукра́|сить (-шу, -сишь; *impf* **разукра́шивать**) *сов перех* to decorate.

ра́зум (-а) *м* reason.

разуме́ть *прил см* **разу́мный**.

разуме́|ться (*3sg* -ется) *сов воз*: **под э́тим ~ется, что** ... by this is meant that ...; (*само́ собо́й*) ~ется that goes without saying; **он, ~ется, не знал об э́том** it goes without saying that he knew nothing about it.

разу́м|ный (-ен, -на, -но) *прил* intelligent; (*посту́пок, реше́ние, до́вод*) reasonable.

разу́т|ый (-, -а, -о) *прил* (*без обу́ви*) barefoot; (*разг: нужда́ющийся в обу́ви*) shoeless.

разу́|ть (-ю; *impf* **разува́ть**) *сов перех*: ~ **кого́-н** to take sb's shoes off

▸ **разу́ться** (*impf* **разува́ться**) *сов воз* to take one's shoes off.

разуч|и́ть (-у́, -у́чишь; *impf* **разу́чивать**) *сов перех* to learn

▸ **разучи́ться** (*impf* **разу́чиваться**) *сов воз*: ~**ся** +*infin* to forget how to do.

разъеда́|ть (*3sg* -ет, *3pl* -ют) *несов от* **разъе́сть** ♦ *перех* (*перен: ду́шу*) to eat away at

▸ **разъеда́ться** *несов от* **разъе́сться**.

разъе́дешься *итп сов см* **разъе́хаться**.

разъеди́м(ся) *сов см* **разъе́сть(ся)**.

разъедин|и́ть (-ю́, -и́шь; *impf* **разъединя́ть**) *сов перех* (*провода́, телефо́н*) to disconnect; (*друзе́й, люби́мых*) to separate.

разъеди́те(сь) *сов см* **разъе́сть(ся)**.

разъеду́сь *итп сов см* **разъе́хаться**.

разъедя́т(ся) *сов см* **разъе́сть(ся)**.

разъе́зд (-а) *м* (*госте́й*) departure; (*для поездо́в*) siding (*BRIT*), sidetrack (*US*); *см также*

разъе́зды.
разъе́зд|ы (-ов) *мн* (*поездки*) travel *ед*; **он всё
вре́мя в ~ах** he does a lot of travelling.
разъезжа́|ть (-ю) *несов неперех* (*по делам, по
городам*) to travel around; (*кататься: на
тройке, на автомобиле*) to ride about; ~ (*impf*)
по гостя́м to go around visiting friends
▸ **разъезжа́ться** *несов от* **разъе́хаться**.
разъе́сть (*как* есть; *см* **Table 15**; *impf*
разъеда́ть) *сов перех* to corrode
▸ **разъе́сться** (*impf* **разъеда́ться**) *сов возв* (*разг*) to get fat.
разъе́|хаться (*как* е́хать; *см* **Table 19**; *impf*
разъезжа́ться) *сов возв* to leave; (*разг*: лыжи,
ноги на льду*) to slide apart; **она́ ~халась с
му́жем/ма́терью** she doesn't live with her
husband/mother any more; **мы с ни́ми ~хались
в темноте́** we missed each other in the darkness;
маши́ны не могли́ ~ the cars couldn't get past
each other.
разъе́шь(ся) *сов см* **разъе́сть(ся)**.
разъярённый *прил* (*зверь, человек, лицо*)
furious; (*перен: река, стихия*) raging.
разъяр|и́ть (-ю́, -и́шь; *impf* **разъяря́ть**) *сов
перех* (*толпу, человека*) to infuriate, enrage;
(*зверя*) to provoke
▸ **разъяри́ться** (*impf* **разъяря́ться**) *сов возв* to
become infuriated.
разъясне́ни|е (-я) *ср* clarification.
разъясн|и́ть (-ю́, -и́шь; *impf* **разъясня́ть**) *сов
перех* to clarify
▸ **разъясни́ться** (*impf* **разъясня́ться**) *сов возв*
to be clarified.
разыгра́|ть (-ю; *impf* **разы́грывать**) *сов перех*
(*МУЗ, СПОРТ*) to play; (*сцену*) to act out; (*в
лотерею, по жребию*) to raffle; (*разг:
подшутить*) to play a joke *или* trick on
▸ **разыгра́ться** (*impf* **разы́грываться**) *сов возв*
(*увлечься игрой*) to get carried away with one's
game; (*начать лучше играть*) to get going;
(*перед концертом*) to warm up; (*перен: буря*)
to rage; (*драма, сражение*) to unfold; **у меня́
~лась мигре́нь** I had a nasty migraine; **по́сле
прогу́лки у него́ ~лся аппети́т** the walk gave
him a big appetite.
разы|ска́ть (-щу́, -щешь; *impf* **разы́скивать**)
сов перех to find
▸ **разыска́ться** (*impf* **разы́скиваться**) *сов возв*
to turn up.
РАИС *ср сокр* (= *Росси́йское аге́нтство
интеллектуа́льной со́бственности*) copyright
protection agency.
рай (-я; *loc sg* -ю́) *м* (*также перен*) paradise.
райко́м (-а) *м сокр* (*ИСТ* = *райо́нный комите́т*)
district committee (*of Communist Party or
Komsomol*).
райо́н (-а) *м* region; (*ПОЛИТ*) district.
райо́нный *прил* district *опред*.

ра́йск|ий (-ая, -ое, -ие) *прил* (*также перен*)
heavenly.
райце́нтр (-а) *м сокр* (= *райо́нный центр*) main
town (*of district*).
рак (-а) *м* (*ЗООЛ: речной*) crayfish (*мн* crayfish);
(: *морской*) crab; (*МЕД*) cancer; (*созвездие*): **Р~**
Cancer.
раке́т|а (-ы) *ж* (*также космос*) rocket; (*ВОЕН*)
missile; (*судно*) hydrofoil.
раке́т|ка (-ки; *gen pl* -ок) *ж* (*СПОРТ*) racket;
пе́рвая ~ (*перен*) the top player.
раке́тный *прил* (*также космос*) rocket *опред*;
(*ВОЕН*) missile *опред*; **раке́тное ору́жие** (*ВОЕН*)
missiles *мн*.
раке́ток *сущ см* **раке́тка**.
ра́ковин|а (-ы) *ж* (*ЗООЛ*) shell; (*для умывания*)
sink; **ушна́я ~** aural cavity.
ра́ковый *прил* (*ЗООЛ, КУЛИН*) crab *опред*; (*МЕД*)
cancer *опред*; **ра́ковая о́пухоль** malignant
tumour.
ра́лли *ср нескл* (*СПОРТ*) rally.
ра́м|а (-ы) *ж* frame; (*АВТ*) chassis; **двойны́е ~ы**
double glazing.
рамаза́н (-а) *м* Ramadan.
ра́м|ка (-ки; *gen pl* -ок) *ж* (*для фотографии, для
картины*) frame; (*текста, рисунка*) border; *см
также* **ра́мки**.
ра́м|ки (-ок) *мн*: ~ +*gen* (*рассказа, разговора,
обязанностей*) framework *ед* of; (*закона,
устава*) limits *мн* of; **в ~ках** +*gen* (*закона,
приличия*) within the bounds of; (*дискуссии,
переговоров*) within the framework of; **за
~ками** +*gen* beyond the bounds of; **держа́ть**
(*impf*) **себя́ в ~ках** to control o.s.
ра́мп|а (-ы) *ж* (*ТЕАТР*): **огни́ ~ы** footlights *мн*.
РАН *м сокр* (= *Росси́йская акаде́мия нау́к*)
Russian Academy of Sciences.
ра́н|а (-ы) *ж* (*также перен*) wound.
Рангу́н (-а) *м* Rangoon.
ра́нен|ая (-ой; *decl like adj*) *ж см* **ра́неный**.
ране́ни|е (-я) *ср* injury.
ра́нен|ый *прил* injured; (*ВОЕН*) wounded ♦ (-ого;
decl like adj) *м* injured person (*мн* people); (*ВОЕН*)
wounded person (*мн* people).
ра́н|ец (-ца) *м* (*школьный*) satchel; (*солдатский,
походный*) backpack.
рани́м|ый (-, -а, -о) *прил* vulnerable.
ра́н|ить (-ю, -ишь) *(не)сов перех* (*также перен*)
to wound; ~ (*impf/perf*) **кого́-н в ру́ку/но́гу** to
wound sb in the arm/leg; ~ (*impf/perf*) **кому́-н
ду́шу** to wound sb (*fig*).
ра́нн|ий (-яя, -ее, -ие) *прил* early.
ра́но *нареч* early ♦ *как сказ* it's early; **ещё ~** (*о
раннем времени*) it's still early; ~ **де́лать** (*impf*)
вы́воды it's too early to draw conclusions; **он
жени́лся/у́мер ~** he married/died young; ~ **и́ли
по́здно** sooner or later.
ра́нца *итп сущ см* **ра́нец**.

ран|ь (-и) ж (*разг*) early morning.

ра́ньше *сравн нареч от* **ра́но** ♦ *нареч* (*прежде*) before; (*снача́ла*) earlier ♦ *предл*: ~ +*gen* before; ~ **он жил в го́роде** he used to live in the city; ~ **поду́май, пото́м отвеча́й** think before you answer; ~ **вре́мени** (*радоваться итп*) too soon; ~ **ве́чера мы не зако́нчим** we won't finish before the evening; **он зако́нчил ~ всех** he finished before everybody else.

папи́р|а (-ы) ж foil (*for fencing*).

ра́порт (-а) м report; **подава́ть** (**пода́ть** *perf*) ~ to submit a report.

рапорт|ова́ть (-у́ю; *perf* **отрапортова́ть**) (*не*)*сов неперех*: ~ (**кому́-н о** +*prp*) to report back (to sb on).

рас- *префикс см* **раз-**.

ра́с|а (-ы) ж race.

раси́зм (-а) м racism.

раси́ст (-а) м racist.

раси́ст|ка (-ки; *gen pl* -ок) ж см **раси́ст**.

раси́стский (-ая, -ое, -ие) *прил* racist *опред*.

раска́ива|ться (-юсь) *несов от* **раска́яться**.

раскалённый *прил* burning hot.

раскал|и́ть (-ю́, -и́шь; *impf* **раскаля́ть**) *сов перех* to bring to a high temperature

▸ **раскали́ться** (*impf* **раскаля́ться**) *сов возв* to get very hot.

раска́лыва|ть (-ю) *несов от* **расколо́ть**

▸ **раска́лываться** *несов от* **расколо́ться** ♦ *возв*: **у меня́** ~**ется голова́** I have a splitting headache.

раскаля́|ть(ся) (-ю(сь)) *несов от* **раскали́ть(ся)**.

раска́пыва|ть (-ю) *несов от* **раскопа́ть**.

раска́рмлива|ть (-ю) *несов от* **раскорми́ть**.

раска́т (-а) м (*обычно мн*: *грома, смеха*) peal.

раската́|ть (-ю; *impf* **раска́тывать**) *сов перех* (*ковёр, рулон*) to unroll; (*тесто*) to roll out; (*дорогу, горку*) to flatten (out); (*брёвна, шары*) to send rolling (*in different directions*).

раска́тист|ый (-, -а, -о) *прил* (*гром, хохот*) booming.

раска́тыва|ть (-ю) *несов от* **раската́ть**.

раскача́|ть (-ю; *impf* **раска́чивать**) *сов перех* to swing; (*качели, ребёнка*) to push

▸ **раскача́ться** (*impf* **раска́чиваться**) *сов возв* (*лодка*) to rock; (*качели*) to swing; (*разг*: *медлить: человек*) to dither.

раска́яни|е (-я) *ср* repentance.

раска́|яться (-юсь; *impf* **раска́иваться**) *сов возв*: ~ (**в** +*prp*) to repent (of).

расквита́|ться (-юсь) *сов возв* (*разг*): ~ +*instr* (*с кредиторами*) to settle up with; (*перен: с врагом, с обидчиком*) to settle a score with.

раскида́|ть (-ю; *impf* **раски́дывать**) *сов перех* to throw around, scatter; **жизнь** ~**ла их по всему́ све́ту** life has scattered them across the globe.

раски́дист|ый (-, -а, -о) *прил* (*дерево*) spreading.

раски́дыва|ть (-ю) *несов от* **раскида́ть**,

раски́нуть.

раски́|нуть (-у, -ешь; *impf* **раски́дывать**) *сов перех* (*руки*) to throw open; (*ковёр, сети*) to spread out; (*лагерь*) to set up; (*палатку, шатёр*) to pitch; ~ (*perf*) ~ **что-н умо́м или мозга́ми** (*разг*) to think sth over

▸ **раски́нуться** (*impf* **раски́дываться**) *сов возв* to stretch out.

раскла́д|ка (-и) ж (*действие*) arranging; (*соотношение: сил, средств*) balance.

раскладно́й *прил* folding *опред*.

расклад|у́шка (-ки; *gen pl* -ек) ж (*разг*) camp bed (*BRIT*), cot (*US*).

раскла́дыва|ть(ся) (-ю(сь)) *несов от* **разложи́ть(ся)**.

раскла́ня|ться (-юсь; *impf* **раскла́ниваться**) *сов возв* (*актёр, выступающий*) to take a bow; (*при встрече, при расставании*) to bow.

раскле́|ить (-ю, -ишь; *impf* **раскле́ивать**) *сов перех* (*конверт*) to unglue; (*плакаты, афиши, рекламы*) to paste up

▸ **раскле́иться** (*impf* **раскле́иваться**) *сов возв* to come unstuck; (*перен: разг: свадьба, дело*) to fall through; **я совсе́м** ~**ился** (*разг*) I feel (like) a complete wreck.

раско́ван|ный (-, -на, -но) *прил* relaxed.

раско́л (-а) м (*организации, движения*) split; (*РЕЛ*) schism.

раскол|о́ть (-о́лю, -о́лешь; *impf* **раска́лывать**) *сов перех* (*дрова, страну, движение*) to split; (*лёд, орех*) to crack

▸ **расколо́ться** (*impf* **раска́лываться**) *сов возв* (*полено, орех*) to split open; (*перен: движение, организация*) to be split.

раскопа́|ть (-ю; *impf* **раска́пывать**) *сов перех* (*также перен*) to dig up.

раско́п|ка (-ки; *gen pl* -ок) ж (*действие*) excavation; см также **раско́пки**.

раско́п|ки (-ок) *мн* (*работы*) excavations *мн*; (*место*) (archaeological) dig *ед*.

раскорм|и́ть (-ормлю́, -о́рмишь; *impf* **раска́рмливать**) *сов перех* to overfeed.

раско́с|ый *прил* (*глаза*) slanting.

раскоше́л|иться (-юсь, -ишься; *impf* **раскоше́ливаться**) *сов возв* (*разг*): ~ (**на** +*acc*) to fork out (for).

раскра́ива|ть (-ю) *несов от* **раскро́йть**.

раскра́|сить (-шу, -сишь; *impf* **раскра́шивать**) *сов перех* (*рисунок, картинку*) to colour (*BRIT*), color (*US*); (*вазу, поделку*) to paint.

раскра́с|ка (-и) ж (*см глаг*) colouring (*BRIT*), coloring (*US*); painting; (*цветовая гамма*) colours *мн* (*BRIT*), colors *мн* (*US*).

раскрасне́|ться (-юсь) *сов возв* to go red.

раскра́шива|ть (-ю) *несов от* **раскра́сить**.

раскра́шу *сов см* **раскра́сить**.

раскритик|ова́ть (-у́ю) *сов перех* to criticize severely.

раскро́|ить (-ю́, -и́шь; *impf* **раскра́ивать**) *сов перех* to cut.

раскр|ути́ть (-учу́, -у́тишь; *impf* **раскру́чивать**)

сов перех (что-н сплетённое) to untwist; *(что-н закрученное)* to unscrew; *(интригу, тайну)* to unravel.

раскры́ть (-о́ю, -о́ешь; *impf* **раскрыва́ть**) *сов перех* to open; *(перен)* to discover; **раскрыва́ть** (~ *perf*) **свои́ ка́рты** *(перен)* to show one's hand

▶ **раскры́ться** (*impf* **раскрыва́ться**) *сов возв* to open; *(перен: характер, дарование)* to be revealed; ~**ся** (*perf*) **пе́ред кем-н** to open up to sb.

раскупи́ть (-уплю́, -у́пишь; *impf* **раскупа́ть**) *сов перех* to buy up.

раскуси́ть (-ушу́, -у́сишь) *сов перех (разг: понять)* to suss out; (*impf* **раску́сывать**; *яблоко, конфету*) to bite into.

ра́совый *прил* racial.

распа́д (-а) *м* break-up, collapse; *(хим)* decomposition.

распада́ться (*3sg* -ется, *3pl* -ются) *несов от* **распа́сться ♦** *возв (состоять из частей)*: ~ **на** +*acc* to be divided into.

распадётся *итп сов см* **распа́сться**.

распа́рывать (-ю; *perf* **распоро́ть**) *несов перех* = **поро́ть**.

распа́сться (*3sg* -дётся, *3pl* -ду́тся, *impf* **распада́ться**) *сов возв* to break up; *(вещество, молекула)* to decompose; **распада́ться** (~ *perf*) **на ча́сти** to fall apart.

распаха́ть (-ашу́, -а́шешь; *impf* **распа́хивать**) *сов перех* to plough (*BRIT*) *или* plow (*US*) up.

распахну́ть (-у́, -ёшь; *impf* **распа́хивать**) *сов перех* to throw open; ~ (*perf*) **ду́шу** to bare one's soul

▶ **распахну́ться** (*impf* **распа́хиваться**) *сов возв (дверь, шуба)* to fly open; *(поля, равнина)* to open out.

распашо́нка (-ки; *gen pl* -ок) *ж cotton baby top without buttons.*

распашу́ *итп сов см* **распаха́ть**.

распева́ть (-ю) *несов неперех (разг)* to sing loudly ♦ *перех (разг)*: ~ **пе́сню** to sing away.

распелена́ть (-ю; *impf* **распелёнывать**) *сов перех* to unwrap.

распеча́тать (-ю; *impf* **распеча́тывать**) *сов перех (письмо, пакет)* to open; *(помещение)* to unseal; *(размножить)* to print off; *(КОМП)* to print out.

распеча́тка (-ки; *gen pl* -ок) *ж (доклада)* print-out; *(КОМП)* hard copy.

распеча́тывать (-ю) *несов от* **распеча́тать**.

распива́ть (-ю) *несов от* **распи́ть**.

распили́ть (-илю́, -и́лишь; *impf* **распи́ливать**) *сов перех* to saw up.

распина́ть (-ю) *несов от* **распя́ть**

▶ **распина́ться** *несов возв (разг)*: ~**ся пе́ред** +*instr* to go out of one's way for.

расписа́ние (-я) *ср* timetable.

расписа́ть (-ишу́, -и́шешь; *impf* **распи́сывать**)

сов перех (дела, мероприятия, расходы итп) to arrange; *(день, месяц)* to fill up; *(стены, шкату́лку, вазу)* to paint; *(перен: разг: будущее, приключения)* to paint a rosy picture of; *(разг: жениха и невесту)* to marry (*in registry office*)

▶ **расписа́ться** (*impf* **распи́сываться**) *сов возв (поставить подпись)* to sign one's name; *(перен)*: ~**ся в** +*prp (в невежестве, в бесси́лии)* to acknowledge; *(разг)*: ~**ся (с** +*instr)* (*зарегистрировать брак*) to get married (to) (*in registry office*); **распи́сываться** (~**ся** *perf*) **в получе́нии чего́-н** to sign for sth.

распи́ска (-ки; *gen pl* -ок) *ж (о получе́нии де́нег)* receipt; *(гара́нтия)* warrant; **принима́ть** (**приня́ть** *perf*) **что-н под** ~**ку** to sign for sth.

расписно́й *прил* painted.

распи́сок *сущ см* **распи́ска**.

распи́сыва(ть)ся (-ю(сь)) *несов от* **расписа́ть(ся)**.

распи́ть (**разопью́, разопьёшь**; *pt* -и́л, -ила́, -и́ло, *impf* **распива́ть**) *сов перех (разг)* to get through.

распиха́ть (-ю; *impf* **распи́хивать**) *сов перех (разг: толпу, о́чередь)* to push through; (: *вещи, бумаги*): ~ **по** +*dat* to stuff into.

распишу́(сь) *итп сов см* **расписа́ть(ся)**.

распла́вить (-лю, -ишь) *сов от* **пла́вить ♦** (*impf* **расплавля́ть**) *перех* to melt

▶ **распла́виться** *сов от* **пла́виться ♦** (*impf* **расплавля́ться**) *возв* to melt.

распла́каться (-чусь, -чешься) *сов возв* to burst into tears.

распласта́ть (-ю; *impf* **распла́стывать**) *сов перех (крылья, руки)* to spread

▶ **распласта́ться** (*impf* **распла́стываться**) *сов возв* to sprawl out.

распла́та (-ы) *ж* payment; *(перен)* retribution; **час** ~**ы** *(перен)* the day of reckoning.

распла́титься (-ачу́сь, -а́тишься; *impf* **распла́чиваться**) *сов возв*: ~ (**с** +*instr)* (*с продавцо́м, с кредито́ром*) to pay; *(перен: с предателем, с негодя́ем)* to get even (with); **распла́чиваться** (~ *perf*) **за оши́бку/преступле́ние** to pay for a mistake/crime.

распла́чусь *итп сов см* **распла́каться**.

расплёл(ся) *итп сов см* **расплести́(сь)**.

распле́скать (-ещу́, -е́щешь; *impf* **расплёскивать**) *сов перех* to spill

▶ **расплеска́ться** (*impf* **расплёскиваться**) *сов возв* to spill.

расплести́ (-ету́, -етёшь; *pt* -ёл, -ела́, -ело́, *impf* **расплета́ть**) *сов перех (плётку)* to untwist; *(косу)* to unplait

▶ **расплести́сь** (*impf* **расплета́ться**) *сов возв* to come untwisted; *(коса)* to come out.

расплещу́(сь) *сов см* **расплеска́ть(ся)**.

расплод|и́ться (*3sg* **-и́тся**, *3pl* **-я́тся**) *сов от*
плоди́ться.
расплыва́|ться (**-юсь**) *несов от* **распль́ться**.
расплыву́сь *итп сов см* **распль́ться**.
распль́вчат|ый (**-**, **-а**, **-о**) *прил* (*рисунок,
очертания*) blurred; (*перен: мысли, ответ,
намёк*) vague.
распль́|ться (**-ву́сь**, **-вёшься**; *pt* **-лся**, **-ла́сь**,
-лось, *impf* **расплыва́ться**) *сов возв* (*утки
итп*) to swim off; (*чернила, краски*) to run;
(*нефть, дым*) to diffuse; (*облака*) to disperse;
(*перен: фигуры, силуэт*) to be blurred; (*разг:
располнеть*) to spread; (: *широко улыбнуться*)
to beam; **он ~лся** *или* **его́ лицо́ ~лось в
улы́бке** a smile spread across his face.
расплю́щ|ить (**-у**, **-ишь**; *impf* **расплю́щивать**)
сов перех to crush.
распну́ *итп сов см* **распя́ть**.
распого́д|иться (*3sg* **-ится**) *сов возв* to clear up
(*weather*).
распозна́|ть (**-ю**; *impf* **распознава́ть**) *сов перех*
to identify.
располага́|ть (**-ю**) *несов от* **расположи́ть** ♦
неперех: ~ **+instr** (*данными, временем итп*) to
have at one's disposal, have available; **Вы
мо́жете мной ~** I am entirely at your disposal
▸ **располага́ться** *несов от* **расположи́ться** ♦
возв (*находиться*) to be situated *или* located.
располага́ющ|ий (**-ая**, **-ее**, **-ие**) *прил*
welcoming.
располз|ти́сь (*3sg* **-ётся**, *3pl* **-у́тся**, *impf*
располза́ться) *сов возв* to crawl off; (*туман,
плющ*) to spread; (*пятно, строчки*) to smudge;
(*разг: ткань, одежда*) to become threadbare.
расположе́ни|е (**-я**) *ср* (*действие: предметов*)
arranging; (*место: отряда, лагеря*) location;
(*комнат*) layout; (*мебели*) arrangement;
(*симпатия*) disposition; ~ **ду́ха** mood; **я
испы́тываю к нему́ ~** I am well-disposed
towards him; **у меня́ нет сейча́с ~я е́хать туда́**
I'm not in the mood for going there right now.
расположен|ный (**-**, **-а**, **-о**) *прил*: ~ **к** +*dat* (*к
челове́ку*) well-disposed towards; (*к инфекции,
к просту́де*) susceptible to; ~ **+infin** (*читать,
работать, играть*) in the mood for doing; **я не
расположе́н э́то сейча́с обсужда́ть** I am not in
the mood to discuss it right now.
распол|ожи́ть (**-ожу́**, **-о́жишь**; *impf*
располага́ть) *сов перех* (*мебель, вещи итп*) to
arrange; (*отряд*) to station; (*лагерь*) to set up;
располага́ть (**~** *perf*) **кого́-н к себе́** to win sb
over
▸ **расположи́ться** (*impf* **располага́ться**) *сов
возв* (*человек: в кресле, под деревом итп*) to
settle down; (*отряд*) to position itself.
распор|о́ть (**-орю́**, **-о́решь**) *сов от* **поро́ть**.
распоряди́тель (**-я**) *м* (*комм*) manager;
(*церемониала, вечера*) organizer.
распоряди́тельный *прил* (*хозяйка,
начальник*) efficient; **распоряди́тельный
дире́ктор** managing director;

распоряди́тельный комите́т management
committee.
распоряд|и́ться (**-жу́сь**, **-ди́шься**; *impf*
распоряжа́ться) *сов возв* to give out
instructions; (**+infin**; **сделать что-н**) to order to
do; (**+instr**; *деньгами, ресурсами*) to manage; **он
~ди́лся, чтобы все яви́лись к шести́** he
instructed everyone to be there by six (o'clock).
распоря́д|ок (**-ка**) *м* routine; **пра́вила
вну́треннего ~ка** regulations *мн*.
распоряжа́|ться (**-юсь**) *несов от*
распоряди́ться ♦ *возв*: ~ (**+instr**) to be in
charge (of).
распоряже́ни|е (**-я**) *ср* (*управление*)
management; (*приказ*) instructions *мн*; (*указ*)
enactment; **ба́нковское ~** banker's order; **в ~**
+gen at sb's/sth's disposal; **предоставля́ть
(предоста́вить** *perf*) **что-н в чьё-н ~** to place
sth at sb's disposal; **я в Ва́шем ~и** I am at your
disposal.
распоряжу́сь *сов см* **распоряди́ться**.
распоя́с|аться (**-юсь**; *impf* **распоя́сываться**)
сов возв (*перен: разг*) to get cocky.
распра́в|а (**-ы**) *ж* reprisals *мн*.
распра́в|ить (**-лю**, **-ишь**; *impf* **расправля́ть**)
сов перех (*складки, смятую бумагу*) to
straighten out; (*грудь, плечи*) to straighten (up);
(*крылья*) to spread
▸ **распра́виться** (*impf* **расправля́ться**) *сов
возв* (*см перех*) to be straightened out; to
straighten up; to spread; (*парус*) to unfurl;
(*наказать*): ~**ся с** +*instr* (*с демонстрантами, с
забастовщиками*) to take reprisals against;
(*перен: разг: с делами, с обедом итп*) to be
finished with.
распределе́ни|е (**-я**) *ср* distribution; (*после
института*) work placement.
распредел|и́ть (**-ю́**, **-и́шь**; *impf* **распределя́ть**)
сов перех (*обязанности, доходы*) to distribute;
(*книги по полкам*) to arrange; (*учеников по
классам*) to divide up; (*разг*): ~ **кого́-н**
(*выпускника*) to give sb a work placement
▸ **распредели́ться** (*impf* **распределя́ться**) *сов
возв* (*разг: выпускники*) to get work
placements; **распределя́ться** (**~ся** *perf*) (**по**
+dat) (*по группам, по бригадам*) to divide up
(into).
распрода|ва́ть (**-ю́**, **-ёшь**) *несов от*
распрода́ть.
распродади́м *итп сов см* **распрода́ть**.
распрода́ж|а (**-и**) *ж* sale.
распрода́ть (*как* **дать**; *см* **Table 14**; *impf*
распродава́ть) *сов перех* (*вещи, имущество,
товар*) to sell off; (*билеты*) to sell out of.
распростёртый *прил* (*руки*) outstretched;
(*тело*) prostrate; **встреча́ть (встре́тить** *perf*)
кого́-н с распростёртыми объя́тиями to
welcome sb with open arms.
распро|сти́ться (**-щу́сь**, **-сти́шься**) *сов возв*: ~
с +*instr* to say *или* bid farewell to.
распростране́ни|е (**-я**) *ср* (*информации,*

опыта, знаний) dissemination; (инфекции)
spreading; (ядерного оружия) proliferation;
(приказа, правила) extension.
распространён|ный (-, -на, -но) прил
widespread.
распространи|ть (-ю, -йшь; impf
распространя́ть) сов перех (информацию,
знания) to disseminate; (опыт) to share;
(сплетни, инфекцию) to spread; (правило,
приказ) to apply; (владения) to widen;
(газеты) to distribute; (запах) to emit
▶ **распространи́ться** (impf
распространя́ться) сов возв to spread; (разг:
подробно говорить) to go into detail; ~ся (perf)
на +acc to extend to; э́тот прика́з ~я́ется на
всех this order applies to everybody.
распроща́|ться (-юсь) сов возв =
распрости́ться.
распрощу́сь сов см **распрости́ться**.
ра́спр|я (-и; gen pl -ей) ж (обычно мн) feud.
распря́г итп сов см **распря́чь**.
распряга́|ть (-ю) несов от **распря́чь**.
распрягу́ итп сов см **распря́чь**.
распряжёшь итп сов см **распря́чь**.
распрям|и́ть (-лю́, -и́шь; impf **распрямля́ть**)
сов перех (проволоку, крючок) to straighten
(out); (спину, грудь, плечи) to straighten (up).
распря́|чь (-гу́, -жёшь итп, -гу́т; pt -г, -гла́, -гло́,
impf **распряга́ть**) сов перех to unharness.
распуга́|ть (-ю; impf **распу́гивать**) сов перех to
scare away или off.
распусти́ть (-ущу́, -у́стишь; impf **распуска́ть**)
сов перех (армию) to disband; (студентов,
школьников) to dismiss; (шнурки, корсет,
ремень) to loosen; (волосы, косу) to let down;
(шов, вязанье) to unpick; (перен): ~ кого́-н
(ребёнка итп) to let sb run wild; **распуска́ть** (~
perf) парла́мент to dissolve parliament;
распуска́ть (~ perf) слу́хи to spread rumours
▶ **распусти́ться** (impf **распуска́ться**) сов возв
(цветы, почки) to open out; (шнуровка,
завязки) to come undone; (дети, люди) to get
out of hand.
распу́та|ть (-ю; impf **распу́тывать**) сов перех
(узел, нитки) to untangle; (перен: дело,
преступление, загадку) to unravel; (лошадь) to
unfetter
▶ **распу́таться** (impf **распу́тываться**) сов возв
(см перех) to come untangled; to unravel itself.
распу́тиц|а (-ы) ж period during autumn and
spring when the roads become impassable.
распу́тник (-а) м libertine.
распу́тниц|а (-ы) ж см **распу́тник**.
распу́т|ный (-ен, -на, -но) прил depraved.
распу́тыва|ть(ся) (-ю(сь)) несов от
распу́тать(ся).
распу́т|ье (-ья; nom pl -ий) ср crossroads; **быть**
(impf) **на** ~ (перен) to be at a crossroads.

распу́хн|уть (-у, -ешь; impf **распуха́ть**) сов
неперех (лицо, нога итп) to swell up;
(бумажник, папка) to bulge.
распу́щен|ный (-, -на, -но) прил unruly;
(безнравственный) dissolute.
распущу́(сь) сов см **распусти́ть(ся)**.
распыли́тель (-я) м spray.
распыл|и́ть (-ю́, -и́шь; impf **распыля́ть**) сов
перех to spray.
распя́ти|е (-я) ср crucifixion.
распн|я́ть (-у́, -нёшь; impf **распина́ть**) сов перех
to crucify.
расса́д|а (-ы) ж собир (бот) seedlings мн.
расса|ди́ть (-ажу́, -а́дишь; impf **расса́живать**)
сов перех (гостей, публику) to seat;
(болтунов) to seat apart; (цветы) to thin out.
расса́дник (-а) м (перен) hotbed.
▶ **расса́жива|ть** (-ю) несов от **рассади́ть**
▶ **расса́живаться** несов от **рассе́сться**.
рассажу́ сов см **рассади́ть**.
расса́сыва|ться (3sg -ется, 3pl -ются) несов
от **рассоса́ться**.
рассве|сти́ (3sg -тёт, pt -ло́, impf **рассвета́ть**)
сов безл: ~та́ет dawn is breaking; уже́ ~ло́ it's
already light.
рассве́т (-а) м daybreak.
рассвета́|ть (3sg -ет) несов от **рассвести́**.
рассветёт сов см **рассвести́**.
рассвирепе́|ть (-ю) сов от **свирепе́ть**.
расседла́|ть (-ю; impf **рассёдлывать**) сов
перех to unsaddle.
рассе́ива|ть(ся) (-ю(сь)) несов от
рассе́ять(ся).
рассе́к итп сов см **рассе́чь**.
рассека́|ть (-ю) несов от **рассе́чь**.
рассеку́ итп сов см **рассе́чь**.
рассе́лин|а (-ы) ж fissure.
рассе|ли́ть (-елю́, -е́лишь; impf **расселя́ть**) сов
перех (по комнатам, по квартирам) to
accommodate, put up; **расселя́ть** (~ perf)
коммуна́льную кварти́ру to move the
occupants of a communal flat into self-contained
accommodation.
рассе́лся итп сов см **рассе́сться**.
рассел|я́ть (-ю) несов от **рассели́ть**.
рассе|рди́ть(ся) (-ержу́(сь), -е́рдишь(ся)) сов
от **серди́ть(ся)**.
рассе́|сться (-я́дусь, -я́дешься; pt -е́лся,
-е́лась, -е́лось) сов возв (по столам, в зале) to
take one's seat; (разг: развалиться: на диване,
в кресле) to slump.
рассе́|чь (-ку́, -чёшь итп, -ку́т; pt -ёк, -екла́,
-екло́, impf **рассека́ть**) сов перех (тушу,
канат) to cut in two; (губу, лоб) to cut;
рассека́ть (~ perf) **во́лны** to cut through the
water.
рассе́ян|ный (-, -на, -но) прил (человек)
absent-minded; (свет) diffuse.

рассе́ять (-ю; *impf* **рассе́ивать**) *сов перех* (*семена, людей*) to scatter; (*свет*) to diffuse; (*перен: сомнения, подозрения*) to dispel; (*горе, тоску*) to alleviate

▸ **рассе́яться** (*impf* **рассе́иваться**) *сов возв* (*люди, семена*) to be scattered; (*тучи, туман, дым*) to disperse; (*сомнения, печаль*) to be dispelled; (*развлечься*) to find a distraction.

расскажу́ *итп сов см* **рассказа́ть**.

расска́з (-а) *м* story; (*свидетеля*) account.

рассказа́ть (-ажу́, -а́жешь; *impf* **расска́зывать**) *сов перех* to tell.

расска́зчик (-а) *м* storyteller; (*автор*) narrator.

расска́зчица (-ы) *ж см* **расска́зчик**.

расска́зывать (-ю) *несов от* **рассказа́ть**.

расслабля́ть (-лю, -ишь; *impf* **расслабля́ть**) *сов перех* (*мышцы, ноги, руки*) to relax; (*ремень, галстук*) to loosen; (*подлеж: болезнь, работа*) to weaken

▸ **рассла́биться** (*impf* **расслабля́ться**) *сов возв* to relax.

рассла́бленный (-, -на, -но) *прил* relaxed.

расслаблю(сь) *сов см* **рассла́бить(ся)**.

расслабля́ть(ся) (-ю(сь)) *несов от* **рассла́бить(ся)**.

рассла́иваться (*3sg* -ется, *3pl* -ются) *несов от* **расслои́ться**.

расследование (-я) *ср* investigation.

рассле́довать (-ую) (*не*)*сов перех* to investigate.

расслои́ться (*3sg* -и́тся, *3pl* -я́тся, *impf* **рассла́иваться**) *сов возв* (*горная порода, общество*) to stratify; (*пирог, фанера*) to split.

рассл́ышать (-у, -ишь) *сов перех* to hear; извини́те, я не ~ал I'm sorry, I didn't catch what you said.

рассма́тривать (-ю) *несов от* **рассмотре́ть** ♦ *перех:* ~ **что-н как** to regard sth as.

рассмеши́ть (-у́, -и́шь) *сов см* **смеши́ть**.

рассмея́ться (-ю́сь, -ёшься) *сов возв* to start laughing.

рассмотре́ние (-я) *ср* examination.

рассмотре́ть (-отрю́, -о́тришь; *impf* **рассма́тривать**) *сов перех* to examine; (*различить: в темноте, вдали*) to discern.

рассова́ть (-ую; *impf* **рассо́вывать**) *сов перех* (*разг*): ~ **что-н в** +*acc или* **по** +*dat* to stuff sth into.

рассо́л (-а; *part gen* -у) *м* brine.

рассо́льник (-а; *part gen* -у) *м* soup made with meat and pickled cucumbers.

рассоса́ться (*3sg* -ётся, *3pl* -у́тся, *impf* **расса́сываться**) *сов возв* (*опухоль*) to go down; (*перен: очередь, пробка*) to ease off; (: *толпа*) to thin out.

расспра́шивать (-ю) *несов от* **расспроси́ть**.

расспро́с (-а) *м* (*действие: свидетелей*) questioning; (*обычно мн: вопросы*) question.

расспроси́ть (-ошу́, -о́сишь; *impf* **расспра́шивать**) *сов перех:* ~ (**о** +*prp*) to question (about).

рассро́чка (-ки; *gen pl* -ек) *ж* installment (*BRIT*), instalment (*US*); **в ~ку** (*купить, продать*) on hire purchase (*BRIT*), on the installment plan (*US*); **выпла́чивать** (**вы́платить** *perf*) **в ~ку** to pay in instal(l)ments.

расстава́ние (-я) *ср* parting.

расстава́ться (-ю́сь, -ёшься) *сов от* **расста́ться**.

расста́вить (-лю, -ишь; *impf* **расставля́ть**) *сов перех* (*книги, мебель итп*) to arrange; (*шахматы*) to set up *или* out; (*знаки препинания, ударения*) to add; (*ножки циркуля*) to open; (*пальцы*) to splay; (*разг: расширить: платье, воротник*) to let out; **расставля́ть** (~ *perf*) **но́ги** to open one's legs.

расстано́вка (-ки; *gen pl* -ок) *ж* (*мебели, книг*) arrangement; ~ **сил** distribution of power; **чита́ть** (*impf*)/**говори́ть** (*impf*) **с ~кой** to read/ speak slowly and clearly.

расста́ться (-нусь, -нешься; *impf* **расстава́ться**) *сов возв:* ~ **с** +*instr* to part with; (*с любимым делом*) to abandon; (*перен: с мечтой, с детством*) to say goodbye to.

расстегну́ть (-у́, -ёшь; *impf* **расстёгивать**) *сов перех* to undo

▸ **расстегну́ться** (*impf* **расстёгиваться**) *сов возв* (*человек*) to unbutton o.s.; (*рубашка, молния, пуговица*) to come undone.

расстели́ть (-елю́, -е́лешь; *impf* **расстила́ть**) *сов перех* to spread out.

расстила́ться (*3sg* -ется, *3pl* -ются) *несов возв* (*равнина, степь*) to extend; (*туман*) to spread.

расстоя́ние (-я) *ср* distance; **держа́ть** (*impf*) **кого́-н на ~и** (*перен*) to keep sb at arm's length; **держа́ться** (*impf*) **на ~и** to keep one's distance.

расстра́ивать(ся) (-ю(сь)) *несов от* **расстро́ить(ся)**.

расстре́л (-а) *м:* ~ +*gen* shooting *или* firing at; (*казнь*) execution (*by firing squad*); **пригова́ривать** (**приговори́ть** *perf*) **кого́-н к ~у** to sentence sb to be shot.

расстреля́ть (-ю; *impf* **расстре́ливать**) *сов перех* (*демонстрацию*) to open fire on; (*казнить*) to shoot; (*патроны, снаряды*) to use up.

расстро́енный (-, -а, -о) *прил* (*здоровье, нервы*) weak; (*человек, вид*) upset; (*рояль, скрипка*) out of tune.

расстро́ить (-ю, -ишь; *impf* **расстра́ивать**) *сов перех* (*планы, дела, свадьбу*) to disrupt; (*нервы*) to unsettle; (*человека, желудок*) to upset; (*здоровье*) to compromise; (*ряды противника*) to throw into confusion *или* disarray; (*муз*) to put out of tune

▸ **расстро́иться** (*impf* **расстра́иваться**) *сов возв* (*поездка, планы*) to fall through; (*дела, бизнес*) to fall apart; (*человек*) to get upset; (*колонна, ряды*) to fall into disarray; (*нервы*) to weaken; (*здоровье*) to become poorly; (*муз*) to go out of tune

расстро́йство (-а) *ср* (*в делах, в хозяйстве*)

disorder; (*в рядах проти́вника*) confusion, disarray; (*огорче́ние*) upset; (*ре́чи, нервно́й систе́мы*) dysfunction; ~ желу́дка stomach upset; **приходи́ть (прийти́** *perf*) в ~ (*дела́, хозя́йство*) to be thrown into confusion; (*челове́к*) to become upset.

расст|упи́ться (*3sg* -у́пится, *impf* **расступа́ться**) *сов возв* (*толпа́*) to make way; (*перен: тайга́, во́лны, земля́*) to part.

расстык|ова́ться (-у́юсь; *impf* **расстыко́вываться**) *сов возв* (*ко́смос*) to undock.

расстыко́в|ка (-ки) *ж* undocking.

расстыко́выва|ться (-юсь) *несов от* **расстыкова́ться**.

рассуди́тел|ьный (-ен, -ьна, -ьно) *прил* judicious.

рассу́д|ок (-ка) *м* reason; **быть** (*impf*) **в своём** ~ке to be in possession of one's facilities.

рассужда́|ть (-ю) *несов непер*ех to reason; ~ (*impf*) **о** +*prp* to debate.

рассужде́ни|е (-я) *ср* (*умозаключе́ние: логи́ческое итп*) judg(e)ment; ~я (*о поли́тике, о мора́ли итп*) reasoning *ед*; **без** ~й without arguing.

рассужу́ *сов см* **рассуди́ть**.

рассчита́|ть (-ю; *impf* **рассчи́тывать**) *сов пер*ех (*сто́имость, трае́кторию, поли́тику*) to calculate; (*рабо́тника*) to lay off; **слова́рь** **рассчи́тан на студе́нтов** the dictionary is designed for students

▶ **рассчита́ться** (*impf* **рассчи́тываться**) *сов возв* (*уво́литься*) to hand in one's notice; (*ВОЕН: в строю́*) to call out one's number; **рассчи́тываться** (~ся *perf*) (**с** +*instr*) (**с** *прода́вцом, в гости́нице*) to settle up (with); (*перен: с враго́м итп*) to settle a score (with).

рассчи́тыва|ть (-ю) *несов от* **рассчита́ть** ◆ *непер*ех: ~ **на** +*acc* (*наде́яться: на уда́чу, на дру́га*) to count *или* rely on; ~ (*impf*) +*infin* to count on doing

▶ **рассчи́тываться** *несов от* **рассчита́ться**.

рассыла́|ть (-ю) *несов от* **разосла́ть**.

рассы́п|ать (-лю, -лешь; *impf* **рассыпа́ть**) *сов пер*ех to spill; (*распредели́ть*) ~ **по** +*dat* to pour into

▶ **рассы́паться** (*impf* **рассыпа́ться**) *сов возв* (*са́хар, песо́к, бу́сы*) to spill; (*стена́, холм*) to crumble; (*во́лосы*) to fall loose; (*толпа́, ста́я*) to scatter; **он** ~ался **в благода́рностях** he was effusive in his thanks.

рассы́пно́й *прил* sold loose.

рассы́пчат|ый (-, -а, -о) *прил* (*ка́ша, рис*) fluffy; (*пече́нье, пиро́г*) crumbly.

расся́дусь *итп сов см* **рассе́сться**.

расста́лкива|ть (-ю) *несов от* **растолка́ть**.

расста́плива|ть (-ю) *несов от* **растопи́ть**.

расста́птыва|ть (-ю) *несов от* **растопта́ть**.

растаска́|ть (-ю; *impf* **раста́скивать**) *сов пер*ех (*ра́зно: по ко́мнатам*) to drag; (: *разворова́ть*) to filch.

раста́щ|ить (-ащу́, -а́щишь) *сов* **растаска́ть** ◆ *пер*ех (*разг: драчуно́в, мальчи́шек*) to drag apart.

раста́|ять (-ю) *сов от* та́ять.

раство́р (-а) *м* (*хим*) solution; (*ци́ркуля*) span, spread; (*строи́тельный*) mortar; **цеме́нтный** ~ cement.

раствори́|мый (-, -а, -о) *прил* soluble; **раствори́мый ко́фе** instant coffee.

раствори́тел|ь (-я) *м* solvent.

раствор|и́ть (-ю́, -и́шь; *impf* **растворя́ть**) *сов пер*ех (*окно́, дверь*) to open; (*порошо́к, са́хар*) to dissolve

▶ **раствори́ться** (*impf* **растворя́ться**) *сов возв* (*см пер*ех) to open; to dissolve; (*перен*): ~ **в** +*prp* (*в темноте́, в тума́не*) to vanish into.

растека́|ться (*3sg* -ется, *3pl* -ются) *несов от* расте́чься.

растёкся *итп сов см* расте́чься.

растеку́тся *итп сов см* расте́чься.

расте́ни|е (-я) *ср* plant.

растениево́дств|о (-а) *ср* horticulture.

раст|ере́ть (разотру́, разотрёшь; *pt* -ёр, -ёрла, -ёрло, *impf* **растира́ть**) *сов пер*ех (*ра́ну, те́ло*) to massage; **растира́ть** (~ *perf*) (**в порошо́к**) to grind (into a powder); **растира́ть** (~ *perf*) **кре́мом/ма́зью** to rub cream/ointment into; **растира́ть** (~ *perf*) **но́гу** to get blisters

▶ **растере́ться** (*impf* **растира́ться**) *сов возв*: ~ся (+*instr*) (*полоте́нцем, мочалкой*) to rub o.s. down (with).

растерза́|ть (-ю) *сов от* терза́ть.

расте́рянност|ь (-и) *ж* confusion; **она́ стоя́ла в** ~и she stood there looking confused.

расте́рян|ный (-, -а, -о) *прил* confused.

растеря́|ться (-юсь) *сов возв* (*челове́к*) to be confused; (*пи́сьма*) to go missing.

расте́|чься (*3sg* -чётся, *3pl* -ку́тся, *pt* -кся, -кла́сь, -екло́сь, *impf* **растека́ться**) *сов возв* (*ру́чьи, вода́*) to spill; (*черни́ла, кра́ска*) to run.

раст|и́ (-у́, -ёшь; *pt* рос, росла́, росло́, *perf* **вы́расти**) *несов непер*ех to grow; (*проводи́ть де́тство*) to grow up; **он вы́рос за грани́цей** he grew up abroad; ~ (**вы́расти** *perf*) **в чьих-н глаза́х** to grow in sb's estimation.

растира́|ть(ся) (-ю(сь)) *несов от* растере́ть(ся).

расти́тельност|ь (-и) *ж собир* vegetation.

расти́тельн|ый *прил* (*бот*) plant *опред*; **расти́тельное ма́сло** vegetable oil; **расти́тельный мир** the plant kingdom;

расти́тельный покро́в vegetation.
ра|сти́ть (-щу́, -сти́шь; *perf* **вы́растить**) *несов перех* (*дете́й*) to raise; (*цветы́*) to grow; (*живо́тных*) to rear; (*перен: ка́дры*) to nurture; (: *тала́нт, дарова́ние*) to cultivate.
растолка́|ть (-ю; *impf* **раста́лкивать**) *сов перех* (*толпу́, люде́й*) to push away; (*разг: разбуди́ть*) to shake.
растолк|ова́ть (-у́ю; *impf* **растолко́вывать**) *сов перех*: ~ что-н (кому́-н) to clarify sth (for sb).
растоло́|чь (-ку́, -чёшь *итп*, -ку́т; *pt* -о́к, -кла́, -кло́) *сов от* **толо́чь**.
растолсте́|ть (-ю) *сов непepex* to put on weight.
раст|опи́ть (-оплю́, -о́пишь; *impf* **раста́пливать**) *сов перех* (*печку́*) to light; (*воск, жир, лёд*) to melt
▶ **растопи́ться** *сов от* **топи́ться**.
раст|опта́ть (-опчу́, -о́пчешь; *impf* **раста́птывать**) *сов перех* (*также перен*) to trample on.
растопы́р|ить (-ю, -ишь; *impf* **растопы́ривать**) *сов перех* to spread.
расто́рг|нуть (-ну, -нешь; *pt* -, -ла, -ло, *impf* **расторга́ть**) *сов перех* to annul.
растормош|и́ть (-у́, -и́шь) *сов перех* (*разг*) to shake.
расторо́п|ный (-ен, -на, -но) *прил* quick, efficient.
расточи́тел|ьный (-ен, -ьна, -ьно) *прил* extravagant.
расточи́тельств|о (-а) *ср* extravagance.
растр|а́вить (-авлю́, -а́вишь; *impf* **растравля́ть**) *сов перех* (*перен*): ~ кому́-н ду́шу to torment sb.
растранжи́р|ить (-ю, -ишь) *сов от* **транжи́рить**.
растра́т|а (-ы) *ж* (*вре́мени, сил, де́нег*) waste; (*хище́ние*) embezzlement; (*растра́ченная сумма́*) loss.
растра́|тить (-чу, -тишь; *impf* **растра́чивать**) *сов перех* to waste; (*расхити́ть*) to embezzle.
растрево́ж|ить (-у, -ишь) *сов перех* to alarm; ~ (*perf*) кому́-н ду́шу to stir sb's emotions
▶ **растрево́житься** *сов возв* to become alarmed.
растрёпан|ный (-, -на, -но) *прил* (*вид, вне́шность*) bedraggled; (*во́лосы*) tousled; (*тетра́дь, кни́га*) tatty; **быть** (*impf*) **в ~ных чу́вствах** (*разг*) to be all confused.
растреп|а́ть (-лю́, -лешь) *сов перех* (*во́лосы*) to mess up; (*тетра́дь, кни́гу*) to tatter; (*разг: разболта́ть*) to blab
▶ **растрепа́ться** *сов возв* (*разг: во́лосы*) to get messed up; (: *тетра́дь, кни́га*) to become tattered.
растро́ган|ный (-, -на, -но) *прил* (*челове́к*) moved, touched; (*го́лос*) full of emotion.
растро́га|ть (-ю) *сов перех*: ~ кого́-н (+*instr*) (*письмо́м, внима́нием*) to touch *или* move sb (by)

▶ **растро́гаться** *сов возв* to be touched *или* moved; ~ся (*perf*) **до слёз** to be moved to tears.
раструб|и́ть (-лю́, -и́шь) *сов от* **труби́ть**.
растя́гива|ть(ся) (-ю(сь)) *несов от* **растяну́ть(ся)**.
растяже́ни|е (-я) *ср* (*МЕД*) strain.
растяжи́м|ый (-, -а, -о) *прил*: ~ое поня́тие a loose concept.
растя́нут|ый (-, -а, -о) *прил* lengthy.
растя́|нуть (-ну́, -нешь; *impf* **растя́гивать**) *сов перех* to stretch; (*ска́терть*) to spread out; (*связки, сухожи́лие*) to strain; (*но́гу, ру́ку*) to sprain; (*докла́д, расска́з*) to drag out; (*удово́льствие*) to prolong; (*сре́дства*) to stretch out
▶ **растяну́ться** (*impf* **растя́гиваться**) *сов возв* to stretch; (*челове́к, обо́з*) to stretch out; (*связки, сухожи́лие*) to be strained; (*собра́ние, рабо́та*) to drag on.
растя́п|а (-ы) *м/ж* (*разг*) bungler.
расфас|ова́ть (-у́ю) *сов от* **фасова́ть**.
расформир|ова́ть (-у́ю; *impf* **расформиро́вывать**) *сов перех* to disband.
расха́жива|ть (-ю) *несов непperex* to saunter.
расхвал|и́ть (-алю́, -а́лишь; *impf* **расхва́ливать**) *сов перех* to enthuse about.
расхвата́|ть (-ю; *impf* **расхва́тывать**) *сов перех* (*разг*) to snatch up.
расхити́тел|ь (-я) *м* embezzler.
расхи́|тить (-щу, -тишь; *impf* **расхища́ть**) *сов перех* to embezzle.
расхище́ни|е (-я) *ср* embezzlement.
расхля́бан|ный (-, -на, -но) *прил* (*жест, движе́ние*) irreverent; (*челове́к, поведе́ние*) lax.
расхо́д (-а) *м* (*эне́ргии, воды́*) consumption; (*обы́чно мн: затра́ты*) expense; (: *КОММ: в бухга́лтерской кни́ге*) expenditure; ~ы **произво́дства** production costs; **вводи́ть** (**ввести́** *perf*) **кого́-н в** ~ to leave sb out of pocket.
расх|оди́ться (-ожу́сь, -о́дишься) *несов от* **разойти́сь**.
расхо́дный *прил*: ~ о́рдер (*КОММ*) expenses form.
расхо́д|овать (-ую; *perf* **израсхо́довать**) *несов перех* (*де́ньги*) to spend; (*материа́лы, эне́ргию*) to expend; (*потребля́ть: бензи́н*) to consume.
расхожде́ни|е (-я) *ср* (*ме́жду сло́вом и де́лом*) discrepancy; (*во взгля́дах*) divergence.
расхо́жий (-ая, -ее, -ие) *прил* (*мне́ние*) widely accepted.
расхожу́сь *несов см* **расходи́ться**.
расхоте́ть (*как* **хоте́ть**; *см* **Table 16**) *сов непperex*: ~ +*infin* (*спать, гуля́ть итп*) to no longer want to do; **я расхоте́л есть** I don't feel hungry any more
▶ **расхоте́ться** *сов безл*: (**мне**) **расхоте́лось спать** I don't feel sleepy any more.
расхох|ота́ться (-очу́сь, -о́чешься) *сов возв* to burst out laughing.

расхочу́(сь) *итп сов см* **расхоте́ть(ся)**.

расцара́па|ть (-ю) *сов перех* to scratch.

расцве|сти́ (-ту́, -тёшь; *pt* -ёл, -ела́, -ело́, *impf* **расцвета́ть**) *сов неперех (также перен)* to blossom; *(от радости)* to light up.

расцве́т (-а) *м (перен: науки, таланта)* blossoming; **он в ~е сил** he is in the prime of life.

расцвета́|ть (-ю) *несов от* **расцвести́**.

расцве́т|ка (-ки; *gen pl* -ок) *ж* colour (*BRIT*) или color (*US*) scheme.

расцвету́ *итп сов см* **расцвести́**.

расцел|ова́ть (-у́ю) *сов перех* to kiss
▶ **расцелова́ться** *сов возв* to kiss each other.

расце́нива|ть (3sg -ется, 3pl -ются) *несов возв*: ~ **как** to be regarded as.

расцени́ть (-еню́, -е́нишь; *impf* **расце́нивать**) *сов перех (состав)* to judge; **расце́нивать** (~ *perf*) **что-н как** to regard sth as.

расцепи́ть (-еплю́, -е́пишь; *impf* **расцепля́ть**) *сов перех (состав)* to uncouple; *(дерущихся, пальцы)* to pull apart.

расч|ерти́ть (-ерчу́, -е́ртишь; *impf* **расче́рчивать**) *сов перех* to rule, line.

расч|еса́ть (-ешу́, -е́шешь; *impf* **расчёсывать**) *сов перех (волосы, гриву)* to comb; *(шерсть, лён)* to card; *(руку, царапину)* to scratch; **расчёсывать** (~ *perf*) **кого-н** to comb sb's hair.

расчёс|ка (-ки; *gen pl* -ок) *ж* comb.

расчёсыва|ть (-ю) *несов от* **расчеса́ть**.

расчёт (-а) *м (налога, стоимости итп)* calculation; *(оплата)* payment; *(предложение)* calculation; *(выгода)* advantage; *(бережливость)* economy; *(увольнение)* dismissal; *(ВОЕН, МОР)* crew; **из ~а** +gen on the basis of; **из ~а 5 проце́нтов годовы́х** at 5 percent per annum; **он ведёт дела́ с ~ом** he runs his business economically; **де́йствовать** *(impf)* **по ~у** to act in a calculated way; **исхо́ди́ть** *(impf)* **из ~а, что ...** to act on the assumption that ...; **брать (взять** *perf***)** или **принима́ть (приня́ть** *perf***) что-н в ~** to take sth into account; **по мойм ~ам мы зако́нчим к ве́черу** by my reckoning we will finish by evening; **я с Ва́ми в ~e** we are all even; **брать (взять** *perf***)** ~ to hand in one's notice.

расчётлив|ый (-, -а, -о) *прил (экономный)* thrifty; *(руководитель, игрок)* calculating; *(движения)* deliberate.

расчётн|ый *прил (ТЕХ: скорость итп)* estimated; **расчётный день** payday; **расчётный счёт** debit account.

расчешу́ *итп сов см* **расчеса́ть**.

расчи́|стить (-щу, -стишь; *impf* **расчища́ть**) *сов перех* to clear
▶ **расчи́ститься** (*impf* **расчища́ться**) *сов возв*

to clear.

расчлен|и́ть (-ю́, -и́шь) *сов от* **расчленя́ть**, **члени́ть**.

расчленя́|ть (-ю) *несов от* **расчлени́ть**.

расчу́вств|оваться (-уюсь) *сов возв (разг)* to be overcome with emotion.

расшата́|ть (-ю; *impf* **расша́тывать**) *сов перех (стол, стул)* to make wobbly; *(здоровье)* to damage; **он ~л себе́ не́рвы** he's become a nervous wreck
▶ **расшата́ться** (*impf* **расша́тываться**) *сов возв (забор, столб)* to become wobbly; *(перен: нервы)* to give out; *(здоровье)* to be damaged.

расшвыря́|ть (-ю) *сов перех (разг)* to hurl around; *(: перен: деньги)* to fritter away.

расшевел|и́ть (-ю́, -и́шь) *сов перех (разг)*: ~ **кого́-н** to give sb a shake; *(перен: слушателей)* to liven sb up
▶ **расшевели́ться** *сов возв* to stir; *(перен: начальство, игроки)* to get moving.

расшиб|и́ть (-у́, -ёшь; *impf* **расшиба́ть**) *сов перех (разг)* to smash
▶ **расшиби́ться** (*impf* **расшиба́ться**) *сов возв (о дверь, при падении)* to hurt o.s.; *(разг: для друга, для семьи)* to put o.s. out.

расшива́|ть (-ю) *несов от* **расши́ть**.

расшире́ни|е (-я) *ср* widening; *(связей, производства)* expansion; *(знаний)* broadening.

расши́рен|ный (-, -на, -но) *прил (проход)* widened; *(комитет, заседание)* expanded; *(зрачки, сосуды)* dilated.

расши́р|ить (-ю, -ишь; *impf* **расширя́ть**) *сов перех* to widen; *(производство)* to expand; **расширя́ть** (~ *perf*) **кругозо́р** to broaden one's horizons
▶ **расши́риться** (*impf* **расширя́ться**) *сов возв* to widen; *(завод, контакты, знания)* to expand; *(зрачки)* to dilate.

расши́тый *прил* embroidered.

ра|сши́ть (-зошью́, -зошьёшь; *impf* **расшива́ть**) *сов перех (вышить)* to embroider.

расшифр|ова́ть (-у́ю; *impf* **расшифро́вывать**) *сов перех (текст, шифро́вку)* to decode, decipher; *(перен: тайну, смысл слов)* to decipher.

расшнур|ова́ть (-у́ю; *impf* **расшнуро́вывать**) *сов перех* to unlace.

расшум|е́ться (-лю́сь, -и́шься) *сов возв (разг)* to make a racket; *(: начать спорить)* to kick up a fuss.

расще́др|иться (-юсь, -ишься; *impf* **расще́дриваться**) *сов возв (разг)* to become generous.

расще́лин|а (-ы) *ж (скалы, горы)* crevice; *(в дереве, в камне)* cleft.

расщеп|и́ть (-лю́, -и́шь; *impf* **расщепля́ть**) *сов перех (также физ)* to split; *(хим)* to decompose
▶ **расщепи́ться** (*impf* **расщепля́ться**) *сов возв*

to splinter; (ФИЗ) to split; (ХИМ) to decompose.
расщепле́ни|е (-я) ср splintering; (ФИЗ) fission; (ХИМ) decomposition.
расщеплю́(сь) сов см **расщепи́ть(ся)**.
расщепля́|ть(ся) (-ю) несов от **расщепи́ть(ся)**.
ратифика́ци|я (-и) ж ratification.
ратифици́р|овать (-ую) (не)сов перех to ratify.
ра́унд (-а) м (СПОРТ) round; (ПОЛИТ): **~ перегово́ров** round of talks.
ра́фик (-а) м (разг) minibus.
рафина́д (-а) м sugar cubes мн.
рафини́рованный прил refined.
рахи́т (-а) м (МЕД) rickets.
рацио́н (-а) м ration.
рациона́лен прил см **рациона́льный**.
рационализа́тор (-а) м innovator.
рационализа́ци|я (-и) ж rationalization.
рационализи́р|овать (-ую) (не)сов перех to rationalize.
рационали́ст (-а) м rationalist.
рациона́л|ьный (-ен, -ьна, -ьно) прил (поступок) rational; (использование ресурсов, организация) effective; **~ьное пита́ние** well-balanced diet.
ра́ци|я (-и) ж walkie-talkie.
рацпредложе́ни|е (-я) ср сокр (= рационализа́торское предложе́ние) innovation proposal.
рачи́тел|ьный (-ен, -ьна, -ьно) прил thrifty.
рван|у́ть (-у, -ёшь) сов перех to pull at; (разг) to explode ♦ неперех (разг: лошадь, бегун) to shoot off; **~** (perf) **кого́-н за пиджа́к/за́ руку** to tug at sb's jacket/arm; **~** (perf) **пе́сню** (разг) to break into song
▶ **рвану́ться** сов возв to tear off.
рва́ный прил torn; (боти́нки) ripped; (ра́на) lacerated.
рв|ать (-у, -ёшь) perf **порва́ть** или **разорва́ть** несов перех (письмо́, оде́жду, кни́гу) to tear, rip; (перен: отношения, дружбу) to break off; (perf **вы́рвать**; предмет из рук) to snatch; (no perf; подлеж: ветер; одежды, занавес) to tear at; (perf **сорва́ть**; цветы, траву) to pick; (ветки) to break off ♦ (perf **вы́рвать**) безл: **его́** итп **~а́ло всю ночь** he was vomiting или being sick all night; **~** (**разорва́ть** perf) **кого́-н/что-н на ча́сти** to tear sb/sth to bits; **меня́ ~ут на ча́сти** (перен) I'm in demand from all sides; **~** (**порва́ть** perf) **с про́шлым** to break with the past; **~** (**вы́рвать** perf) **кому́-н зуб** (разг) to pull sb's tooth out; **~** (impf) **и мета́ть** (impf) (разг) to rant and rave
▶ **рва́ться** (perf **порва́ться** или **разорва́ться**) несов возв (бумага, одежда) to tear, rip; (обувь) to rip; (перен: отношения, связи) to be severed; (perf **разорва́ться**; снаряд) to explode; **~а́ться** (impf) **к приключе́ниям/вла́сти** to be hungry for adventure/power; **~а́ться** (impf) **в дра́ку** to be spoiling for a fight; **у меня́ се́рдце** или **душа́ ~ётся на ча́сти** my heart is being torn in two.

рвач (-а́) м (разг: пренебр) taker.
рве́ни|е (-я) ср (в учёбе, в работе) enthusiasm; (патриотический, религиозный) zeal; **~ +infin** desire to do.
рво́т|а (-ы) ж vomiting.
рво́тн|ый прил: **~ое (сре́дство)** emetic.
ре ср нескл (МУЗ) re.
реабилита́ци|я (-и) ж rehabilitation.
реабилити́р|овать (-ую) (не)сов перех to rehabilitate.
реаги́р|овать (-ую) несов неперех: **~ (на +acc)** (на свет, на раздражение) to react (to); (perf **отреаги́ровать** или **прореаги́ровать**; на критику, на слова) to react или respond (to).
реакти́в (-а) м (ХИМ) reagent.
реакти́вный прил (ХИМ) reactive; (ТЕХ) jet-propelled; **реакти́вный дви́гатель** jet engine; **реакти́вный самолёт** jet (plane).
реа́ктор (-а) м reactor.
реакционе́р (-а) м reactionary.
реакцио́нный прил reactionary.
реа́кци|я (-и) ж reaction.
реа́лен прил см **реа́льный**.
реализа́ци|я (-и) ж (см глаг) implementation; realization.
реали́зм (-а) м realism.
реализ|ова́ть (-у́ю) (не)сов перех (реформы, проект, предложение) to implement; (товар, ценные бумаги) to realize.
реали́ст (-а) м realist.
реалисти́чен прил см **реалисти́чный**.
реалисти́ческ|ий (-ая, -ое, -ие) прил realistic; (искусство) realist опред.
реалисти́ч|ный (-ен, -на, -но) прил realistic.
реа́льност|ь (-и) ж reality; (политики, плана, задачи) practicability, feasibility; **~и на́шего вре́мени** modern-day realities.
реа́л|ьный (-ен, -ьна, -ьно) прил (не воображаемый) real; (осуществимый, практический) realistic; **в ~ьном вре́мени** (КОМП) real-time; **реа́льная за́работная пла́та** (ЭКОН) real wage.
реанима́ци|я (-и) ж resuscitation; **отделе́ние ~и** intensive care unit.
ребён|ок (-ка; nom pl де́ти или **ребя́та)** м child (мн children); (грудной) baby; **дом ~ка** children's home.
ребр|о́ (-а́; nom pl рёбра, gen pl рёбер) ср (АНАТ) rib; (монеты, стола, кубика итп) edge; **ста́вить** (**поста́вить** perf) **вопро́с ~м** to put a question bluntly.
ре́бус (-а) м rebus; (перен) riddle.
ребя́т|а (-) мн от **ребёнок**; (разг: парни) guys мн.
ребя́ческ|ий (-ая, -ое, -ие) прил (душа, сознание) child's опред; (перен: поведение, суждение) childish.
рёв (-а) м roar; (разг: громкий плач) howling.
ревальва́ци|я (-и) ж (ЭКОН) revaluation.
рева́нш (-а) м revenge; (игра) revenge match; **взять** (perf) **~** to take revenge.

реванши́зм (-а) *м* revanchism.
реве́н|ь (-я́) *м* rhubarb.
реве́|ть (-у́, -ёшь) *несов неперех* to roar; (*разг: плакать*) to howl.
ревизио́нн|ый *прил*: ~ая коми́ссия audit commission.
реви́зи|я (-и) *ж* (*комм*) audit; (*взглядов, учения*) revision.
ревиз|ова́ть (-у́ю) (*не*)*сов перех* (*предприятие*) to inspect; (*бухгалтерские книги*) to audit.
ревизо́р (-а) *м* (*комм*) auditor.
ревмати́зм (-а) *м* rheumatism.
ревмати́ческ|ий (-ая, -ое, -ие) *прил* rheumatoid.
ревмато́лог (-а) *м* rheumatologist.
ревни́в|ый (-, -а, -о) *прил* jealous.
ревн|ова́ть (-у́ю) *несов неперех*: ~ (кого́-н) to be jealous (of sb); **он ~у́ет меня́ к своему́ бра́ту** he is jealous of my relationship with his brother.
ре́вностн|ый (-ен, -на, -но) *прил* ardent, zealous.
ре́вност|ь (-и) *ж* jealousy.
револьве́р (-а) *м* revolver.
революционе́р (-а) *м* revolutionary.
революционе́р|ка (-ки; *gen pl* -ок) *ж см* **революционе́р**.
революцио́нный *прил* revolutionary.
револю́ци|я (-и) *ж* revolution.
реви́ю *ср нескл* revue.
рега́ли|я (-и) *ж* (*обычно мн*) regalia *ед*.
рега́т|а (-ы) *ж* regatta.
ре́гби *ср нескл* rugby.
регби́ст (-а) *м* rugby player.
регио́н (-а) *м* region.
региона́льный *прил* regional.
реги́стр (-а) *м* (*муз, комп, мор*) register; (*на пишущей машинке*): **ве́рхний/ни́жний** ~ upper/lower case.
регистра́тор (-а) *м* (*в поликлинике*) receptionist; (*в загсе*) registrar.
регистрату́р|а (-ы) *ж* (*в поликлинике*) reception; (*на предприятии*) records department.
регистра́ци|я (-и) *ж* registration.
регистри́р|овать (-ую; *perf* **регистри́ровать** *или* **зарегистри́ровать**) *несов перех* to register
▶ **регистри́роваться** (*не*)*сов возв* to register; (*оформлять брак*) to get married (*at a registry office*).
регла́мент (-а) *м* (*порядок заседаний*) order of business; (*время для выступления*) speaking time.
регла́н *прил неизм* raglan ◆ (-а) *м*: **(пальто́-)/(пла́тье-)**~ raglan coat/dress.
регули́р|овать (-ую) *несов перех* to regulate; (*perf* **урегули́ровать**; *отношения*) to

normalize; (*perf* **отрегули́ровать**; *мотор, громкость*) to adjust.
регулиро́вщик (-а) *м* traffic policeman (*мн* policemen).
регуля́рен *прил см* **регуля́рный**.
регуля́рно *нареч* regularly.
регуля́рност|ь (-и) *ж* regularity.
регуля́р|ный (-ен, -на, -но) *прил* regular; **регуля́рные войска́** regular army *ед*.
редакти́р|овать (-ую; *perf* **отредакти́ровать**) *несов перех* to edit.
реда́ктор (-а) *м* (*также комп*) editor.
редакцио́нн|ый *прил* (*поправки*): ~ая колле́гия editorial board; **редакцио́нная статья́** editorial.
реда́кци|я (-и) *ж* (*действие: текста, статьи*) editing; (*вариант произведения*) edition; (*формулировка: статьи закона*) wording; (*учреждение*) editorial offices *мн*; (*на радио*) desk; (*на телевидении*) division; **под** ~**ей** +*gen* edited by.
реде́|ть (*3sg* -ет, *3pl* -ют, *perf* **пореде́ть**) *несов неперех* to thin out.
реди́с (-а) *м* radish.
реди́ск|а (-и) *ж* (*разг*) (red) radish ◆ *собир* radishes *мн*.
ре́д|кий (-кая, -кое, -кие; -ок, -ка́, -ко) *прил* rare; (*выстрелы, письма, гость*) occasional; (*волосы*) thin; (*зубы*) gappy; (*лес*) sparse; (*ткань, материал*) loose-weave.
ре́дко *нареч* rarely, seldom; (*расти*) sparsely.
редколле́ги|я (-и) *ж сокр* = **редакцио́нная колле́гия**.
ре́дкост|ь (-и) *ж* rarity; **на** ~ unusually; **он на** ~ **до́брый челове́к** he is a person of uncommon kindness; **таки́е приме́ры не** ~ such examples are not uncommon.
ре́док *прил см* **ре́дкий**.
ре́дьк|а (-и) *ж* (white) radish ◆ *собир* radishes *мн*.
режи́м (-а) *ж* (*питания, также полит*) regime; (*больничный, тюремный итп*) routine; (*условия работы*) conditions *мн*; (*комп*) mode; ~ **безопа́сности** security system; **рабо́чий** ~ **дви́гателя** the operating conditions of the engine.
режиссёр (-а) *м* director (*of film, play etc*); **режиссёр-постано́вщик** (stage) director.
режиссу́р|а (-ы) *ж* (*профессия*) directing; (*фильма, спектакля*) direction.
ре́|зать (-жу, -жешь; *perf* **разре́зать**) *несов перех* (*хлеб*) to slice, cut up; (*металл, кожу*) to cut; (*разг: нарыв, живот*) to cut open; (*perf* **заре́зать**; *разг: гуся, свинью*) to slaughter; (*перен: разг: диссертацию*) to flunk; (*perf* **сре́зать**; *студента*) to fail; (*no perf; ложки, фигурки итп*) to carve; (*причинять боль: подлеж: воротник*) to dig into; (: *дым, ветер*)

to sting; (*наносить изображения*): ~ **по** +*dat*
(*по де́реву, по ка́мню*) to carve; (*по стеклу́*) to
cut; (*по мета́ллу*) to engrave; **ре́зать** (*impf*)
слух *или* **у́хо** to grate

▸ **ре́заться** (*perf* **проре́заться**) *несов возв*
(*зу́бы, рога́*) to come through; (*no perf*; *разг*):
~**ся в** +*acc* (*в ка́рты итп*) to play.

резви́ться (-**лю́сь, -и́шься**) *несов возв* to
frolic, frisk about.

ре́зво *нареч* (*бежа́ть*) energetically.

ре́зв|ый (-, -**а́, -о**) *прил* (*ребёнок*) playful;
(*бы́стрый в бе́ге: конь, за́яц*) frisky.

резе́рв (-**а**) *м* (*СПОРТ*) reserve team; (*обычно мн*:
материа́льные итп) reserve; **ка́ссовый ~**
(*КОММ*) cash reserves.

резе́рвн|ый *прил* reserve *опред*; (*КОМП*) backup
опред; ~**ые войска́** (*army*) reserves;
резе́рвная валю́та reserve currency;
резе́рвный капита́л capital reserve;
резе́рвный фонд reserve fund.

резервуа́р (-**а**) *м* reservoir (*tank*).

рез|е́ц (-**ца́**) *м* (*инструме́нт*) cutting tool; (*АНАТ*)
incisor.

резиде́нт (-**а**) *м* spy.

резиде́нци|я (-**и**) *ж* residence.

рези́н|а (-**ы**) *ж* rubber; **тяну́ть** (*impf*) ~**у** (*разг*) to
drag things out.

рези́н|ка (-**ки**; *gen pl* -**ок**) *ж* (*ла́стик*) rubber
(*BRIT*), eraser (*esp US*); (*тесёмка*) elastic;
(*жва́чка*) chewing gum.

рези́новый *прил* rubber *опред*.

рези́нок *сущ см* **рези́нка**.

ре́зк|ий (-**кая, -кое, -кие; -ок, -ка́, -ко**) *прил*
sharp; (*свет, звук, го́лос*) harsh; (*за́пах*)
pungent; (*стиль, мане́ра*) abrupt.

ре́зко *нареч* sharply; (*встать, вы́сказать*)
abruptly.

ре́зкост|ь (-**и**) *ж* (*поведе́ния, мане́ры*)
abruptness; (*ФОТО*) focus; **говори́ть (сказа́ть**
perf) **кому́-н** ~**и** to be rude to sb.

резно́й *прил* carved.

резн|я́ (-**и́**) *ж* slaughter.

ре́зок *прил см* **ре́зкий**.

резолю́ци|я (-**и**) *ж* (*съе́зда, заседа́ния*)
resolution; (*распоряже́ние*) directive.

резона́нс (-**а**) *м* (*физ*) resonance; (*перен*)
response.

резо́н|ный (-**ен, -на, -но**) *прил* reasonable.

результа́т (-**а**) *м* result; **в** ~**е** as a result; (*в*
ито́ге) in the end.

результати́вн|ый (-**ен, -на, -но**) *прил* (*де́ло,*
встре́ча) productive; (*спортсме́н*) successful.

ре́зче *сравн прил от* **ре́зкий** ♦ *сравн нареч от*
ре́зко.

ре́зус (-**а**) *м* (*та́кже:* ~**-фа́ктор**) rhesus factor.

резца́ *итп сущ см* **резе́ц**.

резь (-**и**) *ж* sharp pain.

резьб|а́ (-**ы́**) *ж* carving; (*ви́нта, шуру́па*) thread;
~ **по де́реву/ка́мню** carving in wood/stone.

резюме́ *ср нескл* resumé, summary.

резюми́р|овать (-**ую**) (*не*)*сов перех* to

summarize.

рейд (-**а**) *м* raid; (*МОР*) anchorage.

ре́|йка (-**йки**; *gen pl* **ек**) *ж* batten;
(*измери́тельная*) measuring rod.

Ре́йкьявик (-**а**) *м* Reykjavik.

Рейн (-**а**) *м* (the) Rhine.

рейнве́йн (-**а**) *м* hock (*wine*).

рейс (-**а**) *м* (*самолёта*) flight; (*авто́буса*) run;
(*паро́хода*) sailing.

ре́йсовый *прил* regular.

ре́йтинг (-**а**) *м* popularity rating.

рейту́з|ы (-) *мн* thermal pants.

рек|а́ (-**и́**; *dat sg* -**е́**, *nom pl* -**и**) *ж* (*та́кже*
перен) river.

ре́квием (-**а**) *м* requiem.

реквизи́р|овать (-**ую**) (*не*)*сов перех* to
requisition.

реквизи́т (-**а**) *м* (*ТЕА́ТР, КИНО́*) props *мн*;
(*обычно мн: в докуме́нте*) stipulation.

рекла́м|а (-**ы**) *ж* (*де́йствие: торго́вая*)
advertising; (*сре́дство*) advert (*BRIT*),
advertisement; (*театра́льная*) publicity;
де́лать (сде́лать *perf*) **себе́** ~**у** to draw attention
to o.s.

реклами́р|овать (-**ую**) (*не*)*сов перех* to
advertise.

рекла́мный *прил* (*отде́л, коло́нка*) advertising
опред; (*статья́, фильм, справо́чник*) publicity
опред; **рекла́мный ро́лик** advertisement;
(*фи́льма*) trailer.

рекоменда́тельн|ый *прил*: ~**ое письмо́** letter
of recommendation.

рекоменда́ци|я (-**и**) *ж* recommendation.

рекоменд|ова́ть (-**у́ю**; *perf* **рекомендова́ть**
или **порекомендова́ть**) *несов перех* to
recommend; ~ (**порекомендова́ть** *perf*) **кого́-н**
кому́-н/на рабо́ту to recommend sb to sb/for a
job; ~ (**порекомендова́ть** *perf*) **кому́-н** +*infin* to
recommend sb to do.

реконструи́р|овать (-**ую**) (*не*)*сов перех*
(*промы́шленность*) to rebuild; (*па́мятник,*
зда́ние) to reconstruct.

реконстру́кци|я (-**и**) *ж* reconstruction.

реко́рд (-**а**) *м* record; **устана́вливать**
(**установи́ть** *perf*)/**поби́ть** (*perf*) ~ to set/break a
record.

реко́рдный *прил* record(-breaking) *опред*.

рекордсме́н (-**а**) *м* recordholder.

рекордсме́н|ка (-**ки**; *gen pl* -**ок**) *ж см*
рекордсме́н.

ре́ктор (-**а**) *м* ≈ principal.

ректора́т (-**а**) *м* principal's office.

религио́з|ный (-**ен, -на, -но**) *прил* religious.

рели́ги|я (-**и**) *ж* religion.

рели́кви|я (-**и**) *ж* relic; (*семе́йная*) heirloom.

релье́ф (-**а**) *м* (*ГЕО, ИСКУ́ССТВО*) relief.

рельс (-**а**) *м* (*обычно мн*) rail; **на ре́льсы** +*gen*
(*перен*) towards.

ре́льсовый *прил*: ~ **путь** railway (*BRIT*) *или*
railroad (*US*) track.

рема́рк|а (-**и**) *ж* (*ТЕА́ТР*) stage directions *мн*;

etc).

(*замечание*) remark.
ремéнь (**-ня́**) *м* (*брюк, платья, также тех*) belt; (*сумки*) strap; **привязны́е ~ни́** seat belt; **приводно́й ~** drive-belt.
ремёсел *сущ см* **ремесло́**.
ремéсленник (**-а**) *м* artisan, craftsman (*мн* craftsmen).
ремéсленный *прил* (*труд, мастерская*) artisan's, craftsman's; (*изделие*) handcrafted; (*перен: не творческий*) mechanical.
ремесл|о́ (**-á**; *nom pl* **ремёсла**, *gen pl* **ремёсел**) *ср* trade; (*перен: нетворческая работа*) hack work.
ремеш|о́к (**-ка́**) *м* strap.
ремня́ *итп сущ см* **ремéнь**.
ремо́нт (**-а**) *м* repair; (*здания*) refurbishment; (: *мелкий*) redecoration; **на ~е** under repair; **теку́щий ~** maintenance; **сдава́ть (сдать** *perf*) **что-н в ~** to put sth in for repair; **у нас до́ма сейча́с идёт ~** our house is being redecorated.
ремонти́р|овать (**-ую**; *perf* **ремонти́ровать** *или* **отремонти́ровать**) *несов перех* to repair; (*квартиру, здание*) to do up.
ремо́нтн|ый *прил*: **~ые рабо́ты** repairs *мн*; **~ая мастерска́я** repair workshop.
рéнт|а (**-ы**) *ж* rent; **земéльная ~** ground rent.
рентáбел|ьный (**-ен, -ьна, -ьно**) *прил* profitable.
рентгéн (**-а**) *м* (*мед*) X-ray; (*физ*) roentgen; **дéлать (сдéлать** *perf*) **кому́-н ~** to X-ray sb.
рентгéновск|ий (**-ая, -ое, -ие**) *прил*: **~ кабинéт/аппара́т** X-ray room/machine; **~ сни́мок** X-ray; **~ие лучи́** X-rays.
рентгено́лог (**-а**) *м* radiologist.
реорганиза́ци|я (**-и**) *ж* reorganization.
реорганиз|ова́ть (**-у́ю**) (*не*)*сов перех* to reorganize.
рéп|а (**-ы**) *ж* (*no pl*) swede (*brit*), rutabaga (*us*).
репатриа́нт (**-а**) *м* repatriate.
репатриа́ци|я (**-и**) *ж* repatriation.
репатрии́р|овать (**-ую**) (*не*)*сов перех* to repatriate.
реп|éй (**-ья́**) *м* (*разг*) = **репéйник**.
репéйник (**-а**) *м* (*бот*) burdock.
репертуа́р (**-а**) *м* repertoire.
репети́р|овать (**-ую**; *perf* **отрепети́ровать** *или* **прорепети́ровать**) *несов* (*не*)*перех* (*диалог, спектакль*) to rehearse.
репети́тор (**-а**) *м* (*преподаватель*) coach, private tutor.
репети́ци|я (**-и**) *ж* rehearsal.
рéплик|а (**-и**) *ж* (*слушателей*) remark; (*театр*) line; (*юр*) objection.
репорта́ж (**-а**) *м* (*статья, передача*) report.
репортёр (**-а**) *м* reporter.
репрéсси|я (**-и**) *ж* (*обычно мн*) repression.
репроду́ктор (**-а**) *м* loudspeaker.
репроду́кци|я (**-и**) *ж* reproduction (*of painting*

репти́ли|я (**-и**) *ж* reptile.
репута́ци|я (**-и**) *ж* reputation.
рéпчатый *прил*: **~ лук** onions *мн*.
репья́ *итп сущ см* **репéй**.
ресни́ц|а (**-ы**) *ж* (*обычно мн*) eyelash.
респекта́бел|ьный (**-ен, -ьна, -ьно**) *прил* respectable.
респондéнт (**-а**) *м* respondent.
респу́блик|а (**-и**) *ж* republic.
республика́нск|ий (**-ая, -ое, -ие**) *прил* republican.
рессо́р|а (**-ы**) *ж* spring.
реставра́тор (**-а**) *м* restorer.
реставра́ци|я (**-и**) *ж* restoration.
реставри́р|овать (**-ую**; *perf* **реставри́ровать** *или* **отреставри́ровать**) *несов перех* to restore.
рестора́н (**-а**) *м* restaurant.
ресу́рс (**-а**) *м* (*обычно мн*) resource; **приро́дные ~ы** natural resources.
рéтро *прил неизм* (*мода, мебель*) retro.
ретрогра́д (**-а**) *м* reactionary.
ретроспекти́вн|а (**-ы**) *ж* retrospective.
рефера́т (**-а**) *м* synopsis (*мн* synopses).
референ|дум (**-а**) *м* referendum (*мн* referenda).
референ|т (**-а**) *м* (*директора, министра*) aide.
рефери́ *м нескл* referee.
рефери́р|овать (**-ую**; *perf* **рефери́ровать** *или* **прорефери́ровать**) (*не*)*сов перех* to summarize.
рефлéкс (**-а**) *м* reflex.
рефлéктор (**-а**) *м* reflector.
рефо́рм|а (**-ы**) *ж* reform.
реформа́тор (**-а**) *м* reformer.
рефрижера́тор (**-а**) *м* (*судно*) refrigerator ship; (*грузовик*) refrigerated lorry (*brit*) *или* truck (*us*).
рехн|у́ться (**-у́сь, -ёшься**) *сов возв* (*разг*) to crack (up), flip; **~ (**perf**) на чём-н** to be nuts about sth.
рецензи́р|овать (**-ую**; *perf* **прорецензи́ровать**) *несов перех* to review.
рецéнзи|я (**-и**) *ж*: **~ (на** +*acc*) review (of).
рецéпт (**-а**) *м* (*мед*) prescription; (*кулин, перен*) recipe.
рециди́в (**-а**) *м* (*преступления*) repetition; (*болезни*) recurrence.
рецидиви́ст (**-а**) *м* recidivist, habitual offender.
речев|о́й *прил* speech *опред*; **~ дефéкт** speech defect; **~ы́е на́выки** speaking skills.
рéч|ка (**-ки**; *gen pl* **-ек**) *ж* stream; (*разг*) river.
речни́к (**-а**) *м* river-transport worker.
речн|о́й *прил* river *опред*; **~а́я ры́ба** freshwater fish; **речно́й трамва́й** river bus.
реч|ь (**-и**) *ж* speech; (*стиль*: разговорная *итп*) language; (*русская, французская*) spoken language; **ру́сская ~** spoken Russian; **часть рéчи** part of speech; **прямáя/ко́свенная ~**

direct/indirect speech; **у́стная/пи́сьменная ~** spoken/written language; **дар ре́чи** the gift of speech; **теря́ть (потеря́ть** *perf)* **дар ре́чи** to be left speechless; **произноси́ть** *(impf)* **у́мные/пусты́е ре́чи** to make clever/empty pronouncements; **~ идёт о** +*prp* ... we are talking about ...; **о чём идёт ~?** what are you talking about?; **~ идёт о том, как/где/кто** *итп* ... the matter in question is how/where/who *итп* ...; **заводи́ть (завести́** *perf)* **~ о** +*prp* to raise the matter of; **об э́том не мо́жет быть и ре́чи** there can be absolutely no question of this; **об э́том ре́чи не́ было** nothing was said about this; **о чём ~!** *(разг)* sure!, of course!

реша́|ть(ся) (-ю(сь)) *несов от* **реши́ть(ся).**

реша́|ющий (-ая, -ее, -ие) *прил* decisive; *(слово, матч)* deciding *опред*; **реша́ющий го́лос** casting vote.

реше́ни|е (-я) *ср (суда, собрания итп)* decision; *(ответ к задаче)* solution; *(действие: вопроса, дела)* solution, solving; *(: судьбы́)* deciding.

решёт|ка (-ки; *gen pl* **-ок) ж** *(садовая)* trellis; *(оконная)* grille; *(в камине)* grate; *(в духовке)* oven rack; **за ~кой** *(разг)* behind bars.

решет|о́ (-а́) *ср* sieve.

решёток *сущ см* **решётка.**

решётчат|ый *прил* lattice *опред*, trellis *опред*; **~ое окно́** lattice window.

реши́мост|ь (-и) ж resolve.

реши́телен *прил см* **реши́тельный.**

реши́тельно *нареч (заявить, отказать)* resolutely; *(действовать)* with resolve, decisively; **я ~ не понима́ю, о чём Вы говори́те** I've got absolutely no idea what you are talking about.

реши́тельн|ый (-ен, -ьна, -ьно) *прил (человек, взгляд)* resolute; *(меры)* drastic; *(решающий)* decisive.

реш|и́ть (-у́, -и́шь; *impf* **реша́ть) сов перех** to decide; *(задачу, вопрос)* to solve; **реша́ть (~** *perf)* +*infin* to decide to do

▶ **реши́ться** *(impf* **реша́ться) сов возв** *(вопрос, судьба)* to be decided; **реша́ться (~ся** *perf)* **на** +*acc*/+*infin* to make up one's mind on/to do.

ре́шк|а (-и) ж *(на монете)* tails *мн*; **орёл или ~?** heads or tails?

реэ́кспорт (-а) м re-export.

реэкспорти́р|овать (-ую) *(не)сов перех* re-export.

ре́|ять (3sg -ет, 3sg -ют) сов неперех *(птица)* to soar; *(флаг)* to fly.

ржа́ве|ть (3sg -ет, 3pl -ют, *perf* **заржа́веть) несов неперех** to rust, go rusty.

ржа́вчин|а (-ы) ж rust.

ржа́в|ый *прил* rusty; *(вода)* brown; *(листва)* rust-coloured *(BRIT)* или -colored *(US)*; **~ое пятно́** rust mark.

ржано́й *прил* rye *опред*.

рж|ать (-у, -ёшь) несов неперех to neigh; *(разг: смеяться)* to roar with laughter.

ржи *итп сущ см* **рожь.**

РЖУ *ср сокр* = **райо́нное жили́щное управле́ние.**

РИА *ср сокр* (= **Росси́йское информацио́нное аге́нтство)** Russian News Agency.

Ривье́р|а (-ы) ж the Riviera.

Ри́г|а (-и) ж Riga.

ри́з|а (-ы) ж *(одежда)* vestments *мн*; *(на иконе)* overlay.

рикоше́т (-а) м ricochet, rebound; **отска́кивать (отскочи́ть** *perf)* **~ом** to ricochet, rebound.

Рим (-а) м Rome.

ри́мск|ий (-ая, -ое, -ие) *прил* Roman; **Па́па Р~** the Pope; **ри́мские ци́фры** Roman numerals.

ри́мско-католи́ческ|ий (-ая, -ое, -ие) *прил* Roman Catholic.

ринг (-а) м (boxing) ring.

ри́|нуться (-усь, -ешься) сов возв to charge; **~ (perf) в рабо́ту** to throw o.s. into one's work.

Рио-де-Жане́йро *м нескл* Rio de Janeiro.

рис. *сокр* (= **рису́нок)** diag. (= *diagram*).

рис (-а) м rice.

риск (-а) м *(no pl)* risk; **на свой страх и ~** at one's own risk.

рискн|у́ть (-у́, -ёшь) сов от **рискова́ть.**

риско́ван|ный (-, -на, -но) *прил* risky; *(перен: разговор, шутка)* risqué.

риск|ова́ть (-у́ю; *perf* **рискну́ть) несов неперех** to take risks; **~ (рискну́ть** *perf)* +*instr (жизнью, здоровьем)* to risk; **~** *(impf)* +*infin* to risk doing; **Вы (си́льно) ~у́ете** you are taking a (big) risk.

ри́слинг (-а) м Riesling.

рисова́ни|е (-я) ср *(карандашом)* drawing; *(красками)* painting.

рис|ова́ть (-у́ю; *perf* **нарисова́ть) несов перех** *(карандашом)* to draw; *(красками)* to paint; *(перен: описывать)* to depict, portray; *(: подлеж: воображение, сознание)* to evoke a picture of

▶ **рисова́ться** *несов возв (виднеться)* to be seen; *(перен: в воображении)* to be conjured up; *(манерничать)* to show off.

ри́сов|ый *прил* rice *опред*.

рису́н|ок (-ка) м drawing; *(на ткани, на обоях)* pattern; *(картины)* sketch; **акваре́льный ~** watercolour *(BRIT)*, watercolor *(US)*.

ритм (-а) м *(сердца, стиха)* rhythm; *(перен: жизни, работы)* pace.

ритми́чен *прил см* **ритми́чный.**

ритми́ческ|ий (-ая, -ое, -ие) *прил* rhythmic(al); **ритми́ческая гимна́стика** aerobics.

ритми́чн|ый (-ен, -на, -но) *прил (музыка, стук)* rhythmic(al); *(работа, процесс)* smooth-running.

рито́рик|а (-и) ж rhetoric.

ритуа́л (-а) м ritual.

риф (-а) м reef.

рифлёный *прил (подошва)* grooved; **рифлёное желе́зо** corrugated iron.

ри́фм|а (-ы) ж rhyme.

рифм|ова́ть (-у́ю; *perf* **срифмова́ть) несов перех (строчки, слова)** to make rhyme

▶ **рифмова́ться** *несов возв* to rhyme.

РКП(б) *ж сокр* (*ИСТ*) = Росси́йская Коммунисти́ческая па́ртия (*большевико́в*).

р-н *сокр* = райо́н.

РНК *ж сокр* (= рибонуклеи́новая кислота́) RNA (= *ribonucleic acid*).

робе́|ть (-ю; *perf* **оробе́ть**) *несов неперех* to go shy.

ро́б|кий (-кая, -кое, -кие; -ок, -ка́, -ко) *прил* shy.

ро́бот (-а) *м* robot.

робототе́хник|а (-и) *ж* robotics.

р|ов (-ва; *loc sg* **-ву**) *м* ditch.

ро́вен *прил см* **ро́вный**.

рове́сник (-а) *м*: **он мой ~** he is the same age as me.

рове́сниц|а (-ы) *ж*: **она́ моя́ ~** she is the same age as me.

ро́вно *нареч* (*писать*) evenly; (*чертить*) straight; (*дышать*) regularly; (*через год*) exactly; **~ в два часа́** at two o'clock sharp; **я ~ ничего́ не по́нял** I didn't understand a thing.

ро́в|ный (-ен, -на́, -но) *прил* even; (*степь*) flat; (*пробор, линия*) straight; (*дыхание, пульс*) regular; (*перен: характер, человек*) stable; **~ счёт** round number; **~ным счётом ничего́** (*разг*) absolutely nothing.

ровня́|ть (-ю; *perf* **сровня́ть** или **вы́ровнять**) *несов перех* (*строй, шеренгу*) to straighten (up); (*perf* **разровня́ть** или **сровня́ть**; *дорожку, площадку*) to level; **сровня́ть** (*perf*) **с землёй** to raze to the ground.

рог (-а; *nom pl* **-á**) *м* (*также муз*) horn; (*полумесяца*) cusp; **оле́ний ~** antler; **~ изоби́лия** horn of plenty; **у черта на ~áх** (*разг*) in the middle of nowhere; **взять** (*perf*) **быка́ за ~á** (*разг*) to take the bull by the horns.

рога́лик (-а) *м* crescent-shaped roll.

рога́т|ка (-ки; *gen pl* **-ок**) *ж* (*для метания камешков*) catapult; (*на дороге*) roadblock; **ста́вить** (*impf*) **~ки кому́-н** to create obstacles for sb.

рога́т|ый (-, -а, -о) *прил* horned; **кру́пный ~ скот** cattle.

рогови́ц|а (-ы) *ж* cornea.

рогово́й *прил* horn *опред*; **рогова́я оболо́чка** cornea.

рого́ж|а (-и) *ж* (*ткань*) sacking.

род (-а; *part gen* **-у**, *loc sg* **-ý**, *nom pl* **-ы́**) *м* clan; (*ряд поколений*) family; (*происхождение*) stock; (*растений, животных*) genus (*мн* genera); (*деятельности, войск*) type; (*линг*) gender; (*одно поколение*) generation; **он ро́дом из По́льши** he comes from Poland; **он ро́дом из дворя́н** he is of noble stock; **своего́ ро́да** a kind of; **в не́котором ро́де** to some extent; **что-то в э́том ро́де** something like that; **вся́кого** или **ра́зного ро́да** all kinds of; **вести́** *perf* **свой ~ от кого́-н** to be descended from sb;

э́то у нас в ~ý it runs in the family; **из ро́да в ~** from generation to generation; **ему́ два́дцать лет от ~у** (*разг*) he is twenty years old; **он от ~у ничего́ тако́го не слы́шал** he had never heard anything like this in his life.

род. *сокр* (= роди́лся) b. (= *born*).

роддо́м (-а) *м сокр* (= роди́льный дом) maternity hospital.

роди́льный *прил*: **~ дом** maternity hospital.

роди́мый *прил* (*разг: край, земля*) native; **~ дом** family home; **роди́мое пятно́** birthmark.

ро́дин|а (-ы) *ж* (*отечество*) homeland; (*место рождения, появления*) birthplace.

ро́дин|ка (-ки; *gen pl* **-ок**) *ж* birthmark.

роди́тел|и (-ей) *мн* parents *мн*.

роди́тельный *прил*: **~ паде́ж** genitive case.

роди́тельский (-ая, -ое, -ие) *прил* (*обязанности, права, дом*) parental; (*деньги*) parents'; **роди́тельское собра́ние** parents' meeting.

ро|ди́ть (-жу́, -ди́шь; *pt perf* **-ди́л, -дила́, -ди́ло**, *pt impf* **-ди́л, -ди́ла, -ди́ло**, *impf* **рожа́ть** или **рожда́ть**) *сов перех* to give birth to; (*подлеж: земля, яблоня*) to bear a crop of;

▶ **роди́ться** (*impf* **рожда́ться**) *сов возв* to be born ◆ (*perf* **уроди́ться**) *несов* (*пшеница, яблоки*) to give a good yield; **у них ~дила́сь дочь** they had a daughter; **~ся** (*perf*) **в руба́шке** (*разг*) to always land on one's feet.

родни́к (-á) *м* spring (*water*).

родн|и́ть (*3sg* **-и́т**, *3pl* **-я́т**) *несов перех*: **~ кого́-н (с** +*instr*) to bring sb closer (to)

▶ **родни́ться** ◆ (-ю́сь, -и́шься; *perf* **породни́ться**) *несов возв*: **~ся (с** +*instr*) to become related (to).

родно́й *прил* (*брат, мать итп*) natural *опред*; (*город, страна*) native; (*в обращении*) dear; **родно́й язы́к** mother tongue; *см также* **родны́е**.

родны́|е (-х; *decl like adj*) *мн* relations *мн*, relatives *мн*.

родн|я́ (-и́) *ж собир* (*родственники*) relations *мн*, relatives *мн* ◆ *ж/м* (*разг*: **ро́дственник**) relative.

родови́т|ый (-, -а, -о) *прил* of noble birth.

родово́й *прил* (*ИСТ: строй, быт*) tribal; (*понятие, признак*) generic; (*линг*) gender *опред*; (*имение*) family *опред*; (*МЕД: судороги, травма*) birth *опред*.

родовспоможе́ние (-я) *ср* midwifery.

родонача́льник (-а) *м* (*семьи, династии*) forefather; (*перен: учения*) founder; (*: теории*) originator.

родосло́ви|е (-я) *ср* genealogy.

родосло́вн|ая (-ой; *decl like adj*) *ж* (*семьи*) ancestry; (*собаки*) pedigree.

родосло́вный *прил*: **~ое де́рево** family tree.

ро́дственник (-а) *м* relation, relative.

ро́дственниц|а (-ы) *ж см* **ро́дственник**.

ро́дствен|ный (-, -на, -но) *прил* family *опред*; (*языки, науки*) related; **ро́дственные свя́зи** family ties.

родств|о́ (-а́) *ср* relationship; (*душ, идей итп*) affinity.

ро́д|ы (-ов) *мн* labour *ед* (*BRIT*), labor *ед* (*US*); **умере́ть** (*perf*) **от ~ов** to die in childbirth; **принима́ть** (**приня́ть** *perf*) **~** to deliver a baby.

ро́ж|а (-и) *ж* (*разг: лицо*) face; (*неприятное лицо*) mug; (*МЕД*) erysipelas (*skin complaint*); **стро́ить** (*impf*) **~** (*разг*) to make faces.

рожа́ть (-ю) *несов от* **роди́ть**.

рожда́емость (-и) *ж* birth rate.

рожда́ть(ся) (-ю(сь)) *несов от* **роди́ть(ся)**.

рожде́ни|е (-я) *ср* birth; **день ~я** birthday.

рожде́ственск|ий (-ая, -ое, -ие) *прил* Christmas *опред*.

Рождеств|о́ (-а́) *ср* (*РЕЛ*) Nativity; (*праздник*) Christmas; **с ~м!** Happy *или* Merry Christmas!

рожени́ц|а (-ы) *ж* (*рожающая женщина*) *woman in labour*; (*только что родившая*) *woman who has given birth*.

рожка́ *итп сущ см* **рожо́к**.

рожна́ *итп сущ см* **рожо́н**.

рож|о́к (-ка́) *м* (*МУЗ*) horn; (*рогалик*) *crescent-shaped roll*; (*для надевания обуви*) shoehorn; (*макароны*) macaroni.

рож|о́н (-на́) *м* (*разг*): **лезть на ~** to ask for trouble; **како́го ~на́ тебе́ на́до?** (*разг*) what the hell do you want?

рожу́(сь) (*не*)*сов см* **роди́ть(ся)**.

рожь (ржи) *ж* rye.

ро́з|а (-ы) *ж* (*растение*) rose(bush); (*цветок*) rose.

роза́рий (-я) *м* rose garden.

ро́з|га (-ги; *gen pl* -ог) *ж* birch (*for punishment*).

розе́т|ка (-ки; *gen pl* -ок) *ж* power point; (*блюдечко*) jam (*BRIT*) *или* jelly (*US*) dish; (*украшение*) rosette.

ро́зниц|а (-ы) *ж* retail goods *мн*; **продава́ть** (*impf*) **в ~у** to retail.

ро́зничный *прил* retail; (**рекомендо́ванная**) **ро́зничная цена́** (recommended) retail price.

розн|ь (-и) *ж*: **студе́нт студе́нту ~** there are students and students.

розове́|ть (-ю; *perf* **порозове́ть**) *несов неперех* to turn *или* go pink; **у него́ на лбу ~л шрам** he had a pink scar on his forehead.

ро́зовый *прил* rose *опред*; (*цвет*) pink; (*ребёнок, мечты*) rosy; **ви́деть** (*impf*) **кого́-н/что-н в ро́зовом све́те** to see sb/sth through rose-coloured spectacles (*BRIT*) *или* rose-colored glasses (*US*).

ро́зог *сущ см* **ро́зга**.

ро́зыгрыш (-а) *м* draw; (*шутка*) prank.

ро́зыск (-а) *м* search; **уголо́вный ~** Criminal Investigation Department (*BRIT*), Federal Bureau of Investigation (*US*).

ро́|иться (*3sg* -и́тся, *3pl* -я́тся) *несов возв* to swarm; (*перен: мысли*) to flood.

ро́|й (-я; *nom pl* -и́) *м* (*пчёл, комаров*) swarm;

(*снежинок, искр*) flurry; (*пыли*) cloud; (*перен: воспоминаний*) flood.

рок (-а) *м* (*злая судьба*) fate; (*рок-музыка*) rock ♦ *прил неизм* (*танец, стиль*) rock *опред*.

ро́кер (-а) *м* (*разг*) rocker.

рок-му́зык|а (-и) *ж* rock music.

рок-н-ро́лл (-а) *м* rock and roll.

роково́й *прил* fatal.

ро́кот (-а) *м* rumble.

рок|ота́ть (*3sg* -о́чет, *3pl* -о́чут) *несов неперех* to rumble.

рокфо́р (-а) *м* Roquefort.

ро́лик (-а) *м* (*вращающийся валик*) roller; (*на ножке*) caster; (*ЭЛЕК*) cleat; (*фотоплёнки, бумаги*) roll; (*обычно мн: разг: коньки на колесиках*) roller skate; **~ новосте́й** newsreel; **рекла́мный ~** advertisement; (*фильма*) trailer; *см также* **ро́лики**.

ро́лик|и (-ов) *мн* roller skates *мн*.

ро́ликовый *прил* (*ТЕХ*) roller *опред*; **~ые конько́** roller skates.

роль (-и; *gen pl* -е́й, *dat pl* -я́м) *ж* role; (*текст*) part; **в ро́ли** +*gen* as; **игра́ть** (*impf*) **~** to play a part; **входи́ть** (**войти́** *perf*) **в ~** to get into the part.

ром (-а) *м* rum.

рома́н (-а) *м* (*исторический, биографический*) novel; (*любовная связь*) affair.

романи́ст (-а) *м* (*писатель*) novelist; (*учёный*) Romance language philologist.

рома́нс (-а) *м* (*МУЗ*) romance.

рома́нский (-ая, -ое, -ие) *прил* Romance *опред*; (*архитектура*) Romanesque.

романти́зм (-а) *м* (*художественное течение*) Romanticism; (*умонастроение*) romantic mood.

рома́нтик (-а) *м* (*мечтатель*) romantic; (*писатель, композитор итп*) romanticist.

рома́нтик|а (-и) *ж* romance.

рома́ш|ка (-ки; *gen pl* -ек) *ж* camomile.

ромб (-а) *м* rhombus.

ро́мовый *прил* rum *опред*; **ро́мовая ба́ба** rum baba.

ромште́кс (-а) *м* rump steak.

РОНО *м сокр* (= *райо́нный отде́л наро́дного образова́ния*) ≈ district education department.

рон|я́ть (-ю; *perf* **урони́ть**) *несов перех* to drop; (*перен: честь, авторитет*) to lose; (*no perf: листву, перья*) to shed; **~** (*impf*) **слёзы** to shed tears; **~** (*impf*) **себя́ в чьих-н глаза́х** to lose face with sb; **~** (*impf*) **слова́** to make haughty remarks.

ро́пот (-а) *м* rumble.

рос *итп несов см* **расти́**.

рос|а́ (-ы́; *nom pl* -ы) *ж* dew.

роси́н|ка (-ки; *gen pl* -ок) *ж* dewdrop.

роско́ш|ный (-ен, -на, -но) *прил* (*наряд, дом*) luxurious; (*еда*) sumptuous; (*разг: волосы, растительность*) luxuriant; (: *день, погода*) splendid; **~ная жизнь** a life of luxury.

ро́скош|ь (-и) *ж* luxury; (*излишества*)

extravagance; (*приро́ды*) luxuriance; **предме́ты**
~и luxury items; **жить** (*impf*) **в ~и** to live in
luxury.
ро́слый *прил* tall.
ро́спис|ь (**-и**) *ж* (*де́йствие: собо́ра, ку́пола*)
painting; (*узо́р: на шкату́лке*) design; (: *на*
сте́нах) mural; (*расхо́дов, иму́щества*) list;
(*по́дпись*) signature.
ро́спуск (**-а**) *м* (*а́рмии*) disbandment;
(*парла́мента*) dissolution.
росси́йский (**-ая, -ое, -ие**) *прил* Russian;
Росси́йская Федера́ция the Russian
Federation.
Росси́|я (**-и**) *ж* Russia.
россия́н|ин (**-ина**; *nom pl* **-е**, *gen pl* **-**) *м* Russian.
россия́н|ка (**-ки**; *gen pl* **-ок**) *ж см* **россия́нин**.
ро́ссказн|и (**-ей**) *мн* (*разг*) old wives' tale.
ро́ссып|и (**-ей**) *мн* (*алма́зов, золоты́е итп*)
deposit *ед*.
ро́ссып|ь (**-и**) *ж* (*грибо́в*) scattering; *см та́кже*
ро́ссыпи.
рост (**-а**) *м* growth; (*перен: ма́стерства,*
производи́тельности) increase; (*разме́р:*
челове́ка) height; (*nom pl* **-а́**; *длина́: пальто́,*
пла́тья) length; **встава́ть (встать** *perf*) **во весь**
~ (*челове́к*) to stand up straight; (*пробле́ма,*
зада́ча) to become fully apparent.
ро́стбиф (**-а**) *м* roast beef.
ростка́ *итп сущ см* **росто́к**.
ростовщи́к (**-а́**) *м* moneylender.
ростовщи́ц|а (**-ы**) *ж см* **ростовщи́к**.
росто́к (**-ка́**) *м* (*БОТ*) shoot; (*перен*): **~ки́** +*gen*
(*демокра́тии, но́вого*) beginnings *мн* of.
ро́счерк (**-а**) *м* stroke; **реша́ть (реши́ть** *perf*)
что-н одни́м ~ом пера́ to decide sth with one
stroke of the pen.
рот (**рта**; *loc sg* **рту́**) *м* mouth; **говори́ть** (*impf*) **не**
закрыва́я рта́ (*разг*) to talk nonstop; **смотре́ть**
(*impf*) **в ~ кому́-н** (*перен*) to hang on sb's every
word; **она́ в ~ не берёт ры́бы** (*разг*) she
doesn't touch fish.
ро́т|а (**-ы**) *ж* (*ВОЕН*) company.
ротапри́нт (**-а**) *м* offset duplicator.
ротозе́й (**-я**) *м* (*разг: безде́льник*) loafer;
(*рази́ня*) scatterbrain.
ро́тор (**-а**) *м* rotor.
Ро́ттердам (**-а**) *м* Rotterdam.
ро́щ|а (**-и**) *ж* grove.
роя́л|ь (**-я**) *м* grand piano.
р-р *сокр* (= **раство́р**) sol. (= *solution*).
р/с *сокр* = **расчётный счёт**.
РСО *ж сокр* (= **раке́та сре́дней да́льности**)
MRBM = *medium-range ballistic missile*.
РСУ *ср сокр* = **ремо́нтно-строи́тельное**
управле́ние.
РСФСР *ж сокр* (*ИСТ*: = **Росси́йская Сове́тская**
Федерати́вная Социалисти́ческая
Респу́блика) RSFSR (= *Russian Soviet Federal*

Socialist Republic).
рта *итп сущ см* **рот**.
рту́тный *прил* mercury *опред*; **~ сто́лбик**
mercury column.
рту́т|ь (**-и**) *ж* mercury.
руб. *сокр* (= **рубль**) R., r., rouble.
руба́н|ок (**-ка**) *м* plane (*tool*).
руба́х|а (**-и**) *ж* (*разг*) shirt; **~-па́рень** (*разг*)
straightforward chap (*BRIT*) *или* guy (*US*).
руба́ш|ка (**-ки**; *gen pl* **-ек**) *ж* (*мужска́я*) shirt;
(*игра́льной ка́рты*) back; **ни́жняя ~** (*же́нская*)
slip; **ночна́я ~** nightshirt; **смири́тельная ~**
(*перен*) straitjacket.
рубе́ж (**-а́**) *м* (*госуда́рства*) border; (: *во́дный,*
лесно́й) boundary; (*ВОЕН*) line; **он живёт за**
рубежо́м he lives abroad; **он уе́хал за ~** he
went abroad; **на рубеже́ эпо́х** between the two
eras.
руб|е́ц (**-ца́**) *м* (*от ран, по́сле опера́ции*) scar;
(*КУЛИН*) tripe.
руби́льник (**-а**) *м* knife switch.
руби́н (**-а**) *м* ruby.
руби́новый *прил* ruby *опред*.
руби́|ть (**-лю́, -ишь**; *perf* **сруби́ть**) *сов перех*
(*де́рево*) to fell; (*ве́тку*) to chop off; (*no perf:*
мя́со, капу́сту) to chop (up); (*го́лову*) to hack
off; (*да́чу, избу́*) to erect; **он ~и́т сплеча́**
(*перен*) he doesn't mince his words.
ру́б|ка (**-и**) *ж* (*де́йствие: дере́вьев*) felling;
(*избы́*) erection; (*мя́са*) chopping; (*на су́дне, на*
радиоста́нции) cabin.
рублёвый *прил* (*моне́та, банкно́та*) rouble
опред; (*пече́нье, конфе́ты*) for one rouble;
(*разг: това́р, пода́рок*) cheap.
ру́блен|ый *прил* (*мя́со, о́вощи*) chopped;
(*амба́р, изба́*) made from logs; **~ые котле́ты**
rissoles.
рубл|ь (**-я́**) *м* rouble; **переводно́й ~** convertible
rouble.
рублю́ *сов см* **руби́ть**.
ру́брик|а (**-и**) *ж* (*разде́л*) column; (*заголо́вок*)
heading.
рубца́ *итп сущ см* **рубе́ц**.
рубцева́ться (*3sg* **-у́ется**, *3pl* **-у́ются**, *perf*
зарубцева́ться) *несов возв* to form a scar.
ру́бчат|ый (**-, -а, -о**) *прил* ribbed.
ру́бчик (**-а**) *м* rib.
ру́ган|ь (**-и**) *ж* bad language.
руга́тельн|ый *прил*: **~ое сло́во** swearword;
пье́са получи́ла мно́го ~ых о́тзывов the play
got a lot of bad reviews.
руга́тельств|о (**-а**) *ср* swearword.
руга́|ть (**-ю**; *perf* **вы́ругать** *или* **отруга́ть**) *несов*
перех (*му́жа, ученика́*) to scold; (*perf* **обруга́ть**;
пье́су, статью́) to take to pieces.
▶ **руга́ться** *несов возв* (*брани́ться*): **~ся с** +*instr*
to scold; (*perf* **вы́ругаться**) to swear; (*perf*
поруга́ться): **~ся с** +*instr* (*с му́жем, с родны́ми*)

to fall out with.

ругну́ться (-у́сь, -ёшься) *сов возв* (*разг*) to swear (*once*).

руд|а́ (-ы́; *nom pl* -ы) *ж* ore.

рудни́к (-а́) *м* mine.

руднико́вый *прил* (*предприятие*) ore-mining.

рудни́чный *прил* = **рудни́ковый**.

руже́йный *прил* rifle *опред*.

руж|ьё (-ья́; *nom pl* -ья, *gen pl* -ей) *ср* rifle.

руи́н|а (-ы) *ж* (*обычно мн*) ruin.

рук|а́ (-и́; *acc sg* -у, *nom pl* -и, *gen pl* -, *dat pl* -а́м) *ж* hand; (*верхняя конечность*) arm; (*разг: в верхах, в руководстве*) contact; **из пе́рвых рук** first hand; **в э́том чу́вствуется ~ ма́стера** one can tell this is the work of clever hands; **у неё на ~х тро́е дете́й** she has three children on her hands; **под руко́й, под ~ми** to hand, handy; **она́ шла с ним по́д ~у** she walked arm in arm with him; **проси́ть** (*impf*) **чьей-н ~и́** to ask for sb's hand (in marriage); **подня́ть** (*perf*) **ру́ку на кого́-н** to raise one's hand to sb; **его́/э́то с ~ми оторву́т** (*разг*) he/it will be snapped up; **у меня́ всё ру́ки не дохо́дят до э́того** I haven't got round to (doing) it; **отсю́да до го́рода ~о́й пода́ть** it's a stone's throw from here to the town; **у меня́ ру́ки че́шутся** +*infin* ... (*разг*) I'm itching to ...; **э́то ему́ на́ ~у** that's what suits him; **брать** (**взять** *perf*) **себя́ в ру́ки** to get a grip of o.s.; **ему́ всё схо́дит с рук** (*разг*) he gets away with everything; **э́то де́ло рук ма́фии** this is the work of the Mafia; **у него́ золоты́е ру́ки** he's very good with his hands; **дела́ иду́т из рук вон пло́хо** things have hit rock bottom; **прибра́ть** (**прибра́ть** *perf*) **что-н к ~м** to get one's hands on sth.

рука́в (-а́) *м* (*одежды*) sleeve; (*реки*) branch; (*пожарный, напорный*) hose; (*зерновой*) chute.

рука́виц|а (-ы) *ж* (*обычно мн*) mitten.

руководи́тел|ь (-я) *м* leader; (*кафедры, предприятия*) head.

руководи́тельниц|а (-ы) *ж см* **руководи́тель**.

руково|ди́ть (-ожу́, -оди́шь) *несов неперех*: ~ +*instr* (*наступлением, действиями*) to lead; (*учреждением, цехом, лабораторией*) to be in charge of; (*страной*) to govern; (*аспирантами*) to supervise; **им ~оди́ла жа́дность** he was governed by greed.

руково́дств|о (-а) *м* (*походом, мероприятием*) leadership; (*заводом, институтом*) management; (*лабораторией*) supervision; (*к действию, в поведении*) guidelines *мн*; (*по рукоделию, по фотографии*) handbook, manual; (*по эксплуатации, по уходу*) instructions *мн* ◆ *собир* (*партии, страны*) leadership (*leaders*); **под ~м** +*gen* under the leadership of.

руково́дств|оваться (-уюсь) *несов возв*: ~ +*instr* to follow; (*здравым смыслом*) to be guided by.

руководя́щ|ий (-ая, -ее, -ие) *прил* (*работник, кадры*) managerial; (*орган*) governing *опред*;

~ие указа́ния instructions.

руковожу́ *несов см* **руководи́ть**.

рукоде́ли|е (-я) *ср* needlework.

рукоде́льниц|а (-ы) *ж* needlewoman (*мн* needlewomen).

рукомо́йник (-а) *м* washstand.

рукопа́шный *прил*: **они́ пошли́ в ~ бой** they went off to fight with their bare hands.

рукопи́сный *прил* (*текст*) handwritten; (*отдел библиотеки*) manuscript *опред*.

ру́копис|ь (-и) *ж* manuscript.

рукоплеска́ть (-ещу́, -е́щешь) *несов неперех*: ~ +*dat* to applaud.

рукопожа́ти|е (-я) *ср* handshake.

рукоприкла́дств|о (-а) *ср* beating.

руко́я́т|ка (-ки; *gen pl* -ок) *ж* (*кинжала, молотка*) handle; (*пульта управления*) crank.

рулев|о́й (-о́го; *decl like adj*) *м* (*МОР*) helmsman (*мн* helmsmen); (*перен: ведущий вперёд*) leader ◆ *прил*: **~о́е колесо́** steering wheel; **~о́е управле́ние** steering.

руле́т (-а) *м* (*картофельный*) croquette; (*с маком, с джемом*) ≈ swiss roll; (*окорок без кости*) boned ham; **мясно́й ~** meat loaf.

руле́т|ка (-ки; *gen pl* -ок) *ж* (*для измерения*) tape measure; (*в игорных домах*) roulette.

рул|и́ть (-ю́, -и́шь) *несов перех* to steer.

руло́н (-а) *м* roll.

рул|ь (-я́) *м* steering wheel; **стоя́ть** (*impf*) **у ~я́** (*перен*) to be at the helm.

румы́н (-а) *м* Romanian.

Румы́ни|я (-и) *ж* Romania.

румы́н|ка (-ки; *gen pl* -ок) *ж см* **румы́н**.

румы́нск|ий (-ая, -ое, -ие) *прил* Romanian; **~ язы́к** Romanian.

румя́н|а (-) *мн* blusher *ед*.

румя́н|ец (-ца) *м* glow.

румя́н|ить (-ю, -ишь; *perf* **нарумя́нить**) *несов перех* (*щёки, лицо*) to put blusher on; (*perf* **разрумя́нить**): **моро́з ~ит ли́ца** the frost makes faces glow

▶ **румя́ниться** (*perf* **разрумя́ниться**) *несов возв* to flush; (*perf* **нарумя́ниться**; *женщина*) to put on blusher; (*perf* **подрумя́ниться**; *пирог*) to brown.

румя́нца *итп сущ см* **румя́нец**.

румя́н|ый (-, -а, -о) *прил* rosy; (*пирог, корочка*) browned.

ру́пор (-а) *м* loudspeaker; ~ +*gen* (*о газете, о журнале*) mouthpiece of.

руса́л|ка (-ки; *gen pl* -ок) *ж* mermaid.

руса́лоч|ий (-ья, -ье, -ьи) *прил* mermaid's *опред*.

ру́сел *сущ см* **ру́сло**.

руси́ст (-а) *м* Russianist.

руси́стик|а (-и) *ж* Russian studies.

руси́ст|ка (-ки; *gen pl* -ок) *ж см* **руси́ст**.

русифика́ци|я (-и) *ж* Russification.

русифици́р|овать (-ую) (*не*)*сов перех* to Russify

▶ **русифици́р|оваться** (*не*)*сов возв* to be

Russified.

рýс|ло (**-ла**; *gen pl* **-ел**) *ср* bed (*of river, stream etc*); (*перен: путь развития чего-н*) course; **жизнь вошла́ в обы́чное ~** life has taken its usual course.

рýсск|ая (**-ой**; *decl like adj*) *ж см* **рýсский**.

рýсск|ий (**-ая, -ое, -ие**) *прил* Russian ♦ (**-ого**; *decl like adj*) *м* Russian; **~ язы́к** Russian.

рýс|ый *прил* (*волосы, борода*) light brown; (*человек*) with light brown hair.

Рýс|ь (**-и**) *ж* Russia.

рути́н|а (**-ы**) *ж* rut (*fig*).

рути́нный *прил* stale.

рýхлядь (**-и**) *ж собир* (*разг*) junk.

рýхн|уть (**-у, -ешь**) *сов* (*дерево, человек итп*) to crash down; (*дом, мост*) to collapse; (*перен: счастье, надежда*) to be shattered.

руча́тельств|о (**-а**) *ср* guarantee.

руча́|ться (**-юсь**; *perf* **поручи́ться**) *несов возв*: **~ за** +*acc* to guarantee; **я голово́й ~юсь, что мы успе́ем** (*разг*) I'll bet my life that we'll do it.

руче́|й (**-ья́**) *м* stream; **~ слёз** floods of tears.

рýч|ка (**-ки**; *gen pl* **-ек**) *ж уменьш от* **рука́**; (*двери, чемодана итп*) handle; (*кресла, дивана*) arm; (*для письма*) pen; **ша́риковая ~** ballpoint (pen).

ручн|о́й *прил* hand *опред*; (*животное, человек*) tame; **~а́я прода́жа** sale without a prescription; **ручна́я кладь, ручно́й бага́ж** hand luggage; **ручны́е часы́** (wrist)watch.

ручь|я́ *сущ см* **руче́й**.

рýш|ить (**-у, -ишь**; *perf* **обру́шить**) *несов перех* (*дома, деревья*) to pull down; (*no perf; разг: счастье, семью*) to wreck.

▶ **рýшиться** *несов возв* (*дом, строение*) to collapse; (*перен: семья, планы*) to be wrecked.

РФ *ж сокр* (= **Росси́йская Федера́ция**) the Russian Federation.

ры́б|а (**-ы**) *м* fish; **ни ~ ни мя́со** neither here nor there; **чу́вствовать** (*impf*) **себя́ как ~ в воде́** to feel at home; *см также* **Ры́бы**.

рыба́к (**-а́**) *м* fisherman (*мн* fishermen).

рыба́л|ка (**-ки**; *gen pl* **-ок**) *ж* fishing.

рыба́цк|ий (**-ая, -ое, -ие**) *прил* fishing *опред*.

рыба́чек *сущ см* **рыба́чка**.

рыба́ч|ий (**-ья, -ье, -ьи**) *прил* = **рыба́цкий**.

рыба́ч|ить (**-у, -ишь**) *несов неперех* to fish.

рыба́|чка (**-чки**; *gen pl* **-ек**) *ж* fisherwoman (*мн* fisherwomen); (*разг: жена рыбака*) fisherman's wife (*мн* wives).

ры́б|ий (**-ья, -ье, -ьи**) *прил* (*чешуя, хвост, клей*) fish *опред*; (*плавник*) fish's; **ры́бий жир** cod-liver oil.

рыбнадзо́р (**-а**) *м* fishing patrol.

ры́бный *прил* (*магазин*) fish *опред*; (*промышленность, хозяйство*) fishing *опред*; (*река, озеро*) full of fish; **ры́бные консе́рвы** tinned (*BRIT*) *или* canned fish; **~ день** day when

only fish is served in a canteen or restaurant.

рыболо́в (**-а**) *м* fisherman (*мн* fishermen), angler.

рыболо́вный *прил* fishing *опред*.

Ры́б|ы (**-**) *мн* (*созвездие*) Pisces.

рыв|о́к (**-ка́**) *м* (*человека, машины*) jerk; (*перен: в работе*) push; (: *бегуна*) dash.

рыга́|ть (**-ю**) *несов неперех* (*разг*) to belch, burp.

рыда́ни|е (**-я**) *ср* sobbing.

рыда́|ть (**-ю**) *несов неперех* to sob.

рыжеволо́с|ый (**-, -а, -о**) *прил* red-haired.

ры́ж|ий (**-ая, -ее, -ие; -, -а́, -е**) *прил* (*усы, волосы, животное*) red *опред*; (*человек*) red-haired.

ры́ка|ть (**-ю**) *несов неперех* to roar.

ры́лец *сущ см* **ры́льце**.

ры́л|о (**-а**) *ср* (*свиное*) snout; (*разг: лицо*) mug.

ры́ль|це (**-ца**; *gen pl* **-ец**) *ср* (*БОТ*) stigma (*мн* stigmata).

ры́н|ок (**-ка**) *м* market; **~ труда́** labour (*BRIT*) *или* labor (*US*) market; **~ки сбы́та** markets.

ры́ночный *прил* (*КОММ*) market *опред*; (*яйца, овощи*) from the market; **ры́ночная цена́** market price; **ры́ночная сто́имость** market value.

рыса́к (**-а́**) *м* trotter (*horse*).

ры́с|ий (**-ья, -ье, -ьи**) *прил* lynx *опред*.

ры́ска|ть (**-щу, -щешь**) *несов неперех* to roam, rove; **~** (*impf*) **глаза́ми** (*перен*) to let one's eyes roam.

рысц|а́ (**-ы́**) *ж* jog trot.

рыс|ь (**-и**) *ж* lynx; (*бег лошади*) trot.

ры́твин|а (**-ы**) *ж* pothole.

рыть (**ро́ю, ро́ешь**; *perf* **вы́рыть**) *несов перех* (*окопы, канал*) to dig; (*картошку итп*) to dig up

▶ **ры́ться** *несов возв* (*в земле, в песке*) to dig; (*в карманах, в шкафу*) to rummage; (*перен: в бумагах, в книгах*) to dig about; **ры́ться** (*impf*) **в па́мяти** to delve into one's memory.

рыхли́|ть (**-ю́, -и́шь**; *perf* **взрыхли́ть** *или* **разрыхли́ть**) *несов перех* to loosen.

ры́хл|ый (**-, -а, -о**) *прил* (*снег, земля*) loose; (*кирпич, камень*) crumbly; (*перен: статья, план*) rough; (: *разг: тело, человек*) podgy (*BRIT*), pudgy (*US*).

ры́царск|ий (**-ая, -ое, -ие**) *прил* (*доспехи, честь долг*) knight's; (*турнир*) jousting *опред*; (*поступок, поведение*) chivalrous, knightly; **ры́царский рома́н** tale of chivalry.

ры́цар|ь (**-я**) *м* knight; **он настоя́щий ~** he's very chivalrous.

рыча́г (**-а́**) *м* (*ТЕХ: управления, скорости*) lever; (*телефона*) cradle; (*перен: воздействия, реформ*) linchpin.

рыча́|ть (**-у́, -и́шь**) *несов неперех* to growl; (*разг*): **~ на** +*acc* (*на подчинённых, на учеников итп*) to snarl at.

рыщу *итп несов см* **ры́скать**.

рья́н|ый (**-, -а, -о**) *прил* zealous.

рэ́кет (-а) *м* racket.

рэкети́р (-а) *м* racketeer.

рюкза́к (-а́) *м* rucksack.

рю́м|ка (-ки; *gen pl* -ок) *ж* (*сосуд*) ≈ liqueur glass; (*водки, коньяка итп*) shot.

рю́мочн|ая (-ой; *decl like adj*) *ж small bar selling alcohol and sandwiches.*

рю́ш|ка (-ки; *gen pl* -ек) *ж* frill.

ряби́н|а (-ы) *ж* (*дерево*) rowan, mountain ash ♦ *собир* (*ягоды*) rowan berry; (*разг: на коже*) pockmark; (*тёмное пятно*) speck.

ряби́новый *прил* (*куст*) rowan *опред*, mountain ash *опред*; (*настойка, варенье*) rowan-berry.

ряби́ть (*3sg* -и́т) *несов перех* (*воду*) to ripple; **у меня́** ~и́т **в глаза́х** I'm seeing stars.

ряб|о́й (-, -á, -о) *прил* (*лицо, тело*) pockmarked; (*курица, скворец*) speckled; (*гладь озера*) rippling; **Ку́рочка-ря́ба** speckled hen (*in fairytales*).

ря́бчик (-а) *м* hazelhen.

рябь (-и) *ж* (*на воде*) ripple; (*в глазах*) stars *мн.*

ря́вка|ть (-ю) *несов неперех* (*разг*): ~ (**на** +*acc*) to bark (at).

ряд (-а; *loc sg* -у́, *nom pl* -ы́) *м* row; (*бойцов*) line; (*явлений, событий*) sequence; (*обычно мн: торговые, овощной*) stalls *мн*; (*prp sg* -е): ~ +*gen* (*вопросов, причин*) a number of; **из ря́да вон выходя́щий** extraordinary; *см также* **ряды́.**

рядов|о́й *прил* (*случай, жизнь, работник итп*) ordinary; (*член партии, боец*) rank-and-file ♦ (-о́го; *decl like adj*) *м* (*ВОЕН*) private.

ря́дом *нареч* close (by), near(by); **они́ сиде́ли** ~ they sat side by side; ~ **с** +*instr* next to; **э́то совсе́м** ~ it's really near.

ряд|ы́ (-о́в) *мн* (*состав: армии, партии*) ranks *мн.*

ря́женк|а (-и) *ж type of yoghurt.*

Ряза́н|ь (-и) *ж* Ryazan.

ря́с|а (-ы) *ж* cassock.

~ С, с ~

С, с сущ нескл (буква) the 18th letter of the Russian alphabet.

с сокр (= се́вер) N (= North;) (= секу́нда) s (= second).

KEYWORD

с предл (+gen) **1** (указывает на объект, от которого что-н отделяется) off; **лист упа́л с де́рева** a leaf fell off the tree; **ма́льчик пры́гнул с кры́ши** the boy jumped off the roof; **письмо́ с ро́дины/Украи́ны** a letter from home/the Ukraine; **с ле́кции/рабо́ты/свида́ния** from a lecture/work/a meeting

2 (следуя чему-н) from; **эски́з с нату́ры** a sketch from nature; **перево́д с ру́сского** a translation from Russian; **ко́пия с докуме́нта** a copy of a document

3 (об источнике) from; **де́ньги с зака́зчика** money from a customer; **с ребёнка спрос ма́ленький** one can't demand much from a child; **с меня́/него́ доста́точно** I've/he's had enough

4 (начиная с) since; **жду тебя́ с утра́** I've been waiting for you since morning; **с января́ по май** from January to May; **с утра́ до ве́чера** from morning till evening

5 (на основании чего-н) with; **зако́н введён с одобре́ния парла́мента** the law was brought in with the approval of parliament

6 (по причине): **с го́лоду/хо́лода/го́ря** of hunger/cold/grief; **с испу́га/доса́ды** with fright/anger; **со зла** out of spite; **я уста́л с доро́ги** I was tired from the journey

◆ предл (+acc; приблизительно) about; **с киломе́тр/то́нну** about a kilometre (BRIT) или kilometer (US)/ton или tonne

◆ предл (+instr) **1** (совместно) with; **я иду́ гуля́ть с дру́гом** I am going for a walk with a friend; **он познако́мился с де́вушкой** he has met a girl; **мы с ним о́чень ра́зные** he and I are very different

2 (о наличии чего-н в чём-н): **пиро́г с мя́сом** a meat pie; **хлеб с ма́слом** bread and butter; **дикта́нт с оши́бками** a dictation containing mistakes; **челове́к с ю́мором** a man with a sense of humour (BRIT) или humor (US)

3 (при указании на образ действия) with; **слу́шать** (impf) **с удивле́нием** to listen with или in surprise; **ждать** (impf) **с нетерпе́нием** to wait impatiently или with impatience; **ждём с нетерпе́нием встре́чи с Ва́ми** we look forward to meeting you; **одева́ться** (impf) **со вку́сом** to dress with (good) taste; **он ел с жа́дностью** he ate greedily

4 (при посредстве): **с курье́ром** by courier; **я уе́хал с пе́рвым по́ездом** I left on the first train

5 (при наступлении чего-н): **с во́зрастом** with age; **мы вы́ехали с рассве́том** we left at dawn; **с отъе́здом госте́й нам ста́ло ску́чно** when the guests left we got bored

6 (об объекте воздействия) with; **поко́нчить** (perf) **с несправедли́востью** to do away with injustice; **поспеши́ть** (perf) **с вы́водами** to draw hasty conclusions; **случа́ться** (случи́ться perf) **с** +instr to happen to; **что с тобо́й?** what's the matter with you?

с. сокр = село́; (= страни́ца) p. (= page).

СА ж сокр (ист) = Сове́тская А́рмия.

са́бл|я (-ли; gen pl **-ель**) ж sabre (BRIT), saber (US).

сабо́ м/ср нескл (обычно мн) clog.

сабота́ж (-а) м sabotage.

саботи́р|овать (-ую) (не)сов перех to sabotage.

са́ван (-а) м shroud.

сава́нн|а (-ы) ж savannah.

са́г|а (-и) ж saga.

сагити́р|овать (-ую) сов от **агити́ровать**.

са́го ср нескл sago.

сад (-а; loc sg **-у́**, nom pl **-ы́**) м garden; (фрукто́вый) orchard; (также: **де́тский ~**) nursery (school) (BRIT), kindergarten (US).

сади́зм (-а) м sadism.

са́дик (-а) м уменьш от **сад**; (разг: детский сад) nursery (BRIT), kindergarten (US).

сади́ст (-а) м sadist.

сади́ться (-жу́сь, -ди́шься) несов от **сесть**.

садо́вник (-а) м (professional) gardener.

садово́д (-а) м (любитель) gardener; (специалист) horticulturalist.

садово́дств|о (-а) ср (хобби) gardening; (наука) horticulture.

садо́в|ый *прил* garden *опред*; **голова́ твоя́ ~ая** (*разг*) you've got a head like a sieve.
са́ек *сущ см* **са́йка.**
са́ж|а (**-и**) *ж* soot.
сажа́|ть (**-ю;** *perf* **посади́ть**) *несов перех* (*человека: на стол, в кресло*) to seat; (: *в поезд, в автобус*) to put; (*растения, дерево*) to plant; (*разг: заключить*) to lock up; (*самолёт*) to land; **~ (посади́ть** *perf*) **кого́-н в по́езд/на самолёт** to put sb on a train/plane; **~ (посади́ть** *perf*) **кого́-н за рабо́ту** to sit sb down to work; **~ (посади́ть** *perf*) **кого́-н в тюрьму́/под аре́ст** to put sb in prison/under arrest.
са́жен|ец (**-ца**) *м* (*дерева*) sapling; (*растения*) seedling.
сажу́сь *несов см* **сади́ться.**
саза́н (**-а**) *м* carp.
са́йка (**-йки;** *gen pl* **-ек**) *ж* (bread) roll.
саквоя́ж (**-а**) *м* travelling (*BRIT*) *или* traveling (*US*) bag.
сакрамента́льный (**-ен, -ьна, -ьно**) *прил* (*РЕЛ*) sacramental; (*перен*) sacred.
саксофо́н (**-а**) *м* saxophone.
сала́з|ки (**-ок**) *мн* (*сани*) toboggan *ед*.
сала́к|а (**-и**) *ж* Baltic herring.
сала́т (**-а**) *м* (*БОТ*) lettuce; (*КУЛИН*) salad.
сала́тница (**-ы**) *ж* salad bowl.
сала́тный *прил* salad *опред*; (*цвет*) pale green.
са́л|о (**-а**) *ср* (*животного*) fat; (*КУЛИН*) lard.
сало́н (**-а**) *м* salon; (*автобуса, самолёта итп*) passenger section; (*в гостинице*) lounge; (*на корабле*) saloon; **худо́жественный ~** art salon.
салфе́т|ка (**-ки;** *gen pl* **-ок**) *ж* (*столовая*) napkin, serviette (*BRIT*); (*маленькая скатерть*) doily.
Сальвадо́р (**-а**) *м* El Salvador.
сальди́р|овать (**-ую**) *несов перех* (*КОММ*) to balance.
са́льдо *ср нескл* (*КОММ*) balance; **~ с перено́са** balance brought forward.
са́льный *прил* greasy; (*шутка, слова*) dirty.
са́льто *ср нескл* somersault.
салю́т (**-а**) *м* salute.
салют|ова́ть (**-у́ю**) (*не)сов неперех* (*+dat*) to salute.
саля́ми *ж нескл* salami.
сам (**-ого́;** *f* **сама́,** *nt* **само́,** *pl* **са́ми**) *мест* (*я*) myself; (*ты*) yourself; (*он*) himself; (*как таково́й*) itself; **он ~ предложи́л э́то** he himself suggested it; **я ~ могу́ прове́рить** I can check it myself; **ты (и) ~ зна́ешь** you know yourself; **~а его́ принципиа́льность важна́** his integrity itself is important; **~ по себе́** (*в отдельности*) per se, by itself; **~ собо́й** (*непроизвольно*) of its own accord, by itself; **фа́кты говоря́т ~а за себя́** the facts speak for themselves.
сам|а́ (**-о́й**) *мест* (*я*) myself; (*ты*) yourself; (*она*) herself; *см также* **сам.**
Сама́р|а (**-ы**) *ж* Samara.
самби́ст (**-а**) *м* sambo wrestler.
са́мбо *ср нескл* sambo (wrestling).

са́м|ец (**-ца́**) *м* male (*ZOOL*).
са́м|и (**-их**) *мест* (*мы*) ourselves; (*они*) themselves; *см также* **сам.**
са́м|ка (**-ки;** *gen pl* **-ок**) *ж* female (*ZOOL*).
само́ (**-ого́**) *мест* itself; **~ собо́й (разуме́ется)** it goes without saying; *см также* **сам.**
самоана́лиз (**-а**) *м* self-analysis.
самобичева́ни|е (**-я**) *ср* (*перен*) self-reproach.
самобы́тен *прил см* **самобы́тный.**
самобы́тность (**-и**) *ж* originality.
самобы́т|ный (**-ен, -на, -но**) *прил* original.
самова́р (**-а**) *м* samovar.
самовлюблённый *прил* (*человек*) vain.
самово́лен *прил см* **самово́льный.**
самово́ли|е (**-я**) *ср* wilfulness (*BRIT*), willfulness (*US*).
самово́л|ьный (**-ен, -ьна, -ьно**) *прил* (*человек*) self-willed; (*уход*) unauthorized.
самого́н (**-а**) *м* home-made vodka.
самоде́л|ка (**-ки;** *gen pl* **-ок**) *ж* (*разг*) home-made thing.
самоде́льный *прил* home-made.
самодержа́ви|е (**-я**) *ср* autocracy.
самодержа́вный *прил* autocratic.
самоде́ятельность (**-и**) *ж* initiative, self-motivation; (*также:* **худо́жественная ~**) amateur art and performance.
самоде́ятельный *прил* (*по личному почину*) self-motivated; (*не профессиональный*) amateur.
самодисципли́н|а (**-ы**) *ж* self-discipline.
самодовле́ющий (**-ая, -ее, -ие**) *прил* self-sufficient.
самодово́л|ьный (**-ен, -ьна, -ьно**) *прил* self-satisfied.
самоду́р (**-а**) *м* tyrant (*fig*).
самозабве́нен *прил см* **самозабве́нный.**
самозабве́ни|е (**-я**) *ср* selflessness.
самозабве́н|ный (**-ен, -на, -но**) *прил* selfless.
самозва́н|ец (**-ца**) *м* impostor.
самозва́н|ка (**-ки;** *gen pl* **-ок**) *ж см* **самозва́нец.**
самозва́нный *прил* self-appointed.
самозва́нок *сущ см* **самозва́нка.**
самозва́н|ца *итп сущ см* **самозва́нец.**
са́мок *сущ см* **са́мка.**
самока́т (**-а**) *м* scooter (*child's*).
самоконтро́л|ь (**-я**) *м* self-control.
самокри́ти|ка (**-и**) *ж* self-criticism.
самокрити́ч|ный (**-ен, -на, -но**) *прил* self-critical.
самолёт (**-а**) *м* (*aero*)plane (*BRIT*), (*air*)plane (*US*).
самолётострое́ни|е (**-я**) *ср* aircraft manufacturing.
самолюби́вый (**-, -а, -о**) *прил* self-enamoured.
самолю́би|е (**-я**) *ср* self-esteem.
самомне́ни|е (**-я**) *ср* self-importance.
самонаде́ян|ный (**-, -на, -но**) *прил* self-important.
самооблада́ни|е (**-я**) *ср* self-possession.
самообма́н (**-а**) *м* self-deception.
самооборо́н|а (**-ы**) *ж* self-defence (*BRIT*), self-

defense (*US*).

самообразова́ни|е (-я) *ср* self-education.

самообслу́живани|е (-я) *ср* self-service.

самоокупа́емост|ь (-и) *ж* (*ЭКОН*) self-sufficiency.

самоопределе́ни|е (-я) *ср* self-determination.

самоопредел|и́ться (-ю́сь, -и́шься; *impf* **самоопределя́ться**) *сов возв* (*человек*) to determine one's position; (*нация*) to make its position clear.

самоотве́ржен|ный (-, -на, -но) *прил* self-sacrificing.

самоотво́д (-а) *м* withdrawal.

самоотрече́ни|е (-я) *ср* self-denial.

самооце́н|ка (-ки; *gen pl* -ок) *ж* self-appraisal.

самоочеви́д|ный (-ен, -на, -но) *прил* self-evident.

самопа́л (-а) *м* (*разг: кустарная вещь*) cheap fake.

самопоже́ртвовани|е (-я) *ср* self-sacrifice.

самопрове́р|ка (-ки; *gen pl* -ок) *ж* (*КОМП*) self-test.

самопроизво́л|ьный (-ен, -ьна, -ьно) *прил* spontaneous.

самореклáм|а (-ы) *ж* self-advertisement.

саморо́д|ок (-ка) *м* (*золотой*) nugget; (*перен: талант*) natural.

самосва́л (-а) *м* dump truck.

самосовершéнствовани|е (-я) *ср* self-improvement.

самосозна́ни|е (-я) *ср* self-awareness.

самосохране́ни|е (-я) *ср* self-preservation.

самостоя́телен *прил см* **самостоя́тельный**.

самостоя́тельно *нареч* (*независимо*) independently; (*без помощи других*) on one's own.

самостоя́тельный (-ен, -ьна, -ьно) *прил* independent.

самосу́д (-а) *м* mob law.

самотёк (-а) *м* (*перен*) chaos; **пуска́ть** (**пусти́ть** *perf*) **де́ло на** ~ to let things slide.

самоуби́йств|о (-а) *ср* suicide; **поко́нчить** (*perf*) **жизнь** ~**м** to commit suicide.

самоуби́йц|а (-ы) *м/ж* suicide (victim).

самоуваже́ни|е (-я) *ср* self-respect.

самоуве́рен|ный (-, -на, -но) *прил* self-confident, self-assured.

самоуниже́ни|е (-я) *ср* self-abasement, self-degradation.

самоуничиже́ни|е (-я) *ср* self-humiliation.

самоуправле́ни|е (-я) *ср* self-administration.

самоупра́вств|о (-а) *ср* (*произвол*) arbitrariness.

самоуспокое́ни|е (-я) *ср* complacency.

самоустран|и́ться (-ю́сь, -и́шься) *сов возв*: ~ **от** +*gen* to evade, dodge.

самоутвержде́ни|е (-я) *ср* self-assertion.

самоу́чек *сущ см* **самоу́чка**.

самоучи́тел|ь (-я) *м* teach-yourself book.

самоу́ч|ка (-ки; *gen pl* -ек) *м/ж*: **он/она́** ~ he/she is self-taught.

самофинанси́ровани|е (-я) *ср* self-financing.

самохо́дный *прил* self-propelled.

самоцве́т (-а) *м* gem.

самоцве́тный *прил*: ~ **ка́мень** gemstone.

самоце́л|ь (-и) *ж* an end in itself.

самочу́встви|е (-я) *ср*: **как Ва́ше** ~? how are you feeling?

самца́ *итп сущ см* **саме́ц**.

са́м|ый (-ая, -ое, -ые) *мест* (+*noun*) the very; (+*adj*: *вкусный, красивый итп*) the most; **на** ~ **верх** to the very top; **в** ~**ом низу́** at the very bottom; **в** ~**ом нача́ле/конце́** right at the beginning/end; ~ **большо́й/ма́ленький/лу́чший/ху́дший** the biggest/smallest/best/worst; **тот же** ~ the same; **э́то тот** ~ **челове́к, о кото́ром мы говори́ли** this is the (same) person that we were talking about; ~**ое вре́мя** *или* ~**ая пора́ уйти́/нача́ть** it is high time to go/start; **в** ~ **раз** (*разг: вовремя*) at just the right time; **э́ти ту́фли в** ~ **раз** (*разг*) these shoes are a perfect fit; ~**ая ма́лость** the tiniest little bit; **в** ~**ом де́ле** really; **на** ~**ом де́ле** in actual fact.

сан (-а) *м* (*звание*) rank; **духо́вный** ~ holy orders *мн*.

санато́рий (-я) *м* sanatorium (*BRIT*), sanitarium (*US*) (*мн* sanatoriums *или* sanatoria).

санда́ли|я (-и) *ж* (*обычно мн*) sandal.

са́н|и (-е́й) *мн* sledge *ед* (*BRIT*), sled *ед* (*US*); (*спортивные*) toboggan *ед*.

санита́р (-а) *м* (*МЕД*) orderly.

санитари́|я (-и) *ж* sanitation.

санита́р|ка (-ки; *gen pl* -ок) *ж* auxiliary.

санита́рный *прил* sanitary; **санита́рная те́хника** = **санте́хника;**; **санита́рное состоя́ние** sanitation; **санита́рный день** cleaning day; **санита́рный инспе́ктор** environmental health officer.

санита́рок *сущ см* **санита́рка**.

са́н|ки (-ок) *мн* sledge *ед* (*BRIT*), sled *ед* (*US*).

Санкт-Петербу́рг (-а) *м* St. Petersburg.

санкт-петербу́ргский (-ая, -ое, -ие) *прил* St. Petersburg *опред*.

санкциони́ровани|е (-я) *ср* sanctioning.

санкциони́р|овать (-ую) (*не)сов перех* to sanction.

са́нкци|я (-и) *ж* (*разрешение*) sanction; (*мера*): **экономи́ческие/полити́ческие** ~ economic/political sanctions; ~ **на о́быск** search warrant; **с** ~**и** +*gen* with the sanction of; **дава́ть** (**дать** *perf*) ~**ю на** +*acc* to sanction.

са́нок *сущ см* **са́нки**.

са́ночник (-а) *м* (*СПОРТ*) tobogganist.

санте́хник (-а) *м сокр* (= **санита́рный те́хник**) plumber.

санте́хник|а (-и) *ж сокр* (= **санита́рная**

те́хника) collective term for plumbing equipment and bathroom accessories.

сантиме́тр (-а) м centimetre (*BRIT*), centimeter (*US*); (*лине́йка*) tape measure.

Сантья́го м *нескл* Santiago.

сану́з|ел (-ла́) м *сокр* (= *санита́рный у́зел*) bathroom facilities *мн*.

Сан-Франци́ско м *нескл* San Francisco.

санча́ст|ь (-и) ж *сокр* = санита́рная часть; (*ВОЕН*) medical unit.

сапёр (-а) м field engineer, sapper.

сапо́г (-а́; *nom pl* -и́, *gen pl* -) м boot.

сапо́жник (-а) м shoemaker; (*разг: пренебр*) bungler.

сапфи́р (-а) м sapphire.

сапфи́ровый *прил* sapphire *опред*.

Сара́ев|о (-а) *ср* Sarajevo.

сара́|й (-я) м (*для дров, скоти́ны*) shed; (*для се́на*) barn.

саранч|а́ (-и́) ж *собир* locusts *мн*.

сарафа́н (-а) м (*пла́тье*) pinafore (dress) (*BRIT*), jumper (*US*).

сарде́л|ька (-ьки; *gen pl* -ек) ж sausage.

сарди́н|а (-ы) ж sardine.

са́рж|а (-и) ж serge.

сарка́зм (-а) м sarcasm.

саркасти́ческ|ий (-ая, -ое, -ие) *прил* sarcastic.

саркофа́г (-а) м sarcophagus (*мн* sarcophaguses *или* sarcophagi).

сары́ч (-а́) м buzzard.

сатан|а́ (-ы́) м Satan.

сателли́т (-а) м (*также ПОЛИТ*) satellite.

сати́н (-а) м sateen.

сати́новый *прил* sateen *опред*.

сати́р|а (-ы) ж satire.

сати́рик (-а) м satirist.

сатири́ческ|ий (-ая, -ое, -ие) *прил* satirical.

Сату́рн (-а) м Saturn.

сау́довск|ий (-ая, -ое, -ие) *прил*: **С~ая Ара́вия** Saudi Arabia.

са́ун|а (-ы) ж sauna.

Сахали́н (-а) м Sakhalin.

са́хар (-а; *part gen* -у) м sugar; **рабо́та у меня́ не** ~ (*разг*) my work is no picnic; **хара́ктер у неё не** ~ (*разг*) she's not all sweetness and light.

Саха́р|а (-ы) ж Sahara.

сахари́н (-а) м saccharin.

са́харниц|а (-ы) ж sugar bowl.

са́харный *прил* sugary; (*перен: бе́лый*) white; (: *сла́щавый*) sugary; **са́харная ва́та** candy floss; **са́харная кость** marrowbone; **са́харная свёкла** sugar beet; **са́харный диабе́т** diabetes; **са́харный песо́к** granulated sugar; **са́харный тростни́к** sugar cane.

сахаро́з|а (-ы) ж sucrose.

сач|о́к (-ка́) м (*для ло́вли рыб*) landing net; (*для ба́бочек*) butterfly net.

СБ ж *сокр* (= *слу́жба бы́та*) service industries *мн*.

сб. *сокр* (= *сбо́рник*) coll. (= *collection*).

сба́в|ить (-лю, -ишь; *impf* **сбавля́ть**) *сов перех* to reduce.

сба́гр|ить (-ю, -ишь) *сов перех* (*разг*) to get rid *или* shot of.

сбаланси́рованный *прил* balanced.

сбаланси́р|овать (-ую) *сов от* **баланси́ровать**.

сба́лтыва|ть (-ю) *несов от* **сболта́ть**.

сбега́|ть (-ю) *сов неперех* (*разг*): ~ **в магази́н/за молоко́м** to run to the shop/for milk.

сбежа́ть (*как* **бежа́ть**; *см* **Table 20**; *impf* **сбега́ть**) *сов неперех* (*убежа́ть*) to run away; **сбега́ть** (~ *perf*) **с** +*gen* (*с горы́ итп*) to run down; **сбега́ть** (~ *perf*) **с ле́стницы** to run downstairs; **сбега́ть** (~ *perf*) **из тюрьмы́** to escape from prison; **улы́бка ~жа́ла с его́ лица́** the smile vanished from his face

▶ **сбежа́ться** (*impf* **сбега́ться**) *сов возв* to come running.

сбе́й(те) *сов см* **сбить**.

сберёг *итп сов см* **сбере́чь**.

сберега́тельный *прил*: ~ **банк** savings bank; **сберега́тельная ка́сса** = **сберка́сса**;; **сберега́тельная кни́жка** = **сберкни́жка**.

сберега́|ть (-ю) *несов от* **сбере́чь**.

сберегу́ *итп сов см* **сбере́чь**.

сбереже́ни|е (-я) *ср* (*де́йствие*) saving; ~**я** savings *мн*.

сбер|е́чь (-егу́, -ежёшь *итп*, -егу́т; *pt* -ёг, -егла́, -егло́, *impf* **сберега́ть**) *сов перех* (*иму́щество*) to protect; (*здоро́вье, любо́вь, отноше́ние*) to preserve; (*де́ньги*) to save (up).

сберка́сс|а (-ы) ж *сокр* (= *сберега́тельная ка́сса*) savings bank.

сберкни́ж|ка (-ки; *gen pl* -ек) ж *сокр* (= *сберега́тельная кни́жка*) savings book.

сбива́|ть(ся) (-ю(сь)) *несов от* **сбить(ся)**.

сби́вчив|ый (-, -а, -о) *прил* confused.

сбить (**собью, собьёшь**; *imper* **сбе́й(те)**, *impf* **сбива́ть**) *сов перех* to knock down; (*пти́цу, самолёт*) to shoot down; (*каблуки́, ту́фли*) to wear down; (*це́ну, температу́ру*) to bring down; (*я́щик из досо́к*) to knock together; (*сли́вки, я́йца*) to beat; **сбива́ть** (~ *perf*) **кого́-н с пути́** (*перен*) to lead sb astray; **сбива́ть** (~ *perf*) **кого́-н с то́лку** to mislead sb

▶ **сби́ться** (*impf* **сбива́ться**) *сов возв* (*ша́пка, повя́зка итп*) to slip; (*каблуки́, копы́та*) to wear down; (*собра́ться вме́сте*) to flock together; (*сли́вки, крем, я́йца*) to stiffen; **сбива́ться** (**сби́ться** *perf*) **с пути́** (*также перен*) to lose one's way; **сбива́ться** (**сби́ться** *perf*) **со счёта** to lose count; **сбива́ться** (**сби́ться** *perf*) **с ног** to be run off one's feet.

сближа́|ть(ся) (-ю(сь)) *несов от* **сбли́зить(ся)**.

сближе́ни|е (-я) *ср* (*ме́жду госуда́рствами*) rapprochement; (*ме́жду людьми́*) closeness.

сбли́|зить (-жу, -зишь; *impf* **сближа́ть**) *сов перех* to bring closer together

▶ **сбли́зиться** (*impf* **сближа́ться**) *сов возв*: ~**ся** (**друг с дру́гом**) to approach (one another); (*лю́ди, госуда́рства*) to become closer.

СБО *м сокр* = спрáвочно-библиографи́ческий отдéл.

сбо́й (-я) *м* (*перебой*) failure; (*в работе людей*) disruption.

сбо́ку *нареч* at the side ♦ *предл*: ~ **от** +*gen* at the side of, beside.

сболтá|**ть** (-ю; *impf* **сбáлтывать**) *сов перех* to shake (up).

сболтн|**ýть** (-ý, -ёшь) *сов перех* (*разг*): ~ ли́шнее/глу́пость to say too much/something stupid.

сбор (-а) *м* (*урожая, данных*) gathering; (*налогов, взносов*) collection; (*валовой, годовой*) yield; (*плата: страховой, аукцио́нный итп*) fee; (*выручка: от концерта, спектакля*) takings *мн*, receipts *мн*; (*собрание*) assembly, gathering; (*обычно мн: армейского запаса, спортсменов*) training *ед*; ~ **фру́ктов** fruit-picking; **тамо́женный/ге́рбовый** ~ customs/stamp duty; ~ **информа́ции** (*КОМП*) data capture; **порто́вые сбо́ры** harbour dues; **все в сбо́ре** everyone is present; *см также* **сбо́ры**.

сбо́рище (-а) *ср* (*разг: пренебр*) gang; (*: собрание*) mob.

сбо́р|**ка** (-ки; *gen pl* -ок) *ж* (*изделия*) assembly; (*обычно мн: на юбке*) gather.

сбо́рн|**ая** (-ой; *decl like adj*) *ж* (*также:* ~ кома́нда) national team.

сбо́рник (-а) *м* collection (*of stories, articles*).

сбо́рный *прил*: ~ **пункт** assembly point; **сбо́рная ме́бель** kit furniture; **сбо́рная мо́дель** model kit.

сбо́рочный *прил* assembly *опред*; ~ **конве́йер** assembly line.

сбо́рщик (-а) *м* (*данных, урожая*) gatherer; (*машин*) assembler; **сбо́рщик нало́гов** tax collector.

сбо́р|**ы** (-ов) *мн* (*приготовления*) preparations *мн*.

сбра́сыва|**ть(ся)** (-ю(сь)) *несов от* **сбро́сить(ся)**.

сбр|**ить** (-е́ю, -е́ешь; *impf* **сбрива́ть**) *сов перех* to shave off.

сброд (-а) *м* (*разг: пренебр*) rabble.

сброс (-а) *м* (*отходов*) discharge; (*воды*) overflow.

сбро́|**сить** (-шу, -сишь; *impf* **сбра́сывать**) *сов перех* (*бросить вниз*) to throw down; (*спустить*) to let down; (*свергнуть*) to overthrow; (*пальто итп*) to throw off; (*скорость, давление*) to reduce; (*карту*) to throw away; (*КОМП*) to reset

▸ **сбро́ситься** (*impf* **сбра́сываться**) *сов возв* (*разг: сложиться*) to chip in; **сбра́сываться** (~**ся** *perf*) **с** +*gen* to throw o.s. from.

сбру́|**я** (-и) *ж* harness.

СБСЕ *ср сокр* (= Совеща́ние по безопа́сности и сотру́дничеству в Евро́пе) CSCE (= *Conference on Security and Cooperation in Europe*).

сбу́ду(сь) *итп сов см* **сбы́ть(ся)**.

сбыва́ть(ся) (-ю(сь)) *несов от* **сбы́ть(ся)**.

сбыт (-а) *м* sale; **ры́нок сбы́та** market; **отде́л сбы́та** sales department.

сбытово́й *прил* retail *опред*.

сб|**ыть** (*как* **быть**; *см* **Table 21**; *impf* **сбыва́ть**) *сов перех* (*товар*) to sell; (*разг: избавиться*) to get rid of; ~ (*perf*) **кого́-н/что-н с рук** to get sb/sth off one's hands

▸ **сбы́ться** (*impf* **сбыва́ться**) *сов возв* (*надежды, предсказания*) to come true.

СВ *сокр* (= сре́дние во́лны) MW= *medium wave ед* ♦ *прил* (*средневолново́й*) MW (= *medium-wave*).

св. *сокр* (= **свято́й**) St (= *Saint*).

сва́деб *сущ см* **сва́дьба**.

сва́дебный *прил*: ~ **пода́рок** wedding present; **сва́дебное пла́тье** wedding dress.

сва́дьб|**а** (-ьбы; *gen pl* -еб) *ж* wedding; **игра́ть** (**сыгра́ть** *perf*) ~**ьбу** to celebrate a wedding.

свал|**и́ть** (-алю́, -а́лишь) *сов от* **вали́ть** ♦ (*impf* **сва́ливать**) *перех* to throw down; (*разг: свергнуть*) to topple; **меня́** ~**али́ла уста́лость** (*разг*) I feel whacked; **её** ~**али́л грипп** (*разг*) she's come down with the flu

▸ **свали́ться** *сов от* **вали́ться** ♦ (*impf* **сва́ливаться**) *возв* (*разг: появиться*) to turn up; (*: заболеть и слечь*) to collapse; **вся рабо́та** ~**али́лась на него́** he was landed with all (of) the work.

сва́л|**ка** (-ки; *gen pl* -ок) *ж* (*действие*) dumping; (*место*) rubbish dump.

сваля́|**ть** (-ю) *сов от* **валя́ть**

▸ **сваля́ться** *сов возв* (*волосы, шерсть*) to become matted.

СВАПО *ж сокр* SWAPO (= *South-West Africa People's Organization*).

свар|**и́ть** (-арю́, -а́ришь) *сов от* **вари́ть** ♦ (*impf* **сва́ривать**) *перех* (*шов*) to weld

▸ **свари́ться** *сов от* **вари́ться**.

сва́р|**ка** (-и) *ж* welding.

сварли́вый (-, -а, -о) *прил* quarrelsome.

сва́рочный *прил* welding *опред*.

сва́рщик (-а) *м* welder.

сва́стик|**а** (-и) *ж* swastika.

сват (-а) *м* (*сватающий*) matchmaker; (*родственник*) the father of one's son-in-law or daughter-in-law.

сва́та|**ть** (-ю; *perf* **посва́тать** *или* **сосва́тать**) *несов перех*: ~ **кого́-н** (**за** +*acc*) (*предлагать в супруги*) to try to marry sb off (to); (*no perf*; *перен*): ~ **кого́-н** (**кому́-н**) to fix sb up (with sb)

▸ **сва́таться** (*perf* **посва́таться**) *несов возв*: ~**ся к** +*dat или* **за** +*acc* to court.

свáть|я (-и) *ж mother of one's son-in-law or daughter-in-law.*

свáх|а (-и) *ж* matchmaker.

свá|я (-и) *ж* (*СТРОИТ*) pile.

свéдени|е (-я) *ср* (*обычно мн: известия, данные*) information *ед*; **доводи́ть (довести́** *perf*) **что-н до ~я кого́-н** to bring sth to sb's attention; **принима́ть (приня́ть** *perf*) **что-н к ~ю** to take sth into consideration; **к Ва́шему ~ю** for your information; *см также* **сведе́ния**.

сведе́ни|е (-я) *ср* (*пятен, грязи*) removal; (*в таблицу, в график итп*) arrangement; **~ к** +*dat* reduction to.

сведе́ни|я (-й) *мн* (*знания*) knowledge *ед*.

сведу́(сь) *итп сов см* **свести́(сь)**.

све́дущ|ий (-ая, -ее, -ие; -, -а, -е) *прил*: **~ (в** +*prp*) knowledgeable (about).

свежезаморо́женный *прил* fresh-frozen.

свежеиспечённый *прил* freshly-baked.

све́жест|ь (-и) *ж* (*продуктов итп*) freshness; (*воздуха, воды*) cleanliness; (*погоды*) briskness; **э́ти о́вощи не пе́рвой ~и** these vegetables aren't very fresh.

свеже́|ть (-ю; *perf* **посвеже́ть**) *несов неперех* (*ветер*) to turn brisk; (*воздух*) to clear; (*человек*) to look fresher.

све́ж|ий (-ая, -ее, -ие; -, -á, -ó, -и) *прил* fresh; (*воздух, вода*) clean; (*ветер*) brisk; (*журнал*) recent; **к ве́черу ста́ло свежо́** it grew chilly towards evening; **обду́мывать (обду́мать** *perf*) **что-н на ~ую го́лову** to come back to sth with a clear head.

свез|ти́ (-у́, -ёшь; *pt* -ёз, -езла́, -езло́, *impf* **свози́ть**) *сов перех*: **~ (с** +*gen*) (*спустить*) to drive down; (*собрать*) to bring; (*разг: отвезти: на дачу*) to take.

свёкл|а (-ы) *ж* beetroot.

свеко́льный *прил* beetroot *опред*; (*цвет*) beetroot(-coloured *или* colored (*US*)).

свёк|ор (-ра) *м* father-in-law, husband's father.

свекро́в|ь (-и) *ж* mother-in-law, husband's mother.

свёл(ся) *итп сов см* **свести́(сь)**.

свергн|уть (-у, -ешь; *impf* **сверга́ть**) *сов перех* to overthrow.

сверже́ни|е (-я) *ср* overthrow.

све́р|ить (-ю, -ишь; *impf* **сверя́ть**) *сов перех*: **~ (с** +*instr*) to check (against)

▶ **све́риться** (*impf* **сверя́ться**) *сов возв*: **~ся с** +*instr* to check in.

сверка́|ть (-ю) *несов неперех* (*звезда, глаза*) to twinkle; (*огни*) to flicker; **~** (*impf*) **умо́м/красото́й** to sparkle with intelligence/beauty.

сверкн|у́ть (-у́, -ёшь) *сов неперех* to flash; **у меня́ ~у́ла мысль** a thought flashed through my mind.

сверли́льный *прил* (*ТЕХ*): **~ стано́к** drill; **~ая голо́вка** drillstock.

сверл|и́ть (-ю́, -и́шь; *perf* **просверли́ть**) *несов перех* to drill, bore; (*no perf; подлеж: сомнения*

итп) to gnaw away at.

сверл|о́ (-ерла́; *nom pl* **свёрла**) *ср* drill.

сверн|у́ть (-у́, -ёшь; *impf* **свёртывать** *или* **свора́чивать**) *сов перех* (*скатать: карту, ковёр итп*) to roll up; (:*сигарету*) to roll; (*сократить*) to cut, reduce; (*временно прекратить*) to hold up ◆ (*impf* **свора́чивать**) *неперех* (*повернуть*) to turn; **~** (*perf*) **себе́ ше́ю** to break one's neck; **~** (*perf*) **кому́-н ше́ю** (*перен*) to wring sb's neck; **свора́чивать (~** *perf*) **напра́во/нале́во** to turn right/left

▶ **сверну́ться** (*impf* **свёртываться** *или* **свора́чиваться**) *сов возв* (*карта, ковёр итп*) to roll up; (*человек, животное*) to curl up; (*молоко*) to curdle; (*кровь*) to clot.

сверста́|ть (-ю) *сов от* **верста́ть**.

све́рстник (-а) *м* peer; **мы с ней ~и** she and I are the same age.

све́рстниц|а (-ы) *ж см* **све́рстник**.

свёрт|ок (-ка) *м* package.

свёртыва|ть(ся) (-ю(сь)) *несов от* **сверну́ть(ся)**.

сверх *предл* (+*gen; нормы*) over and above; **э́то ~ мои́х возмо́жностей** it is out of my reach; **~ ожида́ния** beyond all expectation; **~ обыкнове́ния** unusually; **~ того́** moreover; **~ всего́** on top of everything else.

сверхзвуково́й *прил* supersonic.

сверхпла́новый *прил* over and above the plan.

сверхпри́был|ь (-и) *ж* surplus profit.

сверхсро́чн|ый *прил*: **~ая вое́нная слу́жба** extended military service.

све́рху *нареч* (*о направлении*) from the top; (*в верхней части*) on the surface; **прика́зы ~** orders from above; **смотре́ть** (*impf*) **~ вниз на кого́-н** to look down on sb.

сверхуро́чно *нареч*: **рабо́тать ~** to work overtime.

сверхуро́чн|ые (-ых; *decl like adj*) *мн* (*плата*) overtime pay *ед*.

сверхуро́чн|ый *прил*: **~ая рабо́та** overtime; **рабо́тать** (*impf*) **в ~ые часы́** to work on after hours.

сверхчелове́ческ|ий (-ая, -ое, -ие) *прил* superhuman.

сверхъесте́ственный *прил* (*РЕЛ*) supernatural; (*перен: усилие, терпение итп*) superhuman.

сверч|о́к (-ка́) *м* (*ЗООЛ*) cricket.

сверша́|ть(ся) (-ю(сь)) *несов от* **сверши́ть(ся)**.

сверше́ни|е (-я) *ср* (*надежд*) fulfilment (*BRIT*), fulfillment (*US*); (*дел, подвига итп*) accomplishment; (*кары*) exacting.

сверш|и́ть (-у́, -и́шь; *impf* **сверша́ть**) *сов перех* to accomplish

▶ **сверши́ться** (*impf* **сверша́ться**) *сов возв* (*событие*) to take place; (*надежды, замыслы*) to be fulfilled.

сверя́|ть(ся) (-ю(сь)) *несов от* **све́рить(ся)**.

све́|сить (-шу, -сишь; *impf* **све́шивать**) *сов*

перех to lower
► свé|ситься (impf свéшиваться) сов возв: ~ся из +gen/чéрез +acc to hang from/over; (вéтви, дерéвья) to overhang.
свести́ (-еду́, -едёшь; pt -ёл, -ела́, -ело́, impf своди́ть) сов перех: ~ с +gen to lead down; (напрáвить в другу́ю стóрону) to lead off; (пятно́, грязь) to shift; (познакóмить) to introduce; (собрáть) to arrange; своди́ть (~ perf) к ми́нимуму to minimize; своди́ть (~ perf) когó-н с ума́ to drive sb mad; у меня́ ~éло нóгу I've got cramp in my leg; своди́ть (~ perf) брóви to knit one's brows; своди́ть (~ perf) ру́ки to clasp one's hands (together)
► свести́сь (impf своди́ться) сов возв: ~сь к +dat to be reduced to; своди́ться (~сь perf) к нулю́ to come to nothing.
свет (-а; loc sg -ý) м light; (Земля́) the world; (аристокрáтия) (high) society; при свéте луны́/свечи́ by moonlight/candlelight; в свéте +gen (нóвой поли́тики, послéдних собы́тий) in the light of; в мра́чном/оптимисти́ческом свéте in a gloomy/optimistic light; ни ~ ни заря́ at the crack of dawn; чуть ~ at daybreak; выводи́ть (вы́вести perf) в ~ (кни́га) to be published; выпуска́ть (вы́пустить perf) в ~ (кни́гу) to publish; включа́ть (включи́ть perf)/ выключа́ть (вы́ключить perf) to switch или turn the light on/off; пролива́ть (проли́ть perf) ~ на что-н to shed или throw light on sth; тот ~ (РЕЛ) the next world; ни за что на свéте не сдéлал бы э́то (разг) I wouldn't do it for the world; руга́ть (impf) или брани́ть (impf) когó-н на чём ~ стои́т (разг) to give sb hell.
света́|ть (3sg -ет) несов безл to get или grow light; лéтом ра́но ~ет it gets light early in summer.
свéтел прил см свéтлый.
свети́л|о (-а) ср: небéсное ~ heavenly body; (перен: науки итп) leading light.
свети́льник (-а) м lamp.
свети́|ть (-ечý, -éтишь) несов неперех to shine; (perf посвети́ть): ~ комý-н (фонарём итп) to light the way for sb
► свети́|ться несов возв (также перен) to shine; её глаза́ ~éтились любóвью her eyes shone with love; он ~éтился от ра́дости he was radiant with joy.
светлé|ть (-ю; perf посветлéть или просветлéть) несов неперех (также перен) to lighten; (ткань, вóлосы) to go lighter; (no perf; виднéться) to shine light; за óкнами ~ет it's getting light outside.
светлó как сказ: на у́лице ~ it's light outside.
свéт|лый (-ел, -ла́, -ло) прил bright; (кóмната) light, bright; (вóлосы, глаза́, крáски) light; (ум, мы́сли) lucid; ~ло-кра́сный/-зелёный light-red/-green; у негó ~лая головá he is very

bright.
световóй прил light опред; световóй день time of the day during which it's light.
светопреставлéни|е (-я) ср doomsday.
светофóр (-а) м traffic light.
светочувстви́тельный прил light-sensitive.
свéтск|ий (-ая, -ое, -ие) прил (круг, манéры) refined; (не духóвный) secular; ~ое óбщество high society; ~ человéк man of the world.
свеч|á (-и́; nom pl -и, gen pl -éй) ж candle; (МЕД) suppository; (ТЕХ) spark(ing) plug; (СПОРТ) lob.
свéч|ка (-ки; gen pl -ек) ж candle.
свечý(сь) сов см свети́ть(ся).
свéша|ть (-ю) сов от вéшать.
свéшива|ть(ся) (-ю(сь)) несов от свéсить(ся).
свéшу(сь) сов см свéсить(ся).
свива́|ть (-ю; perf свить) несов перех to weave
► свива́|ться несов от сви́ться.
свида́ни|е (-я) ср rendezvous; (делово́е) appointment; (с заключённым, с больны́м) visit; (влюблённых) date; до ~я goodbye; до скóрого ~я see you soon; назнача́ть (назна́чить perf) комý-н ~ to arrange to meet sb; (о влюблённых) to make a date with sb.
свидéтел|ь (-я) м witness.
свидéтельниц|а (-ы) ж см свидéтель.
свидéтельск|ий (-ая, -ое, -ие) прил witness's.
свидéтельств|о (-а) ср evidence; (докумéнт) certificate; свидéтельство о рождéнии/брáке birth/marriage certificate.
свидéтельств|овать (-ую) несов неперех: ~ о +prp (свидéтель) to give evidence about; (ци́фры, собы́тия) to testify to ◆ (perf засвидéтельствовать) перех (пóдпись) to certify.
свина́рник (-а) м (также перен) pigsty.
свин|éц (-ца́) м lead (metal).
свини́н|а (-ы) ж pork.
свин|ка (-и) ж (МЕД) mumps; морска́я ~ guinea pig.
свиновóдств|о (-а) ср pig farming.
свинóй прил (сáло, корм) pig опред; (из свини́ны) pork опред; свина́я кóжа pigskin.
сви́нск|ий (-ая, -ое, -ие) прил (разг) filthy.
сви́нств|о (-а) ср (разг) filth.
свин|ти́ть (-чý, -ти́шь; impf сви́нчивать) сов перех (соедини́ть) to screw together.
свинц|á итп сущ см свинéц.
свинцóвый прил lead опред; (цвет) leaden.
сви́нчива|ть (-ю) несов от свинти́ть.
свинчý сов см свинти́ть.
свинь|я́ (-и́; nom pl -ьи, gen pl -éй) ж pig; (разг: пренебр) pig, swine; подложи́ть (perf ~ю́) комý-н (разг) to do the dirty on sb.
свирéл|ь (-и) ж (МУЗ) reed pipe.
свирепé|ть (-ю; perf рассвирепéть) несов неперех to turn savage.

свире́пств|овать (-ую) *несов неперех* to rage.
свире́п|ый (-, -а, -о) *прил* fierce, ferocious.
свиса́ть (*3sg* -ет, *3pl* -ют) *несов неперех* to hang.
свист (-а) *м* whistle; (*ветра*) whistling.
сви|сте́ть (-щу́, -сти́шь; *perf* **просвисте́ть**) *несов неперех* to whistle.
свистка́ *сущ см* **свисто́к**.
сви́стн|уть (-у, -ешь) *сов неперех* to give a whistle ◆ *перех* (*разг: украсть*) to nick (*BRIT*), pinch.
свисто́к (-ка́) *м* whistle.
сви́т|а (-ы) *ж* retinue.
сви́тер (-а) *м* sweater.
свить (**совью́, совьёшь**) *сов от* **вить, свива́ть**
  ► **сви́ться** (*impf* **свива́ться**) *сов возв* (*растения*) to intertwine.
свихну́ться (-у́сь, -ёшься) *сов возв* (*разг: помешаться*) to go round the bend *или* twist; ~ (*perf*) **на чём-н** (*на футболе, на кино*) to be mad *или* crazy about sth.
свищ (-а́) *м* (*МЕД*) fistula.
свищу́ *несов от* **свисте́ть**.
свобо́д|а (-ы) *ж* freedom; **лише́ние ~ы** imprisonment; **лиша́ть** (**лиши́ть** *perf*) **кого́-н ~ы** to imprison sb; **выпуска́ть** (**вы́пустить** *perf*) **кого́-н на ~у** to set sb free; **свобо́да ли́чности/печа́ти** freedom of the individual/press; **свобо́да сло́ва** freedom of speech.
свобо́ден *прил см* **свобо́дный**.
свобо́дно *нареч* (*передвигаться*) freely; (*говорить*) fluently; (*облегать*) loosely ◆ *как сказ*: **мне здесь ~** I feel free here; **в до́ме ~** there's a lot of room in the house; **здесь ~?** is this place free?; **он ~ говори́т по-ру́сски** he speaks Russian fluently.
свобо́д|ный (-ен, -на, -но) *прил* free; (*незанятый: место, номер*) vacant; (: *комната*) spare; (*одежда*) loose-fitting; (*помещение*) spacious; (*движение, речь*) fluent; (*дыхание*) unrestricted; ~ **от** +*gen* (*от недостатков итп*) free from *или* of; **вход ~** free admission; **телефо́н ~** the telephone is free; **Вы ~ны, мо́жете идти́** you are free to go; **у меня́ сейча́с нет ~ных де́нег** I don't have any money to spare; **свобо́дный перево́д** free translation; **свобо́дный стиль** (*в плавании*) free style; **свобо́дный уда́р** (*в футболе*) free kick.
свободолюби́в|ый (-, -а, -о) *прил* freedom-loving.
свободомы́сли|е (-я) *ср* free thinking.
свод (-а) *м* (*пятен, грязи*) removal; (*частей в целое, данных в таблицу*) arrangement; (*правил итп*) set; (*летописей*) collection; (*здания, тоннеля*) vaulting; ~ **пра́вил** (*профессиональный*) code of practice; **свод зако́нов** legal code.
свод|и́ть (-ожу́, -о́дишь) *несов от* **свести́** ◆ *сов перех* (*отвести*) to take
  ► **своди́ться** *несов от* **свести́сь**.

сво́д|ка (-ки; *gen pl* -ок) *ж*: ~ **пого́ды/новосте́й** weather/news summary; **операти́вная ~** (*ВОЕН*) situation report.
сво́дный *прил* (*таблица, график*) summary *опред*; **сво́дный брат** stepbrother; **сво́дная сестра́** stepsister.
сво́док *прил см* **сво́дка**.
сво́дчатый *прил* vaulted.
своё (-его́) *мест см* **свой**.
своево́льный (-ен, -ьна, -ьно) *прил* self-willed.
своевре́мен|ный (-ен, -на, -но) *прил* timely.
своём *итп мест см* **свой, своё**.
своенра́в|ный (-ен, -на, -но) *прил* wilful (*BRIT*), willful (*US*).
своеобра́зен *прил см* **своеобра́зный**.
своеобра́зи|е (-я) *ср* distinctiveness.
своеобра́з|ный (-ен, -на, -но) *прил* (*оригинальный*) original; (*no short form*; *своего рода*) peculiar.
свожу́(сь) (*не*)*сов см* **своди́ть(ся)**.
св|ози́ть (-ожу́, -о́зишь) *несов от* **свезти́** ◆ *сов перех* to take; **он ~ози́л нас в кино́** he took us to the cinema.

┌─────────────────┐
│ **KEYWORD** │
└─────────────────┘

свой (-его́; *f* **своя́**, *nt* **своё**, *pl* **свои́**; *как* **мой**; *см* **Table 8**) *мест* **1** (*я*) my; (*ты*) your; (*он*) his; (*она*) her; (*оно*) its; (*мы*) our; (*вы*) your; (*они*) their; **я люблю́ свою́ рабо́ту** I love my work; **мы собра́ли свои́ ве́щи** we collected our things; **де́лать** (**сде́лать** *perf*) **что-н свои́ми рука́ми** to make sth oneself; **жить** (*impf*) **свои́м трудо́м** to live by one's own hard work; **крича́ть** (*impf*) **не свои́м го́лосом** to shout wildly; **называ́ть** (*impf*) **ве́щи свои́ми имена́ми** to call a spade a spade
2 (*собственный*) one's own; **у неё свой компью́тер** she has her own computer; **у меня́ своя́ маши́на** I have my own car
3 (*своеобразный*) its; **э́тот план име́ет свои́ недоста́тки** this plan has its shortcomings
4 (*близкий*): **свой челове́к** one of us; **он сам не свой по́сле случи́вшегося** he is not himself after what happened.

сво́йский|ий (-ая, -ое, -ие) *прил* (*разг*) easy-going, laid-back.
сво́йствен|ный (-, -на, -но) *прил* (+*dat*) characteristic of; **ему́ ~но серди́ться** he has a tendency to get angry.
сво́йств|о (-а) *ср* (*человека*) characteristic; (*предмета*) property.
сво́лочь (-и; *gen pl* -е́й) *ж* (*груб!*) bastard (*!*)
сво́р|а (-ы) *ж собир* (*волков*) pack; (*перен: хулиганов, мошенников*) pack, gang.
свора́чива|ть (-ю) *несов от* **сверну́ть, свороти́ть**
  ► **свора́чиваться** *несов от* **сверну́ться**.
свор|оти́ть (-очу́, -о́тишь; *impf* **свора́чивать**) *сов неперех* (*разг: сдвинуть*) to shift, budge; (: *свернуть*) to turn.
своя́ (-е́й) *мест см* **свой**.

своя́к (-á) *м* brother-in-law (*wife's sister's husband*).

своя́чениц|а (-ы) *ж* sister-in-law (*wife's sister*).

СВЧ *сокр* (= *сверхвысо́кая частота́*) SHF, shf (= *superhigh frequency*) ◆ *прил сокр* (*сверхвысокочасто́тный*) SHF, shf (= *superhigh frequency*).

свы́кн|уться (-усь, -ешься; *impf* свыка́ться) *сов возв*: ~ с +*instr* to get *или* become used to.

свысока́ *нареч* condescendingly; **смотре́ть** (*impf*) на кого́-н ~ to look down on sb.

свы́ше *предл*: в ~ +*gen* (*выше*) beyond; (*бо́льше*) over, more than; э́то ~ мои́х сил it's beyond me.

свяжу́(сь) *итп сов см* связа́ть(ся).

свя́зан|ный (-, -а, -о) *прил*: ~ (с +*instr*) connected (to *или* with); (*име́ющий связи́*): ~ с +*instr* (*с деловы́ми круга́ми, с худо́жниками итп*) associated with; (-, -на, -но; *несвобо́дный*: *движе́ния, речь*) restricted; э́то ~о со значи́тельными расхо́дами it involves considerable expense; он был не́сколько лет свя́зан с э́той фи́рмой he was involved with the company for several years.

связ|а́ть (-жу́, -жешь) *сов от* вяза́ть ◆ (*impf* свя́зывать) *перех* (*верёвку итп*) to tie; (*ве́щи, челове́ка*) to tie up; (*перен: де́йствия, инициати́ву*) to bind; (*установи́ть сообще́ние, зави́симость*): ~ что-н с +*instr* to connect *или* link sth to; с чем Вы э́то свя́зываете? to what do you attribute this?; я могу́ Вас с ним ~ I can put you in touch with him; он ~а́л свою́ жизнь с нау́кой he devoted his life to science; он двух слов ~ не мо́жет (*перен*) he can't string two words together; свя́зывать (~ *perf*) кого́-н по рука́м и нога́м (*перен*) to bind sb hand and foot

► **связ|а́ться** (*impf* свя́зываться) *сов возв*: ~ся с +*instr* to contact; (*разг: с вора́ми итп*) to get mixed up with; (: *с невы́годным де́лом*) to get o.s. caught up in; свя́зываться (~ся *perf*) с кем-н по телефо́ну to get in touch with sb by phone.

свя́з|и (-ей) *мн* (*знако́мства*) connections *мн*.

связи́ст (-а) *м* (*ВОЕН*) signalman (*мн* signalmen).

свя́з|ка (-ки; *gen pl* -ок) *ж* (*ключе́й*) bunch; (*бума́г, дров*) bundle; (*АНАТ*) ligament; (*ЛИНГ*) copula.

связн|о́й (-о́го; *decl like adj*) *м* messenger.

свя́зный *прил* coherent.

свя́зок *сущ см* свя́зка.

связу́ющий (-ая, -ее, -ие) *прил* connecting *опред*.

свя́зывани|е (-я) *ср* tying.

свя́зыва|ть(ся) (-ю(сь)) *несов от* связа́ть(ся).

связ|ь (-и) *ж* (*экономи́ческая, дру́жеская итп*) tie; (*причи́нная*) connection, link; (*телегра́фная, почто́вая итп*) communications *мн*; (*та́кже:* любо́вная ~)

relationship; в ~и с +*instr* (*всле́дствие*) due to; (*по по́воду*) in connection with; в э́той ~й in this regard; **Министе́рство Свя́зи** Ministry of Communications; *см та́кже* свя́зи.

свят|а́я (-о́й; *decl like adj*) *ж см* свято́й.

святи́лищ|е (-а) *ср* (*РЕЛ*) sanctuary.

свя|ти́ть (-щу́, -ти́шь; *perf* освяти́ть) *несов перех* (*РЕЛ*) to sanctify.

свя́т|ки (-ок) *мн* ≈ Christmas(tide) *ед*.

свят|о́й *прил* holy; (-, -а, -о; *де́ло, обя́занность, и́стина*) sacred ◆ (-о́го; *decl like adj*) *м* (*РЕЛ*) saint; ~а́я святы́х the holy of holies; ~ оте́ц father (*used to address a priest*); он/она́ ~ челове́к he/she is a real saint.

свя́ток *сущ см* свя́тки.

свя́тост|ь (-и) *ж* holiness; (*де́ла, чу́вства*) sanctity.

святота́тств|о (-а) *ср* sacrilege.

святы́н|я (-и) *ж* (*ме́сто*) sacred place; (*предме́т*) sacred object.

свяще́нник (-а) *м* priest.

священноде́йстви|е (-я) *ср* religious ceremony.

священноде́йств|овать (-ую) *несов неперех* to conduct a religious ceremony.

священнослужи́тел|ь (-я) *м* clergyman (*мн* clergymen).

свяще́нный *прил* holy, sacred; (*долг, обя́занность*) sacred; **Свяще́нное Писа́ние** Holy Scripture.

свяще́нств|о (-а) *ср собир* the priesthood.

свящу́ *несов см* святи́ть.

с.г. *сокр* = сего́ го́да.

сгиб (-а) *м* bend.

сгиба́|ть (-ю; *perf* согну́ть) *несов перех* to bend

► **сгиба́|ться** (*perf* согну́ться) *несов возв* to bend down.

сги́н|уть (-у, -ешь) *сов неперех* (*разг*) to vanish.

сгла́|дить (-жу, -дишь; *impf* сгла́живать) *сов перех* to smooth out; (*перен: противоре́чия, остроту́ го́ря*) to smooth over; сгла́живать (~ *perf*) углы́ (*перен*) to iron out difficulties

► **сгла́|диться** (*impf* сгла́живаться) *сов возв* to be smoothed out.

сгла́|зить (-жу, -зишь) *сов перех* (*РЕЛ*) to put the evil eye on; (*разг*) to jinx.

сглуп|и́ть (-лю́, -и́шь) *сов от* глупи́ть.

сгнива́|ть (*3sg* -ет, *3pl* -ют) *несов неперех* to rot.

сгни|ть (-ю, -ёшь) *сов от* гнить.

сгно|и́ть (-ю́, -и́шь) *сов от* гнои́ть.

сгова́рива|ться (-юсь) *несов от* сговори́ться.

сго́вор (-а) *м* agreement.

сговор|и́ться (-ю́сь, -и́шься; *impf* сгова́риваться) *сов возв*: ~ с +*instr* (*о встре́че, о сде́лке*) to come to an arrangement with; (*в диску́ссии, в бесе́де*) to reach an agreement with.

сгово́рчив|ый (-, -а, -о) *прил* cooperative.

сгоню́ *итп сов см* **согна́ть**.

сгоня́ть (-ю) *несов от* **согна́ть** ♦ *сов неперех* (*разг: сбегать*) to run ♦ *перех* (*послать*) to send.

сгора́ни|е (-я) *ср* (*ТЕХ*) combustion.

сгора́ть (-ю) *несов от* **сгоре́ть** ♦ *неперех*: ~ **от** **любопы́тства/нетерпе́ния** to be burning with curiosity/impatience.

сго́рб|ить(ся) (-лю(сь), -ишь(ся)) *сов от* **го́рбить(ся)**.

сгор|е́ть (-ю́, -и́шь; *impf* **сгора́ть** *или* **горе́ть**) *сов неперех* to burn; (*impf* **сгора́ть**; *ЭЛЕК*) to fuse; (*на солнце*) to get burnt; (*перен: на работе*) to burn o.s. out.

сгоряча́ *нареч* in the heat of the moment.

сгото́в|ить (-лю, -ишь) *сов от* **гото́вить**.

сгр|ести́ (-ебу́, -ебёшь; *pt* -ёб, -ебла́, -ебло́, *impf* **сгреба́ть**) *сов перех* (*собрать*) to rake up; (*скинуть*): ~ **с** +*gen* to shovel off.

сгруд|и́ться (*3sg* -и́тся, *1pl* -и́мся) *сов неперех* (*разг*) to crowd together.

сгр|узи́ть (-ужу́, -у́зишь; *impf* **сгружа́ть**) *сов перех*: ~ (**с** +*gen*) to unload (from).

сгруппир|ова́ть(ся) (-у́ю(сь)) *сов от* **группирова́ть(ся)**.

сгу́б|ить (-лю́, -ишь, -у́бишь) *сов от* **губи́ть**.

сгу|сти́ть (-щу́, -усти́шь; *impf* **сгуща́ть**) *сов перех* to thicken; **сгуща́ть** (~ *perf*) **кра́ски** (*перен*) to paint an exaggerated picture

▶ **сгусти́ться** (*impf* **сгуща́ться**) *сов возв* to thicken.

сгу́ст|ок (-ка) *м* blob.

сгуща́|ть(ся) (-ю(сь)) *несов от* **сгусти́ть(ся)**.

сгущённый *прил*: ~**ое молоко́** condensed milk.

сгущу́(сь) *сов см* **сгусти́ть(ся)**.

с.-д. *сокр* = **социа́л-демократи́ческий**.

сда|ва́ть (-ю́, -ёшь; *imper* -ва́й(те)) *несов от* **сдать** ♦ *перех*: ~ **экза́мен** to sit an exam

▶ **сдава́ться** *несов от* **сда́ться** ♦ *возв* (*отдаваться внаём*) to be leased out ♦ *безл* (+*dat*; *разг*): ~**ётся мне, что** ... I reckon that ...; **~**ётся внаём**" "to let".

сда|ви́ть (-авлю́, -а́вишь; *impf* **сда́вливать**) *сов перех* to squeeze.

сда́вленный (-, -на, -но) *прил* (*голос, плач*) choked.

сда́влива|ть (-ю) *несов от* **сдави́ть**.

сдавлю́ *сов см* **сдави́ть**.

сда́м(ся) *итп сов см* **сда́ть(ся)**.

сда́тчик (-а) *м* supplier.

сда́ть (*как* **дать**; *см* **Table 14**; *impf* **сдава́ть**) *сов перех* (*пальто, багаж, работу*) to hand in; (*сырьё, продукцию*) to supply; (*дежурство, рабочее место итп*) to hand over; (*дом, комнату итп*) to rent out; (*город, позицию*) to surrender; (*сдачу*) to give (back); (*no impf*; экзамен, зачёт итп) to pass ♦ *неперех* (*ослабеть*) to give out; **сдать** (*perf*) **дела́** to step down; **сдава́ть** (**сдать** *perf*) **ору́жие** to lay down one's arms; **он сдал мне 5 рубле́й** he gave me 5 roubles change

▶ **сда́ться** (*impf* **сдава́ться**) *сов возв* to give up; (*солдат, город*) to surrender; **сдава́ться** (~**ся** *perf*) **на** +*acc* (*на уговоры итп*) to give in to; **на что мне сдали́сь э́ти де́ньги?** (*разг*) what use is this money to me?; **сдава́ться** (~**ся** *perf*) **в плен кому́-н** to give o.s. up to sb.

сда́ч|а (-и) *ж* (*сырья*) supply; (*экзамена*) passing; (*дежурства*) handing over; (*дома*) letting; (*города врагу*) surrender; (*излишек денег*) change; (*КАРТЫ*) deal; **дава́ть (дать** *perf*) **кому́-н** ~**у** (*в магазине*) to give sb his *итп* change; **дать** (*perf*) **кому́-н** ~**и** (*разг*) to match sb blow for blow; ~ **с 10 рубле́й** change from 10 roubles.

сда́шь(ся) *сов см* **сда́ть(ся)**.

сдвиг (-а) *м* (*в работе, в учёбе*) progress; (*в сознании*) change; **у него́** ~ (*разг*) he's not all there.

сдви́|нуть (-у, -ешь; *impf* **сдвига́ть**) *сов перех* (*переместить*) to move; (*сблизить*) to move together; (*заставить тронуться*) to shift

▶ **сдви́нуться** (*impf* **сдвига́ться**) *сов возв*: ~**ся** (**с ме́ста**) to move; (*сместиться*) to shift.

сде́ла|ть(ся) (-ю(сь)) *сов от* **де́лать(ся)**.

сде́л|ка (-ки; *gen pl* -ок) *ж* deal; **заключа́ть (заключи́ть** *perf*) ~**ку (с** +*instr*) to do a deal (with); **пойти́** (*perf*) **на** ~**ку с со́вестью** to do a deal with the devil.

сде́льный *прил*: ~**ая рабо́та** piecework.

сде́льщик (-а) *м* pieceworker.

сде́льщиц|а (-ы) *ж см* **сде́льщик**.

сдёргива|ть (-ю) *несов от* **сдёрнуть**.

сде́ржанно *нареч* (*сказать, плакать итп*) with restraint; (*отнестись, принять*) with reserve.

сде́ржан|ный (-, -на, -но) *прил* (*человек*) reserved; (*чувства*) contained.

сдержа́ть (-ержу́, -е́ржишь; *impf* **сде́рживать**) *сов перех* to contain, hold back; **сде́рживать** (~ *perf*) **себя́** to contain o.s.; **сде́рживать** (~ *perf*) **сло́во/обеща́ние** to keep one's word/promise; **сде́рживать** (~ *perf*) **кля́тву** to honour an oath

▶ **сдержа́ться** (*impf* **сде́рживаться**) *сов возв* to restrain o.s.

сдёрн|уть (-у, -ешь; *impf* **сдёргивать**) *сов перех* to pull off.

сдеру́ *итп сов см* **содра́ть**.

сдира́|ть (-ю; *perf* **содра́ть**) *несов перех* (*кожуру, кору*) to peel off.

сдо́б|а (-ы) *ж* (*добавки*) shortening ♦ *собир* (*булки*) buns *мн*.

сдо́бный *прил* rich.

сдо́хн|уть (-у, -ешь) *сов от* **до́хнуть**.

сдр|ужи́ть (-ужу́, -у́жишь) *сов перех* to bring together

▶ **сдружи́ться** *сов возв* to become friends.

сдубли́р|овать (-ую) *сов от* **дубли́ровать**.

сдува́|ть (-ю) *несов см* **сдуть**.

сду́ру *нареч* (*разг*) stupidly.

сду|ть (-ю; *impf* **сдува́ть**) *сов перех* to blow away; (*разг: списать*) to copy.

сдыха́|ть (-ю) *несов неперех* (*разг: человек*) to

snuff it.

сё (**сего́**) *мест* this; **то да ~** (*разг*) this and that; **ни то ни ~** (*разг*) neither one thing nor the other.

сеа́нс (**-а**) *м* (*кино*) show; (*психотерапии итп*) session.

СЕА́ТО *ср сокр* (= Организа́ция догово́ра Юго-Восто́чной А́зии) SEATO (= *Southeast Asia Treaty Organization*).

себе́ *мест см* **себя́** ♦ *част* (*разг*): **так ~** so-so; **ничего́ ~!** wow!; **иди́ ~, не вме́шивайся!** just stay out of it!

себесто́имост|ь (**-и**) *ж* cost price.

KEYWORD

себя́ *мест* (*я*) myself; (*ты*) yourself; (*он*) himself; (*она*) herself; (*оно*) itself; (*мы*) ourselves; (*вы*) yourselves; (*они*) themselves; **он тре́бователен к себе́** he asks a lot of himself; **она́ вини́т себя́** she blames herself; **представля́ть** (**предста́вить** *perf*) **что-н себе́** to imagine sth; **испы́тывать** (**испыта́ть** *perf*) **что-н на себе́** (*лекарство*) to test sth on o.s.; (*трудности*) to experience sth; **к себе́** (*домой*) home; (*в свою комнату*) to one's room; **„к себе́"** (*на двери*) "pull"; **„от себя́"** (*на двери*) "push"; **по себе́** (*по своим вкусам*) to one's taste; **убира́ть** (**убра́ть** *perf*) **по́сле себя́** to tidy up after o.s.; **приходи́ть** (**прийти́** *perf*) **в себя́** to come to one's senses; **говори́ть** (*impf*)/**чита́ть** (*impf*) **про себя́** to talk/read to o.s.; **она́ себе́ на уме́** (*разг*) she is secretive; **он** (*в своём доме*) he is at home; (*в своём кабинете*) he is in the office.

себялюби́в|ый (**-, -а, -о**) *прил* egotistical.

себялю́би|е (**-я**) *ср* self-love.

сев (**-а**) *м* sowing.

Севасто́пол|ь (**-я**) *м* Sevastopol.

се́вер (**-а**) *м* north; **С~** (*Арктика*) the Arctic North.

се́верн|ый *прил* north *опред*; (*ветер, направление*) northerly; (*климат, полушарие*) northern; **С~ Кавка́з** the Northern Caucasus; **С~ая Коре́я** North Korea; **С~ Ледови́тый океа́н** Arctic Ocean; **се́верное сия́ние** the northern lights *мн*; **Се́верный по́люс** the North Pole.

се́веро-восто́к (**-а**) *м* northeast.

се́веро-за́пад (**-а**) *м* northwest.

северя́н|ин (**-ина**; *nom pl* **-е**, *gen pl* **-**) *м* northerner.

северя́н|ка (**-ки**; *gen pl* **-ок**) *ж см* **северя́нин**.

севрю́г|а (**-и**) *ж* sturgeon.

сегме́нт (**-а**) *м* segment.

сего́ *мест см* **сей, сие́**.

сего́дня *нареч, сущ нескл* today; **~ у́тром/ днём/ве́чером** this morning/afternoon/ evening; **встре́ча назна́чена на ~** this meeting

has been set for today; **на ~ у нас ма́ло ресу́рсов** we currently have very few resources; **не ~~за́втра** any day now.

сего́дняшн|ий (**-яя, -ее, -ие**) *прил* today's; **~ день** today; **на ~ день** at present; **жить** (*impf*) **~им днём** to live for the present.

сегрега́ци|я (**-и**) *ж* segregation.

седе́л *сущ см* **седло́**.

седе́|ть (**-ю**; *perf* **поседе́ть**) *несов неперех* to go grey (*BRIT*) *или* gray (*US*).

седина́ (**-ины́**; *nom pl* **-и́ны**) *ж* grey (*BRIT*) *или* gray (*US*) hair.

седла́|ть (**-ю**; *perf* **оседла́ть**) *несов перех* to saddle.

седл|о́ (**-а́**; *nom pl* **сёдла**, *gen pl* **сёдел**) *ср* saddle; **вы́шибить** (*perf*) *или* **вы́бить** (*perf*) **кого́-н из ~а́** (*перен*) to knock sb out of his *итп* stride.

седовла́с|ый (**-, -а, -о**) *прил* grey-haired (*BRIT*), gray-haired (*US*).

седоволо́с|ый (**-, -а, -о**) *прил* = **седовла́сый**.

сед|о́й (**-, -а́, -о**) *прил* (*волосы*) grey (*BRIT*), gray (*US*); (*человек*) grey-haired (*BRIT*), gray-haired (*US*); **~а́я старина́** ancient times.

седо́|к (**-а́**) *м* (*всадник*) rider; (*пассажир*) passenger.

седьм|о́й (**-а́я, -о́е, -ы́е**) *чис* seventh; **сейча́с ~ час** it's after six; **быть** (*impf*) **на ~о́м не́бе** to be in seventh heaven; *см также* **пя́тый**.

сезо́н (**-а**) *м* season; **~ дожде́й** the rainy season.

сезо́нник (**-а**) *м* seasonal worker.

сезо́нный *прил* seasonal; **сезо́нный биле́т** season ticket.

сей (**сего́**; *см* **Table 12**) *мест* this; **сию́ мину́ту** *или* **секу́нду!** this minute!; **~ раз** on this occasion; **по ~ день** to this day; **5-го ма́я сего́ го́да** on the 5th (of) May this year; **от сих до сих** (*разг*) from here to here.

сейсми́ческ|ий (**-ая, -ое, -ие**) *прил* (*колебания, волны*) seismic; (*станция, прибор*) seismological.

сейсмо́лог (**-а**) *м* seismologist.

сейф (**-а**) *м* (*ящик*) safe; (*помещение*) vault.

сейча́с *нареч* (*теперь*) now; (*скоро*) just now; (*разг: недавно*) (only) just; **он ~ рабо́тает** he's working just now; **~ приду́** I'm just on my way; **~ же!** right now!

сёк *итп сов см* **сечь**.

СЕКА́М *м сокр* (= систе́ма цветно́го телеви́дения) SECAM (= *séquentiel couleur à mémoire*).

сека́тор (**-а**) *м* secateurs *мн*.

секре́т (**-а**) *м* secret; **по ~у** in secret; **под ~ом** confidentially; **держа́ть** (*impf*) **что-н в ~е** to keep sth a secret.

секретариа́т (**-а**) *м* secretariat.

секрета́рш|а (**-и**) *ж* (*разг*) secretary (*female*).

секрета́р|ь (**-я**) *м* secretary; **генера́льный ~** secretary-general; **секрета́рь-машини́стка**

secretary.

секрéтен *прил см* **секрéтный**.

секретéр (-а) *м* bureau (*BRIT*), secretaire.

секрéтничать (-ю) *несов неперех* (*скрытничать*) to be secretive; (*разговаривать по секрету*) to talk secretively.

секрéтный (-ен, -на, -но) *прил* secret.

секс (-а) *м* sex.

сексопúльность (-и) *ж* sex appeal.

сексопúльный *прил* sexy.

сексуáльный *прил* sexual; (-ен, -ьна, -ьно; *эротичный*) sexy; **сексуáльная жизнь** sex life; **сексуáльное образовáние** sex education.

сéкт|а (-ы) *ж* sect.

сектáнт (-а) *м* sect member.

сектáнт|ка (-ки; *gen pl* -ок) *ж см* **сектáнт**.

сектáнтск|ий (-ая, -ое, -ие) *прил* sectarian.

сéктор (-а) *м* (*также* ЭКОН, ГЕОМ) sector; (*здания*) section; (*учреждения*) department.

сéкторный *прил*: **сéкторная диаграмма** pie chart.

секу́ *итп сов см* **сечь**.

секу́нд|а (-ы) *ж* second; **(одну́) ~у!** just one *или* a second!

секундáнт (-а) *м* second (*of boxer, duellist*).

секу́ндный *прил* (*пауза, заминка*) second's; **~ая стрéлка** second hand (*on clock*).

секундомéр (-а) *м* stopwatch.

секциóнный *прил* divided into sections.

сéкци|я (-и) *ж* section.

сел *итп сов см* **сесть**.

селёд|ка (-ки; *gen pl* -ок) *ж* herring.

селезёнк|а (-и) *ж* spleen.

сéлез|ень (-ня) *м* drake.

селéктор (-а) *м* (ТЕЛ) intercom.

селекционéр (-а) *м* breeder.

селéкци|я (-и) *ж* (БИО) selective breeding.

селéни|е (-я) *ср* village.

сел|и́ть (-ю, -ишь; *perf* **посели́ть**) *несов перех* (*в местности*) to settle; (*в доме*) to house

► **сели́ться** (*perf* **посели́ться**) *несов возв* to settle.

сел|ó (-á; *nom pl* **сёла**) *ср* (*селение*) village; (*no pl*; *местность*) the country; **ни к ~у́ ни к гóроду** (*разг*) inappropriately.

сел|ь (-я) *м* mountain torrent.

сельдерé|й (-я) *м* celery.

сельд|ь (-и; *gen pl* -éй) *ж* herring.

сельпó *ср нескл* (= *сéльское потреби́тельское óбщество*) village shop.

сéльск|ий (-ая, -ое, -ие) *прил* (*см сущ*) village *опред*; country *опред*, rural; **сéльское хозя́йство** agriculture.

сельскохозя́йственный *прил* agricultural.

сельчá|нин (-нина; *nom pl* -е, *gen pl* -) *м* villager.

сельчá|нка (-ки; *gen pl* -ок) *ж см* **сельчáнин**.

сём *мест см* **сей, сиé**.

семáнтик|а (-и) *ж* semantics.

семанти́ческий (-ая, -ое, -ие) *прил* semantic.

семафóр (-а) *м* semaphore.

сёмг|а (-и) *ж* salmon.

семéйный *прил* family *опред*; **~ человéк**

family man.

семéйственность (-и) *ж* nepotism.

семéйств|о (-а) *ср* family.

сéмени *итп сущ см* **сéмя**.

семен|и́ть (-ю́, -и́шь) *несов неперех* to mince.

семеннóй *прил* (*для посева*) seed *опред*; (БИО) sperm *опред*.

семёр|ка (-ки; *gen pl* -ок) *ж* (*цифра, карта*) seven; (*группа из семи*) group of seven; (*разг*: *автобус, трамвай итп*) (number) seven (*bus, tram etc*).

сéмер|о (-ы́х; *как* **чéтверо**; *см* **Table 36b**) *чис* seven; *см также* **двóе**.

семёрок *сущ см* **семёрка**.

семéстр (-а) *м* term (*BRIT*), semester (*US*).

сéмеч|ки (-ек) *мн* (*подсолнечника*) sunflower seeds *мн*.

сéмеч|ко (-ка; *gen pl* -ек) *ср* seed; *см также* **сéмечки**.

семи́ *чис см* **семь**.

семи́десяти *чис см* **сéмьдесят**.

семидесятилéти|е (-я) *ср* (*промежуток*) seventy years; (*годовщина*) seventieth anniversary.

семидесятилéтн|ий (-яя, -ее, -ие) *прил* seventy-year; (*человек*) seventy-year-old.

семидеся́т|ый (-ая, -ое, -ые) *чис* seventieth; *см также* **пятидеся́тый**.

семиднéвный *прил* seven-day.

семиклáссник (-а) *м pupil in seventh year at school* (*usually 13 years old*).

семиклáссниц|а (-ы) *ж см* **семиклáссник**.

семикрáтн|ый *прил*: **~ чемпиóн** seven-times champion; **в ~ом размéре** sevenfold.

семилéти|е (-я) *ср* (*срок*) seven years; (*годовщина*) seventh anniversary.

семилéтн|ий (-яя, -ее, -ие) *прил* seven-year; (*ребёнок*) seven-year-old.

семимéсячный *прил* seven-month; (*ребёнок*) seven-month-old.

семинáр (-а) *м* seminar.

семинари́ст (-а) *м* seminarist.

семинáри|я (-и) *ж* seminary.

семинедéльный *прил* seven-week; (*ребёнок*) seven-week-old.

семисóт *чис см* **семьсóт**.

семисотлéти|е (-я) *ср* (*срок*) seven hundred years *мн*; (*годовщина*) seven hundredth anniversary.

семисотлéтн|ий (-яя, -ее, -ие) *прил* (*период*) seven-hundred-year; (*дерево*) seven-hundred-year-old.

семисóт|ый (-ая, -ое, -ые) *чис* seven hundredth.

семиуго́льник (-а) *м* heptagon.

семичасовóй *прил* (*рабочий день*) seven-hour; (*поезд*) seven o'clock.

семнáдцати *чис см* **семнáдцать**.

семнáдцат|ый (-ая, -ое, -ые) *чис* seventeenth; *см также* **пя́тый**.

семнáдцат|ь (-и; *как* **пять**; *см* **Table 27**) *чис* seventeen; *см также* **пять**.

сему́ *мест см* сей, сие́.

семь (-й; *как* пять; *см* Table 27) *чис* seven; *см также* пять.

се́мь|десят (-и́десяти; *как* пятьдеся́т; *см* Table 29) *чис* seventy; *см также* пятьдеся́т.

семьсо́т (-исо́т; *как* пятьсо́т; *см* Table 34) *чис* seven hundred; *см также* сто.

се́мью *нареч*: ~ пять *итп* seven times five *итп*.

семью́ *чис см* семь.

семь|я́ (-й; *nom pl* -и) *ж* family.

семьяни́н (-а) *м* family man.

се́м|я (-ени; *как* вре́мя; *см* Table 4) *ср* (БОТ. *также перен*) seed; (*no pl*; БИО) semen.

Се́н|а (-ы) *ж* Seine.

сена́т (-а) *м* senate.

сена́тор (-а) *м* senator.

Сенега́л (-а) *м* Senegal.

се́н|и (-ей) *мн* hall *ед*.

сенн|о́й *прил*: ~а́я лихора́дка hay fever.

се́н|о (-а) *м* hay.

сенова́л (-а) *м* hayloft.

сенoко́с (-а) *м* (*косьба*) haymaking; (*место*) hayfield.

сенсацио́нный *прил* sensational.

сенса́ци|я (-и) *ж* sensation.

сенте́нци|я (-и) *ж* maxim.

сентимента́л|ьный (-ен, -ьна, -ьно) *прил* sentimental.

сентя́бр|ь (-я́) *м* September; *см также* октя́брь.

сентя́брьск|ий (-ая, -ое, -ие) *прил* September *опред*.

сень (-и; *prp sg* -и́) *ж* canopy; под се́нью +*gen* under the protection of.

сепарати́зм (-а) *м* separatism.

сепара́тный *прил* separate.

се́псис (-а) *м* septicaemia (BRIT), septicemia (US).

септи́ческий (-ая, -ое, -ие) *прил* septic.

се́р|а (-ы) *ж* sulphur (BRIT), sulfur (US); (*в ушах*) earwax.

серб (-а) *м* Serb.

Се́рби|я (-и) *ж* Serbia.

се́рб|ка (-ки; *gen pl* -ок) *ж см* серб.

се́рбский (-ая, -ое, -ие) *прил* Serbian.

серва́нт (-а) *м* buffet unit.

серви́з (-а) *м*: столо́вый/ча́йный ~ dinner/tea service.

сервиро́ва́ть (-у́ю) (*не*)*сов перех*: ~ стол to set *или* lay the table.

се́рвис (-а) *м* service (*in shop, restaurant etc*).

серде́ц *итп сущ см* се́рдце.

серде́чен *прил см* серде́чный.

серде́чник (-а) *м* (ТЕХ) core; (*разг*): он ~ he's got a bad heart.

серде́чниц|а (-ы) *ж* (*разг*) *см* серде́чник.

серде́чный *прил* heart *опред*, cardiac; (*любовный*) loving; (*волнения, обида*) deep-felt; (-ен, -на, -но; *человек*) warm-hearted; (*приём, разговор*) cordial; ~ная тоска́

heartache; серде́чная боле́знь heart disease; серде́чный при́ступ acute angina.

серди́т|ый (-, -а, -о) *прил* angry.

серд|и́ть (-жу́, -дишь; *perf* рассерди́ть) *несов перех* to anger, make angry

▶ серди́ться (*perf* рассерди́ться) *несов возв*: ~ся (на кого́-н/что́-н) to be angry (with sb/about sth).

сердобо́л|ьный (-ен, -ьна, -ьно) *прил* soft-hearted.

сердоли́к (-а) *м* carnelian.

се́рд|це (-ца; *nom pl* -ца́, *gen pl* -е́ц, *dat pl* -ца́м) *ср* (*также перен*) heart; в сердца́х in a fit of temper; в глубине́ ~ца in one's heart of hearts; от всего́ ~ца from the bottom of one's heart; принима́ть (приня́ть *perf*) что-н бли́зко к ~цу to take sth to heart; он мне по́ сердцу he's a man after my own heart; у него́ ~ не лежи́т к э́той рабо́те his heart isn't in the work.

сердцебие́ни|е (-я) *ср* (*нормальное*) heartbeat; (*учащённое*) palpitations *мн*.

сердцеви́н|а (-ы) *ж* (*стебля, плода*) core; (*перен: события*) heart.

серебри́ст|ый (-, -а, -о) *прил* silver(-coloured (BRIT) *или* -colored (US)); (*перен: голос, смех*) silvery.

серебр|и́ть (-ю́, -и́шь; *perf* посеребри́ть) *несов перех* (*покрыть серебром*) to silver-plate; (*перен*) to turn silver.

серебр|о́ (-а́) *ср, собир* silver.

сере́бряник (-а) *м* silversmith.

сере́бряный *прил* silver; сере́бряная сва́дьба silver wedding (anniversary).

серёг *сущ см* серьга́.

середи́н|а (-ы) *ж* middle; в ~е +*gen* in the middle of.

середи́нный *прил* middle-of-the-road.

серёд|ка (-и) *ж* (*разг*) middle.

серёж|ка (-ки; *gen pl* -ек) *ж уменьш от* серьга́; (БОТ) catkin.

серена́д|а (-ы) *ж* serenade.

сере́|ть (-ю; *perf* посере́ть) *несов неперех* to turn grey (BRIT) *или* gray (US); (*no perf*; *цветы*) to show grey.

сержа́нт (-а) *м* sergeant.

сержу́(сь) *несов см* серди́ть(ся).

сери́йный *прил*: ~ое произво́дство serial production; сери́йный но́мер serial number.

се́ри|я (-и) *ж* series *ед*; (*кинофильма*) part.

се́рн|а (-ы) *ж* chamois.

се́рн|ый *прил*: ~ая кислота́ sulphuric (BRIT) *или* sulfuric (US) acid.

серп (-а́) *м* sickle; лу́нный ~ crescent moon.

серпанти́н (-а) *м* (*бумажная лента*) streamer; (*дорога*) sharply winding road (*in the mountains*).

сертифика́т (-а) *м* certificate; (*товара*) guarantee (certificate).

се́р|ый *прил* grey (*BRIT*), gray (*US*); (-, -á, -о; *перен: погода, жизнь*) grey, drab; (*разг: малообразованный*) dim; **се́рый хлеб** brown bread.

серьга́ (-ьги́; *nom pl* -ьги, *gen pl* -ёг, *dat pl* -ьга́м) ж earring.

серьёзен *прил см* **серьёзный**.

серьёзно *нареч, вводн сл* seriously; ~, **ты согла́сен?** do you really agree?

серьёзност|ь (-и) ж seriousness.

серьёз|ный (-ен, -на, -но) *прил* serious.

се́сси|я (-и) ж (*суда, парламента*) session; (*также: экзаменацио́нная* ~) examinations мн.

сестр|а́ (-ы́; *nom pl* **сёстры**, *gen pl* **сестёр**) ж sister; (*также: медицинская* ~) nurse.

сесть (ся́ду, ся́дешь; *pt* сел, се́ла, се́ло, *impf* **сади́ться**) *сов неперех* to sit down; (*птица, самолёт*) to land; (*солнце, луна*) to go down; (*одежда*) to shrink; (*батаре́йка, аккумуля́тор*) to run down; **сади́ться** (~ *perf*) **в по́езд/на самолёт** to get on a train/plane; **сади́ться** (~ *perf*) **за руль** to get behind the wheel; **сади́ться** (~ *perf*) **за рабо́ту** to sit down to work; **сади́ться** (~ *perf*) **в тюрьму́** to go to prison; **сади́ться** (~ *perf*) **под аре́ст** to be placed under arrest; **сади́ться** (~ *perf*) **за стол** to sit down at the table.

сет (-а) м (*ТЕННИС итп*) set.

се́т|ка (-ки; *gen pl* -ок) ж net; (*разг: сумка*) string bag; **тари́фная** ~ scale of charges.

се́товани|е (-я) ср (*обычно мн*) complaint.

се́т|овать (-ую; *perf* **посе́товать**) *несов неперех*: ~ **на** +*acc* to complain about.

се́ток *сущ см* **се́тка**.

сет|ь (-и; *prp sg* -и́, *gen pl* -е́й) ж (*для ловли рыб итп*) net; (*система, также КОМП*) network; **расставля́ть** (**расста́вить** *perf*) **кому́-н се́ти** to set a trap for sb.

Сеу́л (-а) м Seoul.

сече́ни|е (-я) ср (*поперечное, продольное итп*) section; **ке́сарево** ~ Caesarean (*BRIT*) или Cesarean (*US*) (section).

се́чк|а (-и) ж (*крупа*) chaff.

сечь (секу́, сечёшь итп, секу́т; *pt* сёк, секла́, секло́) *несов перех* (*рубить*) to cut up; (*perf* **вы́сечь**; *розгами итп*) to lash, flog.

се́ял|ка (-ки; *gen pl* -ок) ж seed drill.

се́|ять (-ю; *perf* **посе́ять**) *несов перех* (*также перен*) to sow ◆ *неперех* (*no perf*): ~**ет дождь** it's drizzling; ~ (**посе́ять** *perf*) **зна́ния/зло** to sow the seeds of knowledge/evil.

СЖ м *сокр* (= *Сою́з журнали́стов*) ≈ NUJ (= *National Union of Journalists*).

сжа́л|иться (-юсь, ишься) *сов возв*: ~ (**над** +*instr*) to have или take pity (on).

сжа́ти|е (-я) ср (*воздуха, га́за*) compression; (*в груди, в горле*) constriction; (*сердца*) contraction.

сжа́т|ый (-, -а, -о) *прил* (*воздух, газ*) compressed; (*краткий*) condensed; **в** ~**ые сро́ки** in a short space of time.

сжать (сожну́, сожнёшь) *сов от* **жать** ◆ (**сожму́, сожмёшь**; *impf* **сжима́ть**) *перех* to squeeze; (*воздух, газ*) to compress; (*текст, статью́*) to condense; (*срок*) to reduce; **сжима́ть** (~ *perf*) **зу́бы** to grit one's teeth; **сжима́ть** (~ *perf*) **гу́бы** to purse one's lips

► **сжа́ться** (*impf* **сжима́ться**) *сов возв* (*пружина, гу́бка, во́здух*) to contract; (*человек: от бо́ли, испу́га*) to tense up; (*перен: се́рдце*) to seize up.

сжечь (сожгу́, сожжёшь итп, сожгу́т; *pt* сжёг, сожгла́, сожгло́, *impf* **сжига́ть** или **жечь**) *сов перех* to burn; (*impf* **сжига́ть**; *перен: подлеж: страсть, жела́ние*) to consume; (: *со́лнце*) to scorch; **его́ сжига́ла за́висть** he was consumed with envy; ~ (*perf*) **свой корабли́** или **за собо́й мосты́** to burn one's boats или bridges.

сжива́|ть(ся) (-ю(сь)) *несов от* **сжи́ть(ся)**.

сживу́(сь) итп *сов см* **сжи́ть(ся)**.

сжига́|ть (-ю) *несов от* **сжечь**.

сжима́|ть(ся) (-ю(сь)) *несов от* **сжа́ть(ся)**.

сжи́|ть (-ву́, -вёшь; *pt* -л, -ла́, -ло, *impf* **сжива́ть**) *сов перех*: ~ **кого́-н со све́та** или **све́ту** to drive sb to his итп grave.

сжи́|ться (-ву́сь, -вёшься; *pt* -лся, -ла́сь, -лось, *impf* **сжива́ться**) *сов возв*: ~ **с** +*instr* to become close to; (*привы́кнуть*) to grow used to; ~ (*perf*) **с ро́лью** to get inside a role.

сжу́льнича|ть (-ю) *сов от* **жу́льничать**.

сза́ди *нареч* (*подойти́*) from behind; (*находи́ться*) behind ◆ *предл* (+*gen*) behind.

сзыва́|ть (-ю) *несов от* **созва́ть**.

си ср *нескл* (*МУЗ*) te.

сиби́рск|ий (-ая, -ое, -ие) *прил* Siberian.

Сиби́р|ь (-и) ж Siberia.

сибиря́|к (-á) м Siberian.

сибиря́ч|ка (-ки; *gen pl* -ек) ж *см* **сибиря́к**.

си́вый *прил* (*масть лошади*) grey (*BRIT*), gray (*US*).

сига́р|а (-ы) ж cigar.

сигаре́т|а (-ы) ж cigarette.

сигна́л (-а) м signal; (*АВТ*) horn.

сигнализа́тор (-а) м signalling device.

сигнализа́ци|я (-и) ж (*действие*) signalling; (*система*) signalling system; (*в кварти́ре*) burglar alarm; **пожа́рная/автомоби́льная** ~ fire/car alarm.

сигнализи́р|овать (-ую; *perf* **сигнализи́ровать** или **просигнализи́ровать**) *несов неперех*: ~ (**о** +*prp*) to signal.

сигна́л|ить (-ю, -ишь; *perf* **просигна́лить**) *несов неперех* (*флажками, фа́рами*) to signal; (*АВТ*) to honk.

сигна́льный *прил* signal *опред*; **сигна́льный экземпля́р** proof copy; **сигна́льная бу́дка** signal box; **сигна́льные огни́** (*АВТ*) indicators.

СИД м *сокр* (= *светоизлуча́ющий дио́д*) LED (= *light-emitting diode*).

сиде́л|ка (-ки; *gen pl* -ок) ж (sick) nurse.

сиде́ни|е (-я) ср sitting.

сиде́нь|е (-я) ср seat.

сиде́ть (-жу́, -ди́шь) *несов неперех* to sit; (*не*

рабо́тать, *отдыха́ть*) to sit around; (*одежда*) to fit; ~ (*impf*) **до́ма** to stay at home; ~ (*impf*) **в тюрьме́** to be in prison; ~ (*impf*) **с ребёнком** to look after a child; ~ (*impf*) **без де́нег/де́ла** to have no money/nothing to do; **он ~дел за кни́гой/рабо́той** he was sitting reading a book/ doing his work; ~ (*impf*) **на телефо́не** (*разг*) to spend ages on the phone

► **сиде́ться** *безл*: **ему́ не ~ди́тся на ме́сте/до́ма** he can't keep still/bear sitting at home.

Сидне́й (-я) *м* Sydney.

си́дя *нареч*: **рабо́тать/есть** ~ to work/eat sitting down.

сидя́чий (-ая, -ее, -ие) *прил* (*положение*) sitting *опред*; (*образ жизни*) sedentary; **сидя́чая забасто́вка** sit-down strike; **сидя́чие места́** (*разг*) seats *мн*.

сие́ *мест см* **сей**.

сижу́ *несов см* **сиде́ть**.

СИЗО́ *сокр* = **сле́дственный изоля́тор**.

си́з|ый (-, -á, -о) *прил* blue-grey (*BRIT*), blue-gray (*US*).

сий *мест см* **сей**.

си́л|а (-ы) *ж* strength; (*тока, ветра, закона*) force; (*воли, слова*) power; (*обычно мн*: *душевные, творческие*) energy; **в ~у того́, что ...** owing to the fact that ...; **и́зо всей ~ы** *или* **всех сил** as hard as one can; **от ~ы** (*разг*) at (the) most; **э́то зада́ние ему́ по ~м** *или* **под си́лу** he is capable of (doing) this task; **я не в ~х э́то сде́лать** I'm not able to do that; **он всё де́лает че́рез ~у** it's an effort for him to do anything; **он ест че́рез ~у** he's forcing himself to eat; **вступа́ть (вступи́ть** *perf*) *или* **входи́ть (войти́** *perf*) **в ~у** to come into *или* take effect; **теря́ть (потеря́ть** *perf*) *или* **утра́чивать (утра́тить** *perf*) **~у** to cease to be effective; **всё остаётся в ~е** everything will stay as it is; **применя́ть (примени́ть** *perf*) **~у** to use force; *см также* **си́лы**.

сила́ч (-á) *м* strong man (*мн* men).

силён *прил см* **си́льный**.

си́л|иться (-юсь, -ишься) *несов возв*: ~ +*infin* to make an effort to do.

силово́й *прил* power *опред*; **силова́я борьба́** wrestling; **силово́й приём** throw (*in martial arts*).

си́лой *нареч* by force.

си́лос (-а) *м* silage.

силуэ́т (-а) *м* (*контур*) silhouette; (*одежды*) outline.

си́л|ы (-) *мн* forces *мн*; **~ами кого́-н** with the help of; **свои́ми ~ами** by o.s.; **производи́тельные ~** production force; **си́лы бы́строго реаги́рования** quick-deployment forces.

си́льно *нареч* strongly; (*уда́рить*) hard;

(*хоте́ть, понра́виться итп*) very much.

сильноде́йствующ|ий (-ая, -ее, -ие) *прил* (*лекарство, яд*) powerful.

си́л|ьный (-ён, -ьна́, -ьно) *прил* strong; (*мороз*) hard; (*впечатле́ние, жела́ние*) powerful; (*шум*) loud; (*дождь*) heavy.

сим *мест см* **сей, сие́, сий**.

си́мвол (-а) *м* symbol; (*КОМП*) character.

символизи́р|овать (-ую) *несов перех* to symbolize.

символи́зм (-а) *м* (*ИСКУССТВО*) symbolism.

симво́лик|а (-и) *ж* (*символическое значение*) symbolism ♦ *собир* (*военная, морская итп*) symbols *мн*.

символи́ческ|ий (-ая, -ое, -ие) *прил* symbolic.

си́ми *мест см* **сий**.

симметри́ческ|ий (-ая, -ое, -ие) *прил* symmetrical.

симметри́чный *прил* = **симметри́ческий**.

симметри́|я (-и) *ж* symmetry.

симпатизи́р|овать (-ую) *несов неперех*: ~ **кому́-н** to like *или* be fond of sb.

симпати́ч|ный (-ен, -на, -но) *прил* nice, pleasant.

симпа́ти|я (-и) *ж* liking, fondness.

симпо́зиум (-а) *м* symposium.

симпто́м (-а) *м* symptom.

симптомати́ч|ный (-ен, -на, -но) *прил* symptomatic.

симули́р|овать (-ую) (*не*)*сов перех* (*нападение*) to simulate; (*болезнь*) to fake.

симфони́ческ|ий (-ая, -ое, -ие) *прил* symphonic; **симфони́ческий орке́стр** symphony orchestra.

симфо́ни|я (-и) *ж* (*МУЗ*) symphony.

синаго́г|а (-и) *ж* synagogue.

Сингапу́р (-а) *м* Singapore.

синдика́т (-а) *м* (*ЭКОН*) syndicate.

синдро́м (-а) *м* (*МЕД*) syndrome.

синев|а́ (-ы́) *ж* (*синий цвет*) blue; (*моря, неба*) blueness.

сине́|ть (-ю; *perf* **посине́ть)** *несов неперех* to turn blue; (*no perf*; *виднеться*) to show blue.

си́н|ий (-яя, -ее, -ие) *прил* blue; **си́ний чуло́к** bluestocking.

син|и́ть (-ю́, -и́шь; *perf* **посини́ть)** *несов перех* (*красить*) to paint blue.

сини́ц|а (-ы) *ж* tit.

синкрети́зм (-а) *м* syncretism.

сино́д (-а) *м* synod.

сино́ним (-а) *м* synonym.

синоними́ческ|ий (-ая, -ое, -ие) *прил* synonymous.

синоними́|я (-и) *ж* synonimity.

сино́птик (-а) *м* weather forecaster.

си́нтаксис (-а) *м* syntax.

синтакси́ческ|ий (-ая, -ое, -ие) *прил* syntactic; **~ая оши́бка** (*КОМП*) syntax error.

си́нтез (-а) *м* (*также хим*) synthesis (*мн* syntheses).

синтези́р|овать (-ую) (*не*)*сов перех* (*также хим*) to synthesize.

синте́тик|а (-и) *ж собир* (*материалы*) synthetic material; (*изделия*) synthetics *мн*.

синтети́ческий (-ая, -ое, -ие) *прил* (*материал*) synthetic.

синхро́нн|ый *прил* (*движение*) synchronous; (*перевод*) simultaneous; **~ое пла́вание** synchronized swimming.

син|ь (-и) *ж* = **синева́**.

си́нь|ка (-и) *ж* blue.

синя́к (-а́) *м* bruise.

сиони́зм (-а) *м* Zionism.

сиони́ст (-а) *м* Zionist.

сип|е́ть (-лю́, -и́шь) *несов неперех* to croak.

си́плый (-, -а́, -о) *прил* hoarse.

сиплю́ *несов см* **сипе́ть**.

си́пн|уть (-у, -ешь; *perf* **оси́пнуть**) *несов неперех* to grow hoarse.

сире́н|а (-ы) *ж* (*гудок*) siren.

сире́невый *прил* lilac.

сире́н|ь (-и) *ж* (*кустарник*) lilac bush ◆ *собир* (*цветы*) lilac.

сири́ек *сущ см* **сири́йка**.

сири́|ец (-йца) *м* Syrian.

сири́йка (-йки; *gen pl* -ек) *ж см* **сири́ец**.

сири́йский (-ая, -ое, -ие) *прил* Syrian.

сири́йца *итп сущ см* **сири́ец**.

Си́ри|я (-и) *ж* Syria.

сиро́п (-а) *м* syrup.

сирот|а́ (-оты́; *nom pl* -о́ты) *м/ж* orphan.

сироте́|ть (-ю; *perf* **осироте́ть**) *несов неперех* to be orphaned.

сиротли́в|ый (-, -а, -о) *прил* sad and lonely.

систе́м|а (-ы) *ж* system; (*конструкция*) make; **приводи́ть** (**привести́** *perf*) **в ~у** to put into order.

систематизи́р|овать (-ую) (*не*)*сов перех* to order.

системати́ческий (-ая, -ое, -ие) *прил* *following a defined system*; (*регулярный*) regular.

системати́чный *прил* = **системати́ческий**.

систе́мный *прил relating to or based on a system*; **систе́мный ана́лиз** systems analysis; **систе́мный диск** (*комп*) system disk.

си́т|ец (-ца) *м* cotton.

си́теч|ко (-ка; *gen pl* -ек) *ср уменьш от* **си́то**; (*для чая*) (tea) strainer.

си́т|о (-а) *ср* sieve.

ситро́ *ср нескл* soft drink.

ситуа́ци|я (-и) *ж* situation.

си́тца *итп сущ см* **си́тец**.

си́тцевый *прил* (*ткань*) cotton.

СИФ *м сокр* c.i.f. (= *cost, insurance, freight*).

си́филис (-а) *м* syphilis.

сифо́н (-а) *м* siphon.

сих *мест см* **сий**.

сицилиа́нский (-ая, -ое, -ие) *прил* Sicilian.

Сици́ли|я (-и) *ж* Sicily.

сию́ *мест см* **сия́**.

сиюмину́тн|ый (-ен, -на, -но) *прил* immediate.

сия́ *мест см* **сей**.

сия́ни|е (-я) *ср* (*солнца, луны, глаз*) shining; (*лица*) radiance; (*славы, успеха*) dazzle; **се́верное ~** the Northern lights *мн*.

сия́|ть (-ю) *несов неперех* (*солнце, звезда*) to shine; (*огонь*) to glow; **~** (*impf*) **от сча́стья** to beam with happiness; **ко́мната ~ла чистото́й** the room was spotlessly clean; **же́нщина ~ла красото́й** the woman was dazzlingly beautiful.

сия́ющий (-ая, -ее, -ие) *прил* (*глаза*) shining; (*лицо, улыбка*) beaming; (*человек*) radiant.

СК *м сокр* (= *Сою́з компози́торов*) ≈ MU (= *Musicians' Union*).

скажу́(сь) *итп сов см* **сказа́ть(ся)**.

сказа́ни|е (-я) *ср* legend.

сказа́ть (-ажу́, -а́жешь) *сов от* **говори́ть** ◆ *перех*; **~а́жем** (*разг*) let's say; **~ажи́те!** (*разг*) I say!; **как ~** (*разг*) how shall I put it; **кста́ти ~** by the way; **не́чего ~** (*разг: действительно*) indeed; **~ажи́те пожа́луйста** could you please tell me; **~ажи́те пожа́луйста!** well I never!; **так ~** so to speak

► **сказа́ться** (*impf* **ска́зываться**) *сов возв* (*способности, опыт итп*) to show; (*отразиться*): **~ся на** +*prp* to take its toll on; **ска́зываться** (**~ся** *perf*) +*instr* (*родственником, журналистом*) to pose as; **ска́зываться** (**~ся** *perf*) **больны́м** to pretend to be ill (*BRIT*) *или* sick (*US*).

ска́з|ка (-ки; *gen pl* -ок) *ж* fairy tale *или* story.

ска́зочен *прил см* **ска́зочный**.

ска́зочник (-а) *м* story teller.

ска́зочниц|а (-ы) *ж см* **ска́зочник**.

ска́зочн|ый *прил* fairy-tale; (-ен, -на, -но; *перен: необычайный*) fantastic.

сказу́ем|ое (-ого; *decl like adj*) *ср* (*линг*) predicate.

ска́зыва|ться (-юсь) *несов от* **сказа́ться**.

скак *м*: **на** (**всём**) **~у́** at top speed.

скака́л|ка (-ки; *gen pl* -ок) *ж* skipping rope.

ска|ка́ть (-чу́, -́чешь) *несов неперех* (*человек*) to skip; (*животное*) to hop; (*мяч*) to bounce; (*разг: температура, цены итп*) to rise and fall; (*лошадь, всадник*) to gallop.

скакн|у́ть (-у́, -ёшь) *сов неперех* to leap.

скаков|о́й *прил*: **~а́я ло́шадь** racehorse; **скаковы́е соревнова́ния** race meeting.

скаку́н (-а́) *м* racehorse.

скал|а́ (-алы́; *nom pl* -а́лы) *ж* cliff.

скаламбу́р|ить (-ю, -ишь) *сов от* **каламбу́рить**.

скали́ст|ый *прил* rocky; **С~ые го́ры** the Rocky Mountains *или* Rockies.

ска́л|ить (-ю, -ишь; *perf* **оска́лить**) *несов перех*: **~ зу́бы** to bare one's teeth

► **ска́литься** (*perf* **оска́литься**) *несов возв* to bare one's teeth.

ска́л|ка (-ки; *gen pl* -ок) *ж* (*кулин*) rolling-pin.

скалола́з (-а) *м* rock-climber.

скалола́зани|**е** (**-я**) *ср* rock-climbing.
ска́лыва|**ть** (**-ю**) *несов от* **сколо́ть**.
скальки́р|**овать** (**-ую**) *сов от* **кальки́ровать**.
ска́льпел|**ь** (**-я**) *м* scalpel.
скаме́йка (**-йки**; *gen pl* **-ек**) *ж* bench.
скамь|я́ (**-ьи́**; *gen pl* **-е́й**) *ж* (*для сидения*) bench;
~ **подсуди́мых** (*ЮР*) the dock; **сесть** (*perf*) **на**
~**ью́ подсуди́мых** to stand trial; **со**
шко́льной/студе́нческой ~**ьи́** from one's
school/student days.
сканда́л (**-а**) *м* (*политический*) scandal; (*ссора*)
quarrel.
сканда́лен *прил см* **сканда́льный**.
скандализи́р|**овать** (**-ую**) (*не*)*сов перех* to
scandalize.
скандали́ст (**-а**) *м* troublemaker.
скандали́ст|**ка** (**-ки**; *gen pl* **-ок**) *ж см*
скандали́ст.
сканда́л|**ить** (**-ю**, **-ишь**; *perf* **насканда́лить**)
несов неперех to quarrel.
сканда́л|**ьный** (**-ен**, **-ьна**, **-ьно**) *прил* (*история,
поступок*) scandalous; (*no short form*; *человек*)
quarrelsome.
сканди́р|**овать** (**-ую**) (*не*)*сов перех* (*подлеж:
толпа итп*) to chant.
ска́нер (**-а**) *м* scanner.
ска́плива|**ть(ся)** (**-ю(сь)**) *несов от*
скопи́ть(ся).
скарб (**-а**) *м собир* (*разг: вещи*) stuff.
ска́редный (**-ен**, **-на**, **-но**) *прил* (*разг*) mingy.
скарлати́н|**а** (**-ы**) *ж* scarlet fever.
ска́рмлива|**ть** (**-ю**) *несов от* **скорми́ть**.
скат (**-а**) *м* slope; (*АВТ: колесо*) wheel; (*ось*) axle.
ска́та|**ть** (**-ю**) *сов от* **ката́ть** ◆ (*impf* **ска́тывать**)
перех to roll up.
ска́терт|**ь** (**-и**; *gen pl* **-е́й**) *ж* tablecloth; ~**ю**
доро́га (*разг*) good riddance.
ск|**ати́ть** (**-ачу́**, **-а́тишь**; *impf* **ска́тывать**) *сов*
перех to roll down.
▸ **скати́ться** (*impf* **ска́тываться**) *сов возв*
(*слеза*) to roll down; (*перен*): ~**ся к** +*dat*/**на**
+*acc* to slide towards/into; ~**ся** (*perf*) **на**
лы́жах/на са́нях to ski/sledge down.
ска́тыва|**ть** (**-ю**) *несов от* **ската́ть**, **скати́ть**
▸ **ска́тываться** *несов от* **скати́ться**.
скафа́ндр (**-а**) *м* (*водолаза*) diving suit;
(*космонавта*) spacesuit.
ска́чек *итп сущ см* **ска́чки**.
ска́чк|**а** (**-и**) *ж* galloping.
скачка́ *итп сущ см* **скачо́к**.
ска́чк|**и** (**-ек**) *мн* the races *мн*.
скач|о́к (**-ка́**) *м* leap.
скачу́(сь) *сов см* **скати́ть(ся)**.
скачу́ *итп несов см* **скака́ть**.
ска́шива|**ть** (**-ю**) *несов от* **скоси́ть**.
СКВ *ж сокр* (= *свободно конвертируемая
валюта*) convertible currency.
сква́жин|**а** (**-ы**) *ж* (*нефтяная, газовая*) well;

замо́чная ~ keyhole; **бурова́я** ~ borehole.
сквер (**-а**) *м small public garden*.
скве́рен *прил см* **скве́рный**.
скверносло́ви|**е** (**-я**) *ср* foul language.
скверносло́в|**ить** (**-лю**, **-ишь**) *несов неперех*
to use foul language.
скве́рный (**-ен**, **-на́**, **-но**) *прил* foul; (*история,
поступок*) nasty.
сквита́|**ться** (**-юсь**) *сов возв*: ~ (**с** +*instr*)
(*отомстить*) to get even (with);
(*рассчитаться*) to pay in full.
сквоз|**и́ть** (*3sg* **-и́т**, *3pl* **-я́т**) *несов неперех*
(*чувство*) to show ◆ *безл*: **здесь** ~**и́т** it's
draughty here.
сквозн|**о́й** *прил* (*поезд*) through *опред*; **он**
получи́л ~**у́ю ра́ну** the bullet has gone right
through him; ~ **ве́тер** crosswinds *мн*.
сквозн|**я́к** (**-а́**) *м* (*в комнате*) draught (*BRIT*),
draft (*US*).
сквозь *предл* (+*acc*) through; **я слы́шал что́-то**
~ **сон** I heard something in my sleep.
скворе́|**ц** (**-ца́**) *м* starling.
скворе́чник (**-а**) *м* nesting box.
скворца́ *итп сущ см* **скворе́ц**.
скеле́т (**-а**) *м* (*также перен*) skeleton.
ске́псис (**-а**) *м* scepticism.
ске́птик (**-а**) *м* sceptic.
скептици́зм (**-а**) *м* scepticism.
скепти́ческ|**ий** (**-ая**, **-ое**, **-ие**) *прил* sceptical.
ски́д|**ка** (**-ки**; *gen pl* **-ок**) *ж* (*с цены*) discount,
reduction; (*сде́лать perf*) ~**ку на что́-н**
to make an allowance for sth; **со** ~**кой на что-н**
taking sth into account; **нало́говая** ~ tax
allowance.
скин|**уть** (**-у**, **-ешь**; *impf* **ски́дывать**) *сов перех*
(*сбросить*) to throw down; (: *одежду, одеяло*)
to throw off; (*разг: с цены*) to knock off
▸ **ски́нуться** *сов возв* (*разг*) to have a whip-
round.
ски́петр (**-а**) *м* sceptre (*BRIT*), scepter (*US*).
скирд|**а́** (**-ы́**) *ж* stack.
скис|**нуть** (**-ну, -нешь**; *pt* **-, -ла, -ло**) *сов от*
ки́снуть ◆ (*impf* **скиса́ть**) *неперех* to turn sour;
(*перен: разг*) to lose interest.
ски́та́л|**ец** (**-ьца**) *м* wanderer.
скита́ни|**е** (**-я**) *ср* wandering.
скита́|**ться** (**-юсь**) *несов возв* to wander.
склад (**-а**) *м* (*помещение: товарный*) store;
(*жизни*) way; (*оружия итп*) cache; ~ **ума́**
mentality; ~ **боеприпа́сов** ammunition dump.
скла́ден *прил см* **скла́дный**.
склади́р|**овать** (**-ую**) (*не*)*сов перех* to store.
скла́д|**ка** (**-ки**; *gen pl* **-ок**) *ж* (*на одежде*) pleat; (*на
лице*) furrow; (*на ткани*) crease; **ю́бка в** ~**ку**
или **со** ~**ми** pleated skirt.
складно́й *прил* folding.
скла́дный (**-ен**, **-на**, **-но**) *прил* (*статный*) well-
built; (*связный*) coherent.

скла́док *сущ см* **скла́дка**.

складско́й *прил* storage *опред*.

скла́дчин|а (-ы) *ж* (*сбор*) pool; **купи́ть** (*perf*) **что-н в ~у** to pool together to buy sth.

скла́дывани|е (-я) *ср* (*действие: предметов*) stacking; (*чисел*) addition.

скла́дыва|ть(ся) (-ю(сь)) *несов от* **сложи́ть(ся)**.

скле́|ить (-ю, -ишь) *сов от* **кле́ить** ◆ (*impf* **скле́ивать**) *перех* to glue together.

склеп (-а) *м* crypt.

склепа́|ть (-ю) *сов от* **клепа́ть**.

склеро́з (-а) *м* (*сосудов, лёгких*) sclerosis; **~ мо́зга** senility.

склеро́зный *прил* sclerotic.

склеро́тик (-а) *м* sclerotic.

склероти́ческ|ий (-ая, -ое, -ие) *прил* = **склеро́зный**.

скло́к|а (-и) *ж* squabble.

склон (-а) *м* slope; **на скло́не лет** *или* **жи́зни** *или* **дней** in one's later life.

скло́нен *прил см* **скло́нный**.

склоне́ни|е (-я) *ср* (*линг*) declension.

скло́н|и́ть (-оню́, -о́нишь; *impf* **склоня́ть**) *сов перех* (*опустить*) to lower; **склоня́ть** (~ *perf*) **кого́-н к побе́гу/на преступле́ние** to talk sb into escaping/committing a crime; **я ~они́л её на свою́ сто́рону** I talked her over to my side

► **склони́ться** (*impf* **склоня́ться**) *сов возв* (*нагнуться*) to bend; (*перен*): **~ся к** +*dat* to come round to

скло́нность (-и) *ж*: **~ к** +*dat* (*к музыке, к математике*) aptitude for; (*к меланхолии, к полноте*) tendency to.

скло́нный (-ен, -на́, -но) *прил*: **~** +*dat* (*к простудам*) prone *или* susceptible to; **~** +*infin* (*согласиться, помириться*) inclined to do; **он ~ен к фи́зике** he has an aptitude for physics.

склоня́емый *прил* declinable.

склоня́|ть (-ю) *несов от* **склони́ть** ◆ (*perf* **просклоня́ть**) *перех* (*линг*) to decline; **~** (*impf*) **кого́-н** to talk about sb a lot

► **склоня́ться** *несов от* **склони́ться** ◆ *возв* (*линг*) to decline.

скло́чен *прил см* **скло́чный**.

скло́чник (-а) *м* (*разг*) quarrelsome man (*мн* men).

скло́чниц|а (-ы) *ж* (*разг*) quarrelsome woman (*мн* women).

скло́чный (-ен, -на, -но) *прил* quarrelsome.

скля́н|ка (-ки; *gen pl* -ок) *ж* (*разг: сосуд*) bottle.

скоб|а́ (-обы́; *nom pl* -обы) *ж* (*для опоры, для держания*) clamp; (*для крепления*) staple.

скоб|ка (-ки; *gen pl* -ок) *ж уменьш от* **скоба́**; (*обычно мн: знак*) bracket, parentheses *мн*; **кру́глые/квадра́тные ~ки** round/square brackets; **брать (взять** *perf*) **сло́во в ~ки** to put a word in brackets *или* parenthese.

скобл|и́ть (-ю́, -и́шь) *несов перех* to scrape.

скобо́к *сущ см* **ско́бка**.

ско́ван|ный (-, -на, -но) *прил* (*человек,*

движения) inhibited.

ск|ова́ть (-ую́) *сов от* **кова́ть** ◆ (*impf* **ско́вывать**) *перех* (*соединить*) to weld together; **страх ~ова́л его́** he was paralysed with fear; **лёд ~ова́л ре́ку** the river froze over.

сковоро́д|а́ (-ы́; *nom pl* **ско́вороды**) *ж* frying-pan (*вRIT*), skillet (*US*).

сковоро́д|ка (-ки; *gen pl* -ок) *ж* = **сковорода́**.

ско́выва|ть (-ю) *несов от* **скова́ть**.

скол|оти́ть (-очу́, -о́тишь; *impf* **скола́чивать**) *сов перех* to hammer together; (*разг: банду, капитал*) to get together.

ск|оло́ть (-олю́, -о́лешь; *impf* **ска́лывать**) *сов перех* (*снять*) to chop off; (*соединить*) to pin together.

сколочу́ *сов см* **сколоти́ть**.

сколь *нареч* (*как*) how; (*возможно*) as much as; **~ ... сто́ль (же)** ... as much ... as ....

скольз|и́ть (-жу́, -зи́шь) *несов неперех* to glide; (*теряя устойчивость*) to slide.

ско́льз|кий (-кая, -кое, -кие; -ок, -ка, -ко) *прил* slippery; (*ситуация, тема*) tricky; (*вопрос*) sensitive.

скользн|у́ть (-у́, -ёшь) *сов неперех* to glide; (*быстро пройти*) to slip.

скользо́к *прил см* **ско́льзкий**.

скользя́щ|ий (-ая, -ее, -ие) *прил* (*шаг*) gliding; (*непостоянный*) flexible.

KEYWORD

ско́лько (-их) *местоимённое нареч* **1** (+*gen*; *книг, часо́в, дней итп*) how many; (*сахара, сил, работы итп*) how much; **ско́лько люде́й пришло́?** how many people came?; **ско́лько де́нег тебе́ на́до?** how much money do you need?; **ско́лько э́то сто́ит?** how much is it?; **ско́лько тебе́ лет?** how old are you?
2 (*относительное*) as much; **бери́, ско́лько хо́чешь** take as much as you want; **ско́лько уго́дно** as much as you like
◆ *нареч* **1** (*насколько*) as far as; **ско́лько по́мню, он всегда́ был агресси́вный** as far as I remember, he was always aggressive
2 (*много*): **ско́лько люде́й!** what a lot of people!; **ско́лько вре́мени он отня́л у нас!** what a long time he has kept us!; **не сто́лько ... ско́лько ...** not so much ... as ....

скома́ндовать (-ую) *сов от* **кома́ндовать**.

скомбини́р|овать (-ую) *сов от* **комбини́ровать**.

ско́мка|ть (-ю) *сов от* **ко́мкать**.

скоморо́х (-а) *м* (*комедиант*) mummer; (*перен*) buffoon.

скомпили́р|овать (-ую) *сов от* **компили́ровать**.

скомплект|ова́ть (-у́ю) *сов от* **комплектова́ть**.

скомпон|ова́ть (-у́ю) *сов от* **компонова́ть**.

скомпромети́р|овать (-ую) *сов от* **компромети́ровать**.

сконструи́р|овать (-ую) *сов от*

конструи́ровать.

сконфу́зить(ся) (-жу(сь), -зишь(ся)) *сов от* **конфу́зить(ся)**.

сконцентри́р|овать(ся) (-ую(сь)) *сов от* **концентри́ровать(ся)**.

сконча́ни|е (-я) *ср*: **до ~я ве́ка** to the end of time.

сконча́|ться (-юсь) *сов возв* to pass away.

скоордини́ровать (-ую) *сов от* **координи́ровать**.

скопидо́м (-а) *м* miser.

скопи́р|овать (-ую) *сов от* **копи́ровать**.

скоп|и́ть(ся) (-лю́(сь), -ишь(ся)) *сов от* **копи́ть(ся)**.

скóпище (-а) *ср* horde.

скопле́ни|е (-я) *ср* (*людей, предметов*) mass.

скоплю́(сь) *сов см* **скопи́ть(ся)**.

скóпом *нареч* (*разг*) in a crowd.

скóр|ая (-ой; *decl like adj*) *ж* (*разг: также:* ~ **пóмощь**) ambulance.

скóрбен *прил см* **скóрбный**.

скорб|éть (-лю́, -и́шь) *несов неперех*: ~ **о** *+prp* to grieve for.

скóрб|ный (-ен, -на, -но) *прил* sorrowful; **в ~ную мину́ту** at a time of sorrow.

скорб|ь (-и; *gen pl* -éй) *ж* grief.

скоре́е *сравн прил см* **скóрый** ♦ *сравн нареч от* **скóро** ♦ *част* rather; ~...**чем** *или* **нежéли** *от* **бóльшей стéпени**) more likely ... than; (*лучше, охотнее*) rather ... than; ~ **всегó они́ дóма** it's most likely they'll be (at) home; ~ **всегó он сегóдня не придёт** he is most unlikely to come today; ~ **бы он верну́лся** I wish he would come back soon.

скорл|упá (-упы́; *nom pl* -у́пы) *ж* shell; **яи́чная** ~ eggshell; **орéховая** ~ nutshell.

скорм|и́ть (-лю́, -ишь; *impf* **скáрмливать**) *сов перех*: ~ **чтó-н комý-н** to feed sth to sb.

скорня́|жный *прил*: ~**ая мастерскáя** furrier's workshop; ~**ое дéло** furriery.

скорня́к (-á) *м* furrier.

скóро *нареч* soon ♦ *как сказ* it's soon; ~ **зимá** it will soon be winter; **я** ~ **верну́сь** I will be back soon.

скоровáр|ка (-ки; *gen pl* -ок) *ж* pressure cooker.

скороговóр|ка (-ки; *gen pl* -ок) *ж* tongue-twister; (*быстрая речь*) gabble.

скорóм|ный *прил*: ~**ая пи́ща** *food forbidden on fasting days*.

скоропали́тель|ный (-ен, -ьна, -ьно) *прил* hasty.

скоропóртящ|ийся (-аяся, -ееся, -иеся) *прил* (*кулин*) perishable.

скоропости́ж|ный (-ен, -на, -но) *прил*: ~**ная смерть** sudden death.

скороспéлый *прил* (*бот*) early.

скоростнóй *прил* (*поезд*) high-speed; (*строительство*) speedy.

скóрост|ь (-и; *gen pl* -éй) *ж* speed; (*физ*) velocity; **со ~ю 5 киломéтров в час** at (a speed of) 5 kilometres (*BRIT*) *или* kilometers (*US*) per hour; **на (большóй)** ~**и** at (great) speed; ~ **передáчи** (*в бóдах*) (*комп*) baud rate.

скоросшивáтель (-я) *м* (loose-leaf) binder.

скоротá|ть (-ю) *сов от* **коротáть**.

скоротéч|ный (ен, -на, -но) *прил* short-lived.

скорпиóн (-а) *м* scorpion; (*созвездие*): **С~** Scorpio.

скорректи́р|овать (-ую) *сов от* **корректи́ровать**.

скóрч|ить(ся) (-у(сь), -ишь(ся)) *сов от* **кóрчить(ся)**.

скóр|ый (-, -á, -о) *прил* (*езда, движение*) fast; (*разлука, визит*) impending; **до ~ого свидáния** see you soon; **в ~ом вре́мени** shortly; **приготóвить** (*perf*) **чтó-н на ~ую ру́ку** to rustle sth up; **скóрая пóмощь** (*учреждение*) ambulance service; (*автомашина*) ambulance; **скóрый пóезд** express (train).

скос (-а) *м* (*скошенная сторона*) slant; (*склон*) slope.

ск|оси́ть (-ошу́, -óсишь) *сов от* **коси́ть** ♦ (*impf* **скáшивать**) *перех* (*траву*) to mow; (*пшеницу*) to reap; (*крышу*) to set on a slant; **скáшивать** *или* **коси́ть** (~ *perf*) **глазá** to squint

▶ **скоси́ться** *сов от* **коси́ться**.

скот (-á) *м собир* livestock; (*перен: разг*) animal; **молóчный/мяснóй** ~ dairy/beef cattle.

скоти́н|а (-ы) *ж собир* livestock ♦ *ж* (*разг: человек*) swine.

скóтник (-а) *м* herdsman (*мн* herdsmen).

скóтниц|а (-ы) *ж* dairy maid.

скóт|ный *прил*: ~ **двор** cattle-yard.

скотовóдств|о (-а) *ср* livestock farming.

скóтск|ий (-ая, -ое, -ие) *прил* (*подлый*) beastly; (*грязный*) bestial.

скошу́ *сов см* **скоси́ть**.

скрáдыва|ть (*3sg* -ет, *3pl* -ют) *несов перех* (*звуки*) to keep out; (*полноту, морщины*) to conceal.

скрá|сить (-шу, -сишь; *impf* **скрáшивать**) *сов перех* to ease.

скрёб(ся) *итп несов см* **скрести́(сь)**.

скреб|óк (-кá) *м* scraper.

скребу́(сь) *итп несов см* **скрести́(сь)**.

скрéжет (-а) *м* (*металла*) grating; (*колёс*) screech.

скреж|етáть (-ещу́, -éщешь) *несов неперех* (*чтó-н металлическое*) to grate; ~ (*impf*) **зубáми** to grate one's teeth.

скреп|и́ть (-лю́, -и́шь; *impf* **скрепля́ть**) *сов перех* (*соединить*) to fasten together; (*перен: дружбу*) to strengthen; (*удостоверить*) to endorse; ~**я́ сéрдце** reluctantly.

скрéп|ка (-ки; *gen pl* -ок) *ж* paperclip.

скреплю́ *сов см* **скрепи́ть**.

скрепля́|ть (-ю) *несов от* **скрепи́ть**.

скре́пок *сущ см* **скре́пка**.

скр|ести́ (-ебу́, -ебёшь; *pt* -ёб, -ебла́, -ебло́) *несов неперех* (мышь, кошка) to scratch ♦ *перех* (сковоро́дку) to scour; (де́рево) to sand; **~ебёт на душе́** *или* **на се́рдце** he *итп* has a nagging feeling inside

► **скрести́сь** *несов возв* (мышь) to scratch about; **соба́ка ~ебётся в дверь** the dog is scratching at the door.

скре|сти́ть (-щу́, -сти́шь; *impf* **скре́щивать**) *сов перех* to cross

► **скрести́ться** (*impf* **скре́щиваться**) *сов возв* to cross; (*перен:* интере́сы, устремле́ния) to clash.

скреще́ни|е (-я) *ср* crossing; (интере́сов) clash; **~ доро́г** crossroads.

скре́щивани|е (-я) *ср* cross-breeding.

скре́щива|ть(ся) (-ю(сь)) *несов от* **скрести́ть(ся)**.

скрещу́(сь) *сов см* **скрести́ть(ся)**.

скрив|и́ть(ся) (-лю́(сь), -и́шь(ся)) *сов от* **криви́ть(ся)**.

скрип (-а) *м* (две́ри, по́ла) creak; (мета́лла) grate; (сне́га) crunch; **со скри́пом** (*перен: разг*) with a struggle.

скрипа́ч (-á) *м* violinist.

скрипа́ч|ка (-ки; *gen pl* -ек) *ж см* **скрипа́ч**.

скрип|е́ть (-лю́, -и́шь) *несов неперех* to creak; (*перен: разг*) to struggle along.

скри́п|ка (-ки; *gen pl* -ок) *ж* violin; (в наро́дной му́зыке) fiddle; **пе́рвая ~** (в орке́стре) first violin; (в де́ле) first fiddle.

скриплю́ *несов см* **скрипе́ть**.

скри́пок *сущ см* **скри́пка**.

скрипу́ч|ий (-ая, -ее, -ие) *прил* (дверь, пол) creaky; (го́лос) croaky.

скро|и́ть (-ю́, -и́шь) *сов от* **крои́ть**.

скро́мен *прил см* **скро́мный**.

скро́мник (-а) *м* (*разг*) modest lad (*BRIT*) *или* guy (*US*).

скро́мниц|а (-ы) *ж* (*разг*) modest girl.

скро́мност|ь (-и) *ж* modesty; (оде́жды *итп*) plainness.

скро́мн|ый (-ен, -á, -но) *прил* modest; (служа́щий, до́лжность) humble.

скро́ю(сь) *итп сов см* **скры́ть(ся)**.

скрупулёз|ный (-ен, -на, -но) *прил* scrupulous.

скру|ти́ть (-чу́, -у́тишь) *сов от* **крути́ть** ♦ (*impf* **скру́чивать**) *перех* (провода́, во́лосы) to twist together; (*разг:* арестованного) to tie up; (: *подлеж:* боле́знь, го́ре) to take a grip

► **скрути́ться** *сов возв* to twist together.

скрыва́|ть (-ю) *несов от* **скрыть**

► **скрыва́ться** *несов от* **скры́ться** ♦ *возв* (от поли́ции, от власте́й) to hide; (раздраже́ние в го́лосе) to lurk; **~ся** (*impf*) **под чужи́м и́менем** to hide behind another name.

скры́т|ный (-ен, -на, -но) *прил* secretive; (возмо́жности) potent.

скры́тый *прил* (смысл, возмо́жности *итп*) hidden; (не́нависть, оппози́ция) secret; **скры́тая ка́мера** *или* **съёмка** hidden camera.

скры́ть (-о́ю, -о́ешь; *impf* **скрыва́ть**) *сов перех* (спря́тать) to hide; (фа́кты) to conceal

► **скры́ться** (*impf* **скрыва́ться**) *сов возв* (от дождя́, от пого́ни) to take cover; (со́лнце, луна́) to disappear; **от него́ ничего́ не ~о́ется** nothing escapes him.

скрю́ч|ить (-у, -ишь) *сов от* **крю́чить** ♦ (*impf* **скрю́чивать**) *перех* to bend

► **скрю́читься** *сов от* **крю́читься** ♦ (*impf* **скрю́чиваться**) *возв* to be stooped.

скря́г|а (-и) *м/ж* (*разг*) skinflint.

ску́ден *прил см* **ску́дный**.

скуде́|ть (-ю; *perf* **оскуде́ть**) *несов неперех* to run thin.

ску́дн|ый (-ен, -на́, -но) *прил* (запа́сы, сре́дства) meagre (*BRIT*), meager (*US*); (язы́к, све́дения) limited; (расти́тельность) sparse; **~ +instr** (собы́тиями, витами́нами) lacking in.

ску́к|а (-и) *ж* boredom; **там ужа́сная ~** it's dreadfully boring there.

скул|а́ (-ы́; *nom pl* -ы) *ж* (обы́чно мн) cheekbone.

скула́ст|ый (-, -а, -о) *прил*: **~ое лицо́** a face with prominent cheekbones.

скул|и́ть (-ю́, -и́шь) *несов неперех* to whine.

ску́льптор (-а) *м* sculptor.

скульпту́р|а (-ы) *ж* sculpture.

ску́мбри|я (-и) *ж* mackerel.

скупа́|ть (-ю) *несов от* **скупи́ть** ♦ *перех* (для перепрода́жи) to buy up; (кра́деное) to buy.

скуп|и́ть (-лю́, -у́пишь; *impf* **скупа́ть**) *сов перех* to buy up.

скуп|и́ться (-лю́сь, -и́шься; *perf* **поскупи́ться**) *несов возв*: **~ на +**acc to skimp on; **он не ~и́тся на обеща́ния/комплиме́нты** he's generous with his promises/compliments.

ску́п|ля (-и) *ж* (де́йствие) buying up; (магази́н) second-hand shop.

скуплю́ *сов см* **скупи́ть**.

скуп|о́й (-, -á, -о) *прил* mean; (свет) dim; (речь) terse; (расти́тельность) sparse; **он скуп на де́ньги/похвалу́** he's sparing with money/praise.

ску́пщик *прил*: **~ магази́н** second-hand shop; **~ пункт** collection point.

ску́пщик (-а) *м* buyer.

скуфь|я́ (-и́; *gen pl* -е́й) *ж* tall hat *worn by Orthodox priests*.

скуча́|ть (-ю) *несов неперех* to be bored; (тоскова́ть): **~ по +**dat *или* **о +**prp to miss.

ску́чен *прил см* **ску́чный**.

ску́чно *нареч* (жить, расска́зывать *итп*) boringly ♦ *как сказ*: **здесь ~** it's boring here; **мы о́чень ~ живём** we lead a boring life; **как ~!** oh, how boring!; **на уро́ке бы́ло ~** the lesson was boring; **мне ~** I'm bored.

ску́ч|ный (-ен, -на́, -но) *прил* (челове́к, жизнь *итп*) boring, dreary; (испы́тывающий ску́ку: челове́к, го́лос *итп*) bored.

ску́ша|ть (-ю) *сов от* **ку́шать**.

слабе́|ть (-ю; *perf* **ослабе́ть**) *несов неперех* (*человек*) to grow weak; (*здоровье, интерес итп*) to weaken; (*мороз*) to ease off; (*ветер*) to drop; (*дисциплина*) to slacken.

слаби́тельн|ое (-ого; *decl like adj*) *ср* laxative.

слаби́тельный *прил* laxative.

сла́б|ить (*3sg* -ит) *несов перех*: ~ кого́-н to give sb diarrhoea (*BRIT*) *или* diarrhea (*US*); его́ ~ит he has diarrhoea.

сла́б|нуть (-ну, -нешь; *perf* **ослабнуть**) *несов* = **слабе́ть**.

сла́бо *нареч* (*вскрикнуть*) weakly; (*нажать*) lightly; (*знать*) badly.

слабово́л|ьный (-ен, -ьна, -ьно) *прил* weak-willed.

сла́бост|ь (-и) *ж* weakness; (*голоса*) feebleness; (*дисциплины*) slackness; (*пристрастие*): ~ к +*dat* weakness for.

слабоу́мный *прил* feeble-minded.

слабохара́ктер|ный (-ен, -на, -но) *прил* weak.

сла́б|ый (-, -á, -о) *прил* weak; (*ветер*) light; (*голос*) feeble; (*знания, доказательство итп*) poor; (*резинка, дисциплина итп*) slack; **сла́бая сторона́, сла́бое ме́сто** weak spot.

сла́в|а (-ы) *ж* (*героя*) glory; (*писателя, актёра итп*) fame; (*дурная, хорошая*) repute; (*разг: слухи*) rumour (*BRIT*), rumor (*US*); **во ~у** +*gen* to the greater glory of; **на ~у** splendidly; ~ **Бо́гу!** thank God!

сла́вен *прил см* **сла́вный**.

слави́р|овать (-ую) *сов от* **лави́ровать**.

сла́в|ить (-лю, -ишь) *несов от* **просла́вить** ♦ *перех* (*героев*) to glorify

▶ **сла́виться** *несов возв*: ~ся +*instr* to be renowned for.

сла́в|ный (-ен, -на́, -но) *прил* (*человек, отдых*) pleasant; (*подвиг, имя*) famous.

славосло́в|ить (-лю, -ишь) *несов перех* to extol.

сла́в|яни́н (-яни́на; *nom pl* -я́не, *gen pl* -я́н) *м* Slav.

славя́н|ка (-ки; *gen pl* -ок) *ж см* **славяни́н**.

славя́нский (-ая, -ое, -ие) *прил* Slavonic.

слага́ем|ое (-ого; *decl like adj*) *ср* (*МАТ*) item; (*успеха*) component.

слага́|ть (-ю) *несов от* **сложи́ть**.

сла́|дить (-жу, -дишь; *impf* **сла́живать**) *сов неперех*: ~ с +*instr* (*с машиной, с лошадью*) to handle; (*с ребёнком*) to cope with.

сла́дкий (-кая, -кое, -кие; -ок, -ка́, -ко) *прил* sweet; (*жизнь*) pleasant.

сла́дко *нареч* (*пахнуть*) sweet; (*спать*) deeply; (*улыбаться*) sweetly; ♦ *как сказ безл*: **во рту́** I am left with a sweet taste in my mouth; **мне здесь не** ~ (*разг*) I can't stand it here.

сла́дк|ое (-ого; *decl like adj*) *ср* sweet things *мн*; (*разг: десерт*) afters (*BRIT*), dessert (*US*); **что**

сего́дня на ~? what's for afters today?

сладкое́ж|ка (-ки; *gen pl* -ек) *м/ж* (*разг*) = **сласте́на**.

сла́док *прил см* **сла́дкий**.

сла́достен *прил см* **сла́достный**.

сла́дост|и (-ей) *мн* sweet things *мн*.

сла́дост|ный (-ен, -на, -но) *прил* sweet.

сладостра́ст|ный (-ен, -на, -но) *прил* sensual.

сла́дост|ь (-и) *ж* (*см прил*) sweetness; pleasantness; *см также* **сла́дости**.

сла́жен|ный (-, -на, -но) *прил* orderly.

сла́жива|ть (-ю) *несов от* **сла́дить**.

сла́жу *сов от* **сла́дить**.

сла́|зить (-жу, -зишь) *сов неперех* to climb.

слайд (-а) *м* (*ФОТО*) slide.

сла́лом (-а) *м* slalom; **гига́нтский** ~ giant slalom.

сламоми́ст (-а) *м* slalom skier.

сласте́н|а (-ы) *м/ж*: **он/она́** ~ he/she has a sweet tooth.

сла́|стить (-щу́, -стишь) *несов перех* to sweeten.

слать (**шлю, шлёшь**) *несов перех* to send.

слаща́|вый (-, -а, -о) *прил* sugary.

сла́ще *сравн прил от* **сла́дкий** ♦ *сравн нареч от* **сла́дко**.

слащу́ *сов от* **сласти́ть**.

сле́ва *нареч* on the left.

слёг *итп сов см* **слечь**.

слегка́ *нареч* slightly.

след (-а; *nom pl* -ы́) *м* trace; (*колес*) track; (*перен*) sign; (*ноги*) footprint; **пре́жней уста́лости и ~á нет** all traces of my earlier tiredness have gone; **напада́ть** (**напа́сть** *perf*) **на чей-н** ~ (*также перен*) to get on sb's trail.

следи́|ть (-жу, -ди́шь) *несов неперех*: ~ **за** +*instr* to follow; (*заботиться*) to take care of; (*за шпионом*) to watch; (*perf* **наследи́ть**; *грязными ногами*) to leave a trail; ~ (*impf*) **за собо́й** to take care of o.s..

следова́ни|е (-я) *ср* (*моде, советам итп*) following; **по́езд/авто́бус да́льнего** ~я long-distance train/bus.

сле́доватеЛ|ь (-я) *м* detective.

сле́довательно *вводн сл* consequently ♦ *союз* therefore.

сле́д|овать (-ую; *perf* **после́довать**) *несов неперех* (*вывод, неприятность*) to follow ♦ *безл*: **Вам** ~**ует поду́мать** you should think about it; **его́** ~**ует за э́то наказа́ть** he should be punished for this; ~ (**после́довать** *perf*) **за кем-н/чем-н** to follow sb/sth; ~ (**после́довать** *perf*) **чему́-н** (*правилам, советам*) to follow sth; **как** ~**ует** properly.

сле́дом *нареч*: **ходи́ть** ~ **за кем-н** to follow sb ♦ *предл*: ~ **за** +*instr* following.

сле́дственный *прил* investigative, investigatory.

сле́дстви|е (-я) *ср* (*последствие*) consequence;

(ЮР: *после преступления*) investigation.

сле́дующ|ий (**-ая, -ее, -ие**) *прил* next ◆ *мест* following; **на ~ день** the next day; **кто ~?** who is next?

слеже́ни|е (**-я**) *ср* observation.

сле́ж|ка (**-ки**; *gen pl* **-ек**) *ж* shadowing.

слежу́ *сов см* **следи́ть**.

слез *итп сов см* **слезть**.

сле|за́ (**-зы́**; *nom pl* **-ёзы**, *dat pl* **-еза́м**) *ж* tear; **доводи́ть (довести́** *perf*) **кого́-н до ~ёз** to reduce sb to tears; **мне оби́дно до ~ёз** I'm so hurt I could cry.

слеза́|ть (**-ю**) *несов от* **слезть**.

слез|и́ться (*3sg* **-и́тся**, *3pl* **-я́тся**) *несов возв* (*глаза*) to water.

слези́в|ый (**-, -а, -о**) *прил* (*человек*) weepy; (*перен: тон, голос*) tearful.

слёзный *прил* lacrimal; (*жалобный*) pitiful.

слезоточи́в|ый *прил*: **~ газ** tear gas.

слез|ть (**-у, -ешь**; *pt* **-, -ла, -ло**, *impf* **слеза́ть**) *сов непepex*: **~ (с +**gen**)** (*с дерева*) to climb down; (*с лошади, с велосипеда*) to climb off; (*разг: с автобуса, с поезда итп*) to get off; (: *очки, платок*) to slip off; (*кожа, краска*) to peel off.

сле́й(те) *сов см* **слить**.

сленг (**-а**) *м* slang.

слеп|ень (**-ня**) *м* horsefly (*мн* horseflies), cleg.

слеп|и́ть (*3sg* **-и́т**, *3pl* **-я́т**) *сов перех*: **~ глаза́ кому́-н** to blind sb.

слеп|и́ть (**-плю́, -пишь**) *сов от* **лепи́ть** ◆ (*impf* **слепля́ть**) *перех* to stick together

▶ **слепи́ться** (*impf* **слепля́ться**) *сов возв* to stick together.

слеп|ка *итп сущ см* **слепок**.

слеплю́(сь) *сов см* **слепи́ть(ся)**.

слепля́|ть(ся) (**-ю(сь)**) *несов от* **слепи́ть(ся)**.

слеп|нуть (**-у, -ешь**; *perf* **осле́пнуть**) *несов неперех* to go blind.

слепн|я́ *итп сущ см* **слепень**.

слеп|о́й (**-, -а́, -о**) *прил* (*также перен*) blind ◆ (**-о́го**; *decl like adj*) *м* blind person (*мн* people); **слепа́я кишка́** appendix (*мн* appendices); **слепо́й ме́тод печа́тания** touch-typing.

слеп|о́к (**-ка**) *м* cast.

слепот|а́ (**-ы́**) *ж* (*также перен*) blindness.

слеса́рн|ый *прил*: **~ая мастерска́я** metal workshop; **~ стано́к** lathe.

слеса́р|ь (**-я**; *nom pl* **-я́**, *gen pl* **-éй**) *м* maintenance man (*мн* men).

слёт (**-а**) *м* (*пионеров*) rally.

слета́|ть (**-ю**) *несов от* **слете́ть** ◆ *непepex* (*на юг, на море*) to fly; (*разг: сбегать*) to nip

▶ **слета́ться** *несов от* **слете́ться**.

сле|те́ть (**-чу́, -ти́шь**; *impf* **слета́ть**) *сов непepex*: **~ (с +**gen**)** (*птица*) to fly down (from); (*разг: спесь*) to vanish (from); (: *шляпа, ребёнок*) to fall off; **вопро́с ~те́л с губ** *или* **с языка́** the question slipped out

▶ **слете́ться** (*impf* **слета́ться**) *сов возв* (*птицы*) to flock; (*мухи*) to swarm.

сле|чь (**-я́гу, -я́жешь** *итп*, **-я́гут**; *pt* **-ёг, -егла́,**

-егло́) *сов непepex* to take to one's bed.

слив (**-а**) *м* (*действие*) discharge; (*устройство*) drain.

сли́в|а (**-ы**) *ж* (*дерево*) plum (tree); (*плод*) plum.

слива́|ть(ся) (**-ю(сь)**) *несов от* **слить(ся)**.

сли́в|ки (**-ок**) *мн* (*также перен*) cream *ед*.

сли́вовый *прил* plum *опред*.

сли́вок *сущ см* **сли́вки**.

сли́вочный *прил* made with cream; **сли́вочное ма́сло** butter.

слиза́|ть (**-ижу́, -и́жешь**; *impf* **сли́зывать**) *сов перех* (*языком*) to lick off.

сли́зистый *прил* mucous *опред*; **сли́зистая оболо́чка** mucous membrane.

сли́зыва|ть (**-ю**) *несов от* **слиза́ть**.

слиз|ь (**-и**) *ж* mucus; (*от сырости, от грязи*) slime.

слипа́|ться (*3sg* **-ется**, *3pl* **-ются**) *несов от* **сли́пнуться** ◆ *возв* (*перен*): **у меня́ глаза́ ~ются** I can't keep my eyes open.

сли́п|нуться (*3sg* **-нется**, *3pl* **-нутся**, *pt* **-ся, -лась, -лось**, *impf* **слипа́ться**) *сов возв* to stick together.

сли́тка *итп сущ см* **сли́ток**.

сли́тн|ый *прил* (*звучание*) unified; **~ое написа́ние** spelt as one word.

сли́т|ок (**-ка**) *м* (*металлический*) bar; (*золота, серебра*) ingot.

сли|ть (**солью́, сольёшь**; *pt* **-л, -ла́, -ло**, *imper* **сле́й(те)**, *impf* **слива́ть**) *сов перех* to pour; (*вылить*) to pour out; (*перен: соединить*) to merge

▶ **сли́ться** (*impf* **слива́ться**) *сов возв* (*реки*) to flow together; (*голоса, судьбы, компании*) to merge.

сличи́|ть (**-у́, -и́шь**; *impf* **слича́ть**) *сов перех*: **~ что-н с чем-н** to check sth against sth.

сли́шком *нареч* too; **э́то уже́ ~** (*разг*) that's just too much.

слов|а́ (**-**) *мн*: **~ пе́сни** lyrics *мн*.

слова́к (**-а**) *м* Slovak.

Слова́ки|я (**-и**) *ж* Slovakia.

слова́рный *прил* (*работа, статья*) dictionary *опред*, lexicographic(al); (*фонд, состав языка*) lexical; **слова́рный запа́с** vocabulary.

слова́р|ь (**-я́**) *м* (*книга*) dictionary; (*запас слов*) vocabulary.

слова́цкий (**-ая, -ое, -ие**) *прил* Slovak, Slovakian.

слова́ч|ка (**-ки**; *gen pl* **-ек**) *ж см* **слова́к**.

слове́н|ец (**-ца**) *м* Slovene.

Слове́ни|я (**-и**) *ж* Slovenia.

слове́н|ка (**-ки**; *gen pl* **-ок**) *ж см* **слове́нец**.

слове́нск|ий (**-ая, -ое, -ие**) *прил* Slovene, Slovenian.

слове́нца *итп сущ см* **слове́нец**.

слове́сность (**-и**) *ж* literature.

слове́сный *прил* oral; (*заявление, протест*) verbal; **слове́сный портре́т** description.

сло́вно *союз* (*как*) like; (*как будто*) as if.

сло́в|о (**-а**; *nom pl* **-а́**) *ср* word; **~ в ~** word for word; **он двух слов связа́ть не мо́жет** (*разг*) he can't string two words together; **на слова́х** (*переда́ть, согласи́ться*) verbally; **она́ сочу́вствует то́лько на слова́х** her sympathy is just empty words; **со слов свиде́телей/его́ друзе́й** according to witnesses/his friends; **проси́ть (попроси́ть** *perf*) **~a** (*на собра́нии*) to ask to speak; **предоставля́ть (предоста́вить** *perf*) **кому́-н ~** to allow sb to speak; **лаборато́рия обору́дована по после́днему ~у нау́ки** the laboratory is equipped with the latest technology; **к ~у пришло́сь** it sprang to mind; (**одни́м**) **~м** in a word; **слов нет, ты прав** what can I say, you're right; *см та́кже* **слова́**.

словоизмене́ни|е (**-я**) *ср* inflection.

сло́вом *вводн сл* in a word.

словообразова́ни|е (**-я**) *ср* word formation.

словоохо́тлив|ый (**-, -а, -о**) *прил* loquacious.

словосочета́ни|е (**-я**) *ср* word combination.

словоупотребле́ни|е (**-я**) *ср* word usage.

словц|о́ (**-а́**) *ср* witticism; **для кра́сного ~а́** for effect.

слог (**-а**; *nom pl* **-и**, *gen pl* **-о́в**) *м* syllable; (*стиль*) style.

сло́ек *сущ см* **сло́йка**.

слоён|ый *прил*: **~ое те́сто** puff pastry.

сло́жен *прил см* **сло́жный**.

сложе́ни|е (**-я**) *ср* (*в матема́тике*) addition; (*телосложе́ние*) build; (*полномо́чий, обя́занностей*) relinquishing; (*чи́сел*) adding.

сл|ожи́ть (**-ожу́, -о́жишь**; *impf* **скла́дывать**) *сов перех* (*ве́щи*) to put; (*кни́ги*) to stack; (*чемода́н, су́мку итп*) to pack; (*бума́гу, руба́шку итп*) to fold (up); (*impf* **скла́дывать** *или* **слага́ть**; *чи́сла*) to add (up); (*пе́сню, стихи́*) to make up; **~** (*perf*) **го́лову/ору́жие** to lay down one's life/weapons; **~** (*perf*) **ру́ки** to fold one's arms; **слага́ть** (**~** *perf*) **с себя́ полномо́чия/отве́тственность** to relinquish one's authority/responsibility; **сиде́ть** (*impf*) **~ожа́ ру́ки** to sit back and do nothing

▶ **сложи́ться** (*impf* **скла́дываться**) *сов возв* (*колле́ктив*) to come together; (*ситуа́ция, обстоя́тельства*) to turn out; (*хара́ктер*) to form; (*собра́ть де́ньги*) to have a collection; (*зонт, пала́тка*) to fold up; (*впечатле́ние*) to form; **у нас ~ожи́лось хоро́шее впечатле́ние о нём** we formed a good impression of him.

сло́жно *нареч* (*де́лать*) in a complicated way; (*сложи́ться*) in a difficult way ♦ *как сказ* it's difficult; **мне ~ поня́ть его́** I find it difficult to understand him.

сложносокращённ|ый *прил*: **~ое сло́во** compound.

сло́жност|ь (**-и**) *ж* (*многообра́зие*) complexity;

(*зати́ейливость*) intricacy; (*обы́чно мн: тру́дность*) difficulty; **в о́бщей ~и** all in all.

сло́ж|ный (**-ен, -на́, -но**) *прил* (*де́ло, предложе́ние, челове́к*) complex; (*узо́р*) intricate; (*вопро́с, рабо́та*) difficult.

сло́йст|ый (**-, -а, -о**) *прил* stratified.

сло|й (**-я**; *nom pl* **-и́**) *м* layer.

сло́йк|а (**-и**; *gen pl* **-ек**) *ж* sweet pastry.

слом (**-а**) *м*: **на ~** for demolition; **дом идёт на ~** this house is due for demolition.

слома́|ть (**-ю**) *сов от* **лома́ть**

▶ **слома́|ться** *сов от* **лома́ться** ♦ *возв* (*перен: разг: челове́к*) to break.

слом|и́ть (**-лю́, -ишь**) *сов перех* (*сопротивле́ние, во́лю итп*) to break; (*подлеж: боле́знь, уста́лость*) to knock out; **~я́ го́лову** (*разг*) at breakneck speed

▶ **сломи́ться** *сов возв* (*перен: челове́к*) to break.

слон (**-а́**) *м* elephant; (*ша́хматы*) bishop.

слонёнок (**-ёнка**; *nom pl* **-я́та**, *gen pl* **-я́т**) *м* elephant calf (*мн* calves).

слони́х|а (**-и**) *ж* cow (*elephant*).

слоно́в|ый *прил* elephant *опред*; **слоно́вая кость** ivory.

слоня́та *итп сущ см* **слонёнок**.

слоня́|ться (**-юсь**) *несов возв* (*разг*) to loaf around.

сло́па|ть (**-ю**) *сов от* **ло́пать**.

слуг|а́ (**-и́**; *nom pl* **-и**) *м* servant.

служа́к|а (**-и**) *м* (*разг*) trouper.

служа́н|ка (**-ки**; *gen pl* **-ок**) *ж* maid.

слу́жащий (**-его**; *decl like adj*) *м* white collar worker; **госуда́рственный ~** civil servant; **конто́рский ~** clerk.

слу́жб|а (**-ы**) *ж* service; (*рабо́та*) work; **срок ~ы** durability; **Слу́жба бы́та** consumer services; **Слу́жба за́нятости** ≈ Employment Service.

служе́бн|ый *прил* (*дела́, обя́занности итп*) official; (*роль, помеще́ние итп*) auxiliary; **~ое положе́ние** rank; **служе́бное сло́во** connective word; **служе́бная соба́ка** working dog.

служе́ни|е (**-я**) *ср* (*де́йствие: ро́дине*) serving; (*РЕЛ*) service.

служи́тел|ь (**-я**) *м* (*в музе́е, в зоопа́рке*) keeper; (*на автозапра́вке*) attendant; (*нау́ки, иску́сства*) servant; **служи́тель це́ркви** clergyman (*мн* clergymen).

служи́тельниц|а (**-ы**) *ж* keeper.

служ|и́ть (**-у́, -ужишь**) *несов неперех* (*в ба́нке, в конто́ре итп*) to work; (*в а́рмии*) to serve ♦ *перех* (*РЕЛ*) to hear ♦ *неперех* (*соба́ка*) to beg; (*perf* **послужи́ть**; +*instr*) to serve as; **~** (*impf*) **ро́дине/па́ртии** to serve one's country/party; **чем могу́ ~?** what can I do for you?

слука́в|ить (**-лю, -ишь**) *сов от* **лука́вить**.

слух (**-а**) *м* hearing; (*музыка́льный*) ear;

(*известие*) rumour (*BRIT*), rumor (*US*); **на** ~ by hearing; **игра́ть** (*impf*) **по слу́ху** to play by ear; **о нём ни слу́ху ни ду́ху** there's been no word of him; **по слу́хам** from what people are saying.

слуховой *прил* (*нерв, орган*) auditory; **слуховой аппара́т** hearing aid.

случа́ен *прил см* **случа́йный**.

случа|й (**-я**) *м* occasion; (*подходящий момент*) chance, opportunity; (*случайность*) chance; **в ~е** +*gen* in the event of; **в ~е чего** (*разг*) if there is anything; **во вся́ком ~е** in any case; **на ~** +*gen* in case of; **на вся́кий ~** just in case; **по ~ю** +*gen* (*годовщины*) on the occasion of; **при ~е** if the opportunity arises; **несча́стный ~** accident.

случа́йно *нареч* accidentally, by chance ♦ *вводн сл* by any chance; **Вы, ~, не зна́ете, где здесь банк?** you don't by any chance know where there is a bank?; **не ~** not by chance.

случа́йность (**-и**) *ж* (*chance*); **по счастли́вой ~и** by sheer luck.

случа́йный (**-ен, -йна, -йно**) *прил* (*встреча*) accidental, chance *опред*; (*знакомство*) casual; (*КОМП*) random; **~ за́работок** casual earnings.

случа́ть (**-ю**) *несов от* **случи́ть**

► **случа́ться** *несов от* **случи́ться** ♦ *возв:* **он, ~ется, прихо́дит серди́тый** occasionally he arrives in a temper.

случ|и́ть (**-у́, -и́шь**; *impf* **случа́ть**) *сов перех* to mate

► **случи́ться** (*impf* **случа́ться**) *сов возв* (*произойти*) to happen ♦ *безл:* **мне ~и́лось с ним познако́миться** I happened to become acquainted with him.

слу́шани|е (**-я**) *ср* (*ЮР*) hearing.

слу́шател|ь (**-я**) *м* listener; (*ПРОСВЕЩ*) student.

слу́шательниц|а (**-ы**) *ж см* **слу́шатель**.

слу́ша|ть (**-ю**) *несов перех* (*музыку, речь*) to listen to; (*ЮР*) to hear; (*курс лекций*) to attend; (*perf* **послу́шать**; *совет*) to listen to; (*perf* **вы́слушать**; *сердце, лёгкие*) to listen to; **~йте!** (*раза*) listen!

► **слу́шаться** (*perf* **послу́шаться**) *несов возв:* **~ся** +*gen* to obey; (*совета*) to follow; **~юсь!** yes, sir!

слы|ть (**-ву́, -вёшь**; *pt* **-л, -ла́, -ло**) *несов неперех:* **~** +*instr или* **за** +*acc* to be reputed to be.

слы́хан|ный *прил:* **где э́то ~о?** (*разг*) whoever heard of such a thing?

слыха́|ть (*pt* **-л, -ла, -ло**) *несов перех* to hear; **мне ничего́ не ~** (*раза*) I can't hear a thing.

слы́ш|ать (**-у, -ишь**) *несов неперех* to hear ♦ (*perf* **услы́шать**) *перех* to hear; **~** (*impf*) **о** +*prp* to hear about; **и ~ об э́том не хочу́** I won't hear of it; **он пло́хо ~ит** he's hard of hearing

► **слы́шаться** *несов возв* to be heard.

слы́шен *прил см* **слы́шный**.

слы́шимость (**-и**) *ж* (*в зале*) acoustics *мн*; (*радио, телевизора*) audibility.

слы́шно *как сказ* it can be heard; **мне ничего́ не ~** I can't hear a thing; **о ней ничего́ не ~** there's

no news of her; **что у Вас ~?** how are things?

слы́ш|ный (**-ен, -на́, -но**) *прил* (*звук, пение*) audible ♦ *как сказ* (*no full form*): **в его́ го́лосе слышна́ трево́га** anxiety can be heard in his voice.

слюд|а́ (**-ы́**) *ж* mica.

слюн|а́ (**-ы́**) *ж* saliva.

слю́н|ки (**-ок**) *мн:* **у меня́ ~ теку́т** my mouth's watering.

слюня́в|ить (**-лю, -ишь**) *несов перех* (*разг*) to lick.

сля́гу *итп сов см* **слечь**.

сля́кот|ь (**-и**) *ж* slush.

сля́па|ть (**-ю**) *сов от* **ля́пать**.

см *сокр* (= **сантиме́тр**) cm(= *centimetre* (*BRIT*) *или* centimeter (*US*)).

см. *сокр* (= **смотри́**) v. (= *vide,*) qv (= *quod vide*).

с.м. *сокр* (= **сего́ ме́сяца**) inst. (= *instant*).

сма́|зать (**-жу, -жешь**; *impf* **сма́зывать**) *сов перех* (*маслом*) to lubricate; (*разг: испортить впечатление*) to slur; **сма́зывать** (**~** *perf*) **что-н ма́зью** to put ointment on sth.

сма́з|ка (**-и**) *ж* (*действие*) lubrication; (*вещество*) lubricant.

смазли́вый (**-, -а, -о**) *прил* (*разг*) pretty.

сма́зочный *прил* lubricating.

сма́зыва|ть (**-ю**) *несов от* **сма́зать**.

смак|ова́ть (**-у́ю**) *несов перех* (*еду*) to savour (*BRIT*), savor (*US*); (*перен: новость, книгу итп*) to relish.

смалоду́шнича|ть (**-ю**) *сов от* **малоду́шничать**.

сма́льт|а (**-ы**) *ж* smalto.

сманеври́р|овать (**-ую**) *сов от* **маневри́ровать**.

сман|и́ть (**-ю́, -а́нишь**; *impf* **сма́нивать**) *сов перех* (*переманить*) to lure, entice.

смастер|и́ть (**-ю́, -и́шь**) *сов от* **мастери́ть**.

сма́тыва|ть(ся) (**-ю(сь)**) *несов от* **смота́ть(ся)**.

сма́хива|ть (**-ю**) *несов от* **смахну́ть** ♦ *неперех* (*разг*) **~ на** +*acc* (*походить*) to look a bit like.

смахн|у́ть (**-у́, -ёшь**) *сов перех* to brush off.

сма́чен *прил см* **сма́чный**.

сма́чива|ть (**-ю**) *несов от* **смочи́ть**.

сма́ч|ный (**-ен, -на́, -но**) *прил* (*разг: вкусный*) scrumptious; (*перен: слово*) juicy.

сме́жен *прил см* **сме́жный**.

сме́жник (**-а**) *м* (*предприятие*) related company.

сме́ж|ный (**-ен, -на, -но**) *прил* (*с общей границей*) adjoining, adjacent; (*производство, предприятие*) affiliated; (*наука*) related.

смека́листый (**-, -а, -о**) *прил* astute.

смека́л|ка (**-и**) *ж* astuteness.

смека́|ть (**-ю**; *perf* **смекну́ть**) *несов перех* to catch onto.

смеле́|ть (**-ю**; *perf* **осмеле́ть**) *несов неперех* to grow bolder.

сме́ло *нареч* boldly; (*без колебаний*) confidently.

смéлост|ь (-и) ж (*храбрость*) bravery; (*поступка, поведения*) boldness, audacity; **брать** (**взять** *perf*) **на себя́** ~ +*infin* to have the audacity to do.

смéл|ый (-, -á, -о) *прил* (*человек, поступок*) brave; (*идея, проект*) ambitious; (*перен: нескрайный*) risqué.

смельчá|к (-á) *м* brave person (*мн* people).

смелю́ *итп сов см* **смолóть**.

смéн|а (-ы) ж (*руководства*) change; (*караула, одежды*) changing; (*на производстве*) shift; (*молодое поколение мн*; (*также*: ~ **белья́**) change of sheets (*BRIT*) или bed-linen (*US*); **приходи́ть** (**прийти́** *perf*) **на** ~**y** кому́-н/ чему́-н to succeed sb/sth.

см|ени́ть (-еню́, -éнишь; *impf* **сменя́ть**) *сов перех* to change; (*коллегу*) to relieve

▶ **смени́ться** (*impf* **сменя́ться**) *сов возв* (*руководство*) to change; (*радость, день*): ~**ся** +*instr* to give way to; **сменя́ться** (~**ся** *perf*) (**с** +*gen*) (*с дежурства, с вахты*) to go off duty (from).

смéнн|ый *прил* (*работа, задание*) shift *опред*; (*колесо*) spare; (~**ое бельё** a change of sheets (*BRIT*) или bed-linen (*US*); (*нижнее*) a change of underwear.

сменя́|ть(ся) (-ю(сь)) *несов от* **смени́ть(ся)**.

смёрзн|уться (*3sg* -ется, *3pl* -утся) *сов возв* to freeze together.

смéр|ить (-ю, -ишь) *сов от* **мéрить**.

смерка́|ться (*3sg* -ется, *perf* **смéркнуться**) *несов безл* to start to get dark.

смертéл|ьный (-ен, -ьна, -ьно) *прил* mortal; (*рана*) fatal; (*скука, усталость*) deadly; **смертéльный исхóд** fatal ending; **смертéльный слу́чай** fatality.

смéртен *прил см* **смéртный**.

смéртник (-а) *м* (*приговорённый к казни*) prisoner on death row; (*террорист*) kamikaze.

смéртност|ь (-и) ж death-rate, mortality.

смéртн|ый (-ен, -на, -но) *прил* mortal; (*разг: скука*) deadly; ~ **час** hour of death; ~ **бой** (*перен*) fight to the death; **простóй** ~ ordinary mortal; **смéртный пригово́р** death sentence; **смéртная казнь** death penalty.

смертонóсный *прил* lethal.

смерт|ь (-и) ж death; **быть** (*impf*) **при** ~**и** to be at death's door; **умира́ть** (**умерéть** *perf*) **своéй смéртью** to die a natural death; **я до** ~**и боюсь** I'm scared to death.

смерч (-а) *м* tornado.

смеси́тел|ь (-я) *м* mixer.

смеси́ть (-шу́, -сишь) *сов от* **меси́ть**.

сме|сти́ (-ту́, -тёшь; *pt* -ёл, -елá, -елó, *impf* **смета́ть**) *сов перех* to sweep; (*подлеж: ураган, смерч*) to sweep away.

сме|сти́ть (-щу́, -сти́шь; *impf* **смеща́ть**) *сов перех* (*уволить*) to remove; (*сдвинуть*) to shift

▶ **смести́ться** (*impf* **смеща́ться**) *сов возв* to shift.

смес|ь (-и) ж mixture; **моло́чная** ~ powdered baby milk.

смéт|а (-ы) ж (*экон*) estimate.

сметáн|а (-ы) ж sour cream.

сметá|ть (-ю) *несов от* **смести́** ♦ *сов от* **метáть**.

сметли́в|ый (-, -а, -о) *прил* quick.

смéтный *прил* estimated; **смéтная стóимость** estimated cost.

сме|ть (-ю; *perf* **посмéть**) *несов неперех*: ~ +*infin* to dare to do; **как Вы смéете!** how dare you!; **не смéй!** don't you dare!

смету́ *итп сов см* **смести́**.

смех (-а; *part gen* -у) *м* laughter ♦ *как сказ* (*смешно*) it's ridiculous; **слу́шать э́то ~ - ~** it makes me laugh to hear it; **поднимáть** (**подня́ть** *perf*) **кого́-н нá** ~ to make a laughing stock of sb; **и ~ и грех** one can see the funny side of it.

смехотвóр|ный (-ен, -на, -но) *прил* (*смешнóй*) funny; (*жалкий*) ludicrous.

смéшанный *прил* mixed.

смешá|ть (-ю) *сов от* **мешáть** ♦ (*impf* **смéшивать**) *перех* (*спутать*) to mix up; ~ (*perf*) **чьи-н кáрты** to spoil sb's plans

▶ **смешáться** *сов от* **мешáться** ♦ *возв* (*смутиться*) to be taken aback; (*impf* **смéшиваться**; *слиться*) to mingle; (*краски, цвета*) to blend; (*чувства*) to become confused.

смешéни|е (-я) *ср* (*стилей, чувств*) mixture.

смéшивани|е (-я) *ср* mixing.

смéшива|ть(ся) (-ю(сь)) *несов от* **смешáть(ся)**.

смеш|и́ть (-у́, -и́шь; *perf* **насмеши́ть** или **рассмеши́ть**) *несов перех*: ~ **кого́-н** to make sb laugh.

смешкá *итп сущ см* **смешóк**.

смешли́в|ый (-, -а, -о) *прил* (*человек*) jolly; (*настроение*) giggly.

смешнó *нареч* (*смотреться*) funny ♦ *как сказ* it's funny; (*глупо*) it's ludicrous; **мне не** ~ I don't find it funny; ~ **надéяться** it's ludicrous to hope; ~ **сказáть, но ...** it sounds funny, but ...; **э́то прóсто** ~ that's just ridiculous.

смеш|нóй (-óн, -нá, -нó) *прил* funny; (*требования, претензии итп*) ludicrous; **до** ~**нóго** to the point of absurdity; **дохóдит до** ~**нóго** it's a real joke.

смеш|óк (-кá) *м* giggle.

смешóн *прил см* **смешнóй**.

смеща́|ть(ся) (-ю(сь)) *несов от* **смести́ть(ся)**.

смещéни|е (-я) *ср* (*руководства*) removal; (*понятий, критериев*) shift.

смещённый (-ён, -енá, -енó) *прил* upset; (*понятия*) disturbed.

смещу́(сь) *сов см* **смести́ть(ся)**.

смея́|ться (-ю́сь) *несов возв* to laugh;

(*шутить*) to joke; (*perf* **посмеяться**; *насмехаться*): ~ **над** +*instr* to laugh at.

сми́лостив|иться (-люсь, -ишься) *сов возв*: ~ (**над** +*instr*) to take pity (on).

смина́|ть (-ю) *несов от* **смять**.

сми́рен *прил см* **сми́рный**.

смире́ни|е (-я) *ср* (*покорность*) humility.

смире́н|ный (-, -на, -но) *прил* humble.

смири́тельн|ый *прил*: ~**ая руба́шка** strait-jacket.

смири́ть (-ю, -и́шь; *impf* **смиря́ть**) *сов перех* to subdue

► **смири́ться** (*impf* **смиря́ться**) *сов возв* (*покориться*) to submit; (*примириться*): ~**ся с** +*instr* to resign o.s. to.

сми́рно *нареч* (*сидеть, вести себя*) quietly; (*воен*: *команда*) attention; **стоя́ть** (*impf*) **по сто́йке** „~" to stand to attention.

сми́р|ный (-ен, -на́, -но) *прил* docile.

смиря́|ть(ся) (-ю(сь)) *несов от* **смири́ть(ся)**.

смог (-а) *м* smog.

смог *итп сов см* **смочь**.

смогу́ *итп сов см* **смочь**.

модели́р|овать (-ую) *сов от* **модели́ровать**.

смо́жешь *итп сов см* **смочь**.

смол|а́ (-ы́; *nom pl* -ы) *ж* (*дерево*) resin; (*дёготь*) tar.

смоли́ст|ый (-, -а, -о) *прил* (*дерево*) resinous.

смо́лк|нуть (-ну, -нешь; *pt* -, -ла, -ло, *impf* **смолка́ть**) *сов неперех* (*голоса*) to fall silent; (*звуки*) to fade away.

сма́лоду *нареч* from one's youth.

смол|оти́ть (-очу́, -о́тишь) *сов от* **молоти́ть**.

смол|о́ть (-елю́, -е́лешь) *сов от* **моло́ть**.

смолочу́ *сов см* **смолоти́ть**.

смолч|а́ть (-у́, -и́шь) *сов неперех* to keep quiet.

смоль (-и) *ж*: **чёрный как** ~ jet-black.

смонти́р|овать (-ую) *сов от* **монти́ровать**.

сморка́|ть (-ю; *perf* **вы́сморкать**) *несов перех*: ~ **нос** to blow one's nose

► **сморка́ться** (*perf* **вы́сморкаться**) *несов возв* to blow one's nose.

сморо́дин|а (-ы) *ж*: **кра́сная** ~ (*кустарник*) redcurrant bush; (*ягоды*) redcurrants *мн*; **чёрная** ~ (*кустарник*) blackcurrant bush; (*ягоды*) blackcurrants *мн*.

сморо́|зить (-жу, -зишь) *сов перех* to say.

смо́рщенный *прил* wrinkled.

смо́рщ|ить (-у, -ишь) *сов от* **мо́рщить**

► **смо́рщиться** *сов от* **мо́рщиться** ♦ *возв* to become wrinkled.

смота́|ть (-ю; *impf* **сма́тывать**) *сов перех* to wind

► **смота́ться** (*impf* **сма́тываться**) *сов возв* (*нитки*) to wind; (*разг: убежать*) to leg it; (: *быстро пойти*) to nip.

смотр (-а; *loc sg* -у́, *nom pl* -ы́) *м* presentation; (*воен*) inspection.

см|отре́ть (-отрю́, -о́тришь; *perf* **посмотре́ть**) *несов неперех* to look ♦ *перех* (*фильм, игру*) to watch; (*газеты, почту*) to look through;

(*квартиру, картину*) to look at; (*музей, выставку*) to look round; (*пациента*) to examine; (*следить*): ~ **за** +*instr* to look after; ~ (*impf*) **в/на** +*acc* to look onto; ~ (**посмотре́ть** *perf*) **на** +*acc* (*относиться*) to look at; **смотри́те, не упади́те** watch, don't fall; ~**отрю́, ты осво́ился здесь** (*разг*) I see you've settled down here; ~**отря́ по** +*dat* depending on; **Вы хоти́те пойти́ погуля́ть? – ~отря́ куда́** would you like to go for a walk? – it depends where to

► **смотре́ться** (*perf* **посмотре́ться**) *несов возв*: ~**ся в** +*acc* (*в зеркало, в воду*) to look at o.s. in; (*разг: хорошо выглядеть*) to look good; **э́та вы́ставка** ~**о́трится легко́** this exhibition is not too demanding.

смотри́тель (-я) *м* (*в музее*) attendant.

смотри́тельниц|а (-ы) *ж см* **смотри́тель**.

смотров|о́й *прил* (*площадка*) viewing *опред*; ~**а́я ба́шня** watch tower; ~**о́е отве́рстие** peephole; **смотрово́й кабине́т** medical examination room.

смо́ч|ить (-очу́, -о́чишь; *impf* **сма́чивать**) *сов перех* to dampen.

смо́чь (-гу́, -жешь *итп*, -гут; *pt* -г, -гла́, -гло́) *сов от* **мочь**.

смоше́ннича|ть (-ю) *сов от* **моше́нничать**.

смо́ю(сь) *итп сов см* **смы́ть(ся)**.

смрад (-а) *м* (*вонь*) stench.

смра́д|ный (-ен, -на, -но) *прил* stinking.

сму́гл|ый (-, -а́, -о) *прил* swarthy.

сму́т|а (-ы) *ж* (*социальная*) unrest; **у меня́ на душе́** ~ my soul is troubled.

сму́тен *прил см* **сму́тный**.

сму|ти́ть (-щу́, -ти́шь; *impf* **смуща́ть**) *сов перех* to embarrass

► **смути́ться** (*impf* **смуща́ться**) *сов возв* to get embarrassed.

сму́т|ный (-ен, -на, -но) *прил* (*очертания, воспоминания*) vague; (*настроение, время итп*) troubled.

смуща́|ть(ся) (-ю(сь)) *несов от* **смути́ть(ся)**.

смуще́ни|е (-я) *ср* embarrassment.

смущённый *прил* embarrassed.

смущу́(сь) *сов см* **смути́ть(ся)**.

смыва́|ть(ся) (-ю(сь)) *несов от* **смы́ть(ся)**.

смыка́|ть(ся) (-ю(сь)) *несов от* **сомкну́ть(ся)**.

смысл (-а) *м* (*книги, статьи*) point; (*слов*) meaning; (*линг*) sense; **в смы́сле** +*gen* as regards; **здра́вый** ~ common sense; **прямо́й/перено́сный** ~ **сло́ва** the literal/figurative sense of a word; **како́й** ~ **на э́то соглаша́ться?** what is the point of agreeing to that?; **есть** ~ **е́хать сего́дня** it makes sense to go today.

смы́сл|ить (-ю, -ишь) *несов неперех* (*разг: разбираться*): ~ **в** +*prp* (*в технике*) to have a knack for.

смы́|ть (-ю, -ешь; *impf* **смыва́ть**) *сов перех* to wash off; (*подлеж: волна, течение*) to wash away

► **смы́ться** (*impf* **смыва́ться**) *сов возв* to wash

off; (*разг: незаметно уйти*) to do a bunk.
смыч|о́к (-ка́) *м* (*МУЗ*) bow.
смышлён|ый (-, -а, -о) *прил* sharp.
смягча́|ть(ся) (-ю(сь)) *несов от* **смягчи́ть(ся)**.
смягча́ющий (-ая, -ее, -ие) *прил*: ~ие
обстоя́тельства (*ЮР*) extenuating
circumstances *мн*.
смягче́ни|е (-я) *ср* (*действие*) softening;
(: *наказания*) mitigation.
смягч|и́ть (-у́, -и́шь; *impf* **смягча́ть**) *сов перех*
(*кожу, ткань, удар*) to soften; (*боль*) to ease;
(*наказание, приговор*) to mitigate; (*человека*)
to appease
▶ **смягчи́ться** (*impf* **смягча́ться**) *сов возв* to
soften.
смяте́ни|е (-я) *ср* turmoil.
смять (**сомну́, сомнёшь**) *сов от* **мять** ◆ (*impf*
смина́ть) *перех* (*противника, оборону*) to
crush
▶ **смя́ться** *сов от* **мя́ться**.
сна *итп сущ см* **сон**.
снаб|ди́ть (-жу́, -ди́шь; *impf* **снабжа́ть**) *сов
перех*: ~ кого́-н/что-н чем-н to supply sb/sth
with sth.
снабже́ни|е (-я) *ср* supply.
снабжу́ *сов см* **снабди́ть**.
сна́йпер (-а) *м* (*стрелок*) sniper.
снару́жи *нареч* (*покрасить, расположиться*)
on the outside; (*закрыть*) from the outside.
снаря́д (-а) *м* (*ВОЕН*) shell; (*СПОРТ*)
apparatus.
снаря|ди́ть (-жу́, -ди́шь; *impf* **снаряжа́ть**) *сов
перех* to equip.
снаряже́ни|е (-я) *ср* (*действие*) equipping;
(*лыжное, охотничье*) equipment; (*солдата*)
kit.
снаряжу́ *сов см* **снаряди́ть**.
снаст|ь (-и) *ж* (*МОР: обычно мн*) rigging *только
ед*; (*рыболовная*) tackle.
снача́ла *нареч* at first; (*ещё раз*) all over again.
сна́шива|ть (-ю) *несов от* **сноси́ть**.
СНГ *м сокр* (= Содру́жество Незави́симых
Госуда́рств) CIS (= *Commonwealth of
Independent States*).
снег (-а; *part gen* -у, *loc sg* -у́, *nom pl* -а́) *м* snow;
идёт ~ it's snowing; **вы́пал** ~ it's been
snowing; **как** ~ **на́ голову** like a bolt from the
blue.
снеги́р|ь (-я́) *м* bullfinch.
снегови́к (-а́) *м* snowman (*мн* snowmen).
снегоочисти́тел|ь (-я) *м* snowplough (*BRIT*),
snowplow (*US*).
снегопа́д (-а) *м* snowfall.
снегоубо́рочн|ый *прил*: ~ая маши́на
snowplough (*BRIT*), snowplow (*US*).
снегу́роч|ка (-ки; *gen pl* -ек) *ж* Snow Maiden.
снед|ь (-и) *ж собир* food.
снежи́н|ка (-ки; *gen pl* -ок) *ж* snowflake.
снежка́ *итп сущ см* **снежо́к**.

сне́жн|ый *прил* snow *опред*; ~ая зима́ snowy
winter; **сне́жная ба́ба** snowman (*мн* snowmen).
снеж|о́к (-ка́) *м* (*комок*) snowball; **игра́ть** (*impf*) **в**
~ки to have a snowball fight.
сн|ести́ (-есу́, -есёшь; *pt* -ёс, -есла́, -есло́) *сов
от* **нести́** ◆ (*impf* **сноси́ть**) *перех* (*отнести*) to
take; (*подлеж: буря*) to carry away; (*сверху
вниз*) to take down; (*перен: вытерпеть*) to
take; (*дом*) to demolish
▶ **снести́сь** *сов от* **нести́сь** ◆ *возв* (*связаться*):
~сь с +*instr* to contact.
снижа́|ть(ся) (-ю(сь)) *несов от* **сни́зить(ся)**.
сниже́ни|е (-я) *ср* (*цен итп*) lowering;
(*самолёта*) descent; (*производительности
итп*) reduction.
сни́|зить (-жу, -зишь; *impf* **снижа́ть**) *сов перех*
(*цены, давление итп*) to lower; (*самолёт*) to
bring down ; (*скорость*) to reduce
▶ **сни́зиться** (*impf* **снижа́ться**) *сов возв* (*цены,
производительность итп*) to fall; (*самолёт*)
to descend.
снизойти́ (*как* **идти́**; *см* **Table 18**; *impf*
снисходи́ть) *сов неперех*: ~ к кому́-н или до
кого́-н to condescend to sb; **он снизошёл к
мое́й про́сьбе** или **до мое́й про́сьбы** he
condescended to grant my request.
сни́зу *нареч* (*внизу*) at the bottom; (*по
направлению вверх*) from the bottom; (*перен:
со стороны народа*) from the masses; ~
дове́рху from top to bottom.
сни́|кнуть (-ну, -нешь; *pt* -, -ла, -ло) *сов от*
ни́кнуть ◆ *неперех* to flag.
снима́|ть(ся) (-ю(сь)) *несов от* **снять(ся)**.
сни́м|ок (-ка) *м* (*ФОТО*) snap(shot).
сниму́(сь) *итп сов см* **снять(ся)**.
сни|ска́ть (-щу́, -щешь) *сов перех* to win; **э́тот
посту́пок** ~ска́л ему́ большу́ю сла́ву this deed
won him great fame.
снисходи́тельн|ый (-ен, -ьна, -ьно) *прил* (*не
стро́гий*) lenient; (*с оттенком высокомерия*)
condescending.
снисхо|ди́ть (-ожу́, -о́дишь) *несов от*
снизойти́.
снисхожде́ни|е (-я) *ср* leniency.
снисхожу́ *несов см* **снисходи́ть**.
сни́|ться (-юсь, -и́шься; *perf* **присни́ться**)
несов безл: мне ~и́лся стра́шный сон I was
having a terrible dream; мне ~и́лось, что я в
гора́х I dreamt I was in the mountains; **ты ча́сто**
~и́шься мне I often dream of you.
снищу́ *итп сов см* **сниска́ть**.
сноб (-а) *м* snob.
сноби́зм (-а) *м* snobbery.
сно́ва *нареч* again.
снов|а́ть (-у́ю) *несов неперех* (*люди*) to dash
about; (*машины*) to zoom about.
сновиде́ни|е (-я) *ср* dream.
сногсшиба́тельн|ый (-ен, -ьна, -ьно) *прил*

The spelling rules for Russian are shown on page xvii.

(*разг*) stunning.

сноп (**-á**) *м* (*с.-х.*) sheaf; (*перен*) shaft.

сноровк|а (**-и**) *ж* knack.

снос (**-а**) *м* demolition; **дом идёт на ~** the house is due for demolition; **э́тим боти́нкам сно́су нет** these boots are hard-wearing.

сно́сен *прил см* **сно́сный**.

сн|оси́ть (**-ошу́, -о́сишь**) *несов от* **снести́** ◆ (*impf* **сна́шивать**) *сов перех* (*износить*) to wear out.

сно́с|ка (**-ки**; *gen pl* **-ок**) *ж* footnote.

сно́с|ный (**-ен, -на, -но**) *прил* (*разг*) tolerable.

сно́сок *сущ см* **сно́ска**.

снотво́рн|ое (**-ого**; *decl like adj*) *ср* sleeping pill или tablet.

снотво́рн|ый *прил*: **~ое сре́дство** sedative.

снох|á (**-и́**) *ж* daughter-in-law (*of husband's father*).

сноше́ни|е (**-я**) *ср* relations *мн*; **входи́ть** (**войти́** *perf*) **в ~я с** +*instr* to enter into relations with.

сношу́ (**не**)*сов см* **сноси́ть**.

сня́ти|е (**-я**) *ср* removal.

сн|ять (**-иму́, -и́мешь**; *impf* **снима́ть**) *сов перех* to take down; (*плод*) to pick; (*одежду*) to take off; (*запрет, ответственность*) to remove; (*копию*) to make; (*дом, комнату итп*) to rent; (*уволить*) to dismiss; **снима́ть** (**~** *perf*) **фотогра́фию** to take a picture; **снима́ть** (**~** *perf*) **фильм** to shoot a film; **снима́ть** (**~** *perf*) **показа́ния** to take down evidence; **снима́ть** (**~** *perf*) **урожа́й** to gather the harvest

▶ **сня́ться** (*impf* **снима́ться**) *сов возв* (*сфотографироваться*) to have one's photograph taken; (*покинуть: со стоянки*) to move off; (*актёр*) to appear; (*корабль*): **~я́ться с я́коря** to up anchor.

со *предл* = **с**.

соа́втор (**-а**) *м* coauthor.

соа́вторств|о (**-а**) *ср* coauthorship; **в ~е с** +*instr* in coauthorship with.

соба́к|а (**-и**) *ж* dog; (*разг*) rat, dog; **он на э́том ~у съел** (*разг*) he knows it inside out; **вот где ~ зары́та!** so that's what it is!

собаково́д (**-а**) *м* dog-breeder.

собаково́дств|о (**-а**) *ср* dog-breeding.

соба́ч|ий (**-ья, -ье, -ьи**) *прил* (*лай, нюх*) dog's; **~ья жизнь** (*разг*) it's a dog's life; **на у́лице хо́лод ~** (*разг*) it's blooming cold outside.

соба́чник (**-а**) *м* (*ловящий собак*) dog-catcher; (*разг: любитель собак*) dog-lover.

собезья́нничa|ть (**-ю**) *сов от* **обезья́нничать**.

соберу́(сь) *итп сов см* **собра́ть(ся)**.

собе́с (**-а**) *м сокр* (= **социа́льное обеспе́чение**) social security; (*учреждение*) ≈ social security department.

собесе́дник (**-а**) *м* interlocutor; **мой ~ замолча́л** the person I was talking to fell silent.

собесе́дниц|а (**-ы**) *ж см* **собесе́дник**.

собесе́довани|е (**-я**) *ср* interview.

собира́ни|е (**-я**) *ср* (*материала, данных итп*) collection, gathering; (*коллекционирование*)

collecting; (*ягод, грибов*) picking; **~ ма́рок** *итп* stamp *итп* collecting.

собира́телен *прил см* **собира́тельный**.

собира́тел|ь (**-я**) *м* collector.

собира́тел|ьный (**-ен, -ьна, -ьно**) *прил* (*также линг*) collective.

собира́|ть (**-ю**) *несов от* **собра́ть**

▶ **собира́ться** *несов от* **собра́ться** ◆ *возв*: **я ~юсь пойти́ туда́** I'm going to go there.

собко́р (**-а**) *м сокр* = **со́бственный корреспонде́нт**: **э́то сообще́ние от на́шего ~а в Москве́** this report is from our own correspondent in Moscow.

собла́зн (**-а**) *м* temptation; **устоя́ть** (*perf*) **пе́ред ~ом** или **про́тив ~а** to resist temptation; **вводи́ть** (**ввести́** *perf*) **кого́-н в ~** to tempt sb.

соблазни́телен *прил см* **соблазни́тельный**.

соблазни́тел|ь (**-я**) *м* seducer.

соблазни́тел|ьный (**-ен, -ьна, -ьно**) *прил* tempting; (*женщина*) seductive.

соблазн|и́ть (**-ю́, -и́шь**; *impf* **соблазня́ть**) *сов перех* to seduce; (*прельстить*): **~ кого́-н чем-н** to tempt sb with sth

▶ **соблазни́ться** (*impf* **соблазня́ться**) *сов возв*: **~ся** +*instr*/+*infin* to be tempted by/to do.

соблюда́|ть (**-ю**) *несов от* **соблюсти́** ◆ *перех* (*дисциплину, порядок*) to maintain; **~йте чистоту́** "please keep this area tidy"

соблю|сти́ (**-ду́, -дёшь**) *сов от* **блюсти́** ◆ (*impf* **соблюда́ть**) *перех* (*закон, правила*) to observe.

соболе́зновани|е (**-я**) *ср* condolences *мн*; **выража́ть** (**вы́разить** *perf*) **кому́-н ~** to express one's condolences to sb.

соболе́зн|овать (**-ую**) *несов неперех*: **~ кому́-н** to condole with sb.

со́бол|ь (**-оля**; *nom pl* **-оля́**) *м* sable.

собо́р (**-а**) *м* cathedral; (*съезд*) council (*of churches*).

собо́рн|ый *прил* (*здание, колокол*) cathedral *опред*; **~ое постановле́ние** decree of the church council.

собра́ни|е (**-я**) *ср* (*партийное, профсоюзное*) meeting; (*представителей*) assembly; (*картин итп*) collection; **собра́ние сочине́ний** collected works *мн*.

со́бран|ный (**-, -на, -но**) *прил* self-disciplined.

соб|ра́ть (**-еру́, -ерёшь**; *pt* **-ра́л, -рала́, -ра́ло**, *impf* **собира́ть**) *сов перех* to gather (together); (*ягоды, грибы*) to pick; (*урожай*) to gather; (*станок, приёмник итп*) to assemble; (*марки, налоги, подписи*) to collect; (*перен: мужество*) to muster up; (: *силы*) to summon; (*пригото́вить*): **~ кого́-н в** +*acc* (*в школу итп*) to get sb ready for; **собра́ть** (**~** *perf*) **чемода́н/ве́щи** to pack one's suitcase/things

▶ **собра́ться** (*impf* **собира́ться**) *сов возв* (*гости, делегаты*) to assemble, gather; (*в экспедицию, на урок итп*) to get ready to go; (*приготовиться*): **~ся** +*infin* to get ready to do; **собра́ться** (**~ся** *perf*) **с** +*instr* (*с силами, с мыслями*) to gather; **собра́ться** (**~ся** *perf*) **с**

ду́хом to pluck up the courage; **ты куда́ ~ра́лся?** where were you going?; **то́лько ~ра́лся лечь спать, как зазвони́л телефо́н** I was about to go to bed when the telephone rang.

со́бственник (-а) *м (владелец)* owner.

со́бственниц|а (-ы) *ж см* **со́бственник.**

со́бственническ|ий (-ая, -ое, -ие) *прил* proprietorial.

со́бственно *част* actually ♦ *вводн сл:* ~ **(говоря́)** as a matter of fact.

со́бственнору́чный *прил (расписка)* own.

со́бственност|ь (-и) *ж (имущество)* property; *(владение)* ownership; ~ **на** +*acc* right of ownership of; **быть** *(impf) или* **находи́ться** *(impf)* **в чьей-н ~и** to be in sb's possession; **приобрета́ть (приобрести́** *perf)* **в ~ что-н** to become the owner of sth.

со́бственн|ый *прил* (one's) own; **по ~ому жела́нию** of one's own volition; **и́мя ~ое** proper name; **чу́вство ~ого досто́инства** self-respect; **со́бственный корреспонде́нт** *см* **собко́р.**

собуты́льник (-а) *м (разг: пренебр)* drinking mate *(BRIT) или* buddy *(US).*

собы́ти|е (-я) *ср* event.

собью́(сь) *итп сов см* **сбить(ся).**

сов|а́ (-ы́; *nom pl* -ы) *ж* owl.

сова́ть (**сую́, суёшь;** *perf* **су́нуть)** *несов перех* to put in; ~ **(су́нуть** *perf)* **нос во что-н** to poke one's nose into sth

▶ **сова́ться** *(perf* **су́нуться)** *несов возв (разг: лезть):* ~**ся вперёд** to push through; ~**ся (су́нуться** *perf)* **не в своё де́ло** to poke one's nose into other people's business.

сов|ёнок (**-ёнка;** *nom pl* **-я́та,** *gen pl* **-я́т)** *м* owlet.

соверша́|ть(ся) (-ю(сь)) *несов от* **соверши́ть(ся).**

соверше́нен *прил см* **соверше́нный.**

соверше́ни|е (-я) *ср (сделки)* conclusion; *(преступления)* committing.

соверше́нно *нареч (играть, исполнять)* perfectly; *(совсем)* absolutely, completely; **у меня́ ~ нет сил** I have absolutely no energy; **э́то ~ ве́рно** it's absolutely *или* completely true.

совершенноле́ти|е (-я) *ср:* **дости́гнуть ~я** to come of age.

совершенноле́тн|ий (-яя, -ее, -ие) *прил:* **стать ~им** to come of age.

соверше́н|ный (-ен, -на, -но) *прил (безукоризненный)* perfect; *(абсолютный)* absolute, complete; **соверше́нный вид** perfective aspect.

соверше́нств|о (-а) *ср* perfection; **доводи́ть (довести́** *perf)* **что-н до ~а** to do sth to perfection; **в ~е владе́ть** *(impf)* **чем-н** to have a perfect command of sth.

соверше́нств|овать (-ую; *perf* **усоверше́нствовать)** *несов перех* to improve

▶ **соверше́нствоваться** *(perf* **усоверше́нствоваться)** *несов возв:* ~**ся в** +*prp* to improve.

соверш|и́ть (-у́, -и́шь; *impf* **соверша́ть)** *сов перех* to make; *(сделку)* to conclude; *(преступление, проступок итп)* to commit; *(богослужение, обряд, подвиг)* to perform

▶ **соверши́ться** *(impf* **соверша́ться)** *сов возв* to take place.

со́вестлив|ый (-, -а, -о) *прил* conscientious.

со́вестно *как сказ:* **мне ~** +*infin* ... I am ashamed to do; **как ему́ не ~!** he ought to be ashamed of himself!

со́вест|ь (-и) *ж* conscience; **на ~ (сде́ланный)** very well; **по ~и говоря́** to be honest; **поступа́ть (поступи́ть** *perf)* **по ~и** to behave as one's conscience dictates; **со споко́йной ~ю** with a clear conscience.

сове́т (-а) *м* advice *только ед; (семейный)* discussion; *(военный)* council; *(ИСТ)* Soviet; **учёный ~** academic council; **С~ Безопа́сности ООН** United Nations Security Council; **дава́ть (дать** *perf)* **кому́-н ~** to give sb advice; **держа́ть** *(impf)* **~** to hold a council.

сове́тник (-а) *м (юстиции итп)* councillor; *(президента)* adviser.

сове́т|овать (-ую; *perf* **посове́товать)** *несов неперех:* ~ **кому́-н** +*infin* to advise sb to do; ~ *(impf)* **кому́-н что-н** to recommend sth to sb

▶ **сове́товаться** *(perf* **посове́товаться)** *несов возв:* ~**ся с кем-н (с другом)** to ask sb's advice; *(с врачо́м, с юри́стом)* to consult sb.

сове́тск|ий (-ая, -ое, -ие) *прил* Soviet.

сове́тчик (-а) *м* confidant(e); **в да́нном вопро́се я тебе́ не ~** I can't advise you on this subject.

совеща́ни|е (-я) *ср (собрание)* meeting; *(конференция)* conference.

совеща́тельный *прил (орган, голос)* consultative.

совеща́|ться (-юсь) *несов возв* to deliberate.

Совинформбюро́ *ср нескл сокр (ИСТ)* = *Сове́тское информацио́нное бюро́.*

совка́ *итп сущ см* **совок.**

совко́в|ый *прил:* ~**ая лопа́та** shovel.

совлада́|ть (-ю) *сов неперех:* ~ **с** +*instr* to control; ~ *(perf)* **с собо́й** to control o.s.

совладе́л|ец (-ьца) *м* joint owner.

совладе́ни|е (-я) *ср* joint ownership.

совме́стен *прил см* **совме́стный.**

совмести́мост|ь (-и) *ж* compatibility.

совмести́м|ый (-, -а, -о) *прил* compatible.

совмести́тельств|о (-а) *ср:* **я рабо́таю по ~у секретарём** my second job is as a secretary.

совме|сти́ть (-щу́, -сти́шь; *impf* **совмеща́ть)** *сов перех* to combine; **он ~ща́л в себе́ учёного и администра́тора** he was both a scholar and an administrator.

совме́стно *нареч* (*работать, решать итп*) jointly; **~ с** +*instr* jointly with.

совме́ст|ный (**-ен, -на, -но**) *прил* (*общий*) joint; **совме́стное предприя́тие** joint venture.

совмеща́|ть (**-ю**) *несов от* **совмести́ть ♦** *перех* (*две до́лжности*) to combine.

совмеще́ни|е (**-я**) *ср* combining.

совмещу́ *сов см* **совмести́ть.**

сов|о́к (**-ка́**) *м* (*для мусора*) dustpan; (*для муки́*) scoop; (*строи́тельный*) shovel.

совоку́пен *прил см* **совоку́пный.**

совоку́пност|ь (**-и**) *ж* (*факторов, причин*) combination; **в ~и** in total.

совоку́п|ный (**-ен, -на, -но**) *прил* (*усилие*) combined, joint.

совпада́|ть (*3sg* **-ет,** *3pl* **-ют**) *несов от* **совпа́сть.**

совпаде́ни|е (**-я**) *ср* (*собы́тий, обстоя́тельств*) coincidence; (*да́нных, цифр*) tallying; (*интере́сов, мне́ний*) meeting.

совпа́|сть (*3sg* **-дёт,** *3pl* **-ду́т,** *impf* **совпада́ть**) *сов неперех* (*собы́тия*) to coincide; (*да́нные, ци́фры итп*) to agree; (*интере́сы, мне́ния*) to meet.

соврати́тел|ь (**-я**) *м* seducer.

совра|ти́ть (**-щу́, -ти́шь;** *impf* **совраща́ть**) *сов перех* (*сбить с пути́*) to lead astray; (*же́нщину*) to seduce.

совр|а́ть (**-у́, -ёшь**) *сов от* **врать.**

совраща́|ть (**-ю**) *несов от* **соврати́ть.**

совращу́ *сов см* **соврати́ть.**

совреме́нен *прил см* **совреме́нный.**

совреме́нник (**-а**) *м* contemporary.

совреме́нниц|а (**-ы**) *ж см* **совреме́нник.**

совреме́нно *нареч* (*одева́ться*) fashionably; (*звуча́ть*) modern.

совреме́нност|ь (**-и**) *ж* (*взгля́дов, иде́й*) progressiveness; (*совреме́нная эпо́ха*) the present day.

совреме́нный *прил* contemporary; (**-ен, -на, -но:** *те́хника*) up-to-date; (*челове́к, иде́и*) modern.

совсе́м *нареч* (*но́вый, него́дный итп*) completely; (*молодо́й*) very; (*ниско́лько: не приго́дный, не ну́жный*) totally; **не ~** (*не вполне́*) not quite.

совхо́з (**-а**) *м сокр* (= *сове́тское хозя́йство*) Sovkhoz (*state farm in the Soviet Union*).

совью́(сь) *итп сов см* **сви́ть(ся).**

совья́та *итп сущ см* **совёнок.**

согла́сен *прил см* **согла́сный.**

согла́си|е (**-я**) *ср* consent; (*в семье́*) harmony, accord; **в ~и с** +*instr* (*с челове́ком*) in agreement with; **с чьего́-н ~я** with sb's consent; **дава́ть** (**дать** *perf*) **~ на что-н** to give one's consent to sth; **приходи́ть** (**прийти́** *perf*) **к ~ю** to come to an agreement; **жить** (*impf*) **в ~и** to live in harmony.

согла|си́ться (**-шу́сь, -си́шься;** *impf* **соглаша́ться**) *сов возв*: **~ на что-н/** +*infin* to agree to sth/to do; **~** (*perf*) **с** +*instr* (*с мне́нием, с высказыванием*) to agree with; **~** (*perf*) **на чём-н** (*ра́зе*) to agree on sth.

согла́сно *нареч* (*жить, рабо́тать*) in harmony **♦** *предл*: **~** +*dat* и́ли **с** +*instr* in accordance with.

согла́с|ный *прил*: **~ звук** consonant **♦** (**-ного;** *decl like adj*) *м* consonant; (**-ен, -на, -но;** *даю́щий согла́сие*): **~ на** +*acc* (*на усло́вия, на ограниче́ния*) agreeable to; **Вы ~ны (со мной)?** do you agree (with me)?; **все ~ны?** are we all agreed?; **я не ~ен** +*infin* ... I am not prepared to ....

согласова́ни|е (**-я**) *ср* (*де́йствий, мер*) coordinating; (*обсужде́ние: пла́на*) coordination.

согласо́ван|ный (**-, -на, -но**) *прил* (*поли́тика*) concerted; (*страте́гия*) agreed.

соглас|ова́ть (**-у́ю;** *impf* **согласо́вывать**) *сов перех* (*уси́лия, де́йствия*) to coordinate; (*обговори́ть*): **~ что-н с** +*instr* (*план, це́ну*) to agree sth with; **~** (*perf*) **что-н с чем-н** (*спрос с предложе́нием*) to make sth meet sth; (*прилага́тельное с существи́тельным*) to make sth agree with sth

▶ **согласова́ться** (*(не)сов возв*: **~ся с** +*instr* to correspond with.

соглаша́|ться (**-юсь**) *несов от* **согласи́ться.**

соглаше́ни|е (**-я**) *ср* agreement; **приходи́ть** (**прийти́** *perf*) **к ~ю** to come to an agreement; **заключа́ть** (**заключи́ть** *perf*) **~** to conclude an agreement.

соглашу́сь *сов см* **согласи́ться.**

согн|а́ть (**сгоню́, сго́нишь;** *pt* **-а́л, -ала́, -а́ло,** *impf* **сгоня́ть**) *сов перех* (*заста́вить удали́ться*) to drive away; (*собра́ть*) to round up; **сгоня́ть** (**~** *perf*) **улы́бку с лица́** to wipe a smile off somebody's face.

согн|у́ть (**-у́, -ёшь**) *сов от* **гнуть, сгиба́ть.**

согр|ажда́нин (**-ажда́нина;** *nom pl* **-а́ждане,** *gen pl* **-а́ждан**) *м* fellow citizen.

согрева́ни|е (**-я**) *ср* (*воды́, пи́щи*) heating up; (*те́ла*) warming up.

согре́|ть (**-ю;** *impf* **согрева́ть**) *сов перех* (*во́ду*) to heat up; (*зе́млю, но́ги, ру́ки*) to warm up; (*подлеж: мысль, ла́ска*) to warm

▶ **согре́ться** (*impf* **согрева́ться**) *сов возв* (*вода́*) to heat up; (*челове́к, пе́чка*) to warm up.

согреш|и́ть (**-у́, -и́шь**) *сов от* **греши́ть.**

со́д|а (**-ы**) *ж* soda; **питьева́я ~** bicarbonate of soda.

соде́йстви|е (**-я**) *ср* assistance.

соде́йств|овать (**-ую**) (*(не)сов неперех* (+*dat*) to assist.

содержа́ни|е (**-я**) *ср* (*семьи́, дете́й*) upkeep; (*магази́на, фе́рмы*) keeping; (*кни́ги, статьи́*) contents *мн*; (*челове́ка: под аре́стом*) holding; (*са́хара, витами́нов*) content; (*зарабо́тная пла́та*) allowance; (*оглавле́ние*) contents *мн*; **о́тпуск без ~я** unpaid leave.

содержа́телен *прил см* **содержа́тельный.**

содержа́тел|ь (**-я**) *м* (*рестора́на*) owner; (*магази́на, пансио́на*) keeper.

содержа́тел|ьный (-ен, -ьна, -ьно) *прил* (*статья́, докла́д*) informative.

содер|жа́ть (-ержу́, -е́ржишь) *несов перех* (*дете́й, роди́телей, магази́н*) to keep; (*рестора́н*) to own; (*са́хар, оши́бки, информа́цию итп*) to contain; (*челове́ка: под аре́стом*) to hold; ~ (*impf*) **что-н в чистоте́/в поря́дке** to keep sth clean/in order

► **содержа́ться** *несов возв* (*под аре́стом*) to be held; **в кни́ге** ~**е́ржится интере́сная информа́ция** the book contains interesting information; ~**ся** (*impf*) **в чистоте́/в поря́дке** to be kept clean/in order.

содержи́м|ое (-ого; *decl like adj*) *ср* (*ба́нки, су́мки итп*) contents *мн*.

со́довый *прил* (*раство́р*) soda *опред*.

содр|а́ть (сдеру́, сдерёшь; *pt* -а́л, -ала́, -а́ло, *impf* **сдира́ть**) *сов перех* (*слой, оде́жду*) to tear off; **сдира́ть** (~ *perf*) **ко́жу с чего́-н** to skin sth; ~ (*perf*) **что-н с кого́-н** (*разг: до́рого взять*) to sting sb for sth.

содрога́ни|е (-я) *ср* (*стен, стёкол*) shaking; (*от бо́ли, от у́жаса*) shuddering.

содрога́|ться (-юсь; *perf* **содрогну́ться**) *несов возв* (*сте́ны, земля́*) to shake; (*от бо́ли, от стра́ха итп*) to shudder.

содру́жеств|о (-а) *ср* (*дру́жба*) cooperation; (*сою́з*) commonwealth; **Содру́жество Незави́симых Госуда́рств** the Commonwealth of Independent States.

со́евый *прил* soya *опред*.

соедине́ни|е (-я) *ср* (*сил*) joining; (*проводо́в*) connection; (*учёбы с рабо́той*) combination; (*ме́сто соедине́ния*) contact; (*ВОЕН*) formation.

соедини́тел|ь (-я) *м* (*ЭЛЕК*) adaptor.

соедини́тельный *прил* (*про́вод, труба́*) connecting.

соедин|и́ть (-ю́, -и́шь; *impf* **соединя́ть**) *сов перех* (*си́лы, уси́лия, дета́ли*) to join; (*люде́й*) to unite; (*провода́, тру́бы, по телефо́ну*) to connect; (*установи́ть сообще́ние*) to link; (*сочета́ть*) ~ **что-н с** +*instr* to combine sth with; **в ней** ~**ены́ ум и красота́** she is both clever and beautiful

► **соедини́ться** (*impf* **соединя́ться**) *сов возв* (*лю́ди, отря́ды*) to join together; ~**ся** (*perf*) **с кем** to make contact with sb.

сожале́ни|е (-я) *ср* (*сострада́ние*) pity; ~ (**о** +*prp*) (*о про́шлом, о поте́ре*) regret (about); **к** ~**ю** unfortunately; **к мо́ему (вели́кому** *или* **глубо́кому)** ~**ю** to my (great *или* deep) regret.

сожале́|ть (-ю) *несов неперех* ~ (**о** +*prp*) (*об оши́бке, о посту́пке*) to regret.

сожгу́ *итп сов см* **сжечь.**

сожже́ни|е (-я) *ср* (*ерети́ка*) burning.

сожи́тел|ь (-я) *м* cohabiter.

сожи́тельниц|а (-ы) *ж см* **сожи́тель.**

сожму́(сь) *итп сов см* **сжа́ть(ся).**

сожну́ *итп сов см* **сжать.**

сожр|а́ть (-у́, -ёшь) *сов от* **жрать.**

созва́нива|ться (-юсь) *несов см* **созвони́ться.**

соз|ва́ть (-ову́, -овёшь; *pt* -ва́л, -вала́, -ва́ло, *impf* **сзыва́ть**) *сов перех* (*пригласи́ть*) to summon; (*impf* **созыва́ть**; *съезд, конфере́нцию итп*) to convene.

созве́зди|е (-я) *ср* constellation.

созвон|и́ться (-ю́сь, -и́шься; *impf* **созва́ниваться**) *сов возв*: ~ **с** +*instr* to phone (*BRIT*) *или* call (*US*); (*договори́ться*): **нам на́до** ~ we should fix something over the phone.

созву́чен *прил см* **созву́чный.**

созву́чи|е (-я) *ср* (*МУЗ*) sonority.

созву́|чный (-ен, -на, -но) *прил* harmonious; (*слова́*) assonant; ~**но** +*dat* (*соотве́тствующий*) in keeping with; ~**но с** +*instr* in keeping with.

создава́|ть(ся) (-ю́(сь), -ёшь(ся)) *несов от* **созда́ть(ся).**

созда́м(ся) *итп сов см* **созда́ть(ся).**

созда́ни|е (-я) *ср* creation; (*шко́лы*) foundation; (*челове́к, живо́тное*) creature.

созда́ст(ся) *сов см* **созда́ть(ся).**

созда́тел|ь (-я) *м* creator; (*шко́лы*) founder.

созда́тельниц|а (-ы) *ж см* **созда́тель.**

созда́ть (*как* **дать;** *см* **Table 14;** *impf* **создава́ть**) *сов перех* to create; (*шко́лу*) to found

► **созда́ться** (*impf* **создава́ться**) *сов возв* (*обстано́вка*) to emerge; (*впечатле́ние*) to be created.

созерца́ни|е (-я) *ср* (*рассма́тривание*) contemplation; (*душе́вное*) reflection.

созерца́|ть (-ю) *несов перех* (*рассма́тривать*) to contemplate.

созида́тел|ьный (-ен, -ьна, -ьно) *прил* creative.

созна|ва́ть (-ю́, -ёшь) *несов от* **созна́ть** ♦ *перех* to be aware of; ~ (*impf*), **что ...** to realize that ...

► **сознава́ться** *несов от* **созна́ться.**

созна́ни|е (-я) *ср* consciousness; (*вины́, до́лга*) awareness; **приходи́ть (прийти́** *perf*) **в** ~ to come round; **теря́ть (потеря́ть** *perf*) ~ to lose consciousness; **он рабо́тал до поте́ри** ~**я** he worked himself senseless.

созна́телен *прил см* **созна́тельный.**

созна́тельность (-и) *ж* (*полити́ческая, социа́льная*) awareness.

созна́тел|ьный (-ен, -ьна, -ьно) *прил* (*жизнь, во́зраст*) conscious; (*отноше́ние, челове́к*) intelligent; (*обма́н, посту́пок*) deliberate, intentional.

созна́|ть (-ю; *impf* **сознава́ть**) *сов перех* (*вину́, долг*) to realize

► **созна́ться** (*impf* **сознава́ться**) *сов возв*: ~**ся** (**в** +*prp*) (*в оши́бке, в како́м-н наме́рении*) to admit (to); (*преступник*) to confess (to); **надо** ~**ся** admittedly.

созову *итп сов см* **созвать**.

созрева|ть (-ю) *несов неперех* = **зреть**.

созре|ть (-ю) *сов от* **зреть**.

созы́в (-а) *м* (*съезда, собрания*) calling.

созыва́|ть (-ю) *несов от* **созвать**.

СОИ *ж сокр* (= *стратегическая оборонная инициатива*) SDI (*US*) (= *Strategic Defense Initiative*).

соизмери́м|ый (-, -а, -о) *прил* (*величины*) proportional; (*понятия, ценности*) comparable.

соизме́р|ить (-ю, -ишь; *impf* **соизмеря́ть**) *сов перех* to compare.

соиска́ние (-я) *ср*: **на** ~ **чего-н** pursuing sth.

соиска́тель (-я) *м* (*приза, награды*) competitor; (*учёной степени*) candidate.

сой|ти́ (*как* **идти́**; *см* **Table 18**; *impf* **сходи́ть**) *сов неперех* (*с горы, с лестницы*) to go down; (*с дороги*) to leave; (*подлеж: краска, загар итп*) to come off; (*разг*): ~ **с** +*instr* (*с поезда, с автобуса*) to get off; ~ (*perf*) **за** +*acc* (*за актёра, за богача*) to pass as; **сходи́ть** (~ *perf*) **с ума́** to go mad; **фильм** ~**шёл с экра́на** the film is not shown anymore; **с ума́ сойдёшь** *или* ~ (*разг*) the mind boggles; **всё** ~**шло́ благополу́чно** everything's turned out well; ~**йдёт (и так)** (*разг*) it will do (as it is); **ему́ всё схо́дит с рук** he gets away with everything

▶ **сойти́сь** (*impf* **сходи́ться**) *сов возв* (*встретиться*) to meet; (*собраться*) to gather; (*цифры, показания*) to tally; (*перен*): ~**сь с** +*instr* (*подружиться*) to become friendly with; ~**шли́сь на том, что** ... it was agreed that ...; ~**сь** (*perf*) **во взгля́дах/во вку́сах** (*перен*) to have similar views/tastes; **сходи́ться** (~**сь** *perf*) **на цене́/усло́виях** to agree on a price/ conditions; ~**сь** (*perf*) **хара́ктерами** to get on.

сок (-а; *part gen* -**у**, *loc sg* -**у́**) *м* juice; (*также*: **фрукто́вый** ~) (fruit) juice.

соковыжима́л|ка (-ки; *gen pl* -**ок**) *ж* juice extractor.

со́кол (-а) *м* falcon.

соколёнок (-ёнка; *nom pl* -**я́та**, *gen pl* -**я́т**) *ж* falcon chick.

соколи́н|ый *прил* (*гнездо*) falcon's *опред*; ~**ая охо́та** falconry.

соколя́та *итп сущ см* **соколёнок**.

сокра|ти́ть (-щу́, -ти́шь; *impf* **сокраща́ть**) *сов перех* (*путь, рабочий день, статью*) to shorten; (*расходы*) to cut down, reduce

▶ **сократи́ться** (*impf* **сокраща́ться**) *сов возв* (*расстояние, сроки*) to be shortened; (*расходы, снабжение*) to be reduced.

сокраще́ни|е (-я) *ср* (*см глаг*) shortening; cutting down, reduction; (*сокращённое название*) abbreviation; (*также*: ~ **шта́тов**) staff reduction; **попада́ть** (*попа́сть perf*) **под** ~ (**шта́тов**) to be made redundant.

сокращённый *прил* (*вариант текста*) abridged; (*рабочий день*) shortened; (*слово*) abbreviated.

сокращу́(сь) *сов см* **сократи́ть(ся)**.

сокрове́нн|ый (-ен, -на, -но) *прил* (*мысли итп*) innermost; (*смысл, мечта*) intimate.

сокро́вищ|е (-а) *ср* (*обычно мн: также перен*) treasure.

сокро́вищниц|а (-ы) *ж* (*место*) treasury; (*совокупность*): ~ +*gen* wealth.

сокруша́|ть (-ю) *несов от* **сокруши́ть**

▶ **сокруша́ться** *несов возв* (*огорчаться*) to be distressed.

сокруше́ни|е (-я) *ср* (*противника*) destruction; (*огорчение*) distress.

сокруши́тел|ьный (-ен, -ьна, -ьно) *прил* devastating.

сокруш|и́ть (-у́, -и́шь; *impf* **сокруша́ть**) *сов перех* (*армию*) to crush; (*режим*) to overthrow.

соку́рсник (-а) *м*: **он мой** ~ he is in my year.

соку́рсниц|а (-ы) *ж*: **она́ моя́** ~ she is in my year.

сол|га́ть (-гу́, -жёшь итп, -гу́т) *сов от* **лгать**.

солда́т (-а) *м* soldier.

солда́тик (-а) *м уменьш от* **солда́т**; (*игрушка*) toy soldier.

солда́т|ка (-ки; *gen pl* -**ок**) *ж* soldier's wife (*мн* wives).

солда́тск|ий (-ая, -ое, -ие) *прил* soldier's.

солдафо́н (-а) *м* (*разг: пренебр*) squaddie.

соле́ни|е (-я) *ср* (*огурцов*) pickling; (*рыбы*) salting.

солёно|е (-ого; *decl like adj*) *ср* salty food.

солёный *прил* (*ветер*) salty; (*овощи*) pickled in brine; (*вода*) salt *опред*; (*рыба*) salted; (-**он**, -**она́**, -**оно**; *пища*) salty.

соле́нь|е (-я) *ср* (*обычно мн*) ≈ pickle.

солжёшь *итп сов см* **солга́ть**.

солида́рен *прил см* **солида́рный**.

солида́рност|ь (-и) *ж* solidarity.

солида́р|ный (-ен, -на, -но) *прил*: **я с ним** ~**ен** I am on his side.

соли́д|ный (-ен, -на, -но) *прил* (*постройка*) solid; (*знания, работа*) sound; (*фирма, специалист*) established; (*человек, манеры*) respectable; (*мебель, одежда*) quality; ~ **во́зраст** respectable age.

соли́р|овать (-ую) *несов* to play a solo part.

соли́ст (-а) *м* soloist.

соли́ст|ка (-ки; *gen pl* -**ок**) *ж см* **соли́ст**.

сол|и́ть (-ю́, -ишь; *perf* **посоли́ть**) *несов перех* (*суп, рагу*) to salt; (*засаливать*) to preserve in brine.

со́лнечн|ый *прил* (*энергия, лучи итп*) solar; (-ен, -на, -но; *день, погода*) sunny; **со́лнечное сплете́ние** solar plexus; **со́лнечный уда́р** sunstroke; **со́лнечные очки́** sunglasses.

со́лнц|е (-а) *ср* sun.

солнцезащи́тный *прил*: ~ **крем** suncream.

солнцепёк (-а) *м*: **на** ~ in a sunny spot.

солнцестоя́ни|е (-я) *ср* solstice.

со́ло *ср нескл, нареч* solo.

солов|е́й (-ья́) *м* nightingale.

соловÉ|**ть** (-ю; *perf* **осоловÉть**) *несов неперех* (*разг*) to become dazed.
соловЬ́иный *прил* nightingale *опред*.
соловЬ́я *итп сущ см* **соловÉй**.
сó|**лод** (-а) *м* malt.
солóм|**а** (-ы) *ж* straw.
солóменный *прил* (*шляпа*) straw *опред*; (*крыша*) thatched; (*цвет*) straw-coloured (*BRIT*), straw-colored (*US*).
солóмин|**а** (-ы) *ж* straw.
солóмин|**ка** (-ки; *gen pl* -**ок**) *ж уменьш от* **солóмина**; (*перен*): **хватáться за** ~**ку** to clutch at straws.
солóм|**ка** (-ки; *gen pl* -**ок**) *ж уменьш от* **солóма**; (*печенье*) long thin biscuit or bread stick.
сóлон *итп прил см* **солёный**.
солóн|**ка** (-ки; *gen pl* -**ок**) *ж* saltcellar.
солончáк (-á) *м* saltmarsh.
сол|**ь** (-и) *ж* salt; (*gen pl* -**éй**; *хим*) salt; (*перен*): ~ +*gen* (*вопроса, рассказа*) point of ♦ *ср нескл* (*муз*) soh; **столóвая** ~ table salt.
сóльный *прил* solo *опред*.
солью́(**сь**) *сов см* **сли́ть(ся)**.
солян|**ка** (-ки; *gen pl* -**ок**) *ж* spicy meat and vegetable soup; (*рагу*) ragout.
солянóй *прил* (*раствор*) saline; (*промысел, залежи*) salt *опред*.
солянóк *сущ см* **солянка**.
сом (-á) *ср* catfish.
Сомали́ *ср нескл* Somalia.
сомкнý|**ть** (-ý, -ёшь; *impf* **смыкáть**) *сов перех* to close; **я глаз не** ~**ул всю ночь** I didn't sleep a wink all night
▸ **сомкнýться** (*impf* **смыкáться**) *сов возв* to close.
сомневá|**ться** (-юсь) *несов возв*: ~ (**в** +*prp*) to doubt; ~**юсь, что э́то прáвда** I doubt that is true; **не** ~**йся придý** don't worry, I'll come.
сомнéни|**е** (-я) *ср* (*неуверенность*) doubt; **вне** *или* **без (вся́кого)** ~**я** without a doubt; **брать** (**взять** *perf*) **что-н под** ~ to doubt sth.
сомни́телен *прил см* **сомни́тельный**.
сомни́тельно *как сказ* it's doubtful; ~, **чтóбы он согласи́лся** it's doubtful he'll agree; **он придёт?-** ~ he's coming? – it's unlikely *или* not likely.
сомни́тель|**ный** (-ен, -ьна, -ьно) *прил* (*дело, личность*) shady; (*предложение, знакомство*) dubious; (*комплимент, речи*) ambiguous; (*победа*) questionable.
сомнý(**сь**) *итп сов см* **смя́ть(ся)**.
сон (**сна**) *м* sleep; (*сновидение*) dream; **ви́деть** (**уви́деть** *perf*) **что-н во сне** to have a dream about sth; **ви́деть** (*impf*) ~ to have a dream; **сквозь** ~ **слы́шать** (**услы́шать** *perf*) to hear in one's sleep; **со сна** half-awake.
сонáт|**а** (-ы) *ж* sonata.
сонéт (-а) *м* sonnet.

сонли́вый *прил* sleepy.
сóнн|**ый** *прил* (*заспанный*) sleepy, somnolent; (*вялый*) drowsy; ~**ые видéния** dreams.
сóн|**я** (-и) *ж* (*животное*) dormouse (*мн* dormice) ♦ *м/ж* (*разг*) sleepyhead.
сообража́|**ть** (-ю) *несов от* **сообрази́ть** ♦ *неперех* (*разг*: **быть сообрази́тельным**) to be quick; (*смыслить*): ~ **в** +*prp* to be good at; **я сегóдня плóхо** ~**ю** I'm slow on the uptake today.
соображéни|**е** (-я) *ср* (*суждение*) reasoning; (*обычно мн*: *мотивы*) reason; **из финáнсовых/педагоги́ческих** ~**й** for financial/educational reasons.
сооражý *сов см* **сообрази́ть**.
сообрази́тель|**ный** (-ен, -ьна, -ьно) *прил* bright.
сообрази́|**ть** (-жý, -зи́шь; *impf* **сообража́ть**) *сов неперех* to work out; **нам нáдо** ~, **что дéлать дáльше** we've got to work out what to do next.
сообрáзно *предл*: ~ +*dat или* **с** +*instr* in accordance with.
сообрáзный *прил*: ~ **с** +*instr* in agreement with.
сообщá *нареч* together.
сообщá|**ть** (-ю) *несов от* **сообщи́ть**
▸ **сообщá**|**ться** *несов от* **сообщи́ться** ♦ *возв*: ~**ся с** +*instr* (*связываться*) to communicate with.
сообщéни|**е** (-я) *ср* (*действие*: *новостей, результатов*) reporting; (*по радио*) report; (*правительственное*) announcement; (*срочное*) communication; (*автобусное, почтовое*) communications *мн*; ~ **об оши́бке** (*комп*) error message.
сообщéств|**о** (-а) *ср* association; **в** ~**е с** +*instr* in association with; **мировóе** *или* **междунарóдное** ~ international community.
сообщи́|**ть** (-ý, -и́шь; *impf* **сообщáть**) *сов неперех*: ~ **комý-н о** +*prp* to inform sb of ♦ *перех* (*новости, тайну*) to tell
▸ **сообщи́ться** (*impf* **сообщáться**) *сов возв* (+*dat*) to be communicated to.
сообщник (-а) *м* accomplice.
сообщниц|**а** (-ы) *ж см* **сообщник**.
сооруди́|**ть** (-жý, -ди́шь; *impf* **сооружáть**) *сов перех* (*построить*) to erect; (*разг*: **смастери́ть**) to put together; (: *ужин, выпить*) to knock up.
сооружá|**ть** (-ю) *несов от* **сооруди́ть**.
сооружéни|**е** (-я) *ср* (*действие*: *здания*) erection; (*крупная постройка*) structure.
сооружý *сов см* **сооруди́ть**.
соотвéтственно *нареч* (*как следует*) accordingly ♦ *предл*: ~ +*dat* (*обстановке*) according to; ~ **с** +*instr* in accordance with.
соотвéтствен|**ный** (-, -на, -но) *прил* (*оплата*) appropriate; (*результаты*) fitting.
соотвéтстви|**е** (-я) *ср* (*интересов, стилей*

итп) conformity; **в ~и с** +*instr* in accordance with.

соответств|овать (**-ую**) *несов неперех:* ~ +*dat* (*интересам, должности итп*) to correspond with; (*требованиям*) to meet; **это не ~ует действительности** it does not correspond with reality.

соответствующий (**-ая, -ее, -ие**) *прил* appropriate; **~им образом** accordingly.

соотечественник (**-а**) *м* compatriot.

соотечественни|ца (**-ы**) *ж см* **соотечественник.**

соотн|ести (**-есу́, -есёшь;** *pt* **-ёс, -есла́, -есло́,** *impf* **соотноси́ть**) *сов перех:* ~ **что-н с чем-н** to correlate sth with sth.

соотноси́тел|ьный (**-ен, -ьна, -ьно**) *прил* correlating.

соотн|оси́ть (**-ошу́, -о́сишь**) *несов от* **соотнести́**

▶ **соотноси́ться** *несов возв* to correlate.

соотноше́ни|е (**-я**) *ср* correlation.

соотношу́(сь) *несов см* **соотноси́ть(ся).**

со́пел *сущ см* **со́пло.**

сопережива́|ть (**-ю**) *несов неперех* to empathize.

сопе́рник (**-а**) *м* rival; (*в спорте*) competitor.

сопе́рни|ца (**-ы**) *ж см* **сопе́рник.**

сопе́рнича|ть (**-ю**) *несов неперех:* ~ **с кем-н в чём-н** to rival sb in sth.

сопе́|ть (**-лю́, -и́шь**) *несов неперех* to snort.

со́п|ка (**-ки;** *gen pl* **-ок**) *ж* (*холм*) hill; (*вулкан*) volcano.

со́пл|и (**-ей**) *мн* (*разг*) snot *ед.*

сопли́вый *прил* (*разг: ребёнок*) snotty; **он ещё ~ мальчи́шка!** (*разг*) he's still just a young whippersnapper!

со́пл|о (**-а́;** *nom pl* **-а,** *gen pl* **-ел**) *ср* nozzle.

соплю́ *несов см* **сопе́ть.**

со́пок *сущ см* **со́пка.**

сопостави́м|ый (**-, -а, -о**) *прил* comparable.

сопоста́в|ить (**-лю, -ишь;** *impf* **сопоставля́ть**) *сов перех:* ~ **что-н** (**с** +*instr*) to collate sth (with).

сопра́но *ср нескл* soprano.

сопреде́л|ьный (**-ен, -ьна, -ьно**) *прил* (*область, страна итп*) neighbouring *опред* (BRIT), neighboring *опред* (US); (*наука, понятие*) related.

сопре́|ть (**3sg -ет, 3pl -ют**) *сов см* **преть.**

соприкаса́|ться (**-юсь;** *perf* **соприкосну́ться**) *несов возв* (*предметы, участки*) to adjoin; (*интересы*) to cross over; ~ (**соприкосну́ться** *perf*) **с кем-н** to come into contact with sb.

сопроводи́тел|ь (**-я**) *м* escort.

сопроводи́тельный *прил* (*документ*) accompanying *опред*; **сопроводи́тельное письмо́** covering letter.

сопрово|ди́ть (**-жу́, -ди́шь;** *impf* **сопровожда́ть**) *сов перех* to accompany; (*no impf; дополнить*): ~ **что-н чем-н** to attach sth to sth.

сопровожда́|ть (**-ю**) *несов от* **сопроводи́ть** ♦

перех (*рассказ, пение*) to accompany

▶ **сопровожда́ться** *несов возв:* ~**ся** +*instr* to be accompanied by.

сопровожде́ни|е (**-я**) *ср* (*действие*) escorting; (*аккомпанемент*) accompaniment; **в ~и** +*gen* accompanied by.

сопровожу́ *сов см* **сопроводи́ть.**

сопротивле́ни|е (**-я**) *ср* resistance; (*ИСТ*) the Resistance; **ока́зывать** (**оказа́ть** *perf*) ~ **кому́-н** to put up resistance to sb.

сопротивля́емост|ь (**-и**) *ж* resistance.

сопротивля́|ться (**-юсь**) *несов возв* (+*dat*) to resist.

сопру́ *итп сов см* **спере́ть.**

сопряжён|ный (**-, -а́, -о**) *прил:* ~ **с** +*instr* (*с опасностями итп*) involving.

сопу́тств|овать (**3sg -ует, 3pl -уют**) *несов неперех* (+*dat*) to accompany.

сопью́сь *итп сов см* **спи́ться.**

сор (**-а;** *part gen* **-у**) *м* rubbish; **выноси́ть** (*impf*) ~ **из избы́** (*перен*) to wash one's dirty linen in public.

соразме́рен *прил см* **соразме́рный.**

соразме́р|ить (**-ю, -ишь;** *impf* **соразмеря́ть**) *сов перех:* ~ **что-н с чем-н** to measure sth against sth.

соразме́р|ный (**-ен, -на, -но**) *прил:* ~ +*dat* proportionate to; **~но** +*dat или* **с** +*instr* according to.

соразмеря́|ть (**-ю**) *несов от* **соразме́рить.**

сора́тник (**-а**) *м* comrade in arms.

сора́тни|ца (**-ы**) *ж см* **сора́тник.**

сорван|е́ц (**-ца́**) *м* (*разг*) scamp.

сорв|а́ть (**-у́, -ёшь;** *pt* **-а́л, -ала́, -а́ло,** *impf* **срыва́ть**) *сов перех* (*цветок, яблоко*) to pick; (*дверь, крышу, одежду итп*) to tear off; (*лекцию, переговоры*) to sabotage; (*планы*) to frustrate; (*разг: аплодисменты*) to get; (: *перен*): ~ **что-н на ком-н** (*гнев, злобу*) to take sth out on sb; ~ (*perf*) **го́лос** to lose one's voice

▶ **сорва́ться** (*impf* **срыва́ться**) *сов возв:* ~**ся с** +*gen* (*с петель*) to come away from; (*с лестницы*) to fall off; (*перен: потерять самооблада́ние*) to lose one's temper; (*планы*) to be frustrated; (*лекция*) to have to be cancelled; ~ (*perf*) **с ме́ста** to dash off; **у него́ срыва́лся го́лос** his voice was faltering; **он как с цепи ~а́лся** (*пренебр*) he's gone completely berserk.

сорганиз|ова́ться (**-у́юсь**) *сов от* **организова́ться.**

соревнова́ни|е (**-я**) *ср* competition; **кома́ндные ~я** team event; **отбо́рочные ~я** elimination contests.

соревн|ова́ться (**-у́юсь**) *несов возв* to compete.

сориенти́р|оваться (**-уюсь**) *сов от* **ориенти́роваться.**

сори́н|ка (**-ки;** *gen pl* **-ок**) *ж* speck.

сор|и́ть (**-ю́, -и́шь;** *perf* **насори́ть**) *несов неперех* to make a mess; ~ (*impf*) **деньга́ми** to throw one's money about *или* around.

со́рн|ый *прил* refuse *опред*; **~ая трава́** weeds.

сорня́к (-а́) *м* weed.

со́рок (-а́; *см* **Table 28**) *чис* forty; **ему́ за ~** he's over forty; *см также* **пятьдеся́т**.

соро́к|а (-и) *ж* magpie; (*о болтливом человеке*) chatterbox.

сорокале́ти|е (-я) *ср* (*срок*) forty years; (*годовщина события*) fortieth anniversary.

сорокале́тн|ий (-яя, -ее, -ие) *прил* (*период*) forty-year; (*человек*) forty-year-old.

сороков|о́й (-а́я, -о́е, -ы́е) *чис* fortieth; *см также* **пятидеся́тый**.

сороконо́ж|ка (-ки; *gen pl* -ек) *ж* centipede.

соро́ч|ка (-ки; *gen pl* -ек) *ж* (*мужская*) shirt; **ночна́я ~** nightgown; **ни́жняя ~** undergarment.

сорт (-а; *nom pl* -а́) *м* (*товара, продукта*) sort; (*пшеницы*) grade; **пе́рвый ~** Grade 1; (*перен*) first rate; **това́р пе́рвого со́рта** a Grade 1 product.

сорта́мент (-а) *м* assortment.

сортирова́льный *прил* sorting *опред*.

сортир|ова́ть (-у́ю) *несов перех* (*также* КОМП) to sort; (*по сортам, качеству*) to grade.

сортиро́в|ка (-ки; *gen pl* -ок) *ж* (*см глаг*) sorting; grading.

со́ртный *прил* ≈ Grade A *или* 1 *опред*.

сортово́й *прил* = **со́ртный**.

сос|а́ть (-у́, -ёшь) *несов перех* to suck; (*младенец, детёныш*) to suckle; **у меня́ ~ёт под ло́жечкой** (*разг*) I've got a sore stomach.

сосва́та|ть (-ю) *сов от* **сва́тать**.

сосе́д (-а; *nom pl* -и, *gen pl* -ей) *м* neighbour (*BRIT*), neighbor (*US*).

сосе́дн|ий (-яя, -ее, -ие) *прил* neighbouring (*BRIT*), neighboring (*US*).

сосе́дств|о (-а) *ср*: **жить по ~у** to live nearby; **в ~е с** +*instr* near.

со́сен *сущ см* **сосна́**.

соси́с|ка (-ки; *gen pl* -ок) *ж* sausage.

со́с|ка (-ки; *gen pl* -ок) *ж* (*на бутылке*) teat; (*пустышка*) dummy.

соска́ *итп сущ см* **сосо́к**.

соска́блива|ть (-ю) *несов от* **соскобли́ть**.

соска́кива|ть (-ю) *несов от* **соскочи́ть**.

соска́льзыва|ть (-ю) *несов от* **соскользну́ть**.

соскобл|и́ть (-ю́, -и́шь; *impf* **соска́бливать**) *сов перех* to scrape off.

соскользн|у́ть (-у́, -ёшь; *impf* **соска́льзывать**) *сов неперех* (*с горы*) to slide down; (*платок*) to slip off.

соск|очи́ть (-очу́, -о́чишь; *impf* **соска́кивать**) *сов неперех* (*с лошади, с поезда итп*) to jump off; (*с головы, с ноги*) to slip off.

соскреба́|ть (-ю) *несов от* **соскрести́**.

соскр|ести́ (-ебу́, -ебёшь; *pt* -ёб, -ебла́, -ебло́, *impf* **соскреба́ть**) *сов перех* to scrape away *или* off.

соску́ч|иться (-усь, -ишься) *сов возв* (*в чужом городе*) to be bored; (*затосковать*): **~ по** +*dat* to miss.

сослага́тельн|ый *прил*: **~ое наклоне́ние** subjunctive mood.

со|сла́ть (-шлю́, -шлёшь; *impf* **ссыла́ть**) *сов перех* to exile

▶ **сосла́ться** (*impf* **ссыла́ться**) *сов возв*: **~ся на** +*acc* to refer to.

со́слепу *нареч* (*разг*) being unable to see properly.

сосло́ви|е (-я) *ср* social class.

сосло́вный *прил* class *опред*.

сослужи́в|ец (-ца) *м* colleague.

сослужи́виц|а (-ы) *ж см* **сослужи́вец**.

сослужи́вца *итп сущ см* **сослужи́вец**.

сослуж|и́ть (-ужу́, -у́жишь) *сов перех*: **~ слу́жбу кому́-н** (*человек*) to do sb a good turn; (*вещь*) to serve sb well.

сос|на́ (-ны́; *nom pl* -ны, *gen pl* -ен) *ж* pine (tree); **заблуди́ться** (*perf*) **в трёх со́снах** (*перен: разг*) to fail to solve a simple problem; **сиби́рская ~** cedar.

сосно́вый *прил* pine *опред*.

сосн|у́ть (-у́, -ёшь) *сов неперех* to take a nap.

со́сок *сущ см* **со́ска**.

сос|о́к (-ка́) *м* nipple.

сосредота́чива|ть(ся) (-ю(сь)) *несов от* **сосредото́чить(ся)**.

сосредото́ченн|ый (-, -на, -но) *прил* (*атака, взгляд*) concentrated; (*ученик, работник*) attentive.

сосредото́ч|ить (-у, -ишь; *impf* **сосредота́чивать**) *сов перех* (*войска*) to concentrate; (*мысли, внимание*) to concentrate, focus

▶ **сосредото́читься** (*impf* **сосредота́чиваться**) *сов возв* (*войска*) to be concentrated; (*внимание*) to concentrate, focus.

соста́в (-а) *м* (*товарный, пассажирский*) train; (*классовый*) structure; (+*gen* (*комитета, комиссии*) members *мн* of; (*вещества*) composition of; **руководя́щий ~** management (staff); **преподава́тельский ~** teaching staff; **в ~е** +*gen* among(st); **входи́ть** (*impf*) **в ~** +*gen* to be a member of; **войти́** (*perf*) **в ~** +*gen* to become a member of; **гру́ппа верну́лась в по́лном ~е** all members of the group returned; **в ~ делега́ции вошли́ ...** the delegation was made up of ...; **коми́ссия в ~е 10 челове́к** a commission consisting of 10 members; **соста́в преступле́ния** (*ЮР*) constitution of a crime.

состави́тел|ь (-я) *м* (*словаря*) compiler; (*сборника*) editor.

состав|ля́ть (-лю, -ишь; *impf* **составля́ть**) *сов перех* (*фразу*) to make; (*словарь, список*) to compile; (*план*) to draw up; (*коллекцию, мнение, впечатление*) to form; (*какую-нибудь*

сумму) to constitute; (*мебель*) to put together; ~
(*perf*) **себé и́мя** to make a name for o.s.;
составля́ть (~ *perf*) **кому́-н компáнию** to join
sb; **составля́ть** (~ *perf*) **себé представлéние о
чём-н** to form an impression about sth; **э́то не
~ит большо́го труда́** it won't take a lot of
effort

▶ **состáвиться** (*impf* **составля́ться**) *сов возв*
(*коллекция, хор, коллектив*) to be formed;
(*мнение, впечатление*) to form; **у нас ~илось
благоприя́тное мнéние о нём** we formed a
good impression of him.

составлéни|е (-**я**) *ср* (*словаря*) compilation;
(*плана*) drawing up; (*коллекции*) forming;
(*фразы*) making.

составлю́(сь) *сов см* **состáвить(ся)**.

составля́|ть(ся) (-**ю(сь)**) *несов от*
состáвить(ся).

составн|о́й *прил:* ~**áя мéбель** kit furniture;
~**áя часть**, ~ **элемéнт** component.

состáр|ить (-**ю**, -**ишь**) *сов от* **стáрить**

▶ **состáриться** *сов возв* (*человек*) to grow old.

состоя́ни|е (-**я**) *ср* (*экономическое,
эмоциональное*) state; (*больного*) condition;
(*собственность*) capital; **быть** (*impf*) **в ~и**
+*infin* to be able to do.

состоя́тельный (-**ен**, -**ьна**, -**ьно**) *прил* (*идея,
вывод итп*) sound; (*богатый*) well-off.

состоя́|ть (-**ю**, -**ишь**) *несов неперех:* ~ **из** +*gen*
(*книга*) to consist of; (*квартира*) to comprise;
(*заключаться*): ~ **в** +*prp* to be in; (*в партии*) to be
a member of; ~ (*impf*) +*instr* (*директором итп*)
to be; **проблéма ~и́т в том, что** ... the problem
is that ...

▶ **состоя́ться** *несов возв* (*собрание, концерт*)
to take place; **как учёный, он не ~я́лся** he
didn't make it as a scholar.

страдáни|е (-**я**) *ср* compassion.

сострáиг *итп сов см* **состри́чь**.

состригá|ть (-**ю**) *несов от* **состри́чь**.

состригу́ *итп сов см* **состри́чь**.

стри́|ть (-**ю**, -**ишь**) *сов от* **состри́ть**.

состри́|чь (-**гу́**, -**жёшь** *итп*, -**гу́т**; *pt* -**г**, -**гла**, -**гло**,
impf **состригáть**) *сов перех* (*волосы*) to cut off;
(*шерсть*) to shear off.

состро́|ить (-**ю**, -**ишь**) *сов от* **стро́ить**.

состря́па|ть (-**ю**) *несов от* **стря́пать** ♦ *сов
перех* (*перен: сделать плохо*) to concoct.

состык|овáть(ся) (-**у́ю(сь)**) *сов от*
стыковáть(ся).

состязáни|е (-**я**) *ср* contest.

состязá|ться (-**юсь**) *несов возв* to compete; ~
(*impf*) **в бéге**, ~ (*impf*) **в плáвании** to race; **они́
~лись в щéдрости** they were competing to
show who was the most generous.

сосу́д (-**а**) *м* vessel.

сосу́дистый *прил* vascular.

сосу́|лька (-**ьки**; *gen pl* -**ек**) *ж* icicle.

сосуществовáни|е (-**я**) *ср* coexistence.

сосуществ|овáть (-**у́ю**) *несов неперех* to
coexist.

сосчитá|ть (-**ю**) *сов от* **считáть**.

сот *чис см* **сто**.

сóт|ая (-**ой**; *decl like adj*) *ж:* **одна́** ~ one
hundredth.

сотворéни|е (-**я**) *ср:* ~ **ми́ра** Creation.

сотвор|и́ть (-**ю́**, -**и́шь**) *сов от* **твори́ть** ♦ *перех*
to create.

сóтен *сущ см* **сóтня**.

сóт|ка (-**ки**; *gen pl* -**ок**) *ж* one tenth of a hectare.

соткá|ть (-**у́**, -**ёшь**) *сов от* **ткать**.

сóтник (-**а**) *м* sotnik (*lieutenant of Cossack
troops*).

сóт|ня (-**ни**; *gen pl* -**ен**) *ж* (*сто*) a hundred;
(*дéньги*) one hundred roubles; (*войска*) Cossack
squadron; ~**ни людéй/вопро́сов/пи́сем**
hundreds of people/questions/letters.

сóток *сущ см* **сóтка**.

сотру́(сь) *итп сов см* **стерéть(ся)**.

сотру́дник (-**а**) *м* (*служащий*) employee;
(*коллега*) colleague; **нау́чный** ~ research
worker.

сотру́дница (-**ы**) *ж см* **сотру́дник**.

сотру́днича|ть (-**ю**) *несов неперех* (*в газете, в
учреждении*) to work; ~ (*impf*) **с** +*instr* (*с
фирмой*) to work with; (*с секретными
службами*) to collaborate with.

сотру́дничеств|о (-**а**) *ср* (*культурное,
экономическое*) cooperation; (*в газете, в
журнале*) work.

сотрясá|ть(ся) (-**ю(сь)**) *несов от*
сотрясти́(сь).

сотрясéни|е (-**я**) *ср* (*от взрыва, от удара*)
shaking; (*также:* ~ **мóзга**) concussion.

сотряс|ти́ (-**у́**, -**ёшь**; *impf* **сотрясáть**) *сов перех*
(*стены, землю*) to shake.

▶ **сотрясти́сь** (*impf* **сотрясáться**) *сов возв*
(*стены, земля*) to shake.

сóт|ы (-**ов**) *мн:* (*пчелины́е*) ~ honeycomb *ед*.

сóт|ый (-**ая**, -**ое**, -**ые**) *чис* hundredth.

сóус (-**а**) *м* sauce.

сóусник (-**а**) *м* ≈ gravy boat.

соучáсти|е (-**я**) *ср* complicity.

соучáстник (-**а**) *м* accomplice.

соучáстница (-**ы**) *ж см* **соучáстник**.

софá (-**ы́**; *nom pl* -**ы**) *ж* sofa.

Софи́|я (-**и**) *ж* Sofia.

сох|á (-**и́**; *nom pl* -**и**) *ж* wooden plough (*BRIT*) *или*
plow (*US*).

сóх|нуть (-**ну**, -**нешь**; *pt* -, -**ла**, -**ло**, *perf*
вы́сохнуть) *несов неперех* (*мокрое бельё,
кожа*) to dry; (*perf* **вы́сохнуть** *или* **засо́хнуть**;
растения, дерево) to wither; (*от болезни, от
переживаний*) to go thin; (*краска, клей*) to dry;
(*чернила*) to dry up.

сохран|и́ть (-**ю́**, -**и́шь**; *impf* **сохраня́ть**) *сов
перех* to preserve; (*комп*) to save

▶ **сохрани́ться** (*impf* **сохраня́ться**) *сов возв* to
survive, be preserved; **онá хорошо́ ~и́лась**
(*разг*) she's well-preserved.

сохрáнност|ь (-**и**) *ж* (*груза*) good condition;
(*вкладов, документов*) security; **в (по́лной) ~и**

(fully) intact.
сохраня́|ть(ся) (-ю(сь)) *несов от*
сохрани́ть(ся).
соцве́ти|е (-я) *ср* inflorescence.
социа́л-демокра́т (-а) *м* social democrat.
социа́л-демократи́ческ|ий (-ая, -ое, -ие)
прил social democrat *опред*.
социали́зм (-а) *м* socialism.
социали́ст (-а) *м* socialist.
социалисти́ческ|ий (-ая, -ое, -ие) *прил*
socialist.
социа́льный *прил* social; **социа́льная
защищённость** social security.
социо́лог (-а) *м* sociologist.
социоло́ги|я (-и) *ж* sociology.
соче́льник (-а) *м* (*рождественский*) Christmas
Eve; (*крещенский*) Twelfth Night.
со́чный *прил см* **со́чный**.
сочета́ни|е (-я) *ср* (*учёбы и работы*)
combining; (*единство: красок, звуков*)
combination.
сочета́|ть (-ю) (*не*)*сов перех* to combine
▶ **сочета́ться** (*не*)*сов возв* (*соединиться*) to
combine; (*гармонировать*) to match, go with; **в
ней ~ются ум и доброта́** she is both kind and
intelligent.
сочине́ни|е (-я) *ср* (*музыки*) composing;
(*стихов*) writing; (*литературное*) work;
(*музыкальное*) composition; (*ПРОСВЕЩ*) essay.
сочин|и́ть (-ю́, -и́шь; *impf* **сочиня́ть**) *сов перех*
(*музыку*) to compose; (*стихи, песню*) to write;
(*разг: письмо*) to concoct; (: *солгать*) to make
up.
соч|и́ться (*3sg* -и́тся, *3pl* -а́тся) *несов возв* to
ooze; ~ (*impf*) **чем-н** to ooze with sth.
со́ч|ный (-ен, -на́, -но) *прил* (*плод*) juicy;
(*трава*) lush; (*краски*) vibrant; (*язык*)
expressive.
сочту́ *итп сов см* **счесть**.
сочу́вствен|ный (-ен, -на, -но) *прил*
sympathetic.
сочу́встви|е (-я) *ср* sympathy; **встреча́ть
(встре́тить** *perf*) **что-н с ~м** to be sympathetic
to sth.
сочу́вств|овать (-ую) *несов неперех*: ~ +*dat* to
sympathize with.
сочу́вствующ|ий (-его; *decl like adj*) *м*
sympathizer.
сошёл(ся) *итп сов см* **сойти́(сь)**.
сошлю́(сь) *итп сов см* **сосла́ть(ся)**.
сошью́ *итп сов см* **сшить**.
сощу́р|ить(ся) (-ю(сь), -ишь(ся)) *сов от*
щу́рить(ся).
сою́з (-а) *м* alliance; (*республик,
профессиональный*) union; (*линг*) conjunction.
сою́зник (-а) *м* ally.
сою́зническ|ий (-ая, -ое, -ие) *прил* ally's.
сою́зный *прил* (*государство, армия*) allied;

(*слово, связь*) conjunctive.
со́|я (-и) *ж собир* soya beans *мн*.
СП *м сокр* = **Сою́з писа́телей** ◆ *ср сокр* =
совме́стное предприя́тие.
спаге́тти *мн нескл* spaghetti *ед*.
спад (-а) *м* (*температуры, давления*) drop;
экономи́ческий ~ recession; **идти́ (пойти́** *perf*)
на ~ (*температура, давление*) to go down;
(*экономика, производство*) to go into recession.
спада́|ть (*3sg* -ет, *3pl* -ют) *несов от* **спасть** ◆
неперех (*волосы, складки*) to fall.
спадёт *итп сов см* **спасть**.
спа́ек *сущ см* **спа́йка**.
спазм (-а) *м* spasm.
спа́ива|ть (-ю) *несов от* **спои́ть, спая́ть**.
спа́|йка (-йки; *gen pl* -ек) *ж* (*действие*) soldering;
(*место*) join (*from soldering*).
спа́лен *прил см* **спа́льня**.
спал|и́ть (-ю́, -и́шь) *сов от* **пали́ть**.
спа́льник (-а) *м* (*разг*) sleeping bag.
спа́льный *прил* (*место*) sleeping *опред*;
спа́льный ваго́н sleeping car; **спа́льный
мешо́к** sleeping bag.
спа́льн|я (-ьни; *gen pl* -ен) *ж* (*комната*)
bedroom; (*мебель*) bedroom suite.
спа́рж|а (-и) *ж* asparagus.
спа́р|ить (-ю, -ишь; *impf* **спа́ривать**) *сов перех*
(*телефон*) to connect (*to a shared line*);
(*вагоны, трубы*) to couple; (*собак, кошек*) to
mate.
спа́рыва|ть (-ю) *несов от* **споро́ть**.
Спас (-а) *м* (*РЕЛ*) the Day of the Saviour (*in the
Orthodox Church*); (: *икона*) the Saviour.
спас(ся) *итп сов см* **спасти́(сь)**.
спаса́ни|е (-я) *ср* rescue.
спаса́тель (-я) *м* rescuer; (*судно*) lifeboat.
спаса́тельный *прил* (*станция*) rescue *опред*;
спаса́тельная ло́дка lifeboat; **спаса́тельный
жиле́т** lifejacket; **спаса́тельный по́яс** lifebelt.
спаса́|ть(ся) (-ю(сь)) *несов от* **спасти́(сь)**.
спасе́ни|е (-я) *ср* rescue; (*РЕЛ*) Salvation.
спаси́бо *част* ~ (**Вам**) thank you; **большо́е ~!**
thank you very much!; ~ **за по́мощь/сове́т**
thanks for the help/advice; ~, **что мили́ция
во́время пришла́** (*разг*) thank God the police
got here on time.
спаси́телен *прил см* **спаси́тельный**.
спаси́тель (-я) *м* saviour; (*РЕЛ*) the Saviour.
спаси́тельниц|а (-ы) *ж* saviour.
спаси́тельный (-ен, -ьна, -ьно) *прил*
lifesaving.
спас|ова́ть (-у́ю) *сов от* **пасова́ть**.
спас|ти́ (-у́, -ёшь; *pt* -, -ла́, -ло́, *impf* **спаса́ть**) *сов
перех* (*также РЕЛ*) to save; **спаса́ть** (~ *perf*)
кому́-н жизнь to save sb's life; ~ (*perf*)
положе́ние to rescue the situation
▶ **спасти́сь** (*impf* **спаса́ться**) *сов возв*: ~**сь** (**от**
+*gen*) to escape; (*РЕЛ*) to be saved (from).

спа|сть (*3sg* -дёт, *3pl* -ду́т, *impf* спада́ть) *сов непрех* (*вода*) to drop; (*упасть вниз*): ~ с +*gen* (*одежда, покрывало*) to fall off; **жара́ к ве́черу спа́ла** the heat lessened towards evening.

сп|ать (-лю, -ишь; *pt* -ал, -ала́, -а́ло) *несов непрех* to sleep; (*перен: разг: быть невнимательным*) to daydream; **ложи́ться** (**лечь** *perf*) ~ to go to bed; **пора́** ~ it's time for bed; ~ (*impf*) **кре́пким сном** to sleep like a log

▸ спа́ться *несов возв*: **мне не** ~**йтся** I can't (get to) sleep; **по́сле рабо́ты хорошо́** ~**йтся** one sleeps well after working.

спа́ян|ный (-, -на, -но) *прил* (*перен: коллектив*) unified.

спа́я|ть (-ю; *impf* спа́ивать) *сов перех* (*трубы*) to weld; (*перен: сплотить*) to unite.

СПБ *сокр* (= *Санкт-Петербу́рг*) St Petersburg.

СПб *сокр* = **СПБ**.

Спб *сокр* = **СПБ**.

спекта́кл|ь (-я) *м* performance.

спектр (-а) *м* (*также перен*) spectrum.

спекули́р|овать (-ую) *несов непрех* (*дефицитом*) to profiteer; (*КОММ*): ~ +*instr* (*на бирже: ценными бумагами*) to speculate in; (*с дурными целями*): ~ **на** +*prp* (*на трудностях, на слабостях*) to exploit.

спекуля́нт (-а) *м* (*КОММ: биржевой*) speculator; (*дефицитом*) profiteer.

спекуляти́в|ный (-ен, -на, -но) *прил* speculative.

спекуля́ци|я (-и) *ж* (*КОММ*) speculation; (*дефицитом*) profiteering.

спеку́тся *итп сов см* **спе́чься**.

спелена́|ть (-ю) *сов от* пелена́ть.

спе́л|ый (-, -а, -о) *прил* ripe.

сперва́ *нареч* (*разг: вначале*) (at) first.

спе́реди *нареч* in front ♦ *предл* (+*gen*) in front of.

сп|ере́ть (сопру́, сопрёшь; *pt* -ёр, -ёрла, -ёрло) *сов от* пере́ть.

спе́рм|а (-ы) *ж* sperm.

спёрт|ый (-, -а, -о) *прил* (*разг: воздух*) stuffy.

спеси́в|ый (-, -а, -о) *прил* (*человек, тон*) haughty, arrogant.

спес|ь (-и) *ж* haughtiness, arrogance.

сп|еть (*3sg* -е́ет, *3pl* -е́ют, *perf* поспе́ть) *несов непрех* (*фрукты, овощи*) to ripen; ♦ (-ою́, -оёшь) *сов от* петь

▸ спе́ться *сов возв* (*хор, ансамбль*) to achieve a good sound; (*разг: пренебр*): ~**е́ться с** +*instr* (*с ворами, со спекуля́нтами*) to get in with.

спех (-а) *м*: **мне не к спе́ху** (*разг*) I'm in no hurry.

спец *сокр* = **специа́льный**.

спец (-а́) *м* (*разг: мастер, знаток*) buff.

специализа́ци|я (-и) *ж* (*производства*) specialization; (*научная*) specialism.

специализи́рованный *прил* specialized.

специализи́р|оваться (-уюсь) (*не*)*сов возв*: ~ **в** +*prp или* **по** +*dat* to specialize in.

специали́ст (-а) *м*: ~ (**по** +*dat*) specialist (in).

специали́ст|ка (-ки; *gen pl* -ок) *ж см* специали́ст.

специа́льно *нареч* specially; (*намеренно*) on purpose.

специа́льност|ь (-и) *ж* (*профессия*) profession; (*ПРОСВЕЩ*) main subject.

специа́льн|ый *прил* (*помещение, одежда итп*) special; (*образование*) specialist; ~ **те́рмин** technical term; **специа́льный корреспонде́нт** special correspondent.

специ́фик|а (-и) *ж* specific nature.

специфика́ци|я (-и) *ж* specification.

специфици́р|овать (-ую) (*не*)*сов перех* to specify.

специфи́чен *прил см* специфи́чный.

специфи́ческ|ий (-ая, -ое, -ие) *прил* specific.

специфи́чн|ый (-ен, -на, -но) *прил* = специфи́ческий.

спе́ци|я (-и) *ж* spice.

спецко́р (-а) *м сокр* = **специа́льный корреспонде́нт**.

спецку́рс (-а) *м сокр* = специа́льный курс; (*в вузе*) course of lectures in a specialist field.

спецо́вк|а (-и) *ж* (*разг*) workman's jacket.

спецоде́жд|а (-ы) *ж сокр* (= специа́льная оде́жда) work clothes *мн*.

спе́|чься (*3sg* -чётся, *3pl* -ку́тся) *сов* = запе́чься.

спе́шен *прил см* спе́шный.

спеш|и́ть (-у́, -и́шь; *perf* поспеши́ть) *несов непрех* (*часы*) to be fast; (*прийти закончить*): ~ +*infin*/**с** +*instr* to be in a hurry to do/with; ~ (*impf*) **на по́езд/в шко́лу** to rush for the train/to school; **я** ~ **у (домо́й/на рабо́ту)** I am in a hurry (to get home/to work); **поспеши́!** hurry up; **он поспеши́л с отве́том** he gave a rash answer; ~**у сообщи́ть, что ...** I hasten to inform you that ...; **рабо́тать** (*impf*) **не** ~**а́** to work at a relaxed pace.

спе́шк|а (-и) *ж* (*разг*) hurry, rush; **в** ~**е я забы́л ша́пку** in the rush I forgot my hat; **нет никако́й** ~**и** there's no hurry.

спе́шно *нареч* (*уйти, закончить*) hurriedly.

спе́шн|ый (-ен, -на, -но) *прил* (*дело, задание*) urgent.

спива́|ться (-юсь) *несов от* спи́ться.

СПИД (-а) *м сокр* (= *синдро́м приобретённого иммунодефици́та*) AIDS (= *acquired immune deficiency syndrome*).

спидо́метр (-а) *м* speedometer.

спи́кер (-а) *м* speaker.

спики́р|овать (-ую) *сов от* пики́ровать.

спил|и́ть (-ю́, -ишь; *impf* спи́ливать) *сов перех* to saw down.

спин|а́ (-ы́; *acc sg* -у, *dat sg* -е́, *nom pl* -ы) *ж* (*человека, животного*) back; **за** ~**о́й у него́ бога́тая жизнь** he has lead a full life.

спи́н|ка (-ки; *gen pl* -ок) *ж уменьш от* спина́; (*дивана, стула итп*) back; (*кровати*) bedstead.

спи́ннинг (-а) *м* spinner.

спинно́й *прил* (*позвонок*) spinal; **спинно́й мозг**

spinal cord.

спи́нок *сущ см* **спи́нка**.

спира́л|ь (-и) *ж* (*линия*) spiral; (*также:* **внутрима́точная ~**) coil (*contraceptive*).

спира́льный *прил* spiral.

спирт (-а; *loc sg* -у) *м* (*технический, медицинский*) spirit.

спиртн|о́е (-о́го; *decl like adj*) *ср* alcohol.

спиртно́й *прил* (*запах, раствор*) of alcohol; **спиртно́й напи́ток** alcoholic drink.

списа́ни|е (-я) *ср* (*комм*) writing off; (*мор*) discharge.

сп|иса́ть (-ишу́, -и́шешь; *impf* **спи́сывать**) *сов перех* to copy; (*комм*) to write off; (*мор*) to discharge; **спи́сывать** (~ *perf*) **что-н с** +*gen* to copy sth from

▶ **списа́ться** (*impf* **спи́сываться**) *сов возв* (*моряк*) to leave ship; **спи́сываться** (~**ся** *perf*) **с** +*instr* (*со старым другом*) to write to.

спи́с|ок (-ка) *м* (*делегатов, присутствующих*) list; (*документов, романа*) manuscript copy; **кни́га разошла́сь в** ~**ках** the book was distributed in handwritten copies.

спи́сыва|ть(ся) (-ю(сь)) *несов от* **списа́ть(ся)**.

спи́ться (**сопью́сь, сопьёшься**; *impf* **спива́ться**) *сов возв* to take to drink.

спихн|у́ть (-у́, -ёшь; *impf* **спи́хивать**) *сов перех* to push aside *или* down; (*разг: конкурента, начальника*) to oust; **спи́хивать** (~ *perf*) **что-н на кого-н** (*разг: плохой товар, ответственность*) to push sth onto sb.

спи́ц|а (-ы) *ж* (*для вязания*) knitting needle; (*колеса*) spoke.

спи́чек *сущ см* **спи́чка**.

спи́чечн|ый *прил*: ~**ая коро́бка** matchbox; ~**ая голо́вка** matchhead.

спи́ч|ка (-ки; *gen pl* -ек) *ж* match; (*разг: худой человек*) beanpole.

спишу́(сь) *итп сов см* **списа́ть(ся)**.

сплав (-а) *м* ((*не*)*металический*) alloy; (*леса*) floating.

спла́в|ить (-лю, -ишь; *impf* **сплавля́ть**) *сов перех* (*металлы*) to alloy; (*лес*) to float; (*перен: разг: избавиться*) to get rid of.

сплани́р|овать (-ую) *сов от* **плани́ровать**.

спланир|ова́ть (-у́ю) *сов от* **планирова́ть**.

спла́чива|ть(ся) (-ю(сь)) *несов от* **сплоти́ть(ся)**.

сплёвыва|ть (-ю) *несов от* **сплю́нуть**.

спл|ести́ (-ету́, -етёшь; *pt* -ёл, -ела́, -ело́) *сов от* **плести́** ◆ (*impf* **сплета́ть**) *перех* to plait; (*пальцы, ноги, руки*) to intertwine

▶ **сплести́сь** (*impf* **сплета́ться**) *сов возв* (*водоросли*) to be interwoven; (*руки, тела*) to be intertwined.

сплетен *сущ см* **спле́тня**.

сплете́ни|е (-я) *ср* (*лент, верёвок*) interlacing;

(*то, что сплетено*) tissue; (*перен: причин, обстоятельств*) combination.

спле́тник (-а) *м* gossip.

спле́тниц|а (-ы) *ж см* **спле́тник**.

спле́тнича|ть (-ю) *несов неперех* to gossip.

спле́тн|я (-ни; *gen pl* -ен) *ж* gossip; **распуска́ть** (*impf*) ~**ни** to spread gossip; **пуска́ть** (**пусти́ть** *perf*) ~**ню** to start gossip.

сплету́(сь) *итп сов см* **сплести́(сь)**.

сплеча́ *нареч* (*ударить*) straight from the shoulder; (*разг: решать*) impulsively.

спло|ти́ть (-чу́, -ти́шь; *impf* **спла́чивать**) *сов перех* to unite

▶ **сплоти́ться** (*impf* **спла́чиваться**) *сов возв* to unite.

сплох|ова́ть (-у́ю) *сов неперех* (*разг*) to slip up.

сплочённый *прил* united.

сплочу́(сь) *сов см* **сплоти́ть(ся)**.

сплошн|о́й *прил* (*стена, поток итп*) continuous; (*грамотность, перепись*) universal; (*разг: мучение, неудачи*) utter; (: *восторг, маразм*) complete and utter.

сплошь *нареч* (*по всей поверхности*) all over; (*без исключения*) completely; ~ **и ря́дом** (*разг*) more often than not.

сплут|ова́ть (-у́ю) *сов от* **плутова́ть**.

сплы|ть (*3sg* -вёт, *3pl* -ву́т, *impf* **сплыва́ть**) *сов неперех* (*уплыть*) to be carried away; **был да** ~**л** (*разг*) it's gone forever

▶ **сплы́ться** (*impf* **сплыва́ться**) *сов возв* (*буквы, краски итп*) to run together, merge.

сплю *несов см* **спать**.

сплю́н|уть (-у, -ешь; *impf* **сплёвывать**) *сов перех* to spit; (*шелуху*) to spit out.

сплю́щ|ить (-у, -ишь) *сов от* **плю́щить** ◆ (*impf* **сплю́щивать**) *перех* to flatten

▶ **сплю́щиться** (*impf* **сплю́щиваться**) *сов возв* to become flattened.

спл|яса́ть (-яшу́, -я́шешь) *сов от* **пляса́ть**.

сподви́жник (-а) *м* loyal supporter.

сподо́б|иться (-люсь, -ишься) *сов возв*: ~ +*infn* to be honoured (*BRIT*) *или* honored (*US*) to do.

спозара́нку *нареч* (*разг*) very early (*in the morning*).

спо|и́ть (-ю́, -и́шь; *imper* -й(те), *impf* **спа́ивать**) *сов перех*: ~ **кого-н** to get sb drunk; (*приучить пьянствовать*) to make a drunkard of sb.

спо́коен *прил см* **спокойный**.

споко́йно *нареч* (*жить, говорить*) quietly; (*спать*) peacefully ◆ *как сказ безл* it's quiet; **у меня́ на душе́** ~ I feel calm.

споко́йн|ый (-ен, -йна, -йно) *прил* (*море*) calm; (*улица, жизнь*) quiet; (*человек, тон, беседа*) serene; (*характер*) placid; (*цвет*) gentle, restful; ~**йная со́весть** clear conscience.

споко́йстви|е (-я) *ср* (*в городе, в лесу*) calm, tranquillity; (*на душе*) calm; **сохраня́ть** (*impf*) ~

to keep calm.

сполáскива|ть (**-ю**) *несов от* **сполоснýть**.

сполз|тú (**-ý, -ёшь**; *pt* **-, -лá, -лó**, *impf* **сползáть**) *сов неперех* to climb down; (*шапка, платок, чулки*) to slip down; (*перен: к национализму*) to slide

▶ **сползтúсь** (*impf* **сползáться**) *сов возв* to congregate.

сполнá *нареч* in full.

сполосн|ýть (**-ý, -ёшь**; *impf* **сполáскивать**) *сов перех* to rinse.

спóнсор (**-а**) *м* sponsor.

спóнсорск|ий (**-ая, -ое, -ие**) *прил* sponsoring *опред*.

спор (**-а**) *м* debate; (*имущественный*) dispute; (*спортивный*) competition; **вестú** (*impf*) ~ to have an argument; **спóру нет** there is no doubt; **нá ~** (*разг*) as a bet.

спóр|а (**-ы**) *ж* (*БОТ*) spore.

сporaдúческ|ий (**-ая, -ое, -ие**) *прил* sporadic.

спóрен *прил см* **спóрный**.

спóр|ить (**-ю, -ишь**; *perf* **поспóрить**) *несов неперех* (*вести спор*) to argue, debate; (*держать пари*) to bet; ~ (*impf*) **с кем-н о чём-н** *или* **за что-н** (*о наследстве*) to dispute sth with sb; ~**им, ты не посмéешь емý возразúть** I bet you wouldn't dare to contradict him

▶ **спóриться** *несов возв* (*работа, дело*) to go well.

спóр|ный (**-ен, -на, -но**) *прил* (*дело*) disputed; (*победа, преимущество*) doubtful; ~ **вопрóс** moot point.

спор|óть (**-орю́, -óрешь**; *impf* **спáрывать**) *сов перех* to nip off.

спорт (**-а**) *м* sport.

спортзáл (**-а**) *м* sports hall, gymnasium.

спортúвный *прил* (*площадка, комментатор*) sports *опред*; (*фигура, человек*) sporty; **спортúвный костю́м** tracksuit.

спортлотó *ср нескл* sports lottery.

спортсмéн (**-а**) *м* sportsman (*мн* **sportsmen**).

спортсмéн|ка (**-ки**; *gen pl* **-ок**) *ж* sportswoman (*мн* **sportswomen**).

спорттовáр|ы (**-ов**) *мн* sports goods *мн*.

спорхн|ýть (**-ý, -ёшь**) *сов неперех* to flutter off.

спóрщик (**-а**) *м* debater.

спóрщиц|а (**-ы**) *ж см* **спóрщик**.

спóрый *прил* efficient.

спóсоб (**-а**) *м* way.

спосóбен *прил см* **спосóбный**.

спосóбность (**-и**) *ж* ability; (*обычно мн: талант*) aptitude *ед*; **математúческие ~и** aptitude for mathematics; **пропускнáя ~** (*дороги, метро*) capacity; **покупáтельная ~ населéния** purchasing power (of the population).

спосóб|ный (**-ен, -на, -но**) *прил* capable; (*талантливый*) able; ~ **+infin** capable of doing; **он ~ен к матемáтике** he has a gift for mathematics; **онá ~на на всё** she is capable of anything.

спосóбств|овать (**-ую**) *сов неперех*: ~ **+dat** (*успеху, развитию*) to promote.

споткн|ýться (**-ýсь, -ёшься**; *impf* **спотыкáться**) *сов возв* (*при ходьбе, при беге*) to trip; (*при чтении*) to get stuck; (*перен: совершить проступок*) to slip up.

спохв|атúться (**-ачýсь, -áтишься**; *impf* **спохвáтываться**) *сов возв* (*вспомнить*) to remember suddenly; (*понять ошибку*) to realize.

спою́ *итп несов см* **спеть**.

спрáва *нареч* to the right; ~ **от чего́-н** to the right of sth.

справедлúво *нареч* fairly, justly ◆ *как сказ*: **э́то ~** that's fair *или* just.

справедлúв|ость (**-и**) *ж* justice; **отдáть** (*perf*) **комý-н** ~ (*оценить по заслугам*) to do justice to sb; ~ **и рáди** ... to be fair ....

справедлúв|ый (**-, -а, -о**) *прил* just; (*утверждение*) correct; (*подозрение*) justified.

спрáв|ить (**-лю, -ишь**; *impf* **справля́ть**) *сов перех* (*разг: день рождения*) to celebrate; (*шубу, туфли*) to get

▶ **спрáвиться** (*impf* **справля́ться**) *сов возв*: ~**ся с +instr** (*с работой, с заданием*) to manage; (*с противником*) to deal with; (*с волнением, с детьми*) to cope with; (*узнавать*): ~**ся о +prp** to enquire *или* ask about.

спрáв|ка (**-ки**; *gen pl* **-ок**) *ж* (*сведения*) information; (*документ*) certificate; **обращáться** (**обратúться** *perf*) **за ~кой** to apply for information; **наводúть** (**навестú** *perf*) ~**ки** to make enquiries.

спрáвлю(сь) *сов см* **спрáвить(ся)**.

справля́|ть(ся) (**-ю(сь)**) *несов от* **спрáвить(ся)**.

спрáвок *сущ см* **спрáвка**.

спрáвочник (**-а**) *м* (*телефонный*) directory; (*грамматический*) reference book.

спрáвочный *прил* (*литература, пособие*) reference *опред*; **спрáвочное бюрó** information office *или* bureau.

спрáшива|ть (**-ю**) *несов от* **спросúть**

▶ **спрáшиваться** *несов от* **спросúться** ◆ *возв*: ~**ется, где ты был в э́то врéмя** the question is, where were you at that time?

спрессовáть (**-ýю**) *сов от* **прессовáть**.

спринт (**-а**) *м* sprint.

спрúнтер (**-а**) *м* sprinter.

спровá|дить (**-жу, -дишь**; *impf* **спровáживать**) *сов перех* (*разг*) to send off.

спровоцúр|овать (**-ую**) *сов от* **провоцúровать**.

спроектúр|овать (**-ую**) *сов от* **проектúровать**.

спрос (**-а**) *м*: ~ **на +acc** (*на товары, на специалистов*) demand for; (*требование*): ~ **с +gen** (*с родителей, с начальника*) demands *мн* on; **без спрóса** *или* **спрóсу** without permission; **с тебя́ ~ осóбый** there are special demands on you; ~ и предложе́ние (экон) supply and demand.

спр|оси́ть (-ошу́, -о́сишь; impf спра́шивать) сов перех (дорогу, время) to ask; (совета, денег) to ask for; (взыскать): ~ что-н с +gen to call sb to account for; (осведомиться): ~ кого́-н о чём-н to ask sb about sth; спра́шивать (~ perf) ученика́ to question или test a pupil; я ~оси́л, кото́рый час/когда́ по́езд I asked what the time was/when the train would be

▶ спроси́ться (impf спра́шиваться) сов возв: ~ся +gen или у +gen (у родителей, у учителя итп) to ask permission of; с нас ~о́сится за э́то we will be answerable for that.

спросо́нок нареч (разг) half asleep.

спрошу́(сь) сов см спроси́ть(ся).

спрут (-а) м octopus.

спры́г|нуть (-ну, -нешь; impf спры́гивать) сов неперех: ~ с +gen to jump off.

спряга́|ть (-ю; perf проспряга́ть) несов перех (линг) to conjugate.

спряду́ итп сов см спрясть.

спряже́ни|е (-я) ср (линг) conjugation.

спря|сть (-ду́, -дёшь) сов от прясть.

спря́|тать(ся) (-чу(сь), -чешь(ся)) сов от пря́тать(ся).

спуг|ну́ть (-ну́, -нёшь; impf спу́гивать) сов перех to frighten off.

спуд (-а) м: держа́ть что-н под спу́дом (идею, план) to keep sth back; извлека́ть (извле́чь perf) что-н из-под спу́да to bring sth into the light of day.

спуск (-а) м (действие: флага) lowering; (: корабля) launch; (: воды, газа) draining; (место: к реке, с горы) descent; (в оружии) trigger; нажима́ть (нажа́ть perf) (на) ~ to pull the trigger; я не дал ему́ спу́ску (разг) I didn't let him off.

спуска́емый прил: ~ аппара́т (космос) landing gear.

спуска́|ть (-ю) несов от спусти́ть ♦ перех: я не ~л глаз с неё I didn't take my eyes off her

▶ спуска́ться несов от спусти́ться ♦ возв (дорога, берег) to descend, go down; (волосы, фалды) to hang down.

спусково́й прил (трап) exit опред; (механизм) trigger опред.

спу|сти́ть (-щу́, -стишь; impf спуска́ть) сов перех to lower; (директиву, план) to send out; (собаку) to let loose; (газ, воду) to drain; (разг: зарплату, наследство) to squander; (простить): ~ что-н кому́-н to let sb off with sth, forgive sb for sth; ~стя́ рукава́ (разг: небре́жно) carelessly; спуска́ть (~ perf) кора́бль (на́ воду) to launch a ship; спуска́ть (~ perf) куро́к to pull the trigger; спуска́ть (~ perf) кого́-н с ле́стницы to kick sb downstairs; (выгнать) to kick sb out; у мое́й маши́ны

~сти́ла ши́на my car has a flat tyre (BRIT) или tire (US)

▶ спусти́ться (impf спуска́ться) сов возв to go down; (чулки, юбка итп) to slip down; (туман, мгла, ночь итп) to descend.

спустя́ нареч: ~ три дня/год three days/a year later.

спу́танный прил (волосы, верёвки) tangled; (речь) muddled.

спу́та|ть(ся) (-ю(сь)) сов от пу́тать(ся).

спу́тник (-а) м (в пути) travelling (BRIT) или traveling (US) companion; (городок) satellite town; (АСТРОНОМИЯ) satellite; (КОСМОС: также: иску́сственный ~) sputnik, satellite; (перен): ~ +gen (бедности, прогресса итп) concomitant of; ~ жи́зни (муж) life's companion.

спу́тниковый прил (связь) satellite опред; спу́тниковое телеви́дение satellite TV.

спу́тниц|а (-ы) ж (в пути) travelling (BRIT) или traveling (US) companion; ~ жи́зни (жена) life's companion.

спу́тыва|ть (-ю; perf спу́тать) несов перех = пу́тать.

спущу́(сь) сов см спусти́ть(ся).

спя́|тить (-чу, -тишь) сов неперех (разг) to go daft.

спя́чк|а (-и) ж (животных) hibernation; (перен: бездеятельность) lethargy.

спя́чу сов см спя́тить.

ср. сокр (= сравни́) ср. (= compare).

сраба́тыва|ть (3sg -ет, 3pl -ют) несов от срабо́тать.

срабо́танност|ь (-и) ж harmony.

срабо́та|ть (3sg -ет, 3pl -ют, impf сраба́тывать) сов неперех to operate.

сравне́ни|е (-я) ср comparison; в ~и или по ~ю с +instr compared with; не мо́жет быть никако́го ~я с +instr there can be no comparison with; не поддава́ться (impf) никако́му ~ю to be unspeakable.

сра́внива|ть (-ю) несов от сравни́ть, сравня́ть.

сравни́м|ый (-, -а, -о) прил comparable.

сравни́телен прил см сравни́тельный.

сравни́тельно нареч comparatively; ~ с +instr compared to или with.

сравни́тел|ьный (-ен, -ьна, -ьно) прил comparative; сравни́тельная сте́пень (линг) comparative degree.

сравн|и́ть (-ю́, -и́шь; impf сра́внивать) сов перех: ~ что-н/кого́-н (с +instr) to compare sth/sb (with); (уподобить): ~ что-н/кого́-н с +instr to compare sth/sb to

▶ сравни́ться сов возв: ~ся с +instr to compare with.

сравня́|ть (-ю; impf сра́внивать) сов перех (расход с доходом) to balance; сра́внивать (~ perf) счёт to equalize

▶ **сравня́ться** *сов возв*: ~ся с +*instr* to become the equal of.

сража́ть(ся) (-ю(сь)) *несов от* **срази́ть(ся)**.

сраже́ни|е (-я) *ср* (*битва*) battle.

сра|зи́ть (-жу́, -зи́шь; *impf* **сража́ть**) *сов перех* (*пулей, ударом*) to slay; (*подлеж: горе, тяжёлая весть*) to crush

▶ **срази́ться** (*impf* **сража́ться**) *сов возв* to join battle.

сра́зу *нареч* (*немедленно*) straight away; (*в один приём*) (all) at once; (*рядом*) right.

срам (-а) *м* (*разг*) shame; ~ **ви́деть тако́е** it's a disgrace *или* shame.

срам|и́ть (-лю́, -и́шь; *perf* **осрами́ть**) *несов перех* (*позорить*) to shame; (*бранить*) to put to shame

▶ **срами́ться** (*perf* **осрами́ться**) *несов возв* to bring shame on o.s.

сраста́ни|е (-я) *ср* (*костей*) knitting.

сраст|и́сь (*3sg* -ётся, *3pl* -у́тся, *impf* **сраста́ться**) *сов возв* (*кости*) to knit (together); (*стволы*) to grow together; (*перен: компании*) to merge.

сраще́ни|е (-я) *ср* (*костей*) knitting.

среаги́р|овать (-ую) *сов от* **реаги́ровать**.

сред|а́ (-ы́; *nom pl* -ы) *ж* medium; (*no pl*; *природная, социальная*) environment; (*артистическая, литературная*) milieu; (*acc sg* -у; *день недели*) Wednesday; *см также* **пя́тница**; **окружа́ющая ~** environment; **охра́на окружа́ющей ~ы** conservation.

среди́ *предл* (+*gen*) in the middle of; (*в пределах*) in the middle of, amidst; (*в окружении*) amidst; (*в среде, в числе*) among.

средизе́мный *прил*: **С~ое мо́ре** the Mediterranean (Sea).

среди́н|а (-ы) *ж* = **середи́на**.

среди́нный *прил* = **середи́нный**.

среднеазиа́тск|ий (-ая, -ое, -ие) *прил* Central Asian.

средневеко́вый *прил* medieval.

средневеко́вь|е (-я) *ср* the Middle Ages *мн*.

среднево́лновый *прил* medium-wave.

среднегодово́й *прил* average annual.

среднеме́сячный *прил* average monthly.

среднесу́точный *прил* average daily.

сре́дн|ий (-яя, -ее, -ие) *прил* medium; (*комната, окно итп*) middle; (*посредственный*) average; **в ~ем** on average; **вы́ше/ни́же ~его** above/below average; **он ~их лет** he is middle-aged; **сре́днее образова́ние** secondary education; **сре́дние века́** the Middle Ages *мн*; **сре́дний па́лец** middle finger; **сре́дняя шко́ла** secondary school.

средото́чи|е (-я) *ср* focus, centre (*BRIT*), center (*US*).

сре́дств|а (-) *мн* means *мн*; (*деньги*) means *мн*, funds *мн*; **отпуска́ть** (**отпусти́ть** *perf*) *или* **выделя́ть** (**вы́делить** *perf*) ~ **на что-н** to allocate funds to sth; **остава́ться** (**оста́ться** *perf*) **без средств** to be without means;

сре́дства произво́дства (*ЭКОН*) means of production; **сре́дства существова́ния** livelihood.

сре́дств|о (-а) *ср* means *мн*; (*лекарство*) remedy, medicine; **добива́ться** (*impf*) **чего́-н все́ми ~ами** to use all means to get sth; **сре́дство передвиже́ния** means of conveyance; *см также* **сре́дства**.

сре́жу(сь) *итп сов см* **сре́зать(ся)**.

срез (-а) *м* (*место*) cut; (*тонкий слой*) section.

сре́|зать (-жу, -жешь; *impf* **среза́ть**) *сов перех* (*траву, цветок*) to cut; (*разг: дотации, кредиты*) to cut off; (: *студента*) to flunk

▶ **сре́заться** (*impf* **среза́ться**) *сов возв* (*разг: студент*) to flunk.

Сре́тени|е (-я) *ср* (*РЕЛ*) Candlemas, Feast of the Purification.

срис|ова́ть (-у́ю; *impf* **срисо́вывать**) *сов перех* to copy.

срифм|ова́ть (-у́ю) *сов от* **рифмова́ть**.

сровня́|ть (-ю) *сов от* **ровня́ть**.

сродни́ *предл* (+*dat*) akin to.

срод|ни́ть (-ню́, -ни́шь) *сов перех*: ~ **кого́-н с** +*instr* to bring sb close to

▶ **сродни́ться** *сов возв*: ~ся с +*instr* to become close to.

сродств|о́ (-а́) *ср* affinity.

сро́ду *нареч*: ~ **не ви́дел/не слы́шал** ... never in my life have I seen/heard ....

сро|́ться (*3sg* -йтся, *3pl* -йтся) *сов от* **ро́иться**.

срок (-а; *part gen* -у) *м* (*длительность*) time, period; (*дата*) date; (*разг: тюремный*) term; **в ~** (*во время*) in time; **после́дний** *или* **преде́льный ~** deadline; **сро́ком на** +*acc* for a term of; **испыта́тельный ~** trial period; ~ **произво́дства платежа́** due date; **срок го́дности** (*товара*) sell-by date; **срок де́йствия** period of validity.

сро́чен *прил см* **сро́чный**.

сро́чно *нареч* quickly, urgently.

сро́чност|ь (-и) *ж* urgency; **нет никако́й ~и** there's no hurry.

сро́чный (-ен, -на, -но) *прил* (*дело, заказ*) urgent; (*ссуда, вклад*) fixed-term; **сро́чная телегра́мма** express telegram.

сро́ю *итп сов см* **срыть**.

сруб (-а) *м* (*место сруба*) cut; (*постройка*) log shell (*of building, well etc*).

сруба́|ть (-ю; *perf* **сруби́ть**) *несов перех* = **руби́ть**.

сруб|и́ть (-ублю́, -у́бишь) *сов от* **руби́ть**.

срыв (-а) *м* (*плана итп*) disruption; (*с горы, с крыши итп*) fall; (*на экзамене итп*) failure; (*обрыв*) precipice.

срыва́ни|е (-я) *ср* picking.

срыва́|ть (-ю) *несов от* **сорва́ть**, **срыть**

▶ **срыва́ться** *несов от* **сорва́ться**.

срыва́ющийся (-аяся, -ееся, -иеся) *прил* (*голос*) breaking.

ср|ыть (-о́ю, -о́ешь; *impf* **срыва́ть**) *сов перех*

(*насыпь, холм*) to level.
СС *м сокр* SS.
ссадин|а (-ы) *ж* scratch.
сса|дить (-жу, -дишь; *impf* **сса́живать**) *сов*
перех (*со стула, с колен*) to help down;
(*безбилетника*) to put off.
ссо́р|а (-ы) *ж* quarrel.
ссо́р|ить (-ю, -ишь; *perf* **поссо́рить**) *несов*
перех (*друзей, родственников*) to cause to
quarrel; ~ (**поссо́рить** *perf*) **кого́-н с** +*instr* to
make sb quarrel with
▶ **ссо́риться** (*perf* **поссо́риться**) *несов возв* to
quarrel.
СССР *м сокр* (*ист*: = *Сою́з Сове́тских*
Социалисти́ческих Респу́блик) USSR (= *Union*
of Soviet Socialist Republics).
ссу́д|а (-ы) *ж* loan; **брать** (**взять** *perf*) **~у** to take
out a loan; ~ **под проце́нты** interest-bearing
loan; ~ **под зало́г** loan on collateral.
ссу|ди́ть (-жу́, -дишь; *impf* **ссужа́ть**) *сов перех*
(*де́ньги*) to lend.
ссу́дный *прил* (*операция, ведомость*) loan
опред; **ссу́дный банк** lending bank; **ссу́дный**
капита́л (*КОММ*) loan capital.
ссужа́ть (-ю) *несов от* **ссуди́ть**.
ссужу́ *сов см* **ссуди́ть**.
ссуту́л|ить(ся) (-ю(сь), -ишь(ся)) *сов от*
суту́лить(ся).
ссыла́|ть(ся) (-ю(сь)) *несов от* **сосла́ть(ся)** ◆
возв: ~**я́сь на** +*acc* with reference to.
ссы́л|ка (-ки; *gen pl* **-ок**) *ж* exile; (*на автора, на*
источник) reference; (*цитата*) quotation.
ссы́льн|ая (-ой; *decl like adj*) *ж см* **ссы́льный**.
ссы́льн|ый (-ого; *decl like adj*) *м* exile.
ссы́п|ать (-лю, -лешь; *impf* **ссыпа́ть**) *сов перех*
(*насыпать*) to pour.
ст. *сокр* (= **ста́нция**) sta. (= *station*); (=
ста́рший) Sen. (= *senior*); = **ста́рый**.
ста *чис см* **сто**.
стаби́лен *прил см* **стаби́льный**.
стабилиза́тор (-а) *м* (*ТЕХ*) stabilizer.
стабилиза́ци|я (-и) *ж* stabilization.
стабилизи́р|овать (-ую) (*не*)*сов перех* to
stabilize
▶ **стабилизи́роваться** (*не*)*сов возв* to
stabilize.
стаби́льный (-ен, -ьна, -ьно) *прил* stable;
стаби́льный уче́бник standard textbook.
ста́в|ень (-ня) *м* (*обычно мн*) shutter.
ста́в|ить (-лю, -ишь; *perf* **поста́вить**) *несов*
перех to put; (*назначать: министром,*
дежурным) to appoint; (*памятник*) to erect;
(*телефон*) to install; (*парус, сроки*) to set;
(*пятно, оценку*) to make; (*точку, запятую*
итп) to put in; (*оперу, фильм итп*) to stage;
(*выдвигать: задачу, цель*) to present;
(: *вопрос*) to raise; ~ (**поста́вить** *perf*) **де́ньги**
на что-н to put money on sth; ~ (**поста́вить**

perf) **печа́ть на что-н** to stamp sth; ~
(**поста́вить** *perf*) **часы́** to set a clock; ~
(**поста́вить** *perf*) **диа́гноз** to make a diagnosis;
~ (**поста́вить** *perf*) **что-н на голосова́ние** to
put sth to the vote; ~ (**поста́вить** *perf*) **что-н**
кому́-н в вину́ to lay the blame for sth on sb; ~
(**поста́вить** *perf*) **что-н кому́-н в заслу́гу** to put
sth at sb's service; ~ (**поста́вить** *perf*) **что-н**
кому́-н в досто́инство to give sb credit for sth;
~ (**поста́вить** *perf*) **себе́ за пра́вило** to make it
a rule; ~ (**поста́вить** *perf*) **кого́-н в**
изве́стность to fill sb in; ~ (**поста́вить** *perf*)
что-н под контро́ль to bring sth under control;
его́ здесь ни во что не ~ят he counts for
nothing here.
ста́в|ка (-ки; *gen pl* **-ок**) *ж* (*также КОММ*) rate;
(*ВОЕН*) headquarters *мн*; (*в азартных играх*)
stake; (*перен*): ~ **на** +*acc* (*расчёт*) counting on;
проце́нтные ~ки (*КОММ*) interest rates;
ба́зовая ссу́дная ~ base rate; **минима́льная**
ссу́дная ~ minimum lending rate; **учётная** ~
(*банка*) discount rate.
ста́вленник (-а) *м* protégé.
ста́вленниц|а (-ы) *ж* protégée.
ста́влю *сов см* **ста́вить**.
ста́вня (-ни) *сущ см* **ста́вень**.
ста́вок *сущ см* **ста́вка**.
ставри́д|а (-ы) *ж* (*ЗООЛ*) horse mackerel, scad.
стагна́ци|я (-и) *ж* stagnation.
стадио́н (-а) *м* stadium (*мн* stadia).
ста́ди|я (-и) *ж* stage.
ста́дный *прил* (*животное*) herd *опред*; (*перен*:
чувство) gregarious.
ста́д|о (-а; *nom pl* **-а́**) *ср* (*коров*) herd; (*овец*)
flock.
стаж (-а) *м* (*рабочий*) length of service;
испыта́тельный ~ probation.
стажёр (-а) *м* probationer.
стажир|ова́ться (-у́юсь) *несов возв* to work on
probation.
стажиро́в|ка (-ки; *gen pl* **-ок**) *ж* probationary
period.
ста́ива|ть (-ю) *несов от* **ста́ять**.
ста́йер (-а) *м* long-distance runner.
ста́йерск|ий (-ая, -ое, -ие) *прил*: ~**ая**
диста́нция long distance.
стака́н (-а) *м* glass; **бума́жный** ~ paper cup.
стака́нчик (-а) *м* glass; **моро́женое в ~ах** ice
cream in tubs.
стакка́то *нареч* staccato.
сталагми́т (-а) *м* stalagmite.
сталакти́т (-а) *м* stalactite.
сталева́р (-а) *м* steel founder.
сталелите́йный *прил* steel-founding.
сталеплави́льный *прил* steel-smelting.
сталепрока́тный *прил* steel-rolling.
стали́йн|ый *прил*: ~**ое вре́мя** (*КОММ*) lay days
мн.
сталини́зм (-а) *м* Stalinism.

ста́лкива|ть(ся) (-ю(сь)) *несов от* столкну́ть(ся).

стал|ь (-и) *ж* steel.

стально́й *прил* (*кабель, рельсы, решимость*) steel *опред*; (*мускулы, нервы*) of steel; (*воля*) iron *опред*; (*цвет: глаза*) steel-blue; (: *море*) steel-grey (*BRIT*), steel-gray (*US*).

стам *итп чис см* сто.

Стамбу́л (-а) *м* Istanbul.

стаме́с|ка (-ки; *gen pl* **-ок)** *ж* chisel.

стан (-а) *м* (*человека*) torso; (*стоянка*) camp; (*ТЕХ*) mill.

станда́рт (-а) *м* (*также перен*) standard; **по ~у** (*изготовить*) in line with the standard; (*перен: действовать*) conventionally.

станда́ртен *прил см* **станда́ртный**.

стандартиза́ци|я (-и) *ж* standardization; (*личности, отношений*) stereotyping.

стандартизи́р|овать (-ую) (*не)сов перех* to standardize.

станда́рт|ный (-ен, -на, -но) *прил* (*детали, машина*) standard; (*вопросы, тема*) stock.

стани́н|а (-ы) *ж* (*ТЕХ*) bed.

стани́ц|а (-ы) *ж* stanitsa (*large Cossack village*).

станка́ *итп сущ см* **стано́к**.

станко́вый *прил* (*живопись*) easel *опред*.

станкострое́ни|е (-я) *ср* machine-tool construction.

станкостро́ительный *прил* (*завод, промышленность*) machine-tool.

стан|ови́ться (-овлю́сь, -о́вишься) *несов от* **стать**.

становле́ни|е (-я) *ср* formation.

становлю́сь *несов см* **станови́ться**.

стан|о́к (-ка́) *м* (*слесарный итп*) machine (tool); (*искусство*) frame; (*балетный*) barre; **тока́рный ~** lathe.

ста́ну(сь) *итп сов см* **стать(ся)**.

станцио́нный *прил* station *опред*.

ста́нци|я (-и) *ж* station; **запра́вочная ~** filling station; **телефо́нная ~** telephone exchange.

ста́пел|ь (-я; *nom pl* **-я́)** *м* (*МОР*) building berth (*BRIT*), slip (*US*).

ста́плива|ть (-ю) *несов от* **стопи́ть**.

ста́птыва|ть(ся) (-ю(сь)) *несов от* **стопта́ть(ся)**.

стара́ни|е (-я) *ср* effort; **при всём ~и не смогу́ тебе́ помо́чь** no matter how much I try, I can't help you.

стара́телен *прил см* **стара́тельный**.

стара́тел|ь (-я) *м* (*gold*) prospector.

стара́тельност|ь (-и) *ж* (*см прил*) diligence; painstakingness.

стара́тель|ный (-ен, -ьна, -ьно) *прил* (*работник, ученик*) diligent; (*работа, подсчёт*) painstaking.

стара́|ться (-юсь; *perf* **постара́ться)** *несов возв*: **~ +***infin* to try to do.

старе́йш|ий (-ая, -ее, -ие) *превос прил от* **ста́рый**.

старе́йшин|а (-ы) *ж* elder.

старе́ни|е (-я) *ср* ageing.

старе́|ть (-ю; *perf* **постаре́ть)** *несов неперех* (*человек*) to grow old(er), age; (*perf* **устаре́ть**; *оборудование*) to become out of date.

ста́р|ец (-ца) *м* (*РЕЛ*) elderly monk.

стари́|к (-а́) *м* old man (*мн* men); **старики́** old people.

старико́вск|ий (-ая, -ое, -ие) *прил* (*привычки*) old people's.

старин|а́ (-ы́) *ж* (*прошлое*) the olden days *мн* ♦ *м* (*обращение*) old man *или* chap (*BRIT*).

стари́н|ка (-и) *ж*: **по ~е** in the old way.

стари́нный *прил* ancient; (*давний: друг*) old.

ста́р|ить (-ю, -ишь; *perf* **соста́рить)** *несов перех* to age.

ста́рк|а (-и) *ж* (*сорт водки*) starka (*type of vodka*).

старо́ *как сказ*: **э́то всё ~** it's all outdated; (*не ново*) there's nothing new in it; **~ как мир** it's as old as the hills.

старове́р (-а) *м* (*РЕЛ*) Old Believer.

старове́р|ка (-ки; *gen pl* **-ок)** *ж см* **старове́р**.

старожи́л (-а) *м* old resident.

старомо́д|ный (-ен, -на, -но) *прил* old-fashioned.

старообря́д|ец (-ца) *м* (*РЕЛ*) Old Believer.

старообря́д|ка (-ки; *gen pl* **-ок)** *ж см* **старообря́дец**.

старообря́дца *итп сущ см* **старообря́дец**.

старообря́дчеств|о (-а) *ср* Old Belief.

старославя́нск|ий (-ая, -ое, -ие) *прил*: **старославя́нский язы́к** Old Church Slavonic.

ста́рост|а (-ы) *м* (*курса*) senior student; (*класса: мальчик*) head boy; (: *девушка*) head girl; (*клуба*) head, president; (*артели*) foreman (*мн* foremen).

ста́рост|ь (-и) *ж* (*человека*) old age; **на ~лет** in one's old age.

старпо́м (-а) *м* = **ста́рший помо́щник**; (*МОР*) first mate.

старт (-а) *м* (*СПОРТ*) start; (*ракеты*) takeoff point; **дава́ть (дать** *perf*) **~** to start; **брать (взять** *perf*) **~** to start; (*перен*) to take off.

ста́ртер (-а) *м* (*АВТ*) starter.

стартёр (-а) *м* (*СПОРТ*) starter.

старт|ова́ть (-у́ю) (*не)сов неперех* (*спортсмен*) to start; (*ракета*) to take off.

ста́ртовый *прил* starting *опред*.

старух|а (-и) *ж* old woman (*мн* women).

стару́шек *сущ см* **стару́шка**.

стару́шеч|ий (-ья, -ье, -ьи) *прил* old woman's.

стару́ш|ка (-ки; *gen pl* **-ек)** *ж* = **старуха**.

ста́рца *итп сущ см* **ста́рец**.

ста́рческ|ий (-ая, -ое, -ие) *прил* old person's *или* people's; **ста́рческий во́зраст** old age; **ста́рческий мара́зм** (*МЕД*) senility.

ста́рше *сравн прил от* **ста́рый** ♦ *как сказ*: **я ~ сестры́ на́ год** I am a year older than my sister; **я ~ его́ по зва́нию** I am senior to him.

старшекла́ссник (-а) *м* senior pupil.

старшекла́ссниц|а (-ы) *ж см*

старшекла́ссник.

старшеку́рсник (-а) *м* senior student.

старшеку́рсниц|а (-ы) *ж см* **старшеку́рсник.**

ста́рш|**ий** (-ая, -ее, -ие) *прил* senior *опред*; (*сестра, брат*) elder *опред* ♦ (-его; *decl like adj*) *м* (*группы, отделения*) senior; ~**ие** (*взрослые люди*) grown-ups *мн*, adults *мн*.

старшин|а́ (-ы́; *nom pl* -ы) *м* (*ВОЕН*) sergeant major; (*милиции*) sergeant.

старшинств|о́ (-а́) *ср* seniority; **по** ~у́ by seniority.

ста́р|**ый** (-, -а́, -о́, -ы) *прил* old; **и стар и млад** old and young; **ста́рый стиль** (*летосчисления*) Old Style.

старь|ё (-я́) *ср собир* old things *мн*.

старьёвщик (-а) *м* junk dealer.

ста́скива|**ть** (-ю) *несов от* **стащи́ть.**

стас|**ова́ть** (-у́ю) *сов от* **тасова́ть.**

ста́тен *прил см* **ста́тный.**

ста́тик|а (-и) *ж* (*наука*) statics; (*неподвижность*) stasis.

стати́ст (-а) *м* (*ТЕАТР*) extra.

стати́стик (-а) *м* statistician.

стати́стик|а (-и) *ж* statistics.

статисти́ческ|**ий** (-ая, -ое, -ие) *прил* statistical; **Центра́льное** ~**ое управле́ние** *central statistics office.*

стати́чен *прил см* **стати́чный.**

стати́ческ|**ий** (-ая, -ое, -ие) *прил* static.

стати́чн|**ый** (-ен, -на, -но) *прил* static.

ста́тн|**ый** (-ен, -на, -но) *прил* stately.

ста́тус (-а) *м* status.

ста́тус-кво *м нескл* status quo.

стату́т (-а) *м* (*правила*) statute.

статуэ́т|ка (-ки; *gen pl* -ок) *ж* statuette.

ста́ту|я (-и) *ж* statue.

ста|**ть** (-ти) *ж* (*осанка*) bearing; ♦ (-ну, -нешь; *impf* **станови́ться**) *сов неперех* to stand; (**к станку, за прилавок**) to take up position; (*no impf*; *часы, завод, движение*) to stop; (*начать*): ~ +*infin* to begin *или* start doing; (*обойтись*): ~ **в** +*acc* to cost ♦ *безл* (*наличествовать*): **нас ста́ло бо́льше/тро́е** there are more/three of us; **под** ~ **кому́-н/чему́-н** (*подобно*) like sb/sth; **с какой ста́ти?** (*разг*) why?; **станови́ться** (~ *perf*) +*instr* (*учителем*) to become; **его́ не ста́ло** he passed away; **не ста́ло де́нег/сил** I have no more money/energy; **с него́ ста́нет** (*разг*) that's all you can expect from him; **ста́ло быть** (*значит*) so; **во что бы то ни ста́ло** no matter what; **что с ним ста́ло?** what has become of him?; **станови́ться** (~ *perf*) **у вла́сти** to come to power; **станови́ться** (~ *perf*) **на путь чего́-н** to set out on the path of sth

▶ **ста́ться** *сов безл* (*случиться*) to happen; **мо́жет ста́ться** it is possible.

стат|**ья́** (-ьи́; *gen pl* -е́й) *ж* (*в газете, в сборнике*) article; (*в словаре*) entry; (*в законе, в договоре*)

paragraph, clause; (*экспорта, импорта*) type; (*КОММ: расхода, дохода*) item; **по всем** ~**м** (*разг*) in all respects.

стафилоко́кк (-а) *м* (*МЕД*) staphylococcus.

стациона́р (-а) *м* (*МЕД*) hospital.

ста́чек *сущ см* **ста́чка.**

ста́чечник (-а) *м* striker.

ста́чечниц|а (-ы) *ж см* **ста́чечник.**

ста́чива|**ть** (-ю) *несов от* **сточи́ть.**

ста́ч|ка (-ки; *gen pl* -ек) *ж* (*ЭКОН*) strike.

стащ|**и́ть** (-у́, -ишь) *сов от* **тащи́ть** ♦ (*impf* **ста́скивать**) *перех* (*что-н сверху*) to pull down; (*что-н в подвал*) to drag down; (*сапоги, чулки*) to pull off; (*no impf*; *разг: украсть*) to nick.

ста́|я (-и) *ж* (*птиц*) flock; (*волков*) pack; (*рыб*) shoal.

ста́|**ять** (*3sg* -ет, *3pl* -ют, *impf* **ста́ивать**) *сов неперех* to melt.

ствол (-а́) *м* (*дерева*) trunk; (*ружья, пушки*) barrel.

ство́р|ка (-ки; *gen pl* -ок) *ж* door; (*ставней*) shutter; (*зеркала*) leaf.

ство́рчатый *прил* (*окно, шкаф*) double (*opening in the middle*).

сте́бел|ь (-ля) *м* (*цветка*) stem.

стёган|ка (-ки; *gen pl* -ок) *ж* quilted jacket.

стёганый *прил* quilted; **стёганое одея́ло** quilt.

стега́|**ть** (-ю; *perf* **простега́ть**) *несов перех* (*одеяло*) to quilt; (*no perf*; *хлыстом*) to lash.

стегн|**у́ть** (-у́, -ёшь) *сов перех* to lash.

стёж|ка (-ки; *gen pl* -ек) *ж* stitch.

стежо́к (-ка́) *м* stitch.

стез|**я́** (-и́) *ж* path (*fig*).

стёк(ся) *итп сов см* **сте́чь(ся).**

стека́|**ть(ся)** (*3sg* -ет(ся), *3pl* -ют(ся)) *несов от* **сте́чь(ся).**

стеклене́|**ть** (*3sg* -ет, *3pl* -ют, *perf* **остеклене́ть**) *несов неперех* to become glassy.

стекл|**и́ть** (-ю́, -и́шь; *perf* **остекли́ть**) *несов перех* (*окно*) to glaze.

стекл|**о́** (-а́; *nom pl* **стёкла**, *gen pl* **стёкол**) *ср* glass; (*также: око́нное* ~) (window) pane; (*для очков*) lenses *мн* ♦ *собир* (*изделия*) glassware.

стёклыш|ко (-ка; *gen pl* -ек) *ср уменьш от* **стекло́**; (*осколок*) piece of glass.

стекля́нный *прил* glass; (*перен: взгляд, глаза*) glassy.

стекля́рус (-а) *м собир* glass beads *мн*.

стекля́ш|ка (-ки; *gen pl* -ек) *ж* (*осколок*) piece of glass; (*пренебр: изделие*) bauble.

стёкол *сущ см* **стекло́.**

стеко́льный *прил* (*завод*) glass.

стеко́льщик (-а) *м* glazier.

стеку́т(ся) *итп сов см* **сте́чь(ся).**

сте́лек *сущ см* **сте́лька.**

стел|**и́ть** (-ю́, -ишь; *perf* **постели́ть**) *несов перех* (*скатерть, подстилку*) to spread out; (*perf*

настели́ть; *пол, паркет*) to lay; ~ **(постели́ть** *perf*) **посте́ль** to make up a bed

▶ **стели́ться** *несов возв* (*туман*) to spread; (*perf* **постели́ться**; *разг: приготовить постель*) to get ready for bed.

стелла́ж (-а́) *м* shelf (*мн* shelves).

сте́л|ька (-ьки; *gen pl* -ек) *ж* (*в обуви*) insole.

стелю́(сь) *итп несов см* **стла́ть(ся).**

стемне́|ть (*3sg* -ет) *сов от* **темне́ть.**

стен|а́ (-ы́; *acc sg* -у, *dat sg* -е́, *nom pl* -ы, *dat pl* -а́м) *ж* (*также перен*) wall; **в ~х** +*gen* (*школы, учреждения*) within the confines of; **сиде́ть** (*impf*) **в четырёх ~х** to be cooped up indoors.

стена́ни|е (-я) *ср* groan.

стена́|ть (-ю) *несов неперех* to groan.

стенгазе́т|а (-ы) *ж* (= *стенна́я газе́та*) *newsletter displayed on wall in school or place of work.*

стенд (-а) *м* (*выставочный*) display stand; (*испытательный*) test-bed; (*для стрельбы*) rifle range.

сте́ндовый *прил*: **сте́ндовая стрельба́** target practice.

сте́н|ка (-ки; *gen pl* -ок) *ж уменьш от* **стена́**; (*комнаты, желудка, также* ФУТБОЛ) wall; (*разг: мебель*) wall unit; (*ящика*) side; **прижима́ть** (**прижа́ть** *perf*) **кого́-н к ~ке** (*разг*) to push sb to the wall.

стенно́й *прил* wall *опред*; **стенна́я ро́спись** mural.

стеногра́мм|а (-ы) *ж* shorthand record.

стенографи́р|овать (-ую; *perf* **стенографи́ровать** *или* **застенографи́ровать**) *несов перех* to take down in shorthand.

стенографи́ст (-а) *м* shorthand typist (*BRIT*), stenographer (*US*).

стенографи́ст|ка (-ки; *gen pl* -ок) *ж см* **стенографи́ст.**

стеногра́фи|я (-и) *ж* shorthand (*BRIT*), stenography (*US*).

сте́нок *сущ см* **сте́нка.**

стенокарди́|я (-и) *ж* angina.

сте́нопись (-и) *ж* mural painting.

сте́ньг|а (-и) *ж* (*МОР*) topmast.

степе́нный (-ен, -на, -но) *прил* sedate.

сте́пен|ь (-и; *gen pl* -е́й) *ж* (*также* ПРОСВЕЩ) degree; (*МАТ*) power; **в вы́сшей ~и** in the extreme; **до изве́стной** *или* **не́которой ~и** to some *или* a certain extent; **ожо́г пе́рвой** *итп* **~и** first *итп* degree burn.

степно́й *прил* steppe *опред*.

степ|ь (-и; *loc sg* -и́, *gen pl* -е́й) *ж* the steppe.

сте́рв|а (-ы) *ж* (*груб!*) bastard (*!*); (*: женщина*) bitch (*!*)

стервене́|ть (-ю; *perf* **остервене́ть**) *несов неперех* (*разг*) to get mad.

стервя́тник (-а) *м* carrion crow.

стерёг *итп несов см* **стере́чь.**

стерегу́ *итп несов см* **стере́чь.**

стереоза́пис|ь (-и) *ж* stereo recording.

стереозвуча́ни|е (-я) *ср* stereo (*sound*).

стереомагнитофо́н (-а) *м* stereo tape recorder.

стереопрои́грыватель (-я) *м* stereo record player.

стереосисте́м|а (-ы) *ж* stereo.

стереоти́п (-а) *м* (*ТИПОГ, перен*) stereotype.

стереоти́п|ный *прил* (-ен, -на, -но; *ответ, мышление итп*) stereotyped.

стере́ть (**сотру́, сотрёшь**; *pt* **стёр, стёрла, стёрло**, *impf* **стира́ть**) *сов перех* (*грязь, пыль, грим*) to wipe off; (*надпись, память, различия*) to erase; **стира́ть** (~ *perf*) **что-н/кого́-н в порошо́к** (*также перен*) to pulverize sth/sb; **стира́ть** (~ *perf*) **с лица́ земли́** to wipe off the face of the earth

▶ **стере́ться** (*impf* **стира́ться**) *сов возв* (*надпись, краска*) to be worn away; (*подошвы*) to wear down; (*перен: различия, границы*) to be erased; **стира́ться** (~**ся** *perf*) **в па́мяти** to become blurred.

стер|е́чь (-егу́, -ежёшь *итп*, -егу́т; *pt* -ёг, -егла́, -егло́) *несов перех* to watch over; (*подстерегать*) to lie in wait for.

стер́ж|ень (-ня) *м* rod; (*винта*) stem; (*ось*) pivot; (*шариковой ручки*) (ink) cartridge; (*перен: политики, романа*) backbone.

стержнево́й *прил* (*осевой*) pivoted; (*перен: вопрос, проблема*) crucial.

сте́ржня *итп сущ см* **сте́ржень.**

стери́лен *прил см* **стери́льный.**

стерилиза́тор (-а) *м* sterilizer.

стерилиза́ци|я (-и) *ж* sterilization.

стерилиз|ова́ть (-у́ю) (*не*)*сов перех* to sterilize.

стери́льный (-ен, -на, -ьно) *прил* sterile, sterilized.

сте́рлинг (-а) *м* (*ЭКОН*) sterling; **10 фу́нтов ~ов** 10 pounds sterling.

стерля́д|ь (-и; *gen pl* -ей) *ж* sterlet.

стерп|е́ть (-лю́, -ишь) *сов перех* to endure

▶ **стерпе́ться** *сов возв*: ~**ся с** +*instr* to learn to endure.

стёртый (-, -а, -о) *прил* (*надпись*) worn; (*монета*) effaced; (*перен: фразы*) hackneyed.

сте|са́ть (-шу́, -шешь; *impf* **стёсывать**) *сов перех* (*кору*) to strip off.

стесне́ни|е (-я) *ср* constraints *мн*; (*в груди*) constriction; (*смущение*) shyness.

стеснённый *прил* (*дыхание*) constricted; **в ~ых обстоя́тельствах** in financial straits.

стесни́телен *прил см* **стесни́тельный.**

стесни́тельност|ь (-и) *ж* shyness.

стесни́тельный (-ен, -ьна, -ьно) *прил* shy.

стесн|и́ть (-ю́, -и́шь) *сов от* **тесни́ть ♦** (*impf* **стесня́ть**) *перех* (*хозяев*) to inconvenience; (*дыхание*) to constrict; **стесня́ть** (~ *perf*) **кого́-н в расхо́дах** to restrict sb's spending.

стесня́|ться (-юсь; *perf* **постесня́ться**) *несов возв*: ~ (+*gen*) (*женщин, незнакомых*) to be shy (of); (+*infin*; *сказать, просить итп*) to be too

shy to do; ~ (*impf*) **пéред кем-н** to feel shy in sb's presence; **онá не ~ется в срéдствах** she won't stop at anything; **он не ~ется в выражéниях** he doesn't mince his words.
стёсыва|ть (-ю) *несов от* **стесáть**.
стетоскóп (-а) *м* stethoscope.
стечéни|е (-я) *ср* (*нарóда*) gathering; (*случайностей*) combination; ~ **обстоя́тельств** coincidence; **при большóм ~и нарóда** in front of a large number of people.
ст|ечь (*3sg* -ечёт, *3pl* -екýт, *pt* -ёк, -еклá, -еклó, *impf* **стекáть**) *сов непepex*: ~ (**с** +*gen*) to run down (from)
► **стéчься** (*impf* **стекáться**) *сов возв* (*ручьи, реки́*) to flow; (*лю́ди*) to congregate.
стешý *итп сов см* **стесáть**.
стíлен *прил см* **стíльный**.
стилизáци|я (-и) *ж* (*подражáние*) imitation; (*о произведéнии*) stylized work.
стилизóван|ный (-, -на, -но) *прил* stylized.
стилиз|овáть (-ýю) (*не*)*сов перех* to stylize.
стилисти́ческ|ий (-ая, -ое, -ие) *прил* (*приём*) stylistic.
стил|ь (-я) *м* style; (*летосчислéния*) calendar; **он в своём стíле** he's being his usual self; **6 ию́ня по стáрому/нóвому стíлю** 6th June Old Style/New Style.
стíльный (-ен, -ьна, -ьно) *прил* stylish; (*разг: причёска, одéжда*) snazzy.
стиля́г|а (-и) *м/ж* (*разг: пренебр*) fashion victim.
стíмул (-а) *м* incentive, stimulus (*мн* stimuli).
стимули́рование (-я) *ср* stimulation; **материáльное ~** financial incentive.
стимули́р|овать (-ую) (*не*)*сов перех* to stimulate; (*рабóту, прогрéсс*) to encourage; ~ (*impf/perf*) **рост экóномики** to encourage economic growth.
стимуля́ци|я (-и) *ж* stimulation; (*рóдов*) induction.
стипендиáльный *прил*: ~ **фонд** scholarship fund; **стипендиáльная комíссия** grants committee.
стипéнди|я (-и) *ж* (*государственная*) grant; (*за особые достижéния*) scholarship.
стипль-чéз (-а) *м* (*СПОРТ*) steeplechase.
стирáльный *прил*: ~ **порошóк** washing powder; **стирáльная машíна** washing machine.
стирáни|е (-я) *ср* (*надписи*) erasure; (*различий*) erosion.
стíраный *прил* washed.
стирá|ть (-ю) *несов от* **стерéть** ♦ (*perf* **вы́стирать** *или* **постирáть**) *перех* to wash
► **стирáться** *несов от* **стерéться**.
стíр|ка (-ки; *gen pl* -ок) *ж* washing; **отдавáть (отдáть** *perf*) **что-н в ~ку** to put sth in for a service wash.
стíсн|уть (-у, -ешь; *impf* **стíскивать**) *сов перех*

(*в руке́, в зубáх*) to clench; (*подлеж: толпá*) to squeeze; **стíскивать** (~ *perf*) **когó-н в объя́тиях** to clutch sb in one's arms; ~ (*perf*) **зýбы** (*перен*) to grit one's teeth.
стих (-á) *м* verse.
стихá|ть (-ю) *несов от* **стíхнуть**.
стих|í (-ов) *мн* (*поэ́зия*) poetry *ед*; **ромáн в ~áх** novel in verse.
стихíйный (-ен, -йна, -йно) *прил* (*сила*) elemental; (*развитие, становлéние*) uncontrolled; (*протéст, демонстрáции*) spontaneous; **стихíйное бéдствие** natural disaster.
стихí|я (-и) *ж* (*водá, огонь итп*) element; (*ры́нка, инфля́ции*) natural force; **борóться** (*impf*) **со ~ей** to do battle with the elements; **быть** (*impf*) **в своéй ~и** to be in one's element; **бíзнес - егó ~** business is his forte.
стíх|нуть (-ну, -нешь; *pt* -, -ла, -ло, *impf* **стихáть**) *сов непepex* to die down.
стихосложéни|е (-я) *ср* versification.
стихотворéни|е (-я) *ср* poem.
стихотвóрный *прил* (*произведéние*) poetic; (*парóдия*) in verse; **стихотвóрный размéр** metre (*in poetry*).
стлать (стелю́, стéлешь; *perf* **постлáть**) *несов перех* = **стелить**
► **стлáться** *несов возв* = **стели́ться**.
сто (стá; *см* Table 30) *чис* one hundred; (*разг: мнóго*): ~ +*gen* hundreds of; ~ **книг/столóв** a hundred books/tables; **óколо стá** about a hundred; ~ **пéрвый** hundred and first; **я увéрен на ~ процéнтов** I am one hundred percent sure; **мнóго сот** many hundreds; **нéсколько сот** several hundred.
стог (-а; *loc sg* -ý, *nom pl* -á) *м*: ~ **сéна** haystack.
стограммóвый *прил* (*гиря*) one-hundred-gram; ~ **стакáн** ≈ shot glass.
стóек *сущ см* **стóйка** ♦ *прил см* **стóйкий**.
стóимостн|ый *прил* (*ЭКОН*): ~**ые показáтели/отношéния** cost indices/relations.
стóимост|ь (-и) *ж* cost; (*цéнность*) value; ~ **по торгóвым кни́гам** (*КОММ*) book value; ~ **и фрахт** cost and freight.
стó|ить (-ю, -ишь) *несов* (*не*)*перех* (+*acc или* +*gen*; *дéнег*) to cost; (*усилий, трудá итп*) to take ♦ *непepex*: ~ +*gen* (*внимáния, любви́*) to be worth ♦ *безл*: ~**ить** +*infin* to be worth doing; **кни́га ~ит 10 рублéй** the book costs 10 roubles; **дом ~ит большíе дéньги** *или* **больши́х дéнег** the house costs a lot of money; **на э́ту вы́ставку ~ит пойтí** it is worth going to see this exhibition; **мне ничегó не ~ит сдéлать э́то** it's no trouble for me to do it; **спасíбо! – не ~ит** thank you! – don't mention it; **чегó ~ят твои́ обещáния!** what are your promises worth?; ~**ит (тóлько) захотéть/постарáться** (*об усло́вии*) you only have to wish/try; ~**ит мне (тóлько)**

войти́ в дом, как сра́зу начина́ет звони́ть телефо́н the minute I come through the door the phone starts ringing.

стои́чески *нареч* stoically.

стои́ческий (**-ая, -ое, -ие**) *прил* stoical.

стой(те) *несов см* **стоя́ть**.

сто́йбище (**-а**) *ср* (*кочевников*) nomad camp.

сто́йка (**-йки**; *gen pl* **-ек**) *ж* (*положение тела*) stance; (*собаки*) pose; (*подпорка*) prop; (*прилавок*) counter; (*воротник*) stand-up collar; **стоя́ть** (*impf*) **по ~йке сми́рно/во́льно** to stand to attention/at ease; **сто́йка на рука́х** handstand; **сто́йка на голове́** headstand.

сто́йкий (**-йкая, -йкое, -йкие; -ек, -йка, -йко**) *прил* (*человек, характер*) steadfast, resilient; (*краска, материал*) durable, hard-wearing; (*запах*) stubborn.

сто́йко *нареч* steadfastly.

сто́йкость (**-и**) *ж* (*см прил*) resilience; durability; stubborness.

сто́йло (**-а**) *ср* stall (*in a stable*).

стоймя́ *нареч* upright.

сто́йче *сравн прил от* **сто́йкий** ♦ *сравн нареч от* **сто́йко**.

сток (**-а**) *м* (*действие*) drainage; (*приспособление*) drain.

Стокго́льм (**-а**) *м* Stockholm.

стокра́тный *прил* hundredfold.

стол (**-а́**) *м* table; (*письменный*) desk; (*еда*) food; **а́дресный ~** *residents' registration office*; **кру́глый ~** round table (*fig*); **сади́ться (сесть** *perf*) **за ~** to sit down at the table; **за ~о́м** at table; **убира́ть (убра́ть** *perf*) **со ~а́** to clear the table; **встава́ть (встать** *perf*) **из-за ~а́** to get up from the table; **стол нахо́док** lost property (office); **стол перегово́ров** negotiating table.

столб (**-а́**) *м* (*пограничный, указательный*) post; (*телеграфный*) pole; (*перен: пыли, дыма*) cloud.

столбене́ть (**-ю**; *perf* **остолбене́ть**) *несов неперех* to be rooted to the spot.

столбе́ц (**-ца́**) *м* column (*on page*).

сто́лбик (**-а**) *м уменьш от* **столб**; (*бумаг*) ream; (*цифр*) column; **рту́тный ~** mercury column; **~ом** in a column.

столбня́к (**-а́**) *м* tetanus.

столбово́й *прил*: **~ дворяни́н** (*ист*) *a member of the old Russian nobility*; **столбова́я доро́га** (*ист*) highway.

столбца́ *итп сущ см* **столбе́ц**.

столе́тие (**-я**) *ср* (*срок*) century; (*годовщина*): **~ +gen** centenary of.

столе́тний (**-яя, -ее, -ие**) *прил* (*период*) hundred-year; (*старик, дерево*) hundred-year-old.

столе́тник (**-а**) *м* (*БОТ*) aloe.

сто́лечко *нареч* (*разг*) = **сто́лько**.

сто́лик (**-а**) *м уменьш от* **стол**; (*в ресторане, в кафе*) table; **туале́тный ~** dressing table.

столи́ца (**-ы**) *ж* capital (city).

столи́чный *прил* (*газеты, жители, театры*)

of the capital; **столи́чный го́род** capital city.

столкнове́ние (**-я**) *ср* clash; (*машин, судов*) collision; **вооружённое ~** armed clash.

столкну́ть (**-у́, -ёшь**; *impf* **ста́лкивать**) *сов перех*: **~** (**с +gen**) to push off; (*сблизить толчком*) to push together; (*подлеж: случай, судьба*) to bring together; **~** (*perf*) **кого́-н в во́ду** to push sb into the water

▸ **столкну́ться** (*impf* **ста́лкиваться**) *сов возв* (*машины, поезда*) to collide; (*интересы, характеры*) to clash; (*встретиться*): **~ся с +instr** (*встречаться*) to come into contact with; (*случайно*) to bump или run into; (*с трудностями, с непониманием*) to encounter; **я ста́лкивался с ним по рабо́те** I have come into contact with him through work.

столкова́ться (**-у́юсь**; *impf* **столко́вываться**) *сов возв*: **~** (**с +instr**) to come to an agreement (with).

столо́вая (**-ой**; *decl like adj*) *ж* (*заведение*) canteen; (*комната*) dining room.

столо́вка (**-ки**; *gen pl* **-ок**) *ж* (*разг*) canteen.

столо́вый *прил* (*мебель, часы*) dining room *опред*; **столо́вая ло́жка** (*для супа*) tablespoon; **столо́вая соль** table salt; **столо́вое вино́** table wine; **столо́вый серви́з** dinner service.

столп (**-а́**) *м* (*обычно мн: перен*) pillar.

столпи́ться (*3sg* **-и́тся**, *3pl* **-я́тся**) *сов возв* to crowd.

столпотворе́ние (**-я**) *ср* chaos.

столь *нареч* so; **~ же ... ско́лько ... as ... as ...**.

сто́лько *нареч* (*об исчисляемом количестве*) so many; (*о неисчисляемом количестве*) so much ♦ (**-их**) *мест* (*см нареч*) this many; this much; **я не хочу́ дава́ть ему́ ~ де́нег** I don't want to give him that much money; **она́ ~ пережила́!** she has been through so much!; **где ты был ~ вре́мени?** where have you been all this time?; **у меня́ ~ (же) де́нег/пробле́м, ско́лько (и) у тебя́** I've got as much money/as many problems as you; **он не ~ глуп, ско́лько лени́в** he is not so much stupid as lazy.

сто́лько-то *нареч* (*об исчисляемом количестве*) X number of; (*об неисчисляемом количестве*) X amount of; **~ сде́лано, ~ оста́лось** this much has been done and this much is left.

столя́р (**-а́**) *м* joiner.

столя́рничать (**-ю**) *несов неперех* (*разг*) to do carpentry.

столя́рный *прил*: **~ая мастерка́я** joiner's; **столя́рное де́ло** joinery; **столя́рные инструме́нты** carpentry tools; **столя́рный клей** wood glue.

стомати́т (**-а**) *м* mouth ulcer.

стомато́лог (**-а**) *м* dental surgeon.

стоматологи́ческий (**-ая, -ое, -ие**) *прил* dental; **стоматологи́ческий кабине́т/поликли́ника** dental surgery/hospital.

стоматоло́гия (**-и**) *ж* dentistry.

стометро́вка (**-ки**; *gen pl* **-ок**) *ж* (*разг: СПОРТ*) the hundred metres (*BRIT*) *или* meters (*US*).

стометро́в|ый *прил:* ~**ая диста́нция** one hundred metres (*BRIT*) *или* meters (*US*).

стон (-а) *м* (*см глаг*) groan; moan.

стон|а́ть (-у́, -ешь) *несов неперех* to groan; (*перен: жаловаться*) to moan.

стоп *межд* stop.

стоп|а́ (-ы́; *nom pl* -ы) *ж* (*в стихах*) foot; (*nom pl* -ы́; *АНАТ*) sole; **идти́ (пойти́** *perf*) **по чьим-н** ~**м** to follow in sb's footsteps.

стоп|и́ть (-лю́, -ишь; *impf* **ста́пливать**) *сов перех* (*дрова*) to burn up.

сто́п|ка (-ки; *gen pl* -ок) *ж* (*бумаг, писем*) pile; (*стаканчик*) glass (*for vodka etc*).

стоп-кра́н (-а) *м* emergency handle (*on train*).

стоплю́ *сов см* **стопи́ть**.

сто́пок *сущ см* **сто́пка**.

сто́пор (-а) *м* (*ТЕХ*) lock.

сто́пор|ить (-ю, -ишь; *perf* **застопорить**) *несов перех* (*машину*) to stop; (*дело, работу*) to hold up; (*фиксировать*) to lock.

стопроце́нтный *прил* one-hundred percent; (*разг: негодяй, лгун итп*) out-and-out.

стоп|та́ть (-чу́, -чешь; *impf* **ста́птывать**) *сов перех* to wear out.

▸ **стопта́ться** (*impf* **ста́птываться**) *сов возв* to wear out.

сторг|ова́ть(ся) (-у́ю(сь)) *сов от* **торгова́ть(ся)**.

стори́цей *нареч:* **возда́ть** ~ **кому́-н** to reward sb in full.

сто́рож (-а; *nom pl* -а́, *gen pl* -е́й) *м* watchman (*мн* watchmen).

сторожево́й *прил:* ~ **пост** lookout post; **сторожева́я вы́шка** watchtower; **сторожево́й ка́тер** patrol boat.

сторо́жек *сущ см* **сторо́жка**.

сторож|и́ть (-у́, -и́шь) *несов перех* (*дом, сад*) to guard; (*зверя, вора*) to lie in wait for.

сторо́ж|ка (-ки; *gen pl* -ек) *ж* hut.

сторон|а́ (-ы́; *acc sg* -ону, *dat sg* -оне́, *nom pl* -оны, *gen pl* -о́н, *dat pl* -она́м) *ж* side; (*направление: левая, правая*) direction; (*страна*) land; **стоя́ть** (*impf*) **в** ~**оне́ от** +*gen* to stand apart from; **в** ~**оне́** a little way off; **держа́ться** (*impf*) **в** ~**оне́** to keep one's distance; **в сто́рону** +*gen* towards; **смотре́ть (посмотре́ть** *perf*) **в сто́рону** to look away; **на** ~**ону** (*разг: продавать*) on the side; **подраба́тывать** (*impf*) **на** ~**оне́** (*разг*) to work on the side; **брать (взять** *perf*) **кого́-н со** ~**оны́** to bring sb in from outside (*fig*); **со** ~**оны́** +*gen* from; **со** ~**оны́ ма́тери/отца́** on one's mother's/father's side; **э́то о́чень любе́зно с Ва́шей** ~**оны́** that is very good of you; **с одно́й** ~**оны́ ... с друго́й** ~**оны́ ...** on the one hand ... on the other hand ...; **принима́ть (приня́ть** *perf*) **чью-н сто́рону** to take sb's side; **встава́ть**

(**встать** *perf*) **на чью-н сто́рону** to come out in sb's defence (*BRIT*) *или* defense (*US*); **быть** (*impf*) **на чьей-н** ~**оне́** to be on sb's side; **смотре́ть** (*impf*) **по** ~**м** to look around; (*отвлекаться*) to let one's attention wander.

стор|они́ться (-оню́сь, -о́нишься; *perf* **посторони́ться**) *несов возв* (*дать дорогу*) to make way; (*избегать*): ~ +*gen* to avoid.

сторо́нн|ий (-яя, -ее, -ие) *прил* outside *опред*.

сторо́нник (-а) *м* supporter, advocate.

сторо́нниц|а (-ы) *ж см* **сторо́нник**.

сторубл|ёвый *прил* (*ассигнация*) one-hundred-rouble; (*о стоимости*) worth one hundred roubles.

стоск|ова́ться (-у́юсь) *сов возв:* ~ **по** +*dat* to miss.

сточ|и́ть (-у́, -ишь; *impf* **ста́чивать**) *сов перех* to smooth down.

сто́чн|ый *прил:* ~**ая кана́ва** gutter (*in street*); **сто́чная труба́** drainpipe; **сто́чные во́ды** effluent; **сто́чный жёлоб** gutter (*on roof*).

стошн|и́ть (-и́т) *сов от* **тошни́ть**.

стоя́ *нареч* standing up.

стоя́ни|е (-я) *ср* standing.

стоя́н|ка (-ки; *gen pl* -ок) *ж* (*поезда, судна*) stop; (*автомобилей*) car park (*BRIT*), parking lot (*US*); (*геологов, путешественников*) camp; (*первобытного человека*) site; **стоя́нка такси́** taxi rank.

сто|я́ть (-ю́, -и́шь; *imper* **сто́й(те)**) *несов неперех* to stand; (*находиться*) to be; (*полк*) to be stationed; (*бездействовать*) to stand idle; (*сохраняться: цветы*) to last; (*: продукты*) to keep; (*perf* **постоя́ть**; *защищать*): ~ **за** +*acc* (*за друга, за идею*) to stand up for; **пе́ред на́ми** ~**и́т тру́дная зада́ча/интере́сная пробле́ма** we are faced with a difficult task/interesting problem; **на бла́нке** ~**и́т по́дпись дире́ктора** the document bears the director's signature; **по́езд** ~**и́т здесь 15 мину́т** the train stops here for 15 minutes; **ча́йник** ~**и́т на плите́** the kettle is on the stove; **цветы́** ~**я́т в ва́зе** the flowers are in the vase; **посу́да** ~**и́т в шкафу́** the crockery is in the cupboard; ~**я́ла весна́/о́сень** it was spring/autumn (*BRIT*) *или* fall (*US*); **всё ле́то** ~**я́ла жара́** it was hot all through the summer; **в до́ме** ~**я́л шум/смех** the house was full of noise/laughter; ~ (*impf*) **у вла́сти** to be in power; ~ (*impf*) **на свои́х пози́циях** to stand one's ground; **он** ~**и́т на своём** he refuses to budge.

стоя́ч|ий (-ая, -ее, -ие) *прил* (*предложение*) standing *опред*; (*воротник*) stand-up; (*вода*) stagnant.

стоя́щ|ий (-ая, -ее, -ие) *прил* (*дело, предложение*) worthwhile; (*человек*) worthy; (*вещь*) useful.

стр. *сокр* (= **страни́ца**) pg. (= *page*).

страви́ть (-лю́, -ишь) *сов от* **трави́ть** ◆ (*impf* **стра́вливать**) *перех* to set on; **он их ~и́л** he set them on each other.

страда́ (-ы́) *ж* harvesting.

страда́лец (-ьца) *м* martyr.

страда́лица (-ы) *ж см* **страда́лец**.

страда́льца *итп сущ см* **страда́лец**.

страда́льческий (-ая, -ое, -ие) *прил* martyred.

страда́ние (-я) *ср* suffering.

страда́тельный *прил* (*линг*): ~ **зало́г** passive voice.

страда́ть (-ю) *несов неперех* to suffer; (*дисциплина, грамотность итп*) to be poor; (*сочувствовать*): ~ **за** +*acc* to suffer for; (*потерпеть ущерб*): ~ **от** +*gen* (*от засухи, от инфляции итп*) to suffer as a result of; (*perf* **пострада́ть**; *поплатиться*) to suffer; ~ (*impf*) (**от** +*gen*) (*от боли, от голода*) to suffer; ~ (*impf*) +*instr* (*болезнью, самомнением*) to suffer from; ~ (*impf*) **от любви́** to be lovesick.

страж (-а) *м* guardian.

стра́жа (-и) *ж собир* guard; **быть** (*impf*) *или* **стоя́ть** (*impf*) **на ~е** +*gen* to guard; **под ~ей** in custody; **брать** (**взять** *perf*) **кого́-н под ~у** to take sb into custody.

страна́ (-ы́; *nom pl* **-ы**) *ж* country; **стра́ны све́та** cardinal points (*on compass*).

стра́нен *прил см* **стра́нный**.

страни́ца (-ы) *ж* (*также перен*) page; (*перен: истории, жизни*) chapter; **на ~х газе́т** in the papers.

стра́нник (-а) *м* wanderer; (*РЕЛ*) pilgrim.

стра́нница (-ы) *ж см* **стра́нник**.

стра́нно *нареч* strangely ◆ *как сказ* that is strange *или* odd; **он ~ вы́глядит** he looks strange; **~, что её ещё нет** it is strange *или* odd that she isn't here yet; **мне ~, что ...** I find it strange that ....

стра́нность (-и) *ж* strangeness; (*обычно мн: человека, поведения*) oddity.

стра́нный (-ен, -на́, -но) *прил* strange; **~ное де́ло** that's strange *или* odd.

странове́дение (-я) *ср* national studies *мн*.

стра́нствие (-я) *ср* wandering.

стра́нствовать (-ую) *несов неперех* to wander.

Стра́сбург (-а) *м* Strasbourg.

стра́стен *прил см* **стра́стный**.

страстно́й *прил*: **~а́я неде́ля** Holy Week.

стра́стность (-и) *ж* passion.

стра́стный (-ен, -на́, -но) *прил* passionate; (*коллекционер итп*) ardent.

страсть (-и) *ж* passion; (*разг: ужас*) horror; **стра́сти разгоре́лись** passions were running high; **~ к му́зыке/кни́гам** a passion for music/books.

страте́г (-а) *м* strategist.

стратеги́ческий (-ая, -ое, -ие) *прил* strategic.

страте́гия (-и) *ж* strategy.

стратосфе́ра (-ы) *ж* stratosphere.

стра́ус (-а) *м* ostrich.

стра́усовый *прил* ostrich *опред*.

страх (-а) *м* fear; (*разг: обычно мн: страшное событие*) horror; **~ за дете́й/за бли́зких** fear for one's children/loved ones; **~ сме́рти/ разоблаче́ния** fear of death/exposure; **~ пе́ред неизве́стным** fear of the unknown; **со стра́ху** in fright; **нача́льник держа́л их в стра́хе** they lived in fear of their boss; **под стра́хом сме́рти** on pain of death; **на свой ~ (и риск)** at one's own risk.

страхова́ние (-я) *ср* insurance; **~ от** +*gen* insurance against; **госуда́рственное ~** national insurance (*BRIT*); **страхова́ние жи́зни** life insurance; **страхова́ние иму́щества** property insurance.

страхова́тель (-я) *м person taking out insurance*.

страхова́ть (-у́ю) *несов перех* (*гимнаста*) to stand by (*to prevent sb from falling*); (*perf* **застрахова́ть**): ~ (**от** +*gen*) (*имущество, автомобиль*) to insure (against); (*от неожиданностей*) to protect (against)

▶ **страхова́ться** (*perf* **застрахова́ться**) *несов возв*: **~ся** (**от** +*gen*) to insure o.s. (against); (*от неожиданностей*) to protect o.s (from).

страхо́вка (-ки; *gen pl* **-ок**) *ж* insurance; **для ~ки** to be on the safe side.

страхово́й *прил* (*фирма, агент*) insurance *опред*; **~ бро́кер** insurance broker; **страхово́й взнос** *или* **страхова́я пре́мия** insurance premium; **страхово́й по́лис** insurance policy.

страхо́вок *сущ см* **страхо́вка**.

страхо́вщик (-а) *м* insurer.

стра́шен *прил см* **стра́шный**.

страши́ла (-ы) *м/ж* = **страши́лище**.

страши́лище (-а; *gen pl* -) *ср* (*разг*) fright.

страши́ть (-у́, -и́шь) *несов перех* to frighten, scare

▶ **страши́ться** *несов возв*: **~ся** +*gen* to be frightened *или* scared of.

стра́шно *нареч* (*кричать*) in a frightening way; (*разг: усталый, довольный*) terribly ◆ *как сказ* it's frightening; **мне ~** I'm frightened *или* scared; **~ поду́мать** it's frightening to think; **он ~ дово́лен собо́й** (*разг*) he's awfully *или* terribly pleased with himself; **она́ ~ уста́ла** (*разг*) she's awfully *или* terribly tired; **она́ ~ лю́бит болта́ть** (*разг*) she really likes to chat.

стра́шный (-ен, -на́, -но) *прил* terrible, awful; (*фильм, сон, путь*) terrifying; **ничего́ ~ного** it doesn't matter.

стре́жень (-ня) *м* deep part (*of river*).

стрекоза́ (-озы́; *nom pl* **-о́зы**) *ж* dragonfly (*мн* dragonflies); (*ребёнок*) fidget.

стрекота́ть (-очу́, -о́чешь) *несов неперех* to chirp.

стрела́ (-ы́; *nom pl* **-ы**) *ж* (*для стрельбы*) arrow; (*крана, итп*) (*поезд*) express (train).

стреле́ц (-ьца́) *м* Strelets (*regular soldier of special regiment in 16th-17th century*); (*созвездие*): **С~** Sagittarius.

стрéл|**ка** (-ки; *gen pl* -ок) *ж уменьш от* **стрела**; (*часов*) hand; (*компаса, барометра*) needle; (*знак*) arrow; (*железнодорожная*) switch; (*ГЕО*) spit; (*лука*) shoot.

стрелка *итп сущ см* **стрелóк**.

стрелкóвый *прил*: ~ **полк** infantry regiment; **стрелкóвый спорт** shooting.

стрéлок *сущ см* **стрéлка**.

стрел|**óк** (-ка) *м* (*ВОЕН*) rifleman (*мн* riflemen); **он хорóший** ~ he is a good shot.

стрéлочник (-а) *м* signalman (*мн* signalmen).

стрéлочниц|**а** (-ы) *ж см* **стрéлочник**.

стрельб|**á** (-ы́) *ж* shooting, firing.

стрéльбище (-а) *ср* shooting range.

стрельцá *итп сущ см* **стрелéц**.

стрéльчатый *прил* (*окна, свод*) arched.

стрéляный *прил* (*дичь*) shot *опред*; ~ **патрóн** spent cartridge; ~ **солдáт** *soldier who has been under fire*; ~ **воробéй** (*разг*) old hand.

стреля́|**ть** (-ю) *несов неперех*: ~ (**в** +*acc*) (*в цель, во врага*) to shoot (at); (*мотор*) to backfire ♦ *перех* (*убивать: птиц*) to shoot; (*выпрашивать*) to cadge; ~ (*impf*) **из ружья́/пу́шки** to fire a rifle/canon; **у меня́ ~ет в боку́** I have a shooting pain in my side

▶ **стреля́ться** *несов возв* (*самоубийца*) to shoot o.s.; (*на дуэли*) ~**ся с** +*instr* to fight a duel with.

стремглáв *нареч* headlong.

стрéмени *итп сущ см* **стрéмя**.

стреми́тельно *нареч* (*мчаться*) headlong; (*меняться*) rapidly.

стреми́тельность (-и) *ж* (*движений*) swiftness; (*изменений*) rapidity.

стреми́тельный *прил* (*движение, бег, атака*) swift; (*человек*) energetic; (*изменения*) rapid.

стреми́ться (-лю́сь, -и́шься) *несов возв*: ~ **в** +*acc* (*в университет, на родину*) to want to go to; (*добиваться*): ~ **к** +*dat* (*к славе, к добру, к правде*) to strive for.

стремлéни|**е** (-я) *ср*: ~ (**к** +*dat*) striving (for).

стремлю́сь *несов см* **стреми́ться**.

стремни́н|**а** (-ы) *ж* rapid (*in river*).

стрéм|**я** (-ени; *как* **врéмя**; *см* **Table 4**) *ср* stirrup.

стремя́н|**ка** (-ки; *gen pl* -ок) *ж* step-ladder.

стрептокóкк (-а) *м* streptococcus.

стресс (-а) *м* stress.

стрéссовый *прил* (*состояние*) stressed; (*ситуация, нагрузки*) stressful.

стриг(ся) *итп несов см* **стричь(ся)**.

стригу́(сь) *итп несов см* **стричь(ся)**.

стриж (-á) *м* swift.

стри́жек *сущ см* **стри́жка**.

стри́женый *прил* shorn; (*трава*) cut; (*мальчик*) short-haired.

стри́ж|**ка** (-ки; *gen pl* -ек) *ж* (*см глаг*) cutting; shearing; mowing; pruning; (*причёска*) haircut.

стрипти́з (-а) *м* striptease.

стрихни́н (-а) *м* strychnine.

стри́|**чь** (-гу́, -жёшь *итп*, -гу́т; *pt* -г, -гла, -гло, *perf* **постри́чь** *или* **остри́чь**) *несов перех* (*волосы, траву*) to cut; (*овцу*) to shear; (*газон*) to mow; (*кусты*) to prune; ~ (**постри́чь** *perf*) **когó-н** to cut sb's hair; ~ (*impf*) **всех под одну́ гребёнку** to tar everyone with the same brush

▶ **стри́чься** (*perf* **постри́чься** *или* **остри́чься**) *несов возв* (*остричь себе волосы*) to cut one's hair; (*в парикмахерской*) to have one's hair cut; (*no perf; носить короткую стрижку*) to wear one's hair short.

стрóганый *прил* planed.

строгá|**ть** (-ю; *perf* **вы́строгать**) *несов перех* to plane.

стрóгий (-ая, -ое, -ие; -, -á, -о) *прил* strict; (*красота, причёска, наказание, выговор*) severe; (*меры*) harsh; (*черты лица*) regular.

стрóго *нареч* (*воспитывать*) strictly; (*наказать, сказать*) severely; ~-**нáстрого** (*разг*) very strictly; ~ **говоря́** strictly speaking.

стрóгость (-и) *ж* (*см прил*) strictness; severity; harshness; regularity; (*обычно мн: строгие порядки*) harsh regulation.

строевóй *прил* (*ВОЕН: командир*) line *опред*; **строевáя подготóвка** drill; **строевáя часть** line unit; **строевóй лес** timber forest; **строевóй шаг** goose step.

стрóек *сущ см* **стрóйка**.

стрóен *прил см* **стрóйный**.

строéни|**е** (-я) *ср* (*здание*) building; (*организации, вещества*) structure.

стрóже *сравн прил от* **стрóгий** ♦ *сравн нареч от* **стрóго**.

стрóител|**ь** (-я) *м* builder; (+*gen; нового общества*) creator of.

строи́тельный *прил* building *опред*, construction *опред*; **строи́тельный учáсток** building site; **строи́тельные материáлы** building materials.

строи́тельств|**о** (-а) *ср* (*зданий*) building, construction; (*нового общества*) building.

стрó|**ить** (-ю, -ишь; *perf* **вы́строить** *или* **постро́ить**) *несов перех* (*дом, дорогу, мост*) to build, construct; (*perf* **постро́ить**; *общество, быт, семью*) to create; (*фразу, мысль*) to compose; (*план, догадку*) to make; (*полк, отряд*) to draw up; ~ (**постро́ить** *perf*) **ромáн на чём-н** to base a novel on sth; ~ (**состро́ить** *perf*) (**из себя́**) **дуракá** to make o.s. out to be a fool; ~ (**состро́ить** *perf*) **глáзки комý-н** to make eyes at sb; ~ (**состро́ить** *perf*) **гримáсы** to make *или* pull faces

▶ **стрóиться** (*perf* **постро́иться**) *несов возв* to build o.s. a house; (*perf* **вы́строиться**; *солдаты, пленные*) to form up; (*no perf*): ~**ся на** +*prp* (*сюжет, роман*) to be based on.

стрó|**й** (-я) *м* (*социальный*) system; (*языка, предложения*) structure; (*loc sg* -ю́; *ВОЕН*:

шеренга) line; (: *походный, боевой*) formation;
(: *действующие войска*) ranks мн; **входи́ть**
(**войти́** *perf*) в ~ (*завод*) to come into operation;
вводи́ть (**ввести́** *perf*) **что-н в** ~ (*завод*) to put
sth into operation; **выводи́ть** (**вы́вести** *perf*)
что-н из стро́я (*танк, машину*) to put sth out of
commission; **выходи́ть** (**вы́йти** *perf*) **из стро́я**
to fall out; (*перен*) to break down; ~ **мы́шления**
way of thinking.

стро́йка (-йки; *gen pl* -ек) ж (*здания*) building;
(*место*) building *или* construction site.

стройматериа́л|ы (-ов) мн сокр (=
строи́тельные материа́лы) building materials
мн.

стро́йный (-ен, -йна́, -йно) прил (*фигура*)
shapely; (*человек*) well-built; (*ряд, шеренга*)
orderly; (*речь, фраза*) well-constructed; (*пение*)
harmonious.

строк|а́ (-и́; *nom pl* -и, *dat pl* -а́м) ж (*в тексте*)
line; **кра́сная** ~ new paragraph; **чита́ть** (*impf*)
ме́жду строк to read between the lines.

стро́н|уться (-усь, -ешься) *сов возв* to start
moving.

строп (-а) м sling.

стропи́л|о (-а) *ср* beam, rafter.

стропти́вый (-, -а, -о) прил headstrong.

строф|а́ (-ы́; *nom pl* -ы, *dat pl* -а́м) ж stanza.

стро́чек *сущ см* **стро́чка**.

строч|и́ть (-у́, -и́шь; *perf* **прострочи́ть**) несов
перех (*рукав, подол*) to stitch; (*perf* **настрочи́ть**;
сочинение, статью) to scribble; (*no perf; перен*:
из автомата) to fire away.

стро́ч|ка (-ки; *gen pl* -ек) ж уменьш от **строка́**;
(*шов*) stitch.

строчн|о́й прил: ~**а́я бу́ква** small *или* lower
case letter.

струга́|ть (-ю; *perf* **вы́стругать**) несов перех =
строга́ть.

стру́ек *сущ см* **стру́йка**.

стру́ж|ка (-ки; *gen pl* -ек) ж shaving (*of wood,
metal etc*).

стру|и́ться (*3sg* -и́тся, *3pl* -я́тся) несов возв
(*вода, ручей*) to stream; (*пот, дым*) to pour.

стру́й|ка (-йки; *gen pl* -ек) ж trickle.

стру́йный прил: ~ **при́нтер** inkjet printer.

структу́р|а (-ы) ж structure.

структурали́зм (-а) м structuralism.

структу́рный прил structural.

струн|а́ (-ы́; *nom pl* -ы) ж (*скрипки, ракетки*)
string; (*перен: поэтическая*) streak.

стру́н|ка (-ки; *gen pl* -ок) ж string; **стать** (*perf*) *или*
вытя́гиваться (**вы́тянуться** *perf*) **в** ~**ку** to
stand to attention; **ходи́ть** (*impf*) **по** ~**ке у кого́-н**
или **пе́ред кем-н** to be under sb's thumb.

стру́нный прил (*инструмент*) stringed;
стру́нный кварте́т string quartet.

стру́нок *сущ см* **стру́нка**.

струп (-а; *nom pl* -ья, *gen pl* -ьев) м scab.

стру́|сить (-шу, -сишь) *сов от* **тру́сить**.

струхн|у́ть (-у́, -ёшь) *сов неперех* (*разг*) to get a
fright.

стручка́ *итп сущ см* **стручо́к**.

стручко́вый прил: ~ **пе́рец** chilli; **стручко́вая
фасо́ль** runner beans мн; **стручко́вый горо́х**
peas мн in the pod.

стручо́к (-ка́) м pod.

стру́шу *сов см* **стру́сить**.

стру|я́ (-и́; *nom pl* -и) ж (*воды, воздуха*) stream;
(*перен: сатирическая, бодрая*) streak; **попа́сть**
(*perf*) **в** ~**ю́** (*перен*) to fit in.

стря́па|ть (-ю; *perf* **состря́пать**) несов перех
(*разг: еду*) to cook; (: *рассказ, стихи*) to cobble
together.

стряпн|я́ (-и́) ж (*разг*) cooking; (*перен*) rubbish.

стряс|ти́ (-у́, -ёшь; *pt* -, -ла́, -ло́, *impf* **стряса́ть**)
сов перех to shake off

▶ **стрясти́сь** *сов возв* (*разг*) to happen; **с ним
~ла́сь беда́** he's in trouble; **что там** ~**ло́сь?**
what happened here?

стряхн|у́ть (-у́, -ёшь; *impf* **стря́хивать**) *сов
перех* (*также перен*) to shake off.

ст.с *сокр* (= **ста́рого сти́ля**) OS (= *Old Style*).

ст.ст. *сокр* = **ст.с.**

студене́|ть (*3sg* -ет, *3pl* -ют) несов неперех
(*заливное*) to gel.

студени́стый (-, -а, -о) прил gelatinous.

студе́нт (-а) м student.

студе́нт|ка (-ки; *gen pl* -ок) ж см **студе́нт**.

студе́нческ|ий (-ая, -ое, -ие) прил student
опред; **студе́нческий биле́т** student card.

студе́нчеств|о (-а) *ср* student days мн ♦ *собир*
(*студенты*) students мн.

студёный (-, -а, -о) прил icy cold.

сту́д|ень (-ня) м jellied meat.

студи́ек *сущ см* **студи́йка**.

студи́ец (-йца) м student (*at art or drama
school*).

студи́й|ка (-йки; *gen pl* -ек) ж см **студи́ец**.

студи́йца *итп сущ см* **студи́ец**.

студ|и́ть (-жу́, -дишь; *perf* **остуди́ть**) несов
перех to cool.

сту́ди|я (-и) ж studio; (*школа*) school (*for actors,
dancers, artists etc*); (*мастерская*) workshop.

сту́дня *итп сущ см* **сту́день**.

стуж|а (-и) ж severe cold.

стужу́ несов см **студи́ть**.

стук (-а) м (*в дверь*) knock; (*машин, падающего
предмета*) thud; (*сердца*) thump; **входи́ть**
(**войти́** *perf*) **без сту́ка** to enter without
knocking.

сту́ка|ть(ся) (-ю(сь)) несов от **сту́кнуть(ся)**.

стука́ч (-а́) м (*разг: пренебр*) grass (*informer*).

сту́кн|уть (-у, -ешь) *сов неперех* (*в дверь, в
окно́*) to knock; (*по столу*) to bang; (*impf*
сту́кать; *разг: ударить*) to knock ♦ *безл* (*no
impf*): **мне** ~**уло 60** I've hit 60

▶ **сту́кнуться** (*impf* **сту́каться**) *сов возв* to bang
o.s.

стул (-а; *nom pl* -ья, *gen pl* -ьев) м chair; (*no pl*;
физиология) stools мн.

сту́п|а (-ы) ж mortar.

ступа́|ть (-ю) несов от **ступи́ть** ♦ *неперех*

(осторо́жно, ме́дленно) to tread; ~йте! off you go!

ступе́нек *сущ см* **ступе́нька**.

ступе́нчат|**ый** (-, -а, -о) *прил* (спуск, водопад) terraced; (процесс) in stages.

ступе́н|**ь** (-и) *ж* step; (gen pl -е́й, dat pl -я́м; процесса) stage; (МУЗ) degree.

ступе́нь|**ка** (-ьки; gen pl -ек) *ж* step.

ступ|**и́ть** (-лю́, -ишь; impf **ступа́ть**) *сов неперех* to step, tread.

ступи́ц|**а** (-ы) *ж* (ТЕХ) hub.

сту́п|**ка** (-ки; gen pl -ок) *ж* mortar.

ступлю́ *сов см* **ступи́ть**.

ступн|**я́** (-и́) *ж* (стопа) foot (мн feet); (подошва) sole.

сту́пок *сущ см* **сту́пка**.

сту́пор (-а) *м* stupor.

стуч|**а́ть** (-у́, -и́шь; perf **постуча́ть**) *несов неперех* (в дверь, в окно) to knock; (по столу, по доске) to bang; (колёса) to rattle; (сердце) to thump; (зубы) to chatter; (perf **настуча́ть**; разг: доноси́ть) to grass; (у меня́) ~и́т в виска́х my temples are throbbing; ~ (**постуча́ть** perf) **в окно́/в дверь** to bang on the window/door

▶ **стуча́ться** (perf **постуча́ться**) *несов возв*: ~ся (в +acc) to knock (at); ~ся (**постуча́ться** perf) **к кому́-н** to knock at sb's door.

стуш|**ева́ться** (-у́юсь; impf **тушева́ться**) *сов возв* to go shy.

стыд (-а́) *м* shame; **к** ~у́ **своему́** to one's shame; **сгора́ть** (**сгоре́ть** perf) **от** ~а́ to burn with shame; **у тебя́ нет ни** ~а́, **ни со́вести** (разг) you've no shame.

стыд|**и́ть** (-жу́, -ди́шь; perf **пристыди́ть**) *несов перех* to (put to) shame

▶ **стыди́ться** (perf **постыди́ться**) *несов возв*: ~ся +gen/+infin to be ashamed of/to do; ~ся (**постыди́ться** perf) **кого́-н/чего́-н пе́ред кем-н** to be ashamed of sb/sth in front of sb.

стыдли́в|**ый** (-, -а, -о) *прил* bashful.

сты́дно *как сказ* it's a shame; **мне** ~ I am ashamed; **мне** ~ **друзе́й** или **пе́ред друзья́ми** I'm ashamed in front of my friends; **как тебе́ не** ~! you ought to be ashamed of yourself!

стыжу́(сь) *несов см* **стыди́ть(ся)**.

стык (-а) *м* (труб, рельсов) join; (улиц) junction; (перен: двух наук, двух эпох) meeting point.

стык|**ова́ть** (-у́ю; perf **состыкова́ть**) *несов перех* (рельсы, трубы) to join; (космос) to dock

▶ **стыкова́ться** (perf **состыкова́ться**) *несов возв* (космос) to dock.

стыко́в|**ка** (-ки; gen pl -ок) *ж* docking.

сты́н|**уть** (-у, -ешь; perf **осты́нуть**) *несов неперех* = **стыть**.

сты|**ть** (-ну, -нешь; perf **осты́ть**) *несов неперех* to go cold; (perf **просты́ть**; мёрзнуть) to freeze; **кровь сты́нет (в жи́лах)** the blood runs cold.

сты́ч|**ка** (-ки; gen pl -ек) *ж* (военная) clash; (разг: с нача́льником, с мили́цией) run-in.

стю́ард (-а) *м* steward.

стюарде́сс|**а** (-ы) *ж* air hostess.

стяг (-а; nom pl -и) *м* banner.

стя́гива|**ть(ся)** (-ю(сь)) *несов от* **стяну́ть(ся)**.

стяжа́тель (-я) *м* taker.

стяжа́тельниц|**а** (-ы) *ж см* **стяжа́тель**.

стяжа́тельск|**ий** (-ая, -ое, -ие) *прил* grasping.

стян|**у́ть** (-у́, -ешь; impf **стя́гивать**) *сов перех* (пояс, шнуровку) to tighten; (войска) to round up; (no impf; разг: украсть) to nick, pinch; (перевязать): ~ **что-н чем-н** (талию поясом) to pull sth in with sth; (чемодан ремнём) to strap sth up with sth; (обувь, перчатку) to pull off

▶ **стяну́ться** (impf **стя́гиваться**) *сов возв* (узел) to tighten; (войска) to gather; (разг: поясом) to pull o.s. in.

СУ *ср сокр* (= статисти́ческое управле́ние) statistics office.

субаре́нд|**а** (-ы) *ж* sub-lease, sub-let.

суббо́т|**а** (-ы) *ж* Saturday; *см также* **пя́тница**.

суббо́тн|**ий** (-яя, -ее, -ие) *прил* (вечер, работа) Saturday опред; (события) Saturday's.

сублима́ци|**я** (-и) *ж* sublimation.

субордина́ци|**я** (-и) *ж* subordination.

субподря́д (-а) *м* subcontract; **заключа́ть** (**заключи́ть** perf) ~ to subcontract.

субподря́дчик (-а) *м* subcontractor.

субсиди́р|**овать** (-ую) *(не)сов перех* to subsidize.

субси́ди|**я** (-и) *ж* subsidy; **инвестицио́нные** ~**и** (КОММ) investment grant ед.

субстантиви́рованн|**ый** *прил*: ~**ое прилага́тельное** substantivized adjective.

субста́нци|**я** (-и) *ж* substance.

субти́тр (-а) *м* subtitle.

субтро́пик|**и** (-ов) *мн* subtropics мн.

субъе́кт (-а) *м* (индивид, также ЮР) individual; (разг: о мужчине) character.

субъекти́вность (-и) *ж* subjectivity.

субъекти́вный *прил* subjective.

сувени́р (-а) *м* souvenir.

суваре́нн|**ый** *прил см* **суваре́нный**.

сувернитет (-а) *м* sovereignty.

суваре́н|**ный** (-ен, -на, -но) *прил* sovereign.

суглин|**ок** (-ка) *м* loam.

сугро́б (-а) *м* snowdrift.

сугу́бо *нареч* highly.

сугу́бый *прил* particular.

суд (-а́) *м* court session; (орган) court; (процесс) trial; (мнение) judgement, verdict ◆ *собир* the judges мн; **отдава́ть** (**отда́ть** perf) **кого́-н под** ~ to prosecute sb; **подава́ть** (**пода́ть** perf) **на кого́-н в** ~ to take sb to court; **предава́ть** (**преда́ть** perf) **кого́-н** ~у́ (преступника) to prosecute sb; **попада́ть** (**попа́сть** perf) **под** ~ to be taken to court; **встать, ~ идёт!** please stand for the court!; **на нет и ~á нет** oh well, that's that then.

суда́ *итп сущ см* **су́дно**.

суда́к (-á) *м* pike-perch.

Суда́н (-а) *м* (the) Sudan.

суда́рын|я (-и; *gen pl* -ь) *ж* Madame.

су́дар|ь (-я) *м* Sir.

суде́б *сущ см* **судьба́**.

суде́бно-медици́нск|ий (-ая, -ое, -ие) *прил*: **суде́бно-медици́нская эксперти́за** forensics.

суде́бн|ый *прил* (*заседание, органы*) court *опред*; (*издержки, практика*) legal; **~ая оши́бка** miscarriage of justice; **~ое реше́ние** adjudication; **суде́бное де́ло** court case; **суде́бный исполни́тель** bailiff; **суде́бный пригово́р** sentence.

суде́йск|ий (-ая, -ое, -ие) *прил* (*ЮР*) judge's; **суде́йская колле́гия** (*ЮР*) the bench; (*СПОРТ*) panel of judges.

суде́йств|о (-а) *ср* refereeing.

су́ден *сущ см* **су́дно**.

суди́мост|ь (-и) *ж* conviction.

суди́ть (-жу́, -дишь) *несов перех* (*преступника*) to try; (*матч*) to referee; (*укорять*) to judge ♦ *неперех* (*на матче*) to referee; (*на соревнованиях*) to judge; **~** (*impf*) **о ком-н/чём-н** to judge sb/sth; **судя́ по** +*dat* judging by
▶ **суди́ться** *несов возв*: **~ся с кем-н** to take sb to court.

су́дн|о (-на; *nom pl* -á, *gen pl* -о́в) *ср* vessel; (*gen pl* -ен; *МЕД*) bedpan.

су́дный *прил*: **~ день** Judgement Day.

судове́рф|ь (-и) *ж сокр* (= *судострои́тельная верфь*) shipyard.

судовладе́л|ец (-ьца) *м* shipowner.

судовожде́ни|е (-я) *ср* navigation.

судово́й *прил*: **~áя кома́нда** ship's crew; **судово́й журна́л** ship's log.

судопроизво́дств|о (-а) *ср* legal proceedings *мн*.

судоремо́нтн|ый *прил*: **~ые мастерски́е** shipyards *мн*.

су́дорог|а (-и) *ж* (*от боли*) spasm; (*от холода, от отвращения итп*) shudder.

су́дорожный (-ен, -на, -но) *прил* (*движения, плач*) convulsive; (*перен: приготовления*) feverish.

судострое́ни|е (-я) *ср* ship building.

судострои́тельный *прил* ship-building.

судохо́дный *прил* navigable; **~ кана́л** shipping canal.

судохо́дств|о (-а) *ср* navigation.

судьб|а́ (-ы́; *nom pl* -ьбы, *gen pl* -еб) *ж* fate; (*будущее*) destiny; **~ э́той пье́сы о́чень интере́сна** this play has had a very interesting fate; **каки́ми ~ми!** fancy seeing you here!; (**нам**) **не ~ встре́титься** we are not fated to meet.

судь|я́ (-и́; *nom pl* -и, *gen pl* -е́й) *ж* judge; (*СПОРТ*) referee; **я тебе́ не ~** who am I to judge

you?

суве́рен *прил см* **суеве́рный**.

суеве́ри|е (-я) *ср* superstition.

суеве́р|ный (-ен, -на, -но) *прил* superstitious.

суе|та́ (-ы́) *ж* (*житейская, мелочная*) futility; (*хлопоты*) hustle and bustle.

су́етен *прил см* **су́етный**.

суе|ти́ться (-чу́сь, -ти́шься) *несов возв* to fuss (about).

суетли́в|ый (-, -а, -о) *прил* fussy; (*жизнь, работа*) busy.

су́ет|ный (-ен, -на, -но) *прил* (*интересы, желания, жизнь итп*) futile; (*человек*) superficial; (*день, жизнь*) busy.

суечу́сь *несов см* **суети́ться**.

сужа́|ть (-ю) *несов от* **су́зить**.

сужде́ни|е (-я) *ср* (*мнение*) opinion; (*заключение*) judgement.

суждено́ *как сказ*: (**нам**) **не ~ бы́ло встре́титься** we weren't fated to meet.

су́жен|ая (-ой; *decl like adj*) *ж*: **его́ ~** his intended.

суже́ни|е (-я) *ср* (*см глаг*) narrowing; taking in.

су́жен|ый (-ого; *decl like adj*) *м*: **её ~** her intended.

сужу́(сь) *несов см* **суди́ть(ся)**.

су́|зить (-жу, -зишь; *impf* **сужа́ть**) *сов перех* to narrow; (*платье*) to take in
▶ **су́зиться** *сов возв* to narrow.

су|к (-ка́; *loc sg* -ку́, *nom pl* -чья, *gen pl* -чьев) *м* (*дерева*) bough.

су́к|а (-и) *ж* bitch ♦ *м/ж* (*груб!: о женщине*) bitch (*!*); (: *о мужчине*) bastard (*!*); **~ин сын** (*разг*) son of a bitch (*!*)

сукн|о́ (-á; *nom pl* -на, *gen pl* -он) *ср* (*шерстяное*) felt; (*хлопчатобумажное*) coarse cloth; **класть** (**положи́ть** *perf*) **что-н под ~** (*перен*) to shelve sth.

суко́нный *прил* (*см сущ*) felt *опред*; coarse cloth *опред*.

сул|и́ть (-ю́, -и́шь; *perf* **посули́ть**) *несов перех*: **~ что-н кому́-н** (*обещать*) to promise sb sth, promise sth to sb; (*предвещать*) to bode for.

султа́н (-а) *м* (*монарх*) sultan; (*украшение*) plume.

сульфа́т (-а) *м* sulphate.

сум|а́ (-ы́) *ж* (*старушечья*) (tote) bag; (*охотничья*) pouch; **ходи́ть** (*impf*) **с ~о́й** (*перен*) to go begging.

сумасбро́д (-а) *м* maverick.

сумасбро́ден *прил см* **сумасбро́дный**.

сумасбро́д|ка (-ки; *gen pl* -ок) *ж см* **сумасбро́д**.

сумасбро́д|ный (-ен, -на, -но) *прил* (*человек, поведение*) maverick; (*идея*) madcap.

сумасбро́док *сущ см* **сумасбро́дка**.

сумасбро́дств|о (-а) *ср* (*поведение*) maverick behaviour; (*поступок*) exploit.

сумасше́дш|ая (-ей; *decl like adj*) *ж* madwoman (*мн* madwomen).

сумасше́дш|ий (-ая, -ее, -ие) *прил* mad; (*разг: успех*) amazing; (: *скорость*) lunatic ♦ (-его; *decl like adj*) *м* madman (*мн* madmen); **~ие**

де́ньги ridiculous amounts of money;
сумасше́дший дом asylum; (разг) madhouse.
сумасше́стви|е (-я) ср madness, lunacy; до ~я
like mad.
сумато́х|а (-и) ж chaos.
сумато́ш|ный (-ен, -на, -но) прил (разг)
chaotic.
сумбу́р (-а) м muddle.
сумбу́р|ный (-ен, -на, -но) прил muddled.
су́мерек сущ см су́мерки.
су́мереч|ный (-ен, -на, -но) прил twilight.
су́мер|ки (-ек) мн twilight ед, dusk ед.
суме́|ть (-ю) сов неперех: ~ +infin to manage to
do.
су́м|ка (-ки; gen pl -ок) ж bag; (кенгуру) pouch.
су́мм|а (-ы) ж sum.
сумма́р|ный (-ен, -на, -но) прил (количество,
затраты) total опред; (оценка, обзор,
описание) overall.
сумми́р|овать (-ую) (не)сов перех (затраты
итп) to add up; (информацию, данные,
сказанное) to summarize.
су́мок сущ см су́мка.
су́моч|ка (-ки; gen pl -ек) ж уменьш от су́мка;
(дамская, вечерняя) handbag.
су́мрак (-а) м gloom.
су́мрачен прил см су́мрачный.
су́мрачно нареч (посмотреть) gloomily;
(выглядеть) gloomy ♦ как сказ (на улице, в
доме) it's gloomy; у меня́ на душе́ ~ I have a
heavy heart.
су́мрач|ный (-ен, -на, -но) прил (также перен)
gloomy.
су́мчатый прил (зоол) marsupial опред.
сумя́тиц|а (-ы) ж mishmash.
сунду́к (-а́) м trunk, chest.
су́н|уть(ся) (-у(сь), -ешь(ся)) сов от
сова́ть(ся).
суп (-а; part gen -у, nom pl -ы́) м soup.
суперма́ркет (-а) м supermarket.
суперме́н (-а) м superman (мн supermen).
супермо́дный прил very trendy.
суперобло́ж|ка (-ки; gen pl -ек) ж dust jacket.
су́пниц|а (-ы) ж soup tureen.
супру́г (-а; nom pl -и) м spouse; ~и husband and
wife.
супру́г|а (-и) ж spouse.
супру́жеск|ий (-ая, -ое, -ие) прил marital;
(чета) married.
супру́жеств|о (-а) ср matrimony.
сургу́ч (-а́) м sealing wax.
суро́вост|ь (-и) ж (см прил) bleakness; severity;
hardship; harshness; sternness.
суро́в|ый (-, -а, -о) прил (природа, зима) bleak;
(приговор) severe; (жизнь) tough;
(действительность) harsh; (человек, взгляд)
stern; (no short form; ткань, нити) coarse.
суррога́т (-а) м (также перен) substitute.

суррога́тный прил substitute опред.
суса́ль|ный прил: ~ое зо́лото gold leaf.
су́слик (-а) м ground squirrel (BRIT), gopher (US).
суспе́нзи|я (-и) ж suspension.
суста́в (-а) м (АНАТ) joint.
суста́вный прил: ~ ревмати́зм rheumatism of
the joints.
сутенёр (-а) м pimp.
су́т|ки (-ок) мн twenty four hours мн; кру́глые ~
day and night.
су́толок|а (-и) ж hurly-burly.
су́точные (-ых; decl like adj) мн subsistence
allowance ед.
су́точный прил twenty-four-hour.
суту́л|ить (-ю, -ишь; perf ссуту́лить) несов
перех to hunch
► суту́литься (perf ссуту́литься) несов возв to
stoop.
суту́л|ый (-, -а, -о) прил stooped.
сут|ь (-и) ж essence; ~ де́ла the crux of the
matter; по су́ти (де́ла) as a matter of fact ♦ как
сказ: э́то не ~ ва́жно it's not all that important;
таки́е слу́чаи ~ гро́зное предупрежде́ние
such incidents serve as a severe warning.
суфле́ ср нескл soufflé.
суфлёр (-а) м prompter.
суфлёрск|ий (-ая, -ое, -ие) прил: ~ая бу́дка
prompt box.
су́ффикс (-а) м suffix.
суха́р|ь (-я́) м cracker; (разг: о человеке) cold
fish.
су́хо нареч drily ♦ как сказ (о сухой погоде) it is
dry; на у́лице ~ it's dry outside.
сухове́|й (-я) м hot dry wind.
сухогру́з (-а) м dry-cargo ship.
сухожи́ли|е (-я) ср tendon.
сух|о́й (-, -а́, -о) прил dry; (ветка, листья) dried;
(no short form; фру́кты, овощи) dried; сухо́е
вино́ dry wine; сухо́е молоко́ dried milk;
сухо́й зако́н dry law, prohibition; сухо́й счёт
(СПОРТ) lockout.
сухопа́р|ый (-, -а, -о) прил bony.
сухопу́тный прил land опред; сухопу́тные
войска́ ground forces мн.
су́хост|ь (-и) ж dryness.
сухофру́кт|ы (-ов) мн dried fruit ед.
сухоща́в|ый (-, -а, -о) прил lean.
суч|о́к (-ка́) м twig.
су́чья итп сущ см сук.
су́ш|а (-и) ж (dry) land.
су́ше сравн прил от сухо́й ♦ сравн нареч от
су́хо.
су́шек сущ см су́шка.
суше́ный прил dried.
суши́л|ка (-ки; gen pl -ок) ж (помещение) drying
room; (приспособление) dryer.
суш|и́ть (-у́, -ишь; perf вы́сушить) несов перех
(бельё, одежду, сено) to dry; (perf вы́сушить

или **засушúть**; *травы итп)* to dry
► **сушúться** *(perf* **вы́сушиться)** *несов возв* to dry; *(человек)* to dry off.

су́ш|ка (-**ки**; *gen pl* -**ек**) *ж (действие)* drying; *(бублик) small dry biscuit in the shape of a doughnut.*

сушь (-**и**) *ж* dry spell.

суще́ственно *нареч (улучшить, изменить)* substantially.

суще́ствен|ный (-, -**на**, -**но**) *прил (черта, качество)* essential; *(изменения)* substantial; *(замечания)* major; *(вопрос)* important.

существи́тельн|ое (-**ого**; *decl like adj) ср (также:* **и́мя ~)** noun.

существ|о́ (-**а́**) *ср (вопроса, дела итп)* essence; *(nom pl* -**а́**; *животное)* creature; *(человек)* being; **по ~у́** *(говорить)* to the point; *(вводн сл)* essentially; **всем свои́м ~м** with one's whole being.

существова́ни|е (-**я**) *ср* existence; **прекраща́ть (прекрати́ть** *perf)* **~** to cease to exist; **сре́дства к ~ю** livelihood; **отравля́ть (отрави́ть** *perf)* **кому́-н ~** to make sb's life a misery.

существ|ова́ть (-**у́ю**) *несов неперех* to exist; **~** *(impf)* +*instr или* **на** +*acc* to make one's living from.

су́щ|ий (-**ая**, -**ее**, -**ие**) *прил (правда)* honest; *(мучение, пустяки)* utter; **она́ ~ ребёнок** she is a real baby.

су́щность (-**и**) *ж (вопроса, проблемы)* essence; **в ~и (говоря́)** in essence, essentially.

Суэ́ц (-**а**) *м* Suez.

суэ́цк|ий (-**ая**, -**ое**, -**ие**) *прил:* **С~ кана́л** the Suez Canal.

СФ *м сокр* (= **Сове́т Федера́ций)** *upper chamber of the Russian parliament.*

сфабрик|ова́ть (-**у́ю**) *сов от* **фабрикова́ть.**

сфальши́в|ить (-**лю**, -**ишь**) *сов от* **фальши́вить.**

сфантази́р|овать (-**ую**) *сов от* **фантази́ровать.**

сфе́р|а (-**ы**) *ж* sphere; *(производства, торговли, науки)* area; *(театральная, дипломатическая)* circles *мн;* **земна́я ~** the globe; **вы́сшие ~ы** upper echelons; **в ~е** +*gen* in the field of; **сфе́ра обслу́живания** *или* **услу́г** service industry.

сфери́ческ|ий (-**ая**, -**ое**, -**ие**) *прил* spherical.

сфинкс (-**а**) *м* sphinx.

сформир|ова́ть(ся) (-**у́ю(сь)**) *сов от* **формирова́ть(ся).**

сформули́р|овать (-**ую**) *сов от* **формули́ровать.**

сфотографи́р|овать(ся) (-**ую(сь)**) *сов от* **фотографи́ровать(ся).**

схалту́р|ить (-**ю**, -**ишь**) *сов от* **халту́рить.**

схват|и́ть (-**чу́**, -**тишь**) *сов от* **хвата́ть** ♦ *(impf* **схва́тывать)** *перех (скрепить)* to secure; *(разг: простуду)* to catch; *(мысль, смысл)* to grasp; **у меня́ ~и́ло живо́т** I've got stomach cramps

► **схвати́ться** *сов от* **хвата́ться** ♦ *(impf*

схва́тываться) *возв (борцы, оппоненты)* to lock together.

схва́т|ка (-**ки**; *gen pl* -**ок**) *ж* fight; *см также* **схва́тки.**

схва́т|ки (-**ок**) *мн (МЕД)* contractions *мн.*

схва́тыва|ть(ся) (-**ю(сь)**) *несов от* **схвати́ть(ся).**

схвачу́(сь) *сов см* **схвати́ть(ся).**

схе́м|а (-**ы**) *ж (метро, улиц)* plan; *(ЭЛЕК: радио итп)* circuit board; *(статьи итп)* outline.

схематизи́р|овать (-**ую**) *(не)сов перех* to schematize.

схемати́зм (-**а**) *м* schematism.

схемати́чен *прил см* **схемати́чный.**

схемати́ческ|ий (-**ая**, -**ое**, -**ие**) *прил (ТЕХ)* diagrammatic; *(изложение)* sketchy.

схемати́чный (-**ен**, -**на**, -**но**) *прил (изложение)* sketchy.

схи́м|а (-**ы**) *ж* schema (*strict vow taken by orthodox monks).*

схи́мник (-**а**) *м monk who has taken strict vows.*

схитр|и́ть (-**ю**, -**и́шь**) *сов от* **хитри́ть.**

схлестн|у́ться (-**у́сь**, -**ёшься**) *impf* **схлёстываться** *сов возв (разг)* to lock together.

схлоп|ота́ть (-**очу́**, -**о́чешь**) *сов перех (разг):* **~ вы́говор** to get a telling off; **ты у меня́ ~о́чешь!** you're asking for it!

схлы́н|уть (*3sg* -**ет**, *3pl* -**ут**) *сов неперех (вода)* to subside; *(толпа)* to thin out.

сход (-**а**) *м (с горы, с трапа)* descent.

схо́ден *прил см* **схо́дный.**

сход|и́ть (-**жу́**, -**дишь**) *сов от* **ходи́ть** ♦ *неперех (раза: в театр, на прогулку)* to go ♦ *несов от* **сойти́**

► **сходи́ться** *несов от* **сойти́сь.**

схо́д|ка (-**ки**; *gen pl* -**ок**) *ж* assembly.

схо́дн|и (-**ей**) *мн* gangplank *ед.*

схо́дн|ый (-**ен**, -**на**, -**но**) *прил* similar.

схо́док *сущ см* **схо́дка.**

схо́дств|о (-**а**) *ср* similarity.

схо́ж|ий (-**ая**, -**ее**, -**ие**) *прил (разг)* = **схо́дный.**

схожу́(сь) *(не)сов см* **сходи́ть(ся).**

схола́стик|а (-**и**) *ж (философия)* scholasticism; *(отвлечённые знания)* speculation.

схоласти́чный (-**ен**, -**на**, -**но**) *прил* scholastic.

схорон|и́ть (-**ю́**, -**ишь**) *сов от* **хорони́ть.**

сца́па|ть (-**ю**) *сов от* **ца́пать.**

сцед|и́ть (-**жу́**, -**дишь**; *impf* **сце́живать)** *сов перех (жидкость, сок)* to strain off; *(грудное молоко)* to express.

сцементи́р|овать (-**ую**) *сов от* **цементи́ровать.**

сце́н|а (-**ы**) *ж (подмостки)* stage; *(эпизод: в пьесе, на улице)* scene; **сходи́ть (сойти́** *perf)* **со ~ы** to leave the stage; *(политик)* to fade from the scene; **устра́ивать (устро́ить** *perf)* **~у** to make a scene.

сцена́ри|й (-**я**) *м (фильма)* script; *(вечера, праздника)* programme.

сценари́ст (-**а**) *м* scriptwriter.

сцени́чен *прил см* **сцени́чный.**

сцени́ческ|ий (**-ая**, **-ое**, **-ие**) *прил* stage *опред*; **~ое мастерство́** acting skills; **~ о́браз** dramatic character; **сцени́ческое иску́сство** dramatic art.

сцени́ч|ный (**-ен**, **-на**, **-но**) *прил*: **~ная пье́са** play well-suited for the theatre (*BRIT*) *или* theater (*US*).

сце́н|ка (**-ки**; *gen pl* **-ок**) *ж уменьш от* **сце́на**; (*зарисовка*) sketch.

сцеп|и́ть (**-лю́**, **-ишь**; *impf* **сцепля́ть**) *сов перех* (*вагоны, прицепы*) to couple; (*пальцы, руки*) to clasp

► **сцепи́ться** (*impf* **сцепля́ться**) *сов возв* (*ветви*) to be caught together; (*разг*: *схватиться*) **~ся** (**с** +*instr*) (*дети, спорщики*) to get into a fight (with).

сцепле́ни|е (**-я**) *ср* (*вагонов*) coupling; (*ТЕХ*: *механизм*) clutch.

сцепля́|ю(сь) *сов см* **сцепи́ть(ся)**.

сцепля́|ть(ся) (**-ю(сь)**) *несов от* **сцепи́ть(ся)**.

счастли́в|ец (**-ца**) *м* lucky man (*мн* men).

счастли́в|ица (**-ы**) *ж* lucky woman (*мн* women).

сча́стливо *нареч* (*жить, рассмеяться*) happily; **~ отде́латься** (*perf*) to have a lucky escape; **счастли́во!** all the best!; **счастли́во остава́ться!** good luck!

счастли́вца *итп сущ см* **счастли́вец**.

счастли́вчик (**-а**) *м* (*разг*) lucky devil.

счастли́в|ый (**-ив**, **-ива**, **-иво**) *прил* (*человек, жизнь, лицо*) happy; (*делец, игрок, случай*) lucky; **у него́ ~ивая рука́** he's got a lucky touch; **~ивого пути́!** have a good journey!

сча́сть|е (**-я**) *ср* (*личное, семейное*) happiness; (*удача*) luck; **к ~ю** luckily, fortunately; **на на́ше ~** luckily for us; **како́е ~, что ты пришёл** how nice that you've come; **возьми́ э́то на ~** take that for good luck; **твоё ~, что ...** you're lucky that ....

счесть (**сочту́**, **сочтёшь**; *pt* **счёл**, **сочла́**, **сочло́**) *сов от* **счита́ть ♦** *неперех*: **пробле́м у меня́ не ~** I've got countless problems.

счёт (**-а**; *part sg* **-у**, *loc sg* **-у́**, *nom pl* **-а́**) *м* (*действие*) counting; (*КОММ*: *в банке*) account; (: *накладная*) invoice; (*ресторанный, телефонный*) bill; (*no pl*; *СПОРТ*) score; **в ~** +*gen* in lieu of; **за ~** +*gen* (*фирмы*) at the expense of; (*эффективности, внедрений итп*) due to; **на ~ кого́-н** at sb's expense; **на э́тот ~** in this respect; **быть** (*impf*) **на хоро́шем/плохо́м счету́ у** to be in the good/bad books with; **у неё ка́ждая копе́йка на счету́** she counts every penny; **э́то не в ~** that doesn't count; **по большо́му ~у** having set a high standard; **име́ть** (*impf*) **что-н на счету́** (*победы*) to have sth to one's name; **предъявля́ть** (**предъяви́ть** *perf*) **~ кому́-н** to invoice sb; **принима́ть** (**приня́ть** *perf*) **что-н на свой ~** to take sth personally; **он не зна́ет ~а деньга́м** he's rolling

in money; **лицево́й ~** (*КОММ*) personal account; **теку́щий ~** (*КОММ*) current (*BRIT*) *или* checking (*US*) account; **~ поступле́ний** (*КОММ*) revenue account; **ссу́дный ~** (*КОММ*) loan account; **~ ассигнова́ний** (*КОММ*) appropriation account; **счета́ кредито́ров/дебито́ров** (*КОММ*) account payable/receivable; **открыва́ть** (**откры́ть** *perf*) **~ в ба́нке** to open a bank account.

счётн|ый *прил*: **~ая коми́ссия** vote counting committee; **счётная маши́на** calculator.

счётчик (**-а**) *м* (*человек*: *голосов*) counter; (*электричества, в такси*) meter.

счёт|ы (**-ов**) *мн* (*приспособление*) abacus; (*деловые*) dealings *мн*; **поко́нчить** (*perf*) **все ~ с кем-н** (*расчитаться*) to pay off one's debts to sb; (*прекратить связи*) to break off ties with sb; **сбра́сывать** (**сбро́сить** *perf*) **кого́-н/что-н со счето́в** to dismiss sb/sth; **своди́ть** (**свести́** *perf*) **~ с кем-н** to settle a score with sb; **у него́ с ни́ми свои́ ~** he's got his own scores to settle with them.

счи́|стить (**-щу**, **-стишь**; *impf* **счища́ть**) *сов перех* to clean off.

счи́та|лка (**-ки**; *gen pl* **-ок**) *ж* counting rhyme.

счи́танн|ый *прил*: **~ые дни/мину́ты** only a few days/minutes; **~ое коли́чество** very few.

счита́|ть (**-ю**) *несов неперех* to count (*perf* **посчита́ть** *или* **сосчита́ть**) *перех* (*деньги итп*) to count; (*perf* **посчита́ть** *или* **счесть**): **~ что-н/кого́-н** +*instr* to regard sth/sb as; **~** (**посчита́ть** *или* **счесть** *perf*) **что-н необходи́мым** to consider sth (to be) necessary; **~я** +*gen* (*принимая в расчёт*) considering; **не ~я** +*gen* excluding; **~я от** +*gen* *или* **с** +*gen* starting with; **~** (**счесть** *perf*) **кого́-н/кого́-н за** +*acc* to regard sb/sth as; **я ~ю, что ...** I believe *или* think that ...

► **счита́ться** *несов возв*: **~ся** +*instr* to be considered to be; (*уважать*): **~ся с** +*instr* (**с** *родителями, с другом итп*) to be considerate to.

счи́тыва|ть (**-ю**; *perf* **счита́ть**) *несов перех* to read (*meter etc*).

счища́|ть (**-ю**) *несов от* **счи́стить**.

счи́щу *сов см* **счи́стить**.

США *мн сокр* (= *Соединённые Шта́ты Аме́рики*) USA (= *United States of America*).

сшиб|и́ть (**-у́**, **-ёшь**; *pt* **-**, **-ла**, **-ло**, *impf* **сшиба́ть**) *сов перех* (*разг*: *подлеж: машина*) to hit

► **сшиби́ться** (*impf* **сшиба́ться**) *сов возв* (*разг*) to get into a fight.

сшива́|ть (**-ю**) *несов от* **сшить**.

сшить (**сошью́**, **сошьёшь**; *imper* **сше́й(те)**) *сов от* **шить ♦** (*impf* **сшива́ть**) *перех* (*соединить шитьём*) to sew together.

съеда́|ть (**-ю**) *несов от* **съесть**.

съе́дем(ся) *сов см* **съе́хать(ся)**.

съеде́ни|е (**-я**) *ср*: **отдава́ть кого́-н на ~**

кому́-н (*также перен*) to leave sb at the mercy of sb.

съе́дешь(ся) *итп сов см* **съе́хать(ся)**.

съеди́м *итп сов см* **съесть**.

съедо́б|ный (**-ен, -на, -но**) *прил* edible.

съе́ду(сь) *итп сов см* **съе́хать(ся)**.

съедя́т *сов см* **съесть**.

съё́ж|иться (**-усь, -ишься**) *сов от* **ё́житься ♦** *возв* (*от холода, от страха*) to huddle; (*листья*) to shrivel up.

съезд (**-а**) *м* (*действие: гостей, делегатов*) gathering; (*к реке, в долину*) descent; (*партийный*) congress.

съе́з|дить (**-жу, -дишь**) *сов неперех* (*за покупками, к родителям*) to go; ~ (*perf*) +*dat* (*раза: ударить*) to whack.

съе́здовск|ий (**-ая, -ое, -ие**) *прил* (*документы, решения*) congress *опред*.

съезжа́|ть(ся) (**-ю(сь)**) *несов от* **съе́хать(ся)**.

съе́зжу *сов см* **съе́здить**.

съем *сов см* **съесть**.

съё́м|ка (**-ки**; *gen pl* **-ок**) *ж* (*копии*) making, taking; (*местности*) survey; (*обычно мн: фильма*) shooting; (*гипса*) removal.

съё́мный *прил* detachable.

съё́мок *сущ см* **съё́мка**.

съё́моч|ный *прил*: ~**ая площа́дка** film set; **съё́мочная гру́ппа** film crew.

съё́мщик (**-а**) *м* tennant.

съё́мщиц|а (**-ы**) *ж см* **съё́мщик**.

съестн|о́й *прил*: ~**ы́е припа́сы** food supplies *мн*.

съе|сть (*как* **есть**; *см* Table 15; *impf* **есть** или **съеда́ть**) *сов перех* (*хлеб, кашу*) to eat; (*подлеж: моль, ржавчина*) to eat away at; (: *тоска, ревность*) to gnaw at; (*impf* **съеда́ть**; *разг: деньги, зарплату*) to eat up.

съе́хать (*как* **е́хать**; *см* Table 19; *impf* **съезжа́ть**) *сов неперех*: ~ **(с** +*gen*) (*спуститься: с горки*) to go down; (*платок*) to slip; (*шапка*) to tilt; **съезжа́ть** (~ *perf*) **(с кварти́ры)** to move out (of one's flat); ~ (*perf*) **с ле́стницы** (*упасть*) to tumble down the stairs

▶ **съе́хаться** (*impf* **съезжа́ться**) *сов возв* (*гости, делегаты*) to gather.

съехи́дни|ча|ть (**-ю**) *сов от* **ехи́дничать**.

съешь *сов см* **съесть**.

съязв|и́ть (**-лю́, -и́шь**) *сов от* **язви́ть**.

сы́воро́т|ка (**-ки**; *gen pl* **-ок**) *ж* (*молочная*) whey; (*мед*) serum.

сы́гранный *прил* well-coordinated.

сыгра́|ть (**-ю**) *сов от* **игра́ть**

▶ **сыгра́ться** (*impf* **сы́грываться**) *сов возв* (*музыканты*) to play well together; (*спортсмены*) to play well as a team.

сы́змала *нареч* from an early age.

сы́знова *нареч* (*разг*) anew.

сымити́р|овать (**-ую**) *сов от* **имити́ровать**.

сымпровизи́р|овать (**-ую**) *сов от* **импровизи́ровать**.

сын (**-а**; *nom pl* **-овья́**, *gen pl* **-ове́й**, *dat pl* **-овья́м**)

м son; (*nom pl* **-ы́**, *gen pl* **-о́в**; *перен*): ~ +*gen* (*наро́да*) son of.

сынка́ *итп сущ см* **сыно́к**.

сыновья́ *итп сущ см* **сын**.

сыно́вн|ий (**-яя, -ее, -ие**) *прил* (*любовь, долг*) son's.

сыно́к (**-ка́**) *м уменьш от* **сын**; (*как обращение*) son.

сы́п|ать (**-лю, -лешь**; *imper* **сы́пь(те)**) *несов перех* to pour ♦ *неперех*: ~ +*instr* (*цитатами, остротами*) to pour forth with

▶ **сы́паться** *несов возв* (*мука, песок, яблоки итп*) to pour; (*вопросы, письма итп*) to pour forth; **на него́ посы́пались уда́ры со всех сторо́н** blows rained down on him from all sides.

сыпно́й *прил*: ~ **тиф** typhus.

сыпу́ч|ий (**-ая, -ее, -ие**) *прил* (*вещество*) friable; (*грунт*) shifting.

сыпь (**-и**) *ж* rash.

сыр (**-а**; *part gen* **-у**, *nom pl* **-ы́**) *м* cheese; **как ~ в ма́сле ката́ться** (*impf*) to live the life of Riley.

сыре́|ть (*3sg* **-ет**, *3pl* **-ют**) *несов неперех* to get damp.

сыр|е́ц (**-ца́**) *м*: **хло́пок-~** rough cotton; **шёлк-~** raw silk.

сырка́ *итп сущ см* **сыро́к**.

сырко́в|ый *прил*: ~**ая ма́сса** cream cheese.

сы́рник (**-а**) *м small thick pancake made with cream cheese*.

сы́ро *как сказ*: **здесь ~** it's damp here.

сыроёжк|а (**-и**) *ж* russula.

сыр|о́й (**-, -á, -о**) *прил* (*бельё, земля, воздух*) damp; (*статья, стихи*) rough; (*no short form; мясо, овощи*) raw, uncooked; **сыра́я вода́** tap water.

сыр|о́к (**-ка́**) *м*: **творо́жный ~** sweet curd cheese; **пла́вленный ~** processed cheese.

сы́рость (**-и**) *ж* dampness.

сырца́ *итп сущ см* **сыре́ц**.

сырьё (**-я́**) *ср собир* raw material.

сырьево́й *прил* (*ресурсы, база*) raw material *опред*.

сыск (**-а**) *м* criminal detection.

сыска́ть (**-щу́, -щешь**) *сов перех* (*разг: отыскать*) to find

▶ **сыска́ться** *сов возв* (*разг: обнаружиться*) to turn up.

сы́т|ный (**-ен, -нá, -но**) *прил* filling.

сы́т|ый (**-, -á, -о**) *прил* (*не голодный*) full, satisfied; (*откормленный*) well-fed; (*no short form; перен: вид, улыбка*) contented; (: *мещанство*) smug; **спаси́бо, я сыт** thank you, I'm full; **я сыт по го́рло** (*перен*) I'm fed up.

сыч (**-á**) *м* little owl; (*о человеке*) loner.

сы́щик (**-а**) *м* detective.

сыщу́(сь) *итп сов см* **сыска́ть(ся)**.

СЭВ (**-а**) *м сокр* (*ист*: = **Сове́т Экономи́ческой Взаимопо́мощи**) Comecon, CMEA (= *Council for Mutual Economic Assistance*).

СЭЗ *ж сокр* = свободная экономи́ческая зо́на.

сэконо́м|ить (-лю, -ишь) *сов от* **эконо́мить.**

СЭС *м сокр* = Сове́тский Энциклопеди́ческий Слова́рь.

сюда́ *нареч* here; **(и) туда́ и** ~ both here and there; **то туда́, то** ~ sometimes here, sometimes there; **ни туда́ ни** ~ neither here nor there; **туда́-**~ *(туда и обратно)* backwards and forwards; *(в разные стороны)* everywhere; **иди́** ~! come here!; **э́то ещё туда́-**~ that's bearable.

сюже́т (-а) *м* plot.

сюже́тн|ый *прил:* ~**ая ли́ния** storyline; **сюже́тное разви́тие** development of the plot.

сюи́т|а (-ы) *ж (муз)* suite.

сюрпри́з (-а) *м* surprise.

сюрреали́зм (-а) *м* surrealism.

сюрреали́ст (-а) *м* surrealist.

сюрту́к (-а́) *м* frock-coat.

сюсю́кани|е (-я) *ср (см глаг)* lisping; fussing.

сюсю́ка|ть (-ю) *несов неперех (в речи)* to lisp; *(потворствовать):* ~ **с кем-н** to fuss over sb

▸ **сюсю́каться** *несов возв:* ~**ся с кем-н** to fuss over sb.

ся́ду *итп сов см* **сесть.**

сяк *нареч:* **(и) так и** ~ *или* **то так, то** ~ *(разг)* by hook or by crook; **э́то ещё так-**~ *(разг)* it's so-so.

сяко́й *прил:* **ах ты тако́й-**~ *(разг)* you little so-and-so.

сям *нареч:* **(и) там и** ~ *(разг)* here and there; **то там, то** ~ now here, now there.

The spelling rules for Russian are shown on page xvii.

~ T, m ~

Т, т *сущ нескл* (*буква*) the 19th letter of the Russian alphabet.

т *сокр* (= **то́нна**) t (= *tonne*).

т. *сокр* = **това́рищ**; (= **том**) v., vol. (= *volume*); = **ты́сяча**.

та (**той**) *мест см* **тот**.

таба́к (**-а́**; *part gen* **-ý**) *м* tobacco.

табака́ *нескл*: **цыплёнок** ~ char-grilled chicken.

табаке́р|ка (**-ки**; *gen pl* **-ок**) *ж* snuffbox.

табаково́д (**-а**) *м* tobacco grower.

табаково́дств|о (**-а**) *ср* tobacco-growing.

таба́чный *прил* tobacco *опред*.

та́бел|ь (**-я**) *м* (ПРОСВЕЩ) school report (BRIT), report card (US, SCOTTISH); (*на работе*) *board on which employees mark their time of arrival and departure*; (*график*) chart.

табле́т|ка (**-ки**; *gen pl* **-ок**) *ж* tablet.

табли́ц|а (**-ы**) *ж* table; (СПОРТ) (league) table; **табли́ца умноже́ния** multiplication table.

табли́ч|ка (**-ки**; *gen pl* **-ек**) *ж* (*с названием улицы*) street sign; (*экспоната*) plate; (*на двери*) nameplate.

табло́ *ср нескл* (*на вокзале, в аэропорту*) (information) board; (*на стадионе*) scoreboard.

та́бор (**-а**) *м* camp.

табу́ *ср нескл* taboo; **налага́ть** (**наложи́ть** *perf*) **на что-н** ~ to make a taboo of sth.

табу́н (**-а́**) *м* herd.

табуре́т (**-а**) *м* = **табуре́тка**.

табуре́т|ка (**-ки**; *gen pl* **-ок**) *ж* stool.

тавтоло́ги|я (**-и**) *ж* tautology.

таджи́к (**-а**) *м* Tajik.

Таджикиста́н (**-а**) *м* Tajikistan.

таджи́кск|ий (**-ая, -ое, -ие**) *прил* Tajiki.

таджи́ч|ка (**-ки**; *gen pl* **-ек**) *ж см* **таджи́к**.

таёжный *прил* taiga *опред*.

таз (**-а**; *loc sg* **-ý**, *nom pl* **-ы́**) *м* (*сосуд*) basin; (АНАТ) pelvis.

тазобе́дренный *прил*: ~ **суста́в** hip joint.

та́зовый *прил* (АНАТ) pelvic.

Таила́нд (**-а**) *м* Thailand.

таила́нд|ец (**-ца**) *м* Thai.

таила́нд|ка (**-ки**; *gen pl* **-ок**) *ж см* **таила́ндец**.

таила́ндца *итп сущ см* **таила́ндец**.

таи́нствен|ный (**-, -на, -но**) *прил* mysterious; (*цель, намерение*) secret.

таи́нств|о (**-а**) *ср* (РЕЛ) sacrament.

Таи́ти *м нескл* Tahiti.

таи́|ть (**-ю, -ишь**) *несов перех* to conceal;

(*перен*): ~ **в себе́** (*возможности, угрозу итп*) to conceal; ~ (*impf*) **зло́бу на кого́-н** to harbour (BRIT) *или* harbor (US) malice towards sb; **что греха́** ~ (*разг*) there's no point in pretending otherwise

▶ **таи́ться** *несов возв* (*скрывать что-н*) to cover up; (*опасность, неожиданность*) to lurk; **в нём** ~**ится наде́жда/зло́ба** he harbo(u)rs a secret hope/feeling of malice.

таитя́нск|ий (**-ая, -ое, -ие**) *прил* Tahitian.

Тайва́н|ь (**-я**) *м* Taiwan.

тайга́ (**-и́**) *ж* the taiga.

тайко́м *нареч* in secret, secretly.

тайм (**-а**) *м* (СПОРТ) period; **пе́рвый/второ́й** ~ (ФУТБОЛ) the first/second half.

тайм-а́ут (**-а**) *м* (СПОРТ) time-out.

та́йн|а (**-ы**) *ж* (*секрет*) secret; (*загадка*) mystery; **держа́ть** (*impf*) **что-н в** ~**е** to keep sth secret; **храни́ть** (*impf*) ~**у** to keep a secret.

тайни́к (**-а́**) *м* hiding place.

та́йный *прил* secret.

тайфу́н (**-а**) *м* typhoon.

KEYWORD

так *нареч* **1** (*указательное: таким образом*) like this, this way; **де́лайте так** do it like this *или* this way; **пусть бу́дет так** so be it; **так не пойдёт** that won't do; **она́ всё де́лает не так** she does everything wrong

2 (*настолько*) so; **я так испуга́лся, что на́чал крича́ть** I was so frightened I started to shout; **всё случи́лось так неожи́данно!** it all happened so unexpectedly!

3 (*без последствий*) just like that; **так э́то не пройдёт** you won't get away with it

4 (*разг: без какого-н намерения*) for no (special) reason; **я сказа́л э́то про́сто так** I said it for no (special) reason; **почему́ ты пла́чешь? – да так** why are you crying? – for no reason

♦ *част* **1** (*разг: ничего*) nothing; **что с тобо́й? – так** what's wrong? – nothing

2 (*разг: усилительная*): **а она́ так жа́ловалась!** she didn't half complain!; **так я тебе́ и пове́рил!** I'm not falling for that!

3 (*разг: приблизительно*) about; **дня так че́рез два** in about two days

4 (*например*) for example; **поведе́ние у него́ плохо́е; так, вчера́ слома́л окно́** his behaviour is bad, for example, yesterday he broke a window

5 (*да*) OK; **так, всё хорошо́/пра́вильно** OK, that's fine/correct
♦ *союз* **1** (*в таком случае*) then; **пло́хо себя́ чу́вствуешь, так иди́ спать** if you feel ill, (then) go and have a sleep; **е́хать, так е́хать** if we are going, (then) let's go
2 (*таким образом*) so; **так ты пое́дешь?** so, you are going?
3 (*но*) but; **я пыта́лся его́ убеди́ть, так он не слу́шает** I tried to convince him but he wouldn't listen
4 (*в разделительных вопросах*): **э́то поле́зная кни́га, не так ли?** it's a useful book, isn't it?; **он хоро́ший челове́к, не так ли?** he's a good person, isn't he?; **у них есть соба́ка, не так ли?** they have a dog, don't they?
5 (*во фразах*): **и так** (*и без того уже*) anyway; **е́сли** *или* **раз так** in that case; **так и быть!** so be it!; **так и есть** (*разг*) sure enough; **так ему́!** serves him right!; **та́к себе** (*разг*) so-so; **так как** since; **так что** so; **так что́бы** so that.

такела́ж (-а) *м* rigging.
та́кже *союз, нареч* also; **я ~ подде́рживаю Ва́ше предложе́ние** I also *или* too am in favour (*ВRIT*) *или* favor (*US*) of your suggestion; **мне нра́вится ~ и Ва́ше предложе́ние** I like your suggestion too *или* as well; **с Но́вым Го́дом! – и Вас ~** Happy New Year! – the same to you; **а ~** and also.
-таки *част* (*разг: всё же*) *emphatic particle;* **ты~ отказа́лся** so you decided to refuse then; **он~ пришёл** so he did come then; **она́ пря́мо-исхо́дит от гне́ва** she is really furious; **опя́ть~** but having said that; **та́к~** (*разг*) so that's the way it is.
тако́в (-а́, -о́, -ы́) *как сказ* such; **~ тебе́ мой сове́т** that is my advice to you; **ситуа́ция такова́, что ...** the situation is such that ...; **и был ~** (*разг*) and we never saw him again.
таково́й *мест*: **как ~** as such.
тако́е (-о́го) *ср* (*о чём-н интересном, важном итп*) something; **я ~ слы́шала!** I've heard something; **~ происхо́дит** something is going on!; **что тут ~о́го?** what is so special about that?
тако́й *мест* such; **~ие лю́ди встреча́ются ре́дко** you rarely meet such people; **до ~ сте́пени** to such an extent; **~ая жара́!** such heat!; **кто ~?** who is it?; **он сего́дня како́й-то не ~** he is not quite himself today; **что ~о́е?** what is it?; **~-то** (*о лице*) so-and-so; (*о предмете*) such-and-such.
тако́й-сяко́й *мест* (*разг*) **ах ты ~** you little so-and-so.
та́кс|а (-ы) *ж* (*зоол*) dachshund; (*комм*) (fixed) rate; **пла́та по ~е** fixed-rate payment.
такса́ци|я (-и) *ж* rating.
такси́ *ср нескл* taxi.
такси́р|овать (-ую) (*не)сов перех* (*услуги итп*)

to set a rate for.
такси́ст (-а) *м* taxi driver.
таксомото́р (-а) *м* taxicab.
таксопа́рк (-а) *м сокр* (= таксомото́рный парк) taxi depot.
таксофо́н (-а) *м* payphone.
такт (-а) *м* (*тактичность*) tact; (*муз*) bar (*ВRIT*), measure (*US*); (*ритм*) beat; **в ~ му́зыке** in time with the music.
та́ктик (-а) *м* tactician.
та́ктик|а (-и) *ж* tactic; (*воен*) tactics *мн*.
такти́чен *прил см* **такти́чный**.
такти́ческий (-ая, -ое, -ие) *прил* tactical.
такти́ч|ный (-ен, -на, -но) *прил* tactful.
тала́нт (-а) *м* talent.
тала́нтлив|ый (-, -а, -о) *прил* talented.
талисма́н (-а) *м* charm, talisman.
та́ли|я (-и) *ж* waist; **пла́тье в ~ю** dress fitted at the waist.
Та́ллин (-а) *м* Tallin(n).
талму́д (-а) *м* the Talmud.
тало́н (-а) *м* ticket; (*на бензин, на продукты итп*) coupon.
та́лый *прил* (*снег, лёд*) melted.
тальк (-а) *м* talcum powder, talc.
там *нареч* there; **бу́ду ~ ско́ро** I'll be there soon; **~ посмо́трим** (*разг*) we'll see; **каки́е ~ сомне́ния** (*разг*) what's there to be unsure about?; **како́е ~!** (*разг*) not a chance!; **я ду́мал, что он догада́ется – куда́ уж ~!** (*разг*) I thought he'd guess, but not a bit of it!; **что ~ ни говори́, а мы оши́блись** whatever you say, we still made a mistake; **и ~ и сям** (*разг*) here, there and everywhere.
тамад|а́ (-ы́) *ж* (*мужчина*) toastmaster; (*женщина*) toastmistress.
та́мбур (-а) *м section at door of train carriage.*
тамбури́н (-а) *м* (*барабан*) tambourin (*small drum*); (*бубен*) tambourine.
тамо́жен *сущ см* **тамо́жня**.
тамо́женник (-а) *м* customs officer.
тамо́женный *прил* (*досмотр*) customs *опред*; **тамо́женная по́шлина** customs (duty).
тамо́ж|ня (-ни; *gen pl* -ен) *ж* customs.
та́мпекс (-а) *м* Tampax ®.
тампо́н (-а) *м* tampon.
та́нгенс (-а) *м* (*мат*) tangent.
та́нго *ср нескл* tango.
та́н|ец (-ца) *м* dance; *см также* **та́нцы**.
танзани́йский (-ая, -ое, -ие) *прил* Tanzanian.
Танзани́|я (-и) *ж* Tanzania.
тани́н (-а) *м* tannin.
танк (-а) *м* (*воен, тех*) tank.
та́нкер (-а) *м* tanker (*ship*).
танке́т|ка (-ки; *gen pl* -ок) *ж* (*обычно мн: обувь*) wedge heel.
танки́ст (-а) *м* tank crew member.

та́нца *итп сущ см* **та́нец.**

танцева́льный *прил* dance *опред;* ~**зал** dance hall.

танц|ева́ть (**-у́ю**) *несов (не)перех* to dance.

танцо́вщик (**-а**) *м* dancer.

танцо́вщиц|а (**-ы**) *ж см* **танцо́вщик.**

танцпло́ща́д|ка (**-ки**; *gen pl* **-ок**) *ж сокр* (= *танцева́льная площа́дка*) dance floor.

танцо́р (**-а**) *м* dancer.

та́нц|ы (**-ев**) *мн* (*вечер*) dance *ед*; **идти́ (пойти́** *perf*) **на** ~ to go dancing.

та́поч|ка (**-ки**; *gen pl* **-ек**) *ж* (*обычно мн*: *домашняя*, (: *спортивная*) plimsoll (*BRIT*), sneaker (*US*).

та́р|а (**-ы**) *ж собир* containers *мн*.

тараба́н|ить (**-ю, -ишь**) *несов неперех* (*разг*) to rap.

тараба́рщин|а (**-ы**) *ж* (*разг*) gobbledegook.

тарака́н (**-а**) *м* cockroach.

тара́н (**-а**) *м* (*ВОЕН*) ram.

тара́н|ить (**-ю, -ишь**; *perf* **протара́нить**) *несов перех* to ram.

таранта́с (**-а**) *м* tarantass (*large springless carriage*).

тара́нтул (**-а**) *м* tarantula.

тарара́м (**-а**) *м* (*разг*) hullaballoo.

тарато́р|ить (**-ю, -ишь**) *несов неперех* (*разг*) to gabble on.

тарах|те́ть (**-чу́, -ти́шь**) *несов неперех* (*колёса, мотор*) to rattle; (*человек*) to rattle on.

тара́щ|ить (**-у, -ишь**; *perf* **вы́таращить**) *несов перех:* ~ **глаза́** (**на** *+acc*) to stare (at)

► **тара́щиться** (*perf* **вы́таращиться**) *несов возв* (*разг*): ~**ся (на** *+acc*) to gawp *или* gawk (at).

таре́л|ка (**-ки**; *gen pl* **-ок**) *ж* plate; **глубо́кая** ~ soup plate; **лета́ющая** ~ flying saucer; **я здесь не в свое́й** ~**ке** (*разг*) I feel out of place here; *см также* **таре́лки.**

таре́л|ки (**-ок**) *мн* (*МУЗ*) cymbals *мн*.

тари́ф (**-а**) *м* tariff.

тарифика́ци|я (**-и**) *ж* tariffing.

тарифици́р|овать (**-ую**) (*не*)*сов перех* (*перевозки, услуги*) to tariff; ~ (*impf/perf*) **окла́ды/нало́ги** to set the salary/tax scale.

тари́фн|ый *прил:* ~**ая табли́ца/се́тка** list/scale of charges.

таска́|ть (**-ю**) *несов перех* to lug; (*разг*: *воровать*) to pinch; (: *одевать*) to wear; ~ (*impf*) **с собо́й** to carry around; ~ (*impf*) **кого́-н за́ во́лосы** to pull sb's hair

► **таска́ться** *несов возв* (*по магазинам итп*) to traipse around; ~**ся** (*impf*) **за кем-н** to trail around after sb.

Тасма́ни|я (**-и**) *ж* Tasmania.

тас|ова́ть (**-у́ю**; *perf* **стасова́ть**) *несов перех* to shuffle.

ТАСС *м сокр* (= *Телегра́фное аге́нтство Сове́тского Сою́за*) Tass (*main news agency of the Soviet Union*).

тата́рин (**-а**; *nom pl* **тата́ры**) *м* Tatar.

тата́р|ка (**-ки**; *gen pl* **-ок**) *ж см* **тата́рин.**

тата́ры *итп сущ см* **тата́рин.**

татуиро́в|ка (**-ки**; *gen pl* **-ок**) *ж* tattoo.

тахт|а́ (**-ы́**) *ж* divan (*BRIT*), ottoman (*US*).

та́ч|ка (**-ки**; *gen pl* **-ек**) *ж* wheelbarrow.

Ташке́нт (**-а**) *м* Tashkent.

тащ|и́ть (**-у́, -ишь**) *несов перех* (*тянуть*) to pull; (*волочить, также перен*) to drag; (*нести*) to haul; (*perf* **вы́тащить**; *перен: в театр, на прогулку*) to drag out; (*perf* **стащи́ть**; *разг: красть*) to nick; **он та́щит всю рабо́ту на себе́** he is lumbered with (*BRIT*) *или* has got landed with all the work

► **тащи́ться** *несов возв* (*медленно ехать*) to trundle along; (*идти неохотно*) to drag o.s. along; (*волочиться: подол*) to drag; **не хо́чется** ~**ся в таку́ю даль** I don't feel like traipsing all that way.

та́|ять (**-ю**; *perf* **раста́ять**) *несов неперех* to melt; (*перен: силы, деньги*) to dwindle; (: *от любви, от похвал*) to melt; (: *от болезни*) to waste away; ~ (*impf*) **во рту** (*перен*) to melt in the mouth.

Тбили́си *м нескл* Tbilisi.

ТВ *м сокр* (= **телеви́дение**) TV (= *television*).

твар|ь (**-и**) *ж* creature; (*разг: пренебр*) swine.

тверде́|ть (*3sg* **-ет**, *3pl* **-ют**, *perf* **затверде́ть**) *несов неперех* (*также перен*) to harden.

тверд|и́ть (**-жу́, -ди́шь**; *perf* **затверди́ть**) *несов перех* (*стихотворение, урок итп*) to learn by rote; ~ (*impf*) **о** *+prp* (*говорить*) to go on about.

твёрдо *нареч* (*верить, сказать*) firmly; (*заучить, запомнить*) properly; **я** ~ **зна́ю, что** ... I know for sure that ....

твердоло́б|ый (**-, -а, -о**) *прил* hard-headed.

твёрдост|ь (**-и**) *ж* firmness; (*цен*) stability; (*воли, характера*) toughness.

твёрд|ый *прил* (*ФИЗ*) solid; (**-, -á, -о**; *земля, предмет*) hard; (*решение, сторонник, тон итп*) firm; (*цены, ставки*) stable; (*порядок*) set; (*знания*) solid; (*воля, характер*) tough; (*ЛИНГ: звук*) hard, nonpalatalized; **здесь нужна́** ~**ая рука́** a firm hand is needed; **твёрдый знак** (*ЛИНГ*) hard sign.

твердын|я (**-и**) *ж* (*перен*) stronghold.

твёрже *сравн прил от* **твёрдый** ♦ *сравн нареч от* **твёрдо.**

тверж|у́ *несов см* **тверди́ть.**

твид (**-а**) *м* tweed.

твист (**-а**) *м* the twist.

тво|й (**-его́**; *f* **-я́**, *nt* **-ё**, *pl* **-и́**; *как* **мой**; *см* **Table 8**) *притяж мест* your; **вот** ~ **чай** here is your tea; **мой оте́ц врач – а** ~**?** my father is a doctor – what does yours do?; **э́то всё** ~**ё** this is all yours; **приве́т (всем)** ~**и́м** say hello to your folks; **по-**~**ему́ мне́нию** in your opinion; **как по-тво́ему?** what is your opinion?; **дава́й сде́лаем по-тво́ему** let's do it your way.

творе́ни|е (**-я**) *ср* creation.

твор|е́ц (**-ца́**) *м* creator; **Т**~ (*РЕЛ*) the Creator.

твори́тельный *прил:* ~ **паде́ж** (*ЛИНГ*) the instrumental (case).

твор|и́ть (-ю́, -и́шь) *несов неперех* to create ◆ (*perf* **сотвори́ть**) *перех* (*шедевр, симфонию итп*) to create; (*perf* **натвори́ть**; *разг*) to get up to; ~ (**сотвори́ть** *perf*) **чудеса́** to work miracles; ~ (**сотвори́ть** *perf*) **добро́** to do good; ~ (*impf*) **беззако́ния** to commit unjust acts
▸ **твори́ться** *несов возв*: **что тут** ~**и́тся?** what's going on here?; **с ним** ~**и́тся что́-то стра́нное** something strange has come over him.
творо́г (-а́; *part gen* -у́) *м* ≈ curd cheese.
творо́жник (-а) *м* curd pancake.
творо́жный *прил* curd-cheese.
творца́ *итп сущ см* **творе́ц**.
тво́рческ|ий (-ая, -ое, -ие) *прил* creative; **тво́рческий о́тпуск** sabbatical.
тво́рчеств|о (-а) *ср* creative work; (*писателя, композитора*) work; **худо́жественное** ~ artistic creativity; **наро́дное** ~ folk art.
тво|я́ (-е́й) *притяж мест см* **твой**.
ТВЧ *сокр* (= **то́ки высо́кой частоты́**) high frequency currents *мн*.
т.д. *сокр* (= **так да́лее**) etc. (= *et cetera*).
те (**тех**) *мест см* **тот**.
т.е. *сокр* (= **то есть**) i.e. (= *id est*).
теа́тр (-а) *м* theatre (*BRIT*), theater (*US*); ~ **Го́голя/Шекспи́ра** Gogol's/Shakespeare's theatrical works; ~ **вое́нных де́йствий** the theatre of operations.
театра́л (-а) *м* theatregoer (*BRIT*), theatergoer (*US*).
театрализ|ова́ть (-у́ю) (*не*)*сов перех* to dramatize.
театра́л|ка (-ки; *gen pl* -ок) *ж см* **театра́л**.
театра́льный *прил* (*афиша, сезон*) theatre *опред* (*BRIT*), theater *опред* (*US*); (*деятельность, жест*) theatrical; **театра́льная ка́сса** theatre box office; **театра́льная сту́дия** theatre studio; **театра́льный зал** theatre; **театра́льный институ́т** drama school.
театрове́д (-а) *м* theatre (*BRIT*) *или* theater (*US*) specialist.
тебе́ *мест см* **ты** ◆ *как част* (*разг*): **здесь** ~ **и по́мощь и понима́ние** you can get help and understanding here; **я** ~ **поспо́рю!** don't you dare to argue!; **я** ~ **дам** *или* **покажу́!** I'll show you!
тебя́ *мест см* **ты**.
Тегера́н (-а) *м* Teheran.
теза́урус (-а) *м* thesaurus.
те́зис (-а) *м* (*идея*) thesis (*мн* theses); (: *в логике*) proposition; (*обычно мн: доклада, статьи*) abstract.
тёз|ка (-ки; *gen pl* -ок) *м/ж* namesake.
тёк *итп несов см* **течь**.
текст (-а) *м* text; (*песни*) words *мн*, lyrics *мн*.
тексти́л|ь (-я) *м собир* textiles *мн*.
тексти́льный *прил*: ~**ые изде́лия** textiles; ~**ая промы́шленность** textile industry.

теку́т *итп несов см* **течь**.
теку́честь (-и) *ж* fluidity; ~ **ка́дров** high staff turnover.
теку́ч|ий (-ая, -ее, -ие; -, -а, -е) *прил* fluid; ~**ие ка́дры** fluctuating workforce.
теку́ч|ка (-и) *ж* (*разг*) daily routine.
теку́щий (-ая, -ее, -ие) *прил* (*год*) current; (*повседневный*): **дела́** routine; ~**ие обяза́тельства** (*КОММ*) current liabilities *мн*; **теку́щие собы́тия** current affairs; **теку́щий ремо́нт** running repairs, maintenance; **теку́щий счёт** (*КОММ*) current (*BRIT*) *или* checking (*US*) account.
тел. *сокр* (= **телефо́н**) tel. (= *telephone*).
телевеща́ни|е (-я) *ср* television broadcasting.
телеви́дени|е (-я) *ср* television; **по** ~**ю** on television.
телевизио́нный *прил* television *опред*.
телеви́зор (-а) *м* television (set); **смотре́ть** (*impf*) ~ to watch television; **по** ~**у** on television.
теле́г|а (-и) *ж* cart.
телегра́мм|а (-ы) *ж* telegram.
телегра́ф (-а) *м* (*способ связи*) telegraph; (*учреждение*) telegraph office.
телеграфи́р|овать (-ую) (*не*)*сов перех* to wire.
телеграфи́ст (-а) *м* telegraphist.
телеграфи́ст|ка (-ки; *gen pl* -ок) *ж см* **телеграфи́ст**.
телегра́фный *прил* (*также перен*) telegraphic; **телегра́фное аге́нтство** news agency; **телегра́фный де́нежный перево́д** telegraphic transfer; **телегра́фный столб** telegraph pole.
теле́ж|ка (-ки; *gen pl* -ек) *ж уменьш от* **теле́га**; (*для багажа, в супермаркете*) trolley.
телезри́тел|ь (-я) *м* viewer.
телека́мер|а (-ы) *ж* television camera.
те́лекс (-а) *м* telex.
телён|ок (-ёнка; *nom pl* -я́та, *gen pl* -я́т) *м* calf (*мн* calves).
телепа́ти|я (-и) *ж* telepathy.
телепереда́ч|а (-и) *ж* TV programme (*BRIT*) *или* program (*US*).
теле́сен *прил см* **теле́сный**.
телеско́п (-а) *м* telescope.
телескопи́ческ|ий (-ая, -ое, -ие) *прил* (*антенна, очки*) telescopic; (*наблюдения*) long-distance.
теле́с|ный (-ен, -на, -но) *прил* bodily; ~**ного цве́та** flesh-coloured; **теле́сное наказа́ние** corporal punishment.
телеста́нци|я (-и) *ж* television station.
телесту́ди|я (-и) *ж* television studio.
телета́йп (-а) *м* teleprinter (*BRIT*), teletypewriter (*US*), Teletype ®.
телефо́н (-а) *м* telephone; (*разг: номер*) (phone) number.
телефони́ст (-а) *м* telephonist.
телефони́ст|ка (-ки; *gen pl* -ок) *ж см*

The spelling rules for Russian are shown on page xvii.

телефони́ст.

телефо́нный *прил* telephone *опред*; **телефо́нная ста́нция** telephone exchange; **телефо́нная кни́га** telephone book *или* directory.

теле́ц *сущ см* **те́льце.**

Теле́ц (-ца́) *м* (*созвездие*) Taurus.

телеце́нтр (-а) *м* television centre (*BRIT*) *или* center (*US*).

тел|и́ться (*3sg* -ится, *3pl* -ятся, *perf* **отели́ться**) *несов возв* to calve.

тёл|ка (-ки; *gen pl* -ок) *ж* heifer.

те́л|о (-а; *nom pl* -а́) *ср* body; **небе́сные тела́** heavenly bodies; **дрожа́ть** (*impf*) **всем ~м** to tremble all over; **держа́ть** (*impf*) **кого́-н в чёрном ~е** to treat sb badly.

телогре́|йка (-йки; *gen pl* -ек) *ж* body warmer.

телодвиже́ни|е (-я) *ср* movement.

тёлок *сущ см* **тёлка.**

телосложе́ни|е (-я) *ср* physique.

телохрани́тел|ь (-я) *м* bodyguard.

Тель-Ави́в (-а) *м* Tel Aviv.

тельня́ш|ка (-ки; *gen pl* -ек) *ж* sailor top.

Тельца́ *итп сущ см* **Теле́ц.**

те́ль|це (-ьца; *nom pl* -ьца́, *gen pl* -е́ц) *ср уменьш от* **те́ло**; (*ребёнка*) body; (*обычно мн*: *кровяные*) corpuscle.

теля́та *итп сущ см* **телёнок.**

теля́тин|а (-ы) *ж* veal.

теля́тник (-а) *м* (*помещение*) calf shed.

теля́чий (-ья, -ье, -ьи) *прил*: **~ья ко́жа** calfskin *опред*; (*КУЛИН*) veal *опред*; **~ьи не́жности** (*разг*) lovey-dovey behaviour; **~ восто́рг** (*разг*) wide-eyed enthusiasm.

тем *мест см* **тот, то** ♦ *союз* (+*comparative*): **чем бо́льше, ~ лу́чше** the more the better; **~ бо́лее!** all the more so!; **~ бо́лее что ...** especially as ...; **э́то тру́дно, ~ бо́лее для меня́** it's difficult, especially for me; **~ лу́чше/ху́же** that's even better/worse; **~ лу́чше для меня́** all the better for me; **не хо́чет слу́шать? ~ ху́же для него́** if he doesn't want to listen then it's his loss; **~ не ме́нее** nevertheless; **~ са́мым** thus.

те́м|а (-ы) *ж* subject, topic; (*МУЗ, ЛИТЕРАТУРА*) theme.

тема́тик|а (-и) *ж* theme.

темати́ческ|ий (-ая, -ое, -ие) *прил* (*выставка, показ фильмов итп*) theme-based.

тембр (-а) *м* timbre.

тёмен *прил см* **тёмный.**

те́мени *итп сущ см* **те́мя.**

Те́мз|а (-ы) *ж* the Thames.

те́ми *мест см* **тот, то.**

темне́|ть (*3sg* -ет, *3pl* -ют, *perf* **потемне́ть**) *несов неперех* (*небо, краска*) to darken ♦ (*perf* **стемне́ть**) *безл* to get dark; (*no perf*; *виднеться*) to loom dark; **зимо́й ра́но ~ет** it gets dark early in winter.

темн|и́ть (-ю́, -и́шь) *несов неперех* (*разг*) to confuse the issue.

темни́ц|а (-ы) *ж* dungeon.

темно́ *как сказ*: **на у́лице/в ко́мнате ~** it's dark outside/inside; **на душе́ у неё бы́ло ~** she felt gloomy.

темнот|а́ (-ы́) *ж* darkness; (*перен*: *невежество*) ignorance.

тём|ный (-ен, -на́, -но́) *прил* dark; (*смысл, теория*) obscure; (*прошлое, дела*) shady; (*невежественный*: *человек*) ignorant; **~ное пятно́** (*перен*) blemish; **~ные времена́** dark times.

темп (-а) *м* speed; (*МУЗ*) tempo; **в те́мпе** (*разг*) quickly; **ускоря́ть** (**ускорить** *perf*) **~ +***gen* to speed up.

те́мпер|а (-ы) *ж* tempera.

темпера́мент (-а) *м* temperament, disposition; **он челове́к с ~ом** he is a temperamental character.

темпера́мент|ный (-ен, -на, -но) *прил* (*речь, исполнение, человек*) spirited.

температу́р|а (-ы) *ж* temperature; **у меня́ ~** I've got a temperature; **ходи́ть** (*impf*) **с ~ой** (*разг*) to go about with a temperature.

температу́р|ить (-ю, -ишь) *несов неперех* (*разг*) to be running a temperature.

те́м|я (-ени; *как* **вре́мя**; *см* **Table 4**) *ср* crown (*of the head*).

те́нге (-) *м* tenga (*currency unit of Kazakhstan*).

тенденцио́зность (-и) *ж* bias.

тенденцио́зный *прил* bias(s)ed.

тенде́нци|я (-и) *ж*: **~ (к +***dat*) tendency (towards); (*предвзятость*) bias.

теневой *прил* shady; (*перен*: *стороны жизни*) shadowy; **тенева́я эконо́мика** shadow economy; **теневой кабине́т** (*полит*) shadow cabinet.

тенелюби́в|ый (-, -а, -о) *прил* (*БОТ*) shade-loving.

те́н|и (-ей) *мн* (*также:* **~ для век**) eye shadow *ед*.

тени́ст|ый (-, -а, -о) *прил* shady.

те́ннис (-а) *м* tennis.

тенниси́ст (-а) *м* tennis player.

тенниси́ст|ка (-ки; *gen pl* -ок) *ж см* **тенниси́ст.**

те́ннис|ка (-ки; *gen pl* -ок) *ж* polo shirt.

те́ннис|ный *прил*: **~ая раке́тка** tennis racket; **те́ннисный корт/мяч** tennis court/ball.

те́ннисок *сущ см* **те́нниска.**

те́нор (-а; *nom pl* -а́) *м* (*МУЗ*) tenor.

тент (-а) *м* awning.

тен|ь (-и; *prp sg* -и́, *gen pl* -е́й) *ж* (*тенистое место*) shade; (*предмета, человека*) shadow; (+*gen*; *перен*: *волнения, печали итп*) flicker of; **отбра́сывать** (**отбро́сить** *perf*) **~** to cast a shadow; **держа́ться** (*impf*) **в ~и́** (*перен*) to remain in the background; **броса́ть** (**бро́сить** *perf*) **~ на +***acc* (*перен*) to cast a slur on; **без те́ни сомне́ния** without a shadow of a doubt; **нет ни те́ни сомне́ния, что ...** there is not the slightest doubt that ...; *см также* **те́ни.**

теологи́ческ|ий (-ая, -ое, -ие) *прил* theological.

теоло́ги|я (-и) *ж* theology.

теоре́м|а (-ы) ж theorem.
теоре́тик (-а) м theoretician.
теорети́чес|кий (-ая, -ое, -ие) *прил* theoretical.
тео́ри|я (-и) ж theory.
тёпел *прил см* **тёплый**.
тепе́решн|ий (-яя, -ее, -ие) *прил* (*разг*) present.
тепе́рь *нареч* (*сейчас*) now; (*в наше время*) nowadays ♦ *союз*: ~ обсу́дим сле́дующий вопро́с let us now move on to the next question.
тепле́|ть (*3sg* -ет, *3pl* -ют, *perf* **потепле́ть**) *несов неперех* to get warmer; (*отношения*) to become warmer.
тёпл|иться (*3sg* -ится, *3pl* -ятся) *несов возв* to flicker; **в нём ещё ~ится наде́жда** he still holds out a faint hope.
тепли́ц|а (-ы) ж hothouse.
тепли́чный *прил* (*растение*) hothouse *опред*; (*перен: условия*) sheltered.
тепло́ *нареч* warmly ♦ (-á) *ср* (*также перен*) warmth ♦ *как сказ* it's warm; **на у́лице/в ко́мнате** ~ it's warm outside/inside; **нас** ~ **встре́тили** we were given a warm welcome; **10 гра́дусов** ~á 10 degrees (centigrade); **мне** ~ I'm warm.
теплово́з (-а) м locomotive.
теплово́й *прил* (*лучи, энергия*) thermal; **теплово́й дви́гатель** heat engine; **теплово́й уда́р** (*МЕД*) heatstroke.
теплолюби́в|ый (-, -а, -о) *прил* (*БОТ*) heat-loving.
теплообме́н (-а) м (*ФИЗ*) heat exchange.
теплот|а́ (-ы́) ж heat; (*перен: чувств, отношений, красок*) warmth.
теплохо́д (-а) м motor ship *или* vessel.
теплоцентра́л|ь (-и) ж generator plant (*supplying central heating systems*).
тёпл|ый (-ел, -ла́, -ло́) *прил* warm; ~**лое месте́чко** (*разг*) cushy job; **сказа́ть** (*perf*) **кому́-н па́ру** ~**лых слов** (*разг*) to give sb a piece of one's mind.
терапе́вт (-а) м ≈ general practitioner.
терапи́|я (-и) ж (*МЕД: наука*) internal medicine; (*лечение*) therapy; **интенси́вная** ~ intensive care.
тереб|и́ть (-лю́, -и́шь) *несов перех* (*волосы, бороду*) to twiddle; (*разг: надоедать*) to pester.
тере́|ть (**тру, трёшь**, *pt* **тёр, тёрла, тёрло**) *несов перех* to rub; (*чистить*) to scrub; (*овощи*) to grate ♦ *неперех* (*обувь, воротник*) to rub
► **тере́ться** *несов возв* (*человек*): ~**ся о** +*acc* to rub o.s. up against; (*перен: разг*): ~**ся о́коло** *или* **во́зле** +*gen* to hang around.
терза́ни|е (-я) *ср* (*обычно мн: душевные*) torment.
терза́|ть (-ю; *perf* **растерза́ть**) *несов перех* (*добычу*) to savage; (*perf* **истерза́ть**; *перен: упрёками, ревностью*) to torment
► **терза́ться** *несов возв* (+*instr*; *сомнениями,*

раскаянием) to be racked by.
тёрк|а (-ки; *gen pl* -ок) ж grater.
те́рмин (-а) м term.
термина́л (-а) м terminal.
терминологи́чес|кий (-ая, -ое, -ие) *прил*: ~ **слова́рь** specialized dictionary.
терминоло́ги|я (-и) ж terminology.
терми́чес|кий (-ая, -ое, -ие) *прил* thermal.
термо́метр (-а) м thermometer.
те́рмос (-а) м Thermos®.
термоста́т (-а) м thermostat.
термосто́й|кий (-ая, -ое, -ие) *прил* heat-resistant.
термоя́дерный *прил* thermonuclear; **термоя́дерное ору́жие** thermonuclear weapon.
терни́ст|ый (-, -а, -о) *прил*: ~ **путь** (*перен*) difficult path.
терно́вник (-а) м blackthorn.
тёрок *сущ см* **тёрка**.
терпели́в|ый (-, -а, -о) *прил* patient.
терпе́ни|е (-я) *ср* patience; **выводи́ть** (**вы́вести** *perf*) **кого́-н из** ~**я** to exhaust sb's patience; ~ **у меня́ ло́пнуло** I lost my patience; **запаса́ться** (**запасти́сь** *perf*) ~**м** to call on one's reserve of patience.
терп|е́ть (-лю́, -ишь) *несов перех* (*боль, холод итп*) to suffer, endure; (*perf* **потерпе́ть**; *неудачу*) to suffer; (*мириться: грубость, наглеца итп*) to tolerate; ~ (**потерпе́ть** *perf*) **неуда́чу/пораже́ние** to suffer failure/a defeat; ~ (**потерпе́ть** *perf*) **круше́ние** (*корабль*) to be wrecked; (*поезд*) to crash; **вре́мя не те́рпит** time waits for no man; **де́ло не те́рпит отлага́тельств** this matter won't wait; ~ **не могу́ таки́х люде́й** (*разг*) I can't stand people like that; ~ **не могу́ спо́рить** (*разг*) I hate arguing
► **терпе́ться** *несов безл*: (**мне**) **не те́рпится** +*infin* I can't wait to do.
терпи́мост|ь (-и) ж: ~ (**к** +*dat*) tolerance (of).
терпи́м|ый (-, -а, -о) *прил* tolerable; (*человек, отношение*): ~ (**к** +*dat*) tolerant (towards).
те́рп|кий (-кая, -кое, -кие; -ок, -ка, -ко) *прил* tart.
терплю́|(сь) *несов см* **терпе́ть(ся)**.
тёрпок *прил см* **тёрпкий**.
террако́т|а (-ы) ж terracotta.
террако́товый *прил* terracotta.
терра́с|а (-ы) ж (*также ГЕО*) terrace.
территориа́льный *прил* territorial.
террито́ри|я (-и) ж (*страны*) territory; (*школы, усадьбы*) grounds мн; **о́бщая** ~ **заво́да – 100 кв миль** the plant occupies an area of 100 sq miles.
терро́р (-а) м terror.
терроризи́р|овать (-ую) (*не*)*сов перех* to terrorize.
террори́зм (-а) м terrorism.
террори́ст (-а) м terrorist.
террористи́чес|кий (-ая, -ое, -ие) *прил*

terrorist *опред.*

террори́ст|ка (**-ки;** *gen pl* **-ок**) *ж см* **террори́ст**.

тёртый *прил* (*сыр, овощи*) grated; **челове́к он ~** (*разг*) he's been around.

терье́р (**-а**) *м* terrier.

теря́|ть (**-ю;** *perf* **потеря́ть**) *несов перех* to lose; **~ (потеря́ть** *perf*) **го́лову** to lose one's head; **~ (потеря́ть** *perf*) **из ви́ду** (*перестать видеть*) to lose sight of; (*не иметь сведений о*) to lose touch with; **~ (потеря́ть** *perf*) **по́чву под нога́ми** (*перен*) to lose one's way

▸ **теря́ться** (*perf* **потеря́ться**) *несов возв* to get lost; (*робеть*) to lose one's nerve; (*утрачиваться: память, уверенность*) to disappear; **~ся** (*impf*) **в дога́дках** to get caught up in conjecture.

тёс (**-а**) *м собир* planks *мн*.

тёсаный *прил* hewn.

те|са́ть (**-шу́, -шешь**) *несов перех* to hew (out).

тесём|ка (**-ки;** *gen pl* **-ок**) *ж* = **тесьма́;** (*завязка*) drawstring.

тесен *прил см* **те́сный**.

тесн|и́ть (**-ю́, -и́шь;** *perf* **потесни́ть**) *несов перех* (*друг друга в толпе*) to squeeze; (*кого-н к стене*) to press; (*противника*) to press back; (*perf* **стесни́ть;** *перен*): **~и́т в груди́** he *итп* has got a tight feeling in his chest

▸ **тесни́ться** *несов возв* (*люди: в толпе, в тесной комнате*) to be squashed together; (*мысли*) to crowd; **семья́ ~и́тся в одно́й ко́мнате** the whole family lives crammed together in one room; **в голове́ ~я́тся воспомина́ния** his *итп* mind is crowded with memories.

те́сно *нареч* (*стоять, расположить итп*) close together; (*сотрудничать*) closely ♦ *как сказ:* **в кварти́ре о́чень ~** the flat is very cramped; **мы с ним ~ знако́мы** he and I know each other very well.

теснот|а́ (**-ы́**) *ж* (*помещения*) cramped conditions *мн;* (*скопление людей*) crowd; (*в груди*) tightness; **в ~е́, да не в оби́де** ≈ the more the merrier.

те́с|ный (**-ен, -на́, -но**) *прил* (*проход*) narrow; (*помещение*) cramped; (*одежда*) tight; (*дружба, ряды*) close; **мир ~ен** it's a small world.

тест (**-а**) *м* test.

те́ст|о (**-а**) *ср* (*дрожжевое*) dough; (*слоёное, песочное*) pastry (*BRIT*), paste (*US*); (*для блинов*) batter; (*для кекса*) mixture; (*бетонное*) mix.

тест|ь (**-я**) *м* father-in-law, wife's father.

тесьм|а́ (**-ы́**) *ж* tape; (*для украшения*) trimming.

те́терев (**-а**) *м* black grouse.

тетёр|я (**-и**) *ж* (*разг*) clot; **глуха́я ~** cloth-ears; **со́нная ~** sleepyhead.

тетив|а́ (**-ы́**) *ж* (*лука*) bowstring.

тёт|ка (**-ки;** *gen pl* **-ок**) *ж* auntie; (*разг: пренебр: женщина*) old dear.

тетра́д|ка (**-ки;** *gen pl* **-ок**) *ж* exercise book.

тетра́д|ь (**-и**) *ж* exercise book; **но́тная ~**

manuscript book.

тёт|я (**-и;** *gen pl* **-ь**) *ж* aunt; (*разг: женщина*) lady.

те́фтел|и (**-ей**) *мн* meatballs *мн.*

тех *мест см* **те**.

Теха́с (**-а**) *м* Texas.

те́хник (**-а**) *м* technician.

те́хник|а (**-и**) *ж* technology; (*приёмы: музыкальная, плавания итп*) technique ♦ *собир* (*машины*) machinery; (*разг: муз*) hi-fi; **вычисли́тельная ~** (*КОМП*) computers *мн;* **те́хника безопа́сности** industrial safety.

те́хникум (**-а**) *м* technical college.

техни́чек *сущ см* **техни́чка**.

техни́чен *прил см* **техни́чный**.

техни́ческ|ий (**-ая, -ое, -ие**) *прил* technical; (*масло, волокно*) industrial; **техни́ческие нау́ки** engineering sciences; **техни́ческие сре́дства обуче́ния** educational technology; **техни́ческий осмо́тр** (*АВТ*) ≈ MOT (*BRIT*) (*annual roadworthiness check*); **техни́ческий реда́ктор** copy editor; **техни́ческое обслу́живание** maintenance, servicing.

техни́ч|ка (**-ки;** *gen pl* **-ек**) *ж* (*автомобиль*) emergency vehicle; (*уборщица*) cleaner.

техни́ч|ный (**-ен, -на, -но**) *прил* (*спортсмен, музыкант*) technically good.

технокра́т (**-а**) *м* technocrat.

техно́лог (**-а**) *м* technologist; (*производственного процесса*) process engineer.

технологи́ческ|ий (**-ая, -ое, -ие**) *прил* technological; (*не строительный*) engineering *опред;* (*не вспомогательный*) basic, major; **технологи́ческий институ́т** institute of technology.

техноло́ги|я (**-и**) *ж* technology.

тече́ни|е (**-я**) *ср* (*воды, жизни*) flow; (*поток: морское, атмосферное*) current; (*в политике, в искусстве*) trend, current; **в ~** *+gen* during; **с ~м вре́мени** in the course of time; **по ~ю** with the current; **плыть** (*impf*) **по ~ю** (*перен*) to go with the flow; **про́тив ~я** against the current.

те́чк|а (**-и**) *ж* (*ЗООЛ*) heat; **у на́шей соба́ки ~** our dog is on *или* in heat.

те|чь (*3sg* **-чёт,** *3pl* **-ку́т,** *pt* **тёк, текла́, текло́**) *несов неперех* (*вода, кровь итп*) to flow; (*крыша, лодка итп*) to leak; (*перен: жизнь, время*) to go by ♦ (**-чи**) *ж* leak; **дава́ть (дать** *perf*) **~** to spring a leak.

те́ш|ить (**-у, -ишь;** *perf* **поте́шить**) *несов перех* to amuse; (*самолюбие*) to indulge

▸ **те́шиться** (*perf* **поте́шиться**) *несов возв:* **~ся** *+instr* (*игрушкой*) to amuse o.s. with; (*мыслью*) to console o.s. with; (*издеваться*): **~ся над** *+instr* to make fun of.

тёщ|а (**-и**) *ж* mother-in-law, wife's mother.

тешу́ *итп несов см* **теса́ть**.

Тибе́т (**-а**) *м* Tibet.

тибе́тск|ий (**-ая, -ое, -ие**) *прил* Tibetan.

Тибр (**-а**) *м* Tiber (*river*).

Тигр (**-а**) *м* Tigris (*river*).

тигр (-а) *м* tiger.
тигрёнок (-ёнка; *nom pl* **-я́та**, *gen pl* **-я́т**) *м* tiger cub.
тигри́ца (-ы) *ж* tigress.
тигро́вый *прил* tiger *опред*; **тигро́вый глаз** (*камень*) tiger's-eye.
тигря́та *итп сущ см* **тигрёнок**.
тик (-а) *м* (*нервный*) tic; (*ткань*) ticking.
ти́кание (-я) *ср* ticking.
ти́кать (*3sg* **-ет**, *3pl* **-ют**) *несов неперех* to tick.
ти́на (-ы) *ж* slime; (*перен: обывательщины итп*) mire.
тип (-а) *м* type; (*разг: о мужчине*) character; **ти́па** +*gen* (*разг*) sort of.
типа́ж (-а́) *м* character type.
типи́чен *прил см* **типи́чный**.
типи́ческий (-ая, -ое, -ие) *прил* typical.
типи́чный (-ен, -на, -но) *прил*: ~ (**для** +*gen*) typical (of).
типово́й *прил* standard-type.
типогра́фия (-и) *ж* press, printing house.
типогра́фский (-ая, -ое, -ие) *прил* typographical; **типогра́фская кра́ска** printing ink; **типогра́фский стано́к** printing press.
типу́н (-а) *м*: ~ **тебе́ на язы́к!** (*разг*) don't say that!
тир (-а) *м* shooting gallery.
тира́да (-ы) *ж* tirade.
тира́ж (-а́) *м* (*газеты*) circulation; (*книги*) printing; (*лотереи, облигаций*) drawing; **кни́га вы́шла тиражо́м в ты́сячу экземпля́ров** one thousand copies of the book were printed; **выходи́ть** (**вы́йти** *perf*) **в** ~ (*заём, облигации*) to be issued; (*книга*) to be printed; (*перен*) to fade from the scene.
тира́н (-а) *м* tyrant.
Тира́на (-ы) *ж* Tirana.
тира́нить (-ю, -ишь) *несов перех* to tyrannize.
тирани́ческий (-ая, -ое, -ие) *прил* tyrannical.
тирани́я (-и) *ж* tyranny.
тире́ *ср нескл* dash.
тис (-а) *м* yew (tree).
ти́скать (-а) *несов перех* to squeeze.
тиски́ (-о́в) *мн* (*ТЕХ*) vice *ед* (*BRIT*), vise *ед* (*US*); **в** ~**áх** +*gen* (*перен*) in the grip of.
тисне́ние (-я) *ср* (*по коже*) stamping.
тиснёный *прил* (*переплёт*) impressed.
тита́н (-а) *м* (*в мифологии*) titan; (*перен: науки, мысли итп*) giant; (*хим*) titanium; (*для нагрева воды*) boiler, urn.
титани́ческий (-ая, -ое, -ие) *прил* titanic.
титр (-а) *м* (*обычно мн*) credit (*of a film*).
ти́тул (-а) *м* (*также КОММ*) title; ~ **на иму́щество** (*ЮР*) title (*to property*).
ти́тульный *прил*: ~ **лист** title page.
тиф (-а) *м* typhus; **брюшно́й** ~ typhoid fever.
тифо́зн|ый *прил*: ~**ая лихора́дка** typhoid fever ♦ (**-ого**) *decl like adj* м typhus patient.
ти́х|ий (-ая, -ое, -ие; -, -á, -о) *прил* quiet;

(*течение, ход*) gentle; **Ти́хий океа́н** the Pacific (Ocean).
ти́х|нуть (*3sg* **-нет**, *3pl* **-нут**, *pt* **-**, **-ла**, **-ло**) *несов неперех* (*говорить, жить итп*) to go quiet.
ти́хо *нареч* (*говорить, жить итп*) quietly; (*идти*) slowly ♦ *как сказ*: **в до́ме** ~ the house is quiet; ~! (be) quiet!
тихо́ня (-и) *м/ж* (*разг*) quiet operator.
ти́ше *сравн прил от* **ти́хий** ♦ *сравн нареч от* **ти́хо**; ~! quiet!, hush!
тишина́ (-ы́) *ж* quiet.
тишь (-и) *ж* = **тишина́**.
т.к. *сокр* = **так как**.
тка́ный *прил* woven.
ткан|ь (-и) *ж* fabric, material; (*АНАТ*) tissue; (*перен: рассказа*) fabric.
ткать (-у, -ёшь; *perf* **сотка́ть**) *несов перех* to weave; (*паутину*) to spin.
тка́цк|ий (-ая, -ое, -ие) *прил*: ~**ое произво́дство** weaving; **тка́цкая фа́брика** mill (*for fabric production*); **тка́цкий стано́к** loom.
ткач (-а́) *м* weaver.
ткачи́х|а (-и) *ж см* **ткач**.
ткну́ть(ся) (-у(сь), -ёшь(ся)) *сов от* **ты́кать(ся)**.
тлен (-а) *м* decay.
тлетво́рный (-ен, -на, -но) *прил* pernicious.
тле|ть (*3sg* **-ет**, *3pl* **-ют**) *несов неперех* (*навоз, мусор*) to decay; (*дрова, угли*) to smoulder (*BRIT*), smolder (*US*); (*пламя*) to die out; (*перен: надежда*) to flicker.
▶ **тле́ться** *несов возв* (*костёр, угли*) to smo(u)lder; (*надежда*) to flicker.
тл|я (-и) *ж* aphid.
тмин (-а) *м* (*БОТ*) tumin.
т.н. *сокр* = **так называ́емый**.
ТНК *ж сокр* = **транснациона́льная корпора́ция**.
то *союз* (*условный*): **éсли** ... ~ ... if ... then ...; (*разделительный*): ~ ... ~ ... sometimes ... sometimes ...; **éсли его́ не бу́дет там**, ~ **я не**, **пойду́** if he isn't going to be there, (then) I'm not going; ~ **even**; **он** ~ **зна́ет об э́том** even he knows about it; ~ **есть** that is; ~ **и де́ло** time and again.
то (**того́**) *мест см* **тот**.
т.о. *сокр* = **таки́м о́бразом**.
-то *част* (*для выделения*): **письмо́-то ты получи́л?** did you (at least) receive the letter?; **где́-то она́ сейча́с** if only I knew where she is now; **когда́-то мы встре́тимся?** when on earth shall we meet?; **э́тот-то всё съел** this one here has eaten everything.
тобо́й *мест см* **ты**.
тобо́ю *мест* = **тобо́й**.
тов. *сокр* = **това́рищ**.
това́р (-а; *part gen* **-у**) *м* product; (*экон*) commodity ♦ *собир* goods *мн*.
това́рищ (-а) *м* (*приятель*) friend; (*по партии*)

comrade; ~ **по шкóле/рабóте** school-/
workmate.

товáрищеск|ий (**-ая, -ое, -ие**) *прил* comradely;
товáрищеский матч (*СПОРТ*) friendly (match).

товáриществ|о (**-а**) *ср* camaraderie; (*КОММ*)
partnership.

товáрный *прил* (*производство*) goods *опред*;
(*рынок*) commodity *опред*; **товáрная бúржа**
commodity exchange; **товáрный вагóн** goods
wagon (*BRIT*), freight car (*US*); **товáрный знак**
trademark; **товáрный пóезд** goods (*BRIT*) *или*
freight (*US*) train; **товáрный склад** warehouse.

товаровéд (**-а**) *м* merchandiser.

товарообмéн (**-а**) *м* barter.

товарооборóт (**-а**) *м* turnover.

товаропроизводúтель (**-я**) *м* (goods)
manufacturer.

тогдá *нареч* then; ~ **как** (*хотя*) while; (*при
противопоставлении*) whereas; **не хóчешь, ~
не нáдо** if you don't want to, then don't.

тогдáшн|ий (**-яя, -ее, -ие**) *прил* (*разг*): **в ~ие
временá** in those days.

тогó *мест см* **тот, то**.

тождéственный (**-, -на, -но**) *прил* identical.

тóждеств|о (**-а**) *ср* (*также МАТ*) identity.

тóже *нареч* (*также*) too, as well, also ♦ *част* as
if; **я ~ пойдý** I'm going too *или* as well, I'm also
going; ~ **мне поэ́т нашёлся!** as if he's a poet!;
я ~ люблю́ я́блоки I too like apples; **я идý
купáться – я ~!** I'm going swimming – me too!

той *мест см* **та**.

ток (**-а**) *м* (*ЭЛЕК*) current; (*для зерна*) threshing
floor.

токáрный *прил*: ~ **станóк** lathe.

тóкар|ь (**-я**; *nom pl* **-я́**) *м* turner.

Тóкио *м нескл* Tokyo.

токсикóз (**-а**) *м* toxicosis; (*беременной*)
hyperemesis.

токсúчен *прил см* **токсúчный**.

токсúческ|ий (**-ая, -ое, -ие**) *прил* toxic.

токсúчн|ый (**-ен, -на, -но**) *прил* = **токсúческий**.

толк (**-а**; *part gen* **-у**) *м* (*в рассуждениях*) sense;
(*разг*: польза) use; **рассуждáть** (*impf*) *или*
говорúть (*impf*) **с тóлком** to talk sense; **от негó
нет тóлку** (*разг*) he's no use; **всё бéз ~у** it's all
for nothing; **взять** (*perf*) **что-н себé в ~** (*разг*)
to get sth; **знать** (*impf*) *или* **понимáть** (*impf*) ~ **в
чём-н** to have a good understanding of sth;
сбивáть (**сбить** *perf*) **когó-н с тóлку** to confuse
sb.

толкáтел|ь (**-я**) *м*: ~ **ядрá** shot-putter.

толкá|ть (**-ю**; *perf* **толкнýть**) *несов перех* to
push; (*перен*): ~ **когó-н на** +*acc* (*подлеж:
голод*) to force sb into; (: *человек*) to put sb up
to; ~ (*impf*) **лóктем** to nudge; ~ (*impf*) **ядрó** to
put the shot; ~ (*impf*) **штáнгу** to lift weights; ~
(**толкнýть** *perf*) **речь** (*разг*) to have one's say

▶ **толкá|ться** *несов возв* (*в толпе*) to push
(one's way); (*разг: без дела*) to hang about *или*
around; ~**ся** (**толкнýться** *perf*) **в** +*acc* (*разг*: в
дверь) to push; (*перен*: в *учреждения*) to

approach.

тóлк|и (**-ов**) *мн* (*разг*) gossip *ед*.

толкнýть(ся) (**-ý(сь), -ёшь(ся)**) *сов от*
толкáть(ся).

толковáни|е (**-я**) *ср* interpretation; (*слова*)
definition.

толк|овáть (**-ую**) *несов перех* (*явления,
события итп*) to interpret; (*разг*): ~ **что-н** +*dat*
to spell sth out to; ~ (*impf*) **с кем-н о чём-н**
(*разг*) to have a chat with sb about sth.

толкóв|ый (**-, -а, -о**) *прил* (*ученик, работник*)
intelligent; (*объяснение*) clear; **толкóвый
словáрь** dictionary with definitions.

тóлком *нареч* (*разг*) properly; **я ~ ничегó не
узнáл** I didn't manage to find anything out.

толкотн|я́ (**-и́**) *ж* (*разг*: в *толпе*, в *очереди*)
crush.

толкý(сь) *итп несов см* **толóчь(ся)**.

толкý|чка (**-ки**; *gen pl* **-ек**) *ж* (*разг: рынок*) flea
market; (*место скопления людей*) crush.

толóк(ся) *итп несов см* **толóчь(ся)**.

толокн|ó (**-á**) *ср* oatmeal.

тол|óчь (**-кý, -чёшь** *итп*, **-кýт**; *pt* **-óк, -клá, -клó**,
perf **истолóчь** *или* **растолóчь**) *несов перех*
(*зерна, сухари*) to pound; ~ (*impf*) **вóду в стýпе**
(*разг*) to pound the air

▶ **толóчься** *несов возв* (*разг*) to crowd about
или around.

толп|á (**-ы́**; *nom pl* **-ы**) *ж* (*народа*) crowd; (*перен*:
в *противопоставление личности*) the crowd.

толп|úться (*3sg* **-úтся**, *3pl* **-я́тся**) *несов возв* to
crowd around.

толстé|ть (**-ю**; *perf* **потолстéть**) *несов неперех*
to get fatter.

толст|úть (*3sg* **-úт**, *3pl* **-я́т**) *несов перех* (*разг*):
Вас ~úт э́то плáтье that dress makes you look
fat.

толстокóж|ий (**-ая, -ее, -ие; -, -а, -о**) *прил*
(*также перен*) thick-skinned.

толстýх|а (**-и**) *ж* (*разг*) = **толстýшка**.

толстý|шка (**-ки**; *gen pl* **-ек**) *ж* (*разг*) fatty.

тóлст|ый (**-, -á, -о**) *прил* thick; (*человек, ноги
итп*) fat; **тóлстая кишкá** large intestine.

толстя́к (**-á**) *м* (*разг*) fatso.

толчёный *прил* crushed.

толче|я́ (**-и́**) *ж* (*разг*) crush.

толч|óк (**-кá**) *м* (в *спину*, в *грудь*) shove; (*при
торможении, при встряхивании*) jolt; (*при
землятресении*) tremor; (*перен*: к *работе, к
началу*) push; (*СПОРТ*: штанги) thrust; (: *ядра*)
put; (*разг: рынок*) flea market.

тóлщ|а (**-и**) *ж* (*льда, облакое*) mass.

тóлще *сравн прил от* **тóлстый**.

толщин|á (**-ы́**) *ж* (*тела, фигуры*) corpulence;
(*слоя, бревна*) thickness.

толь (**-я**) *м* roofing felt.

KEYWORD

тóлько *част* **1** only; **тóлько 5 книг** only 5
books; **он читáет тóлько газéты** he only reads
newspapers

2 (+*pron*/+*adv*; *усиливает выразительность*):

заче́м то́лько я согласи́лся! why on earth did I agree!; где то́лько он не побыва́л where has he NOT been!; попро́буй то́лько отказа́ться! just try to refuse!; поду́мать то́лько! imagine that!
♦ *союз* **1** (*сразу после*) as soon as; **то́лько напи́шешь, я прие́ду** as soon as you write, I'll come
2 (*однако, но*) only; **позвони́, то́лько разгова́ривай недо́лго** phone (*BRIT*) *или* call (*US*), only don't talk for long
♦ *нареч* **1** (*недавно*) (only) just; **ты давно́ здесь? - нет, то́лько вошла́** have you been here long? – no, I've (only) just come in
2 (*во фразах*): **то́лько лишь** (*разг*) only; **то́лько и всего́** (*разг*) that's all; **как** *или* **лишь** *или* **едва́ то́лько** (*сразу после того, как*) as soon as; **не то́лько ..., но и ...** not only ... but also ...; **то́лько бы** if only; **то́лько бы знать, где он!** if only I knew where he was!; **то́лько что** only just.

том *мест см* **тот, то**.
том (**-а**; *nom pl* **-а́**) *м* volume.
тома́т (**-а**) *м* (*помидор*) tomato (*мн* tomatoes); (*соус*) tomato purée.
тома́тный *прил*: **~ сок/суп** tomato juice/soup.
то́мен *прил см* **то́мный**.
томи́тельн|ый (**-ен, -ьна, -ьно**) *прил* tormenting.
том|и́ть (**-лю́, -и́шь**; *perf* **истоми́ть**) *несов перех* (*расспросами, ожиданием*) to torment
▶ **томи́ться** (*perf* **истоми́ться**) *несов возв* (*ожиданием, жаждой*) to be tormented.
томле́ни|е (**-я**) *ср* languor.
томлю́(сь) *несов см* **томи́ть(ся)**.
то́м|ный (**-ен, -на, -но**) *прил* languid.
тому́ *мест см* **тот, то**.
тон (**-а**) *м* (*также муз. мед*) tone.
тона́льност|ь (**-и**) *ж* (*муз*) key; (*картины*) tones *мн*; (*перен: стихотворения*) tone.
тонзилли́т (**-а**) *м* tonsillitis.
тонизи́рующ|ий (**-ая, -ее, -ие**) *прил* (*прогулка, напиток*) refreshing; **~ее сре́дство** tonic.
то́н|кий (**-кая, -кое, -кие; -ок, -ка́, -ко**) *прил* thin; (*фигура, пальцы*) slender; (*черты лица, работа, ум*) fine; (*запах, вкус*) delicate; (*обращение, различия, намёк*) subtle; (*слух*) sharp; **то́нкая кишка́** small intestine.
то́нко *нареч* (*резать*) thinly; (*пахнуть*) delicately; (*намекать, чувствовать*) subtly; **она́ ~ чу́вствует му́зыку/поэ́зию** she has a fine appreciation of music/poetry.
тонкоко́ж|ий (**-ая, -ее, -ие; -, -а, -о**) *прил* thin-skinned.
то́нкост|ь (**-и**) *ж* (*см прил*) thinness; slenderness; fineness; delicacy; subtlety; sharpness; (*частность*) detail; **до ~ей** down to the last detail; **вдава́ться** (*impf*) **в ~и** to go into detail.

то́нн|а (**-ы**) *ж* tonne.
тонна́ж (**-а**) *м* (*судна*) tonnage; (*вагона*) capacity.
тонне́л|ь (**-я**) *м* tunnel.
то́нок *прил см* **то́нкий**.
то́нус (**-а**) *м* (*сердца, тканей*) tone; **жи́зненный ~** vitality.
тон|у́ть (**-у́, -ешь**; *perf* **утону́ть** *или* **потону́ть**) *несов неперех* (*человек*) to drown; (*perf* **утону́ть**; *дерево, камень*) to sink; (*perf* **затону́ть**; *корабль*) to sink; (*увязать*): **~ в** +*prp* (*в снегу, в грязи*) to get stuck in; (*перен: в делах*) to be up to one's eyes in; (*no perf*; *перен: в зелени*) to get lost; (*в шуме*) to drown.
то́ньше *сравн прил от* **то́нкий** ♦ *сравн нареч от* **то́нко**.
топа́з (**-а**) *м* topaz.
то́па|ть (**-ю**) *несов неперех* (*разг: идти*) to go; **~** (*impf*) **нога́ми** to stamp one's feet; **~й отсю́да!** (*разг*) scram!
топ|и́ть (**-лю́, -ишь**) *несов перех* (*печь*) to stoke (up); (*дом*) to warm (up); (*плавить: масло, воск*) to melt; (*perf* **утопи́ть** *или* **потопи́ть**; *корабль*) to sink; (*человека*) to drown; (*perf* **потопи́ть**; *перен: дело*) to ruin; **~** (**потопи́ть** *perf*) **го́ре** to drown one's sorrows
▶ **топи́ться** *несов возв* (*печь*) to burn; (*помещение*) to be heated; (*perf* **растопи́ться**; *воск*) to melt; (*perf* **утопи́ться**; *лишить себя жизни*) to drown o.s.
то́пк|а (**-и**) *ж* (*действие: печи*) stoking; (*часть печи*) furnace.
то́п|кий (**-кая, -кое, -кие; -ок, -ка́, -ко**) *прил* (*дорога, почва*) muddy.
топлён|ый *прил* (*кулин: масло, жир*) melted; **~ое молоко́** boiled milk.
то́пливо (**-а**) *ср* fuel; **жи́дкое/твёрдое ~** liquid/solid fuel.
топлю́(сь) *несов см* **топи́ть(ся)**.
топогра́фи|я (**-и**) *ж* topography.
то́пок *прил см* **то́пкий**.
то́пол|ь (**-я**) *м* poplar.
топони́мик|а (**-и**) *ж* toponymy.
топо́р (**-а́**) *м* axe (*BRIT*), ax (*US*).
топо́рен *прил см* **топо́рный**.
топори́щ|е (**-а**) *ср* axe (*BRIT*) *или* ax (*US*) handle.
топо́р|ный (**-ен, -на, -но**) *прил* (*перен: работа, стиль*) crude.
топо́рщ|ить (**-у, -ишь**; *perf* **встопо́рщить**) *несов перех* (*перья, шерсть*) to fluff up
▶ **топо́рщиться** (*perf* **встопо́рщиться**) *несов возв* (*разг: усы, хвост*) to bristle; (*платье, складки*) to puff up.
то́пот (**-а**) *м* clatter.
топ|та́ть (**-чу́, -чешь**; *perf* **потопта́ть**) *несов перех* (*траву*) to trample; (*пол*) to dirty
▶ **топта́ться** *несов возв* (*разг*) to shift from one foot to the other; **~ся** (*impf*) **на ме́сте** (*перен*) to

go round in circles.

топ-топ *звукоподражание* pitter-patter.

топча́н (-а́) *м* trestle bed.

топчу́(сь) *итп несов см* **топта́ть(ся).**

топ|ь (-и) *ж* marsh.

торг (-а) *м* trading.

торга́ш (-а́) *м* (*разг: пренебр*) money-grubber.

торг|и́ (-о́в) *мн* (*аукцион*) auction *ед*; (*состязание*) tender *ед*.

торг|ова́ть (-у́ю) *несов неперех* (*перен: совестью, убеждениями*) to forfeit; (*магазин*) to trade; ~ (*impf*) +*instr* (*мясом, мебелью*) to trade in; ~ (*impf*) **с** +*instr* to (do) trade with

▸ **торгова́ться** (*perf* **сторгова́ться**) *несов возв* (*разг: спорить о цене*) to haggle; (*перен: спорить*) to bicker.

торго́в|ец (-ца) *м* merchant; (*мелкий, уличный*) trader.

торго́в|ка (-ки; *gen pl* **-ок**) *ж* (*уличная, базарная*) trader.

торго́вл|я (-и) *ж* trade.

торго́вок *сущ см* **торго́вка.**

торго́вца *итп сущ см* **торго́вец.**

торго́вый *прил* (*договор, прибыль, барьеры*) trade *опред*; (*судно, флот*) merchant *опред*; **торго́вая сеть** retail network; **торго́вая то́чка** retail outlet; **торго́вое представи́тельство** trade mission; **торго́вый рабо́тник** retail industry worker; **торго́вый центр** shopping centre (*BRIT*), mall (*US*).

торгпре́д (-а) *м сокр* (= **торго́вый представи́тель**) head of the trade mission.

торгпре́дств|о (-а) *ср сокр* (= **торго́вое представи́тельство**) trade mission.

тореадо́р (-а) *м* toreador.

тор|е́ц (-ца́) *м* (*доски, книги*) butt; (*здания*) gable end.

торже́ственен *прил см* **торже́ственный.**

торже́ственно *нареч* (*обещать*) solemnly; (*праздновать*) fully.

торже́ствен|ный *прил* (*день, случай*) special; (*собрание*) celebratory; (**-ен, -на, -но**; *вид, обстановка*) festive; (*no short form*; *обещание, клятва*) solemn.

торжеств|о́ (-а́) *ср* (*семейное, национальное*) celebration; (*в голосе, в словах*) triumph; ~ +*gen* (*справедливости итп*) the triumph of.

торжеств|ова́ть (-у́ю) *perf* **восторжествова́ть**) *несов неперех*: ~ (**над** +*instr*) to triumph (over); (*no perf*; *внутренне, открыто*) to rejoice.

торма́ш|ки (-ек) *мн* (*разг*): **вверх ~ками** upside down.

торможе́ни|е (-я) *ср* (*машины*) braking; (*рефлексов*) inhibition.

торможу́(сь) *несов см* **тормози́ть(ся).**

то́рмоз (-а; *nom pl* **-а́)** *м* brake; (*nom pl* **-ы;** *перен: в работе*) hindrance, obstacle.

тормо|зи́ть (-жу́, -зи́шь; *perf* **затормози́ть)** *несов перех* (*машину, поезд*) to slow down; (*перен: движение, работу*) to hamper, impede

◆ *неперех* (*машина, поезд*) to brake

▸ **тормози́ться** (*perf* **затормози́ться**) *несов возв* (*дело, работа итп*) to be hindered *или* impeded.

тормозн|о́й *прил* (*механизм, педаль*) brake *опред*; (*био: рефлекс*) inhibitory; **~а́я жи́дкость** brake fluid.

тормош|и́ть (-у́, -и́шь) *несов перех* to shake; ~ (*impf*) **кого́-н за рука́в** to tug at sb's sleeve; ~ (*impf*) **кого́-н** (*вопросами*) to pester sb.

тор|опи́ть (-оплю́, -о́пишь; *perf* **поторопи́ть**) *несов перех* (*коня*) to urge on; (*ребёнка, события*) to hurry; ~ (**поторопи́ть** *perf*) **кого́-н с чем-н** to hurry sb with sth

▸ **торопи́ться** (*perf* **поторопи́ться**) *несов возв* (*на поезд, в школу итп*) to hurry; (*с работой, с выполнением*): **~ся с** +*instr* to hurry with.

торопли́вый (-, -а, -о) *прил* (*человек*) hasty; (*шаг*) hurried; (*суждение, вывод*) hasty, hurried.

тороплю́(сь) *несов см* **торопи́ть(ся).**

торпе́д|а (-ы) *ж* torpedo (*мн* torpedoes).

торпеди́р|овать (-ую) (*не*)*сов перех* (*также перен*) to torpedo.

торс (-а) *м* torso.

торт (-а) *м* cake.

торф (-а) *м* peat.

торца́ *итп сущ см* **торе́ц.**

торч|а́ть (-у́, -и́шь) *несов неперех* (*вверх*) to stick up; (*в стороны*) to stick out; (*разг: на улице, в ресторане*) to hang around.

торчко́м *нареч* (*разг*) on end.

торше́р (-а) *м* standard lamp.

тоск|а́ (-и́) *ж* (*на сердце, во взгляде*) melancholy; (*скука*) boredom; ~ **по ро́дине** homesickness.

тоскли́вый (-, -а, -о) *прил* (*настроение, музыка итп*) melancholy; (*погода, разговор итп*) dreary.

тоск|ова́ть (-у́ю) *несов неперех* to pine away; ~ (*impf*) **по** +*dat или* +*prp* to miss.

тост (-а) *м* toast; ~ **за** +*acc* toast to.

KEYWORD

то|т (-го́; *f* **та,** *nt* **то,** *pl* **те; см Table 11**) *мест* **1** that; **тот дом** that house; **та ру́чка** that pen; **те кни́ги** those books; **по ту сто́рону** on that side **2** (*указывает на ранее упомянутое*) that; **в тот раз/день** that time/day **3** (*разг: о прошлом*) last; (: *о будущем*) next; **я ви́дел его́ на той неде́ле** I saw him last week; **уви́димся на той неде́ле** we'll meet next week **4** (*в главных предложениях*): **э́то тот челове́к, кото́рый приходи́л вчера́** it's the man who came yesterday; **мы обра́довались тому́, что он ушёл** we were pleased that he had gone **5** (*о последнем из названных лиц*): **я посмотре́л на дру́га, тот стоя́л мо́лча** I looked at my friend, he stood silently **6** (*обычно с отрицанием*): **зашёл не в тот дом** I called at the wrong house; **э́то всё не то** it's not that **7** (*об одном из перечисляемых предметов*): **ни тот, ни друго́й** neither one nor the other; **тем или ины́м спо́собом** by some means or other;

тот же the same; **та же маши́на, что и в про́шлый раз** the same car as last time; **он сказа́л то же са́мое** he said the same thing **8** (*во фра́зах*): **до того́** so; **он до того́ испуга́лся, что не мог усну́ть** he was so frightened he couldn't sleep; **мне не до того́** I have no time for that; **не то что́(бы)** ... , **а** ... not so much that ... but ...; **она́ не то что́(бы) глупа́, а засте́нчива** she's not so much stupid, as just shy; **к тому́ же** moreover; **с тем, что́бы** in order to; **ни с того́ ни с сего́** (*разг*) out of the blue; **тому́ наза́д** ago; **и тому́ подо́бное** et cetera, and so on.

тота́лен *прил см* **тота́льный**.
тотализа́тор (-а) *м* totalizer.
тоталитари́зм (-а) *м* totalitarianism.
тоталита́рный *прил* totalitarian.
тота́л|ьный (-ен, -ьна, -ьно) *прил* total.
то-то *част* (*разг: вот именно*) exactly, that's just it; (*вот почему*) that's why; (*выража́ет удовлетворе́ние*): **~ же** pleased to hear it; **он не сдал экза́мен – ~ он тако́й гру́стный** he didn't pass the exam – that's why he's so sad; **~ он удиви́тся!** he WILL be surprised!
то́тчас *нареч* immediately.
то́чек *сущ см* **то́чка**.
то́чен *прил см* **то́чный**.
точёный *прил* (*о́стрый: нож*) sharpened; (*дета́ль, грань итп*) turned; (*перен: фигу́ра*) shapely; (: *черты́ лица́*) fine.
то́чечн|ый *прил* (*ли́ния*) dotted; **~ масса́ж** shiatsu, acupressure; **~ая электросва́рка** spot-welding.
точи́л|ка (-ки; *gen pl* -ок) *ж* pencil sharpener.
точи́|ть (-у́, -ишь; *perf* **наточи́ть**) *несов перех* (*нож, каранда́ш*) to sharpen; (*perf* **вы́точить**; *дета́ль*) to turn; (*no perf*; *подле́ж: червь, ржа́вчина*) to eat away at; (*перен: подле́ж: боле́знь, тоска́ итп*) to drain.
то́ч|ка (-ки; *gen pl* -ек) *ж* point; (*пятны́шко*) dot; (*линг*) full stop (*BRIT*), period (*esp US*); (*де́йствие: дета́ли, каранда́ша*) sharpening; **~ зре́ния** point of view; **попада́ть** (*попа́сть perf*) **в (са́мую) ~ку** to hit the bull's-eye; **дойти́** (*perf*) **до ~ки** (*разг*) to reach one's limit; **то́чка с запято́й** semicolon.
точне́е *вводн сл* to be exact *или* precise; **приходи́ вечером, ~, в 5 часо́в** come in the evening, at 5 o'clock to be exact *или* precise.
то́чно *нареч* exactly; (*объясни́ть*) exactly, precisely; (*подсчита́ть, перевести́*) accurately ♦ *част* (*действи́тельно*) precisely ♦ *союз* (*как бу́дто*) as if *или* though; **~ тако́й дом** exactly the same house; **он ~ та́к и сде́лал/ сказа́л** that's exactly what he did/said; **~, он уе́хал** that's right, he's gone; **так ~!** yes, sir!; **распла́кался, ~ ребёнок** he burst into tears, just like a child; **он говори́л со мной, ~ я ребёнок** he talked to me as if *или* though I were a child.

то́чность (-и) *ж* (*часо́в, попада́ния*) accuracy; (*рабо́ты*) precision; **я подсчита́л затра́ты с ~ю до рубля́** I counted the expenditure right down to the last rouble; **в ~и** (*разг*) exactly.
то́ч|ный (-ен, -на́, -но) *прил* (*часы́, перево́д, попада́ние*) accurate; (*описа́ние, прика́з*) precise; (*а́дрес, ко́пия*) exact; **то́чное вре́мя** exact time; **то́чные нау́ки** exact sciences.
точь-в-точь *нареч* (*разг*) just like.
тошн|и́ть (*3sg* -и́т, *perf* **стошни́ть**) *несов безл*: **меня́ ~и́т** I feel sick; (*перен*) it makes me sick; **меня́ ~и́т от твоего́ лицеме́рия** your hypocrisy makes me sick.
то́шно *как сказ* (*перен: разг*) it's nauseating *или* sickening.
тошнот|а́ (-ы́) *ж* (*чу́вство*) nausea; **мне э́то до ~ы́ надое́ло** I'm sick to death of it.
тошнотво́р|ный (-ен, -на, -но) *прил* (*та́кже перен*) nauseating, sickening.
то́щ|ий (-ая, -ее, -ие; -, -á, -е) *прил* (*челове́к*) gaunt; (*кошелёк*) empty; (*по́чва*) poor; (*расти́тельность*) sparse.
т.п. *сокр* (= **тому́ подо́бное**) etc. (= *et cetera*).
ТПП *м сокр* (= Торго́во-промы́шленная пала́та) ≈ Chamber of Commerce.
тпру *межд* (*лошадя́м*) whoa.
т-р *сокр* = **теа́тр**.
трав|а́ (-ы́; *nom pl* -ы) *ж* grass; (*лека́рственная*) herb; **со́рная ~** weed; **хоть ~ не расти́** (*разг*) he *итп* couldn't care less.
трави́н|ка (-ки; *gen pl* -ок) *ж* blade of grass.
трав|и́ть (-лю́, -ишь) *несов перех* (*та́кже перен*) to poison; (*perf* **потрави́ть**; *посе́вы*) to damage; (*perf* **затрави́ть**; *дичь*) to hunt; (*перен: ра́за: притесня́ть*) to harass, hound; (*perf* **вы́травить**; *узо́р*) to etch
► **трави́ться** (*perf* **отрави́ться**) *несов возв* to poison o.s.
травле́ни|е (-я) *ср* etching.
травлю́(сь) *несов см* **трави́ть(ся)**.
тра́вл|я (-и) *ж* hunting; (*демокра́тов, радика́лов*) hounding.
тра́вм|а (-ы) *ж* (*физи́ческая*) injury; (*психи́ческая*) trauma.
травмато́лог (-а) *м* specialist in traumatology.
травматологи́ческ|ий (-ая, -ое, -ие) *прил*: **~ отде́л** casualty; **~ пункт** first-aid room.
травматоло́ги|я (-и) *ж* traumatology.
травми́р|овать (-ую) (*не*)*сов перех* (*го́лову*) to injure; (*перен: гру́бостью*) to traumatize.
травоя́д|ный (-ен, -на, -но) *прил* herbivorous.
травяни́ст|ый *прил* herbaceous; (-, -а, -о; *луг*) grassy.
травяно́й *прил* (*насто́йка*) herbal; **~ покро́в** grass.

трагéди|я (-и) *ж* tragedy.
траги́зм (-а) *м* tragedy.
трагикомéди|я (-и) *ж* tragicomedy.
трагикоми́ческ|ий (-ая, -ое, -ие) *прил*
tragicomic.
траги́чен *прил см* **траги́чный**.
траги́ческ|ий (-ая, -ое, -ие) *прил* tragic; ~
актёр (*трагик*) tragedy actor.
траги́ч|ный (-ен, -на, -но) *прил* tragic.
традицио́н|ный (-ен, -на, -но) *прил* traditional.
тради́ци|я (-и) *ж* tradition; **входи́ть** (**войти́** *perf*)
в ~ю to become a tradition.
траекто́ри|я (-и) *ж* trajectory.
тракт (-а) *м* (*ИСТ*) highway; (*АНАТ*):
пищевари́тельный ~ alimentary canal.
тракта́т (-а) *м* treatise.
такти́р (-а) *м* inn.
тракти́рщик (-а) *м* innkeeper.
тракти́рщиц|а (-ы) *ж см* **тракти́рщик**.
тракт|ова́ть (-у́ю) *несов перех* to interpret.
тракто́в|ка (-ки; *gen pl* -ок) *ж* interpretation.
тра́ктор (-а) *м* tractor.
трактори́ст (-а) *м* tractor driver.
трактори́ст|ка (-ки; *gen pl* -ок) *ж см* **трактори́ст**.
трал (-а) *м* (*сеть*) trawl; **ми́нный** ~
minesweeping operation.
тра́л|ить (-ю, -ишь; *perf* **протра́лить**) *несов*
перех to trawl; ~ (**протра́лить** *perf*) **ми́ны** to
sweep for mines.
трамб|ова́ть (-у́ю; *perf* **утрамбова́ть**) *несов*
перех to tamp.
трамва́|й (-я) *м* tram (*BRIT*), streetcar (*US*);
éздить/éхать (*impf*) **на ~е** to go go by tram.
трамва́й|ный *прил* tram *опред* (*BRIT*), streetcar
опред (*US*); **~ые пути́** tramlines; **трамва́йный**
парк tram *или* streetcar depot.
трампли́н (-а) *м* (*также перен*) springboard;
лы́жный ~ ski jump.
транжи́р (-а) *м* spendthrift.
транжи́р|ить (-ю, -ишь; *perf* **растранжи́рить**)
несов перех (*разг: деньги*) to blow.
транжи́р|ка (-ки; *gen pl* -ок) *ж см* **транжи́р**.
транзи́стор (-а) *м* (*усилитель*) transistor;
(*радиоприёмник*) transistor (radio).
транзи́т (-а) *м* transit; (*о грузе*) transit goods.
транзи́тный *прил* transit *опред*.
транквилиза́тор (-а) *м* tranquillizer (*BRIT*),
tranquilizer (*US*).
транс (-а) *м* (*ПСИХОЛ*) trance; (*КОММ: докумен т*)
transport document; **но́мер тра́нса** trans
number.
трансконтинента́льный *прил*
transcontinental.
транскри́пци|я (-и) *ж* transcription.
трансли́р|овать (-ую) (*не*)*сов перех* to
broadcast.
трансля́тор (-а) *м* (*ТЕХ*) translator.
трансля́ци|я (-и) *ж* (*передачи*) transmission,
broadcasting; (*передача*) broadcast; **пряма́я** ~
live broadcast.
транспара́нт (-а) *м* banner.
транспланта́ци|я (-и) *ж* transplant.

тра́нспорт (-а) *м* transport.
транспортёр (-а) *м* (*конвейер*) conveyor belt;
(*ВОЕН*) troop carrier.
транспорти́р|овать (-ую) (*не*)*сов перех* to
transport.
транспортиро́в|ка (-и) *ж* transportation.
тра́нспортный *прил* transport *опред*.
транссексуа́л (-а) *м* transsexual.
трансформа́тор (-а) *м* transformer.
трансформа́ци|я (-и) *ж* transformation.
трансформи́р|овать (-ую) (*не*)*сов перех* to
transform.
траншé|я (-и) *ж* trench.
трап (-а) *м* gangway; **подава́ть** (**пода́ть** *perf*) ~
to put down the gangway.
тра́пез|а (-ы) *ж communal meal in monastery*.
тра́пезн|ая (-ой; *decl like adj*) *ж* refectory.
трапéци|я (-и) *ж* (*ГЕОМ*) trapezium; (*цирковая,*
гимнастическая) trapeze.
тра́сс|а (-ы) *ж* (*лыжная*) run; (*трубопровода,*
канала) route; **автомоби́льная** ~ motorway
(*BRIT*), expressway (*US*); **возду́шная** ~ airway.
трасса́т (-а) *м* (*КОММ*) drawee.
тра́т|а (-ы) *ж* spending; **пуста́я** ~ **врéмени/**
дéнег a waste of time/money.
тра́|тить (-чу, -тишь; *perf* **истра́тить** *или*
потра́тить) *несов перех* to spend
▶ **тра́титься** (*perf* **истра́титься** *или*
потра́титься) *несов возв*: **~ся на** +*acc* to spend
a lot of money on.
тра́улер (-а) *м* trawler.
тра́ур (-а) *м* mourning; ~ **по** +*prp* mourning for;
носи́ть (*impf*) ~ to wear mourning.
тра́ур|ный *прил* (*процессия, платье*) mourning
опред; (-ен, -на, -но; *перен: обстановка, тон*)
mournful.
трафарéт (-а) *м* stencil; **мы́слить** (*impf*) **по ~у**
(*перен*) to think in clichés.
трафарéт|ный (-ен, -на, -но) *прил* (*рисунок,*
черчение) stencilled; (*перен: фразы*) trite.
трах *межд* bang; **а он ~ по столу́** and he banged
against the table.
тра́ха|ть(ся) (-ю(сь)) *несов от* **тра́хнуть(ся)**.
трахé|я (-и) *ж* trachea.
тра́хн|уть (-у, -ешь; *impf* **тра́хать**) *сов неперех*
(*раз: выстрел*) to ring out ♦ *перех* (*ударить*)
to thump; (*переспать: женщину*) to lay
▶ **тра́хнуться** (*impf* **тра́хаться**) *сов возв* (*разг:*
удариться) to bang o.s.; (: *мужчина и женщина*)
to have it off; **тра́хаться** (**~ся** *perf*) **голово́й о**
стéнку to bang one's head against the wall.
тра́чу(сь) *несов см* **тра́тить(ся)**.
трéбовани|е (-я) *ср* (*объяснений, денег*)
request; (*решительное, категорическое*)
demand; (*устава, экзаменационные*)
requirement; (*документ: на книгу*) order; **~я**
(*моральные, эстетические*) needs *мн*.
трéбовател|ный (-ен, -ьна, -ьно) *прил*
demanding; (*тон, голос*) peremptory.
трéб|овать (-ую; *perf* **потрéбовать**) *несов*
перех (*квитанцию*) to ask for; (*в суд, к*

начальнику) to summon; ~ (**потре́бовать** *perf*) **что-н/**+*infin* to demand sth/to do; ~ (**потре́бовать** *perf*) +*gen* (*сочу́вствия, пра́вдивости*) to expect; (*по́мощи, переде́лки*) to need, require

▶ **тре́боваться** (*perf* **потре́боваться**) *несов возв* to be needed *или* required.

требух|а́ (-*и́*) *ж* entrails *мн*.

трево́г|а (-*и*) *ж* (*волне́ние*) anxiety; (*на у́лице, в до́ме*) alarm; **возду́шная** ~ air-raid warning; **поднима́ть** (**подня́ть** *perf*) *или* **бить** (*impf*) ~**у** (*перен*) to raise the alarm.

трево́жен *прил см* **трево́жный**.

трево́ж|ить (-*у*, -*ишь*; *perf* **встрево́жить**) *несов перех* (*роди́телей, прави́тельство*) to alarm; (*perf* **потрево́жить**; *подлеж: шум, посети́тели*) to disturb; (*перен: ра́ну*) to reopen

▶ **трево́житься** (*perf* **встрево́житься**) *несов возв* (*за дете́й*) to be concerned; (*perf* **потрево́житься**; *затрудня́ть себя́*) to trouble o.s.

трево́жно *нареч* (*посмотре́ть*) anxiously ♦ *как сказ*: **на се́рдце** ~ I feel anxious; **в го́роде** ~ there is a sense of alarm in the city.

трево́ж|ный (-*ен*, -*на*, -*но*) *прил* (*го́лос, взгляд*) anxious; (*све́дения*) alarming; ~**ное вре́мя** time of unrest; **трево́жный сигна́л** alarm.

тре́звенник (-*а*) *м* teetotaller.

трезве́|ть (-*ю*; *perf* **отрезве́ть**) *несов неперех* to sober up.

трезво́н (-*а*) *м* (*колоко́льный*) peal; (*разг: то́лки*) gossip.

трезво́н|ить (-*ю*, -*ишь*) *несов неперех* (*ко́локола*) to peal; (*телефо́н, звоно́к*) to ring; (*разг*) to spread gossip.

тре́звость (-*и*) *ж* (*неупотребле́ние алкого́ля*) sobriety; (*перен: взгля́да, сужде́ний*) soberness.

тре́зв|ый (-, -*а́*, -*о*) *прил* (*состоя́ние, челове́к*) sober; (*перен: рассужде́ние, реше́ние*) sensible.

трек (-*а*) *м* track.

трел|ь (-*и*) *ж* warble.

трель*я́ж* (-*а*) *м* (*зе́ркало*) triple mirror.

трём *итп чис см* **три**.

трёмста́м *итп чис см* **три́ста**.

тренажёр (-*а*) *м equipment used for physical training*.

тре́нер (-*а*) *м* coach; **гла́вный** ~ manager (*of sports team*).

тре́ни|е (-*я*) *ср* friction; (*обы́чно мн: перен*) friction *ед*.

трениро́в|ать (-*ую*; *perf* **натренирова́ть**) *несов перех* to train; (*спортсме́нов*) to coach.

▶ **трениров́а́ться** (*perf* **натренирова́ться**) *несов возв* (*спортсме́н*) to train; (*учени́к, рабо́тник*) to train o.s.

трениро́в|ка (-*ки*; *gen pl* -*ок*) *ж* (*па́мяти, ло́шади итп*) training; (*отде́льное заня́тие*) training (session).

трениро́вочный *прил* training *опред*; **трениро́вочный костю́м** tracksuit.

трено́жник (-*а*) *м* tripod.

трёп (-*а*; *part gen* -*у*) *м* (*разг*) blethering, blathering.

трепана́ци|я (-*и*) *ж* (*МЕД*) trepanation.

трёпаный *прил* (*разг*) tattered.

трепа́|ть (-*лю́*, -*лешь*; *perf* **потрепа́ть**) *несов перех* (*подлеж: ве́тер*) to blow about; (*по плечу́*) to pat; (*перен: кора́бль*) to toss; (*perf* **истрепа́ть** *или* **потрепа́ть**; *разг: обувь, кни́ги*) to wear out; ~ (**потрепа́ть** *perf*) **кого́-н за во́лосы/за у́ши** to pull sb's hair/ears; ~ (**потрепа́ть** *perf*) **не́рвы кому́-н** to wear sb's nerves down; ~ (*impf*) **языко́м** (*разг cми*) to chatter

▶ **трепа́ться** *несов возв* (*no perf*; *фла́ги, во́лосы*) to be blown about; (*perf* **истрепа́ться** *или* **потрепа́ться**; *разг: оде́жда, о́бувь*) to wear out; (*perf* **потрепа́ться**; *разг: о пустяка́х*) to chatter.

трепа́ч (-*а́*) *м* (*разг*) chatterbox.

тре́пет (-*а*) *м* (*ли́стьев*) quivering; (*волне́ние*) tremor; (*страх*) trepidation.

трепе|та́ть (-*щу́*, -*щешь*) *несов неперех* (*ли́стья, фла́ги*) to quiver; (*от у́жаса*) to quake, tremble.

тре́пет|ный (-*ен*, -*на*, -*но*) *прил* tremulous.

трепещу́ *итп несов см* **трепета́ть**.

треплю́(сь) *итп несов см* **трепа́ть(ся)**.

трепыха́|ться (-*юсь*) *несов возв* (*разг: живо́тное, ры́ба*) to wriggle; (*флаг, па́рус*) to flutter; (*перен: волнова́ться*) to be in a flutter.

треск (-*а*) *м* (*лома́ющихся су́чьев*) snapping; (*вы́стрелов*) crackling; **с тре́ском прова́ливаться** (**провали́ться** *perf*) (*разг: пье́са*) to be a flop; (: *студе́нт*) to come a cropper.

треск|а́ (-*и́*) *ж* cod.

тре́ска|ться (*3sg* -*ется*, *3pl* -*ются*, *perf* **потре́скаться**) *несов возв* (*земля́, стекло́*) to crack.

трескотн|я́ (-*и́*) *ж* (*разг: кузне́чиков*) chirp; (*перен: болтовня́*) chitchat.

треску́ч|ий (-*ая*, -*ее*, -*ие*; -, -*а*, -*е*) *прил* (*перен: ре́чи, слова́*) bombastic; ~ **моро́з** hard frost.

тре́сн|уть (*3sg* -*ет*, *3pl* -*ут*) *сов неперех* (*ве́тка*) to snap; (*стака́н, ко́жа*) to crack; (*разг*): ~ **чем-н по чему́-н** (*кулако́м: по столу́*) to bang sth on sth ♦ *перех* (*разг*): ~ **кого́-н по** +*dat* (*по ше́е, по руке́*) to thump sb on

▶ **тре́снуться** *сов возв* (*разг*): ~**ся чем-н о** +*acc* to bang sth on.

трест (-*а*) *м* (*ЭКОН*) trust.

тре́т|ий (-*ья*, -*ье*, -*ьи*) *чис* third; **фильм/врач** ~**ьего со́рта** a third-rate film/doctor; ~**ьего дня** the day before yesterday; **Т**~ **мир** the Third World; **тре́тий сорт** (*това́ра*) Grade 3 (*denoting product of inferior quality*); **тре́тье**

лицо́ (*линг*) the third person; **тре́тья сторона́, тре́тьи ли́ца** third party; *см также* **пя́тый**.
трети́р|овать (-ую) *сов перех* to patronize.
трети́чный *прил* tertiary.
трет|ь (-и; *nom pl* -и, *gen pl* -ей) ж third.
тре́ть|е (-его; *decl like adj* ср (*кулин*) sweet (*BRIT*), dessert.
третьекла́ссник (-а) *м pupil in third year at school (usually nine years old)*.
третьекла́ссница (-ы) *ж см* **третьекла́ссник**.
третьесо́рт|ный (-ен, -на, -но) *прил* third-rate.
тре́ть|я (-ей; *decl like adj*) ж: **одна́** ~ one third.
треуго́льник (-а) *м* triangle.
треуго́льный *прил* triangular.
треф|ы (-) *мн* (*карты*) clubs *мн*.
трёх *чис см* **три**.
трёхгоди́чный *прил* three-year.
трёхгодова́лый *прил* three-year-old.
трёхдне́вный *прил* three-day.
трёхкра́т|ный *прил*: ~ **чемпио́н** three-times champion; **в ~ом разме́ре** threefold.
трёхле́ти|е (-я) *ср* (*срок*) three years; (*годовщина*) third anniversary.
трёхле́тн|ий (-яя, -ее, -ие) *прил* (*период*) three-year; (*ребёнок*) three-year-old.
трёхме́рный *прил* 3-D, three-dimensional.
трёхме́сячный *прил* three-month; (*ребёнок*) three-month-old.
трёхнеде́льный *прил* three-week; (*ребёнок*) three-week-old.
трёхсо́т *чис см* **три́ста**.
трёхсотле́ти|е (-я) *ср* (*срок*) three hundred years; (*годовщина*) tercentenary.
трёхсотле́тн|ий (-яя, -ее, -ие) *прил* (*период*) three hundred-year; (*дерево*) three hundred-year-old.
трёхсо́т|ый (-ая, -ое, -ые) *чис* three hundredth.
трёхста́х *чис см* **три́ста**.
трёхсторо́нн|ий (-яя, -ее, -ие) *прил* (*соглашение, союз*) trilateral.
трёхчасово́й *прил* (*операция*) three-hour; (*поезд*) three o'clock.
трёш|ка (-ки; *gen pl* -ек) ж (*разг*) three-rouble note.
трещ|а́ть (-у́, -и́шь) *несов неперех* (*лёд, доски итп*) to crack; (*кузнечики*) to chip; (*пулемёты*) to crackle; (*разг: тараторить*) to jabber (on); **у меня́ ~и́т голова́** I've got a splitting headache; ~ (*impf*) **по швам** (*также перен*) to be falling apart at the seams.
тре́щин|а (-ы) ж (*также перен*) crack; **дава́ть** (**дать** *perf*) ~у to crack.
трещо́т|ка (-ки; *gen pl* -ок) ж rattle ◆ *м/ж* (*перен: болтун*) chatterbox.
тр|и (-ёх; *см* Table 24) *чис* three ◆ *нескл* (*ПРОСВЕЩ*) ≈ C (*school mark*); **ей** ~ **го́да** she is three (years old); **они́ живу́т в до́ме но́мер** ~ they live at number three; **о́коло** ~ёх about three; **кни́га сто́ит** ~ **рубля́** the book costs three roubles; ~ **с полови́ной часа́** three and a half hours; **сейча́с** ~ **часа́** it is three o'clock; **я́блоки**

продаю́тся по ~ **штуки** the apples are sold in threes; **дели́ть** (**раздели́ть** *perf*) **что-н на** ~ to divide sth into three.
трибу́н|а (-ы) ж platform; (*стадиона*) stand.
трибуна́л (-а) *м* tribunal; **вое́нный** ~ military court.
тривиа́льный (-ен, -ьна, -ьно) *прил* trivial.
тригономе́три|я (-и) ж trigonometry.
три́девять: за ~ **земе́ль** (*ФОЛЬКЛОР*) in far off lands.
тридеся́т|ый *прил* (*ФОЛЬКЛОР*): **в** ~ом **госуда́рстве** in a far off country.
три́дцати *чис см* **три́дцать**.
тридцатиле́ти|е (-я) *ср* (*срок*) thirty years; (*годовщина события*) thirtieth anniversary.
тридцатиле́тн|ий (-яя, -ее, -ие) *прил* (*период*) thirty-year; (*человек*) thirty-year-old.
тридца́т|ый (-ая, -ое, -ые) *чис* thirtieth; *см также* **пятидеся́тый**.
три́дцат|ь (-и; *как* пять; *см* Table 27) *чис* thirty; *см также* **пятьдеся́т**.
три́жды *нареч* three times; ~ **два – шесть** three times two is six; **он** ~ **прав** he's absolutely right.
трико́ *ср нескл* leotard.
трикота́ж (-а) *м* (*ткань*) knitted fabric ◆ *собир* (*одежда*) knitwear.
трикота́жный *прил* knitted; ~ **магази́н** knitwear shop.
три́лер (-а) *м* thriller.
трили́стник (-а) *м* trefoil.
триллио́н (-а) *м* trillion.
трило́ги|я (-и) ж trilogy.
трина́дцати *чис см* **трина́дцать**.
трина́дцат|ый (-ая, -ое, -ые) *чис* thirteenth; *см также* **пя́тый**.
трина́дцат|ь (-и; *как* пять; *см* Table 27) *чис* thirteen; *см также* **пять**.
три́|о *ср нескл* trio.
Три́|поли *м нескл* Tripoli.
три́птих (-а) *м* triptych.
три́ста (трёхсо́т; *как* сто; *см* Table 32) *чис* three hundred; *см также* **сто**.
трито́н (-а) *м* newt.
триу́мф (-а) *м* triumph.
триумфа́льный *прил* triumphant; **триумфа́льная а́рка** triumphal arch.
тро́га|ть (-ю; *perf* **тро́нуть**) *несов перех* (*также перен*) to touch; (*разг: беспокоить: вопросами*) to pester; (*подлеж: рассказ, событие*) to move ◆ (*лошадь, повозка*) to start moving; **улы́бка тро́нула её гу́бы** a smile flickered across her lips; **седина́ тро́нула его́ во́лосы** his hair was touched with grey
▸ **тро́гаться** (*perf* **тро́нуться**) *несов возв* (*поезд*) to move off; (*лёд*) to (begin to) break; ~**ся** (**тро́нуться** *perf*) **в путь** to set off.
тр|о́е (-о́их; *см* Table 35a) *чис* three; *см также* **дво́е**.
троеборь|е (-я) *ср* triathlon.
тробек *сущ см* **тро́йка**.

тро́ен *сущ см* **тро́йня**.

тро́йх *чис см* **тро́е**.

тро́иц|**а** (-ы) *ж* (*также: свята́я* ~) the Holy Trinity; (*праздник: также:* Т~ын день) ≈ Trinity Sunday; (*разг: о друзьях*) threesome.

тро́й|**ка** (-ки; *gen pl* -ек) *ж* (*цифра, карта*) three; (*ПРОСВЕЩ*) ≈ C (*school mark*); (*лошадей*) troika; (*группа людей*) threesome; (*разг: автобус, трамвай итп*) (number) three (*bus, tram etc*); (*костюм*) three-piece suit.

тройни́к (-а́) *м* (*ЭЛЕК*) (three-way) adaptor.

тройн|**о́й** *прил* triple; **в** ~**о́м разме́ре** triple the size; **тройно́й прыжо́к** (*СПОРТ*) triple jump.

тро́йня (-йни; *gen pl* -ен) *ж* triplets *мн*.

тро́йствен|**ный** (-ен, -на, -но) *прил* (*связь*) threefold; (*no short form; ПОЛИТ: союз, соглашение*) tripartite.

тройча́т|**ка** (-и) *ж* (*разг*) *mild painkiller taken for headaches etc*.

тролле́йбус (-а) *м* trolleybus.

тромб (-а) *м* blood clot.

тромбо́з (-а) *м* thrombosis.

тромбо́н (-а) *м* trombone.

трон (-а) *м* throne.

тро́нн|**ый** *прил*: ~ **зал** throne room; ~**ая речь** royal address.

тро́н|**уть** (-у, -ешь) *сов от* **тро́гать**

▶ **тро́нуться** *сов от* **тро́гаться** ♦ *возв*: ~**ся** (**умо́м**) (*разг*) to be (a bit) touched.

тропа́ (-ы́; *nom pl* -ы) *ж* pathway.

тро́пик (-а) *м*: **се́верный/ю́жный** ~ the tropic of Cancer/Capricorn; *см также* **тро́пики**.

тро́пик|**и** (-ов) the tropics *мн*.

тропи́н|**ка** (-ки; *gen pl* -ок) *ж* footpath.

тропи́ческ|**ий** (-ая, -ое, -ие) *прил* tropical.

трос (-а) *м* cable.

трости́н|**ка** (-ки; *gen pl* -ок) *ж* (*камыша*) cane; (*травинка*) stem.

тростни́к (-а́) *м* reed; **са́харный** ~ sugar cane.

трост|**ь** (-и; *gen pl* -е́й) *ж* walking stick.

тротуа́р (-а) *м* pavement (*BRIT*), sidewalk (*US*).

трофе́й (-я) *м* trophy.

трою́родный *прил*: ~ **брат** second cousin (*male*); **трою́родная сестра́** second cousin (*female*).

тро́йк|**ий** (-ая, -ое, -ие; -, -а, -о) *прил* triple.

тру(сь) *итп несов см* **тере́ть(ся)**.

труб|**а́** (-ы́; *nom pl* -ы) *ж* (*газовая, водосточная итп*) pipe; (*дымовая*) chimney; (*МУЗ*) trumpet; (*АНАТ*): **фалло́пиева** ~ Fallopian tube; **в** ~**у́ вылета́ть** (**вы́лететь** *perf*) (*разг*) to go to the wall.

труба́ч (-а́) *м* trumpeter.

труб|**и́ть** (-лю́, -и́шь; *perf* **протруби́ть**) *несов неперех*: ~ **в** +*acc* (*МУЗ*) to blow; (*подлеж: труба*) to sound; (*перен: разг*): ~ **о** +*prp* to trumpet ♦ *перех* (*сбор, отбой*) to sound.

тру́б|**ка** (-ки; *gen pl* -ок) *ж* tube; (*курительная*)

pipe; (*телефона*) receiver; (*МЕД*) stethoscope; **брать** (**взять** *perf*) *или* **поднима́ть** (**подня́ть** *perf*) ~**ку** (*ТЕЛ*) to pick up the receiver; **сворáчивать** (**сверну́ть** *perf*) **что-н в** ~**ку** to roll sth into a tube.

трублю́ *несов см* **труби́ть**.

тру́бок *сущ см* **тру́бка**.

трубопрово́д (-а) *м* pipeline.

трубо́чек *сущ см* **тру́бочка**.

трубочи́ст (-а) *м* chimney sweep.

тру́боч|**ка** (-ки; *gen pl* -ек) *ж уменьш от* **тру́бка**; (*кулин*) cream horn.

труд (-а́) *м* work; (*ЭКОН*) labour (*BRIT*), labor (*US*); (*ПРОСВЕЩ*) *home economics and design*; **бескоры́стный** ~ labo(u)r of love; **брать** (**взять** *perf*) **на себя́** ~ +*infin* to take the trouble to do; **без** ~**а́** without any difficulty; **с** (**больши́м**) ~**о́м** with (great) difficulty.

тру́ден *прил см* **тру́дный**.

тру|**ди́ться** (-жу́сь, -дишься) *несов возв* to work hard; ~ (*impf*) **над** +*instr* to labour (*BRIT*) *или* labor (*US*) over; **не** ~**ди́тесь писа́ть мне** don't bother to write.

тру́дно *как сказ* it's hard *или* difficult; **у меня́** ~ **с деньга́ми** I've got money problems; **мне** ~ **поня́ть э́то/найти́ вре́мя** I find it hard to understand/to find the time; (**мне**) ~ **бе́гать/ стоя́ть** I have trouble running/standing up; ~ **сказа́ть** it's hard to say.

трудновоспиту́ем|**ый** (-, -а, -о) *прил*: ~ **ребёнок** problem child (*мн* children).

труднодосту́п|**ный** (-ен, -на, -но) *прил* (*горы, место*) hard to get to.

труднопроходи́м|**ый** (-, -а, -о) *прил* (*дорога*) almost impassable.

тру́дност|**ь** (-и) *ж* difficulty.

тру́дн|**ый** (-ен, -на́, -но) *прил* difficult.

трудов|**о́й** *прил* working; ~**о́е законода́тельство** employment legislation; ~**ые дохо́ды** earned income; ~ **стаж** working life; ~**я́ дисципли́на** discipline in the workplace; **трудова́я кни́жка** employment record book; **трудово́е соглаше́ние** contract (of employment).

трудоёмк|**ий** (-ая, -ое, -ие; -ок, -ка, -ко) *прил* labour-intensive (*BRIT*), labor-intensive (*US*).

трудолюби́в|**ый** (-, -а, -о) *прил* hard-working, industrious.

трудоспосо́бност|**ь** (-и) *ж* fitness to work; **утра́та** ~**и** disablement.

трудоспосо́бный *прил* fit to work.

трудотерапи́|**я** (-и) *ж* occupational therapy.

трудоустро́|**ить** (-ю, -ишь) *impf* **трудоустра́ивать**) *сов перех* to find work for.

трудоустро́йств|**о** (-а) *ср* placement.

трудя́щийся (-аяся, -ееся, -иеся) *прил* working ♦ (-егося; *decl like adj*) *м* worker.

тру́женик (-а) *м* worker.

тру́жениц|**а** (-ы) *ж см* **тру́женик**.

тружу́сь *несов см* **труди́ться**.

труп (-а) *м* corpse; **то́лько че́рез мой ~!** over my dead body!

тру́пп|**а** (-ы) *ж* (*ТЕАТР*) company.

трус (-а) *м* coward.

тру́сик|**и** (-ов) *мн* (*женские, детские*) knickers *мн* (*BRIT*), panties *мн* (*US*).

тру́|**сить** (-шу, -сишь; *perf* **стру́сить**) *несов неперех* to get scared; ~ (*impf*) **пе́ред кем-н** to cower before sb.

тру|**си́ть** (-шу́, -си́шь) *несов неперех* to trot along ♦ *перех* (*содержимое мешка*) to shake out; (*плоды: с дерева*) to shake.

трусли́в|**ый** (-, -а, -о) *прил* cowardly.

тру́сость (-и) *ж* cowardice.

трусц|**а́** (-ы́) *ж* trot; **бег ~о́й** jogging; **бе́гать** (*impf*) ~**о́й** to jog.

трус|**ы́** (-о́в) *мн* (*бельё: обычно мужские*) underpants *мн*; (*спортивные*) shorts *мн*.

тру́т|**ень** (-ня) *м* (*ЗООЛ*) drone; (*перен: человек*) parasite.

трух|**а́** (-и́) *ж* dust.

трухля́в|**ый** (-, -а, -о) *прил* crumbly.

тру́шу *несов см* **тру́сить**.

трушу́ *несов см* **труси́ть**.

трущо́б|**а** (-ы) *ж* (*бедный район*) slum; (*лесная*) jungle (*fig*).

трюк (-а) *м* trick; (*акробатический*) stunt.

трюка́ч (-а́) *м* (*в цирке*) acrobat; (*мошенник*) fraudster.

трюм (-а) *м* hold (*of ship*).

трюмо́ *ср нескл* dresser (*piece of furniture*).

трю́фель (-я; *nom pl* -**я́**) *м* (*также* конфета) truffle.

тряпи́чн|**ый** *прил*: ~**ая ку́кла** rag doll.

тря́п|**ка** (-ки; *gen pl* -**ок**) *ж* (*половая, для пыли*) cloth; (*лоскут*) rag; (*перен: разг: о человеке*) drip; ~**и** (*разг: пренебр*) rags.

тряпьё (-я́) *ср собир* rags *мн*.

тряси́н|**а** (-ы) *ж* quagmire; (*перен*) mire.

тря́с|**кий** (-кая, -кое, -кие; -ок, -ка, -ко) *прил* (*вагон, машина*) rickety; (*дорога*) bumpy.

трясогу́з|**ка** (-ки; *gen pl* -**ок**) *ж* wagtail.

трясо́к *прил см* **тря́ский**.

тряс|**ти́** (-у́, -ёшь) *несов перех* to shake; (*perf* **вы́трясти**; *ковёр, мешок*) to shake down; ~ (*impf*) +*instr* (*головой, кулаком*) to shake; (*гривой*) to toss; **в маши́не ~ёт** the car is jolting; **его́ ~ёт от стра́ха** he's shaking with fear

▶ **трясти́сь** *несов возв* (*машина*) to jolt; (*разг: в машине, в поезде итп*) to rattle along; ~**сь** (*impf*) **пе́ред** +*instr* (*перед начальством*) to tremble before; ~**сь** (*impf*) **над** +*instr* (*разг: над ребёнком, над деньгами*) to fret over *или* about; ~**сь** (*impf*) **от сме́ха/стра́ха/хо́лода** to shake with laughter/fear/cold.

тряхн|**у́ть** (-у́, -ёшь) *сов перех* to shake; ~ (*perf*) **старино́й** (*разг*) to turn the clock back.

т/с *сокр* (= **теку́щий счёт**) C/A (= *current account*).

т/счёт *сокр* = **т/с**.

тт *сокр* = **тома́**.

т.т. *сокр* = **това́рищи**.

ТУ *м сокр* = самолёт констру́кции А.Н.Ту́полева.

Ту *м сокр* = **ТУ**.

туале́т (-а) *м* toilet; (*гардероб*) outfit.

туале́тн|**ый** *прил*: ~**ая бума́га** toilet paper; **туале́тное мы́ло** toilet soap; **туале́тные принадле́жности** toiletries; **туале́тный сто́лик** dressing table.

туберкулёз (-а) *м* TB, tubercolosis.

туберкулёзный *прил* TB, tubercolosis *опред*.

ту́го *нареч* tightly; (*набить*) tight ♦ *как сказ* (*разг*): (**у нас**) ~ **с деньга́ми** money is tight (for us); (**у нас**) ~ **со вре́менем** we're hard-pressed for time; **дела́ иду́т** ~ (*разг*) things aren't going too well.

тугоду́м (-а) *м* dimwit.

туг|**о́й** (-, -а́, -о) *прил* (*струна, пружина*) taut; (*узел, одежда*) tight; (*чемодан*) tightly-packed; (*кошелёк*) bulging; **он туг на́ ухо** (*разг*) he's a bit hard of hearing.

туда́ *нареч* there; ~ **и обра́тно** there and back; **биле́т** ~ **и обра́тно** return (*BRIT*) *или* round-trip (*US*) ticket; **ни** ~ **ни сюда́!** (*разг*) it won't budge!; ~ **ему́ и доро́га** (*разг*) that's the best place for him; **он тако́й молодо́й, а** ~ **же, кома́ндует** (*разг*) he is so young, and look at him ordering everyone around.

туда́-сюда́ *нареч* all over the place; (*раскачиваться*) backwards and forwards ♦ *как сказ* (*разг*) it's so-so.

ту́же *сравн прил от* **туго́й** ♦ *сравн нареч от* **ту́го**.

туж|**и́ть** (-у́, -ишь) *несов неперех*: ~ (**о** +*prp*) to pine (for).

туз (-а́) *м* (*финансовый, городской*) bigwig.

тузе́м|**ец** (-ца) *м* native.

тузе́м|**ка** (-ки; *gen pl* -**ок**) *ж см* **тузе́мец**.

тузе́мный *прил* (*население, обычай*) native *опред*.

тузе́мок *сущ см* **тузе́мка**.

тузе́мца *итп сущ см* **тузе́мец**.

тук *межд* knock.

ту́ловище (-а) *ср* torso.

тулу́п (-а) *м* (*овчинный*) sheepskin coat.

тума́к (-а́) *м* (*разг*) thump, whack.

тума́н (-а; *part gen* -у) *м* mist; (*перен: в голове*) haze.

тума́нен *прил см* **тума́нный**.

тума́н|**ить** (*3sg* -ит, *3pl* -ят *perf* **затума́нить**); *несов перех* (*подлеж: дым, дождь*) to obscure; **слёзы затума́нили ей глаза́** her eyes were misty with tears; **вино́ затума́нило мне го́лову** the wine has addled my brain

▶ **тума́ниться** (*perf* **затума́ниться**) *несов возв* to become shrouded in mist; (*перен: глаза*) to mist over; (: *лицо*) to cloud.

тума́нность (-и) *ж* (*АСТРОНОМИЯ*) nebula; (*перен: в мыслях, в изложении*) cloudiness.

тума́н|ный (-ен, -на, -но) *прил* (*воздух, утро*)
misty; (*перен: взгляд*) dull; (: *смысл,
объясне́ние*) nebulous.

ту́мб|а (-ы) *ж* (*прича́льная, у́личная*) bollard;
(*для цвето́в*) stand; (*для скульпту́ры, стола́*)
pedestal; **афи́шная ~** cylindrical advertising
hoarding.

ту́мблер (-а) *м* (*КОМП*) toggle switch.

ту́мбоч|ка (-ки; *gen pl* -ек) *ж уменьш от* ту́мба;
(*ме́бель*) bedside cabinet.

ту́ндр|а (-ы) *ж* tundra.

ту́ндровый *прил* tundra *опред*.

туне́|ц (-ца́) *м* tuna (*fish*).

туне́я́д|ец (-ца) *м* parasite (*fig*).

туне́я́дство (-а) *ср* parasitism.

туне́я́дца *итп сущ см* туне́я́дец.

Туни́с (-а) *м* (*го́род*) Tunis; (*страна́*) Tunisia.

туни́сский (-ая, -ое, -ие) *прил* Tunisian.

тунне́л|ь (-я) *м =* тонне́ль.

тунца́ *итп сущ см* туне́ц.

тупе́|ть (-ю) *несов непepex* (*боль*) to become less
acute; (*perf* отупе́ть; *разг: челове́к*) to become
stupid; (*чу́вства*) to dull.

тупи́|к (-а́) *м* (*у́лица*) dead end, cul-de-sac; (*для
поездо́в*) siding; (*перен: в перегово́рах итп*)
deadlock; **поста́вить** (*поста́вить perf*) **кого́-н ~**
to stump sb; **стать** (*perf*) **в ~** to be stumped;
заходи́ть (**зайти́** *perf*) **в ~** (*перегово́ры*) to
reach a deadlock.

тупико́вый *прил* (*ситуа́ция*) dead-end;
(*ста́нция*) at the end of the line.

тупи́|ть (-лю́, -ишь; *perf* затупи́ть) *несов перех*
to blunt.

▶ тупи́ться (*perf* затупи́ться) *несов возв* to
become blunt.

тупи́ц|а (-ы) *м/ж* (*разг*) dunce.

тупл|ю́(сь) *несов см* тупи́ть(ся).

туп|о́й (-, -а́, -о) *прил* (*нож, каранда́ш*) blunt;
(*челове́к*) stupid; (*боль, ум*) dull; (*поко́рность,
страх*) blind; **тупо́й у́гол** obtuse angle.

ту́пость (-и) *ж* (*челове́ка, поведе́ния*) stupidity;
(*ума́*) dullness.

тур (-а) *м* (*ко́нкурса, перегово́ров, вы́боров*)
round; (*в та́нце*) turn; (*ЗООЛ*) mountain goat.

тур|а́ (-ы́) *ж* (*разг: в ша́хматах*) castle.

турби́н|а (-ы) *ж* turbine.

туре́цкий (-ая, -ое, -ие) *прил* Turkish; **~ язы́к**
Turkish.

тури́зм (-а) *м* tourism.

тури́ст (-а) *м* tourist; (*в похо́де*) hiker.

туристи́ческий (-ая, -ое, -ие) *прил* tourist
опред.

тури́стский (-ая, -ое, -ие) *прил* tourist's; **~
маршру́т** trail; **~ое снаряже́ние** camping and
walking equipment.

ту́рка *итп сущ см* ту́рок.

туркме́н (-а) *м* Turkmen.

Туркме́ни|я (-и) *ж* Turkmenia.

туркме́н|ка (-ки; *gen pl* -ок) *ж см* туркме́н.

туркме́нский (-ая, -ое, -ие) *прил* Turkmenian.

турне́ *ср нескл* (*ТЕА́ТР, СПОРТ*) tour.

турне́пс (-а) *м* turnip.

турни́к (-а́) *м* horizontal bar.

турнике́т (-а) *м* turnstile.

турни́р (-а) *м* tournament.

ту́р|ок (-ка) *м* Turk.

Ту́рци|я (-и) *ж* Turkey.

турча́н|ка (-ки; *gen pl* -ок) *ж см* ту́рок.

ту́скл|ый (-, -а́, -о) *прил* (*стекло́*) opaque; (*лак,
кра́ска, позоло́та*) matt; (*свет, стиль, взгляд*)
dull.

тускне́|ть (*3sg* -ет, *3pl* -ют, *perf* потускне́ть)
несов непepex (*кра́ска, тала́нт*) to fade;
(*серебро́, позоло́та, кра́ски*) to tarnish.

тут *нареч* here; **что ~ говори́ть!** (*разг*) what is
there to say?; **я ~ ни при чём** it has nothing to
do with me; **и всё ~** (*разг*) and that's that; **он
уже́ ~ как ~** (*разг*) right at that moment he
appeared; **не ~-то бы́ло** (*разг*) it wasn't to be.

ту́товый *прил*: **~ое де́рево** mulberry tree;
ту́товый шелкопря́д silkworm.

ту́фл|я (-ли; *nom pl* -ли, *gen pl* -ель) *ж* (*обы́чно
мн*) shoe.

ту́хл|ый (-, -а́, -о) *прил* (*еда́*) rotten; (*за́пах*)
putrid.

ту́х|нуть (*3sg* -нет, *3pl* -нут, *pt* -, -ла, -ло, *perf*
поту́хнуть) *несов непepex* (*костёр, свет,
свеча́*) to go out; (*perf* проту́хнуть; *мя́со, ры́ба*)
to go off.

ту́ч|а (-и) *ж* rain cloud; (*перен: мух, стрел*)
cloud; **он сего́дня, как ~** he's been in a black
mood all day.

ту́ч|ный (-ен, -на́, -но) *прил* (*челове́к*) stout;
(*по́чва*) fertile; (*трава́, луга́*) lush.

туш (-а) *м* (*МУЗ*) flourish.

ту́ш|а (-и) *ж* carcass; (*разг: о ту́чном челове́ке*)
hulk.

тушева́|ть (-ю́; *perf* затушева́ть) *несов перех*
(*рису́нок, фотогра́фию*) to shade in; (*перен:
ра́зницу, противоре́чия*) to gloss over.

тушева́|ться (-ю́сь) *несов от* стушева́ться.

тушён|ка (-ки; *gen pl* -ок) *ж* (*разг*) tinned (*BRIT*)
или canned meat.

тушёный *прил* (*КУЛИ́Н*) braised.

туши́|ть (-у́, -ишь; *perf* затуши́ть *или* потуши́ть)
несов перех (*свечу́, костёр, пожа́р*) to put out;
(*perf* потуши́ть; *свет*) to put out; (*КУЛИ́Н*) to
braise.

тушка́нчик (-а) *м* jerboa.

тущ|ь (-и) *ж* (*для рисова́ния*) Indian ink; (*для
ресни́ц*) mascara.

ту́|я (-и) *ж* red cedar.

т/х *сокр =* теплохо́д.

тчк *сокр =* то́чка.

тща́тел|ьный (-ен, -ьна, -ьно) *прил* thorough.

тщеду́ш|ный (-ен, -на, -но) *прил* feeble.

тщесла́вен *прил см* **тщесла́вный**.

тщесла́ви|е (-я) *ср* vanity.

тщесла́в|ный (-ен, -на, -но) *прил* vain.

тщётен *прил см* **тщётный**.

тще́тност|ь (-и) *ж* futility.

тще́т|ный (-ен, -на, -но) *прил* futile.

ты (тебя́; *см* Table 5а) *мест* you; (*разг: для усиления*): **ах ~, кака́я жа́лость!** oh, what a pity!; **быть** (*impf*) **с кем-н на ~** to be on familiar terms with sb; **вот тебе́ раз**! good grief!

ты́ка|ть (-чу, -чешь; *perf* ткнуть) *несов перех* (*разг: ударять*): **тыка́ть что-н/кого-н чем-н** to poke sth/sb with sth; (*: вонзать*): **тыка́ть что-н в** +*acc* to stick sth into; (*: обращаться на „ты"*) to address somebody using the informal form of "you"; **~** (*impf*) **кого́-н но́сом во что-н** (*разг*) to rub sb's face in sth; **~** (ткнуть *perf*) **па́льцем на** +*acc* (*разг*) to point at

▶ **ты́каться** (*perf* ткну́ться) *несов возв* (*разг: суетливо двигаться*) to rush about; **~ся** (ткну́ться *perf*) **в** +*acc* (*в стену, в дверь итп*) to bang into; (*соваться*) to nuzzle.

ты́кв|а (-ы) *ж* pumpkin.

тыл (-а; *loc sg* -ý, *nom pl* -ы́) *м* (ВОЕН: *сторона, территория*) the rear; (*: вся страна*) the home front; (*: воинские организации*) rear units.

тылово́й *прил* (ВОЕН) rear.

ты́льн|ый *прил* back; **~ая часть руки́** the back of one's hand.

тыс. *сокр* = **ты́сяча**.

ты́сяч|а (-и; *см* Table 35) *ж чис* thousand.

тысячеле́ти|е (-я) *ср* millenium; (*годовщина*) thousandth anniversary.

тысячеле́т|ний (-яя, -ее, -ие) *прил* (*период*) thousand-year; (*дерево*) thousand-year-old.

ты́сячи *чис см* **ты́сяча**.

ты́сячн|ая (-ой; *decl like adj*) *ж*: **одна́ ~** one thousandth.

ты́сячн|ый (-ая, -ое, -ие) *чис* thousandth; (*толпа, армия*) of many thousands.

ты́сячу *чис см* **ты́сяча**.

тычи́н|ка (-ки; *gen pl* -ок) *ж* stamen.

ты́чу(сь) *итп несов см* **ты́кать(ся)**.

тьм|а (-ы) *ж* (*мрак*) darkness, gloom; (*множество*) swarm.

тьфу *межд* yuk.

ТЭС *ж сокр* = **теплоэлектроста́нция**.

ТЭЦ *ж сокр* = **теплоэлектроцентра́ль**.

тюбете́й|ка (-йки; *gen pl* -ек) *ж* skullcap (*worn in Central Asia*).

тю́бик (-а) *м* tube.

ТЮЗ (-а) *м сокр* (= **теа́тр ю́ного зри́теля**) youth theatre (BRIT) *или* theater (US).

тюз (-а) *м сокр* = **ТЮЗ**.

тюк (-á) *м* bale.

тю́левый *прил* tulle.

тюле́н|ь (-я) *м* (ЗООЛ) seal.

тюл|ь (-я) *м* tulle.

тюльпа́н (-а) *м* tulip.

тюрба́н (-а) *м* turban.

тюре́мный *прил* prison *опред*; **тюре́мное**

заключе́ние imprisonment.

тюрьм|а́ (-ы́) *ж* prison; **сажа́ть** (**посади́ть** *perf*) **кого́-н в ~ý** to put sb in prison.

тюфя́к (-á) *м* straw mattress; (*разг: о человеке*) wimp.

тя́вка|ть (-ю) *несов неперех* to yap.

тя́вкн|уть (-у, -ешь) *сов неперех* to yap.

тя́г|а (-и) *ж* (*в печи*) draught (BRIT), draft (US); (*насоса, пылесоса*) suction; (ТЕХ) traction; (*реактивная*) thrust; **~ к** +*dat* (*перен*) attraction to; **на электри́ческой ~е** powered by electricity; **на ко́нной ~е** horse-drawn.

тяга́|ться (-юсь; *perf* потяга́ться) *несов возв* (*разг*): **~ с кем-н (в** +*prp*) to compete with sb (in); **~** (**потяга́ться** *perf*) **с кем-н умо́м** to pit one's wits against sb.

тяга́ч (-á) *м* tractor.

тя́гост|ный (-ен, -на, -но) *прил* burdensome; (*впечатления*) depressing.

тя́гост|ь (-и) *ж* (*ожидания, зависимости*) burden; (*обычно мн: войны, бедности*) hardship; (*на сердце, на душе*) heavy feeling; **быть** (*impf*) **в ~ кому́-н** to be a burden to sb.

тяготе́ни|е (-я) *ср* (ФИЗ) gravity; (*перен*): **~ к** +*dat* attraction to.

тяготе́|ть (-ю) *несов неперех*: **~ к** +*dat* (*к культуре, к прогрессу, к общению*) to gravitate *или* be drawn towards; (*к мнению*) to tend towards; (*перен*): **~ над** +*instr* (*обвинение, подозрение*) to hang over; (*чья-н власть, воля*) to oppress.

тяготи́|ть (-щу́, -ти́шь) *несов перех* to weigh (heavy) on

▶ **тяготи́ться** *несов возв* (+*instr*) to be weighed down by.

тя́гот|ы (-) *мн* hardships *мн*.

тягощу́(сь) *несов см* **тяготи́ть(ся)**.

тягу́ч|ий (-ая, -ее, -ие; -, -а, -е) *прил* (*клей, краска итп*) viscous; (*резинка, ткань*) stretchy; (*перен: речь, голос*) droning.

тя́жб|а (-ы) *ж* dispute.

тя́жек *прил см* **тя́жкий**.

тяжеле́|ть (-ю; *perf* отяжеле́ть *или* потяжеле́ть) *несов неперех* to get heavier; (*голова, ноги: от усталости*) to grow heavy.

тяжело́ *нареч* heavily; (*больной, раненый*) seriously ◆ *как сказ* (*нести*) it's heavy; (*понять, согласиться*) it's hard; **мне ~ здесь** I find it hard here; **больно́му ~** the patient is suffering.

тяжелоатле́т (-а) *м* weightlifter.

тяжелоатлети́ческ|ий (-ая, -ое, -ие) *прил*: **~ие соревнова́ния** weightlifting competiton.

тяжелове́с (-а) *м* (СПОРТ) heavyweight.

тяжелове́с|ный *прил* (-ен, -на, -но; *перен: речь, шутка, стиль*) laboured (BRIT), labored (US); (*архитектура*) heavy; **~ по́езд** freight train.

тяжёл|ый (-ёл, -ела́, -ело́) *прил* heavy; (*трудный: труд, обязанность, дорога итп*) hard, tough; (*сон*) restless; (*запах*) thick;

(*воздух*) close; (*преступление, болезнь, рана*)
serious; (*горестный: зрелище, день трудный*)
grim; (*мрачный: мысли, настроение*) sombre
(*BRIT*), somber (*US*); (*no short form*; *трудный:
человек, характер*) difficult; **с ~ёлым
се́рдцем** with a heavy heart; **тяжёлая атле́тика**
weightlifting; **тяжёлая промы́шленность**
heavy industry.

тя́жест|ь (**-и**) ж heaviness, weight; (*работы,
задачи*) difficulty; (*болезни, раны,
преступления*) seriousness, severity; (*обычно
мн: тяжёлый предмет*) weight; **си́ла ~и** (*физ*)
gravitational pull; **центр ~и** (*физ*) centre of
gravity.

тя́ж|кий (**-кая, -кое, -кие; -ек, -ка́, -ко**) прил
(*труд*) arduous; (*характер*) oppressive;
(*зрелище*) grim; (*сомнения, подозрение,
преступление*) grave.

тяну́ть (**-у́, -ешь**) несов перех (*канат, сеть
итп*) to pull; (*вытягивать: шею, руку*) to
stretch out; (*дело, разговор, заседание*) to drag
out; (*напиток*) to sip (at); (*perf* **протяну́ть**;
трубопровод, кабель) to lay; (*perf* **вы́тянуть**;

жребий, номер) to draw ◆ неперех: **~ с** +*instr* (*с
ответом, с решением*) to delay; (*разг*): **~ на**
+*acc* (*на килограмм итп*) to weigh; **~**
(**потяну́ть** *perf*) **кого́-н за́ руку** to pull at sb's
arm; **~** (*impf*) **кого́-н в кино́** to tempt sb out to the
cinema; **меня́ тя́нет в Петербу́рг** I want to go to
Petersburg; **меня́ тя́нет ко сну** I'm feeling
drowsy; **он не тя́нет на ли́дера** he is not
leadership material

▶ **тяну́ться** несов возв to stretch; (*заседание,
дни, зима итп*) to drag on; (*дым, запах*) to waft;
~ся (*impf*) **к** +*dat* to be attracted *или* drawn to; **он
тя́нется к зна́ниям** he has a thirst for
knowledge; **~ся** (*impf*) **за кем-н** to try to keep up
with sb.

тяну́ч|ка (**-ки**; *gen pl* **-ек**) ж toffee.

тя́п|ка (**-ки**; *gen pl* **-ок**) ж hoe.

тяп-ля́п нареч (*разг: пренебр*): **де́лать что-н ~**
to do sth in a slapdash way.

тя́пн|уть (**-у, -ешь**) сов неперех (*разг: укусить*)
to nip.

тя́пок сущ см **тя́пка**.

~ У, у ~

У, у *сущ нескл* (*буква*) the 20th letter of the Russian alphabet.

> **KEYWORD**

у *предл* (+*gen*) **1** (*около*) by; **у окна́/стены́** by the window/wall; **у мо́ря/реки́** by the sea/river; **у вхо́да** at the entrance

2 (*обозначает орудие, место работы*) at; **сиде́ть** (*impf*) **у руля́** to sit at the helm; **стоя́ть** (*impf*) **у станка́** to stand at the workbench

3 (*обозначает обладателя чего-н*): **у меня́ есть дом/де́ти** I have a house/children; **у таки́х люде́й быва́ют интере́сные иде́и** people like that have interesting ideas; **голова́ у меня́ совсе́м разболе́лась** I have a terrible headache

4 (*обозначает объект, с которым соотносится действие*): **я живу́ у друзе́й** I live with friends; **я учи́лся у него́** I was taught by him

5 (*указывает на источник получения чего-н*) from; **я взял/попроси́л у дру́га де́нег** I got/asked for money from a friend; **мы получи́ли разреше́ние у нача́льства** we got permission from the authorities

♦ *межд* (*выражает угрозу*) hey; (*выражает испуг, восторг*) oh; **у, негодя́й!** hey, you rascal!; **у, как высоко́!** oh, how high it is!; **у, кака́я красота́!** oh, how beautiful!

УАЗ *м сокр* = **Улья́новский автомоби́льный заво́д**; (*автомобиль*) *vehicle produced at the Ul'ianovskiy car factory.*

уба́в|ить (**-лю, -ишь**; *impf* **убавля́ть**) *сов перех* (*цену, размеры*) to reduce; (*рукава*) to shorten

▶ **уба́виться** (*impf* **убавля́ться**) *сов возв* (*расходы*) to decrease; (*срок*) to be reduced; (*дни*) to get shorter.

убаю́ка|ть (**-ю**) *сов от* **баю́кать**.

убега́|ть (**-ю**) *несов от* **убежа́ть**.

убегу́ *итп сов см* **убежа́ть**.

убеди́тельный (**-ен, -ьна, -ьно**) *прил* (*пример, доказательство*) convincing; (*просьба*) urgent.

убеди́|ть (**-шь, -йт**; *impf* **убежда́ть**) *сов перех*: **~ кого́-н** +*infin* to persuade sb to do; **убежда́ть** (**~** *perf*) **кого́-н в чём-н** to convince sb of sth

▶ **убеди́ться** (*impf* **убежда́ться**) *сов возв*: **~ся в чём-н** to be convinced of sth.

убежа́|ть (*как* **бежа́ть**; *см* **Table 20**; *impf* **убега́ть**) *сов неперех* to run away; **молоко́ ~ло**

(*разг*) the milk has boiled over.

убежда́|ть(ся) (**-ю(сь)**) *несов от* **убеди́ть(ся)**.

убежде́ни|е (**-я**) *ср* (*внушение*) assurance; (*взгляд*) conviction; **поддава́ться** (**подда́ться** *perf*) **~ям** to give in to persuasion.

убеждённость (**-и**) *ж* (*уверенность*) assurance, conviction.

убеждённый (**-ён, -ена́, -ено́**) *прил*: **~ в** +*prp* convinced of; (**-ён, -ённа, -ённо**; *тон*) assured; (*no short form*; *католик*) convinced.

убежи́шь *итп сов см* **убежа́ть**.

убе́жищ|е (**-а**) *ср* (*от дождя, от бомб*) shelter; **полити́ческое ~** political asylum.

убелённый *прил*: **~ седи́нами** silver-haired.

убер|е́чь (**-егу́, -ежёшь** *итп*, **-егу́т**; *pt* **-ёг, -егла́, -егло́**, *impf* **уберега́ть**) *сов перех* to protect

▶ **убере́чься** (*impf* **уберега́ться**) *сов возв* (*от опасности итп*) to protect o.s.; **~ся** (*perf*) **от просту́ды** to avoid catching cold.

уберу́(сь) *итп сов см* **убра́ть(ся)**.

убива́|ть (**-ю**) *несов от* **уби́ть**

▶ **убива́ться** *несов возв* (*разг: страдать*) to grieve; (: *на работе*) to break one's back.

уби́йственный *прил* (*оружие*) deadly; (*новость, результат*) devastating; (*разг: жара, климат*) unbearable.

уби́йств|о (**-а**) *ср* murder.

уби́йц|а (**-ы**) *м/ж* murderer.

убира́|ть(ся) (**-ю(сь)**) *несов от* **убра́ть(ся)**.

уби́т|ая (**-ой**; *decl like adj*) *ж* dead woman (*мн* women).

уби́тый *прил* (*перен: лицо*) crushed ♦ (**-ого**; *decl like adj*) *м* dead man (*мн* men); **спит как ~** (*перен*) he is sleeping like a log.

уб|и́ть (**-ью, -ьёшь**; *impf* **убива́ть**) *сов перех* to kill; (*совершить преступление*) to murder; (*перен: надежды, инициативу*) to destroy; **~** (*perf*) **вре́мя** (*перен*) to kill time.

ублаж|и́ть (**-у́, -и́шь**; *impf* **ублажа́ть**) *сов перех* (*разг*) to please.

убо́г|ий (**-ая, -ое, -ие**) *прил* (*дом, человек*) wretched; (*перен: идеи, фильм*) mediocre.

убо́жеств|о (**-а**) *ср* (*мыслей, идей*) mediocrity; (*обстановки*) wretchedness.

убо́|й (**-я**) *м* slaughter.

убо́р (**-а**) *м*: **головно́й ~** hat.

убо́рист|ый (**-, -а, -о**) *прил* (*почерк, печать*) close, dense.

убо́рк|а (**-и**) *ж* (*помещения*) cleaning;

занима́ться (заня́ться *perf*) ~ to do the cleaning; ~ урожа́я harvest.

убо́рн|ая (-ой; *decl like adj*) ж (*артисти́ческая*) dressing-room; (*туале́т*) toilet, lavatory.

убо́рочн|ый *прил* harvesting *опред*; ~ая маши́на harvester.

убо́рщик (-а) м cleaner.

убо́рщиц|а (-и) ж *см* убо́рщик.

убра́ть (уберу́, уберёшь; *pt* -а́л, -ала́, -а́ло, *impf* убира́ть) *сов перех* (*унести́: ве́щи*) to take away, remove; (*помести́ть*) to put away; (*паруса́, я́корь*) to stow; (*ша́сси*) to retract, draw in; (*ко́мнату*) to tidy; (*разг: пара́граф: из те́кста*) to remove; (*урожа́й*) to gather in; убира́ть (~ *perf*) со стола́ to clear the table

▶ убра́ться (*impf* убира́ться) *сов возв* (*разг: удали́ться*) to get out; (*сде́лать убо́рку*) to clear *или* tidy up; убира́йся отсю́да! get lost!

убу́ду *итп сов см* убы́ть.

убыва́ть (-ю) *несов от* убы́ть.

у́быль (-и) ж (*рабо́чей си́лы*) decrease; идти́ (пойти́ *perf*) на ~ (*дни*) to get shorter; (*боле́знь, эпиде́мия*) to run its course.

убы́т|ок (-ка) м loss; терпе́ть (*impf*) *или* нести́ (*impf*) ~ки to incur losses.

убы́точн|ый (-ен, -на, -но) *прил* unprofitable.

убы́ть (*как* быть; *см* Table 21; *impf* убыва́ть) *сов непepex* to decrease; его́ от э́того не убу́дет he won't be any worse off for it.

убью́ *итп сов см* убы́ть.

уважа́ем|ый *прил* respected, esteemed; у~ые да́мы и господа́! Ladies and Gentlemen!

уважа́ть (-ю) *несов перех* to respect.

уваже́ни|е (-я) *ср* respect.

уважи́тельный (-ен, -ьна, -ьно) *прил* (*отноше́ние*) respectful; (*до́вод, причи́на*) respectable.

ува́ж|ить (-у, -ишь) *сов перех* (*угоди́ть*) to humour (*BRIT*), humor (*US*); ~ (*perf*) чью-н про́сьбу to grant sb's request.

у́вал|ень (-ьня) м lumbering oaf.

ува́р|иться (3sg -арится, 3pl -а́рятся, *impf* ува́риваться) *сов возв* (*сиро́п, щи*) to boil down, reduce.

УВД *ср сокр* (= Управле́ние вну́тренних дел) administration of internal affairs within a town or region.

уве́дом|ить (-лю, -ишь; *impf* уведомля́ть) *сов перех* to inform.

уведомле́ни|е (-я) *ср* (*докуме́нт*) notification.

уведомлю́ *сов см* уве́домить.

уведомля́|ть (-ю) *несов от* уве́домить.

уведу́ *итп сов см* увести́.

увез|ти́ (-у́, -ёшь; *pt* увёз, увезла́, увезло́, *impf* увози́ть) *сов перех* to take away.

увекове́ч|ить (-у, -ишь) *сов перех* (*геро́я*) to immortalize.

увеличе́ни|е (-я) *ср* increase.

увели́чива|ть(ся) (-ю(сь)) *несов от* увели́чить(ся).

увеличи́тельн|ый *прил*: ~ое стекло́ magnifying glass.

увели́ч|ить (-у, -ишь; *impf* увели́чивать) *сов перех* to increase; (*фотогра́фию*) to enlarge

▶ увели́читься (*impf* увели́чиваться) *сов возв* to increase, be increased.

увенча́|ться (-юсь) *сов возв*: ~ успе́хом to result in success.

уве́ренност|ь (-и) ж confidence; ~ в себе́ self-confidence; поколеба́ть (*perf*) чью-н ~ в чём-н/в том, что ... to shake sb's conviction in sth/that ...; я был в по́лной ~и, что ... I was absolutely sure that ....

уве́рен|ный (-, -на, -но, -ы) *прил* (*шаг, отве́т, го́лос*) confident; (*рука́*) sure; ~ в +prp sure of; ~ в себе́ self-confident, sure of o.s.

уве́р|ить (-ю, -ишь) *сов от* уверя́ть.

уверн|у́ться (-у́сь, -ёшься; *impf* увёртываться) *сов возв* to swerve; увёртываться (~ *perf*) от уда́ра to dodge a blow; увёртываться (~ *perf*) от прямо́го отве́та to avoid giving a straight answer.

уве́р|овать (-ую) *сов неперех*: ~ в +acc to (come to) believe in.

увёртлив|ый (-, -а, -о) *прил* (*подви́жный*) nimble; (*перен: хи́трый*) evasive.

увёртыва|ться (-юсь) *несов от* уверну́ться.

увертю́р|а (-ы) ж overture.

увер|я́ть (-ю; *perf* уве́рить) *несов перех*: ~ кого́-н/что-н (в чём-н) to assure sb/sth (of sth); ~ю Вас, что я был про́тив э́того I assure you that I was against it.

увесели́тельн|ый *прил* (*зре́лище*) entertaining; ~ая прогу́лка jaunt.

уве́сист|ый (-, -а, -о) *прил* heavy.

уве|сти́ (-ду́, -дёшь; *pt* -ёл, -ела́, -ело́, *impf* уводи́ть) *сов перех* to lead off *или* away; (*разг: похи́тить*) to nick.

уве́чь|е (-я) *ср* injury; наноси́ть (нанести́ *perf*) кому́-н ~ to maim sb; получа́ть (получи́ть *perf*) ~ to be maimed.

уве́ша|ть (-ю; *impf* уве́шивать) *сов перех*: ~ кого́-н/что-н чем-н to cover sb/sth with sth.

увещева́|ть (-ю) *несов перех* to exhort.

увива́|ться (-юсь) *несов возв* (*уха́живать*): ~ (за кем-н) (*за же́нщиной*) to hang around (sb).

уви́|деть (-жу, -дишь) *сов от* ви́деть ♦ *перех* to catch sight of

▶ уви́деться *сов от* ви́деться.

увильн|у́ть (-у́, -ёшь) *сов неперех*: ~ от +gen (*разг*) to dodge; (*от отве́тственности*) to get *или* wriggle out of.

увлажн|и́ть (-ю́, -и́шь; *impf* увлажня́ть) *сов перех* to moisten

▶ увлажни́ться (*impf* увлажня́ться) *сов возв* to become moist.

увлёк(ся) *итп сов см* **увлечь(ся)**.
увлека́тел|ьный *прил (захватывающий)* absorbing; (-ен, -ьна, -ьно; *занимательный*) entertaining.
увлека́|ть(ся) (-ю(сь)) *несов от* **увлечь(ся)**.
увлека́ющ|ийся (-аяся, -ееся, -иеся) *прил* easily carried away.
увлеку́(сь) *итп сов см* **увлечь(ся)**.
увлече́ни|е (-я) *ср (влюблённость)* infatuation; ~ (+*instr*) (*работой, балетом*) enthusiasm *или* passion (for).
увл|е́чь (-еку́, -ечёшь *итп*, -еку́т; *pt* -ёк, -екла́, -екло́, *impf* **увлека́ть**) *сов перех* to lead away; (*перен*) to captivate
▶ **увле́чься** (*impf* **увлека́ться**) *сов возв*: ~ся +*instr* to get carried away with; (*влюбиться*) to fall for; (*шахматами итп*) to become keen on.
ув|оди́ть (-ожу́, -о́дишь) *несов от* **увести́**.
ув|ози́ть (-ожу́, -о́зишь) *несов от* **увезти́**.
увола́кива|ть (-ю) *несов от* **уволо́чь**.
увол|ить (-ю, -ишь; *impf* **увольня́ть**) *сов перех* (*с работы*) to dismiss, sack; **увольня́ть** (~ *perf*) **в запа́с** to transfer to the reserve
▶ **уво́литься** (*impf* **увольня́ться**) *сов возв*: ~ся **с рабо́ты** to leave one's job.
уволо́чь (-ку́, -чёшь *итп*, -ку́т; *pt* -к, -кла́, -кло́, *impf* **увола́кивать**) *сов перех* to drag away *или* off; (*разг: украсть*) to nick.
увольне́ни|е (-я) *ср (со службы)* dismissal; (*воен*) leave.
увольни́тельн|ая (-ой; *decl like adj*) *ж (воен)* leave-pass.
увольня́|ть(ся) (-ю(сь)) *несов от* **уво́лить(ся)**.
УВЧ *сокр* (= ультравысо́кая частота́) UHF (= *ultrahigh frequency*) ♦ *прил сокр* (ультравысокочасто́тный) UHF (= *ultrahigh-frequency*).
увы́ *межд* alas.
увяда́ни|е (-я) *ср (цветов)* withering; (*красоты*) fading.
увя́дш|ий (-ая, -ее, -ие) *прил (цветок)* withered; (*красота*) faded.
увя|за́ть (-жу́, -жешь; *impf* **увя́зывать**) *сов перех (вещи)* to tie up; (*перен: согласовать*) to tie in
▶ **увяза́ться** *сов возв (разг)*: ~ся (**за** +*instr*) to tag along (behind).
увя́з|нуть (-у, -ешь) *сов от* **вя́знуть**.
увя́зыва|ть (-ю) *несов от* **увяза́ть**.
увя́|нуть (-ну, -ешь) *сов от* **вя́нуть**.
угада́|ть (-ю; *impf* **уга́дывать**) *сов перех* to guess.
Уга́нд|а (-ы) *ж* Uganda.
уга́р (-а) *м (воздух)* fume-filled air; (*отравление*) carbon-monoxide poisoning; **пья́ный** ~ drunken haze.
уга́рный *прил*: ~ **дым** poisonous smoke; **уга́рный газ** carbon monoxide.
угаса́|ть (-ю; *perf* **уга́снуть**) *несов неперех (костёр, закат)* to die down.

уга́с|нуть (-у, -ешь) *сов от* **га́снуть**.
угла́ *итп сущ см* **у́гол**.
углево́д (-а) *м* carbohydrate.
углеводоро́д (-а) *м* hydrocarbon.
углекислот|а́ (-ы́) *ж* carbon dioxide.
углеки́слый *прил*: ~ **газ** carbon dioxide.
углепромы́шленность (-и) *ж* coal industry.
углеро́д (-а) *м (хим)* carbon.
углова́тость (-и) *ж (лица)* angularity; (*человека, движений*) awkwardnes.
углова́тый *прил (лицо)* angular; (*человек, движения*) awkward.
углово́й *прил* corner *опред*; (*также*: ~ **уда́р**: *спорт*) corner.
углуб|и́ть (-лю́, -и́шь; *impf* **углубля́ть**) *сов перех* to deepen
▶ **углуби́ться** (*impf* **углубля́ться**) *сов возв* (*также перен*) to deepen; **углубля́ться** (~ся *perf*) **в** +*acc* (*в книгу, в чтение*) to become absorbed in; ~ся (*perf*) **в воспомина́ния/мы́сли** to become lost in memories/thought; ~ся (*perf*) **в лес** to go deep into the forest.
углубле́ни|е (-я) *ср (кризиса)* deepening; (*впадина*) depression.
углублённый (-ён, -ена́, -ено́) *прил* profound.
углублю́(сь) *сов см* **углуби́ть(ся)**.
углубля́|ть(ся) (-ю(сь)) *несов от* **углуби́ть(ся)**.
угля́ *итп сущ см* **у́голь**.
угля|де́ть (-жу́, -ди́шь) *сов перех (разг: увидеть)* to spot.
угн|а́ть (угоню́, уго́нишь; *pt* -а́л, -ала́, -а́ло, *impf* **угоня́ть**) *сов перех* to drive off; (*разг: украсть*) to steal; (*самолёт*) to hijack
▶ **угна́ться** *сов возв*: ~ся **за** +*instr* (*также перен*) to catch up with.
угнета́тель (-я) *м* oppressor.
угнета́|ть (-ю) *несов перех (притеснять)* to oppress; (*тяготить*) to depress.
угнете́ни|е (-я) *ср (народа)* oppression.
угнетённость (-и) *ж* depression.
угнетённый *прил (народ)* oppressed; (*мед*) depressed.
угова́рива|ть (-ю) *несов от* **уговори́ть** ♦ *перех* to try to persuade.
угово́р (-а) *м (обычно мн: наставление)* persuasion; (*соглашение*) agreement, arrangement; **поддава́ться** (**подда́ться** *perf*) **на** ~**ы** to give in to persuasion.
уговор|и́ть (-ю́, -и́шь; *impf* **угова́ривать**) *сов перех* to persuade.
уго́д|а (-ы) *ж*: **в** ~**у кому́-н** to please sb.
уго́ден *прил см* **уго́дный**.
уго|ди́ть (-жу́, -ди́шь; *impf* **угожда́ть**) *сов неперех*: ~ +*dat*/**на** +*acc* to please; (*попасть*) to end up; ~ (*perf*) **под маши́ну** to get run over; ~ (*perf*) **ного́й в я́му** to put one's foot in a hole.
уго́длив|ый (-, -а, -о) *прил* obsequious.
уго́дник (-а) *м (рел)* saint; **да́мский** ~ ladies' man.
уго́днича|ть (-ю) *несов неперех*: ~ (**пе́ред**

+*instr*) to fawn (on).

угóдно *част*: **что** ~ whatever you like ♦ *как сказ*: **что Вам** ~**?** what can I do for you?; **кто** ~ anyone; **когда́/какóй** ~ whenever/whichever you like; **скóлько** ~ any amount; **комý** ~ **нача́ть?** who would like to start?; **возьми́те всё, что Вам** ~ take whatever you like; **от них мóжно ожида́ть чегó** ~ they might do anything.

угóд|ный (-ен, -на, -но) *прил* (+*dat*; *родителям, властям*) pleasing to.

угóд|ья (-ий) *мн*: **земéльные** ~ arable and pasture land; **лéсные** ~ forestry; **вóдные** ~ fisheries and waterways.

угожда́|ть (-ю) *несов от* угоди́ть.

угожý *сов см* угоди́ть.

ýгол (-ла́; *loc sg* -лý) *м* (ГЕОМ) angle; (*стола, дома, комнаты*) corner; **завора́чивать (заверну́ть** *perf*) **за́ угол** to turn the corner; **за углóм** round the corner; **из-за угла́** from around the corner; ~ **зрéния** perspective, standpoint; **он снима́ет** ~ he's renting a tiny little place.

уголка́ *сущ см* уголóк.

уголóвник (-а) *м* criminal.

уголóвный *прил* criminal *опред*; **уголóвный кóдекс** criminal code; **уголóвный престýпник** criminal; **уголóвный рóзыск** Criminal Investigation Department.

уголóвщин|а (-ы) *ж* (*разг*) crime.

уголó|к (-ка́) *м уменьш от* ýгол; (*место*) corner; **ти́хий** ~ secluded spot.

ýг|оль (-ля́; *nom pl* -ли, *gen pl* -лей) *м* coal.

ýгóльник (-а) *м* (*чертёжный*) set square.

ýгольный *прил* coal.

угомон|и́ться (-ю́сь, -и́шься) *сов возв* (*разг*) to quieten down.

угóн (-а) *м* (*самолёта*) hijacking; (*машины, коня*) theft.

угóнщик (-а) *м* (*самолёта*) hijacker.

угоню́(сь) *итп сов см* угна́ть(ся).

угоня́|ть (-ю) *несов от* угна́ть.

угора́зд|ить (3sg -ит) *сов безл*: ~**ило тебя́ сказа́ть э́то!** what on earth made you say that?; **как э́то тебя́** ~**ило** how on earth did you manage that?

угорéлый *прил*: **бéгать как** ~ to run around like a mad thing.

угорé|ть (-ю́, -и́шь) *сов неперех* to get gas-poisoning.

ýг|орь (-ря́; *nom pl* -ри́) *м* (ЗООЛ) eel; (*на лице*) blackhead.

угости́ть (-щý, -сти́шь; *impf* угоща́ть) *сов перех*: ~ **когó-н чем-н** (*дома*) to offer sb sth; (*в рестора́не*) to treat sb to sth.

угоща́|ться (-юсь) *несов возв*: ~**йтесь!** help yourself!

угощéни|е (-я) *ср* (*гостéй*) entertaining; (*вкусное, изысканное*) food.

угощý *сов см* угости́ть.

угрóб|ить (-лю, -ишь) *сов от* грóбить.

угрожа́|ть (-ю) *несов неперех*: ~ **комý-н (чем-н)** to threaten sb (with sth); **емý** ~**ет банкрóтство** he is threatened with bankruptcy.

угрожа́ющий (-ая, -ее, -ие) *прил* threatening; (*вид*) menacing.

угрóз|а (-ы) *ж* (*обычно мн*) threat.

угрóха|ть (-ю) *сов перех* (*разг*: *дéньги*) to blow; (*продукты*) to use (up).

угрызéни|е (-я) *ср*: ~**я сóвести** pangs *мн* of conscience.

угрю́м|ый (-, -а, -о) *прил* gloomy.

угря́ *итп сущ см* ýгорь.

удáбрива|ть (-ю) *несов от* удóбрить.

удáв (-а) *м* boa constrictor.

удава́|ться (3sg -ётся, 3pl -ю́тся) *несов от* уда́ться.

удади́мся *итп сов см* уда́ться.

удалéц (-ьца́) *м* (*разг*) hero.

удал|и́ть (-ю́, -и́шь; *impf* удаля́ть) *сов перех* (*детей, посторонних*) to send away, remove; (*игрока*: *с поля*) to send off; (*пятно, занозу, орган*) to remove; (*зуб*) to extract; (КОМП) to delete

► **удали́ться** (*impf* удаля́ться) *сов возв* to move away; (*перен*: *от темы*) to digress; (*в свою комнату*) to withdraw.

удалóй *прил* daring.

ýдал|ь (-и) *ж* daring.

удальца́ *итп сущ см* удалéц.

удаля́|ть(ся) (-ю(сь)) *несов от* удали́ть(ся).

удáр (-а) *м* blow; (*ногóй*) kick; (*звук, инсульт*) stroke; (*пульса, сéрдца*) beat; ~ **грóма** clap of thunder; **быть** (*impf*) **в** ~**е** (*разг*) to be on the ball; **ста́вить** (**поста́вить** *perf*) **когó-н под** ~ to put sb in a vulnerable position; **наноси́ть (нанести́** *perf*) ~ **комý-н** to deal a blow to sb.

ударéни|е (-я) *ср* (*также* линг) stress.

удáр|ить (-ю, -ишь; *impf* уда́рять) *сов перех* to hit; (*подлеж*: *часы*) to strike; (: *морóзы*) to set in; **уда́рять** (~ *perf*) **когó-н по головé/спинé** to hit sb on the head/back; **уда́рять** (~ *perf*) **в бараба́н** to beat a drum; ~ (*perf*) **по спекуля́нтам** to crack down on profiteers; **винó** ~**ил емý в гóлову** the wine has gone to his head; ~**ил гром** there was a clap of thunder; **он не** ~**ил лицóм в грязь** he didn't disgrace himself

► **удáриться** (*impf* уда́ряться) *сов возв* (*натолкнуться на что-н*): ~**ся о** +*acc* (*о дверь, о стену итп*) to bang (o.s.) against; ~**ся** (*perf*) **в па́нику** to fly into a panic; ~**ся** (*perf*) **в спорт/в на́уку/в поли́тику** to become obsessed with sport/science/politics; **он** ~**ился головóй о шкаф** he hit his head on *или* against the cupboard.

удáрник (-а) *м* (*музыка́нт*) percussionist; (*ружья́, пистолéта*) striker, firing pin.

уда́рный *прил* (*инструмент*) percussion *опред*; (*войска, труд*) shock *опред*; (*слог*) stressed; **уда́рная волна́** shock wave.

ударя|ть(ся) (-ю(сь)) *несов от* **уда́рить(ся)**.

уда́ться (*как* **дать**; *см* **Table 14**; *impf* **удава́ться**) *сов возв* (*получиться: опыт, испытание*) to be successful, work; (*пирог*) to turn out well; **нам удало́сь/не удало́сь поговори́ть/зако́нчить рабо́ту** we managed/didn't manage to talk to one another/finish the work.

уда́ч|а (-и) *ж* (good) luck; **нам вы́пала больша́я ~** we had a great stroke of luck; **жела́ю ~и!** good luck!

уда́чен *прил см* **уда́чный**.

уда́члив|ый (-, -а, -о) *прил* lucky.

уда́ч|ный (-ен, -на, -но) *прил* successful; (*хороший: выбор, выражение*) good.

удва́ива|ть(ся) (-ю(сь)) *несов от* **удво́ить(ся)**.

удво́ени|е (-я) *ср* doubling.

удво́енный *прил* (*зарплата*) doubled; (*энергия, сила итп*) redoubled.

удво́|ить (-ю, -ишь; *impf* **удва́ивать**) *сов перех* to double; (*внимание, усилия*) to redouble

▶ **удво́иться** (*impf* **удва́иваться**) *сов возв* to double; (*усилия итп*) to be redoubled.

уде́л (-а) *м* (*судьба*) lot, fate.

удел|и́ть (-ю́, -и́шь; *impf* **уделя́ть**) *сов перех*: ~ **что-н кому́-н/чему́-н** to devote sth to sb/sth.

уде́льный *прил*: ~ **вес** (*физ*) specific gravity.

уделя́|ть (-ю) *несов от* **удели́ть**.

у́держ (-у) *м*: **без ~у** uncontrollably; **он не зна́ет ~у в тра́тах** he doesn't know when to stop spending.

удерж|а́ть (-ержу́, -е́ржишь; *impf* **уде́рживать**) *сов перех* to restrain; (*часть зарплаты*) to deduct; (*первенство, позиции*): ~ **(за собо́й)** to retain; ~ (*perf*) **что-н в рука́х** to hold onto sth, not let go of sth; **уде́рживать** (~ *perf*) **кого́-н от пое́здки** to keep sb from going on a journey; **уде́рживать** (~ *perf*) **кого́-н до́ма** to keep sb at home

▶ **удержа́ться** (*impf* **уде́рживаться**) *сов возв* (*остановить себя*) to stop *или* restrain o.s.; (*устоять: на краю обрыва*) to hang on; ~**ся** (*perf*) **на нога́х** to stay on one's feet; ~**ся** (*perf*) **на свои́х пози́циях** to hold one's ground; ~**ся** (*perf*) **от сме́ха** to stop *или* keep o.s. from laughing; ~**ся** (*perf*) **от слёз** to hold back the tears.

удеру́ *итп сов см* **удра́ть**.

удесятер|и́ть (-ю́, -и́шь) *сов перех* to increase tenfold; (*усилия*) to triple.

удешев|и́ть (-лю́, -и́шь; *impf* **удешевля́ть**) *сов перех* to make cheaper

▶ **удешеви́ться** (*impf* **удешевля́ться**) *сов возв* to get cheaper.

удешевле́ни|е (-я) *ср*: ~ **цен** (**на** +*acc*) reduction in the price (of).

удешевлю́(сь) *сов см* **удешеви́ть(ся)**.

удешевля́|ть(ся) (-ю(сь)) *несов от* **удешеви́ть(ся)**.

удиви́телен *прил см* **удиви́тельный**.

удиви́тельно *нареч* (*красивый, вкусный*) amazingly ♦ *как сказ* it's amazing; **мне ~, что ты э́того не понима́ешь** I'm amazed that you don't understand this; ~, **как ты не простуди́лся** it's amazing that you didn't catch (a) cold; **и не ~** and no wonder.

удиви́тел|ьный (-ен, -ьна, -ьно) *прил* amazing.

удив|и́ть (-лю́, -и́шь; *impf* **удивля́ть**) *сов перех* to surprise

▶ **удиви́ться** (*impf* **удивля́ться**) *сов возв*: ~**ся** +*dat* (*известию, приезду итп*) to be surprised at *или* by; **я ~и́лся, что он не позвони́л** I was surprised that he didn't phone.

удивле́ни|е (-я) *ср* surprise; **к на́шему ~ю, она́ ушла́** to our surprise she left; **с ~м** with surprise; **от ~я** in surprise; **краси́вый/у́мный на ~** amazingly beautiful/clever.

удивлённый *прил* surprised.

удивлю́(сь) *сов см* **удиви́ть(ся)**.

удивля́|ть(ся) (-ю(сь)) *несов от* **удиви́ть(ся)**.

удил|а́ (-**у́ил**) *мн* bit *ed* (*of bridle*).

уди́лище (-а) *ср* (*часть удочки*) (fishing-)rod.

удира́|ть (-ю) *несов от* **удра́ть**.

уди́ть (**ужу́, у́дишь**) *несов неперех* to angle.

удлине́ни|е (-я) *ср* (*рукава*) lengthening; (*срока*) extension.

удлинённый *прил* (*пальто*) long; (*лицо*) elongated.

удлин|и́ть (-ю́, -и́шь; *impf* **удлиня́ть**) *сов перех* (*рукав, пальто*) to lengthen; (*рабочий день, срок*) to extend

▶ **удлини́ться** (*impf* **удлиня́ться**) *сов возв* to grow longer.

удо́бен *прил см* **удо́бный**.

удо́бно *нареч* (*усесться, лечь*) comfortably ♦ *как сказ*: **мне здесь** ~ I'm comfortable here; **мне ~ прийти́ ве́чером** it's convenient for me to come in the evening.

удо́б|ный (-ен, -на, -но) *прил* (*мебель*) comfortable; (*время, формат, место*) convenient; **дожида́ться** (**дожда́ться** *perf*) ~**ного слу́чая** to wait for the right opportunity.

удобре́ни|е (-я) *ср* (*действие*) fertilizing; (*минеральное, химическое*) fertilizer.

удо́бр|ить (-ю, -ишь; *impf* **удобря́ть** (или) **уда́бривать**) *сов перех* to fertilize.

удо́бств|о (-а) *ср* comfort; **кварти́ра со все́ми ~ами** a flat with all (modern) conveniences.

удовлетворе́ни|е (-я) *ср* satisfaction; (*требований*) fulfilment.

удовлетворённый *прил* satisfied.

удовлетвори́телен *прил см* **удовлетвори́тельный**.

удовлетвори́тельно *нареч* satisfactorily; (*просвещ*) ≈ satisfactory (*school mark*).

удовлетвори́тел|ьный (-ен, -ьна, -ьно) *прил* satisfactory.

удовлетвор|и́ть (-ю́, -и́шь; *impf* **удовлетворя́ть**) *сов перех* to satisfy;

(*потребности, спрос, просьбу*) to meet; (*жалобу*) to respond to; **удовлетворя́ть** (~ *perf*) +*dat* (*требованиям, вкусам, правилам*) to satisfy

▸ **удовлетвори́ться** (*impf* **удовлетворя́ться**) *сов возв*: ~**ся** +*instr* to be satisfied with.

удово́льстви|е (-я) *ср* pleasure; **получа́ть** (**получи́ть** *perf*) ~ **от чего́-н** to enjoy sth; **доставля́ть** (**доста́вить** *perf*) **кому́-н** ~ to make sb happy; **с** ~**м** with pleasure; **я бы с** ~**м пошёл с Ва́ми** I would love to go with you.

удово́льств|оваться (-уюсь) *сов от* **дово́льствоваться**.

удо́д (-а) *м* (*зоол*) hoopoe.

удо́|й (-я) *м* yield (*of milk*).

удо́йливый (-, -а, -о) *прил*: ~**ая коро́ва** good milking cow.

удорожа́ни|е (-я) *ср*: ~ **проду́ктов пита́ния** rise in food prices.

удоста́ива|ть(ся) (-ю(сь)) *несов от* **удосто́ить(ся)**.

удостовере́ни|е (-я) *ср* (*подписи*) verification; (*документ*) identification (card); **удостовере́ние ли́чности** identity card.

удостове́р|ить (-ю, -ишь; *impf* **удостоверя́ть**) *сов перех* (*факт*) to verify

▸ **удостове́риться** (*impf* **удостоверя́ться**) *сов возв*: ~**ся в** +*prp* (*в чьей-н невиновности, в верности сообщения*) to assure o.s. of; **он** ~**ился, что она́ до́ма** he made sure that she was at home.

удосто́|ить (-ю, -ишь; *impf* **удоста́ивать**) *сов перех*: ~ **кого́-н чего́-н** to bestow sth on sb; **удоста́ивать** (~ *perf*) **кого́-н свои́м визи́том** to honour (*BRIT*) *или* honor (*US*) sb with a visit; ~ (*perf*) **кого́-н улы́бки** to bestow a smile on sb

▸ **удосто́иться** (*impf* **удоста́иваться**) *сов возв*: ~**ся** +*gen* (*награды*) to be honoured (*BRIT*) *или* honored (*US*) with.

удосу́ж|иться (-усь, -ишься; *impf* **удосу́живаться**) *сов возв*: ~ +*infin* to find time to do.

у́дочек *сущ см* **у́дочка**.

удочере́ни|е (-я) *ср* adoption (*of daughter*).

удочер|и́ть (-ю, -и́шь; *impf* **удочеря́ть**) *сов перех* to adopt (*daughter*).

у́доч|ка (-ки; *gen pl* -ек) *ж* (fishing-)rod; **он попа́лся на** ~**ку** (*перен*) he fell for it; **заки́дывать** (**заки́нуть** *perf*) ~**ку** (*рыболов*) to cast; (*перен*) to put out feelers.

удр|а́ть (удеру́, удерёшь; *pt* -а́л, -ала́, -а́ло, *impf* **удира́ть**) *сов неперех* (*разг*) to make off.

удруж|и́ть (-у́, -и́шь) *сов неперех*: ~ **кому́-н** to do sb a favour (*BRIT*) *или* favor (*US*).

удручённый *прил* (*взгляд, лицо, вид*) dejected; (-ён, -ена́, -ено́; *человек*) dejected, depressed.

уду́ш|ить (-у́шу, -у́шишь) *сов от* **души́ть** ◆ (*impf* **удуша́ть**) *перех* (*человека*) to strangle;

(*свободу*) to stifle.

уду́шливый *прил* (*газ, вещество*) suffocating; (*жара*) stifling.

уду́шь|е (-я) *ср* (*no pl*) suffocation.

ужу́ *несов см* **уди́ть**.

уе́дешь *итп сов см* **уе́хать**.

уедине́ни|е (-я) *ср* solitude.

уединён|ный (-, -на, -но) *прил* (*место, остров*) solitary.

уедин|и́ться (-ю́сь, -и́шься; *impf* **уединя́ться**) *сов возв* to go off, withdraw.

уе́ду *итп сов см* **уе́хать**.

уе́зд (-а) *м* (*ист*) uezd (*administrative division in pre-Revolutionary Russia*).

уезжа́й(те) *сов см* **уе́хать**.

уезжа́|ть (-ю) *несов от* **уе́хать**.

УЕФА́ *м сокр* (= Европе́йский сою́з футбо́льных ассоциа́ций) UEFA (= *Union of European Football Associations*).

уе́ха|ть (*как* е́хать; *см* Table 19; *impf* **уезжа́ть**) *сов неперех* to leave, go away; **он** ~**л в о́тпуск/в Москву́** he has gone on holiday/to Moscow; **мы ско́ро уезжа́ем** we are leaving soon.

уж (-а́) *м* (*зоол*) grass snake ◆ *нареч* (*уже*) already ◆ *част* (*выражает усиление*): **здесь не так** ~ **пло́хо** it's not as bad as all that here; **э́то** ~ **о́чень до́рого** it really is too expensive.

ужа́л|ить (-ю, -ишь) *сов от* **жа́лить**.

у́жас (-а) *м* horror; (*страх*) terror ◆ *как сказ* (*разг*): (**э́то**) ~! it's awful *или* terrible! ◆ *нареч*: **он** ~ **како́й бога́тый** (*разг*) he's incredibly rich; ~**ы войны́** horrors of war; **прийти́** (*perf*) **в** ~ **от чего́-н** to be horrified by sth; **к моему́** ~**у** to my horror; **он дрожа́л от** ~**а** he was shaking in terror; ~ **как бы́стро вре́мя идёт** it's awful *или* terrible how time flies; **ти́хий** ~! (*разг*) horror of horrors!; **до** ~**а** (*разг*) terribly.

ужасн|у́ть (-у́, -ёшь; *impf* **ужаса́ть**) *сов перех* to horrify

▸ **ужасну́ться** (*impf* **ужаса́ться**) *сов возв* to be horrified.

ужаса́ющий (-ая, -ее, -ие) *прил* (*крик, зрелище*) horrific; (*запах, холод*) terrible.

ужа́сен *прил см* **ужа́сный**.

ужа́сно *нареч* (*разг*: *умный, краси́вый итп*) terribly ◆ *как сказ*: **здесь сейча́с** ~ it's terrible here now; **он чу́вствует себя́** ~ he feels terrible.

ужа́с|ный (-ен, -на, -но) *прил* terrible, horrible, awful.

у́же *сравн прил от* **у́зкий**.

уже́ *нареч* (*уже*: *тоже* already; **мы не ви́делись** ~ **3 го́да** it's now 3 years since we've seen each other; **ты же** ~ **не ма́ленький** you're not a child any more; ~ **по э́тому мо́жно суди́ть, что ...** one can judge from this alone that ....

ужива́|ться (-юсь) *несов от* **ужи́ться**.

уживу́сь *итп сов см* **ужи́ться.**

ужи́|вчивый (-, -а, -о) *прил (человек)* easy to get along with.

ужи́м|ка (-ки; *gen pl* **-ок)** *ж (обычно мн)* grimace.

у́жин (-а) *м* supper.

у́жина|ть (-ю; *perf* **поу́жинать)** *несов неперех* to have supper.

ужи́|ться (-ву́сь, -вёшься; *pt* **-лся, -ла́сь, -ло́сь,** *impf* **ужива́ться)** *сов возв:* **~ с кем-н** to get on with sb.

узако́ненный *прил (порядок, ритуал)* established.

узако́н|ить (-ю, -ишь; *impf* **узако́нивать)** *сов перех (отношения, порядок)* to legalize.

узбе́к (-а) *м* Uzbek.

Узбекиста́н (-а) *м* Uzbekistan.

узбе́кский (-ая, -ое, -ие) *прил* Uzbek; **~ язы́к** Uzbek.

узбе́ч|ка (-ки; *gen pl* **-ек)** *ж см* **узбе́к.**

узда́ (-ы́; *nom pl* **-ы)** *ж* bridle; **держа́ть** *(impf)* **кого́-н в ~е́** to keep sb in check.

узде́чк|а (-и) *ж* = **узда́.**

узд́цы: под ~ by the bridle.

у́з|ел (-ла́) *м* knot; *(мешок)* bundle; **телефо́нный ~** telephone exchange; **железнодоро́жный ~** railway junction; **санита́рный ~** bathroom and toilet; **морско́й ~** hitch; **не́рвный ~** ganglion; **~ противоре́чий** a mass of contradictions.

у́з|кий (-кая, -кое, -кие; -ок, -ка́, -ко) *прил* narrow; *(тесный)* tight; *(перен: человек, взгляд)* narrow-minded; **~ая специа́льность** narrow specialism; **~ круг друзе́й** small circle of friends.

узкоколе́йн|ый *прил:* **~ая желе́зная доро́га** narrow-gauge railway.

узколо́бый *прил (перен)* narrow-minded.

узла́ *итп сущ см* **у́зел.**

узлова́тый (-, -а, -о) *прил* knotty.

узлов|о́й *прил (перен: вопрос, задачи)* key; **~а́я ста́нция** junction.

узна́|ть (-ю; *impf* **узнава́ть)** *сов перех (знакомого, свою вещь итп)* to recognize; *(новости)* to find out, learn; *(познать: нужду, любовь)* to know; **я ~л, что ты прие́хал** I heard that you had come; **он ~л о состоя́нии дел** he found out how things stood.

у́зник (-а) *м* captive.

у́зок *прил см* **у́зкий.**

узо́р (-а) *м* pattern.

узо́рный *прил* = **узо́рчатый.**

узо́рчатый *прил* patterned.

у́зость (-и) *ж (улиц, взглядов)* narrowness; *(платья)* tightness; *(человека)* narrow-mindedness.

узурпа́тор (-а) *м* usurper.

узурпи́р|овать (-ую) *(не)сов перех* to usurp.

у́з|ы (-) *мн (перен)* bonds *мн.*

уйду́ *итп сов см* **уйти́.**

у́йм|а (-ы) *ж (разг):* **~ де́нег/вре́мени** heaps *или* loads of money/time.

уйму́(сь) *итп сов см* **уня́ть(ся).**

уйти́ (*как* **идти́;** *см* **Table 18;** *impf* **уходи́ть)** *сов неперех (человек)* to go away, leave; *(пароход, поезд)* to go, leave; *(молодость)* to go; *(время, годы)* to pass; *(отдаться):* **~** *+acc (в бизнес)* to go into; *(избежать):* **~ от** *+gen (от опасности итп)* to get away from; *(потребоваться):* **~ на** *+acc (деньги, время)* to be spent on; **уходи́ть (~** *perf)* **из до́ма** to leave the house; **уходи́ть (~** *perf)* **со слу́жбы/со сце́ны** to leave one's job/the stage; **уходи́ть (~** *perf)* **от му́жа** to leave one's husband; **уходи́ть (~** *perf)* **из жи́зни** to pass away; **уходи́ть (~** *perf)* **на пе́нсию** to retire; **у нас ушло́ мно́го де́нег на поку́пки** we spent a lot of money on shopping.

укажу́ *итп сов см* **указа́ть.**

ука́з (-а) *м (президента)* decree; **он мне не ~** *(разг)* I don't take orders from him.

указа́ни|е (-я) *ср* pointing out, indication; *(разъяснение)* instruction; *(: начальства)* directive; **~я врача́** doctor's orders.

указа́тел|ь (-я) *м (дорожный)* sign; *(книга)* guide; *(список в книге)* index; *(прибор)* indicator.

указа́тельный *прил (жест)* pointing; **указа́тельное местоиме́ние** demonstrative pronoun; **указа́тельный па́лец** index finger.

ук|аза́ть (-ажу́, -а́жешь; *impf* **ука́зывать)** *сов перех* to point out; *(дорогу)* to show; *(свой адрес, интересы, срок)* to indicate; *(движением, жестом):* **~ на** *+acc (на дверь, на карти́ну итп)* to point to; *(на ошибки, на недоста́тки)* to point out; **~** *(perf)* **кому́-н на дверь** *(перен)* to show sb the door.

ука́з|ка (-ки; *gen pl* **-ок)** *ж* pointer; **де́лать (сде́лать** *perf)* **что-нибудь по чужо́й ~ке** to blindly follow somebody else's directions.

ука́зыва|ть (-ю) *несов от* **указа́ть ♦** *неперех (свидетельствовать):* **~ на** *+acc (факты, цифры)* to indicate, point to.

ука́лыва|ть (-ю) *несов от* **уколо́ть.**

ука́та|ть (-ю; *impf* **ука́тывать)** *сов перех (дорогу)* to roll, flatten.

ук|ати́ть (-ачу́, -а́тишь) *сов перех (мяч)* to roll away; *(тачку)* to wheel away ♦ *неперех (разг: уехать)* to go off.

ука́тыва|ть (-ю) *несов от* **уката́ть.**

укача́|ть (-ю; *impf* **ука́чивать)** *сов перех (усыпить: ребёнка)* to rock to sleep; *(довести до тошноты):* **его́ ~ло в маши́не/на парохо́де** he got (car-/sea-)sick.

укачу́ *сов см* **укати́ть.**

укла́д (-а) *м (экон: капиталисти́ческий, феода́льный)* order; **~ жи́зни** way of life.

укла́д|ка (-и) *ж (действие: дров, рельс)* laying; *(причёска)* set.

укла́дчик (-а) *м (путей, парке́та)* layer.

укла́дывани|е (-я) *ср (вещей, чемода́на)* packing; *(ребёнка)* putting to bed.

укла́дыва|ть (-ю) *несов от* **уложи́ть**

▶ **укла́дываться** *несов от* **уложи́ться,**

улéчься ♦ *возв:* э́то не ~ется в обы́чные ра́мки this is out of the ordinary; э́то не ~ется в головé *или* в созна́нии it's beyond me.

уклóн (-а) *м* (*также перен*) slant; **пóезд/дорóга идёт под ~** the train/road is going downhill.

уклонéни|е (-я) *ср* (*дороги в сторону*) bending; (*от ответа, от обязанностей*) evasion.

укл|онúться (-онюсь, -óнишься; *impf* **уклоня́ться**) *сов возв* (*отстраниться: в сторону*) to swerve; (*отойти от главного*): ~ **от** +*gen* to dodge; (*от темы, от предмета*) to digress from; (*от поручения*) to evade; **уклоня́ться** (~ *perf*) **от отвéта** to avoid giving an answer.

уклóнчив|ый (-, -а, -о) *прил* (*ответ*) evasive.

уклоня́|ться (-юсь) *несов от* **уклонúться**.

уключин|а (-ы) *ж* rowlock.

укóл (-а) *м* (*иголкой*) prick; (*перен: замечание*) dig; (*МЕД*) injection; **дéлать (сдéлать** *perf*) **комý-н ~** to give sb an injection; **~ самолю́бию** blow to one's ego.

ук|олóть (-олю́, -óлешь) *сов от* **колóть ♦** (*impf* **ука́лывать**) *перех* (*иглой, шипом*) to prick; (*перен: самолюбие*) to wound

▸ **уколóться** *сов от* **колóться**.

укомплектóванный *прил* complete.

укомплект|ова́ть (-у́ю) *сов от* **комплектова́ть**.

укóр (-а) *м* (*упрёк*) reproach; **~ы сóвести** the pangs of conscience; **живóй ~ комý-н** living indictment of sb; **ста́вить (поста́вить** *perf*) **комý-н что-н в ~** to reproach sb with sth.

укора́чива|ть(ся) (-ю(сь)) *несов от* **укороти́ть(ся)**.

укоренéни|е (-я) *ср* taking root, establishment.

укорен|и́ть (-ю́, -и́шь; *impf* **укореня́ть**) *сов перех* (*рассаду*) to allow to take root.

укорен|и́ться (*3sg* -и́тся, *3pl* -я́тся, *impf* **укореня́ться**) *сов возв* (*также перен*) to take root.

укори́зн|а (-ы) *ж* (*укор*) reproach.

укори́зненно *нареч* reproachfully.

укори́зненн|ый (-, -на, -но) *прил* reproachful.

укор|и́ть (-ю́, -и́шь; *impf* **укоря́ть**) *сов перех* to reproach.

укор|оти́ть (-чу́, -ти́шь; *impf* **укора́чивать**) *сов перех* (*платье, палку, путь*) to shorten; (*жизнь, сроки*) to reduce; **~** (*perf*) **ру́ки комý-н** (*перен*) to take sb down a peg

▸ **укор|оти́ться** (*impf* **укора́чиваться**) *сов возв* (*юбка итп*) to be shortened; (*сроки*) to be reduced.

укорóченный *прил* (*пальто, юбка*) short; (*рабочий день*) reduced.

укорчу́(сь) *сов см* **укороти́ть(ся)**.

укоря́|ть (-ю) *несов от* **укори́ть**.

укоря́ющ|ий (-ая, -ее, -ие) *прил* (*взгляд*) reproachful.

укра́дкой *нареч* secretly.

украду́ *итп сов см* **укра́сть**.

Украи́н|а (-ы) *ж* (the) Ukraine.

украи́н|ец (-ца) *м* Ukrainian.

украи́н|ка (-ки; *gen pl* -ок) *ж см* **украи́нец**.

украи́нск|ий (-ая, -ое, -ие) *прил* Ukrainian; **~ язы́к** Ukrainian.

украи́нца *итп сущ см* **украи́нец**.

укра́|сить (-шу, -сишь; *impf* **украша́ть**) *сов перех* (*комнату*) to decorate; (*ёлку*) to decorate (*BRIT*), trim (*US*); (*речь*) to embellish; (*существование, жизнь итп*) to brighten

▸ **укра́|ситься** (*impf* **украша́ться**) *сов возв:* ~ся +*instr* (*деревья, поля*) to be decorated with (*fig*); (*жизнь, существование*) to be brightened up by.

укра́|сть (-ду́, -дёшь) *сов от* **красть**.

украша́|ть (-ю) *несов от* **укра́сить ♦** *перех:* **такóе поведéние тебя́ не ~ет** that kind of behaviour doesn't suit you

▸ **украша́|ться** *несов от* **укра́ситься**.

украшéни|е (-я) *ср* decoration; (*коллектива*) pride; (*коллекции*) jewel; (*также: ювели́рное* ~) jewellery (*BRIT*), jewelry (*US*).

укра́шу(сь) *сов см* **укра́сить(ся)**.

укреп|и́ть (-лю́, -и́шь; *impf* **укрепля́ть**) *сов перех* (*мир, семью, организм*) to strengthen; (*стену, строение, город, перевал*) to fortify; **укрепля́ть** (~ *perf*) **здорóвье** to get fit(ter)

▸ **укреп|и́ться** (*impf* **укрепля́ться**) *сов возв* (*нервы, организм*) to become stronger; (*хозяйство, авторитет*) to become established; (*здоровье*) to improve; (*дисциплина*) to be tightened up; **~ся** (*perf*) **в свои́х убеждéниях** to become surer of one's convictions; **за ним ~и́лась дурна́я репута́ция** he has earned a bad reputation.

укреплéни|е (-я) *ср* (*здоровья*) improving; (*авторитета*) reinforcement; (*ВОЕН: обычно мн*) fortification.

укреплю́(сь) *сов см* **укрепи́ть(ся)**.

укрепля́|ть(ся) (-ю(сь)) *несов от* **укрепи́ть(ся)**.

укрепля́ющ|ий (-ая, -ее, -ие) *прил* fortifying.

укрóмный *прил* (*уголок*) secluded.

укрóп (-а) *м, собир* dill.

укрóпный *прил* dill; **укрóпная вода́** (*МЕД*) gripe water.

укроти́тель| (-я) *м* tamer; **~ львов** lion-tamer.

укроти́тельниц|а (-ы) *ж см* **укроти́тель**.

укро|ти́ть (-щу́, -ти́шь; *impf* **укроща́ть**) *сов перех* (*животного, гнев, страсти*) to tame; (*человека*) to bring to heel.

укрощéни|е (-я) *ср* (*действие*) taming.

укрощу́ *сов см* **укроти́ть**.

укрóю(сь) *итп сов см* **укры́ть(ся)**.

укрупнéни|е (-я) *ср* enlargement.

укрупн|и́ть (-ю́, -и́шь; *impf* **укрупня́ть**) *сов*

перех to enlarge

▶ **укрупни́ться** (*impf* **укрупня́ться**) *сов возв* (*завод, произво́дство*) to get larger; (*черты лица́*) to grow more pronounced.

укрыва́тельство (-а) *ср* (*престу́пника итп*) harbouring.

укрыва́ть(ся) (-ю(сь)) *несов от* **укры́ть(ся)**.

укры́тие (-я) *ср* (*ме́сто: подзе́мное, от бомб*) shelter.

укры́ть (-о́ю, -о́ешь; *impf* **укрыва́ть**) *сов перех* (*закры́ть: платко́м, сне́гом*) to cover; (*спря́тать: престу́пника*) to harbour; (: *бе́женца*) to shelter

▶ **укры́ться** (*impf* **укрыва́ться**) *сов возв* (*одея́лом, платко́м*) to cover o.s.; (*от обстре́ла, от дождя́*) to take cover; (*от пого́ни*) to hide; **от моего́ взгля́да не ~ы́лось, что ...** it has not escaped my notice that ....

у́ксус (-а) *м* vinegar.

у́ксусный *прил* (*за́пах, эссе́нция*) vinegar *опред*; **у́ксусная кислота́** acetic acid.

уку́с (-а) *м* bite.

укуси́ть (-ушу́, -у́сишь) *сов перех* to bite.

уку́тать (-ю; *impf* **уку́тывать**) *сов перех* (*больно́го, ше́ю итп*) to wrap up

▶ **уку́таться** (*impf* **уку́тываться**) *сов возв* to wrap o.s. up.

укушу́ *сов см* **укуси́ть**.

ул. *сокр* (= **у́лица**) St (= *street*).

ула́вливать (-ю) *несов от* **улови́ть**.

ула́дить (-жу, -дишь; *impf* **ула́живать**) *сов перех* to settle

▶ **ула́диться** (*impf* **ула́живаться**) *сов возв* to sort o.s. out.

ула́живание (-я) *ср* (*ссо́ры, конфли́кта*) settling.

ула́живать(ся) (-ю(сь)) *несов от* **ула́дить(ся)**.

ула́жу(сь) *сов см* **ула́дить(ся)**.

ула́мывать (-ю) *несов от* **уломать**.

ула́н (-а) *м* (*ист*) uhlan (*lancer*).

Ула́н-Ба́тор (-а) *м* Ulan Bator.

улёгся *итп сов см* **уле́чься**.

у́лей (-ья) *м* (bee-)hive.

улете́ть (-чу́, -ти́шь; *impf* **улета́ть**) *сов непе́рех* (*пти́ца*) to fly away; (*самолёт*) to leave; (*перен: стреми́тельно уйти́*) to fly off.

улету́читься (-усь, -ишься; *impf* **улету́чиваться**) *сов возв* (*также перен*) to evaporate; (*перен: разг*) to vanish.

улечу́ *сов см* **улете́ть**.

уле́чься (-я́гусь, -я́жешься *итп*, -я́гутся; *pt* -ёгся, -егла́сь, -егло́сь, *impf* **укла́дываться**) *сов возв* to lie down; (*no impf*: *пыль*) to settle; (*перен: бу́ря, стра́сти, гнев*) to subside.

улизну́ть (-у́, -ёшь) *сов непе́рех* (*разг*) to slip away.

ули́ка (-и) *ж* (piece) of evidence (*мн* evidence); **ко́свенная/прямая ~** circumstantial/hard evidence.

ули́тка (-ки; *gen pl* -ок) *ж* snail.

у́лица (-ы) *ж* (*в го́роде, в селе́*) street; (*перен: некульту́рная среда́*) the gutter; **на ~е** outside; **остава́ться** (**оста́ться** *perf*) **на ~е** to be out on the street; **выбра́сывать** (**вы́бросить** *perf*) **на ~у** (*вы́селить*) to throw sb out onto the streets.

уличи́ть (-у́, -и́шь; *impf* **улича́ть**) *сов перех*: **~ кого́-н в чём-н** to face sb with sth.

у́личный *прил* street *опред*; **у́личное движе́ние** traffic.

уло́в (-а) *м* catch (*of fish*).

улови́мый (-, -а, -о) *прил*: **едва́** *или* **чуть** *или* **е́ле ~** barely perceptible.

улови́ть (-овлю́, -о́вишь; *impf* **ула́вливать**) *сов перех* (*зву́ки, шум, за́пах*) to catch, detect; (*перен: мысль, связь*) to catch, grasp; **ула́вливать** (**~** *perf*) **(подходя́щий) моме́нт** to find the right moment.

уло́вка (-ки; *gen pl* -ок) *ж* ruse.

уловлю́ *сов см* **улови́ть**.

уло́вок *сущ см* **уло́вка**.

уложи́ть (-ожу́, -о́жишь; *impf* **укла́дывать**) *сов перех* (*ребёнка*) to put to bed; (*ве́щи, чемода́н*) to pack; (*во́лосы*) to set; (*шпа́лы, ре́льсы*) to lay; (*бельё*) to fold away; (*no impf*: *разг*): **~ кого́-н на ме́сте** to kill sb; **хозя́йка ~ожи́ла нас в гости́ной** our hostess put us (up) in the living room

▶ **уложи́ться** (*impf* **укла́дываться**) *сов возв* (*сложи́ть ве́щи*) to pack; **укла́дываться** (**~ся** *perf*) **в сро́ки** to keep to the deadline; **~ся** (*perf*) **в полчаса́** to keep it down to half an hour.

улома́ть (-ю; *impf* **ула́мывать**) *сов перех* (*разг*): **~ кого́-н** to talk sb round; **ула́мывать** (**~** *perf*) **кого́-н** +*infin* to talk sb into doing.

у́лочка (-ки; *gen pl* -ек) *ж* lane.

улучи́ть (-у́, -и́шь; *impf* **улуча́ть**) *сов перех* (*моме́нт, полчаса́*) to find.

улучша́ть (-ю) *несов от* **улу́чшить**.

улучше́ние (-я) *ср* improvement.

улу́чшить (-у, -ишь; *impf* **улучша́ть**) *сов перех* to improve.

улыба́ться (-юсь; *perf* **улыбну́ться**) *несов возв*: **~** +*dat* to smile at; (*перен: сча́стье, жизнь*) to smile on; **мне не ~ется э́та рабо́та/пое́здка** this work/trip doesn't appeal to me.

улы́бка (-ки; *gen pl* -ок) *ж* smile.

улыбну́ться (-у́сь, -ёшься) *сов от* **улыба́ться**.

улы́бок *сущ см* **улы́бка**.

улы́бчивый (-, -а, -о) *прил* smiley.

ультима́тум (-а) *м* ultimatum; **предъявля́ть** (**предъяви́ть** *perf*) **кому́-н ~** to give sb an ultimatum.

ультразву́к (-а) *м* ultrasound.

ультразвуково́й *прил* ultrasonic.

ультрамари́н (-а) *м* ultramarine.

ультрафиоле́товый *прил*: **~ые лучи́** ultraviolet rays *мн*.

у́лья *итп сущ см* **у́лей**.

улюлю́кать (-ю) *несов непе́рех* to halloo;

(перен) to hoot *(in derision)*.

уля́гусь *итп сов см* **уле́чься**.

ум (-а́) *м* mind; **быть** *(impf)* **без ~а́ от кого́-н/чего́-н** to be wild about sb/sth; **в ~é** *(считать, держать)* in one's head; **в своём ~é** in one's right mind; **бра́ться (взя́ться** *perf)* **за ~** to see sense; **сходи́ть (сойти́** *perf)* **с ~а́** to go mad; **своди́ть (свести́** *perf)* **кого́-н с ~а́** to drive sb mad; *(перен: увлечь)* to drive sb wild; **приро́дный ~** native wit; **~а́ не приложу́, куда́/ско́лько/кто ...** I can't think where/how much/who ...; **с ~óм** *(рассудительно)* sensibly; **приходи́ть (прийти́** *perf)* **на ~ кому́-н** to come into sb's head.

умали́ть (-ю́, -и́шь; *impf* **умаля́ть)** *сов перех* *(значение, роль)* to diminish, belittle.

умалишённый *прил* insane.

ума́лчива|ть (-ю) *несов от* **умолча́ть**.

умаля́|ть (-ю) *несов от* **умали́ть**.

ума́|яться (-юсь) *сов от* **ма́яться**.

уме́ле|ц (-ьца) *м* skilled artisan.

уме́ло *нареч* skilfully (*BRIT*), skillfully (*US*).

уме́л|ый (-, -а, -о) *прил* *(рука, ремесленник, политик)* skilful (*BRIT*), skillful (*US*); *(работник)* able.

уме́льца *итп сущ см* **уме́лец**.

умён *прил см* **у́мный**.

уме́ни|е (-я) *ср* ability, skill; **с ~м** *(делать что-н)* with skill.

уменьша́|ть(ся) (-ю(сь)) *несов от* **уме́ньшить(ся)**.

уменьше́ни|е (-я) *ср* reduction.

уменьши́тельный *прил* *(суффикс)* diminutive.

уме́ньш|ить (-у, -ишь; *impf* **уменьша́ть)** *сов перех* to reduce; **~** *(perf)* **шаг** to slow down

▶ **уме́ньши́ться** *(impf* **уменьша́ться)** *сов возв* *(объём, опасность)* to diminish, decrease.

уме́ренност|ь (-и) *ж* moderateness; *(климата)* temperate nature.

уме́ренн|ый (-, -на, -но) *прил* *(аппетит, скорость, политика)* moderate; *(no short form*; *климат, характер)* temperate.

ум|ере́ть (-ру́, -рёшь; *pt* -ер, -ерла́, -ерло, *impf* **умира́ть)** *сов неперех* to die; *(традиция)* to die out; **хоть ~ри́, но сде́лай** *(разг)* do it, even if it kills you; **~** *(perf)* **от го́лода/ра́ка** to die of hunger/cancer; **со́ смеху ~ мо́жно** *(разг)* I could die laughing.

уме́р|ить (-ю, -ишь; *impf* **умеря́ть)** *сов перех* *(требования, желания)* to moderate; *(гнев)* to restrain.

умер|тви́ть (-щвлю́, -тви́шь; *impf* **умерщвля́ть)** *сов перех* *(также перен)* to kill.

умерщвле́ни|е (-я) *ср* killing.

умерщвлю́ *сов см* **умертви́ть**.

умерщвля́|ть (-ю) *несов от* **умертви́ть**.

умеря́|ть (-ю) *несов от* **уме́рить**.

уме|сти́ть (-щу́, -сти́шь; *impf* **умеща́ть)** *сов перех* to fit, find room for

▶ **умести́ться** *(impf* **умеща́ться)** *сов возв* to fit; **мы все уме́стимся в маши́ну** there's room for all of us in the car; **мои́ ве́щи не ~ща́ются в чемода́н** my things won't fit in my suitcase.

уме́|ть (-ю) *несов неперех* can, to be able to; *(иметь способность)* to know how to; **он ~ет пла́вать/чита́ть** he can swim/read; **Мари́я ~ет хорошо́ одева́ться** Maria knows how to dress well.

умеща́|ть(ся) (-ю(сь)) *несов от* **умести́ть(ся)**.

умещу́(сь) *сов см* **умести́ть(ся)**.

уме́ючи *нареч (разг)*: **э́то на́до де́лать ~** you need to have the knack (to do this).

умиле́ни|е (-я) *ср* tenderness; **слёзы ~я** fond tears.

умили́тельный (-ен, -ьна, -ьно) *прил* touching.

умили́|ть (-ю, -ишь; *impf* **умиля́ть)** *сов перех* to touch

▶ **умили́ться** *(impf* **умиля́ться)** *сов возв* to be touched.

уми́льный *прил (нежный)* touching; *(льстивый)* smarmy.

умиля́|ть(ся) (-ю(сь)) *несов от* **умили́ть(ся)**.

умина́|ть (-ю) *несов от* **умя́ть**.

умира́ни|е (-я) *ср* dying.

умира́|ть (-ю) *несов от* **умере́ть** ◆ *неперех (перен)*: **~ю, как хочу́ есть/спать** I'm dying for something to eat/to go to sleep; **я ~ю от ску́ки** I'm bored to death.

умиротворе́ни|е (-я) *ср (сердца, души)* bringing of peace; *(агрессора)* appeasement.

умиротворённый *прил* serene, tranquil.

умиротвор|и́ть (-ю́, -и́шь; *impf* **умиротворя́ть)** *сов перех (душу)* to bring peace to; *(враждующих)* to pacify; *(агрессора)* to appease

▶ **умиротвори́ться** *(impf* **умиротворя́ться)** *сов возв (враждующие, спорщики итп)* to be pacified.

умне́|ть (-ю; *perf* **поумне́ть)** *несов неперех (человек)* to grow wiser; *(ребёнок)* to become more intelligent; **э́то помо́жет тебе́ поумне́ть** *(перен)* that'll teach you a lesson.

у́мник (-а) *м* clever boy; *(пренебр: умничающий)* clever dick, knowall.

у́мниц|а (-ы) *ж* clever girl ◆ *м/ж (разг)*: **вот ~!** good for you!, well done!; **он ~** he's a clever one.

у́мнича|ть (-ю) *несов неперех (разг: пренебр)* to show off how clever one is, be clever; *(своевольничать)* to try to be clever.

у́мно *нареч (вести себя)* sensibly; *(говорить)* intelligently.

умножа́|ть (-ю) *несов от* **умно́жить**.

умноже́ни|е (-я) *ср (см глаг)* multiplication; increase; **табли́ца ~я** *(МАТ)* multiplication table.

умно́ж|ить (-у, -ишь; *impf* **мно́жить** *или* **умножа́ть**) *сов перех* (МАТ) to multiply; (*доходы, опыт, славу итп*) to increase; **умножа́ть** (~ *perf*) **пять на́ два** to multiply five by two

▶ **умно́житься** *сов от* **мно́житься**.

умну́ *итп сов см* **умя́ть**.

у́м|ный (-ён, -на́, -но́ *или* -но) *прил* (*человек*) clever, intelligent; (*лицо*) intelligent; (*собака, машина, прибор*) clever; (*речи, совет, политика*) sensible.

умозаключе́ни|е (-я) *ср* (*вывод*) deduction.

умозри́тел|ьный (-ен, -ьна, -ьно) *прил* (*построение, рассуждения*) speculative.

умол|и́ть (-ю́, -ишь; *impf* **умоля́ть**) *сов перех*: ~ **кого́-н** (+*infin*) to prevail upon sb (to do) (*by pleading*).

у́молк *м*: **без** ~**у** incessantly.

умо́лк|нуть (-у, -ешь; *impf* **умолка́ть**) *сов неперех* (*голос, скрипка*) to fall silent; (*смех, звон*) to stop.

умолча́ни|е (-я) *ср* (*фактов*) supression, hushing up.

умолч|а́ть (-у́, -и́шь; *impf* **ума́лчивать**) *сов неперех*: ~ **о чём-н** (*о преступлении, о недостатках итп*) to keep quiet about sth.

умоля́|ть (-ю) *несов от* **умоли́ть** ♦ *перех* to implore.

умоля́ющий (-ая, -ее, -ие) *прил* (*взгляд, голос*) pleading.

умонастрое́ни|е (-я) *ср* frame of mind.

умопомеша́тельств|о (-а) *ср* insanity.

умопомраче́ни|е (-я) *ср* temporary loss of one's senses; **до** ~**я** (*устать*) terribly; (*любить, влюбиться*) madly; **рабо́тать** (*impf*)/**танцева́ть** (*impf*) **до** ~**я** to work/dance until one is ready to drop.

умопомрачи́тел|ьный (-ен, -ьна, -ьно) *прил* (*разг: красота, богатство*) staggering.

умо́ра *ж нескл*: **э́то про́сто** ~ (*разг*) it's hilarious.

умори́тел|ьный (-ен, -ьна, -ьно) *прил* (*разг*) hilarious.

умор|и́ть (-ю́, -и́шь) *сов от* **мори́ть**.

умота́|ть (-ю) *сов от* **мота́ть**.

умру́ *итп сов см* **умере́ть**.

умо́ю(сь) *сов см* **умы́ть(ся)**.

у́мственно *нареч*: ~ **отста́лый** mentally retarded.

у́мственный *прил* (*способности*) mental; ~ **труд** brainwork.

умудрённый (-ён, -ена́, -ено́) *прил*: ~ **о́пытом/года́ми** wise from experience/with age.

умудр|и́ться (-ю́сь, -и́шься; *impf* **умудря́ться**) *сов возв* (*разг*) to manage; **я** ~**и́лся простуди́ться/опозда́ть на по́езд** I managed to catch a cold/miss the train.

умч|а́ть (-у́, -и́шь) *сов перех* to whisk off *или* away

▶ **умча́ться** *сов возв* (*кони, всадники, дети*) to

dash off; (*годы, детство*) to fly by.

умыва́льник (-а) *м* washstand.

умыва́льный *прил*: ~**ые принадле́жности** washing things *мн*.

умыва́ни|е (-я) *ср* washing.

умыва́|ть(ся) (-ю(сь)) *несов от* **умы́ть(ся)**.

умы́к|нуть (-у́, -ёшь; *impf* **умыка́ть**) *сов перех* (*разг: украсть*) to nick; (*невесту*) to abduct (*as part of wedding ritual*).

у́мыс|ел (-ла) *м* intent; **де́лать** (**сде́лать** *perf*) **что-н без** ~**ла/с у́мыслом** to do sth without/with intent.

умы́|ть (-о́ю, умо́ешь; *impf* **умыва́ть**) *сов перех* to wash

▶ **умы́ться** (*impf* **умыва́ться**) *сов возв* to wash.

умы́шленно *нареч* deliberately, intentionally.

умы́шленность (-и) *ж* (*поступка*) deliberateness; (*преступления*) premeditated nature.

умы́шлен|ный (-, -на, -но) *прил* (*поступок*) deliberate, intentional; (*преступление, убийство*) premeditated.

ум|я́ть (-ну́, -нёшь; *impf* **умина́ть**) *сов перех* (*снег, землю*) to flatten; (*разг: съесть много*) to stuff down.

унаво́з|ить (-жу, -зишь) *сов от* **навози́ть**.

унасле́д|овать (-ую) *сов от* **насле́довать**.

ун|ести́ (-есу́, -есёшь; *pt* -ёс, -есла́, -есло́, *impf* **уноси́ть**) *сов перех* to take away; (*разг: украсть*) to carry off; (*подлеж: война, эпидемия*) to claim; **ло́дку** ~**есло́ тече́нием** the boat drifted away; **бума́ги** ~**есло́ ве́тром** the papers blew away

▶ **унести́сь** (*impf* **уноси́ться**) *сов возв* (*тучи, кони, поезд*) to speed off; **мои́ мы́сли** ~**ли́сь в про́шлое** his thoughts flashed back to the past; **он** ~**ёсся в мир фанта́зий** he was carried into the world of fantasy.

универма́г (-а) *м* (= **универса́льный магази́н**) department store.

универса́л (-а) *м* all-rounder.

универса́льность (-и) *ж* (*знаний*) breadth; (*средств*) universality.

универса́льный *прил* (*проблема*) universal; (*образование*) all-round; (*человек*) versatile, multitalented; (*знания*) encyclopaedic (*BRIT*), encyclopedic (*US*); (*машина, инструмент*) versatile, multipurpose; ~**ое сре́дство** cure-all; ~**ая вычисли́тельная маши́на** (*КОМП*) mainframe; ~ **си́мвол** (*КОМП*) wildcard; **универса́льный магази́н** department store.

универса́м (-а) *м* supermarket.

университе́т (-а) *м* university.

университе́тск|ий (-ая, -ое, -ие) *прил* university *опред*.

унижа́|ть(ся) (-ю(сь)) *несов от* **уни́зить(ся)**.

униже́ни|е (-я) *ср* humiliation; **идти́** (**пойти́** *perf*) **на** ~ to humble o.s.

уни́жен|ный (-, -на, -но) *прил* (*человек*) humbled; (*взгляд, про́сьба*) humble.

уни́жу(сь) *сов см* **уни́зить(ся)**.

ун|иза́ть (-ижу́, -и́жешь; *impf* **уни́зывать**) *сов перех* to string; (*пояс: жемчугом*) to stud.

унизи́телен *прил см* **унизи́тельный**.

унизи́тельность (-и) *ж* humiliation.

унизи́тел|ьный (-ен, -ьна, -ьно) *прил* humiliating, degrading.

ун|и́зить (-жу, -зишь; *impf* **унижа́ть**) *сов перех* to humiliate; **унижа́ть** (~ *perf*) **себя́** to abase o.s.

▶ **уни́зиться** (*impf* **унижа́ться**) *сов возв*: ~**ся (пе́ред** +*instr*) to abase o.s. (before).

уни́зыва|ть (-ю) *несов от* **униза́ть**.

уника́л|ьный (-ен, -ьна, -ьно) *прил* unique.

у́никум (-а) *м*: **он настоя́щий** ~ he's one of a kind.

унима́|ть(ся) (-ю(сь)) *несов от* **уня́ть(ся)**.

унисо́н (-а) *м* unison; **в** ~ (**с** +*instr*) (*также перен*) in unison (with).

унита́з (-а) *м* toilet.

унифика́ци|я (-и) *ж* standardization.

унифици́р|овать (-ую) (*не*)*сов перех* to standardize.

унифо́рм|а (-ы) *ж* (*одежда*) uniform.

уничижа́|ть (-ю) *несов перех* to disparage.

уничижи́тел|ьный (-ен, -ьна, -ьно) *прил* disparaging.

уничтожа́|ть (-ю) *несов от* **уничто́жить**.

уничтожа́ющий (-ая, -ее, -ие) *прил* (*огонь, удар, критика*) devastating; (*взгляд*) scathing, withering.

уничто́ж|ить (-у, -ишь; *impf* **уничтожа́ть**) *сов перех* to destroy; (*насекомых, вредителей*) to exterminate; (*память о чём-н, следы*) to wipe out; (*безработицу, преступность итп*) to do away with; (*перен: унизить*) to crush.

ун|оси́ть(ся) (-ошу́(сь), -о́сишь(ся)) *несов от* **унести́(сь)**.

у́нтер-офице́р (-а) *м* non-commissioned officer.

у́нци|я (-и) *ж* ounce.

уныва́|ть (-ю) *несов неперех* (*человек*) to be downcast *или* despondent; (*впадать в уныние*) to lose heart.

уны́ло *нареч* despondently.

уны́лый *прил* (*человек*) despondent; (*мысли*) depressing; (*природа*) cheerless, dreary.

уны́ни|е (-я) *ср* despondency.

ун|я́ть (уйму́, уймёшь; *pt* -л, -ла́, -ло, *impf* **унима́ть**) *сов перех* (*ребёнка, хулигана*) to restrain; (*слёзы, волнение*) to suppress.

▶ **уня́ться** (*impf* **унима́ться**) *сов возв* (*ребёнок, шалун итп*) to calm down; (*буря, боль*) to die down.

упа́вший (-ая, -ее, -ие) *прил* (*голос*) fallen.

упа́д (-у) *м*: **мы танцева́ли до** ~**у** (*разг*) we danced till we were ready to drop; **я сме́ялся до** ~**у** (*разг*) I laughed my head off.

упа́д|ок (-ка) *м* decline; ~ **сил** exhaustion; ~ **ду́ха** despondency.

упа́дочническ|ий (-ая, -ое, -ие) *прил* decadent.

упаду́ *итп сов см* **упа́сть**.

упак|ова́ть (-у́ю) *сов от* **пакова́ть**.

упако́вк|а (-и) *ж* packing; (*паковочный материал*) packaging.

упако́вочный *прил* packaging *опред*.

упако́выва|ть (-ю; *perf* **упакова́ть**) *несов* = **пакова́ть** ◆ *перех* (*КОМП*) to pack.

упако́вщик (-а) *м* packer.

упако́вщиц|а (-ы) *ж см* **упако́вщик**.

упасти́ *сов перех*: **упаси́ Бог** *или* **Бо́же** *или* **Го́споди**! God forbid!

упа́|сть (-ду́, -дёшь) *сов от* **па́дать** ◆ *неперех*: ~ **в но́ги кому́-н** to go down on one's knees to sb.

упека́|ть (-ю) *несов от* **упе́чь**.

упеку́ *итп сов см* **упе́чь**.

упере́ть (упру́, упрёшь; *pt* упёр, упёрла, упёрло, *impf* **упира́ть**) *сов перех* (*разг: украсть*) to nick, pinch; (~ *perf*) **что-н в** +*acc* (*в стену итп*) to prop sth against

▶ **упере́ться** (*impf* **упира́ться**) *сов возв*: ~**ся чем-н в** +*acc* (*в землю*) to dig sth into; (*в плот*) to stick sth into; (*натолкнуться на преграду*): ~**ся в** +*acc* (*в ограду, в забор итп*) to come up against; (*перен: взглядом, глазами*) to stare; **упира́ться** (~**ся** *perf*) (**на** +*prp*) (*перен: разг: настоять*) to dig one's heels in (on).

упе́|чь (-ку́, -чёшь *итп*, -ку́т; *impf* **упека́ть**) *сов перех* (*разг: в тюрьму*) to fling.

упива́|ться (-юсь) *несов от* **упи́ться**.

упира́|ть (-ю) *несов от* **упере́ть**.

▶ **упира́ться** *несов от* **упере́ться** ◆ *возв* (*иметь причиной*): ~**ся в** +*prp* to arise from.

упи́танный (-, -на, -но) *прил* plump.

уп|и́ться (-ью́сь, -ьёшься; *impf* **упива́ться**) *сов возв* (*разг: напиться допьяна*) to get very drunk; (*перен*): ~ +*instr* (*счастьем, свободой итп*) to be intoxicated by; (: *чьим-н несчастьем*) to revel in.

УПК *м сокр* (= **Уголо́вно-процессуа́льный ко́декс**) *criminal code*.

упла́т|а (-ы) *ж* payment.

упл|ати́ть (-ачу́, -а́тишь) *сов от* **плати́ть**.

упла́чива|ть (-ю; *perf* **уплати́ть**) *несов перех* = **плати́ть**.

уплачу́ *сов см* **уплати́ть**.

упл|ести́ (-ету́, -етёшь) *сов от* **уплета́ть**.

уплета́|ть (-ю) *несов перех* (*разг*) to tuck *или* get stuck into.

уплотне́ни|е (-я) *ср* (*почвы, снега*) compression; (*под кожей*) lump (*ANAT*).

уплотн|и́ть (-ю́, -и́шь; *impf* **уплотня́ть**) *сов перех* (*также перен*) to compress.

▶ **уплотни́ться** (*impf* **уплотня́ться**) *сов возв* (*песок, грунт*) to become firmer; (*рабочий день, график*) to become busier.

уплы́|ть (-ву́, -вёшь; *pt* -л, -ла́, -ло, *impf*

уплывá|ть) *сов неперех* (*человек, рыба итп*) to swim away *или* off; (*пароход*) to sail away *или* off; (*плавно уйти*) to float away *или* off; (*перен: пройти*) to pass; (*: разг: деньги, наследство итп*) to vanish.

уповáни|е (-я) *ср* hope; **возлагáть** (*impf*) **~я на** +*acc* to set one's hopes on.

уповá|ть (-ю) *несов неперех*: **~ на** +*acc* to count on.

уподóб|ить (-лю, -ишь; *impf* **уподоблять**) *сов перех*: **~ что-н/кого-н** +*dat* to compare sth/sb to

▶ **уподóбиться** (*impf* **уподобля́ться**) *сов возв*: **~ся** +*dat* to become like.

упоéни|е (-я) *ср* elation; **с ~м** with relish.

упоённый (-ён, -енá, -енó) *прил*: **~** +*instr* (*успехом итп*) elated by; (*счастьем*) intoxicated with.

упои́тельный (-ен, -ьна, -ьно) *прил* (*воздух*) intoxicating; (*поцелуй*) rapturous.

упокó|й (-я) *м*: **моли́тва за ~ (души́) когó-н** prayer for sb's eternal rest.

уполз|ти́ (-ý, -ёшь; *pt* -, -лá, -лó) *сов неперех* (*змея*) to slither away; (*червь*) to wriggle away; (*ребёнок*) to crawl away.

уполномóченн|ая (-ой; *decl like adj*) *ж см* **уполномóченный**.

уполномóченн|ый (-ого; *decl like adj*) *м* authorized person (*мн* people).

уполномó|чить (-у, -ишь; *impf* **уполномóчивать**) *сов перех*: **~ когó-н** +*infin* to authorize sb to do.

упоминáни|е (-я) *ср* (*см глаг*) mention; reference.

упоминá|ть (-ю) *несов от* **упомянýть**

▶ **упоминáться** *несов неперех* (*имя, событие*) to be mentioned.

упом|янýть (-янý, -я́нешь; *impf* **упоминáть**) *сов* (*не)перех* (*назвать*): **~** +*acc или* **о** +*prp* to mention; (*коснуться*) to refer to.

упóр (-а) *м* (*для ног, для рук*) rest; **в ~** (*стрелять*) point-blank; (*смотреть*) intently; **дéлать (сдéлать** *perf*) **~ на** +*prp* to put emphasis on.

упóрно *нареч* persistently.

упóр|ный (-ен, -на, -но) *прил* persistent; (*сопротивление*) unrelenting.

упóрств|о (-а) *ср* persistence.

упóрств|овать (-ую) *несов неперех* to persist *или* be persistent.

упорхн|ýть (-ý, -ёшь) *сов неперех* (*также перен*) to flit away.

упорядочени|е (-я) *ср* (*корреспонденции, информации*) sorting; (*торговли, процедуры*) regulation.

упорядоченный *прил* ordered.

упорядоч|ить (-у, -ишь; *impf* **упорядочивать**) *сов перех* to put in order; (*цены, процедуру*) to regulate

▶ **упоря́дочиться** (*impf* **упоря́дочиваться**) *сов возв* (*дела*) to be put in order; (*процедура*) to be regulated.

употреби́телен *прил см* **употреби́тельный**.

употреби́тельность (-и) *ж* frequency (*of use*).

употреби́тель|ный (-ен, -ьна, -ьно) *прил* frequently used.

употреб|и́ть (-лю́, -и́шь; *impf* **употребля́ть**) *сов перех* to use; **употребля́ть (~** *perf*) **что-н в пи́щу** to eat sth.

употреблéни|е (-я) *ср* (*лекарства, наркотиков*) taking; (*алкоголя*) consumption; (*слова, термина*) usage; **находи́ться** (*impf*) **в ~и** to be in use; **выходи́ть (вы́йти** *perf*) **из ~** (*слово*) to go out of usage; **вводи́ть (ввести́** *perf*) **в ~** (*слово*) to introduce; (*одежду, предмет быта*) to bring into use.

употреблю́ *сов см* **употреби́ть**.

употребля́|ть (-ю) *несов от* **употреби́ть**

▶ **употребля́ться** *несов возв* to be used.

упр. *сокр* (= **управлéние**) admin (= *administration*).

упрáв|а (-ы) *ж* (*ист*) office; (*разг: мера пресечéния*): **искáть ~у** to seek justice; **найти́** (*perf*) **~у на когó-н** to make sure that sb is punished; **на негó нет ~ы** there's no control over him.

упрáв|иться (-люсь, -ишься; *impf* **управля́ться**) *сов возв*: **~ с** +*instr* (*разг: с делами, с уборкой*) to manage; (*с шалуном, с плохим учеником*) to deal with.

управлéни|е (-я) *ср* (*судном, самолётом*) navigation; (*делами, финансами*) administration; (*оркестром, хором*) conducting; (*учреждéние*) office; (*система приборов*) controls *мн*; **симфóния испóлнена под ~м áвтора** the symphony was conducted by the composer; **теря́ть (потеря́ть** *perf*) **~** to lose control.

управлéнческ|ий (-ая, -ое, -ие) *прил*: **~ аппарáт** ruling body.

упрáвлюсь *сов см* **упрáвиться**.

управля́ем|ый (-, -а, -о) *прил*: **~ая ракéта** guided missile; **~ (с пóмощью) меню́** (*комп*) menu-driven.

управля́|ть (-ю) *несов неперех*: **~** +*instr* (*автомобилем*) to drive; (*судном*) to navigate; (*конём*) to ride; (*государством*) to govern; (*учреждéнием, фирмой итп*) to manage; (*оркестром, хором*) to conduct

▶ **управля́ться** *несов от* **упрáвиться**.

управля́ющ|ий (-его; *decl like adj*) *м* (*хозя́йством*) manager; (*имéнием, помéстьем*) bailiff.

упражнéни|е (-я) *ср* (*мускулов, памяти*) exercising; (*граммати́ческие, гимнасти́ческие*) exercise.

упражня́|ть (-ю) *несов перех* to exercise

▶ **упражня́ться** *несов возв* to practise.

упраздн|и́ть (-ю́, -и́шь; *impf* **упраздня́ть**) *сов перех* to abolish.

упрáшива|ть (-ю) *несов от* **упроси́ть**.

упрёк (-а) *м* reproach; **бросáть (брóсить** *perf*) **~ комý-н** to reproach sb; **стáвить (постáвить**

perf) **что-н в ~ кому́-н** to hold sth against sb.

упрека́|ть (**-ю**; *perf* **упрекну́ть**) *несов перех*: **~ кого́-н (в** +*prp*) to reproach sb (for).

упр|оси́ть (**-ошу́, -о́сишь**; *impf* **упра́шивать**) *сов перех*: **~ кого́-н** +*infin* to persuade sb to do.

упро|сти́ть (**-щу́, -сти́шь**; *impf* **упроща́ть**) *сов перех* to simplify; (*сделать слишком простым*) to oversimplify

► **упрости́ться** (*impf* **упроща́ться**) *сов возв* to become simpler.

упроче́ние (**-я**) *ср* consolidation.

упро́ч|ить (**-у, -ишь**; *impf* **упро́чивать**) *сов перех* to consolidate

► **упро́читься** (*impf* **упро́чиваться**) *сов возв* (*работник*) to establish o.s.; (*положение, позиции*) to be consolidated; (*перен*): **за ним ~илась репута́ция хоро́шего реда́ктора** his reputation as a good editor was established.

упрошу́ *сов см* **упроси́ть**.

упроща́|ть(ся) (**-ю(сь)**) *несов от* **упрости́ть(ся)**.

упроще́ние (**-я**) *ср* simplification.

упроще́нный *прил* (*простой*) simplified; (*излишне простой*) oversimplified.

упрощу́(сь) *сов см* **упрости́ть(ся)**.

упру́(сь) *итп сов см* **упере́ть(ся)**.

упру́г|ий (**-ая, -ое, -ие; -, -а, -о**) *прил* (*пружина, тело*) elastic; (*походка, движения*) bouncy, springy.

упру́гость (**-и**) *ж* (*пружины, мышц*) elasticity; (*походки*) springiness.

упря́ж|ка (**-ки**; *gen pl* **-ек**) *ж* team (*of horses, dogs etc*); (*упряжь*) harness.

у́пряжь (**-и**) *ж* (*no pl*) harness.

упря́м|ец (**-ца**) *м* stubborn person (*мн* people).

упря́м|иться (**-люсь, -ишься**) *несов возв* to be obstinate *или* stubborn.

упря́мица (**-ы**) *ж см* **упря́мец**.

упря́мо *нареч* (*сказать*) obstinately, stubbornly; (*искать*) persistently.

упря́мств|о (**-а**) *ср* obstinacy, stubbornness.

упря́мица *итп сущ см* **упря́мец**.

упря́м|ый (**-, -а, -о**) *прил* obstinate, stubborn; (*поиски, стремление*) persistent.

упря́|тать (**-чу, -чешь**) *сов перех* (*разг*) to put away.

упуска́|ть (**-ю**; *perf* **упусти́ть**) *несов перех* (*мяч*) to let go of; (*момент, случай*) to miss; **~ (упусти́ть** *perf*) **из ви́ду** to overlook.

упу|сти́ть (**-щу́, -у́стишь**) *сов от* **упуска́ть**.

упуще́ние (**-я**) *ср* omission.

упы́р|ь (**-я́**) *м* vampire.

упью́сь *итп сов см* **упи́ться**.

ура́ *межд* hooray, hurrah; **на ~** (*с энтузиазмом*) enthusiastically; (*без подготовки*) just like that.

уравне́ни|е (**-я**) *ср* (*сил*) equalization; (*МАТ*) equation.

ура́внива|ть (**-ю**) *несов от* **уравня́ть**,

уровня́ть.

уравни́ловк|а (**-и**) *ж* (*разг: пренебр*) *equal rewarding regardless of contribution.*

уравнове́|сить (**-шу, -сишь**; *impf* **уравнове́шивать**) *сов перех* to balance

► **уравнове́ситься** (*impf* **уравнове́шиваться**) *сов возв* (*чаши весов*) to balance; (*силы*) to be counterbalanced.

уравнове́шенность (**-и**) *ж* composure.

уравнове́шен|ный (**-, -на, -но**) *прил* balanced, steady.

уравнове́шива|ть(ся) (**-ю(сь)**) *несов от* **уравнове́сить(ся)**.

уравнове́шу(сь) *сов см* **уравнове́сить(ся)**.

уравня́|ть (**-ю**; *impf* **ура́внивать**) *сов перех* (*размеры, доли итп*) to make equal; **ура́внивать (~** *perf*) **кого́-н в права́х с кем-н** to give sb the same rights as sb.

урага́н (**-а**) *м* hurricane; (*перен: страстей*) storm.

урага́нный *прил*: **~ ве́тер** gale.

Уралма́ш (**-а**) *м сокр* = **Ура́льский машиностро́ительный заво́д**.

ура́н (**-а**) *м* uranium; (*планета*): **У~** Uranus.

ура́новый *прил* uranium.

ура-патрио́т (**-а**) *м* (*пренебр*) jingoist.

ура-патриоти́зм (**-а**) *м* jingoism.

урбаниза́ци|я (**-и**) *ж* urbanization.

урв|а́ть (**-у́, -ёшь**; *impf* **урыва́ть**) *сов перех* (*разг: материальные блага*) to grab; (*: время*) to snatch.

урегули́рование (**-я**) *ср* settlement.

урегули́р|овать (**-ую**) *сов от* **регули́ровать** ◆ *перех* (*отношения*) to put to rights; (*конфликт*) to settle.

уре́жу *итп сов см* **уре́зать**.

уре́занный *прил* (*демократия, свобода*) limited.

уре́|зать (**-жу, -жешь**; *impf* **уреза́ть**) *сов перех* (*расходы, штаты*) to cut down.

урезо́н|ить (**-ю, -ишь**; *impf* **урезо́нивать**) *сов перех*: **~ кого́-н** (*разг*) to make sb see reason.

уреми́|я (**-и**) *ж* uraemia (*BRIT*), uremia (*US*).

уре́тр|а (**-ы**) *ж* urethra.

у́рн|а (**-ы**) *ж* (*погребальная*) urn; (*для мусора, для окурков*) bin; **избира́тельная ~** ballot box.

у́ров|ень (**-ня**) *м* level; (*техники*) standard; (*зарплаты, доходов*) rate; **в ~ с** +*instr* on a level with; **на ~не земли́** at ground level; **встре́ча на вы́сшем ~не** the summit meeting; **вы́ше/ни́же ~ня мо́ря** above/below sea level; **моя́ рабо́та была́ на ~не** my work was up to standard; **у́ровень жи́зни** living standard.

уровня́|ть (**-ю**; *impf* **ура́внивать**) *сов перех* (*дорогу, землю*) to level.

уро́д (**-а**) *м person with a deformity*; (*нравственный*) monster.

уро́дин|а (**-ы**) *м/ж* ugly person (*мн* people).

уро|ди́ться (-жу́сь, -ди́шься) *сов возв*
(*пшеница*) to give a good yield; ~ (*perf*) **в кого́-н**
(*в де́да, в отца́ итп*) to take after sb.

уро́д|ка (-ки; *gen pl* -ок) *ж см* **уро́д**.

уро́дливост|ь (-и) *ж* (*см прил*) deformity;
distortion; ugliness.

уро́длив|ый (-, -а, -о) *прил* (*с уро́дством*)
deformed; (*представле́ние*) distorted;
(*безобра́зный*) ugly.

уро́д|овать (-ую; *perf* **изуро́довать**) *несов*
перех (*кале́чить*) to deform; (*де́лать*
некраси́вым) to make ugly; (*созна́ние*) to
distort; (*ду́шу, молодёжь*) to corrupt.

уро́дств|о (-а) *ср* (*физи́ческий недоста́ток*)
deformity; (*некраси́вая вне́шность*) ugliness.

урожа́|й (-я) *м* (*зерна́, карто́феля итп*) harvest;
(*большо́е коли́чество*) abundance; **снима́ть**
(**снять** *perf*) *или* **собира́ть** (**собра́ть** *perf*) ~ to
gather the harvest; **убира́ть** (**убра́ть** *perf*) ~ to
take in the harvest.

урожа́йност|ь (-и) *ж* yield.

урожа́йный *прил* (*год*) productive.

урождённая *прил* née.

урожён|ец (-ца) *м* native.

урожу́сь *сов см* **уроди́ться**.

уро́к (-а) *м* lesson; (*зада́ние*) task; (*обы́чно мн*:
дома́шняя рабо́та) homework *ед*; **де́лать**
(**сде́лать** *perf*) ~**и** to do one's homework; **э́то**
послу́жит тебе́ хоро́шим ~**ом** let it be a (good)
lesson to you; **брать** (*impf*) ~**и чего́-н у кого́-н** to
take lessons in sth from sb; **дава́ть** (*impf*) ~ to
give a lesson; **дава́ть** (*impf*) ~**и где́-нибудь/**
кому́-н to teach somewhere/sb.

уро́лог (-а) *м* urologist.

урологи́ческ|ий (-ая, -ое, -ие) *прил* urological.

уроло́ги|я (-и) *ж* urology.

уро́н (-а) *м* (*поте́ри*) losses *мн*; **нести́** (**понести́**
perf) ~ to suffer losses; **наноси́ть** (**нанести́** *perf*)
кому́-н ~ to inflict loss on sb.

ур|они́ть (-оню́, -о́нишь) *сов от* **роня́ть**.

уро́чищ|е (-а) *ср* natural boundary.

Уругва́|й (-я) *м* Uruguay.

уругва́йск|ий (-ая, -ое, -ие) *прил* Uruguayan.

урча́ни|е (-я) *ср* (*воды́*) gurgling; (*соба́ки*)
growling; (*ко́шки*) purring.

урч|а́ть (-у́, -и́шь) *несов неперех* (*вода́*) to
gurgle; (*тигр*) to growl; (*ко́шка*) to purr; **у меня́**
~**и́т в желу́дке** my tummy's rumbling.

урыва́|ть (-ю) *несов от* **урва́ть**.

уры́вками *нареч* at odd times.

урю́к (-а) *м собир* dried apricots *мн*.

ус (-а) *м* whisker; *см та́кже* **усы́**.

ус|ади́ть (-ажу́, -а́дишь; *impf* **уса́живать**) *сов*
перех: ~ **госте́й** to show the guests to their
seats; (*заста́вить де́лать*): ~ **кого́-н за**
что-н/+*infin* to sit sb down to sth/to do;
уса́живать (~ *perf*) **сад цвета́ми** to plant the
garden with lots of flowers.

уса́дьб|а (-ы) *ж* (*поме́щичья*) country estate;
(*крестья́нская*) farmstead.

уса́жива|ть (-ю) *несов от* **усади́ть**

▶ **уса́живаться** *несов от* **усе́сться**.

усажу́ *сов см* **усади́ть**.

уса́т|ый (-, -а, -о) *прил*: ~ **мужчи́на** man with a
moustache; ~ **кот** cat with whiskers.

усва́ива|ть (-ю) *несов от* **усво́ить**.

усвое́ни|е (-я) *ср* (*уро́ка, нау́ки*) mastering;
(*пи́щи*) assimilation.

усво́|ить (-ю, -ишь; *impf* **усва́ивать**) *сов перех*
(*привы́чку*) to acquire; (*уро́к*) to master; (*пи́щу,*
лека́рство) to assimilate.

усвоя́емост|ь (-и) *ж* assimilability.

усёк *итп сов см* **усе́чь**.

усека́|ть (-ю) *несов от* **усе́чь**.

усеку́ *итп сов см* **усе́чь**.

усе́рден *прил см* **усе́рдный**.

усе́рди|е (-я) *ср* diligence.

усе́рдный (-ен, -на, -но) *прил* diligent.

усе́рдств|овать (-ую) *несов непере х* to make
an effort.

усе́|сться (-я́дусь, -я́дешься; *pt* -е́лся, -е́лась,
-е́лось, *impf* **уса́живаться**) *сов возв* to settle
down; (*заня́ться чем-н*): ~ **за** +*acc* (*за рабо́ту,*
за письмо́) to sit down to.

усе́|чь (-ку́, -чёшь итп, -ку́т; *pt* -ёк, -екла́,
-екло́, *impf* **усека́ть**) *сов перех* (*укороти́ть*) to
truncate; (*разг: поня́ть*) to catch on to.

усе́|ять (-ю) *сов перех* (*по́ле, не́бо*) to cover

▶ **усе́яться** *сов возв*: ~**ся** +*instr* to be dotted *или*
strewn with; (*цвета́ми*) to be full of.

уси|де́ть (-жу́, -ди́шь) *сов непере х* (*оста́ться*
сиде́ть) to stay sitting; (*не упа́сть*) to stay in
one's seat; **он е́ле** ~**де́л на ме́сте** he could
hardly sit still; **он не мог** ~ **до́ма** he couldn't
just sit at home.

уси́дчивост|ь (-и) *ж* assiduity.

уси́дчив|ый (-, -а, -о) *прил* assiduous.

усижу́ *сов см* **усиде́ть**.

ýси|ки (-ов; *nom sg* -) *мн* (*ма́ленькие усы́*) small
moustache *ед*; (*у расте́ний*) tendril *ед*; (*у*
членистоно́гих) feelers *мн*.

уси́ленн|ый *прил* (*охра́на*) reinforced;
(*про́сьбы, напомина́ния*) persistent; (*внима́ние*)
increased; ~**ое пита́ние** high calorie diet.

усили́ва|ть(ся) (-ю(сь)) *несов от* **уси́лить(ся)**.

уси́ли|е (-я) *ср* effort; (*физи́ческое*) exertion;
де́лать (**сде́лать** *perf*) ~ **над собо́й** to force o.s.

усили́тел|ь (-я) *м* amplifier.

усили́тельный *прил* amplifying.

уси́л|ить (-ю, -ишь; *impf* **уси́ливать**) *сов перех*
to intensify; (*охра́ну*) to reinforce; (*внима́ние*) to
increase; (*звук*) to amplify

▶ **уси́литься** (*impf* **уси́ливаться**) *сов возв*
(*ве́тер*) to get stronger; (*сопротивле́ние*) to
intensify; (*волне́ние*) to increase.

уска|ка́ть (-чу́, -чешь) *сов непере х* (*ко́ни*) to
gallop away *или* off; (*пере́н: разг: челове́к*) to
whizz off.

ускольз|ну́ть (-ну́, -нёшь; *impf* **ускольза́ть**) *сов*
непере х (*ры́ба, змея́ итп*) to slip off; (*пере́н*): ~
из +*gen*/**от** +*gen* to slip out of/away from;
ускольза́ть (~ *perf*) **от чьего́-н внима́ния** to

escape sb's attention.

ускоре́ни|е (-я) *ср* acceleration; (*шага*) quickening.

ускóренный *прил* (*шаг*) quickened; (*дыхание, пульс, темпы*) accelerated; **~ курс** crash course.

ускóритель (-я) *м* accelerator; **ракéтный ~** rocket booster.

ускóр|ить (-ю, -ишь; *impf* **ускоря́ть**) *сов перех* (*шаги*) to quicken; (*ход механизма, прогресс*) to accelerate; (*выздоровление, отъезд*) to be speeded up

▸ **ускóриться** (*impf* **ускоря́ться**) *сов возв* (*ход поезда*) to accelerate; (*шаги*) to quicken; (*отъезд, решение вопроса*) to speed up.

усла́влива|ться (-юсь) *несов от* **усло́виться**.

усла́д|а (-ы) *ж* delight, joy.

услад|и́ть (-жу́, -ди́шь; *impf* **услажда́ть**) *сов перех* (*слух, зрение*) to delight

▸ **услади́ться** (*impf* **услажда́ться**) *сов возв*: **~ся** +*instr* (*зрелищем, ароматом*) to delight in.

усл|а́ть (ушлю́, ушлёшь; *impf* **усыла́ть**) *сов перех* (*курьера, слуг*) to dispatch; (*на каторгу*) to send away.

уследи́ть (-жу́, -ди́шь) *сов неперех*: **~ за** +*instr* (*за ребёнком*) to keep an eye on; (*за ходом разговора*) to follow.

усло́вен *прил см* **усло́вный**.

усло́ви|е (-я) *ср* condition; (*договора, платежа*) term; (*соглашение*) agreement; (*обычно мн: поступления в институт, приёма на работу*) requirement; **ста́вить** (**поста́вить** *perf*) **что-н ~м** to make sth a condition; **при ~и хоро́шей пого́ды** on the condition that the weather is good; **при ~и, что он согласи́тся** on the condition *или* provided that he agrees; *см также* **усло́вия**.

усло́в|иться (-люсь, -ишься; *impf* **усла́вливаться**) *сов возв*: **~ о** +*prp* (*договориться*) to agree on.

усло́ви|я (-й) *мн* (*природные*) conditions *мн*; (*задачи, теоремы*) factors *мн*; (*пользования чем-н, какого-н режима*) terms *мн*; **жили́щные ~** housing; **~ труда́** working conditions; **в ~х** +*gen* in an atmosphere of; **по ~м догово́ра** on the terms of the agreement; **на льго́тных ~х** on special terms; **на сле́дующих ~х** on the following conditions; **для рабо́ты здесь – все ~** (*разг*) everything you need for working here is laid on.

усло́вленный *прил* agreed.

усло́влюсь *сов см* **усло́виться**.

усло́вность (-и) *ж* conditional nature; (*обычай*) convention.

усло́в|ный (-ен, -на, -но) *прил* (*срок, согласие итп*) conditional; (*знак, сигнал*) code *опред*; (*линия*) imaginary; (*no short form*; *линг*) conditional; **усло́вный рефле́кс** conditional reflex; **усло́вный срок** suspended sentence.

усложн|и́ть (-ю́, -и́шь; *impf* **усложня́ть**) *сов перех* to complicate

▸ **усложни́ться** (*impf* **усложня́ться**) *сов возв* to get more complicated.

услу́г|а (-и) *ж* (*одолжение*) favour (*BRIT*), favor (*US*); (*обычно мн: обслуживание*) service; **коммуна́льные ~и** public utilities; **бюро́ (до́брых) услу́г** domestic services agency; **к Ва́шим ~м!** at your service!; **ока́зывать** (**оказа́ть** *perf*) **кому́-н ~у** to do sb a good turn.

услуже́ни|е (-я) *ср*: **быть в ~и** (**у** +*gen*) to be in service (with).

услуж|и́ть (-у́, -у́жишь) *сов неперех*: **~ кому́-н** to do sb a good turn.

услу́жлив|ый (-, -а, -о) *прил* obliging.

услы́ш|ать (-у, -ишь) *сов от* **слы́шать**.

усма́трива|ть (-ю) *несов от* **усмотре́ть**.

усмехн|у́ться (-у́сь, -ёшься; *impf* **усмеха́ться**) *сов возв* to smile slightly.

усме́шк|а (-и) *ж* slight smile; **зла́я ~** sneer.

усмире́ни|е (-я) *ср* (*тигра*) taming; (*страстей, мятежа*) suppression.

усмир|и́ть (-ю́, -и́шь; *impf* **усмиря́ть**) *сов перех* (*льва*) to tame; (*детей*) to discipline; (*страсти, мятеж, восстание*) to suppress

▸ **усмири́ться** (*impf* **усмиря́ться**) *сов возв* (*лев*) to become tame; (*дети*) to calm down.

усмотре́ни|е (-я) *ср* discretion; **предоставля́ть** (**предоста́вить** *perf*) **на ~ нача́льства** to be left to the management's discretion; **де́йствовать** (*impf*) **по своему́ ~ю** to use one's own discretion *или* judgement; **на Ва́ше ~** at your discretion.

усм|отре́ть (-отрю́, -о́тришь; *impf* **усма́тривать**) *сов перех* (*разг*) to spot; (*счесть*): **~ что-н в** +*prp* to see sth in ♦ *неперех* (*разг: уследить*): **~ за** +*instr* to keep an eye on.

усна|сти́ть (-щу́, -сти́шь; *impf* **уснаща́ть**) *сов перех*: **~ что-н чем-н** to pepper sth with sth.

усн|у́ть (-у́, -ёшь) *сов неперех* (*заснуть*) to fall asleep, go to sleep; **~ (**perf**) наве́ки** *или* **ве́чным сном** to go to one's eternal rest.

усоверше́нствовани|е (-я) *ср* improvement, refinement.

усоверше́нств|овать(ся) (-ую(сь)) *сов от* **соверше́нствовать(ся)**.

усо́ве|стить (-щу, -стишь; *impf* **усо́вещивать**) *сов перех*: **~ кого́-н** to make sb (feel) ashamed.

усомн|и́ться (-ю́сь, -и́шься) *сов возв*: **~ в** +*prp* to doubt.

усо́пш|ая (-ей; *decl like adj*) *ж см* **усо́пший**.

усо́пш|ий (-его; *decl like adj*) *м* deceased.

усо́хн|уть (-у, -ешь; *impf* **усыха́ть**) *сов неперех* (*также перен*) to shrivel (up); (*шерсть*) to shrink.

успева́емост|ь (-и) *ж* performance (*in studies*).

успева́|ть (-ю) *несов от* **успе́ть** ♦ *неперех* to make progress (*in one's studies*).

успе́ется *сов безл* there's no hurry *или* rush.

Успе́ни|е (-я) *ср* the Assumption.

успе́|ть (-ю; *impf* **успева́ть**) *сов неперех* (*сделать что-н в срок*) to manage; (*прийти вовремя*) to be *или* make it in time; **я не ~л э́то сде́лать, как ...** I'd hardly done it when ...; **не ~л огляну́ться, как он уже́ ушёл** I hardly had time to blink before he'd already gone.

успе́х (-а) *м* success; (*обычно мн: в спорте, в учёбе*) achievement; **как Ва́ши ~и?** how are you doing?; **с ~ом** (*успешно*) successfully; (*без затрудне́ний*) easily; **добива́ться (доби́ться** *perf*)**~а** to achieve success; **с тем же ~ом** just as well.

успе́шно *нареч* successfully.

успе́ш|ный (-ен, -на, -но) *прил* successful.

успока́ива|ть(ся) (-ю(сь)) *несов от* **успоко́ить(ся)**.

успокое́ни|е (-я) *ср* (*боли, совести*) easing; (*плачущего*) pacifying; **э́ти мы́сли принесли́ ей ~** these thoughts brought her peace of mind.

успоко́енност|ь (-и) *ж* complacency.

успокои́тельн|ое (-ого; *decl like adj*) *ср* sedative.

успокои́тельный *прил* (*известие, ответ*) calming, soothing; (*лекарство*) sedative *опред*.

успоко́|ить (-ю, -ишь; *impf* **успока́ивать**) *сов перех* to calm (down); (*совесть*) to ease; (*боль*) to soothe

▸ **успоко́иться** (*impf* **успока́иваться**) *сов возв* (*человек*) to calm down; (*море*) to calm; (*боль, совесть, волнения*) to be eased; (*ветер*) to drop; **успока́иваться (~ся** *perf*) **на дости́гнутом** to be content with one's achievements; **он не ~ился, пока́ не раскры́ли всё де́ло** he couldn't rest until they'd uncovered the whole business.

уст|а́ (-) *мн* lips *мн*; **в его́ ~х э́то звучи́т стра́нно** it sounds strange coming from him; **из уст в ~** by word of mouth; **из пе́рвых уст** from the horse's mouth; **э́то у всех на ~х** it's on everyone's lips.

уста́в (-а) *м* (*партийный*) rules *мн*; (*воинский*) regulations *мн*; (*корпорации*) statute; **~ акционе́рной компа́нии** (*комм*) articles of association.

устава́|ть (-ю, -ёшь) *несов от* **уста́ть**.

уста́в|ить (-лю, -ишь; *impf* **уставля́ть**) *сов перех* (*разместить*) to place, put; (*занять*): **~ что-н чем-н** (*стол*) to cover sth with; (*полку*) to fill with; (*разг: устремить*): **~ что-н в** +*acc* to fix sth on

▸ **уста́виться** (*impf* **уставля́ться**) *сов возв* (*разг*): **~ся на/в** +*acc* (*на собеседника, в стену*) to gaze at.

уста́вный *прил* statutory; **уста́вный капита́л** (*комм*) authorized capital.

уста́ло *нареч* wearily.

уста́лост|ь (-и) *ж* tiredness, fatigue.

уста́лый *прил* tired, weary.

у́стал|ь (-и) *ж*: **без** *или* **не зна́я ~и** tirelessly, indefatigably.

устан|ови́ть (-овлю́, -о́вишь; *impf* **устана́вливать**) *сов перех* to establish; (*размер оплаты, сроки*) to set; (*прибор, машину*) to install; **устана́вливать (~** *perf*) **реко́рд** to set a record

▸ **установи́ться** (*impf* **устана́вливаться**) *сов возв* to be established; (*погода*) to become settled; (*характер*) to be formed.

устано́вк|а (-и) *ж* installation; (*директива*) directive; (*цель*) objective.

установлю́(сь) *сов см* **установи́ть(ся)**.

уста́ну *итп сов см* **уста́ть**.

устаре́|ть (-ю) *сов от* **старе́ть** ◆ (*impf* **устарева́ть**) *неперех* (*оборудование*) to become obsolete.

уста́|ть (-ну, -нешь; *impf* **устава́ть**) *сов неперех* to get tired.

уст|ла́ть (-елю́, -е́лешь; *impf* **устила́ть**) *сов перех*: **~ что-н (чем-н)** to cover sth (with sth).

у́стный *прил* (*экзамен*) oral; (*обещание, приказ*) verbal; **у́стная речь** spoken language.

усто́|й (-я) *м* (*опора*) support; **~и** (*основы*) foundations.

усто́йчивост|ь (-и) *ж* stability.

усто́йчив|ый (-, -а, -о) *прил* (*также перен*) stable; (*лестница*) steady; **усто́йчивое (слово)сочета́ние** set phrase.

усто|я́ть (-ю́, -и́шь) *сов неперех* (*не упасть*) to remain standing; (*в споре, в борьбе итп*) to stand one's ground; (*не поддаться*) to resist; **~ (** *perf*) **на нога́х** to keep one's balance

▸ **устоя́ться** *сов возв* (*характер*) to be formed; (*жидкость*) to settle; (*взгляды*) to become fixed.

устра́ива|ть(ся) (-ю(сь)) *несов от* **устро́ить(ся)**.

устран|и́ть (-ю́, -и́шь; *impf* **устраня́ть**) *сов перех* (*препятствие*) to remove; (*недостатки, соперника*) to eliminate; (*работника*) to dismiss

▸ **устрани́ться** (*impf* **устраня́ться**) *сов возв* to resign.

устраша́|ть(ся) (-ю(сь)) *несов от* **устраши́ть(ся)**.

устраша́ющ|ий (-ая, -ее, -ие) *прил* frightening.

устраш|и́ть (-у́, -и́шь; *impf* **устраша́ть**) *сов перех* to frighten

▸ **устраши́ться** (*impf* **устраша́ться**) *сов возв*: **~ся** +*gen* to be frightened of.

устрем|и́ть (-лю́, -и́шь; *impf* **устремля́ть**) *сов перех* (*удар, глаза итп*) to direct; (*внимание, помыслы*) to focus

▸ **устреми́ться** (*impf* **устремля́ться**) *сов возв*: **~ся на** +*acc* (*конница, толпа*) to charge at; (*перен: внимание, мысли*) to be focused on; (*взгляд, глаза*) to be fixed on.

устремле́ни|е (-я) *ср* aspiration.

устремлённост|ь (-и) *ж* tendency.

устремлю́(сь) *сов см* **устреми́ть(ся)**.

устремля́|ть(ся) (-ю(сь)) *несов от* **устреми́ть(ся)**.

у́стриц|а (-ы) *ж* oyster.

у́стричный *прил* oyster.

устро́ен|ный (-, -а, -о) *прил* (жизнь) ordered; (кварти́ра) habitable.
устро́итель (-я) *м* organizer.
устро́|ить (-ю, -ишь; *impf* **устра́ивать**) *сов перех* (жизнь, дела) to organize; (спекта́кль, выставку) to arrange; (подлеж: предложе́ние, цена́) to suit; **устра́ивать** (~ *perf*) кого́-н на рабо́ту/кварти́ру to help sb find work/a flat; **устра́ивать** (~ *perf*) сканда́л to make a scene; **э́то меня́ ~ит** that suits me
▸ **устро́иться** (*impf* **устра́иваться**) *сов возв* (расположи́ться) to settle down; (прийти́ в поря́док) to work out; **устра́иваться** (~ся *perf*) **на рабо́ту** to get a job; **он ~ился на заво́д** he got a job in a factory.
устро́йств|о (-а) *ср* (де́йствие: выставки) organization; (: на рабо́ту) finding; (до́ма, прибо́ра) construction; (госуда́рственное, обще́ственное) structure; (техни́ческое) device, mechanism; ~ **опти́ческого счи́тывания си́мволов** (КОМП) optical character reader.
усту́п (-а) *м* ledge.
уступ|и́ть (-уплю́, -у́пишь; *impf* **уступа́ть**) *сов перех*; ~ **что-н кому́-н** to give sth up for sb ♦ *неперех*: ~ **кому́-н/чему́-н** (си́льному, си́ле, жела́нию итп) to give in to sb/sth; **уступа́ть** (~ *perf*) в +*prp* (в си́ле, в уме́) to be inferior in; **уступа́ть** (~ *perf*) **доро́гу кому́-н** to make way for sb; **он ~упи́л мне кни́гу за 10 рубле́й** he let me have the book for 10 roubles.
усту́п|ка (-ки; *gen pl* -ок) *ж* (компроми́сс) compromise; (си́ле, врагу́) surrender; (ски́дка) discount; **пойти́** (*perf*) **на ~ку** to compromise.
уступлю́ *сов см* **уступи́ть**.
усту́пок *сущ см* **усту́пка**.
усту́пчив|ый (-, -а, -о) *прил* compliant.
усты|ди́ть (-жу́, -ди́шь) *сов перех* to shame
▸ **усты́ди́ться** *сов возв*: ~**ся** +*gen* to be ashamed of.
у́сть|е (-я) *ср* (реки́) mouth; (ша́хты) entrance.
усугу́б|ить (-лю, -ишь; *impf* **усугубля́ть**) *сов перех* (вину́, опа́сность) to increase; (боле́знь, положе́ние) to aggravate
▸ **усугу́биться** (*impf* **усугубля́ться**) *сов возв* (вина́) to increase; (страда́ния, боле́знь) to be aggravated.
усу́ш|ка (-и) *ж* (зерна́) loss of weight (through drying).
ус|ы́ (-о́в) *мн* (у челове́ка) moustache *ед*; (у живо́тных) whiskers *мн*; **он (и) в ус (себе́) не ду́ет** (разг) he's completely unruffled; **на ус мота́ть** (намота́ть *perf*) **что-н** (разг) to take good note of sth; **са́ми с ~а́ми** (разг) we weren't born yesterday.
усыла́|ть (-ю) *несов от* **усла́ть**.
усынов|и́ть (-лю́, -и́шь; *impf* **усыновля́ть**) *сов перех* to adopt (son).

усыновле́ни|е (-я) *ср* adoption (son).
усыновлю́ *сов см* **усынови́ть**.
усыновля́|ть (-ю) *несов от* **усынови́ть**.
усыпа́льниц|а (-ы) *ж* burial chamber.
усы́п|ать (-лю, -лешь; *impf* **усыпа́ть**) *сов перех*: ~ **что-н чем-н** (путь, доро́гу) to scatter sth with sth.
усып|и́ть (-лю́, -и́шь; *impf* **усыпля́ть**) *сов перех* (больно́го) to anaesthetize (BRIT), anesthetize (US); (ребёнка) to lull to sleep; (перен: внима́ние, бди́тельность) to weaken; (больну́ю соба́ку итп) to put to sleep; **он ~и́л меня́ свои́ми ску́чными разгово́рами** his boring conversation sent me to sleep.
усы́плю *итп сов см* **усы́пать**.
усыплю́ *сов см* **усыпи́ть**.
усыпля́|ть (-ю) *несов от* **усыпи́ть**.
усыха́|ть (-ю) *несов от* **усо́хнуть**.
уся́дусь *итп сов см* **усе́сться**.
ута|и́ть (-ю́, -и́шь; *impf* **ута́ивать**) *сов перех* (пра́вду) to keep secret; (де́ньги, докуме́нты) to appropriate.
ута́йк|а (-и) *ж*: **без ~и** (разг) openly.
ута́пыва|ть (-ю) *несов от* **утопта́ть**.
ута|щи́ть (-щу́, -а́щешь; *impf* **ута́скивать**) *сов перех* (унести́) to drag away *или* off; (разг: укра́сть) to make off with.
у́тва́р|ь (-и) *ж собир* utensils *мн*.
утверди́тельный (-ен, -ьна, -ьно) *прил* (также линг) affirmative.
утверд|и́ть (-жу́, -ди́шь; *impf* **утвержда́ть**) *сов перех* (прое́кт, гра́фик) to approve; (госпо́дство, демокра́тию итп) to establish; ~ (*perf*) **кого́-н в подозре́ниях** to confirm sb's suspicions; ~ (*perf*) **кого́-н в до́лжности** to approve sb's appointment to office; ~ (*perf*) **кого́-н в мне́нии/наме́рении** to strengthen sb's conviction/intention
▸ **утверди́ться** (*impf* **утвержда́ться**) *сов возв* to be established; (увери́ться): ~**ся в** +*prp* (в наме́рении) to become convinced of.
утвержда́|ть (-ю) *несов от* **утверди́ть** ♦ *перех* (пра́вильность, достове́рность) to maintain; **он ~л, что ничего́ не зна́ет** he maintained that he didn't know anything
▸ **утвержда́ться** *несов от* **утверди́ться**.
утвержде́ни|е (-я) *ср* (см глаг) approval; establishment; (пра́вильное, интере́сное) statement.
утвержу́(сь) *сов см* **утверди́ть(ся)**.
утёк *итп сов см* **утёчь**.
утека́|ть (*3sg* -ет, *3pl* -ют) *несов от* **утёчь**.
утеку́т *итп сов см* **утёчь**.
утёно|к (-ёнка; *nom pl* -я́та, *gen pl* -я́т) *м* duckling.
утеплённый *прил* (гара́ж) insulated; (о́бувь) lined.
утепл|и́ть (-ю́, -и́шь; *impf* **утепля́ть**) *сов перех* to insulate.

утере́ть (-ру́, -рёшь; *pt* -ёр, -ёрла, -ёрло, *impf* **утира́ть**) *сов перех* (*пот*) to wipe off; (*слёзы*) to wipe away; (*лицо, нос*) to wipe; ~ (*perf*) **нос кому́-н** (*перен: разг*) to show sb what's what

► **утере́ться** (*impf* **утира́ться**) *сов возв* to wipe one's face; (*нос*) to wipe one's nose.

уте́р|я (-и) *ж* loss.

утеря́ть (-ю) *сов от* **теря́ть**.

утёс (-а) *м* cliff.

уте́чк|а (-и) *ж* (*также перен*) leak; (*кадров*) turnover; **уте́чка мозго́в** brain drain.

уте́чь (*3sg* -ечёт, *3pl* -еку́т, *pt* -ёк, -екла́, -екло́, *impf* **утека́ть**) *сов неперех* (*вода, газ*) to leak; (*годы*) to go by, pass; (*информация*) to be leaked.

утеша́|ть(ся) (-ю(сь)) *несов от* **уте́шить(ся)**.

утеше́ни|е (-я) *ср* (*плачущего*) comforting; (*о чём-н утешающем*) consolation.

уте́ш|ить (-у, -ишь; *impf* **утеша́ть**) *сов перех* (*плачущего, несчастного*) to comfort, console; (*подлеж: мысль, успехи детей*) to comfort

► **уте́шиться** (*impf* **утеша́ться**) *сов возв* to cheer up.

утилиза́ци|я (-и) *ж* recycling.

утилизи́р|овать (-ую) (*не)сов перех* to recycle.

утилита́р|ный (-ен, -на, -но) *прил* (*взгляды*) utilitarian; (*знания*) practical.

ути́л|ь (-я) *м собир* recyclable waste.

ути́ный *прил* (*гнездо*) duck's; (*яйцо, охота*) duck *опред*.

утира́|ть(ся) (-ю(сь)) *несов от* **утере́ть(ся)**.

утихн|у́ть (-у, -ешь; *impf* **утиха́ть**) *сов неперех* (*спор*) to calm down; (*гром, звон*) to die away; (*ветер*) to drop; (*вьюга*) to die down.

утихоми́р|ить (-ю, -ишь; *impf* **утихоми́ривать**) *сов перех* to pacify

► **утихоми́риться** (*impf* **утихоми́риваться**) *сов возв* to calm down.

у́т|ка (-ки; *gen pl* -ок) *ж* duck; (*ложный слух*) canard; (*сосуд*) bedpan; **пуска́ть** (**пусти́ть** *perf*) ~**ку** to spread a false rumour (*BRIT*) *или* rumor (*US*).

уткн|у́ть (-у́, -ёшь) *сов перех* (*разг: подборо́док*) to bury; ~ (*perf*) **нос в** +*acc* to bury one's nose in; ~ (*perf*) **глаза́ в зе́млю** to fix one's eyes on the ground

► **уткну́ться** *сов возв* (*разг*): ~**ся в** +*acc* (*в кни́гу, в газе́ту*) to bury one's nose in; **она́** ~**у́лась голово́й в поду́шку** she buried her face in the pillow.

утконо́с (-а) *м* duck-billed platypus (*мн* platypus).

у́тлый *прил* (*лодка*) decrepit.

у́ток *сущ см* **у́тка**.

утол|и́ть (-ю́, -и́шь; *impf* **утоля́ть**) *сов перех* (*жажду*) to quench; (*голод, любопытство*) to satisfy; (*боль*) to ease.

утол|сти́ть (-щу́, -сти́шь; *impf* **утолща́ть**) *сов перех* to thicken.

утолще́ни|е (-я) *ср* widening.

утолщу́ *сов см* **утолсти́ть**.

утоля́|ть (-ю) *несов от* **утоли́ть**.

утоми́тельный (-ен, -ьна, -ьно) *прил* tedious, tiresome; (*ребёнок*) tiring.

утом|и́ть (-лю́, -и́шь; *impf* **утомля́ть**) *сов перех* to tire

► **утоми́ться** (*impf* **утомля́ться**) *сов возв* to get tired.

утомле́ни|е (-я) *ср* tiredness, fatigue.

утомлю́(сь) *сов см* **утоми́ть(ся)**.

утомля́емост|ь (-и) *ж* (*также TEX*) fatigue.

утомля́|ть(ся) (-ю(сь)) *несов от* **утоми́ть(ся)**.

утон|у́ть (-ону́, -о́нешь) *сов от* **тону́ть**.

утонче́нность (-и) *ж* refinement.

утончён|ный (-, -на, -но) *прил* refined.

утонч|и́ть (-у́, -и́шь) *сов перех* (*нитку*) to make thinner

► **утончи́ться** *сов возв* (*вкусы, восприя́тие*) to become refined.

утопа́|ть (-ю) *несов неперех* (*тонуть*) to drown; (*перен*): ~ **в** +*prp* (*в кружевах, в цветах*) to be smothered in; (*в роскоши, в разврате*) to wallow in.

утопи́ст (-а) *м* utopian.

утоп|и́ть(ся) (-оплю́(сь), -о́пишь(ся)) *сов от* **топи́ть(ся)**.

утопи́чен *прил см* **утопи́чный**.

утопи́ческ|ий (-ая, -ое, -ие) *прил* utopian.

утопи́ч|ный (-ен, -на, -но) *прил* utopian.

уто́пи|я (-и) *ж* utopia.

уто́пленник (-а) *м* drowned man (*мн* men).

уто́пленниц|а (-ы) *ж* drowned woman (*мн* women).

утоплю́(сь) *сов см* **утопи́ть(ся)**.

ут|опта́ть (-опчу́, -о́пчешь; *impf* **ута́птывать**) *сов перех* to stamp down.

уточне́ни|е (-я) *ср* elaboration; **вноси́ть** (**внести́** *perf*) ~**я в** +*acc* to elaborate on.

уточн|и́ть (-ю́, -и́шь; *impf* **уточня́ть**) *сов перех* (*пункт договора, выводы*) to elaborate on; (*сведения, факты*) to clarify.

утрамб|ова́ть (-у́ю) *сов от* **трамбова́ть**.

утра́т|а (-ы) *ж* loss; ~ **трудоспосо́бности** disablement; **понести́** (*perf*) ~**у** to suffer a loss.

утра́|тить (-чу, -тишь; *impf* **утра́чивать**) *сов перех* (*потерять*) to lose; ~ (*perf*) **си́лу** (*документ итп*) to become invalid.

у́тренн|ий (-яя, -ее, -ие) *прил* morning *опред*; (*событие, известие*) this morning's.

у́тренник (-а) *м* matinée; (*с участием детей*) children's party.

утри́рованный *прил* exaggerated.

утри́р|овать (-ую) (*не)сов перех* to exaggerate.

у́тр|о (-а́; *nom pl* -а, *gen pl* -, *dat pl* -ам) *ср* morning; **до утра́** till morning; **с утра́** since this morning; **дава́й встре́тимся с утра́** let's meet in the morning; **с утра́ до́ ночи** from morn till night; **до́брое** ~**!, с до́брым** ~**м!** good morning!; **на** ~ next morning; **по утра́м** in the mornings; **под** ~, **к утру́** in the early hours of the morning.

утро́б|а (-ы) *ж* (*материнская*) womb; (*брюхо*) belly.

утро́бный *прил* (био) f(o)etal; (*истошный*) hollow.

утро́|ить (**-ю, -ишь**) *сов перех* to treble, triple
▸ **утро́иться** *сов возв* to treble, triple.

у́тром *нареч* in the morning; **ра́но ~** early in the morning.

утру́(сь) *итп сов см* **утере́ть(ся)**.

утружда́|ть (**-ю**) *несов перех*: **~ кого́-н чем-н** to trouble sb with sth; **не ~йте себя́** don't trouble yourself
▸ **утружда́ться** *несов возв* to trouble o.s.

утру́ск|а (**-и**) *ж* spillage.

утр|ясти́ (**-ясу́, -ясёшь;** *impf* **утряса́ть**) *сов перех* (*перен: разг: вопрос, проблему*) to settle; (*муку*) to shake down
▸ **утрясти́сь** *сов возв* (*разг*) to settle.

уты́|кать (**-чу, -чешь;** *impf* **утыка́ть**) *сов перех*: **~ что-н чем-н** to stick sth into sth.

утю́г (**-а́**) *м* iron (*appliance*).

утю́ж|ить (**-у, -ишь;** *perf* **вы́утюжить** *или* **отутю́жить**) *несов перех* to iron.

утяжел|и́ть (**-ю́, -и́шь;** *impf* **утяжеля́ть**) *сов перех* to make heavier, increase the weight of.

утя́та *итп сущ см* **утёнок**.

утя́тин|а (**-ы**) *ж* (*мясо*) duck.

уф *межд*: **~!** phew!

ух *межд*: **~!** ooh!

ух|а́ (**-и́**) *ж* fish broth.

уха́б (**-а**) *м* pothole.

уха́бист|ый (**-, -а, -о**) *прил*: **~ая доро́га** road full of potholes.

ухажёр (**-а**) *м* (*разг*) admirer.

уха́живани|е (**-я**) *ср* courting.

уха́жива|ть (**-ю**) *несов неперех*: **~ за** +*instr* (*за больным, за ранеными*) to nurse; (*за цветами, за садом*) to tend; (*за женщиной*) to court.

у́хань|е (**-я**) *ср* (*no pl*) hooting.

у́ха|ть (**-ю**) *несов от* **у́хнуть**.

ухва́т (**-а**) *м* oven fork.

ухва|ти́ть (**-чу́, -́тишь;** *impf* **ухва́тывать**) *сов перех* (*человека: за руку, за рукав*) to get hold of; (*перен: идею, смысл*) to grasp
▸ **ухвати́ться** (*impf* **ухва́тываться**) *сов возв*: **~ся за** +*acc* (*за перила, за руку*) to grab hold of; (*за дело, за мысль*) to latch onto; (*за предложение*) to jump at.

ухва́т|ки (**-ок**) *мн* manners *мн*.

ухва́тыва|ть(ся) (**-ю(сь)**) *несов от* **ухвати́ть(ся)**.

ухвачу́(сь) *сов см* **ухвати́ть(ся)**.

ухитр|и́ться (**-ю́сь, -и́шься;** *impf* **ухитря́ться**) *сов возв* = **умудри́ться**.

ухищре́ни|е (**-я**) *ср* (*уловка*) trick; **прибега́ть** (**прибе́гнуть** *perf*) **к ра́зным ~ям** to resort to various tricks.

ухищрённый *прил* crafty.

ухищря́|ться (**-юсь**) *несов возв* to contrive.

ухло́па|ть (**-ю;** *impf* **ухло́пывать**) *сов перех*

(*разг: истратить*) to blow.

ухмы́лк|а (**-и**) *ж* (*разг*) smirk.

ухмыля́|ться (**-юсь;** *perf* **ухмыльну́ться**) *несов возв* (*разг*) to smirk.

у́хн|уть (**-у, -ешь;** *impf* **у́хать**) *сов неперех* (*снаряд*) to thud; (*гром*) to rumble; (*филин, сова*) to hoot; (*разг: упасть*) to come a cropper
♦ *перех* (*разг: все де́ньги*) to blow; (: *камень*) to hurl; **~** (*perf*) **кулако́м по столу́** to bang one's fist down on the table.

у́х|о (**-а;** *nom pl* **у́ши,** *gen pl* **уше́й**) *ср* ear; (*у шапки*) flap; **говори́ть** (**сказа́ть** *perf*) **что-н кому́-н на́ ухо** to whisper sth in sb's ear; **не вида́ть тебе́ де́нег как свои́х уше́й** (*разг*) you've got no chance of getting the money; **слу́шать** (*impf*) **во все у́ши** to be all ears; **слы́шать** (**услы́шать** *perf*) **что-н кра́ем ~а** *или* **одни́м ~м** to listen to sth with half an ear; **по́ уши влюби́ться** (*perf*) **в кого́-н** (*разг*) to fall head over heels in love with sb; **уши вя́нут от твои́х шу́ток** your jokes make me sick.

ухо́д (**-а**) *м* (*со слу́жбы, из семьи́*) leaving; (*от пого́ни, от реа́льности*) escape; (*в монасты́рь*) retreat; (*с собра́ния, со сце́ны*) exit; (*за больны́м, за ребёнком*) care; **~ в отста́вку** resignation; **~ на пе́нсию** retirement.

ух|оди́ть (**-ожу́, -о́дишь**) *несов от* **уйти́** ♦ *неперех* (*простира́ться*) to extend.

ухо́женный *прил* (*лицо́, ру́ки*) well-looked-after; (*сад*) well-kept; (*ло́шадь, челове́к*) well-groomed.

ухожу́ *несов см* **уходи́ть**.

ухудша́|ть(ся) (**-ю(сь)**) *несов от* **уху́дшить(ся)**.

ухудше́ни|е (**-я**) *ср* deterioration, worsening.

уху́дш|ить (**-у, -ишь;** *impf* **ухудша́ть**) *сов перех* to make worse
▸ **уху́дшиться** (*impf* **ухудша́ться**) *сов возв* to get worse, deteriorate.

уцеле́|ть (**-ю**) *сов неперех* to survive.

уценённый *прил* reduced.

уцен|и́ть (**-ю́, -ишь;** *impf* **уце́нивать**) *сов перех* to reduce the price of.

уце́н|ка (**-ки;** *gen pl* **-ок**) *ж* reduction.

уцеп|и́ть (**-лю́, -ишь**) *сов перех* to hook
▸ **уцепи́ться** *сов возв* (*ухвати́ться*): **~ся за** +*acc* (*за руку*) to get hold of; (*за предложе́ние, за возмо́жность*) to jump at.

уча́ств|овать (**-ую**) *сов неперех*: **~ в** +*prp* (*в собра́нии, в спекта́кле*) to take part in; (*в предприя́тии, в при́былях*) to have a share in.

уча́сти|е (**-я**) *ср* (*в собра́нии, в спекта́кле итп*) participation; (*в предприя́тии, в при́былях*) share; (*ро́дственное, дру́жеское*) concern; **принима́ть** (**приня́ть** *perf*) **~ в** +*prp* to take part in; **принима́ть** (**приня́ть** *perf*) **~ в ком-н** to show concern for sb.

уча|сти́ть (**-щу́, -сти́шь;** *impf* **учаща́ть**) *сов*

перех *(шаг)* to quicken; *(контакты, встречи)*
to make more frequent

▶ **участи́ться** *(impf* **учаща́ться)** *сов возв*
(пульс, дыхание) to quicken; *(столкновения,*
контакты) to become more frequent.

уча́стка *сущ см* **уча́сток.**

участко́в|ый *прил* local ♦ *(-ого; decl like adj)* м
(разг) local policeman *(мн* policemen); *(также:*
~ **врач)** local GP *или* doctor; *(также:* ~
инспе́ктор) local policeman *(мн* policemen).

уча́стливо *нареч* sympathetically.

уча́стливый *прил* sympathetic.

уча́стник (-а) м *(кружка, экспедиции)* member;
(восстания, репетиции, переговоров)
participant; ~ **соревнова́ния** competitor,
contestant; ~ **вы́ставки** exhibitor; ~ **войны́**
(war) veteran.

уча́стниц|а (-ы) ж см **уча́стник.**

уча́ст|ок (-ка) м *(земли, кожи итп)* area; *(дороги,*
реки, фронта) stretch; *(врачебный)* catchment
area; *(приусадебный, земельный)* plot;
(строительный) site; *(работы,*
деятельности) field; **избира́тельный** ~
polling station; **садо́вый** ~ allotment.

у́част|ь (-и) ж lot; **его́ пости́гла стра́шная** ~ fate
dealt him a terrible blow.

учаща́|ть(ся) (-ю(сь)) *несов от* **участи́ть(ся).**

уча́щаяся (-ейся; *decl like adj)* ж см **уча́щийся.**

уча́щийся (-егося; *decl like adj)* м *(школы)* pupil;
(училища) student.

учащу́(сь) *сов см* **участи́ть(ся).**

учёб|а (-ы) ж studies мн.

учёбник (-а) м textbook; ~ **исто́рии** *или* **по**
исто́рии history textbook.

учёбный *прил (работа)* academic; *(процесс,*
фильм) educational; *(стрельба)* practice; *(бой)*
mock; *(мастерская, судно)* training *опред;*
(методы) teaching *опред;* **учёбная програ́мма**
curriculum; **учёбное заведе́ние** educational
establishment; **учёбный год** academic year;
учёбный план course outline; **учёбный о́тпуск**
block release.

учёл *итп сов см* **уче́сть.**

учён|ая (-ой; *decl like adj)* ж см **учёный.**

уче́ни|е (-я) *ср (в школе, в вузе)* study; *(теория)*
teachings мн; *см также* **уче́ния.**

учени́к (-а́) м *(школы)* pupil; *(училища)* student;
(мастера) apprentice; *(последователь)*
follower.

учени́ц|а (-ы) ж см **учени́к.**

учени́ческий (-ая, -ое, -ие) *прил (дневник,*
тетради) school *опред; (перен: рассуждение,*
работа) primitive.

учени́честв|о (-а) *ср (у мастера)*
apprenticeship; **го́ды** ~**а** schooldays мн.

уче́ни|я (-й) мн exercises мн.

учёност|ь (-и) ж learning.

учён|ый *прил (спор, круги)* academic; *(разг:*
опытом, каким-н событием) educated;
(труды) scholarly; *(кот, собака)* trained; **(-, -а,**
-о; *человек)* learned, scholarly ♦ **(-ого;** *decl like*

adj) м *(научный работник)* academic, scholar;
(: в области точных и естественных наук)
scientist; **учёное зва́ние** academic title;
учёный сове́т academic council.

уч|е́сть (-ту́, -тёшь; *pt* **-ёл, -ла́, -ло́,** *impf*
учи́тывать) *сов перех (обстоятельства,*
сложности) to take into account; *(материал,*
имущество) to make an inventory of;
(присутствующих) to make a list of; ~**ти́те,**
что ... bear in mind that ...; ~ *(perf)* **ве́ксель** to
discount a bill.

учёт (-а) м *(потребностей, обстоятельств)*
consideration; *(товара)* stock-taking; *(военный,*
медицинский) registration; *(векселей)* discount;
(затрат, поступлений) record; **бухга́лтерский** ~ *(учебный предмет)*
accountancy; *(практическая деятельность)*
bookkeeping; **брать (взять** *perf)* **на** ~ to
register; **вести́** *(impf)* ~ to keep a record; **с** ~**ом**
всех обстоя́тельств bearing in mind all the
circumstances; **с** ~**ом сезо́нных колеба́ний**
allowing for seasonal fluctuations.

учётн|ый *прил:* ~**ая ка́рточка** registration form;
~**ая кни́га** record book; ~ **проце́нт** *(КОММ)* rate
of discount; ~ **дом** *(КОММ)* discount house.

учи́лищ|е (-а) *ср* college; **профессиона́льно-**
техни́ческое ~ technical college.

учин|и́ть (-ю́, -и́шь; *impf* **учиня́ть)** *сов перех*
(драку) to start; **учиня́ть (**~ *perf)* **сканда́л** to
make a scene.

учи́тель (-я; *nom pl* **-я́)** м *(школьный)* teacher;
(nom pl **-и;** *мудрости)* master.

учи́тельниц|а (-ы) ж teacher.

учи́тельск|ая (-ой; *decl like adj)* ж staffroom.

учи́тельств|о (-а) *ср (профессия)* teaching ♦
собир (учителя) teachers мн.

учи́тельств|овать (-ую) *несов неперех* to
teach, work as a teacher.

учи́тыва|ть (-ю) *несов от* **уче́сть.**

уч|и́ть (-у́, -ишь; *perf* **вы́учить)** *несов перех*
(урок, роль) to learn; *(perf* **вы́учить** *или*
научи́ть *или* **обучи́ть):** ~ **кого́-н чему́-н/**+*infin*
to teach sb sth/to do; **исто́рия/э́та тео́рия у́чит,**
что ... history/this theory teaches that ...

▶ **учи́ться** *несов возв (в школе, училище)* to
study; *(perf* **вы́учиться** *или* **научи́ться;**
получить навыки) ~**ся чему́-н/**+*infin* to learn
sth/to do.

учреди́тель (-я) м founder.

учреди́тельниц|а (-ы) ж см **учреди́тель.**

учреди́тельн|ый *прил:* ~**ое собра́ние**
inaugural meeting.

учре|ди́ть (-жу́, -ди́шь; *impf* **учрежда́ть)** *сов*
перех (фонд, банк) to set up; *(контроль,*
порядок) to introduce.

учрежде́ни|е (-я) *ср (фонда, организации итп)*
setting up; *(контроля)* introduction; *(научное,*
исследовательское) establishment;
(финансовое, общественное) institution;
(страховое) agency.

учрежу́ *сов см* **учреди́ть.**

учти́вост|ь (-и) *ж* courtesy.
учти́в|ый (-, -а, -о) *прил* courteous, civil.
учту́ *итп сов см* **уче́сть**.
учу́|ять (-ю, -ешь) *сов перех (разг: собака)* to sniff; (: *перен: человек*) to sense.
уша́н|ка (-ки; *gen pl* -ок) *ж cap with ear-flaps*.
уша́ст|ый (-, -а, -о) *прил*: ~ **ма́льчик** boy with big ears.
уша́т (-а) *м* tub.
у́шек *сущ см* **у́шко**.
ушёл *сов см* **уйти́**.
у́ши *итп сущ см* **у́хо**.
уши́б (-а) *м* bruise.
ушиб|и́ть (-у́, -ёшь; *pt* -, -ла, -ло, *impf* **ушиба́ть**) *сов перех* to bang
► **ушиби́ться** *сов возв* to bang o.s.
уш|и́ть (-ью, -ьёшь; *impf* **ушива́ть**) *сов перех* (*сделать уже*) to take in; (*сделать короче*) to shorten, take up.
у́шк|о (-ка; *nom pl* -ки, *gen pl* -ек) *ср уменьш от* **у́хо**; (*медали*) eyelet; (*иголки*) eye.
ушла́ *итп сов см* **уйти́**.
у́шлый *прил* smart.
ушлю́ *итп сов см* **усла́ть**.
ушни́к (-а́) *м (разг)* ear specialist.
ушн|о́й *прил* ear опред; ~**а́я боль** earache; ~**а́я ра́ковина** (АНАТ) auricle.
ушью́ *итп сов см* **уши́ть**.
ущел|ье (-ья; *gen pl* -ий) *ср* gorge, ravine.
ущем|и́ть (-лю́, -и́шь; *impf* **ущемля́ть**) *сов перех* (*права, возможности*) to limit; (*палец*) to trap; **ущемля́ть** (~ *perf*) **чьё-н самолю́бие** to hurt *или* wound sb's pride.
ущемле́ни|е (-я) *ср (прав, возможностей)*

limitation; ~ **чьего́-н самолю́бия** wound to sb's pride.
ущемлённый *прил (самолюбие, гордость)* wounded; (*права*) limited.
ущемлю́ *сов см* **ущеми́ть**.
ущемля́|ть (-ю) *несов от* **ущеми́ть**.
ущерб (-а) *м (материальный)* loss; (*здоровью*) detriment; **в** ~ +*dat* to the detriment of; **на** ~**е** on the wane; **наноси́ть** (**нанести́** *perf*) *или* **причиня́ть** (**причини́ть** *perf*) ~ **кому́-н/чему́-н** to inflict loss on sb/sth.
уще́рбен *прил см* **уще́рбный**.
уще́рбност|ь (-и) *ж (см прил)* waning; abnormality.
уще́рб|ный *прил (луна)* waning; (-ен, -на, -но; *характер, психика*) abnormal.
ущипн|у́ть (-у́, -ёшь) *сов перех* to nip, pinch.
Уэ́льс (-а) *м* Wales.
уэ́льс|кий (-ая, -ое, -ие) *прил* Welsh; ~ **язы́к** Welsh.
ую́т (-а) *м* comfort, cosiness.
ую́тен *прил см* **ую́тный**.
ую́тно *нареч (расположиться)* comfortably ♦ *как сказ*: **здесь** ~ it's cosy here; **мне здесь** ~ I feel comfortable here.
ую́т|ный (-ен, -на, -но) *прил* cosy.
уязви́мост|ь (-и) *ж* vulnerability.
уязви́м|ый (-, -а, -о) *прил* vulnerable; ~**ое ме́сто** weak spot.
уязв|и́ть (-лю́, -и́шь) *сов перех* to wound, hurt.
уясне́ни|е (-я) *ср* clarification.
уясн|и́ть (-ю́, -и́шь; *impf* **уясня́ть**) *сов перех* (*смысл, значение*) to comprehend; **уясня́ть** (~ *perf*) (**себе́**) to clarify for o.s.

~ Ф, ф ~

Ф, ф *сущ нескл (буква)* the 21st letter of the Russian alphabet.

фа *ср нескл (муз)* fa.

фа́брик|а (-и) *ж* factory; *(ткацкая, бумажная)* mill.

фабрик|ова́ть (-у́ю; *perf* сфабрикова́ть) *несов перех (перен)* to fabricate.

фабри́чный *прил* factory *опред;* **фабри́чная ма́рка** trademark.

фа́бул|а (-ы) *ж* plot.

фавори́т (-а) *м (также СПОРТ)* the favourite *(BRIT)* или favorite *(US)*.

фавори́т|ка (-ки; *gen pl* -ок) *ж см* фавори́т.

фаго́т (-а) *м* bassoon.

фа́з|а (-ы) *ж* phase; *(работы, строительства)* stage.

фаза́н (-а) *м* pheasant.

файл (-а) *м (КОМП)* file.

фак. *сокр* (= факульте́т) Fac. (= *Faculty*).

фа́кел (-а) *м* torch; *(дыма, выбросов)* column.

факс (-а) *м* fax; **посыла́ть (посла́ть** *perf)* ~ to send a fax.

факси́миле *ср нескл* facsimile.

факси́мильный *прил* facsimile *опред.*

факт (-а) *м* fact; **ста́вить (поста́вить** *perf)* кого́-н пе́ред фа́ктом to present sb with a fait accompli; **го́лые фа́кты** the bare facts; ~ **тот, что ...** *(разг)* the fact of the matter is that ....

факти́чески *нареч* actually, in fact.

факти́ческ|ий (-ая, -ое, -ие) *прил (материал, данные)* factual; *(руководитель, положение дел)* real, actual.

фа́ктор (-а) *м* factor.

факту́р|а (-ы) *ж* texture; *(КОММ)* invoice.

факультати́в (-а) *м* optional *или* elective course.

факультати́в|ный (-ен, -на, -но) *прил* optional, elective.

факульте́т (-а) *м* faculty.

фала́нг|а (-и) *ж (АНАТ, ВОЕН)* phalanx.

фа́лд|а (-ы) *ж* tail *(of coat)*; *(складка)* crease.

фальсифика́тор (-а) *м* falsifier.

фальсифика́ци|я (-и) *ж* falsification.

фальсифици́р|овать (-ую) *(не)сов перех* to falsify.

фальста́рт (-а) *м (СПОРТ)* false start.

фальце́т (-а) *м* falsetto.

фальши́в|ить (-лю, -ишь; *perf* сфальши́вить) *несов неперех (петь)* to sing out of tune;

(играть) to play out of tune; *(лицемерить)* to pretend, put on an act.

фальши́в|ка (-ки; *gen pl* -ок) *ж (разг)* forgery.

фальши́вл|ю *несов см* фальши́вить.

фальши́вок *сущ см* фальши́вка.

фальшивомоне́тчик (-а) *м* counterfeiter.

фальшивомоне́тчиц|а (-ы) *ж см* фальшивомоне́тчик.

фальши́в|ый *прил (документ, паспорт)* false, forged; *(монета, банкнот)* counterfeit; *(пение, инструмент)* out of tune; *(борода, улыбка, нота)* false; (-, -а, -о; *игра актёра)* unnatural, artificial; *(человек, поведение)* insincere.

фальш|ь (-и) *ж* insincerity.

фами́ли|я (-и) *ж* surname; *(королевская, старинная)* family; **де́вичья** ~ maiden name; **как Ва́ша** ~? what is your surname?; **моя́** ~ **Серо́в** my surname is Serov.

фами́льный *прил* family *опред.*

фамилья́рен *прил см* фамилья́рный.

фамилья́рнича|ть (-ю) *несов неперех:* ~ (с +*instr)* to be too familiar (with).

фамилья́р|ный (-ен, -на, -но) *прил* over(ly)-familiar.

фанати́зм (-а) *м* fanaticism.

фана́тик (-а) *м (также перен)* fanatic.

фанати́ч|ный (-ен, -на, -но) *прил* fanatical.

фане́р|а (-ы) *ж (для облицовки)* veneer; *(древесный материал)* plywood.

фане́рный *прил* plywood *опред.*

фант (-а) *м* forfeit.

фантазёр (-а) *м* dreamer.

фантазёр|ка (-ки; *gen pl* -ок) *ж см* фантазёр.

фантази́р|овать (-ую) *несов неперех (мечтать)* to dream; *(выдумывать)* to make up stories.

фанта́зи|я (-и) *ж (художника, писателя)* imagination; *(мечта)* fantasy; *(выдумка)* fib; *(муз)* fantasia.

фанта́ст (-а) *м* writer of fantasy; *(научный)* science-fiction writer.

фанта́стик|а (-и) *ж (сказок, преданий)* fantastic element ◆ *собир (ЛИТЕРАТУРА)* fantasy; **нау́чная** ~ science fiction; **э́то** ~! *(разг)* it's incredible!

фантасти́ческ|ий (-ая, -ое, -ие) *прил* fantastic; *(причудливый)* fantastical; *(проект)* fantastic, far-fetched.

фа́нтик (-а) *м* wrapper.

фанфа́р|а (-ы) *ж (инструмент)* bugle; *(обычно*

мн: *сигнал*) fanfare.
ФАО *сокр* FAO (= *Food and Agriculture Organization*).
фа́р|а (-ы) ж (*АВТ, АВИА*) light; **пере́дние ~ы** headlights, headlamps; **за́дние ~ы** rear lights (*BRIT*), taillights *или* taillamps (*US*).
фарао́н (-а) м pharaoh.
фарва́тер (-а) м (*МОР*) fairway, channel.
Фаренге́йт (-а) м Fahrenheit; **70 гра́дусов по ~у** 70 degrees Fahrenheit.
фаре́рск|ий (-ая, -ое, -ие) *прил*: Ф~**ие острова́** the Faroe Islands, the Faroes.
фаринги́т (-а) м pharyngitis.
фарисе́|й (-я) м Pharisee.
фарисе́йств|о (-а) *ср* hypocrisy.
фармаколо́ги|я (-и) ж pharmacology.
фармаце́вт (-а) м chemist, pharmacist.
фарс (-а) м farce.
фа́ртук (-а) м apron.
фарфо́р (-а) м, *собир* porcelain, china.
фарфо́ровый *прил* porcelain, china.
фарцо́вщик (-а) м (*разг*) *illegal trader who sells imported goods to Russians*.
фарцо́вщиц|а (-ы) ж *см* **фарцо́вщик**.
фарш (-а) м stuffing, forcemeat; (*мясной*) mince, minced *или* ground (*US*) meat.
фарширо́ванный *прил* (*КУЛИН*) stuffed.
фарширо́ва́ть (-у́ю; *perf* **зафарширова́ть**) *несов перех* to stuff.
ФАС *сокр* f.a.s. (= *free alongside ship*).
фас (-а) м (*ФОТО*) front.
фаса́д (-а) м (*лицевая сторона*) facade, front; **за́дний ~** back; **боково́й ~** side.
фасова́ть (-у́ю; *perf* **расфасова́ть**) *несов перех* to prepack.
фасо́вк|а (-и) ж packing.
фасо́вочн|ый *прил* (*цех, машина*) packing *опред*; **~ая бума́га** wrapping paper.
фасо́л|ь (-и) ж (*растение*) bean plant ◆ *собир* (*БОТ; семена*) beans мн; **кра́сная ~** kidney beans мн.
фасо́н (-а) м style.
фат|а́ (-ы́) ж veil.
фата́льный (-ен, -ьна, -ьно) *прил* fatal, fateful.
фа́ун|а (-ы) ж fauna.
фаши́зм (-а) м fascism.
фаши́ст (-а) м fascist.
фаши́стск|ий (-ая, -ое, -ие) *прил* fascist.
фая́нс (-а) м (*материал*) faïence ◆ *собир* (*изделия*) faïence, glazed earthenware.
фая́нсовый *прил* (*посуда, изделия*) glazed earthenware *опред*.
ФБР *ср сокр* (= *Федера́льное бюро́ рассле́дований (США)*) FBI (= *Federal Bureau of Investigation*).
февра́л|ь (-я́) м February; *см также* **октя́брь**.
февра́льск|ий (-ая, -ое, -ие) *прил* February *опред*.

федера́льный *прил* federal; **Федера́льное бюро́ рассле́дований** Federal Bureau of Investigation; **Федера́льное собра́ние** (*ПОЛИТ*) the Federal Assembly (*upper house of the Russian parliament*).
федерати́вный *прил* federal.
федера́ци|я (-и) ж federation; **Росси́йская Ф~** the Russian Federation; **Сове́т Ф~й** *upper chamber of the Russian parliament*.
фее́ри|я (-и) ж magic show.
фейерве́рк (-а) м firework.
фе́льдшер (-а) м medical assistant.
фельето́н (-а) м satirical article.
фемини́стк|а (-ки; *gen pl* -ок) ж feminist.
фен (-а) м hairdryer.
фено́мен (-а) м phenomenon (*мн* phenomena).
феномена́льный (-ен, -ьна, -ьно) *прил* phenomenal.
феода́л (-а) м feudal lord.
феодали́зм (-а) м feudalism.
феода́льный *прил* feudal.
ферз|ь (-я́) м (*ШАХМАТЫ*) queen.
фе́рм|а (-ы) ж farm.
ферме́нт (-а) м ferment, enzyme.
фе́рмер (-а) м farmer.
фе́рмерск|ий (-ая, -ое, -ие) *прил*: **~ое хозя́йство** farm.
фестива́л|ь (-я) м festival.
фетр (-а) м felt.
фе́тровый *прил* felt.
фехтова́льщик (-а) м fencer.
фехтова́льщиц|а (-ы) ж *см* **фехтова́льщик**.
фехтова́ни|е (-я) *ср* (*СПОРТ*) fencing.
фешене́бельный (-ен, -ьна, -ьно) *прил* fashionable.
фе́|я (-и) ж fairy.
фи *межд*: ~! ugh!
фиа́лк|а (-ки; *gen pl* -ок) ж violet.
фиа́ско *ср нескл* fiasco; **терпе́ть (потерпе́ть** *perf*) ~ to suffer an embarrassment.
фи́г|а (-и) ж (*БОТ*) fig; (*разг*) fig (*gesture of refusal*); **ни фига́ не полу́чишь (от них)** (*разг*) you won't get a thing out of them; **иди́ на́ фиг** (*разг*) get lost, clear off.
фи́говый *прил* fig *опред*.
фи́го́вый *прил* (*разг*) lousy, rotten.
фигу́р|а (-ы) ж (*ГЕОМ, перен*) figure; (*ШАХМАТЫ*) (chess)piece; **фигу́ра вы́сшего пилота́жа** aerobatic figure.
фигура́льный (-ен, -ьна, -ьно) *прил* figurative.
фигури́|ровать (-ую) *несов неперех* (*присутствовать*) to be present; (*имя, тема*) to figure; ~ (*impf*) **на суде́ в ка́честве свиде́теля** to appear as a witness.
фигури́ст (-а) м figure skater.
фигури́стк|а (-ки; *gen pl* -ок) ж *см* **фигури́ст**.
фигу́р|ка (-ки; *gen pl* -ок) ж (*скульптура*) figurine, statuette; (*обычно мн: игральная*) piece.

фигу́рный *прил* (*резьба*) figured; (*СПОРТ*) figure *опред*; **фигу́рное ката́ние** figure skating; **фигу́рные ско́бки** curly *или* brace brackets.

фигу́рок *сущ см* **фигу́рка**.

Фи́джи *ср нескл* Fiji.

фи́зик (-а) *м* physicist.

фи́зик|а (-и) *ж* physics.

физио́лог (-а) *м* physiologist.

физиологи́чес|кий (-ая, -ое, -ие) *прил* physiological.

физиоло́ги|я (-и) *ж* physiology.

физионо́ми|я (-и) *ж* (*разг*) face.

физиотерапе́вт (-а) *м* physiotherapist.

физиотерапевти́чес|кий (-ая, -ое, -ие) *прил* physiotherapy *опред*.

физиотерапи́|я (-и) *ж* physiotherapy.

физи́ческ|ий (-ая, -ое, -ие) *прил* (*также СПОРТ, физ*) physical; (*труд*) manual; **физи́ческая культу́ра** physical education; **физи́ческие упражне́ния** physical exercise *ед*; **физи́ческое лицо́** (*ЮР*) individual; **физи́ческое наси́лие** physical violence.

физкульту́р|а (-ы) *ж сокр* (= **физи́ческая культу́ра**) PE (= *physical education*).

физма́т (-а) *м сокр* = **фи́зико-математи́ческий факульте́т**.

фикс *м*: **иде́я** ~ idée fixe.

фикса́ж (-а) *м* (*ФОТО*) fixer.

фикса́ци|я (-и) *ж* (*ТЕХ*) clamping; (*ФОТО*) fixing.

фикси́р|овать (-ую; *perf* **зафикси́ровать**) *несов перех* (*события, факты, показания*) to record, chronicle; (*срок, да́ту, це́ны*) to fix, set; (*внима́ние, взгляд*) to fix; (*груз, тормоз*) to clamp, fix.

фикти́в|ный (-ен, -на, -но) *прил* fictitious; **фикти́вный брак** (*ЮР*) marriage of convenience.

фи́кус (-а) *м* ficus; (*каучуконосный*) rubber plant.

фи́кци|я (-и) *ж* fiction.

филармо́ни|я (-и) *ж* (*зал*) concert hall; (*организация*) philharmonic society.

филатели́ст (-а) *м* philatelist.

филе́ *ср нескл* (*сорт мяса*) fillet.

филиа́л (-а) *м* branch.

филигра́н|ный (-ен, -на, -но) *прил* (*изделия, орнамент*) filigree; (*перен: работа*) intricate.

фи́лин (-а) *м* eagle owl.

филиппи́н|ец (-ца) *м* Filipino.

филиппи́н|ка (-ки; *gen pl* -ок) *ж см* **филиппи́нец**.

филиппи́нск|ий (-ая, -ое, -ие) *прил* Filipino, Philippine.

филиппи́нца *итп сущ см* **филиппи́нец**.

Филиппи́н|ы (-) *мн* the Philippines *мн*.

фило́лог (-а) *м* philologist (*specialist in languages and literature*).

филологи́чес|кий (-ая, -ое, -ие) *прил* philological; **филологи́ческий факульте́т** faculty of philology.

филоло́ги|я (-и) *ж* philology (*study of language and literature*).

фило́н|ить (-ю, -ишь) *несов неперех* (*разг*) to skive.

фило́соф (-а) *м* philosopher.

филосо́фи|я (-и) *ж* philosophy.

филфа́к (-а) *м сокр* = **филологи́ческий факульте́т**.

фильм (-а) *м* film; **сего́дня идёт хоро́ший** ~ there's a good film on today.

фильмоско́п (-а) *м* slide projector.

фильтр (-а) *м* filter.

фильтр|ова́ть (-у́ю; *perf* **профильтрова́ть**) *несов перех* to filter.

фин. *сокр* (= **фина́нсовый**) fin. (= *financial*).

фина́л (-а) *м* (*спекта́кля, конце́рта*) finale; (*СПОРТ*) final; **выходи́ть (вы́йти** *perf*) **в** ~ to reach the final.

фина́льный *прил* (*также СПОРТ, КОММ*) final *опред*.

финанси́рование (-я) *ср* financing.

финанси́р|овать (-ую) *несов перех* to finance.

финанси́ст (-а) *м* (*предприниматель*) financier; (*специалист*) specialist in financial matters.

фина́нсовый *прил* financial; (*год*) fiscal; (*отдел, инспектор, комиссия*) finance *опред*; ~ **институ́т** institute of finance; ~ **отчёт** financial statement.

фина́нс|ы (-ов) *мн* finances *мн*; (*де́ньги*) cash *ед*; **Министе́рство** ~**ов** ≈ the Treasury (*BRIT*), ≈ the Treasury Department *или* Department of the Treasury (*US*).

фи́ник (-а) *м* (*плод*) date; (*де́рево*) date palm.

фини́фт|ь (-и) *ж, собир decorated Russian enamel*.

фи́ниш (-а) *м* (*СПОРТ*) finish; **приходи́ть (прийти́** *perf*) **к** ~**у** to reach the finish.

финиши́р|овать (-ую) (*не*)*сов неперех* to finish, come in.

фи́нишн|ый *прил* finishing *опред*; **выходи́ть (вы́йти** *perf*) **на** ~**ую прямую** to reach the final straight; (*перен*) to be on the home straight; ~**ая черта́/ле́нточка** finishing line/tape.

фи́н|ка (-ки; *gen pl* -ок) *ж см* **финн**; (*разг: нож*) Finnish knife.

Финля́нди|я (-и) *ж* Finland.

финн (-а) *м* Finn.

фи́нок *сущ см* **фи́нка**.

фи́нск|ий (-ая, -ое, -ие) *прил* Finnish; ~ **язы́к** Finnish; **Фи́нский зали́в** Gulf of Finland.

финт (-а́) *м* (*СПОРТ*) feint; (*разг: уло́вка*) trick.

фин|ти́ть (-чу́, -ти́шь) *несов неперех* (*разг*) to be tricky.

Ф.И.О. *сокр* (= **фами́лия, и́мя, о́тчество**) surname, first name, patronymic.

ф.и.о. *сокр* = **Ф.И.О.**

фиоле́товый *прил* purple.

фи́рм|а (-ы) *ж* firm; (*разг: модная вещь*) quality; **секре́т** ~**ы** (*разг*) trade secret.

фи́рменный *прил* (*марка, ресторан*) firm's, company *опред*; (*магазин*) chain *опред*; (*разг*:

джинсы, юбка, костюм итп) quality *опред* (*usually of imported brand names*); **фи́рменный знак** brand name.

фиста́шк|**а** (**-и**) *ж* pistachio.

фити́л|**ь** (**-я́**) *м* wick; (*взрывных устройств*) fuse.

ФИФА́ *ж сокр* (= *Междунаро́дная федера́ция футбо́ла*) FIFA (= *Fédération Internationale de Football Association*).

фи́фа|**а** (**-ы**) *ж* (*разг*) bimbo, dolly bird.

фи́шк|**а** (**-ки**; *gen pl* **-ек**) *ж* counter, chip.

флаг (**-а**) *м* flag.

фла́гман (**-а**) *м* (*командующий*) flag officer; (*корабль*) flagship.

флагшто́к (**-а**) *м* flagpole.

флаж|**о́к** (**-ка́**) *ж* flag.

флако́н (**-а**) *м* bottle.

флама́нд|**ец** (**-ца**) *м* Fleming.

флама́нд|**ка** (**-ки**; *gen pl* **-ок**) *ж см* **флама́ндец.**

флама́ндск|**ий** (**-ая, -ое, -ие**) *прил* Flemish; ~ **язы́к** Flemish.

флама́ндца *итп сущ см* **флама́ндец.**

флами́нго *м нескл* flamingo.

фланг (**-а**) *м* flank.

Фла́ндри|**я** (**-и**) *ж* Flanders.

фла́нелевый *прил* flannel.

флане́л|**ь** (**-и**) *ж* flannel.

флегма́тик (**-а**) *м*: **он** ~ he is phlegmatic.

флегмати́ч|**ный** (**-ен, -на, -но**) *прил* phlegmatic.

флейт|**а** (**-ы**) *ж* flute.

флейти́ст (**-а**) *м* flautist.

фле́кси|**я** (**-и**) *ж* inflection.

флекти́вный *прил* inflected.

фли́гел|**ь** (**-я**) *м* (*АРХИТ*) wing.

флирт (**-а**) *м* flirtation.

флирт|**ова́ть** (**-у́ю**) *несов неперех*: ~ (**с** +*instr*) to flirt (with).

флокс (**-а**) *м* phlox.

флома́стер (**-а**) *м* felt-tip (pen).

фло́р|**а** (**-ы**) *ж* flora.

флоренти́йский (**-ая, -ое, -ие**) *прил* Florentine.

Флоре́нци|**я** (**-и**) *ж* Florence.

флот (**-а**) *м* (*ВОЕН*) navy; (*МОР*) fleet.

флоти́ли|**я** (**-и**) *ж* flotilla.

флю́гер (**-а**) *м* wind gauge; (*на башне*) weather vane.

флюи́д|**ы** (**-ов**) *мн* (*разг*) vibes *мн*.

флюорогра́фи|**я** (**-и**) *ж* fluorography.

флюс (**-а**) *м* (dental) abscess, gumboil.

фля́г|**а** (**-и**) *ж* (*для воды, спирта*) flask; (*для молока, для сметаны*) churn.

ФНО *м сокр* (= *Фронт национа́льного освобожде́ния*) NLF (= *National Liberation Front*).

ФОБ *сокр* (= *фра́нко-борт*) f.o.b. (= *free on board*).

фойе́ *ср нескл* foyer.

фокстерье́р (**-а**) *м* fox terrier.

фокстро́т (**-а**) *м* foxtrot.

фо́кус (**-а**) *м* trick; (*ТЕХ, перен*) focus; **выки́дывать (вы́кинуть** *perf*) ~ (*перен: разг*) to start some nonsense.

фо́кусник (**-а**) *м* conjurer.

фолкле́ндск|**ий** (**-ая, -ое, -ие**) *прил*: **Ф~ие острова́** the Falkland Islands, the Falklands.

фольг|**а́** (**-и́**) *ж* foil.

фолькло́р (**-а**) *м* folklore.

фолькло́рный *прил* (*фестиваль, ансамбль*) folk *опред*.

фон (**-а**) *м* background; **на фо́не чего́-н** against a background of sth; **на фо́не кого́-н** next to sb, compared to sb.

фона́р|**ь** (**-я́**) *м* (*уличный*) lamp; (*карманный*) torch; (*разг: синяк*) black eye, shiner; **ему́ всё до фонаря́** (*разг*) he doesn't give a toss about anything.

фонд (**-а**) *м* (*организация*) fund, foundation; (*денежные средства, запас*) fund; (*жилищный, семенной, земельный*) resources *мн*; **фо́нды** (*ценные бумаги*) stocks; **уставно́й** ~ (*КОММ*) authorized capital.

фо́ндов|**ый** *прил*: ~**ая би́ржа** stock exchange.

фоне́тик|**а** (**-и**) *ж* phonetics.

фоногра́мм|**а** (**-ы**) *ж* recording; **петь (спеть** *perf*) **под** ~**у** to mime to a recording.

фоноло́ги|**я** (**-и**) *ж* phonology.

фоноте́к|**а** (**-и**) *ж* record and tape collection.

фонта́н (**-а**) *м* fountain; (*нефти*) gusher.

фо́р|**а** (**-ы**) *ж*: **дать кому́-н** ~**у** (*разг*) to give sb a start *или* an advantage; (*перен: разг*) to be miles better than sb.

фо́рвард (**-а**) *м* forward.

форе́л|**ь** (**-и**) *ж* trout.

фо́рм|**а** (**-ы**) *ж* (*также ЛИНГ*) form; (*одежда*) uniform; (*ТЕХ*) mould; (*КУЛИН*) (cake) tin (*BRIT*) *или* pan (*US*); **быть** (*impf*) **в** ~**е** to be in good form; *см также* **фо́рмы.**

форма́лен *прил см* **форма́льный.**

формали́зм (**-а**) *м* (*в искусстве, в науке*) formalism; ~ **в рабо́те** bureaucratic attitude to work.

формали́ст (**-а**) *м* (*бюрократ*) bureaucrat.

формали́стик|**а** (**-и**) *ж* bureaucracy.

форма́льно *нареч* (*относиться*) formally; ~ **он прав** factually he's right.

форма́льност|**ь** (**-и**) *ж* formality.

форма́льн|**ый** (**-ен, -ьна, -ьно**) *прил* (*отношение, подход*) bureaucratic; (*ответ*) nominal; (*no short form; согласие, метод, логика*) formal.

форма́т (**-а**) *м* format.

формати́р|**овать** (**-ую**) (**не**)*сов перех* (*КОМП*) to format.

форма́ци|**я** (**-и**) *ж* (*общественная*) structure; **челове́к но́вой** ~**и** forward-thinking person.

The spelling rules for Russian are shown on page xvii.

фо́рменн|ый *прил (безобразие, негодяй)* absolute; ~ **бланк** official form; **фо́рменная оде́жда** uniform.

формирова́ни|е (-я) *ср* formation; **вое́нное ~** military unit.

формир|ова́ть (-у́ю; *perf* **сформирова́ть**) *несов перех* to form

► **формирова́ться** (*perf* **сформирова́ться**) *несов возв* to form.

фо́рмул|а (-ы) *ж* formula.

формули́р|овать (-ую; *perf* **сформули́ровать**) *несов перех* to formulate.

формулиро́в|ка (-ки; *gen pl* -ок) *ж (мысли, предложения)* formulation; *(определение)* definition.

формуля́р (-а) *м* library ticket *или* card.

фо́рм|ы (-) *мн (разг)* curves *мн*.

форпо́ст (-а) *м (ВОЕН)* outpost; *(перен: демократии, науки)* stronghold.

форс (-а) *м (разг)* swank.

форси́р|овать (-ую) *(не)сов перех* to force.

фор|си́ть (-шу́, -си́шь) *несов неперех (разг)* to show off.

форсу́н|ка (-ки; *gen pl* -ок) *ж (двигателя)* fuel injector.

форт (-а; *loc sg* -у́, *nom pl* -ы́) *м* fort.

фортепья́нный *прил* piano *опред*.

фортепья́но *ср нескл* piano.

фо́рточ|ка (-ки; *gen pl* -ек) *ж* hinged, upper pane for ventilation.

форту́н|а (-ы) *ж* fortune.

фо́рум (-а) *м* forum.

форшу́ *несов см* **форси́ть**.

фосфа́т (-а) *м (обычно мн)* phosphate.

фо́сфор (-а) *м* phosphorous.

фо́то *ср нескл (разг)* photo.

фотоаппара́т (-а) *м* camera.

фотоателье́ *ср нескл* photographic *или* photographer's studio.

фотобума́г|а (-и) *ж* photographic paper.

фотогени́ч|ный (-ен, -на, -но) *прил* photogenic.

фото́граф (-а) *м* photographer.

фотографи́р|овать (-ую; *perf* **сфотографи́ровать**) *несов перех* to photograph

► **фотографи́роваться** (*perf* **сфотографи́роваться**) *несов возв* to have one's photo(graph) taken.

фотогра́фи|я (-и) *ж (занятие)* photography; *(снимок)* photograph; *(учреждение)* photographer's studio.

фотока́рточ|ка (-ки; *gen pl* -ек) *ж* photo.

фотоси́нтез (-а) *м* photosynthesis.

фототелегра́мм|а (-ы) *ж* phototelegram.

фотоэлеме́нт (-а) *м* photocell.

фрагме́нт (-а) *м (фильма, спектакля)* excerpt; *(древних сосудов итп)* fragment.

фрагмента́р|ный (-ен, -на, -но) *прил* fragmentary.

фра́з|а (-ы) *ж* phrase.

фразеоло́ги|я (-и) *ж (линг)* phraseology;

(пустословие) rhetoric.

фрак (-а) *м* tail coat, tails *мн*.

фракцио́нный *прил* factional.

фра́кци|я (-и) *ж* faction.

франк (-а) *м* franc.

фра́нко *прил неизм (КОММ)*: ~ **вдоль бо́рта су́дна** free alongside ship; ~-**железнодоро́жный ваго́н** free on rail.

Фра́нкфурт (-а) *м* Frankfurt.

франт (-а) *м* dandy.

Фра́нци|я (-и) *ж* France.

францу́жен|ка (-ки; *gen pl* -ок) *ж* Frenchwoman *(мн* Frenchwomen).

францу́з (-а) *м* Frenchman *(мн* Frenchmen).

францу́зск|ий (-ая, -ое, -ие) *прил* French; ~ **язы́к** French.

франши́з|а (-ы) *ж (КОММ)* franchise; **держа́тель/предоста́витель ~ы** franchisee/franchiser.

фрахт (-а) *м* freight; ~, **упла́чиваемый по прибы́тие** *(КОММ)* freight inward; ~, **упла́чиваемый в порту́ вы́грузки** *(КОММ)* freight forward.

фрахт|ова́ть (-у́ю; *perf* **зафрахтова́ть**) *несов перех* to charter.

ФРГ *ж сокр (ИСТ:* = Федерати́вная Респу́блика Герма́нии) FRG (= *Federal Republic of Germany*).

фрега́т (-а) *м* frigate.

фре́йлин|а (-ы) *ж* lady-in-waiting *(мн* ladies-in-waiting).

фре́с|ка (-ки; *gen pl* -ок) *ж* fresco.

фриво́лен *прил см* **фриво́льный**.

фриво́льность (-и) *ж* frivolity.

фриво́льный (-ен, -ьна, -ьно) *прил* frivolous.

фриз (-а) *м* frieze.

фрикаде́ль|ка (-ьки; *gen pl* -ек) *ж* meatball.

фронт (-а; *nom pl* -ы́) *м* front; **рабо́тать** *(impf)* **на два фро́нта** *(перен)* to do two things at the same time.

фронта́льный (-ен, -ьна, -ьно) *прил (ВОЕН)* frontal; *(перен)* по́лный, general.

фронтиспи́с (-а) *м* frontispiece.

фронтови́к (-а́) *м* front line soldier; *(ветеран)* war veteran.

фронто́н (-а) *м (АРХИТ)* pediment.

фрукт (-а) *м (БОТ)* fruit; *(разг: пренебр: человек)* suspicious character.

фрукто́вый *прил* fruit *опред*.

фрукто́з|а (-ы) *ж* fructose.

ФСК *ж сокр* (= Федера́льная слу́жба контрразве́дки) *Russian counterespionage intelligence service*.

фтор (-а) *м* fluorin(e).

фу *межд*: ~! ugh!

фу́г|а (-и) *ж* fugue.

фу́ксия (-и) *ж* fuchsia.

фуже́р (-а) *м* wineglass; *(для шампанского)* flute.

фунда́мент (-а) *м (СТРОИТ)* foundation, base; *(перен: семьи, науки)* foundation, basis.

фундамента́л|ьный (-ен, -ьна, -ьно) *прил*
(*здание, мост*) sound, solid; (*перен: знания,
труд*) profound; ~**ьные нау́ки** basic science.
фунду́к (-а́) *м* (*кустарник*) hazel; (*плод*)
hazelnut.
фуникулёр (-а) *м* funicular railway.
функциона́л|ьный (-ен, -ьна, -ьно) *прил*
functional; **функциона́льная кла́виша** (*КОМП*)
function key.
функционе́р (-а) *м* official, functionary.
функциони́р|овать (-ую) *несов неперех* to
function.
фу́нкци|я (-и) *ж* function; (*круг обязанностей*)
function, duties *мн*.
фунт (-а) *м* pound.
фура́ж (-а́) *м* fodder.
фура́ж|ка (-ки; *gen pl* -ек) *ж* cap; (*ВОЕН*) forage
cap.
фурго́н (-а) *м* (*АВТ*) van; (*конная повозка*)
(covered) wagon.
фу́ри|я (-и) *ж* (*разг*) virago.
фуро́р (-а) *м* furore; **производи́ть (произвести́**

perf) ~ to create a furore.
фуру́нкул (-а) *м* boil.
фут (-а) *м* foot.
футбо́л (-а) *м* football (*BRIT*), soccer;
америка́нский ~ (American) football.
футболи́ст (-а) *м* footballer (*BRIT*), soccer
player.
футбо́л|ка (-ки; *gen pl* -ок) *ж* T-shirt, tee shirt.
футбо́льный *прил* football *опред*, soccer
опред; **футбо́льный мяч** football.
футля́р (-а) *м* case.
фуфа́|йка (-йки; *gen pl* -ек) *ж* (*ватник*) padded
jacket; (*вязаная рубашка*) jersey.
фы́рка|ть (-ю) *несов неперех* (*животное*) to
snort; (*разг: смеяться*) to snort with laughter; (:
брюзжать) to complain.
фы́ркн|уть (-у, -ешь) *сов неперех* (*животное*)
to give a snort; (*разг: издать смешок*) to snort
with laughter.
фырч|а́ть (-у́, -и́шь) *несов неперех* (*разг*) to
snort; (*брюзжать*) to whinge.
фью́черс|ы (-ов) *мн* (*КОММ*) futures *мн*.

X, x *сущ нескл (буква)* the 22nd letter of the Russian alphabet.

ха́ки *прил неизм, ср нескл* khaki.

хала́т (-а) *м (домашний)* dressing gown; **ба́нный ~** bathrobe.

хала́тен *прил см* **хала́тный.**

хала́тность (-и) *ж* negligence.

хала́тный (-ен, -на, -но) *прил* negligent.

халв|а́ (-ы́) *ж* halva.

халту́р|а (-ы) *ж (разг: плохая работа)* shoddy work; (: *работа на стороне*) moonlighting.

халту́р|ить (-ю, -ишь); *perf* **схалту́рить** *несов неперех (разг)* to cut corners; (*no perf; разг: работать на стороне*) to moonlight.

хам (-а) *м (разг)* brute, lout.

хамелео́н (-а) *м (также перен)* chameleon.

хаме́|ть (-ю); *perf* **охаме́ть** *несов неперех* to become impudent.

хам|и́ть (-лю́, -и́шь; *perf* **нахами́ть)** *несов неперех:* ~ (+*dat*) *(разг)* to be cheeky (BRIT) или rude (US) (to).

ха́м|ка (-ки; *gen pl* **-ок)** *ж (разг)* hussy.

хамлю́ *сов см* **хамить.**

ха́мок *сущ см* **ха́мка.**

ха́мск|ий (-ая, -ое, -ие) *прил (разг)* brutish, loutish.

ха́мств|о (-а) *ср* rudeness.

хан (-а) *м* khan.

хандр|а́ (-ы́) *ж* depression.

хандр|и́ть (-ю́, -и́шь) *несов неперех* to feel down.

ханж|а́ (-и́; *gen pl* **-е́й)** *м/ж* prude, prig.

ха́нжеств|о (-а) *ср* prudishness, priggishness.

Хано́|й (-я) *м* Hanoi.

ха́ос (-а) *м* chaos.

хаоти́чен *прил см* **хаоти́чный.**

хаоти́ческ|ий (-ая, -ое, -ие) *прил* chaotic.

хаоти́ч|ный (-ен, -на, -но) *прил* = **хаоти́ческий.**

ха́па|ть (-ю, -ешь) *несов перех (разг: хватать)* to grab at; (: *присваивать*) to swipe.

хара́ктер (-а) *м* nature; *(человека)* personality; **он челове́к с ~ом** he has a lot of character; **выде́рживать (вы́держать** *perf*) ~ to hold firm.

характе́рен *прил см* **характе́рный.**

характериз|ова́ть (-у́ю) *несов перех* to be typical of; *(perf* **охарактеризова́ть***; персонаж, эпоху итп)* to characterize; **его́ ~у́ет доброта́** he is a kind person

▶ **характеризова́ться** *несов возв* (+*instr*) to be characterized by.

характери́стик|а (-и) *ж (документ)* (character) reference; *(описание)* description.

характе́р|ный (-ен, -на, -но) *прил (внешность, поведение)* distinctive; *(свойственный):* ~ **(для** +*gen*) characteristic (of); (*no short form; обычаи, танцы итп*) typical; **для него́ ~ перио́ды депре́ссии** he tends to go through bouts of depression.

ха́рка|ть (-ю) *несов неперех* (+*instr; кровью, слизью*) to cough up.

ха́рти|я (-и) *ж (документ)* charter.

харч (-а; *nom pl* **-и́**, *gen pl* **-е́й)** *м (обычно мн: разг)* grub *ед*, chow *ед*.

харчо́ *ср нескл* spicy Georgian meat and vegetable soup.

ха́р|я (-и) *ж (разг)* mug *(face)*.

ха́т|а (-ы) *ж* cottage *(in Southern Russia and Ukraine)*; **моя́ ~ с кра́ю** *(разг)* it's nothing to do with me.

ха-ха *межд* ha-ha.

хачапу́ри *ср нескл* flat Georgian pie filled with cheese.

ха́|ять (-ю) *несов перех (разг)* to slag off.

х/б *сокр* = **хлопчатобума́жный.**

хвал|а́ (-ы́) *ж* praise.

хвале́бный *прил* complimentary.

хвалёный *прил* celebrated.

хвал|и́ть (-ю́, -ишь); *perf* **похвали́ть** *несов перех* to praise

▶ **хвали́ться** *(perf* **похвали́ться***) несов возв:* ~**ся** (+*instr*) *(разг)* to show off (about).

хва́ста|ться (-юсь); *perf* **похва́статься** *несов возв:* ~ (+*instr*) to boast (about).

хвастли́в|ый (-, -а, -о) *прил* boastful.

хвастовств|о́ (-а́) *ср* boasting.

хвасту́н (-а́) *м (разг)* show-off.

хвасту́н|ья (-ьи; *gen pl* **-ий)** *ж см* **хвасту́н.**

хвата́|ть (-ю); *perf* **схвати́ть** *несов перех* to grab (hold of); *(преступника)* to arrest; *(разг: простуду, насморк)* to catch; (: *плохую отме́тку, оплеуху*) to get ◆ *(perf* **хвати́ть)** *безл* (+*gen; денег, времени итп*) to have enough; **мне ~ет де́нег на еду́** I've got enough to buy food; **его́ не хвати́ло на э́то** he wasn't up to it; **он ~л всё подря́д** *(разг)* he grabbed whatever he could; ~ *(impf)* **за́ душу** to tug at one's heartstrings; ~ **(схвати́ть** *perf***) что-н на лету́** to grasp sth in an instant; **э́того ещё не ~ло!**

(*разг*) as if that wasn't enough!; **не ~ет то́лько, что́бы он отказа́лся** (*разг*) now all we need is for him to refuse

▶ **хвата́ться** (*perf* **схвати́ться**) *несов возв*: **~ся за** +*acc* (*за се́рдце*) to clutch at; (*за дверь, за ору́жие*) to grab; **~ся** (*impf*) **за всё сра́зу** (*разг*) to try to do everything at once; **~ся** (**схвати́ться** *perf*) **за соло́минку** to clutch at straws; **~ся** (**схвати́ться** *perf*) **за́ голову** (*перен*) to panic.

хва|ти́ть (-чу́, -тишь) *сов от* **хвата́ть ♦** *перех* (*разг*): **~ по рю́мочке/ча́йку** to have a quick drink/cuppa; (+*gen*; *беды, горя*) to suffer; (*разг*: *уда́рить*) to whack, thump ♦ *безл* (*разг*): **хва́тит!** that's enough!; **его́ ~ти́л парали́ч** he was paralysed; **её ~ти́л уда́р** she had a stroke; **он ~ти́л меня́ по голове́** he thumped me on the head; **он ~ти́л кулако́м по столу́** he banged on the table with his fist; **хва́тит спо́ров** *или* **спо́рить!** (*разг*) that's enough of this arguing!; **~** (*perf*) **че́рез край** to go too far; **с меня́ хва́тит!** I've had enough!

▶ **хвати́ться** *сов возв* (*разг*): **~ся чего́-н/ кого́-н** to notice that sth/sb is gone.

хва́т|ка (-ки; *gen pl* -ок) *ж* grip; (*перен: ло́вкость*) skill; **делова́я ~** business acumen; **вцепля́ться** (**вцепи́ться** *perf*) **в что-н/кого́-н мёртвой ~кой** (*также перен*) to cling onto sth/sb for dear life.

хвать *как сказ* (*разг*): **он меня́ ~ по голове́** he whacked me right in the head; **я поверну́лся, и ~ нет кошелька́** I turned round and my purse (*BRIT*) *или* wallet (*US*) had vanished.

хвачу́(сь) *сов см* **хвати́ть(ся)**.

х-во *сокр* = **хозя́йство**.

хво́йный *прил* coniferous; **хво́йное де́рево** conifer.

хвора́|ть (-ю) *несов неперех* to feel poorly (*BRIT*), to feel sick (*US*).

хво́рост (-а; *part gen* -у) *м собир* firewood; (*кулин*) *sugar-coated strips of dough fried in oil.*

хворости́н|а (-ы) *ж* switch.

хво́рый *прил* (*разг*) ill.

хво́р|ь (-и) *ж* ailment.

хвост (-á) *м* tail; (*по́езда*) tail end; (*перен: пы́ли, зева́к итп*) trail; (*разг: о́чередь*) queue (*BRIT*), line (*US*); (: *по матема́тике итп*) *an exam which has to be taken again.*

хво́стик (-а) *м* (*мы́ши, реди́ски*) tail; **ему́ 50 с ~ом** (*разг*) he's just over 50.

хвостов|о́й *прил* tail *опред*; **~а́я часть** (*самолёта, по́езда*) the tail end.

хвощ (-á) *м* (*БОТ*) horsetail.

хво́|я (-и) *ж собир* needles *мн* (*of a conifer*).

ХДС *м сокр* (= **Христиа́нско-демократи́ческий сою́з**) CDU (= *Christian Democratic Union*).

хек (-а) *м* whiting.

хе́кер (-а) *м* (*КОМП*) hacker.

Хе́льсинки *м нескл* Helsinki.

хе́рес (-а; *part gen* -у) *м* sherry.

хи́жин|а (-ы) *ж* hut.

хи́л|ый (-, -á, -о) *прил* (*мужчи́на, рука́*) puny; (*расте́ние, ребёнок*) sickly; (*дом, постро́йка*) rickety.

хи́мик (-а) *м* chemist.

химика́т (-а) *м* chemical.

химиотерапи́|я (-и) *ж* chemotherapy.

хими́ческ|ий (-ая, -ое, -ие) *прил* chemical *опред*; (*факульте́т, кабине́т*) chemistry *опред*; **хими́ческий каранда́ш** *graphite pencil which writes in purple when moistened.*

хи́ми|я (-и) *ж* chemistry; **бытова́я ~** household chemicals *мн*.

химчи́ст|ка (-ки; *gen pl* -ок) *ж сокр* = **хими́ческая чи́стка**; (*проце́сс*) dry-cleaning; (*пункт приёма*) dry-cleaner('s).

хини́н (-а) *м* quinine.

хи́ппи *м нескл* hippie.

хире́|ть (-ю; *perf* **захире́ть**) *несов неперех* (*челове́к*) to waste away; (*расте́ние*) to wither; (*перен: тво́рчество, тала́нт*) to dry up.

хирома́нти|я (-и) *ж* palmistry.

Хироси́ма (-ы) *ж* Hiroshima.

хиру́рг (-а) *м* surgeon.

хирурги́ческ|ий (-ая, -ое, -ие) *прил* surgical; (*больно́й, кли́ника*) surgery *опред*.

хирурги́|я (-и) *ж* surgery.

хит (-а) *м* (*МУЗ*) hit.

хитёр *прил см* **хи́трый**.

хитре́ц (-á) *м* cunning devil.

хитр|и́ть (-ю́, -и́шь; *perf* **схитри́ть**) *несов неперех* to act slyly.

хи́тро *нареч* cunningly; (*сде́ланный*) intricately.

хи́трост|ь (-и) *ж* slyness; (*уло́вка*) cunning.

хитроу́ми|е (-я) *ср* ingenuity.

хитроу́мный (-ен, -на, -но) *прил* ingenious.

хи́т|рый (-ёр, -ра́, -ро) *прил* sly, cunning; (*изобрета́тельный*) cunning; (*замыслова́тый*) intricate.

хихи́ка|ть (-ю) *несов неперех* (*разг*) to giggle; (: *смея́ться исподтишка́*) to snigger.

хи́щен *прил см* **хи́щный**.

хище́ни|е (-я) *ср* misappropriation.

хи́щник (-а) *м* (*также перен*) predator.

хи́щниц|а (-ы) *ж* (*перен*) predator.

хи́щническ|ий (-ая, -ое, -ие) *прил* (*поли́тика, инсти́нкт*) predatory; (*истребле́ние ле́са, охо́та*) ruthless; (*испо́льзование ресу́рсов*) rapacious.

хи́щ|ный (-ен, -на, -но) *прил* (*также перен*) predatory; (*деле́ц, торга́ш*) cutthroat; **~ная пти́ца** bird of prey.

хладнокро́вен *прил см* **хладнокро́вный**.

хладнокро́ви|е (-я) *ср* composure.

хладнокро́в|ный (-ен, -на, -но) *прил* composed; (*уби́йство итп*) cold-blooded.

хлам (-а) *м собир* (*также перен*) junk.

хлеб (-а) *м* bread; (*зерно́*) grain; (*nom pl* **-ы**;

формово́й, кру́глый) loaf (*мн* loaves); (*nom pl* -а́; озимые, яровые) cereal; **зараба́тывать** (*impf*) **на** ~ to earn a crust; ~ **насу́щный** bread and butter (*fig*); ~**соль** bread and salt (*traditionally offered to guests as a symbol of hospitality*).

хлеба́ть (-ю) *несов перех* (*разг*) to slurp.

хлебе́ц (-ца́) *м* loaf; **хрустя́щие ~цы́** ≈ crispbreads.

хле́бниц|а (-ы) *ж* bread basket; (*для хранения*) bread bin.

хлебну́ть (-у́, -ёшь) *сов перех* (*разг*: чай итп) to take a gulp of; ~ (*perf*) **го́ря** to see a lot of sorrow.

хле́бн|ый *прил* bread *опред*; (*злак, растение*) corn *опред*; (*край, поле*) fertile; (*разг*: местечко) well-paid; **э́то год был** ~ we had a good harvest this year; ~**ые дро́жжи** baker's yeast.

хлебобу́лочн|ый *прил*: ~**ые изде́лия** bread products *мн*.

хлебозаво́д (-а) *м* bakery.

хлебре́з|ка (-ки; gen pl -ок) *ж* bread slicer.

хлеборо́б (-а) *м* harvester.

хлеборо́дный *прил* (*край, земля*) fertile; **э́тот год был** ~ we had a good harvest this year.

хлебосо́льный *прил* hospitable.

хлебца́ *итп сущ см* **хлебе́ц**.

хлев (-а; loc sg -у́, nom pl -а́) *м* cowshed; (*перен: разг*) pigsty.

хлеста́ть (-ещу́, -е́щешь) *несов перех* (ремнём, кнутом) to whip; (*по лицу, по щекам*) to slap; (*разг*: водку, пиво) to knock back ♦ *неперех* (*дождь*) to lash down; (*вода, кровь*) to gush; (*пули*) to rain down; **во́лны** ~**еста́ли о борт ло́дки** the waves lashed against the side of the boat.

хлёст|кий (-кая, -кое, -кие; -ок, -ка́, -ко) *прил* (*перен*) scathing.

хлестну́ть (-у́, -ёшь) *сов перех* to whip; (*по щеке*) to slap.

хлёсток *прил см* **хлёсткий**.

хлещу́ *итп несов см* **хлеста́ть**.

хли́пкий (-ая, -ое, -ие) *прил* (*разг*: здоровье) poor; (: человек, земля) weedy; (: стол, строение) wobbly.

хлоп *как сказ* (*разг*): **он меня́** ~ **по спине́** he whacked me right in the back; **он** ~ **на крова́ть** he flopped onto the bed.

хло́па|ть (-ю) *несов перех* (*ладонью*) to slap; (*кнутом*) to lash ♦ *неперех* (+*instr*; дверью, крышкой) to slam; (+*dat*; артисту, певцу) to clap; (*хлопушка, выстрел*) to go bang; ~ (*impf*) **уша́ми/глаза́ми** to look stupid/baffled.

хло́пка *сущ см* **хло́пок**.

хлопка́ *сущ см* **хлопо́к**.

хлопково́дств|о (-а) *ср* cotton growing.

хло́пковый *прил* cotton.

хло́пнуть (-у, -ешь) *сов перех* (*по спине*) to slap ♦ *неперех* (*в ладони*) to clap; (*дверь*) to slam shut; (*хлопушка, выстрел*) to go bang; (+*instr*; дверью) to slam; (*кнутом*) to crack.

хло́п|ок (-ка) *м* cotton.

хлоп|о́к (-ка́) *м* (*удар в ладоши*) clap; (*выстрела, кнута*) crack; (*по спине, по затылку*) slap.

хлоп|ота́ть (-очу́, -о́чешь) *несов неперех* (по дому, по хозяйству) to busy o.s.; (*добиваться*): ~ **о** +*prp* (о разрешении, о пособии итп) to be busy trying to get; ~ (*impf*) **о ком-н** или **за кого́-н** to trouble o.s. on sb's behalf.

хлопотли́в|ый (-, -а, -о) *прил* (*человек*) busy; (*дело, обязанности*) troublesome.

хло́потный *прил* (*разг*) troublesome.

хло́п|оты (-от; dat pl -отам) *мн* (по хозяйству, по дому итп) things *мн* to do; (*о ком-н*) effort *ед*, trouble *ед*; **все мои́** ~ **бы́ли напра́сны** all of my efforts were in vain; **хлопо́т по́лон рот** he *итп* has troubles galore.

хлопочу́ *итп несов см* **хлопота́ть**.

хлопу́ш|ка (-ки; gen pl -ек) *ж* (*для мух*) fly swatter; (*игрушка*) (Christmas) cracker.

хлопча́тник (-а) *м* (*БОТ: растение*) cotton.

хлопчатобума́жный *прил* cotton.

хло́пь|я (-ев) *мн* (*снега, мыла*) flakes *мн*; (*ваты, овчины*) clumps *мн*; **кукуру́зные** ~ cornflakes.

хлор (-а) *м* chlorine.

хло́рк|а (-и) *ж* (*разг*) bleaching powder.

хло́рн|ый *прил*: ~**ая и́звесть** bleaching powder; **хло́рная кислота́** hydrochloric acid.

хлы́н|уть (3sg -ет, 3pl -ут) *сов неперех* to flood; (*перен: мысли, воспоминания*) to flood back.

хлыст (-а́) *м* whip.

хлыщ (-а́) *м* playboy.

хлю́па|ть (-ю) *несов неперех* (*разг*) to squelch; ~ (*impf*) **но́сом** to sniff.

хля́стик (-а) *м* half-belt.

хмеле́|ть (-ю) *несов неперех* to be drunk; ~ (*impf*) **от сча́стья/свобо́ды** to be drunk with happiness/freedom.

хмел|ь (-я) *м* (*БОТ*) hops *мн*; (*опьянение*) drunkenness; **во-ю́** drunk.

хмельно́й *прил* drunken; (*напиток*) alcoholic; (*воздух, запах*) intoxicating.

хму́р|ить (-ю, -ишь; perf нахму́рить) *несов перех* (*лоб, брови*) to furrow

▸ **хму́риться** *несов возв* to frown; (*небо*) to become overcast; (*погода, день*) to turn gloomy.

хму́ро *нареч* gloomily ♦ *как сказ*: **сего́дня на у́лице** ~ it's very gloomy outside; **у него́ на душе́** ~ he's feeling very gloomy.

хму́рый *прил* gloomy.

хмы́ка|ть (-ю) *несов неперех* (*разг*) *to say "hmm" as a sign of surprise, annoyance etc.*

хмы́кн|уть (-у, -ешь) *сов неперех to say "hmm" as a sign of surprise, annoyance etc.*

хн|а (-ы) *ж* henna.

хны́ка|ть (-ю) *несов неперех* (*разг*: плакать) to whimper; (*перен: жаловаться*) to whine.

хо́бби *ср нескл* hobby.

хо́бот (-а) *м* (*слона*) trunk.

хобот|о́к (-ка́) *м* (*насекомого*) proboscis.

ход (-а; part gen -у, loc sg -у́) *м* (*поезда, машины,*

руля, поршня) movement; (*событий, дела итп*)
course; (*часов, двигателя*) working; (КАРТЫ)
go; (*манёвр, также* ШАХМАТЫ) move;
(*возможность*) chance; (*вход*) entrance;
(*тоннель*) passage; **в хóде** +*gen* in the course
of; ~ **мы́слей** train of thought; **идти́ (пойти́**
perf) **в** ~ to come into use; **пуска́ть (пусти́ть**
perf) **что-н в** ~ (*механизм*) to bring into use;
(*слово, тип одежды*) to popularize; **быть** (*impf*)
в (большо́м) ~**ý** to be (very) popular; **на** ~**ý**
(*есть, разговаривать*) on the move; (*делать
замечания, шутить*) in passing; **с хóду** straight
off; **он с хóду взбежа́л на ле́стницу** he ran
straight upstairs; **до дóма три часá** ~**ý** it's three
hours' walk to the house; **дава́ть (дать** *perf*) ~
де́лу to set things in motion; **дава́ть (дать** *perf*)
~ **нóвым лю́дям/ме́тодам** to give new people/
methods a chance; **дава́ть (дать** *perf*) **за́дний** ~
(АВТ) to reverse; (*человек*) to retreat; **знать**
(*impf*) **все** ~**ы́ и вы́ходы** to know all the ins and
outs; **де́ло идёт свои́м хóдом** events are taking
their natural course; **по хóду де́ла** during the
course of events; **чей** ~**?** (*в игре*) whose go is it?

ходáтайств|о (-а) *ср* petition; **подава́ть
(пода́ть** *perf*) ~ to submit a petition.

ходáтайств|овать (-ую; *perf*
походáтайствовать) *несов неперех*: ~ **о
чём-н/за кого-н** to petition for sth/on sb's
behalf.

хóдик|и (-ов) *мн* wall clock *ед*.

ход|и́ть (-жу́, -дишь) *несов неперех* to walk; (*по
магазинам, в гости, в кино итп*) to go (*on foot*);
(*поезд, автобус итп*) to go; (*слухи, грипп*) to
go round; (*часы*) to work; (+*instr*; *тузом итп*) to
play; (*конём, пешкой итп*) to move; (*носить*):
~ **в** +*prp* (*в пальто, в сапогах итп*) to wear;
(*ухаживать*): ~ **за кем-н** to look after sb.

хóд|кий (-кая, -кое, -кие; -ок, -ка́, -ко) *прил*
(*разг: машина*) speedy; (*: товар*) popular.

ходово́й *прил* popular.

хóдок *прил см* **хóдкий.**

ходо́к (-á) *м*: **он хорóший** ~ he's a good walker;
туда́ я бóльше не ~ (*разг*) I'm not going there
again.

ходу́л|я (-и; *gen pl* **-ей)** *ж* (*обычно мн*) stilt.

ходуно́м *нареч*: **ходи́ть** ~ (*разг*) to shake.

ходьб|а́ (-ы́) *ж* walking; **полчаса́** ~**ы́** half an
hour's walk.

ходя́ч|ий (-ая, -ее, -ие) *прил* trendy; (*избитый*)
hackneyed; (*больной*) able to walk; **он** ~ –**ая
доброде́тель** he is a paragon of virtue.

хожде́ни|е (-я) *ср* walking; (*слухов*) circulation;
име́ть (*impf*) ~ (*валюта*) to be in circulation;
(*выражение, товар*) to be popular.

хожу́ *несов см* **ходи́ть.**

хозрасчёт (-а) *м* (= *хозя́йственный расчёт*)
*system of management based on self-financing
and self- governing principles.*

хозрасчётн|ый *прил*: ~**ое предприя́тие** self-
financing, self-governing enterprise.

хозя́ева *итп сущ см* **хозя́ин.**

хозя́ек *сущ см* **хозя́йка.**

хозя́|ин (-ина; *nom pl* **-ева,** *gen pl* **-ев)** *м*
(*владелец*) owner; (*сдающий жильё*) landlord;
(*пользующийся наёмным трудом*) employer;
(*принимающий гостей*) host; (*ведущий
хозяйство*) manager; (*перен: положения, своей
судьбы*) master.

хозя́|йка (-йки; *gen pl* **-ек)** *ж* (*владелица*) owner;
(*сдающая жильё*) landlady; (*принимающая
гостей*) hostess; (*разг: жена*) missus, old lady;
дома́шняя ~ housewife.

хозя́йнича|ть (-ю) *несов неперех* (*в доме, на
кухне*) to be in charge; (*командовать*) to be
bossy.

хозя́йск|ий (-ая, -ое, -ие) *прил*: (*э́то*) **де́ло** ~**ое**
(*разг*) have it your own way.

хозя́йственник (-а) *м* manager.

хозя́йственный *прил* (*деятельность,
управление*) economic *опред*; (*постройка,
инвентарь*) domestic *опред*; (*человек*) thrifty;
хозя́йственные това́ры hardware;
хозя́йственный магази́н hardware shop.

хозя́йств|о (-а) *ср* (*экон*) economy;
(*производственная единица*) enterprise;
(*оборудование*) equipment; (*предметы быта*)
household goods *мн*; **городско́е/наро́дное** ~
urban/national economy; **дома́шнее** ~
housekeeping; **вести́** (*impf*) ~ to run the house.

хозя́йств|овать (-ую) *несов неперех*: ~ **на
предприя́тии/фи́рме** to manage an enterprise/
firm; **он уме́ло** ~**ует** he is a good manager.

хоккеи́ст (-а) *м* hockey player.

хокке́|й (-я) *м* hockey; ~ **с ша́йбой/на траве́**
ice/field hockey.

хокке́йный *прил* hockey *опред*.

хóлдинг (-а) *м* (КОММ) holding.

хóлдингов|ый *прил*: ~**ая компа́ния** holding
company.

хóленый *прил* (*человек, лошадь*) well-
groomed; (*лицо, руки*) elegant.

холёный *прил* = **хóленый.**

холе́р|а (-ы) *ж* (МЕД) cholera.

холестери́н (-а) *м* cholesterol.

холл (-а) *м* (*театра, гостиницы*) foyer, lobby;
(*в квартире, в доме*) hall.

холм (-á) *м* hill.

хóлмик (-а) *м* hillock.

холми́ст|ый (-, -а, -о) *прил* hilly.

хóлод (-а; *nom pl* **-á)** *м* cold; (*осенний, зимний*)
cold weather; (*перен: равнодушие*) coldness;
(*озноб*) cold shiver.

холода́ть (3sg **-ет,** *perf* **похолода́ть)** *несов безл*
to turn cold.

хóлоден *прил см* **холóдный.**

холоде́ть (-ю; *perf* **похолоде́ть)** *несов неперех*

(*руки, ноги*) to get cold; (*от страха, при
смерти*) to go cold.
холодец (**-ца́**) *м* meat in aspic.
холоди́льник (**-а**) *м* (*домашний*) fridge,
refrigerator; (*промышленный*) refrigerator;
двухка́мерный ~ fridge-freezer.
хо́лодно *нареч* coldly ♦ *как сказ* it's cold;
(*+dat*): **мне** *итп* **~** I'm *итп* cold; **на у́лице
сего́дня ~** it's cold outside today.
хол|о́дный (**-оден, -одна́, -одно**) *прил* cold; **эта
ку́ртка ~о́дная** this jacket isn't very warm;
холо́дная война́ cold war; **холо́дное ору́жие**
side arms *мн.*
холодца́ *итп сущ см* **холоде́ц.**
холост|о́й (**хо́лост**) *прил* (*мужчина*) unmarried,
single; (*no short form; вы́стрел, патро́н*) blank;
рабо́тать (*impf*) **на ~о́м ходу́** (*АВТ, ТЕХ*) to idle,
tick over; **~ прого́н** dry run.
холостя́к (**-а́**) *м* bachelor.
холу́|й (**-я**) *м* sycophant.
холст (**-а́**) *м* canvas.
хому́т (**-а́**) *м* (*коня*) harness collar; (*ТЕХ*) clamp;
(*перен*) bind; **пове́сить** (*perf*) **или наде́ть** (*perf*)
себе́ ~ на ше́ю to weigh o.s. down.
хомя́к (**-а́**) *м* hamster.
хор (**-а**) *м* choir; (*перен*) chorus.
хорва́т (**-а**) *м* Croatian.
Хорва́ти|я (**-и**) *ж* Croatia.
хорва́т|ка (**-ки**; *gen pl* **-ок**) *ж см* **хорва́т.**
хорва́тск|ий (**-ая, -ое, -ие**) *прил* Croatian.
хорёк (**-ька́**) *м* ferret.
хорео́граф (**-а**) *м* choreographer.
хореогра́фи|я (**-и**) *ж* choreography.
хори́ст (**-а**) *м* chorister.
хори́ст|ка (**-ки**; *gen pl* **-ок**) *ж см* **хори́ст.**
хорме́йстер (**-а**) *м* choirmaster.
хорово́д (**-а**) *м* round dance.
хорово́й *прил* choral.
хо́ром *нареч* in unison.
хоро́м|ы (**-**) *мн* mansion *ед.*
хор|они́ть (**-оню́, -о́нишь;** *perf* **похорони́ть**)
несов перех to bury.
хорохо́р|иться (**-юсь, -ишься**) *несов возв*
(*разг*) to brag.
хоро́шеньк|ий (**-ая, -ое, -ие**) *прил*
(*симпатичный*) pretty; (*разг: плохой*) fine, nice.
хоро́шенько *нареч* (*разг*) properly.
хороше́|ть (**-ю;** *perf* **похороше́ть**) *несов
неперех* to become more attractive.
хоро́ш|ий (**-ая, -ее, -ие; -, -а́, -о**) *прил* good; **он
хоро́ш (собо́ю)** he's good-looking; **хоро́ш
друг!** (*разг*) a fine friend!; **всего́ ~его!** all the
best!
хорошо́ *нареч* well ♦ *как сказ* it's good; (*+dat*):
мне ~ I feel good ♦ *част* *вводн сл* okay, all
right ♦ *ср нескл* (*ПРОСВЕЩ*) ≈ good (*school
mark*); **~ отдыха́ть (отдохну́ть** *perf*) to have a
good rest; **на мо́ре ~** it's nice by the sea; **мне
здесь ~** I like it here; **~, я согла́сен** okay, I
agree; **ну, ~!** (*разг: выражение угрозы*) right
then!; **~ бы пое́сть/поспа́ть** (*разг*) I wouldn't

mind a bite to eat/getting some sleep.
хо́р|ы (**-ов**) *мн* (*в церкви, в большом зале*)
gallery *ед.*
хорька́ *итп сущ см* **хорёк.**
хот-дог (**-а**) *м* hot dog.
хо|те́ть (*см* **Table 16**) *несов перех:* **~ +***infin* to
want to do; **как ~ти́те** (*как вам угодно*) as you
wish; (*а всё-таки*) no matter what you say; **~
хо́чешь не хо́чешь** whether you like it or not; **~**
(*impf*) **есть/пить** to be hungry/thirsty
▶ **хоте́ться** *несов безл* (*+infin*): **мне** *итп*
хо́чется пла́кать/есть I *итп* feel like crying/
something to eat; **мне хо́чется ча́ю** I feel like
some tea.

KEYWORD

хоть *союз* **1** (*несмотря на то, что*) (al)though;
хоть я и оби́жен, я помогу́ тебе́ although I am
hurt, I will help you
2 (*до такой степени, что*) even if; **не
соглаша́ется, хоть до утра́ проси́** he won't
agree, even if you ask all night; **хоть умри́, а
де́нег доста́нь** get hold of some money, even if
it kills you; **хоть убе́й, не могу́ пойти́ на э́то** I
couldn't do that to save my life; **хоть..., хоть**
either ..., or; **езжа́й хоть сего́дня, хоть че́рез
ме́сяц** go either today, or in a month's time
♦ *част* **1** (*служит для усиления*) at least;
подвези́ его́ хоть до ста́нции take him to the
station at least; **пойми́ хоть ты** you of all people
should understand
2 (*разг: например*) for example; **взять хоть
Мари́ю: она́ же всё вре́мя рабо́тает** take
Maria for example, she works all the time
3 (*во фразах*): **хоть бы** at least; **хоть бы ты
ему́ позвони́л!** you could at least phone him!;
хоть бы зако́нчить сего́дня! if only we could
get finished today!; **хоть кто** anyone; **хоть
како́й** any; **ему́ хоть бы что** it doesn't bother
him; **хоть куда́!** (*разг*) excellent!; **хоть бы и
так!** so what!

хотя́ *союз* although; **~ и** even though; **~ бы** at
least; **он сра́зу всё по́нял, ~ и не знал
подро́бностей** even without knowing the
details, he was able to understand at once;
возьми́те ~ бы приме́р А́нглии take England
for example.
хотя́т(ся) *несов см* **хоте́ть(ся).**
хохла́ *итп сущ см* **хохо́л.**
хохлом|а́ (**-ы́**) *ж* khokhloma (*traditional wooden
articles decorated in red, gold and black*).
хо́хм|а (**-ы**) *ж* (*разг*) joke; (*что-н смешное*)
laugh.
хох|о́л (**-ла́**) *м* (*клок волос*) tuft of hair; (*разг:
пренебр*) Ukrainian.
хо́хот (**-а**) *м* guffaw; (*шакала*) laugh.
хох|ота́ть (**-очу́, -о́чешь**) *несов неперех* to
laugh (loudly); (*филин, шакал*) to laugh; **~**
(*impf*) **над** *+instr* to laugh at; **я ~ота́л до слёз** I
laughed till the tears ran down my face.
хочу́(сь) *итп несов см* **хоте́ть(ся).**

храбре́ц (-á) м brave person (мн people).
храб|и́ться (-ю́сь, -и́шься) несов возв (разг) to try to appear brave.
хра́бро нареч bravely.
хра́брост|ь (-и) ж bravery, courage.
хра́бр|ый (-, -á, -о) прил brave, courageous.
храм (-а) м (РЕЛ) temple.
хране́ни|е (-я) ср (денег) keeping; ~ ору́жия possession of firearms; ка́мера для ~я багажа́ left-luggage office (BRIT), checkroom (US); сдава́ть (сдать perf) ве́щи на ~ to put things in for safekeeping.
храни́лищ|е (-а) ср store.
храни́тел|ь (-я) м curator, keeper.
хран|и́ть (-ю́, -и́шь) несов перех to keep; (границы, достоинство) to protect; (традиции) to preserve; ~ (impf) что-н в та́йне to keep sth secret
▸ **храни́ться** несов возв to be kept.
храп (-а) м (во сне) snoring.
храп|е́ть (-лю́, -и́шь) несов неперех (человек) to snore; (лошадь) to snort.
хреб|е́т (-та́) м (АНАТ) spine; (разг: спина) back; (ГЕО) ridge.
хребто́вый прил (позвонки) spinal; (перевал, гряда) mountain опред.
хрен (-а) м (БОТ, КУЛИН) horseradish; (груб!) willy (!); ~ его́ зна́ет (разг) who the hell knows; ста́рый ~ (разг) old fool.
хрено́вый прил (БОТ, КУЛИН) horseradish опред; (груб!) crappy (!), lousy (US).
хрестомати́йный прил (идея, образ) basic.
хрестома́ти|я (-и) ж study aid, reader.
хризанте́м|а (-ы) ж chrysanthemum.
хрип (-а) м wheezing; **предсме́ртный** ~ dying gasp.
хрип|е́ть (-лю́, -и́шь) несов неперех (лошадь, больной) to wheeze; (пластинка) to crackle.
хри́пл|ый (-, -á, -о) прил (голос) hoarse; (гармонь, звук) wheezing.
хриплю́ несов см хрипе́ть.
хри́пн|уть (-у, -ешь; perf охри́пнуть) несов неперех to become или grow hoarse.
хрипот|а́ (-ы́) ж hoarseness.
христиан|и́н (-ани́на; nom pl -а́не, gen pl -а́н) м Christian.
христиа́н|ка (-ки; gen pl -ок) ж см христиани́н.
христиа́нск|ий (-ая, -ое, -ие) прил Christian.
христиа́нств|о (-а) ср Christianity.
Христ|о́с (-а́) м Christ; ~а́ ра́ди (разг) for Christ's sake.
хром (-а) м (ХИМ) chrome; (краска) chrome yellow; (кожа) box calf.
хрома́|ть (-ю) несов неперех to limp; (перен: разг: знания, дисциплина) to be weak; **моя́ матема́тика** ~**ет** (разг) my maths is pretty shaky.
хро́мовый прил (ХИМ) chrome; (кожа, сапоги

итп) box-calf.
хром|о́й (-, -á, -о) прил lame; (перен: разг: стол итп) wobbly.
хромосо́м|а (-ы) ж chromosome.
хромот|а́ (-ы́) ж limp.
хро́ник (-а) м (разг) bad case.
хро́ник|а (-и) ж chronicle; (КИНО) film chronicle.
хроника́льный прил chronicle опред.
хроникёр (-а) м (журналист) reporter.
хрони́ческ|ий (-ая, -ое, -ие) прил chronic.
хронологи́ческ|ий (-ая, -ое, -ие) прил chronological; **в** ~**ой после́довательности** in chronological order.
хроноло́ги|я (-и) ж chronology.
хронометра́ж (-а) м time-keeping.
хру́п|кий (-кая, -кое, -кие; -ок, -ка́, -ко) прил (лёд, стекло итп) fragile; (печенье, кости) brittle; (перен: фигура, девушка) delicate; (: здоровье, организм) frail.
хру́пкост|ь (-и) ж (см прил) fragility; brittleness; delicacy; frailty.
хру́пок прил см хру́пкий.
хруст (-а) м crunch.
хруста́лик (-а) м (АНАТ) lens.
хруста́л|ь (-я́) м, собир crystal; **го́рный** ~ rock crystal.
хруста́льный прил crystal опред; (перен: лёд, звон) crystal clear.
хру|сте́ть (-щу́, -сти́шь) несов неперех to crunch; (+instr; редиской, сахаром итп) to crunch.
хрустя́щий (-ая, -ее, -ие) прил crunchy; (скатерть, бельё) crisp; **хрустя́щий карто́фель** potato crisps (BRIT) или chips (US) мн.
хрущу́ несов см хрусте́ть.
хрю́ка|ть (-ю) несов неперех to grunt.
хрящ (-а́) м (АНАТ) cartilage.
ХСС м сокр (= Христиа́нско-социалисти́ческий сою́з) CSU (= Christian Socialist Union).
худе́|ть (-ю) несов неперех to grow thin; (быть на диете) to slim.
худо́жественный прил artistic; (школа, выставка) art опред; **худо́жественная литерату́ра** fiction; **худо́жественная самоде́ятельность** amateur art and performance; **худо́жественный сало́н** (выставка) art exhibition; (магазин) ≈ craft shop; **худо́жественный фильм** feature film.
худо́жеств|о (-а) ср: **акаде́мия худо́жеств** art school.
худо́жник (-а) м artist.
худо́жниц|а (-ы) ж см худо́жник.
худ|о́й (-, -á, -о) прил thin; (разг: плохой) bad; (: дыря́вый) full of holes; **на** ~ **коне́ц** if the worst comes to the worst (BRIT), in the worst case scenario (US).
худоща́в|ый (-, -а, -о) прил thin.

ху́дш|ее (-его; *decl like adj*) *ср* the worst.

ху́дш|ий (-ая, -ее, -ие) *превос прил* the worst
опред.

ху́же *сравн прил, нареч* worse.

ху|й (-я) *м* (*груб!*) cock (*!*), prick (*!*)

хулига́н (-а) *м* hooligan.

хулига́н|ить (-ю, -ишь; *perf* **нахулига́нить**)
несов неперех to act like a hooligan.

хулига́н|ка (-ки; *gen pl* -ок) *ж см* **хулига́н**.

хулига́нск|ий (-ая, -ое, -ие) *прил*: ~ **посту́пок**
act of hooliganism; ~**ое поведе́ние**
hooliganism.

хулига́нств|о (-а) *ср* hooliganism.

хулиганьё (-я́) *ср собир* hooligans *мн*, yobs *мн*
(*BRIT*).

хул|и́ть (-ю́, -ишь) *несов перех* (*порочить*) to
abuse.

ху́нт|а (-ы) *ж* (*ПОЛИТ*) junta.

хурм|а́ (-ы́) *ж* (*дерево*) persimmon tree; (*плод*)
persimmon, sharon fruit.

ху́тор (-а) *м* (*ферма*) farmstead; (*селение*)
village (*in Southern Russia and the Ukraine*).

хуторя́н|ин (-ина; *nom pl* -е, *gen pl* -) *м* (*владелец*
хутора) farmer; (*житель хутора*) villager.

хуторя́н|ка (-ки; *gen pl* -ок) *ж см* **хуторя́нин**.

~ Ц, ц ~

Ц, ц *сущ нескл* (*буква*) the 23rd letter of the Russian alphabet.

ц. *сокр* (= **центр**) ctr. (= *centre*); = **цена́**.

ца́па|ть (**-ю**) *несов перех* (*когтями, зубами*) to seize; (*perf* **сца́пать**; *разг*) to snatch, grab.

ца́пл|я (**-ли**; *gen pl* **-ель**) *ж* heron.

ца́пн|уть (**-у, -ешь**) *сов перех* to seize; (*разг*) to snatch, grab.

цара́пань|е (**-я**) *ср* scratching.

цара́па|ть (**-ю**; *perf* **оцара́пать**) *несов перех* (*раздирать*) to scratch; (*perf* **нацара́пать**; *разг*: *писать*) to scribble

▶ **цара́паться** (*perf* **оцара́паться**) *несов возв* to scratch; (*no perf*; *друг друга*) to scratch one another.

цара́пин|а (**-ы**) *ж* scratch.

царе́вен *сущ см* **царе́вна**.

царе́вич (**-а**) *м* tsarevich (*son of the tsar*).

царе́в|на (**-ны**; *gen pl* **-ен**) *ж* tsarevna (*daughter of the tsar*).

цари́зм (**-а**) *м* tsarism.

цар|и́ть (**-ю́, -и́шь**) *несов неперех* (*также перен*) to reign.

цари́ц|а (**-ы**) *ж* tsarina (*wife of the tsar*), empress; (*перен: бала, моды*) queen.

ца́рск|ий (**-ая, -ое, -ие**) *прил* (*двор, указ, семья*) tsar's, royal; (*режим, правительство*) tsarist; (*перен: роскошь, прием*) regal.

ца́рствен|ный (**-, -на, -но**) *прил* regal.

ца́рств|о (**-а**) *ср* (*государство*) tsardom; (*царствование*) reign; (*перен: любви, природы*) realm; **живо́тное/расти́тельное ~** the animal/plant kingdom.

ца́рствование (**-я**) *ср* reign.

ца́рств|овать (**-ую**) *несов неперех* (*также перен*) to reign.

цар|ь (**-я́**) *м* tsar; (*перен*) king; **без ~я́ в голове́** (*разг*) completely daft.

ЦБ *м сокр* = **центра́льный банк**.

ЦБНТИ *ср сокр* = **Центра́льное бюро́ нау́чно-техни́ческой информа́ции**.

цве|сти́ (**-ту́, -тёшь**) *несов неперех* (*БОТ*) to blossom, flower; (*перен: страна, человек*) to flourish; **~** (*impf*) **здоро́вьем/от ра́дости** to be bursting with health/joy.

цвет (**-а**; *nom pl* **-а́**) *м* (*окраска*) colour (*BRIT*), color (*US*); (*part gen* **-у**, *loc sg* **-у́**; *БОТ*) blossom; **~ о́бщества** the cream of society; **во цве́те лет** in the prime of life.

цвета́ст|ый (**-, -а, -о**) *прил* colourful (*BRIT*), colorful (*US*).

цвете́ни|е (**-я**) *ср* blossoming.

цвети́ст|ый (**-, -а, -о**) *прил* (*узор*) floral; (*луг, поле*) flower-covered; (*речь, стиль*) flowery.

цветка́ *итп сущ см* **цвето́к**.

цветни́к (**-а́**) *м* flowerbed.

цветн|о́й *прил* (*карандаш*) coloured (*BRIT*), colored (*US*); (*одежда*) colourful (*BRIT*), colorful (*US*); (*фотография, фильм*) colour (*BRIT*), color (*US*) ◆ (**-о́го**; *decl like adj*) *м* (*человек*) colo(u)red; **цветна́я капу́ста** cauliflower; **цветно́й телеви́зор** colo(u)r television; **цветны́е мета́ллы** non-ferrous metals.

цвет|о́к (**-ка́**; *nom pl* **-ки́**) *м* flower (*reproductive part of a plant*); (*nom pl* **-ы́**) flower (*bloom*); (*комнатный*) plant.

цветому́зык|а (**-и**) *ж* son et lumière, sound-and-light show (*US*).

цвето́чник (**-а**) *м* florist.

цвето́чниц|а (**-ы**) *ж см* **цвето́чник**.

цвето́чный *прил* flower *опред*; (*духи*) flower-scented; **цвето́чный горшо́к** flowerpot; **цвето́чный магази́н** florist's.

цвету́ *итп несов см* **цвести́**.

цвету́щий (**-ая, -ее, -ие**) *прил* (*вид, женщина*) blossoming; (*область, экономика*) flourishing.

ЦГАЛИ *м сокр* = **Центра́льный госуда́рственный архи́в литерату́ры и иску́сства**.

ЦГИА *м сокр* = **Центра́льный госуда́рственный истори́ческий архи́в**.

це|ди́ть (**-жу́, -дишь**; *perf* **процеди́ть**) *несов перех* (*молоко, отвар*) to strain; (*no perf*; *заливать: в бутылку*) to siphon; (*perf* **процеди́ть**; *перен: слова*) to force out.

це́др|а (**-ы**) *ж* (dried) peel.

цежу́ *несов см* **цеди́ть**.

Цейло́н (**-а**) *м* Ceylon.

цейло́нск|ий (**-ая, -ое, -ие**) *прил* Ceylonese.

цейтно́т (**-а**) *м*: **быть в ~е** (*ШАХМАТЫ*) to be in time-trouble; (*перен: разг*) to be pushed for time.

целе́бен *прил см* **целе́бный**.

целе́бност|**ь** (-**и**) *ж* healing *или* medicinal properties *мн*.

целе́б|**ный** (-**ен**, -**на**, -**но**) *прил* medicinal; (*воздух*) healthy.

целево́й *прил* (*задание, установка*) special; (*финансирование, ссуды*) for a specified purpose; ~ **ры́нок** (*КОММ*) target market.

це́лен *прил см* **це́льный**.

целенапра́вленност|**ь** (-**и**) *ж* single-mindedness.

целенапра́вленный *прил* single-minded.

целесообра́зен *прил см* **целесообра́зный**.

целесообра́зно *нареч* expediently ◆ *как сказ* it makes sense; ~ **заверши́ть рабо́ту сейча́с** it makes sense to finish the work now.

целесообра́зност|**ь** (-**и**) *ж* expediency.

целесообра́з|**ный** (-**ен**, -**на**, -**но**) *прил* expedient.

целеустремлён|**ный** (-, -**на**, -**но**) *прил* purposeful.

целико́м *нареч*: **проглоти́ть/съесть что-н** ~ to swallow/eat sth whole; (*перен: без ограничений*) wholly, entirely.

целин|**а́** (-**ы́**) *ж* (*также перен*) virgin territory; **сне́жная** ~ virgin snow.

цели́нный *прил* (*земля*) virgin *опред*.

цели́тель|**ный** (-**ен**, -**на**, -**ьно**) *прил* (*бальзам*) medicinal; (*действие, свойство*) healing *опред*; (*воздух*) healthy.

це́л|**ить** (-**ю**, -**ишь**; *perf* **наце́лить**) *несов неперех*: ~ **в** +*acc* to aim at; (*перен: в начальники*) to have one's sights set on

► **це́литься** (*perf* **наце́литься**) *несов возв*: ~**ся в** +*acc* to (take) aim at; ~**ся** (**наце́литься** *perf*) +*infin* (*разг*) to aim to do.

целлофа́н (-**а**) *м* cellophane®.

целлофа́новый *прил* cellophane® *опред*.

целлуло́ид (-**а**) *м* celluloid.

целлюло́з|**а** (-**ы**) *ж* cellulose.

цел|**ова́ть** (-**у́ю**; *perf* **поцелова́ть**) *несов перех* to kiss

► **целова́ться** (*perf* **поцелова́ться**) *несов возв* to kiss (each other).

це́л|**ое** (-**ого**; *decl like adj*) *ср* whole; (*МАТ*) integer; **еди́ное** ~ unified whole.

целому́дрен|**ный** (-, -**на**, -**но**) *прил* chaste.

целому́дри|**е** (-**я**) *ср* (*девственность*) chastity; (*нравственность*) chasteness.

це́лостен *прил см* **це́лостный**.

це́лостност|**ь** (-**и**) *ж* integrity.

це́лост|**ный** (-**ен**, -**на**, -**но**) *прил* integrated.

це́лост|**ь** (-**и**) *ж* (*машины, предмета*) safety; (*денег, инвестиций*) security, safety; **в** ~**и и сохра́нности** in one piece; **сохраня́ть** (**сохрани́ть** *perf*) **что-н в** ~**и** to keep sth safe.

це́л|**ый** *прил* whole, entire; (-, -**а́**, -**о**; *неповреждённый: машина, оборудование итп*): **о́**: *одежда*) undamaged; **в** ~**ом** (*целиком*) as a whole; (*в общем*) on the whole; ~ **и невреди́мый** safe and sound; ~ **ряд**

+*gen pl* a whole range of; **це́лое число́** (*МАТ*) whole number.

цел|**ь** (-**и**) *ж* (*при стрельбе*) target; (*перен*) aim, goal; **с це́лью** +*infin* with the object *или* aim of doing; **с це́лью** +*gen* for; **в це́лях** +*gen* for the purpose of; **в воспита́тельных/рекла́мных це́лях** for education/publicity purposes.

це́льност|**ь** (-**и**) *ж* integrity, completeness.

це́л|**ьный** *прил* (*кусок, камень*) solid; (-**ен**, -**ьна**, -**ьно**; *характер, произведение*) complete; (*теория*) integrated; ~**ьное молоко́** full-cream milk.

цеме́нт (-**а**) *м* cement.

цементи́р|**овать** (-**ую**; *perf* **зацементи́ровать**) *несов перех* to cement; (*perf* **сцементи́ровать**; *перен*) to cement.

цеме́нтный *прил* cement *опред*.

цен|**а́** (-**ы́**; *acc sg* -**у**, *dat sg* -**е́**, *nom pl* -**ы**) *ж* price; (*перен: суждения, человека*) value; ~**о́ю** +*gen* at the expense of; **таки́е лю́ди/кни́ги в** ~**е́** such people/books are highly prized; **ему́** ~**ы́ нет** he is invaluable; ~ **продавца́** (*КОММ*) offer price; **торго́вая** ~ (*КОММ*) trade price.

це́нен *прил см* **це́нный**.

ценз (-**а**) *м* requirement.

це́нзор (-**а**) *м* censor.

цензу́р|**а** (-**ы**) *ж* censorship.

цензу́р|**ный** *прил* censorship *опред*; (-**ен**, -**на**, -**но**; *пристойный*) acceptable.

цени́тель|**ь** (-**я**) *м* judge (*of art, character etc*).

цени́тельниц|**а** (-**ы**) *ж см* **цени́тель**.

цен|**и́ть** (-**ю́**, -**ишь**) *несов перех* (*дорожить*) to value; (*помощь, совет*) to appreciate; (*раза: назначать цену*) to name a price for

► **цени́ться** *несов неперех* to be (highly) valued.

це́нник (-**а**) *м* (*бирка*) price tag; (*список*) price list.

це́нност|**ь** (-**и**) *ж* value; (*обычно мн: духовные, культурные*) treasure; ~**и** valuables; **материа́льные** ~**и** commodities.

це́н|**ный** (-**ен**, -**на**, -**но**) *прил* valuable; (*no short form*; *посылка, письмо*) registered; **це́нные бума́ги** (*КОММ*) securities *мн*.

ценообразова́ни|**е** (-**я**) *ср* price formation.

цент (-**а**) *м* cent.

це́нтнер (-**а**) *м* centner (*100kg*).

центр (-**а**) *м* centre (*BRIT*), center (*US*); **в це́нтре внима́ния** in the limelight; **торго́вый центр** shopping centre (*BRIT*) *или* mall (*US*).

централи́зм (-**а**) *м* centralism.

централиз|**ова́ть** (-**у́ю**) (*не*)*сов перех* to centralize.

центра́льный *прил* central; ~ **проце́ссор** (*КОМП*) central processing unit; **центра́льная пре́сса** the national press; **центра́льное отопле́ние** central heating.

центров|**о́й** *прил*: ~ **напада́ющий/круг** centre forward/circle ◆ (-**о́го**; *decl like adj*) *м* (*в баскетболе*) centre (*BRIT*), center (*US*); (*в футболе*) midfielder.

цепене́|**ть** (-**ю**; *perf* **оцепене́ть**) *несов неперех* (*от ужаса, от страха*) to freeze; ~ (**оцепене́ть** *perf*) **от хо́лода** to be frozen stiff.

це́п|кий (**-кая, -кое, -кие; -ок, -ка́, -ко**) *прил* tenacious.

цепля́|ться (**-юсь**) *несов возв*: ~ **за** +*acc* (*также перен*) to cling *или* hang on to; ~ (*impf*) **рукаво́м/ного́й за что-н** to catch one's sleeve/ leg on sth; ~ (*impf*) **к чему́-н** (*перен: разг*) to pick up on sth.

цепно́й *прил* chain *опред*; **цепна́я реа́кция** chain reaction; **цепна́я соба́ка** guard dog; **цепно́й мост** drawbridge.

це́пок *прил см* **це́пкий**.

цепо́ч|ка (**-ки;** *gen pl* **-ек**) *ж* (*тонкая цепь*) chain; (*машин, людей*) line; (*предложений*) string; **идти́** (*impf*) ~**кой** to walk in single file.

цеп|ь (**-и;** *loc sg* **-й**) *ж* (*также перен*) chain; (*ЭЛЕК*) circuit; **го́рная** ~ mountain range; **сажа́ть** (**посади́ть** *perf*) **кого́-н на** ~ to chain sb up; **зако́вывать** (**закова́ть** *perf*) **кого́-н в це́пи** to put sb in chains.

церемо́нен *прил см* **церемо́нный**.

церемо́н|иться (**-юсь, -ишься**) *несов возв* (*стесняться*) to stand on ceremony; (*быть снисходительным*) ~ **с кем-н** to be too soft on sb.

церемо́ни|я (**-и**) *ж* ceremony; **без** ~**й** without ceremony.

церемо́н|ный (**-ен, -на, -но**) *прил* ceremonious.

це́ркви *итп сущ см* **це́рковь**.

церко́вник (**-а**) *м* clergyman *или* clergymen.

церковнослужи́тел|ь (**-я**) *м* junior churchman (*мн* churchmen).

церко́вный *прил* church *опред*.

це́рк|овь (**-ви;** *instr sg* **-овью;** *nom pl* **-ви,** *gen pl* **-ве́й**) *ж* church.

цех (**-а;** *loc sg* **-у́,** *nom pl* **-а́**) *м* (work)shop (*in factory*).

цивилиза́ци|я (**-и**) *ж* civilization.

цивилизо́ванно *нареч* in a civilized manner.

цивилизо́ван|ный (**-, -на, -но**) *прил* civilized.

цивилизов|а́ть (**-у́ю**) (*не*)*сов перех* to civilize.

циге́йк|а (**-и**) *ж* beaver lamb.

циге́йковый *прил* beaver-lamb.

цикл (**-а**) *м* cycle; (*лекций, концертов итп*) series.

циклаconstmе́н (**-а**) *м* cyclamen.

цикли́чен *прил см* **цикли́чный**.

цикли́ческ|ий (**-ая, -ое, -ие**) *прил* cyclical.

цикли́ч|ный (**-ен, -на, -но**) *прил* = **цикли́ческий**.

цикло́н (**-а**) *м* cyclone.

цико́ри|й (**-я**) *м* chicory.

цили́ндр (**-а**) *м* cylinder; (*шляпа*) top hat.

цилиндри́ческ|ий (**-ая, -ое, -ие**) *прил* cylindrical.

цинг|а́ (**-и́**) *ж* scurvy.

цини́зм (**-а**) *м* cynicism.

ци́ник (**-а**) *м* cynic.

цини́чен *прил см* **цини́чный**.

цини́чность (**-и**) *ж* cynicism.

цини́ч|ный (**-ен, -на, -но**) *прил* cynical.

цинк (**-а**) *м* zinc.

ци́нковый *прил* zinc.

цирк (**-а**) *м* circus; (*разг: смешное событие*) farce.

цирка́ч (**-а́**) *м* (*разг*) circus performer.

цирково́й *прил* circus *опред*.

циркули́р|овать (*3sg* **-ует,** *3pl* **-уют**) *несов неперех* to circulate.

ци́ркул|ь (**-я**) *м* (a pair of) compasses.

циркуля́р (**-а**) *м* circular.

циркуля́ци|я (**-и**) *ж* circulation.

цирро́з (**-а**) *м* cirrhosis.

цисте́рн|а (**-ы**) *ж* (*резервуар*) cistern; (*автомобиль*) tanker; (*вагон*) tank wagon (*BRIT*) *или* car (*US*).

цитаде́л|ь (**-и**) *ж* (*также перен*) citadel.

цита́т|а (**-ы**) *ж* quote, quotation.

цити́р|овать (**-ую;** *perf* **процити́ровать**) *несов перех* to quote.

ци́трус (**-а**) *м* (*обычно мн*) citrus fruit.

ци́трусовый *прил* citrus *опред*.

цифербла́т (**-а**) *м* dial; (*на часах*) face.

ци́фр|а (**-ы**) *ж* number; (*арабские, римские*) numeral; (*обычно мн: расчет*) figure.

цифрово́й *прил* numerical.

ЦК *м сокр* = *Центра́льный Комите́т*.

цо́ка|ть (**-ю**) *несов неперех* (*языком*) to tut; (*каблуки, копыта*) to clatter.

ЦП *сокр* (= *центра́льный проце́ссор*) CPU (= *central processing unit*).

ЦПКиО *м сокр* (= *Центра́льный парк культу́ры и о́тдыха*) *park used for recreational purposes*.

ЦПКО *м сокр* = **ЦПКиО**.

ЦРУ *ср сокр* (= *Центра́льное разве́дывательное управле́ние (США*)) CIA (= *Central Intelligence Agency*).

ЦСДФ *ж сокр* = *Центра́льная сту́дия документа́льных фи́льмов*.

ЦСКА *м сокр* = *Центра́льный спорти́вный клуб а́рмии*.

ЦСУ *ср сокр* = *Центра́льное статисти́ческое управле́ние*.

ЦТ *ср сокр* = *Центра́льное телеви́дение*.

цука́т (**-а**) *м* candied fruit.

ЦУМ (**-а**) *м сокр* = *центра́льный универса́льный магази́н*.

цум (**-а**) *м сокр* = **ЦУМ**.

цуна́ми *ср нескл* tidal wave.

цыга́н (**-а;** *nom pl* **-е**) *м* gypsy.

цыга́н|ка (**-ки;** *gen pl* **-ок**) *ж см* **цыга́н**.

цыга́нск|ий (**-ая, -ое, -ие**) *прил* gypsy *опред*.

цы́ка|ть (**-ю**) *несов неперех* (*разг*): ~ **на** +*acc* to snap at.

цыпл|ёнок (**-ёнка;** *nom pl* **-я́та,** *gen pl* **-я́т**) *м* chick.

цыпля́ч|ий (**-ая, -ее, -ие**) *прил* chicken *опред*; (*перен: шея, руки*) scrawny.

цы́почк|и (**-ек**) *мн*: **на** ~**ках** on tiptoe; **встава́ть** (**встать** *perf*) **на** ~ to stand on tiptoe.

Цю́рих (**-а**) *м* Zürich.

~ Ч, ч ~

Ч, ч *сущ нескл* (*буква*) *the 24th letter of the Russian alphabet.*

ча́вка|ть (-ю) *несов неперех* to chomp; (*перен: по грязи*) to squelch.

чад (-а; *loc sg* -у́) *м* fumes *мн.*

чади́ть (-жу́, -ди́шь; *perf* **начади́ть**) *несов неперех* to give off fumes.

ча́д|о (-а) *ср* offspring (*мн* offspring).

чадр|а́ (-ы́) *ж* yashmak.

чаевы́|е (-ы́х; *decl like adj*) *мн* tip *ед*; **дава́ть** (**дать** *perf*) **кому́-н** ~ to tip sb.

чаево́д (-а) *м* tea-grower.

чаево́дств|о (-а) *ср* tea-growing.

ча́ек *сущ см* **ча́йка.**

чаепи́ти|е (-я) *ср* (*занятие*) tea-drinking; (*событие*) tea-party.

чажу́ *несов см* **чади́ть.**

ча́йн|ка (-ки; *gen pl* -ок) *ж* tea leaf.

ча|й (-я; *part gen* -ю, *nom pl* -и́) *м* tea; **зава́ривать** (**завари́ть** *perf*) ~ to make tea; **за ча́ем** over a cup of tea; **ча́шка ча́я** a cup of tea; **дава́ть** (**дать** *perf*) **кому́-н на** ~ to give sb a tip.

ча́йк|а (-йки; *gen pl* -ек) *ж* (sea)gull.

ча́йн|ая (-ой; *decl like adj*) *ж* tearoom, teashop.

ча́йник (-а) *м* kettle; (*для заварки*) teapot.

ча́йн|ый *прил* (*плантация*) tea *опред*; **ча́йная ло́жка** teaspoon; **ча́йный серви́з** tea service *или* set.

чалм|а́ (-ы́) *ж* turban.

чан (-а) *м* (*деревянный*) vat; (*металлический*) tank.

ча́р|ка (-ки; *gen pl* -ок) *ж* chalice.

чар|ова́ть (-у́ю) *несов перех* (*красотой*) to charm; (*умом*) to captivate.

чароде́ек *сущ см* **чароде́йка.**

чароде́|й (-я) *м* sorcerer.

чароде́|йка (-йки; *gen pl* -ек) *ж* sorceress.

ча́рок *сущ см* **ча́рка.**

ча́ртер (-а) *м* (*КОММ*) charter.

ча́ртерный *прил* charter *опред.*

ча́р|ы (-) *мн* (*обаяние*) charms *мн*; (*волшебство*) magic *ед.*

час (-а́; *nom pl* -ы́) *м* hour; **академи́ческий** ~ (*ПРОСВЕЩ*) ≈ period; **кото́рый** ~? what time is it?; **сейча́с 3** ~**а́ но́чи/дня** it's 3 o'clock in the morning/afternoon; **в 9** ~**о́в утра́/ве́чера** at 9 o'clock in the morning/evening; **стоя́ть** (*impf*) **на** ~**а́х** to stand guard; **по** ~**а́м** by the clock; ~ **от** ~**у не ле́гче** it gets worse by the hour; **в**

до́брый ~! Godspeed!; **с ча́су на** ~ any moment; **он помо́г мне в тру́дный** ~ he helped me in my hour of need; *см также* **часы́.**

часо́в|ня (-ни; *gen pl* -ен) *ж* chapel.

часов|о́й *прил* (*лекция, перерыв итп*) one-hour; (*поезд*) one o'clock; (*механизм: ручных часов*) watch *опред*; (: *стенных часов*) clock *опред* ♦ (-о́го; *decl like adj*) *м* sentry; ~**а́я стре́лка** the small hand; ~**а́я опла́та** payment by the hour; **часово́й по́яс** time zone.

часовщи́к (-а́) *м* watchmaker.

ча́сом *нареч* (*разг: иногда*) the odd time ♦ *вводн сл* (*разг: случайно*) by any chance.

часосло́в (-а) *м* (*РЕЛ*) Book of Hours.

часте́нько *нареч* (*разг*) many's the time.

части́ц|а (-ы) *ж* (*маленькая часть*) fragment; (*ФИЗ, ЛИНГ*) particle; (*перен: правды*) grain.

части́чен *прил см* **части́чный.**

части́чно *нареч* partly.

части́чн|ый (-ен, -на, -но) *прил* partial.

ча́стник (-а) *м* (*разг: предприниматель*) entrepreneur; (*собственник*) proprietor.

частновладе́льческ|ий (-ая, -ое, -ие) *прил* privately owned.

ча́стно|е (-го; *decl like adj*) *ср* quotient.

ча́стность (-и) *ж* (*деталь*) detail; **в** ~**и** in particular.

ча́стн|ый *прил* private; (*нехарактерный*) certain; **в** ~**ых рука́х** in private hands; ~ **слу́чай** isolated case; **ча́стная со́бственность** private property; **ча́стное лицо́** individual; **ча́стный капита́л** (*ЭКОН*) private capital; **ча́стный со́бственник** private owner; **ча́стная акционе́рная компа́ния** private limited company.

ча́сто *нареч* (*много раз*) often; (*тесно*) close together.

частоко́л (-а) *м* palings *мн.*

частот|а́ (-оты́) *ж* (*повторяемость*) frequency; (*nom pl* -о́ты; *ТЕХ*) frequency.

часто́тность (-и) *ж* frequency.

часту́ш|ка (-ки; *gen pl* -ек) *ж traditional humorous folk song.*

ча́стый *прил* frequent; (*сито*) fine; (*лес. ряд предметов*) dense.

част|ь (-и; *gen pl* -е́й, *dat pl* -я́м) *ж* part; (*симфонии*) movement; (*отдел*) department; (*ВОЕН*) unit; **хозя́йственная** ~ supply department; **уче́бная** ~ academic studies office;

по ча́сти +gen when it comes to; э́то не по мое́й ча́сти this is not my department; разрыва́ться (impf) на ча́сти to have lots on the go at once; её рву́т на ча́сти she is in constant demand; часть ре́чи part of speech; часть све́та continent.
ча́стью нареч partly.
час|ы́ (-о́в) мн (карманные) watch ед; (стенные) clock ед.
ча́хл|ый (-, -а, -о) прил (цветок) withered; (человек) sickly.
ча́х|нуть (-ну, -нешь; pt -, -ла, -ло, perf зача́хнуть) несов неперех (растения) to wither; (человек, животное) to fade away.
чахо́т|ка (-и) ж consumption.
ча́ш|а (-и) ж bowl; (весов) pan; у них дом – по́лная ~ they've got everything imaginable in their house; ~ терпе́ния перепо́лнилась this is the last straw.
ча́ш|ка сущ см ча́шка.
ча́шеч|ка (-ки; gen pl -ек) ж уменьш от ча́шка; (БОТ) calyx; коле́нная ~ kneecap.
ча́ш|ка (-ки; gen pl -ек) ж cup; (весов) pan.
ча́щ|а (-и) ж (лес) thick forest.
ча́ще сравн прил от ча́стый ◆ сравн нареч от ча́сто.
ча́яни|е (-я) ср (обычно мн) aspiration.
ча́|ять (-ю) несов перех: он в ней души́ не ~ет he dotes on her.
чванли́в|ый (-, -а, -о) прил conceited.
чва́нств|о (-а) ср conceit.
чебуре́к (-а) м ≈ meat pasty.
чего́ мест см что.
чей (чьего́; см Table 7; f чья, nt чьё, pl чьи) мест whose; ~ э́то ребёнок? whose child is this?; ~ бы то ни́ был no matter whose it is.
чей-либо (чьего́-либо; как чей; см Table 7; f чья-либо, nt чьё-либо, pl чьи-либо) мест = чей-нибудь.
чей-нибудь (чьего́-нибудь; как чей; см Table 7; f чья-нибудь, nt чьё-нибудь, pl чьи-нибудь) мест anyone's.
чей-то (чьего́-то; как чей; см Table 7; f чья-то, nt чьё-то, pl чьи-то) мест someone's, somebody's.
чек (-а) м (банковский) cheque (BRIT), check (US); (товарный, кассовый) receipt; выбива́ть (вы́бить perf) ~ to issue a receipt (to be presented as proof of payment in Russian shops).
Чека́ ж сокр (ист: = Чрезвыча́йная коми́ссия по борьбе́ с контрреволю́цией и сабота́жем) Cheka (state security police in Soviet Russia from 1918-1922).
чека́н|ить (-ю, -ишь; perf отчека́нить) несов перех (монеты) to mint; (узор) to enchase; ~ (отчека́нить perf) слова́ to enunciate one's words.
чека́н|ка (-и) ж (монет) minting; (изделие) enchased object.

чеки́ст (-а) м (ист) Cheka officer.
че́ковый прил cheque опред (BRIT), check опред (US); че́ковая кни́жка cheque book.
чёл|ка (-ки; gen pl -ок) ж (человека) fringe (BRIT), bangs мн (US); (лошади) forelock.
челно́к (-а́) м (лодка) dugout; (швейный) shuttle.
челно́чный прил shuttle опред.
челове́к (-а; nom pl лю́ди, gen pl люде́й) м human (being); (некто, личность) person (мн people); два/три/четы́ре ~а two/three/four people; пять/шесть итп ~ five/six итп people; будь ~ом, помоги́ нам! (разг) be a sport and give us a hand!; вот ~! (разг) what a character!
челове́ко-де́нь (-ня; gen pl -ней) м man-day.
человеколю́би|е (-я) ср philanthropy.
человеконенави́стник (-а) м misanthrope.
человеконенави́стническ|ий (-ая, -ое, -ие) прил misanthropic.
челове́ко-час (-а) м man-hour.
челове́чен прил см челове́чный.
челове́ческ|ий (-ая, -ое, -ие) прил human опред; (человечный) humane; по-~и in a humane way.
челове́честв|о (-а) ср humanity, mankind.
челове́ч|ный (-ен, -на, -но) прил humane.
чёлок сущ см чёлка.
че́люст|ь (-и) ж (АНАТ) jaw.
Челя́бинск (-а) м Chelyabinsk.
чем мест см что ◆ союз than; (разг: вместо того чтобы) instead of; бо́льше, ~ де́сять челове́к more than ten people; ~ спо́рить, дава́й спро́сим кого́-нибудь instead of arguing, let's ask someone; ~ бо́льше/ра́ньше итп, тем лу́чше the bigger/earlier итп, the better.
чемода́н (-а) м suitcase; сиде́ть (impf) на ~ах (перен: разг) to have one's bags packed.
чемпио́н (-а) м champion; ~ по те́ннису tennis champion.
чемпиона́т (-а) м championship; ~ страны́ по хокке́ю national hockey championships.
чемпио́н|ка (-ки; gen pl -ок) ж см чемпио́н.
чему́ мест см что.
чепе́ ср нескл (разг) crisis.
чепух|а́ (-и́) ж (разг) rubbish (BRIT), garbage (US).
че́пчик (-а) м bonnet (hat).
че́рв|и (-е́й) мн (КАРТЫ) hearts мн.
черви́в|ый (-, -а, -о) прил maggoty.
черво́н|ец (-ца) м (разг: 10 рублей) ten roubles.
черво́нн|ый прил (КАРТЫ): ~ая да́ма/деся́тка the queen/ten of hearts.
черво́нца итп сущ см черво́нец.
черв|ь (-я́; gen pl -е́й) м worm; (личинка) maggot.
червя́|к (-а́) м worm.
червя́чный прил (ТЕХ) worm опред.
черда́к (-а́) м attic, loft.
черда́чный прил attic опред.
черёд м (разг) turn; всё идёт свои́м чередо́м

everything is going as normal.

череда́ (**-ы́**) ж (*люде́й*) stream; (*собы́тий*) sequence.

череду́|ова́ть (**-ую**) несов перех: ~ что-н с +*instr* to alternate sth with

▸ **череду́ова́ться** несов возв to alternate; **~ся** (*impf*) **с** +*instr* to take turns with.

KEYWORD

че́рез предл (+*acc*) **1** (*поперёк*) across, over; **мост че́рез кана́л/ре́ку** the bridge across или over the canal/river; **переходи́ть** (**перейти́** *perf*) **че́рез доро́гу** to cross the road

2 (*сквозь*) through; **он влез че́рез окно́** he climbed through the window; **че́рез лу́пу** through a magnifying glass

3 (*поверх*) over; **он перелёз че́рез забо́р** he climbed over the fence; **де́ти пры́гают че́рез верёвку** the children are jumping over a rope

4 (*спустя*) in; **че́рез час** in an hour('s time); **че́рез ме́сяц/год** in a month('s)/year('s) (time)

5 (*минуя какое-н простра́нство*): **че́рез три кварта́ла – ста́нция** the station is three blocks away

6 (*при помощи*) via; **он переда́л письмо́ че́рез знако́мого** he sent the letter via a friend

7 (*при повторении де́йствия*) every; **принима́йте табле́тки че́рез ка́ждый час** take the tablets every hour.

черёмух|а (**-и**) ж bird cherry.

чёрен прил см **чёрный**.

черен|о́к (**-ка́**) м (*рукоя́тка*) handle; (*бот*) cutting.

че́реп (**-а**) м skull.

черепа́х|а (**-и**) ж tortoise; (*морска́я*) turtle.

черепа́ховый прил (*суп*) turtle; (*гребень*) tortoiseshell.

черепа́ш|ий (**-ья, -ье, -ьи**) прил tortoise's; (*морско́й*) turtle's; **идти́** (*impf*) **~ьим ша́гом** to go at a snail's pace.

черепи́ц|а (**-ы**) ж tile ◆ собир tiles мн.

черепи́чный прил tiled.

черепи́ц|а сущ см **черепо́к**.

черепно́й прил skull опред; **черепна́я коро́бка** cranium.

череп|о́к (**-ка́**) м pottery fragment.

чересчу́р нареч far too; **э́то уж ~!** that's just too much!

чере́ш|ня (**-ни**; gen pl **-ен**) ж (*де́рево*) cherry (tree); (*плод*) cherry.

черка́|ть (**-ю**; perf **начерка́ть**) несов перех (*разг*) to draw lines on; (*зачёркивать*) to cross out.

черкн|у́ть (**-у́, -ёшь**) сов перех (*разг: написа́ть*) to scribble.

черне́|ть (**-ю**; perf **почерне́ть**) несов неперех (*становиться чёрным*) to turn black; (*no perf*; *виднеться*) to show black.

черни́к|а (**-и**) ж (*куста́рник*) bilberry (bush) ◆ собир bilberries мн.

черни́л|а (**-**) мн ink ед.

черни́льниц|а (**-ы**) ж inkwell.

черни́льный прил ink опред; **черни́льный каранда́ш** *graphite pencil which writes in purple when moistened*.

черн|и́ть (**-ю́, -и́шь**; perf **начерни́ть**) несов перех (*брови*) to tint; (*perf* **очерни́ть**; *имя, репута́цию*) to tarnish; (*no perf*; *сталь, серебро́*) to tarnish.

чёрно-бе́лый прил black-and-white.

чернобу́рк|а (**-и**) ж (*разг: мех*) silver fox.

чёрно-бу́рый прил: **~ая лиса́** silver fox.

чернови́к (**-а́**) м draft.

чернов|о́й прил draft опред; **~а́я рабо́та** rough work.

черноволо́с|ый (**-, -а, -о**) прил black-haired.

черного́р|ец (**-ца**) м Montenegrin.

Черного́ри|я (**-и**) ж Montenegro.

черного́р|ка (**-ки**; gen pl **-ок**) ж см **черного́рец**.

черного́рск|ий (**-ая, -ое, -ие**) прил Montenegrin.

черного́рца итп сущ см **черного́рец**.

чернозём (**-а**) м black earth.

чернокож|ий (**-ая, -ее, -ие**) прил black (*person*) ◆ (**-его**; decl like adj) м black (person) (*мн* people).

чернорабо́ч|ий (**-его**; decl like adj) м unskilled worker.

черносли́в (**-а**) м собир prunes мн.

чернот|а́ (**-ы́**) ж blackness.

чёрн|ый (**-ен, -на́, -но́**) прил black; (*мра́чный*) gloomy; (*no short form*; *престу́пный*) wicked; (*за́дний*) back опред; **держа́ть** (*impf*) **кого́-н в ~ном те́ле** to treat sb badly; **~ным по бе́лому** in black and white; **~ная рабо́та** dirty work; **чёрные мета́ллы** ferrous metals; **чёрный ко́фе** black coffee; **чёрный ры́нок** black market.

че́рпа|ть (**-ю**) несов перех (*жи́дкость*) to ladle; (*песо́к*) to scoop (up); (*перен: зна́ния, си́лы*) to derive.

черпн|у́ть (**-у́, -ёшь**) сов перех (*жи́дкость*) to ladle; (*песо́к*) to scoop (up).

черстве́|ть (**-ю**; perf **зачерстве́ть**) несов неперех (*хлеб*) to go stale; (*perf* **очерстве́ть**; *челове́к, душа́*) to harden.

чёрств|ый (**-, -а́, -о**) прил (*хлеб*) stale; (*челове́к, душа́*) hard.

чёрт (**-а**; nom pl **че́рти**, gen pl **черте́й**) м (*дья́вол*) devil; **у него́ де́нег до ~а** (*разг*) he's rolling in money; **иди́ к ~у!** (*разг*) go to hell!; **к ~у!** *reply to a wish of good luck*; **ни черта́** not a thing; **~ меня́ дёрнул** I don't know what got into me; **чем ~ не шу́тит** you never know; **~ возьми́** или **побери́** или **подери́!** (*разг*) damn it!; **~ его́ зна́ет!** (*разг*) God knows!; **~ зна́ет что!** (*разг*) it's outrageous!; **он мо́жет ~ зна́ет, что наде́лать** it's frightening to think what he might do; **~ с ним!** (*разг*) to hell with him!; **он дал тебе́ де́нег? – ~а с два!** (*разг*) did he give you any money? – like hell he did!

черт|а́ (**-ы́**) ж (*ли́ния*) line; (*грани́ца*) limit; (*при́знак*) trait; **в о́бщих ~х** in general terms; см также **черты́**.

чертёж (-á) *м* draft.
чертёжник (-а) *м* draughtsman (*BRIT*) (*мн* draughtsmen), draftsman (*US*) (*мн* draftsmen).
чертёжный *прил* drawing *опред*.
чер|тúть (-чý, -тишь; *perf* **начертúть**) *несов перех* (*линию*) to draw; (*план, график*) to draw up.
чёртов (-а, -о, -ы) *прил* (*разг: холод, работа итп*) damn(ed); **чёртова дюжина** baker's dozen.
чертóвски *нареч* (*разг*) dreadfully: **я ~ гóлоден** I'm ravenous.
чертóвский (-ая, -ое, -ие) *прил* (*разг*) damn (ed).
чертополóх (-а) *м* thistle.
чёрточ|ка (-ки; *gen pl* -ек) *ж уменьш от* **чертá**; (*дефис*) hyphen; **э́то слóво пúшется чéрез ~ку** this word is written with a hyphen.
черт|ы́ (-) *мн* (*также:* **~ лицá**) features *мн*.
черчéни|е (-я) *ср* (*действие*) drawing; (*ПРОСВЕЩ*) technical drawing.
черчý *несов см* **чертúть**.
че|сáть (-шý, -шешь; *perf* **почесáть**) *несов перех* (*спину*) to scratch; (*no perf; разг: гребнем*) to comb; (: *щёткой*) to brush; **~** (*impf*) **язы́к** *или* **языкóм** to natter
▶ **чесáться** (*perf* **почесáться**) *несов возв* to scratch o.s.; (*зудеть*) to itch; **он и не чéшется** (*разг*) he doesn't lift a finger; **у меня рýки ~шýтся** +*infin* (*разг*) I'm itching to do.
чеснóк (-á) *м* garlic.
чесóт|ка (-и) *ж* (*МЕД*) scabies.
чéствовани|е (-я) *ср* (*действие*) honouring (*BRIT*), honoring (*US*).
чéств|овать (-ую) *несов перех* to honour (*BRIT*), honor (*US*).
чéстен *прил см* **чéстный**.
чéстно *нареч* honestly ♦ *как сказ*: **так бýдет ~** that'll be fair.
чéстность (-и) *ж* honesty.
чéст|ный (-ен, -нá, -но) *прил* honest; (*безупречный*) upright; **~ное úмя** good name; **~ное слóво** honest to God; **держáться** (*impf*) **на ~ном слóве** (*разг*) to hang by a thread.
честолюб|ец (-ца) *м* ambitious person (*мн* people).
честолюбúв|ый (-, -а, -о) *прил* (*человек, план*) ambitious.
честолюби|е (-я) *ср* ambition.
честолюбца *итп сущ см* **честолюбец**.
чест|ь (-и) *ж* honour (*BRIT*), honor (*US*); (*loc sg* -**ú**; *почёт*) glory; **в ~** +*gen* in hono(u)r of; **к чéсти когó-н** to sb's credit; **дéлать** (*impf*) **~ комý-н** to do sb credit; (*оказывать уважение*) to do sb an hono(u)r; **отдавáть** (**отдáть** *perf*) **~ комý-н** to salute sb; **выходúть** (**выйти** *perf*) **с чéстью из чегó-н** to come out of sth with one's hono(u)r intact; **порá и ~ знать** (*разг*) it is time to wind

up.
чет|á (-ы́) *ж* couple; **он мне не ~** he is no match for me.
четвéрг (-á) *м* Thursday; *см также* **вторник**.
четверéн|ьки (-ек) *мн*: **вставáть** (**встать** *perf*) **на ~** to go down on all fours; **ходúть** (*impf*) **на ~ьках** to move on all fours.
четвёр|ка (-ки; *gen pl* -ок) *ж* (*цифра, карта*) four; (*ПРОСВЕЩ*) ≈ B (*school mark*); (*группа людей*) foursome; (*разг: автобус, трамвай итп*) (number) four (*bus, tram etc*).
четверн|я́ (-ú; *gen pl* -éй) *ж* quadruplets *мн*.
чéтвер|о (*см* **Table 36a**; -ы́х) *чис* four; *см также* **двóе**.
четвёрок *сущ см* **четвёрка**.
четвероклáссник (-а) *м* pupil in fourth year at school (*usually ten years old*).
четвероклáссниц|а (-ы) *ж см* **четвероклáссник**.
четвероногий (-ая, -ое, -ие) *прил* four-legged.
четверостúши|е (-я) *ср* quatrain.
четвёрт|ая (-ой; *decl like adj*) *ж*: **однá ~** one quarter.
четвёрт|овáть (-ýю) *несов перех* to quarter (*at execution*).
четвёрт|ый (-ая, -ое, -ые) *чис* fourth; **сейчáс ~ час** it's after three; *см также* **пятый**.
четвéрт|ь (-и) *ж* quarter; (*МУЗ*) crotchet (*BRIT*), quarter note (*US*); (*ПРОСВЕЩ*) term.
четвертьфинáл (-а) *м* (*СПОРТ*) quarter final.
четверы́м *итп чис см* **чéтверо**.
чёт|кий (-кая, -кое, -кие; -ок, -кá, -ко) *прил* clear; (*движения, шаг*) precise.
чёткост|ь (-и) *ж* (*см прил*) clarity; precision.
чётный *прил* (*число*) even.
чёток *сущ см* **чёткий**.
четы́р|е (-ёх; *instr sg* -ьмя́; *см* **Table 25**) *чис* (*цифра, число*) four; (*ПРОСВЕЩ*) ≈ B (*school mark*); **ей ~ гóда** she is four (years old); **онú живýт в дóме нóмер ~** they live at number four; **óколо четырёх** about four; **кнúга стóит ~ рубля́** the book costs four roubles; **~ с половúной часá** four and a half hours; **сейчáс ~ часá** it is four o'clock; **я́блоки продаются по ~ штýки** the apples are sold in fours; **делúть** (**разделúть** *perf*) **что-н на ~** to divide sth into four.
четы́р|еста (-ёхсóт; *см* **Table 33**) *чис* four hundred; *см также* **сто**.
четырёх *чис см* **четы́ре**.
четырёхднéвный *прил* four-day.
четырёхкрáт|ный *прил*: **~ чемпиóн** four-times champion; **в ~ом размéре** fourfold.
четырёхлéти|е (-я) *ср* (*срок*) four years; (*годовщина*) fourth anniversary.
четырёхлéт|ний (-яя, -ее, -ие) *прил* (*период*) four-year; (*ребёнок*) four-year-old.
четырёхмесячный *прил* four-month;

(ребёнок) four-month-old.

четырёхнедёльный *прил* four-week;
(ребёнок) four-week-old.

четырёхсо́т *чис см* **четы́реста.**

четырёхсотлётие (-я) *ср (срок)* four hundred
years; *(годовщина)* quartercentenary.

четырёхсотлётний (-яя, -ее, -ие) *прил
(период)* four-hundred-year; *(дерево)* four-
hundred-year-old.

четырёхсо́т|ый (-ая, -ое, -ые) *чис* four-
hundredth.

четырёхста́х *чис см* **четы́реста.**

четырёхуго́льник (-а) *м* quadrangle.

четырёхуго́льный *прил* quadrangular.

четырёхчасово́й *прил (рабочий день)* four-
hour; *(поезд)* four o'clock.

четы́рнадцатый (-ая, -ое, -ые) *чис* fourteenth;
см также **пя́тый.**

четы́рнадцать (-и; *как* **пять;** *см* **Table 27)** *чис*
fourteen; *см также* **пять.**

четырьмя́ *чис см* **четы́ре.**

четырьмяста́ми *чис см* **четы́реста.**

чех (-а) *м* Czech.

чехарда́ (-ы́) *ж (разг: игра)* leapfrog; *(перен:
путаница)* muddle.

Чёхия (-и) *ж* the Czech Republic.

чех|о́л (-ла́) *м (для мебели)* cover; *(для гитары,
для оружия)* case.

Чехослова́кия (-и) *ж (ист)* Czechoslovakia.

чечеви́ца (-ы) *ж* lentil ♦ *собир* lentils *мн.*

чече́н|ец (-ца) *м* Chechen.

чече́н|ка (-ки; *gen pl* -ок) *ж см* **чече́нец.**

чече́нца *итп сущ см* **чече́нец.**

чечётка (-и) *ж* tap dance.

Чечня (-и́) *ж* Chechenia, Chechnya.

чёш|ка (-ки; *gen pl* -ек) *ж см* **чех.**

чёшский (-ая, -ое, -ие) *прил* Czech; ~ **язы́к**
Czech.

чешу́(сь) *итп несов см* **чеса́ть(ся).**

чешу́йка (-и) *ж* scale.

чешу́йчатый *прил* scaly.

чешу́я (-и́) *ж собир* scales *мн.*

чи́бис (-а) *м* lapwing.

чиж (-а́) *м* siskin.

чи́збургер (-а) *м* cheeseburger.

Чика́го *м нескл* Chicago.

Чи́ли *ср нескл* Chile.

чили́йский (-ая, -ое, -ие) *прил* Chilean.

чин (-а; *nom pl* -ы́) *м* rank; **повы́сить** *(повы́сить
perf)* **кого́-н в чи́не** to promote sb to a higher
rank.

чин|и́ть (-ю́, -ишь; *perf* **почини́ть)** *несов перех*
to mend, repair; *(perf* **очини́ть;** *карандаш)* to
sharpen; (-ю́, -йшь; *perf* **учини́ть;** *насилие,
произвол)* to commit; *(no perf; препятствия)* to
create.

чино́вник (-а) *м (служащий)* official;
(бюрократ) bureaucrat.

чино́внически|й (-ая, -ое, -ие) *прил
(должность)* official; *(аппарат)* bureaucratic.

чи́пс|ы (-ов) *мн* crisps *мн.*

чири́ка|ть (-ю) *несов неперех* to twitter.

чи́рка|ть (-ю) *несов неперех:* ~ **спи́чкой** to
strike a match.

чи́ркн|уть (-у, -ешь) *сов неперех* to strike.

чи́сел *сущ см* **число́.**

чи́сленность (-и) *ж (армии)* numbers *мн;
(учащихся)* number; ~ **населе́ния** population.

чи́сленный *прил (количественный)* numerical;
чи́сленное превосхо́дство numerical
advantage; **чи́сленный соста́в** *(армии)* total
numbers *мн.*

числи́тель (-я) *м* numerator.

числи́тельн|ое (-ого; *decl like adj)* *ср* numeral.

чи́сл|иться (-юсь, -ишься) *несов возв (в
организации)* to be registered; ~ *(impf)* +*instr
(больным, должником итп)* to be registered as;
он ~**ится дире́ктором фи́рмы** he's officially
the director of the firm; **за ним** ~**ится долг** he
owes some money; **в спи́ске его́ фами́лия не**
~**ится** his name is not on the list.

числ|о́ (-а́; *nom pl* -а, *gen pl* -ел) *ср* number;
(день месяца) date; **еди́нственное** ~ singular;
мно́жественное ~ plural; **быть** *(impf)* **в** ~**ле́**
+*gen* to be among(st); **какое сего́дня** ~? what is
the date today?; **прие́ду в пе́рвых чи́слах
ма́рта** I am coming at the beginning of March;
отмеча́ть *(***отме́тить** *perf)* **что-н за́дним** ~**м** to
backdate sth; **узнава́ть** *(***узна́ть** *perf)* **за́дним**
~**м** *(разг)* to find out later; **в том** ~**ле́** including;
оши́бкам нет ~**ла́** there are countless mistakes.

числово́й *прил:* ~**ое програ́ммное
управле́ние** *(КОМП)* numerically programmed
(BRIT) *или* programed *(US)* control.

чисти́лище (-а) *ср* purgatory.

чи́стить (-щу, -стишь; *perf* **вы́чистить** *или*
почи́стить) *несов перех* to clean; *(зубы)* to
brush, clean; *(perf* **почи́стить;** *яблоко,
картошку)* to peel; *(рыбу)* to scale; *(perf*
очи́стить; *дно реки)* to dredge; *(сад)* to clean
up; *(perf* **обчи́стить;** *разг: кассу, человека)* to
clean out.

чи́ст|ка (-ки; *gen pl* -ок) *ж (действие)* cleaning;
(: овощей) peeling; *(в партии)* purge.

чи́сто *нареч (только)* purely; *(убранный,
сделанный)* neatly ♦ *как сказ:* **в до́ме** ~ the
house is clean.

чистови́к (-а́) *м* fair copy.

чистово́й *прил* fair.

чи́сток *сущ см* **чи́стка.**

чистокро́вный *прил* pure-breed; ~**ая ло́шадь**
thoroughbred.

чистопло́тен *прил см* **чистопло́тный.**

чистопло́тность (-и) *ж* cleanliness.

чистопло́тный (-ен, -на, -но) *прил* clean;
(перен: порядочный) decent.

чистопро́бный *прил (золото)* pure.

чистосерде́чный (-ен, -на, -но) *прил* sincere.

чистот|а́ (-ы́) *ж (воздуха, спирта, раствора)*
purity; **у него́ в до́ме всегда́** ~ his house is
always extremely clean.

чи́ст|ый (-, -а́, -о) *прил (одежда, комната)* clean;
(любовь, сердце, человек) pure and innocent;

(*совесть, небо, произношение*) clear; (*золото, спирт*) pure; (*язык*) proper; (*no short form*; *прибыль, вес*) net; (*совпадение, случайность*) pure; **выводи́ть (вы́вести** *perf*) **кого́-н на ~ую во́ду** (*разоблачить*) to expose sb.

читáльный *прил*: ~ **зал** reading room.

читáтел|ь (-я) *м* reader.

читáтельниц|а (-ы) *ж см* **читáтель**.

читá|ть (-ю; *perf* **проче́сть** *или* **прочитáть**) *несов перех* to read; (*декламировать*) to recite; (*курс*) to teach; (*лекцию*) to give.

чихá|ть (-ю; *perf* **чихну́ть**) *несов неперех* to sneeze; (*разг: мотор*) to splutter: **ему́ ~ на прáвила/свои́х роди́телей** he doesn't give a damn about the rules/his parents.

чи́ще *сравн прил от* **чи́стый ♦** *сравн нареч от* **чи́сто**.

чи́щу *несов см* **чи́стить**.

ЧК *ж сокр* = **Чекá**.

член (-а) *м* member; (*обычно мн: конечности*) limb; **половóй ~** penis; **~ предложе́ния** part of a sentence.

член|и́ть (-ю́, -и́шь; *perf* **расчлени́ть**) *несов перех* to break up.

членкóр (-а) *м сокр* = **член-корреспонде́нт**.

член-корреспонде́нт (-а, -а) *м* (*звание*) *academic title junior to academician*.

членоразде́л|ьный (-ен, -ьна, -ьно) *прил* intelligible.

чле́нск|ий (-ая, -ое, -ие) *прил* membership.

чле́нств|о (-а) *ср* membership.

ЧМ *сокр* (= *частóтная модуля́ция*) FM (= *frequency modulation*).

чóка|ться (-юсь; *perf* **чóкнуться**) *несов возв* to clink glasses (*during a toast*).

чóкнут|ый (-, -а, -о) *прил* (*разг: человек*) barmy, crazy.

чóкн|уться (-усь, -ешься) *сов от* **чóкаться**.

чóпор|ный (-ен, -на, -но) *прил* prim.

ЧП *ср сокр* = **чрезвычáйное происше́ствие**.

ЧПУ *ср сокр* = **числовóе прогрáммное управле́ние**.

чрезвычá|ен *прил см* **чрезвычáйный**.

чрезвычáйно *нареч* extremely.

чрезвычá|йный (-ен, -йна, -йно) *прил* (*исключительный*) extraordinary; (*no short form*; *экстренный*) emergency *опред*; **чрезвычáйный и полномóчный посóл** ambassador extraordinary and plenipotentiary; **чрезвычáйное положе́ние** state of emergency; **чрезвычáйное происше́ствие** crisis.

чрезме́р|ный (-ен, -на, -но) *прил* excessive.

чте́ни|е (-я) *ср* reading; *см также* **чте́ния**.

чте́ни|я (-й) *мн* course *ед* of lectures.

чтец (-á) *м* reader.

чт|ить (*см* **Table 17**) *несов перех* to honour (*BRIT*), honor (*US*).

KEYWORD

что (**чего́**; (*см* **Table 6**) *мест* **1** (*вопросительное*) what; **что ты сказáл?** what did you say?; **что с тобóй?** what's the matter (with you)?; **что Вы говори́те?** you don't say!; **к чему́** *или* **на что тебе́ э́то?** what do you need it for?

2 (*относительное*) which; **онá не поздорóвалась, что бы́ло мне неприя́тно** she did not say hello, which was unpleasant for me; **что ни говори́** ... whatever you say ...

3 (*столько сколько*): **онá закричáла что бы́ло сил** she shouted with her all might

4 (*который*) that; **де́рево, что растёт у дóма** the tree that grows by the house

5 (*разг: что-нибудь*) anything; **е́сли что случи́тся** if anything happens, should anything happen; **в слу́чае чего́** if anything crops up; **чуть что – срáзу скажи́ мне** get in touch at the slightest thing

♦ *нареч* (*почему*) why; **что ты грусти́шь?** why are you sad?; **мне не хóчется идти́ – что так?** I don't feel like going – why's that?

♦ *союз* **1** (*при сообщении, высказывании*): **я знáю, что нáдо де́лать** I know what must be done; **я знáю, что он прие́дет** I know that he will come; **стрáнно то, что он молчи́т** it is strange that he remains silent; **что ни день, то нóвые пробле́мы** there isn't a day without new problems

2 (*во фразах*): **а что?** (*разг*) why (do you ask)?; **к чему́** (*зачем*) why; **не́ за что!** not at all! (*BRIT*), you're welcome! (*US*); **ни за что!** (*разг*) no way!; **ни за что ни про что** (*разг*) for no (good) reason; **что ты!** (*при возражении*) what!; **я здесь ни при чём** it has nothing to do with me; **э́то тут ни при чём** that's beside the point; **чегó там!** forget it!; **что ж** (*да*) oh well; **что за чепухá?** what kind of nonsense is this!; **сáмый что ни на есть лу́чший/óпытный** best/most experienced there is; **что к чему́** (*разг*) what's what; **поéхали, что ли?** (*разг*) shall we go or not?

чтоб *союз* = **чтóбы**.

KEYWORD

чтóбы *союз*: **чтóбы** +*infin* (*выражает цель*) in order *или* so as to do; **я бу́ду рабóтать нóчью, чтóбы сдать сочине́ние зáвтра** I will work at night in order *или* so as to hand in the composition tomorrow

♦ *союз* (+*pt*) **1** (*выражает цель*) so that; **учи́тель говори́т ме́дленно, чтóбы мы всё понимáли** the teacher speaks slowly so that we understand everything

2 (*выражает желательность*): **я хочу́, чтóбы онá пришлá** I want her to come

3 (*выражает возможность*): **не мóжет быть,**

чтобы он так поступи́л it can't be possible that
he should have acted like that
♦ част 1 (выражает пожелание): что́бы она́
заболе́ла! I hope she gets ill!
2 (выражает требование): что́бы я его́ здесь
бо́льше не ви́дел! I hope (that) I never see him
here again!

что́-либо (чего́-либо; как что; см Table 6)
мест = что́-нибудь.
что́-нибудь (чего́-нибудь; как что; см Table 6)
мест (в утвердительных предложениях)
something; (в вопросительных предложениях)
anything; скажи́ ~ say something; есть ~
интере́сное? is there anything interesting?
что́-то (чего́-то; как что; см Table 6) мест
something; (приблизительно) something like ♦
нареч (разг: почему́-то) somehow; он
получи́л ~ о́коло ста пи́сем he got something
like a hundred letters; ~ не по́мню тако́го
somehow I don't remember that.
чуб (-а) м forelock.
чува́ш (-а) м Chuvash.
чува́шек сущ см чува́шка.
Чува́ши|я (-и) ж Chuvashia.
чува́ш|ка (-ки; gen pl -ек) ж см чува́ш.
чу́вствен|ный (-, -на, -но) прил (удовольствие,
любовь итп) sensual; (no short form;
восприятия) sensory.
чувстви́телен прил см чувстви́тельный.
чувстви́тельность (-и) ж sensitivity; (стихов,
музыки) sentimentality.
чувстви́тель|ный (-ен, -ьна, -ьно) прил
sensitive; (стихи, музыка) sentimental; (удар)
heavy; (оскорбление) deep; (потери)
considerable.
чу́вств|о (-а) ср (эмоция, ощущение) feeling;
(+gen; юмора, долга, ответственности) sense
of; лиша́ться (лиши́ться perf) чувств to faint,
lose consciousness; приводи́ть (привести́ perf)
кого́-н в ~ to bring sb round.
чу́вств|овать (-ую; perf почу́вствовать) несов
перех to feel; (присутствие, опасность) to
sense; ~ (impf) себя́ хорошо́/пло́хо/нело́вко to
feel good/bad/awkward
▶ чу́вствоваться несов возв (жара,
усталость) to be felt; ~уется, что он
волну́ется you can tell he's worried.
чугу́н (-á) м cast iron.
чугу́нный прил cast-iron.
чуда́к (-á) м eccentric.
чу́ден прил см чу́дный.
чуде́н прил см чудно́й.
чудеса́ итп сущ от чу́до.
чуде́сен прил см чуде́сный.
чуде́сно нареч wonderfully ♦ как сказ it's
wonderful.
чуде́с|ный (-ен, -на, -но) прил (необычный)
miraculous; (очень хороший) marvellous (BRIT),
marvelous (US), wonderful.
чуди́|ть (2sg -ишь, 3sg -ит) несов неперех to
behave oddly.

чу́д|иться (3sg -ится, 3pl -ятся, perf
почу́диться) несов возв (+dat) to appear.
чу́дище (-а) ср monster.
чудно́й (-ён, -на́, -но́) прил (разг) odd.
чу́дный (-ен, -на, -но) прил (великолепный)
marvellous (BRIT), marvelous (US).
чу́д|о (-а; nom pl -еса́) ср miracle.
чудо́вище (-а) ср monster.
чудо́вищ|ный (-ен, -на, -но) прил
(преступление, факт) monstrous; (перен:
ураган, мороз) terrible.
чудоде́йствен|ный (-ен, -на, -но) прил
(средство) miraculous.
чу́дом нареч (спастись) by a miracle.
чужа́к (-á) м stranger.
чужби́н|а (-ы) ж foreign country.
чужда́|ться (-юсь) несов возв: ~ +gen (также
перен) to shun.
чу́жд|ый (-, -á, -о) прил (взгляды, ценности)
alien; ~ +gen devoid of; ему́ чужда́ за́висть he
is devoid of envy.
чужезе́м|ец (-ца) м stranger.
чужезе́мный прил from foreign parts.
чужезе́мца итп сущ см чужезе́мец.
чужеро́дный прил (элемент) alien.
чуж|о́й прил (принадлежащий другому) someone
или somebody else's; (речь, обычай) foreign;
(человек) strange ♦ (-о́го; decl like adj) м
stranger; под ~им и́менем under an assumed
name.
чу́кч|а (-и) м/ж нескл Chukchi.
чула́н (-а) м storeroom.
чул|о́к (-ка́; gen pl -о́к, dat pl -ка́м) м (обычно мн)
stocking.
чум|а́ (-ы́) ж plague.
чума́з|ый (-, -а, -о) прил (разг) mucky.
чур межд (разг): ~ я пе́рвый! mind out, I'm
first!; ~ меня́! get away from me! (to keep evil
at bay).
чурба́н (-а) м (деревянный) block; (разг:
пренебр: человек) blockhead.
чу́т|кий (-кая, -кое, -кие; -ок, -ка́, -ко) прил
sensitive; (натура) sympathetic; ~ сон light
sleep.
чу́ткость (-и) ж (см прил) sensitivity; sympathy.
чу́ток прил см чу́ткий.
чу́точк|а (-и) ж (разг): ~у a bit; ни ~и not a bit.
чуть нареч (разг: едва) hardly; (немного) a little
♦ союз (как только) as soon as; ~ (бы́ло) не
almost, nearly; ~ ли не almost certainly; ~ что
(разг) at the slightest thing.
чутьё (-я) ср (у животных) scent; (у людей)
intuition.
чу́чел|о (-а) ср (также перен) scarecrow; ~
живо́тного/пти́цы stuffed animal/bird.
чушь (-и) ж (разг) rubbish (BRIT), garbage (US).
чу́я|ть (-ю) несов перех (также перен) to scent;
я ног под собо́й не ~ю I'm walking on air; (от
усталости) my legs are giving way beneath me.
чьё (чьего́) мест см чей.
чьи (чьих) мест см чей.
чья (чьей) мест см чей.

~ Ш, ш ~

Ш, ш *сущ нескл* (*буква*) the 25th letter of the Russian alphabet.
ш *сокр* (= **широта́**) w. (= *width*).
ш. *сокр* (= **шту́ка**) ea. (= *each*).
ша́баш (-а) *м* Sabbath.
шаба́ш *част* (*кончено*) that's enough.
шабло́н (-а) *м* (*ТЕХ*) pattern, gauge; (*перен: в речи, в письме*) cliché.
шабло́н|ный *прил* (*об инструменте, о чертеже*) pattern *опред*; (-ен, -на, -но; *перен: фраза, ответ*) trite.
шаг (-а; *part gen* -у, *loc sg* -у́, *nom pl* -и́) *м* (*также перен*) step; **на ка́ждом ~у́** (*перен*) continually; **~ за ша́гом** step by step; **ша́гу не даю́т ступи́ть** (*перен*) one has no freedom of action; **прибавля́ть** (**приба́вить** *perf*) **ша́гу** to quicken one's pace; **предпринима́ть** (**предприня́ть** *perf*) **но́вые ~и** to take a new initiative; **я услы́шал ~и́** I heard footsteps.
шага́ть (-ю) *несов неперех* to march; (*делать шаг*) to step; **~й отсю́да!** (*разг*) get lost!
шагну́ть (-у́, -ёшь) *сов неперех* to step, take a step; **~** (*perf*) **вперёд** (*также перен*) to take a step forward.
ша́гом *нареч* (*идти*) at a walk, at walking pace; **~ марш!** (*ВОЕН*) quick march!
ша́ек *сущ см* **ша́йка**
ша́йб|а (-ы) *ж* (*ТЕХ: прокладка*) spacer; (: *болта*) washer; (*СПОРТ*) puck.
ша́йк|а (-йки; *gen pl* -ек) *ж* (*бандитская*) gang.
шака́л (-а) *м* jackal.
шала́нд|а (-ы) *ж* scow, barge.
шала́ш (-á) *м* hut (*made of branches*).
ша́лев|ый *прил*: **~ плато́к** shawl; **ша́левый воротни́к** shawl collar.
шале́|ть (-ю) *perf* **ошале́ть** *несов неперех* (*разг*) to go crazy; **~** (**ошале́ть** *perf*) **от ра́дости** to go mad with joy.
шал|и́ть (-ю́, -и́шь) *несов неперех* (*дети*) to be mischevious; (*разг: мотор, сердце*) to play up.
шаловли́в|ый (-, -а, -о) *прил* (*ребёнок*) mischevious; (*тон, глаза*) playful.
шалопа́|й (-я) *м* (*разг*) loafer, skiver.
ша́лост|ь (-и) *ж* (*проказа*) mischief.
шалу́н (-á) *м* mischevious boy.
шалу́н|ья (-ьи; *gen pl* -ий) *ж* mischevious girl.

шалфе́|й (-я) *м* (*БОТ*) sage.
шал|ь (-и) *ж* shawl.
шально́й *прил* (*разг*) wild; (*пуля*) stray; (*деньги*) easy.
шаля́й-валя́й *нареч* (*разг: небрежно*) any(old) how.
шама́н (-а) *м* (*колдун*) shaman.
шама́н|ка (-ки; *gen pl* -ок) *ж см* **шама́н**.
ша́мка|ть (-ю) *несов неперех* to mumble.
шампа́нск|ое (-ого; *decl like adj*) *ср* champagne.
шампиньо́н (-а) *м* (*БОТ*) (field) mushroom.
шампу́н|ь (-я) *м* shampoo.
шампу́р (-а) *м* skewer.
шанс (-а) *м* chance; **~ на что-н** chance of sth.
шансоне́т|ка (-ки; *gen pl* -ок) *ж см* **шансонье́**.
шансонье́ *м нескл* singer.
шанта́ж (-á) *м* blackmail.
шантажи́р|овать (-ую) *несов перех* to blackmail.
шантажи́ст (-а) *м* blackmailer.
шантажи́ст|ка (-ки; *gen pl* -ок) *ж см* **шантажи́ст**.
шантрап|а́ (-ы́) *м/ж собир* (*разг*) yobs *мн*.
Шанха́|й (-я) *м* Shanghai.
ша́п|ка (-ки; *gen pl* -ок) *ж* hat; (*перен: снежная*) cap; (*заголовок*) headline; **по ~ке дава́ть** (**дать** *perf*) +*dat* (*перен: разг*) to punish; **по ~ке получа́ть** (**получи́ть** *perf*) (*разг*) to be punished; **на воре́ ~ гори́т** he's given the game away.
ша́почн|ый *прил* of a hat; **~ое знако́мство** nodding acquaintance; **приходи́ть** (**прийти́** *perf*) **к ~ому разбо́ру** (*перен*) to miss the bus.
шар (-а; *nom pl* -ы́) *м* (*ГЕОМ*) sphere; (*кегли, бильярдный итп*) ball; **возду́шный ~** balloon; **земно́й ~** the Earth; **в до́ме хоть ~о́м покати́** the house is completely empty.
шара́д|а (-ы) *ж* charade.
шара́хн|уть (-у, -ешь; *impf* **шара́хать**) *сов* (*не*)*перех* (*разг*): **~** +*acc или* +*instr* (*ударять*) to thump
▶ **шара́хнуться** (*impf* **шара́хаться**) *сов возв* (*разг: отпрянуть*) to leap back; (: *удариться*): **~ся о** +*acc* to bang into.
шара́шкин *прил*: **~а конто́ра** dodgy enterprise; (*несолидное учреждение*) pathetic place.
шарж (-а) *м* caricature.
шаржи́р|овать (-ую) *несов перех* to caricature.

шáрик (-a) м уменьш от шар; (АНАТ): кровянóй ~ blood corpuscule.

шáриковый прил (подшипник) ball опред; ~ая рýчка ballpoint pen.

шарикоподшúпник (-a) м (ТЕХ) ball bearing.

шáрить (-ю, -ишь) несов неперех (разг) to grope; ~ (impf) глазáми to sweep; ~ (impf) по (чужúм) кармáнам (разг) to pick pockets.

шáрканье (-я) ср shuffling.

шáркать (-ю) несов неперех: ~ +instr to shuffle.

шáркнуть (-у, -ешь) сов неперех: ~ ногóй to click one's heels.

шарлатáн (-a) м charlatan.

шарлатáнка (-ки; gen pl -ок) ж см шарлатáн.

шарлатáнство (-a) ср charlatanism.

шарлóтка (-ки; gen pl -ок) ж (КУЛИН) charlotte.

шарм (-a) м (обаяние) charm.

шармáнка (-ки; gen pl -ок) ж (МУЗ) barrel organ.

шарнúр (-a) м (ТЕХ) hinge; (АВТ) (suspension) joint.

шаровáры (-) мн baggy trousers мн.

шаровúдный (-ен, -на, -но) прил spherical.

шаровóй прил (ГЕОМ) spherical; ~ клáпан ball valve; шаровáя мóлния (ГЕО) fireball, globe lightning.

шарообрáзный (-ен, -на, -но) прил = шаровúдный.

шарф (-a) м scarf.

шассú ср нескл (самолёта) landing gear; (автомобиля) chassis.

шáстать (-ю) несов неперех (разг) to mooch about.

шатáние (-я) ср (хождение) mooching about; (раскачивание) swaying; (перен: идейные) vacillation.

шатáть (-ю) несов перех (раскачивать) to rock; меня ~ет от устáлости I am reeling with tiredness

▶ шатáться несов возв (зуб) to be loose или wobbly; (столб) to shake; (от усталости) to reel, stagger; (разг: по городу, по улицам итп) to mooch about.

шатéн (-a) м man with auburn hair.

шатёр (-pá) м tent.

шáткий (-кая, -кое, -кие; -ок, -ка, -ко) прил (стул) wobbly, rickety; (перен: положение) precarious; (: доводы) shaky.

шáткость (-и) ж (см прил) wobbliness; precariousness; shakiness.

шатнýть (-ý, -ёшь) сов перех (столб) to shake

▶ шатнýться сов возв (столб) to be unsteady; (от усталости) to reel.

шáток прил см шáткий.

шатрá итп сущ см шатёр.

шатрóвый прил (крыша, купол) hipped; шатрóвая архитектýра hipped architecture.

шатýн (-á) м (ТЕХ) connecting rod.

шáфер (-a) м best man (мн men).

шафрáн (-a) м (БОТ) saffron.

шах (-a) м (монарх) shah; (в шахматах) check.

шахматúст (-a) м chess player.

шахматúстка (-ки; gen pl -ок) ж см шахматúст.

шáхматный прил (кружок, чемпионат) chess опред; (порядок, рисунок) staggered; шáхматная доскá chessboard.

шáхматы (-) мн (игра) chess ед; (фигуры) chessmen мн.

шáхта (-ы) ж (выработка) mine, pit; (предприятие) mine; (лифта) shaft.

шахтёр (-a) м miner.

шáшек сущ см шáшки.

шашúст (-a) м draughts (BRIT) или checkers (US) player.

шашúстка (-ки; gen pl -ок) ж см шашúст.

шáшка (-и) ж (игральная) draught (BRIT), checker (US); (взрывчатка) blasting cartridge; (оружие) sabre (BRIT), saber (US); см также шáшки.

шáшки (-ек) мн (игра) draughts мн (BRIT), checkers мн (US).

шашлык (-á) м shashlik, kebab.

шашлычная (-ой; decl like adj) ж kebab-house.

шáшни (-ей) мн (разг) affair ед.

шва итп сущ см шов.

швáбра (-ы) ж мор.

швáркнуть (-у, -ешь; impf швáркать) сов перех (разг) to hurl.

швартóв (-a) м (МОР) mooring line; отдавáть (отдáть perf) ~ы to cast off.

швартовáть (-ýю; perf пришвартовáть или ошвартовáть) несов перех (МОР) to moor.

швед (-a) м Swede.

швéдка (-ки; gen pl -ок) ж см швед.

швéдский (-ая, -ое, -ие) прил Swedish; ~ язык Swedish.

швéйный прил (машина, нитки) sewing опред; (фабрика) clothing опред.

швейцáр (-a) м doorman (мн doormen).

швейцáрец (-ца) м Swiss.

Швейцáрия (-и) ж Switzerland.

швейцáрка (-ки; gen pl -ок) ж см швейцáрец.

швейцáрский (-ая, -ое, -ие) прил Swiss.

швейцáрца итп сущ см швейцáрец.

Швéция (-и) ж Sweden.

швея (-и) ж seamstress.

швырнýть (-ý, -ёшь) сов (не)перех: ~ +acc или +instr to hurl.

швырять (-ю) несов перех to hurl, fling; ~ (impf) дéньги или деньгáми (разг) to throw one's money about

▶ швыряться несов возв (разг) to throw at each other; (перен): ~ся +instr (людьми) to treat lightly; ~ся (impf) деньгáми (разг) to throw one's money about.

шевелúть (-ю, -úшь; perf пошевелúть) несов перех (сено) to turn over; (подлеж: ветер) to stir ♦ неперех: ~ +instr (пальцами, губами) to move; ~ (пошевелúть perf) мозгáми (перен: разг) to use one's head

▶ шевелúться (perf пошевелúться) несов возв to stir; ~úсь! (разг) get a move on!

шевельнýть (-ý, -ёшь) сов неперех: ~ +instr

(пальцами, плечом) to move
▶ **шевельну́ться** *сов возв* to stir.
шевелю́р|а (-ы) *ж* (head of) hair.
шевро́н (-а) *м (нашивка)* chevron, long-service stripe.
шеде́вр (-а) *м* masterpiece.
ше́ек *сущ см* **ше́йка**.
шезло́нг (-а) *м* deckchair.
ше́|йка (-йки; *gen pl* **-ек)** *ж уменьш от* **ше́я;** *(рельса)* web; *(гильзы)* neck; **ше́йка ма́тки** *(АНАТ)* cervix.
ше́йный *прил (мышца)* neck *опред; (позвонок)* cervical; ~ **плато́к** neckerchief.
шейх (-а) *м* sheikh.
шёл *несов см* **идти́**.
ше́лест (-а) *м* rustle.
шелест|е́ть (-и́шь) *несов неперех* to rustle.
шёлк (-а; *nom pl* **-а́)** *м* silk.
шелкови́ст|ый (-, -а, -о) *прил (гладкий)* silky.
шелкови́чный *прил:* ~ **червь** silkworm.
шелково́дств|о (-а) *ср* sericulture, silkworm breeding.
шёлковый *прил (нить, одежда)* silk; *(перен: разг: человек)* meek.
шелкопря́д (-а) *м* silkworm.
шелкопряди́льный *прил* silk-spinning.
шелкотка́цк|ий (-ая, -ое, -ие) *прил* silk-weaving.
шелохн|у́ть (-у́, -ёшь) *сов перех* to stir, agitate
▶ **шелохну́ться** *сов возв* to stir, move.
шелух|а́ (-и́) *ж (картофельная)* skin, peel; *(гороховая)* pod; *(семечек)* chaff; *(перен)* dross.
шелуше́ни|е (-я) *ср (зерна)* shelling; *(кожи)* peeling.
шелуш|и́ть (-у́, -и́шь) *несов перех* to shell
▶ **шелуши́ться** *несов возв* to peel.
ше́льм|а (-ы) *м/ж (разг)* rascal.
шельф (-а) *м (ГЕО)* shelf.
шепеля́в|ить (-лю, -ишь) *несов неперех* to lisp.
шепеля́в|ый (-, -а, -о) *прил (человек, речь)* lisping.
шепн|у́ть (-у́, -ёшь) *сов перех* to whisper.
шёпот (-а) *м* whisper; *(перен: ручья, листьев)* murmuring.
шёпотом *нареч (сказать, подсказать)* in a whisper.
шепта́ни|е (-я) *ср (см глаг)* whispering; murmuring.
шеп|та́ть (-чу́, -чешь) *несов перех* to whisper ♦ *неперех (перен: ручей, листья)* to murmur
▶ **шепта́ться** *несов возв* to whisper to each other.
шербе́т (-а) *м* sherbet.
шере́нг|а (-и) *ж (солдат)* rank; *(машин)* line.
шери́ф (-а) *м* sheriff.
шерохова́тост|ь (-и) *ж (см прил)* roughness; uneveness; *(шероховатое место)* rough area.

шерохова́т|ый (-, -а, -о) *прил (доска, кожа)* rough; *(перен: изложение)* uneven.
шерсти́н|ка (-ки; *gen pl* **-ок)** *ж* strand of wool.
шерстопряди́льный *прил* wool-spinning.
шерст|ь (-и) *ж (животного)* hair; *(пряжа, ткань)* wool.
шерстяно́й *прил (пряжа, ткань)* woollen (BRIT), woolen (US).
шерша́в|ый (-, -а, -о) *прил (руки, ткань)* rough.
шест (-а́) *м* pole; **прыжо́к с** ~**о́м** pole vault.
шест|а́я (-о́й; *decl like adj)* *ж:* **одна́** ~ one sixth.
ше́стви|е (-я) *ср* procession.
ше́ств|овать (-ую) *несов неперех* to walk in procession.
шестерён|ка (-ки; *gen pl* **-ок)** *ж (ТЕХ)* gear (wheel).
шестёр|ка (-и) *ж (цифра, карта)* six; *(шлюпка)* six-oar boat; *(группа из шести)* group of six; *(разг: автобус, трамвай итп)* (number) six *(bus, tram etc)*.
ше́стер|о (-ы́х; *см* **Table 36b)** *чис* six; *см также* **дво́е**.
шести́ *чис см* **шесть**.
шести́десяти *чис см* **шестьдеся́т**.
шестидесятиле́ти|е (-я) *ср (срок)* sixty years *мн; (годовщина события)* sixtieth anniversary.
шестидесятиле́тн|ий (-яя, -ее, -ие) *прил (период)* sixty-year; *(юбилей)* sixtieth; *(человек)* sixty-year-old.
шестидеся́т|ый (-ая, -ое, -ые) *чис* sixtieth; *см также* **пятидеся́тый**.
шестидне́вный *прил* six-day.
шестикла́ссник (-а) *м* pupil in sixth year at school (usually twelve years old).
шестикла́ссни|ца (-ы) *ж см* **шестикла́ссник**.
шестикра́тн|ый *прил:* ~ **чемпио́н** six-times champion; **в** ~**ом разме́ре** sixfold.
шестиле́ти|е (-я) *ср (срок)* six years; *(годовщина)* sixth anniversary.
шестиле́тн|ий (-яя, -ее, -ие) *прил (отсутствие)* six-year; *(ребёнок)* six-year-old.
шестиме́сячный *прил* six-month; *(ребёнок)* six-month-old.
шестинеде́льный *прил* six-week; *(ребёнок)* six-week-old.
шестисо́т *чис см* **шестьсо́т**.
шестисотле́ти|е (-я) *ср (срок)* six hundred years *мн; (годовщина)* six hundredth anniversary, sexcentenary.
шестисотле́тн|ий (-яя, -ее, -ие) *прил (период)* six hundred-year; *(дерево)* six hundred-year-old.
шестисо́т|ый (-ая, -ое, -ые) *чис* six-hundredth.
шестиуго́льник (-а) *м* hexagon.
шестичасово́й *прил (рабочий день)* six-hour; *(поезд)* six-o'clock.
шестна́дцати *чис см* **шестна́дцать**.
шестна́дцат|ый (-ая, -ое, -ые) *чис* sixteenth; *см*

также **пя́тый**.

шестна́дцать (-и; *как* **пять**; *см* **Table 27**) *чис* sixteen; *см также* **пять**.

шесто́й (-а́я, -о́е, -ы́е) *чис* sixth; *см также* **пя́тый**.

шесть (-й; *как* **пять**; *см* **Table 27**) *чис* six; *см также* **пять**.

шестьдеся́т (-и́десяти; *как* **пятьдеся́т**; *см* **Table 29**) *чис* sixty; *см также* **пятьдеся́т**.

шестьсо́т (-исо́т; *как* **пятьсо́т**; *см* **Table 34**) *чис* six hundred; *см также* **сто**.

ше́стью *нареч* six times.

шестью́ *чис см* **шесть**.

шестьюста́ми *чис см* **шестьсо́т**.

шетла́ндский (-ая, -ое, -ие) *прил*: **Ш~ие острова́** Shetland Islands.

шеф (-а) *м* (*полиции*) chief; (*разг: начальник*) boss; (*обычно мн: детского дома*) patron.

ше́фский (-ая, -ое, -ие) *прил* (*помощь*) patronal.

ше́фство (-а) *ср*: ~ **над** +*instr* patronage of.

ше́фствовать (-ую) *несов неперех*: ~ **над** +*instr* to be patron of.

ше́я (-и) *ж* (*АНАТ*) neck; **на свою́ ~ю** (*разг*) to our loss; **сиде́ть** (*impf*) *или* **висе́ть** (*impf*) **у кого́-н на ~е** to live off sb; **гнать** (*impf*) **кого́-н в ~ю** (*разг*) to throw sb out on his *итп* ear.

ши́бко *нареч* terribly.

ши́ворот (-а) *м* (*разг*): **за ~** by the collar; **~-навы́ворот** back to front.

шизофре́ник (-а) *м* schizophrenic.

шизофрени́я (-и) *ж* schizophrenia.

шик (-а; *part gen* -у) *м* chic, stylishness.

шика́рен *прил см* **шика́рный**.

шика́рно *нареч* (*разг: жить*) in style; (*обставленный*) stylishly ♦ *как сказ*: **в гости́нице ~** the hotel is stylish.

шика́рный (-ен, -на, -но) *прил* (*разг*) smart, stylish.

ши́кать (-ю) *несов неперех* (*разг*): ~ **на кого́-н** to hush sb.

ши́кнуть (-у, -ешь) *сов неперех*: ~ **на кого́-н** to hush sb.

шикова́ть (-у́ю) *несов неперех* (*разг*) to show off.

ши́ллинг (-а) *м* (*денежная единица*) shilling.

ши́ло (-а; *nom pl* -ья, *gen pl* -ьев) *ср* awl.

шимпанзе́ *м нескл* chimpanzee.

ши́на (-ы) *ж* (*АВТ*) tyre (*BRIT*), tire (*US*); (*МЕД*) splint.

шине́ль (-и) *ж* (*солдатская*) greatcoat, overcoat.

шинкова́ние (-я) *ср* shredding.

шинкова́ть (-у́ю; *perf* **нашинкова́ть**) *несов перех* (*овощи*) to shred.

шиньо́н (-а) *м* chignon.

шип (-а́) *м* (*растения*) thorn; (*соединительный*) tenon, tongue; (*на колесе*) stud; (*на ботинке*) spike.

шипе́ние (-я) *ср* hissing.

шипе́ть (-лю́, -йшь) *несов неперех* (*также*

разг) to hiss; (*шампанское, газировка*) to fizz.

шипо́вки (-ок) *мн* (*СПОРТ*) spikes *мн*.

шипо́вник (-а) *м* (*куст*) wild rose; (*плод*) (rose)hip; (*настой*) rosehip drink.

шипо́вок *сущ см* **шипо́вки**.

шипу́чий (-ая, -ее, -ие; -, -а, -е) *прил* fizzy; (*вино*) sparkling.

шипя́щий (-ая, -ее, -ие) *прил* (*линг*) sibilant *опред*.

ши́ре *сравн прил от* **широ́кий** ♦ *сравн нареч от* **широко́**.

ширина́ (-ы́) *ж* width; **доро́жка метр ~о́й** *или* **в ~у́** a path a metre (*BRIT*) *или* meter (*US*) wide.

шири́нка (-ки; *gen pl* -ок) *ж* (*брюк*) fly.

ши́риться (*3sg* -ится, *3pl* -ятся) *несов возв* (*дела*) to expand; (*движение*) to grow.

ши́рма (-ы) *ж* (*также перен*) screen.

широ́кий (-ая, -ое, -ие; -, -а́, -о́) *прил* wide; (*степи, фронт, планы*) extensive; (*перен: общественность, публика*) general; (: *смысл, интерпретация*) broad; (: *масштабы*) large; (: *натура, жест*) generous; (: *образ жизни*) grand; **това́ры ~ого потребле́ния** (*ЭКОН*) consumer goods; **жить** (*impf*) **на ~ую но́гу** to live in grand style; **широ́кий экра́н** (*КИНО*) wide screen.

широко́ *нареч* (*раскинуться*) widely; (*улыбаться, интерпретировать*) broadly; (*жить*) in grand style; ~ **раскрыва́ть** (**раскры́ть** *perf*) **глаза́** to open one's eyes wide; (*перен*) to be amazed.

широковеща́тельный (-ен, -ьна, -ьно) *прил* broadcasting *опред*; **широковеща́тельная сеть** (*КОМП*) broadcast network.

широкопле́чий (-ая, -ее, -ие; -, -а, -е) *прил* (*человек*) broad-shouldered.

широкопо́лый *прил* (*шляпа*) wide-brimmed; (*пальто*) with a full skirt.

широкоформа́тный *прил* (*экран*) wide-format.

широкофюзеля́жный *прил* (*самолёт*) wide-bodied.

широкоэкра́нный *прил* (*фильм*) wide-screen.

широта́ (-оты́) *ж* breadth; (*nom pl* -о́ты; *ГЕО*) latitude.

ширпотре́б (-а) *м сокр* = **широ́кое потребле́ние**; (*разг: о товарах*) consumer goods *мн*; (: *о плохом товаре*) low-quality goods *мн*.

ширь (-и) *ж* expanse; **развора́чиваться** (**разверну́ться** *perf*) **во всю ~** (*перен*) to develop to one's full potential.

ши́то-кры́то *нареч* (*разг*): **всё ~** it's all being kept under wraps.

ши́тый *прил* embroidered.

шить (**шью, шьёшь**; *perf* **сшить**) *несов перех* (*платье итп*) to sew ♦ *неперех*: ~ +*instr* (*шёлком итп*) to embroider.

шитьё (-я́) *ср* (*см глаг*) sewing; embroidery.

ши́фер (-а) *м* (*натуральный*) slate; (*СТРОИТ*) corrugated asbestos board.

шифо́н (-а) *м* chiffon.

шифонье́р (-а) *м* wardrobe.

шифр (-а) *м* (*для секретного письма*) code, cipher; (*книги, документа*) pressmark.

шифрова́льщик (-а) *м* cipher-clerk; (*расшифровывающий*) code cracker.

шифр|ова́ть (-у́ю; *perf* **зашифрова́ть**) *несов перех* (*донесение*) to encode, encipher.

шифро́в|ка (-ки; *gen pl* -ок) *ж* (*см глаг*) encoding, enciphering; (*сообщение*) coded message.

шиш (-а́) *м* (*разг: кукиш*) fig (*rude gesture*); **ни ~á** (*разг*) damn all; **~ ты от меня полу́чишь** (*разг*) you'll get damn all from me; **на каки́е ~й?** (*разг*) who's paying?

ши́ш|ка (-ки; *gen pl* -ек) *ж* (*БОТ*) cone; (*на лбу*) bump, lump; (*разг: важный человек*) bigwig.

шишкова́т|ый (-, -а, -о) *прил* (*руки*) knobbly; (*лоб*) lumpy; (*доска*) rough.

шкал|а́ (-ы́; *nom pl* -ы) *ж* scale; (*приёмника*) dial.

шкату́л|ка (-ки; *gen pl* -ок) *ж* casket; **музыка́льная ~** musical box.

шкаф (-а; *loc sg* -у́, *nom pl* -ы́) *м* (*для одежды*) wardrobe; (*для посуды*) cupboard; (*ТЕХ: сушильный итп*) oven; **духово́й ~** airing cupboard; **кни́жный ~** bookcase.

шквал (-а) *м* (*ветер*) squall; **~** +*gen* (*оваций, огня*) burst of.

шква́льн|ый *прил* (*ветер*) squally; (*огонь*) heavy.

шкив (-а) *м* (*ТЕХ*) pulley.

шки́пер (-а) *м* (*МОР*) skipper.

шки́р|ка (-и) *ж*: **брать кого́-н за ~у** (*разг*) to take sb by the scruff of the neck; (*перен*) to twist sb's arm.

шко́л|а (-ы) *ж* school; (*милиции*) college, academy; (*выучка*) education, training; (*СПОРТ*) training; **вы́сшая ~** higher education; **нача́льная ~** primary (*BRIT*) *или* elementary (*US*) school; **сре́дняя ~** secondary (*BRIT*) *или* high (*US*) school.

шко́л|а-интерна́т (-ы, -а) *м* boarding school.

шко́льник (-а) *м* schoolboy.

шко́льниц|а (-ы) *ж* schoolgirl.

шко́льн|ый *прил* (*здание*) school *опред*; **шко́льные го́ды** schooldays; **шко́льный во́зраст** school age; **шко́льный уче́бник** school book; **шко́льный учи́тель** school teacher.

шку́р|а (-ы) *ж* (*животного*) fur; (*убитого животного*) skin; (: *обработанная*) hide ◆ *м/ж* (*разг: продажный человек*) self-seeker; **быть** (*impf*) **в чьей-н ~е** to be in sb's shoes (*fig*); **спаса́ть** (*impf*) **свою́ ~у** (*разг*) to save one's (own) skin; **на свое́й ~е узна́ть** (*perf*) (*разг*) to experience first-hand.

шку́р|ить (-ю, -ишь) *сов перех* (*шлифовать*) to sand(paper).

шку́р|ка (-и) *ж уменьш от* **шку́ра**; (*разг: плода*) rind, peel; (*абразив*) sandpaper.

шку́рник (-а) *м* (*разг: пренебр*) self-seeker.

шку́рный *прил* (*интересы*) selfish.

шла *несов см* **идти́**.

шлагба́ум (-а) *м* barrier.

шлак (-а) *м* (*ТЕХ*) slag.

шлакобето́нный *прил* (*панель, кирпич*) slag-concrete.

шланг (-а) *м* hose.

шлейф (-а) *м* (*платья*) train; (*дыма*) trail.

шлем (-а) *м* helmet.

шлёпан|ец (-ца) *м* (*разг: обычно мн*) bedroom slipper.

шлёпа|ть (-ю) *несов перех* (*бить*) to slap ◆ *неперех*: **~ по** +*acc* (*по полу*) to shuffle; (*по воде*) to splash

▶ **шлёпаться** (*perf* **шлёпнуться**) *несов возв* (*разг*) to plop.

шли *несов см* **идти́**.

шлифова́льный *прил* (*ТЕХ*) grinding *опред*.

шлиф|ова́ть (-у́ю; *perf* **отшлифова́ть**) *несов перех* (*ТЕХ*) to grind; (*перен: стиль*) to polish.

шлифо́в|ка (-и) *ж* (*детали*) grinding.

шли́ц|а (-ы) *ж* (*ТЕХ*) spline; (*юбки*) slit.

шло *несов см* **идти́**.

шлю *итп несов см* **слать**.

шлюз (-а) *м* (*на канале*) lock; (*на реке*) sluice.

шлю́п|ка (-ки; *gen pl* -ок) *ж* (*МОР*) dinghy; **спаса́тельная ~** lifeboat.

шлю́х|а (-и) *ж* (*разг*) tart.

шля́гер (-а) *м* (*МУЗ*) hit.

шля́п|а (-ы) *ж* hat ◆ *м/ж* (*перен: разг: человек*) wimp; **де́ло в ~е** (*разг*) it's in the bag.

шля́п|ка (-ки; *gen pl* -ок) *ж* hat; (*гвоздя*) head; (*гриба*) cap.

шля́пник (-а) *м* (*мужской*) hatter; (*женский*) milliner.

шля́пный *прил* hat *опред*.

шля́пок *сущ см* **шля́пка**.

шля́|ться (-юсь) *несов возв* (*разг*) to mooch about.

шмель (-я́) *м* bumblebee.

шмо́т|ки (-ок) *мн* (*разг*) clobber *ед*.

шмыга|ть (-ю) *несов перех* (*разг: шнырять*) to rush; (*исчезнуть*) to slip, dart; **~** (*impf*) **но́сом** to sniff.

шмыгн|у́ть (-у́, -ёшь) *сов неперех* (*быстро пройти*) to dart, nip; (*исчезнуть*) to slip, dart.

шмякн|уть (-у, -ешь; *impf* **шмя́кать**) *сов перех* (*разг: бросить*) to thump down

▶ **шмя́кнуться** (*impf* **шмя́каться**) *сов возв* (*разг: упасть*) to topple over.

шни́цель (-я) *м* (*КУЛИН*) schnitzel.

шнур (-а́) *м* (*верёвка*) cord; (*телефонный, лампы*) flex.

шнурка́ *итп сущ см* **шнуро́к**.

шнур|ова́ть (-у́ю; *perf* **зашнурова́ть**) *несов перех* (*ботинки*) to lace (up); (*perf* **прошнурова́ть**; *прошивать шнуром*) to tie, bind.

шнуро́вк|а (-и) ж (см глаг) lacing up; tying, binding; (на одежде, на обуви) lacing.

шнур|о́к (-ка́) м (ботинка) lace.

шныря́|ть (-ю) несов неперех (разг: в толпе, по улицам) to dash about; **он ~л глаза́ми** (перен: разг) his eyes darted about.

шов (шва) м (швейный) seam; (хирургический) stitch, suture; (намёточный, тамбурный итп) stitch; (кровельный) joint, seam; **сварно́й ~** joint weld, weld seam; **накла́дывать (наложи́ть** perf)/**снима́ть (снять** perf) **швы** (МЕД) to put in/take out stitches; **треща́ть** (impf) **по всем швам** (перен: разг) to fall apart at the seams; **ру́ки по швам** stand at attention.

шовини́зм (-а) м chauvinism.

шовини́ст (-а) м chauvinism.

шовинисти́ческ|ий (-ая, -ое, -ие) прил chauvinist.

шок (-а) м (МЕД, перен) shock.

шоки́р|овать (-ую) (не)сов перех to shock.

шо́ков|ый прил: **~ое состоя́ние** state of shock; **шо́ковая терапи́я** (МЕД, перен) shock therapy.

шокола́д (-а) м chocolate; (напиток) (hot) chocolate.

шокола́д|ка (-ки; gen pl -ок) ж (разг) bar of chocolate.

шокола́дн|ый прил (конфета) chocolate; (цвет) chocolate-brown; **~ая пли́тка** bar of chocolate.

шокола́док сущ см **шокола́дка.**

шо́мпол (-а) м (ВОЕН) cleaning rod.

шо́рох (-а) м rustle.

шо́рт|ы (-) мн shorts мн.

шоссе́ ср нескл highway.

шоссе́йн|ый прил: **~ая доро́га** highway.

шотла́нд|ец (-ца) м Scotsman (мн Scotsmen).

Шотла́нди|я (-и) ж Scotland.

шотла́нд|ка (-ки; gen pl -ок) ж Scotswoman (мн Scotswomen); (ткань) tartan (BRIT), plaid (US).

шотла́ндск|ий (-ая, -ое, -ие) прил Scottish, Scots.

шотла́ндца итп сущ см **шотла́ндец.**

шо́у ср нескл (также перен) show.

шофёр (-а) м driver.

шпа́г|а (-и) ж sword.

шпага́т (-а) м (бечёвка) string, twine; (СПОРТ) the splits.

шпажи́ст (-а) м (СПОРТ) fencer.

шпажи́ст|ка (-ки; gen pl -ок) ж см **шпажи́ст.**

шпакл|ева́ть (-ю́ю; perf **зашпаклева́ть**) несов перех (трещины, дыры) to fill.

шпаклёвк|а (-и) ж (действие) filling; (замазка) filler.

шпа́л|а (-ы) ж sleeper (RAIL).

шпале́р|а (-ы) ж (обои) handpainted wallpaper; (для растений) trellis.

шпан|а́ (-ы́) ж собир (разг) rabble.

шпарга́л|ка (-ки; gen pl -ок) ж (разг: для экзаменов) crib.

шпа́р|ить (-ю, -ишь) несов неперех (разг): **~ на гита́ре** to play away on the guitar; **~** (impf)

по-англи́йски (разг) to speak fluent English; **~** (impf) **по у́лице** (разг) to rush along the street.

шпа́тел|ь (-я) м (для шпаклёвки, для краски) palette knife (мн knives); (МЕД) spatula.

шпиг|ова́ть (-у́ю; perf **нашпигова́ть**) несов перех (КУЛИН, перен) to lard.

шпик (-а; part gen -у) м (сало) lard; (разг: сыщик) detective.

шпи́лек сущ см **шпи́лька.**

шпил|ь (-я) м spire.

шпи́льк|а (-ьки; gen pl -ек) ж (для волос) hairpin; (для шляпы) hatpin; (каблук) stiletto (heel); (перен: разг: замечание) dig; **ту́фли на ~ьке** stilettos.

шпина́т (-а) м spinach.

шпингале́т (-а) м (на окне) catch; (разг: о мальчишке) little boy.

шпио́н (-а) м spy.

шпиона́ж (-а) м espionage.

шпио́н|ить (-ю, -ишь) несов неперех (разг) to spy; **~** (impf) **за** +instr (за врагом, за женой) to spy on.

Шпицбе́рген (-а) м Spitzbergen.

шпо́р|а (-ы) ж spur.

шприц (-а) м syringe.

шпро́т|ы (-ов) мн sprats мн.

шпу́льк|а (-и) ж spool, bobbin.

шрам (-а) м (на теле) scar.

шрапне́л|ь (-и) ж (ВОЕН) shrapnel только ед.

Шри-Ла́нк|а (-и) ж Sri Lanka.

шрифт (-а; nom pl -ы́) м type, print; **жи́рный/ курси́вный ~** bold/italic type; **набо́рный ~** (ТИПОГ) printing type.

шт. сокр = **ш.**

штаб (-а; nom pl -ы́) м headquarters мн; (люди) staff.

шта́бел|ь (-я; nom pl -я́) м (дров) stack.

штаб-кварти́р|а (-ы) ж (ВОЕН) headquarters мн.

штабно́й прил (разведка, офицер) staff опред.

штаке́тник (-а) м (ограда) palings мн.

штамп (-а) м (печать) stamp; (перен: в речи) cliché; (ТЕХ) die, stamp.

штамп|ова́ть (-у́ю; perf **проштампова́ть**) несов перех (справки, документы) to stamp; (perf **отштампова́ть**; детали) to punch, press; (no perf; решения, ответы) to rubber-stamp.

штампо́вочный прил (ТЕХ) punching опред, pressing опред.

шта́нг|а (-и) ж (СПОРТ: в тяжёлой атлетике) weight; (: ворот) post.

штангенци́ркул|ь (-я) м (ТЕХ) sliding calipers мн, slide gauge.

штанги́ст (-а) м (СПОРТ) weightlifter.

штанда́рт (-а) м (ВОЕН) standard.

штани́н|а (-ы) ж (разг) trouser leg.

штан|ы́ (-о́в) мн trousers мн.

шта́пел|ь (-я) м (ткань) viscose manufactured to resemble cotton.

шта́пельный прил (ткань, платье) made with viscose manufactured to resemble cotton.

штат (-а) м (государства) state; (работники)

staff; (*положение*) staff regulations мн; **э́та до́лжность полага́ется по шта́ту** this job is stipulated by the regulations; **зачисля́ть (зачи́слить** *perf*) **кого́-н в ~** to take sb onto the staff.

штати́в (**-а**) м (*ФОТО*) tripod; (*микроскопа*) stand.

шта́тный *прил* (*сотрудник*) permanent; **шта́тная до́лжность** (*АДМИН*) established post; **шта́тное расписа́ние** (*АДМИН*) staff register.

шта́тск|ий (**-ая, -ое, -ие**) *прил* (*одежда*) civilian *опред* ♦ (**-ого;** *decl like adj*) м civilian.

шта́тск|ое (**-ого;** *decl like adj*) *ср* civilian clothes мн, civvies мн (*inf*).

штéмпел|ь (**-я**) м: **почто́вый ~** postmark.

штéпсел|ь (**-я**) м (*ЭЛЕК*) plug.

штéпсельн|ый *прил*: **~ая розéтка** electric socket.

штиблéт|ы (**-**) мн lace-up boots мн.

штилево́й *прил* (*погода*) calm.

штил|ь (**-я**) м (*МОР*) calm.

штифт (**-á**) м (*ТЕХ*) pin.

штол|ьня (**-ьни;** *gen pl* **-ен**) ж (*ГЕО*) gallery.

што́паный *прил* darned.

што́па|ть (**-ю;** *perf* **заштóпать**) *несов перех* to darn.

што́пк|а (**-и**) ж (*действие*) darning; (*нитки*) darning thread; (*разг: заштопанное место*) darn.

што́пор (**-а**) м corkscrew.

што́р|а (**-ы**) ж drapery; (*поднимающаяся*) blind.

шторм (**-а**) м gale.

шторм|и́ть (*3sg* **-и́т**) *несов неперех* (*море*) to be rough; **сего́дня ~и́т** it is rough today.

штормо́в|ка (**-ки;** *gen pl* **-ок**) ж oilskin coat.

штормово́й *прил* (*погода*) stormy; (*ветер*) gale-force; **штормово́е предупрежде́ние** (*МОР*) gale warning.

штормо́вок *сущ см* **штормо́вка**.

штраф (**-а**) м (*денежный*) fine; (*СПОРТ*) punishment; **накла́дывать (наложи́ть** *perf*) **~ на** +*acc* to impose a fine on.

штрафни́к (**-á**) м (*СПОРТ*) *player who has been sent off*; **скамéйка штрафнико́в** penalty box (*in ice-hockey*).

штрафн|о́й *прил* penal ♦ (**-óго;** *decl like adj*) м (*СПОРТ: также:* **~ уда́р**) penalty (kick); **штрафно́е очко́** (*СПОРТ*) penalty point.

штраф|ова́ть (**-у́ю;** *perf* **оштрафова́ть**) *несов перех* to fine; (*СПОРТ*) to penalize.

штрейкбрéхер (**-а**) м strikebreaker, blackleg.

штрек (**-а**) м (*ГЕО*) drift.

штрих (**-á**) м (*черта*) stroke; (*частность*) feature.

штрих|ова́ть (**-у́ю;** *perf* **заштрихова́ть**) *несов перех* (*рисунок*) to shade.

штуди́р|овать (**-ую;** *perf* **проштуди́ровать**) *несов перех* to study.

шту́к|а (**-и**) ж (*отдельный предмет*) item; (*разг: трудная, забавная*) thing; (: *проделка*) trick; **вот так ~!** (*разг*) what do you know!

штукату́р (**-а**) м plasterer.

штукату́р|ить (**-ю, -ишь;** *perf* **отштукату́рить** *или* **оштукату́рить**) *несов перех* to plaster.

штукату́рк|а (**-и**) ж (*действие*) plastering; (*раствор*) plaster; (*на стене*) plaster, stucco.

штукату́рный *прил* (*работы*) plaster *опред*.

штуко́вин|а (**-ы**) ж (*разг*) thing.

штурва́л (**-а**) м (*судна, комбайна*) wheel; (*самолёта*) controls мн.

штурва́льный *прил* steering *опред*.

штурм (**-а**) м (*ВОЕН*) storm; (*перен: горной вершины*) conquest; **брать (взять** *perf*) **что-н штýрмом** to take sth by storm.

штýрман (**-а**) м (*МОР, АВИА*) navigator.

штýрманск|ий (**-ая, -ое, -ие**) *прил* navigator's.

штурм|ова́ть (**-у́ю**) *несов перех* (*ВОЕН*) to storm; (*перен*) to conquer.

штýчный *прил* (*товар, изделие*) sold by the piece; (*работа, оплата*) piece *опред*.

штык (**-á**) м (*ВОЕН*) bayonet; **принима́ть (приня́ть** *perf*) *или* **встреча́ть (встре́тить** *perf*) **что-н/кого́-н в ~й** (*перен*) to give sth/sb a hostile reception; **как ~** (*разг*) on the dot.

штыково́й *прил* (*атака*) bayonet *опред*; **штыкова́я лопа́та** sharp-bladed spade.

штыр|ь (**-я́**) м (*ТЕХ*) pin, pintle.

шýб|а (**-ы**) ж (*меховая*) fur coat; (*разг: животного*) coat; **селёдка под ~ой** (*КУЛИН*) *herring served with an elaborate topping*.

шýлер (**-а**) м cardsharper.

шум (**-а;** *part gen* **-у**) м (*звук*) noise; (*перен: ажиотаж*) stir, sensation; (*МЕД*) murmur; (*разг: ссора*) row, racket; (*суета*) bustle, fuss; **вызыва́ть (вы́звать** *perf*) *или* **наде́лать** (*perf*) **~** to cause a sensation.

шýмен *прил см* **шу́мный**.

шумéть (**-лю́, -и́шь**) *несов неперех* to make a noise; (*разглашать*) to create a scene; (*ссориться*) to kick up a row; **у меня́ ~и́т в голове́/в уша́х** I have a buzzing in my head/ears.

шуми́х|а (**-и**) ж (*разг: пренебр: толки*) sensation, stir; **поднима́ть (подня́ть** *perf*) **~у вокру́г чего́-н** to create a sensation around sth; **газéтная ~** *sensation created by the press*.

шумли́вый (**-, -а, -о**) *прил* noisy.

шумлю́ *несов см* **шуметь**.

шýмно *нареч* noisily ♦ *как сказ* it is noisy.

шýм|ный (**-ен, -на́, -но**) *прил* noisy; (*разговор, компания*) loud; (*оживлённый: улица, залы итп*) bustling; (*перен: успех*) sensational.

шумо́в|ка (**-ки;** *gen pl* **-ок**) ж perforated spoon.

шумово́й *прил* (*оформление*) sound *опред*.

шумо́вок *сущ см* **шумо́вка**.

шумо́к м (*разг*): **под ~** (*разг*) on the quiet.

шу́рин (-а) *м* brother-in-law, wife's brother.

шуру́п (-а) *м* (*ТЕХ*) screw.

шурша́ть (-у́, -и́шь) *несов неперех* to rustle.

шу́ры-му́ры *мн нескл* (*разг*) love affairs *мн*.

шу́стрый (-, -а́, -о) *прил* (*разг*) nimble.

шут (-а́) *м* (*придворный*) jester; (*разг: человек*) fool, clown; ~ **горо́ховый** (*разг*) buffoon; ~ **с ним** (*разг*) forget it.

шу|ти́ть (-чу́, -тишь; *perf* **пошути́ть**) *несов неперех* to joke; (*смеяться*): ~ **над** +*instr* to make fun of; (*no perf; пренебрегать*): ~ +*instr* (*здоровьем*) to disregard; ~ (*impf*) **с огнём** (*перен*) to play with fire; **чем чёрт не шу́тит!** (*разг*) anything might happen!

шу́т|ка (-ки; *gen pl* -ок) *ж* joke; **без** ~**ок** joking apart, seriously; **кро́ме** ~**ок, ты пра́вда согла́сен?** joking apart *или* seriously, do you really agree?; **не на** ~**ку** (*рассердился, испугался итп*) in earnest; **сказа́ть** (*perf*) **что-н в** ~**ку** to say sth as a joke; ~**ки пло́хи с кем-н/чем-н** sb/sth is not to be trifled with.

шутли́в|ый (-, -а, -о) *прил* (*человек, тон, замечание*) humorous (*BRIT*), humorous (*US*); (*настроение*) light-hearted.

шутни́к (-а́) *м* joker.

шутовск|о́й *прил*: ~**йе вы́ходки** buffoonery; ~ **колпа́к** jester's cap.

шутовств|о́ (-а́) *ср* buffoonery.

шу́ток *сущ см* **шу́тка**.

шу́точ|ный (-ен, -на, -но) *прил* (*рассказ*) comic, funny; **э́то де́ло не** ~**ное** it's no laughing matter.

шутя́ *нареч* (*разг: без труда*) easily.

шучу́ *несов см* **шути́ть**.

шу́шер|а (-ы) *ж собир* (*разг*) riffraff.

шушу́ка|ться (-юсь) *несов возв*: ~ (**с** +*instr*) to whisper (to).

шху́н|а (-ы) *ж* (*МОР*) schooner.

ш-ш *межд* sh.

шью *итп несов см* **шить**.

~ Щ, щ ~

Щ, щ *сущ нескл (буква)* the 26th letter of the Russian alphabet.

щаве́л|ь (**-я́**) *м* sorrel.

щад|и́ть (**-жу́**, **-ди́шь**; *perf* **пощади́ть**) *несов перех* to spare; **он на ~дя́щем режи́ме** (*МЕД*) he's not allowed to exert himself.

щам *итп сущ см* **щи**.

щебёнк|а (**-и**) *ж* = **щебень**.

ще́б|ень (**-ня**) *м* (*СТРОИТ*) ballast.

ще́бет (**-а**) *м* twitter.

щебет|а́ть (**-ечу́**, **-е́чешь**) *несов неперех* (*также перен*) to twitter.

ще́бня *итп сущ см* **щебень**.

щег|о́л (**-ла́**) *м* goldfinch.

щегол|ева́т|ый (**-**, **-а**, **-о**) *прил* (*одежда*) fancy; (*мужчина*) stylish.

щёгол|ь (**-я**) *м* dandy.

щегольн|у́ть (**-у́**, **-ёшь**) *сов неперех*: ~ +*instr* to show off.

щегольско́й *прил* stylish.

щегольств|о́ (**-а́**) *ср* dandyism.

щегол|я́ть (**-ю**) *несов неперех* to dress up; ~ (*impf*) +*instr* to show off; ~ (*impf*) **в** +*prp* to rig o.s. out in.

ще́дрост|ь (**-и**) *ж* generosity.

ще́др|ый (**-**, **-а́**, **-о**) *прил* generous; (*природа*) lush; (*климат*) fertile; ~ **на** +*acc* generous with.

щей *сущ см* **щи**.

щек|а́ (**щеки́**; *nom pl* **щёки**, *gen pl* **щёк**, *dat pl* **щека́м**) *ж* cheek; **за о́бе щеки́ есть** (*impf*) *или* **упи́сывать** (*impf*) (*разг*) to gobble one's food up *или* down.

щеко́лд|а (**-ы**) *ж* latch.

щекот|а́ть (**-очу́**, **-о́чешь**; *perf* **пощекота́ть**) *несов неперех* (*пятки итп*) to tickle; ~ (*impf*) **кому́-н не́рвы** to excite sb; **у меня́ ~о́чет в го́рле/носу́** I've got a tickle in my throat/nose.

щеко́тк|а (**-и**) *ж* tickling.

щекотли́в|ый (**-**, **-а**, **-о**) *прил* (*вопрос итп*) delicate.

щеко́тно *как сказ*: **мне ~** it's tickling me; **здесь ~ ходи́ть босико́м** it's ticklish going barefoot here.

щекочу́ *итп несов см* **щекота́ть**.

щёлк|а (**-и**) *ж* small hole.

щёлка|ть (**-ю**) *несов перех* (*человека*) to flick; (*орехи, семечки*) to crack (open) ♦ *неперех*: ~ +*instr* (*языком*) to click; (*кнутом*) to crack.

щёлкн|уть (**-у**, **-ешь**) *сов неперех* to click; (*хлыстом*) to crack.

щелочно́й *прил* alkaline.

щёлоч|ь (**-и**) *ж* alkali.

щелч|о́к (**-ка́**) *м* flick; (*звук*) click; (*перен: оскорбление*) jibe.

щел|ь (**-и**; *loc sg* **-и́**, *gen pl* **-е́й**) *ж* (*отверстие*) crack; (*ТЕХ*) slit; **смотрова́я ~** vision slit.

щем|и́ть (*3sg* **-и́т**, *3pl* **-я́т**) *несов перех* (*перен: тревожить*) to trouble ♦ *безл* (*ныть*): ~**и́т в боку́** his *итп* side is aching; ~**и́т в груди́** his *итп* heart is heavy.

щемя́щ|ий (**-ая**, **-ее**, **-ие**) *прил* aching.

щен|и́ться (*3sg* **-и́тся**, *3pl* **-я́тся**, *perf* **ощени́ться**) *несов возв* (*собака*) to have pups; (*волчица, лиса*) to have cubs.

щен|о́к (**-ка́**; *nom pl* **-я́та**, *gen pl* **-я́т**) *м* (*собаки*) pup; (*лисы, волчицы*) cub; (*перен: разг*) whippersnapper.

щепети́лен *прил см* **щепети́льный**.

щепети́льност|ь (**-и**) *ж* (*в отношении, денежных делах*) scrupulousness.

щепети́льн|ый (**-ен**, **-ьна**, **-ьно**) *прил* scrupulous.

ще́п|ка (**-ки**; *gen pl* **-ок**) *ж* splinter; (*для растопки*): ~**ки** chippings *мн*; **худо́й как ~** thin as a rake.

щепо́т|ка (**-ки**; *gen pl* **-ок**) *ж* (*соли, табака*) pinch.

щерба́т|ый (**-**, **-а**, **-о**) *прил* (*рот*) gap-toothed; (*лицо*) pock-marked.

щерби́н|а (**-ы**) *ж* (*на лице, на коже*) pock-mark; (*во рту*) gap (between teeth); (*на посуде*) chink.

щети́н|а (**-ы**) *ж* (*животных, щётки*) bristle; (*у мужчины*) stubble.

щети́нист|ый (**-**, **-а**, **-о**) *прил* (*жёсткий*) bristly; (*небритый*) stubbly.

щети́н|иться (*3sg* **-ится**, *3pl* **-ятся**, *perf* **ощети́ниться**) *несов возв* (*также перен*) to bristle.

щёт|ка (**-ки**; *gen pl* **-ок**) *ж* brush; **зубна́я ~** toothbrush; ~ **для воло́с** hairbrush.

щи (**щей**; *dat pl* **щам**) *мн* cabbage soup *ед*; **ки́слые ~** sour cabbage soup; **зелёные ~** sorrel soup.

The spelling rules for Russian are shown on page xvii.

щи́колот|ка (-ки; *gen pl* -ок) *ж* ankle.

щип|а́ть (-лю́, -лешь) *несов перех* (защемлять до боли) to nip, pinch; (*no perf*; *подлеж: мороз*) to bite; (: *специя, кислое*) to sting; (*perf* **ощипа́ть**; *волосы, курицу*) to pluck

► **щипа́ться** *несов возв* (*разг*) to nip, pinch.

щипка́ *итп сущ см* **щипо́к.**

щипко́вый *прил* (*муз*): ~ **инструме́нт** plucked (*BRIT*) *или* picked (*US*) instrument.

щиплю́(сь) *итп несов см* **щипа́ть(ся).**

щипну́ть (-у́, -ёшь) *сов перех* to nip, pinch.

щипо́к (-ка́) *м* nip, pinch.

щипц|ы́ (-о́в) *мн*: **ками́нные** ~ tongs *мн*; **кузне́чные** ~ pliers *мн*; **хирурги́ческие** ~ forceps *мн*; ~ **для са́хара** sugar-tongs *мн*.

щи́пчик|и (-ов) *мн уменьш от* **щипцы́**; (*для ногтей, бровей*) tweezers *мн*.

щит (-а́) *м* shield; (*фанерный, металлический*

итп) barrier; (*рекламный, баскетбольный*) board; (*ТЕХ*) panel; ~ **управле́ния** control panel.

щитови́дн|ый *прил*: ~**ая железа́** thyroid gland.

щу́к|а (-и) *ж* pike (*мн* pike).

щуп (-а) *м* (*ТЕХ*) probe.

щу́пал|ьце (-ьца; *nom pl* -ьца, *gen pl* -ец) *ср* (*осьминога*) tentacle; (*насекомых*) feeler.

щу́па|ть (-ю; *perf* **пощу́пать**) *несов перех* (*опухоль, пульс*) to feel for; (*карманы*) to grope in.

щу́пл|ый (-, -а́, -о) *прил* (*разг*) puny.

щу́р|ить (-ю, -ишь; *perf* **сощу́рить**) *несов перех*: ~ **глаза́** to screw up one's eyes

► **щу́риться** (*perf* **сощу́риться**) *несов возв* (*от солнца*) to squint.

щу́ч|ий (-ья, -ье, -ьи) *прил*: **по ~ьему веле́нью** (as if) by magic.

~ Э, э ~

Э, э *сущ нескл (буква)* the 30th letter of the Russian alphabet.

э *межд (выражает недоумение)* er ...; um ...; *(выражает решимость)* oh; **э, нет, я не пойду!** oh, no, I'm not going!

эбони́т (-а) *м* vulcanite, ebonite.

эвакуацио́нный *прил (пункт)* evacuation *опред*; *(госпиталь)* evacuee *опред*.

эвакуа́ци|я (-и) *ж* evacuation.

эваку́и́р|овать (-ую) *(не)сов перех* to evacuate
▸ **эваку́и́роваться** *(не)сов возв* to be evacuated.

Эвере́ст (-а) *м* Mount Everest.

эвкали́пт (-а) *м* eucalyptus.

эвкали́птов|ый *прил*: ~**ое ма́сло** eucalyptus oil.

ЭВМ *ж сокр (= электро́нная вычисли́тельная маши́на)* computer.

эволюциони́р|овать (-ую) *(не)сов непepex* to evolve.

эволюцио́нный *прил* evolutionary.

эволю́ци|я (-и) *ж* evolution.

эвфеми́зм (-а) *м* euphemism.

эвфемисти́ческ|ий (-ая, -ое, -ие) *прил* euphemistic.

эги́д|а (-ы) *ж*: **под** ~**ой** +*gen* under the aegis of.

эгои́зм (-а) *м* egoism.

эгои́ст (-а) *м* egoist.

эгоисти́чен *прил см* **эгоисти́чный**.

эгоисти́ческ|ий (-ая, -ое, -ие) *прил* egotistic(al).

эгоисти́|чный (-ен, -на, -но) *прил* = **эгоисти́ческий**.

эго́ист|ка (-ки; *gen pl* -**ок)** *ж см* **эгои́ст**.

эгоцентри́ст (-а) *м*: **он настоя́щий** ~ he is very egocentric.

эдельве́йс (-а) *м* edelweiss.

Эдинбу́рг (-а) *м* Edinburgh.

эй *межд (разг)* hey; ~, **кто идёт?** hey, who's there?

Эй-би-си *м сокр (= Америка́нская радиовеща́тельная компа́ния)* ABC (= *American Broadcasting Company*).

Эквадо́р (-а) *м* Ecuador.

эквадо́рск|ий (-ая, -ое, -ие) *прил* Ecuadorian.

эква́тор (-а) *м* equator.

экваториа́льный *прил* equatorial.

эквивале́нт (-а) *м* equivalent.

эквивале́нт|ный (-ен, -на, -но) *прил* equivalent.

эквилибри́стик|а (-и) *ж* tightrope walking.

ЭКГ *ж сокр (= электрокардиогра́мма)* ECG (= *electrocardiogram*).

экзальта́ци|я (-и) *ж* exhilaration.

экзальти́рован|ный (-, -на, -но) *прил* exhilarated.

экза́мен (-а) *м*: ~ **(по** +*dat*) (по истории, по языку)* exam(ination) (in); *(для получения звания, должности)*: ~ **на перево́дчика** translator's test; *(перен)*: ~ **(на** +*acc*) test (of); **выпускны́е** ~**ы** Finals *мн*; **сдава́ть** *(impf)* ~ to sit *(BRIT)* или take an exam(ination); **сдать** *(perf)* или **выде́рживать (вы́держать** *perf)* ~ to pass an exam(ination); **прова́ливать (провали́ть** *perf)* ~ to fail an exam(ination); **принима́ть (приня́ть** *perf)* ~ to hold an exam(ination).

экзамена́тор (-а) *м* examiner.

экзаменацио́нный *прил (комиссия, сессия)* examination *опред*; **экзаменацио́нный биле́т** exam(ination) paper.

экзамен|ова́ть (-у́ю; *perf* **проэкзаменова́ть)** *несов перех* to examine.

экзе́м|а (-ы) *ж* eczema.

экземпля́р (-а) *м (рукописи, документа)* copy; *(животного, растения)* specimen; **в двух/трёх** ~**ах** in duplicate/triplicate.

экзистенциали́зм (-а) *м* existentialism.

экзо́тик|а (-и) *ж* exotica *мн*.

экзоти́чен *прил см* **экзоти́чный**.

экзоти́ческ|ий (-ая, -ое, -ие) *прил (растение, страна)* exotic.

экзоти́|чный (-ен, -на, -но) *прил (наряд, декорации)* exotic.

э́к|ий (-ая, -ое, -ие; -а, -о, -и) *мест*: ~**ая незада́ча!** what a nuisance!; ~ **ты стра́нный** what a strange one you are!

экипа́ж (-а) *м (коляска)* carriage; *(команда)* crew.

экипир|ова́ть (-у́ю) *(не)сов перех (бойцов, экспедицию)* to equip.

экипиро́в|ка (-и) *ж (действие)* equipping; *(снаряжение)* equipment.

The spelling rules for Russian are shown on page xvii.

э― экологи́ческ|ий (**-ая, -ое, -ие**) *прил* ecological.
эколо́ги|я (**-и**) *ж* ecology.
эконо́мен *прил см* **эконо́мный**.
эконо́мик|а (**-и**) *ж* (*страны, региона*) economy;
  (*наука*) economics.
экономи́ст (**-а**) *м* economist.
эконо́м|ить (**-лю, -ишь;** *perf* **сэконо́мить**) *несов*
  перех (*энергию, деньги*) to save;
  (*выгадывать*): ~ **на** +*prp* to economize *или*
  save on.
эконо́ми|чен *прил см* **эконо́мичный**.
экономи́ческий (**-ая, -ое, -ие**) *прил* economic.
экономи́ч|ный (**-ен, -на, -но**) *прил* economical.
эконо́ми|я (**-и**) *ж* (*в работе, в использовании
  чего-н*) economy; (*выгода*): ~ **в** +*prp* (*в
  топливе, в ресурсах*) economizing in;
  соблюда́ть (*impf*) ~**ю** to economize;
  полити́ческая ~ political economy.
эконо́м|ка (**-ки;** *gen pl* **-ок**) *ж* housekeeper.
эконо́млю *несов см* **эконо́мить**.
эконо́м|ный (**-ен, -на, -но**) *прил* (*хозяин*) thrifty;
  (*метод*) economical.
эконо́мок *сущ см* **эконо́мка**.
экосисте́м|а (**-ы**) *ж* ecosystem.
экра́н (**-а**) *м* screen.
экраниза́ци|я (**-и**) *ж* screen adaptation.
экранизи́р|овать (**-ую**) (*не*)*сов перех* to screen.
экра́нн|ый *прил*: ~**ая па́мять** (*КОМП*) screen
  memory; ~**ое редакти́рование** (*КОМП*) screen
  editing.
экс- *префикс* ex-; ~**чемпио́н** ex-champion.
экскава́тор (**-а**) *м* excavator, digger.
экскава́торщик (**-а**) *м* excavator operator.
эксклюзи́вный *прил* exclusive.
э́кскурс (**-а**) *м* excursus, digression.
экскурса́нт (**-а**) *м* tour group member.
экскурсио́нный *прил* excursion *опред*.
экску́рси|я (**-и**) *ж* (*посещение*) excursion;
  (*группа*) party.
экскурсово́д (**-а**) *м* guide.
экспанси́в|ный (**-ен, -на, -но**) *прил*
  enthusiastic.
экспа́нси|я (**-и**) *ж* (*полит*) expansion.
экспеди́тор (**-а**) *м* shipping agent.
экспеди́ци|я (**-и**) *ж* (*научная, студенческая*)
  field work; (*группа людей*) expedition;
  (*газетная*) dispatch.
экспериме́нт (**-а**) *м* experiment.
эксперимента́льный *прил* experimental.
эксперименти́р|овать (**-ую**) *несов неперех*: ~
  (**над** *или* **с** +*instr*) to experiment (on *или* with).
экспе́рт (**-а**) *м* expert.
эксперти́з|а (**-ы**) *ж* (*медицинская*) medical
  assessment; (*судебная*) legal evaluation.
экспе́ртный *прил* expert *опред*.
эксплуата́тор (**-а**) *м* exploiter.
эксплуата́ци|я (**-и**) *ж* (*человека, ресурсов*)
  exploitation; (*машин, месторождений*)
  utilization; **сдава́ть** (**сдать** *perf*) **что-н в** ~**ю** to
  put sth into commission.
эксплуати́р|овать (**-ую**) *несов перех* to
  exploit; (*машины, дороги*) to use.

экспози́ци|я (**-и**) *ж* (*музейная*) exhibition;
  (*ФОТО*) exposure.
экспона́т (**-а**) *м* exhibit.
экспони́р|овать (**-ую**) (*не*)*сов перех* to exhibit.
э́кспорт (**-а**) *м* export; **на** ~ for export.
экспортёр (**-а**) *м* exporter.
экспорти́р|овать (**-ую**) *несов перех* to export.
э́кспортный *прил* (*товар*) exported; (*правила*)
  export *опред*.
экспре́сс (**-а**) *м* (*транспорт*) express.
экспресси́в|ный (**-ен, -на, -но**) *прил*
  expressive.
экспре́сси|я (**-и**) *ж* expression.
экспро́мт (**-а**) *м* impromptu.
экспро́мтом *нареч* spontaneously.
экста́з (**-а**) *м* ecstasy.
экстенси́в|ный (**-ен, -на, -но**) *прил* extensive.
экстравага́нт|ный (**-ен, -на, -но**) *прил*
  extravagant.
экстра́кт (**-а**) *м* extract.
экстраордина́р|ный (**-ен, -на, -но**) *прил*
  extraordinary.
экстрасе́нс (**-а**) *м* psychic.
экстрема́л|ьный (**-ен, -ьна, -ьно**) *прил*
  extreme.
экстреми́зм (**-а**) *м* extremism.
экстреми́ст (**-а**) *м* extremist.
экстреми́стск|ий (**-ая, -ое, -ие**) *прил* extremist.
э́кстрен|ный (**-ен, -на, -но**) *прил* (*отъезд,
  вызов*) urgent; (*расходы, заседание*) emergency
  опред.
эксце́нтрик (**-а**) *м* eccentric.
эксцентри́|чен *прил см* **эксцентри́чный**.
эксцентри́ческ|ий (**-ая, -ое, -ие**) *прил*
  eccentric.
эксцентри́ч|ный (**-ен, -на, -но**) *прил* eccentric.
эксце́сс (**-а**) *м* excess.
ЭКЮ *сокр* ECU (= *European Currency Unit*).
эла́стик (**-а**) *м* stretchy material.
эласти́ч|ный (**-ен, -на, -но**) *прил* (*материал*)
  stretchy; (*походка*) springy.
элева́тор (**-а**) *м* (*с.-х.*) grain store *или* elevator
  (*US*); (*ТЕХ*) elevator.
элега́нт|ный (**-ен, -на, -но**) *прил* elegant.
эле́ги|я (**-и**) *ж* elegy.
электриз|ова́ть (**-у́ю;** *perf* **наэлектризова́ть**)
  несов перех (*физ*) to electrify; (*перен*:
  человека, атмосферу) to stir up.
эле́ктрик (**-а**) *м* electrician.
электрифика́ци|я (**-и**) *ж* electrification.
электрифици́р|овать (**-ую**) (*не*)*сов перех* to
  connect an electricity supply to.
электри́чек *сущ см* **электри́чка**.
электри́ческ|ий (**-ая, -ое, -ие**) *прил* electric.
электри́честв|о (**-а**) *ср* (*энергия*) electricity;
  (*освещение*) light; **зажига́ть** (**заже́чь** *perf*) ~ to
  turn on the light.
электри́ч|ка (**-ки;** *gen pl* **-ек**) *ж* electric train.
электробытов|о́й *прил*: ~**ые прибо́ры**
  electrical appliances.
электрово́з (**-а**) *м* electric locomotive.
электрогита́р|а (**-ы**) *ж* electric guitar.

электро́д (-а) *м* electrode.
электрокардиогра́мм|а (-ы) *ж* electrocardiogram.
электромонтёр (-а) *м* electrician.
электромото́р (-а) *м* electric motor.
электро́н (-а) *м* electron.
электро́ник|а (-и) *ж* electronics *мн*.
электро́нн|ый *прил*: ~ **микроско́п** electron microscope; **~ая доска́ объявле́ний** (*комп*) bulletin board; **~ая по́чта** (*комп*) electronic mail; **~ая табли́ца** (*комп*) spreadsheet; **электро́нная вычисли́тельная маши́на** computer.
электропереда́ч|а (-и) *ж* power transmission; **ли́ния ~и** power line.
электропо́езд (-а) *м* electric train.
электроприбо́р (-а) *м* electrical device.
электропрово́дк|а (-и) *ж* (electrical) wiring.
электропрово́дность (-и) *ж* conductivity.
электросва́рк|а (-и) *ж* (electric) welding.
электроста́нци|я (-и) *ж* (electric) power station.
электроте́хник (-а) *м* electrical engineer.
электроте́хник|а (-и) *ж* electrical engineering.
электроэне́рги|я (-и) *ж* electric power.
элеме́нт (-а) *м* (*также* хим. элек) element; **престу́пные ~ы** criminal element; **прогресси́вные ~ы о́бщества** progressive elements in society.
элемента́рн|ый *прил* (*также физ*) elementary; (-ен, -на, -но; *правила, условия*) basic.
эликси́р (-а) *м* elixir.
эли́т|а (-ы) *ж собир* elite.
элита́рный *прил* elite.
э́ллипс (-а) *м* ellipse.
эл|ь (-я) *м* ale.
Эльб|а (-ы) *ж* (*остров*) Elba; (*река*) Elbe.
Эльза́с (-а) *м* Alsace.
эльза́сск|ий (-ая, -ое, -ие) *прил* Alsatian.
эльф (-а) *м* elf.
эма́левый *прил* enamel.
эмали́рованный *прил* enamelled.
эмали́р|ова́ть (-у́ю) *несов перех* to enamel.
эма́л|ь (-и) *ж* enamel.
эмансипа́ци|я (-и) *ж* emancipation.
эмансипи́рованный *прил* emancipated.
эмба́рго *ср нескл* embargo; **налага́ть** (**наложи́ть** *perf*) **~ на** +*acc* to place an embargo on.
эмбле́м|а (-ы) *ж* emblem.
эмбриоло́ги|я (-и) *ж* embryology.
эмбрио́н (-а) *м* embryo.
эмигра́нт (-а) *м* emigrant.
эмигра́нтск|ий (-ая, -ое, -ие) *прил* (*поселение*) emigrant *опред*; (*литература*) emigré *опред*.
эмиграцио́нный *прил* emigration *опред*.
эмигра́ци|я (-и) *ж* emigration ♦ *собир* emigrants *мн*.
эмигри́р|овать (-ую) (*не*)*сов неперех* to

emigrate.
эмоциона́л|ьный (-ен, -ьна, -ьно) *прил* emotional.
эмо́ци|я (-и) *ж* emotion.
эму́льси|я (-и) *ж* emulsion.
эмфати́ческ|ий (-ая, -ое, -ие) *прил* emphatic.
эндокри́нн|ый *прил* (*физиология*) endocrine; **~ые же́лезы** endocrine glands.
эндокриноло́ги|я (-и) *ж* endocrinology.
энерге́тик|а (-и) *ж* (*отдел физики*) energetics; (*промышленность*) power industry; (*наука*) power engineering.
энергети́ческ|ий (-ая, -ое, -ие) *прил* (*проблемы, ресурсы*) energy *опред*; **энергети́ческий кри́зис** energy crisis.
энерги́чн|ый (-ен, -на, -но) *прил* (*человек, движения*) energetic; (*меры*) effective.
эне́рги|я (-и) *ж* energy.
энергонезави́сим|ый *прил*: **~ая па́мять** (*комп*) nonvolatile memory.
э́нн|ый *прил*: **~ое число́/коли́чество вре́мени** X number/amount of time; **в ~ раз** yet again; **в ~ой сте́пени** to the nth degree.
энтузиа́зм (-а) *м* enthusiasm.
энтузиа́ст (-а) *м* enthusiast.
энциклопеди́ческ|ий (-ая, -ое, -ие) *прил* (*ум*) encyclopaedic (*BRIT*), encyclopedic (*US*); **энциклопеди́ческий слова́рь** encyclopaedia (*BRIT*), encyclopedia (*US*).
энциклопе́ди|я (-и) *ж* encyclopaedia (*BRIT*), encyclopedia (*US*).
эпигра́мм|а (-ы) *ж* epigram.
эпи́граф (-а) *м* epigraph.
эпиде́ми|я (-и) *ж* epidemic.
эпизо́д (-а) *м* episode.
эпизоди́ческ|ий (-ая, -ое, -ие) *прил* (*случай, факт*) random.
эпизоди́чный *прил* = **эпизоди́ческий**.
эпиле́пси|я (-и) *ж* epilepsy.
эпиле́птик (-а) *м* epileptic.
эпило́г (-а) *м* epilogue (*BRIT*), epilog (*US*).
эпистоля́рный *прил* epistolary.
эпи́тет (-а) *м* epithet.
эпице́нтр (-а) *м* epicentre (*BRIT*), epicenter (*US*).
эпи́ческ|ий (-ая, -ое, -ие) *прил* epic.
эполе́т|а (-ы) *ж* (*обычно мн*) epaulette.
эпопе́|я (-и) *ж* epic.
э́пос (-а) *м* epic literature.
эпо́х|а (-и) *ж* epoch.
эпоха́л|ьный (-ен, -на, -но) *прил* epochmaking.
э́р|а (-ы) *ж* era; **1-ый век на́шей ~ы/до на́шей ~ы** the first century AD/BC.
эре́кци|я (-и) *ж* (*АНАТ*) erection.
эрза́ц (-а) *м* substitute.
Эритре́|я (-и) *ж* Eritrea.
эритроци́т (-а) *м* erythrocyte, red blood cell.
эро́зи|я (-и) *ж* erosion.
эро́тик|а (-и) *ж* erotica *мн*.

The spelling rules for Russian are shown on page xvii.

эроти́ческ|ий (-ая, -ое, -ие) *прил* erotic.
Эр-Рия́д (-а) *м* Riyadh.
эруди́рован|ный (-, -на, -но) *прил* erudite.
эруди́т (-а) *м*: **он настоя́щий ~** he knows an enormous amount.
эруди́ци|я (-и) *ж* erudition.
эска́др|а (-ы) *ж* squadron (*navy*).
эскадри́ль|я (-и) *ж* squadron (*air force*).
эскадро́н (-а) *м* squadron (*army*).
эскала́тор (-а) *м* escalator.
эскала́ци|я (-и) *ж* escalation.
эскало́п (-а) *м* escalope.
эски́з (-а) *м* (*к картине*) sketch; (*к проекту*) draft.
эскимо́ *ср нескл* choc-ice, Eskimo (*US*).
эскимо́с (-а) *м* Eskimo.
эскимо́с|ка (-ки; *gen pl* -ок) *ж см* **эскимо́с**.
эско́рт (-а) *м* escort.
эсми́н|ец (-ца) *м* (= *эска́дренный миноно́сец*) destroyer.
эссе́ *ср нескл* essay.
эссе́нци|я (-и) *ж* essence.
эстака́д|а (-ы) *ж* (*на автомагистрали*) flyover (*BRIT*), overpass; (*на железной дороге*) viaduct; (*на пристани*) pier.
эста́мп (-а) *м* (*ИСКУССТВО*) print.
эстафе́т|а (-ы) *ж* (*СПОРТ*) relay (race); (: *палочка*) baton.
эсте́тик|а (-и) *ж* aesthetics.
эстети́чен *прил см* **эстети́чный**.
эстети́ческ|ий (-ая, -ое, -ие) *прил* aesthetic.
эстети́ч|ный (-ен, -на, -но) *прил* aesthetic.
эсто́н|ец (-ца) *м* Estonian.
Эсто́ни|я (-и) *ж* Estonia.
эсто́н|ка (-ки; *gen pl* -ок) *ж см* **эсто́нец**.
эсто́нск|ий (-ая, -ое, -ие) *прил* Estonian; **~ язы́к** Estonian.
эсто́нца *итп сущ см* **эсто́нец**.
эстра́д|а (-ы) *ж* (*для оркестра*) platform; (*вид искусства*) variety.
эстра́дный *прил*: **~ концерт** variety show; **~ арти́ст** variety performer.
эт|а (-ой) *мест см* **э́тот**.
эта́ж (-а́) *м* floor, storey (*BRIT*), story (*US*); **пе́рвый/второ́й/тре́тий ~** ground/first/second floor (*BRIT*), first/second/third floor (*US*).
этаже́р|ка (-ки; *gen pl* -ок) *ж* (stack of) shelves.
э́так *нареч* (*разг: таким образом*) in such a way ♦ *вводн сл* (*приблизительно*): **~ 25 лет** 25 years or so; **~ у нас ничего́ не полу́чится** we won't get anywhere this way; **и так и ~** (*разг*) this way and that (way).
э́так|ий (-ая, -ое, -ие) *мест* (*разг*) such.
этало́н (-а) *м* (*веса, меры*) standard; (*перен: красоты, благородства итп*) model; **брать** (**взять** *perf*) **что-н за ~** to use sth as a standard.
эта́п (-а) *м* (*развития, работы*) stage; (*гонки*) lap; **ссы́льный ~** stopping point (*for deported convicts*); **отправля́ть** (*impf*) **~ом** *или* **по ~у** to deport (*under convoy*).
эта́пн|ый *прил* (*работа, произведение*)

prominent; **~ое собы́тие** an event of great significance.
э́ти (*-их*) *мест см* **э́тот**.
э́тик|а (-и) *ж* ethics.
этике́т (-а) *м* etiquette.
этике́т|ка (-ки; *gen pl* -ок) *ж* label.
эти́л (-а) *м* ethyl.
эти́ловый *прил* ethyl *опред*.
э́тим *мест см* **э́тот, э́то, э́ти**.
э́тими *мест см* **э́ти**.
этимоло́ги|я (-и) *ж* etymology.
эти́ч|ный (-ен, -на, -но) *прил* ethical.
этни́ческ|ий (-ая, -ое, -ие) *прил* ethnic.
этнографи́ческ|ий (-ая, -ое, -ие) *прил* ethnographic.
этногра́фи|я (-и) *ж* ethnography.

KEYWORD

э́т|о (-ого; *см* **Table 10**) *мест* **1** (*указательное*) this; **на́до успе́ть к ве́черу; э́то бу́дет тру́дно** we need to finish by this evening, this will be difficult; **он на всё соглаша́ется; э́то о́чень стра́нно** he is agreeing to everything, this is most strange
2 (*связка в сказуемом*): **любо́вь – э́то проще́ние** love is forgiveness
3 (*как подлежащее*): **с кем ты разгова́ривал? – э́то была́ моя́ сестра́** who were you talking to? – that was my sister; **как э́то произошло́?** how did it happen?
4 (*для усиления*): **э́то он во всём винова́т** he is the one who is to blame for everything; **э́то они́ нас подвели́** they are the ones who let us down
♦ *част* **1** (*служит для усиления*): **кто э́то звони́л?** who was it who phoned (*BRIT*) *или* called (*US*)?; **о чём э́то ты так беспоко́ишься?** what is it that you are so worried about?
2 (*указательная*): **э́то ты так крича́л?** was it you who called out?

KEYWORD

э́т|от (-ого; *f* **э́та**, *nt* **э́то**, *pl* **э́ти**; *см* **Table 10**) *мест* **1** (*указательное: о близком предмете*) this; (: *о близких предметах*) these; **э́тот дом** this house; **э́ти кни́ги** these books
2 (*о данном времени*) this; **э́тот год осо́бенно тру́дный** this year is particularly hard; **в э́ти дни я при́нял реше́ние** in the last few days I have come to a decision; **э́тот са́мый** that very
3 (*о чём-то только что упомянутом*) this; **он ложи́лся в 10 часо́в ве́чера; э́та привы́чка меня́ всегда́ удивля́ла** he used to go to bed at 10 pm, this habit always amazed me
♦ *ср* (*как сущ: об одном предмете*) this one; (: *о многих предметах*) these ones; **дай мне вот э́ти** give me these ones; **э́тот не всё спосо́бен** this one is capable of anything; **при э́том** in addition.

этю́д (-а) *м* (*ИСКУССТВО*) sketch; (*ЛИТЕРАТУРА*) study; (*МУЗ*) étude; (*шахматный*) problem.
эфеме́р|ный (-ен, -на, -но) *прил* ephemeral.
эфе́с (-а) *м* (*шпаги, сабли*) hilt.

эфио́п (-а) *м* Ethiopian.
Эфио́пи|я (-и) *ж* Ethiopia.
эфио́п|ка (-ки; *gen pl* -ок) *ж см* **эфио́п**.
эфио́пск|ий (-ая, -ое, -ие) *прил* Ethiopian.
эфи́р (-а) *м* (*хим*) ether; (*воздушное пространство*) air; **выходи́ть** (**вы́йти** *perf*) **в** ~ to go on the air; **прямо́й** ~ live broadcast.
эфи́рн|ый *прил*: ~**ое ма́сло** essential oil; ~**ое вре́мя** airtime.
эффе́кт (-а) *м* effect; (*обычно мн: шумовые, световые*) effects *мн*; **экономи́ческий** ~ economic result; **производи́ть** (**произвести́** *perf*) ~ **на** +*acc* to have an effect on; **дава́ть** (**дать** *perf*) **жела́емый** ~ to have the desired effect.
эффе́ктен *прил см* **эффе́ктный**.
эффекти́вен *прил см* **эффекти́вный**.
эффекти́вность (-и) *ж* effectiveness.
эффекти́в|ный (-ен, -на, -но) *прил* effective.
эффе́кт|ный (-ен, -на, -но) *прил* (*одежда*) striking; (*речь*) impressive.
эх *межд* (*разг*) oh; ~ **ты, лентя́й** ! oh, you're such a lazybones!
э́х|о (-а) *ср* echo (*мн* echoes).
эшафо́т (-а) *м* scaffold; **всходи́ть** (**взойти́** *perf*) **на** ~ to mount the scaffold.
эшело́н (-а) *м* echelon; (*поезд*) special train; ~**ы вла́сти** echelons of power.

~ Ю, ю ~

Ю, ю *сущ нескл (буква)* the 31st letter of the Russian alphabet.

ю. *сокр* (= **юг**) S (= *South*); (= **южный**) S (= *South*).

юа́нь (**-я**) *м* yuan (*мн* yuan).

ЮАР *ж сокр* (= Южно-Африка́нская Респу́блика) RSA (= *Republic of South Africa*).

юбиле́й (**-я**) *м (годовщина)* anniversary; *(празднование)* jubilee.

юбиле́йный *прил (торжество)* anniversary *опред*; *(монета, значок итп)* jubilee *опред*.

юбиля́р (**-а**) *м*: **уче́ный-/заво́д-~** *scientist/factory whose anniversary is being celebrated*.

ю́б|ка (**-ки**; *gen pl* **-ок**) *ж* skirt; **держа́ться** *(impf)* **за чью-н ~ку** *(разг)* to be tied to sb's apron strings.

ювели́р (**-а**) *м* jeweller (*BRIT*), jeweler (*US*).

ювели́рный *прил* jewellery *опред* (*BRIT*), jewelery *опред* (*US*); *(перен: работа, точность)* painstaking; **~ые изде́лия** jewel(l)ery; **~ магази́н** jeweller's (*BRIT*) *или* jeweler's (*US*) (shop).

юг (**-а**) *м* south; **на ю́ге страны́** in the south of the country; **к ю́гу от го́рода** to the south of the town.

ю́го-восто́к (**-а**) *м* south-east.

ю́го-за́пад (**-а**) *м* south-west.

Югосла́вия (**-и**) *ж* (*ИСТ*) Yugoslavia.

южа́н|ин (**-ина**; *nom pl* **-е**, *gen pl* **-**) *м* southerner.

южа́н|ка (**-ки**; *gen pl* **-ок**) *ж см* **южа́нин**.

ю́жный *прил* southern; **Ю́жная Коре́я** South Korea; **Ю́жный по́люс** the South Pole.

юл|а́ (**-ы́**) *ж (игрушка)* (spinning) top ♦ *м/ж (перен: разг)* fidget.

юл|и́ть (**-ю́, -и́шь**) *несов неперех (разг: суетиться)* to fidget; (*: хитрить*) to be shifty; **~** *(impf)* **пе́ред** +*instr (заискивать)* to play up to.

ю́мор (**-а**) *м* humour (*BRIT*), humor (*US*).

юморе́с|ка (**-ки**; *gen pl* **-ок**) *ж (МУЗ)* humoresque; *(ЛИТЕРАТУРА)* short comedy.

юмори́ст (**-а**) *м (автор)* humorist; *(шутливый человек)* comedian.

юмори́стик|а (**-и**) *ж (ЛИТЕРАТУРА)* humour (*BRIT*), humor (*US*).

юмористи́ческий (**-ая, -ое, -ие**) *прил* humorous; **~ журна́л** satirical magazine.

юмори́ст|ка (**-ки**; *gen pl* **-ок**) *ж* comedienne.

ю́нг|а (**-и**) *м* cabin boy; *(младший матрос)* trainee sailor.

ЮНЕ́СКО *ср сокр* UNESCO (= *United Nations*

Educational Scientific and Cultural Organization).

юн|е́ц (**-ца́**) *м (разг: юноша)* youth.

юнио́р (**-а**) *м* junior.

ЮНИСЕ́Ф *м сокр* UNICEF (= *United Nations (International) Children's (Emergency) Fund*).

ю́нкер (**-а**; *nom pl* **-а́**) *м (ИСТ)* cadet.

ю́нкерский (**-ая, -ое, -ие**) *прил* cadet *опред*; **~ое учи́лище** military school.

ю́ность (**-и**) *ж* youth ♦ *собир (юношество)* young people *мн*; **в ~и он был любозна́телен** in his youth he was greedy for knowledge.

ю́нош|а (**-и**; *nom pl* **-и**, *gen pl* **-ей**) *м* young man (*мн* men).

ю́ношеский (**-ая, -ое, -ие**) *прил* youthful; *(журнал)* young person's; *(организация, клуб)* youth; **~ие го́ды** youth.

ю́ношеств|о (**-а**) *ср собир* young people *мн*; *(юность)* youth.

юнца́ *итп сущ см* **юне́ц**.

ю́ный (**-, -а́, -о**) *прил (молодой)* young; *(силы, задор)* youthful; **теа́тр ~ого зри́теля** children's theatre (*BRIT*) *или* theater (*US*).

ЮПИ́ *м сокр* UPI (= *United Press International*).

юпи́тер (**-а**) *м (прибор)* floodlight; **Ю~** Jupiter.

юриди́чески *нареч*: **~ обяза́тельный** legally binding.

юриди́ческий (**-ая, -ое, -ие**) *прил (сила)* juridical; *(образование)* legal; **~ факульте́т** law faculty; **юриди́ческая консульта́ция** ≈ legal advice office; **юриди́ческое лицо́** body corporate.

юрисди́кци|я (**-и**) *ж (ЮР)* jurisdiction; **подлежа́ть** *(impf)* **чьей-н ~и** to come under sb's jurisdiction.

юрисконсу́льт (**-а**) *м* legal adviser.

юриспруде́нци|я (**-и**) *ж (правоведение)* jurisprudence; *(практика юриста)* law.

юри́ст (**-а**) *м* lawyer.

ю́ркий (**-кая, -кое, -кие; -ок, -ка́, -ко**) *прил* nimble.

ю́ркн|уть (**-у, -ешь**) *сов неперех* to scurry away.

юро́дивый *прил (разг)* crazy ♦ (**-ого**; *decl like adj*) *м (РЕЛ)* holy fool.

юро́дств|овать (**-ую**) *несов неперех (перен)* to behave like a lunatic.

ю́рок *прил см* **ю́ркий**.

ю́рский (**-ая, -ое, -ие**) *прил (ГЕО)* Jurassic.

ю́рт|а (**-ы**) *ж* yurt *(skin tent used by nomads in*

Central Asia and Siberia).

ЮСИА *м сокр* USIA (= *United States Information Agency).*

юстúци|я (-**и**) *ж* (*правовые учреждения*) the judiciary; **Министéрство** ~**и** the Ministry of Justice.

ю|тúться (-**чýсь**, -**тúшься**) *несов неперех* (*располагаться*) to huddle together; (*иметь приют*) to live in cramped conditions.

~ Я, я ~

Я, я *сущ нескл (буква)* the 32nd letter of the Russian alphabet.

я (меня; *см* **Table 5a**) *мест* I ♦ *сущ нескл (личность)* the self, the ego; ~ **тебя** *или* **тебе́!** (*разг: угроза*) I'll teach you!; **не ~ бу́ду, е́сли не ...** (*разг*) I'll be damned if I don't ...; **второ́е "я"** alter ego.

я́бед|а (-ы) *м/ж* sneak.

я́бедник (-а) *м* = **я́беда.**

я́бедничá|ть (-ю; *perf* **ная́бедничать**) *несов непереx:* ~ **на** +*acc* (*разг*) to tell tales about.

я́блок|о (-а; *nom pl* -и) *ср* apple; **глазно́е** ~ eyeball; **в ~ах** (*о масти лошадей*) dappled; **~у не́где упа́сть** (*перен*) there's not enough room to swing a cat.

я́блоневый *прил (цвет)* apple-green; **~ая ве́тка** branch of an apple tree.

я́блон|я (-и) *ж* apple tree.

я́блочк|о (-а) *ср уменьш от* **я́блоко;** (*на мишени*) bull's-eye.

я́блочный *прил* apple *опред*.

я́вен *прил см* **я́вный.**

яви́ться (-лю́сь, -ишься; *impf* **явля́ться**) *сов возв (в суд)* to appear; (*на слу́жбу*) to report; (*домой, в гости*) to arrive; (*мысль, образ*) to arise; **явля́ться** (~ *perf*) +*instr* (*причиной, сле́дствием*) to turn out to be.

я́в|ка (-ки; *gen pl* -ок) *ж (действие: в суд, на допрос)* appearance; (: *на интервью итп*) attendance; (*место: конспираторов*) secret meeting place.

явле́ни|е (-я) *ср* phenomenon (*мн* phenomena); (*событие*) occurrence; (*ТЕАТР*) scene; (*РЕЛ*) manifestation.

явлю́сь *сов см* **яви́ться.**

явля́|ться (-юсь) *несов от* **яви́ться** ♦ *возв:* ~ +*instr* to be.

я́вно *нареч (очевидно)* obviously.

я́в|ный (-ен, -на, -но) *прил (вражда, благоскло́нность)* overt; (*ложь, лесть итп*) obvious.

я́вок *сущ см* **я́вка.**

я́вочный *прил;* **~ая кварти́ра** secret meeting place; ~ **пункт** (*ВОЕН*) reporting point; **~ым поря́дком** without permission; **я́вочный лист** attendance sheet.

я́вственн|ый (-, -на, -но) *прил (звук)* distinct; (*сознание, понимание итп*) clear.

я́вств|овать (*3sg* -ует) *несов непереx* to be

obvious; **из показа́ний ~ует, что он невино́вен** from the evidence it is obvious that he is innocent.

явь| (-и) *ж* reality.

яг|а́ (-и́) *ж* Baba-Yaga (*witch in Russian folk tales*).

я́гель (-я) *м* Iceland moss.

ягн|ёнок (-ёнка; *nom pl* -я́та, *gen pl* -я́т) *м* lamb.

ягни́ться (*3sg* -и́тся, *3pl* -я́тся, *perf* **оягни́ться**) *несов возв* to lamb.

ягня́та *итп сущ см* **ягнёнок.**

я́год|а (-ы) *ж* berry; **одного́ по́ля** ~ kindred spirit.

ягоди́ц|а (-ы) *ж* buttock.

я́годник (-а) *м (место)* berry patch; (*кустарник*) berry bush; (*разг: сборщик*) berry picker.

я́годный *прил* berry *опред*.

ягуа́р (-а) *м* jaguar.

яд (-а; *part gen* -у) *м* poison.

я́дер *сущ см* **ядро́.**

я́дерный *прил* nuclear.

я́дерщик (-а) *м (разг)* nuclear physicist.

ядови́тый (-, -а, -о) *прил* poisonous; (*перен: человек, слова*) venomous.

ядохимика́т (-а) *м (обычно мн)* chemical (*used as weedkiller or pesticide*).

ядрён|ый (-, -а, -о) *прил (яблоко)* juicy; (*перен: воздух*) fresh; (: *мороз*) hard.

ядр|о́ (-а́; *nom pl* -а, *gen pl* -ер) *ср* nucleus; (*ореха*) kernel; (*Земли, древесины*) core; (*ВОЕН*) projectile; (*СПОРТ*) shot; **толка́ние ~а́** (*СПОРТ*) shot put.

яз. *сокр* (= **язы́к**) lang. (= *language*).

я́зв|а (-ы) *ж (МЕД)* ulcer; (*перен: общества*) evil ♦ *м/ж (перен: разг)* sarcastic person (*мн* people); **я́зва желу́дка** stomach ulcer.

я́звенный *прил:* ~**ая боле́знь** stomach ulcer.

язви́тельный (-ен, -ьна, -ьно) *прил* scathing.

язв|и́ть (-лю́, -и́шь; *perf* **съязви́ть**) *несов непереx* (+*dat*) to speak sharply to; ~ (**съязви́ть** *perf*) **на чей-н счёт** to be scathing at sb's expense.

язы́к| (-а́) *м* tongue; (*русский, разговорный итп*) language; (*ВОЕН: разг*) *prisoner captured for information;* (*ВОЕН: разг*) *prisoner captured for information;* **держа́ть** (*impf*) ~ **за зуба́ми** (*разг*) to hold one's tongue; **вопро́с (был) у него́ на ~е** (*разг*) the question was on the tip of his tongue; **прикуси́ть** (*perf*) ~ (*разг*) to bite one's tongue; **тяну́ть** (*perf*) **кого́-н за** ~ (*разг*) to make sb talk; ~ **не повернётся сказа́ть/попроси́ть** (*разг*) I could not bring myself to say/ask; **владе́ть** (*impf*) **языко́м** to speak a language; **находи́ть** (**найти́** *perf*) **о́бщий** ~ to find a common language; ~ **программи́рования высо́кого/ни́зкого у́ровня** (*комп*) high-level/low-level language; ~ **ассе́мблера** (*комп*) assembly language.

языка́ст|ый (-, -а, -о) *прил* (*человек*) sharp-tongued.

языкове́д (-а) *м* linguist.

языкове́ди|е (-я) *ср* linguistics.

языков|о́й *прил* (*факульте́т, систе́ма*) language *опред*; ~**о́е пра́ви|ло** rule of a language.

языкозна́ни|е (-я) *ср* linguistics.

язы́ческ|ий (-ая, -ое, -ие) *прил* pagan *опред*.

язы́честв|о (-а) *ср* paganism.

язычка́ *итп сущ см* **язычо́к**.

язы́чник (-а) *м* pagan.

язы́чниц|а (-ы) *ж см* **язы́чник**.

язычо́к (-ка́) *м уменьш от* **язы́к**; (*АНАТ*) uvula; (*боти́нка*) tongue; (*замка́*) catch.

яйц *сущ см* **яйцо́**.

яйч|ко (-ка, *gen pl* -ек) *ср уменьш от* **яйцо́**; (*АНАТ*) testicle.

яи́чник (-а) *м* ovary.

яи́чниц|а (-ы) *ж* fried eggs *мн*.

яи́чн|ый *прил*: ~ **бело́к** egg white; ~**ая скорлупа́** eggshell.

яйцеви́дн|ый (-ен, -на, -но) *прил* egg-shaped.

яйцево́д (-а) *м* oviduct.

яйцекле́т|ка (-ки, *gen pl* -ок) *ж* ovule.

яйц|о́ (*яйца́*; *nom pl* **я́йца**, *gen pl* **яи́ц**, *dat pl* **я́йцам**) *ср* egg; (*АНАТ*) ovum; ~ **всмя́тку/вкруту́ю** soft-boiled/hard-boiled egg.

ЯК (-а) *м сокр* = *самолёт констру́кции А.С. Я́ковлева*.

Як (-а) *м сокр* = **ЯК**.

як (-а) *м* yak.

я́кобы *союз* (*бу́дто бы*) that ♦ *част* supposedly; **он утвержда́ет**, ~ **ничего́ не зна́ет** he claims that he doesn't know anything; **он предлага́ет** ~ **вы́годную сде́лку** he is supposedly proposing a good deal.

я́корный *прил* anchor *опред*.

я́кор|ь (-я; *nom pl* -я́) *м* (*МОР*) anchor; **броса́ть** (**бро́сить** *perf*) ~ to cast anchor; **стоя́ть** (*impf*) **на** ~**е** to ride at anchor; **снима́ться** (**сня́ться** *perf*) **с** ~**я** to weigh anchor.

яку́т (-а) *м* Yakut.

Яку́ти|я (-и) *ж* Yakutia.

яку́т|ка (-ки; *gen pl* -ок) *ж см* **яку́т**.

якша́|ться (-юсь) *несов возв*: ~ **с** +*instr* to consort with.

Я́лт|а (-ы) *ж* Yalta.

я́м|а (-ы) *ж* (*в земле́*) pit; (*разг: впа́дина*) hollow;

рыть (*impf*) ~**у кому́-н** to lay a trap for sb; **возду́шная** ~ air pocket; **оркестро́вая** ~ orchestra pit.

Яма́йк|а (-и) *ж* Jamaica.

яма́йск|ий (-ая, -ое, -ие) *прил* Jamaican.

я́моч|ка (-ки; *gen pl* -ек) *ж* dimple.

ямщи́к (-а́) *м* coachman (*мн* coachmen).

январ|ь (-я́) *м* January; *см также* **октя́брь**.

янта́рный *прил* amber *опред*.

янта́р|ь (-я́) *м* amber.

япо́н|ец (-ца) *м* Japanese.

Япо́ни|я (-и) *ж* Japan.

япо́н|ка (-ки; *gen pl* -ок) *ж см* **япо́нец**.

япо́нск|ий (-ая, -ое, -ие) *прил* Japanese; ~ **язы́к** Japanese.

япо́нца *итп сущ см* **япо́нец**.

ярд (-а) *м* yard.

я́рк|ий (-ая, -кое, -кие; -ок, -ка́, -ко) *прил* bright; (*перен: человек, речь*) brilliant; (: *тала́нт*) outstanding.

я́ркост|ь (-и) *ж* (*цве́та, кра́ски*) brightness; (*челове́ка, ре́чи*) brilliance.

ярлы́к (-а́) *м* label; **ему́ накле́или** ~ **реакционе́ра** he was labelled as a reactionary.

я́рмар|ка (-ки; *gen pl* -ок) *ж* fair; **междунаро́дная** ~ international trade fair.

ярм|о́ (-а́ *также перен*) yoke.

яров|о́й *прил* (*зла́ки*) spring *опред*; ~**о́е по́ле** field sown with spring crops.

я́рок *прил см* **я́ркий**.

я́рост|ный (-ен, -на, -но) *прил* (*взгляд, слова́*) furious; (*перен: ата́ка, кри́тика*) fierce.

я́рост|ь (-и) *ж* fury; **приходи́ть** (**прийти́** *perf*) **в** ~ to fly into a rage.

я́рус (-а) *м* (*в зри́тельном за́ле*) circle; (*ряд*) tier; (*ГЕО*) layer.

я́рый *прил* (*пре́данный*) ardent.

я́сен *прил см* **я́сный**.

я́сен|ь (-я) *м* ash (tree).

я́сл|и (-ей) *мн* (*для скота́*) trough *ед*; (*также:* **де́тские** ~) crèche, day nursery (*БРИТ*).

ясне́|ть (*3sg* -ет, *3pl* -ют) *несов неперех* to clear, become clear.

я́сно *нареч* clearly ♦ *как сказ* (*о пого́де*) it's fine; (*поня́тно*) it's clear; **я** ~ **выража́юсь?** do I make myself clear?; **на у́лице сего́дня** ~ it's fine outside today; **тепе́рь мне всё** ~ it's all clear to me now; ~, **что он недово́лен** it's clear that he's not happy; **с ним всё** ~ nothing more needs to be said about him.

яснови́дени|е (-я) *ср* clairvoyance.

яснови́д|ец (-ца) *м* clairvoyant.

яснови́дящ|ий (-ая, -ее, -ие) *прил* (*человек*) clairvoyant *опред* ♦ (-его; *decl like adj*) *м* clairvoyant.

я́сност|ь (-и) *ж* clarity; **вноси́ть** (**внести́** *perf*) ~ **в что-н** to clarify sth.

я́сн|ый (-ен, -на́, -но) *прил* clear.

я́стреб (-а) *м* (*зоол*) hawk.

ястреби́н|ый *прил* (*клюв*) hawk's; **~ая охо́та** falconry; **~ нос** (*перен*) hooked nose.

я́хонт (-а) *м* (*рубин*) ruby; (*сапфир*) sapphire.

я́хт|а (-ы) *ж* yacht.

яхт-клу́б (-а) *м* yacht club.

яхтсме́н (-а) *м* yachtsman (*мн* yachtsmen).

яче́|йка (-йки; *gen pl* **-ек**) *ж* (*сотовая, партийная*) cell; (*профсоюзная*) branch; (*для почты*) pigeonhole; **яче́йка па́мяти** (*КОМП*) memory cell.

ячме́нный *прил* barley *опред*.

ячме́н|ь (-я́) *м* (*с.-х.*) barley; (*МЕД*) sty(e).

я́чневый *прил* crushed-barley.

я́шм|а (-ы) *ж* jasper.

я́щериц|а (-ы) *ж* lizard.

я́щик (-а) *м* (*вместилище: большой*) chest; (: *маленький*) box; (*в письменном столе итп*) drawer; (*также:* **мусо́рный ~**) dustbin (*BRIT*), garbage can (*US*); **почто́вый ~** (*домашний*) letter box (*BRIT*), mailbox (*US*); (*уличный: как адрес*) post office box; (*разг: об учреждении*) *secret plant, institution etc*; (: *ТЕЛ*) the box; **откла́дывать** (**отложи́ть** *perf*) **что-н в до́лгий ~** (*перен*) to shelve sth.

я́щур (-а) *м* (*болезнь*) foot-and-mouth disease.

GUIDE TO RUSSIAN GRAMMAR

It is not the purpose of this grammar section to attempt to give an exhaustive treatment of Russian grammar. Instead it is intended to outline the basic grammatical principles and to draw the user's attention to the most commonly encountered irregular forms.

NOUNS

1 Gender

A Russian noun has either masculine, feminine or neuter gender. In most cases it is grammatically determinable by its ending:

дом *m*
картѝна *f*
крѐсло *nt*

Gender of nouns is significant since, for example, it determines the ending of a qualifying adjective:

большо́й дом
больша́я карти́на
большо́е кре́сло

1.1 Masculine noun categories

I) All nouns ending in a hard consonant eg. кот, собо́р, а́дрес or in -й eg. кремато́рий, музе́й.
II) Some nouns ending in -а/-я which are natural masculine nouns eg.мужчи́на, дя́дя and masculine first names eg. Са́ша.
III) Numerous nouns ending in a soft sign, including:
    i)   natural masculines eg. па́рень, коро́ль.
    ii) months of the year eg. ию́ль.

1.2 Feminine noun categories

I) The majority of nouns ending in -а/-я, eg. доро́га, ко́мната, тётя.
II) The majority of nouns ending in a soft sign, including:
    i) natural feminines eg. мать
    ii) all nouns ending in -жь,-чь,-шь,-щь,-знь,-мь,-пь,-фь.
    iii) most nouns ending in -сть,-бь,-вь,-дь,-зь,-сь,-ть.

1.3 Neuter noun categories

a) Almost all nouns ending in -о eg. окно́
b) Almost all nouns ending in -е eg. со́лнце
c) Nouns ending in -ё eg. копьё.
d) Nouns ending in -мя eg. вре́мя, пле́мя.
e) Most indeclinable loan words eg. ви́ски, ра́дио (a notable exception being ко́фе, which is masculine).

2 Declension

There are three declension patterns for nouns. The first covers most masculine and neuter nouns, the second most feminine nouns and the third is specific to feminine nouns ending in a soft sign. For the first declension pattern hard-ending masculine and neuter nouns (eg. мост, о́зеро) have the genitive singular ending -a, whereas soft-ending masculine and neuter nouns (eg. кремато́рий, гость, го́ре) have the genitive ending -я. Similarly, the second declension pattern has a split between hard-ending feminine nouns (eg. ла́мпа), which have the genitive singular ending -ы, and soft-ending feminine nouns (eg. ба́шня), which have the genitive ending -и. All nouns in the third declension pattern, as they are soft-ending, have the genitive ending -и.

The genitive singular declension generally sets the pattern for the other oblique cases of a noun, ie. whether these will be hard- or soft-ending. The general pattern followed in all three declensions is illustrated by the following table, using specific noun examples:

[NB. The table does not, of course, cover all the variations in declension or stress that exist]

Nom	Acc	Singular Gen	Dat	Instr	Prp	Nom	Acc	Plural Gen	Dat	Instr	Prp
Masculine											
заво́д	~	~а	~у	~ом	~е	~ы	~ы	~ов	~ам	~ами	~ах
музе́й	~й	~я	~ю	~ем	~е	~и	~и	~ев	~ям	~ями	~ях
гость	~я	~я	~ю	~ем	~е	~и	~ей	~ей	~я́м	~я́ми	~я́х
писа́тель	~я	~я	~ю	~ем	~е	~и	~ей	~ей	~ям	~ями	~ях
дви́гатель	~ь	~я	~ю	~ем	~е	~и	~и	~ей	~ям	~ями	~ях
Neuter											
ме́сто	~о	~а	~у	~ом	~е	~а́	~а́	~	~а́м	~а́ми	~а́х
по́ле	~е	~я	~ю	~ем	~е	~я́	~я́	~ей	~я́м	~я́ми	~я́х
зда́ние	~е	~я	~ю	~ем	~и	~я	~я	~й	~ям	~ями	~ях
Feminine											
ла́мпа	~у	~ы	~е	~ой	~е	~ы	~ы	~	~ам	~ами	~ах
ба́шня	~ню	~ни	~не	~ней	~не	~ни	~ни	~ен	~ням	~нями	~нях
по́весть	~ь	~и	~и	~ью	~и	~и	~и	~ей	~ям	~ями	~ях
ста́нция	~ю	~и	~и	~ей	~и	~и	~и	~й	~ям	~ями	~ях

One particularly important rule to bear in mind is that the accusative case of animate masculine singular nouns and of all animate plural nouns is identical with the genitive.

3 Stress patterns

Stress varies a great deal from one Russian noun to the next, and even oblique cases of a particular noun frequently differ from each other in this respect.

Nouns ending in unstressed -a/-я and in -ия/-ие do not undergo any stress changes.

Fixed stem-stress is found in first declension masculine nouns such as стул, музе́й, локомоти́в, in nouns with medial stress, in nouns of three or more syllables, and in nouns with unstressed prefixes or suffixes.

Fixed end-stress is found in many hard-ending and soft-ending first declension masculine nouns such as стол, дождь, словарь, as well as in almost all nouns with the stressed suffixes -а́к/-я́к,-а́ч, -ёж, -ёж,-и́к,-и́ч,-у́н,-у́х.

A shift of stress from the stem in the singular to the end in the plural is found in first declension masculine nouns such as мост and сад, as well as in many nouns with nominative plural endings -ья́,-а́/-я́. A similar stress shift occurs in neuter nouns such as де́ло and ме́сто. The reverse happens (ie. a shift of stress from the end in the singular to the stem in the plural) in other neuter nouns eg. письмо́, вино́, окно́. This is also true for many second declension feminine nouns eg. война́, игра́, страна́ and others which undergo a vowel mutation in the stress change eg. жена́ » жёны, сестра́ » сёстры.

Irregularity of stress pattern is greatest in end-stressed second declension feminine nouns, where the following patterns are possible: the accusative singular and nominative/accusative plural have stem stress eg. рука́, нога́, сторона́, or only the nominative/accusative plural have stem stress eg. губа́, волна́. Alternatively, stem stress may be confined to: the singular accusative and all plural forms, as in the case of вода́, цена́, стена́; all plural forms with the exception of the genitive and animate accusative, as in the case of семья́, судья́; the accusative singular and all plural forms excepting the genitive, as in the case of земля́.

2 ADJECTIVES

Russian adjectives generally have a long (attributive) form eg. ве́жливый, ве́жливая, ве́жливое, ве́жливые and a short (predicative) form eg. ве́жлив, ве́жлива, ве́жливо, ве́жливы.

1 Long form

Russian long adjectives are mostly used attributively and the majority have hard endings, the first vowel of the ending being -ы,-а or -о. The declension of such adjectives is seen as the regular one for the purposes of this dictionary. Thus, adjectives such as ста́рый decline as follows:

	m	*f*	*nt*	*pl*
Nom	ста́р|ый	ста́р|ая	ста́р|ое	ста́р|ые
Acc	~ый/~ого	~ую	~ое	~ые/~ых
Gen	~ого	~ой	~ого	~ых
Dat	~ому	~ой	~ому	~ым
Instr	~ым	~ой	~ым	~ыми
Prp	о ~ом	о ~ой	о ~ом	о ~ых

(NB. The alternative forms of the accusative are animate and identical with the genitive. The feminine instrumental ending -ою also exists)

End-stressed adjectives with hard endings, eg. живо́й, decline similarly, with the only difference being the masculine nominative singular and inanimate accusative singular, where the ending -о́й replaces -ый. Alternative endings are determined by Russian spelling rules, according to which и replaces ы after г,к,х,ж,ч,ш,щ, and е replaces an unstressed о after ж,ч,ш,щ and ц. Thus, a stem-stressed adjective such as гла́дкий declines as follows:

	m	*f*	*nt*	*pl*
Nom	гла́дкий	гла́дкая	гла́дкое	гла́дкие
Acc	~ий/~ого	~ую	~ое	~ие/~их
Gen	~ого	~ой	~ого	~их
Dat	~ому	~ой	~ому	~им
Instr	~им	~ой	~им	~ими
Prp	о ~ом	о ~ой	о ~ом	о ~их

(NB. The alternative forms of the accusative are animate and identical with the genitive. The feminine instrumental ending -ою also exists)

End-stressed adjectives such as большо́й decline similarly, with only the masculine nominative and inanimate accusative singular differing in that they have the ending -о́й instead of -ий. In stem-stressed adjectives such as хоро́ший, however, the declensions are as follows:

	m	*f*	*nt*	*pl*
Nom	хоро́ший	хоро́шая	хоро́шее	хоро́шие
Acc	~ий/~его	~ую	~ее	~ие/~их
Gen	~его	~ей	~его	~их
Dat	~ему	~ей	~ему	~им
Instr	~им	~ей	~им	~ими
Prp	о ~ем	о ~ей	о ~ем	о ~их

(NB. The alternative forms of the accusative are animate and identical with the genitive. The feminine instrumental ending -ею also exists)

Soft-ending adjectives, ie. those ending in -ний, decline differently again. Thus, adjectives such as о́сенний or сосе́дний decline as follows:

	m	*f*	*nt*	*pl*
Nom	о́сенний	о́сенняя	о́сеннее	о́сенние
Acc	~ий/~его	~юю	~ее	~ие/~их
Gen	~его	~ей	~его	~их
Dat	~ему	~ей	~ему	~им
Instr	~им	~ей	~им	~ими
Prp	о ~ем	о ~ей	о ~ем	о ~их

(NB. The alternative forms of the accusative are animate and, therefore, identical with the genitive. The feminine instrumental ending -ею also exists)

1.1 Possessive adjectives

These follow one of two declension patterns. Possessive adjectives like соба́чий and де́вичий decline as follows:

	m	*f*	*nt*	*pl*
Nom	соба́чий	соба́чья	соба́чье	соба́чьи
Acc	~ий/~ьего	~ью	~ье	~ьи/~ьих
Gen	~ьего	~ьей	~ьего	~ьих
Dat	~ьему	~ьей	~ьему	~ьим
Instr	~ьим	~ьей	~ьим	~ьими
Prp	о ~ьем	о ~ьей	о ~ьем	о ~ьих

(NB. The alternative forms of the accusative are animate and identical with the genitive. The feminine instrumental ending -ьею also exists. The ordinal numeral тре́тий declines according to the above table)

In addition, there are those possessive adjectives formed by adding the suffixes -ин,-нин or -ов to the stems of nouns. This form is mainly used with reference to particular family members, eg. ма́мин, му́жнин, де́дов, but can also be derived from the familiar forms of first names, eg. Ле́нин, Са́шин. These decline as follows:

	m	*f*	*nt*	*pl*
Nom	Са́шин	Са́шин|а	Са́шин|о	Са́шин|ы
Acc	~/~ого	~у	~о	~ы/~ых
Gen	~ого	~ой	~ого	~ых
Dat	~у	~ой	~у	~ым
Instr	~ым	~ой	~ым	~ыми
Prp	о ~ом	о ~ой	о ~ом	о ~ых

(NB. The alternative forms of the accusative are animate and identical with the genitive. The feminine instrumental ending -ою also exists)

Note that the animate accusative/genitive rule which affects nouns also applies to long adjectives.

1.2 Usage

Long adjectives are typically used attributively, for example:

на у́лице стои́т **бе́лая** маши́на "a white car is parked on the street"

or showing the use of the accusative case:

он во́дит **бе́лую** маши́ну "he drives a white car"

Long adjectives may be used predicatively when they denote characteristics inherent to the nouns they refer to.

э́та у́лица – **дли́нная** "this street is long"
э́тот груз – **тяжёлый** "this load is heavy"

2 Short adjectives

Short adjectives can be derived from most long adjectives. They are formed by replacing the long-form endings with contracted ones eg. ве́жливый. This declines as follows:

	Long Form	*Short Form*
m	ве́жлив|ый	ве́жлив
f	~ая	~а
nt	~ое	~о
pl	~ые	~ы

The masculine short form of many adjectives requires a buffer vowel (e,o or ё) to be inserted between the last two consonants or to replace a soft sign. Thus, ва́жный has masculine short form ва́жен, ви́дный has ви́ден, лёгкий лёгок, у́мный умён etc. Masculine short forms of adjectives ending in -енный (ie. unstressed) generally have -ен endings, whereas those in -ённый (ie. stressed) are replaced by the short form -ёнен.

Short-form adjectives have either fixed stem stress, eg. ве́жлив, ве́жлива, ве́жливо, ве́жливы, end stress in feminine, neuter and plural, eg. хоро́ш, хороша́, хорошо́, хоро́ший, end stress in the feminine, eg. жив, жива́, жи́во, жи́вы, or end stress in the feminine and plural, eg. ви́ден, видна́, ви́дно, видны́.

2.1 Usage

In contrast to the predicative use of long adjectives, the short form on the whole is used when talking about a temporary state. For example, он **плох** "he is poorly" contrasts with он – плохо́й "he is bad".

3 VERBS

1 Conjugation

Russian verbs can be divided into two groups, according to their endings when conjugated. The two groups are often referred to as "first-conjugation" and "second-conjugation" verbs, and the following examples – one from either group – show the pattern of endings encountered in the present-tense conjugations of verbs from each group:

	1st Conjugation	*2nd Conjugation*
	рабо́тать	говори́ть
я	рабо́таю	говорю́
ты	рабо́таешь	говори́шь
он/она́	рабо́тает	говори́т
мы	рабо́таем	говори́м
вы	рабо́таете	говори́те
они́	рабо́тают	говоря́т

1.1 First-conjugation verbs

These include verbs with infinitive endings in -ать (eg. рабо́тать: see above), in -ять (eg. стреля́ть: стреля́ю,стреля́ешь etc), in -овать/-евать (eg. интересова́ть: интерес-у́ю,интересу́ешь etc), in -уть (eg. махну́ть: махну́,махнёшь etc), in -авать (eg. узнава́ть: узнаю́,узнаёшь etc), in -ыть (eg. мыть: мо́ю,мо́ешь etc), and in -зть,-оть,-сть and -ти, as well as monosyllabic verbs in -ить (eg. шить: шью,шьёшь etc). Note how under stress e is replaced by ё.

Many first-conjugation verbs – generally those with end-stressed infinitives – undergo consonant mutation in conjugation, which is frequently accompanied by a stress shift from the end to the stem after the first person singular; this is the general pattern for stress changes within the conjugation of first-conjugation verbs. For example:

	писа́ть	иска́ть
я	пишу́	ищу́
ты	пи́шешь	и́щешь
он/она́	пи́шет	и́щет
мы	пи́шем	и́щем
вы	пи́шете	и́щете
они́	пи́шут	и́щут

Stress change does not occur in first-conjugation verbs where the stress falls on the stem of the infinitive, eg. пла́кать: пла́чу, пла́чешь etc, and дви́гать: дви́жу,дви́жешь etc.

1.2 Second-conjugation verbs

These include most verbs with infinitive endings in -ить (the main exception being the monosyllabic ones), many verbs in -еть, some in -ать and two in -ять (боя́ться and стоя́ть).

Note that y replaces ю and a replaces я after ж,ч,ш, or щ. Thus, смотре́ть conjugates: смотрю́,смо́тришь,...смо́трят, whereas слы́шать conjugates: слы́шу,слы́шишь,...слы́шат.

As with first-conjugation verbs, stress change in second-conjugation verbs that are end-stressed in the infinitive is often accompanied by a consonant change in conjunction, eg. плати́ть: плачу́,пла́тишь,...пла́тят and суди́ть: сужу́,су́дишь,...су́дят. However, this mutation applies consistently only to the first person singular of second-conjugation verbs in -ить and -еть. Furthermore, the addition of л in the first person singular of verbs with the stem ending in п, б, в, ф and м is a salient feature of the second conjugation, eg. люби́ть: люблю́,лю́бишь,...лю́бят and корми́ть: кормлю́, ко́рмишь,...ко́рмят. In fact, a consonant change of one form or other, in the first person singular, is found in all second conjugation verbs in -ить whose stems end in -б,-в,-д,-з,-с,-т and -ф, and those in -еть and -ить whose stems end in -м,-п, and -ст.

2 Past Tense

The past tense for most Russian verbs, including all those with infinitive endings in -сть and -ть, is formed by replacing the infinitive ending by -л,-ла,-ло,-ли, giving the masculine, feminine, neuter and plural forms respectively.

For example:

infinitive	*past tense*
молча́ть	он молча́л
	она́ молча́ла
	оно́ молча́ло
	они́ молча́ли
укра́сть	он укра́л
	она́ укра́ла
	оно́ укра́ло
	они́ укра́ли
звони́ть	он звони́л
	она́ звони́ла
	оно́ звони́ло
	они́ звони́ли

The singular past tense always reflects the gender of the subject, so that even after the personal pronouns я and ты the gender is always marked, eg. я сказа́л (masculine subject)
я сказа́ла (feminine subject)

Verbs with infinitives ending in -ереть,-зть,-чь, and many in -ти have no -л in the masculine past tense, eg. умере́ть (у́мер,умерла́), лезть (лез,ле́зла), мочь (мог,могла́), нести́ (нёс,несла́). This is also the case with some verbs in -нуть, привы́кнуть (привы́к, привы́кла).

The verb быть, while not used in the present tense, is encountered frequently in the past tense:

был, былá, бы́ло, бы́ли

Note the stress changes when used in the negative, ie. preceded by не:

нé был, не былá, нé было, нé были

3 Imperative Mood

The imperative mood has two forms – the familiar and the formal - which are used in accordance with the mode of address (ie. the familiar ты or the formal Вы) appropriate in any given situation. The formal imperative is obtained by simply adding -те to the end of the familiar form. The familiar imperative is formed by replacing the third person plural ending of a verb by -й where it is directly preceded by a vowel, eg.:

дéлать (*infin*) » дéлают (*3rd person pl*) » дéлай(те) (*imperative*)

similarly:

читáть » читáют » читáй(те)

Alternatively, -и(те) replaces the third person plural ending where this is directly preceded by a consonant and the verb has mobile or end stress in conjunction, eg.:

подчеркнýть » подчеркнýт » подчеркни́(те)
держáть » дéржат » держи́(те)

The imperative ending -ь(те) replaces the third person plural ending where this is directly preceded by no more than one consonant and the verb has fixed stem stress in conjugation, eg.:

постáвить » постáвят » постáвь(те)
одéть » одéнут » одéнь(те)

Note: stress in imperative forms is identical to that of the first person singular.

- давáйть and its compounds have imperative -й(те).
- пить has imperative пéй(те) (compare петь which has imperative пóй(те)). бить, вить, лить and шить also form the imperative like пить.
- the imperative of быть is бýдь(те).

4 Aspect

The majority of Russian verbs have two verb aspects, the **imperfective** for conveying the **frequency** of an action or describing a **process**, and the **perfective** for emphasis on a **single action** or a **result**. It follows that the perfective can only be used in the past and future, while the imperfective can also be used in the present tense.

Aspectual pairs can be differentiated either by the presence of a prefix in the perfective aspect, eg. сдéлать (cf imperfective дéлать), by the presence of a suffix in the imperfective aspect, eg. покáзывать (cf perfective показáть), or by a change in conjugation, eg. perfective кóнчить (2nd conjugation) and its imperfective counterpart кончáть (1st conjugation).

It should be noted, though, that some aspectual pairs do not follow this pattern, for instance those that derive from different roots, eg. говори́ть (*impf*)/сказáть (*perf*), брать (*impf*)/взять (*perf*). Then there are a minority of verbs which exist in one aspect only, eg. стóить (*impf*), while some verbs incorporate the two aspects in one form, eg. исслéдовать (*impf/perf*).

Aspect also has a bearing on the use of the imperative mood, where, generally speaking, the perfective aspect is used in positive commands (ie. telling someone to do something), while the imperfective is used in negative commands (ie. telling someone not to do something), in other words where the imperative form is preceded by "не".

~ A, a ~

A, a [eɪ] *n* (*letter*) 1-ая бу́ква англи́йского алфави́та; (*SCOL: mark*) ≈ отли́чно; ~ **road** (*BRIT: AUT*) шоссе́ *nt ind* (пе́рвой катего́рии); ~ **shares** (*BRIT: STOCK EXCHANGE*) а́кции *fpl* с ограни́ченным пра́вом го́лоса; **from ~ to Z** от "а" до "я".

A [eɪ] *n* (*MUS*) ля *nt ind*.

KEYWORD

a [eɪ] (*before vowel or silent h* **an**) *indef art*: **1: a book** кни́га; **an apple** я́блоко; **she's a student** она́ студе́нтка
2 (*instead of the number "one"*): **a week ago** неде́лю наза́д; **a hundred/thousand** *etc* **pounds** сто/ты́сяча *etc* фу́нтов
3 (*in expressing time*) в +*acc*: **3 a day/week** 3 в день/неде́лю; **10 km an hour** 10 км в час
4 (*in expressing prices*): **30p a kilo** 30 пе́нсов килогра́мм; **£5 a person** с ка́ждого 5 фу́нтов.

---

a. *abbr* = **acre.**
AA *n abbr* (*BRIT*: = *Automobile Association*) Автомоби́льная ассоциа́ция; (*US*: = *Associate in/of Arts*) член ассоциа́ции рабо́тников иску́сства; (= *Alcoholics Anonymous*) о́бщество анони́много излече́ния от алкоголи́зма; (= *anti-aircraft*) противовозду́шный.
AAA *n abbr* (= *American Automobile Association*) Америка́нская автомоби́льная ассоциа́ция; (*BRIT*: = *Amateur Athletics Association*) Люби́тельская ассоциа́ция лёгкой атле́тики.
A & R *n abbr* (*MUS*: = *artists and repertoire*) исполни́тели и репертуа́р.
AAUP *n abbr* = *American Association of University Professors.*
AB *abbr* (*BRIT*) = **able-bodied seaman**; (*CANADA*) = *Alberta.*
abaci [ˈæbəsaɪ] *npl of* **abacus.**
aback [əˈbæk] *adv*: **I was taken ~** я был поражён.
abacus [ˈæbəkəs] (*pl* **abaci**) *n* счёты *pl*.
abandon [əˈbændən] *vt* (*person*) покида́ть (поки́нуть *perf*); (*car*) броса́ть (бро́сить* *perf*); (*search, research*) прекраща́ть (прекрати́ть* *perf*); (*idea, hope*) отка́зываться (отказа́ться*

perf) от +*gen* ◆ *n* (*wild behaviour*): **with ~** самозабве́нно; **to ~ ship** покида́ть (поки́нуть *perf*) кора́бль.
abandoned [əˈbændənd] *adj* поки́нутый; (*unrestrained*) безу́держный.
abase [əˈbeɪs] *vt*: **to ~ o.s. (before)** унижа́ться (уни́зиться* *perf*) (пе́ред +*instr*).
abashed [əˈbæʃt] *adj* смущённый* (смущён).
abate [əˈbeɪt] *vi* (*storm*) утиха́ть (ути́хнуть* *perf*); (*anger, terror*) ослабева́ть (ослабе́ть *perf*).
abatement [əˈbeɪtmənt] *n*: **noise ~** сниже́ние у́ровня шу́ма.
abattoir [ˈæbətwɑ:ʼ] *n* (*BRIT*) скотобо́йня.
abbey [ˈæbɪ] *n* абба́тство.
abbot [ˈæbət] *n* абба́т.
abbreviate [əˈbri:vɪeɪt] *vt* (*essay, word*) сокраща́ть (сократи́ть* *perf*).
abbreviation [əbri:vɪˈeɪʃən] *n* сокраще́ние.
ABC *n abbr* = *American Broadcasting Company.*
abdicate [ˈæbdɪkeɪt] *vt* (*responsibility, right*) слага́ть (сложи́ть *perf*) с себя́ ◆ *vi* (*monarch*) отрека́ться (отре́чься* *perf*) от престо́ла.
abdication [æbdɪˈkeɪʃən] *n* (*see vb*) скла́дывание; отрече́ние от престо́ла.
abdomen [ˈæbdəmɛn] *n* брюшна́я по́лость *f*, живо́т.
abdominal [æbˈdɔmɪnl] *adj* брюшно́й; ~ **pain** бо́ли *fpl* в брюшно́й по́лости *or* в животе́.
abduct [æbˈdʌkt] *vt* похища́ть (похи́тить* *perf*).
abduction [æbˈdʌkʃən] *n* похище́ние.
Aberdeen [æbəˈdi:n] *n* Абердин.
Aberdonian [æbəˈdəʊnɪən] *adj* аберди́нский ◆ *n* аберди́нец(-нка).
aberration [æbəˈreɪʃən] *n* аберра́ция, отклоне́ние (от но́рмы); **in a moment of mental ~** в мину́ту помраче́ния рассу́дка.
abet [əˈbɛt] *vt see* **aid.**
abeyance [əˈbeɪəns] *n*: **in ~** приостано́вленный (приостано́влен).
abhor [əbˈhɔ:ʼ] *vt* испы́тывать (*impf*) отвраще́ние к +*dat*.
abhorrent [əbˈhɔrənt] *adj* отврати́тельный* (отврати́телен).
abide [əˈbaɪd] *vt*: **I can't ~ it/him** я э́того/его́ не выношу́

---
* marks translations which have irregular inflections. The Russian-English side of the dictionary gives inflectional information.

▶ **abide by** *vt fus* (*law, decision*) соблюда́ть (соблюсти́* *perf*).

abiding [ə'baɪdɪŋ] *adj* неослабева́ющий.

ability [ə'bɪlɪtɪ] *n* (*capacity*) спосо́бность *f*; (*talent, skill*) спосо́бности *fpl*; **to the best of my** ~ в ме́ру мои́х спосо́бностей.

abject ['æbdʒɛkt] *adj* (*poverty, coward*) жа́лкий*; (*apology*) уни́женный*.

ablaze [ə'bleɪz] *adj* (*building etc*) в огне́; **the city was** ~ **with light** го́род был за́лит огня́ми.

able ['eɪbl] *adj* (*capable*) спосо́бный* (спосо́бен); (*skilled*) уме́лый (уме́л); **he is/ was** ~ **to** ... он спосо́бен/был спосо́бен +*infin* ....

able-bodied ['eɪbl'bɔdɪd] *adj* (*person*) кре́пкий*; ~ **seaman** (*BRIT*) матро́с пе́рвого кла́сса.

ablutions [ə'blu:ʃənz] *npl* омове́ние *ntsg*.

ably ['eɪblɪ] *adv* (*skilfully*) уме́ло.

ABM *n abbr* (= *anti-ballistic missile*) ≈ ЗУРС= зени́тный управля́емый реакти́вный снаря́д.

abnormal [æb'nɔ:ml] *adj* ненорма́льный* (ненорма́лен).

abnormality [æbnɔ:'mælɪtɪ] *n* ненорма́льность *f*, анома́лия.

aboard [ə'bɔ:d] *prep* (*position*: *NAUT, AVIAT*) на борту́ +*gen*; (: *train, bus*) в +*prp*; (*motion*: *NAUT, AVIAT*) на борт +*gen*; (: *train, bus*) в +*acc* ◆ *adv*: **to climb** ~ (*ship*) сади́ться (сесть* *perf*) на кора́бль; (*train*) сади́ться (сесть* *perf*) в по́езд.

abode [ə'bəud] *n* (*LAW*): **of no fixed** ~ без постоя́нного местожи́тельства.

abolish [ə'bɔlɪʃ] *vt* отменя́ть (отмени́ть* *perf*).

abolition [æbə'lɪʃən] *n* отме́на.

abominable [ə'bɔmɪnəbl] *adj* отврати́тельный* (отврати́телен).

abominably [ə'bɔmɪnəblɪ] *adv* отврати́тельно.

aborigine [æbə'rɪdʒɪnɪ] *n* абориге́н(ка).

abort [ə'bɔ:t] *vt* (*plan, activity*) прекраща́ть (прекрати́ть* *perf*); (*COMPUT*) прерыва́ть (прерва́ть* *perf*); (*MED*): **to** ~ **a baby** де́лать (сде́лать *perf*) або́рт.

abortion [ə'bɔ:ʃən] *n* (*MED*) або́рт; **to have an** ~ де́лать (сде́лать *perf*) або́рт.

abortionist [ə'bɔ:ʃənɪst] *n человек, де́лающий подпо́льные або́рты*.

abortive [ə'bɔ:tɪv] *adj* неуда́чный* (неуда́чен).

abound [ə'baund] *vi* быть* (*impf*) в изоби́лии; **to** ~ **in** *or* **with** изоби́ловать (*impf*) +*instr*.

KEYWORD

about [ə'baut] *adv* **1** (*approximately: referring to time, price etc*) приблизи́тельно +*acc*, приме́рно +*acc*, о́коло +*gen*; **it will take me about 3 hours** э́то займёт у меня́ приме́рно *or* приблизи́тельно 3 часа́; **at about 2 (o'clock)** приблизи́тельно *or* приме́рно в 2 (часа́), часа́ в 2, о́коло двух (часо́в); **I've just about finished** я почти́ зако́нчил

2 (*approximately: referring to height, size etc*) приме́рно +*nom*, приблизи́тельно +*nom*; **the room is about 10 metres wide** ко́мната

приме́рно *or* приблизи́тельно 10 ме́тров в ширину́; **she is about your height/age** она́ приме́рно *or* приблизи́тельно Ва́шего ро́ста/во́зраста

3 (*referring to place*) повсю́ду; **to leave things lying about** разбра́сывать (разброса́ть *perf*) ве́щи повсю́ду; **to run/walk etc about** бе́гать (*impf*)/ходи́ть* (*impf*) *etc*

4: **to be about to do** собира́ться (собра́ться* *perf*) +*infin*; **he was about to go to bed** он собра́лся лечь спать

◆ *prep* **1** (*relating to*) о(б) +*prp*; **a book about London** кни́га о Ло́ндоне; **what is it about?** о чём э́то?; **we talked about it** мы говори́ли *or* разгова́ривали об э́том; **what** *or* **how about doing this?** как насчёт того́, что́бы +*infin*?

2 (*referring to place*) по +*dat*; **to walk about the town** ходи́ть* (*impf*) по го́роду; **her clothes were scattered about the room** её оде́жда была́ разбро́сана по ко́мнате.

about-face [ə'baut'feɪs] *n* (*MIL*) поворо́т круго́м; (*fig*) поворо́т на 180 гра́дусов.

about-turn [ə'baut'tə:n] *n* = **about-face**.

above [ə'bʌv] *adv* (*higher up*) наверху́; (*greater, more*) вы́ше, свы́ше ◆ *prep* (*higher than*) над +*instr*; (: *in rank etc*) вы́ше +*gen*; (: *in number*) свы́ше +*gen*, бо́лее +*gen*; **from** ~ све́рху; **costing** ~ **£10** стоя́щий свы́ше £10; ~ **the knees** вы́ше коле́н; **mentioned** ~ вышеупомя́нутый; **he's not** ~ **a bit of blackmail** он не погнуша́ется шантажо́м; ~ **suspicion/criticism** вне подозре́ния/кри́тики; ~ **all** пре́жде всего́.

above board *adj* че́стный* (че́стен), откры́тый (откры́т).

abrasion [ə'breɪʒən] *n* тре́ние; (*on skin*) сса́дина.

abrasive [ə'breɪzɪv] *adj* (*substance*) абрази́вный; (*manner*) жёсткий* (жёсток).

abreast [ə'brɛst] *adv* (*people, vehicles*) в ряд; **three** ~ по́ трое в ряд; **to keep** ~ **of** (*fig*) быть* (*impf*) в ку́рсе +*gen*.

abridge [ə'brɪdʒ] *vt* (*novel, play*) сокраща́ть (сократи́ть* *perf*).

abroad [ə'brɔ:d] *adv* (*to be*) за грани́цей *or* рубежо́м; (*to go*) за грани́цу *or* рубе́ж; (*from abroad*) из-за грани́цы *or* рубежа́; **there is a rumour** ~ **that** ... (*fig*) хо́дит слух, что ....

abrupt [ə'brʌpt] *adj* (*action, ending etc*) внеза́пный* (внеза́пен); (*person, manner*) ре́зкий* (ре́зок).

abruptly [ə'brʌptlɪ] *adv* (*leave, end*) внеза́пно; (*speak*) ре́зко.

abscess ['æbsɪs] *n* абсце́сс.

abscond [əb'skɔnd] *vi* (*thief*): **to** ~ **with** скры́ться* (*perf*) с +*instr*; (*prisoner*): **to** ~ **(from)** сбега́ть (сбежа́ть* *perf*) (из +*gen*).

abseil ['æbseɪl] *vi* спуска́ться (спусти́ться* *perf*) при по́мощи кана́та.

absence ['æbsəns] *n* (*of person, thing*)

отсу́тствие; **in the ~ of** (*person*) в отсу́тствие +*gen*; (*thing*) при отсу́тствии +*gen*; **~ without leave** (*MIL*) самово́льная отлу́чка.

absent [*adj* 'æbsənt, *vb* æb'sɛnt] *adj* отсу́тствующий* ♦ *vt*: **to ~ o.s.** отлуча́ться (отлучи́ться *perf*).

absentee [æbsən'tiː] *n* отсу́тствующий*(-ая) *m(f) adj*.

absenteeism [æbsən'tiːɪzəm] *n* прогу́лы *mpl*.

absent-minded ['æbsənt'maɪndɪd] *adj* рассе́янный* (рассе́ян).

absent-mindedly ['æbsənt'maɪndɪdlɪ] *adv* рассе́янно.

absent-mindedness ['æbsənt'maɪndɪdnɪs] *n* рассе́янность *f*.

absolute ['æbsəluːt] *adj* абсолю́тный*.

absolutely [æbsə'luːtlɪ] *adv* (*totally*) абсолю́тно, соверше́нно; (*certainly*) безусло́вно.

absolute monopoly *n* абсолю́тная монопо́лия.

absolution [æbsə'luːʃən] *n* (*REL*) отпуще́ние грехо́в.

absolve [əb'zɔlv] *vt*: **to ~ sb (from sth)** отпуска́ть (отпусти́ть* *perf*) кому́-н (что-н).

absorb [əb'zɔːb] *vt* (*liquid, information*) впи́тывать (впита́ть *perf*); (*light, business*) поглоща́ть (поглоти́ть* *perf*); (*changes, effects*) воспринима́ть (восприня́ть* *perf*); **he is ~ed in a book** он поглощён кни́гой.

absorbent [əb'zɔːbənt] *adj* гигроскопи́чный.

absorbent cotton *n* (*US*) гигроскопи́ческая ва́та.

absorbing [əb'zɔːbɪŋ] *adj* (*book, film etc*) увлека́тельный* (увлека́телен).

absorption [əb'sɔːpʃən] *n* (*see vt*) впи́тывание; поглоще́ние; восприя́тие; (*interest*) увлечённость *f*.

abstain [əb'steɪn] *vi*: **to ~ (from)** возде́рживаться (воздержа́ться* *perf*) (от +*gen*).

abstemious [əb'stiːmɪəs] *adj* (*person*) возде́ржанный* (возде́ржан).

abstention [əb'stɛnʃən] *n* (*refusal to vote*) неуча́стие в голосова́нии.

abstinence ['æbstɪnəns] *n* воздержа́ние.

abstract [*adj, n* 'æbstrækt, *vb* æb'strækt] *adj* абстра́ктный*; (*idea, quality*) отвлечённый ♦ *n* (*summary*) анноти́ция; (*of dissertation*) рефера́т ♦ *vt* (*remove*) извлека́ть (извле́чь* *perf*); (*summarize*) анноти́ровать (проанноти́ровать *perf*).

abstruse [æb'struːs] *adj* замыслова́тый.

absurd [əb'səːd] *adj* абсу́рдный* (абсу́рден), неле́пый (неле́п).

absurdity [əb'səːdɪtɪ] *n* абсу́рдность *f*, неле́пость *f*.

ABTA ['æbtə] *n abbr* = Association of British Travel Agents.

Abu Dhabi ['æbuː'dɑːbɪ] *n* Абу́-Да́би.

abundance [ə'bʌndəns] *n* изоби́лие; **in ~** в изоби́лии.

abundant [ə'bʌndənt] *adj* изоби́льный* (изоби́лен).

abundantly [ə'bʌndəntlɪ] *adv* в изоби́лии; **~ clear/obvious** соверше́нно я́сно/очеви́дно.

abuse [*n* ə'bjuːs, *vb* ə'bjuːz] *n* (*insults*) брань *f*; (*ill-treatment*) жесто́кое обраще́ние; (*misuse: of power, drugs etc*) злоупотребле́ние ♦ *vt* (*insult*) оскорбля́ть (оскорби́ть* *perf*); (*ill-treat*) жесто́ко обраща́ться (*impf*) с +*instr*; (*misuse*) злоупотребля́ть (злоупотреби́ть* *perf*) +*instr*; **this system is open to ~** э́той систе́мой легко́ злоупотребля́ть.

abuser [ə'bjuːzə'] *n*: **drug ~** наркома́н; **child ~** челове́к, подверга́ющий дете́й физи́ческому и́ли сексуа́льному наси́лию.

abusive [ə'bjuːsɪv] *adj* (*person*) гру́бый (груб); **~ language** брань *f*.

abysmal [ə'bɪzməl] *adj* (*performance, failure*) плаче́вный* (плаче́вен); (*ignorance etc*) вопию́щий* (вопию́щ).

abysmally [ə'bɪzməlɪ] *adv* (*see adj*) плаче́вно; вопию́ще.

abyss [ə'bɪs] *n* про́пасть *f*.

AC *abbr* = **alternating current**; (*US*: = **athletic club**) легкоатлети́ческий клуб.

a/c *abbr* (*COMM*) = **account**; (= *account current*) теку́щий* счёт.

academic [ækə'dɛmɪk] *adj* (*system, standards*) академи́ческий*; (*qualifications*) учёный; (*work, books*) нау́чный*; (*person, child*) интеллектуа́льный*; (*pej: issue*) академи́чный (академи́чен) ♦ *n* учёный(-ая) *m(f) adj*.

academic year *n* (*in school*) уче́бный год*; (*in higher education*) академи́ческий* год*.

academy [ə'kædəmɪ] *n* (*learned body*) акаде́мия; (*school*) учи́лище; (: *in Scotland*) сре́дняя шко́ла; **~ of music** консервато́рия; **military/naval ~** вое́нная/вое́нно-морска́я акаде́мия.

ACAS ['eɪkæs] *n abbr* (*BRIT*: = Advisory, Conciliation and Arbitration Service) слу́жба юриди́ческих консульта́ций и арбитра́жа.

accede [æk'siːd] *vi*: **to ~ to** (*request*) удовлетворя́ть (удовлетвори́ть *perf*); (*opinion, contention*) соглаша́ться (согласи́ться* *perf*) с +*instr*.

accelerate [æk'sɛləreɪt] *vt* (*process*) ускоря́ть (уско́рить *perf*) ♦ *vi* (*AUT*) разгоня́ться (разогна́ться *perf*).

acceleration [æksɛlə'reɪʃən] *n* (*see vb*) ускоре́ние; разго́н.

accelerator [æk'sɛləreɪtə'] *n* акселера́тор.

accent ['æksɛnt] *n* акце́нт; (*stress mark*) знак

---

* marks translations which have irregular inflections. The Russian-English side of the dictionary gives inflectional information.

ударе́ния; **to speak with an Irish ~** говори́ть *(impf)* с ирла́ндским акце́нтом; **to have a strong ~** име́ть *(impf)* си́льный акце́нт.

accented [æk'sɛntɪd] *adj* с акце́нтом; **heavily ~** с си́льным акце́нтом.

accentuate [æk'sɛntjueɪt] *vt (syllable)* акценти́ровать *(impf/perf)*, проставля́ть (проста́вить *perf*) ударе́ние на +*acc*; *(need, difference)* подчёркивать (подчеркну́ть *perf*).

accept [ək'sɛpt] *vt (gift, proposal etc)* принима́ть (приня́ть* *perf*); *(fact, situation, risk)* мири́ться (примири́ться *perf*) с +*instr*; *(responsibility, blame)* принима́ть (приня́ть* *perf*) на себя́.

acceptable [ək'sɛptəbl] *adj* прие́млемый (прие́млем).

acceptance [ək'sɛptəns] *n (of gift, offer etc)* приня́тие; *(of fact, situation)* прия́тие; **to meet with general ~** находи́ть* (найти́* *perf*) всео́бщее одобре́ние.

access ['æksɛs] *n* до́ступ ♦ *vt (COMPUT)* испо́льзовать *(impf/perf)* до́ступ к +*dat*; (: *data*) обраща́ться (обрати́ться* *perf*) к +*dat*; **to have ~ to** *(child)* име́ть *(impf)* возмо́жность обще́ния с +*instr*; **the burglars gained ~ through a window** взло́мщики прони́кли че́рез окно́.

accessible [æk'sɛsəbl] *adj* досту́пный* (досту́пен).

accession [æk'sɛʃən] *n* прихо́д к вла́сти; *(of king)* вступле́ние на престо́л; *(to library)* поступле́ние.

accessory [æk'sɛsərɪ] *n (COMM, TECH, AUT)* принадле́жность *f*; *(LAW)*: **~ to** соуча́стник(-ица) +*gen*; **accessories** *npl (DRESS)* аксессуа́ры *mpl*; **toilet accessories** *(BRIT)* туале́тные принадле́жности *fpl*.

access road *n* подъездно́й путь* *m*.

access time *n (COMPUT)* вре́мя* *nt* до́ступа.

accident ['æksɪdənt] *n (chance event)* случа́йность *f*; *(mishap, disaster)* несча́стный слу́чай, ава́рия; **to meet with** *or* **to have an ~** попада́ть (попа́сть *perf*) в ава́рию *or* катастро́фу; **he had an ~** с ним произошёл несча́стный слу́чай; **by ~** *(unintentionally)* неча́янно; *(by chance)* случа́йно.

accidental [æksɪ'dɛntl] *adj* случа́йный* (случа́ен).

accidentally [æksɪ'dɛntəlɪ] *adv* случа́йно, неча́янно.

accident insurance *n* страхова́ние от несча́стных слу́чаев.

accident-prone ['æksɪdənt'prəun] *adj* невезу́чий; **he is ~** его́ пресле́дуют несча́стья.

acclaim [ə'kleɪm] *n* призна́ние ♦ *vt*: **he was ~ed for his achievements** он получи́л призна́ние за свои́ достиже́ния.

acclamation [æklə'meɪʃən] *n (approval)* бу́рное *or* шу́мное одобре́ние; *(applause)* бу́рные аплодисме́нты *mpl*.

acclimate [ə'klaɪmət] *vt (US)* = **acclimatize**.

acclimatize [ə'klaɪmətaɪz] *(US acclimate) vt*: **to become ~d (to)** *(surroundings)* акклиматизи́роваться *(impf/perf)* (в +*prp*), осва́иваться (осво́иться *perf*) (в +*prp*); *(heat, cold)* привыка́ть (привы́кнуть* *perf*) (к +*dat*).

accolade ['ækəleɪd] *n* по́честь *f*.

accommodate [ə'kɔmədeɪt] *vt (subj: person)* предоставля́ть (предоста́вить* *perf*) жильё +*dat*; (: *car, hotel etc*) вмеща́ть (вмести́ть* *perf*); *(oblige, help)* ока́зывать (оказа́ть* *perf*) услу́гу +*dat*; **to ~ one's plans to** приспоса́бливать (приспосо́бить* *perf*) свои́ пла́ны к +*dat*.

accommodating [ə'kɔmədeɪtɪŋ] *adj* услу́жливый (услу́жлив).

accommodation [əkɔmə'deɪʃən] *n (to live in)* жильё; *(to work in)* помеще́ние; **~s** *npl (US: lodgings)* жильё *ntsg*; **"accommodation to let"** *(living)* "сдаётся жильё"; *(office)* "сдаётся помеще́ние"; **they have ~ for 500** они́ мо́гут размести́ть 500 челове́к; **the hall has seating ~ for 600** *(BRIT)* зал расчи́тан на 600 мест; **do you have any ~?** *(for yourself)* Вам есть где жить?; *(for me)* Вы предоставля́ете жильё?

accompaniment [ə'kʌmpənɪmənt] *n* сопровожде́ние; *(MUS)* аккомпанеме́нт.

accompanist [ə'kʌmpənɪst] *n* аккомпаниа́тор.

accompany [ə'kʌmpənɪ] *vt (escort, go along with)* сопровожда́ть (сопроводи́ть* *perf*); *(MUS)* аккомпани́ровать *(impf)* +*dat*.

accomplice [ə'kʌmplɪs] *n* соуча́стник(-ица), соо́бщник(-ица).

accomplish [ə'kʌmplɪʃ] *vt (task)* заверша́ть (заверши́ть *perf*); *(goal)* достига́ть (дости́гнуть* *or* дости́чь* *perf*) +*gen*.

accomplished [ə'kʌmplɪʃt] *adj (person)* тала́нтливый (тала́нтлив); *(performance)* соверше́нный (соверше́нен).

accomplishment [ə'kʌmplɪʃmənt] *n (completion, bringing about)* заверше́ние; *(achievement)* достиже́ние; *(skill: usu pl)* уме́ние.

accord [ə'kɔːd] *n* соглаше́ние ♦ *vt* ока́зывать (оказа́ть* *perf*); **of his own ~** по со́бственному жела́нию; **of its own ~** сам по себе́; **with one ~** единоду́шно; *(movement)* как по кома́нде; **he and I are in ~ on this issue** мы с ним в согла́сии на э́тот счёт *or* по э́тому по́воду.

accordance [ə'kɔːdəns] *n*: **in ~ with** в согла́сии *or* соотве́тствии с +*instr*.

according [ə'kɔːdɪŋ] *prep*: **~ to** согла́сно +*dat*; **~ to plan** по пла́ну.

accordingly [ə'kɔːdɪŋlɪ] *adv (appropriately)* соотве́тствующим о́бразом; *(as a result)* соотве́тственно.

accordion [ə'kɔːdɪən] *n* аккордео́н.

accost [ə'kɔst] *vt* пристава́ть* (приста́ть* *perf*) к +*dat*.

account [ə'kaunt] *n (bill)* счёт*; *(monthly*

account) ежемéсячный счёт; (*in bank*) (расчётный) счёт; (*report*) отчёт; **~s** *npl* (*COMM*) счетá* *mpl*; (*books*) бухгáлтерские кни́ги *fpl*; **"account payee only"** (*BRIT*) "подлежи́т уплáте тóлько на счёт получáтеля"; **to keep an ~ of** вести́* (*impf*) счёт *+gen or +dat*; **to bring sb to ~ for sth** призывáть (призвáть* *perf*) когó-н к отвéту за что-н; **by all ~s** по всем свéдениям; **of no ~** не вáжно; **on ~** в креди́т; **to pay £5 on ~** плати́ть* (заплати́ть* *perf*) £5 в задáток; **to buy sth on ~** покупáть (купи́ть* *perf*) что-н в креди́т; **on no ~** ни в кóем слýчае; **on ~ of** по причи́не *+gen*; **take into ~, take ~ of** принимáть (приня́ть* *perf*) в расчёт

▶ **account for** *vt fus* (*money spent, expenses*) отчи́тываться (отчитáться *perf*) за *+acc*; (*absence, failure*) объясня́ть (объясни́ть *perf*); (*represent*) составля́ть (состáвить* *perf*); **all the children were ~ed for** все дéти бы́ли на мéсте; **four people are still not ~ed for** не досчитáлись четырёх.

accountability [əˈkauntəˈbɪlɪtɪ] *n* отчётность *f*.
accountable [əˈkauntəbl] *adj* подотчётный* (подотчётен); **to be ~ to sb for sth** отвечáть (*impf*) за что-н пéред кем-н.
accountancy [əˈkauntənsɪ] *n* бухгалтéрия.
accountant [əˈkauntənt] *n* бухгáлтер.
account executive *n* делопроизводи́тель *m*.
accounting [əˈkauntɪŋ] *n* бухгáлтерское дéло*.
accounting period *n* отчётный пери́од.
account number *n* (*at bank etc*) нóмер* счёта.
account payable *n* счёт кредитóров (*в балáнсе*).
account receivable *n* счёт дебитóров (*в балáнсе*).
accredited [əˈkrɛdɪtɪd] *adj* (*agent etc*) аккредитóванный.
accretion [əˈkriːʃən] *n* (*process*) нарастáние; (*layer*) нарóст.
accrue [əˈkruː] *vi* (*mount up*) нарастáть (нарасти́* *perf*); **to ~ to** доставáться* (достáться* *perf*) *+dat*.
accrued charges *npl* нарóсшие процéнты *mpl*.
accrued interest *n* нарóсшие процéнты *mpl*.
accumulate [əˈkjuːmjuleɪt] *vt* накáпливать (накопи́ть* *perf*) ♦ *vi* накáпливаться (накопи́ться* *perf*).
accumulation [əkjuːmjuˈleɪʃən] *n* накоплéние.
accuracy [ˈækjurəsɪ] *n* тóчность *f*.
accurate [ˈækjurɪt] *adj* тóчный* (тóчен); (*person, device*) аккурáтный* (аккурáтен); (*shot*) мéткий*.
accurately [ˈækjurɪtlɪ] *adv* тóчно; (*shoot*) мéтко.
accusation [ækjuˈzeɪʃən] *n* обвинéние.
accusative [əˈkjuːzətɪv] *n* (*LING*) вини́тельный падéж*.

accuse [əˈkjuːz] *vt*: **to ~ sb (of sth)** обвиня́ть (обвини́ть *perf*) когó-н (в чём-н).
accused [əˈkjuːzd] *n* (*LAW*): **the ~** обвиня́емый(-ая) *m(f) adj*.
accuser [əˈkjuːzə] *n* обвини́тель *m*.
accusing [əˈkjuːzɪŋ] *adj* обвиня́ющий.
accustom [əˈkʌstəm] *vt* приучáть (приучи́ть* *perf*); **to ~ o.s. to sth** приучáться (приучи́ться *perf*) *or* привыкáть (привы́кнуть* *perf*) к чемý-н.
accustomed [əˈkʌstəmd] *adj* (*usual*) привы́чный*; **I'm ~ to working late/to the heat** я привы́к рабóтать пóздно/к жарé.
AC/DC *abbr* (= *alternating current/direct current*) переменный ток/постоя́нный ток.
ACE [eɪs] *n abbr* = **American Council on Education**.
ace [eɪs] *n* (*CARDS*) туз; (*TENNIS*) вы́игрыш с подáчи.
acerbic [əˈsɔːbɪk] *adj* (*remark*) éдкий* (éдок).
acetate [ˈæsɪteɪt] *n* ацетáт.
ache [eɪk] *n* боль *f* ♦ *vi* (*be painful*) болéть (*impf*); (*yearn*): **to ~ to do** томи́ться* (*impf*) желáнием *+infin*; **I've got stomach ~** *or* **a stomach ~** у меня́ боли́т живóт; **I'm aching all over** у меня́ всё тéло нóет; **my head ~s** у меня́ боли́т головá.
achieve [əˈtʃiːv] *vt* (*aim, result*) достигáть (дости́гнуть* *or* дости́чь* *perf*) *+gen*; (*success, victory*) добивáться (доби́ться* *perf*) *+gen*.
achievement [əˈtʃiːvmənt] *n* достижéние.
Achilles heel [əˈkɪliːz-] *n* Ахиллéсова пятá.
acid [ˈæsɪd] *adj* (*CHEM: soil etc*) кислóтный*; (*taste*) ки́слый* ♦ *n* (*CHEM*) кислотá*; (*inf: DRUGS*) ЛСД (*наркóтик*).
acid house *adj* áсид хáус (*стиль поп-мýзыки*).
acidic [əˈsɪdɪk] *adj* ки́слый* (кисел).
acidity [əˈsɪdɪtɪ] *n* кислóтность *f*.
acid rain *n* кислóтный дождь* *m*.
acid test *n* прóбный кáмень* *m*.
acknowledge [əkˈnɒlɪdʒ] *vt* (*letter etc: also:* **~ receipt of**) подтверждáть (подтверди́ть* *perf*) получéние *+gen*; (*fact, situation*) признавáть (признáть *perf*).
acknowledgement [əkˈnɒlɪdʒmənt] *n* (*of letter etc*) подтверждéние получéния; **~s** *npl* (*in book*) выражéние *ntsg* благодáрности (*в предислóвии кни́ги*).
ACLU *n abbr* = **American Civil Liberties Union**.
acme [ˈækmɪ] *n* верх*, верши́на.
acne [ˈæknɪ] *n* угри́* *mpl*, прыщи́ *mpl*.
acorn [ˈeɪkɔːn] *n* жёлудь *m*.
acoustic [əˈkuːstɪk] *adj* (*guitar etc*) акусти́ческий*.
acoustic coupler *n* (*COMPUT*) акусти́ческий* соедини́тель *m*.
acoustics [əˈkuːstɪks] *n* (*science*) акýстика ♦ *npl* (*of hall, room*) акýстика *fsg*.

---

* marks translations which have irregular inflections. The Russian-English side of the dictionary gives inflectional information.

acquaint [əˈkweɪnt] *vt*: **to ~ sb with sth** (*inform*) ознако́мить* (*perf*) кого́-н с чем-н; **I am/was ~ed with** (*person, fact*) я знако́м/был знако́м с +*instr*.

acquaintance [əˈkweɪntəns] *n* (*person*) знако́мый(-ая) *m(f) adj*; (*with person, subject*) знако́мство; **to make sb's ~** познако́миться* (*perf*) с кем-н.

acquiesce [ækwɪˈɛs] *vi*: **to ~ to** соглаша́ться (согласи́ться* *perf*) на +*acc*.

acquire [əˈkwaɪəʳ] *vt* приобрета́ть (приобрести́* *perf*).

acquired [əˈkwaɪəd] *adj* приобретённый; **it's an ~ taste** к э́тому на́до привы́кнуть.

acquisition [ækwɪˈzɪʃən] *n* приобрете́ние.

acquisitive [əˈkwɪzɪtɪv] *adj* (*greedy*) приобрета́тельский.

acquit [əˈkwɪt] *vt* (*LAW*) опра́вдывать (оправда́ть *perf*); **to ~ o.s. well** хорошо́ проявля́ть (прояви́ть* *perf*) себя́.

acquittal [əˈkwɪtl] *n* оправда́ние.

acre [ˈeɪkəʳ] *n* акр.

acreage [ˈeɪkərɪdʒ] *n* пло́щадь* *f* в а́крах.

acrid [ˈækrɪd] *adj* е́дкий* (е́док).

acrimonious [ækrɪˈməunɪəs] *adj* язви́тельный* (язви́телен).

acrimony [ˈækrɪmənɪ] *n* язви́тельность *f*.

acrobat [ˈækrəbæt] *n* акроба́т.

acrobatic [ækrəˈbætɪk] *adj* (*movement, display*) акробати́ческий; (*person*) ги́бкий* (ги́бок) и ло́вкий* (ло́вок).

acrobatics [ækrəˈbætɪks] *npl* акроба́тика *fsg*.

acronym [ˈækrənɪm] *n* бу́квенная аббревиату́ра.

Acropolis [əˈkrɔpəlɪs] *n*: **the ~** (*GEO*) Акро́поль *m*.

across [əˈkrɔs] *prep* (*from one side to the other of*) че́рез +*acc*; (*on the other side of*) на друго́й стороне́ +*gen*; (*crosswise over*) поперёк +*gen* ♦ *adv* на ту́ *or* другу́ю сто́рону; (*measurement: width*) шириной; **to walk ~ the road** переходи́ть* (перейти́* *perf*) доро́гу; **to take sb ~ the road** переводи́ть* (перевести́* *perf*) кого́-н че́рез доро́гу; **a road ~ the wood** доро́га че́рез лес; **the lake is 12 km ~** ширина́ о́зера – 12 км; **~ from** напро́тив +*gen*; **to get sth ~ (to sb)** втолко́вывать (втолкова́ть *perf*) что-н (кому́-н).

acrylic [əˈkrɪlɪk] *adj* акри́ловый ♦ *n* акри́л; **~s** *npl* (*ART*) акри́ловые кра́ски *fpl*.

ACT *n abbr* = *American College Test*.

act [ækt] *n* (*action, also LAW*) акт; (*deed*) посту́пок*; (*of play*) де́йствие, акт; (*in music-hall etc*) но́мер* ♦ *vi* (*do sth, take action*) де́йствовать* (*impf*); (*behave*) вести́* (*impf*) себя́; (*have effect*) де́йствовать (поде́йствовать *perf*); (*THEAT*) игра́ть (сыгра́ть *perf*); (*pretend*) разы́грывать (разыгра́ть *perf*) ♦ *vt* (*part*) игра́ть (сыгра́ть *perf*); **it's only an ~** э́то всего́ лишь игра́; **~ of God** (*LAW*) стихи́йное бе́дствие; **in the ~ of** в

проце́ссе +*gen*; **to catch sb in the ~** пойма́ть (*perf*) кого́-н на ме́сте преступле́ния; **to ~ as** де́йствовать* (*impf*) в ка́честве +*gen*; **it ~s as a deterrent** э́то де́йствует в ка́честве сде́рживающей си́лы; **~ing in my capacity as chairman, I ...** выступа́я в ка́честве председа́теля, я ...; **to ~ the fool** (*BRIT*) валя́ть (сваля́ть *perf*) дурака́

▶ **act on** *vt*: **to ~ on sth** де́йствовать (поде́йствовать *perf*) на что-н

▶ **act out** *vt* (*event*) разы́грывать (разыгра́ть *perf*); (*fantasies*) выплёскивать (вы́плеснуть *perf*).

acting [ˈæktɪŋ] *adj*: **~ manager/director** исполня́ющий обя́занности управля́ющего/дире́ктора ♦ *n* (*activity, profession*) актёрская профе́ссия.

action [ˈækʃən] *n* (*deed*) де́йствие; (*motion*) движе́ние; (*MIL*) вое́нные де́йствия *ntpl*; (*LAW*) иск; **to bring an ~ against sb** (*LAW*) предъявля́ть (предъяви́ть* *perf*) иск кому́-н; **he was killed in ~** (*MIL*) он был уби́т в бою́; **she/the machine was out of ~ for a week** она́/маши́на вы́шла из стро́я на неде́лю; **to take ~** принима́ть (приня́ть* *perf*) ме́ры; **to put a plan into ~** реализо́вывать (реализова́ть *perf*) план.

action replay *n* (*TV*) повторе́ние ка́дра (*ча́сто заме́дленное*).

activate [ˈæktɪveɪt] *vt* (*mechanism*) приводи́ть* (привести́* *perf*) в де́йствие; (*CHEM*) активи́ровать (*impf/perf*); (*PHYS*) де́лать (сде́лать *perf*) радиоакти́вным.

active [ˈæktɪv] *adj* (*person, life*) акти́вный* (акти́вен); (*volcano*) де́йствующий*; **to play an ~ part in** игра́ть (сыгра́ть *perf*) акти́вную роль в +*prp*.

active duty *n* (*US: MIL*) де́йствующая а́рмия.

actively [ˈæktɪvlɪ] *adv* (*participate*) акти́вно; (*discourage, dislike*) си́льно.

active partner *n* (*COMM*) гла́вный партнёр с ограни́ченной (иму́щественной) отве́тственностью.

active service *n* (*BRIT: MIL*) де́йствующая а́рмия.

active suspension *n* автомати́ческая систе́ма амортиза́ции го́ночного автомоби́ля, реаги́рующая на ка́чество пове́рхности.

activist [ˈæktɪvɪst] *n* активи́ст(ка).

activity [ækˈtɪvɪtɪ] *n* (*being active*) акти́вность *f*; (*action*) де́ятельность *f*; (*pastime, pursuit*) заня́тие.

actor [ˈæktəʳ] *n* актёр.

actress [ˈæktrɪs] *n* актри́са.

actual [ˈæktjuəl] *adj* (*real*) действи́тельный* (действи́телен); (*emphatic use*): **the ~ work hasn't begun yet** сама́ рабо́та ещё не начала́сь.

actually [ˈæktjuəlɪ] *adv* (*really*) действи́тельно; (*in fact*) факти́чески, на са́мом де́ле; (*even*)

да́же.
actuary [ˈæktjuərɪ] *n* (COMM) актуа́рий.
actuate [ˈæktjueɪt] *vt* приводи́ть* (привести́*
perf) в де́йствие.
acuity [əˈkjuːɪtɪ] *n* острота́.
acumen [ˈækjumən] *n* сообрази́тельность *f*;
business ~ делова́я хва́тка*.
acupuncture [ˈækjuprʌŋktʃəˈ] *n*
иглоука́лывание, акупункту́ра.
acute [əˈkjuːt] *adj* (*illness, mind, angle*) о́стрый*
(остр); (*anxiety*) си́льный*; (*person, observer*)
проница́тельный* (проница́телен); (*LING*): ~
accent аку́т.
AD *adv abbr* (= *Anno Domini*) н.э.= *на́шей э́ры* ♦
n abbr (US: MIL) = **active duty**.
ad [æd] *n abbr* (*inf*) = **advertisement**.
adage [ˈædɪdʒ] *n* погово́рка*.
adamant [ˈædəmənt] *adj* непрекло́нный*
(непрекло́нен).
Adam's apple [ˈædəmz-] *n* ада́мово я́блоко*,
кады́к*.
adapt [əˈdæpt] *vt* (*alter, change*)
приспоса́бливать (or приспособля́ть
(приспосо́бить* *perf*) ♦ *vi*: **to** ~ **(to)**
приспоса́бливаться *or* приспособля́ться
(приспосо́биться* *perf*) *or* адапти́роваться
(*impf/perf*) (к +*dat*).
adaptability [ədæptəˈbɪlɪtɪ] *n* приспособ-
ля́емость *f*.
adaptable [əˈdæptəbl] *adj* (*device*)
приспособля́емый; (*person*) легко́
приспоса́бливающийся.
adaptation [ædæpˈteɪʃən] *n* (*of story, novel etc*)
переложе́ние; (*of machine, equipment etc*)
приспособле́ние.
adapter [əˈdæptəˈ] *n* (*ELEC*) ада́птер,
перехо́дник.
adaptor [əˈdæptəˈ] *n* = **adapter**.
ADC *n abbr* (MIL) = **aide-de-camp**; (US: = **Aid to**
Dependent Children) по́мощь нужда́ющимся
де́тям.
add [æd] *vt* (*to a collection etc*) прибавля́ть
(приба́вить* *perf*); (*comment etc*) добавля́ть
(доба́вить* *perf*); (*figures: also*: ~ **up**)
скла́дывать (сложи́ть* *perf*), сумми́ровать
(*impf/perf*) ♦ *vi*: **to** ~ **to** (*increase*) увели́чивать
(увели́чить *perf*)
▶ **add on** *vt*: ~ **on (to)** прибавля́ть (приба́вить*
perf) (к +*dat*)
▶ **add up** *vt* скла́дываться (сложи́ться *perf*) в
+*acc* ♦ *vi* (*fig*): **it doesn't** ~ **up** концы́ не
схо́дятся; **it doesn't** ~ **up to much** (*fig*) э́то не
впечатля́ет.
addenda [əˈdɛndə] *npl of* **addendum**.
addendum [əˈdɛndəm] (*pl* **addenda**) *n*
приложе́ние.
adder [ˈædəˈ] *n* гадю́ка.
addict [ˈædɪkt] *n* (*also*: **drug** ~) наркома́н;

(*enthusiast*) фана́тик.
addicted [əˈdɪktɪd] *adj*: **to be** ~ **to** (*drugs, drink*
etc) пристрасти́ться* (*perf*) к +*dat*; (*fig*): **he's** ~
to football/golf он зая́длый люби́тель
футбо́ла/го́льфа.
addiction [əˈdɪkʃən] *n* пристра́стие; **drug** ~
наркома́ния.
addictive [əˈdɪktɪv] *adj* (*drug*) вызыва́ющий*
привыка́ние; (*activity*) захва́тывающий*.
adding machine [ˈædɪŋ-] *n* счётная маши́на.
Addis Ababa [ˈædɪsˈæbəbə] *n* (GEO)
Адди́с-Абе́ба *f*.
addition [əˈdɪʃən] *n* (MATH) сложе́ние; (*thing*
added) добавле́ние; (*to collection*)
пополне́ние; **in** ~ вдоба́вок; **in** ~ **to** в
дополне́ние к +*dat*.
additional [əˈdɪʃənl] *adj* дополни́тельный*.
additive [ˈædɪtɪv] *n* доба́вка*.
addled [ˈædld] *adj* (BRIT: *egg*) ту́хлый*; **his brain**
is ~ он сбит с то́лку.
address [əˈdrɛs] *n* а́дрес*; (*speech*) речь* *f* ♦ *vt*
(*letter, parcel*) адресова́ть (*impf/perf*); (*person,*
problem) обраща́ться (обрати́ться* *perf*) к
+*dat*; **form of** ~ фо́рма обраще́ния; **absolute/**
relative ~ (COMPUT) абсолю́тный/
относи́тельный а́дрес; **to** ~ **o.s. to**
обраща́ться (обрати́ться* *perf*) к +*dat*.
address book *n* записна́я кни́жка.
addressee [ædrɛˈsiː] *n* адреса́т.
Aden [ˈeɪdən] *n*: **Gulf of** ~ А́денский зали́в.
adenoids [ˈædɪnɔɪdz] *npl* адено́иды *mpl*.
adept [ˈædɛpt] *adj*: ~ **at** иску́сный* (иску́сен)
+*prp*.
adequacy [ˈædɪkwəsɪ] *n* (*in quantity*)
доста́точность *f*; (*in quality*) адеква́тность *f*.
adequate [ˈædɪkwɪt] *adj* (*sufficient*)
доста́точный (доста́точен); (*satisfactory*)
удовлетвори́тельный (удовлетвори́телен),
адеква́тный (адеква́тен).
adequately [ˈædɪkwɪtlɪ] *adv* адеква́тно.
adhere [ədˈhɪəˈ] *vi*: **to** ~ **to** прилипа́ть
(прили́пнуть* *perf*) к +*dat*; (*fig*)
приде́рживаться (*impf*) +*gen*.
adhesion [ədˈhiːʒən] *n* прилипа́ние; (*fig*)
приве́рженность *f*.
adhesive [ədˈhiːzɪv] *adj* кле́йкий* ♦ *n* клей*.
adhesive tape *n* (BRIT) кле́йкая ле́нта; (US:
MED) лейкопла́стырь *m*.
ad hoc [ædˈhɔk] *adj* (*decision*) момента́льный*,
(*committee*) со́зданный на ме́сте ♦ *adv*
(*decide, appoint*) тут же.
ad infinitum [ˈædɪnfɪˈnaɪtəm] *adv* до
бесконе́чности.
adjacent [əˈdʒeɪsənt] *adj*: ~ **(to)** сме́жный*
(сме́жен) (с +*instr*).
adjective [ˈædʒɛktɪv] *n* прилага́тельное *nt adj*.
adjoining [əˈdʒɔɪnɪŋ] *adj* (*room*) сме́жный.
adjourn [əˈdʒəːn] *vt* откла́дывать (отложи́ть*

perf) ◆ *vi*: **the meeting** ~**ed** собрáние бы́ло отло́жено; **to** ~ **a meeting till the following week** отложи́ть* *(perf)* заседáние до слéдующей недéли; **they** ~**ed to the restaurant** *(BRIT: inf)* они́ перебрáлись в рестоpáн.

adjournment [ə'dʒə:nmənt] *n* *(period)* переры́в.

Adjt. *abbr* *(MIL)* = **adjutant**.

adjudicate [ə'dʒu:dɪkeɪt] *vt* *(claim)* pассмáтривать (рассмотрéть* *perf)*; *(competition)* суди́ть* *(impf)* ◆ *vi* суди́ть* *(impf)*.

adjudication [ədʒu:dɪ'keɪʃən] *n* *(LAW)* решéние судá.

adjudicator [ə'dju:dɪkeɪtəʳ] *n* судья́* *m/f*.

adjust [ə'dʒʌst] *vt* *(plans, views)* приспосáбливать (приспосóбить *perf)*; *(clothing)* поправля́ть (попрáвить* *perf)*; *(mechanism)* регули́ровать (отрегули́ровать *perf)* ◆ *vi*: **to** ~ **(to)** приспосáбливаться (приспосóбиться* *perf)* (к +*dat*).

adjustable [ə'dʒʌstəbl] *adj* регули́руемый.

adjuster [ə'dʒʌstəʳ] *n see* **loss**.

adjustment [ə'dʒʌstmənt] *n* *(to surroundings)* адаптáция; *(of prices, wages)* регули́рование; **to make** ~**s to** вноси́ть* (внести́* *perf)* измéнения в +*acc*.

adjutant ['ædʒətənt] *n* адъютáнт.

ad-lib [æd'lɪb] *vti* импровизи́ровать (сымпровизи́ровать *perf)* ◆ *adv*: **ad lib** *(speak)* экспрóмтом.

adman ['ædmæn] *irreg n* *(inf)* реклами́ст.

admin ['ædmɪn] *n abbr* *(inf)* = **administration**.

administer [əd'mɪnɪstəʳ] *vt* *(country, department)* управля́ть *(impf)* +*instr*, руководи́ть* *(impf)* +*instr*; *(justice)* отправля́ть *(impf)*; *(test)* проводи́ть* (провести́* *perf)*; *(drug)* вводи́ть* (ввести́* *perf)*.

administration [ədmɪnɪs'treɪʃən] *n* *(management)* администрáция; **the A~** *(US)* прави́тельство; **the Clinton A~** администрáция Кли́нтона.

administrative [əd'mɪnɪstrətɪv] *adj* админ-истрати́вный.

administrator [əd'mɪnɪstreɪtəʳ] *n* админ-истрáтор.

admirable ['ædmərəbl] *adj* *(quality)* восхити́тельный* (восхити́телен); *(action)* замечáтельный* (замечáтелен).

admiral ['ædmərəl] *n* адмирáл.

Admiralty ['ædmərəltɪ] *n* *(BRIT)*: **the** ~ *(also:* **the** ~ **Board)** ≈ адмиралтéйство *(воéнно-морскóе вéдомство)*.

admiration [ædmə'reɪʃən] *n* восхищéние; **I have great** ~ **for her** онá вызывáет у меня́ большóе восхищéние.

admire [əd'maɪə] *vt* *(respect, appreciate)* восхищáться (восхити́ться *perf)* +*instr*; *(gaze at)* любовáться *(impf)* +*instr*.

admirer [əd'maɪərəʳ] *n* поклóнник(-ица).

admiring [əd'maɪərɪŋ] *adj* восхищённый (восхищён), востóрженный* (востóржен).

admissible [əd'mɪsəbl] *adj* приéмлемый (приéмлем), допусти́мый* (допусти́м); **it is** ~ **evidence** э́то мóжет быть* при́нято в кáчестве доказáтельства.

admission [əd'mɪʃən] *n* *(admittance)* дóпуск; *(entry fee)* входнáя плáта; *(confession)* признáние; **to gain** ~ **to** *(official permission)* получáть (получи́ть* *perf)* дóпуск в/на +*acc*; **"admission free"**, **"free** ~**"** "вход свобóдный"; **by his own** ~ по егó сóбственному признáнию.

admit [əd'mɪt] *vt* *(confess, accept)* признавáть* (признáть* *perf)*; *(permit to enter)* впускáть (впусти́ть* *perf)*; *(to club, organization)* принимáть (приня́ть* *perf)*; *(to hospital)* госпитализи́ровать *(impf/perf)*; **"children not** ~**ted"** "дéтям вход воспрещён"; **this ticket** ~**s two** э́тот билéт нá два лицá

▸ **admit of** *vt fus* *(allow)* допускáть *(impf)*
▸ **admit to** *vt fus* *(murder etc)* сознавáться* (сознáться *perf)* в +*prp*.

admittance [əd'mɪtəns] *n* дóпуск; **no** ~ вход воспрещён.

admittedly [əd'mɪtɪdlɪ] *adv*: ~ **it is not easy** признáться, э́то не легкó.

admonish [əd'mɔnɪʃ] *vt* дéлать (сдéлать *perf)* внушéние +*dat*; *(LAW)* дéлать (сдéлать *perf)* предупреждéние +*dat*.

ad nauseam [æd'nɔ:sɪæm] *adv* бесконéчно.

ado [ə'du:] *n*: **without (any) more** ~ без дальнéйших церемóний.

adolescence [ædəu'lɛsns] *n* подрóстковый вóзраст.

adolescent [ædəu'lɛsnt] *adj* подрóстковый ◆ *n* подрóсток*.

adopt [ə'dɔpt] *vt* *(son)* усыновля́ть (усынови́ть* *perf)*; *(daughter)* удочеря́ть (удочери́ть *perf)*; *(policy)* придéрживаться *(impf)* +*gen*; **to** ~ **sb as a candidate** выдвигáть (вы́двинуть *perf)* когó-н в кандидáты.

adopted [ə'dɔptɪd] *adj* *(child)* приёмный.

adoption [ə'dɔpʃən] *n* *(see vb)* усыновлéние; удочерéние; приня́тие.

adoptive [ə'dɔptɪv] *adj* *(parent)* приёмный.

adorable [ə'dɔ:rəbl] *adj* прелéстный* (прелéстен).

adoration [ædə'reɪʃən] *n* *(of person)* обожáние.

adore [ə'dɔ:ʳ] *vt* обожáть *(impf)*.

adoring [ə'dɔ:rɪŋ] *adj* обожáющий.

adoringly [ə'dɔ:rɪŋlɪ] *adv* с обожáнием.

adorn [ə'dɔ:n] *vt* украшáть (укрáсить* *perf)*.

adornment [ə'dɔ:nmənt] *n* украшéние.

ADP *n abbr* = **automatic data processing**.

adrenalin [ə'drɛnəlɪn] *n* адреналин; **to get the** ~ **going** давáть* (дать* *perf)* заря́д энéргии.

Adriatic [eɪdrɪ'ætɪk] *n*: **the** ~ Адриáтика.

adrift [ə'drɪft] *adv* *(NAUT)*: **to be** ~ дрейфовáть *(impf)*; *(fig)* плыть* *(impf)* по течéнию; **to go** ~

(*plans etc*) расстра́иваться (расстро́иться *perf*); **to come ~** (*boat*) лечь* (*perf*) в дрейф; (*fastening*) расслабля́ться (рассла́биться *perf*).

adroit [əˈdrɔɪt] *adj* ло́вкий* (ло́вок).

adroitly [əˈdrɔɪtlɪ] *adv* ло́вко.

ADT *abbr* (*US*) = **Atlantic Daylight Time**.

adulation [ædjuˈleɪʃən] *n* обожа́ние.

adult [ˈædʌlt] *n* взро́слый(-ая) *m adj ♦ adj* (*grown-up*) взро́слый; (*for adults*) для взро́слых.

adult education *n* образова́ние для взро́слых.

adulterate [əˈdʌltəreɪt] *vt* (*food, drink: with additives*) по́ртить* (испо́ртить* *perf*) (доба́вками); (: *with water*) разбавля́ть (разба́вить* *perf*).

adulterer [əˈdʌltərə*] *n* неве́рный муж.

adulteress [əˈdʌltərɪs] *n* неве́рная жена́.

adultery [əˈdʌltərɪ] *n* супру́жеская неве́рность *f*.

adulthood [ˈædʌlthud] *n* зре́лый во́зраст.

advance [ədˈvɑːns] *n* (*progress*) успе́х; (*MIL*) наступле́ние; (*movement*) продвиже́ние; (*money*) ава́нс ♦ *adj* (*booking*) предвари́тельный ♦ *vt* (*theory, idea*) выдвига́ть (вы́двинуть *perf*) ♦ *vi* (*move forward: also fig*) продвига́ться (продви́нуться *perf*) вперёд; (*MIL*) наступа́ть (*impf*); **in ~** предвари́тельно, зара́нее; **to make ~s (to sb)** заи́грывать (*impf*) (с кем-н); **to give sb ~ notice** *or* **~ warning (of sth)** предупрежда́ть (предупреди́ть* *perf*) кого́-н зара́нее (о чём-н); **to ~ sb money** плати́ть* (заплати́ть* *perf*) кому́-н ава́нсом; **we ~d 20 km** мы продви́нулись на 20 киломе́тров.

advanced [ədˈvɑːnst] *adj* (*studies, course*) для продви́нутого у́ровня; (*child, country*) развито́й (ра́звит); (*ideas, views*) прогресси́вный* (прогресси́вен); **~ maths** вы́сшая матема́тика; **a man of ~ years** *or* **~ in years** челове́к прекло́нного во́зраста.

advancement [ədˈvɑːnsmənt] *n* (*of science*) прогре́сс; (*in job, rank*) продвиже́ние (по слу́жбе).

advancing [ədˈvɑːnsɪŋ] *adj* надвига́ющийся.

advantage [ədˈvɑːntɪdʒ] *n* преиму́щество; (*TENNIS*) "бо́льше"; **to take ~ of** (*person*) испо́льзовать (*perf*); (*sb's hospitality*) злоупотребля́ть (злоупотреби́ть* *perf*) +*instr*; (*opportunity*) воспо́льзоваться (*perf*) +*instr*; **to our/his ~** в на́ших/его́ интере́сах; **to turn sth to one's ~** обраща́ть (обрати́ть* *perf*) что-н в свою́ по́льзу.

advantageous [ædvənˈteɪdʒəs] *adj* (*position, situation*) вы́годный* (вы́годен); **it's ~ to us** нам э́то вы́годно.

advent [ˈædvənt] *n* появле́ние; (*REL*): **A~** *ме́сяц*

до Рождества́.

Advent calendar *n* календа́рь с две́рцами на ка́ждый день ме́сяца до Рождества́.

adventure [ədˈvɛntʃə*] *n* (*exciting event*) приключе́ние; **to look for ~** иска́ть* (*impf*) приключе́ний.

adventure playground *n* де́тская игрова́я площа́дка.

adventurous [ədˈvɛntʃərəs] *adj* (*action*) риско́ванный (риско́ван); (*person*) сме́лый (смел); **an ~ life** жизнь по́лная приключе́ний.

adverb [ˈædvəːb] *n* наре́чие.

adversarial [ædvəˈsɛərɪəl] *adj* противо-бо́рствующий.

adversary [ˈædvəsərɪ] *n* проти́вник(-ница).

adverse [ˈædvəːs] *adj* неблагоприя́тный; **in ~ circumstances** при неблагоприя́тных обстоя́тельствах.

adversity [ədˈvəːsɪtɪ] *n* бе́дствие, несча́стие.

advert [ˈædvəːt] *n abbr* (*BRIT*) = **advertisement**.

advertise [ˈædvətaɪz] *vti* реклами́ровать (*impf*); **to ~ on television/in a newspaper** (дать* *perf*) объявле́ние по телеви́дению/в газе́ту; **to ~ a job** объявля́ть (объяви́ть* *perf*) ко́нкурс на ме́сто; **to ~ for staff/accommodation** дава́ть* (дать* *perf*) объявле́ние, что тре́буются рабо́тники/тре́буется жильё.

advertisement [ədˈvəːtɪsmənt] *n* рекла́ма; (*in classified ads*) объявле́ние.

advertiser [ˈædvətaɪzə*] *n* (*professional*) реклами́ст(ка); (*in newspaper, on television etc*) рекламода́тель *m*.

advertising [ˈædvətaɪzɪŋ] *n* рекла́ма.

advertising agency *n* рекла́мное аге́нтство.

advertising campaign *n* рекла́мная кампа́ния.

advice [ədˈvaɪs] *n* сове́т; (*notification*) уведомле́ние, извеще́ние; **a piece of ~** сове́т; **to ask sb for ~** (*friend*) сове́товаться (посове́товаться *perf*) с кем-н; (*professional*) обраща́ться (обрати́ться* *perf*) (за сове́том) к кому́-н; **to take legal ~** обраща́ться (обрати́ться* *perf*) (за сове́том) к юри́сту.

advice note *n* (*BRIT*) извеще́ние.

advisable [ədˈvaɪzəbl] *adj* целесообра́зный* (целесообра́зен).

advise [ədˈvaɪz] *vt* сове́товать (посове́товать *perf*) +*dat*; (*professionally*) консульти́ровать (проконсульти́ровать *perf*) +*gen*; (*inform*): **to ~ sb of sth** извеща́ть (извести́ть* *perf*) кого́-н о чём-н; **to ~ (sb) against doing** сове́товать (посове́товать *perf*) (кому́-н) +*impf infin*; **you would be well-/ill-~d to go** Вам бы сле́довало пойти́/не сле́довало ходи́ть ....

advisedly [ədˈvaɪzɪdlɪ] *adv* наме́ренно.

adviser [ədˈvaɪzə*] *n* сове́тник, консульта́нт;

---

* marks translations which have irregular inflections. The Russian-English side of the dictionary gives inflectional information.

legal ~ юрисконсульт.
advisor [əd'vaɪzəʳ] n = **adviser.**
advisory [əd'vaɪzərɪ] adj (body, role) консультативный; **in an ~ capacity** в качестве советника or консультанта.
advocate [vb 'ædvəkeɪt, n 'ædvəkɪt] vt выступать (impf) за +acc ♦ n (LAW) защитник, адвокат; (supporter): ~ **of** сторонник(-ица) +gen.
advt. abbr = **advertisement.**
AEA n abbr (BRIT: = Atomic Energy Authority) Управление атомной энергии.
AEC n abbr (US: = Atomic Energy Commission) Комиссия по атомной энергии.
AEEU n abbr (BRIT) = Amalgamated Engineering and Electrical Union.
Aegean [iː'dʒiːən] n: **the ~** Эгейское Море.
aegis ['iːdʒɪs] n: **under the ~ of** под эгидой +gen.
aeon ['iːən] n: **for ~s** целую вечность.
aerial ['ɛərɪəl] n антенна ♦ adj воздушный; ~ **photography** аэрофотосъёмка.
aerobatics ['ɛərəʊ'bætɪks] npl высший пилотаж msg.
aerobics [ɛə'rəʊbɪks] n аэробика.
aerodrome ['ɛərədrəʊm] n (BRIT) аэродром.
aerodynamic ['ɛərəʊdaɪ'næmɪk] adj аэродинамический.
aeronautics [ɛərə'nɔːtɪks] n аэронавтика.
aeroplane ['ɛərəpleɪn] n (BRIT) самолёт.
aerosol ['ɛərəsɒl] n аэрозоль m.
aerospace industry ['ɛərəʊspeɪs-] n аэро-космическая промышленность f.
aesthetic [iːs'θɛtɪk] adj эстетический.
aesthetically [iːs'θɛtɪklɪ] adv эстетически.
afar [ə'fɑːʳ] adv: **from ~** издалека.
AFB n abbr (US) = Air Force Base.
AFDC n abbr (US) = Aid to Families with Dependent Children.
affable ['æfəbl] adj (person) добродушный (добродушен); (behaviour) доброжелательный (доброжелателен).
affair [ə'fɛəʳ] n (matter) дело; (also: **love ~**) роман; ~**s** npl (business) дела ntpl.
affect [ə'fɛkt] vt (influence) действовать (подействовать perf) на +acc, влиять (повлиять perf) на +acc; (afflict) поражать (поразить perf); (move deeply) трогать (тронуть perf); (feign) касаться (коснуться perf); **to ~ an American accent** говорить (impf) с деланным американским акцентом.
affectation [æfɛk'teɪʃən] n (in manner, speech) наигранность f.
affected [ə'fɛktɪd] adj (person) претенциозный (претенциозен); (manner) деланный.
affection [ə'fɛkʃən] n привязанность f.
affectionate [ə'fɛkʃənɪt] adj нежный.
affectionately [ə'fɛkʃənɪtlɪ] adv нежно.
affidavit [æfɪ'deɪvɪt] n (LAW) письменное свидетельство, аффидавит.
affiliated [ə'fɪlɪeɪtɪd] adj (company) дочерний;

to be ~ to (body) являться (impf) филиалом +gen.
affinity [ə'fɪnɪtɪ] n: **to have an ~ with** (bond) ощущать (ощутить perf) близость с +instr; (resemblance) обнаруживать (обнаружить perf) родство с +instr.
affirm [ə'fəːm] vt утверждать (утвердить perf).
affirmation [æfə'meɪʃən] n (of facts) подтверждение; (of ideas) утверждение.
affirmative [ə'fəːmətɪv] adj утвердительный ♦ n: **in the ~** утвердительно.
affix [ə'fɪks] vt прикреплять (прикрепить perf).
afflict [ə'flɪkt] vt постигать (постичь perf); **to be ~ed by** (illness) страдать (impf) от +gen.
affliction [ə'flɪkʃən] n несчастье.
affluence ['æfluəns] n благосостояние.
affluent ['æfluənt] adj благополучный (благополучен); **the ~ society** общество благосостояния.
afford [ə'fɔːd] vt позволить (perf) себе; (provide) предоставлять (предоставить perf); **I can't ~ it** мне это не по карману; **can we ~ a car?** мы можем себе позволить купить машину?; **I can't ~ the time** мне время не позволяет.
affordable [ə'fɔːdəbl] adj доступный по цене.
affray [ə'freɪ] n (BRIT: LAW) драка в общественном месте.
affront [ə'frʌnt] n оскорбление.
affronted [ə'frʌntɪd] adj оскорблённый (оскорблён).
Afghan ['æfgæn] adj афганский ♦ n афганец*(-нка).
Afghanistan [æf'gænɪstæn] n Афганистан.
afield [ə'fiːld] adv: **far ~** вдалеке, вдали; **from far ~** издалека.
AFL-CIO n abbr = American Federation of Labor and Congress of Industrial Organizations.
afloat [ə'fləʊt] adv (floating) на плаву; **to stay ~** (fig) держаться (impf) на поверхности; **to keep a business ~** не давать (дать perf) потонуть предприятию.
afoot [ə'fʊt] adv: **there is something ~** что-то затевается.
aforementioned [ə'fɔːmɛnʃənd] adj вышеупомянутый.
aforesaid [ə'fɔːsɛd] adj вышеупомянутый.
afraid [ə'freɪd] adj (frightened) испуганный (испуган); **to be ~ of sth/sb/of doing** бояться (impf) чего-н/кого-н/+infin; **to be ~ to** бояться (побояться perf) +infin; **I am ~ that** (apology) боюсь, что; **I am ~ that I'll be late** боюсь, что я опоздаю; **I am ~ so/not** боюсь, что да/нет.
afresh [ə'frɛʃ] adv заново.
Africa ['æfrɪkə] n Африка.
African ['æfrɪkən] adj африканский ♦ n африканец*(-нка).
Afrikaans [æfrɪ'kɑːns] n (язык*) африкаанс.
Afrikaner [æfrɪ'kɑːnəʳ] n африканер (урожёнец Южной Африки голландского происхождения).

Afro-American [ˈæfrəuəˈmɛrɪkən] *adj* афро-
американский*.
Afro-Caribbean [ˈæfrəkærɪˈbiːən] *adj* афро-
карибский.
AFT *n abbr* (*US*) = American Federation of
Teachers.
after [ˈɑːftəʳ] *prep* (*time*) после +*gen*, спустя
+*acc*; (*place, order*) за +*instr*; (*style, technique*)
в стиле +*gen* ◆ *adv* потом, после ◆ *conj* после
того как; ~ **dinner** после обеда; **the day** ~
tomorrow послезавтра; ~ **three years they
divorced** спустя три года они развелись;
what/who are you ~? что/кто Вам нужно/
нужен?; **the police are** ~ **him** его разыскивает
полиция; **to name sb** ~ **sb** называть
(назвать* *perf*) кого-н в честь кого-н; **it's
twenty** ~ **eight** (*US*) сейчас двадцать минут
девятого; **to ask** ~ **sb** справляться
(справиться* *perf*) о ком-н; ~ **all** в конце
концов; ~ **you!** после Вас!; ~ **he left** после
того, как он ушёл; ~ **having done this** сделав
это.
afterbirth [ˈɑːftəbəːθ] *n* послед.
aftercare [ˈɑːftəkɛəʳ] *n* (*BRIT: MED*) уход за
выздоравливающим.
after-effects [ˈɑːftərɪfɛkts] *npl* последствия *ntpl.*
afterlife [ˈɑːftəlaɪf] *n* загробная жизнь *f.*
aftermath [ˈɑːftəmɑːθ] *n* последствия *ntpl*; **in
the** ~ **of** после +*gen*.
afternoon [ˈɑːftəˈnuːn] *n* вторая половина
дня; **in the** ~ днём; **good** ~! (*goodbye*) до
свидания!; (*hello*) добрый день!
afters [ˈɑːftəz] *n* (*inf: dessert*): **for** ~ на третье *or*
десерт.
after-sales service [ɑːftəˈseɪlz-] *n* (*BRIT*)
гарантированное техобслуживание.
after-shave (lotion) [ˈɑːftəʃeɪv-] *n* одеколон
после бритья.
aftershock [ˈɑːftəʃɔk] *n* толчок* (*после
основного землетрясения*).
aftertaste [ˈɑːftəteɪst] *n* привкус.
afterthought [ˈɑːftəθɔːt] *n*: **as an** ~
машинально.
afterward [ˈɑːftəwəd] *adv* (*US*) = afterwards.
afterwards [ˈɑːftəwədz] (*US* afterward) *adv*
позже, потом.
again [əˈgɛn] *adv* (*once more*) ещё раз, снова;
(*repeatedly*) опять; **I won't see him/go there** ~
я больше не увижу его/пойду туда; **to do sth**
~ делать (сделать *perf*) что-н ещё раз *or*
снова; **to begin** ~ начать* (*perf*) сначала; **to
see** ~ смотреть* (посмотреть* *perf*) *or*
видеть* (увидеть* *perf*) ещё раз; **he opened
the door** ~ он опять *or* снова открыл дверь;
~ **and** ~ снова и снова; **now and** ~ время от
времени.
against [əˈgɛnst] *prep* (*lean*) к +*dat*; (*hit, rub*) о
+*acc*; (*standing*) у +*gen*; (*in opposition to*)

против +*gen*; (*at odds with*) вопреки +*dat*;
(*compared to*) по сравнению с +*instr*; ~ **a blue
background** на синем фоне; (*as*) ~ в
сравнении с +*instr*.
age [eɪdʒ] *n* (*of person*) возраст; (*period in
history*) век* ◆ *vi* (*person*) стареть (постареть
perf) ◆ *vt* (*subj: hairstyle, dress*) старить (*impf*);
what ~ **is he?** сколько ему лет?; **he is 20 years
of** ~ ему двадцать лет; **under** ~
несовершеннолетний*; **to come of** ~
достигать (достичь* *perf*) совершеннолетия;
it's been ~**s since I saw you** я не видел Вас
целую вечность.
aged[1] [ˈeɪdʒd] *adj*: **a boy** ~ **ten** мальчик десяти
лет.
aged[2] [ˈeɪdʒɪd] *npl*: **the** ~ престарелые *pl adj.*
age group *n* возрастная группа; **the forty to
fifty** ~ ~ люди возрастом от сорока до
пятидесяти лет.
ageing [ˈeɪdʒɪŋ] *adj* стареющий ◆ *n* старение.
ageless [ˈeɪdʒlɪs] *adj* (*building, ritual*) вечный*
(вечен).
age limit *n* возрастной предел.
agency [ˈeɪdʒənsɪ] *n* (*COMM*) агентство, бюро
nt ind; (*government body*) управление;
through *or* **by the** ~ **of** при посредстве +*gen*.
agenda [əˈdʒɛndə] *n* (*of meeting*) повестка*
(дня); **on the** ~ на повестке (дня).
agent [ˈeɪdʒənt] *n* (*representative, spy*) агент;
(*COMM*) посредник; (*CHEM*) реактив; (*fig*)
фактор.
aggravate [ˈægrəveɪt] *vt* (*situation*) усугублять
(усугубить* *perf*); (*person*) раздражать
(раздражить *perf*).
aggravating [ˈægrəveɪtɪŋ] *adj*: **his behaviour is**
~ его поведение раздражает меня.
aggravation [ægrəˈveɪʃən] *n* (*see vt*)
усугубление; раздражение.
aggregate [ˈægrɪgɪt] *n* (*total*) совокупность *f* ◆
vt группировать (сгруппировать *perf*) в +*acc*.
aggression [əˈgrɛʃən] *n* агрессия.
aggressive [əˈgrɛsɪv] *adj* (*belligerent*)
агрессивный* (агрессивен); (*assertive*)
напористый (напорист).
aggressiveness [əˈgrɛsɪvnɪs] *n* агрессивность
f.
aggressor [əˈgrɛsəʳ] *n* агрессор.
aggrieved [əˈgriːvd] *adj* огорчённый*
(огорчён).
aggro [ˈægrəu] *n* (*inf: aggressive behaviour*)
напряжёнка; (*difficulties*) возня.
aghast [əˈgɑːst] *adj*: **to be** ~ **at** быть* (*impf*) в
ужасе от +*gen*.
agile [ˈædʒaɪl] *adj* (*person*) проворный*
(проворен); (*mind*) живой*.
agility [əˈdʒɪlɪtɪ] *n* подвижность *f*; **mental** ~
живость *f* ума.
agitate [ˈædʒɪteɪt] *vt* (*person*) возбуждать

(возбуди́ть* *perf*); (*liquid*) взба́лтывать (взболта́ть *perf*) ◆ *vi*: **to ~ for/against** агити́ровать (сагити́ровать *perf*) за +*acc*/ против +*gen*.

agitated ['ædʒɪteɪtɪd] *adj* возбуждённый* (возбуждён), взволно́ванный (взволно́ван).

agitator ['ædʒɪteɪtə'] *n* агита́тор.

AGM *n abbr* (= *annual general meeting*) ежего́дное о́бщее собра́ние.

agnostic [æg'nɔstɪk] *n* агно́стик.

ago [ə'gəu] *adv*: **two days ~** два дня наза́д; **not long ~** неда́вно; **as long ~ as 1960** ещё в 1960 году́; **how long ~?** как давно́?

agog [ə'gɔg] *adj* (*excited*) взволно́ванный (взволно́ван); **to be (all) ~** (*with anticipation*) сгора́ть (*impf*) от нетерпе́ния.

agonize ['ægənaɪz] *vi*: **he ~d over the problem** он му́чился над пробле́мой.

agonizing ['ægənaɪzɪŋ] *adj* мучи́тельный* (мучи́телен).

agony ['ægənɪ] *n* (*pain*) мучи́тельная боль *f*; (*torment*) му́ка, муче́ние; **to be in ~** му́читься (*impf*) от бо́ли.

agony aunt *n* психо́лог "по́чты дове́рия", отвеча́ющий на вопро́сы чита́телей.

agony column *n* ру́брика "по́чта дове́рия".

agree [ə'gri:] *vt* согласо́вывать (согласова́ть *perf*) ◆ *vi*: **to ~ with** (*have same opinion*) соглаша́ться (согласи́ться *perf*) с +*instr*; (*correspond*) согласо́вываться (*impf/perf*) с +*instr*; **to ~ that** согласи́ться* (*perf*), что; **it was ~d that ...** бы́ло решено́, что ...; **the price is still to be ~d** це́ну всё ещё на́до согласова́ть; **I ~ (with you)** я согла́сен (с Ва́ми); **to ~ (with)** (*LING*) согласо́вывать (согласова́ть* *perf*) (с +*instr*); **garlic doesn't ~ with me** я не переношу́ чеснока́; **to ~ on sth** догова́риваться (договори́ться *perf*) о чём-н; **they ~d on this** они́ сошли́сь на э́том; **they ~d on going/on a price** они́ договор- и́лись пойти́/о цене́; **to ~ to sth/to do** соглаша́ться (согласи́ться* *perf*) на что-н/+*infin*.

agreeable [ə'gri:əbl] *adj* (*pleasant*) прия́тный* (прия́тен); (*willing*) согла́сен; **are you ~ to this?** Вы согла́сны на э́то?

agreed [ə'gri:d] *adj* усло́вленный (усло́влен).

agreement [ə'gri:mənt] *n* (*consent*) согла́сие; (*arrangement*) соглаше́ние, догово́р; **in ~ with** в согла́сии с +*instr*; **we are in complete ~** ме́жду на́ми по́лное согла́сие; **by mutual ~** по взаи́мному соглаше́нию.

agricultural [ægrɪ'kʌltʃərəl] *adj* се́льско- хозя́йственный; **~ land** земе́льные уго́дья *ntpl*.

agriculture ['ægrɪkʌltʃə'] *n* се́льское хозя́йство.

aground [ə'graund] *adv*: **to run ~** сади́ться* (сесть* *perf*) на мель.

ahead [ə'hɛd] *adv* впереди́; (*direction*) вперёд; **~ of** (*more advanced than*) впереди́ +*gen*;

(*earlier than*) ра́ньше +*gen*; **~ of time** *or* **schedule** досро́чно; **go right** *or* **straight ~** иди́те вперёд *or* пря́мо; **go ~!** (*permission*) дава́йте!; **they were (right) ~ of us** они́ бы́ли (пря́мо) пе́ред на́ми.

AI *n abbr* (= *Amnesty International*) Междунаро́дная амни́стия; (*COMPUT*) = **artificial intelligence**.

AIB *n abbr* (*BRIT*) = **Accident Investigation Bureau**.

AID *n abbr* (= *artificial insemination by donor*) иску́сственное оплодотворе́ние се́менем до́нора; (*US*) = **Agency for International Development**.

aid [eɪd] *n* (*assistance*) по́мощь *f*; (*device*) приспособле́ние ◆ *vt* помога́ть (помо́чь* *perf*) +*dat*; **with the ~ of** при по́мощи +*gen*; **in ~ of** в по́мощь +*dat*; **to ~ and abet** (*LAW*) подстрека́ть (*impf*); *see also* **hearing**.

aide [eɪd] *n* помо́щник.

aide-de-camp ['eɪddə'kɔŋ] *n* адьюта́нт.

AIDS [eɪdz] *n abbr* (= *acquired immune deficiency syndrome*) СПИД = *синдро́м приобретённого имму́нодефици́та*.

AIH *n abbr* (= *artificial insemination by husband*) иску́сственное оплодотворе́ние се́менем му́жа.

ailing ['eɪlɪŋ] *adj* больно́й* (бо́лен); **an ~ economy** эконо́мика прише́дшая в упа́док.

ailment ['eɪlmənt] *n* неду́г.

aim [eɪm] *n* (*objective*) цель *f* ◆ *vi* (*also*: **take ~**) це́литься (наце́литься *perf*) ◆ *vt*: **to ~ (at)** (*gun, camera*) наводи́ть* (навести́* *perf*) (на +*acc*); (*missile, blow*) це́лить (*impf*) *or* наце́ливать (наце́лить *perf*) (на +*acc*); (*remark*) направля́ть (напра́вить* *perf*) (на +*acc*); **to ~ at** це́литься (*impf*) в +*acc*, прице́ливаться (прице́литься *perf*) в +*acc*; (*fig*) стреми́ться* (*impf*) к +*dat*; **to ~ to do** ста́вить* (поста́вить* *perf*) свое́й це́лью +*infin*; **he has a good ~** он ме́ткий стрело́к.

aimless ['eɪmlɪs] *adj* бесце́льный* (бесце́лен).

aimlessly ['eɪmlɪslɪ] *adv* бесце́льно.

ain't [eɪnt] (*inf*) = **am not**, **aren't**, **isn't**; *see* **be**.

air [ɛə'] *n* во́здух; (*tune*) моти́в; (*appearance*) вид* ◆ *vt* (*room, bedclothes*) прове́тривать (прове́трить *perf*); (*views*) обнаро́довать (*perf*) ◆ *cpd* (*currents, attack etc*) возду́шный; **to throw sth into the ~** подбра́сывать (подбро́сить* *perf*) что-н в во́здух; **by ~** самолётом; **everything's still very much in the ~** всё до сих пор виси́т в во́здухе; **on the ~** в эфи́ре; **to go on the ~** выходи́ть* (вы́йти* *perf*) в эфи́р.

airbag ['ɛəbæg] *n* возду́шная поду́шка, надува́ющаяся автомати́чески ме́жду рулём и шофёром, в слу́чае ава́рии.

air base *n* авиаба́за.

airbed ['ɛəbɛd] *n* (*BRIT*) надувно́й матра́с.

airborne ['ɛəbɔ:n] *adj* возду́шный* (возду́шен); (*troops*) возду́шно-деса́нтный; (*particles*) летучий*; **as soon as the plane was**

~ как то́лько самолёт подня́лся в во́здух.
air cargo n возду́шный груз.
air-conditioned [ˈɛəkənˈdɪʃənd] adj кондициони́рованный.
air conditioning n кондициони́рование.
air-cooled [ˈɛəkuːld] adj охлажда́емый во́здухом.
aircraft [ˈɛəkrɑːft] n inv самолёт.
aircraft carrier n авиано́сец*.
air cushion n возду́шная поду́шка*.
airfield [ˈɛəfiːld] n аэродро́м.
Air Force n Вое́нно-Возду́шные Си́лы fpl.
air freight n авиагру́з.
air freshener n освежи́тель m во́здуха.
air gun n духово́е ружьё*.
air hostess n (BRIT) бортпроводни́ца, стюарде́сса.
airily [ˈɛərɪlɪ] adv с лёгкостью, небре́жно.
airing [ˈɛərɪŋ] n: **to give an ~ to** (ideas, views etc) обнаро́довать (perf).
air letter n (BRIT) письмо́* а́виа.
airlift [ˈɛəlɪft] n возду́шная перебро́ска ♦ vt перебра́сывать (перебро́сить* perf) по во́здуху.
airline [ˈɛəlaɪn] n авиакомпа́ния.
airliner [ˈɛəlaɪnəʳ] n пассажи́рский* (авиа)ла́йнер.
airlock [ˈɛəlɔk] n возду́шная про́бка.
air mail n: **by ~ ~** авиапо́чтой.
air mattress n надувно́й матра́с.
airplane [ˈɛəpleɪn] n (US) самолёт.
air pocket n возду́шная я́ма.
airport [ˈɛəpɔːt] n аэропо́рт.
air raid n возду́шный налёт.
air rifle n пневмати́ческая винто́вка.
airsick [ˈɛəsɪk] adj: **to be ~** страда́ть (impf) возду́шной боле́знью.
airspace [ˈɛəspeɪs] n возду́шное простра́нство.
airspeed [ˈɛəspiːd] n возду́шная ско́рость f, ско́рость f в во́здухе.
airstrip [ˈɛəstrɪp] n взлётно-поса́дочная полоса́*.
air terminal n аэровокза́л.
airtight [ˈɛətaɪt] adj гермети́ческий.
air time n вре́мя* nt в эфи́ре.
air-traffic control [ˈɛətræfɪk-] n возду́шно-диспе́тчерская слу́жба.
air-traffic controller n возду́шный диспе́тчер.
airway [ˈɛəweɪ] n возду́шная тра́сса.
air waybill n тра́нспортная накладна́я для авиагру́за.
airy [ˈɛərɪ] adj (room) просто́рный* (просто́рен); (manner) беспе́чный* (беспе́чен).
aisle [aɪl] n прохо́д.
ajar [əˈdʒɑːʳ] adj приоткры́тый (приоткры́т).
AK abbr (US: POST) = Alaska.
aka abbr (= also known as) изве́стный та́кже

под и́менем.
akin [əˈkɪn] adj: **~ to** сродни́ +dat.
AL (US: POST) abbr = Alabama.
ALA n abbr = American Library Association.
alabaster [ˈæləbɑːstəʳ] n алеба́стр.
à la carte [ɑːlɑːˈkɑːt] adv: **dinner ~ ~ ~** обе́д с зака́зом блюд по меню́.
alacrity [əˈlækrɪtɪ] n гото́вность f; **with ~** с гото́вностью.
alarm [əˈlɑːm] n (anxiety) трево́га; (device) сигнализа́ция ♦ vt (person) трево́жить (встрево́жить perf); (car, house) устана́вливать (установи́ть* perf) сигнализа́цию в +prp.
alarm call n: **I would like an ~ ~ for 6 a.m.** позвони́те, пожа́луйста, в 6 часо́в и разбуди́те меня́.
alarm clock n буди́льник.
alarmed [əˈlɑːmd] adj встрево́женный* (встрево́жен); **his car is ~** у него́ в маши́не сигнализа́ция.
alarming [əˈlɑːmɪŋ] adj трево́жный* (трево́жен).
alarmist [əˈlɑːmɪst] n паникёр(ша).
alas [əˈlæs] excl увы́.
Alaska [əˈlæskə] n Аля́ска.
Albania [ælˈbeɪnɪə] n Алба́ния.
Albanian [ælˈbeɪnɪən] adj алба́нский* ♦ n алба́нец*(-нка); (LING) алба́нский язы́к*.
albatross [ˈælbətrɔs] n (ZOOL) альбатро́с.
albeit [ɔːlˈbiːɪt] conj хотя́ и.
album [ˈælbəm] n альбо́м.
albumen [ˈælbjumɪn] n бело́к*.
alchemy [ˈælkɪmɪ] n алхи́мия.
alcohol [ˈælkəhɔl] n алкого́ль m.
alcohol-free [ˈælkəhɔlˈfriː] adj безалкого́льный.
alcoholic [ælkəˈhɔlɪk] adj алкого́льный ♦ n алкого́лик(-и́чка).
alcoholism [ˈælkəhɔlɪzəm] n алкоголи́зм.
alcove [ˈælkəuv] n алько́в.
Ald. abbr = **alderman**.
alderman [ˈɔːldəmən] irreg n глава́ муниципалите́та.
ale [eɪl] n пи́во (пригото́вленное без хме́ля).
alert [əˈləːt] adj (attentive) внима́тельный* (внима́телен); (to danger) бди́тельный* (бди́телен) ♦ n (alarm) трево́га ♦ vt (police etc) предупрежда́ть (предупреди́ть* perf); **to be on the ~** (also MIL) быть* (impf) начеку́; **to ~ sb to sth** предупрежда́ть (предупреди́ть perf) кого́-н о чём-н; **to ~ sb to the dangers of sth** предостерега́ть (предостере́чь* perf) кого́-н от опа́сности чего́-н.
Aleutian Islands [əˈluːʃən-] npl Але́утские острова́ mpl.
Alexandria [ælɪgˈzɑːndrɪə] n Александри́я.
alfresco [ælˈfrɛskəu] adj, adv под откры́тым

нёбом.

algebra ['ældʒıbrə] *n* áлгебра.

Algeria [æl'dʒıərıə] *n* Алжи́р.

Algerian [æl'dʒıərıən] *adj* алжи́рский* ♦ *n* алжи́рец*(-рка).

Algiers [æl'dʒıəz] *n* Алжи́р (*го́род*).

algorithm ['ælgərıðəm] *n* алгори́тм.

alias ['eılıəs] *n* (*of criminal*) вы́мышленное и́мя* *nt*; (*of writer*) псевдони́м ♦ *adv*: ~ **John Green** он же Джон Грин.

alibi ['ælıbaı] *n* áлиби *nt ind*.

alien ['eılıən] *n* (*foreigner*) иностра́нец*(-нка); (*extraterrestrial*) инопланетя́нин*(-я́нка) ♦ *adj*: ~ (**to**) чу́ждый* (чужд) (+*dat*); **pity was ~ to his nature** чу́вство жа́лости ему́ бы́ло чу́ждо.

alienate ['eılıəneıt] *vt* (*person*) отчужда́ть (*impf*), отта́лкивать (оттолкну́ть *perf*).

alienation [eılıə'neıʃən] *n* отчужде́ние.

alight [ə'laıt] *adj*: **to be ~** горе́ть (*impf*); (*eyes, face*) сия́ть (*impf*) ♦ *adv*: **to set ~** поджига́ть (подже́чь* *perf*) ♦ *vi*: **to ~ on** опуска́ться (опусти́ться* *perf*) на +*acc*; **to ~ from** (*boat*) сходи́ть* (сойти́* *perf*) с +*gen*; (*bus, train*) выходи́ть* (вы́йти* *perf*) из +*gen*.

align [ə'laın] *vt* (*objects*) выра́внивать (вы́ровнять *perf*); **to ~ o.s. with** присоединя́ться (присоедини́ться *perf*) к +*dat*.

alignment [ə'laınmənt] *n* сою́з; (*POL*) алья́нс; **out of ~** неро́вно.

alike [ə'laık] *adj* одина́ковый (одина́ков) ♦ *adv* одина́ково; **they look ~** они́ похо́жи друг на дру́га; **winter and summer ~** и зимо́й и ле́том.

alimony ['ælımənı] *n* алиме́нты* *pl*.

alive [ə'laıv] *adj* жив; (*place*) оживлённый*; (*active: person*) живо́й; **~ with** по́лон +*gen*; **to be ~ to sth** осознава́ть (осозна́ть *perf*) что-н.

alkali ['ælkəlaı] *n* щёлочь* *f*.

alkaline ['ælkəlaın] *adj* щелочно́й.

KEYWORD

all [ɔ:l] *adj* весь* (*f* вся, *nt* всё, *pl* все); **all day** весь день* *m*; **all night** всю ночь* *f*; **all men are equal** все лю́ди равны́; **all five stayed** все пя́теро оста́лись; **all the books** все кни́ги; **all the time** всё вре́мя; **all his life** всю свою́ жизнь

♦ *pron* **1** всё; **I ate it all, I ate all of it** я всё съел; **all of us stayed** мы все оста́лись; **we all sat down** мы все се́ли; **is that all?** э́то всё?; (*in shop*) всё?

2 (*in phrases*): **above all** пре́жде всего́; **after all** в конце́ концо́в; **all in all** в це́лом *or* о́бщем; **not at all** (*in answer to question*) совсе́м нет, ничу́ть нет; (*in answer to thanks*) не́ за что; **I'm not at all tired** я совсе́м не уста́л

♦ *adv* совсе́м; **I am all alone** я совсе́м оди́н; **I did it all by myself** я всё сде́лал сам; **it's not as hard as all that** э́то совсе́м не так уж тру́дно; **all the more/the better** тем бо́лее/лу́чше; **I have all but finished** я почти́ что зако́нчил; **the score is two all** счёт—два два.

allay [ə'leı] *vt* (*fears etc*) разве́ивать (разве́ять *perf*).

all clear *n* отбо́й.

allegation [ælı'geıʃən] *n* обвине́ние; **according to his ~s** согла́сно его́ утвержде́ниям.

allege [ə'lɛdʒ] *vt* (*claim*) утвержда́ть (*impf*); **he is ~d to have said that ...** утвержда́ют, что он сказа́л что ....

alleged [ə'lɛdʒd] *adj* подозрева́емый.

allegedly [ə'lɛdʒıdlı] *adv* я́кобы.

allegiance [ə'li:dʒəns] *n* (*to people*) ве́рность *f*; (*to ideas*) приве́рженность *f*.

allegory ['ælıgərı] *n* аллего́рия.

all-embracing ['ɔ:lım'breısıŋ] *adj* всеобъе́млющий* (всеобъе́млющ).

allergic [ə'lə:dʒık] *adj* аллерги́ческий*; **he is ~ to** у него́ аллерги́я на +*acc*; (*fig*) он не выно́сит +*gen*.

allergy ['ælədʒı] *n* (*MED*) аллерги́я.

alleviate [ə'li:vıeıt] *vt* облегча́ть (облегчи́ть *perf*).

alley ['ælı] *n* (*street*) переу́лок*.

alleyway ['ælıweı] *n* прою́лок*.

alliance [ə'laıəns] *n* сою́з; (*POL*) алья́нс.

allied ['ælaıd] *adj* (*POL, MIL*) сою́зный; (*industries*) сме́жный*.

alligator ['ælıgeıtə'] *n* аллига́тор.

all-important ['ɔ:lım'pɔ:tnt] *adj* суще́ственный.

all-in ['ɔ:lın] *adj* (*BRIT: cost*) о́бщий*; **it cost me £100 ~** в о́бщей сло́жности мне э́то сто́ило £100.

all-in wrestling *n* во́льная борьба́.

alliteration [əlıtə'reıʃən] *n* аллитера́ция.

all-night ['ɔ:l'naıt] *adj* (*café, cinema*) ночно́й.

allocate ['æləkeıt] *vt* (*money, time, room*) выделя́ть (вы́делить *perf*); (*tasks*) поруча́ть (поручи́ть* *perf*).

allocation [æləu'keıʃən] *n* (*of responsibilty*) распределе́ние; (*of resources*) выделе́ние; (*of money*) ассигнова́ние.

allot [ə'lɔt] *vt*: **to ~ (to)** отводи́ть* (отвести́* *perf*) (+*dat*); **in the ~ted time** в отведённое вре́мя.

allotment [ə'lɔtmənt] *n* (*share*) до́ля*; (*garden*) (земе́льный) уча́сток*.

all-out ['ɔ:laut] *adj* (*effort*) максима́льный; (*attack*) масси́рованный; (*strike*) всео́бщий* ♦ *adv* по́лностью; **to go all out (for)** по́лностью выкла́дываться (вы́ложиться *perf*) (для +*gen*).

allow [ə'lau] *vt* (*permit*) разреша́ть (разреши́ть *perf*); (: *claim, goal*) признава́ть* (призна́ть *perf*) действи́тельным; (*set aside: sum*) выделя́ть (вы́делить *perf*); (*concede*): **to ~ that** допуска́ть (допусти́ть* *perf*), что; **to ~ sb to do** разреша́ть (разреши́ть *perf*) *or* позволя́ть (позво́лить *perf*) кому́-л +*infin*; **he was ~ed to ...** ему́ бы́ло разрешено́ +*infin* ...; **smoking is not ~ed** кури́ть воспреща́ется *or*

запреща́ется; **we must ~ 3 days for the journey** мы должны́ оста́вить три дня на доро́гу
▶ **allow for** *vt fus* учи́тывать (уче́сть* *perf*), принима́ть (приня́ть* *perf*) в расчёт.
allowance [ə'lauəns] *n* (*company expenses*) де́ньги* *pl* на расхо́ды; (*pocket money*) карма́нные де́ньги; (*welfare payment*) посо́бие; (*tax allowance*) нало́говая ски́дка*; **to make ~s for sb/sth** де́лать (сде́лать *perf*) ски́дку для кого́-н/на что-н.
alloy ['ælɔɪ] *n* сплав.
all right *adv* хорошо́, норма́льно; (*as answer: in agreement*) хорошо́, ла́дно ◆ *adj* неплохо́й*, норма́льный; **is everything ~ ~?** всё норма́льно *or* в поря́дке?; **are you ~ ~?** как Вы (себя́ чу́вствуете)?; **do you like him? – he's ~ ~** он Вам нра́вится? – ничего́.
all-rounder [ɔ:l'raundə'] *n* универса́л.
allspice ['ɔ:lspaɪs] *n* души́стый пе́рец*.
all-time ['ɔ:l'taɪm] *adj* (*record*) непревзойдённый; **inflation is at an ~ low** инфля́ция на небыва́ло ни́зком у́ровне.
allude [ə'lu:d] *vi*: **to ~ to** намека́ть (намекну́ть *perf*) на +*acc*.
alluring [ə'ljuərɪŋ] *adj* соблазни́тельный* (соблазни́телен).
allusion [ə'lu:ʒən] *n*: **~ (to)** намёк (на +*acc*); (*LITERATURE*) аллю́зия (на +*acc*).
alluvium [ə'lu:vɪəm] *n* аллю́вий.
ally [*n* 'ælaɪ, *vb* ə'laɪ] *n* сою́зник ◆ *vt*: **to ~ o.s. with** объединя́ться (объедини́ться *perf*) с +*instr*.
Alma-Ata [ælmɑ:ə'tɑ:] *n* А́лма-Ата́ *f ind*.
almighty [ɔ:l'maɪtɪ] *adj* (*omnipotent*) всемогу́щий* (всемогу́щ); (*tremendous*) колосса́льный.
almond ['ɑ:mənd] *n* минда́ль* *m*.
almost ['ɔ:lməust] *adv* почти́; (*all but*) чуть *or* едва́ не; **he ~ fell** он чуть не упа́л.
alms [ɑ:mz] *npl* ми́лостыня *fsg*, подая́ние *ntsg*.
aloft [ə'lɔft] *adv* (*hold, carry*) над голово́й.
alone [ə'ləun] *adj, adv* оди́н (одна́); **to leave sb/sth ~** оставля́ть (оста́вить* *perf*) кого́-н/что-н в поко́е; **let ~ ...** не говоря́ уже́ о +*prp* ....
along [ə'lɔŋ] *prep* (*motion*) по +*dat*, вдоль +*gen*; (*position*) вдоль +*gen* ◆ *adv*: **is he coming ~ (with us)?** он идёт с на́ми?; **he was limping ~** он шёл хрома́я; **~ with** вместе с +*instr*; **all ~** с са́мого нача́ла.
alongside [ə'lɔŋ'saɪd] *prep* (*position*) ря́дом с +*instr*, вдоль +*gen*; (*motion*) к +*dat* ◆ *adv* ря́дом; **we brought our boat ~** мы прича́лили ло́дку.
aloof [ə'lu:f] *adj* отрешённый (отрешён) ◆ *adv*: **to stand ~** держа́ться (*impf*) в стороне́.
aloofness [ə'lu:fnɪs] *n* отрешённость *f*.

aloud [ə'laud] *adv* (*read, speak*) вслух.
alphabet ['ælfəbɛt] *n* алфави́т.
alphabetical [ælfə'bɛtɪkl] *adj* алфави́тный; **in ~ order** в алфави́тном поря́дке.
alphanumeric ['ælfənju:'mɛrɪk] *adj* алфави́тно-цифрово́й.
alpine ['ælpaɪn] *adj* высокого́рный, альпи́йский*.
Alps [ælps] *npl*: **the ~** А́льпы* *pl*.
already [ɔ:l'rɛdɪ] *adv* уже́.
alright ['ɔ:l'raɪt] *adv* (*BRIT*) = **all right**.
Alsace ['ælsæs] *n* Эльза́с.
Alsatian [æl'seɪʃən] *n* (*BRIT: dog*) неме́цкая овча́рка*; (*person*) эльза́сец(-ска).
also ['ɔ:lsəu] *adv* (*referring to subject*) та́кже, то́же; (*referring to object*) та́кже; (*moreover*) кро́ме того́, к тому́ же; **he ~ likes apples** он та́кже *or* то́же лю́бит я́блоки; **he likes apples ~** он лю́бит та́кже я́блоки.
altar ['ɔltə'] *n* алта́рь* *m*.
alter ['ɔltə'] *vt* изменя́ть (измени́ть* *perf*) ◆ *vi* изменя́ться (измени́ться* *perf*).
alteration [ɔltə'reɪʃən] *n* измене́ние; **~s** *npl* (*SEWING*) переде́лки *fpl*; **to make ~s to a building** перестра́ивать (перестро́ить *perf*) зда́ние.
altercation [ɔltə'keɪʃən] *n* препира́тельство.
alternate [*adj* ɔl'tə:nɪt, *vb* 'ɔltə:neɪt] *adj* череду́ющийся; (*US: alternative*) альтернати́вный ◆ *vi*: **to ~ (with)** чередова́ться (*impf*) (с +*instr*); **on ~ days** че́рез день.
alternately [ɔl'tə:nɪtlɪ] *adv* попереме́нно.
alternating current ['ɔltə:neɪtɪŋ-] *n* переме́нный ток*.
alternative [ɔl'tə:nətɪv] *adj* альтернати́вный ◆ *n* альтернати́ва.
alternatively [ɔl'tə:nətɪvlɪ] *adv*: **~ one could ...** кро́ме того́ мо́жно ....
alternative medicine *n* альтернати́вная *or* нетрадицио́нная медици́на.
alternator ['ɔltə:neɪtə'] *n* (*AUT*) генера́тор переме́нного то́ка.
although [ɔ:l'ðəu] *conj* хотя́.
altitude ['æltɪtju:d] *n* (*of plane*) высота́*; (*of place*) высота́ над у́ровнем мо́ря.
alto ['æltəu] *n* (*female*) контра́льто *nt ind*; (*male*) альт*.
altogether [ɔ:ltə'gɛðə'] *adv* (*completely*) соверше́нно; (*in all*) в о́бщем, в о́бщей сло́жности; **how much is that ~?** ско́лько бу́дет в о́бщей сло́жности?
altruism ['æltruɪzəm] *n* альтруи́зм.
altruistic [æltru'ɪstɪk] *adj* (*action*) альтруисти́ческий; (*person*) альтруисти́чный (альтруисти́чен).
aluminium [ælju'mɪnɪəm] *n* (*BRIT*) алюми́ний.

---

* marks translations which have irregular inflections. The Russian-English side of the dictionary gives inflectional information.

aluminum [ə'luːmɪnəm] *n* (*US*) = **aluminium**.
always ['ɔːlweɪz] *adv* всегда́.
Alzheimer's disease ['æltshaɪməz-] *n* боле́знь *f* Алцхе́ймера.
AM *abbr* (= *amplitude modulation*) амплиту́дная модуля́ция.
am [æm] *vb see* **be**.
a.m. *adv abbr* (= *ante meridiem*) до полу́дня.
AMA *n abbr* = *American Medical Association*.
amalgam [ə'mælgəm] *n* амальга́ма.
amalgamate [ə'mælgəmeɪt] *vi* слива́ться (сли́ться *perf*) ◆ *vt* слива́ть (слить *perf*).
amalgamation [əmælgə'meɪʃən] *n* (*of companies*) слия́ние.
amass [ə'mæs] *vt* нака́пливать (накопи́ть* *perf*).
amateur ['æmətə*r*] *n* люби́тель *m*; ~ **sport/dramatics** люби́тельский* спорт/теа́тр; ~ **photographer** фото́граф-люби́тель *m*.
amateurish ['æmətərɪʃ] *adj* (*work, efforts*) непрофессиона́льный (непрофессиона́лен).
amaze [ə'meɪz] *vt* поража́ть (порази́ть* *perf*), изумля́ть (изуми́ть* *perf*); **I was ~d (at)** я был поражён (+*instr*).
amazement [ə'meɪzmənt] *n* изумле́ние.
amazing [ə'meɪzɪŋ] *adj* (*surprising*) порази́тельный* (порази́телен); (*fantastic*) изуми́тельный* (изуми́телен), замеча́тельный* (замеча́телен).
amazingly [ə'meɪzɪŋlɪ] *adv* порази́тельно.
Amazon ['æməzən] *n* (*river*) Амазо́нка; (*woman*) амазо́нка*; **the ~ basin** бассе́йн реки́ Амазо́нки; **the ~ jungle** джу́нгли *pl* Амазо́нки.
Amazonian [æmə'zəunɪən] *adj* (*GEO*) амазо́нский.
ambassador [æm'bæsədə*r*] *n* посо́л*.
amber ['æmbə*r*] *n* янта́рь* *m*; **the lights were at ~** на светофо́ре был жёлтый свет.
ambidextrous [æmbɪ'dɛkstrəs] *adj* одина́ково владе́ющий пра́вой и ле́вой руко́й.
ambience ['æmbɪəns] *n* атмосфе́ра.
ambiguity [æmbɪ'gjuɪtɪ] *n* двусмы́сленность *f*, нея́сность *f*.
ambiguous [æm'bɪgjuəs] *adj* двусмы́сленный, нея́сный*.
ambition [æm'bɪʃən] *n* (*quality: positive*) честолю́бие; (: *negative*) амби́ция; (*aim*) цель *f*; **to achieve one's ~** достига́ть (дости́чь* *perf*) свое́й це́ли.
ambitious [æm'bɪʃəs] *adj* честолюби́вый (честолюби́в); амбицио́зный* (амбицио́зен).
ambivalence [æm'bɪvələns] *n* (*indecision*) дво́йственное отноше́ние; (*ambiguity*) несоотве́тствия *ntpl*.
ambivalent [æm'bɪvələnt] *adj* (*attitude*) дво́йственный (дво́йствен); (*person*) противоречи́вый (противоречи́в).
amble ['æmbl] *vi* прогу́ливаться (прогуля́ться *perf*).

ambulance ['æmbjuləns] *n* ско́рая по́мощь *f*.
ambulanceman ['æmbjulənsmən] *irreg n* фе́льдшер ско́рой по́мощи.
ambush ['æmbuʃ] *n* заса́да ◆ *vt* устра́ивать (устро́ить* *perf*) заса́ду +*dat*.
ameba [ə'miːbə] *n* (*US*) = **amoeba**.
ameliorate [ə'miːlɪəreɪt] *vt* (*situation*) улучша́ть (улу́чшить *perf*).
amen ['ɑː'mɛn] *excl* ами́нь.
amenable [ə'miːnəbl] *adj*: ~ **to** пода́тливый (пода́тлив) на +*acc*; **he's ~ to advice** он прислу́шивается к сове́там; ~ **to the law** отве́тственный (отве́тствен) пе́ред зако́ном.
amend [ə'mɛnd] *vt* пересма́тривать (пересмотре́ть *perf*); (*habits*) исправля́ть (испра́вить* *perf*) ◆ *vi* исправля́ться (испра́виться* *perf*) ◆ *n*: **to make ~s** загла́живать (загла́дить* *perf*) вину́.
amendment [ə'mɛndmənt] *n* попра́вка*.
amenities [ə'miːnɪtɪz] *npl* удо́бства *ntpl*.
amenity [ə'miːnɪtɪ] *n* удо́бство.
America [ə'mɛrɪkə] *n* Аме́рика.
American [ə'mɛrɪkən] *adj* америка́нский* ◆ *n* америка́нец*(-нка).
americanize [ə'mɛrɪkənaɪz] *vt* американизи́ровать (*impf/perf*).
amethyst ['æmɪθɪst] *n* аметйст.
Amex ['æmɛks] *n abbr* = *American Stock Exchange*.
amiable ['eɪmɪəbl] *adj* дружелю́бный* (дружелю́бен).
amiably ['eɪmɪəblɪ] *adv* дружелю́бно.
amicable ['æmɪkəbl] *adj* (*relationship*) дру́жеский*; (*divorce*) ми́рный* (ми́рен).
amicably ['æmɪkəblɪ] *adv* по-дру́жески, ми́рно.
amid(st) [ə'mɪd(st)] *prep* посреди́ +*gen*.
amiss [ə'mɪs] *adj, adv*: **to take sth ~** оши́бочно истолко́вывать (истолкова́ть* *perf*) что-н; **there's something ~** что́-то нела́дно.
ammeter ['æmɪtə*r*] *n* амперме́тр.
ammo ['æməu] *n abbr* (*inf*) = **ammunition**.
ammonia [ə'məunɪə] *n* (*gas*) аммиа́к; (*liquid*) нашаты́рный спирт.
ammunition [æmju'nɪʃən] *n* (*MIL*) боеприпа́сы *pl*; (*for gun*) патро́ны *mpl*; (*fig*) ору́жие.
ammunition dump *n* склад боеприпа́сов.
amnesia [æm'niːzɪə] *n* амнези́я, утра́та па́мяти.
amnesty ['æmnɪstɪ] *n* амни́стия; **to grant an ~ to** объявля́ть (объяви́ть* *perf*) амни́стию +*dat*.
amoeba [ə'miːbə] *n* (*US* **ameba**) *n* амёба.
amok [ə'mɔk] *adv*: **to run ~** (*people*) беснова́ться (*impf*); (*animals*) беси́ться* (взбеси́ться *perf*).
among(st) [ə'mʌŋ(st)] *prep* среди́ +*gen*; (*between*) ме́жду +*instr*.
amoral [æ'mɔrəl] *adj* безнра́вственный* (безнра́вствен), амора́льный* (амора́лен).
amorous ['æmərəs] *adj* любо́вный.

amorphous [ə'mɔ:fəs] *adj* амóрфный* (амóрфен).

amortization [əmɔ:taɪ'zeɪʃən] *n* (*COMM*) амортизáция.

amount [ə'maunt] *n* колúчество; (*sum of money*) сýмма ♦ *vi*: **to ~ to** (*total*) составлять (состáвить* *perf*); **this ~s to a refusal** э́то равносúльно откáзу; **the total ~** (*of money*) óбщая сýмма.

amp(ère) ['æmp(εə')] *n* ампéр*; **a 13 amp plug** вúлка в 13 ампéр.

ampersand ['æmpəsænd] *n* знак "&" (*обозначáющий "и"*).

amphetamine [æm'fεtəmi:n] *n* амфетамúн.

amphibian [æm'fɪbɪən] *n* амфúбия, земновóдное живóтное *nt adj*.

amphibious [æm'fɪbɪəs] *adj* (*animal*) земновóдный; (*vehicle*) амфúбийный; **~ tank** танк-амфúбия.

amphitheatre ['æmfɪθɪətə'] (*US* **amphitheater**) *n* амфитеáтр.

ample ['æmpl] *adj* (*large*) большóй; (*abundant*) обúльный* (обúлен); (*enough*) достáточный (достáточен); **to have ~ time/room** имéть (*impf*) достáточно врéмени/мéста; **this is ~** э́того вполнé достáточно.

amplifier ['æmplɪfaɪə'] *n* усилúтель *m*.

amplify ['æmplɪfaɪ] *vt* усúливать (усúлить *perf*).

amply ['æmplɪ] *adv* вполнé.

ampoule ['æmpu:l] (*US* **ampule**) *n* áмпула.

amputate ['æmpjuteɪt] *vt* ампутúровать (*impf/ perf*).

amputation [æmpju'teɪʃən] *n* ампутáция.

amputee [æmpju'ti:] *n* инвалúд.

Amsterdam ['æmstədæm] *n* Амстердáм.

amt *abbr* (= **amount**) кол-во= *колúчество*.

amuck [ə'mʌk] *adv* = **amok**.

amuse [ə'mju:z] *vt* развлекáть (развлéчь* *perf*); **to ~ o.s. with sth** заняться (*perf*) *or* развлекáться (развлéчься* *perf*) чем-н; **he was ~d at this** его́ э́то позабáвило; **he was not ~d** емý бы́ло не до смéха.

amusement [ə'mju:zmənt] *n* (*mirth*) удовóльствие; (*pastime*) развлечéние; **much to my ~** к моемý осóбенному удовóльствию.

amusement arcade *n* павильóн с развлекáтельными аппарáтами.

amusement park *n* лунá-парк.

amusing [ə'mju:zɪŋ] *adj* забáвный* (забáвен), занимáтельный* (занимáтелен).

an [æn] *indef art see* **a**.

ANA *n abbr* = *American Newspaper Association*; *American Nurses Association*.

anachronism [ə'nækrənɪzəm] *n* анахронúзм.

anaemia [ə'ni:mɪə] (*US* **anemia**) *n* анемúя, малокрóвие.

anaemic [ə'ni:mɪk] (*US* **anemic**) *adj* (*MED, fig*) анемúчный* (анемúчен).

anaesthetic [ænɪs'θεtɪk] (*US* **anesthetic**) *n* наркóз; **under the ~** под наркóзом; **local/ general ~** мéстный/óбщий* наркóз.

anaesthetist [æ'ni:sθɪtɪst] (*US* **anesthetist**) *n* анестезиóлог.

anagram ['ænəgræm] *n* анаграмма.

anal ['eɪnl] *adj* анáльный, заднепроходный.

analgesic [ænæl'dʒi:sɪk] *adj* обезбóливающий* ♦ *n* обезбóливающее срéдство.

analog ['ænəlɒg] *adj* = **analogue**.

analogous [ə'næləgəs] *adj* аналогúчный* (аналогúчен).

analogue ['ænəlɒg] *adj* (*computer*) анáлоговый.

analogy [ə'nælədʒɪ] *n* аналóгия; **to draw an ~ between** проводúть* (провестú* *perf*) аналóгию мéжду +*instr*; **by ~** по аналóгии.

analyse ['ænəlaɪz] (*US* **analyze**) *vt* анализúровать (проанализúровать *perf*); (*PSYCH*): **to ~ sb** подвергáть (подвéргнуть* *perf*) когó-н психоанáлизу.

analyses [ə'næləsi:z] *npl of* **analysis**.

analysis [ə'næləsɪs] (*pl* **analyses**) *n* анáлиз; (*PSYCH*) психоанáлиз; **in the last ~** в конéчном итóге.

analyst ['ænəlɪst] *n* (*political*) комментáтор; (*financial, economic*) экспéрт; (*US*: *psychiatrist*) психиáтр.

analytic(al) [ænə'lɪtɪk(l)] *adj* аналитúческий.

analyze ['ænəlaɪz] *vt* (*US*) = **analyse**.

anarchic [æ'na:kɪk] *adj* анархúческий.

anarchist ['ænəkɪst] *adj* анархúческий ♦ *n* анархúст.

anarchy ['ænəkɪ] *n* анáрхия.

anathema [ə'næθɪmə] *n*: **that is ~ to him** для негó э́то анáфема.

anatomical [ænə'tɔmɪkl] *adj* анатомúческий.

anatomy [ə'nætəmɪ] *n* анатóмия; (*body*) органúзм.

ANC *n abbr* (= *African National Congress*) АНК= *Африкáнский* национáльный конгрéсс.

ancestor ['ænsɪstə'] *n* прéдок*.

ancestral [æn'sεstrəl] *adj* родовóй; **~ home** родовóе помéстье.

ancestry ['ænsɪstrɪ] *n* происхождéние.

anchor ['æŋkə'] *n* я́корь *m* ♦ *vi* (*also*: **to drop ~**) бросáть (брóсить* *perf*) я́корь; **to weigh ~** поднимáть (поднять* *perf*) я́корь.

anchorage ['æŋkərɪdʒ] *n* я́корная стоя́нка*.

anchor man *n* ведýщий* *m adj* (*прогрáммы*).

anchovy ['æntʃəvɪ] *n* анчóус*.

ancient ['eɪnʃənt] *adj* (*civilization, person*) дрéвний*; (*monument*) старúнный.

ancient monument *n* пáмятник старины́.

ancillary [æn'sɪlərɪ] *adj* подсóбный.

---

and [ænd] *conj* и; (*with pronouns*) с +*instr*;
you ~ I мы с Ва́ми; my father ~ I мы с отцо́м;
bread ~ butter хлеб с ма́слом; ~ so on и так
да́лее; try ~ come постара́йтесь прийти́; he
talked ~ talked он всё говори́л и говори́л.

Andes [ˈændi:z] *npl*: the ~ А́нды* *pl*.

Andorra [ænˈdɔ:rə] *n* Андо́рра.

anecdote [ˈænɪkdəut] *n* заба́вная исто́рия.

anemia *etc n* (*US*) = **anaemia** *etc*.

anemone [əˈnɛmənɪ] *n* ве́треница, анемо́на.

anesthetic *etc* (*US*) = **anaesthetic** *etc*.

anew [əˈnju:] *adv* за́ново.

angel [ˈeɪndʒəl] *n* а́нгел.

angel dust *n* (*drug*) „а́нгельская пыль" *f*.

angelic [ænˈdʒɛlɪk] *adj* а́нгельский*.

anger [ˈæŋgə*] *n* гнев, возмуще́ние ◆ *vt*
серди́ть* (рассерди́ть* *perf*), возмуща́ть
(возмути́ть* *perf*).

angina [ænˈdʒaɪmə] *n* грудна́я жа́ба.

angle [ˈæŋgl] *n* (*corner*) у́гол*; (*viewpoint*): from
their ~ с их то́чки зре́ния ◆ *vi*: to ~ for
(*invitation*) напра́шиваться (напроси́ться*
perf) на +*acc* ◆ *vt*: the idea is/was ~d towards *or*
to иде́я рассчи́тана/была́ рассчи́тана на
+*acc*.

angler [ˈæŋglə*] *n* рыболо́в.

Anglican [ˈæŋglɪkən] *adj* англика́нский* ◆ *n*
англика́нец(-а́нка).

anglicize [ˈæŋglɪsaɪz] *vt* англизи́ровать (*impf*).

angling [ˈæŋglɪŋ] *n* ры́бная ло́вля.

Anglo- [ˈæŋgləu] *prefix* а́нгло-.

Anglo-Saxon [ˈæŋgləuˈsæksən] *adj* англо-
саксо́нский; (*LING*) древнеангли́йский ◆ *n*
англосакс; (*LING*) древнеангли́йский язы́к*.

Angola [æŋˈgəulə] *n* Анго́ла.

Angolan [æŋˈgəulən] *adj* анго́льский* ◆ *n*
анго́лец*(-лка*).

angrily [ˈæŋgrɪlɪ] *adv* серди́то, гне́вно.

angry [ˈæŋgrɪ] *adj* серди́тый (серди́т),
гне́вный (гне́вен); (*wound*) воспалённый
(воспалён); to be ~ with sb/at sth серди́ться*
(*impf*) *or* зли́ться (*impf*) на кого́-н/что́-н; to get
~ серди́ться* (рассерди́ться* *perf*), зли́ться
(разозли́ться *perf*); he gets ~ easily его́ легко́
рассерди́ть; to make sb ~ серди́ть*
(рассерди́ть* *perf*) *or* злить (разозли́ть *perf*)
кого́-н.

anguish [ˈæŋgwɪʃ] *n* му́ка.

anguished [ˈæŋgwɪʃt] *adj* страда́льческий*.

angular [ˈæŋgjulə*] *adj* (*person, features*)
углова́тый (углова́т).

animal [ˈænɪməl] *n* живо́тное *nt adj*; (*wild
animal*) зверь* *m*; (*pej: person*) зверь,
живо́тное ◆ *adj* живо́тный.

animal rights [-raɪts] *npl* права́ *ntpl* живо́тных;
the ~ ~ movement движе́ние за права́
живо́тных.

animate [*vb* ˈænɪmeɪt, *adj* ˈænɪmɪt] *vt* оживля́ть
(оживи́ть* *perf*) ◆ *adj* живо́й* (жив); (*LING*)
одушевлённый.

animated [ˈænɪmeɪtɪd] *adj* оживлённый*

(оживлён), живо́й* (жив); (*film*)
мультипликацио́нный.

animation [ænɪˈmeɪʃən] *n* (*CINEMA*)
мультипликация; (*enthusiasm*) оживле́ние.

animosity [ænɪˈmɔsɪtɪ] *n* враждёбность *f*.

aniseed [ˈænɪsi:d] *n* ани́с ◆ *adj* ани́совый.

Ankara [ˈæŋkərə] *n* Анкара́.

ankle [ˈæŋkl] *n* лоды́жка*.

ankle sock *n* носо́к*.

annex [ˈænɛks] *n* (*also*: ~e: *BRIT*) пристро́йка;
(: *separate building*) отде́льный ко́рпус ◆ *vt*
аннекси́ровать (*impf/perf*).

annexation [ænɛkˈseɪʃən] *n* анне́ксия.

annihilate [əˈnaɪɪleɪt] *vt* уничтожа́ть
(уничто́жить *perf*).

annihilation [ənaɪəˈleɪʃən] *n* уничтоже́ние.

anniversary [ænɪˈvə:sərɪ] *n* годовщи́на.

Anno Domini [ˈænəuˈdɔmɪnaɪ] *adv* на́шей э́ры.

annotate [ˈænəuteɪt] *vt* анноти́ровать
(проанноти́ровать *perf*).

announce [əˈnauns] *vt* (*decision, engagement*)
объявля́ть (объяви́ть* *perf*) (о +*prp*); (*birth,
death etc*) извеща́ть (извести́ть* *perf*) о +*prp*;
he ~d that he wasn't going он заяви́л, что не
пойдёт.

announcement [əˈnaunsmənt] *n* объявле́ние;
(*in newspaper etc*) сообще́ние; (*in letter etc*)
извеще́ние; I'd like to make an ~ я бы хоте́л
сде́лать заявле́ние.

announcer [əˈnaunsə*] *n* (*RADIO, TV*) ди́ктор.

annoy [əˈnɔɪ] *vt* раздража́ть (раздражи́ть
perf); I am ~ed with him он меня́ раздража́ет;
don't get ~ed! не раздража́йтесь *or*
серди́тесь!

annoyance [əˈnɔɪəns] *n* (*feeling*) раздраже́ние,
доса́да.

annoyed [əˈnɔɪd] *adj* раздражённый*
(раздражён).

annoying [əˈnɔɪɪŋ] *adj* (*noise*) раздража́ющий;
(*mistake, event*) доса́дный* (доса́ден); he is ~
он меня́ раздража́ет.

annual [ˈænjuəl] *adj* (*meeting*) ежего́дный;
(*income*) годово́й ◆ *n* (*BOT*) одноле́тнее
расте́ние; (*book*) ежего́дник.

annual general meeting *n* (*BRIT*) ежего́дное
о́бщее собра́ние.

annually [ˈænjuəlɪ] *adv* ежего́дно.

annual report *n* годово́й отчёт.

annuity [əˈnju:ɪtɪ] *n* ре́нта; life ~ пожи́зненная
ре́нта.

annul [əˈnʌl] *vt* (*contract*) аннули́ровать (*impf*
perf); (*marriage*) расторга́ть (расто́ргнуть*
perf); (*law*) отменя́ть (отмени́ть* *perf*).

annulment [əˈnʌlmənt] *n* (*see vt*)
аннули́рование; расторже́ние; отме́на.

annum [ˈænəm] *n see* per.

Annunciation [ənʌnsɪˈeɪʃən] *n* Благове́щение.

anode [ˈænəud] *n* ано́д.

anodyne [ˈænədaɪn] *n* успока́ивающее
сре́дство ◆ *adj* нейтра́льный* (нейтра́лен).

anoint [əˈnɔɪnt] *vt* пома́зывать (пома́зать*

anomalous [ə'nɔmələs] *adj* анома́льный*
(анома́лен).

anomaly [ə'nɔmǝlɪ] *n* анома́лия.

anon. [ə'nɔn] *abbr* = **anonymous**.

anonymity [ænə'nɪmɪtɪ] *n* анони́мность *f*.

anonymous [ə'nɔnɪməs] *adj* анони́мный*
(анони́мен); (*place*) безли́кий* (безли́к); **to
remain** ~ сохраня́ть (сохрани́ть *perf*)
анони́мность.

anorak [ˈænɔræk] *n* ку́ртка* с капюшо́ном.

anorexia [ænǝ'rɛksɪǝ] *n* аноре́ксия.

anorexic [ænǝ'rɛksɪk] *adj*: **she is** ~ она́
страда́ет аноре́ксией.

another [ə'nʌðə'] *pron* друго́й ◆ *adj*: ~ **book**
(*additional*) ещё одна́ кни́га; (*different*)
друга́я кни́га; **I waited** ~ **week** я ждал ещё
одну́ неде́лю; ~ **drink?** Вам ещё нали́ть?; **in**
~ **5 years** ещё че́рез 5 лет; *see also* **one**.

ANSI *n abbr* (= *American National Standards
Institute*) Институ́т америка́нских
национа́льных станда́ртов.

answer [ˈɑːnsə'] *n* отве́т; (*to problem*) реше́ние
◆ *vi* отвеча́ть (отве́тить* *perf*) ◆ *vt* (*letter,
question*) отвеча́ть (отве́тить* *perf*) на +*acc*;
(*person*) отвеча́ть (отве́тить* *perf*) +*dat*; **in** ~
to your letter в отве́т на Ва́ше письмо́; **to** ~
the phone подходи́ть (подойти́* *perf*) к
телефо́ну; **to** ~ **the bell** *or* **the door** открыва́ть
(откры́ть* *perf*) дверь; **our prayers were** ~**ed**
на́ши моли́твы бы́ли услы́шаны
▸ **answer back** *vi* огрыза́ться (*impf*)
▸ **answer for** *vt fus* отвеча́ть (отве́тить* *perf*) за
+*acc*
▸ **answer to** *vt fus* (*description*) соотве́тст-
вовать (*impf*) +*dat*.

answerable [ˈɑːnsǝrǝbl] *adj*: ~ **to sb for sth**
отве́тственный* пе́ред кем-н за что-н; **I am** ~
to no-one я не отвеча́ю ни пе́ред кем.

answering machine [ˈɑːnsǝrɪŋ-] *n*
автоотве́тчик.

ant [ænt] *n* мураве́й*.

ANTA *n abbr* = *American National Theater and
Academy.*

antagonism [ænˈtægǝnɪzǝm] *n* антагони́зм.

antagonist [ænˈtægǝnɪst] *n* проти́вник.

antagonistic [æntægǝ'nɪstɪk] *adj* (*feelings*)
вражде́бный* (вражде́бен); **he is** ~ **to the
government** он вражде́бен по отноше́нию к
прави́тельству.

antagonize [ænˈtægǝnaɪz] *vt*: **to** ~ **sb** вызыва́ть
(вы́звать* *perf*) чьё-н вражде́бное
отноше́ние.

Antarctic [æntˈɑːktɪk] *n*: **the** ~ Анта́рктика.

Antarctica [æntˈɑːktɪkǝ] *n* Антаркти́да.

Antarctic Circle *n*: **the** ~ ~ Ю́жный поля́рный
круг.

Antarctic Ocean *n*: **the** ~ ~ Антаркти́ческий*

океа́н.

ante [ˈæntɪ] *n*: **to up the** ~ повыша́ть
(повы́сить* *perf*) ста́вку.

ante... [ˈæntɪ] *prefix* до..., пред....

anteater [ˈænti:tǝ'] *n* муравье́д.

antecedent [æntɪ'si:dǝnt] *n* предше́ственник;
(*ancestor*) пре́док*.

antechamber [ˈæntɪtʃeɪmbǝ'] *n* пере́дняя *f adj*,
прихо́жая *f adj*.

antelope [ˈæntɪlǝup] *n* антило́па.

antenatal [ˈæntɪ'neɪtl] *adj* дородово́й.

antenatal clinic *n* ≈ же́нская консульта́ция.

antenna [ænˈtɛnǝ] (*pl* ~**e**) *n* у́сик; (*RADIO, TV*)
анте́нна.

antennae [ænˈtɛni:] *npl of* **antenna**.

anteroom [ˈæntɪrum] *n* приёмная *f adj*.

anthem [ˈænθǝm] *n*: **national** ~
госуда́рственный гимн.

ant hill *n* мураве́йник.

anthology [ænˈθɔlǝdʒɪ] *n* антоло́гия.

anthropologist [ænθrǝ'pɔlǝdʒɪst] *n*
антропо́лог.

anthropology [ænθrǝ'pɔlǝdʒɪ] *n*
антрополо́гия.

anti... [ˈæntɪ] *prefix* а́нти..., про́тиво....

anti-aircraft [ˈæntɪ'ɛǝkrɑːft] *adj* (*missile*)
противовозду́шный.

anti-aircraft defence *n* противовозду́шная
оборо́на.

antiballistic [ˈæntɪbǝ'lɪstɪk] *adj* (*missile*)
антибаллисти́ческий.

antibiotic [ˈæntɪbaɪ'ɔtɪk] *n* (*MED*) антибио́тик.

antibody [ˈæntɪbɔdɪ] *n* антите́ло*.

anticipate [ænˈtɪsɪpeɪt] *vt* (*expect*) ожида́ть
(*impf*) +*gen*; (*foresee*) предви́деть* (*impf*/*perf*);
(*look forward to*) предвкуша́ть (*impf*);
(*forestall*) предвосхища́ть (предвосхи́тить*
perf); **this is worse than I** ~**d** э́то ху́же, чем я
ожида́л; **as** ~**d** как предполага́лось.

anticipation [æntɪsɪ'peɪʃǝn] *n* (*expectation*)
ожида́ние; (*eagerness*) предвкуше́ние;
thanking you in ~ зара́нее благодарю́ Вас.

anticlimax [ˈæntɪ'klaɪmæks] *n* разочарова́ние.

anticlockwise [ˈæntɪ'klɔkwaɪz] *adv* (*BRIT*)
про́тив часово́й стре́лки.

antics [ˈæntɪks] *npl* (*of animal, child*) ша́лости
fpl; (*of clown*) проде́лки *pl*; (*of politicians etc*)
вы́ходки *pl*.

anticyclone [ˈæntɪ'saɪklǝun] *n* антицикло́н.

antidote [ˈæntɪdǝut] *n* (*also fig*) противоя́дие.

antifreeze [ˈæntɪfri:z] *n* антифри́з.

antihistamine [ˈæntɪ'hɪstǝmɪn] *n*
антигистами́н.

Antilles [ænˈtɪli:z] *npl*: **the** ~ Анти́льские
острова́ *mpl*.

antipathy [ænˈtɪpǝθɪ] *n* антипа́тия.

antiperspirant [ˈæntɪ'pǝ:spɪrǝnt] *n* дезодора́нт.

Antipodean [æntɪpǝ'di:ǝn] *adj* антипо́дный

---

* marks translations which have irregular inflections. The Russian-English side of the dictionary gives inflectional information.

(*обычно о жителях Австра́лии и Но́вой Зела́ндии*).

Antipodes [æn'tɪpədiːz] *npl*: **the ~** Австра́лия и Но́вая Зела́ндия.

antiquarian [æntɪ'kweərɪən] *n* антиква́р ◆ *adj*: **~ bookshop** букинисти́ческий• магази́н.

antiquated ['æntɪkweɪtɪd] *adj* устаре́лый.

antique [æn'tiːk] *n* предме́т старины́ ◆ *adj* (*furniture etc*) антиква́рный•; (*pre-medieval*) анти́чный.

antique dealer *n* антиква́р.

antique shop *n* антиква́рный магази́н.

antiquity [æn'tɪkwɪtɪ] *n* анти́чность *f*.

anti-Semitic ['æntɪsɪ'mɪtɪk] *adj* анти-семи́тский•.

anti-Semitism ['æntɪ'semɪtɪzəm] *n* анти-семити́зм.

antiseptic [æntɪ'septɪk] *n* антисе́птик ◆ *adj* антисепти́ческий•.

antisocial ['æntɪ'səʊʃəl] *adj* (*behaviour*) антиобще́ственный; (*person*) необщи́тельный• (необщи́телен).

antitank ['æntɪ'tæŋk] *adj* противота́нковый.

antitheses [æn'tɪθɪsiːz] *npl of* **antithesis**.

antithesis [æn'tɪθɪsɪs] (*pl* **antitheses**) *n* антите́за.

antitrust ['æntɪ'trʌst] *adj*: **~ legislation** антимонопо́льное законода́тельство.

antlers ['æntləz] *npl* (оле́ньи) рога́• *mpl*.

Antwerp ['æntwəːp] *n* Антве́рпен.

anus ['eɪnəs] *n* за́дний• прохо́д.

anvil ['ænvɪl] *n* накова́льня•.

anxiety [æŋ'zaɪətɪ] *n* (*also MED*) трево́га; **~ to do** стремле́ние +*infin*.

anxious ['æŋkʃəs] *adj* (*person*) беспоко́йный• (беспоко́ен); (*expression*) озабо́ченный• (озабо́чен); (*worrying*) трево́жный• (трево́жен); (*keen*): **she is ~ to do** она́ о́чень хо́чет +*infin*; **to be ~ about** беспоко́иться (*impf*) о +*prp*; **I'm very ~ about you** я о́чень беспоко́юсь за Вас.

anxiously ['æŋkʃəslɪ] *adv* беспоко́йно, трево́жно.

KEYWORD

any ['enɪ] *adj* **1** (*in questions etc*): **have you any butter/children?** у Вас есть ма́сло/де́ти?; **do you have any questions/doubts?** у Вас есть каки́е-нибудь вопро́сы/сомне́ния?; **if there are any tickets left** е́сли ещё оста́лись биле́ты
2 (*with negative*): **I haven't any bread/books** у меня́ нет хле́ба/книг; **I didn't buy/read any newspapers** я не купи́л/не чита́л газе́ты
3 (*no matter which*) любо́й; **any colour will do** любо́й цвет пойдёт; **choose any book you like** выбира́йте любу́ю кни́гу, кака́я Вам понра́вится
4 (*in phrases*): **in any case** в любо́м слу́чае; **any day now** сейча́с в любо́й день; **at any moment** в любо́й моме́нт; **at any rate** во вся́ком слу́чае; (*anyhow*) так и́ли ина́че; **any time** (*at any moment*) в любо́й моме́нт;

(*whenever*) в любо́е вре́мя; (*in answer to thanks*) не́ за что; **I need some black leather boots – have you any?** мне нужны́ чёрные ко́жаные сапоги́ – у Вас таки́е есть?; **I have run out of sugar, you don't have any?** у меня́ ко́нчился са́хар, у Вас не найдётся немно́го?
◆ *pron* **1** (*in questions etc*): **I need some money, have you got any?** мне нужны́ де́ньги, у Вас они́ есть?; **can any of you sing?** кто́-нибудь из Вас уме́ет петь?
2 (*with negative*) ни оди́н (*f* одна́, *nt* одно́, *pl* одни́); **I haven't any (of those)** у меня́ таки́х нет
3 (*no matter which one(s)*) любо́й; **take any you like** возьми́те то, что Вам нра́вится
◆ *adv* **1** (*in questions etc*): **do you want any more soup/sandwiches?** хоти́те ещё су́па/бутербро́ды?; **are you feeling any better?** Вам хоть чуть-чуть лу́чше?
2 (*with negative*): **I can't hear him any more** я бо́льше его́ не слы́шу; **don't wait any longer** не жди́те бо́льше; **he isn't any better** ему́ ниско́лько *or* ничу́ть не лу́чше.

anybody ['enɪbɔdɪ] *pron* = **anyone**.

anyhow ['enɪhaʊ] *adv* (*at any rate*) так и́ли ина́че; (*haphazardly*): **the work is done ~** рабо́та сде́лана ко́е-как *or* как попа́ло; **I shall go ~** я так и́ли ина́че пойду́; **she leaves things just ~** она́ разбра́сывает ве́щи как попа́ло.

anyone ['enɪwʌn] *pron* (*in questions etc*) кто́-нибудь; (*with negative*) никто́; (*no matter who*) кто угодно, любо́й, вся́кий•; **can you see ~?** Вы ви́дите кого́-нибудь?; **I can't see ~** я никого́ не ви́жу; **~ could do it** кто угодно *or* любо́й *or* вся́кий• мо́жет э́то сде́лать; **you can invite ~** Вы мо́жете пригласи́ть кого́ угодно.

anyplace ['enɪpleɪs] *adv* (*US*) = **anywhere**.

KEYWORD

anything ['enɪθɪŋ] *pron* **1** (*in questions etc*) что́-нибудь; **can you see anything?** Вы ви́дите что́-нибудь?
2 (*with negative*) ничего́; **I can't see anything** я ничего́ не ви́жу
3 (*no matter what*) (всё,) что угодно; **anything (at all) will do** всё, (что угодно) подойдёт; **he'll eat anything** он ест всё, что ему́ ни дай.

anyway ['enɪweɪ] *adv* (*at any rate*) всё равно́; (*besides*) всё равно́, в любо́м слу́чае; **I'll be there ~** я всё равно́ там бу́ду; **~, I couldn't stay even if I wanted to** всё равно́ *or* в любо́м слу́чае, я не мог бы оста́ться, да́же е́сли бы я захоте́л; **why are you phoning, ~?** а что Вы звони́те?

KEYWORD

anywhere ['enɪweə'] *adv* **1** (*in questions etc*: *position*) где́-нибудь; (: *motion*) куда́-

нибудь; **can you see him anywhere?** Вы его́ где́-нибудь ви́дите?; **did you walk anywhere yesterday?** Вы вчера́ куда́-нибудь ходи́ли? **2** (with negative: position) нигде́; (: motion) никуда́; **I can't see him anywhere** я нигде́ его́ не ви́жу; **I'm not walking anywhere today** сего́дня я никуда́ не иду́ **3** (no matter where: position) где уго́дно; (: motion) куда́ уго́дно; **anywhere in the world** где уго́дно в ми́ре; **put the books down anywhere** положи́те кни́ги куда́ уго́дно.

Anzac ['ænzæk] n abbr = Australia-New Zealand Army Corps.

apace [ə'peɪs] adv стреми́тельно.

apart [ə'pɑːt] adv (position) в стороне́; (motion) в сто́рону; (separately) разде́льно, врозь; **they are ten miles/a long way** ~ они́ нахо́дятся на расстоя́нии десяти́ миль/на большо́м расстоя́нии друг от дру́га; **they are living** ~ они́ живу́т врозь; **they jumped** ~ они́ отпры́гнули в сто́роны; **with one's legs** ~ с расста́вленными нога́ми; **to take** ~ разбира́ть (разобра́ть* perf) (на ча́сти); ~ **from** кро́ме +gen.

apartheid [ə'pɑːteɪt] n апарте́ид.

apartment [ə'pɑːtmənt] n (US) кварти́ра; (room) ко́мната.

apartment building n (US) многокварти́рный дом*.

apathetic [æpə'θɛtɪk] adj апати́чный* (апати́чен).

apathy ['æpəθɪ] n апа́тия.

APB n abbr (US: = all points bulletin) ≈ сигна́л всем поста́м.

ape [eɪp] n (ZOOL) человекообра́зная обезья́на ◆ vt копи́ровать (скопи́ровать perf).

Apennines ['æpənaɪnz] npl: **the** ~ Апенни́ны pl.

aperitif [ə'pɛrɪtiːf] n аперити́в.

aperture ['æpətʃjuə'] n отве́рстие; (PHOT) диафра́гма.

apex ['eɪpɛks] n (also fig) верши́на.

aphid ['eɪfɪd] n тля*.

aphorism ['æfərɪzəm] n афори́зм.

aphrodisiac [æfrəu'dɪzɪæk] n сре́дство, возбужда́ющее полово́е влече́ние ◆ adj возбужда́ющий* полово́е влече́ние.

API n abbr = American Press Institute.

apiece [ə'piːs] adv (each person) на ка́ждого; (each thing) за шту́ку.

aplomb [ə'plɔm] n апло́мб.

APO n abbr (US) = Army Post Office.

apocalypse [ə'pɔkəlɪps] n (end of world) коне́ц* све́та; (destruction) катастро́фа.

apolitical [eɪpə'lɪtɪkl] adj аполити́чный* (аполити́чен).

apologetic [əpɔlə'dʒɛtɪk] adj (tone) извиня́ющийся*; (person, expression) винова́тый; **an** ~ **letter** письмо́* с

извине́ниями; **he's very** ~ **about** ... он прино́сит свои́ извине́ния за +acc ....

apologize [ə'pɔlədʒaɪz] vi: **to** ~ **(for sth to sb)** извиня́ться (извини́ться perf) (за что́-н пе́ред кем-н).

apology [ə'pɔlədʒɪ] n извине́ние; **to send one's apologies** извиня́ться (извини́ться* perf) за своё отсу́тствие; **please accept my apologies** пожа́луйста, прими́те мои́ извине́ния.

apoplectic [æpə'plɛktɪk] adj (MED) апоплекси́ческий; (fig): ~ **with rage** разъярённый (разъярён).

apoplexy ['æpəplɛksɪ] n апопле́ксия.

apostle [ə'pɔsl] n апо́стол.

apostrophe [ə'pɔstrəfɪ] n апостро́ф.

apotheosis [əpɔθɪ'əusɪs] n (deification) обожествле́ние; (fig) апофео́з.

appal [ə'pɔːl] vt ужаса́ть (ужасну́ть perf); **to be** ~**led by** ужаса́ться (ужасну́ться perf) +dat.

Appalachian Mountains [æpə'leɪʃən-] npl: **the** ~ ~ Аппала́чи pl.

appalling [ə'pɔːlɪŋ] adj (awful) ужа́сный* (ужа́сен); (shocking) ужаса́ющий*; **she's an** ~ **cook** она́ ужа́сно гото́вит.

apparatus [æpə'reɪtəs] n аппарату́ра; (in gymnasium) (гимнасти́ческий) снаря́д; (of organization) аппара́т.

apparel [ə'pærl] n (esp US) одея́ние.

apparent [ə'pærənt] adj (seeming) ви́димый; (obvious) очеви́дный* (очеви́ден); **it is** ~ **that** ... очеви́дно, что ....

apparently [ə'pærəntlɪ] adv по всей ви́димости.

apparition [æpə'rɪʃən] n виде́ние, при́зрак.

appeal [ə'piːl] vi (LAW) апелли́ровать (impf/perf), подава́ть (пода́ть* perf) апелля́цию ◆ n (attraction) привлека́тельность f; (plea) при́зыв; (LAW) апелля́ция, обжа́лование; **to** ~ **(to sb) for** (help, funds) обраща́ться (обрати́ться* perf) (к кому́-н) за +instr; (calm, order) призыва́ть (призва́ть* perf) (кого́-н) к +dat; **to** ~ **(be attractive to)** привлека́ть (привле́чь* perf), нра́виться (понра́виться perf) +dat; **to** ~ **to sb for mercy** взыва́ть (воззва́ть* perf) к кому́-н о милосе́рдии; **the idea doesn't** ~ **to me** э́та иде́я не привлека́ет меня́; **right of** ~ пра́во на апелля́цию or на обжа́лование; **on** ~ (LAW) на апелля́ции.

appealing [ə'piːlɪŋ] adj (attractive) привлека́тельный* (привлека́телен); (touching) тро́гательный* (тро́гателен); (pleading) умоля́ющий*.

appear [ə'pɪə'] vi (come into view, develop) появля́ться (появи́ться* perf); (seem) каза́ться* (показа́ться* perf); (be published) выходи́ть* (вы́йти* perf); **to** ~ **in court** представа́ть* (предста́ть* perf) пе́ред судо́м; **to** ~ **on TV** выступа́ть (вы́ступить* perf) по

---

* marks translations which have irregular inflections. The Russian-English side of the dictionary gives inflectional information.

телеви́дению; **to ~ in "Hamlet"** игра́ть
(сыгра́ть *perf*) в "Га́млете"; **it would ~ that ...**
похо́же (на то), что ....

appearance [ə'pɪərəns] *n* (*arrival*) появле́ние;
(*look, aspect*) вне́шность *f*; (*in public, on TV*)
выступле́ние; **to put in** *or* **make an ~**
появля́ться (появи́ться* *perf*); **cast in** *or* **by
order of ~** (*THEAT*) соста́в исполни́телей в
поря́дке появле́ния; **to keep up ~s**
соблюда́ть (соблюсти́* *perf*) прили́чия; **to** *or*
by all ~s су́дя по всему́.

appease [ə'pi:z] *vt* (*person, country*)
умиротворя́ть (умиротвори́ть *perf*).

appeasement [ə'pi:zmənt] *n* (*POL*)
умиротворе́ние.

append [ə'pɛnd] *vt* (*COMPUT*) добавля́ть
(доба́вить* *perf*) (в коне́ц), присоединя́ть
(присоедини́ть *perf*).

appendage [ə'pɛndɪdʒ] *n* прида́ток*.

appendices [ə'pɛndɪsi:z] *npl of* **appendix**.

appendicitis [əpɛndɪ'saɪtɪs] *n* аппендици́т.

appendix [ə'pɛndɪks] (*pl* **appendices**) *n*
приложе́ние; (*ANAT*) аппе́ндикс; **he had his ~
out** ему́ вы́резали аппенди́цит.

appetite ['æpɪtaɪt] *n* аппети́т; (*fig*) страсть* *f*;
that walk has given me an ~ по́сле прогу́лки
у меня́ разыгра́лся.

appetizer ['æpɪtaɪzə'] *n* (*food*) заку́ска*; (*drink*)
аперити́в.

appetizing ['æpɪtaɪzɪŋ] *adj* (*smell*) аппети́тный.

applaud [ə'plɔ:d] *vi* (*clap*) аплоди́ровать (*impf*),
рукоплеска́ть* (*impf*) ♦ *vt* аплоди́ровать (*impf*)
+*dat*, рукоплеска́ть* (*impf*) +*dat*; (*praise*)
одобря́ть (одо́брить *perf*).

applause [ə'plɔ:z] *n* (*clapping*) аплодисме́нты
pl.

apple ['æpl] *n* я́блоко*; **he's the ~ of her eye**
она́ в нём души́ не ча́ет.

apple tree *n* я́блоня.

apple turnover *n* слоёный пирожо́к с
я́блоком.

appliance [ə'plaɪəns] *n* (*electrical, domestic*)
прибо́р.

applicable [ə'plɪkəbl] *adj*: ~ **(to)** примен́имый
(примени́м) (к +*dat*); **the law is ~ from
January** зако́н вступа́ет в си́лу с января́.

applicant ['æplɪkənt] *n* (*for job, scholarship*)
кандида́т; (*for college*) абитурие́нт.

application [æplɪ'keɪʃən] *n* (*for a job, a grant etc*)
заявле́ние; (*hard work*) стара́ние; (*of cream,
paint*) нанесе́ние; **on** ~ (*of rule, knowledge*) по
зая́вке; (*of methods*) примене́ние.

application form *n* заявле́ние-анке́та.

application program *n* (*COMPUT*) прикладна́я
програ́мма.

applications package *n* (*COMPUT*) паке́т
прикладны́х програ́мм.

applied [ə'plaɪd] *adj* (*science, art*) прикладно́й.

apply [ə'plaɪ] *vt* (*paint, makeup*) наноси́ть*
(нанести́* *perf*); (*bandage*) накла́дывать
(наложи́ть *perf*); (*theory, law*) применя́ть

(примени́ть* *perf*) ♦ *vi*: **to ~ to** (*be applicable*)
применя́ться (*impf*) к +*dat*; (*ask*) обраща́ться
(обрати́ться* *perf*) (с про́сьбой) к +*dat*; **to ~
the brakes** нажима́ть (нажа́ть* *perf*) на
тормоза́; **to ~ o.s. to** сосредота́чиваться
(сосредото́читься *perf*) на +*prp*; **to ~ for a
grant/job** подава́ть* (пода́ть* *perf*) заявле́ние
на стипе́ндию/о приёме на рабо́ту.

appoint [ə'pɔɪnt] *vt* назнача́ть (назна́чить *perf*).

appointed [ə'pɔɪntɪd] *adj*: **at the ~ time** в
назна́ченное вре́мя*.

appointee [əpɔɪn'ti:] *n* получи́вший(-ая) *m(f)*
adj назначе́ние.

appointment [ə'pɔɪntmənt] *n* (*of person*)
назначе́ние; (*post*) до́лжность* *f*; (*arranged
meeting*) приём; **to make an ~ (with sb)**
назнача́ть (назна́чить* *perf*) (кому́-н) встре́чу
or свида́ние; **I have an ~ with the director/the
doctor** я запи́сан на приём к мини́стру/к
врачу́; **to make an ~ with the hairdresser/
doctor** запи́са́ться* (*perf*) в парикма́херскую/
на приём к врачу́; **by ~** по за́писи.

apportion [ə'pɔ:ʃən] *vt* распределя́ть
(распредели́ть *perf*); **to ~ sth to sb** наделя́ть
(надели́ть *perf*) кого́-н чем-н; **to ~ blame to
sb** возлага́ть (возложи́ть *perf*) вину́ на
кого́-н.

apposition [æpə'zɪʃən] *n* приложе́ние.

appraisal [ə'preɪzl] *n* оце́нка*.

appraise [ə'preɪz] *vt* оце́нивать (оцени́ть* *perf*).

appreciable [ə'pri:ʃəbl] *adj* значи́тельный.

appreciably [ə'pri:ʃəblɪ] *adv* заме́тно,
ощути́мо.

appreciate [ə'pri:ʃeɪt] *vt* (*value*) цени́ть* (*impf*);
(*understand*) понима́ть (поня́ть* *perf*) ♦ *vi*
(*COMM*) повыша́ться (повы́ситься* *perf*) в
цене́; **I ~ your help** я благода́рен Вам за
по́мощь; **he ~s good cooking/opera** он
цени́тель хоро́шей ку́хни/о́перы.

appreciation [əpri:ʃɪ'eɪʃən] *n* (*understanding*)
понима́ние; (*gratitude*) призна́тельность *f*;
(*COMM*) повыше́ние сто́имости.

appreciative [ə'pri:ʃɪətɪv] *adj* (*person, audience*)
призна́тельный* (призна́телен); (*comment*)
одобри́тельный* (одобри́телен).

apprehend [æprɪ'hɛnd] *vt* (*arrest*) заде́рживать
(задержа́ть* *perf*); (*understand*) понима́ть
(поня́ть* *perf*).

apprehension [æprɪ'hɛnʃən] *n* опасе́ние; (*of
criminal*) задержа́ние.

apprehensive [æprɪ'hɛnsɪv] *adj* (*glance etc*)
опа́сливый; **to be ~ about sth** опаса́ться
(*impf*) за что-н.

apprentice [ə'prɛntɪs] *n* подмасте́рье*, учени́к*
♦ *vt*: **to be ~d to sb** быть (*impf*) в уче́нии у
кого́-н.

apprenticeship [ə'prɛntɪsʃɪp] *n* (*also fig*)
учени́чество; **to serve one's ~** проходи́ть*
(пройти́* *perf*) обуче́ние.

appro. ['æprəʊ] *abbr* (*BRIT: inf: COMM:*) =
approval): **on ~** на про́бу.

approach [ə'prəutʃ] *vi* приближа́ться
(прибли́зиться* *perf*) ◆ *vt* (*ask, apply to*)
обраща́ться (обрати́ться* *perf*) к +*dat*; (*come
to*) приближа́ться (прибли́зиться* *perf*) к
+*dat*; (*consider*) подходи́ть* (подойти́* *perf*) к
+*dat* ◆ *n* (*advance: also fig*) приближе́ние;
(*access: on foot*) подхо́д; (: *by transport*)
подъе́зд; (*to problem, situation*) подхо́д; **to ~
sb about sth** обраща́ться (обрати́ться* *perf*) к
кому́-н с предложе́нием о чём-н.
approachable [ə'prəutʃəbl] *adj* (*person, place*)
досту́пный* (досту́пен).
approach road *n* подъездно́й путь* *m*.
approbation [æprə'beɪʃən] *n* одобре́ние.
appropriate [*adj* ə'prəuprɪɪt, *vb* ə'prəuprɪeɪt] *adj*
(*behaviour*) подоба́ющий*; (*remarks*)
уме́стный; (*tools*) подходя́щий* ◆ *vt*
присва́ивать (присво́ить *perf*); **it would not
be ~ for me to comment** бы́ло бы неуме́стно
с мое́й стороны́ комменти́ровать; **it is not ~
for you to behave like that** Вам не подоба́ет
вести́ себя́ так.
appropriately [ə'prəuprɪɪtlɪ] *adv* подоба́ющим
or соотве́тствующим о́бразом.
appropriation [əprəuprɪ'eɪʃən] *n* присвое́ние.
appropriation account *n* счёт ассигнова́ний.
approval [ə'pru:vəl] *n* одобре́ние; (*permission*)
согла́сие; **to meet with sb's ~** получа́ть
(получи́ть* *perf*) чьё-н одобре́ние; **on ~**
(*COMM*) на про́бу.
approve [ə'pru:v] *vt* (*motion, decision*)
одобря́ть (одо́брить *perf*); (*publication,
product*) утвержда́ть (утверди́ть* *perf*)
▶ **approve of** *vt fus* одобря́ть (одо́брить *perf*).
approved school [ə'pru:vd-] *n* (*BRIT: formerly*)
исправи́тельная шко́ла.
approvingly [ə'pru:vɪŋlɪ] *adv* одобри́тельно.
approx. *abbr* = **approximately**.
approximate [*adj* ə'prɔksɪmɪt, *vb* ə'prɔksɪmeɪt]
adj приблизи́тельный* (приблизи́телен) ◆ *vi*:
to ~ to приближа́ться (прибли́зиться* *perf*) к
+*dat*.
approximately [ə'prɔksɪmɪtlɪ] *adv* приблиз-
и́тельно.
approximation [ə'prɔksɪ'meɪʃən] *n* приближ-
е́ние.
APR *n abbr* (= *annual percentage rate*) годова́я
проце́нтная ста́вка.
Apr. *abbr* = **April**.
apricot ['eɪprɪkɔt] *n* абрико́с.
April ['eɪprəl] *n* апре́ль *m*; **~ fool!** пе́рвое
Апре́ля – никому́ не ве́рю!; *see also* **July**.
April Fool's Day *n* день *m* дурако́в.
apron ['eɪprən] *n* пере́дник, фа́ртук; (*AVIAT*)
площа́дка пе́ред анга́ром.
apse [æps] *n* апси́да.
APT *n abbr* (*BRIT*: = *advanced passenger train*)
пассажи́рский* суперэкспре́сс.

apt [æpt] *adj* (*suitable: comment, description etc*)
уда́чный (уда́чен), уме́стный (уме́стен); **~
to do** скло́нный +*infin*.
Apt. *abbr* (= **apartment**) кв.= *кварти́ра*.
aptitude ['æptɪtju:d] *n* скло́нность *f*.
aptitude test *n* тест на выявле́ние
скло́нностей.
aptly ['æptlɪ] *adv* уме́стно; (*accurately*) то́чно.
aqualung ['ækwəlʌŋ] *n* аквала́нг.
aquarium [ə'kwɛərɪəm] *n* аква́риум.
Aquarius [ə'kwɛərɪəs] *n* Водоле́й; **he is ~** он –
Водоле́й.
aquatic [ə'kwætɪk] *adj* во́дный.
aqueduct ['ækwɪdʌkt] *n* акведу́к.
AR *abbr* (*US: POST*) = **Arkansas**.
ARA *n abbr* (*BRIT*) = **Associate of the Royal
Academy**.
Arab ['ærəb] *adj* ара́бский* ◆ *n* ара́б(ка).
Arabia [ə'reɪbɪə] *n* Ара́вия.
Arabian [ə'reɪbɪən] *adj* ара́бский*.
Arabian Desert *n*: **the ~~** Арави́йская
пусты́ня.
Arabian Sea *n*: **the ~~** Арави́йское мо́ре*.
Arabic ['ærəbɪk] *adj* ара́бский* ◆ *n* ара́бский*
язы́к*.
arable ['ærəbl] *adj* (*land*) па́хотный; (*farm*)
полево́дческий.
Aral Sea ['ærəl-] *n* Ара́льское мо́ре.
ARAM *n abbr* (*BRIT*) = **Associate of the Royal
Academy of Music**.
arbiter ['ɑ:bɪtə'] *n* арби́тр (*в спо́ре*).
arbitrary ['ɑ:bɪtrərɪ] *adj* произво́льный*
(произво́лен).
arbitrate ['ɑ:bɪtreɪt] *vi* выноси́ть* (вы́нести*
perf) трете́йское реше́ние.
arbitration [ɑ:bɪ'treɪʃən] *n* (*of quarrel*)
трете́йский суд*; (*INDUSTRY*) арбитра́ж; **the
dispute went to ~** спор пе́редан в арбитра́ж.
arbitrator ['ɑ:bɪtreɪtə'] *n* трете́йский судья́*,
арби́тр.
ARC *n abbr* = **American Red Cross**.
arc [ɑ:k] *n* (*also MATH*) дуга́*.
arcade [ɑ:'keɪd] *n* (*round a square*) арка́да;
(*shopping mall*) пасса́ж.
arch [ɑ:tʃ] *n* а́рка*, свод; (*of foot*) свод ◆ *vt*
(*back*) выгиба́ть (вы́гнуть *perf*) ◆ *adj* (*playful*)
игри́вый; (*knowing*) многозначи́тельный ◆
prefix а́рхи-.
archaeological [ɑ:kɪə'lɔdʒɪkl] (*US
archeological*) *adj* археологи́ческий*.
archaeologist [ɑ:kɪ'ɔlədʒɪst] (*US archeologist*) *n*
архео́лог.
archaeology [ɑ:kɪ'ɔlədʒɪ] (*US archeology*) *n*
археоло́гия.
archaic [ɑ:'keɪɪk] *adj* археи́ческий.
Archangel [ɑ:keɪndʒəl] *n* Арха́нгельск.
archangel ['ɑ:keɪndʒəl] *n* арха́нгел.
archbishop [ɑ:tʃ'bɪʃəp] *n* архиепи́скоп.

---

* marks translations which have irregular inflections. The Russian-English side of the dictionary gives inflectional information.

arch-enemy ['ɑːtʃ'ɛnəmɪ] n заклятый враг*.
archeology etc [ɑːkɪ'ɔlədʒɪ] (US) = archaeology etc.
archery ['ɑːtʃərɪ] n стрельба* из лука.
archetypal ['ɑːkɪtaɪpəl] adj типичный*.
archetype ['ɑːkɪtaɪp] n образец.
archipelago [ɑːkɪ'pɛlɪgəu] n архипелаг.
architect ['ɑːkɪtɛkt] n (of building) архитектор.
architectural [ɑːkɪ'tɛktʃərəl] adj архитектурный.
architecture ['ɑːkɪtɛktʃəʳ] n архитектура.
archive ['ɑːkaɪvz] n архив.
archive file n (COMPUT) архивный файл.
archives ['ɑːkaɪvz] npl архив msg.
archivist ['ɑːkɪvɪst] n архивариус.
archway ['ɑːtʃweɪ] n арочный проход.
ARCM n abbr (BRIT) = Associate of the Royal College of Music.
Arctic ['ɑːktɪk] adj арктический* ♦ n: the ~ Арктика*.
Arctic Circle n: the ~ ~ Северный Полярный круг.
Arctic Ocean n: the ~ ~ Северный Ледовитый океан.
ARD n abbr (US: MED: = acute respiratory disease) ОРЗ= острое респираторное заболевание.
ardent ['ɑːdənt] adj пылкий* (пылок).
ardour ['ɑːdəʳ] (US ardor) n пыл*.
arduous ['ɑːdjuəs] adj тяжёлый* (тяжёл).
are [ɑːʳ] vb see be.
area ['ɛərɪə] n (of country, knowledge) область f; (part. of place) участок*; (: of room) часть f; (GEOM etc) площадь* f; in the London ~ в районе Лондона.
area code n код зоны.
arena [ə'riːnə] n (also fig) арена.
aren't [ɑːnt] = are not; see be.
Argentina [ɑːdʒən'tiːnə] n Аргентина.
Argentinian [ɑːdʒən'tɪnɪən] adj аргентинский* ♦ n аргентинец*(-йнка*).
arguable ['ɑːgjuəbl] adj спорный* (спорен); it is ~ whether this is necessary нужно ли это – вопрос спорный; it is ~ that ... можно утверждать, что ....
arguably ['ɑːgjuəblɪ] adv возможно; he is ~ the best in his profession можно утверждать, что он лучший специалист в своей области.
argue ['ɑːgjuː] vi (quarrel) ссориться (поссориться perf); (reason) доказывать (доказать* perf) ♦ vt обсуждать (обсудить* perf); to ~ that ... доказывать (доказать* perf), что ...; to ~ about sth спорить (поспорить perf) о чём-н; to ~ for/against sth приводить* (привести* perf) доводы в пользу/против чего-н.
argument ['ɑːgjumənt] n (quarrel) ссора; (reasons) аргумент, довод; (debate) обсуждение, спор*; ~ for/against аргумент or довод в пользу/против +gen.
argumentative [ɑːgju'mɛntətɪv] adj (person) конфликтный; (voice) вызывающий*.

aria ['ɑːrɪə] n ария.
ARIBA n abbr (BRIT) = Associate of the Royal Institute of British Architects.
arid ['ærɪd] adj безводный* (безводен); (fig) сухой.
aridity [ə'rɪdɪtɪ] n сухость f.
Aries ['ɛərɪz] n Овен*; he is ~ он – Овен.
arise [ə'raɪz] (pt arose, pp arisen) vi (occur) возникать (возникнуть* perf); to ~ from возникать (возникнуть* perf) вследствие +gen; should the need ~ если возникнет необходимость.
arisen [ə'rɪzn] pp of arise.
aristocracy [ærɪs'tɔkrəsɪ] n аристократия.
aristocrat ['ærɪstəkræt] n аристократ(ка*).
aristocratic [ærɪstə'krætɪk] adj (family) аристократический*; (features) аристократичный.
arithmetic [ə'rɪθmətɪk] n (MATH) арифметика; (calculation) подсчёт.
arithmetical [ærɪθ'mɛtɪkl] adj арифметический*.
ark [ɑːk] n: Noah's A~ Ноев ковчег.
arm [ɑːm] n рука*; (of chair) ручка*; (of clothing) рукав*; (of organization) подразделение ♦ vt вооружать (вооружить perf); ~s npl (MIL) вооружение ntsg; (HERALDRY) герб; ~ in ~ под руку.
armaments ['ɑːməmənts] npl вооружение sg.
armband ['ɑːmbænd] n нарукавная повязка.
armchair ['ɑːmtʃɛəʳ] n кресло*.
armed [ɑːmd] adj вооружённый (вооружён); the ~ forces вооружённые силы.
armed robbery n вооружённый грабёж*.
Armenia [ɑː'miːnɪə] n Армения.
Armenian [ɑː'miːnɪən] adj армянский* ♦ n армянин(-нка); (LING) армянский* язык*.
armful ['ɑːmful] n охапка.
armistice ['ɑːmɪstɪs] n перемирие.
armor etc (US) = armour etc.
armour ['ɑːməʳ] (US armor) n (also: suit of ~) доспехи mpl; (also: ~plating) броня; (tanks) бронесилы fpl.
armoured car ['ɑːməd-] n бронемашина.
armoury ['ɑːmərɪ] n (also fig) арсенал.
armpit ['ɑːmpɪt] n подмышка*.
armrest ['ɑːmrɛst] n подлокотник.
arms control [ɑːmz-] n контроль m вооружений.
arms race n: the ~ ~ гонка вооружений.
army ['ɑːmɪ] n (also fig) армия.
aroma [ə'rəumə] n аромат.
aromatherapy [ərəumə'θɛrəpɪ] n ароматерапия.
aromatic [ærə'mætɪk] adj ароматный* (ароматен).
arose [ə'rəuz] pt of arise.
around [ə'raund] adv вокруг ♦ prep (encircling) вокруг +gen; (near, about) около +gen; is he ~? он здесь?; ~ £5/3 o'clock около £5/3 часов; ~ here здесь поблизости.

arousal [əˈrauzəl] *n* возбуждéние.
arouse [əˈrauz] *vt* (*sleeping person*) будúть*
(разбудúть* *perf*); (*interest, passions*)
возбуждáть (возбудúть* *perf*).
arpeggio [ɑːˈpɛdʒɪəu] *n* арпéджио *nt ind.*
arrange [əˈreɪndʒ] *vt* (*organize*) устрáивать
(устрóить *perf*); (*put in order*) расставлять
(расстáвить *perf*); (*MUS*) аранжúровать (*impf/
perf*) ♦ *vi*: **we have ~d for a car to pick you up**
мы договорúлись, чтóбы машúна заéхала
за Вáми; **it was ~d that ...** бы́ло услóвлено,
что ...; **to ~ to do** услáвливаться
(услóвиться* *perf*) +*infin*, договáриваться
(договорúться *perf*) +*infin*.
arrangement [əˈreɪndʒmənt] *n* (*agreement*)
договорённость *f*; (*MUS*) аранжирóвка*;
(*order, layout*) расположéние; **~s** *npl*
(*preparations, plans*) приготовлéния *ntpl*; **to
come to an ~ with sb** приходúть* (прийтú*
perf) к соглашéнию с кем-н; **home deliveries
by ~** достáвка нá дом по договорённости;
I'll make ~s for you to be met я договорю́сь,
чтóбы Вас встрéтили.
arrant [ˈærənt] *adj* отъя́вленный.
array [əˈreɪ] *n* (*MATH, COMPUT*) массúв; **~ of**
мáсса +*gen*, мнóжество +*gen*.
arrears [əˈrɪəz] *npl* задóлженность *fsg*; **to be in
~ with one's rent** имéть (*impf*)
задóлженность по квартплáте.
arrest [əˈrɛst] *vt* (*criminal*) арестóвывать
(арестовáть *perf*); (*sb's attention*)
прикóвывать (приковáть *perf*) ♦ *n* арéст,
задержáние; **under ~** под арéстом.
arresting [əˈrɛstɪŋ] *adj* поразúтельный.
arrival [əˈraɪvl] *n* прибы́тие; (*COMM*) привóз;
new ~ (*person*) новичóк*; (*baby*)
новорождённый(-ая) *m(f) adj.*
arrive [əˈraɪv] *vi* (*traveller*) прибывáть
(прибы́ть* *perf*); (*letter, news*) приходúть*
(прийтú* *perf*); (*baby*) рождáться (родúться*
perf)
▶ **arrive at** *vt fus* (*fig*) приходúть* (прийтú* *perf*)
к +*dat*.
arrogance [ˈærəgəns] *n* высокомéрие.
arrogant [ˈærəgənt] *adj* высокомéрный*
(высокомéрен).
arrow [ˈærəu] *n* (*weapon*) стрелá*; (*sign*)
стрéлка*.
arse [ɑːs] *n* (*BRIT: inf!*) жóпа (*!*)
arsenal [ˈɑːsɪnl] *n* арсенáл.
arsenic [ˈɑːsnɪk] *n* мышья́к*.
arson [ˈɑːsn] *n* поджóг.
art [ɑːt] *n* (*also fig*) искýсство; (*also:* **Fine A~**)
изобразúтельное искýсство; **A~s** *npl*
гуманитáрные наýки *fpl*; **work of ~**
произведéние искýсства.
artefact [ˈɑːtɪfækt] *n* худóжественное издéлие,
подéлка.

arterial [ɑːˈtɪərɪəl] *adj* (*ANAT*) артериáльный; **~
road** магистрáль *f.*
artery [ˈɑːtərɪ] *n* (*also fig*) артéрия.
artful [ˈɑːtful] *adj* лóвкий*.
art gallery *n* (*national*) картúнная галерéя;
(*private*) галерéя.
arthritic [ɑːˈθrɪtɪk] *adj* артритúческий*.
arthritis [ɑːˈθraɪtɪs] *n* артрúт.
artichoke [ˈɑːtɪtʃəuk] *n* (*also:* **globe ~**)
артишóк; (*also:* **Jerusalem ~**) землянáя
грýша.
article [ˈɑːtɪkl] *n* (*object, item*) предмéт; (*LING*)
артúкль *m*; (*in newspaper*) статья́*; (*in
document*) пункт; **~s** *npl* (*BRIT: LAW*) курс
профессионáльной подготóвки адвокáтов; **~
of clothing** предмéт одéжды.
articles of association *npl* (*COMM*) устáв
акционéрной компáнии.
articulate [*adj* ɑːˈtɪkjulɪt, *vb* ɑːˈtɪkjuleɪt] *adj*
(*speech, writing*) вразумúтельный*
(вразумúтелен) ♦ *vt* (*fears, ideas*) выражáть
(вы́разить* *perf*) ♦ *vi*: **to ~ well/badly** чётко/
нечётко выговáривать (вы́говорить *perf*);
she is very ~ онá чётко *or* я́сно выражáет
свои́ мы́сли.
articulated lorry *n* (*BRIT*) грузовúк* с
прицéпом.
artifice [ˈɑːtɪfɪs] *n* (*trick*) приём; (*skill*)
искýсность *f.*
artificial [ɑːtɪˈfɪʃəl] *adj* искýсственный*;
(*affected*) неестéственный* (неестéствен).
artificial insemination [-ɪnsɛmɪˈneɪʃən] *n*
искýсственное оплодотворéние.
artificial intelligence *n* искýсственный
интеллéкт.
artificial respiration *n* искýсственное
дыхáние.
artillery [ɑːˈtɪlərɪ] *n* (*MIL: corps*) артиллéрия.
artisan [ˈɑːtɪzæn] *n* ремéсленник(-ица).
artist [ˈɑːtɪst] *n* худóжник(-ица); (*performer*)
артúст(ка).
artistic [ɑːˈtɪstɪk] *adj* худóжественный; **an ~
person** худóжественная лúчность *f.*
artistry [ˈɑːtɪstrɪ] *n* мастерствó.
artless [ˈɑːtlɪs] *adj* безыскýсный (безыскýсен).
art school *n* худóжественное учúлище.
artwork [ˈɑːtwəːk] *n* оформлéние.
ARV *n abbr* (*BIBLE:* = *American Revised Version*)
америкáнский* вариáнт Бúблии.
AS *n abbr* (*US:* = *Associate in/of Science*) член
ассоциáции наýчных рабóтников ♦ *abbr*
(*POST*) = *American Samoa.*

KEYWORD

as [æz] *conj* **1** (*referring to time*) когдá; **as the
years went by** с годáми; **he came in as I was
leaving** он вошёл, когдá я уходúл; **as from
tomorrow** с зáвтрашнего дня
2 (*in comparisons*): **as big as** такóй же

большо́й, как; **twice as big as** в два ра́за
бо́льше, чем; **as white as snow** бе́лый как
снег; **as much money/many books as** сто́лько
же де́нег/книг, ско́лько; **as soon as** как
то́лько; **as soon as possible** как мо́жно
скоре́е
3 (*since, because*) поско́льку, так как
4 (*referring to manner, way*) как; **do as you
wish** де́лайте как хоти́те; **as she said** как она́
сказа́ла
5 (*concerning*) **as for** *or* **to** что каса́ется +*gen*:
6: **as if** *or* **though** так, как бу́дто бы; **he looked
as if he had been ill** он вы́глядел так, как
бу́дто бы он был бо́лен
◆ *prep* (*in the capacity of*): **he works as a driver/
waiter** он рабо́тает шофёром/официа́нтом;
as chairman of the company, he ... как глава́
компа́нии, он ...; *see also* **long, same, such,
well**.

ASA *n abbr* (= *American Standards Association*)
Америка́нская ассоциа́ция станда́ртов.
a.s.a.p. *adv abbr* (= *as soon as possible*) как
мо́жно скоре́е.
asbestos [æz'bɛstəs] *n* асбе́ст.
ascend [ə'sɛnd] *vt* (*hill*) восходи́ть* (взойти́* *perf*)
на +*acc*; (*stairs*) всходи́ть* (взойти́* *perf*) по
+*dat*; (*throne*) взойти́* (*perf*) на +*acc*.
ascendancy [ə'sɛndənsɪ] *n* госпо́дство; ~ **over
sb** госпо́дство над кем-н.
ascendant [ə'sɛndənt] *n*: **to be in the** ~
госпо́дствовать (*impf*).
ascension [ə'sɛnʃən] *n*: **the A~** (*REL*)
Вознесе́ние.
Ascension Island *n* О́стров Вознесе́ния.
ascent [ə'sɛnt] *n* (*slope*) подъём; (*climb*)
восхожде́ние.
ascertain [æsə'teɪn] *vt* устана́вливать
(установи́ть* *perf*).
ascetic [ə'sɛtɪk] *adj* аскети́ческий*.
asceticism [ə'sɛtɪsɪzəm] *n* аскети́зм.
ASCII ['æski:] *n abbr* (*COMPUT*: = *American
Standard Code for Information Interchange*)
*америка́нский станда́ртный код для обме́на
информа́цией*.
ascribe [ə'skraɪb] *vt*: **to** ~ **sth to** припи́сывать
(приписа́ть* *perf*) что-н +*dat*.
ASCU *n abbr* (*US*) = *Association of State Colleges
and Universities*.
ASEAN ['æsɪæn] *n abbr* (= *Association of South-
East Asian Nations*) АСЕА́Н.
ASH [æʃ] *n abbr* (*BRIT*: = *Action on Smoking and
Health*) О́бщество борьбы́ с куре́нием.
ash [æʃ] *n* (*of fire*) зола́, пе́пел*; (*of cigarette*)
пе́пел; (*wood, tree*) я́сень *m*.
ashamed [ə'ʃeɪmd] *adj*: **to be** ~ (**of**) стыди́ться
(*impf*) (+*gen*); **I'm** ~ **of ...** мне сты́дно +*gen* ...;
I'm ~ **of myself for having done that** мне
сты́дно, что я сде́лал э́то.
ashen ['æʃən] *adj* (*face*) мёртвенно-бле́дный*.
Ashkhabad [aʃxa'bat] *n* Ашхаба́д.

ashore [ə'ʃɔːʳ] *adv* (*be*) на берегу́; (*swim, go*) на
бе́рег.
ashtray ['æʃtreɪ] *n* пе́пельница.
Ash Wednesday *n* пе́рвый день* *m* Вели́кого
Поста́.
Asia ['eɪʃə] *n* А́зия.
Asia Minor *n* Ма́лая А́зия.
Asian ['eɪʃən] *adj* азиа́тский* ◆ *n* азиа́т(ка*).
Asiatic [eɪsɪ'ætɪk] *adj* азиа́тский*.
aside [ə'saɪd] *adv* в сто́рону ◆ *n* ре́плика ◆ *prep*:
~ **from** поми́мо +*gen*; **to brush objections** ~
отмета́ть (отмести́* *perf*) возраже́ния в
сто́рону.
ask [ɑːsk] *vt* (*inquire*) спра́шивать (спроси́ть*
perf); (*invite*) звать* (позва́ть* *perf*); **to** ~ **sb
sth/sb to do** проси́ть* (попроси́ть* *perf*) что-н
у кого́-н/кого́-н +*infin*; **to** ~ **sb the time**
спра́шивать (спроси́ть* *perf*) кого́-н,
кото́рый час; **to** ~ **sb about sth** спра́шивать
(спроси́ть* *perf*) кого́-н о чём-н; **to** ~ **about
the price** спра́шивать (спроси́ть* *perf*) о цене́;
to ~ (**sb**) **a question** задава́ть* (зада́ть* *perf*)
(кому́-н) вопро́с; **to** ~ **sb out to dinner**
приглаша́ть (пригласи́ть* *perf*) кого́-н в
рестора́н
▶ **ask after** *vt fus* (*person*) справля́ться
(спра́виться* *perf*) о +*prp*
▶ **ask for** *vt fus* (*request*) проси́ть* (попроси́ть*
perf); (*look for: trouble*) напра́шиваться
(напроси́ться* *perf*) на +*acc*; **he's just** ~**ing for
trouble** *or* **for it** он про́сто напра́шивается на
неприя́тности.
askance [ə'skɑːns] *adv*: **to look** ~ **at sb/sth**
смотре́ть* (посмотре́ть* *perf*) на кого́-н/
что-н ко́со.
askew [ə'skjuː] *adv* (*clothes*) кри́во, ко́со.
asking price ['ɑːskɪŋ-] *n*: **the** ~ ~
запра́шиваемая цена́*.
asleep [ə'sliːp] *adj* спя́щий; **to be** ~ спать*
(*impf*); **to fall** ~ засыпа́ть (засну́ть *perf*).
ASLEF ['æzlɛf] *n abbr* (*BRIT*) = *Associated Society
of Locomotive Engineers and Firemen*.
asp [æsp] *n* а́спид.
asparagus [əs'pærəgəs] *n* спа́ржа.
asparagus tips *npl* спа́ржевые голо́вки* *fpl*.
ASPCA *n abbr* (= *American Society for the
Prevention of Cruelty to Animals*)
Америка́нское о́бщество защи́ты
живо́тных.
aspect ['æspɛkt] *n* (*element*) аспе́кт, сторона́*;
(*quality, air*) вид*; **a room with a southern** ~
ко́мната с ви́дом на юг.
aspersions [əs'pəːʃənz] *npl*: **to cast** ~ **on**
(*integrity, ability*) ста́вить* (поста́вить* *perf*)
под сомне́ние; (*person*) очерня́ть (очерни́ть
perf).
asphalt ['æsfælt] *n* асфа́льт.
asphyxiate [æs'fɪksɪeɪt] *vt* души́ть* (задуши́ть*
perf).
asphyxiation [æsfɪksɪ'eɪʃən] *n* уду́шье.
aspirate [*vt* 'æspəreɪt, *adj* 'æspərɪt] *vt*

произноси́ть* (произнести́* *perf*) с
придыха́нием ♦ *adj* придыха́тельный.
aspirations [æspə'reɪʃənz] *npl*
устремле́ния *ntpl*.
aspire [əs'paɪəʳ] *vi*: **to ~ to** стреми́ться* (*impf*) к
+*dat*.
aspirin ['æsprɪn] *n* аспири́н.
aspiring [əs'paɪərɪŋ] *adj* начина́ющий*.
ass [æs] *n* (*also fig*) осёл*; (*US: inf!*) жо́па (*!*)
assail [ə'seɪl] *vt* (*person*) напада́ть (напа́сть*
perf) на +*acc*; (*fig*): **he was ~ed by doubts** его́
одоле́ли сомне́ния.
assailant [ə'seɪlənt] *n*: **his/her ~** напа́вший(-ая)
m(f) adj на него́/неё.
assassin [ə'sæsɪn] *n* полити́ческий* уби́йца *m/f*.
assassinate [ə'sæsɪneɪt] *vt* соверша́ть
(соверши́ть *perf*) покуше́ние на +*acc*.
assassination [əsæsɪ'neɪʃən] *n* полити́ческое
уби́йство.
assault [ə'sɔːlt] *n* нападе́ние; (*MIL, fig*) ата́ка ♦
vt напада́ть (напа́сть* *perf*) на +*acc*; (*MIL*)
атакова́ть (*impf/perf*); (*sexually*) наси́ловать
(изнаси́ловать *perf*); **~ and battery** (*LAW*)
оскорбле́ние де́йствием.
assemble [ə'sɛmbl] *vt* собира́ть (собра́ть* *perf*)
♦ *vi* собира́ться (собра́ться* *perf*).
assembly [ə'sɛmblɪ] *n* (*meeting*) собра́ние;
(*institution*) ассамбле́я, законода́тельное
собра́ние; (*construction*) сбо́рка; **General A~
of the UN** Генера́льная Ассамбле́я ООН.
assembly language *n* (*COMPUT*) язы́к*
ассе́мблера.
assembly line *n* сбо́рочный конве́йер.
assent [ə'sɛnt] *n* согла́сие ♦ *vi*: **to ~** (**to**)
соглаша́ться (согласи́ться* *perf*) (на +*acc*).
assert [ə'sɜːt] *vt* (*opinion, authority*)
утвержда́ть (утверди́ть* *perf*); (*rights,
innocence*) отста́ивать (отстоя́ть *perf*); **to ~
o.s.** самоутвержда́ться (самоутверди́ться*
perf).
assertion [ə'sɜːʃən] *n* (*claim*) утвержде́ние.
assertive [ə'sɜːtɪv] *adj* самоуве́ренный
(самоуве́рен).
assess [ə'sɛs] *vt* оце́нивать (оцени́ть* *perf*); **to
~ for tax** оцени́ть (*perf*) сто́имость для це́лей
налогообложе́ния.
assessment [ə'sɛsmənt] *n*: **~ (of)** оце́нка*
(+*gen*); **tax ~** оце́нка сто́имости для це́лей
налогообложе́ния.
assessor [ə'sɛsəʳ] *n* (*LAW*) экспе́рт-
(-консульта́нт).
asset ['æsɛt] *n* (*useful quality*) досто́инство; **~s**
npl (*property, funds*) акти́вы *mpl*; (*COMM*)
акти́в *msg* бала́нса; **he's an ~ to the company**
он представля́ет собо́й большу́ю це́нность
для компа́нии.
asset-stripping ['æsɛt'strɪpɪŋ] *n* (*COMM*)
распрода́жа неприбыльных акти́вов (*при*

поглоще́нии одно́й компа́нии друго́й*).
assiduous [ə'sɪdjuəs] *adj* (*care, work*)
усе́рдный* (усе́рден).
assign [ə'saɪn] *vt* (*task*) поруча́ть (поручи́ть*
perf), предпи́сывать (предписа́ть* *perf*);
(*significance*) придава́ть* (прида́ть* *perf*);
(*resources, role*) предназнача́ть
(предназна́чить *perf*); **to ~ a date for a
meeting** назнача́ть (назна́чить *perf*) да́ту
заседа́ния.
assignment [ə'saɪnmənt] *n* (*task*) предписа́ние;
(*SCOL*) зада́ние.
assimilate [ə'sɪmɪleɪt] *vt* (*ideas*) усва́ивать
(усво́ить *perf*); (*immigrants*): **to be ~d**
ассимили́роваться (*impf/perf*).
assimilation [əsɪmɪ'leɪʃən] *n* усвое́ние; (*of
immigrants etc*) ассимиля́ция.
assist [ə'sɪst] *vt* помога́ть (помо́чь* *perf*) +*dat*;
(*financially*) соде́йствовать (*impf/perf*) +*dat*.
assistance [ə'sɪstəns] *n* по́мощь *f*; (*financial*)
соде́йствие.
assistant [ə'sɪstənt] *n* помо́щник(-ица); (*in
office etc*) ассисте́нт(ка); (*BRIT: also*: **shop ~**)
продаве́ц*(-вщи́ца); **laboratory ~**
лабора́нт(ка).
assistant manager *n* замести́тель *m*
заве́дующего.
assizes [ə'saɪzɪz] *npl* (*BRIT: LAW*) выездна́я
се́ссия суда́ прися́жных.
associate [*n, adj* ə'səuʃɪɪt, *vb* ə'səuʃɪeɪt] *n*
(*colleague*) колле́га *m/f* ♦ *adj* (*member,
director, professor*) ассоции́рованный ♦ *vt*
(*mentally*) ассоции́ровать (*impf/perf*); **to ~
with sb** обща́ться (*impf*) с кем-н.
associated company [ə'səuʃɪeɪtɪd-] *n* доче́рнее
предприя́тие.
association [əsəusɪ'eɪʃən] *n* (*group, PSYCH*)
ассоциа́ция; (*involvement*) связь *f*; **in ~ with**
в сотру́дничестве с +*instr*.
association football *n* футбо́л.
assorted [ə'sɔːtɪd] *adj* разнообра́зный*; **hats in
~ sizes** шля́пы ра́зных разме́ров.
assortment [ə'sɔːtmənt] *n* (*of clothes, colours*)
ассортиме́нт; (*of books, people*) подбо́р.
Asst. *abbr* (= **assistant**) ассисте́нт.
assuage [ə'sweɪdʒ] *vt* (*grief, pain*) смягча́ть
(смягчи́ть *perf*); (*thirst, hunger*) утоля́ть
(утоли́ть *perf*).
assume [ə'sjuːm] *vt* (*suppose*) предполага́ть
(предположи́ть* *perf*), допуска́ть
(допусти́ть* *perf*); (*responsibilities*) брать*
(взять* *perf*) на себя́; (*command, appearance,
air*) принима́ть (приня́ть* *perf*); (*power*)
брать* (взять* *perf*).
assumed name [ə'sjuːmd-] *n* вы́мышленное
и́мя *nt*.
assumption [ə'sʌmpʃən] *n* (*supposition*)
предположе́ние; (*of control, responsibility*)

---

* marks translations which have irregular inflections. The Russian-English side of the dictionary gives inflectional information.

приня́тие на себя́; ~ **of power** прихо́д к вла́сти; **on the** ~ **that** ... предполага́я, что ....

assurance [ə'ʃʊərəns] *n* (*promise*) завере́ние; (*confidence*) уве́ренность *f*; (*insurance*) страхова́ние; **I can give you no** ~**s** я не могу́ дать Вам никаки́х гара́нтий.

assure [ə'ʃʊə'] *vt* (*reassure*) уверя́ть (уве́рить *perf*), заверя́ть (заве́рить *perf*); (*guarantee*) обеспе́чивать (обеспе́чить *perf*).

assured [ə'ʃʊəd] *adj* (*voice*) уве́ренный* (уве́рен); (*success*) несомне́нный* (несомне́нен).

AST *abbr* (*US*) = *Atlantic Standard Time*.

asterisk ['æstərɪsk] *n* звёздочка* (*знак* "*"*).

astern [ə'stə:n] *adv* (*NAUT: on ship: position*) на корме́; (: *motion*) на корму́; (*behind ship*) за кормо́й; **to move** ~ идти́* (*impf*) за́дним хо́дом.

asteroid ['æstərɔɪd] *n* астеро́ид.

asthma ['æsmə] *n* а́стма.

asthmatic [æs'mætɪk] *adj* (*breathing*) астмати́ческий* ◆ *n* астма́тик; ~ **attack** при́ступ а́стмы.

astigmatism [ə'stɪgmətɪzəm] *n* астигмати́зм.

astir [ə'stə:'] *adv* на нога́х.

astonish [ə'stɔnɪʃ] *vt* изумля́ть (изуми́ть* *perf*), поража́ть (порази́ть* *perf*).

astonishing [ə'stɔnɪʃɪŋ] *adj* порази́тельный* (порази́телен); **I find it** ~ **that** ... меня́ поража́ет, что ....

astonishingly [ə'stɔnɪʃɪŋlɪ] *adv* порази́тельно; **the play,** ~, **was successful** порази́тельным о́бразом пье́са была́ уда́чной.

astonishment [ə'stɔnɪʃmənt] *n* удивле́ние, изумле́ние; **to my** ~ к моему́ изумле́нию.

astound [ə'staund] *vt* поража́ть (порази́ть* *perf*), изумля́ть (изуми́ть* *perf*).

astounded [ə'staundɪd] *adj* поражённый (поражён), изумлённый (изумлён).

astounding [ə'staundɪŋ] *adj* порази́тельный* (порази́телен), изуми́тельный* (изуми́телен).

astray [ə'streɪ] *adv*: **to go** ~ (*letter*) затеря́ться (*perf*); (*fig*) сбива́ться (сби́ться* *perf*) с пути́; **to lead** ~ (*fig*) сбива́ть (сбить* *perf*) с пути́; **to go** ~ **in one's calculations** сбива́ться (сби́ться* *perf*) со счёта.

astride [ə'straɪd] *prep* верхо́м на +*prp* ◆ *adv* верхо́м.

astringent [əs'trɪndʒənt] *adj* вя́жущий* ◆ *n* вя́жущее вещество́.

astrologer [əs'trɔlədʒə'] *n* астро́лог.

astrology [əs'trɔlədʒɪ] *n* астроло́гия.

astronaut ['æstrənɔ:t] *n* астрона́вт, космона́вт.

astronomer [əs'trɔnəmə'] *n* астроно́м.

astronomical [æstrə'nɔmɪkl] *adj* (*also fig*) астрономи́ческий*.

astronomy [əs'trɔnəmɪ] *n* астроно́мия.

astrophysics ['æstrəu'fɪzɪks] *n* астрофи́зика.

astute [əs'tju:t] *adj* (*person*) проница́тельный* (проница́телен); (*decision*) дальнови́дный* (дальнови́ден).

asunder [ə'sʌndə'] *adv*: **to tear** ~ разрыва́ть (разорва́ть* *perf*) на куски́.

ASV *n abbr* (*BIBLE*: = *American Standard Version*) америка́нский* станда́ртный вариа́нт Би́блии.

asylum [ə'saɪləm] *n* (*refuge*) убе́жище; (*mental hospital*) сумасше́дший* дом*; **to seek political** ~ иска́ть* (*perf*) полити́ческого убе́жища.

asymmetrical [eɪsɪ'mɛtrɪkl] *adj* ассиметри́чный* (ассиметри́чен).

KEYWORD

at [æt] *prep* **1** (*referring to position*) в/на +*prp*; **at the top** наверху́; **at home** до́ма; **at school** в шко́ле; **at the theatre** в теа́тре; **at the baker's** в бу́лочной; **at a concert** на конце́рте; **at the station** на ста́нции; **they are sitting at the table** они́ сидя́т за столо́м; **at my friend's (house)** у моего́ дру́га; **at the doctor's** у врача́
2 (*referring to direction*) в/на +*acc*; **to look at sb/sth** смотре́ть (посмотре́ть *perf*) на кого́-н/что-н; **to throw sth at sb** (*several objects*) броса́ться (*impf*) чем-н в кого́-н; (*one object*) броса́ть (бро́сить* *perf*) что-н в кого́-н
3 (*referring to time*): **at four o'clock** в четы́ре часа́; **at half past two** в полови́не тре́тьего; **at a quarter to two** без че́тверти два; **at a quarter past two** в че́тверть тре́тьего; **at dawn** на заре́; **at night** но́чью; **at Christmas** на Рождество́; **at lunch** за обе́дом; **at times** времена́ми
4 (*referring to rates*): **at £1 a kilo** по фу́нту за килогра́мм; **two at a time** по два за раз; **at fifty km/h** со ско́ростью пятьдеся́т км/ч; **at full speed** на по́лной ско́рости
5 (*referring to manner*): **at a stroke** одни́м ма́хом; **at peace** в ми́ре
6 (*referring to activity*): **to be at home/work** быть (*impf*) до́ма/на рабо́те; **to play at cowboys** игра́ть (*impf*) в ковбо́и; **to be good at doing sth** хорошо́ уме́ть (*impf*) что-н де́лать (*impf*)
7 (*referring to cause*): **shocked/surprised/ annoyed at sth** шоки́рован/удивлён*/ раздражён* чем-н; **I am surprised at you** Вы меня́ удивля́ете; **I stayed at his suggestion** я оста́лся по его́ предложе́нию.

---

ate [eɪt] *pt of* eat.

atheism ['eɪθɪɪzəm] *n* атеи́зм.

atheist ['eɪθɪɪst] *n* атеи́ст(ка*).

Athenian [ə'θi:nɪən] *adj* афи́нский* ◆ *n* афиня́нин(-нка).

Athens ['æθɪnz] *n* Афи́ны* *pl*.

athlete ['æθli:t] *n* спортсме́н(ка*).

athletic [æθ'lɛtɪk] *adj* спорти́вный*; (*physique*) атлети́ческий*.

athletics [æθ'lɛtɪks] *n* лёгкая атле́тика.

Atlantic [ət'læntɪk] *adj* атланти́ческий* ◆ *n*: **the ~ (Ocean)** Атланти́ческий* Океа́н.
atlas ['ætləs] *n* а́тлас.
Atlas Mountains *npl*: **the ~ ~** Атла́сские Го́ры* *fpl*.
ATM *abbr* (= *Automated Telling Machine*) ба́нковский* автома́т.
atmosphere ['ætməsfɪəʳ] *n* атмосфе́ра; (*air*) во́здух.
atmospheric [ætməs'fɛrɪk] *adj* атмосфе́рный.
atmospherics [ætməs'fɛrɪks] *npl* (*RADIO*) атмосфе́рные поме́хи *fpl*.
atoll ['ætɔl] *n* ато́лл.
atom ['ætəm] *n* а́том.
atomic [ə'tɔmɪk] *adj* а́томный.
atom(ic) bomb *n* а́томная бо́мба.
atomizer ['ætəmaɪzəʳ] *n* (*for perfume*) пульвериза́тор.
atone [ə'təun] *vi*: **to ~ for** искупа́ть (искупи́ть* *perf*).
atonement [ə'təunmənt] *n* искупле́ние.
ATP *n abbr = Association of Tennis Professionals.*
atrocious [ə'trəuʃəs] *adj* ужа́сный* (ужа́сен).
atrocity [ə'trɔsɪtɪ] *n* (*act*) зве́рство.
atrophy ['ætrəfɪ] *n* атрофия́ ◆ *vt* атрофи́ровать (*impf*/*perf*) ◆ *vi* атрофи́роваться (*impf*/*perf*).
attach [ə'tætʃ] *vt* прикрепля́ть (прикрепи́ть* *perf*); (*document, letter*) прилага́ть (приложи́ть* *perf*); **he is/was ~ed to** (*fond of*) он привя́зан/был привя́зан к +*dat*; (*connected with*) он свя́зан/был свя́зан с +*instr*; **to ~ importance to** придава́ть (прида́ть* *perf*) значе́ние +*dat*; **the ~ed letter** прилага́емое письмо́.
attaché [ə'tæʃeɪ] *n* атташе́ *m ind*.
attaché case *n* диплома́т (*портфе́ль*).
attachment [ə'tætʃmənt] *n* (*fastening*) крепле́ние; (*device*) приспособле́ние, наса́дка; (*love*): ~ (**to sb**) привя́занность *f* (к кому́-н).
attack [ə'tæk] *vt* (*MIL, fig*) атакова́ть (*impf*/*perf*); (*assault*) напада́ть (напа́сть* *perf*) на +*acc*; (*tackle: problem*) бра́ться* (взя́ться* *perf*) энерги́чно за +*acc* ◆ *n* (*criticism, MIL*) ата́ка; (*assault*) нападе́ние; (*of illness*) при́ступ*; **heart ~** серде́чный при́ступ.
attacker [ə'tækəʳ] *n*: **his/her ~** напа́вший(-ая) *m(f) adj* на него́/неё.
attain [ə'teɪn] *vt* (*happiness, success*) достига́ть (дости́гнуть* *or* дости́чь* *perf*) +*gen*, добива́ться (доби́ться* *perf*) +*gen*; (*knowledge*) приобрета́ть (приобрести́* *perf*).
attainments [ə'teɪnmənts] *npl* достиже́ния *ntpl*.
attempt [ə'tɛmpt] *n* (*try*) попы́тка* ◆ *vt* (*try*) пыта́ться (попыта́ться *perf*) +*infin*; **to make an ~ on sb's life** соверша́ть (соверши́ть *perf*) покуше́ние на чью-н жизнь; **he made no ~ to help** он соверше́нно не попыта́лся помо́чь.
attempted [ə'tɛmptɪd] *adj*: ~ **murder**

покуше́ние на жизнь; ~ **suicide** попы́тка* самоуби́йства; ~ **burglary** попы́тка* ограбле́ния.
attend [ə'tɛnd] *vt* (*school, church, lectures*) посеща́ть (*impf*); (*patient*) уха́живать (*impf*) за +*instr*; (*course*) слу́шать (прослу́шать *perf*); (*meeting, talk*) прису́тствовать (*impf*) на +*prp*
▶ **attend to** *vt fus* (*needs, patient*) занима́ться (заня́ться* *perf*) +*instr*; (*customer*) обслу́живать (обслужи́ть *perf*).
attendance [ə'tɛndəns] *n* прису́тствие; (*in school*) посеща́емость *f*; (*SPORT: gate*) коли́чество боле́льщиков на ма́тче.
attendant [ə'tɛndənt] *n* сопровожда́ющий(-ая) *m(f) adj*; (*in garage etc*) служи́тель(ница) *m(f)* ◆ *adj* (*dangers, risks*) сопу́тствующий.
attention [ə'tɛnʃən] *n* (*concentration*) внима́ние; (*care*) ухо́д ◆ *excl* (*MIL*) сми́рно; ~**s** *npl* (*acts of courtesy*) зна́ки *mpl* внима́ния; **for the ~ of ...** (*ADMIN*) к све́дению +*gen*; **it has come to my ~ that ...** мне ста́ло изве́стно, что ...; **to stand to/at ~** (*MIL*) стоя́ть (*impf*) по сто́йке "сми́рно".
attentive [ə'tɛntɪv] *adj* (*audience*) внима́тельный* (внима́телен); (*polite*) предупреди́тельный* (предупреди́телен); (*kind*) забо́тливый.
attentively [ə'tɛntɪvlɪ] *adv* внима́тельно, забо́тливо.
attenuate [ə'tɛnjueɪt] *vt* ослабля́ть (осла́бить* *perf*) ◆ *vi* ослабля́ться (осла́биться* *perf*).
attest [ə'tɛst] *vi*: **to ~ to** (*demonstrate*) свиде́тельствовать (*impf*) о +*prp*; (*LAW*) свиде́тельствовать (засвиде́тельствовать *perf*).
attic ['ætɪk] *n* (*living space*) манса́рда; (*storage space*) черда́к*.
attire [ə'taɪəʳ] *n* одея́ние.
attitude ['ætɪtjuːd] *n* (*view, behaviour*): ~ (**to** *or* **towards**) отноше́ние (к +*dat*); (*posture*) по́за.
attorney [ə'təːnɪ] *n* (*US: lawyer*) юри́ст; (*having proxy*) пове́ренный(-ая) *m(f) adj*; **power of ~** дове́ренность *f*.
Attorney General *n* (*BRIT*) мини́стр юсти́ции; (*US*) Генера́льный прокуро́р.
attract [ə'trækt] *vt* привлека́ть (привле́чь* *perf*).
attraction [ə'trækʃən] *n* (*charm, appeal*) привлека́тельность *f*; (*usu pl: amusements*) аттракцио́ны *mpl*; (*PHYS*) притяже́ние; (*fig: towards sb, sth*) влече́ние.
attractive [ə'træktɪv] *adj* привлека́тельный* (привлека́телен).
attribute [*n* 'ætrɪbjuːt, *vb* ə'trɪbjuːt] *n* при́знак, атрибу́т ◆ *vt*: **to ~ sth to** (*cause*) относи́ть* (отнести́* *perf*) что-н за счёт +*gen*; (*painting, quality*) припи́сывать (приписа́ть* *perf*) что-н +*dat*.
attribution [ætrɪ'bjuːʃən] *n* припи́сывание.

---

* marks translations which have irregular inflections. The Russian-English side of the dictionary gives inflectional information.

attrition [əˈtrɪʃən] *n*: **war of ~** война́* на изнуре́ние.

Atty. Gen. *abbr* = **Attorney General**.

ATV *n abbr* (= *all terrain vehicle*) вездехо́д.

atypical [eiˈtɪpɪkl] *adj* нетипи́чный (нетипи́чен).

aubergine [ˈəubəʒiːn] *n* (*vegetable*) баклажа́н; (*colour*) тёмно-лило́вый.

auburn [ˈɔːbən] *adj* (*hair*) тёмно-ры́жий*.

auction [ˈɔːkʃən] *n* (*also*: **sale by ~**) аукцио́н ♦ *vt* продава́ть (прода́ть* *perf*) с аукцио́на.

auctioneer [ɔːkʃəˈnɪəʳ] *n* аукциони́ст.

auction room *n* аукцио́нный зал.

audacious [ɔːˈdeɪʃəs] *adj* (*behaviour*) де́рзкий* (де́рзок).

audacity [ɔːˈdæsɪtɪ] *n* де́рзость *f*.

audible [ˈɔːdɪbl] *adj* слы́шимый* (слы́шен).

audience [ˈɔːdɪəns] *n* аудито́рия, пу́блика; (*with queen etc*) аудие́нция.

audio typist [ˈɔːdɪəu-] *n* фономашини́стка.

audiovisual [ˈɔːdɪəuˈvɪzjuəl] *adj* (*materials, equipment*) а́удио-визуа́льный*.

audiovisual aids [ˈɔːdɪəuˈvɪzjuəl-] *npl* техни́ческие сре́дства *ntpl* обуче́ния.

audit [ˈɔːdɪt] *vt* (*COMM*) проводи́ть* (провести́* *perf*) реви́зию +*gen* ♦ *n* реви́зия, ауди́т.

audition [ɔːˈdɪʃən] *n* (*CINEMA, THEAT etc*) прослу́шивание ♦ *vi*: **to ~ (for)** проходи́ть* (пройти́* *perf*) прослу́шивание (на +*acc*).

auditor [ˈɔːdɪtəʳ] *n* реви́зия, ауди́тор.

auditorium [ɔːdɪˈtɔːrɪəm] *n* зал.

Aug. *abbr* = **August**.

augment [ɔːgˈmɛnt] *vt* (*income etc*) увели́чивать (увели́чить *perf*).

augur [ˈɔːgəʳ] *vi*: **it ~s well** э́то хоро́шее предзнаменова́ние.

August [ˈɔːgəst] *n* а́вгуст; *see also* **July**.

august [ɔːˈgʌst] *adj* (*figure, building*) вели́чественный.

aunt [ɑːnt] *n* тётя*.

auntie [ˈɑːntɪ] *n dimin of* **aunt**.

aunty [ˈɑːntɪ] *n dimin of* **aunt**.

au pair [ˈəuˈpɛəʳ] *n* (*also*: **~ ~ girl**) молода́я ня́ня-иностра́нка, живу́щая в семье́.

aura [ˈɔːrə] *n* (*fig: air*) орео́л.

auspices [ˈɔːspɪsɪz] *npl*: **under the ~ of** под эги́дой +*gen*.

auspicious [ɔːsˈpɪʃəs] *adj* благоприя́тный.

austere [ɔsˈtɪəʳ] *adj* (*room etc*) стро́гий*; (*person, manner*) суро́вый (суро́в).

austerity [ɔsˈtɛrɪtɪ] *n* (*simplicity*) стро́гость *f*; (*ECON: hardship*) лише́ния *ntpl*.

Australasia [ɔːstrəˈleɪzɪə] *n* Австра́лия и Но́вая Зела́ндия.

Australasian [ɔːstrəˈleɪzɪən] *adj* австрало-азиа́тский*.

Australia [ɔsˈtreɪlɪə] *n* Австра́лия.

Australian [ɔsˈtreɪlɪən] *adj* австрали́йский* ♦ *n* австрали́ец*(-и́йка).

Austria [ˈɔstrɪə] *n* А́встрия.

Austrian [ˈɔstrɪən] *adj* австри́йский* ♦ *n* австри́ец*(-и́йка).

AUT *n abbr* (*BRIT*) = *Association of University Teachers*.

authentic [ɔːˈθɛntɪk] *adj* по́длинный*.

authenticate [ɔːˈθɛntɪkeɪt] *vt* удостоверя́ть (удостове́рить *perf*) по́длинность +*gen*.

authenticity [ɔːθɛnˈtɪsɪtɪ] *n* по́длинность *f*.

author [ˈɔːθəʳ] *n* (*of text, plan*) а́втор; (*profession*) писа́тель*(ница).

authoritarian [ɔːθɔrɪˈtɛərɪən] *adj* (*attitudes, conduct*) авторита́рный* (авторита́рен).

authoritative [ɔːˈθɔrɪtətɪv] *adj* авторите́тный* (авторите́тен).

authority [ɔːˈθɔrɪtɪ] *n* (*power*) власть *f*; (*government body*) управле́ние; (*expert*) авторите́т; (*official permission*) полномо́чие; **the authorities** *npl* (*ruling body*) вла́сти* *fpl*; **to have the ~ to do** име́ть (*impf*) полномо́чия +*infin*.

authorization [ɔːθəraɪˈzeɪʃən] *n*: **~ (for)** са́нкция (на +*acc*).

authorize [ˈɔːθəraɪz] *vt* санкциони́ровать (*impf/perf*); **to ~ sb to do** уполномо́чивать (уполномо́чить *perf*) кого́-н +*infin*.

authorized capital [ˈɔːθəraɪzd-] *n* (*COMM*) уста́вный капита́л.

authorship [ˈɔːθəʃɪp] *n* а́вторство.

autistic [ɔːˈtɪstɪk] *adj* (*person*) страда́ющий аути́змом.

auto [ˈɔːtəu] *n* (*US: inf*) авто́ *nt ind*.

autobiographical [ˈɔːtəbaɪəˈgræfɪkl] *adj* автобиографи́ческий*.

autobiography [ɔːtəbaɪˈɔgrəfɪ] *n* автобиогра́фия.

autocracy [ɔːˈtɔkrəsɪ] *n* автокра́тия.

autocratic [ɔːtəˈkrætɪk] *adj* автократи́ческий.

Autocue® [ˈɔːtəukjuː] *n* телесуфлёр.

autograph [ˈɔːtəgrɑːf] *n* авто́граф ♦ *vt* надпи́сывать (надписа́ть* *perf*).

auto-immune [ɔːtəuɪˈmjuːn] *adj* аутоимму́нный.

automat [ˈɔːtəmæt] *n* (*vending machine*) автома́т; (*US: place*) кафе́-автома́т.

automata [ɔːˈtɔmətə] *npl of* **automaton**.

automate [ˈɔːtəmeɪt] *vt* автоматизи́ровать (*impf/perf*).

automated [ˈɔːtəmeɪtɪd] *adj* автоматиз-и́рованный.

automatic [ɔːtəˈmætɪk] *adj* автомати́ческий* ♦ *n* (*US: gun*) (самозаря́дный) пистоле́т; (*car*) автомоби́ль *m* с автомати́ческим переключе́нием скоросте́й; (*washing machine*) стира́льная маши́на-автома́т.

automatically [ɔːtəˈmætɪklɪ] *adv* автомати́чески.

automatic data processing *n* автомати́ческая обрабо́тка да́нных.

automation [ɔːtəˈmeɪʃən] *n* автоматиза́ция.

automaton [ɔːˈtɔmətən] (*pl* **automata**) *n* автома́т.

automobile [ˈɔːtəməbiːl] *n* (*US*) автомоби́ль *m*.

австри́ец*(-и́йка).

autonomous [ɔː'tɒnəməs] *adj* (*region*)
автоно́мный* (автоно́мен); (*person,
organization*) самостоя́тельный*
(самостоя́телен).
autonomy [ɔː'tɒnəmɪ] *n* (*of organization, country
etc*) автоно́мия, самостоя́тельность *f.*
autopsy ['ɔːtɒpsɪ] *n* вскры́тие (*тру́па*).
autumn ['ɔːtəm] *n* о́сень *f;* **in** ~ о́сенью.
autumnal [ɔː'tʌmnəl] *adj* осе́нний*.
auxiliary [ɔːg'zɪlɪərɪ] *adj* вспомога́тельный ♦ *n*
помо́щник.
AV *n abbr* (*BIBLE:* = *Authorized Version*) перево́д
Би́блии, при́нятый в англика́нской це́ркви ♦
abbr = **audiovisual.**
Av. *abbr* = **avenue.**
avail [ə'veɪl] *vt:* **to** ~ **o.s. of** воспо́льзоваться
(*perf*) +*instr* ♦ *n:* **to no** ~ напра́сно.
availability [əveɪlə'bɪlɪtɪ] *n* (*supply*) нали́чие.
available [ə'veɪləbl] *adj* (*article, service*)
име́ющийся в нали́чии, досту́пный*
(досту́пен); (*person, time*) свобо́дный*
(свобо́ден); **every** ~ **means** все досту́пные
сре́дства; **is the manager** ~? заве́дующий *m
adj* свобо́ден?; **to make sth** ~ **to sb**
предоставля́ть (предоста́вить* *perf*) что-н
кому́-н.
avalanche ['ævəlɑːnʃ] *n* (*also fig*) лави́на.
avant-garde ['ævɑ̃ŋ'gɑːd] *adj*
авангарди́стский*.
avarice ['ævərɪs] *n* а́лчность *f.*
avaricious [ævə'rɪʃəs] *adj* а́лчный* (а́лчен).
avdp. *abbr* (= *avoirdupois*) *систе́ма едини́ц
ве́са, испо́льзуемая в англоязы́чных
стра́нах.*
Ave. *abbr* = **avenue.**
avenge [ə'vɛndʒ] *vt* мстить* (отомсти́ть* *perf*)
за +*acc.*
avenue ['ævənjuː] *n* (*street*) у́лица; (*drive*)
алле́я; (*means, solution*) путь* *m.*
average ['ævərɪdʒ] *n* сре́днее *nt adj* ♦ *adj*
сре́дний* ♦ *vt* достига́ть (дости́чь* *perf*) в
сре́днем +*gen,* составля́ть (соста́вить* *perf*) в
сре́днем; **on** ~ в сре́днем; **above/below (the)**
~ вы́ше/ни́же сре́днего у́ровня
▸ **average out** *vi:* **to** ~ **out at** равня́ться (*impf*) в
сре́днем +*dat.*
averse [ə'vɜːs] *adj:* **to be** ~ **to sth/doing** быть*
(*impf*) про́тив чего́-н/того́, что́бы +*infin;* **I
wouldn't be** ~ **to a drink** я непро́чь что́-
нибудь вы́пить.
aversion [ə'vɜːʃən] *n* неприя́знь *f;* **to have an** ~
to sb/sth испы́тывать (*impf*) неприя́знь к
кому́-н/чему́-н.
avert [ə'vɜːt] *vt* (*accident, war*) предотвраща́ть
(предотврати́ть* *perf*); (*blow, eyes*)
отводи́ть* (отвести́* *perf*).
aviary ['eɪvɪərɪ] *n* пти́чий* вольѐр.
aviation [eɪvɪ'eɪʃən] *n* авиа́ция.

avid ['ævɪd] *adj* (*supporter, viewer*) стра́стный.
avidly ['ævɪdlɪ] *adv* стра́стно.
avocado [ævə'kɑːdəʊ] *n* (*also:* ~ **pear:** *BRIT*)
авока́до *nt ind.*
avoid [ə'vɔɪd] *vt* избега́ть* (избежа́ть* *perf*).
avoidable [ə'vɔɪdəbl] *adj* (*death, accident*)
предотврати́мый.
avoidance [ə'vɔɪdəns] *n:* ~ (**of**) (*of tax, issue*)
уклоне́ние (от +*gen*).
avowed [ə'vaʊd] *adj* откры́тый.
AVP *n abbr* (*US:* = *assistant vice-president*)
помо́щник ви́це-президе́нта.
avuncular [ə'vʌŋkjʊlə] *adj* (*expression, tone*)
оте́ческий*; (*person*) забо́тливый.
AWACS ['eɪwæks] *n abbr* (= *airborne warning
and control system*) АВАКС (*авиацио́нная
систе́ма да́льнего радиолокацио́нного
обнаруже́ния и управле́ния*).
await [ə'weɪt] *vt* ожида́ть (*impf*) +*gen;* ~**ing
delivery** (*COMM*) отпра́вка предстои́т; **long**
~**ed** долгожда́нный.
awake [ə'weɪk] (*pt* **awoke,** *pp* **awoken** *or*
awaked) *vt* буди́ть* (разбуди́ть* *perf*) ♦ *vi*
просыпа́ться (просну́ться *perf*) ♦ *adj:* **he is** ~
он просну́лся; **to be** ~ **to** (*dangers,
possibilities*) сознава́ть* (*impf*); **he was still** ~
он ещё не спал.
awakening [ə'weɪknɪŋ] *n* (*also fig*)
пробужде́ние.
award [ə'wɔːd] *n* награ́да; (*LAW*) возмеще́ние
♦ *vt* награжда́ть (награди́ть* *perf*); (*LAW*)
присужда́ть (присуди́ть* *perf*).
aware [ə'wɛə] *adj:* **to be** ~ (**of**) (*realize*)
сознава́ть (*impf*) (+*acc*); **to become** ~ **of/that**
осознава́ть* (осозна́ть* *perf*) +*acc/,* что;
politically/socially ~ полити́чески/социа́льно
созна́тельный; **I am fully** ~ **that** я по́лностью
созна́ю, что.
awareness [ə'wɛənɪs] *n* осозна́ние; **to develop
people's** ~ **of** развива́ть (ра́звить* *perf*)
обще́ственное осозна́ние +*gen.*
awash [ə'wɒʃ] *adj* зато́пленный; (*fig*): ~ **with**
наводнённый (наводнён) +*instr.*
away [ə'weɪ] *adv* (*movement*) в сто́рону;
(*position*) в стороне́, по́одаль; (*far away*)
далеко́; (*in time*): **the holidays are two weeks**
~ до кани́кул (оста́лось) две неде́ли; ~ **from**
(*movement*) от +*gen;* (*position*) по́одаль от
+*gen;* **two kilometres** ~ **from the town** в двух
киломе́трах от го́рода; **two hours** ~ **by car** в
двух часа́х езды́ на маши́не; **he's** ~ **for a
week** он в отъе́зде на неде́лю; **he's** ~ **in Milan**
он в отъе́зде в Мила́н; **to take** ~ (**from**)
(*remove*) забира́ть (забра́ть* *perf*) (у +*gen*);
(*subtract*) отнима́ть (отня́ть* *perf*) (от +*gen*);
he is working ~ он продолжа́ет рабо́тать ; **to
fade** ~ (*colour*) выцвета́ть (вы́цвести* *perf*);
(*enthusiasm, light*) угаса́ть (уга́снуть *perf*).

---

* marks translations which have irregular inflections. The Russian-English side of the dictionary gives inflectional information.

away game n (*SPORT*) игра́ на вы́езде.
awe [ɔ:] n благогове́ние.
awe-inspiring ['ɔ:ɪnspaɪərɪŋ] adj (*person, thing*) внуша́ющий благогове́ние.
awesome ['ɔ:səm] adj = **awe-inspiring**.
awestruck ['ɔ:strʌk] adj охва́ченный (охва́чен) благогове́нием.
awful ['ɔ:fəl] adj ужа́сный* (ужа́сен); **an ~ lot (of)** ужа́сно мно́го (+*gen*).
awfully ['ɔ:fəlɪ] adv ужа́сно.
awhile [ə'waɪl] adv недо́лго, како́е-то вре́мя; **wait ~** подожди́те немно́го.
awkward ['ɔ:kwəd] adj (*clumsy*) неуклю́жий* (неуклю́ж); (*inconvenient*) неудо́бный* (неудо́бен); (*embarrassing*) нело́вкий*.
awkwardness ['ɔ:kwədnɪs] n (*see adj*) неуклю́жесть f; неудо́бство; нело́вкость f.
awl [ɔ:l] n ши́ло*.
awning ['ɔ:nɪŋ] n (*of tent*) наве́с; (*of shop, hotel*) тент.
awoke [ə'wəuk] pt of **awake**.
awoken [ə'wəukən] pp of **awake**.
AWOL ['eɪwɔl] abbr (*MIL*: = *absent without leave*) (находя́щийся) в самово́льной отлу́чке.
awry [ə'raɪ] adv (*crooked*) кри́во, ко́со; **to go ~** (*plan*) спу́тываться (спу́таться perf).
axe [æks] (*US* **ax**) n топо́р* ◆ vt (*employee*) увольня́ть (уво́лить perf); (*project etc*)

урéзывать (урéзать* perf); (*jobs*) сокраща́ть (сократи́ть* perf); **to have an ~ to grind** (*fig*) име́ть (*impf*) коры́стные побужде́ния.
axes[1] ['æksɪz] npl of **ax(e)**.
axes[2] ['æksi:z] npl of **axis**.
axiom ['æksɪəm] n аксио́ма.
axiomatic [æksɪəu'mætɪk] adj аксиомати́чный (аксиомати́чен).
axis ['æksɪs] (pl **axes**) n ось* f.
axle ['æksl] n (*also:* **~-tree**: *AUT*) ось* f.
aye [aɪ] excl да; **the ~s** npl голосу́ющие "за".
AYH n abbr = *American Youth Hostels*.
AZ abbr (*US*: *POST*) = *Arizona*.
azalea [ə'zeɪlɪə] n аза́лия.
Azerbaijan [[ae]zəbaɪ'dʒɑ:n] n Азербайджа́н.
Azerbaijani [[ae]zəbaɪ'dʒɑ:nɪ] n (*person*) азербайджа́нец*(-а́нка*); (*LING*) азербайджа́нский язы́к* ◆ adj азербайджа́нский*.
Azores [ə'zɔ:z] npl: **the ~** Азо́рские острова́ mpl.
Azov ['ɑ:zɔv] n: **Sea of ~** Азо́вское мо́ре.
AZT n abbr (= *azidothymidine*) аздотимиди́н.
Aztec ['æztɛk] n ацте́к ◆ adj: **~ civilization/art** цивилиза́ция/иску́сство ацте́ков.
azure ['eɪʒə'] adj лазу́рный.

~ *B, b* ~

B, b [bi:] *n* (*letter*) 2-ая бу́ква англи́йского
алфави́та; (*SCOL: mark*) ≈ хорошо́; ~ **road**
(*BRIT: AUT*) шоссе́ *nt ind* (второ́й катего́рии).
B [bi:] *n* (*MUS*) си *nt ind*.
b. *abbr* (= **born**) род.= *роди́лся*.
BA *n abbr* (= *Bachelor of Arts*) бакала́вр
гуманита́рных нау́к; (= *British Academy*)
Брита́нская акаде́мия (*гуманита́рных
нау́к*).
babble ['bæbl] *vi* лепета́ть* (залепета́ть* *perf*) ◆
n: **a ~ of voices** го́мон голосо́в.
babe [beɪb] *n* (*inf*) де́тка*, кро́шка*.
baboon [bə'bu:n] *n* бабуи́н.
baby ['beɪbɪ] *n* ребёнок*; (*US: inf*) де́тка*.
baby carriage *n* (*US*) коля́ска*.
baby grand *n* (*also:* ~ ~ **piano**) кабине́тный
роя́ль *m*.
babyhood ['beɪbɪhud] *n* младе́нчество.
babyish ['beɪbɪʃ] *adj* де́тский*.
baby-minder ['beɪbɪ'maɪndə'] *n* (*BRIT*) ня́ня*
(*присма́тривающая за детьми́ у себя́ до́ма*).
baby-sit ['beɪbɪsɪt] *vi* смотре́ть (*impf*) за
детьми́.
baby-sitter ['beɪbɪsɪtə'] *n* приходя́щая ня́ня*.
bachelor ['bætʃələ'] *n* холостя́к*; **B~ of Arts/
Science** ≈ бакала́вр гуманита́рных/
есте́ственных нау́к; **B~ of Arts/Science
degree** ≈ сте́пень* *f* бакала́вра
гуманита́рных/есте́ственных нау́к.
bachelorhood ['bætʃələhud] *n* холостя́цкая
жизнь *f*.
bachelor party *n* (*US*) мальчи́шник.

KEYWORD
---

back [bæk] *n* **1** (*of person, animal*) спина́; **the
back of the hand** ты́льная сторона́ ладо́ни;
he has his back to the wall (*fig*) он прижа́т к
стене́
2 (*of house, car etc*) за́дняя часть *f*; (*of chair*)
спи́нка*; (*of page*) обра́тная сторона́,
оборо́т; (*back cover: of book*) оборо́т; **back to
front** за́дом наперёд; **to break the back of a
job** (*BRIT*) выполня́ть (вы́полнить *perf*)
гла́вную часть рабо́ты; **at the back** (*of
crowd*) в за́дних ряда́х; (*of book*) в конце́
3 (*FOOTBALL*) защи́тник
◆ *vt* **1** (*candidate: also:* **back up**)

подд́ерживать (поддержа́ть *perf*)
2 (*financially: person*) финанси́ровать (*impf*),
ока́зывать (оказа́ть *perf*) фина́нсовую
подд́ержку; (: *horse*) ста́вить* (поста́вить*
perf) на +*acc*
3 (*car*): **he backed the car into the garage** он
дал за́дний ход и поста́вил маши́ну в гара́ж
◆ *vi* (*car etc: also:* **back up**) дава́ть* (дать* *perf*)
за́дний ход
◆ *adv* **1** (*not forward*) обра́тно, наза́д; **he ran
back** он побежа́л обра́тно *or* наза́д
2 (*returned*): **he's back** он верну́лся; **when will
you be back?** когда́ Вы вернётесь?
3 (*restitution*): **to throw the ball back** кида́ть
(ки́нуть *perf*) мяч обра́тно; **can I have the pen
back?** верни́те мне ру́чку, пожа́луйста
4 (*again*): **to call back** (*TEL*) перезва́нивать
(перезвони́ть *perf*); (*visit again*) заходи́ть
(зайти́ *perf*) ещё раз
◆ *cpd* **1** (*payment*) за́дним число́м
2 (*AUT: seat, wheels*) за́дний*; (*room, garden*)
вну́тренний*; **to take a back seat** (*fig*)
станови́ться* (стать* *perf*) пасси́вным
наблюда́телем
▶ **back down** *vi* отступа́ть (отступи́ть* *perf*)
▶ **back on to** *vt fus*: **the house backs on to a park**
дом выхо́дит за́дним фаса́дом в парк
▶ **back out** *vi* (*of promise*) отступа́ться
(отступи́ться* *perf*)
▶ **back up** *vt* (*person, theory etc*) подде́рживать
(поддержа́ть* *perf*); (*COMPUT*) резерви́ровать
(*impf/perf*).

backache ['bækeɪk] *n* простре́лы *mpl*, боль *f* в
пояснице.
backbencher ['bæk'bentʃə'] *n* (*BRIT*)
"заднескаме́ечник".
backbiting ['bækbaɪtɪŋ] *n* злосло́вие.
backbone ['bækbəun] *n* позвоно́чник; **he's the
~ of the organization** на нём де́ржится вся
организа́ция.
backchat ['bæktʃæt] *n* (*BRIT: inf*)
препира́тельство.
backcloth ['bækklɔθ] *n* (*BRIT: THEAT*) за́дник.
backcomb ['bækkəum] *vt* (*BRIT*) начёсывать
(начеса́ть* *perf*).

---

* marks translations which have irregular inflections. The Russian-English side of the dictionary gives inflectional information.

backdate [bæk'deɪt] vt (pay rise) проводи́ть*
(провести́* perf) за́дним число́м; (letter)
помеча́ть (поме́тить* perf) за́дним число́м;
~d pay rise (of 20%) повыше́ние зарпла́ты
за́дним число́м (на 20%).
backdrop ['bækdrɔp] n = **backcloth**.
backer ['bækə'] n (COMM) финанси́рующая
сторона́*.
backfire [bæk'faɪə'] vi (AUT) дава́ть* (дать* perf)
обра́тную вспы́шку; **his plan** ~d его́ план
оберну́лся про́тив него́.
backgammon ['bækgæmən] n триктра́к.
background ['bækgraund] n (of picture)
за́дний* план; (of events) предысто́рия;
(COMPUT) фон; (experience) о́пыт ◆ cpd (noise,
music) посторо́нний*; **he's from a working
class** ~ он из рабо́чей семьи́; **against a** ~ **of ...**
на фо́не +gen ...; ~ **reading (on)**
дополни́тельное чте́ние (по +dat).
backhand ['bækhænd] n (TENNIS) уда́р сле́ва.
backhanded ['bæk'hændɪd] adj (fig)
двусмы́сленный (двусмы́слен).
backhander ['bæk'hændə'] n (BRIT: inf) взя́тка*.
backing ['bækɪŋ] n (support) подде́ржка*;
(COMM) финанси́рование; (MUS)
сопровожде́ние.
back issue n ста́рый но́мер*.
backlash ['bæklæʃ] n (fig) обра́тная реа́кция.
backlog ['bæklɔg] n: ~ **of work** невы́полненная
рабо́та.
back number n = **back issue**.
backpack ['bækpæk] n рюкза́к*.
backpacker ['bækpækə'] n молодо́й челове́к,
путеше́ствующий с рюкзако́м.
back pay n пла́та за́дним число́м.
backpedal ['bækpɛdl] vi (fig) идти́* (пойти́*
perf) на попя́тный.
backseat driver ['bæksi:t-] n пассажи́р,
даю́щий сове́ты шофёру.
backside ['bæksaɪd] n (inf) зад*.
backslash ['bækslæʃ] n коса́я черта́ вле́во.
backslide ['bækslaɪd] vi принима́ться
(приня́ться perf) за ста́рое.
backspace ['bækspeɪs] vi реверси́ровать (impf/
perf).
backstage [bæk'steɪdʒ] adv за кули́сами.
backstreet ['bækstri:t] n окра́ина ◆ cpd: ~
abortionist челове́к, де́лающий подпо́льные
або́рты.
backstroke ['bækstrəuk] n пла́вание на спине́;
to do the ~ пла́вать (impf) на спине́.
backtrack ['bæktræk] vi (fig) идти́* (пойти́* perf)
на попя́тный.
backup ['bækʌp] adj (train, plane)
дополни́тельный*; (COMPUT) резе́рвный ◆ n
(support) подде́ржка*; (also: ~ **disk**)
дублика́т (ги́бкого ди́ска).
backward ['bækwəd] adj (movement)
обра́тный*; (person, country) отста́лый.
backwards ['bækwədz] adv наза́д; (in reverse
order) наоборо́т; (fall) на́взничь; **to know sth**
~ **or (US)** ~ **and forwards** знать (impf) что-н
вдоль и поперёк; **to walk** ~ пя́титься*
(попя́титься* perf).
backwater ['bækwɔ:tə'] n (fig) боло́то.
backyard [bæk'jɑ:d] n (of house) за́дний*
двор*.
bacon ['beɪkən] n беко́н.
bacteria [bæk'tɪərɪə] npl бакте́рии fpl.
bacteriology [bæktɪərɪ'ɔlədʒɪ] n
бактериоло́гия.
bad [bæd] adj плохо́й*; (mistake) серьёзный;
(injury, crash) тяжёлый* (тяжёл); (food)
ту́хлый*; **his** ~ **leg** его́ больна́я нога́; **to go** ~
(food) ту́хнуть (проту́хнуть perf), по́ртиться*
(испо́ртиться* perf); (milk) скиса́ть (ски́снуть
perf); **she's having a** ~ **time of it** у неё тяжёлый
пери́од; **I feel** ~ **about it** я чу́вствую себя́
винова́тым; **in** ~ **faith** неи́скренне.
bad debt n спи́санный долг (по
несостоя́тельности должника́).
baddy ['bædɪ] n (inf) плохо́й* m adj (в кни́ге,
фи́льме).
bade [bæd] pt of **bid**.
badge [bædʒ] n значо́к*; (of policeman) бля́ха;
(sew-on) наши́вка; (fig) си́мвол.
badger ['bædʒə'] n барсу́к ◆ vt пристава́ть*
(приста́ть* perf) к +dat.
badly ['bædlɪ] adv пло́хо; ~ **wounded** тяжело́
ра́неный; **he needs it** ~ он си́льно в э́том
нужда́ется; **to be** ~ **off (for money)** нужда́ться
(impf) (в деньга́х).
bad-mannered ['bæd'mænəd] adj
невоспи́танный.
badminton ['bædmɪntən] n бадминто́н.
bad-tempered ['bæd'tɛmpəd] adj (by nature)
вспы́льчивый (вспы́льчив),
раздражи́тельный (раздражи́телен); (on
one occasion) раздражённый (раздражён).
baffle ['bæfl] vt озада́чивать (озада́чить perf).
baffling ['bæflɪŋ] adj: **I find his behaviour** ~ его́
поведе́ние меня́ озада́чивает.
bag [bæg] n су́мка; (paper, plastic) паке́т;
(handbag) су́мочка*; (satchel) ра́нец; (case)
портфе́ль m; (of hunter) ягдта́ш; (pej:
woman) карга́; ~**s of** (inf) у́йма +gen; **to pack
one's** ~**s** собира́ть (собра́ть* perf) чемода́ны;
~**s under the eyes** мешки́ под глаза́ми.
bagful ['bægful] n (of flour etc) (по́лный) паке́т;
(of shopping) (по́лная) су́мка*.
baggage ['bægɪdʒ] n (US) бага́ж*.
baggage car n (US) бага́жный ваго́н.
baggage claim n (US) вы́дача багажа́.
baggy ['bægɪ] adj мешкова́тый.
Baghdad [bæg'dæd] n Багда́д.
bag lady n (esp US) бездо́мная ни́щая f adj.
bagpipes ['bægpaɪps] npl волы́нка* fsg.
bag-snatcher ['bægsnætʃə'] n (BRIT) вор*,
выхва́тывающий су́мки.
Bahamas [bə'hɑ:məz] npl: **the** ~ Бага́мские
острова́ mpl.
Bahrain [bɑ:'reɪn] n Бахре́йн.

Baikal [baɪˈkɑ:l] *n*: **Lake** ~ Байка́л.
bail [beɪl] *n* (*payment*) зало́г ◆ *vt* (*also*: **to grant** ~ **to**) выпуска́ть (вы́пустить* *perf*) под зало́г; **he was released on** ~ он был вы́пущен на пору́ки
▶ **bail out** *vt* (*LAW*) плати́ть* (заплати́ть* *perf*) зало́говую су́мму за +*acc*; (*boat*) выче́рпывать (вы́черпать *perf*) во́ду из +*gen*; (*firm, friend*) выруча́ть (вы́ручить *perf*) ◆ *vi* выбра́сываться (вы́броситься* *perf*) с парашю́том.
bailiff [ˈbeɪlɪf] *n* (*LAW*: *BRIT*) суде́бный исполни́тель *m*; (: *US*) помо́щник шери́фа; (*BRIT*: *of estate*) управля́ющий(-ая) *m(f) adj* име́нием.
bait [beɪt] *n* (*for fish*) нажи́вка*; (*for animal, criminal*) прима́нка* ◆ *vt* (*hook, trap*) нажива́ть (нажи́ть* *perf*); (*person*) дразни́ть* (*impf*).
baize [beɪz] *n* (зелёное) сукно́.
bake [beɪk] *vt* печь* (испе́чь* *perf*); (*clay etc*) обжига́ть (обже́чь* *perf*) ◆ *vi* (*bread etc*) пе́чься* (испе́чься* *perf*); (*make cakes etc*) печь* (испе́чь* *perf*) пироги́.
baked beans [beɪkt-] *npl* консерви́рованная фасо́ль *fsg*.
baker [ˈbeɪkə] *n* пе́карь* *m*; (*also*: **the** ~**'s**) бу́лочная *f adj*.
baker's dozen *n* чёртова дю́жина.
bakery [ˈbeɪkərɪ] *n* (*factory*) пека́рня*; (*shop*) бу́лочная *f adj*.
baking [ˈbeɪkɪŋ] *n* вы́печка ◆ *adj* (*inf*): **it's** ~ **hot today** сего́дня печёт; **she does her** ~ **once a week** она́ печёт раз в неде́лю.
baking powder *n* разрыхли́тель *m*.
baking tin *n* (*for cake, meat*) фо́рма.
baking tray *n* про́тивень* *m*.
Baku [baˈku] *n* Баку́ *m ind*.
balaclava [bæləˈklɑ:və] *n* (*also*: ~ **helmet**) вя́заный шлем.
balance [ˈbæləns] *n* (*equilibrium*) равнове́сие; (*COMM*: *in account*) бала́нс; (: *remainder*) оста́ток*; (*scales*) весы́ *pl* ◆ *vt* (*budget, account*) баланси́ровать (сбаланси́ровать *perf*); (*make equal*) уравнове́шивать (уравнове́сить* *perf*); **on** ~ по зре́лом размышле́нии; ~ **of trade/payments** торго́вый/платёжный бала́нс; ~ **carried forward** бала́нс к перено́су; ~ **brought forward** бала́нс с перено́са; **to** ~ **the books** баланси́ровать (сбаланси́ровать *perf*) кни́ги; **to** ~ **the pros and cons** взве́шивать (взве́сить* *perf*) все за и про́тив.
balanced [ˈbælənst] *adj* (*report*) взве́шенный (взве́шен); (*diet*) сбаланси́рованный (сбаланси́рован); (*personality*) уравнове́шенный.
balance sheet *n* сво́дный бала́нс.

balcony [ˈbælkənɪ] *n* балко́н.
bald [bɔ:ld] *adj* (*head*) лы́сый*; (*tyre*) стёртый; (*statement*) прямо́й*.
baldness [ˈbɔ:ldnɪs] *n* лы́сина.
bale [beɪl] *n* (*of hay etc*) тюк*; (*of papers etc*) ки́па
▶ **bale out** *vti see* **bail out**.
Balearic Islands [bælɪˈærɪk-] *npl*: **the** ~ ~ Балеа́рские острова́ *mpl*.
baleful [ˈbeɪlful] *adj* (*glance*) злове́щий* (злове́щ).
balk [bɔ:k] *vi*: **he** ~**ed at the idea** ему́ прети́ла э́та иде́я; (*subj*: *horse*): **to** ~ (**at**) заарта́читься (*perf*) (пе́ред +*instr*).
Balkan [ˈbɔ:lkən] *adj* балка́нский; **the** ~**s** *npl* Балка́ны *pl*.
ball [bɔ:l] *n* (*for football*) мяч*; (*for tennis, golf*) мя́чик; (*of wool, string*) клубо́к*; (*dance*) бал*; **to set the** ~ **rolling** (*fig*) пуска́ть (пусти́ть* *perf*) де́ло в ход; **to play** ~ (**with sb**) (*fig*) подъи́грывать (подыгра́ть *perf*) (кому́-н); **to be on the** ~ (*fig*) быть* (*impf*) на коне́; **the** ~ **is in their court** (*fig*) о́чередь за ни́ми.
ballad [ˈbæləd] *n* балла́да.
ballast [ˈbæləst] *n* балла́ст.
ball bearing *n* ша́рик подши́пника.
ballcock [ˈbɔ:lkɔk] *n* шарово́й кла́пан.
ballerina [bæləˈri:nə] *n* балери́на.
ballet [ˈbæleɪ] *n* бале́т.
ballet dancer *n* арти́ст(ка) бале́та.
ballistic [bəˈlɪstɪk] *adj* баллисти́ческий*.
ballistic missile *n* баллисти́ческий* снаря́д.
ballistics [bəˈlɪstɪks] *n* балли́стика.
balloon [bəˈlu:n] *n* возду́шный шар; (*also*: **hot air** ~) аэроста́т; (*in comic strip*) ко́нтур, в кото́рый впи́сываются ре́плики геро́ев ко́миксов.
balloonist [bəˈlu:nɪst] *n* воздухопла́ватель *m*.
ballot [ˈbælət] *n* голосова́ние, баллотиро́вка*.
ballot box *n* избира́тельная у́рна.
ballot paper *n* избира́тельный бюллете́нь *m*.
ballpark [ˈbɔ:lpɑ:k] *n* (*US*) бейсбо́льное по́ле.
ballpark figure *n* (*inf*) приблизи́тельный подсчёт.
ballpoint (pen) [ˈbɔ:lpɔɪnt(-)] *n* ша́риковая ру́чка*.
ballroom [ˈbɔ:lrum] *n* ба́льный зал.
balls [bɔ:lz] *npl* (*infl*) я́йца* *ntpl* (!); (: *nonsense*) фигня́ *fsg* (!)
balm [bɑ:m] *n* бальза́м.
balmy [ˈbɑ:mɪ] *adj* (*breeze*) ласка́ющий (ласка́ющ); (*day*) прия́тный* (прия́тен); (*BRIT*: *inf*) = **barmy**.
BALPA [ˈbælpə] *n abbr* = *British Airline Pilots' Association*.
balsam [ˈbɔ:lsəm] *n* бальза́м.
balsa (wood) [ˈbɔ:lsə-] *n* ба́льзовое де́рево*.

---

* marks translations which have irregular inflections. The Russian-English side of the dictionary gives inflectional information.

Baltic [bɔːltɪk] *n*: **the ~** Балти́йское Мо́ре ◆ *adj*: **the ~ States** прибалти́йские госуда́рства *ntpl*.

balustrade [bæləsˈtreɪd] *n* балюстра́да.

bamboo [bæmˈbuː] *n* бамбу́к.

bamboozle [bæmˈbuːzl] *vt* (*inf*) одура́чивать (одура́чить *perf*).

ban [bæn] *vt* (*prohibit*) запреща́ть (запрети́ть* *perf*); (*suspend, exclude*) отстраня́ть (отстрани́ть *perf*) ◆ *n* (*prohibition*) запре́т; (*suspension*): **~ from** отстране́ние от +*gen*; **he was ~ned from driving** (*BRIT*) у него́ отобра́ли води́тельские права́.

banal [bəˈnɑːl] *adj* (*remark, idea etc*) бана́льный* (бана́лен).

banana [bəˈnɑːnə] *n* бана́н.

band [bænd] *n* (*group: of people, rock musicians*) гру́ппа; (: *of jazz, military musicians*) орке́стр; (*strip: of light, colour*) полоса́*; (: *of cloth*) ле́нта; (*range*) диапазо́н
▸ **band together** *vi* объединя́ться (объедини́ться *perf*).

bandage [ˈbændɪdʒ] *n* повя́зка* ◆ *vt* (*wound, leg*) бинтова́ть (забинтова́ть *perf*); (*person*) перевя́зывать (перевяза́ть* *perf*).

Bandaid® [ˈbændeɪd] *n* (*US*) пла́стырь *m*.

bandit [ˈbændɪt] *n* банди́т.

bandstand [ˈbændstænd] *n* эстра́да.

bandwagon [ˈbændwægən] *n*: **to jump on the ~** примкну́ть (*perf*) к си́льной стороне́ *or* мо́дному тече́нию.

bandy [ˈbændɪ] *vt* (*jokes, ideas*) перебра́сываться (перебро́ситься* *perf*) +*instr*
▸ **bandy about** *vt* бесконе́чно упомина́ть (*impf*).

bandy-legged [ˈbændɪˈlɛgɪd] *adj* (*person*) кривоно́гий*.

bane [beɪn] *n*: **it/he is the ~ of my life** э́то/он несча́стье мое́й жи́зни.

bang [bæŋ] *n* стук; (*explosion*) вы́стрел; (*blow*) уда́р ◆ *excl* бах ◆ *vt* (*door*) хло́пать (хло́пнуть *perf*) +*instr*; (*one's head etc*) ударя́ть (уда́рить *perf*) ◆ *vi* (*door*) захло́пываться (захло́пнуться *perf*); (*fireworks*) хло́пать (*impf*) ◆ *adv*: **~ on time** (*BRIT: inf*) как раз во́ вре́мя; **to ~ at the door** колоти́ть* (*impf*) в дверь; **to ~ into sth** ста́лкиваться (столкну́ться *perf*) с чём-н.

banger [ˈbæŋəʳ] *n* (*BRIT: inf: also:* **old ~**) драндуле́т; (: *sausage*) сарде́лька*; (: *firework*) хлопу́шка.

Bangkok [bæŋˈkɔk] *n* Бангко́к.

Bangladesh [bæŋgləˈdɛʃ] *n* Бангладе́ш.

Bangladeshi [bæŋgləˈdɛʃɪ] *n* (*person*) бангладе́шец(-е́шка*) ◆ *adj* бангладе́шский.

bangle [ˈbæŋgl] *n* брасле́т.

bangs [bæŋz] *npl* (*US*) чёлка* *fsg*.

banish [ˈbænɪʃ] *vt* высыла́ть (вы́слать* *perf*).

banister [ˈbænɪstəʳ] *n* (*usu pl*) пери́ла *pl*.

banjo [ˈbændʒəu] (*pl* **~es** *or* **~s**) *n* ба́нджо *nt ind*.

bank [bæŋk] *n* банк; (*of river, lake*) бе́рег*; (*of*

earth) на́сыпь *f*; (*of switches*) пане́ль *f* ◆ *vi* (*AVIAT*) крени́ться (накрени́ться *perf*); (*COMM*): **they ~ with Pitt's** они́ де́ржат де́ньги в ба́нке Питт
▸ **bank on** *vt fus* полага́ться (положи́ться* *perf*) на +*acc*.

bank account *n* ба́нковский* счёт.

bank balance *n* коли́чество де́нег на ба́нковском счету́.

bank card *n* ба́нковская ка́рточка*.

bank charges *npl* (*BRIT*) *пла́та, взима́емая ба́нком за услу́ги*.

bank draft *n* ба́нковская тра́тта.

banker [ˈbæŋkəʳ] *n* банки́р.

banker's card *n* (*BRIT*) = **bank card**.

banker's order *n* (*BRIT*) ба́нковское поруче́ние.

Bank Giro *n* Жи́ро *nt ind* банк.

bank holiday *n* (*BRIT*) нерабо́чий* день *m* (*обы́чно понеде́льник*).

banking [ˈbæŋkɪŋ] *n* ба́нковское де́ло*.

banking hours *npl* часы́ *mpl* рабо́ты ба́нка.

bank loan *n* ба́нковский* заём*.

bank manager *n* управля́ющий(-ая) *m(f) adj* ба́нком.

banknote [ˈbæŋknəut] *n* банкно́т.

bank rate *n* учётная ста́вка* ба́нка.

bankroll [ˈbæŋkrəul] *vt* обеспе́чивать (обеспе́чить *perf*) деньга́ми ◆ *n* (*esp US*) фина́нсовые ресу́рсы *pl*.

bankrupt [ˈbæŋkrʌpt] *adj* обанкро́тившийся ◆ *n* банкро́т; **to go ~** обанкро́титься* (*perf*); **I am ~** я ‒ банкро́т.

bankruptcy [ˈbæŋkrʌptsɪ] *n* (*COMM, fig*) банкро́тство, несостоя́тельность *f*.

bank statement *n* вы́писка* с ба́нковского счёта.

banner [ˈbænəʳ] *n* транспара́нт.

banner headline *n* (газе́тная) ша́пка*.

bannister [ˈbænɪstəʳ] *n* = **banister**.

banns [bænz] *npl огла́ше́ние в це́ркви имён вступа́ющих в брак*.

banquet [ˈbæŋkwɪt] *n* банке́т.

bantamweight [ˈbæntəmweɪt] *n* (*BOXING*) боксёр лёгкого ве́са.

banter [ˈbæntəʳ] *n* подшу́чивание.

BAOR *n abbr* = *British Army of the Rhine*.

baptism [ˈbæptɪzəm] *n* креще́ние.

Baptist [ˈbæptɪst] *n* бапти́ст(ка).

baptize [bæpˈtaɪz] *vt* крести́ть* (окрести́ть* *perf*).

bar [bɑːʳ] *n* (*pub*) бар; (*counter*) сто́йка; (*rod*) прут; (*cake: of soap*) брусо́к*; (: *of chocolate*) пли́тка*; (*obstacle*) прегра́да; (*prohibition*) запре́т; (*MUS*) такт ◆ *vt* (*door, way*) загора́живать (загороди́ть* *perf*); (*road*) прегражда́ть (прегради́ть *perf*); (*person*) не допуска́ть (допусти́ть* *perf*); (*activity*) запреща́ть (запрети́ть* *perf*); **~s** *npl* (*on window etc*) решётка *fsg*; **behind ~s** за решёткой; **the B~** адвокату́ра; **~ none** без

исключе́ния.
Barbados [bɑːˈbeɪdɔs] *n* Барба́дос.
barbaric [bɑːˈbærɪk] *adj* ва́рварский*.
barbarous [ˈbɑːbərəs] *adj* ва́рварский*.
barbecue [ˈbɑːbɪkjuː] *n* барбекю́ *nt ind.*
barbed wire [ˈbɑːbd-] *n* колю́чая про́волока.
barber [ˈbɑːbə'] *n* парикма́хер.
barbiturate [bɑːˈbɪtjurɪt] *n* барбитура́т.
Barcelona [bɑːsəˈləunə] *n* Барсело́на.
bar chart *n* гистогра́мма.
bar code *n* штрихово́й код.
bare [bɛə'] *adj* (*body*) го́лый*, обнажённый
(обнажён); (*trees*) оголённый (оголён) ♦ *vt*
(*one's body*) обнажа́ть (обнажи́ть *perf*);
(*teeth*) ска́лить (оска́лить *perf*); **in** *or* **with ~**
feet босико́м; **the ~ essentials** предме́ты *mpl*
пе́рвой необходи́мости; **~ minimum** то́лько
ми́нимум; **to ~ one's soul** раскрыва́ть
(раскры́ть* *perf*) свою́ ду́шу.
bareback [ˈbɛəbæk] *adv* без седла́.
barefaced [ˈbɛəfeɪst] *adj* бессты́дный*.
barefoot [ˈbɛəfut] *adj* босо́й* (бос) ♦ *adv*
босико́м.
bareheaded [bɛəˈhɛdɪd] *adj*, *adv* с непокры́той
голово́й.
barely [ˈbɛəlɪ] *adv* едва́.
Barents Sea [ˈbærənts-] *n*: **the ~ ~** Ба́ренцево
мо́ре.
bargain [ˈbɑːgɪn] *n* сде́лка*; (*good buy*)
вы́годная поку́пка* ♦ *vi*: **to ~** (**with sb**)
торгова́ться (сторгова́ться *perf*) (с кем-н);
into the ~ в прида́чу
▸ **bargain for** *vt fus*: **he got more than he ~ed for**
он получи́л бо́льше, чем ожида́л.
bargaining [ˈbɑːgənɪŋ] *n* торг.
bargaining position *n* пози́ция, с кото́рой
предъявля́ются тре́бования и усло́вия
сде́лки и́ли догово́ра.
barge [bɑːdʒ] *n* ба́ржа
▸ **barge in** *vi* (*enter*) вва́ливаться (ввали́ться*
perf); (*interrupt*) влеза́ть (влезть* *perf*)
▸ **barge into** *vt fus* (*person*) ната́лкиваться
(натолкну́ться *perf*) на +*acc*.
bargepole [ˈbɑːdʒpəul] *n*: **I wouldn't touch him**
with a ~ я к нему́ на пу́шечный вы́стрел не
подойду́.
baritone [ˈbærɪtəun] *n* барито́н.
barium meal [ˈbɛərɪəm-] *n* ба́риевая
микстура.
bark [bɑːk] *n* (*of tree*) кора́; (*of dog*) лай ♦ *vi*
(*dog*) ла́ять (*impf*); **she's ~ing up the wrong**
tree она́ обраща́ется не по а́дресу.
barley [ˈbɑːlɪ] *n* ячме́нь* *m.*
barley sugar *n* ≈ леденец*.
barmaid [ˈbɑːmeɪd] *n* буфе́тчица.
barman [ˈbɑːmən] *irreg n* ба́рмен.
barmy [ˈbɑːmɪ] *adj* (*BRIT: inf: person*) чо́кнутый;
(: *idea*) неле́пый.

barn [bɑːn] *n* амба́р.
barn owl *n* сипу́ха.
barnacle [ˈbɑːnəkl] *n* моллю́ск.
barometer [bəˈrɔmɪtə'] *n* баро́метр.
baron [ˈbærən] *n* баро́н; (*of press, industry*)
магна́т.
baroness [ˈbærənɪs] *n* бароне́сса.
baronet [ˈbærənɪt] *n* бароне́т.
barracking [ˈbærəkɪŋ] *n* вы́крики *mpl*,
неодобри́тельные во́згласы *mpl*.
barracks [ˈbærəks] *npl* (*MIL*) каза́рма *fsg.*
barrage [ˈbærɑːʒ] *n* (*MIL*) загради́тельный
ого́нь *m*; (*dam*) да́мба; (*fig*) лави́на.
barrel [ˈbærəl] *n* (*of wine, beer*) бо́чка*; (*of oil*)
барре́ль *m*; (*of gun*) ствол*.
barrel organ *n* шарма́нка*.
barren [ˈbærən] *adj* (*land*) беспло́дный*
(беспло́ден).
barricade [bærɪˈkeɪd] *n* баррика́да ♦ *vt*
баррикади́ровать (забаррикади́ровать
perf); **to ~ o.s. in** баррикади́роваться
(забаррикади́роваться *perf*).
barrier [ˈbærɪə'] *n* (*at entrance*) барье́р; (*at*
frontier) шлагба́ум; (*BRIT: also*: **crash ~**)
предохрани́тельный барье́р на шоссе́ и
доро́гах; (*fig*: *to progress etc*) препя́тствие;
(: *to communication*) поме́ха.
barrier cream *n* (*BRIT*) защи́тный крем.
barring [ˈbɑːrɪŋ] *prep* за исключе́нием +*gen.*
barrister [ˈbærɪstə'] *n* (*BRIT*) адвока́т.
barrow [ˈbærəu] *n* (*also*: **wheelbarrow**) та́чка*;
(*cart*) двухколёсная теле́жка*.
bar stool *n* высо́кое сиде́нье во́зле сто́йки
ба́ра.
Bart. *abbr* (*BRIT*. = *baronet*) бароне́т.
bartender [ˈbɑːtɛndə'] *n* (*US*) ба́рмен.
barter [ˈbɑːtə'] *vi* производи́ть* (произвести́*
perf) ба́ртерный обме́н ♦ *n* ба́ртер.
base [beɪs] *n* основа́ние; (*of monument etc*)
постаме́нт; (*of make up*) осно́ва; (*MIL*) ба́за;
(*for organization*) местонахожде́ние ♦ *adj*
ни́зкий* (ни́зок) ♦ *vt*: **to ~ sth on** (*opinion*,
belief) осно́вывать (*impf*) что-н на +*prp*; **to be**
~d at бази́роваться (*impf*) в/на +*prp*; **the film**
is ~d on the book фильм осно́ван на кни́ге;
I'm ~d in London for now сейча́с я бази́руюсь
в Ло́ндоне (*inf*); **a Paris-~d firm** фи́рма
бази́рующаяся в Пари́же; **computer-~d**
teaching обуче́ние при по́мощи
компью́теров.
baseball [ˈbeɪsbɔːl] *n* бейсбо́л.
baseboard [ˈbeɪsbɔːd] *n* (*US*) пли́нтус.
base camp *n* ба́зовый ла́герь* *m.*
Basel [bɑːl] *n* = **Basle.**
baseline [ˈbeɪslaɪn] *n* (*SPORT*) ли́ния пода́чи;
(*starting point*) исхо́дная черта́.
basement [ˈbeɪsmənt] *n* подва́л.
base rate *n* тари́фная ста́вка.

---

bases[1] ['beɪsɪz] *npl of* **base**.
bases[2] ['beɪsiːz] *npl of* **basis**.
bash [bæʃ] (*inf*) *vt* колоти́ть* (поколоти́ть*
perf) ♦ *n*: **I'll have a ~ (at it)** (*BRIT*) я попыта́юсь
▸ **bash up** *vt* (*car*) разбива́ть (разби́ть* *perf*);
(*BRIT: person*) избива́ть (изби́ть* *perf*).
bashful ['bæʃful] *adj* засте́нчивый (засте́нчив).
bashing ['bæʃɪŋ] *n* (*inf*): **union-~** я́ростные
напа́дки на профсою́зы.
BASIC ['beɪsɪk] *n* (*COMPUT*) Бэ́йсик.
basic ['beɪsɪk] *adj* (*fundamental*)
фундамента́льный; (*elementary*)
нача́льный; (*primitive*) элемента́рный
(элемента́рен).
basically ['beɪsɪklɪ] *adv* по существу́; (*on the
whole*) в основно́м.
basic rate *n* ба́зисная ста́вка.
basics ['beɪsɪks] *npl*: **the ~** осно́вы *fpl*.
basil ['bæzl] *n* базили́к.
basin ['beɪsn] *n* (*also:* **washbasin**) ра́ковина;
(*BRIT: for food*) ми́ска*; (*GEO*) бассе́йн.
basis ['beɪsɪs] (*pl* **bases**) *n* основа́ние; **on a part-
time ~** на непо́лной ста́вке; **on a trial ~** на
испыта́тельный срок; **on the ~ of what
you've said** на осно́ве ска́занного Ва́ми.
bask [bɑːsk] *vi*: **to ~ in the sun** гре́ться (*impf*) на
со́лнце.
basket ['bɑːskɪt] *n* корзи́на.
basketball ['bɑːskɪtbɔːl] *n* баскетбо́л.
basketball player *n* баскетболи́ст(ка).
Basle [bɑːl] *n* Ба́зель *m*.
Basque [bæsk] *adj* ба́скский ♦ *n* баск.
bass [beɪs] *n* бас* ♦ *adj* басо́вый.
bass clef *n* басо́вый ключ*.
bassoon [bə'suːn] *n* фаго́т.
bastard ['bɑːstəd] *n* внебра́чный ребёнок*;
(*infl*)ублю́док* (*!*)
baste [beɪst] *vt* (*CULIN*) полива́ть (поли́ть* *perf*)
жи́ром и со́ком; (*SEWING*) смётывать
(смета́ть* *perf*).
bastion ['bæstɪən] *n* (*fig*) опло́т.
bat [bæt] *n* (*ZOOL*) летуча́я мы́шь *f*; (*SPORT*)
бита́; (*BRIT: TABLE TENNIS*) раке́тка* ♦ *vt*: **he
didn't ~ an eyelid** он и гла́зом не моргну́л;
off one's own ~ по со́бственному почи́ну.
batch [bætʃ] *n* (*of bread*) вы́печка*; (*of papers
etc*) па́чка*; (*of applicants, goods*) па́ртия.
batch processing *n* (*COMPUT*) паке́тная
обрабо́тка (*да́нных*).
bated ['beɪtɪd] *adj*: **with ~ breath** затаи́в
дыха́ние.
bath [bɑːθ] *n* ва́нна ♦ *vt* купа́ть (вы́купать
perf); **to have a ~** принима́ть (приня́ть* *perf*)
ва́нну; *see also* **baths**.
bathe [beɪð] *vi* (*swim*) купа́ться (*impf*); (*US: have
a bath*) принима́ть (приня́ть* *perf*) ва́нну ♦ *vt*
(*wound*) промыва́ть (промы́ть* *perf*).
bather ['beɪðə'] *n* купа́льщик(-ица).
bathing ['beɪðɪŋ] *n* купа́ние.
bathing cap *n* купа́льная ша́почка*.
bathing costume (*US* **bathing suit**) *n*

купа́льный костю́м.
bath mat *n* ко́врик для ва́нной.
bathrobe ['bɑːθrəub] *n* купа́льный хала́т.
bathroom ['bɑːθrum] *n* ва́нная *f adj*.
baths [bɑːðz] *npl* (*also:* **swimming ~**)
пла́вательный бассе́йн *msg*.
bath towel *n* ба́нное полоте́нце.
bathtub ['bɑːθtʌb] *n* ва́нна.
batman ['bætmən] *irreg n* (*BRIT*) денщи́к.
baton ['bætən] *n* (*MUS*) дирижёрская па́лочка*;
(*ATHLETICS*) эстафе́тная па́лочка*; (*POLICE*)
дуби́нка*.
battalion [bə'tælɪən] *n* батальо́н.
batten ['bætn] *n* (*CARPENTRY*) ре́йка; (*NAUT*) ре́я
▸ **batten down** *vt* (*NAUT*): **to ~ down the
hatches** задра́ивать (задра́ить* *perf*) лю́ки.
batter ['bætə'] *vt* (*child, wife*) бить (изби́ть*
perf); (*subj: wind, rain*) бить* (поби́ть* *perf*) ♦ *n*
(*CULIN*) жи́дкое те́сто.
battered ['bætəd] *adj* (*hat*) потрёпанный
(потрёпан); (*pan*) покорёженный (покорё-
жен); **~ wife** подверга́емая побо́ям жена́*.
battering ram ['bætərɪŋ-] *n* тара́н.
battery ['bætərɪ] *n* (*of torch etc*) батаре́йка*;
(*AUT*) аккумуля́тор; (*of tests, reporters*) ряд*.
battery charger *n* заря́дное устро́йство
(батаре́и).
battery farm *n* птицефа́брика.
battery hens *npl* инкуба́торные ку́ры *mpl*.
battle ['bætl] *n* би́тва, бой* ♦ *vi* боро́ться
(*impf*), сража́ться (*impf*); **that's half the ~** э́то
уже́ полде́ла; **it's a** *or* **we're fighting a losing ~**
(*fig*) э́то безнадёжная борьба́, мы ведём
безнадёжную борьбу́.
battle dress *n* похо́дная фо́рма.
battlefield ['bætlfiːld] *n* по́ле* би́твы *or* бо́я.
battlements ['bætlmənts] *npl* сте́ны* *fpl* с
бойни́цами.
battleship ['bætlʃɪp] *n* вое́нный кора́бль* *m*.
batty ['bætɪ] *adj* (*inf*) чо́кнутый (чо́кнут).
bauble ['bɔːbl] *n* безделу́шка*.
baud [bɔːd] *n* (*COMPUT*) бод.
baud rate *n* (*COMPUT*) ско́рость *f* переда́чи (в
бо́дах).
baulk [bɔːlk] *vi* = **balk**.
bauxite ['bɔːksaɪt] *n* бокси́т.
Bavaria [bə'vɛərɪə] *n* Бава́рия.
Bavarian [bə'vɛərɪən] *adj* бава́рский* ♦ *n*
бава́рец(-рка).
bawdy ['bɔːdɪ] *adj* (*joke, song*) скабрёзный*
(скабрёзен).
bawl [bɔːl] *vi* ора́ть* (заора́ть* *perf*).
bay [beɪ] *n* зали́в; (*smaller*) бу́хта; (*horse*)
гнеда́я ло́шадь *f*; **parking ~** (*BRIT*) ме́сто*
парко́вки; **loading ~** погру́зочная
площа́дка*; **to hold sb at ~** держа́ть (*impf*)
кого́-н на расстоя́нии.
bay leaf *n* лавро́вый лист*.
bayonet ['beɪənɪt] *n* штык*.
bay tree *n* ла́вровое де́рево*.
bay window *n* э́ркер.

bazaar [bə'zɑ:'] *n* (*market*) база́р, ры́нок*; (*fete*) благотвори́тельный база́р.

bazooka [bə'zu:kə] *n* базу́ка, гранатомёт.

BB *n abbr* (*BRIT*: = *Boys' Brigade*) ≈ отря́д бойска́утов.

B & B *n abbr* = **bed and breakfast**.

b & b *n abbr* = **B & B**.

BBC *n abbr* (= *British Broadcasting Corporation*) Би-Би-Си *nt ind*.

BC *adv abbr* (= *before Christ*) до рождества́ Христо́ва ♦ *abbr* (*CANADA*) = *British Columbia*.

BCG *n abbr* (= *Bacillus Calmette-Guérin*) БЦЖ.

BD *n abbr* (= *Bachelor of Divinity*) бакала́вр богосло́вия.

B/D *abbr* = **bank draft**.

BDS *n abbr* (= *Bachelor of Dental Surgery*) бакала́вр стоматоло́гии.

KEYWORD
---

be [bi:] (*pt* **was, were**, *pp* **been**) *aux vb* **1** (*with present participle: forming continuous tenses*): **what are you doing?** что Вы де́лаете?; **it is raining** идёт дождь; **they're working tomorrow** они́ рабо́тают за́втра; **the house is being built** дом стро́ится/стро́ят; **I've been waiting for you for ages** я жду Вас уже́ це́лую ве́чность

2 (*with pp: forming passives*): **he was killed** он был уби́т; **the box had been opened** я́щик открыва́ли; **the thief was nowhere to be seen** во́ра нигде́ не́ было ви́дно

3 (*in tag questions*) пра́вда, да; **she's back again, is she?** она́ верну́лась, да?; **she is pretty, isn't she?** она́ хоро́шенькая, пра́вда?

4 (*to +infin*): **the house is to be sold** дом бу́дет про́дан; **you're to be congratulated for all your work** Вы бу́дете отме́чены за всю ва́шу рабо́ту; **he's not to open it** он не до́лжен открыва́ть э́то

♦ *vb* **1** (*+ complement: in present tense*): **he is English** он англича́нин; (*in past/future tense*) быть (*impf*) +*instr or* +*nom*; **he was a doctor** он был врачо́м; **she is going to be very tall** она́ бу́дет о́чень высо́кая *or* высо́кой; **he is going to be an actor** он бу́дет актёром; **I'm tired** я уста́л; **I was hot/cold** мне бы́ло жа́рко/хо́лодно; **two and two are four** два́жды два – четы́ре; **she's tall/pretty** она́ высо́кая/ симпати́чная; **be careful!** бу́дьте осторо́жны!; **be quiet!** ти́ше!

2 (*of health*): **how are you feeling?** как Вы себя́ чу́вствуете?; **he's very ill** он о́чень бо́лен; **I'm better now** мне сейча́с лу́чше

3 (*of age*): **how old are you?** ско́лько Вам лет?; **I'm sixteen (years old)** мне шестна́дцать (лет); **I was only 5 (years old) then** мне тогда́ бы́ло всего́ 5 (лет)

4 (*cost*): **how much is/was the wine?** ско́лько сто́ит/сто́ило вино́?; **that'll be £5.75, please** с Вас £5.75, пожа́луйста

♦ *vi* **1** (*exist*) быть (*impf*); **there are people who...** есть лю́ди, кото́рые...; **there is one drug that...** есть одно́ лека́рство, кото́рое...; **is there a God?** Бог есть на све́те?

2 (*occur*) быва́ть (*impf*); **there are frequent accidents on this road** на э́той доро́ге ча́сто быва́ют ава́рии; **be that as it may** как бы то ни́ было; **so be it** так и бы́ть, быть по сему́

3 (*referring to place*): **I won't be here tomorrow** меня́ здесь за́втра не бу́дет; **Edinburgh is in Scotland** Эдинбу́рг нахо́дится в Шотла́ндии; **the book is on the table** кни́га на столе́; **there are pictures on the wall** на стене́ карти́ны; **there is someone in the house** в до́ме кто-то есть; **we've been here for ages** мы здесь уже́ о́чень давно́

4 (*referring to movement*): **where have you been?** где Вы бы́ли?; **I've been to the post office** я был на по́чте

♦ *impers vb* **1** (*referring to time*): **it's five o'clock (now)** сейча́с пять часо́в; **it's the 28th of April (today)** сего́дня 28-ое апре́ля

2 (*referring to distance, weather*: *in present tense*): **it's 10 km to the village** до дере́вни 10 км; (: *in past/future tense*) **it's too hot/cold (today)** сего́дня сли́шком жа́рко/ хо́лодно; **it was very windy yesterday** вчера́ бы́ло о́чень ве́трено; **it will be sunny tomorrow** за́втра бу́дет со́лнечно

3 (*emphatic*): **it's (only) me/the postman** э́то я/ почтальо́н; **it was Maria who paid the bill** счёт оплати́ла Мари́я.

B/E *abbr* = **bill of exchange**.

beach [bi:tʃ] *n* (*stony*) бе́рег* мо́ря; (*sandy*) пляж ♦ *vt* (*boat*) выта́скивать (вы́тащить *perf*) на бе́рег.

beach buggy *n* пля́жный вездехо́д.

beachcomber ['bi:tʃkəumə'] *n* бич*.

beachwear ['bi:tʃwɛə'] *n* пля́жная оде́жда.

beacon ['bi:kən] *n* (*lighthouse*) мая́к*; (*marker*) сигна́льный огонь* *m*; (*also*: **radio ~**) радиомая́к*.

bead [bi:d] *n* бу́сина; (*of sweat*) ка́пля*; **~s** *npl* (*necklace*) бу́сы *pl*.

beady ['bi:dɪ] *adj*: **~ eyes** глаза́-бу́синки *mpl*.

beagle ['bi:gl] *n* го́нчая *f adj* (соба́ка).

beak [bi:k] *n* клюв.

beaker ['bi:kə'] *n* (*cup*) пластма́ссовый стака́н.

beam [bi:m] *n* (*ARCHIT*) ба́лка*; (*of light*) луч*; (*RADIO*) радиосигна́л ♦ *vi* (*smile*) сия́ть (*impf*) ♦ *vt* (*signal*) передава́ть* (переда́ть* *perf*); **to drive on full** *or* **main** *or* (*US*) **high ~** éхать* (*impf*) с включёнными да́льними фа́рами.

beaming ['bi:mɪŋ] *adj* сия́ющий*.

---

* marks translations which have irregular inflections. The Russian-English side of the dictionary gives inflectional information.

bean [bi:n] *n* боб*; **French** ~ фасо́ль *f no pl*; **runner** ~ фасо́ль о́гненная; **coffee** ~ кофе́йное зерно́.

beanpole ['bi:npəul] *n* (*inf*) каланча́* (*высо́кий челове́к*).

beansprouts ['bi:nsprauts] *npl* побе́ги *mpl* бобо́в.

bear [bɛəʳ] (*pt* **bore**, *pp* **borne**) *n* медве́дь(-дица) *m(f)*; (*STOCK EXCHANGE*) "медве́дь" (*спекуля́нт, игра́ющий на пониже́ние ку́рса*) ♦ *vt* (*responsibility, cost*) нести́* (понести́* *perf*); (*weight*) нести́* (*impf*); (*examination, scrutiny*) выде́рживать (вы́держать* *perf*); (*situation, person*) выноси́ть* (вы́нести* *perf*); (*traces, signs*) нести́* (*impf*) на себе́; (*children*) рожда́ть (роди́ть* *perf*); (*fruit*) приноси́ть* (принести́* *perf*); (*COMM*): **to ~ interest** приноси́ть* (принести́* *perf*) проце́нты ♦ *vi*: **to ~ right/left** (*AUT*) держа́ться (*impf*) пра́вого/ле́вого поворо́та; **to ~ the responsibility of** нести́* (понести́* *perf*) отве́тственность за +*acc*; **to ~ comparison with** выде́рживать (вы́держать* *perf*) сравне́ние с +*instr*; **I can't ~ him** я его́ не выношу́; **the road ~s to the right/left** доро́га идёт впра́во/вле́во; **to bring pressure to ~ on sb** ока́зывать (оказа́ть* *perf*) давле́ние на кого́-н
▸ **bear out** *vt* подде́рживать (поддержа́ть *perf*)
▸ **bear up** *vi* держа́ться (*impf*); **he bore up well** он держа́лся молодцо́м
▸ **bear with** *vt fus* терпе́ть (*impf*) с +*instr*; **~ with me a minute** потерпи́те мину́ту.

bearable ['bɛərəbl] *adj* терпи́мый (терпи́м).

beard [bɪəd] *n* борода́*.

bearded ['bɪədɪd] *adj* борода́тый.

bearer ['bɛərəʳ] *n* (*of letter*) пода́тель(ница) *m(f)*; (*of news*) ве́стник; (*of cheque, passport etc*) владе́лец*, предъяви́тель *m*; (*of title*) носи́тель(ница) *m(f)*.

bearing ['bɛərɪŋ] *n* (*manner*) мане́ра держа́ть себя́; (*connection*) отноше́ние; (*TECH*) подши́пник; **~s** *npl* (*also*: **ball ~s**) ша́рики *mpl* подши́пника; **to take a ~** ориенти́роваться (*impf/perf*); **to get one's ~s** ориенти́роваться (сориенти́роваться *perf*).

beast [bi:st] *n* (*also inf*) зверь* *m*.

beastly ['bi:stlɪ] *adj* ужа́сный (ужа́сен), жу́ткий* (жу́ток).

beat [bi:t] (*pt* **beat**, *pp* **beaten**) *n* (*of heart*) бие́ние; (*MUS: rhythm*) ритм; (: *in bar*) такт; (*POLICE*) уча́сток* ♦ *vt* (*wife, child*) бить* (поби́ть* *perf*); (*eggs etc*) взбива́ть (взби́ть* *perf*); (*opponent, record*) побива́ть (поби́ть* *perf*); (*drum*) бить* (*impf*) в +*acc* ♦ *vi* (*heart*) би́ться* (*impf*); (*rain, wind*) стуча́ть (*impf*); **to ~ time** отбива́ть (*impf*) такт; **~ it!** (*inf*) кати́сь!; **that ~s everything** э́то превосхо́дит всё; **to ~ about the bush** ходи́ть* (*impf*) вокру́г да о́коло; **off the ~en track** по непрото́ренному пути́

▸ **beat down** *vt* (*door*) выла́мывать (вы́ломать *perf*); (*price*) сбива́ть (сбить* *perf*); (*seller*) добива́ться (доби́ться* *perf*) ски́дки у +*gen* ♦ *vi* (*rain*) хлеста́ть* (*impf*); (*sun*) пали́ть (*impf*)
▸ **beat off** *vt* отбива́ть (отби́ть* *perf*)
▸ **beat up** *vt* (*person*) избива́ть (изби́ть* *perf*); (*eggs etc*) взбива́ть (взби́ть* *perf*).

beaten ['bi:tn] *pp of* **beat**.

beater ['bi:təʳ] *n* ве́нчик.

beating ['bi:tɪŋ] *n* (*thrashing*) по́рка*; **to take a ~** (*fig*) терпе́ть* (потерпе́ть* *perf*) пораже́ние.

beat-up ['bi:t'ʌp] *adj* (*inf*) раздо́лбанный (раздо́лбан).

beautician [bju:'tɪʃən] *n* космети́чка*.

beautiful ['bju:tɪful] *adj* (*woman, place*) краси́вый (краси́в); (*day, experience*) прекра́сный* (прекра́сен).

beautifully ['bju:tɪflɪ] *adv* (*play, sing etc*) краси́во, прекра́сно; (*quiet, empty etc*) замеча́тельно.

beautify ['bju:tɪfaɪ] *vt* украша́ть (укра́сить* *perf*).

beauty ['bju:tɪ] *n* красота́*; (*woman*) краса́вица; **the ~ of it is that ...** (*fig*) пре́лесть *f* э́того в том, что ....

beauty contest *n* ко́нкурс красоты́.

beauty queen *n* короле́ва красоты́.

beauty salon *n* сало́н красоты́.

beauty sleep *n* сон до полу́ночи, по пове́рию де́лающий челове́ка молоды́м и здоро́вым.

beauty spot *n* (*BRIT: TOURISM*) живопи́сная ме́стность *f*.

beaver ['bi:vəʳ] *n* (*ZOOL*) бобр*.

becalmed [bɪ'kɑ:md] *adj* заштиле́вший.

became [bɪ'keɪm] *pt of* **become**.

because [bɪ'kɔz] *conj* потому́ что; (*since, as*) так как; **~ of** (*illness etc*) из-за +*gen*.

beck [bɛk] *n*: **to be at sb's ~ and call** быть* (*impf*) у кого́-н на побегу́шках.

beckon ['bɛkən] *vt* (*also*: **~ to**) мани́ть* (помани́ть* *perf*) ♦ *vi* (*fame, glory*) мани́ть* (*impf*).

become [bɪ'kʌm] (*irreg: like* **come**) *vi* станови́ться* (стать* *perf*) +*instr*; **to ~ fat** толсте́ть (потолсте́ть *perf*); **to ~ thin** худе́ть (похуде́ть *perf*); **to ~ angry** серди́ться* (рассерди́ться* *perf*); **it became known that** ста́ло изве́стно, что; **what has ~ of him?** что с ним ста́лось?

becoming [bɪ'kʌmɪŋ] *adj* (*behaviour*) прили́чествующий; (*clothes*): **your dress is ~** э́то пла́тье Вам к лицу́.

BECTU *n abbr* (*BRIT*) = Broadcasting Entertainment Cinematographic and Theatre Union.

BEd *n abbr* (= Bachelor of Education) бакала́вр педаго́гики.

bed [bɛd] *n* крова́ть *f*; (*of coal, clay*) пласт*; (*of river, sea*) дно*; (*of flowers*) клу́мба*; **to go to ~** ложи́ться (лечь* *perf*) спать

► **bed down** *vi* располага́ться (расположи́ться* *perf*) на ночле́г.
bed and breakfast *n* ма́ленькая ча́стная гости́ница с за́втраком; (*terms*) ночле́г и за́втрак.
bedbug ['bɛdbʌg] *n* клоп*.
bedclothes ['bɛdkləuðz] *npl* посте́льное бельё *ntsg*.
bedding ['bɛdɪŋ] *n* посте́льные принадле́жности *fpl*.
bedevil [bɪ'dɛvl] *vt* (*person*) опу́тывать (опу́тать *perf*); (*plans*) спу́тывать (спу́тать *perf*); **to be ~led by** вя́знуть (увя́знуть *perf*) в +*prp*.
bedfellow ['bɛdfɛləu] *n*: **they are strange ~s** (*fig*) они́ стра́нная па́ра.
bedlam ['bɛdləm] *n* бедла́м.
bedpan ['bɛdpæn] *n* (подкладно́е) су́дно*.
bedpost ['bɛdpəust] *n* сто́лбик крова́тного по́лога.
bedraggled [bɪ'drægld] *adj* (*person, clothes*) потрёпанный (потрёпан); (*hair*) всклоко́ченный (всклоко́чен).
bedridden ['bɛdrɪdn] *adj* прико́ванный (прико́ван) к посте́ли.
bedrock ['bɛdrɔk] *n* (*fig*) краеуго́льный ка́мень* *m*; (*GEO*) материко́вая поро́да.
bedroom ['bɛdrum] *n* спа́льня*.
Beds *abbr* (*BRIT*: *POST*) = **Bedfordshire**.
bed settee *n* дива́н-крова́ть *f*.
bedside ['bɛdsaɪd] *n*: **at sb's ~** у посте́ли кого́-н ♦ *cpd* (*lamp, cabinet*) прикрова́тный.
bedsit(ter) ['bɛdsɪt(ə')] *n* (*BRIT*) ко́мната, соединя́ющая в себе́ спа́льню, гости́ную и иногда́ ку́хню.
bedspread ['bɛdsprɛd] *n* покрыва́ло.
bedtime ['bɛdtaɪm] *n* вре́мя* *nt* ложи́ться спа́ть; **it's ~** пора́ (ложи́ться) спа́ть.
bee [bi:] *n* пчела́*; **to have a ~ in one's bonnet about sth** помеша́ться (*impf*) на чём-н.
beech [bi:tʃ] *n* бук.
beef [bi:f] *n* говя́дина; **roast ~** ро́стбиф
► **beef up** *vt* (*inf*: *support*) придава́ть (прида́ть* *perf*) си́лы +*dat*; (: *essay*) напо́лнить (*perf*) +*instr*.
beefburger ['bi:fbə:gə'] *n* говя́жья котле́та, га́мбургер.
Beefeater ['bi:fi:tə'] *n* лейб-гварде́ец охра́ны Та́уэра в Ло́ндоне.
beehive ['bi:haɪv] *n* у́лей*.
beekeeping ['bi:ki:pɪŋ] *n* пчелово́дство.
beeline ['bi:laɪn] *n*: **to make a ~ for** мча́ться (помча́ться *perf*) пря́мо в +*acc*.
been [bi:n] *pp of* **be**.
beep [bi:p] *n* гудо́к* ♦ *vi* сигна́лить (просигна́лить *perf*).
beer [bɪə'] *n* пи́во.
beer belly *n* (*inf*) брю́хо.

beer can *n* ба́нка из-под пи́ва.
beet [bi:t] *n* (*vegetable*) кормова́я свёкла; (*US*: *also*: **red ~**) свёкла.
beetle ['bi:tl] *n* жук*.
beetroot ['bi:tru:t] *n* (*BRIT*) свёкла *no pl*.
befall [bɪ'fɔ:l] (*irreg*: *like* **fall**) *vt* выпада́ть (вы́пасть* *perf*) +*dat*.
befit [bɪ'fɪt] *vt* прили́чествовать (*impf*) +*dat*.
before [bɪ'fɔ:'] *prep* пе́ред +*instr*, до +*gen* ♦ *conj* до того́ *or* пе́ред те́м, как ♦ *adv* (*time*) ра́ньше, пре́жде; (*space*) впереди́; **the day ~ yesterday** позавчера́; **do this ~ you forget** сде́лайте э́то пока́ Вы не забы́ли; **~ going** пе́ред ухо́дом; **~ she goes** до того́ *or* пе́ред тем, как она́ уйдёт; **the week ~** неде́лю наза́д, на про́шлой неде́ле; **I've never seen it ~** я никогда́ э́того ра́ньше не ви́дел.
beforehand [bɪ'fɔ:hænd] *adv* зара́нее.
befriend [bɪ'frɛnd] *vt* подружи́ться (*perf*) с +*instr*.
befuddled [bɪ'fʌdld] *adj* одурма́ненный (одурма́нен).
beg [bɛg] *vi* ни́щенствовать (*impf*) ♦ *vt* (*also*: **~ for**: *food, money*) проси́ть* (*impf*); (: *forgiveness, mercy etc*) умоля́ть (умоли́ть *perf*) о +*prp*; **to ~ sb to do** умоля́ть (умоли́ть *perf*) кого́-н +*infin*; **I ~ your pardon** (*apologizing*) прошу́ проще́ния; (*not hearing*) прости́те, не расслы́шал; **to ~ the question** счита́ть (счесть* *perf*) спо́рный вопро́с решённым; **to ~ a favour of sb** проси́ть* (попроси́ть* *perf*) об одолже́нии у кого́-н.
began [bɪ'gæn] *pt of* **begin**.
beggar ['bɛgə'] *n* ни́щий*(-ая) *m(f) adj*.
begin [bɪ'gɪn] (*pt* **began**, *pp* **begun**) *vt* начина́ть (нача́ть* *perf*) ♦ *vi* начина́ться (нача́ться* *perf*); **to ~ doing** *or* **to do** начина́ть (нача́ть* *perf*) +*impf infin*; **~ning (from) Monday** начина́я с понеде́льника; **I can't ~ to thank you** не зна́ю, как Вас благодарю́; **we'll have soup to ~ with** мы начнём с су́па; **to ~ with, I'd like to know** ... для нача́ла, я бы хоте́л знать ....
beginner [bɪ'gɪnə'] *n* начина́ющий*(-ая) *m(f) adj*.
beginning [bɪ'gɪnɪŋ] *n* нача́ло; **right from the ~** с са́мого нача́ла.
begrudge [bɪ'grʌdʒ] *vt*: **he ~s me my success** он зави́дует моему́ успе́ху.
beguile [bɪ'gaɪl] *vt* соблазня́ть (соблазни́ть *perf*).
beguiling [bɪ'gaɪlɪŋ] *adj* соблазни́тельный, зама́нчивый.
begun [bɪ'gʌn] *pp of* **begin**.
behalf [bɪ'hɑ:f] *n*: **on** *or* (*US*) **in ~ of** от и́мени +*gen*; (*for benefit of*) ра́ди +*gen*, в интере́сах +*gen*; **on my/his ~** от моего́/его́ и́мени.
behave [bɪ'heɪv] *vi* вести́* (*impf*) себя́; (*well*: *also*: **~ o.s.**) вести́* (*impf*) себя́ хорошо́.

---

* marks translations which have irregular inflections. The Russian-English side of the dictionary gives inflectional information.

behaviour [bɪ'heɪvjə^r] (US **behavior**) n
поведе́ние.
behead [bɪ'hɛd] vt обезгла́вливать
(обезгла́вить* perf).
beheld [bɪ'hɛld] pt, pp of **behold**.
behind [bɪ'haɪnd] prep (at the back of) за +instr,
позади́ +gen; (supporting) за +instr; (lower in
rank etc) ни́же +gen ♦ adv сза́ди, позади́ ♦ n
(buttocks) зад*; ~ **the scenes** за кули́сами;
we're ~ them in technology мы отста́ли от
них в техноло́гии; **to be ~ schedule**
отстава́ть* (отста́ть* perf) от гра́фика; **to
leave sth ~** (forget) оставля́ть (оста́вить*
perf) что-н.
behold [bɪ'həuld] (irreg: like **hold**) vt узре́ть
(perf).
beige [beɪʒ] adj бе́жевый.
Beijing ['beɪ'dʒɪŋ] n Пеки́н.
being ['bi:ɪŋ] n (creature) существо́*;
(existence) существова́ние; **to come into ~**
возника́ть (возни́кнуть* perf).
Beirut [beɪ'ru:t] n Бейру́т.
Belarus [bɛlə'rus] n Белару́сь f.
belated [bɪ'leɪtɪd] adj запозда́лый.
belch [bɛltʃ] vi отры́гивать (отрыгну́ть perf) ♦
vt (also: ~ **out**) изверга́ть (изве́ргнуть* perf).
beleaguered [bɪ'li:gɪd] adj (also fig)
осаждённый (осаждён*); (army)
окружённый*.
Belfast ['bɛlfɑ:st] n Бе́лфаст.
belfry ['bɛlfrɪ] n колоко́льня*.
Belgian ['bɛldʒən] adj бельги́йский* ♦ n
бельги́ец*(-и́йка).
Belgium ['bɛldʒəm] n Бе́льгия.
Belgrade [bɛl'greɪd] n Белгра́д.
belie [bɪ'laɪ] vt (give false impression of) дава́ть*
(дать* perf) неве́рное представле́ние о +prp;
(disprove) опроверга́ть (опрове́ргнуть* perf).
belief [bɪ'li:f] n (conviction) убежде́ние; (trust,
faith) ве́ра; **it's beyond ~** э́то невероя́тно; **in
the ~ that** полага́я, что.
believable [bɪ'li:vəbl] adj правдоподо́бный*
(правдоподо́бен).
believe [bɪ'li:v] vt ве́рить (пове́рить perf) +dat
or в(о) +acc ♦ vi ве́рить (impf); **to ~ in** ве́рить
(пове́рить perf) в +acc; **I don't ~ in corporal
punishment** я не ве́рю в теле́сные
наказа́ния; **he is ~d to be abroad** полага́ют,
что он за грани́цей.
believer [bɪ'li:və^r] n сторо́нник(-ица); (REL)
ве́рующий*(-ая) m(f) adj; **she's a great ~ in
healthy eating** она́ – сторо́нница здоро́вого
пита́ния.
belittle [bɪ'lɪtl] vt преуменьша́ть
(преуме́ньшить perf), уничижа́ть (impf).
Belize [bɛ'li:z] n Бели́з.
bell [bɛl] n ко́локол*; (small) колоко́льчик; (on
door) звоно́к*; **that rings a ~** я что́-то
припомина́ю.
bell-bottoms ['bɛlbɔtəmz] npl брю́ки клёш pl.
bellboy ['bɛlbɔɪ] n (BRIT) коридо́рный m adj.

bellhop ['bɛlhɔp] n (US) = **bellboy**.
belligerence [bɪ'lɪdʒərəns] n вой́нственность f.
belligerent [bɪ'lɪdʒərənt] adj (person, attitude)
вой́нственный (вой́нственен).
bellow ['bɛləu] vi реве́ть* (impf) ♦ vt (orders)
пpоpeве́ть* (perf).
bellows ['bɛləuz] npl (for fire) мехá mpl.
bell push n (BRIT) звоно́к*.
belly ['bɛlɪ] n брю́хо.
bellyache ['bɛlɪeɪk] (inf) n бо́ли fpl в животе́ ♦
vi ныть* (impf).
bellybutton ['bɛlɪbʌtn] n пупо́к*.
bellyful ['bɛlɪful] n: **I've had a ~ of it** я сыт по
го́рло э́тим.
belong [bɪ'lɔŋ] vi: **to ~ to** принадлежа́ть (impf)
+dat; (club etc) состоя́ть (impf) в +prp; **this
book ~s here** ме́сто э́той кни́ги здесь.
belongings [bɪ'lɔŋɪŋz] npl ве́щи fpl; **personal ~**
ли́чные принадле́жности fpl.
Belorussia [bɛləu'rʌʃə] n Белору́ссия.
Belorussian [bɛləu'rʌʃən] n (person)
белору́с(ка*); (LING) белору́сский* язы́к* ♦
adj белору́сский.
beloved [bɪ'lʌvɪd] adj люби́мый ♦ n
возлю́бленный(-ая) m(f) adj.
below [bɪ'ləu] prep (position) под(о) +instr;
(motion) под(о) +acc; (less than) ни́же +gen ♦
adv (position) внизу́; (motion) вниз;
temperatures ~ normal температу́ры ни́же
норма́льных; **see ~** смотри́те ни́же.
belt [bɛlt] n (leather etc) реме́нь* m; (cloth)
по́яс*; (of land) по́яс*, зо́на; (TECH)
приводно́й реме́нь* ♦ vt (thrash) поро́ть*
(вы́пороть perf) ♦ vi (BRIT: inf): **to ~ along** or
down the road жа́рить (impf) по доро́ге;
industrial ~ индустриа́льная зо́на
► **belt out** vt горла́нить (impf)
► **belt up** vi (inf. BRIT) заткну́ться* (perf); (: AUT)
застёгиваться (застегну́ться perf).
beltway ['bɛltweɪ] n (US: AUT) кольцева́я
доро́га; (motorway) кольцевáя скоростна́я
автомагистра́ль f.
bemoan [bɪ'məun] vt опла́кивать (опла́кать*
perf).
bemused [bɪ'mju:zd] adj озада́ченный.
bench [bɛntʃ] n скамья́*; (in workshop)
верста́к*; (in laboratory) лаборато́рный
стол*; (BRIT: POL) места́ па́ртий в
Парла́менте; **the B~** (LAW) суде́йская
колле́гия.
benchmark ['bɛntʃmɑ:k] n крите́рий.
bend [bɛnd] (pt, pp **bent**) vt (pipe, leg etc) гнуть
(согну́ть perf), сгиба́ть (impf) ♦ vi (person)
гну́ться (согну́ться* perf) ♦ n (BRIT: in road)
поворо́т; (in pipe) изги́б; (in river) излу́чина;
~s npl (MED): **the ~s** кессо́нная боле́знь fsg
► **bend down** vi наклоня́ться (наклони́ться*
perf), нагиба́ться (нагну́ться perf)
► **bend over** vt fus (book, child) склоня́ться
(склони́ться* perf) над +instr; (fence)
перегиба́ться (перегну́ться perf) че́рез +acc.

beneath [bɪ'ni:θ] *prep* (*position*) под +*instr*; (*motion*) под(о) +*acc*; (*unworthy of*) ни́же +*gen* ♦ *adv* внизу́.

benefactor ['bɛnɪfæktə'] *n* (*to person*) благоде́тель *m*; (*to institution*) благотвори́тель *m*.

benefactress ['bɛnɪfæktrɪs] *n* благоде́тельница; благотвори́тельница.

beneficial [bɛnɪ'fɪʃəl] *adj*: ~ (**to**) благотво́рный* (благотво́рен) (для +*gen*).

beneficiary [bɛnɪ'fɪʃərɪ] *n* (*LAW*) бенефициа́рий.

benefit ['bɛnɪfɪt] *n* (*advantage*) вы́года; (*money*) посо́бие; (*also:* ~ **concert**) благотвори́тельный конце́рт; (*also:* ~ **match**) благотвори́тельный матч ♦ *vt* приноси́ть* (принести́* *perf*) по́льзу +*dat* ♦ *vi*: **he'll ~ from it** он полу́чит от э́того вы́году.

Benelux ['bɛnɪlʌks] *n* Бенилю́кс.

benevolent [bɪ'nɛvələnt] *adj* (*person*) доброжела́тельный* (доброжела́телен); (*organization*) благотвори́тельный* (благотвори́телен).

BEng *n abbr* (= *Bachelor of Engineering*) ≈ бакала́вр инжене́рного де́ла.

Bengal [bɛn'gɔ:l] *n*: **Bay of ~** Бенга́льский зали́в.

Bengali [bɛn'gɔ:lɪ] *n* (*person*) бенга́лец*(-а́лка*); (*LING*) бенга́льский язы́к* ♦ *adj* бенга́льский.

benign [bɪ'naɪn] *adj* добросерде́чный* (добросерде́чен); (*MED*) доброка́чественный.

bent [bɛnt] *pt, pp of* **bend** ♦ *adj* (*wire, pipe*) по́гнутый; (*inf: dishonest*) жуликова́тый (жуликова́т); (: *pej: homosexual*): **he is** ~ он голубо́й ♦ *n*: **a** ~ **for** скло́нность *f* к +*dat*; **he is** ~ **on doing** он реши́тельно настро́ен +*infin*.

bequeath [bɪ'kwi:ð] *vt* завеща́ть (*impf/perf*).

bequest [bɪ'kwɛst] *n* насле́дство.

bereaved [bɪ'ri:vd] *adj* понёсший тяжёлую утра́ту ♦ *n*: **the** ~ друзья́ *mpl* и ро́дственники *mpl* поко́йного.

bereavement [bɪ'ri:vmənt] *n* тяжёлая утра́та.

bereft [bɪ'rɛft] *adj*: ~ **of** лишённый (лишён) +*gen*.

beret ['bɛreɪ] *n* бере́т.

Bering Sea ['bɛɪrɪŋ-] *n*: **the** ~ ~ Бе́рингово мо́ре.

berk [bə:k] *n* (*inf: pej*) крети́н, деби́л.

Berks *abbr* (*BRIT: POST*) = **Berkshire**.

Berlin [bə:'lɪn] *n* Берли́н; **East/West** ~ (*formerly*) Восто́чный/За́падный Берли́н.

Bermuda [bə:'mju:də] *n* Берму́дские острова́ *mpl*.

Bermuda shorts *npl* берму́ды *pl*.

Bern [bə:n] *n* Берн.

berry ['bɛrɪ] *n* я́года.

berserk [bə'sə:k] *adj*: **to go** ~ разъяря́ться (разъяри́ться *perf*).

berth [bə:θ] *n* (*bed: in caravan*) ко́йка*; (: *on ship*) каю́та; (: *on train*) по́лка*; (*mooring*) прича́л ♦ *vi* прича́ливать (прича́лить *perf*); **to give sb/sth a wide** ~ обходи́ть* (обойти́* *perf*) кого́-н/что-н за версту́.

beseech [bɪ'si:tʃ] (*pt, pp* **besought**) *vt* моли́ть* (*impf*).

beset [bɪ'sɛt] (*pt, pp* **beset**) *vt*: **we have been** ~ **with problems** нас одолева́ли пробле́мы.

beside [bɪ'saɪd] *prep* ря́дом с +*instr*, о́коло +*gen*, у +*gen*; (*compared with*) ря́дом с +*instr*; **to be** ~ **o.s. (with)** быть* (*impf*) вне себя́ (от +*gen*); **that's** ~ **the point** э́то к де́лу не отно́сится.

besides [bɪ'saɪdz] *adv* кро́ме того́ ♦ *prep* кро́ме +*gen*, поми́мо +*gen*.

besiege [bɪ'si:dʒ] *vt* (*also fig*) осажда́ть (осади́ть* *perf*).

besmirch [bɪ'smə:tʃ] *vt* очерня́ть (очерни́ть *perf*).

besotted [bɪ'sɔtɪd] *adj* (*BRIT*): ~ **with** опьянённый (опьянён) +*instr*.

besought [bɪ'sɔ:t] *pt, pp of* **beseech**.

bespectacled [bɪ'spɛktɪkld] *adj* в очка́х.

bespoke [bɪ'spəuk] *adj* (*BRIT*) поши́тый (поши́т); ~ **tailor** портно́й, рабо́тающий на зака́з.

best [bɛst] *adj* лу́чший* ♦ *adv* лу́чше всего́; **the** ~ **thing to do is** ... лу́чше всего́ +*infin* ...; **the** ~ **part of** (*quantity*) бо́льшая часть +*gen*; **at** ~ в лу́чшем слу́чае; **to make the** ~ **of sth** испо́льзовать (*impf*) что-н наилу́чшим о́бразом; **to do one's** ~ де́лать (сде́лать *perf*) всё возмо́жное; **to the** ~ **of my knowledge** наско́лько мне изве́стно; **to the** ~ **of my ability** в ме́ру мои́х спосо́бностей; **he's not exactly patient at the** ~ **of times** он не отлича́ется осо́бым терпе́нием.

bestial ['bɛstɪəl] *adj* ско́тский*.

best man *n* ша́фер*.

bestow [bɪ'stəu] *vt*: **to** ~ **sth on sb** (*title*) дарова́ть (*impf/perf*) что-н кому́-н; (*affection*) одаря́ть (одари́ть *perf*) кого́-н чем-н.

bestseller ['bɛst'sɛlə'] *n* бестсе́ллер.

bet [bɛt] (*pt, pp* **bet** *or* **betted**) *n* (*wager*) пари́ *nt ind*; (*in gambling*) ста́вка ♦ *vi* (*wager*) держа́ть (*impf*) пари́; (*expect, guess*) би́ться* (*impf*) об закла́д ♦ *vt*: **to** ~ **sb sth** би́ться* (поби́ться* *perf*) об закла́д с кем-н о чём-н, спо́рить (поспо́рить *perf*) с кем-н на что-н; **it's a safe** ~ (*fig*) э́то ве́рное де́ло; **to** ~ **money on sth** ста́вить* (поста́вить* *perf*) де́ньги на что-н.

Bethlehem ['bɛθlɪhɛm] *n* Вифлее́м.

betray [bɪ'treɪ] *vt* (*friends*) предава́ть* (преда́ть* *perf*); (*trust*) обма́нывать (обману́ть* *perf*); (*emotion*) выдава́ть* (вы́дать* *perf*).

---

* marks translations which have irregular inflections. The Russian-English side of the dictionary gives inflectional information.

betrayal [bɪ'treɪəl] *n* преда́тельство.
better ['bɛtə'] *adj* лу́чший* ◆ *adv* лу́чше ◆ *vt*
(*score*) улучша́ть (улу́чшить *perf*) ◆ *n*: **to get
the ~ of** бра́ть (взя́ть* *perf*) верх над +*instr*; **I
feel ~** я чу́вствую себя́ лу́чше; **to get ~** (*MED*)
поправля́ться (попра́виться* *perf*); **that's ~!**
вот та́к(-то) лу́чше!; **I had ~ go** мне лу́чше
уйти́; **he thought ~ of it** он переду́мал; **a
change for the ~** измене́ние к лу́чшему.
better off *adj* (*wealthier*) бо́лее
состоя́тельный* (состоя́телен); (*more
comfortable etc*) лу́чше; (*fig*): **you'd be ~ ~
this way** так Вам бу́дет лу́чше.
betting ['bɛtɪŋ] *n* пари́ *nt ind.*
betting shop *n* (*BRIT*) *ме́сто, где де́лают
ста́вки.*
between [bɪ'twi:n] *prep* ме́жду +*instr* ◆ *adv*: **in ~**
ме́жду тем; **the road ~ here and London**
доро́га отсю́да до Ло́ндона; **we only had £5
~ us** у нас на двои́х бы́ло всего́ £5.
bevel ['bɛvəl] *n* (*also: ~* **edge**) скос.
bevelled ['bɛvəld] *adj*: **a ~ edge** ско́шенный
край*.
beverage ['bɛvərɪdʒ] *n* напи́ток*.
bevy ['bɛvɪ] *n*: **a ~ of** (*people*) гру́ппа +*gen*;
(*things*) ряд +*gen*.
bewail [bɪ'weɪl] *vt* скорбе́ть (*impf*) о +*prp*.
beware [bɪ'wɛə'] *vi*: **to ~ (of)** остерега́ться
(остере́чься* *perf*) (+*gen*); **"beware of the dog"**
"осторо́жно, (зла́я) соба́ка".
bewildered [bɪ'wɪldəd] *adj* изумлённый
(изумлён).
bewildering [bɪ'wɪldrɪŋ] *adj* изуми́тельный*
(изуми́телен).
bewitching [bɪ'wɪtʃɪŋ] *adj* (*smile, person*)
чару́ющий.
beyond [bɪ'jɔnd] *prep* (*position*) за +*instr*;
(*motion*) за +*acc*; (*understanding*) вы́ше +*gen*;
(*expectations*) сверх +*gen*; (*age*) бо́льше +*gen*;
(*date*) по́сле +*gen* ◆ *adv* (*position*) вдали́;
(*motion*) вда́ль; **~ doubt** вне сомне́ния; **it's ~
repair** э́то невозмо́жно почини́ть; **it's ~ me**
э́то вы́ше моего́ понима́ния.
b/f *abbr* (*COMM*. = **brought forward**)
перенесённый на сле́дующую страни́цу.
BFPO *n abbr* = **British Forces Post Office.**
bhp *n abbr* (*AUT*. = **brake horsepower**)
*эффекти́вная мо́щность дви́гателя
вну́треннего сгора́ния в лошади́ных си́лах.*
bi... [baɪ] *prefix* би..., дву(х)....
biannual [baɪ'ænjuəl] *adj* выходя́щий два ра́за
в год.
bias ['baɪəs] *n* (*against*) предубежде́ние;
(*towards*) пристра́стие.
bias(s)ed ['baɪəst] *adj* (*jury*) пристра́стный*
(пристра́стен); (*judgement*) предвзя́тый
(предвзя́т); **he is/was ~ against** он
предубеждён/был предубеждён про́тив
+*gen*.
bib [bɪb] *n* (*child's*) нагру́дник.
Bible ['baɪbl] *n* Би́блия.

biblical ['bɪblɪkl] *adj* библе́йский*.
bibliography [bɪblɪ'ɔgrəfɪ] *n* библиогра́фия.
bicarbonate of soda [baɪ'kɑ:bənɪt-] *n* питьева́я
or пищева́я со́да.
bicentenary [baɪsɛn'ti:nərɪ] *n* двухсотле́тие.
bicentennial [baɪsɛn'tɛnɪəl] *n* (*US*) =
bicentenary.
biceps ['baɪsɛps] *n* би́цепс.
bicker ['bɪkə'] *vi* препира́ться (*impf*).
bickering ['bɪkərɪŋ] *n* препира́тельство.
bicycle ['baɪsɪkl] *n* велосипе́д.
bicycle path *n* велосипе́дная доро́жка.
bicycle pump *n* велосипе́дный насо́с.
bicycle track *n* велотре́к.
bid [bɪd] (*pt* **bade** *or* **bid**, *pp* **bid(den)**) *n* (*at
auction*) предложе́ние цены́; (*in tender*)
зая́вка*; (*attempt*) попы́тка* ◆ *vt* (*offer*)
предлага́ть (предложи́ть* *perf*) ◆ *vi*: **to ~ for**
(*at auction*) предлага́ть (предложи́ть* *perf*)
це́ну за +*acc*; (*CARDS*) объявля́ть (объяви́ть*
perf) (*масть или коли́чество взя́ток*); **to ~ sb
good day** здоро́ваться (поздоро́ваться *perf*) с
кем-н.
bidden ['bɪdn] *pp* of **bid.**
bidder ['bɪdə'] *n*: **the highest ~** лицо́,
предлага́ющее наивы́сшую це́ну.
bidding ['bɪdɪŋ] *n* (*at auction*) предложе́ние
цены́, торги́ *pl*; (*command*): **to do sb's ~**
исполня́ть (испо́лнить *perf*) чьи-н
приказа́ния.
bide [baɪd] *vt*: **to ~ one's time** дожида́ться
(дожда́ться *perf*) своего́ ча́са.
bidet ['bi:deɪ] *n* биде́ *nt ind.*
bidirectional ['baɪdɪ'rɛkʃənl] *adj* (*COMPUT*.
printing) двунапра́вленный; (: *drive*)
реверси́вный.
biennial [baɪ'ɛnɪəl] *adj* происходя́щий раз в
два го́да ◆ *n* двухлéтник.
bier [bɪə'] *n* катафа́лк.
bifocals [baɪ'fəuklz] *npl* бифока́льные очки́ *pl*.
big [bɪg] *adj* большо́й*; (*important*) ва́жный*
(ва́жен); (*bulky*) кру́пный*; (*older: brother,
sister*) ста́рший*; **to do things in a ~ way**
де́лать (сде́лать *perf*) что-н с широ́ким
разма́хом.
bigamist ['bɪgəmɪst] *n* (*man*) двоеже́нец*.
bigamous ['bɪgəməs] *adj* бига́мный.
bigamy ['bɪgəmɪ] *n* бига́мия.
big dipper [-'dɪpə'] *n* аттракцио́н
"америка́нские го́ры".
big end *n* больша́я голо́вка (шатуна́).
biggish ['bɪgɪʃ] *adj* дово́льно большо́й *or*
кру́пный.
bigheaded ['bɪg'hɛdɪd] *adj* зано́счивый
(зано́счив).
big-hearted ['bɪg'hɑ:tɪd] *adj* великоду́шный*
(великоду́шен).
bigot ['bɪgət] *n* фана́тик.
bigoted ['bɪgətɪd] *adj* фанати́чный*
(фанати́чен).
bigotry ['bɪgətrɪ] *n* фанати́зм.

big toe *n* большо́й па́лец* ноги́.
big top *n* ку́пол* ци́рка.
big wheel *n* колесо́* обозре́ния.
bigwig ['bɪgwɪg] *n* (*inf*) (ва́жная) ши́шка*.
bike [baɪk] *n* (*bicycle*) ве́лик; (*motorcycle*) мотоци́кл.
bikini [bɪ'ki:nɪ] *n* бики́ни *nt ind*.
bilateral [baɪ'lætərl] *adj* двусторо́нний*.
bile [baɪl] *n* жёлчь *f*; (*fig*) жёлчность *f*.
bilingual [baɪ'lɪŋgwəl] *adj* двуязы́чный*.
bilious ['bɪlɪəs] *adj* (*also fig*) тошнотво́рный (тошнотво́рен).
bill [bɪl] *n* (*invoice*) счёт*; (*POL*) законопрое́кт; (*US: banknote*) банкно́та; (*beak*) клюв ◆ *vt* (*item*) реклами́ровать (*impf/perf*); (*customer*) присыла́ть (присла́ть* *perf*) счёт +*dat*; "**post no ~s**" "помеща́ть афи́ши воспреща́ется"; **to fit** *or* **fill the ~** (*fig*) отвеча́ть (*impf*) всем тре́бованиям; **on the ~** (*THEAT*) в афи́шах *or* програ́мме; **~ of exchange** ве́ксель* *m*; **~ of fare** меню́ *nt ind*; **~ of lading** коносаме́нт, (тра́нспортная) накладна́я *f adj*; **~ of sale** ку́пчая *f adj*.
billboard ['bɪlbɔːd] *n* доска́ объявле́ний.
billet ['bɪlɪt] *n* (*MIL*) кварти́ры *fpl* ◆ *vt* расквартиро́вывать (расквартирова́ть *perf*).
billfold ['bɪlfəʊld] *n* (*US*) бума́жник.
billiards ['bɪljədz] *n* билья́рд.
billion ['bɪljən] *n* (*BRIT*) биллио́н; (*US*) миллиа́рд.
billow ['bɪləʊ] *n* (*of smoke, steam*) клуб ◆ *vi* (*smoke*) клуби́ться (*impf*); (*sail*) надува́ться (наду́ться* *perf*).
billy goat ['bɪlɪ-] *n* козёл*.
bimbo ['bɪmbəʊ] *n* (*inf*) ку́кла (*хоро́шенькая, но не у́мная же́нщина*).
bin [bɪn] *n* (*BRIT: also:* **rubbish ~**) му́сорное ведро́*; (*container*) я́щик.
binary ['baɪnərɪ] *adj* (*MATH, COMPUT*) дво́ичный, бина́рный.
bind [baɪnd] (*pt, pp* **bound**) *vt* (*tie*) привя́зывать (привяза́ть* *perf*); (*tie together: hands and feet*) свя́зывать (связа́ть* *perf*); (*oblige*) обя́зывать (обяза́ть* *perf*); (*book*) переплета́ть (переплести́* *perf*) ◆ *n* (*inf*) обу́за
▸ **bind over** *vt* (*LAW*) обя́зывать (обяза́ть* *perf*)
▸ **bind up** *vt* (*wound*) перевя́зывать (перевяза́ть* *perf*); **he is/was bound up in** (*work etc*) он вовлечён/был вовлечён в +*acc*; **he is/was bound up with** (*person*) он свя́зан/был свя́зан с +*instr*.
binder ['baɪndə'] *n* (*file*) скоросшива́тель *m*.
binding ['baɪndɪŋ] *adj* обя́зывающий ◆ *n* (*of book*) переплёт.
binge [bɪndʒ] *n* (*inf*): **to go on a ~** (*drink a lot*) пья́нствовать (*impf*).
bingo ['bɪŋgəʊ] *n* лото́ *nt ind*.
bin-liner ['bɪnlaɪnə'] *n* мешо́к* для му́сора.

binoculars [bɪ'nɒkjuləz] *npl* бино́кль *msg*.
bio... [baɪəʊ] *prefix* био...; **~chemistry** биохи́мия.
biodegradable ['baɪəʊdɪ'greɪdəbl] *adj* биологи́чески разложи́мый (разложи́м).
biodiversity ['baɪəʊdaɪ'və:sɪtɪ] *n* биологи́ческое разнообра́зие.
biographer [baɪ'ɒgrəfə'] *n* био́граф.
biographic(al) [baɪə'græfɪk(l)] *adj* биографи́ческий.
biography [baɪ'ɒgrəfɪ] *n* биогра́фия.
biological [baɪə'lɒdʒɪkl] *adj* (*science*) биологи́ческий*; (*warfare*) бактериологи́ческий*; (*washing powder*) содержа́щий* биопрепара́ты.
biological clock *n* биологи́ческие часы́ *pl*; **to upset sb's ~ ~** наруша́ть (нару́шить *perf*) чей-н режи́м.
biologist [baɪ'ɒlədʒɪst] *n* био́лог.
biology [baɪ'ɒlədʒɪ] *n* биоло́гия.
biophysics ['baɪəʊ'fɪzɪks] *n* биофи́зика.
biopic ['baɪəʊpɪk] *n* (*inf*) биографи́ческий фильм.
biopsy ['baɪɒpsɪ] *n* биопси́я.
biosphere ['baɪəsfɪə'] *n* биосфе́ра.
biotechnology ['baɪəʊtɛk'nɒlədʒɪ] *n* биотехноло́гия.
biped ['baɪpɛd] *n* двуно́гое *nt adj*.
birch [bəːtʃ] *n* берёза.
bird [bəːd] *n* пти́ца; (*BRIT: inf: girl*) деви́ца.
bird of prey *n* хи́щная пти́ца.
bird's-eye view [bə:dzaɪ-] *n* (*aerial view*) вид* с высоты́ пти́чьего полёта; (*overview*) о́бщая карти́на.
bird-watcher ['bə:dwɒtʃə'] *n* орнито́лог-люби́тель *m*.
Birmingham ['bə:mɪŋəm] *n* Бирминге́м.
Biro® ['baɪərəʊ] *n* ша́риковая ру́чка*.
birth [bə:θ] *n* рожде́ние; **to give ~ to** рожа́ть (роди́ть* *perf*).
birth certificate *n* свиде́тельство о рожде́нии.
birth control *n* (*policy*) контро́ль *m* рожда́емости; (*methods*) противозача́точные ме́ры *fpl*.
birthday ['bə:θdeɪ] *n* день* *m* рожде́ния ◆ *cpd* ко дню рожде́ния; *see also* **happy**.
birthmark ['bə:θmɑ:k] *n* (*large*) роди́мое пятно́*; (*small*) роди́нка*.
birthplace ['bə:θpleɪs] *n* (*also fig*) ро́дина.
birth rate *n* рожда́емость *f*.
Biscay ['bɪskeɪ] *n*: **the Bay of ~** Биска́йский зали́в.
biscuit ['bɪskɪt] *n* (*BRIT*) пече́нье; (*US*) ≈ кекс.
bisect [baɪ'sɛkt] *vt* (*MATH*) дели́ть* (раздели́ть* *perf*).
bisexual ['baɪ'sɛksjuəl] *adj* бисексуа́льный* (бисексуа́лен).
bishop ['bɪʃəp] *n* (*REL*) епи́скоп; (*CHESS*) слон*.

---

* marks translations which have irregular inflections. The Russian-English side of the dictionary gives inflectional information.

bistro ['bi:strəu] *n* бистро́ *nt ind.*

bit [bɪt] *pt of* **bite** ◆ *n* (*piece*) кусо́к*, кусо́чек*; (*of tool*) сверло́*; (*COMPUT*) бит; (*of horse*) удила́* *pl*; (*US: coin*) (ме́лкая) моне́та; **a ~ of** немно́го +*gen*; **a ~ dangerous** слегка́ опа́сный; **~ by ~** ма́ло-пома́лу; **to come to ~s** разла́мываться (разлома́ться* *perf*); **bring all your ~s and pieces** принеси́те все Ва́ши пожи́тки; **to do one's ~** вноси́ть* (внести́* *perf*) свой вклад.

bitch [bɪtʃ] *n* (*also inf!*) су́ка (*also !*)

bitching ['bɪtʃɪŋ] *n* хула́.

bite [baɪt] (*pt* bit, *pp* bitten) *vt* куса́ть (укуси́ть* *perf*) ◆ *vi* куса́ться (*impf*) ◆ *n* (*insect bite*) уку́с*; **to ~ one's nails** куса́ть (*impf*) но́гти; **let's have a ~ (to eat)** (*inf*) дава́йте переку́сим; **he had a ~ of cake** он откуси́л кусо́к пирога́.

biting ['baɪtɪŋ] *adj* (*wind*) прони́зывающий; (*wit*) язви́тельный* (язви́телен).

bit part *n* проходна́я роль* *f.*

bitten ['bɪtn] *pp of* **bite**.

bitter ['bɪtə'] *adj* го́рький*; (*wind*) прони́зывающий; (*struggle*) ожесточённый ◆ *n* (*BRIT*) пи́во с горькова́тым при́вкусом; **to the ~ end** до са́мого конца́.

bitterly ['bɪtəlɪ] *adv* го́рько; (*oppose, criticize*) ожесточённо; (*jealous*) ужа́сно; **it's ~ cold today** сего́дня прони́зывающий хо́лод.

bitterness ['bɪtənɪs] *n* (*anger*) го́речь *f*, ожесточённость *f*; (*taste*) го́речь.

bittersweet ['bɪtəswi:t] *adj* горькова́то-сла́дкий*.

bitty ['bɪtɪ] *adj* (*BRIT: inf*) неро́вный* (неро́вен).

bitumen ['bɪtjumɪn] *n* би́тум.

bivouac ['bɪvuæk] *n* бива́к.

bizarre [bɪ'zɑ:'] *adj* стра́нный, причу́дливый.

bk *abbr* = **bank, book**.

BL *n abbr* (= *Bachelor of Law*) ≈ бакала́вр правове́дения; (= *Bachelor of Letters*) ≈ бакала́вр литературове́дения; (*US:* = *Bachelor of Literature*) ≈ бакала́вр литературове́дения.

bl *abbr* (= *bill of lading*) ≈ тра́нспортная накладна́я *f adj.*

blab [blæb] *vi* (*inf*) проба́лтываться (проболта́ться *perf*).

black [blæk] *adj* чёрный*; (*tea, coffee*) без молока́; (*person*) чернoко́жий* ◆ *n* (*colour*) чёрный цвет, чёрное *nt adj*; (*person*): **B~** негр(ити́нка) ◆ *vt* (*BRIT: INDUSTRY*) бойкоти́ровать (*impf/perf*); **to give sb a ~ eye** подбива́ть (подби́ть* *perf*) кому́-н глаз; **~ and blue** в синяка́х; **there it is in ~ and white** (*fig*) вот оно́, чёрным по бе́лому напи́сано; **to be in the ~** име́ть (*impf*) де́ньги в ба́нке
▶ **black out** *vi* па́дать (упа́сть* *perf*) в о́бморок.

black belt *n* (*JUDO*) чёрный по́яс*; (*US: area*) ю́жные райо́ны США, в кото́рых преоблада́ет негритя́нское населе́ние.

blackberry ['blækbərɪ] *n* ежеви́ка *no pl.*

blackbird ['blækbə:d] *n* (чёрный) дрозд*.

blackboard ['blækbɔ:d] *n* кла́ссная доска́*.

black box *n* (*AVIAT*) чёрный я́щик.

black coffee *n* чёрный ко́фе *m ind.*

Black Country *n* (*BRIT*): **the ~~** индустриа́льные райо́ны Се́веро-За́падной А́нглии.

blackcurrant ['blæk'kʌrənt] *n* чёрная сморо́дина.

black economy *n*: **the ~~** теневáя эконо́мика.

blacken ['blækn] *vt* (*fig*) черни́ть (очерни́ть *perf*).

black eye *n* синя́к* *or* фона́рь* *m* под гла́зом.

Black Forest *n*: **the ~~** Шварцва́льд.

blackhead ['blækhɛd] *n* у́горь* *m.*

black hole *n* чёрная дыра́*.

black ice *n* гололе́дица.

blackjack ['blækdʒæk] *n* (*CARDS*) блэкджéк; (*US: truncheon*) дуби́нка.

blackleg ['blæklɛg] *n* (*BRIT: INDUSTRY*) штрейкбре́хер.

blacklist ['blæklɪst] *n* чёрный спи́сок* ◆ *vt* (*person*) заноси́ть* (занести́* *perf*) в чёрный спи́сок.

blackmail ['blækmeɪl] *n* шанта́ж ◆ *vt* шантажи́ровать (*impf*).

blackmailer ['blækmeɪlə'] *n* шантажи́ст.

black market *n* чёрный ры́нок*.

blackout ['blækaut] *n* (*in wartime*) затемне́ние; (*ELEC*) обесто́чка*; (*TV, RADIO*) приостановле́ние переда́ч; (*MED*) о́бморок.

black pepper *n* чёрный пе́рец*.

Black Sea *n*: **the ~~** Чёрное мо́ре.

black sheep *n* (*fig*) парши́вая овца́.

blacksmith ['blæksmɪθ] *n* кузне́ц*.

black spot *n* (*AUT*) ги́блое ме́сто*; (*ECON*) мёртвая зо́на.

bladder ['blædə'] *n* (*ANAT*) мочево́й пузы́рь* *m.*

blade [bleɪd] *n* ле́звие; (*of oar, propeller*) ло́пасть* *f*; **a ~ of grass** трави́нка*.

blame [bleɪm] *n* вина́* ◆ *vt*: **to ~ sb for sth** вини́ть (*impf*) кого́-н в чём-н; **he is/was to ~ (for sth)** он винова́т *or* винóвен/был винова́т *or* винóвен (в чём-н); **who's to ~?** кого́ сле́дует в э́том вини́ть?; **I'm not to ~** э́то не моя́ вина́.

blameless ['bleɪmlɪs] *adj* (*person*) невинóвный, безупре́чный.

blanch [blɑ:ntʃ] *vi* беле́ть (побеле́ть *perf*) ◆ *vt* (*CULIN*) обва́ривать (обвари́ть* *perf*) кипятко́м.

blancmange [blə'mɔnʒ] *n* бланманже́ *nt ind.*

bland [blænd] *adj* (*taste, food*) пре́сный (пре́сен).

blank [blæŋk] *adj* (*paper*) чи́стый* (чист); (*look*) безуча́стный* (безуча́стен) ◆ *n* (*of memory*) пробе́л; (*on form*) про́пуск; (*for gun*) холосто́й патро́н; **we drew a ~** (*fig*) мы оста́лись ни с чем.

blank cheque *n* незапо́лненный чек; **to give sb a ~~** (*fig*) предоставля́ть (предоста́вить*

perf) кому́-н карт-бланш.
blanket ['blæŋkɪt] *n* одея́ло; (*of snow*) покро́в; (*of fog*) пелена́ ♦ *adj* всеобъе́млющий*.
blanket cover *n* (*INSURANCE*) бла́нковый *or* блок по́лис.
blare [blɛəʳ] *vi* реве́ть (*impf*)
▶ **blare out** *vi* прореве́ть (*perf*).
blarney ['blɑːnɪ] *n* лесть *f*.
blasé ['blɑːzeɪ] *adj* пресы́щенный.
blaspheme [blæs'fiːm] *vi* богоху́льствовать (*impf*), святота́тствовать (*impf*).
blasphemous ['blæsfɪməs] *adj* (*words*) богоху́льный; **a ~ person** богоху́льник.
blasphemy ['blæsfɪmɪ] *n* богоху́льство, святота́тство.
blast [blɑːst] *n* (*of wind*) поры́в; (*of air, steam*) волна́*; (*of whistle*) пронзи́тельный свист; (*explosion*) взрыв ♦ *vt* (*blow up*) взрыва́ть (взорва́ть* *perf*) ♦ *excl* (*BRIT: inf*) пропади́ (всё) про́падом; **at full ~** (*play music etc*) на по́лную мо́щность
▶ **blast off** *vi* взлета́ть (взлете́ть* *perf*), взмыва́ть (взмыть* *perf*).
blast furnace *n* до́менная печь* *f*.
blast-off ['blɑːstɔf] *n* старт.
blatant ['bleɪtənt] *adj* я́вный (я́вен), неприкры́тый.
blatantly ['bleɪtəntlɪ] *adv* я́вно, неприкры́то; **it's ~ obvious** э́то я́сно как день.
blaze [bleɪz] *n* (*fire*) пла́мя* *nt*; (*of colour*) полыха́ние; (*of glory*) сия́ние ♦ *vi* (*fire*) пыла́ть (*impf*); (*guns*) пали́ть (*impf*); (*fig: eyes*) сверка́ть (*impf*) ♦ *vt*: **to ~ a trail** прокла́ть (проложи́ть* *perf*) путь; **in a ~ of publicity** в газе́тной шуми́хе.
blazer ['bleɪzəʳ] *n* фо́рменная ку́ртка.
bleach [bliːtʃ] *n* (*also*: **household ~**) отбе́ливатель *m* ♦ *vt* (*fabric*) отбе́ливать (отбели́ть *perf*); (*hair*) обесцве́чивать (обесцве́тить* *perf*).
bleached [bliːtʃt] *adj* (*hair*) обесцве́ченный (обесцве́чен).
bleachers ['bliːtʃəz] *npl* (*US: SPORT*) откры́тая трибу́на *fsg*.
bleak [bliːk] *adj* (*weather, expression*) уны́лый (уны́л); (*prospect*) безра́достный* (безра́достен).
bleary-eyed ['blɪərɪ'aɪd] *adj* с воспалёнными глаза́ми.
bleat [bliːt] *vi* (*animal*) бле́ять (забле́ять *perf*) ♦ *n* (*of animal*) бле́яние.
bled [blɛd] *pt, pp of* **bleed**.
bleed [bliːd] (*pt, pp* **bled**) *vi* кровото́чить (*impf*); (*colour*) течь* (поте́чь* *perf*) ♦ *vt* (*brakes, radiator*) опорожни́ть (опорожня́ть *perf*); **my nose is ~ing** у меня́ идёт кровь из но́са.
bleep [bliːp] *n* сигна́л; (*TEL*) гудо́к* ♦ *vi* сигна́лить (просигна́лить *perf*) ♦ *vt* (*doctor*)

вызыва́ть (вы́звать* *perf*).
bleeper ['bliːpəʳ] *n* переносна́я ра́ция.
blemish ['blɛmɪʃ] *n* пятно́*.
blend [blɛnd] *n* (*of tea, whisky*) буке́т ♦ *vt* (*CULIN*) сме́шивать (смеша́ть *perf*); (*colours, styles etc*) сочета́ть (*impf*) ♦ *vi* (*also*: **~ in**) сочета́ться (*impf*), слива́ться (сли́ться* *perf*).
blender ['blɛndəʳ] *n* смеси́тель *m*, ми́ксер.
bless [blɛs] (*pt, pp* **blessed** *or* **blest**) *vt* (*REL*) благословля́ть (благослови́ть* *perf*); **he is ~ed with** Бог награди́л его́ +*instr*; **~ you!** бу́дьте здоро́вы!
blessed ['blɛsɪd] *adj* блаже́нный; **it rains every ~ day** (*inf*) дождь идёт ка́ждый Бо́жий день.
blessing ['blɛsɪŋ] *n* благослове́ние; (*godsend*) благода́ть *f*; **to count one's ~s** не гневи́ть* (*impf*) Бо́га, не ропта́ть* (*impf*) по́пусту на судьбу́; **it was a ~ in disguise** ≈ не́ бы́ло бы сча́стья, да несча́стье помогло́.
blest [blɛst] *pt, pp of* **bless**.
blew [bluː] *pt of* **blow**.
blight [blaɪt] *vt* губи́ть* (погуби́ть* *perf*) ♦ *n* (*of plants*) головня́*.
blimey ['blaɪmɪ] *excl* (*BRIT: inf*) чтоб мне провали́ться.
blind [blaɪnd] *adj* слепо́й* ♦ *n* што́ра; (*also*: **Venetian ~**) жалюзи́ *pl ind* ♦ *vt* ослепля́ть (ослепи́ть* *perf*); **the ~** *npl* (*blind people*) слепы́е *pl adj*; **to be ~ (to)** (*fig*) не ви́деть* (*impf*) (+*acc*); **to turn a ~ eye (on** *or* **to)** закрыва́ть (закры́ть* *perf*) глаза́ (на +*acc*).
blind alley *n* (*fig*) тупи́к.
blind corner *n* (*BRIT*) непросма́тривающийся поворо́т.
blind date *n* свида́ние с незнако́мцем.
blinders ['blaɪndəz] *npl* (*US*) = **blinkers**.
blindfold ['blaɪndfəuld] *n* повя́зка ♦ *adv* вслепу́ю ♦ *vt* завя́зывать (завяза́ть* *perf*) глаза́ +*dat*.
blinding ['blaɪndɪŋ] *adj* ослепля́ющий (ослепля́ющ), слепя́щий; (*fig*) ослепи́тельный (ослепи́телен).
blindly ['blaɪndlɪ] *adv* (*without seeing*) вслепу́ю; (*without thinking*) сле́по.
blindness ['blaɪndnɪs] *n* слепота́; (*fig*) ослепле́ние.
blind spot *n* (*AUT*) опа́сное ме́сто*; (*fig*) сла́бое ме́сто*.
blink [blɪŋk] *vi* (*person, animal*) морга́ть (*impf*); (*light*) мига́ть (*impf*) ♦ *n*: **the TV's on the ~** (*inf*) телеви́зор барахли́т.
blinkers ['blɪŋkəz] *npl* шо́ры *fpl*.
blinking ['blɪŋkɪŋ] *adj* (*BRIT: inf*): **this ~ weather** прокля́тая пого́да.
blip [blɪp] *n* вспы́шка* (*на экра́не*); (*scientific*) отражённый и́мпульс.
bliss [blɪs] *n* блаже́нство.
blissful ['blɪsful] *adj* блаже́нный (блаже́н);

blissfully ~ blow

(*event*) счастли́вый (сча́стлив); **in ~ ignorance** в счастли́вом неве́дении.

blissfully ['blɪsfəlɪ] *adv* блаже́нно; **~ happy** бесконе́чно счастли́вый; **~ unaware of ...** в счастли́вом неве́дении о +*prp* ....

blister ['blɪstə] *n* (*on skin*) волды́рь* *m*; (*in paint, rubber*) пузы́рь* *m* ♦ *vi* (*paint*) пузыри́ться (*impf*).

blithely ['blaɪðlɪ] *adv* беспе́чно.

blithering ['blɪðərɪŋ] *adj* (*inf*): **this ~ idiot** э́тот зако́нченный дура́к.

BLit(t) *n abbr* = **Bachelor of Literature, Bachelor of Letters**.

blitz [blɪts] *n* (*MIL*) бомбёжка*; **to have a ~ on sth** (*fig*) нава́ливаться (навали́ться* *perf*) на что-н.

blizzard ['blɪzəd] *n* вьюга.

BLM *n abbr* (*US*) = **Bureau of Land Management**.

bloated ['bləutɪd] *adj* (*face, stomach*) взду́тый (вздут); **I feel ~** я весь разду́лся.

blob [blɔb] *n* (*of glue, paint*) сгу́сток*; (*indistinct shape*) сму́тное очерта́ние.

bloc [blɔk] *n* блок; **the Eastern ~** (*formerly*) стра́ны Восто́чного бло́ка.

block [blɔk] *n* (*of buildings*) кварта́л; (*of stone etc*) плита́*; (*in pipe etc*) про́бка; (*toy*) ку́бик ♦ *vt* (*entrance, road*) загора́живать (загороди́ть* *perf*); (*progress*) препя́тствовать (*impf*); (*COMPUT*) блоки́ровать (*impf/perf*); **~ of flats** (*BRIT*) многокварти́рный дом*; **three ~s from here** че́рез три у́лицы; **mental ~** прова́л па́мяти; **~ and tackle** лебёдка*; **to ~ sb's way** прегражда́ть (прегради́ть* *perf*) кому́-н доро́гу

► **block up** *vt* затыка́ть (заткну́ть *perf*) ♦ *vi* засоря́ться (засори́ться *perf*); **my nose is ~ed up** у меня́ нос заложи́ло.

blockade [blɔ'keɪd] *n* блока́да ♦ *vt* блоки́ровать (заблоки́ровать *perf*).

blockage ['blɔkɪdʒ] *n* блоки́рование.

block booking *n* группова́я бронь *f*.

blockbuster ['blɔkbʌstə] *n* боеви́к*.

block capitals *npl* печа́тные бу́квы *fpl*.

blockhead ['blɔkhɛd] *n* (*inf*) болва́н.

block letters *npl* печа́тные бу́квы *fpl*.

block release *n* (*BRIT*) уче́бный о́тпуск.

block vote *n* (*BRIT*) представи́тельное голосова́ние.

bloke [bləuk] *n* (*BRIT: inf*) па́рень* *m*.

blond(e) [blɔnd] *adj* белоку́рый (белоку́р) ♦ *n*: **blonde** (*woman*) блонди́нка*.

blood [blʌd] *n* кровь* *f*; **new ~** (*fig*) све́жие си́лы *fpl*.

blood bank *n* храни́лище кро́ви.

bloodbath ['blʌdbɑ:θ] *n* бо́йня.

blood count *n* о́бщий* ана́лиз кро́ви.

bloodcurdling ['blʌdkə:dlɪŋ] *adj* леденя́щий* кровь.

blood donor *n* до́нор.

blood group *n* гру́ппа кро́ви.

bloodhound ['blʌdhaund] *n* ище́йка*.

bloodless ['blʌdlɪs] *adj* бескро́вный* (бескро́вен).

bloodletting ['blʌdlɛtɪŋ] *n* кровопуска́ние; (*fig*) кровопроли́тие.

blood poisoning *n* зараже́ние кро́ви.

blood pressure *n* кровяно́е давле́ние; **he has high/low ~ ~** у него́ высо́кое/ни́зкое давле́ние.

bloodshed ['blʌdʃɛd] *n* кровопроли́тие.

bloodshot ['blʌdʃɔt] *adj* (*eyes*) нали́тый кро́вью.

blood sport *n* охо́та (*как вид спо́рта*).

bloodstained ['blʌdsteɪnd] *adj* запя́тнанный кро́вью.

bloodstream ['blʌdstri:m] *n* кровообраще́ние.

blood test *n* ана́лиз кро́ви.

bloodthirsty ['blʌdθə:stɪ] *adj* кровожа́дный* (кровожа́ден).

blood transfusion *n* перелива́ние кро́ви.

blood type *n* гру́ппа кро́ви.

blood vessel *n* кровено́сный сосу́д.

bloody ['blʌdɪ] *adj* (*battle*) крова́вый; (*nose*) окрова́вленный (окрова́влен); (*BRIT: inf!*): **this ~ weather** э́та прокля́тая пого́да (*!*); **~ strong/good** (*inf!*) ужа́сно си́льный/хоро́ший*.

bloody-minded ['blʌdɪ'maɪndɪd] *adj* (*BRIT: inf*) по́длый (подл).

bloom [blu:m] *n* (*BOT*) цвето́к ♦ *vi* (*BOT*) цвести́* (*impf*); (*talent, person*) расцвета́ть (расцвести́* *perf*); **to be in ~** быть* (*impf*) в цвету́, цвести́* (*impf*).

blooming ['blu:mɪŋ] *adj* (*BRIT: inf*): **this ~ weather** э́та чёртова пого́да.

blossom ['blɔsəm] *n* цвет ♦ *vi* цвести́* (*impf*); (*fig*): **to ~ into** расцвести́* (*perf*) в +*acc*.

blot [blɔt] *n* (*on text*) кля́кса; (*on name etc*) пятно́* ♦ *vt* (*with ink etc*) ста́вить* (поста́вить* *perf*) кля́ксу на +*acc*; **to be a ~ on the landscape** по́ртить* (*impf*) вид; **to ~ one's copy book** (*fig*) мара́ть (замара́ть *perf*) свою́ репута́цию

► **blot out** *vt* (*view*) заслоня́ть (заслони́ть *perf*); (*memory*) уничтожа́ть (уничто́жить *perf*).

blotchy ['blɔtʃɪ] *adj* (*complexion*) пятни́стый (пятни́ст).

blotter ['blɔtə] *n* бюва́р.

blotting paper ['blɔtɪŋ-] *n* промока́тельная бума́га.

blotto ['blɔtəu] *adj* (*inf*) пья́ный (пьян) в сте́льку.

blouse [blauz] *n* блу́за, блу́зка*.

blow [bləu] (*pt* **blew**, *pp* **blown**) *n* (*also fig*) уда́р ♦ *vi* (*wind, person*) дуть (поду́ть *perf*); (*fuse*) перегора́ть (перегоре́ть *perf*) ♦ *vt* (*subj: wind*) гнать* (*impf*); (*instrument*) дуть (*impf*) в +*acc*; **to ~ one's nose** сморка́ться (вы́сморкаться *perf*); **to ~ a whistle** свисте́ть (просвисте́ть *perf*) в свисто́к; **to come to ~s** доходи́ть* (дойти́* *perf*) до дра́ки

▶ **blow away** vt сдувáть (сдуть perf) ◆ vi уноси́ться* (унести́сь* perf)

▶ **blow down** vt вали́ть* (повали́ть* perf)

▶ **blow off** vt сдувáть (сдуть perf) ◆ vi слетáть (слетéть* perf); (NAUT): **the ship was ~n off course** корáбль снеслó с кýрса

▶ **blow out** vi гáснуть* (погáснуть perf)

▶ **blow over** vi (storm, crisis) проходи́ть* (пройти́* perf)

▶ **blow up** vi (storm, crisis) разражáться (разрази́ться* perf) ◆ vt (bridge) взрывáть (взорвáть* perf); (tyre) надувáть (надýть perf); (PHOT) увели́чивать (увели́чить perf).

blow-dry ['bləʊdraɪ] n уклáдка волóс фéном ◆ vt уклáдывать (уложи́ть* perf) волосы фéном.

blowlamp ['bləʊlæmp] n (BRIT) пая́льная лáмпа.

blown [bləʊn] pp of **blow**.

blow-out ['bləʊaʊt] n (of tyre) разры́в; (of oil well) проры́в; (inf: big meal) кутёж*.

blowtorch ['bləʊtɔ:tʃ] n = **blowlamp**.

blow-up ['bləʊʌp] n увели́ченный сни́мок*.

blowzy ['blaʊzɪ] adj (BRIT) обрю́згший.

BLS n abbr (US) = Bureau of Labor Statistics.

blubber ['blʌbə'] n вы́топленный жир ◆ vi (pej) ревéть* (заревéть* perf).

bludgeon ['blʌdʒən] vt бить* (изби́ть* perf) дуби́нкой; (fig): **to ~ sb into doing** заставля́ть (застáвить* perf) когó-н из-под пáлки +impf infin.

blue [blu:] adj (colour: light) голубóй*; (: dark) си́ний*; (depressed) грýстный, подáвленный; **~s** npl (MUS):**the ~s** блюз msg; **~ film** похáбный фильм; **(only) once in a ~ moon** раз в сто лет; **out of the ~** (fig) как с нéба свали́ться.

blue baby n сини́ошный младéнец*.

bluebell ['blu:bɛl] n колокóльчик.

bluebottle ['blu:bɒtl] n навóзная мýха.

blue cheese n сыр* ти́па рокфóр.

blue-chip ['blu:tʃɪp] adj: **~ investment** надёжное капиталовложéние.

blue-collar worker ['blu:kɔlə'-] n рабóчий*(-ая) m(f) adj.

blue jeans npl джи́нсы pl.

blueprint ['blu:prɪnt] n (fig): **a ~ (for)** проéкт (+gen).

bluff [blʌf] vi (pretend, threaten) блефовáть (impf) ◆ n блеф; (GEO) утёс; **to call sb's ~** заставля́ть (застáвить* perf) когó-н раскры́ть кáрты.

blunder ['blʌndə'] n прóмах ◆ vi (make mistake) допускáть (допусти́ть* perf) прóмах; **to ~ into sb/sth** натыкáться (наткнýться perf) на когó-н/чтó-н.

blunt [blʌnt] adj тупóй* (туп); (person) прямолинéйный* (прямолинéен); (talk) откровéнный* (откровéнен) ◆ vt (chisel etc) затупля́ть (затупи́ть* perf); (feelings) тупи́ть (притупи́ть* perf); **~ instrument** (LAW) тупóе орýдие.

bluntly ['blʌntlɪ] adv пря́мо.

bluntness ['blʌntnɪs] n (of person) прямолинéйность f.

blur [bləː'] n смýтное очертáние; (memory) смýтное воспоминáние ◆ vt (vision) затумáнивать (затумáнить perf); (distinction) стерéть* (стирáть perf).

blurb [bləːb] n (about book etc) реклáма.

blurred [bləːd] adj стёртый.

blurt out [bləː't-] vt выпáливать (вы́палить perf).

blush [blʌʃ] vi краснéть (покраснéть perf) ◆ n румя́нец*.

blusher ['blʌʃə'] n румя́на pl.

bluster ['blʌstə'] n взрыв гнéва ◆ vi разбушевáться* (perf).

blustering ['blʌstərɪŋ] adj (person) бýйный* (бýен); (tone etc) громоглáсный* (громоглáсен).

blustery ['blʌstərɪ] adj вéтреный.

Blvd abbr = **boulevard**.

BM n abbr = British Museum; (= Bachelor of Medicine) ≈ бакалáвр медици́ны.

BMA n abbr = British Medical Association.

BMJ n abbr = British Medical Journal.

BMus n abbr (= Bachelor of Music) ≈ бакалáвр музыковéдения.

BMX n abbr (= bicycle motorcross) велосипéдные гóнки pl; **~ bike** мáрка велосипéда.

BNP n abbr (= British National Party) Бритáнская национáльная пáртия.

BO n abbr (inf: = body odour): **he has ~** от негó пáхнет пóтом; (US) = **box office**.

boar [bɔː'] n бóров; (wild pig) кабáн*.

board [bɔːd] n доскá*; (cardboard) картóн; (committee) комитéт; (in firm) правлéние ◆ vt (ship) сади́ться* (сесть* perf) на +acc; (train) сади́ться* (сесть* perf) в/на +acc; **on ~** (NAUT, AVIAT) на бортý; **full ~** (BRIT) пóлный пансиóн; **half ~** (BRIT) пансиóн с зáвтраком и ýжином; **~ and lodging** проживáние и питáние; **the plan went by the ~** (fig) план был вы́брошенным зá борт; **above ~** (fig) закóнным óбразом; **across the ~** (fig) по всем категóриям.

▶ **board up** vt забивáть (заби́ть* perf), заколáчивать (заколоти́ть* perf).

boarder ['bɔːdə'] n (SCOL) учени́к*(-и́ца) шкóлы-интернáта.

board game n настóльная игрá*.

boarding card ['bɔːdɪŋ-] n (AVIAT, NAUT) = **boarding pass**.

boarding house n пансиóн.

---

* marks translations which have irregular inflections. The Russian-English side of the dictionary gives inflectional information.

boarding party n спецгруппа таможенников или полицейских, проводящая инспекцию судов, подозреваемых в провозе контрабанды и наркотиков.
boarding pass n посадочный талон.
boarding school n школа-интернат.
board meeting n совещание правления.
board room n зал заседаний.
boardwalk ['bɔ:dwɔ:k] n (US) дощатый настил.
boast [bəust] vt гордиться (impf) +instr ♦ vi: **to ~ (about** or **of)** хвастаться (похвастаться perf) (+instr).
boastful ['bəustful] adj хвастливый (хвастлив).
boastfulness ['bəustfulnıs] n хвастовство.
boat [bəut] n (small) лодка*; (large) корабль* m; **to go by ~** плыть* (поплыть* perf); **to be in the same ~** (fig) быть* (impf) товарищами по несчастью.
boater ['bəutə'] n соломенная шляпа.
boating ['bəutıŋ] n катание на лодке.
boatswain ['bəusn] n боцман.
bob [bɔb] vi (boat: also: **~ up and down)** покачиваться (impf) ♦ n (BRIT: inf) = **shilling**
▶ **bob up** vi выскакивать (выскочить perf).
bobbin ['bɔbın] n шпулька.
bobby ['bɔbı] n (BRIT: inf) мент.
bobsleigh ['bɔbsleı] n бобслей.
bode [bəud] vi: **to ~ well/ill** предвещать (impf) or сулить (impf) хорошее/недоброе.
bodice ['bɔdıs] n корсаж.
bodily ['bɔdılı] adj физический* ♦ adv целиком.
body ['bɔdı] n тело*; (torso) туловище; (of speech, document) основная часть* f; (of car) корпус; (of plane) фюзеляж; (fig: group) группа; (: organization) орган, организация; (of information) масса; (of wine) консистенция; (also: **~stocking)** свитергольф (по типу закрытого купальника), трико nt ind; **ruling ~** орган правления; **in a ~** в полном составе.
body blow n сокрушительный удар.
body-building ['bɔdı'bıldıŋ] n боди-билдинг, атлетизм.
body-double ['bɔdıdʌbl] n актёр, снимающийся в обнажённом виде вместо ведущего актёра.
bodyguard ['bɔdıgɑ:d] n телохранитель m.
body language n язык* жестов.
body repairs npl ремонт корпуса.
body search n личный досмотр.
bodywork ['bɔdıwə:k] n корпус.
boffin ['bɔfın] n (BRIT: inf) спец.
bog [bɔg] n (GEO) болото, трясина ♦ vt: **to get ~ged down in** (fig) вязнуть (увязнуть perf) в +prp.
bogey ['bəugı] n (worry) пугало; (also: **~man)** бука m/f.
boggle ['bɔgl] vi: **the mind ~s** уму непостижимо.

bogie ['bəugı] n (RAIL) двухосная тележка*.
Bogotá [bəugə'tɑ:] n Богота.
bogus ['bəugəs] adj (claim) фиктивный* (фиктивен); (person) сомнительный (сомнителен).
Bohemia [bəu'hi:mıə] n Богемия.
Bohemian [bəu'hi:mıən] adj (GEO) богемский ♦ n богемец(ка); (non-conformist: also: **b~)** представитель(ница) m(f) богемы.
boil [bɔıl] vt (water) кипятить* (вскипятить* perf); (eggs, potatoes etc) варить (сварить perf), отваривать (отварить perf) ♦ vi (also fig) кипеть* (вскипеть* perf) ♦ n фурункул; **to come to the** (BRIT) or **a** (US) **~** вскипеть* (perf)
▶ **boil down to** vt fus (fig) сводиться (свестись* perf) к +dat
▶ **boil over** vi (milk) убегать (убежать* perf); (potatoes) выкипать (impf).
boiled egg [bɔıld-] n варёное яйцо*.
boiled potatoes npl варёная картошка fsg.
boiler ['bɔılə'] n (device) паровой котёл*, бойлер.
boiler suit n (BRIT) комбинезон.
boiling ['bɔılıŋ] adj: **I'm ~ (hot)** (inf) я запарился; **it's ~!** (of weather) жара!, жарища!
boiling point n (of liquid) точка кипения.
boisterous ['bɔıstərəs] adj разбитной.
bold [bəuld] adj (brave) смелый* (смел); (pej: cheeky) наглый (нагл); (pattern, colours) броский* (бросок).
boldly ['bəuldlı] adv (bravely) смело; (impudently) нагло.
boldness ['bəuldnıs] n (see adv) смелость f; наглость f.
bold type n жирный шрифт.
Bolivia [bə'lıvıə] n Боливия.
Bolivian [bə'lıvıən] adj боливийский ♦ n боливиец(-ийка).
bollard ['bɔləd] n (BRIT: AUT) тумба; (: NAUT) швартовая тумба.
bolshy ['bɔlʃı] adj (BRIT: inf) агрессивный* (агрессивен), воинственный.
bolster ['bəulstə'] n валик
▶ **bolster up** vt подкреплять (подкрепить* perf).
bolt [bəult] n (lock) засов; (with nut) болт* ♦ vt (lock) запирать (запереть* perf) на засов; (also: **~ together)** скреплять (скрепить* perf) болтами; (devour) заглатывать (заглотнуть* perf) ♦ vi (run away) понестись* (perf) ♦ adv: **~ upright** вытянувшись в струнку; **a ~ of lightning** разряд молнии; **a ~ from the blue** (fig) гром среди ясного неба.
bomb [bɔm] n бомба ♦ vt бомбить* (impf).
bombard [bɔm'bɑ:d] vt (MIL, fig) бомбардировать (impf).
bombardment [bɔm'bɑ:dmənt] n бомбардировка.
bombastic [bɔm'bæstık] adj претенциозный* (претенциозен).

bomb disposal *n*: ~ ~ **unit** отря́д сапёров; ~ **expert** сапёр.
bomber ['bɔmə'] *n* (*AVIAT*) бомбардиро́вщик; (*person*) террори́ст.
bombing ['bɔmɪŋ] *n* бомбардиро́вка, бомбёжка.
bombshell ['bɔmʃɛl] *n* (*fig*): **my sacking was a real** ~ изве́стие о моём увольне́нии произвело́ эффе́кт разорва́вшейся бо́мбы.
bomb site *n* разбомблённый уча́сток*.
bona fide ['bəunə'faɪdɪ] *adj* (*traveller etc*) по́длинный*; (*offer*) настоя́щий*.
bonanza [bə'nænzə] *n* золото́е дно.
bond [bɔnd] *n* у́зы *pl*; (*binding promise*) обяза́тельство; (*FINANCE*) облига́ция; (*COMM*): **goods in** ~ това́ры, неопла́ченные по́шлиной.
bondage ['bɔndɪdʒ] *n* (*slavery*) нево́ля.
bonded goods ['bɔndɪd-] *npl* храня́щиеся това́ры *mpl* на тамо́женных скла́дах.
bonded warehouse *n* тамо́женный склад (*для товаров неопла́ченных по́шлиной*).
bone [bəun] *n* кость* *f* ♦ *vt* отделя́ть (отдели́ть* *perf*) от косте́й; **I've got a** ~ **to pick with you** у меня́ к тебе́ прете́нзия.
bone china *n* костяно́й фарфо́р.
bone-dry ['bəun'draɪ] *adj* соверше́нно сухо́й*.
bone idle *adj* пра́здный* (пра́зден); **he is** ~ ~ он безде́льник.
bone marrow *n* ко́стный мозг.
boner ['bəunə'] *n* (*US*) про́мах*.
bonfire ['bɔnfaɪə'] *n* костёр*.
bonk [bɔŋk] (*inf*) *vt* тра́хать (тра́хнуть *perf*) ♦ *vi* тра́хаться (тра́хнуться *perf*).
bonkers ['bɔŋkəz] *adj* (*inf*) чо́кнутый (чо́кнут).
Bonn [bɔn] *n* Бонн.
bonnet ['bɔnɪt] *n* (*hat*) ка́пор; (*BRIT*: *of car*) капо́т.
bonny ['bɔnɪ] *adj* (*esp SCOTTISH*) краси́вый (краси́в).
bonus ['bəunəs] *n* (*payment*) пре́мия; (*on wages*) премиа́льные *pl adj*; (*fig*) дополни́тельное преиму́щество.
bony ['bəunɪ] *adj* (*person, fingers*) костля́вый (костля́в); (*meat, fish*) кости́стый.
boo [bu:] *excl* фу ♦ *vt* осви́стывать (освиста́ть* *perf*).
boob [bu:b] *n* (*inf*: *breast*) грудь *f*; (*BRIT*: *mistake*) глу́пость *f*.
booby prize ['bu:bɪ-] *n* приз* проигра́вшему игроку́.
booby trap *n* (*MIL*) ми́на-лову́шка*; (*fig*) лову́шка*.
booby-trapped ['bu:bɪtræpt] *adj*: **a** ~ **car** маши́на с подло́женной ми́ной.
book [buk] *n* кни́га; (*of stamps, tickets*) кни́жечка* ♦ *vt* (*ticket, table*) зака́зывать (заказа́ть* *perf*); (*seat, room*) брони́ровать

(заброни́ровать *perf*); (*subj*: *policeman, referee*) штрафова́ть (оштрафова́ть *perf*); ~**s** *npl* (*COMM*: *accounts*) бухга́лтерские кни́ги *fpl*; **to keep the** ~**s** вести́* (*impf*) бухга́лтерские кни́ги; **by the** ~ согла́сно инстру́кции; **to throw the** ~ **at sb** обвиня́ть (обвини́ть *perf*) кого́-н во всех сме́ртных греха́х
► **book in** *vi* (*BRIT*: *at hotel*) регистри́роваться (зарегистри́роваться *perf*)
► **book up** *vt*: **all seats are** ~**ed up** все биле́ты про́даны; **the hotel is** ~**ed up** в гости́нице нет мест; **I'm** ~**ed up that week** у меня́ э́та неде́ля по́лностью за́нята.
bookable ['bukəbl] *adj*: **all seats are** ~ все биле́ты по предвари́тельным зака́зам.
bookcase ['bukkeɪs] *n* кни́жный шкаф*.
book end *n* книгодержа́тель *m*.
booking ['bukɪŋ] *n* (*BRIT*) зака́з.
booking office *n* (*BRIT*) биле́тная ка́сса.
book-keeping ['buk'ki:pɪŋ] *n* бухгалте́рия, счетово́дство.
booklet ['buklɪt] *n* брошю́ра.
bookmaker ['bukmeɪkə'] *n* букме́кер.
bookseller ['buksɛlə'] *n* книготорго́вец*.
bookshelf ['bukʃɛlf] *n* кни́жная по́лка.
bookshop ['bukʃɔp] *n* кни́жный магази́н.
bookstall ['bukstɔ:l] *n* кни́жный кио́ск.
book store *n* = **bookshop**.
book token *n* *пода́рочный тало́н на поку́пку кни́ги*.
book value *n* сто́имость *f* по торго́вым кни́гам.
bookworm ['bukwə:m] *n* кни́жный червь *m*.
boom [bu:m] *n* (*noise*) ро́кот; (*growth*: *in population etc*) бы́стрый рост; (*ECON*) бум ♦ *vi* (*guns, thunder*) грохота́ть* (прогрохота́ть* *perf*); (*voice*) рокота́ть* (пророкота́ть* *perf*); (*business*) процвета́ть (*impf*).
boomerang ['bu:məræŋ] *n* бумера́нг ♦ *vi*: **to** ~ **on sb** верну́ться (*perf*) к кому́-н бумера́нгом.
boom town *n* *го́род, процвета́ющий во вре́мя экономи́ческого подъёма*.
boon [bu:n] *n* бла́го.
boorish ['buərɪʃ] *adj* неотёсанный (неотёсан).
boost [bu:st] *n* (*to confidence etc*) толчо́к*, сти́мул ♦ *vt* стимули́ровать (*impf*), дава́ть (дать* *perf*) толчо́к +*dat*; **to give a** ~ **to sb's spirits** *or* **to sb** окрыля́ть (окрыли́ть *perf*) кого́-н.
booster ['bu:stə'] *n* (*MED*) повто́рная приви́вка*; (*TV, ELEC*) усили́тель *m*; (*also*: ~ **rocket**) раке́та-носи́тель *m*.
booster cushion *n* *сиде́нье для дете́й в маши́не*.
boot [bu:t] *n* (*for winter*) сапо́г*; (*for football*) бу́тса; (*for walking*) боти́нок*; (*BRIT*: *of car*) бага́жник ♦ *vt* (*COMPUT*) загружа́ть (загрузи́ть* *perf*); **... to** ~ (*in addition*) ... в

прида́чу; **to give sb the ~** (inf) вы́турить (perf) кого́-н.

booth [buːð] n (at fair) ларёк*; (TEL, for voting) бу́дка*.

bootleg ['buːtlɛg] adj контраба́ндный.

bootlegger ['buːtlɛgə'] n контрабанди́ст.

booty ['buːtɪ] n трофе́и mpl.

booze [buːz] (inf) n вы́пивка ♦ vi выпива́ть (impf).

boozer ['buːzə'] n (BRIT: inf: pub) пивну́шка*; **he's a real ~** (inf) он настоя́щий* пьянчу́га.

border ['bɔːdə'] n (of a country); (for flowers) бордю́р; (on cloth etc) кайма́* ♦ vt (road, river etc) окаймля́ть (окайми́ть* perf); (another country: also: ~ on) грани́чить (impf) с +instr; **B~s** n: **the B~s** райо́н на грани́це ме́жду А́нглией и Шотла́ндией

▶ **border on** vt fus (fig) грани́чить (impf) с +instr.

borderline ['bɔːdəlaɪn] n: **on the ~** на гра́ни.

borderline case n промежу́точный слу́чай.

bore [bɔː'] pt of **bear** ♦ vt (hole) сверли́ть (просверли́ть perf); (well, tunnel) бури́ть (пробури́ть perf); (person) наску́чить (perf) +dat ♦ n (person) зану́да m/f; (of gun) кана́л ствола́, кали́бр; **to be ~d** скуча́ть (impf); **he's ~d to tears** or **~d to death** or **~d stiff** ему́ сме́ртельно ску́чно.

boredom ['bɔːdəm] n (condition) ску́ка; (boring quality) зану́дство.

boring ['bɔːrɪŋ] adj ску́чный*.

born [bɔːn] adj рождённый; **to be ~** рожда́ться (роди́ться* perf); **I was ~ in 1960** я роди́лся в 1960 году́; **~ blind** слепорождённый; **a ~ comedian** прирождённый ко́мик.

born-again [bɔːnə'gɛn] adj: ~ **Christian** новообращённый(-ая) христиани́н*(-а́нка).

borne [bɔːn] pp of **bear**.

Borneo ['bɔːnɪəu] n Борне́о m ind.

borough ['bʌrə] n администрати́вный о́круг*.

borrow ['bɔrəu] vt: **to ~ sth from sb** занима́ть (заня́ть* perf) что-н у кого́-н; **to ~ books from the library** брать* (взять* perf) кни́ги в библиоте́ке; **may I ~ your car?** мо́жно взять на вре́мя Ва́шу маши́ну?

borrower ['bɔrəuə'] n заёмщик.

borrowing ['bɔrəuɪŋ] n (word, custom) заи́мствование; (of money) заём*.

borstal ['bɔːstl] n (BRIT) исправи́тельная коло́ния для несовершенноле́тних престу́пников.

Bosnia ['bɔznɪə] n Бо́сния; ~**-Herzegovina** Бо́сния-Герцегови́на.

Bosnian ['bɔznɪən] n жи́тель(ница) m(f) Бо́снии.

bosom ['buzəm] n грудь* f; (fig: of family) ло́но.

bosom friend n закады́чный друг*.

Bosphorus ['bɔsfərəs] n: **the ~** Босфо́р.

boss [bɔs] n (employer) хозя́ин*(-я́йка*), босс; (leader) ли́дер, вожа́к* ♦ vt (also: ~ **around**, ~ **about**) распоряжа́ться (impf), кома́ндовать (impf) +instr; **stop ~ing everyone about!**

перестáнь все́ми кома́ндовать!

bossy ['bɔsɪ] adj вла́стный (вла́стен).

bosun ['bəusn] n бо́цман.

botanical [bə'tænɪkl] adj ботани́ческий.

botanist ['bɔtənɪst] n бота́ник.

botany ['bɔtənɪ] n бота́ника.

botch [bɔtʃ] vt (also: ~ **up**) состря́пать (perf).

both [bəuθ] adj, pron о́ба* (f о́бе*) ♦ adv: ~ **A and B** и А, и Б; ~ **(of them)** о́ба (они́); ~ **of us went, we ~ went** мы о́ба пошли́; **they sell ~ meat and poultry** они́ торгу́ют и мя́сом, и пти́цей.

bother ['bɔðə'] vt (worry) беспоко́ить (обеспоко́ить perf); (disturb) беспоко́ить (побеспоко́ить perf) ♦ vi (also: ~ **o.s.**) беспоко́иться (impf) ♦ n (trouble) хло́поты* pl ♦ excl: ~! чёрт возьми́!; **to ~ doing** брать* (взять* perf) на себя́ труд +infin; **I'm sorry to ~ you** извини́те за беспоко́йство; **please don't ~** пожа́луйста, не беспоко́йтесь; **don't ~!** не на́до!; **it is a ~ to have to do** э́то так хло́потно +infin; **it's no ~** э́то меня́ не затрудни́т; **I can't be ~ed** мне лень.

Botswana [bɔt'swɑːnə] n Ботсва́на.

bottle ['bɔtl] n буты́лка*; (for baby) рожо́к*; (BRIT: inf: courage) сме́лость f ♦ vt (beer, wine) разлива́ть (разли́ть* perf) по буты́лкам; (fruit) консерви́ровать (законсерви́ровать perf); ~ **of wine/milk** буты́лка* вина́/молока́; **wine/milk** ~ буты́лка* из-под вина́/молока́

▶ **bottle up** vt скрыва́ть (скрыть* perf).

bottle bank n му́сорный я́щик для стекля́нной та́ры.

bottle-fed ['bɔtlfɛd] adj: ~ **baby** иску́сственник.

bottleneck ['bɔtlnɛk] n (AUT) у́зкий езд; (fig) зато́р.

bottle-opener ['bɔtləupnə'] n што́пор.

bottom ['bɔtəm] n (of container, sea etc) дно*; (ANAT) зад*; (of page, list) низ*; (of class) неуспева́ющий*(-ая) m(f) adj; (of mountain etc) подно́жие ♦ adj (lowest) ни́жний*; (last) после́дний*; **at the ~ of** на дне +gen; **to get to the ~ of sth** (fig) добира́ться (добра́ться* perf) до су́ти чего́-н.

bottomless ['bɔtəmlɪs] adj (funds, store) бездо́нный* (бездо́нен).

bottom line n суть f де́ла.

botulism ['bɔtjulɪzəm] n ботули́зм.

bough [bau] n сук*.

bought [bɔːt] pt, pp of **buy**.

boulder ['bəuldə'] n валу́н*.

boulevard ['buːləvɑːd] n бульва́р.

bounce [bauns] vi (ball) отска́кивать (отскочи́ть perf); (cheque) верну́ться (perf) (о че́ке, ввиду́ отсу́тствия де́нег на счету́) ♦ vt (ball) ударя́ть (уда́рить perf); (signal) отража́ть (отрази́ть* perf) ♦ n (of ball) отско́к; **he's got plenty of ~** (fig) он о́чень живо́й.

bouncer ['baʊnsə'] *n* (*inf*) вышибáла *m*.
bouncy castle ['baʊnsɪ-] *n* надувнáя констрýкция в фóрме зáмка, на котóрой мóгут пры́гать дéти.
bound [baʊnd] *pt, pp of* **bind** ♦ *n* (*leap*) прыжóк*, скачóк* ♦ *vi* (*leap*) пры́гать (пры́гнуть *perf*) ♦ *vt* (*border*) служи́ть (*impf*) грани́цей +*gen* ♦ *adj*: **he is ~ by law to** ... егó обя́зывает закóн +*infin*...; **~s** *npl* (*limits*) предéлы *mpl*; **he is/was ~ to do** он обя́зан/был обя́зан +*infin*; **he's ~ to come** он обязáтельно *or* непремéнно придёт; **~ for** направля́ющийся* в/на +*acc*; **this area is out of ~s** (*fig*: *place*) э́то мéсто явля́ется запрéтным.
boundary ['baʊndrɪ] *n* грани́ца.
boundless ['baʊndlɪs] *adj* безграни́чный* (безграни́чен).
bountiful ['baʊntɪful] *adj* (*person*) щéдрый* (щедр); (*supply*) оби́льный* (оби́лен).
bounty ['baʊntɪ] *n* (*generosity*) щéдрость *f*; (*reward*) вознаграждéние.
bounty hunter *n* охóтник за нагрáдой.
bouquet ['bukeɪ] *n* букéт.
bourbon ['buəbən] *n* (*US*: *also*: **~ whiskey**) кукурýзное ви́ски *nt ind*, бурбóн.
bourgeois ['buəʒwɑ:] *adj* буржуáзный* ♦ *n* буржуá *m ind*.
bout [baʊt] *n* (*of illness*) при́ступ; (*of activity*) всплéск; (*BOXING etc*) схвáтка*.
boutique [bu:'ti:k] *n* лáвка*.
bow[1] [bəʊ] *n* (*knot*) бант; (*weapon*) лук; (*MUS*) смычóк.
bow[2] [baʊ] *n* (*of the head, body*) поклóн; (*NAUT*: *also*: **~s**) нос ♦ *vi* (*with head, body*) клáняться (поклони́ться* *perf*); (*yield*): **to ~ to** *or* **before** поддавáться* (поддáться* *perf*) +*dat or* на +*acc*; **to ~ to the inevitable** покоря́ться (покори́ться *perf*) неизбéжному.
bowels ['baʊəlz] *npl* кишéчник *msg*; (*of the earth etc*) нéдра *pl*.
bowl [bəʊl] *n* ми́ска*, чáша; (*for washing*) таз*; (*ball*) шар*; (*of pipe*) голóвка; (*US*: *stadium*) арéна ♦ *vi* подавáть* (подáть* *perf*) мяч
▶ **bowl over** *vt* (*fig*) сбивáть (сбить* *perf*).
bow-legged ['bəʊ'legɪd] *adj* кривонóгий*.
bowler ['bəʊlə'] *n* бóулер, подаю́щий мяч; (*BRIT*: *also*: **~ hat**) котелóк*.
bowling ['bəʊlɪŋ] *n* (*game*) кегельбáн.
bowling alley *n* кегельбáн.
bowling green *n* площáдка* для игры́ в шары́.
bowls [bəʊlz] *n* игрá* в шары́.
bow tie [bəʊ-] *n* бáбочка*.
box [bɒks] *n* я́щик, корóбка*; (*also*: **cardboard ~**) картóнная корóбка*; (*THEAT*) лóжа; (*BRIT*: *AUT*) разграничи́тельная ли́ния; (*ADMIN*: *on form*) графá* ♦ *vt* (*put in a box*) упакóвывать (упаковáть *perf*) в корóбку; (*SPORT*) ударя́ть

(удáрить *perf*) ♦ *vi* (*SPORT*) бокси́ровать (*impf*); **what's on the ~?** (*inf*: *TV*) что сегóдня по я́щику?; **to ~ sb's ears** надирáть (надрáть* *perf*) комý-н ýши
▶ **box in** *vt* окружáть (окружи́ть *perf*)
▶ **box off** *vt* отгорáживать (отгороди́ть* *perf*).
boxer ['bɒksə'] *n* боксёр.
box file *n* я́щик для хранéния докумéнтов.
boxing ['bɒksɪŋ] *n* бокс.
Boxing Day *n* (*BRIT*) день пóсле Рождествá.
boxing gloves *npl* боксёрские перчáтки* *fpl*.
boxing ring *n* ринг.
box number *n* нóмер* абонéнтского я́щика.
box office *n* театрáльная кáсса.
boxroom ['bɒksrum] *n* чулáн.
boy [bɔɪ] *n* мáльчик; (*son*) сынóк*.
boycott ['bɔɪkɔt] *n* бойкóт ♦ *vt* бойкоти́ровать (*impf/perf*).
boyfriend ['bɔɪfrɛnd] *n* друг*.
boyish ['bɔɪɪʃ] *adj* мальчи́шеский*.
boy scout *n* бойскáут.
Bp *abbr* = **bishop**.
BR *abbr* = **British Rail**.
bra [brɑ:] *n* ли́фчик.
brace [breɪs] *n* (*on leg*) ши́на; (*on teeth*) пласти́нки *pl*; (*tool*) коловорóт; (*also*: **bracket**) скóбка* ♦ *vt* (*knees, shoulders*) напрягáть (напря́чь* *perf*); **~s** *npl* (*BRIT*: *for trousers*) подтя́жки *pl*; **to ~ o.s.** (*for shock*) собирáться (собрáться* *perf*) с дýхом.
bracelet ['breɪslɪt] *n* браслéт.
bracing ['breɪsɪŋ] *adj* бодря́щий.
bracken ['brækən] *n* орля́к.
bracket ['brækɪt] *n* (*TECH*) кронштéйн; (*group, range*) категóрия; (*also*: **brace ~**) скóбка*; (*also*: **round ~**) крýглая скóбка*; (*also*: **square ~**) квадрáтная скóбка* ♦ *vt* (*fig*: *also*: **~ together**) группировáть (сгруппировáть *perf*); (*word, phrase*) заключáть (заключи́ть *perf*) в скóбки; **income ~** ýровень *m* дохóда; **in ~s** в скóбках.
brackish ['brækɪʃ] *adj* солоновáтый (солновáт).
brag [bræg] *vi* хвáстаться (похвáстаться *perf*).
braid [breɪd] *n* (*for clothes etc*) тесьмá; (*of hair*) косá*.
Braille [breɪl] *n* шрифт Брáйля.
brain [breɪn] *n* (*ANAT, fig*) мозг*; **~s** *npl* (*CULIN*) мозги́ *mpl*; (*intelligence*) мозги́ *mpl*, сообрази́тельность *f*; **he's got ~s** он пáрень с головóй.
brainchild ['breɪntʃaɪld] *n* дети́ще.
braindead ['breɪndɛd] *adj*: **the patient was ~** у пациéнта наступи́ла биологи́ческая смерть.
brain drain *n*: **the ~ ~** утéчка мозгóв.
brainless ['breɪnlɪs] *adj* безмóзглый.
brainstorm ['breɪnstɔ:m] *n* (*fig*) умопомрачéние; (*US*: **brainwave**) озарéние.

---

* marks translations which have irregular inflections. The Russian-English side of the dictionary gives inflectional information.

brainwash ['breɪnwɔʃ] *vt* промыва́ть (промы́ть* *perf*) мозги́ +*dat.*
brainwave ['breɪnweɪv] *n* озаре́ние; **he had a ~** на него́ нашло́ озаре́ние.
brainy ['breɪnɪ] *adj* мозгови́тый.
braise [breɪz] *vt* туши́ть* (потуши́ть* *perf*).
brake [breɪk] *n* (*also fig*) то́рмоз* ◆ *vi* тормози́ть* (затормози́ть* *perf*).
brake fluid *n* тормозна́я жи́дкость *f.*
brake light *n* тормозно́й сигна́л.
brake pedal *n* педа́ль *f* тормоза́, то́рмоза* *mpl.*
bramble ['bræmbl] *n* ежеви́ка.
bran [bræn] *n* о́труби *pl.*
branch [brɑːntʃ] *n* (*of tree*) ве́тка*, ветвь* *f*; (*fig: of family, organization*) ветвь*; (*COMM: of bank, company etc*) филиа́л ◆ *vi* разветвля́ться (разветви́ться* *perf*)
▶ **branch out** *vi* (*fig*) разветвля́ться (разветви́ться* *perf*).
branch line *n* (железнодоро́жная) ве́тка*.
branch manager *n* дире́ктор* филиа́ла.
brand [brænd] *n* (*also: ~ name*) фи́рменная ма́рка*; (*fig: type*) сорт ◆ *vt* (*cattle*) клейми́ть* (заклейми́ть* *perf*); (*fig: pej*): **to ~ sb a communist** *etc* клейми́ть* (заклейми́ть* *perf*) кого́-н коммуни́стом *etc.*
brandish ['brændɪʃ] *vt* разма́хивать (*impf*) +*instr*; (*weapon*) потряса́ть (*impf*) +*instr.*
brand name *n* фи́рменная ма́рка.
brand-new ['brænd'njuː] *adj* соверше́нно но́вый*.
brandy ['brændɪ] *n* бре́нди *nt ind*, конья́к*.
brash [bræʃ] *adj* наха́льный* (наха́лен).
Brasilia [brə'zɪlɪə] *n* Брази́лия.
brass [brɑːs] *n* (*metal*) лату́нь *f*; **the ~** (*MUS*) духовы́е инструме́нты *mpl.*
brass band *n* духово́й орке́стр.
brassiere ['bræsɪə'] *n* бюстга́льтер.
brass tacks *npl*: **to get down to ~ ~** доходи́ть* (дойти́* *perf*) до су́ти.
brassy ['brɑːsɪ] *adj* (*colour*) ме́дный; (*sound*) ре́зкий*; (*behaviour*) вызыва́ющий*.
brat [bræt] *n* (*pej*) отро́дье*.
Bratislava [brætɪ'slɑːvə] *n* Братисла́ва.
bravado [brə'vɑːdəʊ] *n* брава́да.
brave [breɪv] *adj* сме́лый (смел), хра́брый (храбр) ◆ *n* инде́йский во́ин ◆ *vt* сме́ло *or* хра́бро встреча́ть (встре́тить* *perf*).
bravely ['breɪvlɪ] *adv* сме́ло, хра́бро.
bravery ['breɪvərɪ] *n* сме́лость *f*, хра́брость *f.*
bravo [brɑː'vəʊ] *excl* бра́во.
brawl [brɔːl] *n* дра́ка ◆ *vi* дра́ться* (подра́ться* *perf*).
brawn [brɔːn] *n* (*strength*) му́скулы *mpl*; (*meat*) зельц, сту́день *m.*
brawny ['brɔːnɪ] *adj* мускули́стый (мускули́ст).
bray [breɪ] *vi* (*donkey*) реве́ть* (*impf*) ◆ *n* рёв осла́.
brazen ['breɪzn] *adj* (*woman*) бессты́жий

(бессты́ж); (*lie, accusation*) на́глый (нагл) ◆ *vt*: **to ~ it out** выкру́чиваться (вы́крутиться* *perf*).
brazier ['breɪzɪə'] *n* жаро́вня*.
Brazil [brə'zɪl] *n* Брази́лия.
Brazilian [brə'zɪljən] *adj* брази́льский* ◆ *n* брази́лец*(-лья́нка*).
Brazil nut *n* америка́нский* оре́х.
breach [briːtʃ] *vt* (*defence, wall*) пробива́ть (проби́ть* *perf*) брешь в +*acc* ◆ *n* (*gap*) брешь *f*; (*estrangement*) разры́в; **~ of contract** наруше́ние догово́ра; **~ of the peace** наруше́ние обще́ственного поря́дка; **~ of trust** злоупотребле́ние дове́рием.
bread [brɛd] *n* хлеб; (*inf: money*) ба́бки *fpl*; **to earn one's daily ~** зараба́тывать (зарабо́тать *perf*) на хлеб *or* на жизнь; **to know which side one's ~ is buttered (on)** знать (*impf*) свою́ вы́году.
bread and butter *n* хлеб с ма́слом; (*fig*) хлеб насу́щный, щи́зненная осно́ва.
breadbin ['brɛdbɪn] *n* (*BRIT*) хле́бница.
breadboard ['brɛdbɔːd] *n* хле́бная доска́*; (*COMPUT*) маке́т, маке́тная пла́та.
breadbox ['brɛdbɔks] *n* (*US*) хле́бница.
breadcrumbs ['brɛdkrʌmz] *npl* кро́шки* *fpl*; (*CULIN*) панирово́чные сухари́ *mpl.*
breadline ['brɛdlaɪn] *n*: **on the ~** за черто́й бе́дности.
breadth [brɛtθ] *n* (*of cloth etc*) ширина́; (*fig: of knowledge, subject*) широта́.
breadwinner ['brɛdwɪnə'] *n* корми́лец*(-лица).
break [breɪk] (*pt* **broke**, *pp* **broken**) *vt* (*cup, glass*) разбива́ть (разби́ть* *perf*); (*leg, arm*) лома́ть (слома́ть *perf*); (*promise, law*) наруша́ть (нару́шить* *perf*); (*record*) побива́ть (поби́ть* *perf*) ◆ *vi* (*crockery*) разбива́ться (разби́ться *perf*); (*storm*) разрази́ться (*perf*); (*weather*) по́ртиться (испо́ртиться *perf*); (*dawn*) бре́зжить (забре́зжить *perf*); (*story, news*) сообща́ть (сообщи́ть *perf*) ◆ *n* (*gap*) пробе́л; (*fracture*) перело́м; (*rest*) переды́шка*; (*interval*) переры́в; (*playtime*) переме́на; (*chance*) шанс; (*holiday*) о́тпуск*, о́тдых; **to ~ the news to sb** сообща́ть (сообщи́ть *perf*) кому́-н но́вость; **to ~ even** (*COMM*) зако́нчить (*perf*) без убы́тка; **to ~ with sb** порыва́ть (порва́ть* *perf*) с кем-н; **to ~ free** *or* **loose** вы́рваться* (*perf*) на свобо́ду; **to take a ~** (*few minutes*) де́лать (сде́лать *perf*) небольшо́й переры́в; (*holiday*) брать* (взять* *perf*) о́тпуск; **without a ~** без переры́ва; **a lucky ~** счастли́вый слу́чай
▶ **break down** *vt* (*figures etc*) разбива́ть (разби́ть* *perf*) по статья́м; (*door etc*) взла́мывать (взлома́ть *perf*) ◆ *vi* (*machine, car*) лома́ться (слома́ться *perf*); (*resistance*) быть* (*impf*) сло́мленным(-ой); (*person*) сломи́ться (*perf*); (*talks*) срыва́ться (сорва́ться* *perf*)
▶ **break in** *vt* (*horse*) обу́здывать (обузда́ть

perf) ◆ *vi* (*burglar*) вламываться (вломиться *perf*); (*interrupt*) вмешиваться (вмешаться *perf*)

▶ **break into** *vt fus* (*house*) вламываться (вломиться* *perf*) в +*acc*

▶ **break off** *vi* (*branch*) отламываться (отломиться* *perf*); (*speaker*) прерываться (прерваться* *perf*) ◆ *vt* (*talks*) прерывать (прервать* *perf*); (*engagement*) расторгать (расторгнуть *perf*)

▶ **break open** *vt* взламывать (взломать *perf*)

▶ **break out** *vi* (*begin*) разражаться (разразиться* *perf*); (*escape*) сбегать (сбежать* *perf*); **to ~ out in spots/a rash** покрываться (покрыться* *perf*) прыщами/сыпью

▶ **break through** *vt fus* прорываться (прорваться* *perf*) сквозь +*acc* ◆ *vi*: **the sun broke through** солнце пробилось сквозь тучи

▶ **break up** *vi* (*ship*) разбиваться (разбиться* *perf*); (*crowd, meeting*) расходиться (разойтись* *perf*); (*marriage, partnership*) распадаться (распасться *perf*); (*SCOL*) закрываться (закрыться* *perf*) на каникулы ◆ *vt* (*rocks etc*) разламывать (разломить* *perf*); (*journey*) прерывать (прервать* *perf*); (*fight etc*) прекращать (прекратить* *perf*); (*meeting*) распускать (распустить* *perf*); (*marriage*) разбивать (разбить* *perf*).

breakable ['breɪkəbl] *adj* хрупкий* (хрупок), ломкий* (ломок) ◆ *n*: **~s** хрупкие предметы *mpl*.

breakage ['breɪkɪdʒ] *n* (*act of breaking*) поломка*; (*object*) бой; **to pay for ~s** платить* (заплатить* *perf*) за бой.

breakaway ['breɪkəweɪ] *adj* (*group etc*) отделившийся, отколовшийся.

break-dancing ['breɪkdɑːnsɪŋ] *n* брейк.

breakdown ['breɪkdaun] *n* (*AUT*) небольшая авария; (*in communications*) нарушение; (*of marriage*) распад*; (*of statistics*) разбивка*; (*also*: **nervous ~**) нервный срыв.

breakdown service *n* (*BRIT*) аварийная служба.

breakdown van *n* (*BRIT*) фургон аварийной службы.

breaker ['breɪkəʳ] *n* вал*.

breakeven ['breɪk'iːvn] *cpd*: **~ chart** график рентабельности; **~ point** точка* безубыточности.

breakfast ['brɛkfəst] *n* завтрак ◆ *vi* завтракать (позавтракать *perf*).

breakfast cereal *n* крупа для завтрака.

break-in ['breɪkɪn] *n* взлом.

breaking and entering ['breɪkɪŋən'ɛntrɪŋ] *n* (*LAW*) вторжение со взломом.

breaking point *n* предел.

breakthrough ['breɪkθruː] *n* (*fig*: *in technology*) переломное открытие.

break-up ['breɪkʌp] *n* (*of partnership, marriage*) распад.

break-up value *n* (*COMM*) ликвидационная стоимость *f*.

breakwater ['breɪkwɔːtəʳ] *n* волнорез, мол*.

breast [brɛst] *n* грудь* *f*; (*of meat*) грудинка; (*of poultry*) белое мясо.

breast-feed ['brɛstfiːd] (*irreg*: *like* **feed**) *vt* кормить* (покормить* *perf*) грудью ◆ *vi* кормить (*impf*) (грудью).

breast pocket *n* (*of jacket etc*) нагрудный карман.

breast-stroke ['brɛststrəuk] *n* брасс.

breath [brɛθ] *n* вдох; (*breathing*) дыхание; **to go out for a ~ of air** выходить* (выйти* *perf*) подышать *or* на свежий воздух; **to be out of ~** запыхиваться (запыхаться *perf*); **to get one's ~ back** отдышаться (*perf*).

breathalyse ['brɛθəlaɪz] *vt* проверять (проверить *perf*) дыхание на алкоголь.

Breathalyser® ['brɛθəlaɪzəʳ] *n* спиртометр.

breathe [briːð] *vt* вдыхать (вдохнуть *perf*) ◆ *vi* дышать* (*impf*); **I won't ~ a word about it** я словом не обмолвлюсь об этом

▶ **breathe in** *vt* вдыхать (вдохнуть *perf*) ◆ *vi* делать (сделать *perf*) вдох

▶ **breathe out** *vt* выдыхать (выдохнуть *perf*) ◆ *vi* делать (сделать *perf*) выдох.

breather ['briːðəʳ] *n* передышка*.

breathing ['briːðɪŋ] *n* дыхание.

breathing space *n* (*fig*) передышка*.

breathless ['brɛθlɪs] *adj* (*from exertion*) запыхавшийся; (*after illness*) бездыханный; **he was ~ with excitement** у него перехватило дыхание от волнения.

breathtaking ['brɛθteɪkɪŋ] *adj* захватывающий* дух.

breath test *n* дыхательная проба.

bred [brɛd] *pt, pp of* **breed**.

-bred [brɛd] *suffix*: **well/ill~** хорошо/плохо воспитанный* (воспитан).

breed [briːd] (*pt, pp* **bred**) *vt* (*animals, plants*) разводить* (развести* *perf*); (*fig*: *give rise to*) порождать (породить* *perf*) ◆ *vi* размножаться (*impf*) ◆ *n* (*ZOOL*) порода; (*type, class*) сорт*, род*.

breeder ['briːdəʳ] *n* (*person*) селекционер; (*PHYS*: *also*: **~ reactor**) реактор-размножитель *m*; **cattle ~** скотовод.

breeding ['briːdɪŋ] *n* воспитание.

breeding ground *n* место* размножения; (*fig*) рассадник.

breeze [briːz] *n* бриз.

breeze block ['briːzblɔk] *n* (*BRIT*) шлако-бетонный кирпич.

breezy ['briːzɪ] *adj* (*manner, tone*) оживлённый

---

* marks translations which have irregular inflections. The Russian-English side of the dictionary gives inflectional information.

(оживлён); (*weather*) прохла́дный*
(прохла́ден).
Bremen ['breɪmən] *n* Бре́мен.
Breton ['brɛtən] *adj* брето́нский ♦ *n*
брето́нец*(-нка*).
brevity ['brɛvɪtɪ] *n* кра́ткость *f*.
brew [bru:] *vt* (*tea*) зава́ривать (завари́ть*
perf); (*beer*) вари́ть* (свари́ть* *perf*) ♦ *vi* (*tea*)
зава́риваться (завари́ться *perf*); (*beer*)
броди́ть* (вы́бродить* *perf*); (*storm*)
надвига́ться (надви́нуться *perf*); (*fig: trouble*)
назрева́ть (назре́ть *perf*).
brewer ['bru:əʳ] *n* пивова́р.
brewery ['bru:ərɪ] *n* пивова́ренный заво́д.
briar ['braɪəʳ] *n* (*thorny bush*) колю́чий*
куста́рник; (*wild rose*) шипо́вник.
bribe [braɪb] *n* взя́тка*, по́дкуп ♦ *vt* (*person*)
подкупа́ть (подкупи́ть* *perf*), дава́ть* (дать*
perf) взя́тку; **to ~ sb to do** подкупа́ть
(подкупи́ть* *perf*) кого́-н +*infin*.
bribery ['braɪbərɪ] *n* по́дкуп.
bric-a-brac ['brɪkəbræk] *n* безделу́шки* *fpl*.
brick [brɪk] *n* кирпи́ч*; (*of ice cream*) брике́т.
bricklayer ['brɪkleɪəʳ] *n* ка́менщик.
brickwork ['brɪkwə:k] *n* (кирпи́чная) кла́дка.
bridal ['braɪdl] *adj* подвене́чный, сва́дебный.
bride [braɪd] *n* неве́ста.
bridegroom ['braɪdgru:m] *n* жени́х*.
bridesmaid ['braɪdzmeɪd] *n* подру́жка*
неве́сты.
bridge [brɪdʒ] *n* (*TECH, ARCHIT, DENTISTRY*) мост*;
(*NAUT*) капита́нский* мо́стик; (*CARDS*)
бридж; (*of nose*) перено́сица ♦ *vt* (*fig: gap,
gulf*) преодолева́ть (преодоле́ть *perf*); **to ~ a
river** стро́ить (постро́ить *perf*) мост че́рез
ре́ку.
bridging loan ['brɪdʒɪŋ-] *n* (*BRIT: COMM*)
промежу́точный заём.
bridle ['braɪdl] *n* узде́чка*, узда́ ♦ *vt* (*horse*)
взну́здывать (взнузда́ть *perf*) ♦ *vi*: **to ~ at**
взвива́ться (взви́ться* *perf*) на дыбы́,
возмуща́ться (возмути́ться* *perf*).
bridle path *n* верхова́я тропа́*.
brief [bri:f] *adj* (*period of time*) коро́ткий*
(ко́роток); (*description*) кра́ткий* (кра́ток) ♦
n (*LAW*) изложе́ние де́ла; (*task*) зада́ние ♦ *vt*
(*inform*) знако́мить* (ознако́мить* *perf*) с
+*instr*; (*MIL etc*): **to ~ sb (about)**
инструкти́ровать (проинструкти́ровать
perf) кого́-н (о +*prp*); **~s** *npl* (*for men*) трусы́ *pl*;
(*for women*) тру́сики *pl*; **in ~** ... вкра́тце ....
briefcase ['bri:fkeɪs] *n* портфе́ль *m*.
briefing ['bri:fɪŋ] *n* инструкта́ж; (*PRESS*)
бри́финг.
briefly ['bri:flɪ] *adv* (*glance, smile*) бе́гло; (*visit*)
на коро́ткое вре́мя; (*explain*) вкра́тце; **to
glimpse ~** броса́ть (бро́сить* *perf*) бе́глый
взгляд.
Brig. *abbr* = **brigadier**.
brigade [brɪ'geɪd] *n* (*MIL*) брига́да.
brigadier [brɪgə'dɪəʳ] *n* бригади́р.

bright [braɪt] *adj* (*light, colour*) я́ркий* (я́рок);
(*room, future*) све́тлый* (све́тел); (*clever:
person, idea*) блестя́щий*; (*lively: person*)
живо́й*, весёлый*; **to look on the ~ side**
ви́деть* (*impf*) све́тлую сто́рону.
brighten ['braɪtn] *vt* (*also: ~ up: room, event*)
оживля́ть (оживи́ть* *perf*); (: *person*)
ра́довать (обра́довать *perf*) ♦ *vi* (*weather*)
проясня́ться (проясни́ться *perf*); (*person*)
оживля́ться (оживи́ться* *perf*); (*face*)
светле́ть (просветле́ть *perf*); (*prospects*)
улучша́ться (улу́чшиться *perf*).
brightly ['braɪtlɪ] *adv* (*shine*) я́рко; (*smile, talk*)
ра́достно.
brill [brɪl] (*inf*) *adj* здо́рово.
brilliance ['brɪljəns] *n* блеск, я́ркость *f*; (*fig: of
person*) гениа́льность *f*.
brilliant ['brɪljənt] *adj* блестя́щий* (блестя́щ);
(*sunshine, light*) я́ркий* (я́рок); (*inf: holiday
etc*) великоле́пный* (великоле́пен).
brilliantly ['brɪljəntlɪ] *adv* (*see adj*) блестя́ще;
я́рко.
brim [brɪm] *n* (*of cup*) край; (*of hat*) поля́ *ntpl*.
brimful ['brɪm'ful] *adj*: **~ (of)** по́лный (по́лон)
до краёв (+*gen*); (*fig*) перепо́лненный
(перепо́лнен) (+*instr*).
brine [braɪn] *n* (*CULIN*) рассо́л.
bring [brɪŋ] (*pt, pp* **brought**) *vt* (*thing*)
приноси́ть* (принести́* *perf*); (*person: on foot*)
приводи́ть* (привести́* *perf*); (: *by transport*)
привози́ть* (привезти́* *perf*); (*fig: satisfaction,
trouble*) доставля́ть (доста́вить* *perf*); **to ~
sth to an end** поко́нчить (*perf*) с чем-н; **I can't
~ myself to tell him** я не могу́ заста́вить себя́
сообщи́ть ему́
▶ **bring about** *vt* (*cause: unintentionally*)
вызыва́ть (вы́звать* *perf*), порожда́ть
(породи́ть* *perf*); (: *intentionally*)
осуществля́ть (осуществи́ть* *perf*)
▶ **bring back** *vt* (*restore*) возрожда́ть
(возроди́ть* *perf*); (*return*) возвраща́ть
(возврати́ть* *perf*), верну́ть (*perf*)
▶ **bring down** *vt* (*government*) сверга́ть
(све́ргнуть* *perf*); (*plane*) сбива́ть (сбить*
perf); (*price*) снижа́ть (сни́зить* *perf*)
▶ **bring forward** *vt* (*meeting*) переноси́ть*
(перенести́* *perf*) на бо́лее ра́нний срок;
(*proposal*) выдвига́ть (вы́двинуть *perf*);
(*BOOKKEEPING*) переноси́ть* (перенести́* *perf*)
на сле́дующую страни́цу
▶ **bring in** *vt* (*money*) приноси́ть* (принести́*
perf); (*person, legislation*) вводи́ть* (ввести́*
perf); (*verdict*) выноси́ть* (вы́нести* *perf*)
▶ **bring off** *vt* (*task, plan*) исполня́ть
(испо́лнить *perf*); (*deal*) заключа́ть
(заключи́ть *perf*)
▶ **bring out** *vt* вынима́ть (вы́нуть *perf*);
(*meaning*) выявля́ть (вы́явить* *perf*);
(*publish*) выпуска́ть (вы́пустить* *perf*)
▶ **bring round** *vt* (*MED*) приводи́ть* (привести́*
perf) в чу́вство

▶ **bring up** *vt* (*carry up*) приноси́ть* (принести́* *perf*) наве́рх; (*educate*) воспи́тывать (воспита́ть *perf*); (*question*) поднима́ть (подня́ть* *perf*); (*vomit*): **he brought up his food** его́ стошни́ло.

bring and buy sale *n* благотвори́тельная перепрода́жа веще́й ме́жду её организа́торами.

brink [brɪŋk] *n* (*of disaster, war etc*) грань *f*; **on the ~ of doing** чуть не +*infin*; **she was on the ~ of tears** она́ е́ле сде́рживала слёзы.

brisk [brɪsk] *adj* (*tone*) отры́вистый (отры́вист); (*person, trade*) оживлённый* (оживлён); **business is ~** дела́ иду́т по́лным хо́дом.

bristle ['brɪsl] *n* щети́на ◆ *vi* (*in anger*) щети́ниться (ощети́ниться *perf*); **bristling with** по́лный (по́лон) +*instr or* +*gen*.

bristly ['brɪslɪ] *adj* щети́нистый; **your chin's all ~** у тебя́ подборо́док щети́нистый.

Brit [brɪt] *n abbr* (*inf*: = *British person*) брита́нец*(-нка*).

Britain ['brɪtən] *n* (*also:* **Great ~**) Брита́ния; **in ~** в Брита́нии.

British ['brɪtɪʃ] *adj* брита́нский*; **the ~** *npl* брита́нцы* *mpl*.

British Isles *npl*: **the ~~** Брита́нские острова́* *mpl*.

British Rail *n* Брита́нская желе́зная доро́га.

British Summer Time *n* Брита́нское ле́тнее вре́мя* *nt*.

Briton ['brɪtən] *n* брита́нец*(-нка*).

Brittany ['brɪtənɪ] *n* Брета́нь *f*.

brittle ['brɪtl] *adj* хру́пкий* (хру́пок), ло́мкий* (ло́мок).

Bro. *abbr* (*REL*) = **brother**.

broach [brəutʃ] *vt* (*subject*) поднима́ть (подня́ть *perf*) вопро́с о +*prp*.

broad [brɔːd] *adj* (*wide*) широ́кий* (широ́к); (*general*) о́бщий*; (*strong*) си́льный* ◆ *n* (*US: inf*) ба́ба; **in ~ daylight** средь бе́ла дня; **~ hint** прозра́чный намёк.

broad bean *n* фасо́ль *f no pl*.

broadcast ['brɔːdkɑːst] (*pt, pp* **broadcast**) *n* (*RADIO*) (ра́дио)переда́ча; (*TV*) (теле)-переда́ча ◆ *vt* (*RADIO*) передава́ть* (переда́ть* *perf*) по ра́дио, трансли́ровать (*impf*); (*TV*) передава́ть* (переда́ть* *perf*) по телеви́дению, трансли́ровать (*impf*) ◆ *vi* трансли́роваться (*impf*).

broadcaster ['brɔːdkɑːstə'] *n* (*RADIO*) ра́дио-журнали́ст; (*TV*) теле-журнали́ст.

broadcasting ['brɔːdkɑːstɪŋ] *n* (*RADIO*) радиовеща́ние; (*TV*) телевеща́ние.

broadcasting station *n* (*RADIO*) радиоста́нция; (*TV*) телеста́нция.

broaden ['brɔːdn] *vt* расширя́ть (расши́рить *perf*) ◆ *vi* расширя́ться (расши́риться *perf*); **to**

~ one's horizons расширя́ть (расши́рить *perf*) свой кругозо́р.

broadly ['brɔːdlɪ] *adv* вообще́.

broad-minded ['brɔːd'maɪndɪd] *adj* с широ́кими взгля́дами.

broadsheet ['brɔːdʃiːt] *n* (*advertisement*) рекла́мный плака́т *or* рекла́мная афи́ша; (*newspaper*) газе́та, отпеча́танная на одно́м развёрнутом листе́ бума́ги.

broccoli ['brɔkəlɪ] *n* бро́кколи *nt ind*.

brochure ['brəuʃjuə'] *n* брошю́ра.

brogue [brəug] *n* (*accent*) провинциа́льный акце́нт (*особенно ирла́ндский или шотла́ндский*); (*shoe*) башма́к.

broil [brɔɪl] *vt* жа́рить (зажа́рить *perf*).

broiler ['brɔɪlə'] *n* бро́йлер.

broke [brəuk] *pt of* **break** ◆ *adj* (*inf*) прогоре́вший; **to go ~** прогора́ть (прогоре́ть *perf*).

broken ['brəukn] *pp of* **break** ◆ *adj* (*window, cup etc*) разби́тый (разби́т); (*machine*) сло́манный (сло́ман); (*promise, vow*) нару́шенный (нару́шен); **a ~ leg** сло́манная нога́*; **a ~ marriage** распа́вшийся брак; **a ~ home** неблагополу́чная семья́; **in ~ English/Russian** на ло́маном англи́йском/ру́сском.

broken-down ['brəukn'daun] *adj* (*car*) сло́манный (сло́ман); (*house*) полу-разру́шенный.

broken-hearted ['brəukn'hɑːtɪd] *adj* уби́тый го́рем, с разби́тым се́рдцем.

broker ['brəukə'] *n* (*COMM: in shares*) бро́кер; (: *in insurance*) страхово́й аге́нт.

brokerage ['brəukrɪdʒ] *n* (*COMM: commission*) брокера́ж; (: *business*) бро́керское аге́нтство.

brolly ['brɔlɪ] *n* (*BRIT: inf*) зонт.

bronchitis [brɔŋ'kaɪtɪs] *n* бронхи́т.

bronze [brɔnz] *n* (*metal*) бро́нза; (*sculpture*) бро́нзовая скульпту́ра.

bronzed [brɔnzd] *adj* (*person, body*) загоре́лый, бро́нзовый.

brooch [brəutʃ] *n* брошь *f*.

brood [bruːd] *n* вы́водок* ◆ *vi* (*hen*) сиде́ть* (*impf*) на я́йцах; (*person*) размышля́ть (*impf*)

▶ **brood on** *or* **over** *vt fus* грусти́ть* (*impf*) *or* размышля́ть (*impf*) о +*prp*.

broody ['bruːdɪ] *adj* (*thoughtful, moody*) угрю́мый (угрю́м); **~ hen** насе́дка*.

brook [bruk] *n* ручей́*.

broom [brum] *n* метла́*; (*BOT*) раки́тник.

broomstick ['brumstɪk] *n* (*broom handle*) ру́чка метлы́.

Bros. *abbr* (*COMM*: = **brothers**) бра́тья* *mpl*.

broth [brɔθ] *n* похлёбка*.

brothel ['brɔθl] *n* публи́чный дом*, борде́ль *m*.

brother ['brʌðə'] *n* (*also REL*) брат*; (*in association*) собра́т*.

---

* marks translations which have irregular inflections. The Russian-English side of the dictionary gives inflectional information.

brotherhood ['brʌðəhud] *n* бра́тство.
brother-in-law ['brʌðərɪn'lɔ:] *n* (*sister's husband*) зять* *m*; (*wife's brother*) шу́рин*; (*husband's brother*) де́верь* *m*.
brotherly ['brʌðəlɪ] *adj* бра́тский*.
brought [brɔ:t] *pt, pp of* **bring**.
brought forward *adj* перенесённый на сле́дующую страни́цу.
brow [brau] *n* (*forehead*) лоб*, чело́*; (*also:* **eyebrow**) бровь *f*; (*of hill*) гре́бень *m*.
browbeat ['braubi:t] *vt:* **to ~ sb (into doing)** запу́гивать (запуга́ть *perf*) кого́-н (для того́, что́бы +*infin*).
brown [braun] *adj* кори́чневый; (*hair*) кашта́новый; (*eyes*) ка́рий*; (*tanned*) загоре́лый ♦ *n* (*colour*) кори́чневый цвет ♦ *vt* (*CULIN*) подрумя́нивать (подрумя́нить *perf*); **to go ~** (*person*) загора́ть (загоре́ть *perf*); (*leaves*) желте́ть (пожелте́ть *perf*).
brown bread *n* чёрный хлеб.
Brownie ['braunɪ] *n* (*also:* **~ Guide**) *мла́дшая де́вочка-ска́ут.*
brownie ['braunɪ] *n* (*US: cake*) *шокола́дное пиро́жное с оре́хами.*
brown paper *n* обёрточная бума́га.
brown rice *n* неочи́щенный рис.
brown sugar *n* неочи́щенный са́хар.
browse [brauz] *vi* (*in shop*) рассма́тривать (*impf*), разгля́дывать (*impf*); (*animal*) пита́ться (*impf*) подно́жным ко́рмом ♦ *n:* **to have a ~ (around)** рассма́тривать (*impf*) *or* разгля́дывать (*impf*); **to ~ through a book** проли́стывать (пролиста́ть *perf*) кни́гу.
bruise [bru:z] *n* (*on face etc*) синя́к*; (*on fruit*) вмя́тина ♦ *vt* ушиба́ть (ушиби́ть* *perf*); (*fruit*) помя́ть* (*perf*) ♦ *vi* (*fruit*) помя́ться* (*perf*).
bruising ['bru:zɪŋ] *n* синяки́* *mpl*.
Brum [brʌm] *n abbr* (*BRIT: inf*) = **Birmingham**.
Brummie ['brʌmɪ] *n* (*inf*) бирминге́мец(-емка).
brunch [brʌntʃ] *n* по́здний* за́втрак.
brunette [bru:'net] *n* брюне́тка*.
brunt [brʌnt] *n:* **to bear the ~ of** принима́ть (приня́ть* *perf*) на себя́ основно́й уда́р +*gen*.
brush [brʌʃ] *n* (*for cleaning*) щётка*; (*for painting*) кисть* *f*; (*for shaving*) помазо́к*; (*quarrel*) столкнове́ние ♦ *vt* (*sweep*) подмета́ть (подмести́* *perf*); (*groom*) чи́стить* (почи́стить* *perf*) щёткой; (*also:* **~ against**) слегка́ задева́ть (заде́ть* *perf*); **to have a ~ with sb** (*verbally*) вздо́рить (повздо́рить *perf*) с ке́м-н; (*physically*) дра́ться* (подра́ться* *perf*) с ке́м-н; **to have a ~ with the police** име́ть (*impf*) столкнове́ние с поли́цией
▸ **brush aside** *vt* (*criticism, emotion*) отмета́ть (отмести́ *perf*)
▸ **brush past** *vt* проноси́ться* (пронести́сь* *perf*) ми́мо +*gen*
▸ **brush up** *vt* (*subject, language*) шлифова́ть (отшлифова́ть *perf*); (*knowledge*) освежа́ть (освежи́ть *perf*).

brushed [brʌʃt] *adj* (*steel, chrome etc*) ма́товый; (*nylon, denim etc*) ворси́стый.
brush-off ['brʌʃɔf] *n* (*inf*): **to give sb the ~** отбрива́ть (отбри́ть* *perf*) кого́-н.
brushwood ['brʌʃwud] *n* хво́рост.
brusque [bru:sk] *adj* бесцеремо́нный*.
Brussels ['brʌslz] *n* Брюссе́ль *m*.
Brussels sprout *n* брюссе́льская капу́ста.
brutal ['bru:tl] *adj* (*person*) жесто́кий*; (*actions*) зве́рский*; (*honesty, frankness*) жёсткий*.
brutality [bru:'tælɪtɪ] *n* (*see adj*) жесто́кость *f*; зве́рство.
brutalize ['bru:təlaɪz] *vt* ожесточа́ть (ожесточи́ть *perf*).
brute [bru:t] *n* зверь* *m* ♦ *adj:* **by ~ force** гру́бой си́лой.
brutish ['bru:tɪʃ] *adj* зве́рский*, ско́тский*.
BS *n abbr* (*US:* = *Bachelor of Science*) ≈ бакала́вр есте́ственный нау́к.
bs *abbr* = **bill of sale**.
BSA *n abbr* (= *Boy Scouts of America*) Сою́з америка́нских бойска́утов.
BSE *n abbr* (= *bovine spongiform encephalopathy*) энцефалопа́тия кру́пного рога́того скота́.
BSc *abbr* (= *Bachelor of Science*) ≈ бакала́вр есте́ственных нау́к.
BSI *n abbr* (= *British Standards Institution*) Брита́нский* институ́т станда́ртов.
BST *abbr* = *British Summer Time*.
Bt. *abbr* (*BRIT*) = **Bart**.
btu *n abbr* (= *British thermal unit*) брита́нская теплова́я едини́ца.
bubble ['bʌbl] *n* пузы́рь* *m* ♦ *vi* (*liquid*) пе́ниться (вспе́ниться *perf*); (*fig*): **to ~ with laughter** залива́ться (*impf*) сме́хом.
bubble bath *n* пе́нистая ва́нна.
bubble gum *n* жева́тельная рези́нка (*образу́ющая пузыри́*).
bubblejet printer ['bʌbldʒet-] *n тип компью́терного при́нтера.*
bubble pack *n* бли́стерная упако́вка*.
bubbly ['bʌblɪ] *adj* (*inf: girl*) живо́й; (*mineral water*) шипу́чий*, газиро́ванный ♦ *n* (*inf*) шипу́чка*.
Bucharest [bu:kə'rest] *n* Бухаре́ст.
buck [bʌk] *n* (*rabbit*) кро́лик*; (*deer*) саме́ц* оле́ня; (*US: inf*) бакс ♦ *vi* (*horse*) брыка́ться (*impf*); **to pass the ~ (to sb)** перекла́дывать (переложи́ть *perf*) отве́тственность (на кого́-н)
▸ **buck up** *vi* (*cheer up*) встряхну́ться (*perf*); (*hurry up*) пошеве́ливаться (*impf*) ♦ *vt:* **to ~ one's ideas up** исправля́ться (испра́виться* *perf*).
bucket ['bʌkɪt] *n* ведро́* ♦ *vi* (*BRIT: inf*): **the rain is ~ing (down)** дождь льёт как из ведра́.
buckle ['bʌkl] *n* пря́жка* ♦ *vt* (*shoe, belt*) застёгивать (застегну́ть *perf*); (*wheel*) деформи́ровать (*impf/perf*) ♦ *vi* (*wheel*) деформи́роваться (*impf/perf*); (*bridge,*

support) прогибáться (прогнýться *perf*);
(*knees, legs*) подгибáться (подогнýться *perf*)
▶ **buckle down** *vi*: **to ~ down (to sth)** засéсть*
(*perf*) (за что-н).
Bucks [bʌks] *abbr* (*BRIT*: *POST*) = Buckingham-
shire.
bud [bʌd] *n* (*of tree*) пóчка*; (*of flower*) бутóн ♦
vi (*flower*) распускáться (распустúться* *perf*);
the trees are ~ding на дерéвьях
распускáются пóчки; **to nip in the ~**
пресекáть (пресéчь* *perf*) в кóрне.
Budapest [bju:də'pɛst] *n* Будапéшт.
Buddha ['budə] *n* Бýдда *m*.
Buddhism ['budɪzəm] *n* буддúзм.
Buddhist ['budɪst] *adj* буддúйский ♦ *n*
буддúст.
budding ['bʌdɪŋ] *adj* подаю́щий надéжды.
buddy ['bʌdɪ] *n* (*US*) прия́тель *m*.
budge [bʌdʒ] *vt* (*object*) сдвигáть (сдвúнуть
perf) (с мéста); (*fig*: *person*) заставля́ть
(застáвить* *perf*) уступúть* ♦ *vi* сдвúнуться
(*perf*) (с мéста).
budgerigar ['bʌdʒərɪgɑ:'] *n* волнúстый
попугáйчик.
budget ['bʌdʒɪt] *n* бюджéт ♦ *vi*: **to ~ for sth**
ассигновáть (*impf/perf*) *or* откла́дывать
(отложúть *perf*) дéньги на что-н; **I'm on a
tight ~** у меня́ тýго с финáнсами; **she works
out her ~ every month** онá рассчúтывает
свой бюджéт кáждый мéсяц.
budgie ['bʌdʒɪ] *n* = budgerigar.
Buenos Aires ['bweɪnɔs'aɪrɪz] *n* Бýэнос-Áйрес.
buff [bʌf] *adj* корúчневый ♦ *n* (*inf*: *enthusiast*)
знатóк*.
buffalo ['bʌfələu] (*pl ~ or ~es*) *n* (*BRIT*) бýйвол;
(*US*: *bison*) бизóн.
buffer ['bʌfə'] *n* бýфер*.
buffering ['bʌfərɪŋ] *n* (*COMPUT*) буферизáция,
испóльзование бýфера.
buffer state *n* бýферное госудáрство.
buffer zone *n* бýферная зóна.
buffet[1] ['bufeɪ] *n* (*BRIT*: *in station*) буфéт; (*food*)
швéдский* стол*.
buffet[2] ['bʌfɪt] *vt* (*subj*: *wind, sea*) трепáть*
(*perf*), швыря́ть (*impf*).
buffet car *n* (*BRIT*: *RAIL*) вагóн-ресторáн.
buffet lunch *n* швéдский* стол*.
buffoon [bə'fu:n] *n* фигля́р.
bug [bʌg] *n* (*esp US*: *insect*) насекóмое *nt adj*;
(*COMPUT*: *of program*) ошúбка*; (*fig*: *germ*)
вúрус, зарáза; (*hidden microphone*)
микрофóн, подслýшивающее устрóйство ♦
vt (*inf*: *annoy*) раздражáть (раздражúть *perf*);
(: *bother*) надоедáть (надоéсть* *perf*) +*dat*;
(*room etc*) прослýшивать (*impf*); **I've got the
travel ~** (*fig*) я помéшан на путешéствиях.
bugbear ['bʌgbɛə'] *n* проблéма.
bugger ['bʌgə'] (*inf!*) *n* свóлочь *m/f* (*!*) ♦ *vb*: ~

~ **off!** катúсь отсю́да! (*!*); ~ **(it)!** твою́ мать! (*!*)
buggy ['bʌgɪ] *n* (*also*: **baby ~**) складнáя
дéтская коля́ска*.
bugle ['bju:gl] *n* горн.
build [bɪld] (*pt, pp* **built**) *n* (*of person*)
телослoжéние ♦ *vt* стрóить (пострóить *perf*)
▶ **build on** *vt fus* (*fig*) пóльзоваться
(воспóльзоваться *perf*) +*instr*
▶ **build up** *vt* (*forces, production*) нарáщивать
(*impf*); (*morale*) укрепля́ть (укрепúть* *perf*);
(*stocks*) накáпливать (накопúть* *perf*);
(*business*) создавáть (создáть* *perf*); **don't ~
your hopes up too soon** не рáдуйтесь рáньше
врéмени.
builder ['bɪldə'] *n* строúтель *m*.
building ['bɪldɪŋ] *n* (*industry, construction*)
стрoúтельство; (*structure*) строéние; (:
residential, offices) здáние.
building contractor *n* строúтельный
подря́дчик.
building industry *n* строúтельная
промы́шленность *f*.
building site *n* строúтельный учáсток*.
building society *n* (*BRIT*) ≈ "строúтельное
óбщество".
building trade *n* = building industry.
build-up ['bɪldʌp] *n* (*of gas etc*) скоплéние;
(*publicity*): **to give sb/sth a good ~**
обеспéчивать (обеспéчить *perf*) комý-н/
чемý-н хорóшую реклáму.
built [bɪlt] *pt, pp of* build ♦ *adj*: **~-in** встрóенный;
well-~ person хорошó сложённый* человéк.
built-in obsolescence ['bɪltɪn-] *n*
заплани́рованное устарéвание.
built-up area ['bɪltʌp-] *n* застрóенный райóн.
bulb [bʌlb] *n* (*BOT*) лýковица; (*ELEC*) лáмпа,
лáмпочка*.
bulbous ['bʌlbəs] *adj* пузáтый (пузáт); (*nose*)
тóлстый (толст).
Bulgaria [bʌl'gɛərɪə] *n* Болгáрия.
Bulgarian [bʌl'gɛərɪən] *adj* болгáрский* ♦ *n*
болгáрин*(-рка*); (*LING*) болгáрский* язы́к*.
bulge [bʌldʒ] *n* (*bump*) вы́пуклость *f*; (*in birth
rate*) врéменное увеличéние ♦ *vi* (*stomach*)
выпя́чиваться (вы́пятиться* *perf*); (*pocket,
file*) трещáть (*impf*) по швам; **her purse is
bulging with money** её кошелёк набúт
деньгáми.
bulimia [bə'lɪmɪə] *n* булимúя.
bulimic [bə'li:mɪk] *adj*: **she is ~** онá страдáет
булимúей.
bulk [bʌlk] *n* громáда; **in ~** óптом; **the ~ of**
бóльшая часть +*gen*.
bulk buying [-'baɪɪŋ] *n* оптóвая закýпка*.
bulk carrier *n* грузовóе сýдно, грузовóй
корáбль *m*.
bulkhead ['bʌlkhɛd] *n* перегорóдка.
bulky ['bʌlkɪ] *adj* громóздкий* (громóздок).

---

* marks translations which have irregular inflections. The Russian-English side of the dictionary gives inflectional information.

bull [bul] *n* (*ZOOL*) бык*; (*male: whale*) самéц* китá; (: *elephant*) слон; (*STOCK EXCHANGE*) *спекулянт, играющий* на повышéние на бирже*; (*REL*) бýлла.
bulldog ['buldɔg] *n* бульдóг.
bulldoze ['buldəuz] *vt* (*flatten*) расчищáть (расчистить* *perf*) бульдóзером; (*knock down*) ломáть (сломáть *perf*) бульдóзером; **I was ~d into it** (*fig: inf*) меня застáвили сдéлать это.
bulldozer ['buldəuzə'] *n* бульдóзер.
bullet ['bulɪt] *n* пýля.
bulletin ['bulɪtɪn] *n*: **news ~** свóдка* новостéй; (*journal*) бюллетéнь *m*.
bulletin board *n* (*COMPUT*) электрóнная доскá объявлéний.
bulletproof ['bulɪtpru:f] *adj* пулене-пробивáемый.
bullfight ['bulfaɪt] *n* бой* быкóв.
bullfighter ['bulfaɪtə'] *n* тореадóр.
bullfighting ['bulfaɪtɪŋ] *n* бой быкóв.
bullion ['buljən] *n* слитóк*.
bullock ['bulək] *n* вол*.
bullring ['bulrɪŋ] *n* арéна (*на котóрой происхóдит бой быкóв*).
bull's-eye ['bulzaɪ] *n* (*on a target*) яблоко* мишéни.
bullshit ['bulʃɪt] (*inf!*) *n* бред (собáчий) (*!*) ♦ *vt* нести* (*impf*) бред (*!*)
bully ['bulɪ] *n* задира *m/f* ♦ *vt* травить* (затравить* *perf*); (*frighten*) запýгивать (запугáть *perf*).
bullying ['bulɪŋ] *n* трáвля, запýгивание.
bum [bʌm] *n* (*inf: backside*) зáдница; (*esp US: tramp*) бродяга *m/f*; (: *good-for-nothing*) бездéльник
▶ **bum around** *vi* (*inf*) шатáться (*impf*).
bumblebee ['bʌmblbi:] *n* шмель* *m*.
bumf [bʌmf] *n* (*inf*) бумáжки* *fpl*.
bump [bʌmp] *n* (*minor accident*) столкновéние; (*jolt*) толчóк; (*swelling*) шишка; (*on road*) ухáб ♦ *vt* (*strike*) удáрить (удáрить *perf*); (*dent*) помять* (*perf*); **he ~ed his head on the door** он удáрился *or* стýкнулся головóй о дверь
▶ **bump along** *vi* трястись* (*impf*) по +*dat*
▶ **bump into** *vt fus* натáлкиваться (натолкнýться *perf*) на +*acc*.
bumper ['bʌmpə'] *n* (*AUT*) бáмпер ♦ *adj*: **~ crop** *or* **harvest** небывáлый урожáй.
bumper cars *npl* (*US*) аттракциóнный электромобиль *m*.
bumper sticker *n* наклéйка на бáмпер.
bumph [bʌmf] *n* = **bumf**.
bumptious ['bʌmpʃəs] *adj* самоувéренный (самоувéрен).
bumpy ['bʌmpɪ] *adj* ухáбистый; **it was a ~ flight** нас всю дорóгу тряслó.
bun [bʌn] *n* (*CULIN*) сдóбная бýлка*; (*of hair*) ýзел*.
bunch [bʌntʃ] *n* (*of flowers*) букéт; (*of keys*) свя́зка*; (*of bananas*) гроздь *f*; (*of people*) компáния; **~es** *npl* (*in hair*) хвóстики *mpl*; **~ of grapes** гроздь *or* кисть* *f* виногрáда.
bundle ['bʌndl] *n* (*of clothes*) ýзел*; (*of sticks*) вязáнка*; (*of papers*) пáчка* ♦ *vt* (*also:* **~ up**) свя́зывать (связáть* *perf*) в ýзел; (*put*): **to ~ sth/sb into** затáлкивать (затолкнýть *perf*) что-н/когó-н в +*acc*
▶ **bundle off** *vt* отсылáть (отослáть* *perf*)
▶ **bundle out** *vt* быстро уходить* (уйти* *perf*).
bun fight *n* (*BRIT: inf: official function*) банкéт; (: *tea party*) чаепитие.
bung [bʌŋ] *n* прóбка* ♦ *vt* (*BRIT: throw*) запихивать (запихáть *perf*); (*also:* **~ up**: *pipe, hole*) затыкáть (заткнýть *perf*); **my nose is ~ed up** у меня заложен нос.
bungalow ['bʌŋgələu] *n* бунгáло *nt ind*.
bungee jumping ['bʌndʒi:'dʒʌmpɪŋ] *n* прыжки́ *с высоты́ вниз головóй, в котóрых человéк привя́зан за нóги к эластичному канáту*.
bungle ['bʌŋgl] *vt* завáливать (завалить* *perf*).
bunion ['bʌnjən] *n* натóптыш.
bunk [bʌŋk] *n* (*bed*) кóйка.
bunk beds *npl* двухъя́русная кровáть *fsg*.
bunker ['bʌŋkə'] *n* бýнкер*; (*GOLF*) я́ма с пескóм (*на пóле для гóльфа*).
bunny ['bʌnɪ] *n* (*also:* **~ rabbit**) зáйчик.
bunny girl *n* (*BRIT*) официáнтка ночнóго клýба, в облегáющем костю́ме с крóличьим хвостóм и ушáми.
bunny hill *n* (*US: SKIING*) лягушáтник.
bunting ['bʌntɪŋ] *n* флажки́ *mpl*.
buoy [bɔɪ] *n* буй*, бáкен
▶ **buoy up** *vt* (*fig*) подбáдривать (подбодрить *perf*).
buoyancy ['bɔɪənsɪ] *n* плавýчесть *f*.
buoyant ['bɔɪənt] *adj* (*ship*) плавýчий*; (*economy, market*) оживлённый (оживлён); (*prices, currency*) твёрдый; (*fig: person*) жизнерáдостный* (жизнерáдостен).
burden ['bə:dn] *n* (*responsibility*) брéмя* *nt*; (*load*) нóша ♦ *vt* (*trouble*): **to ~ sb with** обременя́ть (обременить *perf*) когó-н +*instr*; **to be a ~ to sb** быть* (*impf*) в тя́гость комý-н.
bureau ['bjuərəu] (*pl* **~x**) *n* (*BRIT*) бюрó *nt ind*; (*US*) комóд.
bureaucracy [bjuə'rɔkrəsɪ] *n* (*POL, COMM*) бюрокрáтия; (*system*) бюрократизм.
bureaucrat ['bjuərəkræt] *n* бюрокрáт.
bureaucratic [bjuərə'krætɪk] *adj* бюрократический*.
bureaux ['bjuərəuz] *npl of* **bureau**.
burgeon ['bə:dʒən] *vi* (*fig*) расцветáть (расцвести* *perf*).
burger ['bə:gə'] *n* бýргер.
burglar ['bə:glə'] *n* взлóмщик.
burglar alarm *n* сигнализáция.
burglarize ['bə:gləraɪz] *vt* (*US*) совершáть (совершить *perf*) крáжу со взлóмом.
burglary ['bə:glərɪ] *n* (*crime*) крáжа со взлóмом; (*act*) взлом.

burgle [ˈbəːgl] *vt* соверша́ть (соверши́ть *perf*)
кра́жу со взло́мом.
Burgundy [ˈbəːgəndɪ] *n* (*GEO*) Бургу́ндия.
burial [ˈbɛrɪəl] *n* погребе́ние, по́хороны *pl*.
burial ground *n* ме́сто* погребе́ния.
burlesque [bəːˈlɛsk] *n* паро́дия.
burly [ˈbəːlɪ] *adj* дю́жий.
Burma [ˈbəːmə] *n* Би́рма.
Burmese [bəːˈmiːz] *adj* бирма́нский ♦ *n inv*
бирма́нец*(-нка*); (*LING*) бирма́нский язы́к*.
burn [bəːn] (*pt, pp* **burned** *or* **burnt**) *vt* жечь*
(сжечь* *perf*), сжига́ть (сжечь* *perf*); (*arson*)
поджига́ть (подже́чь* *perf*) ♦ *vi* (*house, wood*)
горе́ть (сгоре́ть *perf*), сгора́ть (сгоре́ть *perf*);
(*cakes*) подгора́ть (подгоре́ть *perf*) ♦ *n* ожо́г;
the cigarette ~t a hole in her dress сигаре́та
прожгла́ ды́рку в её пла́тье; **she always ~s
the meat** у неё всегда́ подгора́ет мя́со; **I've
~t myself!** я обжёгся.
▶ **burn down** *vt* сжига́ть (сжечь* *perf*) дотла́
▶ **burn out** *vt*: **to ~ o.s. out** выма́тываться
(вы́мотаться *perf*); **the fire ~t itself out** ого́нь
догоре́л.
burner [ˈbəːnə] *n* горе́лка*.
burning [ˈbəːnɪŋ] *adj* (*building, forest*)
горя́щий; (*sand, desert*) раскалённый; (*issue,
ambition*) жгу́чий*.
burnish [ˈbəːnɪʃ] *vt* полирова́ть
(отполирова́ть *perf*).
burnt [bəːnt] *pt, pp of* **burn**.
burnt sugar *n* (*BRIT*) жжёный са́хар.
burp [bəːp] *n* отры́жка* ♦ *vt*: **to ~ a baby**
вызыва́ть (вы́звать* *perf*) отры́жку у
ребёнка ♦ *vi* отры́гивать (отрыгну́ть *perf*).
burrow [ˈbʌrəu] *n* нора́* ♦ *vi* (*dig*) рыть*
(вы́рыть* *perf*) нору́; (*rummage*) ры́ться*
(*impf*).
bursar [ˈbəːsə] *n* казначе́й.
bursary [ˈbəːsərɪ] *n* (*BRIT*) стипе́ндия.
burst [bəːst] (*pt, pp* **burst**) *vt* (*bag etc*) разрыва́ть
(разорва́ть* *perf*) ♦ *vi* (*pipe*) прорыва́ться
(прорва́ться* *perf*); (*tyre, balloon*) ло́паться
(ло́пнуть *perf*) ♦ *n* (*of gunfire*) залп; (*of
shelling*) разры́в; (*also*: **~ pipe**) проры́в; **the
river has ~ its banks** река́ вы́шла из берего́в;
to ~ into flames вспы́хивать (вспы́хнуть
perf); **to ~ into tears** распла́каться* (*perf*); **to ~
out laughing** расхохота́ться* (*perf*); **to ~ into a
room** врыва́ться (ворва́ться* *perf*) в
ко́мнату; **~ blood vessel** разо́рванный
кровено́сный сосу́д; **the room is/was ~ing
with people** ко́мната наби́та/была́ наби́та
до отка́за людьми́; **to be ~ing with** (*pride,
anger*) раздува́ться (разду́ться *perf*) от +*gen*;
a ~ of energy/enthusiasm прили́в эне́ргии/
энтузиа́зма; **~ of laughter/applause** взрыв
сме́ха/рукоплеска́ний; **~ of machine gun fire**
пулемётная о́чередь *f*

▶ **burst into** *vt fus* (*room*) врыва́ться
(ворва́ться* *perf*).
▶ **burst open** *vi* (*door etc*) распа́хиваться
(распахну́ться *perf*).
bury [ˈbɛrɪ] *vt* (*object*) зарыва́ть (зары́ть* *perf*),
зака́пывать (закопа́ть *perf*); (*person*)
хорони́ть* (похорони́ть* *perf*); **many people
were buried in the rubble** мно́го люде́й бы́ло
зары́то под обло́мками; **to ~ one's face in
one's hands** пря́тать* (спря́тать* *perf*) лицо́ в
ладо́ни; **to ~ one's head in the sand** (*fig*)
зарыва́ть (зары́ть* *perf*) го́лову в песо́к; **to ~
the hatchet** (*fig*) забыва́ть (забы́ть* *perf*)
раздо́ры, мири́ться (помири́ться *perf*).
bus [bʌs] *n* авто́бус; (*double decker*)
(двухэта́жный) авто́бус.
bus boy *n* (*US*) *помо́щник официа́нта,
убира́ющий гря́зную посу́ду со стола́.*
bush [buʃ] *n* куст*; (*scrubland*) *простра́нства,
покры́тые куста́рниками (в Австра́лии и
т.п.*); **to beat about the ~** ходи́ть* (*impf*)
вокру́г да о́коло.
bushed [buʃt] *adj* (*inf*) вы́мотанный
(вы́мотан).
bushel [ˈbuʃl] *n* бу́шель *m*.
bush fire *n* лесно́й пожа́р.
bushy [ˈbuʃɪ] *adj* (*tail*) пуши́стый (пуши́ст);
(*hair, eyebrows*) густо́й* (густ); (*plant*)
кусти́стый.
busily [ˈbɪzɪlɪ] *adv* (*actively*) делови́то,
энерги́чно; **to be ~ing sth** энерги́чно
занима́ться (*impf*) чем-н.
business [ˈbɪznɪs] *n* (*matter*) де́ло*; (*trading*)
би́знес; (*firm*) предприя́тие, фи́рма;
(*occupation*) заня́тие; **to be away on ~** быть
(*impf*) в командиро́вке; **I'm here on ~** я здесь
по де́лу; **he's in the insurance/transport ~** он
рабо́тает в страхово́м/тра́нспортном
би́знесе; **to do ~ with sb** име́ть (*impf*) дела́ с
кем-н; **it's my ~ to ...** э́то моя́ обя́занность
+*infin* ...; **it's none of my ~** э́то не моё де́ло; **he
means** ~ он серьёзно настро́ен.
business address *n* а́дрес* фи́рмы.
business card *n* визи́тная ка́рточка*.
businesslike [ˈbɪznɪslaɪk] *adj* делови́тый
(делови́т).
businessman [ˈbɪznɪsmən] *irreg n* бизнесме́н.
business trip *n* командиро́вка*.
businesswoman [ˈbɪznɪswumən] *irreg n*
же́нщина-бизнесме́н, делова́я же́нщина.
busker [ˈbʌskə] *n* (*BRIT*) у́личный музыка́нт.
bus lane *n* (*BRIT*) *часть доро́ги, отведённая
для движе́ния авто́бусов.*
bus shelter *n* авто́бусная остано́вка (*с
наве́сом*).
bus station *n* авто́бусная ста́нция,
автовокза́л.
bus-stop [ˈbʌsstɔp] *n* авто́бусная остано́вка*.

* marks translations which have irregular inflections. The Russian-English side of the dictionary gives inflectional information.

bust [bʌst] n (ANAT) бюст, грудь* f;
(measurement) объём груди; (sculpture)
бюст ♦ adj (inf: broken) сломанный (сломан)
♦ vt (inf: arrest) накрывать (накрыть* perf); **to
go ~** (company etc) прогорать (прогореть
perf), вылетать (вылететь* perf) в трубу.
bustle ['bʌsl] n (activity) суматоха, суета ♦ vi
(person) суетиться* (impf).
bustling ['bʌslɪŋ] adj (place) оживлённый,
шумный*.
bust-up ['bʌstʌp] n (BRIT: inf) скандал, ссора.
BUSWE n abbr (BRIT) = British Union of Social
Work Employees.
busty ['bʌstɪ] adj (inf) грудастый (грудаст).
busy ['bɪzɪ] adj (person) занятой; (street)
оживлённый (оживлён), шумный* (шумен);
(TEL): **the line is ~** линия занята ♦ vt: **to ~ o.s.
with** занимать (занять* perf) себя +instr,
заниматься (заняться* perf) +instr; **he's a ~
man** (normally) он занятой человек; **he's ~**
(temporarily) он занят; **it's usually a very ~
shop** в этом магазине обычно много
народу.
busybody ['bɪzɪbɒdɪ] n: **he is a ~** он суёт нос в
чужие дела.
busy signal n (US: TEL) короткие гудки mpl.

KEYWORD

but [bʌt] conj **1** (yet) но; (: in contrast) а; **he's not
very bright, but he's hard-working** он не очень
умён, но усерден; **I'm tired but Paul isn't** я
устал, а Павел не устал
2 (however) но; **I'd love to come, but I'm busy**
я бы с удовольствием пришёл, но я занят
3 (showing disagreement, surprise etc) но; **but
that's fantastic!** но это же потрясающе!
♦ prep (apart from, except): **no-one but him can
do it** никто, кроме него, не может это
сделать; **nothing but trouble/bad luck**
сплошные неприятности/неудачи; **but for
you/your help** если бы не Вы/ваша помощь;
I'll do anything but that я сделаю всё, что
угодно, но только не это
♦ adv (just, only): **she's but a child** она всего
лишь ребёнок; **had I but known** если бы
только я знал; **I can but try** ну я, конечно,
могу попробовать; **the work is all but
finished** работа почти закончена.

butane ['bjuːteɪn] n (also: ~ **gas**) бутан.
butch [bʊtʃ] adj (pej: woman) мужеподобный*
(мужеподобен); **he's very ~** он (настоящий)
мужик.
butcher ['bʊtʃə'] n мясник*; (pej: murderer)
палач* ♦ vt (cattle) бить* (забить* perf),
резать (зарезать* perf); (prisoners)
вырезать* (вырезать* perf).
butcher's (shop) ['bʊtʃəz-] n мясной магазин.
butler ['bʌtlə'] n дворецкий m adj.
butt [bʌt] n (large barrel) бочка*; (thick end)
утолщённый конец*; (of rifle) приклад*; (of
pistol) рукоятка; (of cigarette) окурок*; (BRIT:

of teasing) посмешище; (: of criticism)
предмет; (US: inf!) задница (!) ♦ vt (subj:
goat) бодать (impf)
► **butt in** vi встревать (встрять* perf).
butter ['bʌtə'] n (сливочное) масло* ♦ vt
(bread) намазывать (намазать* perf)
(сливочным) маслом.
buttercup ['bʌtəkʌp] n лютик.
butter dish n маслёнка*.
butterfingers ['bʌtəfɪŋgəz] n (inf) растяпа m/f.
butterfly ['bʌtəflaɪ] n бабочка*; (also: ~ **stroke**)
баттерфляй.
buttocks ['bʌtəks] npl ягодицы fpl.
button ['bʌtn] n (on clothes) пуговица; (on
machine) кнопка*; (US: badge) значок* ♦ vt
(also: ~ **up**) застёгивать (застегнуть* perf).
buttonhole ['bʌtnhəʊl] n петля*, петлица ♦ vt:
to ~ sb приставать (пристать* perf) к
кому-н с разговорами.
buttress ['bʌtrɪs] n контрфорс.
buxom ['bʌksəm] adj (woman) полногрудый
(полногруд).
buy [baɪ] (pt, pp **bought**) vt покупать (купить*
perf); (COMM) приобретать (приобрести* perf)
♦ n покупка*; **to ~ sb sth/sth from sb**
покупать (купить* perf) кому-н что-н/что-н у
кого-н; **to ~ sb a drink** покупать (купить*
perf) кому-н выпить что-нибудь; **that was a
good/bad ~** это была удачная/неудачная
покупка
► **buy back** vt выкупать (выкупить* perf)
► **buy in** vt (BRIT) закупать (закупить* perf)
► **buy into** vt fus (BRIT) покупать (купить* perf)
часть +gen, входить (войти* perf) в долю с
+instr
► **buy off** vt подкупать (подкупить* perf)
► **buy out** vt выкупать (выкупить* perf)
► **buy up** vt скупать (скупить* perf).
buyer ['baɪə'] n покупатель(ница) m(f); (COMM)
закупщик(-ица).
buyer's market ['baɪəz-] n рынок, выгодный
для покупателя.
buy-out ['baɪaʊt] n: **management ~** выкуп
частной фирмы у её владельца членами
администрации, работающими на фирме.
buzz [bʌz] n жужжание ♦ vi (insect, saw)
жужжать* (прожужжать* perf); (inf: place)
гудеть* (impf) ♦ vt (call on intercom) звонить
(позвонить perf) по внутреннему телефону;
(with buzzer) звонить (позвонить perf);
(AVIAT) совершать (совершить perf)
бреющий полёт над +instr; **to give sb a ~** (inf:
TEL) звякнуть (perf) кому-н; **my head is ~ing** у
меня голова гудит
► **buzz off** vi (inf) отваливать (отвалить* perf).
buzzard ['bʌzəd] n канюк*, сарыч*.
buzzer ['bʌzə'] n зуммер, звонок.
buzz word n (inf) модное словечко*.

KEYWORD

by [baɪ] prep **1** (referring to cause, agent): **he was
killed by lightning** он был убит молнией; **a**

painting by Van Gogh картина Ван Гога; **it's by Shakespeare** это Шекспир
2 (*referring to manner, means*): **by bus/train** на автобусе/поезде, автобусом/поездом; **by car** на машине; **by phone** по телефону; **to pay by cheque** платить* (заплатить* *perf*) чеком; **by moonlight** при свете луны; **by candlelight** при свечах; **by working constantly, he...** благодаря тому, что он работал без остановки, он...
3 (*via, through*) через +*acc*; **by land/sea** по суше/морю; **by the back door** через заднюю дверь
4 (*close to*) около +*gen*, у +*gen*; **the house is by the river** дом* находится около *or* у реки; **a holiday by the sea** отпуск на море
5 (*past*) мимо +*gen*; **she rushed by me** она пронеслась мимо меня
6 (*not later than*) к +*dat*; **by four o'clock** к четырём часам; **by the time I got here it was too late** к тому времени, когда я добрался сюда, было слишком поздно
7 (*during*): **by day** днём; **by night** ночью
8 (*amount*): **to sell by the kilo/metre** продавать* (*impf*) в килограммах/метрах; **she is paid by the hour** у неё почасовая оплата
9 (*MATH, measure*) на +*acc*; **to divide/multiply by three** делить* (разделить* *perf*)/умножать (умножить *perf*) на три; **a room three metres by four** комната размером три метра на четыре
10 (*according to*) по +*dat*; **to play by the rules** играть (*impf*) по правилам; **it's all right by me** я не возражаю; **by law** по законам
11: **(all) by oneself** (*alone*) (совершенно) один

(*f* одна, *nt* одно, *pl* одни); (*unaided*) сам (*f* сама, *nt* само, *pl* сами); **I did it all by myself** я сделал всё сам; **he was standing by himself in the corner** он стоял в углу один/сам по себе
12: **by the way** кстати, между прочим; **this wasn't my idea by the way** кстати *or* между прочим, это была не моя идея
♦ *adv* **1** *see* go, pass *etc*
2: **by and by** вскоре; **by and large** в целом.

bye(-bye) ['baɪ('baɪ)] *excl* пока, всего.
by(e)-law ['baɪlɔ:] *n* постановление местной власти.
by-election ['baɪɪlɛkʃən] *n* (*BRIT*) дополнительные выборы *mpl*.
Byelorussia [bjɛləu'rʌʃə] *n* Белоруссия.
bygone ['baɪgɔn] *adj* минувший* ♦ *n*: **let ~s be ~s** что было, то прошло.
bypass ['baɪpɑ:s] *n* (*AUT*) объезд; (*MED*) обходное шунтирование (*обычно в кардиохирургии*) ♦ *vt* (*town*) объезжать (объехать* *perf*); (*fig*) обходить* (обойти* *perf*).
by-product ['baɪprɔdʌkt] *n* (*of industrial process*) побочный продукт; (*of situation*) побочный результат.
byre ['baɪə'] *n* (*BRIT*) коровник.
bystander ['baɪstændə'] *n* свидетель(ница) *m(f)*, прохожий(-ая) *m(f) adj*.
byte [baɪt] *n* (*COMPUT*) байт.
byway ['baɪweɪ] *n* (*in country*) просёлочная дорога; (*in city*) улочка.
byword ['baɪwə:d] *n*: **to be a ~ for** быть* (*impf*) олицетворением *or* символом +*gen*.
by-your-leave ['baɪjɔ:'li:v] *n*: **without so much as a ~** без всякого разрешения.

~ C, c ~

C, c [siː] n (letter) 3-ья бу́ква англи́йского
алфави́та; (SCOL: mark) ≈
удовлетвори́тельный.

C [siː] n (MUS) до nt ind.

C. abbr = **Celsius, centigrade**.

c abbr (= **century**) в.= век; (= circa) о́коло +gen;
(US etc: = cents) це́нты mpl.

CA n abbr (BRIT) = **chartered accountant** ♦ abbr =
Central America; (US: POST) = **California**.

ca. abbr (= circa) о́коло +gen.

c/a abbr (COMM) = **capital account, credit
account, current account**.

CAA n abbr (BRIT: = Civil Aviation Authority)
Управле́ние гражда́нской авиа́ции; (US) =
Civil Aeronautics Authority.

CAB n abbr (BRIT: = Citizens' Advice Bureau)
бюро́, даю́щее беспла́тные сове́ты по
широ́кому спе́ктру пробле́м.

cab [kæb] n такси́ nt ind; (of truck etc) каби́на;
(horse-drawn) экипа́ж, кэб.

cabaret ['kæbəreɪ] n кабаре́ nt ind.

cabbage ['kæbɪdʒ] n капу́ста.

cabbie ['kæbɪ] n такси́ст.

cab driver n шофёр такси́.

cabin ['kæbɪn] n (on ship) каю́та; (on plane)
каби́на; (house) хи́жина.

cabin cruiser n пассажи́рский* ка́тер*.

cabinet ['kæbɪnɪt] n шкаф*; (also: **display ~**)
го́рка; (POL) кабине́т (мини́стров).

cabinet-maker ['kæbɪnɪt'meɪkə^r] n красно-
деревщик.

cabinet minister n член кабине́та
мини́стров.

cable ['keɪbl] n (strong rope) кана́т; (metal)
трос; (ELEC, TEL, TV) ка́бель m; (also: **~gram**)
каблогра́мма, телегра́мма ♦ vt (message)
телеграфи́ровать (impf/perf); (money)
посыла́ть (посла́ть* perf) телегра́фом.

cable car n кана́тная доро́га.

cable railway n фуникулёр.

cable television n ка́бельное телеви́дение.

cache [kæʃ] n та́йный склад; **a ~ of food** запа́с
продово́льствия.

cackle ['kækl] vi (person) хихи́кать (impf); (hen)
куда́хтать* (impf).

cacti ['kæktaɪ] npl of **cactus**.

cactus ['kæktəs] n (pl **cacti**) n ка́ктус.

CAD n abbr (= computer-aided design)
автоматизи́рованное проекти́рование.

caddie ['kædɪ] n (GOLF) подру́чный m adj
игрока́ в гольф.

caddy ['kædɪ] n = **caddie**.

cadence ['keɪdəns] n (of voice) интона́ция.

cadet [kə'dɛt] n курса́нт; **police ~** курса́нт
полице́йской шко́лы.

cadge [kædʒ] vt (inf): **to ~ (from or off)**
выкля́нчивать (вы́клянчить perf) (у +gen).

cadger ['kædʒə^r] n (BRIT: inf) попроша́йка m/f.

cadre ['kædrɪ] n ка́дры mpl.

Caesarean [siː'zɛərɪən] n (also: **~ section**)
ке́сарево сече́ние.

CAF abbr (BRIT: = cost and freight) КАФ
(сто́имость и фра́хт).

café ['kæfeɪ] n кафе́ nt ind.

cafeteria [kæfɪ'tɪərɪə] n кафете́рий.

caffein(e) ['kæfiːn] n кофеи́н.

cage [keɪdʒ] n (of animal) кле́тка; (of lift)
каби́на ♦ vt сажа́ть (посади́ть* perf) в кле́тку.

cagey ['keɪdʒɪ] adj (inf: person) скры́тный*
(скры́тен); (: answer) укло́нчивый
(укло́нчив).

cagoule [kə'guːl] n дождеви́к.

cahoots [kə'huːts] npl: **to be in ~ with sb** быть*
(impf) в сго́воре с кем-н.

CAI n abbr (= computer-aided instruction)
автоматизи́рованное обуче́ние.

Cairo ['kaɪərəu] n Каи́р.

cajole [kə'dʒəul] vt: **to ~ sb** склоня́ть
(склони́ть perf) ле́стью кого́-н.

cake [keɪk] n (large) торт; (small) пиро́жное nt
adj; (of soap) брусо́к*; **it's a piece of ~** (inf) э́то
пустяко́вое де́ло*; **his books sell like hot ~s**
его́ кни́ги иду́т нарасхва́т.

caked [keɪkt] adj: **~ with** облеплённый +instr.

cake shop n бу́лочная-конди́терская f adj.

calamine lotion ['kæləmaɪn-] n калами́нный
лосьо́н.

calamitous [kə'læmɪtəs] adj бе́дственный.

calamity [kə'læmɪtɪ] n бе́дствие.

calcium ['kælsɪəm] n ка́льций.

calculate ['kælkjuleɪt] vt (work out: numbers,
cost) подсчи́тывать (подсчита́ть perf);
(: distance) вычисля́ть (вы́числить perf);
(estimate) рассчи́тывать (рассчита́ть perf).

▶ **calculate on** vt fus: **to ~ on sth** рассчи́тывать
(impf) на что-н.

calculated ['kælkjuleɪtɪd] adj наме́ренный
(наме́рен); **a ~ risk** созна́тельный риск.

calculating ['kælkjuleɪtɪŋ] *adj* расчётливый (расчётлив).

calculation [kælkju'leɪʃən] *n* (*see vb*) подсчёт; вычисление; расчёт.

calculator ['kælkjuleɪtə˚] *n* калькулятор.

calculus ['kælkjuləs] *n* исчисление; **integral/differential** ~ интегральное/дифференциальное исчисление.

Calcutta [kæl'kʌtə] *n* Калькутта.

calendar ['kæləndə˚] *n* календарь* *m* ♦ *cpd*: ~ **month/year** календарный месяц*/год*.

calf [kɑːf] (*pl* **calves**) *n* (*of cow*) телёнок*; (*of elephant, seal*) детёныш; (*also*: ~**skin**) телячья кожа; (*ANAT*) икра*.

caliber ['kælɪbə˚] (*US*) *n* = **calibre**.

calibrate ['kælɪbreɪt] *vt* калибровать (*impf*).

calibre ['kælɪbə˚] (*US* **caliber**) *n* (*of gun, person*) калибр.

calico ['kælɪkəu] *n* (*BRIT*) миткаль* *m*; (*US*) ситец*.

California [kælɪ'fɔːnɪə] *n* Калифорния.

calipers ['kælɪpəz] (*US*) *npl* = **callipers**.

call [kɔːl] *vt* (*name, label*) называть* *perf*; (*TEL*) звонить (позвонить *perf*) +*dat*; (*summon*) вызывать (вызвать* *perf*); (*arrange*) созывать (созвать* *perf*); (*announce*) объявлять (объявить* *perf*) ♦ *vi* (*shout*) кричать (крикнуть *perf*); (*telephone*) звонить (позвонить *perf*); (*visit: also*: ~ **in**, ~ **round**) заходить* (зайти* *perf*) ♦ *n* (*shout, cry*) крик; (*TEL*) звонок*; (*visit*) посещение; (*demand*) призыв; (*summons: for flight*) объявление; (*fig: lure*) зов*; **she is** ~**ed Suzanne** её зовут Сюзанна; **the mountain is** ~**ed Ben Nevis** гора называется Бен Невис; **to** ~ **sb as a witness** призывать (призвать* *perf*) кого-н в свидетели; **who is** ~**ing?** (*TEL*) кто звонит?; **London** ~**ing** (*RADIO*) говорит Лондон; **please give me a** ~ **at 7** позвоните мне, пожалуйста, в 7 часов; **to make a** ~ звонить (позвонить *perf*); **to pay a** ~ **on sb** навещать (навестить* *perf*) кого-н; **there's not much** ~ **for these items** на эти предметы нет большого спроса; **to be on** ~ (*nurse, doctor*) дежурить (*impf*); (*army, fire brigade*) быть* (*impf*) наготове

▶ **call at** *vt fus* (*subj: ship*) заходить* (зайти* *perf*) в +*prp*; (: *train*) останавливаться (остановиться* *perf*) в +*prp*

▶ **call back** *vi* (*return*) заходить* (зайти* *perf*) опять; (*TEL*) перезванивать (перезвонить *perf*) ♦ *vt* (*TEL*) перезванивать (перезвонить *perf*) +*dat*

▶ **call for** *vt fus* (*demand*) призывать (призвать* *perf*) к +*dat*; (*fetch*) заходить* (зайти* *perf*) за +*instr*

▶ **call in** *vt* (*doctor*) вызывать (вызвать* *perf*) ♦ *vi* (*visit*) заходить* (зайти* *perf*); **to** ~ **sth in**

(*books, stock*) отзывать (отозвать* *perf*)

▶ **call off** *vt* отменять (отменить* *perf*); **the strike was** ~**ed off** забастовка была отменена

▶ **call on** *vt fus* (*visit*) заходить* (зайти* *perf*) к +*dat*; (*appeal to*) призывать (призвать* *perf*) к +*dat*; (*request*): **to** ~ **on sb to do** призывать (призвать* *perf*) кого-н +*infin*

▶ **call out** *vi* кричать (крикнуть *perf*) ♦ *vt* (*doctor, police*) вызывать (вызвать* *perf*)

▶ **call up** *vt* (*MIL*) призывать (призвать* *perf*) (в армию); (*TEL*) звонить (позвонить *perf*) +*dat*.

Callanetics® [kælə'nɛtɪks] *n* калланетика (*вид оздоровительной гимнастики*).

call box *n* (*BRIT*) телефонная будка.

caller ['kɔːlə˚] *n* (*visitor*) посетитель(ница) *m(f)*; (*TEL*) звонящий(-ая) *m(f) adj*; **hold the line,** ~! не кладите трубку!

call girl *n* проститутка* (*которую вызывают по телефону*).

call-in ['kɔːlɪn] *n* (*US*) программа, приглашающая звонки (*от телезрителей или радиослушателей*).

calling ['kɔːlɪŋ] *n* призвание.

calling card *n* (*US*) визитная карточка*.

callipers ['kælɪpəz] (*US* **calipers**) *npl* (*MATH*) штангенциркуль *msg*.

callous ['kæləs] *adj* (*heartless*) бездушный (бездушен).

callousness ['kæləsnɪs] *n* бездушие.

callow ['kæləu] *adj*: ~ **youth** птенец*.

calm [kɑːm] *adj* спокойный* (спокоен); (*place*) тихий*; (*weather*) безветренный ♦ *n* тишина, покой; (*at sea*) штиль *m* ♦ *vt* успокаивать (успокоить *perf*)

▶ **calm down** *vt* (*person, animal*) успокаивать (успокоить *perf*) ♦ *vi* (*person*) успокаиваться (успокоиться *perf*).

calmly ['kɑːmlɪ] *adv* спокойно.

calmness ['kɑːmnɪs] *n* спокойствие.

Calor gas® ['kælə˚-] *n* фирменная марка баллонного газа.

calorie ['kælərɪ] *n* калория; **low-~ product** низкокалорийный продукт.

calve [kɑːv] *vi* (*cow*) телиться (отелиться* *perf*); (*elephant, seal*) рождать (родить* *perf*) детёныша.

calves [kɑːvz] *npl of* **calf**.

CAM *n abbr* (= *computer-aided manufacturing*) автоматизированное производство.

camber ['kæmbə˚] *n* поперечный уклон.

Cambodia [kæm'bəudɪə] *n* Камбоджа.

Cambodian [kæm'bəudɪən] *adj* камбоджийский* ♦ *n* камбоджиец(-ийка).

Cambridge ['keɪmbrɪdʒ] *n* Кембридж.

Cambs *abbr* (*BRIT: POST*) = **Cambridgeshire**.

camcorder ['kæmkɔːdə˚] *n* видеокамера.

came [keɪm] *pt of* **come**.

---

* marks translations which have irregular inflections. The Russian-English side of the dictionary gives inflectional information.

camel ['kæməl] *n* верблю́д.
cameo ['kæmɪəu] *n* (*jewellery*) каме́я; (*THEAT, LITERATURE*) миниатю́ра.
camera ['kæmərə] *n* (*PHOT*) фотоаппара́т; (*also:* **cine ~, movie ~**) кинока́мера; (*TV*) телека́мера; **35 mm ~** кинока́мера для 35-мм плёнки; **in ~** (*LAW*) при закры́тых дверя́х.
cameraman ['kæmərəmæn] *irreg n* (*CINEMA*) (кино)опера́тор; (*TV*) (теле)опера́тор.
Cameroon [kæmə'ruːn] *n* Камеру́н.
Cameroun [kæmə'ruːn] *n* = **Cameroon**.
camomile ['kæməumaɪl] *n* рома́шка; **~ tea** рома́шковый чай*.
camouflage ['kæməflɑːʒ] *n* (*MIL*) камуфля́ж, маскиро́вка; (*ZOOL*) защи́тная окра́ска ♦ *vt* (*also MIL*) маскирова́ть (замаскирова́ть *perf*).
camp [kæmp] *n* ла́герь* *m*; (*MIL*) вое́нный городо́к* ♦ *vi* (*set up camp*) разбива́ть (разби́ть* *perf*) ла́герь; (*go camping*) жить* (*impf*) в пала́тках ♦ *adj* (*effeminate*) женоподо́бный.
campaign [kæm'peɪn] *n* кампа́ния ♦ *vi*: **to ~ (for/against)** вести́* (*impf*) кампа́нию (за +*acc*/про́тив +*gen*).
campaigner [kæm'peɪnəʳ] *n*: **~ (for/against)** боре́ц* (за +*acc*/про́тив +*gen*).
camp bed *n* (*BRIT*) раскладу́шка*.
camper ['kæmpəʳ] *n* (*person*) тури́ст(ка) (*живу́щий* в пала́тке*); (*vehicle*) фурго́н (*оборудованный для походно́й жи́зни*).
camping ['kæmpɪŋ] *n* ке́мпинг; **to go ~** отправля́ться (отпра́виться* *perf*) в похо́д.
camping site *n* = **camp site**.
camp site *n* ке́мпинг.
campus ['kæmpəs] *n* университе́тский* *or* студе́нческий* городо́к*.
camshaft ['kæmʃɑːft] *n* кулачко́вый вал*.
can[1] [kæn] *n* (*for foodstuffs*) консе́рвная ба́нка; (*for oil, beer*) ба́нка ♦ *vt* консерви́ровать (законсерви́ровать *perf*); **a ~ of beer** ба́нка пи́ва; **he had to carry the ~** (*BRIT: inf*) ему́ пришло́сь за всё отдува́ться.

KEYWORD

can[2] (*negative* **cannot, can't**, *conditional, pt* **could**) *aux vb* **1** (*be able to*) мочь* (смочь* *perf*); **you can do it** (**if you try**) Вы смо́жете э́то сде́лать(, е́сли Вы постара́етесь); **I'll help you all I can** я помогу́ Вам всем, чем могу́; **I can't go on any longer** я бо́льше не могу́; **I can't see/hear you** я не ви́жу/слы́шу Вас; **she couldn't sleep that night** в ту ночь она́ не могла́ усну́ть
2 (*know how to*) уме́ть (*impf*); **I can swim** я уме́ю пла́вать; **can you speak Russian?** Вы говори́те *or* уме́ете говори́ть по-ру́сски?
3 (*may*) мо́жно; **can I use your phone?** мо́жно от Вас позвони́ть?; **could I have a word with you?** мо́жно с Ва́ми поговори́ть?; **you can smoke if you like** Вы мо́жете кури́ть, е́сли хоти́те; **can I help you with that?** могу́ я Вам

в э́том помо́чь?
4 (*expressing disbelief, puzzlement*): **it can't be true!** не мо́жет быть!; **what CAN he want?** что ему́ ну́жно?
5 (*expressing possibility, suggestion etc*): **he could be in the library** он мо́жет быть в библиоте́ке, возмо́жно, он в библиоте́ке; **she could have been delayed** возмо́жно, её что-то задержа́ло.

Canada ['kænədə] *n* Кана́да.
Canadian [kə'neɪdɪən] *adj* кана́дский* ♦ *n* кана́дец*(-дка*).
canal [kə'næl] *n* кана́л.
Canaries [kə'nɛərɪz] *npl* = **Canary Islands**.
canary [kə'nɛərɪ] *n* канаре́йка*.
Canary Islands *npl*: **the ~ ~** Кана́рские острова́ *mpl*.
Canberra ['kænbərə] *n* Канбе́рра.
cancel ['kænsəl] *vt* отменя́ть (отмени́ть* *perf*); (*contract, cheque, visa*) аннули́ровать (*impf/ perf*); (*words, figures*) вычёркивать (вы́черкнуть *perf*); (*stamp*) погаша́ть (погаси́ть* *perf*)
▸ **cancel out** *vt* нейтрализова́ть (*impf/perf*); **they ~ each other out** они нейтрализу́ют друг дру́га.
cancellation [kænsə'leɪʃən] *n* отме́на, аннули́рование.
cancer ['kænsəʳ] *n* (*MED*) рак; (*fig*) бич; **C~** (*ASTROLOGY*) Рак; **he is C~** он – Рак.
cancerous ['kænsrəs] *adj* ра́ковый.
cancer patient *n* ра́ковый(-ая) больно́й(-а́я) *m(f) adj*.
cancer research *n* онкологи́ческие иссле́дования *ntpl*.
C and F *abbr* (*BRIT: COMM*) = **CAF**.
candid ['kændɪd] *adj* и́скренний (и́скренен), чистосерде́чный* (чистосерде́чен).
candidacy ['kændɪdəsɪ] *n* кандидату́ра.
candidate ['kændɪdeɪt] *n* (*for job*) претенде́нт; (*in exam*) экзамену́емый(-ая) *m(f) adj*; (*POL*) кандида́т.
candidature ['kændɪdətʃəʳ] (*BRIT*) *n* = **candidacy**.
candied ['kændɪd] *adj*: **~ fruit** цука́ты *mpl*; **~ apple** (*US*) я́блочный цука́т.
candle ['kændl] *n* свеча́*; (*smaller*) све́чка*.
candleholder ['kændlhəuldəʳ] *n* = **candlestick**.
candlelight ['kændllaɪt] *n*: **by ~** при свеча́х.
candlestick ['kændlstɪk] *n* подсве́чник.
candour ['kændəʳ] (*US* **candor**) *n* и́скренность *f*.
candy ['kændɪ] *n* (*also:* **sugar-~**) караме́ль *f*, леденец́*; (*US*) конфе́та.
candyfloss ['kændɪflɔs] *n* (*BRIT*) са́харная ва́та.
candy store *n* (*US*) конди́терская *f adj*.
cane [keɪn] *n* (*BOT*) тростни́к*; (*stick*) ро́зга*; (*for walking*) трость* *f* ♦ *vt* (*BRIT*) нака́зывать (наказа́ть* *perf*) ро́згами.
canine ['keɪnaɪn] *adj* соба́чий*.
canister ['kænɪstəʳ] *n* (*for tea etc*) жестяна́я ба́нка*; (*pressurized container*) балло́н; (*of chemicals etc*) кани́стра.

cannabis [ˈkænəbɪs] n гашúш; (also: ~ **plant**) конопля́.

canned [kænd] adj (fruit, vegetables etc) консервúрованный; (inf: music) в за́писи; (BRIT: inf: drink) ба́ночный; (: drunk) наклюка́вшийся.

cannibal [ˈkænɪbəl] n (animal) канниба́л; (person) канниба́л, людое́д.

cannibalism [ˈkænɪbəlɪzəm] n каннибалúзм, людое́дство.

cannon [ˈkænən] (pl ~ or ~**s**) n (gun) пу́шка*.

cannonball [ˈkænənbɔːl] n пу́шечное ядро́*.

cannon fodder n пу́шечное мя́со.

cannot [ˈkænɔt] = **can not**; see **can²**.

canny [ˈkænɪ] adj смека́листый (смека́лист).

canoe [kəˈnuː] n (boat) челно́к*; (for competition) кано́э nt ind.

canoeing [kəˈnuːɪŋ] n гре́бля на кано́э.

canon [ˈkænən] n (clergyman) кано́ник; (rule) кано́н; (standard) крите́рий.

canonize [ˈkænənaɪz] vt канонизи́ровать (impf/ perf).

can-opener [ˈkænəupnə'] n консе́рвный нож* or ключ*.

canopy [ˈkænəpɪ] n (above bed etc) балдахи́н, по́лог; (of leaves etc) свод.

cant [kænt] n ха́нжество.

can't [kænt] = **can not**; see **can²**.

Cantab. abbr (BRIT: in degree titles) = Cantabrigiensis.

cantankerous [kænˈtæŋkərəs] adj сварли́вый (сварли́в), приди́рчивый (приди́рчив).

canteen [kænˈtiːn] n столо́вая f adj; (mobile) похо́дная ку́хня*; (BRIT): ~ **of cutlery** похо́дный я́щик со столо́выми принадле́жностями.

canter [ˈkæntə'] vi ездúть*/е́хать* (impf) лёгким гало́пом ◆ n лёгкий* гало́п.

cantilever [ˈkæntɪliːvə'] n консо́ль f, кронште́йн; ~ **bridge** консо́льный мост*.

canvas [ˈkænvəs] n (fabric, also ART) холст*; (for tents) брезе́нт; (NAUT) парусúна ◆ adj (shoes, bag) парусúновый; **under** ~ (camping) в пала́тках.

canvass [ˈkænvəs] vi: **to** ~ **for** агити́ровать (impf/perf) за +acc ◆ vt (opinions) собира́ть (impf).

canvasser [ˈkænvəsə'] n агита́тор.

canvassing [ˈkænvəsɪŋ] n предвы́борная агита́ция.

canyon [ˈkænjən] n каньо́н.

CAP n abbr (= Common Agricultural Policy) о́бщая сельскохозя́йственная полúтика (в стра́нах Общего ры́нка).

cap [kæp] n (hat) ке́пка*; (of uniform) фура́жка*; (of pen) колпачо́к*; (of bottle) кры́шка*; (also: **Dutch** ~: contraceptive) колпачо́к*; (for toy gun) писто́н; (FOOTBALL) футбо́льный игро́к,

кото́рый получа́ет ке́пку как знак отлúчия ◆ vt (outdo) превосходи́ть* (превзойтú* perf); (SPORT): **he was** ~**ped ten times** он игра́л в сбо́рной кома́нде страны́ де́сять раз; **swimming** ~ купа́льная ша́почка; **to be** ~**ped with** уве́нчиваться (увенча́ться perf) +instr; **and to** ~ **it all, he ...** в доверше́ние ко всему́, он ....

capability [keɪpəˈbɪlɪtɪ] n (competence) спосо́бность f; (MIL) потенциа́л.

capable [ˈkeɪpəbl] adj (person) спосо́бный* (спосо́бен); ~ **of sth/doing** (person, object) спосо́бен к чему́-н/+infin.

capacious [kəˈpeɪʃəs] adj вмести́тельный* (вмести́телен).

capacity [kəˈpæsɪtɪ] n (of container) ёмкость f; (of ship, theatre etc) вмести́тельность f; (of lift) подъёмная спосо́бность f; (of person: capability) спосо́бность f; (: role) роль* f; (of factory) произво́дственная мо́щность f; **filled to** ~ запо́лнен до преде́ла; **in his** ~ **as** в ро́ли +gen; **in an advisory** ~ в ро́ли сове́тника; **this work is beyond my** ~ э́та рабо́та вне мое́й компете́нции; **to work at full** ~ рабо́тать (impf) на по́лную мо́щность.

cape [keɪp] n (GEO) мыс*; (cloak) плащ.

Cape of Good Hope n: **the** ~~~~ Мыс До́брой Наде́жды.

caper [ˈkeɪpə'] n (CULIN: usu pl) ка́персы mpl; (prank) ро́зыгрыш.

Cape Town n Кейпта́ун.

capita [ˈkæpɪtə] see **per capita**.

capital [ˈkæpɪtl] n (also: ~ **city**) столúца; (money) капита́л; (also: ~ **letter**) загла́вная бу́ква.

capital account n бала́нс движе́ния капита́ла.

capital allowance n нало́говая скúдка, свя́занная с инвестúциями в основно́й капита́л.

capital assets npl основно́й капита́л msg, основны́е фо́нды mpl.

capital employed n применя́емый капита́л.

capital expenditure n капиталовложе́ние.

capital gains tax n нало́г на реализо́ванный прирост капита́ла.

capital goods npl капита́льные това́ры mpl, сре́дства ntpl произво́дства.

capital-intensive [ˈkæpɪtlɪnˈtɛnsɪv] adj капиталоёмкий.

capital investment n капиталовложе́ние.

capitalism [ˈkæpɪtəlɪzm] n капиталúзм.

capitalist [ˈkæpɪtəlɪst] adj капиталисти́ческий* ◆ n капиталúст.

capitalize [ˈkæpɪtəlaɪz] vt (COMM) капитализи́ровать (impf/perf) ◆ vi: **to** ~ **on** извлека́ть (извле́чь* perf) вы́году из +gen.

capital punishment n сме́ртная казнь f.

---

* marks translations which have irregular inflections. The Russian-English side of the dictionary gives inflectional information.

capital transfer tax *n* (*BRIT*) налог на перевод капитала.
Capitol ['kæpɪtl] *n*: **the ~** Капитолий.
capitulate [kə'pɪtjuleɪt] *vi*: **to ~ (to)** капитулировать (*impf/perf*) (перед +*instr*).
capitulation [kəpɪtju'leɪʃən] *n* капитуляция.
capricious [kə'prɪʃəs] *adj* (*person*) капризный* (капризен), прихотливый (прихотлив).
Capricorn ['kæprɪkɔ:n] *n* (*ASTROLOGY*) Козерог; **he is ~** он – Козерог.
caps [kæps] *abbr* = **capital letters**.
capsize [kæp'saɪz] *vt* опрокидывать (опрокинуть *perf*) ◆ *vi* опрокидываться (опрокинуться *perf*).
capstan ['kæpstən] *n* (*NAUT*) кабестан.
capsule ['kæpsju:l] *n* капсула.
Capt. *abbr* (*MIL*) = **captain**.
captain ['kæptɪn] *n* (*of ship, plane*) командир; (*of team, army*) капитан ◆ *vt* (*ship*) командовать (*impf*) +*instr*; (*team*) являться (*impf*) капитаном +*gen*.
caption ['kæpʃən] *n* подпись *f*.
captivate ['kæptɪveɪt] *vt* пленять (пленить *perf*).
captive ['kæptɪv] *adj* пленный ◆ *n* пленник(-ица).
captivity [kæp'tɪvɪtɪ] *n* плен*; **in ~** (*animal*) в неволе; (*person*) в плену.
captor ['kæptə'] *n* (*unlawful*) похититель(ница) *m(f)*; (*lawful*) взявший(-ая) *m(f) adj* в плен; **his ~s** взявшие его в плен.
capture ['kæptʃə'] *vt* (*animal*) ловить* (поймать *perf*); (*person, city, also COMM*) захватывать (захватить* *perf*); (*attention*) приковывать (приковать* *perf*) ◆ *n* (*of person, town etc*) захват; (*of animal*) поимка*; (*COMPUT*): **data ~** сбор информации; **to ~ the screen** (*COMPUT*) хватать (хватить* *perf*) or фиксировать (зафиксировать *perf*) изображение с экрана.
car [kɑ:'] *n* автомобиль *m*, машина; (*RAIL*) вагон; **by ~** на автомобиле or машине; **dining ~** (*BRIT*) вагон-ресторан.
Caracas [kə'rækəs] *n* Каракас.
carafe [kə'ræf] *n* графин.
caramel ['kærəməl] *n* (*sweet*) карамель *f*; (*burnt sugar*) жжёный сахар*.
carat ['kærət] *n* (*of diamond, gold*) карат; **24 ~ gold** чистое золото.
caravan ['kærəvæn] *n* (*BRIT*) жилой-автоприцеп; (*in desert*) караван.
caravan site *n* (*BRIT*) площадка для стоянки жилых-автоприцепов.
caraway ['kærəweɪ] *n*: **~ seeds** тмин *msg*.
carbohydrate [kɑ:bəu'haɪdreɪt] *n* углевод.
carbolic acid [kɑ:'bɔlɪk-] *n* карболовая кислота.
car bomb *n* бомба, подложенная в or под машину.
carbon ['kɑ:bən] *n* углерод.
carbonated ['kɑ:bəneɪtɪd] *adj* газированный.

carbon copy *n* копия (*сделанная под копирку*).
carbon dioxide *n* двуокись *f* углерода.
carbon monoxide [mɔ'nɔksaɪd] *n* моноксид углерода.
carbon paper *n* копировальная бумага, копирка.
carbon ribbon *n* лента (*для пишущей машинки или принтера*).
car boot sale *n* барахолка, на которой товар разложен на капотах машин.
carburettor [kɑ:bju'rɛtə'] (*US* **carburetor**) *n* карбюратор.
carcass ['kɑ:kəs] *n* туша.
carcinogenic [kɑ:sɪnə'dʒɛnɪk] *adj* канцерогенный.
card [kɑ:d] *n* (*material*) картон; (*also*: **record ~**) карточка*; (*also*: **membership ~**) членский* билет; (*also*: **playing ~**) игральная карта; (*also*: **greetings ~**) открытка; (*also*: **visiting ~, business ~**) визитная карточка*; **to play ~s** играть (*impf*) в карты.
cardamom ['kɑ:dəməm] *n* кардамон.
cardboard ['kɑ:dbɔ:d] *n* картон.
cardboard box *n* картонная коробка*.
cardboard city (*inf*) *n* район города, занятый бездомными, живущими в картонных ящиках.
card-carrying ['kɑ:d'kærɪŋ] *adj*: **~ member** полноправный член политической организации.
card game *n* игра* в карты.
cardiac ['kɑ:dɪæk] *adj* сердечный; (*unit*) кардиологический.
Cardiff ['kɑ:dɪf] *n* Кардифф.
cardigan ['kɑ:dɪgən] *n* жакет (*вязаный*).
cardinal ['kɑ:dɪnl] *adj* (*also*: **~ number**) количественное числительное *nt adj*; (*sin*) смертный; (*principle, importance*) кардинальный ◆ *n* кардинал.
card index *n* картотека.
cardsharp ['kɑ:dʃɑ:p] *n* шулер*.
card vote *n* (*BRIT*) мандатное голосование.
CARE [kɛə'] *n abbr* = *Cooperative for American Relief Everywhere*.
care [kɛə'] *n* (*worry*) забота; (*of the ill*) уход; (*attention*) внимание ◆ *vi*: **to ~ about** (*person, animal*) заботиться* (позаботиться* *perf*) о +*prp*; (*in sb's*) ~ на чьём-н попечении; **the child has been taken into ~** ребёнок был взят в детский дом; **"handle with ~"** "не кантовать"; **to take ~ (to do)** позаботиться (*perf*) (+*infin*); **to take ~ of** (*patient, child etc*) заботиться* (позаботиться* *perf*) о +*prp*; (*problem, situation*) заниматься (заняться* *perf*) +*instr*; **~ of** для передачи +*dat*; **he ~s about environmental issues** его волнуют проблемы защиты окружающей среды; **would you ~ to/for ...?** не хотите ли +*infin*/+*acc*; **I wouldn't ~ to repeat the experience** мне бы не хотелось испытать это снова; **I**

don't ~ мне всё равно; **I couldn't** ~ **less** мне наплевать
► **care for** *vt fus* (*look after*) заботиться* (позаботиться* *perf*) о +*prp*; (*like*): **he** ~**s for her** он неравнодушен к ней.
career [kə'pɪə'] *n* карьера ♦ *vi* мчаться* (помчаться* *perf*); **my school** ~ (*life*) мои школьные годы.
career girl *n* = **career woman.**
careers officer [kə'pəz-] *n консультант по профессиональной ориентации.*
career woman *irreg n* деловая женщина.
carefree ['kɛəfriː] *adj* беззаботный* (беззаботен).
careful ['kɛəful] *adj* (*cautious*) осторожный* (осторожен); (*thorough*) тщательный* (тщателен); (**be**) ~! осторожно!, берегись!; **he is/was** ~ **with his money** он экономен/был экономен.
carefully ['kɛəfəlɪ] *adv* (*see adj*) осторожно; тщательно.
careless ['kɛəlɪs] *adj* (*negligent*) невнимательный* (невнимателен); (*casual*: *remark*) небрежный* (небрежен); (*untroubled*) беззаботный* (беззаботен).
carelessly ['kɛəlɪslɪ] *adv* (*see adj*) невнимательно; небрежно; беззаботно.
carelessness ['kɛəlɪsnɪs] *n* (*negligence*) невнимательность *f*; (*casualness*) небрежность *f*; (*lack of concern*) беззаботность *f*.
carer ['kɛərə'] *n человек, ухаживающий за больными, престарелыми и т.п.*
caress [kə'rɛs] *n* ласка* ♦ *vt* ласкать (*impf*).
caretaker ['kɛəteɪkə'] *n* (*of building*) завхоз.
caretaker government *n* (*BRIT*) временное правительство.
car ferry *n* автомобильный паром.
cargo ['kɑːgəu] (*pl* ~**es**) *n* груз.
cargo boat *n* грузовое судно*.
cargo plane *n* грузовой самолёт.
car hire *n* (*BRIT*) прокат автомобилей.
Caribbean [kærɪ'biːən] *adj* карибский ♦ *n*: **the** ~ (**Sea**) Карибское море*.
caricature ['kærɪkətjuə'] *n* карикатура; ~ **of the truth** карикатура на правду.
caring ['kɛərɪŋ] *adj* заботливый (заботлив).
carjack ['kɑːdʒæk] *n* домкрат.
carnage ['kɑːnɪdʒ] *n* резня.
carnal ['kɑːnl] *adj* плотский*.
carnation [kɑː'neɪʃən] *n* гвоздика.
carnival ['kɑːnɪvl] *n* карнавал; (*US: funfair*) аттракционный городок*.
carnivorous [kɑː'nɪvərəs] *adj* (*animal*) плотоядный*; (*plant*) насекомоядный.
carol ['kærəl] *n* (*also:* **Christmas** ~) Рождественский* гимн.
carouse [kə'rauz] *vi* бражничать (*impf*).

carousel [kærə'sɛl] *n* (*US*) карусель *f*.
carp [kɑːp] *n* карп
► **carp at** *vt fus* придираться (придраться* *perf*) к +*dat*.
car park *n* (*BRIT*) автостоянка*.
Carpathian Mountains [kɑː'peɪθɪən-] *npl* Карпаты *pl*.
carpenter ['kɑːpɪntə'] *n* плотник.
carpentry ['kɑːpɪntrɪ] *n* плотницкое дело.
carpet ['kɑːpɪt] *n* (*also fig*) ковёр*; (*of snow*) покров ♦ *vt* (*room*) устилать (устлать* *perf*) коврами; **fitted** ~ (*BRIT*) ковровое покрытие.
carpet bombing *n* ковровый налёт.
carpet slippers *npl* шлёпанцы *mpl*.
carpet sweeper [-'swiːpə'] *n* щётка для ковра.
car phone *n* радио-телефон (*в машине*).
carport ['kɑːpɔːt] *n* навес для машины.
car rental *n* прокат автомобилей.
carriage ['kærɪdʒ] *n* (*BRIT*: *RAIL*) (пассажирский*) вагон; (*horse-drawn*) экипаж; (*of goods*) перевозка; (*of typewriter*) каретка*; (*transport costs*) стоимость *f* перевозки; ~ **forward** стоимость перевозки подлежит оплате получателем; ~ **free** перевозка осуществляется бесплатно; ~ **inwards** сумма, оплачиваемая покупателем за доставку полученного груза; ~ **outwards** сумма, представленная продавцом к оплате на покрытие расходов по доставке; ~ **paid** за перевозку уплачено.
carriage return *n* перевод каретки.
carriageway ['kærɪdʒweɪ] *n* (*BRIT*) проезжая часть* *f* дороги.
carrier ['kærɪə'] *n* (*transporter*) транспортировщик; (*MED*) носитель *m*.
carrier bag *n* (*BRIT*) пакетик (*для покупок*).
carrier pigeon *n* почтовый голубь* *m*.
carrion ['kærɪən] *n* падаль *f*.
carrot ['kærət] *n* морковь *f*; (*fig*): ~ **and stick policy** политика кнута и пряника.
carry ['kærɪ] *vt* (*take*) носить*/нести* (*impf*); (*transport*) возить*/везти* (*impf*); (*a motion, bill*) проводить* (провести* *perf*); (*involve*) влечь* (повлечь* *perf*); (*MED*) переносить* (*impf*); (*have: picture, slogan*) содержать* (*impf*) ♦ *vi* (*sound*) передаваться* (*impf*); **he carries the virus** он носитель вируса; **this loan carries 10% interest per annum** этот заём предоставляется под 10% годовых; **to get carried away (by)** (*fig*) увлекаться (увлечься* *perf*) (+*instr*)
► **carry forward** *vt* (*also COMM*) переносить* (перенести* *perf*) на другую страницу
► **carry on** *vi* продолжаться (продолжиться* *perf*); (*inf. make a fuss*) заводиться* (завестись* *perf*) ♦ *vt* продолжать (продолжить *perf*); **to** ~ **on with sth/doing** продолжать (продолжить *perf*) что-н/+*impf*

---

* marks translations which have irregular inflections. The Russian-English side of the dictionary gives inflectional information.

infin

▶ **carry out** *vt* (*orders*) выполня́ть (вы́полнить *perf*), исполня́ть (испо́лнить *perf*); (*investigation*) проводи́ть* (провести́* *perf*); (*threat*) осуществля́ть (осуществи́ть* *perf*).

carrycot ['kærɪkɔt] *n* (*BRIT*) переносна́я колыбе́ль *f*.

carry-on ['kærɪ'ɔn] *n* (*inf: fuss*) суматóха, суетá; (: *annoying behaviour*) капри́зы *mpl*; **I've had enough of your ~!** надое́ли мне твои́ капри́зы!; **what a ~!** кака́я суматóха *or* суетá!

cart [kɑːt] *n* телéга, повóзка; (*handcart*) телéжка* ◆ *vt* (*inf: people, objects*) таска́ть/тащи́ть* (*impf*).

carte blanche ['kɑːt'blɒnʃ] *n*: **to give sb ~ ~** предоставля́ть (предоста́вить* *perf*) комý-н пóлную свобóду дéйствий.

cartel [kɑː'tɛl] *n* карте́ль *m*.

cartilage ['kɑːtɪlɪdʒ] *n* хрящ*.

cartographer [kɑː'tɔgrəfə'] *n* карто́граф.

cartography [kɑː'tɔgrəfɪ] *n* картогра́фия.

carton ['kɑːtən] *n* (*large box*) карто́нная коро́бка*; (*container*) паке́т.

cartoon [kɑː'tuːn] *n* (*drawing*) карикату́ра; (*BRIT: comic strip*) кóмикс; (*TV*) мультфи́льм= *мультипликацио́нный фи́льм*.

cartoonist [kɑː'tuːnɪst] *n* карикатури́ст(ка).

cartridge ['kɑːtrɪdʒ] *n* (*for gun*) ги́льза; (*for camera*) кассéта с фотоплёнкой; (*music tape*) кассéта; (*of record-player*) голóвка*; (*of pen*) (черни́льный) баллóнчик; (*of printer*) ка́ртридж.

cartwheel ['kɑːtwiːl] *n* колесó* телéги; **to turn a ~** дéлать (сдéлать *perf*) колесó.

carve [kɑːv] *vt* (*meat*) нареза́ть (нарéзать* *perf*); (*initials, design*) выреза́ть (вы́резать* *perf*); (*wood, stone*) выреза́ть* (*impf*)

▶ **carve up** *vt* (*land, property*) раздробля́ть (раздроби́ть* *perf*); (*meat*) разреза́ть (разрéзать* *perf*).

carving ['kɑːvɪŋ] *n* (*object*) резнóе издéлие; (*design*) резьба́; (*art*) иску́сство резьбы́.

carving knife *n* разде́лочный нож*.

car wash *n* мóйка автомоби́лей.

Casablanca [kæsə'blæŋkə] *n* Касабла́нка.

cascade [kæs'keɪd] *n* (*waterfall*) каска́д ◆ *vi* (*water*) низверга́ться (*impf*); (*hair*) ниспада́ть (*impf*).

case [keɪs] *n* (*instance, problem*) слу́чай; (*MED: patient*) больнóй(-áя) *m(f) adj*; (*LAW*) (судéбное) дéло*; (*criminal investigation*) расслéдование; (*for spectacles etc*) футля́р; (*BRIT: also: suitcase*) чемода́н; (*of wine etc*) я́щик (*содержа́щий* 12 буты́лок); (*TYP*): **lower/upper ~** ни́жный/вéрхний* реги́стр; **to have a good ~** имéть (*impf*) убеди́тельные дóводы; **there's a strong ~ for reform** есть все основа́ния для проведéния рефóрмы; **in ~ (of)** (*fire, emergency*) в слу́чае (+*gen*); **in ~ he**

comes в слу́чае, éсли он придёт; **in any ~** во вся́ком слу́чае; **just in ~** на вся́кий слу́чай.

case history *n* (*MED*) истóрия болéзни.

case study *n* изучéние конкрéтного слу́чая.

cash [kæʃ] *n* нали́чные *pl adj* (дéньги) ◆ *vt*: **to ~ a cheque** обмéнивать (обменя́ть *perf*) чек на дéньги; **to pay (in) ~** плати́ть* (заплати́ть* *perf*) нали́чными; **~ on delivery** налóженный платёж; **~ with order** опла́та при совершéнии зака́за.

▶ **cash in** *vt* получа́ть (получи́ть* *perf*) дéньги по +*dat*

▶ **cash in on** *vt fus* испóльзовать (*impf*) в свои́х интерéсах.

cash account *n* нали́чный счёт*.

cash-and-carry [kæʃən'kærɪ] *n* мелкоопто́вый магази́н.

cash-book ['kæʃbuk] *n* ка́ссовая кни́га.

cash box *n* коро́бка для хранéния ка́ссы.

cash card *n* (*BRIT*) ка́рточка для получéния нали́чных из автома́та.

cash cow *n* (*enterprise*) хлéбное дéло*; (*product*) золотóе днó*.

cash crop *n* това́рная культу́ра.

cash desk *n* (*BRIT*) ка́сса.

cash discount *n* ски́дка с цены́ това́ра в слу́чае упла́ты нали́чными.

cash dispenser *n* (*BRIT*) автома́т для вы́дачи нали́чных с ба́нковского счёта.

cashew [kæ'ʃuː] *n* (*also: ~ nut*) орéх кéшью *m ind*.

cash flow *n* движéние дéнежной нали́чности.

cashier [kæ'ʃɪə'] *n* касси́р.

cashmere ['kæʃmɪə'] *n* (*wool, jersey*) кашеми́р.

cash point *n* автома́т для вы́дачи нали́чных с ба́нковского счёта.

cash price *n* цена́ това́ра при прода́же за нали́чные.

cash register *n* ка́ссовый аппара́т.

cash reserves *npl* ка́ссовый резéрв *msg*.

cash sale *n* прода́жа за нали́чные *pl adj*.

casing ['keɪsɪŋ] *n* оболóчка*, футля́р.

casino [kə'siːnəu] *n* казинó *nt ind*.

cask [kɑːsk] *n* бочóнок*.

casket ['kɑːskɪt] *n* шкату́лка; (*US: coffin*) гроб*.

Caspian Sea ['kæspɪən-] *n* (*GEO*): **the ~ ~** Каспи́йское мóре*.

casserole ['kæsərəul] *n* рагу́ *nt ind*; (*also: ~ dish*) ла́тка*.

cassette [kæ'sɛt] *n* кассéта.

cassette deck *n* кассéтный магнитофóн (*стациона́рный*).

cassette player *n* кассéтный плéйер.

cassette recorder *n* кассéтный магнитофóн (*портати́вный*).

cast [kɑːst] (*pt, pp* **cast**) *vt* (*light, shadow, glance*) броса́ть (брóсить* *perf*); (*net, fishing line*) забра́сывать (забрóсить* *perf*); (*doubts*) сéять (посéять *perf*); (*spell*) околдóвывать (околдова́ть *perf*); (*skin*) сбра́сывать (сбрóсить* *perf*); (*statue*) отлива́ть (отли́ть*

perf) ♦ *vi (FISHING)* забра́сывать (забро́сить*
perf) се́ти ♦ *n (THEAT)* соста́в (исполни́телей);
(mould) фо́рма *(для отли́вки)*; *(also: plaster*
~) ги́псовый слепо́к*; **to ~ one's vote (for sb)**
отдава́ть* (отда́ть* *perf)* свой го́лос (за
кого́-н); **to ~ sb as Hamlet** *(THEAT)* назнача́ть
(назна́чить *perf)* кого́-н на роль Га́млета;
the ~ was full of celebrities в спекта́кле
игра́ло мно́го знамени́тостей
► **cast aside** *vt* отверга́ть (отве́ргнуть *perf)*
► **cast off** *vi (NAUT)* отча́ливать (отча́лить
perf); *(KNITTING)* сбра́сывать (сбро́сить* *perf)*
пе́тлю ♦ *vt (KNITTING)* сбра́сывать (сбро́сить*
perf) (пе́тлю)
► **cast on** *vi (KNITTING)* набира́ть (набра́ть*
perf) пе́тли ♦ *vt* набира́ть (набра́ть* *perf)*
(пе́тли).
castaway ['kɑːstəweɪ] *n попа́вший по́сле
кораблекруше́ния на необита́емый о́стров.*
caste [kɑːst] *n* ка́ста; **the ~ system** ка́стовая
систе́ма.
caster sugar ['kɑːstə-] *n (BRIT)* са́харная пу́дра.
casting vote ['kɑːstɪŋ-] *n (BRIT)* реша́ющий*
го́лос *(при ра́вном числе́ голосо́в "за" и
"про́тив")*.
cast iron *n* чугу́н* ♦ *adj:* ~~~ *(fig)* желе́зный.
castle ['kɑːsl] *n* за́мок*; *(fortified)* кре́пость *f*;
(CHESS) ладья́*, тура́.
cast-offs ['kɑːstɔfs] *npl* обно́ски *mpl.*
castor ['kɑːstə] *n (wheel)* ро́лик.
castor oil *n* касто́ровое ма́сло.
castrate [kæs'treɪt] *vt* кастри́ровать *(impf/perf).*
casual ['kæʒjul] *adj (meeting)* случа́йный*
(случа́ен); *(attitude)* небре́жный* (небре́жен);
(clothes) повседне́вный; **to do ~ work** де́лать
(impf) случа́йную рабо́ту; ~ **wear**
повседне́вная оде́жда.
casual labour *n* вре́менные рабо́тники *mpl.*
casually ['kæʒjulɪ] *adv (behave)* небре́жно;
(dress) повседне́вно; *(by chance)* случа́йно;
he was ~ dressed он был оде́т в повсе-
дне́вную оде́жду.
casualty ['kæʒjultɪ] *n (sb injured)*
пострада́вший(-ая) *m(f) adj*; *(sb killed, victim)*
же́ртва; *(MED: department)* травматоло́гия;
heavy casualties тяжёлые поте́ри *fpl.*
casualty ward *n (BRIT)* травматологи́ческое
отделе́ние.
cat [kæt] *n (pet)* ко́шка*; *(tomcat)* кот; **big ~s**
ко́шачьи *pl adj.*
catacombs ['kætəkuːmz] *npl* катако́мбы *fpl.*
catalogue ['kætəlɔg] *(US* **catalog)** *n* катало́г; *(of
events, faults)* пе́речень *m* ♦ *vt (books,
collection)* каталогизи́ровать *(impf/perf)*;
(events) перечисля́ть (перечи́слить *perf).*
catalyst ['kætəlɪst] *n (CHEM, fig)* катализа́тор.
catalytic converter [kætə'lɪtɪk kən'vɜːtə'] *n
(AUT)* катали́тический нейтрализа́тор.

catapult ['kætəpʌlt] *n (BRIT)* рога́тка*; *(MIL)*
катапу́льта ♦ *vi* катапульти́роваться *(impf/
perf)* ♦ *vt* катапульти́ровать *(impf/perf).*
cataract ['kætərækt] *n* катара́кта.
catarrh [kə'tɑː'] *n* ката́р.
catastrophe [kə'tæstrəfɪ] *n* катастро́фа.
catastrophic [kætə'strɔfɪk] *adj*
катастрофи́ческий*.
catcall ['kætkɔːl] *n* осви́стывание.
catch [kætʃ] *(pt, pp* **caught)** *vt* лови́ть* (пойма́ть
perf); *(bus etc)* сади́ться (сесть* *perf)* на +*acc*;
(breath) зата́ивать (затаи́ть *perf)*; *(attention)*
привлека́ть (привле́чь *perf)*; *(hit)* ударя́ть
(уда́рить *perf)*; *(hear)* ула́вливать (улови́ть*
perf); *(illness)* подхва́тывать (подхвати́ть*
perf); *(person)* застава́ть (заста́ть* *perf)* ♦ *vi
(become trapped)* застрева́ть (застря́ть *perf)*
♦ *n (of fish)* уло́в; *(criminal caught)*
заде́ржанный(-ая) *m(f) adj*; *(of ball)* захва́т;
(hidden problem) подво́х; *(of lock)* защёлка;
(game) пятна́шки *pl*; **to ~ sb's attention** *or* **eye**
привлека́ть (привле́чь* *perf)* чьё-н внима́ние;
to ~ sight of уви́деть* *(perf)*; **to ~ fire**
загоре́ться *(perf)*
► **catch on** *vi (grow popular)* прижива́ться
(прижи́ться* *perf)*; *(understand):* **to ~ on (to
sth)** понима́ть (поня́ть *perf)* (что-н)
► **catch out** *vt (BRIT: fig)* лови́ть* (пойма́ть *perf)*
► **catch up** *vi (fig)* нагоня́ть (нагна́ть* *perf)* ♦ *vt
(also:* ~ **up with)** догоня́ть (догна́ть* *perf).*
catching ['kætʃɪŋ] *adj (fig)* зарази́тельный*;
(MED) зара́зный*.
catchment area ['kætʃmənt-] *n (BRIT: of school
etc)* микрорайо́н; *(GEO)* бассе́йн.
catch phrase *n* мо́дное выраже́ние.
catch-22 ['kætʃtwɛntɪ'tuː] *n*: **it's a ~ situation**
э́то безвы́ходная ситуа́ция.
catchy ['kætʃɪ] *adj* легко́ запомина́ющийся.
catechism ['kætɪkɪzəm] *n* катехи́зис.
categoric(al) [kætɪ'gɔrɪk(l)] *adj*
категори́ческий*.
categorize ['kætɪgəraɪz] *vt (classify)*
классифици́ровать *(impf/perf).*
category ['kætɪgərɪ] *n* катего́рия.
cater ['keɪtə'] *vi (provide food):* **to ~ (for)**
организо́вывать (организова́ть *perf)*
пита́ние *(для* +*gen)*
► **cater for** *vt fus (BRIT: needs, tastes)*
удовлетворя́ть (удовлетвори́ть *perf)*;
(: readers, consumers) обслу́живать
(обслужи́ть* *perf).*
caterer ['keɪtərə'] *n* организа́тор пита́ния.
catering ['keɪtərɪŋ] *n (trade, business)*
обще́ственное пита́ние.
caterpillar ['kætəpɪlə'] *n* гу́сеница ♦ *cpd
(vehicle)* гу́сеничный.
caterpillar track *n* гу́сеница *(TEX)*
cat flap *n* коша́чий* лаз* *(в две́ри)*, коша́чья

две́рца.
cathedral [kə'θi:drəl] *n* собо́р.
cathode ['kæθəud] *n* като́д.
cathode-ray tube [kæθəud'reɪ-] *n*
электроннолучева́я тру́бка*.
Catholic ['kæθəlɪk] *adj* католи́ческий* ♦ *n*
като́лик(-и́чка).
catholic *adj* (*tastes, interests*) разно-
сторо́нний*.
CAT scanner *n abbr* (*MED*: = *computerized axial
tomography scanner*) аксиа́льный
компью́терный томо́граф.
Catseye® ['kæts'aɪ] *n* (*BRIT*: *AUT*) "коша́чий
глаз" (*вмонти́рованный в доро́гу
отража́тель све́та фар*).
catsup ['kætsəp] *n* (*US*) ке́тчуп.
cattle ['kætl] *npl* скот* *msg*.
catty ['kætɪ] *adj* ехи́дный*.
catwalk ['kætwɔ:k] *n* (*at fashion show*) помо́ст
or эстра́да (*для демонстра́ции моде́лей
оде́жды*).
Caucasian [kɔ:'keɪzɪən] *adj* кавка́зский ♦ *n*
кавка́зец*(-зка).
Caucasus ['kɔ:kəsəs] *n* Кавка́з.
caucus ['kɔ:kəs] *n* (*POL*: *group*) влия́тельная
группиро́вка внутри́ па́ртии; (: *US*)
предвы́борный ми́тинг сторо́нников па́ртии.
caught [kɔ:t] *pt, pp of* **catch**.
cauliflower ['kɔlɪflauə'] *n* цветна́я капу́ста.
cause [kɔ:z] *n* (*reason*) причи́на; (*aim*) де́ло* ♦
vt явля́ться (яви́ться* *perf*) причи́ной +*gen*;
there is no ~ for concern нет причи́н для
беспоко́йства; **to ~ sb trouble/harm**
причиня́ть (причини́ть *perf*) кому́-н
неприя́тности/вред; **to ~ sb to do** (*force*)
заставля́ть (заста́вить* *perf*) кого́-н +*infin*.
causeway ['kɔ:zweɪ] *n* доро́га (*проло́женная
че́рез то́пкое ме́сто*).
caustic ['kɔ:stɪk] *adj* каусти́ческий*; (*fig*)
е́дкий*.
cauterize ['kɔ:təraɪz] *vt* прижига́ть (прижечь*
perf).
caution ['kɔ:ʃən] *n* осторо́жность *f*; (*warning*)
предупрежде́ние, предостереже́ние ♦ *vt*
предупрежда́ть (предупреди́ть *perf*).
cautious ['kɔ:ʃəs] *adj* осторо́жный*
(осторо́жен).
cautiously ['kɔ:ʃəslɪ] *adv* осторо́жно.
cautiousness ['kɔ:ʃəsnɪs] *n* осторо́жность *f*.
cavalier [kævə'lɪə'] *adj* надме́нный*,
пренебрежи́тельный.
cavalry ['kævəlrɪ] *n* кавале́рия; (*mechanized*)
мотопехо́та.
cave [keɪv] *n* пеще́ра ♦ *vi*: **to go caving**
занима́ться (*impf*) спелеоло́гией
▶ **cave in** *vi* (*roof etc*) обва́ливаться
(обвали́ться *perf*); (*inf*: *give in*) сдава́ться*
(сда́ться* *perf*).
caveman ['keɪvmæn] *irreg n* пеще́рный
челове́к*.
cavern ['kævən] *n* пеще́ра.

caviar(e) ['kævɪɑ:'] *n* икра́*.
cavity ['kævɪtɪ] *n* по́лость* *f*; (*in tooth*) дупло́*.
cavity wall insulation *n* двойна́я стена́ с
изоля́цией.
cavort [kə'vɔ:t] *vi* скака́ть* (*impf*).
cayenne [keɪ'ɛn] *n* (*also*: ~ **pepper**) кра́сный
стручко́вый пе́рец.
CB *n abbr* (= *Citizens' Band (Radio)*) диапазо́н
часто́т *люби́тельской радиосвя́зи*; (*BRIT*: =
Companion of (the Order of) the Bath) кавале́р
о́рдена Ба́ни.
CBC *n abbr* = *Canadian Broadcasting
Corporation*.
CBE *n abbr* (*BRIT*: = *Companion of (the Order of)
the British Empire*) кавале́р о́рдена
Брита́нской Импе́рии.
CBI *n abbr* (= *Confederation of British Industries*)
Конфедера́ция брита́нской
промы́шленности.
CBS *n abbr* (*US*: = *Columbia Broadcasting
System*).
CC *abbr* (*BRIT*: = *county council*) ≈ сове́т
гра́фства.
cc *abbr* (= *cubic centimetre*) куби́ческий*
сантиме́тр; = **carbon copy**.
CCA *n abbr* (*US*: = *Circuit Court of Appeals*)
Окружно́й апелляцио́нный суд.
CCU *n abbr* (*US*: = *coronary care unit*) отделе́ние
интенси́вной терапи́и для больны́х с о́строй
серде́чной недоста́точностью.
CD *n abbr* (*BRIT*: = *Corps Diplomatique*)
дипко́рпус= *дипломати́ческий ко́рпус* ♦ *n
abbr* (*MIL*: *BRIT*: = *Civil Defence (Corps)*)
гражда́нская оборо́на; (: *US*: = *Civil Defense*)
гражда́нская оборо́на; = **compact disc**; ~
player прои́грыватель *m* для
компа́кт-ди́сков.
CDC *n abbr* (*US*) = *Center for Disease Control*.
CD-I *n abbr* (= *compact disc interactive*)
компа́ктный диск-интеракти́вный
(*устро́йство, позволя́ющее передава́ть
содержа́ние компа́ктного ди́ска на
телеэкра́н*).
Cdr. *abbr* (*MIL*) = **commander**.
CD-ROM *abbr* (= *compact disc read-only
memory*) па́мять, счи́тывающая
информа́цию с компа́кт-ди́ска.
CDT *abbr* (*US*) = *Central Daylight Time*.
cease [si:s] *vt* прекраща́ть (прекрати́ть* *perf*) ♦
vi прекраща́ться (прекрати́ться* *perf*).
cease-fire ['si:sfaɪə'] *n* прекраще́ние огня́.
ceaseless ['si:slɪs] *adj* непреры́вный*.
CED *n abbr* (*US*) = *Committee for Economic
Development*.
cedar ['si:də'] *n* кедр.
cede [si:d] *vt* уступа́ть (уступи́ть* *perf*).
cedilla [sɪ'dɪlə] *n* седи́ль *m* (*орфографи́ческий
знак*).
CEEB *n abbr* (*US*) = *College Entry Examination
Board*.
Ceefax ['si:fæks] *n* информацио́нная слу́жба

БиБиСи, осуществля́емая путём вы́вода на экра́н телеви́зора информа́ции, классифици́рованной по разли́чным направле́ниям.

ceilidh ['keɪlɪ] *n* ве́чер с наро́дной му́зыкой и та́нцами в Шотла́ндии и́ли Ирла́ндии.

ceiling ['si:lɪŋ] *n* (*also fig*) потоло́к*.

celebrate ['sɛlɪbreɪt] *vt* пра́здновать (отпра́здновать *perf*) ♦ *vi* весели́ться (повесели́ться *perf*); **to ~ mass** отправля́ть (*impf*) церко́вную слу́жбу.

celebrated ['sɛlɪbreɪtɪd] *adj* знамени́тый (знамени́т).

celebration [sɛlɪ'breɪʃən] *n* (*event*) пра́здник; (*of anniversary etc*) пра́зднование.

celebrity [sɪ'lɛbrɪtɪ] *n* знамени́тость *f*.

celeriac [sə'lɛrɪæk] *n* корнепло́д сельдере́я.

celery ['sɛlərɪ] *n* сельдере́й.

celestial [sɪ'lɛstɪəl] *adj* небе́сный.

celibacy ['sɛlɪbəsɪ] *n* сексуа́льное воздержа́ние; (*unmarried state*) безбра́чие.

cell [sɛl] *n* (*in prison*) ка́мера; (*in monastery*) ке́лья*; (*of revolutionaries etc*) яче́йка*; (*BIO*) кле́тка*; (*ELEC*) элеме́нт.

cellar ['sɛlə'] *n* подва́л; (*also:* **wine ~**) ви́нный по́греб*.

cellist ['tʃɛlɪst] *n* виолончели́ст(ка).

cello ['tʃɛləʊ] *n* виолонче́ль *f*.

cellophane ['sɛləfeɪn] *n* целлофа́н.

cellphone ['sɛlfəʊn] *n* портати́вный телефо́н.

cellular ['sɛljulə'] *adj* (*BIO*) кле́точный; (*fabrics*) се́тчатый.

celluloid ['sɛljulɔɪd] *n* целлуло́ид.

cellulose ['sɛljuləʊs] *n* клетча́тка, целлюло́за.

Celsius ['sɛlsɪəs] *adj:* **30 degrees ~** 30 гра́дусов по Це́льсию.

Celt [kɛlt] *n* кельт.

Celtic ['kɛltɪk] *adj* ке́льтский* ♦ *n* (*LING*) ке́льтский* язы́к*.

cement [sə'mɛnt] *n* цеме́нт; (*glue*) клей* ♦ *vt* (*also fig*) цементи́ровать (*impf/perf*); (*stick, glue*): **to ~ to** прикле́ивать (прикле́ить *perf*) *or* прикрепля́ть (прикрепи́ть* *perf*) к +*dat*.

cement mixer *n* бето́номеша́лка*.

cemetery ['sɛmɪtrɪ] *n* кла́дбище.

cenotaph ['sɛnətɑ:f] *n* па́мятник поги́бшим солда́там.

censor ['sɛnsə'] *n* це́нзор ♦ *vt* подверга́ть (подве́ргнуть* *perf*) цензу́ре.

censorship ['sɛnsəʃɪp] *n* цензу́ра.

censure ['sɛnʃə'] *vt* осужда́ть (осуди́ть* *perf*), порица́ть (*impf*) ♦ *n* осужде́ние, порица́ние.

census ['sɛnsəs] *n* (*of population*) пе́репись *f*.

cent [sɛnt] *n* (*US etc: coin*) цент; *see also* **per**.

centenary [sɛn'ti:nərɪ] *n* столе́тие.

centennial [sɛn'tɛnɪəl] *n* (*US*) столе́тие.

center *etc n* (*US*) = **centre** *etc*.

centigrade ['sɛntɪgreɪd] *adj:* **30 degrees ~** 30

гра́дусов по Це́льсию.

centilitre ['sɛntɪli:tə'] (*US* **centiliter**) *n* центили́тр.

centimetre ['sɛntɪmi:tə'] (*US* **centimeter**) *n* сантиме́тр.

centipede ['sɛntɪpi:d] *n* многоно́жка*.

central ['sɛntrəl] *adj* центра́льный*; **this flat is very ~** э́та кварти́ра располо́жена бли́зко к це́нтру го́рода.

Central African Republic *n* Центра́льно-Африка́нская респу́блика.

Central America *n* Центра́льная Аме́рика.

central heating *n* центра́льное отопле́ние.

centralize ['sɛntrəlaɪz] *vt* централизова́ть (*impf/perf*).

central processing unit *n* центра́льный проце́ссор.

central reservation *n* (*BRIT: AUT*) раздели́тельная полоса́.

centre ['sɛntə'] (*US* **center**) *n* центр ♦ *vt* (*PHOT, TYP*) центри́ровать (*impf/perf*); (*SPORT: ball*) подава́ть* (пода́ть* *perf*) в центр; (*concentrate on*): **to ~ (on)** сосредото́чиваться (сосредото́читься *perf*) (на +*prp*); **to ~ sth on** сосредото́чивать (сосредото́чить *perf*) что-н на +*acc*.

centrefold ['sɛntəfəʊld] (*US* **centerfold**) *n* центра́льная вкла́дка*.

centre forward *n* (*SPORT*) центра́льный напада́ющий* *m adj*, центр-фо́рвард.

centre half *n* (*SPORT*) центра́льный полузащи́тник.

centrepiece ['sɛntəpi:s] (*US* **centerpiece**) *n* декорати́вный предме́т, вы́ставленный посереди́не стола́, по́лки итд; (*fig*) гла́вное украше́ние.

centre spread *n* (*BRIT: PRESS*) разворо́т.

centre-stage [sɛntə'steɪdʒ] *n* центр сце́ны.

centrifugal [sɛn'trɪfjugl] *adj* (*PHYS*) центробе́жный.

centrifuge ['sɛntrɪfju:ʒ] *n* центрифу́га.

century ['sɛntjurɪ] *n* век*; (*CRICKET*) сто очко́в; **twentieth ~** двадца́тый век; **in the twentieth ~** в двадца́том ве́ке.

CEO *n abbr* (*US:* = chief executive officer) гла́вный администра́тор.

ceramic [sɪ'ræmɪk] *adj* керами́ческий*.

ceramics [sɪ'ræmɪks] *npl* кера́мика *fsg*.

cereal ['si:rɪəl] *n* (*plant, crop*): **~s** зерновы́е *pl adj*; (*also:* **breakfast ~**) хло́пья *pl* к за́втраку.

cerebral ['sɛrɪbrəl] *adj* (*MED*) мозгово́й, церебра́льный; (*intellectual*) умозри́тельный* (умозри́телен); **~ palsy** церебра́льный парали́ч.

ceremonial [sɛrɪ'məʊnɪəl] *n* церемониа́л ♦ *adj* обря́довый.

ceremony ['sɛrɪmənɪ] *n* церемо́ния; (*behaviour*) церемо́нии *fpl*; **with ~** со все́ми

формáльностями; **to stand on** ~ настáивать
(настоя́ть* *perf*) на соблюде́нии
формáльностей.
cert [sə:t] *n* (*BRIT*: *inf*): **it's a dead** ~ э́то де́ло
ве́рное.
certain ['sə:tən] *adj* (*sure*): **I'm** ~ **(that)** я уве́рен
(что); (*particular*): ~ **days** определённые дни;
(*some*): **a** ~ **pleasure** не́которое
удово́льствие; **it's** ~ **(that)** несомне́нно
(что); **in** ~ **circumstances** при определённых
обстоя́тельствах; **a** ~ **Mr Smith** не́кий
Ми́стер Смит; **to make** ~ **of/that**
удостоверя́ться (удостове́риться *perf*) в
+*prp*/что; **for** ~ наверняка́.
certainly ['sə:tənlɪ] *adv* (*undoubtedly*)
несомне́нно; (*of course*) коне́чно.
certainty ['sə:təntɪ] *n* (*assurance*) уве́ренность
f; (*inevitability*) несомне́нность *f*.
certificate [sə'tɪfɪkɪt] *n* (*doctor's etc*) спрáвка;
(*diploma*) дипло́м; (*birth* ~ свиде́тельство
рожде́нии; **marriage** ~ свиде́тельство о
заключе́нии брáка.
certified letter ['sə:tɪfaɪd-] *n* (*US*)
гаранти́рованное письмо́.
certified mail *n* (*US*) гаранти́рованная по́чта.
certified public accountant *n* (*US*) бухгáлтер
высшей квалификáции.
certify ['sə:tɪfaɪ] *vt* (*fact*) удостоверя́ть
(удостове́рить *perf*); (*after studies*) выдавáть*
(вы́дать* *perf*) дипло́м +*dat*; (*also:* ~ **insane**)
признавáть* (призна́ть* *perf*)
душевнобольны́м(-ой); **he is a certified
lawyer** он дипломи́рованный юри́ст.
cervical ['sə:vɪkl] *adj*: ~ **cancer** рак ше́йки
мáтки; ~ **smear** мазо́к* с ше́йки мáтки.
cervix ['sə:vɪks] *n* ше́йка мáтки.
Cesarean [si:'zɛərɪən] *adj*, *n* (*US*) = **Caesarean**.
cessation [sə'seɪʃn] *n* прекращéние.
cesspit ['sɛspɪt] *n* выгребнáя я́ма.
CET *abbr* (= *Central European Time*)
центральноевропе́йское вре́мя* *nt*.
Ceylon [sɪ'lɔn] *n* Цейло́н.
cf. *abbr* = **compare**.
c/f *abbr* (*COMM*: = *carried forward*) перенесено́
на сле́дующую страни́цу.
CFC *n abbr* (= *chlorofluorocarbon*) хлор-
фтороуглеро́д.
CG *n abbr* (*US*) = **coastguard**.
cg *abbr* (= *centigram*) сантигрáмм.
CH *n abbr* (*BRIT*: = *Companion of Honour*)
кавалéр óрдена.
ch. *abbr* (= *chapter*) гл.= *глава́*.
c.h. *abbr* (*BRIT*) = **central heating**.
Chad [tʃæd] *n* Чад.
chafe [tʃeɪf] *vt* (*rub*) натирáть (натере́ть *perf*) ◆
vi (*fig*): **to** ~ **at/under** раздражáться (*impf*)
из-за +*gen*.
chaffinch ['tʃæfɪntʃ] *n* зя́блик.
chagrin ['ʃægrɪn] *n* (*annoyance*) досáда;
(*disappointment*) огорчéние.
chain [tʃeɪn] *n* (*also fig*) цепь* *f*; (*decorative, on*

bicycle) цепо́чка*; (*of shops, hotels*) сеть* *f*; (*of
events, ideas*) верени́ца ◆ *vt* (*also:* ~ **up**:
person) прико́вывать (прикова́ть *perf*); (*dog*)
сажáть (посади́ть* *perf*) на цепь; **a** ~ **of
mountains** го́рная цепь.
chain reaction *n* цепнáя реáкция.
chain-smoke ['tʃeɪnsməuk] *vi* кури́ть* (*impf*)
одну́ сигаре́ту за друго́й.
chain store *n* филиáл (*магази́на*).
chair [tʃɛə'] *n* стул*; (*also:* **armchair**) кре́сло*;
(*of university*) кáфедра; (*of meeting: also:*
~**person**) председáтель *m* ◆ *vt*
председáтельствовать (*impf*) на +*prp*; **the** ~
(*US: also:* **the electric** ~) электри́ческий*
стул*; **to take the** ~ председáтельствовать
(*impf*).
chair lift *n* канáтный подъёмник.
chairman ['tʃɛəmən] *irreg n* председáтель *m*;
(*BRIT: of company*) президéнт.
chairperson ['tʃɛəpə:sn] *n* председáтель *m*.
chairwoman ['tʃɛəwumən] *irreg n*
председáтель *m*.
chalet ['ʃæleɪ] *n* ≈ котте́дж.
chalice ['tʃælɪs] *n* (*REL*) поти́р.
chalk [tʃɔ:k] *n* мел*
► **chalk up** *vt* (*fig: success etc*) заноси́ть*
(занести́* *perf*) в спи́сок свои́х достижéний.
challenge ['tʃælɪndʒ] *n* вы́зов; (*challenging
task*) испытáние ◆ *vt* (*rival: also SPORT*)
бросáть (бро́сить* *perf*) вы́зов +*dat*;
(*authority, right etc*) оспáривать (оспо́рить
perf); **to** ~ **sb to sth** вызывáть (вы́звать* *perf*)
кого́-н на что-н.
challenger ['tʃælɪndʒə'] *n* (*in sport*)
претендéнт(ка).
challenging ['tʃælɪndʒɪŋ] *adj* (*task*) трýдный*
(трýден); (*tone, look*) вызывáющий*; **this
work is very** ~ э́та рабо́та трéбует большо́й
отдáчи.
chamber ['tʃeɪmbə'] *n* (*room*) кáмера; (*POL*)
палáта; (*BRIT: LAW: usu pl*) адвокáтская
конто́ра; ~ **of commerce** Торго́вая Палáта.
chambermaid ['tʃeɪmbəmeɪd] *n* го́рничная *f*
adj.
chamber music *n* кáмерная мýзыка.
chamber pot *n* ночно́й горшо́к*.
chameleon [kə'mi:lɪən] *n* хамелео́н.
chamois ['ʃæmwɑ:] *n* (*ZOOL*) сéрна; (*also:* ~
leather) зáмша.
champagne [ʃæm'peɪn] *n* шампáнское *nt adj*.
champers ['ʃæmpəz] *n* (*inf*) шампáнское *nt adj*.
champion ['tʃæmpɪən] *n* (*SPORT*) чемпио́н; (*of
cause*) побо́рник(-ица); (*of person*)
защи́тник(-ица) ◆ *vt* защищáть (защити́ть*
perf).
championship ['tʃæmpɪənʃɪp] *n* (*contest*)
чемпионáт; (*title*) звáние чемпио́на.
chance [tʃɑ:ns] *n* (*hope, possibility*) шанс;
(*opportunity*) возмо́жность *f*; (*risk*) риск ◆ *vt*
(*risk*) рискова́ть (*impf*) +*instr* ◆ *adj* случáйный;
the ~**s are that** ... все шáнсы за то, что ...;

there is little ~ of his coming маловероя́тно, что он придёт; **to take a ~** рискну́ть *(perf)*; **by ~** случа́йно; **to leave to ~** оставля́ть (оста́вить* *perf)* на во́лю слу́чая; **it's the ~ of a lifetime** така́я возмо́жность представля́ется раз в жи́зни; **to ~ it** рискну́ть *(perf)*; **to ~ to overhear/see** *(happen)* случа́йно подслу́шать *(perf)*/уви́деть *(perf)*
▶ **chance (up)on** *vt fus* случа́йно наткну́ться *(perf)* на +*acc*.

chancel ['tʃɑːnsəl] *n* алта́рная часть *f*.

chancellor ['tʃɑːnsələ'] *n* (*POL*) ка́нцлер; (*BRIT: of university*) почётный ре́ктор (*номина́льный пост*).

Chancellor of the Exchequer *n* (*BRIT*) ка́нцлер казначе́йства (*мини́стр фина́нсов*).

chancy ['tʃɑːnsɪ] *adj* риско́ванный (риско́ван).

chandelier [ʃændə'lɪə'] *n* лю́стра.

change [tʃeɪndʒ] *vt* меня́ть (поменя́ть *perf*); (*wheel, bulb etc*) заменя́ть (замени́ть* *perf*); (*job, address*) сменя́ть (смени́ть* *perf*); (*money: to different currency*) обме́нивать (обменя́ть *perf*); (: *for smaller notes or coins*) разме́нивать (разменя́ть *perf*) ♦ *vi* (*alter*) меня́ться (*impf*), изменя́ться (измени́ться* *perf*); (*one's clothes*) переодева́ться (переоде́ться* *perf*); (*change trains, buses*) де́лать (сде́лать *perf*) переса́дку ♦ *n* (*alteration*) измене́ние; (*difference*) переме́на; (*replacement*) сме́на; (*coins: also: small or* **loose ~**) ме́лочь *f*, (*money returned*) сда́ча; **to ~ sb into** превраща́ть (преврати́ть* *perf*) кого́-н в +*acc*; **to ~ one's mind** переду́мывать (переду́мать *perf*); **to ~ gear** (*AUT*) переключа́ть (переключи́ть *perf*) ско́рость; **to ~ a baby's nappy** перепелёнывать (перепелена́ть *perf*) ребёнка; **to ~ into** (*be transformed*) превраща́ться (преврати́ться* *perf*) в +*acc*; **a ~ of clothes** сме́на оде́жды; **to give sb ~ for** *or* **of ten pounds** дава́ть* (дать* *perf*) кому́-н сда́чу с десяти́ фу́нтов; **keep the ~** сда́чи не на́до; **for a ~** для разнообра́зия.

changeable ['tʃeɪndʒəbl] *adj* (*weather, mood*) изме́нчивый (изме́нчив); (*person*) непостоя́нный* (непостоя́нен).

change machine *n* разме́нный автома́т.

changeover ['tʃeɪndʒəuvə'] *n*: **~ (to)** (*to new system*) перехо́д (к +*dat*).

changing ['tʃeɪndʒɪŋ] *adj* (*world*) изменя́ющийся; (*colours*) меня́ющийся.

changing room *n* (*BRIT: in shop*) приме́рочная *f adj*; (: *SPORT*) раздева́лка*.

channel ['tʃænl] *n* кана́л; (*for shipping*) тра́сса; (*groove*) жёлоб* ♦ *vt*: **to ~ into** (*money, interest*) направля́ть (напра́вить* *perf*) на +*acc*; **through the usual ~s** че́рез обы́чные кана́лы; **~s of communication** кана́лы свя́зи; **green/red ~** зелёный/кра́сный кана́л (*при*

тамо́женном контро́ле); **the (English) C~** Ла-Ма́нш; **the C~ Islands** Норма́ндские острова́ *mpl*.

Channel Tunnel *n* тунне́ль *m* под Ла-Ма́ншем.

chant [tʃɑːnt] *n* (*of crowd, fans etc*) сканди́рование; (*REL: song*) пе́ние ♦ *vti* (*shout*) сканди́ровать (*impf*); **the demonstrators ~ed their disapproval** демонстра́нты хо́ром выража́ли неодобре́ние.

chaos ['keɪɔs] *n* ха́ос.

chaos theory *n*: **the ~ ~** тео́рия ха́оса.

chaotic [keɪ'ɔtɪk] *adj* (*mess, situation*) хаоти́чный* (хаоти́чен).

chap [tʃæp] *n* (*BRIT: inf*) па́рень* *m*; (*term of address*): **old ~** старина́ *m*, стари́к.

chapel ['tʃæpl] *n* (*in church*) приде́л; (*in hospital, prison, school etc*) це́рковь* *f*; (*BRIT: also: non-conformist ~*) протеста́нтская нон-конформи́стская це́рковь*; (: *of trade union*) отделе́ние профсою́за рабо́тников изда́тельства.

chaperone ['ʃæpərəun] *n* (*for woman*) компаньо́нка ♦ *vt* сопровожда́ть (сопроводи́ть* *perf*).

chaplain ['tʃæplɪn] *n* капелла́н.

chapped [tʃæpt] *adj* (*skin, lips etc*) потре́скавшийся.

chapter ['tʃæptə'] *n* (*of book*) глава́*; (*of life, history*) страни́ца; **a ~ of accidents** череда́ неуда́ч.

char [tʃɑː'] *vt* (*burn*) обу́гливать (обу́глить *perf*) ♦ *vi* (*BRIT*) рабо́тать (*impf*) убо́рщицей ♦ *n* (*BRIT*) = **charlady**.

character ['kærɪktə'] *n* (*personality*) ли́чность *f*; (*nature, strength of character*) хара́ктер; (*in novel, film*) персона́ж; (*eccentric*) оригина́л; (*letter, symbol*) знак; (: *COMPUT*) си́мвол; **a person of good ~** досто́йный челове́к.

character code *n* (*COMPUT*) код си́мвола.

characteristic ['kærɪktə'rɪstɪk] *n* характе́рная черта́ ♦ *adj*: **~ (of)** характе́рный (характе́рен) (для +*gen*); **it is ~ of him** э́то характе́рно для него́.

characterize ['kærɪktəraɪz] *vt* (*typify*) характеризова́ть (*impf/perf*); (*describe*): **to ~ (as)** характеризова́ть* (*impf/perf*) (как); **to be ~d by** характеризова́ться (*impf*) +*instr*.

charade [ʃə'rɑːd] *n* шара́да; (*fig*) коме́дия.

charcoal ['tʃɑːkəul] *n* (*fuel*) древе́сный у́голь* *m*; (*for drawing*) у́голь.

charge [tʃɑːdʒ] *n* (*fee*) пла́та; (*LAW: accusation*) обвине́ние; (*responsibility*) отве́тственность *f*; (*of gun, battery*) заря́д; (*MIL: attack*) ата́ка ♦ *vi* (*also MIL*) атакова́ть (*impf/perf*); (*rush*) кида́ться (ки́нуться *perf*), броса́ться (бро́ситься *perf*) ♦ *vt* (*battery, gun*) заряжа́ть

---

* marks translations which have irregular inflections. The Russian-English side of the dictionary gives inflectional information.

(заряди́ть* *perf*); (*LAW: accuse*): **to ~ sb with** обвиня́ть (обвини́ть *perf*) кого́-н в +*prp*; (*entrust*) поруча́ть (поручи́ть* *perf*) кому́-н +*acc*; **~s** *npl* (*bank charges*) де́нежный сбор *msg*; (*telephone charges*) телефо́нный тари́ф *msg*; **labour ~s** сто́имость *fsg* рабо́чей си́лы; **to reverse the ~s** (*TEL*) звони́ть (*impf*) по колле́кту; **is there a ~?** за э́то ну́жно плати́ть?; **at no extra ~** без дополни́тельной опла́ты; **free of ~** беспла́тно; **to take ~ of** (*child*) брать* (взять* *perf*) на попече́ние; (*company*) брать* (взять* *perf*) на себя́ руково́дство +*instr*; **to be in ~ of** отвеча́ть (*impf*) за +*acc*; **who's in ~ here?** кто здесь гла́вный?; **to ~ (sb) (for)** (*demand fee*) проси́ть* (попроси́ть* *perf*) (у кого́-н) пла́ту (за +*acc*); **they ~d us £10 for the meal** с нас взя́ли £10 за еду́; **how much do you ~ for?** ско́лько Вы про́сите за +*acc*?; **to ~ an expense (up) to sb's account** переводи́ть* (перевести́* *perf*) расхо́ды на чей-н счёт.

charge account *n* креди́т по откры́тому счёту.

charge card *n* креди́тная ка́рточка* (*определённого магази́на*).

chargé d'affaires ['ʃɑ:ʒeɪ dæ'feə] *n* пове́ренный* *m adj* в дела́х.

charge hand *n* (*BRIT*) ма́стер* (*на произво́дстве*).

charger ['tʃɑ:dʒə'] *n* (*also: battery ~*) заря́дное устро́йство; (*warhorse*) боево́й конь *m*.

chariot ['tʃærɪət] *n* колесни́ца.

charisma [kæ'rɪsmə] *n* обая́ние.

charitable ['tʃærɪtəbl] *adj* (*organization*) благотвори́тельный; (*person*) милосе́рдный* (милосе́рден).

charity ['tʃærɪtɪ] *n* (*organization*) благотвори́тельная организа́ция; (*kindness*) милосе́рдие; (*money, gifts*) ми́лостыня.

charlady ['tʃɑ:leɪdɪ] *n* (*BRIT*) убо́рщица.

charlatan ['ʃɑ:lətən] *n* шарлата́н.

charm [tʃɑ:m] *n* (*attractiveness*) обая́ние, очарова́ние; (*spell*) заклина́ние; (*talisman*) амуле́т; (*on bracelet etc*) брело́к ♦ *vt* (*please, delight*) очаро́вывать (очарова́ть* *perf*).

charm bracelet *n* брасле́т с брелка́ми.

charming ['tʃɑ:mɪŋ] *adj* очарова́тельный* (очарова́телен).

chart [tʃɑ:t] *n* (*graph, diagram*) гра́фик; (*NAUT*) навигацио́нная ка́рта; (*ASTRONOMY*) ка́рта звёздного не́ба; (*weather chart*) синопти́ческая ка́рта ♦ *vt* (*put on map*) наноси́ть* (нанести́* *perf*) на ка́рту; (*keep track of*) фикси́ровать (*impf*); **~s** *npl* (*hit parade*) хит-пара́д *msg*; **to be in the ~s** (*record*) быть в спи́ске наибо́лее популя́рных ди́сков.

charter ['tʃɑ:tə'] *vt* (*plane, ship etc*) фрахтова́ть (зафрахтова́ть* *perf*) ♦ *n* (*of company*) уста́в; (*document, constitution*) ха́ртия; **on ~** (*plane,*

train etc) по ча́ртеру.

chartered accountant ['tʃɑ:təd-] *n* (*BRIT*) бухга́лтер вы́сшей квалифика́ции.

charter flight *n* ча́ртерный рейс.

charwoman ['tʃɑ:wumən] *irreg n* = **charlady**.

chary ['tʃɛərɪ] *adj*: **to be ~ of** остерега́ться (*impf*) +*gen*.

chase [tʃeɪs] *vt* (*pursue: also fig*) гна́ться*/ гоня́ться (*impf*) за +*instr* ♦ *n* пого́ня; **to ~ away** *or* **off** прогоня́ть (прогна́ть* *perf*)
▶ **chase down** *vt* (*US*) = **chase up**
▶ **chase up** *vt* (*BRIT: information*) разы́скивать (разыска́ть* *perf*); (: *person: remind*) напомина́ть (напо́мнить *perf*) +*dat*.

chasm ['kæzəm] *n* (*GEO*) уще́лье; (*between people*) про́пасть* *f*.

chassis ['ʃæsɪ] *n* шасси́ *nt ind*.

chaste [tʃeɪst] *adj* (*person, relationship etc*) целому́дренный*.

chastened ['tʃeɪsnd] *adj* присты́женный (присты́жен).

chastening ['tʃeɪsnɪŋ] *adj* (*sobering*) отрезвля́ющий.

chastise [tʃæs'taɪz] *vt* отчи́тывать (отчита́ть *perf*).

chastity ['tʃæstɪtɪ] *n* целому́дрие.

chat [tʃæt] *vi* болта́ть (поболта́ть *perf*) ♦ *n* бесе́да; **idle ~** болтовня́
▶ **chat up** *vt* (*BRIT: inf*) заи́грывать (*impf*) с +*instr*.

chatline ['tʃætlaɪn] *n* телефо́нная слу́жба, предоставля́ющая собесе́дника.

chat show *n* (*BRIT*) ≈ шо́у с уча́стием знамени́тостей.

chattel ['tʃætl] *n see* **goods**.

chatter ['tʃætə'] *vi* (*person, monkey, parrot*) треща́ть (*impf*); (*magpie*) стрекота́ть* (*impf*); (*teeth*) стуча́ть (*impf*) ♦ *n* (*of people*) болтовня́; (*of birds, animals*) трескотня́; **my teeth are ~ing** я стучу́ зуба́ми.

chatterbox ['tʃætəbɔks] *n* (*inf*) трещо́тка.

chattering classes ['tʃætərɪŋ 'klɑ:sɪz] *npl*: **the ~** ~ псевдоинтеллиге́нция, лю́бящая обсужда́ть совреме́нные полити́ческие и обще́ственные пробле́мы.

chatty ['tʃætɪ] *adj* (*letter*) живо́й; (*person*) говорли́вый (говорли́в).

chauffeur ['ʃəufə'] *n* (персона́льный) шофёр.

chauvinism ['ʃəuvɪnɪzəm] *n* (*also: male ~*) мужско́й шовини́зм; (*nationalism*) шовини́зм.

chauvinist ['ʃəuvɪnɪst] *n* (*also: male ~*) шовини́ст.

chauvinistic [ʃəuvɪ'nɪstɪk] *adj* (*ideas, views*) шовинисти́ческий*.

ChE *abbr* = **chemical engineer**.

cheap [tʃi:p] *adj* (*also fig*) дешёвый*; (*reduced*) со ски́дкой ♦ *adv*: **to buy/sell sth ~** дёшево покупа́ть (купи́ть* *perf*)/продава́ть* (прода́ть* *perf*) что-н.

cheapen ['tʃi:pn] *vt* (*person*) унижа́ть

(уни́зить* *perf*).
cheaper ['tʃiːpə'] *adj* деше́вле.
cheaply ['tʃiːplɪ] *adv* дёшево.
cheap money *n*: ~ ~ **policy** *ситуа́ция, когда́ вла́сти стремя́тся стимули́ровать экономи́ческий рост с по́мощью ни́зких ста́вок.*
cheat [tʃiːt] *vi* (*at cards*) жу́льничать (*impf*); (*in exam*) спи́сывать (списа́ть* *perf*) ♦ *n* (*person*) жу́лик ♦ *vt*: **to ~ sb** (*out of £10*) наду́ть (*perf*) кого́-н (на £10); **to ~ on sb** (*inf*: *husband, wife etc*) изменя́ть (измени́ть* *perf*) кому́-н.
cheating ['tʃiːtɪŋ] *n* жу́льничество, надува́тельство.
check [tʃɛk] *vt* проверя́ть (прове́рить *perf*); (*halt*) приостана́вливать (приостанови́ть* *perf*); (*restrain*) сде́рживать (сдержа́ть* *perf*); (*US*: *items on list*) отмеча́ть (отме́тить* *perf*) ♦ *vi* проверя́ть (прове́рить *perf*) ♦ *n* (*inspection*) прове́рка*; (*US*: *bill*) счёт*; (: *COMM*) = **cheque**; (*pattern*: *usu pl*) кле́тка* ♦ *adj* (*cloth, skirt*) кле́тчатый; **to ~ with sb** посове́товаться (*perf*) с кем-н; **to keep a ~ on sb/sth** контроли́ровать (*impf*) кого́-н/что-н; **to act as a ~ on** (*curb*) явля́ться (яви́ться* *perf*) ме́рой контро́ля +*gen*
▶ **check in** *vi* (*at hotel, airport*) регистри́роваться (зарегистри́роваться *perf*) ♦ *vt* (*luggage*) сдава́ть (сдать* *perf*)
▶ **check off** *vt* (*items on list etc*) отмеча́ть (отме́тить* *perf*)
▶ **check out** *vi* (*of hotel*) выпи́сываться (вы́писаться* *perf*) ♦ *vt* (*investigate*: *story*) проверя́ть (прове́рить *perf*); (: *building*) прочёсывать (прочеса́ть *perf*)
▶ **check up** *vi*: **to ~ up on sb/sth** наводи́ть (навести́* *perf*) спра́вки о ком-н/чём-н.
checkered ['tʃɛkəd] *adj* (*US*) = **chequered**.
checkers ['tʃɛkəz] *npl* (*US*: *draughts*) ша́шки *pl*.
check guarantee card *n* (*US*) = **cheque card**.
check-in (desk) ['tʃɛkɪn-] *n* (*at airport*) сто́йка регистра́ции.
checking account ['tʃɛkɪŋ-] *n* (*US*: *current account*) теку́щий* счёт*.
check list *n* контро́льный спи́сок*.
checkmate ['tʃɛkmeɪt] *n* (*CHESS*) мат.
checkout ['tʃɛkaut] *n* (*in shop*) контро́ль *m*, ка́сса.
checkpoint ['tʃɛkpɔɪnt] *n* (*on border*) контро́льно-пропускно́й пункт.
checkroom ['tʃɛkrum] *n* (*US*) ка́мера хране́ния.
checkup ['tʃɛkʌp] *n* (*MED*) осмо́тр.
cheek [tʃiːk] *n* (*ANAT*) щека́*; (*impudence*) на́глость *f*; (*nerve*) де́рзость *f*.
cheekbone ['tʃiːkbəun] *n* скула́*.
cheeky ['tʃiːkɪ] *adj* наха́льный* (наха́лен), на́глый (нагл).

cheep [tʃiːp] *vi* пища́ть* (*impf*) ♦ *n* писк.
cheer [tʃɪə'] *vt* (*encourage*) приве́тствовать (поприве́тствовать *perf*); (*gladden*) ободря́ть (ободри́ть *perf*) ♦ *vi* одобри́тельно восклица́ть (*impf*); ~**s** *npl* (*of crowd*: *of welcome*) приве́тственные во́згласы *mpl*; (: *of approval*) одобри́тельные во́згласы *mpl*; ~**s!** (*toast*) (за) Ва́ше здоро́вье!
▶ **cheer on** *vt* ободря́ть (ободри́ть *perf*)
▶ **cheer up** *vi* развесели́ться (*perf*), повеселе́ть (*perf*) ♦ *vt* (*person*) развесели́ть (*perf*); ~ **up!** не грусти́(те)!
cheerful ['tʃɪəful] *adj* весёлый* (ве́сел).
cheerfulness ['tʃɪəfulnɪs] *n* весёлость *f*.
cheerio ['tʃɪərɪ'əu] *excl* (*BRIT*) пока́.
cheerleader ['tʃiːəliːdə'] *n* заводи́ла (*де́вушка, подстрека́ющая боле́льщиков в спорти́вных состяза́ниях*).
cheerless ['tʃɪəlɪs] *adj* уны́лый* (уны́л).
cheese [tʃiːz] *n* сыр*.
cheeseboard ['tʃiːzbɔːd] *n* доска́* для сы́ра; (*with cheese on it*) доска́* с сы́ром.
cheeseburger ['tʃiːzbɔːgə'] *n* чи́збургер.
cheesecake ['tʃiːzkeɪk] *n* ≈ творо́жный кекс.
cheetah ['tʃiːtə] *n* гепа́рд.
chef [ʃɛf] *n* шеф-по́вар*.
chemical ['kɛmɪkl] *adj* хими́ческий* ♦ *n* химика́т; (*in laboratory*) реакти́в.
chemical engineering *n* хими́ческая техноло́гия.
chemist ['kɛmɪst] *n* (*BRIT*: *pharmacist*) фармаце́вт; (*scientist*) хи́мик.
chemistry ['kɛmɪstrɪ] *n* хи́мия.
chemist's (shop) ['kɛmɪsts-] *n* (*BRIT*) апте́ка.
chemotherapy [kiːməu'θɛrəpɪ] *n* химотерапи́я.
cheque [tʃɛk] *n* (*BRIT*) чек; **to pay by** ~ плати́ть* (заплати́ть* *perf*) че́ком.
chequebook ['tʃɛkbuk] *n* (*BRIT*) че́ковая кни́жка*.
cheque card *n* (*BRIT*) ка́рточка, подтвержда́ющая платёжеспосо́бность владе́льца.
chequered ['tʃɛkəd] (*US* **checkered**) *adj* (*fig*: *career*) пёстрый.
cherish ['tʃɛrɪʃ] *vt* леле́ять (взлеле́ять *perf*).
cheroot [ʃə'ruːt] *n* сига́ра (*с уплощёнными конца́ми*).
cherry ['tʃɛrɪ] *n* (*fruit, tree*) чере́шня*; (: *sour variety*) ви́шня.
chervil ['tʃə:vɪl] *n* купы́рь *m*.
Ches *abbr* (*BRIT*: *POST*) = **Cheshire**.
chess [tʃɛs] *n* ша́хматы *pl*.
chessboard ['tʃɛsbɔːd] *n* ша́хматная доска́*.
chessman ['tʃɛsmən] *irreg n* ша́хматная фигу́ра.
chess player *n* ша́хматист.
chest [tʃɛst] *n* (*ANAT*) грудь* *f*; (*box*) сунду́к*;

---

* marks translations which have irregular inflections. The Russian-English side of the dictionary gives inflectional information.

I'm glad I got it off my ~ (*inf*) я рад, что облегчи́л ду́шу.
chest measurement *n* окру́жность *f* груди́.
chestnut ['tʃɛsnʌt] *n* кашта́н ◆ *adj* (*hair*) кашта́новый; (*horse*) гнедо́й.
chest of drawers *n* комо́д.
chesty ['tʃæstɪ] *adj* грудно́й.
chew [tʃuː] *vt* (*food*) жева́ть (*impf*); (*nails*) грызть* (*impf*); (*a hole*) прогрыза́ть (прогры́зть* *perf*).
chewing gum ['tʃuːɪŋ-] *n* жева́тельная рези́нка.
chic [ʃiːk] *adj* шика́рный*, элега́нтный* (элега́нтен).
Chicago [ʃɪ'kɑːgəu] *n* Чика́го *m ind*.
chick [tʃɪk] *n* (*of hen*) цыплёнок; (*of wild bird*) птене́ц*; (*inf: girl*) пта́шка.
chicken ['tʃɪkɪn] *n* (*bird, meat*) ку́рица; (*inf: coward*) труси́шка *m/f*
▸ **chicken out** *vi* (*inf*) тру́сить (стру́сить* *perf*);
he ~ed out of going он стру́сил и не пошёл.
chicken feed *n* (*fig*) гроши́ *mpl*.
chickenpox ['tʃɪkɪnpɔks] *n* ветря́нка.
chickpeas ['tʃɪkpiːz] *npl* туре́цкий горо́х* *msg*.
chicory ['tʃɪkərɪ] *n* цико́рий.
chide [tʃaɪd] *vt* (*person*): **to ~ sb (for)** брани́ть (вы́бранить *perf*) кого́-н (за +*acc*).
chief [tʃiːf] *n* (*of tribe*) вождь* *m*; (*of organization, department*) нача́льник ◆ *adj* гла́вный, основно́й.
chief constable *n* (*BRIT*) нача́льник поли́ции.
chief executive (*US* **chief executive officer**) *n* гла́вный исполни́тельный дире́ктор.
chiefly ['tʃiːflɪ] *adv* гла́вным о́бразом.
Chief of Staff *n* (*MIL*) нача́льник шта́ба.
chiffon ['ʃɪfɔn] *n* шифо́н.
chilblain ['tʃɪlbleɪn] *n* обморо́женное ме́сто* (на па́льцах).
child [tʃaɪld] (*pl* **~ren**) *n* ребёнок*; (*fig*): **~ (of)** дитя́ (+*gen*); **do you have any ~ren?** у Вас есть де́ти?
child benefit *n* (*BRIT*) *де́нежное посо́бие на ребёнка*.
childbirth ['tʃaɪldbəːθ] *n* ро́ды *pl*.
childhood ['tʃaɪldhud] *n* де́тство.
childish ['tʃaɪldɪʃ] *adj* (*games, attitude*) ребя́ческий*; (*person*) ребя́чливый (ребя́лчив).
childless ['tʃaɪldlɪs] *adj* безде́тный* (безде́тен).
childlike ['tʃaɪldlaɪk] *adj* (*smile, figure*) де́тский*.
child minder *n* (*BRIT*) ня́ня.
child prodigy *n* вундерки́нд.
children ['tʃɪldrən] *npl of* **child**.
children's home ['tʃɪldrənz-] *n* де́тский* дом*.
child's play ['tʃaɪldz-] *n*: **it was ~ ~** (*fig*) э́то бы́ло пустяко́вое де́ло.
Chile ['tʃɪlɪ] *n* Чи́ли *nt ind*.
Chilean ['tʃɪlɪən] *adj* чили́йский* ◆ *n* чили́ец(-и́йка).
chili ['tʃɪlɪ] *n* (*US*) = **chilli**.

chill [tʃɪl] *n* (*coldness*) прохла́да; (*MED*) простуда ◆ *adj* холо́дный* ◆ *vt* (*food, drinks*) охлажда́ть (охлади́ть* *perf*); **to catch a ~** простужа́ться (простуди́ться* *perf*); **his words sent a ~ down my spine** от его́ слов у меня́ пробежа́л холодо́к по спине́; **a ~ reminder** (*fig*) злове́щее предзнаменова́ние; **I'm ~ed to the bone** я промёрз до косте́й; **"serve ~ed"** "подава́ть в охлаждённом ви́де"
▸ **chill out** *vi* (*inf*) кайфова́ть (*impf*).
chilli ['tʃɪlɪ] (*US* **chili**) *n* (*CULIN*) кра́сный стручко́вый пе́рец*.
chilling ['tʃɪlɪŋ] *adj* (*wind*) прохла́дный* (прохла́ден), холо́дный* (хо́лоден); (*tale*) ужаса́ющий*.
chilly ['tʃɪlɪ] *adj* (*weather*) холо́дный, промо́зглый; (*response, person*) холо́дный* (хо́лоден); **to feel ~** зя́бнуть* (*impf*).
chime [tʃaɪm] *n* (*of bell*) звон; (*of clock*) бой* ◆ *vi* (*bell*) звони́ть (*impf*); (*clock*) бить* (проби́ть* *perf*).
chimney ['tʃɪmnɪ] *n* (дымова́я) труба́.
chimney sweep *n* трубочи́ст.
chimpanzee [tʃɪmpæn'ziː] *n* шимпанзе́ *m ind*.
chin [tʃɪn] *n* подборо́док*.
China ['tʃaɪnə] *n* Кита́й.
china ['tʃaɪnə] *n* фарфо́р.
Chinese [tʃaɪ'niːz] *adj* кита́йский* ◆ *n inv* (*person*) кита́ец(-ая́нка); (*LING*) кита́йский язы́к*.
chink [tʃɪŋk] *n* (*crack*) щель* *f*; (*clink*) звя́канье.
chintz [tʃɪnts] *n* набивно́й си́тец.
chinwag ['tʃɪnwæg] *n* (*inf*) дру́жеская болтовня́; **we had a good ~** мы хорошо́ поболта́ли.
chip [tʃɪp] *n* (*of wood*) ще́пка*; (*of glass, stone*) оско́лок*; (*in glass, cup etc*) щерби́нка; (*in gambling*) фи́шка*; (*COMPUT: also:* **microchip**) микросхе́ма ◆ *vt* (*cup, plate*) обива́ть (оби́ть* *perf*); **~s** *npl* (*BRIT: CULIN*) карто́фель *msg*-фри; (*US: also:* **potato ~s**) чи́псы *mpl*; **when the ~s are down** (*fig*) когда́ уда́ча отвернётся
▸ **chip in** *vi* (*inf: contribute*) сбра́сываться (сбро́ситься* *perf*); (: *interrupt*) встрева́ть (встрять* *perf*).
chipboard ['tʃɪpbɔːd] *n* древесно-стру́жечная плита́.
chipmunk ['tʃɪpmʌŋk] *n* бурунду́к.
chippings ['tʃɪpɪŋz] *npl*: **loose ~** ще́пки *fpl*.
chiropodist [kɪ'rɔpədɪst] *n* (*BRIT*) мозо́льный опера́тор *m/f*.
chiropody [kɪ'rɔpədɪ] *n* (*BRIT*) *ухо́д за нога́ми*.
chirp [tʃəːp] *vi* (*bird*) чири́кать (*impf*); (*cricket, grasshopper*) стрекота́ть* (*impf*).
chirpy ['tʃəːpɪ] *adj* (*inf*) жизнера́достный* (жизнера́достен).
chisel ['tʃɪzl] *n* (*for wood*) долото́*; (*for stone*) зуби́ло*; (*of sculptor*) резе́ц*.
chit [tʃɪt] *n* (*note*) запи́ска*; (*receipt*) распи́ска.
chitchat ['tʃɪttʃæt] *n* болтовня́.

chivalrous ['ʃɪvəlrəs] *adj* галáнтный* (галáнтен).

chivalry ['ʃɪvəlrɪ] *n* галáнтность *f*.

chives [tʃaɪvz] *npl* лук-рéзанец *msg*.

chloride ['klɔːraɪd] *n* хлорúд.

chlorinate ['klɔrɪneɪt] *vt* хлорúровать *(impf)*.

chlorine ['klɔːriːn] *n* хлор.

chock [tʃɔk] *n* (AUT, AVIAT) тормознáя колóдка*.

chock-a-block ['tʃɔkə'blɔk] *adj* биткóм набúтый (набúт).

chock-full [tʃɔk'ful] *adj* = chock-a-block.

chocolate ['tʃɔklɪt] *n* шоколáд; *(sweet)* шоколáдная конфéта ◆ *cpd* шоколáдный.

choice [tʃɔɪs] *n* (*selection*) вы́бор ◆ *adj* (*cut of meat, fruit etc*) отбóрный; **this is a possible ~** э́то возмóжный вариáнт; **by** *or* **from ~** добровóльно; **a wide ~** большóй вы́бор; **to have first ~** выбирáть (вы́брать *perf*) пéрвым; **I have no ~, but/but to** у меня́ нет другóго вы́хода крóме +*gen*/крóме как +*infin*.

choir ['kwaɪə'] *n* хор*; *(area of church)* хóры *pl*.

choirboy ['kwaɪə'bɔɪ] *n* пéвчий* *m adj*.

choke [tʃəuk] *vi* (*on food, drink*) давúться* (подавúться* *perf*); *(with smoke, anger)* задыхáться (задохну́ться *perf*) ◆ *vt* (*strangle*) душúть* (задушúть* *or* удушúть* *perf*) ◆ *n* (AUT) возду́шная заслóнка; **~d (with)** *(blocked)* засорённый (засорён) (+*instr*).

cholera ['kɔlərə] *n* холéра.

cholesterol [kə'lɛstərɔl] *n* холестерúн; **high/low ~** с высóким/нúзким содержáнием холестерúна.

choose [tʃuːz] *(pt* chose, *pp* chosen*) *vt* выбирáть (вы́брать *perf*); (*elect*) избирáть (избрáть* *perf*) ◆ *vi*: **to ~ between/from** выбирáть (вы́брать* *perf*) мéжду +*instr*/из +*gen*; **to ~ to do** решáть (решúть *perf*) +*infin*.

choosy ['tʃuːzɪ] *adj* привередливый (привередлив); **he is ~ about his food** он привередлив в едé.

chop [tʃɔp] *vt* (*wood*) рубúть* (нарубúть* *perf*); *(also:~* **up**: *vegetables, meat*) рéзать* (нарéзать* *or* порéзать* *perf*) ◆ *n* (CULIN) ≈ отбивнáя (котлéта); **~s** *npl* (*inf: jaws*): **to lick one's ~s** облúзываться (облизáться* *perf*); **he got the ~** (BRIT: *inf*) егó вы́гнали с рабóты

▶ **chop down** *vt* (*tree*) рубúть* (срубúть* *perf*).

chopper ['tʃɔpə'] *n* (*helicopter*) вертолёт.

choppy ['tʃɔpɪ] *adj* (*sea*) неспокóйный* (неспокóен).

chopsticks ['tʃɔpstɪks] *npl* пáлочки* *fpl* для еды́.

choral ['kɔːrəl] *adj* хоровóй; (*in church*) хорáльный.

chord [kɔːd] *n* (MUS) аккóрд; (MATH) хóрда.

chore [tʃɔː'] *n* (*domestic task*) рабóта по дóму;

(routine task) повседнéвная обя́занность *f*; **household ~s** домáшние хлóпоты.

choreographer [kɔn'ɔgrəfə'] *n* хореóграф; (*of ballet*) балетмéйстер*.

choreography [kɔn'ɔgrafɪ] *n* хореогрáфия.

chorister ['kɔrɪstə'] *n* пéвчий* *m adj*, хорúст.

chortle ['tʃɔːtl] *vi* хохотáть* *(impf)*.

chorus ['kɔːrəs] *n* (*choir, song, also fig*) хор*; (*church song*) хорáл; (*refrain*) припéв; **in ~** хóром.

chose [tʃəuz] *pt of* **choose**.

chosen ['tʃəuzn] *pp of* **choose**.

chow [tʃau] *n* (*dog*) чáу-чáу *m/f ind*.

chowder ['tʃaudə'] *n* ≈ похлёбка.

Christ [kraɪst] *n* Христóс.

christen ['krɪsn] *vt* крестúть* (окрестúть* *perf*); (*with nickname*) окрестúть* *(perf)* +*instr*.

christening ['krɪsnɪŋ] *n* крещéние.

Christian ['krɪstɪən] *adj* христиáнский* ◆ *n* христианúн*(-áнка).

Christianity [krɪstɪ'ænɪtɪ] *n* христиáнство.

Christian name *n* úмя* *nt*.

Christmas ['krɪsməs] *n* Рождествó; **Happy** *or* **Merry ~!** Счастлúвого Рождествá!

Christmas card *n* рождéственская откры́тка*.

Christmas Day *n* день *m* Рождествá.

Christmas Eve *n* сочéльник.

Christmas Island *n* óстров* Рождествá.

Christmas tree *n* рождéственская ёлка*.

chrome [krəum] *n* = chromium.

chromium ['krəumɪəm] *n* хром; (*also:~* plating) хромúрование.

chromosome ['krəuməsəum] *n* хромосóма.

chronic ['krɔnɪk] *adj* хронúческий*.

chronicle ['krɔnɪkl] *n* (*of events*) хрóника.

chronological [krɔnə'lɔdʒɪkl] *adj* (*order*) хронологúческий*.

chrysanthemum [krɪ'sænθəməm] *n* хризантéма.

chubby ['tʃʌbɪ] *adj* пу́хлый*.

chuck [tʃʌk] (*inf*) *vt* швыря́ть (швырну́ть *perf*); (BRIT: *also:~* **up**, **~ in**: *job, girlfriend*) бросáть (брóсить* *perf*)

▶ **chuck out** *vt* (*person, rubbish*) вышвы́ривать (вы́швырнуть *perf*).

chuckle ['tʃʌkl] *vi* посмéиваться (*impf*); **"Yes", he ~d** Да, – сказáл он, посмéиваясь.

chuffed [tʃʌft] *adj* (*inf*) довóльный* (довóлен).

chug [tʃʌg] *vi* пыхтéть* (*impf*); (*also:~* along) пыхтéть* (пропыхтéть* *perf*).

chum [tʃʌm] *n* (*inf: friend*) закады́чный друг*.

chump [tʃʌmp] *n* (*inf*) болвáн.

chunk [tʃʌŋk] *n* (*of meat*) кусóк*; (*of bread*) лóмоть* *m*.

chunky ['tʃʌŋkɪ] *adj* (*furniture etc*) громóздкий* (громóздок); (*person*) коренáстый (коренáст); (*knitwear*) тóлстый.

church [tʃəːtʃ] *n* цéрковь* *f*; **the C~ of England**

---

* marks translations which have irregular inflections. The Russian-English side of the dictionary gives inflectional information.

Англикáнская Цéрковь*.

churchyard ['tʃə:tʃjɑ:d] *n* погóст.

churlish ['tʃə:lɪʃ] *adj* грýбый (груб).

churn [tʃə:n] *n* (*machine*) маслобóйка; (*also: milk* ~) бидóн

▶ **churn out** *vt* производи́ть* (произвести́* *perf*) в большóм коли́честве.

chute [ʃu:t] *n* (*also: rubbish* ~) мусоропровóд; (*for parcels etc*) жёлоб*; (*BRIT: slide*) гóрка*.

chutney ['tʃʌtnɪ] *n* чáтни *nt ind* (*индúйская припрáва*).

CIA *n abbr* (*US:* = *Central Intelligence Agency*) ЦРУ.

cicada [sɪ'kɑ:də] *n* цикáда.

CID *n abbr* (*BRIT:* = *Criminal Investigation Department*) Уголóвный рóзыск.

cider ['saɪdə'] *n* сидр.

c.i.f. *abbr* (*COMM:* = *cost, insurance and freight*) СИФ (*стóимость, страховáние, фрахт*).

cigar [sɪ'gɑ:'] *n* сигáра.

cigarette [sɪgə'rɛt] *n* сигарéта.

cigarette case *n* портсигáр.

cigarette end *n* окýрок*.

cigarette holder *n* мундштýк*.

C-in-C *abbr* (*MIL:* = *commander in chief*) главнокомáндующий*.

cinch [sɪntʃ] *n* (*inf*): **it's a** ~ э́то пустя́к.

Cinderella [sɪndə'rɛlə] *n* Зóлушка.

cinders ['sɪndəz] *npl* золá *fsg*.

cine camera ['sɪnɪ-] *n* (*BRIT*) кинокáмера.

cine film *n* (*BRIT*) киноплёнка*.

cinema ['sɪnəmə] *n* кинотеáтр; (*film-making*) кинематогрáфия.

cine projector *n* (*BRIT*) кинопроéктор.

cinnamon ['sɪnəmən] *n* кори́ца.

cipher ['saɪfə'] *n* шифр; (*fig*) пéшка*; **a letter in** ~ зашифрóванное письмó.

circa ['sə:kə] *prep* óколо +*gen*.

circle ['sə:kl] *n* круг*; (*THEAT*) балкóн; (*of trees*) кольцó ◆ *vi* (*bird, plane*) кружи́ть* (*impf*) ◆ *vt* (*move round*) дви́гаться* (*impf*) вокрýг +*gen*; (*surround*) окружáть (окружи́ть *perf*); **to form a** ~ вставáть* (встать* *perf*) в круг.

circuit ['sə:kɪt] *n* (*ELEC*) цепь *f*; (*tour*) турнé *nt ind*; (*track*) трек; (*lap*) заéзд.

circuit board *n* монтáжная плáта.

circuitous [sə:'kjuɪtəs] *adj* окóльный.

circular ['sə:kjulə'] *adj* (*plate, pond etc*) крýглый*; (*route*) окружнóй; (*argument*) нескóнчаемый ◆ *n* (*letter*) циркуля́р; (*advertisement*) проспéкт.

circulate ['sə:kjuleɪt] *vi* (*blood, traffic*) циркули́ровать (*impf*); (*news, rumour etc*) передавáться* (передáться* *perf*) ◆ *vt* передавáть (передáть* *perf*); **to** ~ **amongst the guests** переходи́ть (*impf*) от одногó гóстя к другóму.

circulating capital [sə:kju'leɪtɪŋ-] *n* оборóтный капитáл.

circulation [sə:kju'leɪʃən] *n* (*of newspaper*) тирáж*; (*MED*) кровообращéние; (*of money*)

обращéние; (*of air, traffic*) циркуля́ция.

circumcise ['sə:kəmsaɪz] *vt* обрезáть (обрéзать* *perf*) (*РЕЛ*).

circumference [sə'kʌmfərəns] *n* окрýжность *f*.

circumflex ['sə:kəmflɛks] *n* (*also:* ~ **accent**) циркумфлéкс.

circumscribe ['sə:kəmskraɪb] *vt* (*GEOM*) впи́сывать (вписáть* *perf*) в окрýжность; (*fig*) ограни́чивать (ограни́чить *perf*).

circumspect ['sə:kəmspɛkt] *adj* осмотри́тельный* (осмотри́телен).

circumstances ['sə:kəmstənsɪz] *npl* обстоя́тельства *ntpl*; **in** *or* **under the** ~ в дáнных обстоя́тельствах; **under no** ~ ни в кóем слýчае.

circumstantial [sə:kəm'stænʃl] *adj* обстоя́тельный* (обстоя́телен); ~ **evidence** кóсвенные ули́ки *fpl*.

circumvent [sə:kəm'vɛnt] *vt* обходи́ть* (обойти́* *perf*).

circus ['sə:kəs] *n* цирк; (*also:* **C**~: *in place names*) ≈ плóщадь *f*.

cirrhosis [sɪ'rəusɪs] *n* циррóз.

CIS *n abbr* (= *Commonwealth of Independent States*) СНГ= *Содрýжество Незави́симых Госудáрств*.

cissy ['sɪsɪ] *n* (*boy*) девчóнка*; (*girl*) нéженка*.

cistern ['sɪstən] *n* (*water tank*) цистéрна; (*of toilet*) бак.

citation [saɪ'teɪʃən] *n* (*from book etc*) цитáта; (*for bravery etc*) благодáрность *f*; (*US: LAW*) повéстка (*в суд*).

cite [saɪt] *vt* (*quote*) цити́ровать (процити́ровать *perf*); (*LAW*) вызывáть (вы́звать* *perf*) в суд.

citizen ['sɪtɪzn] *n* (*of a country*) граждани́н*(-áнка); (*of town*) жи́тель(ница) *m(f)*.

Citizens' Advice Bureau ['sɪtɪznz-] *n* бюрó, *даю́щее беспла́тные совéты по широ́кому крýгу вопро́сов*.

citizenship ['sɪtɪznʃɪp] *n* (*of a country*) граждáнство.

citric acid ['sɪtrɪk-] *n* лимóнная кислотá*.

citrus fruit ['sɪtrəs-] *n* ци́трус.

city ['sɪtɪ] *n* гóрод*; **the C**~ Си́ти *nt ind*.

city centre *n* центр (гóрода).

City Hall *n* рáтуша.

civic ['sɪvɪk] *adj* муниципáльный; (*duties, pride*) граждáнский*.

civic centre *n* (*BRIT*) ≈ Дом* Культýры.

civil ['sɪvɪl] *adj* граждáнский*; (*authorities*) госудáрственный; (*polite*) учти́вый (учти́в).

Civil Aviation Authority *n* (*BRIT*) Управлéние граждáнской авиáции.

civil defence *n* граждáнская оборóна.

civil disobedience *n* граждáнское неповиновéние.

civil engineer *n* инженéр-строи́тель *m*.

civil engineering *n* граждáнское строи́тельство.

civilian [sɪ'vɪlɪən] *adj* (*life*) обще́ственный ◆ *n*
ми́рный(-ая) жи́тель(ница) *m(f)*; ~ **casualties**
же́ртвы среди́ ми́рного населе́ния.

civilization [sɪvɪlaɪ'zeɪʃən] *n* цивилиза́ция.

civilized ['sɪvɪlaɪzd] *adj* (*society*)
цивилизо́ванный; (*person*) культу́рный;
(*place*) комфорта́бельный.

civil law *n* Гражда́нское пра́во.

civil liberties *npl* гражда́нские свобо́ды *fpl*.

civil rights *npl* гражда́нские права́ *ntpl*.

civil servant *n* госуда́рственный слу́жащий*
m adj.

Civil Service *n* госуда́рственная слу́жба.

civil war *n* гражда́нская война́*.

civvies ['sɪvɪz] *npl* (*inf*) циви́льная оде́жда *fsg*.

cl *abbr* = **centilitre**.

clad [klæd] *adj*: ~ (**in**) облачённый (облачён) (в
+*acc*).

claim [kleɪm] *vt* (*responsibility, credit*)
припи́сывать (приписа́ть* *perf*) себе́; (*rights,
inheritance*) претендова́ть (*impf*) *or* притяза́ть
(*impf*) на +*acc*; (*compensation, damages*)
тре́бовать (потре́бовать *perf*) ◆ *vi* (*for
insurance*) де́лать (сде́лать *perf*) страхову́ю
зая́вку ◆ *n* (*assertion*) утвержде́ние; (*for
compensation, pension*) тре́бование; (*right*)
пра́во; (*to inheritance, land*) прете́нзия,
притяза́ние; (*for expenses*) зая́вка; **to** ~ (**that**)
or **to be** (*assert*) утвержда́ть (*impf*), что;
(**insurance**) ~ страхова́я зая́вка; **to put in a** ~
for (*expenses*) подава́ть* (пода́ть* *perf*)
зая́вку на +*acc*.

claimant ['kleɪmənt] *n* (*LAW*) претенде́нт;
(*ADMIN*) пода́тель(ница) *m(f)* заявле́ния.

claim form *n* бланк заявле́ния.

clairvoyant [klɛə'vɔɪənt] *n* яснови́дец*(-дица).

clam [klæm] *n* двухство́рчатый моллю́ск
▸ **clam up** *vi* (*inf*) уходи́ть* (уйти́* *perf*) в себя́.

clamber ['klæmbəʳ] *vi* кара́бкаться
(вскара́бкаться *perf*).

clammy ['klæmɪ] *adj* (*hands*) ли́пкий*;
(*weather*) ду́шный*.

clamour ['klæməʳ] (*US* **clamor**) *n* (*noise*) гул;
(*protest*) ро́пот ◆ *vi*: **to** ~ **for** шу́мно
тре́бовать (*impf*) +*gen*.

clamp [klæmp] *n* зажи́м ◆ *vt* зажима́ть
(зажа́ть* *perf*)
▸ **clamp down on** *vt fus* повести́* (*perf*)
наступле́ние про́тив +*gen*.

clampdown ['klæmpdaun] *n*: ~ (**on**) стро́гие
ме́ры *fpl* (про́тив +*gen*); **there was a** ~ **on drug
dealing in the area** в райо́не прикры́ли
торго́влю нарко́тиками.

clan [klæn] *n* клан.

clandestine [klæn'dɛstɪn] *adj* подпо́льный.

clang [klæŋ] *vi* (*bell*) звене́ть (*impf*); (*metal
object*) ля́згать (*impf*) ◆ *n* (*see vi*) звон; лязг.

clanger ['klæŋəʳ] *n* (*inf*) ля́псус.

clansman ['klænzmən] *irreg n* член кла́на.

clap [klæp] *vi* хло́пать (*impf*) ◆ *vt*: **to** ~ **one's
hands** хло́пать (*impf*) в ладо́ши; **a** ~ **of
thunder** уда́р гро́ма.

clapping ['klæpɪŋ] *n* хлопки́ *mpl*,
аплодисме́нты *fpl*.

claptrap ['klæptræp] *n* (*inf*) белиберда́.

claret ['klærət] *n* бордо́ *nt ind*.

clarification [klærɪfɪ'keɪʃən] *n* (*fig*)
разъясне́ние.

clarify ['klærɪfaɪ] *vt* (*fig*) разъясня́ть
(разъясни́ть *perf*).

clarinet [klærɪ'nɛt] *n* кларне́т.

clarity ['klærɪtɪ] *n* (*of explanation, thought*)
я́сность *f*.

clash [klæʃ] *n* столкнове́ние; (*of events etc*)
совпаде́ние; (*of metal objects*) звя́канье ◆ *vi*
(*gangs*) име́ть (*impf*) столкнове́ние; (*political
opponents*) вступа́ть (вступи́ть* *perf*) в
столкнове́ние; (*beliefs*) ста́лкиваться
(столкну́ться *perf*); (*colours*) не совмеща́ться
(*impf*); (*events etc*) совпада́ть (совпа́сть* *perf*)
(по вре́мени); (*metal objects*) звя́кать (*impf*).

clasp [klɑ:sp] *n* (*hold*) хва́тка*; (*of necklace,
bag*) застёжка* ◆ *vt* сжима́ть (сжать* *perf*).

class [klɑ:s] *n* (*in school, society*) класс; (*lesson*)
уро́к; (*of goods: type*) разря́д; (: *quality*) сорт
◆ *adj* кла́ссовый ◆ *vt* классифици́ровать (*impf/
perf*).

class-conscious ['klɑ:s'kɔnʃəs] *adj* (*person*)
осознаю́щий кла́ссовое разли́чие.

class-consciousness ['klɑ:s'kɔnʃəsnɪs] *n*
кла́ссовое созна́ние.

classic ['klæsɪk] *adj* класси́ческий* ◆ *n* (*film,
novel etc*) класси́ческое произведе́ние;
(*author*) кла́ссик; **C**~**s** *npl* (*SCOL*)
класси́ческая филоло́гия *fsg*.

classical ['klæsɪkl] *adj* класси́ческий*.

classification [klæsɪfɪ'keɪʃən] *n*
классифика́ция; (*category*) разря́д.

classified ['klæsɪfaɪd] *adj* засекре́ченный.

classified advertisement *n* объявле́ния под
ру́брикой.

classify ['klæsɪfaɪ] *vt* классифици́ровать (*impf/
perf*).

classless ['klɑ:slɪs] *adj* бескла́ссовый.

classmate ['klɑ:smeɪt] *n* однокла́ссник(-ица).

classroom ['klɑ:srum] *n* класс.

classy ['klɑ:sɪ] *adj* (*inf*: *car, flat*) кла́ссный.

clatter ['klætəʳ] *n* (*of dishes etc*) звя́канье; (*of
hooves*) цо́канье ◆ *vi* (*see n*) звя́кать (*impf*);
цо́кать (*impf*).

clause [klɔ:z] *n* (*LAW*) пункт; (*LING*): **principal/
subordinate** ~ гла́вное/прида́точное
предложе́ние.

claustrophobia [klɔ:strə'fəubɪə] *n*
клаустрофо́бия.

claustrophobic [klɔ:strə'fəubɪk] *adj*: **she is** ~

---

* marks translations which have irregular inflections. The Russian-English side of the dictionary gives inflectional information.

она́ страда́ет клаустрофо́бией, у неё
клаустрофо́бия.

claw [klɔ:] n (of animal, bird) ко́готь* m;
(of lobster) клешня́*
► **claw at** vt fus цепля́ться (impf) за +acc.

clay [kleɪ] n гли́на.

clean [kli:n] adj чи́стый*; (fight) че́стный*;
(reputation) незапя́тнанный (незапя́тан);
(joke) прили́чный* (прили́чен); (edge,
fracture) ро́вный* (ро́вен) ♦ vt (hands, face)
мыть* (вы́мыть* perf); (car, cooker) чи́стить*
(почи́стить* perf) ♦ adv: **he ~ forgot** он
на́чисто забы́л; **~ driving licence** or (US)
record чи́стые води́тельские права́ ntpl; **to ~
one's teeth** (BRIT) чи́стить* (почи́стить perf)
зу́бы; **the thief got ~ away** во́ра и след
просты́л; **to come ~** (inf) выкла́дывать
(вы́ложить perf) всё начисту́ю
► **clean off** vt (wash) смыва́ть (смыть* perf);
(brush, dust etc) счища́ть (счи́стить* perf)
► **clean out** vt (cupboard etc) вычища́ть
(вы́чистить* perf); (inf: person) обчища́ть
(обчи́стить* perf)
► **clean up** vt (room) убира́ть (убра́ть* perf);
(child) мыть* (помы́ть* perf); (fig) проводи́ть*
(провести́* perf) чи́стку в +prp ♦ vi убира́ться
(убра́ться* perf); (fig) загреба́ть (загрести́*
perf) больши́е де́ньги; **to ~ up after sb/sth**
убира́ть (убра́ть* perf) за кем-н/чем-н.

clean-cut ['kli:n'kʌt] adj (person) опря́тный*
(опря́тен); (situation) я́сный* (я́сен).

cleaner ['kli:nə'] n (person) убо́рщик(-ица);
(substance) мо́ющее сре́дство.

cleaner's ['kli:nəz] n (also: dry ~) химчи́стка*.

cleaning ['kli:nɪŋ] n убо́рка*.

cleaning lady n убо́рщица.

cleanliness ['klɛnlɪnɪs] n чистопло́тность f.

cleanly ['kli:nlɪ] adv чи́сто.

cleanse [klɛnz] vt (purify) очища́ть (очи́стить*
perf); (face) мыть* (вы́мыть* perf); (cut)
промыва́ть (промы́ть* perf).

cleanser ['klɛnzə'] n (for face) очища́ющий
лосьо́н.

clean-shaven ['kli:n'ʃeɪvn] adj чи́сто
вы́бритый.

cleansing department ['klɛnzɪŋ-] n (BRIT)
санита́рное управле́ние.

clean sweep n: **to make a ~ ~** (in tournaments)
забира́ть (забра́ть* perf) все призы́.

cleanup ['kli:nʌp] n (of house, room) убо́рка*;
(of river, air) очи́стка.

clear [klɪə'] adj я́сный* (я́сен); (report,
argument) я́сный* (я́сен), поня́тный*;
(footprint) чёткий*; (writing) разбо́рчивый
(разбо́рчив); (majority) подавля́ющий*;
(glass, water) прозра́чный* (прозра́чен);
(road) свобо́дный* (свобо́ден); (conscience,
profit) чи́стый* ♦ vt (space, room)
освобожда́ть (освободи́ть* perf); (ground)
расчища́ть (расчи́стить* perf); (weeds, slums)
убира́ть (убра́ть* perf); (suspect)

опра́вдывать (оправда́ть perf); (fence etc)
брать* (взять* perf); (goods) распродава́ть*
(распрода́ть* perf) ♦ vi (sky) проясня́ться
(проясни́ться perf); (fog, smoke)
рассе́иваться (рассе́яться perf); (room etc)
обезлю́деть (perf) ♦ adv: **~ of** (trouble, ground)
пода́льше от +gen ♦ n: **he is/was in the ~** (out
of debt) он свобо́ден/был свобо́ден от
долго́в; **to be in the ~** (free of suspicion)
быть* (impf) вне подозре́ния; (out of danger)
быть* (impf) вне опа́сности; **have I made
myself ~?** я я́сно вы́разился?; **to make it ~ to
sb that ...** дава́ть* (дать* perf) кому́-н поня́ть,
что ...; **I have a ~ day tomorrow** (BRIT) у меня́
за́втра свобо́дный день; **to ~ the table**
убира́ть (убра́ть* perf) со стола́; **to ~ one's
throat** прочища́ть (прочи́стить* perf) го́рло;
to ~ a cheque выпла́чивать (вы́платить* perf)
де́ньги по че́ку; **to ~ a profit** получа́ть
(получи́ть* perf) чи́стую при́быль; **to keep ~
of sb/sth** держа́ться* (impf) пода́льше от
кого́-н/чего́-н
► **clear off** vi (inf: leave) убира́ться (убра́ться*
perf)
► **clear up** vt (room) убира́ть (убра́ть* perf);
(mystery, problem) разреша́ть (разреши́ть
perf) ♦ vi убира́ться (убра́ться* perf); (illness)
проходи́ть* (пройти́* perf); (weather)
проясня́ться (проясни́ться perf).

clearance ['klɪərəns] n (removal) расчи́стка*;
(permission) разреше́ние; (above vehicle)
габари́тная высота́*.

clearance sale n распрода́жа.

clear-cut ['klɪə'kʌt] adj (decision, issue) я́сный*
(я́сен); (division) чёткий*.

clearing ['klɪərɪŋ] n поля́на; (BRIT: COMM)
кли́ринг.

clearing bank n (BRIT) кли́ринговый банк.

clearing house n кли́ринговая пала́та.

clearly ['klɪəlɪ] adv (distinctly) я́сно, отчётливо;
(obviously) я́вно, очеви́дно; (coherently)
я́сно, поня́тно.

clearway ['klɪəweɪ] n (BRIT) автодоро́га, где
остано́вка тра́нспорта запрещена́.

cleavage ['kli:vɪdʒ] n я́мка*.

cleaver ['kli:və'] n (for meat) топо́рик.

clef [klɛf] n (MUS) ключ*.

cleft [klɛft] n рассе́лина.

cleft palate n за́ячья губа́.

clemency ['klɛmənsɪ] n милосе́рдие.

clement ['klɛmənt] adj мя́гкий.

clench [klɛntʃ] vt сжима́ть (сжать* perf).

clergy ['klə:dʒɪ] n духове́нство.

clergyman ['klə:dʒɪmən] irreg n свяще́нник,
священнослужи́тель m.

clerical ['klɛrɪkl] adj (job, error) канцеля́рский*;
(skills) секрета́рский*; (REL) церко́вный.

clerk [klɑ:k, (US) klə:rk] n (BRIT: office worker)
клерк, делопроизводи́тель*(ница) m(f); (US:
sales person) продаве́ц*(-вщи́ца).

Clerk of Court n секрета́рь* m суда́.

clever ['klɛvə'] *adj* (*intelligent*) у́мный* (умён); (*deft, crafty*) ло́вкий* (ло́вок).

cleverly ['klɛvəlɪ] *adv* ло́вко.

clew [klu:] *n* (*US*) = **clue.**

cliché ['kli:ʃeɪ] *n* клише́ *nt ind*, штамп.

click [klɪk] *vt* (*tongue, heels*) щёлкать (щёлкнуть *perf*) +*instr* ◆ *vi* (*device, switch etc*) щёлкать (щёлкнуть *perf*).

client ['klaɪənt] *n* клие́нт.

clientele [kli:ã:n'tɛl] *n* клиенту́ра.

cliff [klɪf] *n* скала́*, утёс.

cliffhanger ['klɪfhæŋə'] *n* (*TV, also fig*) напряжённый моме́нт.

climactic [klaɪ'mæktɪk] *adj* кульминацио́нный.

climate ['klaɪmɪt] *n* (*weather, fig*) кли́мат; **~ of opinion** состоя́ние обще́ственного мне́ния.

climax ['klaɪmæks] *n* кульмина́ция; (*during sex*) орга́зм.

climb [klaɪm] *vi* (*sun*) поднима́ться (подня́ться* *perf*); (*plant*) ви́ться (*impf*); (*plane*) набира́ть (набра́ть* *perf*) высоту́; (*prices, shares*) поднима́ться (подня́ться* *perf*) ◆ *vt* (*stairs, ladder*) взбира́ться (взобра́ться* *perf*) по +*prp*; (*tree, hill*) взбира́ться (взобра́ться* *perf*) *or* поднима́ться (подня́ться* *perf*) на +*acc* ◆ *n* подъём; **to ~ over a wall** перелеза́ть (переле́зть* *perf*) че́рез сте́ну.

► **climb down** *vi* (*BRIT: fig*) уступа́ть (уступи́ть *perf*).

climb-down ['klaɪmdaun] *n* (*BRIT*) усту́пка*.

climber ['klaɪmə'] *n* (*mountaineer*) альпини́ст(ка*); (*plant*) вью́щееся расте́ние.

climbing ['klaɪmɪŋ] *n* альпини́зм.

clinch [klɪntʃ] *vt* (*deal*) заключа́ть (заключи́ть *perf*); (*argument*) разреша́ть (разреши́ть *perf*).

clincher ['klɪntʃə'] *n* реша́ющий* до́вод.

cling [klɪŋ] (*pt, pp* clung) *vi* (*clothes, dress*) облега́ть (*impf*); **to ~ to** (*mother, support*) вцепля́ться (вцепи́ться* *perf*) в +*acc*; (*idea, belief*) цепля́ться (*impf*) за +*acc*.

clingfilm ['klɪŋfɪlm] *n* обёрточная плёнка для проду́ктов.

clinic ['klɪnɪk] *n* (*medical centre*) кли́ника; (*session*) консульта́ция.

clinical ['klɪnɪkl] *adj* (*MED*) клини́ческий*; (*fig: attitude*) бесстра́стный (бесстра́стен); (*: room*) стери́льный.

clink [klɪŋk] *vi* звене́ть (*impf*) ◆ *vt* (*glasses*) чо́каться (чо́кнуться *perf*).

clip [klɪp] *n* (*also:* **paper ~**) скре́пка*; (*BRIT: also:* **bulldog ~**) зажи́м; (*for hair*) зако́лка*; (*TV, CINEMA*) клип ◆ *vt* (*fasten*) прикрепля́ть (прикрепи́ть* *perf*); (*also: ~* **together**) papers) скрепля́ть (скрепи́ть* *perf*); (*cut*) подстрига́ть (подстри́чь* *perf*).

clippers ['klɪpəz] *npl* (*for gardening*) сека́тор *msg*; (*also:* **nail ~**) щи́пчики *pl*.

clipping ['klɪpɪŋ] *n* (*PRESS*) вы́резка*.

clique [kli:k] *n* кли́ка.

clitoris ['klɪtərɪs] *n* кли́тор.

cloak [kləuk] *n* (*cape*) плащ* ◆ *vt* (*fig: in mist*) оку́тывать (оку́тать *perf*); **~ed in** оку́танный (оку́тан) +*instr*.

cloakroom ['kləukrum] *n* (*for coats*) гардеро́б; (*BRIT: toilet*) убо́рная *f adj*.

clobber ['klɔbə'] (*inf*) *n* мона́тки *pl* ◆ *vt* (*hit*) колошма́тить (исколошма́тить* *perf*); (*defeat*) отколошма́тить* (*perf*).

clock [klɔk] *n* часы́ *pl*; (*of taxi*) счётчик; **to sleep/work round the ~** спать* (*impf*)/ рабо́тать (*impf*) кру́глые су́тки; **this car has 30,000 miles on the ~** (*BRIT*) э́та маши́на нае́здила 30,000 миль; **to work against the ~** рабо́тать (*impf*) наперегонки́ со вре́менем

► **clock in** *vi* (*BRIT: for work*) отмеча́ться (отме́титься* *perf*) (*приходя́ на рабо́ту*)

► **clock off** *vi* (*BRIT: from work*) отмеча́ться (отме́титься* *perf*) (*уходя́ с рабо́ты*)

► **clock on** *vi* (*BRIT*) = **clock in**

► **clock out** *vi* (*BRIT*) = **clock off**

► **clock up** *vt* (*debts*) нака́пливать (накопи́ть* *perf*); (*miles*) накру́чивать (накрути́ть* *perf*); (*hours*) набира́ть (набра́ть* *perf*).

clockwise ['klɔkwaɪz] *adv* по часово́й стре́лке.

clockwork ['klɔkwə:k] *n* заво́д ◆ *adj* (*toy*) заводно́й.

clog [klɔg] *n* сабо́* *nt ind* ◆ *vt* (*drain*) засоря́ть (засори́ть *perf*) ◆ *vi* (*also: ~* **up**: *sink*) засоря́ться (засори́ться *perf*); **my nose is ~ged (up)** у меня́ зало́жен нос.

cloister ['klɔɪstə'] *n* кры́тая галере́я.

clone [kləun] *n* (*BIO*) клон.

close¹ [kləus] *adj* (*near*) бли́зкий* (бли́зок); (*writing*) убо́ристый (убо́рист); (*contact, ties*) те́сный* (те́сен); (*watch, attention*) при́стальный* (при́стален); (*weather, room*) ду́шный* (ду́шен) ◆ *adv* бли́зко; **~ to** (*near*) бли́зкий* (бли́зок) к +*dat*; **~ to** *or* **on** (*almost*) бли́зко к +*dat*; **how ~ is Edinburgh to Glasgow?** как бли́зко от Эдинбу́рга нахо́дится Гла́зго?; **a ~ friend** бли́зкий* друг*; **a ~ contest** борьба́ на ра́вных; **I had a ~ shave** (*fig*) я был на волосо́к от э́того; **to keep a ~ eye on sb/sth** внима́тельно следи́ть (*impf*) за +*instr*; **at ~ quarters** на бли́зком расстоя́нии.

close² [kləuz] *vt* (*shut*) закрыва́ть (закры́ть* *perf*); (*finalize*) заключа́ть (заключи́ть *perf*); (*end*) заверша́ть (заверши́ть *perf*) ◆ *vi* (*shut*) закрыва́ться (закры́ться* *perf*); (*end*) заверша́ться (заверши́ться *perf*) *n* коне́ц*; **to bring sth to a ~** заверша́ть (заверши́ть *perf*) что-н

► **close down** *vt* закрыва́ть (закры́ть* *perf*) ◆ *vi* закрыва́ться (закры́ться* *perf*)

---

* marks translations which have irregular inflections. The Russian-English side of the dictionary gives inflectional information.

▶ **close in** *vi* (*night, fog*) опуска́ться (опусти́ться* *perf*); (*hunters*): **to ~ in (on sb/ sth)** окружа́ть (окружи́ть *perf*) (кого́-н/ что́-н); **the days are closing in** дни стано́вятся коро́че

▶ **close off** *vt* (*area*) огора́живать (огороди́ть* *perf*); (*road*) блоки́ровать (*impf/perf*).

closed [kləuzd] *adj* закры́тый (закры́т).

closed-circuit ['kləuzd'sə:kɪt] *adj*: **~ television** за́мкнутая телевизио́нная систе́ма.

closed shop *n* (*union*) *предприя́тие, на кото́ром рабо́тают то́лько чле́ны определённого профсою́за*.

close-knit ['kləus'nɪt] *adj* сплочённый (сплочён).

closely ['kləuslɪ] *adv* (*watch, examine*) при́стально; (*connected, related*) те́сно; **he ~ resembles his father** он о́чень похо́ж на отца́; **we are ~ related** мы бли́зкие ро́дственники; **a ~ guarded secret** тща́тельно оберега́емый секре́т.

close season ['kləus-] *n* закры́тый сезо́н.

closet ['klɔzɪt] *n* (*cupboard*) шкаф*; (*room*) чула́н.

close-up ['kləusʌp] *n* (*PHOT*) кру́пный план.

closing ['kləuzɪŋ] *adj* (*stages, remarks*) заключи́тельный.

closing price *n* (*COMM*) после́дняя цена́ *or* ста́вка*.

closing time *n* вре́мя* *nt* закры́тия (*ба́ра*).

closure ['kləuʒə'] *n* (*of factory*) закры́тие; (*of road*) блоки́рование.

clot [klɔt] *n* (*of blood etc*) сгу́сток*; (*inf*) балда́ *m/f* ◆ *vi* (*blood*) свора́чиваться (сверну́ться* *perf*).

cloth [klɔθ] *n* (*material*) ткань *f*; (*for cleaning etc*) тря́пка*; (*BRIT: also: teacloth*) ку́хонное полоте́нце*; (*also: tablecloth*) ска́терть* *f*.

clothe [kləuð] *vt* одева́ть (оде́ть* *perf*).

clothes [kləuðz] *npl* оде́жда *fsg*; **to put one's ~ on** одева́ться (оде́ться* *perf*); **to take one's ~ off** раздева́ться (разде́ться* *perf*); **to change one's ~** переодева́ться (переоде́ться* *perf*).

clothes brush *n* оде́жная щётка*.

clothesline ['kləuðzlaɪn] *n* бельева́я верёвка*.

clothes peg (*US* **clothes pin**) *n* прище́пка*.

clothing ['kləuðɪŋ] *n* = **clothes**.

clotted cream ['klɔtɪd-] *n* (*BRIT*) густы́е сли́вки *pl*.

cloud [klaud] *n* о́блако* ◆ *vt* (*liquid*) мути́ть* (замути́ть* *perf*); **every ~ has a silver lining** нет ху́да без добра́; **to ~ the issue** запу́тывать (запу́тать *perf*) де́ло

▶ **cloud over** *vi* (*sky*) покрыва́ться (покры́ться* *perf*) облака́ми; (*face*) тума́ниться (затума́ниться *perf*).

cloudburst ['klaudbə:st] *n* ли́вень* *m*.

cloud-cuckoo-land [klaud'kuku:lænd] *n* (*BRIT*): **he is living in ~** он живёт в безо́блачном ца́рстве.

cloudy ['klaudɪ] *adj* (*sky*) о́блачный* (о́блачен); (*liquid*) му́тный* (му́тен).

clout [klaut] *vt* (*inf*) долбану́ть (*perf*) ◆ *n* (*fig*) влия́ние.

clove [kləuv] *n* гвозди́ка; **~ of garlic** до́лька чеснока́.

clover ['kləuvə'] *n* кле́вер.

cloverleaf ['kləuvəli:f] *n* лист* кле́вера; (*AUT*) кле́верный лист* (*о констру́кции пересече́ния автомоби́льных доро́г*).

clown [klaun] *n* кло́ун ◆ *vi* (*also:* **~ about, ~ around**) пая́сничать (*impf*).

cloying ['klɔɪɪŋ] *adj* (*taste, smell*) при́торный* (при́торен).

club [klʌb] *n* (*society, place*) клуб; (*weapon*) дуби́нка; (*implement: also:* **golf ~**) клю́шка* ◆ *vt* (*hit*) избива́ть (изби́ть* *perf*) ◆ *vi*: **to ~ together** скла́дываться (сложи́ться* *perf*); **~s** *npl* (*CARDS*) тре́фы *fpl*; **king of ~s** трефо́вый коро́ль *m*.

club car *n* (*US: RAIL*) ваго́н-рестора́н.

club class *n* осо́бый класс (*в самолётах*).

clubhouse ['klʌbhaus] *n* спорти́вный клуб (*зда́ние*).

club soda *n* со́довая вода́.

cluck [klʌk] *vi* (*hen*) куда́хтать* (*impf*).

clue [klu:] *n* ключ*; (*for police*) ули́ка; **I haven't a ~** я поня́тия не име́ю.

clued-up ['klu:dʌp] (*US* **clued in**) *adj* (*inf*): **to be ~** быть* (*impf*) в ку́рсе (дел).

clueless ['klu:lɪs] *adj* без поня́тия.

clump [klʌmp] *n* (*of trees, plants*) за́росли *fpl*; (*of buildings*) скопле́ние.

clumsy ['klʌmzɪ] *adj* (*person, movement*) неуклю́жий* (неуклю́ж); (*object*) неудо́бный (неудо́бен).

clung [klʌŋ] *pt, pp* of **cling**.

cluster ['klʌstə'] *n* (*of people, stars*) скопле́ние; (*of flowers*) пучо́к* ◆ *vi* (*people*) сгруди́ться (*perf*); (*things*) ска́пливаться (скопи́ться* *perf*).

clutch [klʌtʃ] *n* (*grip*) хва́тка; (*AUT*) сцепле́ние ◆ *vt* сжима́ть (сжать* *perf*) ◆ *vi*: **to ~ at** цепля́ться (*impf*) за +*acc*; **he has me in his ~es** я у него́ в рука́х.

clutter ['klʌtə'] *vt* (*also:* **~ up**: *room, table*) захламля́ть (захлами́ть* *perf*) ◆ *n* хлам.

CM *abbr* (*US: POST*) = North Mariana Islands.

cm *abbr* (= **centimetre**) см= *сантиме́тр*.

CNAA *n abbr* (*BRIT*) = Council for National Academic Awards.

CND *n abbr* = Campaign for Nuclear Disarmament.

CO *n abbr* = **commanding officer**; (*BRIT*: = **Commonwealth Office**) *отде́л по дела́м на́ций брита́нского Содру́жества* ◆ *abbr* (*US: POST*) = Colorado.

Co. *abbr* = **company, county**.

c/o *abbr* (= **care of**) для переда́чи +*dat*.

coach [kəutʃ] *n* (*bus*) авто́бус; (*horse-drawn*) каре́та; (*of train*) ваго́н; (*SPORT*) тре́нер; (*SCOL*) репети́тор ◆ *vt* (*SPORT*) тренирова́ть

(натренировáть *perf*); (*SCOL*): **to ~ sb for sth** готóвить* (подготóвить* *perf*) когó-н к чемý-н.
coach trip *n* автóбусная экскýрсия.
coagulate [kəu'ægjuleɪt] *vi* (*blood*) сворáчиваться (свернýться *perf*); (*paint*) сгущáться (сгустúться* *perf*).
coal [kəul] *n* ýголь* *m*.
coalface ['kəulfeɪs] *n* забóй.
coalfield ['kəulfi:ld] *n* каменноýгольный бассéйн.
coalition [kəuə'lɪʃən] *n* (*also POL*) коалúция.
coalman ['kəulmən] *irreg n* ýгольщик.
coalmine ['kəulmaɪn] *n* ýгольная шáхта.
coal miner *n* шахтёр.
coal mining *n* добыча ýгля.
coarse [kɔ:s] *adj* грýбый*; (*hair*) жёсткий*; (*salt, sand etc*) крýпный*.
coast [kəust] *n* бéрег*; (*area*) побережье ♦ *vi* (*car etc*) катúться* (покатúться* *perf*) по инéрции.
coastal ['kəustl] *adj* прибрéжный; (*services*) береговóй.
coaster ['kəustə'] *n* (*NAUT*) каботáжное сýдно*; (*for glass*) подстáвка* для стакáна.
coastguard ['kəustgɑ:d] *n* (*officer*) офицéр береговóй слýжбы; **the ~ (service)** береговáя слýжба.
coastline ['kəustlaɪn] *n* береговáя лúния.
coat [kəut] *n* пальтó *nt ind*; (*on animal: fur*) мех*; (: *wool*) шерсть*; (*of paint*) слой* ♦ *vt* покрывáть (покрыть* *perf*).
coat hanger *n* вéшалка*.
coating ['kəutɪŋ] *n* слой.
coat of arms *n* герб*.
coauthor ['kəu'ɔ:θə'] *n* соáвтор.
coax [kəuks] *vt* угровáривать (уговорúть *perf*) лáской.
cob [kɔb] *n see* **corn**.
cobbler ['kɔblə'] *n* сапóжник.
cobbles ['kɔblz] *npl* булыжники *mpl*.
cobblestones ['kɔblstəunz] *npl* = **cobbles**.
COBOL ['kəubɔl] *n* Кóбол.
cobra ['kəubrə] *n* кóбра.
cobweb ['kɔbwɛb] *n* паутúна.
cocaine [kə'keɪn] *n* кокаúн.
cock [kɔk] *n* (*rooster*) петýх*; (*male bird*) самéц* ♦ *vt* (*gun*) взводúть* (взвестú* *perf*); **to ~ one's ears** (*fig*) навострúть (*perf*) ýши.
cock-a-hoop [kɔkə'hu:p] *adj*: **to be ~** балдéть (*impf*).
cockerel ['kɔkərl] *n* петýх*.
cockeyed ['kɔkaɪd] *adj* (*fig*) дурáцкий*.
cockle ['kɔkl] *n* моллюск.
cockney ['kɔknɪ] *n* (*person*) кóкни *m/f ind* (*уроженец райóна Ист-Энд в Лóндоне*); (*LING*) кóкни *m ind* (*диалéкт уроженцев Ист-Энда*).

cockpit ['kɔkpɪt] *n* кабúна.
cockroach ['kɔkrəutʃ] *n* таракáн.
cocktail ['kɔkteɪl] *n* (*drink*) коктéйль *m*; (*with fruit, prawns etc*) салáт, закýска.
cocktail cabinet *n* бар (*в сервáнте*).
cocktail party *n* приём.
cocktail shaker [-'ʃeɪkə'] *n* мúксер.
cockup ['kɔkʌp] *n* (*infl*) лáжа (*!*).
cocky ['kɔkɪ] *adj* дéрзкий* (дéрзок), задúристый (задúрист).
cocoa ['kəukəu] *n* какáо *nt ind*.
coconut ['kəukənʌt] *n* (*fruit*) кокóсовый орéх; (*flesh*) кокóс.
cocoon [kə'ku:n] *n* (*of butterfly*) кóкон; (*fig*) оболóчка.
COD *abbr* (= *cash on delivery*) налóженный платёж; (*US*: = *collect on delivery*) налóженный платёж.
cod [kɔd] *n* трескá *f no pl*.
code [kəud] *n* (*of behaviour*) кóдекс; (*cipher, TEL*) код; **post ~** почтóвый úндекс; **~ of practice** свод прáвил (*профессионáльной дéятельности*).
codeine ['kəudi:n] *n* кодеúн.
codger ['kɔdʒə'] *n* чудáк*.
codicil ['kɔdɪsɪl] *n* (*LAW*) дополнúтельный парáграф завещáния.
codify ['kəudɪfaɪ] *vt* кодифицúровать (*impf/perf*).
cod-liver oil ['kɔdlɪvə-] *n* рыбий* жир*.
co-driver ['kəu'draɪvə'] *n* (*in race*) штýрман; (*of lorry*) смéнный водúтель.
co-ed ['kəu'ɛd] *adj abbr* (*SCOL*) = **coeducational** ♦ *n abbr* (*US*: *female student*) студéнтка (*в учéбных заведéниях смéшанного типа*); (*BRIT*: *school*) смéшанная шкóла.
coeducational ['kəuɛdju'keɪʃənl] *adj* (*school*) смéшанный.
coerce [kəu'ə:s] *vt* принуждáть (принýдить* *perf*).
coercion [kəu'ə:ʃən] *n* принуждéние.
coexistence ['kəuɪg'zɪstəns] *n* сосуществовáние.
C. of C. *n abbr* (= *chamber of commerce*) Торгóвая палáта.
C of E *abbr* = **Church of England**.
coffee ['kɔfɪ] *n* кóфе *m ind*; **black ~** чёрный кóфе; **white ~** кóфе с молокóм; **~ with cream** кóфе со слúвками.
coffee bar *n* (*BRIT*) кофéйня.
coffee beans *npl* кофéйные зёрна *ntpl*.
coffee break *n* перерыв на кóфе.
coffee cake *n* (*US*) торт к кóфе.
coffee cup *n* кофéйная чáшка*.
coffeepot ['kɔfɪpɔt] *n* кофéйник.
coffee table *n* кофéйный стóлик.
coffin ['kɔfɪn] *n* гроб*.
C of I *abbr* = **Church of Ireland**.
C of S *abbr* = **Church of Scotland**.

---

* marks translations which have irregular inflections. The Russian-English side of the dictionary gives inflectional information.

cog [kɔg] *n* (*wheel*) зубча́тое колесо́*; (*tooth*) зубе́ц*.

cogent ['kəudʒənt] *adj* внуши́тельный* (внуши́телен).

cognac ['kɔnjæk] *n* конья́к*.

cogwheel ['kɔgwi:l] *n* зу́бчатое колесо́*.

cohabit [kəu'hæbɪt] *vi*: **to ~ (with sb)** сожи́тельствовать (*impf*) (с кем-н).

coherent [kəu'hɪərənt] *adj* свя́зный; **she was very ~** её речь была́ о́чень свя́зной.

cohesion [kəu'hi:ʒən] *n* це́льность *f*.

cohesive [kə'hi:sɪv] *adj* (*fig*) це́льный* (це́лен).

COI *n abbr* (*BRIT*: = *Central Office of Information*) Центра́льное управле́ние информа́ции.

coil [kɔɪl] *n* (*of rope, wire*) мото́к*; (*one loop*) вито́к*; (*of smoke*) кольцо́*; (*AUT*) кату́шка*; (*contraceptive*) спира́ль *f* ♦ *vt* (*rope*) сма́тывать (смота́ть *perf*).

coin [kɔɪn] *n* моне́та ♦ *vt* (*phrase*) приду́мывать (приду́мать *perf*).

coinage ['kɔɪnɪdʒ] *n* (*money*) де́нежные зна́ки *mpl*; (*system*) де́нежная систе́ма; (*LING*) неологи́зм.

coin box *n* (*BRIT*) телефо́н-автома́т.

coincide [kəun'saɪd] *vi* совпада́ть (совпа́сть* *perf*).

coincidence [kəu'ɪnsɪdəns] *n* совпаде́ние.

coin-operated ['kɔɪn'ɔpəreɪtɪd] *adj*: **~ machine** автома́т.

Coke® [kəuk] *n* (*drink*) ко́ка-ко́ла; **I would like a ~, please** да́йте пожа́луйста ко́ка-ко́лу.

coke [kəuk] *n* (*coal*) кокс.

Col. *abbr* = **colonel**.

COLA *n abbr* (*US*: = *cost-of-living adjustment*) индекса́ция за́работной пла́ты.

colander ['kɔləndə'] *n* (*CULIN*) дуршла́г.

cold [kəuld] *adj* холо́дный* ♦ *n* хо́лод; (*MED*) просту́да; **it's ~** хо́лодно; **I am** *or* **feel ~** мне хо́лодно; **the wall is ~** э́та стена́ холо́дная; **to catch ~** *or* **a ~** простужа́ться (простуди́ться* *perf*); **in ~ blood** хладнокро́вно; **to have ~ feet** (*fig*) тру́сить* (стру́сить* *perf*); **I gave her the ~ shoulder** я был неприве́тлив с ней.

cold-blooded ['kəuld'blʌdɪd] *adj* (*ZOOL*) холоднокро́вный (холоднокро́вен); (*callous*) хладнокро́вный* (хладнокро́вен).

cold cream *n* ко́льд крем.

coldly ['kəuldlɪ] *adv* хо́лодно.

cold-shoulder [kəuld'ʃəuldə'] *vt* относи́ться* (отнести́сь* *perf*) неприве́тливо к +*dat*.

cold sore *n* лихора́дка* (*на губе́ и́ли носу́*).

cold sweat *n* холо́дный пот.

cold turkey *n* (*inf*): **he is going through ~ ~** у него́ ло́мка.

cold war *n*: **the ~ ~** холо́дная война́.

coleslaw ['kəulslɔ:] *n* капу́стный сала́т с майоне́зом.

colic ['kɔlɪk] *n* ко́лики *pl*.

colicky ['kɔlɪkɪ] *adj* страда́ющий ко́ликами.

collaborate [kə'læbəreɪt] *vi* сотру́дничать

(*impf*).

collaboration [kəlæbə'reɪʃən] *n* сотру́дничество.

collaborator [kə'læbəreɪtə'] *n* (*on book etc*) соа́втор; (*with enemy*) коллаборациони́ст.

collage [kɔ'lɑ:ʒ] *n* (*ART*) колла́ж.

collagen ['kɔlədʒən] *n* коллаге́н.

collapse [kə'læps] *vi* (*building, system, plans*) ру́шиться (ру́хнуть *perf*); (*table etc*) скла́дываться (сложи́ться *perf*); (*company*) разоря́ться (разори́ться *perf*); (*government*) разва́ливаться (развали́ться *perf*); (*resistance*) сломи́ться (*perf*); (*MED: person*) свали́ться (*perf*) ♦ *n* (*of building*) обва́л; (*of system, plans*) круше́ние; (*of company*) разоре́ние; (*of government*) паде́ние; (*MED*) упа́док сил, колла́пс; **a ~d lung** колла́пс лёгкого.

collapsible [kə'læpsəbl] *adj* складно́й.

collar ['kɔlə'] *n* (*of shirt etc*) воротни́к*; (*of dog etc*) оше́йник; (*TECH*) ше́йка* ♦ *vt* (*inf: physically*) схва́тывать (схвати́ть* *perf*); (*to speak to*) заде́рживать (задержа́ть* *perf*).

collarbone ['kɔləbəun] *n* ключи́ца.

collate [kɔ'leɪt] *vt* сопоставля́ть (сопоста́вить* *perf*).

collateral [kə'lætərl] *n* (*COMM*) обеспече́ние креди́та.

collateral damage *n* сопу́тствующее разруше́ние.

collation [kɔ'leɪʃən] *n* сопоставле́ние, слличе́ние; (*CULIN*): **a cold ~** холо́дный буфе́т.

colleague ['kɔli:g] *n* колле́га *m/f*.

collect [kə'lɛkt] *vt* (*gather*) собира́ть (собра́ть* *perf*); (*stamps etc*) коллекциони́ровать (*impf*); (*BRIT: on foot*) заходи́ть* (зайти́* *perf*) за +*instr*; (: *by vehicle*) заезжа́ть* (зае́хать* *perf*) за +*instr*; (*debts etc*) взы́скивать (взыска́ть* *perf*); (*mail*) забира́ть (забра́ть* *perf*) ♦ *vi* (*crowd*) собира́ться (собра́ться* *perf*); **to call ~** (*US*) звони́ть (*impf*) по колле́кту; **to ~ one's thoughts** собира́ться (собра́ться *perf*) с мы́слями; **~ on delivery** (*US*) нало́женный платёж.

collected [kə'lɛktɪd] *adj*: **~ works** собра́ние сочине́ний.

collection [kə'lɛkʃən] *n* (*of stamps etc*) колле́кция; (*of poems etc*) сбо́рник; (*for charity, also REL*) поже́ртвования *ntpl*; (*of mail*) вы́емка.

collective [kə'lɛktɪv] *adj* коллекти́вный ♦ *n* коллекти́в.

collective bargaining *n* перегово́ры ме́жду предпринима́телем и профсою́зами об опла́те труда́ рабо́чих.

collector [kə'lɛktə'] *n* (*of stamps etc*) коллекционе́р; (*of taxes etc*) сбо́рщик(-ица); (*of cash*) инкасса́тор; **~'s item** *or* **piece** вещь, представля́ющая интере́с для коллекционе́ра.

college ['kɔlɪdʒ] *n* (*of university*) ко́лледж; (*of*

technology etc) институ́т; **to go to ~** поступа́ть (поступи́ть* *perf*) в институ́т; **~ of education** уче́бное заведе́ние.

collide [kə'laɪd] *vi (cars, people)* ста́лкиваться (столкну́ться *perf*); **to ~ with sth** ната́лкиваться (натолкну́ться *perf*) на что-н.

collie ['kɔlɪ] *n* ко́лли *m ind*.

colliery ['kɔlɪərɪ] *n (BRIT)* у́гольная ша́хта.

collision [kə'lɪʒən] *n (of vehicles)* столкнове́ние; **to be on a ~ course** находи́ться* (*impf*) на пути́, веду́щем к столкнове́нию; (*fig*) встава́ть* (встать* *perf*) на путь конфронта́ции.

collision damage waiver *n страхо́вка, освобожда́ющая от вы́платы компенса́ции за поврежде́ние взя́той напрока́т маши́ны.*

colloquial [kə'ləukwɪəl] *adj* разгово́рный.

collusion [kə'luːʒən] *n (collaboration)* сго́вор; **in ~ with** в сго́воре с +*instr*.

Cologne [kə'ləun] *n* Кёльн.

cologne [kə'ləun] *n (also: eau de ~)* одеколо́н.

Colombia [kə'lɔmbɪə] *n* Колу́мбия.

Colombian [kə'lɔmbɪən] *adj* колумби́йский* ♦ *n* колумби́ец(-и́йка).

colon ['kəulən] *n (LING)* двоето́чие; (*ANAT*) пряма́я кишка́.

colonel ['kəːnl] *n* полко́вник.

colonial [kə'ləunɪəl] *adj* колониа́льный.

colonize ['kɔlənaɪz] *vt (country etc)* колонизи́ровать (*impf/perf*).

colony ['kɔlənɪ] *n (of people, animals)* коло́ния.

color *etc (US)* = **colour** *etc*.

Colorado beetle [kɔlə'rɑːdəu-] *n* колора́дский жук*.

colossal [kə'lɔsl] *adj* колосса́льный* (колосса́лен).

colour ['kʌləʳ] (*US* color) *n* цвет*; (*of spectacle etc*) кра́сочность *f* ♦ *vt (paint)* раскра́шивать (раскра́сить* *perf*); (*dye*) кра́сить* (покра́сить* *perf*); (*fig: judgement etc*) окра́шивать (окра́сить* *perf*) ♦ *vi (blush)* красне́ть (покрасне́ть *perf*) ♦ *cpd* цветно́й; **~s** *npl (of club etc)* эмбле́ма *fsg*; (*MIL*) флаг *msg*; **skin ~** цвет ко́жи; **in ~** в цве́те; **with flying ~s** с триу́мфом

► **colour in** *vt* раскра́шивать (раскра́сить* *perf*).

colour bar *n* ра́ссовый барье́р.

colour-blind ['kʌləblaɪnd] *adj*: **he is ~** он дальто́ник.

coloured ['kʌləd] *adj* цветно́й.

colour film *n* цветна́я плёнка.

colourful ['kʌləful] *adj (cloth)* цвети́стый (цвети́ст); (*story*) кра́сочный* (кра́сочен); (*personality*) я́ркий*.

colouring ['kʌlərɪŋ] *n (complexion)* цвет лица́; (*in food*) краси́тель *m*.

colour scheme *n* цветова́я га́мма.

colour supplement *n (BRIT: PRESS)* иллюстри́рованное приложе́ние.

colour television *n* цветно́й телеви́зор.

colt [kəult] *n* жеребёнок*.

column ['kɔləm] *n (of people, also ARCHIT)* коло́нна; (*of smoke*) столб*; (*PRESS*) ру́брика; **the editorial ~** реда́кторская статья́*.

columnist ['kɔləmnɪst] *n (PRESS)* обозрева́тель *m*.

coma ['kəumə] *n (MED)*: **to be in a ~** находи́ться* (*impf*) в ко́ме.

comb [kəum] *n (for hair)* расчёска; (: *ornamental*) гре́бень* *m* ♦ *vt (hair)* расчёсывать (расчеса́ть* *perf*); (*area*) прочёсывать (прочеса́ть* *perf*).

combat [*n* 'kɔmbæt, *vt* kɔm'bæt] *n (fighting)* бой*; (*battle*) би́тва ♦ *vt* боро́ться* (*impf*) про́тив +*gen*.

combination [kɔmbɪ'neɪʃən] *n (mixture)* сочета́ние, комбина́ция; (*code*) код.

combination lock *n* замо́к* с ши́фром.

combine [*vb* kəm'baɪn, *n* 'kɔmbaɪn] *vt* комбини́ровать (скомбини́ровать *perf*) ♦ *vi (groups)* объединя́ться (объедини́ться *perf*); (*CHEM*) вступа́ть (вступи́ть* *perf*) в соедине́ние ♦ *n (ECON)* объедине́ние; (*also: ~ harvester*) комба́йн; **to ~ sth with sth** (*qualities*) сочета́ть *perf* что-н с чем-н; (*activities*) совмеща́ть (совмести́ть* *perf*) что-н с чем-н; **a ~d effort** совме́стное уси́лие.

combo ['kɔmbəu] *n (JAZZ)* ко́мбо.

combustible [kəm'bʌstɪbl] *adj* горю́чий*.

combustion [kəm'bʌstʃən] *n (act)* сгора́ние; (*process*) горе́ние.

KEYWORD

come [kʌm] (*pt* **came**, *pp* **come**) *vi* **1** (*move towards: on foot*) подходи́ть* (подойти́* *perf*); (: *by transport*) подъезжа́ть (подъе́хать* *perf*); **they came to a river** (*on foot*) они́ подошли́ к реке́; (*by transport*) они́ подъе́хали к реке́; **he came running up to us** он побежа́л к нам; **to come running** подбега́ть (подбежа́ть* *perf*) **2** (*arrive: on foot*) приходи́ть* (прийти́* *perf*); (: *by transport*) приезжа́ть (прие́хать* *perf*); **to come home** (*on foot*) приходи́ть* (прийти́* *perf*) домо́й; (*by transport*) приезжа́ть (прие́хать* *perf*) домо́й; **he came running to tell us** он прибежа́л, сказа́ть нам; **are you coming to my party?** Вы придёте ко мне на вечери́нку?; **I've only come for an hour** я зашёл то́лько на час **3** (*reach: power, decision, conclusion*): **to come to** приходи́ть* (прийти́* *perf*) к +*dat*; **the bill came to £40** счёт был £40; **her hair came to her waist** у неё бы́ли во́лосы до по́яса **4** (*occur*): **an idea came to me** мне в го́лову

---

* marks translations which have irregular inflections. The Russian-English side of the dictionary gives inflectional information.

пришла́ иде́я
5 (*be, become*): **to come into being** возника́ть
(возни́кнуть *perf*); **to come loose** отходи́ть*
(отойти́* *perf*); **I've come to like him** он стал
мне нра́виться
► **come about** *vi*: **how did it come about?**
каки́м о́бразом э́то получи́лось?; **it came
about through...** э́то получи́лось из-за +*gen*
► **come across** *vt fus* ната́лкиваться
(натолкну́ться *perf*) на +*acc*
◆ *vi*: **to come across well/badly** производи́ть*
(произвести́* *perf*) хоро́шее/плохо́е
впечатле́ние
► **come along** *vi* (*pupil, work*) продвига́ться
(продви́нуться *perf*); **come along!** идёмте!,
пошли́!
► **come apart** *vi* (*break*) лома́ться (слома́ться
perf); (*can be dismantled*) разбира́ться (*impf*);
(*tear*) рва́ться* (разорва́ться* *perf*)
► **come away** *vi* (*leave*) уходи́ть* (уйти́* *perf*);
(*to become detached*) отходи́ть* (отойти́*
perf)
► **come back** *vi* (*return*) возвраща́ться
(верну́ться *perf*); (*inf*): **can I come back to you
on that one?** я ещё верну́сь к Вам с э́тим,
ла́дно?
► **come by** *vt fus* (*acquire*) достава́ть* (доста́ть*
perf)
► **come down** *vi* (*price*) понижа́ться
(пони́зиться* *perf*); **the tree came down in the
storm** де́рево снесло́ бу́рей; **the building will
have to come down soon** зда́ние должны́
ско́ро снести́
► **come forward** *vi* (*volunteer*) вызыва́ться
(вы́зваться* *perf*)
► **come from** *vt fus* (*place, source etc*): **she
comes from India** она́ из Йнди́и
► **come in** *vi* (*person*) входи́ть* (войти́* *perf*);
(*on deal etc*): **to come in on** вступа́ть
(вступи́ть* *perf*) в +*acc*; **where does he come
in?** в чём его́ роль?
► **come in for** *vt fus* подверга́ться
(подве́ргнуться* *perf*) +*dat*
► **come into** *vt fus* (*fashion*) входи́ть* (войти́*
perf) в +*acc*; (*be involved in*) игра́ть (*impf*) роль
в +*prp*; **to come into money** получа́ть
(получи́ть* *perf*) су́мму де́нег
► **come off** *vi* (*button*) отрыва́ться
(оторва́ться *perf*); (*handle*) отла́мываться
(отлома́ться *perf*); (*can be taken off*)
снима́ться (*impf*); (*attempt*) удава́ться*
(уда́ться* *perf*)
► **come on** *vi* (*pupil*) де́лать (сде́лать *perf*)
успе́хи; (*work etc*) продвига́ться (*impf*); (*lights
etc*) включа́ться (включи́ться* *perf*); **come
on!** (ну,) дава́йте!
► **come out** *vi* (*fact*) станови́ться (стать* *perf*)
изве́стным(-ой); (*book, sun*) выходи́ть*
(вы́йти* *perf*); (*stain*) сходи́ть* (сойти́* *perf*);
(*person*) выходи́ть* (вы́йти* *perf*); (*workers*):
to come out on strike выходи́ть* (вы́йти* *perf*)

на забасто́вку
► **come over** *vt fus*: **I don't know what's come
over him!** я не зна́ю, что с ним тако́е!
► **come round** *vi* (MED) очну́ться (*perf*),
приходи́ть* (прийти́* *perf*) в себя́
► **come through** *vt fus* (*survive*) пережи́ть*
(*perf*); (: *operation*) переноси́ть* (перенести́*
perf)
◆ *vi*: **his visa came through yesterday** его́ ви́за
пришла́ вчера́
► **come to** *vi* (MED) очну́ться (*perf*), приходи́ть*
(прийти́* *perf*) в себя́
◆ *vt fus*: **how much does it come to?** ско́лько
э́то всё бу́дет?
► **come under** *vt fus*: **to come under (the
heading)** идти́* (*impf*) под заголо́вком; **to
come under criticism from ...** подверга́ться
(подве́ргнуться *perf*) кри́тике со стороны́
+*gen* ...; **he has come under pressure from his
boss** его́ нача́льник ока́зывал на него́
давле́ние
► **come up** *vi* (*sun*) всходи́ть* (взойти́* *perf*);
(*approach: event*) приближа́ться (*impf*); (*arise:
questions*) встава́ть (встать* *perf*); (*to be
mentioned*) быть (*impf*) затро́нутым; **I can't
come with you, something important has
come up** я не смогу́ пойти́ с тобо́й, у меня́
возни́кло ва́жное де́ло
► **come up against** *vt fus* ната́лкиваться
(натолкну́ться *perf*) на +*acc*
► **come up to** *vt fus*: **the film didn't come up to
our expectations** фи́льм не оправда́л на́ши
ожида́ния
► **come up with** *vt fus* (*idea, solution*)
приду́мывать (приду́мать *perf*); (*money*)
найти́* (*perf*)
► **come upon** *vt fus* ната́лкиваться
(натолкну́ться *perf*) на +*acc*.

comeback ['kʌmbæk] *n* (*reaction*)
язви́тельный отве́т; (*response*) возраже́ние;
to make a ~ (*of actor etc*) обрета́ть (обрести́*
perf) но́вую популя́рность.
Comecon ['kɔmɪkɔn] *n abbr* (= *Council for
Mutual Economic Aid*) ≈ СЭВ= *Сове́т
Экономи́ческой Взаимопо́мощи.*
comedian [kə'miːdɪən] *n* ко́мик.
comedienne [kəmiːdɪ'ɛn] *n* коми́ческая
актри́са.
comedown ['kʌmdaun] *n* (*inf: humiliation*)
униже́ние; (: *demotion*) пониже́ние.
comedy ['kɔmɪdɪ] *n* (*play, film*) коме́дия;
(*humour*) коми́зм.
comet ['kɔmɪt] *n* коме́та.
comeuppance [kʌm'ʌpəns] *n*: **to get one's ~**
получа́ть (получи́ть* *perf*) по заслу́гам.
comfort ['kʌmfət] *n* (*well-being*) комфо́рт;
(*solace*) утеше́ние; (*relief*) облегче́ние ◆ *vt*
утеша́ть (уте́шить *perf*); **~s** *npl* (*luxuries*)
удо́бства *ntpl*.
comfortable ['kʌmfətəbl] *adj* (*furniture, room*)

удо́бный* (удо́бен), комфорта́бельный*
(комфорта́белен); (*walk etc*) лёгкий*;
(*majority*) прили́чный* (прили́чен); **to be ~**
(*person: physically*) чу́вствовать (*impf*) себя́
удо́бно; (: *financially*) жить (*impf*) в доста́тке;
(*patient*) чу́вствовать (*impf*) себя́ норма́льно;
I don't feel very ~ about it я чу́вствую себя́
нело́вко в да́нном слу́чае; **make yourself ~**
располага́йтесь поудо́бнее.
comfortably [ˈkʌmfətəblɪ] *adv* удо́бно.
comforter [ˈkʌmfətəʳ] *n* (*US*) со́ска-пусты́шка*.
comfort station *n* (*US*) обще́ственный туале́т.
comic [ˈkɒmɪk] *adj* коми́ческий*, смешно́й ♦ *n*
(*comedian*) ко́мик; (*BRIT: magazine*) ко́микс.
comical [ˈkɒmɪkl] *adj* смешно́й* (смешо́н),
коми́чный* (коми́чен).
comic strip *n* ко́микс (*се́рия рису́нков*).
coming [ˈkʌmɪŋ] *n* прибы́тие ♦ *adj*
(*approaching*) приближа́ющийся; (*next*)
сле́дующий*; (*future*) бу́дущий*; **in the ~
weeks** в тече́ние сле́дующих неде́ль.
coming(s) and going(s) *n(pl)* прихо́д *msg* и
ухо́д *msg*.
Comintern [ˈkɒmɪntəːn] *n* (*POL*) Коминте́рн.
comma [ˈkɒmə] *n* (*LING*) запята́я *f adj*.
command [kəˈmɑːnd] *n* (*order*) кома́нда;
(*control*) контро́ль *m*; (*MIL*) кома́ндование;
(*mastery*) владе́ние; (*COMPUT*) кома́нда,
директи́ва ♦ *vt* (*troops*) кома́ндовать (*impf*)
+*instr*; (*be able to get*) располага́ть (*impf*)
+*instr*; (*deserve*) заслу́живать (*impf*) +*gen*; **to
be in ~ of** (*situation*) владе́ть (овладе́ть *perf*)
+*instr*; **to take ~ of** (*MIL*) принима́ть (приня́ть*
perf) кома́ндование +*instr*; **to have at one's ~**
(*resources etc*) име́ть (*impf*) в своём
распоряже́нии; **he has a good ~ of English** он
хорошо́ владе́ет англи́йским языко́м; **to ~
sb to do** прика́зывать (приказа́ть* *perf*)
кому́-н +*infin*.
commandant [ˈkɒməndænt] *n* коменда́нт.
command economy *n* кома́ндная
эконо́мика.
commandeer [kɒmənˈdɪəʳ] *vt* (*requisition*)
реквизи́ровать (*impf/perf*); (*fig*) присва́ивать
(присво́ить *perf*).
commander [kəˈmɑːndəʳ] *n* (*MIL: of troops*)
кома́ндующий *m adj*; (: *of batallion*)
команди́р.
commander in chief *n* главнокома́ндующий
m adj.
commanding [kəˈmɑːndɪŋ] *adj* (*appearance*)
внуши́тельный*; (*voice etc*) вла́стный*;
(*situation*) госпо́дствующий*.
commanding officer *n* команди́р.
commandment [kəˈmɑːndmənt] *n* за́поведь *f*.
command module *n* (*SPACE*) кома́ндный
отсе́к корабля́.
commando [kəˈmɑːndəu] *n* (*group*) деса́нтные

войска́ *ntpl*; (*soldier*) деса́нтник.
commemorate [kəˈmɛməreɪt] *vt* (*with statue
etc*) увекове́чивать (увекове́чить *perf*); (*with
celebration etc*) отмеча́ть (отме́тить* *perf*).
commemoration [kəmɛməˈreɪʃən] *n*
ознаменова́ние.
commemorative [kəˈmɛmərətɪv] *adj* (*stamp*)
юбиле́йный; (*plaque*) мемориа́льный.
commence [kəˈmɛns] *vt* приступа́ть
(приступи́ть* *perf*) к +*dat* ♦ *vi* начина́ться
(нача́ться* *perf*).
commend [kəˈmɛnd] *vt* хвали́ть* (похвали́ть*
perf); (*recommend*): **to ~ sth to sb**
рекомендова́ть (порекомендова́ть *perf*)
что-н кому́-н.
commendable [kəˈmɛndəbl] *adj* похва́льный*
(похва́лен).
commendation [kɒmɛnˈdeɪʃən] *n*
благода́рность *f*.
commensurate [kəˈmɛnʃərɪt] *adj*: **~ with**
соразме́рный* (соразме́рен) +*dat or c* +*instr*.
comment [ˈkɒmɛnt] *n* (*remark*) замеча́ние; (*on
situation*) коммента́рий ♦ *vi*: **to ~ (on)**
комменти́ровать (прокомменти́ровать *perf*)
(+*acc*); **to ~ that** поясня́ть (поясни́ть *perf*),
что; **"no ~"** "возде́рживаюсь от
коммента́риев".
commentary [ˈkɒməntərɪ] *n* репорта́ж; (*book,
article*) коммента́рий.
commentator [ˈkɒmənteɪtəʳ] *n* (*TV, RADIO*)
коммента́тор; (**sports**) **~** спорти́вный
коммента́тор.
commerce [ˈkɒməːs] *n* комме́рция.
commercial [kəˈməːʃəl] *adj* (*organization*)
комме́рческий*; (*success, failure*)
фина́нсовый ♦ *n* (*TV, RADIO*) рекла́ма.
commercial bank *n* комме́рческий банк.
commercial break *n* рекла́мная па́уза.
commercial college *n* институ́т комме́рции.
commercialism [kəˈməːʃəlɪzəm] *n*
меркантили́зм.
commercialized [kəˈməːʃəlaɪzd] *adj* (*pej*)
поста́вленный на комме́рческую осно́ву.
commercial radio *n* комме́рческое ра́дио.
commercial television *n* комме́рческое
телеви́дение.
commercial traveller *n* коммивояжёр.
commercial vehicle *n* комме́рческий
тра́нспорт.
commiserate [kəˈmɪzəreɪt] *vi*: **to ~ with**
сочу́вствовать (посочу́вствовать *perf*) +*dat*.
commission [kəˈmɪʃən] *n* (*order for work*)
зака́з; (*COMM*) комиссио́нные *pl adj*,
комиссио́нное вознагражде́ние; (*committee*)
коми́ссия; (*MIL*) офице́рский* чин ♦ *vt* (*order*)
зака́зывать (заказа́ть* *perf*); (*MIL*)
присва́ивать (присво́ить *perf*) офице́рский*
чин +*dat*; **out of ~** (*NAUT*) не приго́дный

---

* marks translations which have irregular inflections. The Russian-English side of the dictionary gives inflectional information.

(приго́ден) к пла́ванию; (*machine*)
неиспра́вный* (неиспра́вен); **I get 10% ~** я
получа́ю 10% комиссио́нных; **~ of inquiry**
сле́дственная коми́ссия; **to ~ sb to do**
sth поруча́ть (поручи́ть* *perf*) кому́-н +*infin*; **to ~**
sth from sb зака́зывать (заказа́ть* *perf*) что-н
кому́-н.

commissionaire [kəmɪʃə'nɛəʳ] *n* (*BRIT*)
швейца́р.

commissioner [kə'mɪʃənəʳ] *n*: (**police**) ~
полице́йский* комисса́р.

commit [kə'mɪt] *vt* (*crime*) соверша́ть
(соверши́ть *perf*); (*money*) выделя́ть
(вы́делить *perf*); (*entrust*) вверя́ть (вве́рить
perf); **to ~ o.s.** принима́ть (приня́ть* *perf*) на
себя́ обяза́тельства; **to ~ suicide** соверша́ть
(соверши́ть *perf*) самоуби́йство; **to ~ to**
writing запи́сывать (записа́ть* *perf*); **to ~ to**
memory запомина́ть (запо́мнить *perf*); **to ~**
sb for trial отдава́ть* (отда́ть* *perf*) кого́-н
под суд.

commitment [kə'mɪtmənt] *n* (*belief*)
пре́данность *f*; (*obligation*) обяза́тельство.

committed [kə'mɪtɪd] *adj* (*supporter*)
приве́рженный (приве́ржен).

committee [kə'mɪtɪ] *n* комите́т; **to be on a ~**
входи́ть* (*impf*) в соста́в комите́та.

committee meeting *n* заседа́ние комите́та.

commodity [kə'mɔdɪtɪ] *n* (*saleable item*) това́р;
(*food*) проду́кт.

commodity exchange *n* това́рная би́ржа.

common ['kɔmən] *adj* (*shared*) о́бщий*; (*usual*,
ordinary) обы́чный; (*vulgar*) вульга́рный*
(вульга́рен) ♦ *n* обще́ственный луг*; **the C~s**
npl (*also*: **the House of C~s**: *BRIT*) Пала́та *fsg*
О́бщин; **to have sth in ~ (with sb)** име́ть (*impf*)
что-н о́бщее (с кем-н); **in ~ use** в широ́ком
употребле́нии; **it's ~ knowledge that**
общеизве́стно, что; **to** *or* **for the ~ good** для
всео́бщего бла́га.

common cold *n* обыкнове́нная просту́да.

common denominator *n* (*MATH*) о́бщий*
знамена́тель *m*; (*characteristic*) о́бщая черта́;
(*attitude*) о́бщее* мне́ние.

commoner ['kɔmənəʳ] *n* простолюди́н.

common ground *n* (*fig*) то́чки *fpl*
соприкоснове́ния.

common land *n* обще́ственная земля́*.

common law *n* обы́чное пра́во.

common-law ['kɔmənlɔ:] *adj* гражда́нский*.

commonly ['kɔmənlɪ] *adv* обы́чно.

Common Market *n*: **the ~ ~** О́бщий* ры́нок*.

commonplace ['kɔmənpleɪs] *adj* обы́чный,
обы́денный.

common room *n* ко́мната о́тдыха (*для*
студе́нтов, учителе́й и т.д.).

common sense *n* здра́вый смысл.

Commonwealth ['kɔmənwɛlθ] *n* (*BRIT*): **the ~**
Содру́жество.

commotion [kə'məuʃən] *n* сумато́ха.

communal ['kɔmju:nl] *adj* (*shared*) о́бщий*;

(*life*) обще́ственный; **a ~ flat** коммуна́льная
кварти́ра.

commune [*n* 'kɔmju:n, *vi* kə'mju:n] *n* комму́на
♦ *vi*: **to ~ with** обща́ться (*impf*) с +*instr*.

communicate [kə'mju:nɪkeɪt] *vt* передава́ть*
(переда́ть* *perf*) ♦ *vi*: **to ~ (with)** обща́ться
(*impf*) (с +*instr*); **to ~ (by letter)** обраща́ться
(обрати́ться* *perf*) пи́сьменно.

communication [kəmju:nɪ'keɪʃən] *n* (*process*)
коммуника́ция; (*letter etc*) сообще́ние.

communication cord *n* (*BRIT*) авари́йный
сигна́л "стоп".

communications network [kəmju:nɪ'keɪʃənz-]
n систе́ма коммуника́ций.

communications satellite *n* спу́тник свя́зи.

communicative [kə'mju:nɪkətɪv] *adj* (*person*)
общи́тельный* (общи́телен).

communion [kə'mju:nɪən] *n* (*also*: **Holy C~**)
Свято́е Прича́стие.

communiqué [kə'mju:nɪkeɪ] *n* коммюнике́ *nt*
ind.

communism ['kɔmjunɪzəm] *n* коммуни́зм.

communist ['kɔmjunɪst] *adj* коммунист-
и́ческий* ♦ *n* коммуни́ст(ка).

community [kə'mju:nɪtɪ] *n* (*public*)
обще́ственность *f*; (*within larger group*)
общи́на; **the business ~** деловы́е круги́ *mpl*.

community centre *n* ≈ обще́ственный центр.

community charge *n* (*BRIT*: *formerly*)
поду́шный нало́г.

community chest *n* (*US*) объединённый
благотвори́тельный фонд.

community health centre *n* райо́нная
поликли́ника.

community home *n* (*BRIT*: *for children*)
де́тский* дом.

community service *n* трудова́я пови́нность *f*
(*как фо́рма наказа́ния*).

community spirit *n* чу́вство о́бщности *or*
това́рищества.

commutation ticket [kɔmju'teɪʃən-] *n* (*US*)
сезо́нный биле́т.

commute [kə'mju:t] *vi* (*to work*) е́здить на
рабо́ту из при́города в го́род ♦ *vt* (*LAW*)
смягча́ть (смягчи́ть *perf*) наказа́ние.

commuter [kə'mju:təʳ] *n* челове́к, кото́рый
е́здит на рабо́ту из при́города в го́род; **~**
train при́городный по́езд.

compact [*adj* kəm'pækt, *n* 'kɔmpækt] *adj*
компа́ктный* (компа́ктен) ♦ *n* (*also*: **powder**
~) пу́дреница.

compact disc *n* компа́кт-диск.

compact-disc player [kɔmpækt'dɪsk-] *n*
прои́грыватель *m* для компа́кт-ди́сков.

companion [kəm'pænjən] *n* спу́тник(-ица).

companionship [kəm'pænjənʃɪp] *n* обще́ние.

companionway [kəm'pænjənweɪ] *n* (*NAUT*)
трап.

company ['kʌmpənɪ] *n* (*COMM*) компа́ния;
(*THEAT*) тру́ппа; (*MIL*) ро́та; (*companionship*)
компа́ния, о́бщество; **he's good ~** его́

о́бщество прия́тно; **we have** ~ у нас го́сти;
to keep sb ~ составля́ть (соста́вить* *perf*)
кому́-н компа́нию; **to part** ~ **with**
расходи́ться* (разойти́сь* *perf*) с +*instr*; **Smith and C**~ Смит и Компа́ния.
company car *n* служе́бная маши́на.
company director *n* дире́ктор* компа́нии.
company secretary *n* (*BRIT*) секрета́рь* *m(f)* фи́рмы.
comparable ['kɔmpərəbl] *adj* (*size*) сравни́мый (сравни́м); (*style*) сопостави́мый (сопостави́м); (*car, property etc*) подо́бный* (подо́бен).
comparative [kəm'pærətɪv] *adj* (*also LING*) сравни́тельный; (*relative*) относи́тельный (относи́телен).
comparatively [kəm'pærətɪvlɪ] *adv* (*relatively*) относи́тельно.
compare [kəm'pɛəʳ] *vt*: **to** ~ **sb/sth with** *or* **to** (*liken*) сра́внивать (сравни́ть *perf*) кого́-н/что-н с +*instr*; (*set side by side*) сопоставля́ть (сопоста́вить* *perf*) кого́-н/что-н с +*instr* ◆ *vi*: **to** ~ (**with**) соотноси́ться (*impf*) (с +*instr*); **how do the prices** ~? как соотно́сятся це́ны?; ~**d with** *or* **to** по сравне́нию *or* в сравне́нии с +*instr*.
comparison [kəm'pærɪsn] *n* (*see vt*) сравне́ние; сопоставле́ние; **in** ~ (**with**) по сравне́нию *or* в сравне́нии (с +*instr*).
compartment [kəm'pɑ:tmənt] *n* (*RAIL*) купе́ *nt ind*; (*section*) отделе́ние.
compass ['kʌmpəs] *n* (*instrument*) ко́мпас; (*fig*) диапазо́н; ~**es** *npl* (*also*: **pair of** ~**es**) ци́ркуль *msg*; **beyond the** ~ **of** за преде́лами +*gen*; **within the** ~ **of** в преде́лах +*gen*.
compassion [kəm'pæʃən] *n* сострада́ние.
compassionate [kəm'pæʃənɪt] *adj* сострада́тельный* (сострада́телен); **on** ~ **grounds** по состоя́нию здоро́вья; ~ **leave** о́тпуск по семе́йным обстоя́тельствам.
compatibility [kəmpætɪ'bɪlɪtɪ] *n* совмести́мость *f*.
compatible [kəm'pætɪbl] *adj* (*also COMPUT*) совмести́мый (совмести́м).
compel [kəm'pɛl] *vt* вынужда́ть (вы́нудить* *perf*).
compelling [kəm'pɛlɪŋ] *adj* (*fig: argument*) убеди́тельный* (убеди́телен); (*: reason*) настоя́тельный.
compendium [kəm'pɛndɪəm] *n* (*summary*) резюме́ *nt ind*.
compensate ['kɔmpənseɪt] *vt*: **to** ~ **sb for sth** компенси́ровать (*impf/perf*) кому́-н что-н ◆ *vi*: **to** ~ **for** (*loss, distress etc*) компенси́ровать (*impf/perf*).
compensation [kɔmpən'seɪʃən] *n* компенса́ция; (*money*) де́нежная компенса́ция.

compère ['kɔmpɛəʳ] *n* (*TV, RADIO*) веду́щий*(-ая) *m(f) adj*.
compete [kəm'pi:t] *vi* (*in contest etc*) соревнова́ться (*impf*); **to** ~ (**with**) (*companies*) конкури́ровать (*impf*) (с +*instr*); (*rivals*) сопе́рничать (*impf*) (с +*instr*); **to** ~ (**with one another**) (*theories etc*) сопе́рничать (*impf*) друг с дру́гом.
competence ['kɔmpɪtəns] *n* компете́нция.
competent ['kɔmpɪtənt] *adj* (*person*) компете́нтный* (компете́нтен); (*piece of work*) иску́сный.
competing [kəm'pi:tɪŋ] *adj* (*firms*) конкури́рующий; (*claims, explanations*) разноречи́вый* (разноречи́в).
competition [kɔmpɪ'tɪʃən] *n* (*contest*) соревнова́ние; (*between firms*) конкуре́нция; (*between rivals*) сопе́рничество; **to be in** ~ **with** конкури́ровать (*impf*) с +*instr*.
competitive [kəm'pɛtɪtɪv] *adj* (*industry*) осно́ванный на конкуре́нции; (*person*) честолюби́вый (честолюби́в); (*price etc*) конкурентоспосо́бный* (конкурентоспосо́бен); (*sport*) состяза́тельный.
competitive examination *n* ко́нкурс.
competitor [kəm'pɛtɪtəʳ] *n* (*rival*) сопе́рник, конкуре́нт; (*in musical competition*) конкурса́нт; (*participant*) уча́стник(-ица) соревнова́ния.
compile [kəm'paɪl] *vt* составля́ть (соста́вить* *perf*).
complacency [kəm'pleɪsnsɪ] *n* безмяте́жность *f*.
complacent [kəm'pleɪsnt] *adj* безмяте́жный (безмяте́жен).
complain [kəm'pleɪn] *vi*: **to** ~ (**about**) жа́ловаться (пожа́ловаться *perf*) (на +*acc*); **to** ~ **of a pain** жа́ловаться (пожа́ловаться *perf*) на боль.
complaint [kəm'pleɪnt] *n* жа́лоба; **to make a** ~ **against** подава́ть* (пода́ть* *perf*) жа́лобу на +*acc*.
complement [*n* 'kɔmplɪmənt, *vb* 'kɔmplɪmɛnt] *n* (*supplement*) дополне́ние; (*ship's crew*) экипа́ж ◆ *vt* (*enhance*) дополня́ть (*impf*); **to have a full** ~ **of** име́ть (*impf*) по́лный компле́кт +*gen*.
complementary [kɔmplɪ'mɛntərɪ] *adj*: **they are** ~ (**to one another**) они́ дополня́ют друг дру́га.
complete [kəm'pli:t] *adj* по́лный*; (*finished*) заверше́нный (заверше́н) ◆ *vt* (*building, task*) заверша́ть (заверши́ть *perf*); (*set etc*) комплектова́ть (укомплектова́ть *perf*); (*a form*) заполня́ть (запо́лнить *perf*); **it's a** ~ **disaster** э́то по́лный прова́л.
completely [kəm'pli:tlɪ] *adv* по́лностью,

совершённо.
completion [kəm'pli:ʃən] *n* (*of building*)
завершёние; (*of contract*) совершёние; **to be**
nearing ~ блйзиться (*impf*) к завершёнию; **on**
~ по завершёнии.
complex ['kɔmplɛks] *adj* слóжный*,
кóмплексный; (*also PSYCH*) кóмплекс.
complexion [kəm'plɛkʃən] *n* (*of face*) цвет*
лицá; (*nature*) харáктер.
complexity [kəm'plɛksɪtɪ] *n* слóжность *f*.
compliance [kəm'plaɪəns] *n* (*submission*)
послушáние; (*agreement*) соглáсие; **~ with**
слéдование +*dat*; **in ~ with** в соотвéтствии с
+*instr*.
compliant [kəm'plaɪənt] *adj* послýшный*
(послýшен).
complicate ['kɔmplɪkeɪt] *vt* усложнять
(усложнйть *perf*).
complicated ['kɔmplɪkeɪtɪd] *adj* слóжный*
(слóжен).
complication [kɔmplɪ'keɪʃən] *n* (*also MED*)
осложнéние.
complicity [kəm'plɪsɪtɪ] *n* соучáстие.
compliment [*n* 'kɔmplɪmənt, *vb* 'kɔmplɪmɛnt] *n*
комплимéнт, хвалá ♦ *vt* хвалйть (похвалйть
perf); **~s** *npl* (*regards*) привéты *mpl*; **to ~ sb,**
pay sb a ~ дéлать (сдéлать *perf*) комý-н
комплимéнт; **to ~ sb (on sth** *or* **on doing)**
поздравлять (поздрáвить* *perf*) когó-н (с
чем-н).
complimentary [kɔmplɪ'mɛntərɪ] *adj* (*remark*)
лéстный* (лéстен); (*ticket etc*) дáрственный.
compliments slip *n* фúрменный бланк для
неофициáльных запúсок.
comply [kəm'plaɪ] *vi*: **to ~ (with)** подчиняться
(подчинйться *perf*) (+*dat*).
component [kəm'pəunənt] *adj* составнóй ♦ *n*
компонéнт.
compose [kəm'pəuz] *vt* (*write*) сочинять
(сочинйть *perf*); (*form*): **to be ~d of** состоять
(*impf*) из +*gen*; **to ~ o.s.** успокáиваться
(успокóиться *perf*).
composed [kəm'pəuzd] *adj* спокóйный*
(спокóен).
composer [kəm'pəuzə'] *n* композúтор.
composite ['kɔmpəzɪt] *adj* составнóй; (*BOT*)
сложноцвéтный; (*MATH*) слóжный.
composition [kɔmpə'zɪʃən] *n* (*structure*)
состáв; (*essay*) сочинéние; (*MUS*)
композúция.
compositor [kəm'pɔzɪtə'] *n* нарóбщик.
compos mentis ['kɔmpɔs 'mɛntɪs] *adj*
вменяемый (вменяем).
compost ['kɔmpɔst] *n* компóст; (*also:* **potting**
~) удóбренная земля.
composure [kəm'pəuʒə'] *n* самооблáдание.
compound [*n, adj* 'kɔmpaund, *vt* kəm'paund] *n*
(*CHEM*) соединéние; (*enclosure*) укреплённый
кóмплекс; (*LING*) слóжное слóво* ♦ *adj*
слóжный ♦ *vt* (*problem etc*) осложнять
(осложнйть *perf*).

compound fracture *n* открытый перелóм.
compound interest *n* слóжные процéнты *pl*.
comprehend [kɔmprɪ'hɛnd] *vt* постигáть
(постúгнуть *or* постúчь* *perf*).
comprehension [kɔmprɪ'hɛnʃən] *n* понимáние.
comprehensive [kɔmprɪ'hɛnsɪv] *adj*
исчéрпывающий* (исчéрпывающ) ♦ *n* =
comprehensive school; ~ insurance
всеобъéмлющее страховáние.
comprehensive school *n* (*BRIT*) срéдняя
шкóла.
compress [*vt* kəm'prɛs, *n* 'kɔmprɛs] *vt* (*air*)
сжимáть (сжать* *perf*); (*cotton, paper*)
прессовáть (спрессовáть *perf*); (*text etc*)
сокращáть (сократúть* *perf*) ♦ *n* компрéсс.
compressed air [kəm'prɛst-] *n* сжáтый вóздух.
compression [kəm'prɛʃən] *n* (*of air*) сжáтие; (*of*
text) сокращéние.
comprise [kəm'praɪz] *vt* (*also:* **be ~d of**)
включáть (*impf*) в себя, состоять (*impf*) из
+*gen*; (*constitute*) составлять (состáвить*
perf).
compromise ['kɔmprəmaɪz] *n* компромúсс ♦ *vt*
компрометúровать (скомпрометúровать
perf) ♦ *vi* (*make concessions*) идтú* (пойтú*
perf) на компромúсс ♦ *cpd* компромúссный.
compulsion [kəm'pʌlʃən] *n* (*desire*) влечéние;
(*force*) принуждéние; **under ~** по
принуждéнию.
compulsive [kəm'pʌlsɪv] *adj* (*gambler etc*)
безрассýдный; (*behaviour*) маниакáльный;
(*reading etc*) захвáтывающий*
(захвáтывающ); **he's a ~ liar** он
неисправúмый лгун.
compulsory [kəm'pʌlsərɪ] *adj* (*attendance*)
обязáтельный (обязáтелен); (*redundancy*)
принудúтельный* (принудúтелен).
compulsory purchase *n* обязáтельная
покýпка*.
compunction [kəm'pʌŋkʃən] *n* раскáяние; **to**
have no ~ about doing дéлать (сдéлать *perf*)
что-н без всякого сожалéния.
computer [kəm'pju:tə'] *n* компьютер ♦ *cpd*
компьютерный; **the process is done by ~**
процéсс выполняется при пóмощи
компьютера.
computer game *n* компьютерная игрá*.
computerization [kəmpju:təraɪ'zeɪʃən] *n*
компьютеризáция.
computerize [kəm'pju:təraɪz] *vt*
компьютеризовáть (*impf/perf*); **to ~**
information обрабáтывать (обрабóтать *perf*)
информáцию на компьютере.
computer literate *adj*: **to be ~ ~** умéть (*impf*)
пóльзоваться компьютером.
computer peripheral *n* периферúйное
устрóйство (*компьютера*). .
computer programmer *n* программúст.
computer programming *n* программú-
рование.
computer science *n* электрóнно-

вычисли́тельная нау́ка.
computer scientist n специали́ст в о́бласти ЭВМ.
computing [kəm'pju:tɪŋ] n (activity) рабо́та на компью́тере; (science) электро́нно-вычисли́тельная нау́ка; **I've never done any ~** я никогда́ не рабо́тал на компью́тере.
comrade ['kɔmrɪd] n (POL, MIL) сора́тник; (friend) това́рищ.
comradeship ['kɔmrɪdʃɪp] n това́рищество.
Comsat® ['kɔmsæt] n abbr = **communications satellite.**
con [kɔn] vt надува́ть (наду́ть perf) ♦ n (trick) обма́н; **to ~ sb into doing** обма́ном заста́вля́ть (заста́вить* perf) кого́-н +infin.
concave ['kɔnkeɪv] adj (mirror etc) во́гнутый; (cheeks) впа́лый.
conceal [kən'si:l] vt (hide) укрыва́ть (укры́ть* perf); (keep back) скрыва́ть (скрыть* perf).
concede [kən'si:d] vt признава́ть* (призна́ть perf) ♦ vi (admit error) признава́ться (призна́ться perf); (admit defeat) сдава́ться* (сда́ться* perf).
conceit [kən'si:t] n высокоме́рие.
conceited [kən'si:tɪd] adj высокоме́рный.
conceivable [kən'si:vəbl] adj мы́слимый (мы́слим); **it is ~ that** ... вполне́ допусти́мо, что ....
conceivably [kən'si:vəblɪ] adv: **he may ~ be right** возмо́жно, что он прав.
conceive [kən'si:v] vt (child) зача́ть* (perf); (idea) заду́мывать (заду́мать perf) ♦ vi (BIO) забере́менеть (perf); **to ~ of sth** представля́ть (предста́вить* perf) что-н.
concentrate ['kɔnsəntreɪt] vi сосредото́чиваться (сосредото́читься perf), концентри́роваться (сконцентри́роваться perf) ♦ vt: **to ~ (on)** (energies etc) сосредото́чивать (сосредото́чить perf) or концентри́ровать (сконцентри́ровать perf) (на +prp).
concentration [kɔnsən'treɪʃən] n сосредото́чение, концентра́ция; (attention) сосредото́ченность f; (CHEM) концентра́ция.
concentration camp n концентрацио́нный ла́герь* m.
concentric [kɔn'sɛntrɪk] adj концентри́ческий*.
concept ['kɔnsɛpt] n поня́тие.
conception [kən'sɛpʃən] n (idea) конце́пция; (BIO) зача́тие.
concern [kən'sə:n] n (affair) де́ло*; (worry) озабо́ченность f; (COMM) предприя́тие ♦ vt (worry) беспоко́ить (impf); (involve) вовлека́ть (вовле́чь* perf); (relate to) каса́ться (impf) +gen; **to be ~ed (about)** беспоко́иться (impf) (о +prp); **"to whom it may ~"** "надлежа́щему лицу́"; **as far as I am ~ed** что каса́ется меня́; **the department ~ed** (relevant)

отде́л, о кото́ром идёт речь; (involved) отде́л, кото́рый э́тим занима́ется.
concerning [kən'sə:nɪŋ] prep относи́тельно +gen.
concert ['kɔnsət] n конце́рт; **to be in ~** (MUS) дава́ть* (impf) конце́рт; **in ~ with** (activities etc) совме́стно or во взаимоде́йствии с +instr.
concerted [kən'sə:tɪd] adj совме́стный.
concert hall n конце́ртный зал.
concertina [kɔnsə'ti:nə] n гармо́ника ♦ vi (fig) скла́дываться (сложи́ться* perf) гармо́никой.
concerto [kən'tʃə:təu] n (MUS) конце́рт; **piano/violin ~** конце́рт для фортепья́но/скри́пки с орке́стром.
concession [kən'sɛʃən] n (compromise) усту́пка*; (right) конце́ссия; (for pensioners, the unemployed) льго́та; **tax ~** нало́говая ски́дка*.
concessionaire [kənsɛʃə'nɛə'] n концессионе́р.
concessionary [kən'sɛʃənrɪ] adj льго́тный.
conciliation [kənsɪlɪ'eɪʃən] n примире́ние.
conciliatory [kən'sɪlɪətrɪ] adj примири́тельный* (примири́телен).
concise [kən'saɪs] adj кра́ткий*.
conclave ['kɔnkleɪv] n та́йное совеща́ние; (REL) конкла́в.
conclude [kən'klu:d] vt (speech, chapter) зака́нчивать (зако́нчить perf); (treaty, deal etc) заключа́ть (заключи́ть perf); (decide) приходи́ть* (прийти́* perf) к заключе́нию or вы́воду ♦ vi (speaker) заключа́ть (заключи́ть perf) речь; (events): **to ~ (with)** заверша́ться (заверши́ться perf) (+instr); **"that", he ~d, "is why we did it"** "вот почему́, – заключи́л он, – мы сде́лали э́то"; **I ~ that** ... я прихожу́ к заключе́нию, что ....
concluding [kən'klu:dɪŋ] adj заключи́тельный.
conclusion [kən'klu:ʒən] n заключе́ние; (of speech) оконча́ние; (of events) заверше́ние; **to come to the ~ that** приходи́ть* (прийти́* perf) к заключе́нию, что.
conclusive [kən'klu:sɪv] adj (evidence) неопровержи́мый (неопровержи́м); (defeat) оконча́тельный* (оконча́телен).
concoct [kən'kɔkt] vt (excuse) приду́мывать (приду́мать perf); (meal) гото́вить* (пригото́вить* perf).
concoction [kən'kɔkʃən] n смесь f.
concord ['kɔŋkɔ:d] n (harmony) согла́сие; (treaty) соглаше́ние.
concourse ['kɔŋkɔ:s] n (hall) вестибю́ль m; (crowd) стече́ние.
concrete ['kɔŋkri:t] n бето́н ♦ adj бето́нный; (fig) конкре́тный* (конкре́тен).
concrete mixer n бетономеша́лка.
concur [kən'kə:'] vi (events) совпада́ть

---

* marks translations which have irregular inflections. The Russian-English side of the dictionary gives inflectional information.

(совпа́сть* *perf*); **to ~ (with)** соглаша́ться (согласи́ться* *perf*) (с +*instr*).
concurrently [kən'kʌrntlɪ] *adv* одновреме́нно.
concussion [kən'kʌʃən] *n* сотрясе́ние мо́зга.
condemn [kən'dɛm] *vt* осужда́ть (осуди́ть* *perf*); (*building*) бракова́ть (забракова́ть *perf*).
condemnation [kɔndɛm'neɪʃən] *n* (*criticism*) осужде́ние.
condensation [kɔndɛn'seɪʃən] *n* конденса́ция.
condense [kən'dɛns] *vi* конденси́роваться (*impf/perf*) ♦ *vt* сжима́ть (сжать* *perf*).
condensed milk [kən'dɛnst-] *n* сгущённое молоко́.
condescend [kɔndɪ'sɛnd] *vi* вести́ (*impf*) себя́ снисходи́тельно; **to ~ to do** соизволя́ть (соизво́лить *perf*) +*infin*.
condescending [kɔndɪ'sɛndɪŋ] *adj* снисходи́тельный* (снисходи́телен).
condition [kən'dɪʃən] *n* (*also MED*) состоя́ние; (*requirement*) усло́вие ♦ *vt* (*person*) формирова́ть (сформирова́ть *perf*); (*hair, skin*) обраба́тывать (обрабо́тать *perf*); **~s** *npl* (*circumstances*) обстоя́тельства *ntpl*; **in good/poor ~** в хоро́шем/плохо́м состоя́нии; **a heart ~** боле́знь *f* се́рдца; **weather ~s** пого́дные усло́вия; **~s of sale** усло́вия прода́жи; **on ~ that** при усло́вии, что.
conditional [kən'dɪʃənl] *adj* усло́вный; **to be ~ upon** зави́сеть* (*impf/perf*) от +*gen*.
conditioner [kən'dɪʃənəʳ] *n* (*for hair*) бальза́м; (*for fabrics*) смягча́ющий* раство́р.
condo ['kɔndəu] *n abbr* (*US: inf*) = **condominium**.
condolences [kən'dəulənsɪz] *npl* соболе́знования *ntpl*.
condom ['kɔndəm] *n* презервати́в.
condominium [kɔndə'mɪnɪəm] *n* (*US: building*) кооперати́вный многокварти́рный дом; (: *rooms*) кооперати́вная кварти́ра.
condone [kən'dəun] *vt* мири́ться (примири́ться *perf*) с +*instr*.
conducive [kən'dju:sɪv] *adj*: **~ to** спосо́бствующий +*dat*.
conduct [*n* 'kɔndʌkt, *vt* kən'dʌkt] *n* (*of person*) поведе́ние ♦ *vt* (*survey etc*) проводи́ть* (провести́* *perf*); (*MUS*) дирижи́ровать (*impf*); (*PHYS*) проводи́ть* (*impf*); **to ~ o.s.** (*behave*) вести́* (повести́* *perf*) себя́.
conducted tour [kən'dʌktɪd-] *n* (*of museum etc*) экску́рсия с ги́дом.
conductor [kən'dʌktəʳ] *n* (*MUS*) дирижёр; (*US: RAIL*) контролёр; (*PHYS*) проводни́к*; (*on bus*) конду́ктор.
conductress [kən'dʌktrɪs] *n* конду́ктор.
conduit ['kɔndjuɪt] *n* (*ELEC*) труба́ для электропрово́дки; (*TECH*) трубопрово́д.
cone [kəun] *n* (*shape*) ко́нус; (*on road*) конусообра́зное доро́жное загражде́ние; (*BOT*) ши́шка*; (*CULIN*) ва́фельная тру́бочка* (для моро́женого).

confectioner [kən'fɛkʃənəʳ] *n* конди́тер.
confectioner's (shop) [kən'fɛkʃənəz-] *n* конди́терская *f adj*.
confectionery [kən'fɛkʃənrɪ] *n* конди́терские изде́лия *ntpl*.
confederate [kən'fɛdrɪt] *adj* конфедерати́вный ♦ *n* (*pej*) соо́бщник; (*US*) конфедера́т.
confederation [kənfɛdə'reɪʃən] *n* конфедера́ция.
confer [kən'fə:ʳ] *vi* совеща́ться (*impf*) ♦ *vt*: **to ~ sth (on sb)** (*honour*) ока́зывать (оказа́ть* *perf*) что-н (кому́-н); (*degree*) присужда́ть (присуди́ть* *perf*) что-н (кому́-н); (*advantage*) дава́ть* (дать* *perf*) что-н (кому́-н); **to ~ (with sb about sth)** совеща́ться (*impf*) (с кем-н о чём-н).
conference ['kɔnfərəns] *n* конфере́нция; **to be in ~** быть* (*impf*) на совеща́нии.
conference room *n* зал заседа́ний, конфере́нцзал.
confess [kən'fɛs] *vt* (*guilt, ignorance*) признава́ть* (призна́ть *perf*); (*sin*) испове́доваться (испове́даться *perf*) в +*prp*; (*crime*) сознава́ться* (созна́ться *perf*) в +*prp* ♦ *vi* (*admit to crime*) признава́ться* (призна́ться *perf*); **to ~ to sth** сознава́ться* (созна́ться *perf*) в чём-н; **I must ~ that I didn't enjoy it at all** до́лжен призна́ться, мне э́то соверше́нно не понра́вилось.
confession [kən'fɛʃən] *n* призна́ние; (*REL*) и́споведь *f*; **to make a ~** де́лать (сде́лать *perf*) призна́ние.
confessor [kən'fɛsəʳ] *n* испове́дник.
confetti [kən'fɛtɪ] *n* конфетти́ *nt ind*.
confide [kən'faɪd] *vi*: **to ~ in** доверя́ться (дове́риться *perf*) +*dat*.
confidence ['kɔnfɪdns] *n* (*faith*) уве́ренность *f*; (*self-assurance*) уве́ренность в себе́; (*secret*) секре́т; **I have ~ in him** я уве́рен в нём; **she has (every) ~ that** она́ по́лностью уве́рена в том, что; **motion of no ~** выраже́ние недове́рия; **in ~** конфиденциа́льно; **to tell sb sth in strict ~** рассказа́ть* (*perf*) кому́-н что-н стро́го конфиденциа́льно.
confidence trick *n* моше́нничество.
confident ['kɔnfɪdənt] *adj* (*positive*) уве́ренный (уве́рен); (*self-assured*) уве́ренный (уве́рен) в себе́.
confidential [kɔnfɪ'dɛnʃəl] *adj* (*report etc*) конфиденциа́льный* (конфиденциа́лен); (*tone*) довери́тельный (довери́телен); (*secretary*) по́льзующийся дове́рием.
confidentiality [kɔnfɪdɛnʃɪ'ælɪtɪ] *n* конфиденциа́льность *f*.
configuration [kənfɪgju'reɪʃən] *n* (*also COMPUT*) конфигура́ция.
confine [kən'faɪn] *vt* (*lock up*) запира́ть (запере́ть* *perf*); (*limit*): **to ~ (to)** ограни́чивать (ограни́чить *perf*) (+*instr*); **to ~ o.s. to sth** ограни́чиваться (ограни́читься *perf*) чем-н.

confined [kən'faɪnd] adj закры́тый.
confinement [kən'faɪnmənt] n (тюре́мное) заключе́ние; (MED) ро́ды pl.
confines ['kɒnfaɪnz] npl (also fig) преде́лы mpl.
confirm [kən'fɜːm] vt подтвержда́ть (подтверди́ть* perf); **to be ~ed** (REL) получа́ть (получи́ть* perf) конфирма́цию.
confirmation [kɒnfə'meɪʃən] n подтвержде́ние; (REL) конфирма́ция.
confirmed [kən'fɜːmd] adj убеждённый.
confiscate ['kɒnfɪskeɪt] vt конфиско́вывать (конфискова́ть perf).
confiscation [kɒnfɪs'keɪʃən] n конфиска́ция.
conflagration [kɒnflə'greɪʃən] n пожа́рище.
conflict [n 'kɒnflɪkt, vi kən'flɪkt] n конфли́кт; (of interests) столкнове́ние ◆ vi противоре́чить (impf) друг дру́гу; **to ~ with sth** противоре́чить (impf) чему́-н.
conflicting [kən'flɪktɪŋ] adj (reports) противоречи́вый (противоречи́в); (interests) противополо́жный* (противополо́жен).
conform [kən'fɔːm] vi: **to ~ (to)** подчиня́ться (подчини́ться perf) (+dat).
conformist [kən'fɔːmɪst] n конформи́ст.
confound [kən'faund] vt (confuse) озада́чивать (озада́чить perf); (amaze) поража́ть (порази́ть* perf).
confounded [kən'faundɪd] adj (nuisance) прокля́тый; (idiot) зако́нченный.
confront [kən'frʌnt] vt (problems) ста́лкиваться (столкну́ться perf) с +instr; (enemy) противостоя́ть (impf) +dat.
confrontation [kɒnfrən'teɪʃən] n конфронта́ция.
confuse [kən'fjuːz] vt (perplex, complicate) запу́тывать (запу́тать perf); (mix up: two things, people etc) пу́тать (спу́тать perf).
confused [kən'fjuːzd] adj (person) озада́ченный (озада́чен); (situation) запу́танный (запу́тан); **to get ~** запу́тываться (запу́таться perf).
confusing [kən'fjuːzɪŋ] adj запу́танный.
confusion [kən'fjuːʒən] n (mix-up) пу́таница; (perplexity) замеша́тельство; (disorder) беспоря́док.
congeal [kən'dʒiːl] vi (blood) запека́ться (запе́чься* perf); (sauce, fat) застыва́ть (засты́ть* perf).
congenial [kən'dʒiːnɪəl] adj (atmosphere) благоприя́тный* (благоприя́тен); (person) ро́дственный; (place, job etc) подходя́щий*.
congenital [kən'dʒɛnɪtl] adj (MED) врождённый.
conger eel ['kɒŋgər-] n морско́й у́горь* m.
congested [kən'dʒɛstɪd] adj (road) перегру́женный (перегру́жен); (area) перенаселённый (перенаселён); (MED) засто́йный.

congestion [kən'dʒɛstʃən] n (of road) перегру́женность f; (of area) перенаселённость f; (MED) засто́й.
conglomerate [kən'glɒmərɪt] n (COMM) конгломера́т.
conglomeration [kənglɒmə'reɪʃən] n конгломера́ция.
Congo ['kɒŋgəu] n Ко́нго ind.
congratulate [kən'grætjuleɪt] vt: **to ~ sb (on)** поздравля́ть (поздра́вить* perf) кого́-н (с +instr).
congratulations [kəngrætju'leɪʃənz] npl поздравле́ния ntpl; **~ (on)** (from one person) поздравля́ю (с +instr); (from several people) поздравля́ем (с +instr).
congregate ['kɒŋgrɪgeɪt] vi собира́ться (собра́ться* perf).
congregation [kɒŋgrɪ'geɪʃən] n прихожа́не* mpl.
congress ['kɒŋgrɛs] n (conference) конгре́сс; (US): **C~** конгре́сс США.
congressman ['kɒŋgrɛsmən] irreg n (US) конгрессме́н.
congresswoman ['kɒŋgrɛswumən] irreg n (US) конгрессме́н.
conical ['kɒnɪkl] adj кони́ческий*.
conifer ['kɒnɪfə'] n хво́йное де́рево*.
coniferous [kə'nɪfərəs] adj хво́йный.
conjecture [kən'dʒɛktʃə'] n предположе́ние ◆ vi предполага́ть (предположи́ть perf).
conjugal ['kɒndʒugl] adj супру́жеский*.
conjugate ['kɒndʒugeɪt] vt (LING) спряга́ть (проспряга́ть perf).
conjugation [kɒndʒə'geɪʃən] n (LING) спряже́ние.
conjunction [kən'dʒʌŋkʃən] n (LING) сою́з; **in ~ with** совме́стно с +instr.
conjunctivitis [kəndʒʌŋktɪ'vaɪtɪs] n (MED) конъюнктиви́т.
conjure ['kʌndʒə'] vt (fig) создава́ть* (созда́ть* perf) из ничего́ ◆ vi (magician) пока́зывать (показа́ть* perf) фо́кусы
► **conjure up** vt (ghost) вызыва́ть* (вы́звать* perf); (memories) пробужда́ть (пробуди́ть* perf).
conjurer ['kʌndʒərə'] n фо́кусник.
conjuring trick ['kʌndʒərɪŋ-] n фо́кус.
conker ['kɒŋkə'] n (BRIT) ко́нский кашта́н.
conk out [kɒŋk-] vi (inf) сдыха́ть (сдо́хнуть perf).
con man irreg n моше́нник.
connect [kə'nɛkt] vt (ELEC) подсоединя́ть (подсоедини́ть perf); (TEL: subscriber) подключа́ть (подключи́ть perf); (fig: associate) свя́зывать (связа́ть* perf) ◆ vi: **to ~ with** согласо́вываться (согласова́ться perf) по расписа́нию с +instr; **to ~ sb/sth (to)** (also TEL) соединя́ть (соедини́ть perf) кого́-н/что-н

(c +*instr*); **he is/was ~ed with** он свя́зан/был свя́зан с +*instr*; **I am trying to ~ you** (*TEL*) я пыта́юсь нала́дить связь.

connection [kə'nɛkʃən] *n* (*also fig, ELEC*) связь* *f*; (*train etc*) переса́дка*; (*TEL: caller*) соедине́ние; (: *subscriber*) подключе́ние; **in ~ with** в связи́ с +*instr*; **what is the ~ between them?** кака́я связь ме́жду ни́ми?; **business ~s** деловы́е свя́зи; **to miss one's ~** опа́здывать (опозда́ть *perf*) на переса́дку; **to get one's ~** де́лать (сде́лать *perf*) переса́дку.

connexion [kə'nɛkʃən] *n* (*BRIT*) = **connection.**

conning tower ['kɔnɪŋ-] *n* (*NAUT*) ру́бка*.

connive [kə'naɪv] *vi*: **to ~ at** потво́рствовать (*impf*) +*dat*.

connoisseur [kɔnɪ'sə:ʳ] *n* знато́к*.

connotation [kɔnə'teɪʃən] *n* коннота́ция.

connubial [kə'nju:bɪəl] *adj* бра́чный.

conquer ['kɔŋkəʳ] *vt* (*MIL*) завоёвывать (завоева́ть* *perf*); (*overcome*) поборо́ть* (*perf*).

conqueror ['kɔŋkərə] *n* завоева́тель *m*.

conquest ['kɔŋkwɛst] *n* (*MIL*) завоева́ние; (*prize*) побе́да; (*of space*) покоре́ние.

cons [kɔnz] *npl see* **convenience, pro.**

conscience ['kɔnʃəns] *n* со́весть *f*; **he has a guilty/clear ~** у него́ со́весть нечиста́/чиста́; **in all ~** по со́вести.

conscientious [kɔnʃɪ'ɛnʃəs] *adj* добро-со́вестный* (добросо́вестен).

conscientious objector *n* отка́зывающийся от призы́ва в а́рмию по убежде́нию.

conscious ['kɔnʃəs] *adj* (*deliberate*) созна́тельный (созна́телен); (*aware*): **to be ~ of sth/that** сознава́ть* (*impf*) что-н/, что; (*awake*): **the patient was ~** пацие́нт находи́лся в созна́нии; **to become ~ of sth/that** осознава́ть (осозна́ть *perf*) что-н/, что.

consciousness ['kɔnʃəsnɪs] *n* (*also MED*) созна́ние; (*of society etc*) самосозна́ние; **to lose ~** теря́ть (потеря́ть *perf*) созна́ние; **to regain ~** приходи́ть* (прийти́* *perf*) в созна́ние.

conscript ['kɔnskrɪpt] *n* призывни́к*, новобра́нец*.

conscription [kən'skrɪpʃən] *n* во́инская пови́нность *f*.

consecrate ['kɔnsɪkreɪt] *vt* (*building etc*) освяща́ть (освяти́ть* *perf*).

consecutive [kən'sɛkjutɪv] *adj*: **on three ~ occasions** в трёх слу́чаях подря́д; **on three ~ days** три дня подря́д.

consensus [kən'sɛnsəs] *n* (*medical, scientific*) еди́ное мне́ние; (*of opinion*) консе́нсус.

consent [kən'sɛnt] *n* согла́сие ♦ *vi*: **to ~ to** соглаша́ться (согласи́ться* *perf*) на +*acc*; **age of ~** совершенноле́тие; **by common ~** с о́бщего согла́сия.

consenting [kən'sɛntɪŋ] *adj*: **~ adult** совершенноле́тний*(-яя) *m(f) adj*.

consequence ['kɔnsɪkwəns] *n* (*result*)

сле́дствие; (*significance*): **of ~** значи́тельный (значи́телен); **it's of little ~** э́то не име́ет большо́го значе́ния; **in ~** (*consequently*) всле́дствие.

consequently ['kɔnsɪkwəntlɪ] *adv* сле́довательно.

conservation [kɔnsə'veɪʃən] *n* (*preservation*) сохране́ние; (*also*: **nature ~**) охра́на приро́ды, природоохра́на; **energy ~** эконо́мия эне́ргии.

conservationist [kɔnsə'veɪʃnɪst] *n* челове́к, выступа́ющий за природоохра́ну.

conservative [kən'sə:vətɪv] *adj* (*person*) консервати́вный*; (*estimate*) скро́мный*; (*BRIT*): **C~** консервати́вный ♦ *n* (*BRIT*): **C~** консерва́тор.

conservatory [kən'sə:vətrɪ] *n* застеклённая вера́нда; (*MUS*) консервато́рия.

conserve [kən'sə:v] *vt* (*preserve*) сохраня́ть (сохрани́ть *perf*); (*energy*) рациона́льно испо́льзовать (*impf*) ♦ *n* варе́нье*.

consider [kən'sɪdə] *vt* (*believe*) счита́ть (посчита́ть *perf*); (*study*) рассма́тривать (рассмотре́ть* *perf*); (*take into account*) учи́тывать (уче́сть* *perf*); (*regard*): **to ~ that ...** полага́ть (*impf*), что ...; **to ~ sth** поду́мывать (*impf*) о чём-н; **they ~ themselves to be superior** они́ счита́ют себя́ вы́ше; **she ~ed it a disaster** она́ счита́ла, что э́то катастро́фа; **~ yourself lucky** счита́йте, что Вам повезло́; **all things ~ed** приня́в всё во внима́ние.

considerable [kən'sɪdərəbl] *adj* значи́тельный* (значи́телен).

considerably [kən'sɪdərəblɪ] *adv* (*improve, deteriorate etc*) значи́тельно; (*bigger, smaller etc*) гора́здо.

considerate [kən'sɪdərɪt] *adj* (*person*) забо́тливый (забо́тлив); (*action*) внима́тельный (внима́телен).

consideration [kənsɪdə'reɪʃən] *n* (*deliberation*) рассмотре́ние, обду́мывание; (*factor*) соображе́ние; (*thoughtfulness*) внима́ние; (*reward*) вознагражде́ние; **out of ~ for** из уваже́ния к +*dat*; **to take sth into ~** принима́ть (приня́ть *perf*) что-н во внима́ние; **under ~** на рассмотре́нии; **my first ~ is my family** я пре́жде всего́ забо́чусь о свое́й семье́.

considered [kən'sɪdəd] *adj* (*approach, answer*) обду́манный; **it is my ~ opinion that ...** у меня́ сложи́лось мне́ние, что ....

considering [kən'sɪdərɪŋ] *prep* учи́тывая +*acc*; **~ (that)** учи́тывая (, что).

consign [kən'saɪn] *vt* (*send: goods*) отправля́ть (отпра́вить* *perf*); **to ~ to** (*thing: to place*) забра́сывать (забро́сить* *perf*) в +*acc*; (*person: to sb's care*) поруча́ть (поручи́ть *perf*) +*dat*; (: *to poverty*) обрека́ть (обре́чь* *perf*) на +*acc*.

consignee [kɔnsaɪ'ni:] *n* грузополуча́тель *m*.

consignment [kən'saɪnmənt] *n* (*COMM*) па́ртия.

consignment note n (COMM) тра́нспортная накладна́я f adj.

consignor [kən'saɪnəʳ] n грузоотправи́тель m.

consist [kən'sɪst] vi: **to ~ of** состоя́ть (impf) из +gen.

consistency [kən'sɪstənsɪ] n (of actions etc) после́довательность f; (of yoghurt etc) консисте́нция.

consistent [kən'sɪstənt] adj (person, argument) после́довательный* (после́дователен); **~ with** соотве́тствующий* +dat.

consolation [kɔnsə'leɪʃən] n утеше́ние.

console [vt kən'səul, n 'kɔnsəul] vt утеша́ть (уте́шить perf) ♦ n (panel) пане́ль f.

consolidate [kən'sɔlɪdeɪt] vt (position, power) укрепля́ть (укрепи́ть* perf).

consolidated balance sheet [kən'sɔlɪdeɪtɪd-] n сво́дный бала́нсовый отчёт.

consols ['kɔnsɔlz] npl (BRIT) консо́ли fpl (прави́тельственные облига́ции).

consommé [kən'sɔmeɪ] n прозра́чный бульо́н*.

consonant ['kɔnsənənt] n согла́сный m adj.

consort [n 'kɔnsɔ:t, vb kən'sɔ:t] n супру́г(а) ♦ vi: **to ~ with sb** свя́зываться (связа́ться* perf) с кем-н; **prince ~** принц-консо́рт, супру́г ца́рствующей короле́вы.

consortium [kən'sɔ:tɪəm] n консо́рциум.

conspicuous [kən'spɪkjuəs] adj (person, feature) заме́тный (заме́тен); **to make o.s. ~** обраща́ть (обрати́ть* perf) на себя́ внима́ние.

conspiracy [kən'spɪrəsɪ] n за́говор.

conspiratorial [kən'spɪrə'tɔ:rɪəl] adj загово́рщический.

conspire [kən'spaɪəʳ] vi (people) устра́ивать (устро́ить perf) за́говор; **circumstances ~d against us** обстоя́тельства скла́дывались про́тив нас.

constable ['kʌnstəbl] (BRIT) n полице́йский m adj; **chief ~** нача́льник поли́ции.

constabulary [kən'stæbjulərɪ] n (BRIT) поли́ция.

constant ['kɔnstənt] adj (continuous) постоя́нный*; (fixed) неизме́нный*.

constantly ['kɔnstəntlɪ] adv (continually) постоя́нно.

constellation [kɔnstə'leɪʃən] n (ASTRONOMY) созве́здие.

consternation [kɔnstə'neɪʃən] n смяте́ние.

constipated ['kɔnstɪpeɪtɪd] adj: **he/she is ~** у него́/неё запо́р.

constipation [kɔnstɪ'peɪʃən] n запо́р.

constituency [kən'stɪtjuənsɪ] n (area) избира́тельный о́круг*; (electors) избира́тели mpl о́круга.

constituency party n ме́стная парти́йная организа́ция.

constituent [kən'stɪtjuənt] n (POL) избира́тель(ница) m(f); (component) компоне́нт.

constitute ['kɔnstɪtju:t] vt (represent) явля́ться (яви́ться* perf) +instr; (make up) составля́ть (соста́вить* perf).

constitution [kɔnstɪ'tju:ʃən] n (of country) конститу́ция; (of organization) уста́в; (health) органи́зм; (of committee etc) строе́ние.

constitutional [kɔnstɪ'tju:ʃənl] adj конституцио́нный; **~ monarchy** конституцио́нная мона́рхия.

constrain [kən'streɪn] vt (force) вынужда́ть (вы́нудить* perf); (limit) сде́рживать (сдержа́ть* perf).

constrained [kən'streɪnd] adj принуждённый*.

constraint [kən'streɪnt] n (restriction) ограниче́ние; (compulsion) принужде́ние; (embarrassment) стесне́ние.

constrict [kən'strɪkt] vt (squeeze) сжима́ть (сжать* perf); (limit) стесня́ть (стесни́ть perf).

constriction [kən'strɪkʃən] n (in throat) стесне́ние; (restriction) ограниче́ние.

construct [kən'strʌkt] vt (build) сооружа́ть (сооруди́ть* perf); (formulate) стро́ить (постро́ить perf).

construction [kən'strʌkʃən] n (of building etc) сооруже́ние; (structure) констру́кция; (fig: interpretation) истолкова́ние; **the building is under ~** зда́ние стро́ится.

construction industry n строи́тельная промы́шленность f.

constructive [kən'strʌktɪv] adj конструкти́вный* (конструкти́вен).

construe [kən'stru:] vt истолко́вывать (истолкова́ть perf).

consul ['kɔnsl] n ко́нсул.

consulate ['kɔnsjulɪt] n ко́нсульство.

consult [kən'sʌlt] vt (friend) сове́товаться (посове́товаться perf) с +instr; (book, map etc) справля́ться (спра́виться* perf) с +instr; **to ~ sb (about sth)** (doctor etc) консульти́роваться (проконсульти́роваться perf) с кем-н (о чём-н).

consultancy [kən'sʌltənsɪ] n (company) консульти́рующая фи́рма; (MED) до́лжность f врача́-консульта́нта.

consultant [kən'sʌltənt] n (MED) врач-консульта́нт; (other specialist) консульта́нт ♦ cpd: **~ engineer/paediatrician** инжене́р-/педиа́тр-консульта́нт; **legal ~** юрисконсу́льт; **management ~** консульта́нт по ме́неджменту.

consultation [kɔnsəl'teɪʃən] n (MED) консульта́ция; (discussion) совеща́ние; (LAW) юриди́ческая консульта́ция; **in ~ with** с по́мощью +gen.

consultative [kən'sʌltətɪv] adj консультати́вный.

---

* marks translations which have irregular inflections. The Russian-English side of the dictionary gives inflectional information.

consulting room [kən'sʌltɪŋ-] *n* (*BRIT*)
врачебный кабинет.
consume [kən'sju:m] *vt* (*food, drink*)
потреблять (потребить* *perf*); (*fuel, energy
etc*) расходовать (израсходовать *perf*); (*subj:
emotion, fire etc*) охватывать (охватить*
perf).
consumer [kən'sju:mə'] *n* (*COMM, also of gas etc*)
потребитель *m*.
consumer credit *n* потребительский* кредит.
consumer durables *npl* потребительские
товары *mpl* длительного пользования.
consumer goods *npl* потребительские
товары *mpl*.
consumerism [kən'sju:mərɪzəm] *n* защита
прав потребителей.
consumer society *n* общество потребления.
consummate ['kɔnsʌmeɪt] *vt* (*marriage,
ambition etc*) осуществлять (осуществить*
perf).
consumption [kən'sʌmpʃən] *n* потребление;
(*amount consumed*) расход; (*MED*)
туберкулёз лёгких; **not fit for human** ~ не
годен к потреблению.
cont. *abbr* (= *continued*): ~ **on** продолжение на
+*prp*.
contact ['kɔntækt] *n* (*communication*) контакт;
(*touch*) соприкосновение; (*person*)
деловой(-ая) знакомый(-ая) *m(f) adj* ♦ *vt*
связываться (связаться* *perf*) с +*instr*; **to
lose/be in** ~ **with sb/sth** терять (потерять
perf)/поддерживать (*impf*) контакт с кем-н/
чем-н; **business** ~**s** деловые связи.
contact lenses *npl* контактные линзы *fpl*.
contagious [kən'teɪdʒəs] *adj* (*disease*)
заразный* (заразен); (*fig*) заразительный*
(заразителен).
contain [kən'teɪn] *vt* (*hold*) вмещать
(вместить* *perf*); (*include*) содержать* (*impf*);
(*curb*) сдерживать (сдержать* *perf*); **to** ~ **o.s.**
сдерживаться (сдержаться* *perf*).
container [kən'teɪnə'] *n* (*also COMM*) контейнер
♦ *cpd* (*ship, lorry etc*) контейнерный.
containerization [kənteɪnəraɪ'zeɪʃən] *n*
упаковка* грузов в контейнеры.
containerize [kən'teɪnəraɪz] *vt* осуществлять
(осуществить* *perf*) контейнерные
перевозки.
contaminate [kən'tæmɪneɪt] *vt* загрязнять
(загрязнить* *perf*).
contamination [kəntæmɪ'neɪʃən] *n*
загрязнение.
cont'd *abbr* (= *continued*): ~ **on** продолжение
на +*prp*; **to be** ~ продолжение следует.
contemplate ['kɔntəmpleɪt] *vt* (*consider*)
размышлять (*impf*) о +*prp*; (*look at*)
созерцать (*impf*).
contemplation [kɔntəm'pleɪʃən] *n* (*see vb*)
размышление; созерцание.
contemporary [kən'tɛmpərərɪ] *adj* (*present-day*)
современный*; (*belonging to same time*)

относящийся к тому времени ♦ *n*
современник(-ица); **Samuel Pepys and his
contemporaries** Самюель Пипс и его
современники.
contempt [kən'tɛmpt] *n* презрение; ~ **of court**
оскорбление суда; **to have** ~ **for sb/sth, to
hold sb/sth in** ~ презирать (*impf*) кого-н/
что-н.
contemptible [kən'tɛmptəbl] *adj* (*conduct*)
презренный.
contemptuous [kən'tɛmptjuəs] *adj*
презрительный* (презрителен).
contend [kən'tɛnd] *vt*: **to** ~ **that** утверждать
(*impf*), что ♦ *vi* (*struggle*): **to** ~ **with** (*problem
etc*) бороться* (*impf*) с +*instr*; (*compete*): **to** ~
for (*power etc*) бороться* (*impf*) за +*acc*; **to
have to** ~ **with** сталкиваться (столкнуться
perf) с +*instr*; **he has a lot to** ~ **with** ему
приходится справляться со многим.
contender [kən'tɛndə'] *n* претендент(ка).
content [*n* 'kɔntɛnt, *adj, vt* kən'tɛnt] *n*
содержание ♦ *adj* довольный* (доволен) ♦ *vt*
(*satisfy*) удовлетворять (удовлетворить*
perf); ~**s** *npl* (*of bottle etc*) содержимое *ntsg adj*;
(*of book*) содержание *ntsg*; (**table of**) ~**s**
оглавление; **she is** ~ **with her life** она
довольна жизнью; **to** ~ **o.s. with sth**
довольствоваться (*impf*) чем-н.
contented [kən'tɛntɪd] *adj* довольный*
(доволен).
contentedly [kən'tɛntɪdlɪ] *adv* довольно,
удовлетворённо.
contention [kən'tɛnʃən] *n* (*assertion*)
утверждение; (*argument*) разногласие; **bone
of** ~**s** яблоко* раздора.
contentious [kən'tɛnʃəs] *adj* спорный*
(спорен).
contentment [kən'tɛntmənt] *n* удовлетворённость *f*.
contest [*n* 'kɔntɛst, *vt* kən'tɛst] *n* (*competition:
sport*) соревнование; (: *beauty*) конкурс; (*for
power etc*) борьба* ♦ *vt* (*statement, decision,
LAW*) оспаривать (оспорить* *perf*); (*compete
for*) бороться* (*impf*) за +*acc*; (*election,
competition*) бороться* (*impf*) на +*prp*.
contestant [kən'tɛstənt] *n* (*in competition*)
участник(-ница); (*in fight*)
противник(-ница).
context ['kɔntɛkst] *n* контекст; **in** ~ в
контексте; **out of** ~ вне контекста.
continent ['kɔntɪnənt] *n* континент, материк;
the C~ (*BRIT*) Европа (*кроме Британских
островов*); **on the C**~ в Европе (*кроме
британских островов*).
continental [kɔntɪ'nɛntl] (*BRIT*) *adj*
европейский* ♦ *n* европеец*(-ейка).
continental breakfast *n* европейский*
завтрак (*лёгкий завтрак из кофе и булочки*).
continental quilt *n* (*BRIT*) стёганое одеяло.
contingency [kən'tɪndʒənsɪ] *n* возможность *f*.
contingency plan *n* план действий на случай

непредвиденных обстоятельств.
contingent [kən'tɪndʒənt] *n* (*also MIL*)
контингент ♦ *adj*: **to be ~ upon** зависеть*
(*impf*) от +*gen.*
continual [kən'tɪnjuəl] *adj* непрерывный*.
continually [kən'tɪnjuəlɪ] *adv* непрерывно,
постоянно.
continuation [kəntɪnju'eɪʃən] *n* продолжение.
continue [kən'tɪnju:] *vi* (*carry on*)
продолжаться (*impf*); (*after interruption: talk*)
продолжаться (продолжиться *perf*);
(: *person*) продолжать (продолжить *perf*) ♦ *vt*
продолжать (продолжить *perf*); **to ~ to do**
продолжать (продолжить *perf*) +*impf infin*; **to
be ~d** продолжение следует; **~d on page 10**
продолжение на странице 10.
continuing education [kən'tɪnjuɪŋ-] *n* курсы
mpl вечернего обучения.
continuity [kɒntɪ'nju:ɪtɪ] *n* (*in management*)
преемственность *f*; (*TV, CINEMA*)
непрерывность *f* (*телевизионных программ
и фильмов*); **~ announcer** диктор,
заполняющий пробелы; **~ department** *отдел,
обеспечивающий непрерывность
телевизионных программ.*
continuous [kən'tɪnjuəs] *adj* (*process, growth
etc*) непрерывный*; (*line*) сплошной; (*LING*)
длительный*; **~ performance** (*CINEMA*) *показ
кинофильма без перерыва между сеансами.*
continuously [kən'tɪnjuəslɪ] *adv* (*repeatedly*)
неоднократно, постоянно; (*uninterruptedly*)
непрерывно.
continuous stationery *n* (*COMPUT*) рулонная
бумага (*для печатающего устройства*).
contort [kən'tɔ:t] *vt* (*body*) искривлять
(искривить* *perf*); (*face*) кривить* (скривить*
perf).
contortion [kən'tɔ:ʃən] *n* искривление.
contortionist [kən'tɔ:ʃənɪst] *n*
пластический*(-ая) акробат(ка).
contour ['kɒntuəʳ] *n* (*also:* **~ line**) контурная
линия; (*outline: usu pl*) контур.
contraband ['kɒntrəbænd] *n* контрабанда ♦ *adj*
контрабандный.
contraception [kɒntrə'sɛpʃən] *n* предупреждение беременности.
contraceptive [kɒntrə'sɛptɪv] *adj* противо-
зачаточный ♦ *n* противозачаточное
средство, контрацептив.
contract [*n, cpd* 'kɒntrækt, *vb* kən'trækt] *n* (*LAW,
COMM*) договор, контракт ♦ *vi* (*become
smaller*) сжиматься (сжаться* *perf*) ♦ *vt*
(*illness*) заболевать (заболеть* *perf*) +*instr* ♦
cpd (*price, date*) договорный; **~ of
employment** служебный контракт; **~ of
service** *договор между компанией и
руководящим сотрудником*; **to ~ to do**
(*COMM*) обязывать (обязать* *perf*) +*infin*; **~**

work работа по контракту
▶ **contract in** *vi* (*BRIT*) официально заявлять
(заявить* *perf*) о желании участвовать в +*prp*
▶ **contract out** *vi* (*BRIT*) официально
отказываться (отказаться* *perf*) от участия
в +*prp.*
contraction [kən'trækʃən] *n* (*of metal*) сжатие;
(*LING*) сокращение; (*MED*) родовая потуга.
contractor [kən'træktəʳ] *n* подрядчик.
contractual [kən'træktʃuəl] *adj* (*agreement etc*)
договорный.
contradict [kɒntrə'dɪkt] *vt* (*person*) возражать
(возразить* *perf*) +*dat*; (*statement*) возражать
(возразить* *perf*) на +*acc*; (*be contrary to*)
противоречить (*impf*) +*dat.*
contradiction [kɒntrə'dɪkʃən] *n* противоречие;
to be in ~ with находиться* (*impf*) в
противоречии с +*instr*; **a ~ in terms**
логическое противоречие.
contradictory [kɒntrə'dɪktərɪ] *adj*
противоречивый (противоречив).
contralto [kən'træltəu] *n* (*MUS*) контральто *nt
ind.*
contraption [kən'træpʃən] *n* дурацкая вещь *f.*
contrary[1] ['kɒntrərɪ] *adj* (*opposite, different*)
противоположный*; (*unfavourable*)
неблагоприятный ♦ *n* противоположность
f; **~ to what we thought** в противоположность тому, что мы думали; **on the ~**
напротив, наоборот; **unless you hear to the
~** если не будет других инструкций.
contrary[2] [kən'trɛərɪ] *adj* своенравный*.
contrast [*n* 'kɒntrɑ:st, *vt* kən'trɑ:st] *n* (*difference*)
контраст ♦ *vt* сопоставлять (сопоставить*
perf); **in ~ to** *or* **with** по контрасту с +*instr.*
contrasting [kən'trɑ:stɪŋ] *adj* (*colours*)
контрастирующий; (*attitudes, views*)
противоположный.
contravene [kɒntrə'vi:n] *vt* преступать
(преступить* *perf*).
contravention [kɒntrə'vɛnʃən] *n*: **in ~ of** в
нарушение +*gen.*
contribute [kən'trɪbju:t] *vi* (*give*) делать
(сделать *perf*) вклад ♦ *vt* (*money, an article*)
вносить* (внести* *perf*); **to ~ to** (*to charity*)
жертвовать (пожертвовать *perf*) на +*acc or
для* +*gen*; (*to newspaper*) писать* (написать*
perf) для +*gen*; (*to discussion*) участвовать
(*impf*) в +*prp*; (*to problem*) усугублять
(усугубить* *perf*).
contribution [kɒntrɪ'bju:ʃən] *n* (*donation*)
пожертвование; (*BRIT: for social security*)
взнос; (*to debate, campaign*) вклад; (*to
journal*) публикация.
contributor [kən'trɪbjutə] *n* (*to appeal*)
жертвователь *m*; (*to newspaper*) автор.
contributory [kən'trɪbjutərɪ] *adj*
способствующий; **it was a ~ factor in ...** это

---

* marks translations which have irregular inflections. The Russian-English side of the dictionary gives inflectional information.

явилось одним из способствующих
факторов в ....

contributory pension scheme *n* (*BRIT*)
пенсионный договор, по которому работник
принимает частичное участие в
формировании своей будущей пенсии.

contrite ['kɒntraɪt] *adj* (*person*) виноватый; **she
looked** ~ у неё был виноватый вид.

contrivance [kən'traɪvəns] *n* (*scheme*) уловка;
(*device*) приспособление.

contrive [kən'traɪv] *vt* (*meeting*) затевать
(затеять *perf*) ♦ *vi*: **to** ~ **to do** ухитряться
(ухитриться *perf*) +*infin*.

control [kən'trəul] *vt* контролировать (*impf*) ♦ *n*
(*of country, organization*) контроль *m*; (*of
oneself*) самообладание; (*also:* ~ **group**)
контрольная группа; ~**s** *npl* (*of vehicle*)
рычаги *mpl* управления; (*on radio etc*) ручки
fpl настройки; **to** ~ **o.s.** сохранять
(сохранить *perf*) самообладание; **to take** ~ **of**
брать* (взять* *perf*) в свои руки управление
+*instr*; (*COMM*) брать* (взять* *perf*) под
контроль +*acc*; **to be in** ~ **of** контролировать
(*impf*); **under** ~ спокойный; **everything is
under** ~ всё под контролем; **out of** ~
неуправляемый; **the car went out of** ~
машина потеряла управление;
circumstances beyond our ~ не зависящие от
нас обстоятельства; **governmental** ~**s**
государственный контроль *msg*.

control key *n* управляющая клавиша,
клавиша управления.

controller [kən'trəulə'] *n* (*head*) руководитель
m.

controlling interest [kən'trəulɪŋ-] *n* (*COMM*)
контрольный пакет акций.

control panel *n* пульт управления.

control point *n* контрольный пункт.

control room *n* (*NAUT, MIL*) пункт управления;
(*RADIO, TV*) аппаратная *f adj*.

control tower *n* контрольно-диспетчерский*
пункт.

control unit *n* (*COMPUT*) блок управления.

controversial [kɒntrə'və:ʃl] *adj* (*topic etc*)
спорный* (спорен); (*person, writer*)
неоднозначный* (неоднозначен).

controversy ['kɒntrəvə:sɪ] *n* дискуссия, спор.

conurbation [kɒnə'beɪʃən] *n* агломерация.

convalesce [kɒnvə'lɛs] *vi* выздоравливать
(выздороветь *perf*).

convalescence [kɒnvə'lɛsns] *n* вы-
здоровление.

convalescent [kɒnvə'lɛsnt] *n* вы-
здоравливающий*(-ая)*m(f) adj* ♦ *adj*: ~ **home**
санаторий; ~ **leave** отпуск* по
выздоровлению.

convector [kən'vɛktə'] *n* (*also:* ~ **heater**)
конвектор.

convene [kən'vi:n] *vt* (*meeting*) созывать
(созвать* *perf*) ♦ *vi* (*parliament etc*)
собираться (собраться* *perf*).

convener [kən'vi:nə'] *n* (*ADMIN*) человек,
ответственный за подготовку и созыв
собрания, заседания итп.

convenience [kən'vi:nɪəns] *n* удобство; **at your**
~ когда *or* как Вам будет удобно; **at your
earliest** ~ при первой возможности; **a flat
with all modern** ~**s** *or* (*BRIT*) **all mod cons**
квартира со всеми удобствами.

convenience foods *npl* пищевые
полуфабрикаты.

convenient [kən'vi:nɪənt] *adj* удобный*
(удобен); **if it is** ~ **to you** если Вам удобно.

conveniently [kən'vi:nɪəntlɪ] *adv* (*happen*) как
раз; (*situated*) удобно.

convenor [kən'vi:nə'] *n* = **convener**.

convent ['kɒnvənt] *n* (*REL*) (женский*)
монастырь* *m*.

convention [kən'vɛnʃən] *n* (*custom*)
условность *f*; (*conference*) конференция;
(*agreement*) конвенция; (*in art, literature*)
приём.

conventional [kən'vɛnʃənl] *adj* обычный.

convent school *n* монастырская школа.

converge [kən'və:dʒ] *vi* (*roads*) сходиться*
(сойтись* *perf*); (*people*) съезжаться
(съехаться* *perf*); (*ideas*) совпадать
(совпасть* *perf*).

conversant [kən'və:snt] *adj*: **he is/was** ~ **with**
он сведущ/был сведущ в +*prp*.

conversation [kɒnvə'seɪʃən] *n* беседа,
разговор; **to have a** ~ **with sb** разговаривать
(*impf*) *or* беседовать (*perf*) с кем-н.

conversational [kɒnvə'seɪʃənl] *adj*
разговорный; (*COMPUT*) диалоговый.

conversationalist [kɒnvə'seɪʃnəlɪst] *n*: **a good** ~
интересный(-ая) собеседник(-ница).

converse [*n* 'kɒnvə:s, *vb* kən'və:s] *n* (*of
statement*) противоположность *f* ♦ *vi*: **to** ~
(**with sb**) (**about sth**) беседовать
(побеседовать *perf*) (с кем-н) (о чём-н).

conversely [kɒn'və:slɪ] *adv* наоборот.

conversion [kən'və:ʃən] *n* (*of weights*) перевод;
(*of substances*) превращение; (*of currency,
REL*) обращение; (*BRIT: of house*)
перестройка; (*RUGBY*) один из приёмов
получения очков.

conversion table *n* таблица преобразования.

convert [*vt* kən'və:t, *n* 'kɒnvə:t] *vt* (*person: REL,
POL*) обращать (обратить* *perf*); (*building,
vehicle*) преобразовывать (преобразовать
perf); (*COMM*) переводить* (перевести* *perf*) ♦
n (*REL, POL*) новообращённый(-ая)*m(f) adj*; **to**
~ **sth into** превращать (превратить* *perf*)
что-н в +*acc*.

convertible [kən'və:təbl] *adj* (*currency*)
конвертируемый ♦ *n* автомобиль *m* с
откидным верхом; ~ **loan stock** (*COMM*)
конвертабельные акции.

convex ['kɒnvɛks] *adj* выпуклый.

convey [kən'veɪ] *vt* (*information, idea, thanks*)
передавать* (передать* *perf*); (*cargo, person*)

перевози́ть* (перевезти́* *perf*).

conveyance [kən'veɪəns] *n* (*of goods*) перево́зка*; (*vehicle*) тра́нспортное сре́дство.

conveyancing [kən'veɪənsɪŋ] *n* (LAW) составле́ние нотариа́льного а́кта о переда́че прав на недви́жимость.

conveyor belt [kən'veɪəʳ-] *n* конве́йер.

convict [*vt* kən'vɪkt, *n* 'kɒnvɪkt] *vt* осужда́ть (осуди́ть* *perf*) ◆ *n* ка́торжник.

conviction [kən'vɪkʃən] *n* (*belief*) убежде́ние; (*certainty*) убеждённость *f*; (LAW: *decision*) осужде́ние; (*previous*) суди́мость *f*.

convince [kən'vɪns] *vt* (*assure*) уверя́ть (уве́рить *perf*); (*persuade*) убежда́ть (убеди́ть* *perf*); **to ~ sb (of sth/that)** убежда́ть (убеди́ть* *perf*) кого́-н (в чём-н/, что).

convinced [kən'vɪnst] *adj*: **~ of/that** убеждённый в +*prp*/, что.

convincing [kən'vɪnsɪŋ] *adj* убеди́тельный* (убеди́телен).

convincingly [kən'vɪnsɪŋlɪ] *adv* убеди́тельно.

convivial [kən'vɪvɪəl] *adj* (*atmosphere*) дру́жеский*; (*person*) дружелю́бный* (дружелю́бен).

convoluted ['kɒnvəluːtɪd] *adj* замыслова́тый (замыслова́т).

convoy ['kɒnvɔɪ] *n* (*of trucks*) коло́нна; (*of ships*) конво́й.

convulse [kən'vʌls] *vt*: **to be ~d with laughter/ pain** содрога́ться (*impf*) от сме́ха/бо́ли.

convulsion [kən'vʌlʃən] *n* су́дорога, конву́льсия.

coo [kuː] *vi* (*dove, person*) воркова́ть (*impf*).

cook [kuk] *vt* (*food*) гото́вить* (пригото́вить* *perf*) ◆ *vi* (*person*) гото́вить* (*impf*); (*food*) гото́виться* (*impf*) ◆ *n* по́вар*

► **cook up** *vt* (*inf*) стря́пать (состря́пать *perf*).

cookbook ['kukbuk] *n* пова́ренная *or* кулина́рная кни́га.

cook-chill ['kuktʃɪl] *adj*: **~ food** заморо́женные полуфабрика́ты *mpl*.

cooker ['kukəʳ] *n* (*stove*) плита́*.

cookery ['kukərɪ] *n* кулинари́я.

cookery book *n* (BRIT) = **cookbook**.

cookie ['kukɪ] *n* (US) пече́нье*.

cooking ['kukɪŋ] *n* гото́вка ◆ *cpd* (*apples, chocolate*) испо́льзуемый в кулинари́и; **her ~ is very good** она́ хорошо́ гото́вит; **Italian ~** италья́нская ку́хня; **~ utensils** ку́хонные принадле́жности.

cookout ['kukaut] *n* (US) приготовле́ние пи́щи на откры́том во́здухе.

cool [kuːl] *adj* (*temperature, drink etc*) прохла́дный*; (*dress, clothes*) лёгкий* (лёгок); (*person: calm, unemotional*) невозмути́мый (невозмути́м); (: *unfriendly*) холо́дный* (хо́лоден) ◆ *vt* (*tea, room*)

охлажда́ть (охлади́ть* *perf*) ◆ *vi* (*water, air*) остыва́ть (осты́ть* *perf*); **it's ~** прохла́дно; **to keep sth ~** *or* **in a ~ place** держа́ть* (*impf*) что-н в прохла́дном ме́сте; **to keep one's ~** сохраня́ть (сохрани́ть *perf*) хладнокро́вие; **to lose one's ~** теря́ть (потеря́ть *perf*) самооблада́ние

► **cool down** *vi* остыва́ть (осты́ть* *perf*); (*situation*) нормализова́ться (*impf/perf*).

coolant ['kuːlənt] *n* хладоаге́нт.

cool box (US **cooler**) *n* холоди́льный я́щик.

cooler ['kuːləʳ] *n* (US) = **cool box**.

cooling ['kuːlɪŋ] *n* охлажде́ние ◆ *adj* прохлади́тельный, освежа́ющий (освежа́ющ).

cooling tower *n* гради́рня*.

coolly ['kuːlɪ] *adv* (*calmly*) невозмути́мо; (*coldly*) хо́лодно.

coolness ['kuːlnɪs] *n* (*see adj*) прохла́да; лёгкость *f*; невозмути́мость *f*; хо́лодность *f*.

coop [kuːp] *n* кле́тка* ◆ *vt*: **to ~ up** (*fig*) запира́ть (запере́ть* *perf*).

co-op ['kəuɒp] *n abbr* (= **cooperative** (**society**)) кооперати́вное о́бщество.

cooperate [kəu'ɒpəreɪt] *vi* (*collaborate*) сотру́дничать (*impf*); (*assist*) соде́йствовать (*impf*); **to ~ with sb** сотру́дничать (*impf*) с кем-н.

cooperation [kəuɒpə'reɪʃən] *n* (*see vb*) коопера́ция, сотру́дничество; соде́йствие.

cooperative [kəu'ɒpərətɪv] *adj* кооперати́вный ◆ *n* кооперати́в; **he is very ~** он всегда́ гото́в оказа́ть по́мощь.

coopt [kəu'ɒpt] *vt*: **to ~ sb onto a committee** кооп́тировать (*impf/perf*) кого́-н в чле́ны комите́та.

coordinate [*vt* kəu'ɔːdɪneɪt, *n* kəu'ɔːdɪnət] *vt* (*activity, attack*) согласо́вывать (согласова́ть *perf*); (*movements*) координи́ровать (*impf/perf*) ◆ *n* (MATH) координа́та; **~s** *npl* (*clothes*) предме́ты оде́жды, составля́ющие оди́н анса́мбль.

coordination [kəuɔːdɪ'neɪʃən] *n* координа́ция.

co-ownership ['kəu'əunəʃɪp] *n* совме́стное владе́ние.

cop [kɒp] *n* (*inf*) мент.

cope [kəup] *vi*: **to ~ with** справля́ться (спра́виться* *perf*) с +*instr*.

Copenhagen ['kəupn'heɪgən] *n* Копенга́ген.

copier ['kɒpɪəʳ] *n* (*also*: **photocopier**) (фо́то)копирова́льная маши́на.

co-pilot ['kəu'paɪlət] *n* второ́й пило́т.

copious ['kəupɪəs] *adj* оби́льный* (оби́лен).

copper ['kɒpəʳ] *n* (*metal*) медь *f*; (BRIT: *inf*) лега́вый *m adj*; **~s** *npl* (*small change*) медяки́* *mpl*.

coppice ['kɒpɪs] *n* ро́щица.

copse [kɒps] *n* = **coppice**.

---

* marks translations which have irregular inflections. The Russian-English side of the dictionary gives inflectional information.

copulate ['kɔpjuleɪt] *vi* совокупля́ться (совокупи́ться* *perf*).

copy ['kɔpɪ] *n* (*duplicate*) ко́пия; (*of book etc*) экземпля́р; (*material: for printing*) пи́сьменный экземпля́р, ру́копись *f* ♦ *vt* (*person, idea, text*) копи́ровать (скопи́ровать *perf*); **to make good ~** (*PRESS*) составля́ть (соста́вить* *perf*) хоро́ший материа́л (для печа́ти)

▶ **copy out** (*text*) копи́ровать (скопи́ровать *perf*)

▶ **copy down** (*text*) копи́ровать (скопи́ровать *perf*).

copycat ['kɔpɪkæt] *n* (*inf*) обезья́на *m/f*.

copyright ['kɔpɪraɪt] *n* а́вторское пра́во*; **~ reserved** а́вторское пра́во сохранено́.

copy typist *n* машини́стка*.

copywriter ['kɔpɪraɪtə'] *n* реклами́ст.

coral ['kɔrəl] *n* кора́лл.

coral reef *n* кора́лловый риф.

Coral Sea *n*: **the ~ ~** Кора́лловое мо́ре*.

cord [kɔːd] *n* (*string*) верёвка*; (*ELEC*) шнур*; (*fabric*) вельве́т; **~s** *npl* (*trousers*) вельве́товые брю́ки *pl*.

cordial ['kɔːdɪəl] *adj* (*friendly*) серде́чный* ♦ *n* (*BRIT*) фрукто́вый напи́ток*.

cordless ['kɔːdlɪs] *adj* переносно́й.

cordon ['kɔːdn] *n* кордо́н, оцепле́ние

▶ **cordon off** *vt* оцепля́ть (оцепи́ть* *perf*).

cordon bleu ['kɔːdɔn 'blɜː] *adj* (*cookery, cook*) вы́сшего кла́сса (*о кулина́рном иску́сстве*).

corduroy ['kɔːdərɔɪ] *n* вельве́т*.

CORE [kɔː'] *n abbr* (*US*) = *Congress of Racial Equality*.

core [kɔː'] *n* (*of fruit, organization*) сердцеви́на; (*of earth*) ядро́*; (*of nuclear reactor*) серде́чник; (*of problem*) суть *f* ♦ *vt* выреза́ть (вы́резать* *perf*) сердцеви́ну +*gen*; **rotten to the ~** (*fig*) прогни́вший до основа́ния.

Corfu [kɔː'fuː] *n* Ко́рфу *m ind*.

coriander [kɔrɪ'ændə'] *n* (*spice*) ки́нза, кориа́ндр.

cork [kɔːk] *n* про́бка*.

corkage ['kɔːkɪdʒ] *n* дополни́тельная опла́та в рестора́не за отку́поривание и пода́чу принесённого с собо́й вина́.

corked [kɔːkt] (*US* **corky**) *adj* пропа́хший про́бкой.

corkscrew ['kɔːkskruː] *n* што́пор.

corky ['kɔːkɪ] *adj* (*US*) = **corked**.

cormorant ['kɔːmərnt] *n* бакла́н.

Corn *abbr* (*BRIT: POST*) = **Cornwall**.

corn [kɔːn] *n* (*BRIT*) зерно́; (*US: maize*) кукуру́за; (*on foot*) мозо́ль *f*; **~ on the cob** поча́ток* кукуру́зы.

cornea ['kɔːnɪə] *n* рогова́я оболо́чка*.

corned beef ['kɔːnd-] *n* консерви́рованная говя́дина.

corner ['kɔːnə'] *n* у́гол*; (*SPORT: also:* ~ **kick**) углово́й *m adj* (уда́р) ♦ *vt* (*trap*) загоня́ть (загна́ть* *perf*) в у́гол; (*COMM: market*) приобрета́ть (приобрести́* *perf*) контро́ль над +*instr* ♦ *vi* (*in car*) де́лать (сде́лать *perf*) поворо́т; **to cut ~s** (*fig*) среза́ть (*impf*) углы́.

corner flag *n* углово́й флажо́к*.

corner kick *n* углово́й уда́р.

cornerstone ['kɔːnəstəun] *n* (*fig*) краеуго́льный ка́мень* *m*.

cornet ['kɔːnɪt] *n* (*MUS*) корне́т; (*BRIT: of ice-cream*) моро́женое в ва́фельной тру́бочке.

cornflakes ['kɔːnfleɪks] *npl* кукуру́зные хло́пья* *pl*.

cornflour ['kɔːnflauə'] *n* (*BRIT*) кукуру́зная мука́.

cornice ['kɔːnɪs] *n* карни́з.

Cornish ['kɔːnɪʃ] *adj* корнуэ́льский.

corn oil *n* кукуру́зное ма́сло*.

cornstarch ['kɔːnstɑːtʃ] *n* (*US*) = **cornflour**.

cornucopia [kɔːnju'kəupɪə] *n* рог* изоби́лия.

Cornwall ['kɔːnwəl] *n* Ко́рнуолл.

corny ['kɔːnɪ] *adj* (*inf*) пло́ский* (пло́сок).

corollary [kə'rɔlərɪ] *n* сле́дствие.

coronary ['kɔrənərɪ] *n* (*also:* ~ **thrombosis**) корона́рный тромбо́з.

coronation [kɔrə'neɪʃən] *n* корона́ция.

coroner ['kɔrənə'] *n* (*LAW*) ко́ронер (*судья́, рассле́дующий причи́ны сме́рти, происше́дшей при подозри́тельных обстоя́тельствах*).

coronet ['kɔrənɪt] *n* диаде́ма.

Corp. *abbr* = **corporation**; (*MIL*) = **corporal**.

corporal ['kɔːpərl] *n* капра́л ♦ *adj*: **~ punishment** теле́сное наказа́ние.

corporate ['kɔːpərɪt] *adj* (*COMM*) корпорати́вный; (*ownership, effort*) о́бщий*; (*identity*) корпорати́вный.

corporate hospitality *n* спецобслу́живание и привиле́гии, ока́зываемые корпора́цией осо́бо ва́жным и́ли це́нным клие́нтам.

corporation [kɔːpə'reɪʃən] *n* (*COMM*) корпора́ция; (*of town*) муниципалите́т.

corporation tax *n* корпорацио́нный нало́г.

corps [kɔː'] (*pl* ~) *n* (*also MIL*) ко́рпус*; **the press ~** корреспонде́нтский ко́рпус.

corpse [kɔːps] *n* труп.

corpuscle ['kɔːpʌsl] *n* (*BIO*) те́льце* (*кровяны́е*).

corral [kə'rɑːl] *n* заго́н.

correct [kə'rɛkt] *adj* (*accurate*) пра́вильный* (пра́вилен); (*proper*) соотве́тствующий* ♦ *vt* (*mistake, fault*) исправля́ть (испра́вить* *perf*); (*exam*) проверя́ть (прове́рить *perf*); **you are ~** Вы пра́вы.

correction [kə'rɛkʃən] *n* (*act of correcting*) исправле́ние; (*mistake corrected*) попра́вка*; (*of proofs*) корректу́ра.

correctly [kə'rɛktlɪ] *adv* пра́вильно.

correlate ['kɔrɪleɪt] *vt* соотноси́ть* (соотнести́* *perf*) ♦ *vi*: **to ~ with** соотноси́ться* (*impf*) *or* коррели́ровать (*impf*) с +*instr*.

correlation [kɔrɪ'leɪʃən] *n* соотноше́ние, корреля́ция.

correspond [kɔrɪs'pɔnd] *vi*: **to ~ (with)** (*write*)

перепи́сываться (*impf*) (с +*instr*); (*tally*) согласо́вываться (*impf*) (с +*instr*); (*equate*): to ~ **(to)** соотве́тствовать (*impf*) (+*dat*).

correspondence [kɔrɪsˈpɔndəns] *n* (*letters*) корреспонде́нция, пе́репи́ска; (*relationship*) соотноше́ние.

correspondence course *n* зао́чный курс.

correspondent [kɔrɪsˈpɔndənt] *n* (*PRESS*) корреспонде́нт(ка).

corresponding [kɔrɪsˈpɔndɪŋ] *adj* соотве́тствующий*.

corridor [ˈkɔrɪdɔːʳ] *n* (*in building etc*) коридо́р; (*in train*) прохо́д.

corroborate [kəˈrɔbəreɪt] *vt* подтвержда́ть (подтверди́ть* *perf*).

corrode [kəˈrəud] *vt* (*metal*) разъеда́ть (разъе́сть* *perf*) ♦ *vi* (*metal*) ржаве́ть (заржаве́ть* *perf*).

corrosion [kəˈrəuʒən] *n* (*damage*) ржа́вчина; (*process*) корро́зия.

corrosive [kəˈrəuzɪv] *adj* коррози́йный.

corrugated [ˈkɔrəgeɪtɪd] *adj* рифлёный.

corrugated iron *n* рифлёное желе́зо.

corrupt [kəˈrʌpt] *adj* (*person*) прода́жный* (прода́жен), коррумпи́рованный; (*COMPUT*) испо́рченный, искажённый ♦ *vt* развраща́ть (разврати́ть* *perf*); (*COMPUT*) искажа́ть (искази́ть* *perf*); ~ **practices** бесче́стные приёмы.

corruption [kəˈrʌpʃən] *n* (*see adj*) корру́пция, прода́жность *f*; искаже́ние.

corset [ˈkɔːsɪt] *n* (*also MED*) корсе́т.

Corsica [ˈkɔːsɪkə] *n* Ко́рсика.

Corsican [ˈkɔːsɪkən] *adj* корсика́нский ♦ *n* корсика́нец*(-нка*).

cortège [kɔːˈteɪʒ] *n* (*also:* **funeral** ~) проце́ссия.

cortisone [ˈkɔːtɪzəun] *n* кортизо́н.

coruscating [ˈkɔrəskeɪtɪŋ] *adj* сверка́ющий.

c.o.s. *abbr* (= *cash on shipment*) опла́та нали́чными при отпра́вке.

cosh [kɔʃ] *n* (*BRIT*) дуби́нка*.

cosignatory [kəuˈsɪɡnətərɪ] *n* одна́ из сторо́н, подпи́сывающих докуме́нт.

cosiness [ˈkəuzɪnɪs] *n* ую́т.

cos lettuce [ˈkɔs-] *n* лату́к (сала́т).

cosmetic [kozˈmetɪk] *n* (*usu pl*) косме́тика ♦ *adj* (*fig*) космети́ческий*; ~ **surgery** космети́ческая хирурги́я.

cosmic [ˈkɔzmɪk] *adj* косми́ческий*.

cosmonaut [ˈkɔzmənɔːt] *n* космона́вт.

cosmopolitan [kɔzməˈpɔlɪtn] *adj* (*place*) космополити́ческий.

cosmos [ˈkɔzmɔs] *n*: **the** ~ ко́смос.

cosset [ˈkɔsɪt] *vt* балова́ть (избалова́ть* *perf*).

cost [kɔst] (*pt, pp* **cost**) *n* сто́имость *f*; (*fig*) цена́* ♦ *vt* (*be priced at*) сто́ить (*impf*); (*pt, pp* **costed**): *find out cost of*) оце́нивать (оцени́ть* *perf*) сто́имость +*gen*; ~**s** *npl* (*COMM*) расхо́ды *mpl*;

(*LAW*) суде́бные изде́ржки* *fpl*; **how much does it** ~? ско́лько э́то сто́ит?; **it** ~**s £5/too much** э́то сто́ит £5/сли́шком до́рого; **what will it** ~ **to have it repaired?** ско́лько бу́дет сто́ить ремо́нт?; **to** ~ **sb time/effort** сто́ить (*impf*) кому́-н вре́мени/уси́лий; **it** ~ **him his life/job** э́то сто́ило ему́ жи́зни/рабо́ты; **the** ~ **of living** сто́имость жи́зни; **to sell/buy at** ~ продава́ть* (прода́ть* *perf*)/покупа́ть (купи́ть* *perf*) по себесто́имости; **at all** ~**s** любо́й цено́й.

cost accountant *n* бухга́лтер (*веду́щий учёт затра́т*).

co-star [ˈkəustɑːʳ] *n* партнёр (*гла́вной ро́ли*).

Costa Rica [ˈkɔstəˈriːkə] *n* Ко́ста-Ри́ка.

cost-benefit analysis [ˈkɔstbɛnɪfɪt-] *n* ана́лиз изде́ржек и при́были.

cost centre *n* счёт, фикси́рующий произво́дственные изде́ржки.

cost control *n* контро́ль *m* за у́ровнем изде́ржек.

cost-effective [ˈkɔstɪˈfɛktɪv] *adj* вы́годный* (вы́годен); (*COMM*) рента́бельный.

cost-effectiveness [ˈkɔstɪˈfɛktɪvnɪs] *n* (*see adj*) вы́годность *f*; рента́бельность *f*.

costing [ˈkɔstɪŋ] *n* (*COMM*) оце́нка сто́имости.

costly [ˈkɔstlɪ] *adj* (*expensive*) дорого́й* (до́рог); (*in time, effort*) дорогосто́ящий*.

cost of living *n* сто́имость *f* жи́зни.

cost price *n* (*BRIT*) себесто́имость *f*; **to sell/buy at** ~ ~ продава́ть* (прода́ть* *perf*)/покупа́ть (купи́ть* *perf*) по себесто́имости.

costume [ˈkɔstjuːm] *n* костю́м; (*BRIT: also:* **swimming** ~) купа́льник, купа́льный костю́м.

costume jewellery *n* бижуте́рия.

cosy [ˈkəuzɪ] (*US* **cozy**) *adj* (*room, atmosphere*) ую́тный* (ую́тен); (*bed*) удо́бный* (удо́бен); (*scarf, gloves*) тёплый*; (*person*) забо́тливый; (*chat, evening*) прия́тный* (прия́тен).

cot [kɔt] *n* (*BRIT: for baby*) де́тская крова́тка*; (*US: camp bed*) ко́йка*.

cot death *n* внеза́пная сме́рть здоро́вого грудно́го ребёнка во сне.

Cotswolds [ˈkɔtswəuldz] *npl*: **the** ~ Ко́тсвольд *msg*.

cottage [ˈkɔtɪdʒ] *n* котте́дж.

cottage cheese *n* творо́г.

cottage industry *n* надо́мный труд*.

cottage pie *n* запека́нка из мя́са и карто́феля.

cotton [ˈkɔtn] *n* (*fabric*) хло́пок*, хлопчатобума́жная ткань *f*; (*plant*) хлопча́тник; (*thread*) (швейная) ни́тка*; ~ **dress** *etc* хлопчатобума́жное пла́тье* *etc*

▶ **cotton on** *vi* (*inf*): **he has** ~**ed on to the fact that** ... до него́ дошло́, что ....

---

* marks translations which have irregular inflections. The Russian-English side of the dictionary gives inflectional information.

cotton candy n (US) cáхарная вáта.
cotton wool n (BRIT) вáта.
couch [kautʃ] n тахтá, дивáн; (for patients) кушéтка* ♦ vt излагáть (изложи́ть* perf).
couchette [ku:'ʃɛt] n спáльное мéсто*, пóлка*.
couch potato n лежебóка m/f.
cough [kɔf] vi (person) кáшлять (impf); (engine) тарахтéть (impf) ♦ n кáшель m.
cough drop n таблéтка* от кáшля.
cough mixture n микстýра от кáшля.
cough syrup n = cough mixture.
could [kud] pt of can².
couldn't ['kudnt] = could not; see can².
council ['kaunsl] n совéт; city or town ~ городскóй совéт, муниципалитéт; C~ of Europe Совéт Еврóпейского Соóбщества.
council estate n (BRIT) жилóй массив, принадлежáщий муниципалитéту.
council house n (BRIT) дом, принадлежáщий муниципалитéту.
council housing n (BRIT) жильё, принадлежáщее муниципалитéту и сдавáемое в арéнду.
councillor ['kaunslə'] n ≈ член муниципалитéта.
council tax n муниципáльный налóг.
counsel ['kaunsl] n (advice) совéт; (lawyer) адвокáт, юрискóнсульт ♦ vt: to ~ sth/sb to do совéтовать (посовéтовать perf) что-н/ кóму-н +infin; ~ for the defence защи́тник; ~ for the prosecution обвини́тель m.
counsellor ['kaunslə'] n (advisor) совéтник; (US: lawyer) адвокáт.
count [kaunt] vt (add up) считáть (посчитáть perf); (include) считáть (impf) ♦ vi пересчи́тывать (пересчитáть perf); (qualify) считáться (impf); (matter) имéть (impf) значéние ♦ n (of things, people) подсчёт; (level) ýровень* m; (nobleman) граф; to ~ (up) to 10 считáть (посчитáть perf) до 10; not ~ing the children не считáя детéй; 10 ~ing him 10, считáя егó; to ~ the cost of оцéнивать (оцени́ть perf) стóимость +gen; it ~s for very little это имéет óчень мáленькое значéние; ~ yourself lucky считáйте, что Вам повезлó; to keep/lose ~ of sth вести́* (impf)/ теря́ть (потеря́ть perf) счёт чегó-н
▶ **count on** vt fus рассчи́тывать (impf) на +acc; to ~ on doing рассчи́тывать (impf) +infin
▶ **count up** vt подсчи́тывать (подсчитáть perf).
countdown ['kauntdaun] n счёт в обрáтном направлéнии.
countenance ['kauntɪnəns] n лицó* ♦ vt одобря́ть (одóбрить perf).
counter ['kauntə'] n (in shop, café) прилáвок*; (in bank, post office) стóйка*; (in game) фи́шка*; (TECH) счётчик ♦ vt (oppose) опроверга́ть (опровéргнуть perf); (blow) отража́ть (отрази́ть perf) ♦ adv: ~ to в противовéс +dat; to buy under the ~ (fig) покупáть (купи́ть* perf) из-под прилáвка; to

~ sth with sth противостоя́ть (impf/perf) чемý-н чем-н.
counteract ['kauntər'ækt] vt (effect etc) противодéйствовать (impf) +dat; (poison etc) нейтрализовáть (impf/perf), обезврéживать (обезврéдить* perf).
counterattack ['kauntərə'tæk] n контратáка ♦ vi контратаковáть (impf/perf).
counterbalance ['kauntə'bæləns] vt уравновéшивать (уравновéсить* perf).
counterclockwise ['kauntə'klɔkwaiz] adv прóтив часовóй стрéлки.
counterespionage ['kauntər'ɛspɪənɑ:ʒ] n контрразвéдка*.
counterfeit ['kauntəfit] n поддéлка* ♦ vt поддéлывать (поддéлать perf) ♦ adj (coin) фальши́вый.
counterfoil ['kauntəfɔil] n (of cheque, money order) корешóк*.
counterintelligence ['kauntərɪn'tɛlɪdʒəns] n контрразвéдка*.
countermand ['kauntəmɑ:nd] vt (order) отменя́ть (отмени́ть* perf).
countermeasure ['kauntəmɛʒə'] n контрмéра.
counteroffensive ['kauntərə'fɛnsɪv] n контрнаступлéние.
counterpane ['kauntəpein] n покрывáло.
counterpart ['kauntəpɑ:t] n (of person) коллéга m/f; (of document etc) кóпия.
counterproductive ['kauntəprə'dʌktɪv] adj непродукти́вный* (непродукти́вен).
counterproposal ['kauntəprə'pəuzl] n встрéчное предложéние.
countersign ['kauntəsain] vt заверя́ть (завéрить perf), засвидéтельствовать (perf).
countersink ['kauntəsiŋk] vt зенковáть (impf).
countess ['kauntɪs] n графи́ня.
countless ['kauntlɪs] adj несчётный*, бесчи́сленный.
countrified ['kʌntrɪfaid] adj деревéнский*.
country ['kʌntrɪ] n (state, nation) странá*; (native land) рóдина; (rural area) дерéвня*; (region) райóн; in the ~ в дерéвне; mountainous ~ гóристая мéстность f.
country and western (music) n кáнтри nt ind.
country dancing n (BRIT) нарóдные тáнцы mpl.
country house n зáгородный дом*, ≈ дáча.
countryman ['kʌntrɪmən] irreg n (compatriot) земля́к*, соотéчественник; (country dweller) деревéнский* or сéльский* жи́тель m.
countryside ['kʌntrɪsaid] n сéльская мéстность f.
countrywide ['kʌntrɪ'waid] adj общенационáльный ♦ adv по всéй странé.
county ['kaunti] n грáфство.
county council n ≈ областнóй совéт, совéт грáфства.
county town n (BRIT) глáвный гóрод* грáфства.
coup [ku:] n (pl ~s) n (also: ~ d'état)

государственный переворо́т; (*fig*)
переворо́т.
coupé [ku:'peɪ] *n* (*AUT*) закры́тый автомоби́ль
с двумя́ дверя́ми и накло́нным ку́зовом.
couple ['kʌpl] *n* (*married couple*) супру́ги *pl*; (*of
people, things*) па́ра ♦ *vt* (*ideas, names*)
свя́зывать (связа́ть* *perf*); (*machinery*)
сцепля́ть (сцепи́ть* *perf*); **a ~ of** (*two, a few*)
па́ра +*gen*.
couplet ['kʌplɪt] *n* двусти́шие.
coupling ['kʌplɪŋ] *n* (*RAIL*) сцепле́ние.
coupon ['ku:pɒn] *n* (*voucher*) купо́н;
(*detachable form*) тало́н; (*COMM*) отрывно́й
бланк.
courage ['kʌrɪdʒ] *n* сме́лость *f*, хра́брость *f*,
му́жество.
courageous [kə'reɪdʒəs] *adj* сме́лый* (смел),
хра́брый (храбр), му́жественный
(му́жественен).
courgette [kuə'ʒet] *n* (*BRIT*) молодо́й кабачо́к*.
courier ['kurɪə'] *n* (*messenger*) курье́р; (*for
tourists*) руководи́тель *m* гру́ппы.
course [kɔ:s] *n* (*SCOL, MED, NAUT*) курс; (*of
events, time etc*) ход; (*of argument, action*)
направле́ние; (*of river*) тече́ние; (*part of
meal*): **first/next/last ~** пе́рвое/второ́е/
сла́дкое блю́до; **~ of lectures/treatment** курс
ле́кций/лече́ния; **in the ~ of the next few days**
в тече́ние сле́дующих не́скольких дней; **in
due ~** в своё вре́мя; **~ (of action)** ли́ния
поведе́ния; **the best ~ would be ...** лу́чшим
вы́ходом бы́ло бы ...; **we have no other ~ but
to ...** у нас нет друго́го вы́хода, кро́ме как ...;
of ~ (*naturally*) коне́чно; (*certainly*)
безусло́вно; **of ~!** коне́чно!; **(no) of ~ not!**
(нет,) коне́чно, нет!; **golf ~** *по́ле для игры́ в
гольф*.
court [kɔ:t] *n* (*LAW*) суд*; (*SPORT*) корт; (*royal*)
двор* ♦ *vt* (*woman*) уха́живать (*impf*) за +*instr*;
(*fig: favour*) добива́ться (доби́ться* *perf*)
+*gen*; (: *death, disaster*) заи́грывать (*impf*) с
+*instr*; **to settle out of ~** приходи́ть* (прийти́*
perf) к соглаше́нию без суде́бного
разбира́тельства; **to take sb to ~** подава́ть*
(пода́ть* *perf*) на кого́-н в суд.
courteous ['kə:tɪəs] *adj* ве́жливый (ве́жлив).
courtesan [kɔ:tɪ'zæn] *n* куртиза́нка*.
courtesy ['kə:təsɪ] *n* ве́жливость *f*; **(by) ~ of**
благодаря́ любе́зности +*gen*.
courtesy light *n* *ла́мпочка в сало́не
автомоби́ля*.
courthouse ['kɔ:thaus] *n* (*US*) зда́ние суда́.
courtier ['kɔ:tɪə'] *n* придво́рный *m adj*.
court martial (*pl* ~**s** ~) *n* вое́нный трибуна́л.
court of appeal (*pl* ~**s** ~ ~) *n* апелляцио́нный
суд*.
court of inquiry (*pl* ~**s** ~ ~) *n* сле́дственная
коми́ссия.

courtroom ['kɔ:trum] *n* зал суда́.
court shoe *n* ло́дочки *pl*.
courtyard ['kɔ:tjɑ:d] *n* вну́тренний* двор*.
cousin ['kʌzn] *n* (*relative: male*) неродно́й
брат*; (: *female*) неродна́я сестра́*; **first ~**
(*male*) двою́родный брат*; (*female*)
двою́родная сестра́*.
cove [kəuv] *n* (*bay*) бу́хточка*.
covenant ['kʌvənənt] *n* (*promise*)
обяза́тельство ♦ *vt*: **to ~ £200 per year to
charity** обя́зываться (обяза́ться* *perf*)
перечисля́ть £200 в год в благо-
твори́тельный фонд.
Coventry ['kɔvəntrɪ] *n*: **send sb to ~** (*fig*)
бойкоти́ровать (*impf/perf*) кого́-н.
cover ['kʌvə'] *vt* (*protect, hide*) закрыва́ть
(закры́ть* *perf*), укрыва́ть (укры́ть* *perf*);
(*distance*) покрыва́ть (покры́ть* *perf*); (*MIL*)
прикрыва́ть (прикры́ть* *perf*); (*INSURANCE*)
предусма́тривать (предусмотре́ть* *perf*);
(*topic*) рассма́тривать (рассмотре́ть* *perf*);
(*include*) охва́тывать (охвати́ть* *perf*);
(*PRESS*) освеща́ть (освети́ть* *perf*) ♦ *n* (*for
furniture, machinery etc*) чехо́л*; (*of book,
magazine*) обло́жка*; (*shelter*) укры́тие;
(*INSURANCE*) покры́тие; (*MIL*) прикры́тие;
(*fig*) прикры́тие; **~s** *npl* (*bedclothes*)
посте́льные принадле́жности *fpl*; **he was ~ed
in** *or* **with** (*mud*) он был весь в +*prp*; **to take ~**
укрыва́ться (укры́ться* *perf*); **under ~** в
укры́тии; **under ~ of darkness** под покро́вом
темноты́; **under separate ~** (*COMM*) в
отде́льном паке́те; **£10 will ~ my expenses**
£10 покро́ют мои́ расхо́ды.
▶ **cover up** *vt* (*protect, hide*) закрыва́ть
(закры́ть* *perf*); (*fig: facts, feelings*) скрыва́ть
(скры́ть* *perf*) ♦ *vi* (*fig*): **to ~ up for sb**
покрыва́ть (покры́ть* *perf*) кого́-н.
coverage ['kʌvərɪdʒ] *n* (*TV, PRESS*) освеще́ние;
television ~ of the conference освеще́ние
конфере́нции по телеви́дению; **to give full ~
to** дава́ть* (дать* *perf*) по́лное освеще́ние
+*gen*.
coveralls ['kʌvərɔ:lz] *npl* (*US*) рабо́чий*
комбинезо́н *msg*.
cover charge *n* (*in restaurant*) наце́нка.
covering ['kʌvərɪŋ] *n* (*layer*) пласт*; (*of snow,
dust etc*) слой*; (*on floor*) насти́л.
covering letter (*US* **cover letter**) *n*
сопроводи́тельное письмо́*.
cover note *n* докуме́нт, удостоверя́ющий
факт страхова́ния.
cover price *n* цена́, ука́занная на обло́жке.
covert ['kʌvət] *adj* (*threat*) скры́тый; (*attack*)
неожи́данный*; **she gave me a ~ glance** она́
укра́дкой на меня́ посмотре́ла.
cover-up ['kʌvərʌp] *n* ши́рма, прикры́тие.
covet ['kʌvɪt] *vt* жа́ждать (*impf*) +*gen*.

---

* marks translations which have irregular inflections. The Russian-English side of the dictionary gives inflectional information.

cow [kau] *n* (*also inf!*) коро́ва (*also !*) ♦ *vt* запу́гивать (запуга́ть *perf*).

coward ['kauəd] *n* трус(и́ха).

cowardice ['kauədɪs] *n* тру́сость *f*.

cowardly ['kauədlɪ] *adj* трусли́вый (трусли́в).

cowboy ['kaubɔɪ] *n* (*in US*) ковбо́й; (*pej: tradesman*) шаба́шник.

cow elephant *n* слони́ха.

cower ['kauə] *vi* съёживаться (съёжиться *perf*).

cow shed *n* коро́вник.

cowslip ['kauslɪp] *n* первоцве́т (настоя́щий* *or* весе́нний*).

cox [kɔks] *n abbr* = **coxswain**.

coxswain ['kɔksn] *n* (*ROWING*) старшина́ (байда́рки).

coy [kɔɪ] *adj* (*shy*) засте́нчивый (засте́нчив).

coyote [kɔɪ'əutɪ] *n* койо́т.

cozy ['kəuzɪ] *adj* (*US*) = **cosy**.

CP *n abbr* = *Communist Party*.

cp. *abbr* (= **compare**) ср. = *сравни*.

c/p *abbr* (*BRIT*: = *carriage paid*) с опла́ченной доста́вкой.

CPA *n abbr* (*US*) = *certified public accountant*.

CPI *n abbr* (= *Consumer Price Index*) и́ндекс потреби́тельских цен.

Cpl. *abbr* (*MIL*) = **corporal**.

CP/M *n abbr* (= *Central Program for Microprocessors*) СРМ (*операцио́нная систе́ма для микроЭВМ*).

c.p.s. *abbr* (*COMPUT, TYP*: = *characters per second*) зна́ков в секу́нду.

CPSA *n abbr* (*BRIT*) = *Civil and Public Services Association*.

CPU *n abbr* (*COMPUT*) (= **central processing unit**) ЦП= *центра́льный проце́ссор*.

cr. *abbr* = **credit, creditor**.

crab [kræb] *n* краб.

crab apple *n* ди́кое я́блоко*.

crack [kræk] *n* (*noise*) треск; (*gap*) щель* *f*; (*in bone, dish, wall*) тре́щина; (*joke*) хо́хма; (*DRUGS*) крэк (*фо́рма кокаи́на*) ♦ *vt* (*whip, twig*) щёлкать (щёлкнуть *perf*) +*instr*; (*bone, dish etc*) раска́лывать (расколо́ть* *perf*); (*nut*) коло́ть* (расколо́ть* *perf*); (*problem*) реша́ть (реши́ть *perf*); (*code*) разга́дывать (разгада́ть *perf*); (*joke*) отпуска́ть (отпусти́ть* *perf*) ♦ *adj* первокла́ссный*; **at the ~ of dawn** на заре́; **to have a ~ (at sth)** (*inf*) пыта́ться (попыта́ть *perf*) свои си́лы (в чём-н); **to get ~ing** (*inf*) пошеве́ливаться (*impf*)

▸ **crack down on** *vt fus* расправля́ться (распра́виться* *perf*) с +*instr*

▸ **crack up** *vi* (*with laughter*) пры́скать (пры́снуть *perf*) со́ смеху; **she ~ed up** (*under strain*) у неё был не́рвный срыв.

crackdown ['krækdaun] *n*: **~ (on)** распра́ва (с +*instr*).

cracked [krækt] *adj* (*inf*) сло́манный (сло́ман).

cracker ['krækə] *n* (*biscuit*) кре́кер; (*Christmas cracker*) хлопу́шка*; (*firework*) шути́ха; **a ~ of**

a goal (*BRIT*: *inf*) сногсшиба́тельный гол; **she's a ~** (*BRIT*: *inf*) она́ сногсшиба́тельная же́нщина; **he's ~s** (*BRIT*: *inf*) он спя́тил.

crackle ['krækl] *vi* потре́скивать (*impf*).

crackling ['kræklɪŋ] *n* треск; (*of pork*) шква́рки* *fpl*.

crackpot ['krækpɔt] *n* (*inf*) полоу́мный(-ая) *m(f)* *adj* ♦ *adj* полоу́мный.

cradle ['kreɪdl] *n* (*for baby*) колыбе́ль *f* ♦ *vt* прижима́ть (*impf*) к груди́.

craft [krɑːft] *n* (*skill*) мастерство́; (*trade*) ремесло́*; (*boat: pl inv*) кора́бль* *f*.

craftsman ['krɑːftsmən] *irreg n* (*artisan*) реме́сленник.

craftsmanship ['krɑːftsmənʃɪp] *n* (*quality*) вы́делка; (*skill*) мастерство́.

crafty ['krɑːftɪ] *adj* лука́вый (лука́в).

crag [kræg] *n* утёс.

craggy ['krægɪ] *adj* (*mountain, cliff*) отве́сный*; (*face*) с ре́зкими черта́ми.

cram [kræm] *vi* (*for exams*) зубри́ть (вы́зубрить *perf*) ♦ *vt* (*fill*): **to ~ sth with** набива́ть (наби́ть* *perf*) что-н +*instr*; (*put*): **to ~ sth into** вти́скивать (вти́снуть *perf*) что-н в +*acc*.

cramming ['kræmɪŋ] *n* зубрёжка.

cramp [kræmp] *n* су́дорога ♦ *vt* стесня́ть (стесни́ть *perf*).

cramped [kræmpt] *adj* (*accommodation*) те́сный (те́сен).

crampon ['kræmpən] *n* (*CLIMBING*) клещи́ *pl*.

cranberry ['krænbərɪ] *n* клю́ква.

crane [kreɪn] *n* (*machine*) (подъёмный) кран; (*bird*) жура́вль* *m* ♦ *vt*: **to ~ one's neck** вытя́гивать (вы́тянуть *perf*) ше́ю ♦ *vi*: **to ~ forward** высо́вываться (вы́сунуться *perf*).

crania ['kreɪnɪə] *npl of* **cranium**.

cranium ['kreɪnɪəm] (*pl* **crania**) *n* че́реп*.

crank [kræŋk] *n* (*person*) чуда́к*; (*handle*) заводна́я рукоя́тка.

crankshaft ['kræŋkʃɑːft] *n* коле́нчатый вал*.

cranky ['kræŋkɪ] *adj* чудакова́тый (чудакова́т).

cranny ['krænɪ] *n see* **nook**.

crap [kræp] (*inf!*) *n* дерьмо́ (*!*) ♦ *vi* срать* (*impf*) (*!*); **to have a ~** посра́ть* (*perf*) (*!*)

crappy ['kræpɪ] *adj* (*inf!*) дерьмо́вый (*!*)

crash [kræʃ] *n* (*noise*) гро́хот; (*of car*) ава́рия; (*of plane, train*) круше́ние; (*COMM*) крах ♦ *vt* (*car, plane*) разбива́ть (разби́ть* *perf*) ♦ *vi* (*car, plane*) разбива́ться (разби́ться* *perf*); (*two cars*) ста́лкиваться (столкну́ться *perf*); (*COMM*) потерпе́ть* (*perf*) крах; **to ~ into** вреза́ться (вре́заться* *perf*) в +*acc*; **he ~ed the car into a wall** он вре́зался на маши́не в сте́ну.

crash barrier *n* (*BRIT*) предохрани́тельный барье́р (на доро́ге).

crash course *n* интенси́вный курс.

crash helmet *n* защи́тный шлем.

crash landing *n* вы́нужденная поса́дка*.

crass [kræs] *adj* тупо́й (туп).
crate [kreɪt] *n* (*box*) деревя́нный я́щик; (*for bottles*) упако́вочный я́щик (*для буты́лок*); (*inf: car*) драндуле́т.
crater ['kreɪtə'] *n* (*of volcano*) кра́тер; (*of bomb blast*) воро́нка*.
cravat [krə'væt] *n* ше́йный плато́к*.
crave [kreɪv] *vti*: **to ~ sth** *or* **for sth** жа́ждать (*impf*) чего́-н.
craven ['kreɪvən] *adj* трусли́вый (трусли́в).
craving ['kreɪvɪŋ] *n*: **~ (for)** жа́жда (+*gen*).
crawl [krɔːl] *vi* по́лзать/ползти́* (*impf*); (*inf: grovel*) пресмыка́ться (*impf*) ◆ *n* (*SWIMMING*) кроль *f*; **to ~ to sb** (*inf*) пресмыка́ться (*impf*) пе́ред кем-н; **I was driving along at a ~** моя́ маши́на е́ле ползла́.
crayfish ['kreɪfɪʃ] *n inv* (*freshwater*) речно́й рак; (*saltwater*) лангу́ст.
crayon ['kreɪən] *n* цветно́й мело́к*.
craze [kreɪz] *n* пова́льное увлече́ние.
crazed [kreɪzd] *adj* (*look, person*) безу́мный*; (*pottery etc*) потре́скавшийся.
crazy ['kreɪzɪ] *adj* сумасше́дший*; (*inf*): **he's ~ about skiing** (*inf*) он поме́шан на лы́жах; **to go ~** помеша́ться (*perf*).
crazy paving *n* (*BRIT*) насти́л из ка́менных плит разли́чной фо́рмы.
creak [kriːk] *vi* скрипе́ть* (*impf*).
cream [kriːm] *n* (*of milk*) сли́вки* *pl*; (*made artificially*) (иску́сственные) сли́вки*; (*cosmetic*) крем ◆ *adj* (*colour*) кре́мовый; **whipped ~** взби́тые сли́вки*; **soured ~** смета́на; **the ~ of society** сли́вки* о́бщества
▶ **cream off** *vt* (*fig: best talents*) отбира́ть (отобра́ть* *perf*); (*part of profits*) снима́ть (*impf*) пе́нки.
cream cake *n* пиро́жное *nt adj* с кре́мом.
cream cheese *n* сли́вочный сыр*.
creamery ['kriːmərɪ] *n* (*shop*) моло́чный магази́н; (*factory*) маслобо́йный заво́д.
creamy ['kriːmɪ] *adj* (*colour*) кре́мовый; (*taste*) сли́вочный.
crease [kriːs] *n* (*fold*) скла́дка*; (: *in trousers*) стре́лка*; (*wrinkle: in dress, on brow*) морщи́на ◆ *vt* мять* (помя́ть* *perf*) ◆ *vi* мя́ться* (помя́ться* *perf*).
crease-resistant ['kriːsrɪzɪstənt] *adj* немну́щийся*.
create [kriː'eɪt] *vt* (*cause to happen, exist*) твори́ть (сотвори́ть* *perf*), порожда́ть (породи́ть* *perf*); (*produce: impression*) создава́ть* (созда́ть* *perf*).
creation [kriː'eɪʃən] *n* созда́ние; (*REL*) сотворе́ние.
creative [kriː'eɪtɪv] *adj* (*artistic*) тво́рческий*; (*inventive*) изобрета́тельный* (изобрета́телен).
creativity [kriːeɪ'tɪvɪtɪ] *n* тво́рчество.

creator [kriː'eɪtə'] *n* созда́тель *m*.
creature ['kriːtʃə'] *n* (*animal*) существо́; (*person*) созда́ние.
creature comforts [- 'kʌmfəts] *npl* удо́бства *ntpl*.
crèche [krɛʃ] *n* (де́тские) я́сли *pl*.
credence ['kriːdns] *n*: **to lend** *or* **give ~ to** придава́ть* (прида́ть* *perf*) правдо-подо́бность +*dat*.
credentials [krɪ'dɛnʃlz] *npl* (*references*) квалифика́ция *fsg*, достиже́ния *ntpl*; (*identity papers*) рекоменда́ция, рекоменда́тельное письмо́.
credibility [krɛdɪ'bɪlɪtɪ] *n* (*of fact*) правдоподо́бность *f*; (*of person*) авторите́т.
credible ['krɛdɪbl] *adj* (*thing*) вероя́тный* (вероя́тен), правдоподо́бный* (правдоподо́бен); (*person*) авторите́тный* (авторите́тен).
credit ['krɛdɪt] *n* (*COMM*) креди́т; (*recognition*) до́лжное *nt adj*; (*SCOL*) курс, необходи́мый для получе́ния дипло́ма ◆ *vt* (*COMM*) кредитова́ть (*impf/perf*); (*believe: also*: **give ~ to**) ве́рить (пове́рить *perf*) +*dat*; **~s** *npl* (*CINEMA, TV*) (вступи́тельные) ти́тры *mpl*; **he is/was in ~** он платёжеспосо́бен/был платёжеспосо́бен; **on ~** в креди́т; **to sb's ~** к чьей-н че́сти; **to take the ~ for** припи́сывать (приписа́ть* *perf*) себе́ +*acc*; **it does him ~** э́то де́лает ему́ честь; **he's a ~ to his family** он де́лает честь свое́й семье́; **to ~ sb with sth** (*fig*) припи́сывать (приписа́ть* *perf*) кому́-н что-н; **he ~s £5 to sb** вноси́ть* (внести́* *perf*) £5 на чей-н счёт.
creditable ['krɛdɪtəbl] *adj* (*behaviour*) досто́йный; (*mark*) похва́льный* (похва́лен).
credit account *n* креди́тный счёт (*в отде́льном магази́не*).
credit agency *n* (*BRIT*) кредитно-информацио́нное бюро́.
credit balance *n* креди́тный оста́ток* на счёте.
credit bureau *n* (*US*) = **credit agency**.
credit card *n* креди́тная ка́рточка*.
credit control *n* (*ECON*) креди́тный контро́ль *m*.
credit facilities *npl* креди́тный лими́т (*креди́тной ка́рточки заёмщика*).
credit limit *n* креди́тный лими́т (*в примене́нию к индивидуа́льному заёмщику и́ли определя́емый креди́тной ли́нией ба́нка*).
credit note *n* (*BRIT*) докуме́нт, позволя́ющий купи́ть това́р взаме́н неиспра́вного.
creditor ['krɛdɪtə'] *n* кредито́р.
credit transfer *n* креди́тный перево́д, жи́ро.
creditworthy ['krɛdɪt'wə:ðɪ] *adj* кредитоспосо́бный*.

---

* marks translations which have irregular inflections. The Russian-English side of the dictionary gives inflectional information.

credulity [krɪ'dju:lɪtɪ] *n* дове́рчивость *f.*
creed [kri:d] *n* (*REL*) вероуче́ние.
creek [kri:k] *n* у́зкий* зали́в; (*US*) руче́й*; **to be up the ~** (*inf*) вли́пнуть (*perf*) в исто́рию.
creel [kri:l] *n* (*also:* **lobster ~**) кле́тка для ло́вли *лангу́стов.*
creep [kri:p] (*pt, pp* **crept**) *vi* (*person, animal*) кра́сться* (*impf*); (*plant*) ви́ться* (*impf*) ♦ *n* (*inf*) подхали́м(ка); **it gives me the ~s** от э́того у меня́ моро́з по ко́же подира́ет; **to ~ up on sb** подкра́дываться (подкра́сться* *perf*) к кому́-н.
creeper ['kri:pə'] *n* ползу́чее расте́ние.
creepers ['kri:pəz] *npl* (*US*) ползунки́ *pl.*
creepy ['kri:pɪ] *adj* жу́ткий*.
creepy-crawly ['kri:pɪ'krɔ:lɪ] *n* (*inf*) бука́шка*.
cremate [krɪ'meɪt] *vt* креми́ровать (*impf/perf*).
cremation [krɪ'meɪʃən] *n* крема́ция.
crematoria [krɛmə'tɔ:rɪə] *npl of* **crematorium**.
crematorium [krɛmə'tɔ:rɪəm] (*pl* **crematoria**) *n* кремато́рий.
creosote ['krɪəsəut] *n* креозо́т.
crêpe [kreɪp] *n* (*fabric*) креп; (*rubber*) *copm каучу́ка.*
crêpe bandage *n* (*BRIT*) эласти́чная повя́зка*.
crêpe paper *n* крепи́рованная бума́га.
crêpe sole *n* каучу́ковая подо́шва.
crept [krɛpt] *pt, pp of* **creep**.
crescendo [krɪ'ʃɛndəu] *n* (*MUS*) креще́ндо *nt ind*; **the noise reached a ~** шум нараста́л креще́ндо.
crescent ['krɛsnt] *n* (*shape*) полуме́сяц; (*street*) серпообра́зная у́лица.
cress [krɛs] *n* кресс-сала́т.
crest [krɛst] *n* (*of hill*) гре́бень* *m*; (*of bird*) хохоло́к*, гребешо́к; (*coat of arms*) герб.
crestfallen ['krɛstfɔ:lən] *adj* удручённый* (удручён); **he looked ~** у него́ был удручённый вид.
Crete [kri:t] *n* Крит.
crevasse [krɪ'væs] *n* рассе́лина *or* расще́лина (*в ледникé*).
crevice ['krɛvɪs] *n* щель *f.*
crew [kru:] *n* (*NAUT, AVIAT*) экипа́ж; (*TV, CINEMA*) съёмочная гру́ппа; (*gang*) компа́ния.
crew cut *n* ёжик; **to have a ~~** стри́чься (постри́чься* *perf*) под ёжик.
crew neck *n* вы́рез под го́рло.
crib [krɪb] *n* (*cot*) де́тская крова́тка*; (*REL*) я́сли *pl* ♦ *vt* (*inf*) сдува́ть (сдуть* *perf*).
cribbage ['krɪbɪdʒ] *n* кри́ббидж.
crick [krɪk] *n* (*in back*) боле́зненный спазм; **~ in the neck** вы́вих шéйного позвонка́.
cricket ['krɪkɪt] *n* (*game*) кри́кет; (*insect*) сверчо́к*.
cricketer ['krɪkɪtə'] *n* игро́к* в кри́кет.
crime [kraɪm] *n* (*also fig*) преступле́ние; (*illegal activity*) престу́пность *f*; **petty ~** мéлкое хулига́нство.
Crimea [kraɪ'mɪə] *n*: **the ~** Крым.
crime wave *n* волна́* престу́пности.
criminal ['krɪmɪnl] *n* престу́пник*(-ица) ♦ *adj*

(*illegal*) кримина́льный, уголо́вный; (*morally wrong*) престу́пный*; **~ law** уголо́вное пра́во; **C~ Investigation Department** Уголо́вный ро́зыск.
criminal code *n* уголо́вный ко́декс.
crimp [krɪmp] *vt* (*fabric*) гофрирова́ть (*impf/ perf*); (*pastry*) защи́пывать (защипну́ть *perf*); (*hair*) завива́ть (зави́ть* *perf*).
crimson ['krɪmzn] *adj* мали́новый, тёмно-кра́сный*.
cringe [krɪndʒ] *vi* съёживаться (съёжиться *perf*).
crinkle ['krɪŋkl] *vt* мять* (измя́ть* *perf*).
cripple ['krɪpl] *n* калéка *m/f* ♦ *vt* (*person*) калéчить (искалéчить *perf*); (*ship, plane*) поврежда́ть (повреди́ть* *perf*); (*production, exports*) наноси́ть* (нанести́* *perf*) вред +*dat*; **~d with rheumatism** искалéченный ревмати́змом.
crippling ['krɪplɪŋ] *adj* (*disease*) веду́щий* к инвали́дности; (*taxation, debts*) разори́тельный (разори́телен).
crises ['kraɪsi:z] *npl of* **crisis**.
crisis ['kraɪsɪs] (*pl* **crises**) *n* кри́зис.
crisp [krɪsp] *adj* (*vegetables*) хрустя́щий*; (*weather*) свéжий* (свеж); (*reply*) чёткий* (чёток).
crisps [krɪsps] *npl* (*BRIT*) чи́псы *pl.*
crisscross ['krɪskrɔs] *adj* перекрёстный ♦ *vt* пересека́ть (пересéчь* *perf*).
criteria [kraɪ'tɪərɪə] *npl of* **criterion**.
criterion [kraɪ'tɪərɪən] (*pl* **criteria**) *n* крите́рий.
critic ['krɪtɪk] *n* кри́тик.
critical ['krɪtɪkl] *adj* (*time, situation, analysis*) крити́ческий*; (*person, opinion*) крити́чный* (крити́чен); **he is ~** (*MED*) он в крити́ческом состоя́нии; **she is ~ of him/the system** она́ крити́чна по отношéнию к нему́/системе.
critically ['krɪtɪklɪ] *adv* (*speak, look*) крити́чески; (*ill*) опа́сно; (*examine*) крити́чно.
criticism ['krɪtɪsɪzəm] *n* кри́тика; (*of book, play*) крити́ческий* разбо́р.
criticize ['krɪtɪsaɪz] *vt* (*find fault with*) критикова́ть (*impf*).
critique [krɪ'ti:k] *n* крити́ческий* ана́лиз.
croak [krəuk] *vi* (*frog*) ква́кать (*impf*); (*bird*) ка́ркать (*impf*); (*person*) хрипéть (*impf*) ♦ *n* (*see vi*) ква́канье; ка́рканье; хрип.
Croatia [krəu'eɪʃə] *n* Хорва́тия.
Croatian [krəu'eɪʃən] *n* (*person*) хорва́т(ка*) ♦ *adj* хорва́тский*.
crochet ['krəuʃeɪ] *n* вяза́ние крючко́м.
crock [krɔk] *n* гли́няный кувши́н; (*inf: also:* **old ~**) разва́лина.
crockery ['krɔkərɪ] *n* гли́няная *or* фая́нсовая посу́да.
crocodile ['krɔkədaɪl] *n* крокоди́л.
crocus ['krəukəs] *n* шафра́н.
croft [krɔft] *n* (*BRIT: small farm*) ху́тор*.
crofter ['krɔftə'] *n* (*BRIT*) хуторя́нин(-нка*).

crone [krəun] *n* карга́.

crony ['krəunı] *n* (*inf*) закады́чный друг*.

crook [kruk] *n* (*criminal*) жу́лик; (*of shepherd*) по́сох; **the ~ of the arm** вну́тренний* сгиб ло́ктя.

crooked ['krukıd] *adj* криво́й* (крив); (*dishonest*) нече́стный*.

crop [krɔp] *n* (*produce grown*) (сельскохозя́йственная) культу́ра; (*amount produced: cereals etc*) урожа́й; (: *honey, herbs*) сбор; (*also: riding ~*) плеть *f*; (*of bird*) зоб* ♦ *vt* (*hair*) ко́ротко подстрига́ть (подстри́чь* *perf*); (*subj: animal*) щипа́ть* (*impf*)

► **crop up** *vi* неожи́данно возника́ть (возни́кнуть* *perf*).

crop circle *n* таи́нственные *круги из сло́манных коло́сьев, появля́ющиеся на засе́янных зерновы́ми поля́х*.

cropper ['krɔpə'] *n* (*inf*): **to come a ~** (*fail*) сади́ться* (сесть *perf*) в лу́жу *or* в кало́шу; (*fall*) шлёпаться (шлёпнуться *perf*).

crop spraying [-'spreıŋ] *n* опры́скивание посе́вов.

croquet ['krəukeı] *n* (*BRIT*) кроке́т.

croquette [krə'kεt] *n* (*CULIN*) кроке́ты *pl*.

cross [krɔs] *n* (*shape, also REL*) крест; (*mark*) кре́стик; (*BIO*) по́месь *f*; (*BOT*) гибри́д ♦ *vt* (*street, room etc*) пересека́ть (пересе́чь* *perf*), переходи́ть* (перейти́* *perf*); (*cheque*) кросси́ровать (*impf/perf*); (*BIO, BOT, also arms etc*) скре́щивать (скрести́ть* *perf*); (*thwart: person, plan*) препя́тствовать* (*impf*) +*dat* ♦ *adj* серди́тый ♦ *vi*: **the boat ~es from ... to ...** кора́бль плывёт из +*gen*... в +*acc*...; **to ~ o.s.** крести́ться* (перекрести́ться* *perf*); **we have a ~ed line** (*BRIT: TEL*) кто́-то подсоедини́лся к на́шей ли́нии; **they've got their lines** *or* **wires ~ed** (*fig*) они́ совсе́м запу́тались; **the thought did not ~ my mind** э́та мысль не приходи́ла мне в го́лову; **to be/get ~ with sb (about sth)** серди́ться (*impf*)/рассерди́ться* *perf* на кого́-н (из-за чего́-н)

► **cross out** *vt* вычёркивать (вы́черкнуть *perf*).

crossbar ['krɔsbɑː'] *n* (*FOOTBALL*) перекла́дина; (*on bicycle*) попере́чная пла́нка.

crossbow ['krɔsbəu] *n* самостре́л, арбале́т.

crossbreed ['krɔsbriːd] *n* по́месь *f*.

cross-Channel ferry ['krɔs'tʃænl-] *n* паро́м, че́рез Ла-Ма́нш.

crosscheck ['krɔst[εk] *n* перепрове́рка ♦ *vt* перепроверя́ть (перепрове́рить *perf*).

cross-country (race) ['krɔs'kʌntrı-] *n* бег по пересечённой ме́стности.

cross-dressing [krɔs'drεsıŋ] *n переодева́ние в оде́жду противополо́жного по́ла*.

cross-examination ['krɔsıgzæmı'neıʃən] *n* перекрёстный допро́с.

cross-examine ['krɔsıg'zæmın] *vt* (*LAW*) подверга́ть (подве́ргнуть* *perf*) перекрёстному допро́су.

cross-eyed ['krɔsaıd] *adj* косогла́зый.

crossfire ['krɔsfaıə'] *n* перекрёстный ого́нь* *m*; **to get caught in the ~** (*MIL*) оказа́ться (*perf*) под перекрёстным огнём; (*fig*) оказа́ться (*perf*) ме́жду двух огне́й.

crossing ['krɔsıŋ] *n* (*sea passage*) перепра́ва; (*also*: **pedestrian ~**) перехо́д.

crossing guard *n* (*US*) *регулиро́вщик или регулиро́вщица движе́ния, кото́рый обеспе́чивает безопа́сный перехо́д у́лицы шко́льниками*.

cross-purposes ['krɔs'pə:pəsız] *npl*: **to be at ~ with sb** не находи́ть* (*impf*) о́бщего языка́ с кем-н; **we're (talking) at ~** мы говори́м о ра́зных веща́х.

cross-question ['krɔs'kwεstʃən] *vt* подверга́ть (подве́ргнуть *perf*) перекрёстному допро́су.

cross-reference ['krɔs'rεfrəns] *n* перекрёстная ссы́лка*.

crossroads ['krɔsrəudz] *n* перекрёсток*.

cross section *n* (*of population*) про́филь *m*; (*of object*) попере́чное сече́ние; (*BIO*) попере́чный разре́з *or* срез.

crosswalk ['krɔswɔ:k] *n* (*US*) перехо́д.

crosswind ['krɔswınd] *n* боково́й ве́тер*.

crosswise ['krɔswaız] *adv* крест-на́крест.

crossword ['krɔswə:d] *n* кроссво́рд.

crotch [krɔtʃ] *n* (*ANAT*) про́межность *f*; **the trousers are tight in the ~** брю́ки жмут в шагу́.

crotchet ['krɔtʃıt] *n* четвертна́я но́та.

crotchety ['krɔtʃıtı] *adj* раздражи́тельный* (раздражи́телен), брюзгли́вый (брюзгли́в).

crouch [krautʃ] *vi* (*person, animal*) приседа́ть (присе́сть* *perf*).

croup [kru:p] *n* круп.

croupier ['kru:pıə'] *n* крупье́ *m ind*.

crouton ['kru:tɔn] *n* грено́к*.

crow [krəu] *n* (*bird*) воро́на; (*of cock*) кукаре́канье ♦ *vi* (*cock*) кукаре́кать (*impf*); (*fig: boast*): **to ~ about** хва́статься (*impf*) +*instr*.

crowbar ['krəuba:'] *n* лом*.

crowd [kraud] *n* толпа́*; (*clique*) компа́ния ♦ *vt* (*fill*) заполня́ть (запо́лнить *perf*); (*cram*): **to ~ sb/sth into sth** набива́ть (наби́ть* *perf*) что́-н кем-н/чем-н ♦ *vi* (*gather*): **to ~ round** толпи́ться (*impf*); (*cram*): **to ~ into sth** набива́ться (наби́ться* *perf*) в что́-н; **~s of people** то́лпы люде́й.

crowded ['kraudıd] *adj* (*overpopulated*) перенаселённый (перенаселён); (*full*): **the room was ~** ко́мната была́ запо́лнена наро́дом; **~ with** по́лный +*gen*, напо́лненный +*instr*.

---

* marks translations which have irregular inflections. The Russian-English side of the dictionary gives inflectional information.

crowd scene *n* массовка*, массовая сцена.
crown [kraun] *n* (*of monarch*) корона; (*of head*) макушка; (*of hill*) вершина; (*of tooth*) коронка*; (*of hat*) тулья* ♦ *vt* (*monarch*) короновать (*impf/perf*); (*tooth*) ставить* (поставить* *perf*) коронку на +*acc*; (*fig*) венчать (увенчать *perf*); **the C~** (*monarchy*) корона; **and to ~ it all ...** (*fig*) и в довершение всего ....
crown court *n* (*BRIT*) коронный суд (*в отличие от магистратур с постоянными судьями и присяжными заседателями*).
crowning ['kraunɪŋ] *adj* блистательный*.
crown jewels *npl* королевские регалии *fpl*.
crown prince *n* кронпринц.
crow's-feet ['krəuzfi:t] *npl* гусиные лапки* *fpl*, морщинки* *fpl* (*в уголках глаз*).
crow's-nest ['krəuznɛst] *n* (*NAUT*) воронье гнездо.
crucial ['kru:ʃl] *adj* (*event, moment*) решающий*; (*work*) важный* (важен); **~ to** важный (важен) для +*gen*.
crucifix ['kru:sɪfɪks] *n* распятие.
crucifixion [kru:sɪ'fɪkʃən] *n* распятие на кресте.
crucify ['kru:sɪfaɪ] *vt* (*also fig*) распинать (распять* *perf*).
crude [kru:d] *adj* (*materials*) сырой; (*fig: basic*) примитивный* (примитивен); (: *vulgar*) грубый* (груб).
crude (oil) *n* сырая нефть *f*.
cruel ['kruəl] *adj* жестокий* (жесток).
cruelty ['kruəltɪ] *n* жестокость *f*.
cruet ['kru:ɪt] *n* судок*.
cruise [kru:z] *n* (*on ship*) круиз ♦ *vi* (*ship, aircraft*) крейсировать (*impf*).
cruise missile *n* управляемый снаряд с ядерной боеголовкой.
cruiser ['kru:zə'] *n* (*motorboat*) катер*; (*warship*) крейсер*.
cruising speed ['kru:zɪŋ-] *n* средняя (экономическая) скорость *f*.
crumb [krʌm] *n* (*of bread, cake*) крошка*; (*fig: of information*) обрывок*; (: *of sympathy, hope*) крупица.
crumble ['krʌmbl] *vt* (*bread, biscuit etc*) крошить* (раскрошить* *perf*) ♦ *vi* осыпаться (осыпаться* *perf*); (*fig*) рушиться (*impf*), рухнуть (*perf*).
crumbly ['krʌmblɪ] *adj* рассыпчатый.
crummy ['krʌmɪ] *adj* (*inf*) задрипанный.
crumpet ['krʌmpɪt] *n* ≈ блин.
crumple ['krʌmpl] *vt* мять* (измять* *perf*).
crunch [krʌntʃ] *vt* (*food etc*) грызть* (сгрызть* *perf*) ♦ *vi* (*stones, glass etc*) скрипеть* (*impf*), хрустеть* (*impf*) ♦ *n* (*fig*): **the ~** критический* *or* решающий* момент; **if it comes to the ~** если наступит критический момент; **when the ~ comes** когда наступит критический момент.
crunchy ['krʌntʃɪ] *adj* хрустящий*.

crusade [kru:'seɪd] *n* (*campaign*) крестовый поход ♦ *vi* (*fig*): **to ~ for/against** бороться* (*impf*) за +*acc*/против +*gen*.
crusader [kru:'seɪdə'] *n* крестоносец*; (*fig*): **~ (for)** борец* (за +*acc*).
crush [krʌʃ] *vt* (*squash*) выжимать (выжать* *perf*); (: *grapes*) давить* (*impf*); (*crumple*) мять* (смять* *perf*); (*grind: garlic, ice*) размельчать (размельчить* *perf*); (*defeat*) сокрушать (сокрушить* *perf*); (*devastate*) уничтожать (уничтожить* *perf*) ♦ *n* (*crowd*) давка; (*infatuation*): **to have a ~ on sb** сходить* (сойти* *perf*) с ума по кому-н; (*drink*): **lemon ~** лимонный напиток*.
crush barrier *n* (*BRIT*) ограждение (*сдерживающее толпу*).
crushing ['krʌʃɪŋ] *adj* сокрушительный*.
crust [krʌst] *n* корка*; (*of earth*) кора.
crustacean [krʌs'teɪʃən] *n* ракообразное *nt adj* (*животное*).
crusty ['krʌstɪ] *adj* хрустящий*; (*fig*) раздражительный* (раздражителен); (*bread*) корочкой; (*old gentleman*) жёлчный.
crutch [krʌtʃ] *n* (*MED*) костыль* *m*; (*support, TECH*) опора; (*ANAT, in garment*) *see* **crotch**.
crux [krʌks] *n* суть *f*.
cry [kraɪ] *vi* (*weep*) плакать* (*impf*); (*also: ~ out*) кричать* (*impf*) ♦ *n* крик; **what are you ~ing about?** почему Вы плачете?; **he began to ~** он заплакал *or* начал плакать; **to ~ for help** звать* (позвать* *perf*) на помощь; **she cried out suddenly in pain** она вскрикнула от боли; **she had a good ~** она выплакалась; **it's a far ~ from ...** (*fig*) это сильно отличается от +*gen*
▶ **cry off** *vi* (*inf*) отказываться (отказаться* *perf*).
crying ['kraɪɪŋ] *adj* (*fig: need*) острый*; **it's a ~ shame** это весьма прискорбно.
crypt [krɪpt] *n* склеп.
cryptic ['krɪptɪk] *adj* (*remark*) загадочный* (загадочен); (*clue*) зашифрованный.
crystal ['krɪstl] *n* горный хрусталь* *m*; (*glass*) хрусталь*; (*CHEM*) кристалл.
crystal clear *adj* (*water, air*) кристально чистый*; (*sound, idea*) совершенно ясный.
crystallize ['krɪstəlaɪz] *vt* (*opinion etc*) формировать (сформировать *perf*) ♦ *vi* (*sugar etc*) кристаллизоваться (*impf/perf*); **~d fruits** (*BRIT*) засахаренные фрукты.
CSA *n abbr* = *Confederate States of America*.
CSC *n abbr* (= *Civil Service Commission*) Комиссия гражданской службы.
CSE *n abbr* (*BRIT*: *formerly*: = *Certificate of Secondary Education*) аттестат о среднем образовании.
CS gas *n* (*BRIT*) слезоточивый газ*.
CST *abbr* (*US*) = *Central Standard Time*.
CT *abbr* (*US*: *POST*) = *Connecticut*.
ct *abbr* = **carat**.
CTC *n abbr* (*BRIT*: = *city technology college*)

тéхникум.
cu. *abbr* (= **cubic**) куб.= *куби́ческий*.
cub [kʌb] *n* детёныш; (*also:* ~ **scout**) член
мла́дшего отря́да бойска́утов.
Cuba ['kjuːbə] *n* Кýба.
Cuban ['kjuːbən] *adj* куби́нский* ◆ *n*
куби́нец*(-нка*).
cubbyhole ['kʌbɪhəʊl] *n* закутóк*.
cube [kjuːb] *n* (*also* MATH) куб* ◆ *vt* возводи́ть*
(возвести́* *perf*) в куб; **the ~ of 4 is 64** 4 в кýбе
равня́ется 64.
cube root *n* куби́ческий* кóрень* *m*.
cubic ['kjuːbɪk] *adj* куби́ческий*; ~ **metre** *etc*
куби́ческий* метр *etc*.
cubic capacity *n* куби́ческий* объём.
cubicle ['kjuːbɪkl] *n* (*at pool*) каби́нка*; (*in
hospital*) бокс.
cuckoo ['kukuː] *n* кукýшка*.
cuckoo clock *n* часы́ *pl* с кукýшкой.
cucumber ['kjuːkʌmbəʳ] *n* огурéц*.
cud [kʌd] *n*: **to chew the ~** жева́ть* (*impf*) жва́чку.
cuddle ['kʌdl] *vt* обнима́ть (обня́ть* *perf*) ◆ *vi*
обнима́ться (обня́ться* *perf*) ◆ *n* ла́ска.
cuddly ['kʌdlɪ] *adj* ми́ленький*.
cudgel ['kʌdʒl] *n* дуби́на ◆ *vt*: **to ~ one's brains
about sth** лома́ть (*impf*) гóлову над чем-н.
cue [kjuː] *n* (SNOOKER *etc*) кий*; (THEAT *etc*)
рéплика.
cuff [kʌf] *n* (*of sleeve*) манжéта; (*US: of
trousers*) отворóт; (*blow*) шлепóк* ◆ *vt* (*hit*)
шлёпать (шлёпнуть *perf*); **off the ~**
экспрóмтом.
cuff links *npl* за́понки* *fpl*.
cu. in. *abbr* (= *cubic inches*) куби́ческие дю́ймы.
cuisine [kwɪ'ziːn] *n* кýхня* (*кýшанья*).
cul-de-sac ['kʌldəsæk] *n* (*road*) тупи́к*.
culinary ['kʌlɪnərɪ] *adj* кулина́рный*.
cull [kʌl] *vt* (*story, idea*) отбира́ть (отобра́ть*
perf); (*animals*) отбракóвывать
(отбракова́ть* *perf*) ◆ *n* отбракóвка*.
culminate ['kʌlmɪneɪt] *vi*: **to ~ in** заверша́ться
(заверши́ться *perf*) +*instr*.
culmination [kʌlmɪ'neɪʃən] *n* кульмина́ция.
culottes [kjuː'lɔts] *npl* ю́бка-брю́ки *pl*.
culpable ['kʌlpəbl] *adj*: ~ (**of**) винóвный
(вино́вен) (в +*prp*).
culprit ['kʌlprɪt] *n* (*of crime*) винóвник(-ница).
cult [kʌlt] *n* (*also* REL) культ.
cult figure *n* куми́р.
cultivate ['kʌltɪveɪt] *vt* (*crop, feeling*)
культиви́ровать (*impf*); (*land*) возде́лывать
(*impf*); (*person*) обха́живать (*impf*).
cultivation [kʌltɪ'veɪʃən] *n* (AGR) культива́ция.
cultural ['kʌltʃərəl] *adj* культýрный*.
culture ['kʌltʃəʳ] *n* (*also* BIO) культýра.
cultured ['kʌltʃəd] *adj* (*individual*) культýрный;
(*pearl*) культиви́рованный.
cumbersome ['kʌmbəsəm] *adj* (*object, process*)

громóздкий* (громóздок).
cumin ['kʌmɪn] *n* (*spice*) тмин*.
cumulative ['kjuːmjulətɪv] *adj* (*effect, result*)
сумма́рный; (*process*) нараста́ющий.
cunning ['kʌnɪŋ] *n* хи́трость *f* ◆ *adj* (*crafty*)
хи́трый* (хитёр).
cunt [kʌnt] *n* (*inf!*) пизда́ (*!*)
cup [kʌp] *n* ча́шка*; (*as prize*) кýбок*; (*of bra*)
ча́шечка*; **a ~ of tea** ча́шка* ча́я.
cupboard ['kʌbəd] *n* шкаф*; (*built-in*) стеннóй
шкаф*.
cup final *n* (BRIT: SPORT) фина́л рóзыгрыша
кýбка.
cupful ['kʌpful] *n* пóлная ча́шка*.
cupid ['kjuːpɪd] *n* (*figurine*) пýтти *pl ind*; **C~**
Купидóн, Амýр.
cupidity [kjuː'pɪdɪtɪ] *n* а́лчность *f*.
cupola ['kjuːpələ] *n* кýпол*.
cuppa ['kʌpə] *n* (*inf*) ча́шка ча́я.
cup tie *n* (BRIT: SPORT) кýбковый матч.
curable ['kjuərəbl] *adj* излечи́мый (излечи́м).
curate ['kjuərɪt] *n* вика́рий.
curator [kjuə'reɪtəʳ] *n* (*in museum*) храни́тель *m*.
curb [kəːb] *vt* (*powers, expenditure*)
обу́здывать (обузда́ть *perf*); (*person*)
сде́рживать (сдержа́ть* *perf*) ◆ *n*
ограничéние; (*US*) бордю́р (*тротуа́ра*).
curd cheese [kəːd-] *n* творóг*.
curdle ['kəːdl] *vi* (*milk*) свёртываться
(сверну́ться *perf*).
curds [kəːdz] *npl* простоква́ша *fsg*.
cure [kjuə] *vt* (*illness, patient*) вылéчивать
(вы́лечить *perf*); (CULIN) обраба́тывать
(обрабóтать *perf*); (*problem*) устраня́ть
(устрани́ть *perf*) ◆ *n* (MED) лека́рство;
(*solution*) срéдство; **to be ~d of sth**
вы́лечиться (*perf*) *or* излечи́ться* (*perf*) от
чегó-н.
cure-all ['kjuərɔːl] *n* (*also fig*) панацéя.
curfew ['kəːfjuː] *n* комендáнтский час*.
curio ['kjuərɪəu] *n* рéдкая антиква́рная вещь* *f*.
curiosity [kjuərɪ'ɔsɪtɪ] *n* (*see adj*)
любознáтельность *f*; любопы́тство.
curious ['kjuərɪəs] *adj* (*interested*)
любознáтельный* (любознáтелен); (*nosy,
strange*) любопы́тный* (любопы́тен); **I'm ~
about him** он меня́ интересýет.
curiously ['kjuərɪəslɪ] *adv* стрáнно;
(*inquisitively*) с любопы́тством; ~ **enough, ...**
как ни стрáнно, ...
curl [kəːl] *n* (*of hair*) лóкон, зави́ток; (*of smoke
etc*) кольцó* ◆ *vt* (*hair: loosely*) завива́ть
(зави́ть* *perf*); (: *tightly*) закру́чивать
(закрути́ть* *perf*) ◆ *vi* (*hair*) ви́ться* (*impf*);
(*smoke*) клуби́ться (*impf*)
▶ **curl up** *vi* свора́чиваться (сверну́ться *perf*);
to ~ up into a ball свора́чиваться
(сверну́ться *perf*) клубкóм.

---

* marks translations which have irregular inflections. The Russian-English side of the dictionary gives inflectional information.

curler ['kə:lə'] n бигуди́ ntpl ind; (SPORT) игро́к в
ке́рлинг.

curlew ['kə:lu:] n большо́й кроншне́п.

curling ['kə:lɪŋ] n (SPORT) ке́рлинг (игра́ на
льду, в кото́рой игроки́ сбива́ют цель при
по́мощи специа́льных камне́й).

curling tongs (US **curling irons**) npl щипцы́ pl
для зави́вки.

curly ['kə:lɪ] adj вью́щийся; (tightly curled)
кудря́вый.

currant ['kʌrnt] n (dried grape) изю́минка;
(bush, fruit) сморо́динка; ~s (dried grapes)
изю́м msg; (fruit) сморо́дина fsg.

currency ['kʌrnsɪ] n (system) де́ньги pl в
обраще́нии; (money) валю́та; **to gain** ~ (fig)
получа́ть (получи́ть perf) распростране́ние.

current ['kʌrnt] n (of air, water) струя́*, пото́к;
(ELEC) ток*; (of opinion) направле́ние ♦ adj
(present) теку́щий*, совреме́нный;
(accepted) общепри́нятый; **direct/alternating**
~ постоя́нный/переме́нный ток*; **the ~ issue
of a magazine** теку́щий* но́мер* журна́ла;
this word is in ~ use э́то сло́во явля́ется
общепри́нятым.

current account n (BRIT) теку́щий* счёт*.

current affairs npl теку́щие собы́тия ntpl.

current assets npl теку́щие оборо́тные
акти́вы mpl.

current liabilities npl теку́щие обяза́тельства
ntpl.

currently ['kʌrntlɪ] adv в да́нный or настоя́щий
моме́нт.

curricula [kə'rɪkjulə] npl of **curriculum**.

curriculum [kə'rɪkjuləm] (pl ~s or **curricula**) n
(SCOL) уче́бный план.

curriculum vitae [-'vi:taɪ] n автобиогра́фия
(обы́чно пи́шущаяся при поступле́нии на
учёбу и́ли рабо́ту *).

curry ['kʌrɪ] n блю́до, с ке́рри ♦ vt: **to ~ favour
with** зайи́скивать (impf) пе́ред +instr.

curry powder n порошо́к* ке́рри nt ind.

curse [kə:s] vi (swear) руга́ться (impf) ♦ vt
проклина́ть (прокля́сть* perf) ♦ n (spell,
problem) прокля́тие; (swearword)
руга́тельство.

cursor ['kə:sə'] n ку́рсор.

cursory ['kə:sərɪ] adj (glance, examination)
бе́глый.

curt [kə:t] adj ре́зкий*.

curtail [kə:'teɪl] vt (freedom, rights)
ограни́чивать (ограни́чить perf); (expenses,
visit) сокраща́ть (сократи́ть* perf).

curtain ['kə:tn] n (light) занаве́ска*; (heavy, also
THEAT) за́навес; **to draw the ~s** (together)
заде́ргивать (задёрнуть perf) занаве́ски;
(apart) отдёргивать (отдёрнуть perf)
занаве́ски.

curtain call n (THEAT) покло́ны mpl; **they took
four ~ ~s** их вызыва́ли четы́ре ра́за.

curts(e)y ['kə:tsɪ] vi де́лать (сде́лать perf)
револа́нс, приседа́ть (присе́сть* perf) в

револа́нсе ♦ n револа́нс.

curvature ['kə:vətʃə'] n (of the earth) кривизна́;
(of curve) изги́б; (of spine) искривле́ние.

curve [kə:v] n изги́б ♦ vi изгиба́ться
(изогну́ться perf) ♦ vt сгиба́ть (согну́ть perf),
изгиба́ть (изогну́ть perf).

curved [kə:vd] adj изо́гнутый, со́гнутый.

cushion ['kuʃən] n поду́шка* ♦ vt (collision,
effect) смягча́ть (смягчи́ть perf); (seat)
подкла́дывать (подложи́ть perf) поду́шку
под +acc.

cushy ['kuʃɪ] adj (inf): **a ~ job** тёпленькое
месте́чко*; **to have a ~ time** бить* (impf)
баклу́ши.

cussed ['kʌsɪd] adj упря́мый (упря́м).

custard ['kʌstəd] n заварно́й крем.

custard powder n (BRIT) заварно́й крем
(порошо́к).

custodial [kʌs'təudɪəl] adj: ~ **care** опеку́нство;
he was given a ~ sentence он был
приговорён к тюре́мному заключе́нию.

custodian [kʌs'təudɪən] n попечи́тель m.

custody ['kʌstədɪ] n (of child) опе́ка; (for
offenders) содержа́ние под стра́жей,
заключе́ние; **to take into ~** (suspect) брать*
(взять* perf) под стра́жу, аресто́вывать
(арестова́ть perf); **he was remanded in ~** он
был оста́влен под стра́жей; **in the ~ of** под
опе́кой +gen; **the mother has ~ of the children**
де́ти нахо́дятся под опе́кой ма́тери.

custom ['kʌstəm] n (traditional) тради́ция;
(convention) обы́чай; (habit) привы́чка*; **we
get a lot of ~ from the locals** бо́льшая часть
на́ших покупа́телей or на́шей клиенту́ры —
ме́стные жи́тели.

customary ['kʌstəmərɪ] adj обы́чный*,
традицио́нный; **it is ~ to** при́нято +infin.

custom-built ['kʌstəm'bɪlt] adj изгото́вленный
на зака́з.

customer ['kʌstəmə'] n (of shop)
покупа́тель*(ница) m(f); (of small business)
клие́нт; (of large company) зака́зчик; **he's an
awkward ~** (inf) он тру́дный тип.

customer profile n про́филь m покупа́теля.

customized ['kʌstəmaɪzd] adj изгото́вленный
на зака́з.

custom-made ['kʌstəm'meɪd] adj
изгото́вленный на зака́з.

customs ['kʌstəmz] npl тамо́жня fsg; **to go
through (the)** ~ проходи́ть* (пройти́* perf)
тамо́женный досмо́тр.

Customs and Excise n (BRIT)
тамо́женно-акци́зное управле́ние.

customs officer n тамо́женник.

cut [kʌt] (pt, pp **cut**) vt (bread, meat) ре́зать*
(разре́зать* perf); (hand, knee) ре́зать*
(поре́зать* perf); (grass, hair) стричь*
(постри́чь* perf); (text, spending, supply)
уре́зывать (уре́зать* perf); (prices) снижа́ть
(сни́зить* perf); (cloth) крои́ть (раскрои́ть
perf); (inf: lecture, appointment) прогу́ливать

(прогуля́ть *perf*) ♦ *vi* (*knife, scissors*) ре́зать* (*impf*); (*lines*) пересека́ться (пересе́чься* *perf*) ♦ *n* (*in skin*) поре́з; (*in salary, spending etc*) сниже́ние; (*of meat*) кусо́к*; (*of garment*) покро́й; (*of jewel*) отде́лка*; **she is ~ting a tooth** у неё прореза́ется зуб; **to ~ one's finger** ре́зать (поре́зать* *perf*) па́лец*; **to get one's hair ~** стри́чься* (постри́чься* *perf*); **to ~ sth short** прерыва́ть (прерва́ть* *perf*) что-н; **to ~ sb short** обрыва́ть (оборва́ть* *perf*) кого́-н; **to ~ sb dead** соверше́нно игнори́ровать (*impf/perf*) кого́-н; **cold ~s** (*US*) холо́дные мясны́е заку́ски*; **we had a power ~** у нас отключи́лось электри́чество
► **cut back** *vt* (*plants*) подреза́ть (подреза́ть* *perf*); (*production, expenditure*) сокраща́ть (сократи́ть* *perf*)
► **cut down** *vt* (*tree*) сруба́ть (сруби́ть* *perf*); (*consumption*) сокраща́ть (сократи́ть* *perf*); **to ~ sb down to size** (*fig*) поста́вить* (*perf*) кого́-н на ме́сто
► **cut down on** *vt fus*: **to ~ down on smoking/drinking** ме́ньше кури́ть (*impf*)/пить (*impf*)
► **cut in** *vi* (*AUT*) пересека́ть (пересе́чь* *perf*) путь*; (*interrupt*): **to ~ in on** вме́шиваться (вмеша́ться *perf*) в +*acc*
► **cut off** *vt* (*also fig*) отреза́ть (отре́зать* *perf*); (*water, electricity*) отключа́ть (отключи́ть *perf*); (*food*) прекраща́ть (прекрати́ть *perf*) снабже́ние +*gen*; (*TEL*) разъединя́ть (разъедини́ть *perf*); **we've been ~ off** (*TEL*) нас разъедини́ли
► **cut out** *vt* (*remove*) выреза́ть (вы́резать* *perf*); (*stop*) прекраща́ть (прекрати́ть* *perf*)
► **cut up** *vt* разреза́ть (разре́зать* *perf*); **it really ~ me up** (*inf*) э́то о́чень подкоси́ло меня́; **she still feels ~ up about her sister's death** (*inf*) она́ всё ещё не опра́вилась по́сле сме́рти свое́й сестры́.
cut-and-dried ['kʌtən'draɪd] *adj* (*answer, solution*) гото́вый.
cut-and-dry ['kʌtən'draɪ] *adj* = **cut-and-dried**.
cutaway ['kʌtəweɪ] *n* (*coat*) визи́тка*; (*of machine, engine etc*): **a ~ model** моде́ль *f* в разре́зе; (*CINEMA, TV*) вста́вка*.
cutback ['kʌtbæk] *n* сокраще́ние.
cute [kju:t] *adj* (*sweet*) ми́лый (мил), преле́стный* (преле́стен); (*clever*) у́мный (умён).
cut glass *n* гранёное стекло́*.
cuticle ['kju:tɪkl] *n* (*of nail*) ко́жица; **~ remover** *жи́дкость и́ли крем размягча́ющий и уничтожа́ющий ко́жицу вокру́г ногтево́й лу́нки*.
cutlery ['kʌtlərɪ] *n* столо́вый прибо́р.
cutlet ['kʌtlɪt] *n* котле́та.
cutoff ['kʌtɔf] *n* (*also:* ~ **point**) преде́л ♦ *cpd*: ~ **date** преде́льный срок.

cutoff switch *n* автомати́ческий* выключа́тель *m*.
cutout ['kʌtaut] *n* (*switch*) автомати́ческий* выключа́тель *m*; (*shape*) вы́резанная фигу́ра; (*paper figure*) апплика́ция.
cut-price ['kʌt'praɪs] (*US* **cut-rate**) *adj* по сни́женной цене́.
cut-rate ['kʌt'reɪt] *adj* (*US*) = **cut-price**.
cutthroat ['kʌtθrəut] *n* головоре́з* ♦ *adj* (*fig*) беспоща́дный; ~ **competition** жёсткая конкуре́нция.
cutting ['kʌtɪŋ] *adj* (*edge*) о́стрый*; (*remark etc*) язви́тельный* ♦ *n* (*BRIT: PRESS*) вы́резка*; (: *RAIL*) вы́емка*; (*from plant*) черено́к*.
cutting edge *n* острие́.
cuttlefish ['kʌtlfɪʃ] *n* карака́тица.
CV *n abbr* = **curriculum vitae**.
C & W *n abbr* = **country and western (music)**.
c.w.o. *abbr* (*COMM*: = *cash with order*) вы́дача това́ра по нали́чному расчёту.
cwt. *abbr* = **hundredweight**.
cyanide ['saɪənaɪd] *n* циа́н, циа́нистый ка́лий.
cybernetics [saɪbə'netɪks] *n* киберне́тика.
cyclamen ['sɪkləmən] *n* (*BOT*) цикламе́н.
cycle ['saɪkl] *n* (*bicycle*) велосипе́д; (*series, also TECH*) цикл ♦ *vi* е́здить* (*impf*) на велосипе́де.
cycle race *n* велого́нка*.
cycle rack *n* металли́ческая ра́ма для *сто́янки велосипе́дов*.
cycling ['saɪklɪŋ] *n* езда́ на велосипе́де; (*in competition*) велоспо́рт; **to go on a ~ holiday** (*BRIT*) е́хать (пое́хать* *perf*) в о́тпуск на велосипе́де.
cyclist ['saɪklɪst] *n* велосипеди́ст.
cyclone ['saɪkləun] *n* цикло́н.
cygnet ['sɪgnɪt] *n* (*ZOOL*) лебедёнок*.
cylinder ['sɪlɪndə^r] *n* (*also TECH*) цили́ндр; (*of gas*) балло́н; **a five ~ engine** пятицили́ндровый дви́гатель *m*.
cylinder head *n* кры́шка* цили́ндра.
cylinder-head gasket ['sɪlɪndəhed-] *n* прокла́дка* кры́шки цили́ндра.
cymbals ['sɪmblz] *npl* (*MUS*) таре́лки* *fpl*.
cynic ['sɪnɪk] *n* ци́ник.
cynical ['sɪnɪkl] *adj* цини́чный* (цини́чен).
cynicism ['sɪnɪsɪzəm] *n* цини́зм.
CYO *n abbr* (*US*) = *Catholic Youth Organization*.
cypress ['saɪprɪs] *n* (*tree*) кипари́с.
Cypriot ['sɪprɪət] *adj* ки́прский ♦ *n* киприо́т(ка).
Cyprus ['saɪprəs] *n* Кипр.
cyst [sɪst] *n* киста́.
cystitis [sɪs'taɪtɪs] *n* цисти́т.
CZ *n abbr* (*US*) = *Canal Zone*.
czar [zɑ:'] *n* царь *m*.
Czech [tʃɛk] *adj* че́шский* ♦ *n* чех (че́шка*); (*LING*) че́шский* язы́к*.
Czech Republic *n* Че́шская Респу́блика.

~ D, d ~

D, d [diː] n (letter) 4-ая бу́ква англи́йского
алфави́та; (SCOL) ≈ неудовлетвори́тельный.
D [diː] n (MUS) ре.
D abbr (US: POL) = **democrat(ic)**.
d abbr (BRIT: formerly) = **penny**.
d. abbr = **died**.
DA n abbr (US) = **district attorney**.
dab [dæb] vt (eyes, wound) промокну́ть* (perf);
(paint, cream) наноси́ть* (нанести́* perf) ♦ n
мазо́к*; **she's a ~ hand at sth/doing** она́ до́ка
в чём-н/+infin
  ▶ **dab at** vt fus промокну́ть (perf).
dabble ['dæbl] vi: **to ~ in** (politics, antiques etc)
балова́ться (impf) +instr.
dachshund ['dækshund] n та́кса.
dad [dæd] n (inf) па́па m, па́почка* m.
daddy ['dædɪ] n (inf) = **dad**.
daddy-longlegs [dædɪ'lɒŋlɛgz] n (inf)
долгоно́жка*.
daffodil ['dæfədɪl] n нарци́сс.
daft [dɑːft] adj (ideas) дура́цкий*; (person)
чо́кнутый, ненорма́льный; **to be ~ about**
sb/sth рехну́ться (perf) на ком-н/чём-н.
dagger ['dægə'] n кинжа́л; **to be at ~s drawn**
with sb быть* (impf) на ножа́х с кем-н; **to look**
~s at sb пронза́ть (пронзи́ть* perf) кого́-н
зло́бным взгля́дом.
dahlia ['deɪljə] n георги́н.
daily ['deɪlɪ] adj (dose) су́точный; (routine)
повседне́вный; (wages) дневно́й ♦ n (also: ~
paper) ежедне́вная газе́та; (BRIT: also: ~ **help**)
приходя́щая домрабо́тница ♦ adv
ежедне́вно; **twice ~** два ра́за or два́жды в
день.
dainty ['deɪntɪ] adj изя́щный* (изя́щен).
dairy ['dɛərɪ] n (BRIT: shop) моло́чный
магази́н; (company) ≈ моло́чная фи́рма; (on
farm: for making butter) маслоде́льня*; (: for
making cheese) сырова́рня* ♦ cpd моло́чный.
dairy farm n моло́чная фе́рма.
dairy products npl моло́чные проду́кты mpl.
dairy store n (US) моло́чный магази́н.
dais ['deɪs] n помо́ст.
daisy ['deɪzɪ] n маргари́тка*.
daisywheel ['deɪzɪwiːl] n лепестко́вый
шрифтоноси́тель m.
daisywheel printer n (COMPUT) лепестко́вый
при́нтер.
Dakar ['dækə'] n Дака́р.

dale [deɪl] n (BRIT) доли́на.
dally ['dælɪ] vi болта́ться (impf) без де́ла; **to ~**
with (idea, plan) носи́ться* (impf) с +instr.
dalmatian [dæl'meɪʃən] n далма́тский дог.
dam [dæm] n (on river) да́мба; (reservoir)
водохрани́лище ♦ vt перекрыва́ть
(перекры́ть* perf) да́мбой.
damage ['dæmɪdʒ] n (harm) уще́рб*,
поврежде́ние; (fig) вред* ♦ vt (object)
поврежда́ть (повреди́ть perf); (reputation,
economy) вреди́ть (повреди́ть perf) +dat; **~s**
npl (LAW) компенса́ция fsg; **~ to property**
иму́щественный уще́рб; **to pay £5,000 in ~s**
выпла́чивать (вы́платить* perf)
компенса́цию в разме́ре £5.000.
damaging ['dæmɪdʒɪŋ] adj: **~ (to)** вре́дный*
(для +gen).
Damascus [də'mɑːskəs] n Дама́ск.
dame [deɪm] n (US: inf) ба́ба; (THEAT)
коми́ческая стару́ха; (title): **D~** Ле́ди f ind.
damn [dæm] vt (condemn) осужда́ть (осуди́ть*
perf); (curse at) проклина́ть (прокля́сть* perf)
♦ adj (inf: also: ~ed) прокля́тый ♦ n (inf): **I**
don't give a ~ мне плева́ть; **~ (it)!** чёрт
возьми́ or побери́!; **~ good** (inf) черто́вски
хоро́ший.
damnable ['dæmnəbl] adj отвра́тный*
(отвра́тен).
damnation [dæm'neɪʃən] n, excl (REL: also inf)
прокля́тие.
damning ['dæmɪŋ] adj изобличи́тельный.
damp [dæmp] adj (building, wall) сыро́й*;
(cloth) вла́жный* ♦ n сы́рость f ♦ vt (also: ~**en**:
cloth etc) сма́чивать (смочи́ть* perf);
(: enthusiasm etc) охлажда́ть (охлади́ть*
perf).
dampcourse ['dæmpkɔːs] n гидроизоля́ция.
damper ['dæmpə'] n (MUS) де́мпфер; (of fire)
засло́нка*; **to put a ~ on** (fig: atmosphere)
по́ртить* (испо́ртить* perf); (enthusiasm)
охлажда́ть (охлади́ть* perf).
dampness ['dæmpnɪs] n сы́рость f.
damson ['dæmzən] n (fruit) терносли́ва.
dance [dɑːns] n та́нец*; (social event) та́нцы*
mpl ♦ vi танцева́ть (impf); **to ~ about** скака́ть*
(impf).
dance hall n танцева́льный зал.
dancer ['dɑːnsə'] n (for pleasure) танцо́р(ка*);
(professional) танцо́вщик(-ица).

dancing ['dɑːnsɪŋ] *n* та́нец.
D and C *n abbr* (*MED*: = *dilation and curettage*)
расшире́ние ше́йки ма́тки и
выска́бливание.
dandelion ['dændɪlaɪən] *n* одува́нчик.
dandruff ['dændrəf] *n* пе́рхоть *f*.
dandy ['dændɪ] *n* де́нди *m ind*, щёголь *m* ♦ *adj*
(*US: inf*) кла́ссный.
Dane [deɪn] *n* датча́нин*(-а́нка*).
danger ['deɪndʒə'] *n* опа́сность *f*; **there is a ~**
of ... есть *or* существу́ет опа́сность +*gen* ...;
"danger!" "опа́сно!"; **in/out of ~** в/вне
опа́сности; **he is in ~ of losing his job** ему́
грози́т поте́ря рабо́ты.
danger list *n*: **on the ~ ~** (*MED*) в спи́ске *or*
числе́ осо́бо тяжёлых больны́х.
dangerous ['deɪndʒrəs] *adj* опа́сный* (опа́сен).
dangerously ['deɪndʒrəslɪ] *adv* с ри́ском; ~
close (to) в опа́сной бли́зости (к +*dat*); **he is ~**
ill он опа́сно бо́лен.
danger zone *n* опа́сная зо́на.
dangle ['dæŋgl] *vt* болта́ть (*impf*) +*instr* ♦ *vi*
болта́ться (*impf*).
Danish ['deɪnɪʃ] *adj* да́тский* ♦ *n* (*LING*)
да́тский* язы́к*; **the ~** *npl* датча́не.
Danish pastry *n* пиро́жное *nt adj* по-да́тски (*с*
откры́той начи́нкой из фру́ктов и́ли
оре́хов).
dank [dæŋk] *adj* сыро́й*.
Danube ['dænjuːb] *n*: **the ~** Дуна́й.
dapper ['dæpə'] *adj* щеголева́тый (щеголева́т).
Dardanelles [dɑːdə'nɛlz] *npl*: **the ~**
Дардане́ллы *pl*.
dare [dɛə'] *vt*: **to ~ sb to do** вызыва́ть
(вы́звать* *perf*) кого́-н +*infin* ♦ *vi*: **to ~ (to) do**
сметь (посме́ть *perf*) +*infin*; **I ~n't tell him**
(*BRIT*) я не могу́ осме́литься сказа́ть ему́;
how ~ you say that! как Вы сме́ете так
говори́ть!; **I ~ say** сме́ю заме́тить.
daredevil ['dɛədɛvl] *n* сорвиголова́* *m/f*.
Dar es Salaam ['dɑːrɛssə'lɑːm] *n* Да́р-
эс-Сала́м.
daring ['dɛərɪŋ] *adj* (*audacious*) де́рзкий*
(де́рзок); (*bold*) сме́лый* (смел) ♦ *n* де́рзость
f.
dark [dɑːk] *adj* тёмный* (тёмен); (*complexion*)
сму́глый*; (*fig: deed*) чёрный ♦ *n*: **in the ~** в
темноте́; **~ blue** *etc* тёмно-си́ний* *etc*; **it is**
getting ~ темне́ет; **it is ~** темно́; **~ chocolate**
чёрный шокола́д*; **to be in the ~ about** (*fig*)
быть* (*impf*) в неве́дении относи́тельно +*gen*;
after ~ по́сле наступле́ния темноты́.
Dark Ages *npl*: **the ~ ~** ра́ннее средневеко́вье
ntsg.
darken [dɑːkn] *vt* затемня́ть (затемни́ть *perf*) ♦
vi (*sky, room*) темне́ть (потемне́ть *perf*).
dark glasses *npl* тёмные очки́ *pl*.
dark horse *n* тёмная лоша́дка*.

darkly ['dɑːklɪ] *adv* мра́чно.
darkness ['dɑːknɪs] *n* темнота́.
darkroom ['dɑːkrum] *n* тёмная ко́мната,
прояви́тельная лаборато́рия.
darling ['dɑːlɪŋ] *adj* (*child, spouse*) люби́мый ♦
n дорого́й(-а́я) *m(f) adj*; (*favourite*): **he is the ~**
of он люби́мец +*gen*; **she is a ~** она́ пре́лесть.
darn [dɑːn] *vt* што́пать (зашто́пать *perf*).
dart [dɑːt] *n* (*in game*) стре́лка* (*для игры́ в*
дарт); (*in sewing*) вы́тачка* ♦ *vi*: **to (make a)**
~ towards броса́ться (бро́ситься* *perf*)
навстре́чу +*dat*; **to ~ along** промча́ться (*perf*);
to ~ away умча́ться (*perf*).
dartboard ['dɑːtbɔːd] *n* мише́нь *f* в да́рте.
darts [dɑːts] *n* дарт.
dash [dæʃ] *n* (*drop*) ка́пелька*; (*pinch*)
щепо́тка*; (*sign*) тире́ *nt ind*; (*rush*) рыво́к* ♦ *vt*
(*throw*) швыря́ть (швырну́ть *perf*); (*shatter:*
hopes) разруша́ть (разру́шить *perf*),
разбива́ть (разби́ть* *perf*) ♦ *vi*: **to ~ towards**
рвану́ться (*perf*) к +*dat*; **we'll have to make a ~**
for the house мы должны́ бежа́ть к до́му
► **dash away** *vi* умча́ться (*perf*)
► **dash off** *vi* = **dash away**.
dashboard ['dæʃbɔːd] *n* (*AUT*) прибо́рная
пане́ль *f*.
dashing ['dæʃɪŋ] *adj* шика́рный* (шика́рен).
dastardly ['dæstədlɪ] *adj* по́длый*, ме́рзкий*.
DAT *n abbr* (= *digital audio tape*)
дискретизи́рованная аудиокассе́та.
data ['deɪtə] *npl* да́нные *pl adj*.
database ['deɪtəbeɪs] *n* ба́за да́нных.
data capture *n* сбор да́нных.
data processing *n* обрабо́тка да́нных.
data transmission *n* переда́ча да́нных.
date [deɪt] *n* (*day*) число́*, да́та; (*with friend*)
свида́ние; (*fruit*) фи́ник ♦ *vt* дати́ровать (*impf/*
perf); (*person*) встреча́ться (*impf*) с +*instr*;
what's the ~ today? како́е сего́дня число́?; **~**
of birth да́та рожде́ния; **the closing ~ for**
applications is ... срок пода́чи заявле́ний
истека́ет +*gen* ...; **to ~** на сего́дняшний* день;
out of ~ (*old-fashioned*) устаре́лый
(устаре́л); (*expired*) просро́ченный
(просро́чен); **up to ~** совреме́нный; **to bring**
up to ~ (*method*) обновля́ть (обнови́ть* *perf*);
(*correspondence, information*) пополня́ть
(попо́лнить *perf*); (*person*) вводи́ть* (ввести́*
perf) в курс де́ла; **letter ~d 5th July** *or* (*US*) **July**
5th письмо́, дати́рованное 5-ым ию́ля.
dated ['deɪtɪd] *adj* устаре́лый.
dateline ['deɪtlaɪn] *n* указа́ние ме́ста и да́ты
(*опи́сываемого собы́тия*).
date rape *n* изнаси́лование во вре́мя свида́ния.
date stamp *n* календа́рный штемпель* *m*.
dative ['deɪtɪv] *n* (*also*: **~ case**) да́тельный
паде́ж*.
daub [dɔːb] *vt* разма́зывать (разма́зать* *perf*);

---

* marks translations which have irregular inflections. The Russian-English side of the dictionary gives inflectional information.

(*wall, face*): **to ~ with** ма́зать* (нама́зать* *perf*) +*instr*.
daughter ['dɔːtə'] *n* дочь* *f*.
daughter-in-law ['dɔːtərɪnlɔː] *n* неве́стка*, сноха́*.
daunt [dɔːnt] *vt* страши́ть (*impf*).
daunting ['dɔːntɪŋ] *adj* устраша́ющий*.
dauntless ['dɔːntlɪs] *adj* бесстра́шный* (бесстра́шен).
dawdle ['dɔːdl] *vi* копа́ться (*impf*), вози́ться* (*impf*); **to ~ over one's work** вози́ться* (*impf*) с рабо́той.
dawn [dɔːn] *n* (*of day*) рассве́т; (*of period, situation*) заря́ ♦ *vi* рассвета́ть (рассвести́* *perf*), света́ть (*impf*); (*fig*): **it ~ed on him that ...** его́ осени́ло, что ...; **from ~ to dusk** с рассве́та до зака́та, от зари́ до зари́.
dawn chorus *n* (*BRIT*) пе́ние птиц на рассве́те.
day [deɪ] *n* (*period*) су́тки *pl*, день* *m*; (*daylight*) день*; (*working day*) рабо́чий* день*; (*heyday*) вре́мя *nt*; **the ~ before** накану́не; **the ~ after** на сле́дующий* день; **the ~ after tomorrow** послеза́втра; **the ~ before yesterday** позавчера́; **the following ~** на сле́дующий* день; **the ~ that ...** в тот день, когда́ ...; **~ by ~** ка́ждый день; **~ after ~** изо дня́ в день; **by ~** днём; **he is paid by the ~** ему́ пла́тят подённо; **I have a ~ off tomorrow** за́втра у меня́ отгу́л; **to work an 8 hour ~** рабо́тать (*impf*) 8 часо́в в день; **these ~s, in the present ~** в на́ши дни, в настоя́щее вре́мя.
daybook ['deɪbuk] *n* (*BRIT: ADMIN*) журна́л.
dayboy ['deɪbɔɪ] *n* приходя́щий учени́к* (*в интерна́те*).
daybreak ['deɪbreɪk] *n* рассве́т.
day-care centre ['deɪkɛə-] *n* (*BRIT*) дневно́й це́нтр по ухо́ду за больны́ми и престаре́лыми.
daydream ['deɪdriːm] *vi* предава́ться (*impf*) мечта́ниям, гре́зить* (*impf*) ♦ *n* мечта́ние, грёза.
daygirl ['deɪɡəːl] *n* приходя́щая учени́ца (*в интерна́те*).
daylight ['deɪlaɪt] *n* дневно́й свет*.
daylight robbery *n* грабёж средь бе́ла дня.
Daylight Saving Time *n* (*US*) ле́тнее вре́мя* *nt*.
day release *n*: **to be on ~ ~** находи́ться на дневны́х ку́рсах по повыше́нию квалифика́ции.
day return *n* (*BRIT*) обра́тный биле́т (*действи́тельный в тече́ние одного́ дня*).
day shift *n* дневна́я сме́на.
daytime ['deɪtaɪm] *n* день* *m*.
day-to-day ['deɪtə'deɪ] *adj* (*life, organization*) повседне́вный*, ежедне́вный; **on a ~ basis** ежедне́вно.
day trip *n* однодне́вная экску́рсия.
day-tripper ['deɪ'trɪpə'] *n* челове́к на однодне́вной экску́рсии.
daze [deɪz] *vt* (*stun*) ошеломля́ть (ошеломи́ть*

perf); (*subj: drug*) тума́нить (затума́нить *perf*) созна́ние +*dat*; (*: blow*) ошеломля́ть (ошеломи́ть *perf*) ♦ *n*: **in a ~** как в тума́не.
dazed [deɪzd] *adj* ошеломлённый.
dazzle ['dæzl] *vt* (*bewitch*) завора́живать (заворожи́ть *perf*); (*blind*) ослепля́ть (ослепи́ть* *perf*).
dazzling ['dæzlɪŋ] *adj* (*also fig*) ослепи́тельный* (ослепи́телен).
DC *abbr* = **direct current**; (*US: POST*) = **District of Columbia**.
DD *n abbr* (= **Doctor of Divinity**) ≈ до́ктор богосло́вия.
dd. *abbr* (*COMM*) = **delivered**.
D/D *abbr* = **direct debit**.
D-day ['diːdeɪ] *n* пе́рвый день генера́льного сраже́ния.
DDS *n abbr* (*US*: = **Doctor of Dental Surgery**) до́ктор стоматоло́гии.
DDT *n abbr* (= **dichlorodiphenyltrichloroethane**) ДДТ = *дихлордифени́л трихлорэта́н*.
DE *abbr* (*US: POST*) = **Delaware**.
DEA *n abbr* (*US*: = **Drug Enforcement Administration**) Управле́ние по соблюде́нию зако́нов о нарко́тиках.
deacon ['diːkən] *n* дья́кон*.
dead [dɛd] *adj* (*person, place, flowers*) мёртвый* (мёртв); (*silence*) мёртвый*; (*arm, leg*) онеме́лый; (*centre*) са́мый ♦ *adv* (*completely*) внеза́пно; (*inf: directly*) пря́мо ♦ *npl*: **the ~** мёртвые *pl adj*; (*in an accident, war*) поги́бшие *pl adj*; **the battery is ~** батаре́йка се́ла; **the telephone is ~** телефо́н отключи́лся; **to shoot sb ~** застрели́ть* (*perf*) кого́-н; **~ on time** то́чно во́время; **to stop ~** (*person*) остана́вливаться (останови́ться* *perf*) как вко́панный; **~ tired** смерте́льно уста́лый* (уста́л); **the line has gone ~** телефо́н замолча́л.
dead-beat ['dɛdbiːt] *adj* смерте́льно уста́вший, соверше́нно вы́мотанный (вы́мотан).
deaden [dɛdn] *vt* (*pain, sound*) заглуша́ть (заглуши́ть *perf*).
dead end *n* тупи́к*.
dead-end ['dɛdɛnd] *adj*: **a ~ job** бесперспекти́вная рабо́та.
dead heat *n*: **to finish in a ~ ~** приходи́ть (прийти́* *perf*) к фи́нишу одновреме́нно.
dead-letter office [dɛd'lɛtə-] *n* отде́л невостре́бованной или недоста́вленной корреспонде́нции.
deadline ['dɛdlaɪn] *n* после́дний* *or* преде́льный срок; **to work to a ~** рабо́тать (*impf*) в ра́мках ограни́ченного сро́ка.
deadlock ['dɛdlɔk] *n* тупи́к; **the meeting ended in ~** собра́ние зашло́ в тупи́к.
dead loss *n* (*inf*): **she is a ~ ~** она́ никчёмна.
deadly ['dɛdlɪ] *adj* (*poison, weapon*) смертоно́сный* (смертоно́сен); (*insult*) смерте́льный* (смерте́лен); (*accuracy*)

ги́бельный ♦ *adv* (*dull*) смерте́льно.
deadpan ['dɛdpæn] *adj* невозмути́мый (невозмути́м).
Dead Sea *n*: the ~~ Мёртвое мо́ре.
dead season *n* мёртвый сезо́н.
deaf [dɛf] *adj* (*totally*) глухо́й* (глух); (*partially*) тугоу́хий (тугоу́х); **to turn a ~ ear to sth** игнори́ровать (*impf*) что-н.
deaf aid *n* (*BRIT*) слуховой аппара́т.
deaf-and-dumb ['dɛfən'dʌm] *adj* глухонемо́й; **~ alphabet** алфави́т для глухонемы́х.
deafen [dɛfn] *vt* оглуша́ть (оглуши́ть *perf*).
deafening ['dɛfnɪŋ] *adj* оглуши́тельный* (оглуши́телен).
deaf-mute ['dɛfmjuːt] *n* глухонемо́й(-а́я) *m(f) adj*.
deafness ['dɛfnɪs] *n* глухота́.
deal [diːl] (*pt*, *pp* dealt) *n* (*agreement*) сде́лка* ♦ *vt* (*blow*) наноси́ть* (нанести́* *perf*); (*cards*) сдава́ть* (сдать* *perf*); **to strike a ~ with sb** заключа́ть (заключи́ть *perf*) сде́лку с кем-н; **it's a ~!** (*inf*) по рука́м!; **he got a fair/bad ~ from them** с ним обошли́сь че́стно/нече́стно; **a good ~ (of)** мно́го (+*gen*); **a great ~ (of)** о́чень мно́го (+*gen*)
▶ **deal in** *vt fus* (*COMM*) торгова́ть (*impf*) +*instr*; (*drugs*) занима́ться (*impf*) прода́жей +*gen*
▶ **deal with** *vt fus* (*person, company*) име́ть (*impf*) де́ло с +*instr*; (*problem*) реша́ть (реши́ть *perf*); (*subject*) занима́ться (заня́ться* *perf*) +*instr*.
dealer ['diːlə'] *n* (*COMM*) торго́вец*; (*also*: **art ~**) ди́лер; (*CARDS*) сдаю́щий(-ая) *m(f) adj* ка́рты, банкомёт; ~ **drug** торго́вец* нарко́тиками.
dealership ['diːləʃɪp] *n* (*COMM*) аге́нтство (*по прода́же проду́кции определённой фи́рмы*).
dealings ['diːlɪŋz] *npl* (*transactions*) опера́ции *fpl*; (*in business*) дела́ *ntpl*.
dealt [dɛlt] *pt*, *pp* of **deal**.
dean [diːn] *n* (*REL*) настоя́тель *m*; (*SCOL*) дека́н.
dear [dɪə'] *adj* (*person*) дорого́й*, ми́лый*; (*expensive*) дорого́й* ♦ *n*: (**my**) ~ (*to man, boy*) дорого́й (мой); (*to woman, girl*) дорога́я (моя) ♦ *excl*: ~ **me!** о, Го́споди!; **D~ Sir** уважа́емый господи́н; **D~ Madam** уважа́емая госпожа́; **D~ Mr Smith** дорого́й *or* уважа́емый ми́стер Смит; **D~ Mrs Smith** дорога́я *or* уважа́емая ми́ссис Смит.
dearly ['dɪəlɪ] *adv* (*love*) о́чень; (*pay*) до́рого.
dear money *n* (*COMM*) "дороги́е" де́ньги *pl*.
dearth [dəːθ] *n*: **a ~ of** нехва́тка +*gen*, недоста́ток* +*gen*.
death [dɛθ] *n* смерть* *f*.
deathbed ['dɛθbɛd] *n*: **to be on one's ~** быть* (*impf*) на сме́ртном одре́.
death certificate *n* свиде́тельство о сме́рти.
deathly ['dɛθlɪ] *adj* (*colour*) смерте́льный*; (*silence*) мёртвый ♦ *adv* смерте́льно.

death penalty *n* сме́ртная казнь *f*.
death rate *n* сме́ртность *f*.
death row [-rəu] *n* часть тюрьмы́, где располо́жены ка́меры приговорённых к сме́ртной ка́зни; **prisoners on ~~** заключённые *pl adj*, ожида́ющие сме́ртной ка́зни.
death sentence *n* сме́ртный пригово́р.
death toll *n* число́* поги́бших.
deathtrap ['dɛθtræp] *n* ги́блое ме́сто*.
deb [dɛb] *n abbr* (*inf*) = **debutante**.
debacle [deɪ'baːkl] *n* (*defeat*) разгро́м; (*failure*) фиа́ско *nt ind*.
debar [dɪ'baː'] *vt*: **to ~ sb from doing** лиша́ть (лиши́ть *perf*) кого́-н возмо́жности +*infin*; **to ~ sb from a club** изгоня́ть (изгна́ть* *perf*) кого́-н из клу́ба.
debase [dɪ'beɪs] *vt* (*value, quality*) снижа́ть (сни́зить* *perf*); (*person*) унижа́ть (уни́зить* *perf*); **to ~ o.s.** унижа́ться (уни́зиться* *perf*).
debatable [dɪ'beɪtəbl] *adj* спо́рный*; **it is ~ whether he can come** смо́жет ли он прийти́ – вопро́с спо́рный.
debate [dɪ'beɪt] *n* деба́ты *pl* ♦ *vt* (*topic*) обсужда́ть (обсуди́ть* *perf*); (*course of action*) обду́мывать (обду́мать *perf*); **he ~d whether to stay** он размышля́л, сле́дует ли оста́ться.
debauchery [dɪ'bɔːtʃərɪ] *n* (*drunkenness etc*) распу́щенность *f*.
debenture [dɪ'bɛntʃə'] *n* (*bond*) це́нная бума́га; **~ capital** ссу́да, обеспе́ченная фикси́рованными и́ли други́ми акти́вами компа́нии.
debilitate [dɪ'bɪlɪteɪt] *vt* истоща́ть (истощи́ть *perf*).
debilitating [dɪ'bɪlɪteɪtɪŋ] *adj* изнури́тельный* (изнури́телен).
debit ['dɛbɪt] *n* де́бет ♦ *vt*: **to ~ a sum to sb** *or* **to sb's account** дебетова́ть (*impf/perf*) су́мму с кого́-н *or* с чьего́-н счёта; *see also* **direct debit**.
debit balance *n* дебето́вый оста́ток*.
debit note *n* дебето́вое ави́зо.
debonaire [dɛbə'nɛə'] *adj* гала́нтный.
debrief [diː'briːf] *vt* опра́шивать (опроси́ть* *perf*).
debriefing [diː'briːfɪŋ] *n* расспро́с.
debris ['dɛbriː] *n* (*rubble*) обло́мки *mpl*, разва́лины *fpl*.
debt [dɛt] *n* (*sum*) долг*; (*state of owing money*) задо́лженность *f*; **to be in ~** быть* (*impf*) в долгу́; **bad ~** безнадёжный долг*.
debt collector *n* челове́к, взы́скивающий долги́.
debtor ['dɛtə'] *n* должни́к*.
debug ['diː'bʌg] *vt* отла́живать (отла́дить* *perf*).
debunk [diː'bʌŋk] *vt* (*claim*) опроверга́ть (опрове́ргнуть *perf*); (*person, institution,*

---

myth) развенчивать (развенчать *perf*).
début ['deɪbjuː] *n* дебют.
debutante ['dɛbjutænt] *n* девушка, выходящая в (высший) свет.
Dec. *abbr* = **December.**
decade ['dɛkeɪd] *n* десятилетие.
decadence ['dɛkədəns] *n* упадок*.
decadent ['dɛkədənt] *adj* (*sentiments*) упадочнический*; (*class*) упадочный.
de-caff ['diːkæf] (*inf*) *adj* без кофейна ♦ *n* кофе без кофейна.
decaffeinated [dɪ'kæfɪneɪtɪd] *adj* без кофейна.
decamp [dɪ'kæmp] *vi* (*inf*) удирать (удрать* *perf*).
decant [dɪ'kænt] *vt* переливать (перелить* *perf*).
decanter [dɪ'kæntə'] *n* графин.
decarbonize [diː'kɑːbənaɪz] *vt* очищать (очистить* *perf*) от нагара.
decathlon [dɪ'kæθlən] *n* десятиборье.
decay [dɪ'keɪ] *n* разрушение*; (*of society*) разложение ♦ *vi* (*body, leaves, society etc*) разлагаться (разложиться* *perf*); (*teeth*) разрушаться (разрушиться *perf*).
decease [dɪ'siːs] *n* (*LAW*): **upon your ~** по Вашей кончине.
deceased [dɪ'siːst] *n*: **the ~** покойный(-ая) *m(f) adj*.
deceit [dɪ'siːt] *n* обман.
deceitful [dɪ'siːtful] *adj* лживый (лжив).
deceive [dɪ'siːv] *vt* обманывать (обмануть* *perf*); **to ~ o.s.** обманываться (обмануться* *perf*).
decelerate [diː'sɛləreɪt] *vi* замедлять (замедлить *perf*) скорость.
December [dɪ'sɛmbə'] *n* декабрь* *m*; *see also* **July.**
decency ['diːsənsɪ] *n* (*propriety*) благопристойность *f*; (*kindness*) порядочность *f*.
decent ['diːsənt] *adj* (*wages, meal, sleep*) приличный* (приличен); (*interval, behaviour, person*) порядочный* (порядочен); **we expect you to do the ~ thing** мы ожидаем, что Вы поступите порядочно; **they were very ~ about it** они отреагировали на это очень благородно; **it was very ~ of him** это было очень порядочно с его стороны; **are you ~?** Вы прилично одеты?
decently ['diːsəntlɪ] *adv* (*respectably*) прилично; (*kindly*) порядочно.
decentralization ['diːsɛntrəlaɪ'zeɪʃən] *n* децентрализация.
decentralize [diː'sɛntrəlaɪz] *vt* децентрализовать (*impf/perf*).
deception [dɪ'sɛpʃən] *n* обман.
deceptive [dɪ'sɛptɪv] *adj* обманчивый* (обманчив).
decibel ['dɛsɪbɛl] *n* децибел.
decide [dɪ'saɪd] *vt* (*person: persuade*) убеждать (убедить *perf*); (*settle*) решать (решить *perf*)

♦ *vi*: **to ~ to do/that** решать (решить *perf*) +*infin*/, что; **to ~ on sth** останавливаться (остановиться* *perf*) на чём-н; **to ~ on doing/against doing** решать (решить *perf*) +*infin*/не +*infin*.
decided [dɪ'saɪdɪd] *adj* (*character*) решительный* (решителен); (*views, opinions*) определённый; (*dangers, improvement*) несомненный* (несомненен).
decidedly [dɪ'saɪdɪdlɪ] *adv* (*distinctly*) несомненно; (*emphatically*) решительно.
deciding [dɪ'saɪdɪŋ] *adj* решающий*.
deciduous [dɪ'sɪdjuəs] *adj* листопадный.
decimal ['dɛsɪməl] *adj* десятичный ♦ *n* десятичная дробь *f*; **to three ~ places** с точностью до третьего знака.
decimalize ['dɛsɪməlaɪz] *vt* переводить* (перевести* *perf*) в метрическую систему мер.
decimal point *n* точка* *or* запятая *f adj* (*отделяющая целое от дроби*).
decimate ['dɛsɪmeɪt] *vt* истреблять (истребить* *perf*).
decipher [dɪ'saɪfə'] *vt* (*message etc: enigmatic*) расшифровывать (расшифровать *perf*); (: *illegible*) разбирать (разобрать* *perf*).
decision [dɪ'sɪʒən] *n* решение; (*decisiveness*) решимость *f*; **to make a ~** принимать (принять* *perf*) решение.
decisive [dɪ'saɪsɪv] *adj* решительный* (решителен).
deck [dɛk] *n* (*NAUT*) палуба; (*of cards*) колода; (*also: record ~*) проигрыватель *m*; (*of bus*): **top ~** верхний* этаж*; **to go up on ~** подниматься (подняться* *perf*) на палубу; **below ~** под палубой; **cassette ~** кассетная дека.
deck chair *n* шезлонг.
deck hand *n* матрос.
declaration [dɛklə'reɪʃən] *n* (*statement*) декларация; (*public announcement*) заявление.
declare [dɪ'klɛə'] *vt* (*state*) объявлять (объявить* *perf*); (*for tax*) декларировать (*impf/perf*).
declassify [diː'klæsɪfaɪ] *vt* рассекречивать (рассекретить* *perf*).
decline [dɪ'klaɪn] *n* (*drop*) падение; (*lessening*) уменьшение; (*decay*) упадок* ♦ *vt* (*invitation*) отклонять (отклонить* *perf*) ♦ *vi* (*strength*) падать (impf); (*business*) приходить* (прийти* *perf*) в упадок; **~ in living standards** снижение уровня жизни; **to be in** *or* **on the ~** быть* (*impf*) в упадке.
declutch [diː'klʌtʃ] *vi* выключать (выключить *perf*) сцепление.
decode ['diː'kəud] *vt* (*message*) декодировать (*impf/perf*), расшифровывать (расшифровать* *perf*).
decoder [diː'kəudə'] *n* (*person*) человек, обращающийся к словарю с целью понять

смысл слóва в инострáнном языкé;
(machine) декóдер.
decompose [di:kəm'pəuz] vi разлагáться
(разложи́ться* perf).
decomposition [di:kɔmpə'zɪʃən] n
разложéние.
decompression [di:kəm'prɛʃən] n
декомпрéссия.
decompression chamber n
декомпрессиóнная кáмера.
decongestant [di:kən'dʒɛstənt] n
сосудосужáющее срéдство.
decontaminate [di:kən'tæmɪneɪt] vt
обеззарáживать (обеззарáзить* perf).
decontrol [di:kən'trəul] vt освобождáть
(освободи́ть* perf) от (госудáрственного)
контрóля.
décor ['deɪkɔː'] n отдéлка*; (THEAT) декорáция.
decorate ['dɛkəreɪt] vt (room etc) отдéлывать
(отдéлать perf); (adorn): **to ~ (with)** украшáть
(укрáсить* perf) +instr.
decoration [dɛkə'reɪʃən] n (on tree, dress etc)
украшéние; (of room) отдéлка*; (medal)
нагрáда.
decorative ['dɛkərətɪv] adj декорати́вный*.
decorator ['dɛkəreɪtə'] n обóйщик; **painter and
~** маля́р и обóйщик.
decorum [dɪ'kɔːrəm] n благопристóйность f,
декóрум.
decoy ['di:kɔɪ] n примáнка*.
decrease ['di:kri:s] vt уменьшáть (умéньшить
perf) ♦ vi уменьшáться (умéньшиться perf) ♦
n: **~ (in)** уменьшéние (+gen); **to be on the ~**
идти́* (пойти́* perf) на у́быль.
decreasing [di:'kri:sɪŋ] adj уменьшáющийся.
decree [dɪ'kri:] n (ADMIN, LAW) постановлéние;
(POL, REL) укáз ♦ vt: **to ~ (that)** (ADMIN, LAW)
постановля́ть (постанови́ть* perf)(, что).
decree absolute n окончáтельное решéние о
развóде.
decree nisi [-'naɪsaɪ] n услóвно-окончáтельное
решéние судá о развóде.
decrepit [dɪ'krɛpɪt] adj дря́хлый* (дряхл).
decry [dɪ'kraɪ] vt порицáть (impf).
dedicate ['dɛdɪkeɪt] vt: **to ~ to** посвящáть
(посвяти́ть* perf) +dat.
dedicated ['dɛdɪkeɪtɪd] adj (person)
прéданный* (прéдан); (COMPUT)
вы́деленный, назнáченный; **~ word
processor** специализи́рованный процéссор
для обрабóтки тéкстов.
dedication [dɛdɪ'fi:ʃən] n (devotion)
прéданность f; (in book etc) посвящéние.
deduce [dɪ'dju:s] vt: **to ~ that** заключáть
(заключи́ть perf), что.
deduct [dɪ'dʌkt] vt вычитáть (вы́честь* perf); **to
~ sth (from)** (from wage etc) вычитáть
(вы́честь* perf) что-н (из +gen).

deduction [dɪ'dʌkʃən] n (conclusion)
умозаключéние; (subtraction) вычитáние;
(amount) вы́чет.
deed [di:d] n (feat) дея́ние, постýпок*; (LAW)
акт; **~ of covenant** акт о передáче.
deem [di:m] vt (formal) полагáть (impf); **to ~ it
wise to do** полагáть (impf) целесообрáзным
+infin.
deep [di:p] adj глубóкий* (глубóк); (voice)
ни́зкий* (ни́зок) ♦ adv: **the spectators stood 20
~** зри́тели стоя́ли в 20 рядóв; **the lake is 4
metres ~** глубинá óзера – 4 мéтра; **knee-~ in
water** по колéно в водé; **he took a ~ breath**
он сдéлал глубóкий вздóх; **~ blue** тёмно-
си́ний*.
deepen [di:pn] vt (hole etc) углубля́ть
(углуби́ть* perf) ♦ vi (crisis, mystery)
углубля́ться (углуби́ться* perf).
deepfreeze ['di:p'fri:z] n морози́льная
кáмера.
deep-fry ['di:p'fraɪ] vt жáрить (зажáрить perf)
во фритю́ре.
deeply ['di:plɪ] adv глубокó.
deep-rooted ['di:p'ru:tɪd] adj (prejudice)
глубокó укорени́вшийся; (affection)
глубóкий* (глубóк); (habit) закоренéлый
(закоренéл).
deep-sea ['di:p'si:] cpd (fishing)
глубоковóдный*; **~ diver** водолáз.
deep-seated ['di:p'si:tɪd] adj укорени́вшийся.
deep-set ['di:psɛt] adj глубокó посáженный
(посáжен).
deer [dɪə'] n inv олéнь m; (red) ~ благорóдный
олéнь; (roe) ~ косýля; (fallow) ~ лань f.
deerskin ['dɪəskɪn] n зáмша.
deerstalker ['dɪəstɔ:kə'] n (hat) охóтничья
вóйлочная шля́па.
deface [dɪ'feɪs] vt обезобрáживать
(обезобрáзить* perf).
defamation [dɛfə'meɪʃən] n клеветá,
диффамáция.
defamatory [dɪ'fæmətrɪ] adj клеветни́ческий*.
default [dɪ'fɔ:lt] n (COMPUT: also: ~ value)
значéние по умолчáнию ♦ vi: **to ~ on a debt**
не выплáчивать (вы́платить* perf) долг; **by ~**
(win) за нея́вкой проти́вника.
defaulter [dɪ'fɔ:ltə'] n неплатéльщик.
default option n (COMPUT) парáметр or
вариáнт, выбирáемый по умолчáнию.
defeat [dɪ'fi:t] n поражéние ♦ vt наноси́ть*
(нанести́* perf) поражéние +dat.
defeatism [dɪ'fi:tɪzəm] n поражéнчество.
defeatist [dɪ'fi:tɪst] adj поражéнческий ♦ n
поражéнец.
defecate ['dɛfəkeɪt] vi испражня́ться
(испражни́ться perf).
defect ['di:fɛkt] n (of product) дефéкт*; (of plan,
society) недостáток* ♦ vi: **to ~ to the enemy**

перебегáть (перебежáть* *perf*) на стóрону
врагá; **physical/mental** ~ физи́ческий*/
ýмственный недостáток*.
defective [dɪ'fɛktɪv] *adj* (*goods*) дефéктный
(дефéктен).
defector [dɪ'fɛktə^r] *n* перебéжчик(-ица).
defence [dɪ'fɛns] *n* (*protection,
justification*) защи́та; (*MIL*) оборóна; **in ~ of** в
защи́ту +*gen*; **witness for the** ~ свидéтель *m*
защи́ты; **the Ministry of D~** Министéрство
оборóны; **the Department of Defense** (*US*)
Департáмент по оборóне.
defenceless [dɪ'fɛnslɪs] *adj* беззащи́тный*
(беззащи́тен).
defend [dɪ'fɛnd] *vt* (*also SPORT*) защищáть
(защити́ть* *perf*); (*LAW*) защищáть (*impf*).
defendant [dɪ'fɛndənt] *n* (*in criminal case*)
подсуди́мый(-ая) *m(f) adj*, обвиня́емый(-ая)
m(f) adj; (*in civil case*) отвéтчик(-ица).
defender [dɪ'fɛndə^r] *n* (*also fig*)
защи́тник(-ица); (*SPORT*) защи́тник.
defending champion [dɪ'fɛndɪŋ-] *n* чемпиóн,
защища́ющий своё зва́ние.
defending counsel *n* адвокáт подсуди́мого.
defense *etc* (*US*) = **defence** *etc*.
defensive [dɪ'fɛnsɪv] *adj* (*weapons, measures*)
оборони́тельный; (*behaviour, manner*)
вызывáющий* ◆ *n*: **he was on the** ~ он был
готóв к оборóне.
defer [dɪ'fə:^r] *vt* отсрóчивать (отсрóчить *perf*).
deference ['dɛfərəns] *n* почтéние; **out of** *or* **in** ~
to из почтéния к +*dat*.
deferential [dɛfə'rɛnʃəl] *adj* почти́тельный*
(почти́телен).
deferred creditor [dɪ'fə:d-] *n* кредитóр,
получи́вший отсрóчку.
defiance [dɪ'faɪəns] *n* вы́зов; **in** ~ **of** вопреки́
+*dat*.
defiant [dɪ'faɪənt] *adj* (*person, reply*) дéрзкий*
(дéрзок); (*tone*) вызывáющий*.
defiantly [dɪ'faɪəntlɪ] *adv* дéрзко, вызывáюще.
deficiency [dɪ'fɪʃənsɪ] *n* (*lack*) нехвáтка*;
(*inadequacy*) недостáток*; (*COMM*) дефици́т.
deficiency disease *n* авитаминóз.
deficient [dɪ'fɪʃənt] *adj* (*inadequate*)
несовершéнный* (несовершéнен); (*lacking*):
to be ~ **in** испы́тывать (*impf*) недостáток в
+*prp*.
deficit ['dɛfɪsɪt] *n* (*COMM*) дефици́т.
defile [dɪ'faɪl] *vt* осквернять (оскверни́ть *perf*)
◆ *n* ущéлье*.
define [dɪ'faɪn] *vt* (*limits etc*) определя́ть
(определи́ть *perf*); (*word etc*) давáть* (дать*
perf) определéние +*dat*.
definite ['dɛfɪnɪt] *adj* определённый*
(определён); **he was** ~ **about it** егó мнéние
на э́тот счёт бы́ло определённым.
definite article *n* определённый арти́кль *m*.
definitely ['dɛfɪnɪtlɪ] *adv* (*positively*)
определённо; (*certainly*) несомнéнно.
definition [dɛfɪ'nɪʃən] *n* (*of word*) определéние;

(*of photograph etc*) чёткость *f*.
definitive [dɪ'fɪnɪtɪv] *adj* окончáтельный*
(окончáтелен).
deflate [di:'fleɪt] *vt* (*tyre, balloon*) спускáть
(спусти́ть* *perf*); (*person*) сбивáть (сбить*
perf) спесь с +*gen*; (*ECON*): **to** ~ **the money
supply** осуществля́ть (осуществи́ть* *perf*)
дефля́цию.
deflation [di:'fleɪʃən] *n* (*ECON*) дефля́ция.
deflationary [di:'fleɪʃənrɪ] *adj* дефляцио́нный.
deflect [dɪ'flɛkt] *vt* (*criticism, shot*) отклоня́ть
(отклони́ть* *perf*); (*attention*) отвлекáть
(отвлéчь* *perf*).
defog ['di:'fɔg] *vt* (*US*) устраня́ть (устрани́ть*
perf) запотевáние +*gen*.
defogger ['di:'fɔgə^r] *n* (*US: AUT*) *устрóйство,
устраня́ющее запотева́ние стекла́.*
deform [dɪ'fɔ:m] *vt* (*damage*) деформи́ровать
(*impf/perf*); (*distort*) искажáть (искази́ть* *perf*).
deformed [dɪ'fɔ:md] *adj* (*see vt*)
деформи́рованный (деформи́рован);
искажённый (искажён).
deformity [dɪ'fɔ:mɪtɪ] *n* (*distorted part*)
физи́ческий* недостáток; (*condition*)
деформáция.
defraud [dɪ'frɔ:d] *vt*: **to** ~ **sb of sth** обмáном
лишáть (лиши́ть *perf*) когó-н чегó-н.
defray [dɪ'freɪ] *vt*: **to** ~ **sb's expenses**
возмещáть (возмести́ть* *perf*) чьи-н
расхóды.
defrost [di:'frɔst] *vt* (*fridge, food*)
размора́живать (разморóзить* *perf*);
(*windscreen*) очищáть (очи́стить* *perf*) ото
льда́.
defroster [di:'frɔstə^r] *n* (*US: demister*)
дефрóстер.
deft [dɛft] *adj* лóвкий* (лóвок).
defunct [dɪ'fʌŋkt] *adj* бездéйственный
(бездéйствен).
defuse [di:'fju:z] *vt* (*also fig*) разряжáть
(разряди́ть* *perf*).
defy [dɪ'faɪ] *vt* (*resist*) оспáривать (оспóрить
perf); (*fig: description, explanation*) не
поддавáться* (*impf*) +*dat*; (*challenge*): **to** ~ **sb
to do** призывáть (призвáть* *perf*) когó-н
+*infin*.
degenerate [*vb* dɪ'dʒɛnəreɪt, *adj* dɪ'dʒɛnərɪt] *vi*
ухудшáться (уху́дшиться *perf*) ◆ *adj*
растлéнный (растлён).
degradation [dɛgrə'deɪʃən] *n* деградáция.
degrade [dɪ'greɪd] *vt* (*debase: person*) унижáть
(уни́зить* *perf*); (*worsen*) ухудшáть
(уху́дшить* *perf*).
degrading [dɪ'greɪdɪŋ] *adj* унизи́тельный*
(унизи́телен).
degree [dɪ'gri:] *n* (*extent*) стéпень* *f*; (*unit of
measurement*) грáдус; (*SCOL*) (учёная)
стéпень*; **10 ~s below (zero)** 10 грáдусов
ни́же нуля́; **a considerable** ~ **of risk**
значи́тельная стéпень* ри́ска; **by ~s**
постепéнно; **to some** ~, **to a certain** ~

до не́которой сте́пени.

dehydrated [di:haɪ'dreɪtɪd] *adj* (*MED*)
обезво́женный (обезво́жен); (*milk, eggs*)
порошко́вый.

dehydration [di:haɪ'dreɪʃən] *n* обезво́живание.

de-ice ['di:'aɪs] *vt* удаля́ть (удали́ть *perf*)
обледене́ние +*gen*.

de-icer ['di:'aɪsə'] *n* антиобледени́тель *m*.

deign [deɪn] *vi*: **to ~ to do** соизволя́ть
(соизво́лить *perf*) +*infin*.

deity ['di:ɪtɪ] *n* божество́*.

déjà vu [deɪʒɑ:'vu:] *n* чу́вство узнава́ния в
незнако́мом ме́сте; **I had a sense of ~ ~** у
меня́ бы́ло тако́е чу́вство, бу́дто я здесь
уже́ был.

dejected [dɪ'dʒɛktɪd] *adj* уны́лый.

dejection [dɪ'dʒɛkʃən] *n* уны́ние.

del. *abbr* = **delete**.

delay [dɪ'leɪ] *vt* (*decision, ceremony etc*)
откла́дывать (отложи́ть* *perf*); (*person,
plane etc*) заде́рживать (задержа́ть* *perf*) ◆ *vi*
ме́длить (*impf*) ◆ *n* заде́ржка*; **to be ~ed**
заде́рживаться (*impf*); **without ~** без
отлага́тельств.

delayed-action [dɪ'leɪd'ækʃən] *adj*: **~ device**
приспособле́ние с регули́руемой заде́ржкой
де́йствия.

delectable [dɪ'lɛktəbl] *adj* (*person*)
притяга́тельный* (притяга́телен); (*food*)
ла́комый (ла́ком).

delegate [*n* 'dɛlɪgɪt, *vt* 'dɛlɪgeɪt] *n* делега́т ◆ *vt*
(*person*) делеги́ровать (*impf/perf*); (*task*)
поруча́ть (поручи́ть *perf*); **to ~ sth to sb/sb to
do** поруча́ть (поручи́ть *perf*) что-н кому́-н/
кому́-н +*infin*.

delegation [dɛlɪ'geɪʃən] *n* (*group*) делега́ция;
(*by manager, leader*) переда́ча.

delete [dɪ'li:t] *vt* вычёркивать (вы́черкнуть
perf); (*COMPUT*) удаля́ть (удали́ть *perf*).

Delhi ['dɛlɪ] *n* Де́ли *m ind*.

deli ['dɛlɪ] (*inf*) *n* магази́н "деликате́сы".

deliberate [*adj* dɪ'lɪbərɪt, *vi* dɪ'lɪbəreɪt] *adj*
(*intentional*) наме́ренный* (наме́рен); (*slow*)
нетороли́вый (нетороли́в) ◆ *vi*
обду́мывать (обду́мать *perf*).

deliberately [dɪ'lɪbərɪtlɪ] *adv* (*see adj*)
наме́ренно, наро́чно; нетороли́во.

deliberation [dɪlɪbə'reɪʃən] *n* (*consideration*)
размышле́ние; (*usu pl: discussion*)
обсужде́ние.

delicacy ['dɛlɪkəsɪ] *n* то́нкость *f*; (*food*)
деликате́с.

delicate ['dɛlɪkɪt] *adj* то́нкий* (то́нок); (*colour*)
не́жный (не́жен); (*approach, problem*)
деликат́ный* (деликат́ен); (*health*) хру́пкий*
(хру́пок).

delicately ['dɛlɪkɪtlɪ] *adv* то́нко.

delicatessen [dɛlɪkə'tɛsn] *n* магази́н

деликате́сов.

delicious [dɪ'lɪʃəs] *adj* (*food*) о́чень вку́сный*
(вку́сен); (*smell, feeling, person*)
восхити́тельный* (восхити́телен).

delight [dɪ'laɪt] *n* (*feeling*) восто́рг; (*person,
experience etc*) пре́лесть *f* ◆ *vt* ра́довать
(пора́довать *perf*); **to take (a) ~ in** находи́ть*
(найти́* *perf*) удово́льствие в +*prp*; **her son
was her ~** она́ души́ не ча́яла в своём сы́не;
she was a ~ to interview брать (*impf*) у неё
интервью́ бы́ло и́стинным удово́льствием;
the ~s of country life пре́лести дереве́нской
жи́зни.

delighted [dɪ'laɪtɪd] *adj*: **(to be) ~ (at** *or* **with)**
(быть (*impf*)) в восто́рге (от +*gen*); **he was ~
to see her** он был рад ви́деть её; **I'd be ~ to
help** я с ра́достью помогу́; **I am ~ to meet
you** о́чень прия́тно познако́миться.

delightful [dɪ'laɪtful] *adj* восхити́тельный*
(восхити́телен).

delimit [di:'lɪmɪt] *vt* определя́ть (определи́ть
perf) грани́цы +*gen*.

delineate [dɪ'lɪnɪeɪt] *vt* оче́рчивать (очерти́ть*
perf).

delinquency [dɪ'lɪŋkwənsɪ] *n*
правонаруше́ние.

delinquent [dɪ'lɪŋkwənt] *adj* престу́пный ◆ *n*
несовершеннолéтний(-яя)
правонаруши́тель(ница) *m(f)*.

delirious [dɪ'lɪrɪəs] *adj*: **to be ~** (*with fever*)
быть* (*impf*) в бреду́; (*with excitement*) быть*
(*impf*) в забытьé.

delirium [dɪ'lɪrɪəm] *n* (*MED*) бред*.

deliver [dɪ'lɪvə'] *vt* (*goods*) доставля́ть
(доста́вить* *perf*); (*letter*) вруча́ть (вручи́ть*
perf); (*message*) передава́ть* (переда́ть* *perf*);
(*speech*) произноси́ть* (произнести́* *perf*);
(*blow*) наноси́ть* (нанести́* *perf*); (*baby*)
принима́ть (приня́ть* *perf*); (*warning,
ultimatum*) предъявля́ть (предъяви́ть* *perf*);
(*person*): **to ~ (from)** избавля́ть (изба́вить*
perf) (от +*gen*); **to ~ the goods** (*fig*) выполня́ть
(вы́полнить *perf*) обе́щанное.

deliverance [dɪ'lɪvrəns] *n* избавле́ние.

delivery [dɪ'lɪvərɪ] *n* (*of goods*) доста́вка*; (*of
speaker*) стиль *m* изложе́ния; (*MED*) ро́ды *pl*;
to take ~ of получа́ть (получи́ть* *perf*).

delivery note *n* тра́нспортная накладна́я *f adj*.

delivery van (*US* **delivery truck**) *n* автофурго́н
для доста́вки това́ров.

delouse ['di:'laus] *vt* избавля́ть (изба́вить*
perf) от вшей.

delta ['dɛltə] *n* (*GEO*) де́льта.

delude [dɪ'lu:d] *vt* вводи́ть* (ввести́* *perf*) в
заблужде́ние; **to ~ o.s.** заблужда́ться (*impf*).

deluge ['dɛlju:dʒ] *n* ли́вень *m*; (*fig*) лави́на.

delusion [dɪ'lu:ʒən] *n* заблужде́ние; **he has ~s
of grandeur** у него́ ма́ния вели́чия.

---

* marks translations which have irregular inflections. The Russian-English side of the dictionary gives inflectional information.

de luxe [də'lʌks] *adj* роско́шный* (роско́шен);
a ~ ~ **car/hotel** маши́на/гости́ница люкс.

delve [dɛlv] *vi*: **to ~ into** (*subject*) углубля́ться
(углуби́ться* *perf*) в +*acc*; (*handbag etc*)
ры́ться* (*impf*) в +*acc*.

Dem. *abbr* (*US: POL*) = **democrat(ic)**.

demagogue ['dɛməgɔg] *n* демаго́г.

demand [dɪ'mɑ:nd] *vt* тре́бовать
(потре́бовать *perf*) +*gen* ♦ *n* (*request, claim*)
тре́бование; (*ECON*): ~ **(for)** спрос (на +*acc*);
to ~ sth (from *or* **of sb)** тре́бовать
(потре́бовать *perf*) чего́-н (от кого́-н); **to be
in ~** (*commodity*) по́льзоваться (*impf*)
спро́сом; **specialists are in great ~** на
специали́стов большо́й спрос; **on ~**
(*available, payable*) по тре́бованию.

demand draft *n* (*COMM*) ве́ксель,
опла́чиваемый при предъявле́нии.

demanding [dɪ'mɑ:ndɪŋ] *adj* (*boss, parents*)
тре́бовательный* (тре́бователен); (*child*)
тру́дный; (*work: involving responsibility*)
отве́тственный; (: *requiring effort*) тяжёлый.

demarcation [di:mɑ:'keɪʃən] *n* разграниче́ние.

demarcation dispute *n* (*INDUSTRY*)
разногла́сие по по́воду разделе́ния.

demean [dɪ'mi:n] *vt*: **to ~ o.s.** унижа́ться
(уни́зиться *perf*).

demeanour [dɪ'mi:nəʳ] (*US* **demeanor**) *n*
мане́ра поведе́ния.

demented [dɪ'mɛntɪd] *adj* (*person*)
поме́шанный* (поме́шан).

demilitarized zone [di:'mɪlɪtəraɪzd-] *n* (*MIL*)
демилитаризо́ванная зо́на.

demise [dɪ'maɪz] *n* упа́док; (*death*) кончи́на.

demist [di:'mɪst] *vt* (*BRIT: AUT*): **to ~ the
windscreen** суши́ть обогрева́телем
запоте́вшое лобово́е стекло́.

demister [di:'mɪstəʳ] *n* (*BRIT: AUT*) обогрева́тель
для су́шки запоте́вших стёкол.

demiveg ['dɛmɪvɛdʒ] *n* полу-
вегитариа́нец*(-нка*).

demo ['dɛməu] *n abbr* (*inf*) = **demonstration**.

demob [de:'mɔb] *vt* (*MIL*: *inf*) демобилизова́ть
(*impf/perf*).

demobilize [di:'məubɪlaɪz] *vt* (*MIL*)
демобилизова́ть (*impf/perf*).

democracy [dɪ'mɔkrəsɪ] *n* (*system*)
демокра́тия; (*country*) демократи́ческая
страна́*.

democrat ['dɛməkræt] *n* демокра́т; **D~** (*US*)
член па́ртии демокра́тов.

democratic [dɛmə'krætɪk] *adj*
демократи́ческий*; **D~ Party** (*US*) па́ртия
демокра́тов.

demography [dɪ'mɔgrəfɪ] *n* демогра́фия.

demolish [dɪ'mɔlɪʃ] *vt* (*building*) сноси́ть*
(снести́* *perf*); (*argument*) разгроми́ть* (*perf*).

demolition [dɛmə'lɪʃən] *n* (*of building*) снос; (*of
argument*) разгро́м.

demon ['di:mən] *n* де́мон ♦ *adj* (*skilled*)
гениа́льный* (гениа́лен).

demonstrate ['dɛmənstreɪt] *vt*
демонстри́ровать (продемонстри́ровать
perf) ♦ *vi* (*POL*): **to ~ (for/against)**
демонстри́ровать (*impf*) (за +*acc*/про́тив
+*gen*).

demonstration [dɛmən'streɪʃən] *n*
демонстра́ция; **to hold a ~** (*POL*) проводи́ть*
(провести́* *perf*) демонстра́цию.

demonstrative [dɪ'mɔnstrətɪv] *adj* (*LING*)
указа́тельный; **she's very ~** она́ откры́то
выража́ет свои́ чу́вства.

demonstrator ['dɛmənstreɪtəʳ] *n* (*POL*)
демонстра́нт; (*sales person*) демонстра́тор.

demoralize [dɪ'mɔrəlaɪz] *vt* деморализова́ть
(*impf/perf*).

demote [dɪ'məut] *vt* понижа́ть (пони́зить* *perf*)
в до́лжности.

demotion [dɪ'məuʃən] *n* пониже́ние в
до́лжности.

demur [dɪ'məːʳ] *vi* (*formal*) возража́ть
(возрази́ть* *perf*) ♦ *n*: **without ~** без
возраже́ний; **they ~red at his suggestion** они́
возрази́ли на его́ предложе́ние.

demure [dɪ'mjuəʳ] *adj* (*smile, person*) чи́нный;
(*dress*) скро́мный* (скро́мен).

demurrage [dɪ'mʌrɪdʒ] *n* (*COMM*) пла́та за
просто́й су́дна.

den [dɛn] *n* (*of animal, person*) ло́гово; (*of
thieves*) прито́н.

denationalization ['di:næʃnəlaɪ'zeɪʃən] *n*
денационализа́ция.

denationalize ['di:'næʃnəlaɪz] *vt*
денационализи́ровать (*impf/perf*).

denatured alcohol [di:'neɪtʃəd-] *n* (*US*)
денатура́т.

denial [dɪ'naɪəl] *n* отрица́ние; (*refusal*) отка́з.

denier ['dɛnɪəʳ] *n* (*of tights, stockings*) денье́ *nt
ind*.

denigrate ['dɛnɪgreɪt] *vt* принижа́ть
(прини́зить* *perf*).

denim ['dɛnɪm] *n* джи́нсовая ткань *f*; **~s** *npl*
(*jeans*) джи́нсы *pl*.

denim jacket *n* джи́нсовая ку́ртка*.

denizen ['dɛnɪzn] *n* (*inhabitant*)
обита́тель(ница) *m(f)*.

Denmark ['dɛnmɑ:k] *n* Да́ния.

denomination [dɪnɔmɪ'neɪʃən] *n* (*of money*)
досто́инство; (*REL*) испове́дание.

denominator [dɪ'nɔmɪneɪtəʳ] *n* (*MATH*)
знамена́тель *m*.

denote [dɪ'nəut] *vt* (*indicate*) ука́зывать
(указа́ть* *perf*) на +*acc*; (*represent*)
обознача́ть (обозна́чить *perf*).

denounce [dɪ'nauns] *vt* (*condemn*) осужда́ть
(осуди́ть* *perf*); (*give information against*)
доноси́ть* (донести́* *perf*) на +*acc*.

dense [dɛns] *adj* (*crowd*) пло́тный*; (*smoke,
foliage etc*) густо́й* (густ); (*inf: person*)
тупо́й* (туп).

densely ['dɛnslɪ] *adv*: **~ populated** гу́сто
населённый; **~ wooded** покры́тый (покры́т)

густы́м ле́сом.

density ['dɛnsɪtɪ] n (of population: also PHYS) пло́тность f; **single/double-~ disk** (COMPUT) диск с одина́рной/двойно́й пло́тностью.

dent [dɛnt] n (in metal) вмя́тина ♦ vt (also: **make a ~ in**: car etc) оставля́ть (оста́вить* perf) вмя́тину в +acc; (ego) уда́рить (perf) по +dat.

dental ['dɛntl] adj зубно́й.

dental floss [-flɔs] n нить для чи́стки межзу́бных промежу́тков.

dental surgeon n зубно́й врач*, стомато́лог.

dentifrice ['dɛntɪfrɪs] n (MED: paste) зубна́я па́ста; (: powder) зубно́й порошо́к*.

dentist ['dɛntɪst] n зубно́й врач*, стомато́лог; (also: **~'s surgery**) зубоврача́чебный кабине́т, стоматологи́ческий* кабине́т.

dentistry ['dɛntɪstrɪ] n стоматоло́гия.

dentures ['dɛntʃəz] npl зубно́й проте́з sg.

denuded [di:'nju:dɪd] adj оголённый* (оголён); **~ of** (fig) лишённый (лишён) +gen.

denunciation [dɪnʌnsɪ'eɪʃən] n (accusation) обличе́ние; (condemnation) осужде́ние.

deny [dɪ'naɪ] vt (refute) отрица́ть (impf); (allegation) отверга́ть (отве́ргнуть perf); (disown) отрека́ться (отре́чься* perf) от +gen; (refuse): **to ~ sb sth** отка́зывать (отказа́ть* perf) кому́-н в чём-н; **he denies having said it** он отрица́ет, что он э́то сказа́л.

deodorant [di:'əudərənt] n дезодора́нт.

depart [dɪ'pɑ:t] vi (person) отбыва́ть (отбы́ть* perf); (bus, train) отправля́ться (отпра́виться* perf); (plane) улета́ть (улете́ть* perf); **to ~ from** (fig) отклоня́ться (отклони́ться* perf) от +gen.

departed [dɪ'pɑ:tɪd] adj поко́йный ♦ n поко́йный(-ая) m(f) adj, у́мерший*(-ая) m(f) adj.

department [dɪ'pɑ:tmənt] n (in shop) отде́л; (in university, school) отделе́ние; (POL) ве́домство, департа́мент; **D~ of Trade and Industry** Министе́рство торго́вли и промы́шленности; **that's not my ~** (fig) я не специали́ст в э́том де́ле; **D~ of State** (US) Госуда́рственный департа́мент.

departmental [di:pɑ:t'mɛntl] adj (COMM, ADMIN): **~ meeting/activities** собра́ние/ де́ятельность f отде́ла; **~ manager** заве́дующий*(-ая) m(f) adj отде́лом.

department store n универса́льный магази́н.

departure [dɪ'pɑ:tʃəʳ] n (of visitor etc) отъе́зд; (of employee) ухо́д; (of bus, train) отправле́ние; (of plane) отлёт; (fig): **~ from** отклоне́ние от +gen; **a new ~** но́вое направле́ние.

departure lounge n (at airport) зал отлёта.

depend [dɪ'pɛnd] vi: **to ~ on** зави́сеть* (impf) от +gen; (trust) полага́ться (положи́ться* perf) на +acc; **it ~s** смотря́ по обстоя́тельствам,

как полу́чится; **~ing on the outcome** ... в зави́симости от исхо́да ....

dependable [dɪ'pɛndəbl] adj надёжный* (надёжен).

dependant [dɪ'pɛndənt] n иждиве́нец(-нка).

dependence [dɪ'pɛndəns] n зави́симость f.

dependent [dɪ'pɛndənt] adj: **~ (on)** зави́симый (зави́сим) (от +gen) ♦ n = **dependant**.

depict [dɪ'pɪkt] vt изобража́ть (изобрази́ть* perf).

depilatory [dɪ'pɪlətrɪ] n (also: **~ cream**) крем для удале́ния воло́с.

depleted [dɪ'pli:tɪd] adj истощённый* (истощён).

deplorable [dɪ'plɔ:rəbl] adj (conditions) плаче́вный* (плаче́вен); (behaviour) возмути́тельный* (возмути́телен).

deplore [dɪ'plɔ:ʳ] vt (condemn) негодова́ть (impf) по по́воду +gen.

deploy [dɪ'plɔɪ] vt (troops) дислоци́ровать (impf/perf).

depopulate [di:'pɔpjuleɪt] vt обезлю́дить (perf).

depopulation ['di:pɔpju'leɪʃən] n опустоше́ние.

deport [dɪ'pɔ:t] vt департи́ровать (impf/perf), высыла́ть (вы́слать* perf).

deportation [di:pɔ:'teɪʃən] n депорта́ция, высы́лка*.

deportation order n (LAW) прика́з о депорта́ции.

deportee [di:pɔ:'ti:] n департи́рованный(-ая) m(f) adj.

deportment [dɪ'pɔ:tmənt] n оса́нка.

depose [dɪ'pəuz] vt (remove) смеща́ть (смести́ть* perf); (overthrow) низлага́ть (низложи́ть perf).

deposit [dɪ'pɔzɪt] n (in account) депози́т, вклад; (down payment) пе́рвый взнос, зада́ток*; (: when hiring, renting) зало́г; (on bottle etc) сто́имость f посу́ды; (CHEM) оса́док*; (of ore, oil) за́лежь f ♦ vt (money) помеща́ть (помести́ть* perf); (subj: river: sand, silt etc) намыва́ть (намы́ть* perf); (case, bag) сдава́ть* (сдать* perf); **to put down a ~ of £50** дава́ть* (дать* perf) зада́ток £50.

deposit account n депози́тный счёт*.

depositor [dɪ'pɔzɪtəʳ] n вкла́дчик* m/f.

depository [dɪ'pɔzɪtərɪ] n (person) дове́ренное лицо́*; (place) храни́лище.

depot ['dɛpəu] n (storehouse) склад; (for buses) парк; (for trains) депо́ nt ind; (US: station) ста́нция.

depraved [dɪ'preɪvd] adj развращённый (развращён).

depravity [dɪ'prævɪtɪ] n развращённость f.

deprecate ['dɛprɪkeɪt] vt порица́ть (impf).

deprecating ['dɛprɪkeɪtɪŋ] adj неодобри́тельный (неодобри́телен).

---

* marks translations which have irregular inflections. The Russian-English side of the dictionary gives inflectional information.

depreciate [dɪˈpriːʃɪeɪt] *vi* обесце́ниваться (обесце́ниться *perf*).
depreciation [dɪpriːʃɪˈeɪʃən] *n* обесце́нивание.
depress [dɪˈprɛs] *vt* (*PSYCH*) подавля́ть (*impf*), угнета́ть (*impf*); (*prices, profits*) снижа́ть (сни́зить* *perf*); (*lever, pedal*) нажима́ть (нажа́ть* *perf*) на +*acc*.
depressant [dɪˈprɛsnt] *n* (*MED*) депресса́нт, успокои́тельное сре́дство.
depressed [dɪˈprɛst] *adj* (*person*) пода́вленный* (пода́влен), угнетённый* (угнетён); (*prices*) сни́женный*; (*industry*): **to be** ~ находи́ться* (*impf*) в состоя́нии спа́да; **to get** ~ впада́ть (впасть* *perf*) в депре́ссию; ~ **area** райо́н, находя́щийся в состоя́нии экономи́ческого упа́дка.
depressing [dɪˈprɛsɪŋ] *adj* (*time*) тяжёлый; (*news, outlook*) удруча́ющий.
depression [dɪˈprɛʃən] *n* (*PSYCH, ECON*) депре́ссия; (*METEOROLOGY*) о́бласть *f* ни́зкого давле́ния; (*hollow*) углубле́ние; (: *in landscape*) впа́дина.
deprivation [dɛprɪˈveɪʃən] *n* (*poverty*) нужда́; (*depriving*) лише́ние.
deprive [dɪˈpraɪv] *vt*: **to** ~ **sb of** лиша́ть (лиши́ть* *perf*) кого́-н +*gen*.
deprived [dɪˈpraɪvd] *adj* (*area, family*) бе́дный* (бе́ден); ~ **child** ребёнок из бе́дной семьи́.
dept. *abbr* = **department**.
depth [dɛpθ] *n* глубина́*; **in the** ~**s of despair/a crisis** в глубо́ком отча́янии/кри́зисе; **in the** ~**s of winter** глубо́кой зимо́й; **at a** ~ **of three metres** на глубине́ трёх ме́тров; **to be out of one's** ~ (*in water*) не достава́ть* (*impf*) до дна; **I'm out of my** ~ **with this job** мне э́та рабо́та не по плечу́; **to study sth in** ~ изуча́ть (изучи́ть* *perf*) что-н углублённо.
depth charge *n* глуби́нная бо́мба.
deputation [dɛpjuˈteɪʃən] *n* депута́ция.
deputize [ˈdɛpjutaɪz] *vi*: **to** ~ **for sb** замеща́ть (*impf*) кого́-н.
deputy [ˈdɛpjutɪ] *n* замести́тель *m*; (*POL*) депута́т; (*US: also:* ~ **sheriff**) исполня́ющий обя́занности шери́фа ♦ *cpd*: ~ **leader/ chairman** замести́тель ли́дера/ председа́теля; ~ **head** (*BRIT: SCOL*) замести́тель дире́ктора.
derail [dɪˈreɪl] *vt*: **to be** ~**ed** сходи́ть* (сойти́* *perf*) с ре́льсов.
derailment [dɪˈreɪlmənt] *n*: **the cause of the** ~ **is unknown** причи́на, по кото́рой по́езд сошёл с ре́льсов неизве́стна.
deranged [dɪˈreɪndʒd] *adj* (*person*) психи́чески больно́й; **he is** ~ он психи́чески бо́лен.
derby [ˈdɑːrbɪ] *n* (*US: bowler hat*) котело́к.
Derbys *abbr* (*BRIT: POST*) = **Derbyshire**.
deregulate [dɪˈrɛgjuleɪt] *vt* (*INDUSTRY*) ослабля́ть (осла́бить* *perf*) госуда́р-ственного регули́рования +*gen*.
deregulation [dɪˈrɛgjuˈleɪʃən] *n* ослабле́ние госуда́рственного контро́ля.

derelict [ˈdɛrɪlɪkt] *adj* забро́шенный* (забро́шен).
deride [dɪˈraɪd] *vt* насмеха́ться (*impf*) над +*instr*.
derision [dɪˈrɪʒən] *n* презре́ние.
derisive [dɪˈraɪsɪv] *adj* презри́тельный* (презри́телен).
derisory [dɪˈraɪsərɪ] *adj* (*ridiculous*) смехотво́рный* (смехотво́рен); (*derisive*) презри́тельный* (презри́телен).
derivation [dɛrɪˈveɪʃən] *n* происхожде́ние.
derivative [dɪˈrɪvətɪv] *n* (*CHEM*) дерива́т; (*LING*) произво́дное сло́во, дерива́т ♦ *adj* (*word, form*) произво́дный; (*not original*) неоригина́льный* (неоригина́лен).
derive [dɪˈraɪv] *vt* (*get*): **to** ~ (**from**) (*pleasure*) получа́ть (получи́ть* *perf*) (от +*gen*); (*benefit*) извлека́ть (извле́чь* *perf*) (из +*gen*) ♦ *vi* (*originate in*): **to** ~ **from** происходи́ть* (*impf*) от +*gen*.
derived demand [dɪˈraɪvd-] *n* ко́свенный *or* произво́дственный спрос.
dermatitis [dəːməˈtaɪtɪs] *n* дермати́т.
dermatology [dəːməˈtɔlədʒɪ] *n* дерматоло́гия.
derogatory [dɪˈrɔgətərɪ] *adj* пренебрежи́тельный* (пренебрежи́телен).
derrick [ˈdɛrɪk] *n* (*on ship*) де́ррик; (*on well*) бурова́я вы́шка*.
derv [dəːv] *n* (*BRIT: AUT*) ди́зельное то́пливо.
DES *n abbr* (*BRIT: formerly:* = *Department of Education and Science*) Министе́рство просвеще́ния и нау́ки.
desalination [diːsælɪˈneɪʃən] *n* опресне́ние.
descend [dɪˈsɛnd] *vt* (*stairs*) спуска́ться (спусти́ться* *perf*) по +*dat*; (*hill*) спуска́ться (спусти́ться* *perf*) с +*gen* ♦ *vi* (*go down*) спуска́ться (спусти́ться* *perf*); **to** ~ **from** (*family, person*) происходи́ть* (*impf*) из +*gen*; **to** ~ **to** (*lying, begging etc*) опуска́ться (опусти́ться* *perf*) до +*gen*; **in** ~**ing order of importance** в нисходя́щем поря́дке
▶ **descend on** *vt fus* (*subj: enemy, misfortune*) обру́шиваться (обру́шиться *perf*) на +*acc*; (: *gloom, darkness*) опуска́ться (опусти́ться* *perf*) на +*acc*; (: *silence*) воцаря́ться (воцари́ться *perf*) на +*acc*; **visitors** ~**ed (up)on us** к нам нагря́нули го́сти.
descendant [dɪˈsɛndənt] *n* пото́мок*.
descent [dɪˈsɛnt] *n* спуск; (*AVIAT*) сниже́ние; (*origin*) происхожде́ние.
describe [dɪsˈkraɪb] *vt* опи́сывать (описа́ть* *perf*).
description [dɪsˈkrɪpʃən] *n* описа́ние; (*sort*) род*; **of every** ~ всевозмо́жного ро́да.
descriptive [dɪsˈkrɪptɪv] *adj* (*writing, passage*) описа́тельный.
desecrate [ˈdɛsɪkreɪt] *vt* оскверня́ть (оскверни́ть* *perf*).
desegregate [diːˈsɛgrɪgeɪt] *vt*: **to** ~ **a society/ school** ликвиди́ровать (*impf/perf*) сегрега́цию в о́бществе/шко́ле.
desert [*n* ˈdɛzət, *vb* dɪˈzəːt] *n* (*also fig*) пусты́ня ♦

vt покида́ть (поки́нуть *perf*) ◆ *vi* (*MIL*) дезерти́ровать (*impf/perf*); *see also* **deserts**.
deserter [dɪ'zə:tə^r] *n* (*MIL*) дезерти́р.
desertion [dɪ'zə:ʃən] *n* (*MIL*) дезерти́рство; (*LAW*) оставле́ние.
desert island *n* необита́емый о́стров*.
deserts [dɪ'zə:ts] *npl*: **to get one's just** ~ получа́ть (получи́ть* *perf*) по заслу́гам.
deserve [dɪ'zə:v] *vt* заслу́живать (заслужи́ть* *perf*).
deservedly [dɪ'zə:vɪdlɪ] *adv* заслу́женно.
deserving [dɪ'zə:vɪŋ] *adj* досто́йный*.
desiccated ['dɛsɪkeɪtɪd] *adj* (*coconut*) сушёный.
design [dɪ'zaɪn] *n* диза́йн; (*process: of dress*) модели́рование; (*sketch: of building*) прое́кт; (*type: of appliance etc*) моде́ль *f*; (*pattern*) рису́нок*; (*intention*) за́мысел* ◆ *vt* (*house, kitchen*) проекти́ровать (спроекти́ровать *perf*); (*product, test*) разраба́тывать (разрабо́тать *perf*); **to have ~s on** име́ть (*impf*) ви́ды на +*acc*; **by ~** с у́мыслом.
designate [*vt* 'dɛzɪgneɪt, *adj* 'dɛzɪgnɪt] *vt* (*nominate*) назнача́ть (назна́чить *perf*); (*indicate*) обознача́ть (обозна́чить *perf*) ◆ *adj*: **minister ~** назна́ченный мини́стр (*до вступле́ния в до́лжность*).
designation [dɛzɪg'neɪʃən] *n* (*description, name*) обозначе́ние.
designer [dɪ'zaɪnə^r] *n* (*ART*) диза́йнер; (*of program*) разрабо́тчик; (*of building*) проекти́ровщик; (*of machine*) констру́ктор; (*also: fashion ~*) модельер ◆ *adj* (*clothes*) моде́льный*; **~ label** фи́рменный знак (модельера).
desirability [dɪzaɪərə'bɪlɪtɪ] *n*: **the ~ of** жела́тельность *f* +*gen*.
desirable [dɪ'zaɪərəbl] *adj* (*proper*) жела́тельный* (жела́телен); (*attractive*) привлека́тельный* (привлека́телен); **it is ~ that** жела́тельно, что́бы.
desire [dɪ'zaɪə^r] *n* жела́ние ◆ *vt* (*want*) жела́ть (*impf*); **to ~ to do/that** жела́ть (*impf*) +*infin*/, что́бы.
desirous [dɪ'zaɪərəs] *adj*: **to be ~ of doing** жела́ть (*impf*) +*infin*.
desist [dɪ'zɪst] *vi*: **to ~ (from)** возде́рживаться (воздержа́ться *perf*) (от +*gen*).
desk [dɛsk] *n* (*in office, study*) (пи́сьменный) стол*; (*for pupil*) па́рта; (*in hotel, at airport*) сто́йка*; (*BRIT: also: cash-~*) ка́сса.
desk job *n* канцеля́рская рабо́та.
desktop ['dɛsktɔp] *adj* насто́льный.
desktop publishing *n* (*COMPUT*) насто́льное изда́тельство, насто́льная типогра́фия.
desolate ['dɛsəlɪt] *adj* (*place*) забро́шенный*; (*person*) поки́нутый.
desolation [dɛsə'leɪʃən] *n* (*action*) опустоше́ние; (*quality*) опустошённость *f*.

despair [dɪs'pɛə^r] *n* отча́яние ◆ *vi*: **to ~ of sth/doing** отча́иваться (отча́яться *perf*) в +*prp*/+*infin*; **to be in ~** быть* (*impf*) в отча́янии.
despatch [dɪs'pætʃ] *n*, *vt* = **dispatch**.
desperate ['dɛspərɪt] *adj* (*action, situation*) отча́янный* (отча́ян); (*criminal*) отъя́вленный; (*person*): **he/she is ~** он/она́ в отча́янии; **to be ~ to do** жа́ждать (*impf*) +*infin*; **to be ~ for money** стра́шно нужда́ться (*impf*) в деньга́х.
desperately ['dɛspərɪtlɪ] *adv* отча́янно; (*very*) чрезвыча́йно.
desperation [dɛspə'reɪʃən] *n* отча́яние; **in (sheer) ~** в (по́лном) отча́янии.
despicable [dɪs'pɪkəbl] *adj* презре́нный* (презре́нен).
despise [dɪs'paɪz] *vt* презира́ть (*impf*).
despite [dɪs'paɪt] *prep* несмотря́ на +*acc*.
despondent [dɪs'pɔndənt] *adj* уны́лый (уны́л).
despot ['dɛspɔt] *n* де́спот.
dessert [dɪ'zə:t] *n* десе́рт.
dessertspoon [dɪ'zə:tspu:n] *n* десе́ртная ло́жка*.
destabilize [di:'steɪbɪlaɪz] *vt* (*also fig*) дестабилизи́ровать (*impf/perf*).
destination [dɛstɪ'neɪʃən] *n* (*of traveller*) цель *f*; (*of mail*) ме́сто* назначе́ния.
destined ['dɛstɪnd] *adj*: **he/she is ~ to do** ему́/ей суждено́ +*infin*; **to be ~ for** предназнача́ться (*impf*) для +*gen*.
destiny ['dɛstɪnɪ] *n* судьба́*.
destitute ['dɛstɪtju:t] *adj* (*person*) обездо́ленный (обездо́лен).
destroy [dɪs'trɔɪ] *vt* (*also fig*) уничтожа́ть (уничто́жить *perf*), разруша́ть (разру́шить *perf*); (*kill: pet*) усыпля́ть (усыпи́ть* *perf*); (: *farm animal*) забива́ть (заби́ть* *perf*).
destroyer [dɪs'trɔɪə^r] *n* (*NAUT*) миноно́сец*.
destruction [dɪs'trʌkʃən] *n* уничтоже́ние, разруше́ние; (*fig: of reputation etc*) ги́бель *f*.
destructive [dɪs'trʌktɪv] *adj* (*capacity, force*) разруши́тельный; (*criticism*) деструкти́вный; (*emotion*) губи́тельный* (губи́телен); (*child*): **he's very ~** он всё лома́ет.
desultory ['dɛsəltərɪ] *adj* (*attempt*) сла́бый (слаб); (*reading, work*) беспоря́дочный (беспоря́дочен).
detach [dɪ'tætʃ] *vt* снима́ть (снять* *perf*); (*unstick*) отделя́ть (отдели́ть *perf*).
detachable [dɪ'tætʃəbl] *adj* съёмный.
detached [dɪ'tætʃt] *adj* (*objective*) беспристра́стный* (беспристра́стен); **~ house** особня́к*.
detachment [dɪ'tætʃmənt] *n* (*aloofness*) отдалённость *f*; (*MIL*) отря́д.
detail ['di:teɪl] *n* дета́ль *f*, подро́бность *f* ◆ *vt* (*list*) перечисля́ть (перечи́слить *perf*); **in ~**

подро́бно, в дета́лях; **to go into ~s**
вдава́ться* *(impf)* в дета́ли *or* подро́бности.
detailed ['di:teɪld] *adj* дета́льный* (дета́лен),
подро́бный* (подро́бен).
detain [dɪ'teɪn] *vt (delay, confine)* заде́рживать
(задержа́ть* *perf);* **to ~ in hospital** оставля́ть
(оста́вить* *perf)* в больни́це.
detainee [di:teɪ'ni:] *n (POL)* у́зник(-ица).
detect [dɪ'tɛkt] *vt (sense)* чу́вствовать
(почу́вствовать *perf);* *(discover)*
обнару́живать (обнару́жить *perf).*
detection [dɪ'tɛkʃən] *n (discovery)*
обнаруже́ние; **crime ~** уголо́вный ро́зыск;
the criminal escaped ~ престу́пник не
обнару́жен; **the mistake escaped ~** оши́бка
оста́лась незаме́ченной.
detective [dɪ'tɛktɪv] *n (POLICE)* сы́щик,
детекти́в.
detective story *n* детекти́в.
detector [dɪ'tɛktəʳ] *n (TECH)* дете́ктор.
détente [deɪ'tɑ:nt] *n (POL)* разря́дка.
detention [dɪ'tɛnʃən] *n (arrest)* задержа́ние;
(imprisonment) содержа́ние под стра́жей;
(SCOL): **to give sb ~** оставля́ть (оста́вить*
perf) кого́-н по́сле уро́ков.
deter [dɪ'tə:ʳ] *vt* уде́рживать (удержа́ть *perf).*
detergent [dɪ'tə:dʒənt] *n* мо́ющее сре́дство.
deteriorate [dɪ'tɪərɪəreɪt] *vi* ухудша́ться
(уху́дшиться *perf).*
deterioration [dɪtɪərɪə'reɪʃən] *n* ухудше́ние.
determination [dɪtə:mɪ'neɪʃən] *n (resolve)*
реши́мость *f; (establishment)* установле́ние.
determine [dɪ'tə:mɪn] *vt (find out)*
устана́вливать (установи́ть* *perf);* *(establish,*
dictate) определя́ть (определи́ть *perf);* **to ~**
that *(establish)* устана́вливать (установи́ть*
perf), что; **to ~ to do** *(decide)* реша́ть (реши́ть
perf) +*infin.*
determined [dɪ'tə:mɪnd] *adj (person, effort)*
реши́тельный* (реши́телен); *(quantity)*
определённый*; **~ to do** по́лный (по́лон*)
реши́мости +*infin.*
deterrence [dɪ'tɛrəns] *n* сде́рживание.
deterrent [dɪ'tɛrənt] *n* сре́дство сде́рживания,
сде́рживающее сре́дство; **nuclear ~**
сре́дство я́дерного сде́рживания; **to act as a**
~ явля́ться (яви́ться* *perf)* сре́дством
сде́рживания.
detest [dɪ'tɛst] *vt* ненави́деть* *(impf).*
detestable [dɪ'tɛstəbl] *adj* отврати́тельный*
(отврати́телен).
detonate ['dɛtəneɪt] *vi* взрыва́ться
(взорва́ться* *perf)* ◆ *vt* взрыва́ть (взорва́ть*
perf).
detonator ['dɛtəneɪtəʳ] *n* детона́тор.
detour ['di:tuəʳ] *n (in vehicle, also US)* объе́зд;
(on foot) обхо́д; **to make a ~** *(in vehicle)*
пое́хать* *(perf)* в объе́зд; *(on foot)* пойти́*
(perf) в обхо́д.
detract [dɪ'trækt] *vi:* **to ~ from** умаля́ть
(умали́ть *perf).*

detractor [dɪ'træktəʳ] *n* недоброжела́тель *m.*
detriment ['dɛtrɪmənt] *n:* **to the ~ of** в уще́рб
+*dat;* **without ~ to** без уще́рба для +*gen.*
detrimental [dɛtrɪ'mɛntl] *adj:* **~ to** вре́дный*
(вре́ден) для +*gen.*
deuce [dju:s] *n (TENNIS)* „ро́вно".
devaluation [dɪvælju'eɪʃən] *n (ECON)*
девальва́ция.
devalue ['di:'vælju:] *vt (currency)*
обесце́нивать (обесце́нить *perf);* *(person,*
work) недооце́нивать (недооцени́ть *perf).*
devastate ['dɛvəsteɪt] *vt* опустоша́ть
(опустоши́ть *perf);* *(fig):* **she is ~d by** она́
потрясена́ +*instr.*
devastating ['dɛvəsteɪtɪŋ] *adj (weapon, storm)*
разруши́тельный* (разруши́телен); *(news,*
effect) ошеломля́ющий*.
devastation [dɛvəs'teɪʃən] *n* разруше́ние,
опустоше́ние.
develop [dɪ'vɛləp] *vt (idea, industry)* развива́ть
(разви́ть* *perf);* *(plan, resource)*
разраба́тывать (разрабо́тать *perf);* *(land)*
застра́ивать (застро́ить *perf);* *(PHOT)*
проявля́ть (прояви́ть* *perf);* *(disease)*
заболева́ть (заболе́ть *perf)* +*instr* ◆ *vi (evolve,*
advance) развива́ться (разви́ться* *perf);*
(appear) проявля́ться (прояви́ться* *perf);* **the**
machine ~ed a fault в маши́не возни́кли
непола́дки; **to ~ a taste for sth**
пристрасти́ться* *(perf)* к чему́-н; **to ~ into**
превраща́ться (преврати́ться* *perf)* в +*acc.*
developer [dɪ'vɛləpəʳ] *n (also:* **property ~:**
company) строи́тельная фи́рма; *(: person)*
разрабо́тчик.
developing country [dɪ'vɛləpɪŋ-] *n*
развива́ющаяся страна́*.
development [dɪ'vɛləpmənt] *n* разви́тие; *(of*
resources) разрабо́тка; *(of land)* застро́йка;
housing ~ жили́щный ко́мплекс.
development area *n* террито́рия, на
развитие кото́рой напра́влены
дополни́тельные прави́тельственные
сре́дства.
deviant ['di:vɪənt] *adj* отклоня́ющийся от
но́рмы.
deviate ['di:vɪeɪt] *vi:* **to ~ (from)** отклоня́ться
(отклони́ться *perf)* (от +*gen).*
deviation [di:vɪ'eɪʃən] *n:* **~ (from)** отклоне́ние
(от +*gen).*
device [dɪ'vaɪs] *n* устро́йство, прибо́р; *(ploy,*
stratagem) сре́дство; **explosive ~** взры́вчатое
устро́йство.
devil ['dɛvl] *n* дья́вол, чёрт*; **go on, be a ~!**
дава́й, позво́ль себе́!; **talk of the ~!** лёгок* на
поми́не!
devilish ['dɛvlɪʃ] *adj* дья́вольский*.
devil's advocate [dɛvlz-] *n* провока́тор.
devious ['di:vɪəs] *adj* лука́вый (лука́в); *(route,*
path) изви́листый (изви́лист).
devise [dɪ'vaɪz] *vt* разраба́тывать
(разрабо́тать *perf).*

devoid [dɪ'vɔɪd] *adj*: ~ **of** лишённый (лишён) +*gen*.

devolution [di:və'lu:ʃən] *n* (*POL*) переда́ча вла́сти (*ме́стным о́рганам*).

devolve [dɪ'vɔlv] *vt* (*power, duty etc*) передава́ть* (переда́ть* *perf*) ♦ *vi*: **to** ~ **(up)on** переходи́ть* (перейти́* *perf*) к +*dat*.

devote [dɪ'vəut] *vt*: **to** ~ **sth to** посвяща́ть (посвяти́ть* *perf*) что-н +*dat*.

devoted [dɪ'vəutɪd] *adj* (*admirer, partner*) пре́данный* (пре́дан); (*service, friendship*) ве́рный; **he is** ~ **to her** он пре́дан ей; **his book is** ~ **to the history of Scotland** его́ кни́га посвящена́ исто́рии Шотла́ндии.

devotee [dɛvəu'ti:] *n* (*fan*) приве́рженец*; (*REL*) правове́рный*(-ая) *m(f) adj*.

devotion [dɪ'vəuʃən] *n* пре́данность *f*; (*REL*) поклоне́ние.

devour [dɪ'vauəʳ] *vt* (*also fig*) пожира́ть (пожра́ть* *perf*).

devout [dɪ'vaut] *adj* (*REL*) благочести́вый (благочести́в).

dew [dju:] *n* роса́*.

dexterity [dɛks'tɛrɪtɪ] *n* (*manual*) ло́вкость *f*; (*mental*) сообрази́тельность *f*.

dext(e)rous ['dɛkstrəs] *adj* (*see n*) ло́вкий* (ло́вок); сообрази́тельный* (сообрази́телен).

dg *abbr* (= *decigram*) дециѓра́мм.

DH *n abbr* (*BRIT*. = *Department of Health*) Министе́рство здравоохране́ния.

Dhaka ['dækə] *n* Да́ка.

DHSS *n abbr* (*BRIT*: *formerly*: = *Department of Health and Social Security*) Министе́рство здравоохране́ния и социа́льного обеспе́чения.

diabetes [daɪə'bi:ti:z] *n* диабе́т.

diabetic [daɪə'bɛtɪk] *n* диабе́тик ♦ *adj* диабети́ческий.

diabolical [daɪə'bɔlɪkl] *adj* дья́вольский*; (*inf. dreadful*) жу́ткий*.

diaeresis [daɪ'ɛrɪsɪs] *n* диере́за.

diagnose [daɪəg'nəuz] *vt* (*illness*) диагности́ровать (*impf/perf*); (*problem*) определя́ть (определи́ть* *perf*).

diagnoses [daɪəg'nəusi:z] *npl of* **diagnosis**.

diagnosis [daɪəg'nəusɪs] (*pl* **diagnoses**) *n* диа́гноз.

diagonal [daɪ'ægənl] *adj* диагона́льный ♦ *n* (*MATH*) диагона́ль *f*.

diagram ['daɪəgræm] *n* схе́ма.

dial ['daɪəl] *n* (*of clock*) цифербла́т; (*of indicator*) шкала́; (*of phone*) диск; (*of radio*) регуля́тор настро́йки ♦ *vt* (*number*) набира́ть (набра́ть* *perf*); **a wrong number** не туда́ попада́ть (попа́сть* *perf*); **can I ~ London direct?** могу́ я набра́ть в Ло́ндон по автома́ту?

dial. *abbr* = **dialect.**

dial code *n* (*US*) = **dialling code.**

dialect ['daɪəlɛkt] *n* диале́кт.

dialling code ['daɪəlɪŋ-] (*US* **dial code**) *n* код; **the ~ ~ for London** код Ло́ндона.

dialling tone (*US* **dial tone**) *n* непреры́вный гудо́к*.

dialogue ['daɪəlɔg] (*US* **dialog**) *n* диало́г.

dial tone *n* (*US*) = **dialling tone.**

dialysis [daɪ'ælɪsɪs] *n* (*MED*) диа́лиз.

diameter [daɪ'æmɪtəʳ] *n* диа́метр.

diametrically [daɪə'mɛtrɪklɪ] *adv*: ~ **opposed (to)** диаметра́льно противополо́жный* (противополо́жен) (+*dat*).

diamond ['daɪəmənd] *n* алма́з; (*cut diamond*) бриллиа́нт; (*shape*) ромб; **~s** *npl* (*CARDS*) бу́бны* *fpl*.

diamond ring *n* бриллиа́нтовое кольцо́*.

diaper ['daɪəpəʳ] *n* (*US*) подгу́зник.

diaphragm ['daɪəfræm] *n* диафра́гма.

diarrhoea [daɪə'ri:ə] (*US* **diarrhea**) *n* поно́с.

diary ['daɪərɪ] *n* (*journal*) дневни́к*; (*engagements book*) записна́я кни́жка*; **to keep a ~** вести́* (*impf*) дневни́к.

diatribe ['daɪətraɪb] *n* ре́зкая кри́тика.

dice [daɪs] *npl of* **die**; (*in game*) ку́бик; (*game*) ко́сти* *fpl* ♦ *vt* (*CULIN*) ре́зать (наре́зать* *perf*) ку́биками.

dicey ['daɪsɪ] *adj* (*inf*): **it's a bit ~** э́то немно́го риско́ванно.

dichotomy [daɪ'kɔtəmɪ] *n* дихотоми́я.

dickhead ['dɪkhɛd] *n* (*inf*) пень* *m*.

Dictaphone® ['dɪktəfəun] *n* диктофо́н.

dictate [dɪk'teɪt] *vt* диктова́ть (продиктова́ть* *perf*) ♦ *n* веле́ние ♦ *vi*: **to ~ to** диктова́ть (продиктова́ть *perf*) +*dat*; **the ~s of** веле́ние +*gen*; **I won't be ~d to by him** я не позволю́, что́бы он мне диктова́л.

dictation [dɪk'teɪʃən] *n* (*of letter*) дикто́вка*; (*SCOL*) дикта́нт; **at ~ speed** со ско́ростью дикто́вки.

dictator [dɪk'teɪtəʳ] *n* дикта́тор.

dictatorship [dɪk'teɪtəʃɪp] *n* диктату́ра.

diction ['dɪkʃən] *n* ди́кция.

dictionary ['dɪkʃənrɪ] *n* слова́рь* *m*.

did [dɪd] *pt of* **do.**

didactic [daɪ'dæktɪk] *adj* дидакти́ческий*, поучи́тельный* (поучи́телен).

diddle ['dɪdl] *vt* (*inf*) надува́ть (наду́ть* *perf*).

didn't ['dɪdnt] = **did not.**

die [daɪ] *n* (*pl* **dice**; *in game*) игра́льная кость* *f*; (*pl* ~**s**; *TECH*) ма́трица, штамп ♦ *vi* (*person, emotion*) умира́ть (умере́ть* *perf*); (*smile, light*) угаса́ть (уга́снуть* *perf*); **to ~ of** *or* **from** умира́ть (умере́ть* *perf*) от +*gen*; **to be dying** умира́ть (*impf*); **to be dying for sth/to do** до́ смерти хоте́ть* (*impf*) чего́-н/+*infin*

▶ **die away** *vi* (*sound*) замира́ть (замере́ть*

perf); (*light*) угаса́ть (уга́снуть* *perf*)
► **die down** *vi* (*wind, noise*) утиха́ть
(ути́хнуть* *perf*); (*fire*) потуха́ть (поту́хнуть*
perf); (*excitement*) улёчься* (*perf*)
► **die out** *vi* (*custom*) умира́ть (умере́ть* *perf*);
(*species*) вымира́ть (вы́мереть* *perf*).
diehard ['daɪhɑːd] *n* ретрогра́д ◆ *adj*
непрекло́нный.
diesel ['diːzl] *n* ди́зель* *m*; (*also:* ~ **oil**)
ди́зельное то́пливо.
diesel engine *n* ди́зельный мото́р.
diet ['daɪət] *n* дие́та ◆ *vi* (*also:* **be on a** ~) быть*
(*impf*) на дие́те; **to live on a** ~ **of** пита́ться
(*impf*) одни́м(-о́й) +*instr*.
dietician [daɪə'tɪʃən] *n* дието́лог.
differ ['dɪfəʳ] *vi*: **to** ~ (**from**) отлича́ться (*impf*)
(от +*gen*); (*disagree*): **to** ~ **about** расходи́ться*
(разойти́сь* *perf*) в вопро́се +*gen*; **we agreed
to** ~ ка́ждый из нас оста́лся при своём
мне́нии.
difference ['dɪfrəns] *n* (*dissimilarity*) разли́чие;
(: *in size, age*) ра́зница; (*disagreement*)
разногла́сие; **it makes no** ~ **to me** мне всё
равно́; **a** ~ **of opinion** расхожде́ние во
мне́ниях; **to settle one's** ~**s** ула́живать
(ула́дить* *perf*) разногла́сия.
different ['dɪfrənt] *adj* (*other*) друго́й, ино́й;
(*various*) разли́чный, ра́зный; **to be** ~ **from**
отлича́ться (*impf*) от +*gen*.
differential [dɪfə'rɛnʃəl] *n* (MATH)
дифференциа́л; (BRIT: *in wages*) ра́зница в
тари́фах.
differentiate [dɪfə'rɛnʃɪeɪt] *vi*: **to** ~ (**between**)
проводи́ть* (провести́* *perf*) разли́чие
(ме́жду +*instr*) ◆ *vt*: **to** ~ **from** отлича́ть
(отличи́ть *perf*) от +*gen*.
differently ['dɪfrəntlɪ] *adv* (*otherwise*) ина́че,
по-друго́му; (*in different ways*) по-ра́зному.
difficult ['dɪfɪkəlt] *adj* тру́дный* (тру́ден);
(*person*) тяжёлый*; ~ **to understand/see**
тру́дно поня́ть/ви́деть.
difficulty ['dɪfɪkəltɪ] *n* тру́дность *f*,
затрудне́ние; **to have difficulties** испы́тывать
(испыта́ть *perf*) тру́дности; **to be in
difficulties** находи́ться* (*impf*) в тру́дном
положе́нии.
diffidence ['dɪfɪdəns] *n* засте́нчивость *f*.
diffident ['dɪfɪdənt] *adj* засте́нчивый
(засте́нчив).
diffuse [*vt* dɪ'fjuːz, *adj* dɪ'fjuːs] *vt* (*information*)
распространя́ть (распространи́ть *perf*) ◆ *adj*
(*idea, sense*) расплы́вчатый (расплы́вчат);
(*light*) рассе́янный*.
dig [dɪg] (*pt, pp* **dug**) *vt* (*hole*) копа́ть (вы́копать
perf), рыть* (вы́рыть* *perf*); (*garden*)
вска́пывать (вскопа́ть *perf*) ◆ *n* (*prod*)
толчо́к*; (*archaeological excavation*)
раско́пки* *fpl*; (*remark*): **to have a** ~ **at sb**
подка́лывать (подколо́ть *perf*) кого́-н; **to** ~
one's nails/claws into sth впива́ться
(впи́ться* *perf*) ногтя́ми/когтя́ми во что-н

► **dig in** *vi* (*inf*: *eat*): **to** ~ **in** (**to**) налега́ть
(налёчь* *perf*) (на +*acc*) ◆ *vt*: **to** ~ **in** (**to**)
(*compost*) вка́пывать (вкопа́ть *perf*) (в +*acc*);
(*knife*) вонза́ть (вонзи́ть* *perf*) (в +*acc*); **to** ~ **in
one's heels** (*fig*) упира́ться (упере́ться* *perf*)
► **dig into** *vt fus* (*snow, soil*) зарыва́ть (зары́ть*
perf), зака́пывать (закопа́ть* *perf*); **to** ~ **into
one's savings** нача́ть (*perf*) тра́тить
сбереже́ния; **to** ~ **into one's pockets** (**for sth**)
запуска́ть (запусти́ть* *perf*) ру́ку в карма́н
(за чем-н)
► **dig out** *vt* (*from snow, earth*) отка́пывать
(откопа́ть *perf*)
► **dig up** *vt* (*plant*) выка́пывать (вы́копать
perf); (*information*) раска́пывать (раскопа́ть
perf).
digest [*vt* daɪ'dʒɛst, *n* 'daɪdʒɛst] *vt* (*food*)
перева́ривать (перевари́ть* *perf*); (*facts*)
усва́ивать (усво́ить *perf*) ◆ *n* (*book*) сбо́рник
(адапти́рованных произведе́ний).
digestible [dɪ'dʒɛstəbl] *adj* удобовари́мый
(удобовари́м).
digestion [dɪ'dʒɛstʃən] *n* пищеваре́ние.
digestive [dɪ'dʒɛstɪv] *adj* пищевари́тельный ◆
n (*also:* ~ **biscuit**) *пече́нье из муки́ гру́бого
помо́ла*.
digit ['dɪdʒɪt] *n* (*number*) ци́фра; (*finger*)
па́лец*.
digital ['dɪdʒɪtl] *adj*: ~ **watch** электро́нные
часы́ *mpl*; ~ **recording** электро́нная за́пись.
digital compact cassette *n*
дисккретизи́рованная компа́ктная кассе́та.
digital computer *n* электро́нно-
вычисли́тельная маши́на.
dignified ['dɪgnɪfaɪd] *adj* по́лный* (по́лон)
досто́инства.
dignitary ['dɪgnɪtərɪ] *n* высокопоста́вленное
лицо́*.
dignity ['dɪgnɪtɪ] *n* досто́инство.
digress [daɪ'grɛs] *vi*: **to** ~ (**from**) отступа́ть
(отступи́ть* *perf*) (от +*gen*).
digression [daɪ'grɛʃən] *n* отступле́ние.
digs [dɪgz] *npl* (BRIT: *inf*) жили́ще.
dike [daɪk] *n* = **dyke**.
dilapidated [dɪ'læpɪdeɪtɪd] *adj* ве́тхий*.
dilate [daɪ'leɪt] *vi* расширя́ться (расши́риться
perf) ◆ *vt* расширя́ть (расши́рить *perf*).
dilatory ['dɪlətərɪ] *adj* (*influence*)
замедля́ющий; (*person*) медли́тельный*
(медли́телен).
dilemma [daɪ'lɛmə] *n* диле́мма; **to be in a** ~
стоя́ть (*impf*) пе́ред диле́ммой.
diligence ['dɪlɪdʒəns] *n* усе́рдие, прилежа́ние.
diligent ['dɪlɪdʒənt] *adj* (*worker*) усе́рдный*
(усе́рден), приле́жный* (приле́жен); (*work*)
тща́тельный* (тща́телен).
dill [dɪl] *n* укро́п*; (*seed*) укро́пное се́мя*.
dilly-dally ['dɪlɪ'dælɪ] *vi* ме́шкать (*impf*).
dilute [daɪ'luːt] *vt* (*liquid*) разбавля́ть
(разба́вить* *perf*); (*belief, principle*)
ослабля́ть (осла́бить* *perf*) ◆ *adj*

разбáвленный (разбáвлен).

dim [dɪm] *adj* (*outline, feeling, memory*)
смýтный* (смýтен); (*light*) тýсклый* (тускл);
(*room*) плóхо освещённый (освещён);
(*eyesight*) слáбый* (слаб); (*future, prospects*)
мрáчный* (мрáчен); (*inf: person*) тупóй*
(туп) ♦ *vt* (*also US: light*) приглушáть
(приглушúть* *perf*); **to take a ~ view of sth**
неодобрúтельно смотрéть* (*impf*) на что-н.

dime [daɪm] *n* (*US*) десятицéнтовая монéта.

dimension [daɪ'mɛnʃən] *n* (*measurement*)
измерéние; (*also pl: scale, size*) размéры *mpl*;
(*aspect*) аспéкт.

diminish [dɪ'mɪnɪʃ] *vi* уменьшáться
(умéньшиться *perf*) ♦ *vt* (*belittle*) принижáть
(принúзить* *perf*).

diminished [dɪ'mɪnɪʃt] *adj*: ~ **responsibility**
(*LAW*) огранúченная отвéтственность *f*.

diminutive [dɪ'mɪnjutɪv] *adj* крóшечный ♦ *n*
(*LING*) уменьшúтельно-ласкáтельное слóво.

dimly ['dɪmlɪ] *adv* (*glow, illuminate*) тýскло;
(*see, remember*) смýтно.

dimmer ['dɪmə^r] *n* (*also:* ~ **switch**) регулятор
освещённости.

dimmers ['dɪməz] *npl* (*US: dipped headlights*)
блúжний* свет *msg* фар; (*parking lights*)
стоя́ночный свет *msg*.

dimple ['dɪmpl] *n* ямочка*.

dim-witted ['dɪm'wɪtɪd] *adj* (*inf*) тупоýмный*
(тупоýмен).

din [dɪn] *n* грóхот ♦ *vt* (*inf*): **to ~ sth into sb**
вдáлбливать (вдолбúть* *perf*) что-н в
когó-н.

dine [daɪn] *vi* обéдать (пообéдать *perf*).

diner ['daɪnə^r] *n* (*person*) обéдающий(-ая) *m(f)*
adj; (*US*) дешёвый рестора́нчик.

dinghy ['dɪŋgɪ] *n* (*also:* **sailing ~**) шлю́пка*;
(*also:* **rubber ~**) надувная лóдка.

dingy ['dɪndʒɪ] *adj* (*streets, room*) мрáчный*
(мрáчен); (*clothes, curtains etc*)
замýзганный.

dining car ['daɪnɪŋ-] *n* (*BRIT*) вагóн-рестора́н.

dining room *n* столóвая *f adj*.

dinner ['dɪnə^r] *n* (*evening meal*) ýжин; (*lunch,
banquet*) обéд.

dinner jacket *n* смóкинг.

dinner party *n* зва́ный обéд.

dinner service *n* столóвый сервúз.

dinner time *n* (*midday*) обéденное врéмя* *nt*;
(*evening*) врéмя* ýжина.

dinosaur ['daɪnəsɔː^r] *n* динозáвр.

dint [dɪnt] *n*: **by ~ of** посрéдством +*gen*.

diocese ['daɪəsɪs] *n* епáрхия.

dioxide [daɪ'ɔksaɪd] *n* двуóкись *f*.

dip [dɪp] *n* (*slope*) уклóн; (*depression*) впáдина;
(*CULIN*) сóус*; (*AGR: for sheep*)
дезинфицúрующий раствóр ♦ *vt* (*immerse*)
погружáть (погрузúть* *perf*), окунáть

(окунýть *perf*); (: *in liquid*) обмáкивать
(обмакнýть *perf*); (*BRIT: AUT: lights*) приглушáть (приглушúть* *perf*) ♦ *vi* (*ground, road*)
идтú* (пойтú* *perf*) пóд уклóн; **to go for a ~ in
the sea** окунáться (окунýться *perf*) в мóре.

Dip. *abbr* (*BRIT*) = **diploma.**

diphtheria [dɪf'θɪərɪə] *n* дифтерúт.

diphthong ['dɪfθɔŋ] *n* дифтóнг.

diploma [dɪ'pləumə] *n* диплóм.

diplomacy [dɪ'pləuməsɪ] *n* дипломáтия.

diplomat ['dɪpləmæt] *n* дипломáт.

diplomatic [dɪplə'mætɪk] *adj* (*POL*)
дипломатúческий*; (*tactful*)
дипломатúчный* (дипломатúчен); **to break
off ~ relations (with)** (*POL*) разрывáть
(разорвáть* *perf*) дипломатúческие
отношéния (с +*instr*).

diplomatic corps *n* дипломатúческий*
кóрпус*.

diplomatic immunity *n* дипломатúческая
неприкоснове́нность *f*.

dip stick *n* (*BRIT: AUT*) *щуп для измерéния
ýровня мáсла.*

dip switch *n* (*BRIT: AUT*) переключáтель *m*
свéта фар.

dire [daɪə^r] *adj* (*consequences*) зловéщий*;
(*poverty, situation*) жýткий*.

direct [daɪ'rɛkt] *adj* прямóй ♦ *adv* прямо ♦ *vt*
(*company, project etc*) руководúть* (*impf*)
+*instr*; (*play, film, programme*) ста́вить*
(поста́вить* *perf*); (*letter*): **to ~ to** направля́ть
(напра́вить* *perf*) +*dat*; (*attention, remark*): **to
~ (towards** *or* **at)** направля́ть (напра́вить*
perf) (на +*acc*); (*order*): **to ~ sb to do** велéть
(*impf*) комý-н +*infin*; **can you ~ me to ...?** Вы не
укáжете, где нахóдится ...?

direct access *n* (*COMPUT*) прямóй дóступ.

direct cost *n* (*COMM*) прямы́е затрáты *fpl*.

direct current *n* постоя́нный ток.

direct debit *n* (*BRIT: COMM*) прямóе
дебетова́ние.

direct dialling *n* автоматúческая телефóнная
связь *f*.

direct hit *n* (*MIL*) прямóе попада́ние.

direction [dɪ'rɛkʃən] *n* (*way*) направлéние; (*TV,
CINEMA*) постанóвка; **~s** *npl* (*instructions*)
указáния *ntpl*; **to have a good sense of ~**
хорошó ориентúроваться (*impf/perf*); **~s for
use** инстрýкция (по эксплуатáции); **to ask for
~s (to)** спрáшивать (спросúть* *perf*) дорóгу
(к +*dat*); **in the ~ of** в направлéнии +*gen*.

directional [dɪ'rɛkʃənl] *adj* (*TECH*)
напра́вленный.

directive [dɪ'rɛktɪv] *n* (*POL, ADMIN*) директúва,
постановлéние; **a government ~**
прави́тельственное постановлéние.

direct labour *n* (*BRIT*) постоя́нная рабóчая
сúла.

---

* marks translations which have irregular inflections. The Russian-English side of the dictionary gives inflectional information.

directly [dɪ'rɛktlɪ] *adv* пря́мо; (*at once*) сейча́с же; (*as soon as*) как то́лько.
direct mail *n* прода́жа това́ров по по́чте.
direct-mail shot [dɪ'rɛkt'meɪl-] *n* (*BRIT*) почто́вая рекла́ма.
directness [daɪ'rɛktnɪs] *n* прямота́.
director [dɪ'rɛktə'] *n* (*COMM*) дире́ктор*; (*of project*) руководи́тель(ница) *m(f)*; (*TV, RADIO, CINEMA*) режиссёр.
Director of Public Prosecutions *n* (*BRIT*) Гла́вный прокуро́р.
directory [dɪ'rɛktərɪ] *n* (*also COMPUT*) спра́вочник; (*also*: **street** ~) указа́тель *m*.
directory enquiries (*US* **directory assistance**) *n* (телефо́нная) спра́вочная *f adj*.
dirt [də:t] *n* грязь* *f*; **to treat sb like** ~ ни во что́ не ста́вить (*impf*) кого́-н.
dirt-cheap ['də:t'tʃi:p] *adv* по дешёвке.
dirt road *n* грунтова́я доро́га.
dirty ['də:tɪ] *adj* гря́зный* ♦ *vt* па́чкать (испа́чкать *perf*).
dirty trick *n* зла́я шу́тка*.
disability [dɪsə'bɪlɪtɪ] *n* (*physical*) инвали́дность *f no pl*; (*mental*) у́мственная неполноце́нность *f*; **physical disabilities** физи́ческие недоста́тки.
disability allowance *n* посо́бие по инвали́дности.
disable [dɪs'eɪbl] *vt* (*subj*: *illness, accident*) кале́чить (искале́чить *perf*); (*tank, gun*) выводи́ть* (вы́вести* *perf*) из стро́я.
disabled [dɪs'eɪbld] *adj* (*mentally*) у́мственно неполноце́нный; (*physically*): ~ **person** инвали́д ♦ *npl*: **the** ~ инвали́ды *mpl*.
disabuse [dɪsə'bju:z] *vt*: **to** ~ **sb (of)** разуверя́ть (разуве́рить *perf*) кого́-н (в +*prp*).
disadvantage [dɪsəd'vɑ:ntɪdʒ] *n* недоста́ток*; **to be at a** ~ быть* (*impf*) в невы́годном положе́нии.
disadvantaged [dɪsəd'vɑ:ntɪdʒd] *adj* (*person, region*) обездо́ленный* (обездо́лен).
disadvantageous [dɪsædvə:n'teɪdʒəs] *adj* невы́годный* (невы́годен).
disaffected [dɪsə'fɛktɪd] *adj* разочаро́в-а́вшийся.
disaffection [dɪsə'fɛkʃən] *n*: ~ **(with)** поте́ря дове́рия (к +*dat*).
disagree [dɪsə'gri:] *vi* (*differ*) расходи́ться* (разойти́сь* *perf*); (*be against, think otherwise*): **to** ~ **(with)** не соглаша́ться (согласи́ться* *perf*) (с +*instr*); **I** ~ **with you** я с Ва́ми не согла́сен; **we** ~ **on many things** мы во мно́гом расхо́димся; **garlic** ~**s with me** я пло́хо переношу́ чесно́к.
disagreeable [dɪsə'gri:əbl] *adj* неприя́тный* (неприя́тен).
disagreement [dɪsə'gri:mənt] *n* (*lack of consensus, argument*) разногла́сие; (*opposition*): ~ **with sb/sth** несогла́сие с кем-н/чем-н; **to have a** ~ **with sb** име́ть (*impf*) разногла́сие с кем-н.

disallow ['dɪsə'lau] *vt* (*appeal*) отклоня́ть (отклони́ть *perf*); (*goal*) не засчи́тывать (засчита́ть *perf*).
disappear [dɪsə'pɪə'] *vi* исчеза́ть (исче́знуть* *perf*).
disappearance [dɪsə'pɪərəns] *n* исчезнове́ние.
disappoint [dɪsə'pɔɪnt] *vt* разочаро́вывать (разочарова́ть *perf*).
disappointed [dɪsə'pɔɪntɪd] *adj* разочаро́ванный* (разочаро́ван).
disappointing [dɪsə'pɔɪntɪŋ] *adj*: **the film is rather** ~ э́тот фильм разочаро́вывает; **the election results were** ~ **for the Democrats** демокра́ты бы́ли разочаро́ваны результа́тами вы́боров.
disappointment [dɪsə'pɔɪntmənt] *n* разочарова́ние.
disapproval [dɪsə'pru:vəl] *n* неодобре́ние.
disapprove [dɪsə'pru:v] *vi*: **to** ~ **(of)** не одобря́ть (*impf*) (+*acc*).
disapproving [dɪsə'pru:vɪŋ] *adj* неодобри́тельный* (неодобри́телен).
disarm [dɪs'ɑ:m] *vt* (*MIL*) разоружа́ть (разоружи́ть *perf*); (*fig*) обезору́живать (обезору́жить *perf*) ♦ *vi* разоружа́ться (разоружи́ться *perf*).
disarmament [dɪs'ɑ:məmənt] *n* разоруже́ние.
disarming [dɪs'ɑ:mɪŋ] *adj* обезору́живающий.
disarray [dɪsə'reɪ] *n*: **in** ~ (*army, organization, thoughts*) в смяте́нии; (*hair, clothes*) в беспоря́дке; **to throw into** ~ приводи́ть* (привести́* *perf*) в смяте́ние.
disaster [dɪ'zɑ:stə'] *n* (*natural*) бе́дствие; (*man-made, also fig*) катастро́фа.
disaster area *n* (*also fig*) зо́на бе́дствия.
disastrous [dɪ'zɑ:strəs] *adj* губи́тельный* (губи́телен).
disband [dɪs'bænd] *vt* распуска́ть (распусти́ть* *perf*) ♦ *vi* расформиро́вываться (расформирова́ться *perf*).
disbelief ['dɪsbə'li:f] *n* неве́рие; **in** ~ с неве́рием.
disbelieve ['dɪsbə'li:v] *vt* (*person*) не ве́рить (*impf*) +*dat*; (*story*) не ве́рить (*impf*) +*dat or* в +*acc*; **I don't** ~ **you** я не могу́ сказа́ть, что не ве́рю Вам.
disc [dɪsk] *n* (*ANAT*) межпозвоно́чный хрящ*; (*record*) диск; (*COMPUT*) = **disk**.
disc. *abbr* (*COMM*) = **discount**.
discard [dɪs'kɑ:d] *vt* (*old things*) выбра́сывать (вы́бросить* *perf*); (*idea, plan*) отбра́сывать (отбро́сить* *perf*).
disc brake *n* ди́сковый то́рмоз*.
discern [dɪ'sə:n] *vt* (*see*) различа́ть (различи́ть *perf*); (*identify*) определя́ть (определи́ть *perf*).
discernible [dɪ'sə:nəbl] *adj* различи́мый.
discerning [dɪ'sə:nɪŋ] *adj* разбо́рчивый (разбо́рчив); **he has** ~ **tastes** он то́нкий* цени́тель.
discharge [*vt* dɪs'tʃɑ:dʒ, *n* 'dɪstʃɑ:dʒ] *vt* (*duties*) выполня́ть (вы́полнить *perf*); (*debt*)

распла́чиваться (расплати́ться* *perf*) с +*instr*; (*waste*) выбра́сывать (вы́бросить* *perf*); (*ELEC*) разряжа́ть (разряди́ть* *perf*); (*pus etc*) выделя́ть (*impf*); (*patient*) выпи́сывать (вы́писать* *perf*); (*employee*) увольня́ть (уво́лить *perf*); (*soldier*) демобилизова́ть (*impf/perf*); (*defendant*) опра́вдывать (оправда́ть *perf*) ◆ *n* (*CHEM, MED*) выделе́ние; (*ELEC*) разря́д; (*of patient*) вы́писка; (*of employee*) увольне́ние; (*of soldier*) демобилиза́ция; (*of defendant*) оправда́ние; **to ~ a gun** разряжа́ть (разряди́ть* *perf*) ружьё.

discharged bankrupt [dɪs'tʃɑːdʒd-] *n лицо́, восстано́вленное в права́х по́сле банкро́тства.*

disciple [dɪ'saɪpl] *n* (*REL*) апо́стол; (*fig*) учени́к*(-и́ца).

disciplinary ['dɪsɪplɪnərɪ] *adj* (*code, measures*) дисциплина́рный; **~ problems** пробле́мы с дисципли́ной; **to take ~ action against sb** принима́ть (приня́ть* *perf*) дисциплина́рные ме́ры к кому́-н.

discipline ['dɪsɪplɪn] *n* дисципли́на ◆ *vt* (*train*) дисциплини́ровать (*impf/perf*); (*punish*) налага́ть (наложи́ть* *perf*) дисциплина́рное взыска́ние на +*acc*; **to ~ o.s. to do** приуча́ться (приучи́ться* *perf*) +*impf infin*.

disc jockey *n* диск-жоке́й.

disclaim [dɪs'kleɪm] *vt* отрица́ть (*impf*).

disclaimer [dɪs'kleɪmə'] *n* отка́з от отве́тственности; **to issue a ~** обнаро́довать (*perf*) отка́з *or* отрече́ние от отве́тственности.

disclose [dɪs'kləuz] *vt* раскрыва́ть (раскры́ть* *perf*).

disclosure [dɪs'kləuʒə'] *n* раскры́тие.

disco ['dɪskəu] *n abbr* = **discotheque.**

discolour [dɪs'kʌlə'] (*US* **discolor**) *vt* обесцве́чивать (обесцве́тить* *perf*) ◆ *vi* обесцве́чиваться (обесцве́титься* *perf*).

discolouration [dɪskʌlə'reɪʃən] (*US* **discoloration**) *n* обесцве́чивание.

discoloured [dɪs'kʌləd] (*US* **discolored**) *adj* вы́цветший.

discomfort [dɪs'kʌmfət] *n* (*unease*) нело́вкость *f*; (*pain etc*) недомога́ние.

disconcert [dɪskən'sə:t] *vt* смуща́ть (смути́ть* *perf*).

disconcerting [dɪskən'sə:tɪŋ] *adj* вызыва́ющий* чу́вство нело́вкости.

disconnect [dɪskə'nɛkt] *vt* (*pipe, telephone*) разъединя́ть (разъедини́ть* *perf*); (*ELEC, RADIO*) отключа́ть (отключи́ть *perf*).

disconnected [dɪskə'nɛktɪd] *adj* (*speech, thoughts*) бессвя́зный* (бессвя́зен).

disconsolate [dɪs'kɔnsəlɪt] *adj* неуте́шный* (неуте́шен), безуте́шный* (безуте́шен).

discontent [dɪskən'tɛnt] *n* недово́льство.

discontented [dɪskən'tɛntɪd] *adj*: **~ (with)** недово́льный* (недово́лен) (+*instr*).

discontinue [dɪskən'tɪnju:] *vt* прекраща́ть (прекрати́ть* *perf*); **"discontinued"** (*COMM*) "сня́то с произво́дства".

discord ['dɪskɔːd] *n* разла́д; (*MUS*) диссона́нс.

discordant [dɪs'kɔːdənt] *adj* (*fig: note*) несогласу́ющийся; (*MUS*) диссони́рующий.

discotheque ['dɪskəutɛk] *n* дискоте́ка.

discount [*n* 'dɪskaunt, *vt* dɪs'kaunt] *n* ски́дка* ◆ *vt* (*COMM*) снижа́ть (сни́зить* *perf*) це́ну на +*acc*; (*idea, fact*) не принима́ть (приня́ть* *perf*) в расчёт; **to give sb a ~ on sth** де́лать (сде́лать *perf*) кому́-н ски́дку на что-н; **~ for cash** ски́дка* при усло́вии опла́ты нали́чными; **at a ~** со ски́дкой.

discount house *n* (*esp BRIT: FINANCE*) учётный дом*; (*esp US: also:* **discount store**) магази́н, торгу́ющий по сни́женным це́нам.

discount rate *n* сни́женная цена́.

discourage [dɪs'kʌrɪdʒ] *vt* (*dishearten*) отбива́ть (отби́ть* *perf*) жела́ние у +*gen*; (*advise against*): **to ~ sb from doing** отгова́ривать (отговори́ть *perf*) кого́-н +*infin*.

discouragement [dɪs'kʌrɪdʒmənt] *n* (*feeling*) разочарова́ние; **to act as a ~ to sb** отбива́ть (отби́ть* *perf*) охо́ту у кого́-н *or* +*infin or* к +*dat*.

discouraging [dɪs'kʌrɪdʒɪŋ] *adj* расхола́живающий.

discourteous [dɪs'kə:tɪəs] *adj* нелюбе́зный* (нелюбе́зен).

discover [dɪs'kʌvə'] *vt* обнару́живать (обнару́жить *perf*).

discovery [dɪs'kʌvərɪ] *n* (*of object etc*) откры́тие; (*thing found*) обнаруже́ние.

discredit [dɪs'krɛdɪt] *vt* дискредити́ровать (*impf/perf*) ◆ *n*: **it is to his ~ that he ...** его́ дискредити́рует то, что он ....

discreet [dɪs'kri:t] *adj* (*tactful*) такти́чный* (такти́чен); (*careful*) осмотри́тельный* (осмотри́телен); (*barely noticeable*) неприме́тный* (неприме́тен).

discreetly [dɪs'kri:tlɪ] *adv* (*see adj*) такти́чно; осмотри́тельно; неприме́тно.

discrepancy [dɪs'krɛpənsɪ] *n* расхожде́ние.

discretion [dɪs'krɛʃən] *n* (*tact*) такти́чность *f*; **at the ~ of** на усмотре́ние +*gen*; **use your (own) ~** поступа́йте, по своему́ усмотре́нию.

discretionary [dɪs'krɛʃənrɪ] *adj* (*powers etc*) дискрецио́нный.

discriminate [dɪs'krɪmɪneɪt] *vi*: **to ~ between** различа́ть (различи́ть *perf*); **to ~ against** дискримини́ровать (*impf/perf*).

discriminating [dɪs'krɪmɪneɪtɪŋ] *adj* (*discerning*)

---

* marks translations which have irregular inflections. The Russian-English side of the dictionary gives inflectional information.

разбо́рчивый (разбо́рчив); (*tax etc*) дифференциа́льный.

discrimination [dɪskrɪmɪ'neɪʃən] *n* (*bias*) дискримина́ция; (*discernment*) разбо́рчивость *f*; **racial ~** ра́совая дискримина́ция; **sexual ~** дискримина́ция по полово́му при́знаку.

discus ['dɪskəs] *n* (*object*) диск; (*event*) мета́ние ди́ска.

discuss [dɪs'kʌs] *vt* обсужда́ть (обсуди́ть* *perf*).

discussion [dɪs'kʌʃən] *n* (*talk*) обсужде́ние; (*debate*) диску́ссия; **the matter is under ~** э́тот вопро́с обсужда́ется.

disdain [dɪs'deɪn] *n* презре́ние ◆ *vt* презира́ть (*impf*) ◆ *vi*: **to ~ to do** счита́ть (посчита́ть *perf*) ни́же своего́ досто́инства +*infin*.

disease [dɪ'zi:z] *n* боле́знь *f*.

diseased [dɪ'zi:zd] *adj* (*also fig*) больно́й* (бо́лен).

disembark [dɪsɪm'bɑ:k] *vt* (*goods*) выгружа́ть (вы́грузить* *perf*); (*passengers*) выса́живать (вы́садить* *perf*) ◆ *vi* выса́живаться (вы́садиться* *perf*).

disembarkation [dɪsɛmbɑ:'keɪʃən] *n* (*see vt*) вы́грузка*; вы́садка*.

disembodied ['dɪsɪm'bɔdɪd] *adj* (*limb, head*) отчленённый; (*voice*) бестеле́сный.

disembowel ['dɪsɪm'bauəl] *vt* потроши́ть (вы́потрошить *perf*).

disenchanted ['dɪsɪn'tʃɑ:ntɪd] *adj*: **~ (with)** разочаро́ванный* (разочаро́ван) (+*instr*).

disenfranchise ['dɪsɪn'fræntʃaɪz] *vt* (*POL*) лиша́ть (лиши́ть *perf*) избира́тельных прав; (*COMM*) лиша́ть (лиши́ть *perf*) франши́зы.

disengage [dɪsɪn'geɪdʒ] *vt* (*TECH*) расцепля́ть (расцепи́ть* *perf*); (*AUT*): **to ~ the clutch** выключа́ть (вы́ключить *perf*) сцепле́ние.

disengagement [dɪsɪn'geɪdʒmənt] *n* освобожде́ние; **military ~** вы́вод вооружённых сил.

disentangle [dɪsɪn'tæŋgl] *vt* (*from wreckage*) высвобожда́ть (вы́свободить* *perf*); (*wool, wire*) распу́тывать (распу́тать *perf*); **to ~ o.s. (from)** выпу́тываться (вы́путаться *perf*) (из +*gen*).

disfavour [dɪs'feɪvə^r] (*US* **disfavor**) *n* неми́лость *f*.

disfigure [dɪs'fɪgə^r] *vt* уро́довать (изуро́довать *perf*).

disgorge [dɪs'gɔ:dʒ] *vt* (*subj: river*) выбра́сывать (вы́бросить* *perf*); (: *building, vehicle*) изверга́ть (изве́ргнуть* *perf*).

disgrace [dɪs'greɪs] *n* позо́р ◆ *vt* позо́рить (опозо́рить *perf*).

disgraceful [dɪs'greɪsful] *adj* позо́рный* (позо́рен).

disgruntled [dɪs'grʌntld] *adj* недово́льный* (недово́лен).

disguise [dɪs'gaɪz] *n* (*make-up, costume*) маскиро́вка*; (*art*) гримиро́вка, маскиро́вка

◆ *vt* (*object*) маскирова́ть (замаскирова́ть *perf*); (*feelings*) скрыва́ть (скрыть* *perf*); (*person*): **to ~ (as)** (*dress up*) переодева́ть (переоде́ть* *perf*) (+*instr*); (*make up*) гримирова́ть (загримирова́ть *perf*) (под +*acc*); **in ~** (*person*) переоде́тый; **to ~ o.s. as** переодева́ться (переоде́ться* *perf*) +*instr*; **there's no disguising the fact that ...** нельзя́ скрыть того́, что ....

disgust [dɪs'gʌst] *n* отвраще́ние ◆ *vt* внуша́ть (внуши́ть *perf*) отвраще́ние +*dat*; **she walked off in ~** она́ с возмуще́нием ушла́.

disgusting [dɪs'gʌstɪŋ] *adj* отврати́тельный* (отврати́телен).

dish [dɪʃ] *n* (*plate, food*) блю́до; (*also:* **satellite ~**) параболи́ческая анте́нна; **to do** *or* **wash the ~es** мыть* (вы́мыть* *perf*) посу́ду

▶ **dish out** *vt* (*money, advice etc*) раздава́ть* (разда́ть* *perf*); (*food*) раскла́дывать (разложи́ть* *perf*) (по таре́лкам)

▶ **dish up** *vt* (*food*) подава́ть* (пода́ть* *perf*) к столу́; (*inf: facts*) преподноси́ть* (преподнести́* *perf*).

dishcloth ['dɪʃklɔθ] *n* тря́пка* для мытья́ посу́ды.

dishearten [dɪs'hɑ:tn] *vt* приводи́ть* (привести́* *perf*) в уны́ние.

dishevelled [dɪ'ʃɛvəld] (*US* **disheveled**) *adj* растрёпанный* (растрёпан).

dishonest [dɪs'ɔnɪst] *adj* нече́стный* (нече́стен).

dishonesty [dɪs'ɔnɪstɪ] *n* нече́стность *f*.

dishonour [dɪs'ɔnə^r] (*US* **dishonor**) *n* бесче́стье.

dishonourable [dɪs'ɔnərəbl] *adj* бесче́стный* (бесче́стен).

dish soap *n* (*US*) хозя́йственное мы́ло*.

dishtowel ['dɪʃtauəl] *n* (*esp US*) ку́хонное *or* посу́дное полоте́нце*.

dishwasher ['dɪʃwɔʃə^r] *n* (*machine*) посудомо́ечная маши́на.

dishy [dɪʃɪ] *adj* (*inf*): **~ bloke** клёвый па́рень *m*.

disillusion [dɪsɪ'lu:ʒən] *vt* разочаро́вывать (разочарова́ть *perf*) ◆ *n* разочарова́ние; **to become ~ed (with)** разочаро́вываться (разочарова́ться *perf*) (в +*prp*).

disillusionment [dɪsɪ'lu:ʒənmənt] *n* разочарова́ние.

disincentive [dɪsɪn'sɛntɪv] *n* сде́рживающее обстоя́тельство; **to be a ~ to sb** явля́ться (*impf*) сде́рживающим обстоя́тельством для кого́-н.

disinclined [dɪsɪn'klaɪnd] *adj*: **I am ~ to do it** мне не хо́чется э́то де́лать.

disinfect [dɪsɪn'fɛkt] *vt* дезинфици́ровать (*impf/ perf*).

disinfectant [dɪsɪn'fɛktənt] *n* дезинфиц-и́рующее сре́дство.

disinflation [dɪsɪn'fleɪʃən] *n* (*ECON*) дез-инфля́ция.

disinformation [dɪsɪnfə'meɪʃən] *n* дезинформа́ция.

disingenuous [dɪsɪn'dʒɛnjuəs] *adj*
неискренний* (неискренен).
disinherit [dɪsɪn'hɛrɪt] *vt:* **to ~ sb** лишать
(лишить *perf*) кого-н наследства.
disintegrate [dɪs'ɪntɪɡreɪt] *vi (break up)*
распадаться (распасться* *perf*) на части;
(*decay*) разлагаться (разложиться* *perf*).
disinterested [dɪs'ɪntrəstɪd] *adj (impartial)*
бескорыстный* (бескорыстен).
disjointed [dɪs'dʒɔɪntɪd] *adj* бессвязный*
(бессвязен).
disk [dɪsk] *n (COMPUT)* диск; **single-/double-
sided ~** односторонний/двусторонний
диск.
disk drive *n* дисковод.
diskette [dɪs'kɛt] *n (US)* **= disk.**
disk operating system *n* дисковая
операционная система.
dislike [dɪs'laɪk] *n (feeling)* неприязнь *f;* (*usu pl:
object of dislike*) нелюбимая вещь *f* ♦ *vt* не
любить* (*impf*) +*gen;* **to take a ~ to sb/sth**
невзлюбить* (*perf*) кого-н/что-н; **I ~ the idea**
мне не нравится идея; **he ~s cooking** он не
любит готовить.
dislocate ['dɪsləkeɪt] *vt* вывихнуть (*perf*); **he has
~d his shoulder** он вывихнул плечо.
dislodge [dɪs'lɔdʒ] *vt* смещать (сместить* *perf*).
disloyal [dɪs'lɔɪəl] *adj:* **~ (to)** неверный*
(неверен) (+*dat*).
dismal ['dɪzml] *adj* унылый (уныл), мрачный*
(мрачен); **a ~ failure** ужасная неудача.
dismantle [dɪs'mæntl] *vt* разбирать
(разобрать* *perf*).
dismast [dɪs'mɑːst] *vt (NAUT)* снимать (снять*
perf) мачты с +*gen.*
dismay [dɪs'meɪ] *n* смятение ♦ *vt* приводить*
(привести* *perf*) в смятение; **much to my ~** к
моему смятению; **he gasped in ~** он ахнул в
смятении.
dismiss [dɪs'mɪs] *vt (worker)* увольнять
(уволить* *perf*); (*pupils, soldiers*) распускать
(распустить* *perf*); (*LAW: case*) прекращать
(прекратить* *perf*); (*possibility, idea*)
отбрасывать (отбросить* *perf*).
dismissal [dɪs'mɪsl] *n (sacking)* увольнение.
dismount [dɪs'maunt] *vi (from horse)*
спешиваться (спешиться *perf*); (*from bicycle*)
слезать (слезть *perf*).
disobedience [dɪsə'biːdɪəns] *n* непослушание.
disobedient [dɪsə'biːdɪənt] *adj* непослушный*
(непослушен).
disobey [dɪsə'beɪ] *vt* не слушаться
(послушаться *perf*).
disorder [dɪs'ɔːdə'] *n* беспорядок*; (*MED*)
расстройство; **civil ~** социальные
беспорядки.
disorderly [dɪs'ɔːdəlɪ] *adj (room etc)*
беспорядочный; (*meeting*)

неорганизованный* (неорганизован);
(*behaviour*) бесчинствующий.
disorderly conduct *n* нарушение
общественного порядка.
disorganize [dɪs'ɔːɡənaɪz] *vt* дезорганизовать
(*impf/perf*).
disorganized [dɪs'ɔːɡənaɪzd] *adj*
неорганизованный.
disorientated [dɪs'ɔːrɪenteɪtɪd] *adj* лишённый
(лишён) чувства ориентации.
disown [dɪs'əun] *vt (action)* отказываться
(отказаться* *perf*) от +*gen;* (*person*)
отрекаться (отречься* *perf*) от +*gen.*
disparaging [dɪs'pærɪdʒɪŋ] *adj* пренебрежительный* (пренебрежителен); **to be ~ about
sb/sth** относиться* (отнестись* *perf*)
пренебрежительно к кому-н/чему-н.
disparate ['dɪspərɪt] *adj* несравнимый.
disparity [dɪs'pærɪtɪ] *n* неравенство.
dispassionate [dɪs'pæʃənət] *adj* бесстрастный*
(бесстрастен).
dispatch [dɪs'pætʃ] *vt (send)* отправлять
(отправить* *perf*); (*deal with*) разделываться
(разделаться *perf*) с +*instr;* (*kill*) покончить
(*perf*) с +*instr* ♦ *n (sending)* отправка; (*PRESS*)
сообщение; (*MIL*) донесение.
dispatch department *n* отдел отправки.
dispatch rider *n (MIL)* мотоциклист связи.
dispel [dɪs'pɛl] *vt* рассеивать (рассеять *perf*).
dispensary [dɪs'pɛnsərɪ] *n* аптека.
dispensation [dɪspən'seɪʃən] *n (of justice,
treatment)* осуществление; (*permission*):
(**special) ~** особое разрешение.
dispense [dɪs'pɛns] *vt (medicines)*
приготовлять (приготовить* *perf*) и
отпускать (отпустить* *perf*); (*charity, advice*)
раздавать* (раздать* *perf*); **to ~ justice**
отправлять (*impf*) правосудие
  ▶ **dispense with** *vt fus (do without)*
обходиться* (обойтись* *perf*) без +*gen;* (*make
unnecessary*) освобождать (освободить*
perf) от необходимости +*gen.*
dispenser [dɪs'pɛnsə'] *n (machine)* торговый
автомат.
dispensing chemist [dɪs'pɛnsɪŋ-] *n (BRIT: shop)*
аптека.
dispersal [dɪs'pəːsl] *n* рассеивание.
disperse [dɪs'pəːs] *vt (objects)* рассеивать
(рассеять *perf*); (*crowd*) разгонять (разо-
гнать* *perf*); (*knowledge*) распространять
(распространить *perf*) ♦ *vi (crowd, clouds*)
рассеиваться (рассеяться *perf*).
dispirited [dɪs'pɪrɪtɪd] *adj* удручённый*
(удручён).
displace [dɪs'pleɪs] *vt* замещать (заместить*
perf).
displaced person [dɪs'pleɪst-] *n* перемещённое
лицо*.

---

* marks translations which have irregular inflections. The Russian-English side of the dictionary gives inflectional information.

displacement [dɪs'pleɪsmənt] n замещéние; (PHYS) вытеснéние.

display [dɪs'pleɪ] n демонстрáция; (exhibition) выставка*; (pej: bad manners) выставлéние напокáз; (COMPUT, TECH) дисплéй ♦ vt (emotion, quality) выкáзывать (вы́казать* perf); (goods, exhibits) выставля́ть (вы́ставить* perf) (напокáз); (results, departure times) покáзывать (показáть* perf); **on ~** (exhibits) на вы́ставке; (goods in window) на витрńне.

display advertising n витрńнно-вы́ставочная реклáма.

displease [dɪs'pli:z] vt раздражáть (раздражńть perf).

displeased [dɪs'pli:zd] adj: **~ with** раздражённый* (раздражён) +instr.

displeasure [dɪs'plɛʒə'] n неудовóльствие.

disposable [dɪs'pəuzəbl] adj (lighter, bottle) однорáзового употреблéния; (syringe) однорáзовый; **~ income** дохóд, котóрым населéние располагáет пóсле уплáты налóгов.

disposable nappy n (BRIT) однорáзовая пелёнка*.

disposal [dɪs'pəuzl] n (of goods for sale) реализáция; (of property etc: by selling) распродáжа; (: by giving away) удалéние; (of rubbish) удалéние; **to have sth at one's ~** располагáть (impf) чем-н; **to put sth at sb's ~** предоставля́ть (предостáвить* perf) что-н в чьё-н распоряжéние.

dispose [dɪs'pəuz] vi: **~ of** (body, unwanted goods) избавля́ться (избáвиться* perf) от +gen; (problem, task) управля́ться (упрáвиться* perf) с +instr; (COMM: stock) реализóвывать (реализовáть perf).

disposed [dɪs'pəuzd] adj: **I am ~ to do я** настрóен +infin; **to be well ~ towards sb** хорошó относńться* (impf) к комý-н.

disposition [dɪspə'zɪʃən] n (nature) нрав; (inclination) склóнность f.

dispossess ['dɪspə'zɛs] vt: **to ~ sb (of)** лишáть (лишńть perf) когó-н (+gen).

disproportion [dɪsprə'pɔ:ʃən] n диспропóрция.

disproportionate [dɪsprə'pɔ:ʃənət] adj (excessive) неопрáвданно большóй; **our income is ~ to our expenditure** нáши дохóды не соизмерńмы с нáшими расхóдами.

disprove [dɪs'pru:v] vt опровергáть (опровéргнуть* perf).

dispute [dɪs'pju:t] n (domestic) ссóра; (POL, MIL, INDUSTRY) спор; (LAW) тя́жба ♦ vt оспáривать (оспóрить perf); **to be in** или **under ~** (matter) оспротестóвываться (impf); (territory) оспáриваться (impf).

disqualification [dɪskwɔlɪfɪ'keɪʃən] n: **~ from sth** лишéние прáва на учáстие в чём-н; **~ from driving** (BRIT) лишéние водńтельских прав.

disqualify [dɪs'kwɔlɪfaɪ] vt (SPORT)

дисквалифицńровать (impf/perf); **to ~ sb for sth/from doing** (status, situation) лишáть (лишńть perf) когó-н прáва на учáстие в чём-н/+infin; (authority) лишáть (лишńть perf) +gen; **to ~ sb from driving** (BRIT) лишáть (лишńть perf) когó-н водńтельских прав.

disquiet [dɪs'kwaɪət] n беспокóйство.

disquieting [dɪs'kwaɪətɪŋ] adj тревóжный* (тревóжен).

disregard [dɪsrɪ'gɑ:d] vt пренебрегáть (пренебрéчь* perf) ♦ n: **~ (for)** пренебрежéние (к +dat).

disrepair ['dɪsrɪ'pɛə'] n: **to fall into ~** приходńть* (прийтń* perf) в негóдность.

disreputable [dɪs'rɛpjutəbl] adj (person, behaviour) недостóйный.

disrepute ['dɪsrɪ'pju:t] n дурнáя слáва; **to fall into ~** приобретáть (приобрестń* perf) дурнýю слáву; **to bring sb/sth into ~** навлекáть (навлéчь* perf) на когó-н/что-н дурнýю слáву.

disrespectful [dɪsrɪ'spɛktful] adj непочтńтельный* (непочтńтелен).

disrupt [dɪs'rʌpt] vt нарушáть (нарýшить perf).

disruption [dɪs'rʌpʃən] n (interruption) нарушéние; (disturbance) социáльные беспоря́дки mpl.

disruptive [dɪs'rʌptɪv] adj (influence) подрывнóй; (action) разрушńтельный.

dissatisfaction [dɪssætɪs'fækʃən] n недовóльство, неудовлетворённость f.

dissatisfied [dɪs'sætɪsfaɪd] adj: **~ (with)** недовóльный* (недовóлен) (+instr).

dissect [dɪ'sɛkt] vt (ANAT) вскрывáть (вскрыть* perf); (theory, article) анализńровать (проанализńровать perf).

disseminate [dɪ'sɛmɪneɪt] vt распространя́ть (распространńть perf).

dissent [dɪ'sɛnt] n инакомы́слие; **~ from the party line** отхóд от партńйной лńнии.

dissenter [dɪ'sɛntə'] n (REL, POL) инакомы́слящий*(-ая) m(f) adj.

dissertation [dɪsə'teɪʃən] n диссертáция.

disservice [dɪs'sə:vɪs] n: **to do sb a ~** окáзывать (оказáть* perf) комý-н плохýю услýгу.

dissident ['dɪsɪdnt] adj (faction, voice) диссидéнтский ♦ n (POL, REL) диссидéнт.

dissimilar [dɪ'sɪmɪlə'] adj: **~ (to)** несхóдный (с +instr); **this is not ~ to ...** э́то схóдно с +instr ....

dissipate ['dɪsɪpeɪt] vt (heat, clouds) рассéивать (рассéять* perf); (money, effort) растрáчивать (растрáтить* perf).

dissipated ['dɪsɪpeɪtɪd] adj (debauched) распýщенный* (распýщен).

dissociate [dɪ'səuʃɪeɪt] vt: **to ~ from** отделя́ть (отделńть* perf) от +gen; **to ~ o.s. from** отмежёвываться (отмежевáться perf) от +gen.

dissolute ['dɪsəlu:t] adj разврáтный* (разврáтен).

dissolution [dɪsə'lu:ʃən] n (of parliament,

organization) ро́спуск; (*of marriage*) расторже́ние.

dissolve [dɪ'zɔlv] *vt* (*substance*) растворя́ть (раствори́ть *perf*); (*organization, parliament*) распуска́ть (распусти́ть* *perf*); (*marriage*) расторга́ть (расто́ргнуть* *perf*) ♦ *vi* растворя́ться (раствори́ться *perf*); **to ~ in(to) tears** залива́ться (зали́ться* *perf*) слеза́ми.

dissuade [dɪ'sweɪd] *vt*: **to ~ sb (from sth)** отгова́ривать (отговори́ть *perf*) кого́-н (от чего́-н).

distaff ['dɪstɑːf] *n*: **on the ~ side** по же́нской ли́нии.

distance ['dɪstns] *n* (*in space*) расстоя́ние; (*in sport*) диста́нция; (*in time*) отдалённость *f*; (*reserve*) сде́ржанность *f* ♦ *vt*: **to ~ o.s. (from)** отдаля́ться (отдали́ться *perf*) (от +*gen*); **in the ~** вдалеке́, вдали́; **from a ~** издалека́, и́здали; **what's the ~ to London?** каково́ расстоя́ние до Ло́ндона; **into the ~** вдаль; **it's within walking ~** туда́ мо́жно дойти́ пешко́м; **the town is some ~ from the sea** го́род нахо́дится в не́котором отдале́нии от мо́ря; **at a ~ of two metres** на расстоя́нии двух ме́тров; **keep your ~!** соблюда́йте диста́нцию!; **to keep sb at a ~** держа́ть (*impf*) кого́-н на расстоя́нии.

distant ['dɪstnt] *adj* (*place, time*) далёкий*; (*relative*) да́льний*; (*manner*) сде́ржанный*; **in the ~ past/future** в далёком про́шлом/-бу́дущем.

distaste [dɪs'teɪst] *n* неприя́знь *f*.

distasteful [dɪs'teɪstful] *adj* неприя́тный* (неприя́тен).

Dist. Atty. *abbr* (*US*) = **district attorney**.

distemper [dɪs'tɛmpə*] *n* (*paint*) те́мпера; (*disease: of dogs*) (соба́чья) чума́.

distend [dɪs'tɛnd] *vt* расширя́ть (расши́рить *perf*), раздува́ть (разду́ть *perf*) ♦ *vi* раздува́ться (разду́ться *perf*).

distended [dɪs'tɛndɪd] *adj* (*stomach*) взду́тый.

distil [dɪs'tɪl] (*US* **distill**) *vt* (*water*) дистилли́ровать (*impf/perf*); (*whisky*) перегоня́ть (перегна́ть* *perf*); (*information etc*) извлека́ть (извле́чь* *perf*).

distillery [dɪs'tɪlərɪ] *n* спи́рто-во́дочный заво́д.

distinct [dɪs'tɪŋkt] *adj* (*clear*) отчётливый (отчётлив); (*unmistakable*) определённый; (*different*): **~ (from)** отли́чный* (отли́чен) (от +*gen*); **as ~ from** в отли́чие от +*gen*.

distinction [dɪs'tɪŋkʃən] *n* (*difference*) отли́чие; (*honour*) честь *f*; (*in exam*) ≈ "отли́чно"; **to draw a ~ between** проводи́ть* (провести́* *perf*) разли́чие ме́жду +*instr*; **to pass an exam with ~** сдава́ть* (сдать* *perf*) экза́мен на отли́чно; **he is a writer of ~** он выдаю́щийся писа́тель.

distinctive [dɪs'tɪŋktɪv] *adj* (*voice, walk etc*)

своеобра́зный* (своеобра́зен), характе́рный* (характе́рен); (*feature*) отличи́тельный.

distinctly [dɪs'tɪŋktlɪ] *adv* (*remember, specify*) отчётливо; (*unhappy, better*) определённо.

distinguish [dɪs'tɪŋgwɪʃ] *vt* различа́ть (различи́ть *perf*); **to ~ (between)** проводи́ть* (провести́* *perf*) разли́чие (ме́жду +*instr*); **to ~ o.s.** отлича́ться (отличи́ться *perf*).

distinguished [dɪs'tɪŋgwɪʃt] *adj* (*eminent*) выдаю́щийся*; (*in appearance*) благоро́дный* (благоро́ден).

distinguishing [dɪs'tɪŋgwɪʃɪŋ] *adj* (*feature*) отличи́тельный.

distort [dɪs'tɔːt] *vt* искажа́ть (искази́ть* *perf*).

distortion [dɪs'tɔːʃən] *n* искаже́ние.

distract [dɪs'trækt] *vt* отвлека́ть (отвле́чь* *perf*).

distracted [dɪs'træktɪd] *adj* (*dreaming*) невнима́тельный* (невнима́телен); (*look*) отсу́тствующий*; (*anxious*) встрево́женный* (встрево́жен).

distraction [dɪs'trækʃən] *n* (*inattention*) отвлече́ние; (*confusion*) пу́таница; (*amusement*) развлече́ние; **to drive sb to ~** доводи́ть* (довести́* *perf*) кого́-н до безу́мия.

distraught [dɪs'trɔːt] *adj*: **~ (with)** (*pain, worry*) обезу́мевший (от +*gen*).

distress [dɪs'trɛs] *n* (*extreme worry, hardship*) отча́яние; (*through pain*) страда́ние ♦ *vt* огорча́ть (огорчи́ть *perf*); **the ship is in ~** кора́бль те́рпит бе́дствие; **he is in ~** он в бе́дственном положе́нии; **~ed area** (*BRIT*) райо́н бе́дствия.

distressing [dɪs'trɛsɪŋ] *adj* огорчи́тельный* (огорчи́телен).

distress signal *n* сигна́л бе́дствия.

distribute [dɪs'trɪbjuːt] *vt* (*leaflets, prizes etc*) раздава́ть* (разда́ть* *perf*); (*profits, weight*) распределя́ть (распредели́ть* *perf*).

distribution [dɪstrɪ'bjuːʃən] *n* (*of goods*) распростране́ние; (*of profits, weight*) распределе́ние.

distribution cost *n* изде́ржки *fpl* обраще́ния.

distributor [dɪs'trɪbjutə*] *n* (*COMM*) дистрибью́тер; (*AUT, TECH*) распредели́тель *m* зажига́ния.

district ['dɪstrɪkt] *n* райо́н.

district attorney *n* (*US*) ≈ окружно́й прокуро́р.

district council *n* (*BRIT*) райо́нный сове́т.

district nurse *n* (*BRIT*) участко́вая медсестра́*.

distrust [dɪs'trʌst] *n* недове́рие ♦ *vt* не доверя́ть (*impf*) +*dat*.

distrustful [dɪs'trʌstful] *adj*: **~ (of)** недове́рчивый (недове́рчив) (к +*dat*).

disturb [dɪs'təːb] *vt* (*person*) беспоко́ить (побеспоко́ить *perf*); (*interrupt: thoughts*,

---

peace etc) мешáть (помешáть *perf)* +*dat*;
(*disorganize)* наруша́ть (нару́шить *perf)*;
sorry to ~ you извини́те за беспоко́йство.

disturbance [dɪsˈtə:bəns] *n* расстро́йство;
(*political etc)* волне́ния *npl*; (*violent event)*
беспоря́дки *mpl*; (*of mind)* расстро́йство; (*by
drunks etc)* наруше́ние (обще́ственного)
поря́дка; **to cause a ~** (*in street etc)* вызыва́ть
(вы́звать *perf)* беспоря́дки; **~ of the peace**
наруше́ние обще́ственного поря́дка.

disturbed [dɪsˈtə:bd] *adj* (*person: upset)*
расстро́енный* (расстро́ен); (*childhood)*
неспоко́йный; **mentally ~** душевнобольно́й;
emotionally ~ психи́чески неуравно-
ве́шенный.

disturbing [dɪsˈtə:bɪŋ] *adj* трево́жный*
(трево́жен).

disuse [dɪsˈju:s] *n*: **to fall into ~** выходи́ть*
(вы́йти* *perf)* из употребле́ния.

disused [dɪsˈju:zd] *adj* забро́шенный*
(забро́шен).

ditch [dɪtʃ] *n* ров, кана́ва; (*for irrigation)* кана́л
◆ *vt* (*inf: person, car)* броса́ть (бро́сить* *perf)*;
(: *plan)* забра́сывать (забро́сить* *perf)*.

dither [ˈdɪðə'] *vi* колеба́ться* (*impf)*.

ditto [ˈdɪtəu] *adv* так же.

divan [dɪˈvæn] *n* (*also: ~ bed)* тахта́.

dive [daɪv] *n* (*from board)* прыжо́к* (*в во́ду)*;
(*underwater)* ныря́ние; (*of submarine)*
погруже́ние; (*pej: place)* забега́ловка ◆ *vi*
ныря́ть (*impf)*; (*submarine)* погружа́ться
(погрузи́ться* *perf)*; **to ~ into** (*bag, drawer etc)*
запуска́ть (запусти́ть* *perf)* ру́ку в +*acc*;
(*shop, car etc)* ныря́ть (нырну́ть *perf)* в +*acc*.

diver [ˈdaɪvə'] *n* водола́з.

diverge [daɪˈvə:dʒ] *vi* расходи́ться (разойти́сь*
perf).

divergent [daɪˈvə:dʒənt] *adj* расходя́щийся*.

diverse [daɪˈvə:s] *adj* разнообра́зный*
(разнообра́зен).

diversification [daɪvə:sɪfɪˈkeɪʃən] *n*
диверсифика́ция.

diversify [daɪˈvə:sɪfaɪ] *vi* разнообра́зить* (*impf)*;
(*COMM)* расширя́ть (расши́рить *perf)* вы́бор.

diversion [daɪˈvə:ʃən] *n* (*BRIT: AUT)* объе́зд; (*of
attention, funds)* отвлече́ние.

diversionary [daɪˈvə:ʃənrɪ] *adj* диверсио́нный.

diversity [daɪˈvə:sɪtɪ] *n* разнообра́зие,
многообра́зие.

divert [daɪˈvə:t] *vt* (*funds, attention)* отвлека́ть
(отвле́чь* *perf)*; (*traffic)* отводи́ть* (отвести́*
perf).

divest [daɪˈvɛst] *vt*: **to ~ sb of** лиша́ть (лиши́ть
perf) кого́-н +*gen*.

divide [dɪˈvaɪd] *vt* (*separate)* разделя́ть
(раздели́ть* *perf)*; (*MATH)* дели́ть*
(раздели́ть* *perf)*; (*share out)* дели́ть*
(подели́ть* *perf)* ◆ *vi* (*cells etc)* дели́ться*
(раздели́ться* *perf)*; (*road)* разделя́ться
(раздели́ться* *perf)*; (*people, groups)*
дели́ться* *or* разделя́ться (раздели́ться* *perf)*

◆ *n* расхожде́ние; **to ~ (between** *or* **among)**
дели́ть* (подели́ть* *perf)* (ме́жду +*instr)*; **40
~d by 5** 40 раздели́ть на 5

▶ **divide out** *vt*: **to ~ out (between** *or* **among)**
разделя́ть (раздели́ть* *perf)* (ме́жду +*instr)*.

divided [dɪˈvaɪdɪd] *adj* (*fig: country, couple)*
разделённый* (разделён); **opinions were ~**
мне́ния раздели́лись.

divided highway *n* (*US)* шоссе́ *nt ind*.

dividend [ˈdɪvɪdɛnd] *n* (*COMM)* дивиде́нд; (*fig)*:
to pay ~s окупа́ться (окупи́ться *perf)*.

dividend cover *n* (*COMM)* покры́тие
дивиде́нда.

dividers [dɪˈvaɪdəz] *npl* (*MATH, TECH)*
раздели́тельный ци́ркуль *msg*.

divine [dɪˈvaɪn] *adj* (*also fig)* боже́ственный ◆ *vt*
(*future, truth)* уга́дывать (угада́ть *perf)*;
(*water, metal)* иска́ть* (*impf)*.

diving [ˈdaɪvɪŋ] *n* ныря́ние; (*SPORT)* прыжки́
mpl в во́ду.

diving board *n* вы́шка* (*для прыжко́в в во́ду)*.

diving suit *n* гидрокостю́м.

divinity [dɪˈvɪnɪtɪ] *n* (*holiness)* боже́ственность
f; (*god)* божество́*; (*SCOL)* богосло́вие.

divisible [dɪˈvɪzəbl] *adj* (*MATH)*: **~ (by)** дели́мый
(на +*acc)*; **to be ~ into** подразделя́ться (*impf)*
на +*acc*.

division [dɪˈvɪʒən] *n* (*also MATH)* деле́ние;
(*sharing out)* разделе́ние; (*disagreement)*
разногла́сие; (*BRIT: POL)* *парла́ментское
голосова́ние, соверша́емое в ра́зных
ко́мнатах*; (*COMM)* подразделе́ние,
отделе́ние; (*MIL)* диви́зия; (*SPORT)* ли́га; **~ of
labour** разделе́ние труда́.

divisive [dɪˈvaɪsɪv] *adj* (*tactics, system etc)*
вызыва́ющий* разногла́сия.

divorce [dɪˈvɔ:s] *n* разво́д ◆ *vt* (*spouse)*
разводи́ться* (развести́сь* *perf)* с +*instr*;
(*dissociate)* отделя́ть (отдели́ть* *perf)*.

divorced [dɪˈvɔ:st] *adj* разведённый*
(разведён).

divorcee [dɪvɔ:ˈsi:] *n* разведённый(-ая) *m(f) adj*.

divot [ˈdɪvət] *n* вы́рванный кусо́к* дёрна.

divulge [daɪˈvʌldʒ] *vt* разглаша́ть
(разгласи́ть* *perf)*.

DIY *n abbr* (*BRIT)* = **do-it-yourself**.

dizziness [ˈdɪzɪnɪs] *n* головокруже́ние.

dizzy [ˈdɪzɪ] *adj* (*height)* головокружи́тельный;
~ turn *or* **spell** при́ступ головокруже́ния; **I
feel ~** у меня́ кру́жится голова́; **to make sb ~**
приводи́ть* (привести́* *perf)* кого́-н в
смяте́ние.

DJ *n abbr* = **disc jockey**.

d.j. *n abbr* = **dinner jacket**.

Djakarta [dʒəˈkɑ:tə] *n* Джака́рта.

DJIA *n abbr* (*US:* = *Dow-Jones Industrial
Average)* и́ндекс Доу Джо́нса.

dl *abbr* (= *decilitre)* децили́тр.

DLit(t) *n abbr* (= *Doctor of Literature, Doctor of
Letters)* до́ктор филоло́гии.

DLO *n abbr* (= *dead-letter office)* Отде́л

недоста́вленной корреспонде́нции.

dm *abbr* (= *decimetre*) дм= *дециме́тр*.

DMus *n abbr* (= *Doctor of Music*) до́ктор
музыкове́дения.

DMZ *n abbr* (= *demilitarized zone*)
демилитаризо́ванная зо́на.

DNA *n abbr* (= *deoxyribonucleic acid*) ДНК=
дезоксирибонуклеи́новая кислота́.

Dnieper ['dni:pə'] *n*: **the ~** Днепр.

KEYWORD
---

do [du:] (*pt* **did**, *pp* **done**) *aux vb* **1** (*in negative
constructions and questions*); **I don't
understand** я не понима́ю; **she doesn't want it**
она́ не хо́чет э́то; **didn't you know?** ра́зве Вы
не зна́ли?; **what do you think?** что Вы
ду́маете?

2 (*for emphasis*) да; **she does look rather pale**
да, она́ вы́глядит о́чень бле́дной; **oh do shut
up!** ну, замолчи́те же!

3 (*in polite expressions*) пожа́луйста; **do sit
down/help yourself** пожа́луйста, сади́тесь/-
угоща́йтесь; **do take care!** пожа́луйста,
береги́те себя́!

4 (*used to avoid repeating vb*): **she swims
better than I** она́ пла́вает лу́чше меня́ *or*
чем я; **do you read/buy newspapers? – yes, I
do/no, I don't** Вы чита́ете/покупа́ете газе́ты?
– да, (чита́ю/покупа́ю)/нет, (не чита́ю/-
покупа́ю); **she lives in Glasgow – so do I** она́
живёт в Гла́зго – а, я то́же; **he didn't like it
and neither did we** ни ему́, ни нам, э́то не
понра́вилось; **who made this mess? – I did**
кто за́дел насори́л? – я; **he asked me to help
him and I did** он попроси́л меня́ помо́чь ему́,
что я и сде́лал

5 (*in question tags*) ве́рно, ведь; **you like him,
don't you?** он Вам нра́вится, ве́рно?, он ведь
Вам нра́вится; **I don't know him, do I?** я ведь
его́ не зна́ю

♦ *vt* **1** де́лать (сде́лать *perf*); **what are you
doing tonight?** что Вы де́лаете сего́дня
ве́чером?; **I've got nothing to do** мне не́чего
де́лать; **what can I do for you?** чем я могу́
Вам помо́чь?; **we're doing "Othello" at school**
(*studying*) мы прохо́дим "Оте́лло" в шко́ле;
(*performing*) мы ста́вим "Оте́лло" в шко́ле;
to do one's teeth чи́стить* (почи́стить* *perf*)
зу́бы; **to do one's hair** причёсываться
(причеса́ться *perf*); **to do the washing-up**
мыть (помы́ть *perf*) посу́ду

2 (*AUT etc*): **the car was doing 100 (km/h)**
маши́на шла со ско́ростью 100 км/ч; **we've
done 200 km already** мы уже́ прое́хали 200
км; **he can do 100 mph in that car** на э́той
маши́не он мо́жет е́хать со ско́ростью 100
миль в час

♦ *vi* **1** (*act, behave*) де́лать (сде́лать *perf*); **do**

as I do де́лайте, как я; **you did well to react so
quickly** Вы молоде́ц, что так бы́стро
среаги́ровали

2 (*get on, fare*): **he's doing well/badly at school**
он хорошо́/пло́хо у́чится; **the firm is doing
well** дела́ в фи́рме иду́т успе́шно; **how do
you do?** о́чень прия́тно

3 (*be suitable*) подходи́ть (подойти́ *perf*); **will
it do?** э́то подойдёт?

4 (*be sufficient*) хвата́ть (хва́тить *perf*) +*gen*;
will ten pounds do? десяти́ фу́нтов хва́тит?;
that'll do ла́дно, хорошо́; **that'll do!** (*in
annoyance*) дово́льно!, хва́тит!; **to make do
(with)** обходи́ться (обойти́сь *perf*) (+*instr*)

♦ *n* (*inf*): **we're having a bit of a do on Saturday**
у нас бу́дет вечери́нка в суббо́ту; **it was a
formal do** э́то был официа́льный приём

▶ **do away with** *vt fus* (*kill*) прико́нчить (*perf*);
(*abolish*) поко́нчить (*perf*) с +*instr*

▶ **do for** *vt fus* (*BRIT: inf*) убира́ть (*impf*) у +*gen*

▶ **do up** *vt* (*laces*) завя́зывать (завяза́ть* *perf*);
(*dress, buttons*) застёгивать (застегну́ть
perf); (*renovate, house*) ремонти́ровать*
(отремонти́ровать* *perf*)

▶ **do with** *vt fus*: **I could do with a drink** я бы
вы́пил чего́-нибудь; **I could do with some
help** по́мощь мне бы не помеша́ла; **what has
it got to do with you?** како́е э́то к Вам име́ет
отноше́ние?; **I won't have anything to do with
it** я не жела́ю име́ть к э́тому никако́го
отноше́ния; **it has to do with money** э́то
относи́тельно де́нег

▶ **do without** *vt fus* обходи́ться* (обойти́сь*
perf) без +*gen*; **if you're late for tea then you'll
do without** е́сли Вы опозда́ете, то
оста́нетесь без ча́я.

do. *abbr* = **ditto**.

DOA *abbr* (= *dead on arrival*): **he was ~** по
прибы́тии в больни́цу он был мёртв.

d.o.b. *abbr* = **date of birth**.

doc [dɔk] *n* (*inf*) до́ктор.

docile ['dəusaɪl] *adj* кро́ткий* (кро́ток).

dock [dɔk] *n* (*NAUT*) док; (*LAW*) скамья́
подсуди́мых; (*BOT*) щаве́ль *m* ♦ *vi* (*NAUT*)
прича́ливать (прича́лить *perf*); (*SPACE*)
стыкова́ться (состыкова́ться *perf*) ♦ *vt*: **they
~ed a third of his wages** они́ удержа́ли треть
его́ зарпла́ты; ~ *s npl* (*NAUT*) док, верфь *f*.

dock dues [-dju:z] *npl* (*COMM*) пла́та за
по́льзование до́ком.

docker ['dɔkə'] *n* до́кер.

docket ['dɔkɪt] *n* (*ADMIN, COMM: certificate*)
квита́нция; (*on parcel*) о́пись *f*.

dockyard ['dɔkjɑːd] *n* док, верфь *f*.

doctor ['dɔktə'] *n* (*MED*) врач*; (*SCOL*) до́ктор* ♦
vt: **I ~ed his coffee with arsenic** я подмеша́л в
его́ ко́фе мышья́к; ~**'s office** (*US*) враче́бный

---

* marks translations which have irregular inflections. The Russian-English side of the dictionary gives inflectional information.

кабинéт.

doctorate ['dɔktərɪt] n (*thesis*) дóкторская
рабóта; (*degree*) дóкторская стéпень* f.

Doctor of Philosophy n (*degree, person*)
дóктор филосóфии or филосóфских наýк.

doctrine ['dɔktrɪn] n доктрúна.

docudrama ['dɔkjudrɑːmə] n фильм úли
прогрáмма, в оснóву котóрых вошлú
реáльные собы́тия.

document [n 'dɔkjumənt, vb 'dɔkjumɛnt] n
докумéнт ♦ vt документúровать (*impf/perf*).

documentary [dɔkju'mɛntərɪ] adj
документáльный ♦ n (*TV, CINEMA*)
документáльный фильм.

documentation [dɔkjumən'teɪʃən] n (*also
COMPUT*) документáция.

DOD n abbr (*US: = Department of Defense*)
Департáмент оборóны.

doddering ['dɔdərɪŋ] adj дря́хлый* (дряхл).

doddery ['dɔdərɪ] adj = **doddering**.

doddle ['dɔdl] n (*inf*) пустя́к, пáра пустякóв.

Dodecanese [dəudɪkə'niːz] n: **the ~ (Islands)**
Докеданéзские островá* mpl.

dodge [dɔdʒ] n (*trick*) увéртка*, улóвка ♦ vt
увёртываться (увернýться perf) от +gen ♦ vi
увёртываться (увернýться perf); (*SPORT*)
дéлать (сдéлать perf) обмáнное движéние;
to ~ out of the way отскáкивать (отскочúть*
perf) в стóрону; **to ~ through the traffic**
лавúровать (*impf*) в потóке машúн.

dodgems ['dɔdʒəmz] npl (*BRIT*)
аттракциóнный электромобúль msg.

dodgy ['dɔdʒɪ] adj (*inf: plan*) рискóванный*
(рискóван); (: *person*): ~ **character**
подозрúтельный тип.

DOE n abbr (*BRIT: = Department of the
Environment*) Департáмент охрáны
окружáющей среды́; (*US: = Department of
Energy*) Департáмент энергéтики.

doe [dəu] n (*deer*) сáмка* олéня; (*rabbit*) сáмка*
крóлика.

does [dʌz] vb see **do**.

doesn't ['dʌznt] = **does not**.

dog [dɔg] n собáка ♦ vt преслéдовать (*impf*); **to
go to the ~s** (*fig*) приходúть* (прийтú* perf) в
упáдок.

dog biscuits npl галéты fpl для собáк.

dog collar n ошéйник; (*REL*) высóкий жёсткий
воротнúк у свящéнников.

dog-eared ['dɔgɪəd] adj потрёпанный*
(потрёпан).

dog food n корм* для собáк.

dogged ['dɔgɪd] adj упóрный.

doggy bag ['dɔgɪ-] n пакéт, в котóром
посетúтели ресторáна мóгут унестú
объéдки.

dogma ['dɔgmə] n дóгма.

dogmatic [dɔg'mætɪk] adj догматúческий*.

do-gooder [duː'gudə*] n (*pej*) благо-
дéтель(ница) m(f).

dogsbody ['dɔgzbɔdɪ] n (*BRIT: inf*) ишáк*.

doily ['dɔɪlɪ] n ажýрная or кружевнáя
салфéточка.

doing ['duɪŋ] n: **this is your ~** э́то твоúх рук
дéло.

doings ['duɪŋz] npl (*activities*) дéйствия ntpl.

do-it-yourself ['duːɪtjɔː'sɛlf] n сдéлай сам.

doldrums ['dɔldrəmz] npl: **to be in the ~**
(*person*) хандрúть (*impf*); (*business*)
находúться (*impf*) в упáдке.

dole [dəul] n (*BRIT*) посóбие по безрабóтице; **to
be on the ~** получáть (*impf*) посóбие по
безрабóтице

▶ **dole out** vt (*food, money*) раздавáть*
(раздáть* perf).

doleful ['dəulful] adj скóрбный* (скóрбен).

doll [dɔl] n (*also US: inf*) кýкла*.

dolled up adj (*inf*) разря́женный (разря́жен).

dollar ['dɔlə*] n дóллар.

dollar area n дóлларовая зóна.

dollop ['dɔləp] n: **a ~ (of)** лóжка (+gen).

dolly ['dɔlɪ] n кýкла.

Dolomites ['dɔləmaɪts] npl: **the ~**
Доломúтовые Áльпы fpl.

dolphin ['dɔlfɪn] n дельфúн.

domain [də'meɪn] n (*sphere*) сфéра; (*empire*)
владéние.

dome [dəum] n кýпол*.

domestic [də'mɛstɪk] adj домáшний*; (*trade,
politics*) внýтренний*; (*happiness*) семéйный.

domesticated [də'mɛstɪkeɪtɪd] adj (*animal*)
одомáшненный; (*person*) домовúтый
(домовúт); **he's very ~** он óчень домовúтый.

domesticity [dəumɛs'tɪsɪtɪ] n домáшняя жизнь
f.

domestic servant n прислýга.

domicile ['dɔmɪsaɪl] n (*LAW, ADMIN*) мéсто*
жúтельства.

dominant ['dɔmɪnənt] adj (*share, role*)
преоблáдающий, доминúрующий; (*partner*)
влáстный* (влáстен).

dominate ['dɔmɪneɪt] vt доминúровать (*impf*)
над +instr.

domination [dɔmɪ'neɪʃən] n преоблáдание,
доминúрование.

domineering [dɔmɪ'nɪərɪŋ] adj влáстный
(влáстен).

Dominican Republic [də'mɪnɪkən-] n: **the ~ ~**
Доминикáнская Респýблика.

dominion [də'mɪnɪən] n (*territory*) доминиóн;
(*authority*): **to have ~ over** влады́чествовать
(*impf*) над +instr.

domino ['dɔmɪnəu] (*pl ~es*) n доминó nt ind.

domino effect n цепнáя реáкция.

dominoes ['dɔmɪnəuz] n (*game*) доминó nt ind.

don [dɔn] n (*BRIT: SCOL*) преподавáтель(ница)
m(f) ♦ vt (*clothing*) надевáть (надéть* perf).

donate [də'neɪt] vt: **to ~ (to)** жéртвовать
(пожéртвовать perf) (+dat или на +acc).

donation [də'neɪʃən] n пожéртвование.

done [dʌn] pp of **do**.

donkey ['dɔŋkɪ] n осёл*.

donkey-work ['dɒŋkɪwɜːk] n (*BRIT: inf*) ишáчья рабóта.
donor ['dəʊnəʳ] n (*MED: of blood, heart etc*) дóнор; (*to charity*) жéртвователь(ница) m(f).
donor card n дóнорская кáрточка.
don't [dəʊnt] = **do not**.
donut ['dəʊnʌt] n (*US*) = **doughnut**.
doodle ['duːdl] vi чúркать (*impf*) ♦ n карáкули* fpl.
doom [duːm] n рок ♦ vt: **the plan was ~ed to failure** план был обречён на провáл.
doomsday ['duːmzdeɪ] n стрáшный суд*.
door [dɔː'] n дверь* f; **to go from ~ to ~** ходúть* (*impf*) от дóма к дóму.
doorbell ['dɔːbɛl] n (дверной) звонóк*.
door handle n двернáя рýчка*; (*of car*) рýчка* двéри.
doorman ['dɔːmən] irreg n (*in hotel*) швейцáр; (*in block of flats*) приврáтник.
doormat ['dɔːmæt] n (*mat*) половúк*; (*inf: person*) трáпка* m/f.
doorpost ['dɔːpəʊst] n дверной косáк*.
doorstep ['dɔːstɛp] n порóг; **on the ~** на порóге.
door-to-door ['dɔːtə'dɔː'] adj: **~ salesman** агéнт, сбывáющий товáры и различные вúды услýг непосрéдственно в домáх потребúтелей; **~ selling** продáжа вразнóс.
doorway ['dɔːweɪ] n дверной проём; **in the ~** в дверáх.
dope [dəʊp] n (*inf: drug*) наркóтик; (*: in sport*) дóпинг; (*: person*) придýрок*; (*: information*) секрéтная информáция ♦ vt (*horse, person*) вводúть* (ввестú* perf) наркóтик +dat.
dopey ['dəʊpɪ] adj (*inf: groggy*) одурмáненный; (*: stupid*) одурéлый.
dormant ['dɔːmənt] adj (*plant*) покóящийся; (*volcano*) спáщий; (*idea, report etc*): **to lie ~** бездéйствовать (*impf*).
dormer ['dɔːməʳ] n (*also: ~ window*) мансáрдное окнó*.
dormice ['dɔːmaɪs] npl of **dormouse**.
dormitory ['dɔːmɪtrɪ] n (*room*) óбщая спáльня*; (*US: building*) общежúтие.
dormouse ['dɔːmaʊs] (*pl dormice*) n (*ZOOL*) сóня.
Dors abbr (*BRIT: POST*) = **Dorset**.
DOS [dɒs] n abbr (*COMPUT: = disk operating system*) ДОС= дúсковая операцóнная систéма.
dosage ['dəʊsɪdʒ] n дóза.
dose [dəʊs] n дóза; (*BRIT: bout*) прúступ ♦ vt: **to ~ o.s. with** принимáть (принять* perf); **I had a ~ of flu last week** на прóшлой недéле у меня был грипп.
dosh [dɒʃ] n (*inf*) бáбки pl.
dosser ['dɒsəʳ] (*inf*) n (*tramp*) бомж; (*layabout*) разгильдáй.

doss house ['dɒs-] n (*BRIT: inf*) ночлéжка*.
dossier ['dɒsɪeɪ] n досьé nt ind.
DOT n abbr (*US: = Department of Transportation*) департáмент путéй сообщéния.
dot [dɒt] n тóчка*; (*speck*) пятнышко* ♦ vt: **~ted with** усéянный (усéян) +instr; **on the ~** минýта в минýту.
dote [dəʊt]: **to ~ on** vt fus душú не чáять (*impf*) в +prp.
dot-matrix printer [dɒt'meɪtrɪks-] n (*COMPUT*) мáтричный прúнтер.
dotted line ['dɒtɪd-] n пунктúрная лúния; **to sign on the ~ ~** (*fig*) окончáтельно соглашáться (согласúться perf).
dotty ['dɒtɪ] adj (*inf*) трóнутый.
double ['dʌbl] adj двойнóй ♦ adv: **to cost ~** стóить (*impf*) вдвóе дорóже ♦ n двойнúк* ♦ vt удвáивать (удвóить perf); (*fold in two*) склáдывать (сложúть* perf) вдвóе ♦ vi (*increase*) удвáиваться (удвóиться perf); **to ~ as** (*person*) совмещáть (*impf*) обязанности +gen; (*object*) служúть* (*impf*) одновремéнно +instr; **he ~s as a servant in this play** он тáкже исполняет роль слугú в этом спектáкле; **on the ~, (*BRIT*) at the ~** бегóм; **~ five two six (5526)** (*BRIT: TEL*) пятьдесят пять двáдцать шесть; **it's spelt with a ~ "l"** пúшется с двумя „л"
► **double back** vi разворáчиваться (развернýться perf) и идтú* (пойтú* perf) назáд
► **double up** vi (*bend over*) скóрчиваться (скóрчиться perf); (*share room*) делúть (*impf*).
double bass n контрабáс.
double bed n двуспáльная кровáть f.
double bend n (*BRIT*) извúлистая дорóга.
double blind n сравнúтельный эксперимéнт, в котóром лúчность учáстников неизвéстна ни эксперименáторам ни эксперименúруемым.
double-breasted ['dʌbl'brɛstɪd] adj двубóртный.
double-check ['dʌbl'tʃɛk] vti перепроверять (перепровéрить perf).
double cream (*BRIT*) n густые слúвки* pl.
double-cross ['dʌbl'krɒs] vt надувáть (надýть perf).
double-decker ['dʌbl'dɛkəʳ] n (*also: double-decker bus*) двухэтáжный автóбус.
double exposure n (*PHOT*) двойнáя экспозúция.
double glazing [-'gleɪzɪŋ] n (*BRIT*) двойные рáмы fpl.
double indemnity n (*US*) выплата страховóй сýммы в двойнóм размéре.
double-page spread ['dʌblpeɪdʒ-] n двойнóй разворóт (*газéты, журнáла*).
double parking n паркóвка вторым рядом.

---

* marks translations which have irregular inflections. The Russian-English side of the dictionary gives inflectional information.

double room n (*in hotel*) двухме́стный но́мер*; (*in house*) ко́мната на двои́х.
doubles ['dʌblz] n (*TENNIS*) па́ры fpl.
double time n двойна́я опла́та.
double whammy [-'wæmɪ] n двойно́й уда́р.
doubly ['dʌblɪ] adv вдвойне́.
doubt [daut] n сомне́ние ♦ vt сомнева́ться (*impf*); (*mistrust*) сомнева́ться (*impf*) в +prp, недоверя́ть (*impf*) +dat; **without (a)** ~ без сомне́ния; **I** ~ **it (very much)** я (о́чень) сомнева́юсь; **I** ~ **if** or **whether she'll come** я сомнева́юсь, что она́ придёт; **I don't** ~ **that** ... я не сомнева́юсь, что ....
doubtful ['dautful] adj сомни́тельный; **to be** ~ **about sth** сомнева́ться (*impf*) насчёт чего́-н; **I'm a bit** ~ я не́сколько сомнева́юсь; **it's** ~ **whether** ... сомни́тельно, что ....
doubtless ['dautlɪs] adv несомне́нно.
dough [dəu] n те́сто; (*inf: money*) ба́бки* fpl.
doughnut ['dəunʌt] (*US* **donut**) n по́нчик.
dour [duə*] adj суро́вый* (суро́в).
douse [dauz] vt: **to** ~ **(with)** облива́ть (обли́ть* perf) (+instr) ♦ vt (*extinguish*) туши́ть (потуши́ть perf), гаси́ть (погаси́ть perf).
dove [dʌv] n го́лубь m.
Dover ['dəuvə*] n Ду́вр; **Straits of** ~ Па-де--Кале́ m ind.
dovetail ['dʌvteɪl] vi (*fig*) совпада́ть (совпа́сть* perf); (*schedules*) дополня́ть (допо́лнить perf) друг дру́га ♦ n (*TECH*): ~ **joint** ла́сточкин хвост*.
dowager ['dauədʒə*] n престаре́лая све́тская да́ма; **the** ~ **duchess** вдо́вствующая герцоги́ня.
dowdy ['daudɪ] adj неказ́истый* (неказ́ист).
Dow-Jones average ['dau'dʒəunz-] n (*US*) и́ндекс веду́щих монопо́лий До́у Джо́нса.
down [daun] n пух*; (*hill*) холм* ♦ adv (*motion*) вниз; (*position*) внизу́ ♦ prep (*towards lower level*) (вниз) с +gen or по +dat; (*movement along*) (вдоль) по +dat ♦ vt (*inf: drink*) прогла́тывать (проглоти́ть* perf); ~ **here** вот там; ~ **here** вот здесь; **the price of meat is** ~ цена́ на мя́со упа́ла; **I've got it** ~ **somewhere** у меня́ где́-то э́то запи́сано; **to pay £2** ~ плати́ть* (заплати́ть* perf) пе́рвый взнос £2; **England is two goals** ~ А́нглия прои́грывает на два очка́; **to** ~ **tools** (*BRIT*) прекраща́ть (прекрати́ть perf) рабо́ту; ~ **with the government!** доло́й прави́тельство!
down-and-out ['daunəndaut] n бездо́мный(-ая) m(f) adj.
down-at-heel ['daunət'hi:l] adj (*shoes etc*) сто́птанный (сто́птан); (*appearance, person*) потрёпанный* (потрёпан).
downbeat ['daunbi:t] n (*MUS*) си́льная до́ля ♦ adj небре́жный* (небре́жен).
downcast ['daunkɑ:st] adj (*person*) пода́вленный (пода́влен); (*eyes*) опу́щенный (опу́щен).
downer ['daunə*] n (*inf: drug*) успокои́тельное

nt adj; **to be on a** ~ (*depressed*) быть* (*impf*) в депре́ссии.
downfall ['daunfɔ:l] n паде́ние; (*from drinking, gambling etc*) ги́бель f.
downgrade ['daungreɪd] vt: **he was** ~**d** его́ пони́зили.
downhearted ['daun'hɑ:tɪd] adj упа́вший* ду́хом.
downhill ['daun'hɪl] n (*also:* ~ **race**: *SKIING*) скоростно́й спуск ♦ adv (*face, look*) вниз; **to go** ~ (*person*) идти́* (пойти́* perf) под го́ру; (*road*) идти́* (пойти́* perf) под укло́н; (*car*) е́хать* (пое́хать* perf) под го́ру; (*fig: person*) кати́ться (покати́ться perf) по накло́нной пло́скости; (: *business*) идти́* (пойти́* perf) под го́ру or под укло́н.
Downing Street ['daunɪŋ-] n (*BRIT: POL*) Да́унинг Стрит.
download ['daunləud] vt (*COMPUT*) загружа́ть (загрузи́ть* perf) (*в па́мять*).
down-market ['daun'mɑ:kɪt] adj (*product*) дешёвый.
down payment n пе́рвый взнос.
downplay ['daunpleɪ] vt (*US*) преуменьша́ть (преуме́ньшить perf).
downpour ['daunpɔ:'] n ли́вень* m.
downright ['daunraɪt] adj я́вный; (*refusal*) по́лный ♦ adv соверше́нно.
Downs [daunz] npl (*BRIT: GEO*): **the** ~ Да́унз (*известко́вые холмы́ на ю́ге А́нглии*).
Down's syndrome [daunz-] n синдро́м Да́уна.
downstairs ['daun'stɛəz] adv (*position*) внизу́; (*motion*) вниз.
downstream ['daunstri:m] adv вниз по тече́нию.
downtime ['dauntaɪm] n просто́й.
down-to-earth ['dauntu'ə:θ] adj (*person*) просто́й; (*solution*) практи́чный* (практи́чен).
downtown ['daun'taun] adv (*position*) в це́нтре; (*motion*) в центр ♦ adj (*US*): ~ **Chicago** центр Чика́го.
downtrodden ['dauntrɔdn] adj (*person*) заби́тый (заби́т).
down under adv (*BRIT: inf: Australia etc*) друго́й коне́ц све́та (*Австра́лия и Но́вая Зела́ндия*); **he lives** ~ ~ он живёт на друго́м конце́ све́та.
downward ['daunwəd] adj напра́вленный вниз ♦ adv вниз; **a** ~ **trend** понижа́тельная тенде́нция.
downwards ['daunwədz] adv = **downward**.
dowry ['dauri] n прида́ное nt adj.
doz. abbr = **dozen**.
doze [dəuz] vi дрема́ть* (*impf*)
▶ **doze off** vi задрема́ть* (*perf*).
dozen ['dʌzn] n дю́жина; **a** ~ **books** дю́жина книг; **80 pence a** ~ 80 пе́нсов за дю́жину; ~**s of** деся́тки +gen.
DPh n abbr (= *Doctor of Philosophy*) до́ктор

философии.
DPhil *n abbr* (= *Doctor of Philosophy*) доктор философии.
DPP *n abbr* (*BRIT:* = *Director of Public Prosecutions*) Генеральный прокурор.
DPT *n abbr* (= *diphtheria, pertussis, tetanus*) коклюшно-дифтерийно-столбнячная вакцина.
DPW *n abbr* (*US:* = *Department of Public Works*) Департамент общественного строительства.
Dr *abbr* = **doctor**.
Dr. *abbr* (*in street names*) = **Drive**.
dr *abbr* (*COMM*) = **debtor**.
drab [dræb] *adj* (*weather, building, clothes*) серый (сер), унылый (уныл).
draft [drɑːft] *n* (*first version*) черновик*, набросок*; (*POL: of bill*) проект; (*COMM*) тратта; (*US: MIL*) призыв ♦ *vt* (*plan*) составлять (составить* *perf*); (*write roughly*) писать* (написать* *perf*) начерно; *see also* **draught**.
draftsman ['drɑːftsmən] *irreg n* (*US*) = **draughtsman**.
draftsmanship ['drɑːftsmənʃɪp] *n* (*US*) = **draughtsmanship**.
drag [dræg] *vt* тащить* (*impf*); (*lake, pond*) прочёсывать (прочесать* *perf*) ♦ *vi* (*time, a concert etc*) тянуться* (*impf*) ♦ *n* (*inf: person*) обуза; (: *task*) бремя* *nt*; (*NAUT, AVIAT*) лобовое сопротивление; **in** ~ в костюме женщины (*о мужчине*)
▶ **drag away** *vt*: **to** ~ **sb away (from)** оттаскивать (оттащить* *perf*) кого-н (от +*gen*)
▶ **drag on** *vi* тянуться* (*impf*).
dragnet ['drægnɛt] *n* невод*, бредень* *m*; (*fig*) облава.
dragon ['drægn] *n* дракон.
dragonfly ['drægənflaɪ] *n* стрекоза*.
dragoon [drə'guːn] *n* драгун* ♦ *vt*: **to** ~ **sb into sth** (*BRIT*) втягивать (втянуть* *perf*) кого-н во что-н.
drain [dreɪn] *n* (*in street*) водосток, водоотвод; (*on resources, manpower*) утечка*; (*on health, energy*) расход ♦ *vt* (*land, glass etc*) осушать (осушить* *perf*); (*vegetables*) сливать (слить* *perf*) ♦ *vi* (*liquid*) стекать (стечь* *perf*); **I feel** ~**ed** я истощён; **I feel** ~**ed of emotion** у меня истощились эмоции.
drainage ['dreɪnɪdʒ] *n* (*system*) канализация; (*process*) дренаж, осушение.
drainboard ['dreɪnbɔːd] *n* (*US*) = **draining board**.
draining board ['dreɪnɪŋ-] (*US* **drainboard**) *n* сушка*.
drainpipe ['dreɪnpaɪp] *n* водосточная труба*.
drake [dreɪk] *n* селезень* *m*.
dram [dræm] *n* (*SCOTTISH: drink*) глоток* (*о*

спиртном).
drama ['drɑːmə] *n* (*also fig*) драма.
dramatic [drə'mætɪk] *adj* драматический*; (*increase etc*) резкий*; (*change*) разительный.
dramatically [drə'mætɪklɪ] *adv* драматически; (*increase, change*) резко.
dramatist ['dræmətɪst] *n* драматург.
dramatize ['dræmətaɪz] *vt* (*exaggerate*) драматизировать (*impf/perf*); (*adapt: for TV, cinema*) инсценировать (*impf/perf*).
drank [dræŋk] *pt of* **drink**.
drape [dreɪp] *vt* драпировать (задрапировать* *perf*).
drapes [dreɪps] *npl* (*US: curtains*) занавески* *fpl*.
drastic ['dræstɪk] *adj* (*measure*) решительный* (решителен); (*change*) коренной.
drastically ['dræstɪklɪ] *adv* (*change*) коренным образом; (*reduce*) резко.
draught [drɑːft] (*US* **draft**) *n* (*of air*) сквозняк*; (*NAUT*) осадка*; (*of chimney*) тяга; **on** ~ (*beer*) из бочки.
draught beer *n* бочковое пиво.
draughtboard ['drɑːftbɔːd] *n* (*BRIT*) шашечная доска*.
draughts [drɑːfts] *n* (*BRIT*) шашки* *pl*.
draughtsman ['drɑːftsmən] *irreg n* (*US* **draftsman**) *n* чертёжник(-ица).
draughtsmanship ['drɑːftsmənʃɪp] (*US* **draftsmanship**) *n* черчение; (*art*) искусство черчения.
draw [drɔː] (*pt* **drew**, *pp* **drawn**) *vt* (*ART*) рисовать (*impf*); (*TECH*) чертить* (*impf*); (*pull: cart*) тащить* (*impf*); (: *curtains*) задёргивать (задёрнуть* *perf*); (*gun, tooth*) вырывать (вырвать* *perf*); (*attention*) привлекать (привлечь* *perf*); (*crowd*) собирать (собрать* *perf*); (*money*) снимать (снять* *perf*); (*wages*) получать (получить* *perf*) ♦ *vi* (*SPORT*) играть (сыграть* *perf*) в ничью ♦ *n* (*SPORT*) ничья*; (*lottery*) лотерея; (: *of teams*) жеребьёвка*; **to** ~ **near** приближаться (приблизиться* *perf*); **to** ~ **to a close** подходить* (подойти* *perf*) к концу; **to** ~ **a conclusion** делать (сделать* *perf*) вывод; **to** ~ **a comparison between** проводить* (провести* *perf*) сравнение между +*instr*
▶ **draw back** *vi*: **to** ~ **back (from)** отпрянуть (*perf*) (от +*gen*)
▶ **draw in** *vi* (*BRIT: car*) останавливаться (остановиться* *perf*); (: *train*) подъезжать (подъехать* *perf*); (*nights*) становиться* (стать* *perf*) длиннее
▶ **draw on** *vt* использовать (*impf/perf*)
▶ **draw out** *vi* (*lengthen*) растягивать (растянуть* *perf*) ♦ *vt* (*money*) снимать (снять* *perf*)
▶ **draw up** *vi* (*train, bus etc*) подъезжать

---

* marks translations which have irregular inflections. The Russian-English side of the dictionary gives inflectional information.

(подъе́хать* *perf*) ♦ *vt* (*chair etc*) придвига́ть (придви́нуть *perf*); (*document*) составля́ть (соста́вить* *perf*).

drawback ['drɔːbæk] *n* недоста́ток*.

drawbridge ['drɔːbrɪdʒ] *n* подъёмный *or* разводно́й мост*.

drawee [drɔːˈiː] *n* трасса́т.

drawer [drɔːʳ] *n* я́щик.

drawing ['drɔːɪŋ] *n* (*picture*) рису́нок*; (*act*) рисова́ние.

drawing board *n* чертёжная доска́*; **to go back to the ~ ~** (*fig*) всё начина́ть (нача́ть* *perf*) снача́ла.

drawing pin *n* (*BRIT*) (канцеля́рская) кно́пка*.

drawing room *n* гости́ная *f adj*.

drawl [drɔːl] *n* протя́жное произноше́ние ♦ *vi* протя́гивать (протяну́ть* *perf*).

drawn [drɔːn] *pp of* **draw** ♦ *adj* изму́ченный* (изму́чен).

drawstring ['drɔːstrɪŋ] *n* шнур* (*кото́рый продёрнут во что́-нибудь*).

dread [drɛd] *n* у́жас ♦ *vt* боя́ться (*impf*) +*gen*.

dreadful ['drɛdful] *adj* ужа́сный*; **I feel ~!** я ужа́сно себя́ чу́вствую!

dream [driːm] (*pt, pp* **dreamed** *or* **dreamt**) *n* сон*; (*ambition*) мечта́ ♦ *vt*: **I must have ~t it** мне, наве́рное, э́то присни́лось ♦ *vi* ви́деть (*impf*) сон*; (*wish*) мечта́ть (*impf*); **I had a ~ about you** ты мне присни́лся; **sweet ~s!** прия́тных сновиде́ний!

▶ **dream up** *vt* выду́мывать (вы́думать *perf*).

dreamer ['driːməʳ] *n* (*fig*) мечта́тель*(ница) *m(f)*.

dreamt [drɛmt] *pt, pp of* **dream**.

dream world *n*: **to live in a ~ ~** жить* (*impf*) в приду́манном ми́ре.

dreamy ['driːmɪ] *adj* (*expression, person*) мечта́тельный* (мечта́телен); (*music*) убаю́кивающий.

dreary ['drɪərɪ] *adj* тоскли́вый (тоскли́в).

dredge [drɛdʒ] *vt* драги́ровать (*impf/perf*).

▶ **dredge up** *vt* драги́ровать (*impf/perf*); (*fig: facts*) выта́скивать (вы́тащить *perf*).

dredger ['drɛdʒəʳ] *n* (*ship*) землечерпа́лка, дра́га; (*BRIT: also:* **sugar ~**) сосу́д с ма́ленькими ды́рочками в кры́шке для са́хара.

dregs [drɛgz] *npl* муть* *fsg*; **~ of society** отбро́сы о́бщества.

drench [drɛntʃ] *vt*: **to be ~ed** мо́кнуть (промо́кнуть* *perf*); **~ed to the skin** наскво́зь промо́кший.

Dresden ['drɛzdən] *n* Дре́зден.

dress [drɛs] *n* (*frock*) пла́тье*; (*no pl: clothing*) оде́жда ♦ *vt* одева́ть (оде́ть* *perf*); (*wound*) перевя́зывать (перевяза́ть* *perf*) ♦ *vi* одева́ться (оде́ться* *perf*); **she ~es very well** она́ о́чень хорошо́ одева́ется; **to ~ a shop window** оформля́ть (офо́рмить* *perf*) витри́ну; **to get ~ed** одева́ться (оде́ться* *perf*)

▶ **dress up** *vi* наряжа́ться (наряди́ться* *perf*).

dress circle *n* (*BRIT*) бельэта́ж.

dress designer *n* модельер.

dresser ['drɛsəʳ] *n* (*BRIT*) ку́хонный шкаф*; (*US: chest of drawers*) туале́тный сто́лик; (*also:* **window ~**) оформи́тель(ница) *m(f)* витри́н.

dressing ['drɛsɪŋ] *n* (*MED*) повя́зка*; (: *process*) перевя́зка*; (*CULIN*) запра́вка*.

dressing gown *n* (*BRIT*) хала́т.

dressing room *n* (*THEAT*) артисти́ческая убо́рная *f adj*; (*SPORT*) раздева́лка*.

dressing table *n* туале́тный сто́лик.

dressmaker ['drɛsmeɪkəʳ] *n* портни́ха.

dressmaking ['drɛsmeɪkɪŋ] *n* поши́в же́нского пла́тья.

dress rehearsal *n* генера́льная репети́ция.

dressy ['drɛsɪ] *adj* (*inf*) наря́дный* (наря́ден).

drew [druː] *pt of* **draw**.

dribble ['drɪbl] *vi* (*liquid*) ка́пать (*impf*); (*baby*) пуска́ть (пусти́ть* *perf*) слю́ни; (*SPORT*) вести́* (*impf*) мяч ♦ *vt* (*ball*) вести́* (*impf*).

dried [draɪd] *adj* (*fruit*) сушёный; (*milk*) сухо́й.

drier ['draɪəʳ] *n* = **dryer**.

drift [drɪft] *n* (*of current etc*) ско́рость* *f*; (*of snow*) зано́с, сугро́б; (*meaning*) смысл ♦ *vi* (*boat*) дрейфова́ть (*impf*); **sand/snow had ~ed over the road** доро́гу занесло́ песко́м/-сне́гом; **to let things ~** пуска́ть (пусти́ть* *perf*) всё на самотёк; **to ~ apart** расходи́ться* (разойти́сь* *perf*); **I get** *or* **catch your ~** я понима́ю куда́ Вы кло́ните.

drifter ['drɪftəʳ] *n* (*person*) бродя́га *m/f*.

driftwood ['drɪftwud] *n* плавни́к.

drill [drɪl] *n* (*drill bit*) сверло́*; (*machine*) дрель *f*; (: *for mining etc*) бура́в*; (*MIL*) уче́ние ♦ *vt* (*hole*) сверли́ть (просверли́ть* *perf*); (*troops*) муштрова́ть (вы́муштровать *perf*); (*pupils*) ната́скивать (натаска́ть *perf*) ♦ *vi* (*for oil*) бури́ть (*impf*).

drilling ['drɪlɪŋ] *n* (*for oil*) буре́ние.

drilling rig *n* бурова́я устано́вка*.

drily ['draɪlɪ] *adv* = **dryly**.

drink [drɪŋk] (*pt* **drank**, *pp* **drunk**) *n* напи́ток*; (*alcoholic drink*) (спиртно́й) напи́ток*; (*sip*) глото́к* ♦ *vt* пить (вы́пить* *perf*) ♦ *vi* пить* (*impf*); **to have a ~** попи́ть* (*perf*); (*alcohol*) вы́пить* (*perf*); **a ~ of water** глото́к* воды́; (*glassful*) стака́н воды́; **would you like something to ~?** хоти́те чего́-нибудь вы́пить?; **we had ~s before lunch** мы вы́пили пе́ред обе́дом

▶ **drink in** *vt* упива́ться (*impf*) +*instr*.

drinkable ['drɪŋkəbl] *adj* (*water*) питьево́й; (*palatable: wine etc*) неплохо́й (непло́х), прия́тный* (прия́тен).

drink-driving ['drɪŋkˈdraɪvɪŋ] *n* вожде́ние в нетре́звом состоя́нии ♦ *cpd*: **they are running a ~ campaign** они́ веду́т кампа́нию про́тив води́телей, садя́щихся за руль в нетре́звом состоя́нии.

drinker ['drɪŋkəʳ] *n* (*of alcohol*) пью́щий*(-ая)

drinking ['drɪŋkɪŋ] *n* питьё*; **there was a lot of ~ at the party** на вечери́нке мно́го пи́ли.
drinking fountain *n* питьево́й фонта́нчик.
drinking water *n* питьева́я вода́*.
drip [drɪp] *n* ка́панье; (*one drip*) ка́пля*; (*MED*) ка́пельница ♦ *vi* (*water, rain*) ка́пать* (*impf*); **the tap is ~ping** кран течёт; **the washing is ~ping** с белья́ ка́пает.
drip-dry ['drɪp'draɪ] *adj*: ~ **material** ткань, кото́рой даю́т стечь по́сле сти́рки и кото́рую не гла́дят.
drip-feed ['drɪpfi:d] *vt* (*MED*) влива́ть (влить* *perf*) че́рез ка́пельницу ♦ *n*: **to be on a ~** быть* (*impf*) на ка́пельнице.
dripping ['drɪpɪŋ] *n* (*CULIN*) (то́пленый) жир ♦ *adj* (*very wet*) мо́крый (мокр); **I'm ~** с меня́ течёт; ~ **wet** соверше́нно мо́крый (мокр).
drive [draɪv] (*pt* **drove**, *pp* **driven**) *n* (*journey*) пое́здка*; (*also*: ~**way**) подъе́зд; (*energy*) напо́ристость *f*; (*campaign*) кампа́ния; (*FOOTBALL*) уда́р; (*TENNIS*) драйв; (*COMPUT*: *also*: **disk** ~) дисково́д; (*in street names*): **Rose D~** Ро́уз Драйв ♦ *vt* (*vehicle*) води́ть*/вести́* (*impf*); (*TECH*: *machine, motor, wheel*) приводи́ть (привести́* *perf*) в движе́ние; (*animal*) гнать* (*impf*); (*ball*) ударя́ть (уда́рить *perf*) (пло́ско); (*nail, stake etc*): **to ~ sth into sth** вбива́ть (вбить* *perf*) что-н во что-н ♦ *vi* (*AUT*: *at controls*) води́ть* (вести́* *perf*) (маши́ну); (*travel*) е́здить*/е́хать* (*impf*); **to go for a ~** пое́хать (*perf*) поката́ться; **the town is three hours' ~ from London** го́род в трёх часа́х езды́ от Ло́ндона; **right-/left-hand ~** (*AUT*) пра́во-/левосторо́нее управле́ние; **front-/rear-wheel ~** (*AUT*) при́вод на пере́дние/за́дние колёса; **economy ~** борьба́ за эконо́мию; **he ~s a taxi** он во́дит такси́; **to ~ at 50 km an hour** е́здить*/е́хать* (*impf*) со ско́ростью 50 км в час; **to ~ sb home/to the airport** отвози́ть* (отвезти́* *perf*) кого́-н домо́й/в аэропо́рт; **to ~ sb mad** своди́ть* (свести́* *perf*) кого́-н с ума́; **to ~ sb to sth** доводи́ть* (довести́* *perf*) кого́-н до чего́-н; **what are you driving at?** куда́ Вы кло́ните?
▸ **drive off** *vt* (*repel*) отбра́сывать (отбро́сить* *perf*)
▸ **drive out** *vt* (*force to leave*) вытесня́ть (вы́теснить *perf*); (*person, animal, evil*) выгоня́ть (вы́гнать* *perf*).
drive-by shooting ['draɪvbaɪ-] *n* стрельба́ из дви́жущегося автомоби́ля.
drive-in ['draɪvɪn] *n* (*esp US*: *restaurant*) кафе́, где мо́жно купи́ть еду́ не выходя́ из маши́ны.
drivel ['drɪvl] *n* (*inf*) чушь *f*.
driven ['drɪvn] *pp of* **drive**.
driver ['draɪvə'] *n* води́тель *m*; (*of train*)

машини́ст.
driver's license ['draɪvəz-] *n* (*US*) води́тельские права́ *nt pl*.
driveway ['draɪvweɪ] *n* подъе́зд.
driving ['draɪvɪŋ] *n* вожде́ние ♦ *adj*: ~ **rain** проливно́й дождь* *m*; ~ **snow** мете́ль *f*.
driving belt *n* приводно́й реме́нь* *m*.
driving force *n* дви́жущая си́ла.
driving instructor *n* инстру́ктор* по вожде́нию.
driving lesson *n* уро́к по вожде́нию.
driving licence *n* (*BRIT*) води́тельские права́ *ntpl*.
driving mirror *n* зе́ркало за́днего ви́да.
driving school *n* автошко́ла.
driving test *n* экза́мен по вожде́нию.
drizzle ['drɪzl] *n* моросящий дождь* *m* ♦ *vi* мороси́ть (*impf*).
droll [drəul] *adj* заба́вный.
dromedary ['drɒmədərɪ] *n* одного́рбый верблю́д.
drone [drəun] *n* (*noise*) гуде́ние; (*male bee*) тру́тень* *m* ♦ *vi* (*bee*) жужжа́ть (*impf*); (*engine etc*) гуде́ть (*impf*); (*also*: ~ **on**) бубни́ть (*impf*).
drool [dru:l] *vi*: **he is ~ing** у него́ теку́т слю́ни; **to ~ over sth/sb** (*inf*) роня́ть (*impf*) слю́ни по по́воду чего́-н/кого́-н.
droop [dru:p] *vi* (*flower, head*) поника́ть (пони́кнуть *perf*); (*shoulders*) ссуту́литься (*perf*).
drop [drɒp] *n* (*of water*) ка́пля*; (*reduction*) паде́ние; (*fall: distance*) расстоя́ние (све́рху вниз); (: *in salary*) сниже́ние; (*also*: **parachute** ~) сбра́сывание на парашю́те (*продово́льствия, боеприпа́сов*) ♦ *vt* (*allow to fall: object*) роня́ть (урони́ть* *perf*); (*eyes*) опуска́ть (опусти́ть* *perf*); (*voice, price*) понижа́ть (пони́зить* *perf*); (*set down from car*) выса́живать (вы́садить* *perf*); (*exclude*) исключа́ть (исключи́ть *perf*) ♦ *vi* па́дать (упа́сть* *perf*); (*wind*) стиха́ть (сти́хнуть* *perf*); ~**s** *npl* (*MED*) ка́пли* *fpl*; **cough** ~**s** леденцы́ от ка́шля; **there is a 30 ft ~ from the window to the ground** высота́ от окна́ до земли́ 30 фу́тов; **there's been a ~ of 10% in profits** при́быль упа́ла на 10%; **to ~ anchor** броса́ть (бро́сить* *perf*) я́корь; **to ~ sb a line** черкну́ть* (*perf*) кому́-н не́сколько стро́чек
▸ **drop in** *vi* (*inf*): **to ~ in on sb** загля́дывать (загляну́ть* *perf*) к кому́-н
▸ **drop off** *vi* (*go to sleep*) засыпа́ть (засну́ть *perf*) ♦ *vt* (*passenger*) выса́живать (вы́садить* *perf*)
▸ **drop out** *vi* (*of game, agreement*) выходи́ть* (вы́йти* *perf*); **to ~ out of college** броса́ть (бро́сить* *perf*) ко́лледж.
droplet ['drɒplɪt] *n* ка́пелька*.
drop-out ['drɒpaut] *n* (*from society*)

отщепе́нец*(-нка*); (SCOL) недоу́чка* m/f.
dropper ['drɔpə'] n пипе́тка*.
droppings ['drɔpɪŋz] npl помёт msg.
dross [drɔs] n шлак; (rubbish) му́сор.
drought [draut] n за́суха.
drove [drəuv] pt of **drive** ◆ n: ~s of people то́лпы fpl люде́й.
drown [draun] vt топи́ть* (утопи́ть* perf); (also: ~ out: sound, voice) заглуша́ть (заглуши́ть perf) ◆ vi тону́ть* (утону́ть* perf).
drowse [drauz] vi дрема́ть* (impf).
drowsy ['drauzɪ] adj со́нный.
drudge [drʌdʒ] n (person) работя́га m/f.
drudgery ['drʌdʒərɪ] n тяжёлая, ну́дная рабо́та; **housework is sheer** ~ рабо́та по до́му – тяжёлый труд.
drug [drʌg] n (MED) лека́рство; (narcotic) нарко́тик ◆ vt (person, animal) вводи́ть* (ввести́* perf) нарко́тик +dat; **to be on** ~s быть* (impf) на нарко́тиках; **hard/soft** ~s си́льные/сла́бые нарко́тики.
drug addict n наркома́н.
druggist ['drʌgɪst] n (US) апте́карь m.
drug peddler n торго́вец наркоти́ками.
drugstore ['drʌgstɔ:'] n (US) апте́ка (иногда с небольши́м кафе́)
drum [drʌm] n бараба́н; (for oil) бо́чка* ◆ vi бараба́нить (impf); ~s npl (kit) уда́рные инструме́нты mpl
▶ **drum up** vt (support) призыва́ть (призва́ть* perf).
drummer ['drʌmə'] n (with military band) бараба́нщик; (in rock group) уда́рник.
drum roll n бараба́нный бой*.
drumstick ['drʌmstɪk] n бараба́нная па́лочка*; (of chicken) но́жка*.
drunk [drʌŋk] pp of **drink** ◆ adj пья́ный* ◆ n пья́ный*(-ая) m(f) adj; (also: ~ard) пья́ница m/f; **to get** ~ напива́ться (напи́ться* perf); ~ **driving** вожде́ние в нетре́звом состоя́нии.
drunken ['drʌŋkən] adj пья́ный* (пьян); ~ **driving** вожде́ние в нетре́звом состоя́нии.
drunkenness ['drʌŋkənnɪs] n пья́нство.
dry [draɪ] adj (also fig) сухо́й* (сух); (lake, riverbed) вы́сохший; (humour) сде́ржанный* (сде́ржан); (lecture, subject) ску́чный* (ску́чен) ◆ vt (clothes, ground) суши́ть* (вы́сушить perf); (surface) вытира́ть (вы́тереть* perf) ◆ vi (paint, washing) со́хнуть (вы́сохнуть perf); **on** ~ **land** на су́ше; **to** ~ **one's hands/eyes** вытира́ть (вы́тереть* perf) ру́ки/глаза́; **to** ~ **one's hair** (with towel) вытира́ть (вы́тереть* perf) во́лосы; (with hairdryer) суши́ть* (вы́сушить perf) во́лосы; **to** ~ **the dishes** вытира́ть (вы́тереть* perf) посу́ду
▶ **dry up** vi (river, well) высыха́ть (вы́сохнуть* perf); (resources, speaker) иссяка́ть (исся́кнуть* perf).
dry clean vt чи́стить* (почи́стить* perf) (в химичи́стке).

dry cleaner n рабо́тник химчи́стки.
dry-cleaner's ['draɪ'kli:nəz] n химчи́стка*.
dry-cleaning ['draɪ'kli:nɪŋ] n хими́ческая чи́стка.
dry dock n (NAUT) сухо́й док.
dryer ['draɪə'] n (for clothes) суши́лка*.
dry goods npl (US) галантере́я fsg и тка́ни fpl.
dry ice n сухо́й лёд*.
dryly ['draɪlɪ] adv ирони́чно.
dryness ['draɪnɪs] n су́хость f.
dry rot n суха́я гниль f (боле́знь древеси́ны).
dry run n (fig: inf) холосто́й прого́н.
dry ski slope n склон с иску́сственным покры́тием.
DSc n abbr (= Doctor of Science) до́ктор естествозна́ния.
DSS n abbr (BRIT: = Department of Social Security) Министе́рство социа́льного обеспе́чения.
DST abbr (US: = Daylight Saving Time) ле́тнее вре́мя* nt.
DT n abbr (COMPUT: = data transmission) переда́ча да́нных.
DTI n abbr (BRIT: = Department of Trade and Industry) Министе́рство промы́шленности и торго́вли.
DTP n abbr = **desktop publishing**.
DT's npl abbr (inf: = delirium tremens) бе́лая горя́чка; **to have the** ~ страда́ть (impf) бе́лой горя́чкой.
dual ['djuəl] adj двойно́й; (function, number) дво́йственный.
dual carriageway n (BRIT) шоссе́ nt ind.
dual nationality n двойно́е гражда́нство.
dual-purpose ['djuəl'pə:pəs] adj двойно́го назначе́ния.
dubbed [dʌbd] adj (CINEMA) дубли́рованный (дубли́рован); (nicknamed) про́званный (про́зван).
dubious ['dju:bɪəs] adj сомни́тельный; **I'm very** ~ **about it** у меня́ серьёзные сомне́ния на э́тот счёт.
Dublin ['dʌblɪn] n Ду́блин.
Dubliner ['dʌblɪnə'] n ду́блинец*(-нка*).
duchess ['dʌtʃɪs] n герцоги́ня.
duck [dʌk] n у́тка* ◆ vi (also: ~ **down**) пригиба́ться (пригну́ться perf) ◆ vt (blow) увёртываться (уверну́ться perf) от +gen; (responsibility etc) увиля́ть (увильну́ть perf) от +gen.
duckling ['dʌklɪŋ] n утёнок*.
duct [dʌkt] n (ELEC) ка́бельный кана́л; (TECH) трубопрово́д; (ANAT) прото́к, кана́л.
dud [dʌd] adj (object, tool) бесполе́зный (беспо́лезен); (grenade) неразорва́вшийся; (BRIT: cheque) недействи́тельный ◆ n (note, coin) подде́лка*.
due [dju:] adj (expected) предполага́емый; (attention, consideration) до́лжный; (owed): **I am** ~ **£20** мне должны́ or прилага́ются £20 ◆ n: **to give sb his** (or **her**) ~ отдава́ть*

(отда́ть* *perf*) кому́-н до́лжное ♦ *adv*: ~ **north** пря́мо на се́вер; **~s** *npl* (*for club, union*) взно́сы *mpl*; (*in harbour*) порто́вые сбо́ры *mpl*; **in ~ course** в своё вре́мя; ~ **to** из-за +*gen*; **he is ~ to go** он до́лжен идти́; **the rent is ~ on the 30th** за кварти́ру должно́ быть* запла́чено 30-ого числа́; **the train is ~ at 8** по́езд до́лжен прийти́ в 8 часо́в; **she is ~ back tomorrow** она́ должна́ верну́ться за́втра; **I am ~ 6 days' leave** мне причита́ется 6 свобо́дных дней.

due date *n* срок произво́дства платежа́.
duel ['dju:əl] *n* дуэ́ль *f*; (*fig*) поеди́нок.
duet [dju:'ɛt] *n* дуэ́т.
duff [dʌf] *adj* (*BRIT*: *inf*) дрянно́й*
▶ **duff up** *vt* (*inf*) колошма́тить* (исколошма́тить* *perf*).
duffel bag ['dʌfl-] *n* су́мка-мешо́к*.
duffel coat *n* шерстяно́е пальто́ с капюшо́ном.
duffer ['dʌfə'] *n* (*inf*) тупи́ца *m/f*.
dug [dʌg] *pt, pp of* **dig**.
dugout ['dʌgaut] *n* (*canoe*) челно́к; (*shelter*) земля́нка.
duke [dju:k] *n* ге́рцог.
dull [dʌl] *adj* (*light, colour*) ту́склый* (ту́скл); (*weather, day*) се́рый* (сер); (*sound*) глухо́й* (глух); (*pain, wit*) тупо́й* (туп); (*event*) ску́чный* (ску́чен) ♦ *vt* притупля́ть (притупи́ть* *perf*).
duly ['dju:lɪ] *adv* (*properly*) до́лжным о́бразом; (*on time*) своевре́менно.
dumb [dʌm] *adj* (*mute*) немо́й*; (*inf*: *pej*: *stupid*: *person*) тупо́й*; (: *idea*) дура́цкий*; **to be struck ~** онеме́ть (*perf*).
dumbbell ['dʌmbel] *n* (*SPORT*) ганте́ль *f*.
dumbfounded [dʌm'faundɪd] *adj* ошеломлённый (ошеломлён).
dummy ['dʌmɪ] *n* (*tailor's model*) манеке́н; (*TECH*) маке́т; (*COMM*) моде́ль *f*; (*SPORT*) обма́нный приём; (*BRIT*: *for baby*) со́ска*, пусты́шка* ♦ *adj* (*bullet*) холосто́й; (*firm*) фикти́вный.
dummy run *n* испыта́тельный прого́н.
dump [dʌmp] *n* (*also*: *rubbish* ~) сва́лка*; (*inf*: *pej*: *place*) дыра́*; (*MIL*) полево́й склад ♦ *vt* (*put down*) сва́ливать (свали́ть* *perf*), выбра́сывать (вы́бросить* *perf*); (*car*) броса́ть (бро́сить* *perf*); (*COMPUT*: *data*) выгружа́ть (вы́грузить* *perf*), сбра́сывать (сбро́сить* *perf*); **to be down in the ~s** (*inf*) хандри́ть (*impf*); "**no ~ing**" "сва́лка му́сора запрещена́".
dumpling ['dʌmplɪŋ] *n* (*CULIN*) клёцка*.
dumpy ['dʌmpɪ] *adj* кря́жистый* (кря́жист).
dunce [dʌns] *n* тупи́ца *m/f*.
Dundee [dʌn'di:] *n* Данди́ *m ind*.
Dundonian [dʌn'dəunɪən] *adj* го́рода Данди́ ♦

n жи́тель(ница) *m(f)* го́рода Данди́.
dune [dju:n] *n* дю́на.
dung [dʌŋ] *n* наво́з*.
dungarees [dʌŋgə'ri:z] *npl* комбинезо́н *msg*.
dungeon ['dʌndʒən] *n* темни́ца.
dunk [dʌŋk] *vt* мака́ть (макну́ть *perf*).
Dunkirk [dʌn'kə:k] *n* Данке́рк.
duo ['dju:əu] *n* дуэ́т.
duodenal [dju:əu'di:nl] *adj* дуодена́льный; ~ **ulcer** я́зва двенадцатипёрстной кишки́.
duodenum [dju:əu'di:nəm] *n* двенадцатипёрстная кишка́.
dupe [dju:p] *n* проста́к*, простофи́ля* *m/f* ♦ *vt* надува́ть (наду́ть* *perf*).
duplex ['dju:plɛks] *n* (*US*: *also*: ~ **house**) одна́ из часте́й двухкварти́рного до́ма; (*also*: ~ **apartment**) двухэта́жная кварти́ра.
duplicate [*n, adj* 'dju:plɪkət, *vt* 'dju:plɪkeɪt] *n* (*of document, key etc*) дублика́т, ко́пия ♦ *adj* (*key, copy etc*) запасно́й ♦ *vt* копи́ровать (скопи́ровать *perf*); (*repeat*) дубли́ровать (продубли́ровать *perf*); **in ~** в двойно́м экземпля́ре.
duplicating machine ['dju:plɪkeɪtɪŋ-] *n* копирова́льная маши́на.
duplicator ['dju:plɪkeɪtə'] *n* копирова́льная маши́на.
duplicity [dju:'plɪsɪtɪ] *n* двули́чие.
Dur *abbr* (*BRIT*: *POST*) = Durham.
durability [djuərə'bɪlɪtɪ] *n* про́чность *f*.
durable ['djuərəbl] *adj* про́чный*.
duration [djuə'reɪʃən] *n* продолжи́тельность *f*.
duress [djuə'rɛs] *n*: **under** ~ под давле́нием.
Durex® ['djuərɛks] *n* (*BRIT*) ма́рка презервати́ва.
during ['djuərɪŋ] *prep* (*in the course of*) во вре́мя +*gen*, в тече́ние +*gen*; (*from beginning to end*) в тече́ние +*gen*.
Dushanbe [du:'ʃɑ:nbɪ] *n* Душанбе́ *m ind*.
dusk [dʌsk] *n* су́мерки* *pl*.
dusky ['dʌskɪ] *adj* (*light*) су́меречный*; (*room*) тёмный.
dust [dʌst] *n* пыль* *f* ♦ *vt* вытира́ть (вы́тереть* *perf*) пыль с +*gen*; (*cake etc*): **to ~ with** посыпа́ть (посы́пать* *perf*) +*instr*
▶ **dust off** *vt* (*also fig*) стря́хивать (стряхну́ть *perf*) пыль с +*gen*.
dustbin ['dʌstbɪn] *n* (*BRIT*) му́сорное ведро́*.
dustbin liner *n* целофа́новая прокла́дка для му́сорного ведра́.
duster ['dʌstə'] *n* (*cloth*) тря́пка* для пы́ли.
dust jacket *n* суперобло́жка*.
dustman ['dʌstmən] *irreg n* (*BRIT*) му́сорщик.
dustpan ['dʌstpæn] *n* сово́к* для му́сора.
dusty ['dʌstɪ] *adj* пы́льный*.
Dutch [dʌtʃ] *adj* голла́ндский* ♦ *n* (*LING*) голла́ндский* язы́к*; **the** ~ *npl* (*people*) голла́ндцы *mpl*; **they decided to go ~** (*inf*) они́ реши́ли, что ка́ждый пла́тит за себя́.

---

* marks translations which have irregular inflections. The Russian-English side of the dictionary gives inflectional information.

Dutch auction *n* "голла́ндский" аукцио́н" (*аукцио́н со сниже́нием цен, пока́ не найдётся покупа́тель*).
Dutchman ['dʌtʃmən] *irreg n* голла́ндец*.
Dutchwoman ['dʌtʃwumən] *irreg n* голла́ндка*.
dutiable ['dju:tɪəbl] *adj* (*COMM: goods*) облага́емый по́шлиной.
dutiful ['dju:tɪful] *adj* (*son, daughter*) послу́шный* (послу́шен); (*husband, wife*) поко́рный* (поко́рен); (*employee*) исполни́тельный* (исполни́телен).
duty ['dju:tɪ] *n* (*responsibility*) обя́занность *f*; (*obligation*) долг; (*tax*) по́шлина; **duties** *npl* (*functions*) обя́занности *fpl*; **to make it one's ~ to do** счита́ть (посчита́ть *perf*) свои́м до́лгом +*infin*; **to pay ~ on sth** плати́ть* (заплати́ть* *perf*) по́шлину за что-н; **on ~** на дежу́рстве; **off ~** вне слу́жбы.
duty-free ['dju:tɪ'fri:] *adj* беспо́шлинный; **~ shop** магази́н това́ров не облага́емых по́шлиной.
duty officer *n* (*MIL*) дежу́рный офице́р.
duvet ['du:veɪ] *n* (*BRIT*) пухо́вое одея́ло.
DV *abbr* (= *Deo volente*) Бог даст.
DVLA *n abbr* (*BRIT*) = *Driver and Vehicle Licensing Authority*.
DVLC *n abbr* (*BRIT*) = *Driver and Vehicle Licensing Centre*.
DVM *n abbr* (*US*: = *Doctor of Veterinary Medicine*) до́ктор ветерина́рных нау́к.
dwarf [dwɔ:f] (*pl* **dwarves**) *n* ка́рлик ♦ *vt* де́лать (сде́лать *perf*) кро́хотным.
dwarves [dwɔ:vz] *npl of* **dwarf**.
dwell [dwɛl] (*pt, pp* **dwelt**) *vi* прожива́ть

(прожи́ть* *perf*)
▶ **dwell on** *vt fus* заде́рживаться (задержа́ться* *perf*) на +*prp*.
dweller ['dwɛlə'] *n* жи́тель(ница) *m(f)*, обита́тель(ница) *m(f)*; **city ~** городско́й(-а́я) жи́тель(ница).
dwelling ['dwɛlɪŋ] *n* (*house*) жили́ще.
dwelt [dwɛlt] *pt, pp of* **dwell**.
dwindle ['dwɪndl] *vi* (*interest, attendance*) сокраща́ться (сократи́ться* *perf*).
dwindling ['dwɪndlɪŋ] *adj* (*strength, interest*) убыва́ющий; (*resources, supplies*) сокраща́ющийся.
dye [daɪ] *n* (*for hair, cloth*) краси́тель *m*, кра́ска* ♦ *vt* кра́сить* (покра́сить* *perf*).
dyestuffs ['daɪstʌfs] *npl* краси́тели *mpl*.
dying ['daɪɪŋ] *adj* умира́ющий; (*moments, words*) предсме́ртный.
dyke [daɪk] *n* (*BRIT: wall*) да́мба; (*channel*) кана́ва; (*causeway*) насы́пь *f*.
dynamic [daɪ'næmɪk] *adj* (*leader, force*) динами́чный.
dynamics [daɪ'næmɪks] *n or npl* (*TECH*) дина́мика *fsg*.
dynamite ['daɪnəmaɪt] *n* динами́т ♦ *vt* взрыва́ть (взорва́ть* *perf*) динами́том.
dynamo ['daɪnəməu] *n* (*ELEC*) дина́мо-маши́на.
dynasty ['dɪnəstɪ] *n* дина́стия.
dysentery ['dɪsntrɪ] *n* дизентери́я.
dyslexia [dɪs'lɛksɪə] *n* дисле́ксия.
dyslexic [dɪs'lɛksɪk] *adj* дислекти́ческий ♦ *n* дисле́ктик.
dyspepsia [dɪs'pɛpsɪə] *n* диспепси́я.

~ *E, e* ~

E, e [i:] *n* (*letter*) 5-ая бу́ква англи́йского
алфави́та; (*SCOL: mark*) ≈ о́чень пло́хо.
E [i:] *n* (*MUS*) ми *nt ind.*
E *abbr* (= *east*) В= восто́к ◆ *n abbr* (= *Ecstasy*)
"Экста́з" (*нарко́тик*).
E111 *n abbr* (*also:* **form ~**) спра́вка,
обеспе́чивающая медици́нскую по́мощь за
преде́лами Великобрита́нии.
ea. *abbr* = **each.**
E.A. *n abbr* (*US*) = *educational age.*
each [i:tʃ] *adj* ка́ждый ◆ *pron* (*each one*)
ка́ждый; **~ other** друг дру́га; **they hate ~
other** они́ ненави́дят друг дру́га; **they don't
talk to ~ other** они́ не разгова́ривают друг с
дру́гом; **they think about ~ other** они́
ду́мают друг о дру́ге; **they are jealous of ~
other** они́ зави́дуют дру́г дру́гу; **~ day**
ка́ждый де́нь; **they have two books ~** у
ка́ждого из них по две кни́ги; **they cost £5 ~**
они́ сто́ят £5 шту́ка *or* за шту́ку; **~ of us**
ка́ждый из нас.
eager ['i:gə^r] *adj* (*keen*) нетерпели́во
ожида́ющий; **to be ~ for** жа́ждать (*impf*) +*gen*;
he is ~ to ... он по́лон жела́ния +*infin* ....
eagerly ['i:gəlɪ] *adv* с воодушевле́нием;
(*awaited*) с нетерпе́нием.
eagle ['i:gl] *n* орёл*.
ear [ɪə^r] *n* (*ANAT*) у́хо*; (*of corn*) ко́лос*; **up to
one's ~s in debt/work/paint** по́ уши в долга́х/
в рабо́те/в кра́ске; **to give sb a thick ~** дать*
(*perf*) кому́-н в у́хо; **we'll play it by ~** (*fig*) мы
посмо́трим по ситуа́ции.
earache ['ɪəreɪk] *n* боль *f* в у́хе; **I have ~** у меня́
боли́т у́хо.
eardrum ['ɪədrʌm] *n* бараба́нная перепо́нка*.
earful ['ɪəful] *n* (*inf*): **to give sb an ~** устра́ивать
(устро́ить *perf*) разно́с кому́-н.
earl [ə:l] *n* (*BRIT*) граф.
earlier ['ə:lɪə^r] *adj* бо́лее ра́нний* ◆ *adv* ра́ньше;
I can't come any ~ я не могу́ прийти́ ра́ньше.
early ['ə:lɪ] *adv* ра́но ◆ *adj* ра́нний*; (*death,
departure*) преждевре́менный*; (*quick: reply*)
незамедли́тельный; (*Christians, settlers*)
пе́рвый; **~ in the morning** ра́но у́тром; **to
have an ~ night** ра́но ложи́ться (лечь* *perf*)
спать; **in the ~ spring, ~ in the spring** ра́нней

весно́й; **in the ~ 19th century, ~ in the 19th
century** в нача́ле 19-го ве́ка; **you need to take
the ~ train** Вам на́до е́хать* ра́нним
по́ездом; **you're ~!** Вы пришли́ ра́но!; **she's
in her ~ forties** ей немно́го за со́рок; **at your
earliest convenience** в ближа́йшее удо́бное
для Вас вре́мя.
early retirement *n*: **to take ~ ~** ра́но уходи́ть*
(уйти́* *perf*) на пе́нсию.
early warning system *n* (*MIL*) систе́ма
ра́ннего предупрежде́ния.
earmark ['ɪəmɑ:k] *vt*: **to ~ for** (*funds*)
предназнача́ть (предназна́чить *perf*) для
+*gen*.
earn [ə:n] *vt* (*salary*) зараба́тывать
(зарабо́тать *perf*); (*interest*) приноси́ть*
(принести́* *perf*); (*praise*) заслу́живать
(заслужи́ть* *perf*); **to ~ one's living**
зараба́тывать (*impf*) на жизнь; **this ~ed him
much praise, he ~ed much praise for this** э́то
принесло́ ему́ мно́го похва́л, он заслужи́л
мно́го похвала́ за э́то; **he's ~ed his rest/
reward** он заслужи́л свой о́тдых/свою́
награ́ду.
earned income [ə:nd-] *n* (*COMM*) трудово́й
дохо́д.
earnest ['ə:nɪst] *adj* (*person, manner*)
серьёзный* (серьёзен); (*wish, desire*)
и́скренний* ◆ *n* (*also:* **~ money**) зада́ток*; **in ~**
всерьёз; **work on the tunnel soon began in ~**
рабо́та по прокла́дке тунне́ля вско́ре
начала́сь всерьёз; **is he in ~ about these
proposals?** всерьёз ли он говори́т об э́тих
предложе́ниях?
earnings ['ə:nɪŋz] *npl* (*personal*) за́работок*
msg; (*of company etc*) при́быль *fsg*.
ear nose and throat specialist *n* (*MED*)
отоларинго́лог*, врач* у́хо-го́рло-нос.
earphones ['ɪəfəunz] *npl* нау́шники *mpl*.
earplugs ['ɪəplʌgz] *npl* заты́чки* *fpl* для уше́й.
earring ['ɪərɪŋ] *n* серьга́*.
earshot ['ɪəʃɔt] *n*: **within/out of ~** в преде́лах/
вне преде́лов слы́шимости.
earth [ə:θ] *n* земля́*; (*BRIT: ELEC*) заземле́ние;
(*of fox*) нора́* ◆ *vt* (*BRIT: ELEC*) заземля́ть
(заземли́ть *perf*); **E~** (*planet*) Земля́*.

---

earthenware ['ə:θnwɛə'] *n* кера́мика, гонча́рные изде́лия *pl* ♦ *adj* гли́няный.
earthly ['ə:θlɪ] *adj* земно́й; ~ **paradise** земно́й рай*; **there is no ~ reason to think** ... нет ни мале́йшей причи́ны ду́мать ....
earthquake ['ə:θkweɪk] *n* землетрясе́ние.
earthshattering ['ə:θʃætərɪŋ] *adj* (*surprising*) потряса́ющий* (потряса́ющ).
earth tremor *n* подзе́мный толчо́к*.
earthworks ['ə:θwə:ks] *npl* земляны́е рабо́ты *fpl*.
earthworm ['ə:θwə:m] *n* земляно́й червь* *m*.
earthy ['ə:θɪ] *adj* (*humour*) грубова́тый (грубова́т).
earwig ['ɪəwɪg] *n* ухове́ртка*.
ease [i:z] *n* лёгкость *f*; (*comfort*) поко́й* ♦ *vt* (*pain*) облегча́ть (облегчи́ть *perf*); (*problem*) уменьша́ть (уме́ньшить *perf*; (*tension*) ослабля́ть (осла́бить* *perf*); (*loosen: grip, belt*) отпуска́ть (отпусти́ть* *perf*) ♦ *vi* (*situation*) упроща́ться (упрости́ться* *perf*); (*pain, grief, grip*) слабе́ть (ослабе́ть *perf*); (*rain, snow*) станови́ться* (стать* *perf*) ти́ше; **to ~ sth into sth** вставля́ть (вста́вить* *perf*) что-н в что-н; **to ~ sth out of sth** выдвига́ть (вы́двинуть *perf*) что-н из чего́-н; **to ~ o.s. into** опуска́ться (опусти́ться *perf*) в +*acc*; **at ~!** (*MIL*) во́льно!; **with ~** с лёгкостью; **life of ~** жизнь в поко́е и дово́льстве
▶ **ease off** *vi* станови́ться* (стать* *perf*) ти́ше; (*slow down*) замедля́ться (заме́длиться *perf*)
▶ **ease up** *vi* = **ease off**
easel ['i:zl] *n* мольбе́рт.
easily ['i:zɪlɪ] *adv* легко́; (*in a relaxed manner*) непринуждённо; (*without doubt*) несомне́нно.
easiness ['i:zɪnɪs] *n* лёгкость *f*; (*of manner*) непринуждённость *f*.
east [i:st] *n* восто́к ♦ *adj* восто́чный ♦ *adv* на восто́к; **the E~** Восто́к.
Easter ['i:stə'] *n* па́сха ♦ *adj* пасха́льный.
Easter egg *n* (*painted*) пасха́льное яйцо́*; (*chocolate*) шокола́дное пасха́льное яйцо́*.
Easter Island *n* о́стров Па́схи.
easterly ['i:stəlɪ] *adj* восто́чный.
Easter Monday *n* ≈ све́тлый понеде́льник.
eastern ['i:stən] *adj* восто́чный; (*POL*) восто́чно-европе́йский; **E~ Europe** Восто́чная Евро́па; **the E~ bloc** (*formerly*) Восто́чно-Европе́йский блок.
Easter Sunday *n* ≈ све́тлое *or* христо́во воскресе́нье.
East Germany *n* (*formerly*) Восто́чная Герма́ния.
eastward(s) ['i:stwəd(z)] *adv* на восто́к.
easy ['i:zɪ] *adj* лёгкий*; (*manner*) непринуждённый* ♦ *adv*: **to take it** *or* **things ~** не напряга́ться (*impf*); (*not worry*) не волнова́ться (*impf*); **payment on ~ terms** (*COMM*) платёж* на лёгких усло́виях; **that's easier said than done** ле́гче сказа́ть, чем

сде́лать; **I'm ~** (*inf*) мне всё равно́.
easy chair *n* удо́бное кре́сло*.
easy-going ['i:zɪ'gəuɪŋ] *adj* с лёгким хара́ктером.
easy touch *n* (*inf*): **she is an ~~** её легко́ убеди́ть.
eat [i:t] (*pt* **ate**, *pp* **eaten**) *vt* есть* (съесть* *perf*) ♦ *vi* есть* (*impf*)
▶ **eat away** *vt* (*rock, metal*) разъеда́ть (разъе́сть* *perf*); (*savings*) съеда́ть (съесть* *perf*)
▶ **eat away at** *vt fus* = **eat away**
▶ **eat into** *vt fus* = **eat away**
▶ **eat out** *vi* (*in restaurant*) есть* (*impf*) в рестора́не
▶ **eat up** *vt* (*food*) доеда́ть (дое́сть* *perf*); **it ~s up electricity** э́то потребля́ет мно́го электроэне́ргии.
eatable ['i:təbl] *adj* съедо́бный*.
eaten ['i:tn] *pp of* **eat**.
eau de Cologne ['əudəkə'ləun] *n* одеколо́н*.
eaves [i:vz] *npl* (*of house*) карни́з *msg*.
eavesdrop ['i:vzdrɒp] *vi*: **to ~ (on)** подслу́шивать (подслу́шать *perf*).
ebb [ɛb] *n* отли́в ♦ *vi* (*tide, sea*) отлива́ть (*impf*); (*fig: also: ~ away*) угаса́ть (уга́снуть *perf*); **the ~ and flow** отли́в и прили́в; **to be at a low ~** (*fig*) находи́ться* (*impf*) в состоя́нии упа́дка.
ebb tide *n* отли́в.
ebony ['ɛbənɪ] *n* эбе́новое *or* чёрное де́рево.
ebullient [ɪ'bʌlɪənt] *adj* по́лный* (по́лон) энтузиа́зма.
EC *n abbr* (= *European Community*) ЕС = *Европе́йское соо́бщество*.
eccentric [ɪk'sɛntrɪk] *adj* (*choice, views*) эксцентри́чный* ♦ *n* эксцентри́чный челове́к.
ecclesiastic(al) [ɪkli:zɪ'æstɪk(l)] *adj* духо́вный.
ECG *n abbr* = **electrocardiogram**.
echo ['ɛkəu] (*pl* ~**es**) *n* э́хо *no pl* ♦ *vt* (*repeat*) вто́рить (*impf*) +*dat* ♦ *vi* (*sound*) отдава́ться* (*impf*); **the room ~ed with her laughter** в ко́мнате раздава́лся её смех.
éclair ['eɪkleə'] *n* экле́р.
eclipse [ɪ'klɪps] *n* затме́ние ♦ *vt* (*also fig*) затмева́ть (затми́ть* *perf*).
ECM *n abbr* (*US*: = *European Common Market*) О́бщий* ры́нок*.
eco- ['i:kəu] *prefix* э́ко-.
eco-friendly ['i:kəu'frɛndlɪ] *adj* экологи́чески безопа́сный* (безопа́сен).
ecological [i:kə'lɒdʒɪkəl] *adj* экологи́ческий*.
ecologist [ɪ'kɒlədʒɪst] *n* эко́лог.
ecology [ɪ'kɒlədʒɪ] *n* (*SCOL*) эколо́гия; (*environment*) окружа́ющая среда́.
economic [i:kə'nɒmɪk] *adj* экономи́ческий*; (*profitable*) рента́бельный* (рента́белен).
economical [i:kə'nɒmɪkl] *adj* (*cheap to run*) экономи́чный* (экономи́чен); (*thrifty*) эконо́мный*.
economically [i:kə'nɒmɪklɪ] *adv* эконо́мно;

(*regarding economics*) экономи́чески.
economics [i:kə'nɒmɪks] *n* эконо́мика ♦ *npl* (*of project, situation*) экономи́ческий* расчёт *msg*.
economic warfare *n* экономи́ческая война́.
economist [ɪ'kɒnəmɪst] *n* экономи́ст.
economize [ɪ'kɒnəmaɪz] *vi* эконо́мить* (сэконо́мить* *perf*).
economy [ɪ'kɒnəmɪ] *n* эконо́мика, хозя́йство; (*financial prudence*) эконо́мия; **economies of scale** (*COMM*) эконо́мичность за счёт кру́пных объёмов опера́ций.
economy class *n* (*AVIAT*) наибо́лее дешёвые поса́дочные места́.
economy size *n* (*COMM*) больша́я упако́вка како́го-либо това́ра, сто́ящая деше́вле, чем ма́ленькая.
ecosystem ['i:kəʊsɪstəm] *n* экосисте́ма.
ECSC *n abbr* (= *European Coal & Steel Community*) европе́йское соо́бщество производи́телей угля́ и ста́ли.
ecstasy ['ɛkstəsɪ] *n* экста́з; **to go into ecstasies over** впада́ть (впасть* *perf*) в экста́з от +*gen*; **in ecstasy** в экста́зе.
ecstatic [ɛks'tætɪk] *adj* восто́рженный*.
ECT *n abbr* = **electroconvulsive therapy**.
ECU *n abbr* (= *European Currency Unit*) экю́ *ind*.
Ecuador ['ɛkwədɔ:'] *n* Эквадо́р.
ecumenical [i:kju'mɛnɪkl] *adj* вселе́нский.
eczema ['ɛksɪmə] *n* экзе́ма.
eddy ['ɛdɪ] *n* (*of water*) водоворо́т; (*of air*) вихрь *m*.
edge [ɛdʒ] *n* край*; (*of knife etc*) остриё* ♦ *vt* (*trim*) окаймля́ть (окайми́ть* *perf*) ♦ *vi*: **to ~ forward** ме́дленно продвига́ться (продви́нуться *perf*); **on ~** (*fig*) = **edgy**; **to have the ~ on** име́ть (*impf*) преиму́щество пе́ред +*instr*; **to ~ past** протисну́ться (*perf*); **to ~ away from** отходи́ть* (отойти́* *perf*) бочко́м от +*gen*; **to ~ up** (*COMM*) незначи́тельно изменя́ться.
edgeways ['ɛdʒweɪz] *adv*: **he couldn't get a word in ~** он не мог слове́чка ввернуть *or* сло́ва вста́вить.
edging ['ɛdʒɪŋ] *n* кайма́*.
edgy ['ɛdʒɪ] *adj* (*nervous, agitated*) раздражённый*.
edible ['ɛdɪbl] *adj* съедо́бный* (съедо́бен).
edict ['i:dɪkt] *n* ука́з.
edifice ['ɛdɪfɪs] *n* вели́чественное зда́ние.
edifying ['ɛdɪfaɪŋ] *adj* поучи́тельный* (поучи́телен).
Edinburgh ['ɛdɪnbərə] *n* Эдинбу́рг.
edit ['ɛdɪt] *vt* (*text, newspaper, COMPUT*) редакти́ровать (отредакти́ровать *perf*); (*book*) гото́вить* (подгото́вить* *perf*) к печа́ти; (*film, broadcast*) монти́ровать (смонти́ровать *perf*).

edition [ɪ'dɪʃən] *n* (*of book*) изда́ние; (*of newspaper, TV programme*) вы́пуск.
editor ['ɛdɪtə'] *n* реда́ктор*; **foreign/political ~** (*PRESS*) реда́ктор* отде́ла зарубе́жных новосте́й/поли́тики.
editorial [ɛdɪ'tɔ:rɪəl] *adj* редакцио́нный ♦ *n* передови́ца, передова́я статья́*.
EDP *n abbr* (*COMPUT*) = **electronic data processing**.
EDT *abbr* (*US*) = *Eastern Daylight Time*.
educate ['ɛdjukeɪt] *vt* (*teach*) дава́ть* (дать* *perf*) образова́ние +*dat*; (*instruct*) просвеща́ть (просвети́ть* *perf*); **to be ~d at ...** получа́ть (получи́ть *perf*) образова́ние в +*prp*.
educated guess ['ɛdjukeɪtɪd-] *n* дога́дка располага́ющего предвари́тельной информа́цией.
education [ɛdju'keɪʃən] *n* (*schooling*) образова́ние; (*teaching*) обуче́ние; (*knowledge*) образо́ванность *f*; **primary or** (*US*) **elementary/secondary ~** нача́льное/ сре́днее образова́ние.
educational [ɛdju'keɪʃənl] *adj* (*institution*) уче́бный; (*staff*) преподава́тельский; (*policy, practice*) уче́бный, воспита́тельный; (*toy*) обуча́ющий; **~ system** систе́ма образова́ния; **~ technology** техни́ческие сре́дства обуче́ния.
Edwardian [ɛd'wɔ:dɪən] *adj* эпо́хи англи́йского короля́ Эдуа́рда VII.
EE *abbr* = **electrical engineer**.
EEC *n abbr* (= **European Economic Community**) ЕЭС= *Европе́йское экономи́ческое соо́бщество*.
EEG *n abbr* = **electroencephalogram**.
eel [i:l] *n* у́горь* *m*.
EENT *n abbr* (*US: MED*: = *eye, ear, nose and throat*) ≈ у́хо-го́рло-нос.
EEOC *n abbr* (*US*: = *Equal Employment Opportunity Commission*) коми́ссия ра́вных возмо́жностей при на́йме на рабо́ту.
eerie ['ɪərɪ] *adj* жу́ткий*.
EET *abbr* (= *Eastern European Time*) восточноевропе́йское вре́мя* *nt*.
efface [ɪ'feɪs] *vt* (*erase*) стира́ть (стере́ть* *perf*); **to ~ o.s.** держа́ться* (*impf*) в тени́.
effect [ɪ'fɛkt] *n* (*result*) эффе́кт, после́дствие; (*impression*) впечатле́ние, эффе́кт ♦ *vt* (*carry out*) производи́ть* (произвести́* *perf*); **~s** *npl* (*property*) иму́щество *ntsg*; (*THEAT, CINEMA*) эффе́кты *mpl*; **to take ~** (*drug*) де́йствовать (поде́йствовать *perf*); (*law*) вступа́ть (вступи́ть* *perf*) в си́лу; **to put into ~** осуществля́ть (осуществи́ть* *perf*); **to have an ~ on sb/sth** де́йствовать (поде́йствовать *perf*) на кого́-н/что-н; **in ~** в су́щности; **his letter is to the ~ that ...** суть его́ письма́ заключа́ется в том, что ....

---

* marks translations which have irregular inflections. The Russian-English side of the dictionary gives inflectional information.

effective [ɪ'fɛktɪv] *adj* (*successful*) эффекти́вный* (эффекти́вен); (*actual*) действи́тельный*; **to become ~** (*LAW*) входи́ть* (войти́* *perf*) в си́лу; **~ date** да́та вступле́ния в си́лу.

effectively [ɪ'fɛktɪvlɪ] *adv* (*successfully*) эффекти́вно; (*in reality*) факти́чески.

effectiveness [ɪ'fɛktɪvnɪs] *n* (*success*) эффекти́вность *f*.

effeminate [ɪ'fɛmɪnɪt] *adj* женоподо́бный* (женоподо́бен).

effervescent [ɛfə'vɛsnt] *adj* (*drink*) шипу́чий*.

efficacy ['ɛfɪkəsɪ] *n* эффекти́вность *f*.

efficiency [ɪ'fɪʃənsɪ] *n* (*see adj*) эффекти́вность *f*; делови́тость *f*.

efficiency apartment *n* (*US*) кварти́ра, соединя́ющая в себе́ спа́льную, гости́ную и иногда́ ку́хню.

efficient [ɪ'fɪʃənt] *adj* (*organization, method, machine*) эффекти́вный* (эффекти́вен); (*person*) делови́тый.

efficiently [ɪ'fɪʃəntlɪ] *adv* эффекти́вно.

effigy ['ɛfɪdʒɪ] *n* (*dummy*) чу́чело; (*image*) изображе́ние.

effluent ['ɛfluənt] *n* сток, жи́дкие отхо́ды *mpl*.

effort ['ɛfət] *n* (*attempt*) попы́тка*; (*exertion, concerted attempt*) уси́лие; **to make an ~ to do** прикла́дывать (приложи́ть* *perf*) уси́лия, чтобы +*infin*.

effortless ['ɛfətlɪs] *adj* (*achievement*) не тре́бующий уси́лий; (*style*) лёгкий*.

effrontery [ɪ'frʌntərɪ] *n* наха́льство, на́глость *f*; **to have the ~ to do** име́ть (*impf*) наха́льство *or* на́глость, чтобы +*infin*.

effusive [ɪ'fju:sɪv] *adj* экспанси́вный*.

EFL *n abbr* (*SCOL*) = English as a Foreign Language.

EFTA ['ɛftə] *n abbr* (= European Free Trade Association) ЕАСТ= *Европе́йская ассоциа́ция свобо́дной торго́вли.*

e.g. *adv abbr* (*for example*: = exempli gratia) наприме́р.

egalitarian [ɪgælɪ'tɛərɪən] *adj* эгалита́рный ♦ *n* (*person*) побо́рник(-ица) равнопра́вия.

egg [ɛg] *n* яйцо́; **hard-boiled/soft-boiled ~** яйцо́ вкруту́ю/всмя́тку

▶ **egg on** *vt* (*encourage*) подстрека́ть (подстрекну́ть *perf*).

egg cup *n* рю́мка* для яйца́.

eggplant ['ɛgplɑ:nt] *n* (*esp US*) баклажа́н*.

eggshell ['ɛgʃɛl] *n* яи́чная скорлупа́* ♦ *adj* (*paint*) ма́товый.

egg timer *n* та́ймер.

egg white *n* яи́чный бело́к*.

egg yolk *n* яи́чный желто́к*.

ego ['i:gəu] *n* (*self-esteem*) самолю́бие.

egoism ['ɛgəuɪzəm] *n* эгои́зм.

egoist ['ɛgəuɪst] *n* эгои́ст(ка*).

egotism ['ɛgəutɪzəm] *n* эготи́зм.

egotist ['ɛgəutɪst] *n* эготи́ст(ка*).

ego trip *n* (*pej*) самоублаже́ние.

Egypt ['i:dʒɪpt] *n* Еги́пет*.

Egyptian [ɪ'dʒɪpʃən] *adj* еги́петский* ♦ *n* египтя́нин*(-я́нка*).

eiderdown ['aɪdədaun] *n* (*quilt*) ва́тное одея́ло.

eight [eɪt] *n* во́семь*; *see also* **five**.

eighteen [eɪ'ti:n] *n* восемна́дцать*; *see also* **five**.

eighteenth [eɪ'ti:nθ] *adj* восемна́дцатый; *see also* **fifth**.

eighth [eɪtθ] *adj* восьмо́й ♦ *n* (*fraction*) восьма́я *f adj*; *see also* **fifth**.

eightieth ['eɪtɪəθ] *adj* восьмидеся́тый; *see also* **fifth**.

eighty ['eɪtɪ] *n* во́семьдесят*; *see also* **fifty**.

Eire ['ɛərə] *n* Эйре *nt ind*.

EIS *n abbr* = Educational Institute of Scotland.

either ['aɪðə*] *adj* (*one or other*) любо́й (из двух); (*both, each*) ка́ждый* ♦ *adv* та́кже ♦ *pron*: **~** (*of them*) любо́й (из них) ♦ *conj*: **~ yes or no** ли́бо "да", ли́бо "нет"; **on ~ side** на обе́их сторона́х; **I don't smoke – I don't ~** я не курю́ – я то́же; **I don't like ~** мне не нра́вится ни то, ни друго́е; **there was no sound from ~ of the flats** не бы́ло зву́ка ни из одно́й из кварти́р; **I haven't seen ~** я не ви́дел ни того́, ни друго́го.

ejaculation [ɪdʒækju'leɪʃən] *n* (*PHYSIOL*) эякуля́ция.

eject [ɪ'dʒɛkt] *vt* выбра́сывать (вы́бросить* *perf*); (*tenant*) выселя́ть (вы́селить *perf*); (*gate-crasher*) выгоня́ть (вы́гнать* *perf*) ♦ *vi* (*pilot*) катапульти́роваться (*impf/perf*).

ejector seat [ɪ'dʒɛktə-] *n* (*AVIAT*) катапульти́руемое кре́сло*.

Ekaterinburg [jɪkətɪrɪn'burk] *n* Екатеринбу́рг.

eke [i:k] *vi*: **to ~ out** растя́гивать (растяну́ть *perf*); **to ~ out a living from** существова́ть (*impf*) за счёт +*gen*.

EKG *n abbr* (*US*) = **electrocardiogram**.

el [ɛl] *n abbr* (*US*: *inf*: = elevated railroad) *надзе́мная желе́зная доро́га.*

elaborate [*adj* ɪ'læbərɪt, *vb* ɪ'læbəreɪt] *adj* сло́жный* ♦ *vt* (*expand*) развива́ть (разви́ть* *perf*); (*refine*) тща́тельно разраба́тывать (разрабо́тать *perf*) ♦ *vi*: **to ~ on** (*idea, plan etc*) рассма́тривать (рассмотре́ть* *perf*) в дета́лях.

elapse [ɪ'læps] *vi* (*time*) проходи́ть* (пройти́* *perf*).

elastic [ɪ'læstɪk] *n* (*material*) рези́нка ♦ *adj* (*stretchy*) эласти́чный* (эласти́чен); (*adaptable*) ги́бкий* (ги́бок).

elastic band *n* (*BRIT*) рези́нка*.

elasticity [ɪlæs'tɪsɪtɪ] *n* эласти́чность *f*.

elated [ɪ'leɪtɪd] *adj*: **to be ~** быть* (*impf*) в припо́днятом настрое́нии.

elation [ɪ'leɪʃən] *n* припо́днятое настрое́ние.

elbow ['ɛlbəu] *n* ло́коть* *m* ♦ *vt*: **to ~ one's way through the crowd** прота́лкиваться (*impf*) в толпе́.

elbow grease *n*: **a lot of ~ ~ is required** придётся хороше́нько потруди́ться.

elbowroom ['ɛlbəurum] *n* простóр.
elder ['ɛldə'] *adj* (*brother, sister etc*) стáрший* ◆ *n* (*tree*) бузинá; (*older person*): ~**s** стáршие *pl adj.*
elderly ['ɛldəlɪ] *adj* пожилóй; **the** ~ *npl* стáрые лю́ди *pl*, престарéлые *pl adj.*
elder statesman *irreg n* заслýженный полити́ческий* дéятель *m.*
eldest ['ɛldɪst] *adj* (*child*) (сáмый) стáрший* ◆ *n* стáрший*(-ая) *m(f) adj.*
elect [ɪ'lɛkt] *vt* избирáть (избрáть* *perf*) ◆ *adj*: **the president** ~ и́збранный президéнт; **to** ~ **to do** (*choose*) предпочитáть (предпочéсть* *perf*) +*infin.*
election [ɪ'lɛkʃən] *n* (*voting*) вы́боры *pl*; (*installation*) избрáние; **to hold an** ~ проводи́ть* (провести́* *perf*) вы́боры.
election campaign *n* избирáтельная кампáния.
electioneering [ɪlɛkʃə'nɪərɪŋ] *n* агитáция.
elector [ɪ'lɛktə'] *n* избирáтель(ница) *m(f).*
electoral [ɪ'lɛktərəl] *adj* избирáтельный.
electoral college *n* коллéгия вы́борщиков.
electorate [ɪ'lɛktərɪt] *n*: **the** ~ избирáтели *mpl.*
electric [ɪ'lɛktrɪk] *adj* электри́ческий*.
electrical [ɪ'lɛktrɪkl] *adj* электри́ческий*; ~ **failure** отключéние тóка.
electrical engineer *n* инженéр-элéктрик.
electric blanket *n* одеялó-грéлка*.
electric chair *n* (*US*) электри́ческий* стул*.
electric cooker *n* электри́ческая плитá*.
electric current *n* электри́ческий* ток.
electric fire *n* (*BRIT*) электри́ческий* ками́н.
electrician [ɪlɛk'trɪʃən] *n* электромонтёр, элéктрик.
electricity [ɪlɛk'trɪsɪtɪ] *n* электри́чество ◆ *cpd* электри́ческий*; **to switch on/off the** ~ подключáть (подключи́ть *perf*)/отключáть (отключи́ть *perf*) электри́чество; ~ **bill** счёт* за электри́чество.
electricity board *n* (*BRIT*) управлéние по электрификáции.
electric light *n* электри́ческий* свет.
electric shock *n* удáр тóком.
electrify [ɪ'lɛktrɪfaɪ] *vt* (*fence, rail network*) электрифици́ровать (*impf/perf*); (*thrill*) электризовáть (наэлектризовáть *perf*).
electro... [ɪ'lɛktrəu] *prefix* элéктро....
electrocardiogram [ɪ'lɛktrə'kɑːdɪəgræm] *n* электрокардиогрáмма.
electroconvulsive therapy [ɪ'lɛktrəkən'vʌlsɪv-] *n* электротóковая терапи́я.
electrocute [ɪ'lɛktrəkjuːt] *vt* (*person: kill*) убивáть (уби́ть* *perf*) электри́ческим тóком; (: *injure*) ударя́ть (удáрить *perf*) электри́ческим тóком.
electrode [ɪ'lɛktrəud] *n* электрóд.

electroencephalogram [ɪ'lɛktrəuɛn'sɛfələgræm] *n* электро- энцефалогрáмма.
electrolysis [ɪlɛk'trɔlɪsɪs] *n* электрóлиз.
electromagnetic [ɪ'lɛktrəmæg'nɛtɪk] *adj* электромагни́тный.
electron [ɪ'lɛktrɔn] *n* электрóн.
electronic [ɪlɛk'trɔnɪk] *adj* электрóнный.
electronic data processing *n* электрóнная обрабóтка информáции.
electronic mail *n* (*COMPUT*) электрóнная пóчта.
electronics [ɪlɛk'trɔnɪks] *n* электрóника.
electron microscope *n* электрóнный микроскóп.
electroplated [ɪ'lɛktrə'pleɪtɪd] *adj* покры́тый метáллом с пóмощью электрóлиза.
electrotherapy [ɪ'lɛktrə'θɛrəpɪ] *n* электро- терапи́я.
elegance ['ɛlɪgəns] *n* элегáнтность *f.*
elegant ['ɛlɪgənt] *adj* элегáнтный* (элегáнтен).
element ['ɛlɪmənt] *n* (*also CHEM*) элемéнт; (*of heater, kettle etc*) электронагревáтельный элемéнт; **the** ~**s** *npl* стихи́я *fsg*; **you are in your** ~ Вы в своéй стихи́и.
elementary [ɛlɪ'mɛntərɪ] *adj* элементáрный* (элементáрен); (*school, education*) начáльный.
elephant ['ɛlɪfənt] *n* слон*(и́ха).
elevate ['ɛlɪveɪt] *vt* (*in rank*) повышáть (повы́сить* *perf*); (*in importance*) возводи́ть* (возвести́* *perf*); (*physically*) поднимáть (подня́ть* *perf*).
elevated railroad ['ɛlɪveɪtɪd-] *n* (*US*) надзéмная желéзная дорóга.
elevation [ɛlɪ'veɪʃən] *n* (*see vb*) повышéние; возведéние; подня́тие; (*height*) высотá*; (*ARCHIT*) фасáд.
elevator ['ɛlɪveɪtə'] *n* (*US*) лифт; (*in warehouse etc*) грузоподъёмник.
eleven [ɪ'lɛvn] *n* оди́ннадцать*; *see also* **five.**
elevenses [ɪ'lɛvnzɪz] *npl* (*BRIT*) лёгкий зáвтрак óколо оди́ннадцати часóв утрá.
eleventh [ɪ'lɛvnθ] *adj* оди́ннадцатый; **at the** ~ **hour** в послéднюю мину́ту; *see also* **fifth.**
elf [ɛlf] (*pl* **elves**) *n* эльф.
elicit [ɪ'lɪsɪt] *vt*: **to** ~ (**from**) (*information*) извлекáть (извлéчь* *perf*) (из +*gen*); (*response, reaction*) вызывáть (вы́звать* *perf*) (от +*gen*); **to** ~ **a reply** добивáться (доби́ться* *perf*) отвéта; **to** ~ **applause from the audience** вызывáть (вы́звать* *perf*) аплодисмéнты аудитóрии.
eligible ['ɛlɪdʒəbl] *adj* (*for marriage*) подходя́щий*; **to be** ~ **for sth** (*qualified, suitable*) быть* (*impf*) подходя́щей кандидатýрой для чего-н; **to be** ~ **for a pension** имéть (*impf*) прáво на пéнсию.

---

* marks translations which have irregular inflections. The Russian-English side of the dictionary gives inflectional information.

eliminate [ɪ'lɪmɪneɪt] *vt* ликвиди́ровать (*impf/ perf*), исключа́ть (исключи́ть *perf*); (*candidate, team, contestant*) отсе́ивать (отсе́ять *perf*); **they were ~d in the first round** они́ бы́ли отсе́яны на пе́рвом ту́ре.

elimination [ɪlɪmɪ'neɪʃən] *n* ликвида́ция, исключе́ние; (*of team, candidate*) устране́ние; **by process of ~** путём исключе́ния *or* ликвида́ции.

élite [eɪ'li:t] *n* эли́та.

élitist [eɪ'li:tɪst] *adj* (*pej*) элита́рный.

elixir [ɪ'lɪksə'] *n* эликси́р.

Elizabethan [ɪlɪzə'bi:θən] *adj* (*house, music, period*) эпо́хи короле́вы Елизаве́ты.

ellipse [ɪ'lɪps] *n* (*MATH*) э́ллипс.

elliptical [ɪ'lɪptɪkl] *adj* (*MATH*) эллипти́ческий.

elm [ɛlm] *n* вяз.

elocution [ɛlə'kju:ʃən] *n* ора́торское иску́сство.

elongated ['i:lɒŋgeɪtɪd] *adj* удлинённый* (удлинён).

elope [ɪ'ləʊp] *vi*: **to ~ (with)** та́йно сбежа́ть* (*impf*) (с +*instr*).

elopement [ɪ'ləʊpmənt] *n* та́йное бе́гство.

eloquence ['ɛləkwəns] *n* (*see adj*) красноре́чие; я́ркость *f*.

eloquent ['ɛləkwənt] *adj* (*description, person*) красноречи́вый; (*speech*) я́ркий*.

El Salvador [ɛl'sælvədɔ:'] *n* Сальвадо́р.

else [ɛls] *adv* (*other*) ещё; **nothing ~** бо́льше ничего́; **somewhere ~** (*be*) где-нибудь ещё; (*go*) куда́-нибудь ещё; (*come from*) отку́да-то ещё; **everywhere ~** везде́; **where ~?** (*position*) где ещё?; (*motion*) куда́ ещё?; **is there anything ~ I can do to help?** я могу́ чём-нибудь ещё помо́чь?; **there was little ~ to do** ма́ло, что мо́жно бы́ло де́лать; **everyone ~** все остальны́е; **nobody ~ spoke** бо́льше никто́ не выступа́л; **or ~ ...** не то (бу́дет ху́же) ....

elsewhere [ɛls'wɛə'] *adv* (*be*) где́-нибудь ещё (*в друго́м ме́сте*); (*go*) куда́-нибудь ещё (*в друго́е ме́сто*).

ELT *n abbr* (*SCOL*) = *English Language Teaching*.

elucidate [ɪ'lu:sɪdeɪt] *vt* разъясня́ть (разъясни́ть *perf*).

elude [ɪ'lu:d] *vt* (*captor, capture*) ускольза́ть (ускользну́ть *perf*) от +*gen*; (*subj: fact, idea*): **to ~ sb** не приходи́ть (*impf*) кому́-н на ум.

elusive [ɪ'lu:sɪv] *adj* (*person, animal*) неулови́мый; (*quality*) не поддаю́щийся описа́нию; **he's very ~** он о́чень за́мкнутый.

elves [ɛlvz] *npl of* **elf**.

emaciated [ɪ'meɪsɪeɪtɪd] *adj* (*person, animal*) истощённый*.

E-mail *n abbr* (= *electronic mail*) электро́нная по́чта.

emanate ['ɛməneɪt] *vi*: **to ~ from** исходи́ть (*impf*) от +*gen*.

emancipate [ɪ'mænsɪpeɪt] *vt* освобожда́ть (освободи́ть* *perf*), эмансипи́ровать (*impf/ perf*).

emancipation [ɪmænsɪ'peɪʃən] *n* освобожде́ние, эмансипа́ция.

emasculate [ɪ'mæskjuleɪt] *vt* (*weaken*) ослабля́ть (осла́бить* *perf*).

embalm [ɪm'ba:m] *vt* бальзами́ровать (забальзами́ровать *perf*).

embankment [ɪm'bæŋkmənt] *n* (*of road, railway*) на́сыпь *f*; (*of river*) на́бережная *f adj*.

embargo [ɪm'ba:gəʊ] (*pl* **~es**) *n* эмба́рго *nt ind* ◆ *vt* запреща́ть (запрети́ть* *perf*); **to put** *or* **impose** *or* **place an ~ on sth** накла́дывать (наложи́ть* *perf*) эмба́рго на что-н; **to lift an ~ from** снима́ть (снять* *perf*) эмба́рго с +*gen*.

embark [ɪm'ba:k] *vi*: **to ~ (on)** (*ship*) грузи́ться* (погрузи́ться* *perf*) (на +*acc*); **to ~ on** (*journey*) отправля́ться (отпра́виться* *perf*) в +*acc*; (*task, course of action*) предпринима́ть (предприня́ть* *perf*).

embarkation [ɛmba:'keɪʃən] *n* (*of people*) поса́дка; (*of cargo*) погру́зка.

embarkation card *n* поса́дочный тало́н.

embarrass [ɪm'bærəs] *vt* смуща́ть (смути́ть* *perf*); (*politician, government*) затрудня́ть (затрудни́ть *perf*).

embarrassed [ɪm'bærəst] *adj* (*laugh, silence*) смущённый*; **to be ~** смуща́ться (смути́ться* *perf*).

embarrassing [ɪm'bærəsɪŋ] *adj* вызыва́ющий* смуще́ние, щекотли́вый.

embarrassment [ɪm'bærəsmənt] *n* (*feeling*) смуще́ние; (*problem*) стыд*.

embassy ['ɛmbəsɪ] *n* посо́льство; **the French E~** Францу́зское посо́льство, посо́льство Фра́нции.

embedded [ɪm'bɛdɪd] *adj* (*object*) заде́ланный; (*attitude, belief*) устоя́вшийся.

embellish [ɪm'bɛlɪʃ] *vt* (*story*) приукра́шивать (приукра́сить* *perf*); (*place, dress*): **~ed with** укра́шенный +*instr*.

embers ['ɛmbəz] *npl* тле́ющие уголька́ *mpl*.

embezzle [ɪm'bɛzl] *vt* присва́ивать (присво́ить *perf*).

embezzlement [ɪm'bɛzlmənt] *n* растра́та.

embezzler [ɪm'bɛzlə'] *n* растра́тчик(-ица).

embitter [ɪm'bɪtə'] *vt* (*fig*) озлобля́ть (озло́бить* *perf*).

embittered [ɪm'bɪtəd] *adj* (*person*) озло́бленный*.

emblem ['ɛmbləm] *n* эмбле́ма.

embodiment [ɪm'bɒdɪmənt] *n*: **she is the ~ of** она́ – воплоще́ние +*gen*.

embody [ɪm'bɒdɪ] *vt* (*incarnate*) воплоща́ть (воплоти́ть* *perf*); (*include, contain*) содержа́ть (*impf*) (в себе́).

embolden [ɪm'bəʊldn] *vt* ободря́ть (ободри́ть *perf*).

embolism ['ɛmbəlɪzəm] *n* эмболи́я.

embossed [ɪm'bɒst] *adj* (*design, word*) релье́фный*; **~ with his initials** с релье́фными инициа́лами.

embrace [ɪm'breɪs] *vt* обнима́ть (обня́ть* *perf*);
(*include*) охва́тывать (охвати́ть* *perf*) ♦ *vi*
обнима́ться (*impf*) ♦ *n* объя́тие.

embroider [ɪm'brɔɪdə'] *vt* (*cloth*) вышива́ть
(вы́шить* *perf*); (*fig: story*) приукра́шивать
(приукра́сить* *perf*).

embroidery [ɪm'brɔɪdərɪ] *n* (*stitching*)
вы́шивка; (*activity*) вышива́ние.

embroil [ɪm'brɔɪl] *vt*: **to become ~ed (in sth)**
ока́зываться (оказа́ться* *perf*)
вовлечённым(-ой) (во что-н).

embryo ['ɛmbrɪəu] *n* (*BIO*) эмбрио́н; (*fig*)
заро́дыш.

emend [ɪ'mɛnd] *vt* (*text*) исправля́ть
(испра́вить* *perf*).

emerald ['ɛmərəld] *n* изумру́д.

emerge [ɪ'mə:dʒ] *vi* (*fact*) всплыва́ть (всплыть*
perf); (*new industry, society*) появля́ться
(появи́ться* *perf*); **to ~ from** (*from room,
imprisonment*) выходи́ть* (вы́йти* *perf*) из
+*gen*; (*from sleep*) пробужда́ться
(пробуди́ться* *perf*) от +*gen*; **it ~s that** (*BRIT*)
вы́яснилось, что.

emergence [ɪ'mə:dʒəns] *n* (*of new idea etc*)
появле́ние.

emergency [ɪ'mə:dʒənsɪ] *n* (*crisis*) кра́йняя
необходи́мость *f* ♦ *cpd*: **~ repair** сро́чный
ремо́нт; **in an ~** в слу́чае опа́сности; **state of
~** чрезвыча́йное положе́ние; **~ talks**
экстренные перегово́ры.

emergency cord *n* (*US*) ≈ стоп-кра́н.

emergency exit *n* запа́сный вы́ход.

emergency landing *n* (*AVIAT*) вы́нужденная
поса́дка.

emergency lane *n* (*US: AUT*) авари́йная
полоса́*.

emergency road service *n* (*US*) авари́йная
доро́жная слу́жба.

emergency services *npl*: **the ~ ~** авари́йная
слу́жба *fsg*.

emergency stop *n* (*BRIT: AUT*) внеза́пная
остано́вка (*в крити́ческой ситуа́ции*).

emergent [ɪ'mə:dʒənt] *adj* (*nation, group*)
получи́вший незави́симость,
образова́вшийся; **an ~ industrial class**
заяви́вший о себе́ промы́шленный класс.

emeritus [ɪ'mɛrɪtəs] *adj*: **professor ~**
заслу́женный профе́ссор в отста́вке.

emery board ['ɛmərɪ-] *n* па́лочка для ногте́й
(*покры́тая кору́ндом*).

emery paper *n* нажда́чная бума́га.

emetic [ɪ'mɛtɪk] *n* (*MED*) рво́тное *nt adj*.

emigrant ['ɛmɪɡrənt] *n* эмигра́нт(ка*).

emigrate ['ɛmɪɡreɪt] *vi* эмигри́ровать (*impf/
perf*).

emigration [ɛmɪ'ɡreɪʃən] *n* эмигра́ция.

émigré ['ɛmɪɡreɪ] *n* полити́ческий*
эмигра́нт(ка).

eminence ['ɛmɪnəns] *n* (*importance*)
знамени́тость *f*.

eminent ['ɛmɪnənt] *adj* (*scientist, writer*)
знамени́тый (знамени́т).

eminently ['ɛmɪnəntlɪ] *adv* (*practical etc*)
весьма́.

emirate ['ɛmɪrɪt] *n* эмира́т.

emission [ɪ'mɪʃən] *n* (*of gas, heat*) выделе́ние *nt
no pl*; (*of light, radiation*) излуче́ние.

emit [ɪ'mɪt] *vt* (*smoke, smell*) испуска́ть
(испусти́ть* *perf*); (*sound*) издава́ть* (изда́ть*
perf); (*light, heat*) излуча́ть (*impf*).

emolument [ɪ'mɔljumənt] *n* (*usu pl*) дохо́д;
(*fee*) вознагражде́ние; (*salary*) жа́лованье*.

emotion [ɪ'məuʃən] *n* чу́вство; (*as opposed to
reason*) эмо́ция.

emotional [ɪ'məuʃənl] *adj* эмоциона́льный*
(эмоциона́лен); (*issue*) волну́ющий.

emotionally [ɪ'məuʃnəlɪ] *adv* (*behave, speak*)
эмоциона́льно; **~ disturbed** эмоциона́льно
неуравнове́шенный*.

emotive [ɪ'məutɪv] *adj* (*subject, language*)
вызыва́ющий эмо́ции; (*person, manner*)
волну́ющий; **~ power** эмоциона́льная си́ла.

empathy ['ɛmpəθɪ] *n* сочу́вствие; **to feel ~ with
sb** сочу́вствовать (*impf*) кому́-н.

emperor ['ɛmpərə'] *n* импера́тор.

emphases ['ɛmfəsi:z] *npl of* **emphasis**.

emphasis ['ɛmfəsɪs] (*pl* **emphases**) *n* значе́ние;
(*in speaking*) ударе́ние, акце́нт; **to lay** *or* **place
~ on sth** (*fig*) подчёркивать (подчеркну́ть*
perf) что-н; **the ~ is on reading** наибо́льшее
значе́ние придаётся чте́нию.

emphasize ['ɛmfəsaɪz] *vt* подчёркивать
(подчеркну́ть* *perf*); **I must ~ that ...** я до́лжен
подчеркну́ть, что ....

emphatic [ɛm'fætɪk] *adj* (*statement, denial*)
убеди́тельный* (убеди́телен); (*person,
manner*) насто́йчиво убежа́ющий; **to be ~
about sth** насто́йчиво убежда́ть (*impf*) в
чем-н.

emphatically [ɛm'fætɪklɪ] *adv* насто́йчиво;
(*certainly*) убеди́тельно.

emphysema [ɛmfɪ'si:mə] *n* эмфизе́ма.

empire ['ɛmpaɪə'] *n* (*also fig*) импе́рия.

empirical [ɛm'pɪrɪkl] *adj* (*knowledge, study*)
эмпири́ческий.

employ [ɪm'plɔɪ] *vt* (*workforce, person*)
нанима́ть (наня́ть* *perf*), трудоустра́ивать
(трудоустро́ить* *perf*), дава́ть* (дать* *perf*)
рабо́ту +*dat*; (*tool, weapon*) применя́ть
(примени́ть* *perf*); **he's ~ed in a bank** он
рабо́тает в ба́нке.

employee [ɪmplɔɪ'i:] *n* рабо́тник.

employer [ɪm'plɔɪə'] *n* работода́тель *m*.

employment [ɪm'plɔɪmənt] *n* рабо́та; **to find ~**
трудоустра́иваться (трудоустро́иться *perf*);
without ~ без рабо́ты; **place of ~** ме́сто

---

* marks translations which have irregular inflections. The Russian-English side of the dictionary gives inflectional information.

работы.
employment agency n бюро́ nt ind по трудоустро́йству.
employment exchange n (BRIT: formerly) би́ржа труда́.
empower [ɪm'pauə'] vt: **to ~ sb to do** уполномо́чивать (уполномо́чить perf) кого́-н +infin.
empress ['ɛmprɪs] n императри́ца.
empties ['ɛmptɪz] npl (bottles) та́ра fsg.
emptiness ['ɛmptɪnɪs] n пустота́.
empty ['ɛmptɪ] adj (also fig) пусто́й* ♦ vt (container) опорожня́ть (опорожни́ть perf); (place, house etc) опустоша́ть (опустоши́ть perf) ♦ vi (house, container) пусте́ть (опусте́ть perf); (liquid) вытека́ть (вы́течь* perf); **on an ~ stomach** на пусто́й желу́док; **to ~ into** (river) впада́ть (impf) в +acc.
empty-handed ['ɛmptɪ'hændɪd] adj с пусты́ми рука́ми; **he returned ~** он верну́лся с пусты́ми рука́ми.
empty-headed ['ɛmptɪ'hɛdɪd] adj (person) пустоголо́вый.
EMS n abbr (= European Monetary System) ЕВС= Европе́йская валю́тная систе́ма.
EMT n abbr = emergency medical technician.
EMU n abbr = economic and monetary union.
emu ['iːmjuː] n стра́ус э́му m ind.
emulate ['ɛmjuleɪt] vt (hero, idol) подража́ть (impf) +dat.
emulsion [ɪ'mʌlʃən] n (liquid) эму́льсия; (also: ~ paint) эму́льсия, эмульсио́нная кра́ска*.
enable [ɪ'neɪbl] vt (make possible) спосо́бствовать (impf) +dat; **to ~ sb to do** (permit, allow) дава́ть* (дать* perf) возмо́жность кому́-н +infin.
enact [ɪ'nækt] vt (law) вводи́ть* (ввести́* perf); (play) ста́вить* (поста́вить* perf); (role) игра́ть (сыгра́ть perf).
enamel [ɪ'næməl] n эма́ль f; (also: ~ paint) эма́ль, эма́левая кра́ска*.
enamoured [ɪ'næməd] (US enamored) adj: **to be ~ of** (pastime, idea, belief) пита́ть (impf) сла́бость к +dat.
encampment [ɪn'kæmpmənt] n ла́герная стоя́нка.
encased [ɪn'keɪst] adj: **~ in** (in plaster, armour) зако́ванный в +acc; (in shell) заключённый в +acc.
encash [ɪn'kæʃ] vt инкасси́ровать perf.
enchant [ɪn'tʃɑːnt] vt (delight) очаро́вывать (очарова́ть perf).
enchanted [ɪn'tʃɑːntɪd] adj (under a spell) заколдо́ванный, зачаро́ванный.
enchanting [ɪn'tʃɑːntɪŋ] adj обворожи́тельный* (обворожи́телен).
encircle [ɪn'səːkl] vt (place, prisoner) окружа́ть (окружи́ть perf).
encl. abbr (on letters etc: = enclosed, enclosure) приложе́ние.
enclave ['ɛnkleɪv] n: **an ~ of** анкла́в +gen,

о́стров +gen.
enclose [ɪn'kləuz] vt (land, space) огора́живать (огороди́ть* perf); (object) заключа́ть (заключи́ть perf); (letter etc): **to ~ (with)** прилага́ть (приложи́ть perf) (к +dat); **please find ~d a cheque for £100** здесь прилага́ется чек на £100.
enclosure [ɪn'kləuʒə'] n (area of land) огоро́женное ме́сто*; (in letter etc) приложе́ние.
encoder [ɪn'kəudə'] n (COMPUT) коди́рующее устро́йство, ко́дер.
encompass [ɪn'kʌmpəs] vt (include) охва́тывать (охвати́ть* perf).
encore [ɔŋ'kɔː'] excl бис ♦ n: **as an ~** на "бис".
encounter [ɪn'kauntə'] n встре́ча; (problem) столкнове́ние ♦ vt (person) встре́титься (perf) с +instr; (new experience, problem) ста́лкиваться (столкну́ться perf) с +instr.
encourage [ɪn'kʌrɪdʒ] vt поощря́ть (поощри́ть perf); (growth) спосо́бствовать (impf) +dat; **to ~ sb to do** убежда́ть (impf) кого́-н +infin.
encouragement [ɪn'kʌrɪdʒmənt] n (see vt) поощре́ние; подде́ржка.
encouraging [ɪn'kʌrɪdʒɪŋ] adj (situation, meeting, news) обнадёживающий.
encroach [ɪn'krəutʃ] vi: **to ~ (up)on** (rights, property, time) покуша́ться (покуси́ться* perf) or посяга́ть (посягну́ть perf) на +acc.
encrusted [ɪn'krʌstɪd] adj: **~ with** покры́тый +instr.
encumber [ɪn'kʌmbə'] vt: **~ed with** (suitcase, baggage etc) загромождённый (загромождён) +instr; (debts) обременённый (обременён) +instr.
encyclop(a)edia [ɛnsaɪkləu'piːdɪə] n энциклопе́дия.
end [ɛnd] n коне́ц*; (of town) часть f; (aim) цель f ♦ vt (also: **bring to an ~, put an ~ to**) зака́нчивать (зако́нчить perf), прекраща́ть (прекрати́ть* perf) ♦ vi (situation, activity, period etc) конча́ться (ко́нчиться perf); **from ~ to ~** с нача́ла до конца́; **to come to an ~** подходи́ть* (подойти́* perf) к концу́, конча́ться (ко́нчиться perf); **to be at an ~** зака́нчиваться (зако́нчиться perf); **in the ~** в конце́ концо́в; **on ~** (object) стойма́; **to stand on ~** (hair) стоя́ть (стать* perf) ды́бом; **for hours on ~** часа́ми; **for 5 hours on ~** 5 часо́в подря́д; **at the ~ of the street** в конце́ у́лицы; **at the ~ of the day** (BRIT: fig) в конце́ концо́в; **to this ~, with this ~ in view** с э́той це́лью
▶ **end up** vi: **to ~ up in** (place) конча́ть (ко́нчить perf) в +prp; **we ~ed up taking a taxi** мы ко́нчили тем, что взя́ли такси́.
endanger [ɪn'deɪndʒə'] vt подверга́ть (подве́ргнуть* perf) опа́сности; **an ~ed species** вымира́ющий вид.
endear [ɪn'dɪə'] vt: **to ~ o.s. to sb** внуша́ть (внуши́ть perf) кому́-н симпа́тию к себе́.
endearing [ɪn'dɪərɪŋ] adj (personality, conduct)

покоря́ющий.

endearment [ɪn'dɪəmənt] n: **to whisper ~s**
шепта́ть* (impf) ла́сковые слова́; **term of ~**
ла́сковое обраще́ние.

endeavour [ɪn'dɛvə'] (US **endeavor**) n (attempt)
попы́тка*; (effort) стара́ние ♦ vi: **to ~ to do**
(attempt) стара́ться (постара́ться perf) +infin;
(strive) стреми́ться* (impf) +infin.

endemic [ɛn'dɛmɪk] adj эндеми́ческий.

ending ['ɛndɪŋ] n (of book, play etc) коне́ц*;
(LING) оконча́ние.

endive ['ɛndaɪv] n (curly) энди́вый сала́т;
(chicory) цико́рный сала́т.

endless ['ɛndlɪs] adj бесконе́чный*
(бесконе́чен); (forest, beach) бескра́йний;
(patience, resources) беспреде́льный*
(беспреде́лен); (possibilities)
неограни́ченный* (неограни́чен).

endorse [ɪn'dɔ:s] vt (cheque, document)
распи́сываться (расписа́ться* perf) на +prp;
(approve: proposal, candidate) подде́рживать
(поддержа́ть* perf).

endorsee [ɪndɔ:'si:] n индосса́т.

endorsement [ɪn'dɔ:smənt] n (approval)
индоссаме́нт; (BRIT: on driving licence)
отме́тка*.

endorser [ɪn'dɔ:sə'] n индосса́нт.

endow [ɪn'dau] vt (provide with money)
обеспе́чивать (обеспе́чить perf); **~ed with**
(talent, quality) наделён (наделён) +instr.

endowment [ɪn'daumənt] n (money)
поже́ртвование (для обеспече́ния
ежего́дным дохо́дом); (quality) спосо́бности
fpl.

endowment mortgage n ипоте́чная ссу́да в
сочета́нии со страхова́нием жи́зни.

endowment policy n по́лис, включа́ющий
страхова́ние жи́зни.

end product n (INDUSTRY) коне́чный проду́кт;
(fig) результа́т.

end result n коне́чный результа́т.

endurable [ɪn'djuərəbl] adj терпи́мый.

endurance [ɪn'djuərəns] n вы́носливость f.

endurance test n испыта́ние на про́чность.

endure [ɪn'djuə'] vt (bear) переноси́ть*
(перенести́* perf) ♦ vi (last) выде́рживать
(вы́держать perf) (испыта́ние вре́менем).

enduring [ɪn'djuərɪŋ] adj (lasting) про́чный*
(про́чен).

end user n (COMPUT) коне́чный по́льзователь
m.

enema ['ɛnɪmə] n (MED) кли́зма.

enemy ['ɛnɪmɪ] adj (forces, strategy)
неприя́тельский, вра́жеский ♦ n враг*;
(opponent) проти́вник; (MIL) враг*,
неприя́тель m; **to make an ~ of sb** нажива́ть
(нажи́ть* perf) врага́ в ком-н.

energetic [ɛnə'dʒɛtɪk] adj энерги́чный*

(энерги́чен).

energy ['ɛnədʒɪ] n эне́ргия; **Department of E~**
Управле́ние по энергоснабже́нию.

energy crisis n энергети́ческий кри́зис.

energy-saving ['ɛnədʒɪ'seɪvɪŋ] adj (device)
сокраща́ющий расхо́д эне́ргии; **~ policy**
поли́тика эконо́мии эне́ргии.

enervating ['ɛnəveɪtɪŋ] adj обесси́ливающий,
отнима́ющий си́лы.

enforce [ɪn'fɔ:s] vt (law) следи́ть* (impf) за
соблюде́нием +gen.

enforced [ɪn'fɔ:st] adj (inactivity,
unemployment) вы́нужденный.

enfranchise [ɪn'fræntʃaɪz] vt предоставля́ть
(предоста́вить perf) избира́тельные права́
+dat.

engage [ɪn'geɪdʒ] vt (attention, interest)
привлека́ть (привле́чь* perf); (employ)
нанима́ть (наня́ть* perf); (AUT: clutch)
зацепля́ть (зацепи́ть* perf); (MIL: enemy)
вступа́ть (вступи́ть* perf) в бой с +instr ♦ vi
(TECH) входи́ть* (войти́* perf) в зацепле́ние;
to ~ in занима́ться (заня́ться* perf) +instr; **to
~ sb in conversation** вовлека́ть (вовле́чь*
perf) кого́-н в разгово́р.

engaged [ɪn'geɪdʒd] adj обручённый
(обручён); (BRIT: busy) за́нят; **~ to** обручён с
+instr; **to get ~** обручи́ться (perf); **he is ~ in
research** он занима́ется иссле́дованием.

engaged tone n (BRIT: TEL) гудки́ pl "за́нято".

engagement [ɪn'geɪdʒmənt] n (appointment)
договорённость f; (hiring) контра́кт; (to
marry) обруче́ние; (MIL) бой*; **I have a
previous ~** у меня́ уже́ есть договорённость.

engagement ring n обруча́льное кольцо́*.

engaging [ɪn'geɪdʒɪŋ] adj привлека́тельный*
(привлека́телен).

engender [ɪn'dʒɛndə'] vt порожда́ть
(породи́ть* perf).

engine ['ɛndʒɪn] n (AUT) дви́гатель m, мото́р;
(RAIL) локомоти́в.

engine driver n (BRIT) машини́ст.

engineer [ɛndʒɪ'nɪə'] n (designer) инжене́р; (for
repairs, also NAUT) меха́ник; (US: RAIL)
машини́ст; **civil ~** инжене́р-строи́тель m;
mechanical ~ инжене́р-меха́ник.

engineering [ɛndʒɪ'nɪərɪŋ] n (science)
инжене́рное де́ло; (design) техни́ческий*
диза́йн; (construction: of roads, ships)
строи́тельство; (of cars, machines)
произво́дство ♦ cpd: **~ works** or **factory**
машинострои́тельный заво́д.

engine failure n отка́з дви́гателя.

engine trouble n неиспра́вность f дви́гателя.

England ['ɪŋglənd] n А́нглия.

English ['ɪŋglɪʃ] adj англи́йский* ♦ n (LING)
англи́йский* язы́к; **the ~** npl (people)
англича́не mpl; **an ~ speaker**

англоговоря́щий(-ая) *m(f) adj.*

English Channel *n*: the ~ ~ Ла-Ма́нш.

Englishman ['ɪŋɡlɪʃmən] *irreg n* англича́нин*.

English-speaking ['ɪŋɡlɪʃ'spi:kɪŋ] *adj* англоговоря́щий.

Englishwoman ['ɪŋɡlɪʃwumən] *irreg n* англича́нка*.

engrave [ɪn'ɡreɪv] *vt* гравирова́ть (вы́гравировать *perf*).

engraving [ɪn'ɡreɪvɪŋ] *n* гравю́ра.

engrossed [ɪn'ɡrəust] *adj*: ~ in поглощённый (поглощён) +*instr*.

engulf [ɪn'ɡʌlf] *vt* (*subj*: *water*) поглоща́ть (поглоти́ть* *perf*); (: *panic, fear, fire*) охва́тывать (охвати́ть* *perf*).

enhance [ɪn'hɑːns] *vt* (*enjoyment*) увели́чивать (увели́чить *perf*); (*beauty, reputation*) улучша́ть (улу́чшить *perf*).

enigma [ɪ'nɪɡmə] *n* зага́дка.

enigmatic [ɛnɪɡ'mætɪk] *adj* зага́дочный* (зага́дочен).

enjoy [ɪn'dʒɔɪ] *vt* люби́ть (*impf*); (*have benefit of*) облада́ть (*impf*) +*instr*; **to ~ o.s.** хорошо́ проводи́ть* (провести́* *perf*) вре́мя; **I ~ dancing** я люблю́ танцева́ть.

enjoyable [ɪn'dʒɔɪəbl] *adj* прия́тный* (прия́тен).

enjoyment [ɪn'dʒɔɪmənt] *n* (*feeling of pleasure*) удово́льствие.

enlarge [ɪn'lɑːdʒ] *vt* увели́чивать (увели́чить *perf*) ♦ *vi*: **to ~ on** распространя́ться (*impf*) о +*prp*.

enlarged [ɪn'lɑːdʒd] *adj* (*edition*) допо́лненный; (*MED, PHOT*) увели́ченный (увели́чен).

enlargement [ɪn'lɑːdʒmənt] *n* (*PHOT*) увеличе́ние.

enlighten [ɪn'laɪtn] *vt* просвеща́ть (просвети́ть* *perf*).

enlightened [ɪn'laɪtnd] *adj* просвещённый.

enlightening [ɪn'laɪtnɪŋ] *adj* просвеща́ющий.

enlightenment [ɪn'laɪtnmənt] *n*: **the E~** Просвеще́ние.

enlist [ɪn'lɪst] *vt* (*person*) вербова́ть (завербова́ть *perf*); (*support*) заруча́ться (заручи́ться *perf*) +*instr* ♦ *vi*: **to ~ in** (*army, navy etc*) идти́* (пойти́* *perf*) в +*acc*; **~ed man** (*US: MIL*) военнослу́жащий* *m adj* (*рядово́го или сержа́нтского соста́ва*).

enliven [ɪn'laɪvn] *vt* (*events*) оживля́ть (оживи́ть* *perf*); (*people*) подбодря́ть (подбодри́ть *perf*).

enmity ['ɛnmɪtɪ] *n* вражде́бность *f*.

ennoble [ɪ'nəubl] *vt* возводи́ть* (возвести́* *perf*) в ти́тул; (*fig*) облагора́живать (облагоро́дить* *perf*).

enormity [ɪ'nɔːmɪtɪ] *n* (*of problem, danger*) величина́.

enormous [ɪ'nɔːməs] *adj* грома́дный* (грома́ден).

enormously [ɪ'nɔːməslɪ] *adv* чрезвыча́йно.

enough [ɪ'nʌf] *adj* (*time, books, people etc*) доста́точно +*gen* ♦ *pron* доста́точно ♦ *adv*: **big ~** доста́точно большо́й; **I've had ~!** с меня́ хва́тит!; **have you got ~ work to do?** у Вас доста́точно рабо́ты?; **have you had ~ to eat?** Вы нае́лись?; **that's ~, thanks** доста́точно, спаси́бо; **I've had ~ of him** он мне надое́л; **he has not worked ~** он недоста́точно рабо́тал; **will five pounds be ~?** пяти́ фу́нтов бу́дет доста́точно?; **I do not have ~ money to buy it** у меня́ не хвата́ет де́нег, чтобы купи́ть э́то; **it's hot ~ as it is** и та́к дово́льно жа́рко; **he was kind ~ to lend me the money** он был насто́лько добр, чтобы одолжи́ть мне де́ньги; **~! дово́льно!; strangely** *or* **oddly ~** ... как э́то ни стра́нно ....

enquire [ɪn'kwaɪəʳ] *vti* = **inquire.**

enrage [ɪn'reɪdʒ] *vt* беси́ть* (взбеси́ть* *perf*).

enrich [ɪn'rɪtʃ] *vt* обогаща́ть (обогати́ть *perf*).

enrol [ɪn'rəul] (*US* **enroll**) *vt* (*subj*: *administrator*) зачисля́ть (зачи́слить *perf*); (: *parents etc*) запи́сывать (записа́ть* *perf*) ♦ *vi* (*see vt*) зачисля́ться (зачи́слиться *perf*); запи́сываться (записа́ться* *perf*).

enrolment [ɪn'rəulmənt] (*US* **enrollment**) *n* (*registration*) зачисле́ние; (*for course, club*) за́пись *f*.

en route [ɔn'ruːt] *adv* по пути́; **~ ~ for** *or* **to/ from** по пути́ в +*acc*/из +*gen*.

ensconce [ɪn'skɔns] *vt*: **to ~ o.s. in** устра́иваться (устро́иться *perf*) в +*prp*.

ensemble [ɔn'sɔmbl] *n* анса́мбль *m*.

enshrine [ɪn'ʃraɪm] *vt* (*belief, right*) храни́ть (*impf*); **to be ~d in** сохраня́ться (сохрани́ться *perf*) в +*prp*.

ensue [ɪn'sjuː] *vi* сле́довать (после́довать *perf*); **a terrible argument ~d** (за э́тим) после́довала ужа́сная ссо́ра.

ensuing [ɪn'sjuːɪŋ] *adj* после́дующий*.

ensure [ɪn'ʃuəʳ] *vt* обеспе́чивать (обеспе́чить *perf*); **to ~ that** обеспе́чивать (обеспе́чить *perf*), что.

ENT *n abbr* (*MED*: = *Ear, Nose and Throat*) у́хо-го́рло-нос.

entail [ɪn'teɪl] *vt* влечь* (повле́чь* *perf*) за собо́й.

entangled [ɪn'tæŋɡld] *adj*: **to become ~ (in)** (*in net, rope etc*) запу́тываться (запу́таться *perf*) (в +*prp*).

enter ['ɛntəʳ] *vt* (*room, building*) входи́ть* (войти́* *perf*) в +*acc*; (*university, college*) поступа́ть (поступи́ть* *perf*) в +*acc*; (*club, profession, contest*) вступа́ть (вступи́ть* *perf*) в +*acc*; (*in book*) запи́сывать (записа́ть* *perf*); (*COMPUT*) вводи́ть* (ввести́* *perf*) ♦ *vi* входи́ть* (войти́* *perf*); **I ~ed my son in the marathon** я по́дал зая́вку на включе́ние моего́ сы́на в марафо́н

▶ **enter for** *vt fus* (*competition, examination*) подава́ть* (пода́ть* *perf*) зая́вку на уча́стие в +*prp*

▶ **enter into** *vt fus* (*discussion, correspondence, agreement*) вступа́ть (вступи́ть* *perf*) в +*acc*
▶ **enter (up)on** *vt fus* (*career, policy*) начина́ть (нача́ть* *perf*).
enteritis [ɛntəˈraɪtɪs] *n* энтери́т.
enterprise [ˈɛntəpraɪz] *n* (*company, undertaking*) предприя́тие; (*initiative*) предприи́мчивость *f*; **free/private ~** свобо́дное/ча́стное предпринима́тельство.
enterprising [ˈɛntəpraɪzɪŋ] *adj* (*person*) предприи́мчивый (предприи́мчив); (*scheme*) предпринима́тельский*.
entertain [ɛntəˈteɪn] *vt* (*amuse*) развлека́ть (развле́чь* *perf*); (*play host to*) принима́ть (приня́ть* *perf*); (*idea*) разду́мывать (*impf*) над +*instr*.
entertainer [ɛntəˈteɪnə'] *n* веду́щий*(-ая) *m(f) adj* развлека́тельной програ́ммы.
entertaining [ɛntəˈteɪnɪŋ] *adj* занима́тельный* (занима́телен), развлека́тельный ♦ *n*: **we do a lot of ~** мы ча́сто приглаша́ем к себе́ госте́й.
entertainment [ɛntəˈteɪnmənt] *n* (*amusement*) развлече́ние; (*show*) представле́ние.
entertainment allowance *n* сре́дства на представи́тельские расхо́ды.
enthral [ɪnˈθrɔ:l] (*US* **enthrall**) *vt* приводи́ть* (привести́* *perf*) в восто́рг.
enthralled [ɪnˈθrɔ:ld] *adj* увлечённый (увлечён); **he was ~ by** *or* **with the book** он был увлечён кни́гой.
enthralling [ɪnˈθrɔ:lɪŋ] *adj* увлека́тельный* (увлека́телен).
enthuse [ɪnˈθu:z] *vi*: **to ~ about** *or* **over** приходи́ть* (прийти́* *perf*) в восто́рг от +*gen*.
enthusiasm [ɪnˈθu:zɪæzəm] *n* энтузиа́зм.
enthusiast [ɪnˈθu:zɪæst] *n* энтузиа́ст; **a jazz** *etc* **~** энтузиа́ст джа́за *etc*.
enthusiastic [ɪnθu:zɪˈæstɪk] *adj* по́лный* (по́лон) энтузиа́зма; (*response, reception*) восто́рженный; **he is ~ about** он по́лон энтузиа́зма по по́воду +*gen*.
entice [ɪnˈtaɪs] *vt* (*lure*) зама́нивать (замани́ть* *perf*); (*tempt*) соблазня́ть (соблазни́ть *perf*).
enticing [ɪnˈtaɪsɪŋ] *adj* (*offer, food*) соблазни́тельный.
entire [ɪnˈtaɪə'] *adj* весь*.
entirely [ɪnˈtaɪəlɪ] *adv* по́лностью; (*for emphasis*) соверше́нно; **~ different** соверше́нно разли́чный.
entirety [ɪnˈtaɪərətɪ] *n*: **in its ~** весь целико́м.
entitle [ɪnˈtaɪtl] *vt*: **to ~ sb to sth/to do** (дать* *perf*) пра́во кому́-н на что-н/+*infin*.
entitled [ɪnˈtaɪtld] *adj* (*book, film etc*) озагла́вленный; **to be ~ to sth/to do** (*impf*) пра́во на что-н, что́бы +*infin*.
entity [ˈɛntɪtɪ] *n* (еди́ная) су́щность *f*; **a separate ~** (*person*) отде́льная ли́чность.

entourage [ɔntuˈrɑ:ʒ] *n* антура́ж, окруже́ние.
entrails [ˈɛntreɪlz] *npl* вну́тренности *fpl*.
entrance [*n* ˈɛntrns, *vt* ɪnˈtrɑ:ns] *n* (*way in*) вход; (*arrival*) вступле́ние, появле́ние; (*THEAT*) вы́ход (на сце́ну) ♦ *vt* (*enchant*) очаро́вывать (очарова́ть *perf*); **to gain ~ to** (*university*) поступа́ть (поступи́ть* *perf*) в +*acc*; (*profession*) получа́ть (получи́ть *perf*) до́ступ к +*dat*; **to make an ~** вступа́ть (вступи́ть* *perf*).
entrance examination *n* вступи́тельный экза́мен.
entrance fee *n* (*for museum etc*) входна́я пла́та.
entrance ramp *n* (*US: AUT*) въезд на автостра́ду.
entrancing [ɪnˈtrɑ:nsɪŋ] *adj* восхити́тельный* (восхити́телен).
entrant [ˈɛntrnt] *n* уча́стник(-ица).
entreat [ɛnˈtri:t] *vt* (*implore*): **to ~ sb to do** умоля́ть (умоли́ть *perf*) кого́-н +*infin*.
entreaty [ɛnˈtri:tɪ] *n* мольба́.
entrée [ˈɔntreɪ] *n* (*CULIN: main course*) гла́вное блю́до.
entrenched [ɛnˈtrɛntʃt] *adj* (*ideas etc*) укорени́вшийся.
entrepreneur [ˈɔntrəprəˈnə:'] *n* пред-принима́тель(ница) *m(f)*.
entrepreneurial [ˈɔntrəprəˈnə:rɪəl] *adj* предпринима́тельский*.
entrust [ɪnˈtrʌst] *vt* (*possessions, task*): **to ~ sth to sb** доверя́ть (дове́рить *perf*) что-н кому́-н; **to ~ sb with sth** (*task*) возлага́ть (возложи́ть* *perf*) на кого́-н что-н.
entry [ˈɛntrɪ] *n* (*way in*) вход; (*in register, account book*) за́пись *f*; (*in reference book*) статья́*; (*in competition: participants*) число́ уча́стников; (*arrival: in country*) въезд; (: *in room*) вход; **"no ~"** (*to room, building*) "нет вхо́да"; (*AUT*) "нет въе́зда"; **single/double ~ book-keeping** (*COMM*) проста́я/двойна́я бухгалте́рия.
entry form *n* зая́вка* на уча́стие.
entry phone *n* (*BRIT*) входно́е переговорное устро́йство.
entwine [ɪnˈtwaɪn] *vt*: **to ~ (with)** переплета́ть (переплести́* *perf*) (с +*instr*).
enumerate [ɪˈnju:məreɪt] *vt* перечисля́ть (перечи́слить *perf*).
enunciate [ɪˈnʌnsɪeɪt] *vt* (*word*) произноси́ть* (произнести́* *perf*); (*principle, plan etc*) излага́ть (изложи́ть* *perf*).
envelop [ɪnˈvɛləp] *vt* (*cover, enclose*) облега́ть (обле́чь* *perf*).
envelope [ˈɛnvələup] *n* конве́рт.
enviable [ˈɛnvɪəbl] *adj* зави́дный* (зави́ден).
envious [ˈɛnvɪəs] *adj* зави́стливый (зави́стлив); **to be ~ of sth/sb** зави́довать

---

* marks translations which have irregular inflections. The Russian-English side of the dictionary gives inflectional information.

(impf) чему-н/кому-н.

environment [ɪn'vaɪərnmənt] *n* среда; **the ~**
окружающая среда; **Department of the E~**
(*BRIT*) отдел охраны окружающей среды.

environmental [ɪnvaɪərn'mɛntl] *adj* связанный
с окружающей средой, экологический*;
children respond to ~ stimuli дети реагируют
на стимулы предлагаемые средой; **~
studies** экология.

environmentalist [ɪnvaɪərn'mɛntlɪst] *n*
сторонник(-ица) защиты окружающей
среды.

environmentally [ɪnvaɪərn'mɛntlɪ] *adv*
экологически.

Environmental Protection Agency *n* (*US*)
агентство по охране окружающей среды.

envisage [ɪn'vɪzɪdʒ] *vt* (*foresee*) предвидеть*
(impf); **I ~ that ...** я предвижу, что ....

envision [ɪn'vɪʒən] *vt* (*US*) = **envisage**.

envoy ['ɛnvɔɪ] *n* посланник.

envy ['ɛnvɪ] *n* зависть *f* ♦ *vt* завидовать
(позавидовать *perf*) +*dat*; **to ~ sb sth**
завидовать (позавидовать *perf*) кому-н
из-за чего-н.

enzyme ['ɛnzaɪm] *n* (*BIO, MED*) энзим.

EPA *n abbr* (*US*: = *Environmental Protection
Agency*) *агентство по охране окружающей
среды.*

ephemeral [ɪ'fɛmərl] *adj* эфемерный*
(эфемерен).

epic ['ɛpɪk] *n* эпопея; (*poem*) эпическая поэма
♦ *adj* (*journey*) эпохальный* (эпохален).

epicentre ['ɛpɪsɛntə] (*US* **epicenter**) *n*
эпицентр.

epidemic [ɛpɪ'dɛmɪk] *n* эпидемия.

epigram ['ɛpɪgræm] *n* эпиграмма.

epilepsy ['ɛpɪlɛpsɪ] *n* эпилепсия.

epileptic [ɛpɪ'lɛptɪk] *adj* эпилептический ♦ *n*
эпилептик.

epilogue ['ɛpɪlɔg] *n* эпилог.

Epiphany [ɪ'pɪfənɪ] *n* Богоявление, Крещение.

episcopal [ɪ'pɪskəpl] *adj* (*REL*) епископский; **the
E~ Church** Епископальная Церковь*.

episode ['ɛpɪsəʊd] *n* эпизод.

epistle [ɪ'pɪsl] *n* послание.

epitaph ['ɛpɪtɑːf] *n* эпитафия.

epithet ['ɛpɪθɛt] *n* эпитет.

epitome [ɪ'pɪtəmɪ] *n* воплощение.

epitomize [ɪ'pɪtəmaɪz] *vt* воплощать
(воплотить* *perf*).

epoch ['iːpɔk] *n* эпоха.

epoch-making ['iːpɔkmeɪkɪŋ] *adj* эпохальный*
(эпохален).

eponymous [ɪ'pɔnɪməs] *adj*: **~ hero** герой,
именем которого названо произведение.

EPOS *n abbr* (= *electronic point of sale*)
*электронное считывание информации с
товарных этикеток.*

equable ['ɛkwəbl] *adj* ровный* (ровен).

equal ['iːkwl] *adj* равный* (равен); (*intensity,
quality*) одинаковый ♦ *n* равный(-ая) *m(f)* ♦ *adj*

♦ *vt* (*number*) равняться *(impf)* +*dat*; (*quality*)
не уступать (уступить* *perf*) +*dat or* по +*dat*;
they are roughly ~ in size они примерно
равны по размеру; **the number of exports
should be ~ to imports** количество экспорта
должно быть* равно количеству импорта;
he is ~ to (*task*) он может справиться с +*instr*.

**Equal Employment Opportunity
Commission** *n* (*US*) = **Equal Opportunities
Commission**.

equality [iː'kwɔlɪtɪ] *n* равенство, равноправие;
~ of opportunity равенство возможностей.

equalize ['iːkwəlaɪz] *vt* уравнивать (уравнять
perf) ♦ *vi* (*SPORT*) сравнивать (сравнять *perf*)
счёт.

equally ['iːkwəlɪ] *adv* (*share etc*) равно; (*good,
bad*) одинаково; **they are ~ clever** они в
равной степени умны.

Equal Opportunities Commission (*US* **Equal
Employment Opportunity Commission**) *n
комиссия равных возможностей при найме
на работу.*

equal(s) sign *n* знак равенства.

equanimity [ɛkwə'nɪmɪtɪ] *n* (*calm*)
хладнокровие; **with ~** хладнокровно.

equate [ɪ'kweɪt] *vt*: **to ~ sth with sth, ~ sth to
sth** приравнивать (приравнять *perf*) что-н к
чему-н.

equation [ɪ'kweɪʃən] *n* (*MATH*) уравнение.

equator [ɪ'kweɪtə[r]] *n* экватор.

equatorial [ɛkwə'tɔːrɪəl] *adj* экваториальный.

Equatorial Guinea *n* Экваториальная
Гвинея.

equestrian [ɪ'kwɛstrɪən] *adj* конный ♦ *n*
всадник(-ица).

equilibrium [iːkwɪ'lɪbrɪəm] *n* равновесие.

equinox ['iːkwɪnɔks] *n* равноденствие; **the
spring/autumn ~** весеннее/осеннее
равноденствие.

equip [ɪ'kwɪp] *vt*: **to ~ (with)** (*person, army*)
снаряжать (снарядить* *perf*) (+*instr*); (*room,
car etc*) оборудовать (*impf/perf*) (+*instr*); **to ~
sb for** (*prepare*) готовить* (подготовить*
perf) кого-н к +*dat*.

equipment [ɪ'kwɪpmənt] *n* оборудование.

equitable ['ɛkwɪtəbl] *adj* справедливый
(справедлив).

equities ['ɛkwɪtɪz] *npl* (*BRIT*) обыкновенные
акции *fpl*.

equity ['ɛkwɪtɪ] *n* справедливость *f*.

equity capital *n* капитал в форме акций.

equivalent [ɪ'kwɪvələnt] *n* эквивалент ♦ *adj*: **~
(to)** эквивалентный* (эквивалентен) (+*dat*); **it
is ~ to** это эквивалентно +*dat*.

equivocal [ɪ'kwɪvəkl] *adj* (*ambiguous*)
двусмысленный* (двусмыслен); (*open to
suspicion*) сомнительный* (сомнителен).

equivocate [ɪ'kwɪvəkeɪt] *vi* говорить *(impf)*
двусмысленно.

equivocation [ɪkwɪvə'keɪʃən] *n* уклончивость
f.

ER *abbr* (*BRIT*) = *Elizabeth Regina.*
ERA *n abbr* (*US*: *POL*: = *Equal Rights Amendment*) поправка о равных правах (*к конституции США*).
era ['ɪərə] *n* эра.
eradicate [ɪ'rædɪkeɪt] *vt* искоренять (искоренить *perf*).
erase [ɪ'reɪz] *vt* стирать (стереть* *perf*).
eraser [ɪ'reɪzə'] *n* резинка*, ластик для стирания.
erect [ɪ'rɛkt] *adj* (*posture*) прямой* (прям), вертикальный* (вертикален); (*tail, ears*) поднятый (поднят) ♦ *vt* (*build*) возводить* (возвести* *perf*); (*assemble*) ставить* (поставить* *perf*).
erection [ɪ'rɛkʃən] *n* возведение; (*of tent, machinery*) установка*; (*PHYSIOL*) эрекция.
ergonomics [ə:gə'nɔmɪks] *n* эргономика.
ERISA *n abbr* (*US*) = *Employee Retirement Income Security Act.*
ERM *n abbr* (= *Exchange Rate Mechanism*) МВК = *механизм валютных курсов.*
ermine ['ə:mɪn] *n* горностай.
ERNIE ['ə:nɪ] *n abbr* (*BRIT*: = *Electronic Random Number Indicator Equipment*) ЭВМ, определяющая выигрышные номера государственного выигрышного займа.
erode [ɪ'rəud] *vt* (*soil, rock: subj: wind*) выветривать (выветрить *perf*); (: *water*) размывать (размыть* *perf*); (*metal*) разъедать (разъесть* *perf*); (*confidence, power*) подрывать (подорвать* *perf*).
erogenous [ɪ'rɔdʒənəs] *adj* эрогенный.
erosion [ɪ'rəuʒən] *n* эрозия.
erotic [ɪ'rɔtɪk] *adj* эротический*.
eroticism [ɪ'rɔtɪsɪzəm] *n* эротизм.
err [ə:'] *vi* допускать (допустить* *perf*) ошибку; **to ~ on the side of** ... слишком склоняться (*impf*) к +*dat* ....
errand ['ɛrənd] *n* поручение; **to run ~s** выполнять (*impf*) поручения; **~ of mercy** поездка* с доброй миссией.
erratic [ɪ'rætɪk] *adj* (*attempts*) беспорядочный* (беспорядочен); (*behaviour*) сумасбродный* (сумасброден).
erroneous [ɪ'rəunɪəs] *adj* ошибочный* (ошибочен).
error ['ɛrə'] *n* ошибка*; **typing ~** опечатка*; **spelling ~** орфографическая ошибка*; **in ~** по ошибке; **~s and omissions excepted** не считая ошибок и пропусков.
error message *n* (*COMPUT*) сообщение об ошибке.
erstwhile ['ə:stwaɪl] *adj* бывший*.
erudite ['ɛrjudaɪt] *adj* (*person*) эрудированный* (эрудирован).
erupt [ɪ'rʌpt] *vi* (*war, crisis*) разражаться (разразиться* *perf*); **the volcano ~ed**

произошло извержение вулкана.
eruption [ɪ'rʌpʃən] *n* (*of volcano*) извержение; (*of fighting*) взрыв.
ESA *n abbr* (= *European Space Agency*) ЕКА = *Европейское космическое агентство.*
escalate ['ɛskəleɪt] *vi* обостряться (обостриться *perf*).
escalation [ɛskə'leɪʃən] *n* обострение, эскалация.
escalation clause *n* оговорка о скользящих ценах или скользящей зарплате.
escalator ['ɛskəleɪtə'] *n* эскалатор.
escapade [ɛskə'peɪd] *n* (*adventure*) эскапада, авантюра.
escape [ɪs'keɪp] *n* (*from prison*) побег; (*from person*) избегание; (*TECH*) выход; (*of gas*) выделение, выпуск ♦ *vi* (*get away*) убегать (убежать* *perf*); (*from jail*) бежать* (*impf/perf*); (*leak*) утекать (утечь* *perf*), давать* (дать* *perf*) утечку ♦ *vt* (*avoid: consequences etc*) избегать (избежать* *perf*) +*gen*; (*elude*): **his name ~s me** его имя выпало у меня из памяти; **to ~ from** (*place*) сбегать (сбежать* *perf*) *or* убегать (убежать* *perf*) из/от +*gen*; (*person*) сбегать (сбежать* *perf*) *or* убегать (убежать* *perf*) от +*gen*; **he ~d with minor injuries** он спасся отделавшись небольшими повреждениями; **to ~ to** (*another place*) сбегать (сбежать* *perf*) *or* убегать (убежать* *perf*) в/на +*prp*; **to ~ to safety** скрываться (скрыться* *perf*) в безопасном месте; **to ~ notice** ускользать (ускользнуть *perf*) незамеченным.
escape artist *n* трюкач.
escape clause *n* пункт договора, избавляющий сторону от ответственности.
escapee [ɪskeɪ'pi:] *n* сбежавший(-ая) *m(f) adj*.
escape hatch *n* аварийный люк.
escape key *n* (*COMPUT*) клавиша выхода.
escape route *n* (*from fire*) запасной (пожарный) выход; (*of prisoners etc*) маршрут побега.
escapism [ɪs'keɪpɪzəm] *n* бегство от действительности, эскапизм.
escapist [ɪs'keɪpɪst] *adj* (*literature*) уводящий от острых проблем жизни, эскапистский.
escapologist [ɛskə'pɔlədʒɪst] *n* (*BRIT*) = **escape artist.**
escarpment [ɪs'ka:pmənt] *n* откос.
eschew [ɪs'tʃu:] *vt* (*company, violence*) сторониться (*impf*) +*gen*.
escort [*n* 'ɛskɔ:t, *vt* ɪs'kɔ:t] *n* (*companion: male*) сопровождающий *m adj*; (: *female*) сопровождающая *f adj*; (*MIL, POLICE*) конвой ♦ *vt* сопровождать (*impf*); **his/her ~** его/её сопровождающий(-ая).
escort agency *n* бюро *nt ind* по найму

сопровождáющих.

Eskimo ['eskɪməu] n эскимóс(ка*).

ESL n abbr (SCOL) = English as a Second Language.

esophagus [i:'sɔfəgəs] n (US) = oesophagus.

esoteric [esə'tɛrɪk] adj эзотерúческий.

ESP n abbr = extrasensory perception; (SCOL) = English for Special Purposes.

esp. abbr = especially.

especially [ɪs'pɛʃlɪ] adv осóбенно.

espionage ['espɪənɑː3] n шпионáж.

esplanade [esplə'neɪd] n эспланáда.

espouse [ɪs'pauz] vt (policy, idea) (целикóм) отдавáться* (отдáться* perf) +dat, поддéрживать (impf).

Esq. abbr = Esquire.

Esquire [ɪs'kwaɪə⁺] n: **J. Brown, ~** Дж. Брáун, эсквáйр.

essay ['eseɪ] n (SCOL) сочинéние; (LITERATURE) óчерк.

essence ['esns] n сýщность f; (CULIN) эссéнция; **in ~** в сýщности; **speed is of the ~** всё дéло в скóрости.

essential [ɪ'senʃl] adj (vital) существéнно необходúмый* (необходúм); (basic) основнóй ♦ n (see adj) существéнно необходúмая вещь f; основнóе nt adj; **it is ~ that** существéнно вáжно, чтóбы.

essentially [ɪ'senʃəlɪ] adv в сýщности.

EST abbr (US) = Eastern Standard Time.

est. abbr = established; estimate(d).

establish [ɪs'tæblɪʃ] vt (organization) учреждáть (учредúть* perf); (facts, contact) устанáвливать (установúть* perf); (reputation) утверждáть (утвердúть* perf) за собóй.

established [ɪs'tæblɪʃt] adj (business) упрóченный; (custom, practice) прúзнанный.

establishment [ɪs'tæblɪʃmənt] n (see vb) учреждéние; установлéние; утверждéние; (shop etc) заведéние; **the E~** истéблишмент.

estate [ɪs'teɪt] n (land) помéстье*; (BRIT: also: **housing ~**) жилóй кóмплекс; (LAW) состоя́ние.

estate agency n (BRIT) агéнтство по продáже недвúжимости.

estate agent n (BRIT) агéнт по продáже недвúжимости.

estate car n (BRIT) автомобúль m-пикáп.

esteem [ɪs'ti:m] n: **to hold sb in high ~** относúться* (отнестúсь* perf) к комý-н с большúм почтéнием.

esthetic [ɪs'θetɪk] adj (US) = aesthetic.

estimate [vb 'estɪmeɪt, n 'estɪmət] vt (reckon, calculate) предварúтельно подсчúтывать (подсчитáть perf); (: chances) оценивать (оценúть perf) ♦ n (calculation) подсчёт; (assessment) оцéнка*; (builder's etc) смéта ♦ vi (BRIT: COMM): **to ~ for** составля́ть (состáвить* perf) смéту +gen; **I ~ that** я полагáю, что; **to give sb an ~** давáть (дать*

perf) комý-н оцéнку стóимости; **at a rough ~** по грýбым подсчётам.

estimation [estɪ'meɪʃən] n (opinion) оцéнка*; (calculation) подсчёт; **in my ~** по моúм подсчётам.

estimator ['estɪmeɪtə⁺] n оцéнщик.

Estonia [es'təunɪə] n Эстóния.

Estonian [es'təunɪən] n (person) эстóнец*- (-óнка*); (LING) эстóнский* язы́к* ♦ adj эстóнский*.

estranged [ɪs'treɪndʒd] adj (from spouse, family) отчуждённый* (отчуждён); **his ~ wife** ушéдшая от негó женá; **he is ~ from his wife** он разошёлся с женóй.

estrangement [ɪs'treɪndʒmənt] n отчуждéние.

estrogen ['i:strəudʒən] n (US) = oestrogen.

estuary ['estjuərɪ] n ýстье*.

ET n abbr (BRIT: = Employment Training) профессионáльная подготóвка ♦ abbr (US) = Eastern Time.

ETA n abbr (= estimated time of arrival) ожидáемое врéмя* nt прибы́тия.

et al. abbr (and others: = et alii) и другúе.

etc. abbr (= et cetera) и т.д. = и так дáлее.

etch [etʃ] vt (surface) гравировáть (вы́гравировать perf); (design): **to ~ (on)** травúть* (вы́травить* perf) (на +prp); **it will be ~ed on my memory** это запечатлéется в моéй пáмяти.

etching ['etʃɪŋ] n (craft) гравирóвка*; (product) гравю́ра, офóрт.

ETD n abbr (= estimated time of departure) ожидáемое врéмя* nt отправлéния.

eternal [ɪ'tə:nl] adj вéчный* (вéчен).

eternity [ɪ'tə:nɪtɪ] n вéчность f.

ether ['i:θə⁺] n эфúр*.

ethereal [ɪ'θɪərɪəl] adj (delicate) эфúрный.

ethical ['eθɪkl] adj (relating to ethics) этúческий; (morally worthy) этúчный* (этúчен).

ethics ['eθɪks] n, npl этика fsg.

Ethiopia [i:θɪ'əupɪə] n Эфиóпия.

Ethiopian [i:θɪ'əupɪən] adj эфиóпский* ♦ n эфиóп(ка).

ethnic ['eθnɪk] adj этнúческий*.

ethnic cleansing n этнúческая чúстка*.

ethnology [eθ'nɔlədʒɪ] n этнолóгия.

ethos ['i:θɔs] n этос.

etiquette ['etɪket] n этикéт.

ETV n abbr (US) = Educational Television.

etymology [etɪ'mɔlədʒɪ] n этимолóгия.

eucalyptus [ju:kə'lɪptəs] n эвкалúпт.

Eucharist ['ju:kərɪst] n (REL): **the ~** евхарúстия, причáстие.

eulogy ['ju:lədʒɪ] n восхвалéние.

euphemism ['ju:fəmɪzəm] n эвфемúзм.

euphemistic [ju:fə'mɪstɪk] adj эвфемистúческий*.

euphoria [ju:'fɔ:rɪə] n эйфорúя.

Eurasia [juə'reɪʃə] n Еврáзия.

Eurasian [juə'reɪʃən] adj евразúйский ♦ n евразúец* (úйка*).

Euratom [juə'rætəm] *n abbr* (= *European Atomic Energy Community*) Европейский* комитет по атомной энергии.
Euro- ['juərəu] *prefix* евро-.
eurocheque ['juərəutʃɛk] *n* еврочек.
Eurocrat ['juərəukræt] *n* служащий в организации Европейского Сообщества.
Eurodollar ['juərəudɔlə'] *n* евродоллар.
Europe ['juərəp] *n* Европа.
European [juərə'pi:ən] *adj* европейский* ♦ *n* европеец(-ейка).
European Community *n*: the ~ ~ Европейское Сообщество.
European Court of Justice *n*: the ~ ~ ~ ~ Европейский* Суд*.
European Economic Community *n*: the ~ ~ ~ Европейское Экономическое Сообщество.
Euro-sceptic ['juərəuskɛptɪk] *n* евроскептик (человек, относящийся с недоверием к идее Европейского Союза).
euthanasia [ju:θə'neɪzɪə] *n* эйтаназия (безнадёжно больных).
evacuate [ɪ'vækjueɪt] *vt* (*people*) эвакуировать (*impf/perf*); (*place*) очищать (очистить* *perf*).
evacuation [ɪvækju'eɪʃən] *n* (*see vb*) эвакуация; очистка*.
evacuee [ɪvækju'i:] *n* эвакуированный(-ая) *m(f) adj*.
evade [ɪ'veɪd] *vt* (*duties, question*) уклоняться (уклониться* *perf*) от +*gen*; (*person*) избегать (*impf*) +*gen*.
evaluate [ɪ'væljueɪt] *vt* оценивать (оценить* *perf*).
evangelical [i:væn'dʒɛlɪkl] *adj* евангелический*.
evangelist [ɪ'vændʒəlɪst] *n* евангелист.
evangelize [ɪ'vændʒəlaɪz] *vi* проповедовать (*impf*) евангелизм.
evaporate [ɪ'væpəreɪt] *vi* испаряться (испариться* *perf*); (*feeling, attitude*) пропадать (пропасть* *perf*).
evaporated milk [ɪ'væpəreɪtɪd-] *n* сгущённое молоко (без сахара).
evaporation [ɪvæpə'reɪʃən] *n* испарение.
evasion [ɪ'veɪʒən] *n* (*of responsibility, tax etc*) уклонение.
evasive [ɪ'veɪsɪv] *adj* (*reply, action*) уклончивый (уклончив).
eve [i:v] *n*: on the ~ of накануне +*gen*; **Christmas E~** канун Рождества; **New Year's E~** канун Нового года.
even ['i:vn] *adj* (*level, smooth*) ровный* (ровен); (*equal*) равный* (равен); (*number*) чётный ♦ *adv* даже; ~ **if** даже если; ~ **though** хотя и; ~ **more** ещё больше; **he loves her ~ more** он любит её ещё больше; **the work is going ~ better/faster** работа идёт ещё

лучше/быстрее; ~ **so** всё же; **not** ~ даже не; ~ **he was there** даже он там был; ~ **on Sundays** даже по воскресеньям; **I am ~ more likely to leave now** теперь даже ещё более вероятно, что я уеду; **to break** ~ работать на уровне самоокупаемости (*но без дохода*); **to get** ~ **with sb** (*inf*) расквитаться (*perf*) с кем-н
▸ **even out** *vt* выравнивать (выровнять *perf*) ♦ *vi* выравниваться (выровняться *perf*).
even-handed ['i:vnhændɪd] *adj* беспристрастный* (беспристрастен).
evening ['i:vnɪŋ] *n* вечер*; **in the** ~ вечером; **this** ~ сегодня вечером; **tomorrow/yesterday** ~ завтра/вчера вечером.
evening class *n* вечерние курсы *mpl*.
evening dress *n* (*no pl: formal clothes*) вечерний туалет*; (*gown*) вечернее платье*.
evenly ['i:vnlɪ] *adv* (*distribute*) равномерно; (*divide, breathe*) ровно.
evensong ['i:vnsɔŋ] *n* вечерня*.
event [ɪ'vɛnt] *n* (*occurrence*) событие; (*SPORT: competition*) соревнование, вид; **in the normal course of** ~s при нормальном течении событий; **in the** ~ **of** в случае +*gen*; **in the** ~ в конечном счёте; **at all** ~s (*BRIT*), **in any** ~ во всяком *or* любом случае.
eventful [ɪ'vɛntful] *adj* насыщенный* (насыщен) событиями.
eventing [ɪ'vɛntɪŋ] *n* (*HORSE-RIDING*) участие в ряде состязаний по верховой езде.
eventual [ɪ'vɛntʃuəl] *adj* (*outcome, goal*) конечный.
eventuality [ɪvɛntʃu'ælɪtɪ] *n* (*possibility*) возможность *f*.
eventually [ɪ'vɛntʃuəlɪ] *adv* в конце концов.
ever ['ɛvə'] *adv* (*always*) всегда; (*at any time*) когда-либо, когда-нибудь; **why** ~ **not?** почему же нет?; **the best** ~ самый лучший*; **have you** ~ **been to Russia?** Вы когда-либо *or* когда-нибудь были в России?; **for** ~ навсегда; **hardly** ~ почти никогда; **I hardly** ~ **read** я почти никогда не читаю; **better than** ~ лучше чем бы то ни было *or* чем когда-либо; ~ **since** с тех пор, как; ~ **since that day** с того дня; ~ **so pretty** ужасно симпатичная; **thank you** ~ **so much** я Вам так благодарен; **yours** ~ (*BRIT: in letters*) преданный Вам.
Everest ['ɛvərɪst] *n* (*also*: **Mount** ~) Эверест.
evergreen ['ɛvəgri:n] *n* вечнозелёный.
everlasting [ɛvə'lɑ:stɪŋ] *adj* (*love, life etc*) вечный* (вечен).

───── **KEYWORD** ─────

every ['ɛvrɪ] *adj* **1** (*each*) каждый; **every child will receive a present** каждый ребёнок получит подарок; **every one of them** каждый из них; **every shop in the town was closed** все

---

* marks translations which have irregular inflections. The Russian-English side of the dictionary gives inflectional information.

магази́ны в го́роде бы́ли закры́ты
2 (*all possible*): **I gave you every assistance** я
помо́г Вам, всем чем то́лько мо́жно; **I tried
every option** я испро́бовал все пути́; **I have
every confidence in him** я в нём соверше́нно
уве́рен; **we wish you every success** мы
жела́ем Вам вся́ческого успе́ха; **he's every
bit as clever/stupid as his brother** он столь же
умён/глуп, как и его́ брат
3 (*showing recurrence*) ка́ждый; **every week**
ка́ждую неде́лю; **every other car** ка́ждая
втора́я маши́на; **she visits me every third/
other day** она прихо́дит ко мне́ ка́ждые два
дня́/че́рез день; **every now and then** вре́мя*
от вре́мени.

everybody ['ɛvrɪbɒdɪ] *pron* (*each*) ка́ждый; (*all*)
все *pl*; ~ **knows about it** об э́том ка́ждый
зна́ет; ~ **else** все остальны́е.
everyday ['ɛvrɪdeɪ] *adj* (*daily*) ежедне́вный;
(*common*) повседне́вный*.
everyone ['ɛvrɪwʌn] *pron* = **everybody**.
everything ['ɛvrɪθɪŋ] *pron* всё; ~ **is ready** всё
гото́во; **he did** ~ **possible** он сде́лал всё
возмо́жное; **you think of** ~ Вы ду́маете обо
всём; **I don't agree with** ~ **he says** я не
согла́сен со всем, что он говори́т.
everywhere ['ɛvrɪwɛəʳ] *adv* везде́, повсю́ду; ~
you go you meet ... куда́ ни пойдёшь, везде́ *or*
повсю́ду встреча́ешь ....
evict [ɪ'vɪkt] *vt* выселя́ть (вы́селить *perf*).
eviction [ɪ'vɪkʃən] *n* выселе́ние.
eviction notice *n* предупрежде́ние о
выселе́нии.
eviction order *n* прика́з о выселе́нии.
evidence ['ɛvɪdns] *n* (*proof*) доказа́тельство;
(*testimony*) показа́ние; (*indication*) при́знаки
mpl; **to give** ~ дава́ть* (дать* *perf*)
(свиде́тельские) показа́ния; **to show** ~ **of**
проявля́ть (прояви́ть* *perf*) при́знаки +*gen*; **in**
~ (*obvious*) заме́тен.
evident ['ɛvɪdnt] *adj* заме́тный* (заме́тен).
evidently ['ɛvɪdntlɪ] *adv* очеви́дно.
evil ['iːvl] *adj* (*person, spirit*) злой* (зол);
(*system, influence*) дурно́й* ♦ *n* зло.
evocative [ɪ'vɒkətɪv] *adj* (*description, music*)
навева́ющий чу́вства и воспомина́ния.
evoke [ɪ'vəuk] *vt* вызыва́ть (вы́звать* *perf*).
evolution [iːvə'luːʃən] *n* эволю́ция.
evolve [ɪ'vɒlv] *vt* развива́ть (разви́ть* *perf*) ♦ *vi*
(*animal, plant*) эволюциони́ровать (*impf/perf*);
(*plan, idea*) развива́ться (разви́ться* *perf*).
ewe [juː] *n* овца́*.
ewer ['juːəʳ] *n* кувши́н*.
ex- [ɛks] *prefix* (*former*) экс-, бы́вший*; (*out of*):
the price ex works цена́ с предприя́тия.
exacerbate [ɛks'æsəbeɪt] *vt* (*situation, pain*)
обостря́ть (обостри́ть *perf*).
exact [ɪg'zækt] *adj* то́чный* (то́чен) ♦ *vt*: **to** ~
sth from (*obedience*) тре́бовать
(потре́бовать *perf*) чего́-н от +*gen*; (*payment*)
взы́скивать (взыска́ть* *perf*) что-н с +*gen*.

exacting [ɪg'zæktɪŋ] *adj* (*task*) тру́дный*;
(*person*) взыска́тельный* (взыска́телен).
exactly [ɪg'zæktlɪ] *adv* то́чно; ~! вот и́менно!
exaggerate [ɪg'zædʒəreɪt] *vti* преувели́чивать
(преувели́чить *perf*).
exaggerated [ɪg'zædʒəreɪtɪd] *adj* пре-
увели́ченный (преувели́чен).
exaggeration [ɪgzædʒə'reɪʃən] *n* пре-
увеличе́ние.
exalt [ɪg'zɔːlt] *vt* превозноси́ть* (превознести́*
perf).
exalted [ɪg'zɔːltɪd] *adj* (*prominent*) высо́кий*
(высо́к); (*elated*) восто́рженный*
(восто́ржен).
exam [ɪg'zæm] *n abbr* = **examination**.
examination [ɪgzæmɪ'neɪʃən] *n* (*inspection*)
изуче́ние; (*plan*) рассмотре́ние; (*SCOL*)
экза́мен; (*LAW*) допро́с; (*MED*) осмо́тр; **to
take** *or* (*BRIT*) **sit an** ~ сдава́ть* (сдать* *perf*)
экза́мен; **the matter is under** ~ де́ло
нахо́дится на рассмотре́нии.
examine [ɪg'zæmɪn] *vt* (*scrutinize*) смотре́ть
(посмотре́ть *perf*) на +*acc*; (*inspect*)
осма́тривать (осмотре́ть *perf*); (*plan*)
рассма́тривать (рассмотре́ть *perf*); (*SCOL*)
экзаменова́ть (проэкзаменова́ть *perf*); (*LAW*)
допра́шивать (допроси́ть* *perf*); (*MED*)
осма́тривать (осмотре́ть* *perf*).
examiner [ɪg'zæmɪnəʳ] *n* (*SCOL*) экзамена́тор.
example [ɪg'zɑːmpl] *n* приме́р; **for** ~
наприме́р; **to set a good/bad** ~ подава́ть*
(пода́ть* *perf*) хоро́ший*/плохо́й приме́р.
exasperate [ɪg'zɑːspəreɪt] *vt* изма́тывать
(измота́ть *perf*); ~**d by** *or* **with** изма́танный
+*instr*.
exasperating [ɪg'zɑːspəreɪtɪŋ] *adj* раз-
дража́ющий.
exasperation [ɪgzɑːspə'reɪʃən] *n* раздраже́ние;
in ~ в раздраже́нии.
excavate ['ɛkskəveɪt] *vt* (*site*) раска́пывать
(раскопа́ть *perf*); (*hole*) выка́пывать
(вы́копать *perf*) ♦ *vi* производи́ть*
(произвести́* *perf*) раско́пки.
excavation [ɛkskə'veɪʃən] *n* (*activity*)
раска́пывание; (*archeological dig*): ~**s**
раско́пки *fpl*.
excavator ['ɛkskəveɪtəʳ] *n* экскава́тор.
exceed [ɪk'siːd] *vt* превыша́ть (превы́сить*
perf); (*hopes*) превосходи́ть* (превзойти́*
perf).
exceedingly [ɪk'siːdɪŋlɪ] *adv* чрезвыча́йно.
excel [ɪk'sɛl] *vt* превосходи́ть* (превзойти́*
perf) ♦ *vi*: **to** ~ (**in** *or* **at**) отлича́ться
(отличи́ться *perf*) (в +*prp*); **to** ~ **o.s.** (*BRIT*)
превосходи́ть* (превзойти́* *perf*) самого́
себя́.
excellence ['ɛksələns] *n* (*in sport, business*)
мастерство́; (*superiority*) превосхо́дство.
Excellency ['ɛksələnsɪ] *n*: **His** ~ его́
Превосходи́тельство.
excellent ['ɛksələnt] *adj* отли́чный* (отли́чен),

превосхо́дный* (превосхо́ден) ♦ *excl:* ~!
отли́чно!, превосхо́дно!

except [ɪk'sɛpt] *prep (also:* ~ **for)** кро́ме +*gen* ♦
vt: **to** ~ **sb (from)** исключа́ть (исключи́ть *perf)*
кого́-н (из +*gen*); ~ **if/when** кро́ме *or* за
исключе́нием тех слу́чаев е́сли/когда́; ~ **that**
кро́ме того́, что.

excepting [ɪk'sɛptɪŋ] *prep* за исключе́нием
+*gen.*

exception [ɪk'sɛpʃən] *n* исключе́ние; **to take** ~
to оби́жа́ться (оби́деться* *perf)* на +*acc*; **with**
the ~ **of** за исключе́нием +*gen.*

exceptional [ɪk'sɛpʃənl] *adj* исключи́тельный*
(исключи́телен).

excerpt ['ɛksə:pt] *n* отры́вок*.

excess [ɪk'sɛs] *n* избы́ток*; (*INSURANCE*)
превыше́ние; ~**es** *npl (of cruelty etc)* эксце́ссы
mpl, кра́йности *fpl*; **an** ~ **of £15, a £15** ~
изли́шек* в £15; **in** ~ **of** сверх +*gen*, свы́ше
+*gen*; **to drink to** ~ пить (*impf)* сверх ме́ры.

excess baggage *n* изли́шек* багажа́.

excess fare *n* (*BRIT*) допла́та (*за биле́т*).

excessive [ɪk'sɛsɪv] *adj* чрезме́рный*
(чрезме́рен).

excess supply *n* избы́точное предложе́ние.

exchange [ɪks'tʃeɪndʒ] *n* (*conversation*) обме́н
мне́ниями; (*argument*) перепа́лка*; (*also:*
telephone ~) коммута́тор ♦ *vt:* **to** ~ **(for)**
(*goods etc*) обме́нивать (обменя́ть *perf)* (на
+*acc*); ~ **(of)** обме́н (+*instr*); **in** ~ **for** в обме́н
на +*acc*; **foreign** ~ валю́тная би́ржа.

exchange control *n* валю́тный контро́ль *m*.

exchange market *n* валю́тный ры́нок*.

exchange rate *n* валю́тный *or* обме́нный
курс.

Exchequer [ɪks'tʃɛkə'] *n* (*BRIT*): **the** ~
казначе́йство.

excisable [ɪk'saɪzəbl] *adj (goods)* облага́емый
акци́зным сбо́ром.

excise [*n* 'ɛksaɪz, *vt* ɛk'saɪz] *n* акци́з, акци́зный
сбор ♦ *vt (remove)* выреза́ть (вы́резать* *perf)*.

excise duties *npl* акци́зный сбор *msg*.

excitable [ɪk'saɪtəbl] *adj (*легко́*) возбуди́мый.

excite [ɪk'saɪt] *vt* возбужда́ть (возбуди́ть* *perf)*;
(*stimulate*) заинтересо́вывать
(заинтересова́ть *perf)*; **to get** ~**d** волнова́ться
(взволнова́ться *perf)*.

excitement [ɪk'saɪtmənt] *n* (*agitation*)
возбужде́ние; (*exhilaration*) оживле́ние.

exciting [ɪk'saɪtɪŋ] *adj* восхити́тельный.

excl. *abbr* = **excluding, exclusive (of)**

exclaim [ɪks'kleɪm] *vi* восклица́ть
(воскли́кнуть *perf)*.

exclamation [ɛksklə'meɪʃən] *n* восклица́ние.

exclamation mark *n* восклица́тельный знак.

exclude [ɪks'klu:d] *vt* исключа́ть (исключи́ть
perf).

excluding [ɪks'klu:dɪŋ] *prep* исключа́я +*acc*.

exclusion [ɪks'klu:ʒən] *n* исключе́ние; **to the** ~
of исключа́я +*acc*.

exclusion clause *n* статья́* об исключе́ниях.

exclusion zone *n* запре́тная зо́на.

exclusive [ɪks'klu:sɪv] *adj (select)*
недосту́пный (недосту́пен), для
и́збранных; (*use*) исключи́тельный*
(исключи́телен); (*interview*) уника́льный
(уника́лен) ♦ *n* (*PRESS*) эксклюзи́вный
материа́л (*напеча́танный то́лько в одно́й
газе́те*) ♦ *adv:* ~ **of** (*COMM*) не счита́я +*gen*;
mutually ~ взаимоисключа́ющие; ~ **of**
postage без сто́имости почто́вых расхо́дов;
from the 1st to the 15th March ~ с 1-ого до
15-ого ма́рта, включи́тельно; ~ **of tax** не
счита́я нало́га.

exclusively [ɪks'klu:sɪvlɪ] *adv* исключи́тельно.

exclusive rights *npl* исключи́тельные права́
ntpl.

excommunicate [ɛkskə'mju:nɪkeɪt] *vt*
отлуча́ть (отлучи́ть *perf)* от це́ркви.

excrement ['ɛkskrəmənt] *n* экскреме́нты *mpl*.

excruciating [ɪks'kru:ʃieɪtɪŋ] *adj* мучи́тельный*
(мучи́телен).

excursion [ɪks'kə:ʃən] *n* экску́рсия.

excursion ticket *n* дешёвый биле́т на
коро́ткую экску́рсию.

excusable [ɪks'kju:zəbl] *adj* прости́тельный*
(прости́телен).

excuse [*n* ɪks'kju:s, *vt* ɪks'kju:z] *n* оправда́ние ♦
vt (justify) опра́вдывать (оправда́ть *perf)*;
(*forgive*) проща́ть (прости́ть* *perf)*; **to make**
~**s for sb** находи́ть* (найти́* *perf)* оправда́ние
кому́-н; **that's no** ~ э́то не причи́на!; **to** ~ **sb**
from sth/doing освобожда́ть (освободи́ть*
perf) кого́-н от чего́-н/от того́, что́бы +*infin*;
~ **me!** (*attracting attention*) извини́те!,
прости́те!; (*as apology*) извини́те *or*
прости́те (меня́)!; **if you will** ~ **me, I have to ...**
Вы прости́те, мне на́до ...; **to** ~ **o.s. for sth/**
for having done sth извиня́ться (извини́ться
perf) за что-то за то, что сде́лал что-н.

ex-directory ['ɛksdɪ'rɛktərɪ] *adj (BRIT: number*)
не включённый (включён) в телефо́нный
спра́вочник; **she's** ~ её но́мер не включён в
телефо́нный спра́вочник.

execrable ['ɛksɪkrəbl] *adj* отврати́тельный*
(отврати́телен).

execute ['ɛksɪkju:t] *vt (kill)* казни́ть (*impf/perf)*;
(*carry out, perform*) выполня́ть (вы́полнить
perf).

execution [ɛksɪ'kju:ʃən] *n (see vb)* казнь *f*;
выполне́ние.

executioner [ɛksɪ'kju:nə'] *n* пала́ч*.

executive [ɪg'zɛkjutɪv] *n (person)*
руководи́тель *m*; (*committee*)
исполни́тельный о́рган ♦ *adj (board, role)*
руководя́щий*; (*secretary*) отве́тственный;

---

* marks translations which have irregular inflections. The Russian-English side of the dictionary gives inflectional information.

(*car, plane, chair, toys*) для руководя́щих рабо́тников.

executive director *n* дире́ктор*-распоряди́тель *m*.

executor [ɪgˈzɛkjutəʳ] *n* (*LAW*) исполни́тель *m*.

exemplary [ɪgˈzɛmplərɪ] *adj* приме́рный* (приме́рен).

exemplify [ɪgˈzɛmplɪfaɪ] *vt* (*typify*) служи́ть* (послужи́ть *perf*) приме́ром +*gen*; (*illustrate*) поясня́ть (пояснить *perf*) приме́ром.

exempt [ɪgˈzɛmpt] *adj*: ~ **from** освобожд-ённый (освобождён) от +*gen* ♦ *vt*: **to ~ sb from** освобожда́ть (освободи́ть* *perf*) кого́-н от +*gen*.

exemption [ɪgˈzɛmpʃən] *n* освобожде́ние.

exercise [ˈɛksəsaɪz] *n* (*no pl*) гимна́стика; (*keep-fit*) заря́дка*; (*SCOL, MUS*) упражне́ние; (*of authority etc*) проявле́ние ♦ *vt* (*patience, authority*) проявля́ть (прояви́ть* *perf*); (*right*) осуществля́ть (осуществи́ть* *perf*); (*dog*) выгу́ливать (*impf*); (*mind*) занима́ть (*impf*) ♦ *vi* (*also*: **to take ~**) упражня́ться (*impf*); **military ~s** вое́нные уче́ния; **you need more ~** Вам на́до бо́льше дви́гаться.

exercise bike *n* велосипе́д-тренажёр.

exercise book *n* тетра́дь *f*.

exert [ɪgˈzəːt] *vt* (*influence, pressure*) ока́зывать (оказа́ть* *perf*); (*authority*) применя́ть (примени́ть* *perf*); **to ~ o.s.** напряга́ться (напря́чься* *perf*).

exertion [ɪgˈzəːʃən] *n* (*effort*) уси́лие; (*strain*) напряже́ние.

ex gratia [ˈɛksˈgreɪʃə] *adj*: **~ ~ payment** де́нежное вознагражде́ние.

exhale [ɛksˈheɪl] *vti* выдыха́ть (вы́дохнуть *perf*).

exhaust [ɪgˈzɔːst] *n* (*also*: **~ pipe**) выхлопна́я труба́; (*fumes*) выхлопны́е га́зы *mpl* ♦ *vt* (*person*) изнуря́ть (изнури́ть *perf*); (*money, resources etc*) истоща́ть (истощи́ть *perf*); (*topic*) исче́рпывать (исче́рпать *perf*); **to ~ o.s.** доводи́ть* (довести́* *perf*) себя́ до изнеможе́ния *or* изнуре́ния.

exhausted [ɪgˈzɔːstɪd] *adj* (*person*) изнурённый* (изнурён), изнеможённый* (изнеможён).

exhausting [ɪgˈzɔːstɪŋ] *adj* изнури́тельный* (изнури́телен).

exhaustion [ɪgˈzɔːstʃən] *n* (*tiredness*) изнеможе́ние; **nervous ~** не́рвное истоще́ние.

exhaustive [ɪgˈzɔːstɪv] *adj* исче́рпывающий*.

exhibit [ɪgˈzɪbɪt] *n* экспона́т; (*LAW*) веще́ственное доказа́тельство ♦ *vt* (*paintings*) экспони́ровать (*impf*/*perf*); (*quality, emotion*) проявля́ть (прояви́ть* *perf*).

exhibition [ɛksɪˈbɪʃən] *n* (*of paintings etc*) вы́ставка*; (*of ability, emotion*) проявле́ние; **to make an ~ of o.s.** выставля́ть (вы́ставить* *perf*) себя́ на посме́шище.

exhibitionist [ɛksɪˈbɪʃənɪst] *n* эксгибициони́ст;

(*show-off*): **he's a real ~** он всё де́лает напока́з.

exhibitor [ɪgˈzɪbɪtəʳ] *n* экспоне́нт.

exhilarating [ɪgˈzɪləreɪtɪŋ] *adj* волну́ющий.

exhilaration [ɪgzɪləˈreɪʃən] *n* взволно́ванность *f*.

exhort [ɪgˈzɔːt] *vt*: **to ~ sb to do** увещева́ть (*impf*) кого́-н +*infin*.

exile [ˈɛksaɪl] *n* (*banishment*) ссы́лка*, изгна́ние; (*person*) ссы́льный(-ая) *m(f)* adj, изгна́нник ♦ *vt* ссыла́ть (сосла́ть* *perf*); (*abroad*) высыла́ть (вы́слать* *perf*); **in ~** в ссы́лке *or* изгна́нии.

exist [ɪgˈzɪst] *vi* существова́ть (*impf*).

existence [ɪgˈzɪstəns] *n* существова́ние; **to be in ~** существова́ть (*impf*).

existentialism [ɛgzɪsˈtɛnʃlɪzəm] *n* экзистенциали́зм.

existing [ɪgˈzɪstɪŋ] *adj* существу́ющий.

exit [ˈɛksɪt] *n* (*way out*) вы́ход; (*on motorway*) вы́езд; (*departure*) ухо́д ♦ *vi* (*THEAT*) уходи́ть* (уйти́* *perf*); (*COMPUT*) выходи́ть* (вы́йти* *perf*); (*leave*): **to ~ from** (*room*) выходи́ть* (вы́йти* *perf*) из +*gen*; (*motorway*) съезжа́ть (съе́хать* *perf*) с +*gen*.

exit poll *n* предвари́тельный подсчёт голосо́в.

exit ramp *n* (*US*: *AUT*) съезд с автостра́ды.

exit visa *n* выездна́я ви́за.

exodus [ˈɛksədəs] *n* ма́ссовое бе́гство; **the ~ to the cities** ма́ссовое переселе́ние в города́.

ex officio [ˈɛksəˈfɪʃɪəu] *adv* по до́лжности.

exonerate [ɪgˈzɔnəreɪt] *vt*: **to ~ sb from guilt/responsibility** снима́ть (снять* *perf*) с кого́-н обвине́ние/отве́тственность.

exorbitant [ɪgˈzɔːbɪtnt] *adj* непоме́рный* (непоме́рен).

exorcize [ˈɛksɔːsaɪz] *vt* (*person, place*) изгоня́ть (изгна́ть* *perf*) дья́вола из +*gen*; (*spirit*) изгоня́ть (изгна́ть* *perf*).

exotic [ɪgˈzɔtɪk] *adj* экзоти́ческий*.

expand [ɪksˈpænd] *vt* (*area, business, influence*) расширя́ть (расши́рить *perf*); (*numbers*) увели́чивать (увели́чить *perf*) ♦ *vi* (*gas, metal, business*) расширя́ться (расши́риться *perf*); (*population*) увели́чиваться (увели́читься *perf*); **to ~ on** (*story, idea etc*) подро́бно разъясня́ть (разъясни́ть *perf*).

expanse [ɪksˈpæns] *n*: **an ~ of sea/sky** морско́й/небе́сный просто́р.

expansion [ɪksˈpænʃən] *n* расшире́ние; (*of population*) увеличе́ние; (*of economy*) рост.

expansionism [ɪksˈpænʃənɪzəm] *n* (*ECON*) экспансиони́зм.

expansionist [ɪksˈpænʃənɪst] *adj* (*policy*) экспансиони́стский.

expatriate [ɛksˈpætrɪət] *n* эмигра́нт(ка*).

expect [ɪksˈpɛkt] *vt* (*anticipate, hope for, await*) ожида́ть (*impf*); (*baby*) ждать (*impf*); (*suppose*) полага́ть (*impf*) ♦ *vi*: **to be ~ing** (*be pregnant*) ждать* (*impf*) ребёнка; **he ~s me to**

finish by Tuesday он ожида́ет, что я зако́нчу ко вто́рнику; **to ~ to do** рассчи́тывать *(impf)* +*infin*; **as ~ed** как и ожида́лось; **I ~ so** я полага́ю.

expectancy [ɪksˈpɛktənsɪ] *n* предвкуше́ние; **life ~** сре́дняя продолжи́тельность *f* жи́зни.

expectant [ɪksˈpɛktənt] *adj* (*silence, crowd*) выжида́ющий.

expectantly [ɪksˈpɛktəntlɪ] *adv* с наде́ждой.

expectant mother *n* бере́менная же́нщина.

expectation [ɛkspɛkˈteɪʃən] *n* (*hope*) ожида́ние; **in ~ of** в ожида́нии +*gen*; **contrary to** *or* **against all ~(s)** вопреки́ всем ожида́ниям; **to come** *or* **live up to sb's ~s** опра́вдывать (оправда́ть *perf*) чьи-н ожида́ния.

expedience [ɪksˈpiːdɪəns] *n* = **expediency**.

expediency [ɪksˈpiːdɪənsɪ] *n* вы́года; **for the sake of ~** ра́ди вы́годы.

expedient [ɪksˈpiːdɪənt] *adj* целесообра́зный* (целесообра́зен) ◆ *n* уло́вка.

expedite [ˈɛkspədaɪt] *vt* ускоря́ть (ускори́ть *perf*).

expedition [ɛkspəˈdɪʃən] *n* экспеди́ция; (*for shopping etc*) похо́д.

expeditionary force [ɛkspəˈdɪʃənrɪ-] *n* экспедицио́нные войска́* *pl*.

expeditious [ɛkspəˈdɪʃəs] *adj* эффекти́вный* (эффекти́вен).

expel [ɪksˈpɛl] *vt* (*person: from school, organization*) исключа́ть (исключи́ть *perf*); (: *from place*) изгоня́ть (изгна́ть* *perf*); (*substance: from body etc*) выводи́ть* (вы́вести* *perf*).

expend [ɪksˈpɛnd] *vt* расхо́довать (израсхо́довать *perf*), тра́тить (затра́тить* *perf*).

expendable [ɪksˈpɛndəbl] *adj* (*resources*) подлежа́щий списа́нию; **he is entirely ~** его́ мо́жно сбро́сить со счётов.

expenditure [ɪksˈpɛndɪtʃəʳ] *n* (*money spent*) затра́ты *fpl*; (*of money*) расхо́дование; (*of energy, time*) затра́та.

expense [ɪksˈpɛns] *n* (*cost*) сто́имость *f*; **~s** *npl* (*travelling expenses etc*) расхо́ды *mpl*; (*expenditure*) затра́ты *fpl*; **at the ~ of** за счёт +*gen*; **to go to the ~ of doing** тра́титься* (потра́титься* *perf*) +*infin*; **at great/little ~** с больши́ми/небольши́ми затра́тами.

expense account *n* счёт подотчётных сумм.

expensive [ɪksˈpɛnsɪv] *adj* дорого́й* (до́рог); **to be ~** до́рого сто́ить *(impf)*; **to have ~ tastes** име́ть *(impf)* вкус к дороги́м веща́м.

experience [ɪksˈpɪərɪəns] *n* (*in job, situation*) о́пыт; (*event, activity*) слу́чай; (: *difficult, painful*) испыта́ние; (*of emotion*) пережива́ние ◆ *vt* испы́тывать (испыта́ть *perf*), пережива́ть (пережи́ть* *perf*); **to know**

by *or* **from ~** знать *(impf)* по о́пыту; **to learn by ~** учи́ться *(impf)* на о́пыте.

experienced [ɪksˈpɪərɪənst] *adj* о́пытный* (о́пытен).

experiment [ɪksˈpɛrɪmənt] *n* экспериме́нт, о́пыт ◆ *vi*: **to ~ (with/on)** эксперименти́ровать *(impf)* (с +*instr*/на +*prp*); **to carry out** *or* **perform an ~** проводи́ть* (провести́* *perf*) экспериме́нт; **as an ~** в ка́честве экспериме́нта; **to ~ with a new vaccine** проводи́ть* (провести́* *perf*) о́пыты с но́вой вакци́ной.

experimental [ɪksˈpɛrɪˈmɛntl] *adj* (*methods, ideas*) эксперимента́льный; (*tests*) про́бный; **at the ~ stage** на ста́дии экспериме́нта.

expert [ˈɛkspəːt] *n* экспе́рт, специали́ст ◆ *adj* (*person*) уме́лый; **~ opinion/advice** мне́ние/ сове́т экспе́рта *or* специали́ста; **an ~ on sth** специали́ст по чему́-н; **she is ~ at resolving disputes** она́ прекра́сно уме́ет разреша́ть спо́ры; **~ witness** (*LAW*) суде́бный экспе́рт.

expertise [ɛkspəːˈtiːz] *n* зна́ния *ntpl* и о́пыт.

expire [ɪksˈpaɪəʳ] *vi* истека́ть (исте́чь* *perf*); **my passport ~s in January** срок де́йствия моего́ па́спорта истека́ет в январе́.

expiry [ɪksˈpaɪərɪ] *n* истече́ние сро́ка.

expiry date *n* да́та истече́ния сро́ка.

explain [ɪksˈpleɪn] *vt* объясня́ть (объясни́ть *perf*)

▶ **explain away** *vt* (*mistake, situation*) находи́ть* (найти́* *perf*) оправда́ние +*gen*.

explanation [ɛkspləˈneɪʃən] *n* объясне́ние; **to find an ~ for sth** находи́ть* (найти́* *perf*) объясне́ние чему́-н.

explanatory [ɪksˈplænətrɪ] *adj* (*comment etc*) объясни́тельный; **~ notes** примеча́ния *ntpl*.

expletive [ɪksˈpliːtɪv] *n* бра́нное сло́во*, руга́тельство.

explicable [ɪksˈplɪkəbl] *adj* объясни́мый; **for no ~ reason** по необъясни́мой причи́не.

explicit [ɪksˈplɪsɪt] *adj* я́вный* (я́вен); (*sex, violence*) открове́нный.

explode [ɪksˈpləud] *vi* (*bomb, person*) взрыва́ться (взорва́ться* *perf*); (*population*) ре́зко возраста́ть (возрасти́* *perf*) ◆ *vt* (*bomb*) взрыва́ть (взорва́ть* *perf*); (*myth, theory*) опроверга́ть* (опрове́ргнуть* *perf*); **to ~ with laughter** разража́ться (разрази́ться* *perf*) сме́хом.

exploit [*vt* ɪksˈplɔɪt, *n* ˈɛksplɔɪt] *vt* (*resources, also pej: person, idea*) эксплуати́ровать *(impf)*; (*opportunity*) испо́льзовать *(impf/perf)* ◆ *n* по́двиг.

exploitation [ɛksplɔɪˈteɪʃən] *n* (*see vb*) эксплуата́ция; испо́льзование.

exploration [ɛkspləˈreɪʃən] *n* (*of place*) иссле́дование; (*of idea*) изуче́ние.

exploratory [ɪksˈplɔrətrɪ] *adj* (*expedition*)

---

* marks translations which have irregular inflections. The Russian-English side of the dictionary gives inflectional information.

исслéдовательский*; (*talks, operation*) предвари́тельный.

explore [ɪks'plɔːʳ] *vt* (*place*) иссле́довать (*impf/ perf*); (*with hands etc*) ощу́пывать (ощу́пать *perf*); (*idea, suggestion*) изуча́ть (изучи́ть* *perf*).

explorer [ɪks'plɔːrəʳ] *n* иссле́дователь(ница) *m(f)*.

explosion [ɪks'pləuʒən] *n* взрыв; **population** ~ демографи́ческий взрыв.

explosive [ɪks'pləusɪv] *adj* (*device, effect*) взрывно́й; (*situation*) взрывоопа́сный* (взрывоопа́сен) ♦ *n* (*substance*) взры́вчатое вещество́*; (*device*) взрывно́е устро́йство; **he has an ~ temper** он о́чень вспы́льчивый.

exponent [ɪks'pəunənt] *n* (*of idea, theory*) сторо́нник(-ица); (*of skill, activity*) ма́стер; (*MATH*) показа́тель *m* сте́пени.

exponential [ɛkspəu'nɛnʃl] *adj* (*growth*) стреми́тельный* (стреми́телен); (*MATH*) экспоненциа́льный ♦ *n* (*MATH*) экспоне́нта.

export [*n, cpd* 'ɛkspɔːt, *vt* ɛks'pɔːt] *n* (*process*) э́кспорт, вы́воз; (*product*) предме́т э́кспорта ♦ *vt* экспорти́ровать (*impf/perf*), вывози́ть* (вы́везти* *perf*) ♦ *cpd* (*duty, licence*) э́кспортный.

exportation [ɛkspɔː'teɪʃən] *n* э́кспорти́рование.

exporter [ɛks'pɔːtəʳ] *n* экспортёр.

expose [ɪks'pəuz] *vt* (*object*) обнажа́ть (обнажи́ть* *perf*); (*truth, plot*) раскрыва́ть (раскры́ть* *perf*); (*person*) разоблача́ть (разоблачи́ть* *perf*); (*PHOT*) экспони́ровать (*impf/perf*); **to ~ sb to sth** подверга́ть (подве́ргнуть* *perf*) кого́-н чему́-н; **to ~ o.s.** (*LAW*) демонстри́ровать (*impf*) половы́е о́рганы.

exposé [ɪks'pəuzeɪ] *n* разоблаче́ние.

exposed [ɪks'pəuzd] *adj* (*wire*) оголённый; (*place*): ~ (**to**) откры́тый (откры́т) (+*dat*).

exposition [ɛkspə'zɪʃən] *n* (*explanation*) изложе́ние; (*exhibition*) экспози́ция.

exposure [ɪks'pəuʒəʳ] *n* (*of culprit*) разоблаче́ние; (*PHOT*) экспози́ция, вы́держка; (*: shot*) кадр; ~ **to radiation** пребыва́ние под возде́йствием радиа́ции; **to suffer/die from** ~ (*MED*) страда́ть (пострада́ть *perf*)/умира́ть (умере́ть* *perf*) от переохлажде́ния.

exposure meter *n* (*PHOT*) экспоно́метр.

expound [ɪks'paund] *vt* излага́ть (изложи́ть* *perf*).

express [ɪks'prɛs] *adj* (*clear*) чёткий*; (*BRIT: service*) сро́чный ♦ *n* (*train, coach etc*) экспре́сс ♦ *adv* (*send*) экспре́ссом ♦ *vt* выража́ть (вы́разить* *perf*); **to ~ o.s.** выража́ть (вы́разить* *perf*) себя́.

expression [ɪks'prɛʃən] *n* выраже́ние; (*expressiveness*) вырази́тельность *f*.

expressionism [ɪks'prɛʃənɪzəm] *n* экспрессиони́зм.

expressive [ɪks'prɛsɪv] *adj* вырази́тельный* (вырази́телен).

expressly [ɪks'prɛslɪ] *adv* (*clearly*) определённо; (*intentionally*) специа́льно.

expressway [ɪks'prɛsweɪ] *n* (*esp US*) скоростна́я автостра́да.

expropriate [ɛks'prəuprɪeɪt] *vt* (*money, property*) экспроприи́ровать (*impf/perf*).

expulsion [ɪks'pʌlʃən] *n* (*from school*) исключе́ние; (*from country*) изгна́ние; (*of substance*) вы́вод.

expurgate ['ɛkspɔːgeɪt] *vt*: **to ~ a text** вычёркивать (вы́черкнуть *perf*) нежела́тельные места́ из те́кста; **the ~d version** вариа́нт с купю́рами.

exquisite [ɛks'kwɪzɪt] *adj* (*face, lace, taste, workmanship*) изы́сканный* (изы́скан); (*pain, pleasure*) о́стрый.

exquisitely [ɛks'kwɪzɪtlɪ] *adv* (*dressed, polite, carved*) изы́сканно; (*sensitive*) обострённо.

ex-serviceman ['ɛks'sɔːvɪsmən] *irreg n* бы́вший* военнослу́жащий* *m adj*.

ext. *abbr* (*TEL*) = **extension**.

extemporize [ɪks'tɛmpəraɪz] *vi* импровизи́ровать (*impf*).

extend [ɪks'tɛnd] *vt* (*visit, deadline*) продлева́ть (продли́ть *perf*); (*building*) расширя́ть (расши́рить *perf*); (*arm, hand*) протя́гивать (протяну́ть* *perf*); (*offer*) ока́зывать (оказа́ть* *perf*); (*credit, help*) предоставля́ть (предоста́вить* *perf*) ♦ *vi* (*land, road*) простира́ться (*impf*); (*period*) продолжа́ться (продо́лжиться *perf*); **to ~ an invitation to sb** приглаша́ть (пригласи́ть* *perf*) кого́-н.

extension [ɪks'tɛnʃən] *n* (*of time*) продле́ние; (*of campaign, rights*) расшире́ние; (*of building*) пристро́йка*; (*of road*) продолже́ние; (*ELEC*) удлини́тель *m*; (*TEL: in house*) паралле́льный телефо́н; (: *in office*) доба́вочный телефо́н; (: **3718** (*TEL*) доба́вочный (но́мер) 3718.

extension cable *n* удлини́тель *m*.

extension lead *n* = **extension cable**.

extensive [ɪks'tɛnsɪv] *adj* обши́рный* (обши́рен); ~ **damage** значи́тельный уще́рб.

extensively [ɪks'tɛnsɪvlɪ] *adv*: **he has travelled** ~ он мно́го путеше́ствовал.

extent [ɪks'tɛnt] *n* (*size: of area etc*) протяжённость *f*; (: *of problem etc*) масшта́б; (*degree: of damage, loss*) разме́р; **to some** ~ до не́которой сте́пени; **to a large** ~ в значи́тельной сте́пени; **to go to the** ~ **of** ... доходи́ть* (дойти́* *perf*) до того́, что ...; **to such an** ~ **that** ... до тако́й сте́пени, что ...; **to what** ~? до како́й сте́пени?

extenuating [ɪks'tɛnjueɪtɪŋ] *adj*: ~ **circumstances** смягча́ющие обстоя́тельства *ntpl*.

exterior [ɛks'tɪərɪəʳ] *adj* (*drain, light, paint*) нару́жный; (*world*) вне́шний* ♦ *n* (*outside*) вне́шняя сторона́*; (*appearance*) вне́шность *f*.

exterminate [ɪksˈtə:mɪneɪt] *vt* истреблять (истребить* *perf*).

extermination [ɪkstə:mɪˈneɪʃən] *n* истребление.

external [ɛksˈtə:nl] *adj* внешний*; **the ~s** *npl* внешняя сторона* *sg*; "**for ~ use only**" "для наружного употребления"; ~ **affairs** (*POL*) внешняя политика*; ~ **evidence** свидетельство со стороны.

externally [ɛksˈtə:nəlɪ] *adv* внешне.

extinct [ɪksˈtɪŋkt] *adj* (*animal*) вымерший; (*plant*) исчезнувший; (*volcano*) потухший; **to become ~** вымирать (вымереть* *perf*).

extinction [ɪksˈtɪŋkʃən] *n* (*see adj*) вымирание; исчезновение.

extinguish [ɪksˈtɪŋgwɪʃ] *vt* (*fire*) тушить* (потушить* *perf*); (*light*) гасить* (погасить* *perf*); (*memory, hope*) уничтожать (уничтожить* *perf*).

extinguisher [ɪksˈtɪŋgwɪʃə*r*] *n* (*also*: **fire ~**) огнетушитель *m*.

extol [ɪksˈtəul] (*US* **extoll**) *vt* превозносить* (превознести* *perf*).

extort [ɪksˈtɔ:t] *vt*: **to ~ sth (from)** вымогать (*impf*) что-н (у +*gen*).

extortion [ɪksˈtɔ:ʃən] *n* вымогательство.

extortionate [ɪksˈtɔ:ʃnɪt] *adj* (*price*) грабительский*; (*demands*) вымогательский.

extra [ˈɛkstrə] *adj* (*additional*) дополнительный; (*spare*) лишний ♦ *adv* (*in addition*) дополнительно; (*especially*) особенно ♦ *n* (*luxury*) излишество; (*surcharge*) доплата; (*CINEMA*) статист(ка*); **wine will cost ~** за вино нужно будет заплатить отдельно; **the room charge does not include ~s** цена номера не включает плату за дополнительные услуги и удобства.

extra... [ˈɛkstrə] *prefix* экстра..., особо..., сверх....

extract [*vt* ɪksˈtrækt, *n* ˈɛkstrækt] *vt* (*tooth*) удалять (удалить* *perf*); (*mineral*) добывать (добыть* *perf*); (*money, promise*) вытягивать (вытянуть* *perf*) ♦ *n* (*from novel, recording*) отрывок*; (*CULIN*) экстракт; **to ~ sth (from)** извлекать (извлечь* *perf*) что-н (из +*gen*).

extraction [ɪksˈtrækʃən] *n* (*of object*) извлечение; (*of tooth*) удаление; (*of minerals etc*) добыча; (*descent*): **of Scottish ~** шотландец(-дка) по происхождению.

extractor fan [ɪksˈtræktə-] *n* вытяжное устройство, вентилятор.

extracurricular [ˈɛkstrəkəˈrɪkjulə*r*] *adj* внеклассный, внеучебный.

extradite [ˈɛkstrədaɪt] *vt*: **to ~ sb to/from** выдавать* (выдать* *perf*) кого-н +*dat*/из +*gen*.

extradition [ɛkstrəˈdɪʃən] *n* выдача (*преступника*) ♦ *cpd*: ~ **order/treaty** просьба/

соглашение о выдаче.

extramarital [ˈɛkstrəˈmærɪtl] *adj* внебрачный.

extramural [ˈɛkstrəˈmjuərl] *adj* заочный.

extraneous [ɛksˈtremɪəs] *adj* посторонний*.

extraordinary [ɪksˈtrɔ:dnrɪ] *adj* незаурядный* (незауряден), необычайный* (необычаен); (*meeting*) чрезвычайный; **the ~ thing is that** ... самое удивительное в том, что ....

extraordinary general meeting *n* чрезвычайное общее собрание.

extrapolation [ɛkstræpəˈleɪʃən] *n* экстраполяция.

extrasensory perception [ˈɛkstrəˈsɛnsərɪ-] *n* сверхчувственное *or* экстрасенсорное восприятие.

extra time *n* дополнительное время* *nt*.

extravagance [ɪksˈtrævəgəns] *n* (*of behaviour*) экстравагантность *f*; (*with money*) расточительство.

extravagant [ɪksˈtrævəgənt] *adj* (*lavish*) экстравагантный* (экстравагантен); (*wasteful*: *person*) расточительный* (расточителен); (: *machine*) неэкономный* (неэкономен); (*wild*: *ideas, claims*) сумасбродный* (сумасброден).

extreme [ɪksˈtri:m] *adj* крайний*; (*heat, cold*) сильнейший ♦ *n* (*of behaviour*) крайность *f*; **the ~ right/left** (*POL*) крайне правые *pl adj*/ левые *pl adj*; ~**s of temperature** перепады температуры.

extremely [ɪksˈtri:mlɪ] *adv* крайне.

extremist [ɪksˈtri:mɪst] *n* экстремист(ка*) ♦ *adj* экстремистский.

extremities [ɪksˈtrɛmɪtɪz] *npl* (*ANAT*) конечности *fpl*.

extremity [ɪksˈtrɛmɪtɪ] *n* конечность *f*; (*of situation*) крайность *f*.

extricate [ˈɛkstrɪkeɪt] *vt*: **to ~ sb/sth (from)** высвобождать (высвободить* *perf*) кого-н/ что-н (из +*gen*); **to ~ o.s. (from)** выпутываться (выпутаться *perf*) (из +*gen*).

extrovert [ˈɛkstrəvə:t] *n* экстроверт.

exuberance [ɪgˈzju:bərns] *n* экспансивность *f*.

exuberant [ɪgˈzju:bərnt] *adj* (*person, behaviour*) экспансивный* (экспансивен); (*imagination*) буйный* (буен).

exude [ɪgˈzju:d] *vt* (*confidence, enthusiasm*) источать (*impf*); (*liquid*) выделять (выделить* *perf*); (*smell*) издавать* (*impf*).

exult [ɪgˈzʌlt] *vi* (*rejoice*): **to ~ (in)** ликовать* (*impf*) (по поводу +*gen*).

exultant [ɪgˈzʌltənt] *adj* ликующий, торжествующий; **to be ~** ликовать (*impf*), торжествовать (*impf*).

exultation [ɛgzʌlˈteɪʃən] *n* экзальтация, ликование.

eye [aɪ] *n* (*ANAT*) глаз*; (*of needle*) ушко* ♦ *vt* разглядывать (разглядеть* *perf*); **to keep an**

---

* marks translations which have irregular inflections. The Russian-English side of the dictionary gives inflectional information.

~ on (*person, object*) присма́тривать (присмотре́ть* *perf*) за +*instr*; (*time*) следи́ть* (*impf*) за +*instr*; **in the public ~** на виду́, в це́нтре внима́ния; **to have an ~ for sth** знать (*impf*) толк в чём-н; **with an ~ to doing** (*BRIT*) с расчётом +*infin*; **as far as the ~ can see** наско́лько мо́жно охвати́ть взгля́дом; **there's more to this than meets the ~** э́то не так про́сто, как ка́жется на пе́рвый взгляд.

eyeball ['aıbɔ:l] *n* глазно́е я́блоко*.

eyebath ['aıbɑ:θ] *n* (*BRIT*) глазна́я ва́нночка*.

eyebrow ['aıbrau] *n* бровь* *f*.

eyebrow pencil *n* каранда́ш* для брове́й.

eye-catching ['aıkætʃıŋ] *adj* броса́ющийся в глаза́.

eyecup ['aıkʌp] *n* (*US*) = **eyebath**.

eye drops *npl* глазны́е ка́пли *fpl*.

eyeful ['aıful] *n*: **an ~ of sand/dust** по́лные глаза́ песка́*/пы́ли; **to get an ~ of sb/sth** (*inf*) разгляде́ть* (*perf*) кого́-н/что́-н.

eyeglass ['aıglɑ:s] *n* моно́кль *m*.

eyelash ['aılæʃ] *n* ресни́ца.

eyelet ['aılıt] *n* фесто́н.

eye level *n*: **at ~~** на у́ровне глаз.

eyelevel ['aılɛvl] *adj* (*grill*) располо́женный на у́ровне глаз.

eyelid ['aılıd] *n* ве́ко*.

eyeliner ['aılaınə'] *n* каранда́ш* для глаз.

eye-opener ['aıəupnə'] *n* открове́ние.

eye shadow *n* те́ни* *fpl* (для век).

eyesight ['aısaıt] *n* зре́ние.

eyesore ['aısɔ:'] *n*: **that building is a real ~** э́то зда́ние как бельмо́ на глазу́.

eyestrain ['aıstreın] *n* чрезме́рное напряже́ние глаз.

eyeteeth ['aıti:θ] *npl of* **eyetooth**.

eyetooth ['aıtu:θ] (*pl* **eyeteeth**) *n* глазно́й зуб; **to give one's eyeteeth for sth/to do** же́ртвовать (поже́ртвовать *perf*) всем за что-н/за то, что́бы +*infin*.

eyewash ['aıwɔʃ] *n* примо́чка* для глаз; (*fig*: *inf*) очковтира́тельство.

eyewitness ['aiwıtnıs] *n* очеви́дец ♦ *cpd*: **an ~ account** свиде́тельство очеви́дца.

eyrie ['ıərı] *n* (*nest*) орли́ное гнездо́*.

~ F, f ~

F, f [ɛf] *n* (*letter*) 6-ая бу́ква англи́йского алфави́та.
F [ɛf] *n* (*MUS*) фа.
F *abbr* = **Fahrenheit**.
FA *n abbr* (*BRIT*: = Football Association) Футбо́льная ассоциа́ция.
FAA *n abbr* (*US*: = Federal Aviation Administration*) Федера́льное управле́ние авиа́цией.
fable ['feɪbl] *n* ба́сня*.
fabric ['fæbrɪk] *n* (*cloth*) ткань *f*; (*of society*) структу́ра; (*of building*) констру́кция.
fabricate ['fæbrɪkeɪt] *vt* (*make up*) фабрикова́ть (сфабрикова́ть *perf*); (*make*) производи́ть* (произвести́* *perf*).
fabrication [fæbrɪ'keɪʃən] *n* (*lie*) фабрика́ция; (*making*) произво́дство.
fabric ribbon *n* (*for typewriter*) печа́тная ле́нта.
fabulous ['fæbjuləs] *adj* (*extraordinary*) невероя́тный* (невероя́тен); (*mythical*) ска́зочный*; (*inf*: *super*) ска́зочный* (ска́зочен).
façade [fə'sɑːd] *n* фаса́д; (*fig*: *pretence*) ви́димость *f*; **a ~ of gaiety/indifference** фаса́д весе́лья/равноду́шия.
face [feɪs] *n* (*of person, organization*) лицо́*; (*grimace*) грима́са; (*of clock*) цифербла́т; (*of mountain, cliff*) склон; (*of building*) фаса́д; (*surface*: *of cube etc*) сторона́* ◆ *vt* (*fact*) признава́ть* (призна́ть* *perf*); **the house is facing the sea** дом обращён к мо́рю; **he was facing the door** он был обращён лицо́м к две́ри; **we are facing difficulties** нам предстоя́т тру́дности; **~ down** лицо́м вниз; **to lose/save ~** теря́ть (потеря́ть *perf*)/спаса́ть (спасти́* *perf*) репута́цию; **to make** *or* **pull a ~** де́лать (сде́лать *perf*) грима́су; **in the ~ of** (*difficulties etc*) несмотря́ на +*acc*; **on the ~ of it** на пе́рвый взгляд; **~ to ~ (with)** (*with person, problem*) лицо́м к лицу́ (с +*instr*); **to ~ the fact that ...** признава́ть* (призна́ть* *perf*) тот факт, что ...
► **face up to** *vt fus* (*obligations, responsibility*) признава́ть* (призна́ть* *perf*); (*difficulties*) справля́ться (спра́виться* *perf*) с +*instr*.

face cloth *n* (*BRIT*) махро́вая салфе́тка (*для обтира́ния лица́*).
face cream *n* крем* для лица́.
faceless ['feɪslɪs] *adj* безли́кий*.
face-lift ['feɪslɪft] *n* подтя́жка* ко́жи на лице́; (*of building etc*) облицо́вка*.
face powder *n* пу́дра для лица́.
face-saving ['feɪs'seɪvɪŋ] *adj* для спасе́ния репута́ции.
facet ['fæsɪt] *n* (*also fig*) грань *f*.
facetious [fə'siːʃəs] *adj* остроу́мный.
face to face *adv* лицо́м к лицу́.
face value *n* номина́льная сто́имость *f*; **to take sth at ~ ~** (*fig*) принима́ть (приня́ть* *perf*) что-н за чи́стую моне́ту.
facia ['feɪʃə] *n* = **fascia**.
facial ['feɪʃl] *n* космети́ческая обрабо́тка лица́ ◆ *adj*: **~ expression** выраже́ние лица́; **~ hair** во́лосы, расту́щие на лице́.
facile ['fæsaɪl] *adj* пове́рхностный*.
facilitate [fə'sɪlɪteɪt] *vt* спосо́бствовать (*impf*/ *perf*) +*dat*.
facilities *npl* (*buildings*) помеще́ние *ntsg*; (*equipment*) обору́дование *ntsg*; **credit ~** креди́тный лими́т (*креди́тной ка́рточки заёмщика*); **cooking ~** усло́вия *ntpl* для приготовле́ния пи́щи.
facility [fə'sɪlɪtɪ] *n* (*feature*) приспособле́ние; (*service*) услу́га; (*aptitude*): **to have a ~ for** име́ть (*impf*) спосо́бности к +*dat*.
facing ['feɪsɪŋ] *prep* (*opposite*) напро́тив +*gen* ◆ *n* (*SEWING*) отде́лка*.
facsimile [fæk'sɪmɪlɪ] *n* факси́миле *nt ind*; (*machine, document*) факс.
fact [fækt] *n* факт; **in ~** факти́чески; **to know for a ~ that ...** знать (*impf*) наверняка́, что ...; **the ~ (of the matter) is that ...** де́ло в том, что ...; **the ~s of life** (*sex*) полова́я сторона́ жи́зни; (*fig*) реа́льности *fpl* жи́зни.
fact-finding ['fæktfaɪndɪŋ] *adj* для рассле́дования фа́ктов.
faction ['fækʃən] *n* (*group*) фра́кция.
factor ['fæktə] *n* фа́ктор; (*COMM*) комиссионе́р; (: *agent*) аге́нт; **safety ~** фа́ктор безопа́сности; **human ~** челове́ческий* фа́ктор.

---

* marks translations which have irregular inflections. The Russian-English side of the dictionary gives inflectional information.

factory ['fæktərɪ] *n* (*for textiles etc*) фа́брика; (*for machinery etc*) заво́д.

factory farming *n* (*BRIT*) веде́ние животново́дства промы́шленными ме́тодами.

factory floor *n* (*fig: workers*) рабо́чие *pl adj* у станка́.

factory ship *n* плаву́чая фа́брика.

factual ['fæktjuəl] *adj* факти́ческий*.

faculty ['fækəltɪ] *n* спосо́бность *f*; (*of university*) факульте́т; (*US: teaching staff*) профе́ссорско-преподава́тельский соста́в.

fad [fæd] *n* причу́да.

fade [feɪd] *vi* (*colour*) выцвета́ть (вы́цвести* *perf*); (*light*) угаса́ть (уга́снуть* *perf*); (*sound*) замира́ть (замере́ть* *perf*); (*flower*) вя́нуть* (завя́нуть* *perf*); (*hope, smile*) угаса́ть (уга́снуть* *perf*); (*memory*) сгла́живаться (сгла́диться* *perf*)

▶ **fade in** *vt*: **to ~ the picture/sound in** постепе́нно увели́чивать (*impf*) чёткость изображе́ния/си́лу зву́ка

▶ **fade out** *vt*: **to ~ the picture/sound out** постепе́нно уменьша́ть (*impf*) чёткость изображе́ния/си́лу зву́ка.

faeces ['fi:si:z] (*US* **feces**) *npl* фека́лии *fpl*.

fag [fæg] (*inf*) *n* (*BRIT: cigarette*) сигаре́та; (*US: pej: homosexual*) го́мик; (*BRIT: chore*): **what a ~!** ну и рабо́тёнка!

Fahrenheit ['færənhaɪt] *n* Фаренге́йт.

fail [feɪl] *vt* (*exam, candidate*) прова́ливать (провали́ть* *perf*); (*subj: person, memory*) изменя́ть (измени́ть *perf*) +*dat*, подводи́ть (подвести́ *perf*); (: *courage*) покида́ть (поки́нуть *perf*) ♦ *vi* (*candidate, attempt*) прова́ливаться (провали́ться* *perf*); (*brakes*) отка́зывать (отказа́ть* *perf*); **my eyesight/ health is ~ing** у меня́ слабе́ет зре́ние/ здоро́вье; **to ~ to do** не смочь* (*perf*) +*infin*; **without ~** обяза́тельно; **the light is ~ing** смерка́ется.

failing ['feɪlɪŋ] *n* недоста́ток* ♦ *prep* за неиме́нием +*gen*; **~ that** за неиме́нием э́того.

fail-safe ['feɪlseɪf] *adj* (*device*) предохрани́тельный.

failure ['feɪljə'] *n* неуда́ча; (*mechanical*) поврежде́ние; (*of crops*) неурожа́й; (*in exam*) прова́л; (*person*) неуда́чник(-ица); **his ~ to complete the work** то, что он не смог вы́полнить рабо́ту; **the evening was a complete ~** ве́чер был по́лным прова́лом.

faint [feɪnt] *adj* сла́бый* (слаб); (*recollection*) сму́тный* (сму́тен); (*mark*) едва́ заме́тный* (заме́тен); (*breeze, trace*) лёгкий* ♦ *n* (*MED*) о́бморок ♦ *vi* (*MED*) па́дать (упа́сть* *perf*) в о́бморок; **to feel ~** чу́вствовать (почу́вствовать *perf*) сла́бость.

faintest ['feɪntɪst] *adj* мале́йший*; **I haven't the ~ idea** я не име́ю ни мале́йшего поня́тия.

faint-hearted ['feɪnt'hɑːtɪd] *adj* малоду́шный* (малоду́шен).

faintly ['feɪntlɪ] *adv* (*a bit*) сла́бо; (*hardly*) едва́.

fair [fɛə'] *adj* (*person, decision*) справедли́вый (справедли́в); (*size, number*) значи́тельный; (*chance, guess*) хоро́ший*; (*skin, hair*) све́тлый* (све́тел); (*weather*) хоро́ший*, я́сный* ♦ *n* (*also*: **trade ~**) я́рмарка*; (*BRIT: also*: **funfair**) аттракцио́ны *mpl* ♦ *adv*: **to play ~** вести́* (*impf*) дела́ разу́мно *or* че́стно; **it's not ~!** э́то нече́стно!; **a ~ amount of money** значи́тельная су́мма де́нег; **a ~ amount of success** значи́тельный успе́х; **I had a pretty ~ idea** у меня́ была́ дово́льно хоро́шая иде́я; **~ wear and tear** обосно́ванный изно́с.

fair copy *n* чистово́й экземпля́р.

fair game *n*: **he is ~ ~** он зако́нная добы́ча.

fairground ['fɛəgraʊnd] *n* лу́на-парк.

fair-haired [fɛə'hɛəd] *adj* светловоло́сый (светлово́лос).

fairly ['fɛəlɪ] *adv* (*justly*) справедли́во; (*quite*) дово́льно; **I'm ~ sure** я почти́ уве́рен.

fairness ['fɛənɪs] *n* (*justice*) справедли́вость *f*; **in all ~** со всей справедли́востью.

fair play *n* че́стная игра́.

fairway ['fɛəweɪ] *n* (*GOLF*): **the ~** *травяни́стая доро́жка ме́жду лу́нками в го́льфе.*

fairy ['fɛərɪ] *n* фе́я.

fairy godmother *n* до́брая волше́бница.

fairy lights *npl* (*BRIT*) электри́ческая гирля́нда *fsg*.

fairy tale *n* ска́зка*.

faith [feɪθ] *n* (*also REL*) ве́ра; **to have ~ in sb/sth** ве́рить (*impf*) в кого́-н/что-н.

faithful ['feɪθful] *adj*: **~ (to)** ве́рный* (ве́рен) (+*dat*).

faithfully ['feɪθfəlɪ] *adv* ве́рно.

faith healer *n* зна́харь(-рка*) *m(f)*.

fake [feɪk] *n* (*painting, document*) подде́лка*; (*person*) притво́рщик(-ица) ♦ *adj* фальши́вый, подде́льный ♦ *vt* (*painting, document*) подде́лывать (подде́лать *perf*); (*illness, emotion*) симули́ровать (*impf*); **his illness is a ~** его́ боле́знь – симуля́ция.

falcon ['fɔːlkən] *n* со́кол.

Falkland Islands ['fɔːlklənd-] *npl*: **the ~ ~** Фолкле́ндские острова́* *mpl*.

fall [fɔːl] (*pt* **fell**, *pp* **fallen**) *n* паде́ние; (*US: autumn*) о́сень *f* ♦ *vi* па́дать (упа́сть* *perf*); (*government, country*) пасть* (*perf*); (*rain, snow*) па́дать (вы́пасть* *perf*); (*silence, hush, night*) наступа́ть (наступи́ть* *perf*); (*sadness*) охва́тывать (охвати́ть *perf*); **~s** *npl* (*waterfall*) водопа́д; **a ~ of snow** снегопа́д; **a ~ of earth** обва́л; **to ~ flat** (*plan*) не удава́ться* (уда́ться* *perf*); (*joke*) не име́ть (*impf*) успе́ха; **to ~ flat (on one's face)** па́дать (упа́сть* *perf*) ничко́м; **to ~ in love (with sb/sth)** влюбля́ться (влюби́ться* *perf*) (в кого́-н/во что-н); **to ~ short of (sb's expectations)** не опра́вдывать (оправда́ть *perf*) (чьих-н ожида́ний); **a lot of rain/snow fell yesterday** вчера́ вы́пало мно́го сне́га/дождя́; **darkness/**

night fell наступи́ла темнота́/ночь
▶ **fall apart** *vi* разва́ливаться (развали́ться*
perf); (*inf: emotionally*) раскле́иваться
(раскле́иться *perf*)
▶ **fall back** *vt fus* (MIL) отступа́ть (отступи́ть*
perf)
▶ **fall back on** *vt fus* прибега́ть (прибе́гнуть*
perf) к +*dat*; **to have sth to ~ back on** (*money,
job etc*) име́ть (*impf*) что-н в запа́се
▶ **fall behind** *vi* отстава́ть* (отста́ть* *perf*); **to ~
behind with the payments** просро́чивать
(просро́чить *perf*) платежи́
▶ **fall down** *vi* (*person*) па́дать (упа́сть* *perf*);
(*building*) ру́шиться (ру́хнуть *perf*)
▶ **fall for** *vt fus* (*trick etc*) попада́ться
(попа́сться* *perf*) на +*acc*; (*story*) ве́рить
(пове́рить *perf*) +*dat*; (*person*) влюбля́ться
(влюби́ться* *perf*) в +*acc*
▶ **fall in** *vi* (*roof*) обва́ливаться (обвали́ться
perf); (MIL) стро́иться (постро́иться *perf*)
▶ **fall in with** *vt fus* (*sb's plans etc*) соглаша́ться
(согласи́ться* *perf*) с +*instr*
▶ **fall off** *vi* па́дать (упа́сть* *perf*)
▶ **fall out** *vi* (*hair, teeth*) выпада́ть (вы́пасть*
perf); (*friends etc*): **to ~ out with sb** ссо́риться
(поссо́риться *perf*) с кем-н
▶ **fall over** *vi* упа́сть* (*perf*) ♦ *vt*: **to ~ over o.s. to
do** лезть* (вы́лезть* *perf*) из ко́жи вон, что́бы
+*infin*
▶ **fall through** *vi* (*plan*) прова́ливаться
(провали́ться* *perf*).
fallacy [ˈfæləsɪ] *n* (*misconception*)
заблужде́ние.
fall-back [ˈfɔːlbæk] *adj*: **~ position** пози́ция для
отступле́ния.
fallen [ˈfɔːlən] *pp of* **fall**.
fallible [ˈfæləbl] *adj* спосо́бный* (спосо́бен)
ошиба́ться (ошиби́ться *perf*).
falling [ˈfɔːlɪŋ] *adj*: **~ market** (COMM)
понижа́тельная ры́ночная конъюнкту́ра.
falling off *n* сниже́ние.
falling out *n* размо́лвка.
Fallopian tube [fəˈləupɪən-] *n* фалло́пиевы
тру́бы *fpl*.
fallout [ˈfɔːlaut] *n* радиоакти́вные оса́дки *pl*.
fallout shelter *n* убе́жище от радиоакти́вных
оса́дков.
fallow [ˈfæləu] *adj* (*land, field*) парово́й.
false [fɔːls] *adj* (*untrue, wrong*) ло́жный*
(ло́жен); (*insincere, artificial*) фальши́вый
(фальши́в); **~ imprisonment** незако́нное
лише́ние свобо́ды.
false alarm *n* ло́жная трево́га.
falsehood [ˈfɔːlshud] *n* ложь* *f*.
falsely [ˈfɔːlslɪ] *adv* (*accuse*) ло́жно.
false pretences *npl*: **under ~ ~** под ло́жным
предло́гом.
false teeth *npl* (BRIT) иску́сственные зу́бы* *mpl*.

falsify [ˈfɔːlsɪfaɪ] *vt* фальсифици́ровать (*impf/
perf*), подде́лывать (подде́лать *perf*).
falter [ˈfɔːltə*] *vi* (*engine*) ка́шлять (*impf*);
(*person: hesitate*) замя́ться* (*perf*); (: *in
speech*) запина́ться (запну́ться *perf*); (: *while
moving*) спотыка́ться (споткну́ться *perf*).
fame [feɪm] *n* сла́ва.
familiar [fəˈmɪlɪə*] *adj* (*well-known*) знако́мый
(знако́м); (*intimate*) дру́жеский*; **he is/was ~
with** (*subject*) он знако́м/был знако́м с +*instr*;
to make o.s. ~ with sth знако́миться*
(ознако́миться* *perf*) с чем-н; **to be on ~
terms with sb** быть* (*impf*) в прия́тельских *or*
дру́жеских отноше́ниях с кем-н.
familiarity [fəmɪlɪˈærɪtɪ] *n* (*knowledge*) зна́ние;
(*informality*) фамилья́рность *f*.
familiarize [fəˈmɪlɪəraɪz] *vt*: **to ~ o.s. with sth**
ознакомля́ться (ознако́миться* *perf*) с
чем-н.
family [ˈfæmɪlɪ] *n* семья́*; (*children*) де́ти* *pl*.
family business *n* семе́йный би́знес.
family credit *n* де́нежное посо́бие,
выпла́чиваемое госуда́рством се́мьям с
ни́зким у́ровнем дохо́дов.
family doctor *n* семе́йный врач*.
family life *n* семе́йная жизнь *f*.
family man *n* семьяни́н*, семе́йный челове́к*.
family planning *n* контро́ль *m* рожда́емости;
~ ~ clinic ≈ же́нская консульта́ция.
family tree *n* родосло́вное де́рево*.
famine [ˈfæmɪn] *n* го́лод*.
famished [ˈfæmɪʃt] (*inf*) *adj* голо́дный; **I'm ~** я
умира́ю с го́лоду.
famous [ˈfeɪməs] *adj* знамени́тый (знамени́т).
famously [ˈfeɪməslɪ] *adv* (*get on*) великоле́пно.
fan [fæn] *n* (*folding*) ве́ер*; (ELEC) вентиля́тор;
(*of famous person*) покло́нник(-ица); (*of
sports team*) боле́льщик(-ица) ♦ *vt* (*face*)
обма́хивать (обмахну́ть *perf*); (*fire, quarrel*)
раздува́ть (разду́ть *perf*)
▶ **fan out** *vi* (*people*) развёртываться
(разверну́ться *perf*) ве́ером; (*roads*)
расходи́ться* (разойти́сь* *perf*) ве́ером.
fanatic [fəˈnætɪk] *n* (*extremist*) фана́тик.
fanatical [fəˈnætɪkl] *adj* (*support, dedication*)
фанати́чный* (фанати́чен).
fan belt *n* (AUT) вентиля́торный реме́нь* *m*.
fanciful [ˈfænsɪful] *adj* причу́дливый
(причу́длив).
fan club *n* клуб покло́нников.
fancy [ˈfænsɪ] *n* (*whim*) при́хоть *f*; (*imagination*)
воображе́ние; (*fantasy*) фанта́зия ♦ *adj*
изы́сканный ♦ *vt* (*feel like, want*) хоте́ть*
(захоте́ть* *perf*); (*imagine*) вообража́ть
(вообрази́ть* *perf*); (*think*) ду́мать (*impf*); **to
take a ~ to** увлека́ться (увле́чься* *perf*) +*instr*;
when the ~ takes him когда́ ему́ взду́мается;
the idea took *or* **caught my ~** иде́я пришла́сь

---

* marks translations which have irregular inflections. The Russian-English side of the dictionary gives inflectional information.

мне по вкусу; **to ~ that** ду́мать *(impf)*, что; **he fancies her** *(inf)* она́ ему́ нра́вится; **~ that!** предста́вьте себе́.

fancy dress *n* маскара́дный костю́м.

fancy-dress ball ['fænsɪdrɛs-] *n* костюм-и́рованный бал*.

fancy goods *npl* украше́ния *ntpl* *(обычно для до́ма)*.

fanfare ['fænfɛə*] *n* фанфа́ра.

fanfold paper ['fænfəuld-] *n* перфори́рованная *or* фальцо́ванная бума́га.

fang [fæŋ] *n* клык*; *(of snake)* ядови́тый зуб*.

fan heater *n (BRIT)* электрообогрева́тель *m (нагнета́ющий тёплый во́здух при по́мощи вентиля́тора)*.

fanlight ['fænlaɪt] *n* веерообра́зное окно́ над две́рью.

fanny ['fænɪ] *n (inf)* за́дница.

fantasize ['fæntəsaɪz] *vi* фантази́ровать *(impf)*.

fantastic [fæn'tæstɪk] *adj* фантасти́ческий*; **that's ~!** э́то фанта́стика!

fantasy ['fæntəsɪ] *n* фанта́зия.

fanzine ['fænziːn] *n* журна́л и́ли газе́та, самоде́ятельно издава́емый покло́нниками попгру́ппы, телепрогра́ммы, спо́рта итп.

FAO *n abbr (= Food and Agriculture Organization)* ФАО *(продово́льственная и сельскохозя́йственная организа́ция ООН)*.

f.a.q. *abbr (= free alongside quay)* фра́нко на́бережная.

far [fɑː*] *adj (distant)* да́льний* ◆ *adv (a long way)* далеко́; *(much)* гора́здо; **at the ~ end** в да́льнем конце́; **at the ~ side** на друго́й стороне́; **the ~ left/right** *(POL)* кра́йне ле́вый/пра́вый; **~ away, ~ off** далеко́; **~ better** гора́здо лу́чше; **he was ~ from poor** он был далеко́ *or* отню́дь не бе́ден; **by ~** намно́го; **is it ~ to London?** далеко́ ли до Ло́ндона?; **it's not ~ from here** э́то недалеко́ отсю́да; **go as ~ as the post office** дойди́те до по́чты; **as ~ back as the 13th century** ещё в 13-ом ве́ке; **as ~ as I know** наско́лько мне изве́стно; **as ~ as possible** наско́лько возмо́жно; **how ~?** *(distance)* как далеко́?; *(to what extent)* наско́лько?; **how ~ have you got with your work?** наско́лько Вы продви́нулись в свое́й рабо́те?

faraway ['fɑːrəweɪ] *adj (place)* да́льний*, далёкий*; *(look)* отсу́тствующий*.

farce [fɑːs] *n (also fig)* фарс.

farcical ['fɑːsɪkl] *adj (fig)* неле́пый.

fare [fɛə*] *n (on trains, buses)* пла́та за прое́зд; *(in taxi)* сто́имость *f* прое́зда; *(: passenger)* пассажи́р; *(food)* еда́ ◆ *vi*: **how did you ~?** как успе́хи?; **half/full ~** полсто́имости/по́лная сто́имость прое́зда; **bus/train ~** пла́та за прое́зд в авто́бусе/на по́езде; **they ~ better than we do under the present system** с ни́ми обраща́ются лу́чше, чем с на́ми при ны́нешней систе́ме; **they ~d well/badly in the recent elections** им повезло́/не повезло́ на

неда́вних вы́борах.

Far East *n*: **the ~ ~** Да́льний* Восто́к.

farewell [fɛə'wɛl] *excl* проща́йте ◆ *n* проща́ние ◆ *cpd (party etc)* проща́льный.

far-fetched ['fɑː'fɛtʃt] *adj* неправдоподо́бный, невероя́тный.

farm [fɑːm] *n* фе́рма ◆ *vt (land)* обраба́тывать (обрабо́тать *perf*)
▶ **farm out** *vt* отдава́ть* (отда́ть* *perf*).

farmer ['fɑːmə*] *n* фе́рмер.

farm hand *n* рабо́тник(-ица) фе́рмы.

farmhouse ['fɑːmhaus] *n* фе́рмерский дом*.

farming ['fɑːmɪŋ] *n (agriculture)* се́льское хозя́йство; *(of crops)* выра́щивание; *(of animals)* разведе́ние; **sheep ~** разведе́ние ове́ц, овцево́дство; **intensive ~** интенси́вное веде́ние се́льского хозя́йства.

farm labourer *n* рабо́тник на фе́рме.

farmland ['fɑːmlænd] *n* сельско-хозя́йственные уго́дья* *ntpl*.

farm produce *n* проду́кты *mpl* се́льского хозя́йства.

farm worker *n* = **farm hand**.

farmyard ['fɑːmjɑːd] *n* фе́рмерский двор*.

Faroe Islands ['fɛərəu-] *npl*: **the ~ ~** Фаре́рские острова́* *mpl*.

Faroes ['fɛərəuz] *npl* = **Faroe Islands**.

far-reaching ['fɑː'riːtʃɪŋ] *adj (reform)* далеко́ иду́щий; *(effect)* глубо́кий*.

far-sighted ['fɑː'saɪtɪd] *adj (US)* дальнозо́ркий* (дальнозо́рок); *(fig)* дальнови́дный* (дальнови́ден); **he is ~** *(US)* у него́ дальнозо́ркость.

fart [fɑːt] *(inf!)* *vi* перде́ть* (пёрнуть *perf*) (!) ◆ *n* перде́ние (!)

farther ['fɑːðə*] *adv* да́льше ◆ *adj* бо́лее да́льний*, далёкий*.

farthest ['fɑːðɪst] *superl of* **far**.

f.a.s. *abbr (BRIT: = free alongside ship)* ФАС *(свобо́дно вдоль бо́рта су́дна)*.

fascia ['feɪʃə] *n (AUT)* пане́ль *f*.

fascinate ['fæsɪneɪt] *vt* захва́тывать (захвати́ть* *perf*); *(subj: person)* очаро́вывать (очарова́ть *perf*).

fascinating ['fæsɪneɪtɪŋ] *adj (story)* захва́тывающий*; *(person)* очарова́тельный* (очарова́телен).

fascination [fæsɪ'neɪʃən] *n* очарова́ние.

fascism ['fæʃɪzəm] *n (POL)* фаши́зм.

fascist ['fæʃɪst] *adj* фаши́стский* ◆ *n* фаши́ст(ка).

fashion ['fæʃən] *n (trend)* мо́да; *(fashion industry)* инду́стрия мо́ды ◆ *vt (make)* мастери́ть (смастери́ть *perf*); **in/out of ~** в/не в мо́де; **in an animated ~** оживлённо; **in a friendly ~** по-дру́жески; **he did it after a ~** он сде́лал э́то ко́е-ка́к; **in the Greek ~** в гре́ческом сти́ле.

fashionable ['fæʃnəbl] *adj* мо́дный* (мо́ден).

fashion designer *n* моделье́р.

fashion show *n* пока́з *or* демонстра́ция мод.

fast [fɑ:st] adv (quickly) бы́стро; (firmly: stick) про́чно; (: hold) кре́пко ♦ n (REL) пост* ♦ vi (REL) пости́ться* (impf) ♦ adj бы́стрый* (быстр); (progress) стреми́тельный*; (car) скоростно́й; (dye, colour) про́чный; (clock): **to be ~** спеши́ть (impf); **he is ~ asleep** он кре́пко спит; **as ~ as possible** как мо́жно быстре́е; **to make a boat ~** (BRIT) кре́пко привяза́ть* (perf) ло́дку; **my watch is 5 minutes ~** мои́ часы́ спеша́т на 5 мину́т.

fasten ['fɑ:sn] vt закрепля́ть (закрепи́ть* perf); (door) запира́ть (запере́ть* perf); (shoe) завя́зывать (завяза́ть perf); (coat, dress) застёгивать (застегну́ть perf); (seat belt) пристёгивать (пристегну́ть perf) ♦ vi (coat, belt) застёгиваться (застегну́ться perf); (door) запира́ться (запере́ться* perf)
► **fasten (up)on** vt fus (idea etc) сосредото́чиваться (сосредото́читься perf) на +acc.

fastener ['fɑ:snə] n (for clothing) застёжка*.

fastening ['fɑ:snɪŋ] n = **fastener**.

fast food n быстропригота́вливаемая еда́ ♦ cpd: **~~ restaurant** рестора́н быстро-приготáвливаемой еды.

fastidious [fæs'tɪdɪəs] adj (fussy) скрупулёзный (скрупулёзен).

fast lane n (BRIT: AUT): **the ~~** скоростно́й ряд*.

fat [fæt] adj то́лстый* (толст); (inf: profit) соли́дный* ♦ n жир*; **that's a ~ lot of use to us** (inf) нам э́то нигде́ не на́до; **to live off the ~ of the land** как сыр в ма́сле ката́ться (impf).

fatal ['feɪtl] adj (mistake) фата́льный* (фата́лен), роково́й; (injury, illness) смерте́льный* (смерте́лен).

fatalistic [feɪtə'lɪstɪk] adj (attitude) фаталисти́ческий.

fatality [fə'tælɪtɪ] n (death) смерте́льный слу́чай.

fatally ['feɪtəlɪ] adv (injured) смерте́льно; (flawed) фата́льно, роковы́м о́бразом.

fate [feɪt] n судьба́*, рок; **to meet one's ~** находи́ть* (найти́* perf) свой коне́ц.

fated ['feɪtɪd] adj обречённый* (обречён); **it seemed ~** каза́лось, э́то бы́ло су́ждено случи́ться.

fateful ['feɪtful] adj роково́й.

fat-free ['fæt'fri:] adj обезжи́ренный.

father ['fɑ:ðə] n оте́ц*.

Father Christmas n ≈ Дед Моро́з.

fatherhood ['fɑ:ðəhud] n отцо́вство.

father-in-law ['fɑ:ðərənlɔ:] n (wife's father) свёкор*; (husband's father) тесть m.

fatherland ['fɑ:ðəlænd] n оте́чество.

fatherly ['fɑ:ðəlɪ] adj оте́ческий*.

fathom ['fæðəm] n (NAUT) фа́том, морска́я са́жень f ♦ vt (understand: also: ~ out)

постига́ть (пости́чь* perf).

fatigue [fə'ti:g] n утомле́ние; **~s** npl (MIL) солда́тская рабо́чая оде́жда fsg; **metal ~** уста́лость f мета́лла.

fatness ['fætnɪs] n (of person) полнота́; (of wallet) толщина́.

fatten ['fætn] vt (animal) отка́рмливать (откорми́ть* perf) ♦ vi жире́ть (разжире́ть perf); **chocolate is ~ing** от шокола́да толсте́ют.

fatty ['fætɪ] adj (food) жи́рный* ♦ n (inf) толстя́к*.

fatuous ['fætjuəs] adj бессмы́сленный*.

faucet ['fɔ:sɪt] n (US) (водопрово́дный) кран.

fault [fɔ:lt] n (blame) вина́*; (defect: in person) недоста́ток*; (: in machine) дефе́кт; (GEO) разло́м; (TENNIS) оши́бка* при пода́че ♦ vt (criticize) придира́ться (impf) к +dat; **it's my ~** э́то моя́ вина́; **to find ~ with** придира́ться (придра́ться* perf) к +dat; **I am at ~** я винова́т; **if my memory is not at ~** е́сли мне не изменя́ет па́мять; **generous to a ~** чрезме́рно ще́дрый*.

faultless ['fɔ:ltlɪs] adj безупре́чный* (безупре́чен).

faulty ['fɔ:ltɪ] adj (goods) испо́рченный*; (machine) повреждённый*.

fauna ['fɔ:nə] n фа́уна.

faux pas ['fəu'pɑ:] n inv неве́рный шаг*.

favour ['feɪvə] (US favor) n (approval) расположе́ние; (help) одолже́ние ♦ vt (prefer: solution) ока́зывать (оказа́ть* perf) предпочте́ние +dat; (: pupil etc) выделя́ть (вы́делить perf); (assist) благоприя́тствовать (impf) +dat; **to ask a ~ of sb** проси́ть* (попроси́ть* perf) кого́-н об одолже́нии; **to do sb a ~** ока́зывать (оказа́ть* perf) кому́-н услу́гу; **in ~ of** в по́льзу +gen; **to be in ~ of sth/doing** быть* (impf) за что-н/за то, что́бы +infin; **to find ~ with sb** (subj: person) завоёвывать (завоева́ть* perf) расположе́ние кого́-н; (: suggestion) находи́ть* (найти́* perf) подде́ржку у кого́-н.

favourable ['feɪvrəbl] (US favorable) adj благоприя́тный* (благоприя́тен).

favourably ['feɪvrəblɪ] (US favorably) adv (react) положи́тельно, благоприя́тно; **to compare ~ with** вы́игрывать (impf) в сравне́нии с +instr.

favourite ['feɪvrɪt] (US favorite) adj люби́мый ♦ n (of teacher, parent) люби́мец*; (SPORT) фавори́т.

favouritism ['feɪvrɪtɪzəm] (US favoritism) n фавори́тизм.

fawn [fɔ:n] n молодо́й оле́нь m ♦ adj (also: ~-coloured) желтова́то-кори́чневый ♦ vi: **to ~ (up)on** зайскивать (impf) пе́ред +instr.

fax [fæks] n факс ♦ vt (letter, document)

---

* marks translations which have irregular inflections. The Russian-English side of the dictionary gives inflectional information.

посылáть (послáть* *perf*) фáксом.
FBI *n abbr* (*US*: = *Federal Bureau of Investigation*)
ФБР= *Федерáльное бюрó расслéдований*.
FCC *n abbr* (*US*: = *Federal Communications
Commission*) Федерáльная комúссия свя́зи.
FCO *n abbr* (*BRIT*: = *Foreign and Commonwealth
Office*) *Министéрство инострáнных дел и
сношéний со стрáнами Британского
содрýжества.*
FD *n abbr* (*US*) = **fire department**.
FDA *n abbr* (*US*: = *Food and Drug Administration*)
*управлéние по контрóлю за продýктами и
медикамéнтами.*
FE *abbr* (= *Further Education*) ≈ профессионáльно-
технúческое образовáние.

fear [fɪə^r] *n* страх; (*less strong*) боя́знь *f*;
(*worry*) опасéние ♦ *vt* боя́ться (*impf*) +*gen* ♦ *vi*
боя́ться (*impf*); **to ~ for** боя́ться (*impf*) за +*acc*;
to ~ that боя́ться (*impf*), что; **~ of heights**
боя́знь высоты́; **for ~ of missing my flight** (*in
case*) боя́сь опоздáть на самолёт.
fearful ['fɪəful] *adj* (*person*) боязлúвый
(боязлúв); (*sight*) ужасáющий*; (*risk, noise*)
стрáшный* (стрáшен); **to be ~ of**
страшúться (*impf*) +*gen*.
fearfully ['fɪəfəlɪ] *adv* (*timidly*) боязлúво; (*inf*:
very) ужáсно.
fearless ['fɪəlɪs] *adj* бесстрáшный*
(бесстрáшен).
fearsome ['fɪəsəm] *adj* (*opponent*)
внушáющий страх; (*sight*) устрашáющий.
feasibility [fi:zə'bɪlɪtɪ] *n* (*of plan*)
осуществúмость *f*.
feasibility study *n* тéхнико-экономúческое
обоснóвание.
feasible ['fi:zəbl] *adj* осуществúмый
(осуществúм).
feast [fi:st] *n* (*banquet*) пир*; (*REL*: *also*: ~ **day**)
прáздник ♦ *vi* пировáть (*impf*); **to ~ on**
лáкомиться* (*impf*) +*instr*; **to ~ one's eyes on**
sth любовáться (*impf*) чем-н.
feat [fi:t] *n* пóдвиг.
feather ['fɛðə^r] *n* перó* ♦ *vt*: **to ~**
one's nest набивáть (набúть* *perf*) себé
кармáн; **~ bed** перúна.
featherweight ['fɛðəweɪt] *n* (*BOXING*) боксёр
полулёгкого вéса.
feature ['fi:tʃə^r] *n* чертá, осóбенность *f*; (*of
landscape*) осóбенность; (*PRESS*) óчерк; (*TV,
RADIO*) передáча ♦ *vi*: **to ~ in** фигурúровать
(*impf*) в +*prp* ♦ *vt*: **the film ~s 2 famous actors** в
фúльме снимáются 2 извéстных актёра; **~s**
npl (*of face*) черты́ *fpl*; **a film featuring ...**
фильм с учáстием +*gen*...; **his article ~d in all
the newspapers** егó статья́ фигурúровала во
всех газéтах; **a special ~ on sth/sb**
специáльная передáча о чём-н/ком-н.
feature film *n* худóжественный фильм.
featureless ['fi:tʃəlɪs] *adj* невыразúтельный*
(невыразúтелен).

Feb. *abbr* = **February**.
February ['fɛbruərɪ] *n* феврáль* *m*; *see also* **July**.
feces ['fi:si:z] *npl* (*US*) = **faeces**.
feckless ['fɛklɪs] *adj* безответственный.
Fed *abbr* (*US*) = **federal, federation**.
fed [fɛd] *pt, pp of* **feed**.
Fed. *n abbr* (*US*: *inf*: = *Federal Reserve Board*)
*совéт, управля́ющий федерáльной резéрвной
систéмой.*
federal ['fɛdərəl] *adj* федерáльный.
Federal Republic of Germany *n*
Федератúвная Респýблика Гермáнии.
Federal Reserve Board *n* (*US*) Федерáльное
резéрвное правлéние.
Federal Trade Commission *n* (*US*)
Федерáльная торгóвая комúссия.
federation [fɛdə'reɪʃən] *n* федерáция.
fed up *adj*: **he is ~ ~** емý надоéло.
fee [fi:] *n* плáта; (*of doctor, lawyer*) плáта,
гонорáр; **school ~s** плáта за обучéние;
entrance ~ входнáя плáта; **membership ~**
члéнский* взнос; **for a small ~** за небольшóе
вознаграждéние.
feeble ['fi:bl] *adj* хúлый (хил); (*joke*) слáбый.
feeble-minded ['fi:bl'maɪndɪd] *adj*
слабоýмный.
feed [fi:d] (*pt, pp* fed) *n* (*feeding*) кормлéние;
(*fodder*) корм*; (*on printer*) загрýзка ♦ *vt*
кормúть* (накормúть* *perf*); **to ~ sth into sth**
(*data, information*) загружáть (загрузúть*
perf) что-н во что-н; (*material*) подавáть*
(подáть* *perf*) что-н во что-н
▶ **feed back** *vt* (*results*) подавáть* (подáть*
perf) обрáтно
▶ **feed on** *vt fus* питáться (*impf*) +*instr*.
feedback ['fi:dbæk] *n* (*response*) обрáтная
связь *f*; (*from person*) óтзыв.
feeding bottle ['fi:dɪŋ-] *n* (*BRIT*) бутылочка*
(*для кормлéния младéнца*).
feel [fi:l] (*pt, pp* felt) *n* ощущéние ♦ *vt* (*touch*)
трóгать (потрóгать *perf*); (*experience*)
чýвствовать (*impf*); (*think, believe*): **to ~** (**that**)
считáть (*impf*) (, что); **to get the ~ of sth**
освáиваться (освóиться *perf*) с чем-н; **I ~ that
you ought to do it** я считáю, что Вы должны́
это сдéлать; **he ~s hungry** он гóлоден; **she
~s cold** ей хóлодно; **to ~ lonely/better**
чýвствовать (*impf*) себя́ одинóким/лýчше; **I
don't ~ well** я плóхо себя́ чýвствую; **he ~s
sorry for me** емý меня́ жáлко *or* жаль; **the
material ~s soft/like velvet** э́тот материáл на
óщупь мя́гкий/как бáрхат; **it ~s colder here**
здесь холоднéе; **I ~ like ... (**want**)** мне хóчется
...; **I'm still ~ing my way** я всё ещё освáиваюсь
or присмáтриваюсь
▶ **feel about** *vi*: **to ~ about for sth** искáть (*impf*)
что-н на óщупь; **to ~ about** *or* **around in one's
pocket for** шáрить (пошáрить *perf*) в
кармáне в пóисках +*gen*
▶ **feel around** *vi* = **feel about**.
feeler ['fi:lə^r] *n* (*of insect*) ýсик, щýпальце*;

to put out a ~ *or* ~**s** (*fig*) зонди́ровать
(прозонди́ровать *perf*) по́чву.
feeling ['fi:lɪŋ] *n* (*emotion, impression*)
чу́вство; (*physical sensation*) ощуще́ние; ~**s**
ran high стра́сти разгоре́лись; **what are your**
~**s about the matter?** каково́ Ва́ше
отноше́ние к э́тому вопро́су?; **I have a** ~ **that**
... у меня́ тако́е ощуще́ние, что ...; **my** ~ **is**
that ... по-мо́ему мне́нию ...; **to hurt sb's** ~**s**
задева́ть (заде́ть* *perf*) чьи-н чу́вства.
fee-paying ['fi:peɪɪŋ] *adj*: ~ **school** пла́тная
шко́ла; ~ **student** студе́нт, платя́щий за
обуче́ние.
feet [fi:t] *npl of* **foot**.
feign [feɪn] *vt* (*injury, interest*) симули́ровать
(*impf/perf*).
feigned [feɪnd] *adj* притво́рный* (притво́рен).
feint [feɪnt] *n* (*of paper*) лино́вка; **a pad of**
narrow ~ блокно́т в у́зкую лине́йку.
felicitous [fɪ'lɪsɪtəs] *adj* уда́чный* (уда́чен).
feline ['fi:laɪn] *adj* коша́чий*.
fell [fɛl] *pt of* **fall** ♦ *vt* вали́ть (свали́ть *perf*) ♦ *n*
(*BRIT*) *гора́, холм и́ли боло́то в назва́ниях* ♦
adj: **in one** ~ **swoop** одни́м ма́хом; **the** ~**s** *npl*
(*moorland*) боло́тистая ме́стность *fsg*.
fellow ['fɛləu] *n* (*man*) па́рень *m*; (*comrade*)
това́рищ; (*of learned society*)
действи́тельный член; (*of university*) член
сове́та ♦ *cpd*: **their** ~ **prisoners/students** их
сока́мерники/соку́рсники; **his** ~ **workers** его́
това́рищи по рабо́те.
fellow citizens *npl* согра́ждане* *mpl*.
fellow countryman *irreg n* соотéчественник.
fellow men *npl* бли́жние *pl adj*.
fellowship ['fɛləuʃɪp] *n* (*comradeship*)
содру́жество; (*society*) чле́нство; (*SCOL*)
стипе́ндия аспира́нта (*зва́ние чле́на сове́та*
колле́джа и́ли нау́чного о́бщества).
fell-walking ['fɛlwɔ:kɪŋ] *n* (*BRIT*) *хожде́ние по*
гора́м, боло́тистой ме́стности итп.
felon ['fɛlən] *n* (*LAW*) уголо́вный престу́пник.
felony ['fɛlənɪ] *n* (*LAW*) уголо́вное
преступле́ние.
felt [fɛlt] *pt, pp of* **feel** ♦ *n* (*fabric*) фетр.
felt-tip pen ['fɛltɪp-] *n* флома́стер.
female ['fi:meɪl] *n* (*also pej*) са́мка ♦ *adj* (*sex,*
character, profession) же́нский*; (*child*)
же́нского по́ла; (*ELEC*) охва́тывающий; ~
suffrage избира́тельное пра́во для же́нщин;
male and ~ **students** студе́нты и студе́нтки.
female impersonator *n* (*THEAT*) актёр,
игра́ющий* же́нщин.
Femidom® ['fɛmɪdɒm] *n* фемидо́м (*же́нский*
презервати́в).
feminine ['fɛmɪnɪn] *adj* (*clothes, behaviour*)
же́нственный* (же́нственен); (*LING*)
же́нского ро́да ♦ *n* (*LING*) же́нский* род.
femininity [fɛmɪ'nɪnɪtɪ] *n* же́нственность *f*.

feminism ['fɛmɪnɪzəm] *n* femини́зм.
feminist ['fɛmɪnɪst] *n* femини́ст(ка).
fen [fɛn] (*BRIT*) *n* (*marsh*) боло́та; **the F**~**s**
ни́зкая боло́тистая ме́стность в
Ке́ймбредшире и Ли́нкольншире.
fence [fɛns] *n* (*barrier*) забо́р, и́згородь *f*;
(*SPORT*) препя́тствие ♦ *vt* (*also:* ~ **in**)
огора́живать (огороди́ть* *perf*) ♦ *vi* (*SPORT*)
фехтова́ть (*impf*); **to sit on the** ~ (*fig*)
занима́ть (*impf*) выжида́тельную пози́цию в
спо́ре.
fencing ['fɛnsɪŋ] *n* (*SPORT*) фехтова́ние.
fend [fɛnd] *vi*: **to** ~ **for o.s.** забо́титься*
(позабо́титься* *perf*) о себе́
► **fend off** *vt* отража́ть (отрази́ть* *perf*).
fender ['fɛndə'] *n* (*of fireplace*) ками́нная
решётка*; (*on boat*) кра́нец*; (*US: of car*)
крыло́*.
fennel ['fɛnl] *n* фе́нхель *m* обыкнове́нный,
сла́дкий* укро́п*.
ferment [*n* 'fə:mɛnt, *vi* fə'mɛnt] *n* (*unrest*)
броже́ние ♦ *vi* броди́ть* (*impf*).
fermentation [fə:mɛn'teɪʃən] *n* броже́ние.
fern [fə:n] *n* па́поротник.
ferocious [fə'rəuʃəs] *adj* (*animal*) свире́пый
(свире́п); (*behaviour*) ди́кий* (дик);
(*competition, opposition, criticism*) жесто́кий*
(жесто́к); (*heat*) ужа́сный* (ужа́сен).
ferocity [fə'rɒsɪtɪ] *n* жесто́кость *f*; (*of*
opposition) я́рость *f*; **the** ~ **of the sun**
невыноси́мое пе́кло.
ferret ['fɛrɪt] *n* хорёк*
► **ferret about** *vi* ша́рить (*impf*)
► **ferret around** *vi* = **ferret about**
► **ferret out** *vt* выве́дывать (вы́ведать *perf*).
ferry ['fɛrɪ] *n* (*also:* ~**boat**) паро́м ♦ *vt*
перевози́ть* (перевезти́* *perf*); **to** ~ **sth/sb**
across *or* **over** переправля́ть (переправи́ть
perf) что-н/кого́-н.
ferryman ['fɛrɪmən] *irreg n* паро́мщик.
fertile ['fə:taɪl] *adj* (*land, soil*) плодоро́дный*
(плодоро́ден); (*imagination*) бога́тый
(бога́т); (*woman*) спосо́бный к зача́тию; ~
period плодотво́рный пери́од.
fertility [fə'tɪlɪtɪ] *n* (*see adj*) плодоро́дие;
бога́тство; спосо́бность *f* к зача́тию.
fertility drug *n* препара́т от беспло́дия.
fertilization [fə:tɪlar'zeɪʃən] *n* (*of egg*)
оплодотворе́ние.
fertilize ['fə:tɪlaɪz] *vt* (*land*) удобря́ть
(удо́брить *perf*); (*egg*) оплодотворя́ть
(оплодотвори́ть *perf*); (*plant*) опыля́ть
(опыли́ть *perf*).
fertilizer ['fə:tɪlaɪzə] *n* удобре́ние.
fervent ['fə:vənt] *adj* (*admirer, belief*) пы́лкий*.
fervour ['fə:və'] (*US* **fervor**) *n* пыл*.
fester ['fɛstə'] *vi* (*wound*) гнои́ться
(загнои́ться *perf*); (*insult, row*) разраста́ться

---

* marks translations which have irregular inflections. The Russian-English side of the dictionary gives inflectional information.

(разрости́сь* *perf*).

festival ['fɛstɪvəl] *n* (*REL*) пра́здник; (*ART, MUS*) фестива́ль *m*.

festive ['fɛstɪv] *adj* (*mood, atmosphere*) пра́здничный* (пра́здничен); **the ~ season** (*BRIT*) свя́тки* *pl*.

festivities [fɛs'tɪvɪtɪz] *npl* пра́зднества *ntpl*.

festoon [fɛs'tu:n] *vt*: **to ~ with** украша́ть (укра́сить* *perf*) +*instr*.

fetch [fɛtʃ] *vt* (*object*) приноси́ть* (принести́* *perf*); (*person*) приводи́ть* (привести́* *perf*); (*by transport*) привози́ть* (привезти́* *perf*); **would you ~ me a jug of water please?** принеси́те мне, пожа́луйста, кувши́н воды́; **how much did the book ~?** ско́лько Вы вы́ручили за кни́гу?; **his pictures ~ very high prices** его́ карти́ны продаю́тся по высо́ким це́нам

▶ **fetch up** *vi* (*BRIT*) оказа́ться* (*perf*).

fetching ['fɛtʃɪŋ] *adj* преле́стный* (преле́стен).

fête [feɪt] *n* благотвори́тельный пра́здник-- база́р.

fetid ['fɛtɪd] *adj* воню́чий*.

fetish ['fɛtɪʃ] *n* (*also fig*) фети́ш*.

fetter ['fɛtə'] *vt* (*person*) зако́вывать (закова́ть *perf*); (*horse*) спу́тывать (спу́тать *perf*); (*fig*) ско́вывать (скова́ть *perf*).

fetters ['fɛtəz] *npl* (*also fig*) око́вы *pl*.

fettle ['fɛtl] *n* (*BRIT*): **in fine ~** (*person*) в прекра́сной фо́рме.

fetus ['fi:təs] *n* (*US*) = **foetus**.

feud [fju:d] *n* вражда́ ♦ *vi* враждова́ть (*impf*); **a family ~** фами́льная вражда́ (*ме́жду двумя́ семья́ми*).

feudal ['fju:dl] *adj* феода́льный.

feudalism ['fju:dlɪzəm] *n* феодали́зм.

fever ['fi:və'] *n* (*temperature*) жар; (*disease*) лихора́дка*; **he has a ~** у него́ жар.

feverish ['fi:vərɪʃ] *adj* (*also fig*) лихора́дочный* (лихора́дочен); (*person: with excitement*) возбуждённый* (возбуждён); **he is ~** у него́ жар, его́ лихора́дит.

few [fju:] *adj* (*not many*) немно́гие; (*several*): **a ~** (*number*) не́сколько +*gen*; (*some*) не́которые *pl adj* ♦ *pron*: **(a) ~** немно́гие *pl adj*; **a ~ more** ещё не́сколько; **for a ~ days** на не́сколько дней; **with a ~ of them** с не́которыми из них; **they were ~** их бы́ло ма́ло *or* немно́го; **~ succeed** немно́гим удаётся; **very ~ survive** о́чень немно́гие выжива́ют; **I know a ~** я зна́ю не́скольких; **a good ~** дово́льно мно́гие; **quite a ~** дово́льно мно́го; **in the next ~ days** в ближа́йшие не́сколько дней; **in the past ~ days** за после́дние не́сколько дней; **every ~ days/months** че́рез ка́ждые не́сколько дней/ме́сяцев.

fewer ['fju:ə'] *adj* ме́ньше +*gen*; **they are ~** их ме́ньше; **there are ~ buses on Sundays** по воскресе́ньям хо́дит ме́ньше авто́бусов.

fewest ['fju:ɪst] *adj* ме́ньше всего́ +*gen*.

FFA *n abbr* = *Future Farmers of America*.

FH *n abbr* (*BRIT*) = **fire hydrant**.

FHA *n abbr* (*US*) = *Federal Housing Administration*.

fiancé [fɪ'ɑ̃:ŋseɪ] *n* жени́х*.

fiancée [fɪ'ɑ̃:ŋseɪ] *n* неве́ста.

fiasco [fɪ'æskəu] *n* фиа́ско *nt ind*.

fib [fɪb] *n* враньё *nt no pl*; **to tell ~s** привира́ть (привра́ть* *perf*); **a few small ~s don't hurt** немно́жко привра́ть не повреди́т.

fibre ['faɪbə'] (*US* **fiber**) *n* волокно́*; (*dietary*) клетча́тка.

fibreboard ['faɪbəbɔ:d] (*US* **fiberboard**) *n* фи́бровый карто́н*.

fibreglass ['faɪbəglɑ:s] (*US* **fiberglass**) *n* стекловолокно́.

fibrositis [faɪbrə'saɪtɪs] *n* фибро́з.

FICA *n abbr* (*US*) = *Federal Insurance Contributions Act*.

fickle ['fɪkl] *adj* непостоя́нный* (непостоя́нен).

fiction ['fɪkʃən] *n* (*LITERATURE*) худо́жественная литерату́ра; (*invention*) вы́мысел*; (*lie*) вы́думка*.

fictional ['fɪkʃənl] *adj* (*character, event*) вы́мышленный (вы́мылен); (*relating to fiction*) беллетристи́ческий.

fictionalize ['fɪkʃnəlaɪz] *vt* беллетризи́ровать (*impf/perf*).

fictitious [fɪk'tɪʃəs] *adj* (*false, invented*) фикти́вный* (фикти́вен); (*character, event*) вы́мышленный* (вы́мышлен).

fiddle ['fɪdl] *n* (*MUS*) скри́пка*; (*swindle*) обма́н ♦ *vt* (*BRIT*: *accounts*) подде́лывать (подде́лать *perf*); **tax ~** махина́ции с нало́гами; **to work a ~** моше́нничать (смоше́нничать *perf*).

▶ **fiddle with** *vt fus* верте́ть* (*impf*) в рука́х.

fiddler ['fɪdlə'] *n* скрипа́ч*(ка*).

fiddly ['fɪdlɪ] *adj* (*task*) трудновыполни́мый; (*object*) неудо́бный в обраще́нии.

fidelity [fɪ'dɛlɪtɪ] *n* ве́рность *f*; (*accuracy*) то́чность *f*.

fidget ['fɪdʒɪt] *vi* ёрзать (*impf*).

fidgety ['fɪdʒɪtɪ] *adj* беспоко́йный* (беспоко́ен).

fiduciary [fɪ'dju:ʃɪərɪ] *n* (*LAW*) дове́ренное лицо́*.

field [fi:ld] *n* (*also ELEC, COMPUT*) по́ле; (*SPORT*) по́ле, площа́дка*; (*fig: area of interest*) о́бласть* *f* ♦ *cpd* (*study, trip, scientist etc*) полево́й; **the ~** (*competitors, entrants*) уча́стники *mpl* состяза́ния; **they lead the ~** (*COMM*) они́ веду́щие в свое́й о́бласти.

field day *n*: **to have a ~ ~** (*fig*) пра́здновать (*impf*), торжествова́ть (*impf*).

field glasses *npl* полево́й бино́кль *msg*.

field hospital *n* полево́й го́спиталь *m*.

field marshal *n* фельдма́ршал.

field work *n* полевы́е иссле́дования *ntpl*; (*GEO*) рабо́та в по́ле.

fiend [fi:nd] *n* злоде́й.

fiendish ['fi:ndɪʃ] *adj* дья́вольский*.

fierce [fɪəs] *adj* (*animal, person, look*) свире́пый; (*fighting*) я́ростный; (*loyalty*) горя́чий* (горя́ч); (*enemy, cold, hatred*) лю́тый* (лют); (*wind, heat, storm*) стра́шный* (стра́шен).

fiery ['faɪərɪ] *adj* (*burning*) жгу́чий*; (*sunset*) о́гненный; (*taste*) обжига́ющий; (*temperament*) горя́чий* (горя́ч); ~ **red** о́гненно-кра́сный.

FIFA ['fi:fə] *n abbr* (= *Fédération Internationale de Football Association*) ФИФА.

fifteen [fɪf'ti:n] *n* пятна́дцать*; *see also* **five**.

fifteenth [fɪf'ti:nθ] *adj* пятна́дцатый; *see also* **fifth**.

fifth [fɪfθ] *adj* пя́тый ♦ *n* (*fraction*) пя́тая *f adj*; (*AUT*: *also*: ~ **gear**) пя́тая ско́рость *f*; **he came** ~ **in the competition** он за́нял пя́тое ме́сто в соревнова́нии; ~ **form** (*BRIT*: *SCOL*) пя́тый класс; **I was** (**the**) ~ **to arrive** я пришёл пя́тым; **Henry the F**~ Ге́нрих Пя́тый; **the** ~ **of July, July the** ~ пя́тое ию́ля; **I wrote to him on the** ~ я написа́л ему́ пя́того числа́.

fifth column *n* пя́тая коло́нна (*преда́тели внутри́ страны́ и́ли организа́ции*).

fiftieth ['fɪftɪəθ] *adj* пятидеся́тый; *see also* **fifth**.

fifty ['fɪftɪ] *n* пятьдеся́т*; **there are about** ~ **people here** здесь о́коло пяти́десяти челове́к; **he'll be** ~ (**years old**) **next week** на сле́дующей неде́ле ему́ бу́дет пятьдеся́т (лет); **he's about** ~ ему́ о́коло пяти́десяти; **the Fifties** (*1950s*) пятидеся́тые го́ды; **he is in his fifties** ему́ за пятьдеся́т лет; **the temperature was in the fifties** температу́ра была́ вы́ше пяти́десяти гра́дусов; **to do** ~ (**miles per hour**) (*AUT*) е́хать (*impf*) со ско́ростью пятьдеся́т миль в час.

fifty-fifty ['fɪftɪ'fɪftɪ] *adj* (*deal, split*) ра́вный* ♦ *adv* попола́м, по́ровну; **to share** ~ **with sb** дели́ть* (раздели́ть* *perf*) попола́м с кем-н; **to have a** ~ **chance** (**of success**) име́ть (*impf*) ра́вные ша́нсы (на успе́х).

fig [fɪg] *n* инжи́р*.

fight [faɪt] (*pt, pp* **fought**) *n* дра́ка; (*MIL*) бой*; (*campaign, struggle*) борьба́ ♦ *vt* (*person*) дра́ться* (подра́ться* *perf*) с +*instr*; (*MIL*) воева́ть* (*impf*) с +*instr*; (*illness, problem, emotion*) боро́ться* (*impf*) с +*instr*; (*POL*: *election*) уча́ствовать (*impf*) в +*prp*; (*LAW*: *case*) защища́ть (*impf*) ♦ *vi* (*people*) дра́ться* (*impf*); (*MIL*) воева́ть* (*impf*); **to put up a** ~ упо́рно сопротивля́ться (*impf*); **to** ~ **one's way through a crowd/the undergrowth** прокла́дывать (*impf*) себе́ доро́гу че́рез толпу́/за́росли; **to** ~ **with sb** дра́ться* (*impf*) с кем-н; **to** ~ (**for/against**) боро́ться* (*impf*) (за +*acc*/про́тив +*gen*)

► **fight back** *vi* защища́ться (защити́ться *perf*); (*SPORT, after illness*) верну́ть (*perf*) себе́ спорти́вную фо́рму ♦ *vt fus* (*tears, fear etc*)

сде́рживать (сдержа́ть* *perf*)

► **fight down** *vt* (*urge, emotion*) подавля́ть (подави́ть* *perf*)

► **fight off** *vt* (*attacker*) отбива́ть (отби́ть* *perf*); (*sleep*) отгоня́ть (отогна́ть* *perf*)

► **fight out** *vt*: **to** ~ **it out** отста́ивать (отстоя́ть *perf*) что́-нибудь в борьбе́.

fighter [faɪtə] *n* (*also fig*) боре́ц*; (*MIL*: *soldier*) бое́ц*; (: *plane*) истреби́тель *m*.

fighter pilot *n* лётчик-истреби́тель *m*.

fighting ['faɪtɪŋ] *n* (*battle*) бой*; (*brawl*) дра́ка.

figment ['fɪgmənt] *n*: **a** ~ **of the imagination** плод* воображе́ния.

figurative ['fɪgjurətɪv] *adj* (*style*) о́бразный*; (*sense*) перено́сный.

figure ['fɪgə*] *n* (*shape, body, also GEOM*) фигу́ра; (*number*) ци́фра; (*personality*) ли́чность *f* ♦ *vt* (*esp US*: *think*) счита́ть (*impf*) ♦ *vi* (*appear*) фигури́ровать (*impf*); **to put a** ~ **on** назнача́ть (назна́чить *perf*) це́ну +*gen or* на +*acc*; **public** ~ изве́стная ли́чность

► **figure out** *vt* понима́ть (поня́ть* *perf*); (*cost*) подсчи́тывать (подсчита́ть *perf*).

figurehead ['fɪgəhed] *n* (*NAUT*) фигу́ра на носу́ корабля́; (*pej*: *leader*) номина́льный глава́ *m*.

figure of speech *n* фигу́ра ре́чи.

figure skating *n* фигу́рное ката́ние.

Fiji (Islands) ['fi:dʒi:-] *n*(*pl*) Фи́джи *ntpl ind*.

filament ['fɪləmənt] *n* (*ELEC, TECH*) нить *f* нака́ла; (*BIO*) тычи́ночная нить.

filch [fɪltʃ] *vt* (*inf*) стяну́ть (*perf*).

file [faɪl] *n* (*dossier*) де́ло*; (*in cabinet*) картоте́ка; (*folder*) скоросшива́тель *m*; (: *for loose leaf*) па́пка*; (*COMPUT*) файл; (*row*) коло́нна; (*tool*) напи́льник ♦ *vt* (*papers, document*) подшива́ть (подши́ть* *perf*); (*in card index*) вноси́ть* (внести́* *perf*); (*LAW*: *claim*) подава́ть* (пода́ть* *perf*); (*wood, fingernails*) шлифова́ть (отшлифова́ть *perf*) ♦ *vi*: **to** ~ **in/out/past** входи́ть* (войти́* *perf*)/ выходи́ть* (вы́йти* *perf*)/проходи́ть* (пройти́* *perf*) коло́нной; **in single** ~ в коло́нну по одному́; **to** ~ **a suit against sb** подава́ть* (пода́ть* *perf*) в суд на кого́-н; **to** ~ **for divorce** подава́ть* (пода́ть* *perf*) на разво́д.

filename ['faɪlneɪm] *n* (*COMPUT*) и́мя *nt* фа́йла.

filibuster ['fɪlɪbʌstə*] *n* (*esp US*: *POL*) *n* (*also*: ~**er**) обструкциони́ст ♦ *vi* тормози́ть (*impf*) приня́тие зако́на путём обстру́кции.

filing ['faɪlɪŋ] *n* (*ADMIN*) систематиза́ция.

filing cabinet *n* картоте́чный шкаф*, шкаф* с картоте́кой.

filing clerk *n* делопроизводи́тель *m*.

Filipino [fɪlɪ'pi:nəu] *n* филиппи́нец*(-нка*); (*LING*) филиппи́нский* язы́к*.

fill [fɪl] *vi* (*room, hall*) наполня́ться

---

* marks translations which have irregular inflections. The Russian-English side of the dictionary gives inflectional information.

(напо́лниться *perf*) ◆ *vt* (*tooth*) пломбирова́ть (запломбирова́ть *perf*); (*vacancy*) заполня́ть (запо́лнить *perf*); (*need*) удовлетворя́ть (удовлетвори́ть *perf*) ◆ *n*: **to eat one's ~** наеда́ться (нае́сться* *perf*); **to ~ (with)** (*container*) наполня́ть (напо́лнить *perf*) (+*instr*); (*space, area*) заполня́ть (запо́лнить *perf*) (+*instr*)

▶ **fill in** *vt* (*cavity, form*) заполня́ть (запо́лнить *perf*); (*time*) корота́ть (*impf*) ◆ *vi*: **to ~ in for sb** замеща́ть (*impf*) кого́-н вре́менно; **to ~ sb in** (*inf*) вводи́ть* (ввести́* *perf*) кого́-н в курс де́ла

▶ **fill out** *vt* (*form, receipt*) заполня́ть (запо́лнить *perf*)

▶ **fill up** *vt* (*container*) наполня́ть (напо́лнить *perf*); (*space*) заполня́ть (запо́лнить *perf*) ◆ *vi* (*AUT*) заправля́ться (запра́виться* *perf*); **~ it up, please** (*AUT*) запра́вьте мне маши́ну, пожа́луйста.

fillet ['fɪlɪt] *n* филе́ *nt ind* ◆ *vt* отделя́ть (отдели́ть *perf*) от косте́й.

fillet steak *n* вы́резка.

filling ['fɪlɪŋ] *n* (*for tooth*) пло́мба; (*of pie*) начи́нка; (*of layer cake*) просло́йка.

filling station *n* запра́вочная ста́нция.

fillip ['fɪlɪp] *n* (*fig*) толчо́к.

filly ['fɪlɪ] *n* молода́я кобы́ла.

film [fɪlm] *n* (*CINEMA*) фи́льм; (*PHOT, COMM*) плёнка*; (*of powder, liquid etc*) то́нкий* слой ◆ *vti* снима́ть (снять *perf*).

film star *n* кинозвезда́* *m/f*.

film strip *n* диафи́льм.

film studio *n* киносту́дия.

Filofax® ['faɪleufæks] *n записна́я кни́жка и́ли дневни́к.*

filter ['fɪltə^r] *n* фильтр ◆ *vt* (*liquid*) фильтрова́ть (профильтрова́ть *perf*)

▶ **filter in** *vi* (*news*) проса́чиваться (просочи́ться *perf*)

▶ **filter through** *vi* = **filter in**.

filter coffee *n ко́фе то́нкого помо́ла для кофева́рок с фи́льтром.*

filter lane *n* (*BRIT: AUT*) *полоса́, по кото́рой Вы должны́ е́хать, что́бы поверну́ть по указа́нию стре́лки светофо́ра.*

filter tip *n* фильтр (*сигаре́ты*).

filter-tipped ['fɪltə'tɪpt] *adj* с фи́льтром.

filth [fɪlθ] *n* грязь *f*; (*fig: on TV etc*) непристо́йность *f*.

filthy ['fɪlθɪ] *adj* гря́зный* (гря́зен); (*fig*) ме́рзкий* (ме́рзок).

fin [fɪn] *n* (*of fish*) плавни́к*; (*TECH: of rocket*) стабилиза́тор.

final ['faɪnl] *adj* (*last*) после́дний*; (*SPORT*) фина́льный; (*ultimate*) заключи́тельный; (*definitive*) оконча́тельный* ◆ *n* (*SPORT*) фина́л; **~s** *npl* (*SCOL*) выпускны́е экза́мены *mpl*.

final demand *n* (*for bill etc*) оконча́тельное тре́бование.

final dividend *n* оконча́тельный дивиде́нд.

finale [fɪ'nɑ:lɪ] *n* фина́л.

finalist ['faɪnəlɪst] *n* финали́ст.

finality [faɪ'nælɪtɪ] *n* оконча́тельность *f*; **to speak with an air of ~** говори́ть (*impf*) то́ном, не допуска́ющим возраже́ния.

finalize ['faɪnəlaɪz] *vt* (*arrangements, plans*) оконча́тельно уточня́ть (уточни́ть *perf*).

finally ['faɪnəlɪ] *adv* (*eventually*) в конце́ концо́в; (*lastly*) наконе́ц; (*irrevocably*) оконча́тельно.

finance [faɪ'næns] *n* фина́нсы *pl* ◆ *vt* (*back, fund*) финанси́ровать (*impf/perf*); **~s** *npl* (*personal finances*) фина́нсы *pl*.

financial [faɪ'nænʃəl] *adj* (*difficulties, venture*) фина́нсовый; **~ statement** фина́нсовый отчёт.

financially [faɪ'nænʃəlɪ] *adv* в фина́нсовом отноше́нии.

financial management *n* фина́нсовое руково́дство.

financial year *n* фина́нсовый год*.

financier [faɪ'nænsɪə^r] *n* финанси́ст.

find [faɪnd] (*pt, pp* **found**) *vt* находи́ть* (найти́* *perf*); (*discover*) обнару́живать (обнару́жить *perf*) ◆ *n* нахо́дка*; **to ~ sb at home** застава́ть* (заста́ть* *perf*) кого́-н до́ма; **to ~ sb guilty** (*LAW*) признава́ть* (призна́ть* *perf*) кого́-н вино́вным(-ой)

▶ **find out** *vt* (*fact, truth*) узнава́ть* (узна́ть* *perf*); (*person*) разоблача́ть (разоблачи́ть *perf*) ◆ *vi*: **to ~ out about** узнава́ть* (узна́ть* *perf*) о +*prp*.

findings ['faɪndɪŋz] *npl* (*LAW*) заключе́ние *ntsg*; (*in research*) результа́ты *mpl*.

fine [faɪn] *adj* (*quality, performance etc*) прекра́сный* (прекра́сен); (*hair, features*) то́нкий*; (*sand, powder, detail*) ме́лкий*; (*adjustment*) то́чный* (то́чен) ◆ *adv* (*well*) прекра́сно; (*small*) ме́лко ◆ *n* штраф ◆ *vt* штрафова́ть (оштрафова́ть *perf*); **he's ~** (*not ill*) он чу́вствует себя́ хорошо́; (*without problems*) у него́ всё в поря́дке; **the weather is ~** пого́да хоро́шая; **to cut it ~** (*of time*) оставля́ть (оста́вить* *perf*) сли́шком ма́ло вре́мени; **you're doing ~** у Вас всё в поря́дке.

fine arts *npl* изя́щные иску́сства *nt pl*.

finely ['faɪnlɪ] *adv* (*splendidly*) превосхо́дно; (*chop*) ме́лко; (*adjust: instrument*) то́нко.

fine print *n* напи́санное *or* напеча́танное ме́лким шри́фтом.

finery ['faɪnərɪ] *n* (*dress*) наря́д; (*jewellery*) украше́ния *ntpl*.

finesse [fɪ'nɛs] *n* то́нкость *f*, изя́щество.

fine-tooth comb ['faɪntu:θ-] *n*: **to go through sth with a ~ ~** (*fig*) скрупулёзно изуча́ть (изучи́ть* *perf*) что-н.

finger ['fɪŋgə^r] *n* па́лец* ◆ *vt* тро́гать (потро́гать *perf*); **little ~** мизи́нец*; **index ~** указа́тельный па́лец*.

fingernail ['fɪŋgəneɪl] *n* но́готь* *m*.

fingerprint ['fɪŋgəprɪnt] *n* отпеча́ток* па́льца ♦ *vt* (*person*) брать* (взять* *perf*) отпеча́тки па́льцев у +*gen*.

fingerstall ['fɪŋgəstɔːl] *n* напа́льчник.

fingertip ['fɪŋgətɪp] *n* ко́нчик па́льца; **to have sth at one's ~s** (*at one's disposal*) име́ть (*impf*) что-н под руко́й; (*know well*) знать* (*impf*) что-н как свои пять па́льцев.

finicky ['fɪnɪkɪ] *adj* приверéдливый (приверéдлив).

finish ['fɪnɪʃ] *n* коне́ц*; (*SPORT*) фи́ниш; (*polish etc*) отде́лка* ♦ *vt* зака́нчивать (зако́нчить *perf*), конча́ть (ко́нчить *perf*) ♦ *vi* зака́нчиваться (зако́нчиться *perf*); (*person*) зака́нчивать (зако́нчить *perf*); **have you ~ed?** Вы уже́ зако́нчили?; **to ~ doing** конча́ть (ко́нчить *perf*) +*infin*; **he ~ed third** (*in race etc*) он зако́нчил тре́тьим; **to ~ with sth** поко́нчить (*perf*) с чем-н; **she's ~ed with him** у неё с ним всё ко́нчено

▸ **finish off** *vt* (*complete*) зака́нчивать (зако́нчить *perf*); (*kill*) прика́нчивать (прико́нчить *perf*)

▸ **finish up** *vt* (*food*) доеда́ть (дое́сть* *perf*); (*drink*) допива́ть (допи́ть* *perf*) ♦ *vi* (*end up*) конча́ть (ко́нчить *perf*).

finished ['fɪnɪʃt] *adj* (*product*) отде́ланный (отде́лан); (*performance*) отто́ченный (отто́чен); (*inf: tired*) измо́танный (измо́тан).

finishing line ['fɪnɪʃɪŋ-] *n* (*SPORT*) фи́нишная черта́.

finishing school *n* ча́стный же́нский пансио́н.

finishing touches *npl* после́дние штрихи́* *mpl*.

finite ['faɪnaɪt] *adj* (*time, space*) ограни́ченный* (ограни́чен), коне́чный* (коне́чен); (*verb*) ли́чный.

Finland ['fɪnlənd] *n* Финля́ндия; **Gulf of ~** Фи́нский* зали́в.

Finn [fɪn] *n* финн (фи́нка).

Finnish ['fɪnɪʃ] *adj* фи́нский* ♦ *n* фи́нский* язы́к*.

fiord [fjɔːd] *n* = **fjord**.

fir [fəː] *n* ель *f*.

fire ['faɪə] *n* (*flames*) пла́мя* *nt*; (*in hearth*) ого́нь* *m*; (*accidental*) пожа́р; (*bonfire*) костёр* ♦ *vt* (*shoot: gun, cannon etc*) вы́стрелить (*perf*) из +*gen*; (*stimulate: imagination etc*) разжига́ть (разже́чь* *perf*); (*inf: dismiss*) увольня́ть (уво́лить *perf*) ♦ *vi* (*shoot*) вы́стрелить (*perf*); **the house is on ~** дом* гори́т; **to set ~ to sth, set sth on ~** поджига́ть (подже́чь* *perf*) что-н; **the house is insured against ~** дом* застрахо́ван на слу́чай пожа́ра; **electric ~** электро-обогрева́тель *m*; **to come under ~ (from)** (*fig*) ока́зываться (оказа́ться* *perf*) под обстре́лом (со стороны́ +*gen*); **to be under ~**

быть* (*impf*) под обстре́лом; **to ~ a gun** стреля́ть (вы́стрелить *perf*) из пу́шки.

fire alarm *n* пожа́рная сигнализа́ция.

firearm ['faɪərɑːm] *n* огнестре́льное ору́жие *nt no pl*.

fire brigade *n* пожа́рная кома́нда.

fire chief *n* нача́льник пожа́рной кома́нды.

fire department *n* (*US*) = **fire brigade**.

fire door *n* пожа́рная дверь* *f*.

fire drill *n* пожа́рное уче́ние.

fire engine *n* пожа́рная маши́на.

fire escape *n* пожа́рная ле́стница.

fire-extinguisher ['faɪərɪk'stɪŋgwɪʃə'] *n* огнетуши́тель *m*.

fireguard ['faɪəgɑːd] *n* (*BRIT*) ками́нная решётка*.

fire hazard *n*: **that's a ~ ~** это огнеопа́сно.

fire hydrant *n* пожа́рный насо́с.

fire insurance *n* страхова́ние на слу́чай пожа́ра.

fireman ['faɪəmən] *irreg n* пожа́рный *m adj*, пожа́рник.

fireplace ['faɪəpleɪs] *n* ками́н.

fireplug ['faɪəplʌg] *n* (*US*) = **fire hydrant**.

fire practice *n* = **fire drill**.

fireproof ['faɪəpruːf] *adj* (*objects*) несгора́емый; (*materials*) огнеупо́рный*.

fire regulations *npl* пра́вила *ntpl* пожа́рной безопа́сности.

fire screen *n* (*decorative*) ками́нный экра́н; (*for protection*) противопожа́рное загражде́ние.

fireside ['faɪəsaɪd] *n*: **by the ~** (*indoors*) у ками́на.

fire station *n* пожа́рное депо́ *nt ind*.

firewood ['faɪəwud] *n* дрова́ *pl*.

fireworks ['faɪəwəːks] *npl* фейерве́рк *msg*; (*display*) фейерве́рк *msg*, салю́т *msg*.

firing line ['faɪərɪŋ-] *n* ли́ния огня́; **to be in the ~ ~** (*fig*) находи́ться* (*impf*) на ли́нии огня́.

firing squad *n* взвод, наря́женный для расстре́ла.

firm [fəːm] *adj* (*ground, decision, faith*) твёрдый* (твёрд); (*mattress*) жёсткий*; (*grasp, body, muscles*) кре́пкий (кре́пок); (*offer*) оконча́тельный* (оконча́телен) ♦ *n* фи́рма; **to be a ~ believer in sth** твёрдо ве́рить (*impf*) во что-н.

firmly ['fəːmlɪ] *adv* (*believe, stand*) твёрдо; (*grasp, shake hands*) кре́пко.

firmness ['fəːmnɪs] *n* (*of ground, decision, faith*) твёрдость *f*; (*of mattress*) жёсткость *f*; (*of grip, hold*) кре́пость *f*.

first [fəːst] *adj* пе́рвый ♦ *adv* (*before all others*) пе́рвый; (*before other things*) снача́ла; (*when listing reasons etc*) во-пе́рвых; (*for the first time*) впервы́е ♦ *n* (*person: in race*) пе́рвый(-ая) *m(f) adj*; (*AUT: also: ~* **gear**)

---

* marks translations which have irregular inflections. The Russian-English side of the dictionary gives inflectional information.

пе́рвая ско́рость f; (BRIT: SCOL: degree) дипло́м пе́рвой сте́пени; **the ~ of January** пе́рвое января́; **at ~** снача́ла; **~ of all** пре́жде всего́; **in the ~ instance** в пе́рвую о́чередь; **I'll do it ~ thing (tomorrow)** я сде́лаю э́то за́втра в пе́рвую о́чередь; **from the very ~** с са́мого нача́ла; see also **fifth**.

first aid n пе́рвая по́мощь f.

first-aid kit [fə:st'eɪd-] n паке́т пе́рвой по́мощи.

first-class ['fə:st'klɑ:s] adj пе́рвого кла́сса; (excellent) первокла́ссный ◆ adv пе́рвым кла́ссом.

first-hand ['fə:st'hænd] adj (experience, knowledge) ли́чный; **a ~ account** расска́з очеви́дца.

first lady n (US) пе́рвая ле́ди f ind; **the ~ ~ of jazz** короле́ва джа́за.

firstly ['fə:stlɪ] adv во-пе́рвых.

first name n и́мя* nt.

first night n (THEAT) премье́ра.

first-rate ['fə:st'reɪt] adj первокла́ссный*; (liar) отме́нный.

first-time buyer ['fə:sttaɪm-] n челове́к, впервы́е покупа́ющий дом и́ли кварти́ру.

fir tree n ель f.

FIS n abbr (BRIT: = Family Income Supplement) дополне́ние к семе́йному дохо́ду (пособие для малоиму́щих).

fiscal ['fɪskl] adj фиска́льный; **~ year** фиска́льный or фина́нсовый год.

fish [fɪʃ] n ры́ба ◆ vt (river, area) лови́ть* (impf) ры́бу в +prp ◆ vi (commercially) занима́ться (impf) рыболо́вством; (as sport, hobby) занима́ться (impf) ры́бной ло́влей; **to go ~ing** ходи́ть*/идти́* (пойти́* perf) на рыба́лку.

▶ **fish out** vt (from water) выу́живать (вы́удить* perf); (from box etc) выта́скивать (вы́тащить perf).

fishbone ['fɪʃbəun] n ры́бья кость* f.

fish cake n ры́бная котле́та.

fisherman ['fɪʃəmən] irreg n рыба́к*.

fishery ['fɪʃərɪ] n (fishing ground) ры́бные места́ ntpl; (fish farm) рыбово́дческое хозя́йство.

fish factory n (BRIT) рыбозаво́д.

fish farm n рыбово́дческая фе́рма.

fish fingers npl (BRIT) ры́бные па́лочки* fpl.

fish hook n рыболо́вный крючо́к*.

fishing boat ['fɪʃɪŋ-] n рыболо́вное су́дно*.

fishing line n (on rod) ле́са*.

fishing net n рыболо́вная сеть f.

fishing rod n у́дочка*.

fishing tackle n рыболо́вная снасть f.

fish market n ры́бный ры́нок*.

fishmonger ['fɪʃmʌŋgə'] n (esp BRIT) торго́вец* ры́бой.

fishmonger's (shop) ['fɪʃmʌŋgəz-] n (esp BRIT) ры́бный магази́н.

fish slice n (BRIT) лопа́точка для

перевора́чивания ры́бы на сковороде́.

fish sticks npl (US) = **fish fingers**.

fishy ['fɪʃɪ] adj (inf: tale, story etc) сомни́тельный.

fission ['fɪʃən] n расщепле́ние; **atomic** or **nuclear ~** а́томное or я́дерное расщепле́ние.

fissure ['fɪʃə'] n (in rock) расще́лина; (in ground) щель* f, тре́щина.

fist [fɪst] n кула́к*.

fistfight ['fɪstfaɪt] n дра́ка, кула́чный бой*.

fit [fɪt] adj (suitable) приго́дный* (приго́ден); (healthy) в хоро́шей фо́рме ◆ vt (be the right size for) быть* (impf) впо́ру +dat, подходи́ть* (подойти́* perf) по разме́ру +dat; (adjust to the right size) подгоня́ть (подогна́ть* perf); (: clothes) примеря́ть (приме́рить perf); (match: facts, description) соотве́тствовать (impf) +dat; (put in: kitchen etc) устана́вливать (установи́ть* perf); (equip) обору́довать (impf); (suit: person) подходи́ть (подойти́* perf) +dat ◆ vi (clothes) подходи́ть* (подойти́* perf) по разме́ру, быть* (impf) впо́ру; (parts) подходи́ть* (подойти́* perf) ◆ n (MED) припа́док*; (of coughing, giggles) при́ступ; **~ to do** (ready) гото́вый (гото́в) +infin; **~ to keep** приго́дный (приго́ден) для хране́ния; **~ for** (suitable for) приго́дный (приго́ден) для +gen; **to keep ~** сохраня́ть (impf) фо́рму; **~ for work** го́дный (го́ден) к рабо́те; **she's not ~ to be a teacher** рабо́та учи́теля ей не подхо́дит; **do as you think** or **see ~** де́лайте так, как Вы счита́ете ну́жным; **the suit ~s her** костю́м сиди́т на ней хорошо́; **to ~ into** входи́ть* (войти́* perf) в +acc; **a ~ of anger** при́ступ гне́ва; **a ~ of pride** поры́в го́рдости; **he had a ~** (MED) у него́ был припа́док; **he nearly had a ~ when he learned about it** (fig: inf) его́ чуть уда́р не хвати́л когда́ он об э́том узна́л; **this dress is a good ~** э́то пла́тье хорошо́ сиди́т; **by ~s and starts** уры́вками

▶ **fit in** vi (person, object) впи́сываться (вписа́ться* perf) ◆ vt (fig: appointment, visitor) находи́ть* (найти́* perf) вре́мя для +gen; **to ~ in with sb's plans** совпада́ть (совпа́сть* perf) с чьи́ми-н пла́нами.

fitful ['fɪtful] adj (sleep) преры́вистый (преры́вист).

fitment ['fɪtmənt] n (in room, cabin) предме́т обстано́вки, обору́дование.

fitness ['fɪtnɪs] n (MED) состоя́ние здоро́вья.

fitted carpet ['fɪtɪd-] n ковро́вое покры́тие.

fitted cupboards npl встро́енные шкафы́ mpl.

fitted kitchen n (BRIT) по́лностью обору́дованная ку́хня.

fitter ['fɪtə'] n (of machinery) меха́ник; (of equipment) устано́вщик.

fitting ['fɪtɪŋ] adj (thanks) надлежа́щий ◆ n (of dress) приме́рка*; (of piece of equipment) устано́вка; **~s** npl (in building) обстано́вка fsg.

fitting room n (in shop) приме́рочная f adj.

five [faɪv] *n* пять*; **she is ~ (years) old** ей пять
лет; **they live at number 5/at 5 Green Street**
они́ живу́т в до́ме но́мер 5/в до́ме но́мер 5
по Зелёной у́лице; **there are ~ of us** нас
пя́теро; **all ~ of them came** все пя́теро
пришли́; **about ~** о́коло пяти́; **the book costs
~ pounds** кни́га сто́ит пять фу́нтов; **~ and a
half/quarter** пять с полови́ной/и одна́
че́тверть; **it's ~ (o'clock)** сейча́с пять часо́в;
to divide sth into ~ дели́ть (раздели́ть *perf*)
что-н на пять; **they are sold in ~s** они́
продаю́тся по пять.

five-day week ['faɪvdeɪ-] *n* пятидне́вная
рабо́чая неде́ля.

fiver ['faɪvə'] *n* (*inf: money: BRIT*) пять фу́нтов;
(: *US*) пять до́лларов.

fix [fɪks] *vt* (*sort out, arrange: amount*)
устана́вливать (установи́ть* *perf*); (: *date*)
назнача́ть (назна́чить *perf*); (*mend*)
нала́живать (нала́дить* *perf*); (*inf: meal,
drink*) организова́ть (*impf/perf*); (: *game etc*)
подстра́ивать (подстро́ить *perf*) ♦ *n* (*inf*): **to
be in a ~** быть* (*impf*) в тру́дном положе́нии;
to ~ sth to (*attach*) прикрепля́ть (прикрепи́ть
perf) что-н к +*dat*; **to ~ one's eyes on**
остана́вливать (останови́ть* *perf*) глаза́ на
+*prp*; **to ~ one's attention on**
сосредота́чивать (сосредото́чить *perf*)
внима́ние на +*prp*; **the fight was a ~** (*inf*)
исхо́д поеди́нка был предрешён

▶ **fix up** *vt* (*meeting*) устра́ивать (устро́ить
perf); **to ~ sb up with sth** устра́ивать
(устро́ить *perf*) кому́-н что-н.

fixation [fɪk'seɪʃən] *n* помеша́тельство; (*fig*):
she has a ~ about cleanliness чистота́ – её
пу́нктик.

fixative ['fɪksətɪv] *n* фиксати́в.

fixed [fɪkst] *adj* (*price*) твёрдый*; (*amount*)
устано́вленный; (*ideas*) навя́зчивый; (*smile*)
засты́вший*; **there's a ~ charge** существу́ет
устано́вленная пла́та; **how are you ~ for
money?** как у тебя́ с деньга́ми?

fixed assets *npl* недви́жимое иму́щество *ntsg*.

fixed charge *n* (*COMM*) постоя́нные изде́ржки*
pl.

fixed-price contract [['fɪkstpraɪs-]] *n* контра́кт
с фикси́рованной цено́й.

fixture ['fɪkstʃə'] *n* (*fitting*) обору́дование;
(*SPORT*) назна́ченный матч.

fizz [fɪz] *vi* (*drink*) шипе́ть (*impf*).

fizzle out ['fɪzl-] *vi* (*event*) ока́нчиваться
(око́нчиться *perf*) неуда́чей; (*interest*)
угаса́ть (уга́снуть* *perf*); (*plan*)
прова́ливаться (провали́ться *perf*).

fizzy ['fɪzɪ] *adj* (*drink*) шипу́чий*,
газиро́ванный.

fjord [fjɔ:d] *n* фьорд, фио́рд.

FL *abbr* (*US: POST*) = *Florida.*

flabbergasted ['flæbəgɑ:stɪd] *adj* изумлённый
(изумлён).

flabby ['flæbɪ] *adj* дря́блый*.

flag [flæg] *n* флаг; (*for signalling*) флажо́к*;
(*also:* ~**stone**) ка́менная плита́* ♦ *vi* (*person*)
выдыха́ться (вы́дохнуться *perf*); (*spirits*)
пропада́ть* (пропа́сть* *perf*); **~ of
convenience** "удо́бный" флаг (*пла́вание под
кото́рым явля́ется осо́бенно вы́годным*); **to
~ down** (*taxi, car etc*) остана́вливать
(останови́ть* *perf*).

flagging ['flægɪn] *adj*: **~ spirits** упа́док ду́ха.

flagon ['flægən] *n* буты́ль *f*; (*for cider, wine*)
кувши́н.

flagpole ['flægpəʊl] *n* флагшто́к.

flagrant ['fleɪgrənt] *adj* (*injustice*) вопию́щий*.

flagship ['flægʃɪp] *n* (*also fig*) фла́гман.

flagstone ['flægstəʊn] *n* ка́менная плита́.

flag stop *n* (*US: for bus*) остано́вка* по
тре́бованию.

flair [fleə'] *n* (*style*) стиль *m*; (*talent*): **a ~ for**
скло́нность *f* к +*dat*; **political ~**
полити́ческий* тала́нт.

flak [flæk] *n* (*MIL*) зени́тная артилле́рия; (*inf:
criticism*) нахлобу́чка*.

flake [fleɪk] *n* (*of snow, soap powder, cereal*)
хло́пья* *pl*; (*of rust, paint*) слой ♦ *vi* (*also:* ~
off: *enamel*) лупи́ться (облупи́ться *perf*);
(: *paint*) тре́скаться (потре́скаться *perf*);
(*skin*) шелуши́ться (*impf*)

▶ **flake out** *vi* (*inf: person*) отключа́ться
(отключи́ться *perf*).

flaky ['fleɪkɪ] *adj* (*paintwork*) облу́пленный;
(*skin*) шелуша́щийся.

flaky pastry *n* слоёное те́сто.

flamboyant [flæm'bɔɪənt] *adj* (*dress, design*)
бро́ский* (бро́сок); (*person*) колори́тный*
(колори́тен).

flame [fleɪm] *n* (*of fire*) пла́мя* *nt*; **to burst into
~s** вспы́хнуть (*perf*); **to be in ~s** пыла́ть (*impf*);
an old ~ (*inf*) ста́рая страсть.

flaming ['fleɪmɪŋ] *adj* (*inf*) дья́вольский*.

flamingo [flə'mɪŋgəʊ] *n* флами́нго *m ind*.

flammable ['flæməbl] *adj* легко́
воспламеня́ющийся.

flan [flæn] *n* (*BRIT*) откры́тый кру́глый пиро́г*.

Flanders ['flɑ:ndəz] *n* Фла́ндрия.

flange [flændʒ] *n* кро́мка*.

flank [flæŋk] *n* (*of animal*) бок*; (*of army*) фланг
♦ *vt* окаймля́ть (*impf*); **~ed by** ме́жду +*instr*.

flannel ['flænl] *n* (*fabric*) флане́ль *f*; (*BRIT: also:
face* ~) махро́вая салфе́тка для лица́; ~**s** *npl*
(*trousers*) флане́левые брю́ки; **to give sb
some** ~ (*BRIT: inf*) моро́чить (*impf*) кому́-н
го́лову.

flannelette [flænə'lɛt] *n* ба́йка.

flap [flæp] *n* (*of envelope*) отворо́т; (*of pocket*)
кла́пан; (*of jacket*) пола́* ♦ *vt* (*arms*) маха́ть*

(*impf*) +*instr*; (*wings*) хло́пать (*impf*) +*instr* ◆ *vi* (*sail, flag*) колыха́ться* (*impf*); (*inf: also:* **be in a ~**) волнова́ться (*impf*).

flapjack ['flæpdʒæk] *n* (*US: pancake*) ола́дья*; (*BRIT: biscuit*) овся́ное пече́нье*.

flare [flɛə*] *n* (*signal*) сигна́льная раке́та; (*in skirt etc*) клёш
► **flare up** *vi* (*fire*) вспы́хивать (вспы́хнуть *perf*) я́рким пла́менем; (*fig: person, fighting, trouble*) вспы́хивать (вспы́хнуть *perf*).

flared ['flɛəd] *adj*: ~ **trousers** брю́ки-клёш; ~ **skirt** ю́бка-клёш.

flash [flæʃ] *n* (*of light, also* PHOT) вспы́шка*; (*also:* **news ~**) "мо́лния"; (*US: torch*) фона́рик ◆ *vt* (*light*) внеза́пно освеща́ть (освети́ть* *perf*); (*send: news, message*) посыла́ть (посла́ть* *perf*) мо́лнией; (*look*) мета́ть* (метну́ть *perf*) ◆ *vi* (*lightning, light, eyes*) сверка́ть (сверкну́ть* *perf*); (*light on ambulance etc*) мига́ть (*impf*); **in a ~** мгнове́нно; **quick as a ~** с быстрото́й мо́лнии; **~ of inspiration** поры́в вдохнове́ния; **to ~ one's headlights** сигна́лить (просигна́лить *perf*); **to ~ a smile at sb** улыба́ться (улыбну́ться *perf*) мимохо́дом кому́-н; **the thought ~ed through his mind** у него́ промелькну́ла мысль; **to ~ by** *or* **past** (*person*) мча́ться (промча́ться *perf*) ми́мо +*gen*.

flashback ['flæʃbæk] *n* (CINEMA) ретроспекти́вный кадр.

flashbulb ['flæʃbʌlb] *n* фотовспы́шка*, ла́мпа-вспы́шка*.

flash card *n* (SCOL) ка́рточка со сло́вом или бу́квой, испо́льзуемая при обуче́нии чте́нию.

flashcube ['flæʃkju:b] *n* фотовспы́шка.

flasher ['flæʃə*] *n* (AUT) поворо́та; (*inf: man*) эксгибициони́ст.

flashlight ['flæʃlaɪt] *n* фона́рь* *m*, прожектор.

flash point *n* (*fig*): **to be at ~ ~** находи́ться* (*impf*) на гра́ни взры́ва.

flashy ['flæʃɪ] *adj* (*pej*) крича́щий*.

flask [flɑ:sk] *n* (*bottle*) фля́жка*; (CHEM) ко́лба; (*also:* **vacuum ~**) те́рмос.

flat [flæt] *adj* (*surface*) пло́ский*; (*tyre*) спу́щенный; (*battery*) се́вший; (*beer*) вы́дохшийся; (*refusal, denial*) категори́ческий*; (MUS: *note*) бемо́льный; (*voice*) однотонный; (*rate, fee*) еди́ный (еди́н) ◆ *n* (BRIT: *apartment*) кварти́ра; (AUT: *also:* **~ tyre**) спу́щенная ши́на; (MUS) бемо́ль *m*; **to work ~ out** выкла́дываться (*impf*) по́лностью, рабо́тать (*impf*) на изно́с; **~ rate of pay** еди́ная ста́вка.

flat-footed ['flæt'futɪd] *adj*: **he is ~** у него́ плоскосто́пие.

flatly ['flætlɪ] *adv* (*deny*) на́чисто; (*refuse*) наотре́з.

flatmate ['flætmeɪt] *n* (BRIT) сосе́д*(ка*) по кварти́ре.

flatness ['flætnɪs] *n* (*of land*) ро́вность *f*.

flat-screen ['flætskri:n] *adj*: ~ **TV set** телеви́зор с пло́ским экра́ном.

flatten ['flætn] *vt* (*also:* **~ out**) выра́внивать (вы́ровнять *perf*); (*building*) сноси́ть* (снести́* *perf*); (*crop*) побива́ть (поби́ть* *perf*); (*city*) сравня́ть (*perf*) с землёй; (*fig: inf: person*) разбива́ть (разби́ть* *perf*) в пух и прах; **to ~ o.s. against a wall/door** *etc* пло́тно прижима́ться (прижа́ться* *perf*) к стене́/две́ри *etc*.

flatter ['flætə*] *vt* льсти́ть* (польсти́ть* *perf*) +*dat*.

flatterer ['flætərə*] *n* льсте́ц*.

flattering ['flætərɪŋ] *adj* (*comment*) ле́стный* (ле́стен); (*clothes*): **that dress is very ~** э́то пла́тье скрыва́ет все недоста́тки.

flattery ['flætərɪ] *n* лесть *f*.

flatulence ['flætjuləns] *n* (MED) метеори́зм.

flaunt [flɔ:nt] *vt* щеголя́ть (*impf*) +*instr*.

flavour ['fleɪvə*] (*US* **flavor**) *vt* (*soups etc*) приправля́ть (припра́вить* *perf*) ◆ *n* (*of food, drink*) вкус; (*of ice-cream etc*) сорт*; (*fig*): **music with an African ~** му́зыка с африка́нскими моти́вами *or* в африка́нском сти́ле; **strawberry-~ed** с клубни́чным при́вкусом; **to give** *or* **add ~ to** придава́ть* (прида́ть* *perf*) вкус +*dat*.

flavouring ['fleɪvərɪŋ] *n* аромати́ческое вещество́.

flaw [flɔ:] *n* (*in argument, character*) недоста́ток*, изъя́н; (*in cloth, glass*) дефе́кт.

flawless ['flɔ:lɪs] *adj* безупре́чный*.

flax [flæks] *n* лён*.

flaxen ['flæksən] *adj* (*hair*) льняно́й.

flea [fli:] *n* блоха́*.

flea market *n* барахо́лка*.

fleck [flɛk] *n* (*mark*) кра́пинка* ◆ *vt*: **to ~ (with)** забры́згивать (*perf*) (+*instr*); **brown ~ed with white** кори́чневый в бе́лую кра́пинку.

fled [flɛd] *pt, pp of* **flee**.

fledg(e)ling ['flɛdʒlɪŋ] *n* (опери́вшийся) птене́ц*.

flee [fli:] (*pt, pp* **fled**) *vt* (*danger, famine*) бежа́ть* (*impf*) от +*gen*; (*country*) бежа́ть* (*impf/perf*) из +*gen* ◆ *vi* (*refugees, escapees*) спаса́ться (*impf*) бе́гством.

fleece [fli:s] *n* (*sheep's coat*) руно́*; (*sheep's wool*) ове́чья шерсть *f* ◆ *vt* (*inf: cheat*) обира́ть (обобра́ть* *perf*).

fleecy ['fli:sɪ] *adj* пуши́стый.

fleet [fli:t] *n* (*of ships*) флот*; (*of lorries, cars*) парк.

fleeting ['fli:tɪŋ] *adj* мимолётный*.

Flemish ['flɛmɪʃ] *adj* флама́ндский* ◆ *n* (LING) флама́ндский* язы́к; **the ~** *npl* (GEO) Флама́ндцы *mpl*.

flesh [flɛʃ] *n* (ANAT) плоть *f*; (*skin*) те́ло; (*of fruit*) мя́коть *f*
► **flesh out** *vt* излага́ть (изложи́ть* *perf*) во всех дета́лях.

flesh wound [-wu:nd] *n* пове́рхностная ра́на.

flew [flu:] *pt of* **fly**.
flex [flɛks] *n* ги́бкий* шнур* ♦ *vt* (*leg, muscles*) размина́ть (размя́ть* *perf*).
flexibility [flɛksɪ'bɪlɪtɪ] *n* ги́бкость *f*.
flexible ['flɛksəbl] *adj* ги́бкий*.
flexitime ['flɛksɪtaɪm] *n* ги́бкий* гра́фик (*рабо́чего дня*).
flick [flɪk] *n* щелчо́к* ♦ *vt* (*with finger*) сма́хивать (смахну́ть *perf*); (*ash*) стря́хивать (стряхну́ть *perf*); (*towel, whip*) хлестну́ть (*perf*) +*instr*; (*switch*) щёлкнуть (*perf*) +*instr*; ~**s** *npl* (*inf*) кино́шка *fsg*
► **flick through** *vt fus* просма́тривать (просмотре́ть *perf*).
flicker ['flɪkə'] *vi* (*light, flame*) мерца́ть (*impf*); (*eyelids*) трепета́ть (*impf*) ♦ *n* (*of light*) мерца́ние; (*of pain, fear*) вспы́шка*; (*of suspicion, doubt*) тень *f*; (*of interest, hope*) про́блеск; (*of eyelid*) трепета́ние.
flick knife *n* (*BRIT*) кно́почный нож.
flier ['flaɪə'] *n* (*pilot*) лётчик.
flight [flaɪt] *n* полёт; (*escape*) бе́гство; (*of steps*) пролёт (*ле́стницы*); **to take ~** обраща́ться (обрати́ться* *perf*) в бе́гство; **to put to ~** обраща́ть (обрати́ть* *perf*) в бе́гство.
flight attendant *n* (*US*) стюа́рд(е́сса).
flight crew *n* экипа́ж самолёта.
flight deck *n* (*AVIAT*) каби́на экипа́жа; (*NAUT*) взлётно-поса́дочная полоса́ на па́лубе.
flight path *n* (*of plane*) курс полёта; (*of rocket*) траекто́рия полёта.
flight recorder *n* "чёрный я́щик".
flimsy ['flɪmzɪ] *adj* (*shoes, clothes*) лёгкий*; (*building, structure*) непро́чный*; (*excuse, evidence*) сла́бый*.
flinch [flɪntʃ] *vi* (*in pain, shock*) вздра́гивать (вздро́гнуть *perf*); **to ~ from** (*unpleasant duty*) уклоня́ться (уклони́ться* *perf*) от +*gen*.
fling [flɪŋ] (*pt, pp* **flung**) *vt* (*throw*) швыря́ть (швырну́ть *perf*) ♦ *n* (*love affair*) рома́н; **to ~ one's arms around sb's neck** обнима́ть (обня́ть* *perf*) кого́-н за ше́ю; **to ~ o.s.** (*move quickly*) кида́ться (ки́нуться *perf*), броса́ться (бро́ситься* *perf*).
flint [flɪnt] *n* креме́нь* *m*.
flip [flɪp] *vt* (*switch*) щёлкать (щёлкнуть *perf*) +*instr*; (*coin*) подбра́сывать (подбро́сить* *perf*) щелчко́м; (*US: pancake*) подбра́сывать (подбро́сить* *perf*) ♦ *vi*: **to ~ for sth** (*US*) броса́ть (бро́сить* *perf*) моне́ту
► **flip through** *vt fus* просма́тривать (просмотре́ть *perf*).
flippant ['flɪpənt] *adj* несерьёзный*.
flipper ['flɪpə'] *n* (*of seal etc*) плавни́к*; (*for swimming*) ласт*.
flip side *n* оборо́т.
flirt [flɜːt] *vi* (*with person*) флиртова́ть (*impf*),

зай́грывать (*impf*); (*with idea*) зай́грывать (*impf*) ♦ *n* коке́тка*, люби́тель(ница) *m(f)* пофлиртова́ть.
flirtation [flɜː'teɪʃən] *n* флирт.
flit [flɪt] *vi* (*birds*) перелета́ть (перелете́ть* *perf*); (*butterfly*) порха́ть (*impf*); (*expression, smile*) мелька́ть (*impf*).
float [fləut] *n* (*for fishing*) поплаво́к*; (*for swimming*) пенопла́стовая доска́ для обуча́ющихся пла́вать; (*lorry*) укра́шенная платфо́рма на колёсах в пра́здничной проце́ссии; (*money*) разме́нные де́ньги *pl* ♦ *vi* (*object: on water*) пла́вать (*impf*), держа́ться (*impf*) на пове́рхности; (*swimmer*) плыть* (*impf*); (*sound, smell, cloud*) плыть* (*impf*); (*paper*) лета́ть (*impf*); (*COMM: currency*) свобо́дно колеба́ться (*impf*) ♦ *vt* (*idea, plan*) пуска́ть (пусти́ть* *perf*) в ход; **to ~ currency** вводи́ть (ввести́* *perf*) пла́вающий валю́тный курс; **to ~ a company** выпуска́ть (вы́пустить* *perf*) а́кции компа́нии че́рез би́ржу
► **float around** *vi* (*idea, rumour*) носи́ться (*impf*) в во́здухе; (*person, object*) пла́вать (*impf*).
flock [flɔk] *n* (*of sheep*) ста́до; (*of birds*) ста́я; (*REL*) па́ства ♦ *vi*: **to ~ to** (*place, event*) стека́ться (сте́чься *perf*) в +*prp*.
floe [fləu] *n* (*also: ice ~*) плавучая льди́на.
flog [flɔg] *vt* (*whip*) сечь* (вы́сечь* *perf*); (*inf: sell*) сплавля́ть (спла́вить* *perf*).
flood [flʌd] *n* (*of water*) наводне́ние; (*of letters, imports etc*) пото́к ♦ *vt* (*subj: water*) залива́ть (зали́ть* *perf*); (: *people*) наводня́ть (наводни́ть *perf*); (*AUT: carburettor*) наполня́ть (напо́лнить *perf*) ♦ *vi* (*place*) наполня́ться (напо́лниться *perf*) водо́й; (*people, goods*): **to ~ into** хлы́нуть (*perf*) в/на +*acc*; **the river is in ~** река́ вы́шла из берего́в; **to ~ the market with** (*COMM*) наводня́ть (наводни́ть *perf*) ры́нок +*instr*.
flooding ['flʌdɪŋ] *n* наводне́ние.
floodlight ['flʌdlaɪt] *n* прожектор* ♦ *vt* освеща́ть (освети́ть* *perf*) прожектором.
floodlit ['flʌdlɪt] *pt, pp of* **floodlight** ♦ *adj* освещённый прожектором.
flood tide *n* прили́в.
flood water *n* (*разли́вшаяся*) вода́* (*во вре́мя наводне́ния*).
floor [flɔː'] *n* (*of room*) пол*; (*storey*) эта́ж*; (*of sea, valley*) дно* ♦ *vt* (*subj: blow*) вали́ть* (повали́ть* *perf*) на́ пол, сбива́ть (сбить* *perf*) с ног; (: *question, remark*) сража́ть (срази́ть* *perf*); **on the ~** на полу́; **ground** *or* (*US*) **first ~** пе́рвый эта́ж*; **first** *or* (*US*) **second ~** второ́й эта́ж*; **top ~** после́дний эта́ж*; **to take the ~** (*fig*) брать (взять* *perf*) сло́во; **to have the ~** (*speaker*) получа́ть (получи́ть *perf*) сло́во.

---

* marks translations which have irregular inflections. The Russian-English side of the dictionary gives inflectional information.

floorboard ['flɔ:bɔ:d] *n* половица.
flooring ['flɔ:rɪŋ] *n* (*floor*) пол*; (*material to make floor*) настил; (*covering*) настилка полов.
floor lamp *n* (*US*) торшёр.
floor show *n* (*in nightclub*) развлекательная программа.
floorwalker ['flɔ:wɔ:kəʳ] *n* (*esp US*) дежурный администратор магазина.
floozy ['flu:zɪ] *n* (*inf*) шлюха.
flop [flɔp] *n* (*failure*) провал ◆ *vi* (*fail*) проваливаться (провалиться* *perf*); (*fall: into chair, onto floor etc*) шлёпаться (шлёпнуться* *perf*).
floppy ['flɔpɪ] *adj* свисающий, отвислый ◆ *n* (*also:~ disk*) гибкий* диск, дискета, флоппи-диск; **~ hat** шляпа с отвислыми полями.
flora ['flɔ:rə] *n* флора.
floral ['flɔ:rl] *adj* (*pattern*) цветистый.
Florence ['flɔrəns] *n* Флоренция.
Florentine ['flɔrəntaɪn] *adj* флорентийский*.
florid ['flɔrɪd] *adj* (*style*) цветистый; (*complexion*) красный*.
florist ['flɔrɪst] *n* торговец* цветами; (*female*) цветочница.
florist's (shop) ['flɔrɪsts-] *n* цветочный магазин.
flotation [fləu'teɪʃən] *n* (*of shares*) свободная продажа; (*of company*) распродажа акций компании.
flotsam ['flɔtsəm] *n* (*also: ~ and jetsam: rubbish*) мусор; (*: people*) бродяги *pl*.
flounce [flauns] *n* (*frill*) оборка*
▶ **flounce out** *vi*: **she ~d out of the room** она бросилась вон из комнаты.
flounder ['flaundəʳ] *vi* (*in water*) барахтаться (*impf*); (*fig*) спотыкаться (*impf*), путаться (*impf*) ◆ *n* (*ZOOL*) камбала.
flour ['flauəʳ] *n* мука.
flourish ['flʌrɪʃ] *vi* (*business*) процветать (*impf*); (*plant*) пышно расти* (*impf*) ◆ *vt* (*document, handkerchief*) размахивать (*impf*) +*instr* ◆ *n* (*in writing*) завитушка; (*bold gesture*): **with a ~** демонстративно.
flourishing ['flʌrɪʃɪŋ] *adj* (*company, trade*) процветающий.
flout [flaut] *vt* (*law, rules*) пренебрегать (пренебречь* *perf*).
flow [fləu] *n* (*of blood, river*) течение; (*ELEC*) поток; (*of traffic, orders, information*) поток; (*of tide*) прилив ◆ *vi* течь* (*impf*); (*clothes, hair*) ниспадать (*impf*), падать (*impf*).
flow chart *n* блок-схема.
flow diagram *n* = flow chart.
flower ['flauəʳ] *n* цветок* ◆ *vi* (*plant, tree*) цвести* (*impf*); **~s** цветы; **in ~** в цвету.
flowerbed ['flauəbɛd] *n* клумба.
flowerpot ['flauəpɔt] *n* цветочный горшок*.
flowery ['flauərɪ] *adj* (*perfume*) цветочный; (*pattern, speech*) цветистый.

flown [fləun] *pp of* **fly**.
flu [flu:] *n* (*MED*) грипп*.
fluctuate ['flʌktjueɪt] *vi* (*price, rate, temperature*) колебаться* (*impf*); (*opinions, attitudes*) меняться (*impf*).
fluctuation [flʌktju'eɪʃən] *n*: **~ (in)** колебание (в +*prp*).
flue [flu:] *n* дымоход.
fluency ['flu:ənsɪ] *n* беглость *f*; **his ~ in Russian** его беглость в русском языке.
fluent ['flu:ənt] *adj* (*linguist*) бегло говорящий; (*speech, writing etc*) беглый, плавный*; **he's a ~ speaker** он очень красноречив; **he's a ~ reader** он быстро читает; **he speaks ~ Russian, he's ~ in Russian** он свободно *or* бегло говорит по-русски.
fluently ['flu:əntlɪ] *adv* (*speak*) бегло; (*read, write*) свободно.
fluff [flʌf] *n* (*on jacket, carpet*) ворс; (*fur, down*) пух* ◆ *vt* (*inf: do badly: lines*) спутывать (спутать *perf*; (*: exam*) заваливать (завалить* *perf*); (*also: ~ out: hair*) взбивать (взбить* *perf*); (*: feathers*) распушать (распушить *perf*).
fluffy ['flʌfɪ] *adj* пушистый; **~ toy** мягкая игрушка*.
fluid ['flu:ɪd] *adj* (*movement*) текучий*; (*situation, arrangement*) переменчивый (переменчив); (*opinion*) неустойчивый (неустойчив) ◆ *n* жидкость *f*.
fluid ounce *n* (*BRIT*: = 0.028l; 0.05 pints) жидкая унция.
fluke [flu:k] *n* (*inf*) везение.
flummox ['flʌməks] *vt* сбивать (сбить* *perf*) с толку.
flung [flʌŋ] *pt, pp of* **fling**.
flunky ['flʌŋkɪ] *n* лакей.
fluorescent [fluə'rɛsnt] *adj* (*dial, light*) флюоресцирующий; (*paint*) флюорес-центный.
fluoride ['fluəraɪd] *n* фторид.
fluorine ['fluəri:n] *n* фтор.
flurry ['flʌrɪ] *n* (*of wind*) порыв; **snow ~** снежный вихрь *m*; **a ~ of activity** бурная деятельность *f*; **a ~ of excitement** бурное возбуждение*.
flush [flʌʃ] *n* (*on face*) румянец*; (*fig: of youth, beauty etc*) расцвет ◆ *vt* (*drains, pipe*) промывать (промыть* *perf*) ◆ *vi* (*become red: face*) заардеться (*perf*) ◆ *adj*: **~ with** (*level*) на одном уровне с +*instr*; **~ against** вплоть до +*gen*; **in the first ~ of youth/freedom** в упоении молодостью/свободой; **hot ~es** (*BRIT: MED*) приливы крови; **to ~ the toilet** спускать (спустить* *perf*) воду в туалете
▶ **flush out** *vt* (*game, birds*) вспугивать (вспугнуть *perf*); (*criminal*) спугивать (спугнуть *perf*).
flushed ['flʌʃt] *adj* раскрасневшийся.
fluster ['flʌstəʳ] *vt* (*person*) смущать (смутить* *perf*) ◆ *n*: **in a ~** в смущении.
flustered ['flʌstəd] *adj* смущённый* (смущён).

flute [flu:t] *n* флéйта.
fluted ['flu:tɪd] *adj* рифлёный, гофрирóванный.
flutter ['flʌtə'] *n* (*of wings*) взмах; (*of panic, excitement*) трéпет ♦ *vi* (*bird*) взмáхивать (*impf*) крЫльями; (*person*) метáться* (*impf*).
flux [flʌks] *n*: **in a state of** ~ в состоЯнии непрерЫвного изменéния.
fly [flaɪ] (*pt* **flew**, *pp* **flown**) *n* (*insect*) мýха; (*on trousers: also:* **flies**) ширИнка ♦ *vt* (*plane*) водИть/вестИ* (*impf*); (*passengers, cargo*) перевозИть* (перевезтИ* *perf*); (*distances*) пролетáть (пролетéть *perf*), преодолевáть (преодолéть* *perf*); (*kite*) запускáть (запустИть* *perf*) ♦ *vi* (*also fig*) летáть/летéть (*impf*); (*escape*) спасáться (спастИсь* *perf*) бéгством, сбегáть (сбежáть *perf*); (*flag*) развевáться (*impf*); **to** ~ **open** распáхиваться (распахнýться *perf*); **to** ~ **off the handle** (*inf*) срывáться (сорвáться *perf*); **pieces of metal went** ~**ing everywhere** оскóлки метáлла полетéли во все стóроны; **she came** ~**ing into the room** онá влетéла в комнáту; **her glasses flew off** у неё слетéли очкИ
▸ **fly away** *vi* улетáть (улетéть *perf*)
▸ **fly in** *vi* (*plane, person*) прилетáть (прилетéть* *perf*)
▸ **fly off** *vi* = **fly away**
▸ **fly out** *vi* (*person, plane*) вылетáть (вЫлететь* *perf*).
fly-fishing ['flaɪfɪʃɪŋ] *n* ужéние на блеснý.
flying ['flaɪɪŋ] *n* (*activity*) лётное дéло; (*action*) полёт ♦ *adj*: **a** ~ **visit** крáткий* визИт; **he doesn't like** ~ он не лЮбит летáть самолётом; **with** ~ **colours** блестЯще.
flying buttress *n* áрочный контрфóрс.
flying picket *n* грýппа профсоЮзных агитáторов, объезжáющая фáбрики с цéлью убедИть рабóчих принЯть учáстие в забастóвка.
flying saucer *n* летáющая тарéлка*.
flying squad *n* полицéйский спецотрЯд (*для бЫстрого налёта*).
flying start *n*: **to get off to a** ~ ~ начинáть (начáть* *perf*) óчень успéшно.
flyleaf ['flaɪli:f] *n* фóрзац.
flyover ['flaɪəʊvə'] *n* (*BRIT: overpass*) эстакáда.
fly-past ['flaɪpɑ:st] *n* воздýшный парáд.
fly sheet *n* (*for tent*) навéс.
flyweight ['flaɪweɪt] *n* боксёр лёгкой весовóй категóрии.
flywheel ['flaɪwi:l] *n* маховóе колесó*.
FM *abbr* (*BRIT: MIL*) = **field marshal**; (*RADIO:* = *frequency modulation*) ЧМ= *частóтная модулЯция*.
FMB *n abbr* (*US*) = *Federal Maritime Board*.
FMCS *n abbr* (*US*: = *Federal Mediation and Conciliation Services*) слýжба

посрéдничества мéжду предпринимáтелями и рабóчими.
FO *n abbr* (*BRIT*) = **Foreign Office**.
foal [fəʊl] *n* жеребёнок*.
foam [fəʊm] *n* пéна; (*also:* ~ **rubber**) пенорезИна ♦ *vi* пéниться (*impf*).
fob [fɒb] *n* (*also:* **watch** ~) цепóчка* для кармáнных часóв ♦ *vt*: **to** ~ **sb off (with sth)** всучивать (всучИть *perf*) *or* подсóвывать (подсýнуть *perf*) комý-н что-н.
f.o.b. *abbr* (*COMM*: = *free on board*) ФОБ= *фрáнко-бóрт*.
foc *abbr* (*COMM: BRIT*: = *free of charge*) беcплáтно.
focal point ['fəʊkl-] *n* средотóчие; (*PHOT*) фокáльная тóчка.
focus ['fəʊkəs] (*pl* ~**es**) *n* (*PHOT*) фóкус; (*of attention, interest, argument*) центр ♦ *vt* (*camera*) настрáивать* (настрóить* *perf*); (*light rays*) фокусИровать (сфокусИровать *perf*) ♦ *vi*: **to** ~ (**on**) (*PHOT*) настрáиваться (настрóиться *perf*) (на +*acc*); (*fig*): **to** ~ **on** сосредотóчиваться (сосредотóчиться *perf*) на +*prp*; **in** ~ в фóкусе; **out of** ~ не в фóкусе.
fodder ['fɒdə'] *n* корм*.
FOE *n abbr* (= *Friends of the Earth*) ОДЗ= *Óбщество "ДрузьЯ ЗемлИ"*; (*US*: = *Fraternal Order of Eagles*) Брáтский óрден орлóв.
foe [fəʊ] *n* нéдруг.
foetus ['fi:təs] (*US* **fetus**) *n* плод, зарóдыш.
fog [fɒg] *n* тумáн.
fogbound ['fɒgbaʊnd] *adj* закрЫтый Или задержáнный из-за тумáна.
foggy ['fɒgɪ] *adj* тумáнный (тумáнен); **it's** ~ стоИт тумáн.
fog lamp (*US* **fog light**) *n* (*AUT*) фáра для тумáна.
foible ['fɔɪbl] *n* причýда.
foil [fɔɪl] *vt* (*plan*) расстрáивать (расстрóить* *perf*); (*attempt, attack*) срывáть (сорвáть* *perf*) ♦ *n* (*metal*) фольгá; (*FENCING*) рапИра; **to act as a** ~ **to** (*fig*) служИть* (*impf*) контрáстом +*dat*.
foist [fɔɪst] *vt*: **to** ~ **sth on sb** навЯзывать (навязáть* *perf*) что-н комý-н.
fold [fəʊld] *n* (*crease*) склáдка*; (: *in paper*) сгиб; (*AGR*) загóн; (*fig*) лóно ♦ *vt* (*clothes, paper*) склáдывать (сложИть* *perf*); (*arms*) скрéщивать (скрестИть* *perf*) ♦ *vi* (*business*) сворáчиваться (свернýться *perf*)
▸ **fold up** *vi* склáдываться (сложИться* *perf*); (*business*) сворáчиваться (свернýться *perf*) ♦ *vt* (*object*) склáдывать (сложИть* *perf*).
folder ['fəʊldə'] *n* (*for papers*) пáпка*, скоросшивáтель *m*; (: *binder*) пáпка* (*с металлИческим зажИмом*); (*brochure*) брошЮра.
folding ['fəʊldɪŋ] *adj* (*chair, bed*) складнóй.

---

* marks translations which have irregular inflections. The Russian-English side of the dictionary gives inflectional information.

foliage ['fəulɪdʒ] *n* листва́.
folk [fəuk] *npl* лю́ди *pl*, наро́д* *msg* ♦ *cpd (art, music)* наро́дный; ~**s** *npl (inf: relatives)* бли́зкие *pl adj*.
folklore ['fəuklɔ:'] *n* фолькло́р.
folk music *n* наро́дная му́зыка.
folk song *n* наро́дная пе́сня*.
follow ['fɒləu] *vt (leader, person)* сле́довать (после́довать *perf)* за +*instr; (example, advice)* сле́довать (после́довать *perf)* +*dat; (event, story)* следи́ть* *(impf)* за +*instr; (route, path)* держа́ться* *(impf)* +*gen; (with eyes)* провожа́ть (проводи́ть* *perf)* взгля́дом ♦ *vi* сле́довать (после́довать *perf)*; **to ~ in sb's footsteps** идти́* (пойти́* *perf)* по чьи́м-н стопа́м; **I don't quite ~ you** я не совсе́м Вас понима́ю; **to ~ sb's advice** сле́довать (после́довать *perf)* чьему́-н сове́ту; **I left the room, and he ~ed** я вы́шел из ко́мнаты и он после́довал за мно́й; **it ~s that he** ... отсю́да сле́дует, что он ...; **to ~ suit** *(fig)* сле́довать (после́довать *perf)* приме́ру
▶ **follow on** *vi (continue)*: **to ~ on from** сле́довать (после́довать *perf)* за +*instr*
▶ **follow out** *vt (idea, plan)* приводи́ть* (привести́* *perf)* в исполне́ние
▶ **follow through** *vt* = **follow out**
▶ **follow up** *vt (letter, offer)* рассма́тривать (рассмотре́ть* *perf)*; *(case)* рассле́довать *(impf)*.
follower ['fɒləuə'] *n (of person)* после́дователь(ница) *m(f); (of belief)* сторо́нник(-ица).
following ['fɒləuɪŋ] *adj* сле́дующий* ♦ *n (followers)* сторо́нники *mpl*; **a large ~** мно́го сторо́нников.
follow-up ['fɒləuʌp] *n* продолже́ние ♦ *adj (treatment, survey)* после́дующий*.
folly ['fɒlɪ] *n (foolishness)* глу́пость *f; (building)* декорати́вное па́рковое сооруже́ние.
fond [fɒnd] *adj (smile, look, parents)* ла́сковый* (ла́сков); *(memory)* прия́тный* (прия́тен); *(hopes, dreams)* тще́тный* (тще́тен); **to be ~ of** люби́ть* *(impf)*; **she's ~ of swimming** она́ лю́бит пла́вать.
fondle ['fɒndl] *vt* ласка́ть *(impf)*.
fondly ['fɒndlɪ] *adv (lovingly)* ла́сково; *(naïvely)* наи́вно; **he ~ believed that** ... он наи́вно ве́рил, что ....
fondness ['fɒndnɪs] *n* любо́вь* *f*; **a special ~ for** осо́бенная любо́вь к +*dat*.
font [fɒnt] *n (in church)* купе́ль *f; (TYP)* компле́кт (шри́фта).
food [fu:d] *n* еда́, пи́ща.
food chain *n* пищево́й симбио́з.
food mixer *n* ми́ксер.
food poisoning *n* пищево́е отравле́ние.
food processor *n* кухо́нный комба́йн.
food stamp *n* продукто́вый тало́н.
foodstuffs ['fu:dstʌfs] *npl* проду́кты *mpl* пита́ния.

fool [fu:l] *n (male)* дура́к*; *(female)* ду́ра; *(CULIN)* сла́дкое блю́до из сли́вок и фру́ктов ♦ *vt (deceive)* обма́нывать (обману́ть* *perf)*, одура́чивать (одура́чить *perf)* ♦ *vi (be silly)* дура́читься *(impf)*; **to make a ~ of sb** *(ridicule)* выставля́ть (вы́ставить* *perf)* кого́-н на посме́шище; *(trick)* одура́чивать (одура́чить *perf)* кого́-н; **to make a ~ of o.s.** ста́вить* (поста́вить* *perf)* себя́ в глу́пое положе́ние; **you can't ~ me** меня́ не проведёте
▶ **fool about** *vi (pej: waste time)* валя́ть *(impf)* дурака́; *(behave foolishly)* дура́читься *perf*
▶ **fool around** *vi* = **fool about**.
foolhardy ['fu:lhɑ:dɪ] *adj* безрассу́дный* (безрассу́ден).
foolish ['fu:lɪʃ] *adj (stupid)* глу́пый* (глуп); *(rash)* опроме́тчивый (опроме́тчив).
foolishly ['fu:lɪʃlɪ] *adv (see adj)* глу́по; опроме́тчиво.
foolishness ['fu:lɪʃnɪs] *n* дура́чество.
foolproof ['fu:lpru:f] *adj (plan)* надёжный* (надёжен).
foolscap ['fu:lskæp] *n бумага формата: 34 см х 43 см.*
foot [fut] *(pl feet) n (of person)* нога́*, ступня́; *(of animal)* нога́*; *(of bed)* коне́ц*; *(of cliff)* подно́жие; *(measure)* фут; *(of page, stairs etc)* низ ♦ *vt*: **to ~ the bill** плати́ть* *(perf)*; **on ~** пешко́м; **at the ~ of the page/stairs** внизу́ страни́цы/ле́стницы; **to find one's feet** *(fig)* встава́ть* (встать* *perf)* на́ ноги; **to put one's ~ down** *(AUT)* нажима́ть (нажа́ть* *perf)* на педа́ль; *(assert authority)* занима́ть (заня́ть* *perf)* твёрдую пози́цию.
footage ['futɪdʒ] *n (CINEMA: material)* ка́дры *mpl*; *(: length)* ≈ метра́ж.
foot-and-mouth [futən'mauθ] *n (also: ~ disease)* я́щур.
football ['futbɔ:l] *n (ball)* футбо́льный мяч*; *(sport: BRIT)* футбо́л; *(: US)* америка́нский* футбо́л.
footballer ['futbɔ:lə'] *n (BRIT)* футболи́ст.
football ground *n* футбо́льное по́ле.
football match *n (BRIT)* футбо́льный матч.
football player *n* футболи́ст.
foot brake *n* ножно́й то́рмоз*.
footbridge ['futbrɪdʒ] *n* пешехо́дный мост*.
foothills ['futhɪlz] *npl* предго́рья* *ntpl*.
foothold ['futhəuld] *n* опо́ра; *(fig)*: **to get a ~** укрепля́ться (укрепи́ться* *perf)*, утверди́ться* *(perf)*.
footing ['futɪŋ] *n (fig: basis, relationship)* осно́ва; **to be on a friendly ~** быть* *(impf)* на дру́жеской ноге́; **to lose one's ~** *(fall)* теря́ть (потеря́ть *perf)* опо́ру; **on an equal ~** на ра́вных (основа́ниях).
footlights ['futlaɪts] *npl* огни́ *mpl* ра́мпы.
footman ['futmən] *irreg n* лаке́й.
footnote ['futnəut] *n* сно́ска*.
footpath ['futpɑ:θ] *n* тропи́нка*, доро́жка*; *(in street)* тротуа́р.

footprint ['futprɪnt] *n* след*, опеча́ток ноги́.
footrest ['futrɛst] *n* скаме́ечка* для ног.
footsie ['futsɪ] *n*: **to play ~ with sb** толка́ть (толкну́ть *perf*) но́жкой кого́-н.
footsore ['futsɔ:'] *adj*: **I am ~** у меня́ боля́т но́ги.
footstep ['futstɛp] *n* (*sound*) шаг*; (*footprint*) след*; (*fig*): **to follow in sb's ~s** идти́* (пойти́* *perf*) по чьим-н стопа́м.
footwear ['futwɛə'] *n* о́бувь *f*.
footwork ['futwə:k] *n* фигу́ры *fpl* (*движе́ния ног в та́нце*).

KEYWORD
---

for [fɔ:'] *prep* **1** (*indicating destination, intention*): **the train for London/Paris** по́езд в Ло́ндон/Пари́ж; **he left for Rome/work** он уе́хал в Рим/на рабо́ту; **when does the train for Moscow leave?** когда́ отправля́ется по́езд на Москву́?; **he went for the paper/the doctor** он пошёл за газе́той/врачо́м; **is this for me?** э́то мне *or* для меня́?; **there's a letter for you** Вам письмо́; **it's time for lunch/bed** пора́ обе́дать (*impf*)/спать (*impf*)
2 (*indicating purpose*) для +*gen*; **what's it for?** для чего́ э́то?; **give it to me – what for?** да́йте э́то мне – заче́м?; **to pray for forgiveness** моли́ть* (*impf*) о проще́нии; **to pray for peace** моли́ться* (*impf*) о ми́ре
3 (*on behalf of, representing*): **to speak for sb** говори́ть (*impf*) от лица́ кого́-н; **MP for Brighton** член *m* парла́мента представля́ющий Бра́йтон; **he works for the government** он на госуда́рственной слу́жбе; **he works for a local firm** он рабо́тает в ме́стной фи́рме; **I'll ask him for you** я спрошу́ его́ от ва́шего и́мени; **to do sth for sb** (*on behalf of*) де́лать (сде́лать *perf*) что-н за кого́-н
4 (*because of*) из-за +*gen*; **for lack of funds** из-за отсу́тствия средств; **for this reason** по э́той причи́не; **for some reason, for whatever reason** почему́-то; **for fear of being criticized** боя́сь кри́тики; **to be famous for sth** быть (*impf*) изве́стным чем-н
5 (*with regard to*): **it's cold for July** для ию́ля сейча́с хо́лодно; **he's tall for fourteen/for his age** для четы́рнадцати лет/для своего́ во́зраста он высо́кий; **a gift for languages** спосо́бности к языка́м; **for everyone who voted yes, 50 voted no** на ка́ждый го́лос „за“, прихо́дится 50 голосо́в „про́тив“
6 (*in exchange for, in favour of*) за +*acc*; **I sold it for £5** я про́дал э́то за £5; **I'm all for it** я целико́м и по́лностью за э́то
7 (*referring to distance*): **there are roadworks for five miles** доро́жные рабо́ты на протяже́нии пяти́ миль; **to stretch for miles** простира́ться (*impf*) на мно́го миль; **we**

walked for miles/for ten miles мы прошли́ мно́го миль/де́сять миль
8 (*referring to time*) на +*acc*; (: *in past*): **he was away for 2 years** он был в отъе́зде 2 го́да; **she will be away for a month** она́ уезжа́ет на ме́сяц; **can you do it for tomorrow?** Вы мо́жете сде́лать э́то на за́втра; **it hasn't rained for 3 weeks** уже́ 3 неде́ли не́ было дождя́; **for hours** часа́ми
9 (*with infinite clause*): **it is not for me to decide** не мне реша́ть; **there is still time for you to do it** у Вас ещё есть вре́мя сде́лать э́то; **for this to be possible** ... чтобы э́то осуществи́ть ...
10 (*in spite of*) несмотря́ на +*acc*; **for all his complaints** несмотря́ на все его́ жа́лобы
11 (*in phrases*): **for the first/last time** в пе́рвый/после́дний раз; **for the time being** пока́

♦ *conj* (*rather formal*) и́бо.

f.o.r. *abbr* (*COMM*: = *free on rail*) фра́нко-ваго́н.
forage ['fɔrɪdʒ] *n* корм ♦ *vi*: **to ~ for sth** ры́скать* (*impf*) по́исках чего́-н.
forage cap *n* фура́жка, пило́тка.
foray ['fɔreɪ] *n* (*raid*) набе́г.
forbad(e) [fə'bæd] *pt of* **forbid**.
forbearing [fɔ:'bɛərɪŋ] *adj* сде́ржанный.
forbid [fə'bɪd] (*pt* **forbad(e)**, *pp* **forbidden**) *vt* запреща́ть (запрети́ть* *perf*); **to ~ sb to do** запреща́ть (запрети́ть* *perf*) кому́-н +*infin*.
forbidden [fə'bɪdn] *pp of* **forbid** ♦ *adj* (*entry, activity*) запрещённый* (запрещён); (*place*) запре́тный; **it's ~ to** ... запрещено́ +*infin* ....
forbidding [fə'bɪdɪŋ] *adj* (*look etc*) неприя́зненный; (*prospect*) мучи́тельный* (мучи́телен).
force [fɔ:s] *n* (*also PHYS*) си́ла; (*influence*) возде́йствие ♦ *vt* (*compel*) заставля́ть (заста́вить* *perf*), принужда́ть (прину́дить* *perf*); (*push*) толка́ть (толкну́ть* *perf*); (*break open*) взла́мывать (взлома́ть* *perf*); **the F~s** *npl* (*BRIT: MIL*) вооружённые си́лы *fpl*; **in ~** в большо́м числе́; **to come into ~** вступа́ть (вступи́ть* *perf*) в си́лу; **to join ~s** объединя́ть (объедини́ть* *perf*) уси́лия; **it's a ~ five wind** си́ла ве́тра – пять ба́ллов; **the sales ~** (*COMM*) торго́вые аге́нты; **to ~ o.s. to do** заставля́ть (заста́вить* *perf*) себя́ +*infin*; **to ~ sb to do** заставля́ть (заста́вить* *perf*) *or* вынужда́ть (вы́нудить* *perf*) кого́-н +*infin*.
▸ **force back** *vt* (*enemy*) отража́ть (отрази́ть* *perf*); (*crowd, tears*) сде́рживать (сдержа́ть* *perf*)
▸ **force down** *vt* (*food*) есть* (съесть* *perf*) с трудо́м.
forced [fɔ:st] *adj* (*landing*) вы́нужденный; (*smile*) натя́нутый (натя́нут); **~ labour** принуди́тельный труд.

---

* marks translations which have irregular inflections. The Russian-English side of the dictionary gives inflectional information.

force-feed ['fɔ:sfi:d] vt насильно кормить* (impf).

forceful ['fɔ:sful] adj сильный* (силён).

forceps ['fɔ:sɛps] npl щипцы pl.

forcible ['fɔ:səbl] adj (action) насильственный; (reminder, lesson) убедительный.

forcibly ['fɔ:səblɪ] adv (remove) насильно; (express) с силой.

ford [fɔ:d] n (in river) брод* ◆ vt переходить* (перейти* perf) вброд.

fore [fɔ:'] n: **to come to the ~** выдвигаться (выдвинуться perf).

forearm ['fɔ:rɑ:m] n предплечье*.

forebear ['fɔ:bɛə'] n предок*.

foreboding [fɔ:'bəudɪŋ] n предчувствие.

forecast ['fɔ:kɑ:st] (irreg: like cast) n прогноз ◆ vt (predict) предсказывать (предсказать* perf).

foreclose [fɔ:'kləuz] vt (LAW: also: ~ on) лишать (лишить perf) прав собственности.

foreclosure [fɔ:'kləuʒə'] n (COMM) лишение прав собственности.

forecourt ['fɔ:kɔ:t] n (of garage) передняя площадка.

forefathers ['fɔ:fɑ:ðəz] npl предки* mpl.

forefinger ['fɔ:fɪŋgə'] n указательный палец*.

forefront ['fɔ:frʌnt] n: **in** or **at the ~ of** (industry, movement) в авангарде +gen.

forego [fɔ:'gəu] (irreg: like go) vt поступаться (поступиться* perf) +instr.

foregoing ['fɔ:gəuɪŋ] adj предшествующий* ◆ n: **the ~** вышеупомянутое nt adj.

foregone ['fɔ:gɔn] adj: **it's a ~ conclusion** это предрешённый исход.

foreground ['fɔ:graund] n (also COMPUT) передний* план.

forehand ['fɔ:hænd] n (TENNIS) удар справа.

forehead ['fɔrɪd] n лоб*.

foreign ['fɔrɪn] adj (person, language) иностранный; (country) зарубежный; (trade) внешний*; (object) посторонний*.

foreign body n инородное тело.

foreign currency n иностранная валюта.

foreigner ['fɔrɪnə'] n иностранец*(-нка*).

foreign exchange n (system) обмен валюты; (money) валюта.

foreign-exchange market [fɔrnɪks'tʃeɪndʒ-] n валютный рынок*.

foreign-exchange rate n валютный курс.

foreign investment n иностранные капиталовложения ntpl.

foreign minister n министр иностранных дел.

Foreign Office n (BRIT) министерство иностранных дел.

Foreign Secretary n (BRIT) министр иностранных дел.

foreleg ['fɔ:lɛg] n (of animal) передняя нога*.

foreman ['fɔ:mən] irreg n (in factory, on building site etc) мастер*; (of jury) старшина m присяжных.

foremost ['fɔ:məust] adj (most important) наиболее важный* ◆ adv: **first and ~** в первую очередь, прежде всего.

forename ['fɔ:neɪm] n имя* nt.

forensic [fə'rɛnsɪk] adj (medicine, test) судебный*; **~ expert** специалист по судебной медицине.

foreplay ['fɔ:pleɪ] n возбуждающие ласки fpl.

forerunner ['fɔ:rʌnə'] n предшественник(-ница).

foresee [fɔ:'si:] (irreg: like see) vt предвидеть* (impf/perf).

foreseeable [fɔ:'si:əbl] adj предвидимый; **in the ~ future** в обозримом будущем.

foreseen [fɔ:'si:n] pp of **foresee**.

foreshadow [fɔ:'ʃædəu] vt (event) предзнаменовать (impf).

foreshore ['fɔ:ʃɔ:'] n береговая полоса, затопляемая приливом.

foreshortened [fɔ:'ʃɔ:tnd] adj (figure, scene) в ракурсе.

foresight ['fɔ:saɪt] n предусмотрительность f.

foreskin ['fɔ:skɪn] n крайняя плоть f.

forest ['fɔrɪst] n лес*.

forestall [fɔ:'stɔ:l] vt (person) приостанавливать (приостановить* perf); (discussion) опережать (опередить* perf).

forestry ['fɔrɪstrɪ] n лесоводство, лесничество.

foretaste ['fɔ:teɪst] n: **a ~ of** представление о +prp.

foretell [fɔ:'tɛl] (irreg: like tell) vt предсказывать (предсказать* perf).

forethought ['fɔ:θɔ:t] n предусмотрительность f.

foretold [fɔ:'təuld] pt, pp of **foretell**.

forever [fə'rɛvə'] adv (for good) навсегда; (endlessly) вечно; **that time has gone ~** то время ушло навсегда; **it will last ~** это будет длиться вечно; **you're ~ finding difficulties** Вы вечно находите трудности.

forewarn [fɔ:'wɔ:n] vt предупреждать (предупредить* perf).

foreword ['fɔ:wə:d] n (in book) предисловие.

forfeit ['fɔ:fɪt] n (penalty) штраф ◆ vt (right, friendship etc) терять (потерять perf); (one's happiness, health) поплатиться* (perf) +instr.

forgave [fə'geɪv] pt of **forgive**.

forge [fɔ:dʒ] n кузница ◆ vt (signature, money) подделывать (подделать perf); (metal) ковать (impf); **to ~ documents/a will** подделывать (подделать perf) документы/завещание.

▶ **forge ahead** vi (country, person) вырываться (вырваться* perf) вперёд.

forger ['fɔ:dʒə'] n (of documents, paintings) подделыватель m; (of money) фальшивомонетчик.

forgery ['fɔ:dʒərɪ] n подделка*.

forget [fə'gɛt] (pt forgot, pp forgotten) vt забывать (забыть* perf); (appointment) забывать (забыть* perf) о +prp ◆ vi забывать

(забы́ть* *perf*); **to ~ o.s.** забы́ться* (*perf*).
forgetful [fəˈgɛtful] *adj* (*person*) забы́вчивый (забы́вчив); **~ of** забы́в о +*prp*.
forgetfulness [fəˈgɛtfulnɪs] *n* забы́вчивость *f*; (*oblivion*) забве́ние.
forget-me-not [fəˈgɛtmɪnɔt] *n* незабу́дка*.
forgive [fəˈgɪv] (*pt* **forgave**, *pp* **forgiven**) *vt* (*pardon*) проща́ть (прости́ть* *perf*) +*dat or* +*gen*; **to ~ sb for sth** (*excuse*) проща́ть (прости́ть* *perf*) кому́-н *or* кого́-н за что-н; **I forgave him for doing it** я прости́л ему́ *or* его́ за то, что он э́то сде́лал; **~ my ignorance, but** ... прости́те моё неве́жество, но ...; **they could be ~n for thinking that** ... их мо́жно прости́ть за то, что они́ ду́мают, что ....
forgiven [fəˈgɪvn] *pp of* **forgive**.
forgiveness [fəˈgɪvnɪs] *n* проще́ние.
forgiving [fəˈgɪvɪŋ] *adj* великоду́шный* (великоду́шен).
forgo [fɔːˈgəu] *vt* = **forego**.
forgot [fəˈgɔt] *pt of* **forget**.
forgotten [fəˈgɔtn] *pp of* **forget**.
fork [fɔːk] *n* ви́лка*; (*for gardening*) ви́лы *pl*; (*in road*) развѝлка*; (*in railway*) стык; (*in river, tree*) разветвле́ние ♦ *vi* (*road*) разветвля́ться (*impf*)
►**fork out** (*inf*) ♦ *vt* выкла́дывать (вы́ложить* *perf*) ♦ *vi* раскоше́ливаться (раскоше́литься *perf*).
forked [fɔːkt] *adj* (*lightning*) зигзагообра́зный.
fork-lift truck [ˈfɔːklɪft-] *n* грузоподъёмник.
forlorn [fəˈlɔːn] *adj* (*person*) несча́стный; (*place*) поки́нутый; (*hope, attempt*) сла́бый.
form [fɔːm] *n* (*type*) вид; (*shape*) фо́рма; (*SCOL*) класс; (*questionnaire*) анке́та ♦ *vt* (*make*) образо́вывать (образова́ть *perf*); (*set up: organization, group*) формирова́ть (сформирова́ть *perf*); (*idea, habit*) выраба́тывать (вы́работать *perf*); **in the ~ of** в фо́рме +*gen*; **to be in good ~** (*SPORT, fig*) быть* (*impf*) в хоро́шей фо́рме; **in top ~** в лу́чшей фо́рме; **on ~** в фо́рме; **~ part of sth** явля́ться (яви́ться* *perf*) ча́стью чего́-н; **I ~ed a good impression of her** у меня́ созда́лось хоро́шее впечатле́ние о ней.
formal [ˈfɔːməl] *adj* форма́льный; (*statement*) форма́льный* (форма́лен); (*person, behaviour*) церемо́нный* (церемо́нен); (*occasion, dinner*) официа́льный* (официа́лен); (*garden*) англи́йский*; **~ clothes** официа́льная фо́рма оде́жды; **~ dress** (*evening dress*) вече́рняя оде́жда.
formalities [fɔːˈmælɪtɪz] *npl* форма́льности *fpl*.
formality [fɔːˈmælɪtɪ] *n* форма́льность *f*; (*of person, behaviour*) церемо́нность *f*; (*of occasion*) официа́льность *f*.
formalize [ˈfɔːməlaɪz] *vt* (*plan, arrangement*) оформля́ть (офо́рмить* *perf*).

formally [ˈfɔːməlɪ] *adv* форма́льно; (*behave*) церемо́нно; **to be ~ invited** получа́ть (получи́ть* *perf*) официа́льное приглаше́ние.
format [ˈfɔːmæt] *n* (*form, style*) форма́т ♦ *vt* (*COMPUT: disk*) формати́ровать (*impf/perf*).
formation [fɔːˈmeɪʃən] *n* формирова́ние; (*of rocks*) форма́ция; (*of clouds*) скопле́ние.
formative [ˈfɔːmətɪv] *adj*: **in his ~ years** в го́ды формирова́ния его́ хара́ктера.
former [ˈfɔːmə*] *adj* (*one-time*) бы́вший*; (*earlier*) пре́жний*; **the ~ ... the latter** ... пе́рвый ... после́дний*; **the ~ president** бы́вший* президе́нт.
formerly [ˈfɔːməlɪ] *adv* ра́ньше, до э́того.
form feed *n* (*on printer*) пода́ча страни́ц.
Formica® [fɔːˈmaɪkə] *n* форма́йка (*огнеупо́рная пластма́сса*).
formidable [ˈfɔːmɪdəbl] *adj* (*task*) чрезвыча́йно тру́дный* (тру́ден); (*opponent*) гро́зный* (гро́зен).
formula [ˈfɔːmjulə] (*pl* **~e** *or* **~s**) *n* (*MATH, CHEM*) фо́рмула; (*plan*) схе́ма; **F~ One** (*AUT*) обозначе́ние го́ночной маши́ны.
formulae [ˈfɔːmjuliː] *npl of* **formula**.
formulate [ˈfɔːmjuleɪt] *vt* (*plan, strategy*) выраба́тывать (вы́работать *perf*), разраба́тывать (разрабо́тать *perf*); (*opinion, thought*) формули́ровать (сформули́ровать *perf*).
fornicate [ˈfɔːnɪkeɪt] *vi* прелюбоде́йствовать (*impf*).
forsake [fəˈseɪk] (*pt* **forsook**, *pp* **forsaken**) *vt* (*abandon*) покида́ть (поки́нуть *perf*).
forsaken [fəˈseɪkən] *pp of* **forsake**.
forsook [fəˈsuk] *pt of* **forsake**.
fort [fɔːt] *n* кре́пость *f*, форт*; **to hold the ~** (*fig*) стоя́ть (*impf*) на стра́же.
forte [ˈfɔːtɪ] *n* (*strength*) си́льная сторона́.
forth [fɔːθ] *adv* (*out*): **to go ~** идти́* (*impf*) вперёд; **to send ~** посла́ть* (*perf*); **to go back and ~** ходи́ть* (*impf*) взад и вперёд; **to bring ~** вынима́ть (вы́нуть *perf*); **and so ~** и так да́лее.
forthcoming [fɔːθˈkʌmɪŋ] *adj* предстоя́щий; (*person*) общи́тельный; **to be ~** (*help, evidence*) ожида́ться (*impf*), появля́ться (*impf*).
forthright [ˈfɔːθraɪt] *adj* (*condemnation, opposition*) прямо́й.
forthwith [ˈfɔːθˈwɪθ] *adv* то́тчас.
fortieth [ˈfɔːtɪθ] *adj* сороково́й*; *see also* **fifth**.
fortification [fɔːtɪfɪˈkeɪʃən] *n* (*MIL*) укрепле́ние.
fortified wine [ˈfɔːtɪfaɪd-] *n* креплёное вино́*.
fortify [ˈfɔːtɪfaɪ] *vt* (*city*) укрепля́ть (укрепи́ть* *perf*); (*person*) придава́ть* (прида́ть* *perf*) си́лы +*dat*.
fortitude [ˈfɔːtɪtjuːd] *n* сто́йкость *f*.
fortnight [ˈfɔːtnaɪt] (*BRIT*) *n* две неде́ли; **it's a ~**

---

* marks translations which have irregular inflections. The Russian-English side of the dictionary gives inflectional information.

since ... прошло́ две неде́ли с тех пор, как ....

fortnightly ['fɔ:tnaɪtlɪ] *adv* раз в две неде́ли ♦ *adj*: ~ **magazine** журна́л, выходя́щий раз в две неде́ли.

FORTRAN ['fɔ:træn] *n* ФОРТРА́Н.

fortress ['fɔ:trɪs] *n* кре́пость *f*.

fortuitous [fɔ:'tju:ɪtəs] *adj* случа́йный* (случа́ен).

fortunate ['fɔ:tʃənɪt] *adj* (*person*) счастли́вый (счастли́в); (*event*) счастли́вый; **he is/was ~** ему́ везёт/повезло́; **he is ~ to have** ... ему́ хорошо́, что у него́ есть ...; **it is ~ that** ... уда́чно, что ....

fortunately ['fɔ:tʃənɪtlɪ] *adv* к сча́стью.

fortune ['fɔ:tʃən] *n* (*wealth*) состоя́ние; (*also: good* ~) сча́стье, уда́ча; **bad** *or* **ill ~** несча́стье, неуда́ча; **to make a ~** нажива́ть (нажи́ть* *perf*) себе́ состоя́ние; **to tell sb's ~** гада́ть (*impf*) кому́-н, предска́зывать (предсказа́ть* *perf*) чью-н судьбу́.

fortune-teller ['fɔ:tʃəntɛlə'] *n* гада́лка, предсказа́тель(ница) *m(f)*.

forty ['fɔ:tɪ] *n* со́рок*; *see also* **fifty**.

forum ['fɔ:rəm] *n* фо́рум.

forward ['fɔ:wəd] *adv* вперёд ♦ *n* (*SPORT*) напада́ющий*(-ая) *m(f) adj* ♦ *vt* (*letter, parcel*) пересыла́ть (пересла́ть* *perf*); (*career*) продвига́ть (продви́нуть *perf*) ♦ *adj* (*position*) пере́дний*; (*not shy*) де́рзкий* (де́рзок); (*COMM: delivery, sales*) заблаговре́менный; **to move ~** (*progress*) продвига́ться (продви́нуться *perf*); **"please ~"** „перешли́те адреса́ту"; **~ movement** движе́ние вперёд; **~ planning** предвари́тельное плани́рование.

forward contract *n* фо́рвардный *or* сро́чный контра́кт.

forward rate *n* фо́рвардный *or* сро́чный валю́тный курс, по кото́рому заключа́ется сро́чная валю́тная сде́лка.

forwards ['fɔ:wədz] *adv* вперёд.

fossil ['fɔsl] *n* окамене́лость *f*, ископа́емое *nt adj*.

fossil fuel *n* то́пливо (*образова́вшееся из окамене́лых оста́нков расте́ний и живо́тных*).

foster ['fɔstə'] *vt* (*child*) брать* (взять* *perf*) на воспита́ние; (*activity*) поощря́ть (*impf*); (*hope*) пита́ть (*impf*); **to ~ an idea** вына́шивать (*impf*) мысль.

foster child *n* ребёнок*.

foster mother *n* приёмная мать* *f*.

fought [fɔ:t] *pt, pp of* **fight**.

foul [faul] *adj* отврати́тельный* (отврати́телен); (*language*) непристо́йный* (непристо́ен); (*temper*) гневли́вый (гневли́в) ♦ *n* (*SPORT*) нaруше́ние ♦ *vt* га́дить* (зага́дить* *perf*); (*SPORT*) наруша́ть (нару́шить *perf*) пра́вила про́тив +*gen*; (*entangle: anchor, propeller*) опу́тывать (опу́тать *perf*).

foul play *n* (*LAW*) престу́пные де́йствия *ntpl*; ~

~ **is not suspected** нет подозре́ния о престу́пных де́йствиях.

found [faund] *pt, pp of* **find** ♦ *vt* (*establish*) осно́вывать (основа́ть *perf*).

foundation [faun'deɪʃən] *n* (*act*) основа́ние; (*base*) осно́ва; (*fig*) осно́ва, усто́и *mpl*; (*organization*) о́бщество, фонд; (*also:* ~ **cream**) крем под макия́ж; **~s** *npl* (*of building*) фунда́мент *msg*; **the rumours are without ~** слу́хи не име́ют основа́ний; **to lay the ~s** (*fig*) закла́дывать (заложи́ть* *perf*) осно́вы.

foundation stone *n* краеуго́льный ка́мень* *m*.

founder ['faundə'] *n* (*of firm, college*) основа́тель(ница) *m(f)* ♦ *vi* (*ship*) идти́* (пойти́* *perf*) ко дну́.

founder member *n* член-учреди́тель(ница) *m(f)*.

founding fathers ['faundɪŋ-] *npl* (*esp US*) основополо́жники *mpl*.

foundry ['faundrɪ] *n* лите́йная *f adj*, лите́йный цех.

fount [faunt] *n* исто́чник; (*TYP*) компле́кт шри́фта.

fountain ['fauntɪn] *n* фонта́н.

fountain pen *n* черни́льная ру́чка*.

four [fɔ:'] *n* четы́ре*; **on all ~s** на четвере́ньках; *see also* **five**.

four-letter word ['fɔ:lɛtə-] *n* ≈ мат.

four-poster ['fɔ:'pəustə'] *n* (*also:* ~ **bed**) крова́ть *f* с по́логом.

foursome ['fɔ:səm] *n* четвёрка*.

fourteen ['fɔ:'ti:n] *n* четы́рнадцать*; *see also* **five**.

fourteenth ['fɔ:'ti:nθ] *adj* четы́рнадцатый*; *see also* **fifth**.

fourth ['fɔ:θ] *adj* четвёртый ♦ *n* (*AUT: also:* ~ **gear**) четвёртая ско́рость *f*; *see also* **fifth**.

four-wheel drive ['fɔ:wi:l-] *n* (*AUT*): **with ~ ~** с приво́дом на четы́ре колеса́.

fowl [faul] *n* пти́ца; (*wild*) дичь *f*.

fox [fɔks] *n* лиса́* ♦ *vt* озада́чивать (озада́чить *perf*).

foxglove ['fɔksglʌv] *n* (*BOT*) наперстя́нка*.

fox-hunting ['fɔkshʌntɪŋ] *n* охо́та на лис.

foxtrot ['fɔkstrɔt] *n* (*dance*) фокстро́т.

foxy ['fɔksɪ] *adj*: ~ **lady** шика́рная же́нщина.

foyer ['fɔɪeɪ] *n* фойе́ *nt ind*.

FPA *n abbr* (*BRIT:* = *Family Planning Association*) организа́ция, обеспе́чивающая консульта́ции по плани́рованию дето-рожде́ния.

Fr. *abbr* (*REL*) = **father, friar**.

fr. *abbr* = *franc*.

fracas ['fræka:] *n* сканда́л.

fraction ['frækʃən] *n* (*portion*) небольша́я часть *f*; (*MATH*) дробь* *f*; **a ~ of a second** до́ля секу́нды.

fractionally ['frækʃnəlɪ] *adv*: ~ **smaller** *etc* незначи́тельно ме́ньше *etc*.

fractious ['frækʃəs] *adj* капри́зный* (капри́зен); **she was ~** она́ капри́зничала.

fracture ['fræktʃə'] *n* (*of bone*) перело́м ◆ *vt* (*bone*) лома́ть (слома́ть *perf*).
fragile ['frædʒaıl] *adj* хру́пкий* (хру́пок).
fragment ['frægmənt] *n* фрагме́нт; (*of stone, glass*) оско́лок*, обло́мок*.
fragmentary ['frægməntərı] *adj* (*evidence, knowledge*) отры́вочный* (отры́вочен).
fragrance ['freıgrəns] *n* благоуха́ние.
fragrant ['freıgrənt] *adj* души́стый (души́ст).
frail [freıl] *adj* (*person*) сла́бый* (слаб); (*structure*) хру́пкий* (хру́пок), непро́чный* (непро́чен).
frame [freım] *n* (*of building, structure*) карка́с; (*of car, human, animal*) о́стов; (*of picture, door, window*) ра́ма; (*of spectacles*: *also*: ~s) опра́ва ◆ *vt* обрамля́ть (обра́мить* *perf*); (*reply, law, theory*) формули́ровать (сформули́ровать *perf*); ~ **of mind** настрое́ние; **to ~ sb** (*inf*) подста́вить* (*perf*) кого́-н.
framework ['freımwə:k] *n* (*structure*) карка́с; (*fig*) ра́мки *fpl*.
France [frɑ:ns] *n* Фра́нция.
franchise ['fræntʃaız] *n* (*POL*) пра́во го́лоса; (*COMM*) франши́за.
franchisee [fræntʃaı'zi:] *n* держа́тель *m* франши́зы.
franchiser ['fræntʃaızə'] *n* предостави́тель *m* франши́зы.
frank [fræŋk] *adj* (*discussion, person*) открове́нный* (открове́нен); (*look*) откры́тый ◆ *vt* (*letter*) франки́ровать (зафранки́ровать *perf*).
Frankfurt ['fræŋkfə:t] *n* Фра́нкфурт.
frankfurter ['fræŋkfə:tə'] *n* соси́ска*.
franking machine ['fræŋkıŋ-] *n* франкирова́льная маши́на.
frankly ['fræŋklı] *adv* открове́нно.
frankness ['fræŋknıs] *n* открове́нность *f*.
frantic ['fræntık] *adj* (*distraught*) обезу́мевший; (*hectic*) сумато́шный*; (*desperate: need, desire*) безу́мный*; (: *cry*) неи́стовый; **we were ~ with worry** мы обезу́мели от волне́ния.
frantically ['fræntıklı] *adv* отча́янно.
fraternal [frə'tə:nl] *adj* бра́тский*.
fraternity [frə'tə:nıtı] *n* (*feeling*) бра́тство; (*club*) содру́жество.
fraternize ['frætənaız] *vi* обща́ться (*impf*).
fraud [frɔ:d] *n* (*crime*) моше́нничество; (*person*) моше́нник.
fraudulent ['frɔ:djulənt] *adj* (*scheme, claim*) моше́ннический*.
fraught [frɔ:t] *adj* (*person*) не́рвный* (не́рвен); (*situation*) ~ **with** (*danger, problems*) чрева́тый (чрева́т) +*instr*.
fray [freı] *vi* обтрёпываться (обтрепа́ться *perf*) ◆ *n* (*battle, fight*): **the ~** бой, дра́ка; **tempers**

were ~ed все бы́ли на гра́ни от изде́рганных не́рвов; **her nerves were ~ed** у неё бы́ли истрёпаны не́рвы; **to return to the ~** сно́ва ри́нуться (*perf*) в бой *or* дра́ку.
FRB *n abbr* (*US*: = *Federal Reserve Board*) федера́льное резе́рвное правле́ние.
FRCM *n abbr* (*BRIT*) = *Fellow of the Royal College of Music*.
FRCO *n abbr* (*BRIT*) = *Fellow of the Royal College of Organists*.
FRCP *n abbr* (*BRIT*) = *Fellow of the Royal College of Physicians*.
FRCS *n abbr* (*BRIT*) = *Fellow of the Royal College of Surgeons*.
freak [fri:k] *adj* (*event, accident*) стра́нный ◆ *n* (*person: in appearance*) уро́дец*(-дица), вы́родок* *m/f*; (: *in attitude, behaviour*): **he is a ~** он со стра́нностями; (*pej: fanatic*): **she's an aerobics ~** она́ помеша́лась на аэро́бике
▸ **freak out** *vi* (*inf: on drugs*) входи́ть* (войти́* *perf*) в раж.
freakish ['fri:kıʃ] *adj* стра́нный.
freckle ['frɛkl] *n* весну́шка*.
freckled ['frɛkld] *adj* весну́шчатый.
free [fri:] *adj* свобо́дный* (свобо́ден); (*costing nothing*) беспла́тный* (беспла́тен) ◆ *vt* (*prisoner etc*) освобожда́ть (освободи́ть* *perf*), выпуска́ть (вы́пустить* *perf*) (на свобо́ду); (*jammed object*) высвобожда́ть (вы́свободить* *perf*), выта́скивать (вы́тащить *perf*); **to give sb a ~ hand** предоставля́ть (предоста́вить* *perf*) кому́-н свобо́ду де́йствовать по-сво́ему; ~ **and easy** непринуждённый; **admission** ~ свобо́дный вход; ~ (**of charge**), **for** ~ беспла́тно; ~ **alongside ship** фра́нко вдоль бо́рта су́дна; ~ **of tax** освобождённый от упла́ты нало́гов; ~ **on rail** фра́нко – железнодоро́жный ваго́н.
free agent *n*: **he's a ~ ~** он сам себе́ хозя́ин.
freebie ['fri:bı] *n* (*inf: gift*) пода́рок*.
freedom ['fri:dəm] *n* свобо́да.
freedom fighter *n* боре́ц* за свобо́ду.
freedom of association *n* свобо́да объедине́ния *or* ассоциа́ции.
free enterprise *n* свобо́дное предпринима́тельство.
Freefone® ['fri:fəun] *n* систе́ма, позволя́ющая звони́ть беспла́тно в определённые организа́ции.
free-for-all ['fri:fərɔ:l] *n* (*fight*) всео́бщая дра́ка.
free gift *n* пода́рок*.
freehold ['fri:həuld] *n* (*of property*) по́лное пра́во на владе́ние.
free kick *n* (*FOOTBALL*) свобо́дный уда́р.
freelance ['fri:lɑ:ns] *adj* внешта́тный, рабо́тающий по договора́м.
freelance work *n* рабо́та по контра́кту *or*

---

* marks translations which have irregular inflections. The Russian-English side of the dictionary gives inflectional information.

договора́м.
freeloader ['fri:ləudə'] *n* (*pej*) дармоéд(ка*).
freely ['fri:lɪ] *adv* (*without restriction*) свобóдно; (*liberally*) обúльно; **drugs are ~ available in the city** наркóтики мóжно легкó достáть в гóроде.
free-market economy ['fri:'mɑ:kɪt-] *n* рыночная экономика.
Freemason ['fri:meɪsn] *n* масóн.
Freemasonry ['fri:meɪsnrɪ] *n* масóнство.
Freepost® ['fri:pəust] *n* (*BRIT*) бесплáтная пóчта.
free-range ['fri:'reɪndʒ] *adj*: ~ **eggs** я́йца от кур свобóдно-вы́гульного содержáния.
free sample *n* бесплáтный образéц*.
freesia ['fri:zɪə] *n* фрéзия.
free speech *n* свобóда слóва.
freestyle ['fri:staɪl] *n* (*in swimming*) кроль *m*.
free trade *n* неограни́ченная беспóшлинная торгóвля.
freeway ['fri:weɪ] *n* (*US*: *AUT*) скоростнáя автострáда.
freewheel [fri:'wi:l] *vi* (*on bicycle*) катúться* (покатúться* *perf*); (*in car*) идтú* (пойтú* *perf*) свобóдным хóдом.
free will *n* свобóда вóли; **of one's own ~~** по дóброй вóле.
freeze [fri:z] (*pt* **froze**, *pp* **frozen**) *vi* (*weather*) холодáть (похолодáть *perf*); (*liquid, pipe, person*) замерзáть (замёрзнуть* *perf*); (*person: stop moving*) застывáть (засты́ть* *perf*) ♦ *vt* замораживать (заморóзить* *perf*) ♦ *n* (*weather*) зáморозки *pl*; (*on arms, wages*) заморáживание; **it's freezing** óчень хóлодно
▸ **freeze over** *vi* замерзáть (замёрзнуть* *perf*)
▸ **freeze up** *vi* замерзáть (замёрзнуть* *perf*).
freeze-dried ['fri:zdraɪd] *adj* обрабóтанный мéтодом заморáживания-высýшивания.
freeze-dry ['fri:zdraɪ] *vt* бы́стро заморáживать и затéм высýшивать в вáкуме.
freezer ['fri:zə'] *n* морозúльник.
freezing ['fri:zɪŋ] *adj*: ~ (**cold**) ледянóй ♦ *n*: **3 degrees below** ~ мúнус 3 грáдуса, 3 грáдуса морóза; **I'm** ~ я замёрз.
freezing point *n* температýра замерзáния.
freight [freɪt] *n* фрахт; ~ **forward** фрахт уплáчиваемый в портý вы́грузки; ~ **inward** фрахт, уплáчиваемый по прибы́тии.
freight car *n* (*US*) товáрный вагóн.
freighter ['freɪtə'] *n* (*NAUT*) грузовóе сýдно*; (*AVIAT*) грузовóй самолёт.
freight forwarder [-'fɔ:wədə'] *n* экспедúтор.
freight train *n* (*US*) товáрный пóезд*.
French [frentʃ] *adj* французский* ♦ *n* (*LING*) французский* язы́к*; **the** ~ *npl* (*people*) французы *mpl*.
French bean *n* (*BRIT*) стручкóвая фасóль *f*.
French Canadian *n* франкоязы́чный(-ая) канáдец*(-дка).
French-Canadian [frentʃkə'neɪdʒən] *adj*

франко-канáдский*.
French dressing *n* сóус для салáта из растúтельного мáсла и ýксуса.
French fried potatoes *npl* чúпсы *mpl*.
French fries [-fraɪz] *npl* (*US*) = **French fried potatoes**.
French Guiana [-gar'ænə] *n* Французская Гвиáна.
Frenchman ['frentʃmən] *irreg n* француз.
French Riviera *n*: **the** ~~ Французская Ривьéра.
French stick *n* длúнный французский батóн.
French window *n* двуствóрчатое окнó до пóла.
Frenchwoman ['frentʃwumən] *irreg n* французенка*.
frenetic [frə'netɪk] *adj* лихорáдочный* (лихорáдочен).
frenzied ['frenzɪd] *adj* (*person*) бéшеный, взбешённый; (*behaviour*) нéистовый.
frenzy ['frenzɪ] *n* (*of violence*) бéшенство, нéистовство; ~ **of joy** безýмная рáдость; ~ **of excitement** безýмное возбуждéние; **to drive sb into a** ~ довестú* (*perf*) когó-н до бéшенства, привестú* (*perf*) когó-н в бéшенство; **to be in a** ~ быть* (*impf*) в бéшенстве.
frequency ['fri:kwənsɪ] *n* (*also RADIO*) частотá*.
frequency modulation *n* частóтная модуляция.
frequent [*adj* 'fri:kwənt, *vt* frɪ'kwent] *adj* чáстый ♦ *vt* (*pub, restaurant*) посещáть (посетúть* *perf*).
frequently ['fri:kwəntlɪ] *adv* (*often*) чáсто.
fresco ['freskəu] *n* фрéска*.
fresh [freʃ] *adj* свéжий* (свеж); (*instructions, approach*) нóвый* (нов); (*cheeky: person*) нахáльный* (нахáлен), фамильярный* (фамильярен); **to make a** ~ **start** начáть* *perf* зáново; ~ **in one's mind** свежó в пáмяти.
freshen ['freʃən] *vi* (*wind, air*) свежéть (*impf*)
▸ **freshen up** *vi* (*person*) освежáться (освежúться *perf*).
freshener ['freʃnə'] *n*: **skin** ~ лосьóн для освежéния кóжи; **air** ~ освежúтель *m* вóздуха.
fresher ['freʃə'] *n* (*BRIT*: *inf*) первокýрсник.
freshly ['freʃlɪ] *adv*: ~ **made** свéжеприготóвленный; ~ **painted** свéжепокрáшенный.
freshman ['freʃmən] *irreg n* (*US*) = **fresher**.
freshness ['freʃnɪs] *n* свéжесть *f*.
freshwater ['freʃwɔ:tə'] *adj* (*lake*) прéсный; (*fish*) пресновóдный.
fret [fret] *vi* волновáться (*impf*).
fretful ['fretful] *adj* (*child*) беспокóйный*.
Freudian ['frɔɪdɪən] *adj* фрейдúстский; ~ **slip** оговóрка по Фрéйду.
FRG *n abbr* (= *Federal Republic of Germany*) ФРГ = *Федератúвная Респýблика Гермáнии*.

Fri. *abbr* = **Friday**.
friar ['fraɪəʳ] *n* монáх.
friction ['frɪkʃən] *n* трéние; (*fig*) трéния *ntpl*.
friction feed *n* (*on printer*) подáча бумáги с пóмощью вáлика.
Friday ['fraɪdɪ] *n* пя́тница; *see also* **Tuesday**.
fridge [frɪdʒ] *n* (*BRIT*) холодúльник.
fridge-freezer ['frɪdʒ'friːzəʳ] *n* холодúльник с большóй морозúльной кáмерой.
fried [fraɪd] *pt, pp of* **fry** ◆ *adj* жáреный.
friend [frɛnd] *n* (*male*) друг*; (*female*) подрýга; **to make ~s with** подружúться (*perf*) с *+instr*.
friendliness ['frɛndlɪnɪs] *n* дружелю́бие.
friendly ['frɛndlɪ] *adj* (*person, smile etc*) дружелю́бный* (дружелю́бен); (*government, country*) дрýжественный* (дрýжествен); (*place, restaurant*) прия́тный* (прия́тен); (*game, match*) товáрищеский* ◆ *n* (*also: ~* **match**) товáрищеская встрéча; **to be ~ with** дружúть* (*impf*) с *+instr*; **to be ~ to sb** относúться* (отнестúсь* *perf*) к комý-н дружелю́бно.
friendly fire *n* огóнь* *m* со своúх позúций.
friendly society *n* óбщество *or* кáсса взаимопóмощи.
friendship ['frɛndʃɪp] *n* дрýжба.
frieze [friːz] *n* фриз, бордю́р.
frigate ['frɪgɪt] *n* фрегáт.
fright [fraɪt] *n* испýг; **to take ~** испугáться (*perf*); **she looks a ~** онá вы́глядит как пýгало.
frighten ['fraɪtn] *vt* пугáть (испугáть *or* напугáть *perf*)
▶ **frighten away** *vt* (*birds, children etc*) спýгивать (спугнýть *perf*)
▶ **frighten off** *vt* = **frighten away**.
frightened ['fraɪtnd] *adj* (*afraid*) испýганный* (испýган); **I am ~** я бою́сь; **to be ~ (of)** боя́ться (*impf*) (*+gen*); **he is ~ by change** егó пугáют изменéние.
frightening ['fraɪtnɪŋ] *adj* (*experience, prospect*) стрáшный.
frightful ['fraɪtful] *adj* (*dreadful*) кошмáрный* (кошмáрен), ужáсный* (ужáсен).
frightfully ['fraɪtfəlɪ] *adv* ужáсно; **I'm ~ sorry** мне ужáсно сты́дно.
frigid ['frɪdʒɪd] *adj* (*woman*) фригúдный.
frigidity [frɪ'dʒɪdɪtɪ] *n* фригúдность *f*.
frill [frɪl] *n* (*of dress, shirt*) обóрка*; **without ~s** (*fig*) без прикрáс.
frilly ['frɪlɪ] *adj* с обóрками.
fringe [frɪndʒ] *n* (*BRIT: of hair*) чёлка*; (*on shawl, lampshade etc*) бахромá*; (*of forest etc*) край*, окрáина; (*fig: of activity, organization etc*) периферúя.
fringe benefits *npl* дополнúтельные льгóты *fpl*.
fringe theatre *n* эксперのментáльный теáтр.

Frisbee® ['frɪzbɪ] *n* тарéлки *fpl* (*летáющий диск*).
frisk [frɪsk] *vt* (*search*) обы́скивать (обыскáть* *perf*) ◆ *vi* (*animal*) резвúться (порезвúться *perf*).
frisky ['frɪskɪ] *adj* игрúвый (игрúв).
fritter ['frɪtəʳ] *n* (*CULIN*) лóмтик чегó-нибудь, обжáренный в кипя́щем мáсле
▶ **fritter away** *vt* (*money*) растрáчивать (растрáтить* *perf*) по мелочáм; (*time*) пóпусту теря́ть (потеря́ть *perf*).
frivolity [frɪ'vɔlɪtɪ] *n* легкомы́слие.
frivolous ['frɪvələs] *adj* (*conduct, person*) легкомы́сленный* (легкомы́слен); (*object, activity*) пусты́чный.
frizzy ['frɪzɪ] *adj* (*hair*) курчáвый, мéлко-вью́щийся.
fro [frəu] *adv*: **to and ~** тудá-сюдá.
frock [frɔk] *n* плáтье*.
frog [frɔg] *n* лягýшка*; **to have a ~ in one's throat** хрипéть* (*impf*).
frogman ['frɔgmən] *irreg n* водолáз, ныря́льщик.
frogmarch ['frɔgmɑːtʃ] *vt* (*BRIT*): **to ~ sb in/out** втáскивать (втащúть *perf*)/вытáскивать (вы́тащить *perf*) когó-н за рýки лицóм вниз.
frolic ['frɔlɪk] *vi* (*animals, children*) веселúться (*impf*) ◆ *n* весéлье*.

KEYWORD

from [frɔm] *prep* **1** (*indicating starting place, origin etc*): **where do you come from?** откýда Вы?; **from London to Glasgow** из Лóндона в Глáзго; **a letter from my sister** письмó от моéй сестры́; **a quotation from Dickens** цитáта из Дúккенса; **to drink from the bottle** пить* (*impf*) из буты́лки
2 (*indicating movement: from inside*) из *+gen*; (*: away from*) от *+gen*; (*: off*) с (со) *+gen*; (*: from behind*) из-за *+gen*; **she ran from the house** онá вы́бежала из дóма; **the car drove away from the house** машúна отъéхала от дóма; **he took the magazine from the table** он взял журнáл со столá; **they got up from the table** онú встáли из-за столá
3 (*indicating time*) с *+gen*; **from two o'clock to** *or* **until** *or* **till three** с двух часóв до трёх (часóв); **from January (to August)** с января́ (по áвгуст)
4 (*indicating distance: position*) от *+gen*; (*: motion*) до *+gen*; **the hotel is 1 km from the beach** гостúница нахóдится в киломéтре от пля́жа; **we're still a long way from home** нам ещё далекó до дóма
5 (*indicating price, number etc: range*) от *+gen*; (*: change*) с *+gen*; **prices range from £10 to £50** цéны от £10 до £50; **the interest rate was increased from nine per cent to ten per cent** процéнты на вклáды повы́сили с девя́ти до

десяти (процéнтов)
6 (*indicating difference*) от +*gen*; **to be different from sb/sth** отличáться (*impf*) от когó-н/чегó-н
7 (*because of, on the basis of*): **from what he says** из тогó, что он говорил; **from what I understand** нáсколько я знáю; **to act from conviction** дéйствовать* (*impf*) по убеждéнию; **he is weak from hunger** он слаб от гóлода.

frond [frɒnd] *n* ветвь *f*; **palm** ~ лист* пáльмы.
front [frʌnt] *n* (*of house, also fig*) фасáд; (*of dress*) пéред; (*of train, car*) передняя часть *f*; (*promenade: also:* **sea** ~) нáбережная *f adj*; (*MIL, METEOROLOGY*) фронт ♦ *adj* передний* ♦ *vi*: **to** ~ **onto sth** выходить* (*impf*) фасáдом на что-н; **in** ~ вперёд; **in** ~ **of** перед +*instr*; **on the political** ~ на политическом фрóнте.
frontage ['frʌntɪdʒ] *n* фасáд.
frontal ['frʌntl] *adj* (*attack*) лобовóй, фронтáльный; ~ **view** вид спéреди.
front bench *n* (*POL: BRIT*) министры прáвящей пáртии и руководители пáртии оппозиции.
front desk *n* (*US: in hotel*) стóйка администрáтора; (: *in doctor's surgery*) регистратýра.
front door *n* входнáя дверь* *f*.
frontier ['frʌntɪə'] *n* граница.
frontispiece ['frʌntɪspiːs] *n* фронтиспис.
front page *n* пéрвая страница (*газéты*).
front room *n* гостиная *f adj*.
frontrunner ['frʌntrʌnə'] *n* (*fig*) претендéнт.
front-wheel drive ['frʌntwiːl-] *n* (*AUT*) передний* привод.
frost [frɒst] *n* морóз; (*also:* **hoarfrost**) иней.
frostbite ['frɒstbaɪt] *n* обморожéние.
frosted ['frɒstɪd] *adj* (*glass*) мáтовый; (*esp US: cake*) глазирóванный.
frosting ['frɒstɪŋ] *n* (*esp US: on cake*) глазýрь *f*.
frosty ['frɒstɪ] *adj* (*weather, night*) морóзный* (морóзен); (*welcome, look*) ледянóй; (*window*) покрытый (покрыт) инеем, замёрзший.
froth ['frɒθ] *n* (*on liquid*) пéна.
frothy ['frɒθɪ] *adj* (*liquid*) пéнистый.
frown [fraun] *n* хмýренный взгляд ♦ *vi* хмýриться (нахмýриться *perf*).
► **frown on** *vt fus* (*fig*) смотрéть* (*impf*) с неодобрéнием на +*acc*.
froze [frəuz] *pt of* **freeze**.
frozen ['frəuzn] *pp of* **freeze** ♦ *adj* (*food*) морóженый; (*COMM: assets*) заморóженный.
FRS *n abbr* (*BRIT*) = Fellow of the Royal Society; (*US*: = Federal Reserve System) Федерáльная резéрвная система.
frugal ['fruːgl] *adj* (*person*) бережливый (бережлив); (*meal*) скýдный* (скýден).
fruit [fruːt] *n inv* (*AGR*) фрукт; (*BOT*) плод; (*fig: results*) плоды *mpl*.
fruiterer ['fruːtərə'] *n* торгóвец* фрýктами.
fruit fly *n* фруктóвая мýшка*.

fruitful ['fruːtful] *adj* плодотвóрный* (плодотвóрен).
fruition [fru:'ɪʃən] *n*: **to come to** ~ осуществляться (осуществиться *perf*), реализóвываться (реализовáться *perf*).
fruit juice *n* фруктóвый сок.
fruitless ['fruːtlɪs] *adj* (*fig*) бесплóдный* (бесплóден).
fruit machine *n* (*BRIT*) игрáльный автомáт.
fruit salad *n* фруктóвый салáт.
fruity ['fruːtɪ] *adj* фруктóвый; (*voice, laugh*) зычный* (зычен).
frump [frʌmp] *n* (*woman*) замухрышка.
frustrate [frʌs'treɪt] *vt* (*person*) расстрáивать (расстрóить *perf*); (*plan, attempt*) срывáть (сорвáть *perf*).
frustrated [frʌs'treɪtɪd] *adj* (*person*) неудовлетворённый (неудовлетворён); (*plan, attempt*) сóрванный (сóрван); ~ **artist/poet** неудáвшийся худóжник/поэт.
frustrating [frʌs'treɪtɪŋ] *adj* (*day*) неудáчный* (неудáчен); **I find this job very** ~ я óчень неудовлетворён этой рабóтой.
frustration [frʌs'treɪʃən] *n* (*irritation*) досáда; (*thwarting*) крушéние.
fry [fraɪ] (*pt, pp* **fried**) *vt* жáрить (пожáрить *or* поджáрить *perf*); *see also* **small**.
frying pan ['fraɪŋ-] (*US* **fry-pan**) *n* сковородá*.
fry-pan ['fraɪpæn] *n* (*US*) = frying pan.
FT *n abbr* (= Financial Times; **the** ~ **index** фóндовый индекс „Фáйнэншл Тáймс".
ft. *abbr* = **feet, foot**.
FTC *n abbr* (*US*: = Federal Trade Commission) Федерáльная торгóвая комиссия.
FTSE 100 Index *n* (*COMM*) показáтель состояния фóндовой биржи, публикуемый в газéте „Финáншл Таймс".
fuchsia ['fjuːʃə] *n* фýксия.
fuck [fʌk] (*infl*) *vti* трáхать (*impf*) (*!*); ~ **off!** иди нá фиг! (*!*)
fuddled ['fʌdld] *adj* одурмáненный.
fuddy-duddy ['fʌdɪdʌdɪ] *n* (*pej*) стáрый занýда *m*.
fudge [fʌdʒ] *n* ≈ сливочная помáдка ♦ *vt* (*issue, problem*) уклоняться (уклониться *perf*) от +*gen*.
fuel ['fjuəl] *n* (*for heating*) тóпливо; (*for plane, car*) горючее *nt adj* ♦ *vt* (*furnace etc*) топить* (*impf*); (*aircraft, ship*) заправлять (запрáвить* *perf*).
fuel oil *n* мазýт.
fuel pump *n* тóпливный насóс.
fuel tank *n* тóпливный бак; (*in car*) бензобáк.
fug [fʌg] *n* (*BRIT*) духотá.
fugitive ['fjuːdʒɪtɪv] *n* беглéц*(-лянка*).
fulfil [ful'fɪl] (*US* **fulfill**) *vt* (*function*) исполнять (исполнить *perf*); (*ambition*) реализóвывать (реализовáть *perf*).
fulfilled [ful'fɪld] *adj* (*person*) состоявшийся; (*life*) напóлненный.
fulfilment [ful'fɪlmənt] (*US* **fulfillment**) *n* (*of*

promise, desire) исполне́ние; (*satisfaction*) удовлетворе́ние; (*of ambitions*) реализа́ция.

full [ful] *adj* по́лный* (по́лон); (*skirt*) широ́кий*; (*life*) напо́лненный; (*maximum*): **at ~ volume/power** на по́лную гро́мкость/мо́щность ◆ *adv*: **to know ~ well that** прекра́сно знать (*impf*), что; **I'm ~ (up)** я сыт; **he is ~ of enthusiasm/hope** он по́лон энтузиа́зма/наде́жды; **~ details** все дета́ли; **~ marks** отли́чные оце́нки; **at ~ speed** на по́лной ско́рости; **a ~ two hours** це́лых два часа́; **in ~** по́лностью.
fullback ['fulbæk] *n* (*SPORT*) защи́тник.
full-blooded ['ful'blʌdɪd] *adj* энерги́чный*.
full board *n*: **hotel with ~** гости́ница с трёхра́зовым пита́нием.
full-cream ['ful'kri:m] *adj*: **~ milk** (*BRIT*) несня́тое молоко́.
full employment *n* по́лная за́нятость *f*.
full-grown ['ful'grəun] *adj* (*animal, person*) взро́слый; (*plant*) вы́росший.
full-length ['ful'lɛŋθ] *adj* (*film, novel*) полнометра́жный; (*coat*) дли́нный; (*portrait*) во весь рост.
full moon *n* по́лная луна́*.
fullness ['fulnɪs] *n*: **in the ~ of time** по проше́ствии вре́мени.
full-page ['fulpeɪdʒ] *adj* (*advertisement, picture*) на всю страни́цу.
full-scale ['ful'skeɪl] *adj* (*model*) в натура́льную величину́; (*attack, war, search*) широко-масшта́бный.
full-sized ['ful'saɪzd] *adj* (*portrait*) в по́лную величину́.
full stop *n* (*BRIT*) то́чка*.
full-time ['ful'taɪm] *adj, adv* (*study*) на дне́вном отделе́нии; (*work*) на по́лной ста́вке, на по́лную ста́вку.
fully ['fulɪ] *adv* (*completely*) по́лностью, вполне́; (*at least*): **~ as big as** по кра́йней ме́ре тако́й же величины́, как.
fully fledged [-'flɛdʒd] *adj* (*teacher, barrister*) вполне́ сложи́вшийся; (*citizen, member*) полнопра́вный*; (*bird*) опери́вшийся.
fully-paid share ['fulpeɪd-] *n* по́лностью опла́ченная а́кция.
fulsome ['fulsəm] *adj* (*praise*) чрезме́рный.
fumble ['fʌmbl] *vi*: **to ~ with** (*catch, key*) вози́ться (*impf*) с +*instr* ◆ *vt*: **to ~ the ball** неуклю́же стара́ться (*impf*) пойма́ть (*perf*) мяч; **to ~ in** (*pocket*) ры́ться (*impf*) в +*prp*; **she ~d for the switch in the dark** она́ ша́рила в темноте́ в по́исках выключа́теля.
fume [fju:m] *vi* дыми́ть (*impf*); **he was fuming** он был разъя́рён.
fumes [fju:mz] *npl* пары́ *mpl*, испаре́ния *ntpl*.
fumigate ['fju:mɪgeɪt] *vt* оку́ривать (окури́ть* *perf*).

fun [fʌn] *n*: **what ~!** как ве́село!; **to have ~** весели́ться (повесели́ться *perf*); **he's good ~ (to be with)** с ним ве́село; **for ~** для заба́вы; **it's not much ~** э́то дово́льно ску́чно; **to make ~ of** подшу́чивать (подшути́ть *perf*) над +*instr*; **to poke ~ at** насмеха́ться (*impf*) над +*instr*.
function ['fʌŋkʃən] *n* (*also* MATH) фу́нкция; (*product*) произво́дная *f adj*; (*social occasion*) приём ◆ *vi* (*operate*) функциони́ровать (*impf*); **to ~ as** выполня́ть (вы́полнить *perf*) *or* исполня́ть (испо́лнить *perf*) фу́нкции +*gen*.
functional ['fʌŋkʃənl] *adj* (*operational*) де́йствующий*; (*practical*) функциона́льный.
function key *n* (*COMPUT*) функциона́льная кла́виша.
fund [fʌnd] *n* (*of money*) фонд; (*of knowledge etc*) запа́с; **~s** *npl* (*money*) (де́нежные) сре́дства *ntpl*, фо́нды *mpl*.
fundamental [fʌndə'mɛntl] *adj* фундамента́льный*.
fundamentalism [fʌndə'mɛntəlɪzəm] *n* фундаментали́зм.
fundamentalist [fʌndə'mɛntəlɪst] *n* фундаментали́ст.
fundamentally [fʌndə'mɛntəlɪ] *adv* в свое́й осно́ве; **they are ~ different** они́ коренны́м о́бразом различа́ются.
fundamentals [fʌndə'mɛntlz] *npl* осно́вы *fpl*.
funding ['fʌndɪŋ] *n* финанси́рование.
fund raising [-reɪzɪŋ] *n* сбор средств.
funeral ['fju:nərəl] *n* по́хороны* *pl*.
funeral director *n* распоряди́тель *m* на похорона́х.
funeral parlour *n* похоро́нное бюро́ *nt ind*.
funeral service *n* панихи́да.
funereal [fju:'nɪərɪəl] *adj* тра́урный.
funfair ['fʌnfɛəʳ] *n* (*BRIT*) я́рмарка*.
fungi ['fʌŋgaɪ] *npl of* **fungus**.
fungus ['fʌŋgəs] (*pl* fungi) *n* (*plant*) гриб*; (*mould*) пле́сень *f*.
funicular [fju:'nɪkjuləʳ] *n* (*also:* **~ railway**) фуникулёр.
funky ['fʌŋkɪ] *adj о* му́зыке с си́льным синкопи́рованным ри́тмом; (*inf*) клёвый.
funnel ['fʌnl] *n* (*for pouring*) воро́нка*; (*of ship*) труба́*.
funnily ['fʌnɪlɪ] *adv* (*strangely*) стра́нно; **~ enough** как ни стра́нно.
funny ['fʌnɪ] *adj* (*comical*) смешно́й* (смешо́н); (*amusing*) заба́вный* (заба́вен); (*strange*) стра́нный* (стра́нен), чудно́й.
funny bone *n* (*inf*) локтева́я кость *f*.
fun run *n* благотвори́тельный пробе́г.
fur [fəʳ] *n* мех*; (*BRIT: in kettle*) на́кипь *f*.
fur coat *n* мехова́я шу́ба.
furious ['fjuərɪəs] *adj* (*person*) взбешённый (взбешён); (*exchange, argument*) бу́рный*

---

* marks translations which have irregular inflections. The Russian-English side of the dictionary gives inflectional information.

(бу́рен); (*effort, speed*) нейстовый; **I am ~
with her** я о́чень серди́т на неё.
furiously ['fjuərɪəslɪ] *adv* нейстово.
furl [fəːl] *vt* свёртывать (сверну́ть *perf*).
furlong ['fəːlɒŋ] *n 201.2 метр в ко́нных
ска́чках.*
furlough ['fəːləu] *n* (*MIL*) увольне́ние.
furnace ['fəːnɪs] *n* печь* *f*.
furnish ['fəːnɪʃ] *vt* (*room, building*) обставля́ть
(обста́вить* *perf*); (*supply*): **to ~ sb with sth**
предоставля́ть (предоста́вить* *perf*) что-н
кому́-н; **~ed flat** *or* (*US*) **apartment**
мебели́рованная кварти́ра.
furnishings ['fəːnɪʃɪŋz] *npl* обстано́вка *fsg.*
furniture ['fəːnɪtʃəʳ] *n* ме́бель *f*; **piece of ~**
предме́т ме́бели.
furniture polish *n* сре́дство для полиро́вки
ме́бели.
furore [fjuə'rɔːrɪ] *n* (*protests*) негодова́ние.
furrier ['fʌrɪəʳ] *n* (*fur seller*) меховщи́к*;
(*artisan*) скорня́к*.
furrow ['fʌrəu] *n* борозда́* ◆ *vt*: **to ~ one's brow**
хму́рить (нахму́рить *perf*) бро́ви.
furry ['fəːrɪ] *adj* пуши́стый (пуши́ст).
further ['fəːðəʳ] *adj* (*additional*)
дополни́тельный ◆ *adv* (*farther*) да́льше;
(*moreover*) бо́лее того́ ◆ *vt* (*career, project*)
соде́йствовать (*impf/perf*) +*dat*; **until ~ notice**
впредь до дальне́йшего уведомле́ния; **how
much ~ is it to the station?** ско́лько ещё до
вокза́ла?; ~ **to your letter of ...** (*formal*)
ссыла́ясь на Ва́ше письмо́ от +*gen* ...; **to ~
one's interests** пресле́довать (*impf*) свой
интере́сы.
further education *n* (*BRIT*) дальне́йшее
обуче́ние (*не включа́я вы́сшее образова́ние*).
furthermore [fəːðə'mɔːʳ] *adv* (*moreover*) бо́лее
того́.
furthermost ['fəːðəməust] *adj* са́мый
да́льний*.
furthest ['fəːðɪst] *superl of* **far**.
furtive ['fəːtɪv] *adj*: ~ **glance/movement** взгляд/
движе́ние укра́дкой.
furtively ['fəːtɪvlɪ] *adv* укра́дкой.
fury ['fjuərɪ] *n* (*anger, rage*) я́рость *f*,
бе́шенство; **to be in a ~** быть* (*impf*) в
бе́шенстве *or* в я́рости.
fuse [fjuːz] (*US* **fuze**) *n* (*ELEC*) предохрани́тель
m; (*for bomb*) фити́ль* *m* ◆ *vt* (*metal*) пла́вить*
(распла́вить* *perf*); (*ideas, systems*) слива́ть
(слить* *perf*) ◆ *vi* (*see vt*) пла́виться

(распла́виться *perf*); слива́ться (сли́ться
perf); **a ~ has blown** предохрани́тель
перегоре́л; **to ~ the lights** (*BRIT*) вызыва́ть
(вы́звать* *perf*) коро́ткое замыка́ние.
fuse box *n* блок предохрани́телей.
fuselage ['fjuːzəlɑːʒ] *n* фюзеля́ж.
fuse wire *n* пла́вкая про́волока (*для
предохрани́телей*).
fusillade [fjuːzɪ'leɪd] *n* залп.
fusion ['fjuːʒən] *n* (*of ideas, qualities*) слия́ние;
(*also:* **nuclear ~**) я́дерный си́нтез.
fuss [fʌs] *n* (*excitement*) сумато́ха; (*anxiety*)
суета́; (*trouble*) шум ◆ *vi* суети́ться* (*impf*) ◆ *vt*
надоеда́ть (*impf*) +*dat*; **to make** *or* **kick up a ~**
поднима́ть (подня́ть* *perf*) шум; **to make a ~
of sb** носи́ться* (*impf*) с кем-н
▸ **fuss over** *vt fus* (*person*) трясти́сь* (*impf*) над
+*instr*.
fusspot ['fʌspɒt] *n* (*inf*) хлопоту́н(ья).
fussy ['fʌsɪ] *adj* (*nervous*) суетли́вый; (*choosy*)
ме́лочный* (ме́лочен), су́етный; (*clothes,
room*) вы́чурный*; **I'm not ~** мне всё равно́.
fusty ['fʌstɪ] *adj* (*pej: archaic*) старомо́дный*
(старомо́ден); (*musty*) за́тхлый.
futile ['fjuːtaɪl] *adj* (*attempt*) тще́тный*
(тще́тен); (*comment, existence*) беспло́дный*
(беспло́ден).
futility [fjuː'tɪlɪtɪ] *n* (*see adj*) тще́тность *f*;
беспло́дность *f*.
futon ['fuːtɒn] *n* фу́тон (*япо́нский матра́с*).
future ['fjuːtʃəʳ] *adj* бу́дущий* ◆ *n* бу́дущее *nt
adj*; (*LING: also:* ~ **tense**) бу́дущее вре́мя* *nt*;
~s *npl* (*COMM*) фью́черсы *pl*, фью́черский
това́р *msg* (*с согласо́ванной да́той
прода́жи*); **in (the) ~** в бу́дущем; **be more
careful in ~** в бу́дущем бу́дьте осторо́жнее;
in the near/immediate ~ в недалёком/
ближа́йшем бу́дущем.
futuristic [fjuːtʃə'rɪstɪk] *adj* футуристи́ческий.
fuze [fjuːz] (*US*) = **fuse**.
fuzz [fʌz] *n* (*inf: police*): **the ~** менты́ *mpl*.
fuzzy ['fʌzɪ] *adj* (*thoughts, also PHOT*)
расплы́вчатый (расплы́вчат); (*hair*)
кудря́вый (кудря́в).
fwd. *abbr* = **forward**.
f-word ['ɛfwɔːd] *n*: **the ~** ≈ сло́во на́ три
бу́квы.
fwy *abbr* (*US*) = **freeway**.
FY *abbr* = *fiscal year*.
FYI *abbr* (= *for your information*) к Ва́шему
све́дению.

~ G, g ~

G, g [dʒi:] n (letter) 7-áя бу́ква англи́йского алфави́та.

G [dʒi:] n (MUS) соль nt ind.

G n abbr (BRIT: SCOL) = good; (US: CINEMA: = general (audience)) фильм, приго́дный для пока́за всем возрастны́м гру́ппам; (PHYS): **G-force** си́ла тя́жести.

g. abbr (= gram) г = грамм; (PHYS) = **gravity**.

G7 n abbr (POL: = Group of Seven) „больша́я семёрка".

GA n abbr (US: POST) = Georgia.

gab [gæb] n (inf): **he has the gift of the ~** у него́ хорошо́ подве́шен язы́к.

gabble ['gæbl] vi тарато́рить (протарато́рить (perf)).

gaberdine [gæbə'di:n] n сукно́*, габарди́н.

gable ['geɪbl] n фронто́н.

Gabon [gə'bɔn] n Габо́н.

gad about [gæd-] vi (inf) болта́ться (impf) без де́ла.

gadget ['gædʒɪt] n приспособле́ние.

gadgetry ['gædʒɪtrɪ] n приспособле́ния ntpl.

Gaelic ['geɪlɪk] adj гэ́льский ♦ n (LING) гэ́льский язы́к* (язы́к ке́льтского происхожде́ния).

gaff [gæf] n (NAUT) га́фель m; (inf: nonsense): **he made a real ~** он тако́е ля́пнул.

gaffe [gæf] n опло́шность f.

gaffer ['gæfə'] (inf) n (supervisor) старшо́й m adj; (fellow) стари́к*.

gag [gæg] n (on mouth) кляп; (joke) хо́хма ♦ vt вставля́ть (вста́вить* perf) кляп +dat, завя́зывать (завяза́ть* perf) рот +dat; (fig) затыка́ть (заткну́ть perf) рот +dat ♦ vi: **the smell made him ~** у него́ го́рло перехвати́ло от за́паха.

gaga ['gɑːgɑ:] adj: **he is ~** у него́ не все до́ма.

gage [geɪdʒ] n, vt (US) = **gauge**.

gaiety ['geɪtɪ] n весе́лье.

gaily ['geɪlɪ] adv ве́село; (coloured) я́рко.

gain [geɪn] n (increase) увеличе́ние; (profit) при́быль f ♦ vt (confidence, experience) приобрета́ть (приобрести́* perf); (speed) набира́ть (набра́ть* perf) ♦ vi (clock, watch) спеши́ть (impf); (benefit): **to ~ from sth** извлека́ть (извле́чь* perf) по́льзу из чего́-н; **to do sth for ~** де́лать (сде́лать perf) что-н ра́ди вы́годы; **what will you ~ by that?** чего́ Вы э́тим добьётесь?; **to ~ ground** получа́ть (получи́ть perf) большо́е распростране́ние; **to ~ 3 pounds (in weight)** попра́виться (perf) на 3 фу́нта; **to ~ on sb** догоня́ть (догна́ть* perf) кого́-н.

gainful ['geɪnful] adj (employment) вы́годный* (вы́годен).

gainfully ['geɪnfəlɪ] adv: **~ employed** по опла́чиваемой рабо́те.

gainsay [geɪn'seɪ] (irreg: like say) vt отрица́ть (impf).

gait [geɪt] n по́ступь f; **to walk with a slow/ confident ~** идти́* (impf) ме́дленной/ уве́ренной по́ступью.

gala ['gɑːlə] n (festival) пра́зднество; **swimming ~** пра́здник на воде́.

Galapagos Islands [gə'læpəgəs-] npl: **the ~ ~** Галапаго́сские острова́* mpl.

galaxy ['gæləksɪ] n гала́ктика.

gale [geɪl] n (wind) си́льный ве́тер*; **~ force ten** поры́вы ве́тра в де́сять ба́ллов.

gall [gɔ:l] n (ANAT) жёлчь f; (fig: impudence) на́глость f ♦ vt раздража́ть (impf).

gall. abbr = **gallon**.

gallant ['gælənt] adj (brave) до́блестный*; (chivalrous) гала́нтный*.

gallantry ['gæləntrɪ] n (see adj) до́блесть f; гала́нтность f.

gall bladder n жёлчный пузы́рь* m.

galleon ['gælɪən] n галео́н.

gallery ['gælərɪ] n (also: art ~) галере́я; (in hall, church, theatre) балко́н.

galley ['gælɪ] n (ship's kitchen) ка́мбуз; (ship) гале́ра; (PUBLISHING: also: ~ proof) гра́нка*.

Gallic ['gælɪk] adj га́лльский.

galling ['gɔ:lɪŋ] adj раздража́ющий.

gallon ['gælən] n галло́н (4,5 ли́тра).

gallop ['gæləp] n гало́п ♦ vi (horse) скака́ть* (impf) (гало́пом), галопи́ровать (impf); (person) носи́ться*/нести́сь* (impf); **~ing** inflation галопи́рующая инфля́ция.

gallows ['gæləuz] n ви́селица.

gallstone ['gɔ:lstəun] n жёлчный ка́мень* m.

Gallup Poll ['gæləp-] n оди́н из ви́дов опро́сов обще́ственного мне́ния.

---

* marks translations which have irregular inflections. The Russian-English side of the dictionary gives inflectional information.

galore [gə'lɔːʳ] *adv* в изоби́лии.
galvanize ['gælvənaɪz] *vt* (*person*) возбужда́ть (возбуди́ть* *perf*); (*support*) обеспе́чивать (обеспе́чить* *perf*); **to ~ sb into action** побужда́ть (побуди́ть* *perf*) кого́-н к де́йствию.
Gambia ['gæmbɪə] *n* Га́мбия.
gambit ['gæmbɪt] *n* (*fig*): (*opening*) ~ пе́рвый ход.
gamble ['gæmbl] *n* риск, риско́ванное предприя́тие ♦ *vt* (*money*) ста́вить* (поста́вить* *perf*) ♦ *vi* (*take a risk*) рискова́ть (рискну́ть *perf*); (*bet*) игра́ть (*impf*) в аза́ртные и́гры; **to ~ on the Stock Exchange** игра́ть (*impf*) на би́рже; **to ~ on sth** (*also fig*) де́лать (сде́лать *perf*) ста́вку на что-н.
gambler ['gæmbləʳ] *n* игро́к*.
gambling ['gæmblɪŋ] *n* аза́ртные и́гры *fpl*.
gambol ['gæmbl] *vi* резви́ться* (*impf*).
game [geɪm] *n* игра́*; (*match*) матч; (*esp TENNIS*) гейм; (*also:* **board ~**) насто́льная игра́; (*CULIN, HUNTING*) дичь *f* ♦ *adj* (*willing*): ~ **(for)** гото́вый (гото́в) (на +*acc*); **~s** *npl* (*SCOL*) спорти́вные и́гры *fpl*; **a ~ of football/tennis** футбо́льный/те́ннисный матч; **a ~ of chess** ша́хматная па́ртия; **big ~** (*lions, tigers etc*) кру́пный зверь.
game bird *n* перна́тая дичь *f*.
gamekeeper ['geɪmkiːpəʳ] *n* е́герь *m*.
gamely ['geɪmlɪ] *adv* хра́бро.
game reserve *n* охо́тничий* запове́дник.
games console ['geɪmz-] *n* пане́ль управле́ния компью́терными и́грами.
gamesmanship ['geɪmzmənʃɪp] *n* трюка́чество.
gaming ['geɪmɪŋ] *n* аза́ртные и́гры *fpl*.
gammon ['gæmən] *n* (*bacon*) о́корок*; (*ham*) ветчина́.
gamut ['gæmət] *n* (*range*) га́мма; **to run the ~ of emotions** пережива́ть (пережи́ть* *perf*) це́лую га́мму эмо́ций.
gander ['gændəʳ] *n* гусь* *m*.
gang [gæŋ] *n* ба́нда; (*of friends*) компа́ния; (*of workmen*) кома́нда.
▸ **gang up** *vi*: **to ~ up on sb** ополча́ться (ополчи́ться *perf*) на *or* про́тив кого́-н.
Ganges ['gændʒiːz] *n*: **the ~** Ганг.
gangland ['gæŋlænd] *adj* (*boss, killers*) мафио́зный.
gangling ['gæŋglɪŋ] *adj* долговя́зый (долговя́з).
gangly ['gæŋglɪ] (*inf*) *adj* = **gangling**.
gangplank ['gæŋplæŋk] *n* трап.
gangrene ['gæŋgriːn] *n* гангре́на.
gangster ['gæŋstəʳ] *n* га́нгстер.
gangway ['gæŋweɪ] *n* (*from ship*) трап; (*BRIT: in cinema, bus etc*) прохо́д.
gantry ['gæntrɪ] *n* (*for crane*) порта́л; (*for railway signal*) сигна́льный мо́стик; (*for rocket*) раке́тная устано́вка.
GAO *n abbr* (*US:* = *General Accounting Office*) Центра́льное фина́нсово-контро́льное управле́ние.
gaol *etc* [dʒeɪl] (*BRIT*) = **jail** *etc*.
gap [gæp] *n* (*space*) промежу́ток*; (: *between teeth*) щерби́на; (: *in time*) интерва́л; (: *in market, records etc*) пробе́л; (*difference*) расхожде́ния *ntpl*; **generation ~** разногла́сия ме́жду поколе́ниями.
gape [geɪp] *vi* (*person*) рази́нуть (*perf*) рот от удивле́ния; (*hole*) зия́ть (*perf*); (*shirt*) распа́хиваться (распахну́ться *perf*).
gaping ['geɪpɪŋ] *adj* (*hole*) зия́ющий; (*shirt*) распа́хнутый (распа́хнут).
garage ['gærɑːʒ] *n* гара́ж*; (*petrol station*) запра́вочная ста́нция, бензоколо́нка*.
garb [gɑːb] *n* оде́жда.
garbage ['gɑːbɪdʒ] *n* (*US: rubbish*) му́сор*; (*inf: nonsense*) ерунда́*; (*fig: film, book*) дрянь *f*.
garbage can *n* (*US*) помо́йный я́щик.
garbage collector *n* (*US*) му́сорщик.
garbage disposal (unit) *n* (*US*) мусоро-прово́д.
garbage truck *n* (*US*) мусороубо́рочная маши́на.
garbled ['gɑːbld] *adj* (*account, message*) запу́танный* (запу́тан).
garden ['gɑːdn] *n* сад* ♦ *vi* занима́ться (заня́ться* *perf*) садово́дством; **~s** *npl* (*park*) парк *msg*; (*in street names*): **Rose G~s** Роуз Га́рденз; **she was busy ~ing** она́ рабо́тала в саду́.
garden centre *n* магази́н садо́вых принадле́жностей.
garden city *n* го́род*-сад*, зелёный го́род*.
gardener ['gɑːdnəʳ] *n* садово́д; (*employee*) садо́вник(-ица).
gardening ['gɑːdnɪŋ] *n* садово́дство.
gargle ['gɑːgl] *vi* полоска́ть* (прополоска́ть* *perf*) го́рло ♦ *n* полоска́ние.
gargoyle ['gɑːgɔɪl] *n* (*ARCHIT*) гарго́йл.
garish ['gɛərɪʃ] *adj* (*light*) ре́жущий глаз; (*dress, colour*) крича́щий.
garland ['gɑːlənd] *n* гирля́нда.
garlic ['gɑːlɪk] *n* чесно́к*.
garment ['gɑːmənt] *n* (*dress etc*) предме́т оде́жды.
garner ['gɑːnəʳ] *vt* добыва́ть (добы́ть* *perf*).
garnish ['gɑːnɪʃ] *vt* украша́ть (укра́сить* *perf*).
garret ['gærɪt] *n* камо́рка*.
garrison ['gærɪsn] *n* гарнизо́н.
garrulous ['gærjuləs] *adj* болтли́вый, говорли́вый.
garter ['gɑːtəʳ] *n* подвя́зка*.
garter belt *n* (*US*) по́яс* (*с подвя́зками*).
gas [gæs] *n* газ*; (*US: gasoline*) бензи́н*; (*as anaesthetic*) ингаляцио́нный анесте́тик ♦ *vt* (*kill*) удуша́ть (удуши́ть* *perf*); (*MIL*) отравля́ть (отрави́ть* *perf*) га́зом.
gas cooker *n* (*BRIT*) га́зовая плита́*.
gas cylinder *n* га́зовый балло́н.
gaseous ['gæsɪəs] *adj* газообра́зный.

gas fire n (BRIT) газовый камин.
gas-fired ['gæsfaɪəd] adj газовый,
работающий на газе.
gash [gæʃ] n (wound) глубокая рана; (cut,
slash) глубокий порез ♦ vt (person)
наносить* (нанести* perf) глубокую рану
+dat; (object) распарывать (распороть perf);
наносить* (нанести* perf) глубокий порез
+dat.
gasket ['gæskɪt] n (AUT) прокладка*.
gas mask n противогаз.
gas meter n газовый счётчик.
gasoline ['gæsəli:n] n (US) бензин*.
gasp [gɑ:sp] n (breath) вдох ♦ vi (pant) тяжело
дышать* (impf); (in surprise) издавать*
(издать* perf) вздох; **I am ~ing for a smoke** я
умираю от желания курить
▸ **gasp out** vt выпаливать (выпалить perf).
gas ring n конфорка*.
gas station n (US) заправочная станция,
бензоколонка*.
gas stove n (cooker) газовая плита*.
gassy ['gæsɪ] adj (beer etc) газированный*
(газирован).
gas tank n бензобак.
gastric ['gæstrɪk] adj желудочный.
gastric ulcer n язва желудка.
gastroenteritis ['gæætrəυεntə'raɪtɪs] n
гастроэнтерит.
gastronomy [gæs'trɔnəmɪ] n кулинарное
искусство.
gasworks ['gæswə:ks] n газовый завод.
gate [geɪt] n (single) калитка*; (double) ворота
mpl; (at airport) выход; (of lock, level crossing
etc) шлагбаум.
gateau ['gætəu] (pl ~**x**) n торт.
gateaux ['gætəuz] npl of **gateau**.
gate-crash ['geɪtkræʃ] vt (BRIT): **to ~ a party**
приходить* (прийти* perf) на вечеринку без
приглашения.
gate-crasher ['geɪtkræʃəʳ] n (to party)
незваный гость m.
gatehouse ['geɪthəus] n сторожка* у ворот.
gateway ['geɪtweɪ] n (also fig) ворота mpl.
gather ['gæðəʳ] vt собирать (собрать* perf);
(understand) полагать (impf); (SEWING)
собирать (собрать* perf) в складки ♦ vi
собираться (собраться* perf); (clouds)
скапливаться (скопиться* perf); (dust)
собираться (собраться* perf), оседать
(осесть* perf); **to ~ from sb** выяснять
(выяснить perf) у кого-н; **I ~ that ... я**
полагаю, что ...; **as far as I can ~** насколько я
понимаю; **to ~ speed** набирать (набрать*
perf) скорость.
gathering ['gæðərɪŋ] n собрание.
GATT [gæt] n abbr (= General Agreement on
Tariffs and Trade) ГАТТ (Генеральное

соглашение по тарифам и торговле).
gauche [gəuʃ] adj неловкий*.
gaudy ['gɔ:dɪ] adj пёстрый*.
gauge [geɪdʒ] n (instrument) измерительный
прибор; (RAIL) ширина колей ♦ vt (amount,
quantity) измерять (измерить perf); (fig:
feelings, character etc) оценивать (оценить*
perf), получать (получить* perf)
представление о +prp; **petrol ~**, **fuel ~**, (US)
gas ~ указатель m уровня бензина; **to ~ the
right moment** выбирать (выбрать* perf)
подходящий момент.
Gaul [gɔ:l] n (country) Галлия; (person) галл.
gaunt [gɔ:nt] adj (haggard) изможденный*
(изможден); (bare, stark) угрюмый*
(угрюм).
gauntlet ['gɔ:ntlɪt] n перчатка*; (fig): **to run the
~** подвергаться (подвергнуться perf)
нападкам; **to throw down the ~** бросать
(бросить* perf) перчатку.
gauze [gɔ:z] n (fabric) марля.
gave [geɪv] pt of **give**.
gavel ['gævl] n молоток (председателя
собрания, судьи или аукциониста).
gawk [gɔ:k] vi (inf): **to ~ at** таращить
(вытаращить perf) глаза на +acc.
gawky ['gɔ:kɪ] adj неотёсанный* (неотёсан).
gawp [gɔ:p] vi: **to ~ at** таращить (вытаращить
perf) глаза на +acc.
gay [geɪ] adj (cheerful) весёлый* (весел);
(homosexual): **he is ~** он голубой or
гомосексуалист; **~ bar** бар
гомосексуалистов or голубых.
gaze [geɪz] n (look, stare) (пристальный)
взгляд ♦ vi: **to ~ at sth** глядеть* (impf) на
что-н.
gazelle [gə'zɛl] n газель f.
gazette [gə'zɛt] n (newspaper) газета; (official
publication) орган.
gazetteer [gæzə'tɪəʳ] n географический
справочник.
gazumping [gə'zʌmpɪŋ] n (BRIT: pej)
увеличение цены дома в последний момент.
gazundering [gə'zʌndərɪŋ] n (BRIT: pej)
понижение предложенной цены на покупку
дома до подписания контракта.
GB abbr = **Great Britain**.
GBH n abbr (BRIT: LAW: = grievous bodily harm)
тяжёлые телесные повреждения ntpl.
GC n abbr (BRIT: = George Cross) ≈
Георгиевский крест.
GCE n abbr (BRIT: = General Certificate of
Education) ≈ аттестат о среднем
образовании.
GCHQ n abbr (BRIT: = Government
Communications Headquarters) Главный
штаб служб правительственной связи.
GCSE n abbr (BRIT: = General Certificate of

---

* marks translations which have irregular inflections. The Russian-English side of the dictionary gives inflectional information.

Secondary Education) ≈ аттестáт о срéднем образовáнии.

Gdansk [gdænsk] *n* Гдáньск.

Gdns. *abbr* (*in street names*) = **Gardens.**

GDP *n abbr* (= **gross domestic product**) ВВП= *валовóй внýтренний продýкт.*

GDR *n abbr* (*formerly:* = *German Democratic Republic*) ГДР= *Гермáнская Демократúческая Респýблика.*

gear [gɪə'] *n* (*equipment, belongings etc*) принадлéжности *fpl*; (*for hunting*) снаряжéние; (*for fishing*) снáсти *fpl*; (*TECH*) зубчáтое колесó; (*AUT*) скóрость *f* ♦ *vt* (*fig*): **to ~ sth to** приспосáбливать (приспосóбить* *perf*) что-н к +*dat*; **top** *or* (*US*) **high/low/bottom ~** вы́сшая/нúзкая/сáмая мáлая передáча *or* скóрость; **in ~** на передáче *or* скóрости, включённый (включён); **out of ~** не на передáче *or* скóрости, невключённый (невключён); **our service is ~ed to meet the needs of the disabled** нáши услýги напрáвлены на удовлетворéние потрéбностей инвалúдов.

▸ **gear up** *vi*: **to ~ up (to do)** готóвиться* (приготóвиться* *or* подготóвиться* *perf*) (+*infin*) ♦ *vt*: **to ~ o.s. up (to do)** готóвить* (приготóвить* *or* подготóвить* *perf*) себя́ (+*infin*)

gearbox ['gɪəbɔks] *n* корóбка* передáч *or* скоростéй.

gear lever (*US* **gear shift**) *n* переключáтель *m* скоростéй.

GED *n abbr* (*US: SCOL*) = *general educational development.*

geek [gi:k] *n* (*inf*) придýрок*.

geese [gi:s] *npl of* **goose.**

geezer ['gi:zə'] *n* (*inf*) чувáк.

Geiger counter ['gaɪgə-] *n* счётчик Гéйгера (*для измерéния радиоактúвности*).

gel [dʒɛl] *n* (*also CHEM*) гель *m*.

gelatin(e) ['dʒɛləti:n] *n* желатúн*.

gelignite ['dʒɛlɪgnaɪt] *n* гелигнúт.

gem [dʒɛm] *n* (*stone*) драгоцéнный кáмень *m*, самоцвéт; (*fig*) сокрóвище.

Gemini ['dʒɛmɪnaɪ] *n* Близнецы́ *mpl*; **he is ~** он – Близнéц.

gen [dʒɛn] *n* (*BRIT: inf*): **to give sb the ~ on sth** опúсывать (описáть* *perf*) комý-н что-н в óбщих чертáх.

Gen. *abbr* (*MIL*) = **general.**

gen. *abbr* = **general, generally.**

gender ['dʒɛndə'] *n* (*sex*) пол; (*LING*) род.

gene [dʒi:n] *n* ген.

genealogy [dʒi:nɪ'ælədʒɪ] *n* генеалóгия.

general ['dʒɛnərl] *n* (*MIL*) генерáл ♦ *adj* óбщий*; (*widespread: movement, interest*) всеóбщий*; **in ~** в óбщем; **the ~ public** широкая пýблика; **~ audit** (*COMM*) аудитóрская провéрка.

general anaesthetic *n* óбщий* наркóз.

general delivery *n* (*US*) пóчта „до вострéбования".

general election *n* всеóбщие вы́боры *mpl*.

generalization ['dʒɛnrəlaɪ'zeɪʃən] *n* обобщéние.

generalize ['dʒɛnrəlaɪz] *vi* обобщáть (обобщúть *perf*).

generally ['dʒɛnrəlɪ] *adv* вообщé; (+*vb*) обы́чно; **it is ~ accepted that ...** обы́чно считáется, что ...; **to become ~ available** становúться* (стать* *perf*) общедостýпным(-ой).

general manager *n* глáвный управляющий* *m adj*.

general practitioner *n* врач-терапéвт.

general strike *n* всеóбщая забастóвка*.

generate ['dʒɛnəreɪt] *vt* (*power, electricity*) производúть* (произвестú* *perf*); (*excitement, interest*) вызывáть (вы́звать* *perf*); (*jobs*) создавáть* (создáть* *perf*).

generation [dʒɛnə'reɪʃən] *n* поколéние; (*of electricity etc*) генерúрование; **for ~s** из поколéния в поколéние.

generator ['dʒɛnəreɪtə'] *n* генерáтор.

generic [dʒɪ'nɛrɪk] *adj* óбщий*.

generosity [dʒɛnə'rɔsɪtɪ] *n* щéдрость *f*; (*of spirit*) великодýшие.

generous ['dʒɛnərəs] *adj* (*person: lavish*) щéдрый (щедр); (: *unselfish*) великодýшный* (великодýшен); (*amount of money*) изря́дный.

genesis ['dʒɛnɪsɪs] *n* гéнезис, истóки *mpl*; **the ~ of an idea** возникновéние идéи.

genetic [dʒɪ'nɛtɪk] *adj* генетúческий*.

genetic engineering *n* генетúческая инженéрия.

genetic fingerprinting [-'fɪŋgəprɪntɪŋ] *n* установлéние лúчности человéка по егó генетúческим осóбенностям (*по ДНК*).

genetics [dʒɪ'nɛtɪks] *n* генéтика.

Geneva [dʒɪ'ni:və] *n* Женéва.

genial ['dʒi:nɪəl] *adj* (*smile, expression etc*) привéтливый; (*host*) радýшный*; (*climate*) мя́гкий*.

genitals ['dʒɛnɪtlz] *npl* половы́е óрганы *mpl*.

genitive ['dʒɛnɪtɪv] *n* (*LING*) родúтельный падéж*.

genius ['dʒi:nɪəs] *n* (*skill*) талáнт; (*person*) гéний.

Genoa ['dʒɛnəuə] *n* Гéнуя.

genocide ['dʒɛnəusaɪd] *n* геноцúд.

Genoese [dʒɛnəu'i:z] *adj* генуэ́зский ♦ *n inv* генуэ́зец*(-зка*).

gent [dʒɛnt] *n abbr* (*BRIT: inf*) = **gentleman.**

genteel [dʒɛn'ti:l] *adj* (*family*) благорóдный*, благорóдного происхождéния; (*person*) свéтский*.

gentle ['dʒɛntl] *adj* нéжный* (нéжен); (*movement, breeze, landscape, nature*) мя́гкий* (мя́гок); **a ~ hint** тóнкий* намёк.

gentleman ['dʒɛntlmən] *irreg n* (*man*) джентльмéн; (*referring to social position*)

дворянин*; ~'s agreement джентльменское
соглашение.
gentlemanly ['dʒɛntlmənlɪ] adj
джентльменский.
gentleness ['dʒɛntlnɪs] n (see adj) нежность f;
мягкость f.
gently ['dʒɛntlɪ] adv (smile, treat) нежно; (curve,
slope, move) мягко; (speak) ласково.
gentry ['dʒɛntrɪ] n inv: the ~ дворянство.
gents [dʒɛnts] n: the ~ мужская уборная f adj.
genuine ['dʒɛnjuɪn] adj (person, feeling)
искренний*; (painting etc) подлинный*.
genuinely ['dʒɛnjuɪnlɪ] adv (sincerely)
искренне; (truly) по-настоящему.
geographer [dʒɪ'ɒɡrəfə*] n географ.
geographic(al) [dʒɪə'ɡræfɪk(l)] adj
географический.
geography [dʒɪ'ɒɡrəfɪ] n география.
geological [dʒɪə'lɒdʒɪkl] adj геологический.
geologist [dʒɪ'ɒlədʒɪst] n геолог.
geology [dʒɪ'ɒlədʒɪ] n геология.
geometric(al) [dʒɪə'mɛtrɪk(l)] adj
геометрический.
geometry [dʒɪ'ɒmətrɪ] n геометрия.
Geordie ['dʒɔːdɪ] n (GEO: inf) уроженец города
Нюкасл в Англии.
Georgia ['dʒɔːdʒə] n Грузия.
Georgian ['dʒɔːdʒən] adj грузинский* ◆ n
грузин(ка*); (LING) грузинский* язык*.
geranium [dʒɪ'reɪnɪəm] n герань f.
geriatric [dʒɛrɪ'ætrɪk] adj гериатрический ◆ n
дряхлый старик.
germ [dʒəːm] n (MED) микроб; (BOT, fig)
зачаток; the ~ of an idea зачаток идеи.
German ['dʒəːmən] adj немецкий* ◆ n
немец*(-мка*); (LING) немецкий* язык*.
German Democratic Republic n (formerly)
Германская Демократическая Республика.
germane [dʒəː'meɪn] adj: ~ to релевантный
для +gen.
German measles n (BRIT) краснуха.
Germany ['dʒəːmənɪ] n Германия.
germinate ['dʒəːmɪneɪt] vi (BOT) прорастать
(прорасти* perf); (fig) давать* (дать* perf)
ростки.
germination [dʒəːmɪ'neɪʃən] n (BOT)
прорастание.
germ warfare n бактериологическая война.
gerrymandering ['dʒɛrɪmændərɪŋ] n изменение
границ избирательных округов с целью дать
преимущество определённой политической
партии.
gestation [dʒɛs'teɪʃən] n созревание плода.
gesticulate [dʒɛs'tɪkjuleɪt] vi жестикулировать
(impf).
gesture ['dʒɛstjə*] n (movement, token) жест; as
a ~ of friendship в знак дружбы.

KEYWORD

get [ɡɛt] (pt, pp got; US) (pp gotten) vi 1 (become,
be): it's getting late становится* (impf)
поздно; to get old стареть (постареть perf);
to get tired уставать* (устать* perf); to get
cold мёрзнуть (замёрзнуть perf); to get
annoyed easily часто раздражаться (impf); he
was getting bored ему стало скучно; he gets
drunk quickly он быстро пьянеет; he gets
drunk every weekend он напивается каждый
выходной; he got killed его убили; when do I
get paid? когда мне заплатят?
2 (go): to get to/from добираться
(добраться* perf) до +gen/от +gen; to get
home приходить* (прийти* perf) домой; how
did you get here/there? как Вы сюда/туда
добрались?
3 (begin): to get to know sb (become
acquainted) познакомиться* (perf) с кем-н; to
get to know sb well близко познакомиться*
(perf) с кем-н; I'm getting to like him он
начинает мне нравиться; let's get started
давайте начнём
◆ modal aux vb: you've got to do it Вы должны
это сделать (perf)
◆ vt: 1: to get sth done сделать (perf) что-н; to
get the washing done постирать (perf); to get
the dishes done помыть* (perf) or вымыть
(perf) посуду; to get the car started or to start
завести* (perf) машину; to get sb to do
заставлять (заставить* perf) кого-н +infin; to
get sb ready собрать* (perf) кого-н; to get sth
ready приготовить* (perf) что-н; to get sb
drunk напоить* (perf) кого-н; she got me into
trouble я влип с ней в неприятности
2 (obtain: permission, results) получать
(получить* perf); (: money) доставать*
(достать* perf); (find: job, flat) находить*
(найти* perf); (person: call) звать* (позвать*
perf); (: pick up) забирать (забрать* perf); (call
out: doctor, plumber etc) вызывать (вызвать*
perf); (object: carry) приносить* (принести*
perf); (: buy) покупать (купить* perf); I'll get
the car я схожу за машиной; can I get you
something to drink? что Вам можно
предложить (perf)?
3 (receive) получать (получить* perf); to get a
reputation for sth заработать (perf) дурную
репутацию чем-н; what did you get for your
birthday? что Вам подарили на день
рождения?
4 (grab) хватать (схватить* perf); (hit): the
bullet got him in the leg пуля попала ему в
ногу; I'll get you there somehow я Вас
как-нибудь туда доставлю; do you think
we'll get the piano through the door? как Вы
думаете, пианино пройдёт через дверь?; we
must get him to hospital мы должны отвезти

его в больни́цу; **I'll get the book to you tomorrow** за́втра кни́га бу́дет у Вас
5 (*catch, take*): **we got a taxi** мы взя́ли такси́; **did she get her plane?** она́ успе́ла на самолёт?; **what train are you getting?** каки́м по́ездом Вы е́дете?; **where do I get the train?** где мне сади́ться на по́езд?
6 (*understand*) понима́ть (поня́ть* *perf*); (*hear*) расслы́шать (*perf*); **(do you) get it?** (*inf*) сечёшь?; **I've got it!** тепе́рь поня́тно!; **I'm sorry, I didn't get your name** прости́те, я не расслы́шал Ва́ше и́мя
7 (*have, possess*): **how many children have you got?** ско́лько у Вас дете́й?; **I've got very little time** у меня́ о́чень ма́ло вре́мени
▶ **get about** *vi* (*after illness*) ходи́ть* (*impf*); (*news*) распространя́ться (распространи́ться *perf*); **I don't get about much now** (*go to places*) тепе́рь я ма́ло где быва́ю
▶ **get across** *vt* (*subj: speaker*) объясня́ть (объясни́ть *perf*); **it's important to get this message across to them** ва́жно, что́бы они́ э́то по́няли
▶ **get along** *vi* (*agree*) ла́дить* (*impf*) с +*instr*; (*manage*) = **get by**; **I'd better be getting along** мне пора́
▶ **get around** *vt* = **get round**
▶ **get at** *vt fus* (*criticize*) придира́ться (придра́ться* *perf*) к +*dat*; (*reach*) дотя́гиваться (дотяну́ться* *perf*) до +*gen*; **what are you getting at?** ну что Вы хоти́те сказа́ть?
▶ **get away** *vi* (*leave*) уйти́* (*perf*); (*on holiday*) уе́хать* (*perf*); (*escape*) убежа́ть* (*impf*)
▶ **get away with** *vt fus*: **he always gets away with it** ему́ всё схо́дит с рук; **he'll never get away with it!** э́то ему́ да́ром не пройдёт!
▶ **get back** *vi* (*return*) возвраща́ться (верну́ться *perf*)
◆ *vt* (*book, car*) получи́ть* (*perf*) обра́тно *or* наза́д; **get back!** отойди́те!
▶ **get back at** *vt fus* (*inf*): **I'll get back at you (for that)** ты у меня́ (за э́то) полу́чишь
▶ **to get back to** *vt fus* (*return to*) возвраща́ться (верну́ться *perf*) к +*dat*; (*contact again*) связа́ться* (*perf*) с +*instr*; **to get back to sleep** сно́ва засыпа́ть (засну́ть *perf*)
▶ **get by** *vi* (*pass: on foot*) проходи́ть* (пройти́* *perf*); (*manage*): **to get by without** обходи́ться* (обойти́сь* *perf*) без +*gen*; **I can/will get by** (*with little food, money*) мне хвата́ет/хва́тит; **I can get by in Dutch** я могу́ объясни́ться по-голла́ндски
▶ **get down** *vi*: **to get down from** слеза́ть (слезть* *perf*) с +*gen*
◆ *vt* (*depress*) де́йствовать* (*impf*) угнета́юще; (*write*) запи́сывать (записа́ть* *perf*); (*swallow*) впи́хивать (впихну́ть *perf*) в себя́; **to get down on your hands and knees** встава́ть (встать* *perf*) на четвере́ньки
▶ **get down to** *vt fus* (*work, business*) сади́ться*

(засе́сть* *perf*) *or* бра́ться* (взя́ться* *perf*) за +*acc*
▶ **get in** *vi* (*train*) прибыва́ть (прибы́ть* *perf*), приходи́ть* (прийти́* *perf*); (*arrive home: on foot*) приходи́ть* (прийти́* *perf*); (*by transport*) приезжа́ть (прие́хать* *perf*); (*be elected*): **he got in by ten votes** его́ избра́ли большинство́м в де́сять голосо́в; **as soon as the bus pulled up we all got in** как то́лько авто́бус подошёл, мы се́ли в него́; **we queued for a long time for the concert but couldn't get in** мы до́лго стоя́ли в о́череди, но так и не попа́ли на конце́рт
◆ *vt* (*harvest*) собира́ть (собра́ть* *perf*); (*coal, supplies*) загота́вливать (загото́вить* *perf*); (*shopping*) закупа́ть (закупи́ть* *perf*); (*into conversation*) вставля́ть (вста́вить* *perf*)
▶ **get into** *vt fus* (*building*) входи́ть* (войти́* *perf*) в +*acc*; (*subj: train*) прибыва́ть (прибы́ть* *perf*) в/на +*acc*; (*vehicle*) сади́ться* (сесть* *perf*) в +*acc*; (*clothes*) влеза́ть (влезть* *perf*) в +*acc*; (*fight, argument*) вступа́ть (вступи́ть* *perf*) в +*acc*; (*university, college*) поступа́ть (поступи́ть* *perf*) в +*acc*; **to get into bed** ложи́ться (лечь* *perf*) в посте́ль; **I can't get into this skirt** э́та ю́бка на меня́ не налеза́ет; **she has got into the habit of going for a walk before breakfast** у неё вошло́ в привы́чку выходи́ть гуля́ть до за́втрака
▶ **get off** *vi* (*escape*): **to get off lightly/with sth** отде́лываться (отде́латься *perf*) легко́/чем-н
◆ *vt* (*clothes*) снима́ть (снять* *perf*); (*stain*) выводи́ть* (вы́вести* *perf*); (*letter etc*) отправля́ть (отпра́вить* *perf*); (*day, time*): **we got 2 days/2 weeks off last month** у нас бы́ло два выходны́х дня/две свобо́дных неде́ли в про́шлом ме́сяце
◆ *vt fus* (*train, bus*) сходи́ть* (сойти́* *perf*) с +*gen*; (*horse, bicycle*) слеза́ть (слезть* *perf*) с +*gen*; **to get off and walk** (*bicycle*) слеза́ть (слезть* *perf*) и идти́* (пойти́* *perf*) пешко́м; **you should get off at the next station** Вам на́до сойти́ (*perf*) на сле́дующей ста́нции; **to get off to a good/poor start** (*fig*) с бле́ском/пло́хо начина́ть (нача́ть* *perf*); **I'd better be getting off** (*departing*) мне пора́
▶ **get on** *vi* (*age*) старе́ть (*impf*); (*progress*): **how are you getting on?** у тебя́ подвига́ется де́ло?; **to get on (with)** ла́дить* (*impf*) (с +*instr*); (*manage*) справля́ться (спра́виться* *perf*) (с +*instr*)
◆ *vt fus* (*train, bus*) сади́ться* (сесть* *perf*) в +*acc*; (*horse, bicycle*) сади́ться* (сесть* *perf*) на +*acc*; **time is getting on** вре́мя идёт
▶ **get on to** *vt fus* (BRIT: *from one subject to another*) переходи́ть* (перейти́* *perf*) +*instr*; (*person*) связыва́ться (связа́ться* *perf*) с +*instr*; **how did we get on to this?** как мы к э́тому пришли́
▶ **get out** *vi* (*leave: building, vehicle*) выходи́ть* (вы́йти* *perf*); (*by transport*) выезжа́ть

(вы́ехать* *perf*); (: *city*) уезжа́ть (уе́хать* *perf*); (*socialize*) выбира́ться (вы́браться* *perf*) из до́ма
♦ *vt* (*stain*) выводи́ть* (вы́вести* *perf*); (*object*) достава́ть (доста́ть* *perf*); (*report*) публикова́ть* (опубликова́ть* *perf*); **get out!** убира́йся!; **the news got out that...** ста́ло изве́стно, что...; **the news got out in the end** но́вости разошли́сь в конце́ концо́в
► **get out of** *vt fus* (*duty etc*) отде́лываться (отде́латься *perf*) от +*gen*
♦ *vt* (*pleasure, satisfaction*) получа́ть (получи́ть* *perf*) от +*gen*; (*money*): **to get out (of)** (*from bank*) бра́ть* (взять* *perf*) (в +*prp*); (*from account*) снима́ть (снять* *perf*) с +*gen*; **I couldn't get a word out of him** я не мог и сло́ва доби́ться от него́
► **get over** *vt fus* (*illness*) поправля́ться (попра́виться* *perf*)
♦ *vt*: **to get sth over with** зако́нчить (*perf*) что-н; **to get the message over that...** объясни́ть (*perf*), что...; **let's get it over with!** дава́йте поко́нчим с э́тим де́лом!
► **get round** *vt fus* (*law, rule*) обходи́ть* (обойти́* *perf*); (*fig: person*) добива́ться (доби́ться* *perf*) своего́ от +*gen*
► **get round to** *vt fus*: **to get round to doing** собира́ться (собра́ться* *perf*) +*infin*; **I'll get around to it some day** когда́-н я доберу́сь до э́того
► **get through** *vi* (*TEL*) дозвони́ться (*perf*)
♦ *vt fus* (*work, book*) зака́нчивать (зако́нчить *perf*)
► **get through to** *vt fus* (*TEL*) дозвони́ться (*perf*) до +*gen*
► **get together** *vi* (*several people*) собира́ться (собра́ться* *perf*); (*two people*) встреча́ться (встре́титься* *perf*)
♦ *vt* (*people*) собира́ть (собра́ть *perf*); (*project, plan etc*) составля́ть (соста́вить* *perf*)
► **get up** *vi* встава́ть* (встать* *perf*)
♦ *vt* (*person*) поднима́ть (подня́ть* *perf*); **I can't get up any enthusiasm for it** у меня́ не возника́ет энтузиа́зма на э́тот счёт
► **get up to** *vt fus* (*BRIT: prank etc*) занима́ться (заня́ться* *perf*) +*instr*; **they're always getting up to mischief** они́ всегда́ прока́зничают.

getaway ['gɛtəweɪ] *n*: **to make a** *or* **one's ~** бежа́ть* (*impf*).
getaway car *n* маши́на, испо́льзованная при побе́ге.
get-together ['gɛttəgɛðəʳ] *n* (*meeting*) неофициа́льное собра́ние; (*party*) вечери́нка*.
get-up ['gɛtʌp] *n* (*inf*) наря́д.
get-well card [gɛt'wɛl-] *n* откры́тка* с

пожела́ниями выздоровле́ния.
geyser ['giːzəʳ] *n* ге́йзер; (*BRIT: water heater*) га́зовая коло́нка*.
Ghana ['gɑːnə] *n* Га́на.
Ghanaian [gɑːˈneɪən] *adj* га́нский ♦ *n* жи́тель(ница) *m(f)* Га́ны.
ghastly ['gɑːstlɪ] *adj* (*horrible: person, situation*) ужа́сный* (ужа́сен), отврати́тельный* (отврати́телен); (: *building, appearance, behaviour*) безобра́зный* (безобра́зен); (*pale: complexion*) мёртвенно-бле́дный* (мёртвенно-бле́ден); (*ill*): **you look ~!** Вы ужа́сно вы́глядите!
gherkin ['gəːkɪn] *n* ме́лкий огуре́ц для марина́вания.
ghetto ['gɛtəu] *n* ге́тто *nt ind.*
ghetto blaster [-'blɑːstəʳ] *n* переносно́й радиомагнитофо́н.
ghost [gəust] *n* (*spirit*) привиде́ние, при́зрак ♦ *vt* явля́ться (яви́ться* *perf*) та́йным а́втором +*gen*; **to give up the ~** (*fig*) приказа́ть* (*perf*) до́лго жить.
ghost town *n* забро́шенный го́род.
ghostwriter ['gəustraɪtəʳ] *n* та́йный а́втор, писа́тель-невиди́мка *m.*
ghoul [guːl] *n* (*ghost*) вурдала́к.
ghoulish ['guːlɪʃ] *adj* (*tastes etc*) ме́рзкий* (ме́рзок).
GHQ *n abbr* (*MIL*) = **general headquarters.**
GI *n abbr* (*US*: *inf*) = **government issue.**
giant ['dʒaɪənt] *n* (*in myths, stories*) велика́н; (*fig: large company etc*) гига́нт ♦ *adj* огро́мный.
giant killers *npl* кома́нда без и́мени, оде́рживающая побе́ды над кома́ндами мирово́го кла́сса.
gibber ['dʒɪbəʳ] *vi* говори́ть (проговори́ть *perf*) невня́тно.
gibberish ['dʒɪbərɪʃ] *n* тараба́рщина.
gibe [dʒaɪb] *n* насме́шка* ♦ *vi*: **to ~ at** смея́ться (*impf*) *or* издева́ться (*impf*) над +*instr.*
giblets ['dʒɪblɪts] *npl* (*of chicken etc*) потроха́ *mpl.*
Gibraltar [dʒɪˈbrɔːltəʳ] *n* Гибралта́р.
giddiness ['gɪdɪnɪs] *n* головокруже́ние.
giddy ['gɪdɪ] *adj* (*height*) голово-кружи́тельный* (головокружи́телен); (*dizzy*): **I feel ~** у меня́ кру́жится голова́; **~ with success** опьянённый (опьянён) успе́хом.
gift [gɪft] *n* (*present*) пода́рок*; (*donation*) дар*; (*COMM: also:* **free ~**) беспла́тный пода́рок*; (*ability*) дар*, тала́нт; **to have a ~ for sth** облада́ть (*impf*) тала́нтом чего́-н.
gifted ['gɪftɪd] *adj* одарённый*.
gift token *n* пода́рочный купо́н.
gift voucher *n* = **gift token.**
gig [gɪg] *n* (*inf: concert*) конце́рт (*рок- и́ли*

---

* marks translations which have irregular inflections. The Russian-English side of the dictionary gives inflectional information.

поп-гру́ппы).

gigabyte [ˈdʒɪɡəbaɪt] *n* едини́ца измере́ния мо́щности па́мяти компью́тера.

gigantic [dʒaɪˈɡæntɪk] *adj* гига́нтский*.

giggle [ˈɡɪɡl] *vi* хихи́кать *(impf)* ♦ *n*: **it was just a ~!** э́то был про́сто смех!; **to do sth for a ~** де́лать (сде́лать *perf*) что-н для сме́ха.

GIGO [ˈɡaɪɡəʊ] *abbr (COMPUT. inf.* = *garbage in, garbage out)* МЗМП= *мя́кину зало́жишь – мя́кину полу́чишь*.

gild [ɡɪld] *vt* золоти́ть* (позолоти́ть* *perf*).

gill [dʒɪl] *n* ме́ра жи́дкости.

gills [ɡɪlz] *npl (of fish)* жа́бры *fpl*.

gilt [ɡɪlt] *adj* позоло́ченный ♦ *n* позоло́та; **~s** *npl (COMM)* = **gilt-edged securities**.

gilt-edged [ˈɡɪltɛdʒd] *adj*: **~ securities** золотообре́зные це́нные бума́ги *fpl (о надёжных а́кциях)*.

gimlet [ˈɡɪmlɪt] *n* бура́вчик.

gimmick [ˈɡɪmɪk] *n (sales)* уло́вка; *(electoral)* трюк.

gin [dʒɪn] *n* джин *(можжеве́ловая во́дка)*.

ginger [ˈdʒɪndʒəˈ] *n (spice)* имби́рь* *m* ♦ *adj (in colour)* ры́жий*.

ginger ale *n* имби́рный эль.

ginger beer *n* имби́рное пи́во.

gingerbread [ˈdʒɪndʒəbrɛd] *n (cake)* ≈ коври́жка, имби́рный пиро́г*; *(biscuit)* ≈ пря́ник, имби́рное пече́нье*.

ginger group *n (BRIT)* гру́ппа чле́нов организа́ции, наста́ивающая на бо́лее реши́тельных де́йствиях.

ginger-haired [ˈdʒɪndʒəˈhɛəd] *adj* рыжеволо́сый.

gingerly [ˈdʒɪndʒəlɪ] *adv* опа́сливо.

gingham [ˈɡɪŋəm] *n* хлопчатобума́жная ткань в кле́тку.

ginseng [ˈdʒɪnsɛŋ] *n* женьше́нь *m*.

gipsy [ˈdʒɪpsɪ] *n* цыга́н*(ка*).

gipsy caravan *n* цыга́нская киби́тка.

giraffe [dʒɪˈrɑːf] *n* жира́ф.

girder [ˈɡəːdəˈ] *n* металли́ческая ба́лка*.

girdle [ˈɡəːdl] *n (corset)* корсе́т ♦ *vt (encircle)* опоя́сывать (опоя́сать* *perf*).

girl [ɡəːl] *n (child)* де́вочка*; *(young unmarried woman)* де́вушка*; *(daughter)* до́чка*; **this is my little ~** э́то моя́ до́чка; **an English ~** англича́нка*.

girlfriend [ˈɡəːlfrɛnd] *n (of girl)* подру́га; *(of boy)* де́вушка*, подру́га.

Girl Guide *n* де́вочка*-ска́ут *f*.

girlish [ˈɡəːlɪʃ] *adj* деви́чий*.

Girl Scout *n (US)* = **Girl Guide**.

Giro [ˈdʒaɪrəʊ] *n*: **the National ~** *(BRIT)* спо́соб перево́да де́нег че́рез банк и́ли по по́чте.

giro [ˈdʒaɪrəʊ] *n (bank giro)* перево́д де́нег че́рез банк; *(post office giro)* перево́д де́нег че́рез по́чту; *(BRIT. welfare cheque)* чек, по кото́рому получа́ют посо́бия по безрабо́тице.

girth [ɡəːθ] *n (circumference)* окру́жность *f*; *(of*

horse) подпру́га.

gist [dʒɪst] *n (of speech, programme)* суть *f*.

KEYWORD

give [ɡɪv] *(pt* **gave**, *pp* **given)** *vt* **1** *(hand over)*: **to give sb sth** *or* **sth to sb** дава́ть* (дать* *perf)* кому́-н что-н; **they gave her a book for her birthday** они́ подари́ли ей кни́гу на день рожде́ния

2 *(used with noun to replace a verb)*: **to give a sigh** вздохну́ть *(perf)*; **to give a push** толкну́ть *(perf)*; **to give a shrug** передёрнуть *(perf)* плеча́ми; **to give a speech** выступа́ть (вы́ступить* *perf)* с ре́чью; **to give a lecture** чита́ть (прочита́ть *perf)* ле́кцию; **to give three cheers** три́жды крича́ть (прокрича́ть *perf)* „ура́“

3 *(tell, deliver. news)* сообща́ть (сообщи́ть *perf)*; *(advice)* дава́ть* (дать* *perf)*; **could you give him a message for me please? tell him that...** переда́йте ему́, пожа́луйста, от меня́, что...; **I've got a message to give you from your brother** я тебе́ до́лжен что-то переда́ть от твоего́ бра́та; **let me give you some advice** разреши́те мне дать Вам сове́т; **he gave me his new address over the phone** он дал мне свой но́вый а́дрес по телефо́ну;

4: **to give sb sth** *(clothing, food, right)* дава́ть* (дать* *perf)* кому́-н что-н; *(title)* присва́ивать (присво́ить *perf)* кому́-н что-н; *(honour, responsibility)* возлага́ть (возложи́ть* *perf)* на кого́-н что-н; **to give sb a surprise** удиви́ть* (perf\ кого́-н; **that's given me an idea** э́то навело́ меня́ на мысль

5 *(dedicate: one's life)* отдава́ть* (отда́ть* *perf)*; *(allow: time, attention)* уделя́ть (удели́ть* *perf)*; **you'll need to give me more time** Вы должны́ дать мне бо́льше вре́мени; **she gave it all her attention** она́ отнесла́сь к э́тому с больши́м внима́нием

6 *(organize)*: **to give a party** устра́ивать (устро́ить *perf)* ве́чер, приглаша́ть (пригласи́ть* *perf)* госте́й; **to give a dinner** *etc* дава́ть* (дать* *perf)* обе́д

♦ *vi* **1** *(stretch: fabric)* растя́гиваться (растяну́ться* *perf)*

2 *(break, collapse)* = **give way**

▶ **give away** *vt (money, object)* отдава́ть* (отда́ть* *perf)*; *(betray: secret, information)* выдава́ть* (вы́дать* *perf)*; *(: person)* выдава́ть* (вы́дать* *perf)*; *(bride)* отдава́ть* *(impf)* за́муж

▶ **give back** *vt* отдава́ть* (отда́ть* *perf)* обра́тно

▶ **give in** *vi (yield)* сдава́ться* (сда́ться* *perf)* ♦ *vt (essay etc)* сдава́ть* (сдать* *perf)*

▶ **give off** *vt fus (smoke)* дыми́ть* *(impf)*; **the radiator/coal fire gives off a lot of heat** от батаре́и/ками́на идёт тепло́

▶ **give out** *vt (distribute)* раздава́ть* (разда́ть* *perf)*; *(make known)* объявля́ть (объяви́ть*

perf)
◆ vi (be exhausted) конча́ться (ко́нчиться perf); (fail) лома́ться (слома́ться perf)
▶ **give up** vi (stop trying) сдава́ться (сда́ться* perf)
◆ vt (job, boyfriend, habit) броса́ть (бро́сить* perf); (idea, hope) оставля́ть (оста́вить* perf); **to give up smoking** броса́ть (бро́сить* perf) кури́ть; **to give o.s. up** сдава́ться* (сда́ться* perf)
▶ **give way** vi (rope, ladder etc) не выде́рживать (вы́держать perf); (wall, roof) обва́ливаться (обвали́ться* perf); (chair, floor) прола́мываться (проломи́ться* perf); (BRIT: AUT) уступа́ть (уступи́ть* perf) доро́гу; **his legs gave way beneath him** его́ но́ги подогну́лись; **to give way (to)** (to demands) уступа́ть (уступи́ть* perf) +dat.

give-and-take ['gɪvənd'teɪk] n ги́бкость f, свобо́да.
giveaway ['gɪvəweɪ] (inf) n: **her expression was a ~** выраже́ние (её) лица́ вы́дало её ◆ adj: **~ prices** даровы́е це́ны; **the exam was a ~!** экза́мен был сру́ндо́вый!
given ['gɪvn] pp of **give** ◆ adj да́нный ◆ conj: **~ the circumstances ...** с учётом обстоя́тельств ..., учи́тывая обстоя́тельства ...; **~ that** учи́тывая, что.
glacial ['gleɪsɪəl] adj (also fig) ледяно́й.
glacier ['glæsɪə'] n ледни́к*.
glad [glæd] adj: **I am ~** я рад; **I was ~ of his help** я был рад его́ по́мощи.
gladden ['glædn] vt (heart) ра́довать (пора́довать perf); (person) обра́довать (perf); **it ~ed his heart to see her well again** у него́ пора́довалось се́рдце, когда́ он уви́дел, что ей ста́ло лу́чше.
glade [gleɪd] n поля́на.
gladioli [glædɪ'əʊlaɪ] npl гладио́лусы mpl.
gladly ['glædlɪ] adv (willingly) с ра́достью.
glamorous ['glæmərəs] adj очарова́тельный* (очарова́телен).
glamour ['glæmə'] n очарова́ние.
glance [glɑːns] n (look) взгляд ◆ vi: **to ~ at** взгля́дывать (взгляну́ть* perf) на +acc
▶ **glance off** vt fus отска́кивать (отскочи́ть* perf) от +gen.
glancing ['glɑːnsɪŋ] adj (blow) боково́й.
gland [glænd] n железа́*.
glandular ['glændjulə'] adj: **~ fever** (BRIT) (инфекцио́нный) мононуклео́з.
glare [gleə'] n (angry) свире́пый взгляд; (hostile) вражде́бный взгляд; (of light) ослепи́тельное сия́ние ◆ vi (light) ослепи́тельно сия́ть (impf); **she lives in the full ~ of publicity** все подро́бности её жи́зни стано́вятся достоя́нием пре́ссы; **to ~ at**

свире́по or при́стально смотре́ть* (посмотре́ть* perf) на +acc.
glaring ['gleərɪŋ] adj (mistake) я́вный, очеви́дный.
Glasgow ['glɑːzgəu] n Гла́зго m ind.
glasnost ['glæznɒst] n гла́сность f.
glass [glɑːs] n (substance) стекло́; (container, contents) стака́н; **~es** npl (spectacles) очки́ ntpl.
glass-blowing ['glɑːsbləʊɪŋ] n стеклоду́вное де́ло.
glass fibre n стекловолокно́.
glasshouse ['glɑːshaus] n тепли́ца, парни́к.
glassware ['glɑːsweə'] n стекля́нная посу́да.
glassy ['glɑːsɪ] adj (eyes, stare) безжи́зненный* (безжи́зен).
Glaswegian [glæs'wiːdʒən] adj гла́зговский ◆ n жи́тель(ница) m(f) Гла́зго.
glaze [gleɪz] vt (window) застекля́ть (застекли́ть perf); (pottery) покрыва́ть (покры́ть* perf) глазу́рью ◆ n (on pottery) глазу́рь f.
glazed [gleɪzd] adj (eyes) му́тный*, ту́склый*; (pottery) покры́тый глазу́рью.
glazier ['gleɪzɪə'] n стеко́льщик.
gleam [gliːm] vi сия́ть (засия́ть perf) ◆ n: **a ~ of hope** луч наде́жды.
gleaming ['gliːmɪŋ] adj сия́ющий*.
glean [gliːn] vt (information) добыва́ть (добы́ть* perf), собира́ть (собра́ть* perf).
glee [gliː] n (joy) ликова́ние.
gleeful ['gliːful] adj лику́ющий.
glen [glɛn] n (SCOTTISH, IRISH) доли́на реки́.
glib [glɪb] adj (person) льсти́вый (болтли́в); (promise, response) бо́йкий* (бо́ек).
glibly ['glɪblɪ] adv (talk, answer) бо́йко.
glide [glaɪd] vi скользи́ть* (impf); (AVIAT) плани́ровать (impf); (bird) пари́ть (impf) ◆ n скольже́ние.
glider ['glaɪdə'] n (AVIAT) планёр.
gliding ['glaɪdɪŋ] n (AVIAT) плани́рование.
glimmer ['glɪmə'] n (of light) мерца́ние; (of interest, hope) про́блеск ◆ vi (light) мерца́ть (impf).
glimpse [glɪmps] n мимолётное впечатле́ние ◆ vt ви́деть* (уви́деть* perf) ме́льком; **to catch a ~ of** уви́деть* (perf) ме́льком.
glint [glɪnt] vi блесте́ть* (блесну́ть perf), сверка́ть (сверкну́ть perf) ◆ n (of metal, light) блеск, сверка́ние; (in eyes) блеск.
glisten ['glɪsn] vi (with sweat, rain etc) блесте́ть* (impf).
glitter ['glɪtə'] vi сверка́ть (сверкну́ть perf) ◆ n сверка́ние.
glittering ['glɪtərɪŋ] adj (eyes, career) блестя́щий*; (stars) сия́ющий*; (diamonds) сверка́ющий.
glitz [glɪts] n (inf) блеск.

---

* marks translations which have irregular inflections. The Russian-English side of the dictionary gives inflectional information.

gloat [gləʊt] vi: **to ~ (over)** злора́дствовать (impf) (над +instr).
global ['gləʊbl] adj (interest, attention) всео́бщий*; (overall: picture) о́бщий*.
global warming [-'wɔːmɪŋ] n всеми́рное or глоба́льное потепле́ние.
globe [gləʊb] n (world) земно́й шар*; (model of world) гло́бус; (shape) шар*.
globetrotter ['gləʊbtrɒtəʳ] n путеше́ственник(-ица).
globule ['glɒbjuːl] n ка́пля*.
gloom [gluːm] n (dark) мрак; (sadness) уны́ние.
gloomily ['gluːmɪlɪ] adv уны́ло.
gloomy ['gluːmɪ] adj мра́чный.
glorification [glɔːrɪfɪ'keɪʃən] n прославле́ние; **the ~ of war** прославле́ние войны́.
glorified ['glɔːrɪfaɪd] adj: **she is merely a ~ secretary** она́ по су́ти де́ла про́сто секрета́рша.
glorify ['glɔːrɪfaɪ] vt (praise) прославля́ть (просла́вить* perf).
glorious ['glɔːrɪəs] adj (sunshine, flowers, weather) великоле́пный* (великоле́пен); (victory) сла́вный; (future) прекра́сный* (прекра́сен).
glory ['glɔːrɪ] n (prestige) сла́ва; (splendour) великоле́пие ♦ vi: **to ~ in** упива́ться (impf) +instr.
glory hole n (inf) кладо́вка.
Glos abbr (BRIT: POST) = Gloucestershire.
gloss [glɒs] n блеск; (also: ~ **paint**) лак*
▶ **gloss over** vt fus (error, problem) зама́зывать (зама́зать perf).
glossary ['glɒsərɪ] n глосса́рий.
glossy ['glɒsɪ] adj (photograph, magazine) гля́нцевый; (hair) блестя́щий* ♦ n (also: ~ **magazine**) журна́л в гля́нцевой обло́жке.
glove [glʌv] n перча́тка*.
glove compartment n (AUT) перча́точный я́щик, бардачо́к* (разг).
glow [gləʊ] vi (embers, stars) свети́ться (impf); (face, eyes) горе́ть (impf) ♦ n (of eyes, stars) свет; (of face) румя́нец.
glower ['glaʊəʳ] vi: **to ~ at sb** смотре́ть* (посмотре́ть* perf) с негодова́нием на кого́-н.
glowing ['gləʊɪŋ] adj (fire) я́рко светя́щийся; (complexion) румя́ный; (fig: report etc) блестя́щий*.
glow-worm ['gləʊwɜːm] n светлячо́к*.
glucose ['gluːkəʊs] n глюко́за.
glue [gluː] n клей* ♦ vt: **to ~ sth onto sth** прикле́ивать (прикле́ить perf) что-н на что-н.
glue-sniffing ['gluːsnɪfɪŋ] n токсикома́ния.
glum [glʌm] adj мра́чный*.
glut [glʌt] n переизбы́ток* ♦ vt: **to be ~ted (with)** (market, economy etc) быть* (impf) зава́ленным(-ой) (+instr).
glutinous ['gluːtɪnəs] adj кле́йкий*.

glutton ['glʌtn] n обжо́ра m/f; **he is a ~ for work** он охо́ч до рабо́ты; **he is a ~ for punishment** он жа́ден до рабо́ты.
gluttonous ['glʌtənəs] adj (person, habits) ненасы́тный* (ненасы́тен).
gluttony ['glʌtənɪ] n ненасы́тность f.
glycerin(e) ['glɪsəriːn] n глицери́н*.
gm abbr (= gram) г = грамм.
GMAT n abbr (US) = Graduate Management Admissions Test.
GMB n abbr (BRIT) = General Municipal and Boilermakers (Union).
GMT abbr (= Greenwich Mean Time) сре́днее вре́мя* nt по Гри́нвичу.
gnarled [nɑːld] adj (tree) сучкова́тый (сучкова́т); (hand) скрю́ченный (скрю́чен).
gnash [næʃ] vt: **to ~ one's teeth** скрежета́ть* (impf) зуба́ми.
gnat [næt] n мо́шка*.
gnaw [nɔː] vt грызть* (impf) ♦ vi (doubts, suspicions): **to ~ at** терза́ть (impf).
gnome [nəʊm] n гном.
GNP n abbr (= gross national product) ВНП= валово́й национа́льный проду́кт.

KEYWORD
---

go [gəʊ] (pt **went**, pp **gone**, pl **goes**) vi **1** (move: on foot) ходи́ть*/идти́* (пойти́* perf); (travel: by transport) е́здить*/е́хать (пое́хать* perf); **she went into the kitchen** она́ пошла́ на ку́хню; **he often goes to China** он ча́сто е́здит в Кита́й; **they are going to the theatre tonight** сего́дня ве́чером они́ иду́т в теа́тр **2** (depart: on foot) уходи́ть* (уйти́* perf); (: by plane) улета́ть (улете́ть* perf); (: by train, car) уезжа́ть (уе́хать* perf); **the plane goes at 6am** самолёт улета́ет в 6 часо́в утра́; **the train/bus goes at 6pm** по́езд/авто́бус ухо́дит в 6 часо́в; **now I must go** тепе́рь я до́лжен идти́ **3** (attend): **to go to** ходи́ть* (impf) в/на +acc; **she went to university in Aberdeen** она́ учи́лась в Аберди́нском университе́те; **she doesn't go to lectures** она́ не хо́дит на ле́кции **4** (take part in an activity) ходи́ть*/идти́* (пойти́* perf) **5** (work): **is your watch going** ва́ши часы́ иду́т?; **the clock stopped going** часы́ останови́лись; **the bell went just then** зазвони́л звоно́к; **the tape recorder was still going** магнитофо́н не был вы́ключен **6** (become): **to go pale** бледне́ть (побледне́ть perf); **to go mouldy** пле́сневеть (запле́сневеть perf) **7** (be sold): **the books went for £10** кни́ги бы́ли про́даны за £10 **8** (fit, suit): **to go with** подходи́ть* (подойти́* perf) к +dat **9** (be about to, intend to) собира́ться (собра́ться* perf) +infin **10** (time: slowly) тяну́ться (impf); (quickly) проходи́ть* (пройти́* perf) **11** (event, activity) проходи́ть* (пройти́* perf);

12 (*be given*): **the job is to go to someone else** рабо́ту должны́ отда́ть кому́-то друго́му; **the proceeds will go to charity** при́быль пойдёт на благотвори́тельные це́ли

13 (*break etc*): **the fuse went** предохрани́тель *m* перегоре́л; **the leg of the chair went** но́жка сту́ла слома́лась

14 (*be placed*): **the milk goes in the fridge** молоко́ ну́жно поста́вить в холоди́льник; **where does this cup go?** куда́ поста́вить э́ту ча́шку?; **the suitcase goes on top of the wardrobe** чемода́н обы́чно лежи́т на шкафу́

◆ *n* **1** (*try*): **to have a go (at sth/at doing sth)** про́бовать* (попро́бовать* *perf*) (что-н/+*perf infin*)

2 (*turn*): **whose go is it?** (*in board games*) чей ход?; (*in sports*) чья (сейча́с) о́чередь?

3 (*move*): **to be on the go** быть (*impf*) на нога́х

▶ **go about** *vi* (*also:* **go around:** *rumour*) ходи́ть* (*impf*)

◆ *vt fus*: **to go about one's business** занима́ться (заня́ться* *perf*) свои́ми дела́ми; **how do I go about (doing) this?** как мне э́то сде́лать?

▶ **go after** *vt fus* (*person*) бежа́ть (побежа́ть* *perf*) (вдого́нку) за +*instr*; **to go after a job** стреми́ться* (*impf*) получи́ть рабо́ту

▶ **go against** *vt fus* (*subj: decision, verdict*): **to go against sb** быть (*impf*) не в чью-н по́льзу

▶ **go ahead** *vi* (*proceed*) продвига́ться (продви́нуться *perf*); (*event*): **to go ahead with** (*project*) приступи́ть* (*perf*) к +*dat*; **may I begin? – yes, go ahead!** мо́жно нача́ть? – да, пожа́луйста!

▶ **go along** *vi* идти́ (пойти́* *perf*); **I went along with his/his decision** (*agree with*) я не стал проти́виться ему́/его́ реше́нию; **to go along with sb** (*accompany*) идти́* (пойти́* *perf*) с кем-н

▶ **go away** *vi* (*leave: on foot*) уходи́ть* (уйти́* *perf*); (: *by transport*) уезжа́ть* (уе́хать* *perf*); **go away and think about it for a while** пойди́ и поду́май немно́жко на э́тот счёт

▶ **go back** *vi* (*return*) возвраща́ться (верну́ться* *perf*); (*go again: on foot*) идти́* (пойти́* *perf*) ещё раз *or* опя́ть; (: *by transport*) е́хать* (пое́хать* *perf*) ещё раз *or* опя́ть; **we went back into the house** мы пошли́ обра́тно в дом; **I am never going back to her house again** я никогда́ бо́льше не пойду́ к ней; **to go back to** (*date from*) относи́ться (*impf*) к +*dat*

▶ **go back on** *vt fus* (*promise, word*) не сде́рживать (сдержа́ть* *perf*) +*gen*

▶ **go by** *vi* (*years, time*) проходи́ть* (пройти́* *perf*)

◆ *vt fus* (*book, rule*) де́лать (сде́лать *perf*) всё по +*dat*; **as time goes by** ... вре́мя идёт, и ...

▶ **go down** *vi* (*descend*) спуска́ться (спусти́ться* *perf*); (*ship*) тону́ть* (затону́ть* *perf*); (*sun*) заходи́ть* (зайти́* *perf*); (*prices, temperature*) па́дать (упа́сть* *perf*); (*swelling*) спада́ть (спасть* *perf*)

◆ *vt fus* (*stairs, ladder*) спуска́ться (спусти́ться* *perf*) с +*gen*; **that should go down well with him** э́то ему́ должно́ понра́вится; **he went to London/to see his sister** он пое́хал в Ло́ндон/в го́сти к свое́й сестре́

▶ **go for** *vt fus* (*fetch: paper, doctor*) идти́* (пойти́* *perf*) за +*instr*; (*choose, like*) люби́ть* (*impf*); (*attack*) набра́сываться (набро́ситься* *perf*) на +*acc*; **that goes for me too** и я то́же

▶ **go in** *vi* (*enter*) входи́ть* (войти́* *perf*); **it's time to go in** пора́ идти́ внутрь

▶ **go in for** *vt fus* принима́ть (приня́ть* *perf*) уча́стие в +*prp*; (*take up*) заня́ться* (*perf*) +*instr*

▶ **go into** *vt fus* (*enter*) входи́ть* (войти́* *perf*) в +*acc*; (*investigate*) рассма́тривать (рассмотре́ть* *perf*); (*take up*) заня́ться* (*perf*) +*instr*; **to go into detail** вдава́ться* (*impf*) в подро́бности

▶ **go off** *vi* (*leave: on foot*) уходи́ть* (уйти́* *perf*); (: *by transport*) уезжа́ть (уе́хать* *perf*); (*food*) по́ртиться* (испо́ртиться* *perf*); (*bomb*) взрыва́ться (взорва́ться* *perf*); (*gun*) вы́стрелить (*perf*); (*alarm*) звони́ть (зазвони́ть *perf*); (*event*) проходи́ть* (пройти́* *perf*); (*lights*) выключа́ться (вы́ключиться *perf*)

◆ *vt fus* разлюби́ть* (*perf*); **to go off to sleep** засыпа́ть (засну́ть *perf*)

▶ **go on** *vi*: **to go on (doing)** (*continue*) продолжа́ть (*impf*) (+*infin*); (*happen: discussion, argument*) идти́* (*impf*); **life goes on** жизнь продолжа́ется; **what's going on here?** что здесь происхо́дит?; **we don't have enough evidence/information to go on** у нас нет доста́точных доказа́тельств/информа́ции

▶ **go on at** *vt fus* пристава́ть* (*impf*) к +*dat*

▶ **go on with** *vt fus* продолжа́ть (продо́лжить* *perf*)

▶ **go out** *vi* (*fire, light*) га́снуть* (пога́снуть* *perf*); (*leave*): **to go out of** выходи́ть* (вы́йти* *perf*) из +*gen*; **are you going out tonight?** (*for entertainment*) Вы сего́дня ве́чером куда́-нибудь идёте?

▶ **go over** *vi* идти́* (пойти́* *perf*)

◆ *vt fus* (*check*) просма́тривать (просмотре́ть* *perf*); **to go over sth in one's mind** повторя́ть (повтори́ть *perf*) что-н в уме́

▶ **go round** *vi* (*circulate*) ходи́ть* (*impf*); (*revolve*) враща́ться (*impf*); (*suffice*) хвата́ть (хвати́ть *perf*) на всех; (*visit*): **to go round (to sb's)** заходи́ть* (зайти́* *perf*) (к кому́-н);

---

* marks translations which have irregular inflections. The Russian-English side of the dictionary gives inflectional information.

(*make a detour*): **to go round (by)** (*on foot*)
идти* (пойти* *perf*) кругóм (чéрез +*acc*); (*by
transport*) éхать (поéхать *perf*) кругóм (чéрез
+*acc*)
▶ **go through** *vt fus* (*town etc: on foot*)
проходи́ть* (пройти́* *perf*) чéрез +*acc*; (: *by
transport*) проезжáть (проéхать* *perf*) чéрез
+*acc*; (*files, papers*) просмáтривать
(просмотрéть* *perf*); (*aloud: list*) читáть
(прочитáть *perf*); (*practice*) продéлывать
(проделáть *perf*)
▶ **go through with** *vt fus* (*plan, crime*)
осуществля́ть (осуществи́ть* *perf*); **I couldn't
go through with it** я не мог осуществи́ть э́то
▶ **go under** *vi* (*also fig*) идти́* (пойти́* *perf*) под
вóду
▶ **go up** *vi* (*ascend*) поднимáться (подня́ться*
perf); (*price, level*) расти́* (вы́расти* *perf*);
(*buildings*) вырастáть (вы́расти* *perf*); **to go
up in flames** загорáться (*impf*)
▶ **go with** *vt fus* (*match*) подходи́ть* (подойти́*
perf) к +*dat*
▶ **go without** *vt fus* (*treats*) оставáться*
(остáться* *perf*) без +*gen*; **I can go without food
for 24 hours** я могу́ сýтки не есть.

goad [gəud] *vt* (*person*) подстрекáть (*impf*)
▶ **goad on** *vt* (*person*) подгоня́ть (*impf*).
go-ahead ['gəuhɛd] *adj* предприи́мчивый
(предприи́мчив) ♦ *n* (*for project*) добрó; **to
give sb the** ~ давáть (дать* *perf*) комý-н
добрó.
goal [gəul] *n* (*SPORT*) гол; (: *goal posts*) ворóта
mpl; (*aim*) цель *f*; **to score a** ~ забивáть
(заби́ть* *perf*) гол.
goal difference *n* рáзница мячéй.
goalie ['gəulɪ] *n* (*inf*) вратáрь* *m*, голки́пер.
goalkeeper ['gəulkiːpə'] *n* вратáрь* *m*,
голки́пер.
goal post *n* боковáя штáнга, стóйка* ворóт.
goat [gəut] *n* (*billy*) козёл*; (*nanny*) козá.
gobble ['gɔbl] *vt* (*also:* ~ **down**, ~ **up**) лóпать
(слóпать *perf*), жрать* (сожрáть* *perf*).
go-between ['gəubɪtwiːn] *n* посрéдник(-ица).
Gobi Desert ['gəubɪ-] *n*: **the** ~ ~ пусты́ня
Гóби.
goblet ['gɔblɪt] *n* кýбок*.
goblin ['gɔblɪn] *n* гóблин.
gobsmacked ['gɔbsmækt] *adj*: **I was** ~ (*inf*) я
совершéнно обалдéл.
go-cart ['gəukɑːt] *n* карт.
God [gɔd] *n* Бог ♦ *excl* Гóсподи!, о Бóже!
god [gɔd] *n* (*MYTHOLOGY, fig*) божествó*, бог*.
god-awful [gɔd'ɔːfəl] *adj* (*inf!*) жýткий*,
кошмáрный*.
godchild ['gɔdtʃaɪld] *n* крéстник(-ица).
goddam ['gɔddæm] *adj* (*inf!*) прокля́тый (*!*)
goddamned ['gɔddæmd] *adj* (*inf!*) прокля́тый.
goddaughter ['gɔddɔːtə'] *n* крéстница.
goddess ['gɔdɪs] *n* боги́ня.
godfather ['gɔdfɑːðə'] *n* крёстный отéц*.
God-fearing ['gɔdfɪərɪŋ] *adj* богобоя́зненный.

godforsaken ['gɔdfəseɪkən] *adj* забы́тый
Бóгом, забрóшенный*.
godmother ['gɔdmʌðə'] *n* крёстная мать* *f*.
godparent ['gɔdpɛərənt] *n* крёстный(-ая) *m(f)*
adj.
godsend ['gɔdsɛnd] *n* благодáть *f*.
godson ['gɔdsʌn] *n* крéстник.
goes [gəuz] *vb see* **go**.
gofer ['gəufə'] *n* (*inf*) мáльчик на побегýшках.
go-getter ['gəugɛtə'] *n* предприи́мчивый
человéк*.
goggle ['gɔgl] *vi* (*inf*): **to** ~ **at** тарáщиться
(вы́тарáщиться *perf*) на +*acc*.
goggles ['gɔglz] *npl* защи́тные очки́ *ntpl*.
going ['gəuɪŋ] *n* (*conditions*): **the** ~
обстоя́тельства *ntpl* ♦ *adj*: **the** ~ **rate**
существýющие расцéнки *fpl*; **this book is
heavy** ~ э́та кни́га трýдно читáется; **it was
hard** ~ поначáлу приходи́лось трýдно; **a** ~
concern дéйствующее предприя́тие.
going-over [gəuɪŋ'əuvə'] *n* (*inf: examination*)
осмóтр; (*physical attack*) трёпка.
goings-on ['gəuɪŋz'ɔn] *npl* (*inf*) делá *ntpl*.
go-kart ['gəukɑːt] *n* = **go-cart**.
gold [gəuld] *n* зóлото; (*SPORT: also:* ~ **medal**)
зóлото, золотáя медáль *f* ♦ *adj* золотóй; ~
reserves золотóй запáс.
golden ['gəuldən] *adj* (*made of gold*) золотóй;
(*gold in colour*) золоти́стый; (*opportunity,
future*) прекрáсный*.
golden age *n* золотóй век*.
golden handshake *n* (*BRIT*) дéнежное
вознаграждéние при ухóде на пéнсию.
golden rule *n* золотóе прáвило.
goldfish ['gəuldfɪʃ] *n* золотáя ры́бка*.
gold leaf *n* сусáльное зóлото.
gold medal *n* (*SPORT*) золотáя медáль *f*.
gold mine *n* золотóй при́иск *or* рудни́к*; (*fig*)
золотóе дно*.
gold-plated ['gəuld'pleɪtɪd] *adj* позолóченный.
goldsmith ['gəuldsmɪθ] *n* золоты́х дел
мáстер*.
gold standard *n* золотóй стандáрт.
golf [gɔlf] *n* гольф.
golf ball *n* мяч для игры́ в гольф; (*on
typewriter*) *металли́ческий шар с бýквами в
электри́ческой печáтной маши́нке*.
golf club *n* (*organization*) клуб люби́телей
игры́ в гольф; (*stick*) клю́шка* для игры́ в
гольф.
golf course *n* пóле для игры́ в гольф.
golfer ['gɔlfə'] *n* игрóк* в гольф.
golfing ['gɔlfɪŋ] *adj* для игры́ в гольф.
gondola ['gɔndələ'] *n* гондóла.
gondolier [gɔndə'lɪə'] *n* гондольéр.
gone [gɔn] *pp of* **go** ♦ *adj* уéхавший, ушéдший.
goner ['gɔnə'] *n* (*inf*) *n*: **I was a** ~ со мной бы́ло
всё покóнчено.
gong [gɔŋ] *n* гонг.
good [gud] *adj* хорóший*; (*pleasant*)
прия́тный*; (*kind*) дóбрый*; (*morally correct*)
прáвильный* ♦ *n* (*virtue*) добрó; (*benefit*)

по́льза; ~s npl (COMM) това́ры mpl; ~! хорошо́!; **to be ~ at** име́ть (impf) спосо́бности к +dat; **to be ~ for** (useful) быть* (impf) поле́зным(-ой) для +dat; **it's ~ for you** э́то Вам поле́зно (для здоро́вья); **it's a ~ thing you were there** хорошо́, что Вы бы́ли там; **she is ~ with children** она́ уме́ет обраща́ться с детьми́; **she is ~ with her hands** у неё золоты́е ру́ки; **to feel ~** чу́вствовать (impf) себя́ хорошо́; **it's ~ to see you** о́чень прия́тно Вас ви́деть; **would you be ~ enough to ...?** не бу́дете ли Вы так добры́ +perf infin ...?; **that's very ~ of you** э́то о́чень ми́ло с Ва́шей стороны́; **is this any ~?** (will it do?) э́то пойдёт?; (what's it like?) понра́вилось ли э́то Вам?; **a ~ deal (of)** большо́е коли́чество (+gen); **a ~ many мно́го** +gen; **to take a ~ look** смотре́ть* (посмотре́ть* perf) хороше́нько; **a ~ while ago** о́чень давно́; **to make ~** (damage) ремонти́ровать (отремонти́ровать perf); (loss) восполня́ть (воспо́лнить perf); **~ afternoon/evening!** до́брый день/ве́чер!; **~ morning!** до́брое у́тро!; **~ night!** (on leaving) до свида́ния!; (on going to bed) споко́йной or до́брой но́чи!; **he's up to no ~** он заду́мал что́-то (плохо́е); **for the common ~** для о́бщего бла́га; **it's no ~ complaining** что то́лку жа́ловаться; **for ~** навсегда́; **~s and chattels** ли́чные ве́щи*.

goodbye [gud'baɪ] excl до свида́ния; **to say ~ (to)** проща́ться (попроща́ться perf) (c +instr).

good-for-nothing ['gudfənʌθɪŋ] adj никчёмный*.

Good Friday n Страстна́я пя́тница.

good-humoured ['gud'hju:məd] (US **good-humored**) adj (person) добродушный*; (remark, joke) до́брый*.

good-looking ['gud'lukɪŋ] adj краси́вый.

good-natured ['gud'neɪtʃəd] adj (person) добродушный*; (pet) послу́шный; (discussion) споко́йный*.

goodness ['gudnɪs] n доброта́; **for ~ sake!** ра́ди Бо́га!; **~ gracious!** Го́споди!

goods train n (BRIT) това́рный по́езд*.

goodwill [gud'wɪl] n (of person) доброжела́тельность f; (COMM) прести́ж фи́рмы.

goody-goody ['gudɪgudɪ] n (pej) па́инька* m/f.

gooey ['gu:ɪ] (inf) adj ли́пкий* (ли́пок).

goose [gu:s] (pl **geese**) n (male) гусь* m; (female) гусы́ня.

gooseberry ['guzbərɪ] n крыжо́вник no pl; **he is playing ~** (BRIT) он тре́тий ли́шний.

goose flesh n = **goose pimples**.

goose pimples npl гуси́ная ко́жа fsg.

goose step n (MIL) гуси́ный шаг.

GOP n abbr (US: POL: inf: = Grand Old Party)

неофициа́льное назва́ние Республика́нской па́ртии США.

gopher ['gəufə'] n го́фер (колумби́йский су́слик).

gore [gɔ:'] vt бода́ть (забода́ть perf) ♦ n (запёкшаяся) кровь f.

gorge [gɔ:dʒ] n тесни́на, (у́зкое) ущелье* ♦ vt: **to ~ o.s. (on)** наеда́ться (нае́сться* perf) (+gen).

gorgeous ['gɔ:dʒəs] adj великоле́пный, прекра́сный.

gorilla [gə'rɪlə] n гори́лла.

gormless ['gɔ:mlɪs] adj (BRIT: inf) тупо́й*.

gorse [gɔ:s] n (BOT) утёсник.

gory ['gɔ:rɪ] adj (details) крова́вый; (situation) кровопроли́тный*.

go-slow ['gəu'sləu] n (BRIT) сниже́ние те́мпа рабо́ты (как вид забасто́вки).

gospel ['gɔspl] n (REL) ева́нгелие; (doctrine) про́поведь f.

gossamer ['gɔsəmə'] n (cobweb) паути́нка; (light fabric) газ.

gossip ['gɔsɪp] n (rumours) спле́тня*; (chat) разгово́ры mpl; (person) спле́тник(-ица) ♦ vi болта́ть (поболта́ть perf); **a piece of ~** спле́тня*, слух.

gossip column n коло́нка* све́тской хро́ники.

got [gɔt] pt, pp of **get**.

Gothic ['gɔθɪk] adj готи́ческий*.

gotten ['gɔtn] pp (US) of **get**.

gouge [gaudʒ] vt (also: **~ out**: hole etc) выда́лбливать (вы́долбить* perf); (: initials) выреза́ть (вы́резать* perf); **to ~ sb's eyes out** выка́лывать (вы́колоть perf) кому́-н глаза́.

gourd [guəd] n ты́ква.

gourmet ['guəmeɪ] n гурма́н.

gout [gaut] n (MED) пода́гра.

govern ['gʌvən] vt (country, also LING) управля́ть (impf) +instr; (event, conduct) руководи́ть* (impf) +instr.

governess ['gʌvənɪs] n гуверна́нтка*.

governing ['gʌvənɪŋ] adj (POL) пра́вящий*, руководя́щий*.

governing body n (of party) руководя́щий* о́рган; (of university) о́рган управле́ния.

government ['gʌvnmənt] n (act of governing) управле́ние; (governing body) прави́тельство ♦ cpd прави́тельственный; **local ~** ме́стное самоуправле́ние.

governmental [gʌvn'mɛntl] adj прави́тельственный.

government housing n (US) жили́щный ко́мплекс, постро́енный на госуда́рственные сре́дства.

government stock n прави́тельственные облига́ции и це́нные бума́ги.

governor ['gʌvənə'] n (of state, colony) губерна́тор; (of bank, school, hospital)

---

* marks translations which have irregular inflections. The Russian-English side of the dictionary gives inflectional information.

дире́ктор*; (*BRIT*: *of prison*) нача́льник.
Govt *abbr* = **government**.
gown [gaun] *n* (*dress*) пла́тье*; (*of teacher*: *BRIT*:
of judge) ма́нтия.
GP *n abbr* = **general practitioner**.
GPO *n abbr* (*BRIT*: *formerly*) = *General Post
Office*; (*US*) *Government Printing Office*.
gr. *abbr* (*COMM*) = **gross**.
grab [græb] *vt* (*seize, also fig*) хвата́ть
(схвати́ть* *perf*); (*food*) перехва́тывать
(перехвати́ть* *perf*); (*sleep*) урыва́ть (урва́ть*
perf) ♦ *vi*: **to ~ at** хвата́ться (ухвати́ться* *perf*)
за +*acc*.
grace [greɪs] *n* гра́ция; (*REL*) моли́тва (*пе́ред
едо́й*) ♦ *vt* (*honour*) удоста́ивать (удосто́ить
perf); (*adorn*) украша́ть (укра́сить* *perf*); **5
days' ~** 5 дней отсро́чки; **with (a) good ~**
любе́зно, с досто́инством; **with (a) bad ~**
нелюбе́зно, бех досто́инства; **his sense of
humour is his saving ~** его́ спаса́ет чу́вство
ю́мора; **to say ~** моли́ться* (помоли́ться*
perf) пе́ред едо́й.
graceful ['greɪsful] *adj* (*animal, person*)
грацио́зный*; (*style, shape*) изя́щный*;
(*refusal, behaviour*) досто́йный*.
gracious ['greɪʃəs] *adj* (*person, smile*)
любе́зный*; (*house*) прекра́сный*; (*living*)
краси́вый ♦ *excl*: **(good) ~!** Бо́же мой!
gradation [grə'deɪʃən] *n* града́ция.
grade [greɪd] *n* (*COMM*: *quality*) сорт*; (*in
hierarchy*) ра́нг; (*SCOL*: *mark*) оце́нка*; (*US*:
school year) класс; (: *gradient*) укло́н ♦ *vt*
(*rank, class*) распределя́ть (распредели́ть
perf); (*products*) сортирова́ть
(рассортирова́ть *perf*); **to make the ~** (*fig*)
добива́ться (доби́ться* *perf*) своего́ *or*
успе́ха.
grade crossing *n* (*US*) железнодоро́жный
перее́зд.
grade school *n* (*US*) нача́льная шко́ла.
gradient ['greɪdɪənt] *n* (*of hill*) укло́н; (*GEOM*)
градие́нт.
gradual ['grædjuəl] *adj* постепе́нный*.
gradually ['grædjuəlɪ] *adv* постепе́нно.
graduate [*n* 'grædjuɪt, *vi* 'grædjueɪt] *n*
выпускни́к*(-и́ца) ♦ *vi*: **to ~ from**
зака́нчивать (зако́нчить *perf*); **I ~d last year** я
зако́нчил университе́т в про́шлом году́.
graduated pension ['grædjueɪtɪd-] *n* пе́нсия,
*увели́чивающаяся в зави́симости от ста́жа
рабо́ты*.
graduation [grædju'eɪʃən] *n* (*ceremony*: *at
university*) церемо́ния вруче́ния дипло́ма; (:
US) ≈ церемо́ния вруче́ния аттеста́та.
graffiti [grə'fi:tɪ] *n, npl* графи́ти *nt ind*.
graft [grɑ:ft] *n* (*AGR*) приви́вка*; (*MED*)
переса́дка* (*ко́жи или ко́стной тка́ни*);
(*BRIT*: *inf*: *hard work*) тяжёлая рабо́та;
(*bribery*) взя́точничество ♦ *vt*: **to ~ (onto)**
(*AGR, also fig*) привива́ть (приви́ть* *perf*) (к
+*dat*); (*MED*) переса́живать (пересади́ть* *perf*)

(на +*acc*).
grain [greɪn] *n* (*seed*) зерно́*; (*no pl*: *cereals*)
хле́бные зла́ки *mpl*; (*US*: *corn*) зерно́; (*of
sand*) песчи́нка*; (*of salt*) крупи́ца; (*of wood*)
волокно́*; **however much it goes against the
~, I ...** (*fig*) как бы э́то ни противоре́чило
мои́м при́нципам, я ....
gram [græm] *n* гра́мм.
grammar ['græmə'] *n* грамма́тика; (*book*)
уче́бник грамма́тики.
grammar school *n* (*BRIT*) сре́дняя шко́ла (*для
одарённых дете́й*).
grammatical [grə'mætɪkl] *adj*
граммати́ческий*.
gramme [græm] *n* = **gram**.
gramophone ['græməfəun] *n* (*BRIT*)
граммофо́н.
granary ['grænərɪ] *n* амба́р; (*larger*)
зернохрани́лище.
Granary bread *or* **loaf®** *n* хлеб и́ли буха́нка из
*муки́ кру́пного помо́ла с це́лыми зёрнами
внутри́*.
grand [grænd] (*pl ~*) *adj* грандио́зный*;
(*gesture*) вели́чественный*; (*inf*: *wonderful*)
великоле́пный*, восхити́тельный* ♦ *n* (*inf*)
ты́сяча.
grandchild ['græntʃaɪld] (*pl ~ren*) *n*
внук(-у́чка*).
grandchildren ['græntʃɪldrən] *npl of* **grandchild**.
granddad ['grændæd] *n* (*inf*) де́душка* *m*.
granddaughter ['grændɔ:tə'] *n* вну́чка*.
grandeur ['grændjə'] *n* великоле́пие.
grandfather ['grændfɑ:ðə'] *n* де́душка* *m*.
grandiose ['grændɪəus] *adj* грандио́зный*.
grand jury *n* (*US*) прися́жные, реша́ющие
вопро́с о преда́нии суду́.
grandma ['grænmɑ:] *n* (*inf*) ба́бушка*.
grandmother ['grænmʌðə'] *n* (*inf*) ба́бушка*.
grandpa ['grænpɑ:] *n* (*inf*) = **granddad**.
grandparents ['grændpɛərənts] *npl* де́душка* *m*
и ба́бушка*.
grand piano *n* роя́ль *m*.
Grand Prix ['grɑ:'pri:] *n* гран-при́ *m ind*.
grandson ['grænsʌn] *n* внук.
grandstand ['grændstænd] *n* (*SPORT*)
центра́льная трибу́на.
grand total *n* о́бщая су́мма.
granite ['grænɪt] *n* грани́т.
granny ['grænɪ] *n* (*inf*) ба́бушка*.
grant [grɑ:nt] *vt* (*money, visa*) выдава́ть*
(вы́дать* *perf*); (*pension*) назнача́ть
(назна́чить *perf*); (*request*) удовлетворя́ть
(удовлетвори́ть *perf*); (*admit*) признава́ть*
(призна́ть* *perf*) ♦ *n* (*SCOL*) стипе́ндия;
(*ADMIN*) субси́дия; **to take sb/sth for ~ed**
принима́ть (приня́ть* *perf*) кого́-н/что́-н как
до́лжное; **to ~ that** признава́ть* (призна́ть*
perf), что.
granulated sugar ['grænjuleɪtɪd-] *n* са́харный
песо́к*.
granule ['grænju:l] *n* (*of coffee*) гра́нула; (*of

salt) крупи́ца.

grape [greɪp] *n* виногра́д* *no pl*; **a bunch of** ~**s** кисть* *f or* гроздь* *f* виногра́да.

grapefruit ['greɪpfruːt] (*pl* ~ *or* ~**s**) *n* грейпфру́т.

grapevine ['greɪpvaɪn] *n* виногра́дная лоза́*; **I heard on the** ~ **that** ... я слы́шал, что ..., говоря́т, что ....

graph [grɑːf] *n* (*diagram*) гра́фик.

graphic ['græfɪk] *adj* (*account, description*) я́ркий*; (*design*) изобрази́тельный; ~ **art** гра́фика; *see also* **graphics**.

graphic designer *n* худо́жник-оформи́тель *m*.

graphic equalizer *n* графи́ческий* выра́вниватель *m*.

graphics ['græfɪks] *n* гра́фика ♦ *npl* рису́нки *mpl*.

graphite ['græfaɪt] *n* графи́т.

graph paper *n* миллиметро́вка.

grapple ['græpl] *vi*: **to** ~ **with sb** схва́тываться (схвати́ться* *perf*) с кем-н; **to** ~ **with a problem** би́ться* (*impf*) над пробле́мой.

grasp [grɑːsp] *vt* (*also fig*) схва́тывать (схвати́ть* *perf*) ♦ *n* (*grip*) хва́тка; (*understanding*) понима́ние; **the vase slipped from my** ~ ва́за вы́скользнула из мои́х рук; **success was now within his** ~ успе́х был тепе́рь в его́ рука́х; **to have a good** ~ **of sth** (*fig*) хорошо́ разбира́ться (*impf*) в чём-н

▸ **grasp at** *vt fus* (*rope etc*) хвата́ться (ухвати́ться* *perf*) за +*acc*; (*fig: opportunity*) цепля́ться (уцепи́ться* *perf*) за +*acc*.

grasping ['grɑːspɪŋ] *adj* (*greedy*) жа́дный*.

grass [grɑːs] *n* трава́*; (*lawn*) газо́н; (*BRIT: inf: informer*) стука́ч*; (: *ex-terrorist*) доно́счик.

grasshopper ['grɑːshɔpəʳ] *n* кузне́чик.

grass-roots ['grɑːsruːts] *adj* (*support*) низово́й; (*member*) рядово́й.

grass snake *n* уж*.

grassy ['grɑːsɪ] *adj* (*bank, slope*) травяни́стый.

grate [greɪt] *n* ками́нная решётка* ♦ *vt* (*CULIN*) тере́ть* (натере́ть* *perf*) ♦ *vi* (*metal, chalk*): **to** ~ (**on**) скрипе́ть* (*impf*) (по +*dat*).

grateful ['greɪtful] *adj* (*person*) благода́рный* (благода́рен); ~ **thanks** и́скренняя благода́рность.

gratefully ['greɪtfəlɪ] *adv* благода́рно.

grater ['greɪtəʳ] *n* тёрка*.

gratification [grætɪfɪ'keɪʃən] *n* удовлетворе́ние.

gratify ['grætɪfaɪ] *vt* (*person*) ра́довать (пора́довать *perf*); (*whim, desire*) удовлетворя́ть (удовлетвори́ть *perf*).

gratifying ['grætɪfaɪŋ] *adj* (*pleasing*) прия́тный* (прия́тен).

grating ['greɪtɪŋ] *n* решётка* ♦ *adj* (*noise*) ре́зкий*.

gratitude ['grætɪtjuːd] *n* благода́рность *f*.

gratuitous [grə'tjuːɪtəs] *adj* (*violence, cruelty*) бессмы́сленный* (бессмы́слен).

gratuity [grə'tjuːɪtɪ] *n* (*tip*) чаевы́е *pl adj*.

grave [greɪv] *n* моги́ла ♦ *adj* серьёзный* (серьёзен); (*mistake*) роково́й.

grave digger *n* моги́льщик.

gravel ['grævl] *n* гра́вий.

gravely ['greɪvlɪ] *adv* серьёзно; ~ **ill** тяжело́ больно́й* (бо́лен).

gravestone ['greɪvstəun] *n* надгро́бие.

graveyard ['greɪvjɑːd] *n* кла́дбище.

gravitas ['grævitæs] *n* многозначи́тельность *f*.

gravitate ['grævɪteɪt] *vi*: **to** ~ **towards** стреми́ться* (*impf*) *or* тяну́ться* (*impf*) к +*dat*.

gravity ['grævɪtɪ] *n* (*PHYS*) си́ла тя́жести; (*seriousness*) серьёзность *f*.

gravy ['greɪvɪ] *n* (*meat juices*) подли́вка; (*sauce*) со́ус*.

gravy boat *n* со́усник.

gravy train *n* (*inf*): **to ride the** ~ ~ име́ть (*impf*) лёгкий за́работок.

gray [greɪ] *adj* (*US*) = **grey**.

graze [greɪz] *vi* пасти́сь* (*impf*) ♦ *vt* (*touch lightly*) задева́ть (заде́ть* *perf*); (*scrape*) цара́пать (оцара́пать *perf*) ♦ *n* цара́пина.

grazing ['greɪzɪŋ] *n* (*pasture*) па́стбище.

grease [griːs] *n* (*lubricant*) сма́зка*; (*fat*) жир* ♦ *vt* сма́зывать (сма́зать* *perf*); **to** ~ **sb's palm** (*fig*) дава́ть* (дать* *perf*) кому́-н взя́тку.

grease gun *n* сма́зочный шприц.

greasepaint ['griːspeɪnt] *n* (театра́льный) грим.

greaseproof paper ['griːspruːf-] *n* (*BRIT*) жиронепроница́емая бума́га.

greasy ['griːsɪ] *adj* жи́рный*; (*clothes*) заса́ленный* (заса́лен); (*BRIT: road, surface*) ско́льзкий*.

great [greɪt] *adj* (*large*) большо́й*; (*heat, pain*) си́льный*; (*city*) знамени́тый; (*man*) вели́кий*, знамени́тый; (*inf: terrific*) замеча́тельный*; **they're** ~ **friends** они́ больши́е друзья́*; **we had a** ~ **time** мы замеча́тельно провели́ вре́мя; **it was** ~! э́то бы́ло замеча́тельно *or* здо́рово!; **the** ~ **thing is that** ... са́мое гла́вное то, что ....

Great Barrier Reef *n*: **the** ~ ~ ~ Большо́й Барье́рный риф.

Great Britain *n* Великобрита́ния.

greater ['greɪtəʳ] *adj*: ~ **Calcutta** больша́я Калькутта; **G**~ **Manchester** большо́й Манче́стер.

great-grandchild [greɪt'græntʃaɪld] (*pl* ~**ren**) *n* пра́внук*(-учка).

great-grandchildren [greɪt'græntʃɪldrən] *npl of* **great-grandchild**.

great-grandfather [greɪt'grænfɑːðəʳ] *n* праде́душка* *m*.

great-grandmother [greɪt'grænmʌðəʳ] *n*

прабабушка*.

Great Lakes npl: **the** ~~ Большие Озёра ntpl.

greatly ['greɪtlɪ] adv очень; (influenced) в значительной степени.

greatness ['greɪtnɪs] n (importance) величие.

Grecian ['gri:ʃən] adj греческий*.

Greece [gri:s] n Греция.

greed [gri:d] n (greediness) жадность f; (for power, wealth) жажда.

greedily ['gri:dɪlɪ] adv жадно.

greedy ['gri:dɪ] adj жадный* (жаден).

Greek [gri:k] adj греческий ♦ n (person) грек (гречанка*); (LING) греческий* язык*; **ancient/modern** ~ древнегреческий*/современный греческий* язык*.

green [gri:n] adj зелёный ♦ n (colour) зелёный цвет; (stretch of grass) лужайка*; (on golf course) площадка вокруг лунки, покрытая травой; (also: village ~) газон в центре деревни; ~**s** npl (vegetables) овощи mpl; (POL) :the G~s зелёные pl adj; the G~ Party партия зелёных; he has ~ fingers or (US) a ~ thumb (fig) что он ни посадит, всё у него растёт; to give sb the ~ light давать* (дать* perf) кому-н зелёную улицу.

green belt n (round town) зелёная зона, зелёный пояс*.

green card n (BRIT: AUT) зелёная карточка (для страховки автомобиля за рубежом); (US: ADMIN) зелёная карточка (необходимая для трудоустройства).

greenery ['gri:nərɪ] n зелень f.

greenfly ['gri:nflaɪ] n (BRIT) тля.

greengage ['gri:ngeɪdʒ] n слива-венчерка.

greengrocer ['gri:ngrəusə'] n (BRIT) зеленщик* (продавец овощей и фруктов).

greenhouse ['gri:nhaus] n теплица.

greenhouse effect n: **the** ~~ парниковый эффект.

greenhouse gas n один из газов, вызывающий тепличный эффект.

greenish ['gri:nɪʃ] adj зеленоватый.

Greenland ['gri:nlənd] n Гренландия.

Greenlander ['gri:nləndə'] n житель(ница) m(f) Гренландии.

green pepper n зелёный перец*.

greet [gri:t] vt (person) приветствовать* (поприветствовать perf), здороваться (поздороваться perf); (receive: news) встречать (встретить* perf).

greeting ['gri:tɪŋ] n (welcome) приветствие; **Christmas/birthday** ~**s** поздравляю с Рождеством/с днём рождения; **Season's** ~**s** поздравляю с Рождеством и Новым годом.

greeting(s) card n поздравительная открытка*.

gregarious [grə'gɛərɪəs] adj общительный* (общителен).

Grenada [grə'neɪdə] n Гренада.

grenade [grə'neɪd] n (also: hand ~) граната.

grew [gru:] pt of **grow**.

grey [greɪ] (US **gray**) adj серый* (сер); (hair) седой; (dismal) мрачный* (мрачен); to go ~ седеть (поседеть perf).

grey-haired [greɪ'hɛəd] adj седой*.

greyhound ['greɪhaund] n борзая f adj.

grid [grɪd] n (pattern) сетка*, сеть f; (grating) решётка*; (ELEC) энергосистема; (US: AUT) решётка радиатора.

griddle [grɪdl] n (on cooker) плоский металлический диск, используемый как сковорода.

gridiron ['grɪdaɪən] n решётка гриля.

gridlock ['grɪdlɔk] n (US: of traffic etc) затор.

grief [gri:f] n горе; **to come to** ~ (plan) рушиться (рухнуть perf); (person) терпеть* (потерпеть* perf) неудачу; **good** ~! Боже мой!

grievance ['gri:vəns] n (complaint) жалоба.

grieve [gri:v] vi горевать* (impf) ♦ vt огорчать (огорчить perf); **to** ~ **for** горевать (impf) о +prp.

grievous ['gri:vəs] adj (mistake, injury) серьёзный*; (shock) сильный.

grievous bodily harm n (LAW) тяжёлые телесные повреждения ntpl.

grill [grɪl] n (on cooker) гриль m; (grilled food: also: **mixed** ~) жаренные на гриле продукты mpl; (restaurant) = **grillroom** ♦ vt (BRIT) жарить (пожарить perf) (на гриле); (inf: question) допрашивать (допросить* perf) с пристрастием.

grille [grɪl] n решётка*; (AUT) решётка радиатора.

grillroom ['grɪlrum] n ≈ гриль-бар.

grim [grɪm] adj (place, person) мрачный* (мрачен); (situation) тяжёлый* (тяжёл).

grimace [grɪ'meɪs] n гримаса ♦ vi гримасничать (impf).

grime [graɪm] n (from soot, smoke) копоть f; (from mud) грязь f.

grimy ['graɪmɪ] adj (dirty) грязный* (грязен).

grin [grɪn] n ухмылка* ♦ vi: **to** ~ (**at**) (широко) улыбаться (улыбнуться perf) (+dat).

grind [graɪnd] (pt, pp **ground**) vt (coffee, pepper etc) молоть (смолоть* perf); (US: meat) пропускать (пропустить* perf) через мясорубку; (make sharp: knife etc) точить* (наточить* perf); (polish: gem, lens) шлифовать (отшлифовать perf) ♦ vi (car gears) скрежетать* (impf) ♦ n (work) изнурительная работа; **to** ~ **one's teeth** скрежетать* (impf) зубами; **to** ~ **one's heel into the ground** вдавливать (вдавить* perf) каблук в землю; **to** ~ **to a halt** (vehicle) останавливаться (остановиться* perf) с лязгом; (fig) застопориться (perf); **the daily** ~ (inf) рутина будней.

grinder ['graɪndə'] n (for coffee) кофемолка*; (for waste disposal etc) дробилка*.

grindstone ['graɪndstəun] n: **to keep one's nose**

to the ~ рабо́тать *(impf)* без переды́шки.
grip [grɪp] *n* (*of person*) хва́тка; (: *control,
grasp*) схва́тывание; (*of tyre*) сцепле́ние;
(*handle*) ру́чка*; (*holdall*) доро́жная су́мка* ◆
vt (*object*) схва́тывать (схвати́ть* *perf*);
(*audience, attention*) захва́тывать
(захвати́ть* *perf*); **to come to** ~**s with**
(*problem, difficulty*) бра́ться* (взя́ться* *perf*)
за реше́ние +*gen*; **to** ~ **the road** (*car*) име́ть
(impf) хоро́шее сцепле́ние с доро́гой; **to lose
one's** ~ (*tyres*) стира́ться (стере́ться* *perf*);
(*shoes*) изна́шиваться (износи́ться* *perf*);
(*fig*) теря́ть (потеря́ть *perf*) хва́тку.
gripe [graɪp] *n* (*inf: complaint*) жа́лоба ◆ *vi* (*inf*)
ворча́ть *(impf)*; **the** ~**s** (*MED*) ко́лики *pl*.
gripping ['grɪpɪŋ] *adj* захва́тывающий*.
grisly ['grɪzlɪ] *adj* ужа́сный*.
grist [grɪst] *n* (*fig*): **it's all** ~ **to the mill** э́то
принесёт по́льзу.
gristle ['grɪsl] *n* (*on meat*) хрящ*.
grit [grɪt] *n* (*sand*) песо́к*; (*stone*) гра́вий;
(*determination, courage*) вы́держка ◆ *vt* (*road*)
посыпа́ть (посы́пать* *perf*) гра́вием; ~ *npl*
(*US*) дроблёная кукуру́за *fsg*; **to** ~ **one's teeth**
сти́скивать (сти́снуть *perf*) зу́бы; **I've got a
piece of** ~ **in my eye** мне в глаз попа́ла
сори́нка.
grizzle ['grɪzl] *vi* (*BRIT*) хны́кать* *(impf)*.
grizzly ['grɪzlɪ] *n* (*also:* ~ **bear**) гри́зли *m ind*.
groan [grəʊn] *n* (*of person*) стон ◆ *vi* (*person: in
pain*) стона́ть* *(impf)*; (: *in disapproval*) тяжело́
вздыха́ть (вздохну́ть *perf*); (*tree, floorboard*)
скрипе́ть *(impf)*.
grocer ['grəʊsə'] *n* бакале́йщик.
groceries ['grəʊsərɪz] *npl* бакале́я *fsg*.
grocer's (shop) *n* бакале́йный магази́н.
grog [grɔg] *n* (*drink*) грог*.
groggy ['grɔgɪ] *adj*: **I feel** ~ у меня́
подка́шиваются но́ги.
groin [grɔɪn] *n* пах*.
groom [gruːm] *n* (*for horse*) ко́нюх; (*also:
bridegroom*) жени́х* ◆ *vt* (*horse*) уха́живать
(impf) за +*instr*; (*fig*): **to** ~ **sb for** (*job*)
гото́вить* (пригото́вить* *perf*) кого́-н к +*dat*;
well-~**ed** (*person*) ухо́женный* (ухо́жен).
groove [gruːv] *n* желобо́к*; (*habit*) рути́на.
grope [grəʊp] *vi*: **to** ~ **for** иска́ть* *(impf)*
о́щупью; (*fig*) нащу́пывать *(impf)*; **to** ~ **one's
way to** дви́гаться *(impf)* о́щупью к +*dat*.
gross [grəʊs] *adj* (*vulgar*) вульга́рный*;
(*flagrant: neglect, injustice*) вопию́щий*;
(*COMM: income*) валово́й ◆ *n inv* (*twelve
dozen*) гросс (*12 дю́жин*) ◆ (*COMM*): **to** ~
£500,000 получа́ть (получи́ть* *perf*) о́бщую
при́быль в £500.000; ~ **weight** вес бру́тто.
gross domestic product *n* валово́й
вну́тренний* проду́кт.
grossly ['grəʊslɪ] *adv* (*greatly*) чрезме́рно.

gross national product *n* валово́й
национа́льный проду́кт.
gross profit *n* валова́я при́быль *f*.
gross sales *npl* валово́й объём *msg* прода́жи.
grotesque [grə'tɛsk] *adj* гроте́скный*.
grotto ['grɔtəʊ] *n* грот.
grotty ['grɔtɪ] *adj* (*inf: dreadful*) парши́вый
(парши́в).
grouch [graʊtʃ] (*inf*) *vi* брюзжа́ть *(impf)* ◆ *n*
(*person*) брюзга́ *m/f*.
ground [graʊnd] *pt, pp of* **grind** ◆ *n* (*earth, land*)
земля́*; (*floor*) пол; (*SPORT*) по́ле; (*US: also:* ~
wire) заземле́ние; (*reason: usu pl*) основа́ние
◆ *vt* (*US: ELEC*) заземля́ть (заземли́ть *perf*) ◆
adj (*coffee etc*) мо́лотый ◆ *vi* (*ship*) сади́ться*
(сесть* *perf*) на мель; ~**s** *npl* (*of coffee*) гу́ща
fsg; **school** ~**s** пришко́льный уча́сток*; **sports**
~ спорти́вная площа́дка*; **on the** ~ на
земле́; **to the** ~ (*burnt*) дотла́; **below** ~ под
землёй; **to gain** ~ продвига́ться
(продви́нуться *perf*) вперёд; **to lose** ~
отступа́ть (отступи́ть* *perf*); **common** ~
вопро́с, в кото́ром спо́рящие сто́роны
схо́дятся; **on the** ~**s that** на том основа́нии,
что; **the plane was** ~**ed by the fog** самолёт не
мог подня́ться в во́здух из-за тума́на.
ground cloth *n* (*US*) = **groundsheet**.
ground control *n* (*AVIAT, SPACE*) слу́жбы *fpl*
назе́много контро́ля *or* управле́ния.
ground floor *n* пе́рвый эта́ж*.
grounding ['graʊndɪŋ] *n* (*in education*)
подгото́вка.
groundless ['graʊndlɪs] *adj* беспо́чвенный*,
необосно́ванный*.
groundnut ['graʊndnʌt] *n* земляно́й оре́х.
ground rent *n* (*BRIT*) земе́льная ре́нта.
ground rule *n* основно́е пра́вило.
groundsheet ['graʊndʃiːt] *n* (*BRIT*)
водонепроница́емая ткань *f* (*испо́льзуемая
в похо́дах для подкла́дки под спа́льные
мешки́*).
groundskeeper ['graʊndzkiːpə'] *n* (*US*) =
groundsman.
groundsman ['graʊndzmən] *irreg n* (*SPORT*)
слу́жащий стадио́на и́ли па́рка
подде́рживающий поря́док.
ground staff *n* (*AVIAT*) назе́мный персона́л.
ground swell *n*: ~ ~ **of opinion (against)**
нараста́ющее чу́вство проте́ста (про́тив
+*gen*).
ground-to-air ['graʊntu'ɛə'] *adj*
противовозду́шный.
ground-to-ground ['graʊntə'graʊnd] *adj*: ~
missile управля́емая раке́та кла́сса
„земля́-земля́“.
groundwork ['graʊndwəːk] *n* (*preparation*)
фунда́мент, осно́ва.
group [gruːp] *n* гру́ппа ◆ *vt* (*also:* ~ **together**:

---

people, things etc) группирова́ть
(сгруппирова́ть *perf*) ◆ *vi* (*also*: ~ **together**)
группирова́ться (сгруппирова́ться *perf*).
groupie ['gru:pɪ] *n* деви́ца из антура́жа (*поп-группы, певца́ итп*).
group therapy *n* группова́я терапи́я.
grouse [graus] *n inv* (*bird*) (шотла́ндская)
куропа́тка* ◆ *vi* (*complain*) ворча́ть (*impf*).
grove [grəuv] *n* ро́ща.
grovel ['grɒvl] *vi* (*crawl*) по́лзать (*impf*); (*fig*): **to**
~ **(before)** заи́скивать (*impf*) (пе́ред +*instr*).
grow [grəu] (*pt* **grew**, *pp* **grown**) *vi* расти́*
(вы́расти* *perf*); (*increase*) увели́чиваться
(увели́читься *perf*); (*become*): **to** ~ **rich/weak**
станови́ться* (стать* *perf*) бога́тым(-ой)/
сла́бым(-ой) ◆ *vt* (*roses, vegetables*)
выра́щивать (вы́растить* *perf*); (*beard, hair*)
отра́щивать (отрасти́ть* *perf*); **to** ~ **(out of** *or*
from) (*city, society*) выраста́ть (вы́расти* *perf*)
(из +*gen*); (*idea, plan*) возника́ть (возни́кнуть
perf) (из +*gen*); **to** ~ **tired of waiting** устава́ть*
(уста́ть* *perf*) от ожида́ния
▶ **grow apart** *vi* (*fig*) отдаля́ться (отдали́ться
perf) друг от дру́га
▶ **grow away from** *vt fus* (*fig*) отдаля́ться
(отдали́ться *perf*) от +*gen*
▶ **grow on** *vt fus*: **that painting is** ~**ing on me** э́та
карти́на нра́вится мне всё бо́льше
▶ **grow out of** *vt fus* (*clothes*) выраста́ть
(вы́расти* *perf*) из +*gen*; (*habit*) перераста́ть
(перерасти́* *perf*); **he'll** ~ **out of it** он
перерастёт э́то
▶ **grow up** *vi* (*child*) расти́* (вы́расти* *perf*),
взросле́ть (повзросле́ть *perf*); (*develop: idea,
friendship*) возника́ть (возни́кнуть *perf*).
grower ['grəuə'] *n* (*BOT*) садово́д; **lily/rose** ~
садово́д, разводя́щий ли́лии/ро́зы.
growing ['grəuɪŋ] *adj* (*increasing*) расту́щий; ~
pains (*MED*) невралги́ческие и́ли
ревмати́ческие бо́ли в де́тском во́зрасте;
(*fig*) боле́знь *f* ро́ста.
growl [graul] *vi* (*dog*) рыча́ть (зарыча́ть *perf*);
(*person*) рыча́ть (прорыча́ть *perf*).
grown [grəun] *pp* of **grow**.
grown-up [grəun'ʌp] *n* (*adult*) взро́слый(-ая)
m(f) adj ◆ *adj* (*son, daughter*) взро́слый.
growth [grəuθ] *n* (*development*) рост;
(*increase*) приро́ст; (*of weeds*) за́росли *fpl*; (*of
beard*) щети́на; (*MED*) о́пухоль *f*.
growth rate *n* темп ро́ста.
grub [grʌb] *n* (*larva*) личи́нка*; (*inf: food*)
жратва́ ◆ *vi*: **to** ~ **about** *or* **around (for)**
ры́ться* (*impf*) (в по́исках +*gen*).
grubby ['grʌbɪ] *adj* (*also fig*) гря́зный* (гря́зен).
grudge [grʌdʒ] *n* (*grievance*) недово́льство ◆
vt: **to** ~ **sb sth** жале́ть (пожале́ть *perf*) что-н
для кого́-н; **to bear sb a** ~ быть* (*impf*) на
кого́-н в оби́де.
grudging ['grʌdʒɪŋ] *adj* (*respect, silence*)
вы́нужденный; (*praise*) скупо́й.
grudgingly ['grʌdʒɪŋlɪ] *adv* неохо́тно.

gruelling ['gruəlɪŋ] (*US* **grueling**) *adj*
изнури́тельный* (изнури́телен), тяжёлый*
(тяжёл).
gruesome ['gru:səm] *adj* (*tale, scene*) жу́ткий*.
gruff [grʌf] *adj* (*voice*) хри́плый* (хрипл);
(*manner*) ре́зкий* (ре́зок).
grumble ['grʌmbl] *vi* ворча́ть (*impf*).
grumpy ['grʌmpɪ] *adj* сварли́вый (сварли́в).
grunge [grʌndʒ] *n* стиль *m* грюндж.
grunt [grʌnt] *vi* (*pig*) хрю́кать (хрю́кнуть *perf*);
(*person*) бурча́ть (бу́ркнуть *perf*) ◆ *n* (*see vb*)
хрю́канье; бурча́ние.
G-string ['dʒi:strɪŋ] *n* (*garment*) тип
откры́тых пла́вок.
GSUSA *n abbr* (= Girl Scouts of the United States
of America) организа́ция де́вочек-ска́утов
США.
GT *abbr* (*AUT*: = gran turismo) дорого́й
двухме́стный закры́тый автомоби́ль.
GU *abbr* (*US: POST*) = Guam.
guarantee [gærən'ti:] *n* (*assurance*)
поручи́тельство; (*COMM: warranty*) гара́нтия
◆ *vt* гаранти́ровать (*impf/perf*); **he can't** ~
(that) he'll come он не мо́жет поручи́ться за
то, что он придёт.
guarantor [gærən'tɔ:'] *n* (*COMM*) поручи́тель
(ница) *m(f)*.
guard [ga:d] *n* (*one person*) часово́й,
охра́нник; (*squad*) охра́на; (*MIL*) карау́л;
(*BOXING, FENCING*) оборони́тельная сто́йка;
(*BRIT: RAIL*) проводни́к*(-и́ца); (*on machine*)
предохрани́тельное устро́йство; (*also*:
fireguard) предохрани́тельная решётка*
(пе́ред ками́ном) ◆ *vt* (*prisoner*) охраня́ть
(*impf*); (*secret*) храни́ть (сохрани́ть *perf*);
(*place, person*): **to** ~ **(against)** охраня́ть (*impf*)
(от +*gen*); **to be on one's** ~ быть* (*impf*)
насторожé *or* начекý
▶ **guard against** *vt fus* (*prevent: disease,
damage etc*) предохраня́ть (*impf*) от +*gen*.
guard dog *n* сторожева́я соба́ка.
guarded ['ga:dɪd] *adj* (*statement, reply*)
осторо́жный* (осторо́жен).
guardian ['ga:dɪən] *n* (*LAW: of minor*) опеку́н*;
(*defender*) защи́тник(-ица).
guardrail ['ga:dreɪl] *n* пери́ла *pl*.
guard's van *n* (*BRIT: RAIL*) бага́жный ваго́н.
Guatemala [gwa:tɪ'ma:lə] *n* Гватема́ла.
Guatemalan [gwa:tɪ'ma:lən] *adj*
гватема́льский.
Guernsey ['gə:nzɪ] *n* Ге́рнси.
guerrilla [gə'rɪlə] *n* партиза́н*(ка*).
guerrilla warfare *n* партиза́нская война́*.
guess [gɛs] *vt* (*estimate: number etc*) счита́ть
(подсчита́ть *perf*) приблизи́тельно;
(: *distance*) рассчи́тывать (рассчита́ть *perf*)
приблизи́тельно; (*correct answer*)
уга́дывать (угада́ть *perf*) ◆ *vi* дога́дываться
(*impf*) *n* (*attempt at correct answer*) дога́дка;
to take *or* **have a** ~ отга́дывать (отгада́ть
perf); **my** ~ **is that ...** мне сдаётся, что́ ...; **I** ~ ...

(US) мне ка́жется ...; **I ~ you're right** Вы, наве́рное, пра́вы; **to keep sb ~ing** держа́ть* (impf) кого́-н в неве́дении.

guesstimate ['gɛstɪmɪt] n (inf) прики́дка.

guesswork ['gɛswə:k] n (speculation) дога́дки fpl, предположе́ния ntpl; **I got the answer by ~** я угада́л отве́т.

guest [gɛst] n (visitor) гость*(я) m(f); (in hotel) постоя́лец*, прожива́ющий(-ая) m(f) adj; **be my ~** (inf) пожа́луйста.

guesthouse ['gɛsthaus] n пансио́н.

guest room n ко́мната для госте́й.

guff [gʌf] n (inf) трёп.

guffaw [gʌˈfɔ:] vi гогота́ть* (impf) ◆ n го́гот.

guidance ['gaɪdəns] n (advice) сове́т; **under the ~ of** с по́мощью +gen, под руково́дством +gen; **vocational ~** сове́т по профориента́ции; **marriage ~** сове́т по вопро́сам семьи́ и бра́ка.

guide [gaɪd] n (in museum, on tour) гид, экскурсово́д; (mountain guide) проводни́к*; (also: ~**book**) путеводи́тель m; (handbook) руково́дство; (BRIT: also: **Girl G~**) де́вочка*-ска́ут f ◆ vt (show around) води́ть* (impf), вести́* (провести́* perf); (direct) направля́ть (напра́вить* perf); **to be ~d by sb/sth** (fig) руково́дствоваться (impf) чьим-н сове́том/чем-н.

guidebook ['gaɪdbuk] n путеводи́тель m.

guided missile n управля́емая раке́та.

guide dog n соба́ка-поводы́рь* f.

guidelines ['gaɪdlaɪnz] npl директи́ва fsg.

guild [gɪld] n ассоциа́ция; (HISTORY) ги́льдия.

guildhall ['gɪldhɔ:l] n (BRIT: in London): **the G~** Ги́льдхолл (зда́ние ра́туши ло́ндонского Си́ти).

guile [gaɪl] n хи́трость f.

guileless ['gaɪlɪs] adj бесхи́тростный*.

guillotine ['gɪləti:n] n гильоти́на; (for paper) ре́зальная маши́на.

guilt [gɪlt] n (remorse) вина́; (culpability) вино́вность f.

guilty ['gɪltɪ] adj (person, expression) винова́тый; (of crime) вино́вный*; (secret) позо́рный*; **to plead ~/not guilty** признава́ть* (призна́ть* perf) себя́ вино́вным(-ой)/невино́вным(-ой); **to feel ~ about sth** чу́вствовать (impf) себя́ винова́тым(-ой) в чём-н.

Guinea ['gɪnɪ] n: **Republic of ~** Гвине́я.

guinea ['gɪnɪ] n (BRIT) гине́я.

guinea pig n (animal) морска́я сви́нка*; (fig) „подо́пытный кро́лик".

guise [gaɪz] n: **in** or **under the ~ of** под ви́дом +gen.

guitar [gɪˈtɑːˈ] n гита́ра.

guitarist [gɪˈtɑːrɪst] n гитари́ст(ка).

gulch [gʌltʃ] n (US) (у́зкое) уще́лье*.

gulf [gʌlf] n (GEO) зали́в; (also fig) про́пасть f; **the (Persian) G~** Перси́дский* зали́в.

Gulf States npl: **the ~ ~** стра́ны fpl Перси́дского зали́ва.

Gulf Stream n: **the ~ ~** Гольфстри́м.

gull [gʌl] n ча́йка*.

gullet ['gʌlɪt] n пищево́д.

gullibility [gʌlɪˈbɪlɪtɪ] n легкове́рие.

gullible ['gʌlɪbl] adj (naive, trusting) легкове́рный* (легкове́рен).

gully ['gʌlɪ] n (ravine) глубо́кий* овра́г.

gulp [gʌlp] vi (swallow: from nerves, excitement) сгла́тывать (сглотну́ть perf) не́рвно ◆ vt (also: ~ **down**: food, drink) прогла́тывать (проглоти́ть* perf) ◆ n: **to drink at one ~** вы́пить* (perf) за́лпом.

gum [gʌm] n (ANAT) десна́*; (glue) клей*; (sweet: also: ~**drop**) желе́йный мармела́д (конфе́та); (also: **chewing ~**) жева́тельная рези́нка*, жва́чка* (разг) ◆ vt (stick): **to ~ (together)** скле́ивать (скле́ить perf)

▶ **gum up** vt: **to ~ up the works** (inf) засто́порить (perf) рабо́ту.

gumboots ['gʌmbu:ts] npl (BRIT) рези́новые сапоги́* mpl.

gumption ['gʌmpʃən] n (sense, wit) сообрази́тельность f, нахо́дчивость f.

gumtree ['gʌmtri:] n: **to be up a ~** (fig: inf) попада́ть (попа́сть* perf) впроса́к.

gun [gʌn] n (revolver, pistol) пистоле́т; (rifle, airgun) ружьё*; (cannon) пу́шка* ◆ vt (also: ~ **down**) расстре́ливать (расстреля́ть perf), застрели́ть* (perf); **to stick to one's ~s** (fig) не скла́дывать (сложи́ть* perf) ору́жия.

gunboat ['gʌnbəut] n каноне́рская ло́дка*.

gun dog n охо́тничья соба́ка.

gunfire ['gʌnfaɪəˈ] n оруди́йный ого́нь* m.

gung ho [gʌŋ həu] adj (inf) безрассу́дный*, фанати́чный.

gunk [gʌŋk] n (inf) га́дость f.

gunman ['gʌnmən] irreg n вооружённый банди́т*.

gunner ['gʌnəˈ] n (MIL) артиллери́ст.

gunpoint ['gʌnpɔɪnt] n: **at ~** под ду́лом пистоле́та, под прице́лом.

gunpowder ['gʌnpaudəˈ] n по́рох*.

gunrunner ['gʌnrʌnəˈ] n контрабанди́ст, торгу́ющий ору́жием.

gunrunning ['gʌnrʌnɪŋ] n контраба́нда ору́жием.

gunshot ['gʌnʃɔt] n вы́стрел.

gunsmith ['gʌnsmɪθ] n оруже́йный ма́стер*.

gurgle ['gə:gl] vi (baby) гу́кать (impf); (water) журча́ть (impf).

guru ['guru:] n (REL) гуру́ m ind; (fig) духо́вный наста́вник.

gush [gʌʃ] vi хлы́нуть (perf); (enthuse) захлёбываться (захлебну́ться perf) от

востóрга ◆ *n* (*of water etc*) потóк.
gushing [ˈgʌʃɪŋ] *adj* (*female*) востóрженный* (востóржен); (*admiration, reverence*) неуёмный* (неуёмен).
gusset [ˈgʌsɪt] *n* клин*.
gust [gʌst] *n* (*of wind*) порьíв.
gusto [ˈgʌstəu] *n*: **with ~** (*eat*) с удовóльст-вием; (*work*) с жáром.
gusty [ˈgʌstɪ] *adj* (*wind*) порьíвистый (порьíвист); (*day*) вéтреный (вéтрен).
gut [gʌt] *n* кишкá*; (*MUS, SPORT*) струнá* (*из кишóк живóтных*) ◆ *vt* (*poultry, fish*) потрошúть (вьíпотрошить *perf*); (*building*) удалять все внýтренние чáсти дóма; **~s** *npl* (*ANAT*) кишкú* *fpl*, внýтренности *fpl*; (*inf: courage*) мýжество *ntsg*; **the house was ~ted by fire** дом сгорéл пóлностью; **to hate sb's ~s** (*inf*) не принимáть (принять* *perf*) когó-н нá дух, смертéльно ненавúдеть* (*impf*) когó-н.
gut reaction *n* инстинктúвная реáкция.
gutsy [ˈgʌtsɪ] (*inf*) *adj* напóристый.
gutted [ˈgʌtɪd] (*inf*) *adj*: **I was ~** (*very disappointed*) я был совершéнно убúт.
gutter [ˈgʌtə] *n* (*in street*) стóчная канáва; (*of roof*) водостóчный жёлоб*.
gutter press (*inf. pej*) *n* бульвáрная прéсса.
guttural [ˈgʌtərl] *adj* гортáнный.

guy [gaɪ] *n* (*inf: man*) пáрень* *m*; (*also:* **~rope**) шнурьí *mpl* для натягивания палáтки; (*effigy of Guy Fawkes*) изображéние Гáя Фóкса, сжигáемое 5 ноября.
Guyana [gaɪˈænə] *n* Гайáна.
guzzle [ˈgʌzl] *vt* (*drink*) пить* (вьíпить* *perf*) с жáдностью; (*food*) есть* (съесть* *perf*) с жáдностью.
gym [dʒɪm] *n* (*also:* **~nasium**) гимнастúческий зал; (*also:* **~nastics**) гимнáстика.
gymkhana [dʒɪmˈkɑ:nə] *n* конноспортúвные состязáния *ntpl*.
gymnasium [dʒɪmˈneɪzɪəm] *n* гимнастúческий зал.
gymnast [ˈdʒɪmnæst] *n* гимнáст(ка*).
gymnastics [dʒɪmˈnæstɪks] *n* гимнáстика.
gym shoes *npl* спортúвные тáпочки* *fpl*.
gymslip [ˈdʒɪmslɪp] *n* (*BRIT: tunic*) шкóльное плáтье без рукавóв.
gynaecologist [gaɪnɪˈkɔlədʒɪst] (*US* **gynecologist**) *n* гинекóлог.
gynaecology [gaɪnəˈkɔlədʒɪ] (*US* **gynecology**) *n* гинекологúя.
gypsy [ˈdʒɪpsɪ] *n* = **gipsy**.
gyrate [dʒaɪˈreɪt] *vi* (*revolve*) вращáться (*impf*) по крýгу.
gyroscope [ˈdʒaɪərəskəup] *n* гироскóп.

~ H, h ~

H, h [eɪtʃ] n (letter) 8-áя бýква англи́йского алфави́та.

habeas corpus ['heɪbɪəs'kɔːpəs] n (LAW) Хáбеас Ко́рпус (зако́н о неприкоснове́нности ли́чности).

haberdashery [hæbə'dæʃərɪ] n (BRIT) галантере́йные товáры mpl.

habit ['hæbɪt] n (custom) привы́чка*; (addiction) пристрáстие; (REL: costume) облаче́ние; **to get out of the ~ of doing** отвыкáть (отвы́кнуть* perf) +infin; **to get into the ~ of doing** привыкáть (привы́кнуть perf) +infin; **to be in the ~ of doing** име́ть (impf) обыкнове́ние +infin.

habitable ['hæbɪtəbl] adj (house etc) приго́дный* для жилья́.

habitat ['hæbɪtæt] n (BOT, ZOOL) есте́ственная средá* обитáния.

habitation [hæbɪ'teɪʃən] n (house etc) жили́ще; **fit for human ~** приго́дный* для жилья́.

habitual [hə'bɪtjuəl] adj (action) привы́чный* (привы́чен); (drinker) запо́йный; (liar) отъя́вленный.

habitually [hə'bɪtjuəlɪ] adv (late, untidy) обы́чно.

hack [hæk] vt (cut, slice) отрубáть (отруби́ть perf) ◆ n (pej: writer) писáка* m/f; (horse) ло́шадь, сдавáемая напрокáт для верхово́й езды́ ◆ vi: **to ~ into** (COMPUT) нелегáльно входи́ть* (войти́* perf) в +acc.

hacker ['hækə'] n (COMPUT) хáкер.

hackles ['hæklz] npl: **to make sb's ~ rise** (fig) приводи́ть* (привести́ perf) в состоя́ние раздраже́ния.

hackney cab ['hæknɪ-] n наёмный экипáж.

hackneyed ['hæknɪd] adj изби́тый.

hacksaw ['hæksɔː] n ножо́вка.

had [hæd] pt, pp of **have**.

haddock ['hædək] (pl ~ or ~s) n трескá; **smoked ~** копчёная трескá.

hadn't ['hædnt] = **had not**.

haematology ['hiːmə'tɔlədʒɪ] (US **hematology**) n гематоло́гия.

haemoglobin ['hiːmə'gləubɪn] (US **hemoglobin**) n гемоглоби́н.

haemophilia ['hiːmə'fɪlɪə] (US **hemophilia**) n гемофили́я.

haemorrhage ['hɛmərɪdʒ] (US **hemorrage**) n кровотече́ние; **brain ~** кровоизлия́ние (в мозг).

haemorrhoids ['hɛmərɔɪdz] (US **hemorroids**) npl геморро́й msg.

hag [hæg] n (woman) кargá; (witch) ве́дьма.

haggard ['hægəd] adj (face, look) изможднённый*.

haggis ['hægɪs] n (SCOTTISH) хáггис (шотлáндское блю́до из барáньей или теля́чьей требухи́ с овся́ной крупо́й и спе́циями).

haggle ['hægl] vi (bargain) торговáться (сторговáться perf); **to ~ over** спо́рить (impf) о +prp.

haggling ['hæglɪŋ] n торго́вля.

Hague [heɪg] n: **The ~** (GEO) Гáага.

hail [heɪl] n (also fig) град ◆ vt (call) окликáть (окли́кнуть perf); (flag down) подзывáть (подозвáть* perf); (acclaim) превозноси́ть* (превознести́* perf) ◆ vi: **it's ~ing** идёт град; **he ~s from Scotland** он ро́дом из Шотлáндии.

hailstone ['heɪlstəun] n грáдина.

hailstorm ['heɪlstɔːm] n грозá* с грáдом.

hair [hɛə'] n во́лосы* pl; (of animal) шерсть f; (single hair) во́лос*; **to do one's ~** причёсываться (причесáться* perf); **to miss by a ~'s breadth** (fig) чуть-чуть промахну́ться (perf).

hairbrush ['hɛəbrʌʃ] n щётка* для воло́с.

haircut ['hɛəkʌt] n стри́жка*.

hairdo ['hɛəduː] n причёска*.

hairdresser ['hɛədrɛsə'] n парикмáхер.

hairdresser's ['hɛədrɛsəz] n парикмáхерская f adj.

hair dryer n фен.

-haired [hɛəd] suffix: **fair/long-~** светло-/ длинноволо́сый.

hairgrip ['hɛəgrɪp] n невиди́мка.

hairline ['hɛəlaɪn] n ли́ния воло́с.

hairline fracture n тре́щина.

hairnet ['hɛənɛt] n се́тка* для воло́с.

hair oil n мáсло* для воло́с.

hairpiece ['hɛəpiːs] n накладны́е во́лосы* mpl.

---

* marks translations which have irregular inflections. The Russian-English side of the dictionary gives inflectional information.

hairpin [ˈhɛəpɪn] n шпи́лька*.
hairpin bend (US **hairpin curve**) n круто́й поворо́т.
hair-raising [ˈhɛəreɪzɪŋ] adj (experience, tale) жу́ткий*.
hair remover n (cream) крем для удале́ния воло́с.
hair slide n зако́лка* для воло́с.
hair spray n лак для воло́с.
hairstyle [ˈhɛəstaɪl] n причёска*.
hairy [ˈhɛərɪ] adj (person) волоса́тый; (animal) мохна́тый (мохна́т); (inf: situation) риско́ванный*.
Haiti [ˈheɪtɪ] n Гаи́ти m ind.
hake [heɪk] (pl ~ or ~s) n серебри́стый хек.
halcyon [ˈhælsɪən] adj: ~ **days** безмяте́жные дни.
hale [heɪl] adj: ~ **and hearty** здоро́вый* (здоро́в) и бо́дрый* (бодр).
half [hɑːf] (pl **halves**) n полови́на; (also: ~ **pint**: of beer etc) полпи́нты f; (RAIL, bus) биле́т за полцены́ ♦ adv (empty, closed, open, asleep) наполови́ну; **first/second** ~ (SPORT) пе́рвый/ второ́й тайм; **one and a** ~ (with m nouns) полтора́ +gen sg; (with f nouns) полторы́ +gen sg; **three and a** ~ три с полови́ной; ~**-an-hour** полчаса́* m; ~ **a dozen (of)** полдю́жины f (+gen); ~ **a pound (of)** полфу́нта m (+gen); **a week and a** ~ полторы́* f неде́ли; ~ **(of)** полови́на (+gen); ~ **the amount of** полови́на +gen; **to cut sth in** ~ разреза́ть (разре́зать* perf) что-н попола́м; ~ **past three** полови́на четвёртого; **to go halves (with sb)** дели́ть* (подели́ть* perf) попола́м (с кем-н); **she never does things by halves** она́ никогда́ не остана́вливается на полпути́; **he's too clever by** ~ он чересчу́р уж у́мный; ~ **empty/closed** наполови́ну пусто́й*/закры́тый; **a** ~ **bottle (of)** полбуты́лки (+gen).
half-baked [ˈhɑːfˈbeɪkt] adj (idea, scheme) непроду́манный.
half board n пансио́н с за́втраком и у́жином.
half-breed [ˈhɑːfbriːd] n = **half-caste**.
half-brother [ˈhɑːfbrʌðəʳ] n (with same mother) единоутро́бный брат*; (with same father) единокро́вный брат*.
half-caste [ˈhɑːfkɑːst] n челове́к сме́шанной ра́сы.
half-day [hɑːfˈdeɪ] n коро́ткий* день* m.
half-hearted [ˈhɑːfˈhɑːtɪd] adj лени́вый.
half-hour [hɑːfˈauəʳ] n полчаса́* m.
half-life [ˈhɑːflaɪf] n (TECH) пери́од полураспа́да.
half-mast [ˈhɑːfˈmɑːst] adv: **at** ~ (flag) приспу́щенный (приспу́щен).
halfpenny [ˈheɪpnɪ] n (BRIT) полпе́нса* m.
half-price [ˈhɑːfˈpraɪs] adj, adv за полцены́.
half-sister [ˈhɑːfsɪstəʳ] n (with same mother) единоутро́бная сестра́*; (with same father) единокро́вная сестра́*.
half term n (BRIT: SCOL) кани́кулы в середи́не

шко́льного триме́стра.
half-timbered [hɑːfˈtɪmbəd] adj деревя́нно-кирпи́чный.
half-time [hɑːfˈtaɪm] n (SPORT) переры́в ме́жду та́ймами.
halfway [ˈhɑːfˈweɪ] adv на полпути́; **I am prepared to meet you** ~ (fig) я гото́в пойти́ Вам навстре́чу.
halfway house n дом* на полпути́; (fig) середи́на.
halfwit [ˈhɑːfwɪt] n приду́рок*, полоу́мный(-ая) m(f) adj.
half-yearly [hɑːfˈjɪəlɪ] adv раз в полго́да ♦ adj полугодово́й.
halibut [ˈhælɪbət] n inv па́лтус.
halitosis [hælɪˈtəusɪs] n дурно́й за́пах изо рта́.
hall [hɔːl] n (entrance way) прихо́жая f adj; (corridor) коридо́р; (mansion) уса́дьба; (for concerts, meetings etc) зал; **to live in** ~s (BRIT: students) жить* (impf) в общежи́тии.
hallmark [ˈhɔːlmɑːk] n (fig) про́ба; (fig) отличи́тельная черта́*.
hallo [həˈləu] excl = **hello**.
hall of residence (pl ~s ~ ~) n (BRIT) общежи́тие.
hallowed [ˈhæləud] adj (REL) свято́й*; (fig: respected, revered) почита́емый.
Hallowe'en [ˈhæləuˈiːn] n кану́н Дня всех святы́х.
hallucination [həluːsɪˈneɪʃən] n галлюцина́ция.
hallucinogenic [həluːsɪnəuˈdʒɛnɪk] adj галлюцинато́рный.
hallway [ˈhɔːlweɪ] n (entrance hall) прихо́жая f adj.
halo [ˈheɪləu] n (REL) нимб; (circle of light) орео́л.
halt [hɔːlt] n остано́вка* ♦ vt остана́вливать (останови́ть* perf) ♦ vi остана́вливаться (останови́ться* perf); **to call a** ~ **to sth** (fig) дава́ть* (дать* perf) отбо́й чему́-н.
halter [ˈhɔːltəʳ] n (for horse) по́вод*.
halterneck [ˈhɔːltənɛk] adj: ~ **dress** пла́тье с откры́той спино́й и завя́зками вокру́г ше́и.
halve [hɑːv] vt (reduce) сокраща́ть (сократи́ть* perf) наполови́ну; (divide) дели́ть* (раздели́ть* perf) попола́м.
halves [hɑːvz] pl of **half**.
ham [hæm] n ветчина́*; (inf: also: **radio** ~) радиолюби́тель m; (: actor) безда́рный(-ая) актёр(-три́са) ♦ vt: **to** ~ **it up** переи́грывать (переигра́ть perf).
Hamburg [ˈhæmbəːg] n Га́мбург.
hamburger [ˈhæmbəːgəʳ] n га́мбургер.
ham-fisted [hæmˈfɪstɪd] adj нело́вкий*.
ham-handed [hæmˈhændɪd] adj = **ham-fisted**.
hamlet [ˈhæmlɪt] n дереву́шка*.
hammer [ˈhæməʳ] n молото́к*, мо́лот ♦ vi (on door etc) колоти́ть* (impf) ♦ vt (criticize severely) критикова́ть (раскритикова́ть perf); (nail): **to** ~ **in** забива́ть (заби́ть* perf), вбива́ть (вбить* perf); (fig: force): **to** ~ **sth into**

sb вдалбливать (вдолбить* *perf*) что-н кому-н

▶ **hammer out** *vt* (*metal*) расплющивать (расплющить *perf*); (*fig: solution, agreement*) вырабатывать (выработать *perf*).

hammock ['hæmək] *n* (*on ship*) койка*; (*in garden*) гамак*.

hamper ['hæmpə'] *vt* мешать (помешать *perf*) +*dat* ◆ *n* (*basket*) большая корзина с крышкой.

hamster ['hæmstə'] *n* хомяк*.

hamstring ['hæmstrɪŋ] *n* (*ANAT*) подколенное сухожилие ◆ *vt* (*restrict*) ограничивать (ограничить *perf*).

hand [hænd] *n* (*ANAT*) рука*, кисть *f* руки; (*of clock*) стрелка*; (*handwriting*) почерк; (*worker*) рабочий* *m adj*; (*of cards*) карты *fpl* (*находящиеся на руках у игрока*); (*measurement: of horse*) ладонь *f* (*мера при измерении роста лошади*) ◆ *vt* (*pass*) передавать* (передать* *perf*); (*give*) вручать (вручить *perf*); **to give** *or* **lend sb a** ~ помогать (помочь* *perf*) кому-н; **at** ~ под рукой; **by** ~ вручную; **in** ~ (*time*) в распоряжении; (*situation*) под контролем; **the job in** ~ текущее дело; **on** ~ (*person, services etc*) в распоряжении; **to get out of** ~ (*child*) отбиваться (отбиться* *perf*) от рук; (*situation*) выходить* (выйти* *perf*) из-под контроля; **to dismiss out of** ~ отвергнуть (*perf*) сразу; **I have the information to** ~ я располагаю информацией; **on the one** ~ ..., **on the other** ~ ... с одной стороны ..., с другой стороны; **to force sb's** ~ заставлять (заставить* *perf*) кого-н раскрыть свои карты; **he has a free** ~ у него развязаны руки; **to change** ~**s** (*be sold etc*) переходить* (перейти* *perf*) из рук в руки; **to have in one's** ~ (*fig*) держать* (*impf*) под контролем; ~**s off!** руки прочь!

▶ **hand down** *vt* (*knowledge, possessions*) передавать* (передать* *perf*); (*LAW: judgement, sentence*) выносить* (вынести* *perf*)

▶ **hand in** *vt* (*essay, work*) сдавать* (сдать* *perf*)

▶ **hand out** *vt* раздавать* (раздать* *perf*)

▶ **hand over** *vt* передавать* (передать* *perf*)

▶ **hand round** *vt* (*BRIT*) раздавать* (раздать* *perf*); (*subj: hostess*) разносить* (разнести* *perf*).

handbag ['hændbæg] *n* (дамская) сумочка*.

hand baggage *n* ручной багаж*.

handball ['hændbɔːl] *n* гандбол.

hand basin *n* таз*.

handbook ['hændbuk] *n* руководство.

handbrake ['hændbreɪk] *n* ручной тормоз*.

h & c *abbr* (*BRIT*) = **hot and cold (water)**.

hand cream *n* крем для рук.

handcuff ['hændkʌf] *vt* надевать (надеть* *perf*) наручники +*dat or* на +*acc*.

handcuffs ['hændkʌfs] *npl* наручники *mpl*.

handful ['hændful] *n* горсть* *f*; (*fig: of people*) горстка*.

hand-held ['hænd'hɛld] *adj* ручной.

handicap ['hændɪkæp] *n* (*disability*) физическая неполноценность *f*; (*disadvantage*) препятствие; (*SPORT*) гандикап ◆ *vt* препятствовать (воспрепятствовать *perf*) +*dat*; **mentally/physically** ~**ped** умственно/физически неполноценный.

handicraft ['hændɪkrɑːft] *n* рукоделие; (*objects*) изделие ручной работы.

handiwork ['hændɪwəːk] *n* ручные изделия *ntpl*; **this looks like his** ~ (*pej*) похоже, что это его рук дело.

handkerchief ['hæŋkətʃɪf] *n* носовой платок*.

handle ['hændl] *n* ручка*; (*CB RADIO: name*) прозвище ◆ *vt* (*touch*) держать* (*impf*) в руках; (*deal with*) справляться (справиться* *perf*) с +*instr*; (*treat: people*) обращаться (*impf*) с +*instr*; **to fly off the** ~ (*inf*) срываться (сорваться* *perf*); **to get a** ~ **on a problem** (*inf*) браться* (взяться* *perf*) за решение проблемы; **"handle with care"** „обращаться осторожно".

handlebar(s) ['hændlbɑː(z)] *n(pl)* руль* *msg* (*велосипеда или мотоцикла*).

handling ['hændlɪŋ] *n*: ~ **of** (*of situation, problem etc*) подход к +*dat*; (*luggage*) обращение с +*instr*; (*LAW*) ведение +*gen*.

handling charges *npl* (*COMM*) плата *fsg* за услуги.

hand luggage *n* ручной багаж*.

handmade ['hænd'meɪd] *adj* ручной работы; **it's** ~ это — ручная работа.

hand-out ['hændaut] *n* (*money, clothing, food*) благотворительная помощь *f*; (*publicity leaflet*) рекламный листок*; (*summary: of lecture*) проспект.

hand-picked ['hænd'pɪkt] *adj* (*produce*) собранный вручную; (*staff etc*) специально подобранный.

handrail ['hændreɪl] *n* перила *pl*.

handset ['hændsɛt] *n* телефонная трубка*.

handshake ['hændʃeɪk] *n* рукопожатие.

handsome ['hænsəm] *adj* (*man*) красивый (красив); (*woman*) интересный (интересен); (*building*) внушительный*; (*gift*) щедрый (щедр); (*fig: profit, return*) внушительный* (внушителен).

hands-on ['hændz'ɔn] *adj* практический*.

handstand ['hændstænd] *n*: **to do a** ~ делать (сделать *perf*) стойку на руках.

hand-to-mouth ['hændtə'mauθ] *adj*: **they live a** ~ **existence** они живут впроголодь.

handwriting ['hændraɪtɪŋ] *n* почерк.

---

* marks translations which have irregular inflections. The Russian-English side of the dictionary gives inflectional information.

handwritten ['hændrɪtn] *adj* напи́санный от руки́.

handy ['hændɪ] *adj* (*useful*) удо́бный*; (*skilful*) ло́вкий*; (*close at hand*) побли́зости; **to come in ~** пригожда́ться* (пригоди́ться* *perf*).

handyman ['hændɪmæn] *irreg n* (*at home*) ма́стер* на все ру́ки; (*in hotel etc*) подру́чный *m adj*.

hang [hæŋ] (*pt, pp* **hung**) *vt* ве́шать (пове́сить* *perf*); (*pt, pp* **hanged**; *execute*) ве́шать (пове́сить* *perf*) ♦ *vi* висе́ть* (*impf*) ♦ *n*: **to get the ~ of sth** (*inf*) разбира́ться (разобра́ться* *perf*) в чём-н; **to ~ one's head** ве́шать (пове́сить* *perf*) го́лову

▸ **hang about** *vi* слоня́ться (*impf*)

▸ **hang around** *vi* = **hang about**

▸ **hang back** *vi* (*hesitate*): **to ~ back (from doing)** быть* (*impf*) в нереши́тельности (+*infin*)

▸ **hang on** *vi* (*wait*) подожда́ть* (*impf*) ♦ *vt fus* (*depend on*) зави́сеть (*impf*) от +*gen*; **to ~ on to** (*keep hold of*) цепля́ться (*impf*) за +*acc*; (*keep*) держа́ть (*impf*) у себя́

▸ **hang out** *vt* (*washing*) выве́шивать (вы́весить* *perf*) ♦ *vi* высо́вываться (вы́сунуться *perf*); **this is where the students always ~ out** (*inf*) студе́нты всегда́ там окола́чиваются

▸ **hang together** *vi* (*argument*) быть* (*impf*) убеди́тельным(-ой)

▸ **hang up** *vi* (*TEL*) ве́шать (пове́сить* *perf*) тру́бку ♦ *vt* ве́шать (пове́сить* *perf*).

hangar ['hæŋəʳ] *n* анга́р.

hangdog ['hæŋdɔg] *adj* (*look, expression*) винова́тый.

hanger ['hæŋəʳ] *n* (*for clothes*) ве́шалка*.

hanger-on [hæŋər'ɔn] *n* прихлеба́тель(ница) *m(f)*.

hang-glider ['hæŋglaɪdəʳ] *n* (*craft*) дельтапла́н; (*pilot*) дельтапланери́ст.

hang-gliding ['hæŋglaɪdɪŋ] *n* дельта-планери́зм.

hanging ['hæŋɪŋ] *n* (*execution*) пове́шение; (*for wall*) портье́ра.

hangman ['hæŋmən] *irreg n* пала́ч*.

hangover ['hæŋəuvəʳ] *n* (*after drinking*) похме́лье; (*from past*) пережи́ток*.

hang-up ['hæŋʌp] *n* (*inhibition*) ко́мплекс.

hank [hæŋk] *n* мото́к*.

hanker ['hæŋkəʳ] *vi*: **to ~ after** (*desire, long for*) мечта́ть (*impf*) о +*prp*.

hankering ['hæŋkərɪŋ] *n*: **I have a ~ for a beer** мне бы сейча́с пивка́.

hankie ['hæŋkɪ] *n abbr* = **handkerchief**.

hanky ['hæŋkɪ] *n abbr* = **handkerchief**.

Hanoi [hæ'nɔɪ] *n* Хано́й.

Hants *abbr* (*BRIT: POST*) = **Hampshire**.

haphazard [hæp'hæzəd] *adj* бессисте́мный*.

hapless ['hæplɪs] *adj* несча́стный*.

happen ['hæpən] *vi* случа́ться (случи́ться *perf*), происходи́ть* (произойти́* *perf*); (*chance*): **I**

~ed to meet him in the park я случа́йно встре́тил его́ в па́рке; **as it ~s** кста́ти; **what's ~ing?** что происхо́дит?; **she ~ed to be free** она́ оказа́лась свобо́дной; **if anything ~ed to him** е́сли с ним что-н случи́тся

▸ **happen (up)on** *vt fus* натыка́ться (наткну́ться *perf*) на +*acc*.

happening ['hæpnɪŋ] *n* слу́чай.

happily ['hæpɪlɪ] *adv* (*luckily*) к сча́стью; (*cheerfully*) ра́достно.

happiness ['hæpɪnɪs] *n* сча́стье.

happy ['hæpɪ] *adj* (*pleased*) счастли́вый (счастли́в); (*cheerful*) весёлый (ве́сел); (*apt*) уда́чный* (уда́чен); **I am ~ (with it)** (*content*) я дово́лен (э́тим); **he is always ~ to help** (*willing*) он всегда́ с удово́льствием помога́ет; **~ birthday!** с днём рожде́ния!

happy-go-lucky ['hæpɪgəu'lʌkɪ] *adj* беспе́чный* (беспе́чен).

happy hour *n* вре́мя, в тече́ние кото́рого спиртны́е напи́тки в ба́рах продаю́тся по сни́женным це́нам.

harangue [hə'ræŋ] *vt* (*audience, class*) увещева́ть (*impf*).

harass ['hærəs] *vt* изводи́ть* (извести́* *perf*).

harassed ['hærəst] *adj* (*person*) изнурённый* (изнурён).

harassment ['hærəsmənt] *n* пресле́дование; **sexual ~** злоупотребле́ние служе́бным положе́нием по отноше́нию к сотру́днику противополо́жного по́ла.

harbour ['hɑ:bəʳ] (*US* **harbor**) *n* га́вань *f* ♦ *vt* (*hope, fear etc*) зата́ивать (затаи́ть *perf*); (*criminal, fugitive*) укрыва́ть (укры́ть* *perf*); **to ~ a grudge against sb** держа́ть* (*impf*) зло на кого́-н.

harbour dues *npl* порто́вые сбо́ры *mpl*.

harbour master *n* нача́льник по́рта.

hard [hɑ:d] *adj* (*surface, object*) твёрдый (твёрд); (*question, problem*) тру́дный* (тру́ден); (*work, life*) тяжёлый (тяжёл); (*person*) суро́вый (суро́в); (*facts, evidence*) неопровержи́мый (неопровержи́м); (*drink*) кре́пкий*; (*drugs*) си́льный ♦ *adv*: **to work ~** мно́го и усе́рдно рабо́тать (*impf*); **~ luck!** не везёт!; **no ~ feelings!** не держи́те зла!; **I don't have any ~ feelings** я не держу́ зла; **he is ~ of hearing** он туг на́ ухо; **to think ~** хорошо́ поду́мать (*perf*); **to try ~ to win** упо́рно добива́ться (*impf*) побе́ды; **to look ~ at** смотре́ть* (посмотре́ть* *perf*) при́стально на +*acc*; **I felt ~ done by** я почу́вствовал, что со мной обошли́сь несправедли́во; **I find it ~ to believe that ...** мне тру́дно пове́рить, что ....

hard-and-fast ['hɑ:dən'fɑ:st] *adj* неукосни́-тельный*.

hardback ['hɑ:dbæk] *n* (*book*) кни́га в твёрдом переплёте.

hardboard ['hɑ:dbɔ:d] *n* древе́сно-стру́жечная плита́.

hard-boiled egg ['hɑ:d'bɔɪld-] *n* яйцо́*

вкруту́ю.

hard cash *n* нали́чные де́ньги* *pl.*

hard copy *n* (*COMPUT*) печа́тная ко́пия, распеча́тка.

hard core *n* (*of group*) гру́ппа пре́данных сторо́нников.

hard-core ['hɑːd'kɔː'] *adj* (*pornography*) преде́льно открове́нный*; (*supporters*) ве́рный*.

hard court *n* (*TENNIS*) твёрдый корт.

hard disk *n* (*COMPUT*) жёсткий* диск.

harden ['hɑːdn] *vt* (*substance*) де́лать (сде́лать *perf*) твёрдым(-ой); (*attitude, person*) ожесточа́ть (ожесточи́ть *perf*) ◆ *vi* (*substance*) тверде́ть (затверде́ть *perf*); (*attitude, person*) ожесточа́ться (ожесточи́ться *perf*).

hardened ['hɑːdnd] *adj* (*criminal*) закорен́е́лый; **to be ~ to sth** быть* (*impf*) нечувстви́тельным(-ой) к чему́-н.

hardening ['hɑːdnɪŋ] *n* зака́ливание; (*of opposition*) усиле́ние.

hard graft *n:* **by sheer ~ ~** то́лько благодаря́ упо́рной рабо́те.

hard-headed ['hɑːd'hɛdɪd] *adj* (*businessman*) расчётливый (расчётлив).

hardhearted ['hɑːd'hɑːtɪd] *adj* бессерде́чный* (бессерде́чен).

hard-hitting ['hɑːd'hɪtɪŋ] *adj* (*report, speech, article*) бьющий напрями́к.

hard labour *n* (*punishment*) принуди́тельные рабо́ты *fpl.*

hardliner [hɑːd'laɪnə'] *n* сторо́нник(-ица) жёсткой ли́нии (*в поли́тике*).

hard-luck story ['hɑːdlʌk-] *n* жа́лостливая исто́рия.

hardly ['hɑːdlɪ] *adv* (*scarcely*) едва́; (*no sooner*) как то́лько; (*harshly*) суро́во; **~ anywhere/ ever** почти́ нигде́/никогда́; **it's ~ the case** э́то не тот слу́чай; **I ~ think so** я так не ду́маю; **I can ~ believe it** я с трудо́м могу́ пове́рить в э́то.

hard-nosed [hɑːd'nəuzd] *adj* трёзвый.

hard-pressed [hɑːd'prɛst] *adj:* **I am ~ for time/ money** у меня́ ту́го со вре́менем/деньга́ми.

hard sell *n* (*COMM*) уси́ленное реклам-и́рование това́ров.

hardship ['hɑːdʃɪp] *n* (*difficulty*) тру́дности *fpl.*

hard shoulder *n* (*BRIT: AUT*) обо́чина с твёрдым покры́тием, на кото́рой разреше́на остано́вка тра́нспорта.

hard up *adj* (*inf*) на мели́.

hardware ['hɑːdwɛə'] *n* скобяны́е изде́лия *ntpl*; (*COMPUT*) обору́дование, аппарату́ра; (*MIL*) вое́нная те́хника.

hardware shop *n* магази́н скобяны́х изде́лий.

hard-wearing [hɑːd'wɛərɪŋ] *adj* (*clothes, shoes*)

кре́пкий* (кре́пок).

hard-won [hɑːd'wʌn] *adj* с трудо́м завоёванный (завоёван); (*victory*) с трудо́м оде́ржанный (оде́ржан).

hard-working [hɑːd'wəːkɪŋ] *adj* (*employee, student*) усе́рдный* (усе́рден).

hardy ['hɑːdɪ] *adj* (*animals, people*) выно́сливый (выно́слив); (*plant*) морозо-усто́йчивый (морозоусто́йчив).

hare [hɛə'] *n* за́яц*.

harebrained ['hɛəbreɪnd] *adj* (*scheme, idea*) несура́зный* (несура́зен).

harelip ['hɛəlɪp] *n* за́ячья губа́*.

harem ['hɑːˈriːm] *n* гаре́м.

hark back [hɑːk-] *vi:* **to ~ ~ to** (*be reminiscent of*) напомина́ть (напо́мнить *perf*) о +*prp*; (*remember*) вспомина́ть (вспо́мнить *perf*) о +*prp*.

harm [hɑːm] *n* (*injury*) теле́сное поврежде́ние; (*damage*) уще́рб ◆ *vt* (*thing*) поврежда́ть (повреди́ть* *perf*); (*person*) наноси́ть* (нанести́* *perf*) вред +*dat*; **to mean no ~** не хоте́ть* (*impf*) оби́деть; **to come to no ~** зако́нчиться (*perf*) благополу́чно; **out of ~'s way** от греха́ пода́льше; **there's no ~ in trying** попы́тка – не пы́тка.

harmful ['hɑːmful] *adj* (*toxin, influence etc*) вре́дный* (вре́ден).

harmless [hɑːmlɪs] *adj* (*animal, person*) безоби́дный* (безоби́ден); (*joke, activity*) неви́нный* (неви́нен).

harmonic [hɑːˈmɔnɪk] *adj* гармони́ческий.

harmonica [hɑːˈmɔnɪkə] *n* губна́я гармо́ника.

harmonics [hɑːˈmɔnɪks] *npl* гармо́ния *fsg.*

harmonious [hɑːˈməuniəs] *adj* гармони́чный* (гармони́чен).

harmonium [hɑːˈməuniəm] *n* фисгармо́ния.

harmonize ['hɑːmənaɪz] *vi* (*MUS*) гармон-и́ровать (*impf*); (*colours, ideas*): **to ~ (with)** гармони́ровать (*impf*) (с +*instr*).

harmony ['hɑːmənɪ] *n* (*accord*) гармо́ния; (*MUS*) созву́чие.

harness ['hɑːnɪs] *n* (*for horse*) у́пряжь *f*; (*for child*) постро́мки* *fpl*; (*safety harness*) привязны́е ремни́ *mpl* ◆ *vt* (*horse, dog*) запряга́ть (запря́чь* *perf*); (*resources, energy etc*) обу́здывать (обузда́ть *perf*).

harp [hɑːp] *n* а́рфа ◆ *vi:* **to ~ on about** (*pej*) заводи́ть* (завести́* *perf*) волы́нку о +*prp*.

harpist ['hɑːpɪst] *n* арфи́ст(ка*).

harpoon [hɑːˈpuːn] *n* гарпу́н*.

harpsichord ['hɑːpsɪkɔːd] *n* клавеси́н.

harried ['hærɪd] *adj* заму́ченный (заму́чен).

harrow ['hærəu] *n* (*AGR*) борона́.

harrowing ['hærəuɪŋ] *adj* душераздира́ющий*.

harry ['hærɪ] *vt* изводи́ть* (извести́* *perf*).

harsh [hɑːʃ] *adj* (*sound, light, criticism*) ре́зкий* (ре́зок); (*person*) жёсткий* (жёсток);

---

* marks translations which have irregular inflections. The Russian-English side of the dictionary gives inflectional information.

(*remark*) стро́гий* (строг); (*life, winter*) суро́вый (суро́в).

harshly ['hɑːʃlɪ] *adv* (*criticize*) ре́зко; (*mark, speak*) стро́го; (*act*) жёстко.

harshness ['hɑːʃnɪs] *n* (*see adj*) ре́зкость *f*; жёсткость *f*; стро́гость *f*; суро́вость *f*.

harvest ['hɑːvɪst] *n* (*harvest time*) жа́тва; (*of barley, fruit etc*) урожа́й ◆ *vt* убира́ть (убра́ть *perf*).

harvester ['hɑːvɪstəʳ] *n* (*machine: also:* **combine** ~) комба́йн.

has [hæz] *vb see* **have**.

has-been ['hæzbiːn] *n* (*inf: person*): **he's/she's a** ~ его́/её вре́мя прошло́.

hash [hæʃ] *n* (*CULIN*) мясно́е рагу́ *nt ind*; (*fig: mess*): **to make a** ~ **of sth** запа́рывать (запоро́ть *perf*) что-н.

hash [hæʃ] *n abbr* (*inf*) = **hashish**.

hashish ['hæʃɪʃ] *n* гаши́ш.

hasn't ['hæznt] = **has not**.

hassle ['hæsl] (*inf*) *n* моро́ка ◆ *vt* надоеда́ть (*impf*) +*dat*.

haste [heɪst] *n* спе́шка; **in** ~ в спе́шке; **to make** ~ (**to do**) торопи́ться (поторопи́ться *perf*) (+*infin*).

hasten ['heɪsn] *vt* (*speed up*) торопи́ть* (поторопи́ть* *perf*) ◆ *vi* (*hurry*): **to** ~ **to do** торопи́ться (поторопи́ться* *perf*) +*infin*; **I** ~ **to add ...** спешу́ доба́вить ...; **she** ~**ed back to the house** она́ поспеши́ла обра́тно к до́му.

hastily ['heɪstɪlɪ] *adv* (*hurriedly*) поспе́шно; (*rashly*) опроме́тчиво.

hasty ['heɪstɪ] *adj* (*hurried*) поспе́шный* (поспе́шен); (*rash*) опроме́тчивый* (опроме́тчив).

hat [hæt] *n* шля́па; (*woolly, furry*) ша́пка*; **to keep sth under one's** ~ держа́ть* (*impf*) что-н в секре́те.

hatbox ['hætbɔks] *n* шля́пная коро́бка*.

hatch [hætʃ] *n* (*NAUT: also:* ~**way**) люк; (*also:* **service** ~) разда́точное *or* буфе́тное окно́* ◆ *vi* (*also:* ~ **out**: *chick, egg*) вылупля́ться (вы́лупиться* *perf*) ◆ *vt* (*egg, chick etc*) выси́живать (вы́сидеть* *perf*); (*plot*) вына́шивать (вы́носить* *perf*).

hatchback ['hætʃbæk] *n* (*AUT*) маши́на-пика́п *f*.

hatchet ['hætʃɪt] *n* (*axe*) топо́рик; **to bury the** ~ мири́ться (помири́ться *perf*).

hatchet job (*inf*) *n* напа́дки* *pl*; **to do a** ~ ~ **on sb** разноси́ть* (разнести́* *perf*) кого́-н в пух и прах.

hatchet man *n* (*US: inf*) наёмник.

hate [heɪt] *vt* ненави́деть* (*impf*) ◆ *n* не́нависть *f*; **to** ~ **to do** *or* **doing** ненави́деть* (*impf*) +*infin*; **I** ~ **to trouble you, but ...** мне о́чень не хо́чется беспоко́ить Вас, но ....

hateful ['heɪtful] *adj* ненави́стный* (ненави́стен).

hatred ['heɪtrɪd] *n* не́нависть *f*.

hat trick *n* (*SPORT, also fig*) побе́да три ра́за подря́д.

haughty ['hɔːtɪ] *adj* надме́нный*.

haul [hɔːl] *vt* (*pull*) таска́ть/тащи́ть* (*impf*); (*transport*) перевози́ть* (перевезти́* *perf*) ◆ *n* (*of stolen goods etc*) добы́ча; (*of fish*) уло́в; **he** ~**ed himself out of the pool** он с трудо́м вы́брался из бассе́йна.

haulage ['hɔːlɪdʒ] *n* перево́зка.

haulage contractor *n* (*BRIT: COMM: firm*) фи́рма, производя́щая перево́зки; (: *person*) руководи́тель *m* фи́рмы, производя́щей перево́зки.

hauler ['hɔːləʳ] *n* (*US*) = **haulage contractor**.

haulier ['hɔːlɪəʳ] *n* (*BRIT*) руководи́тель *m* фи́рмы, производя́щей перево́зки.

haunch [hɔːntʃ] *n* бедро́*; (*of meat*) бе́дренная часть* *f*.

haunt [hɔːnt] *n* (*of crooks*) прито́н; (*in childhood etc*) люби́мое ме́сто* ◆ *vt* (*subj: problem, memory, fear*) пресле́довать (*impf*); **to** ~ **sb/a house** явля́ться (яви́ться* *perf*) кому́-н/в до́ме.

haunted ['hɔːntɪd] *adj* (*expression, look*) встрево́женный* (встрево́жен); **a** ~ **house** дом* с привиде́ниями; **this house is** ~ в э́том до́ме есть привиде́ния.

haunting ['hɔːntɪŋ] *adj* (*sight, music*) пресле́дующий.

Havana [hə'vænə] *n* Гава́на.

KEYWORD
---

have [hæv] (*pt, pp* **had**) *aux vb*: **1**: **to have arrived** прие́хать (*perf*); **have you already eaten?** ты уже́ пое́л?; **he has been kind to me** он прояви́л доброту́ по отноше́нию ко мне; **he has been promoted** он получи́л повыше́ние по слу́жбе; **has he told you?** он Вам сказа́л?; **having finished** *or* **when he had finished, he went to bed** зако́нчив *or* когда́ он зако́нчил, он пошёл спать

2 (*in tag questions*): **you've done it, haven't you?** Вы сде́лали э́то, да?; **he hasn't done it, has he?** он ведь э́то не сде́лал, ве́рно?

3 (*in short answers and questions*): **you've made a mistake – no I haven't/so I have** Вы оши́блись – нет, не оши́бся/да, оши́бся; **we haven't paid – yes we have!** мы не заплати́ли – нет, заплати́ли!; **I've been there before, have you?** я там был, а Вы?

◆ *modal aux vb* (*be obliged*): **to have (got) to do** быть (*impf*) до́лжным(-ой) +*infin*; **I have (got) to finish this work** я до́лжен зако́нчить э́ту рабо́ту; **you haven't to tell her** Вы не должны́ говори́ть ей; **I haven't got** *or* **I don't have to wear glasses** я могу́ не носи́ть очки́; **this has to be a mistake** э́то, наверняка́, оши́бка

◆ *vt* **1** (*possess*): **I** *etc* **have** у меня́ *etc*; **he has (got) blue eyes/dark hair** у него́ голубы́е глаза́/тёмные во́лосы; **do you have** *or* **have you got a car/phone?** у Вас есть маши́на/телефо́н?

2 (*referring to meals etc*): **to have breakfast** за́втракать (поза́втракать *perf*); **to have**

dinner обéдать (пообéдать *perf*); **to have a cigarette** выкýривать (вы́курить *perf*) сигарéту; **to have a glass of wine** выпивáть (вы́пить* *perf*) стакáн винá
3 (*receive, obtain etc*): **may I have your address?** Вы мне мóжете дать свой áдрес?; **you can have the book for £5** э́та кни́га вáша за £5; **I must have it by tomorrow** э́то должнó быть у меня́ к зáвтрашнему дню; **she is having a baby in March** у неё в мáрте бýдет ребёнок
4 (*maintain, allow*): **he will have it that he is right** он настáивает на том, что он прав; **I won't have it!** я э́того не допущý!
5: I am having my television repaired мне должны́ починúть телевúзор; **to have sb do** попросúть* (*perf*) когó-н +*infin*; **he soon had them all laughing/working** онú у негó все тут же стáли смея́ться/рабóтать
6 (*experience, suffer*): **I have flu/a headache** у меня́ грипп/болúт головá; **to have a cold** простужáться (простудúться* *perf*); **she had her bag stolen** у неё украли́ сýмку; **he had an operation** емý сдéлали опéрацию
7 (+*n*): **to have a swim** плáвать (поплáвать *perf*); **to have a rest** отдыхáть (отдохнýть *perf*); **let's have a look** давáйте посмóтрим; **we are having a meeting/party tomorrow** зáвтра у нас бýдет собрáние/бýдут гóсти; **let me have a try** дайте мнé попрóбовать
8 (*inf: dupe*) провестú* (*perf*); **he's been had** егó провелú; **to have sb on** (*BRIT: inf*) водúть* (*impf*) когó-н зá нос
▶ **have in** *vt* (*inf*): **he has got it in for me** у негó прóтив меня́ зуб
▶ **have on** *vt*: **have you anything on tomorrow?** у Вас есть на зáвтра какúе-нибудь плáны?; **I don't have any money on me** у меня́ нет при себé дéнег; **he had a black sweater on** на нём был чёрный свúтер
▶ **have out** *vt*: **to have it out with sb** объясня́ться (объяснúться *perf*) с кем-н; **she had her tooth out** ей удалúли зуб; **she had her tonsils/appendix out** ей вы́резали глáнды/ аппендицúт.

haven ['heɪvn] *n* гáвань *f*; (*fig*) убéжище.
haven't ['hævnt] = **have not**.
haversack ['hævəsæk] *n* (*of hiker*) рюкзáк*; (*of soldier*) рáнец*.
haves [hævz] *npl* (*inf*): **the ~ and the have-nots** имýщие *pl adj* и неимýщие *pl adj*.
havoc ['hævək] *n* (*chaos*) хáос; **to play ~ with** (*plans etc*) игрáть (*impf*) злы́е шýтки над +*instr*.
Hawaii [hə'waɪiː] *n* Гавáйи *m ind*.
Hawaiian [hə'waɪjən] *adj* гавáйский ◆ *n* гавáец*(-áйка*); (*LING*) гавáйский язы́к*.

hawk [hɔːk] *n* я́стреб*.
hawker ['hɔːkə'] *n* (*COMM*) ýличный(-ая) торгóвец*(-вка*).
hawkish ['hɔːkɪʃ] *adj* хúщный.
hawthorn ['hɔːθɔːn] *n* боя́рышник.
hay [heɪ] *n* сéно.
hay fever *n* сеннáя лихорáдка*.
haystack ['heɪstæk] *n* стог* сéна; **it's like looking for a needle in a ~** э́то как искáть игóлку в стóге сéна.
haywire ['heɪwaɪə'] (*inf*) *adj*: **to go ~** (*machine*) барахлúть (забарахлúть *perf*); (*plans*) нарушáться (нарýшиться *perf*).
hazard ['hæzəd] *n* (*danger*) опáсность *f* ◆ *vt* (*risk*): **to ~ a guess** осмéливаться (осмéлиться *perf*) предположúть; **it's a health ~** э́то опáсно для здорóвья; **smoking is a fire ~** курéние мóжет служúть причúной пожáра.
hazard lights *npl* = **hazard warning lights**.
hazardous ['hæzədəs] *adj* опáсный* (опáсен).
hazard pay *n* (*US*) дополнúтельная плáта за труд в опáсных услóвиях.
hazard warning lights *npl* (*AUT*) аварúйные огнú *mpl*.
haze [heɪz] *n* ды́мка*; **heat ~** мáрево.
hazel [heɪzl] *n* лещúна ◆ *adj* (*eyes*) зеленовáто-кáрий*.
hazelnut ['heɪzlnʌt] *n* леснóй орéх.
hazy ['heɪzɪ] *adj* тумáнный* (тумáнен); **I'm rather ~ about the details** у меня́ довóльно смýтное представлéние о подрóбностях.
H-bomb ['eɪtʃbɒm] *n* водорóдная бóмба.
HE *abbr* (*REL, DIPLOMACY*): = *His/Her Excellency*) Егó/Её Превосходúтельство; = *high explosive*.
he [hiː] *pron* он.
head [hɛd] *n* (*ANAT*) головá*; (*mind*) ум*; (*of list, queue*) начáло; (*of table*) главá; (*of company, organization*) руководúтель(ница) *m(f)*; (*of school*) дирéктор*; (*on tape recorder etc*) голóвка ◆ *vt* (*list, queue*) стоя́ть (*impf*) пéрвым(-ой) в +*prp*; (*group, company*) возглавля́ть (возглáвить* *perf*); **~s or tails** ≈ орёл úли рéшка; **~ over heels in love** влюблён пó уши; **to ~ a ball** забивáть (забúть* *perf*) мяч головóй; **£10 a** *or* **per ~** по £10 кáждому *or* на кáждого; **to sit at the ~ of the table** сидéть* (сесть* *perf*) во главé столá; **he has a ~ for business** у негó спосóбности к бúзнесу; **I have no ~ for heights** у меня́ крýжится головá от высоты́; **to come to a ~** (*fig: situation etc*) доходúть* (дойтú* *perf*) до крити́ческой тóчки; **let's put our ~s together** давáйте обсýдим э́то вмéсте; **to say sth off the top of one's ~** говорúть (сказáть* *perf*) что-н не задýмываясь; **on your own ~ be it!** пусть э́то бýдет на Вáшей сóвести!; **to bite**

---

or **snap sb's ~ off** огрыза́ться (огрызну́ться *perf*) кому́-н, гру́бо обрыва́ть (обры́ть* *perf*) кого́-н; **to go to sb's ~** (*alcohol*) ударя́ть (уда́рить *perf*) кому́-н в го́лову; (*success, power*) кружи́ть (вскружи́ть *perf*) кому́-н го́лову; **to keep/lose one's ~** не теря́ть (потеря́ть *perf*)/теря́ть (потеря́ть *perf*) го́лову; **I can't make ~ nor tail of this** я ничего́ не могу́ поня́ть в э́том; **he's off his ~!** (*inf*) он рехну́лся!

▸ **head for** *vt fus* (*place*) направля́ться (напра́виться* *perf*) в/на +*acc or* к +*dat*; (*disaster*) обрека́ть (обре́чь* *perf*) себя́ на +*acc*

▸ **head off** *vt* (*threat, danger*) отводи́ть* (отвести́* *perf*).

headache ['hɛdeɪk] *n* головна́я боль* *f*; (*fig: problem*) неприя́тность *f*; **I've got a ~** у меня́ боли́т голова́.

headband ['hɛdbænd] *n* о́бруч* для воло́с.

headboard ['hɛdbɔ:d] *n* спи́нка* крова́ти.

head cold *n* на́сморк.

headdress ['hɛddrɛs] *n* головно́е украше́ние.

headed notepaper ['hɛdɪd-] *n* бланк; (*personal*) бланк для письма́ со шта́мпом *отправи́теля*.

header ['hɛdə'] *n* (*BRIT: inf: FOOTBALL*) уда́р голово́й.

headfirst ['hɛd'fə:st] *adv* (*dive, fall*) голово́й вниз; (*rush*) сломя́ го́лову.

headgear ['hɛdgɪə'] *n* головно́й убо́р.

head-hunt ['hɛdhʌnt] *vi* сма́нивать (смани́ть* *perf*) лу́чших специали́стов ♦ *vt* сма́нивать (смани́ть *perf*).

head-hunter ['hɛdhʌntə'] *n* (*COMM*) челове́к, кото́рый перема́нивает сотру́дников из одно́й фи́рмы в другу́ю.

heading ['hɛdɪŋ] *n* (*of chapter, article*) заголо́вок*.

headlamp ['hɛdlæmp] *n* (*BRIT*) = **headlight**.

headland ['hɛdlənd] *n* мыс*.

headlight ['hɛdlaɪt] *n* фа́ра.

headline ['hɛdlaɪn] *n* (*PRESS, TV, RADIO*) заголо́вок*.

headlong ['hɛdlɔŋ] *adv* (*headfirst*) голово́й вперёд; (*hastily*) опроме́тчиво.

headmaster [hɛd'ma:stə'] *n* дире́ктор* шко́лы.

headmistress [hɛd'mɪstrɪs] *n* дире́ктор* шко́лы.

head office *n* (*of company etc*) дире́кция.

head of state (*pl ~s ~ ~*) *n* глава́* госуда́рства.

head-on [hɛd'ɔn] *adj* (*collision, confrontation*) лобово́й ♦ *adv* но́сом к но́су.

headphones ['hɛdfəunz] *npl* нау́шники *mpl*.

headquarters ['hɛdkwɔ:təz] *npl* (*of company, organization*) гла́вное управле́ние *ntsg*; (*MIL*) штаб-кварти́ра *fsg*.

headrest ['hɛdrɛst] *n* подголо́вник.

headroom ['hɛdrum] *n* (*in car*) вну́тренняя высота́ (*ку́зова*); (*under bridge*) просве́т.

headscarf ['hɛdska:f] *n* косы́нка*; (*square*) головно́й плато́к*.

headset ['hɛdsɛt] *n* = **headphones**.

head start *n*: **to have/get a ~ ~** име́ть (*impf*)/получа́ть (получи́ть* *perf*) исхо́дное преиму́щество.

headstone ['hɛdstəun] *n* (*on grave*) надгро́бный ка́мень* *m*.

headstrong ['hɛdstrɔŋ] *adj* упо́рный* (упо́рен).

head teacher *n* дире́ктор* шко́лы.

head waiter *n* (*in restaurant*) гла́вный официа́нт.

headway ['hɛdweɪ] *n*: **to make ~** продвига́ться (продви́нуться *perf*) вперёд.

headwind ['hɛdwɪnd] *n* встре́чный ве́тер*.

heady ['hɛdɪ] *adj* (*experience, time*) головокружи́тельный; (*drink*) хмельно́й; (*atmosphere*) взбудора́женный.

heal [hi:l] *vt* (*patient*) изле́чивать (излечи́ть* *perf*); (*injury*) заживля́ть (заживи́ть* *perf*); (*damage*) восстана́вливать (восстанови́ть* *perf*) ♦ *vi* (*injury*) зажива́ть (зажи́ть *perf*); (*damage*) восстана́вливаться (восстанови́ться* *perf*).

health [hɛlθ] *n* (*also MED*) здоро́вье; **good ~** кре́пкое здоро́вье.

health care *n* здравоохране́ние.

health centre *n* (*BRIT*) поликли́ника.

health food *n* здоро́вая пи́ща.

health-food shop ['hɛlθfu:d-] *n* магази́н здоро́вого пита́ния.

health hazard *n* опа́сность *f* для здоро́вья.

Health Service *n* (*BRIT*): **the ~ ~** слу́жба здравоохране́ния.

healthy ['hɛlθɪ] *adj* (*person*) здоро́вый* (здоро́в); (*economy, appetite*) здоро́вый; (*pursuit, pastime*) поле́зный* (поле́зен); (*profit*) доста́точно хоро́ший*; **it's not ~ to drink too much** сли́шком мно́го пить — вре́дно для здоро́вья.

heap [hi:p] *n* (*small*) ку́ча; (*large*) гру́да ♦ *vt* (*stones, sand*): **to ~ (up)** сва́ливать (свали́ть* *perf*) в ку́чу; (*plate, sink*): **to ~ with sth** наполня́ть (напо́лнить *perf*) чем-н; (*food, books*): **to ~ sth on** нава́ливать (навали́ть* *perf*) что-н на +*acc*; **~s of** (*inf*) ку́ча *fsg* +*gen*; **to ~ favours/praise/gifts on sb** осыпа́ть (осы́пать* *perf*) кого́-н ми́лостями/ похвала́ми/пода́рками.

hear [hɪə'] (*pt, pp* **heard**) *vt* слы́шать (услы́шать *perf*); (*lecture, concert*) слу́шать (*impf*); (*LAW: case*) слу́шать (*impf*); **to ~ about** слы́шать (услы́шать *perf*) о +*prp*; **did you ~ about the move?** Вы слы́шали о перее́зде?; **to ~ from sb** слы́шать (услы́шать *perf*) от кого́-н; **I can't ~ you** Вас не слы́шно; **I've never ~d of that book** я никогда́ не слы́шал об э́той кни́ге; **I wouldn't ~ of it!** я и слы́шать об э́том не хочу́!

▸ **hear out** *vt* выслу́шивать (вы́слушать *perf*).

heard [hə:d] *pt, pp of* **hear**.

hearing ['hɪərɪŋ] *n* (*sense*) слух; (*LAW, POL*) слушание; **she is a bit hard of** ~ она́ тугова́та на́ ухо; **within/out of** ~ **distance** в преде́лах/ за преде́лами слы́шимости; **to give sb a (fair)** ~ (*BRIT*) дать* (*perf*) кому́-н вы́сказаться.

hearing aid *n* слухово́й аппара́т.

hearsay ['hɪəseɪ] *n* слух; **by** ~ по слу́хам.

hearse [hə:s] *n* катафа́лк.

heart [hɑ:t] *n* се́рдце*; (*of lettuce*) сердцеви́на; (*of problem, matter*) суть *f*; ~**s** *npl* (*CARDS*) че́рви *fpl*; **to lose/take** ~ пасть* (*perf*)/не па́дать (*impf*) ду́хом; **at** ~ в глубине́ души́; (**off**) **by** ~ наизу́сть; **he has a weak** ~ у него́ сла́бое се́рдце; **to set one's** ~ **on sth/on doing** стреми́ться* (*impf*) всей душо́й к чему́-н/ +*infin*; **to pour one's** ~ **out to sb** излива́ть (изли́ть* *perf*) кому́-н ду́шу; **he's a man after my own** ~ он мне по́ се́рдцу; **the** ~ **of the matter** суть де́ла.

heartache ['hɑ:teɪk] *n* серде́чная боль *f*.

heart attack *n* серде́чный при́ступ.

heartbeat ['hɑ:tbi:t] *n* (*one pulsation*) серде́чное сокраще́ние; (*rhythm*) сердцебие́ние.

heartbreak ['hɑ:tbreɪk] *n* большо́е го́ре.

heartbreaking ['hɑ:tbreɪkɪŋ] *adj* душераздира́ющий* (душераздира́ющ).

heartbroken ['hɑ:tbrəukən] *adj*: **he is** ~ (*sad*) он уби́т го́рем.

heartburn ['hɑ:tbə:n] *n* изжо́га.

-hearted ['hɑ:tɪd] *suffix*: **kind-**~ добро- серде́чный.

hearten ['hɑ:tn] *vt* воодушевля́ть (воодушеви́ть* *perf*).

heart failure *n* (*resulting in death*) остано́вка се́рдца.

heartfelt ['hɑ:tfɛlt] *adj* и́скренний*.

hearth [hɑ:θ] *n* оча́г*.

heartily ['hɑ:tɪlɪ] *adv* (*thank, welcome*) серде́чно; (*dislike*) всем се́рдцем; **to laugh** ~ смея́ться (*impf*) от души́.

heartland ['hɑ:tlænd] *n* (*of country*) се́рдце; **Britain's industrial** ~ промы́шленный центр Брита́нии.

heartless ['hɑ:tlɪs] *adj* бессерде́чный* (бессерде́чен).

heartstrings ['hɑ:tstrɪŋz] *npl* душе́вные стру́ны* *ntpl*; **the film really tugs at your** ~ фильм берёт за́ душу.

heartthrob ['hɑ:tθrɔb] *n* сердцее́д.

heart-to-heart ['hɑ:t'tə'hɑ:t] *adj* серде́чный; **to have a** ~ говори́ть (*impf*) по душа́м.

heart transplant *n* переса́дка* се́рдца.

heartwarming ['hɑ:twɔ:mɪŋ] *adj* (*sight*) тро́гательный* (тро́гателен).

hearty ['hɑ:tɪ] *adj* (*person, laugh*) весёлый* (ве́сел); (*welcome, support*) серде́чный; (*appetite*) здоро́вый; (*dislike*) глубо́кий*.

heat [hi:t] *n* тепло́; (*extreme*) жар; (*of weather*) жара́; (*temperature*) температу́ра; (*excitement*) пыл*; (*also*: **qualifying** ~: *in race etc*) забе́г; (: *in swimming*) заплы́в; (*ZOOL*): **our dog is in** *or* (*US*) **on** ~ у на́шей соба́ки те́чка ♦ *vt* (*water, food*) греть *or* нагрева́ть (нагре́ть *perf*); (*house*) ота́пливать (отопи́ть* *perf*)

▶ **heat up** *vi* (*water, house*) согрева́ться (согре́ться *perf*) ♦ *vt* (*food, water*) подогрева́ть (подогре́ть *perf*); (*room*) обогрева́ть (обогре́ть *perf*); (*engine*) разогрева́ть (разогре́ть *perf*).

heated ['hi:tɪd] *adj* ота́пливаемый; (*argument*) горя́чий*; (*pool*) обогрева́емый.

heater ['hi:tə'] *n* обогрева́тель *m*.

heath [hi:θ] *n* (*BRIT*) (ве́ресковая) пу́стошь *f*.

heathen ['hi:ðn] *n* язы́чник(-ица).

heather ['hɛðə'] *n* ве́реск.

heating ['hi:tɪŋ] *n* отопле́ние.

heat-resistant ['hi:trɪzɪstənt] *adj* жаро- про́чный* (жаропро́чен), термосто́йкий* (термосто́ек).

heat-seeking ['hi:tsi:kɪŋ] *adj* тепло- ула́вливающий.

heatstroke ['hi:tstrəuk] *n* теплово́й уда́р.

heat wave ['hi:tweɪv] *n* пери́од си́льной жары́.

heave [hi:v] *vt* (*pull*) выта́гивать (вы́тянуть *perf*); (*push*) толка́ть (толкну́ть *perf*); (*lift*) взва́ливать (взвали́ть* *perf*); (*throw*) швыря́ть (швырну́ть *perf*) ♦ *vi* (*chest*) вздыма́ться (*impf*); (*retch*) чу́вствовать (почу́вствовать *perf*) тошноту́ ♦ *n* (*upwards*) подъём; (*sideways*) рыво́к; **to** ~ **a sigh** глубоко́ вздохну́ть (*perf*)

▶ **heave to** ♦ (*pt, pp* **hove**) *vi* (*NAUT*) ложи́ться (лечь* *perf*) в дрейф.

heaven ['hɛvn] *n* (*also fig*) рай*; **thank** ~(**s**)! сла́ва Бо́гу!; ~ **forbid!** Бо́же упаси́!; **for** ~'**s sake!** ра́ди Бо́га!

heavenly ['hɛvnlɪ] *adj* небе́сный; (*fig*) ра́йский.

heaven-sent [hɛvn'sɛnt] *adj* благода́тный* (благода́тен).

heavily ['hɛvɪlɪ] *adv* (*fall, sigh*) тяжело́; (*drink, smoke, depend*) си́льно; (*sleep*) кре́пко; (*say*) весо́мый (весо́м).

heavy ['hɛvɪ] *adj* тяжёлый* (тяжёл); (*rain, blow, fall*) си́льный* (си́лен); (*breathing, sleep*) тяжёлый*; (*build: of person*) гру́зный; (*sea*) бу́рный* (бу́рен); **he is a** ~ **drinker/ smoker** он мно́го пьёт/ку́рит; **the work is** ~ **going** рабо́та идёт тяжело́; **he is** ~ **going** с ним тру́дно име́ть де́ло.

heavy cream *n* (*US*) жи́рные сли́вки* *pl*.

heavy-duty ['hɛvɪ'dju:tɪ] *adj* сверхпро́чный.

heavy goods vehicle *n* (*BRIT*) грузови́к, перевозя́щий тяжёлые гру́зы.

---

heavy-handed ['hɛvɪ'hændɪd] *adj* вла́стный* (вла́стен).

heavy industry *n* тяжёлая промы́шленность *f*.

heavy metal *n* (*MUS*) хэ́ви ме́тал, (тяжёлый) мета́лл.

heavy-set ['hɛvɪ'sɛt] *adj* (*esp US*) корена́стый (корена́ст).

heavy user *n* лицо́/компа́ния, покупа́ющее/-ая больши́е па́ртии определённого това́ра.

heavyweight ['hɛvɪweɪt] *n* боксёр тяжёлого ве́са.

Hebrew ['hi:bru:] *adj* древнееврейский ♦ *n* (*LING*: *ancient*) древнееврейский язы́к*; (*modern*) иври́т.

Hebrides ['hɛbrɪdi:z] *npl*: **the** ~ Гебри́дские острова́* *mpl*.

heck [hɛk] *excl* (*inf*) чёрт.

heckle ['hɛkl] *vt* перебива́ть (переби́ть* *perf*).

heckler ['hɛklə'] *n*: **there were several ~s in the audience** не́которые лю́ди в за́ле перебива́ли.

hectare ['hɛktɑː'] *n* (*BRIT*) гекта́р.

hectic ['hɛktɪk] *adj* (*day*) сумато́шный* (сумато́шен); (*actions, activities*) лихора́дочный* (лихора́дочен).

hector ['hɛktə'] *vt* запу́гивать (запуга́ть *perf*).

he'd [hi:d] = **he would, he had.**

hedge [hɛdʒ] *n* жива́я и́згородь *f* ♦ *vi* (*stall*) уви́ливать (увильну́ть *perf*) ♦ *vt*: **to ~ one's bets** подстрахо́вываться (подстрахова́ться *perf*); **as a ~ against inflation** как страхо́вка от инфля́ции
► **hedge in** *vt* ограни́чивать (ограни́чить *perf*).

hedgehog ['hɛdʒhɔg] *n* ёж*.

hedgerow ['hɛdʒrəu] *n* жива́я и́згородь *f*.

hedonism ['hi:dənɪzəm] *n* гедони́зм.

heed [hi:d] *vt* (*also*: **take ~ of**) принима́ть (приня́ть* *perf*) во внима́ние ♦ *n*: **to pay (no) ~ to, take (no) ~ of** (не) принима́ть (приня́ть* *perf*) во внима́ние.

heedless ['hi:dlɪs] *adj*: ~ **of** не обраща́я внима́ния на +*acc*.

heel [hi:l] *n* (*of foot*) пя́тка*; (*of shoe*) каблу́к* ♦ *vt* (*shoe*) подбива́ть (подби́ть* *perf*); **to bring to ~** (*dog*) заставля́ть (заста́вить* *perf*) идти́ *or* стоя́ть ря́дом; (*person*) подчиня́ть (подчини́ть *perf*); **to take to one's ~s** (*inf*) пуска́ться (пусти́ться* *perf*) наутёк.

hefty ['hɛftɪ] *adj* (*person, object*) здорове́нный*; (*profit, fine*) изря́дный*.

heifer ['hɛfə'] *n* тёлка*.

height [haɪt] *n* (*of tree, of plane*) высота́*; (*of person*) рост; (*of power*) верши́на; (*of mountain*) возвы́шенность *f*; (*of season*) разга́р; (*of luxury, taste*) верх; **what ~ are you?** како́й у Вас рост?; **of average ~** сре́днего ро́ста; **to be afraid of ~s** боя́ться (*impf*) высоты́; **it's the ~ of fashion** э́то верх мо́ды; **at the ~ of the tourist season** в разга́р туристи́ческого сезо́на.

heighten ['haɪtn] *vt* уси́ливать (уси́лить *perf*).

heinous ['heɪnəs] *adj* (*crime*) чудо́вищный.

heir [ɛə'] *n* насле́дник.

heir apparent *n* прямо́й насле́дник.

heiress ['ɛərɛs] *n* насле́дница.

heirloom ['ɛəlu:m] *n* семе́йная рели́квия.

heist [haɪst] *n* (*US*: *inf*) грабёж*.

held [hɛld] *pt, pp of* **hold.**

helicopter ['hɛlɪkɔptə'] *n* вертолёт.

heliport ['hɛlɪpɔ:t] *n* вертодро́м.

helium ['hi:lɪəm] *n* ге́лий.

hell [hɛl] *n* (*also fig*) ад*; ~**!** (*inf*) чёрт!; **a** *or* **one ~ of a mess** (*inf*) кошма́рный беспоря́док*; **a** *or* **one ~ of a party** (*inf*) кла́ссная вечери́нка.

he'll [hi:l] = **he will, he shall;** *see* **will.**

hellish ['hɛlɪʃ] *adj* (*inf*: *awful*) кошма́рный* (кошма́рен).

hello [hə'ləu] *excl* здра́вствуйте; (*informal*) приве́т; (*TEL*: *on answering*) алло́; (*to attract attention*) эй; (*in surprise*): ~**(, what's this!)** эй (что э́то!).

helm [hɛlm] *n* (*NAUT*) руль* *m*; **man at the ~** (*fig*) рулево́й *m adj*; **at the ~ of** у корми́ла +*gen*.

helmet ['hɛlmɪt] *n* (*of policeman, miner*) ка́ска*; (*also*: **crash ~**) шлем.

helmsman ['hɛlmzmən] *n* рулево́й *m adj*.

help [hɛlp] *n* по́мощь *f*; (*charwoman*) прислу́га ♦ *vt* помога́ть (помо́чь* *perf*) +*dat*; **with the ~ of** (*person*) с по́мощью +*gen*; (*tool*) при по́мощи +*gen*; **can I be of (any) ~?** я могу́ Вам чем-нибу́дь помо́чь?; ~**!** помоги́те!; **can I ~ you?** (*in shop*) чем могу́ быть* поле́зен?; ~ **yourself** угоща́йтесь; **he can't ~ it** он ничего́ не мо́жет поде́лать с э́тим; **I can't ~ thinking that ...** я не могу́ не ду́мать, что ....

helper ['hɛlpə'] *n* помо́щник(-ица).

helpful ['hɛlpful] *adj* поле́зный* (поле́зен).

helping ['hɛlpɪŋ] *n* по́рция.

helping hand *n*: **to lend a ~ ~** протя́гивать (протяну́ть *perf*) ру́ку по́мощи.

helpless ['hɛlplɪs] *adj* беспо́мощный* (беспо́мощен).

helplessly ['hɛlplɪslɪ] *adv* беспо́мощно.

helpline ['hɛlplaɪn] *n* телефо́н дове́рия.

Helsinki ['hɛlsɪŋkɪ] *n* Хе́льсинки *m ind*.

helter-skelter ['hɛltə'skɛltə'] *n* (*BRIT*) спира́льная го́рка (*аттракцио́н*).

hem [hɛm] *n* (*of dress*) подо́л; (*of curtains*) низ ♦ *vt* подшива́ть (подши́ть* *perf*)
► **hem in** *vt* пло́тно окружа́ть (окружи́ть *perf*); **city life made him feel ~med in** жизнь в го́роде стесня́ла его́.

hematology ['hi:mə'tɔlədʒɪ] *n* (*US*) = **haematology.**

hemisphere ['hɛmɪsfɪə'] *n* полуша́рие.

hemlock ['hɛmlɔk] *n* (*BOT*) болиголо́в.

hemoglobin ['hi:mə'gləubɪn] *n* (*US*) = **haemoglobin.**

hemophilia ['hi:mə'fɪlɪə] *n* (*US*) = **haemophilia.**

hemorrhage ['hɛmərɪdʒ] *n* (*US*) = **haemorrhage.**

hemorrhoids ['hɛmərɔɪdz] *npl* (*US*) =

haemorrhoids.
hemp [hɛmp] *n* конопля́.
hen [hɛn] *n* (*chicken*) ку́рица*; (*female bird*) са́мка*.
hence [hɛns] *adv* (*therefore*) сле́довательно; (*from now*): **2 years ~** (*formal*) по истече́нии двух лет.
henceforth [hɛns'fɔ:θ] *adv* впредь.
henchman ['hɛntʃmən] *irreg n* приспе́шник.
henna ['hɛnə] *n* хна.
hen party *n* (*inf*) деви́чник.
henpecked ['hɛnpɛkt] *adj* (*husband*) поко́рный* (поко́рен).
hepatitis [hɛpə'taɪtɪs] *n* гепати́т.
her [hə:'] *pron* (*direct*) её; (*indirect*) ей; (*after prep*: +*instr*, +*dat*, +*prp*) ней; (: +*gen*) неё; *see also* **me** ♦ *adj* её; (*referring to subject of sentence*) свой; *see also* **my**.
herald ['hɛrəld] *n* (*precursor*) предве́стник ♦ *vt* (*event*) предвеща́ть (*impf*).
heraldic [hɛ'rældɪk] *adj* геральди́ческий.
heraldry ['hɛrəldrɪ] *n* (*study*) гера́льдика; (*coat of arms*) герб.
herb [hə:b] *n* (*BOT*, *CULIN*) трава́*; (*MED*) лека́рственная трава́; ~**s** *npl* (*CULIN*) зе́лень *fsg*.
herbaceous [hə:'beɪʃəs] *adj*: ~ **plant** цвето́чное расте́ние; ~ **border** клу́мба.
herbal ['hə:bl] *adj*: ~ **medicine** лече́ние тра́вами; ~ **remedy** лека́рство из трав; ~ **tea** чай* из трав.
herbicide ['hə:bɪsaɪd] *n* гербици́д.
herd [hə:d] *n* ста́до* ♦ *vt* (*drive*: *animals, people*) гнать* (*impf*); (*gather*) сгоня́ть (согна́ть* *perf*).
here [hɪə'] *adv* (*location*) здесь; (*destination*) сюда́; (*departure point*): **from ~** отсю́да; (*at this point*: *in past*) тут; *"here!"* (*present*) „здесь!"; ~ **is ...**, ~ **are ...** вот ...; ~ **you are** (*giving*) вот, пожа́луйста; **where are my keys? ~ we are!** (*finding sth*) где мои́ ключи́? вот они́!; ~**'s my sister** вот моя́ сестра́; ~ **she comes** вот она́ идёт; **come ~!** иди́те сюда́!; **she left ~ yesterday** она́ уе́хала отсю́да вчера́; ~ **and there** (*location*) там и сям; (*motion*) туда́ и сюда́; *"here's to ...!"* (*toast*) „за +*acc* ...!".
hereabouts ['hɪərə'bauts] *adv* побли́зости.
hereafter [hɪər'ɑ:ftə'] *adv* в дальне́йшем.
hereby [hɪə'baɪ] *adv* (*formal*: *in letter*): **we ~ acknowledge ...** настоя́щим подтвержда́ем ....
hereditary [hɪ'rɛdɪtrɪ] *adj* насле́дственный.
heredity [hɪ'rɛdɪtɪ] *n* насле́дственность *f*.
heresy ['hɛrəsɪ] *n* е́ресь *f*.
heretic ['hɛrətɪk] *n* ерети́к*(-и́чка*).
heretical [hɪ'rɛtɪkl] *adj* ерети́ческий*.
herewith ['hɪə'wɪð] *adv* (*formal*: *letter*): **please find enclosed ~ ...** при сём прилага́ется ....
heritage ['hɛrɪtɪdʒ] *n* насле́дие; **our national ~**

на́ше национа́льное бога́тство.
hermetically [hə:'mɛtɪklɪ] *adv*: ~ **sealed** гермети́чески закры́тый.
hermit ['hə:mɪt] *n* отше́льник(-ица).
hernia ['hə:nɪə] *n* гры́жа.
hero ['hɪərəu] (*pl* ~**es**) *n* геро́й.
heroic [hɪ'rəuɪk] *adj* герои́ческий*.
heroin ['hɛrəuɪn] *n* герои́н.
heroin addict *n* наркома́н (*принима́ющий герои́н*).
heroine ['hɛrəuɪn] *n* герои́ня.
heroism ['hɛrəuɪzəm] *n* герои́зм.
heron ['hɛrən] *n* ца́пля*.
hero worship *n* культ героя́.
herring ['hɛrɪŋ] *n* (*ZOOL*) сельдь* *f*; (*CULIN*) селёдка.
hers [hə:z] *pron* её; (*referring to subject of sentence*) свой; *see also* **mine**.
herself [hə:'sɛlf] *pron* (*reflexive, after prep*: +*acc*, +*gen*) себя́; (: +*dat*, +*prp*) себе́; (: +*instr*) собой; (*emphatic*) сама́; (*alone*): **by ~** одна́; *see also* **myself**.
Herts *abbr* (*BRIT*: *POST*) = Hertfordshire.
he's [hi:z] = **he is**, **he has**; *see* **be**, **have**.
hesitant ['hɛzɪtənt] *adj* нереши́тельный (нереши́телен); **to be ~ about doing** не реша́ться (*impf*) or колеба́ться (*impf*) +*infin*.
hesitate ['hɛzɪteɪt] *vi* (*pause*) колеба́ться* (поколеба́ться* *perf*); (*be unwilling*) не реша́ться (*impf*); **to ~ (about/to do)** не реша́ться (*impf*) (на +*acc*/+*infin*); **don't ~ to see a doctor if you are worried** е́сли Вы обеспоко́ены (э́тим), без колеба́ний обрати́тесь к врачу́.
hesitation [hɛzɪ'teɪʃən] *n* (*pause*) колеба́ние; **I have no ~ in saying (that) ...** я говорю́ не колебля́сь(, что) ....
hessian ['hɛsɪən] *n* мешкови́на.
heterogeneous ['hɛtərə'dʒi:nɪəs] *adj* разноро́дный* (разноро́ден).
heterosexual ['hɛtərəu'sɛksjuəl] *adj* гетеросексуа́льный ♦ *n* гетеросексуа́льный челове́к*.
het up [hɛt-] *adj* (*inf*): **to get ~ ~ (about)** заводи́ться* (завести́сь* *perf*) (из-за +*gen*).
HEW *n abbr* (*US*) = Department of Health, Education and Welfare.
hew [hju:] (*pp* **hewed** *or* **hewn**) *vt* (*stone*) выда́лбливать (вы́долбить* *perf*); (*wood*) выруба́ть (вы́рубить* *perf*).
hewn [hju:n] *pp of* **hew**.
hex [hɛks] (*US*) *n* колду́нья*, ве́дьма ♦ *vt* завора́живать (заворожи́ть* *perf*).
hexagon ['hɛksəgən] *n* шестиуго́льник.
hexagonal [hɛk'sægənl] *adj* шестиуго́льный.
hey [heɪ] *excl* эй.
heyday ['heɪdeɪ] *n*: **the ~ of** расцве́т +*gen*.
HF *n abbr* (= *high frequency*) ВЧ= *высо́кая*

---

* marks translations which have irregular inflections. The Russian-English side of the dictionary gives inflectional information.

частота́.

HGV *n abbr* (*BRIT*: = heavy goods vehicle) грузово́й автомоби́ль *m*.

HI *abbr* (*US*: *POST*) = Hawaii.

hi [haɪ] *excl* (*as greeting*) приве́т; (*to attract attention*) эй.

hiatus [haɪˈeɪtəs] *n* (*in activity*) пробе́л; (*in conversation*) па́уза.

hibernate [ˈhaɪbəneɪt] *vi* впада́ть (впасть* *perf*) в зи́мнюю спя́чку.

hibernation [haɪbəˈneɪʃən] *n* зи́мняя спя́чка.

hick [hɪk] *n* (*US*: inf: pej) дереве́нщина *m/f*.

hiccough *etc* = hiccup *etc*.

hiccup [ˈhɪkʌp] *vi* ика́ть (*impf*).

hiccups [ˈhɪkʌps] *npl* ико́та *fsg*; **she's got (the) ~** у неё ико́та.

hid [hɪd] *pt of* hide.

hidden [ˈhɪdn] *pp of* hide ♦ *adj*: **there are no ~ extras** здесь нет скры́тых доба́вочных расхо́дов; **there is a ~ agenda** за э́тим что-то кро́ется.

hide [haɪd] (*pt* hid, *pp* hidden) *n* (*skin*) шку́ра; (*of birdwatcher*) укры́тие ♦ *vt* (*object, person*) пря́тать* (спря́тать* *perf*); (*feeling, information*) скрыва́ть (скрыть* *perf*); (*sun, view*) закрыва́ть (закры́ть* *perf*) ♦ *vi*: **to ~ (from sb)** пря́таться* (спря́таться* *perf*) (от кого́-н); **to ~ sth (from sb)** (*object, person*) пря́тать* (спря́тать* *perf*) что-н (от кого́-н); (*information*) скрыва́ть (скрыть* *perf*) что-н (от кого́-н).

hide-and-seek [ˈhaɪdənˈsiːk] *n* пря́тки* *fpl*.

hideaway [ˈhaɪdəweɪ] *n* убе́жище.

hideous [ˈhɪdɪəs] *adj* (*painting, conditions*) жу́ткий* (жу́ток); (*face*) омерзи́тельный* (омерзи́телен).

hideously [ˈhɪdɪəslɪ] *adv* (*ugly*) омерзи́тельно; (*difficult*) жу́тко.

hide-out [ˈhaɪdaut] *n* укры́тие; (*of criminals*) ло́говище.

hiding [ˈhaɪdɪŋ] *n* (*beating*) по́рка*; (*concealed*): **to be in ~** скрыва́ться (*impf*).

hiding place *n* (*for person*) укры́тие; (*for money etc*) тайни́к*, потайно́е ме́сто*.

hierarchy [ˈhaɪərɑːkɪ] *n* иера́рхия.

hieroglyphic [haɪərəˈglɪfɪk] *adj* иероглифи́ческий.

hieroglyphics [haɪərəˈglɪfɪks] *npl* иеро́глифы *mpl*.

hi-fi [ˈhaɪfaɪ] *n abbr* (= high fidelity) высо́кая ве́рность звуковоспроизведе́ния ♦ *adj* (*equipment, system*): **~ equipment** аппарату́ра с высо́кой ве́рностью звуковоспроизведе́ния.

higgledy-piggledy [ˈhɪgldɪˈpɪgldɪ] (*inf*) *adj* беспоря́дочный* (бесоря́дочен) ♦ *adv* ко́е-ка́к, беспоря́дочно.

high [haɪ] *adj* высо́кий* (высо́к); (*wind*) си́льный*; (*BRIT*: meat) вы́держанный (вы́держан) ♦ *adv* (*climb, aim etc*) высоко́ ♦ *n*: **exports have reached a new ~** э́кспорт дости́г

но́вой высоты́; **the building is 20 m ~** высота́ зда́ния – 20 м; **to be ~** (*inf*: on drugs, drink) кайфова́ть (*impf*); **~ risk** высо́кая сте́пень *f* ри́ска; **~ in the air** (*position*) высоко́ в во́здухе; (*motion*) высоко́ в во́здух; **to pay a ~ price for sth** плати́ть* (заплати́ть* *perf*) высо́кую це́ну за что-н; **it's ~ time you learned how to do it** Вам давно́ пора́ научи́ться де́лать э́то.

highball [ˈhaɪbɔːl] *n* (*US*) ви́ски с со́довой и льдо́м (в высо́ком стака́не).

highboy [ˈhaɪbɔɪ] *n* (*US*) высо́кий комо́д.

highbrow [ˈhaɪbrau] *adj* (*subjects*) учёный; (*person*) интеллектуа́льный* (интеллектуа́лен).

highchair [ˈhaɪtʃɛəʳ] *n* высо́кий* сту́льчик (для ма́леньких дете́й).

high-class [ˈhaɪˈklɑːs] *adj* (*hotel, performance*) первокла́ссный, высо́кого кла́сса; (*neighbourhood*) прести́жный* (прести́жен).

High Court *n* (*BRIT*): **the ~** ~ Верхо́вный суд*.

higher [ˈhaɪəʳ] *adj* вы́сший* ♦ *adv* вы́ше.

higher education *n* вы́сшее образова́ние.

highfalutin [haɪfəˈluːtɪn] *adj* (*inf*) высоко-па́рный* (высокопа́рен).

high finance *n*: **the world of ~** ~ мир вы́сших фина́нсовых круго́в.

high-five [haɪˈfaɪv] *n* пятерня́ (хлопо́к ладо́нью по чьей-нибудь ладо́ни).

high-flier [haɪˈflaɪəʳ] *n* пти́ца высо́кого полёта.

high-flying [haɪˈflaɪɪŋ] *adj* (*person*) честолюби́вый; (*lifestyle*) шика́рный.

high-handed [haɪˈhændɪd] *adj* (*decision, person*) своево́льный* (своево́лен).

high-heeled [haɪˈhiːld] *adj* на высо́ком каблуке́.

high heels *npl* ту́фли* *fpl* на высо́ком каблуке́.

high jump *n* прыжо́к* в высоту́.

Highlands [ˈhaɪləndz] *npl*: **the ~** Высокого́рья* *ntpl* (Шотла́ндии).

high-level [ˈhaɪlɛvl] *adj* (*talks etc*) на вы́сшем у́ровне; **~ language** (*COMPUT*) язы́к* высо́кого у́ровня.

highlight [ˈhaɪlaɪt] *n* (*of event*) кульмина́ция ♦ *vt* (*problem, need*) выявля́ть (вы́явить* *perf*); **~s** *npl* (*in hair*) пря́ди *fpl*; **the match ~s were shown on TV** кульминацио́нные моме́нты ма́тча бы́ли пока́заны по телеви́дению.

highlighter [ˈhaɪlaɪtəʳ] *n* (*also*: **~ pen**) флома́стер (для выделе́ния часте́й те́кста).

highly [ˈhaɪlɪ] *adv* о́чень; (*paid*) высоко́; **to speak ~ of** высоко́ отзыва́ться (отозва́ться* *perf*) о +*prp*; **to think ~ of** быть* (*impf*) высо́кого мне́ния о +*prp*.

highly strung *adj* нерво́зный* (нерво́зен).

High Mass *n* торже́ственная ме́сса.

highness [ˈhaɪnɪs] *n*: **Her/His H~** Её/Его́ Высо́чество.

high-pitched [haɪˈpɪtʃt] *adj* пронзи́тельный* (пронзи́телен).

high point *n* кульмина́ция.

high-powered ['haɪ'pauəd] adj (engine) мо́щный*; (job) отве́тственный; (course, person) высо́кого у́ровня.
high-pressure ['haɪprɛʃə'] adj высо́кого давле́ния.
high-rise ['haɪraɪz] adj (buildings, flats) высо́тный.
high school n (BRIT) сре́дняя шко́ла (для 11-18ти ле́тних); (US) сре́дняя шко́ла (для 15-18ти ле́тних).
high season n (BRIT) разга́р сезо́на.
high spirits npl припо́днятое настрое́ние ntsg.
high street n (BRIT) центра́льная у́лица.
high-strung ['haɪ'strʌŋ] adj (US) = **highly strung**
high tide n прили́в.
highway ['haɪweɪ] n (US: between towns, states) шоссе́ nt ind, автостра́да; (main road) автостра́да.
Highway Code n (BRIT) ≈ пра́вила ntpl доро́жного движе́ния.
highwayman ['haɪweɪmən] irreg n разбо́йник с большо́й доро́ги.
hijack ['haɪdʒæk] vt угоня́ть (угна́ть* perf); (fig) перехва́тывать (перехвати́ть* perf) ♦ n (also: ~ing) уго́н.
hijacker ['haɪdʒækə'] n уго́нщик.
hike [haɪk] vi ходи́ть*/идти́* (impf) в похо́д ♦ vt (inf: prices) взви́нчивать (взвинти́ть* perf) ♦ n: **to go for a** ~ идти́* (пойти́* perf) на дли́тельную прогу́лку; (inf): **a** ~ **in prices** скачо́к* цен.
hiker ['haɪkə'] n тури́ст(ка).
hiking ['haɪkɪŋ] n: **to go** ~ ходи́ть*/идти́* (impf) в похо́д.
hilarious [hɪ'lɛərɪəs] adj чрезвыча́йно смешно́й* (смешо́н).
hilarity [hɪ'lærɪtɪ] n бу́йное весе́лье.
hill [hɪl] n (small) холм*; (fairly high) (небольша́я) гора́*; (slope) склон; (on road) подъём.
hillbilly ['hɪlbɪlɪ] n (US) го́рец*; (: pej) дереве́нщина m/f.
hillock ['hɪlək] n приго́рок*.
hillside ['hɪlsaɪd] n склон.
hill start n (AUT) заво́д и управле́ние автомоби́лей на подъёме.
hilltop ['hɪltɔp] n верши́на (холма́, горы́)
hilly ['hɪlɪ] adj холми́стый (холми́ст).
hilt [hɪlt] n рукоя́тка*; **to back sb to the** ~ подде́рживать (impf) кого́-н по́лностью.
him [hɪm] pron (direct) его́; (indirect) ему́; (after prep: +gen) него́; (: +dat) нему́; (: +instr) ним; (: +prp) нём; see also **me**.
Himalayas [hɪmə'leɪəz] npl: **the** ~ Гимала́и pl.
himself [hɪm'sɛlf] pron (reflexive, after prep: +acc, +gen) себя́; (: +dat, +prp) себе́; (: +instr) собо́й; (emphatic) сам; (alone): **by** ~ оди́н; see

also **myself**.
hind [haɪnd] adj за́дний* ♦ n са́мка* оле́ня.
hinder ['hɪndə'] vt (progress, movement) препя́тствовать (воспрепя́тствовать perf) or меша́ть (помеша́ть perf) +dat; **to** ~ **sb from doing** меша́ть (помеша́ть perf) кому́-н +infin.
hindquarters ['haɪnd'kwɔ:təz] npl (of animal) зад msg.
hindrance ['hɪndrəns] n (nuisance, interruption) поме́ха.
hindsight ['haɪndsaɪt] n: **with** ~ ретроспекти́вным взгля́дом.
Hindu ['hɪndu:] adj инду́сский.
hinge [hɪndʒ] n (on door) петля́* ♦ vi (fig): **to** ~ **on** зави́сеть (impf) от +gen.
hint [hɪnt] n (suggestion) намёк; (tip) сове́т; (sign, glimmer) подо́бие ♦ vt: **to** ~ **that** намека́ть (намекну́ть perf) что ♦ vi: **to** ~ **at** намека́ть (намекну́ть perf) на +acc; **to drop a** ~ оброни́ть* (perf) намёк; **to give sb a** ~ подска́зывать (подсказа́ть* perf) кому́-н; **white with a** ~ **of pink** бе́лый с намёком на ро́зовый.
hip [hɪp] n бедро́*.
hip flask n набе́дренная фля́га.
hip hop n стиль поп-му́зыки.
hippie ['hɪpɪ] n хи́ппи m/f ind.
hippo ['hɪpəu] n гиппопота́м.
hip pocket n за́дний* карма́н.
hippopotami [hɪpə'pɔtəmaɪ] npl of **hippopotamus**.
hippopotamus [hɪpə'pɔtəməs] (pl ~es or **hippopotami**) n гиппопота́м.
hippy ['hɪpɪ] n = **hippie**.
hire ['haɪə'] vt (BRIT: car, equipment) брать* (взять* perf) напрока́т; (venue) снима́ть (снять* perf), арендова́ть (impf/perf); (worker) нанима́ть (наня́ть* perf) ♦ n (BRIT: of car) прока́т; (venue) аре́нда; **for** ~ напрока́т; **on** ~ взя́тый напрока́т
▸ **hire out** vt (car, equipment) дава́ть* (дать* perf) напрока́т; (venue) сдава́ть* (сдать* perf) внаём.
hire(d) car n (BRIT) маши́на, взя́тая напрока́т.
hire-purchase [haɪə'pə:tʃɪs] n (BRIT): **to buy sth on** ~ покупа́ть (купи́ть* perf) что-н в рассро́чку.
Hiroshima [hɪ'rɔʃɪmə] n Хироси́ма.
his [hɪz] adj его́; (referring to subject of sentence) свой; see also **my** ♦ pron его́; see also **mine**[1].
hiss [hɪs] vi (snake, gas, fat) шипе́ть* (impf); (person, audience) осви́стывать (освиста́ть* perf), ши́кать (оши́кать perf) ♦ n (see vb) шипе́ние; свист, ши́кание.
histogram ['hɪstəgræm] n гистогра́мма.
historian [hɪ'stɔ:rɪən] n исто́рик.
historic [hɪ'stɔrɪk] adj (agreement, achievement)

---

* marks translations which have irregular inflections. The Russian-English side of the dictionary gives inflectional information.

истори́ческий*.
historical [hɪˈstɔrɪkl] *adj* (*event, film*)
истори́ческий*.
history [ˈhɪstərɪ] *n* исто́рия; **medical ~** (*of patient*) исто́рия боле́зни; **there's a long ~ of illness in his family** боле́знь передава́лась в его́ семье́ по насле́дству.
hit [hɪt] (*pt* **hit**) *vt* ударя́ть (уда́рить *perf*); (*reach: target*) попада́ть (попа́сть* *perf*) в +*acc*; (*collide with: car*) ста́лкиваться (столкну́ться *perf*) с +*instr*; (*affect: person, services*) ударя́ть (уда́рить *perf*) по +*dat* ♦ *n* (*knock*) уда́р; (*success*): **the play was a big ~** пье́са по́льзовалась больши́м успе́хом; **to ~ it off (with sb)** (*inf*) найти́* (*perf*) о́бщий язы́к (с кем-н); **to ~ the headlines** попа́сть* (*perf*) на пе́рвые страни́цы газе́т; **to ~ the road** (*inf*) отправля́ться (отпра́виться* *perf*) в путь; **he'll ~ the roof when he finds out about it** (*inf*) он всё здесь разнесёт, когда́ узна́ет об э́том
▶ **hit back** *vi*: **to ~ back at sb** (*in fight, argument*) наноси́ть* (нанести́* *perf*) отве́тный уда́р кому́-н
▶ **hit out at** *vt fus* (*also fig*) набра́сываться (набро́ситься* *perf*) на +*acc*
▶ **hit (up)on** *vt fus* (*answer, solution etc*) оты́скивать (отыска́ть* *perf*).
hit and miss *adj* (*unpredictable*) непред-ска́зуемый (непредска́зуем).
hit-and-run driver [ˈhɪtənˈrʌn-] *n* води́тель, кото́рый, сбив пешехо́да, уезжа́ет с ме́ста происше́ствия.
hitch [hɪtʃ] *vt* (*also:* **~ up**: *trousers, skirt*) подтя́гивать (подтяну́ть* *perf*) ♦ *n* (*difficulty*) поме́ха; **to ~ sth to** (*fasten*) привя́зывать (привяза́ть* *perf*) что-н к +*dat*; (*hook*) прицепля́ть (прицепи́ть* *perf*) что-н к +*dat*; **~ a lift** лови́ть* (пойма́ть *perf*) попу́тку; **technical ~** техни́ческая неувя́зка*
▶ **hitch up** *vt* (*horse, cart*) запряга́ть (запря́чь* *perf*); *see also* **hitch**.
hitchhike [ˈhɪtʃhaɪk] *vi* е́здить*/е́хать* (пое́хать* *perf*) автосто́пом.
hitchhiker [ˈhɪtʃhaɪkəʳ] *n* путеше́ственник (-ица) автосто́пом.
hi-tech [ˈhaɪˈtɛk] *adj* высокотехни́ческий.
hitherto [hɪðəˈtuː] *adv* (*formal*) до настоя́щего вре́мени.
hit list *n* спи́сок* наме́ченных жертв.
hit man *irreg n* наёмный уби́йца *m*.
hit-or-miss [ˈhɪtəˈmɪs] *adj* сде́ланный (сде́лан) наугад́; (*casual*) сде́ланный как попа́ло *or* ко́е-как; (*unpredictable*) непредска́зуемый (непредска́зуем); **it's ~ whether I'll be able to come** тру́дно предсказа́ть, смогу́ ли я прийти́.
hit parade *n* (*formerly*) хит-пара́д.
HIV *n abbr* (= *human immunodeficiency virus*) ВИЧ= *ви́рус иммунодефици́та челове́ка*; **~-negative** с отрица́тельной реа́кцией на ВИЧ; **~-positive** с положи́тельной реа́кцией

на ВИЧ.
hive [haɪv] *n* (*of bees*) у́лей*; (*fig*): **Moscow is a ~ of activity** жизнь в Москве́ кипи́т
▶ **hive off** *vt* отделя́ть (отдели́ть* *perf*).
hl *abbr* (= *hectolitre*) гектоли́тр.
HM *abbr* (= *His/Her Majesty*) Его́/Её Вели́чество.
HMG *abbr* (*BRIT*) = *His (or Her) Majesty's Government*.
HMI *n abbr* (*BRIT*: *SCOL*) = *His (or Her) Majesty's Inspector*.
HMO *n abbr* (*US*) = *health maintenance organization*.
HMS *abbr* (*BRIT*) = *His (or Her) Majesty's Ship*.
HMSO *n abbr* (*BRIT*) = *His (or Her) Majesty's Stationery Office*.
HNC *n abbr* (*BRIT*: = *Higher National Certificate*) свиде́тельство о сре́днем техни́ческом образова́нии.
HND *n abbr* (*BRIT*: = *Higher National Diploma*) дипло́м о сре́днем техни́ческом образова́нии.
hoard [hɔːd] *n* (*of food*) (та́йный) запа́с; (*of treasure*) клад ♦ *vt* (*provisions*) запаса́ть (запасти́* *perf*); (*money*) копи́ть* (скопи́ть* *perf*).
hoarding [ˈhɔːdɪŋ] *n* (*BRIT*) рекла́мный щит*.
hoarfrost [ˈhɔːfrɔst] *n* и́ней.
hoarse [hɔːs] *adj* (*voice*) хри́плый* (хрипл.)
hoax [həuks] *n* (*trick*) мистифика́ция; (*false alarm*) ло́жная трево́га*.
hob [hɔb] *n* ве́рхняя часть плиты́ с конфо́рками.
hobble [ˈhɔbl] *vi* ковыля́ть (*impf*).
hobby [ˈhɔbɪ] *n* хо́бби *nt ind*.
hobbyhorse [ˈhɔbɪhɔːs] *n* (*fig*) люби́мый конёк*; **he is on his ~** он сел на своего́ люби́мого конька́.
hobnail boot [ˈhɔbneɪl-] *n* подко́ванный сапо́г.
hobnob [ˈhɔbnɔb] *vi* (*inf*): **to ~ with** води́ться (*impf*) с +*instr*.
hobo [ˈhəubəu] *n* (*US*) бродя́га *m/f*.
hock [hɔk] *n* (*BRIT*: *wine*) рейнве́йн; (*of horse*) скака́тельный суста́в ♦ *vt* (*inf*) закла́дывать (заложи́ть *perf*); **to be in ~** (*inf*: *person*) быть* (*impf*) в долга́х; (: *object*) быть* (*impf*) в закла́де.
hockey [ˈhɔkɪ] *n* хокке́й (на траве́).
hocus-pocus [ˈhəukəsˈpəukəs] *n* (*trickery*) очковтира́тельство; (*words: of magician*) фо́кус-по́кус; (*jargon*) белиберда́.
hod [hɔd] *n* лото́к* (*для перено́ски кирпиче́й*).
hodgepodge [ˈhɔdʒpɔdʒ] *n* (*US*) = **hotchpotch**.
hoe [həu] *n* моты́га, тя́пка* ♦ *vt* моты́жить (*impf*).
hog [hɔg] *n* бо́ров ♦ *vt* (*inf*: *road, telephone*) завладева́ть (завладе́ть *perf*) +*instr*; **to go the whole ~** (*inf*) гуля́ть (*impf*) на всю кату́шку.
Hogmanay [hɔgməˈneɪ] *n* (*SCOTTISH*) кану́н Но́вого го́да.

hogwash ['hɔgwɔʃ] *n* (*inf*) чушь *f*.

hoist [hɔɪst] *n* подъёмник, лебёдка* ♦ *vt* поднима́ть (подня́ть* *perf*); **to ~ sth on to one's shoulders** взва́ливать (взвали́ть* *perf*) что-н на пле́чи.

hoity-toity [hɔɪtɪ'tɔɪtɪ] *adj* (*inf: pej*) кичли́вый (кичли́в).

hold [həuld] (*pt, pp* **held**) *vt* (*grip*) держа́ть* (*impf*); (*contain*) вмеща́ть (вмести́ть* *perf*); (*power, qualification*) облада́ть (*impf*) +*instr*; (*opinion*) приде́рживаться (*impf*) +*gen*; (*post*) занима́ть (заня́ть* *perf*); (*conversation, meeting*) вести́* (провести́* *perf*); (*party*) устра́ивать (устро́ить *perf*); (*detain*) держа́ть* (*impf*) ♦ *vi* (*withstand pressure*) выде́рживать (вы́держать *perf*); (*be valid*) остава́ться (оста́ться* *perf*) в си́ле; (*weather*) держа́ться* (продержа́ться* *perf*) ♦ *n* (*grasp*) захва́т; (*NAUT*) трюм; (*AVIAT*) грузово́й отсе́к; **to ~ one's head up** высоко́ держа́ть* (*impf*) го́лову; **to ~ sb hostage** держа́ть* (*impf*) кого́-н в ка́честве зало́жника(-ицы); **~ the line!** (*TEL*) не клади́те тру́бку!; **to ~ one's own** не ударя́ть (уда́рить *perf*) лицо́м в грязь; **he ~s you responsible for her death** он счита́ет тебя́ вино́вным в её сме́рти; **~ it!** подожди́те!; **he ~s the view that ...** он приде́рживается того́ мне́ния, что ...; **to ~ firm** *or* **fast** не кре́пко держа́ться* (*impf*); **~ still, ~ steady** не дви́гайтесь; **if my luck ~s ...** е́сли мне бу́дет продолжа́ть везти́ ...; **I don't ~ with ...** я не одобря́ю ...; **to get ~ of** (*obtain*) достава́ть* (доста́ть* *perf*); **to get ~ of o.s.** сде́рживать (сдержа́ть *perf*) себя́, сде́рживаться (сдержа́ться *perf*); **to catch** *or* **grab ~ of** хвата́ться (схвати́ться* *perf*) за +*acc*; **to have a ~ over sb** держа́ть (*impf*) кого́-н в рука́х
► **hold back** *vt* (*thing*) приде́рживать (придержа́ть* *perf*); (*person*) уде́рживать (удержа́ть* *perf*); (*information*) скрыва́ть (скрыть* *perf*)
► **hold down** *vt* (*person*) уде́рживать (удержа́ть* *perf*); **to ~ down a job** уде́рживаться (удержа́ться*) на рабо́те
► **hold forth** *vi*: **to ~ forth (on** *or* **about)** увлечённо говори́ть (*impf*) (о +*prp*)
► **hold off** *vt* (*enemy*) сде́рживать (сдержа́ть* *perf*) ♦ *vi* (*weather*): **if the rain ~s off** е́сли не пойдёт дождь
► **hold on** *vi* (*hang on*) держа́ться* (*impf*); (*wait*) ждать (подожда́ть* *perf*); **~ on!** (*TEL*) не ве́шайте тру́бку!
► **hold on to** *vt fus* (*for support*) держа́ться* (*impf*) за +*acc*; (*keep: an object*) приде́рживать (придержа́ть *perf*); (: *beliefs*) сохраня́ть (сохрани́ть *perf*)
► **hold out** *vt* (*hand*) протя́гивать (протяну́ть

perf); (*hope, prospect*) сохраня́ть (сохрани́ть *perf*) ♦ *vi* (*resist*) держа́ться (продержа́ться *perf*)
► **hold over** *vt* (*meeting*) откла́дывать (отложи́ть* *perf*)
► **hold up** *vt* (*raise*) поднима́ть (подня́ть* *perf*); (*support*) подде́рживать (поддержа́ть* *perf*); (*delay*) заде́рживать (задержа́ть* *perf*); (*rob*) гра́бить* (огра́бить* *perf*).

holdall ['həuldɔ:l] *n* (*BRIT*) доро́жная су́мка*.

holder ['həuldə] *n* (*container*) держа́тель *m*; (*of ticket, record*) облада́тель(ница) *m(f)*; **post ~** занима́ющий(-ая) *m(f) adj* пост; **title ~** нося́щий(-ая) *m(f) adj* ти́тул.

holding ['həuldɪŋ] *n* (*share*) вклад; (*farm*) уча́сток земли́ ♦ *adj*: **~ operation/tactic** опера́ция/та́ктика сде́рживания.

holding company *n* хо́лдинг-компа́ния.

hold-up ['həuldʌp] *n* (*robbery*) ограбле́ние; (*delay*) заде́ржка*; (*BRIT: in traffic*) про́бка*.

hole [həul] *n* (*in wall*) дыра́*; (*in road*) я́ма; (*burrow*) нора́*; (*in clothing*) ды́рка*; (*in argument*) брешь *f*; (*inf: place*) дыра́* ♦ *vt* (*ship, building*) пробива́ть (проби́ть* *perf*); **~ in the heart** поро́к се́рдца; **to pick ~s (in)** находи́ть* (найти́* *perf*) сла́бое ме́сто (в +*prp*)
► **hole up** *vi* уединя́ться (уедини́ться *perf*).

holiday ['hɔlɪdeɪ] *n* (*BRIT: from school*) кани́кулы *mpl*; (: *from work*) о́тпуск*; (*day off*) выходно́й день* *m*; (*also*: **public ~**) пра́здник; **on ~** (*from school*) на кани́кулах; (*from work*) в о́тпуске; **tomorrow is a (public) ~** за́втра – пра́здник.

holiday camp *n* (*for children*) молодёжный ла́герь *m*; (*BRIT: also*: **holiday centre**) ба́за о́тдыха.

holiday-maker ['hɔlədɪmeɪkə'] *n* (*BRIT*) отпускни́к(-и́ца), отдыха́ющий*(-ая) *m(f) adj*.

holiday pay *n* отпускны́е *pl adj*.

holiday resort *n* куро́рт.

holiday season *n* куро́ртный сезо́н.

holiness ['həulɪnɪs] *n* свя́тость *f*.

holistic [həu'lɪstɪk] *adj* це́лостный.

Holland ['hɔlənd] *n* Голла́ндия.

holler ['hɔlə'] *vt* (*inf*) ора́ть (заора́ть *perf*).

hollow ['hɔləu] *adj* (*container*) по́лый; (*log, tree*) дупли́стый; (*cheeks*) впа́лый (впал); (*eyes*) ввали́вшийся; (*laugh*) неи́скренний* (неи́скренен); (*claim, sound*) пусто́й* (пуст); (*doctrine, opinion*) пове́рхностный* (пове́рхностен) ♦ *n* (*in ground*) впа́дина; (*in tree*) дупло́* ♦ *vt*: **to ~ out** выка́пывать (вы́копать *perf*).

holly ['hɔlɪ] *n* остроли́ст.

hollyhock ['hɔlɪhɔk] *n* алте́й ро́зовый.

Hollywood ['hɔlɪwud] *n* Голливу́д.

holocaust ['hɔləkɔ:st] *n* (*nuclear*) истребле́ние;

(Jewish) холоко́ст.
hologram ['hɔləgræm] n голограмма.
hols [hɔlz] (inf) npl (for students, pupils etc) кани́кулы pl; (for working people) о́тпуск* msg.
holster ['həulstə'] n кобура́*.
holy ['həulɪ] adj свято́й* (свят).
Holy Communion n Свято́е Прича́стие.
Holy Father n Его́ святе́йшество m (nána ри́мский).
Holy Ghost n свято́й дух.
Holy Land n: the ~ ~ свята́я земля́*.
holy orders npl духо́вный сан msg.
Holy Spirit n = Holy Ghost.
homage ['hɔmɪdʒ] n почте́ние; **to pay ~ to** воздава́ть* (возда́ть* perf) по́чести +dat.
home [həum] n (house, institution, family) дом*; (area, country) ро́дина ♦ cpd (domestic) дома́шний*; (ECON, POL) вну́тренний*; (SPORT): ~ **team** хозя́ева* mpl по́ля ♦ adv (go, come) домо́й; (right in) в цель or то́чку; **at ~** (house) до́ма; (country) на ро́дине; (in situation) как у себя́ до́ма; **make yourself at ~** чу́вствуйте себя́ как до́ма; **to make one's ~ somewhere** поселя́ться (посели́ться perf) где-то; **the ~ of free enterprise/jazz** etc ро́дина свобо́дного предпринима́тельства/джа́за etc; **a ~ from ~** второ́й дом; ~ **match/win** матч/вы́игрыш на своём по́ле; ~ **and dry** цел и невреди́м; **to bring sth ~ to sb** доводи́ть* (довести́* perf) что-н до чьего́-н созна́ния
▶ **home in on** vt fus (subj: missile) осуществля́ть (осуществи́ть* perf) самонаведе́ние на +acc.
home address n дома́шний* а́дрес*.
home-brew [həum'bru:] n дома́шнее пи́во.
homecoming ['həumkʌmɪŋ] n возвраще́ние домо́й.
home computer n дома́шний компью́тер.
Home Counties npl (BRIT): **the ~ ~** гра́фства прилега́ющие к Ло́ндону.
home economics n домово́дство.
home ground n: **to be on ~ ~** (in place) чу́вствовать (impf) себя́ как до́ма.
home-grown ['həumgrəun] adj (from garden) дома́шний*; (not foreign) оте́чественный.
home help n рабо́тник собе́са ока́зывающий по́мощь по до́му больны́м и престаре́лым.
homeland ['həumlænd] n ро́дина.
homeless ['həumlɪs] adj (family, refugee) бездо́мный* (бездо́мен) ♦ npl: **the ~** бездо́мные pl adj.
home loan n ба́нковская ссу́да на поку́пку до́ма.
homely ['həumlɪ] adj просто́й* (прост), ую́тный* (ую́тен).
home-made [həum'meɪd] adj (food) дома́шний*; (bomb) самоде́льный.
Home Office n (BRIT): **the ~ ~** ≈ Министе́рство вну́тренних дел.

homeopathy etc (US) = **homoeopathy** etc.
home rule n самоуправле́ние.
Home Secretary n (BRIT) ≈ мини́стр вну́тренних дел.
homesick ['həumsɪk] adj: **to be ~** (for family) скуча́ть (impf) по до́му; (for country) скуча́ть по ро́дине.
homestead ['həumstɛd] n уса́дьба.
home stretch n (of race) фи́нишная пряма́я.
home town n родно́й го́род*.
home truth n: **he needs to learn some ~ ~s** ему́ пора́ объясни́ть, что к чему́.
homeward ['həumwəd] adj (journey) обра́тный ♦ adv: ~**(s)** домо́й.
homework ['həumwə:k] n дома́шняя рабо́та, дома́шнее зада́ние.
homicidal [hɔmɪ'saɪdl] adj предрасполо́женный к убийству.
homicide ['hɔmɪsaɪd] n (esp US) убийство.
homily ['hɔmɪlɪ] n (tirade) тира́да; (sermon) нравоуче́ние.
homing ['həumɪŋ] adj: ~ **device** голо́вка* самонаведе́ния; ~ **pigeon** почто́вый го́лубь* m.
homoeopath ['həumɪəupæθ] (US homeopath) n гомеопа́т.
homoeopathy [həumɪ'ɔpəθɪ] (US homeopathy) n гомеопа́тия.
homogeneous [hɔməu'dʒi:nɪəs] adj одноро́дный* (одноро́ден).
homogenize [hə'mɔdʒənaɪz] vt гомогенизи́ровать (impf/perf).
homosexual [hɔməu'sɛksjuəl] adj гомосексуа́льный ♦ n гомосексуали́ст(ка*).
Hon. abbr = **honorary**, **honourable**.
Honduras [hɔn'djuərəs] n Гондура́с.
hone [həun] n точи́льный ка́мень* m ♦ vt точи́ть (наточи́ть* perf); (TECH) хонингова́ть (impf/perf); (fig) отта́чивать (отточи́ть* perf).
honest ['ɔnɪst] adj че́стный* (че́стен); **to be quite ~ (with you)** ... че́стно говоря́, ...
honestly ['ɔnɪstlɪ] adv че́стно.
honesty ['ɔnɪstɪ] n че́стность f.
honey ['hʌnɪ] n мёд*; (esp US: inf: darling) ми́лый(-ая) m(f) adj, голу́бчик.
honeycomb ['hʌnɪkəum] n (пчели́ные) со́ты fpl; (pattern) шестиуго́льный моза́ичный узо́р ♦ vt: **to ~ with** кише́ть (impf) +instr.
honeymoon ['hʌnɪmu:n] n медо́вый ме́сяц.
honeysuckle ['hʌnɪsʌkl] n жи́молость f.
Hong Kong ['hɔŋ'kɔŋ] n Гонко́нг.
honk [hɔŋk] vi (AUT) гуде́ть* (прогуде́ть* perf).
Honolulu [hɔnə'lu:lu:] n Гонолу́лу m ind.
honor etc (US) = **honour** etc.
honorary ['ɔnərərɪ] adj почётный* (почётен).
honour ['ɔnə'] (US honor) vt (person) почита́ть (impf), чтить* (impf); (commitment) выполня́ть (вы́полнить perf); (pride) честь f; (tribute, distinction) по́честь f; **in ~ of** в честь +gen.
honourable ['ɔnərəbl] adj благоро́дный* (благоро́ден); (BRIT: POL) уважа́емый (o

чле́нах парла́мента).

honour-bound [ˈɔnəˈbaund] *adj*: **he is ~ to keep his word** сдержа́ть сло́во явля́ется для него́ де́лом че́сти.

honours degree [ˈɔnəz-] *n* учёная сте́пень *f* (*обы́чно бакала́вра*).

honours list *n* (*BRIT*) спи́сок* предста́вленных к награ́де.

Hons. *abbr* (*SCOL*) = **honours degree**.

hood [hud] *n* капюшо́н; (*AUT*: *BRIT*: *folding roof*) откидно́й верх*; (: *US*: *bonnet*) капо́т; (*of cooker*) вытяжно́й колпа́к.

hooded [ˈhudɪd] *adj* (*robber*) в ма́ске; (*jacket*) с капюшо́ном.

hoodlum [ˈhuːdləm] *n* (*inf*) громи́ла *m*.

hoodwink [ˈhudwɪŋk] *vt* (*inf*) одура́чивать (одура́чить *perf*).

hoof [huːf] (*pl* **hooves**) *n* копы́то.

hook [huk] *n* крючо́к* ◆ *vt* прицепля́ть (прицепи́ть* *perf*); (*fish*) пойма́ть (*perf*) (на крючо́к); **by ~ or by crook** все́ми пра́вдами и непра́вдами; **he is ~ed on her/sweets** (*inf*) он поме́шан на ней/конфе́тах; **to get ~ed (on)** (*on drugs*) пристрасти́ться* *perf* (к +*dat*)

▸ **hook up** *vt* (*dress*) застёгивать (застегну́ть *perf*) на крючо́к; (*COMPUT, TV*): **to ~ up to the main network** подключа́ть (подключи́ть* *perf*) к центра́льной се́ти.

hook and eye (*pl* **~s ~ ~s**) *n* крючо́к* и петля́* (*на оде́жде*).

hooligan [ˈhuːlɪgən] *n* хулига́н.

hooliganism [ˈhuːlɪgənɪzəm] *n* хулига́нство.

hoop [huːp] *n* о́бруч*; (*for croquet*) воро́та *pl*.

hooray [huːˈreɪ] *excl* = **hurrah**.

hoot [huːt] *vi* (*AUT*: *horn*) гуде́ть* (прогуде́ть* *perf*); (*siren*) выть (*impf*); (*owl*) у́хать (*impf*); (*laugh, jeer*) улюлю́кать (*impf*) ◆ *vt* (*horn*) гуде́ть* (прогуде́ть* *perf*) в +*acc* ◆ *n* (*see vi*) гудо́к*; вой; у́ханье; улюлю́канье; **to ~ with laughter** разража́ться (разрази́ться* *perf*) оглуши́тельным сме́хом.

hooter [ˈhuːtə²] *n* (*BRIT*) гудо́к*.

hoover® [ˈhuːvə²] (*BRIT*) *n* пылесо́с ◆ *vt* пылесо́сить (пропылесо́сить *perf*).

hooves [huːvz] *npl of* **hoof**.

hop [hɔp] *vi* скака́ть* (*impf*) на одно́й ноге́; (*bird*) скака́ть (*impf*) ◆ *n* скачо́к*.

hope [həup] *vti* наде́яться (*impf*) ◆ *n* наде́жда; **to ~ that/to do** наде́яться (*impf*), что/+*infin*; **I ~ so/not** наде́юсь, что да/нет; **to ~ for the best** наде́яться (*impf*) на лу́чшее; **I have no ~ of sth/doing** у меня́ нет никако́й наде́жды на что-н/+*infin*; **in the ~ of/that** в наде́жде на +*acc*/что.

hopeful [ˈhəupful] *adj* (*person*) по́лный* (по́лон) наде́жд; (*situation etc*) обнадёживающий; **to be ~ of sth** наде́яться (*impf*) на что-н; **I'm ~ that she'll manage to**

come я наде́юсь, что она́ смо́жет прийти́.

hopefully [ˈhəupfulɪ] *adv* (*expectantly*) с наде́ждой; (*one hopes*): **~, he'll come back** бу́дем наде́яться, что он вернётся.

hopeless [ˈhəuplɪs] *adj* (*situation, person*) безнадёжный* (безнадёжен); (*incorrigible*) неисправи́мый (неисправи́м); **I'm ~ at names** я не в состоя́нии запомина́ть имена́.

hopper [ˈhɔpə²] *n* бу́нкер*.

hops [hɔps] *npl* хмель *msg*.

horde [hɔːd] *n* по́лчище.

horizon [həˈraɪzn] *n* горизо́нт.

horizontal [hɔrɪˈzɔntl] *adj* горизонта́льный* (горизонта́лен).

hormone [ˈhɔːməun] *n* гормо́н.

hormone replacement therapy *n* гормона́льная терапи́я.

horn [hɔːn] *n* (*of animal*) рог*; (*also*: **French ~**) валто́рна; (*AUT*) гудо́к*.

horned [hɔːnd] *adj* рога́тый.

hornet [ˈhɔːnɪt] *n* (*insect*) ше́ршень* *m*.

horn-rimmed [ˈhɔːnˈrɪmd] *adj*: **~ spectacles** очки́ в рогово́й опра́ве.

horny [ˈhɔːnɪ] *adj* (*inf*: *aroused*) (сексуа́льно) возбуждённый* (возбуждён).

horoscope [ˈhɔrəskəup] *n* гороско́п.

horrendous [həˈrɛndəs] *adj* ужаса́ющий*.

horrible [ˈhɔrɪbl] *adj* ужа́сный* (ужа́сен).

horrid [ˈhɔrɪd] *adj* проти́вный* (проти́вен), ме́рзкий* (ме́рзок).

horrific [hɔˈrɪfɪk] *adj* ужа́сный* (ужа́сен); **it was simply ~** э́то бы́ло про́сто ужа́сно.

horrify [ˈhɔrɪfaɪ] *vt* ужаса́ть (ужасну́ть *perf*).

horrifying [ˈhɔrɪfaɪɪŋ] *adj* ужаса́ющий*.

horror [ˈhɔrə²] *n* (*alarm*) у́жас; (*abhorrence*) отвраще́ние; (*of war*) у́жасы *mpl*.

horror film *n* фильм у́жасов.

horror-stricken [ˈhɔrəstrɪkn] *adj* = **horror-struck**.

horror-struck [ˈhɔrəstrʌk] *adj* объя́тый (объя́т) у́жасом.

hors d'oeuvre [ɔːˈdəːvrə] *n* заку́ска*.

horse [hɔːs] *n* ло́шадь* *f*; (*male*) конь* *m*.

horseback [ˈhɔːsbæk] *adj* верхово́й ◆ *adv*: **on ~** верхо́м; **police on ~** ко́нная поли́ция.

horsebox [ˈhɔːsbɔks] *n* (*BRIT*) ваго́н для лошаде́й.

horse chestnut *n* ко́нский* кашта́н.

horse-drawn [ˈhɔːsdrɔːn] *adj* ко́нный*; (*transport*) гужево́й.

horsefly [ˈhɔːsflaɪ] *n* слепе́нь* *m*.

horseman [ˈhɔːsmən] *irreg n* вса́дник.

horsemanship [ˈhɔːsmənʃɪp] *n* иску́сство верхово́й езды́.

horseplay [ˈhɔːspleɪ] *n* возня́.

horsepower [ˈhɔːspauə²] *n* лошади́ная си́ла; **a 30 ~ engine** дви́гатель *m* мо́щностью в 30 лошади́ных сил.

---

* marks translations which have irregular inflections. The Russian-English side of the dictionary gives inflectional information.

horse racing *n* ска́чки* *fpl.*
horseradish ['hɔ:srædɪʃ] *n* хрен*.
horseshoe ['hɔ:sʃu:] *n* подко́ва.
horse show *n* соревнова́ния по вы́ездке.
horse trading *n* закули́сные сде́лки *fpl.*
horse trials *npl* = **horse show.**
horsewhip ['hɔ:swɪp] *n* хлыст* ◆ *vt* хлеста́ть* (отхлеста́ть* *perf).*
horsewoman ['hɔ:swumən] *irreg n* вса́дница.
horsey ['hɔ:sɪ] *adj (person)* увлека́ющийся* лошадьми́; *(features)* лошади́ный.
horticulture ['hɔ:tɪkʌltʃə] *n* садово́дство.
hose [həuz] *n (also: ~pipe)* шланг
► **hose down** *vt* полива́ть (поли́ть *perf)* из шла́нга.
hosepipe ['həuzpaɪp] *n* шланг.
hosiery ['həuzɪərɪ] *n* чуло́чные изде́лия *ntpl.*
hospice ['hɔspɪs] *n* больни́ца *(для безнадёжно больны́х).*
hospitable ['hɔspɪtəbl] *adj (person, behaviour)* гостеприи́мный* (гостеприи́мен); *(climate)* благоприя́тный* (благоприя́тен).
hospital ['hɔspɪtl] *n* больни́ца; **to be in ~** *or (US)* **in the ~** лежа́ть* *(impf)* в больни́це.
hospitality [hɔspɪ'tælɪtɪ] *n* гостеприи́мство.
hospitalize ['hɔspɪtəlaɪz] *vt* госпитализи́ровать *(impf/perf).*
host [həust] *n (at party, dinner)* хозя́ин*; *(TV, RADIO)* веду́щий* *m adj* ◆ *adj (country, organization)* принима́ющий* ◆ *vt (programme)* вести́* *(impf); (event)* проводи́ть* (провести́* *perf);* **the H~** *(REL)* просвира́*; **a ~ of** ма́сса +*gen,* мно́жество +*gen.*
hostage ['hɔstɪdʒ] *n* зало́жник(-ица); **he was taken/held ~** его́ взя́ли/держа́ли в ка́честве зало́жника.
hostel ['hɔstl] *n* общежи́тие; *(for homeless)* прию́т; *(also:* **youth ~)** молодёжная гости́ница.
hostelling ['hɔstlɪŋ] *n:* **to go (youth) ~** путеше́ствовать *(impf),* остана́вливаясь в молодёжных гости́ницах.
hostess ['həustɪs] *n (at party, dinner etc)* хозя́йка*; *(BRIT: also:* **air ~)** стюарде́сса; *(TV, RADIO)* веду́щая *f adj; (in club, restaurant) же́нщина, развлека́ющая посети́телей но́чного клу́ба, рестора́на итп.*
hostile ['hɔstaɪl] *adj (person, attitude)* вражде́бный* (вражде́бен); *(conditions, environment)* неблагоприя́тный* (неблагоприя́тен); *(troops)* вра́жеский; **~ to** *or* **towards** вражде́бный* (вражде́бен) по отноше́нию к +*dat.*
hostility [hɔ'stɪlɪtɪ] *n* вражде́бность *f;* **hostilities** *npl (fighting)* вое́нные де́йствия *ntpl.*
hot [hɔt] *adj (object, temper, argument etc)* горя́чий* (горя́ч); *(weather)* жа́ркий*; *(spicy: food)* о́стрый* (остр); **she is ~** ей жа́рко; **it's ~** *(weather)* жа́рко; **I'm not too ~ on**

mathematics я не о́чень разбира́юсь в матема́тике
► **hot up** *vi (BRIT: inf: situation)* накаля́ться (накали́ться *perf); (: party)* разгора́ться (разгоре́ться *perf)* ◆ *vt (engine)* разогрева́ть (разогре́ть* *perf); (race)* ускоря́ть (ускори́ть *perf).*
hot air *n (fig)* пустосло́вие, болтовня́.
hot-air balloon [hɔt'εə-] *n* возду́шный шар*.
hotbed ['hɔtbɛd] *n (fig)* расса́дник.
hot-blooded [hɔt'blʌdɪd] *adj* пы́лкий* (пы́лок).
hotchpotch ['hɔtʃpɔtʃ] *n (BRIT)* сбо́рная соля́нка *(также перен).*
hot dog *n* ≈ соси́ска* в бу́лке.
hotel [həu'tɛl] *n* гости́ница, оте́ль *m.*
hotelier [həu'tɛlɪə] *n (owner)* владе́лец* (-е́лица) гости́ницы; *(manager)* администра́тор гости́ницы.
hot flush *n (esp BRIT)* прили́в.
hotel industry *n* гости́ничный би́знес.
hotel room *n* гости́ничный но́мер*.
hotfoot ['hɔtfut] *adv (inf)* стремгла́в.
hothead ['hɔthɛd] *n (inf)* горя́чая голова́*.
hot-headed [hɔt'hɛdɪd] *adj (person)* поры́вистый (поры́вист); *(remark)* необду́манный (необду́ман).
hothouse ['hɔthaus] *n* оранжере́я, тепли́ца.
hot line *n (POL)* пря́мая телефо́нная связь ме́жду прави́тельствами ра́зных стран.
hotly ['hɔtlɪ] *adv* горячо́.
hotplate ['hɔtpleɪt] *n* конфо́рка*.
hotpot ['hɔtpɔt] *n (BRIT)* жарко́е *nt adj.*
hot potato *n (inf)* больно́й вопро́с.
hot seat *n (inf):* **to be in the ~ ~** занима́ть (заня́ть* *perf)* отве́тственный пост.
hot spot *n (war zone)* горя́чая то́чка*.
hot spring *n* горя́чий* исто́чник.
hot stuff *n (inf: woman)* красо́тка*; *(: film, book)* кла́ссная вещь *f.*
hot-tempered ['hɔt'tɛmpəd] *adj* вспы́льчивый (вспы́льчив).
hot-water bottle ['hɔt'wɔ:tə-] *n* гре́лка*.
hound [haund] *vt* трави́ть* (затрави́ть* *perf)* ◆ *n (dog)* го́нчая *f adj.*
hour ['auə] *n* час*; **at 60 miles an** *or* **per ~** со ско́ростью 60 миль в час; **24 ~ job** круглосу́точная рабо́та; **I am paid by the ~** я получа́ю почасову́ю опла́ту.
hourly ['auəlɪ] *adj (rate)* почасово́й; *(service)* ежеча́сный; ◆ *adv (each hour)* ежеча́сно; *(soon)* с ча́су на час.
house [*n* haus, *vt* hauz] *n* дом*; *(company)* фи́рма; *(THEAT)* зал ◆ *vt (person)* сели́ть (посели́ть* *perf); (collection)* размеща́ть (размести́ть* *perf);* **at my ~** у меня́ до́ма; **to my ~** ко мне домо́й; **the H~ of Commons/ Lords** *(BRIT)* пала́та о́бщин/ло́рдов; **the H~ (of Representatives)** *(US)* пала́та представи́телей; **the H~s of Parliament** зда́ние *ntsg* парла́мента; **on the ~** *(inf)* беспла́тно.
house arrest *n* дома́шний* аре́ст.

houseboat [ˈhausbəut] *n* плаву́чий* дом*.
housebound [ˈhausbaund] *adj*: **she is ~** она́ не мо́жет выходи́ть из до́ма.
housebreaking [ˈhausbreɪkɪŋ] *n* грабёж со взло́мом.
house-broken [ˈhausbrəukn] *adj* (*US*) = **house-trained**.
housecoat [ˈhauskəut] *n* дома́шний* хала́т.
household [ˈhaushəuld] *n* (*home, inhabitants*) дом*; **~ name** (*brand*) изве́стная ма́рка*; (*person*) широко́ изве́стная ли́чность *f*.
householder [ˈhaushəuldəʳ] *n* домовладе́лец*.
house-hunting [ˈhaushʌntɪŋ] *n*: **to go ~** занима́ться (заня́ться* *perf*) по́исками до́ма.
housekeeper [ˈhauskiːpəʳ] *n* эконо́мка*.
housekeeping [ˈhauskiːpɪŋ] *n* (*work*) дома́шние дела́ *ntpl*; (*also:* **~ money**) де́ньги* *pl* на хозя́йственные ну́жды.
houseman [ˈhausmən] *irreg n* (*BRIT*) врач-стажёр, интéрн.
house-owner [ˈhausəunəʳ] *n* домовладе́лец* (-лица).
house-party [ˈhauspɑːtɪ] *n приглаше́ние люде́й в го́сти с ночёвкой.*
house plant *n* ко́мнатное расте́ние.
house-proud [ˈhauspraud] *adj* домови́тый (домови́т).
house-to-house [ˈhaustəˈhaus] *adj*: **to make ~ enquiries** проводи́ть* (провести́* *perf*) покварти́рный опро́с.
house-train [ˈhaustreɪn] *vt*: **to ~ a pet** приуча́ть (приучи́ть* *perf*) дома́шнего живо́тного не га́дить в до́ме.
house-trained [ˈhaustreɪnd] *adj* (*BRIT*): **our dog is fully ~** на́ша соба́ка приу́чена к туале́ту.
house-warming [ˈhauswɔːmɪŋ] *n* (*also:* **~ party**) новосе́лье*.
housewife [ˈhauswaɪf] *irreg n* дома́шняя хозя́йка*, домохозя́йка.
housework [ˈhauswəːk] *n* дома́шнее хозя́йство.
housing [ˈhauzɪŋ] *n* жили́ще, жильё; (*provision*) жили́щное снабже́ние; (*TECH*) ко́рпус, кожу́х* ◆ *cpd* жили́щный; **~ shortage** недоста́ток жилья́.
housing association *n* (*BRIT*) ассоциа́ция домовладе́льцев (*предоставля́ющая жильё по бо́лее вы́годным це́нам*).
housing benefit *n де́нежное посо́бие неиму́щим се́мьям по вы́плате квартпла́ты.*
housing conditions *npl* жили́щные усло́вия *ntpl*.
housing development *n* = **housing estate**.
housing estate (*US* **housing project**) *n* жили́щный ко́мплекс; (*larger*) жило́й масси́в.
housing project *n* (*US*) = **housing estate**.
hove [həuv] *pt, pp of* **heave**.

hovel [ˈhɔvl] *n* лачу́га.
hover [ˈhɔvəʳ] *vi* (*bird, insect*) пари́ть (*impf*); (*person*) мя́ться (*impf*); **to ~ round sb** увива́ться (*impf*) вокру́г кого́-н.
hovercraft [ˈhɔvəkrɑːft] *n* су́дно на возду́шной поду́шке.
hoverport [ˈhɔvəpɔːt] *n* порт для су́ден на возду́шной поду́шке.

KEYWORD

---

how [hau] *adv* **1** (*in what way*) как; **to know how to do** знать *perf*, как +*infin*; уме́ть (*impf*) +*infin*; **how did you like the film?** как Вам понра́вился фильм?; **how are you?** как дела́? **2** ско́лько; **how much milk/many people?** ско́лько молока́/челове́к?; **how long have you been here?** ско́лько Вы уже́ здесь?; **how old are you?** ско́лько Вам лет?; **how tall is he?** како́го он ро́ста?; **how lovely/awful!** как чуде́сно/ужа́сно!

---

however [hauˈɛvəʳ] *conj* одна́ко ◆ *adv* (*no matter how*) как бы ... ни; (*in questions*) как же; **~ did you find me?** как же Вы меня́ нашли́?
howl [haul] *vi* (*animal, wind*) выть* (*impf*); (*baby, person*) реве́ть* (*impf*) ◆ *n* (*see vb*) вой; рёв.
howler [ˈhaulə] *n* (*inf: mistake*) ля́псус.
howling [ˈhaulɪŋ] *adj* невероя́тный* (невероя́тен), фантасти́ческий*.
HP *n abbr* (*BRIT*) = **hire-purchase**.
h.p. *abbr* (*AUT*) (= **horsepower**) л.с.= *лошади́ная си́ла*.
HQ *abbr* = **headquarters**.
HR *n abbr* (*US: POL*: = *House of Representatives*) пала́та представи́телей.
HRH *abbr* (*BRIT*: = *His/Her Royal Highness*) Его́/Её Короле́вское Высо́чество.
hr(s) *abbr* = **hour(s)**.
HS *abbr* (*US*) = **high school**.
HST *abbr* (*US*) = *Hawaiian Standard Time*.
hub [hʌb] *n* (*of wheel*) ступи́ца; (*fig*) средото́чие.
hubbub [ˈhʌbʌb] *n* гам, го́мон.
hubcap [ˈhʌbkæp] *n* (*AUT*) покры́шка.
HUD *n abbr* (*US*) = *Department of Housing and Urban Development*.
huddle [ˈhʌdl] *vi*: **to ~ together** прижима́ться (прижа́ться* *perf*) друг к дру́гу ◆ *n*: **to lie in a ~** лежа́ть* (*impf*) в ку́че.
hue [hjuː] *n* тон, отте́нок*.
hue and cry *n* шум; (*pej*) шуми́ха.
huff [hʌf] *n*: **he's in a ~** он оби́жен ◆ *vi*: **to ~ and puff** (*also fig*) пыхте́ть* (*impf*).
huffy [ˈhʌfɪ] *adj* (*inf*) наду́тый (наду́т).
hug [hʌg] *vt* (*person*) обнима́ть (обня́ть* *perf*); (*thing*) обхва́тывать (обхвати́ть* *perf*) ◆ *n* объя́тие; **to give sb a ~** обнима́ть (обня́ть* *perf*) кого́-н.

---

* marks translations which have irregular inflections. The Russian-English side of the dictionary gives inflectional information.

huge [hju:dʒ] *adj* огро́мный* (огро́мен), грома́дный* (грома́ден).

hugely ['hju:dʒlɪ] *adv* чрезвыча́йно.

hulk [hʌlk] *n* (NAUT) ко́рпус* (*затону́вшего кораб ля́*); (*building, person*) грома́дина.

hulking ['hʌlkɪŋ] *adj* здорове́нный; **a ~ great oaf** у́валень *m*.

hull [hʌl] *n* (NAUT) ко́рпус*; (*of seeds*) шелуха́; (*of strawberries*) ча́шечка ♦ *vt* (*fruit*) лущи́ть (облущи́ть *perf*).

hullabal(l)oo ['hʌləbə'lu:] *n* (*inf*) шуми́ха.

hullo [hə'ləu] *excl* = **hello.**

hum [hʌm] *vt* напева́ть (*impf*) (*без слов*) ♦ *vi* (*person*) напева́ть (*impf*); (*machine*) гуде́ть* (прогуде́ть* *perf*); (*insect*) жужжа́ть (*impf*) ♦ *n* (*of wires*) гуде́ние; (*of voices, machines*) гул.

human ['hju:mən] *adj* челове́ческий* ♦ *n* (*also:* ~ **being**) челове́к*.

humane [hju:'meɪn] *adj* (*treatment*) челове́чный* (челове́чен); (*slaughter*) гума́нный* (гума́нен).

humanely [hju:'meɪnlɪ] *adv* по-челове́чески, гума́нно.

humanism ['hju:mənɪzəm] *n* гумани́зм.

humanitarian [hju:mænɪ'teərɪən] *adj* (*aid*) гуманита́рный; (*principles*) гума́нный*.

humanity [hju:'mænɪtɪ] *n* (*mankind*) челове́чество; (*humaneness*) челове́чность *f*, гума́нность *f*; (*human nature*) челове́ческая суть *f*; **the humanities** *npl* гума́нитарные нау́ки *fpl*.

humanly ['hju:mənlɪ] *adv*: **it's not ~ possible** э́то вне челове́ческих возмо́жностей; **it is ~ possible** э́то в преде́лах челове́ческих возмо́жностей.

humanoid ['hju:mənɔɪd] *adj* человеко-подо́бный* ♦ *n* гумано́ид.

human relations *npl* (COMM) обще́ственные отноше́ния *ntpl*.

human rights *npl* права́ *ntpl* челове́ка.

humble ['hʌmbl] *adj* (*modest, simple*) скро́мный* (скро́мен) ♦ *vt* сбива́ть (сбить* *perf*) спесь с +*gen*.

humbly ['hʌmblɪ] *adv* скро́мно, смире́нно.

humbug ['hʌmbʌg] *n* (*of statement*) надува́тельство; (BRIT: *sweet*) чёрно-бе́лый мя́тный леденец.

humdrum ['hʌmdrʌm] *adj* ну́дный* (ну́ден).

humid ['hju:mɪd] *adj* вла́жный* (вла́жен).

humidifier [hju:'mɪdɪfaɪə'] *n* увлажни́тель *m* во́здуха.

humidity [hju:'mɪdɪtɪ] *n* вла́жность *f*.

humiliate [hju:'mɪlɪeɪt] *vt* унижа́ть (уни́зить* *perf*).

humiliating [hju:'mɪlɪeɪtɪŋ] *adj* унизи́тельный* (унизи́телен).

humiliation [hju:mɪlɪ'eɪʃən] *n* униже́ние.

humility [hju:'mɪlɪtɪ] *n* (*modesty*) скро́мность *f*; (*humbleness*) смире́ние.

humming bird ['hʌmɪŋ-] *n* коли́бри *m/f ind*.

humor *etc* (US) = **humour** *etc*.

humorist ['hju:mərɪst] *n* юмори́ст(ка*).

humorous ['hju:mərəs] *adj* (*book*) юмористи́ческий*; (*remark*) шутли́вый (шутли́в); (*person*) с ю́мором.

humour ['hju:mə'] (US **humor**) *n* (*mood*) настрое́ние ♦ *vt* ублажа́ть (ублажи́ть *perf*); **sense of** ~ чу́вство ю́мора; **to be in good/bad** ~ быть* (*impf*) в хоро́шем/плохо́м настрое́нии.

humourless ['hju:mələs] *adj* лишённый (лишён) чу́вства ю́мора.

hump [hʌmp] *n* (*in ground*) буго́р*; (*on back*) горб*.

humpbacked ['hʌmpbækt] *adj*: ~ **bridge** горба́тый мост.

humus ['hju:məs] *n* перегно́й.

hunch [hʌntʃ] *n* (*premonition*) дога́дка*; **I have a ~ that** ... я предчу́вствую, что ....

hunchback ['hʌntʃbæk] *n* горбу́н*(ья*).

hunched [hʌntʃt] *adj* суту́лый (суту́л).

hundred ['hʌndrəd] *n* сто*; **a** *or* **one ~ books/people/dollars** сто* книг/люде́й/до́лларов; **about a ~** о́коло ста; ~ **and first** сто* пе́рвый; **to live to be a ~** жить* (дожи́ть* *perf*) до ста лет; ~**s of** со́тни* +*gen pl*; **people came in their** ~**s** *or* **by the** ~ пришли́ со́тни люде́й; **I'm a ~ per cent sure** я уве́рен на сто проце́нтов.

hundredth ['hʌndrədθ] *adj* со́тый ♦ *n* (*fraction*) одна́ со́тая *f adj*.

hundredweight ['hʌndrɪdweɪt] *n* (BRIT) ме́ра ве́са, равня́ющаяся 50.8 килогра́ммов; (US) ме́ра ве́са, равня́ющаяся 45.3 килогра́ммов.

hung [hʌŋ] *pt, pp of* **hang.**

Hungarian [hʌŋ'geərɪən] *adj* венге́рский* ♦ *n* венгр(-ге́рка*); (LING) венге́рский язы́к*.

Hungary ['hʌŋgərɪ] *n* Ве́нгрия.

hunger ['hʌŋgə'] *n* го́лод* ♦ *vi*: **to ~ for** жа́ждать* (*impf*) +*gen*.

hunger strike *n* голодо́вка*.

hung over *adj* (*inf*): **I'm feeling ~ ~** у меня́ похме́лье.

hungrily ['hʌŋgrəlɪ] *adv* (*also fig*) жа́дно.

hungry ['hʌŋgrɪ] *adj* голо́дный* (го́лоден); (*keen*): ~ **for** жа́ждущий +*gen*; **he is** ~ он го́лоден; **to go** ~ голода́ть (*impf*).

hung up *adj* (*inf*): **to be** ~ ~ **about** *or* **on** зацикливаться (зацикли́ться *perf*) на +*prp*.

hunk [hʌŋk] *n* (большо́й) кусо́к*; (*of bread*) ломо́ть* *m*; (*inf: man*) краса́вчик.

hunt [hʌnt] *vt* (*animal*) охо́титься* (*impf*) на +*acc*; (*criminal*) охо́титься* (*impf*) за +*instr* ♦ *vi* (SPORT) охо́титься* (*impf*) ♦ *n* охо́та; (*for criminal*) ро́зыск; **to ~ (for)** (*search*) иска́ть* (*impf*).

► **hunt down** *vt* высле́живать (вы́следить* *perf*).

hunter ['hʌntə'] *n* охо́тник(-ица).

hunting ['hʌntɪŋ] *n* охо́та.

hurdle ['hə:dl] *n* (*difficulty*) препя́тствие; (SPORT) препя́тствие, барье́р.

hurl [hə:l] *vt* (*object*) швыря́ть (швырну́ть *perf*);

to ~ abuse *or* **insults at sb** осыпа́ть (осы́пать *perf*) кого́-н руга́нью.
hurling ['hə:lɪŋ] *n* (*SPORT*) ирла́ндский* хокке́й на траве́.
hurly-burly ['hə:lɪ'bə:lɪ] *n* сумато́ха.
hurrah [hu'rɑ] *excl* ура́.
hurray [hu'reɪ] *excl* = **hurrah**.
hurricane ['hʌrɪkən] *n* урага́н.
hurried ['hʌrɪd] *adj* поспе́шный* (поспе́шен).
hurriedly ['hʌrɪdlɪ] *adv* поспе́шно.
hurry ['hʌrɪ] *n* спе́шка ♦ *vi* спеши́ть (поспеши́ть *perf*), торопи́ться* (потороп́иться* *perf*) ♦ *vt* (*person*) подгоня́ть (подогна́ть* *perf*), торопи́ть* (поторопи́ть* *perf*); (*work*) ускоря́ть (ускори́ть *perf*); **to be in a ~** спеши́ть (*impf*); **to do sth in a ~** де́лать (сде́лать *perf*) что-н в спе́шке; **there's no ~** нет никако́й спе́шки; **what's the ~?** почему́ така́я спе́шка?; **to ~ in/out** поспе́шно входи́ть* (войти́* *perf*)/выходи́ть* (вы́йти* *perf*); **they hurried to help him** они́ поспеши́ли ему́ на по́мощь; **to ~ home** спеши́ть (поспеши́ть *perf*) домо́й.
► **hurry along** *vi* поспе́шно проходи́ть* (пройти́* *perf*)
► **hurry away** *vi* поспе́шно уходи́ть* (уйти́* *perf*)
► **hurry off** *vi* = **hurry away**
► **hurry up** *vt* (*person*) подгоня́ть (подогна́ть* *perf*), торопи́ть* (поторопи́ть* *perf*); (*process*) ускоря́ть (ускори́ть *perf*) ♦ *vi* торопи́ться* (потороп́иться* *perf*); **~ up!** поторопи́сь!
hurt [hə:t] (*pt, pp* **hurt**) *vt* (*also fig*) причиня́ть (причини́ть *perf*) боль +*dat*; (*injure*) ушиба́ть (ушиби́ть* *perf*); (*offend*) обижа́ть (оби́деть* *perf*); (*chances, reputation*) поврежда́ть (повреди́ть *perf*) ♦ *vi* (*be painful*) боле́ть (*impf*) ♦ *adj* (*offended*) оби́женный* (оби́жен); (*injured*) уши́бленный (уши́блен); **to ~ o.s.** ушиба́ться (ушиби́ться *perf*); **I've ~ my arm** я уши́б ру́ку; **where does it ~?** где боли́т?; **nobody was ~ in the crash** в ава́рии никто́ не пострада́л.
hurtful ['hə:tful] *adj* оби́дный* (оби́ден).
hurtle ['hə:tl] *vi*: **to ~ past** проноси́ться* (пронести́сь* *perf*); **to ~ down** ска́тываться (скати́ться* *perf*).
husband ['hʌzbənd] *n* муж*.
hush [hʌʃ] *n* тишина́ ♦ *vt* заставля́ть (заста́вить* *perf*) замолча́ть; **~!** ти́хо!, ти́ше!
► **hush up** *vt* (*scandal*) замина́ть (замя́ть* *perf*).
hushed [hʌʃt] *adj* (*place*) ти́хий* (тих); (*voice*) приглушённый (приглушён).
hush-hush [hʌʃ'hʌʃ] *adj* (*inf*) сугу́бо секре́тный* (секре́тен).
husk [hʌsk] *n* шелуха́.
husky ['hʌskɪ] *adj* (*voice*) хри́плый* (хрипл) ♦ *n* ездова́я соба́ка.

hustings ['hʌstɪŋz] *npl* (*BRIT: POL*) пред-вы́борные собра́ния *ntpl*.
hustle ['hʌsl] *vt* (*hurry*) подта́лкивать (подтолкну́ть *perf*) ♦ *n*: **~ and bustle** сумато́ха.
hut [hʌt] *n* (*house*) избу́шка*, хи́жина; (*shed*) сара́й.
hutch [hʌtʃ] *n* кле́тка* (*для кро́ликов итп*).
hyacinth ['haɪəsɪnθ] *n* гиаци́нт.
hybrid ['haɪbrɪd] *n* (*BIO*) гибри́д; (*fig*) смесь *f* ♦ *adj* (*see n*) гибри́дный; сме́шанный.
hydrant ['haɪdrənt] *n* (*also*: **fire ~**) ≈ пожа́рный кран.
hydraulic [haɪ'drɔ:lɪk] *adj* гидравли́ческий*.
hydraulics [haɪ'drɔ:lɪks] *n* гидра́влика.
hydrochloric acid ['haɪdrəu'klɔrɪk-] *n* соля́ная кислота́.
hydroelectric ['haɪdrəuɪ'lɛktrɪk] *adj* гидро-электри́ческий.
hydrofoil ['haɪdrəfɔɪl] *n* су́дно на подво́дных кры́льях.
hydrogen ['haɪdrədʒən] *n* водоро́д.
hydrogen bomb *n* водоро́дная бо́мба.
hydrophobia ['haɪdrə'fəubɪə] *n* водобоя́знь *f*.
hydroplane ['haɪdrəpleɪn] *n* (*boat*) гли́ссер; (*plane*) гидросамолёт ♦ *vi* (*boat*) глисси́ровать (*impf*).
hyena [haɪ'i:nə] *n* гие́на.
hygiene ['haɪdʒi:n] *n* гигие́на.
hygienic [haɪ'dʒi:nɪk] *adj* (*product*) гигиени́ческий*; (*habits*) гигиени́чный* (гигиени́чен).
hymn [hɪm] *n* церко́вный гимн.
hype [haɪp] *n* (*inf*) ажиота́ж.
hyperactive ['haɪpər'æktɪv] *adj* (*MED*) гиперакти́вный.
hyper-inflation ['haɪpərɪn'fleɪʃən] *n* гипер-инфля́ция.
hypermarket ['haɪpəmɑ:kɪt] *n* (*BRIT*) кру́пный универса́м.
hypertension ['haɪpə'tɛnʃən] *n* гипертони́я.
hyphen ['haɪfn] *n* дефи́с.
hyphenated ['haɪfəneɪtɪd] *adj*: **this word is ~** э́то сло́во пи́шется че́рез дефи́с.
hypnosis [hɪp'nəusɪs] *n* гипно́з.
hypnotic [hɪp'nɔtɪk] *adj* (*trance etc*) гипноти́ческий.
hypnotism ['hɪpnətɪzəm] *n* гипноти́зм.
hypnotist ['hɪpnətɪst] *n* гипноти́зёр.
hypnotize ['hɪpnətaɪz] *vt* (*also fig*) гипнотизи́ровать (загипнотизи́ровать *perf*).
hypoallergenic ['haɪpəuælə'dʒɛnɪk] *adj* не вызыва́ющий* аллерги́ческой реа́кции.
hypochondriac [haɪpə'kɔndrɪæk] *n* ипохо́ндрик.
hypocrisy [hɪ'pɔkrɪsɪ] *n* лицеме́рие.
hypocrite ['hɪpəkrɪt] *n* лицеме́р(ка*).
hypocritical [hɪpə'krɪtɪkl] *adj* лицеме́рный*

---

* marks translations which have irregular inflections. The Russian-English side of the dictionary gives inflectional information.

(лицеме́рен).

hypodermic [haɪpə'də:mɪk] *adj* подко́жный ♦ *n* (*also*: ~ **syringe**) шприц для подко́жных инъе́кций.

hypotenuse [haɪ'pɔtɪnjuːz] *n* гипотену́за.

hypothermia [haɪpə'θə:mɪə] *n* гипотерми́я.

hypotheses [haɪ'pɔθɪsiːz] *npl of* **hypothesis**.

hypothesis [haɪ'pɔθɪsɪs] (*pl* **hypotheses**) *n* гипо́теза.

hypothesize [haɪ'pɔθɪsaɪz] *vi* предполага́ть (предположи́ть* *perf*).

hypothetic(al) [haɪpəu'θɛtɪk(l)] *adj* гипотети́ческий*.

hysterectomy [hɪstə'rɛktəmɪ] *n* удале́ние ма́тки.

hysteria [hɪ'stɪərɪə] *n* истери́я.

hysterical [hɪ'stɛrɪkl] *adj* (*uncontrolled*) истери́ческий*; (*funny*) умори́тельный* (умори́телен); **to become** ~ впада́ть (впасть* *perf*) в исте́рику.

hysterically [hɪ'stɛrɪklɪ] *adv* истери́чески; ~ **funny** о́чень смешно́й* (смешо́н).

hysterics [hɪ'stɛrɪks] *npl*: **to be in** *or* **have** ~ быть* (*impf*) в исте́рике.

Hz *abbr* (= *hertz*) Гц= *герц*.

~ I, i ~

I, i [aɪ] n (letter) 9-ая бу́ква англи́йского
  алфави́та.
I [aɪ] pron я.
I abbr (= **island, isle**) о.= о́стров.
IA abbr (US: POST) = **Iowa.**
IAEA n abbr = **International Atomic Energy
  Agency.**
IBA n abbr (BRIT) = **Independent Broadcasting
  Authority.**
Iberian [aɪˈbɪərɪən] adj: **the ~ Peninsula**
  Пирене́йский полуо́стров.
IBEW n abbr (US) = **International Brotherhood of
  Electrical Workers.**
ib(id) abbr (from the same source: = **ibidem**) там
  же.
i/c abbr (BRIT) = **in charge.**
ICBM n abbr (= **intercontinental ballistic missile**)
  МБР= межконтинента́льная
  баллисти́ческая раке́та.
ICC n abbr = **International Chamber of
  Commerce**; (US: = **Interstate Commerce
  Commission**) Коми́ссия по торго́вле ме́жду
  шта́тами.
ice [aɪs] n лёд*; (portion of ice cream)
  моро́женое nt adj ♦ vt (cake) покрыва́ть
  (покры́ть* perf) глазу́рью; **to put sth on ~**
  (fig) заморо́зить* (perf) что-н
  ▸ **ice over** vi (road, window etc) обледене́ть
  (perf), покрыва́ться (покры́ться* perf) льдом
  ▸ **ice up** vi = **ice over.**
Ice Age n леднико́вый пери́од.
ice axe n ледору́б.
iceberg [ˈaɪsbəːg] n а́йсберг; **the tip of the ~**
  (fig) верху́шка а́йсберга.
icebox [ˈaɪsbɒks] n (US: fridge) холоди́льник;
  (BRIT: compartment) морози́льник; (insulated
  box) су́мка-холоди́льник f.
ice breaker n ледоко́л.
ice bucket n ведёрко* со льдом.
ice-cap [ˈaɪskæp] n леднико́вый покро́в.
ice-cold [aɪsˈkəuld] adj ледяно́й.
ice cream n моро́женое nt adj.
ice-cream soda [ˈaɪskriːm-] n со́довая вода́ с
  моро́женым.
ice cube n ку́бик льда.
iced [aɪst] adj (cake) покры́тый глазу́рью; ~

tea холо́дный чай со льдом; ~ **beer**
  холо́дное пи́во.
ice hockey n (SPORT) хокке́й (на льду).
Iceland [ˈaɪslənd] n Исла́ндия.
Icelander [ˈaɪsləndə'] n исла́ндец*(-дка*).
Icelandic [aɪsˈlændɪk] adj исла́ндский* ♦ n
  (LING) исла́ндский* язы́к*.
ice lolly n (BRIT) фрукто́вое моро́женое на
  па́лочке.
ice pick n топо́рик для льда.
ice rink n като́к*.
ice-skate [ˈaɪsskeɪt] n конёк* ♦ vi ката́ться (impf)
  на конька́х.
ice-skating [ˈaɪsskeɪtɪŋ] n (SPORT) ката́ние на
  конька́х.
icicle [ˈaɪsɪkl] n сосу́лька*.
icing [ˈaɪsɪŋ] n (on cake) глазу́рь f; (on window
  etc) обледене́ние.
icing sugar n (BRIT) са́харная пу́дра для
  приготовле́ния глазу́ри.
ICJ n abbr = **International Court of Justice.**
icon [ˈaɪkɒn] n (REL) ико́на.
ICR n abbr (US) = **Institute for Cancer Research.**
ICU n abbr (MED: = **intensive care unit**)
  отделе́ние интенси́вной терапи́и.
icy [ˈaɪsɪ] adj (cold) ледяно́й; (covered in ice)
  покры́тый (покры́т) льдом.
ID abbr (US: POST) = **Idaho.**
I'd [aɪd] = **I would, I had.**
ID card n = **identity card.**
IDD n abbr (BRIT: TEL: = **international direct
  dialling**) пряма́я междунаро́дная связь f.
idea [aɪˈdɪə] n (scheme, opinion) иде́я; (notion)
  представле́ние; (objective) зада́ча; **good ~!**
  прекра́сная иде́я!; **to have an ~ that**
  подозрева́ть (impf) что; **I haven't the least ~** я
  не име́ю ни мале́йшего представле́ния.
ideal [aɪˈdɪəl] n идеа́л ♦ adj идеа́льный*
  (идеа́лен).
idealist [aɪˈdɪəlɪst] n идеали́ст(ка*).
ideally [aɪˈdɪəlɪ] adv идеа́льно; ~ **the work
  should be done by tomorrow** в идеа́ле,
  рабо́та должна́ быть зако́нчена к
  за́втрашнему дню; **she's ~ suited for the job**
  она́ идеа́льно подхо́дит для э́той рабо́ты.
identical [aɪˈdɛntɪkl] adj одина́ковый

(одинаков), иденти́чный* (иденти́чен).

identification [aɪdɛntɪfɪ'keɪʃən] n определе́ние; (*process*) выявле́ние; (*of person, dead body*) опозна́ние; (**means of**) ~ удостовере́ние ли́чности.

identify [aɪ'dɛntɪfaɪ] vt (*recognize*) определя́ть (определи́ть perf); (: *person*) узнава́ть* (узна́ть* perf); (: *body*) опознава́ть* (опозна́ть* perf); (*distinguish*) отлича́ть (отличи́ть perf); **he is identified with radical politics** он отлича́ется радика́льными полити́ческими взгля́дами.

Identikit® [aɪ'dɛntɪkɪt] n: ~ (**picture**) портре́т-ро́бот престу́пника, соста́вленный по описа́нию свиде́телей.

identity [aɪ'dɛntɪtɪ] n (*of person, suspect etc*) ли́чность f; (*of group, culture, nation etc*) самосозна́ние.

identity card n удостовере́ние ли́чности.

identity papers npl докуме́нты mpl, удостоверя́ющие ли́чность.

identity parade n (BRIT) процеду́ра опозна́ния подозрева́емого в гру́ппе люде́й.

ideological [aɪdɪə'lɒdʒɪkl] adj идеологи́ческий*.

ideology [aɪdɪ'ɔlədʒɪ] n идеоло́гия.

idiocy ['ɪdɪəsɪ] n идиоти́зм.

idiom ['ɪdɪəm] n (*style*) стиль m; (*phrase*) идио́ма.

idiomatic [ɪdɪə'mætɪk] adj идиомати́чный* (идиомати́чен).

idiosyncrasy [ɪdɪəu'sɪŋkrəsɪ] n (*foible*) осо́бенность f, характе́рная черта́.

idiosyncratic [ɪdɪəusɪŋ'krætɪk] adj индивидуа́льный* (индивидуа́лен), осо́бенный.

idiot ['ɪdɪət] n идио́т(ка*).

idiotic [ɪdɪ'ɔtɪk] adj идио́тский*.

idle ['aɪdl] adj пра́здный; (*lazy*) лени́вый (лени́в); (*unemployed*) безрабо́тный; (*machinery, factory*) безде́йствующий ◆ vi (*machine*) проста́ивать (impf); (*engine*) рабо́тать (impf) на холосто́м ходу́; **to be ~** безде́йствовать (impf); **to lie ~** быть* (impf) неиспо́льзованным(-ой); **an ~ hour** час досу́га

▶ **idle away** vt: **to ~ away the time** корота́ть (impf) вре́мя.

idle capacity n неиспо́льзуемая произво́дственная мо́щность f.

idle money n неинвести́рованные де́ньги* pl.

idleness ['aɪdlnɪs] n (*inactivity*) безде́лье; (*laziness*) лень f.

idler ['aɪdlə] n безде́льник(-ица), лентя́й(ка*).

idle time n (COMM) просто́й.

idly ['aɪdlɪ] adv пра́здно, лени́во.

idol ['aɪdl] n (*hero*) куми́р; (REL) и́дол.

idolize ['aɪdəlaɪz] vt боготвори́ть (impf).

idyllic [ɪ'dɪlɪk] adj (*place, holiday*) идилли́ческий*.

i.e. abbr (*that is*: = id est) т.е.= *то есть.*

KEYWORD

if [ɪf] conj **1** (*conditional use*) е́сли; **if I finish early today, I will ring you** е́сли я зако́нчу ра́но сего́дня, я тебе́ позвоню́; **if I were you (I would ...)** на Ва́шем ме́сте (я бы ...)
2 (*whenever*) когда́
3 (*although*): (**even**) **if** (да́же) е́сли; **I'll get it done, even if it takes all night** я сде́лаю э́то, е́сли да́же э́то займёт у меня́ всю ночь; **I like it, (even) if you don't** хоть Вам и не нра́вится э́то, а мне (всё равно́) нра́вится
4 (*whether*): **I don't know if he is here** я не зна́ю, здесь ли он; **ask him if he can stay** спроси́те, смо́жет ли он оста́ться
5: **if so/not** е́сли да/нет; **if only** е́сли то́лько; **if only I could** е́сли бы я то́лько мог; *see also* **as**.

iffy ['ɪfɪ] adj (*inf: scheme, suggestion*) подозри́тельный; **I'm feeling a bit ~ today** я сего́дня фиго́во себя́ чу́вствую.

igloo ['ɪgluː] n и́глу nt ind (*жили́ще эскимо́сов*).

ignite [ɪg'naɪt] vt (*set fire to*) зажига́ть (заже́чь* perf) ◆ vi воспламеня́ться (воспламени́ться perf), загора́ться (загоре́ться perf).

ignition [ɪg'nɪʃən] n (AUT) зажига́ние; **to switch on/off the ~** включа́ть (включи́ть perf)/ выключа́ть (вы́ключить perf) зажига́ние.

ignition key n (AUT) ключ* зажига́ния.

ignoble [ɪg'nəubl] adj недосто́йный* (недосто́ен).

ignominious [ɪgnə'mɪnɪəs] adj позо́рный* (позо́рен).

ignoramus [ɪgnə'reɪməs] n неве́жда m/f.

ignorance ['ɪgnərəns] n неве́жество; ~ **of the facts** незна́ние фа́ктов; **to keep sb in ~ of sth** держа́ть* (impf) кого́-н в неве́дении по по́воду чего́-н.

ignorant ['ɪgnərənt] adj (*uninformed, unaware*) несве́дущий* (несве́дущ); (*badly educated*) неве́жественный* (неве́жествен); **to be ~ of** (*subject, events etc*) быть* (impf) неосведомлённым(-ой) относи́тельно +gen.

ignore [ɪg'nɔː] vt (*pay no attention to*) игнори́ровать* (impf/perf); (*fail to take into account*) упуска́ть (упусти́ть* perf) из ви́ду.

ikon ['aɪkɒn] n = **icon**.

IL abbr (US: POST) = *Illinois*.

ILA n abbr (US) = *International Longshore Association*.

I'll [aɪl] = **I will, I shall**.

ill [ɪl] adj (*child etc*) больно́й*; (*harmful: effects*) дурно́й ◆ n (*evil*) зло; (*trouble*) беда́ ◆ adv: **to speak/think ~ (of sb)** пло́хо говори́ть (impf)/ ду́мать (impf) (о ком-н); **he is ~** он бо́лен; **to be taken ~** заболева́ть (заболе́ть perf).

ill-advised [ɪləd'vaɪzd] adj опроме́тчивый (опроме́тчив).

ill-at-ease [ɪlət'iːz] adj (*awkward, uncomfortable*) нело́вкий*.

ill-considered [ɪlkən'sɪdəd] adj необду́манный* (необду́ман).

ill-disposed [ˌɪldɪsˈpəuzd] *adj*: **to be ~ towards sb/sth** недоброжелательно относиться* (*impf*) к кому-н/чему-н.

illegal [ɪˈliːgl] *adj* нелегальный* (нелегален), незаконный* (незаконен).

illegally [ɪˈliːgəlɪ] *adv* нелегально, незаконно.

illegible [ɪˈlɛdʒɪbl] *adj* неразборчивый (неразборчив).

illegitimate [ˌɪlɪˈdʒɪtɪmət] *adj* (*child*) внебрачный; (*activity, treaty*) незаконный* (незаконен).

ill-fated [ɪlˈfeɪtɪd] *adj* (*doomed*) злополучный* (злополучен).

ill-favoured [ɪlˈfeɪvəd] (*US* **ill-favored**) *adj* некрасивый (некрасив).

ill feeling *n* неприязнь *f*.

ill-gotten [ˈɪlgɔtn] *adj*: **~ gains** добытый нечестным путём доход.

ill-health [ɪlˈhɛlθ] *n* плохое здоровье.

illicit [ɪˈlɪsɪt] *adj* незаконный* (незаконен).

ill-informed [ɪlɪnˈfɔːmd] *adj* неосведомлённый* (неосведомлён).

illiterate [ɪˈlɪtərət] *adj* неграмотный* (неграмотен).

ill-mannered [ɪlˈmænəd] *adj* невоспитанный* (невоспитан), невежливый (невежлив).

illness [ˈɪlnɪs] *n* болезнь *f*.

illogical [ɪˈlɔdʒɪkl] *adj* нелогичный* (нелогичен).

ill-suited [ɪlˈsuːtɪd] *adj*: **they are ~** они не подходят друг к другу; **he is ~ to the job** он не годится для этой работы.

ill-timed [ɪlˈtaɪmd] *adj* несвоевременный* (несвоевремен); **her comments were ~** её замечания были не к месту.

ill-treat [ɪlˈtriːt] *vt* плохо обращаться (*impf*) с +*instr*.

ill-treatment [ɪlˈtriːtmənt] *n* жестокость *f*.

illuminate [ɪˈluːmɪneɪt] *vt* (*light up*) освещать (осветить* *perf*).

illuminated sign [ɪˈluːmɪneɪtɪd-] *n* освещённая вывеска*.

illuminating [ɪˈluːmɪneɪtɪŋ] *adj* (*report, book etc*) разъясняющий; (*person*) просвещённый* (просвещён), познавательный* (познавателен).

illumination [ɪluːmɪˈneɪʃən] *n* (*lighting*) освещение; **~s** *npl* (*decorative lights*) иллюминация *fsg*.

illusion [ɪˈluːʒən] *n* (*false idea*) иллюзия; (*trick*) фокус; **to be under the ~ that ...** находиться (*impf*) под впечатлением, что ....

illusive [ɪˈluːsɪv] *adj* = **illusory**.

illusory [ɪˈluːsərɪ] *adj* иллюзорный* (иллюзорен), обманчивый (обманчив).

illustrate [ˈɪləstreɪt] *vt* иллюстрировать (проиллюстрировать *perf*).

illustration [ɪləˈstreɪʃən] *n* (*example, picture*)

иллюстрация; (*act*) иллюстрирование.

illustrator [ˈɪləstreɪtə] *n* иллюстратор.

illustrious [ɪˈlʌstrɪəs] *adj* (*career*) блестящий* (блестящ); (*predecessor, partner*) прославленный* (прославлен).

ill will *n* неприязнь *f*.

ILO *n abbr* = **International Labour Organization**.

ILWU *n abbr* (*US*) = **International Longshoremen's and Warehousemen's Union**.

I'm [aɪm] = **I am**.

image [ˈɪmɪdʒ] *n* (*picture*) образ; (*public face*) имидж; (*reflection*) отражение.

imagery [ˈɪmɪdʒərɪ] *n* (*ART, LITERATURE*) образность *f*, образный мир.

imaginable [ɪˈmædʒɪnəbl] *adj* воображаемый; **we've tried every ~ solution** мы перепробовали все воображаемые решения; **she had the prettiest hair ~** у неё были невообразимо красивые волосы.

imaginary [ɪˈmædʒɪnərɪ] *adj* (*creature, land*) воображаемый; (*danger, illness*) мнимый.

imagination [ɪmædʒɪˈneɪʃən] *n* воображение; (*illusion*) фантазия; **it's just your ~** это просто плод Вашего воображения.

imaginative [ɪˈmædʒɪnətɪv] *adj* (*person*) обладающий богатым *or* творческим воображением; (*solution*) хитроумный* (хитроумен).

imagine [ɪˈmædʒɪn] *vt* (*visualize*) представлять (представить* *perf*); (*self*), воображать (вообразить* *perf*); (*dream*) воображать (вообразить* *perf*); (*suppose*) полагать (*impf*).

imbalance [ɪmˈbæləns] *n* несоответствие, неравновесие.

imbecile [ˈɪmbəsiːl] *n* ненормальный(-ая) *m(f) adj*.

imbue [ɪmˈbjuː] *vt*: **to ~ sb with sth** вдохновлять (вдохновить* *perf*) кого-н чем-н; **to ~ sth with sth** наполнять (наполнить *perf*) что-н чем-н.

IMF *n abbr* (= *International Monetary Fund*) МВФ= *Международный валютный фонд*.

imitate [ˈɪmɪteɪt] *vt* (*copy*) копировать (скопировать *perf*); (*mimic*) подражать (*impf*) +*dat*, имитировать (*impf*).

imitation [ɪmɪˈteɪʃən] *n* (*see vb*) копирование; подражание; (*instance*) имитация.

imitator [ˈɪmɪteɪtə] *n* подражатель(ница) *m(f)*.

immaculate [ɪˈmækjulət] *adj* безупречный* (безупречен); (*REL*) непорочный.

immaterial [ɪməˈtɪərɪəl] *adj* (*unimportant*) несущественный* (несущественен).

immature [ɪməˈtjuə] *adj* (*fruit*) неспелый (неспел); (*cheese*) незрелый; (*organism*) недоразвившийся; (*person*) незрелый (незрел).

immaturity [ɪməˈtjuərɪtɪ] *n* незрелость *f*.

immeasurable [ɪˈmɛʒərəbl] *adj* неизмеримый

---

* marks translations which have irregular inflections. The Russian-English side of the dictionary gives inflectional information.

(неизмери́м).

immediacy [ɪˈmiːdɪəsɪ] *n* (*of events etc*) непосре́дственность *f*; (*of needs*) безотлага́тельность *f*.

immediate [ɪˈmiːdɪət] *adj* (*reaction, answer*) неме́дленный, мгнове́нный; (*pressing: need*) безотлага́тельный* (безотлага́телен); (*nearest: neighbourhood, family etc*) ближа́йший*.

immediately [ɪˈmiːdɪətlɪ] *adv* (*at once*) неме́дленно; (*directly*) непосре́дственно; ~ **next to** непосре́дственно ря́дом с +*instr*.

immense [ɪˈmɛns] *adj* (*huge: size*) необъя́тный* (необъя́тен); (: *progress, importance*) огро́мный* (огро́мен).

immensely [ɪˈmɛnslɪ] *adv* (*grateful etc*) бесконе́чно; (*difficult*) необыча́йно; **I enjoyed it** ~ мне э́то о́чень понра́вилось.

immensity [ɪˈmɛnsɪtɪ] *n* необъя́тность *f*.

immerse [ɪˈməːs] *vt* (*submerge*) погружа́ть (погрузи́ть* *perf*); **to** ~ **sth in** погружа́ть (погрузи́ть* *perf*) что-н в +*acc*; **to be ~d in** (*fig*) быть* (*impf*) погружённым(-ой) в +*acc*.

immersion heater [ɪˈməːʃən-] *n* (*BRIT*) бо́йлер.

immigrant [ˈɪmɪɡrənt] *n* иммигра́нт(ка*).

immigration [ɪmɪˈɡreɪʃən] *n* (*process*) иммигра́ция; (*also*: ~ **control**: *at airport etc*) пограни́чный контро́ль *m* ♦ *cpd*: ~ **laws** зако́ны *mpl* об иммигра́ции; ~ **authorities** пограни́чная слу́жба.

imminent [ˈɪmɪnənt] *adj* (*arrival, departure*) немину́емый (немину́ем).

immobile [ɪˈməʊbaɪl] *adj* неподви́жный* (неподви́жен).

immobilize [ɪˈməʊbɪlaɪz] *vt* (*person, machine*) остана́вливать (останови́ть* *perf*), свя́зывать (связа́ть* *perf*).

immoderate [ɪˈmɔdərət] *adj* неуме́ренный* (неуме́рен).

immodest [ɪˈmɔdɪst] *adj* нескро́мный* (нескро́мен).

immoral [ɪˈmɔrl] *adj* амора́льный* (амора́лен), безнра́вственный* (безнра́вствен).

immorality [ɪmɔˈrælɪtɪ] *n* амора́льность *f*, безнра́вственность *f*.

immortal [ɪˈmɔːtl] *adj* (*also fig*) бессме́ртный* (бессме́ртен).

immortality [ɪmɔːˈtælɪtɪ] *n* бессме́ртие.

immortalize [ɪˈmɔːtlaɪz] *vt* увекове́чивать (увекове́чить *perf*).

immovable [ɪˈmuːvəbl] *adj* (*object*) неподви́жный* (неподви́жен); (*opinion*) неизме́нный* (неизме́нен).

immune [ɪˈmjuːn] *adj*: ~ (**to**) (*disease*) облада́ющий иммуните́том (к +*dat*); **he is** ~ **to ...** (*flattery, criticism etc*) он неподве́ржен влия́нию +*gen* ....

immune system *n* имму́ная систе́ма.

immunity [ɪˈmjuːnɪtɪ] *n* (*to disease*) иммуните́т; (*to criticism*) невос-

при́мчивость *f*; (*of diplomat, from prosecution*) неприкоснове́нность *f*.

immunization [ɪmjunaɪˈzeɪʃən] *n* иммуниза́ция, приви́вка*.

immunize [ˈɪmjunaɪz] *vt* (*MED*): **to** ~ (**against**) привива́ть (приви́ть* *perf*) (про́тив +*gen*).

imp [ɪmp] *n* бесёнок*.

impact [ˈɪmpækt] *n* (*of bullet*) моме́нт попада́ния; (*of crash*) уда́р; (*of law, measure*) возде́йствие.

impair [ɪmˈpɛəˈ] *vt* (*vision, judgement*) ослабля́ть (осла́бить* *perf*).

impaired [ɪmˈpɛəd] *adj* осла́бленный (осла́блен).

impale [ɪmˈpeɪl] *vt* нака́лывать (наколо́ть* *perf*); **to** ~ **sth on** наса́живать (насади́ть* *perf*) что-н на +*acc*.

impart [ɪmˈpɑːt] *vt*: **to** ~ **sth** (**to**) (*information*) передава́ть* (переда́ть* *perf*) (+*dat*); (*flavour*) придава́ть* (прида́ть* *perf*) (+*dat*).

impartial [ɪmˈpɑːʃl] *adj* беспристра́стный* (беспристра́стен).

impartiality [ɪmpɑːʃɪˈælɪtɪ] *n* беспристра́стие.

impassable [ɪmˈpɑːsəbl] *adj* непроходи́мый (непроходи́м).

impasse [æmˈpɑːs] *n* тупи́к*; **to reach an** ~ зайти́* (*perf*) в тупи́к.

impassive [ɪmˈpæsɪv] *adj* бесстра́стный* (бесстра́стен).

impatience [ɪmˈpeɪʃəns] *n* нетерпели́вость *f*.

impatient [ɪmˈpeɪʃənt] *adj* нетерпели́вый (нетерпели́в); **to get** *or* **grow** ~ начина́ть (нача́ть* *perf*) теря́ть терпе́ние; **she was** ~ **to leave** ей не терпе́лось уйти́.

impatiently [ɪmˈpeɪʃəntlɪ] *adv* нетерпели́во.

impeach [ɪmˈpiːtʃ] *vt* привлека́ть (привле́чь* *perf*) к отве́тственности.

impeachment [ɪmˈpiːtʃmənt] *n* привлече́ние к отве́тственности.

impeccable [ɪmˈpɛkəbl] *adj* безупре́чный* (безупре́чен).

impecunious [ɪmpɪˈkjuːnɪəs] *adj* (*formal*) нужда́ющийся.

impede [ɪmˈpiːd] *vt* затрудня́ть (затрудни́ть *perf*).

impediment [ɪmˈpɛdɪmənt] *n* (*obstacle*) препя́тствие; **speech** ~ дефе́кт ре́чи.

impel [ɪmˈpɛl] *vt*: **to** ~ **sb to do** вынужда́ть (вы́нудить* *perf*) кого́-н +*infin*.

impending [ɪmˈpɛndɪŋ] *adj* надвига́ющийся.

impenetrable [ɪmˈpɛnɪtrəbl] *adj* (*jungle, fortress*) непроходи́мый (непроходи́м); (*look, expression*) непроница́емый (непроница́ем); (*darkness, fog*) непрогля́дный* (непрогля́ден); (*fig: law, text*) недосту́пный* (недосту́пен) (для понима́ния).

imperative [ɪmˈpɛrətɪv] *adj* (*tone*) вла́стный* (вла́стен); (*need etc*) настоя́тельный* (настоя́телен) ♦ *n* (*LING*) повели́тельное наклоне́ние; **it is** ~ **that ...** необходи́мо,

чтóбы ....
imperceptible [ɪmpə'sɛptɪbl] *adj* незамéтный*
(незамéтен).
imperfect [ɪm'pə:fɪkt] *adj* (*system etc*)
несовершéнный* (несовершéнен); (*goods*)
дефéктный ♦ *n* (*LING: also:* ~ **tense**)
имперфéкт.
imperfection [ɪmpə'fɛkʃən] *n* (*failing*)
недостáток*; (*blemish*) изъя́н.
imperial [ɪm'pɪərɪəl] *adj* (*history, power*)
импéрский*; (*BRIT: measure*): ~ **system**
британская система меры и веса.
imperialism [ɪm'pɪərɪəlɪzəm] *n* империалúзм.
imperil [ɪm'pɛrɪl] *vt* подвергáть (подвéргнуть*
perf) опáсности.
imperious [ɪm'pɪərɪəs] *adj* (*person*) влáстный*
(влáстен).
impersonal [ɪm'pə:sənl] *adj* (*organization,
place*) безлúкий*.
impersonate [ɪm'pə:səneɪt] *vt* (*pass o.s. off as*)
выдавáть* (вы́дать *perf*) себя́ за +*acc*; (*THEAT*)
изображáть (изобразúть* *perf*).
impersonation [ɪmpə:sə'neɪʃən] *n*
изображéние; (*LAW*) самозвáнство; (*THEAT*)
исполнéние рóли.
impertinent [ɪm'pə:tɪnənt] *adj* (*pupil, question*)
дéрзкий* (дéрзок), нахáльный* (нахáлен).
imperturbable [ɪmpə'tə:bəbl] *adj* невоз-
мутúмый (невозмутúм).
impervious [ɪm'pə:vɪəs] *adj* (*fig*): **he is** ~ **to** ... на
негó не дéйствует ....
impetuous [ɪm'pɛtjuəs] *adj* порúвистый
(порúвист).
impetus ['ɪmpətəs] *n* (*momentum*) инéрция;
(*fig*) стúмул.
impinge [ɪm'pɪndʒ]: **to** ~ **on** *vt fus* (*person*)
посягáть (посягнýть *perf*) на +*acc*; (*rights*)
попирáть (попрáть* *perf*).
impish ['ɪmpɪʃ] *adj* озорнóй.
implacable [ɪm'plækəbl] *adj* непримирúмый
(непримирúм).
implant [ɪm'plɑ:nt] *vt* (*MED*) пересáживать
(пересадúть* *perf*); (*fig: idea, principle*)
внушáть (внушúть *perf*).
implausible [ɪm'plɔ:zɪbl] *adj* неправдо-
подóбный* (неправдоподóбен).
implement [*vt* 'ɪmplɪmɛnt, *n* 'ɪmplɪmənt] *vt* (*plan,
regulation*) проводúть* (провестú* *perf*) в
жизнь ♦ *n*: **gardening** ~ садóвый
инструмéнт; **farming** ~**s** сельско-
хозя́йственные орýдия; **cooking** ~**s**
кýхонные принадлéжности.
implicate ['ɪmplɪkeɪt] *vt* (*in crime, error*)
вовлекáть (вовлéчь* *perf*).
implication [ɪmplɪ'keɪʃən] *n* (*inference*) вы́вод;
(*involvement*) причáстность *f*; **by** ~ судя́ по
всемý.
implicit [ɪm'plɪsɪt] *adj* (*inferred*) подраз-

умевáющийся; (*unquestioning*)
безоговóрочный.
implicitly [ɪm'plɪsɪtlɪ] *adv* (*totally*)
безоговóрочно.
implore [ɪm'plɔ:ʳ] *vt* (*beg*) умоля́ть (*impf*); **to** ~
sb to do умоля́ть (*impf*) когó-н +*infin*.
imply [ɪm'plaɪ] *vt* (*hint*) намекáть (намекнýть
perf) на +*acc*; (*mean*) подразумевáть (*impf*).
impolite [ɪmpə'laɪt] *adj* (*rude, offensive*)
невéжливый (невéжлив).
imponderable [ɪm'pɒndərəbl] *adj* неуловúмый
(неуловúм) ♦ *n* вещь, не поддаю́щаяся
определéнию.
import [*vb* ɪm'pɔ:t, *n, cpd* 'ɪmpɔ:t] *vt*
импортúровать (*impf/perf*), ввозúть* (ввезтú*
perf) ♦ *n* (*article*) импортúруемый товáр;
(*importation*) úмпорт ♦ *cpd*: ~ **duty** пóшлина
на ввоз; ~ **licence** лицéнзия на ввоз; ~ **quota**
úмпортная квóта.
importance [ɪm'pɔ:tns] *n* вáжность *f*; **it is of
great/little** ~ э́то óчень/не óчень вáжно.
important [ɪm'pɔ:tnt] *adj* вáжный* (вáжен);
(*influential: person*) вáжный*; **it's not** ~ э́то
невáжно.
importantly [ɪm'pɔ:tntlɪ] *adv* вáжно; **but more**
~ ... но ещё важнéе ..., но сáмое глáвное ....
importation [ɪmpɔ:'teɪʃən] *n* úмпорт.
imported [ɪm'pɔ:tɪd] *adj* úмпортный.
importer [ɪm'pɔ:təʳ] *n* импортёр.
impose [ɪm'pəuz] *vt* (*sanctions, restrictions,
discipline etc*) налагáть (наложúть* *perf*) ♦ *vi*:
to ~ **on sb** навя́зываться (навязáться* *perf*)
комý-н.
imposing [ɪm'pəuzɪŋ] *adj* внушúтельный*
(внушúтелен), велúчественный*
(велúчествен).
imposition [ɪmpə'zɪʃən] *n* (*of tax etc*)
обложéние; **to be an** ~ **on sb** быть* (*impf*)
обýзой комý-н.
impossibility [ɪmpɒsə'bɪlɪtɪ] *n* невозмóжность
f.
impossible [ɪm'pɒsɪbl] *adj* (*task, demand,
person*) невозмóжный* (невозмóжен);
(*situation*) невероя́тный* (невероя́тен); **it's** ~
for me to leave now я не могý сейчáс уйтú.
impossibly [ɪm'pɒsɪblɪ] *adv* невозмóжно.
imposter [ɪm'pɒstəʳ] *n* = **impostor**.
impostor [ɪm'pɒstəʳ] *n* самозвáнец*(-нка*).
impotence ['ɪmpətns] *n* бессúлие; (*MED*)
импотéнция.
impotent ['ɪmpətnt] *adj* бессúльный*
(бессúлен); (*MED*) импотéнтный*
(импотéнтен).
impound [ɪm'paund] *vt* конфисковáть
(конфисковáть *perf*).
impoverished [ɪm'pɒvərɪʃt] *adj* (*country*)
обеднéвший*.
impracticable [ɪm'præktɪkəbl] *adj*

---

* marks translations which have irregular inflections. The Russian-English side of the dictionary gives inflectional information.

неосуществимый (неосуществим).

impractical [ɪm'præktɪkl] *adj* (*plan etc*)
нереальный* (нереален); (*person*)
непрактичный* (непрактичен).

imprecise [ɪmprɪ'saɪs] *adj* неточный*
(неточен).

impregnable [ɪm'prɛgnəbl] *adj* (*castle, fortress*)
неприступный* (неприступен); (*fig: person*)
неуязвимый (неуязвим).

impregnate ['ɪmprɛgneɪt] *vt* (*saturate*)
пропитывать (пропитать *perf*); (*fertilize*)
оплодотворять (оплодотворить *perf*).

impresario [ɪmprɪ'sɑːrɪəu] *n* импресарио *m ind*.

impress [ɪm'prɛs] *vt* (*person*) производить*
(произвести* *perf*) впечатление на +*acc*;
(*mark*) отпечатывать (отпечатать *perf*); **to ~
sth on sb** внушать (внушить *perf*) что-н
кому-н.

impression [ɪm'prɛʃən] *n* впечатление; (*of
stamp, seal*) отпечаток*; (*imitation*)
имитация; **to make a good/bad ~ on sb**
производить* (произвести* *perf*) хорошее/
плохое впечатление на кого-н; **he is under
the ~ that** ... у него создалось впечатление,
что ....

impressionable [ɪm'prɛʃnəbl] *adj*
впечатлительный* (впечатлителен).

impressionist [ɪm'prɛʃənɪst] *n* (*ART*)
импрессионист; (*entertainer*) имитатор.

impressive [ɪm'prɛsɪv] *adj* впечатляющий.

imprest system ['ɪmprɛst-] *n система
денежного аванса.*

imprint ['ɪmprɪnt] *n* отпечаток*; (*PUBLISHING*)
выходные данные *pl adj*; (: *label*) *печать на
переплёте с именем владельца или
издателя.*

imprinted [ɪm'prɪntɪd] *adj*: **~ on** (*surface*)
отпечатавшийся в/на +*prp*; (*memory*)
запечатлённый (запечатлён) в +*prp*.

imprison [ɪm'prɪzn] *vt* (*criminal*) заключать
(заключить *perf*) в тюрьму.

imprisonment [ɪm'prɪznmənt] *n* (тюремное)
заключение.

improbable [ɪm'prɔbəbl] *adj* (*outcome*)
маловероятный* (маловероятен); (*story*)
неправдоподобный* (неправдоподобен).

impromptu [ɪm'prɔmptjuː] *adj* (*celebration,
party*) импровизированный
(импровизирован); (*tactics*) неплановый.

improper [ɪm'prɔpə] *adj* (*unsuitable: conduct*)
неуместный* (неуместен); (: *procedure*)
неправильный* (неправилен); (*dishonest:
activities*) незаконный* (незаконен).

impropriety [ɪmprə'praɪətɪ] *n* (*indecency*)
неприличие; **the ~ of his conduct**
непристойность *f* его поведения.

improve [ɪm'pruːv] *vt* улучшать (улучшить
perf) ◆ *vi* улучшаться (улучшиться *perf*);
(*pupil*) становиться* (стать* *perf*) лучше;
(*patient*) начинать (начать *perf*)
выздоравливать

▶ **improve (up)on** *vt fus* (*work, achievement etc*)
делать (сделать *perf*) лучше.

improvement [ɪm'pruːvmənt] *n*: ~ **(in)**
улучшение (+*gen*); **to make ~s to** вносить*
(внести* *perf*) улучшения в +*acc*.

improvisation [ɪmprəvaɪ'zeɪʃən] *n* (*THEAT*)
импровизация.

improvise ['ɪmprəvaɪz] *vt* (*meal*) наскоро
готовить* (приготовить* *perf*); (*bed, shelter*)
наскоро устраивать (устроить *perf*) ◆ *vi*
(*THEAT, MUS*) импровизировать
(сымпровизировать *perf*).

imprudence [ɪm'pruːdns] *n* неблагоразумное
поведение.

imprudent [ɪm'pruːdnt] *adj* неблагоразумный*
(неблагоразумен); **it would be ~ of you to
insult him** оскорбить его будет
неблагоразумием с Вашей стороны.

impudent ['ɪmpjudnt] *adj* наглый* (нагл).

impugn [ɪm'pjuːn] *vt* подвергать
(подвергнуть* *perf*) сомнению.

impulse ['ɪmpʌls] *n* (*urge*) порыв; (*ELEC*)
импульс; **to act on ~** поддаваться*
(поддаться* *perf*) порыву.

impulse buy *n* случайная покупка*.

impulsive [ɪm'pʌlsɪv] *adj* (*purchase*) случай-
ный* (случаен); (*person*) импульсивный*
(импульсивен); (*gesture*) порывистый
(порывист).

impunity [ɪm'pjuːnɪtɪ] *n*: **with ~** безнаказанно.

impure [ɪm'pjuə] *adj* нечистый (нечист);
(*sinful*) непристойный* (непристоен).

impurity [ɪm'pjuərɪtɪ] *n* (*foreign substance*)
примесь *f*.

IN *abbr* (*US: POST*) = **Indiana**.

KEYWORD

in [ɪn] *prep* **1** (*indicating place, position*) в/на
+*prp*; **in the house/garden** в доме/саду; **in the
street/Ukraine/north** на улице/Украине/
севере; **in London/Canada** в Лондоне/
Канаде; **in the country** загородом; **in town** в
городе; **in here** здесь; **in there** там
2 (*indicating motion*) в +*acc*; **in the house/
room** в дом/комнату
3 (*indicating time: during*) в +*prp*; **in spring/
summer/autumn/winter** весной/летом/
осенью/зимой; **in the morning/afternoon/
evening** утром/днём/вечером; **they often
play cards in the evening** они часто играют в
карты по вечерам; **at 4 o'clock in the
afternoon** в 4 часа дня
4 (*indicating time: in the space of*) за +*acc*; (:
after a period of) через +*acc*; **I did it in 3 hours** я
сделал это за 3 часа; **I'll see you in 2 weeks**
увидимся через 2 недели
5 (*indicating manner etc*): **in a loud/quiet voice**
громким/тихим голосом; **in English/Russian**
по-английски/по-русски, на английском/
русском языке; **the boy in the blue shirt**
мальчик в голубой рубашке
6 (*indicating circumstances*): **in the sun** на

со́лнце; **in the rain** под дождём; **in the shade** в тени́; **there has been a change in public opinion** обще́ственное мне́ние перемени́лось; **a rise in prices** повыше́ние цен

7 (*indicating mood, state*) в +*prp*

8 (*with ratios, numbers*): **one in ten households have a second car** одна́ из десяти́ семе́й име́ет втору́ю маши́ну; **20 pence in the pound** 20 пе́нсов с фу́нта; **they lined up in twos** они́ вы́строились по́ дво́е; **a gradient of one in five** укло́н оди́н к пяти́

9 (*referring to people, works*): **the disease is common in children** э́то заболева́ние ча́сто встреча́ется у дете́й; **in Dickens** у Ди́ккенса; **you have a good friend in him** он тебе́ хоро́ший друг

10 (*indicating profession etc*): **to be in teaching** рабо́тать (*impf*) учи́телем; **to be in publishing** занима́ться (*impf*) изда́тельским де́лом; **to be in the army** быть* (*impf*) в а́рмии

11 (*after superlative*) в +*prp*; **the best doctor in the city** лу́чший* врач в го́роде

12 (*with present participle*): **in saying this** говоря́ э́то; **in behaving like this, she ...** поступа́я таки́м о́бразом, она́ ...

♦ *adv*: **to be in** (*train, ship, plane*) прибы́ть* (*perf*); (*in fashion*) быть* (*impf*) в мо́де; **is he in today? – yes, he's in/no, he's not in** (*at work*) он сего́дня на рабо́те? – да, он на рабо́те/ нет, его́ сего́дня нет; (*at home*) он сего́дня до́ма? – да, он до́ма/нет, его́ сего́дня нет; **he wasn't in yesterday** его́ вчера́ не́ было; **he'll be in later today** он бу́дет сего́дня по́зже; **to ask sb in** предложи́ть* (*perf*) кому́-н зайти́; **to run/walk** *etc* **in** вбега́ть (вбежа́ть* *perf*)/ входи́ть* (войти́* *perf*) *etc*

♦ *n*: **to know all the ins and outs** знать (*impf*) все ходы́.

in. *abbr* = **inch**.

inability [ɪnə'bɪlɪtɪ] *n* (*incapacity*): ~ **(to do)** неспосо́бность *f* (+*infin*).

inaccessible [ɪnək'sɛsɪbl] *adj* (*also fig*) недосту́пный* (недосту́пен).

inaccuracy [ɪn'ækjurəsɪ] *n* (*quality*) нето́чность *f*; (*mistake*) оши́бка*.

inaccurate [ɪn'ækjurət] *adj* нето́чный* (нето́чен).

inaction [ɪn'ækʃən] *n* безде́йствие.

inactive [ɪn'æktɪv] *adj* (*person*) безде́ятельный* (безде́ятелен), пасси́вный* (пасси́вен); (*animal*) пасси́вный* (пасси́вен); (*volcano*) поту́хший.

inactivity [ɪnæk'tɪvɪtɪ] *n* (*idleness*) безде́ятельность *f*.

inadequacy [ɪn'ædɪkwəsɪ] *n* недоста́точность *f*; (*of person*) неполноце́нность *f*.

inadequate [ɪn'ædɪkwət] *adj* (*income, amount, preparation*) недоста́точный* (недоста́точен); (*reply*) неадеква́тный* (неадеква́тен); (*work, result*) неудовле- твори́тельный* (неудовлетвори́телен); (*person*) неполноце́нный (неполноце́н).

inadmissible [ɪnəd'mɪsəbl] *adj* недопусти́мый (недопусти́м); (*LAW: evidence*) неприе́м- лемый (неприе́млем).

inadvertently [ɪnəd'vɜːtntlɪ] *adv* неумы́шленно.

inadvisable [ɪnəd'vaɪzəbl] *adj* (*course of action*) нецелесообра́зный* (нецелесообра́зен); **it is ~ to ...** не рекоменду́ется +*infin* ....

inane [ɪ'neɪn] *adj* (*smile*) глупый* (глуп); (*remark etc*) бессмы́сленный* (бессмы́слен).

inanimate [ɪn'ænɪmət] *adj* (*object*) неодушевлённый* (неодушевлён).

inapplicable [ɪn'æplɪkəbl] *adj* (*description, comment*) неподходя́щий*; (*rule*) непримени́мый (непримени́м).

inappropriate [ɪnə'prəuprɪət] *adj* (*unsuitable*) неподходя́щий*; (*improper*) неуме́стный* (неуме́стен).

inapt [ɪn'æpt] *adj* неуме́стный* (неуме́стен).

inarticulate [ɪnɑː'tɪkjulət] *adj* (*person*) косноязы́чный* (косноязы́чен); (*speech*) невня́тный* (невня́тен).

inasmuch as [ɪnəz'mʌtʃ-] *adv* (*in that*) посто́льку поско́льку; (*insofar as*) насто́лько наско́лько.

inattention [ɪnə'tɛnʃən] *n* невнима́ние.

inattentive [ɪnə'tɛntɪv] *adj* невнима́тельный* (невнима́телен).

inaudible [ɪn'ɔːdɪbl] *adj* неслы́шный* (неслы́шен).

inaugural [ɪ'nɔːgjurəl] *adj* (*speech*) вступи́тельный; (*meeting*) пе́рвый.

inaugurate [ɪ'nɔːgjureɪt] *vt* (*president, official*) вводи́ть* (ввести́* *perf*) в до́лжность; (*system, measure*) вводи́ть* (ввести́* *perf*); (*organization*) открыва́ть (откры́ть* *perf*).

inauguration [ɪnɔːgju'reɪʃən] *n* (*see vb*) вступле́ние в до́лжность; введе́ние; откры́тие.

inauspicious [ɪnɔːs'pɪʃəs] *adj* (*occasion*) неблагоприя́тный* (неблагоприя́тен).

in-between [ɪnbɪ'twiːn] *adj* (*intermediate*) промежу́точный; **~ stage** промежу́точная ста́дия.

inborn [ɪn'bɔːn] *adj* врождённый, приро́дный.

inbred [ɪn'brɛd] *adj* (*quality*) врождённый, приро́дный; **an ~ family** семья́, в кото́рой де́ти рождены́ от роди́телей, состоя́щих в кро́вном родстве́.

inbreeding [ɪn'briːdɪŋ] *n* (*among animals*) ро́дственное спа́ривание; (*among people*) узкоро́дственные бра́чные отноше́ния *ntpl*.

---

inbuilt [ɪn'bɪlt] adj (quality, feeling etc)
врождённый.

Inc. abbr = **incorporated**.

Inca ['ɪŋkə] adj: **the** ~ or ~**n civilization** и́нки fpl.

incalculable [ɪn'kælkjuləbl] adj (effect)
огро́мный* (огро́мен); (loss) неисчисли́мый
(неисчисли́м); (consequences) непред-
ви́денный.

incapable [ɪn'keɪpəbl] adj (helpless) бес-
по́мощный* (беспо́мощен); (unable to): ~ **of**
sth/doing неспосо́бный* (неспосо́бен) на
что-н/+infin.

incapacitate [ɪnkə'pæsɪteɪt] vt: **to** ~ **sb**
выводи́ть* (вы́вести* perf) кого́-н из стро́я;
to ~ **sb for work** де́лать (сде́лать perf) кого́-н
нетрудоспосо́бным(-ой).

incapacitated [ɪnkə'pæsɪteɪtɪd] adj (LAW)
лишённый (лишён) пра́ва.

incapacity [ɪnkə'pæsɪtɪ] n (weakness)
беспо́мощность f; (inability) неспосо́бность
f.

incarcerate [ɪn'kɑːsəreɪt] vt заключа́ть
(заключи́ть perf) в тюрьму́.

incarnate [ɪn'kɑːnɪt] adj воплощённый
(воплощён), олицетворённый
(олицетворён); **evil** ~ воплоще́ние or
олицетворе́ние зла.

incarnation [ɪnkɑː'neɪʃən] n воплоще́ние,
олицетворе́ние; (REL) инкарна́ция.

incendiary [ɪn'sɛndɪərɪ] adj (device, bomb)
зажига́тельный.

incense [n 'ɪnsɛns, vt ɪn'sɛns] n (also REL) ла́дан
♦ vt (anger) приводи́ть* (привести́* perf) в
я́рость.

incense burner n кури́льница.

incentive [ɪn'sɛntɪv] n (inducement) сти́мул ♦
cpd: ~ **scheme** систе́ма поощре́ния; ~ **bonus**
материа́льное поощре́ние.

inception [ɪn'sɛpʃən] n (of institution)
откры́тие, основа́ние; (of activity) нача́ло.

incessant [ɪn'sɛsnt] adj бесконе́чный*
(бесконе́чен), постоя́нный* (постоя́нен).

incessantly [ɪn'sɛsntlɪ] adv бесконе́чно,
постоя́нно.

incest ['ɪnsɛst] n кровосмеше́ние.

inch [ɪntʃ] n (measurement) дюйм; **he was**
within an ~ **of succeeding** он был уже́ бли́зок
к успе́ху; **to be within an** ~ **of one's life** быть*
(impf) на волосо́к от сме́рти; **he didn't give an**
~ (fig: back down, yield) он не уступи́л ни на
йо́ту

▶ **inch forward** vi ме́дленно тро́гаться
(тро́нуться perf) с ме́ста.

incidence ['ɪnsɪdns] n (of crime, disease)
чи́сленность f.

incident ['ɪnsɪdnt] n (event) слу́чай; (MIL)
инциде́нт; **without** ~ без происше́ствий.

incidental [ɪnsɪ'dɛntl] adj (additional,
supplementary) дополни́тельный; **these**
duties are ~ **to the job** э́ти обя́занности
сопряжены́ с рабо́той; **ills** ~ **to old age**

неду́ги, прису́щие ста́рости; ~ **expenses**
побо́чные расхо́ды.

incidentally [ɪnsɪ'dɛntəlɪ] adv (by the way)
кста́ти, ме́жду про́чим.

incidental music n (CINEMA) му́зыка к
кинофи́льму.

incident room n диспе́тчерская f adj (в
полице́йском управле́нии).

incinerate [ɪn'sɪnəreɪt] vt (rubbish, paper etc)
сжига́ть (сжечь* perf).

incinerator [ɪn'sɪnəreɪtə'] n мусоросжига́тель
m.

incipient [ɪn'sɪpɪənt] adj (baldness)
начина́ющийся*; (madness) в нача́льной
ста́дии.

incision [ɪn'sɪʒən] n (also MED) разре́з.

incisive [ɪn'saɪsɪv] adj (comment) о́стрый*
(остёр), ре́зкий* (ре́зок); (criticism) ре́зкий*
(ре́зок).

incisor [ɪn'saɪzə'] n резе́ц*.

incite [ɪn'saɪt] vt (rioters) подстрека́ть
(подстрекну́ть perf); (violence, hatred)
вызыва́ть (вы́звать* perf).

incl. abbr = **including**, **inclusive (of)**.

inclement [ɪn'klɛmənt] adj (weather)
нена́стный* (нена́стен).

inclination [ɪnklɪ'neɪʃən] n (tendency)
скло́нность f; (disposition, desire) жела́ние.

incline [n 'ɪnklaɪn, vb ɪn'klaɪn] n (slope) укло́н,
накло́н ♦ vt (bend: head) наклоня́ть
(наклони́ть* perf) ♦ vi (surface) наклоня́ться
(наклони́ться* perf); **to be** ~**d to sth/to do**
быть* (impf) скло́нным(-ой) к чему́-н/+infin;
to be well ~**d towards sb** быть* (impf)
благоскло́нным(-ой) к кому́-н.

include [ɪn'kluːd] vt включа́ть (включи́ть perf);
to be ~**d (in)** быть* (impf) включённым(-ой) (в
+acc); **to** ~ **sth in the price** включа́ть
(включи́ть perf) в це́ну.

including [ɪn'kluːdɪŋ] prep включа́я +acc; ~
service charge включа́я пла́ту за
обслу́живание.

inclusion [ɪn'kluːʒən] n включе́ние.

inclusive [ɪn'kluːsɪv] adj (price, terms)
включа́ющий в себя́ все услу́ги; ~ **of**
включа́я +acc; **from March 1st to 5th** ~ с 1-ого
до 5-ое ма́рта включи́тельно.

incognito [ɪnkɔg'niːtəu] adv инко́гнито.

incoherent [ɪnkəu'hɪərənt] adj (argument)
непосле́довательный* (непосле́довател(ен));
(speech) несвя́зный* (несвя́зен); (person)
косноязы́чный* (косноязы́чен).

income ['ɪnkʌm] n (earned) за́работок*; (from
property, investment) дохо́д; **gross/net** ~
валово́й/чи́стый дохо́д; ~ **and expenditure**
account прихо́дно-расхо́дный счёт*; **high/**
low ~ **bracket** гру́ппа населе́ния с высо́ким/
ни́зким у́ровнем дохо́да.

income support n де́нежное посо́бие.

income tax n подохо́дный нало́г ♦ cpd (COMM)
нало́говый.

incoming ['ɪnkʌmɪŋ] adj (flight, passenger)
прибыва́ющий; (call) поступа́ющий; (mail)
входя́щий; (government) новои́збранный;
(official) вступа́ющий* в до́лжность; ~ **tide**
прили́в.

incommunicado ['ɪnkəmjunɪ'kɑ:dəu] adj: **to
hold sb ~** держа́ть* (impf) кого́-н взаперти́.

incomparable [ɪn'kɔmpərəbl] adj несрав-
не́нный*.

incompatible [ɪnkəm'pætɪbl] adj (lifestyles)
соверше́нно ра́зный; (systems, aims)
несовмести́мый (несовмести́м); **they are ~**
они́ соверше́нно ра́зные.

incompetence [ɪn'kɔmpɪtns] n некомпете́нт-
ность f.

incompetent [ɪn'kɔmpɪtnt] adj (person)
некомпете́нтный* (некомпете́нтен); (work)
неуме́лый (неуме́л).

incomplete [ɪnkəm'pli:t] adj (unfinished)
незако́нченный* (незако́нчен); (partial)
непо́лный* (непо́лон).

incomprehensible [ɪnkɔmprɪ'hɛnsɪbl] adj
непоня́тный* (непоня́тен).

inconceivable [ɪnkən'si:vəbl] adj немы́слимый
(немы́слим); **it is ~ that** ... немы́слимо,
что ....

inconclusive [ɪnkən'klu:sɪv] adj (evidence)
недоста́точный* (недоста́точен); (result)
неоконча́тельный* (неоконча́телен);
(argument) неубеди́тельный*
(неубеди́телен); **the experiment was ~**
эксперимент не дал определённых
результа́тов; **the discussion was ~** диску́ссия
зако́нчилась ниче́м.

incongruous [ɪn'kɔŋgruəs] adj (strange)
неле́пый (неле́п); (inappropriate)
неуме́стный* (неуме́стен).

inconsequential [ɪnkɔnsɪ'kwɛnʃl] adj
несуще́ственный* (несуще́ственен),
незначи́тельный* (незначи́телен).

inconsiderable [ɪnkən'sɪdərəbl] adj: **not ~**
значи́тельный* (значи́телен).

inconsiderate [ɪnkən'sɪdərət] adj (person) не
счита́ющийся ни с ке́м; (action) безду́мный*
(безду́мен); **~ towards** невнима́тельный к
+dat.

inconsistency [ɪnkən'sɪstənsɪ] n (of behaviour)
непосле́довательность f; (of statement)
противоречи́вость f.

inconsistent [ɪnkən'sɪstnt] adj (behaviour,
person) непосле́довательный*
(непосле́дователен); (work) неро́вный*
(неро́вен); (statement) противоречи́вый
(противоречи́в); **~ with** (beliefs, values)
несовмести́мый (несовмести́м) с +instr.

inconsolable [ɪnkən'səuləbl] adj безуте́шный*
(безуте́шен).

inconspicuous [ɪnkən'spɪkjuəs] adj незаме́т-

ный* (незаме́тен), непримéтный*
(непримéтен); **to make o.s. ~** стара́ться
(постара́ться perf) не привлека́ть к себе́
внима́ния.

incontinence [ɪn'kɔntɪnəns] n (MED)
недержа́ние (мочи́ или ка́ла).

incontinent [ɪn'kɔntɪnənt] adj (MED)
страда́ющий недержа́нием (мочи́ или ка́ла).

inconvenience [ɪnkən'vi:njəns] n (problem)
неудо́бство; (trouble) беспоко́йство ♦ vt
причиня́ть (причини́ть perf) неудо́бство
+dat; **don't ~ yourself** не утружда́йте себя́;
sorry about the ~ извини́те за причинённое
неудо́бство.

inconvenient [ɪnkən'vi:njənt] adj неудо́бный*
(неудо́бен); (visitor) прише́дший не ко
вре́мени; **that time is very ~ for me** э́то о́чень
неудо́бное для меня́ вре́мя.

incorporate [ɪn'kɔ:pəreɪt] vt (contain)
содержа́ть* (impf); **to ~ (into)** включа́ть
(включи́ть perf) (в +acc); **safety features have
been ~d in the design** предохрани́тельные
устро́йства бы́ли внесены́ в прое́кт; **the coat
of arms ~s three lions** на гербе́ изображены́
три льва́.

incorporated company [ɪn'kɔ:pəreɪtɪd-] n (US)
компа́ния, зарегистри́рованная как
корпора́ция.

incorrect [ɪnkə'rɛkt] adj неве́рный* (неве́рен),
непра́вильный* (непра́вилен).

incorrigible [ɪn'kɔrɪdʒɪbl] adj (liar, crook)
неисправи́мый (неисправи́м).

incorruptible [ɪnkə'rʌptɪbl] adj (not open to
bribes) неподку́пный* (неподку́пен).

increase [n 'ɪnkri:s, vb ɪn'kri:s] n: **~ (in), ~ (of)**
увеличе́ние (+gen) ♦ vi увели́чиваться
(увели́читься perf) ♦ vt увели́чивать
(увели́чить perf); (price) поднима́ть
(подня́ть* perf); (knowledge) расширя́ть
(расши́рить perf); **an ~ of 5%** увеличе́ние на
5%; **to be on the ~** увели́чиваться (impf),
расти́* (impf).

increasing [ɪn'kri:sɪŋ] adj увели́чивающийся,
возраста́ющий.

increasingly [ɪn'kri:sɪŋlɪ] adv (more intensely)
всё бо́лее; (more often) всё ча́ще.

incredible [ɪn'krɛdɪbl] adj (unbelievable)
неправдоподо́бный* (неправдоподо́бен),
невероя́тный* (невероя́тен); (enormous)
невероя́тный* (невероя́тен); (amazing,
wonderful) потряса́ющий* (потряса́ющ); **it
was an ~ experience** э́то бы́ло потряса́юще.

incredulity [ɪnkrɪ'dju:lɪtɪ] n недове́рие.

incredulous [ɪn'krɛdjuləs] adj недове́рчивый
(недове́рчив).

increment ['ɪnkrɪmənt] n (in salary) приба́вка*.

incriminate [ɪn'krɪmɪneɪt] vt изоблича́ть
(изобличи́ть perf).

---

* marks translations which have irregular inflections. The Russian-English side of the dictionary gives inflectional information.

incriminating [ɪnˈkrɪmɪneɪtɪŋ] *adj* изоблич-
áющий.
incrusted [ɪnˈkrʌstɪd] *adj* = **encrusted**.
incubate [ˈɪnkjubeɪt] *vt* (*egg*) выси́живать
(вы́сидеть* *perf*) ♦ *vi* (*chickens*) вылупля́ться
(вы́лупиться *perf*); (*disease*) развива́ться
(разви́ться* *perf*).
incubation [ɪnkjuˈbeɪʃən] *n* (*by bird*) выведе́ние
цыпля́т; (*of illness*) инкубацио́нный пери́од.
incubation period *n* инкубацио́нный пери́од.
incubator [ˈɪnkjubeɪtə'] *n* (*for babies*)
инкубáтор.
inculcate [ˈɪnkʌlkeɪt] *vt*: **to ~ sth in sb** внушáть
(внуши́ть *perf*) что-н кому́-н.
incumbent [ɪnˈkʌmbənt] *n* (*official*)
отвéтственное лицó* ♦ *adj*: **it is ~ on him to ...**
он обя́зан +*infin* ....
incur [ɪnˈkə:'] *vt* (*expenses, loss*) нести́*
(понести́* *perf*); (*debt*) надéлать (*perf*) +*gen*;
(*disapproval, anger*) навлекáть (навлéчь* *perf*)
на себя́.
incurable [ɪnˈkjuərəbl] *adj* (*disease*)
неизлечи́мый (неизлечи́м).
incursion [ɪnˈkə:ʃən] *n* (*MIL*) вторжéние.
indebted [ɪnˈdɛtɪd] *adj*: **to be ~ to sb** (*grateful*)
быть* (*impf*) обя́занным(-ой) кому́-н.
indecency [ɪnˈdi:snsɪ] *n* непристóйность *f*.
indecent [ɪnˈdi:snt] *adj* непристóйный*
(непристóен); (*haste*) неприли́чный*
(неприли́чен).
indecent assault *n* (*BRIT*) (сексуáльное)
оскорблéние дéйствием.
indecent exposure *n* обнажéние половы́х
óрганов.
indecipherable [ɪndɪˈsaɪfərəbl] *adj* (*writing*)
неразбóрчивый (неразбóрчив); (*expression,
glance etc*) загáдочный* (загáдочен).
indecision [ɪndɪˈsɪʒən] *n* нереши́тельность *f*.
indecisive [ɪndɪˈsaɪsɪv] *adj* нереши́тельный*
(нереши́телен).
indeed [ɪnˈdi:d] *adv* (*certainly*) конéчно,
безуслóвно; (*in fact, furthermore*) на сáмом
дéле; (*rather*) скорéе дáже; **I'm upset, ~
shocked** я расстрóен, пожáлуй дáже
шоки́рован; **this book is very interesting ~**
эта кни́га чрезвычáйно интерéсная; **thank
you very much ~** большóе Вам спаси́бо; **he is
~ very talented** он и впрáвду *or* на сáмом
дéле о́чень талáнтлив; **yes ~**! ну конéчно!
indefatigable [ɪndɪˈfætɪgəbl] *adj* (*person*)
неутоми́мый (неутоми́м); (*rhythm, pulse etc*)
неослабевáющий.
indefensible [ɪndɪˈfɛnsɪbl] *adj* (*conduct*)
непрости́тельный* (непрости́телен).
indefinable [ɪndɪˈfaməbl] *adj* (*quality*) не
поддаю́щийся определéнию.
indefinite [ɪnˈdɛfɪnɪt] *adj* (*answer, view*)
неопределéнный* (неопределéнен); (*period,
number*) неограни́ченный* (неограни́чен).
indefinite article *n* (*LING*) неопределéнный
арти́кль *m*.

indefinitely [ɪnˈdɛfɪnɪtlɪ] *adv* (*continue, wait*)
бесконéчно; (*be closed, postponed*) на
неопределéнное врéмя.
indelible [ɪnˈdɛlɪbl] *adj* (*mark, stain: on clothes*)
неотсти́рывающийся; (: *on hands, furniture*)
несмывáемый; (*fig: memory, impact*)
неизглади́мый.
indelicate [ɪnˈdɛlɪkɪt] *adj* нетакти́чный*
(нетакти́чен).
indemnify [ɪnˈdɛmnɪfaɪ] *vt* (*COMM*) гарант-
и́ровать (*impf*) возмещéние убы́тков +*dat*.
indemnity [ɪnˈdɛmnɪtɪ] *n* (*insurance*) гарáнтия
возмещéния убы́тков; (*compensation*)
возмещéние.
indent [ɪnˈdɛnt] *vt* (*line of text*) писáть*
(написáть* *perf*) с крáсной строки́.
indentation [ɪndɛnˈteɪʃən] *n* углублéние; (*TYP*)
абзáц; (*on metal*) зазýбрина.
indenture [ɪnˈdɛntʃə'] *n* договóр* (*мéжду
подмастéрьем и́ли ученикóм и хозя́ином*).
independence [ɪndɪˈpɛndns] *n* незави́симость
f.
independent [ɪndɪˈpɛndnt] *adj* незави́симый
(незави́сим).
independently [ɪndɪˈpɛndntlɪ] *adv* незави́симо;
~ of незави́симо от +*gen*.
in-depth [ˈɪndɛpθ] *adj* детáльный, глубóкий*.
indescribable [ɪndɪsˈkraɪbəbl] *adj* неописýемый
(неописýем).
indestructible [ɪndɪsˈtrʌktəbl] *adj* (*object*)
неразруши́мый (неразруши́м); (*friendship,
alliance*) неруши́мый (неруши́м); (*army*)
непобеди́мый (непобеди́м).
indeterminate [ɪndɪˈtə:mɪnɪt] *adj* неопределéнный* (неопределéнен).
index [ˈɪndɛks] (*pl ~es*) *n* (*in book*)
(словáрь*-)указáтель *m*; (*in library etc*)
катáлог; (*pl indices; MATH*) показáтель* *msg*.
index card *n* (картотéчная) кáрточка*.
indexed [ˈɪndɛkst] *adj* (*US*) = **index-linked**.
index finger *n* указáтельный пáлец*.
index-linked [ˈɪndɛksˈlɪŋkt] *adj* (*income,
payment*) изменя́ющийся в соотвéтствии с
и́ндексом инфля́ции.
India [ˈɪndɪə] *n* Индия.
Indian [ˈɪndɪən] *adj* инди́йский* ♦ *n* инди́ец*
(индиáнка*); **Red ~** индéец* (индиáнка*).
Indian Ocean *n*: **the ~** Инди́йский* океáн.
Indian Summer *n* индéйское *or* бáбье лéто.
India paper *n* китáйская бумáга.
India rubber *n* рези́на, каучýк.
indicate [ˈɪndɪkeɪt] *vt* (*point to: also fig*)
укáзывать (указáть* *perf*) на +*acc*; (*mention*)
давáть* (дать* *perf*) знать о +*prp* ♦ *vi*: **to ~
that** (*show*) покáзывать (показáть* *perf*), что;
(*BRIT: AUT*): **to ~ left/right** включáть
(включи́ть *perf*) лéвый/прáвый указáтель
поворóта.
indication [ɪndɪˈkeɪʃən] *n* знак; **all the ~s are
that ...** всё укáзывает на то, что ....
indicative [ɪnˈdɪkətɪv] *n* (*LING*) изъяви́тельное

наклоне́ние ♦ *adj*: **to be ~ of**
свиде́тельствовать *(impf)* о +*prp*, ука́зывать
(impf) на +*acc*.

indicator ['ɪndɪkeɪtəʳ] *n (marker, signal)*
указа́тель *m*; (*AUT*) указа́тель поворо́та; *(fig)*
показа́тель *m*.

indices ['ɪndɪsi:z] *npl of* **index**.

indict [ɪn'daɪt] *vt* (*LAW*) предъявля́ть
(предъяви́ть* *perf*) обвине́ние +*dat*.

indictable [ɪn'daɪtəbl] *adj* подлежа́щий
уголо́вному рассмотре́нию; **~ offence**
уголо́вное преступле́ние.

indictment [ɪn'daɪtmənt] *n (denunciation)*
осужде́ние; *(charge)* обвини́тельный акт.

indie ['ɪndɪ] *adj (music, chart etc)* вы́пущенный
ма́ленькой незави́симой сту́дией
звукоза́писи.

indifference [ɪn'dɪfrəns] *n (lack of interest)*
безразли́чие, равноду́шие.

indifferent [ɪn'dɪfrənt] *adj* безразли́чный*
(безразли́чен), равноду́шный*
(равноду́шен); *(mediocre)* посре́дственный*
(посре́дствен).

indigenous [ɪn'dɪdʒɪnəs] *adj (wildlife,
population)* коренно́й; *(culture)* ме́стный.

indigestible [ɪndɪ'dʒɛstɪbl] *adj* тру́дно
перева́риваемый (перева́риваем).

indigestion [ɪndɪ'dʒɛstʃən] *n* расстро́йство
желу́дка.

indignant [ɪn'dɪgnənt] *adj* возмущённый*
(возмущён); **to be ~ at sth/with sb** быть*
(impf) возмущённым(-ой) чем-н/кем-н.

indignation [ɪndɪg'neɪʃən] *n* возмуще́ние,
негодова́ние.

indignity [ɪn'dɪgnɪtɪ] *n* униже́ние.

indigo ['ɪndɪgəu] *n (colour)* инди́го *nt ind*.

indirect [ɪndɪ'rɛkt] *adj (way, route)* око́льный,
обхо́дный; *(answer)* укло́нчивый
(укло́нчив); *(effect)* побо́чный; (*LING*): **~
object** ко́свенное дополне́ние.

indirectly [ɪndɪ'rɛktlɪ] *adv* ко́свенно.

indiscreet [ɪndɪs'kri:t] *adj* неосмотри́тельный*
(неосмотри́телен), неблагоразу́мный*
(неблагоразу́мен).

indiscretion [ɪndɪs'krɛʃən] *n* неосмотри́тель-
ность *f*; *(indiscreet act)* неблагоразу́мный
посту́пок*.

indiscriminate [ɪndɪs'krɪmɪnət] *adj (bombing)*
беспоря́дочный* (беспоря́дочен); *(taste,
reader, love)* неразбо́рчивый (неразбо́рчив);
(criticism) огу́льный.

indispensable [ɪndɪs'pɛnsəbl] *adj (object)*
необходи́мый (необходи́м); *(person)*
незамени́мый (незамени́м).

indisposed [ɪndɪs'pəuzd] *adj (unwell)*
нездоро́вый (нездоро́в).

indisputable [ɪndɪs'pju:təbl] *adj (undeniable)*
неоспори́мый (неоспори́м).

indistinct [ɪndɪs'tɪŋkt] *adj (image, noise)*
нея́сный* (нея́сен); *(memory)* сму́тный*
(сму́тен).

indistinguishable [ɪndɪs'tɪŋgwɪʃəbl] *adj*: **~ from**
неотличи́мый (неотличи́м) от +*gen*.

individual [ɪndɪ'vɪdjuəl] *n (person)* ли́чность *f*,
индиви́дуум ♦ *adj (personal)* индивид-
уа́льный* (индивидуа́лен), ли́чный; *(single)*
отде́льный; *(particular: characteristic)*
своеобра́зный* (своеобра́зен),
индивидуа́льный* (индивидуа́лен); **certain
~s** не́которые лю́ди.

individualist [ɪndɪ'vɪdjuəlɪst] *n* индивид-
уали́ст(ка*).

individuality [ɪndɪvɪdju'ælɪtɪ] *n* индивид-
уа́льность *f*.

individually [ɪndɪ'vɪdjuəlɪ] *adv* отде́льно; **he is
~ responsible** он несёт ли́чную
отве́тственность; **we'll help each of you ~** мы
помо́жем ка́ждому из Вас.

indivisible [ɪndɪ'vɪzɪbl] *adj* недели́мый
(недели́м).

Indo-China ['ɪndəu'tʃaɪnə] *n* Индокита́й.

indoctrinate [ɪn'dɔktrɪneɪt] *vt* подверга́ть
(подве́ргнуть* *perf*) идеологи́ческой
обрабо́тке.

indoctrination [ɪndɔktrɪ'neɪʃən] *n* идеолог-
и́ческая обрабо́тка.

indolence ['ɪndələns] *n* ле́ность *f*.

indolent ['ɪndələnt] *adj* лени́вый (лени́в).

Indonesia [ɪndə'ni:zɪə] *n* Индоне́зия.

Indonesian [ɪndə'ni:zɪən] *adj* индонези́йский* ♦
n индонези́ец*(-и́йка*).

indoor ['ɪndɔ:ʳ] *adj (plant, games for children)*
ко́мнатный; *(swimming pool)* закры́тый; **~
games** спорти́вные и́гры в закры́том
помеще́нии.

indoors [ɪn'dɔ:z] *adv (go)* в помеще́ние; *(be)* в
помеще́нии; **he stayed ~ all morning** он
проси́дел до́ма всё у́тро.

indubitable [ɪn'dju:bɪtəbl] *adj* несомне́нный*
(несомне́нен).

indubitably [ɪn'dju:bɪtəblɪ] *adv* несомне́нно.

induce [ɪn'dju:s] *vt (bring about)* вызыва́ть
(вы́звать* *perf*); *(persuade)* побужда́ть
(побуди́ть* *perf*); (*MED: birth*) стимули́ровать
(impf/perf); **to ~ sb to do** побужда́ть
(побуди́ть* *perf*) кого́-н +*infin*.

inducement [ɪn'dju:smənt] *n (incentive)*
сти́мул; *(pej: bribe)* по́дкуп.

induct [ɪn'dʌkt] *vt* назнача́ть (назна́чить *perf*)
на до́лжность; *(fig)* посвяща́ть (посвяти́ть*
perf) в(о) +*acc*.

induction [ɪn'dʌkʃən] *n* (*MED: of birth*)
стимуля́ция.

induction course *n* (*BRIT*) вво́дный курс.

indulge [ɪn'dʌldʒ] *vt (desire, whim etc)*
потво́рствовать *(impf)* +*dat*, потака́ть *(impf)*

---

* marks translations which have irregular inflections. The Russian-English side of the dictionary gives inflectional information.

+dat; (person, child) баловáть (избаловáть perf) ◆ vi: **to ~ in** баловáться (побаловáться perf) +instr.

indulgence [ɪn'dʌldʒəns] n (pleasure) прúхоть f; (leniency) потвóрство.

indulgent [ɪn'dʌldʒənt] adj (smile) снис-ходúтельный* (снисходúтелен); **he has very ~ parents** егó родúтели (во всём) емý потакáют.

industrial [ɪn'dʌstrɪəl] adj индустриáльный, промúшленный; **~ accident** несчáстный слýчай на произвóдстве.

industrial action n забастóвка.

industrial design n промúшленный дизáйн.

industrial estate n (BRIT) промúшленный кóмплекс.

industrialist [ɪn'dʌstrɪəlɪst] n промúшленник.

industrialize [ɪn'dʌstrɪəlaɪz] vt (country) индустриализúровать (impf/perf).

industrial park n (US) = **industrial estate**.

industrial relations npl произвóдственные отношéния ntpl.

industrial tribunal n (BRIT) суд, занимáющийся рассмотрéнием произ-вóдственных конфлúктов.

industrial unrest n (BRIT) рабóчие волнéния ntpl.

industrious [ɪn'dʌstrɪəs] adj трудолюбúвый (трудолюбúв).

industry ['ɪndəstrɪ] n (manufacturing) индустрúя, промúшленность f no pl; (diligence) трудолюбие; **industries** óтрасли pl промúшленности; **the oil/textile ~** нефтянáя/текстúльная промúшленность.

inebriated [ɪ'niːbrɪeɪtɪd] adj нетрéзвый (нетрéзв).

inedible [ɪn'ɛdɪbl] adj несъедóбный* (несъедóбен).

ineffective [ɪnɪ'fɛktɪv] adj неэффектúвный* (неэффектúвен).

ineffectual [ɪnɪ'fɛktʃuəl] adj = **ineffective**.

inefficiency [ɪnɪ'fɪʃənsɪ] n неэффектúвность f; непроизводúтельность f.

inefficient [ɪnɪ'fɪʃənt] adj неэффектúвный* (неэффектúвен); (machine) непроиз-водúтельный* (непроизводúтелен).

inelegant [ɪn'ɛlɪɡənt] adj неэлегáнтный* (неэлегáнтен).

ineligible [ɪn'ɛlɪdʒɪbl] adj (candidate) неподходящий*; **to be ~ for sth** не имéть (impf) прáво на что-н.

inept [ɪ'nɛpt] adj (management etc) неумéлый (неумéл).

ineptitude [ɪ'nɛptɪtjuːd] n неумéние, неумéлость f.

inequality [ɪnɪ'kwɔlɪtɪ] n (of system) нерáвенство; (of amount, share) рáзница.

inequitable [ɪn'ɛkwɪtəbl] adj несправедлúвый (несправедлúв).

inert [ɪ'nɜːt] adj (immobile) неподвúжный* (неподвúжен); (gas) инéртный.

inertia [ɪ'nɜːʃə] n (laziness) инéртность f; (PHYS) инéрция.

inertia-reel seat belt [ɪ'nɜːʃə'riːl-] n инерциóнный ремéнь* m безопáсности.

inescapable [ɪnɪ'skeɪpəbl] adj неизбéжный* (неизбéжен).

inessential [ɪnɪ'sɛnʃl] adj несущéственный* (несущéственен).

inessentials [ɪnɪ'sɛnʃlz] npl рóскошь fsg.

inestimable [ɪn'ɛstɪməbl] adj (value) неоценúмый (неоценúм); (cost) неподдающийся* оцéнке.

inevitability [ɪnɛvɪtə'bɪlɪtɪ] n неизбéжность f; **the ~ of change** неизбéжность изменéний; **it is an ~** это неизбéжность.

inevitable [ɪn'ɛvɪtəbl] adj неизбéжный* (неизбéжен).

inevitably [ɪn'ɛvɪtəblɪ] adv неизбéжно; **as ~ happens, ...** как это неизбéжно случáется, ...

inexact [ɪnɪɡ'zækt] adj нетóчный* (нетóчен).

inexcusable [ɪnɪks'kjuːzəbl] adj непростúтельный* (непростúтелен).

inexhaustible [ɪnɪɡ'zɔːstɪbl] adj (wealth, resources) неисчерпáемый (неисчерпáем).

inexorable [ɪn'ɛksərəbl] adj (progress) неотвратúмый (неотвратúм); (decline) неумолúмый (неумолúм).

inexpensive [ɪnɪk'spɛnsɪv] adj недорогóй* (недóрог).

inexperience [ɪnɪk'spɪərɪəns] n неóпытность f.

inexperienced [ɪnɪk'spɪərɪənst] adj неóпытный* (неóпытен); **to be ~ in sth** не имéть (impf) óпыта в чём-н.

inexplicable [ɪnɪk'splɪkəbl] adj необъяснúмый (необъяснúм).

inexpressible [ɪnɪk'sprɛsɪbl] adj невыразúмый (невыразúм).

inextricable [ɪnɪk'strɪkəbl] adj (union, knot, tangle) неразрúвный* (неразрúвен); (dilemma) безвúходный* (безвúходен).

inextricably [ɪnɪk'strɪkəblɪ] adv неразрúвно.

infallibility [ɪnfælə'bɪlɪtɪ] n непогрешúмость f.

infallible [ɪn'fælɪbl] adj (person) непогрешúмый (непогрешúм); (guide) надёжный* (надёжен).

infamous ['ɪnfəməs] adj бесчéстный* (бесчéстен).

infamy ['ɪnfəmɪ] n бесчéстие.

infancy ['ɪnfənsɪ] n (of person) младéнчество; (of movement, firm) перúод становлéния.

infant ['ɪnfənt] n (baby) младéнец*; (young child) ребёнок* ◆ cpd дéтский*.

infantile ['ɪnfəntaɪl] adj (disease) дéтский*; (childish) инфантúльный* (инфантúлен).

infantry ['ɪnfəntrɪ] n пехóта.

infantryman ['ɪnfəntrɪmən] irreg n пехотúнец*.

infant school n (BRIT) ≈ начáльная шкóла (для детéй от 5-и до 7-и лет).

infatuated [ɪn'fætjueɪtɪd] adj: **~ with** увлечённый (увлечён) +instr; **to become ~ with** увлекáться (увлéчься* perf) +instr.

infatuation [ɪnfætju'eɪʃən] *n* увлечéние*.

infect [ɪn'fɛkt] *vt* (*also fig*) заражáть (заразúть* *perf*); **to become ~ed** (*wound*) заражáться (заразúться* *perf*).

infection [ɪn'fɛkʃən] *n* инфéкция.

infectious [ɪn'fɛkʃəs] *adj* (*person, animal*) зарáзный* (зарáзен); (*disease*) инфекциóнный; (*fig*) заразúтельный* (заразúтелен).

infer [ɪn'fə:'] *vt* (*deduce*) заключáть (заключúть* *perf*); (*imply*) подразумевáть (*impf*).

inference ['ɪnfərəns] *n* (*deduction*) заключéние; (*implication*) вы́вод.

inferior [ɪn'fɪərɪə'] *adj* (*position, status*) подчинённый; (*goods*) нúзкого кáчества ♦ *n* (*subordinate*) подчинённый(-ая) *m(f) adj*; (*junior*) млáдший* по чúну; **to feel ~ (to)** ощущáть (ощутúть* *perf*) свою́ неполноцéнность (по сравнéнию с +*instr*); **he is ~ to me in rank** он нúже меня́ по дóлжности; **the second model is ~ to the first** вторáя модéль уступáет пéрвой по кáчеству.

inferiority [ɪnfɪərɪ'ɔrətɪ] *n* (*of position, status*) подчинённое положéние; (*of goods*) низкосóртность *f*.

inferiority complex *n* кóмплекс неполноцéнности.

infernal [ɪn'fə:nl] *adj* áдский*.

inferno [ɪn'fə:nəʊ] *n* (*also fig*) ад.

infertile [ɪn'fə:taɪl] *adj* (*soil*) неплодорóдный* (неплодорóден); (*person, animal*) бесплóдный* (бесплóден).

infertility [ɪnfə:'tɪlɪtɪ] *n* (*see adj*) неплодорóдность *f*; бесплóдие.

infested [ɪn'fɛstɪd] *adj*: **the house is ~ with rats** дом кишúт кры́сами.

infidelity [ɪnfɪ'dɛlɪtɪ] *n* невéрность *f*.

infighting ['ɪnfaɪtɪŋ] *n* внýтренний* конфлúкт.

infiltrate ['ɪnfɪltreɪt] *vt* проникáть (проникнуть* *perf*) в +*acc*.

infinite ['ɪnfɪnɪt] *adj* бесконéчный* (бесконéчен); (*resources*) несмéтный* (несмéтен).

infinitely ['ɪnfɪnɪtlɪ] *adv* бесконéчно.

infinitesimal [ɪnfɪnɪ'tɛsɪməl] *adj* бесконéчно мáлый* (мал).

infinitive [ɪn'fɪnɪtɪv] *n* инфинитúв, неопределённая фóрма глагóла.

infinity [ɪn'fɪnɪtɪ] *n* бесконéчность *f*.

infirm [ɪn'fə:m] *adj* нéмощный* (нéмощен).

infirmary [ɪn'fə:mərɪ] *n* больнúца.

infirmity [ɪn'fə:mɪtɪ] *n* нéмощь *f*.

inflame [ɪn'fleɪm] *vt* (*person, crowd*) распаля́ть (распалúть* *perf*); (*situation, emotions*) накаля́ть (накалúть* *perf*).

inflamed [ɪn'fleɪmd] *adj* (*throat, appendix*) воспалённый (воспалён).

inflammable [ɪn'flæməbl] *adj* (*fabric*) легкó воспламеня́ющийся; (*chemical*) горю́чий* (горю́ч).

inflammation [ɪnflə'meɪʃən] *n* воспалéние.

inflammatory [ɪn'flæmətərɪ] *adj* (*speech*) подстрекáтельский.

inflatable [ɪn'fleɪtəbl] *adj* надувнóй.

inflate [ɪn'fleɪt] *vt* (*tyre*) накáчивать (накачáть* *perf*); (*balloon*) надувáть (надýть* *perf*); (*price*) вздувáть (вздуть* *perf*); (*expectation, position, ideas*) раздувáть (раздýть* *perf*).

inflated [ɪn'fleɪtɪd] *adj* (*style*) напы́щенный* (напы́щен); (*prices*) взду́тый (вздут).

inflation [ɪn'fleɪʃən] *n* (*ECON*) инфля́ция.

inflationary [ɪn'fleɪʃənərɪ] *adj* инфляциóнный.

inflationist [ɪn'fleɪʃənɪst] *n* сторóнник(-ица) полúтики инфля́ции.

inflexible [ɪn'flɛksɪbl] *adj* (*rule, timetable*) жёсткий* (жёсток); (*person*) негúбкий* (негúбок).

inflict [ɪn'flɪkt] *vt*: **to ~ sth on sb** причиня́ть (причинúть* *perf*) что-н комý-н; (*penalty*) налагáть (наложúть* *perf*) что-н на когó-н.

infliction [ɪn'flɪkʃən] *n* (*of pain*) причинéние; (*of penalty*) наложéние.

in-flight ['ɪnflaɪt] *adj* (*meal, entertainment*) на бортý самолёта; **~ refuelling** дозапрáвка в полёте.

inflow ['ɪnfləʊ] *n* притóк.

influence ['ɪnfluəns] *n* (*power*) влия́ние; (*effect*) воздéйствие ♦ *vt* (*person, situation, choice etc*) влия́ть (повлия́ть* *perf*) на +*acc*, окáзывать (оказáть* *perf*) влия́ние на +*acc*; **under the ~ of alcohol** под воздéйствием алкогóля.

influential [ɪnflu'ɛnʃl] *adj* влия́тельный* (влия́телен).

influenza [ɪnflu'ɛnzə] *n* грипп.

influx ['ɪnflʌks] *n* (*of people, funds*) притóк.

inform [ɪn'fɔ:m] *vt*: **to ~ sb of sth** (*tell*) сообщáть (сообщúть *perf*) комý-н о чём-н, информúровать (проинформúровать *perf*) когó-н о чём-н ♦ *vi*: **to ~ on sb** доносúть* (донестú* *perf*) на когó-н.

informal [ɪn'fɔ:ml] *adj* (*visit, meeting, invitation*) неофициáльный* (неофициáлен); (*manner, discussion*) непринуждённый* (непринуждён); (*clothes*) бýдничный, повседнéвный* (повседнéвен); (*language*) разговóрный.

informality [ɪnfɔ:'mælɪtɪ] *n* непринуждённость *f*.

informally [ɪn'fɔ:məlɪ] *adv* неофициáльно; (*discuss*) непринуждённо; (*dress*) бýднично; (*invite*) без церемóний.

informant [ɪn'fɔ:mənt] *n* (*source*) информáнт.

information [ɪnfə'meɪʃən] *n* информáция; **to get ~ on** получáть (получúть* *perf*) информáцию о +*prp*; **a piece of ~** сообщéние; **for your ~** к Вáшему свéдению.

---

* marks translations which have irregular inflections. The Russian-English side of the dictionary gives inflectional information.

information bureau *n* = information office.
information office *n* спра́вочное бюро́ *nt ind*.
information processing *n* обрабо́тка
информа́ции.
information retrieval *n* (*COMPUT*) по́иск
информа́ции, информацио́нный по́иск.
information science *n* информа́тика.
information technology *n* информацио́нная
техноло́гия.
informative [ɪn'fɔ:mətɪv] *adj* содержа́тельный*
(содержа́телен).
informed [ɪn'fɔ:md] *adj* осведомлённый*
(осведомлён), информи́рованный*
(информи́рован); **well/ill ~** хорошо́/пло́хо
информи́рованный (информи́рован); **an ~
guess** обосно́ванная дога́дка*.
informer [ɪn'fɔ:mə'] *n* (*also:* **police ~**)
осведоми́тель(ница) *m(f)*.
infra dig ['ɪnfrə'dɪg] *adj abbr* (*inf:* = *beneath one's
dignity:* = *infra dignitatem*) ни́же чьего́-н
досто́инства.
infrared [ɪnfrə'rɛd] *adj* инфракра́сный.
infrastructure ['ɪnfrəstrʌktʃə'] *n*
инфраструкту́ра.
infrequent [ɪn'fri:kwənt] *adj* ре́дкий* (ре́док).
infringe [ɪn'frɪndʒ] *vt* (*law*) преступа́ть
(преступи́ть* *perf*) ♦ *vi:* **to ~ on** (*rights*)
ущемля́ть (ущеми́ть* *perf*), посяга́ть
(посягну́ть *perf*) на +*acc*.
infringement [ɪn'frɪndʒmənt] *n* (*see vb*)
наруше́ние; ущемле́ние, посяга́тельство.
infuriate [ɪn'fjuərɪeɪt] *vt* (*person*) приводи́ть*
(привести́* *perf*) в я́рость *or* бе́шенство,
беси́ть* (взбеси́ть* *perf*).
infuriating [ɪn'fjuərɪeɪtɪŋ] *adj* приводя́щий в
я́рость *or* бе́шенство; **the noise is ~** шум
приво́дит меня́ *etc* в я́рость.
infuse [ɪn'fju:z] *vt* (*tea, herbs*) наста́ивать
(настоя́ть *perf*); (*person*): **to ~ sb with sth**
вселя́ть (всели́ть* *perf*) что-н в кого́-н.
infusion [ɪn'fju:ʒən] *n* (*tea*) насто́йка*.
ingenious [ɪn'dʒi:njəs] *adj* хитроу́мный*
(хитроу́мен); (*person*) изобрета́тельный*
(изобрета́телен).
ingenuity [ɪndʒɪ'nju:ɪtɪ] *n* хитроу́мность *f*; (*of
person*) изобрета́тельность *f*.
ingenuous [ɪn'dʒɛnjuəs] *adj* бесхи́тростный*
(бесхи́тростен).
ingot ['ɪŋgət] *n* сли́ток*.
ingrained [ɪn'greɪnd] *adj* закорене́лый.
ingratiate [ɪn'greɪʃɪeɪt] *vt:* **to ~ o.s. with**
зайскивать (impf) пе́ред +*instr*.
ingratiating [ɪn'greɪʃɪeɪtɪŋ] *adj* (*smile, speech*)
заи́скивающий*; (*person*) льсти́вый
(льстив).
ingratitude [ɪn'grætɪtju:d] *n* неблагода́р-
ность *f*.
ingredient [ɪn'gri:dɪənt] *n* (*CULIN*) ингредие́нт;
(*of situation*) составна́я часть* *f*.
ingrowing ['ɪngrəuɪŋ] *adj:* **~ toenail**
враста́ющий но́готь* *m* (*на па́льце ноги́*).

inhabit [ɪn'hæbɪt] *vt* населя́ть (*impf*).
inhabitant [ɪn'hæbɪtnt] *n* жи́тель(ница) *m(f)*.
inhale [ɪn'heɪl] *vt* вдыха́ть (вдохну́ть* *perf*) ♦ *vi*
вдыха́ть (вдо́хнуть* *perf*); (*when smoking*)
затя́гиваться (затяну́ться* *perf*).
inhaler [ɪn'heɪlə'] *n* ингаля́тор.
inherent [ɪn'hɪərənt] *adj* (*laziness*)
прирождённый* ♦ **~ in** *or* **to** сво́йственный*
(сво́йствен) +*dat*, прису́щий* (прису́щ) +*dat*.
inherently [ɪn'hɪərəntlɪ] *adv* (*easy, difficult*) по
приро́де; (*lazy*) по нату́ре.
inherit [ɪn'hɛrɪt] *vt* насле́довать (*impf/perf*),
унасле́довать (*perf*).
inheritance [ɪn'hɛrɪtəns] *n* насле́дство;
(*cultural, political etc*) насле́дие; **right of ~**
пра́во насле́дования.
inhibit [ɪn'hɪbɪt] *vt* (*impulse*) ско́вывать
(скова́ть *perf*); (*growth*) заде́рживать
(задержа́ть* *perf*).
inhibited [ɪn'hɪbɪtɪd] *adj* (*see vb*) ско́ванный*
(ско́ван); заде́ржанный.
inhibiting [ɪn'hɪbɪtɪŋ] *adj* (*situation*)
ско́вывающий; (*factor*) препя́тствующий.
inhibition [ɪnhɪ'bɪʃən] *n* (*see vb*) ско́ванность *f*
no pl; заде́ржка*.
inhospitable [ɪnhɔs'pɪtəbl] *adj* (*person*)
негостеприи́мный* (негостеприи́мен);
(*place*) неприве́тливый (неприве́тлив).
inhuman [ɪn'hju:mən] *adj* (*behaviour*)
бесчелове́чный* (бесчелове́чен);
(*appearance*) нечелове́ческий*.
inhumane [ɪnhju:'meɪn] *adj* негума́нный*
(негума́нен).
inimitable [ɪ'nɪmɪtəbl] *adj* неподража́емый
(неподража́ем).
iniquitous [ɪ'nɪkwɪtəs] *adj* (*see n*) чудо́вищный*
(чудо́вищен); чудо́вищно несправедли́вый
(несправедли́в).
iniquity [ɪ'nɪkwɪtɪ] *n* (*wickedness*) чудо́вищ-
ность *f*; (*injustice*) несправедли́вость *f*.
initial [ɪ'nɪʃl] *adj* первонача́льный, нача́льный
♦ *n* (*also:* **~ letter**) нача́льная бу́ква ♦ *vt*
ста́вить* (поста́вить* *perf*) инициа́лы на
+*prp*; **~s** *npl* инициа́лы *mpl*.
initialize [ɪ'nɪʃəlaɪz] *vt* (*COMPUT*) инициализ-
и́ровать (*impf/perf*).
initially [ɪ'nɪʃəlɪ] *adv* (*at first*) внача́ле, снача́ла;
(*first*) первонача́льно.
initiate [ɪ'nɪʃɪeɪt] *vt* (*talks, process*) класть*
(положи́ть *perf*) нача́ло +*dat*; (*new member*)
посвяща́ть (посвяти́ть* *perf*); **to ~ sb into a
secret** посвяща́ть (посвяти́ть* *perf*) кого́-н в
та́йну; **to ~ proceedings against sb**
возбужда́ть (возбуди́ть* *perf*) де́ло про́тив
кого́-н.
initiation [ɪnɪʃɪ'eɪʃən] *n* (*beginning*) основа́ние;
(*into secret etc*) посвяще́ние; **~ ceremony**
церемо́ния посвяще́ния.
initiative [ɪ'nɪʃətɪv] *n* (*move*) инициати́ва,
начина́ние; (*enterprise*) инициати́вность *f*; **to
take the ~** брать* (взять* *perf*) на себя́

инициати́ву.

inject [ɪn'dʒɛkt] vt (*drugs, poison*) вводи́ть*
(ввести́* *perf*); (*patient*): **to ~ sb with sth**
де́лать (сде́лать *perf*) уко́л *or* инъе́кцию
чего́-н кому́-н; (*money*): **to ~ into** влива́ть
(влить* *perf*) в +*acc.*

injection [ɪn'dʒɛkʃən] n уко́л, инъе́кция; (*of
money*) влива́ние; **to give an ~** де́лать
(сде́лать *perf*) уко́л *or* инъе́кцию; **I had an ~**
мне сде́лали уко́л.

injudicious [ɪndʒu'dɪʃəs] adj неразу́мный*
(неразу́мен).

injunction [ɪn'dʒʌŋkʃən] n (*LAW*) (суде́бный)
запре́т.

injure ['ɪndʒəʳ] vt (*person, limb, feelings*) ра́нить
(*impf/perf*); (*reputation*) поврежда́ть
(повреди́ть* *perf*); **to ~ o.s.** пора́ниться (*perf*),
ушиба́ться (ушиби́ться* *perf*).

injured ['ɪndʒəd] adj (*see vb*) ра́неный;
повреждённый (повреждён); уши́бленный
(уши́блен); **~ party** (*LAW*) потерпе́вшая
сторона́*.

injurious [ɪn'dʒuərɪəs] adj: **~ to** вре́дный*
(вре́ден) для +*gen*, губи́тельный*
(губи́телен) для +*gen.*

injury ['ɪndʒərɪ] n поврежде́ние; (*more serious*)
ране́ние; (*industrial, sports*) тра́вма; (*to
reputation, feelings*) оскорбле́ние; **to escape
without ~** избега́ть (избежа́ть* *perf*)
ране́ний.

injury time n (*SPORT*) доба́вочное вре́мя* nt.

injustice [ɪn'dʒʌstɪs] n несправедли́вость f; **you
do me an ~** Вы ко мне несправедли́вы.

ink [ɪŋk] n (*in pen*) черни́ла pl; (*for printing*)
типогра́фская кра́ска*.

ink-jet printer ['ɪŋkdʒɛt-] n (*COMPUT*)
струйный при́нтер.

inkling ['ɪŋklɪŋ] n (*idea, clue*): **to have an ~ of**
име́ть (*impf*) поня́тие о +*prp.*

ink pad n штемпельная поду́шечка*.

inky ['ɪŋkɪ] adj (*blackness, sky*) черни́льный;
(*fingers*) запа́чканный (запа́чкан)
черни́лами.

inlaid ['ɪnleɪd] adj: **~ (with)** инкрусти́рованный
(инкрусти́рован) (+*instr*).

inland ['ɪnlənd] adj вну́тренний* ♦ adv (*travel*)
вглубь.

Inland Revenue n (*BRIT*) ≈ Гла́вное нало́говое
управле́ние.

in-laws ['ɪnlɔ:z] npl родня́ со стороны́ му́жа
и́ли жены́.

inlet ['ɪnlɛt] n (у́зкий*) зали́в.

inlet pipe n впускна́я труба́*.

inmate ['ɪnmeɪt] n (*of prison*)
заключённый(-ая) m(f) adj; (*of asylum*)
пацие́нт(ка*).

inmost ['ɪnməust] adj сокрове́ннейший*.

inn [ɪn] n тракти́р.

innards ['ɪnədz] npl (*inf*) вну́тренности fpl.

innate [ɪ'neɪt] adj врождённый.

inner ['ɪnəʳ] adj вну́тренний*.

inner city n центра́льная часть* f го́рода.

innermost ['ɪnəməust] adj = **inmost**.

inner tube n ка́мера (*шины*).

innings ['ɪnɪŋz] n *серия атаку́ющих уда́ров в
кри́кете*; **he's had a good ~** (*BRIT: inf*) он
прожи́л до́лгую и счастли́вую жизнь.

innocence ['ɪnəsns] n (*LAW*) невино́вность f;
(*naivety*) неви́нность f.

innocent ['ɪnəsnt] adj (*also LAW*) невино́вный*
(невино́вен); (*naive*) неви́нный* (неви́нен).

innocuous [ɪ'nɔkjuəs] adj (*substance*)
безвре́дный* (безвре́ден); (*remarks*)
безоби́дный* (безоби́ден).

innovation [ɪnəu'veɪʃən] n но́вшество.

innuendo [ɪnju'ɛndəu] (*pl* **~es**) n инсинуа́ция.

innumerable [ɪ'nju:mrəbl] adj бесчи́сленный*
(бесчи́слен).

inoculate [ɪ'nɔkjuleɪt] vt: **to ~ sb against sth**
де́лать (сде́лать *perf*) кому́-н приви́вку
про́тив чего́-н; **to ~ sb with sth** привива́ть
(приви́ть* *perf*) кому́-н что-н.

inoculation [ɪnɔkju'leɪʃən] n приви́вка*.

inoffensive [ɪnə'fɛnsɪv] adj безоби́дный*
(безоби́ден).

inopportune [ɪn'ɔpətju:n] adj (*moment*)
неподходя́щий*; (*event*) несвоевре́менный*
(несвоевре́менен).

inordinate [ɪ'nɔ:dɪnət] adj необыча́йный*
(необыча́ен).

inordinately [ɪ'nɔ:dɪnətlɪ] adv необыча́йно.

inorganic [ɪnɔ:'gænɪk] adj неоргани́ческий*.

inpatient ['ɪnpeɪʃənt] n стациона́рный(-ая)
больно́й(-а́я) m(f) adj.

input ['ɪnput] n (*resources, money*) вложе́ние;
(*COMPUT*) ввод ♦ vt (*COMPUT*): **to ~ (into)**
вводи́ть* (ввести́* *perf*) (в +*acc*).

inquest ['ɪnkwɛst] n (*on sb's death*) (суде́бное)
рассле́дование.

inquire [ɪn'kwaɪəʳ] vt спра́шивать (спроси́ть*
perf) ♦ vi: **to ~ (about)** справля́ться
(справи́ться* *perf*) (о +*prp*); **to ~ when/where**
справля́ться (справи́ться* *perf*) когда́/где; **he
~d whether he could go** он спроси́л, мо́жет
ли он идти́

▶ **inquire after** vt fus спра́шивать (спроси́ть*
perf) о +*prp*

▶ **inquire into** vt fus рассле́довать (*impf/perf*).

inquiring [ɪn'kwaɪərɪŋ] adj пытли́вый.

inquiry [ɪn'kwaɪərɪ] n (*question*) вопро́с; (: *more
official*) запро́с; (*investigation*)
рассле́дование; (: *LAW*) сле́дствие; **to make
inquiries about sth** наводи́ть* (навести́* *perf*)
спра́вки о чём-н; **to hold an ~ into sth** вести́*
(*impf*) рассле́дование чего́-н.

inquiry desk n (*BRIT*) спра́вочный стол*.

---

* marks translations which have irregular inflections. The Russian-English side of the dictionary gives inflectional information.

inquiry office n (BRIT) спра́вочное бюро́ nt ind.
inquisition [ɪnkwɪ'zɪʃən] n сле́дствие no pl;
(REL): **the I~** Инквизи́ция.
inquisitive [ɪn'kwɪzɪtɪv] adj любопы́тный*
(любопы́тен).
inroads ['ɪnrəudz] npl: **to make ~ into** (savings,
resources) тра́тить* (потра́тить* perf).
ins abbr = inches.
ins and outs ['ɪnzən'auts] npl: **to know all the ~
~ ~** знать (impf) все ходы́.
insane [ɪn'seɪn] adj (foolish, crazy) безу́мный*
(безу́мен); (PSYCH) душевнобольно́й.
insanitary [ɪn'sænɪtərɪ] adj антисанита́рный*
(антисанита́рен).
insanity [ɪn'sænɪtɪ] n (also fig) безу́мие,
сумасше́ствие.
insatiable [ɪn'seɪʃəbl] adj ненасы́тный*
(ненасы́тен).
inscribe [ɪn'skraɪb] vt надпи́сывать
(надписа́ть* perf).
inscription [ɪn'skrɪpʃən] n на́дпись f.
inscrutable [ɪn'skru:təbl] adj зага́дочный*
(зага́дочен).
inseam measurement ['ɪnsi:m-] n (US) =
inside leg measurement.
insect ['ɪnsɛkt] n насеко́мое nt adj.
insect bite n уку́с насеко́мого.
insecticide [ɪn'sɛktɪsaɪd] n инсектици́д.
insect repellent n сре́дство от насеко́мых.
insecure [ɪnsɪ'kjuə'] adj (structure, border)
ненадёжный* (ненадёжен); (person)
неуве́ренный* (неуве́рен) в себе́.
insecurity [ɪnsɪ'kjuərɪtɪ] n (of structure)
ненадёжность f; неуве́ренность f в себе́.
insemination [ɪnsɛmɪ'neɪʃən] n: **artificial ~**
иску́сственное оплодотворе́ние.
insensible [ɪn'sɛnsɪbl] adj (unconscious) без
созна́ния; (unable to feel): **~ to**
нечувстви́тельный* (нечувстви́телен) к +dat;
(unaware): **~ of** не осознаю́щий +gen.
insensitive [ɪn'sɛnsɪtɪv] adj бесчу́вственный*
(бесчу́вствен).
insensitivity [ɪnsɛnsɪ'tɪvɪtɪ] n (of person)
бесчу́вственность f.
inseparable [ɪn'sɛprəbl] adj (ideas, elements)
нераздели́мый (нераздели́м); (friends)
неразлу́чный (неразлу́чен).
insert [vt ɪn'sə:t, n 'ɪnsə:t] vt: **to ~ (into)**
вставля́ть (вста́вить* perf) (в +acc); (piece of
paper) вкла́дывать (вложи́ть* perf) ♦ n
вкла́дыш, вкла́дка.
insertion [ɪn'sə:ʃən] n (in book, file) вста́вка*;
(of needle) введе́ние; (of peg) вбива́ние.
in-service ['ɪn'sə:vɪs] adj: **~ training**
произво́дственное обуче́ние.
inshore [ɪn'ʃɔ:'] adj (fishing, waters) при-
бре́жный ♦ adv (be) у бе́рега; (go) к бе́регу.
inside ['ɪn'saɪd] n вну́тренняя часть* f; (of coat
etc) изна́нка; (of road: BRIT) ле́вая сторона́;
(: US, Europe etc) пра́вая сторона́ ♦ adj
вну́тренний* ♦ adv (go) внутрь; (be) внутри́ ♦

prep (position) внутри́ +gen; (motion) внутрь
+gen; (of time): **~ ten minutes** в преде́лах
десяти́ мину́т; **~s** npl (inf: stomach)
вну́тренности fpl.
inside forward n (FOOTBALL) полусре́дний
напада́ющий* m adj.
inside information n информа́ция,
полу́ченная из вну́тренних исто́чников.
inside lane n (AUT: BRIT) ле́вый ряд*; (: US,
Europe etc) пра́вый ряд*.
inside leg measurement n (BRIT) вну́тренняя*
длина́ ноги́.
inside out adv (be, wear, turn) наизна́нку;
(know) вдоль и поперёк.
insider [ɪn'saɪdə'] n свой челове́к; (COMM)
инса́йдер.
insider dealing n (STOCK EXCHANGE)
незако́нное испо́льзование делово́й
информа́ции при сде́лках на би́рже.
insider trading n = **insider dealing.**
inside story n информа́ция из пе́рвых рук.
insidious [ɪn'sɪdɪəs] adj кова́рный* (кова́рен).
insight ['ɪnsaɪt] n: **(into)** понима́ние no pl
(+gen); **to gain (an) ~ into sth** вника́ть
(вни́кнуть perf) в что-н.
insignia [ɪn'sɪgnɪə] n inv зна́ки mpl отли́чия.
insignificant [ɪnsɪg'nɪfɪknt] adj
незначи́тельный* (незначи́телен).
insincere [ɪnsɪn'sɪə'] adj нейскренний*
(нейскренен).
insincerity [ɪnsɪn'sɛrɪtɪ] n нейскренность f.
insinuate [ɪn'sɪnjueɪt] vt намека́ть (намекну́ть*
perf) на +acc.
insinuation [ɪnsɪnju'eɪʃən] n инсинуа́ция.
insipid [ɪn'sɪpɪd] adj (person) бесцве́тный*
(бесцве́тен); (colour) блёклый; (food, drink)
пре́сный* (пре́сен).
insist [ɪn'sɪst] vi: **to ~ (on)** наста́ивать
(настоя́ть perf) (на +prp); **to ~ that** (demand)
наста́ивать (настоя́ть perf) на том, что́бы
+past tense; (claim) наста́ивать (настоя́ть perf)
на том, что.
insistence [ɪn'sɪstəns] n настоя́ние; **at his ~** по
его́ настоя́нию.
insistent [ɪn'sɪstənt] adj насто́йчивый
(насто́йчив).
insofar as [ɪnsəu'fɑ:'-] adv поско́льку.
insole ['ɪnsəul] n сте́лька*.
insolence ['ɪnsələns] n на́глость f.
insolent ['ɪnsələnt] adj (attitude, remark)
на́глый* (нагл).
insoluble [ɪn'sɔljubl] adj неразреши́мый
(неразреши́м).
insolvency [ɪn'sɔlvənsɪ] n неплатёже-
спосо́бность f.
insolvent [ɪn'sɔlvənt] adj неплатёже-
спосо́бный* (неплатёжеспосо́бен).
insomnia [ɪn'sɔmnɪə] n бессо́нница.
insomniac [ɪn'sɔmnɪæk] n страда́ющий(-ая)
m(f) adj бессо́нницей.
inspect [ɪn'spɛkt] vt (premises, equipment)

осма́тривать (осмотре́ть* *perf*); (*BRIT: ticket, luggage*) проверя́ть (прове́рить *perf*).

inspection [ɪnˈspɛkʃən] *n* (*see vb*) осмо́тр; прове́рка*.

inspector [ɪnˈspɛktə'] *n* (*ADMIN, POLICE*) инспе́ктор*; (*BRIT: on buses, trains*) контролёр.

inspiration [ɪnspəˈreɪʃən] *n* вдохнове́ние.

inspire [ɪnˈspaɪə'] *vt* (*workers, troops*) вдохновля́ть (вдохнови́ть* *perf*); **to ~ sth (in sb)** внуша́ть (внуши́ть *perf*) что-н (кому́-н).

inspired [ɪnˈspaɪəd] *adj* (*writer etc*) вдохновлённый (вдохновлён); (*book*) вдохнове́нный (вдохнове́нен); **in an ~ moment** в моме́нт вдохнове́ния.

inspiring [ɪnˈspaɪərɪŋ] *adj* вдохновля́ющий*.

inst. *abbr* (*BRIT: COMM:* = *instant*) с.м.= *сего́ ме́сяца.*

instability [ɪnstəˈbɪlɪtɪ] *n* нестаби́льность *f*.

install [ɪnˈstɔːl] *vt* (*machine*) устана́вливать (установи́ть* *perf*); (*official*) ста́вить* (поста́вить* *perf*).

installation [ɪnstəˈleɪʃən] *n* (*of machine, plant*) устано́вка; (*MIL*) объе́кт.

installment plan *n* (*US*) рассро́чка.

instalment [ɪnˈstɔːlmənt] (*US* **installment**) *n* (*of payment*) взнос; (*of story, TV serial*) часть *f*; **to pay in ~s** плати́ть* (заплати́ть* *perf*) в рассро́чку.

instance [ˈɪnstəns] *n* (*example*) приме́р; **for ~** наприме́р; **in this** *or* **that ~** в да́нном слу́чае; **in many ~s** во мно́гих слу́чаях; **in the first ~** в пе́рвую о́чередь.

instant [ˈɪnstənt] *n* мгнове́ние, миг ◆ *adj* (*reaction, success*) мгнове́нный* (мгнове́нен); **come here this ~!** иди́ сюда́ сию́ мину́ту!; **the 10th ~** (*COMM, ADMIN*) 10-ое число́ сего́ ме́сяца; **~ coffee** раствори́мый ко́фе; **~ food** пищево́й концентра́т.

instantaneous [ɪnstənˈteɪnɪəs] *adj* (*immediate*) мгнове́нный* (мгнове́нен).

instantly [ˈɪnstəntlɪ] *adv* неме́дленно, сра́зу.

instant replay *n* (*TV*) повто́р.

instead [ɪnˈstɛd] *adv* взаме́н ◆ *prep*: **~ of** вме́сто +*gen*, взаме́н +*gen*; **~ of sb** вме́сто кого́-н.

instep [ˈɪnstɛp] *n* подъём (*ноги́, ту́фли*).

instigate [ˈɪnstɪgeɪt] *vt* (*rebellion, strike etc*) подстрека́ть (*impf*) к +*dat*; **to ~ talks** дава́ть* (дать* *perf*) толчо́к перегово́рам.

instigation [ɪnstɪˈgeɪʃən] *n* подстрека́тельство; **at my ~** по мое́й инициати́ве.

instil [ɪnˈstɪl] *vt*: **to ~ sth in(to) sb** (*confidence, fear etc*) вселя́ть (всели́ть *perf*) что-н в кого́-н.

instinct [ˈɪnstɪŋkt] *n* инсти́нкт; **by ~** инстинкти́вно; **maternal ~** матери́нский инсти́нкт.

instinctive [ɪnˈstɪŋktɪv] *adj* инстинкти́вный*

(инстинкти́вен).

instinctively [ɪnˈstɪŋktɪvlɪ] *adv* инстинкти́вно.

institute [ˈɪnstɪtjuːt] *n* (*for research, teaching*) институ́т; (*professional body*) ассоциа́ция ◆ *vt* (*system, rule*) учрежда́ть (учреди́ть* *perf*); (*inquiry*) назнача́ть (назна́чить *perf*); **to ~ proceedings (against)** возбужда́ть (возбуди́ть* *perf*) суде́бное де́ло (про́тив +*gen*).

institution [ɪnstɪˈtjuːʃən] *n* учрежде́ние; (*custom, tradition*) институ́т.

institutional [ɪnstɪˈtjuːʃənl] *adj* (*value, quality etc*) закреплённый (закреплён); (*education*) осуществля́емый кру́пными учрежде́ниями; **~ care** попече́ние (*осуществля́емое учрежде́ниями*); **~ reform** рефо́рма социа́льных учрежде́ний.

instruct [ɪnˈstrʌkt] *vt*: **to ~ sb in sth** обуча́ть (обучи́ть* *perf*) кого́-н чему́-н; **to ~ sb to do** поруча́ть (поручи́ть* *perf*) кому́-н +*infin*.

instruction [ɪnˈstrʌkʃən] *n* (*teaching*) обуче́ние ◆ *cpd*: **~ manual**, **~ leaflet** инстру́кция; **~s** *npl* (*orders*) указа́ния *ntpl*; **~s (for use)** инстру́кция *or* руково́дство (по примене́нию).

instructive [ɪnˈstrʌktɪv] *adj* поучи́тельный* (поучи́телен).

instructor [ɪnˈstrʌktə'] *n* преподава́тель(ница) *m(f)*; (*for skiing, driving etc*) инстру́ктор*.

instrument [ˈɪnstrumənt] *n* инструме́нт.

instrumental [ɪnstruˈmɛntl] *adj* (*MUS*) инструмента́льный; (*important*): **to be ~ in** игра́ть (сыгра́ть *perf*) суще́ственную роль в +*prp*.

instrumentalist [ɪnstruˈmɛntəlɪst] *n* инструментали́ст.

instrument panel *n* прибо́рная пане́ль *f*.

insubordination [ɪnsəbɔːdəˈneɪʃən] *n* неповинове́ние.

insufferable [ɪnˈsʌfrəbl] *adj* невыноси́мый (невыноси́м).

insufficient [ɪnsəˈfɪʃənt] *adj* недоста́точный* (недоста́точен).

insufficiently [ɪnsəˈfɪʃəntlɪ] *adv* недоста́точно.

insular [ˈɪnsjulə'] *adj* ограни́ченный* (ограни́чен).

insulate [ˈɪnsjuleɪt] *vt* (*protect: person, group, also ELEC*) изоли́ровать (*impf/perf*); (*against cold*) утепля́ть (утепли́ть *perf*); (*against sound*) (звуко)изоли́ровать (*impf/perf*).

insulating tape [ˈɪnsjuleɪtɪŋ-] *n* (*BRIT*) изоляцио́нная ле́нта.

insulation [ɪnsjuˈleɪʃən] *n* (*see vb*) изоля́ция; (тепло)изоля́ция; (звуко)изоля́ция.

insulator [ˈɪnsjuleɪtə'] *n* (*material*) изоля́тор.

insulin [ˈɪnsjulɪn] *n* инсули́н.

insult [*vt* ɪnˈsʌlt, *n* ˈɪnsʌlt] *vt* оскорбля́ть (оскорби́ть* *perf*) ◆ *n* оскорбле́ние.

---

* marks translations which have irregular inflections. The Russian-English side of the dictionary gives inflectional information.

insulting [ɪnˈsʌltɪŋ] *adj* оскорбительный*
(оскорбителен).

insuperable [ɪnˈsjuːprəbl] *adj* непреодолимый
(непреодолим).

insurance [ɪnˈʃuərəns] *n* страхование; **life/fire
~** страхование жизни/на случай пожара; **to
take out ~ (against)** брать* (взять* *perf*)
страховку (от +*gen*).

insurance agent *n* страховой агент.

insurance broker *n* страховой брокер.

insurance policy *n* страховой полис.

insurance premium *n* страховая премия.

insure [ɪnˈʃuə^r] *vt*: **to ~ (against)** страховать
(застраховать *perf*) (от +*gen*); **to ~ (o.s.)
against** страховаться (застраховаться *perf*)
от +*gen*; **the car is ~d for £5,000** машина
застрахована на сумму в £5.000.

insured [ɪnˈʃuəd] *n*: **the ~** страхователь(ница)
m(f).

insurer [ɪnˈʃuərə^r] *n* (*insurance company*)
страховщик.

insurgent [ɪnˈsəːdʒənt] *adj* восставший ♦ *n*
повстанец*.

insurmountable [ɪnsəˈmauntəbl] *adj*
непреодолимый (непреодолим).

insurrection [ɪnsəˈrɛkʃən] *n* восстание.

intact [ɪnˈtækt] *adj* (*whole*) нетронутый
(нетронут); (*unharmed*) неповреждённый
(неповреждён).

intake [ˈɪnteɪk] *n* (*of food, drink*) потребление;
(*of air*) поглощение; (BRIT: *of pupils, recruits*)
набор.

intangible [ɪnˈtændʒɪbl] *adj* неощутимый
(неощутим).

integer [ˈɪntɪdʒə^r] *n* целое число*.

integral [ˈɪntɪgrəl] *adj* (*feature, element*)
неотъемлемый (неотъемлем) ♦ *n* (MATH)
интеграл.

integrate [ˈɪntɪgreɪt] *vt* интегрировать (*impf/
perf*) ♦ *vi* (*groups, individuals*) объединяться
(объединиться *perf*).

integrated circuit [ˈɪntɪgreɪtɪd-] *n* (COMPUT)
интегральная схема.

integration [ɪntɪˈgreɪʃən] *n* интеграция; **racial ~**
расовая интеграция.

integrity [ɪnˈtɛgrɪtɪ] *n* (*morality*) честность *f*,
порядочность *f*; (*wholeness*) целостность *f*.

intellect [ˈɪntəlɛkt] *n* интеллект.

intellectual [ɪntəˈlɛktjuəl] *adj*
интеллектуальный* (интеллектуален) ♦ *n*
интеллектуал.

intelligence [ɪnˈtɛlɪdʒəns] *n* (*cleverness*) ум*;
(*thinking power*) умственные способности
fpl; (MIL etc) разведка.

intelligence quotient *n* коэффициент
умственного развития.

intelligence service *n* разведывательная
служба.

intelligence test *n* *тест, определяющий
уровень умственных способностей.*

intelligent [ɪnˈtɛlɪdʒənt] *adj* умный* (умён);

(*animal*) разумный* (разумен).

intelligently [ɪnˈtɛlɪdʒəntlɪ] *adv* умно.

intelligentsia [ɪntɛlɪˈdʒɛntsɪə] *n*: **the ~**
интеллигенция.

intelligible [ɪnˈtɛlɪdʒɪbl] *adj* понятный*
(понятен).

intemperate [ɪnˈtɛmpərət] *adj* несдержанный*
(несдержан).

intend [ɪnˈtɛnd] *vt*: **to ~ sth for** предназначать
(предназначить *perf*) что-н для +*gen*; **to ~ to
do** намереваться (*impf*) +*infin*.

intended [ɪnˈtɛndɪd] *adj* (*effect, route*)
запланированный (запланирован); (*victim*)
предполагаемый (предполагаем); (*insult*)
преднамеренный* (преднамерен).

intense [ɪnˈtɛns] *adj* (*heat, emotion*) сильный*
(силён); (*look*) напряжённый; (*noise, activity*)
интенсивный* (интенсивен); **she is very ~**
она всё очень серьёзно воспринимает.

intensely [ɪnˈtɛnslɪ] *adv* (*see adj*) сильно;
напряжённо.

intensify [ɪnˈtɛnsɪfaɪ] *vt* усиливать (усилить
perf).

intensity [ɪnˈtɛnsɪtɪ] *n* (*of effort, sun*)
интенсивность *f*; (*of look*) напряжённость *f*.

intensive [ɪnˈtɛnsɪv] *adj* интенсивный*
(интенсивен).

intensive care *n* интенсивная терапия.

intensive care unit *n* отделение интенсивной
терапии.

intent [ɪnˈtɛnt] *n* (*also* LAW) намерение ♦ *adj*: **~
(on)** сосредоточенный* (сосредоточен) (на
+*prp*); **to all ~s and purposes** что бы там ни
было; **to be ~ on doing** (*determined*)
стремиться* (*impf*) +*infin*.

intention [ɪnˈtɛnʃən] *n* намерение.

intentional [ɪnˈtɛnʃnl] *adj* намеренный
(намерен); (LAW) преднамеренный*
(преднамерен).

intentionally [ɪnˈtɛnʃnəlɪ] *adv* (*see adj*)
намеренно; преднамеренно.

intently [ɪnˈtɛntlɪ] *adv* пристально.

inter [ɪnˈtəː^r] *vt* погребать (погрести* *perf*).

interact [ɪntərˈækt] *vi*: **to ~ (with)**
взаимодействовать (*impf*) (с +*instr*).

interaction [ɪntərˈækʃən] *n* взаимодействие.

interactive [ɪntərˈæktɪv] *adj* взаимо-
действующий; (COMPUT) интерактивный,
диалоговый.

intercede [ɪntəˈsiːd] *vi*: **to ~ (with sb/on behalf
of sb)** ходатайствовать (*impf*) (перед кем-н/
за кого-н).

intercept [ɪntəˈsɛpt] *vt* перехватывать
(перехватить* *perf*).

interception [ɪntəˈsɛpʃən] *n* перехват.

interchange [ˈɪntətʃeɪndʒ] *n* (*on motorway*)
транспортная развязка*; **~ (of)** (*exchange*)
обмен (+*instr*)

interchangeable [ɪntəˈtʃeɪndʒəbl] *adj*
взаимозаменяемый (взаимозаменяем).

intercity [ɪntəˈsɪtɪ] *adj* междугородный.

intercom ['ɪntəkɔm] *n* селе́ктор.
interconnect [ɪntəkə'nɛkt] *vi* соединя́ться *(impf)*
(ме́жду собо́й).
intercontinental ['ɪntəkɔntɪ'nɛntl] *adj*
межконтинента́льный.
intercourse ['ɪntəkɔːs] *n (sexual)* половóе
сношéние; *(social, verbal)* общéние.
interdependence [ɪntədɪ'pɛndəns] *n*
взаимозави́симость *f.*
interdependent [ɪntədɪ'pɛndənt] *adj*
взаимозави́симый (взаимозави́сим).
interest ['ɪntrɪst] *n*: ~ (in) интерéс (к +*dat*);
(COMM: in company) дóля*; (: *sum of money*)
процéнты *mpl* ◆ *vt* интересовáть *(impf)*;
compound/simple ~ слóжные/простые
процéнты *mpl*; **it is in our ~s** *(to our
advantage)* э́то в нáших интерéсах; **British ~s
in the Middle East** бритáнские интерéсы на
Бли́жнем Востóке; **his main ~ is history** егó
основнóй интерéс – э́то истóрия.
interested ['ɪntrɪstɪd] *adj* заинтересóванный
(заинтересóван); **to be ~ (in sth)** *(music etc)*
интересовáться *(impf)* (чем-н); **they are ~ in
increasing production** они́ заинтересóваны в
увеличéнии производи́тельности; **she is ~ in
becoming a nurse** онá хóчет стать
медсестрóй.
interest-free ['ɪntrɪst'friː] *adj* беспроцéнтный ◆
adv без упла́ты процéнтов.
interesting ['ɪntrɪstɪŋ] *adj* интерéсный*
(интерéсен).
interest rate *n* процéнтная стáвка*.
interface ['ɪntəfeɪs] *n (COMPUT)* интерфéйс;
(area of contact): ~ **between technology and
design** соприкосновéние технолóгии с
дизáйном.
interfere [ɪntə'fɪə˞] *vi*: **to ~ in** вмéшиваться
(вмешáться *perf*) в +*acc*; **to ~ with** *(object)*
трóгать *(impf)*; *(plans, career, duty, decision)*
мешáть (помешáть *perf*) +*dat*; **don't ~** не
вмéшивайтесь.
interference [ɪntə'fɪərəns] *n* вмешáтельство;
(RADIO, TV) помéхи *fpl.*
interfering [ɪntə'fɪərɪŋ] *adj* назóйливый
(назóйлив).
interim ['ɪntərɪm] *adj (government)* врéменный;
(report) промежýточный ◆ *n*: **in the ~** тем
врéменем.
interim dividend *n* промежýточный
дивидéнд.
interior [ɪn'tɪərɪə˞] *n (of building)* интерьéр; *(of
car, box etc)* внýтренность *f*; *(of country)*
глуби́нные райóны *mpl* ◆ *adj (door, room etc)*
внýтренний*; ~ **minister/department**
мини́стр/департáмент внýтренних дел.
interior decorator *n* худóжник(-ица) по
интерьéру.
interior designer *n* дизáйнер интерьéра.

interjection [ɪntə'dʒɛkʃən] *n* перебивáющий
вóзглас; *(LING)* междомéтие.
interlock [ɪntə'lɔk] *vi* сцепля́ться (сцепи́ться*
perf).
interloper ['ɪntələupə˞] *n* наруши́тель *m.*
interlude ['ɪntəluːd] *n* перерыв; *(THEAT)*
антрáкт.
intermarry [ɪntə'mærɪ] *vi* вступáть (вступи́ть*
perf) в смéшанный брак.
intermediary [ɪntə'miːdɪərɪ] *n* посрéдник
(-ица).
intermediate [ɪntə'miːdɪət] *adj (stage)*
промежýточный; ~ **student** студéнт срéдней
ступéни обучéния.
interment [ɪn'təːmənt] *n* погребéние.
interminable [ɪn'təːmɪnəbl] *adj* бесконéчный*
(бесконéчен).
intermission [ɪntə'mɪʃən] *n* перерыв.
intermittent [ɪntə'mɪtnt] *adj* периоди́ческий*.
intermittently [ɪntə'mɪtntlɪ] *adv* периоди́чески.
intern [*vt* ɪn'təːn, *n* 'ɪntəːn] *vt* интерни́ровать
(impf/perf) ◆ *n (US: MED)* врач-стажёр.
internal [ɪn'təːnl] *adj* внýтренний*.
internally [ɪn'təːnəlɪ] *adv*: "**not to be taken ~**"
„внутрь не принимáть".
Internal Revenue Service *n (US)* ≈ Глáвное
налóговое управлéние.
international [ɪntə'næʃənl] *adj* междунарóдный ◆ *n (BRIT: SPORT: also: ~* **match**)
междунарóдная встрéча.
International Atomic Energy Agency *n*
Междунарóдное агéнтство по áтомной
энéргии.
International Chamber of Commerce *n*
Междунарóдная торгóвая палáта.
International Court of Justice *n* Междунарóдный суд*.
International Date Line *n* ли́ния перемéны
дат.
International Labour Organization *n*
Междунарóдная организáция трудá.
internationally [ɪntə'næʃnəlɪ] *adv* в междунарóдном масштáбе.
International Monetary Fund *n* Междунарóдный валю́тный фонд.
international relations *npl* междунарóдные
отношéния *ntpl.*
internecine [ɪntə'niːsaɪn] *adj* междоусóбный.
internee [ɪntəː'niː] *n* интерни́рованный(-ая)
m(f) adj.
internment [ɪn'təːnmənt] *n* интерни́рование.
interplay ['ɪntəpleɪ] *n*: ~ **(of** *or* **between)**
взаимодéйствие (+*gen*).
Interpol ['ɪntəpɔl] *n* интерпóл.
interpret [ɪn'təːprɪt] *vt (explain)* интерпрети́ровать *(impf/perf)*, толковáть *(impf)*;
(translate) переводи́ть* (перевести́* *perf*);
(ýстно) ◆ *vi* переводи́ть* (перевести́* *perf*)

(*ýстно*).

interpretation [ɪntə:prɪ'teɪʃən] *n* интерпретáция, толковáние.

interpreter [ɪn'tə:prɪtə'] *n* перевóдчик(-ица).

interpreting [ɪn'tə:prɪtɪŋ] *n* (ýстный) перевóд.

interrelated [ɪntərɪ'leɪtɪd] *adj* взаимо-свя́занный (взаимосвя́зан).

interrogate [ɪn'tɛrəugeɪt] *vt* допрáшивать (допроси́ть* *perf*).

interrogation [ɪntɛrəu'geɪʃən] *n* допрóс.

interrogative [ɪntə'rɔgətɪv] *adj* (*LING*) вопроси́тельный.

interrogator [ɪn'tɛrəgeɪtə'] *n* слéдователь *m*.

interrupt [ɪntə'rʌpt] *vti* прерывáть (прервáть* *perf*).

interruption [ɪntə'rʌpʃən] *n* (*act*) прерывáние; **I hate ~s when I'm working** я ненави́жу, когдá меня́ прерывáют во врéмя рабóты.

intersect [ɪntə'sɛkt] *vi* пересекáться (пересéчься* *perf*) ◆ *vt* пересекáть (пересéчь* *perf*).

intersection [ɪntə'sɛkʃən] *n* (*of roads*) пересечéние; (*MATH*) тóчка пересечéния.

intersperse [ɪntə'spə:s] *vt*: **to ~ with** перемежáть (*impf*) с +*instr*.

intertwine [ɪntə'twaɪn] *vi* переплетáться (переплести́сь* *perf*).

interval ['ɪntəvl] *n* (*also MUS*) интервáл; (*BRIT: SPORT*) перерыв; (: *THEAT*) антрáкт; **bright ~s** (*in weather*) прояснéния *ntpl*; **at ~s** врéмя от врéмени.

intervene [ɪntə'vi:n] *vi* (*in conversation, situation*) вмéшиваться (вмешáться *perf*); (*event*) мешáть (помешáть *perf*); (*time*) проходи́ть* (пройти́* *perf*).

intervening [ɪntə'vi:nɪŋ] *adj* (*period*) про-межýточный.

intervention [ɪntə'vɛnʃən] *n* (*interference*) вмешáтельство; (*mediation*) посрéдничество; **military ~** воéнная интервéнция.

interview ['ɪntəvju:] *n* (*for job*) собесéдование; (*RADIO, TV etc*) интервью́ *nt ind* ◆ *vt* (*see n*) проводи́ть* (провести́* *perf*) собесéдование с +*instr*; интервью́и́ровать (*impf/perf*), брать* (взять* *perf*) интервью́ у +*gen*; **to give an ~** давáть* (дать* *perf*) интервью́.

interviewee [ɪntəvju:'i:] *n* интервью́и́руемый (-ая) *m(f) adj*.

interviewer ['ɪntəvjuə'] *n* (*of candidate*) проводя́щий(-ая) *m(f) adj* собесéдование; (*RADIO, TV etc*) интервью́éр.

intestate [ɪn'tɛsteɪt] *adj*: **to die ~** скончáться (*perf*), не остáвив завещáния.

intestinal [ɪn'tɛstɪnl] *adj* кишéчный.

intestine [ɪn'tɛstɪn] *n* кишкá*; **large/small ~** тóлстая/тóнкая кишкá; **~s** кишéчник *msg*.

intimacy ['ɪntɪməsɪ] *n* инти́мность *f*.

intimate [*adj* 'ɪntɪmət, *vt* 'ɪntɪmeɪt] *adj* (*very close*) бли́зкий* (бли́зок); (*relationship, conversation, atmosphere*) инти́мный*

(инти́мен); (*knowledge*) глубóкий* (глубóк) ◆ *vt* намекáть (намекнýть *perf*) на +*acc*; **to ~ that** намекáть (намекнýть *perf*), что.

intimately ['ɪntɪmətlɪ] *adv* (*see adj*) инти́мно; глубокó.

intimation [ɪntɪ'meɪʃən] *n* намёк.

intimidate [ɪn'tɪmɪdeɪt] *vt* запýгивать (запугáть *perf*).

intimidation [ɪntɪmɪ'deɪʃən] *n* запýгивание.

KEYWORD
---

into ['ɪntu] *prep* **1** (*indicating motion or direction*) в/на +*acc*; **into the house/garden** в дом/сад; **into the post office/factory** на пóчту/фáбрику; **research into cancer** исслéдования *ntpl* в óбласти рáковых заболевáний; **he worked late into the night** он рабóтал до пóздней нóчи

2 (*indicating change of condition, result*): **she has translated the letter into Russian** онá перевелá письмó на рýсский язы́к; **the vase broke into pieces** вáза разби́лась вдрéбезги *or* на кусóчки; **they got into trouble for it** им попáло за э́то; **he lapsed into silence** он погрузи́лся в молчáние; **to burst into tears** расплáкаться* (*perf*); **to burst into flames** загорáться (загорéться *perf*).

---

intolerable [ɪn'tɔlərəbl] *adj* нетерпи́мый (нетерпи́м), невыноси́мый (невыноси́м).

intolerance [ɪn'tɔlərns] *n* нетерпи́мость *f*.

intolerant [ɪn'tɔlərnt] *adj*: **~ (of)** нетерпи́мый (нетерпи́м) (к +*dat*).

intonation [ɪntəu'neɪʃən] *n* интонáция.

intoxicated [ɪn'tɔksɪkeɪtɪd] *adj* (*drunk*) опьянéвший; (*fig*) опьянённый (опьянён).

intoxication [ɪntɔksɪ'keɪʃən] *n* (*also fig*) опьянéние.

intractable [ɪn'træktəbl] *adj* (*person, temper*) неподáтливый (неподáтлив); (*problem*) труднорешими́мый (труднорешими́м); (*illness*) трудноизлечи́мый (трудно-излечи́м).

intransigence [ɪn'trænsɪdʒəns] *n* упóрство.

intransigent [ɪn'trænsɪdʒənt] *adj* упóрный* (упóрен).

intransitive [ɪn'trænsɪtɪv] *adj* (*LING*) неперехóдный.

intrauterine device ['ɪntrə'ju:tərɪn-] *n* внутримáточное противозачáточное срéдство.

intravenous [ɪntrə'vi:nəs] *adj* внутривéнный.

in-tray ['ɪntreɪ] *n* (*in office*) корзи́на для входя́щих бумáг.

intrepid [ɪn'trɛpɪd] *adj* неустраши́мый (неустраши́м).

intricacy ['ɪntrɪkəsɪ] *n* (*of situation*) слóжность *f*; (*of pattern, design*) замыслова́тость *f*.

intricate ['ɪntrɪkət] *adj* замыслова́тый (замыслова́т).

intrigue [ɪn'tri:g] *n* интри́га ◆ *vt* интриговáть (заинтриговáть *perf*).

intriguing [ɪnˈtriːgɪŋ] *adj* (*fascinating*)
интригу́ющий.
intrinsic [ɪnˈtrɪnsɪk] *adj* неотъе́млемый
(неотъе́млем).
introduce [ɪntrəˈdjuːs] *vt* (*new idea, measure
etc*) вводи́ть* (ввести́* *perf*); (*speaker, TV show
etc*) представля́ть (предста́вить* *perf*); **to ~
sb (to sb)** представля́ть (предста́вить* *perf*)
кого́-н (кому́-н); **to ~ sb to** (*pastime,
technique*) знако́мить* (познако́мить* *perf*)
кого́-н с +*instr*; **may I ~ ...?** разреши́те Вам
предста́вить ....
introduction [ɪntrəˈdʌkʃən] *n* введе́ние; (*to
person, new experience*) знако́мство; **a letter
of ~** рекоменда́тельное письмо́*.
introductory [ɪntrəˈdʌktərɪ] *adj* (*lesson*)
вступи́тельный; **~ remarks** вступи́тельные
замеча́ния; **an ~ offer** предвари́тельная
цена́*.
introspection [ɪntrəuˈspɛkʃən] *n* самоана́лиз.
introspective [ɪntrəuˈspɛktɪv] *adj*
самосозерца́тельный.
introvert [ˈɪntrəuvəːt] *n* интрове́рт.
introverted [ˈɪntrəuvəːtɪd] *adj* само-
углублённый (самоуглублён).
intrude [ɪnˈtruːd] *vi*: **to ~ (on)** вторга́ться
(вто́ргнуться* *perf*) (в/на +*acc*); **am I
intruding?** я не помеша́ю?
intruder [ɪnˈtruːdər] *n*: **there is an ~ in our house**
к нам в дом кто́-то вто́ргся.
intrusion [ɪnˈtruːʒən] *n* вторже́ние.
intrusive [ɪnˈtruːsɪv] *adj* назо́йливый
(назо́йлив).
intuition [ɪntjuːˈɪʃən] *n* интуи́ция.
intuitive [ɪnˈtjuːɪtɪv] *adj* интуити́вный*
(интуити́вен).
inundate [ˈɪnʌndeɪt] *vt*: **to ~ with** (*calls, letters
etc*) зава́ливать (завали́ть* *perf*) +*instr*;
Moscow is ~d with visitors Москва́
наводнена́ прие́зжими.
inure [ɪnˈjuər] *vt*: **to ~ o.s. to** приуча́ть
(приучи́ть* *perf*) себя́ к +*dat*.
invade [ɪnˈveɪd] *vt* (*MIL*) вторга́ться
(вто́ргнуться* *perf*) в +*acc*; (*fig: subj: people,
animals etc*) наводня́ть (наводни́ть* *perf*).
invader [ɪnˈveɪdər] *n* (*MIL*) захва́тчик.
invalid [*n* ˈɪnvəlɪd, *adj* ɪnˈvælɪd] *n* (*MED*) инвали́д
♦ *adj* (*not valid*) недействи́тельный*
(недействи́телен).
invalidate [ɪnˈvælɪdeɪt] *vt* (*argument, result etc*)
дока́зывать (доказа́ть* *perf*) несостоя́тель-
ность *f* +*gen*; (*law, marriage, election*) де́лать
(сде́лать *perf*) недействи́тельным.
invaluable [ɪnˈvæljuəbl] *adj* (*person, thing*)
неоцени́мый (неоцени́м).
invariable [ɪnˈvɛərɪəbl] *adj* (*amount, result,
routine*) неизме́нный* (неизме́нен).
invariably [ɪnˈvɛərɪəblɪ] *adv* неизме́нно; **she is**

~ late она́ неизме́нно опа́здывает.
invasion [ɪnˈveɪʒən] *n* (*MIL*) вторже́ние; (*fig*)
посяга́тельство; **an ~ of privacy** вторже́ние в
ли́чную жизнь.
invective [ɪnˈvɛktɪv] *n* оскорбле́ние.
inveigle [ɪnˈviːgl] *vt*: **to ~ sb into sth** вовлека́ть
(вовле́чь* *perf*) кого́-н во что́-н.
invent [ɪnˈvɛnt] *vt* (*machine, game, phrase etc*)
изобрета́ть (изобрести́* *perf*); (*fabricate: lie,
excuse*) выду́мывать (вы́думать *perf*).
invention [ɪnˈvɛnʃən] *n* изобрете́ние; (*untrue
story*) вы́думка.
inventive [ɪnˈvɛntɪv] *adj* (*person*)
изобрета́тельный* (изобрета́телен).
inventiveness [ɪnˈvɛntɪvnɪs] *n*
изобрета́тельность *f*.
inventor [ɪnˈvɛntər] *n* (*of machines, systems*)
изобрета́тель *m*.
inventory [ˈɪnvəntrɪ] *n* (*of house, ship etc*)
(инвентаризацио́нная) о́пись *f*.
inventory control *n* (*COMM*) управле́ние
запа́сами.
inverse [ɪnˈvəːs] *adj* (*relationship*) обра́тный; **in
~ proportion to** в обра́тной пропорциона́ль-
ности к +*dat*.
invert [ɪnˈvəːt] *vt* (*turn upside down*)
перевора́чивать (переверну́ть *perf*).
invertebrate [ɪnˈvəːtɪbrət] *n* беспозвоно́чное *nt
adj*.
inverted commas [ɪnˈvəːtɪd-] *npl* (*BRIT: LING*)
кавы́чки *fpl*.
invest [ɪnˈvɛst] *vt* (*money*) инвести́ровать*
(*impf/perf*) в(о) +*acc*; (*fig: time, energy*)
вкла́дывать (вложи́ть* *perf*) ♦ *vi*: **~ in** (*COMM*)
помеща́ть (помести́ть* *perf*) капита́л в +*acc*;
(*fig: sth useful*) вкла́дывать (вложи́ть* *perf*)
де́ньги в +*acc*; **to ~ sb with sth** облека́ть
(обле́чь* *perf*) кого́-н чем-н.
investigate [ɪnˈvɛstɪgeɪt] *vt* (*accident, crime*)
рассле́довать* (*impf/perf*); (*person*)
иссле́довать* (*impf/perf*).
investigation [ɪnvɛstɪˈgeɪʃən] *n* рассле́дование.
investigative [ɪnˈvɛstɪgeɪtɪv] *adj*: **~ journalism**
журнали́стское рассле́дование.
investigator [ɪnˈvɛstɪgeɪtər] *n* (*of events, people
etc*) иссле́дователь(ница) *m(f)*; **private ~**
ча́стный сле́дователь *m*.
investiture [ɪnˈvɛstɪtʃər] *n* (*of chancellor*)
введе́ние в до́лжность *f*; (*of prince*)
пожа́лование зва́ния.
investment [ɪnˈvɛstmənt] *n* (*activity*)
инвести́рование; (*amount of money*)
инвести́ция, вклад.
investment grant *n* (*COMM*) инвестицио́нные
субси́дии *fpl*.
investment income *n* (*COMM*) дохо́д с
инвести́ций.
investment portfolio *n* (*COMM*) портфе́ль *m*

---

* marks translations which have irregular inflections. The Russian-English side of the dictionary gives inflectional information.

це́нных бума́г.

investment trust *n* (*COMM*) инвестицио́нный трест.

investor [ɪnˈvɛstəʳ] *n* (*COMM*) инве́стор, вкла́дчик.

inveterate [ɪnˈvɛtərət] *adj* (*liar, cheat etc*) неисправи́мый (неисправи́м); (*smoker*) зая́длый; (*dislike etc*) да́вний*.

invidious [ɪnˈvɪdɪəs] *adj* (*task, job*) неприя́тный* (неприя́тен); (*comparison, decision*) несправедли́вый (несправедли́в).

invigilator [ɪnˈvɪdʒɪleɪtəʳ] *n* (*in exam*) экзамена́тор, следя́щий за тем, чтобы студе́нты не спи́сывали во вре́мя экза́менов.

invigorating [ɪnˈvɪgəreɪtɪŋ] *adj* (*air*) бодря́щий (бодря́щ); (*experience*) воодушевля́ющий.

invincible [ɪnˈvɪnsɪbl] *adj* (*army, team*) непобеди́мый (непобеди́м); (*belief, conviction*) неукроти́мый (неукроти́м).

inviolate [ɪnˈvaɪələt] *adj* ненару́шенный (ненару́шен).

invisible [ɪnˈvɪzɪbl] *adj* неви́димый (неви́дим) ◆ *cpd* (*COMM*: *exports, earnings, assets*) неви́димый.

invisible mending *n* худо́жественная што́пка.

invitation [ɪnvɪˈteɪʃən] *n* приглаше́ние; **by ~ only** то́лько по приглаше́нию; **at sb's ~** по приглаше́нию кого́-н.

invite [ɪnˈvaɪt] *vt* (*to party, meal, meeting etc*) приглаша́ть (пригласи́ть* *perf*); (*discussion, criticism*) побужда́ть (побуди́ть* *perf*); **to ~ sb to do** предлага́ть (предложи́ть* *perf*) кому́-н +*infin*; **to ~ sb to dinner** приглаша́ть (пригласи́ть* *perf*) кого́-н на обе́д

▸ **invite out** *vt* приглаша́ть (пригласи́ть* *perf*).

inviting [ɪnˈvaɪtɪŋ] *adj* (*attractive, desirable*) соблазни́тельный* (соблазни́телен).

invoice [ˈɪnvɔɪs] *n* (*COMM*) счёт, факту́ра ◆ *vt* выпи́сывать (вы́писать* *perf*) счёт *or* факту́ру +*dat*; **to ~ sb for goods** выпи́сывать (вы́писать* *perf*) счёт *or* факту́ру кому́-н за това́ры.

invoke [ɪnˈvəʊk] *vt* (*law, principle*) обраща́ться (обрати́ться* *perf*) к +*dat*; (*feelings, memories etc*) взыва́ть (воззва́ть* *perf*) к +*dat*.

involuntary [ɪnˈvɔləntrɪ] *adj* (*action, reflex etc*) непроизво́льный* (непроизво́лен).

involve [ɪnˈvɔlv] *vt* (*person, thing*: *include, use*) вовлека́ть (вовле́чь* *perf*); (: *concern, affect*) включа́ть (включи́ть* *perf*); **to ~ sb (in sth)** вовлека́ть (вовле́чь* *perf*) кого́-н (во что́-н).

involved [ɪnˈvɔlvd] *adj* (*complicated*) запу́танный* (запу́тан); (*thing required*: *in task, situation etc*) включённый (включён); **to be ~ in** (*in activity etc*) быть* (*impf*) вовлечённым(-ой) в(о) +*acc*; **to feel ~** быть* (*impf*) вовлечённым; **to become ~ with sb** (*socially*) свя́зываться (связа́ться *perf*) с кем-н; (*emotionally*) увлека́ться (увле́чься*

perf) кем-н.

involvement [ɪnˈvɔlvmənt] *n* (*participation*) прича́стность *f*; (*concern, enthusiasm*) вовлечённость *f*; (*relationship*) связь *f*.

invulnerable [ɪnˈvʌlnərəbl] *adj* (*person, ship, building etc*) неуязви́мый (неуязви́м).

inward [ˈɪnwəd] *adj* (*thought, feeling*) вну́тренний*; (*movement*) напра́вленный внутрь ◆ *adv* = **inwards**.

inwardly [ˈɪnwədlɪ] *adv* внутри́.

inwards [ˈɪnwədz] *adv* (*move, face*) внутрь.

I/O *abbr* (*COMPUT*: = *input/output*) ввод-вы́вод.

IOC *n abbr* = *International Olympic Committee*.

iodine [ˈaɪəʊdiːn] *n* йод.

IOM *abbr* (*BRIT*: *POST*) = *Isle of Man*.

ion [ˈaɪən] *n* (*ELEC*) ио́н.

Ionian Sea [aɪˈəʊnɪən-] *n*: **the ~ ~** Иони́ческое мо́ре.

ioniser [ˈaɪənaɪzəʳ] *n* ионизи́рующая устано́вка*.

iota [aɪˈəʊtə] *n* йо́та.

IOU *n abbr* (= *I owe you*) просте́йший долгово́й докуме́нт.

IOW *abbr* (*BRIT*: *POST*) = *Isle of Wight*.

IPA *n abbr* (= *International Phonetic Alphabet*) Междунаро́дная систе́ма транскри́пции.

IQ *n abbr* (= *intelligence quotient*) коэффицие́нт у́мственного разви́тия.

IRA *n abbr* (= *Irish Republican Army*) ИРА= *Ирла́ндская респу́бликанская а́рмия*; (*US*) *individual retirement account*.

Iran [ɪˈrɑːn] *n* Ира́н.

Iranian [ɪˈreɪnɪən] *adj* ира́нский* ◆ *n* ира́нец(-нка).

Iraq [ɪˈrɑːk] *n* Ира́к.

Iraqi [ɪˈrɑːkɪ] *adj* ира́кский* ◆ *n* жи́тель(ница) *m(f)* Ира́ка.

irascible [ɪˈræsɪbl] *adj* (*person*) вспы́льчивый (вспы́льчив).

irate [aɪˈreɪt] *adj* (*person, letter etc*) разгне́ванный* (разгне́ван).

Ireland [ˈaɪələnd] *n* Ирла́ндия; **the Republic of ~** Ирла́ндская Респу́блика.

iris [ˈaɪrɪs] (*pl* **~es**) *n* (*ANAT*) ра́дужная оболо́чка* (гла́за); (*BOT*) и́рис.

Irish [ˈaɪrɪʃ] *adj* ирла́ндский*; **the ~** ирла́ндцы.

Irishman [ˈaɪrɪʃmən] *irreg n* ирла́ндец*.

Irish Sea *n*: **the ~ ~** Ирла́ндское мо́ре.

Irishwoman [ˈaɪrɪʃwumən] *irreg n* ирла́ндка.

irk [əːk] *vt* (*person*) раздража́ть (*impf*).

irksome [ˈəːksəm] *adj* надое́дливый (надое́длив).

IRN *n abbr* = *Independent Radio News*.

IRO *n abbr* (*US*) = *International Refugee Organization*.

iron [ˈaɪən] *n* (*metal*) желе́зо *no pl*; (*for clothes*) утю́г ◆ *cpd* желе́зный ◆ *vt* (*clothes*) гла́дить* (погла́дить* *perf*).

▸ **iron out** *vt* (*fig*: *problems*) ула́живать (ула́дить* *perf*).

Iron Curtain *n* (*POL*: *formerly*): **the ~ ~**

желе́зный за́навес.
iron foundry *n* чугунолите́йный цех.
ironic(al) [aɪˈrɒnɪk(l)] *adj* ирони́ческий.
ironically [aɪˈrɒnɪklɪ] *adv* (*say, enquire etc*)
ирони́чно; ~, **the intelligence chief was the
last to find out** иро́ния в том, что шеф
разве́дки узна́л после́дним.
ironing [ˈaɪənɪŋ] *n* (*activity*) гла́женье; (*clothes*)
бельё для гла́женья.
ironing board *n* глади́льная доска́.
iron lung *n* (*MED*) аппара́т (для)
иску́сственного дыха́ния.
ironmonger [ˈaɪənmʌŋgəʳ] *n* (*BRIT*) торго́вец
скобяны́ми изде́лиями.
ironmonger's (shop) [ˈaɪənmʌŋgəz-] *n*
магази́н скобяны́х изде́лий.
iron ore *n* желе́зная руда́.
irons [ˈaɪəns] *npl* (*chains*) кандалы́ *pl*; **to clap sb
in** ~ зако́вывать (закова́ть *perf*) кого́-н в
кандалы́.
ironworks [ˈaɪənwəːks] *n* чугунолите́йный
заво́д.
irony [ˈaɪrənɪ] *n* иро́ния.
irrational [ɪˈræʃənl] *adj* (*feelings, behaviour*)
нерациона́льный* (нерациона́лен),
неразу́мный* (неразу́мен).
irreconcilable [ɪrɛkənˈsaɪləbl] *adj* (*ideas,
conflict*) непримири́мый (непримири́м).
irredeemable [ɪrɪˈdiːməbl] *adj* (*COMM*) не
подлежа́щий погаше́нию *or* вы́купу; (*fault,
character*) неисправи́мый (неисправи́м).
irrefutable [ɪrɪˈfjuːtəbl] *adj* (*fact, argument*)
неопровержи́мый (неопровержи́м).
irregular [ɪˈrɛgjuləʳ] *adj* (*surface*) неро́вный*
(неро́вен); (*pattern*) непра́вильной фо́рмы;
(*action, event*) нерегуля́рный* (нерегуля́рен);
(*behaviour*) распу́щенный; (*LING: verb etc*)
непра́вильный.
irregularity [ɪrɛgjuˈlærɪtɪ] *n* (*see adj*) неро́в-
ность *f*; непра́вильность *f*; нерегуля́рность *f*;
распу́щенность *f*.
irrelevance [ɪˈrɛləvəns] *n* неуме́стность *f*.
irrelevant [ɪˈrɛləvənt] *adj* (*fact, information*)
неуме́стный.
irreligious [ɪrɪˈlɪdʒəs] *adj* неве́рующий*.
irreparable [ɪˈrɛprəbl] *adj* (*harm, damage etc*)
непоправи́мый (непоправи́м).
irreplaceable [ɪrɪˈpleɪsəbl] *adj* (*antique, wedding
ring etc*) незамени́мый (незамени́м).
irrepressible [ɪrɪˈprɛsəbl] *adj* (*person, good
humour, enthusiasm etc*) неудержи́мый
(неудержи́м).
irreproachable [ɪrɪˈprəutʃəbl] *adj* (*behaviour,
character*) безупре́чный* (безупре́чен).
irresistible [ɪrɪˈzɪstɪbl] *adj* (*urge, desire*)
непреодоли́мый (непреодоли́м); (*person,
thing*) неотрази́мый (неотрази́м).
irresolute [ɪˈrɛzəluːt] *adj* (*person*)

нереши́тельный* (нереши́телен).
irrespective [ɪrɪˈspɛktɪv] *prep*: ~ **of** незави́симо
от +*gen*.
irresponsible [ɪrɪˈspɒnsɪbl] *adj* (*person, action*)
безотве́тственный* (безотве́тствен).
irretrievable [ɪrɪˈtriːvəbl] *adj* (*object*)
безвозвра́тный* (безвозвра́тен); (*loss,
damage*) непоправи́мый (непоправи́м).
irreverent [ɪˈrɛvərnt] *adj* (*person, behaviour,
comment etc*) непочти́тельный*
(непочти́телен).
irrevocable [ɪˈrɛvəkəbl] *adj* (*action, decision*)
бесповоро́тный* (бесповоро́тен).
irrigate [ˈɪrɪgeɪt] *vt* (*AGR: land*) ороша́ть
(ороси́ть* *perf*).
irrigation [ɪrɪˈgeɪʃən] *n* (*AGR*) ороше́ние,
иррига́ция.
irritable [ˈɪrɪtəbl] *adj* раздражи́тельный*
(раздражи́телен).
irritant [ˈɪrɪtənt] *n* раздражи́тель *m*.
irritate [ˈɪrɪteɪt] *vt* (*also MED*) раздража́ть
(раздражи́ть *perf*).
irritating [ˈɪrɪteɪtɪŋ] *adj* (*person, sound etc*)
раздража́ющий.
irritation [ɪrɪˈteɪʃən] *n* (*also MED*) раздраже́ние;
(*annoying thing*) раздража́ющий фа́ктор.
IRS *n abbr* (*US*) = **Internal Revenue Service**.
is [ɪz] *vb see* **be**.
ISBN *n abbr* (= *International Standard Book
Number*) ISBN.
Islam [ˈɪzlɑːm] *n* (*REL*) исла́м; (*Islamic
countries*) мусульма́нские стра́ны *fpl*.
Islamic [ɪzˈlæmɪk] *adj* мусульма́нский*.
island [ˈaɪlənd] *n* о́стров*; (*also*: **traffic** ~)
остро́вок безопа́сности.
islander [ˈaɪləndəʳ] *n* островитя́нин*(-нка).
isle [aɪl] *n* о́стров*.
isn't [ˈɪznt] = **is not**.
isobar [ˈaɪsəubɑː] *n* изоба́ра.
isolate [ˈaɪsəleɪt] *vt* (*set apart*) изоли́ровать*
(*impf/perf*); (*substance*) выделя́ть (вы́делить
perf).
isolated [ˈaɪsəleɪtɪd] *adj* (*place, person*)
изоли́рованный* (изоли́рован); (*incident*)
отде́льный.
isolation [aɪsəˈleɪʃən] *n* изоля́ция.
isolationism [aɪsəˈleɪʃənɪzəm] *n*
изоляциони́зм.
isotope [ˈaɪsəutəup] *n* (*PHYS*) изото́п.
Israel [ˈɪzreɪl] *n* Изра́иль *m*.
Israeli [ɪzˈreɪlɪ] *adj* изра́ильский* ◆ *n* (*person*)
израильтя́нин*(-нка).
issue [ˈɪʃuː] *n* (*problem, subject*) вопро́с; (*most
important part*) суть *f*; (*of book, stamps etc*)
вы́пуск; (*LAW, old: offspring*) пото́мок* ◆ *vt*
(*statement, newspaper*) издава́ть* (изда́ть*
perf); (*rations, equipment, documents*)
выдава́ть* (вы́дать* *perf*) ◆ *vi*: **to** ~ **from**

---

* marks translations which have irregular inflections. The Russian-English side of the dictionary gives inflectional information.

(*liquid, gas*) вытека́ть (вы́течь* *perf*) из +*gen*; (*sound, smell*) исходи́ть* (*impf*) из/от +*gen*; **to be at** ~ быть* (*impf*) предме́том обсужде́ния; **to avoid the** ~ обходи́ть* (обойти́* *perf*) суть де́ла; **to confuse** *or* **obscure the** ~ затемня́ть (затемни́ть *perf*) суть вопро́са; **to** ~ **sth to sb** выдава́ть* (вы́дать* *perf*) что-н кому́-н; **to** ~ **sb with sth** снабжа́ть (снабди́ть* *perf*) кого́-н чем-н; **to take** ~ **with sb** (**over**) начина́ть (нача́ть* *perf*) спо́рить с кем-н (о +*prp*); **to make an** ~ **of sth** де́лать (сде́лать *perf*) исто́рию из чего́-н.

issued capital [ˈɪʃuːd-] *n* (*COMM*) вы́пущенный акционе́рный капита́л.

Istanbul [ɪstænˈbuːl] *n* Стамбу́л.

isthmus [ˈɪsməs] *n* переше́ек.

IT *n abbr* = **information technology**.

KEYWORD

it [ɪt] *pron* **1** (*specific subject*) он (*f* она́, *nt* оно́); (*direct object*) его́ (*f* её); (*indirect object*) ему́ (*f* ей); (*after prep*: +*gen*) его́ (*f* её); (: +*dat*) ему́ (*f* ей); (: +*instr*) им (*f* ей); (: +*prp*) нём (*f* ней); **where is your car? - it's in the garage** где Ва́ша маши́на? - она́ в гараже́; **I like this hat, whose is it?** мне нра́вится э́та шля́па, чья она́?; **have you got the dictionary with you? - no, I gave it to Mary** у Вас с собо́й слова́рь? - нет, я дал его́ Мэ́ри; **this pen is fine, I wrote with it yesterday** э́та ру́чка рабо́тает, я писа́л е́ю вчера́

2 э́то; (: *indirect object*) э́тому; **what kind of car is it? - it's a Lada** кака́я э́то маши́на? - э́то Ла́да; **who is it? - it's me** кто э́то? - э́то я

3 (*after prep*: +*gen*) э́того; (: +*dat*) э́тому; (: +*instr*) э́тим; (: +*prp*) э́том; **I spoke to him about it** я говори́л с ним об э́том; **that's just it!** вот и́менно!; **why is it that ...** почему́ же тогда́ ...; **what is it?** (*what's wrong*) что тако́е?; **that's it for today** на сего́дняя всё

4 (*impersonal*): **it's raining** идёт дождь; **it's cold today** сего́дня хо́лодно; **it's interesting that ...** интере́сно, что ...; **it's 6 o'clock** сейча́с 6 часо́в; **it's the 10th of August** сего́дня 10-ое а́вгуста.

ITA *n abbr* (*BRIT*: = *initial teaching alphabet*)

алфави́т, испо́льзуемый при обуче́нии чте́нию.

Italian [ɪˈtæljən] *adj* италья́нский* ♦ *n* (*person*) италья́нец(-нка); (*LING*) италья́нский* язы́к*; **the** ~**s** италья́нцы.

italics [ɪˈtælɪks] *npl* (*TYP*) курси́в *msg*.

Italy [ˈɪtəlɪ] *n* Ита́лия.

itch [ɪtʃ] *n* (*irritation*) зуд ♦ *vi* (*part of body*) чеса́ться* (*impf*); **I am** ~**ing all over** у меня́ всё че́шется; **he was** ~**ing to know our secret** ему́ не терпе́лось узна́ть наш секре́т.

itchy [ˈɪtʃɪ] *adj* (*skin*) зудя́щий; **I feel all** ~ у меня́ всё че́шется; **my back is** ~ у меня́ че́шется спина́.

it'd [ˈɪtd] = **it had**, **it would**.

item [ˈaɪtəm] *n* (*one thing*: *of list, collection*) предме́т; (*on agenda*) пункт; (*also*: **news** ~) сообще́ние; ~**s of clothing** предме́ты оде́жды.

itemize [ˈaɪtəmaɪz] *vt* (*list*) составля́ть (соста́вить* *perf*) спи́сок +*gen*.

itemized bill [ˈaɪtəmaɪzd-] *n* счёт с указа́нием сто́имости ка́ждой ве́щи или ка́ждого ви́да услу́г.

itinerant [ɪˈtɪnərənt] *adj* (*labourer, salesman, priest etc*) стра́нствующий.

itinerary [aɪˈtɪnərərɪ] *n* маршру́т.

it'll [ˈɪtl] = **it shall**, **it will**.

ITN *n abbr* (*BRIT*: *TV*) = *Independent Television News*.

its [ɪts] *adj* его́/её; свой/своя́/своё; *see also* **my** ♦ *pron* его́/её; свой/своя́/своё; *see also* **mine**[1].

it's [ɪts] = **it has**, **it is**.

itself [ɪtˈsɛlf] *pron* (*reflexive*) себя́*; (*emphatic*) он сам/она́ сама́/оно́ само́.

ITV *n abbr* (*BRIT*: *TV*) = *Independent Television*.

IUD *n abbr* (= *intrauterine device*) внутри-ма́точное противозача́точное сре́дство.

I've [aɪv] = **I have**.

ivory [ˈaɪvərɪ] *n* (*substance*) слоно́вая кость* *f*; (*colour*) цвет слоно́вой ко́сти.

Ivory Coast *n* Бе́рег Слоно́вой Ко́сти.

ivory tower *n* (*fig*) ба́шня из слоно́вой ко́сти.

ivy [ˈaɪvɪ] *n* (*BOT*) плющ*.

Ivy League *n* (*US*: *SCOL*) гру́ппа старе́йших университе́тов США.

~ J, j ~

J, j [dʒeɪ] n (letter) 10-ая бу́ква англи́йского алфави́та.
JA n abbr = **judge advocate**.
J/A abbr = **joint account**.
jab [dʒæb] vt (with finger, stick etc) ты́кать* (ткну́ть perf) ♦ n (BRIT: inf: MED) уко́л ♦ vi: **to ~ at** стуча́ть (impf) по +dat; **to ~ sth into sth** втыка́ть* (воткну́ть perf) что-н в что-н.
jack [dʒæk] n (AUT) домкра́т; (SPORT) ма́лый шар, слу́жащий мише́нью для игро́ков в шары́; (CARDS) вале́т.
▶ **jack in** vt (inf) завя́зывать (завяза́ть* perf) с +instr
▶ **jack up** vt (AUT) поднима́ть (подня́ть* perf) домкра́том.
jackal ['dʒækl] n шака́л.
jackass ['dʒækæs] n (also fig) осёл*.
jackdaw ['dʒækdɔ:] n га́лка*.
jacket ['dʒækɪt] n (of suit) пиджа́к*; (casual) ку́ртка*; (of book) суперобло́жка; **potatoes in their ~s, jacket potatoes** карто́шка в мунди́ре.
jack-in-the-box ['dʒækɪnðəbɔks] n чёртик в табаке́рке.
jackknife ['dʒæknaɪf] n складно́й нож* ♦ vi: **the lorry ~d** грузови́к заноси́ло.
jack of all trades n: **he's a ~ ~ ~ ~** он ма́стер на все ру́ки.
jack plug n штéккер.
jackpot ['dʒækpɔt] n куш; **to hit the ~** (fig) срыва́ть (сорва́ть perf) куш.
jacuzzi [dʒə'ku:zɪ] n „джаку́зи" m ind (ва́нна, в кото́рой под напо́ром циркули́рует вода́).
jade [dʒeɪd] n нефри́т.
jaded ['dʒeɪdɪd] adj утомлённый (утомлён) и равноду́шный (равноду́шен).
JAG n abbr (= Judge Advocate General) гла́вный прави́тельственный сове́тник по вое́нно-юриди́ческим вопро́сам.
jagged ['dʒægɪd] adj зу́бчатый.
jaguar ['dʒægjuə] n ягуа́р.
jail [dʒeɪl] n тюрьма́* ♦ vt заключа́ть (заключи́ть perf) в тюрьму́.
jailbird ['dʒeɪlbə:d] n (inf) уголо́вник.
jailbreak ['dʒeɪlbreɪk] n побе́г из тюрьмы́.
jalopy [dʒə'lɔpɪ] n (inf) драндуле́т.

jam [dʒæm] n (preserve) джем; (conserve) варе́нье; (also: **traffic ~**) про́бка* ♦ vt (passage) забива́ть (заби́ть* perf); (mechanism) закли́нивать (закли́нить perf); (RADIO) глуши́ть (заглуши́ть perf) ♦ vi (drawer) застрева́ть (застря́ть* perf); (mechanism): **the engine/rifle has ~med** зае́ло or закли́нило мото́р/ружьё; **I'm in a real ~** (inf: difficulty) я (здо́рово) влип; **to get sb out of a ~** (inf) помога́ть (помо́чь perf) кому́-н вы́браться из переде́лки; **to ~ sth into sth** запи́хивать (запихну́ть perf) что-н во что-н; **the telephone lines are ~med** все ли́нии (свя́зи) перегру́жены.
Jamaica [dʒə'meɪkə] n Яма́йка.
Jamaican [dʒə'meɪkən] adj яма́йский* ♦ n жи́тель(ница) m(f) Яма́йки.
jamb ['dʒæm] n кося́к*.
jamboree [dʒæmbə'ri:] n гуля́нье*.
jam-packed [dʒæm'pækt] adj: **~ (with)** битко́м наби́тый (наби́т) (+instr).
jam session n джем-се́йшен.
Jan. abbr = **January**.
jangle ['dʒæŋgl] vi (keys, bracelets etc) бренча́ть (impf).
janitor ['dʒænɪtə] n (caretaker) вахтёр(ша).
January ['dʒænjuərɪ] n янва́рь* m; see also **July**.
Japan [dʒə'pæn] n Япо́ния.
Japanese [dʒæpə'ni:z] adj япо́нский* ♦ n inv (person) япо́нец*(-нка*); (LING) япо́нский* язы́к*.
jar [dʒɑ:ᵣ] n ба́нка* ♦ vi (sound) ре́зать* (impf) слух; (colours) ре́зать* (impf) глаза́ ♦ vt (fig) потряса́ть (потрясти́* perf).
jargon ['dʒɑ:gən] n жарго́н.
jarring ['dʒɑ:rɪŋ] adj (sound) ре́жущий у́хо; (colour) ре́жущий глаз.
Jas. abbr = **James**.
jasmine ['dʒæzmɪn] n жасми́н.
jaundice ['dʒɔ:ndɪs] n желтуха́.
jaundiced ['dʒɔ:ndɪst] adj: **he has a very ~ view of politics** он смо́трит на поли́тику весьма́ пессимисти́чески.
jaunt [dʒɔ:nt] n вы́лазка*.
jaunty ['dʒɔ:ntɪ] adj (tone, step) бо́йкий*.
Java ['dʒɑ:və] n Я́ва.

* marks translations which have irregular inflections. The Russian-English side of the dictionary gives inflectional information.

javelin ['dʒævlɪn] *n* копьё*.
jaw [dʒɔ:] *n* чéлюсть* *f*.
jawbone ['dʒɔ:bəun] *n* челюстнáя кость* *f*.
jay [dʒeɪ] *n* сóйка*.
jaywalker ['dʒeɪwɔ:kəʳ] *n*
недисциплинúрованный пешехóд.
jazz [dʒæz] *n* джаз
▸ **jazz up** (*inf*) ◆ *vt* (*party, image etc*) оживлять
(оживúть* *perf*); (*food*) придавáть* (придáть*
perf) пикáнтность +*dat*.
jazz band *n* джáзовый оркéстр, джаз-бáнд.
JCB® *n* (колёсный) экскавáтор.
JCS *n abbr* (*US*: = *Joint Chiefs of Staff*) Комитéт
начáльников штабóв.
JD *n abbr* (*US*: = *Doctor of Laws*) доктóр
правовéдения; (= *Justice Department*)
Министéрство юстúции.
jealous ['dʒɛləs] *adj* ревнúвый (ревнúв); **to be**
~ **of** (*possessive*) ревновáть (*impf*) к +*dat*;
(*envious*) завúдовать (*impf*) +*dat*.
jealously ['dʒɛləslɪ] *adv* (*enviously*) ревнúво;
(*watchfully*) рéвностно.
jealousy ['dʒɛləsɪ] *n* (*resentment*) рéвность *f*;
(*envy*) зáвисть *f*.
jeans [dʒi:nz] *npl* джúнсы *pl*.
Jeep® [dʒi:p] *n* джип.
jeer [dʒɪəʳ] *vi*: **to** ~ (**at**) (*mock, scoff*)
насмехáться (*impf*) (над +*instr*), высмéивать
(вы́смеять *perf*).
jeering ['dʒɪərɪŋ] *adj* насмéшливый ◆ *n*
насмéшки* *fpl*.
jeers ['dʒɪəz] *npl* улюлю́канье *ntsg*.
jelly ['dʒɛlɪ] *n* желé *nt ind*; (*US*) джем.
jellyfish ['dʒɛlɪfɪʃ] *n* медýза.
jeopardize ['dʒɛpədaɪz] *vt* подвергáть
(подвéргнуть* *perf*) опáсности, стáвить*
(постáвить* *perf*) под угрóзу.
jeopardy ['dʒɛpədɪ] *n*: **to be in** ~ быть* (*impf*) в
опáсности.
jerk [dʒə:k] *n* (*jolt*) толчóк*, рывóк*; (*inf*: *idiot*)
болвáн ◆ *vt* дёргать (дёрнуть *perf*), рвануть
(*perf*) ◆ *vi* дёргаться (дёрнуться *perf*); **the car**
~**ed to a halt** машúна рéзко затормозúла.
jerkin ['dʒə:kɪn] *n* безрукáвка.
jerky ['dʒə:kɪ] *adj* сýдорожный (сýдорожен).
jerry-built ['dʒɛrɪbɪlt] *adj* пострóенный
(пострóен) кóе-как *or* на скóрую рýку.
jerry can ['dʒɛrɪ-] *n* канúстра.
Jersey ['dʒə:zɪ] *n* Джéрси *nt ind*.
jersey ['dʒə:zɪ] *n* (*pullover*) свúтер; (*fabric*)
джéрси *nt ind*.
Jerusalem [dʒə'ru:sləm] *n* Иерусалúм.
jest [dʒɛst] *n* шýтка.
jester ['dʒɛstəʳ] *n* (*HISTORY*) шут*.
Jesus ['dʒi:zəs] *n* (*REL*) Иисýс; ~ **Christ** Иисýс
Христóс.
jet [dʒɛt] *n* (*of gas, liquid*) струя́*; (*AVIAT*)
реактúвный самолёт; (*MINERALOGY*) гагáт.
jet-black ['dʒɛt'blæk] *adj* (*hair*) чёрный как
смоль; (*eyes*) агáтовый.
jet engine *n* реактúвный двúгатель *m*.

jet lag *n* нарушéние сýточного режúма
органúзма пóсле длúтельного полёта.
jet-propelled ['dʒɛt'prəpɛld] *adj* реактúвный.
jetsam ['dʒɛtsəm] *n* плавнúк.
jet-setter ['dʒɛtsɛtəʳ] *n* человéк, разъезжáющий
по свéту.
jettison ['dʒɛtɪsn] *vt* выбрáсывать
(вы́бросить* *perf*) за борт.
jetty ['dʒɛtɪ] *n* причáл.
Jew [dʒu:] *n* еврéй(ка*).
jewel ['dʒu:əl] *n* (*also fig*) драгоцéнный
кáмень* *m*; (*in watch*) кáмень.
jeweller ['dʒu:ələʳ] (*US* **jeweler**) *n* ювелúр.
jeweller's (shop) *n* ювелúрный магазúн.
jewellery ['dʒu:əlrɪ] (*US* **jewelry**) *n*
драгоцéнности *fpl*.
Jewess ['dʒu:ɪs] *n* еврéйка, жидóвка (*пренебр*).
Jewish ['dʒu:ɪʃ] *adj* еврéйский*.
JFK *n abbr* (*US*) = *John Fitzgerald Kennedy
International Airport*.
jib [dʒɪb] *n* (*NAUT*) клúвер*; (*of crane*) стрелá* ◆
vi (*horse*) упирáться (упереться* *perf*),
артáчиться (*impf*); **to** ~ **at doing** наотрéз
отказáться (*perf*) +*infin*.
jibe [dʒaɪb] *n* = **gibe**.
jiffy ['dʒɪfɪ] *n* (*inf*): **in a** ~ мúгом.
jig [dʒɪg] *n* джúга.
jigsaw ['dʒɪgsɔ:] *n* (*also*: ~ **puzzle**)
головолóмка (*в виде картúны, кусóчки
котóрой нýжно сложúть вмéсте*); (*tool*)
ажýрная пилá*.
jilt [dʒɪlt] *vt* (*person*) бросáть (брóсить* *perf*).
jingle ['dʒɪŋgl] *n* (*for advert*) корóткая
незамыслóватая мелóдия в реклáме ◆ *vi*
звенéть (*impf*).
jingoism ['dʒɪŋgəuɪzəm] *n* ура-патриотúзм.
jinx [dʒɪŋks] *n* (*inf*): **he is a** ~ у негó дурнóй
глаз.
jitters ['dʒɪtəz] *npl* (*inf*): **she's got the** ~ её
трясёт.
jittery ['dʒɪtərɪ] *adj* (*inf*) нéрвный* (нéрвен).
jiujitsu [dʒu:'dʒɪtsu:] *n* джúу-джúтсу *nt ind*.
job [dʒɔb] *n* (*employment*) рабóта; (*task*) дéло*;
(*inf*: *difficulty*): **I had a** ~ **getting here!** я с
трудóм добрáлся сюдá!; **it's not my** ~ э́то не
моё дéло; **a part-time/full-time** ~ рабóта на
почасовóй/пóлной стáвке; **he's only doing his**
~ он всегó-нáвсего выполня́ет свой
обя́занности; **it's a good** ~ **that** ... хорошó
ещё, что ...; **just the** ~**!** сáмое то!
jobber ['dʒɔbəʳ] *n* (*BRIT*) джóббер.
jobbing ['dʒɔbɪŋ] *adj* (*BRIT*): ~ **workman**
шабáшник.
Jobcentre ['dʒɔbsɛntəʳ] *n* (*BRIT*) бюрó *nt ind* по
трудоустрóйству.
job creation scheme *n* прогрáмма
зáнятости.
job description *n* описáние служéбных
обя́занностей.
jobless ['dʒɔblɪs] *adj* безрабóтный*; **the** ~ *npl*
безрабóтные *pl adj*.

job lot n па́ртия дешёвых това́ров, продаю́щихся о́птом.

job satisfaction n удовлетворённость f рабо́той.

job security n гара́нтия рабо́ты.

job sharing n ситуа́ция, когда́ два челове́ка деля́т рабо́чее ме́сто.

job specification n пе́речень m служе́бных обя́занностей.

jock [dʒɔk] n (US: inf) спортсме́н.

jockey ['dʒɔkɪ] n жоке́й ♦ vi: **to ~ for position** сопе́рничать (impf).

jockey box n (US: AUT) перча́точный я́щик, бардачо́к (разг).

jocular ['dʒɔkjʊlə'] adj (person) весёлый* (ве́сел); (remark) шутли́вый (шутли́в).

jog [dʒɔg] vt толка́ть (толкну́ть perf) ♦ vi бе́гать (impf) трусцо́й; **to ~ sb's memory** подстёгивать (подстегну́ть perf) чью-н па́мять

▸ **jog along** vi ме́дленно продвига́ться (impf).

jogger ['dʒɔgə'] n бегу́н* (трусцо́й).

jogging ['dʒɔgɪŋ] n бег трусцо́й.

Johannesburg [dʒəʊ'hænɪsbə:g] n Йоха́ннесбург.

john [dʒɔn] n (inf: US) туале́т.

join [dʒɔɪn] vt (queue) встава́ть* (встать* perf) в +acc; (organization) вступа́ть (вступи́ть* perf) в +acc; (put together: things, places) соединя́ть (соедини́ть perf); (meet: group of people) присоединя́ться (присоедини́ться perf) к +dat ♦ vi (rivers) слива́ться (сли́ться* perf); (roads) сходи́ться (сойти́сь* perf) ♦ n соедине́ние; **to ~ forces (with)** (fig) объединя́ть (объедини́ть perf) уси́лия (с +instr); **will you ~ us for dinner?** не хоти́те с на́ми поу́жинать?; **I'll ~ you later** я присоединю́сь к Вам по́зже

▸ **join in** vi присоединя́ться (присоедини́ться perf) ♦ vt fus (work, discussion etc) принима́ть (приня́ть* perf) уча́стие в +prp

▸ **join up** vi (meet) соединя́ться (соедини́ться perf); (MIL) поступа́ть (поступи́ть* perf) на вое́нную слу́жбу.

joiner ['dʒɔɪnə'] n (BRIT) столя́р*.

joinery ['dʒɔɪnərɪ] n (BRIT) столя́рное ремесло́*.

joint [dʒɔɪnt] n (TECH) сочлене́ние, стык; (ANAT) суста́в; (BRIT: CULIN) кусо́к* (мя́са); (inf: place) прито́н*; (: of cannabis) скру́тка с марихуа́ной ♦ adj совме́стный.

joint account n совме́стный счёт (в ба́нке).

jointly ['dʒɔɪntlɪ] adv совме́стно.

joint owners npl совладе́льцы mpl.

joint ownership n совме́стное владе́ние.

joint-stock bank ['dʒɔɪntstɔk-] n акционе́рный банк.

joint-stock company n акционе́рная компа́ния.

joint venture n совме́стное предприя́тие.

joist [dʒɔɪst] n ба́лка*.

joke [dʒəʊk] n (gag) шу́тка*, анекдо́т; (also: **practical ~**) ро́зыгрыш ♦ vi шути́ть* (пошути́ть* perf); **to play a ~ on** шути́ть* (пошути́ть* perf) над +instr, сыгра́ть (perf) шу́тку с +instr.

joker ['dʒəʊkə'] n (person) шу́тник; (CARDS) джо́кер.

joking ['dʒəʊkɪŋ] adj (remark) шу́точный.

jokingly ['dʒəʊkɪŋlɪ] adv в шу́тку.

jollity ['dʒɔlɪtɪ] n жизнера́достность f.

jolly ['dʒɔlɪ] adj (merry) весёлый* (ве́сел) ♦ adv (BRIT: inf) о́чень ♦ vt (BRIT): **to ~ sb along** ободря́ть (impf) кого́-н; **~ good!** о́чень хорошо́!, здо́рово!

jolt [dʒəʊlt] n (jerk) толчо́к*; (shock) потрясе́ние ♦ vt (physically) тряхну́ть or встря́хивать (встряхну́ть perf); (emotionally) потряса́ть (потрясти́* perf).

Jordan ['dʒɔːdən] n (country) Иорда́ния; (river) Иорда́н.

Jordanian [dʒɔː'deɪnɪən] adj иорда́нский* ♦ n иорда́нец*(-нка*).

joss stick ['dʒɔs-] n аромати́ческая па́лочка*.

jostle ['dʒɔsl] vt (subj: passers-by etc) толка́ть (толкну́ть perf), раста́лкивать (растолка́ть perf) ♦ vi толка́ться (impf).

jot [dʒɔt] n: **not one ~** ни ка́пли, ниско́лько

▸ **jot down** vt помеча́ть (поме́тить* perf).

jotter ['dʒɔtə'] n (BRIT) блокно́т.

journal ['dʒəːnl] n (periodical) журна́л; (diary) дне́вник*.

journalese [dʒəːnə'liːz] n (pej) газе́тный штамп.

journalism ['dʒəːnəlɪzəm] n журнали́стика.

journalist ['dʒəːnəlɪst] n журнали́ст(ка*).

journey ['dʒəːnɪ] n (trip, route) путь* m, доро́га ♦ vi путеше́ствовать (impf); **a five-hour ~** пятичасова́я пое́здка; **return ~** обра́тный путь*, обра́тная доро́га.

jovial ['dʒəʊvɪəl] adj бо́дрый, жизнера́достный.

jowl [dʒaʊl] n че́люсть* f.

joy [dʒɔɪ] n ра́дость f.

joyful ['dʒɔɪful] adj ра́достный* (ра́достен).

joyride ['dʒɔɪraɪd] n ката́ние на укра́денной маши́не.

joyrider ['dʒɔɪraɪdə'] n челове́к, кото́рый угоня́ет маши́ны и ката́ется на них.

joyriding ['dʒɔɪraɪdɪŋ] n езда́ (обы́чно на у́гнанном автомоби́ле).

joystick ['dʒɔɪstɪk] n (AVIAT) рыча́г* управле́ния; (COMPUT) джо́йстик.

JP n abbr = **Justice of the Peace**.

Jr. abbr (in names) = **junior**.

JTPA n abbr (US) = **Job Training Partnership Act**.

---

* marks translations which have irregular inflections. The Russian-English side of the dictionary gives inflectional information.

jubilant ['dʒu:bɪlnt] *adj* ликýющий.
jubilation [dʒu:bɪ'leɪʃən] *n* ликовáние.
jubilee ['dʒu:bɪli:] *n* (*anniversary*) юбилéй;
silver/golden ~ 25-лéтний/50-лéтний
юбилéй.
judge [dʒʌdʒ] *n* судья́* *m* ♦ *vt* (*LAW*) выноси́ть*
(вы́нести* *perf*) пригово́р; (*competition,
person etc*) суди́ть* (*impf*); (*consider, estimate*)
оцéнивать (оцени́ть* *perf*) ♦ *vi*: **judging** *or* **to ~
by his expression** су́дя по его́ выраже́нию;
she's a good ~ of character она́ хорошо́
разбира́ется в лю́дях; **I'll be the ~ of that** ну
это уж мне суди́ть; **I ~d it necessary to inform
him** я посчита́л ну́жным сообщи́ть ему́ об
э́том; **as far as I can ~** наско́лько я могу́
суди́ть.
judge advocate *n* (*MIL*) вое́нный прокуро́р.
judg(e)ment ['dʒʌdʒmənt] *n* (*LAW*) пригово́р,
решéние суда́; (*view*) сужде́ние;
(*discernment*) рассуди́тельность *f*; **in my ~**
по моему́ мне́нию; **to pass ~ (on)** (*LAW*)
выноси́ть* (вы́нести* *perf*) реше́ние (на +*acc*);
(*fig*) суди́ть* (*impf*).
judicial [dʒu:'dɪʃl] *adj* (*LAW*) судéбный; (*fig*)
рассуди́тельный* (рассуди́телен); **~ review**
судéбное разбира́тельство.
judiciary [dʒu:'dɪʃɪərɪ] *n*: **the ~** судéбные
о́рганы *mpl*.
judicious [dʒu:'dɪʃəs] *adj* благоразу́мный*
(благоразу́мен).
judo ['dʒu:dəu] *n* дзюдо́ *nt ind*.
jug [dʒʌg] *n* кувши́н.
jugged hare ['dʒʌgd-] *n* (*BRIT*) ≈ жарко́е *nt adj*
из за́йца.
juggernaut ['dʒʌgənɔ:t] *n* (*BRIT*) многото́нный
грузови́к*.
juggle ['dʒʌgl] *vi* (*also fig*) жонгли́ровать (*impf*)
♦ *vt* (*fig*) жонгли́ровать (*impf*) +*instr*; **to ~ with
sth** жонгли́ровать (*impf*) чем-н.
juggler ['dʒʌglə'] *n* жонглёр.
Jugoslav *etc* ['ju:gəu'slɑ:v] = **Yugoslav** *etc*.
jugular ['dʒʌgjulə'] *n* (*also*: **~ vein**) яре́мная
ве́на.
juice [dʒu:s] *n* сок*; (*inf*: *petrol*) бензи́н.
juicy ['dʒu:sɪ] *adj* со́чный* (со́чен).
jukebox ['dʒu:kbɔks] *n* музыка́льный
автома́т.
Jul. *abbr* = **July**.
July [dʒu:'laɪ] *n* ию́ль *m*; **the first of ~** пéрвое
ию́ля; **on the eleventh of ~** оди́ннадцатого
ию́ля; **in the month of ~** в ию́ле ме́сяце; **at
the beginning/end of ~** в нача́ле/концé ию́ля;
in the middle of ~ в середи́не ию́ля; **during ~**
в тече́ние ию́ля; **in ~** в ию́ле; **in ~ of next year**
в ию́ле сле́дующего го́да; **each** *or* **every ~**
ка́ждый ию́ль; **~ was wet this year** в э́том
году́ ию́ль был дождли́вым.
jumble ['dʒʌmbl] *n* нагроможде́ние; (*BRIT*:
items for sale) старьё ♦ *vt* (*also*: **~ up**)
переме́шивать (перемеша́ть *perf*).
jumble sale *n* (*BRIT*) благотвори́тельная

распрода́жа поде́ржанных веще́й.
jumbo ['dʒʌmbəu] *n* (*also*: **~ jet**) реакти́вный
аэро́бус.
jumbo-size ['dʒʌmbəusaɪz] *adj* гига́нтский*.
jump [dʒʌmp] *vi* пры́гать (пры́гнуть *perf*);
(*start*) подпры́гивать (подпры́гнуть *perf*);
(*increase*) подска́кивать (подскочи́ть* *perf*) ♦
vt (*fence*) перепры́гивать (перепры́гнуть
perf), переска́кивать (перескочи́ть* *perf*) ♦ *n*
прыжо́к*; (*increase*) скачо́к*; **to ~ the queue**
(*BRIT*) идти́* (пойти́* *perf*) без о́череди
▶ **jump about** *vi* суети́ться* (*impf*)
▶ **jump at** *vt fus* (*seize*) ухва́тываться
(ухвати́ться *perf*) за +*acc*
▶ **jump down** *vi* спры́гивать (спры́гнуть *perf*)
▶ **jump up** *vi* (*from a seat*) вска́кивать
(вскочи́ть* *perf*); (*into the air*) подпры́гивать
(подпры́гнуть *perf*).
jumped-up ['dʒʌmptʌp] *adj* (*BRIT*: *pej*): **~ office
boy** вы́скочка *m*.
jumper ['dʒʌmpə'] *n* (*BRIT*: *pullover*) сви́тер,
джéмпер; (*US*: *dress*) сарафа́н; (*SPORT*)
прыгу́н*(ья*).
jumper cables *npl* (*US*) = **jump leads**.
jump leads *npl* (*BRIT*) про́вод большо́го
сече́ния (*для пу́ска дви́гателя*).
jump-start ['dʒʌmpstɑ:t] *vt*: **to ~ a car**
подта́лкивать (подтолкну́ть *perf*) маши́ну,
чтобы завести́ её.
jump suit *n* комбинезо́н.
jumpy ['dʒʌmpɪ] *adj* не́рвный.
Jun. *abbr* = **June**.
junction ['dʒʌŋkʃən] *n* (*BRIT*: *of roads*)
пересече́ние; (*RAIL*) у́зел*.
juncture ['dʒʌŋktʃə'] *n*: **at this ~** в да́нный
моме́нт.
June [dʒu:n] *n* ию́нь *m*; *see also* **July**.
jungle ['dʒʌŋgl] *n* (*also fig*) джу́нгли *pl*.
junior ['dʒu:nɪə'] *adj* мла́дший* ♦ *n*
мла́дший*(-ая) *m(f) adj*; **he's ~ to me (by 2
years), he's my ~ (by 2 years)** он мла́дше
меня́ (на 2 го́да); **he's ~ to me** (*seniority*) он
мой подчинённый.
junior executive *n* мла́дший* руководя́щий*
рабо́тник.
junior high school *n* (*US*) ≈ непо́лная срéдняя
шко́ла.
junior minister *n* (*BRIT*) мла́дший* мини́стр.
junior partner *n* мла́дший* партнёр.
junior school *n* (*BRIT*) шко́ла для дете́й в
во́зрасте от 7 до 11 лет.
junior sizes *npl* де́тские разме́ры *mpl*.
juniper ['dʒu:nɪpə'] *n*: **~ berry** можжеве́льник.
junk [dʒʌŋk] *n* барахло́, хлам; (*ship*) джо́нка*
♦ *vt* (*inf*) выки́дывать (вы́кинуть *perf*).
junk bond *n* облига́ции, обеща́ющие высо́кие
проце́нты, но не даю́щие гара́нтий.
junket ['dʒʌŋkɪt] *n* (*CULIN*) сла́дкое моло́чное
блю́до; (*US*: *inf*: *pej*): **to go on a ~**
прокати́ться* (*perf*) за казённый счёт.
junk food *n* еда́, содержа́щая ма́ло

питательных веществ.
junkie [ˈdʒʌŋkɪ] *n* (*inf*) наркома́н.
junk mail *n* незапро́шенная рекла́ма,
доставля́емая по по́чте.
junk room *n* чула́н.
junk shop *n* ла́вка* старьёвщика.
Junr *abbr* (*in names*) = **junior**.
junta [ˈdʒʌntə] *n* ху́нта.
Jupiter [ˈdʒuːpɪtə*] *n* Юпи́тер.
jurisdiction [dʒuərɪsˈdɪkʃən] *n* (*LAW*)
юрисди́кция; (*ADMIN*) сфе́ра полномо́чий; **it
is within/outside my ~** э́то вхо́дит/не вхо́дит
в мой полномо́чия.
jurisprudence [dʒuərɪsˈpruːdəns] *n*
юриспруде́нция.
juror [ˈdʒuərə*] *n* прися́жный заседа́тель *m*.
jury [ˈdʒuərɪ] *n* прися́жные *pl adj* (заседа́тели).
jury box *n* скамья́* прися́жных.
juryman [ˈdʒuərɪmən] *irreg n* = **juror**.
just [dʒʌst] *adj* справедли́вый (справедли́в) ♦
adv (*exactly*) как раз, и́менно; (*only*) то́лько;
(*barely*) едва́; **he's ~ left/done it** он то́лько
что ушёл/э́то сде́лал; **~ as I expected** как я и
ожида́л; **it's ~ right** э́то как раз то, что на́до;
~ two o'clock ро́вно два часа́; **we were ~
going** *or* **about to go** мы как раз собира́лись
уходи́ть; **I was ~ about to phone** я уже́
собра́лся позвони́ть; **she's ~ as clever as you**
она́ столь же умна́, как и ты; **it's ~ as well
(that)** ... даже и хорошо́, (что) ...; **~ as he was
leaving** как раз когда́ он собра́лся уходи́ть;
~ before Christmas пе́ред са́мым
Рождество́м; **there was ~ enough petrol** едва́
хвати́ло бензи́на; **~ here** вот здесь; **he (only)
~ missed** он чуть не попа́л; **it's ~ me** э́то
(то́лько) я; **it's ~ a mistake** э́то про́сто
оши́бка; **~ listen!** ты то́лько послу́шай!; **~
ask someone the way** про́сто спроси́ у кого́-
нибудь доро́гу; **not ~ now** то́лько не сейча́с;

~ a minute!, ~ one moment! подожди́те!,
〈одну́〉 мину́ту!
justice [ˈdʒʌstɪs] *n* (*LAW: system*) правосу́дие;
(*rightness*) справедли́вость *f*; (*US: judge*)
судья́* *m*; **Lord Chief J~** (*BRIT*) второ́й по
значе́нию судья́ в брита́нской систе́ме
правосу́дия; **to do ~ to** (*fig: task, meal, person*)
отдава́ть (отда́ть* *perf*) до́лжное +*dat*.
Justice of the Peace *n* (*BRIT*) мирово́й судья́*
m.
justifiable [dʒʌstɪˈfaɪəbl] *adj* опра́вданный*
(опра́вдан), обосно́ванный (обосно́ван).
justifiably [dʒʌstɪˈfaɪəblɪ] *adv* опра́вданно,
обосно́ванно.
justification [dʒʌstɪfɪˈkeɪʃən] *n* (*of action*)
оправда́ние; (*reason*) основа́ние; (*TYP*)
выра́внивание строки́.
justify [ˈdʒʌstɪfaɪ] *vt* опра́вдывать (оправда́ть
perf); (*text*) выра́внивать (вы́ровнять *perf*); **to
~ o.s.** опра́вдываться (оправда́ться *perf*); **to
be justified in doing** име́ть (*impf*) все
основа́ния +*infin*.
justly [ˈdʒʌstlɪ] *adv* справедли́во.
jut [dʒʌt] *vi* (*also: ~* **out**) выступа́ть (*impf*).
jute [dʒuːt] *n* джут.
juvenile [ˈdʒuːvənaɪl] *n* (*LAW, ADMIN*)
подро́сток*, несовершенноле́тний*(-яя) *m(f)*
adj ♦ *adj* (*humour, mentality*) де́тский*.
juvenile court *n* суд для несовершенно-
ле́тних.
juvenile delinquency *n* престу́пность *f* среди́
несовершенноле́тних.
juvenile delinquent *n* несовершенно-
ле́тний(-яя) правонаруши́тель(-ница) *m(f)*.
juxtapose [ˈdʒʌkstəpəuz] *vt* сопоставля́ть
(сопоста́вить* *perf*).
juxtaposition [ˈdʒʌkstəpəˈzɪʃən] *n*
сопоставле́ние.

---

* marks translations which have irregular inflections. The Russian-English side of the dictionary gives inflectional information.

~ K, k ~

K, k [keɪ] n (letter) 11-ая бу́ква англи́йского алфави́та.

K abbr = one thousand; (COMPUT) (= **kilobyte**) K= килоба́йт; (BRIT: in titles) = **knight**.

Kabul ['kɑ:bul] n Кабу́л.

kaftan ['kæftæn] n кафта́н.

Kalahari Desert [kælə'hɑ:rɪ-] n: **the ~ ~** пусты́ня Калаха́ри.

kale [keɪl] n капу́ста кормова́я.

kaleidoscope [kə'laɪdəskəup] n калейдоско́п.

kamikaze [kæmɪ'kɑ:zɪ] n камика́дзе m ind, лётчик-сме́ртник.

Kampala [kæm'pɑ:lə] n Кампа́ла.

Kampuchea [kæmpu'tʃɪə] n Кампучи́я.

Kampuchean [kæmpu'tʃɪən] adj кампучи́йский*.

kangaroo [kæŋgə'ru:] n кенгуру́ m ind.

kaput [kə'put] (inf) adj: **the TV is ~**! телеви́зору капу́т!

karaoke [kɑ:rə'əukɪ] n карио́ки ind (самоде́ятельное пе́ние под за́пись профессиона́льного анса́мбла).

karate [kə'rɑ:tɪ] n карата́ё nt ind.

Kashmir [kæʃ'mɪə] n Кашми́р.

kayak ['kaɪæk] n кая́к*.

Kazakh ['kæzæk] n (person) каза́х(-а́шка*); (LING) каза́хский* язы́к* ◆ adj каза́хский*.

Kazakhstan [kæzæk'stɑ:n] n Казахста́н.

KC n abbr (BRIT: LAW: = King's Counsel) короле́вский* адвока́т (адвока́тский ранг).

kd abbr (US: COMM: = knocked down) в разо́бранном ви́де.

kebab [kə'bæb] n шашлы́к*.

keel [ki:l] n киль m; **on an even ~** (fig) в состоя́нии стаби́льности.
► **keel over** vi опроки́дываться (опроки́нуться perf).

keen [ki:n] adj о́стрый; (eager) стра́стный* (стра́стен), увлечённый; **to be ~ to do** or **on doing** о́чень хоте́ть* (impf) +infin; **to be ~ on sth** увлека́ться (impf) чем-н; **he is ~ on her** он увлечён е́ю; **I'm not ~ on going** мне не о́чень хо́чется идти́; **~ competition** напряжённая конкуре́нтая борьба́.

keenly ['ki:nlɪ] adv (enthusiastically) увлечённо; (intently) при́стально; **to feel sth ~** глубоко́ пережива́ть (impf) что-н.

keenness ['ki:nnɪs] n (eagerness) увлечённость f; **~ to do** стремле́ние +infin.

keep [ki:p] (pt, pp **kept**) vt (receipt, money) оставля́ть (оста́вить* perf) себе́; (store) храни́ть (impf); (preserve) сохраня́ть (сохрани́ть perf); (house, garden, shop, family) содержа́ть (impf); (prisoner, chickens, bees) держа́ть* (impf); (accounts, diary) вести́* (impf); (promise) сде́рживать (сдержа́ть* perf) ◆ vi (in a certain state or place) остава́ться* (оста́ться* perf); (food) сохраня́ться (impf); (continue): **to ~ doing** продолжа́ть (impf) +impf infin ◆ n (of castle) центра́льная ба́шня*; (food etc): **he has enough for his ~** ему́ доста́точно на прожи́тие; **he kept the job** он сохрани́л э́ту рабо́ту; **where do you ~ the salt?** где у Вас соль?; **he tries to ~ her happy** он де́лает всё для того́, чтобы она́ была́ дово́льна; **to ~ the house tidy** содержа́ть* (impf) дом в поря́дке; **to ~ sb waiting** заставля́ть (заста́вить* perf) кого́-н ждать; **to ~ sb from doing** не дава́ть* (дать* perf) кому́-н +infin; **to ~ an appointment** прийти́* (perf) в назна́ченное вре́мя; **to ~ a record** вести́* (impf) учёт; **to ~ sth to o.s.** держа́ть (impf) что-н при себе́; **to ~ sth (back) from sb** скрыва́ть (скрыть* perf) что-н от кого́-н; **to ~ sth from happening** не дава́ть* (дать* perf) чему́-н случи́ться; **to ~ time** (clock) идти́* (impf) то́чно
► **keep away** vt: **to ~ sth/sb away from sb/sth** держа́ть (impf) что-н/кого́-н пода́льше от кого́-н/чего́-н ◆ vi: **to ~ away (from)** держа́ться* (impf) пода́льше (от +gen)
► **keep back** vt (crowds, tears) сде́рживать (сдержа́ть* perf); (money) уде́рживать (удержа́ть* perf) ◆ vi держа́ться* (impf) на расстоя́нии
► **keep down** vt (prices, spending) сде́рживать (сдержа́ть* perf); (retain): **she can't ~ her food down** что бы она́ ни съе́ла, её всё вре́мя рвёт ◆ vi: **~ down!** ложи́сь!
► **keep in** vt (person) держа́ть (impf) до́ма ◆ vi (inf): **to ~ in with sb** подде́рживать (impf) хоро́шие отноше́ния с кем-н
► **keep off** vt (hold back) не подпуска́ть (подпусти́ть* perf); (abstain) избега́ть (impf) +gen ◆ vi держа́ться* (impf) в стороне́; "**keep off the grass**" „по газо́нам не ходи́ть"; **~ your hands off** рука́ми не тро́гать
► **keep on** vi: **to ~ on doing** продолжа́ть (impf)

+*impf infin*; **to ~ on (about sth)** не переставая говорить (*impf*) (о чём-н)
► **keep out** *vt* не впускать (впустить* *perf*); **"keep out"** „посторонним вход воспрещён"
► **keep up** *vt* (*payments, standards*) поддерживать (*impf*) ◆ *vi*: **to ~ up (with)** (*pace*) поспевать (поспеть *perf*) (за +*instr*); (*level*) идти* (*impf*) в ногу (с +*instr*).
keeper ['ki:pə^r] *n* (*of zoo, park*) смотритель (ница) *m(f)*.
keep fit *n* аэробика.
keeping ['ki:pɪŋ] *n* (*care*) присмотр; **I'll leave this in your ~** оставляю это под Вашим присмотром; **in ~ with** в соответствии с +*instr*; **out of ~ with** несовместимый (несовместим) с +*instr*.
keeps [ki:ps] *n*: **for ~** (*inf*) на совсем.
keepsake ['ki:pseɪk] *n* памятный подарок.
keg [kɛg] *n* бочонок*; **~ beer** бочковое пиво.
kennel ['kɛnl] *n* конура*.
kennels ['kɛnlz] *npl* гостиница *fsg or* платный приют *msg* для собак.
Kenya ['kɛnjə] *n* Кения.
Kenyan ['kɛnjən] *adj* кенийский* ◆ *n* кениец*(-ийка*).
kept [kɛpt] *pt, pp of* **keep**.
kerb [kə:b] *n* (*BRIT*) бордюр.
kerb crawler [-'krɔ:lə^r] *n* шофёр, выбирающий себе проституток из окна медленно ползущего автомобиля.
kernel ['kə:nl] *n* (*of nut*) ядро*; (*of idea*) суть *f*.
kerosene ['kɛrəsi:n] *n* керосин.
kestrel ['kɛstrəl] *n* пустельга*.
ketchup ['kɛtʃəp] *n* кетчуп.
kettle ['kɛtl] *n* чайник.
kettledrum ['kɛtldrʌm] *n* литавра.
key [ki:] *n* ключ*; (*MUS*) тональность *f*; (*of piano, computer*) клавиш(а) ◆ *cpd* (*issue etc*) ключевой ◆ *vt* (*also:~ in*) набирать (набрать* *perf*) на клавиатуре.
keyboard ['ki:bɔ:d] *n* клавиатура.
keyboarder ['ki:bɔ:də^r] *n* машинист(ка), оператор клавиатуры.
keyed up [ki:d'] *adj*: **he was all ~~** он был очень взвинчен.
keyhole ['ki:həul] *n* замочная скважина.
keyhole surgery *n* полостная операция, осуществляемая через минимальный разрез.
keynote ['ki:nəut] *n* (*MUS*) тоника; (*of speech*) лейтмотив.
keypad ['ki:pæd] *n* (*COMPUT*) (малая) клавиатура, клавишная панель *f*.
keyring ['ki:rɪŋ] *n* брелок*.
keystroke ['ki:strəuk] *n* (*COMPUT*) нажатие клавиши.
kg *abbr* (= **kilogram(me)**) кг= *килограмм*.
KGB *n abbr* (*POL: formerly*) КГБ.

khaki ['kɑ:kɪ] *n, adj* хаки *nt, adj ind*.
kHz *abbr* (= **kilohertz**) кГц= *килогерц*.
kibbutz [kɪ'buts] *n* киббуц.
kick [kɪk] *vt* (*person, table*) ударять (ударить *perf*) ногой; (*ball*) ударять (ударить *perf*) ногой по +*dat*; (*inf: habit, addiction*) побороть (*perf*) ◆ *vi* (*horse*) лягаться (*impf*) ◆ *n* удар; (*of rifle*) отдача; (*thrill: inf*): **he does it for ~s** он делает это, чтобы пощекотать себе нервы
► **kick around** *vi* (*inf*) валяться (*impf*)
► **kick off** *vi*: **the match ~s off at 3pm** матч начинается в 3 часа (*в футболе*).
kickoff ['kɪkɔf] *n* начало (футбольного) матча.
kick-start ['kɪkstɑ:t] *n* (*also:~er: BRIT*) ножной стартёр.
kid [kɪd] *n* (*inf: child*) ребёнок*; (*goat*) козлёнок*; (*leather*) лайка ◆ *vt* (*inf*) водить* (*impf*) за нос, дурачить (*impf*); ~ **brother** младший* братишка* *m*; ~ **sister** младшая сестрёнка*; **you're ~ding!** ты шутишь!
kid gloves *n*: **to handle sb with ~ ~** бережно обращаться (*impf*) с кем-н.
kidnap ['kɪdnæp] *vt* похищать (похитить* *perf*).
kidnapper ['kɪdnæpə^r] *n* похититель(ница) *m(f)*.
kidnapping ['kɪdnæpɪŋ] *n* похищение.
kidney ['kɪdnɪ] *n* (*MED*) почка*; (*CULIN*) почки *fpl*.
kidney bean *n* красная фасоль *f no pl*.
kidney machine *n* искусственная почка*.
Kiev ['ki:ɛf] *n* Киев.
Kilimanjaro [kɪlɪmən'dʒɑ:rəu] *n*: **Mount ~** Килиманджаро *nt ind*.
kill [kɪl] *vt* убивать (убить* *perf*); (*proposal*) губить (загубить *perf*); (*rumour*) пресекать (пресечь* *perf*) ◆ *n* (*prey*) добыча; **to ~ time** (*inf*) убивать (убить* *perf*) время; **to ~ o.s. to be ~ed** (*in war, accident*) погибать (погибнуть* *perf*); **to ~ o.s. to do** (*fig*) надрываться (*impf*), чтобы +*perf infin*; **to ~ o.s. (laughing)** помирать (*impf*) (со смеху).
► **kill off** *vt* (*also fig*) уничтожать (уничтожить *perf*).
killer ['kɪlə^r] *n* убийца *m/f*.
killer instinct *n* смертельная *or* мёртвая хватка.
killing ['kɪlɪŋ] *n* убийство; (*profit*): **to make a ~** (*inf*) срывать (сорвать* *perf*) куш.
killjoy ['kɪldʒɔɪ] *n*: **don't be such a ~!** не отравляй другим удовольствие!
kiln [kɪln] *n* печь* *f* (*для обжига*).
kilo ['ki:ləu] *n* кило *nt ind*.
kilobyte ['ki:ləubaɪt] *n* килобайт.
kilogram(me) ['kɪləugræm] *n* килограмм.
kilohertz ['kɪləuhə:ts] *n inv* килогерц.
kilometre ['kɪləmi:tə^r] (*US* **kilometer**) *n*

---

* marks translations which have irregular inflections. The Russian-English side of the dictionary gives inflectional information.

киломе́тр.

kilowatt ['kɪləuwɒt] *n* килова́тт.

kilt [kɪlt] *n* шотла́ндская ю́бка*.

kilter ['kɪltə'] *n*: **out of** ~ в беспоря́дке.

kimono [kɪ'məunəu] *n* кимоно́ *nt ind*.

kin [kɪn] *n see* **kith, next.**

kind [kaɪnd] *adj* до́брый* (добр*) ◆ *n* род*; **would you be ~ enough** *or* **so ~ as to ...?** не бу́дете ли Вы так добры́ *or* любе́зны +*perf infin* ...?; **it's very ~ of you to help me** о́чень любе́зно с Ва́шей стороны́, что Вы мне помогли́; **he seemed ~ of unhappy** он был вро́де бы недово́лен; **in ~** (*COMM*) това́рами и услу́гами; **a ~ of** род +*gen*; **two of a ~** две ве́щи одного́ ти́па; **what ~ of person is he?** что он за челове́к?; **she has a strange ~ of smile** у неё стра́нная улы́бка.

kindergarten ['kɪndəgɑːtn] *n* де́тский сад*.

kind-hearted [kaɪnd'hɑːtɪd] *adj* до́брый* (добр*), добросерде́чный* (добросерде́чен).

kindle ['kɪndl] *vt* (*also fig*) разжига́ть (разже́чь* *perf*).

kindling ['kɪndlɪŋ] *n* ще́пки* *fpl*, расто́пка.

kindly ['kaɪndlɪ] *adj* (*smile*) до́брый* (добр*); (*person, tone*) доброжела́тельный* (доброжела́телен) ◆ *adv* (*smile, behave*) любе́зно, доброжела́тельно; **will you ~ ...** бу́дьте добры́ ...; **he didn't take it ~** он был далеко́ не рад э́тому.

kindness ['kaɪndnɪs] *n* (*quality*) доброта́; (*act*) любе́зность *f*.

kindred ['kɪndrɪd] *adj*: **~ spirit** ро́дственная душа́*.

kinetic [kɪ'nɛtɪk] *adj* кинети́ческий*.

king [kɪŋ] *n* коро́ль* *m*.

kingdom ['kɪŋdəm] *n* короле́вство; **the animal/ plant ~** живо́тное/расти́тельное ца́рство.

kingfisher ['kɪŋfɪʃə'] *n* зиморо́док*.

kingpin ['kɪŋpɪn] *n* (*TECH*) шкво́рень* *m*; (*fig*) ва́жная ши́шка*.

king-size(d) ['kɪŋsaɪz(d)] *adj* са́мого большо́го разме́ра.

kink [kɪŋk] *n* (*in rope*) у́зел; (*in hair*) завито́к*; (*in character*) причу́да, стра́нность *f*.

kinky ['kɪŋkɪ] *adj* (*inf*) поро́чный* (поро́чен).

kinship ['kɪnʃɪp] *n* родство́.

kinsman ['kɪnzmən] *irreg n* ро́дич.

kinswoman ['kɪnzwumən] *irreg n* кро́вная ро́дственница.

kiosk ['kiːɔsk] *n* кио́ск; (*BRIT*: *TEL*) телефо́нная бу́дка*; (*also*: **newspaper ~**) газе́тный кио́ск.

kipper ['kɪpə'] *n* ≈ копчёная селёдка*.

Kirghiz ['kəːgɪz] *n* (*person*) кирги́з(ка*); (*LING*) кирги́зский* язы́к* ◆ *adj* кирги́зский*.

Kirghizia [kəː'gɪzɪə] *n* Кирги́зия.

Kishinev [kɪʃɪ'njɔf] *n* Кишинёв.

kiss [kɪs] *n* поцелу́й ◆ *vt* целова́ть (поцелова́ть *perf*) ◆ *vi* целова́ться (поцелова́ться *perf*); **to ~ sb goodbye** целова́ть (поцелова́ть *perf*) кого́-н на проща́ние.

kissagram ['kɪsəgr[+e]m] *n* сюрпри́зная

доста́вка поздравле́ний, сопровожда́ющаяся поцелу́ем доста́вщика и́ли доста́вщицы.

kiss of life *n* (*BRIT*): **the ~ ~ ~** иску́сственное дыха́ние.

kit [kɪt] *n* (*also*: **sports ~**) костю́м; (*equipment*) снаряже́ние; (*set of tools*) набо́р; (*for assembly*) компле́кт.

▶ **kit out** *vt* (*BRIT*) снаряжа́ть (снаряди́ть* *perf*).

kitbag ['kɪtbæg] *n* вещмешо́к*= веще́вой мешо́к.

kitchen ['kɪtʃɪn] *n* ку́хня*.

kitchen garden *n* огоро́д.

kitchen sink *n* (ку́хонная) мо́йка* *or* ра́ковина.

kitchen unit *n* (*BRIT*) ку́хонный шкаф.

kitchenware ['kɪtʃɪnwɛə'] *n* ку́хонные принадле́жности *fpl*, (ку́хонная) у́тварь *f*.

kite [kaɪt] *n* (*toy*) возду́шный змей; (*ZOOL*) ко́ршун.

kith [kɪθ] *n*: **~ and kin** родны́е *pl adj* и бли́зкие *pl adj*.

kitten ['kɪtn] *n* котёнок*.

kitty ['kɪtɪ] *n* (*pool of money*) о́бщая ка́сса.

kiwi ['kiːwiː] *n* ки́ви *f ind*.

KKK *n abbr* (*US*: = *Ku Klux Klan*) ку-клукс-кла́н.

Kleenex® ['kliːnɛks] *n inv* бума́жный носово́й плато́к*.

kleptomaniac [klɛptəu'meɪnɪæk] *n* клептома́н(ка*).

km *abbr* (= **kilometre**) км= *киломе́тр.*

km/h *abbr* (= *kilometres per hour*) км/ч= *киломе́тров в час.*

knack [næk] *n*: **he has the ~ of imitating other people** он о́чень ло́вко имити́рует други́х люде́й; **there's a ~ to doing this** тут есть оди́н секре́т *or* осо́бая хи́трость.

knackered ['nækəd] *adj* (*inf*: *tired*) вы́мотанный (вы́мотан).

knapsack ['næpsæk] *n* (небольшо́й) рюкза́к.

knead [niːd] *vt* меси́ть* (смеси́ть* *perf*).

knee [niː] *n* коле́но*.

kneecap ['niːkæp] *n* коле́нная ча́шечка*.

kneecapping ['niːkæpɪŋ] *n* вы́стрел по коле́нной ча́шечке (*фо́рма ме́сти, применя́емой террори́стами*).

knee-deep ['niː'diːp] *adj, adv* по коле́но.

knee-jerk ['niːdʒəːk] *n* коле́нный рефле́кс ◆ *adj*: **~ reaction** (*fig*) рефле́кс.

kneel [niːl] (*pt, pp* **knelt**) *vi* (*also*: **~ down**: *action*) встава́ть* (встать* *perf*) на коле́ни; (: *state*) стоя́ть (*impf*) на коле́нях.

kneepad ['niːpæd] *n* наколе́нник.

knell [nɛl] *n* погреба́льный звон; (*fig*) коне́ц*.

knelt [nɛlt] *pt, pp of* **kneel**.

knew [njuː] *pt of* **know**.

knickers ['nɪkəz] *npl* (*BRIT*) (же́нские) тру́сики *mpl*.

knick-knacks ['nɪknæks] *npl* безделу́шки* *fpl*.

knife [naɪf] (*pl* **knives**) *n* нож* ◆ *vt* ра́нить (*impf*) ножо́м.

knight [naɪt] *n* рыцарь *m*; (*CHESS*) конь* *m*.
knighthood ['naɪthud] *n* (*BRIT*) рыцарство (*полученное от монарха за заслуги перед страной*).
knit [nɪt] *vt* (*garment*) вязать (связать *perf*) ◆ *vi* (*with wool etc*) вязать (*impf*); (*bones*) срастаться (срастись* *perf*); **to ~ one's brows** хмурить (нахмурить *perf*) брови.
knitted ['nɪtɪd] *adj* (*garment*) вязаный.
knitting ['nɪtɪŋ] *n* вязанье.
knitting machine *n* вязальная машина.
knitting needle *n* вязальная спица.
knitting pattern *n* вязка*.
knitwear ['nɪtwɛə'] *n* трикотаж.
knives [naɪvz] *npl of* **knife.**
knob [nɔb] *n* (*of door*) ручка*; (*on radio etc*) кнопка*; (*of stick*) набалдашник; **a ~ of butter** (*BRIT*) кусочек (сливочного) масла.
knobbly ['nɔblɪ] (*US* **knobby**) *adj* (*surface*) бугристый (бугрист*); (*hand*) узловатый (узловат*); (*knee*) шишковатый.
knobby ['nɔbɪ] *adj* (*US*) = **knobbly.**
knock [nɔk] *vt* (*strike*) ударять (ударить *perf*); (*bump into*) сталкиваться (столкнуться *perf*) с +*instr*; (*inf: criticize*) критиковать (*impf*) ◆ *vi* (*engine*) стучать (*impf*) ◆ *n* (*blow, bump*) удар, толчок*; (*on door*) стук; **to ~ a nail into sth** вбивать (вбить* *perf*) гвоздь во что-н; **to ~ some sense into sb** учить* (научить* *perf*) кого-н уму-разуму; **he ~ed at** *or* **on the door** он постучал в дверь
▶ **knock about** (*inf*) ◆ *vt* (*hit*) колотить* (поколотить* *perf*) ◆ *vi* (*travel*) шататься (*impf*) по свету; (*hang out*): **~ about (with)** водиться (*impf*) (с +*instr*)
▶ **knock around** *vti* = **knock about**
▶ **knock back** *vt* (*inf: drink*) пропускать (пропустить* *perf*)
▶ **knock down** *vt* (*person, price*) сбивать (сбить* *perf*); (*building*) сносить (снести* *perf*)
▶ **knock off** *vi* (*inf: finish*) закругляться (закруглиться *perf*) ◆ *vt* (*from price*) сбавлять (сбавить* *perf*); (*inf: steal*) стянуть* (*perf*)
▶ **knock out** *vt* (*subj: person, drug*) оглушать (оглушить* *perf*); (*BOXING*) нокаутировать (*perf*); (*defeat*) выбивать (выбить* *perf*)
▶ **knock over** *vt* (*person, object*) сбивать (сбить* *perf*).
knockdown ['nɔkdaun] *adj*: **~ price** сниженная цена.
knocker ['nɔkə'] *n* дверной молоток*.
knocking ['nɔkɪŋ] *n* стук.
knock-kneed [nɔk'niːd] *adj* с вывернутыми внутрь коленями.
knockout ['nɔkaut] *n* (*BOXING*) нокаут ◆ *cpd* (*competition*) отборочный.
knock-up ['nɔkʌp] *n* (*TENNIS*): **to have a ~** разминаться (размяться* *perf*).

knot [nɔt] *n* (*also NAUT*) узел*; (*in wood*) сучок* ◆ *vt* завязывать (завязать* *perf*) узлом; **to tie/untie a ~** завязывать (завязать* *perf*)/развязывать (развязать* *perf*) узел.
knotty ['nɔtɪ] *adj* (*fig*) запутанный.
know [nəu] (*pt* **knew**, *pp* **known**) *vt* (*facts, people*) знать (*impf*); **to ~ how to do** уметь (*impf*) +*infin*; **to ~ about** *or* **of sth/sb** знать (*impf*) о чём-н/ком-н; **to get to ~ sth** (*news*) узнавать* (узнать* *perf*) что-н; **to get to ~ sb** (*more intimately*) узнавать* (узнать* *perf*) кого-н поближе; (*get acquainted*) знакомиться* (познакомиться* *perf*) с кем-н; **to get to ~ about** узнать (*perf*) о +*prp*; **as far as I ~** насколько мне известно; **yes, I ~** да, знаю; **I don't ~** не знаю.
know-all ['nəuɔːl] *n* (*BRIT: inf: pej*) всезнайка* *m/f*.
know-how ['nəuhau] *n* ноу-хау *nt ind*.
knowing ['nəuɪŋ] *adj* (*look*) понимающий.
knowingly ['nəuɪŋlɪ] *adv* (*purposely*) сознательно; (*smile, look*) понимающе.
know-it-all ['nəuɪtɔːl] *n* (*US*) = **know-all.**
knowledge ['nɔlɪdʒ] *n* (*abstract concept*) знание; (*things learnt*) знания *ntpl*; (*awareness*) представление; **to have no ~ of** не иметь (*impf*) никакого представления о +*prp*; **not to my ~** насколько мне известно – нет; **without my ~** без моего ведома; **to have a working ~ of Russian** неплохо владеть (*impf*) русским (языком); **it is common ~ that** ... общеизвестно, что ...; **it has come to my ~ that** ... мне стало известно, что ....
knowledgeable ['nɔlɪdʒəbl] *adj* знающий*; **he is very ~ about art** он большой знаток искусства.
known [nəun] *pp of* **know** ◆ *adj* (*thief, facts*) известный* (известен).
knuckle ['nʌkl] *n* костяшка*
▶ **knuckle down** *vi* браться* (взяться* *perf*) за дело
▶ **knuckle under** *vi* (*inf*) подчиняться (подчиниться *perf*).
knuckleduster ['nʌkldʌstə'] *n* кастет.
KO *n abbr* (= *knockout*) нокаут ◆ *vt* нокаутировать (*impf/perf*).
koala [kəu'ɑːlə] *n* (*also:* **~ bear**) коала *f ind*.
kook [kuːk] *n* (*US: inf*) помешанный(-ая) *m(f) adj*.
Koran [kɔ'rɑːn] *n*: **the ~** Коран.
Korea [kə'rɪə] *n* Корея; **North/South ~** Северная/Южная Корея.
Korean [kə'rɪən] *adj* корейский* ◆ *n* кореец(-еянка*).
kosher ['kəuʃə'] *adj* (*food*) кошерный.
kowtow ['kau'tau] *vi*: **to ~ to sb** заискивать (*impf*) *or* угодничать (*impf*) перед кем-н.
Kremlin ['krɛmlɪn] *n*: **the ~** Кремль* *m*.

KS *abbr* (*US*: *POST*) = *Kansas*.

Kt *abbr* (*BRIT*: *in titles*) = **knight**.

Kuala Lumpur ['kwɑ:lə'lumpuə'] *n* Куала-Лумпу́р.

kudos ['kju:dɔs] *n* прести́жность *f*.

Kurd [kə:d] *n* курд(ка*).

Kuwait [ku'weɪt] *n* Куве́йт.

Kuwaiti [ku'weɪtɪ] *adj* куве́йтский ◆ *n* жи́тель(ница) *m(f)* Куве́йта.

kW *abbr* (= **kilowatt**) кВт= *килова́тт*.

KY *abbr* (*US*: *POST*) = *Kentucky*.

~ L, l ~

L, l [εl] *n* (*letter*) 12-ая бу́ква англи́йского алфави́та.

L *abbr* (*BRIT: AUT.* = *learner*) уче́бная *f adj*; (= **lake**) о. = о́зеро; = **large, left**.

l. *abbr* (= *litre*) л = *литр*.

LA *n abbr* (*US*) = *Los Angeles* ◆ *abbr* (*POST*) = *Louisiana*.

lab [læb] *n abbr* = **laboratory**.

label ['leɪbl] *n* этике́тка*, ярлы́к; (*on suitcase*) би́рка*; (*also:* **record** ~) знак фи́рмы грамза́писи ◆ *vt* (*suitcase*) прикрепля́ть (прикрепи́ть* *perf*) би́рку к +*dat*; (*merchandise*) прикрепля́ть (прикрепи́ть* *perf*) ярлы́к на +*acc*; (*fig*) накле́ивать (накле́ить *perf*) ярлы́к на +*acc*.

labor *etc* ['leɪbə'] *n* (*US*) = **labour** *etc*.

laboratory [lə'bɔrətərɪ] *n* лаборато́рия.

Labor Day *n* (*US*) День* *m* Труда́.

laborious [lə'bɔːrɪəs] *adj* трудоёмкий* (трудоёмок).

labor union *n* (*US*) профсою́з.

labour ['leɪbə'] (*US* **labor**) *n* (*work*) труд*; (*workforce*) рабо́чая си́ла; (*MED*): **to be in** ~ рожа́ть (*impf*) ◆ *vi*: **to** ~ (**at sth**) труди́ться* (*impf*) (над чем-н) ◆ *vt*: **to** ~ **the point** входи́ть* (*impf*) в изли́шние подро́бности; **L~, the L~ Party** (*BRIT*) лейбори́сты *mpl*, Лейбори́стская Па́ртия; **hard** ~ ка́торжные рабо́ты *pl*.

labour camp *n* исправи́тельно-трудово́й ла́герь* *m*.

labour cost *n* сто́имость *f* рабо́чей си́лы.

labour dispute *n* трудово́й конфли́кт.

laboured ['leɪbəd] *adj* (*breathing, movement*) затруднённый (затруднён); (*style, joke*) вы́мученный (вы́мучен).

labourer ['leɪbərə'] *n* (неквалифици́рованный) рабо́чий *m adj*; **farm** ~ се́льско-хозя́йственный рабо́чий.

labour force *n* рабо́чая си́ла.

labour-intensive [leɪbərɪn'tɛnsɪv] *adj* трудоёмкий* (трудоёмок).

labour market *n* ры́нок* труда́.

labour pains *npl* родовы́е схва́тки *fpl*.

labour relations *npl* трудовы́е отноше́ния *ntpl*.

labour-saving ['leɪbəseɪvɪŋ] *adj* облегча́ющий

труд.

labour unrest *n* рабо́чие волне́ния *ntpl*.

laburnum [lə'bəːnəm] *n* (*BOT*) золото́й дождь* *m*.

labyrinth ['læbɪrɪnθ] *n* лабири́нт.

lace [leɪs] *n* (*fabric*) кру́жево*; (*of shoe*) шнуро́к* ◆ *vt* (*shoe: also:* ~ **up**) шнурова́ть (зашнурова́ть *perf*); **I ~d his coffee with arsenic** я подмеша́л в его́ ко́фе мышья́к.

lacemaking ['leɪsmeɪkɪŋ] *n* плете́ние кру́жев.

lacerate ['læsəreɪt] *vt* раздира́ть (разодра́ть* *perf*).

laceration [læsə'reɪʃən] *n* рва́ная ра́на.

lace-up ['leɪsʌp] *adj* шнуро́ванный.

lack [læk] *n* (*absence*) отсу́тствие; (*shortage*) недоста́ток*, нехва́тка ◆ *vt*: **she** ~**ed self-confidence** ей не хвата́ло *or* не достава́ло уве́ренности в себе́; **he is** ~**ing in experience** ему́ не хвата́ет *or* не достаёт о́пыта; **through** *or* **for** ~ **of** из-за недоста́тка +*gen*.

lackadaisical [lækə'deɪzɪkl] *adj* вя́лый (вял).

lackey ['lækɪ] *n* (*pej*) лаке́й.

lacklustre ['læklʌstə'] (*US* **lackluster**) *adj* ту́склый* (тускл).

laconic [lə'kɔnɪk] *adj* лакони́чный* (лакони́чен).

lacquer ['lækə'] *n* лак*.

lacrosse [lə'krɔs] *n* (*SPORT*) лакро́сс.

lacy ['leɪsɪ] *adj* кружевно́й.

lad [læd] *n* па́рень* *m*.

ladder ['lædə'] *n* (*also fig*) ле́стница; (*BRIT: in tights*) спусти́вшиеся пе́тли *fpl* ◆ *vti*: **I've** ~**ed my tights, my tights have** ~**ed** у меня́ пе́тли на колго́тках спусти́лись.

laden ['leɪdn] *adj*: **to be** ~ (**with**) ломи́ться (*impf*) от +*gen*; (*person*): ~ (**with**) нагру́женный (нагру́жен) (+*instr*); **fully** ~ по́лностью нагру́женный; **the trees were** ~ **with fruit** дере́вья ломи́лись от плодо́в.

ladle ['leɪdl] *n* поло́вник ◆ *vt* (*soup, stew*) разлива́ть (разли́ть* *perf*)

▶ **ladle out** *vt* (*advice, money*) раздава́ть* (разда́ть* *perf*) напра́во и нале́во.

Ladoga ['lædəgə] *n*: **Lake** ~ Ла́дожское о́зеро.

lady ['leɪdɪ] *n* да́ма; (*BRIT: title*) ле́ди *f ind*; **ladies and gentlemen ...** да́мы и господа́ ...; **young** ~

---

* marks translations which have irregular inflections. The Russian-English side of the dictionary gives inflectional information.

молода́я же́нщина; (*younger*) де́вушка*; **old ~** пожила́я же́нщина; **the ladies' (room)** же́нский туале́т.
ladybird ['leɪdɪbə:d] *n* бо́жья коро́вка.
ladybug ['leɪdɪbʌg] *n* (*US*) = **ladybird**.
lady-in-waiting ['leɪdɪn'weɪtɪŋ] *n* фре́йлина.
lady-killer ['leɪdɪkɪlə'] *n* (*fig*) сердцее́д.
ladylike ['leɪdɪlaɪk] *adj* элега́нтный* (элега́нтен).
ladyship ['leɪdɪʃɪp] *n*: **your ~** Ва́ша ми́лость *f*.
lag [læg] *n* (*period of time*) заде́ржка ♦ *vi* (*also*: **~ behind**: *person*) тащи́ться* (*impf*) (позади́); (: *trade, investment*) отстава́ть* (отста́ть* *perf*) ♦ *vt* (*pipes etc*) покрыва́ть (покры́ть* *perf*) теплоизоля́цией; **old ~** (*inf*: *prisoner*) рецидиви́ст; **to ~ behind** (*trade, development*) отстава́ть* (отста́ть* *perf*) от +*gen*.
lager ['lɑ:gə'] *n* све́тлое пи́во.
lager lout *n* (*inf*) пья́ная шпана́ *f no pl*.
lagging ['lægɪŋ] *n* (*for pipes*) теплоизоля́ция.
lagoon [lə'gu:n] *n* лагу́на.
Lagos ['leɪgɔs] *n* Ла́гос.
laid [leɪd] *pt, pp of* **lay**.
laid-back [leɪd'bæk] *adj* (*inf*) споко́йный* (споко́ен).
laid up *adj*: **~ ~ (with)** прико́ванный (прико́ван) к посте́ли (+*instr*).
lain [leɪn] *pp of* **lie**.
lair [lɛə'] *n* ло́гово, ло́говище.
laissez faire [lɛseɪ'fɛə'] *n* (*ECON*) экономи́ческое невмеша́тельство.
laity ['leɪətɪ] *n or npl* (*REL*) миря́не *mpl*; (*non-professionals*) не профессиона́лы *mpl*.
lake [leɪk] *n* о́зеро*.
Lake District *n* (*BRIT*): **the ~ ~** Озёрный край.
lamb [læm] *n* (*ZOOL*) ягнёнок*; (*CULIN*) (молода́я) бара́нина.
lambada [læm'bɑ:də] *n* ламба́да.
lamb chop *n* бара́нья котле́та.
lambskin ['læmskɪn] *n* овчи́на.
lambswool ['læmzwul] *n* поя́рок* ♦ *cpd* поя́рковый.
lame [leɪm] *adj* (*person, animal*) хромо́й* (хром); (*excuse, argument*) сла́бый* (слаб).
lame duck *n* неуда́чник(-ица).
lamely ['leɪmlɪ] *adv* неубеди́тельно.
lament [lə'mɛnt] *n* плач ♦ *vt* опла́кивать (опла́кать* *perf*).
lamentable ['læməntəbl] *adj* плаче́вный* (плаче́вен).
laminated ['læmɪneɪtɪd] *adj* (*layered*) сло́истый; (*plastic coated*) с пла́стиковым покры́тием.
lamp [læmp] *n* (*electric, gas, oil*) ла́мпа; (*street lamp*) фона́рь* *m*.
lamplight ['læmplaɪt] *n*: **by ~** (*indoors*) при све́те ла́мпы.
lampoon [læm'pu:n] *n* па́сквиль *m* ♦ *vt* писа́ть* (написа́ть* *perf*) па́сквиль на +*acc*.
lamppost ['læmppəust] *n* (*BRIT*) фона́рный столб*.
lampshade ['læmpʃeɪd] *n* абажу́р.

lance [lɑ:ns] *n* пи́ка ♦ *vt* (*MED*) вскрыва́ть (вскрыть* *perf*).
lance corporal *n* (*BRIT*) мла́дший* капра́л.
lancet ['lɑ:nsɪt] *n* ланце́т.
Lancs [læŋks] *abbr* (*BRIT*: *POST*) = **Lancashire**.
land [lænd] *n* земля́*; (*not sea*) су́ша; (*country*) страна́* ♦ *vi* (*from ship*) выса́живаться (вы́садиться* *perf*); (*AVIAT*) приземля́ться (приземли́ться* *perf*); (*fig*: *arrive unexpectedly*) очути́ться* (*perf*) ♦ *vt* (*plane*) посади́ть* (*perf*); (*passengers*) выса́живать (вы́садить* *perf*); (*goods*) выгружа́ть (вы́грузить* *perf*); **to own ~** владе́ть (*impf*) землёй; **to go by ~** е́хать*/е́здить* (*impf*) по су́ше; **he always ~s on his feet** (*fig*) в конце́ концо́в ему́ везёт; **she ~ed (herself) a good job** (*inf*) она́ доби́лась хоро́шей рабо́ты; **to ~ sb with sth** (*inf*) нава́ливать (навали́ть* *perf*) что-н на кого́-н
▸ **land up** *vi*: **to ~ up (in/at)** очути́ться* (*perf*) (в/на +*prp*).
landed gentry ['lændɪd-] *n* земле-владе́льческая аристокра́тия.
landfill site ['lændfɪl-] *n* ме́сто захороне́ния отхо́дов.
landing ['lændɪŋ] *n* (*of house*) ле́стничная площа́дка*; (*of plane*) поса́дка*, приземле́ние.
landing card *n* ка́рта, заполня́емая прибыва́ющими в страну́ иностра́нцами.
landing craft *n inv* деса́нтное су́дно*.
landing gear *n* (*AVIAT*) шасси́ *nt ind*.
landing stage *n* при́стань* *f*.
landing strip *n* взлётно-поса́дочная полоса́*.
landlady ['lændleɪdɪ] *n* (*of house, flat*) домовладе́лица, хозя́йка*; (*of pub*) хозя́йка*.
landlocked ['lændlɔkt] *adj* без вы́хода к мо́рю.
landlord ['lændlɔ:d] *n* (*of house, flat*) домовладе́лец*, хозя́ин*; (*of pub*) хозя́ин*.
landlubber ['lændlʌbə'] *n*: **to be a ~** не люби́ть (*impf*) путеше́ствовать мо́рем.
landmark ['lændmɑ:k] *n* (назе́мный) ориенти́р; (*fig*) ве́ха.
landowner ['lændəunə'] *n* землевладе́лец (-лица).
landscape ['lænskeɪp] *n* (*view, painting*) пейза́ж; (*terrain*) ландша́фт ♦ *vt*: **to ~ an area** (иску́сственно) создава́ть* (созда́ть* *perf*) ландша́фт.
landscape architect *n* = **landscape gardener**.
landscape gardener *n* ландша́фтный архите́ктор.
landscape painting *n* (*picture*) пейза́ж; (*art*) пейза́жная жи́вопись *f*.
landslide ['lændslaɪd] *n* (*GEO*) о́ползень* *m*; (*POL*: *also*: **~ victory**) реши́тельная побе́да.
lane [leɪn] *n* (*in country*) тропи́нка*; (*in town*) переу́лок*; (*of carriageway*) полоса́*; (*SPORT*) доро́жка*; **shipping ~** морска́я тра́сса.
language ['læŋgwɪdʒ] *n* язы́к*; **bad ~** скверносло́вие.

language laboratory *n* лингафо́нный кабине́т.

languid ['læŋgwɪd] *adj* то́мный* (то́мен).

languish ['læŋgwɪʃ] *vi* (*person*) томи́ться* (истоми́ться* *perf*); (*project, case*) тяну́ться* (*impf*).

lank [læŋk] *adj* (*hair*) дли́нный* и са́льный*.

lanky ['læŋkɪ] *adj* долгов́язый (долгов́яз).

lanolin(e) ['lænəlɪn] *n* ланоли́н.

lantern ['læntən] *n* фона́рь* *m*.

Laos [laus] *n* Лао́с.

lap [læp] *n* коле́ни* *ntpl*; (*SPORT*) круг* ♦ *vt* (*also*: ~ **up**) лака́ть (вы́лакать *perf*) ♦ *vi* (*water*) плеска́ться* (*impf*); **in his/my** ~ у него́/меня́ на коле́нях

▶ **lap up** *vt* (*fig: flattery*) упива́ться (упи́ться* *perf*) +*instr*.

La Paz [læ'pæz] *n* Ла-Па́с.

lapdog ['læpdɔg] *n* боло́нка*.

lapel [lə'pɛl] *n* ла́цкан.

Lapland ['læplænd] *n* Лапла́ндия.

Lapp [læp] *adj* лапла́ндский ♦ *n* (*person*) лапла́ндец*(-дка), саа́м(ка); (*LING*) саа́мский язы́к*.

lapse [læps] *n* (*bad behaviour*) про́мах*; (*of time*) промежу́ток*; (*of concentration*) поте́ря ♦ *vi* (*law, membership*) теря́ть (потеря́ть *perf*) си́лу; **memory** ~ прова́л в па́мяти; **to** ~ **into bad habits** усва́ивать (усво́ить *perf*) дурны́е привы́чки.

lap-top ['læptɔp] *n*: ~ **computer** портати́вный компью́тер.

larceny ['lɑ:sənɪ] *n* (*esp US*) воровство́.

larch [lɑ:tʃ] *n* ли́ственница.

lard [lɑ:d] *n* свино́й жир*.

larder [lɑ:də'] *n* кладова́я *f adj*.

large [lɑ:dʒ] *adj* большо́й; (*major*) кру́пный*; **to make** ~**r** увели́чивать (увели́чить *perf*); **this coat is too** ~ **for me** э́то пальто́ мне велико́; **a** ~ **number of people** большо́е число́ люде́й; **on a** ~ **scale** в кру́пном масшта́бе; **at** ~ (*as a whole*) в це́лом; (*at liberty*) на во́ле; **by and** ~ вообще́.

largely ['lɑ:dʒlɪ] *adv* по бо́льшей ча́сти; ~ **because ...** в основно́м, потому́ что ....

large-scale ['lɑ:dʒ'skeɪl] *adj* крупномасшта́бный.

largesse [lɑ:'ʒɛs] *n* ще́дрость* *f*.

lark [lɑ:k] *n* (*bird*) жа́воронок*; (*BRIT: inf: joke*) прока́за

▶ **lark about** *vi* (*BRIT: inf*) прока́зничать (напрока́зничать *perf*).

larva ['lɑ:və] (*pl* ~**e**) *n* личи́нка.

larvae ['lɑ:vi:] *npl of* **larva**.

laryngitis [lærɪn'dʒaɪtɪs] *n* ларинги́т.

larynx ['lærɪŋks] *n* горта́нь *f*.

lasagne [lə'zænjə] *n* лаза́нья (*италья́нское блю́до*).

lascivious [lə'sɪvɪəs] *adj* похотли́вый (похотли́в).

laser ['leɪzə'] *n* ла́зер.

laser beam *n* ла́зерный луч*.

laser printer *n* ла́зерный при́нтер.

lash [læʃ] *n* (*eyelash*) ресни́ца; (*of whip*) уда́р (*хлыста́*) ♦ *vt* (*whip*) хлеста́ть* (*impf*), стега́ть (*impf*); (*also*: ~ **against**: *subj: rain, wind*) хлеста́ть* (*impf*) о +*acc*; (*tie*): **to** ~ **to** привя́зывать (привяза́ть* *perf*) к +*dat*; **to** ~ **together** свя́зывать (связа́ть* *perf*)

▶ **lash down** *vt* привя́зывать (привяза́ть* *perf*) ♦ *vi* (*rain*) хлеста́ть* (*impf*)

▶ **lash out** *vi*: **to** ~ **out at** (*also fig*) наки́дываться (наки́нуться* *perf*) на +*acc*; **to** ~ **out (on sth)** (*inf*) разоря́ться (разори́ться* *perf*) (на что-н.)

lashing ['læʃɪŋ] *n*: ~**s of** (*BRIT: inf: cream etc*) ку́ча +*gen*.

lass [læs] *n* (*BRIT: girl*) де́вочка*; (: *young woman*) де́вушка*.

lasso [læ'su:] *n* лассо́ *nt ind*, арка́н ♦ *vt* аркани́ть (заарка́нить *perf*).

last [lɑ:st] *adj* (*most recent*) про́шлый; (*final*) после́дний* ♦ *adv* в после́дний раз; (*finally*) в конце́ ♦ *vi* (*continue*) дли́ться (продли́ться *perf*), продолжа́ться (продо́лжиться* *perf*); (*keep: thing*) сохраня́ться (сохрани́ться *perf*); (: *person*) держа́ться (продержа́ться* *perf*); (*suffice*): **we had enough money to** ~ **us** нам хвати́ло де́нег; ~ **year** в про́шлом году́; ~ **week** на про́шлой неде́ле; ~ **night** (*early*) вчера́ ве́чером; (*late*) про́шлой но́чью; **at** ~ наконе́ц; ~ **but one** предпосле́дний*; **the** ~ **time** в после́дний раз; **the film** ~**s (for) 2 hours** фильм дли́тся 2 часа́.

last-ditch ['lɑ:st'dɪtʃ] *adj* (*attempt*) отча́янный*.

lasting ['lɑ:stɪŋ] *adj* (*friendship*) продолжи́тельный* (продолжи́телен), дли́тельный* (дли́телен); (*solution*) долговре́менный* (долговре́менен).

lastly ['lɑ:stlɪ] *adv* наконе́ц.

last-minute ['lɑ:stmɪnɪt] *adj* (*attempt*) сде́ланный в после́днюю мину́ту; (*details, meeting*) после́дний*.

latch [lætʃ] *n* (*on gate*) задви́жка*; (*on front door*) замо́к* *m*; **to leave the door on the** ~ оставля́ть (оста́вить* *perf*) замо́к на предохрани́теле

▶ **latch on to** *vt fus* (*person*) прилипа́ть (прили́пнуть *perf*) к +*dat*; (*idea*) привя́зываться (привяза́ться* *perf*) к +*dat*.

latchkey ['lætʃki:] *n* ключ от замка́ (*к вхо́дной две́ри*).

latchkey child *n* ребёнок, находя́щийся до́ма в то вре́мя когда́ роди́тели рабо́тают.

late [leɪt] *adj* (*far on in time, process, work etc*) по́здний*; (*former*) бы́вший*; (*dead*)

---

* marks translations which have irregular inflections. The Russian-English side of the dictionary gives inflectional information.

поко́йный ◆ *adv* по́здно; (*behind time*) с опозда́нием; **to be ~** опа́здывать (опозда́ть *perf*); **I was 10 minutes ~** я опозда́л на 10 мину́т; **in the ~ 1970s** к концу́ семидеся́тых годо́в; **he is in his ~ thirties** ему́ далеко́ за три́дцать; **in ~ May** в конце́ ма́я; **to work ~** рабо́тать (*impf*) допоздна́; **~ in life** в пожило́м во́зрасте; **of ~** в после́днее вре́мя.

latecomer ['leɪtkʌmə'] *n* опозда́вший(-ая)*m(f) adj.*

lately ['leɪtlɪ] *adv* в после́днее вре́мя.

lateness ['leɪtnɪs] *n* опозда́ние; **owing to the ~ of the hour** из-за по́зднего ча́са.

latent ['leɪtnt] *adj* скры́тый (скрыт); **~ defect** скры́тый дефе́кт.

later ['leɪtə'] *adj* (*time, date*) бо́лее по́здний*; (*meeting, version*) после́дующий* ◆ *adv* по́зже, поздне́е; **~ on** в после́дствии, пото́м; **he arrived ~ than me** он пришёл по́зже меня́.

lateral ['lætərl] *adj* боково́й; **~ thinking** нестанда́ртное мы́шление.

latest ['leɪtɪst] *adj* са́мый по́здний*; (*most recent*) (са́мый) но́вый *or* после́дний*; (*news*) после́дний*; **at the ~** са́мое по́зднее.

latex ['leɪteks] *n* ла́текс.

lathe [leɪð] *n* тока́рный стано́к*.

lather ['lɑ:ðə'] *n* (мы́льная) пе́на ◆ *vt* мы́лить (намы́лить *perf*).

Latin ['lætɪn] *n* (*LING*) лати́нский* язы́к*; (*person*) жи́тель(ница) *m(f)* ю́жной Евро́пы ◆ *adj*: **~ languages** рома́нские языки́; **~ countries** стра́ны ю́жной Евро́пы.

Latin America *n* Лати́нская Аме́рика.

Latin American *adj* латиноамерика́нский ◆ *n* латиноамерика́нец*(-а́нка*).

latitude ['lætɪtju:d] *n* (*GEO*) широта́*; (*fig*) свобо́да.

latrine [lə'tri:n] *n* отхо́жее ме́сто*.

latter ['lætə'] *adj* после́дний* ◆ *n*: **the ~** после́дний*(-яя) *m(f)*; **the ~ part of the week** втора́я полови́на неде́ли.

latter-day ['lætədeɪ] *adj* совреме́нный.

latterly ['lætəlɪ] *adv* неда́вно, в после́днее вре́мя.

lattice ['lætɪs] *n* решётка*.

lattice window *n* решётчатое окно́*.

Latvia ['lætvɪə] *n* Ла́твия.

Latvian ['lætvɪən] *adj* латви́йский ◆ *n* латы́ш(ка); (*LING*) латы́шский язы́к*.

laudable ['lɔ:dəbl] *adj* похва́льный* (похва́лен).

laudatory ['lɔ:dətrɪ] *adj* хвале́бный* (хвале́бен).

laugh [lɑ:f] *n* смех* ◆ *vi* смея́ться* (*impf*); **(to do sth) for a ~** (*inf*) (де́лать (*impf*) что-н) для сме́ха

► **laugh at** *vt fus* смея́ться* (посмея́ться *perf*) над +*instr*

► **laugh off** *vt*: **to ~ sth off** отде́лываться (отде́латься *perf*) от чего́-н шу́ткой.

laughable ['lɑ:fəbl] *adj* смехотво́рный*

(смехотво́рен).

laughing gas ['lɑ:fɪŋ-] *n* веселя́щий газ*.

laughing matter *n*: **this is no ~ ~** э́то де́ло нешу́точное.

laughing stock *n* посме́шище; **to be the ~ ~ of** служи́ть (*impf*) посме́шищем для +*gen*.

laughter ['lɑ:ftə'] *n* смех*.

launch [lɔ:ntʃ] *n* (*of rocket, product*) за́пуск; (*motorboat*) мото́рный ка́тер* ◆ *vt* (*ship*) спуска́ть (спусти́ть* *perf*) на́ воду; (*rocket*) запуска́ть (запусти́ть* *perf*); (*campaign, attack*) начина́ть (нача́ть* *perf*); (*product*) пуска́ть (пусти́ть* *perf*) в прода́жу

► **launch into** *vt fus* (*speech, activity*) пуска́ться (пусти́ться* *perf*) в +*acc*

► **launch out** *vi*: **to ~ out into** бра́ться* (взя́ться* *perf*) за +*acc.*

launching ['lɔ:ntʃɪŋ] *n* (*of ship*) спуск (на́ воду); (*of rocket, product*) за́пуск; (*of campaign, attack*) нача́ло.

launch(ing) pad *n* ста́ртовая площа́дка*.

launder ['lɔ:ndə'] *vt* (*clothes, sheets*) стира́ть (вы́стирать *perf*); (*money*) отмыва́ть (отмы́ть* *perf*).

Launderette® [lɔ:n'drɛt] *n* (*BRIT*) пра́чечная *f adj* самообслу́живания.

Laundromat® ['lɔ:ndrəmæt] *n* (*US*) = **Launderette®**.

laundry ['lɔ:ndrɪ] *n* (*washing*) сти́рка; (*place*) пра́чечная *f adj*; **to do the ~** стира́ть (вы́стирать *perf*).

laureate ['lɔ:rɪət] *adj see* **poet laureate.**

laurel ['lɔrl] *n* (*tree*) лавр, ла́вровое де́рево; **to rest on one's ~s** почива́ть (почи́ть* *perf*) на ла́врах.

Lausanne [ləu'zæn] *n* Лоза́нна.

lava ['lɑ:və] *n* ла́ва.

lavatory ['lævətərɪ] *n* туале́т.

lavatory paper *n* туале́тная бума́га.

lavender ['lævəndə'] *n* лава́нда.

lavish ['lævɪʃ] *adj* (*amount, hospitality*) ще́дрый* (щедр); (*meal*) оби́льный* (оби́лен); (*surroundings*) пы́шный* (пы́шен); (*person*): **~ with** ще́дрый* (щедр) на +*acc* ◆ *vt*: **to ~ sth on sb** осыпа́ть (осы́пать* *perf*) кого́-н чем-н.

lavishly ['lævɪʃlɪ] *adv* (*generously*) ще́дро; (*sumptuously*) пы́шно.

law [lɔ:] *n* зако́н; (*professions*): **(the) ~** юриспруде́нция; (*SCOL*) пра́во; **it's against the ~** э́то противозако́нно; **to study ~** изуча́ть (*impf*) пра́во; **to go to ~** обраща́ться (обрати́ться* *perf*) в суд; **to break the ~** наруша́ть (нару́шить *perf*) зако́н.

law-abiding ['lɔ:əbaɪdɪŋ] *adj* законопослу́шный.

law and order *n* правопоря́док*.

lawbreaker ['lɔ:breɪkə'] *n* правонаруши́тель-(ница) *m(f)*.

law court *n* суд*.

lawful ['lɔ:ful] *adj* зако́нный.

lawfully ['lɔ:fəlɪ] *adv* зако́нно.
lawless ['lɔ:lɪs] *adj* (*action*) беззако́нный.
Law Lord *n* (*BRIT*) член пала́ты ло́рдов, состоя́щий в апелляцио́нном суде́.
lawmaker ['lɔ:meɪkə'] *n* законода́тель(ница) *m(f)*.
lawn [lɔ:n] *n* газо́н.
lawn mower ['lɔ:nməuə'] *n* газонокоси́лка*.
lawn tennis *n* те́ннис (*на травяно́м ко́рте*).
law school *n* (*US*) юриди́ческий институ́т.
law student *n* студе́нт(ка) юриди́ческого факульте́та.
lawsuit ['lɔ:su:t] *n* суде́бный иск.
lawyer ['lɔ:jə'] *n* (*solicitor, barrister*) адвока́т; (*legal specialist*) юри́ст.
lax [læks] *adj* (*discipline, standards*) нестро́гий (нестро́г); (*morals, behaviour*) распу́щенный (распу́щен).
laxative ['læksətɪv] *n* слаби́тельное *nt adj*.
laxity ['læksɪtɪ] *n* небре́жность *f*; (*moral*) распу́щенность *f*.
lay [leɪ] (*pt, pp* **laid**) *pt of* **lie** ♦ *adj* (*REL*) мирско́й; (*not expert*) непрофессиона́льный ♦ *vt* (*place*) класть* (положи́ть* *perf*); (*table*) накрыва́ть (накры́ть* *perf*) (на +*acc*); (*carpet*) стлать (настла́ть *or* настели́ть* *perf*); (*cable*) прокла́дывать (проложи́ть* *perf*); (*plans*) составля́ть (соста́вить* *perf*); (*trap*) ста́вить* (поста́вить* *perf*); (: *fig*) подстра́ивать (подстро́ить* *perf*); (*egg*) откла́дывать (отложи́ть* *perf*); **to ~ facts/proposals before sb** излага́ть (изложи́ть* *perf*) фа́кты/предложе́ния пе́ред кем-н; **to ~ one's hands on sth** (*inf*) достава́ть* (доста́ть* *perf*) что-н; **to get laid** (*inf!*) тра́хаться (тра́хнуться *perf*) (*!*)
► **lay aside** *vt* откла́дывать (отложи́ть* *perf*)
► **lay by** *vt* = **lay aside**
► **lay down** *vt* (*object*) класть* (положи́ть* *perf*); (*rules, laws*) устана́вливать (установи́ть* *perf*); (*weapons*) скла́дывать (сложи́ть* *perf*); **to ~ down the law** прика́зывать (*impf*); **to ~ down one's life** положи́ть* (*perf*) жизнь
► **lay in** *vt* (*supplies*) запаса́ть (запасти́* *perf*)
► **lay into** *vt fus* (*also fig*) набра́сываться (набро́ситься* *perf*) на +*acc*
► **lay off** *vt* (*workers*) увольня́ть (уво́лить *perf*)
► **lay on** *vt* (*meal, entertainment*) устра́ивать (устро́ить *perf*); (*water, gas*) прокла́дывать (проложи́ть* *perf*); (*paint*) наноси́ть* (нанести́* *perf*)
► **lay out** *vt* раскла́дывать (разложи́ть* *perf*); (*inf*): **to ~ out money on sth** выкла́дывать (вы́ложить* *perf*) де́ньги на что-н
► **lay up** *vt* (*ship*) ста́вить* (поста́вить* *perf*) на прико́л; (*sick person*): **to be laid up with** валя́ться (*impf*) с +*instr*; **the car was laid up all**

year маши́на простоя́ла весь год.
layabout ['leɪəbaut] *n* (*inf*) безде́льник(-ица).
lay-by ['leɪbaɪ] *n* (*BRIT*) площа́дка для вре́менной стоя́нки (*на автодоро́ге*).
lay days *npl* (*NAUT*) сталийное вре́мя* *ntsg*.
layer ['leɪə'] *n* слой*.
layette [leɪ'ɛt] *n* прида́ное *nt adj* (*для новорождённого*).
layman ['leɪmən] *irreg n* (*non-expert*) неспециали́ст.
lay-off ['leɪɔf] *n* увольне́ние.
layout ['leɪaut] *n* (*of garden, building*) планиро́вка*; (*of page*) компано́вка*.
laze [leɪz] *vi* (*also:* **~ about**) безде́льничать (*impf*); **to ~ about in bed/the sun** не́житься (*impf*) в посте́ли/на со́лнце.
laziness ['leɪzɪnɪs] *n* лень *f*.
lazy ['leɪzɪ] *adj* лени́вый (лени́в).
LB *abbr* (*CANADA*) = **Labrador**.
lb. *abbr* (= *pound (weight)*) фунт.
lbw *abbr* (*CRICKET*) = **leg before wicket**.
LC *n abbr* (*US*) = **Library of Congress**.
lc *abbr* (*TYP*: = *lower case*) строчна́я бу́ква.
L/C *abbr* (= *letter of credit*) аккредити́в.
LCD *n abbr* = **liquid crystal display**.
Ld *abbr* (*BRIT*: *in titles*) = **lord**.
LDS *n abbr* (*BRIT*: = *Licentiate in Dental Surgery*) лице́нзия на стоматологи́ческую пра́ктику ♦ *abbr* = *Latter-day Saints*) „Святы́е после́днего дня" (*официа́льное назва́ние се́кты мормо́нов*).
LEA *n abbr* (*BRIT*: = *Local Education Authority*) ме́стное управле́ние по дела́м просвеще́ния.
lead[1] [li:d] (*pt, pp* **led**) *n* (*front position*) пе́рвенство, ли́дерство; (*clue*) нить *f*; (*in play, film*) гла́вная роль *f*; (*for dog*) поводо́к*; (*ELEC*) про́вод* ♦ *vt* (*competition, market*) лиди́ровать (*impf*) в +*prp*; (*opponent*) опережа́ть (*impf*); (*person, group: guide*) вести́* (повести́* *perf*); (*activity, organization etc*) руководи́ть* (*impf*) +*instr*, возглавля́ть (возгла́вить* *perf*) ♦ *vi* (*road, pipe etc*) вести́* (*impf*); (*SPORT*) лиди́ровать (*impf*); **to take the ~** (*SPORT*) выходи́ть* (вы́йти* *perf*) вперёд; (*fig*) брать* (взять* *perf*) на себя́ веду́щую роль; **to ~ the way** (*also fig*) ука́зывать (указа́ть* *perf*) путь; **to ~ sb astray** вводи́ть* (ввести́* *perf*) кого́-н в заблужде́ние; **to ~ sb to do** приводи́ть* (привести́* *perf*) кого́-н к чему́-н; **to ~ sb to believe that ...** дава́ть* (дать* *perf*) кому́-н поня́ть, что ...; **to ~ an interesting life** вести́* (*impf*) интере́сную жизнь; **to ~ an orchestra** (*BRIT*) исполня́ть (испо́лнить *perf*) пе́рвую скри́пку
► **lead away** *vt* уводи́ть* (увести́* *perf*)
► **lead back** *vt* приводи́ть* (привести́* *perf*) обра́тно
► **lead into** *vt fus* вводи́ть* (ввести́* *perf*) в +*acc*

---

* marks translations which have irregular inflections. The Russian-English side of the dictionary gives inflectional information.

► **lead off** *vi* (*in game, conversation*) начина́ть (нача́ть *perf*); (*road, corridor*) отходи́ть* (*impf*) ♦ *vt fus* отходи́ть* (*impf*) от +*gen*
► **lead on** *vt* (*tease*) води́ть* (*impf*) за́ нос
► **lead out of** *vt fus* выводи́ть* (вы́вести* *perf*) из +*gen*
► **lead to** *vt fus* вести́* (привести́* *perf*) к +*dat*
► **lead up to** *vt fus* (*events*) приводи́ть* (привести́* *perf*) к +*dat*; (*topic*) подводи́ть* (подвести́* *perf*) к +*dat*.
lead² [lɛd] *n* (*metal*) свине́ц*; (*in pencil*) графи́т.
leaded ['lɛdɪd] *adj* (*window, glass*) со свинцо́выми крепле́ниями; (*petrol*) содержа́щий свине́ц.
leaden ['lɛdn] *adj* (*sky, sea*) свинцо́вый; (*movements*) ско́ванный (ско́ван).
leader ['li:dəʳ] *n* (*of group, SPORT*) ли́дер; (*in newspaper*) передова́я статья́; **the L~ of the House (of Commons/Lords)** (*BRIT*) *представи́тель пра́вящей па́ртии в пала́те Общин/Ло́рдов, наделённый осо́быми полномо́чиями*.
leadership ['li:dəʃɪp] *n* (*position, process*) руково́дство; (*quality*) ли́дерские ка́чества *ntpl*.
lead-free ['lɛdfri:] *adj* (*petrol*) не содержа́щий свинца́.
leading ['li:dɪŋ] *adj* (*most important*) веду́щий*; (*first, front*) пере́дний*; (*winning*) лиди́рующий; **~ role** (*in film, play*) гла́вная роль *f*.
leading lady *n* (*THEAT*) исполни́тельница гла́вной ро́ли.
leading light *n* (*person*) свети́ло.
leading man *irreg n* (*THEAT*) исполни́тель *m* гла́вной ро́ли.
leading question *n* наводя́щий* вопро́с.
lead pencil [lɛd-] *n* гри́фельный каранда́ш*.
lead poisoning [lɛd-] *n* отравле́ние свинцо́м.
lead singer [li:d-] *n* соли́ст(ка).
lead time [li:d-] *n* (*COMM*) вре́мя* *ntsg* реализа́ции зака́за.
lead-up ['li:dʌp] *n*: **in the ~ to** незадо́лго до +*gen*.
leaf [li:f] (*pl* **leaves**) *n* (*BOT, of book*) лист*; (*of table*) откидна́я доска́* ♦ *vi*: **to ~ through** листа́ть (пролиста́ть *perf*); **to turn over a new ~** (*perf*) но́вую жизнь; **to take a ~ out of sb's book** сле́довать (после́довать *perf*) приме́ру кого́-н.
leaflet ['li:flɪt] *n* листо́вка*.
leafy ['li:fɪ] *adj* (*trees, vegetables*) покры́тый (покры́т) листво́й; (*place*) зелёный* (зе́лен).
league [li:g] *n* ли́га; **to be in ~ with sb** быть* (*impf*) в сго́воре с кем-н.
league table *n* (*BRIT: SPORT*) табли́ца результа́тов спортклу́бов одно́й из лиг; (*fig: of wages, prices*) сравни́тельная табли́ца.
leak [li:k] *n* (*hole*) течь *f*; (*seepage*) уте́чка*; (*fig*): **(information) ~** уте́чка* информа́ции ♦

vi (*pipe, roof, shoes*) протека́ть (проте́чь* *perf*); (*ship*) дава́ть* (дать* *perf*) течь; (*liquid, gas*) проса́чиваться (просочи́ться *perf*) ♦ *vt* (*information*) разглаша́ть (разгласи́ть* *perf*)
► **leak out** *vi* (*liquid*) вытека́ть (вы́течь* *perf*); (*information*) проса́чиваться (просочи́ться *perf*).
leakage ['li:kɪdʒ] *n* уте́чка*.
leaky ['li:kɪ] *adj* (*roof etc*) дыря́вый, проху́дившийся.
lean [li:n] (*pt, pp* **leaned** *or* **leant**) *adj* (*person*) поджа́рый (поджа́р); (*meat*) по́стный; (*period*) ску́дный* (ску́ден) ♦ *vt*: **to ~ sth on** *or* **against sth** прислоня́ть (прислони́ть* *perf*) что-н к чему́-н ♦ *vi*: **to ~ (forward/back)** наклоня́ться (наклони́ться* *perf*) (вперёд/наза́д); **to ~ against** (*wall*) прислоня́ться (прислони́ться* *perf*) к +*dat*; (*person*) опира́ться (опере́ться* *perf*) на +*acc*; **to ~ on** (*chair*) опира́ться (опере́ться* *perf*) о +*acc*; (*rely on*) опира́ться (опере́ться* *perf*) на +*acc*; (*pressurize*) нажима́ть (нажа́ть* *perf*) на +*acc*; **to ~ towards** (*idea, belief*) склоня́ться (склони́ться* *perf*) к +*dat*
► **lean out** *vi*: **to ~ out (of)** высо́вываться (вы́сунуться *perf*) (из +*gen*)
► **lean over** *vi* наклоня́ться (наклони́ться* *perf*).
leaning ['li:nɪŋ] *n*: **~ (towards)** скло́нность *f* (к +*dat*).
leant [lɛnt] *pt, pp of* **lean**.
lean-to ['li:ntu:] *n* пристро́йка*.
leap [li:p] (*pt, pp* **leaped** *or* **leapt**) *n* прыжо́к*, скачо́к*; (*increase*) скачо́к* ♦ *vi* пры́гать (пры́гнуть *perf*); (*price, number*) подска́кивать (подскочи́ть *perf*); **to ~ at** (*offer, opportunity*) ухвати́ться* (*perf*) за +*acc*; **to ~ to one's feet** вска́кивать (вскочи́ть *perf*) на́ ноги
► **leap up** *vi* подпры́гивать (подпры́гнуть *perf*).
leapfrog ['li:pfrɒg] *n* чехарда́.
leapt [lɛpt] *pt, pp of* **leap**.
leap year *n* високо́сный год*.
learn [lə:n] (*pt, pp* **learned** *or* **learnt**) *vt* (*skill*) учи́ться* (научи́ться* *perf*) +*dat*; (*facts, poem*) учи́ть* (вы́учить* *perf*) ♦ *vi* учи́ться* (*impf*); **to ~ about** *or* **of/that ...** (*hear, read*) узнава́ть* (узна́ть* *perf*) о +*prp*/, что ...; **to ~ about sth** (*study*) изуча́ть (изучи́ть* *perf*) что-н; **to ~ (how) to do** учи́ться* (научи́ться* *perf*) +*impf infin*.
learned ['lə:nɪd] *adj* учёный.
learner ['lə:nəʳ] *n* учени́к*(-и́ца).
learning ['lə:nɪŋ] *n* учёность *f*; **person of ~** учёный челове́к.
learnt [lə:nt] *pt, pp of* **learn**.
lease [li:s] *n* аре́ндный догово́р ♦ *vt*: **to ~ sth (to sb)** сдава́ть* (сдать* *perf*) что-н в аре́нду (кому́-н); **to ~ sth from sb** арендова́ть (*impf/ perf*) *or* брать* (взять* *perf*) в аре́нду у кого́-н;

on ~ **(to sb)** сда́нный (сдан) в аре́нду (кому́-н)
► **lease back** vt сдава́ть* (сдать* perf) в аре́нду пре́жнему владе́льцу (*для мобилиза́ции де́нежных средств*).
leaseback ['li:sbæk] n сда́ча со́бственности в аре́нду её пре́жнему владе́льцу.
leasehold ['li:shəuld] n (also: ~ **property**) арендо́ванная со́бственность f ♦ adj арендо́ванный (арендо́ван).
leash [li:ʃ] n поводо́к*.
least [li:st] adj: **the** ~ (+noun: smallest) наиме́ньший*; (: slightest) мале́йший* ♦ adv (+vb) ме́ньше всего́; (+adj): **the** ~ наиме́нее; **the** ~ **possible effort** наиме́ньшее уси́лие; **I don't have the** ~ **idea about it** я не име́ю ни мале́йшего представле́ния об э́том; **at** ~ по кра́йней ме́ре; **you could at** ~ **have written** Вы могли́ бы по кра́йней ме́ре написа́ть; **not in the** ~ совсе́м нет; (+vb, +adj) совсе́м or во́все не.
leather ['lɛðəʳ] n ко́жа.
leather goods npl ко́жаные изде́лия ntpl.
leave [li:v] (pt, pp left) vt оставля́ть (оста́вить* perf); (go away from: on foot) уходи́ть* (уйти́* perf) из +gen; (: by transport) уезжа́ть (уе́хать* perf) из +gen; (party, committee) выходи́ть* (вы́йти* perf) из +gen ♦ vi (on foot) уходи́ть* (уйти́* perf); (by transport) уезжа́ть (уе́хать* perf); (bus, train) уходи́ть* (уйти́* perf) ♦ n о́тпуск*; **to** ~ **sth to sb** (money, property) оставля́ть (оста́вить* perf) что-н кому́-н; (responsibility) оставля́ть (оста́вить* perf) что-н под чью-н отве́тственность; **to be left (over)** остава́ться* (оста́ться* perf); **to take one's** ~ **of sb** проща́ться (попроща́ться perf) с кем-н; **on** ~ в о́тпуске
► **leave behind** vt оставля́ть (оста́вить* perf)
► **leave off** vt (heating, light) не включа́ть (включи́ть perf) ♦ vi (stop: inf) отстава́ть* (отста́ть* perf); **he left the lid off** он не положи́л кры́шку
► **leave on** vt (coat) не снима́ть (снять* perf); (light, heating) оставля́ть (оста́вить* perf)
► **leave out** vt (omit) пропуска́ть (пропусти́ть* perf); **he was left out** его́ пропусти́ли.
leave of absence n о́тпуск без содержа́ния.
leaves [li:vz] npl of **leaf**.
Lebanese [lɛbə'ni:z] adj лива́нский* ♦ n inv лива́нец(-нка).
Lebanon ['lɛbənən] n Лива́н.
lecherous ['lɛtʃərəs] adj развра́тный* (развра́тен).
lectern ['lɛktə:n] n ка́федра.
lecture ['lɛktʃəʳ] n ле́кция ♦ vi чита́ть (impf) ле́кции ♦ vt (scold): **to** ~ **sb on** or **about sth** чита́ть (impf) кому́-н ле́кцию по по́воду чего́-н; **to give a** ~ **on** чита́ть (прочита́ть perf)

ле́кцию о +prp.
lecture hall n аудито́рия, лекцио́нный зал.
lecturer ['lɛktʃərəʳ] n (BRIT: at university) преподава́тель(ница) m(f); (speaker) ле́ктор.
LED n abbr (ELEC: = light-emitting diode) СИД= светоизлуча́ющий дио́д.
led [lɛd] pt, pp of **lead**[1].
ledge [lɛdʒ] n (of mountain) вы́ступ; (of window) подоко́нник; (on wall) по́лка*.
ledger ['lɛdʒəʳ] n расхо́дно-прихо́дная кни́га.
lee [li:] n (shelter) покро́в.
leech [li:tʃ] n (also fig) пия́вка*.
leek [li:k] n лук-поре́й no pl.
leer [lɪəʳ] vi: **to** ~ **at sb** похотли́во смотре́ть (посмотре́ть perf) на кого́-н.
leeward ['li:wəd] (NAUT) adj подве́тренный ♦ adv с подве́тренной стороны́ ♦ n подве́тренная сторона́*; **to** ~ на подве́тренную сто́рону.
leeway ['li:weɪ] n (fig): **to allow o.s. some** ~ дава́ть (дать* perf) себе́ свобо́ду; **we have a lot of** ~ **to make up** нам ну́жно мно́гое наверста́ть.
left [lɛft] pt, pp of **leave** ♦ adj (remaining) оста́вшийся; (of direction, position) ле́вый ♦ n ле́вая сторона́* ♦ adv (motion): **(to the)** ~ нале́во; (position): **(on the)** ~ сле́ва; **the L~** (POL) ле́вые pl adj.
left-hand drive ['lɛfthænd-] adj (AUT) с рулём на ле́вой стороне́.
left-handed [lɛft'hændɪd] adj: **he/she is** ~ он/она́ левша́.
left-hand side n: **the** ~ ~ ле́вая сторона́.
leftie ['lɛftɪ] n (inf. pej: BRIT: left winger) ле́вый(-ая) m/f adj.
leftist ['lɛftɪst] n ле́вый(-ая) m(f) adj ♦ adj ле́вый.
left-luggage (office) [lɛft'lʌgɪdʒ(-)] n (BRIT) ка́мера хране́ния.
leftovers ['lɛftəuvəz] npl оста́тки mpl.
left-wing ['lɛft'wɪŋ] adj (POL) ле́вый.
left-winger ['lɛft'wɪŋəʳ] n (BRIT: POL) ле́вый(-ая) m(f) adj, представи́тель m ле́вого крыла́.
lefty ['lɛftɪ] n = **leftie**.
leg [lɛg] n (ANAT, also CULIN: of lamb) нога́*; (of insect, furniture, also CULIN: of chicken) но́жка*; (also: **trouser** ~) штани́на; (of journey, race) эта́п; **to stretch one's** ~**s** размина́ть (размя́ть* perf) но́ги.
legacy ['lɛgəsɪ] n (in will) насле́дство; (fig) насле́дие.
legal ['li:gl] adj (advice, requirement) юриди́ческий*; (system, action) суде́бный; (lawful) зако́нный* (зако́нен); **to take** ~ **action** or **proceedings against sb** возбужда́ть (возбуди́ть* perf) суде́бное де́ло про́тив кого́-н.
legal adviser n юрисконсу́льт.

---

* marks translations which have irregular inflections. The Russian-English side of the dictionary gives inflectional information.

legal holiday n (US) непрису́тственный день* m.

legality [lɪ'gælɪtɪ] n зако́нность f.

legalize ['li:gəlaɪz] vt узако́нивать (узако́нить* perf); (party, group) легализова́ть (impf/perf).

legally ['li:gəlɪ] adv юриди́чески; (act) зако́нно; (by law) по зако́ну; ~ **binding** юриди́чески обяза́тельный* (обяза́телен).

legal tender n зако́нное сре́дство платежа́ (обы́чно о бума́жных и металли́ческих деньга́х).

legatee [lɛgə'ti:] n насле́дник.

legation [lɪ'geɪʃən] n ми́ссия, представи́тельство.

legend ['lɛdʒənd] n (story) леге́нда; (person) легенда́рная ли́чность f.

legendary ['lɛdʒəndərɪ] adj легенда́рный* (легенда́рен).

-legged ['lɛgɪd] suffix -но́гий*.

leggy ['lɛgɪ] adj длинноно́гий* (длинноно́г).

leggings ['lɛgɪnz] npl лоси́ны fpl.

legibility [lɛdʒɪ'bɪlɪtɪ] n разбо́рчивость f.

legible ['lɛdʒəbl] adj разбо́рчивый (разбо́рчив).

legibly ['lɛdʒəblɪ] adv разбо́рчиво.

legion ['li:dʒən] n легио́н ♦ adj (numerous): **their problems are** ~ у них легио́н пробле́м.

legionnaire [li:dʒə'nɛə'] n легионе́р.

legionnaire's disease n боле́знь f „легионе́ров".

legislate ['lɛdʒɪsleɪt] vi издава́ть* (изда́ть* perf) зако́н(ы).

legislation [lɛdʒɪs'leɪʃən] n законода́тельство.

legislative ['lɛdʒɪslətɪv] adj (POL) законода́тельный.

legislator ['lɛdʒɪsleɪtə'] n (POL) законода́тель m.

legislature ['lɛdʒɪslətʃə'] n законода́тельные о́рганы mpl.

legitimacy [lɪ'dʒɪtɪməsɪ] n зако́нность f.

legitimate [lɪ'dʒɪtɪmət] adj зако́нный* (зако́нен).

legitimize [lɪ'dʒɪtɪmaɪz] vt узако́нивать (узако́нить perf).

legless ['lɛglɪs] adj (without legs) безно́гий* (безно́г); (very drunk: inf: BRIT) пья́ный в сте́льку.

legroom ['lɛgru:m] n (in car etc) простра́нство для ног.

Leics abbr (BRIT: POST) = Leicestershire.

Leipzig ['laɪpsɪg] n Ле́йпциг.

leisure ['lɛʒə'] n (also: ~ **time**) досу́г, свобо́дное вре́мя* nt; **to do sth at (one's)** ~ де́лать (сде́лать perf) что-н не спеша́.

leisure centre n спорти́вно-оздорови́тельный ко́мплекс.

leisurely ['lɛʒəlɪ] adj неторопли́вый (неторопли́в).

leisure suit n спорти́вный костю́м.

lemon ['lɛmən] n лимо́н ♦ adj лимо́нный.

lemonade [lɛmə'neɪd] n лимона́д.

lemon cheese n = lemon curd.

lemon curd n (CULIN) сла́дкое лимо́нное пови́дло.

lemon juice n лимо́нный сок*.

lemon squeezer n (ручна́я) соковыжима́лка*.

lemon tea n чай* с лимо́ном.

lend [lɛnd] (pt, pp lent) vt: **to** ~ **sth to sb**, ~ **sb sth** ода́лживать (одолжи́ть perf) что́-н кому́-н; **it ~s itself to ...** э́то поддаётся +dat ...; **to** ~ **sb a hand** выруча́ть (вы́ручить perf) кого́-н.

lender ['lɛndə'] n кредито́р.

lending library ['lɛndɪŋ-] n библиоте́ка, выдаю́щая кни́ги на́ дом.

length [lɛŋθ] n (measurement) длина́; (distance) протяжённость f; (piece: of wood, cloth etc) кусо́к*; (duration) продолжи́тельность f; (of book) объём; **2 metres in** ~ длино́й в 2 ме́тра; **he walked the (whole)** ~ **of the island** он прошёл че́рез весь о́стров; **I swam three ~s** я проплы́л три длины́ пла́вательного бассе́йна; **at** ~ (at last) наконе́ц; (for a long time) до́лго; **to lie full** ~ растя́гиваться (растяну́ться* perf) во весь рост; **to go to any ~(s) to do** прикла́дывать (приложи́ть* perf) все уси́лия что́бы +perf infin.

lengthen ['lɛŋθn] vt удлиня́ть (удлини́ть perf) ♦ vi удлиня́ться (удлини́ться perf).

lengthways ['lɛŋθweɪz] adv вдоль.

lengthy ['lɛŋθɪ] adj (text) дли́нный* (дли́нен); (meeting) продолжи́тельный* (продолжи́телен); (explanation) до́лгий*.

leniency ['li:nɪənsɪ] n мя́гкость f.

lenient ['li:nɪənt] adj мя́гкий* (мя́гок).

leniently ['li:nɪəntlɪ] adv мя́гко.

Leningrad ['lɛnɪngræd] n Ленингра́д.

lens [lɛnz] n (of spectacles, camera) ли́нза; (of telescope) объекти́в.

Lent [lɛnt] n Вели́кий* пост*.

lent [lɛnt] pt, pp of **lend**.

lentil ['lɛntl] n чечеви́ца no pl.

Leo ['li:əu] n Лев*; **he is** ~ он – Лев.

leopard ['lɛpəd] n леопа́рд.

leotard ['li:əta:d] n трико́ nt ind.

leper ['lɛpə'] n прокажённый(-ая) m(f) adj.

leper colony n лепрозо́рий.

leprosy ['lɛprəsɪ] n прока́за.

lesbian ['lɛzbɪən] adj лесби́йский ♦ n лесбия́нка*.

lesion ['li:ʒən] n поврежде́ние.

Lesotho [lɪ'su:tu:] n Лесо́то.

less [lɛs] adj (in size, degree, amount) ме́ньше; (in quality) ме́нее ♦ adv ме́ньше ♦ prep: ~ **tax/10% discount** ми́нус нало́г/ски́дка на 10%; ~ **than half** ме́ньше полови́ны; ~ **than ever** ме́ньше, чем когда́-либо; ~ **and** ~ всё ме́ньше и ме́ньше; **the** ~ ... **the more** ... чем ме́ньше ..., тем бо́льше ...; **the Prime Minister, no** ~ никто́ ино́й как премье́р-мини́стр.

lessee [lɛ'si:] n (of premises) съёмщик; (of land) аренда́тор.

lessen ['lɛsn] *vt* уменьша́ть (уме́ньшить *perf*)
♦ *vi* уменьша́ться (уме́ньшиться *perf*).
lesser ['lɛsə'] *adj* ме́ньший*; **to a ~ extent** в
ме́ньшей сте́пени.
lesson ['lɛsn] *n* (*also fig*) уро́к; **to teach sb a ~**
(*fig*) проучи́ть* (*perf*) кого́-н.
lessor ['lɛsə'] *n* лицо́*, сдаю́щее со́бствен-
ность в аре́нду.
lest [lɛst] *conj*: **~ you (should) forget** что́бы Вы
не забы́ли.
let [lɛt] (*pt, pp* **let**) *vt* (*BRIT*: *lease*) сдава́ть*
(сдать* *perf*) (внаём); (*allow*) разреша́ть
(разреши́ть *perf*) *or* позволя́ть
(позво́лить *perf*) кому́-н +*infin*; **~ me try**
да́йте я попро́бую; **~ him come** пусть он
придёт; **to ~ sb know about ...** дава́ть* (дать*
perf) кому́-н знать о +*prp* ...; **~'s go** пошли́,
пойдёмте; **"to ~"** „сдаётся внаём"; **to ~ go of**
отпуска́ть (отпусти́ть* *perf*); **~ go!** (от)пусти́!;
to ~ sth drop роня́ть (урони́ть* *perf*) что-н; **to
~ o.s. go** (*relax*) расслабля́ться
(рассла́биться* *perf*); (*neglect o.s.*)
опуска́ться (опусти́ться* *perf*)
▶ **let down** *vt* (*tyre etc*) спуска́ть (спусти́ть*
perf); (*fig: person*) подводи́ть* (подвести́*
perf); (*hair*) распуска́ть (распусти́ть* *perf*);
(*dress, hem*) отпуска́ть (отпусти́ть* *perf*)
▶ **let in** *vt* (*water, air*) пропуска́ть (пропусти́ть*
perf); (*person*) впуска́ть (впусти́ть* *perf*)
▶ **let off** *vt* (*culprit, schoolchildren*) отпуска́ть
(отпусти́ть* *perf*); (*bomb*) взрыва́ть
(взорва́ть* *perf*); (*gun*) выстре́ливать
(вы́стрелить *perf*) из +*gen*; (*smell*) испуска́ть
(испусти́ть* *perf*); **to ~ off steam** (*inf*)
выпуска́ть (вы́пустить *perf*) пар
▶ **let on** *vi* прогова́риваться (проговори́ться
perf)
▶ **let out** *vt* (*person, dog, water, air*) выпуска́ть
(вы́пустить* *perf*); (*passenger*) выса́живать
(вы́садить* *perf*); (*sound*) издава́ть* (изда́ть*
perf); (*house, room*) сдава́ть* (сдать* *perf*)
▶ **let up** *vi* (*cease*) перестава́ть* (переста́ть*
perf); (*diminish*) ослабева́ть (ослабе́ть* *perf*).
letdown ['lɛtdaun] *n* разочарова́ние.
lethal ['li:θl] *adj* (*weapon, chemical*)
смертоно́сный* (смертоно́сен); (*dose*)
смерте́льный (смерте́лен).
lethargic [lɛ'θɑːdʒɪk] *adj* вя́лый* (вял),
со́нный (со́нен).
lethargy ['lɛθədʒɪ] *n* вя́лость *f*.
letter ['lɛtə'] *n* (*correspondence*) письмо́*; (*of
alphabet*) бу́ква; **small/capital ~** строчна́я/
прописна́я бу́ква.
letter bomb *n* бо́мба, при́сланная по по́чте.
letter box *n* (*BRIT*) почто́вый я́щик.
letterhead ['lɛtəhɛd] *n* ша́пка (*в письме́*).
lettering ['lɛtərɪŋ] *n* шрифт.
letter of credit *n* аккредити́в.

letter opener *n* нож для разреза́ния бума́ги.
letterpress ['lɛtəprɛs] *n* (*method*) высо́кая
печа́ть *f*.
letter quality *n* (*of printer*) ка́чество печа́ти.
letters patent *npl* пате́нт.
lettuce ['lɛtɪs] *n* сала́т* лату́к.
let-up ['lɛtʌp] *n* ослабле́ние.
leukaemia [luː'kiːmɪə] (*US* **leukemia**) *n*
белокро́вие, лейкеми́я.
level ['lɛvl] *adj* (*flat*) ро́вный* (ро́вен) ♦ *n*
у́ровень *m*; (*also*: **spirit ~**) ватерпа́с ♦ *vt*
(*land*) ровня́ть (сровня́ть *perf*); (*building*)
сровня́ть* (*perf*) с землёй ♦ *vi* (*inf*): **to ~ with
sb** объясня́ться (объясни́ться *perf*) с кем-н
начистоту́ ♦ *adv*: **to draw ~ with** (*person,
vehicle*) поравня́ться (*perf*) с +*instr*; **to be ~
with** быть* (*impf*) на одно́м у́ровне с +*instr*;
"A" ~s (*BRIT: exams*) выпускны́е экза́мены (*в
сре́дней шко́ле*); (: *qualification*)
квалифика́ция, получа́емая при успе́шной
сда́че выпускно́го экза́мена; **on the ~** (*inf*)
че́стный* (че́стен); **to ~ a gun at sb** наводи́ть*
(навести́ *perf*) ружьё на кого́-н; **to ~ an
accusation/a criticism at** *or* **against sb**
направля́ть (напра́вить* *perf*) обвине́ние/
кри́тику про́тив кого́-н
▶ **level off** *vi* (*prices etc*) выра́вниваться
(вы́ровняться* *perf*)
▶ **level out** *vi* = **level off**.
level crossing *n* (*BRIT*) железнодоро́жный
перее́зд.
level-headed [lɛvl'hɛdɪd] *adj* уравнове́шенный
(уравнове́шен).
levelling ['lɛvlɪŋ] *n* выра́внивание.
level playing field *n* ра́вные пози́ции *fpl*.
lever ['liːvə'] *n* (*also fig*) рыча́г*; (*bar*) лом ♦ *vt*:
to ~ up/out поднима́ть (подня́ть *perf*)/
тащи́ть (вы́тащить *perf*) с уси́лием.
leverage ['liːvərɪdʒ] *n* рыча́жная си́ла; (*fig:
influence*) влия́ние.
levity ['lɛvɪtɪ] *n* легкомы́слие.
levy ['lɛvɪ] *n* нало́г ♦ *vt* взима́ть (*impf*).
lewd [luːd] *adj* (*look*) похотли́вый (похотли́в);
(*remark*) непристо́йный* (непристо́ен).
lexicographer [lɛksɪ'kɔɡrəfə'] *n* лексико́граф.
lexicography [lɛksɪ'kɔɡrəfɪ] *n* лексикогра́фия.
LI *abbr* (*US*) = **Long Island**.
liability [laɪə'bɪlɪtɪ] *n* (*LAW: responsibility*)
отве́тственность *f*; (*person, thing*) обу́за *m/f*;
liabilities *npl* (*COMM*) обяза́тельства *ntpl*.
liable ['laɪəbl] (*LAW*) *adj* (*responsible*): **~ for** (*for
actions*) отве́тственный (отве́тствен) за
+*acc*; (*legally responsible*) подсу́дный*
(подсу́ден) за +*acc*; (*subject*): **~ to**
подлежа́щий +*dat*; **to be ~ for** нести́* (*impf*)
отве́тственность за +*acc*; **to be ~ to**
подлежа́ть (*impf*) +*dat*; **he's ~ to take offence**
возмо́жно, что он оби́дится.

---

* marks translations which have irregular inflections. The Russian-English side of the dictionary gives inflectional information.

liaise [lɪ'eɪz] *vi*: **to ~ (with)** коопери́роваться (скоопери́роваться *perf*) (с +*instr*).

liaison [lɪ'eɪzɒn] *n* (*cooperation*) коопера́ция; (*sexual*) связь *f*.

liar ['laɪə] *n* лжец*, лгун*(ья).

libel ['laɪbl] *n* клевета́ ◆ *vt* клевета́ть* (оклевета́ть* *perf*).

libellous ['laɪbləs] (*US* **libelous**) *adj* (*comment etc*) клеветни́ческий*.

liberal ['lɪbərl] *adj* (*tolerant, also* POL) либера́льный* (либера́лен); (*large, generous*) ще́дрый; ~ **with** ще́дрый* (щедр) на +*acc* ◆ *n* (*tolerant person*) либера́л; (POL): **L~** либера́л.

liberalize ['lɪbərəlaɪz] *vt* либерализова́ть (*impf/perf*).

liberally ['lɪbrəlɪ] *adv* (*see adj*) либера́льно; ще́дро.

Liberal Democrat *n* либера́л-демокра́т; **the ~ ~s** (*party*) па́ртия Либера́л-демокра́тов.

liberal-minded ['lɪbərl'maɪndɪd] *adj* либера́льно-настро́енный (либера́льно-настро́ен).

liberate ['lɪbəreɪt] *vt* освобожда́ть (освободи́ть* *perf*).

liberation [lɪbə'reɪʃən] *n* освобожде́ние.

Liberia [laɪ'bɪərɪə] *n* Либе́рия.

Liberian [laɪ'bɪərɪən] *adj* либери́йский ◆ *n* либери́ец*(-и́йка*).

liberty ['lɪbətɪ] *n* свобо́да; **to be at ~** (*criminal*) быть* (*impf*) на свобо́де; **I'm not at ~ to comment** я не во́лен комменти́ровать; **to take the ~ of doing** позволя́ть (позво́лить* *perf*) себе́ +*infin*.

libido [lɪ'biːdəu] *n* либи́до *nt ind*.

Libra ['liːbrə] *n* Весы́ *pl*; **he is** ~ он – Весы́.

librarian [laɪ'brɛərɪən] *n* библиоте́карь *m*.

library ['laɪbrərɪ] *n* библиоте́ка.

library book *n* библиоте́чная кни́га.

libretto [lɪ'brɛtəu] *n* либре́тто *nt ind*.

Libya ['lɪbɪə] *n* Ли́вия.

Libyan ['lɪbɪən] *adj* ливи́йский ◆ *n* ливи́ец*(-и́йка*).

lice [laɪs] *npl of* **louse**.

licence ['laɪsns] (*US* **license**) *n* (*permit*) лице́нзия; (AUT: *also*: **driving ~**) (води́тельские) права́ *ntpl*; (*freedom*) во́льность *f*; **under ~** (COMM) по лице́нзии.

license ['laɪsns] *n* (*US*) = **licence** ◆ *vt* выдава́ть* (вы́дать* *perf*) лице́нзию на +*acc*.

licensed ['laɪsnst] *adj* (*car etc*) зарегистри́рованный (зарегистри́рован); (*restaurant*) с лице́нзией на прода́жу спиртны́х напи́тков.

licensed trade *n* организа́ции, торгу́ющие алкого́льными напи́тками.

licensee [laɪsən'siː] *n* держа́тель *m* лице́нзии.

license plate *n* (*US*) номерно́й знак (*на автомоби́ле*).

licensing hours ['laɪsnsɪŋ] *npl* (BRIT) *часы́, в кото́рые разрешена́ торго́вля спиртны́ми напи́тками*.

licentious [laɪ'sɛnʃəs] *adj* распу́щенный (распу́щен).

lichen ['laɪkən] *n* лиша́йник.

lick [lɪk] *vt* (*stamp, fingers etc*) лиза́ть* (*impf*), обли́зывать (облиза́ть* *perf*); (*inf: defeat*) положи́ть* (*perf*) на лопа́тки ◆ *n*: **to give sth a ~** лизну́ть (*perf*) что-н; **to give sth a ~ of paint** подкра́шивать (подкра́сить* *perf*) что-н; **to one's lips** обли́зываться (облиза́ться* *perf*); (*fig*) обли́зываться (*impf*).

licorice ['lɪkərɪs] *n* (*US*) = **liquorice**.

lid [lɪd] *n* кры́шка; (*also*: **eyelid**) ве́ко; **to take the ~ off sth** (*fig*) выта́скивать (вы́тащить *perf*) что-н на свет бо́жий.

lido ['laɪdəu] *n* (BRIT: *pool*) бассе́йн на откры́том во́здухе.

lie [laɪ] (*pt* **lay**, *pp* **lain**) *vi* (*be horizontal*) лежа́ть* (*impf*); (*be situated*) лежа́ть* (*impf*), находи́ться* (*impf*); (*problem, cause*) заключа́ться (*impf*); (*be untruthful*) (*pt, pp* **lied**) лгать* (солга́ть* *perf*), врать* (совра́ть* *perf*) ◆ *n* (*untrue statement*) ложь* *f no pl*; **to ~ or be lying in first/last place** быть* (*impf*) на пе́рвом/после́днем ме́сте; **to ~ low** (*fig*) пережида́ть (пережда́ть* *perf*); **to tell ~s** говори́ть (*impf*) непра́вду

► **lie about** *vi* валя́ться (*impf*)

► **lie around** *vi* = **lie about**

► **lie back** *vi* отки́дываться (отки́нуться *perf*); (*fig*) успока́иваться (успоко́иться *perf*)

► **lie down** *vi* ложи́ться (лечь* *perf*); **to be lying down** лежа́ть* (*impf*)

► **lie up** *vi* (*hide*) скрыва́ться (скры́ться* *perf*).

Liechtenstein ['lɪktənstaɪn] *n* Лихтенште́йн.

lie detector *n* дете́ктор лжи.

lie-down ['laɪdaun] *n* (BRIT): **to have a ~** полежа́ть* (*perf*).

lie-in ['laɪɪn] *n* (BRIT): **to have a ~** вставать* (встать* *perf*) попо́зже.

lieu [luː]: **in ~ of** *prep* вме́сто +*gen*.

Lieut. *abbr* (MIL) = **lieutenant**.

lieutenant [lɛf'tɛnənt, (*US*) luː'tɛnənt] *n* лейтена́нт.

lieutenant colonel *n* подполко́вник.

life [laɪf] (*pl* **lives**) *n* жизнь *f no pl*; **true to ~** правдоподо́бный* (правдоподо́бен); **to paint from ~** писа́ть* (написа́ть* *perf*) с нату́ры; **to be sent to prison for ~** получа́ть (получи́ть* *perf*) пожи́зненное заключе́ние; **to come to ~** (*fig: person*) ожива́ть (ожи́ть* *perf*); (: *party*) оживля́ться (оживи́ться* *perf*).

life annuity *n* пожи́зненный аннуите́т.

life assurance *n* (BRIT) = **life insurance**.

life belt *n* (BRIT) спаса́тельный круг*.

lifeblood ['laɪfblʌd] *n* (*fig*) жи́зненная осно́ва.

lifeboat ['laɪfbəut] *n* (*rescue launch*) спаса́тельное су́дно*; (*on ship*) спаса́тельная шлю́пка.

life buoy *n* = **life belt**.

life expectancy *n* продолжи́тельность *f* жи́зни.

lifeguard ['laɪfgɑ:d] *n* спаса́тель(ница) *m(f)*.
life imprisonment *n* пожи́зненное заключе́ние.
life insurance *n* страхова́ние жи́зни.
life jacket *n* спаса́тельный жиле́т.
lifeless ['laɪflɪs] *adj* (*also fig*) безжи́зненный (безжи́знен).
lifelike ['laɪflaɪk] *adj* (*model, robot*) как живо́й; (*performance*) реалисти́чный* (реалисти́чен).
lifeline ['laɪflaɪn] *n* (*fig*) сре́дство вы́живания; (*rope*) спаса́тельный кана́т.
lifelong ['laɪflɔŋ] *adj* (*friend, habit*) неизме́нный; **it was a ~ ambition of his** э́то бы́ло мечто́й всей его́ жи́зни.
life preserver *n* (*US*) = **life belt**, **life jacket**.
lifer ['laɪfə'] *n* бессро́чник(-ица).
life raft *n* спаса́тельный плот*.
life-saver ['laɪfseɪvə'] *n* спасе́ние.
life science *n* есте́ственные нау́ки *fpl*.
life sentence *n* пригово́р к пожи́зненному заключе́нию.
life-size(d) ['laɪfsaɪz(d)] *adj* в натура́льную величину́.
life span *n* (*of living thing*) продолж-и́тельность *f* жи́зни; (*of product*) срок* слу́жбы; (*of idea, organization*) долгове́чность *f*.
lifestyle ['laɪfstaɪl] *n* о́браз жи́зни.
life-support system ['laɪfsəpɔ:t-] *n* систе́ма жизнеобеспе́чения.
lifetime ['laɪftaɪm] *n* (*of person*) жизнь *f*; (*of institution*) вре́мя* *nt* существова́ния; **the chance of a ~** уника́льный шанс.
lift [lɪft] *vt* поднима́ть (подня́ть* *perf*); (*ban, sanctions*) снима́ть (снять* *perf*); (*inf: steal*) тащи́ть (стащи́ть* *perf*) ♦ *vi* (*fog*) рассе́иваться (рассе́яться *perf*) ♦ *n* (*BRIT*) лифт; **to give sb a ~** (*BRIT: AUT*) подвози́ть* (подвезти́* *perf*) кого́-н.
► **lift in** *vt* (*goods, people*) ввози́ть* (ввезти́* *perf*) самолётом.
► **lift off** *vi* (*rocket*) отрыва́ться (оторва́ться* *perf*) от земли́, стартова́ть (*impf/perf*).
► **lift out** *vt* (*goods, people*) вывози́ть* (вы́везти* *perf*) самолётом.
► **lift up** *vt* (*object, person*) поднима́ть (подня́ть* *perf*).
liftoff ['lɪftɔf] *n* старт.
ligament ['lɪgəmənt] *n* (*ANAT*) свя́зка*.
light [laɪt] (*pt, pp* **lit**) *n* свет*; (*AUT*) фа́ра ♦ *vt* (*candle, cigarette, fire*) зажига́ть (заже́чь* *perf*); (*place*) освеща́ть (освети́ть* *perf*) ♦ *adj* (*pale, bright*) све́тлый* (све́тел); (*not heavy*) лёгкий* (лёгок) ♦ *adv* (*travel*) налегке́; **~s** *npl* (*also*: **traffic ~s**) светофо́р *msg*; **to turn the ~ on/off** включа́ть (включи́ть *perf*)/выключа́ть (вы́ключить *perf*) свет; **have you got a ~?** (*for*

cigarette) мо́жно у Вас прикури́ть?; **to come to ~** выясня́ться (вы́ясниться *perf*); **to cast** *or* **shed** *or* **throw ~ on** пролива́ть (проли́ть* *perf*) свет на +*acc*; **in the ~ of** (*discussions, new evidence*) в све́те +*gen*; **to make ~ of** не заостря́ть (*impf*) внима́ние на +*acc*; **the house is lit by electricity** дом освещён электри́чеством
► **light up** *vi* (*face*) светле́ть (просветле́ть *perf*) ♦ *vt* (*illuminate*) освеща́ть (освети́ть* *perf*).
light bulb *n* ла́мпочка*.
lighten ['laɪtn] *vi* (*become less dark*) светле́ть (посветле́ть *perf*) ♦ *vt* (*make less heavy*) облегча́ть (облегчи́ть *perf*).
lighter ['laɪtə'] *n* (*also*: **cigarette ~**) зажига́лка*; (*boat*) ли́хтер.
light-fingered [laɪt'fɪŋgəd] *adj* нечи́стый* (нечи́ст) на́ руку.
light-headed [laɪt'hɛdɪd] *adj*: **she felt ~** у неё кружи́лась голова́.
light-hearted [laɪt'hɑ:tɪd] *adj* (*person*) беспе́чный* (беспе́чен); (*question, remark*) несерьёзный* (несерьёзен).
lighthouse ['laɪthaus] *n* маяк*.
lighting ['laɪtɪŋ] *n* освеще́ние.
lighting-up time [laɪtɪŋ'ʌp-] *n* вре́мя* *nt* включе́ния у́личного освеще́ния.
lightly ['laɪtlɪ] *adv* (*touch, kiss*) слегка́; (*eat, treat*) легко́; (*sleep*) неглубоко́; **to get off ~** легко́ отде́лываться (отде́латься *perf*).
light meter *n* экспоно́метр.
lightness ['laɪtnɪs] *n* (*in weight*) лёгкость *f*.
lightning ['laɪtnɪŋ] *n* мо́лния ♦ *adj* (*rapid*) молниено́сный* (молниено́сен).
lightning conductor *n* (*BRIT*) громоотво́д.
lightning rod *n* (*US*) = **lightning conductor**.
light pen *n* прибо́р, счи́тывающий штрихово́й код.
lightship ['laɪtʃɪp] *n* плаву́чий* маяк*.
lightweight ['laɪtweɪt] *adj* (*suit*) лёгкий* ♦ *n* (*BOXING*) бо́ксер лёгкого ве́са.
light year *n* светово́й год*.
like [laɪk] *prep* как +*acc*; (*similar to*) похо́жий на +*acc* ♦ *adj* подо́бный (подо́бен) ♦ *vt* (*sweets, reading*) люби́ть* (*impf*); (*find attractive, acceptable*) **I ~ him** он мне нра́вится ♦ *n*: **and the ~** тому́ подо́бное; **to be** *or* **look ~** походи́ть* (*impf*) на +*acc*; **he looks ~ his father** он похо́ж на своего́ отца́; **what does she look ~?** как она́ вы́глядит?; **what's he ~?** что он за челове́к?; **what's the weather ~?** кака́я сего́дня пого́да?; **something ~ that** что́-то в э́том ро́де; **I feel ~ a drink** я хочу́ что́-нибудь вы́пить; **there's nothing ~ ...** ничто́ не мо́жет сравни́ться с +*instr* ...; **do it ~ this** де́лайте (сде́лайте *perf*) э́то так; **that's just ~ him** (*typical*) это на него́ похо́же; **it is nothing ~ ...** э́то совсе́м не то, что ...; **I would ~**, **I'd ~** мне

хоте́лось бы, я бы хоте́л; **would you ~ a coffee?** хоти́те ко́фе?; **I ~d him** он мне понра́вился; **I don't ~ his behaviour** мне не нра́вится его́ поведе́ние; **if you ~** е́сли хоти́те; **his ~s and dislikes** его́ вку́сы.

likeable ['laɪkəbl] *adj* симпати́чный* (симпати́чен).

likelihood ['laɪklɪhud] *n* вероя́тность *f*; **in all ~** по все́й вероя́тности; **there is every ~ that ...** о́чень вероя́тно, что ....

likely ['laɪklɪ] *adj* вероя́тный* (вероя́тен); **she is ~ to agree** она́ вероя́тно согласи́тся; **not ~!** (*inf*) ни за что!

like-minded ['laɪk'maɪndɪd] *adj*: **a ~ person** единомы́шленник; **~ friends/colleagues** друзья́/колле́ги – единомы́шленники.

liken ['laɪkən] *vt*: **to ~ sth/sb to** уподобля́ть (уподо́бить* *perf*) что-н/кого́-н +*dat*.

likeness ['laɪknɪs] *n* схо́дство; **the portrait is a good ~ of her** портре́т обнару́живает большо́е схо́дство с ней.

likewise ['laɪkwaɪz] *adv* та́кже; **to do ~** поступа́ть (поступи́ть* *perf*) таки́м же о́бразом.

liking ['laɪkɪŋ] *n*: **~ (for)** (*person*) симпа́тия (к +*dat*); (*thing*) вкус (к +*dat*); **to be to sb's ~** быть* (*impf*) *or* приходи́ться* (прийти́сь* *perf*) кому́-н по вку́су; **I took an instant ~ to him** он мне сра́зу понра́вился.

lilac ['laɪlək] *n* сире́нь *f no pl* ♦ *adj* сире́невый.

Lilo® ['laɪləu] *n* надувно́й рези́новый матра́ц.

lilt [lɪlt] *n* (*in voice*) перели́вы *mpl*.

lilting ['lɪltɪŋ] *adj* (*voice*) мелоди́чный* (мелоди́чен).

lily ['lɪlɪ] *n* ли́лия.

lily of the valley *n* ла́ндыш.

Lima ['liːmə] *n* Ли́ма.

limb [lɪm] *n* (*ANAT*) коне́чность *f*; (*of tree*) ветвь* *f*; **to be out on a ~** быть* (*impf*) *or* находи́ться* (*impf*) в крити́ческом положе́нии.

limber up ['lɪmbə'-] *vi* размина́ться (размя́ться* *perf*).

limbo ['lɪmbəu] *n*: **to be in ~** (*fig*) находи́ться* (*impf*) в состоя́нии неопределённости.

lime [laɪm] *n* (*fruit*) лайм; (*tree*) ли́па*; (*also*: **~ juice**) сок ла́йма; (*chemical*) и́звесть *f*; (*rock*) известня́к*.

limelight ['laɪmlaɪt] *n*: **to be in the ~** быть* (*impf*) в це́нтре внима́ния.

limerick ['lɪmərɪk] *n* лиме́рик (юмористи́ческое пятистро́чное стихотворе́ние).

limestone ['laɪmstəun] *n* известня́к*.

limit ['lɪmɪt] *n* преде́л; (*restriction*) лими́т, ограниче́ние ♦ *vt* (*production, expense etc*) лими́ровать (*impf/perf*), ограни́чивать (ограни́чить *perf*); **speed ~** преде́льная ско́рость *f*; **within ~s** в преде́лах допусти́мого; **that's the ~!** э́то перехо́дит все грани́цы!

limitation [lɪmɪ'teɪʃən] *n* ограниче́ние; **~s** *npl* недоста́тки *mpl*.

limited ['lɪmɪtɪd] *adj* ограни́ченный (ограни́чен); **to be ~ to** ограни́чиваться (ограни́читься *perf*) +*instr*.

limited edition *n* малотира́жное изда́ние.

limited (liability) company *n* (*BRIT*) компа́ния с ограни́ченной отве́тственностью.

limitless ['lɪmɪtlɪs] *adj* беспреде́льный* (беспреде́лен).

limousine ['lɪməziːn] *n* лимузи́н.

limp [lɪmp] *vi* хрома́ть (*impf*) ♦ *adj* (*person, limb*) бесси́льный* (бесси́лен); (*material*) мя́гкий* (мя́гок) ♦ *n*: **to have a ~** хрома́ть (*impf*).

limpet ['lɪmpɪt] *n* блю́дечко* (*моллю́ск*).

limpid ['lɪmpɪd] *adj* прозра́чный* (прозра́чен).

limply ['lɪmplɪ] *adv* (*lie*) бесси́льно; (*fall*) мя́гко.

linchpin ['lɪntʃpɪn] *n* опо́ра.

Lincs [lɪŋks] *abbr* (*BRIT: POST*) = Lincolnshire.

line [laɪn] *n* (*also TEL, RAIL*) ли́ния; (*row*) ряд*; (*US: queue*) о́чередь *f*; (*of writing, song*) строка́*, стро́чка*; (*wrinkle*) морщи́на; (*rope*) верёвка*; (*for fishing*) ле́ска*; (*wire*) про́вод; (*route*) маршру́т; (*fig: attitude, policy*) ли́ния; (: *of thought, reasoning*) ход; (*of business, work*) о́бласть *f*; (*of product(s)*) моде́ль *f*, тип ♦ *vt* (*stand along*) выстра́иваться (вы́строиться *perf*) вдоль +*gen*; (*clothing*) подбива́ть (подби́ть* *perf*); (*container*) выкла́дывать (вы́ложить* *perf*) изнутри́; **hold the ~ please!** (*TEL*) пожа́луйста, не клади́те тру́бку!; **to cut in ~** (*US*) идти́* (пойти́* *perf*) без о́череди; **to stand in ~** (*in a row*) стоя́ть (*impf*) в шере́нге *or* ряд; **in ~ with** (*in keeping with*) в соотве́тствии с +*instr*; **to bring sth into ~ with sth** приводи́ть* (привести́* *perf*) что-н в соотве́тствие с чем-н; **on the right ~s** на ве́рном пути́; **to draw the ~ at sth** ограни́чиваться (ограни́читься *perf*) чем-н; **he is in ~ for a pay rise** он ско́ро до́лжен получи́ть повыше́ние зарпла́ты; **the streets are ~d with trees** у́лицы обса́жены дере́вьями; **the walls were ~d with pictures** сте́ны бы́ли заве́шены карти́нами.

▶ **line up** *vi* выстра́иваться (вы́строиться *perf*) ♦ *vt* (*place in order*) выстра́ивать (вы́строить *perf*); (*prepare*) подгота́вливать (подгото́вить* *perf*); **she has a new job ~d up** она́ устро́илась на но́вую рабо́ту.

linear ['lɪnɪə] *adj* лине́йный*.

lined [laɪnd] *adj* (*paper*) линованный; (*face*) морщи́нистый (морщи́нист); (*skirt, jacket*) на подкла́дке, с подкла́дкой.

line editing *n* (*COMPUT*) постро́чное редакти́рование.

line feed *n* (*COMPUT*) перево́д *or* прого́н строки́.

lineman ['laɪnmən] *n* (*US: workman*) инжене́р телефо́нной свя́зи; (: *SPORT*) боково́й судья́.

linen ['lɪnɪn] *n* (*material*) лён*; (*sheets etc*)

бельё.

line printer *n* (*COMPUT*) постро́чно-печата́ющее устро́йство, устро́йство постро́чной печа́ти.

liner ['laɪnə'] *n* (*ship*) ла́йнер; (*also:* **bin** ~) целофа́новый мешо́к для му́сорного ведра́.

linesman ['laɪnzmən] *irreg n* судья́* *m* на ли́нии.

line-up ['laɪnʌp] *n* (*also:* **team** ~) соста́в кома́нды; (*at event*) соста́в уча́стников; (*US:* *queue*) о́чередь* *f*; (*identity parade*) опозна́ние (*престу́пника*).

linger ['lɪŋgə'] *vi* (*smell, tradition*) уде́рживаться (удержа́ться* *perf*); (*person*) заде́рживаться (задержа́ться* *perf*).

lingerie ['lænʒəri:] *n* же́нское ни́жнее бельё.

lingering ['lɪŋgərɪŋ] *adj* (*sense, feeling, doubt*) усто́йчивый.

lingo ['lɪŋgəu] (*pl* ~**es**) *n* (*inf: language*) (иностра́нный) язы́к.

linguist ['lɪŋgwɪst] *n* (*language specialist*) лингви́ст; **he is a good** ~ (*speaks several languages*) он спосо́бен к языка́м.

linguistic [lɪŋ'gwɪstɪk] *adj* лингвисти́ческий*.

linguistics [lɪŋ'gwɪstɪks] *n* языкозна́ние, лингви́стика.

liniment ['lɪnɪmənt] *n* жи́дкая мазь *f*.

lining ['laɪnɪŋ] *n* (*cloth*) подкла́дка*; (*TECH*) прокла́дка*; (*of stomach etc*) вы́стилка.

link [lɪŋk] *n* связь *f*; (*of a chain*) звено́* ◆ *vt* (*join*) соединя́ть (соедини́ть *perf*); (*associate*): **to** ~ **with** *or* **to** свя́зывать (связа́ть* *perf*) с +*instr*; ~**s** *npl* (*GOLF*) по́ле для игры́ в гольф; **rail** ~ железнодоро́жная связь

▶ **link up** *vt* (*machines, systems*) соединя́ть (соедини́ть *perf*) ◆ *vi* соединя́ться (соедини́ться *perf*).

linkup ['lɪŋkʌp] *n* соедине́ние; (*of spaceships*) стыко́вка*; (*RADIO, TV*) свя́зка*, связна́я часть* *f*; (*between studios: RADIO*) радиомо́ст; (*: TV*) телемо́ст.

lino ['laɪnəu] *n* = **linoleum**.

linoleum [lɪ'nəulɪəm] *n* лино́леум.

linseed oil ['lɪnsi:d-] *n* льняно́е ма́сло.

lint [lɪnt] *n* ма́рля.

lintel ['lɪntl] *n* при́толока.

lion ['laɪən] *n* лев*.

lion cub *n* львёнок*.

lioness ['laɪənɪs] *n* льви́ца.

lip [lɪp] *n* (*ANAT*) губа́*; (*of container*) край*; (*inf: insolence*) гру́бости *fpl*.

liposome ['lɪpəusəum] *n* липосо́ма.

liposuction ['lɪpəusʌkʃən] *n* липоса́кция, отса́сывание жирово́й тка́ни.

lip-read ['lɪpri:d] *vi* чита́ть (*impf*) с губ.

lip salve *n* мазь *f* для смягче́ния губ.

lip service *n*: **to pay** ~ ~ **to sth** признава́ть* (призна́ть *perf*) что-н то́лько на слова́х.

lipstick ['lɪpstɪk] *n* губна́я пома́да.

liquefy ['lɪkwɪfaɪ] *vt* превраща́ть (преврати́ть* *perf*) в жи́дкость ◆ *vi* переходи́ть* (перейти́* *perf*) в жи́дкое состоя́ние.

liqueur [lɪ'kjuə'] *n* ликёр.

liquid ['lɪkwɪd] *n* жи́дкость *f* ◆ *adj* жи́дкий* (жи́док).

liquid assets *npl* ликви́дные акти́вы *mpl*.

liquidate ['lɪkwɪdeɪt] *vt* ликвиди́ровать (*impf/perf*).

liquidation [lɪkwɪ'deɪʃən] *n* ликвида́ция; **to go into** ~ ликвиди́роваться (*impf*).

liquidation sale *n* (*US*) распрода́жа иму́щества ликвиди́рованного предприя́тия.

liquidator ['lɪkwɪdeɪtə'] *n* ликвида́тор.

liquid crystal display *n* жидкокристалли́ческий индика́тор.

liquidity [lɪ'kwɪdɪtɪ] *n* ликви́дность *f*.

liquidize ['lɪkwɪdaɪz] *vt* пропуска́ть (пропусти́ть* *perf*) че́рез ми́ксер.

liquidizer ['lɪkwɪdaɪzə'] *n* ми́ксер, смеси́тель *m*.

liquor ['lɪkə'] *n* (*esp US*) спиртно́е *nt adj*, спиртно́й напи́ток*.

liquorice ['lɪkərɪs] *n* (*BRIT: sweet*) лакри́ца.

liquor store *n* (*US*) магази́н спиртны́х напи́тков.

Lisbon ['lɪzbən] *n* Лиссабо́н.

lisp [lɪsp] *n* шепеля́вость *f* ◆ *vi* шепеля́вить* (*impf*).

lissom(e) ['lɪsəm] *adj* изя́щный* (изя́щен).

list [lɪst] *n* (*also COMPUT*) спи́сок* ◆ *vt* (*enumerate*) перечисля́ть (перечи́слить *perf*); (*write down*) составля́ть (соста́вить* *perf*) спи́сок +*gen*; (*put on list*) включа́ть (включи́ть* *perf*) в спи́сок ◆ *vi* (*ship*) крени́ться (накрени́ться *perf*).

listed building *n* (*BRIT*) зда́ние, охраня́емое госуда́рством.

listed company *n* официа́льно зарегистри́рованная компа́ния.

listen ['lɪsn] *vi*: **to** ~ (**to sb/sth**) слу́шать (*impf*) (кого́-н/что-н); **to** ~ **to sb** *or* **sb's advice** слу́шать (послу́шать *perf*) кого́-н; **I'm** ~**ing out for him** я прислу́шиваюсь, не идёт ли он; ~! послу́шайте!

listener ['lɪsnə'] *n* слу́шатель(ница) *m(f)*; (*RADIO*) радиослу́шатель(ница) *m(f)*.

listeria [lɪs'tɪərɪə] *n* листе́рия.

listing ['lɪstɪŋ] *n* (*COMPUT*) распеча́тка, ли́стинг.

listless ['lɪstlɪs] *adj* вя́лый (вял).

listlessly ['lɪstlɪslɪ] *adv* вя́ло.

list price *n* прейскура́нтная цена́*.

lit [lɪt] *pt, pp of* **light**.

litany ['lɪtənɪ] *n* (*REL: Catholic*) лита́ния; (*: Orthodox*) ектенья́; (*list*) моното́нное перечисле́ние.

liter ['li:tə'] *n* (*US*) = **litre**.

literacy ['lɪtərəsɪ] *n* гра́мотность *f*.

literacy campaign *n* борьба́ с

---

* marks translations which have irregular inflections. The Russian-English side of the dictionary gives inflectional information.

неграмотностью.
literal [ˈlɪtərl] *adj* буква́льный* (буква́лен).
literally [ˈlɪtrəlɪ] *adv* буква́льно.
literary [ˈlɪtərərɪ] *adj* литерату́рный*.
literate [ˈlɪtərət] *adj* (able to read and write) гра́мотный* (гра́мотен); (educated) образо́ванный (образо́ван).
literature [ˈlɪtrɪtʃə] *n* литерату́ра.
lithe [laɪð] *adj* ги́бкий* (ги́бок).
lithograph [ˈlɪθəɡrɑːf] *n* литогра́фия.
lithography [lɪˈθɒɡrəfɪ] *n* литогра́фия.
Lithuania [lɪθjuˈeɪnɪə] *n* Литва́.
Lithuanian [lɪθjuˈeɪnɪən] *adj* лито́вский* ♦ *n* (person) лито́вец*(-вка*); (LING) лито́вский язы́к.
litigation [lɪtɪˈɡeɪʃən] *n* тя́жба.
litmus paper [ˈlɪtməs-] *n* ла́кмусовая бума́га.
litre [ˈliːtə] (US **liter**) *n* литр.
litter [ˈlɪtə] *n* (rubbish) му́сор; (young animals) помёт.
litter bin *n* (BRIT) у́рна (для му́сора).
litterbug [ˈlɪtəbʌɡ] *n* (inf) челове́к, кото́рый сори́т в обще́ственных места́х.
littered [ˈlɪtəd] *adj*: ~ **with** зава́ленный (зава́лен) +instr.
litter lout *n* (inf) = **litterbug**.
little [ˈlɪtl] *adj* (small, young) ма́ленький*; (younger) мла́дший*; (short) коро́ткий* ♦ *adv* ма́ло; **a** ~ (bit) немно́го; **I have** ~ **time/money** у меня́ ма́ло вре́мени/де́нег; **to make** ~ **of** не заостря́ть (impf) внима́ние на +prp; ~ **by** ~ ма́ло-пома́лу, понемно́гу.
little finger *n* мизи́нец* (на руке́).
little-known [ˈlɪtlˈnəun] *adj* малоизве́стный* (малоизве́стен).
liturgy [ˈlɪtədʒɪ] *n* литурги́я.
live [vb lɪv, adj laɪv] *vi* жить* (impf) ♦ *adj* (animal, plant) живо́й*; (broadcast) прямо́й; (performance) пе́ред пу́бликой; (ELEC) под напряже́нием; (bullet) боево́й; (bomb) не взорва́вшийся; **to** ~ **with sb** жить* (impf) с кем-н; **he** ~**d to (be) a hundred** он прожи́л до ста лет
▸ **live down** *vt* загла́живать (загла́дить* perf)
▸ **live for** *vt* жить* (impf) для +gen
▸ **live in** *vi*: **most students** ~ **in** большинство́ студе́нтов живёт в общежи́тии
▸ **live off** *vt fus* (survive on): **we** ~**d off fish** мы жи́ли на одно́й ры́бе; (pej: parents etc) жить* (impf) за счёт +gen
▸ **live on** *vt fus* (food) жить* (impf) на одно́м(-ой) +prp; (salary) жить* (impf) на +acc
▸ **live out** *vi*: **postgraduates usually** ~ **out** аспира́нты обы́чно не живу́т в общежи́тии ♦ *vt*: **to** ~ **out one's days** or **life** прожива́ть (прожи́ть* perf) оста́ток свое́й жи́зни
▸ **live together** *vi* жить* (impf) вме́сте
▸ **live up** *vt*: **to** ~ **it up** жить* (impf) широко́
▸ **live up to** *vt fus* опра́вдывать (оправда́ть* perf).
live-in [ˈlɪvɪn] *adj*: ~ **lover** сожи́тель(ница) *m(f)*;

they have a ~ **nanny** с ни́ми живёт ня́ня.
livelihood [ˈlaɪvlɪhud] *n* сре́дства *ntpl* к существова́нию.
liveliness [ˈlaɪvlɪnɪs] *n* жи́вость *f*.
lively [ˈlaɪvlɪ] *adj* (person, book, interest, mind) живо́й*; (place, event) оживлённый (оживлён).
liven up [ˈlaɪvn-] *vt* (person) ободря́ть (ободри́ть* perf); (discussion, evening) оживля́ть (оживи́ть* perf) ♦ *vi* оживля́ться (оживи́ться* perf).
liver [ˈlɪvə] *n* (ANAT) пе́чень *f*; (CULIN) печёнка.
liverish [ˈlɪvərɪʃ] *adj*: **he is feeling** ~ его́ подта́шнивает.
Liverpool [ˈlɪvəpuːl] *n* Ли́верпуль *m*.
Liverpudlian [lɪvəˈpʌdlɪən] *adj* ливерпу́льский ♦ *n* ливерпу́лец*(-лька*).
livery [ˈlɪvərɪ] *n* (of servant) ливре́я.
lives [laɪvz] *npl of* **life**.
livestock [ˈlaɪvstɒk] *n* скот*.
live wire *n* (inf): **he's a real** ~ ~ он ужа́сно заводно́й.
livid [ˈlɪvɪd] *adj* (colour) серова́то-си́ний*; (inf: furious): **she was** ~ она́ была́ в я́рости.
living [ˈlɪvɪŋ] *adj* живо́й* ♦ *n*: **to earn** or **make a** ~ зараба́тывать (зарабо́тать perf) на жизнь; **within** ~ **memory** на па́мяти живу́щих; **the cost of** ~ сто́имость *f* жи́зни.
living conditions *npl* усло́вия *ntpl* жи́зни.
living expenses *npl* расхо́ды *mpl* на жизнь.
living room *n* гости́ная *f adj*.
living standards *npl* жи́зненный у́ровень *msg*.
living wage *n* прожи́точный ми́нимум.
lizard [ˈlɪzəd] *n* я́щерица.
Ljubljana [luːˈbljɑːnə] *n* Любля́на.
llama [ˈlɑːmə] *n* ла́ма (ЗООЛ).
LLB *n abbr* (= Bachelor of Laws) ≈ бакала́вр правове́дения.
LLD *n abbr* (= Doctor of Laws) ≈ до́ктор правове́дения.
LMT *abbr* (US) = Local Mean Time.
load [ləud] *n* (of person, animal) но́ша; (of vehicle) груз; (weight, also ELEC, TECH) нагру́зка* ♦ *vt* (also: ~ **up**: cargo, goods) грузи́ть* (погрузи́ть* perf); (COMPUT) загружа́ть (загрузи́ть* perf); (gun, camera) заряжа́ть (заряди́ть* perf); (tape recorder) ста́вить* (поста́вить* perf) кассе́ту в +prp; **to** ~ (**with**) (also: ~ **up**: vehicle, ship) нагружа́ть (нагрузи́ть* perf) (+instr); ~**s of**, **a** ~ **of** (inf) ку́ча +gen; **a** ~ **of rubbish** (inf) сплошна́я чепуха́.
loaded [ˈləudɪd] *adj* (gun) заря́женный (заря́жен); (dice) утяжелённый (утяжелён); (vehicle): ~ (**with**) нагру́женный (нагру́жен) (+instr); (inf): **he's** ~ у него́ ку́ча де́нег; ~ **question** вопро́с с подво́хом.
loading bay [ˈləudɪŋ-] *n* погру́зочная площа́дка*.
loaf [ləuf] (pl **loaves**) *n* буха́нка* ♦ *vi* (also: ~ **about** or **around**: inf) болта́ться (impf) без

дéла; **use your ~!** (*inf*) шевелúте мозгáми!
loam [ləum] *n* суглúнок*.
loan [ləun] *n* заём*; (*money*) ссýда* ◆ *vt* давáть*
(дать* *perf*) взаймы́; (*money*) ссужáть
(ссудúть* *perf*); **to take sth on ~** брать*
(взять* *perf*) чтó-н на врéмя.
loan account *n* ссýдный счёт*.
loan capital *n* заёмный *or* ссýдный капитáл.
loan shark *n* (*inf: pej*) ростовщúк
(*ссужáющий дéньги под óчень высóкие
процéнты*).
loath [ləuθ] *adj*: **he is ~ to ...** емý óчень не
хóчется +*infin* ....
loathe [ləuð] *vt* ненавúдеть* (*impf*).
loathing [ˈləuðɪŋ] *n* отвращéние, омерзéние.
loathsome [ˈləuðsəm] *adj* отвратúтельный*
(отвратúтелен), омерзúтельный*
(омерзúтелен).
loaves [ləuvz] *npl of* **loaf**.
lob [lɔb] *vt* (*ball*) перебрáсывать (перебро́сить*
perf).
lobby [ˈlɔbɪ] *n* (*of building*) вестибю́ль *m*;
(*pressure group*) ло́бби *nt ind* ◆ *vt* (*politician*)
склоня́ть (склони́ть *perf*) на свою́ сто́рону.
lobbyist [ˈlɔbɪɪst] *n* лобби́ст.
lobe [ləub] *n* (*of ear*) мо́чка*.
lobster [ˈlɔbstəʳ] *n* ома́р.
lobster pot *n* ве́рша* для ома́ров.
local [ˈləukl] *adj* ме́стный ◆ *n* (*BRIT: inf*): **this is
my ~** э́то мой люби́мый ме́стный паб; **the
~s** *npl* ме́стные жи́тели *mpl*.
local anaesthetic *n* ме́стный нарко́з.
local authority *n* ме́стные вла́сти* *fpl*.
local call *n* (*TEL*) ме́стный (телефо́нный)
разгово́р.
locale [ləuˈkɑ:l] *n* ме́сто*.
local government *n* ме́стные вла́сти* *fpl*.
locality [ləuˈkælɪtɪ] *n* ме́стность *f*.
localize [ˈləukəlaɪz] *vt* (*limit*) локализова́ть
(*impf/perf*).
locally [ˈləukəlɪ] *adv* (*live*) побли́зости; (*solve
problems*) на места́х.
locate [ləuˈkeɪt] *vt* определя́ть (определи́ть
perf) местонахожде́ние +*gen*; (*situate*): **to be
~d in** находи́ться* (*impf*) в *or* на +*prp*.
location [ləuˈkeɪʃən] *n* (*place*)
местонахожде́ние; (*finding*): **~ (of)** лока́ция
(+*gen*); **on ~** (*CINEMA*) на нату́ре.
loch [lɔx] *n* (*SCOTTISH*) о́зеро*.
lock [lɔk] *n* (*on door etc*) замо́к*; (*on canal*)
шлюз; (*of hair*) ло́кон ◆ *vt* запира́ть
(запере́ть* *perf*); (*immobilize*) фикси́ровать
(зафикси́ровать *perf*) ◆ *vi* (*door*) запира́ться
(запере́ться* *perf*); (*jaw, mechanism*)
смыка́ться (сомкну́ться *perf*); (*wheels*)
тормози́ть* (затормози́ть* *perf*); **the steering
wheel was on full ~** (*AUT*) руль был повёрнут
до отка́за; **~, stock and barrel** всё целико́м

▶ **lock away** *vt* (*valuables*) пря́тать* (спря́тать*
perf) под замо́к; (*criminal*) заключа́ть
(заключи́ть *perf*) под стра́жу
▶ **lock in** *vt*: **to ~ sb in** запира́ть (запере́ть* *perf*)
кого́-н
▶ **lock out** *vt* (*person*) запира́ть (запере́ть* *perf*)
дверь и не впуска́ть (впусти́ть* *perf*);
(*INDUSTRY*) объявля́ть (объяви́ть* *perf*)
лока́ут +*dat*
▶ **lock up** *vt* (*criminal, mental patient*)
упря́тывать (упря́тать* *perf*); (*house*)
запира́ть (запере́ть* *perf*) ◆ *vi* запира́ться
(запере́ться* *perf*).
locker [ˈlɔkəʳ] *n* шка́фчик.
locker room *n* раздева́лка*.
locket [ˈlɔkɪt] *n* медальо́н.
lockjaw [ˈlɔkdʒɔ:] *n* (*trismus*) тризм; (*tetanus*)
столбня́к.
lockout [ˈlɔkaut] *n* (*INDUSTRY*) лока́ут.
locksmith [ˈlɔksmɪθ] *n* сле́сарь* *m*.
lockup [ˈlɔkʌp] *n* (*jail*) куту́зка*; (*BRIT: also:
lock-up garage) гара́ж.
locomotive [ləukəˈməutɪv] *n* локомоти́в.
locum [ˈləukəm] *n* (*MED*) *врач, вре́менно
замеща́ющий друго́го врача́*.
locust [ˈləukəst] *n* саранча́* *f no pl*.
lodge [lɔdʒ] *n* привра́тницкая *f adj*; (*also:
hunting ~*) охо́тничий* дом*; (*also:* **masonic
~**) масо́нская ло́жа ◆ *vt* (*complaint*)
подава́ть* (пода́ть* *perf*) ◆ *vi* (*bullet*)
застрева́ть (застря́ть* *perf*); (*person*): **to ~
(with)** (вре́менно) жить* (*impf*) на кварти́ре (у
+*gen*).
lodger [ˈlɔdʒəʳ] *n* кварти́рант(ка).
lodging [ˈlɔdʒɪŋ] *n* (вре́менное) жильё.
lodging house *n* меблиро́ванные ко́мнаты
fpl.
lodgings [ˈlɔdʒɪŋz] *npl* кварти́ра *fsg*.
loft [lɔft] *n* черда́к*.
lofty [ˈlɔftɪ] *adj* (*high*) высо́кий* (высо́к);
(*noble*) возвы́шенный (возвы́шен); (*self-
important*) высокоме́рный* (высокоме́рен).
log [lɔg] *n abbr* = **logarithm**.
log [lɔg] *n* (*piece of wood*) бревно́*; (: *for fire*)
поле́но*; (*account*) журна́л ◆ *vt* (*event, fact*)
регистри́ровать (зарегистри́ровать *perf*)
▶ **log in** *vi* (*COMPUT*) входи́ть* (войти́* *perf*) в
систе́му
▶ **log into** *vt fus* (*COMPUT*) входи́ть* (войти́* *perf*)
в +*acc*
▶ **log off** *vi* (*COMPUT*) выходи́ть* (вы́йти* *perf*)
из систе́мы
▶ **log on** *vi* = **log in**
▶ **log out** *vi* = **log off**.
logarithm [ˈlɔgərɪðm] *n* логари́фм.
logbook [ˈlɔgbuk] *n* (*NAUT*) ва́хтенный
журна́л; (*AVIAT*) бортово́й журна́л; (*of car,
lorry*) формуля́р; (*of events, movement of*

---

* marks translations which have irregular inflections. The Russian-English side of the dictionary gives inflectional information.

goods) журна́л.

log fire n дровяно́й ками́н.

logger ['lɔgə'] n лесору́б.

loggerheads ['lɔgəhedz] npl: **to be at** ~ **(with)** конфликтова́ть (impf) (с +instr).

logic ['lɔdʒɪk] n ло́гика.

logical ['lɔdʒɪkl] adj (based on logic) логи́ческий*; (reasonable) логи́чный* (логи́чен).

logically ['lɔdʒɪkəlɪ] adv (see adj) логи́чески; логи́чно.

logistics [lɔ'dʒɪstɪks] npl организа́ция fsg.

log jam ['lɔgdʒæm] n (fig) тупи́к.

logo ['ləugəu] n эмбле́ма.

loin [lɔɪn] n (of meat) филе́йная часть* f; ~**s** npl (ANAT) чре́сла pl.

loincloth ['lɔɪnklɔθ] n набе́дренная повя́зка*.

Loire [lwɑ:] n: **the** ~ Луа́ра.

loiter ['lɔɪtə'] vi слоня́ться (impf).

loll [lɔl] vi (person: also: ~ **about**) разва́ливаться (развали́ться* perf); (head, tongue) све́шиваться (све́ситься* perf).

lollipop ['lɔlɪpɔp] n ледене́ц* на па́лочке ♦ cpd: ~ **man/lady** (BRIT) регулиро́вщик/ регулиро́вщица движе́ния, кото́рый обеспе́чивает безопа́сный перехо́д у́лицы шко́льниками.

lollop ['lɔləp] vi бе́гать/бежа́ть* (impf) вперева́лку.

lolly ['lɔlɪ] n (inf: lollipop) ледене́ц на па́лочке; (: also: **ice** ~) моро́женое на па́лочке; (: money) деньжа́та pl.

London ['lʌndən] n Ло́ндон.

Londoner ['lʌndənə'] n ло́ндонец*(-донка).

lone [ləun] adj (person, parent) одино́кий*; (thing) еди́нственный.

loneliness ['ləunlɪnɪs] n одино́чество.

lonely ['ləunlɪ] adj (person, childhood) одино́кий* (одино́к); (place) уединённый (уединён).

lonely hearts n одино́кие сердца́ nt pl.

lone parent n (father) оте́ц*-одино́чка; (mother) мать* f-одино́чка.

loner ['ləunə'] n одино́чка* m/f.

long [lɔŋ] adj (in time) до́лгий* (до́лог); (road, book) дли́нный* (дли́нен); (clothes) дли́нен ♦ adv (see adj) до́лго; дли́нно ♦ vi: **to** ~ **for sth/to do** жа́ждать (impf) чего́-н/+infin; **in the** ~ **run** в коне́чном ито́ге; **so** or **as** ~ **as you don't mind** е́сли то́лько Вы не возража́ете; **don't be** ~! не заде́рживайтесь!; **how** ~ **is the street?** какова́ длина́ э́той у́лицы?; **how** ~ **is the lesson?** ско́лько дли́тся уро́к?; **6 metres** ~ длино́й в 6 ме́тров; **6 months** ~ продолжи́тельностью в 6 ме́сяцев; **all night (long)** всю ночь (напролёт); **he no** ~**er comes** он бо́льше не прихо́дит; ~ **ago** давно́; ~ **before** задо́лго до +gen; ~ **after** до́лгое вре́мя по́сле +gen; **before** ~ вско́ре; **at** ~ **last** наконе́ц; **the** ~ **and the short of it is that ...** коро́че говоря́ ....

long-distance [lɔŋ'dɪstəns] adj (travel) да́льний* (да́лен); ~ **race** забе́г на дли́нную диста́нцию; ~ **runner** бегу́н на дли́нные диста́нции.

long-distance call n (within same country) междугоро́дный (телефо́нный) разгово́р; (international) междунаро́дный (телефо́нный) разгово́р.

longevity [lɔn'dʒevɪtɪ] n (of person) долголе́тие; (of scheme, marriage etc) долгове́чность f.

long-haired ['lɔŋ'hɛəd] adj (person) длинноволо́сый (длинноволо́с); (animal) длинношёрстый.

longhand ['lɔŋhænd] n: **in** ~ (write) от руки́.

longing ['lɔŋɪŋ] n: ~ **(for)** тоска́ (по +dat).

longingly ['lɔŋɪŋlɪ] adv с тоско́й.

longitude ['lɔŋgɪtju:d] n долгота́.

long johns [-dʒɔnz] npl кальсо́ны* pl.

long jump n прыжо́к* в длину́.

long-life ['lɔŋlaɪf] adj (milk etc) консерви́рованный; (battery) продлённого де́йствия.

long-lost ['lɔŋlɔst] adj (relative etc) давно́ утра́ченный (утра́чен) or поте́рянный (поте́рян).

long-playing record ['lɔŋpleɪŋ-] n долгоигра́ющая пласти́нка.

long-range ['lɔŋ'reɪndʒ] adj (plan, forecast) долгосро́чный* (долгосро́чен); (missile) дальнобо́йный.

longshoreman ['lɔŋʃɔ:mən] n (US) порто́вый гру́зчик.

long-sighted ['lɔŋ'saɪtɪd] adj дальнозо́ркий* (дальнозо́рок).

long-standing ['lɔŋ'stændɪŋ] adj долголе́тний.

long-suffering ['lɔŋ'sʌfərɪŋ] adj много-страда́льный* (многострада́лен).

long-term ['lɔŋtə:m] adj долгосро́чный* (долгосро́чен).

long wave n (RADIO) дли́нные во́лны fpl.

long-winded [lɔŋ'wɪndɪd] adj многосло́вный* (многосло́вен).

loo [lu:] n (BRIT: inf) туале́т.

loofah ['lu:fə] n люфа́ (гу́бка).

look [luk] vi (see) смотре́ть* (посмотре́ть* perf); (glance) взгля́нуть (perf); (seem, appear) вы́глядеть* (impf) ♦ n (glance) взгляд; (appearance) вид; (expression) выраже́ние; ~**s** npl: **good** ~**s** краси́вая вне́шность fsg; **to** ~ **south/(out) onto the sea** (face) выходи́ть* (impf) на юг/на мо́ре; ~ **(here)!** (expressing annoyance) послу́шайте!; ~**!** (expressing surprise) смотри́те!; **to** ~ **like sb/sth** походи́ть* (impf) на кого́-н/что-н; **the wall** ~**s about 4 metres long** похо́же, что длина́ э́той стены́ 4 ме́тра; **everything** ~**s all right to me** мне ка́жется, что всё в поря́дке; **it** ~**s as if he's not coming** похо́же, что он не придёт; **to** ~ **ahead** смотре́ть* (посмотре́ть* perf) вперёд; **to have a** ~ посмотре́ть* (perf),

взгляну́ть *(perf)*; **to ~ around** осма́триваться
(осмотре́ться* *perf*); **to have a ~ at sth** *(glance
at)* взгляну́ть* *(perf)* на что-н; *(study)*
рассма́тривать (рассмотре́ть* *(perf))* что-н;
to have a ~ for sth иска́ть* (поиска́ть* *perf)*
что-н; **you can't tell by ~s alone** нельзя́
суди́ть то́лько по вне́шности
▶ **look after** *vt fus (care for)* уха́живать *(impf)* за
+*instr*; *(deal with)* забо́титься* *(impf)* о +*prp*
▶ **look (a)round** *vt fus (castle, museum etc)*
осма́тривать (осмотре́ть* *perf)*
▶ **look at** *vt fus (see)* смотре́ть* (посмотре́ть*
perf) на +*acc*; *(study)* рассма́тривать
(рассмотре́ть* *perf)*; *(read quickly)*
просма́тривать (просмотре́ть* *perf)*
▶ **look back** *vi (turn around)*: **to ~ back (at sth/
sb)** огля́дываться (огляну́ться* *perf)* (на
что-н/кого́-н); **to ~ back (at** *or* **on the past)**
огля́дываться (огляну́ться* *perf)* (на
про́шлое)
▶ **look down on** *vt fus (fig)* смотре́ть* *(impf)*
свысока́ на +*acc*
▶ **look for** *vt fus* иска́ть* (поиска́ть* *perf)*
▶ **look forward to** *vt fus*: **to ~ forward to sth**
ждать* *(impf)* чего́-н с нетерпе́нием; *(in
letters)*: **we ~ forward to hearing from you** (с
нетерпе́нием) ждём Ва́шего отве́та
▶ **look in** *vi*: **to ~ in on sb** загля́дывать
(загляну́ть* *perf)* к кому́-н
▶ **look into** *vt fus* рассле́довать *(impf/perf)*
▶ **look on** *vi (watch)* наблюда́ть *(impf)*
▶ **look out** *vi (beware)*: **to ~ out (for)**
остерега́ться *(impf)* (+*gen)*; *(glance out)*: **to ~
out (of)** выгля́дывать (вы́глянуть *perf)* (в
+*acc)*
▶ **look out for** *vt fus (search for)* стара́ться
(постара́ться* *perf)* найти́
▶ **look over** *vt (essay)* просма́тривать
(просмотре́ть* *perf)*; *(town, building)*
осма́тривать (осмотре́ть* *perf)*; *(person)*
проверя́ть (прове́рить *perf)*
▶ **look round** *vi* осма́триваться (осмотре́ться*
perf)
▶ **look through** *vt fus (papers)* просма́тривать
(просмотре́ть* *perf)*; *(window)* смотре́ть*
(посмотре́ть* *perf)* в +*acc*
▶ **look to** *vt fus (rely on)* ждать* *(impf)* от +*gen*
▶ **look up** *vi (with eyes)* поднима́ть (подня́ть*
perf) глаза́; *(situation)* идти́* *(impf)* к лу́чшему
◆ *vt (piece of information)* посмотре́ть* *(perf)*
▶ **look up to** *vt fus* почита́ть *(impf)*.
lookalike ['lukəlaɪk] *n* двойни́к*.
look-in ['lukɪn] *n*: **to get a ~** *(inf)* получи́ть*
(perf) свой кусо́к пирога́; **I couldn't get a ~** *(in
conversation)* я не мог вста́вить слова́.
lookout ['lukaut] *n (person)* наблюда́тель
(ница) *m(f)*; *(point)* наблюда́тельный пункт;
to be on the ~ быть* *(impf)* начеку́ *or*

насторо́же; **to be on the ~ for sth**
присма́тривать *(impf)* что-н.
LOOM *n abbr* (*US*: = *Loyal Order of Moose*)
та́йное о́бщество.
loom [lu:m] *vi (also:* **~ up**: *object)* нея́сно
вырисо́вываться *(impf)*; *(event)* надвига́ться
(impf) ◆ *n* тка́цкий* стано́к*.
loony ['lu:nɪ] *(inf) adj* чо́кнутый ◆ *n*
чо́кнутый(-ая) *m(f) adj*.
loop [lu:p] *n (also COMPUT)* пе́тля*;
(contraceptive) спира́ль *f* ◆ *vt*: **to ~ sth round
sth** завя́зывать (завяза́ть* *perf)* что-н пе́тлей
вокру́г чего́-н.
loophole ['lu:phəul] *n* лазе́йка*.
loose [lu:s] *adj* свобо́дный (свобо́ден); *(knot,
grip)* сла́бый (слаб); *(hair)* распу́щенный
(распу́щен); *(definition, translation)*
приблизи́тельный (приблизи́телен); *(weave)* непло́тный (непло́тен);
(promiscuous) распу́щенный; *(ELEC)*: **~
connection** сла́бый конта́кт ◆ *n*: **to be on the
~** быть* *(impf)* в бега́х; **the handle is ~** ру́чка
расшата́лась; **to set ~** *(prisoner)*
освобожда́ть (освободи́ть* *perf)*; *(unleash)*
высвобожда́ть (вы́свободить* *perf)*; **to come
~** расша́тываться (расшата́ться* *perf)*.
loose change *n* ме́лочь *f*.
loose chippings *npl (on road)* щебёнка *fsg*.
loose end *n*: **to be at a ~ ~** *or (US)* **at ~ ~s**
шата́ться *(impf)* без де́ла; **to tie up (the) ~ ~s**
заверша́ть (заверши́ть *perf)* все ме́лочи.
loose-fitting ['lu:sfɪtɪŋ] *adj* просто́рный*
(просто́рен).
loose-leaf ['lu:sli:f] *adj* отрывно́й.
loose-limbed [lu:s'lɪmd] *adj* ги́бкий* (ги́бок).
loosely ['lu:slɪ] *adv (freely)* свобо́дно; *(vaguely)*
приблизи́тельно.
loosely-knit ['lu:slɪ'nɪt] *adj* ре́дко свя́занный.
loosen ['lu:sn] *vt (belt, screw, grip)* ослабля́ть
(осла́бить* *perf)*; *(by shaking)* расша́тывать
(расшата́ть* *perf)*.
▶ **loosen up** *vi (before game)* разогрева́ться
(разогре́ться *perf)*; *(inf: relax)* расслабля́ться
(рассла́биться* *perf)*.
loot [lu:t] *n (inf)* награ́бленное *nt adj* ◆ *vt (shops,
homes)* разграбля́ть (разгра́бить* *perf)*.
looter ['lu:tə] *n (during riot)* граби́тель(ница)
m(f); *(during war)* мародёр.
looting ['lu:tɪŋ] *n* разграбле́ние; *(during war)*
мароде́рство.
lop off [lɔp-] *vt (branches etc)* отреза́ть
(отре́зать* *perf)*.
lopsided ['lɔp'saɪdɪd] *adj* кривобо́кий
(кривобо́к); *(smile)* криво́й* (крив).
lord [lɔ:d] *n (BRIT: peer)* лорд; *(REL)*: **the L~**
Госпо́дь* *m*; **my L~** *(to bishop, noble, judge)*
мило́рд; **good L~!** Бо́же мой!; **the (House of)
L~s** *(BRIT)* пала́та ло́рдов.

---

* marks translations which have irregular inflections. The Russian-English side of the dictionary gives inflectional information.

lordly ['lɔ:dlɪ] *adj* бáрственный.
lordship ['lɔ:dʃɪp] *n*: **your L~** Вáша свéтлость *f*.
lore [lɔ:ʳ] *n* предáния *ntpl*.
lorry ['lɒrɪ] *n* (*BRIT*) грузовúк*.
lorry driver *n* (*BRIT*) водúтель *m* грузовикá.
Los Angeles [lɒs 'ændʒɪli:z] *n* Лос-Áнджелес.
lose [lu:z] (*pt, pp* **lost**) *vt* терять (потерять *perf*); (*contest, argument*) прóигрывать (проигрáть *perf*); (*pursuers*) избавляться (избáвиться* *perf*) от +*gen* ♦ *vi* (*in contest, argument*) прóигрывать (проигрáть *perf*); **to ~ (time)** (*clock*) отставáть* (отстáть* *perf*); **to ~ sight of sth** терять (потерять *perf*) из вúду что-н; (*fig*) упускáть (упустúть* *perf*) из вúду что-н.
loser ['lu:zəʳ] *n* (*in contest*) проигрáвший(-ая) *m(f) adj*; (*inf: failure*) неудáчник(-ица); **to be a good/bad ~** умéть (*impf*)/не умéть достóйно прóигрывать (*impf*).
loss [lɒs] *n* потéря; (*sense of bereavement*) утрáта; (*COMM*): **to make a ~** терпéть* (потерпéть* *perf*) убы́ток; **to sell sth at a ~** продавáть* (продáть* *perf*) что-н в убы́ток; **heavy ~es** тяжёлые потéри *fpl*; **to cut one's ~es** сокращáть (сократúть* *perf*) потéри; **to be at a ~** терять́ся (растеряться *perf*); **to be at a ~ for words** не найтúсь* (*perf*), что сказáть.
loss adjuster *n* специалúст по оцéнке убы́тков.
loss leader *n* *товáр, продавáемый в убы́ток для привлечéния покупáтелей.*
lost [lɒst] *pt, pp of* **lose** ♦ *adj* (*person, animal*) пропáвший; (*object*) потéрянный (потéрян); **to get ~** заблудúться* (*perf*); **get ~!** (*inf*) провáливай!; **he was ~ in thought** он был погружён в свой мы́сли.
lost and found *n* (*US*) стол *or* бюрó *nt ind* нахóдок.
lost cause *n* прóигранное дéло*.
lost property *n* потéрянные вéщи *fpl*; (*BRIT: also: ~ ~ office*) стол *or* бюрó *nt ind* нахóдок.
lot [lɒt] *n* (*of people, goods*) пáртия; (*at auction*) лот; (*destiny*) ýчасть *f*; (*at US: ground*) (*земéльный*) учáсток*; (*large number, amount*): **a ~ (of)** мнóго (+*gen*); **the ~** (*everything*) всё; **~s of ...** мнóго +*gen* ...; **I see a ~ of him** мы с ним чáсто вúдимся; **I read/don't read a ~** я мнóго/мáло читáю; **a ~ bigger/louder/more expensive** намнóго *or* горáздо бóльше/грóмче/дорóже; **to draw ~s (for sth)** тянýть (*impf*) жрéбий (для чегó-н).
lotion ['ləuʃən] *n* (*for skin, hair*) лосьóн.
lottery ['lɒtərɪ] *n* лотерéя.
loud [laud] *adj* (*noise, voice, laugh*) грóмкий* (грóмок); (*support, condemnation*) шýмный* (шýмен); (*clothes*) кричáщий* ♦ *adv* грóмко; **out ~** вслух.
loud-hailer [laud'heɪləʳ] *n* (*BRIT*) рýпор.
loudly ['laudlɪ] *adv* (*see adj*) грóмко; шýмно.
loudmouthed ['laudmauθt] *adj* горлáстый (горлáст).
loudspeaker [laud'spi:kəʳ] *n* громко-

говорúтель *m*.
lounge [laundʒ] *n* (*in house, hotel*) гостúная *f adj*; (*at airport*) зал ожидáния; (*BRIT: also: ~ bar*) часть бáра, где посетúтели сидя́т ♦ *vi* (*in chair*) развалúться (*perf*)
▶ **lounge about** *vi* болтáться (*impf*) (без дéла)
▶ **lounge around** *vi* = **lounge about.**
lounge suit *n* (*BRIT*) пиджáчный костю́м.
louse [laus] (*pl* **lice**) *n* (*insect*) вошь* *f*
▶ **louse up** *vt* (*inf*) напóртить* (*perf*) +*dat*.
lousy ['lauzɪ] *adj* (*inf: bad quality*) паршúвый; (*: ill*): **to feel ~** чýвствовать (*impf*) себя́ паршúво.
lout [laut] *n* (*inf*) хам.
louvre ['lu:vəʳ] (*US* **louver**) *n* жалюзú *nt ind*.
lovable ['lʌvəbl] *adj* мúлый* (мил).
love [lʌv] *vt* любúть* (*impf*) ♦ *n*: ~ **(for)** любóвь* *f* (к +*dat*); **to ~ to do** любúть* (*impf*) +*infin*; **I ~ chocolate** я люблю́ шоколáд; **I'd ~ to come** я с удовóльствием пришёл бы; **"love (from) Anne"** (*in letter*) „любящая Вас Áнна"; **to fall in ~ with** влюбляться (влюбúться* *perf*) в +*acc*; **he is in ~ with her** он в неё влюблён; **to make ~** занимáться (заняться* *perf*) любóвью; ~ **at first sight** любóвь* с пéрвого взгля́да; **to send one's ~ to sb** передавáть (передáть* *perf*) привéт комý-н; **"fifteen ~"** (*TENNIS*) „пятнáдцать – ноль".
love affair *n* ромáн.
love child *n* дитя́* *nt* любвú.
loved ones ['lʌvdwʌnz] *npl* любúмые *pl adj*.
love-hate relationship ['lʌvheɪt-] *n* любóвь *f*-нéнависть *f*.
love letter *n* любóвное письмó*.
love life *n* интúмная жизнь *f*.
lovely ['lʌvlɪ] *adj* (*beautiful*) красúвый (красúв); (*delightful*) чудéсный* (чудéсен).
lover ['lʌvəʳ] *n* (*sexual partner*) любóвник (-ица); (*person in love*) влюблённый(-ая)*m(f) adj*; **a ~ of art/music** любúтель(ница) *m(f)* искýсства/мýзыки.
lovesick ['lʌvsɪk] *adj* томúмый любóвью; **to be ~** томúться* (*impf*) от любвú.
love song *n* любóвная пéсня*.
loving ['lʌvɪŋ] *adj* (*person*) любящий*, нéжный* (нéжен); (*actions*) нéжный* (нéжен).
low [ləu] *adj* нúзкий* (нúзок); (*sound: quiet*) тúхий* (тих); (*depressed*) подáвленный (подáвлен); (*ill*) нездорóвый (нездорóв) ♦ *adv* (*sing: deeply*) нúзким гóлосом; (*: quietly*) тúхо; (*fly*) нúзко ♦ *n* (*METEOROLOGY*) нúзкое давлéние; **we are (running) ~ on milk** у нас остаётся мéло молокá; **to reach a new** *or* **an all-time ~** (*morale, profits*) опускáться (опустúться* *perf*) на небывáло нúзкий ýровень.
low-alcohol ['ləu'ælkəhɒl] *adj*: ~ **wine/beer** винó/пúво с нúзким содержáнием алкогóля.
lowbrow ['ləubrau] *adj* низкопрóбный.
low-calorie ['ləu'kælərɪ] *adj* низко-

калори́йный* (низкокалори́ен).
low-cut ['ləukʌt] *adj* с глубо́ким вы́резом.
lowdown ['ləudaun] *n* (*inf*): **to give sb the ~ on
sth** раскрыва́ть (раскры́ть* *perf*) пе́ред кем-н
всю подного́тную чего́-н.
lower ['ləuə^r] *adj* (*bottom: of two things*)
ни́жний*; (*less important*) ни́зший* ♦ *vt*
(*object*) спуска́ть (спусти́ть* *perf*); (*level,
price*) снижа́ть (сни́зить* *perf*); (*voice*)
понижа́ть (пони́зить* *perf*); (*eyes*) опуска́ть
(опусти́ть* *perf*).
low-fat ['ləu'fæt] *adj* обезжи́ренный
(обезжи́рен).
low-key ['ləu'ki:] *adj* сде́ржанный (сде́ржан).
lowlands ['ləuləndz] *npl* ни́зменность *fsg*.
low-level language ['ləulɛvl-] *n* (*COMPUT*)
язы́к* программи́рования ни́зкого у́ровня.
low-loader ['ləuləudə^r] *n* автомоби́ль *m* с
погру́зочным приспособле́нием.
lowly ['ləulı] *adj* (*position, origin*) ни́зкий*
(ни́зок).
low-lying [ləu'laıŋ] *adj* ни́зменный.
low-paid [ləu'peıd] *adj* низкоопла́чиваемый
(низкоопла́чиваем).
low-rise ['ləuraız] *adj* ни́зкий* (ни́зок).
low-tech ['ləutɛk] *adj*: **their office is very ~** у
них в о́фисе техноло́гия на о́чень ни́зком
у́ровне.
loyal ['lɔıəl] *adj* ве́рный* (ве́рен); (*POL*)
лоя́льный* (лоя́лен).
loyalist ['lɔıəlıst] *n* лоялист(ка).
loyalty ['lɔıəltı] *n* ве́рность *f*; (*POL*) лоя́льность
f.
lozenge ['lɔzındʒ] *n* (*shape*) ромб; (*pastille*):
throat ~ табле́тка* от ка́шля.
LP *n abbr* = **long-playing record**.
L-plate ['ɛlpleıt] *n* (*BRIT*) *знак на маши́не,
обознача́ющий "учени́к"*.
LPN *n abbr* (*US*) = **Licensed Practical Nurse**.
LRAM *n abbr* (*BRIT*) = **Licentiate of the Royal
Academy of Music**.
LSAT *n abbr* (*US*) = **Law School Admissions Test**.
LSD *n abbr* (= *lysergic acid diethylamide*) ЛСД;
(*BRIT*: = *pounds, shillings and pence*) *фу́нты,
ши́ллинги и пе́нсы*.
LSE *n abbr* (*BRIT*) = **London School of Economics**.
LT *abbr* (*ELEC*: = *low tension*) ни́зкое
напряже́ние.
Lt *abbr* (*MIL*) = **lieutenant**.
Ltd *abbr* (*COMM*) = **limited (liability) company**.
lubricant ['lu:brıkənt] *n* сма́зка, лубрика́тор.
lubricate ['lu:brıkeıt] *vt* сма́зывать (сма́зать*
perf).
lucid ['lu:sıd] *adj* (*writing, speech*) я́сный*
(я́сен); (*thinking*): **I'm not feeling very ~ today**
я сего́дня пло́хо сообража́ю.
lucidity [lu:'sıdıtı] *n* я́сность *f*.
luck [lʌk] *n* (*also*: **good ~**) уда́ча; **bad ~**

неуда́ча; **good ~!** уда́чи (Вам)!; **bad** *or* **hard** *or*
tough ~! не повезло́!; **we are in ~/out of ~**
нам везёт/не везёт; **to push one's ~**
искуша́ть (*impf*) судьбу́.
luckily ['lʌkılı] *adv* к сча́стью.
luckless ['lʌklıs] *adj* невезу́чий (невезу́ч).
lucky ['lʌkı] *adj* (*situation, event, object*)
счастли́вый; (*person*) уда́чливый (уда́члив);
he is ~ at cards/in love ему́ везёт в ка́ртах/
любви́; **how did you manage it? – I was ~** как
Вам э́то удало́сь? – мне повезло́.
lucrative ['lu:krətıv] *adj* (*profitable*)
при́быльный* (при́былен), дохо́дный*
(дохо́ден); (*job*) высокоопла́чиваемый.
ludicrous ['lu:dıkrəs] *adj* смехотво́рный*
(смехотво́рен).
ludo ['lu:dəu] *n насто́льная игра́ с фи́шками и
броса́нием косте́й*.
lug [lʌg] *vt* (*inf*) волочи́ть* (*impf*).
luggage ['lʌgıdʒ] *n* бага́ж*.
luggage car *n* = **luggage van**.
luggage rack *n* (*in train*) бага́жная по́лка.
luggage van *n* (*BRIT*) бага́жный ваго́н.
lugubrious [lu'gu:brıəs] *adj* ско́рбный*
(ско́рбен).
lukewarm ['lu:kwɔ:m] *adj* (*liquid*) слегка́
тёплый; (*reaction*) прохла́дный*
(прохла́ден).
lull [lʌl] *n* зати́шье ♦ *vt*: **to ~ sb to sleep**
убаю́кивать (убаю́кать *perf*) кого́-н; **to ~ sb
into a false sense of security** усыпля́ть
(усыпи́ть* *perf*) чью-н бди́тельность.
lullaby ['lʌləbaı] *n* колыбе́льная *f adj*.
lumbago [lʌm'beıgəu] *n* люмба́го *nt ind*.
lumber ['lʌmbə^r] *n* (*esp US: wood*) лесо-
материа́лы *mpl*; (*junk*) ру́хлядь *f* ♦ *vi*: **to ~
about/along** *etc* тащи́ться (*impf*)
▸ **lumber with** *vt*: **to ~ sb with sth** навя́зывать
(навяза́ть* *perf*) кому́-н что-н; **he was ~ed
with all the work** ему́ навяза́ли всю рабо́ту.
lumberjack ['lʌmbədʒæk] *n* лесору́б.
lumber room *n* (*BRIT*) чула́н.
lumberyard ['lʌmbəjɑ:d] *n* (*US*) склад
лесоматериа́лов.
luminous ['lu:mınəs] *adj* (*fabric, colour*)
блестя́щий*; (*digit, star*) светя́щийся.
lump [lʌmp] *n* (*of clay, snow*) ком; (*of butter,
sugar etc*) кусо́к*; (*swelling*) ши́шка; (*growth*)
о́пухоль *f* ♦ *vt*: **to ~ together** меша́ть
(смеша́ть *perf*) в (одну́) ку́чу; **a ~ sum**
единовре́менно выпла́чиваемая су́мма.
lumpy ['lʌmpı] *adj* (*sauce*) комкова́тый; (*bed*)
бугри́стый (бугри́ст).
lunacy ['lu:nəsı] *n* (*fig*) безу́мие; (*mental illness*)
помеша́тельство.
lunar ['lu:nə^r] *adj* лу́нный.
lunatic ['lu:nətık] *adj* (*behaviour*) безу́мный*
(безу́мен) ♦ *n* (*also fig*) сумасше́дший*(-ая)

---

* marks translations which have irregular inflections. The Russian-English side of the dictionary gives inflectional information.

m(f) adj.

lunatic asylum *n* сумасше́дший* дом*.

lunatic fringe *n*: **the** ~~ ку́чка фана́тиков.

lunch [lʌntʃ] *n* обе́д ◆ *vi* обе́дать (пообе́дать *perf).*

lunch break *n* переры́в на обе́д, обе́денный переры́в.

luncheon [ˈlʌntʃən] *n (formal meal)* за́втрак.

luncheon meat *n* свина́я тушёнка.

luncheon voucher *n (BRIT)* тало́н на обе́д.

lunch hour *n* = **lunch break**.

lunch time *n* обе́денное вре́мя* *nt.*

lung [lʌŋ] *n* лёгкое *nt adj*; ~ **cancer** рак лёгких.

lunge [lʌndʒ] *vi (also:* ~ **forward)** рвану́ться *(perf);* (*SPORT)* де́лать (сде́лать *perf)* вы́пад; **to** ~ **at** ри́нуться *(perf)* на +*acc;* (*SPORT)* де́лать (сде́лать *perf)* вы́пад про́тив +*gen.*

lupin [ˈluːpɪn] *n (BOT)* люпи́н.

lurch [ləːtʃ] *vi (person)* покачну́ться *(perf);* (*vehicle)* рвану́ть *(perf);* (*ship):* **to** ~ **sideways** крени́ться* (накрени́ться* *perf)* ◆ *n (of ship)* крен; *(of vehicle)* бросо́к*; **the car** ~**ed forward** маши́ну бро́сило вперёд; **to leave sb in the** ~ (*inf)* броса́ть (бро́сить* *perf)* кого́-н в беде́.

lure [luəʳ] *n* прима́нка ◆ *vt* зама́нивать (замани́ть* *perf);* **to** ~ **sb away from** отвлека́ть (отвле́чь* *perf)* кого́-н от +*gen.*

lurid [ˈluərɪd] *adj (garish)* аляпова́тый (аляпова́т).

lurk [ləːk] *vi (animal, person, also fig)* тайться *(impf).*

luscious [ˈlʌʃəs] *adj (person, thing)* притяга́тельный* (притяга́телен); (*food)* со́чный* (со́чен).

lush [lʌʃ] *adj (fields, gardens)* пы́шный* (пы́шен); *(restaurant, lifestyle)* роско́шный* (роско́шен).

lust [lʌst] *n (sexual desire)* по́хоть *f*; (*greed):* ~ **(for)** жа́жда (к +*dat)*

▶ **lust after** *vt fus (desire sexually)* испы́тывать (испыта́ть *perf)* вожделе́ние к +*dat*; (*crave)* жа́ждать* *(impf)* +*gen*

▶ **lust for** *vt fus* = **lust after**.

lustful [ˈlʌstful] *adj* похотли́вый (похотли́в).

lustre [ˈlʌstəʳ] (*US* **luster**) *n* блеск.

lusty [ˈlʌstɪ] *adj* по́лный* (по́лон) жи́зни и здоро́вья.

lute [luːt] *n* лю́тня*.

luvvie [ˈlʌvɪ] *n (inf)* дорогу́ша *m/f.*

luvvy [ˈlʌvɪ] *n* = **luvvie.**

Luxembourg [ˈlʌksəmbəːg] *n* Люксембу́рг.

luxuriant [lʌgˈzjuərɪənt] *adj (plants, gardens)* бу́йный* (бу́ен); *(hair)* пы́шный* (пы́шен).

luxuriate [lʌgˈzjuərɪeɪt] *vi*: **to** ~ **in** наслажда́ться (наслади́ться* *perf)* +*instr.*

luxurious [lʌgˈzjuərɪəs] *adj* роско́шный* (роско́шен).

luxury [ˈlʌkʃərɪ] *n (great comfort)* ро́скошь *f*; (*treat)* роско́шество ◆ *cpd* роско́шный.

luxury tax *n* нало́г на предме́ты ро́скоши.

LV *n abbr* = **luncheon voucher**.

Lvov [ljvɔf] *n* Льво́в.

LW *abbr (RADIO)* (= **long wave**) ДВ= *дли́нные во́лны.*

lycra® [ˈlaɪkrə] *n синтети́ческий эласти́чный материа́л, испо́льзуемый при изготовле́нии трикота́жной оде́жды.*

lying [ˈlaɪɪŋ] *n* ложь *f* ◆ *adj* лжи́вый.

lynch [lɪntʃ] *vt* линчева́ть* *(impf/perf).*

lynx [lɪŋks] *n (ZOOL)* рысь *f.*

Lyon [ˈliːɔ̃] *n* Лио́н.

lyric [ˈlɪrɪk] *adj*: ~ **poetry** ли́рика, лири́ческая поэ́зия.

lyrical [ˈlɪrɪkl] *adj (poem)* лири́ческий*; (*fig: praise, comment)* восто́рженный (восто́ржен).

lyricism [ˈlɪrɪsɪzəm] *n* лири́зм.

lyrics [ˈlɪrɪks] *npl* слова́ *ntpl or* текст *msg (пе́сни).*

~ M, m ~

M, m [ɛm] n (letter) 13-ая бу́ква англи́йского
алфави́та.
M n abbr (BRIT: = motorway) автомагистра́ль f ◆
abbr = **medium**.
m. abbr (= **metre**) м= ме́тр; = **mile, million**.
MA n abbr (= Master of Arts) ≈ маги́стр
гуманита́рных нау́к; (= military academy)
Вое́нная акаде́мия ◆ abbr (US: POST) =
Massachusetts.
mac [mæk] n (BRIT: inf) макинто́ш.
macabre [məˈkɑːbrə] adj жу́ткий* (жу́ток).
macaroni [mækəˈrəunɪ] n макаро́ны* pl.
macaroon [mækəˈruːn] n минда́льное безе́ nt
ind.
mace [meɪs] n (weapon) булава́*; (ceremonial)
жезл*; (spice) муска́т.
Macedonia [mæsɪˈdəunɪə] n Македо́ния.
Macedonian [mæsɪˈdəunɪən] adj македо́нский*.
machinations [mækɪˈneɪʃənz] npl (plot) ко́зни*
pl; (scheme) махина́ция fsg.
machine [məˈʃiːn] n (also fig) маши́на ◆ vt
(TECH) подверга́ть (подве́ргнуть* perf)
маши́нной обрабо́тке; (dress etc) шить*
(сшить* perf) на маши́не.
machine code n (COMPUT) маши́нный код.
machine gun n пулемёт.
machine language n (COMPUT) маши́нный
язы́к*.
machine readable adj (COMPUT) маши́но-
чита́емый.
machinery [məˈʃiːnərɪ] n обору́дование; (of
government) механи́зм.
machine shop n механи́ческий* цех*.
machine tool n стано́к*.
machine washable adj (garment) приго́дный
к маши́нной сти́рке.
machinist [məˈʃiːnɪst] n стано́чник(-ица).
macho [ˈmætʃəu] adj мужи́цкий.
mackerel [ˈmækrl] n inv ску́мбрия.
mackintosh [ˈmækɪntɔʃ] n (BRIT) макинто́ш.
macro... [ˈmækrəu] prefix ма́кро....
macroeconomics [ˈmækrəuiːkəˈnɔmɪks] npl
макроэконо́мика fsg.
mad [mæd] adj (also fig) сумасше́дший*,
поме́шанный (поме́шан); (angry) бе́шеный;
(keen): **he is ~ about** он поме́шан на +prp; **to**

go ~ (insane) сходи́ть* (сойти́* perf) с ума́;
(angry) беси́ться* (взбеси́ться* perf).
Madagascar [mædəˈgæskə'] n Мадагаска́р.
madam [ˈmædəm] n (form of address) мада́м f
ind, госпожа́; **yes, ~** да, мада́м; **Dear M~** (in
formal letter) уважа́емая госпожа́; **M~
Chairman** госпожа́ председа́тель.
madcap [ˈmædkæp] adj сумасбро́дный*.
mad cow disease n (inf) энцефалопа́тия
кру́пного рога́того скота́.
madden [ˈmædn] vt (make angry) беси́ть*
(взбеси́ть* perf).
maddening [ˈmædnɪŋ] adj невыноси́мый
(невыноси́м).
made [meɪd] pt, pp of **make**.
Madeira [məˈdɪərə] n (GEO) Маде́йра; (wine)
маде́ра.
made-to-measure [ˈmeɪdtəˈmɛʒə'] adj (BRIT)
индивидуа́льного поши́ва.
madhouse [ˈmædhaus] n (inf: asylum)
сумасше́дший* дом*, психу́шка*; (state of
uproar) сумасше́дший дом.
madly [ˈmædlɪ] adv безу́мно; **she is ~ in love
with him** она́ безу́мно влюблена́ в него́; **to
fall ~ in love with sb** безу́мно влюби́ться*
(perf) в кого́-н.
madman [ˈmædmən] irreg n сумасше́дший* m
adj.
madness [ˈmædnɪs] n (insanity) безу́мие,
сумасше́ствие; (foolishness) безу́мие.
Madrid [məˈdrɪd] n Мадри́д.
madwoman [ˈmædwumən] irreg n
сумасше́дшая* f adj.
Mafia [ˈmæfɪə] n: **the ~** ма́фия.
mag [mæg] n abbr (BRIT: inf) = **magazine**.
magazine [mægəˈziːn] n (RADIO)
радиожурна́л; (TV) тележурна́л; (MIL: store)
склад боеприпа́сов; (: of firearm) магази́н.
maggot [ˈmægət] n личи́нка* му́хи.
magic [ˈmædʒɪk] n ма́гия; (conjuring) фо́кусы
mpl ◆ adj (powers, ritual) маги́ческий*; (fig:
place, moment, experience) волше́бный
(волше́бен); **~ wand** волше́бная па́лочка*.
magical [ˈmædʒɪkl] adj (powers, ritual)
маги́ческий*; (experience, evening)
волше́бный* (волше́бен).

---

* marks translations which have irregular inflections. The Russian-English side of the dictionary gives inflectional information.

magician [mə'dʒɪʃən] *n* (*wizard*) маг; (*conjurer*) фо́кусник.
magistrate ['mædʒɪstreɪt] *n* (*LAW*) мирово́й судья́* *m*.
magistrates' court *n* магистрату́ра.
magnanimous [mæg'nænɪməs] *adj* великоду́шный* (великоду́шен).
magnate ['mægneɪt] *n* магна́т.
magnesium [mæg'ni:zɪəm] *n* ма́гний.
magnet ['mægnɪt] *n* магни́т.
magnetic [mæg'nɛtɪk] *adj* магни́тный; (*personality*) притяга́тельный* (притяга́телен).
magnetic disk *n* (*COMPUT*) магни́тный диск.
magnetic tape *n* магни́тная плёнка*.
magnetism ['mægnɪtɪzəm] *n* магнети́зм.
magnetize ['mægnɪtaɪz] *vt* намагни́чивать (намагни́тить* *perf*).
magnification [mægnɪfɪ'keɪʃən] *n* увеличе́ние.
magnificence [mæg'nɪfɪsns] *n* великоле́пие.
magnificent [mæg'nɪfɪsnt] *adj* великоле́пный* (великоле́пен).
magnify ['mægnɪfaɪ] *vt* увели́чивать (увели́чить *perf*); (*sound*) уси́ливать (уси́лить *perf*); (*exaggerate*) преувели́чивать (преувели́чить *perf*).
magnifying glass ['mægnɪfaɪɪŋ-] *n* увеличи́тельное стекло́*, лу́па.
magnitude ['mægnɪtju:d] *n* (*size*) величина́; (*importance*) масшта́б.
magnolia [mæg'nəʊlɪə] *n* магно́лия.
magpie ['mægpaɪ] *n* соро́ка.
mahogany [mə'hɒgənɪ] *n* кра́сное де́рево ◆ *cpd* кра́сного де́рева.
maid [meɪd] *n* (*in private house*) служа́нка*; (*in hotel*) го́рничная *f adj*; **old ~** (*pej*) ста́рая де́ва.
maiden ['meɪdn] *n* (*literary*) де́ва ◆ *adj* (*aunt etc*) незаму́жняя; (*speech, voyage*) пе́рвый.
maiden name *n* де́вичья фами́лия.
mail [meɪl] *n* по́чта ◆ *vt* отправля́ть (отпра́вить* *perf*) по по́чте; **by ~** по по́чте.
mailbox ['meɪlbɒks] *n* (*US: letter box, also COMPUT*) почто́вый я́щик.
mailing list ['meɪlɪŋ-] *n* спи́сок* адреса́тов.
mailman ['meɪlmæn] *irreg n* (*US*) почтальо́н.
mail order *n* систе́ма зака́за това́ров по по́чте ◆ *cpd*: **~~ catalogue** катало́г „Това́ры по́чтой"; **~~ firm** фи́рма, продаю́щая това́ры по по́чте.
mailshot ['meɪlʃɒt] *n* рассы́лка объявле́ний по по́чте.
mail train *n* почто́вый по́езд*.
mail truck *n* (*US*) почто́вый фурго́н.
mail van *n* (*BRIT: AUT*) почто́вый фурго́н; (: *RAIL*) почто́вый ваго́н.
maim [meɪm] *vt* кале́чить (искале́чить *perf*).
main [meɪn] *adj* (*reason, point, door*) гла́вный ◆ *n* (*pipe*): **gas/water ~** газопрово́дная/ водопрово́дная магистра́ль *f*; **the ~s** *npl* сеть *fsg*; **~ meal** обе́д; **in the ~** в основно́м.

main course *n* основно́е *or* второ́е блю́до.
mainframe ['meɪnfreɪm] *n* (*COMPUT*) (универса́льная) вычисли́тельная маши́на.
mainland ['meɪnlənd] *n*: **the ~** матери́к, больша́я земля́*.
main line *n* (*RAIL*) железнодоро́жная магистра́ль *f*.
mainline ['meɪnlaɪn] *adj* (*RAIL: station*) магистра́льный ◆ *vt* (*DRUGS*) вка́лывать (вколо́ть* *perf*) ◆ *vi* (*DRUGS*) коло́ться* (*impf*).
mainly ['meɪnlɪ] *adv* гла́вным о́бразом.
main road *n* шоссе́ *nt ind*; (*in town, village*) гла́вная у́лица.
mainstay ['meɪnsteɪ] *n* гла́вная опо́ра.
mainstream ['meɪnstri:m] *n* госпо́дствующая тенде́нция ◆ *adj* госпо́дствующий*.
maintain [meɪn'teɪn] *vt* (*friendship, system, momentum*) подде́рживать (поддержа́ть* *perf*); (*dependant*) содержа́ть* (*impf*); (*building*) обслу́живать (*impf*); (*affirm: belief, opinion*) утвержда́ть (*impf*); **to ~ (that ...)** утвержда́ть (*impf*) (, что ...).
maintenance ['meɪntənəns] *n* (*see vb*) подде́ржание; содержа́ние; обслу́живание; утвержде́ние; (*LAW: alimony*) алиме́нты* *pl*.
maintenance contract *n* контра́кт по обслу́живанию.
maintenance grant *n* стипе́ндия.
maintenance order *n* (*LAW*) постановле́ние о вы́плате алиме́нтов.
maisonette [meɪzə'nɛt] *n* (*BRIT*) двухэта́жная кварти́ра.
maize [meɪz] *n* кукуру́за, ма́ис.
Maj. *abbr* (*MIL*) = **major**.
majestic [mə'dʒɛstɪk] *adj* вели́чественный* (вели́чествен).
majesty ['mædʒɪstɪ] *n* (*sovereignty*) короле́в-ская власть *f*; (*splendour*) вели́чественность *f*; (*form of address*): **Your M~** Ва́ше Вели́чество.
major ['meɪdʒə᷈] *n* (*MIL*) майо́р ◆ *adj* (*important*) гла́вный; (*MUS*) мажо́рный ◆ *vi* (*US: SCOL*): **to ~ in** специализи́роваться (*impf/perf*) в +*prp*; **a ~ operation** (*also fig*) кру́пная опера́ция.
Majorca [mə'jɔ:kə] *n* Мальо́рка, Майо́рка.
major general *n* генера́л-майо́р.
majority [mə'dʒɒrɪtɪ] *n* большинство́ ◆ *cpd*: **~ verdict** пригово́р, вы́несенный большинство́м (голосо́в); **~ (share)holding** контро́льный паке́т а́кций.
make [meɪk] (*pt, pp* **made**) *vt* де́лать (сде́лать *perf*); (*clothes*) шить* (сшить* *perf*); (*manufacture*) изготовля́ть (изгото́вить* *perf*); (*meal*) гото́вить* (пригото́вить* *perf*); (*money*) зараба́тывать (зарабо́тать *perf*) ◆ *n* (*brand*) ма́рка*; **to ~ sb do** (*force*) заставля́ть (заста́вить* *perf*) кого́-н +*infin*; **two and two ~ four** (*equal*) два плюс два – четы́ре; **to ~ sb unhappy** расстра́ивать (расстро́ить *perf*) кого́-н; **to ~ a noise** шуме́ть* (*impf*); **to ~ the bed** стели́ть* (постели́ть* *perf*) посте́ль; **to ~**

a fool of sb де́лать (сде́лать *perf*) из кого́-н дурака́; **to ~ a profit** получа́ть (получи́ть* *perf*) при́быль; **to ~ a loss** нести́* (понести́* *perf*) убы́ток; **to ~ it** (*succeed*) преуспева́ть (преуспе́ть* *perf*); (*arrive*) успева́ть (успе́ть* *perf*); **what time do you ~ it?** ско́лько на ва́ших (часа́х)?; **let's ~ it Monday** дава́йте договори́мся на понеде́льник; **to ~ good ♦** *vi* (*succeed*) преуспева́ть (преуспе́ть* *perf*) **♦** *vt* (*deficit*) возмеща́ть (возмести́ть* *perf*); (*damage*) исправля́ть (испра́вить* *perf*); **to ~ do with/without** обходи́ться* (обойти́сь* *perf*) +*instr*/без +*gen*
► **make for** *vt fus* (*place*) направля́ться (напра́виться* *perf*) к +*dat*/в +*acc*
► **make off** *vi* (*escape*) скрыва́ться (скры́ться* *perf*)
► **make out** *vt* (*decipher*) разбира́ть (разобра́ть* *perf*); (*see*) различа́ть (различи́ть *perf*); (*write out*) выпи́сывать (вы́писать* *perf*); (*claim*) утвержда́ть (*impf*); (*understand*) разбира́ться (разобра́ться* *perf*) в +*prp*; (*claim, imply*) де́лать (сде́лать *perf*) вид; **to ~ out a case for sth** обосно́вывать (обоснова́ть *perf*) что-н
► **make over** *vt* (*assign*): **to ~ over (to)** передава́ть* (переда́ть* *perf*) (+*dat*)
► **make up** *vt fus* (*constitute*) составля́ть (соста́вить* *perf*) **♦** *vt* (*invent*) выду́мывать (вы́думать *perf*); (*prepare: bed, parcel*) гото́вить* (пригото́вить* *perf*); (*with cosmetics*) де́лать (сде́лать *perf*) макия́ж +*dat* **♦** *vi* (*after quarrel*) мири́ться (помири́ться *perf*); (*with cosmetics*): **to ~ (o.s.) up** де́лать (сде́лать *perf*) макия́ж; **to be made up of** состоя́ть (*impf*) из +*gen*
► **make up for** *vt fus* (*mistake, misdemeanour*) загла́живать (загла́дить* *perf*); (*loss*) восполня́ть (воспо́лнить *perf*); **to ~ up for lost time** навёрстывать (наверста́ть *perf*) упу́щенное вре́мя.
make-believe ['meɪkbɪliːv] *n* фанта́зии *fpl*; **a world of ~** мир фанта́зий; **it's just ~** э́то – про́сто фанта́зия.
maker ['meɪkə'] *n* (*of programme, film*) созда́тель(ница) *m(f)*; (*of goods*) изготови́тель *m*.
makeshift ['meɪkʃɪft] *adj* (*temporary*) вре́менный.
make-up ['meɪkʌp] *n* косме́тика, макия́ж; (*THEAT*) грим.
make-up bag *n* косме́тичка*.
make-up remover *n* сре́дство для сня́тия макия́жа.
making ['meɪkɪŋ] *n* (*of programme*) созда́ние; (*of goods*) изготовле́ние; (*fig*): **in the ~** в проце́ссе созда́ния; **to have the ~s of** име́ть (*impf*) зада́тки +*gen*; **the problem is of your**

own ~ пробле́ма Ва́ми же и со́здана.
maladjusted [mælə'dʒʌstɪd] *adj* (*child*) трудновоспиту́емый.
maladroit [mælə'drɔɪt] *adj* (*behaviour*) неуме́лый (неуме́л); (*comment*) беста́ктный* (беста́ктен).
malaise [mæ'leɪz] *n* (*of society*) неду́г.
malaria [mə'lɛərɪə] *n* маляри́я.
Malawi [mə'lɑːwɪ] *n* Мала́ви *nt ind*.
Malay [mə'leɪ] *adj* мала́йский* **♦** *n* (*person*) мала́ец*(-а́йка*); (*LING*) мала́йский* язы́к*.
Malaya [mə'leɪə] *n* Мала́йя.
Malayan [mə'leɪən] *adj, n* = **Malay**.
Malaysia [mə'leɪzɪə] *n* Мала́йзия.
Malaysian [mə'leɪzɪən] *adj* малайзи́йский **♦** *n* малайзи́ец*(-и́йка*).
Maldives ['mɔːldaɪvz] *npl*: **the ~** Мальди́вские острова́* *mpl*.
male [meɪl] *n* (*human*) мужчи́на *m*; (*animal*) саме́ц* **♦** *adj* (*sex, attitude*) мужско́й; (*child etc*) мужско́го по́ла; (*ELEC*) охва́тываемый; **~ and female students** студе́нты: ю́ноши и де́вушки*.
male chauvinist *n*: **he's a ~~** он о́чень пренебрежи́тельно отно́сится к же́нщинам.
male nurse *n* медбра́т*.
malevolence [mə'lɛvələns] *n* (*act*) злодея́ние; (*feeling*) зло́ба.
malevolent [mə'lɛvələnt] *adj* зло́бный* (зло́бен).
malformed [mæl'fɔːmd] *adj* непра́вильно сформирова́вшийся.
malfunction [mæl'fʌŋkʃən] *n* неиспра́вность *f*.
Mali ['mɑːli] *n* Мали́ *nt ind*.
Malian ['mɑːlɪən] *adj* мали́йский **♦** *n* мали́ец*(-и́йка*).
malice ['mælɪs] *n* зло́ба.
malicious [mə'lɪʃəs] *adj* (*person, gossip*) зло́бный (зло́бен), злой* (зол); (*LAW*) злонаме́ренный (злонаме́рен).
malign [mə'laɪn] *vt* клевета́ть* (оклевета́ть* *perf*) **♦** *adj* па́губный* (па́губен).
malignant [mə'lɪgnənt] *adj* (*MED*) злока́чественный*; (*behaviour, intention*) зло́стный* (зло́стен).
malingerer [mə'lɪŋgərə'] *n* симуля́нт(ка*).
mall [mɔːl] *n* (*also:* **shopping ~**) ≈ торго́вая у́лица.
malleable ['mælɪəbl] *adj* (*clay, substance*) пода́тливый (пода́тлив); (*person*) поко́рный* (поко́рен).
mallet ['mælɪt] *n* деревя́нный молото́к*.
malnutrition [mælnjuː'trɪʃən] *n* недоеда́ние.
malpractice [mæl'præktɪs] *n* злоупотребле́ние служе́бным положе́нием.
malt [mɔːlt] *n* (*grain*) со́лод*; (*also:* **~ whisky**) соло́довое ви́ски *nt ind*.
Malta ['mɔːltə] *n* Ма́льта.

---

* marks translations which have irregular inflections. The Russian-English side of the dictionary gives inflectional information.

Maltese [mɔːlˈtiːz] *adj* мальти́йский* ♦ *n inv*
мальти́ец*(-и́йка*); (*LING*) мальти́йский*
язы́к*.
maltreat [mælˈtriːt] *vt* пло́хо обраща́ться (*impf*)
с +*instr*.
mammal [ˈmæml] *n* млекопита́ющее *nt adj*.
mammoth [ˈmæməθ] *n* ма́монт ♦ *adj* (*task*)
колосса́льный* (колосса́лен).
man [mæn] (*pl* **men**) *n* (*adult male*) мужчи́на *m*;
(*person, mankind*) челове́к*; (*CHESS*) фигу́ра ♦
vt (*machine*) обслу́живать (*impf*); (*post*)
занима́ть (заня́ть* *perf*); (*NAUT*): **to ~ a ship**
набира́ть (набра́ть* *perf*) кома́нду корабля́;
an old ~ стари́к*; **~ and wife** муж и жена́.
manage [ˈmænɪdʒ] *vi* (*get by*) обойди́ться*
(обойти́сь* *perf*) ♦ *vt* (*business, organization*)
руководи́ть* (*impf*) +*instr*, управля́ть (*impf*)
+*instr*; (*shop, restaurant*) заве́довать (*impf*)
+*instr*; (*economy*) управля́ть (*impf*) +*instr*;
(*control*) кома́ндовать (*impf*) +*instr*; (*workload,
task*) справля́ться (*impf*) с +*instr*; **to ~ without
sb/sth** обходи́ться* (обойти́сь* *perf*) без
кого́-н/чего́-н; **I ~d to convince him** мне
удало́сь убеди́ть его́; **I ~d to finish in time** я
успе́л зако́нчить во́время.
manageable [ˈmænɪdʒəbl] *adj* (*task*)
выполни́мый (выполни́м); (*number, size*)
удо́бный.
management [ˈmænɪdʒmənt] *n* (*body*)
руково́дство; (*act*): **~ (of)** управле́ние
(+*instr*); **"under new ~"** "под но́вым
руково́дством".
management accounting *n* управле́нческий*
учёт.
management consultant *n* консульта́нт по
вопро́сам ме́неджмента.
manager [ˈmænɪdʒə^r] *n* (*of business,
organization*) управля́ющий* *m adj*,
ме́неджер; (*of estate*) управля́ющий; (*of
shop*) заве́дующий*(-ая) *m(f) adj*; (*of pop star*)
ме́неджер; (*SPORT*) гла́вный тре́нер; **sales ~**
нача́льник по сбы́ту.
manageress [mænɪdʒəˈrɛs] *n* (*of shop*)
заве́дующая *f adj*.
managerial [mænɪˈdʒɪərɪəl] *adj* (*role*)
управле́нческий*; **~ staff** управле́нческий*
аппара́т; **~ decisions** реше́ния, при́нятые
руково́дством.
managing director [ˈmænɪdʒɪŋ-] *n*
дире́ктор*-распоряди́тель *m*.
Managua [məˈnægwə] *n* Мана́гуа.
Manchester [ˈmæntʃɪstə^r] *n* Манче́стер.
Manchuria [mænˈtʃuərɪə] *n* Маньчжу́рия.
Mancunian [mænˈkjuːnɪən] *n* жи́тель(ница)
m(f) Манче́стера.
mandarin [ˈmændərɪn] *n* (*also:* **~ orange**)
мандари́н; (*BRIT: POL*) кру́пный чино́вник;
(*LING*): **M~ (Chinese)** мандари́нское наре́чие
кита́йского языка́.
mandate [ˈmændeɪt] *n* (*POL: from electorate*)
полномо́чие; (: *from UN etc*) манда́т; (*task*)

поруче́ние.
mandatory [ˈmændətərɪ] *adj* обяза́тельный*
(обяза́телен).
mandolin(e) [ˈmændəlɪn] *n* мандоли́на.
mane [meɪn] *n* гри́ва.
maneuver *etc* (*US*) = **manoeuvre** *etc*.
manfully [ˈmænfəlɪ] *adv* му́жественно.
manganese [mæŋɡəˈniːz] *n* ма́рганец*.
mangetout [ˈmɒnʒˈtuː] *n* стручко́вый горо́х
(*со съедо́бными стру́чками*).
mangle [ˈmæŋɡl] *vt* корёжить (искорёжить
perf) ♦ *n* пресс для отжима́ния белья́.
mango [ˈmæŋɡəu] (*pl* **~es**) *n* ма́нго *nt ind*.
mangrove [ˈmæŋɡrəuv] *n* ма́нгровое де́рево*.
mangy [ˈmeɪndʒɪ] *adj* (*diseased*) парши́вый
(парши́в); (*scruffy*) обле́злый (обле́зл).
manhandle [ˈmænhændl] *vt* (*mistreat*) гру́бо
обраща́ться (*impf*) с +*instr*; (*move by hand*)
приводи́ть* (привести́* *perf*) в де́йствие
вручну́ю.
manhole [ˈmænhəul] *n* люк.
manhood [ˈmænhud] *n* (*state*) возмужа́лость *f*;
(*age*) зре́лость *f*.
man-hour [ˈmænauə^r] *n* челове́ко-час*.
manhunt [ˈmænhʌnt] *n* ро́зыск.
mania [ˈmeɪnɪə] *n* (*also PSYCH*) ма́ния.
maniac [ˈmeɪnɪæk] *n* (*also fig*) манья́к; **he's a
football ~** он стра́стный люби́тель футбо́ла.
manic [ˈmænɪk] *adj* безу́мный* (безу́мен).
manic-depressive [ˈmænɪkdɪˈprɛsɪv] *adj*
маниака́льно-депресси́вный* ♦ *n* челове́к,
*страда́ющий маниака́льно-депресси́вным
психо́зом.*
manicure [ˈmænɪkjuə^r] *n* маникю́р ♦ *vt* (*person*)
де́лать (сде́лать *perf*) маникю́р +*dat*.
manicure set *n* маникю́рный набо́р.
manifest [ˈmænɪfɛst] *vt* проявля́ть (прояви́ть*
perf) ♦ *adj* очеви́дный* (очеви́ден), я́вный*
(я́вен) ♦ *n* (*NAUT*) деклара́ция (судово́го
гру́за); (*AVIAT*) манифе́ст.
manifestation [mænɪfɛsˈteɪʃən] *n*: **a ~ of**
проявле́ние +*gen*.
manifesto [mænɪˈfɛstəu] *n* манифе́ст.
manifold [ˈmænɪfəuld] *adj* многообра́зный*
(многообра́зен) ♦ *n* (*AUT*): **exhaust ~**
выхлопно́й колле́ктор.
Manila [məˈnɪlə] *n* Мани́ла.
manila [məˈnɪlə] *adj*: **~ paper** пло́тная
кори́чневая бума́га.
manipulate [məˈnɪpjuleɪt] *vt* манипули́ровать
(*impf*) +*instr*.
manipulation [mənɪpjuˈleɪʃən] *n* манипуля́ция.
mankind [mænˈkaɪnd] *n* челове́чество.
manliness [ˈmænlɪnɪs] *n* му́жественность *f*.
manly [ˈmænlɪ] *adj* му́жественный*
(му́жествен).
man-made [ˈmænˈmeɪd] *adj* иску́сственный*.
manna [ˈmænə] *n* ма́нна небе́сная.
mannequin [ˈmænɪkɪn] *n* (*dummy*) манеке́н;
(*fashion model*) манеке́нщица.
manner [ˈmænə^r] *n* (*way*) о́браз; (*behaviour*)

мане́ра; ~s *npl* мане́ры *fpl*; **bad** ~s плохи́е мане́ры; **all** ~ **of things/people** всевозмо́жные ве́щи/лю́ди; **in a** ~ **of speaking** в некото́ром ро́де.
mannerism ['mænərɪzəm] *n* осо́бенность *f* мане́ра.
mannerly ['mænəlɪ] *adj* учти́вый (учти́в).
manning ['mænɪŋ] *n* набо́р рабо́чей си́лы.
manoeuvrable [mə'nu:vrəbl] (*US* **maneuvrable**) *adj* мане́вренный.
manoeuvre [mə'nu:və'] (*US* **maneuver**) *vt* (*move*) уме́ло передвига́ть (передви́нуть *perf*); (*manipulate*) маневри́ровать (*impf*) +*instr* ♦ *vi* маневри́ровать (*impf*) ♦ *n* манёвр; ~s *npl* (*MIL*) манёвры *mpl*; **to** ~ **sb into doing** подводи́ть* (подвести́* *perf*) кого́-н к тому́, чтобы сде́лал что-н.
manor ['mænə'] *n* (*also:* ~ **house**) уса́дебный дом*.
manpower ['mænpauə'] *n* рабо́чая си́ла.
manservant ['mænsə:vənt] (*pl* **menservants**) *n* слуга́* *m*.
mansion ['mænʃən] *n* особня́к*.
manslaughter ['mænslɔ:tə'] *n* непредумы́шленное уби́йство.
mantelpiece ['mæntlpi:s] *n* ками́нная доска́*.
mantle ['mæntl] *n* (*cloak*) ма́нтия; (*fig: covering*) покро́в.
man-to-man ['mæntə'mæn] *adj* мужско́й ♦ *adv* по-мужски́, как мужчи́на с мужчи́ной.
manual ['mænjuəl] *adj* ручно́й ♦ *n* (*book*) посо́бие; ~ **worker** чернорабо́чий*(-ая) *m(f) adj*.
manufacture [mænju'fæktʃə'] *vt* (*goods*) изготовля́ть (изгото́вить* *perf*), производи́ть* (произвести́* *perf*) ♦ *n* изготовле́ние, произво́дство.
manufactured goods *npl* промы́шленные това́ры *mpl*.
manufacturer [mænju'fæktʃərə'] *n* изготови́тель *m*, производи́тель *m*.
manufacturing [mænju'fæktʃərɪŋ] *n* изготовле́ние, произво́дство.
manure [mə'njuə'] *n* наво́з.
manuscript ['mænjuskrɪpt] *n* (*author's draft*) ру́копись *f*; (*old document*) манускри́пт, ру́копись.
many ['menɪ] *adj* (*a lot of*) мно́го +*gen* ♦ *pron* (*several*) мно́гие; **a great** ~ о́чень мно́го +*gen*, мно́жество +*gen*; **how** ~? ско́лько?; **how** ~ **people/times?** ско́лько люде́й/раз?; **too** ~ **difficulties** сли́шком мно́го тру́дностей; **twice as** ~ вдво́е бо́льше, в два ра́за бо́льше; ~ **a time** мно́го раз; **in** ~ **cases** во мно́гих слу́чаях; ~ **of us** мно́гие из нас.
Maori ['mauri] *n* ма́ори *m/f ind*.
map [mæp] *n* ка́рта; (*of town*) план ♦ *vt* составля́ть (соста́вить* *perf*) ка́рту +*gen*

▸ **map out** *vt* (*plan*) составля́ть (соста́вить* *perf*); (*task, holiday, career*) плани́ровать (*impf*).
maple ['meɪpl] *n* клён ♦ *cpd* клено́вый.
mar [mɑ:'] *vt* по́ртить* (испо́ртить* *perf*).
Mar. *abbr* = **March**.
marathon ['mærəθən] *n* марафо́н ♦ *adj* (*fig*) марафо́нский.
marathon runner *n* марафо́нец*.
marauder [mə'rɔ:də'] *n* мароде́р.
marble ['mɑ:bl] *n* (*stone*) мра́мор; (*toy*) стекля́нный ша́рик ♦ *adj* мра́морный.
marbles ['mɑ:blz] *n* (*game*) де́тская игра́* в стекля́нные ша́рики.
March [mɑ:tʃ] *n* март; *see also* **July**.
march [mɑ:tʃ] *vi* марширова́ть (промарширова́ть *perf*); (*protesters*) проходи́ть* (пройти́* *perf*) ма́ршем ♦ *n* марш ♦ *vt*: **to** ~ **sb out of** выдворя́ть (вы́дворить *perf*) кого́-н из +*gen*; **to** ~ **out of** демонстрати́вно выходи́ть* (вы́йти* *perf*) из +*gen*; **to** ~ **into** реши́тельно входи́ть* (войти́* *perf*) в +*acc*.
marcher ['mɑ:tʃə'] *n* (*demonstrator*) уча́стник(-ица) ма́рша.
marching orders ['mɑ:tʃɪŋ-] *npl*: **to give sb his** ~ ~ увольня́ть (уво́лить *perf*) кого́-н.
march past *n* (*MIL*) строево́й смотр.
mare [mɛə'] *n* кобы́ла.
marge [mɑ:dʒ] *n abbr* (*BRIT*: *inf*) = **margarine**.
margarine [mɑ:dʒə'ri:n] *n* маргари́н.
margin ['mɑ:dʒɪn] *n* (*on page*) поля́ *ntpl*; (*of group*) перифери́я; (*of area*) край*; (*difference: of victory*) преиму́щество; (: *of defeat*) меньшинство́; (*also:* **profit** ~) чи́стая при́быль *f no pl*; **safety** ~ запа́с про́чности; ~ **of error** преде́л допусти́мой погре́шности; **they won by a** ~ **of five votes** они́ победи́ли с большинство́м в пять голосо́в.
marginal ['mɑ:dʒɪnl] *adj* незначи́тельный* (незначи́телен) ♦ *n* (*also:* ~ **seat** *or* **constituency**: *BRIT*: *POL*) избира́тельный *уча́сток где пра́вящая па́ртия име́ет незначи́тельное большинство́ голосо́в.
marginally ['mɑ:dʒɪnəlɪ] *adv* незначи́тельно.
marigold ['mærɪɡəuld] *n* (*BOT*) ноготки́ *mpl*.
marijuana [mærɪ'wɑ:nə] *n* марихуа́на.
marina [mə'ri:nə] *n* мари́на *or* при́стань* *f* для яхт.
marinade [mærɪ'neɪd] *n* марина́д ♦ *vt* = **marinate**.
marinate ['mærɪneɪt] *vt* маринова́ть (замаринова́ть *perf*).
marine [mə'ri:n] *adj* морско́й; (*engineer*) судово́й ♦ *n* (*BRIT*) служа́щий* *m adj* вое́нно-морско́го фло́та; (*US*) морско́й пехоти́нец*.
marine insurance *n* морско́е страхова́ние.

---

* marks translations which have irregular inflections. The Russian-English side of the dictionary gives inflectional information.

marital ['mærɪtl] *adj* супру́жеский*; ~ **status** семе́йное положе́ние.

maritime ['mærɪtaɪm] *adj* морско́й; ~ **law** морско́е пра́во.

Mariupol [mɑri'upəlj] *n* Мариу́поль *m*.

marjoram ['mɑ:dʒərəm] *n* души́ца, майора́н.

mark [mɑ:k] *n* (*written symbol*) значо́к*, поме́тка*; (*stain*) пятно́*; (*trace*) след*; (*of friendship, respect*) знак; (*BRIT: SCOL*) отме́тка*, оце́нка*; (*level*) отме́тка*; (*currency*) ма́рка* ♦ *vt* (*with pen*) помеча́ть (поме́тить* *perf*); (*subj: shoes, tyres*) оставля́ть (оста́вить* *perf*) след на +*prp*; (*furniture etc*) поврежда́ть (повреди́ть* *perf*); (*clothes, carpet*) ста́вить* (поста́вить* *perf*) пятно́ на +*prp*; (*place, time*) ука́зывать (указа́ть* *perf*); (*characterize*) отмеча́ть (отме́тить* *perf*); (*BRIT: SCOL*) проверя́ть (прове́рить *perf*); (*SPORT: player*) блоки́ровать (*impf*); **punctuation** ~ знак препина́ния; **M~ 2/3** (*BRIT: TECH*) второ́го/тре́тьего вы́пуска; **up to the** ~ на высоте́; **to be quick off the** ~ **to do** (*fig*) сразу́ де́лить (*perf*) +*infin*; **to** ~ **the price on sth** ста́вить* (поста́вить* *perf*) це́ну на чём-н; **to** ~ **time** (*MIL*) марширова́ть (*impf*) на ме́сте; (*fig*) топта́ться* (*impf*)

▸ **mark down** *vt* (*price*) снижа́ть (сни́зить* *perf*); (*goods*) уце́нивать (уцени́ть* *perf*)

▸ **mark off** *vt* (*tick off*) отмеча́ть (отме́тить* *perf*)

▸ **mark out** *vt* (*area, road*) размеча́ть (разме́тить* *perf*); (*person*) выделя́ть (вы́делить *perf*)

▸ **mark up** *vt* (*price*) повыша́ть (повы́сить* *perf*).

marked [mɑ:kt] *adj* заме́тный* (заме́тен).

markedly ['mɑ:kɪdlɪ] *adv* заме́тно.

marker ['mɑ:kə'] *n* (*sign*) знак; (*bookmark*) закла́дка*; (*pen*) флома́стер.

market ['mɑ:kɪt] *n* (*also COMM*) ры́нок* ♦ *vt* выпуска́ть (вы́пустить* *perf*) в прода́жу; **to be on the** ~ быть* (*impf*) в прода́же; **on the open** ~ в свобо́дной прода́же; **to play the** ~ игра́ть (*impf*) на би́рже.

marketable ['mɑ:kɪtəbl] *adj* по́льзующийся спро́сом; **to be** ~ по́льзоваться (*impf*) спро́сом.

market analysis *n* ана́лиз ры́нка.

market day *n* база́рный день* *m*.

market demand *n* ры́ночный спрос.

market economy *n* ры́ночная эконо́мика.

market forces *npl* ры́ночные си́лы *fpl*.

market garden *n* (*BRIT*) огоро́д (*для выра́щивания овоще́й на прода́жу*).

marketing ['mɑ:kɪtɪŋ] *n* ма́ркетинг.

marketing manager *n* ме́неджер по ма́ркетингу.

marketplace ['mɑ:kɪtpleɪs] *n* ры́ночная *or* база́рная пло́щадь* *f*; (*COMM*) ры́нок*.

market price *n* ры́ночная цена́.

market research *n* иссле́дование ры́нка.

market value *n* ры́ночная сто́имость *f*.

marking ['mɑ:kɪŋ] *n* (*on animal*) расцве́тка; (*on road*) разме́тка.

marksman ['mɑ:ksmən] *irreg n* ме́ткий* стрело́к*.

marksmanship ['mɑ:ksmənʃɪp] *n* ме́ткая стрельба́.

mark-up ['mɑ:kʌp] *n* (*margin*) ра́зница (*ме́жду себесто́имостью и прода́жной цено́й*); (*increase*) наце́нка*.

marmalade ['mɑ:məleɪd] *n* джем (*ци́трусовый*).

maroon [mə'ru:n] *adj* бордо́вый ♦ *vt*: **we were ~ed** мы бы́ли отре́заны от вне́шнего ми́ра; (*fig*) мы бы́ли в изоля́ции.

marquee [mɑ:'ki:] *n* марки́за, пала́точный павильо́н, шатёр.

marquess ['mɑ:kwɪs] *n* (*BRIT*) марки́з.

marquis ['mɑ:kwɪs] *n* = **marquess**.

Marrakech [mærə'keʃ] *n* = **Marrakesh**.

Marrakesh [mærə'keʃ] *n* Марраке́ш.

marriage ['mærɪdʒ] *n* брак; (*wedding*) сва́дьба*.

marriage bureau *n* бюро́ *nt ind* знако́мств.

marriage certificate *n* свиде́тельство о бра́ке.

marriage guidance (*US* **marriage counselling**) *n* консульта́ция по вопро́сам семьи́ и бра́ка.

marriage of convenience *n* фикти́вный брак.

married ['mærɪd] *adj* (*man*) жена́тый (жена́т); (*woman*) заму́жняя; (*couple*) жена́тые (жена́ты); (*life*) супру́жеский*; **he is** ~ **to** он жена́т на +*prp*; **she is** ~ **to** она́ за́мужем за +*instr*; **they are** ~ они́ жена́ты.

marrow ['mærəu] *n* (*vegetable*) кабачо́к*; (*also:* **bone** ~) ко́стный мозг.

marry ['mærɪ] *vt* (*subj: man*) жени́ться* (*impf/perf*) на +*prp*; (: *woman*) выходи́ть* (вы́йти* *perf*) за́муж за +*acc*; (*also:* ~ **off:** *son*) жени́ть* (*impf/perf*); (: *daughter*) выдава́ть* (вы́дать* *perf*) за́муж; (: *priest*) венча́ть (обвенча́ть *perf*) ♦ *vi* (*get married: man*) жени́ться (*impf*); (: *woman*) выходи́ть* (вы́йти* *perf*) за́муж; (: *couple*) жени́ться (пожени́ться *perf*).

Mars [mɑ:z] *n* Марс.

Marseilles [mɑ:'seɪlz] *n* Марсе́ль *m*.

marsh [mɑ:ʃ] *n* боло́то; **salt** ~ солонча́ковое боло́то.

marshal ['mɑ:ʃl] *n* (*MIL*) ма́ршал; (*at public event*) распоряди́тель(ница) *m(f)* ♦ *vt* (*thoughts, support*) упоря́дочить (*perf*); (*soldiers*) выстра́ивать (вы́строить *perf*); **police/fire** ~ (*US*) нача́льник полице́йского уча́стка/пожа́рной ча́сти.

marshalling yard ['mɑ:ʃlɪŋ-] *n* (*RAIL*) сортиро́вочная ста́нция.

marshmallow [mɑ:ʃ'mæləu] *n* (*BOT*) мушмула́; (*sweet*) ≈ зефи́р.

marshy ['mɑ:ʃɪ] *adj* боло́тистый (боло́тист).

marsupial [mɑ:'su:pɪəl] *n* су́мчатое *nt adj*

(живо́тное) ◆ *adj* су́мчатый.
marten ['mɑ:tɪn] *n* куни́ца.
martial ['mɑ:ʃl] *adj* вое́нный.
martial art *n* восто́чное единобо́рство.
martial law *n* вое́нное положе́ние.
Martian ['mɑ:ʃən] *n* марсиа́нин*(-а́нка*).
martin ['mɑ:tɪn] *n*: **house/sand** ~ городска́я/ берегова́я ла́сточка*.
martyr ['mɑ:tə'] *n* му́ченик(-ица) ◆ *vt* му́чить (замучить *perf*).
martyrdom ['mɑ:tədəm] *n* му́ченичество.
marvel ['mɑ:vl] *n* чу́до* ◆ *vi*: **to** ~ **(at)** восхища́ться (восхити́ться* *perf*) (+*instr*).
marvellous ['mɑ:vləs] (*US* **marvelous**) *adj* восхити́тельный* (восхити́телен), изуми́тельный* (изуми́телен).
Marxism ['mɑ:ksɪzəm] *n* маркси́зм.
Marxist ['mɑ:ksɪst] *adj* маркси́стский ◆ *n* маркси́ст(ка*).
marzipan ['mɑ:zɪpæn] *n* марципа́н.
mascara [mæs'kɑ:rə] *n* тушь *f* для ресни́ц.
mascot ['mæskət] *n* талисма́н.
masculine ['mæskjʊlɪn] *adj* мужско́й; (*woman*) мужеподо́бный* (мужеподо́бен); ~ **noun/ pronoun** существи́тельное/местоиме́ние мужско́го ро́да.
masculinity [mæskjʊ'lɪnɪtɪ] *n* му́жественность *f*.
MASH [mæʃ] *n abbr* (*US*: = *mobile army surgical hospital*) ≈ ПП Г= *полево́й подви́жный го́спиталь.*
mash [mæʃ] *vt* де́лать (сде́лать *perf*) пюре́ из +*gen*.
mashed potatoes [mæʃt-] *npl* карто́фельное пюре́ *nt ind*.
mask [mɑ:sk] *n* ма́ска* ◆ *vt* (*face*) закрыва́ть (закры́ть* *perf*); (*feelings*) маскирова́ть (*impf*).
masking tape ['mɑ:skɪŋ-] *n* кле́йкая ле́нта.
masochism ['mæsəʊkɪzəm] *n* мазохи́зм.
masochist ['mæsəʊkɪst] *n* мазохи́ст(ка*).
mason ['meɪsn] *n* (*also*: **stone** ~) ка́менщик; (*also*: **freemason**) масо́н.
masonic [mə'sɔnɪk] *adj* масо́нский*.
masonry ['meɪsnrɪ] *n* (*stonework*) (ка́менная) кла́дка.
masquerade [mæskə'reɪd] *n* маскара́д ◆ *vi*: **to** ~ **as** выдава́ть* (*impf*) себя́ за +*acc*.
mass [mæs] *n* (*also PHYS*) ма́сса; (*REL*: *Orthodox*) обе́дня*; (: *Catholic*) ме́сса ◆ *cpd* ма́ссовый ◆ *vi* сосредото́чиваться (сосредото́читься *perf*); **the** ~**es** *npl* (наро́дные) ма́ссы *fpl*; **to go to M**~ идти́* (пойти́* *perf*) к обе́дне/ме́ссе; ~**es of** (*inf*) ма́сса *fsg* +*gen*, у́йма *fsg* +*gen*.
massacre ['mæsəkə'] *n* ма́ссовое уби́йство ◆ *vt* зве́рски убива́ть (уби́ть* *perf*).
massage ['mæsɑ:ʒ] *n* масса́ж ◆ *vt* (*rub*) масси́ровать (*impf*).

masseur [mæ'sə:'] *n* массажи́ст.
masseuse [mæ'sə:z] *n* массажи́стка*.
massive ['mæsɪv] *adj* (*furniture, person*) масси́вный* (масси́вен); (*support, changes*) огро́мный* (огро́мен).
mass market *n* ма́ссовый спрос.
mass media *n inv* сре́дства *ntpl* ма́ссовой информа́ции.
mass meeting *n* ма́ссовый ми́тинг.
mass-produce ['mæsprə'dju:s] *vt* ма́ссово производи́ть* (произвести́* *perf*).
mass production *n* ма́ссовое произво́дство.
mast [mɑ:st] *n* ма́чта.
mastectomy [mæs'tɛktəmɪ] *n* мастэктоми́я.
master ['mɑ:stə'] *n* (*also fig*) хозя́ин; (*BRIT*: *SCOL*) учи́тель* *m*; (*expert*) ма́стер ◆ *cpd* (*baker, craftsman*) уме́лый ◆ *vt* (*control*) владе́ть (овладе́ть *perf*) +*instr*; (*learn, understand*) овладева́ть (овладе́ть *perf*) +*instr*; **M**~ **Smith** (*title for boys*) господи́н *or* ма́стер Смит; **M**~**'s degree** сте́пень *f* маги́стра; **M**~ **of Arts/Science** маги́стр гуманита́рных/есте́ственных нау́к; **M**~ **of Ceremonies** церемоиймейстер.
master disk *n* (*COMPUT*) оригина́л ди́ска.
masterful ['mɑ:stəfʊl] *adj* вла́стный* (вла́стен).
master key *n* универса́льный ключ (*подходя́ющий ко всем дверя́м зда́ния*).
masterly ['mɑ:stəlɪ] *adj* ма́стерский.
mastermind ['mɑ:stəmaɪnd] *n* (*of plan*) созда́тель(ница) *m(f)* ◆ *vt* разраба́тывать (разрабо́тать *perf*).
masterpiece ['mɑ:stəpi:s] *n* шеде́вр.
master plan *n* гениа́льный план.
masterstroke ['mɑ:stəstrəʊk] *n* гениа́льный ход*.
mastery ['mɑ:stərɪ] *n* (*excellence: skill*) мастерство́; ~ **of** (*skill, language*) владе́ние +*instr*.
mastiff ['mæstɪf] *n* (*dog*) ма́стифф.
masturbate ['mæstəbeɪt] *vi* мастурби́ровать (*impf*).
masturbation [mæstə'beɪʃən] *n* мастурба́ция.
mat [mæt] *n* ко́врик; (*also*: **doormat**) дверно́й ко́врик; (*also*: **table** ~) подста́вка* ◆ *adj* = **matt**.
match [mætʃ] *n* спи́чка; (*SPORT*) матч; (*equal*) ро́вня *m/f* ◆ *vt* (*subj: colours*) сочета́ться (*impf*) с +*instr*; (*equal*) сравня́ться (*perf*) с +*instr*; (*correspond to*) соотве́тствовать (*impf*) +*dat* ◆ *vi* (*colours, materials*) сочета́ться (*impf*); **to be a good** ~ (*colours, clothes*) сочета́ться (*impf*); **they make** *or* **are a good** ~ они́ хоро́шая па́ра; **I'm no** ~ **for him** я ему́ не ро́вня; **to** ~ **sth (up) with sth** (*pair*) подбира́ть (подобра́ть* *perf*) что-н к чему́-н
▶ **match up** *vi* совпада́ть (совпа́сть* *perf*).

---

* marks translations which have irregular inflections. The Russian-English side of the dictionary gives inflectional information.

matchbox ['mætʃbɔks] *n* спи́чечная коро́бка*.
matching ['mætʃɪŋ] *adj* (*clothes, colours*)
сочета́ющийся.
matchless ['mætʃlɪs] *adj* несравне́нный*
(несравне́нен).
mate [meɪt] *n* (*inf: friend*) друг* (подру́га);
(*animal*) саме́ц*(-мка*); (*workman's assistant*)
подру́чный *m adj*; (*NAUT*) помо́щник
(*капита́на*) ◆ *vi* спа́риваться (спа́риться
perf).
material [mə'tɪərɪəl] *n* (*substance, information*)
материа́л; (*cloth*) материа́л, ткань *f* ◆ *adj*
(*possessions, existence*) материа́льный*;
(*evidence*) веще́ственный*; ~**s** *npl*
принадле́жности *fpl*; **building** ~**s**
строи́тельные материа́лы; **reading** ~
материа́л для чте́ния.
materialistic [mətɪərɪə'lɪstɪk] *adj* (*person etc*)
материалисти́ческий.
materialize [mə'tɪərɪəlaɪz] *vi*
материализова́ться (*impf/perf*),
осуществля́ться (осуществи́ться* *perf*).
maternal [mə'təːnl] *adj* матери́нский*.
maternity [mə'təːnɪtɪ] *n* матери́нство ◆ *cpd*
(*hospital, ward*) роди́льный; ~ **care** ухо́д за
роже́ницами.
maternity benefit *n* декре́тные *pl adj*.
maternity dress *n* пла́тье* для бере́менной
(же́нщины).
maternity hospital *n* роди́льный дом*,
роддо́м*.
maternity leave *n* декре́тный о́тпуск.
matey ['meɪtɪ] *adj* (*BRIT: inf*) дружелю́бный*
(дружелю́бен).
math [mæθ] *n abbr* (*US*) = **mathematics**.
mathematical [mæθə'mætɪkl] *adj*
математи́ческий*.
mathematician [mæθəmə'tɪʃən] *n* матема́тик.
mathematics [mæθə'mætɪks] *n* матема́тика.
maths [mæθs] *n abbr* (*BRIT*) = **mathematics**.
matinée ['mætɪneɪ] *n* (*CINEMA*) дневно́й сеа́нс;
(*THEAT*) дневно́й спекта́кль *m*.
mating ['meɪtɪŋ] *n* спа́ривание, слу́чка.
mating call *n* бра́чный призы́в.
mating season *n* бра́чный сезо́н.
matriarchal [meɪtrɪ'ɑːkl] *adj* матриарха́льный.
matrices ['meɪtrɪsiːz] *npl of* **matrix**.
matriculation [mətrɪkju'leɪʃən] *n* (*enrolment*)
зачисле́ние в университе́т.
matrimonial [mætrɪ'məunɪəl] *adj*
матримониа́льный, бра́чный.
matrimony ['mætrɪmənɪ] *n* супру́жество.
matrix ['meɪtrɪks] (*pl* **matrices**) *n* ма́трица.
matron ['meɪtrən] *n* (*in hospital*) ста́ршая
медсестра́*; (*in school*) (шко́льная)
медсестра́*.
matronly ['meɪtrənlɪ] *adj* пы́шный* (пы́шен).
matt [mæt] *adj* ма́товый.
matted ['mætɪd] *adj* (*hair*) спу́танный (спу́тан).
matter ['mætəʳ] *n* де́ло*, вопро́с; (*PHYS*)
мате́рия; (*substance, material*) вещество́*;

(*MED: pus*) гной ◆ *vi* име́ть (*impf*) значе́ние; ~**s**
npl (*affairs, situation*) дела́ *ntpl*; **printed** ~
печа́тный материа́л; **reading** ~ (*BRIT*)
материа́л для чте́ния; **what's the** ~? в чём
де́ло?; **no** ~ **what** несмотря́ ни на что́, что́
бы то ни бы́ло; **that's another** ~ э́то друго́е
де́ло; **as a** ~ **of course** как само́ собо́й
разуме́ющееся; **as a** ~ **of fact** со́бственно
говоря́; **it's a** ~ **of habit** э́то де́ло привы́чки; **it
doesn't** ~ э́то не ва́жно.
matter-of-fact ['mætərəv'fækt] *adj*
безразли́чный* (безразли́чен).
matting ['mætɪŋ] *n* цино́вка; **rush** ~
камышо́вая цино́вка.
mattress ['mætrɪs] *n* матра́с, матра́ц.
mature [mə'tjuə] *adj* (*person*) зре́лый* (зрел);
(*cheese, wine*) вы́держанный* (вы́держан) ◆
vi (*develop*) развива́ться (разви́ться* *perf*);
(*grow up*) взросле́ть (повзросле́ть *perf*);
(*cheese*) зреть *or* созрева́ть (созре́ть *perf*);
(*wine*) выста́иваться (вы́стояться *perf*);
(*COMM*): **this policy is due to** ~ **next year** в
сле́дующем году́ начина́ются вы́платы по
э́тому по́лису.
mature student *n* студе́нт, начина́ющий
вы́сшее образова́ние в во́зрасте 23 лет и́ли
ста́рше.
maturity [mə'tjuərɪtɪ] *n* зре́лость *f*.
maudlin ['mɔːdlɪn] *adj* плакси́вый (плакси́в),
слезли́вый (слезли́в).
maul [mɔːl] *vt* (*physically*) терза́ть (растерза́ть
perf).
Mauritania [mɔːrɪ'teɪnɪə] *n* Маврита́ния.
Mauritius [mə'rɪʃəs] *n* Маври́кий.
mausoleum [mɔːsə'lɪəm] *n* мавзоле́й.
mauve [məuv] *adj* сире́невый.
maverick ['mævrɪk] *n* индивидуали́ст.
mawkish ['mɔːkɪʃ] *adj* слаща́вый (слаща́в).
max. *abbr* (= **maximum**) макс(им).,
масима́льный.
maxim ['mæksɪm] *n* ма́ксима.
maxima ['mæksɪmə] *npl of* **maximum**.
maximize ['mæksɪmaɪz] *vt* максима́льно
увели́чивать (увели́чить *perf*).
maximum ['mæksɪməm] (*pl* **maxima** *or* ~**s**) *adj*
максима́льный* (максима́лен) ◆ *n*
ма́ксимум.
May [meɪ] *n* май; *see also* **July**.
may [meɪ] (*conditional* **might**) *vi* (*indicating
possibility*): **I** ~ **go to Russia** я, мо́жет быть,
пое́ду в Росси́ю; (*indicating permission*): ~ **I
smoke/sit here** мо́жно закури́ть/здесь
присе́сть; (*indicating wishes*): ~ **God bless
you!** да благослови́т Вас Бог!; **it** ~ *or* **might
rain** мо́жет пойти́ дождь; **he might be there**
возмо́жно, что он там; **you might like to try**
мо́жет быть, Вы хоти́те попро́бовать; **you**
~ *or* **might as well go now** Вы, пожа́луй,
мо́жете уйти́ сейча́с; **come what** ~ будь что
бу́дет.
maybe ['meɪbiː] *adv* мо́жет быть; ~ **he'll** ...

мо́жет быть, он +*infin* ...; ~ **not** мо́жет быть, нет.

mayday ['meɪdeɪ] *n* сигна́л бе́дствия.

May Day *n* Пе́рвое Ма́я.

mayhem ['meɪhɛm] *n* погро́м.

mayonnaise [meɪə'neɪz] *n* майоне́з.

mayor [mɛə^r] *n* мэр.

mayoress ['mɛərɛs] *n* (*partner*) жена́* мэ́ра.

maypole ['meɪpəul] *n* укра́шенный цвета́ми столб.

maze [meɪz] *n* (*labyrinth*) лабири́нт; (*puzzle*) головоло́мка*; (*of ideas*) пу́таница.

MB *abbr* (COMPUT) (= **megabyte**) M= мегаба́йт; (CANADA) = Manitoba.

MBA *n abbr* (= Master of Business Administration) маги́стрская сте́пень по менеджме́нту.

MBBS *n abbr* (BRIT: = Bachelor of Medicine and Surgery) бакала́вр медици́нских нау́к и хирурги́и.

MBChB *n abbr* (BRIT: = Bachelor of Medicine and Surgery) бакала́вр медици́нских нау́к и хирурги́и.

MBE *n abbr* (BRIT) = Member of the Order of the British Empire.

MC *n abbr* = **Master of Ceremonies**.

MCAT *n abbr* (US) = Medical College Admissions Test.

MCP *n abbr* (BRIT: inf) = male chauvinist pig.

MD *n abbr* (= Doctor of Medicine) до́ктор медици́ны *or* медици́нских нау́к; (COMM) = **managing director** ◆ *abbr* (US: POST) = Maryland.

MDT *abbr* (US) = Mountain Daylight Time.

ME *n abbr* (US: = medical examiner) суде́бно-медици́нский экспе́рт; (MED: = myalgic encephalomyelitis) миалги́ческий энцефаломиели́т ◆ *abbr* (US: POST) = Maine.

KEYWORD
---

me [mi:] *pron* **1** (*direct*) меня́; **he loves me** он лю́бит меня́; **it's me** э́то я
2 (*indirect*) мне; **give me them** *or* **them to me** да́йте их мне
3 (*after prep: +gen*) меня́; (: *+dat, +prp*) мне; (: *+instr*) мной; **it's for me** (*on answering phone*) э́то мне *or* для меня́; **this kind of work is not for me** э́та рабо́та не для меня́
4 (*referring to subject of sentence: after prep: +gen*) себя́; (: *+dat*) себе́; (: *+instr*) собо́й; (: *+prp*) себе́; **I took him with me** я взял его́ с собо́й.

meadow ['mɛdəu] *n* луг*.

meagre ['mi:gə^r] (US **meager**) *adj* ску́дный* (ску́ден).

meal [mi:l] *n* еда́ *no pl*; (*afternoon*) обе́д; (*evening*) у́жин; (*flour*) мука́ гру́бого помо́ла; **during** ~**s** во вре́мя еды́; **to go out**

for a ~ (*in the evening*) у́жинать (поу́жинать *perf*) в рестора́не; **to eat** ~**s a day** есть* (*impf*) 3 ра́за в день; **to make a** ~ **of sth** безоснова́тельно усложня́ть (усложни́ть *perf*) что-н.

meals on wheels *npl* доста́вка обе́дов на́ дом инвали́дам и престаре́лым.

meal time *n* вре́мя* *nt* еды́; **during** ~ ~**s** во вре́мя еды́, за едо́й.

mealy-mouthed ['mi:lɪmauðd] *adj* чрезме́рно деликатный* (деликатен) в вы́боре слов.

mean [mi:n] (*pt, pp* **meant**) *adj* (*miserly*) скупо́й* (скуп); (*unkind*) по́длый* (подл); (US: *inf: animal*) зло́бный* (зло́бен); (*shabby*) убо́гий* (убо́г); (*average*) сре́дний ◆ *vt* (*signify*) зна́чить (*impf*), означа́ть (*impf*); (*refer to*) име́ть (*impf*) в виду́ ◆ *n* (*average*) середи́на; ~**s** *npl* (*way*) спо́соб *msg*, сре́дство *ntsg*; (*money*) сре́дства *ntpl*; **by** ~**s of** посре́дством +*gen*, с по́мощью +*gen*; **by all** ~**s**! пожа́луйста!; **do you** ~ **it?** Вы говори́те об э́том всерьёз?, Вы э́то серьёзно?; **what do you** ~? что Вы име́ете в виду́?; **to** ~ **to do** (*intend*) намерева́ться (*impf*) +*infin*; **to be** ~**t for sb/sth** предназнача́ться (*impf*) кому́-н/ чему́-н.

meander [mɪ'ændə^r] *vi* (*river*) извива́ться (*impf*); (*person*) броди́ть* (*impf*).

meaning ['mi:nɪŋ] *n* (*purpose, value*) смысл; (*definition*) значе́ние; **this word has two** ~**s** э́то сло́во име́ет два значе́ния; **his words have no** ~ его́ слова́ не име́ют смы́сла.

meaningful ['mi:nɪŋful] *adj* (*result, occasion*) значи́тельный* (значи́телен); (*explanation*) вразуми́тельный* (вразуми́телен); (*glance, remark*) многозначи́тельный* (многозначи́телен); (*relationship*) серьёзный* (серьёзен).

meaningless ['mi:nɪŋlɪs] *adj* бессмы́сленный (бессмы́слен).

meanness ['mi:nnɪs] *n* (*with money*) ску́пость *f*; (*unkindness*) по́длость *f*; (*shabbiness*) убо́гость *f*.

means test [mi:nz-] *n* (ADMIN) прове́рка* дохо́дов (*при получе́нии социа́льного посо́бия*).

meant [mɛnt] *pt, pp of* **mean**.

meantime ['mi:ntaɪm] *adv* (*also:* **in the** ~) тем вре́менем, ме́жду тем.

meanwhile ['mi:nwaɪl] *adv* = **meantime**.

measles ['mi:zlz] *n* корь *f*.

measly ['mi:zlɪ] *adj* (*inf*) жа́лкий*.

measurable ['mɛʒərəbl] *adj* измери́мый (измери́м).

measure ['mɛʒə^r] *vt* измеря́ть (изме́рить *perf*) ◆ *n* (*action, amount*) ме́ра; (*of whisky etc*) по́рция; (*also:* **tape** ~) руле́тка*, сантиме́тр; (*of achievement*) мери́ло; (*of performance*)

---

* marks translations which have irregular inflections. The Russian-English side of the dictionary gives inflectional information.

критéрий ♦ *vi*: **the room ~s 10 feet by 20**
плóщадь э́той кóмнаты 10 фýтов на 20; **in
some/great ~** (*extent*) в какóй-то/
значи́тельной мéре; **a litre ~** (*vessel*)
литрóвый сосýд; **to take ~s** (**to do**)
принима́ть (приня́ть* *perf*) мéры (чтóбы
+*infin*)
▶ **measure up** *vi*: **to ~ up to** (*to standard*)
отвеча́ть (*impf*) +*dat*; (*to expectations*)
опра́вдывать (оправда́ть* *perf*).
measured ['mɛʒəd] *adj* (*tone*) сде́ржанный*
(сде́ржан); (*step*) разме́ренный* (разме́рен);
(*opinion*) взве́шенный (взве́шен).
measurement ['mɛʒəmənt] *n* разме́р;
(*process*) измере́ние; **chest/hip ~** объём
груди́/бёдер.
measurements ['mɛʒəmənts] *npl* разме́ры *mpl*;
to take sb's ~ снима́ть (снять* *perf*) с когó-н
ме́рки.
meat [mi:t] *n* мя́со; **cold ~s** (*BRIT*) холóдные
мясны́е заку́ски* *fpl*; **crab ~** мя́со кра́ба.
meatball ['mi:tbɔ:l] *n* фрикаде́лька*.
meat pie *n* пирóг* с мя́сом.
meaty ['mi:tɪ] *adj* (*hand, face*) мяси́стый
(мяси́ст); (*stew*) мяснóй; (*discussion*)
содержа́тельный* (содержа́телен).
Mecca ['mɛkə] *n* (*also fig*) Мéкка.
mechanic [mɪ'kænɪk] *n* меха́ник.
mechanical [mɪ'kænɪkl] *adj* механи́ческий*.
mechanical engineering *n* машинострое́ние.
mechanics [mɪ'kænɪks] *n* (*PHYS*) меха́ника ♦ *npl*
(*of reading, government*) меха́ника *fsg*.
mechanism ['mɛkənɪzəm] *n* механи́зм.
mechanization [mɛkənaɪ'zeɪʃən] *n*
механиза́ция.
mechanize ['mɛkənaɪz] *vt* механизи́ровать
(*impf/perf*) ♦ *vi* проводи́ть* (провести́* *perf*)
механиза́цию.
MEd *n abbr* (= *Master of Education*) маги́стр
педагоги́ческих нау́к.
medal ['mɛdl] *n* меда́ль *f*.
medalist ['mɛdlɪst] *n* (*US*) = **medallist**.
medallion [mɪ'dæljən] *n* медальóн.
medallist ['mɛdlɪst] (*US* **medalist**) *n*
медали́ст(ка*).
meddle ['mɛdl] *vi*: **to ~ in** вме́шиваться
(вмеша́ться *perf*) в +*acc*; **to ~ with sth**
вторга́ться (вто́ргнуться *perf*) в что-н.
meddlesome ['mɛdlsəm] *adj* назóйливый
(назóйлив).
media ['mi:dɪə] *n or npl*: **the ~** срéдства *ntpl*
ма́ссовой информа́ции ♦ *npl see* **medium**.
mediaeval [mɛdɪ'i:vl] *adj* = **medieval**.
median ['mi:dɪən] *n* медиа́на.
median strip ['mi:dɪən-] *n* (*US*)
раздели́тельная полоса́ (*автостра́ды*).
media research *n* иссле́дование *or* опрóс
срéдствами ма́ссовой информа́ции.
mediate ['mi:dɪeɪt] *vi* (*arbitrate*) посре́дничать
(*impf*).
mediation [mi:dɪ'eɪʃən] *n* посре́дничество.

mediator ['mi:dɪeɪtə'] *n* посре́дник(-ица).
Medicaid ['mɛdɪkeɪd] *n* (*US*) госуда́рственная
програ́мма, субсиди́рующая медици́нское
обслу́живание малоиму́щей ча́сти
населе́ния.
medical ['mɛdɪkl] *adj* медици́нский* ♦ *n*
(*examination*) медосмóтр= *медици́нский*
осмóтр.
medical certificate *n* медици́нская спра́вка*.
medical examiner *n* (*US*) судéбно-
медици́нский* экспéрт.
medical student *n* студéнт – мéдик.
Medicare ['mɛdɪkɛə'] *n* (*US*) госуда́рственная
програ́мма медици́нского страхова́ния для
людéй в во́зрасте от 65 лет и ста́рше.
medicated ['mɛdɪkeɪtɪd] *adj* содержа́щий
лека́рственное вещество́.
medication [mɛdɪ'keɪʃən] *n* лека́рство,
лека́рственный препара́т; **to be on ~**
проходи́ть* (пройти́* *perf*) лека́рственную
терапи́ю.
medicinal [mɛ'dɪsɪnl] *adj* (*substance, qualities*)
лека́рственный; (*purposes, reasons*)
лечéбный.
medicine ['mɛdsɪn] *n* (*science*) медици́на;
(*drug*) лека́рство.
medicine ball *n* (*SPORT*) ≈ ги́ря.
medicine chest *n* апте́чка*.
medicine man *n* зна́харь *m*.
medieval [mɛdɪ'i:vl] *adj* средневекóвый.
mediocre [mi:dɪ'əukə'] *adj* заура́дный*
(заура́ден), посре́дственный* (посре́дствен).
mediocrity [mi:dɪ'ɔkrɪtɪ] *n* заура́дность *f*,
посре́дственность *f*.
meditate ['mɛdɪteɪt] *vi* размышля́ть (*impf*);
(*REL*) занима́ться (заня́ться* *perf*)
медита́цией.
meditation [mɛdɪ'teɪʃən] *n* (*see vb*)
размышле́ние; медита́ция.
Mediterranean [mɛdɪtə'reɪnɪən] *adj*
средиземномóрский; **the ~** (**Sea**)
Средизéмное мóре.
medium ['mi:dɪəm] (*pl* **media** *or* **~s**) *adj*
срéдний* ♦ *n* (*means*) срéдство; (*substance*)
материа́л; (*environment*) среда́; (*pl* **~s**;
person) мéдиум; **a happy ~** золота́я
середи́на.
medium-dry ['mi:dɪəm'draɪ] *adj* полусухóй.
medium-sized ['mi:dɪəm'saɪzd] *adj* (*tin etc*)
срéдней величины́.
medium wave *n* (*RADIO*) срéдние вóлны *fpl*.
medley ['mɛdlɪ] *n* (*mixture*) смесь *f*; (*MUS*)
попурри́ *r. ind*.
meek [mi:k] *adj* крóткий* (крóток).
meet [mi:t] (*pt, pp* **met**) *vt* (*friend, opponent etc*)
встреча́ть (встрéтить* *perf*); (*obligations*)
выполня́ть (вы́полнить *perf*); (*problem*)
ста́лкиваться (столкну́ться *perf*) с +*instr*;
(*need*) удовлетворя́ть (удовлетвори́ть *perf*);
(*expenses, bill*) опла́чивать (оплати́ть* *perf*) ♦
vi (*people*) встреча́ться (встрéтиться* *perf*);

(*lines, roads*) пересека́ться (пересе́чься* *perf*)
♦ *n* (*BRIT: hunting*) сбор; (*US: SPORT*) встре́ча;
pleased to ~ you! рад (с Ва́ми)
познако́миться!, о́чень прия́тно!
▶ **meet up** *vi*: **to ~ up with sb** сходи́ться*
(сойти́сь* *perf*) с кем-н
▶ **meet with** *vt fus* (*difficulty*) ста́лкиваться
(столкну́ться *perf*) с +*instr*; (*success*)
по́льзоваться (*impf*) +*instr*; (*approval*)
находи́ть* (найти́* *perf*).
meeting [ˈmiːtɪŋ] *n* встре́ча; (*of club,
committee etc*) собра́ние; (*POL: also:* **mass ~**)
ми́тинг; **she's at a ~** она́ на заседа́нии; **to call
a ~** созыва́ть (созва́ть* *perf*) собра́ние.
meeting place *n* ме́сто* встре́чи.
megabyte [ˈmɛgəbaɪt] *n* мегаба́йт.
megadrive [ˈmɛgədraɪv] *n* ме́гадрайв (*игрова́я
систе́ма*).
megalomania [mɛgələˈmeɪnɪə] *n* ма́ния
вели́чия.
megaphone [ˈmɛgəfəun] *n* мегафо́н.
megawatt [ˈmɛgəwɔt] *n* мегава́тт.
melancholy [ˈmɛlənkəlɪ] *n* меланхо́лия ♦ *adj*
(*smile*) меланхоли́ческий; (*person*)
меланхоли́чный* (меланхоли́чен).
Melbourne [ˈmɛlbən] *n* Ме́льбурн.
mellow [ˈmɛləu] *adj* (*sound, colour, light*)
бархати́стый (бархати́ст); (*taste*) мя́гкий*
(мя́гок); (*stone, building*) *приобре́тший с
года́ми гла́дкую пове́рхность и мя́гкий цвет*
♦ *vi* (*person*) смягча́ться (смягчи́ться *perf*).
melodious [mɪˈləudɪəs] *adj* мелоди́чный*
(мелоди́чен).
melodrama [ˈmɛlədrɑːmə] *n* мелодра́ма.
melodramatic [mɛlədrəˈmætɪk] *adj* (*situation*)
мелодрамати́ческий; (*behaviour, person*)
мелодрамати́чный* (мелодрамати́чен).
melody [ˈmɛlədɪ] *n* мело́дия.
melon [ˈmɛlən] *n* ды́ня.
melt [mɛlt] *vi* (*metal*) пла́виться* (рас-
пла́виться* *perf*); (*snow, butter, also fig*) та́ять
(раста́ять *perf*) ♦ *vt* (*metal*) пла́вить*
(распла́вить* *perf*); (*snow, butter*) топи́ть*
(растопи́ть* *perf*)
▶ **melt down** *vt* (*metal*) расплавля́ть
(распла́вить* *perf*).
meltdown [ˈmɛltdaun] *n* (*in nuclear reactor*)
расплавле́ние сте́ржня (*в а́томном
реа́кторе*).
melting point [ˈmɛltɪŋ-] *n* то́чка* плавле́ния.
melting pot *n* (*fig*) смеше́ние; **to be in the ~ ~**
вари́ться* (*impf*) в одно́м котле́.
member [ˈmɛmbəʳ] *n* (*also ANAT*) член ♦ *cpd*: **~
country** *or* **state** госуда́рство-член; **M~ of
Parliament** (*BRIT*) член парла́мента.
membership [ˈmɛmbəʃɪp] *n* (*members*) чле́ны
mpl; (*status*) чле́нство; (*number of members*)
число́* чле́нов.

membership card *n* чле́нский* биле́т.
membrane [ˈmɛmbreɪn] *n* мембра́на.
memento [məˈmɛntəu] *n* сувени́р.
memo [ˈmɛməu] *n* (*ADMIN: report*) докладна́я
запи́ска; (: *instruction*) отноше́ние, запи́ска.
memoir [ˈmɛmwɑː] *n* биографи́ческий о́черк.
memoirs [ˈmɛmwɑːz] *npl* мемуа́ры *pl*.
memo pad *n* записна́я кни́жка*.
memorable [ˈmɛmərəbl] *adj* па́мятный*
(па́мятен).
memoranda [mɛməˈrændə] *npl of*
memorandum.
memorandum [mɛməˈrændəm] (*pl*
memoranda) *n* мемора́ндум.
memorial [mɪˈmɔːrɪəl] *n* па́мятник ♦ *cpd*
(*service*) мемориа́льный; ... **M~ Prize** пре́мия
и́мени +*gen* ....
Memorial Day *n* (*US*) *30 ма́я – день па́мяти
поги́бших*.
memorize [ˈmɛməraɪz] *vt* зау́чивать (заучи́ть
perf) (наизу́сть).
memory [ˈmɛmərɪ] *n* (*ability to remember*)
па́мять *f no pl*; (*COMPUT*) па́мять *f*,
запомина́ющее устро́йство; (*recollection*)
воспомина́ние; **in ~ of** в па́мять +*gen*; **I have a
good/bad ~** у меня́ хоро́шая/плоха́я
па́мять; **loss of ~** поте́ря па́мяти.
men [mɛn] *npl of* **man**.
menace [ˈmɛnɪs] *n* (*threat*) угро́за; (*nuisance*)
наказа́ние ♦ *vt* угрожа́ть (*impf*) +*dat*, грози́ть*
(*impf*) +*dat*; **a public ~** угро́за о́бществу.
menacing [ˈmɛnɪsɪŋ] *adj* угрожа́ющий*
(угрожа́ющ).
menagerie [mɪˈnædʒərɪ] *n* звери́нец*.
mend [mɛnd] *vt* ремонти́ровать
(отремонти́ровать *perf*), чини́ть* (почини́ть*
perf); (*clothes*) чини́ть* (почини́ть* *perf*) ♦ *n*: **to
be on the ~** идти́* (*impf*) на попра́вку; **to ~
one's ways** исправля́ться (испра́виться*
perf).
mending [ˈmɛndɪŋ] *n* (*of machine etc*) ремо́нт;
(*of clothes*) почи́нка.
menial [ˈmiːnɪəl] *adj* (*work, tasks*) чёрный.
meningitis [mɛnɪnˈdʒaɪtɪs] *n* менинги́т.
menopause [ˈmɛnəupɔːz] *n*: **the ~**
климактери́ческий пери́од, кли́макс.
menservants [ˈmɛnsəːvənts] *npl of* **manservant**.
men's room *n* (*US*): **the ~ ~** мужска́я
раздева́лка.
menstrual [ˈmɛnstruəl] *adj* менструа́льный.
menstruate [ˈmɛnstrueɪt] *vi* менструи́ровать
(*impf*).
menstruation [mɛnstruˈeɪʃən] *n* менструа́ция.
menswear [ˈmɛnzwɛəʳ] *n* мужска́я оде́жда.
mental [ˈmɛntl] *adj* (*ability, exhaustion*)
у́мственный; (*image*) мы́сленный; (*illness*)
душе́вный, психи́ческий*; (*arithmetic,
calculation*) в уме́; **~ healthcare** забо́та о

---

* marks translations which have irregular inflections. The Russian-English side of the dictionary gives inflectional information.

душевнобольны́х.
mental hospital *n* психиатри́ческая
больни́ца.
mentality [mɛn'tælɪtɪ] *n* менталите́т,
умонастрое́ние; (*way of thinking*) склад ума́.
mentally ['mɛntlɪ] *adv* (*see adj*) у́мственно;
мы́сленно; ~ **ill** душевнобольно́й.
mentally handicapped *adj* у́мственно
отста́лый.
menthol ['mɛnθɔl] *n* менто́л.
mention ['mɛnʃən] *n* упомина́ние ◆ *vt*
упомина́ть (упомяну́ть* *perf*); **don't ~ it!**
ничего́!, не за что!; **I need hardly ~ that ...**
вряд ли сто́ит упомина́ть, что ...; **not to ~ ...,
without ~ing ...** не говоря́ уж о +*prp* ....
mentor ['mɛntɔ:'] *n* наста́вник.
menu ['mɛnju:] *n* (*also COMPUT*) меню́ *nt ind*.
menu-driven ['mɛnju:drɪvn] *adj* (*COMPUT*)
управля́емый меню́.
MEP *n abbr* (*BRIT*: = *Member of the European
Parliament*) член Европе́йского парла́мента.
mercantile ['mə:kəntaɪl] *adj* (*society, law*)
торго́вый.
mercenary ['mə:sɪnərɪ] *adj* коры́стный*
(коры́стен) ◆ *n* (*soldier*) наёмник.
merchandise ['mə:tʃəndaɪz] *n* това́ры *mpl*.
merchandiser ['mə:tʃəndaɪzə'] *n* торго́вец*.
merchant ['mə:tʃənt] *n* (*trader*) торго́вец*,
купе́ц* (*ИСТ*); **timber/wine ~** торго́вец*
ле́сом/вино́м.
merchant bank *n* (*BRIT*) торго́вый банк.
merchantman ['mə:tʃəntmən] *irreg n* торго́вое
су́дно*.
Merchant Navy (*US* **merchant marine**) *n*
торго́вый флот.
merciful ['mə:sɪful] *adj* (*person*) милосе́рдный*
(милосе́рден); (*fortunate*) благо́й.
mercifully ['mə:sɪflɪ] *adv* милосе́рдно;
(*fortunately*) к сча́стью.
merciless ['mə:sɪlɪs] *adj* беспоща́дный*
(беспоща́ден).
mercurial [mə:'kjuərɪəl] *adj* изме́нчивый
(изме́нчив).
mercury ['mə:kjurɪ] *n* ртуть *f*; (*planet*): **M~**
Мерку́рий.
mercy ['mə:sɪ] *n* милосе́рдие; **to have ~ on sb**
проявля́ть (прояви́ть* *perf*) милосе́рдие к
кому́-н; **to be at sb's ~** быть* (*impf*) *or*
находи́ться* (*impf*) во вла́сти кого́-н.
mercy killing *n* уби́йство из милосе́рдия.
mere [mɪə'] *adj*: **she's a ~ child** она́ всего́ лишь
ребёнок; **his ~ presence irritates her** само́ его́
прису́тствие раздража́ет её; **by a ~ chance**
по чи́стой случа́йности.
merely ['mɪəlɪ] *adv* (*simply*) про́сто; (*just*)
то́лько.
merge [mə:dʒ] *vt* (*also COMPUT*) слива́ть
(слить* *perf*), объединя́ть (объедини́ть* *perf*)
◆ *vi* (*also COMM*) слива́ться (сли́ться* *perf*);
(*roads*) сходи́ться* (сойти́сь* *perf*).
merger ['mə:dʒə'] *n* (*COMM*) слия́ние.

meridian [mə'rɪdɪən] *n* меридиа́н.
meringue [mə'ræŋ] *n* безе́ *nt ind*.
merit ['mɛrɪt] *n* (*worth, value*) досто́инство ◆ *vt*
заслу́живать (заслужи́ть* *perf*); **to judge sth
on its ~s** оце́нивать (оцени́ть *perf*) что-н по
досто́инству.
meritocracy [mɛrɪ'tɔkrəsɪ] *n* о́бщество, в
кото́ром положе́ние челове́ка определя́ется
его́ спосо́бностями.
mermaid ['mə:meɪd] *n* руса́лка*.
merrily ['mɛrɪlɪ] *adv* ве́село.
merriment ['mɛrɪmənt] *n* весе́лье.
merry ['mɛrɪ] *adj* весёлый* (ве́сел); **M~
Christmas!** С Рождество́м!
merry-go-round ['mɛrɪgəuraund] *n* карусе́ль *f*.
mesh [mɛʃ] *n* (*net*) сеть *f*; **wire ~** про́волочная
се́тка.
mesmerize ['mɛzməraɪz] *vt* гипнотизи́ровать
(загипнотизи́ровать *perf*).
mess [mɛs] *n* (*muddle: in room*) беспоря́док*; (:
of situation) неразбери́ха; (*dirt*) грязь *f*; (*MIL*)
столо́вая *f adj*; **to be in a ~** (*untidy*) быть*
(*impf*) в беспоря́дке; **to get o.s. into a ~** (*inf*)
влипа́ть (вли́пнуть* *perf*); **my life is in a real ~**
(*inf*) у меня́ в жи́зни всё идёт вверх дном
▶ **mess about** *vi* (*inf: fool around*) дура́читься
(*impf*), валя́ть (*impf*) дурака́
▶ **mess about with** *vt fus* (*inf: play around with*)
вози́ться* (*impf*) с +*instr*
▶ **mess around** *vi* (*inf*) = **mess about**
▶ **mess around with** *vt fus* (*inf*) = **mess about
with**
▶ **mess up** *vt* (*spoil*) по́ртить* (испо́ртить*
perf); (*dirty*) па́чкать (испа́чкать *perf*).
message ['mɛsɪdʒ] *n* (*piece of information*)
сообще́ние; (*note*) запи́ска*; (*of play, book*)
иде́я; **to leave sb a ~** (*note*) оставля́ть
(оста́вить* *perf*) кому́-н запи́ску; **can I give
him a ~?** ему́ что́-нибудь переда́ть?; **he got
the ~** (*fig: inf*) до него́ дошло́.
message switching [-'swɪtʃɪŋ] *n* (*COMPUT*)
коммута́ция сообще́ний.
messenger ['mɛsɪndʒə'] *n* курье́р, посы́льный
m adj.
Messiah [mɪ'saɪə] *n* Месси́я *m*.
Messrs *abbr* (*on letters*: = *messieurs*) гг.=
господа́.
Messrs. *abbr* = **Messrs**.
messy ['mɛsɪ] *adj* (*untidy*) неу́бранный
(неу́бран); (*dirty*) гря́зный* (гря́зен).
Met [mɛt] *n abbr* (*US*) = *Metropolitan Opera*.
met [mɛt] *pt, pp of* **meet**.
met *adj abbr* = *meteorological*: **the M~** Office
метеоце́нтр.
metabolism [mɛ'tæbəlɪzəm] *n* метаболи́зм,
обме́н веще́ств.
metal ['mɛtl] *n* мета́лл.
metal fatigue *n* уста́лость *f* мета́лла.
metalled ['mɛtld] *adj*: **~ road** доро́га, с
щебёночным покры́тием.
metallic [mɪ'tælɪk] *adj* металли́ческий*.

metallurgy [mɛ'tælədʒɪ] n металлурги́я.
metalwork ['mɛtlwə:k] n рабо́та по мета́ллу.
metamorphoses [mɛtə'mɔ:fəsi:z] npl of
metamorphosis.
metamorphosis [mɛtə'mɔ:fəsɪs] (pl
metamorphoses) n метаморфо́за.
metaphor ['mɛtəfə'] n мета́фора.
metaphorical [mɛtə'fɔrɪkl] adj
метафори́ческий.
metaphysics [mɛtə'fɪzɪks] n метафи́зика.
meteor ['mi:tɪə'] n метео́р.
meteoric [mi:tɪ'ɔrɪk] adj (fig) метеори́ческий.
meteorite ['mi:tɪəraɪt] n метеори́т.
meteorological [mi:tɪərə'lɔdʒɪkl] adj
метеорологи́ческий.
meteorology [mi:tɪə'rɔlədʒɪ] n метеороло́гия.
mete out [mi:t-] vt отмеря́ть (отме́рить perf).
meter ['mi:tə'] n (instrument) счётчик; (US: unit)
= **metre**.
methane ['mi:θeɪn] n мета́н.
method ['mɛθəd] n (way) ме́тод, спо́соб; ~ **of**
payment спо́соб опла́ты.
methodical [mɪ'θɔdɪkl] adj методи́чный*
(методи́чен).
Methodist ['mɛθədɪst] n (REL) методи́ст(ка*).
methodology [mɛθə'dɔlədʒɪ] n методоло́гия.
meths [mɛθs] n (BRIT: inf) = **methylated spirit**.
methylated spirit ['mɛθɪleɪtɪd-] n (BRIT)
денатура́т.
meticulous [mɪ'tɪkjuləs] adj тща́тельный*
(тща́телен).
metre ['mi:tə'] (US **meter**) n метр.
metric ['mɛtrɪk] adj метри́ческий*; **to go** ~
переходи́ть* (перейти́* perf) на метри́ческую
систе́му мер.
metrical ['mɛtrɪkl] adj метри́ческий*.
metrication [mɛtrɪ'keɪʃən] n введе́ние
метри́ческой систе́мы мер.
metric system n метри́ческая систе́ма мер.
metric ton n (метри́ческая) то́нна.
metronome ['mɛtrənəum] n метроно́м.
metropolis [mɪ'trɔpəlɪs] n столи́ца.
metropolitan [mɛtrə'pɔlɪtn] adj столи́чный.
Metropolitan Police n (BRIT): **the** ~ ~
Ло́ндонская поли́ция.
mettle ['mɛtl] n: **to show one's** ~ проявля́ть
(прояви́ть* perf) (свой) хара́ктер.
mew [mju:] vi мяу́кать (impf).
mews [mju:z] n (BRIT) переу́лок в жило́е
помеще́ние.
Mexican ['mɛksɪkən] adj мексика́нский* ♦ n
мексика́нец*(-нка*).
Mexico ['mɛksɪkəu] n Ме́ксика.
Mexico City n Ме́хико m ind.
mezzanine ['mɛtsəni:n] n (also: ~ **floor**)
мезони́н, полуэта́ж.
MFA n abbr (US: = Master of Fine Arts) маги́стр
иску́сств.
mfr abbr = **manufacture**, **manufacturer**.

mg abbr (= **milligram(me)**) мг.= миллигра́мм.
Mgr abbr (= Monseigneur, Monsignor)
монсенье́р; (COMM) = **manager**.
MHR n abbr (US: = Member of the House of
Representatives) член пала́ты
представи́телей.
MHz abbr (= megahertz) МГц= мегаге́рц.
MI abbr (US: POST) = Michigan.
MI5 n abbr (BRIT: = Military Intelligence 5)
вне́шняя разве́дка Великобрита́нии.
MI6 n abbr (BRIT: = Military Intelligence 6)
вну́тренняя разве́дка Великобрита́нии.
MIA abbr (MIL: = missing in action) пропа́вший
бёз вести.
miaow [mi:'au] vi мяу́кать (impf).
mice [maɪs] npl of **mouse**.
micro... ['maɪkrəu] prefix микро....
microbe ['maɪkrəub] n микро́б.
microbiology [maɪkrəbaɪ'ɔlədʒɪ] n микро-
биоло́гия.
microchip ['maɪkrəutʃɪp] n микрочи́п.
micro(computer) ['maɪkrəu(kəm'pju:tə')] n
микрокомпью́тер.
microcosm ['maɪkrəukɔzəm] n микроко́смос,
микроко́см.
microeconomics ['maɪkrəui:kə'nɔmɪks] n
микроэконо́мика.
microelectronics ['maɪkrəuɪlɛk'trɔnɪks] n
микроэлектро́ника.
microfiche ['maɪkrəufi:ʃ] n микрофи́ша.
microfilm ['maɪkrəufɪlm] n микрофи́льм,
микроплёнка*.
microlight ['maɪkrəulaɪt] n сверхлёгкий
самолёт.
micrometer [maɪ'krɔmɪtə'] n микро́метр.
microphone ['maɪkrəfəun] n микрофо́н.
microprocessor ['maɪkrəu'prəusɛsə'] n
микропроце́ссор.
microscope ['maɪkrəskəup] n микроско́п;
under the ~ под микроско́пом.
microscopic [maɪkrə'skɔpɪk] adj микро-
скопи́ческий*.
microsurgery [maɪkrəusə:dʒərɪ] n микро-
хирурги́я.
microwave ['maɪkrəuweɪv] n (also: ~ **oven**)
микроволно́вая печь* f.
mid [mɪd] adj: **in** ~ **May/afternoon** в середи́не
ма́я/дня; **in** ~ **air** в во́здухе; **he's in his** ~
thirties ему́ за три́дцать.
midday [mɪd'deɪ] n по́лдень* m.
middle ['mɪdl] n середи́на; (waist) по́яс* ♦ adj
сре́дний*; **in the** ~ **of the night** посреди́ но́чи;
I'm in the ~ **of reading it** я как раз сейча́с э́то
чита́ю.
middle age n сре́дний* во́зраст.
middle-aged [mɪdl'eɪdʒd] adj сре́дних лет.
Middle Ages npl: **the** ~ ~ сре́дние века́* mpl.
middle class n: **the** ~ ~ сре́дний* класс.

---

* marks translations which have irregular inflections. The Russian-English side of the dictionary gives inflectional information.

middle-class [mɪdl'klɑːs] *adj* принадлежа́щий к сре́днему кла́ссу.
middle classes *npl* = **middle class.**
Middle East *n*: **the ~ ~** Бли́жний* Восто́к.
middleman ['mɪdlmæn] *irreg n* посре́дник.
middle management *n* сре́днее руководя́щее звено́.
middle name *n* второ́е и́мя* *nt*.
middle-of-the-road ['mɪdləvðə'rəud] *adj* (*politician*) уме́ренный; (*music*) лёгкий*.
middleweight ['mɪdlweɪt] *n* (*BOXING*) боксёр сре́днего ве́са.
middling ['mɪdlɪŋ] *adj* сре́дний*.
Middx *abbr* (*BRIT: POST*) = *Middlesex.*
midge [mɪdʒ] *n* мо́шка*.
midget ['mɪdʒɪt] *n* ка́рлик(-ица).
midi system ['mɪdɪ-] *n* МИДИ (*электро́нный контро́ль для синтеза́торов*).
Midlands ['mɪdləndz] *npl*: **the ~** Центра́льные райо́ны *mpl* А́нглии.
midnight ['mɪdnaɪt] *n* по́лночь* *f* ♦ *cpd* (*party, feast*) полно́чный; **at ~** в по́лночь.
midriff ['mɪdrɪf] *n* живо́т.
midst [mɪdst] *n*: **in the ~ of** посреди́ +*gen*.
midsummer [mɪd'sʌməʳ] *n* середи́на ле́та; **M~'s Day** день* *m* ле́тнего солнцестоя́ния.
midway [mɪd'weɪ] *adv*: **~ (between)** на полпути́ (ме́жду +*instr*); **~ through** в середи́не +*gen*; **to turn back ~** верну́ться (*perf*) с полпути́.
midweek [mɪd'wiːk] *adj, adv* в середи́не неде́ли.
midwife ['mɪdwaɪf] (*pl* **midwives**) *n* акуше́рка*.
midwifery ['mɪdwɪfərɪ] *n* акуше́рство.
midwinter [mɪd'wɪntəʳ] *n* середи́на зимы́.
midwives ['mɪdwaɪvz] *npl of* **midwife**.
miffed [mɪft] *adj* (*inf*) оби́женный (оби́жен).
might [maɪt] *vb see* **may** ♦ *n* (*power*) мощь *f*.
mighty ['maɪtɪ] *adj* мо́щный* (мо́щен).
migraine ['miːgreɪn] *n* мигре́нь *f*.
migrant ['maɪgrənt] *adj* (*bird*) перелётный ♦ *n* (*bird*) перелётная пти́ца; (*animal*) мигри́рующее живо́тное *nt adj*; (*person*) переселе́нец*(-нка*); **~ worker** рабо́чий*-мигра́нт.
migrate [maɪ'greɪt] *vi* мигри́ровать (*impf/perf*).
migration [maɪ'greɪʃən] *n* мигра́ция.
mike [maɪk] *n abbr* = **microphone.**
Milan [mɪ'læn] *n* Мила́н.
mild [maɪld] *adj* (*character, climate, taste, reproach*) мя́гкий* (мя́гок); (*infection, illness*) лёгкий* (лёгок); (*interest*) незначи́тельный* (незначи́телен).
mildew ['mɪldjuː] *n* пле́сень *f*.
mildly ['maɪldlɪ] *adv* (*see adj*) мя́гко; легко́; слегка́; **to put it ~** мя́гко говоря́.
mildness ['maɪldnɪs] *n* (*see adj*) мя́гкость *f*; лёгкость *f*; незначи́тельность *f*.
mile [maɪl] *n* ми́ля*; **this car does 30 ~s to the gallon** э́тот автомоби́ль затра́чивает галло́н бензи́на ка́ждый 30 миль; **~s better**

(*inf*) намно́го лу́чше.
mileage ['maɪlɪdʒ] *n* (*number of miles*) пробе́г в ми́лях; (*distance*) расстоя́ние в ми́лях.
mileage allowance *n* покры́тие доро́жных расхо́дов (*в расчёте на ка́ждую ми́лю*).
mileometer [maɪ'lɔmɪtəʳ] *n* счётчик (*про́йденных миль*).
milestone ['maɪlstəun] *n* ≈ километро́вый столб; (*fig*) ве́ха.
milieu [miː'ljəː] *n* среда́*.
militant ['mɪlɪtnt] *adj* войнству́ющий ♦ *n* радика́л.
militarism ['mɪlɪtərɪzəm] *n* милитари́зм.
militaristic [mɪlɪtə'rɪstɪk] *adj* милитаристи́ческий.
military ['mɪlɪtərɪ] *adj* вое́нный ♦ *n*: **the ~** вое́нные *pl adj*.
military police *n* вое́нная поли́ция.
military service *n* вое́нная слу́жба.
militate ['mɪlɪteɪt] *vi*: **to ~ against** препя́тствовать (*impf*) +*dat*.
militia [mɪ'lɪʃə] *n* (*MIL*) (наро́дное) ополче́ние.
milk [mɪlk] *n* молоко́ ♦ *vt* (*cow*) дои́ть* (подои́ть* *perf*); (*fig: situation, person*) эксплуати́ровать (*impf*).
milk chocolate *n* моло́чный шокола́д.
milk float *n* (*BRIT*) моло́чный фурго́н.
milking ['mɪlkɪŋ] *n* дое́ние.
milkman ['mɪlkmən] *irreg n* разно́счик молока́.
milk shake *n* моло́чный кокте́йль *m*.
milk tooth *n* моло́чный зуб*.
milk truck *n* (*US*) = **milk float.**
milky ['mɪlkɪ] *adj* моло́чный.
Milky Way *n*: **the ~ ~** Мле́чный путь* *m*.
mill [mɪl] *n* (*windmill*) ме́льница; (*factory: making cloth*) фа́брика; (: *making steel*) заво́д; (*also: coffee ~*) кофемо́лка* ♦ *vt* моло́ть* (смоло́ть* *perf*) ♦ *vi* (*also: ~ about*) толо́чься* (*impf*).
millennia [mɪ'lɛnɪə] *npl of* **millennium.**
millennium [mɪ'lɛnɪəm] (*pl* **~s** *or* **millennia**) *n* тысячеле́тие.
miller ['mɪləʳ] *n* ме́льник.
millet ['mɪlɪt] *n* пшено́.
milli... ['mɪlɪ] *prefix* милли....
milligram(me) ['mɪlɪgræm] (*US* **milligram**) *n* миллигра́м.
millilitre ['mɪlɪliːtəʳ] (*US* **milliliter**) *n* миллили́тр.
millimetre ['mɪlɪmiːtəʳ] (*US* **millimeter**) *n* миллиме́тр.
millinery ['mɪlɪnərɪ] *n* да́мские шля́пы *fpl*.
million ['mɪljən] *n* миллио́н.
millionaire [mɪljə'nɛəʳ] *n* миллионе́р.
millipede ['mɪlɪpiːd] *n* тысячено́жка*.
millstone ['mɪlstəun] *n* (*fig*): **a ~ around one's neck** ка́мень *m* на ше́е.
millwheel ['mɪlwiːl] *n* ме́льничное колесо́*.
milometer [maɪ'lɔmɪtəʳ] *n* = **mileometer.**
mime [maɪm] *n* (*art*) пантоми́ма; (*also: ~ artist*) мим ♦ *vt* изобража́ть (изобрази́ть* *perf*) же́стами.

mimic ['mɪmɪk] n пароди́ст ◆ vt (subj: comedian) пароди́ровать (impf/perf); (animal, person) имити́ровать (impf).

mimicry ['mɪmɪkrɪ] n имита́ция.

Min. abbr (BRIT: POL) = ministry.

min. abbr (= minute) мин(.)= мину́та; (= minimum) мин.= минима́льный.

minaret [mɪnə'rɛt] n минаре́т.

mince [mɪns] vt (meat) пропуска́ть (пропусти́ть* perf) че́рез мясору́бку ◆ vi (in walking) семени́ть (impf) ◆ n (BRIT: (мясно́й) фарш; **he doesn't ~ (his) words** он не выбира́ет выраже́ний.

mincemeat ['mɪnsmiːt] n (BRIT: fruit) начи́нка из сухофру́ктов (для пирожко́в); (US: meat) (мясно́й) фарш; **to make ~ of sb** разбива́ть (разби́ть* perf) кого́-н в пух и прах.

mince pie n (BRIT: sweet) пирожо́к* с начи́нкой из сухофру́ктов.

mincer ['mɪnsə'] n мясору́бка*.

mincing ['mɪnsɪŋ] adj (walk) семеня́щий; (voice) жема́нный* (жема́нен).

mind [maɪnd] n (intellect) ум*; (thoughts) голова́* ◆ vt (look after) смотре́ть* (impf) за +instr; (object to): **I don't ~ the noise** меня́ не беспоко́ит шум; **to be out of one's ~** быть* (impf) не в своём уме́; **it's constantly on my ~** э́то не выхо́дит у меня́ из головы́; **to keep** or **bear sth in ~** по́мнить (impf) что-н, име́ть (impf) что-н в виду́; **to make up one's ~** реша́ться (реши́ться perf); **to change one's ~** переду́мывать (переду́мать perf); **to my ~ ...** (opinion) по моему́ мне́нию ...; **to be in two ~s about sth** сомнева́ться (impf) в чём-н; **to have in ~ to do sth** намерева́ться (impf) +infin; **I have somebody in ~** у меня́ есть ко́е-кто на приме́те; **it went right out of my ~** э́то совсе́м вы́летело у меня́ из головы́; **to bring** or **call to ~** напомина́ть (напо́мнить perf) о +prp; **she doesn't ~ the cold** она́ не бои́тся хо́лода; **do you ~ if ...?** Вы не возража́ете, е́сли ...?; **I don't ~** мне всё равно́; **~ you, ...** име́йте в виду́ ...; **never ~!** ничего́!; **"mind the step"** "осторо́жно, не споткни́тесь".

mind-boggling ['maɪndbɒglɪŋ] adj (inf) уму́ непостижи́мый.

-minded ['maɪndɪd] adj: **fair-~** справедли́вый (справедли́в); **an industrially-~ nation** наро́д, скло́нный к индустриа́льной де́ятельности.

minder ['maɪndə'] n (childminder) ня́ня*; (inf: bodyguard) телохрани́тель m.

mindful ['maɪndful] adj: **to be ~ of** име́ть (impf) в виду́.

mindless ['maɪndlɪs] adj (violence) безду́мный* (безду́мен); (job) механи́ческий*.

┌─────────────┐
│ **KEYWORD** │
└─────────────┘

mine¹ [maɪn] pron **1** мой; **that book is mine** э́та

кни́га моя́, э́то моя́ кни́га; **this is mine** э́то моё; **an uncle of mine** мой дя́дя
2 (referring back to subject) свой; **may I borrow your pen? I have forgotten mine** мо́жно взять Ва́шу ру́чку? я забы́л свою́.

mine² [maɪn] n (coal) ша́хта; (gold, diamonds) при́иск; (copper, tin) рудни́к; (explosive) ми́на ◆ vt (coal) добыва́ть (добы́ть* perf); (beach) мини́ровать (замини́ровать perf).

mine detector n миноиска́тель m.

minefield ['maɪnfiːld] n (also fig) ми́нное по́ле*.

miner ['maɪnə'] n шахтёр.

mineral ['mɪnərəl] n (crystalline) минера́л; (ore) поле́зное ископа́емое nt adj ◆ adj минера́льный; **~s** npl (BRIT: soft drinks) прохлади́тельные напи́тки mpl.

mineralogy [mɪnə'rælədʒɪ] n минерало́гия.

mineral water n минера́льная вода́.

minesweeper ['maɪnswiːpə'] n ми́нный тра́льщик.

mingle ['mɪŋgl] vi: **to ~ with** сме́шиваться (смеша́ться perf) с +instr.

mingy ['mɪndʒɪ] adj (inf: person) прижи́мистый (прижи́мист); (: amount) ми́зерный* (ми́зерен).

mini... ['mɪnɪ] prefix мини́....

miniature ['mɪnətʃə'] adj миниатю́рный* (миниатю́рен) ◆ n миниатю́ра.

minibus ['mɪnɪbʌs] n микроавто́бус.

minicab ['mɪnɪkæb] n (BRIT) такси́ nt ind.

minicomputer ['mɪnɪkəm'pjuːtə'] n мини-компью́тер.

minim ['mɪnɪm] n полови́нная но́та.

minima ['mɪnɪmə] npl of **minimum**.

minimal ['mɪnɪml] adj минима́льный* (минима́лен).

minimalist ['mɪnɪməlɪst] adj минимали́ст(-ка).

minimize ['mɪnɪmaɪz] vt (reduce) своди́ть* (свести́* perf) к ми́нимуму; (play down) преуменьша́ть (преуме́ньшить perf).

minimum ['mɪnɪməm] (pl **minima**) n ми́нимум ◆ adj минима́льный; **to reduce to a ~** своди́ть* (свести́* perf) к ми́нимуму; **~ wage** минима́льная зарпла́та.

minimum lending rate n минима́льная ссу́дная ста́вка.

mining ['maɪnɪŋ] n (process) добы́ча; (science) го́рное де́ло; (industry) у́гольная промы́шленность f ◆ cpd (industry) горнодобыва́ющий*; (region) шахтёрский.

minion ['mɪnjən] n (pej) подчинённый m adj.

mini-series ['mɪnɪsɪərɪːz] n минисериа́л.

miniskirt ['mɪnɪskəːt] n ми́ни ю́бка*.

minister ['mɪnɪstə'] n (BRIT: POL) мини́стр; (REL) свяще́нник ◆ vi: **to ~ to** (people, needs) служи́ть (impf) +dat.

ministerial [mɪnɪs'tɪərɪəl] adj (BRIT: POL) министе́рский*; **~ post** пост мини́стра.

---

* marks translations which have irregular inflections. The Russian-English side of the dictionary gives inflectional information.

ministry ['mɪnɪstrɪ] n (BRIT: POL) министе́рство; (REL): **to go into the ~** принима́ть (приня́ть* perf) духо́вный сан.
Ministry of Defence n Министе́рство оборо́ны.
mink [mɪŋk] n но́рка*.
mink coat n но́рковая шу́ба.
minnow ['mɪnəu] n пескарь m.
minor ['maɪnə'] adj (injuries, poet) незначи́тельный; (repairs) ме́лкий*; (MUS) мино́рный ♦ n (LAW) несовершенноле́тний* (-яя) m(f) adj.
Minorca [mɪ'nɔ:kə] n Мино́рка.
minority [maɪ'nɔrɪtɪ] n меньшинство́*; **to be in a ~** быть* (impf) в меньшинстве́; **~ interest** (COMM) неконтро́льный паке́т а́кций.
Minsk [mɪnsk] n Минск.
minster ['mɪnstə'] n собо́р.
minstrel ['mɪnstrəl] n менестре́ль m.
mint [mɪnt] n (BOT) мя́та; (sweet) мя́тная конфе́та ♦ vt (coins) чека́нить (отчека́нить perf); **the (Royal) M~,** (US) **the (US) M~ ≈** Моне́тный двор; **in ~ condition** как но́венький*.
mint sauce n со́ус из мя́ты.
minuet [mɪnju'ɛt] n менуэ́т.
minus ['maɪnəs] n (also: ~ **sign**) ми́нус ♦ prep: **12 ~ 6 equals 6** 12 ми́нус 6 равня́ется 6; (temperature): **~ 24 (degrees)** ми́нус 24 гра́дуса.
minuscule ['mɪnəskju:l] adj кро́хотный* (кро́хотен), кро́шечный* (кро́шечен).
minute[1] [maɪ'nju:t] adj (search) тща́тельный; **in ~ detail** до мале́йших подро́бностей.
minute[2] ['mɪnɪt] n (also fig) мину́та; (official record) за́пись f; **~s** npl (of meeting) протоко́л msg; **it's five ~s past three** сейча́с пять мину́т четвёртого ...; **wait a ~!, just a ~!** подожди́те мину́точку!; **up to the ~** (fashion, news) са́мый после́дний*; (technology) нове́йший; **at the last ~** в после́днюю мину́ту.
minute book n кни́га протоко́лов.
minute hand n мину́тная стре́лка*.
minutely [maɪ'nju:tlɪ] adv (by a small amount) едва́ заме́тно; (in detail) подро́бно, подро́бнейшим о́бразом.
minutiae [mɪ'nju:ʃiː] npl мельча́йшие дета́ли fpl.
miracle ['mɪrəkl] n чу́до*.
miraculous [mɪ'rækjuləs] adj чуде́сный* (чуде́сен).
mirage ['mɪrɑ:ʒ] n мира́ж.
mire ['maɪə'] n тряси́на.
mirror ['mɪrə'] n зе́ркало*; (also: **hand-~**) зе́ркальце ♦ vt отража́ть (отрази́ть* perf).
mirror image n зерка́льное отраже́ние.
mirth [mə:θ] n весе́лье.
misadventure [mɪsəd'vɛntʃə'] n злоключе́ние; **death by ~** (BRIT) смерть* f в результа́те несча́стного слу́чая.
misanthropist [mɪ'zænθrəpɪst] n мизантро́п.

misapply [mɪsə'plaɪ] vt непра́вильно применя́ть (примени́ть perf).
misapprehension ['mɪsæprɪ'hɛnʃən] n ло́жное представле́ние.
misappropriate [mɪsə'prəuprɪeɪt] vt незако́нно присва́ивать (присво́ить perf).
misappropriation ['mɪsəprəuprɪ'eɪʃən] n назако́нное присвое́ние.
misbehave [mɪsbɪ'heɪv] vi пло́хо себя́ вести́* (impf).
misbehaviour [mɪsbɪ'heɪvjə'] (US **misbehavior**) n плохо́е поведе́ние.
misc. abbr = **miscellaneous**.
miscalculate [mɪs'kælkjuleɪt] vt неве́рно оце́нивать (оцени́ть perf) ♦ vi просчи́тываться (просчита́ться perf).
miscalculation ['mɪskælkju'leɪʃən] n просчёт.
miscarriage ['mɪskærɪdʒ] n (MED) вы́кидыш; (LAW): **~ of justice** суде́бная оши́бка.
miscarry [mɪs'kærɪ] vi (plans) не удава́ться* (уда́ться* perf); **she miscarried** у неё был вы́кидыш.
miscellaneous [mɪsɪ'leɪnɪəs] adj (collection, group) разноро́дный* (разноро́ден); (subjects, items) разнообра́зный* (разнообра́зен); **~ expenses** ме́лкие расхо́ды; **~ files** ра́зное nt adj.
mischance [mɪs'tʃɑ:ns] n (misfortune) невезе́ние; **by (some) ~** по несча́стной случа́йности.
mischief ['mɪstʃɪf] n (naughtiness, playfulness) озо́рство; (maliciousness) зло; **to get into ~** прока́зничать (напрока́зничать perf); **to do sb a ~** причиня́ть (причини́ть perf) кому́-н зло.
mischievous ['mɪstʃɪvəs] adj (naughty, playful) озорно́й; (malicious) зло́бный.
misconception ['mɪskən'sɛpʃən] n ло́жное представле́ние.
misconduct [mɪs'kɔndʌkt] n дурно́е поведе́ние; **professional ~** наруше́ние профессиона́льной э́тики.
misconstrue [mɪskən'stru:] vt неве́рно истолко́вывать (истолкова́ть* perf).
miscount [mɪs'kaunt] vt неве́рно счита́ть (сосчита́ть perf) ♦ vi ошиба́ться (ошиби́ться* perf) в подсчётах.
misdemeanour [mɪsdɪ'mi:nə'] (US **misdemeanor**) n просту́пок*.
misdirect [mɪsdɪ'rɛkt] vt (person) оши́бочно направля́ть (напра́вить perf); (letter) непра́вильно адресова́ть (impf/perf).
miser ['maɪzə'] n скря́га m/f.
miserable ['mɪzərəbl] adj (unhappy: person, expression) несча́стный (несча́стен); (unpleasant: weather, person) скве́рный* (скве́рен); (donation, conditions) жа́лкий* (жа́лок); (failure) позо́рный*; **to feel ~** чу́вствовать (impf) себя́ о́чень пло́хо; **she looked ~** у неё был несча́стный вид.
miserably ['mɪzərəblɪ] adv (live, pay) ску́дно;

(*smile*) жа́лко; (*small*) ничто́жно; (*fail*) позо́рно.

miserly ['maɪzəlɪ] *adj* (*person*) скупо́й* (скуп); (*amount*) ми́зерный* (ми́зерен).

misery ['mɪzərɪ] *n* (*unhappiness*) невзго́да; (*pain*) страда́ние; (*wretchedness*) бе́дственное положе́ние.

misfire [mɪs'faɪə'] *vi* (*plan*) прова́ливаться (провали́ться *perf*); (*car engine*) пропуска́ть (пропусти́ть* *perf*) вспы́шку.

misfit ['mɪsfɪt] *n* (*person*): **he was a ~ in our community** он не подходи́л к на́шему о́бществу.

misfortune [mɪs'fɔ:tʃən] *n* несча́стье*.

misgiving [mɪs'gɪvɪŋ] *n* опасе́ния *ntpl*; **I have ~s about it** у меня́ есть опасе́ния на э́тот счёт.

misguided [mɪs'gaɪdɪd] *adj* (*person*) неве́рно ориенти́рованный (ориенти́рован); (*ideas*) оши́бочный* (оши́бочен).

mishandle [mɪs'hændl] *vt* (*problem, situation*) не справля́ться (спра́виться* *perf*) с +*instr*.

mishap ['mɪshæp] *n* неприя́тность *f*.

mishear [mɪs'hɪə'] (*irreg: like* **hear**) *vt* не рассл́ышать (*perf*) ◆ *vi* осл́ышаться (*perf*).

misheard [mɪs'hə:d] *pt, pp of* **mishear**.

mishmash ['mɪʃmæʃ] *n* (*inf*) неразбери́ха.

misinform [mɪsɪn'fɔ:m] *vt* неве́рно информи́ровать (проинформи́ровать *perf*); (*deliberately*) дезинформи́ровать (*impf/perf*).

misinterpret [mɪsɪn'tə:prɪt] *vt* неве́рно интерпрети́ровать (*impf/perf*) *or* истолко́вывать (истолкова́ть *perf*).

misinterpretation ['mɪsɪntə:prɪ'teɪʃən] *n* неве́рная интерпрета́ция.

misjudge [mɪs'dʒʌdʒ] *vt* неве́рно оце́нивать (оцени́ть *perf*).

mislay [mɪs'leɪ] *irreg* *vt* (*lose*) дева́ть (подева́ть *perf*).

mislead [mɪs'li:d] (*irreg: like* **lead**[1]) *vt* вводи́ть* (ввести́* *perf*) в заблужде́ние.

misleading [mɪs'li:dɪŋ] *adj* обма́нчивый (обма́нчив).

misled [mɪs'lɛd] *pt, pp of* **mislead**.

mismanage [mɪs'mænɪdʒ] *vt* (*business, institution*) неуме́ло руководи́ть* (*impf*) +*instr*; (*problem, situation*) неуме́ло справля́ться (спра́виться* *perf*) с +*instr*.

mismanagement [mɪs'mænɪdʒmənt] *n* (*of company*) неуме́лое руково́дство; (*of situation*) неуме́лое реше́ние.

misnomer [mɪs'nəumə'] *n* непра́вильное назва́ние.

misogynist [mɪ'sɔdʒɪnɪst] *n* женоненави́стник.

misplace [mɪs'pleɪs] *vt* (*lose*) дева́ть (подева́ть *perf*).

misplaced [mɪs'pleɪst] *adj* (*unwarranted*) неуме́стный* (неуме́стен).

misprint ['mɪsprɪnt] *n* опеча́тка*.

mispronounce [mɪsprə'nauns] *vt* непра́вильно произноси́ть* (произнести́* *perf*).

misquote ['mɪs'kwəut] *vt* неве́рно цити́ровать (процити́ровать *perf*).

misread [mɪs'ri:d] *irreg* *vt* непра́вильно чита́ть (прочита́ть *or* проче́сть* *perf*).

misrepresent [mɪsrɛprɪ'zɛnt] *vt* преподноси́ть* (преподнести́* *perf*) в ло́жном све́те.

misrepresentation [mɪsrɛprɪzɛn'teɪʃən] *n* искаже́ние; (*LAW*) умы́шленный обма́н.

Miss [mɪs] *n* мисс *f ind*; **Dear ~ Smith** (*formal*) Госпожа́ Смит; (*informal*) Мисс Смит.

miss [mɪs] *vt* (*train, bus, class etc*) пропуска́ть (пропусти́ть* *perf*); (*fail to hit*) не попада́ть (попа́сть* *perf*) в +*acc*; (*notice loss of: money etc*) обнару́живать (обнару́жить *perf*) пропа́жу +*gen*; (*pine for*) скуча́ть (*impf*) по +*dat*; (*chance, opportunity*) упуска́ть (упусти́ть* *perf*) ◆ *vi* (*subj: person*) прома́хиваться (промахну́ться* *perf*); (: *missile, object*) не достига́ть (дости́чь* *or* дости́гнуть* *perf*) це́ли ◆ *n* (*failure to hit*) про́мах; **you can't ~ my house** мой дом невозмо́жно не заме́тить; **the bus just ~ed the wall** авто́бус чуть не вре́зался в сте́ну; **I ~ him** я скуча́ю по нему́; **nobody will ~ us** никто́ не заме́тит, что нас нет; **you're ~ing the point** Вы не понима́ете су́ти де́ла

▶ **miss out** *vt* (*BRIT*) пропуска́ть (пропусти́ть* *perf*)

▶ **miss out on** *vt fus* (*fun, party*) пропуска́ть (пропусти́ть* *perf*); (*chance, bargain*) упуска́ть (упусти́ть* *perf*).

missal ['mɪsl] *n* моли́твенник.

misshapen [mɪs'ʃeɪpən] *adj* деформи́рованный (деформи́рован).

missile ['mɪsaɪl] *n* (*MIL*) раке́та; (*projectile*): **demonstrators threw ~s at the police** демонстра́нты забра́сывали поли́цию разли́чными предме́тами.

missile base *n* раке́тная ба́за.

missile launcher [-'lɔ:ntʃə'] *n* раке́тная пускова́я устано́вка*.

missing ['mɪsɪŋ] *adj* (*lost*) пропа́вший; (*removed: tooth, wheel*) недостаю́щий*; (*absent*): **who is ~ today?** кто сего́дня отсу́тствует?; **to be ~, go ~** пропада́ть (пропа́сть* *perf*) без ве́сти; **~ person** пропа́вший(-ая) *m(f) adj* без ве́сти.

mission ['mɪʃən] *n* (*also POL, REL*) ми́ссия; (*MIL*) зада́ние; **on a ~ to sb** с ми́ссией к кому́-н.

missionary ['mɪʃənrɪ] *n* миссионе́р(ка*).

Mississippi [mɪsɪ'sɪpɪ] *n*: **the ~** Миссиси́пи *f ind*.

missive ['mɪsɪv] *n* посла́ние.

misspell ['mɪs'spɛl] (*irreg: like* **spell**) *vt* писа́ть* (написа́ть* *perf*) с оши́бками.

misspent ['mɪs'spɛnt] *adj*: **a ~ youth**

---

* marks translations which have irregular inflections. The Russian-English side of the dictionary gives inflectional information.

растра́ченная ю́ность *f*.

mist [mɪst] *n* (*heavy*) тума́н; (*light*) ды́мка ♦ *vi* (*also:* ~ **over**: *eyes*) затума́ниваться (затума́ниться *perf*); (*BRIT: also:* ~ **over** *or* **up**: *windows*) запотева́ть (запоте́ть *perf*).

mistake [mɪsˈteɪk] *n* (*irreg: like* **take**) *n* оши́бка* ♦ *vt* (*be wrong about*) ошиба́ться (ошиби́ться* *perf*) в +*prp*; (*intentions*) непра́вильно понима́ть (поня́ть* *perf*); **by** ~ по оши́бке; **to make a** ~ ошиба́ться (ошиби́ться* *perf*), де́лать (сде́лать *perf*) оши́бку; **to make a** ~ **about sb/sth** ошиба́ться (ошиби́ться* *perf*) в ком-н/чём-н; **to** ~ **A for B** принима́ть (приня́ть* *perf*) А за Б.

mistaken [mɪsˈteɪkən] *pp of* **mistake** ♦ *adj* оши́бочный* (оши́бочен); **to be** ~ ошиба́ться (ошиби́ться* *perf*).

mistaken identity *n*: **a case of** ~ ~ слу́чай оши́бочного опозна́ния.

mistakenly [mɪsˈteɪkənlɪ] *adv* оши́бочно.

mister [ˈmɪstə'] *n* (*inf*) дя́дя *m* (*обраще́ние*); *see* **Mr**.

mistletoe [ˈmɪsltəu] *n* (*BOT*) оме́ла.

mistook [mɪsˈtuk] *pt of* **mistake**.

mistranslation [mɪstrænsˈleɪʃən] *n* непра́вильный перево́д.

mistreat [mɪsˈtriːt] *vt* пло́хо обраща́ться (*impf*) с +*instr*.

mistress [ˈmɪstrɪs] *n* (*lover*) любо́вница; (*also* *fig*) хозя́йка*; (*BRIT: SCOL*) учи́тельница.

mistrust [mɪsˈtrʌst] *vt* не доверя́ть (*impf*) +*dat*, испы́тывать (испыта́ть *perf*) недове́рие к +*dat* ♦ *n*: ~ (**of**) недове́рие (к +*dat*).

mistrustful [mɪsˈtrʌstful] *adj* недове́рчивый (недове́рчив); **to be** ~ **of** не доверя́ть (*impf*) +*dat*.

misty [ˈmɪstɪ] *adj* (*day*) тума́нный* (тума́нен); (*eyes*) затума́ненный (затума́нен); (*glasses, window*) запоте́вший*.

misty-eyed [ˈmɪstɪˈaɪd] *adj* (*girl*) с глаза́ми по́лными слёз; (*fig: girl*) с затума́ненным взгля́дом.

misunderstand [mɪsʌndəˈstænd] (*irreg: like* **understand**) *vt* непра́вильно понима́ть (поня́ть* *perf*) ♦ *vi* не понима́ть (поня́ть* *perf*).

misunderstanding [ˈmɪsʌndəˈstændɪŋ] *n* недоразуме́ние.

misunderstood [mɪsʌndəˈstud] *pt, pp of* **misunderstand**.

misuse [*n* mɪsˈjuːs, *vb* mɪsˈjuːz] *n* (*of power, funds*) злоупотребле́ние; (*of word*) непра́вильное употребле́ние ♦ *vt* (*see n*) злоупотребля́ть (злоупотреби́ть* *perf*) +*instr*; непра́вильно употребля́ть (употреби́ть* *perf*).

MIT *n abbr* (*US*) = *Massachusetts Institute of Technology*.

mite [maɪt] *n* (*small quantity*) ка́пля*; (*BRIT: small child*) кро́шка* *m/f*.

miter [ˈmaɪtə'] *n* (*US*) = **mitre**.

mitigate [ˈmɪtɪgeɪt] *vt* смягча́ть (смягчи́ть

perf); **mitigating circumstances** смягча́ющие обстоя́тельства.

mitigation [mɪtɪˈgeɪʃən] *n* смягче́ние; **in** ~ (*LAW*) в оправда́ние.

mitre [ˈmaɪtə'] (*US* **miter**) *n* ми́тра; (*also:* ~ **joint**) соедине́ние в ус.

mitt [mɪt] *n* (*inf*) = **mitten**.

mitten [ˈmɪtn] *n* ва́режка*, рукави́ца.

mix [mɪks] *vt* (*cake, cement*) заме́шивать (замеси́ть* *perf*) ♦ *n* смесь *f* ♦ *vi* (*people*): **to** ~ (**with**) обща́ться (*impf*) (с +*instr*); **to** ~ **sth (with sth)** сме́шивать (смеша́ть *perf*) что-н (с чем-н); **to** ~ **business with pleasure** сочета́ть (*impf*) прия́тное с поле́зным; **cake** ~ гото́вая смесь для то́рта

▸ **mix in** *vt* (*eggs etc*) вме́шивать (вмеша́ть *perf*)

▸ **mix up** *vt* (*combine*) переме́шивать (перемеша́ть *perf*); (*confuse: people*) пу́тать (спу́тать *perf*); (: *things*) пу́тать (перепу́тать *perf*); **to get** ~**ed up in sth** впу́тываться (впу́таться *perf*) во что-н; **he's** ~**ed up in this business too** он то́же заме́шан в э́том де́ле.

mixed [mɪkst] *adj* сме́шанный.

mixed-ability [ˈmɪkstəˈbɪlɪtɪ] *adj* с ра́зными спосо́бностями.

mixed bag *n* (*of people*) разношёрстная гру́ппа; (*of activities*) всего́ понемно́жку.

mixed blessing *n*: **it was a** ~ ~ э́то бы́ло ба́бушка на́двое сказа́ла.

mixed doubles *npl* (*TENNIS etc*) игра́ *fsg* сме́шанных пар.

mixed economy *n* сме́шанная эконо́мика.

mixed grill *n* (*BRIT*) *ассорти́ из жа́реного мя́са и овоще́й*.

mixed marriage *n* сме́шанный брак.

mixed-up [ˈmɪkstˈʌp] *adj* (*confused*) сби́тый (сбит) с то́лку.

mixer [ˈmɪksə'] *n* (*for food*) ми́ксер; (*for drinks*) смеси́тель *m*; (*person*): **she is a good** ~ она́ о́чень общи́тельна.

mixer tap *n* кран со смеси́телем.

mixture [ˈmɪkstʃə'] *n* смесь *f*; (*MED*) миксту́ра.

mix-up [ˈmɪksʌp] *n* пу́таница.

Mk *abbr* (*BRIT: TECH*) = **mark**.

mk *abbr* (*COMM*) = **mark**.

mkt *abbr* = **market**.

MLitt *n abbr* (= *Master of Literature, Master of Letters*) ≈ маги́стр литературове́дения.

MLR *n abbr* (*BRIT*: = *minimum lending rate*) минима́льная ссу́дная ста́вка.

mm *abbr* (= *millimetre*) мм= *миллиме́тр*.

MN *abbr* (*BRIT*) = **Merchant Navy**; (*US: POST*) = *Minnesota*.

MO *n abbr* = *medical officer*; (*US: inf*. = *modus operandi*) при́нцип рабо́ты ♦ *abbr* (*US: POST*) = *Missouri*.

m.o. *abbr* = **money order**.

moan [məun] *n* (*cry*) стон ♦ *vi* (*inf*. *complain*): **to** ~ (**about**) ныть* (*impf*) (о +*prp*).

moaner [ˈməunə'] *n* (*inf*. *pej*) ны́тик.

moat [məut] n ров*.
mob [mɔb] n толпа*; (inf: group of friends) компания ♦ vt осаждать (осадить* perf).
mobile ['məubaɪl] adj подвижный* (подвижен); (population, forces) мобильный* (мобилен) ♦ n (decoration) подвесное декоративное украшение; **applicants must be** ~ кандидаты должны быть готовы к смене местожительства.
mobile home n дом* на колёсах.
mobile phone n портативный телефон.
mobile shop n (BRIT) автолавка*.
mobility [məu'bɪlɪtɪ] n (see adj) подвижность f; мобильность f; (of applicant) готовность f менять местожительство.
mobility allowance n (BRIT) пособие, выплачиваемое инвалидам для покрытия дополнительных дорожных расходов.
mobilize ['məubɪlaɪz] vt мобилизовать (impf/perf) ♦ vi мобилизоваться (impf/perf).
moccasin ['mɔkəsɪn] n мокасин.
mock [mɔk] vt (ridicule) издеваться (impf) над +instr; (laugh at) насмехаться (impf) над +instr ♦ adj (fake) ложный* (ложен); (: emotion) притворный; ~ (exam) (BRIT) пробный экзамен (для подготовки к основному); ~ **battle** инсценировка боя.
mockery ['mɔkərɪ] n издевательство; **to make a ~ of sb/sth** выставлять (выставить* perf) кого-н/что-н на посмешище.
mocking ['mɔkɪŋ] adj издевательский*.
mockingbird ['mɔkɪŋbə:d] n пересмешник.
mock-up ['mɔkʌp] n макет.
MOD n abbr (BRIT: = Ministry of Defence) Министерство обороны.
mod cons ['mɔd'kɔnz] npl abbr (BRIT: = modern conveniences) современные удобства ntpl.
mode [məud] n (form: of life) образ; (: of transport) вид; (COMPUT) режим.
model ['mɔdl] n модель f, макет; (also: fashion ~) манекенщик(-ица); (also: artist's ~) натурщик(-ица) ♦ adj (small scale) модельный; (ideal) образцовый ♦ vt (clothes) демонстрировать (impf/perf); (with clay etc) лепить* (вылепить* perf) ♦ vi (for designer, photographer) позировать (impf); **to ~ o.s. on** (copy) копировать (impf).
modeller ['mɔdlə] (US **modeler**) n (model maker) моделист(ка)*.
model railway n макет железной дороги.
modem ['məudɛm] n (COMPUT) модем.
moderate [adj, n 'mɔdərət, vb 'mɔdəreɪt] adj (views, amount) умеренный* (умерен); (change) незначительный ♦ n человек* умеренных взглядов ♦ vt умерять (умерить perf) ♦ vi (storm, wind etc) утихать (утихнуть* perf).
moderately ['mɔdərətlɪ] adv (act) умеренно; ~

expensive/pleased довольно дорого/рад; ~ **priced** по умеренной цене.
moderation [mɔdə'reɪʃən] n умеренность f; **in** ~ в умеренных количествах.
moderator ['mɔdəreɪtə] n (mediator) посредник; (chairman) председатель m.
modern ['mɔdən] adj современный; ~ **languages** современные языки mpl.
modernization [mɔdənaɪ'zeɪʃən] n модернизация.
modernize ['mɔdənaɪz] vt модернизировать (impf/perf).
modest ['mɔdɪst] adj скромный* (скромен).
modestly ['mɔdɪstlɪ] adv скромно.
modesty ['mɔdɪstɪ] n скромность f.
modicum ['mɔdɪkəm] n: **a** ~ **of** толика +gen.
modification [mɔdɪfɪ'keɪʃən] n (of vehicle, engine) модификация; (of plan) видоизменение; **to make ~s to** вносить* (внести* perf) видоизменения в +acc.
modify ['mɔdɪfaɪ] vt (see n) модифицировать (impf/perf); видоизменять (видоизменить* perf).
modish ['məudɪʃ] adj модный* (моден).
Mods [mɔdz] n abbr (BRIT: SCOL: = (Honour) Moderations) экзамен, позволяющий перейти на курс, необходимый для получения степени бакалавра в Оксфордском университете.
modular ['mɔdjulə] adj (filing, unit) модульный.
modulate ['mɔdjuleɪt] vt (voice) модулировать (impf).
modulation [mɔdju'leɪʃən] n (MUS, RADIO) модуляция.
module ['mɔdju:l] n модуль m; (SPACE) отсек; (BRIT: SCOL) курс.
modus operandi ['məudəsɔpə'rændi:] n принцип работы.
Mogadishu [mɔgə'dɪʃu:] n Могадишу m ind.
mogul ['məugl] n (fig) магнат.
MOH n abbr (BRIT) = Medical Officer of Health.
mohair ['məuhɛə] n мохер.
Mohammed [mə'hæmɛd] n Магомет.
moist [mɔɪst] adj влажный* (влажен).
moisten ['mɔɪsn] vt (lips) увлажнять (увлажнить* perf); (: with tongue) облизывать (облизать perf); (sponge) мочить* (намочить* perf).
moisture ['mɔɪstʃə] n влага.
moisturize ['mɔɪstʃəraɪz] vt увлажнять (увлажнить perf).
moisturizer ['mɔɪstʃəraɪzə] n увлажняющий крем.
molar ['məulə] n коренной зуб*.
molasses [məu'læsɪz] n патока.
mold etc [məuld] (US) = **mould** etc.
Moldavian [mɔl'deɪvɪən] n (person)

---

* marks translations which have irregular inflections. The Russian-English side of the dictionary gives inflectional information.

молдова́нин*(-а́нка*) ◆ *adj* молдо́вский.

Moldova [mɔl'dəuvə] *n* Молдо́ва.

mole [məul] *n* (*spot*) ро́динка*; (*ZOOL*) крот*; (*spy*) доно́счик(-ица), стука́ч*(ка).

molecular [məu'lɛkjulə^r] *adj* молекуля́рный.

molecule ['mɔlɪkjuːl] *n* моле́кула.

molehill ['məulhɪl] *n* крото́вая нора́*.

molest [mə'lɛst] *vt* (*assault sexually*) надруга́ться (*perf*) над +*instr*; (*harass*) трави́ть* (затрави́ть* *perf*).

mollusc ['mɔləsk] *n* моллю́ск.

mollycoddle ['mɔlɪkɔdl] *vt* трясти́сь* (*impf*) над +*instr*.

Molotov cocktail ['mɔlətɔf-] *n* кокте́йль *m* Мо́лотова (*буты́лка с зажига́тельной сме́сью*).

molt [məult] *vi* (*US*) = **moult**.

molten ['məultən] *adj* распла́вленный.

mom [mɔm] *n* (*US*) = **mum**.

moment ['məumənt] *n* моме́нт, мгнове́ние; (*PHYS*) моме́нт; **for a** ~ на мгнове́ние *or* мину́ту; **at that** ~ в э́тот моме́нт; **at the** ~ в настоя́щий* моме́нт; **for the** ~ пока́; **in a** ~ че́рез мину́ту; (**at**) **any** ~ (**now**) в любо́й моме́нт; **"one** ~ **please"** „одну́ мину́точку".

momentarily ['məuməntrɪlɪ] *adv* на мгнове́ние; (*US: very soon*) в любо́й моме́нт.

momentary ['məuməntərɪ] *adj* (*brief*) мгнове́нный.

momentous [məu'mɛntəs] *adj* важне́йший.

momentum [məu'mɛntəm] *n* (*PHYS*) и́мпульс; (*fig*) дви́жущая си́ла; **to gather** *or* **gain** ~ набира́ть (набра́ть* *perf*) си́лу.

mommy ['mɔmɪ] *n* (*US: mother*) = **mummy**.

Mon. *abbr* = **Monday**.

Monaco ['mɔnəkəu] *n* Мона́ко *nt ind*.

monarch ['mɔnək] *n* мона́рх.

monarchist ['mɔnəkɪst] *n* монархи́ст(ка*).

monarchy ['mɔnəkɪ] *n* мона́рхия.

monastery ['mɔnəstərɪ] *n* монасты́рь* *m*.

monastic [mə'næstɪk] *adj* (*vows, order, also fig*) мона́шеский*; (*building*) монасты́рский.

Monday ['mʌndɪ] *n* понеде́льник; *see also* **Tuesday**.

Monegasque [mɔnə'gæsk] *adj* мона́кский ◆ *n* жи́тель(ница) *m(f)* Мона́ко.

monetarist ['mʌnɪtərɪst] *n* монетари́ст ◆ *adj* монетари́стский.

monetary ['mʌnɪtərɪ] *adj* де́нежный.

money ['mʌnɪ] *n* де́ньги* *pl*; **to make** ~ (*person*) зараба́тывать (зарабо́тать *perf*); (*business*) приноси́ть* (принести́* *perf*) дохо́д; **danger** ~ (*BRIT*) надба́вка за вре́дность; **I've got no** ~ **left** у меня́ совсе́м не оста́лось де́нег.

moneyed ['mʌnɪd] *adj* де́нежный.

moneylender ['mʌnɪlɛndə^r] *n* ростовщи́к*.

money-maker ['mʌnɪmeɪkə^r] *n* (*person*) кру́пный деле́ц*; (*project, investment*) при́быльное де́ло.

moneymaking ['mʌnɪmeɪkɪŋ] *adj* при́быльный.

money market *n* де́нежный ры́нок*.

money order *n* де́нежный перево́д.

money-spinner ['mʌnɪspɪnə^r] *n* (*inf*): **this business/idea will be a real** ~ э́тот би́знес/э́та иде́я бу́дет де́лать больши́е де́ньги.

money supply *n* де́нежная ма́сса.

Mongol ['mɔŋgəl] *n* (*LING*) монго́льский* язы́к*; (*HISTORY*): **the** ~**s** монго́ло-тата́ры.

mongol ['mɔŋgəl] *n* (*pej*) челове́к, страда́ющий боле́знью Да́уна.

Mongolia [mɔŋ'gəulɪə] *n* Монго́лия.

Mongolian [mɔŋ'gəulɪən] *adj* монго́льский* ◆ *n* (*person*) монго́л(ка*); (*LING*) монго́льский* язы́к*.

mongoose ['mɔŋguːs] *n* мангу́ст.

mongrel ['mʌŋgrəl] *n* дворня́га.

monitor ['mɔnɪtə^r] *n* монито́р ◆ *vt* (*broadcasts*) контроли́ровать (*impf*); (*heartbeat, pulse*) наблюда́ть (*impf*) за +*instr*; (*progress*) следи́ть* (*impf*) за +*instr*; (*foreign station*) прослу́шивать (*impf*).

monk [mʌŋk] *n* мона́х.

monkey ['mʌŋkɪ] *n* обезья́на.

monkey business *n* (*inf*) проде́лки* *fpl*.

monkey nut *n* (*BRIT*) ара́хис *no pl*.

monkey tricks *npl* = **monkey business**.

monkey wrench *n* разводно́й га́ечный ключ*.

mono ['mɔnəu] *adj* (*recording*) мо́но *ind*.

monochrome ['mɔnəkrəum] *adj* черно-бе́лый; (*COMPUT*) монохро́мный.

monogamous [mə'nɔgəməs] *adj* монога́мный* (монога́мен).

monogamy [mə'nɔgəmɪ] *n* монога́мия, единобра́чие.

monogram ['mɔnəgræm] *n* моногра́мма.

monolith ['mɔnəlɪθ] *n* моноли́т.

monolithic [mɔnə'lɪθɪk] *adj* моноли́тный.

monologue ['mɔnəlɔg] *n* моноло́г.

monoplane ['mɔnəpleɪn] *n* монопла́н.

monopolist [mə'nɔpəlɪst] *n* монополи́ст.

monopolize [mə'nɔpəlaɪz] *vt* (*ECON*) монополизи́ровать (*impf/perf*); (*place, conversation*) завладева́ть (завладе́ть *perf*) +*instr*; (*person*) захва́тывать (захвати́ть* *perf*).

monopoly [mə'nɔpəlɪ] *n* (*also ECON*) монопо́лия; **Monopolies and Mergers Commission** (*BRIT*) Коми́ссия по монопо́лиям и слия́ниям.

monorail ['mɔnəureɪl] *n* моноре́льсовая доро́га.

monosodium glutamate [mɔnə'səudɪəm 'gluːtəmeɪt] *n* глутамина́т на́трия.

monosyllabic [mɔnəsɪ'læbɪk] *adj* (*word*) односло́жный; (*person*) немногосло́вный*.

monosyllable ['mɔnəsɪləbl] *n* односло́жное сло́во*.

monotone ['mɔnətəun] *n*: **to speak in a** ~ говори́ть (*impf*) моното́нно.

monotonous [mə'nɔtənəs] *adj* (*life, job etc*)

однообра́зный* (однообра́зен); (*voice, sound*) моното́нный* (моното́нен).

monotony [mə'nɔtənɪ] *n* (*see adj*) однообра́зие; моното́нность *f*.

monsoon [mɔn'su:n] *n* муссо́н.

monster ['mɔnstə'] *n* (*also fig*) чудо́вище, монстр.

monstrosity [mɔn'strɔsɪtɪ] *n* (*object, building*) чу́дище, монстр.

monstrous ['mɔnstrəs] *adj* чудо́вищный* (чудо́вищен).

montage [mɔn'tɑ:ʒ] *n* монта́ж*.

Mont Blanc [mɔ̃ blɑ̃] *n* Монбла́н.

Montenegrin [mɔntə'ni:grɪn] *n* черного́рец*(-о́рка*) ♦ *adj* черного́рский*.

Montenegro [mɔntə'ni:grəʊ] *n* Черного́рия.

month [mʌnθ] *n* ме́сяц; **every ~** ка́ждый ме́сяц; **300 dollars a ~** 300 до́лларов в ме́сяц.

monthly ['mʌnθlɪ] *adj* ежеме́сячный; (*ticket*) ме́сячный ♦ *adv* ежеме́сячно; **twice ~** два́жды в ме́сяц.

Montreal [mɔntrɪ'ɔ:l] *n* Монреа́ль *m*.

monument ['mɔnjumənt] *n* (*memorial*) па́мятник, монуме́нт; (*historical building*) па́мятник.

monumental [mɔnju'mɛntl] *adj* (*building, book*) монумента́льный* (монумента́лен); (*storm, row*) колосса́льный.

moo [mu:] *vi* мыча́ть* (*impf*).

mood [mu:d] *n* настрое́ние; (*of group, crowd*) настро́й; **to be in a good/bad ~** быть* (*impf*) в хоро́шем/плохо́м настрое́нии; **I'm in the ~ for a drink/to watch TV** у меня́ есть настрое́ние вы́пить/смотре́ть телеви́зор.

moodily ['mu:dɪlɪ] *adv* мра́чно, угрю́мо.

moody ['mu:dɪ] *adj* (*sullen*) угрю́мый (угрю́м); (*temperamental*): **she is a very ~ person** у неё о́чень переме́нчивое настрое́ние.

moon [mu:n] *n* луна́*.

moonlight ['mu:nlaɪt] *n* лу́нный свет ♦ *vi* (*inf*) рабо́тать (*impf*) на стороне́.

moonlighting ['mu:nlaɪtɪŋ] *n* (*inf*) рабо́та по совмести́тельству.

moonlit ['mu:nlɪt] *adj*: **a ~ night** лу́нная ночь*.

moonshot ['mu:nʃɔt] *n* полёт на Луну́.

moor [muə'] *n* ве́ресковая пу́стошь *f* ♦ *vt* (*ship*) пришварто́вывать (пришвартова́ть *perf*) ♦ *vi* пришварто́вываться (пришвартова́ться *perf*).

mooring ['muərɪŋ] *n* прича́л; **~s** *npl* (*chains*) шварто́вые це́пи *fpl*.

Moorish ['muərɪʃ] *adj* маврита́нский.

moorland ['muələnd] *n* ве́ресковая пу́стошь *f*.

moose [mu:s] *n inv* лось* *m*.

moot [mu:t] *vt*: **it was ~ed that ...** бы́ло предло́жено, что ... ♦ *adj*: **~ point** спо́рный вопро́с.

mop [mɔp] *n* (*for floor*) шва́бра; (*for dishes*) щётка*; (*of hair*) копна́ ♦ *vt* (*floor*) мыть* (вы́мыть* *or* помы́ть* *perf*) (шва́брой); (*eyes, face*) вытира́ть (вы́тереть* *perf*)

► **mop up** *vt* (*liquid*) вытира́ть (вы́тереть* *perf*).

mope [məup] *vi* хандри́ть (*impf*)

► **mope about** *vi* слоня́ться (*impf*)

► **mope around** *vi* = **mope about**.

moped ['məupɛd] *n* мопе́д.

moquette [mɔ'kɛt] *n* ≈ плюш.

MOR *adj abbr* (*MUS*: = *middle-of-the-road*) лёгкий*.

moral ['mɔrl] *adj* нра́вственный, мора́льный; (*person*) нра́вственный* (нра́вствен) ♦ *n* (*of story*) мора́ль *f*; **~s** *npl* нра́вы *mpl*; **~ support/dilemma/victory** мора́льная подде́ржка/диле́мма/побе́да; **~ courage** душе́вное му́жество.

morale [mɔ'rɑ:l] *n* мора́льный дух.

morality [mɔ'rælɪtɪ] *n* нра́вственность *f*.

moralize ['mɔrəlaɪz] *vi*: **to ~ (about)** морализи́ровать (*impf*) (о +*prp*).

morally ['mɔrəlɪ] *adv* (*wrong, responsible*) мора́льно; (*live, behave*) нра́вственно.

moral victory *n* мора́льная побе́да.

morass [mɔ'ræs] *n* (*also fig*) тряси́на.

moratorium [mɔrə'tɔ:rɪəm] *n* морато́рий.

morbid ['mɔ:bɪd] *adj* (*imagination*) ненорма́льный; (*ideas*) жу́ткий*.

KEYWORD

more [mɔ:'] *adj* **1** (*greater in number etc*) бо́льше +*gen*; **I have more friends than enemies** у меня́ бо́льше друзе́й, чем враго́в **2** (*additional*) ещё; **do you want (some) more tea?** хоти́те ещё ча́ю?; **is there any more wine?** ещё есть вино́?; **I have no** *or* **I don't have any more money** у меня́ бо́льше нет де́нег; **it'll take a few more weeks** э́то займёт ещё не́сколько неде́ль

♦ *pron* **1** (*greater amount*): **more than ten** бо́льше десяти́; **we've sold more than a hundred tickets** мы прода́ли бо́лее ста биле́тов; **it cost more than we expected** э́то сто́ило бо́льше, чем мы ожида́ли **2** (*further or additional amount*): **is there any more?** ещё есть?; **there's no more** бо́льше ничего́ нет; **a little more** ещё немно́го *or* чуть-чу́ть; **many/much more** намно́го/ гора́здо бо́льше

♦ *adv* **1** (+*vb*) бо́льше; **I like this one more** мне э́то бо́льше нра́вится **2** (+*adj*): **more dangerous/difficult** *etc* (**than**) бо́лее опа́сный/тру́дный *etc*, (чем) **3** (+*adv*): **more economically (than)** бо́лее экономи́чно (чем); **more easily/quickly (than)** ле́гче/быстре́е (чем); **he became more and more excited/friendly** он станови́лся всё бо́лее и бо́лее возбуждённым/ дружелю́бным; **he grew to like her more and**

---

* marks translations which have irregular inflections. The Russian-English side of the dictionary gives inflectional information.

more она нравилась ему всё больше и больше; **more or less** более или менее; **it should cost £500, more or less** это должно стоить приблизительно £500; **she is more beautiful than ever** она прекраснее, чем когда-либо; **he loved her more than ever** он любил её больше, чем когда-либо; **the more ..., the better** чем больше ..., тем лучше; **once more** ещё раз; **I'd like to see more of you** хотелось бы почаще Вас видеть.

moreover [mɔːˈrəuvəˈ] *adv* более того.

morgue [mɔːg] *n* морг.

MORI [ˈmɔːrɪ] *n abbr* (*BRIT*: = Market & Opinion Research Institute) научно-исследовательский институт изучения рынка и общественного мнения.

moribund [ˈmɔːrɪbʌnd] *adj* (*industry*) отживший своё.

Mormon [ˈmɔːmən] *n* мормон(ка*).

morning [ˈmɔːnɪŋ] *n* утро*; (*between midnight and 3 a.m.*) ночь *f* ♦ *cpd* (*paper, sun, walk*) утренний*; **in the ~** утром; **3 o'clock in the ~** 3 часа ночи; **7 o'clock in the ~** 7 часов утра; **this ~** сегодня утром.

morning-after pill [ˈmɔːnɪŋˈɑːftə-] *n* противозачаточная таблетка с высоким содержанием гормональных препаратов (*обычно принимается в экстренных случаях после полового акта*).

morning sickness *n* утренняя тошнота (*у беременных*).

Moroccan [məˈrɔkən] *adj* марокканский ♦ *n* марокканец*(-нка*).

Morocco [məˈrɔkəu] *n* Морокко *nt ind.*

moron [ˈmɔːrɔn] *n* (*inf*) кретин(ка*).

moronic [məˈrɔnɪk] *adj* (*inf*) кретинский.

morose [məˈrəus] *adj* (*miserable*) угрюмый (угрюм).

morphine [ˈmɔːfiːn] *n* морфий.

morris dancing [ˈmɔrɪs-] *n* (*BRIT*) моррис (*народный английский танец*).

Morse [mɔːs] *n* (*also:* ~ **code**) азбука Морзе.

morsel [ˈmɔːsl] *n* (*of food*) кусочек*.

mortal [ˈmɔːtl] *adj* (*human*) смертный* (смертен); (*deadly*) смертельный* (смертелен); (*sin*) смертный* ♦ *n*: **mere ~** простой(-ая) смертный(-ая) *m(f) adj*; **~ remains** бренные останки.

mortality [mɔːˈtælɪtɪ] *n* (*death*) смертность *f.*

mortality rate *n* смертность *f.*

mortar [ˈmɔːtəˈ] *n* (*cannon*) миномёт; (*cement*) цементный раствор; (*bowl*) ступка*.

mortgage [ˈmɔːgɪdʒ] *n* ипотечная ссуда ♦ *vt* закладывать (заложить* *perf*); **to take out a ~** брать* (взять* *perf*) ссуду (*для покупки дома*).

mortgage company *n* (*US*) ипотечная компания.

mortgagee [mɔːgəˈdʒiː] *n* кредитор (*при ипотечном кредите*).

mortgagor [ˈmɔːgədʒəˈ] *n* заёмщик (*при*

ипотечном кредите).

mortician [mɔːˈtɪʃən] *n* (*US*) работник похоронного бюро.

mortified [ˈmɔːtɪfaɪd] *adj*: **to be ~** быть* (*impf*) в смертельном ужасе.

mortify [ˈmɔːtɪfaɪ] *vt* приводить* (привести* *perf*) в полный ужас.

mortise lock [ˈmɔːtɪs-] *n* врезной замок*.

mortuary [ˈmɔːtjuərɪ] *n* морг (*при больнице*), покойницкая *f adj.*

mosaic [məuˈzeɪɪk] *n* мозаика.

Moscow [ˈmɔskəu] *n* Москва.

Moslem [ˈmɔzləm] *adj, n* = **Muslim**.

mosque [mɔsk] *n* мечеть *f.*

mosquito [mɔsˈkiːtəu] (*pl* ~**es**) *n* комар*.

mosquito net *n* москитная сетка*.

moss [mɔs] *n* мох*.

mossy [ˈmɔsɪ] *adj* поросший мхом.

KEYWORD

most [məust] *adj* **1** (*almost all: countable nouns*) большинство +*gen*; (*: uncountable and collective nouns*) по большей части; **most people/cars** большинство людей/машин; **most milk** молоко, по большей части; **in most cases** в большинстве случаев **2** (*largest, greatest*): **who has the most money?** у кого больше всего денег?; **this book has attracted the most interest among the critics** эта книга вызвала наибольший интерес у критиков

♦ *pron* (*greatest quantity, number: countable nouns*) большинство; (*: uncountable and collective nouns*) большая часть *f*; **most of the houses/her friends** большинство домов/её друзей; **most of the cake** большая часть торта; **do the most you can** делайте всё, что можете; **I ate the most** я съел больше всех; **to make the most of sth** максимально использовать (*impf*) что-н; **at the (very) most** самое большее

♦ *adv* (+*vb*) больше всего; (+*adv*) исключительно; **the most interesting/expensive** наиболее *or* самый интересный/дорогой; **I liked him the most** он понравился мне больше всех; **what do you value most, wealth or health?** что Вы больше цените, богатство или здоровье?

mostly [ˈməustlɪ] *adv* в основном, главным образом.

MOT *n abbr* (*BRIT*: = Ministry of Transport) Министерство транспорта; ~ (**test**) техосмотр= *технический осмотр.*

motel [məuˈtɛl] *n* мотель *m.*

moth [mɔθ] *n* мотылёк*; (*also:* **clothes ~**) моль *f no pl.*

mothballs [ˈmɔθbɔːlz] *npl* нафталиновые шарики *mpl.*

moth-eaten [ˈmɔθiːtn] *adj* (*also fig*) изъеденный (изъеден).

mother [ˈmʌðəˈ] *n* мать* *f* ♦ *vt* (*raise*)

выра́щивать (вы́растить* *perf*); (*pamper*)
ня́нчиться (*impf*) с +*instr* ◆ *adj*: ~ **country**
ро́дина; ~ **company** матери́нская компа́ния.
motherboard ['mʌðəbɔ:d] *n* (*COMPUT*)
объедини́тельная пла́та.
motherhood ['mʌðəhud] *n* матери́нство.
mother-in-law ['mʌðərɪnlɔ:] *n* (*wife's mother*)
тёща; (*husband's mother*) свекро́вь *f*.
motherly ['mʌðəlɪ] *adj* матери́нский*.
mother-of-pearl ['mʌðərəv'pɜ:l] *n* перламу́тр
◆ *adj* перламу́тровый.
Mother's Day *n* пра́здник посвящённый
матеря́м.
mother's help *n* ня́ня.
mother-to-be ['mʌðətə'bi:] *n* бу́дущая мать* *f*.
mother tongue *n* родно́й язы́к*.
mothproof ['mɔθpru:f] *adj* (*fabric etc*)
молесто́йкий.
motif [məu'ti:f] *n* (*design*) орна́мент; (*theme*)
моти́в.
motion ['məuʃən] *n* (*movement, gesture*)
движе́ние; (*proposal*) предложе́ние; (*BRIT*:
bowel movement) стул *no pl* ◆ *vti*: **he ~ed (to)**
her to sit down он же́стом предложи́л ей
сесть; **to be in** ~ быть* (*impf*) в движе́нии; **to**
set in ~ приводи́ть* (привести́* *perf*) в
де́йствие; **to go through the ~s** (*fig*:
formalities) исполня́ть (испо́лнить *perf*)
форма́льности.
motionless ['məuʃənlɪs] *adj* неподви́жный*
(неподви́жен).
motion picture *n* кинокарти́на.
motivate ['məutɪveɪt] *vt* (*act, decision*)
мотиви́ровать (*impf*); (*person*)
заинтересо́вывать (заинтересова́ть *perf*); **he**
is ~d by ambition им дви́жет честолю́бие.
motivated ['məutɪveɪtɪd] *adj* (*enthusiastic*)
заинтересо́ванный (заинтересо́ван);
(*impelled*): ~ **by envy/greed** движи́мый
чу́вством за́висти/жа́дности.
motivation [məutɪ'veɪʃən] *n* (*drive*)
целеустремлённость *f*.
motivational research *n* иссле́дование
мотива́ций.
motive ['məutɪv] *n* моти́в, побужде́ние ◆ *adj*: ~
power *or* **force** дви́жущая си́ла; **from the best**
(**of**) ~**s** из лу́чших побужде́ний.
motley ['mɔtlɪ] *adj* пёстрый* (пёстр).
motor ['məutə˥] *n* (*also BRIT*: *inf*) мото́р ◆ *cpd*
(*industry, trade*) автомоби́льный.
motorbike ['məutəbaɪk] *n* мотоци́кл.
motorboat ['məutəbəut] *n* мото́рная ло́дка*.
motorcade ['məutəkeɪd] *n* корте́ж
автомоби́лей.
motorcar ['məutəkɑ:] *n* (*BRIT*) автомоби́ль *m*.
motorcoach ['məutəkəutʃ] *n* (*BRIT*) авто́бус.
motorcycle ['məutəsaɪkl] *n* мотоци́кл.
motorcycle racing *n* мотого́нки *fpl*.

motorcyclist ['məutəsaɪklɪst] *n*
мотоцикли́ст(ка*).
motoring ['məutərɪŋ] (*BRIT*) *n* езда́ на
автомоби́ле ◆ *cpd*: ~ **accident**
автомоби́льная ава́рия; ~ **offence**
наруше́ние пра́вил доро́жного движе́ния;
we went on a ~ holiday in France мы провели́
о́тпуск путеше́ствуя по Фра́нции на
маши́не.
motorist ['məutərɪst] *n* автомобили́ст.
motorized ['məutəraɪzd] *adj*: ~ **transport**
автотра́нспорт; ~ **vehicle** автомаши́на; ~
regiment моторизо́ванный полк*.
motor oil *n* мото́рное ма́сло.
motor racing *n* (*BRIT*) автого́нки* *fpl*=
автомоби́льные го́нки.
motor scooter *n* моторо́ллер.
motor vehicle *n* автомаши́на.
motorway ['məutəweɪ] *n* (*BRIT*)
автомагистра́ль *f*, автостра́да.
mottled ['mɔtld] *adj* пятни́стый.
motto ['mɔtəu] (*pl* ~**es**) *n* деви́з.
mould [məuld] (*US* **mold**) *n* (*cast*) фо́рма;
(*mildew*) пле́сень *f* ◆ *vt* (*substance*) лепи́ть*
(слепи́ть* *or* вы́лепить* *perf*); (*fig*: *opinion*,
character) формирова́ть (сформирова́ть
perf).
moulder ['məuldə˥] *vi* разлага́ться
(разложи́ться* *perf*).
moulding ['məuldɪŋ] *n* (*ARCHIT*) лепно́е
украше́ние.
mouldy ['məuldɪ] *adj* (*food*) заплесневе́лый;
(*smell*) за́тхлый (за́тхл).
moult [məult] (*US* **molt**) *vi* линя́ть (*impf*).
mound [maund] *n* (*hillock*) холм, приго́рок*;
(*heap*) ку́ча.
mount [maunt] *n* (*horse*) ло́шадь* *f*; (*for picture*,
photograph) паспарту́ *nt ind* ◆ *vt* (*horse*)
сади́ться* (сесть* *perf*) на +*acc*; (*exhibition*,
display) устра́ивать (устро́ить *perf*); (*jewel*)
оправля́ть (опра́вить* *perf*); (*picture*)
обрамля́ть (обрами́ть* *perf*; (*staircase*)
всходи́ть* (взойти́* *perf*) по +*dat*; (*attack*)
предпринима́ть (предприня́ть* *perf*) ◆ *vi*
(*increase*) расти́* (*impf*); (*get on a horse*)
сади́ться* (сесть* *perf*) на ло́шадь; **M~**
Ararat/Kilimanjaro гора́ Арара́т/
Килиманджа́ро
▸ **mount up** *vi* (*bills, costs*) нака́пливаться
(накопи́ться* *perf*).
mountain ['mauntɪn] *n* (*also fig*) гора́* ◆ *cpd*
го́рный; **to make a ~ out of a molehill** де́лать
(сде́лать *perf*) из му́хи слона́*.
mountain bike *n* велосипе́д, приспосо́бленный
для испо́льзования на пересечённой
ме́стности.
mountaineer [mauntɪ'nɪə˥] *n* альпини́ст(ка*).
mountaineering [mauntɪ'nɪərɪŋ] *n* альпини́зм;

---

* marks translations which have irregular inflections. The Russian-English side of the dictionary gives inflectional information.

to go ~ ходи́ть* (*impf*) в го́ры.
mountainous ['mauntɪnəs] *adj* гори́стый (гори́ст).
mountain range *n* го́рная цепь* *f*.
mountain rescue team *n* горноспаса́тельный отря́д.
mountainside ['mauntɪnsaɪd] *n* склон горы́.
mounted ['mauntɪd] *adj* (*on horseback*) ко́нный.
Mount Everest *n* гора́ Эвере́ст.
mourn [mɔːn] *vt* опла́кивать (*impf*) ◆ *vi*: **to** ~ **for** скорбе́ть (*impf*) по +*dat or* о +*prp*.
mourner ['mɔːnə'] *n* прису́тствующий(-ая) *m(f)* *adj* на похорона́х.
mournful ['mɔːnful] *adj* (*sad*) ско́рбный* (ско́рбен).
mourning ['mɔːnɪŋ] *n* тра́ур; **in** ~ в тра́уре.
mouse [maus] (*pl* **mice**) *n* (*also fig, COMPUT*) мышь* *f*.
mousetrap ['maustræp] *n* мышело́вка*.
moussaka [mu'sɑːkə] *n* мусса́ка (*гре́ческое блю́до*).
mousse [muːs] *n* мусс.
moustache [məs'tɑːʃ] (*US* **mustache**) *n* усы́ *mpl*.
mousy ['mausɪ] *adj* (*hair*) мыши́ного цве́та.
mouth [mauθ] (*pl* ~**s**) *n* рот*; (*of cave, hole*) вход; (*of river*) у́стье*; (*of bottle*) го́рлышко*.
mouthful ['mauθful] *n* (*of food*) кусо́чек*; (*of drink*) глото́к*.
mouth organ *n* губна́я гармо́шка*.
mouthpiece ['mauθpiːs] *n* (*of musical instrument*) мундшту́к*; (*of telephone*) микрофо́н; (*spokesman, newspaper*) глаша́тай.
mouth-to-mouth ['mauθə'mauθ] *adj*: ~ **resuscitation** иску́сственное дыха́ние.
mouthwash ['mauθwɔʃ] *n* жи́дкость *f* для полоска́ния рта.
mouthwatering ['mauθwɔːtərɪŋ] *adj* о́чень аппети́тный* (аппети́тен).
movable ['muːvəbl] *adj* подвижно́й; **Easter is a** ~ **feast** в ра́зные го́ды Па́сха прихо́дится на ра́зные чи́сла.
move [muːv] *n* (*movement*) движе́ние; (*in game*) ход*; (*change: of house*) перее́зд; (: *of job*) перехо́д (*на другу́ю рабо́ту*) ◆ *vt* передвига́ть (передви́нуть *perf*); (*piece: in game*) ходи́ть* (пойти́* *perf*) +*instr*; (*part of body*) дви́гать (дви́нуть *perf*) +*instr*; (*person: emotionally*) тро́гать (тро́нуть *perf*), растро́гать (*perf*); (*resolution etc*) предлага́ть (предложи́ть* *perf*) ◆ *vi* дви́гаться (дви́нуться *perf*); (*in game*) де́лать (сде́лать *perf*) ход; (*of things*) дви́гаться (*impf*); (*also:* ~ **house**) переезжа́ть (перее́хать* *perf*); **get a** ~ **on!** поторо́пливайтесь!; **to** ~ **to a new job** переходи́ть* (перейти́* *perf*) на но́вую рабо́ту; **to** ~ **sb to sth** подви́гнуть* (*perf*) кого́-н на что-н; **to** ~ **towards** дви́гаться (дви́нуться *perf*) к +*dat*
▶ **move about** *vi* (*change position*)

передвига́ться (передви́нуться *perf*); (*travel, change residence*) переезжа́ть (*impf*) с ме́ста на ме́сто; (*change job*) переходи́ть* (*impf*) с рабо́ты на рабо́ту
▶ **move along** *vi* проходи́ть* (пройти́* *perf*)
▶ **move around** *vi* = **move about**
▶ **move away** *vi*: **to** ~ **away (from)** (*leave*) уезжа́ть (уе́хать* *perf*) (из +*gen*); (*step away*) отходи́ть* (отойти́* *perf*) (от +*gen*)
▶ **move back** *vi* переезжа́ть (перее́хать* *perf*) обра́тно
▶ **move forward** *vi* продвига́ться (продви́нуться *perf*)
▶ **move in** *vi* (*police, soldiers*) входи́ть* (войти́* *perf*); **to** ~ **in(to)** (*house*) въезжа́ть (въе́хать* *perf*) (в +*acc*)
▶ **move off** *vi* отъезжа́ть (отъе́хать* *perf*)
▶ **move on** *vi* (*leave*) направля́ться (напра́виться* *perf*) да́льше ◆ *vt* (*onlookers*) продвига́ть (продви́нуть *perf*)
▶ **move out** *vi* (*of house*) выезжа́ть (вы́ехать* *perf*)
▶ **move over** *vi* (*to make room*) подвига́ться (подви́нуться *perf*)
▶ **move up** *vi* (*be promoted*) продвига́ться (продви́нуться *perf*).
moveable ['muːvəbl] *adj* = **movable**.
movement ['muːvmənt] *n* (*action, also POL, REL*) движе́ние; (*between two fixed points*) передвиже́ние; (*transportation: of goods etc*) перево́зка*; (*shift: in attitude, policy*) сдвиг; (*MUS*) часть* *f*.
mover ['muːvə'] *n* (*of proposal*) инициа́тор.
movie ['muːvɪ] *n* фильм, кинофи́льм; **to go to the** ~**s** ходи́ть*/идти́* (пойти́* *perf*) в кино́.
movie camera *n* кинока́мера.
moviegoer ['muːvɪɡəuə'] *n* (*US*) кинолюби́тель *m*.
moving ['muːvɪŋ] *adj* (*emotional*) тро́гательный* (тро́гателен); (*mobile*) подви́жный* (подви́жен); (*spirit, force*) дви́жущий* ◆ *n* (*US*) перее́зд.
mow [məu] (*pt* **mowed**, *pp* **mowed** *or* **mown**) *vt* (*grass*) подстрига́ть (подстри́чь* *perf*); (*hay*) коси́ть* (скоси́ть* *perf*)
▶ **mow down** *vt* (*kill*) коси́ть* (скоси́ть* *perf*).
mower ['məuə'] *n* коси́лка*.
mown [məun] *pp of* **mow**.
Mozambique [məuzəm'biːk] *n* Мозамби́к.
MP *n abbr* (= *Member of Parliament*) член парла́мента; (= *Military Police*) вое́нная поли́ция; (*CANADA*: = *Mounted Police*) ко́нная поли́ция.
mpg *n abbr* = *miles per gallon*.
mph *abbr* = *miles per hour*.
MPhil *n abbr* (= *Master of Philosophy*) ≈ маги́стр филосо́фии.
MPS *n abbr* (*BRIT*) = *Member of the Pharmaceutical Society*.
Mr ['mɪstə'] (*US* **Mr.**) *n*: ~ **Smith** (*informal*) ми́стер Смит; (*formal*) г-н Смит= *господи́н*

Смит.
MRC *n abbr* (*BRIT*) = *Medical Research Council.*
MRCP *n abbr* (*BRIT*) = *Member of the Royal College of Physicians.*
MRCS *n abbr* (*BRIT*) = *Member of the Royal College of Surgeons.*
MRCVS *n abbr* (*BRIT*) = *Member of the Royal College of Veterinary Surgeons.*
Mrs ['mɪsɪz] (*US* **Mrs.**) *n*: ~ **Smith** (*informal*) ми́ссис Смит; (*formal*) г-жа Смит= *госпожа́ Смит.*
Ms [mɪz] (*US* **Ms.**) *n* (= *Miss or Mrs*): ~ **Smith** г-жа Смит= *госпожа́ Смит.*
MS *n abbr* = **multiple sclerosis**; (*US*: = *Master of Science*) ≈ маги́стр есте́ственных нау́к ♦ *abbr* (*US*: *POST*) = *Mississippi.*
MS. *n abbr* = **manuscript.**
MSA *n abbr* (*US*: = *Master of Science in Agriculture*) ≈ маги́стр сельско-хозя́йственных нау́к.
MSc *n abbr* (= *Master of Science*) ≈ маги́стр есте́ственных нау́к.
MSG *n abbr* = *monosodium glutamate.*
MST *abbr* (*US*) = *Mountain Standard Time.*
MSW *n abbr* (*US*: = *Master of Social Work*) ≈ маги́стр социоло́гии.
MT *n abbr* (*COMPUT*, *LING*: = *machine translation*) МП= *маши́нный перево́д* ♦ *abbr* (*US*: *POST*) = *Montana.*
Mt *abbr* (*GEO*) = **mount.**
MTV *n abbr* (*US*) = *music television.*

┌ KEYWORD ┐

much [mʌtʃ] *adj* (*time, money, effort*) мно́го *+gen*; **we haven't got much time/money** у нас не так мно́го вре́мени/де́нег; **how much money/time do you need?** ско́лько де́нег/вре́мени Вам ну́жно?; **he's spent so much money today** он сего́дня потра́тил сто́лько де́нег; **I have as much money as you (do)** у меня́ сто́лько же де́нег, ско́лько у Вас; **I don't have as much time as you do** у меня́ нет сто́лько вре́мени, ско́лько у Вас
♦ *pron*: **there isn't much to do here** здесь не́чего де́лать; **much is still unclear** мно́гое ещё нея́сно; **much has been gained from our discussions** на́ша диску́ссия дала́ больши́е результа́ты *or* мно́гое; **how much does it cost?** ско́лько э́то сто́ит? – **too much** ско́лько э́то сто́ит? – сли́шком до́рого; **how much is it?** почём э́то?
♦ *adv* **1** (*greatly, a great deal*): **thank you very much** большо́е спаси́бо; **we are very much looking forward to your visit** мы о́чень ждём Ва́шего прие́зда; **he is very much a gentleman/politician** он настоя́щий джентльме́н/поли́тик; **however much he tries** ско́лько бы он ни стара́лся; **I try to help**

as much as possible *or* **as much as I can** я стара́юсь помога́ть как мо́жно бо́льше *or* ско́лько могу́; **I read as much as ever** я чита́ю сто́лько же, ско́лько пре́жде; **he is as much a member of the family as you** он тако́й же член семьи́, как и Вы
2 (*by far*) намно́го, гора́здо; **I'm much better now** мне намно́го *or* гора́здо лу́чше; **it's much the biggest publishing company in Europe** э́то са́мое кру́пное изда́тельство в Евро́пе
3 (*almost*) почти́; **the view from my window today is much as it was 10 years ago** вид из моего́ окна́ сего́дня сейча́с почти́ тако́й же, как и 10 лет наза́д; **how are you feeling?** – **much the same** как Вы себя́ чу́вствуете? – всё та́к же.

muck [mʌk] *n* (*dirt*) грязь* *f*; (*manure*) наво́з
▶ **muck about** *vi* (*inf*) валя́ть (*impf*) дурака́; (*tinker*): **to ~ about with** вози́ться* (*impf*) с +*instr*
▶ **muck around** *vi* = **muck about**
▶ **muck in** *vi* (*inf*) впряга́ться (впря́чься* *perf*)
▶ **muck out** *vt* (*stable*) выгреба́ть (вы́грести* *perf*) наво́з из +*gen*
▶ **muck up** *vt* (*inf*) зава́ливать (завали́ть* *perf*).
muckraking ['mʌkreɪkɪŋ] *n* (*fig: inf*) копа́ние в гря́зном белье́.
mucky ['mʌkɪ] *adj* гря́зный* (гря́зен).
mucus ['mju:kəs] *n* слизь *f*.
mud [mʌd] *n* грязь* *f*.
muddle ['mʌdl] *n* (*mess*) беспоря́док*; (*mix-up*) неразбери́ха, пу́таница ♦ *vt* (*also:* ~ **up**: *person*) запу́тывать (запу́тать *perf*); (: *things*) переме́шивать (перемеша́ть *perf*); (: *story, names*) пу́тать (перепу́тать *perf*); **to get in(to) a ~** (*while explaining etc*) запу́тываться (запу́таться *perf*); **I'm in a real ~** я соверше́нно запу́тался
▶ **muddle along** *vi* справля́ться (*impf*) кое-как
▶ **muddle through** *vi* выкара́бкиваться (вы́карабкаться *perf*).
muddleheaded [mʌdl'hɛdɪd] *adj* бестолко́вый (бестолко́в).
muddy ['mʌdɪ] *adj* гря́зный* (гря́зен).
mud flats *npl* и́листые уча́стки *mpl* (*вскрыва́ющиеся во вре́мя отли́ва*).
mudguard ['mʌdgɑ:d] *n* (*on vehicle*) крыло́*.
mudpack ['mʌdpæk] *n* грязева́я ма́ска*.
mudslinging ['mʌdslɪŋɪŋ] *n* (*fig*) полива́ние гря́зью.
muesli ['mju:zlɪ] *n* смесь овся́ных хло́пьев и сухофру́ктов.
muffin ['mʌfɪn] *n* (*BRIT*) (сдо́бная) бу́лочка; (*US*) кекс.
muffle ['mʌfl] *vt* (*sound*) приглуша́ть (приглуши́ть *perf*); (*against cold*: *also:* ~ **up**)

---

* marks translations which have irregular inflections. The Russian-English side of the dictionary gives inflectional information.

закутывать (закутать *perf*).
muffled ['mʌfld] *adj* (*see vb*) приглушённый (приглушён); (*also*: ~ **up**) закутанный.
muffler ['mʌflə'] *n* (*US*: *AUT*) глушитель *m*; (*scarf*) шарф.
mufti ['mʌfti] *n*: **in** ~ в штатском.
mug [mʌg] *n* кружка*; (*inf*: *face*) морда; (: *fool*) дурак* (дура) ◆ *vt* (*assault*) грабить* (ограбить* *perf*) (*на улице*); **it's a ~'s game** (*BRIT*: *inf*) это никчёмное дело
▶ **mug up** *vt* (*BRIT*: *inf*: *also*: ~ **up on**) зубрить* (вызубрить *perf*).
mugger ['mʌgə'] *n* уличный грабитель *m*.
mugging ['mʌgɪŋ] *n* грабёж* (*на улице*).
muggins ['mʌgɪnz] *n* (*inf*) простак*.
muggy ['mʌgɪ] *adj* душный* (душен).
mug shot *n* (*inf*) фотография подозреваемого в преступлении.
mulatto [mju:'lætəu] (*pl* **—es**) *n* мулат(ка*).
mulberry ['mʌlbri] *n* (*fruit*) тутовая ягода; (*tree*) тутовое дерево*, шелковица.
mule [mju:l] *n* (*ZOOL*) мул.
mulled wine [mʌld-] *n* глинтвейн.
mullioned ['mʌliənd] *adj* (*ARCHIT*): ~ **window** окно сп средником.
mull over [mʌl-] *vt* размышлять (*impf*) над +*instr*.
multi... [['mʌlti] *prefix* много..., мульти....
multiaccess ['mʌlti'ækses] *adj* (*COMPUT*) многопользовательский*.
multicoloured ['mʌltikʌləd] (*US* **multicolored**) *adj* многоцветный* (многоцветен).
multifarious [mʌlti'fɛəriəs] *adj* многообразный* (многообразен).
multilateral [mʌlti'lætərl] *adj* многосторонний*.
multilevel ['mʌltilɛvl] *adj* (*US*) = **multistorey**
multimillionaire [mʌltimiljə'nɛə'] *n* мультимиллионер.
multinational [mʌlti'næʃənl] *adj* международный ◆ *n* международная корпорация.
multiple ['mʌltipl] *adj* (*injuries*) многочисленный; (*interests*) разнообразный* (разнообразен) ◆ *n* (*MATH*) кратное число*; (*BRIT*: *also*: ~ **store**) филиал сети (*магазинов*); ~ **collision** столкновение нескольких автомобилей.
multiple-choice ['mʌltiplt∫ɔis] *adj*: ~ (**exam**) тест на выбор, *правильного ответа из нескольких предложенных вариантов*.
multiple sclerosis *n* рассеянный склероз.
multiplication [mʌltipli'keiʃən] *n* умножение.
multiplication table *n* таблица умножения.
multiplicity [mʌlti'plisiti] *n*: **a** ~ **of** множество +*gen*.
multiply ['mʌltiplai] *vt* умножать (умножить *perf*) ◆ *vi* размножаться (размножиться *perf*).
multiracial [mʌlti'reiʃl] *adj* многонациональный* (многонационален).
multistorey ['mʌlti'stɔ:ri] *adj* (*BRIT*)

многоэтажный.
multitude ['mʌltitju:d] *n* (*crowd*) массы *fpl*; (*large number*): **a** ~ **of** множество +*gen*.
mum [mʌm] (*BRIT*: *inf*) *n* мама ◆ *adj*: **to keep** ~ **about sth** помалкивать (*impf*) о чём-н; **"mum's the word!"** „молчу!".
mumble ['mʌmbl] *vt* бормотать* (пробормотать* *perf*) ◆ *vi* бормотать (*impf*).
mumbo jumbo ['mʌmbəu-] *n* (*inf*) тарабарщина.
mummify ['mʌmifai] *vt* мумифицировать (*impf/perf*).
mummy ['mʌmi] *n* (*BRIT*: *inf*: *mother*) мама; (*embalmed corpse*) мумия.
mumps [mʌmps] *n* свинка.
munch [mʌnt∫] *vti* (*chew*) жевать (*impf*).
mundane [mʌn'dein] *adj* обыденный (обыден).
Munich ['mju:nik] *n* Мюнхен.
municipal [mju:'nisipl] *adj* муниципальный.
municipality [mju:nisi'pæliti] *n* город*; (*authority*) муниципалитет.
munitions [mju:'niʃənz] *npl* боеприпасы *mpl*.
mural ['mjuərl] *n* настенная роспись *f*, фреска.
murder ['mə:də'] *n* убийство (*умышленное*) ◆ *vt* (*kill*) убивать (убить* *perf*) (*умышленно*); (*fig*: *inf*) угробить* (*perf*); **to commit** ~ совершать (совершить *perf*) убийство.
murderer ['mə:dərə'] *n* убийца *m/f*.
murderess ['mə:dəris] *n* убийца *m/f*.
murderous ['mə:dərəs] *adj* (*dictator, regime*) кровавый; (*look*) убийственный; (*attack*) смертоносный* (смертоносен); ~ **tendencies** склонность *f* к убийству.
murk [mə:k] *n* мгла.
murky ['mə:ki] *adj* (*street, night*) мрачный* (мрачен); (*water*) мутный* (мутен).
murmur ['mə:mə'] *n* (*of voices, waves*) ропот; (*of wind*) шелест ◆ *vti* шептать* (*impf*); **heart** ~ шумы *mpl* в сердце.
MusB(ac) *n abbr* (= *Bachelor of Music*) бакалавр музыковедения.
muscle ['mʌsl] *n* (*ANAT*) мышца, мускул; (*fig*: *strength*) сила.
▶ **muscle in** *vi* пролезать (пролезть* *perf*).
Muscovite ['mʌskəvait] *n* москвич*(ка*).
muscular ['mʌskjulə'] *adj* (*pain, injury*) мышечный; (*person, build*) мускулистый (мускулист).
muscular dystrophy *adj* мускульная дистрофия.
MusD(oc) *n abbr* (= *Doctor of Music*) доктор музыковедения.
muse [mju:z] *vi* размышлять (*impf*) ◆ *n* муза.
museum [mju:'ziəm] *n* музей.
mush [mʌ∫] *n* месиво; (*pej*) масса.
mushroom ['mʌ∫rum] *n* гриб* ◆ *vi* (*fig*) быстро разрастаться (разрастись* *perf*).
mushroom cloud *n* атомный гриб*.
mushy ['mʌ∫i] *adj* разварившийся, как каша; (*inf*: *pej*: *story, fiction*) слащавый (слащав); ~

peas горо́шек.
music ['mjuːzɪk] *n* му́зыка; **sheet** ~ но́ты *fpl*.
musical ['mjuːzɪkl] *adj* (*career, skills*) музыка́льный; (*person*) музыка́льный* (музыка́лен); (*sound, tune*) мелоди́чный* (мелоди́чен) ◆ *n* (*show, film*) мю́зикл.
music(al) box *n* музыка́льная шкату́лка*.
musical chairs *n* ≈ тре́тий* ли́шний* *m adj* (*игра́*).
musical instrument *n* музыка́льный инструме́нт.
music centre *n* де́ка с прои́грывателем и магнитофо́ном.
music hall *n* (BRIT: *vaudeville*) мю́зик-холл.
musician [mjuː'zɪʃən] *n* музыка́нт.
music stand *n* пюпи́тр.
musk [mʌsk] *n* му́скус.
musket ['mʌskɪt] *n* мушке́т.
muskrat ['mʌskræt] *n* онда́тра.
musk rose *n* му́скусная ро́за.
Muslim ['mʌzlɪm] *n* мусульма́нин*(-нка*) ◆ *adj* мусульма́нский*.
muslin ['mʌzlɪn] *n* ма́рля.
musquash ['mʌskwɔʃ] *n* = **muskrat**.
mussel ['mʌsl] *n* ми́дия.
must [mʌst] *n* (*necessity*) необходи́мость *f* ◆ *aux vb* (*necessity*): **I ~ do it** я до́лжен э́то сде́лать; (*probability*): **he ~ be there by now** он до́лжен уже́ там быть; **it's (simply) a ~** э́то про́сто необходи́мость; **you ~ come and see me soon** Вы обяза́тельно должны́ ско́ро ко мне зайти́; **why ~ he behave so badly?** отчего́ он так пло́хо себя́ веде́т?; **I ~ have made a mistake** я, должно́ быть, оши́бся.
mustache ['mʌstæʃ] *n* (US) = **moustache**.
mustard ['mʌstəd] *n* горчи́ца.
mustard gas *n* иприт, горчи́чный газ.
muster ['mʌstə] *vt* (*support, energy*) собира́ть (собра́ть* *perf*); (*troops*) набира́ть (набра́ть* *perf*); (*also:* ~ **up**: *strength, courage*) набира́ться (набра́ться* *perf*) +*gen*.
mustiness ['mʌstɪnɪs] *n* за́тхлость *f*.
mustn't ['mʌsnt] = **must not**.
musty ['mʌstɪ] *adj* (*smell*) за́тхлый (затхл).
mutant ['mjuːtənt] *n* мута́нт.
mutate [mjuː'teɪt] *vi* (BIO) мути́ровать (*impf*).
mutation [mjuː'teɪʃən] *n* (BIO) мута́ция; (*change*) преобразова́ния *ntpl*.
mute [mjuːt] *adj* (*silent*) безмо́лвный* (безмо́лвен) ◆ *n* (MUS) сурди́нка.
muted ['mjuːtɪd] *adj* (*reaction, criticism*) сде́ржанный* (сде́ржан); (*colour, noise*) приглушённый (приглушён); ~ **strings** стру́ны под сурди́нкой.
mutilate ['mjuːtɪleɪt] *vt* (*person*) уве́чить (изуве́чить *perf*); (*thing*) уро́довать (изуро́довать *perf*).
mutilation [mjuːtɪ'leɪʃən] *n* (*injury*) уве́чье*;

(*maiming*) нанесе́ние уве́чья.
mutinous ['mjuːtɪnəs] *adj* (*troops, attitude*) мяте́жный*.
mutiny ['mjuːtɪnɪ] *n* мяте́ж*, бунт ◆ *vi* бунтова́ть (*impf*).
mutter ['mʌtə] *vti* бормота́ть* (*impf*).
mutton ['mʌtn] *n* бара́нина.
mutual ['mjuːtʃuəl] *adj* (*feeling*) взаи́мный* (взаи́мен); (*help*) взаи́мный; (*friend, interest*) о́бщий*; ~ **understanding** взаимопонима́ние; ~ **aid** взаимопо́мощь *f*.
mutually ['mjuːtʃuəlɪ] *adv* взаи́мно; ~ **beneficial** взаимовы́годный* (взаимовы́годен).
Muzak® ['mjuːzæk] *n* бессодержа́тельная лёгкая му́зыка, испо́льзуемая в магази́нах и рестора́нах как фон.
muzzle ['mʌzl] *n* (*mouth: of dog*) мо́рда; (: *of gun*) ду́ло; (*guard: for dog*) намо́рдник ◆ *vt* (*dog*) надева́ть (наде́ть* *perf*) намо́рдник на +*acc*; (*fig: press, person*) затыка́ть (заткну́ть *perf*) рот +*dat*.
MV *abbr* = motor vessel.
MVP *n abbr* (US: SPORT: = most valuable player) са́мый це́нный игро́к.
MW *abbr* (RADIO) (= medium wave) СВ= сре́дние во́лны.

KEYWORD
my [maɪ] *adj* **1** (*with objects, possessions*) мой; **this is my house/car** э́то мой дом/моя́ маши́на; **is this my pen or yours?** э́то моя́ ру́чка и́ли ва́ша?
2 (*with parts of the body etc*): **I've washed my hair/cut my finger** я помы́л го́лову/поре́зал па́лец
3 (*referring to subject of sentence*) свой; **I've lost my key** я потеря́л свой ключ.

myopic [maɪ'ɔpɪk] *adj* (*also fig*) близору́кий* (близору́к).
myriad ['mɪrɪəd] *n* мириа́ды *mpl*.
myrrh [məː'] *n* ми́рра.
KEYWORD
myself [maɪ'sɛlf] *pron* **1** (*reflexive*): **I've hurt myself** я уши́бся; **I consider myself clever** я счита́ю себя́ у́мным
2 (*complement*): **she's the same age as myself** она́ одного́ во́зраста со мной
3 (*after prep: +gen*) себя́; (: +*dat, +prp*) себе́; (: +*instr*) собо́й; **I wanted to keep the book for myself** я хоте́л оста́вить кни́гу себе́; **I sometimes talk to myself** иногда́ я сам с собо́й разгова́риваю; **(all) by myself** (*alone*) сам; **I made it all by myself** я всё э́то сде́лал сам; **4** (*emphatic*) сам; **I myself chose the flowers** я сам выбира́л цветы́.

mysterious [mɪs'tɪərɪəs] *adj* таи́нственный* (таи́нствен).
mysteriously [mɪs'tɪərɪəslɪ] *adv* (*disappear, die*)

---

* marks translations which have irregular inflections. The Russian-English side of the dictionary gives inflectional information.

таи́нственно; (*smile*) зага́дочно.
mystery ['mɪstərɪ] *n* (*strangeness*) та́йна;
   (*puzzle*) зага́дка* ♦ *cpd* (*tour, guest, voice*)
   зага́дочный.
mystery story *n* детекти́в.
mystic ['mɪstɪk] *n* ми́стик ♦ *adj* мисти́ческий.
mystical ['mɪstɪkl] *adj* = **mystic**.
mystify ['mɪstɪfaɪ] *vt* (*perplex*) озада́чивать

(озада́чить *perf*).
mystique [mɪs'tiːk] *n* ми́стика.
myth [mɪθ] *n* миф.
mythical ['mɪθɪkl] *adj* (*also fig*) мифи́ческий*.
mythological [mɪθə'lɔdʒɪkl] *adj*
   мифологи́ческий.
mythology [mɪ'θɔlədʒɪ] *n* мифоло́гия.

~ *N, n* ~

N, n [εn] *n* (*letter*) 14-ая бу́ква англи́йского алфави́та.

N *abbr* (= **north**) C= *се́вер*.

NA *n abbr* (*US*: = *Narcotics Anonymous*) о́бщество анони́много излече́ния от наркома́нии; = **National Academy**.

n/a *abbr* (= *not applicable*) не применя́ется; (*COMM etc*: = *no account*) счёт отсу́тствует.

NAACP *n abbr* (*US*) = **National Association for the Advancement of Colored People**.

NAAFI ['næfɪ] *n abbr* (*BRIT*: = *Navy, Army & Air Force Institute*) Институ́т а́рмии, вое́нно-морского и вое́нно-возду́шного фло́та.

NACU *n abbr* (*US*) = **National Association of Colleges and Universities**.

nadir ['neɪdɪə'] *n* (*ASTRONOMY*) нади́р; (*fig*) ни́зшая то́чка.

nag [næg] *vt* (*scold*) пили́ть* (*impf*) ◆ *vi*: **to ~ at** ныть (*impf*) (из-за +*gen*) ◆ *n* (*pej: horse*) кля́ча; (: *person*): **she's an awful ~** она́ жу́ткая зану́да.

nagging ['nægɪŋ] *adj* (*pain*) ною́щий; (*suspicion, doubt*) неотвя́зный.

nail [neɪl] *n* (*on finger etc*) но́готь* *m*; (*metal*) гвоздь* *m* ◆ *vt* (*inf: catch*) засту́кивать (засту́кать *perf*); **to ~ sth to sth** прибива́ть (приби́ть* *perf*) что-н к чему́-н; **to ~ sb down to doing** (*inf*) прижима́ть (прижа́ть* *perf*) кого́-н к сте́нке и заста́вить* +*infin*.

nailbrush ['neɪlbrʌʃ] *n* щёточка* для ногте́й.

nailfile ['neɪlfaɪl] *n* пи́лка* (*для ногте́й*).

nail polish *n* лак для ногте́й.

nail polish remover *n* жи́дкость *f* для сня́тия ла́ка.

nail scissors *npl* маникю́рные но́жницы *pl*.

nail varnish *n* (*BRIT*) = **nail polish**.

Nairobi [naɪˈrəubɪ] *n* Найро́би *m ind*.

naive [naɪˈiːv] *adj* наи́вный* (наи́вен).

naiveté [naɪˈiːvteɪ] *n* = **naivety**.

naivety [naɪˈiːvteɪ] *n* наи́вность *f*.

naked ['neɪkɪd] *adj* (*also fig*) го́лый* (гол); (*anger*) не скрыва́емый; **with the ~ eye** невооружённым гла́зом.

nakedness ['neɪkɪdnɪs] *n* нагота́.

NAM *n abbr* (*US*) = **National Association of Manufacturers**.

name [neɪm] *n* (*of person*) и́мя* *nt*; (*of place, object, species*) назва́ние; (*of pet*) кли́чка* ◆ *vt* называ́ть (назва́ть* *perf*); **what's your ~?** как Вас зову́т?; **my ~ is Peter** меня́ зову́т Пи́тер; **what's the ~ of this place?** как называ́ется э́то ме́сто?; **by ~** по и́мени; **in the ~ of** во и́мя +*gen*; **to give one's ~ and address** (*to police etc*) дава́ть* (дать* *perf*) своё и́мя и а́дрес; **to make a ~ for o.s.** создава́ть* (созда́ть* *perf*) себе́ и́мя; **to get (o.s.) a bad ~** зараба́тывать (зарабо́тать (*perf*)) себе́ дурну́ю репута́цию; **to call sb ~s** обзыва́ть (обозва́ть* *perf*) кого́-н.

name-dropping ['neɪmdrɔpɪŋ] *n* упомина́ние изве́стных имён.

nameless ['neɪmlɪs] *adj* (*unknown*) безымя́нный* (безымя́нен); (*anonymous*) неизве́стный* (неизве́стен).

namely ['neɪmlɪ] *adv* а и́менно.

nameplate ['neɪmpleɪt] *n* табли́чка* (*с и́менем*).

namesake ['neɪmseɪk] *n* тёзка* *m/f*.

Namibia [nəˈmɪbɪə] *n* Нами́бия.

nan bread [nɑː-] *n* инди́йский* хлеб в фо́рме лепёшки.

nanny ['nænɪ] *n* ня́ня.

nanny goat *n* коза́*.

nap [næp] *n* коро́ткий* сон; (*of fabric*) ворс ◆ *vi*: **he was caught ~ping** (*fig*) его́ заста́ли врасплёх; **to have or take a ~** вздремну́ть (*perf*).

NAPA *n abbr* (*US*) = **National Association of Performing Artists**.

napalm ['neɪpɑːm] *n* напа́лм.

nape [neɪp] *n*: **~ of the neck** за́дняя часть *f* ше́и.

napkin ['næpkɪn] *n* (*also: table ~*) салфе́тка*.

Naples ['neɪplz] *n* Неа́поль *m*.

Napoleonic [nəpəulɪˈɔnɪk] *adj* наполео́новский.

nappy ['næpɪ] *n* (*BRIT*) подгу́зник.

nappy liner *n* (*BRIT*) прокла́дка для подгу́зника.

nappy rash *n* (*BRIT*) потни́ца.

narcissi [nɑːˈsɪsaɪ] *npl of* **narcissus**.

narcissistic [nɑːsɪˈsɪstɪk] *adj* само-влюблённый.

---

* marks translations which have irregular inflections. The Russian-English side of the dictionary gives inflectional information.

narcissus [naː'sɪsəs] (*pl* **narcissi**) *n* (*BOT*)
нарци́сс.
narcotic [naː'kɔtɪk] *adj* наркоти́ческий ♦ *n*
(*MED*) снотво́рное *nt adj*; ~**s** *npl* (*drugs*)
нарко́тики *mpl*.
nark [naːk] *vt* (*BRIT*: *inf*) раздража́ть
(раздражи́ть *perf*).
narrate [nə'reɪt] *vt* (*story, novel*) расска́зывать
(рассказа́ть* *perf*); **to ~ a film/programme**
чита́ть (*impf*) текст фи́льма/переда́чи.
narration [nə'reɪʃən] *n* повествова́ние.
narrative ['nærətɪv] *n* исто́рия.
narrator [nə'reɪtə'] *n* (*in book*)
расска́зчик(-ица); (*in film*) ди́ктор.
narrow ['nærəu] *adj* (*also fig*) у́зкий* (у́зок);
(*majority, advantage*) незначи́тельный*
(незначи́телен) ♦ *vi* (*road*) сужа́ться
(су́зиться* *perf*); (*gap, difference*)
уменьша́ться (уме́ньшиться *perf*) ♦ *vt*: **to ~**
sth down to своди́ть* (свести́* *perf*) что-н к
+*dat*; **to have a ~ escape** едва́ спасти́сь* (*perf*).
narrow-gauge ['nærəugeʊɪdʒ] *adj* (*RAIL*)
узкоколе́йный.
narrowly ['nærəulɪ] *adv* (*miss*) чуть не;
(*interpret*) у́зко; **he only ~ avoided injury/**
defeat он чуть не покале́чился/проигра́л; **he**
only ~ missed the target он почти́ попа́л в
цель.
narrow-minded [nærəu'maɪndɪd] *adj*
ограни́ченный (ограни́чен).
narrowness ['nærəunɪs] *n* у́зость *f*.
NAS *n abbr* (*US*) = National Academy of Sciences.
NASA ['næsə] *n abbr* (*US*: = National Aeronautics
and Space Administration) НАСА.
nasal ['neɪzl] *adj* (*ANAT*) носово́й; (*tone, voice*)
гнуса́вый.
Nassau ['næsɔː] *n* Нaccáу *m ind*.
nastily ['naːstɪlɪ] *adv* зло́бно.
nastiness ['naːstɪnɪs] *n* (*unpleasantness*)
проти́вность *f*; (*spitefulness*) зло́бность *f*.
nasturtium [nəs'təːʃəm] *n* насту́рция.
nasty ['naːstɪ] *adj* (*unpleasant*) проти́вный*
(проти́вен); (*malicious*) зло́бный* (зло́бен);
(*situation, wound*) скве́рный* (скве́рен); **to**
say ~ things about sb говори́ть (*impf*) га́дости
о ком-н; **to turn ~** (*situation*) принима́ть
(приня́ть* *perf*) скве́рный оборо́т; (*weather*)
де́латься (сде́латься *perf*) скве́рным;
(*person*) озлобля́ться (озло́биться* *perf*); **it's**
a ~ business э́то ме́рзкое де́ло.
NAS/UWT *n abbr* (*BRIT*) = National Association
of Schoolmasters/Union of Women Teachers.
nation ['neɪʃən] *n* (*POL*) на́ция; (*people*) наро́д;
(*state*) страна́, госуда́рство.
national ['næʃənl] *adj* национа́льный ♦ *n*
граждани́н*(-да́нка*).
national anthem *n* госуда́рственный гимн.
national curriculum *n* (*BRIT*) всео́бщая
програ́мма (обуче́ния) (*в шко́лах*).
national debt *n* госуда́рственный долг*.
national dress *n* национа́льная оде́жда.

National Guard *n* (*US*) Национа́льная
гва́рдия.
National Health Service *n* (*BRIT*)
Госуда́рственная слу́жба здравоохране́ния.
National Insurance *n* (*BRIT*) госуда́рственное
страхова́ние.
nationalism ['næʃnəlɪzəm] *n* национали́зм.
nationalist ['næʃnəlɪst] *adj* националист-
и́ческий ♦ *n* национали́ст(ка*).
nationality [næʃə'nælɪtɪ] *n* (*status*)
гражда́нство; (*ethnic group*) наро́дность *f*.
nationalization [næʃnəlaɪ'zeɪʃən] *n*
национализа́ция.
nationalize ['næʃnəlaɪz] *vt* национализ-
и́ровать (*impf/perf*).
nationalized industry ['næʃnaɪzd-] *n*
национализи́рованная промы́шленность *f*.
nationally ['næʃnəlɪ] *adv* (*nationwide*) в
национа́льном всей страны́.
national park *n* национа́льный па́рк.
national press *n* национа́льная пре́сса.
National Security Council *n* (*US*) Сове́т
национа́льной безопа́сности.
national service *n* (*MIL*: *esp BRIT*) во́инская
пови́нность *f*.
National Trust *n* (*BRIT*) *организа́ция,*
занима́ющаяся охра́ной архитекту́рных
па́мятников и приро́дных запове́дников.
nationwide ['neɪʃənwaɪd] *adj* общенаро́дный
♦ *adv* по всей стране́.
native ['neɪtɪv] *n* (*local inhabitant*)
ме́стный(-ая) жи́тель(ница) *m(f)* ♦ *adj*
(*indigenous*) коренно́й, иско́нный; (*of one's*
birth) родно́й; (*innate*) врождённый; **a ~ of**
Russia урожéнец(-нка*) Росси́и; **a ~ speaker**
of Russian носи́тель(ница) *m(f)* ру́сского
языка́.
Native American *n потóмок коренно́го*
населе́ния Се́веро-Америка́нского
контине́нта.
native language *n* родно́й язы́к*.
Nativity [nə'tɪvɪtɪ] *n*: **the ~** Рождество́
Христо́во.
nativity play *n* Рожде́ственская мисте́рия
(*обы́чно разы́грываемая детьми́*).
NATO ['neɪtəu] *n abbr* (= North Atlantic Treaty
Organization) НАТО.
natter ['nætə'] (*BRIT*) *vi* трепа́ться* (*impf*) ♦ *n*: **to**
have a ~ трепа́ться* (потрепа́ться* *perf*).
natural ['nætʃrəl] *adj* (*behaviour*) есте́ственный
(есте́ствен); (*aptitude, materials*) приро́дный;
(*foods*) натура́льный; (*disaster*) стихи́йный;
to die of ~ causes умира́ть (умере́ть* *perf*)
есте́ственной сме́ртью.
natural childbirth *n* есте́ственные ро́ды *pl*.
natural gas *n* приро́дный газ.
natural history *n* естествозна́ние.
naturalist ['nætʃrəlɪst] *n* натурали́ст.
naturalize ['nætʃrəlaɪz] *vt*: **to become ~d**
(*person*) получа́ть (получи́ть* *perf*)
гражда́нство; (*plant*) акклиматизи́роваться

(impf/perf).

naturally ['nætʃrəlɪ] *adv* естéственно; (*innately*) от прирóды; (*in nature*) в прирóде; ~, **I refused** естéственно, я отказáлся.

naturalness ['nætʃrəlnɪs] *n* естéственность *f*.

natural resources *npl* прирóдные ресýрсы *mpl*.

natural selection *n* (*BIO*) естéственный отбóр.

natural wastage *n* (*INDUSTRY*) естéственная ýбыль* *f* (*рабóчей сúлы*).

nature ['neɪtʃə'] *n* (*also:* **N~**) прирóда; (*character*) натýра; (*sort*) харáктер; **by ~** (*person*) по натýре; (*event, thing*) по прирóде; **documents of a confidential ~** докумéнты конфиденциáльного харáктера.

-natured ['neɪtʃəd] *suffix*: **ill-~** злóбный по натýре.

nature reserve *n* (*BRIT*) заповéдник.

nature trail *n* размéченная трóпа, проходящая чéрез сéльскую мéстность, заповéдник итп.

naturist ['neɪtʃərɪst] *n* нудúст(ка*).

naught [nɔːt] *n* = **nought**.

naughtiness ['nɔːtɪnɪs] *n* (*see adj*) непослушáние, озорствó; пикáнтность *f*.

naughty ['nɔːtɪ] *adj* (*child*) непослýшный* (непослýшен), озорнóй; (*story, film*) пикáнтный* (пикáнтен).

nausea ['nɔːsɪə] *n* тошнотá.

nauseate ['nɔːsɪeɪt] *vt* (*also fig*) вызывáть (вýзвать* *perf*) тошнотý в +*prp* или у +*gen*.

nauseating ['nɔːsɪeɪtɪŋ] *adj* (*also fig*) тошнотвóрный* (тошнотвóрен).

nauseous ['nɔːsɪəs] *adj* тошнотвóрный* (тошнотвóрен); **he's feeling ~** егó тошнúт.

nautical ['nɔːtɪkl] *adj* морскóй.

naval ['neɪvl] *adj* воéнно-морскóй; (*battle, power*) морскóй.

naval officer *n* морскóй офицéр.

nave [neɪv] *n* неф.

navel ['neɪvl] *n* пупóк*.

navigable ['nævɪgəbl] *adj* судохóдный* (судохóден).

navigate ['nævɪgeɪt] *vt* (*NAUT, AVIAT*) управлять (*impf*) +*instr* ◆ *vi* определять (определúть *perf*) маршрýт; **to ~ a ship through/around** вестú* (провестú* *perf*) корáбль чéрез +*acc*/вокрýг +*gen*.

navigation [nævɪ'geɪʃən] *n* (*science*) навигáция; (*action*): **~ (of)** управлéние (+*instr*).

navigator ['nævɪgeɪtə'] *n* штýрман.

navvy ['nævɪ] *n* (*BRIT*) чернорабóчий* *m adj*.

navy ['neɪvɪ] *n* воéнно-морскóй флот; **Department of the N~** (*US*) ≈ Министéрство воéнно-морскóго флóта.

navy(-blue) ['neɪvɪ('bluː)] *adj* тёмно-сúний*.

Nazareth ['næzərɪθ] *n* Назарéт.

Nazi ['nɑːtsɪ] *n* нацúст(ка*).

NB *abbr* = *nota bene*; (*note well*) NB, нотабéне; (*CANADA*) = *New Brunswick*.

NBA *n abbr* (*US*) = *National Basketball Association*; *National Boxing Association*.

NBC *n abbr* (*US*) = *National Broadcasting Company*.

NBS *n abbr* (*US*) = *National Bureau of Standards*.

NC *abbr* (*COMM etc*: = *no charge*) беспл́тно; (*US*: *POST*) = *North Carolina*.

NCC *n abbr* (*BRIT*) = *Nature Conservancy Council*; (*US*) *National Council of Churches*.

NCCL *n abbr* (*BRIT*: = *National Council for Civil Liberties*) Национáльный совéт по граждáнским правáм.

NCO *n abbr* (*MIL*) = **noncommissioned officer**.

ND *abbr* (*US*: *POST*) = *North Dakota*.

NE *abbr* (*US*: *POST*) = *New England*; *Nebraska*.

NEA *n abbr* (*US*) = *National Education Association*.

neap [niːp] *n* (*also:* **~ tide**) квадратýрный прилúв.

Neapolitan [nɪə'pɔlɪtən] *adj* неаполитáнский* ◆ *n* неаполитáнец(-нка*).

near [nɪə'] *adj* блúзкий* (блúзок) ◆ *adv* блúзко ◆ *prep* (*also:* **~ to**: *space*) вóзле +*gen*, óколо +*gen*; (: *time*) к +*dat*, óколо +*gen* ◆ *vt* приближáться (приблúзиться* *perf*) к +*dat*; **~ here/there** недалекó отсю́да/отту́да; **£25,000 or ~est offer** (*BRIT*) цена́ £25.000 и́ли по договорённости; **in the ~ future** в ближáйшем бýдущем; **~er (to) the time** óколо положéнной дáты; **to come ~ (to)** (*also fig*) приближáться (приблúзиться* *perf*) (к +*dat*); **he was ~ to despair/victory** он был блúзок к отчáянию/побéде; **the building is ~ing completion** стрóительство приближáется к завершéнию.

nearby [nɪə'baɪ] *adj* близлежáщий ◆ *adv* поблúзости.

Near East *n*: **the ~ ~** Блúжний* Востóк.

nearer ['nɪərə'] *adj, adv* блúже.

nearly ['nɪəlɪ] *adv* почтú; **I ~ fell** я чуть (бы́ло) не упáл; **she was ~ crying** онá почтú плáкала; **it's not ~ as easy as it looks** э́то отню́дь не так прóсто, как кáжется; **the house is not ~ big enough** дом совсéм мал.

near miss *n* (*failed attempt*): **that was a ~ ~!** промахнýлся!; **we had a ~ ~ in the car today** мы сегóдня чуть не попáли в авáрию.

nearness ['nɪənɪs] *n* блúзость *f*.

nearside ['nɪəsaɪd] *n* (*AUT*: *in Britain*) лéвая сторонá; (: *in US, Europe etc*) прáвая сторонá.

near-sighted [nɪə'saɪtɪd] *adj* близорýкий* (близорýк).

neat [niːt] *adj* (*person, place*) опрятный* (опрятен); (*work*) аккурáтный* (аккурáтен);

(*clear: categories*) чёткий* (чёток); (*esp US: inf*) кла́ссный* (кла́ссен); (*alcohol*) неразба́вленный.

neatly ['ni:tlɪ] *adv* (*dress*) опря́тно; (*work*) аккура́тно; (*sum up*) чётко.

neatness ['ni:tnɪs] *n* (*see adv*) опря́тность *f*; аккура́тность *f*; чёткость *f*.

nebulous ['nɛbjuləs] *adj* (*concept, proposal*) тума́нный* (тума́нен).

necessarily ['nɛsɪsrɪlɪ] *adv* неизбе́жно; **not ~** не обяза́тельно.

necessary ['nɛsɪsrɪ] *adj* необходи́мый (необходи́м); (*inevitable*) обяза́тельный, неизбе́жный; **if ~** е́сли необходи́мо; **it's not ~** э́то не обяза́тельно; **it is ~ to/that ...** необходи́мо +*infin*/чтóбы ....

necessitate [nɪ'sɛsɪteɪt] *vt* обусло́вливать (обусло́вить* *perf*).

necessity [nɪ'sɛsɪtɪ] *n* необходи́мость *f*; **necessities** *npl* (*essentials*) предме́ты *mpl* пе́рвой необходи́мости; **in case of ~** в слу́чае необходи́мости.

neck [nɛk] *n* (*ANAT*) ше́я; (*of garment*) во́рот; (*of bottle*) гóрлышко* ♦ *vi* (*inf*) милова́ться (*impf*); **~ and ~** вро́вень; **to stick one's ~ out** (*inf*) лезть* (*impf*) на рожóн; **to risk one's ~** (*inf*) рискова́ть (рискну́ть *perf*) головóй.

necklace ['nɛklɪs] *n* ожере́лье.

neckline ['nɛklaɪn] *n* вы́рез.

necktie ['nɛktaɪ] *n* (*US*) га́лстук.

nectar ['nɛktə] *n* некта́р.

nectarine ['nɛktərɪn] *n* нектари́н.

NEDC *n abbr* (*BRIT*: = *National Economic Development Council*) Националь́ный совéт экономи́ческого развити́я.

Neddy ['nɛdɪ] *n abbr* (*BRIT*: *inf*) = **NEDC**.

née [neɪ] *adj*: **~ Scott** урождённая Скотт.

need [ni:d] *n* (*thing needed*) потре́бность *f*; (*deprivation*) нужда́; (*necessity*): **~ (for)** нужда́ (в +*prp*) ♦ *vt*: **I ~ time/money** мне ну́жно вре́мя/нужны́ де́ньги; **there's no ~ to worry** нéзачем волновáться; **to be in ~ of, have ~ of** нужда́ться (*impf*) в +*prp*; **in case of ~** в слу́чае необходи́мости; **the ~s of industry** потре́бности промы́шленности; **£10 will meet my immediate ~s** £10 удовлетворя́т мои́ ну́жды на да́нный момéнт; **I ~ to see him** мне на́до *or* ну́жно с ним уви́деться; **you don't ~ to leave yet** Вам ещё не порá идти́; **a signature is ~ed** трéбуется пóдпись.

needle ['ni:dl] *n* игла́, иго́лка*; (*for knitting*) спи́ца ♦ *vt* (*fig: inf*) подка́лывать (подколóть *perf*).

needlecord ['ni:dlkɔ:d] *n* (*BRIT*) тóнкий* вельве́т.

needless ['ni:dlɪs] *adj* изли́шний* (изли́шен); **~ to say** само́ собóй разуме́ется.

needlessly ['ni:dlɪslɪ] *adv* напра́сно.

needlework ['ni:dlwə:k] *n* рукоде́лие.

needn't ['ni:dnt] = **need not**; *see* **need**.

needy ['ni:dɪ] *adj* нужда́ющийся; **the ~** *npl*

нужда́ющиеся *pl adj*.

negation [nɪ'geɪʃən] *n* отрица́ние.

negative ['nɛgətɪv] *adj* (*also ELEC*) отрица́тельный ♦ *n* (*LING*) отрица́ние; (*PHOT*) негати́в; **to answer in the ~** дава́ть* (дать* *perf*) отрица́тельный отве́т.

negative cash flow *n* отрица́тельный потóк нали́чности.

negative equity *n* (*COMM*) отрица́тельная *or* негати́вная ма́ржа.

neglect [nɪ'glɛkt] *vt* (*child, work*) забра́сывать (забрóсить* *perf*); (*garden, area, health*) запуска́ть (запусти́ть* *perf*); (*duty*) пренебрега́ть (пренебре́чь* *perf*) ♦ *n*: **~ (of)** невнима́ние (к +*dat*); (*duty*) пренебреже́ние (+*instr*); **in a state of ~** в запустéнии.

neglected [nɪ'glɛktɪd] *adj* (*animal, child*) забрóшенный (забрóшен).

neglectful [nɪ'glɛktful] *adj* небре́жный* (небре́жен); **to be ~ of sb** относи́ться* (*impf*) к кому́-н без внима́ния; **to be ~ of sth** пренебрега́ть (пренебре́чь* *perf*) чем-н.

negligee ['nɛglɪʒeɪ] *n* пеньюáр.

negligence ['nɛglɪdʒəns] *n* хала́тность *f*.

negligent ['nɛglɪdʒənt] *adj* хала́тный* (хала́тен); **to be ~ in** хала́тно относи́ться* (*impf*) к +*dat*.

negligently ['nɛglɪdʒəntlɪ] *adv* (*irresponsibly*) хала́тно; (*offhandedly*) небре́жно.

negligible ['nɛglɪdʒɪbl] *adj* ничтóжный* (ничтóжен).

negotiable [nɪ'gəuʃɪəbl] *adj*: **the price/contract is ~** це́ну/контра́кт мóжно обсуди́ть; (*road*) проходи́мый (проходи́м); (*cheque, assets*): **~/not negotiable** с пра́вом/без пра́ва переда́чи.

negotiate [nɪ'gəuʃɪeɪt] *vt* (*treaty, transaction*) заключа́ть (заключи́ть *perf*); (*obstacle*) преодолева́ть (преодоле́ть *perf*); (*bend in road*) огиба́ть (обогну́ть *perf*) ♦ *vi*: **to ~ (with sb for sth)** вести́* (*impf*) перегово́ры (с кем-н о чём-н).

negotiating table [nɪ'gəuʃɪeɪtɪŋ-] *n* стол* перегово́ров.

negotiation [nɪgəuʃɪ'eɪʃən] *n* (*see vb*) заключе́ние; преодоле́ние; перегово́ры *mpl*; **to enter into ~s with sb** вступа́ть (вступи́ть* *perf*) в перегово́ры с кем-н.

negotiator [nɪ'gəuʃɪeɪtə] *n* уча́стник перегово́ров.

Negress ['ni:grɪs] *n* негритя́нка*.

Negro ['ni:grəu] (*pl ~es*) *adj* негритя́нский* ♦ *n* (*old-fashioned*) негр(итя́нка*); (*pej*) чёрный(-ая) *m(f) adj*.

neigh [neɪ] *vi* ржать* (*impf*).

neighbor *etc* (*US*) = **neighbour** *etc*.

neighbour ['neɪbə] (*US* **neighbor**) *n* сосе́д*(ка*).

neighbourhood ['neɪbəhud] *n* (*place*) райóн; (*people*) сосéди *mpl*.

neighbourhood watch *n система, при которой сосéди договáриваются смотрéть*

за домáми друг дрýга.
neighbouring ['neɪbərɪŋ] adj сосéдний*.
neighbourly ['neɪbəlɪ] adj доброcосéдский.
neither ['naɪðəʳ] adj ни тот, ни другóй ♦ conj: I didn't move and ~ did John ни я, ни Джон не двúнулись с мéста ♦ pron: ~ of them came ни одúн из них не пришёл, ни тот, ни другóй не пришлú; ~ version is true ни та, ни другáя вéрсия не вернá; ~ ... nor ... ни ..., ни ...; ~ good nor bad ни хорошó, ни плóхо.
neo... ['niːəu] prefix нео....
neolithic [niːəu'lɪθɪk] adj неолитúческий.
neologism [nɪ'ɔlədʒɪzəm] n неологúзм.
neon ['niːɔn] n неóн.
neon light n неóновый свет.
neon sign n неóновая вúвеска.
Nepal [nɪ'pɔːl] n Непáл.
Nepalese [nɛpə'liːz] adj непáльский*.
nephew ['nɛvjuː] n племя́нник.
nepotism ['nɛpətɪzəm] n непотúзм, кумовствó.
Neptune ['nɛptjuːn] n (planet) Нептýн.
nerd [nəːd] n (inf) придýрок*.
nerve [nəːv] n (ANAT) нерв; (courage) вúдержка; (impudence) нáглость f; to have a fit of ~s перенéрвничать (perf); he gets on my ~s он дéйствует мне на нéрвы; she lost her ~ у неё сдáли нéрвы.
nerve centre n (ANAT) нéрвный центр; (fig) мозговóй центр.
nerve gas n нéрвный газ.
nerve-racking ['nəːvrækɪŋ] adj (period) нéрвный; (situation) нервóзный* (нервóзен).
nervous ['nəːvəs] adj нéрвный* (нéрвен); (ANAT) нéрвный; to be or feel ~ нéрвничать (impf).
nervous breakdown n нéрвный срыв.
nervously ['nəːvəslɪ] adv нéрвно.
nervousness ['nəːvəsnɪs] n нéрвность f.
nervous wreck n (inf) комóк нéрвов.
nervy ['nəːvɪ] n нéрвный*.
nest [nɛst] n гнездó* ♦ vi гнездúться* (impf); ~ of tables комплéкт стóликов (вставляющихся одúн в другóй).
nest egg n заначка*.
nestle ['nɛsl] vi (snuggle) приютúться (perf).
nestling ['nɛstlɪŋ] n птенéц*.
net [nɛt] n (fabric) тюль m; (netting, also SPORT) сéтка*; (for fish, game: also fig) сеть* f ♦ adj (COMM) чúстый ♦ vt (fish) ловúть* (поймáть* perf) в сеть; (profit) приносúть* (принестú* perf); (deal, sale) провора́чивать (провернýть perf); ~ of tax пóсле вúчета налóгов; ~ assets нéтто-актúвы; he earns ten thousand ~ per year он зарабáтывает чúстыми дéсять тúсяч в год.
netball ['nɛtbɔːl] n нетбóл.
net curtains npl тюлевые занавéски fpl.

Netherlands ['nɛðələndz] npl: the ~ Нидерлáнды pl.
nett [nɛt] adj = **net**.
netting ['nɛtɪŋ] n сéтка*.
nettle ['nɛtl] n крапúва; to grasp the ~ (fig) без промедлéния взя́ться (perf) за дéло.
network ['nɛtwəːk] n сеть* f ♦ vt (RADIO, TV) транслúровать (impf/perf) по разлúчным канáлам; (COMPUT) подключáть (подключúть* perf) к системе.
neuralgia [njuə'rældʒə] n невралгúя.
neurosis [njuə'rəusɪs] n неврóз.
neurological [njuərə'lɔdʒɪkl] n неврологúческий.
neurotic [njuə'rɔtɪk] adj неврастенúчный* (неврастенúчен) ♦ n неврастéник.
neuter ['njuːtəʳ] vt (cat etc) кастрúровать (impf/perf) ♦ adj (LING): ~ noun существúтельное nt adj срéднего рóда.
neutral ['njuːtrəl] adj нейтрáльный* (нейтрáлен) ♦ n (AUT) холостóй ход*.
neutrality [njuː'trælɪtɪ] n нейтралитéт.
neutralize ['njuːtrəlaɪz] vt нейтрализовáть (impf/perf).
neutron ['njuːtrɔn] n нейтрóн.
neutron bomb n нейтрóнная бóмба.
Neva ['niːvə] n: the ~ Невá.
never ['nɛvəʳ] adv никогдá; ~ in my life никогдá в жúзни; ~ again бóльше никогдá; I ~ went я не ходúл; see also **mind**.
never-ending [nɛvər'ɛndɪŋ] adj несконча́емый (несконча́ем).
nevertheless [nɛvəðə'lɛs] adv тем не мéнее.
new [njuː] adj (brand new) нóвый* (нов); (recent) недáвний*; I'm ~ to this business я в э́том дéле новичóк; as good as ~ совсéм как нóвый.
New Age adj (PHILOSOPHY) филосóфская система, базúрующаяся на вéре в альтернатúвную медицúну, астролóгию итп; ~ ~ (music) тип мýзыки, включáющий элемéнты джáза, нарóдной и класúческой мýзыки.
newborn ['njuːbɔːn] adj новорóжденный.
newcomer ['njuːkʌməʳ] n новичóк*.
newfangled ['njuːfæŋgld] adj (pej) новомóдный* (новомóден).
new-found ['njuːfaund] adj недáвно обретённый.
Newfoundland ['njuːfənlənd] n Нью-фáундлéнд.
New Guinea n Нóвая Гвинéя.
newly ['njuːlɪ] adv недáвно.
newlyweds ['njuːlɪwɛdz] npl новобрáчные pl adj.
new moon n молодóй мéсяц; (time) новолýние.
newness ['njuːnɪs] n новизнá.

New Orleans [-'ɔ:li:ənz] *n* Но́вый Орлеа́н.
news [nju:z] *n* (*good, bad*) но́вость* *f*,
изве́стие; **a piece of** ~ но́вость*; **the** ~ (*RADIO,
TV*) но́вости *fpl*; **what's the** ~? каки́е
но́вости?; **financial** ~ фина́нсовые но́вости*.
news agency *n* информацио́нное аге́нтство.
newsagent ['nju:zeɪdʒənt] *n* (*BRIT: also:* ~'s) ≈
газе́тный кио́ск; (*person*) владе́лец*(-лица)
газе́тного кио́ска.
news bulletin *n* сво́дка* новосте́й.
newscaster ['nju:zkɑːstə^r] *n* ди́ктор
(*програ́ммы новосте́й*).
newsdealer ['nju:zdi:lə^r] *n* (*US*) = **newsagent**.
newsflash ['nju:zflæʃ] *n* э́кстренное
сообще́ние.
newsletter ['nju:zlɛtə^r] *n* информацио́нный
бюллете́нь *m*.
newspaper ['nju:zpeɪpə^r] *n* газе́та; **daily/
weekly** ~ ежедне́вная/еженеде́льная газе́та.
newsprint ['nju:zprɪnt] *n* (*paper*) газе́тная
бума́га.
newsreader ['nju:zri:də^r] *n* = **newscaster**.
newsreel ['nju:zri:l] *n* информацио́нный
киножурна́л.
newsroom ['nju:zru:m] *n* (*PRESS*) отде́л
новосте́й; (*RADIO, TV*) сту́дия новосте́й.
newsstand ['nju:zstænd] *n* газе́тный кио́ск.
newsworthy ['nju:zwə:ðɪ] *adj* досто́йный*
(досто́ен) интере́са.
newt [nju:t] *n* трито́н.
new town *n* но́вый го́род*.
New Year *n* Но́вый год*; **Happy** ~~! С
Но́вым го́дом!; **to wish sb a Happy** ~~ (*for
the festive season*) поздравля́ть
(поздра́вить* *perf*) кого́-н с Но́вым го́дом;
(*for the coming year*) жела́ть (пожела́ть *perf*)
кому́-н счастли́вого но́вого го́да.
New Year's Day *n* пе́рвое января́.
New Year's Eve *n* кану́н Но́вого го́да.
New York [-'jɔ:k] *n* Нью-Йо́рк.
New Zealand [-'zi:lənd] *n* Но́вая Зела́ндия ♦
adj новозела́ндский*.
New Zealander [-'zi:ləndə^r] *n*
новозела́ндец*(-дка*).
next [nɛkst] *adj* сле́дующий*; (*neighbouring*)
сосе́дний* ♦ *adv* пото́м, зате́м ♦ *prep*: ~ **to**
ря́дом с +*instr*, во́зле +*gen*; ~ **time** в
сле́дующий* раз; **the** ~ **day** на сле́дующий*
день; **the** ~ **week** на сле́дующей неде́ле; **the
week after** ~ че́рез неде́лю; ~ **year** в
бу́дущем *or* сле́дующем году́; **in the** ~ **15
minutes** в ближа́йшие 15 мину́т; ~ **to
nothing** почти́ ничего́; ~ **please!** сле́дующий,
пожа́луйста!; **who's** ~? кто сле́дующий?;
"**turn to the** ~ **page**" "переверни́те
страни́цу"; **when do we meet** ~? когда́ мы
сно́ва встре́тимся?
next door *adv* по сосе́дству, ря́дом ♦ *adj* (*flat,
house*) сосе́дний*; ~~ **neighbour**
ближа́йший* сосе́д*.
next of kin *n* ближа́йший* ро́дственник.

NF *n abbr* (*BRIT: POL:* = *National Front*) НФ=
Национа́льный фронт ♦ *abbr* (*CANADA*) =
Newfoundland.
NFL *n abbr* (*US*) = *National Football League*.
NG *abbr* (*US*) = **National Guard**.
NGO *n abbr* (*US:* = *non-governmental
organization*) неправи́тельственная
организа́ция.
NH *abbr* (*US: POST*) = *New Hampshire*.
NHL *n abbr* (*US:* = *National Hockey League*)
НХЛ= *Национа́льная хокке́йная ли́га*.
NHS *n abbr* (*BRIT*) = **National Health Service**.
NI *abbr* = **Northern Ireland**; (*BRIT*) = **National
Insurance**.
Niagara Falls [naɪ'ægərə-] *npl*: **the** ~~
Ниага́рский водопа́д *msg*.
nib [nɪb] *n* перо́*.
nibble ['nɪbl] *vt* надку́сывать (надкуси́ть* *perf*)
♦ *vi*: **to** ~ **at** (*mice*) грызть* (*impf*); (*at grass*)
щипа́ть* (*impf*).
NICAM *n abbr* = *near-instantaneous companding
system*: ~ **stereo** систе́ма стереозвуча́ния.
Nicaragua [nɪkə'rægjuə] *n* Никара́гуа *f ind*.
Nicaraguan [nɪkə'rægjuən] *adj*
никарагуа́нский* ♦ *n* никарагуа́нец*(-нка*).
Nice [ni:s] *n* Ни́цца.
nice [naɪs] *adj* прия́тный* (прия́тен), хоро́ший*
(хоро́ш); (*attractive*) симпати́чный*
(симпати́чен); **to look** ~ хорошо́ вы́глядеть*
(*impf*); **that's very** ~ **of you** о́чень ми́ло с
ва́шей стороны́.
nicely ['naɪslɪ] *adv* прия́тно, хорошо́; **that will
do** ~ э́то вполне́ подойдёт.
niceties ['naɪsɪtɪz] *npl* то́нкости *fpl*.
niche [ni:ʃ] *n* (*also fig*) ни́ша.
nick [nɪk] *n* (*in skin*) поре́з; (*in surface*) зару́бка*
♦ *vt* (*inf: steal*) переть* (спереть* *perf*); (: *BRIT:
arrest*) ца́пать (сца́пать *perf*); (*cut*): **to** ~ **o.s.**
поре́заться* (*perf*); **in the** ~ **of time** как раз
во́время; **in good** ~ (*BRIT: inf: condition*) в
хоро́шем состоя́нии.
nickel ['nɪkl] *n* ни́кель *m*; (*US: coin*) моне́та в 5
це́нтов.
nickname ['nɪkneɪm] *n* кли́чка*, про́звище ♦ *vt*
прозыва́ть (прозва́ть* *perf*).
Nicosia [nɪkə'si:ə] *n* Никоси́я.
nicotine ['nɪkəti:n] *n* никоти́н.
niece [ni:s] *n* племя́нница.
nifty ['nɪftɪ] *adj* (*inf: car, jacket*) сти́льный*
(сти́лен); (: *gadget, tool*) ло́вко
приду́манный (приду́ман).
Niger ['naɪdʒə^r] *n* Ни́гер.
Nigeria [naɪ'dʒɪərɪə] *n* Ниге́рия.
Nigerian [naɪ'dʒɪərɪən] *adj* нигери́йский* ♦ *n*
нигери́ец(-и́йка).
niggardly ['nɪgədlɪ] *adj* (*person*) ска́редный;
(*amount*) ску́дный.
nigger [nɪgə^r] *n* (*inf!*) чернома́зый(-ая) *m(f) adj*
(*!*)
niggle ['nɪgl] *vt* задева́ть (заде́ть* *perf*) ♦ *vi* (*find
fault*) придира́ться (придра́ться* *perf*).

niggling ['nɪglɪŋ] *adj* (*trifling*) придирчивый (придирчив); (*annoying*) навязчивый (навязчив).

night [naɪt] *n* ночь* *f*; (*evening*) вечер*; **at ~, by ~** ночью; **all ~ long** всю ночь напролёт; **in** *or* **during the ~** ночью; **last ~** вчера ночью; (*evening*) вчера вечером; **the ~ before last** позапрошлой ночью; (*evening*) позавчера вечером.

nightcap ['naɪtkæp] *n* (*drink*) стаканчик на ночь.

nightclub ['naɪtklʌb] *n* ночной клуб.

nightdress ['naɪtdrɛs] *n* ночная рубашка*.

nightfall ['naɪtfɔ:l] *n* сумерки* *pl*.

nightgown ['naɪtgaun] *n* = **nightdress**.

nightie ['naɪtɪ] *n* (*inf*) = **nightdress**.

nightingale ['naɪtɪŋgeɪl] *n* соловей*.

nightlife ['naɪtlaɪf] *n* ночная жизнь *f*.

nightly ['naɪtlɪ] *adj* (*every night*) еженощный; (*by night*) ночной ♦ *adv* еженощно.

nightmare ['naɪtmɛəʳ] *n* (*also fig*) кошмар.

nightmarish ['naɪtmɛərɪʃ] *adj* кошмарный*.

night porter *n* ночной портье *m ind*.

night safe *n* ночной сейф (*в банке*).

night school *n* вечерняя школа.

nightshade ['naɪtʃeɪd] *n*: **deadly ~** белладонна, красавка.

night shift *n* ночная смена.

night-time ['naɪttaɪm] *n* ночное время* *nt*.

night watchman *n* ночной сторож*.

nihilism ['naɪɪlɪzəm] *n* нигилизм.

nil [nɪl] *n* нуль* *m*; (*BRIT: SPORT*) ноль* *m* ♦ *cpd* нулевой.

Nile [naɪl] *n*: **the ~** Нил.

nimble ['nɪmbl] *adj* (*agile*) проворный* (проворен); (*alert*) сообразительный* (сообразителен).

nine [naɪn] *n* девять*; *see also* **five**.

nineteen ['naɪn'ti:n] *n* девятнадцать*; *see also* **five**.

nineteenth ['naɪn'ti:nθ] *adj* девятнадцатый; *see also* **fifth**.

ninetieth ['naɪntɪɪθ] *adj* девяностый; *see also* **fifth**.

ninety ['naɪntɪ] *n* девяносто*; *see also* **fifty**.

ninth [naɪnθ] *adj* девятый; *see also* **fifth**.

nip [nɪp] *vt* (*pinch*) щипать* (ущипнуть *perf*); (*bite*) кусать* (*impf*) ♦ *n* (*pinch*) щипок*; (*bite*) укус; (*drink*) рюмочка* ♦ *vi* (*BRIT: inf*): **to ~ out** выскакивать (выскочить *perf*); **to ~ into a shop** заскакивать (заскочить *perf*) в магазин.

nipple ['nɪpl] *n* (*ANAT*) сосок*; (*TECH*) ниппель* *m*.

nippy ['nɪpɪ] *adj* (*BRIT: inf*) проворный* (проворен); (: *weather*) холодноватый (холодноват).

nit [nɪt] *n* (*in hair*) гнида; (*BRIT: inf: idiot*) олух.

nit-pick ['nɪtpɪk] *vi* (*inf*) придираться (придраться* *perf*).

nitrogen ['naɪtrədʒən] *n* азот.

nitroglycerin(e) ['naɪtrəu'glɪsəri:n] *n* нитроглицерин.

nitty-gritty ['nɪtɪ'grɪtɪ] *n* (*inf*): **to get down to the ~** переходить* (перейти* *perf*) к сути дела.

nitwit ['nɪtwɪt] *n* (*inf*) олух.

Nizhni Novgorod ['nɪʒnij 'nɔvgərət] *n* Нижний Новгород.

NJ *abbr* (*US: POST*) = **New Jersey**.

NLF *n abbr* (= *National Liberation Front*) ФНО= Фронт национального освобождения.

NLQ *abbr* (*COMPUT, TYP*: = *near letter quality*) повышенное качество печати.

NLRB *n abbr* (*US*) = **National Labor Relations Board**.

NM *abbr* (*US: POST*) = **New Mexico**.

KEYWORD

no [nəu] (*pl* **noes**) *adv* (*opposite of "yes"*) нет; **are you coming? – no (I'm not)** Вы придёте? -нет(, не приду); **no thank you** нет, спасибо
♦ *adj* (*not any*): **I have no money/time/books** у меня нет денег/времени/книг; **there is no bread left** хлеб кончился; **there is no one here** здесь никого нет; **it is of no importance at all** это не имеет никакого значения; **no system is totally fair** никакая система не является полностью справедливой; **"no entry"** "вход воспрещён"; **"no smoking"** "не курить"
♦ *n*: **there were twenty noes** двадцать (человек) были "против".

no. *abbr* = **number**.

nobble ['nɔbl] *vt* (*BRIT: inf: bribe*) покупать (купить* *perf*); (: *to speak to*) подлавливать (подловить* *perf*); (: *RACING*) портить* (испортить* *perf*).

Nobel Prize [nəu'bɛl-] *n* Нобелевская премия.

nobility [nəu'bɪlɪtɪ] *n* (*social class*) знать *f*, дворянство; (*quality*) благородство.

noble ['nəubl] *adj* (*aristocratic*) дворянский; (*high-minded*) благородный* (благороден); (*impressive*) величавый (величав).

nobleman ['nəublmən] *irreg n* дворянин*.

noblewoman ['nəublwumən] *irreg n* дворянка*.

nobly ['nəublɪ] *adv* (*behave, act*) благородно.

nobody ['nəubədɪ] *pron* никто*.

no-claim(s) bonus ['nəukleɪmz-] *n* (*INSURANCE*) скидка со следующей страховой премии (*предоставляется страхователю в случае отсутствия страховых претензий в предыдущем году*).

nocturnal [nɔk'tə:nl] *adj* ночной.

nod [nɔd] *vi* (*gesture*) кивать (*impf*); (*doze*) клевать* (*impf*) носом ♦ *n* кивок* ♦ *vt*: **to ~ one's head** кивать (*impf*) головой; **they ~ded their agreement** они кивнули в знак

---

* marks translations which have irregular inflections. The Russian-English side of the dictionary gives inflectional information.

согла́сия

▶ **nod off** *vi* задрема́ть* *(perf)*.

no-fly zone [nəu'flaɪ-] *n* запре́тная возду́шная зо́на.

noise [nɔɪz] *n* шум.

noiseless ['nɔɪzlɪs] *adj* бесшу́мный* (бесшу́мен).

noisily ['nɔɪzɪlɪ] *adv* шу́мно.

noisy ['nɔɪzɪ] *adj* шу́мный* (шу́мен).

nomad ['nəumæd] *n* коче́вник(-ица).

nomadic [nəu'mædɪk] *adj* кочево́й.

no-man's-land ['nəumænzlænd] *n* (MIL) ниче́йная полоса́; *(fig)* тума́нность *f*.

nominal ['nɔmɪnl] *adj* номина́льный* (номина́лен); *(value)* номина́льный.

nominate ['nɔmɪneɪt] *vt (propose)*: **to ~ sb (for)** выставля́ть (вы́ставить* *perf)* кандидату́ру кого́-н (на +*acc*); *(appoint)*: **to ~ sb (to/as)** назнача́ть (назна́чить *perf)* кого́-н (на +*acc*/ +*instr*).

nomination [nɔmɪ'neɪʃən] *n* (*see vb*) выставле́ние; назначе́ние.

nominee [nɔmɪ'niː] *n* кандида́т.

non... [nɔn] *prefix* не....

nonalcoholic [nɔnælkə'hɔlɪk] *adj (drink)* безалкого́льный* (безалкого́лен).

nonaligned *adj* неприсоедини́вшийся.

nonbreakable [nɔn'breɪkəbl] *adj* небью́щийся.

nonce word ['nɔns-] *n* окказионали́зм.

nonchalant ['nɔnʃələnt] *adj* беспе́чный* (беспе́чен).

noncommissioned officer [nɔnkə'mɪʃənd-] *n* у́нтер-офице́р.

noncommittal [nɔnkə'mɪtl] *adj* укло́нчивый (укло́нчив).

nonconformist [nɔnkən'fɔːmɪst] *n* нон-конформи́ст(ка*); *(BRIT: REL)*: **N~** нон-конформи́ст(ка) ◆ *adj* нонконформи́стский.

non-contributory pension scheme *n* пенсио́нные схе́мы, по кото́рым рабо́тники не должны́ де́лать регуля́рных взно́сов.

noncooperation ['nɔnkəuɔpə'reɪʃən] *n* отка́з в сотру́дничестве.

nondescript ['nɔndɪskrɪpt] *adj (person, clothing)* невзра́чный* (невзра́чен); *(colour)* небро́ский*.

none [nʌn] *pron (person)* никто́*, ни оди́н*; *(thing)* ничто́*, ни оди́н*; **~ of you** никто́ *or* ни оди́н из Вас; **I've ~ left** у меня́ ничего́ не оста́лось; **~ at all** совсе́м ничего́; **he's ~ the worse for it** ему́ от э́того отню́дь не ху́же.

nonentity [nɔ'nɛntɪtɪ] *n* ничто́жество.

nonessential [nɔnɪ'sɛnʃl] *adj (items)* несуще́ственный (несуще́ствен) ◆ *n*: **~s** несуще́ственные ве́щи *fpl*.

nonetheless ['nʌnðə'lɛs] *adv* тем не ме́нее, всё же.

non-event [nɔnɪ'vɛnt] *n* бессмы́сленное мероприя́тие.

nonexecutive [nɔnɪg'zɛkjutɪv] *adj*: **~ director** дире́ктор* без распоряди́тельных

полномо́чий.

nonexistent [nɔnɪg'zɪstənt] *adj* несущест-ву́ющий.

nonfiction [nɔn'fɪkʃən] *n* документа́льная литерату́ра.

nonflammable [nɔn'flæməbl] *adj* невоспламеня́ющийся*.

nonintervention ['nɔnɪntə'vɛnʃən] *n* невмеша́тельство.

no-no ['nəunəu] *n (inf)* запре́тная те́ма.

non obst. *abbr (notwithstanding*: = *non obstante)* несмотря́ на +*acc*.

no-nonsense [nəu'nɔnsəns] *adj* делово́й.

nonpayment [nɔn'peɪmənt] *n* неупла́та.

nonplussed [nɔn'plʌst] *adj* ошеломлённый (ошеломлён).

non-profit-making [nɔn'prɔfɪtmeɪkɪŋ] *adj*: **~ organization** некомме́рческая организа́ция.

nonsense ['nɔnsəns] *n (rubbish)* ерунда́, чепуха́; **it is ~ to say that ...** говори́ть (сказа́ть* *perf)*, что ... -- про́сто глу́пость.

nonsensical [nɔn'sɛnsɪkl] *adj* бессмы́сленный* (бессмы́слен).

nonshrink [nɔn'ʃrɪŋk] *adj (BRIT)*: **nylon is (a) ~ (fabric)** нейло́н не сади́тся.

nonskid [nɔn'skɪd] *adj* нескользя́щий.

nonsmoker ['nɔn'sməukə*] *n* некуря́щий*(-ая) *m(f) adj*.

nonstarter [nɔn'stɑːtə*] *n* мёртвый но́мер *no pl*.

nonstick ['nɔn'stɪk] *adj* непригора́ющий.

nonstop ['nɔn'stɔp] *adj (conversation)* беспреры́вный* (беспреры́вен); *(flight)* беспоса́дочный; *(train, bus)* иду́щий без остано́вок ◆ *adv (see adj)* беспреры́вно; без поса́дки; без остано́вок.

nontaxable [nɔn'tæksəbl] *adj* необлага́емый (необлага́ем) нало́гом.

non-U *adj abbr (BRIT: inf*: = *non-upper class)* не принадлежа́щий к вы́сшему (социа́льному) кла́ссу.

nonvolatile [nɔn'vɔlətaɪl] *adj*: **~ memory** *(COMPUT)* энергонезави́симая па́мять *f*.

nonvoting [nɔn'vəutɪŋ] *adj*: **~ shares/member** а́кции/член без пра́ва голосова́ния.

non-white ['nɔn'waɪt] *adj (person)* цветно́й ◆ *n*: **non-White** цветно́й(-а́я) *m(f) adj*.

noodles ['nuːdlz] *npl* вермише́ль *fsg*.

nook [nuk] *n*: **in every ~ and cranny** во всех угла́х.

noon [nuːn] *n* по́лдень* *m*.

no-one ['nəuwʌn] *pron* = **nobody**.

noose [nuːs] *n* пе́тля*.

nor [nɔː*] *conj* = **neither** ◆ *adv see* **neither**.

Norf *abbr (BRIT: POST)* = Norfolk.

norm [nɔːm] *n* но́рма.

normal ['nɔːml] *adj* норма́льный* (норма́лен) ◆ *n*: **to return to ~** возвраща́ться (верну́ться *perf)* в норма́льное состоя́ние.

normality [nɔː'mælɪtɪ] *n* норма́льность *f*.

normally ['nɔːməlɪ] *adv (usually)* обы́чно; *(properly)* норма́льно.

Normandy ['nɔ:məndɪ] *n* Норма́ндия.
north [nɔ:θ] *n* се́вер ◆ *adj* се́верный ◆ *adv* (*go*) на се́вер; (*be*) к се́веру.
North Africa *n* Се́верная А́фрика.
North African *adj* североафрика́нский ◆ *n* жи́тель(ница) *m(f)* Се́верной А́фрики.
North America *n* Се́верная Аме́рика.
North American *adj* североамерика́нский ◆ *n* североамерика́нец*(-нка*).
Northants [nɔ:'θænts] *abbr* (*BRIT*: *POST*) = *Northamptonshire*.
northbound ['nɔ:θbaund] *adj* (*traffic, carriageway*) на се́вер; (*platform*) се́верного направле́ния.
Northd *abbr* (*BRIT*: *POST*) = *Northumberland*.
northeast [nɔ:θ'i:st] *n* се́веро-восто́к.
northerly ['nɔ:ðəlɪ] *adj* се́верный.
northern ['nɔ:ðən] *adj* се́верный.
northerner ['nɔ:ðənər] *n* северя́нин*(-я́нка*).
Northern Ireland *n* Се́верная Ирла́ндия.
North Korea *n* Се́верная Коре́я.
North Pole *n* Се́верный по́люс.
North Sea *n* Се́верное мо́ре.
North-Sea oil ['nɔ:θsi:-] *n* нефть *f* Се́верного мо́ря.
northward(s) ['nɔ:θwəd(z)] *adv* к се́веру.
northwest [nɔ:θ'wɛst] *n* се́веро-за́пад.
Norway ['nɔ:weɪ] *n* Норве́гия.
Norwegian [nɔ:'wi:dʒən] *adj* норве́жский* ◆ *n* норве́жец*(-жка*); (*LING*) норве́жский* язы́к*.
nos. *abbr* = *numbers*.
nose [nəuz] *n* нос*; (*sense of smell*) нюх, чутьё ◆ *vi*: **to ~ forward** осторо́жно пробира́ться (пробра́ться* *perf*) вперёд; **he has a ~ for danger/scandal** у него́ нюх на опа́сность/ сканда́л; **to pay through the ~ (for sth)** (*inf*) плати́ть* (заплати́ть* *perf*) втри́дорога (за что-н)
▶ **nose about** *vi* выню́хивать (вы́нюхать *perf*)
▶ **nose around** *vi* = **nose about**.
nosebleed ['nəuzbli:d] *n* носово́е кровоте́чение.
nose dive *n* (круто́е) пики́рование.
nose drops *npl* ка́пли *fpl* для но́са.
nosey ['nəuzɪ] *adj* (*inf*) = **nosy**.
nostalgia [nɔs'tældʒɪə] *n* ностальги́я.
nostalgic [nɔs'tældʒɪk] *adj* (*film, memory*) ностальги́ческий*; (*person*): **to be ~ (for)** испы́тывать (*impf*) ностальги́ю (по +*dat*).
nostril ['nɔstrɪl] *n* ноздря́*.
nosy ['nəuzɪ] *adj* (*inf*): **to be ~** сова́ть* (*impf*) нос в чужи́е дела́.

KEYWORD

not [nɔt] *adv* нет; (*before verbs*) не; **he is not** *or* **isn't at home** его́ нет до́ма; **he asked me not to do it** он попроси́л меня́ не де́лать э́того; **you must not** *or* **you mustn't do that** (*forbidden*) э́того нельзя́ де́лать; (*should not*)

Вы не должны́ э́то де́лать; **it's too late, isn't it?** уже́ сли́шком по́здно, да?; **not that ...** не то, что́бы ...; **not yet** нет ещё, ещё нет; **not now** не сейча́с; *see also* **all, only**.

---

notable ['nəutəbl] *adj* примеча́тельный* (примеча́телен).
notably ['nəutəblɪ] *adv* (*particularly*) осо́бенно; (*markedly*) заме́тно.
notary ['nəutərɪ] *n* (*also:* **~ public**) нота́риус.
notation [nəu'teɪʃən] *n* (*MUS etc*) нота́ция.
notch [nɔtʃ] *n* (*on the edge*) зазу́брина; (*on the surface*) вы́емка*
▶ **notch up** *vt* (*victory*) добива́ться (доби́ться* *perf*) +*instr*; (*score*) набира́ть (набра́ть* *perf*).
note [nəut] *n* (*record*) за́пись *f*; (*letter*) запи́ска*; (*also:* **footnote**) примеча́ние; (*also:* **banknote**) банкно́та; (*MUS*) но́та; (*tone*) тон ◆ *vt* (*observe*) замеча́ть (заме́тить* *perf*); (*also:* **~ down**) запи́сывать (записа́ть* *perf*); **of ~** примеча́тельный (примеча́телен).
notebook ['nəutbuk] *n* записна́я кни́жка; (*exercise book*) тетра́дь *f*.
notecase ['nəutkeɪs] *n* (*BRIT*) бума́жник.
noted ['nəutɪd] *adj* изве́стный* (изве́стен).
notepad ['nəutpæd] *n* блокно́т.
notepaper ['nəutpeɪpər] *n* пи́счая бума́га.
noteworthy ['nəutwə:ðɪ] *adj* досто́йный* (досто́ен) внима́ния; **it is ~ that** ... досто́йно внима́ния что ....
nothing ['nʌθɪŋ] *n* ничто́*; (*zero*) ноль *m*; **he does ~** он ничего́ не де́лает; **there is ~ to do/be said** де́лать/сказа́ть не́чего; **~ new/ much/of the sort** ничего́ но́вого/осо́бенного/ подо́бного; **for ~** да́ром; **think ~ of it!, it was ~!** не́ за что!; **~ like as ... as ...** совсе́м не так ..., как ...; **to say ~ of ...** не говоря́ уже́ о +*prp* ...; **it has ~ to do with you** э́то Вас не каса́ется.
notice ['nəutɪs] *n* (*announcement*) объявле́ние; (*official letter, circular*) уведомле́ние, извеще́ние; (*warning*) предупрежде́ние; (*BRIT*: *review*) о́тзыв ◆ *vt* замеча́ть (заме́тить* *perf*); **to take ~ of** обраща́ть (обрати́ть* *perf*) внима́ние на +*acc*; **to bring sth to sb's ~** (*attention*) обраща́ть (обрати́ть* *perf*) внима́ние кого́-н на что-н; **to escape** *or* **avoid ~** остава́ться* (оста́ться* *perf*) незаме́ченным; **it has come to my ~ that** ... мне ста́ло изве́стно, что ...; **to hand in one's ~** подава́ть (пода́ть* *perf*) заявле́ние об ухо́де с рабо́ты; **he was given 2 weeks ~** его́ предупреди́ли, что он бу́дет уво́лен че́рез 2 неде́ли; **advance ~** заблаговре́менное предупрежде́ние; **without ~** без предупрежде́ния; **at short ~** без предупрежде́ния; **until further ~** впредь до дальне́йшего уведомле́ния.

---

* marks translations which have irregular inflections. The Russian-English side of the dictionary gives inflectional information.

noticeable ['nəutɪsəbl] *adj* заме́тный* (заме́тен).

notice board *n* (*BRIT*) доска́* объявле́ний.

notification [nəutɪfɪ'keɪʃən] *n* уведомле́ние.

notify ['nəutɪfaɪ] *vt*: **to ~ sb (of sth)** уведомля́ть (уведо́мить* *perf*) кого́-н (о чём-н).

notion ['nəuʃən] *n* (*idea*) поня́тие; (*opinion*) представле́ние; **~s** *npl* (*US*: *haberdashery*) галантере́я *fsg*.

notoriety [nəutə'raɪətɪ] *n* дурна́я сла́ва.

notorious [nə'tɔ:rɪəs] *adj* (*criminal, liar*) изве́стен* (изве́стен); (*place*) печа́льно изве́стный* (изве́стен).

notoriously [nə'tɔ:rɪəslɪ] *adv*: **she is ~ unreliable** у неё дурна́я сла́ва ненадёжного челове́ка; **this word is ~ difficult to translate** э́то сло́во изве́стно тем, что его́ тру́дно перевести́.

Notts [nɔts] *abbr* (*BRIT*: *POST*) = **Nottinghamshire.**

notwithstanding [nɔtwɪθ'stændɪŋ] *adv* тем не ме́нее ♦ *prep* несмотря́ на +*acc*.

nougat ['nu:gɑ:] *n* нуга́.

nought [nɔ:t] *n* ноль* *m*.

noun [naun] *n* (и́мя* *nt*) существи́тельное *nt adj*.

nourish ['nʌrɪʃ] *vt* (*feed*) пита́ть (*impf*); (*fig*: *foster*) взра́щивать (взрасти́ть* *perf*).

nourishing ['nʌrɪʃɪŋ] *adj* пита́тельный* (пита́телен).

nourishment ['nʌrɪʃmənt] *n* (*food*) пита́ние.

Nov. *abbr* = **November.**

Nova Scotia ['nəuvə'skəuʃə] *n* Но́вая Шотла́ндия.

Novaya Zemlya ['nɔvəjə zɪm'lja] *n* Но́вая Земля́.

novel ['nɔvl] *n* рома́н ♦ *adj* оригина́льный* (оригина́лен).

novelist ['nɔvəlɪst] *n* романи́ст(ка*).

novelty ['nɔvəltɪ] *n* (*newness*) новизна́; (*object*) нови́нка*.

November [nəu'vɛmbəʳ] *n* ноя́брь* *m*; *see also* **July.**

novice ['nɔvɪs] *n* новичо́к*; (*REL*) по́слушник(-ица).

Novosibirsk [nɔvəsɪ'bɪrsk] *n* Новосиби́рск.

NOW [nau] *n abbr* (*US*) = **National Organization for Women.**

now [nau] *adv* тепе́рь, сейча́с ♦ *conj*: **~ (that)** ... тепе́рь, когда́ ...; **right ~** пря́мо сейча́с; **by ~** к настоя́щему вре́мени; **~ and then** *or* **again** вре́мя от вре́мени; **from ~ on** впредь; **until ~** до сих пор; **that's the fashion just ~** э́то сейча́с в мо́де; **I saw her just ~** я то́лько что её ви́дел; **in 3 days from ~** че́рез 3 дня; **between ~ and Monday** ме́жду сего́дняшним днём и понеде́льником; **that's all for ~** пока́ всё.

nowadays ['nauədeɪz] *adv* в на́ши дни.

nowhere ['nəuwɛəʳ] *adv* (*be*) нигде́; (*go*) никуда́; **~ else** (*be*) бо́льше нигде́; (*go*) бо́льше никуда́; **I have ~ else to go** мне бо́льше не́куда идти́.

no-win situation [nəu'wɪn-] *n* безвы́игрышное положе́ние.

noxious ['nɔkʃəs] *adj* вредоно́сный; (*smell*) проти́вный* (проти́вен).

nozzle ['nɔzl] *n* (*TECH*) сопло́*; (*of hose, vacuum cleaner*) наса́дка*; (*of fire extinguisher*) брандспо́йт.

NP *n abbr* (*LAW*) = **notary public.**

NS *abbr* (*CANADA*) = **Nova Scotia.**

NSC *n abbr* (*US*: = **National Security Council**) Сове́т национа́льной безопа́сности.

NSF *n abbr* (*US*) = **National Science Foundation.**

NSPCC *n abbr* (*BRIT*) = **National Society for the Prevention of Cruelty to Children.**

NSW *abbr* (*AUSTRALIA*) = **New South Wales.**

NT *n abbr* (*BIBLE*: = **New Testament**) Но́вый заве́т.

nth [enθ] *adj*: **for the ~ time** (*inf*) в э́нный раз.

nuance ['nju:ɑ̃:ns] *n* нюа́нс.

nubile ['nju:baɪl] *adj* (*woman*) зре́лый*; (*attractive*) прельсти́тельный*.

nuclear ['nju:klɪəʳ] *adj* я́дерный.

nuclear disarmament *n* я́дерное разоруже́ние.

nuclear-free zone ['nju:klɪə'fri:-] *n* внея́дерная зо́на.

nuclear reactor *n* я́дерный реа́ктор.

nuclei ['nju:klɪaɪ] *npl of* **nucleus.**

nucleus ['nju:klɪəs] (*pl* **nuclei**) *n* (*also fig*) ядро́*.

NUCPS *n abbr* (*BRIT*) = **National Union of Civil and Public Servants.**

nude [nju:d] *adj* обнажённый (обнажён), наго́й* (наг) ♦ *n* обнажённая фигу́ра; **in the ~** в обнажённом ви́де.

nudge [nʌdʒ] *vt* подта́лкивать (подтолкну́ть* *perf*).

nudist ['nju:dɪst] *n* нуди́ст(ка*).

nudist colony *n* коло́ния нуди́стов.

nudity ['nju:dɪtɪ] *n* нагота́.

nugget ['nʌgɪt] *n* (*of gold*) саморо́док*; **~ of information** це́нная информа́ция.

nuisance ['nju:sns] *n* (*state of affairs, thing*) доса́да; (*person*) доку́чливый челове́к*; **what a ~!** кака́я доса́да!; **that noise is a real ~** э́тот шум си́льно раздража́ет; **he is a real ~** он о́чень надое́дливый.

NUJ *n abbr* (*BRIT*) = **National Union of Journalists.**

nuke [nju:k] *n* (*inf*) я́дерное ору́жие.

null [nʌl] *adj*: **to be ~ and void** потеря́ть (*perf*) зако́нную си́лу.

nullify ['nʌlɪfaɪ] *vt* (*efforts*) своди́ть* (свести́* *perf*) к нулю́; (*LAW*) аннули́ровать (*impf/perf*).

NUM *n abbr* (*BRIT*) = **National Union of Mineworkers.**

numb [nʌm] *adj*: **~ (with)** онеме́вший (от +*gen*) ♦ *vt*: **the cold ~ed his fingers** его́ па́льцы онеме́ли от хо́лода; **to go ~** онеме́ть (*perf*).

number ['nʌmbəʳ] *n* но́мер*; (*MATH*) число́*; (*written figure*) ци́фра; (*quantity*) коли́чество ♦ *vt* (*pages etc*) нумерова́ть (пронумерова́ть

perf); (*amount to*) насчи́тывать (*impf*); **a ~ of**
не́сколько +*gen*; **in a ~ of cases** в ря́де
слу́чаев; **they were ten in ~** их бы́ло де́сять;
you've got the wrong ~ (*TEL*) Вы не туда́
попа́ли; **he is ~ed among ...** его́ причисля́ют
к +*dat* ...; **~ed (bank) account** номерно́й счёт в
ба́нке.
numberplate ['nʌmbəpleɪt] *n* (*BRIT*: *AUT*)
номерно́й знак.
Number Ten *n* (*BRIT*: *also:* ~ ~ **Downing Street**)
но́мер 10 по Да́унинг Стри́т (*резиде́нция
премье́р-мини́стра*).
numbness ['nʌmnɪs] *n* (*due to cold*) онеме́ние;
(*due to fear, shock*) оцепене́ние.
numbskull ['nʌmskʌl] *n* (*inf*) тупи́ца *m/f*.
numeral ['njuːmərəl] *n* ци́фра.
numerate ['njuːmərɪt] *adj* (*BRIT*): **to be ~** знать
(*impf*) арифме́тику.
numerical [njuː'mɛrɪkl] *adj* (*value*) числово́й;
(*superiority*) чи́сленный; (*data*) цифрово́й; **in
~ order** по номера́м.
numerous ['njuːmərəs] *adj* многочи́сленный
(многочи́слен); **on ~ occasions** много-
кра́тно.
nun [nʌn] *n* мона́хиня.
nunnery ['nʌnərɪ] *n* же́нский* монасты́рь *m*.
nuptial ['nʌpʃəl] *adj* бра́чный.
nurse [nəːs] *n* медсестра́*; (*also:* **male ~**)
медбра́т; (*also:* **~maid**) ня́ня ♦ *vt* (*patient*)
уха́живать (*impf*) за +*instr*; (*desire, also BRIT*:
cuddle) леле́ять (взлеле́ять *perf*); (*grudge*)
таи́ть (*impf*); (*US*: *suckle*) корми́ть (*impf*)
гру́дью; **to ~ a cold** сиде́ть* (*impf*) до́ма с
просту́дой.
nursery ['nəːsərɪ] *n* (*institution*) я́сли* *pl*; (*room*)
де́тская *f adj*; (*for plants*) пито́мник.
nursery rhyme *n* пе́сенка для дете́й.
nursery school *n* де́тский* сад*.
nursery slope *n* (*BRIT*) спуск для начина́ющих
лы́жников.
nursing ['nəːsɪŋ] *n* (*profession*) профе́ссия

медсестры́; (*care*) ухо́д.
nursing home *n* ча́стный дом* (*для
престаре́лых*).
nursing mother *n* кормя́щая мать* *f*.
nurture ['nəːtʃə] *vt* (*child, plant*) выра́щивать
(вы́растить* *perf*).
NUS *n abbr* (*BRIT*) = *National Union of Students*.
NUT *n abbr* (*BRIT*) = *National Union of Teachers*.
nut [nʌt] *n* (*BOT*) оре́х; (*TECH*) га́йка; (*inf*) =
nutcase.
nutcase ['nʌtkeɪs] *n* (*inf*) псих.
nutcrackers ['nʌtkrækəz] *npl* щипцы́* *pl* для
оре́хов.
nutmeg ['nʌtmɛg] *n* муска́тный оре́х.
nutrient ['njuːtrɪənt] *n* пита́тельное вещество́.
nutrition [njuː'trɪʃən] *n* (*diet*) пита́ние;
(*nourishment*) пита́тельность *f*.
nutritionist [njuː'trɪʃənɪst] *n* дието́лог.
nutritious [njuː'trɪʃəs] *adj* пита́тельный*
(пита́телен).
nuts [nʌts] (*inf*) *adj*: **he's ~** он чо́кнутый; **to be
~ about sb** с ума́ сходи́ть* (*impf*) по кому́-н.
nutshell ['nʌtʃɛl] *n* оре́ховая скорлупа́*; **in a ~**
(*fig*) в двух слова́х.
nutty ['nʌtɪ] *adj* (*flavour*) похо́жий* (по вку́су)
на оре́хи; (*inf*: *person*) чо́кнутый (чо́кнут);
(*idea*) бредо́вый.
nuzzle ['nʌzl] *vi*: **to ~ up to** тере́ться*
(потере́ться* *perf*) но́сом о +*acc*.
NV *abbr* (*US*: *POST*) = *Nevada*.
NWT *abbr* (*CANADA*) = *Northwest Territories*.
NY *abbr* (*US*: *POST*) = *New York*.
NYC *abbr* (*US*: *POST*) = *New York City*.
nylon ['naɪlən] *n* нейло́н ♦ *adj* нейло́новый; **~s**
npl нейло́новые чулки́* *mpl*.
nymph [nɪmf] *n* (*MYTHOLOGY*) ни́мфа; (*ZOOL*)
личи́нка*.
nymphomaniac ['nɪmfəu'meɪnɪæk] *n*
нимфома́нка*.
NYSE *n abbr* (*US*) = *New York Stock Exchange*.
NZ *abbr* = *New Zealand*.

---

* marks translations which have irregular inflections. The Russian-English side of the dictionary gives inflectional information.

~ O, o ~

O, o [əu] n (letter) 15-ая бу́ква англи́йского алфави́та; (number: TEL etc) ноль* m.
O abbr = outstanding; (US: SCOL) ≈ отл.= отли́чно.
oaf [əuf] n чурба́н, дуби́на m/f.
oak [əuk] n дуб* ♦ adj дубо́вый.
O & M n abbr = organization and method.
OAP n abbr (BRIT) = old age pensioner.
oar [ɔ:ʳ] n весло́*; **to put** or **shove one's ~ in** (fig: inf) встрева́ть (встрять* perf).
oarsman ['ɔ:zmən] n гребе́ц*.
OAS n abbr = Organization of American States.
oases [əu'eɪsi:z] npl of **oasis**.
oasis [əu'eɪsɪs] (pl **oases**) n (also fig) оа́зис.
oath [əuθ] n (promise) кля́тва; (: LAW) прися́га; (swear word) прокля́тие; **on** (BRIT) or **under ~** под прися́гой; **to take the ~** принима́ть (приня́ть* perf) прися́гу.
oatmeal ['əutmi:l] n овся́ная мука́.
oats [əuts] npl овёс*.
OAU n abbr = Organization of African Unity.
obdurate ['ɔbdjurɪt] adj непрекло́нный* (непрекло́нен).
OBE n abbr (BRIT: = Order of the British Empire) о́рден Брита́нской импе́рии.
obedience [ə'bi:dɪəns] n повинове́ние, послуша́ние; **in ~ to** повину́ясь +dat.
obedient [ə'bi:dɪənt] adj послу́шный* (послу́шен); **to be ~ to sb/sth** слу́шаться (послу́шаться perf) кого́-н/чего́-н.
obelisk ['ɔbɪlɪsk] n обели́ск.
obese [əu'bi:s] adj ту́чный* (ту́чен).
obesity [əu'bi:sɪtɪ] n ожире́ние, ту́чность f.
obey [ə'beɪ] vt подчиня́ться (подчини́ться perf) +dat, повинова́ться (impf/perf) +dat ♦ vi подчиня́ться (подчини́ться perf), повинова́ться (impf).
obituary [ə'bɪtjuərɪ] n некроло́г.
object [n 'ɔbdʒɪkt, vi əb'dʒɛkt] n (thing) предме́т; (aim, purpose) цель f; (of affection, desires) объе́кт; (LING) дополне́ние ♦ vi: **to ~ (to)** возража́ть (возрази́ть* perf) (про́тив +gen); **expense is no ~** де́ньги – не пробле́ма; **what's the ~ of doing that?** для чего́ де́лать э́то?; **he ~ed that ...** он возрази́л, что ...; **I ~!** я возража́ю!; **do you ~ to my smoking?** Вы не возража́ете е́сли я бу́ду кури́ть?
objection [əb'dʒɛkʃən] n возраже́ние; **I have no ~ to ...** я не име́ю никаки́х возраже́ний про́тив +gen ...; **if you have no ~** е́сли Вы не возража́ете; **to make** or **raise an ~** выдвига́ть (вы́двинуть perf) возраже́ние.
objectionable [əb'dʒɛkʃənəbl] adj (language, conduct) возмути́тельный* (возмути́телен); (person) неприя́тный* (неприя́тен).
objective [əb'dʒɛktɪv] adj объекти́вный* (объекти́вен) ♦ n (aim, purpose) цель f.
objectively [əb'dʒɛktɪvlɪ] adv объекти́вно.
objectivity [ɔbdʒɪk'tɪvɪtɪ] n объекти́вность f.
object lesson n: **an ~ ~ in** нагля́дный приме́р +gen.
objector [əb'dʒɛktəʳ] n протесту́ющий*(-ая) m(f) adj.
obligation [ɔblɪ'geɪʃən] n обяза́тельство; **we are under no ~ to them** мы им ниче́м не обя́заны; **we are under (an) ~ to give him what he needs** мы обя́заны дать ему́ всё, что потре́буется; **"without ~"** (COMM) „без обяза́тельств".
obligatory [ə'blɪgətərɪ] adj обяза́тельный* (обяза́телен).
oblige [ə'blaɪdʒ] vt (do a favour for) обя́зывать (обяза́ть perf); (force): **to ~ sb to do** обя́зывать (обяза́ть* perf) кого́-н +infin; **I'm much ~d to you for your help** (grateful) я о́чень обя́зан Вам за ва́шу по́мощь; **anything to ~!** (inf) (я весь) к ва́шим услу́гам!
obliging [ə'blaɪdʒɪŋ] adj (helpful) любе́зный* (любе́зен).
oblique [ə'bli:k] adj (line) накло́нный; (comment, reference) ко́свенный ♦ n (BRIT: TYP): **~ (stroke)** накло́нная черта́.
obliterate [ə'blɪtəreɪt] vt (destroy) уничтожа́ть (уничто́жить perf); (from mind) стира́ть (стере́ть* perf).
oblivion [ə'blɪvɪən] n забве́ние; **these events have sunk into ~** э́ти собы́тия пре́даны забве́нию.
oblivious [ə'blɪvɪəs] adj: **to be ~ of** or **to** не сознава́ть* (impf) +gen.
oblong ['ɔblɔŋ] adj продолгова́тый ♦ n продолгова́тый предме́т.
obnoxious [əb'nɔkʃəs] adj отврати́тельный* (отврати́телен).
o.b.o. abbr (US: in classified ads: = or best offer) и́ли по договорённости.
oboe ['əubəu] n гобо́й.

333

obscene ~ occupy

obscene [əb'si:n] *adj* непристо́йный*
(непристо́ен).

obscenity [əb'sɛnɪtɪ] *n* непристо́йность *f*.

obscure [əb'skjuəʳ] *adj* (*little known*) мало-
изве́стный* (малоизве́стен); (*difficult to
understand*) нея́сный* (нея́сен), сму́тный*
(сму́тен) ♦ *vt* (*view, sun etc*) загора́живать
(загороди́ть* *perf*); (*truth, meaning etc*)
затемня́ть (затемни́ть *perf*).

obscurity [əb'skjuərɪtɪ] *n* (*see adj*) безве́стность
f; нея́сность *f*.

obsequious [əb'si:kwɪəs] *adj* подобо-
стра́стный* (подобостра́стен).

observable [əb'zə:vəbl] *adj* наблюда́емый;
(*appreciable*) заме́тный* (заме́тен).

observance [əb'zə:vns] *n* (*of law, custom*)
соблюде́ние; **religious ~s** религио́зные
обря́ды.

observant [əb'zə:vnt] *adj* наблюда́тельный*
(наблюда́телен).

observation [ɔbzə'veɪʃən] *n* (*remark*)
замеча́ние; (*surveillance, also* MED)
наблюде́ние.

observation post *n* наблюда́тельный пост* *or*
пункт.

observatory [əb'zə:vətrɪ] *n* обсервато́рия.

observe [əb'zə:v] *vt* (*watch*) наблюда́ть (*impf*)
за +*instr*; (*comment*) замеча́ть (заме́тить*
perf); (*abide by*) соблюда́ть (соблюсти́* *perf*).

observer [əb'zə:vəʳ] *n* наблюда́тель *m*.

obsess [əb'sɛs] *vt* владева́ть (владе́ть *perf*);
you are ~ed by the idea Вы одержи́мы э́той
иде́ей; **he is totally ~ed with this woman** он
соверше́нно поме́шан на э́той же́нщине.

obsession [əb'sɛʃən] *n* навя́зчивая иде́я; **she
has an ~ for cats** она́ поме́шана на ко́шках.

obsessive [əb'sɛsɪv] *adj* одержи́мый
(одержи́м).

obsolescence [ɔbsə'lɛsns] *n* устаре́лость *f*.

obsolete ['ɔbsəli:t] *adj* (*words*) устаре́вший;
(*technology*) устаре́лый.

obstacle ['ɔbstəkl] *n* (*also fig*) препя́тствие.

obstacle race *n* бег с препя́тствиями.

obstetrician [ɔbstə'trɪʃən] *n* врач-акуше́р.

obstetrics [ɔb'stɛtrɪks] *n* акуше́рство.

obstinacy ['ɔbstɪnəsɪ] *n* (*of person*) упря́мство.

obstinate ['ɔbstɪnɪt] *adj* (*person, behaviour*)
упря́мный* (упря́м); (*cold, pain*) упо́рный.

obstruct [əb'strʌkt] *vt* (*road, path*)
загора́живать (загороди́ть* *perf*); (*traffic,
progress*) препя́тствовать
(воспрепя́тствовать *perf*) +*dat*.

obstruction [əb'strʌkʃən] *n* (*action*)
препя́тствование; (: *of law*) обстру́кция;
(*object*) препя́тствие.

obstructive [əb'strʌktɪv] *adj* (*behaviour*)
обструкцио́нный; **he is ~** он чи́нит
препя́тствия.

obtain [əb'teɪn] *vt* (*get hold of*) достава́ть*
(доста́ть* *perf*); (*gain*) получа́ть (получи́ть*
perf) ♦ *vi* (*formal: exist*) существова́ть (*impf*); **to
~ sth (for o.s.)** добива́ться (доби́ться* *perf*)
чего́-н (для себя́).

obtainable [əb'teɪnəbl] *adj* достижи́мый
(достижи́м).

obtrusive [əb'tru:sɪv] *adj* навя́зчивый
(навя́зчив).

obtuse [əb'tju:s] *adj* (*person, remark*)
бестолко́вый (бестолко́в); (MATH) тупо́й.

obverse ['ɔbvə:s] *n*: **the ~** обра́тное *nt adj*.

obviate ['ɔbvɪeɪt] *vt* устраня́ть (устрани́ть
perf).

obvious ['ɔbvɪəs] *adj* очеви́дный* (очеви́ден).

obviously ['ɔbvɪəslɪ] *adv* очеви́дно; (*of course*)
разуме́ется; **he was ~ not drunk** бы́ло
очеви́дно, что он не пьян; **he was not ~
drunk** он не был очеви́дным о́бразом пьян;
~ not разуме́ется, нет.

OCAS *n abbr* = *Organization of Central American
States*.

occasion [ə'keɪʒən] *n* (*time*) раз*; (*case*)
слу́чай; (*event*) собы́тие; (*opportunity*)
возмо́жность *f* ♦ *vt* (*cause*) вызыва́ть
(вы́звать* *perf*); **on this ~** на э́тот раз; **on that
~** в тот раз; **to rise to the ~** ока́зываться
(оказа́ться* *perf*) на высоте́.

occasional [ə'keɪʒənl] *adj* ре́дкий*, неча́стый.

occasionally [ə'keɪʒənəlɪ] *adv* вре́мя от
вре́мени, и́зредка; **very ~** о́чень ре́дко.

occasional table *n* запасно́й сто́лик.

occult [ɔ'kʌlt] *n*: **the ~** окку́льтные нау́ки *fpl*.

occupancy ['ɔkjupənsɪ] *n* пребыва́ние.

occupant ['ɔkjupənt] *n* (*long-term*)
обита́тель(ница) *m(f)*; (*temporary*): **the ~s of
the car/room** находя́щиеся *pl adj* в маши́не/
ко́мнате.

occupation [ɔkju'peɪʃən] *n* заня́тие;
(*occupancy*) пребыва́ние; (MIL) оккупа́ция;
unfit for ~ (*house*) неприго́дный*
(неприго́ден) для жилья́.

occupational accident [ɔkju'peɪʃənl-] *n*
произво́дственный несча́стный слу́чай.

occupational guidance *n* (BRIT) консульта́ция
по по́иску ме́ста рабо́ты.

occupational hazard *n* произво́дственный
риск.

occupational pension scheme *n* пенсио́нный
план, по кото́рому пенсио́нный фонд
форми́руется за счёт взно́сов рабо́тника и
его́ работода́теля.

occupational therapy *n* трудотерапи́я.

occupier ['ɔkjupaɪəʳ] *n* прожива́ющий(-ая) *m(f)
adj*; **"to the ~"** „прожива́ющему" (*обраще́ние
в письме́*).

occupy ['ɔkjupaɪ] *vt* занима́ть (заня́ть* *perf*);
(*country, attention*) захва́тывать (захвати́ть*

* marks translations which have irregular inflections. The Russian-English side of the dictionary gives inflectional information.

perf); **to ~ o.s. (with sth)** занима́ться
(заня́ться *perf*) (чем-н); **all of the rooms are
occupied** все ко́мнаты за́няты; **he was
occupied with his work** он был за́нят
рабо́той.

occur [ə'kə:ʳ] *vi* (*take place*) происходи́ть*
(произойти́* *perf*), случа́ться (случи́ться
perf); (*exist*) встреча́ться (встре́титься *perf*);
to ~ to sb приходи́ть* (прийти́* *perf*) кому́-н
в го́лову.

occurrence [ə'kʌrəns] *n* (*event*) происше́ствие;
(*existence*) слу́чай.

ocean ['əuʃən] *n* океа́н; **~s of** (*fig: inf*) мо́ре
+*gen*.

ocean bed *n* дно* океа́на.

ocean-going ['əuʃəngəuɪŋ] *adj* (*ship etc*)
океа́нский.

Oceania [əuʃi'emɪə] *n* Океа́ния.

ocean liner *n* океа́нский ла́йнер.

ochre ['əukəʳ] (*US* **ocher**) *adj* (*colour*) о́хровый.

o'clock [ə'klɔk] *adv*: **it is five ~** сейча́с пять
часо́в.

OCR *n abbr* (*COMPUT*) = **optical character
recognition, optical character reader.**

Oct. *abbr* = **October.**

octagonal [ɔk'tægənl] *adj* восьмиуго́льный.

octane ['ɔkteɪn] *n* окта́н; **high-~ petrol** *or* (*US*)
gas бензи́н с высо́ким окта́новым число́м.

octave ['ɔktɪv] *n* окта́ва.

October [ɔk'təubəʳ] *n* октя́брь* *m*; *see also* **July.**

octogenarian ['ɔktəudʒɪ'nɛərɪən] *n*: **he is an ~**
ему́ за во́семьдесят.

octopus ['ɔktəpəs] *n* осьмино́г.

odd [ɔd] *adj* (*strange*) стра́нный* (стра́нен),
необы́чный* (необы́чен); (*uneven*)
нечётный; (*not paired*) непа́рный; (*rare*)
ре́дкий*; **60-~** шестьдеся́т с ли́шним; **at ~
times** вре́мя от вре́мени; **I was the ~ one out**
я был ли́шний.

oddball ['ɔdbɔ:l] *n* (*inf*) чуда́к*.

oddity ['ɔdɪtɪ] *n* (*thing*) дико́винка; (*person*)
ре́дкость *f*; (*characteristic*) стра́нность *f*.

odd-job man [ɔd'dʒɔb-] *n* разнорабо́чий* *m adj*.

odd jobs *npl* случа́йные рабо́ты *fpl*.

oddly ['ɔdlɪ] *adv* (*strangely: behave, dress*)
стра́нно; *see also* **enough.**

oddments ['ɔdmənts] *npl* оста́тки *mpl*.

odds [ɔdz] *npl* (*in betting*) ста́вки* *fpl*; **the ~ are
against him** обстоя́тельства про́тив него́; **to
succeed against all the ~** добива́ться
(доби́ться* *perf*) успе́ха напереко́р всему́; **it
makes no ~** всё равно́; **to be at ~ (with)** быть*
(*impf*) не в лада́х (с +*instr*).

odds and ends *npl* ме́лочи* *fpl*.

odds-on [ɔdz'ɔn] *adj* (*inf: favourite*)
абсолю́тный; **he is ~ to win the election** он
наверняка́ победи́т на вы́борах.

ode [əud] *n* о́да.

Odessa [əu'dɛsə] *n* Оде́сса.

odious ['əudɪəs] *adj* одио́зный* (одио́зен).

odometer [ɔ'dɒmɪtəʳ] *n* одо́метр.

odour ['əudəʳ] (*US* **odor**) *n* за́пах.

odourless ['əudəlɪs] *adj* без за́паха.

OECD *n abbr* = *Organization for Economic
Cooperation and Development.*

oesophagus [i:'sɔfəgəs] (*US* **esophagus**) *n*
пищево́д.

oestrogen ['i:strəudʒən] (*US* **estrogen**) *n*
эстроге́н.

KEYWORD

---

of [ɔv] *prep*: **1:** **the history of Russia** исто́рия
Росси́и; **a friend of ours** наш друг*; **a boy of 10**
ма́льчик десяти́ лет; **that was kind of you** э́то
бы́ло о́чень любе́зно с ва́шей стороны́; **a
man of great ability** челове́к больши́х
спосо́бностей; **the city of New York** го́род
Нью-Йо́рк; **south of London** к ю́гу от
Ло́ндона

2 (*expressing quantity, amount, dates etc*): **a
kilo of flour** килогра́мм муки́; **how much of
this material do you need?** ско́лько тако́й
тка́ни Вам ну́жно?; **there were three of them**
(*people*) их бы́ло тро́е; (*objects*) их бы́ло
три; **3 of us stayed** тро́е из нас оста́лись; **the
5th of July** 5-ое ию́ля; **on the 5th of July** 5-ого
ию́ля

3 (*from, out of*) из +*gen*; **the house is made of
wood** дом* сде́лан из де́рева.

KEYWORD

---

off [ɔf] *adv* **1** (*referring to distance, time*): **it's a
long way off** э́то далеко́ отсю́да; **the city is
five miles off** до го́рода пять миль; **the game
is 3 days off** до игры́ оста́лось 3 дня́

2 (*departure*): **to go off to Paris/Italy** уезжа́ть
(уе́хать* *perf*) в Пари́ж/Ита́лию; **I must be off**
мне пора́ идти́*

3 (*removal*): **to take off one's hat/coat/clothes**
снима́ть (снять* *perf*) шля́пу/пальто́/оде́жду;
the button came off пу́говица оторвала́сь;
10% off (*COMM*) ски́дка в 10%

4: to be off (*on holiday*) быть (*impf*) в о́тпуске;
I'm off on Fridays у меня́ выходно́й по
пя́тницам; **he was off on Friday** в пя́тницу его́
не́ было на рабо́те; **I have a day off** у меня́
отгу́л; **to be off sick** не рабо́тать (*impf*) по
боле́зни

♦ *adj* **1** (*not turned on*) вы́ключенный
(вы́ключен); (: *tap*) закры́тый (закры́т);
(*disconnected*) отключённый (отключён)

2 (*cancelled: meeting, match*) отменённый
(отменён); (*agreement*) расто́ргнутый
(расто́ргнут)

3 (*BRIT*): **to go off** (*milk*) прокиса́ть
(проки́снуть* *perf*); (*cheese, meat*) по́ртиться
(испо́ртиться *perf*); **the milk has gone off**
молоко́ проки́сло:

4: on the off chance на вся́кий* слу́чай; **to
have an off day** встава́ть* (встать* *perf*) с
ле́вой ноги́

♦ *prep* **1** (*indicating motion, removal etc*) с
+*gen*; **to fall off a cliff** упа́сть (*perf*) со скалы́

2 (*distant from*) от +*gen*; **it's just off the M1** это недалеко от автострады M1; **it's five km off the main road** это в пяти км от шоссе; **to be off meat** (*no longer eat it*) не есть* (*impf*) мясо; (*no longer like it*) разлюбить* (*perf*) мясо.

offal ['ɔfl] *n* потроха* *pl*.

offbeat ['ɔfbi:t] *adj* нетривиальный* (нетривиален).

off-centre [ɔf'sɛntə'] (*US* **off-center**) *adj* смещённый* (смещён) ♦ *adv* не по центру.

off colour *adj* (*BRIT: inf*): **I feel ~~** мне нездоровится.

offence [ə'fɛns] (*US* **offense**) *n* (*crime*) право-нарушение; (*insult*) оскорбление; **to commit an ~** совершать (совершить *perf*) правонарушение; **to take ~ at** обижаться (обидеться* *perf*) на +*acc*; **to give ~ to** обижать (обидеть* *perf*), оскорблять (оскорбить* *perf*); **"no ~, but ..."** „не в обиду будет сказано, но ...".

offend [ə'fɛnd] *vt* (*person*) обижать (обидеть* *perf*); (*feelings*) оскорблять (оскорбить* *perf*) ♦ *vi*: **to ~ against** (*law, rule*) нарушать (нарушить *perf*).

offender [ə'fɛndə'] *n* правонарушитель(ница) *m(f)*.

offending [ə'fɛndɪŋ] *adj* соответствующий*.

offense [ə'fɛns] *n* (*US*) = **offence**.

offensive [ə'fɛnsɪv] *adj* (*remark, behaviour*) оскорбительный* (оскорбителен); (*smell etc*) отвратительный* (отвратителен) ♦ *n* (*MIL*) наступление; **~ weapon** орудие нападения.

offer ['ɔfə'] *n* предложение ♦ *vt* предлагать (предложить* *perf*); **to make an ~ for sth** предлагать (предложить* *perf*) цену за что-н; **to ~ sth to sb** предлагать (предложить* *perf*) кому-н что-н; **to ~ to do** предлагать (предложить* *perf*) +*infin*; **"on ~"** (*COMM*) „продаётся со скидкой".

offering ['ɔfərɪŋ] *n* (*also REL*) подношение.

offer price *n* цена продовца.

offhand [ɔf'hænd] *adj* (*unfriendly*) пренебрежительный* (пренебрежителен); (*easy-going*) непринуждённый* (непринуждён) ♦ *adv* сразу, не думая; **I can't tell you ~** я не могу Вам сказать сразу.

office ['ɔfɪs] *n* офис; (*room*) кабинет; (*position*) пост, должность *f*; **doctor's ~** (*US*) кабинет врача; **to take ~** (*person*) вступать (вступить* *perf*) в должность; (*political party*) приходить* (прийти* *perf*) к власти; **through his good ~s** (*fig*) благодаря его услугам; **the O~ of Fair Trading** (*BRIT*) Управление добросовестной конкуренции.

office automation *n* автоматизация делопроизводства.

office bearer *n* должностное лицо*.

office block (*US* **office building**) *n* административное здание.

office boy *n* посыльный *m adj*.

office hours *npl* часы *mpl* работы; (*US: MED*) приёмные часы *mpl*.

office manager *n* начальник конторы.

officer ['ɔfɪsə'] *n* (*MIL*) офицер; (*also*: **police ~**) полицейский* *m adj*; (: *in Russia*) милиционер; (*of organization*) заведующий* *m adj*.

office work *n* канцелярская работа.

office worker *n* канцелярский*(-ая) *or* конторский*(-ая) служащий*(-ая) *m(f) adj*.

official [ə'fɪʃl] *adj* официальный ♦ *n* должностное лицо*; **government ~** официальное лицо*.

officialdom [ə'fɪʃldəm] *n* (*pej*) бюрократия.

officially [ə'fɪʃəlɪ] *adv* официально.

Official Receiver *n* (*COMM*) официальное лицо, назначенное для проведения ликвидации неплатёжеспособной компании.

official strike *n* официальная забастовка.

officiate [ə'fɪʃɪeɪt] *vi* распоряжаться (*impf*); (*REL*) совершать (совершить *perf*) богослужение; **to ~ as Mayor** исполнять (*impf*) обязанности мэра; **to ~ at a marriage** совершать (совершить *perf*) брако-сочетание.

officious [ə'fɪʃəs] *adj* придирчивый.

offing ['ɔfɪŋ] *n*: **war is in the ~** война грядёт.

off-key [ɔf'ki:] *adj* (*MUS*) фальшивый.

off-licence ['ɔflaɪsns] *n* (*BRIT*) винный магазин.

off-limits [ɔf'lɪmɪts] *adj* (*esp US*) закрытый (закрыт).

off-line [ɔf'laɪn] *adj* (*COMPUT*) автономный, независимый ♦ *adv* (*COMPUT*) автономно, независимо; (: *switched off*) отключено.

off-load ['ɔfləud] *vt* сваливать (свалить *perf*).

off-peak ['ɔf'pi:k] *adj* (*heating, electricity*) непиковый; (*train, ticket*) со скидкой.

off-putting ['ɔfputɪŋ] *adj* (*BRIT*) нерасполагающий.

off-season ['ɔf'si:zn] *adj* (*booking etc*) несезонный ♦ *adv* не в сезон.

offset ['ɔfsɛt] *irreg vt* уравновешивать (*impf*).

offshoot ['ɔfʃu:t] *n* (*fig*) ответвление; (: *of discussion*) последствие.

offshore [ɔf'ʃɔ:'] *adj* (*oilrig, fishing*) морской; **there was a gentle ~ breeze** на море дул лёгкий бриз.

offside ['ɔf'saɪd] *n* (*AUT: in Britain*) правая сторона ♦ *adj* (*SPORT*): **to be ~** быть (*impf*) в офсайде.

offspring ['ɔfsprɪŋ] *n inv* отпрыск.

offstage [ɔf'steɪdʒ] *adv* (*sounds*) за сценой.

off-the-cuff [ɔfðə'kʌf] *adj* импровиз-ированный.

---

* marks translations which have irregular inflections. The Russian-English side of the dictionary gives inflectional information.

off-the-job ['ɔfðə'dʒɔb] *adj*: ~ **training** обуче́ние с отры́вом от произво́дства.
off-the-peg ['ɔfðə'pɛg] (*US* **off-the-rack**) *adj*: ~ **clothing** гото́вая оде́жда.
off-the-rack ['ɔfðə'ræk] *adj* (*US*) = **off-the-peg**.
off-the-record ['ɔfðə'rɛkɔːd] *adj* неофициа́льный* (неофициа́лен) ♦ *adv* неофициа́льно.
off-white ['ɔfwaɪt] *adj* белова́тый.
Ofgas ['ɔfgæs] *n* (*BRIT*) управле́ние по контро́лю за газоснабже́нием.
Oftel ['ɔftɛl] *n* (*BRIT*) управле́ние по контро́лю за телефо́нной се́тью.
Ofwat ['ɔfwɔt] *n* (*BRIT*) управле́ние по контро́лю за водоснабже́нием.
often ['ɔfn] *adv* ча́сто; **how** ~ ...? как ча́сто ...?; **more** ~ **than not** ча́ще всего́; **as** ~ **as not** дово́льно ча́сто; **every so** ~ вре́мя от вре́мени.
ogle ['əugl] *vt* глазе́ть (*impf*) на +*acc*.
ogre ['əugə'] *n* велика́н-людое́д.
OH *abbr* (*US*: *POST*) = Ohio.
oh [əu] *excl* о, а; ~ **really!** да!; ~ **no!** (о) нет!
ohm [əum] *n* (*ELEC*) ом.
OHMS *abbr* (*BRIT*: = **On His/Her Majesty's Service**) на слу́жбе у Его́/Её Короле́вского Вели́чества.
oil [ɔɪl] *n* (*CULIN*) ма́сло; (*petroleum*) нефть *f*; (*for heating*) печно́е то́пливо ♦ *vt* (*engine, gun etc*) сма́зывать (сма́зать* *perf*); ~**s** *npl* (*ART*) ма́сляные кра́ски *fpl*.
oilcan ['ɔɪlkæn] *n* маслёнка*.
oil change *n* (*AUT*) сме́на ма́сла (*в мото́ре*).
oilcloth ['ɔɪlklɔθ] *n* клеёнка*.
oilfield ['ɔɪlfiːld] *n* месторожде́ние не́фти.
oil filter *n* (*AUT*) ма́сляный фильтр.
oilfired ['ɔɪlfaɪəd] *adj* ма́сляный.
oil gauge *n* (*AUT*) индика́тор у́ровня ма́сла.
oil industry *n* нефтяна́я промы́шленность *f*.
oil painting *n* карти́на, напи́санная ма́слом.
oil refinery *n* нефтеперераба́тывающий заво́д.
oil rig *n* нефтяна́я платфо́рма.
oilseed rape ['ɔɪlsiː-d-] *n* рапс, суре́пка.
oilskins ['ɔɪlskɪnz] *npl* водонепроница́емая оде́жда *fsg*.
oil slick *n* нефтяно́е пятно́*.
oil tanker *n* (*ship*) та́нкер; (*truck*) нефтево́з.
oil well *n* нефтяна́я сква́жина.
oily ['ɔɪlɪ] *adj* (*rag*) прома́сленный (прома́слен); (*substance*) масляни́стый; (*food*) жи́рный* (жи́рен).
ointment ['ɔɪntmənt] *n* мазь *f*.
OK *abbr* (*US*: *POST*) = Oklahoma.
O.K. ['əu'keɪ] *excl* (*inf*) хорошо́, ла́дно ♦ *adj* (*film, meal etc*) сре́дний ♦ *vt* (*approve*) одобря́ть (одо́брить *perf*) ♦ *n*: **to give sth the** ~ дава́ть* (дать* *perf*) (что-н; **is it** ~? (э́то) норма́льно?; **is everything** ~? всё в поря́дке?; **are you (feeling)** ~? Вы себя́ норма́льно чу́вствуете?; **are you** ~ **for**

money? у Вас нет пробле́м с деньга́ми?; **it's** ~ **with** *or* **by me** я не про́тив.
okay ['əu'keɪ] *excl* = **O.K.**.
old [əuld] *adj* (*aged*) ста́рый* (стар); (*former*) ста́рый; **how** ~ **are you?** ско́лько Вам лет?; **he's 10 years** ~ ему́ 10 лет; ~ **man** стари́к; ~ **woman** стару́ха; ~**er brother** ста́рший* брат*; **any** ~ **rag will do** сойдёт люба́я тря́пка.
old age *n* ста́рость *f*.
old age pension *n* пе́нсия по ста́рости.
old age pensioner *n* (*BRIT*) пенсионе́р(ка*).
old-fashioned ['əuld'fæʃnd] *adj* старомо́дный* (старомо́ден).
old hand *n* о́пытный челове́к.
old hat *adj* (*inf*): **this is very** ~ ~ э́то ужа́сно неново́.
old maid *n* ста́рая де́ва.
old people's home *n* дом* для престаре́лых.
old-style ['əuldstaɪl] *adj* в стари́нном сти́ле.
old-time ['əuld'taɪm] *adj* (*dancing*) старомо́дный.
old-timer [əuld'taɪmə'] *n* (*inf*) старожи́л(ка*).
old wives' tale *n* ба́бушкины ска́зки* *fpl*.
oleander [əulɪ'ændə'] *n* олеа́ндр.
O-level ['əulɛvl] *n* (*formerly*) ≈ экза́мены в 8-ом кла́ссе сре́дней шко́лы.
olive ['ɔlɪv] *n* (*fruit*) масли́на, оли́вка* ♦ *adj* (*also*: ~**-green**) оли́вковый; ~ **tree** оли́вковое де́рево*; **to offer an** ~ **branch** (*fig*) предлага́ть (предложи́ть* *perf*) переми́рие.
olive oil *n* оли́вковое ма́сло.
Olympic [əu'lɪmpɪk] *adj* олимпи́йский*.
Olympic Games *npl*: **the** ~ ~ (*also*: **the Olympics**) Олимпи́йские и́гры *fpl*.
OM *n abbr* (*BRIT*: = *Order of Merit*) о́рден "За заслу́ги".
Oman [əu'mɑːn] *n* Ома́н.
OMB *n abbr* (*US*) = *Office of Management and Budget*.
ombudsman ['ɔmbudzmən] *n* официа́льное лицо́, рассма́тривающее жа́лобы ча́стных лиц на госуда́рственные учережде́ния.
omelet(te) ['ɔmlɪt] *n* омле́т; **ham/cheese** ~ омле́т с ветчино́й/сы́ром.
omen ['əumən] *n* предзнаменова́ние.
ominous ['ɔmɪnəs] *adj* злове́щий* (злове́щ).
omission [əu'mɪʃən] *n* про́пуск.
omit [əu'mɪt] *vt* пропуска́ть (пропусти́ть* *perf*) ♦ *vi*: **he** ~**ted to inform me of this** он не проинформи́ровал меня́ об э́том.
omnipotent [ɔm'nɪpətnt] *adj* всемогу́щий* (всемогу́щ).
omnivorous [ɔm'nɪvrəs] *adj* всея́дный* (всея́ден).
ON *abbr* (*CANADA*) = Ontario.

KEYWORD

on [ɔn] *prep* **1** (*position*) на +*prp*; (*motion*) на +*acc*; **the book is on the table** кни́га на столе́; **to put the book on the table** класть* (положи́ть* *perf*) кни́гу на стол; **on the left**

слéва; **the house is on the main road** дом
стои́т у шоссé

2 (*indicating means, method, condition etc*): **on
foot** пешко́м; **on the train/plane** (*go*) на по́езде/
самолёте; (*be*) в по́езде/самолёте; **on the
telephone/radio/television** по телефо́ну/
ра́дио/телеви́зору; **she's on the telephone**
она́ разгова́ривает по телефо́ну; **to be on
drugs** принима́ть (*impf*) лека́рства; **to be on
holiday/business** быть (*impf*) в о́тпуске/
командиро́вке

3 (*referring to time*): **on Friday** в пя́тницу; **on
Fridays** по пя́тницам; **on June 20th** 20-го
ию́ня; **a week on Friday** че́рез неде́лю, счита́я
с пя́тницы; **on arrival** по прие́зде; **on seeing
this** уви́дев э́то

4 (*about, concerning*) о +*prp*, по +*dat*;
information on train services информа́ция о
расписа́нии поездо́в; **a book on physics**
кни́га по фи́зике

♦ *adv* **1** (*referring to dress*) в +*prp*; **to have
one's coat on** быть (*impf*) в пальто́; **what's she
got on?** во что она́ была́ оде́та?; **she put her
boots/gloves/hat on** она́ наде́ла сапоги́/
перча́тки/шля́пу

2 (*further, continuously*) да́льше, да́лее; **to
walk on** идти́* (*impf*) да́льше

♦ *adj* **1** (*functioning, in operation*)
включённый (включён), (: *tap*) откры́тый
(откры́т); **is the meeting still on?** (*in progress*)
собра́ние ещё идёт?; (*not cancelled*)
собра́ние не отмени́ли?; **there's a good film
on at the cinema** в кинотеа́тре идёт хоро́ший
фильм

2: **that's not on!** (*inf: of behaviour*) так не
пойдёт *or* не годи́тся!

ONC *n abbr* (*BRIT*. = *Ordinary National Certificate*)
≈ свиде́тельство об оконча́нии нача́льной
шко́лы.

once [wʌns] *adv* (*on one occasion*) (оди́н) раз;
(*formerly*) когда́-то, одна́жды ♦ *conj*
(*immediately afterwards*) как то́лько; ~ **he
had left** как то́лько он ушёл; **at** ~
(*immediately*) сра́зу же; (*simultaneously*)
вме́сте; **come here at** ~! сейча́с же подойди́
сюда́!; (**all**) **at** ~ все вме́сте; ~ **a week** (оди́н)
раз в неде́лю; ~ **more** ещё раз; ~ **and for all**
раз и навсегда́; **I knew him** ~ я когда́-то был
знако́м с ним; ~ **upon a time there lived** ...
жил-был ....

oncoming [ˈɒnkʌmɪŋ] *adj* (*traffic etc*)
встре́чный.

OND *n abbr* (*BRIT*. = *Ordinary National Diploma*)
дипло́м о сре́днем техни́ческом
образова́нии.

one [wʌn] *n* оди́н* (*f* одна́*, *nt* одно́*, *pl* одни́*);
one hundred and fifty сто пятьдеся́т; **one day
there was a sudden knock at the door**
одна́жды неожи́данно разда́лся стук в
дверь; **one by one** по одному́, оди́н за
други́м; *see also* **five**

♦ *adj* **1** (*sole*) еди́нственный; **the one book
which** еди́нственная кни́га, кото́рая
2 (*same*) оди́н; **they all belong to the one
family** они́ все из одно́й семьи́

♦ *pron* **1**: **I'm the one who did it** э́то я сде́лал;
this one э́тот (*f* э́та, *nt* э́то); **that one** тот (*f* та,
nt то); **I've already got one** у меня́ уже́ есть:
2: **one another** друг дру́га; **do you two ever
see one another?** Вы когда́-нибудь
ви́дитесь?; **the boys didn't dare look at one
another** ма́льчики не сме́ли взгляну́ть друг
на дру́га

3 (*impersonal*): **one never knows** никогда́ не
зна́ешь; **to cut one's finger** поре́зать (*perf*)
(себе́) па́лец; **one needs to eat** на́до *or* ну́жно
есть.

one-day excursion [ˈwʌndeɪ-] *n* (*US*)
обра́тный биле́т (*действи́тельный в
тече́ние одного́ дня*).

One-hundred share index [ˈwʌnhʌndrəd-] *n*
и́ндекс ста́ а́кций (*публику́емый ежедне́вно
и пока́зывающий состоя́ние фо́ндовой
би́ржи*).

one-man [ˈwʌnˈmæn] *adj* (*business*)
индивидуа́льный; (*canoe*) одноме́стный.

one-man band *n* челове́к-орке́стр.

one-off [wʌnˈɔf] *n* (*BRIT*: *inf*) едини́чный
слу́чай.

one-parent family [ˈwʌnpɛərənt-] *n* непо́лная
семья́*.

one-piece [ˈwʌnpiːs] *adj*: ~ **bathing suit**
це́льный купа́льник.

onerous [ˈɒnərəs] *adj* тя́гостный* (тя́гостен),
обремени́тельный* (обремени́телен).

one's [wʌnz] *adj*: **to dry** ~ **hands** вытира́ть
(вы́тереть* *perf*) ру́ки; *see also* **my**.

oneself [wʌnˈself] *pron* (*reflexive*) себя́;
(*emphatic*) сам; (*after prep*: +*acc*, +*gen*)
самого́ себя́; (: +*dat*) самому́ себе́; (: +*instr*)
сами́м собо́й; (: +*prp*) само́м себе́; **to hurt** ~
ушиби́ться (ушиби́ться *perf*); **to keep sth for**
~ держа́ть* (*impf*) что-н при себе́; **to talk to** ~
разгова́ривать (*impf*) с сами́м собо́й.

one-shot [ˈwʌnʃɔt] *n* (*US*) = **one-off**.

one-sided [wʌnˈsaɪdɪd] *adj* односторо́нний
(односторо́нен); (*contest*) нера́вный*
(нера́вен).

one-time [ˈwʌntaɪm] *adj* бы́вший*.

one-to-one [ˈwʌntəwʌn] *adj* (*tuition etc*)
индивидуа́льный ♦ *adv* оди́н на оди́н.

---

* marks translations which have irregular inflections. The Russian-English side of the dictionary gives inflectional information.

one-upmanship [wʌn'ʌpmənʃɪp] *n*: **the art of ~** уме́ние вы́делиться и показа́ть своё превосхо́дство.

one-way ['wʌnweɪ] *adj* (*traffic*) одно-сторо́нний*; **~ street** у́лица с односторо́нним движе́нием.

ongoing ['ɒngəuɪŋ] *adj* продолжа́ющийся.

onion ['ʌnjən] *n* лук*.

on-line ['ɒnlaɪn] (*COMPUT*) *adj* неавтоно́мный; (*switched on*) подключённый ♦ *adv* неавтоно́мно.

onlooker ['ɒnlukə'] *n* зри́тель(ница) *m(f)*.

only ['əunlɪ] *adv* то́лько ♦ *adj* еди́нственный ♦ *conj* (*but*) то́лько; **an ~ child** еди́нственный ребёнок*; **I ~ bought one bottle** я купи́л то́лько одну́ буты́лку; **I saw her ~ yesterday** я то́лько вчера́ ви́дел её; **I'd be ~ too pleased to help** я был бы о́чень рад помо́чь; **I would come, ~ I'm too busy** я бы пришёл, то́лько я сли́шком за́нят; **not ~ ... but also ...** не то́лько ..., но и ....

o.n.o. *abbr* (*BRIT: in classified ads*) = **or near(est) offer.**

onset ['ɒnsɛt] *n* наступле́ние.

onshore ['ɒnʃɔ:'] *adj*: **~ wind** ве́тер с мо́ря; (*oil rig, drilling*) назе́мный.

onslaught ['ɒnslɔ:t] *n* нападе́ние.

on-the-job ['ɒnðə'dʒɒb] *adj*: **~ training** обуче́ние без отры́ва от произво́дства.

onto ['ɒntu] *prep* = **on to.**

onus ['əunəs] *n*: **the ~ is on him to prove it** его́ долг – доказа́ть э́то.

onward(s) ['ɒnwəd(z)] *adv* вперёд, да́льше; **from that time ~** с тех пор.

onyx ['ɒnɪks] *n* о́никс.

oops [ups] *excl* (*inf*) ой!

ooze [u:z] *vi* сочи́ться (*impf*) ♦ *vt*: **to ~ confidence** излуча́ть (*impf*) уве́ренность.

opacity [əu'pæsɪtɪ] *n* непрозра́чность *f*.

opal ['əupl] *n* опа́л.

opaque [əu'peɪk] *adj* непрозра́чный* (непрозра́чен).

OPEC ['əupɛk] *n abbr* (= *Organization of Petroleum-Exporting Countries*) ОПЕ́К.

open ['əupn] *adj* (*also fig*) откры́тый; (*enemy, hostility*) открове́нный; (*vacancy*) свобо́дный* ♦ *vt* открыва́ть (откры́ть* *perf*) ♦ *vi* открыва́ться (откры́ться* *perf*); (*flower*) раскрыва́ться (раскры́ться* *perf*); (*book, debate etc*: *commence*) начина́ться (нача́ться* *perf*); **in the ~** (*air*) на откры́том во́здухе; **the ~ sea** откры́тое мо́ре; **~ ground** (*among trees*) поля́на; (*waste ground*) пусты́рь* *m*; **to have an ~ mind on sth** подходи́ть* (*impf*) к чему́-н без предубежде́ния

▶ **open on to** *vt fus* (*subj: room, door*) выходи́ть* (*impf*) в/на +*acc*

▶ **open out** *vt* раскрыва́ть (раскры́ть* *perf*) ♦ *vi* раскрыва́ться (раскры́ться* *perf*)

▶ **open up** *vt* открыва́ть (откры́ть* *perf*) ♦ *vi* открыва́ться (откры́ться* *perf*).

open-air ['əupn'ɛə'] *adj* (*concert*) на откры́том во́здухе; (*swimming pool*) откры́тый.

open-and-shut ['əupnən'ʃʌt] *adj*: **~ case** элемента́рное де́ло.

open day *n* день* *m* откры́тых двере́й.

open-ended [əupn'ɛndɪd] *adj* (*fig: question*) откры́тый; (: *discussion*) незавершённый.

opener ['əupnə'] *n* (*also: tin or can ~*) открыва́лка*.

open-heart [əupn'hɑ:t] *adj*: **~ surgery** откры́тая опера́ция на се́рдце.

opening ['əupnɪŋ] *adj* (*speech, remarks etc*) вступи́тельный ♦ *n* (*gap, hole*) отве́рстие; (*start*) нача́ло; (*opportunity*) возмо́жность *f*; (*job*) вака́нсия.

opening night *n* (*THEAT*) премье́ра.

open learning *n* самообуче́ние (*по подгото́вленным посо́биям*).

openly ['əupnlɪ] *adv* откры́то.

open-minded [əupn'maɪndɪd] *adj* (*person*) откры́тый; (*approach*) непредвзя́тый.

open-necked ['əupnnɛkt] *adj* расстёгнутый.

openness ['əupnnɪs] *n* (*frankness*) откры́тость *f*.

open-plan ['əupn'plæn] *adj*: **~ office** о́фис с откры́той планиро́вкой.

open prison *n* тюрьма́ свобо́дного режи́ма.

open sandwich *n* бутербро́д.

open shop *n* (*TRADE UNIONS*) *предприя́тие, на кото́рое нанима́ют рабо́чих незави́симо от чле́нства в профсою́зе.*

Open University *n* (*BRIT*): **the ~ ~** Откры́тый университе́т.

open verdict *n* (*LAW*): **an ~ ~ was passed** объяви́ли, что причи́на сме́рти неустано́влена.

opera ['ɒpərə] *n* о́пера.

opera glasses *npl* театра́льный бино́кль *msg*.

opera house *n* о́перный теа́тр.

opera singer *n* о́перный(-ая) певе́ц*(-ви́ца).

operate ['ɒpəreɪt] *vt* управля́ть (*impf*) +*instr* ♦ *vi* де́йствовать (*impf*); (*drug*) де́йствовать (поде́йствовать *perf*); (*MED*): **to ~ (on sb)** опери́ровать (проопери́ровать *perf*) (кого́-н).

operatic [ɒpə'rætɪk] *adj* о́перный.

operating costs *n* эксплуатацио́нные затра́ты *fpl*.

operating profit *n* при́быль *f* от произ-во́дственной де́ятельности.

operating room ['ɒpəreɪŋ-] *n* (*US*) операцио́нная *f adj*.

operating statement *n* отчёт о при́были и убы́тках; (*esp US*) теку́щий бала́нс.

operating system *n* (*COMPUT*) операцио́нная систе́ма.

operating table *n* операцио́нный стол*.

operating theatre *n* операцио́нная *f adj*.

operation [ɒpə'reɪʃən] *n* (*of machine: functioning*) рабо́та; (: *controlling*) управле́ние; (*MED, MIL, COMM*) опера́ция; **to be in ~** де́йствовать (*impf*); **he had an ~** (*MED*) ему́ сде́лали опера́цию; **to perform an ~** (*MED*) де́лать (сде́лать *perf*) опера́цию.

operational [ɔpə'reɪʃənl] *adj* (*working*) функциони́рующий; **the machine was ~** маши́на функциони́ровала.

operative ['ɔpərətɪv] *adj* (*law etc*) де́йствующий*; (*position*) операти́вный ♦ *n* (*in factory*) опера́тор; **the ~ word** ключево́е сло́во*.

operator ['ɔpəreɪtə'] *n* (*TEL*) телефони́ст(ка*); (*of machine*) опера́тор.

operetta [ɔpə'retə] *n* опере́тта.

ophthalmic [ɔf'θælmɪk] *adj* офтальмологи́ческий.

ophthalmic optician *n* окули́ст.

ophthalmologist [ɔfθæl'mɔlədʒɪst] *n* офтальмо́лог.

opinion [ə'pɪnjən] *n* мне́ние; **in my ~** по-мо́ему, по моему́ мне́нию; **to seek a second ~** запра́шивать (запроси́ть* *perf*) дополни́тельное мне́ние.

opinionated [ə'pɪnjəneɪtɪd] *adj* самоуве́ренный.

opinion poll *n* опро́с обще́ственного мне́ния.

opium ['əupɪəm] *n* о́пиум.

opponent [ə'pəunənt] *n* оппоне́нт, проти́вник(-ница); (*MIL, SPORT*) проти́вник.

opportune ['ɔpətju:n] *adj* подходя́щий*.

opportunism [ɔpə'tju:nɪzəm] *n* оппортуни́зм.

opportunist [ɔpə'tju:nɪst] *n* оппортуни́ст.

opportunity [ɔpə'tju:nɪtɪ] *n* возмо́жность *f*; **to take the ~ of doing** по́льзоваться (воспо́льзоваться *perf*) слу́чаем чтобы +*infin*.

oppose [ə'pəuz] *vt* проти́виться* (воспроти́виться* *perf*) +*dat*; **to be ~d to sth** проти́виться (*impf*) чему́-н; **as ~d to в** противополо́жность +*dat*.

opposing [ə'pəuzɪŋ] *adj* (*ideas, forces*) противополо́жный; **the ~ team** кома́нда проти́вника.

opposite ['ɔpəzɪt] *adj* противополо́жный ♦ *adv* напро́тив ♦ *prep* напро́тив +*gen* ♦ *n*: **the ~** (*say, think, do etc*) противополо́жное *nt adj*; **the ~ sex** противополо́жный пол; **"see ~ page"** „см. на противополо́жной страни́це".

opposite number *n* (*person*) лицо́, занима́ющее соотве́тствующую до́лжность в друго́й организа́ции.

opposition [ɔpə'zɪʃən] *n* оппози́ция; **the O~** (*POL*) оппозицио́нная па́ртия.

oppress [ə'prɛs] *vt* угнета́ть (*impf*).

oppression [ə'prɛʃən] *n* угнете́ние.

oppressive [ə'prɛsɪv] *adj* (*régime*) угнета́тельский; (*weather, heat*) гнету́щий*.

opprobrium [ə'prəubrɪəm] *n* (*formal*) осужде́ние.

opt [ɔpt] *vi*: **to ~ for** избира́ть (избра́ть* *perf*); **to ~ to do** реша́ть (реши́ть *perf*) +*infin*
▶ **opt out** *vi* (*school, hospital etc*) выходи́ть* (вы́йти* *perf*) из-под госуда́рственного контро́ля; **to ~ out of sth** выходи́ть* (вы́йти* *perf*) из чего́-н.

optical ['ɔptɪkl] *adj* опти́ческий*.

optical character reader *n* (*COMPUT*) устро́йство опти́ческого счи́тывания си́мволов.

optical character recognition *n* (*COMPUT*) опти́ческое распознава́ние си́мволов.

optical fibre *n* опти́ческое волокно́.

optical illusion *n* опти́ческий* обма́н.

optician [ɔp'tɪʃən] *n* окули́ст.

optics ['ɔptɪks] *n* (*PHYS*) о́птика.

optimism ['ɔptɪmɪzəm] *n* оптими́зм.

optimist ['ɔptɪmɪst] *n* оптими́ст(ка*).

optimistic [ɔptɪ'mɪstɪk] *adj* оптимисти́чный* (оптимисти́чен).

optimum ['ɔptɪməm] *adj* оптима́льный.

option ['ɔpʃən] *n* (*choice*) вариа́нт; (*SCOL*) предме́т по вы́бору; (*COMM*) опцио́н; **to keep one's ~s open** оставля́ть (оста́вить* *perf*) за собо́й пра́во вы́бора; **I have no ~** у меня́ нет вы́бора.

optional ['ɔpʃənl] *adj* (*also COMM*) необяза́тельный*; **~ extras** дополни́тельные, но необяза́тельные това́ры и́ли услу́ги.

opulence ['ɔpjuləns] *n* бога́тство.

opulent ['ɔpjulənt] *adj* (*person, society etc*) бога́тый.

OR *abbr* (*US: POST*) = Oregon.

or [ɔː'] *conj* и́ли; (*otherwise*): **~ (else)** а то, ина́че; (*with negative*): **he hasn't seen ~ heard anything** он ничего́ не ви́дел и не слы́шал.

oracle ['ɔrəkl] *n* (*prophet*) ора́кул; (*prophecy*) прорица́ние.

oral ['ɔːrəl] *adj* (*test, report*) у́стный; (*vaccine, medicine*) ора́льный ♦ *n* (*exam*) у́стный экза́мен.

orange ['ɔrɪndʒ] *n* апельси́н ♦ *adj* (*colour*) ора́нжевый.

orangeade [ɔrɪndʒ'eɪd] *n* апельси́новый напи́ток*.

oration [ɔː'reɪʃən] *n* торже́ственная речь *f*.

orator ['ɔrətə'] *n* ора́тор.

oratorio [ɔrə'tɔːrɪəu] *n* орато́рия.

orb [ɔːb] *n* шар*.

orbit ['ɔːbɪt] *n* орби́та ♦ *vt* обраща́ться (*impf*) вокру́г +*gen*.

orchard ['ɔːtʃəd] *n* сад* (*фрукто́вый*); **apple ~** я́блоневый сад*.

orchestra ['ɔːkɪstrə] *n* орке́стр; (*US: seating*) парте́р.

orchestral [ɔː'kɛstrəl] *adj* оркестро́вый; **~ musician** оркестра́нт(ка*).

---

* marks translations which have irregular inflections. The Russian-English side of the dictionary gives inflectional information.

orchestrate ['ɔ:kɪstreɪt] *vt* (*stage-manage*) организо́вывать (организова́ть *perf*); (*MUS*) оркестрова́ть (*impf/perf*).

orchid ['ɔ:kɪd] *n* орхиде́я.

ordain [ɔ:'deɪn] *vt* (*REL*) посвяща́ть (посвяти́ть* *perf*) в сан; (*decide*) предпи́сывать (предписа́ть* *perf*).

ordeal [ɔ:'di:l] *n* испыта́ние.

order ['ɔ:dəʳ] *n* (*command*) прика́з; (*from shop, company, in restaurant*) зака́з; (*sequence, discipline*) поря́док* ◆ *vt* (*command*) прика́зывать (приказа́ть* *perf*) +*dat*; (*from shop, company, in restaurant*) зака́зывать (заказа́ть* *perf*); (*also:* put in ~) располага́ть (расположи́ть* *perf*) по поря́дку; **in ~** в поря́дке; **in** (*working*) **~** испра́вный* (испра́вен); **in ~ to do** для того́ чтобы +*infin*; **in ~ of size** по разме́ру; **it is already on ~** (*COMM*) э́то уже́ зака́зано; **out of ~** (*not in sequence*) не по поря́дку; (*not working*) неиспра́вный* (неиспра́вен); **to place an ~ for sth with sb** зака́зывать (заказа́ть* *perf*) что-н кому́-н; **made to ~** сде́лан на зака́з; **she is under ~s to remain silent** ей прика́зано молча́ть; **a point of ~** вопро́с о наруше́нии регла́мента; **to the ~ of** (*BANKING*) опла́чиваемый по ве́кселю на и́мя +*gen*; **to ~ sb to do** прика́зывать (приказа́ть* *perf*) кому́-н +*infin*.

order book *n* кни́га зака́зов.

order form *n* бланк зака́за.

orderly ['ɔ:dəlɪ] *n* (*MIL*) ордина́рец*; (*MED*) санита́р ◆ *adj* (*room*) опря́тный* (опря́тен); (*person*) организо́ванный* (организо́ван); (*system*) упоря́доченный* (упоря́дочен).

order number *n* но́мер* зака́за.

ordinal ['ɔ:dɪnl] *adj*: ~ **number** поря́дковое числи́тельное *nt adj*.

ordinarily ['ɔ:dnrɪlɪ] *adv* обы́чно.

ordinary ['ɔ:dnrɪ] *adj* (*everyday, usual*) обыкнове́нный* (обыкнове́нен), обы́чный* (обы́чен); (*mediocre*) заура́дный* (заура́ден); **out of the ~** (*exceptional*) необыкнове́нный* (необыкнове́нен).

ordinary seaman *n* (*BRIT*) мла́дший* матро́с.

ordinary shares *npl* обыкнове́нные а́кции *fpl*.

ordination [ɔ:dɪ'neɪʃən] *n* (*REL*) посвяще́ние в духо́вный сан.

ordnance ['ɔ:dnəns] *n* (*MIL*) ору́дие ◆ *adj* (*factory, supplies*) оруже́йный.

Ordnance Survey *n* (*BRIT*) ≈ Госуда́рственное Управле́ние по геоде́зии и картогра́фии.

ore [ɔ:ʳ] *n* руда́*.

Orenburg ['ɔrənbə:g] *n* Оренбу́рг.

organ ['ɔ:gən] *n* (*ANAT*) о́рган; (*MUS*) орга́н.

organic [ɔ:'gænɪk] *adj* (*fertilizer*) органи́ческий*; (*food*) вы́ращенный без примене́ния химика́тов.

organism ['ɔ:gənɪzəm] *n* органи́зм.

organist ['ɔ:gənɪst] *n* органи́ст(ка*).

organization [ɔ:gənaɪ'zeɪʃən] *n* организа́ция.

organization chart *n* организацио́нная структу́ра.

organize ['ɔ:gənaɪz] *vt* организо́вывать (организова́ть *perf*), устра́ивать (устро́ить *perf*); **to get ~d** организо́вываться (организова́ться *perf*).

organized crime *n* организо́ванная престу́пность *f*.

organized labour *n* чле́ны *mpl* профсою́зов.

organizer ['ɔ:gənaɪzəʳ] *n* организа́тор, устро́итель(ница) *m(f)*.

orgasm ['ɔ:gæzəm] *n* орга́зм.

orgy ['ɔ:dʒɪ] *n* о́ргия, разгу́л.

Orient ['ɔ:rɪənt] *n*: **the ~** Восто́к.

orient ['ɔ:rɪənt] *vt* ориенти́ровать (сориенти́ровать *perf*).

oriental [ɔ:rɪ'ɛntl] *adj* восто́чный.

orientate ['ɔ:rɪənteɪt] *vt*: **to ~ o.s.** ориент-и́роваться (сориенти́роваться *perf*).

orifice ['ɔrɪfɪs] *n* отве́рстие.

origin ['ɔrɪdʒɪn] *n* происхожде́ние; **country of ~** ме́сто* рожде́ния.

original [ə'rɪdʒɪnl] *adj* (*new*) оригина́льный* (оригина́лен); (*genuine*) по́длинный* (по́длинен); (*imaginative: writer, artist etc*) самобы́тный* (самобы́тен) ◆ *n* по́длинник, оригина́л.

originality [ərɪdʒɪ'nælɪtɪ] *n* (*of artist etc*) самобы́тность *f*, оригина́льность *f*.

originally [ə'rɪdʒɪnəlɪ] *adv* первонача́льно.

originate [ə'rɪdʒɪneɪt] *vi*: **to ~ from** происходи́ть* (произойти́* *perf*) от/из +*gen*; **to ~ in** зарожда́ться (зароди́ться* *perf*) в +*prp*.

originator [ə'rɪdʒɪneɪtəʳ] *n* созда́тель *m*.

Orkneys ['ɔ:knɪz] *npl*: **the ~** (*also:* **the Orkney Islands**) Оркне́йские острова́* *mpl*.

ornament ['ɔ:nəmənt] *n* (*decorative object*) украше́ние; (*on building, dress etc*) орна́мент.

ornamental [ɔ:nə'mɛntl] *adj* (*decorative: garden, pond*) декорати́вный.

ornamentation [ɔ:nəmɛn'teɪʃən] *n* украше́ние.

ornate [ɔ:'neɪt] *adj* декорати́вный.

ornithologist [ɔ:nɪ'θɔlədʒɪst] *n* орнито́лог.

ornithology [ɔ:nɪ'θɔlədʒɪ] *n* орнитоло́гия.

orphan ['ɔ:fn] *n* сирота́* *m/f* ◆ *vt*: **to be ~ed** оста́ться* (*perf*) сирото́й (*perf*).

orphanage ['ɔ:fənɪdʒ] *n* де́тский* дом*.

orthodox ['ɔ:θədɔks] *adj* (*also fig*) ортодокса́льный* (ортодокса́лен); **the Russian O~ Church** Ру́сская Правосла́вная це́рковь.

orthodoxy ['ɔ:θədɔksɪ] *n* ортодокса́льные воззре́ния *ntpl*.

orthopaedic [ɔ:θə'pi:dɪk] (*US* **orthopedic**) *adj* ортопеди́ческий*.

OS *abbr* (*BRIT*) = **Ordnance Survey**; (*NAUT*) = **ordinary seaman**; (*DRESS*) = **outsize**.

O/S *abbr* (*COMM*: = *out of stock*) нет в прода́же.

Oscar ['ɔskəʳ] *n* О́скар (*приз*).

oscillate ['ɔsɪleɪt] *vi* (*ELEC, PHYS*) колеба́ться*
(*impf*), осцилли́ровать (*impf*); (*fig*)
колеба́ться* (*impf*).
OSHA *n abbr* (*US*) = Occupational Safety and
Health Administration.
Oslo ['ɔzləu] *n* О́сло *nt ind*.
ostensible [ɔs'tɛnsɪbl] *adj* мни́мый.
ostensibly [ɔs'tɛnsɪblɪ] *adv* я́кобы.
ostentation [ɔstɛn'teɪʃən] *n* показна́я ро́скошь
f.
ostentatious [ɔstɛn'teɪʃəs] *adj* (*building, car*)
бро́ский*; (*behaviour*) показно́й; **he is very ~**
он выставля́ет себя́ напока́з.
osteopath ['ɔstɪəpæθ] *n* остеопа́т.
ostracize ['ɔstrəsaɪz] *vt* подверга́ть
(подве́ргнуть* *perf*) остраки́зму.
ostrich ['ɔstrɪtʃ] *n* стра́ус.
OT *abbr* (*BIBLE:* = Old Testament) Ве́тхий* заве́т.
OTB *n abbr* (*US:* = off-track betting)
внеиппподро́мный тотализа́тор.
OTE *abbr* (*COMM:* = on-target earnings)
предполага́емый дохо́д.
other ['ʌðə'] *adj* друго́й ♦ *pron*: **the ~ (one)**
друго́й(-а́я) *m(f) adj*, тот (*f* та) ♦ *adv*: **~ than**
кро́ме +*gen*; **~s** (*other people*) други́е *pl adj*;
the ~s остальны́е *pl adj*; **the ~ day** на днях;
some ~ people have still to arrive прие́дет ещё
не́сколько челове́к; **some actor or ~** како́й-
то из актёров; **somebody or ~** кто-
нибу́дь, кто-то; **it was none ~ than the prime
minister** э́то был ни кто ино́й как
премье́р-мини́стр.
otherwise ['ʌðəwaɪz] *adv* (*differently*) ина́че,
по-друго́му; (*apart from that*) в остально́м ♦
conj а то, ина́че; **it is an ~ good piece of work** в
остально́м э́то о́чень хоро́шая рабо́та.
OTT *abbr* (*inf*) = **over the top** *see* **top**.
Ottawa ['ɔtəwə] *n* Отта́ва.
otter ['ɔtə'] *n* вы́дра.
OU *n abbr* (*BRIT*) = **Open University**.
ouch [autʃ] *excl* ай, ой.
ought [ɔːt] (*pt* ought) *aux vb*: **I ~ to do it** мне
сле́довало бы э́то сде́лать; **this ~ to have
been corrected** э́то сле́довало испра́вить; **he
~ to win** он до́лжен вы́играть; **you ~ to go
and see this film** Вы обяза́тельно должны́
посмотре́ть э́тот фильм.
ounce [auns] *n* у́нция.
our ['auə'] *adj* наш; *see also* **my**.
ours [auəz] *pron* наш; (*referring to subject of
sentence*) свой; *see also* **mine**[1].
ourselves [auə'sɛlvz] *pl pron* (*reflexive*) себя́;
(*complement*) себя́; (*after prep: +acc, +gen*)
себя́; (*: +dat*) себе́; (*: +instr*) собо́й; (*: +prp*)
себе́; (*emphatic*) са́ми; (*alone*): (**all**) **by ~**
са́ми; **let's keep it between ~** дава́йте
оста́вим э́то ме́жду на́ми; *see also* **myself**.
oust [aust] *vt* изгоня́ть (изгна́ть* *perf*).

out [aut] *adv* **1** (*not in*): **they're out in the garden**
они́ в саду́; **out in the rain/snow** под дождём/
сне́гом; **out here** здесь; **out there** там; **to go
out** выходи́ть* (вы́йти* *perf*); **out loud** гро́мко
2 (*not at home, absent*): **he is out at the
moment** его́ сейча́с нет (до́ма); **let's have a
night out on Friday!** дава́йте пойдём
куда́-нибудь в пя́тницу ве́чером!
3 (*indicating distance*) в +*prp*; **the boat was 10
km out (from the shore)** кора́бль находи́лся в
10 км от бе́рега; **three days out from
Plymouth** в трёх днях пла́вания от Пли́мута
4 (*SPORT*): **the ball is out** мяч за преде́лами
по́ля; **out!** (*TENNIS etc*) а́ут!
♦ *adj*: **1: to be out** (*unconscious*) быть (*impf*)
без созна́ния; (*out of game*) быть (*impf*)
удалённым(-ой) с по́ля; (*have appeared:
flowers*) распуска́ться (распусти́ться* *perf*);
(: *news, secret*) станови́ться* (стать* *perf*)
изве́стным(-ой); (*extinguished: fire, light, gas*)
ту́хнуть* (поту́хнуть* *perf*), га́снуть*
(пога́снуть* *perf*); (*fashion*): **to go out**
выходи́ть* (вы́йти* *perf*) из мо́ды
2 (*finished*): **before the week was out** до
оконча́ния неде́ли;
3: to be out to do (*intend*) намерева́ться (*impf*)
+*infin*; **to be out in one's calculations** (*wrong*)
ошиба́ться (ошиби́ться* *perf*) в расчётах
♦ *prep* **1** (*outside, beyond*) из +*gen*; **to go out of
the house** выходи́ть* (вы́йти* *perf*) из до́ма;
to be out of danger (*safe*) быть (*impf*) вне
опа́сности
2 (*cause, motive*): **out of curiosity** из
любопы́тства; **out of fear** от стра́ха; **out of
boredom** от *or* со ску́ки; **out of grief/joy** с
го́ря/ра́дости; **out of necessity** по
необходи́мости
3 (*from, from among*) из +*gen*
4 (*without*): **we are out of sugar/petrol** *etc* у нас
ко́нчился са́хар/бензи́н *etc*.

outage ['autɪdʒ] *n* (*esp US: power failure*)
отключе́ние электри́чества.
out-and-out ['autəndaut] *adj* отъя́вленный.
outback ['autbæk] *n* (*in Australia*): **the ~**
необжиты́е райо́ны *mpl*.
outbid [aut'bɪd] *vt*: **to ~ sb** перебива́ть
(переби́ть* *perf*) чью-н це́ну.
outboard ['autbɔːd] *n* (*also: ~ motor*)
подвесно́й мото́р.
outbreak ['autbreɪk] *n* (*of disease, violence*)
вспы́шка*; (*of war*) нача́ло.
outbuilding ['autbɪldɪŋ] *n* надво́рная
постро́йка*.
outburst ['autbəːst] *n* вспы́шка*, взрыв.
outcast ['autkɑːst] *n* изго́й.
outclass [aut'klɑːs] *vt* превосходи́ть*

---

* marks translations which have irregular inflections. The Russian-English side of the dictionary gives inflectional information.

(превзойти́* *perf*).
outcome ['autkʌm] *n* исхо́д, результа́т.
outcrop ['autkrɔp] *n* (*of rock*) обнаже́ние.
outcry ['autkraı] *n* негодова́ние, проте́ст.
outdated [aut'deıtıd] *adj* (*customs, ideas*) отжи́вший; (*clothes*) старомо́дный*; (*technology*) устаре́лый.
outdo [aut'du:] *irreg vt* превосходи́ть* (превзойти́* *perf*).
outdoor [aut'dɔ:] *adj* на откры́том во́здухе; (*swimming pool*) откры́тый; ~ **clothes** ве́рхняя оде́жда.
outdoors [aut'dɔ:z] *adv* на у́лице, на откры́том во́здухе.
outer ['autə] *adj* нару́жный; ~ **suburbs** да́льние предме́стья; **the ~ office** кра́йний* кабине́т.
outer space *n* косми́ческое простра́нство.
outfit ['autfıt] *n* (*set of clothes*) компле́кт (оде́жды); (*inf: organization*) компа́ния.
outfitter's ['autfıtəz] *n* (*BRIT*) торго́вец* мужско́й оде́ждой.
outgoing ['autgəuıŋ] *adj* (*extrovert*) общи́тельный* (общи́телен); (*president, mayor etc*) уходя́щий; (*mail etc*) исходя́щий*.
outgoings ['autgəuıŋz] *npl* (*BRIT*) расхо́ды *mpl*.
outgrow [aut'grəu] *irreg vt* (*one's clothes*) выраста́ть (вы́расти* *perf*) из +*gen*; (*friends, habits*) перераста́ть (перерасти́* *perf*).
outhouse ['authaus] *n* надво́рная постро́йка*.
outing ['autıŋ] *n* похо́д.
outlandish [aut'lændıʃ] *adj* дико́винный.
outlast [aut'lɑ:st] *vt* пережива́ть (пережи́ть* *perf*).
outlaw ['autlɔ:] *n* челове́к вне зако́на ♦ *vt* объявля́ть (объяви́ть* *perf*) вне зако́на.
outlay ['autleı] *n* (*expenditure*) затра́ты *fpl*; (*investment*) вложе́ния *ntpl*.
outlet ['autlɛt] *n* (*hole*) выходно́е отве́рстие; (*pipe*) сток; (*US: ELEC*) розе́тка*; (*COMM: also:* **retail** ~) торго́вая то́чка*; (*for emotions*) вы́ход.
outline ['autlaın] *n* (*shape*) очерта́ния *ntpl*; (*sketch, explanation*) набро́сок* ♦ *vt* (*fig: theory, plan etc*) набра́сывать (наброса́ть* *perf*).
outlive [aut'lıv] *vt* пережива́ть (пережи́ть* *perf*).
outlook ['autluk] *n* (*attitude*) взгля́ды *mpl*, воззре́ния *ntpl*; (*prospects*) перспекти́вы *fpl*; (*: for weather*) прогно́з.
outlying ['autlaıŋ] *adj* отдалённый.
outmanoeuvre [autmə'nu:və] (*US* **outmaneuver**) *vt* перехитри́ть (*perf*).
outmoded [aut'məudıd] *adj* устаре́вший.
outnumber [aut'nʌmbə] *vt* превосходи́ть* (превзойти́* *perf*) чи́сленно; **they were ~ed by 5 to 1** их бы́ло в пять раз ме́ньше.
out of bounds *adj*: **this area is** ~ ~ ~ э́та ме́сто явля́ется запре́тным.
out-of-court [autəv'kɔ:t] *adv*: **to settle** ~

приходи́ть* (прийти́* *perf*) к соглаше́нию без обраще́ния в суд.
out-of-date [autəv'deıt] *adj* (*clothes etc*) немо́дный; (*dictionary*) устаре́вший; (*equipment*) устаре́лый; (*passport*) просро́ченный.
out-of-doors [autəv'dɔ:z] *adv* на у́лице, на откры́том во́здухе.
out-of-the-way ['autəvðə'weı] *adj* (*place*) глуби́нный; (*fig*) глухо́й.
out of touch *adj*: **to be** ~ ~ ~ отстава́ть* (отста́ть* *perf*) от вре́мени.
out-of-work ['autəvwə:k] *adj* безрабо́тный.
outpatient ['autpeıʃənt] *n* амбулато́рный(-ая) больно́й(-а́я) *m(f) adj*.
outpouring ['autpɔ:rıŋ] *n* (*of emotions*) излия́ние.
outpost ['autpəust] *n* аванпо́ст.
output ['autput] *n* (*production*) вы́работка; (*COMPUT*) выходны́е да́нные *pl adj* ♦ *vt* (*COMPUT*) выводи́ть* (вы́вести* *perf*) (*да́нные*).
outrage ['autreıdʒ] *n* (*action: scandalous*) возмути́тельный посту́пок*; (*: violent*) акт наси́лия; (*emotion*) возмуще́ние ♦ *vt* (*shock, anger*) возмуща́ть (возмути́ть* *perf*); **his behaviour is an** ~ его́ поведе́ние про́сто возмути́тельно.
outrageous [aut'reıdʒəs] *adj* возмути́тельный* (возмути́телен).
outrider ['autraıdə] *n* (*on motorcycle, horse*) эско́рт.
outright [aut'raıt] *adv* (*win, own*) абсолю́тно; (*refuse, deny*) наотре́з; (*ask*) пря́мо; (*kill*) напова́л ♦ *adj* (*winner, victory*) абсолю́тный; (*refusal, hostility*) откры́тый; **to be killed** ~ погиба́ть (поги́бнуть *perf*) сра́зу.
outrun [aut'rʌn] *irreg vt* обгоня́ть (обогна́ть* *perf*), опережа́ть (опереди́ть* *perf*).
outset ['autsɛt] *n* нача́ло; **from the** ~ с са́мого нача́ла; **at the** ~ внача́ле.
outshine [aut'ʃaın] *irreg vt* (*fig*) затмева́ть (затми́ть *perf*).
outside [aut'saıd] *n* нару́жная сторона́* ♦ *adj* нару́жный, вне́шний ♦ *adv* (*be*) снару́жи; (*go*) нару́жу ♦ *prep* вне +*gen*, за преде́лами +*gen*; (*next to: building*) у +*gen*; (*: London etc*) под +*instr*; **at the** ~ (*with times*) са́мое по́зднее; (*of size*) са́мое бо́льшее; **an** ~ **chance** ничто́жный шанс; **it's cold** ~ на у́лице хо́лодно.
outside broadcast *n* (*RADIO, TV*) репорта́ж *or* трансля́ция с ме́ста собы́тий.
outside lane *n* (*AUT: in Britain*) пра́вый ряд; (*: in US, Europe*) ле́вый ряд.
outside left *n* (*FOOTBALL*) ле́вый кра́йний* напада́ющий* *m adj*.
outside line *n* (*TEL*) городско́й телефо́н; **dial "9" for an** ~ ~ го́род – че́рез девя́тку.
outsider [aut'saıdə] *n* (*person not involved*) посторо́нний*(-яя) *m(f) adj*; (*in race etc*) аутса́йдер.

outside right n (FOOTBALL) пра́вый кра́йний* напада́ющий* m adj.

outsize ['autsaɪz] adj: ~ **clothes** оде́жда fsg больши́х разме́ров.

outskirts ['autskɔ:ts] npl окра́ины fpl.

outsmart [aut'smɑ:t] vt перехитри́ть (perf).

outspoken [aut'spəukən] adj открове́нный* (открове́нен).

outspread [aut'sprɛd] adj (wings) распростёртый (распростёрт).

outstanding [aut'stændɪŋ] adj (exceptional) выдаю́щийся*; (unfinished) незако́нченный (незако́нчен); (unpaid) неопла́ченный (неопла́чен); **your account is still** ~ Вы до сих пор не уплати́ли по счёту.

outstay [aut'steɪ] vt: **to** ~ **one's welcome** заси́живаться (засиде́ться* perf) в гостя́х.

outstretched [aut'strɛtʃt] adj (hand) протя́нутый; (arms) вы́тянутый; (body) вы́тянувшийся.

outstrip [aut'strɪp] vt превосходи́ть* (превзойти́* perf).

out tray n корзи́на для исходя́щих докуме́нтов.

outvote [aut'vəut] vt: **to** ~ **sb by 3 votes** победи́ть (perf) кого́-н с переве́сом в 3 го́лоса.

outward ['autwəd] adj (sign, appearances) вне́шний*, нару́жный*; **the** ~ **journey was much quicker** пое́здка туда́ намно́го быстре́е, чем пое́здка обра́тно.

outwardly ['autwədlɪ] adv вне́шне.

outweigh [aut'weɪ] vt переве́шивать (переве́сить* perf).

outwit [aut'wɪt] vt перехитри́ть (perf).

ova ['əuvə] npl of **ovum**.

oval ['əuvl] adj ова́льный ♦ n ова́л.

ovarian [əu'vɛərɪən] adj: ~ **cyst** кисты́ я́ичника; ~ **cancer** рак я́ичника.

ovary ['əuvərɪ] n я́ичник.

ovation [əu'veɪʃən] n ова́ция.

oven ['ʌvn] n (domestic) духо́вка*; (baker's, industrial) печь* f.

ovenproof ['ʌvnpru:f] adj жаросто́йкий, жаропро́чный*.

oven-ready ['ʌvnrɛdɪ] adj (chicken, chips etc) гото́вый для жа́рения в духо́вке.

ovenware ['ʌvnwɛə'] n жаросто́йкая or жаропро́чная посу́да.

KEYWORD

over ['əuvə'] adv **1** (across): **to cross over (to the other side of the road)** переходи́ть* (перейти́* perf) (на другу́ю сто́рону доро́ги); **over here** здесь; **over there** там; **to ask sb over** (to one's house) приглаша́ть (пригласи́ть* perf) кого́-н в го́сти or к себе́
2 (indicating movement from upright): **to knock/turn sth over** сбива́ть (сбить* perf)/

перевора́чивать (переверну́ть perf) что-н; **to fall over** па́дать (упа́сть* perf); **to bend over** нагиба́ться (нагну́ться perf)
3 (finished): **the game is over** игра́ око́нчена; **his life is over** его́ жизнь око́нчена
4 (excessively) сли́шком, чересчу́р
5 (remaining: money, food etc): **there are 3 over** 3 оста́лось:
6: **all over** (everywhere) везде́, повсю́ду; **over and over (again)** сно́ва и сно́ва
♦ prep **1** (on top of) на +prp; (above) над +instr
2 (on the other side of) че́рез +acc; **the pub over the road** паб че́рез доро́гу; **he jumped over the wall** он перепры́гнул че́рез сте́ну
3 (more than) свы́ше +gen; **over and above** бо́льше (чем); **this is over and above what we have already ordered** э́то бо́льше, чем мы уже́ заказа́ли
4 (in the course of) в тече́ние +gen, за +acc; **over the winter** за зи́му, в тече́ние зимы́; **let's discuss it over dinner** дава́йте обсу́дим э́то за обе́дом; **the work is spread over two weeks** рабо́та рассчи́тана на две неде́ли.

over... ['əuvə'] prefix пере....

overact [əuvər'ækt] vi переи́грывать (переигра́ть perf).

overall ['əuvərɔ:l] adj о́бщий* ♦ adv (in general) в це́лом or о́бщем; (entirely) целико́м ♦ n (BRIT: child's, painter's etc) хала́т; ~**s** npl (clothing) комбинезо́н msg.

overall majority n большинство́.

overanxious [əuvər'æŋkʃəs] adj весьма́ встрево́женный* (встрево́жен).

overawe [əuvər'ɔ:] vt вызыва́ть (вы́звать* perf) благогове́ние в +prp.

overbalance [əuvə'bæləns] vi теря́ть (потеря́ть perf) равнове́сие.

overbearing [əuvə'bɛərɪŋ] adj вла́стный* (вла́стен).

overboard ['əuvəbɔ:d] adv: **to fall** ~ па́дать (упа́сть* perf) за́ борт; **man** ~! челове́к за борто́м!; **to go** ~ (fig) перебра́щивать (перебороди́ть perf).

overbook [əuvə'buk] vt: **the play is** ~**ed** на пье́су про́дали сли́шком мно́го биле́тов; **the hotel is** ~**ed** гости́ница перепо́лнена.

overcame [əuvə'keɪm] pt of **overcome**.

overcapitalize [əuvə'kæpɪtəlaɪz] vt: **to** ~ **a project** вкла́дывать (вложи́ть* perf) в прое́кт неопра́вданно большо́й капита́л.

overcast ['əuvəkɑ:st] adj па́смурный (па́смурен), хму́рый (хмур).

overcharge [əuvə'tʃɑ:dʒ] vt обсчи́тывать (обсчита́ть perf).

overcoat ['əuvəkəut] n пальто́ nt ind.

overcome [əuvə'kʌm] irreg vt (opponent, enemy) одолева́ть (одоле́ть perf);

---

* marks translations which have irregular inflections. The Russian-English side of the dictionary gives inflectional information.

(*difficulties, problems*) преодолева́ть
(преодоле́ть *perf*) ♦ *adj*: ~ **by** (*fear, suspicion*)
одолева́емый (одолева́ем) +*instr*; ~ **with**
(*joy*) охва́ченный (охва́чен) +*instr*; **he was ~
with grief** он был уби́т го́рем.

overconfident [əuvə'kɔnfɪdənt] *adj* (*person*)
самонаде́янный (самонаде́ян).

overcrowded [əuvə'kraudɪd] *adj* пере-
по́лненный (перепо́лнен).

overcrowding [əuvə'kraudɪŋ] *n* перенаселённость *f*; (*in bus*) теснота́.

overdo [əuvə'du:] *irreg vt* (*work, exercise*)
перестара́ться (*perf*) в +*prp*; (*interest, concern*)
утри́ровать (*impf*); (*overcook: boil*) пере-
ва́ривать (перевари́ть* *perf*); (: *fry, bake*)
пережа́ривать (пережа́рить *perf*); **don't ~ it!**
(*compliments etc*) не переусе́рдствуйте!;
(*work etc*) не перестара́йтесь!

overdose ['əuvədəus] *n* передозиро́вка*.

overdraft ['əuvədra:ft] *n* (*COMM*) овердра́фт.

overdrawn [əuvə'drɔ:n] *adj*: **he is** *or* **his account
is** ~ он превы́сил креди́т своего́ теку́щего
счёта.

overdrive ['əuvədraɪv] *n* (*AUT*) ускоря́ющая
переда́ча.

overdue [əuvə'dju:] *adj* (*change, reform etc*)
запозда́лый; (*account*) просро́ченный
(просро́чен); **he/the bus is an hour ~** он/
автобус опа́здывает на час; **these changes
were long ~** э́тих переме́н давно́ жда́ли.

overemphasis [əuvər'εmfəsɪs] *n*: ~ **on**
изли́шнее ударе́ние на +*prp*.

overestimate [əuvər'εstɪmeɪt] *vt*
переоце́нивать (переоцени́ть* *perf*).

overexcited [əuvərɪk'saɪtɪd] *adj* чрезме́рно
возбуждённый* (возбуждён).

overexertion [əuvərɪg'zə:ʃən] *n*
перенапряже́ние.

overexpose [əuvərɪk'spəuz] *vt* (*PHOT*)
переде́рживать (передержа́ть* *perf*).

overflow [əuvə'fləu] *vi* (*river*) разлива́ться
(разли́ться* *perf*); (*sink, vase etc*) пере-
полня́ться (перепо́лниться *perf*) ♦ *n* (*also:*
pipe) сливна́я труба́.

overfly [əuvə'flaɪ] *irreg vt* (*fly past*) пролета́ть
(пролете́ть* *perf*).

overgenerous [əuvə'dʒεnərəs] *adj* сли́шком
ще́дрый* (щедр).

overgrown [əuvə'grəun] *adj* (*garden*)
заро́сший; **he's just an ~ schoolboy** он
про́сто переро́сток.

overhang [əuvə'hæŋ] *irreg vt* нависа́ть
(нави́снуть* *perf*) над +*instr* ♦ *vi* нависа́ть
(нави́снуть* *perf*) ♦ *n* наве́с.

overhaul [əuvə'hɔ:l] *vt* (*engine, equipment*)
производи́ть* (произвести́* *perf*) по́лную
прове́рку и ремо́нт +*gen* ♦ *n* по́лная
прове́рка и ремо́нт.

overhead [*adv* əuvə'hεd, *adj, n* 'əuvəhεd] *adv*
(*above*) наверху́, над голово́й; (*in the sky*) в
не́бе ♦ *adj* (*lighting*) ве́рхний*; (*cable, railway*)
надзе́мный ♦ *n* (*US*) = **overheads**; ~**s** *npl*
(*expenses*) накладны́е расхо́ды *mpl*.

overhear [əuvə'hɪə] *irreg vt* (*случа́йно*)
подслу́шать* (*perf*).

overheat [əuvə'hi:t] *vi* перегрева́ться
(перегре́ться *perf*).

overjoyed [əuvə'dʒɔɪd] *adj*: **to be ~ (at)** о́чень
ра́доваться (обра́доваться *perf*) (+*dat*); **she
was ~ to see him** она́ была́ о́чень ра́да его́
ви́деть.

overkill ['əuvəkɪl] *n* (*fig*): **it would be ~** э́то
бу́дет я́вный перебо́р.

overland ['əuvəlænd] *adj* сухопу́тный ♦ *adv*
(*travel*) по су́ше.

overlap [əuvə'læp] *vi* (*edges*) находи́ть* (*impf*)
оди́н на друго́й; (*fig: ideas, activities etc*)
части́чно совпада́ть (совпа́сть* *perf*).

overleaf [əuvə'li:f] *adv* на оборо́те.

overload [əuvə'ləud] *vt* (*also ELEC, fig*)
перегружа́ть (перегрузи́ть* *perf*); **to ~ with
work/problems** перегружа́ть (перегрузи́ть*
perf) рабо́той/пробле́мами.

overlook [əuvə'luk] *vt* (*have view into*)
выходи́ть* (*impf*) на +*acc*; (*fail to consider*)
упуска́ть (упусти́ть* *perf*) из ви́ду; (*excuse*)
закрыва́ть (закры́ть* *perf*) глаза́ на +*acc*.

overlord ['əuvəlɔ:d] *n* повели́тель *m*.

overmanning [əuvə'mænɪŋ] *n* (*INDUSTRY*)
избы́ток* рабо́чей си́лы.

overnight [əuvə'naɪt] *adv* (*for the night*) на́
ночь; (*during the night*) за́ ночь; (*fig:
suddenly*) за́ день, сра́зу же ♦ *adj* (*train,
journey*) ночно́й; **to travel ~** путеше́ствовать
(*impf*) но́чью; **to stay ~** (*переночева́ть
perf); **he'll be away ~** он е́дет с
ночёвкой.

overpass ['əuvəpɑ:s] *n* (*esp US*) путепрово́д.

overpay [əuvə'peɪ] *vt*: **to ~ sb by £50**
перепла́чивать (переплати́ть* *perf*) кому́-н
£50.

overplay [əuvə'pleɪ] *vt* преувели́чивать
(преувели́чить *perf*) значе́ние +*gen*.

overpower [əuvə'pauə] *vt* переси́ливать
(переси́лить *perf*).

overpowering [əuvə'pauərɪŋ] *adj* (*heat, stench*)
невыноси́мый (невыноси́м).

overproduction ['əuvəprə'dʌkʃən] *n* пере-
произво́дство.

overrate [əuvə'reɪt] *vt* переоце́нивать
(переоцени́ть* *perf*).

overreach [əuvə'ri:tʃ] *vt*: **to ~ o.s.** пере-
напряга́ться (перенапря́чься* *perf*).

overreact [əuvəri:'ækt] *vi* горячи́ться
(погорячи́ться *perf*).

override [əuvə'raɪd] *irreg vt* (*order, objection*)
отверга́ть (отве́ргнуть* *perf*).

overriding [əuvə'raɪdɪŋ] *adj* (*importance*)
первостепе́нный; (*factor, consideration*)
реша́ющий*.

overrule [əuvə'ru:l] *vt* (*decision*) отменя́ть
(отмени́ть* *perf*); (*objection*) отверга́ть

(отве́ргнуть* *perf*); **the judge ~d the defence** судья́ отклони́л тре́бования защи́тника.

overrun [əuvə'rʌn] *irreg vt* (*country*) бы́стро овладева́ть (овладе́ть *perf*) +*instr*; (*time limit*) превыша́ть (превы́сить* *perf*) ♦ *vi* дли́ться* (*impf*) до́льше поло́женного (вре́мени); **the town is ~ with tourists** го́род наводнён тури́стами.

overseas [əuvə'si:z] *adv* (*live, travel, work*) за рубежо́м *or* грани́цей; (*to go*) за рубе́ж *or* грани́цу ♦ *adj* (*market, trade*) вне́шний*; (*student, visitor*) иностра́нный; **to trade ~** торгова́ть (*impf*) с иностра́нными госуда́рствами.

oversee [əuvə'si:] *vt* следи́ть* (*impf*) за +*instr*.

overseer ['əuvəsɪə'] *n* (*in factory*) контролёр.

overshadow [əuvə'ʃædəu] *vt* (*place, building etc*) возвыша́ться (*impf*) над +*instr*; (*fig*) затмева́ть (затми́ть* *perf*).

overshoot [əuvə'ʃu:t] *irreg vt* проезжа́ть (прое́хать* *perf*).

oversight ['əuvəsaɪt] *n* недосмо́тр; **due to an ~** по недосмо́тру.

oversimplify [əuvə'sɪmplɪfaɪ] *vt* сли́шком упроща́ть (упрости́ть* *perf*).

oversleep [əuvə'sli:p] *irreg vi* просыпа́ть (проспа́ть* *perf*).

overspend [əuvə'spɛnd] *irreg vi* перерасхо́довать (*impf/perf*); **we have overspent by 5,000 dollars** наш перерасхо́д соста́вил 5,000 до́лларов.

overspill ['əuvəspɪl] *n* (*excess population*) избы́точное населе́ние.

overstaffed [əuvə'stɑ:ft] *adj*: **this office is ~** в э́том отде́ле сли́шком мно́го рабо́тников.

overstate [əuvə'steɪt] *vt* преувели́чивать (преувели́чить *perf*).

overstatement [əuvə'steɪtmənt] *n* преувеличе́ние.

overstay [əuvə'steɪ] *vt*: **to ~ one's welcome** загости́ться* (*perf*).

overstep [əuvə'stɛp] *vt*: **to ~ the mark** переходи́ть* (перейти́* *perf*) грани́цы.

overstock [əuvə'stɔk] *vt* затова́ривать (затова́рить *perf*).

overstretched [əuvə'strɛtʃt] *adj* (*at work*) перегру́женный (перегру́жен); (*funds*) переизрасхо́дованный (переизрасхо́дован).

overstrike ['əuvəstraɪk] *irreg n* (*on printer*) набо́р ли́шних си́мволов ♦ *vt* набира́ть (набра́ть* *perf*) (*на клавиату́ре*).

oversubscribed [əuvəsəb'skraɪbd] *adj*: **this product is ~** коли́чество зая́вок на э́тот това́р превыша́ет предложе́ние.

overt [əu'və:t] *adj* открове́нный* (открове́нен).

overtake [əuvə'teɪk] *irreg vt* (*AUT*) обгоня́ть (обогна́ть* *perf*); (*subj: event, change*)

застига́ть (засти́гнуть* *perf*) враспло́х; (: *emotion, weakness*) овладева́ть (овладе́ть *perf*) +*instr*.

overtaking [əuvə'teɪkɪŋ] *n* (*AUT*) обго́н.

overtax [əuvə'tæks] *vt* (*ECON*) облага́ть (обложи́ть* *perf*) сли́шком высо́ким нало́гом; (*strength, patience*) истоща́ть (истощи́ть *perf*); **to ~ o.s.** перенапряга́ться (перенапря́чься* *perf*).

overthrow [əuvə'θrəu] *irreg vt* сверга́ть (све́ргнуть* *perf*).

overtime ['əuvətaɪm] *n* сверхуро́чное вре́мя* *nt*; **to do** *or* **work ~** рабо́тать (*impf*) в сверхуро́чное вре́мя.

overtime ban *n* запре́т на сверхуро́чную рабо́ту.

overtone ['əuvətəun] *n* (*also*: ~**s**): ~ **of** намёк на +*acc*.

overture ['əuvətʃuə'] *n* (*MUS*) увертю́ра; (*fig*) подгото́вка*.

overturn [əuvə'tə:n] *vt* (*car, chair*) перевора́чивать (переверну́ть *perf*); (*decision, plan*) отверга́ть (отве́ргнуть *perf*); (*government, system*) сверга́ть (све́ргнуть *perf*) ♦ *vi* перевора́чиваться (переверну́ться *perf*).

overview ['əuvəvju:] *n* (*summary*) обзо́р; (*general understanding*) о́бщее представле́ние.

overweight [əuvə'weɪt] *adj* (*person*) ту́чный* (ту́чен); **your luggage is ~** у Вас переве́с.

overwhelm [əuvə'wɛlm] *vt* (*opponent, enemy etc*) оде́рживать (одержа́ть *perf*) верх над +*instr*; (*subj: feelings, emotions*) переполня́ть (перепо́лнить *perf*).

overwhelming [əuvə'wɛlmɪŋ] *adj* (*victory, defeat*) по́лный; (*majority*) подавля́ющий; (*feeling, desire*) всепобежда́ющий*; (*heat*) невыноси́мый (невыноси́м); ~ **impression** о́бщее впечатле́ние.

overwhelmingly [əuvə'wɛlmɪŋlɪ] *adv* (*vote, win*) по́лностью; (*appreciative, generous etc*) безграни́чно; (*predominantly: opposed etc*) в основно́м.

overwork [əuvə'wə:k] *n* перегру́зка ♦ *vt* (*person*) перегружа́ть (перегрузи́ть* *perf*); (*cliché etc*) зата́скивать (затаска́ть *perf*) ♦ *vi* (*person*) переутомля́ться (переутоми́ться* *perf*).

overwrite [əuvə'raɪt] *vt* (*COMPUT*) перепи́сывать (переписа́ть* *perf*).

overwrought [əuvə'rɔ:t] *adj* (*person*) переутомлённый (переутомлён).

ovulate ['ɔvjuleɪt] *vi* овули́ровать (*impf/perf*).

ovulation [ɔvju'leɪʃən] *n* овуля́ция.

ovum ['əuvəm] (*pl* **ova**) *n* яйцо́* (*АНАТ*).

owe [əu] *vt*: **she ~s me £500** она́ мне должна́ £500; **we ~ him our gratitude** мы должны́

---

* marks translations which have irregular inflections. The Russian-English side of the dictionary gives inflectional information.

быть* благода́рны ему́; **he ~s his talent/life to that man** он обя́зан свои́м тала́нтом/ свое́й жи́знью э́тому челове́ку.

owing to [ˈəuɪŋ-] *prep* всле́дствие +*gen*.

owl [aul] *n* сова́*.

own [əun] *vt* владе́ть *(impf)* +*instr* ♦ *vi* (*BRIT*): **to ~ to sth** признава́ться* (призна́ться *perf*) в чём-н ♦ *adj* (*house, work, style etc*) со́бственный; **a room of one's ~** своя́ со́бственная ко́мната; **he lives on his ~** он живёт оди́н; **to come into one's ~** быть* *(impf)* в свое́й стихи́и; **to get one's ~ back** отыгрываться (отыгра́ться *perf*)

▶ **own up** *vi*: **to ~ up to sth** признава́ться* (призна́ться *perf*) в чём-н.

own brand *n* (*COMM*) това́р с ма́ркой продаю́щей его́ торго́вой компа́нии.

owner [ˈəunəʳ] *n* владе́лец*(-лица).

owner-occupier [ˈəunərˈɔkjupaɪəʳ] *n* домо-владе́лец(-лица).

ownership [ˈəunəʃɪp] *n*: **~ (of)** владе́ние (+*instr*); **under new ~** в но́вом владе́нии.

own goal *n* (*SPORT*): **to score an ~ ~** забива́ть (заби́ть* *perf*) гол в свой воро́та.

ox [ɔks] (*pl* ~**en**) *n* бык*.

oxen [ˈɔksn] *npl of* **ox**.

Oxfam [ˈɔksfæm] *n abbr* (*BRIT*: = *Oxford Committee for Famine Relief*) Óксфордский комите́т по́мощи голода́ющим.

Oxford [ˈɔksfəd] *n* Óксфорд.

oxide [ˈɔksaɪd] *n* о́кись *f*, окси́д.

oxidize [ˈɔksɪdaɪz] *vi* окисля́ться (окисли́ться *perf*).

Oxon. [ˈɔksn] *abbr* (*BRIT*: *POST*) = *Oxfordshire*; (*in degree titles*) *Oxoniensis*.

oxtail [ˈɔksteɪl] *n*: **~ soup** суп из бы́чьего хвоста́.

oxyacetylene [ˈɔksɪəˈsɛtɪliːn] *adj* (*flame*) ацетиле́новый.

oxygen [ˈɔksɪdʒən] *n* кислоро́д.

oxygen mask *n* кислоро́дная ма́ска*.

oxygen tent *n* кислоро́дная пала́тка*.

oyster [ˈɔɪstəʳ] *n* у́стрица.

oz. *abbr* = **ounce**.

ozone [ˈəuzəun] *n* озо́н.

ozone layer *n* озо́новый слой*.

ozonosphere [əuˈzəunəsfɪəʳ] *n* озо́нный слой.

~ P, p ~

P, p [pi:] *n* (*letter*) 16-ая бу́ква англи́йского алфави́та.
P. *abbr* = **president, prince.**
p *abbr* (*BRIT*) = **penny, pence.**
p. *abbr* (= **page**) стр.= *страни́ца.*
PA *n abbr* = **personal assistant, public-address system** ◆ *abbr* (*US: POST*) = **Pennsylvania.**
pa [pɑː] *n* (*inf*) па́па.
p.a. *abbr* (= **per annum**) в год.
PAC *n abbr* (*US*) = **political action committee.**
pace [peɪs] *n* (*step*) шаг*; (*speed*) темп ◆ *vi*: **to ~ up and down** ходи́ть* (*impf*) взад вперёд; **to keep ~ with** (*person, events*) идти́* (*impf*) в но́гу с +*instr*; **to set the ~** (*also fig*) определя́ть (определи́ть *perf*); **I put him through his ~s** (*fig*) я посмотре́л, на что он спосо́бен.
pacemaker [ˈpeɪsmeɪkəʳ] *n* (*MED*) ритмиза́тор се́рдца; (*SPORT*) ли́дер.
Pacific [pəˈsɪfɪk] *n*: **the ~ (Ocean)** Ти́хий* океа́н.
pacific [pəˈsɪfɪk] *adj* (*intentions etc*) миролюби́вый.
pacifier [ˈpæsɪfaɪəʳ] *n* (*US: dummy*) со́ска*(-пусты́шка*).
pacifist [ˈpæsɪfɪst] *n* пацифи́ст(ка*).
pacify [ˈpæsɪfaɪ] *vt* умиротворя́ть (умиротвори́ть *perf*).
pack [pæk] *n* (*packet*) па́чка*; (*of hounds*) сво́ра; (*of wolves*) ста́я; (*of people*) компа́ния; (*also:* **backpack**) рюкза́к*; (*of cards*) коло́да ◆ *vt* (*fill*) накова́ть *or* упако́вывать (упакова́ть *perf*); (*press down*) уплотня́ть (уплотни́ть *perf*); (*COMPUT*) упако́вывать (упакова́ть *perf*); (*cram*): **to ~ into** набива́ть (наби́ть* *perf*) в +*acc* ◆ *vi*: **to ~ (one's bags)** накова́ть *or* упако́вывать (упакова́ть *perf*) чемода́ны; **to ~ sb off** отправля́ть (отпра́вить* *perf*) кого́-н; **to send sb ~ing** (*inf*) посыла́ть (посла́ть* *perf*) кого́-н пода́льше
▶ **pack in** (*BRIT: inf*) ◆ *vi* (*machine*) разва́ливаться (развали́ться *perf*) ◆ *vt* (*boyfriend*) завя́зывать (завяза́ть* *perf*) с +*instr*; **~ it in!** прекрати́!
▶ **pack off** *vt* отправля́ть (отпра́вить* *perf*)
▶ **pack up** *vi* (*BRIT: inf: machine*) разва́ливаться

(развали́ться *perf*); (*: person*) закругля́ться (закругли́ться *perf*) ◆ *vt* накова́ть *or* упако́вывать (упакова́ть *perf*).
package [ˈpækɪdʒ] *n* (*parcel, also COMPUT*) паке́т; (*also:* **~ deal**) паке́т предложе́ний ◆ *vt* (*goods*) накова́ть *or* упако́вывать (упакова́ть *perf*).
package holiday *n* (*BRIT*) организо́ванный о́тдых по путёвке.
package tour *n* (*BRIT*) туристи́ческая пое́здка* по путёвке.
packaging [ˈpækɪdʒɪŋ] *n* упако́вка.
packed [pækt] *adj* (*crowded*) наби́тый (наби́т).
packed lunch *n* (*BRIT*) за́втрак в паке́те.
packer [ˈpækəʳ] *n* упако́вщик(-ица).
packet [ˈpækɪt] *n* (*of cigarettes, washing powder etc*) па́чка*; (*of crisps*) паке́т.
packet switching *n* (*COMPUT*) коммута́ция паке́тов, паке́тная коммута́ция.
pack ice [ˈpækaɪs] *n* пак, па́ковый лёд*.
packing [ˈpækɪŋ] *n* (*act*) упако́вка; (*material*) прокла́дочный материа́л.
packing case *n* упако́вочный я́щик.
pact [pækt] *n* пакт.
pad [pæd] *n* (*of paper*) блокно́т; (*soft material*) прокла́дка*; (*for inking*) поду́шечка*; (*inf: home*) (свой) у́гол* ◆ *vt* (*cushion, soft toy etc*) набива́ть (наби́ть* *perf*); (*shoulder, suit*) подбива́ть (подби́ть* *perf*) ◆ *vi*: **to ~ about** ступа́ть (*impf*).
padded cell [ˈpædɪd-] *n* пала́та, оби́тая во́йлоком (*в психиатри́ческой больни́це*).
padding [ˈpædɪŋ] *n* (*material*) наби́вочный материа́л, наби́вка; (*in speech*) вода́*.
paddle [ˈpædl] *n* (*oar*) байда́рочное весло́*; (*US: for table tennis*) раке́тка* ◆ *vt* (*boat, canoe etc*) управля́ть (*impf*) +*instr* ◆ *vi* (*with feet*) шлёпать (*impf*).
paddle steamer *n* колёсный парохо́д.
paddling pool [ˈpædlɪŋ-] *n* (*BRIT*) лягуша́тник.
paddock [ˈpædək] *n* (*field*) вы́гон; (*at racecourse*) заго́н.
paddy field [ˈpædɪ-] *n* ри́совое по́ле*.
padlock [ˈpædlɔk] *n* (*вися́чий**) замо́к* ◆ *vt* запира́ть (запере́ть* *perf*) на вися́чий замо́к.
padre [ˈpɑːdrɪ] *n* (*REL*) па́дре *m ind*.

---

* marks translations which have irregular inflections. ◆ The Russian-English side of the dictionary gives inflectional information.

paediatrician [pi:dɪə'trɪʃən] (*US* **pediatrician**) *n* педиа́тр, де́тский* врач.

paediatrics [pi:dɪ'ætrɪks] (*US* **pediatrics**) *n* педиатри́я.

paedophile ['pi:dəufaɪl] (*US* **pedophile**) *n* педофи́л.

paedophilia [pi:dəu'fɪlɪə] (*US* **pedophilia**) *n* педофили́я.

pagan ['peɪgən] *adj* язы́ческий* ◆ *n* язы́чник(-ица).

page [peɪdʒ] *n* страни́ца; (*also:* ~**boy**) паж*; (: *at wedding*) ма́льчик, несу́щий шлейф неве́сты ◆ *vt* (*in hotel etc*) вызыва́ть (вы́звать* *perf*).

pageant ['pædʒənt] *n* театрализо́ванное представле́ние.

pageantry ['pædʒəntrɪ] *n* пы́шное зре́лище.

pageboy ['peɪdʒbɔɪ] *n see* **page**.

pager ['peɪdʒə'] *n* портати́вное электро́нное устро́йство для вы́зова полице́йского, врача́ итп.

page three girl *n* де́вушка, снима́ющаяся в полуобнажённом ви́де для фотогра́фий в бульва́рных газе́тах.

paginate ['pædʒɪneɪt] *vt* нумерова́ть* (пронумерова́ть* *perf*) страни́цы +*gen*.

pagination [pædʒɪ'neɪʃən] *n* нумера́ция страни́ц, пагина́ция.

pagoda [pə'gəudə] *n* па́года.

paid [peɪd] *pt, pp of* **pay** ◆ *adj* опла́чиваемый; **to put ~ to** (*BRIT*) класть* (положи́ть* *perf*) коне́ц +*dat*.

paid-in ['peɪdɪn] *adj* (*US*) = **paid-up**.

paid-up ['peɪdʌp] (*US* **paid-in**) *adj* (*COMM: shares*) опла́ченный; **he is a ~ member** он уплати́л чле́нский* взнос; ~ **capital** (*COMM*) опла́ченная часть объя́вленного акционе́рного капита́ла.

pail [peɪl] *n* ведро́*.

pain [peɪn] *n* (*also fig*) боль *f*; **to be in ~** страда́ть (*impf*) от бо́ли; **to have a ~ in** чу́вствовать (*impf*) боль в +*prp*; **to take ~s do** стара́ться (постара́ться *perf*) изо всех сил, что́бы +*infin*; **on ~ of death** под стра́хом сме́рти.

pained [peɪnd] *adj* оби́женный (оби́жен).

painful ['peɪnful] *adj* (*upsetting, unpleasant, laborious*) мучи́тельный* (мучи́телен); (*sore*): **my back is ~** спина́ причиня́ет мне боль.

painfully ['peɪnfəlɪ] *adv* (*fig: very*) глубоко́; (: *aware, familiar*) до бо́ли; (: *dull, obvious*) мучи́тельно.

painkiller ['peɪnkɪlə'] *n* болеутоля́ющее *nt adj* (сре́дство).

painless ['peɪnlɪs] *adj* безболе́зненный* (безболе́знен).

painstaking ['peɪnzteɪkɪŋ] *adj* кропотли́вый (кропотли́в).

paint [peɪnt] *n* кра́ска* ◆ *vt* (*wall, door, house etc*) краси́ть* (вы́красить* *or* покра́сить*

perf); (*picture, portrait*) рисова́ть (нарисова́ть *perf*); (*about artists*) писа́ть* (написа́ть* *perf*); (*fig*) изобража́ть (изобрази́ть* *perf*); **a tin of ~** ба́нка* кра́ски; **to ~ the door blue** кра́сить* (вы́красить* *or* покра́сить* *perf*) дверь в голубо́й цвет; **to ~ in oils** писа́ть* (написа́ть* *perf*) ма́слом.

paintbox ['peɪntbɔks] *n* набо́р кра́сок.

paintbrush ['peɪntbrʌʃ] *n* кисть* *f*.

painter ['peɪntə'] *n* (*artist*) худо́жник(-ица); (*decorator*) маля́р*.

painting ['peɪntɪŋ] *n* (*activity: of artist*) жи́вопись *f*; (: *of decorator*) маля́рное де́ло; (*picture*) карти́на.

paint stripper *n* сре́дство для сня́тия кра́ски.

paintwork ['peɪntwə:k] *n* кра́ска.

pair [pɛə'] *n* па́ра; **a ~ of scissors** но́жницы *pl*; **a ~ of trousers** па́ра брюк

▶ **pair off** *vi*: **to ~ off with sb** объединя́ться (объедини́ться* *perf*) в па́ре с кем-н.

pajamas [pə'dʒɑ:məz] *npl* (*US*) пижа́ма *fsg*.

Pakistan [pɑ:kɪ'stɑ:n] *n* Пакиста́н.

Pakistani [pɑ:kɪ'stɑ:nɪ] *adj* пакиста́нский* ◆ *n* пакиста́нец*(-нка*).

PAL *n abbr* (*TV:* = *phase alternation line*) ПАЛ.

pal [pæl] *n* (*inf*) ко́реш.

palace ['pæləs] *n* дворе́ц*.

palaeontology [pælɪən'tɔlədʒɪ] *n* палеонтоло́гия.

palatable ['pælɪtəbl] *adj* (*food, drink*) вку́сный* (вку́сен); (*idea, fact*) прие́млемый.

palate ['pælɪt] *n* (*ANAT*) нёбо; (*fig*) вкус.

palatial [pə'leɪʃəl] *adj* роско́шный* (роско́шен).

palaver [pə'lɑ:və'] *n* (*inf*) суетня́.

pale [peɪl] *adj* бле́дный* (бле́ден) ◆ *vi* бледне́ть (побледне́ть *perf*) ◆ *n*: **his behaviour is beyond the ~** (*unacceptable*) его́ поведе́ние перехо́дит все гра́ницы; **to grow** *or* **turn ~** бледне́ть (побледне́ть *perf*); ~ **blue** бле́дно-голубо́й; **to ~ into insignificance beside** бледне́ть (побледне́ть *perf*) пе́ред +*instr*.

paleness ['peɪlnɪs] *n* бле́дность *f*.

Palestine ['pælɪstaɪn] *n* Палести́на.

Palestinian [pælɪs'tɪnɪən] *adj* палести́нский* ◆ *n* палести́нец*(-нка*).

palette ['pælɪt] *n* (*ART*) пали́тра.

palings ['peɪlɪŋz] *npl* частоко́л *msg*.

palisade [pælɪ'seɪd] *n* крепостна́я огра́да.

pall [pɔ:l] *n* (*cloud of smoke*) покро́в ◆ *vi* приеда́ться (прие́сться* *perf*).

pallet ['pælɪt] *n* (*for goods*) поддо́н.

palliative ['pælɪətɪv] *n* (*MED*) паллиати́вное сре́дство; (*fig*) полуме́ра.

pallid ['pælɪd] *adj* бле́дный* (бле́ден).

pallor ['pælə'] *n* бле́дность *f*.

pally ['pælɪ] *adj* (*inf*) сво́йский*.

palm [pɑ:m] *n* (*also:* ~ **tree**) па́льма; (*of hand*) ладо́нь *f* ◆ *vt*: **to ~ sth off on sb** (*inf*) подсо́вывать (подсу́нуть *perf*) что-н кому́-н.

palmist ['pɑ:mɪst] *n* хиромáнт(ка*).
Palm Sunday *n* ≈ Вéрбное воскресéнье.
palpable ['pælpəbl] *adj* ощутúмый (ощутúм).
palpitations [pælpɪ'teɪʃənz] *npl* (учащённое) сердцебиéние *ntsg*.
paltry ['pɔ:ltrɪ] *adj* (*amount*) ничтóжный* (ничтóжен).
pamper ['pæmpə'] *vt* баловáть (избаловáть *perf*).
pamphlet ['pæmflət] *n* (*leaflet*) брошю́ра; (: *political, literary etc*) памфлéт.
pan [pæn] *n* (*also*: **saucepan**) кастрю́ля; (*also*: **frying** ~) сковородá ♦ *vi* (*CINEMA, TV*) панорамúровать (*impf/perf*) ♦ *vt* (*inf*: *book, film*) разносúть* (разнестú* *perf*); **to ~ for gold** намывáть (намы́ть* *perf*) зóлото.
panacea [pænə'sɪə] *n* панацéя.
panache [pə'næʃ] *n* щегольствó.
Panama ['pænəmɑ:] *n* Панáма.
panama *n* (*also*: ~ **hat**) панáма.
Panama Canal *n*: **the** ~ ~ Панáмский* канáл.
Panamanian [pænə'meɪnɪən] *adj* панáмский* ♦ *n* панáмец*(-мка).
pancake ['pænkeɪk] *n* (*thin*) блин*; (*thick*) олáдья.
Pancake Day *n* (*BRIT*) *втóрник во врéмя мáсленицы, в котóрый пекýт блины́*.
pancake roll *n* блúнчик с начúнкой (*свёрнутый в трýбочку*).
pancreas ['pæŋkrɪəs] *n* поджелýдочная железá*.
panda ['pændə] *n* бамбýковый медвéдь *m*.
panda car *n* (*BRIT*) полицéйская машúна.
pandemonium [pændɪ'məunɪəm] *n* столпотворéние.
pander ['pændə'] *vi*: **to** ~ **to** потвóрствовать (*impf*) +*dat*.
p & h *abbr* (*US*: = **postage and handling**) почтóвые расхóды *pl*.
P & L *abbr* (= **profit and loss**) прúбыль *f* и убы́ток.
p & p *abbr* (*BRIT*: = **postage and packing**) почтóвые расхóды и упакóвка.
pane [peɪn] *n*: ~ (**of glass**) (*in window*) окóнное стеклó*.
panel ['pænl] *n* (*of wood, metal, glass*) панéль *f*; (*of judges, experts*) комúссия.
panel game *n* (*BRIT*: *TV, RADIO*) викторúна.
panelling ['pænəlɪŋ] (*US* **paneling**) *n* деревя́нная обшúвка.
panellist ['pænəlɪst] (*US* **panelist**) *n* (*TV, RADIO*) учáстник(-ица) прогрáммы.
pang [pæŋ] *n*: ~ **of jealousy** укóл рéвности; ~**s of conscience** укóры сóвести; ~ **of regret** мýки сожалéния; **hunger** ~**s** голóдные бóли.
panhandler ['pænhændlə'] *n* (*US*: *inf*) нúщий* *m adj*.
panic ['pænɪk] *n* пáника ♦ *vi* паниковáть (*impf*).

panic buying [-baɪɪŋ] *n* скýпка дефицúтных товáров.
panicky ['pænɪkɪ] *adj* (*feeling, reaction*) панúческий*; (*person*): **he is very** ~ он паникýет.
panic-stricken ['pænɪkstrɪkən] *adj* (*person, crowd*) охвáченный (охвáчен) пáникой.
pannier ['pænɪə'] *n* (*on bicycle*) корзúнка*-багáжник; (*on animal*) корзúна.
panorama [pænə'rɑ:mə] *n* панорáма.
panoramic [pænə'ræmɪk] *adj* панорáмный.
pansy ['pænzɪ] *n* аню́тины глáзки *mpl*; (*inf*: *pej*) флунтя́й.
pant [pænt] *vi* задыхáться (задохнýться *perf*).
pantechnicon [pæn'teknɪkən] *n* (*BRIT*: *AUT*) *автофургóн для перевóзки мéбели or оборýдования*.
panther ['pænθə'] *n* пантéра.
panties ['pæntɪz] *npl* трýсики *pl*.
pantihose ['pæntɪhəuz] *npl* (*US*) колгóтки* *pl*.
panto ['pæntəu] *n* = **pantomime**.
pantomime ['pæntəmaɪm] *n* (*BRIT*) *рождéственское представлéние для детéй*; (: *fig*) фарс.
pantry ['pæntrɪ] *n* кладовáя *f adj*, кладóвка; (*room*) буфéтная *f adj*.
pants [pænts] *npl* (*BRIT*: *underwear*) трусы́ *pl*; (*US*: *trousers*) брю́ки *pl*.
pantsuit ['pæntsu:t] *n* (*US*) брю́чный костю́м.
papacy ['peɪpəsɪ] *n* пáпство.
papal ['peɪpəl] *adj* пáпский.
paparazzi [pæpə'rætsɪ:] *npl* *фотóграфы, гоня́ющиеся за знаменúтостями и фотографúрующие их для бульвáрной прéссы*.
paper ['peɪpə'] *n* бумáга; (*also*: **newspaper**) газéта; (*exam*) пúсьменный экзáмен; (*academic essay*: *at conference*) доклáд; (: *in journal*) статья́*; (*also*: **wallpaper**) обóи *pl* ♦ *adj* бумáжный ♦ *vt* (*room*) оклéивать (оклéить* *perf*) обóями; ~**s** *npl* (*also*: **identity** ~**s**) докумéнты *mpl*; **a piece of** ~ (*odd bit*) клочóк бумáги, бумáжка; (*sheet*) лист* бумáги; **to put** *or* **get sth down on** ~ запúсывать (записáть* *perf*) что-н на бумáге.
paper advance *n* (*on printer*) продвижéние бумáги.
paperback ['peɪpəbæk] *n* кнúга в мя́гкой облóжке ♦ *adj*: ~ **edition** издáние в мя́гкой облóжке.
paper bag *n* бумáжный пакéт.
paperboy ['peɪpəbɔɪ] *n* мáльчик-разнóсчик газéт.
paperclip ['peɪpəklɪp] *n* (канцеля́рская) скрéпка*.
papergirl ['peɪpəgə:l] *n* дéвочка-разнóсчица газéт.

---

* marks translations which have irregular inflections. The Russian-English side of the dictionary gives inflectional information.

paper hankie *n* бума́жный носово́й плато́к*.
paper mill *n* бума́жная фа́брика.
paper profit *n* бума́жная *or* нереализо́ванная при́быль *f*.
paper shop *n* ≈ газе́тный кио́ск.
paperweight ['peɪpǝweɪt] *n* пресс-папье́ *nt ind*.
paperwork ['peɪpǝwǝ:k] *n* канцеля́рская рабо́та.
papier-mâché ['pæpɪeɪ'mæʃeɪ] *n* папье́-маше́ *nt ind*.
paprika ['pæprɪkǝ] *n* кра́сный мо́лотый пе́рец*.
Pap smear ['pæp-] *n* мазо́к* с ше́йки ма́тки.
Pap test *n* = **Pap smear**.
par [pɑ:ʰ] *n* (*equality of value*) ра́венство; (*GOLF*) коли́чество уда́ров, допусти́мое для ка́ждой лу́нки и́ли для всего́ по́ля; **to be on a ~ with** быть* (*impf*) на одно́м у́ровне с +*instr*; **at ~** (*COMM*) по номина́лу; **to feel below** *or* **under ~** чу́вствовать (*impf*) себя́ нева́жно.
parable ['pærǝbl] *n* при́тча.
parabola [pǝ'ræbǝlǝ] *n* пара́бола.
parachute ['pærǝʃu:t] *n* парашю́т.
parachute jump *n* прыжо́к* с парашю́том.
parachutist ['pærǝʃu:tɪst] *n* парашюти́ст(ка*).
parade [pǝ'reɪd] *n* (*public procession*) ше́ствие; (*MIL*) пара́д ♦ *vt* (*troops etc*) выстра́ивать (вы́строить* *perf*); (*show off: wealth, knowledge etc*) выставля́ть (вы́ставить* *perf*) напока́з ♦ *vi* (*MIL*) идти́* (*impf*) стро́ем; **fashion ~** пока́з мод.
parade ground *n* (уче́бный) плац*.
paradise ['pærǝdaɪs] *n* (*also fig*) рай*.
paradox ['pærǝdɔks] *n* парадо́кс.
paradoxical [pærǝ'dɔksɪkl] *adj* парадокса́льный* (парадокса́лен).
paradoxically [pærǝ'dɔksɪklɪ] *adv* как э́то ни парадокса́льно.
paraffin ['pærǝfɪn] *n* (*BRIT: also: ~ oil*) кероси́н; **liquid ~** (*BRIT*) вазели́новое ма́сло.
paraffin heater *n* (*BRIT*) обогрева́тель *m* на твёрдом парафи́не.
paraffin lamp *n* (*BRIT*) кероси́новая ла́мпа.
paragon ['pærǝgǝn] *n* (*of honesty, virtue etc*) образе́ц*.
paragraph ['pærǝgrɑ:f] *n* абза́ц; (*of document*) пара́граф; **to begin a new ~** начина́ть (нача́ть* *perf*) писа́ть с абза́ца.
Paraguay ['pærǝgwaɪ] *n* Парагва́й.
Paraguayan [pærǝ'gwaɪǝn] *adj* парагва́йский ♦ *n* парагва́ец*(-а́йка*).
parallel ['pærǝlɛl] *adj* паралле́льный* (паралле́лен); (*fig: similar*) аналоги́чный* (аналоги́чен); (*COMPUT*) паралле́льный ♦ *n* (*GEO, fig*) паралле́ль *f*; **to draw ~s between/with** проводи́ть* (провести́* *perf*) паралле́ль ме́жду +*instr*/с +*instr*; **~ (with** *or* **to)** паралле́льно (с +*instr*); **in ~** (*ELEC*) паралле́льно.
paralyse ['pærǝlaɪz] *vt* (*BRIT: also fig*) парализова́ть (*impf/perf*); **he is ~d** (*BRIT*) он парализо́ван.

paralyses [pǝ'rælɪsi:z] *npl of* **paralysis**.
paralysis [pǝ'rælɪsɪs] (*pl* **paralyses**) *n* (*MED*) парали́ч*.
paralytic [pærǝ'lɪtɪk] *adj* (*MED*) парализо́ванный (парализо́ван); (*BRIT: inf: drunk*) упи́вшийся.
paralyze ['pærǝlaɪz] *vt* (*US*) = **paralyse**.
paramedic [pærǝ'mɛdɪk] *n* парамедик; **~s** кома́нда ско́рой по́мощи.
parameter [pǝ'ræmɪtǝ'] *n* пара́метр.
paramilitary [pærǝ'mɪlɪtǝrɪ] *adj* военизи́рованный.
paramount ['pærǝmaunt] *adj* первостепе́нный.
paranoia [pærǝ'nɔɪǝ] *n* парано́йя.
paranoid ['pærǝnɔɪd] *adj* (*person*) парано́идный; (*feeling*) парано́ический.
paranormal [pærǝ'nɔ:ml] *adj* не поддаю́щийся объясне́нию ♦ *n*: **the ~** явле́ния *ntpl*, не поддаю́щиеся объясне́нию.
parapet ['pærǝpɪt] *n* парапе́т.
paraphernalia [pærǝfǝ'neɪlɪǝ] *n* (*gear*) принадле́жности *fpl*.
paraphrase ['pærǝfreɪz] *vt* перефрази́ровать (*impf/perf*).
paraplegic [pærǝ'pli:dʒɪk] *n* страда́ющий(-ая) *m(f) adj* параличо́м ни́жней ча́сти те́ла.
parapsychology [pærǝsaɪ'kɔlǝdʒɪ] *n* парапсихоло́гия.
parasite ['pærǝsaɪt] *n* (*also fig*) парази́т.
parasol ['pærǝsɔl] *n* зо́нтик (*защища́ющий от со́лнца*); (*at café etc*) тент.
paratrooper ['pærǝtru:pǝ'] *n* деса́нтник.
parcel ['pɑ:sl] *n* (*package*) свёрток*; (*sent by post*) посы́лка* ♦ *vt* (*also: ~ up*) завёртывать (заверну́ть* *perf*).
► **parcel out** *vt* раздава́ть* (разда́ть* *perf*).
parcel bomb *n* (*BRIT*) бо́мба, спря́танная в паке́т.
parcel post *n* почто́во-посы́лочная слу́жба.
parch [pɑ:tʃ] *vt* (*crops, land*) выжига́ть (вы́жечь* *perf*).
parched [pɑ:tʃt] *adj*: **I'm ~** у меня́ пересо́хло в го́рле.
parchment ['pɑ:tʃmǝnt] *n* перга́мент.
pardon ['pɑ:dn] *n* (*LAW*) поми́лование ♦ *vt* проща́ть (прости́ть* *perf*); (*LAW*) поми́ловать (*perf*); **~ me!, I beg your ~!** прошу́ проще́ния!; **(I beg your) ~?**, (*US*) **~ me?** (*what did you say?*) прости́те, не рассл́ышал.
pare [pɛǝ'] *vt* (*BRIT: nails*) стричь* (остри́чь* *perf*); (*fruit*) чи́стить* (очи́стить* *perf*); (*costs*) уре́зывать *or* уреза́ть (уре́зать* *perf*).
parent [ˈpɛǝrǝnt] *n* роди́тель(ница) *m(f)*; **~s** *npl* (*mother and father*) роди́тели *mpl*.
parentage ['pɛǝrǝntɪdʒ] *n* происхожде́ние; **she is of unknown ~** её происхожде́ние неизве́стно.
parental [pǝ'rɛntl] *adj* роди́тельский*.
parent company *n* (*COMM*) матери́нская компа́ния.
parentheses [pǝ'rɛnθɪsi:z] *npl of* **parenthesis**.

parenthesis [pə'rɛnθɪsɪs] (*pl* **parentheses**) *n* (*word*) вво́дное сло́во*; (*phrase*) вво́дное предложе́ние; **in** ~ в ско́бках.
parenthood ['pɛərənthud] *n* (*motherhood*) матери́нство; (*fatherhood*) отцо́вство.
parenting ['pɛərəntɪŋ] *n* воспита́ние.
Paris ['pærɪs] *n* Пари́ж.
parish ['pærɪʃ] *n* (*REL*) прихо́д; (*BRIT: civil*) о́круг*.
parish council *n* (*BRIT*) прихо́дский* сове́т.
parishioner [pə'rɪʃənər] *n* (*REL*) прихожа́нин*(-а́нка*).
Parisian [pə'rɪzɪən] *adj* пари́жский* ◆ *n* парижа́нин*(-нка*).
parity ['pærɪtɪ] *n* (*equality: of pay, conditions etc*) парите́т.
park [pɑːk] *n* парк ◆ *vt* (*AUT*) ста́вить* (поста́вить* *perf*), паркова́ть (припаркова́ть *perf*) ◆ *vi* (*AUT*) паркова́ться (припаркова́ться *perf*).
parka ['pɑːkə] *n* стёганая ку́ртка на меху́.
parking ['pɑːkɪŋ] *n* (*of vehicle*) паркова́ние; (*space to park*) стоя́нка*; "**no** ~" „стоя́нка запрещена́".
parking lights *npl* подфа́рники *mpl*.
parking lot *n* (*US*) (авто)стоя́нка.
parking meter *n* счётчик на (авто)стоя́нке.
parking offence *n* (*BRIT*) наруше́ние пра́вил стоя́нки.
parking place *n* ме́сто* на автостоя́нке.
parking ticket *n* штраф за наруше́ние пра́вил паркова́ния.
parking violation *n* (*US*) = **parking offence**.
Parkinson's ['pɑːkɪnsənz] *n* (*also:* ~ **disease**) боле́знь *f* Паркинсона.
parkway ['pɑːkweɪ] *n* (*US*) доро́га, обса́женная дере́вьями.
parlance ['pɑːləns] *n*: **in common/modern** ~ говоря́ обы́чным/совреме́нным языко́м.
parliament ['pɑːləmənt] *n* парла́мент.
parliamentary [pɑːlə'mɛntərɪ] *adj* парла́ментский*.
parlour ['pɑːlər] (*US* **parlor**) *n* гости́ная *f adj*.
parlous ['pɑːləs] *adj* бе́дственный.
Parmesan [pɑːmɪ'zæn] *n* (*also:* ~ **cheese**) сыр пармеза́н.
parochial [pə'rəukɪəl] *adj* (*pej*) ограни́ченный* (ограни́чен).
parody ['pærədɪ] *n* паро́дия ◆ *vt* пароди́ровать (*impf/perf*).
parole [pə'rəul] *n*: **he is/was released on** ~ (*LAW*) он освобождён/был освобождён под че́стное сло́во.
paroxysm ['pærəksɪzəm] *n* (*also MED*) парокси́зм.
parquet ['pɑːkeɪ] *n*: ~ **floor(ing)** парке́тный пол*.
parrot ['pærət] *n* попуга́й.

parrot-fashion ['pærətfæʃən] *adv* как попуга́й.
parry ['pærɪ] *vt* (*blow*) отража́ть (отрази́ть* *perf*); (*question*) пари́ровать (*impf/perf*).
parsimonious [pɑːsɪ'məunɪəs] *adj* (*person*) скупо́й* (скуп).
parsley ['pɑːslɪ] *n* петру́шка.
parsnip ['pɑːsnɪp] *n* пастерна́к (посевно́й).
parson ['pɑːsn] *n* прихо́дский* свяще́нник; (*Church of England*) па́стор.
part [pɑːt] *n* (*section, division*) часть* *f*; (*component*) дета́ль* *f*; (*role*) роль* *f*; (*episode*) се́рия; (*MUS*) па́ртия; (*US: in hair*) пробо́р ◆ *adv* = **partly** ◆ *vt* разделя́ть (раздели́ть* *perf*); (*hair*) расчёсывать (расчеса́ть* *perf*) на пробо́р ◆ *vi* (*people*) расстава́ться* (расста́ться* *perf*); (*crowd*) расступа́ться (расступи́ться* *perf*); (*roads*) расходи́ться* (разойти́сь* *perf*); **to take** ~ **in** принима́ть (приня́ть* *perf*) уча́стие в +*prp*; **to take sth in good** ~ не обижа́ться (оби́деться* *perf*) на что-н; **to take sb's** ~ (*support*) станови́ться* (стать* *perf*) на чью-н сто́рону; **on his/for my** ~ с его́/мое́й стороны́; **for the most** ~ бо́льшей ча́стью; **for the better** ~ **of the day** бо́льшую часть дня; **to be** ~ **and parcel of** явля́ться (*impf*) неотъе́млемой ча́стью +*gen*; ~ **of speech** (*LING*) часть ре́чи.
► **part with** *vt fus* (*money, possessions*) расстава́ться* (расста́ться* *perf*) с +*infin*.
partake [pɑː'teɪk] *irreg vi* (*formal*): **to** ~ **of sth** отве́дывать (отве́дать* *perf*) чего́-н.
part exchange *n* (*BRIT: COMM*) рассчёт, при кото́ром де́нежный взнос сочета́ется с обме́ном ста́рого това́ра на но́вый.
partial ['pɑːʃl] *adj* (*not complete*) части́чный*; (*biased*) пристра́стный* (пристра́стен); **I am** ~ **to chocolate** (*like*) я пристра́стен к шокола́ду.
partially ['pɑːʃəlɪ] *adv* части́чно.
participant [pɑː'tɪsɪpənt] *n* уча́стник(-ица).
participate [pɑː'tɪsɪpeɪt] *vi*: **to** ~ **in** уча́ствовать (*impf*) в +*prp*.
participation [pɑːtɪsɪ'peɪʃən] *n* уча́стие.
participle ['pɑːtɪsɪpl] *n* прича́стие.
particle ['pɑːtɪkl] *n* (*also PHYS*) части́ца.
particular [pə'tɪkjulər] *adj* (*distinct, special*) осо́бый; (*demanding*) привере́дливый (привере́длив); ~**s** *npl* (*specifics*) ча́стности *fpl*; (*personal details*) да́нные *pl adj*; **he is very** ~ **about what he eats** он о́чень привере́длив в еде́; **in** ~ в ча́стности.
particularly [pə'tɪkjulərlɪ] *adv* осо́бенно.
parting ['pɑːtɪŋ] *n* (*action*) разделе́ние; (*farewell*) проща́ние; (*BRIT: in hair*) пробо́р ◆ *adj* (*words, gift etc*) проща́льный; ~ **shot** проща́льное замеча́ние.
partisan [pɑːtɪ'zæn] *adj* (*politics, views*) пристра́стный* (пристра́стен) ◆ *n* (*supporter*)

---

* marks translations which have irregular inflections. The Russian-English side of the dictionary gives inflectional information.

приве́рженец*; (*resistance fighter*)
партиза́н(ка*).

partition [pɑːˈtɪʃən] *n* (*wall, screen*)
перегоро́дка*; (*of country*) разде́л ♦ *vt*
разделя́ть (раздели́ть* *perf*).

partly [ˈpɑːtlɪ] *adv* части́чно.

partner [ˈpɑːtnəʳ] *n* (*spouse*) супру́г(а);
(*girlfriend*) де́вушка*; (*boyfriend*) па́рень* *m*;
(*COMM, SPORT, CARDS*) партнёр ♦ *vt*: **I used to ~
him** я был его́ партнёром.

partnership [ˈpɑːtnəʃɪp] *n* (*COMM: company*)
това́рищество; (: *with person*) партнёрство;
(*POL*) сою́з; **to go into** *or* **form a ~ (with)**
устана́вливать (установи́ть* *perf*)
партнёрство (с +*instr*).

part payment *n* части́чная опла́та.

partridge [ˈpɑːtrɪdʒ] *n* (*се́рая*) куропа́тка*.

part-time [ˈpɑːtˈtaɪm] *adj* (*work*) почасово́й;
(*staff*) за́нятый* (за́нят) непо́лный рабо́чий*
день* ♦ *adv*: **to work ~** быть* (*impf*) на
почасово́й ста́вке; **to study ~** обуча́ться
(*impf*) по непо́лной програ́мме.

part-timer [ˈpɑːtˈtaɪməʳ] *n* (*also*: **part-time
worker**) рабо́тник(-ица) на почасово́й
ста́вке, почасови́к.

party [ˈpɑːtɪ] *n* (*POL*) па́ртия; (*celebration:
formal*) ве́чер*; (: *informal*) вечери́нка*;
(*group of people: surveying etc*) па́ртия;
(: *rescue etc*) отря́д; (: *tourists etc*) гру́ппа;
(*LAW*) сторона́* ♦ *cpd* (*POL*) парти́йный;
dinner ~ зва́ный обе́д; **to give** *or* **throw a ~**
(*official*) устра́ивать (устро́ить* *perf*) ве́чер;
we're having a ~ next Saturday в сле́дующую
суббо́ту у нас вечери́нка; **birthday ~**
пра́зднование дня рожде́ния; **he was (a) ~ to
the crime** он явля́лся соуча́стником
преступле́ния.

party dress *n* вече́рнее пла́тье*.

party line *n* (*TEL*) о́бщая телефо́нная ли́ния;
(*POL*) парти́йная ли́ния.

party piece *n* коро́нный но́мер*.

party-political [ˈpɑːtɪpəˈlɪtɪkl] *adj* парти́йный
полити́ческий*.

party-political broadcast *n* рекла́ма
*полити́ческой па́ртии по ра́дио и
телеви́дению.*

pass [pɑːs] *vt* (*spend: time*) проводи́ть*
(провести́* *perf*); (*hand over*) передава́ть*
(переда́ть* *perf*); (*go past: on foot*) проходи́ть*
(пройти́* *perf*); (: *by transport*) проезжа́ть
(прое́хать* *perf*); (*overtake: vehicle*) обгоня́ть
(обогна́ть* *perf*); (*fig: surpass*) превосходи́ть*
(превзойти́* *perf*); (*exam*) сдава́ть* (сдать*
perf); (*approve: law, proposal*) принима́ть
(приня́ть* *perf*) ♦ *vi* (*go past: on foot*)
проходи́ть* (пройти́* *perf*); (: *by transport*)
проезжа́ть (прое́хать* *perf*); (*in exam*)
сдава́ть* (сдать* *perf*) ♦ *n* (*permit*) про́пуск*;
(*membership card*) чле́нский биле́т*; (*GEO*)
перева́л; (*SPORT*) пас, переда́ча; (*SCOL: also*:
~ mark): **to get a ~** получа́ть (получи́ть* *perf*)

зачёт; **to ~ sth through sth** просо́вывать
(просу́нуть* *perf*) что-н че́рез что-н; **could you
~ the vegetables round?** переда́йте,
пожа́луйста, о́вощи всем; **she could ~ for 25**
она́ могла́ бы сойти́ за 25-ле́тнюю; **things
have come to a pretty ~** (*BRIT*) дела́ пло́хи; **to
make a ~ at sb** (*inf*) пристава́ть* (приста́ть*
perf) к кому́-н
▶ **pass away** *vi* (*die*) сконча́ться (*perf*)
▶ **pass by** *vi* (*on foot*) проходи́ть* (пройти́*
perf); (*by transport*) проезжа́ть (прое́хать*
perf) ♦ *vt* (*ignore*) не обраща́ть (обрати́ть*
perf) внима́ния на +*acc*
▶ **pass down** *vt* (*customs, inheritance*)
передава́ть* (переда́ть* *perf*)
▶ **pass on** *vt* передава́ть* (переда́ть* *perf*);
(*price rises*) перекла́дывать (переложи́ть*
perf) ♦ *vi* (*die*) сконча́ться (*perf*)
▶ **pass out** *vi* (*faint*) теря́ть (потеря́ть *perf*)
созна́ние; (*BRIT: MIL*) успе́шно проходи́ть*
(пройти́* *perf*) подгото́вку
▶ **pass over** *vt* (*ignore*) оставля́ть (оста́вить*
perf) без внима́ния ♦ *vi* (*die*) сконча́ться (*perf*)
▶ **pass up** *vt* (*opportunity*) упуска́ть (упусти́ть*
perf).

passable [ˈpɑːsəbl] *adj* (*road*) проходи́мый
(проходи́м); (*acceptable: work*) сно́сный*
(сно́сен).

passage [ˈpæsɪdʒ] *n* (*also ANAT*) прохо́д; (*in
book*) отры́вок*; (*act of passing*)
прохожде́ние; (*journey: on boat*)
путеше́ствие.

passenger [ˈpæsɪndʒəʳ] *n* пассажи́р(ка*).

passer-by [ˈpɑːsəˈbaɪ] (*pl* **passers-by**) *n*
прохо́жий*(-ая) *m(f) adj*.

passers-by [ˈpɑːsəzˈbaɪ] *npl of* **passer-by**.

passing [ˈpɑːsɪŋ] *adj* мимолётный*
(мимолётен) ♦ *n*: **in ~** мимохо́дом; **to
mention sth in ~** замеча́ть (заме́тить* *perf*)
что-н мимохо́дом.

passing place *n* (*AUT*) расшире́ние на доро́ге.

passion [ˈpæʃən] *n* (*also fig*) страсть* *f*; **she has
a ~ for history** у неё страсть к исто́рии.

passionate [ˈpæʃənɪt] *adj* стра́стный*
(стра́стен).

passion fruit *n* плод* страстоцве́та.

Passion play *n* мисте́рия, в кото́рой
представля́ются стра́сти Госпо́дни.

passive [ˈpæsɪv] *adj* пасси́вный* (пасси́вен);
(*LING*) пасси́вный, страда́тельный ♦ *n* (*LING*):
the ~ страда́тельный зало́г.

passive smoking *n* пасси́вное куре́ние.

passkey [ˈpɑːskiː] *n* отмы́чка*.

Passover [ˈpɑːsəuvəʳ] *n* евре́йская Па́сха.

passport [ˈpɑːspɔːt] *n* (*official document*)
па́спорт*; (*fig*) ключ*.

passport control *n* па́спортный контро́ль *m*.

password [ˈpɑːswəːd] *n* паро́ль *m*.

past [pɑːst] *prep* (*in front of*) ми́мо +*gen*;
(*beyond*) за +*instr*; (*later than*) по́сле +*gen* ♦ *adj*
(*previous: government etc*) бы́вший*; (: *week*,

month etc) прóшлый ◆ *n* прóшлое *nt adj*; (*LING*): **the ~ (tense)** прошéдшее врéмя* *nt* ◆ *adv*: **to run ~** пробегáть (пробежáть* *perf*) мúмо; **he's ~ forty** (*older than*) емý за сóрок; **it's ~ midnight** ужé зá пóлночь; **ten/quarter ~ eight** дéсять минýт/чéтверть девя́того; **he ran ~ me** он пробежáл мúмо меня́; **I'm ~ caring** мне ýже всё равнó; **he's ~ it** (*BRIT: inf*) он вы́дохнулся; **for the ~ few/3 days** за послéдние нéсколько днéй/3 дня́; **in the ~** в прóшлом; (*LING*) в прошéдшем врéмени.
pasta ['pæstə] *n* макарóнные издéлия *ntpl*.
paste [peɪst] *n* (*wet mixture*) пáста; (*glue*) клéйстер; (*jewellery*) страз; (*fish, meat paste*) паштéт ◆ *vt* (*paper etc*) наносúть* (нанестú* *perf*) клей на +*acc*; **tomato ~** томáтная пáста; **to ~ sth onto sth** наносúть* (нанестú* *perf*) что-н на что-н.
pastel ['pæstl] *adj* (*colour*) пастéльный.
pasteurized ['pæstʃəraɪzd] *adj* (*milk etc*) пастеризóванный.
pastille ['pæstl] *n* пастилá.
pastime ['pɑːstaɪm] *n* (*hobby*) врéмя-препровождéние.
past master *n* (*BRIT*) непревзойдённый мáстер.
pastor ['pɑːstəʳ] *n* пáстор.
pastoral ['pɑːstərl] *adj* (*REL*) пáсторский.
pastry ['peɪstrɪ] *n* (*dough*) тéсто; (*cake*) пирóжное *nt adj*.
pasture ['pɑːstʃəʳ] *n* пáстбище.
pasty [*adj* 'peɪstɪ, *n* 'pæstɪ] *adj* (*complexion, face*) блéдный* (блéден) ◆ *n* пирожóк*.
pat [pæt] *n* (*answer, remark*) стандáртный* (стандáртен) ◆ *vt* (*dog*) ласкáть (приласкáть* *perf*) ◆ *n*: **to give sb/o.s. a ~ on the back** (*fig*) хвалúть* (похвалúть* *perf*) когó-н/себя́ ◆ *adv*: **to know sth off ~**, (*US*) **have sth down ~** знать (*impf*) что-н назубóк; **to ~ sb's back** похлóпывать (похлóпать *perf*) когó-н по спинé.
patch [pætʃ] *n* (*piece of material*) заплáта; (*also*: **eye ~**) повя́зка*; (*area: damp, black etc*) пятнó*; (*repair: on tyre etc*) заплáта, заплáтка*; (*of land*) учáсток* ◆ *vt* (*clothes*) латáть (залатáть *perf*); **to go through a bad ~** попадáть (попáсть* *perf*) в полосý невезéния; **bald ~** лы́сина
▸ **patch up** *vt* (*mend temporarily*) задéлывать (задéлать *perf*); (*quarrel*) улáживать (улáдить* *perf*).
patchwork ['pætʃwəːk] *n* (*SEWING*) лоскýтная рабóта.
patchy ['pætʃɪ] *adj* (*uneven: colour*) пятнúстый (пятнúст); (*incomplete: information, knowledge etc*) отры́вочный* (отры́вочен).
pate [peɪt] *n*: **a bald ~** лы́сина на макýше.
pâté ['pæteɪ] *n* (*CULIN*) паштéт.

patent ['peɪtnt] *n* (*COMM*) патéнт ◆ *vt* (*COMM*) патентовáть* (запатентовáть* *perf*) ◆ *adj* (*obvious*) я́вный* (я́вен).
patent leather *n* лакирóванная кóжа.
patently ['peɪtntlɪ] *adv* (*obvious, wrong*) очевúдно.
patent medicine *n* патентóванное лекáрство.
Patent Office *n* патéнтное бюрó *nt ind*.
patent rights *npl* патéнтное прáво *ntsg*.
paternal [pə'təːnl] *adj* (*love, duty*) отцóвский*; (*grandmother etc*) по отцý.
paternalistic [pətəːnə'lɪstɪk] *adj* (*society, attitudes*) патерналистúческий.
paternity [pə'təːnɪtɪ] *n* отцóвство.
paternity leave *n* óтпуск отцá по ухóду за ребёнком.
paternity suit *n* (*LAW*) установлéние отцóвства.
path [pɑːθ] *n* (*trail, track*) тропá*, тропúнка*; (*concrete path, gravel path etc*) дорóжка*; (*trajectory*) путь* *m* движéния; (*fig*) путь*.
pathetic [pə'θɛtɪk] *adj* (*pitiful: sight, cries*) жáлостный* (жáлостен); (*very bad*) жáлкий* (жáлок).
pathological [pæθə'lɔdʒɪkl] *adj* (*liar, hatred*) патологúческий*; (*MED: work*) в óбласти патолóгии.
pathologist [pə'θɔlədʒɪst] *n* (*MED*) патóлог.
pathology [pə'θɔlədʒɪ] *n* (*MED*) патолóгия.
pathos ['peɪθɔs] *n* пáфос.
pathway ['pɑːθweɪ] *n* (*path*) тропá; (*route, fig*) путь* *m*.
patience ['peɪʃns] *n* (*personal quality*) терпéние; (*BRIT: CARDS*) пасья́нс; **to lose one's ~** теря́ть (потеря́ть *perf*) терпéние.
patient ['peɪʃnt] *n* (*MED*) пациéнт(ка) ◆ *adj* (*person*) терпелúвый (терпелúв); **he is ~ with me** он терпелúв со мной.
patiently ['peɪʃntlɪ] *adv* терпелúво.
patio ['pætɪəu] *n* пáтио *m ind*, внýтренний двóрик.
patriot ['peɪtrɪət] *n* патриóт(ка).
patriotic [pætrɪ'ɔtɪk] *adj* (*person*) патриотúчный* (патриотúчен); (*song, speech etc*) патриотúческий, патриотúчный* (патриотúчен).
patriotism ['pætrɪətɪzəm] *n* патриотúзм.
patrol [pə'trəul] *n* (*MIL, POLICE*) патрýль *m* ◆ *vt* (*MIL, POLICE: city, streets etc*) патрулúровать* (*impf*); **to be on ~** быть* (*impf*) в дозóре; (*POLICE*) быть* (*impf*) на дежýрстве.
patrol boat *n* (*NAUT, MIL, CUSTOMS etc*) сторожевóй кáтер.
patrol car *n* (*POLICE*) полицéйская патрýльная машúна.
patrolman [pə'trəulmən] *irreg n* (*US: POLICE*) дежýрный полицéйский *m adj*.
patron ['peɪtrən] *n* (*customer, client*)

(постоя́нный) клие́нт; (*benefactor: of charity*) спо́нсор, шеф; ~ **of the arts** покрови́тель (ница) *m(f)* иску́сств.

patronage ['pætrənɪdʒ] *n* (*of artist etc*) покрови́тельство; (*of charity*) спо́нсорство, ше́фство.

patronize ['pætrənaɪz] *vt* (*pej: look down on*) относи́ться* (отнести́сь* *perf*) свысока́; (*artist, writer*) покрови́тельствовать (*impf*) +*dat*; (*shop, club, firm*) постоя́нно посеща́ть (*impf*).

patronizing ['pætrənaɪzɪŋ] *adj* (*pej: person, tone, comment etc*) снисходи́тельный* (снисходи́телен).

patron saint *n* (*REL*) засту́пник(-ица).

patter ['pætə'] *n* (*sound: of feet, rain*) топота́ние; (*of rain*) сту́к; (*sales talk etc*) речитати́в ♦ *vi* (*footsteps*) топота́ть (*impf*); (*rain*) бараба́нить (*impf*).

pattern ['pætən] *n* (*design*) узо́р; (*SEWING*) вы́кройка*; (*sample*) образе́ц*; **behaviour ~s** мане́ры *fpl* поведе́ния.

patterned ['pætənd] *adj* (*fabric, wallpaper, carpet etc*) узо́рчатый; ~ **with flowers** с узо́ром из цвето́в.

paucity ['pɔːsɪtɪ] *n* недоста́ток*.

paunch [pɔːntʃ] *n* брюшко́*.

pauper ['pɔːpə'] *n* ни́щий*(-ая) *m(f) adj*; ~**'s grave** бедня́цкая моги́ла.

pause [pɔːz] *n* (*temporary halt*) переры́в; (*MUS*) па́уза ♦ *vi* (*stop temporarily*) де́лать (сде́лать *perf*) переры́в; (: *while speaking*) де́лать (сде́лать *perf*) па́узу; **to ~ for breath** переводи́ть* (перевести́* *perf*) дыха́ние; (*fig*) передохну́ть (*perf*).

pave [peɪv] *vt* (*street, yard etc*) мости́ть* (вы́мостить* *perf*); **to ~ the way for** (*fig*) прокла́дывать (проложи́ть* *perf*) путь к +*dat*.

pavement ['peɪvmənt] *n* (*BRIT: for pedestrians*) тротуа́р; (*US: roadway*) доро́жное покры́тие.

pavilion [pə'vɪlɪən] *n* (*SPORT*) павильо́н.

paving ['peɪvɪŋ] *n* (*material*) доро́жное покры́тие.

paving stone *n* брусча́тка*.

paw [pɔː] *n* (*of animal*) ла́па* ♦ *vt* (*animal*) тро́гать (потро́гать *perf*) ла́пой *or* ла́пами; (*horse, bull*) бить* (*impf*) копы́том *or* копы́тами; (*pej: touch*) ла́пать (*impf*).

pawn [pɔːn] *n* (*CHESS, fig*) пе́шка ♦ *vt* закла́дывать (заложи́ть* *perf*).

pawnbroker ['pɔːnbrəukə'] *n* ростовщи́к(-и́ца).

pawnshop ['pɔːnʃɒp] *n* ломба́рд.

pay [peɪ] (*pt, pp* **paid**) *n* (*wage, salary etc*) зарпла́та ♦ *vt* (*sum of money, wage*) плати́ть* (заплати́ть* *perf*); (*debt, bill*) плати́ть* (уплати́ть* *perf*); (*be profitable to: also fig*) окупа́ть (окупи́ть* *perf*) ♦ *vi* (*be profitable*) окупа́ться (окупи́ться* *perf*); **how much did you ~ for it?** ско́лько Вы за него́/неё/э́то заплати́ли?; **I paid £5 for that record** я заплати́л £5 за ту пласти́нку; **to ~ one's way**

обеспе́чивать (обеспе́чить *perf*) себя́; **to ~ dividends** (*fig*) вознагражда́ться (вознагради́ться* *perf*); **it won't ~ you to do that** э́то де́ло не принесёт вам успе́ха; **to ~ attention (to)** обраща́ть (обрати́ть* *perf*) внима́ние (на +*acc*); **to ~ sb a visit** наноси́ть* (нанести́* *perf*) кому́-н визи́т; **to ~ one's respects to sb** свиде́тельствовать* (засвиде́тельствовать* *perf*) кому́-н (своё) почте́ние

▸ **pay back** *vt* (*money*) возвраща́ть (возврати́ть* *or* верну́ть *perf*); (*person*) отплати́ть* (*perf*)

▸ **pay for** *vt fus* (*purchases*) опла́чивать (оплати́ть* *perf*); (*fig*) поплати́ться* (*perf*) за +*acc*

▸ **pay in** *vt* (*money, cheque etc*) вноси́ть* (внести́* *perf*)

▸ **pay off** *vt* (*debt, creditor, mortgage*) распла́чиваться (расплати́ться* *perf*) с +*instr*; (*person*) рассчи́тывать (рассчита́ть *perf*) ♦ *vi* (*also fig*) окупа́ться (окупи́ться* *perf*); **to ~ sth off in instalments** распла́чиваться (расплати́ться* *perf*) за что-н в рассро́чку

▸ **pay out** *vt* (*money*) выпла́чивать (вы́платить* *perf*); (*rope*) трави́ть* (потрави́ть* *perf*)

▸ **pay up** *vt* (*money*) выпла́чивать (вы́платить* *perf*) ♦ *vi* (*person, company etc*) рассчи́тываться (рассчита́ться *perf*) (сполна́).

payable ['peɪəbl] *adj* (*sum of money*) подлежа́щий упла́те; (*cheque*): ~ **to** подлежа́щий упла́те на и́мя +*gen*.

pay award *n* повыше́ние зарпла́ты.

payday ['peɪdeɪ] *n* день* *m* зарпла́ты.

PAYE *n abbr* (*BRIT:* = *pay as you earn*) *отчисле́ние подохо́дного нало́га из зарпла́ты*.

payee [peɪ'iː] *n* (*of cheque, postal order*) получа́тель(ница) *m(f)*.

pay envelope *n* (*US*) = **pay packet**.

paying guest ['peɪŋ-] *n* постоя́лец(-лица).

payload ['peɪləud] *n* (*COMM*) поле́зная нагру́зка*.

payment ['peɪmənt] *n* (*act*) платёж*, упла́та; (*of bill*) опла́та; (*amount of money*) вы́плата; **advance ~** (*part sum*) внесе́ние ава́нса; (*total sum*) платёж ава́нсом; **deferred ~** отсро́ченный платёж; ~ **by instalments** платёж в рассро́чку; **monthly ~** ме́сячный платёж; **in ~ for, in ~ of** в опла́ту за +*acc*; **on ~ of five pounds** по упла́те пяти́ фу́нтов.

pay packet *n* (*BRIT*) паке́т с зарпла́той.

payphone ['peɪfəun] *n* (*TEL*) телефо́н-автома́т.

payroll ['peɪrəul] *n* платёжная ве́домость *f*; **to be on a firm's ~** быть* (*impf*) в спи́сочном соста́ве фи́рмы.

pay slip *n* (*BRIT*) извеще́ние о зарпла́те.

pay station *n* (*US*) телефо́н-автома́т.

PBS *n abbr* (*US:* = *Public Broadcasting Service*)

Госуда́рственная слу́жба радиовеща́ния.

PC *n abbr* (= **personal computer**) ПК= *персона́льный компью́тер*; (*BRIT*) = **police constable** ♦ *adj abbr* = **politically correct** ♦ *abbr* (*BRIT*) = **Privy Councillor**.

pc *abbr* = **per cent, postcard**.

p/c *abbr* = **petty cash**.

PCB *n abbr* (*ELEC, COMPUT*: = *printed circuit board*) печа́тная пла́та; (= *polychlorinated biphenyl*) полихлори́рованный дифени́л.

pcm *abbr* (= *per calendar month*) в ме́сяц.

PD *n abbr* (*US*) = **police department**.

pd *abbr* = **paid**.

PDQ *adv abbr* (*inf*: = *pretty damn quick*) чертовски бы́стро.

PDSA *n abbr* (*BRIT*: = *People's Dispensary for Sick Animals*) *благотвори́тельное о́бщество, организу́ющее ветерина́рную по́мощь живо́тным*.

PDT *abbr* (*US*) = *Pacific Daylight Time*.

PE *n abbr* (*SCOL*) (= **physical education**) физкульту́ра= *физи́ческая культу́ра* ♦ *abbr* (*CANADA*) = *Prince Edward Island*.

pea [pi:] *n* (*BOT, CULIN*) горо́х *no pl*.

peace [pi:s] *n* (*not war*) мир; (*calm: of place, surroundings*) поко́й, споко́йствие; (: *personal*) поко́й; **to be at ~ with sb** быть* (*impf*) в ми́ре с ке́м-н; **to be at ~ with sth** смиря́ться (смири́ться* *perf*) с чем-н; **to keep the ~** (*policeman*) подде́рживать (поддержа́ть* *perf*) споко́йствие; (*citizen*) соблюда́ть (*impf*) споко́йствие.

peaceable ['pi:səbl] *adj* миролюби́вый (миролюби́в).

peaceful ['pi:sful] *adj* (*calm*) ми́рный* (ми́рен).

peacekeeper ['pi:ski:pə'] *n* член ми́рных войск.

peacekeeping force ['pi:ski:pɪŋ-] *n* миро-тво́рческие си́лы *fpl*.

peace offering *n* зада́бривание.

peach [pi:tʃ] *n* пе́рсик.

peacock ['pi:kɔk] *n* павли́н.

peak [pi:k] *n* верши́на, пик; (*of cap*) козырёк*.

peak hours *npl* часы́ *mpl* пик.

peak period *n* пи́ковый пери́од.

peak rate *n* (*TEL*) *расце́нки, применя́емые в пи́ковый пери́од*.

peaky ['pi:kɪ] *adj* (*BRIT*: *inf*) до́хлый.

peal [pi:l] *n* (*of bells*) перезво́н; **~ of laughter** раска́т сме́ха.

peanut ['pi:nʌt] *n* ара́хис.

peanut butter *n* ара́хисовая па́ста.

pear [pɛə'] *n* гру́ша.

pearl [pə:l] *n* жемчу́жина; **~s** жемчу́г.

peasant ['pɛznt] *n* крестья́нин*(-нка*).

peat [pi:t] *n* торф.

pebble ['pɛbl] *n* га́лька* *no pl*.

peck [pɛk] *vt* (*subj: bird*) клева́ть* (*impf*); (: *once*) клю́нуть (*perf*); (*also*: **~ at**: *food*) поклева́ть* (*impf*) ♦ *n* (*of bird*) клево́к*; (*kiss*) чмо́канье.

pecking order ['pɛkɪŋ-] *n* старшинство́.

peckish ['pɛkɪʃ] *adj* (*BRIT*: *inf*): **I'm feeling ~** мне хо́чется пожева́ть.

peculiar [pɪ'kju:lɪə'] *adj* (*strange*) своеобра́зный* (своеобра́зен); (*belonging exclusively*): **~ to** сво́йственный* (сво́йствен) +*dat*.

peculiarity [pɪkju:lɪ'ærɪtɪ] *n* (*strange habit*) стра́нность *f*; (*distinctive feature*) осо́бенность *f*.

peculiarly [pɪ'kju:lɪəlɪ] *adv* (*oddly*) стра́нно; (*distinctively*) осо́бенно.

pecuniary [pɪ'kju:nɪən] *adj* де́нежный.

pedal ['pɛdl] *n* педа́ль *f* ♦ *vi* крути́ть* (*impf*) педа́ли.

pedal bin *n* (*BRIT*) му́сорное ведро́* с педа́лью.

pedant ['pɛdənt] *n* педа́нт(ка*).

pedantic [pɪ'dæntɪk] *adj* педанти́чный* (педанти́чен).

peddle ['pɛdl] *vt* (*goods, drugs*) торгова́ть (*impf*) +*instr*; (*gossip*) разноси́ть* (разнести́* *perf*).

peddler ['pɛdlə'] *n*: (**drug**) **~** торго́вец* нарко́тиками.

pedestal ['pɛdəstl] *n* пьедеста́л.

pedestrian [pɪ'dɛstrɪən] *n* пешехо́д ♦ *adj* пешехо́дный; (*fig*) ску́чный.

pedestrian crossing *n* (*BRIT*) пешехо́дный перехо́д.

pedestrian precinct *n* (*BRIT*) пешехо́дная зо́на.

pediatrics [pi:dɪ'ætrɪks] *n* (*US*) = **paediatrics**.

pedigree ['pɛdɪgri:] *n* (*also fig*) родосло́вная *f* ♦ *cpd* (*animal*) поро́дистый (поро́дист).

pee [pi:] *vi* (*inf*) пи́сать (попи́сать *perf*).

peek [pi:k] *vi*: **to ~ at/over** взгля́дывать (взгляну́ть* *perf*) на +*acc*/пове́рх +*gen* ♦ *n*: **to have** *or* **take a ~ (at)** взгля́дывать (взгляну́ть* *perf*) (на +*acc*); **to ~ into** загля́дывать (загляну́ть* *perf*) в +*acc*.

peel [pi:l] *n* кожура́ ♦ *vt* (*vegetables, fruit*) чи́стить (почи́стить* *perf*), очища́ть (очи́стить* *perf*) ♦ *vi* (*paint*) лупи́ться* (облупи́ться* *perf*); (*wallpaper*) отстава́ть* (отста́ть* *perf*); (*skin*) шелуши́ться (*impf*).

▶ **peel back** *vt* оття́гивать (оттяну́ть* *perf*).

peeler ['pi:lə'] *n* (*for potatoes etc*) *нож для очи́стки овоще́й и фру́ктов*.

peelings ['pi:lɪŋz] *npl* очи́стки *pl*.

peep [pi:p] *n* (*look*) взгляд укра́дкой; (*sound*) писк ♦ *vi* взгля́дывать (взгляну́ть* *perf*); **to have** *or* **take a ~ (at)** взгля́дывать (взгляну́ть* *perf*) (на +*acc*)

▶ **peep out** *vi* (*be visible*) пока́зываться (показа́ться* *perf*), выгля́дывать (вы́глянуть* *perf*).

---

* marks translations which have irregular inflections. The Russian-English side of the dictionary gives inflectional information.

peephole ['pi:phəul] *n* глазо́к*.
peer [pɪə'] *n* (*BRIT: noble*) пэр; (*equal*) ро́вня *m/f*; (*contemporary*) рове́сник(-ица) ♦ *vi:* **to ~ at** всма́триваться (всмотре́ться* *perf*) в +*acc.*
peerage ['pɪərɪdʒ] *n* (*title, position*) пэ́рство; **the ~** пэ́ры.
peerless ['pɪəlɪs] *adj* несравне́нный* (несравне́нен).
peeved [pi:vd] *adj* (*inf*) злой* (зол).
peevish ['pi:vɪʃ] *adj* капри́зный* (капри́зен), сварли́вый (сварли́в).
peg [pɛg] *n* (*for coat etc*) крючо́к*; (*BRIT: also:* **clothes ~**) прище́пка*; (*also:* **tent ~**) ко́лышек* (*для натя́гивания пала́тки*) ♦ *vt* (*clothes: on line*) прикрепля́ть (прикрепи́ть* *perf*) прище́пками; (*prices*) замора́живать (заморо́зить* *perf*); **off the ~ clothing** гото́вая оде́жда.
pejorative [pɪ'dʒɔrətɪv] *adj* уничижи́тельный* (уничижи́телен).
Pekin [pi:'kɪn] *n* = **Peking**.
Pekinese [pi:kɪ'ni:z] *n* = **Pekingese**.
Peking [pi:'kɪŋ] *n* Пеки́н.
Pekingese [pi:kɪ'ni:z] *n* (*dog*) кита́йский* мопс.
pelican ['pɛlɪkən] *n* пелика́н.
pelican crossing *n* (*BRIT*) пешехо́дный *перехо́д, на кото́ром переключе́ние светофо́ра регули́руется нажа́тием кно́пки.*
pellet ['pɛlɪt] *n* (*of paper, mud*) ша́рик, ка́тышек*; (*for shotgun*) дроби́на.
pell-mell ['pɛl'mɛl] *adv* очертя́ го́лову.
pelmet ['pɛlmɪt] *n* ламбреке́н.
pelt [pɛlt] *n* (*animal skin*) шку́ра ♦ *vi* (*rain: also:* **~ down**) лить* (*impf*) как из ведра́; (*inf: run*) проноси́ться* (пронести́сь* *perf*) ♦ *vt:* **to ~ sb with sth** забра́сывать (заброса́ть *perf*) кого́-н чем-н.
pelvis ['pɛlvɪs] *n* таз* *no pl.*
pen [pɛn] *n* ру́чка*; (*felt-tip*) флома́стер; (*enclosure*) заго́н; (*US: inf: prison*) тюрьма́*; **to put ~ to paper** бра́ться* (взя́ться* *perf*) за перо́.
penal ['pi:nl] *adj* (*colony, institution*) исправ- и́тельный; (*system*) кара́тельный; **~ code** уголо́вный ко́декс.
penalize ['pi:nəlaɪz] *vt* (*also fig*) нака́зывать (наказа́ть* *perf*); (*SPORT*) штрафова́ть (оштрафова́ть *perf*).
penal servitude [-'sə:vɪtjuːd] *n* ка́торжные рабо́ты *fpl.*
penalty ['pɛnltɪ] *n* (*punishment*) наказа́ние; (*fine*) штраф; (*RUGBY*) штрафно́й *m adj* (уда́р); (*FOOTBALL*) штрафно́й (уда́р), пена́льти *m ind.*
penalty area *n* (*BRIT: SPORT*) штрафна́я *f adj* (площа́дка*).
penalty clause *n* (*COMM*) пункт, предус- ма́тривающий вид и разме́р штра́фа за наруше́ние усло́вий контра́кта.

penalty kick *n* (*RUGBY*) штрафно́й *m adj* (уда́р); (*FOOTBALL*) штрафно́й (уда́р), пена́льти *m ind.*
penalty shoot-out [-'ʃuːtaut] *n* определе́ние кома́нды-победи́теля путём забива́ния се́рии штрафны́х уда́ров по́сле ма́тча око́нчившегося ничье́й.
penance ['pɛnəns] *n* ка́ра.
pence [pɛns] *npl of* **penny**.
penchant ['pɑ̃:ʃɑ̃:ŋ] *n* скло́нность *f*; **to have a ~ for** име́ть (*impf*) скло́нность к +*dat.*
pencil ['pɛnsl] *n* каранда́ш* ♦ *vt:* **to ~ sth in** впи́сывать (вписа́ть* *perf*) что-н карандашо́м; (*fig*) помеча́ть (поме́тить* *perf*) что-н.
pencil case *n* пена́л.
pencil sharpener *n* точи́лка.
pendant ['pɛndnt] *n* куло́н.
pending ['pɛndɪŋ] *prep* впредь до +*gen*, в ожида́нии +*gen* ♦ *adj* (*lawsuit, exam etc*) предстоя́щий*.
pendulum ['pɛndjuləm] *n* ма́ятник.
penetrate ['pɛnɪtreɪt] *vt* (*subj: person, light*) проника́ть (прони́кнуть* *perf*) в/на +*acc.*
penetrating ['pɛnɪtreɪtɪŋ] *adj* (*sound, glance*) пронзи́тельный* (пронзи́телен); (*mind*) проница́тельный* (проница́телен); (*observation*) глубо́кий*.
penetration [pɛnɪ'treɪʃən] *n* проникнове́ние.
pen friend *n* (*BRIT*) друг* (подру́га) по перепи́ске.
penguin ['pɛŋgwɪn] *n* пингви́н.
penicillin [pɛnɪ'sɪlɪn] *n* пеницилли́н.
peninsula [pə'nɪnsjulə] *n* полуо́стров*.
penis ['pi:nɪs] *n* пе́нис, мужско́й полово́й член.
penitence ['pɛnɪtns] *n* раска́яние.
penitent ['pɛnɪtnt] *adj* ка́ющийся.
penitentiary [pɛnɪ'tɛnʃərɪ] *n* (*US*) тюрьма́*.
penknife ['pɛnnaɪf] *n* перочи́нный нож*.
pen name *n* (литерату́рный) псевдони́м.
pennant ['pɛnənt] *n* (*NAUT*) сигна́льный флажо́к*.
penniless ['pɛnɪlɪs] *adj* без гроша́; **she is ~** у неё нет ни гроша́.
Pennines ['pɛnaɪnz] *npl:* **the ~** Пени́нские го́ры *fpl.*
penny ['pɛnɪ] (*pl* **pennies** *or* (*BRIT*) **pence**) *n* пе́нни *nt ind*, пенс; (*US*) цент.
pen pal *n* = **pen friend**.
penpusher ['pɛnpuʃə'] *n* занима́ющийся ну́дной пи́сьменной рабо́той/пи́сарь *m.*
pension ['pɛnʃən] *n* пе́нсия
▶ **pension off** *vt* отправля́ть (отпра́вить* *perf*) на пе́нсию.
pensionable ['pɛnʃnəbl] *adj* (*age*) пенсио́нный*; (*job*) даю́щий пра́во на пе́нсию.
pensioner ['pɛnʃənə'] *n* (*BRIT: also:* **old age ~**) пенсионе́р(ка*).
pension fund *n* пенсио́нный фонд.
pensive ['pɛnsɪv] *adj* заду́мчивый (заду́мчив).

pentagon ['pɛntəgən] *n* пятиуго́льник; (*US*): **the P~** Пентаго́н.

Pentecost ['pɛntɪkɔst] *n* (*Jewish*) пятидеся́тница; (*Christian*) Тро́ицын день* *m*.

penthouse ['pɛnthaus] *n* (*flat*) „пе́нтхаус" *(фешенебельная кварти́ра, располо́женная на кры́ше*).

pent-up ['pɛntʌp] *adj* (*feelings*) сде́рживаемый.

penultimate [pɛ'nʌltɪmət] *adj* предпосле́дний*.

penury ['pɛnjurɪ] *n* нужда́, бе́дность *f*.

people ['pi:pl] *npl* (*persons*) лю́ди* *pl*; (*nation, race*) наро́д; **old ~** старики́ *mpl*; **young ~** молодёжь *fsg*; **the ~** (*POL*) наро́д; **~ at large** лю́ди в ма́ссе свое́й; **a man of the ~** челове́к из наро́да; **several ~ came** пришло́ не́сколько челове́к; **the room was full of ~** в ко́мнате бы́ло полно́ наро́ду; **~ say that ...** говоря́т, что ....

pep [pɛp] (*inf*) *n* бо́дрость *f*
▸ **pep up** *vt* (*enliven*) оживи́ть* (*perf*); (*food*) де́лать (сде́лать *perf*) остре́е.

pepper ['pɛpəʳ] *n* пе́рец* ♦ *vt* (*fig*): **to ~ with** забра́сывать (заброса́ть *perf*) +*instr*.

peppercorn ['pɛpəkɔ:n] *n* перчи́нка*.

pepper mill *n* ме́льница для пе́рца.

peppermint ['pɛpəmɪnt] *n* (*sweet*) мя́тная конфе́та; (*plant*) мя́та пе́речная.

pepperoni [pɛpə'rəunɪ] *n* пеперо́ни *f ind* (*итальянская колбаса́*).

pepper pot *n* пе́речница.

pep talk *n* (*inf*) нака́чка*.

per [pə:ʳ] *prep* (*for each: of amounts*) на +*acc*; (: *of price*) за +*acc*; (: *of charge*) с +*gen*; **~ annum/day/hour** в год/день/час; **~ person** на челове́ка; **~ kilo** за килогра́мм; **as ~ your instructions** согла́сно ва́шим инстру́кциям; **as ~ usual** по обыкнове́нию.

per capita *adj, adv* (*income*) на ду́шу населе́ния.

perceive [pə'si:v] *vt* (*sound, light, idea*) воспринима́ть (восприня́ть* *perf*); (*realize*) понима́ть (поня́ть* *perf*).

per cent *n* проце́нт; **a twenty ~ ~ discount** двадцатипроце́нтная ски́дка.

percentage [pə'sɛntɪdʒ] *n* (*of income*) проце́нт; (*of immigrants etc*) до́ля; (*of substances*) (проце́нтное) содержа́ние; **on a ~ basis** на основа́нии проце́нтного отчисле́ния.

percentage point *n* проце́нт.

perceptible [pə'sɛptɪbl] *adj* ощути́мый (ощути́м).

perception [pə'sɛpʃən] *n* (*faculty*) восприя́тие; (*insight*) понима́ние *no pl*; (*opinion, understanding*) ощуще́ние.

perceptive [pə'sɛptɪv] *adj* проница́тельный* (проница́телен).

perch [pə:tʃ] *n* (*for bird*) насе́ст ♦ *n inv* (*fish*)

о́кунь* *m* ♦ *vi*: **to ~ (on)** (*bird*) сади́ться* (сесть* *perf*) (на +*acc*); (*person*) прися́живаться (присе́сть* *perf*) (на +*acc*).

percolate ['pə:kəleɪt] *vt* (*coffee*) вари́ть* (свари́ть* *perf*) в кофева́рке ♦ *vi* (*coffee*) вари́ться (свари́ться *perf*) в кофева́рке; (*idea, information, light etc*): **to ~ through/into** проса́чиваться (просочи́ться *perf*) сквозь +*acc*/в +*acc*.

percolator ['pə:kəleɪtəʳ] *n* (*also*: **coffee ~**) кофева́рка.

percussion [pə'kʌʃən] *n* уда́рные инструме́нты *mpl*.

peremptory [pə'rɛmptərɪ] *adj* (*pej: person*) вла́стный* (вла́стен), категори́чный* (категори́чен); (: *order, instruction*) категори́ческий*.

perennial [pə'rɛnɪəl] *adj* (*plant*) многоле́тний*; (*fig: problem, feature etc*) ве́чный* (ве́чен) ♦ *n* (*BOT*) многоле́тнее *nt adj* (*расте́ние*).

perfect [*adj, n* 'pə:fɪkt, *vt* pə'fɛkt] *adj* (*person, behaviour etc*) безупре́чный* (безупре́чен); (*weather*) прекра́сный* (прекра́сен); (*utter: nonsense etc*) соверше́нный ♦ *n* (*also*: **~ tense**) перфе́кт ♦ *vt* (*technique*) соверше́нствовать (усоверше́нствовать *perf*); **he's a ~ stranger to me** он мне соверше́нно незнако́м.

perfection [pə'fɛkʃən] *n* соверше́нство.

perfectionist [pə'fɛkʃənɪst] *n* взыска́тельный* челове́к*.

perfective [pə'fɛktɪv] *n* (*also*: **~ aspect**) соверше́нный вид.

perfectly ['pə:fɪktlɪ] *adv* (*emphatic*) вполне́, соверше́нно; (*faultlessly*) безупре́чно; (*completely*) вполне́, прекра́сно; **I'm ~ happy with the situation** я вполне́ дово́лен положе́нием дел; **you know ~ well** Вы прекра́сно зна́ете.

perforate ['pə:fəreɪt] *vt* перфори́ровать (*impf/ perf*).

perforated ulcer ['pə:fəreɪtəd-] *n* перфорати́вная я́зва желу́дка.

perforation [pə:fə'reɪʃən] *n* перфора́ция.

perform [pə'fɔ:m] *vt* (*task, operation*) выполня́ть (вы́полнить *perf*); (*ceremony, experiment*) проводи́ть* (провести́* *perf*); (*piece of music*) исполня́ть (испо́лнить *perf*); (*play*) игра́ть (сыгра́ть *perf*); (*subj: mechanism*) рабо́тать (*impf*) ♦ *vi* (*well, badly*) спра́виться* (*perf*).

performance [pə'fɔ:məns] *n* (*of actor, athlete etc*) выступле́ние; (*of musical work*) исполне́ние; (*of play, show*) представле́ние; (*of car, engine, company*) рабо́та; (*of economy*) эффекти́вность *f*; **the team put up a good ~** кома́нда хорошо́ вы́ступила.

performer [pə'fɔ:məʳ] *n* исполни́тель(ница)

m(f).

performing [pə'fɔːmɪŋ] *adj* (*animal*) дрессир-
óванный.

perfume ['pəːfjuːm] *n* духи́ *pl*; (*aroma*) аромáт
◆ *vt* (*air, room etc*) ароматизи́ровать (*impf/
perf*).

perfunctory [pə'fʌŋktərɪ] *adj* (*kiss, remark etc*)
небрéжный* (небрéжен).

perhaps [pə'hæps] *adv* мóжет бы́ть,
возмóжно; ~ **he'll come** мóжет бы́ть, *or*
возмóжно он придёт; ~ **so** мóжет бы́ть; ~
not мóжет быть* и нет.

peril ['pɛrɪl] *n* опáсность *f*.

perilous ['pɛrɪləs] *adj* опáсный* (опáсен).

perilously ['pɛrɪləslɪ] *adv*: **they came ~ close to
being caught** они́ находи́лись на грáни
разоблачéния.

perimeter [pə'rɪmɪtə'] *n* пери́метр.

perimeter wall *n* стенá по пери́метру.

period ['pɪərɪəd] *n* (*length of time*) пери́од;
(*SCOL*) урóк; (*esp US: full stop*) тóчка*; (*MED*)
менструáция ◆ *adj* (*costume, furniture*)
стари́нный; ~ **of validity** срок дéйствия; **for a
~ of three weeks** (*go*) на три недéли; (*be*) три
недéли; **the holiday ~** (*BRIT*) врéмя* *or* пери́од
отпускóв.

periodic [pɪərɪ'ɔdɪk] *adj* периоди́ческий*.

periodical [pɪərɪ'ɔdɪkl] *n* (*magazine*)
периоди́ческое издáние ◆ *adj*
периоди́ческий*.

periodically [pɪərɪ'ɔdɪklɪ] *adv* периоди́чески.

period pains *npl* (*BRIT: MED*) менструáльные
бóли *fpl*.

peripatetic [pɛrɪpə'tɛtɪk] *adj* (*salesman*)
бродя́чий*; (*BRIT: teacher*) приходя́щий*.

peripheral [pə'rɪfərəl] *adj* (*also COMPUT*)
перифери́йный ◆ *n* (*COMPUT*) перифери́я.

periphery [pə'rɪfərɪ] *n* перифери́я.

periscope ['pɛrɪskəup] *n* перискóп.

perish ['pɛrɪʃ] *vi* (*person*) погибáть
(поги́бнуть* *perf*); (*fabric*) приходи́ть*
(прийти́* *perf*) в негóдность.

perishable ['pɛrɪʃəbl] *adj* (*food, goods*)
скоропóртящийся*.

perishables ['pɛrɪʃəblz] *npl* (*food*)
скоропóртящиеся продýкты *mpl*.

perishing ['pɛrɪʃɪŋ] *adj* (*BRIT: inf*): **it's ~ (cold)**
ужáсно хóлодно.

peritonitis [pɛrɪtə'naɪtɪs] *n* перитони́т.

perjure ['pəːdʒə'] *vt*: **~ o.s.** давáть* (дать*
perf) лóжные показáния.

perjury ['pəːdʒərɪ] *n* (*LAW*) лжесвидéтельство.

perk [pəːk] *n* (*inf*) льгóта.

perk up *vi* (*inf*) оживля́ться (оживи́ться* *perf*).

perky ['pəːkɪ] *adj* (*cheerful*) весёлый* (вéсел),
бóйкий* (бóек).

perm [pəːm] *n* (*for hair*) перманéнт,
хими́ческая зави́вка* ◆ *vt*: **to have one's hair
~ed** дéлать (сдéлать *perf*) себé хими́ческую
зави́вку *or* хи́мию.

permanence ['pəːmənəns] *n* постоя́нство.

permanent ['pəːmənənt] *adj* постоя́нный*
(постоя́нен); (*job, position*) постоя́нный;
(*dye, ink*) стóйкий*; **~ address** постоя́нное
местожи́тельство; **I'm not ~ here** я нахожýсь
здесь врéменно.

permanently ['pəːmənəntlɪ] *adv* постоя́нно.

permeable ['pəːmɪəbl] *adj* водопроницáемый
(водопроницáем).

permeate ['pəːmɪeɪt] *vt* (*subj: liquid*)
пропи́тывать (пропитáть *perf*); (: *idea*)
прони́зывать (пронизáть *perf*) ◆ *vi*: **to ~ into/
through** проникáть (прони́кнуть* *perf*) в +*acc*/
сквозь +*acc*.

permissible [pə'mɪsɪbl] *adj* (*action, behaviour*)
допусти́мый (допусти́м), позволи́тельный*
(позволи́телен).

permission [pə'mɪʃən] *n* (*consent*) позволéние;
(*official authorization*) разрешéние; **to give sb
~ to do** разрешáть (разреши́ть *perf*) комý-н
+*infin*.

permissive [pə'mɪsɪv] *adj* (*person*) терпи́мый
(терпи́м); (*behaviour*) вóльный* (вóлен); **the
~ society** óбщество вседозвóленности.

permit [*vt* pə'mɪt, *n* 'pəːmɪt] *vt* (*allow*) позволя́ть
(позвóлить *perf*), разрешáть (разреши́ть
perf); (*make possible*) давáть* (дать* *perf*)
возмóжность +*dat* ◆ *n* (*official authorization*)
разрешéние; (*entrance pass*) прóпуск*; **to ~
sb to do** разрешáть (разреши́ть *perf*) комý-н
+*infin*; **weather ~ting** éсли погóда позволя́ет;
fishing ~ разрешéние на ры́бную лóвлю.

permutation [pəːmju'teɪʃən] *n* (*MATH*)
перестанóвка*; (*fig*) перемещéние.

pernicious [pəː'nɪʃəs] *adj* (*attitude, influence
etc*) пáгубный* (пáгубен); (*MED*)
перници́зный.

pernickety [pə'nɪkɪtɪ] *adj* (*inf*) привередли́вый
(привередли́в).

perpendicular [pəːpən'dɪkjulə'] *adj* (*line,
surface*) перпендикуля́рный*
(перпендилуля́рен); (*cliff, slope*) отвéсный*
(отвéсен).

perpetrate ['pəːpɪtreɪt] *vt* совершáть
(соверши́ть *perf*).

perpetual [pə'pɛtjuəl] *adj* (*motion, questions*)
вéчный* (вéчен); (*darkness, noise*)
постоя́нный* (постоя́нен).

perpetuate [pə'pɛtjueɪt] *vt* увековéчивать
(увековéчить *perf*).

perpetuity [pəːpɪ'tjuːɪtɪ] *n*: **in ~** навсегдá,
навéчно.

perplex [pə'plɛks] *vt* озадáчивать (озадáчить
perf).

perplexing [pəː'plɛksɪŋ] *adj* запýтанный*
(запýтан), слóжный* (слóжен).

perquisites ['pəːkwɪzɪts] *npl* (*formal*) льгóты
fpl.

per se [-seɪ] *adv* (*as such*) как таковóй*; (*in
itself*) самó по себé.

persecute ['pəːsɪkjuːt] *vt* преслéдовать (*impf*),
подвергáть (подвéргнуть* *perf*) гонéниям

+dat.
persecution [pə:sɪ'kju:ʃən] *n* преслéдование.
perseverance [pə:sɪ'vɪərns] *n* настóйчивость *f*.
persevere [pə:sɪ'vɪəʳ] *vi* упóрно добивáться
(*impf*).
Persia ['pə:ʃə] *n* Пéрсия.
Persian ['pə:ʃən] *adj*: **the (Persian) Gulf**
Перси́дский* зали́в.
Persian cat *n* перси́дский*(-ая) кот* (кóшка).
persist [pə'sɪst] *vi*: **to ~ (in doing)** настáивать
(настоя́ть *perf*) (на том, чтóбы +*infin*).
persistence [pə'sɪstəns] *n* упóрство.
persistent [pə'sɪstənt] *adj* (*noise*) непре-
кращáющийся*; (*smell*) стóйкий* (стóек);
(*cough*) непроходя́щий; (*person*) упóрный*
(упóрен); (*lateness*) постоя́нный*
(постоя́нен); (*rain*) непрерьívный*
(непрерьíвен); **~ offender** рециди́вист(ка*).
persnickety [pə'snɪkɪtɪ] *adj* (*US*: *inf*) =
pernickety.
person ['pə:sn] *n* человéк*; **in ~** ли́чно; **to have
sth on** *or* **about one's ~** (*weapon*) носи́ть*
(*impf*) что-н при себé; **~ to ~ call** (*TEL*)
*междугорóдный телефóнный разговóр с
вьíзовом абонéнта.*
personable ['pə:snəbl] *adj* (*adult*)
представи́тельный* (представи́телен).
personal ['pə:snl] *adj* ли́чный; (*car*)
персонáльный.
personal allowance *n* (*COMM*) ли́чные ски́дки
fpl с подохóдного налóга.
personal assistant *n* ли́чный секретáрь* *m*.
personal column *n* колóнка* для чáстных
объявлéний.
personal computer *n* персонáльный
компью́тер.
personal details *npl* биографи́ческие дáнные
pl adj.
personal effects *npl* ли́чные вéщи *fpl or*
принадлéжности *fpl*.
personal hygiene *n* ли́чная гигиéна.
personal identification number *n* (*BANKING*)
ли́чный идентификацио́нный нóмер*
(*владéльца плáстиковой кáрточки*);
(*COMPUT*) персонáльный *or* ли́чный
идентификацио́нный нóмер*.
personality [pə:sə'nælɪtɪ] *n* харáктер; (*famous
person*) знамени́тость *f*.
personal loan *n* (*COMM*) ли́чная ссýда.
personally ['pə:snəlɪ] *adv* ли́чно; **to take sth ~**
принимáть (приня́ть* *perf*) что-н на свой
счёт.
personal organizer *n* ежеднéвник.
personal property *n* ли́чное имýщество.
personal stereo *n* персонáльное стéрео *nt ind*.
personify [pə:'sɔnɪfaɪ] *vt* олицетворя́ть
(олицетвори́ть* *perf*), воплощáть
(воплоти́ть* *perf*).

personnel [pə:sə'nɛl] *n* персонáл, штáт; (*MIL*)
ли́чный состáв.
personnel department *n* отдéл кáдров.
personnel management *n* руковóдство
кáдрами.
personnel manager *n* начáльник отдéла
кáдров.
perspective [pə'spɛktɪv] *n* (*ARCHIT, ART*)
перспекти́ва; (*way of thinking*) ви́дение; **to
get sth into ~** (*fig*) смотрéть* (посмотрéть*
perf) на что-н в и́стинном свéте.
Perspex® ['pə:spɛks] *n* плексиглáс.
perspicacity [pə:spɪ'kæsɪtɪ] *n* прониц-
áтельность *f*.
perspiration [pə:spɪ'reɪʃən] *n* пот*.
perspire [pə'spaɪəʳ] *vi* потéть (вспотéть *perf*).
persuade [pə'sweɪd] *vt*: **to ~ sb to do** убеждáть
(убеди́ть* *perf*) *or* угова́ривать (уговори́ть
perf) когó- н +*infin*; **to ~ sb of/that** убеждáть
(убеди́ть* *perf*) когó-н в +*prpl*/, что.
persuasion [pə'sweɪʒən] *n* убеждéние;
(*religious*) вероисповéдание.
persuasive [pə'sweɪsɪv] *adj* (*argument*)
убеди́тельный* (убеди́телен); (*person*)
настóйчивый (настóйчив).
pert [pə:t] *adj* (*impudent*) дéрзкий* (дéрзок);
(*jaunty: hat etc*) кокéтливый.
pertaining [pə:'teɪnɪŋ]: **~ to** *prep* относя́щийся
к +*dat*, касáющийся +*gen*.
pertinent ['pə:tɪnənt] *adj* умéстный* (умéстен).
perturb [pə'tə:b] *vt* тревóжить (встревóжить
perf).
Peru [pə'ru:] *n* Перý *f ind*.
perusal [pə'ru:zl] *n* прочтéние.
peruse [pə'ru:z] *vt* просмáтривать
(просмотрéть* *perf*).
Peruvian [pə'ru:vjən] *adj* перуáнский* ◆ *n*
перуáнец*(-нка*).
pervade [pə'veɪd] *vt* (*subj: smell, feeling*)
наполня́ть (напóлнить *perf*).
pervasive [pə'veɪsɪv] *adj* (*smell, influence,
ideas*) всепроника́ющий; (*gloom*)
прони́цивающий.
perverse [pə'və:s] *adj* (*contrary*) врéдный*
(врéден).
perversion [pə'və:ʃən] *n* извращéние.
perversity [pə'və:sɪtɪ] *n* врéдность *f*.
pervert [*vt* pə'və:t, *n* 'pə:və:t] *vt* (*person, mind*)
развращáть (разврати́ть* *perf*), растлевáть
(растли́ть *perf*); (*truth, sb's words*) извращáть
(изврати́ть* *perf*) ◆ *n* (*also:* **sexual ~**)
(половóй) извращéнец.
pessimism ['pɛsɪmɪzəm] *n* пессими́зм.
pessimist ['pɛsɪmɪst] *n* пессими́ст(ка*).
pessimistic [pɛsɪ'mɪstɪk] *adj* пессимисти́чный*
(пессимисти́чен).
pest [pɛst] *n* (*insect*) вреди́тель *m*; (*fig:
nuisance*) занýда *m/f*.

---

* marks translations which have irregular inflections. The Russian-English side of the dictionary gives inflectional information.

pest control *n* борьба́ с вреди́телями.
pester ['pɛstə'] *vt* приставáть* (пристáть* *perf*) к +*dat*.
pesticide ['pɛstɪsaɪd] *n* пестици́д.
pestilence ['pɛstɪləns] *n* мор.
pestle ['pɛsl] *n* пе́стик.
pet [pɛt] *n* домáшнее живо́тное *nt adj* ◆ *cpd* излю́бленный ◆ *vt* (*stroke*) ласкáть (*impf*) ◆ *vi* (*inf: sexually*) обнимáться (*impf*), целовáться (*impf*); ~ **lion** *etc* ручно́й лев *etc*; **teacher's** ~ люби́мчик.
petal ['pɛtl] *n* лепесто́к*.
peter out ['pi:tə-] *vi* (*road*) исчезáть (исче́знуть* *perf*); (*stream, conversation*) иссякáть (исся́кнуть* *perf*); (*meeting*) закáнчиваться (закóнчиться *perf*).
petite [pə'ti:t] *adj* миниатю́рный* (миниатю́рен).
petition [pə'tɪʃən] *n* (*signed document*) пети́ция; (*LAW*) ходáтайство ◆ *vt* обращáться (обрати́ться* *perf*) с пети́цией к +*dat* ◆ *vi*: **to ~ for divorce** подавáть* (подáть* *perf*) заявле́ние о разво́де.
pet name *n* (*BRIT*) ласкáтельное и́мя* *nt*.
petrified ['pɛtrɪfaɪd] *adj* (*fig*) оцепене́вший.
petrify ['pɛtrɪfaɪ] (*fig*) *vt* приводи́ть* (привести́* *perf*) в оцепене́ние.
petrochemical [pɛtrə'kɛmɪkl] *adj* нефтехими́ческий.
petrodollars ['pɛtrəudɔləz] *npl* (*COMM*) нефтедо́ллары *mpl*.
petrol ['pɛtrəl] (*BRIT*) *n* бензи́н; **two/four-star** ~ ни́зкооктановый/высóкооктановый бензи́н; **unleaded** ~ бензи́н не содержáщий свинцá.
petrol bomb *n* бáнка со взрывчáтой сме́сью.
petrol can *n* (*BRIT*) кани́стра для бензи́на.
petrol engine *n* (*BRIT*) бензи́новый дви́гатель *m*.
petroleum [pə'trəulɪəm] *n* нефть *f*.
petroleum jelly *n* вазели́н*.
petrol pump *n* (*BRIT: in garage*) бензо-колóнка*; (: *in engine*) бензонасóс.
petrol station *n* (*BRIT*) бензозапрáвочная стáнция.
petrol tank *n* (*BRIT*) бензобáк.
petticoat ['pɛtɪkəut] *n* (*full-length*) комбинáция; (*waist slip*) ни́жняя ю́бка*.
pettifogging ['pɛtɪfɔgɪŋ] *adj* ме́лочный* (ме́лочен).
pettiness ['pɛtɪnɪs] *n* (*of actions*) ме́лочность *f*; (*of mind*) ограни́ченность *f*.
petty ['pɛtɪ] *adj* (*small, unimportant*) ме́лкий* (ме́лок); (*small-minded*) ограни́ченный* (ограни́чен).
petty cash *n* (*in office*) де́ньги* *pl* на ме́лкие расхóды.
petty officer *n* старшинá *m* (*во флóте*).
petulant ['pɛtjulənt] *adj* оби́дчивый (оби́дчив).
pew [pju:] *n* скамья́* (*в це́ркви*).
pewter ['pju:tə'] *n* сплав о́лова со свинцóм.

Pfc *abbr* (*US: MIL*: = *private first class*) рядово́й 1-го клáсса.
PG *n abbr* (*CINEMA*: = *parental guidance*) фильм до 16-ти лет.
PGA *n abbr* = *Professional Golfers Association*.
PH *n abbr* (*US: MIL*: = *Purple Heart*) ≈ медáль *f* „За отвáгу".
pH *n abbr* (= *potential of hydrogen*) pH (*водорóдный показáтель*).
PHA *n abbr* (*US*) = *Public Housing Administration*.
phallic ['fælɪk] *adj* фалли́ческий.
phantom ['fæntəm] *n* фантóм ◆ *adj* (*fig*) при́зрачный* (при́зрачен).
Pharaoh ['fɛərəu] *n* фараóн.
pharmaceutical [fɑ:mə'sju:tɪkl] *adj* фармацевти́ческий ◆ *n*: ~**s** медикаме́нты *mpl*.
pharmacist ['fɑ:məsɪst] *n* фармаце́вт.
pharmacy ['fɑ:məsɪ] *n* (*profession*) фармаце́втика; (*shop*) апте́ка.
phase [feɪz] *n* фáза ◆ *vt*: **to ~ sth in** поэтáпно вводи́ть* (ввести́* *perf*) что-н; **to ~ sth out** ликвиди́ровать (*impf/perf*) что-н.
PhD *n abbr* (= *Doctor of Philosophy*) дóктор филосóфии.
pheasant ['fɛznt] *n* фазáн.
phenomena [fə'nɔmɪnə] *npl of* **phenomenon**.
phenomenal [fə'nɔmɪnl] *adj* феноменáльный* (феноменáлен).
phenomenon [fə'nɔmɪnən] (*pl* **phenomena**) *n* явле́ние, фенóмен.
phew [fju:] *excl* уф.
phial ['faɪəl] *n* скля́нка*.
philanderer [fɪ'lændərə'] *n* волоки́та *m*.
philanthropic [fɪlən'θrɔpɪk] *adj* филантроп-и́ческий.
philanthropist [fɪ'lænθrəpɪst] *n* филантрóп (ка*).
philatelist [fɪ'lætəlɪst] *n* филатели́ст(ка*).
philately [fɪ'lætəlɪ] *n* филатели́я.
Philippines ['fɪlɪpi:nz] *npl*: **the** ~ Филиппи́ны *pl*, Филиппи́нские островá* *mpl*.
philosopher [fɪ'lɔsəfə'] *n* филóсоф.
philosophical [fɪlə'sɔfɪkl] *adj* филосóфский.
philosophize [fɪ'lɔsəfaɪz] *vi* филосóфствовать (*impf*).
philosophy [fɪ'lɔsəfɪ] *n* филосóфия.
phlegm [flɛm] *n* (*MED*) мокрóта.
phlegmatic [flɛg'mætɪk] *adj* флегмати́чный* (флегмати́чен).
phobia ['fəubjə] *n* (*MED*) фóбия, страх.
phone [fəun] *n* телефóн ◆ *vt* звони́ть (позвони́ть *perf*) (по телефóну) +*dat*; **to be on the** ~ (*possess a phone*) име́ть (*impf*) телефóн; (*be calling*) говори́ть (*impf*) по телефóну
▶ **phone back** *vt* перезвáнивать (перезвони́ть *perf*) +*dat* ◆ *vi* перезвáнивать (перезвони́ть *perf*)
▶ **phone up** *vt* звони́ть (позвони́ть *perf*) +*dat* ◆ *vi* звони́ть (позвони́ть *perf*).
phone book *n* телефóнная кни́га.

phone booth n телефо́н-автома́т.
phone box n (BRIT) телефо́нная бу́дка*, телефо́н-автома́т.
phone call n телефо́нный звоно́к*.
phone-card ['fəʊnkɑːd] n телефо́нная ка́рточка (*испо́льзуется в автома́тах для безнали́чной опла́ты перегово́ров*).
phone-in ['fəʊnɪn] n (BRIT: RADIO, TV) програ́мма „звони́те-отвеча́ем".
phone tapping [-tæpɪŋ] n прослу́шивание телефо́нных разгово́ров.
phonetics [fə'nɛtɪks] n фоне́тика.
phoney ['fəʊnɪ] adj фальши́вый (фальши́в).
phonograph ['fəʊnəgrɑːf] n (US) про́-игрыватель m.
phony ['fəʊnɪ] adj = **phoney**.
phosphate ['fɔsfeɪt] n фосфа́т.
phosphorus ['fɔsfərəs] n фо́сфор.
photo ['fəʊtəʊ] n фотогра́фия.
photo... ['fəʊtəʊ] prefix фото....
photocopier ['fəʊtəʊkɔpɪəʳ] n (machine) ксе́рокс, копирова́льная маши́на.
photocopy ['fəʊtəʊkɔpɪ] n ксероко́пия, фотоко́пия ◆ vt фотокопи́ровать (сфотокопи́ровать perf), ксерокопи́ровать (impf/perf).
photoelectric [fəʊtəʊɪ'lɛktrɪk] adj фото-электри́ческий; ~ **cell** фотоэлеме́нт.
photo finish n фотофи́ниш.
Photofit® ['fəʊtəʊfɪt] n фотореконстру́кция.
photogenic [fəʊtəʊ'dʒɛnɪk] adj фотогени́чный* (фотогени́чен).
photograph ['fəʊtəgræf] n фотогра́фия ◆ vt фотографи́ровать (сфотографи́ровать perf); **to take a ~ of sb** фотографи́ровать (сфотографи́ровать perf) кого́-н.
photographer [fə'tɔgrəfəʳ] n фото́граф.
photographic [fəʊtə'græfɪk] adj фото-графи́ческий.
photography [fə'tɔgrəfɪ] n фотогра́фия.
photo opportunity n ситуа́ция, даю́щая возмо́жность знамени́тостям быть предста́вленным в вы́годном све́те на фотогра́фии.
Photostat® ['fəʊtəʊstæt] n фотоко́пия.
photosynthesis [fəʊtəʊ'sɪnθəsɪs] n (BIO) фотоси́нтез.
phrase [freɪz] n (also LING, MUS) фра́за ◆ vt формули́ровать (сформули́ровать perf); (letter) составля́ть (соста́вить* perf).
phrase book n разгово́рник.
physical ['fɪzɪkl] adj физи́ческий*; (world, universe, object) материа́льный* (материа́лен); ~ **examination** медосмо́тр= медици́нский* осмо́тр; ~ **exercises** физи́ческие упряжне́ния.
physical education n физи́ческое воспита́ние, физкульту́ра.

physically ['fɪzɪklɪ] adv физи́чески.
physician [fɪ'zɪʃən] n (esp US) врач*.
physicist ['fɪzɪsɪst] n фи́зик.
physics ['fɪzɪks] n фи́зика.
physiological ['fɪzɪə'lɔdʒɪkl] adj физиолог-и́ческий*.
physiology [fɪzɪ'ɔlədʒɪ] n физиоло́гия.
physiotherapist [fɪzɪəʊ'θɛrəpɪst] n физио-терапе́вт.
physiotherapy [fɪzɪəʊ'θɛrəpɪ] n физиотерапи́я.
physique [fɪ'ziːk] n (build) телосложе́ние; (health) физи́ческие да́нные pl adj.
pianist ['piːənɪst] n пиани́ст(ка*).
piano [pɪ'ænəʊ] n пиани́но, фортепья́но nt ind; **grand ~** роя́ль m.
piano accordion n (BRIT) аккордео́н.
piccolo ['pɪkələʊ] n пи́кколо nt ind.
pick [pɪk] n (also: ~**axe**) кирка́* ◆ vt (select) выбира́ть (вы́брать* perf); (gather: fruit, flowers) собира́ть (собра́ть* perf); (pluck) рвать* (impf); (lock) взла́мывать (взлома́ть perf); (scab, spot) сковы́ривать (сковырну́ть perf); **take your ~** выбира́йте; **the ~ of the bunch** (best) са́мое лу́чшее; **to ~ one's nose/ teeth** ковыря́ть (impf) в носу́/зуба́х; **to ~ sb's brains** обраща́ться (обрати́ться* perf) к кому́-н за сове́том; **to ~ pockets** ла́зать (impf) карма́нам; **to ~ a quarrel (with sb)** иска́ть* (impf) по́вод для ссо́ры (с кем-н)
▶ **pick at** vt fus (food) ковыря́ть (impf)
▶ **pick off** vt (planes) методи́чно сбива́ть (сбить* perf); (people) методи́чно стреля́ть (impf) по +dat
▶ **pick on** vt fus (criticize) придира́ться (придра́ться* perf) к +dat; (treat badly) цепля́ться (impf) к +dat
▶ **pick out** vt (distinguish) разгляде́ть (perf); (select) выбира́ть (вы́брать* perf)
▶ **pick up** vi (improve: health, economy) улучша́ться (улу́чшиться perf) ◆ vt (lift) поднима́ть (подня́ть* perf); (POLICE: arrest) забира́ть (забра́ть* perf); (collect: person: on foot) заходи́ть* (зайти́* perf) за +instr; (: with transport) заезжа́ть (зае́хать* perf) за +instr; (: parcel) забира́ть (забра́ть* perf); (AUT: passenger) подбира́ть (подобра́ть* perf); (inf: person: for sexual encounter) подцепи́ть* (perf); (language, skill etc) усва́ивать (усво́ить perf); (RADIO) лови́ть* (пойма́ть perf); **to ~ up speed** набира́ть (набра́ть* perf) ско́рость; **to ~ o.s. up** (after falling etc) поднима́ться (подня́ться* perf); **we ~ed up where we left off** мы на́чали с того́ ме́ста, где останови́лись.
pickaxe ['pɪkæks] (US **pickax**) n кирка́*.
picket ['pɪkɪt] n (in strike) пике́т ◆ vt пикети́ровать (impf).
picketing ['pɪkɪtɪŋ] n пикети́рование.
picket line n ли́ния пике́тов.

---

pickings ['pɪkɪŋz] *npl*: **there are good ~ to be had here** на э́том мо́жно хорошо́ нажи́ться.

pickle ['pɪkl] *n* (*marinade*) марина́д; (*also:* **~s**) соле́нья *ntpl*; (*fig: inf*) переде́лка* ♦ *vt* (*in vinegar*) маринова́ть (замаринова́ть *perf*); (*in salt water*) соли́ть* (засоли́ть* *perf*); **to be in a ~** (*fig: inf*) попада́ть (попа́сть* *perf*) в переде́лку.

pick-me-up ['pɪkmiːʌp] *n* тонизи́рующий* напи́ток*.

pickpocket ['pɪkpɒkɪt] *n* вор*-карма́нник.

pick-up ['pɪkʌp] *n* (*also:* **~ truck** *or* **van**) пика́п; (*BRIT: on record player*) звукоснима́тель *m*.

picnic ['pɪknɪk] *n* пикни́к* ♦ *vi* устра́ивать (устро́ить *perf*) пикни́к.

picnicker ['pɪknɪkəʳ] *n* уча́стник(-ица) пикника́.

pictorial [pɪk'tɔːrɪəl] *adj* иллюстри́рованный (иллюстри́рован).

picture ['pɪktʃəʳ] *n* (*also fig*) карти́на; (*photograph*) фотогра́фия; (*TV*) изображе́ние; (*film*) (кино)карти́на ♦ *vt* (*imagine*) рисова́ть (нарисова́ть *perf*) карти́ну +*gen*; **the ~s** *npl* (*BRIT: inf*) кино́ *nt ind*; **to take a ~ of sb/sth** фотографи́ровать (сфотографи́ровать *perf*) кого́-н/что-н; **the overall ~** о́бщая карти́на; **to put sb in the ~** вводи́ть* (ввести́* *perf*) кого́-н в курс де́ла.

picture book *n* кни́га* с карти́нками.

picturesque [pɪktʃə'rɛsk] *adj* живопи́сный* (живопи́сен).

picture window *n* (*ARCHIT*) *большо́е окно́, из кото́рого открыва́ется краси́вый вид*.

piddling ['pɪdlɪŋ] *adj* (*inf*) пустя́чный*.

pidgin ['pɪdʒɪn] *adj*: **~ English** пи́джин-и́нглиш.

pie [paɪ] *n* пиро́г*; (*small*) пирожо́к*.

piebald ['paɪbɔːld] *adj* пе́гий* (пег).

piece [piːs] *n* (*portion, part*) кусо́к*; (*component*) дета́ль *f*; (*CHESS*) фигу́ра; (*DRAUGHTS*) ша́шка* ♦ *vt*: **to ~ together** (*information*) свя́зывать (связа́ть* *perf*); (*parts of a whole*) соединя́ть (соедини́ть *perf*); **a ~ of clothing** вещь* *f*; **a ~ of advice** сове́т; **in ~s** (*broken*) вдре́безги; (*not yet assembled*) разо́бранный (разо́бран); **to take to ~s** (*dismantle*) разбира́ть (разобра́ть* *perf*); **in one ~** в це́лости и сохра́нности; **to get back all in one ~** возвраща́ться (верну́ться *perf*) це́лым и невреди́мым; **a 10p ~** (*BRIT*) моне́та в 10 пе́нсов; **~ by ~** по частя́м; **a six-~ band** анса́мбль *m* из шести́ музыка́льных инструме́нтов; **to say one's ~** выска́зывать (вы́сказать* *perf*) своё мне́ние.

piecemeal ['piːsmiːl] *adv* понемно́гу.

piece rate *n* тари́ф *or* ста́вка за едини́цу вы́полненных рабо́т.

piecework ['piːswəːk] *n* сде́льная рабо́та.

pie chart *n* се́кторная диагра́мма.

pier [pɪəʳ] *n* пирс.

pierce [pɪəs] *vt* протыка́ть (проткну́ть *perf*), прока́лывать (проколо́ть* *perf*); **to have one's**

ears ~d прока́лывать (проколо́ть* *perf*) у́ши.

piercing ['pɪəsɪŋ] *adj* (*cry, eyes, stare*) пронзи́тельный* (пронзи́телен); (*wind*) прони́зывающий.

piety ['paɪətɪ] *n* на́божность *f*.

piffling ['pɪflɪŋ] *adj* (*inf*) никчёмный* (никчёмен).

pig [pɪg] *n* (*also fig*) свинья́*.

pigeon ['pɪdʒən] *n* го́лубь* *m*.

pigeonhole ['pɪdʒənhəul] *n* (*in office, bureau*) яче́йка (*для корреспонде́нции*); (*fig*) ни́ша ♦ *vt* (*person*) накле́ивать (накле́ить *perf*) ярлыки́ на +*acc*.

pigeon-toed ['pɪdʒəntəud] *adj* косола́пый (косола́п).

piggy bank ['pɪgɪ-] *n* копи́лка*.

pig-headed ['pɪg'hɛdɪd] *adj* (*inf*) упря́мый (упря́м).

piglet ['pɪglɪt] *n* поросёнок*.

pigment ['pɪgmənt] *n* пигме́нт.

pigmentation [pɪgmən'teɪʃən] *n* пигмента́ция.

pigmy ['pɪgmɪ] *n* = **pygmy**.

pigskin ['pɪgskɪn] *n* свина́я ко́жа.

pigsty ['pɪgstaɪ] *n* (*also fig*) свина́рник.

pigtail ['pɪgteɪl] *n* коси́чка*.

pike [paɪk] *n inv* (*fish*) щу́ка ♦ *n* (*spear*) пи́ка.

pilchard ['pɪltʃəd] *n* сарди́на.

pile [paɪl] *n* (*large heap*) ку́ча, гру́да; (*neat stack*) сто́пка*; (*pillar*) сва́я; (*of carpet, cloth*) ворс ♦ *vi*: **to ~ into** (*vehicle*) набива́ться (наби́ться* *perf*) в +*acc*; **in a ~** в ку́че; **to ~ out of** (*vehicle*) выва́ливаться (вы́валиться *perf*) из +*gen*

▶ **pile on** *vt*: **to ~ it on** (*inf*) переба́рщивать (переборщи́ть* *perf*)

▶ **pile up** *vt* (*objects*) сва́ливать (свали́ть* *perf*) в ку́чу ♦ *vi* громозди́ться* (*impf*); (*problems, work*) нака́пливаться (накопи́ться *perf*).

piles [paɪlz] *npl* (*MED*) геморро́й *msg*.

pile-up ['paɪlʌp] *n* (*AUT*) столкнове́ние не́скольких маши́н.

pilfer ['pɪlfəʳ] *vti* ворова́ть (*impf*).

pilfering ['pɪlfərɪŋ] *n* ме́лкое воровство́.

pilgrim ['pɪlgrɪm] *n* пало́мник(-ица), пилигри́м.

pilgrimage ['pɪlgrɪmɪdʒ] *n* пало́мничество.

pill [pɪl] *n* табле́тка*; **the ~** (*contraceptive*) противозача́точные *pl adj* (табле́тки); **to be on the ~** принима́ть (*impf*) противозача́точные табле́тки.

pillage ['pɪlɪdʒ] *n* грабёж*.

pillar ['pɪləʳ] *n* (*ARCHIT*) столб*, коло́нна; **a ~ of society** (*fig*) столп о́бщества.

pillar box *n* (*BRIT*) почто́вый я́щик*.

pillion ['pɪljən] *n*: **to ride ~** (*on motorcycle*) е́хать*/е́здить* (*impf*) на за́днем сиде́нье мотоци́кла; (*on horse*) е́хать*/е́здить* (*impf*) верхо́м на ло́шади сза́ди вса́дника.

pillory ['pɪlərɪ] *vt* выставля́ть (вы́ставить* *perf*) на осмея́ние ♦ *n* позо́рный столб*.

pillow ['pɪləu] *n* поду́шка*.

pillowcase ['pɪləukeɪs] *n* наволочка*.
pillowslip ['pɪləuslɪp] *n* = **pillowcase**.
pilot ['paɪlət] *n* (*AVIAT*) пилот, лётчик; (*NAUT*) лоцман ♦ *cpd* (*scheme, study etc*) экспериментальный ♦ *vt* (*aircraft*) управлять (*impf*) +*instr*; (*fig: new law, scheme*) апробировать (*impf*/*perf*).
pilot boat *n* лоцманский катер*.
pilot light *n* запальник.
pimento [pɪ'mentəu] *n* душистый перец.
pimp [pɪmp] *n* сутенёр.
pimple ['pɪmpl] *n* прыщ*, прыщик.
pimply ['pɪmplɪ] *adj* прыщавый (прыщав).
PIN *n abbr* = **personal identification number**.
pin [pɪn] *n* булавка*; (*TECH*) штифт*; (*BRIT: also:* **drawing ~**) кнопка*; (*of grenade*) чека*; (*BRIT: ELEC: of plug*) штырь* *m* ♦ *vt* прикалывать (приколоть* *perf*); **~s and needles** (*fig*) колотьё; **to ~ sb against** *or* **to** прижимать (прижать* *perf*) кого-н к +*dat*; **to ~ sth on sb** (*fig*) возлагать (возложить* *perf*) на кого-н вину за что-н
▶ **pin down** *vt* (*fig*): **to ~ sb down** припирать (припереть* *perf*) кого-н к стенке; **there's something strange here but I can't quite ~ it down** что-то здесь не так, но не пойму что.
pinafore ['pɪnəfɔː] *n* (*also:* **~ dress**) сарафан.
pinball ['pɪnbɔːl] *n* китайский* бильярд.
pincers ['pɪnsəz] *npl* (*TECH*) клещи* *pl*; (*of crab etc*) клешни *fpl*.
pinch [pɪntʃ] *n* (*small amount*) щепотка* ♦ *vt* щипать* (ущипнуть* *perf*); (*inf: steal*) стащить* (*perf*) ♦ *vi* (*shoe*) жать* (*impf*); **at a ~** в крайнем случае; **to feel the ~** (*fig*) оказываться (оказаться* *perf*) в стеснённых обстоятельствах.
pinched [pɪntʃt] *adj* (*drawn*) осунувшийся; **~ with cold** съёжившийся от холода; **I am ~ for money** у меня туго с деньгами; **we're ~ for space here** у нас здесь мало места.
pincushion ['pɪnkuʃən] *n* игольник.
pine [paɪn] *n* (*tree, wood*) сосна* ♦ *vi*: **to ~ for** тосковать (*impf*) по +*dat*
▶ **pine away** *vi* (*gradually die*) чахнуть* (зачахнуть* *perf*).
pineapple ['paɪnæpl] *n* ананас *m no pl*.
pine cone *n* сосновая шишка.
pine needles *npl* сосновые иголки *fpl*.
ping [pɪŋ] *n* (*noise*) звон.
Ping-Pong® ['pɪŋpɔŋ] *n* настольный теннис, пинг-понг.
pink [pɪŋk] *adj* розовый ♦ *n* (*colour*) розовый цвет*; (*BOT*) гвоздика.
pinking shears *npl* зубчатые ножницы *pl*.
pin money *n* (*BRIT*) деньги* *pl* на булавки.
pinnacle ['pɪnəkl] *n* (*of building*) шпиц; (*of mountain, also fig*) вершина.
pinpoint ['pɪnpɔɪnt] *vt* (*discover*) точно

определять (определить *perf*); (*explain*) точно объяснять (объяснить *perf*); (*position of sth*) точно указывать (указать* *perf*).
pinstripe ['pɪnstraɪp] *n* полоска*; **~ suit** костюм в полоску.
pint [paɪnt] *n* пинта.
pin-up ['pɪnʌp] *n* (*picture*) журнальная вырезка с изображением красивых девушек.
pioneer [paɪə'nɪə] *n* (*initiator: of scheme, science, method*) первооткрыватель *m*, новатор; (*early settler, also fig*) первопроходец*, пионер ♦ *vt* (*initiate*) прокладывать (проложить* *perf*) путь к +*dat*.
pious ['paɪəs] *adj* набожный* (набожен).
pip [pɪp] *n* (*of grape, melon*) косточка*; (*of apple, orange*) зёрнышко; **the ~s** *npl* (*BRIT: RADIO*) сигнал *msg* (точного времени).
pipe [paɪp] *n* (*for water, gas*) труба*; (*for smoking*) трубка*; (*MUS*) дудка* ♦ *vt* (*water, gas, oil*) подавать* (подать* *perf*); **~s** *npl* (*also:* **bagpipes**) волынка* *fsg*
▶ **pipe down** *vi* (*inf: be quiet*) затыкаться (заткнуться *perf*).
pipe cleaner *n* ёршик (*для трубки*).
piped music [paɪpt-] *n* музыка из громкоговорителя.
pipe dream *n* пустые мечты *fpl*.
pipeline ['paɪplaɪn] *n* трубопровод; **oil ~** нефтепровод; **gas ~** газопровод; **a new project is in the ~** (*fig*) дан ход новому проекту.
piper ['paɪpə] *n* (*bagpipe player*) волынщик.
pipe tobacco *n* трубочный табак*.
piping ['paɪpɪŋ] *adv*: **~ hot** очень горячий*.
piquant ['piːkənt] *adj* (*also fig*) пикантный* (пикантен).
pique ['piːk] *n* задетое самолюбие.
piracy ['paɪərəsɪ] *n* пиратство.
pirate ['paɪərət] *n* (*sailor*) пират ♦ *vt* (*video tape, cassette*) незаконно распространять (распространить *perf*); (*book*) незаконно переиздавать* (переиздать* *perf*).
pirate radio *n* (*BRIT*): **~ ~ station** пиратская радиостанция.
pirouette [pɪru'et] *n* пируэт.
Pisces ['paɪsiːz] *n* (*ASTROLOGY*) Рыбы; **he is ~** он – Рыба.
piss [pɪs] (*infl*) *vi* писать (пописать *perf*) (*!*); **~ off!** пошёл ты! (*!*)
pissed [pɪst] *adj* (*infl: drunk*) пьяный* (пьян) в стельку (*!*)
pistol ['pɪstl] *n* пистолет.
piston ['pɪstən] *n* поршень* *m*.
pit [pɪt] *n* (*in ground*) яма; (*in surface of sth*) ямка*; (*also:* **coal ~**) шахта; (*also:* **orchestra ~**) оркестровая яма; (*quarry*) карьер ♦ *vt*: **to ~ one's wits against sb** состязаться (*impf*) в эрудиции с кем-н; **~s** *npl* (*in motor racing*)

пункт *msg* ремо́нта и запра́вки; **to ~ sb against sb** направля́ть (напра́вить* *perf*) кого́-н на кого́-н.

pitapat ['pɪtə'pæt] *adv* (*BRIT*: *of heart*) тук-ту́к; (: *of rain*) кап-кап.

pitch [pɪtʃ] *n* (*BRIT*: *SPORT*) по́ле*; (*MUS*) высота́; (*fig*: *level, degree*) у́ровень *m*; (*tar*) смола́; (*also*: **sales ~**) рула́да; (*NAUT*) килева́я ка́чка ♦ *vt* (*throw*) подава́ть (пода́ть* *perf*), гнать* (погна́ть* *perf*); (*set*: *price*) устана́вливать (установи́ть* *perf*); (: *message*) подстра́ивать (подстро́ить* *perf*) ♦ *vi* (*fall*) па́дать (упа́сть* *perf*); (*NAUT*) испы́тывать (испыта́ть* *perf*) килеву́ю ка́чку; **at this ~** (*fig*) на тако́м у́ровне; **to ~ a tent** ста́вить* (поста́вить* *perf*) пала́тку; **he was ~ed forward** его́ бро́сило вперёд.

pitch-black ['pɪtʃ'blæk] *adj* о́чень тёмный.

pitched battle [pɪtʃt-] *n* ожесточённая схва́тка*.

pitcher ['pɪtʃə*] *n* (*jug*) кувши́н; (*US*: *BASEBALL*) подаю́щий *m adj*.

pitchfork ['pɪtʃfɔ:k] *n* ви́лы *pl*.

piteous ['pɪtɪəs] *adj* (*sound etc*) жа́лобный* (жа́лобен); (*sight*) несча́стный* (несча́стен).

pitfall ['pɪtfɔ:l] *n* (*difficulty, danger*) лову́шка, подво́дные ка́мни *mpl*.

pith [pɪθ] *n* (*of orange, lemon etc*) паренхи́ма; (*of plant*) сердцеви́на; (*fig*) суть *f*.

pithead ['pɪthed] *n* (*BRIT*) копёр (*над ша́хтой*).

pithy ['pɪθɪ] *adj* (*saying etc*) содержа́тельный* (содержа́телен).

pitiable ['pɪtɪəbl] *adj* (*sight, person*) жа́лкий* (жа́лок).

pitiful ['pɪtɪful] *adj* жа́лкий* (жа́лок).

pitifully ['pɪtɪfəlɪ] *adv* жа́лобно; **it's ~ obvious** к несча́стью, э́то очеви́дно.

pitiless ['pɪtɪlɪs] *adj* безжа́лостный* (безжа́лостен).

pittance ['pɪtns] *n* гроши́ *mpl*.

pitted ['pɪtɪd] *adj*: **~ with** (*holes, acne*) изры́тый (изры́т) +*instr*; (*rust*) изъе́денный (изъе́ден) +*instr*.

pity ['pɪtɪ] *n* жа́лость *f* ♦ *vt* жале́ть (пожале́ть* *perf*); **what a ~!** кака́я жа́лость!; **it is a ~ that you can't come** жа́лко, что Вы не смо́жете прийти́; **to have** *or* **take ~ on sb** сжа́литься (*perf*) над кем-н.

pitying ['pɪtɪɪŋ] *adj* жа́лостливый (жа́лостлив).

pivot ['pɪvət] *n* (*TECH*: *pin*) ось *f*; (: *point*) то́чка* враще́ния; (*fig*) центр ♦ *vi*: **to ~ on** (*balance*) держа́ться* (*perf*) на +*prp*; (*turn*) враща́ться (*impf*) вокру́г +*gen*; (*fig*: *depend on*) зави́сеть* (*impf*) от +*gen*.

pixel ['pɪksl] *n* (*COMPUT*) пи́ксель *m*, элеме́нт изображе́ния.

pixie ['pɪksɪ] *n* эльф.

pizza ['pi:tsə] *n* пи́цца.

placard ['plæka:d] *n* плака́т.

placate [plə'keɪt] *vt* (*person*) умиротворя́ть (умиротвори́ть *perf*); (*anger*) усмиря́ть (усмири́ть *perf*).

placatory [plə'keɪtərɪ] *adj* примири́тельный* (примири́телен).

place [pleɪs] *vt* (*put*) помеща́ть (помести́ть* *perf*); (*identify*: *person*) вспомина́ть (вспо́мнить *perf*) ♦ *n* ме́сто*; (*home*): **at his ~** у него́; (*in street names*): **Laurel P~** Ло́рел Плейс; **to ~ an order with sb for sth** (*COMM*) зака́зывать (заказа́ть* *perf*) что-н у кого́-н; **to be ~d** (*in race, exam*) быть* (*impf*) на како́м-н ме́сте; **how are you ~d next week?** как у Вас со сле́дующей неде́лей?; **to take ~** происходи́ть* (произойти́* *perf*); **from ~ to ~** с ме́ста на ме́сто; **all over the ~** повсю́ду; **out of ~** (*not suitable*) неуме́стный* (неуме́стен); **I feel out of ~ here** я чу́вствую себя́ не в свое́й таре́лке/не на ме́сте здесь; **in the first ~** (*first of all*) во-пе́рвых; **to put sb in his ~** (*fig*) ста́вить* (поста́вить* *perf*) кого́-н на ме́сто; **he's going ~s** он далеко́ пойдёт; **it's not my ~** э́то не моё де́ло; **to change ~s with sb** меня́ться (поменя́ться *perf*) места́ми с кем-н.

placebo [plə'si:bəu] *n* (*MED*) плаце́бо *nt ind*; (*fig*) успокои́тельное сре́дство.

place mat *n* подста́вка* (*для столо́вых прибо́ров*); (*in linen etc*) салфе́тка*.

placement ['pleɪsmənt] *n* (*action*) размеще́ние; (*job*) ме́сто*.

place name *n* географи́ческое назва́ние, топони́м.

placenta [plə'sentə] *n* плаце́нта.

place of birth *n* ме́сто* рожде́ния.

place setting *n* столо́вый прибо́р.

placid ['plæsɪd] *adj* споко́йный* (споко́ен); (*place*) ти́хий* (тих).

plagiarism ['pleɪdʒjərɪzəm] *n* плагиа́т.

plagiarist ['pleɪdʒjərɪst] *n* плагиа́тор.

plagiarize ['pleɪdʒjəraɪz] *vt* красть* (укра́сть* *perf*), спи́сывать (списа́ть* *perf*).

plague [pleɪg] *n* (*MED*) чума́; (*fig*: *of locusts etc*) наше́ствие ♦ *vt* (*fig*: *subj*: *problems, difficulties*) осажда́ть (осади́ть* *perf*); **to ~ sb with questions** донима́ть (*impf*) кого́-н вопро́сами.

plaice [pleɪs] *n inv* ка́мбала.

plaid [plæd] *n* шотла́ндка* (*ткань*).

plain [pleɪn] *adj* (*simple, not beautiful*) просто́й* (прост); (*unpatterned*) гла́дкий* (гла́док); (*clear, easily understood*) я́сный* (я́сен), поня́тный* (поня́тен); (*frank*) прямо́й* (прям) ♦ *adv* (*wrong, stupid etc*) я́вно ♦ *n* (*GEO*) равни́на; (*KNITTING*) чуло́чная вя́зка; **to make sth ~ to sb** разъясня́ть (разъясни́ть* *perf*) что-н кому́-н.

plain chocolate *n* го́рький* шокола́д.

plain-clothes ['pleɪnkləuðz] *adj*: **~ policeman** полице́йский* *m adj* в шта́тском.

plain flour *n* мука́ без дрожжевы́х доба́вок.

plainly ['pleɪnlɪ] *adv* я́сно.

365

plainness ['pleɪnnɪs] n (simplicity) простота́; (clarity) я́сность f.
plaintiff ['pleɪntɪf] n исте́ц*(-ти́ца).
plain speaking n прямота́.
plaintive ['pleɪntɪv] adj (voice, look, song) жа́лобный* (жа́лобен).
plait [plæt] n (of hair) коса́* ♦ vt (hair) заплета́ть (заплести́* perf); (rope) плести́ (сплести́* perf).
plan [plæn] n план ♦ vt плани́ровать (заплани́ровать perf); (draw up plans for) плани́ровать (impf) ♦ vi плани́ровать (impf); **to ~ to do** плани́ровать (заплани́ровать perf) +infin; **how long do you ~ to stay?** как до́лго Вы плани́руете пробы́ть здесь?; **to ~ for sth** (anticipate) рассчи́тывать (impf) на что-н.
plane [pleɪn] n (AVIAT) самолёт; (MATH) пло́скость f; (fig: level) план; (tool) руба́нок*; (BOT) плата́н ♦ vt (wood) строга́ть (вы́стругать perf) ♦ vi (NAUT, AUT): **to ~ across** скользи́ть* (impf) по +dat.
planet ['plænɪt] n плане́та.
planetarium [plænɪ'tɛərɪəm] n планета́рий.
plank [plæŋk] n доска́*; (fig: of policy etc) при́нцип.
plankton ['plæŋktən] n планкто́н.
planned economy ['plænd-] n пла́новая эконо́мика.
planner ['plænə'] n (of towns) планиро́вщик; (of TV programme, project) состави́тель m.
planning ['plænɪŋ] n (of future, event) плани́рование; (of programme etc) составле́ние; (also: **town ~**) планиро́вка.
planning permission n (BRIT) разреше́ние на строи́тельство.
plant [plɑ:nt] n (BOT) расте́ние; (factory) заво́д; (machinery) устано́вка* ♦ vt (seed, plant, garden) сажа́ть (посади́ть* perf); (field) засе́ивать (засе́ять perf); (bomb, evidence) подкла́дывать (подложи́ть* perf); (fig: kiss) запечатлева́ть (запечатле́ть perf).
plantation [plæn'teɪʃən] n (of tea, rubber, sugar etc) планта́ция; (of trees) лесонасажде́ние.
plant pot n (BRIT) цвето́чный горшо́к*.
plaque [plæk] n (on building etc) мемори́альная доска́*; (on teeth) налёт.
plasma ['plæzmə] n пла́зма.
plaster ['plɑ:stə'] n (for walls) штукату́рка*; (also: **~ of Paris**) гипс; (BRIT: also: **sticking ~**) пла́стырь m ♦ vt (wall, ceiling) штукату́рить (оштукату́рить perf); (cover): **to ~ with** залепля́ть (залепи́ть* perf) +instr; **in ~** (BRIT) в ги́псе.
plasterboard ['plɑ:stəbɔ:d] n ги́псовые щиты́ (для обши́вки стен и потолка́).
plaster cast n (MED) гипс; (model, statue) ги́псовый слепо́к*.
plastered ['plɑ:stəd] adj (inf: drunk): **he is ~** он

нажра́лся.
plasterer ['plɑ:stərə'] n штукату́р.
plastic ['plæstɪk] n пластма́сса ♦ adj (made of plastic) пластма́ссовый; (flexible) пласти́чный*; (art) пласти́ческий*.
plastic bag n полиэтиле́новый мешо́к*.
plastic bullet n пластма́ссовая пу́ля*.
plastic explosive n синтети́ческая взрывча́тка консисте́нции пластили́на.
Plasticine® ['plæstɪsi:n] n пластили́н.
plastic surgery n (science) пласти́ческая хирурги́я; (operation) пласти́ческая опера́ция.
plate [pleɪt] n (dish) таре́лка*; (metal cover: on building, machinery) пласти́на; (TYP) печа́тная фо́рма; (PHOT) фотопласти́нка*; (AUT: number plate) но́мер*; (in book) вкладна́я иллюстра́ция; (also: **dental ~**) вставна́я че́люсть* f; (on door) табли́чка*; **gold ~** позоло́та; **silver ~** серебре́ние.
plateau ['plætəu] (pl **~s** or **~x**) n (GEO, also fig) плато́ nt ind.
plateaux ['plætəuz] npl of **plateau**.
plateful ['pleɪtful] n: **a ~ of** таре́лка* +gen.
plate glass n (for window, door) зерка́льное стекло́.
platen ['plætən] n (TYP) ва́лик.
plate rack n суши́лка* (для посу́ды).
platform ['plætfɔ:m] n (at meeting) трибу́на; (at concert) помо́ст; (for landing, loading on etc) площа́дка; (RAIL, POL) платфо́рма; (BRIT: of bus) подно́жка*; **the train leaves from ~ seven** по́езд отправля́ется с седьмо́го пути́.
platform ticket n (BRIT: RAIL) перро́нный биле́т.
platinum ['plætɪnəm] n пла́тина.
platitude ['plætɪtju:d] n пло́скость f, бана́льность f.
platonic [plə'tɔnɪk] adj платони́ческий.
platoon [plə'tu:n] n взвод.
platter ['plætə'] n блю́до.
plaudits ['plɔ:dɪts] npl похвала́ fsg.
plausible ['plɔ:zɪbl] adj (theory, excuse etc) правдоподо́бный* (правдоподо́бен); (person) убеди́тельный*.
play [pleɪ] n пье́са ♦ vt (subj: children: game) игра́ть (impf) в +acc; (sport, cards) игра́ть (сыгра́ть perf) в +acc; (opponent) игра́ть (сыгра́ть perf) с +instr; (part, role, piece of music) игра́ть (сыгра́ть perf); (instrument) игра́ть (impf) на +prp; (listen to: tape, record) ста́вить* (поста́вить* perf) ♦ vi игра́ть (impf); **a ~ on words** игра́* слов; **to bring** or **call into ~** вводи́ть* (ввести́* perf) в де́йствие; **to ~ a trick on sb** сыгра́ть (perf) шу́тку над кем-н; **they're ~ing at soldiers** они́ игра́ют в солда́тики; **to ~ for time** тяну́ть (impf) вре́мя; **to ~ safe** де́йствовать (impf) осторо́жно; **to ~**

---

* marks translations which have irregular inflections. The Russian-English side of the dictionary gives inflectional information.

into sb's hands играть (сыграть *perf*) кому́-н
на́ руку
► **play about** *vi*: **to ~ about with** (*feelings*)
игра́ть (*impf*) +*instr*; (*object*) вози́ться (*impf*) с
+*instr*
► **play along** *vi* (*fig*): **to ~ along with** (*person,
plan, idea*) поды́грывать (подыгра́ть *perf*)
+*dat* ♦ *vt* (*fig*): **to ~ sb along** испо́льзовать
(*impf*) кого́-н в свои́х це́лях
► **play around** *vi* = **play about**
► **play back** *vt* (*recording*) прои́грывать
(проигра́ть *perf*) (*повто́рно*)
► **play down** *vt* не заостря́ть (*impf*) внима́ние
на +*prp*
► **play on** *vt fus* (*sb's feelings etc*) игра́ть (*impf*)
на +*prp*; **to ~ on sb's nerves** де́йствовать
(*impf*) кому́-н на не́рвы
► **play up** *vi* (*machine*) барахли́ть* (*impf*);
(*children*) шали́ть (*impf*), прики́дываться
(*impf*).
play-act ['pleɪækt] *vi* де́лать (сде́лать *perf*) вид.
playboy ['pleɪbɔɪ] *n* хлыщ.
player ['pleɪə'] *n* (*SPORT*) игро́к*; (*MUS, THEAT*)
исполни́тель(ница) *m(f)*.
playful ['pleɪful] *adj* (*person*) игри́вый (игри́в).
playgoer ['pleɪgəuə'] *n* театра́л.
playground ['pleɪgraund] *n* (*in park*) (де́тская)
площа́дка*; (*in school*) (игрова́я) площа́дка*.
playgroup ['pleɪgru:p] *n* де́тская гру́ппа.
playing card ['pleɪɪŋ-] *n* игра́льная ка́рта.
playing field *n* игрово́е по́ле*.
playmate ['pleɪmeɪt] *n* прия́тель(ница) *m(f)*.
play-off ['pleɪɔf] *n* (*SPORT*) игра́ за призово́е
ме́сто.
playpen ['pleɪpɛn] *n* (де́тский*) мане́ж.
playroom ['pleɪru:m] *n* де́тская *f adj*.
playschool ['pleɪsku:l] *n* = **playgroup**.
plaything ['pleɪθɪŋ] *n* игру́шка*.
playtime ['pleɪtaɪm] *n* (*SCOL*) переме́на.
playwright ['pleɪraɪt] *n* драмату́рг.
plc *abbr* (*BRIT*: = *public limited company*)
публи́чная компа́ния с ограни́ченной
отве́тственностью.
plea [pli:] *n* (*personal request*) мольба́; (*public
request*) призы́в; (*LAW*) заявле́ние; (*excuse*)
предло́г.
plea bargaining *n* призна́ние вино́вности в
*обме́н на бо́лее коро́ткое тюре́мное
заключе́ние.*
plead [pli:d] *vt* (*ignorance, ill health etc*)
ссыла́ться (сосла́ться* *perf*) на +*acc* ♦ *vi* (*LAW*)
признава́ть* (призна́ть* *perf*) себя́; (*beg*): **to ~
with sb** умоля́ть (*impf*) кого́-н, моли́ть* (*impf*)
кого́-н; **to ~ sb's case** (*LAW*) защища́ть (*impf*)
кого́-н (*в суде́*); **to ~ for sth** призыва́ть
(призва́ть* *perf*) к чему́-н; **to ~ guilty/not
guilty** признава́ть* (призна́ть* *perf*) себя́
вино́вным(-ой)/невино́вным(-ой).
pleasant ['plɛznt] *adj* прия́тный* (прия́тен).
pleasantly ['plɛzntlɪ] *adv* прия́тно.
pleasantries ['plɛzntrɪz] *npl* любе́зности *fpl*.

please [pli:z] *excl* пожа́луйста ♦ *vt* угожда́ть
(угоди́ть* *perf*) +*dat* ♦ *vi* (*give pleasure,
satisfaction*) угожда́ть (угоди́ть* *perf*); **yes, ~**
да, спаси́бо; **my bill, ~** получи́те (с меня́),
пожа́луйста; **~ don't cry!** не пла́чь,
пожа́луйста!; **~ yourself!** (*inf*) как Вам
уго́дно!; **do as you ~** де́лайте как хоти́те; **he
is difficult/easy to ~** ему́ тру́дно/легко́
угоди́ть (*perf*).
pleased [pli:zd] *adj*: **~ (with)** дово́льный*
(дово́лен) (+*instr*); **~ to meet you** о́чень
прия́тно; **we are ~ to inform you that ...** мы
ра́ды сообщи́ть Вам, что ....
pleasing ['pli:zɪŋ] *adj* прия́тный* (прия́тен).
pleasurable ['plɛʒərəbl] *adj* ра́достный*
(ра́достен).
pleasure ['plɛʒə'] *n* удово́льствие; **it's a ~** не
сто́ит; **with ~** с удово́льствием; **to take ~ in**
получа́ть (получи́ть *perf*) удово́льствие от
+*gen*; **is this trip for business or ~?** э́та пое́здка
делова́я и́ли развлека́тельная?
pleasure boat *n* прогу́лочный ка́тер.
pleasure cruise *n* круи́з.
pleat [pli:t] *n* скла́дка*.
plebiscite ['plɛbɪsɪt] *n* плебисци́т.
plebs [plɛbz] *npl* (*pej*) плебе́и *mpl*, плебс *msg*.
plectrum ['plɛktrəm] *n* плектр.
pledge [plɛdʒ] *n* (*promise*) обяза́тельство ♦ *vt*
(*promise: money, support, help*) обяза́ться
(*perf*); **to ~ sb to secrecy** брать* (взять* *perf*) с
кого́-н сло́во молча́ть.
plenary ['pli:nərɪ] *adj*: **in ~ session** на
плена́рном заседа́нии.
plentiful ['plɛntɪful] *adj* оби́льный* (оби́лен).
plenty ['plɛntɪ] *n* (*sufficient*) доста́точное
коли́чество; **~ of** (*food, money etc*) мно́го
+*gen*; (*jobs, people, houses etc*) мно́жество
+*gen*; **we've got ~ of time to get there** у нас
дово́льно вре́мени, что́бы туда́ добра́ться.
plethora ['plɛθərə] *n*: **a ~ of** вели́кое
мно́жество +*gen*.
pleurisy ['pluərɪsɪ] *n* плеври́т.
Plexiglas® ['plɛksɪglɑ:s] *n* (*US*) плексигла́с.
pliable ['plaɪəbl] *adj* (*material*) ги́бкий* (ги́бок);
(*fig: person*) усту́пчивый (усту́пчив),
пода́тливый (пода́тлив).
pliant ['plaɪənt] *adj* = **pliable**.
pliers ['plaɪəz] *npl* плоскогу́бцы* *pl*.
plight [plaɪt] *n* мучи́тельное положе́ние.
plimsolls ['plɪmsolz] *npl* (*BRIT*) паруси́новые
ту́фли *pl*, ке́ды *fpl*.
plinth [plɪnθ] *n* постаме́нт.
PLO *n abbr* (= *Palestine Liberation Organization*)
ООП= *Организа́ция освобожде́ния
Палести́ны.*
plod [plod] *vi* (*walk, also fig*) тащи́ться* (*impf*).
plodder ['plodə'] *n* (*pej: slow worker*)
болоки́тчик; **he is a real ~** (*pej*) он тако́й
медли́тельный.
plonk [plonk] *n* (*inf: BRIT: wine*) дешёвое вино́ ♦
vt (*inf*): **to ~ sth down** бу́хать (бу́хнуть *perf*)

что-н.

plot [plɔt] *n* (*conspiracy*) за́говор; (*of story*) сюже́т; (*of land*) уча́сток* ◆ *vt* (*sb's downfall etc*) замышля́ть (*impf*); (*AVIAT, NAUT*) прокла́дывать (проложи́ть *perf*); (*MATH*) наноси́ть* (нанести́* *perf*) ◆ *vi* (*conspire*) составля́ть (соста́вить* *perf*) за́говор; **a vegetable ~** (*BRIT*) садо́вый уча́сток*, огоро́д.

plotter ['plɔtə'] *n* (*instrument*) графопостро́итель *m*; (: *AVIAT, NAUT*) курсопрокла́дчик; (*COMPUT*) пло́ттер, графопостро́итель *m*.

plough [plau] (*US* **plow**) *n* плуг* ◆ *vt* паха́ть* (вспаха́ть* *perf*); **to ~ money into** вкла́дывать (вложи́ть *perf*) де́ньги в +*acc*
► **plough back** *vt* (*COMM*) реинвести́ровать (*impf/perf*)
► **plough through** *vt fus* (*crowd*) продира́ться (продра́ться* *perf*) сквозь +*acc*; (*snow etc*) пробира́ться (пробра́ться* *perf*) че́рез +*acc*.

ploughman ['plaumən] (*US* **plowman**) *irreg n* па́харь *m*.

ploughman's lunch ['plaumənz-] *n* (*BRIT*) ≈ крестья́нский* обе́д.

plow *etc* (*US*) = **plough** *etc*.

ploy [plɔɪ] *n* уло́вка*.

pluck [plʌk] *n* (*courage*) му́жество ◆ *vt* (*fruit, flower*) срыва́ть (сорва́ть *perf*); (*bird*) ощи́пывать (ощипа́ть* *perf*); (*eyebrows*) выщи́пывать (вы́щипать* *perf*); (*string instrument*): **to ~ (the strings of) sth** перебира́ть (*impf*) стру́ны чего́-н; **to ~ up courage** набира́ться (набра́ться* *perf*) хра́брости *or* му́жества.

plucky ['plʌkɪ] *adj* му́жественный* (му́жествен), отва́жный* (отва́жен).

plug [plʌg] *n* (*ELEC*) ви́лка*; (*in sink, bath*) про́бка*; (*AUT: also:* **spark(ing) ~**) свеча́ (зажига́ния) ◆ *vt* (*hole*) затыка́ть (заткну́ть *perf*); (*inf: advertise*) реклами́ровать (разреклами́ровать *perf*); **to give sb/sth a ~** реклами́ровать (разреклами́ровать *perf*) кого́-н/что-н
► **plug in** *vt* (*ELEC*) включа́ть (включи́ть *perf*) в розе́тку ◆ *vi* включа́ться (включи́ться *perf*).

plughole ['plʌghəul] *n* (*BRIT*) сток.

plum [plʌm] *n* сли́ва ◆ *cpd* (*inf*): **~ job** мирова́я рабо́та.

plumage ['plu:mɪdʒ] *n* опере́ние.

plumb [plʌm] *vt*: **to ~ the depths of** (*fig*) достига́ть (дости́чь* *perf*) глуби́н +*gen*
► **plumb in** *vt* (*washing machine*) подключа́ть (подключи́ть *perf*), подсоединя́ть (подсоедини́ть *perf*).

plumber ['plʌmə'] *n* водопрово́дчик.

plumbing ['plʌmɪŋ] *n* (*piping*) водопрово́д и канализа́ция; (*trade, work*) слеса́рное де́ло.

plumb line *n* отве́с.

plume [plu:m] *n* (*of bird*) перо́*; (*on helmet, horse's head*) плюма́ж; (*fig*): **~ of smoke** струя́* ды́ма.

plummet ['plʌmɪt] *vi*: **to ~ (down)** (*bird, aircraft*) ру́хнуть (*perf*); (*price, amount*) ре́зко па́дать (упа́сть* *perf*).

plump [plʌmp] *adj* (*adult*) по́лный*; (*child*) пу́хлый* (пухл) ◆ *vi*: **to ~ for** (*inf*) выбира́ть (вы́брать* *perf*)
► **plump up** *vt* взбива́ть (взбить* *perf*).

plunder ['plʌndə'] *n* (*activity*) грабёж*; (*stolen things*) награ́бленное *nt adj* ◆ *vt* гра́бить* (разгра́бить* *perf*).

plunge [plʌndʒ] *n* (*dive: of bird, person*) бросо́к*; (*fig: of prices, rates etc*) ре́зкое паде́ние ◆ *vt* (*knife*) мета́ть (метну́ть *perf*); (*hand*) выбра́сывать (вы́бросить* *perf*) ◆ *vi* (*fall: person, thing*) ру́хнуть (*perf*); (*dive: bird, person*) броса́ться (бро́ситься* *perf*); (*fig: prices, rates etc*) ре́зко па́дать (упа́сть* *perf*); **to take the ~** (*fig*) отва́живаться (отва́житься *perf*); **the room was ~d into darkness** ко́мната погрузи́лась во тьму.

plunger ['plʌndʒə'] *n* (*for sink*) плу́нжер.

plunging ['plʌndʒɪŋ] *adj*: **~ neckline** декольте́ *nt ind*.

pluperfect [plu:'pə:fɪkt] *n* плюсквамперфе́кт.

plural ['pluərl] *adj* мно́жественный* ◆ *n* мно́жественное число́*.

plus [plʌs] *n, adj* плюс *ind* ◆ *prep*: **ten ~ ten is twenty** де́сять плюс де́сять – два́дцать; **ten/ twenty ~** (*more than*) де́сять/два́дцать с ли́шним; **we discussed the ~es of the plan** (*fig*) мы обсужда́ли плю́сы прое́кта.

plus fours *npl* бри́джи *pl*.

plush [plʌʃ] *adj* шика́рный* (шика́рен), роско́шный* (роско́шен) ◆ *n* (*fabric*) плюш.

Pluto ['plu:təu] *n* (*planet*) Плуто́н.

plutonium [plu:'təunɪəm] *n* плуто́ний.

ply [plaɪ] *vt* (*a trade*) занима́ться (заня́ться* *perf*) +*instr*; (*tool*) ору́довать (*impf*) +*instr* ◆ *vi* (*ship*) курси́ровать (*impf*) ◆ *n* (*of wool, rope*) нить *f*; (*of wood*) слой*; **to ~ sb with sth** (*food, drink*) по́тчевать (*perf*) кого́-н чем-н; **to ~ sb with questions** засыпа́ть (засы́пать* *perf*) кого́-н вопро́сами; **two/three ~** двойна́я/ тройна́я нить.

Plymouth ['plɪməθ] *n* Пли́мут.

plywood ['plaɪwud] *n* фане́ра.

PM *abbr* (*BRIT*) = **Prime Minister**.

p.m. *adv abbr* (= *post meridiem*) по́сле полу́дня.

PMT *abbr* = **premenstrual tension**.

pneumatic [nju:'mætɪk] *adj* пневмати́ческий*.

pneumatic drill *n* пневмати́ческая дрель *f*.

pneumonia [nju:'məunɪə] *n* воспале́ние лёгких, пневмони́я.

Pnomh Penh [nɔm pɛn] *n* Пномпе́нь *m*.

PO *n abbr* = **Post Office**; (*MIL*) = **petty officer**.

---

* marks translations which have irregular inflections. The Russian-English side of the dictionary gives inflectional information.

p.o. *abbr* = **postal order.**
POA *n abbr* (*BRIT*) = *Prison Officers' Association.*
poach [pəutʃ] *vt* (*steal: fish etc*) охо́титься (*impf*)
без лице́нзии на +*acc*; (*cook: fish*) вари́ть*
(свари́ть* *perf*) ♦ *vi* (*steal*) охо́титься (*impf*) без
лице́нзии; **to ~ an egg** вари́ть* (свари́ть* *perf*)
яйцо́-пашо́т.
poached [pəutʃt] *adj*: **~ egg** яйцо́-пашо́т *ind.*
poacher ['pəutʃə'] *n* браконье́р.
PO Box *n abbr* = **Post Office Box.**
pocket ['pɒkɪt] *n* (*on clothes*) карма́н; (*on
suitcase, car door*) отделе́ние; (*fig: small area*)
уголо́к* ♦ *vt* класть* (положи́ть* *perf*) себе́ в
карма́н; **to be out of ~** (*BRIT*) быть* (*impf*) в
убы́тке на чём-н.
pocketbook ['pɒkɪtbuk] *n* (*US: wallet*)
бума́жник; (*handbag*) (да́мская) су́мочка*;
(*notebook*) записна́я кни́жка*.
pocket calculator *n* карма́нный
калькуля́тор.
pocketknife ['pɒkɪtnaɪf] *n* перочи́нный нож*.
pocket money *n* карма́нные де́ньги* *pl.*
pocket-sized ['pɒkɪtsaɪzd] *adj* (*book*)
карма́нный; (*nation*) кро́хотный.
pockmarked ['pɒkmɑ:kt] *adj* рябо́й* (ряб).
pod [pɒd] *n* (*BOT*) стручо́к*.
podgy ['pɒdʒɪ] *adj* (*inf*) то́лстый* (толст).
podiatrist [pə'di:ətrɪst] *n* (*US*) ортопе́д.
podiatry [pə'di:ətrɪ] *n* (*US*) ортопеди́я.
podium ['pəudɪəm] *n* по́диум.
POE *n abbr* (= *port of embarkation*) порт
вы́садки; (= *port of entry*) порт захо́да.
poem ['pəuɪm] *n* (*short*) стихотворе́ние; (*long*)
поэ́ма.
poet ['pəuɪt] *n* (*male*) поэ́т; (*female*) поэте́сса.
poetic [pəu'etɪk] *adj* (*also fig*) поэти́ческий*.
poetic justice *n* воздая́ние.
poetic licence *n* поэти́ческая во́льность *f.*
poet laureate *n* придво́рный поэ́т.
poetry ['pəuɪtrɪ] *n* поэ́зия.
poignant ['pɔɪnjənt] *adj* жа́лостный*
(жа́лостен).
point [pɔɪnt] *n* (*of needle, knife etc*) острие́*,
ко́нчик; (*purpose*) цель *f*; (*significant part*)
смысл; (*subject, idea*) предме́т; (*detail,
aspect, quality*) аспе́кт; (*particular place or
position*) то́чка*, ме́сто*; (*moment*) моме́нт;
(*stage in development*) ста́дия; (*score: in
competition, game, sport*) очко́*; (*ELEC: also:
power ~*) розе́тка* ♦ *vt* (*show, mark*)
ука́зывать (указа́ть* *perf*); (*gun etc*): **to ~ sth
at sb** наце́ливать (наце́лить *perf*) что-н на
кого́-н ♦ *vi*: **to ~ at** ука́зывать (указа́ть* *perf*)
на +*acc*; **~s** *npl* (*AUT*) конта́кт *msg*
(зажига́ния), (*RAIL*) стре́лка* *fsg*; **good ~s** (*of
person, plan*) досто́инства; **2 ~ 3 (2.3)** 2 и 3
деся́тых; **to be on the ~ of doing** собира́ться
(*impf*) +*infin*; **I made a ~ of visiting him** я счёл
необходи́мым посети́ть его́; **to get/miss the
~** понима́ть (поня́ть* *perf*)/не понима́ть
(поня́ть* *perf*) суть; **to come to the ~**

доходи́ть* (дойти́* *perf*) до су́ти; **when it
comes to the ~** когда́ дохо́дит до де́ла; **that's
the whole ~!** в э́том-то и де́ло!; **that's beside
the ~** не в э́том де́ло; **there's no ~ in doing**
нет смы́сла +*infin*; **you've got a ~ there!** в
э́том Вы пра́вы!; **in ~ of fact** на де́ле; **~ of
departure** (*also fig*) отправно́й пункт; **~ of
sale** (*COMM*) торго́вая то́чка*
▶ **point out** *vt* ука́зывать (указа́ть* *perf*) на
+*acc*
▶ **point to** *vt fus* (*also fig*) ука́зывать (указа́ть*
perf) на +*acc*.
point-blank ['pɔɪnt'blæŋk] *adv* (*refuse*)
наотре́з; (*say, ask*) напрями́к ♦ *adj*: **at ~ range**
в упо́р.
point duty *n* (*BRIT*): **to be on ~ ~** находи́ться*
(*impf*) на посту́ реглиро́вщика.
pointed ['pɔɪntɪd] *adj* о́стрый* (остёр); (*fig:
remark*) язви́тельный.
pointedly ['pɔɪntɪdlɪ] *adv* язви́тельно.
pointer ['pɔɪntə'] *n* (*on chart, machine*)
стре́лка*; (*stick*) ука́зка*; (*fig*) намёк; (*dog*)
по́йнтер.
pointing ['pɔɪntɪŋ] *n* (*CONSTR*) заме́на
раство́ра в швах.
pointless ['pɔɪntlɪs] *adj* бессмы́сленный*
(бессмы́слен).
point of order *n* вопро́с по поря́дку веде́ния.
point-of-sale advertising ['pɔɪntəv'seɪl-] *n*
рекла́ма в места́х соверше́ния поку́пок.
point of view *n* то́чка* зре́ния.
poise [pɔɪz] *n* (*composure, balance*)
равнове́сие; (*of head, body*) оса́нка* ♦ *vt*: **to
be ~d for** (*fig*) наце́ливаться (наце́литься
perf) на +*acc*.
poison ['pɔɪzn] *n* яд, отра́ва ♦ *vt* отравля́ть
(отрави́ть* *perf*).
poisoning ['pɔɪznɪŋ] *n* отравле́ние.
poisonous ['pɔɪznəs] *adj* ядови́тый (ядови́т);
(*fig*) гну́сный* (гну́сен).
poison-pen letter [pɔɪzn'pɛn] *n* анони́мка*.
poke [pəuk] *vt* (*with finger, stick etc*) ты́кать*
(ткнуть *perf*); (*fire*) вороши́ть (*impf*), меша́ть
(*impf*) ♦ *n* (*jab*) толчо́к*; (*to fire*) поме́ши-
вание; **to ~ sth in(to)** (*put*) втыка́ть
(воткну́ть *perf*) что-н в +*acc*; **to ~ one's head
out of the window** высо́вываться
(вы́сунуться *perf*) из окна́; **to ~ fun at sb**
подка́лывать (подколо́ть* *perf*) кого́-н
▶ **poke about** *vi* ша́рить (поша́рить *perf*)
▶ **poke out** *vi* высо́вывать (вы́сунуть *perf*).
poker ['pəukə'] *n* кочерга́*; (*CARDS*) по́кер.
poker-faced ['pəukə'feɪst] *adj* невозмути́мый
(невозмути́м).
poky ['pəukɪ] *adj* (*room, house*) убо́гий* (убо́г).
Poland ['pəulənd] *n* По́льша.
polar ['pəulə'] *adj* поля́рный.
polar bear *n* бе́лый медве́дь* *m.*
polarize ['pəuləraɪz] *vt* раска́лывать
(расколо́ть *perf*), поляризи́ровать (*impf/perf*).
Pole [pəul] *n* поля́к(-лька*).

pole [pəul] *n* (*stick, staff*) шест*; (*for flag*)
дре́вко; (*telegraph pole*) столб; (*GEO, ELEC*)
по́люс.

poleaxe ['pəulæks] *n* (*butcher's*) топо́р;
(*HISTORY*) секи́ра ♦ *vt* (*hit*) тре́снуть (*perf*);
(*surprise*) ошеломля́ть (ошеломи́ть* *perf*).

pole bean *n* (*US*) стручко́вая фасо́ль *f*.

polecat ['pəulkæt] *n* (чёрный) хорёк*.

Pol. Econ. ['pɔlɪkən] *n abbr* (= *political economy*)
политэконо́мия= *полити́ческая эконо́мия*.

polemic [pɔ'lɛmɪk] *n* поле́мика.

Pole Star *n* поля́рная звезда́*.

pole vault ['pəulvɔ:lt] *n* прыжо́к* с шесто́м.

police [pə'li:s] *npl* поли́ция *fsg*; (*in Russia*)
мили́ция *fsg* ♦ *vt* следи́ть* (*impf*) за поря́дком;
a large number of ~ **were hurt** бы́ло ра́нено
мно́го полице́йских.

police car *n* полице́йская маши́на.

police constable *n* (*BRIT*) полице́йский* *m adj*.

police department *n* (*US*) полице́йский*
уча́сток*.

police force *n* поли́ция.

policeman [pə'li:smən] *irreg n* полице́йский* *m
adj*.

police officer *n* = **police constable**.

police record *n*: **to have a** ~ ~ состоя́ть (*impf*)
на учёте в поли́ции.

police state *n* (*POL*) полице́йское
госуда́рство.

police station *n* полице́йский* уча́сток*; (*in
Russia*) отделе́ние мили́ции.

policewoman [pə'li:swumən] *irreg n* (же́нщина-)
полице́йский* *m adj*.

policy ['pɔlɪsɪ] *n* поли́тика; (*also:* **insurance** ~)
по́лис; **to take out a** ~ (*INSURANCE*)
застрахо́вываться (застрахова́ться *perf*).

policyholder ['pɔlɪsɪ'həuldə'] *n* (*INSURANCE*)
держа́тель *m* страхово́го по́лиса.

policymaking ['pɔlɪsɪmeɪkɪŋ] *n* разрабо́тка
страте́гии.

polio ['pəulɪəu] *n* полиомиели́т.

Polish ['pəulɪʃ] *adj* по́льский* ♦ *n* (*LING*)
по́льский* язы́к*.

polish ['pɔlɪʃ] *n* (*for shoes*) гутали́н; (*for
furniture etc*) лак*; (*for floors*) масти́ка; (*shine,
also fig*) лоск ♦ *vt* (*shoes*) вычища́ть
(вы́чистить* *perf*); (*floors*) натира́ть
(натере́ть *perf*); (*furniture etc*) полирова́ть
(отполирова́ть *perf*); (*fig: improve*)
шлифова́ть (отшлифова́ть *perf*)

▶ **polish off** *vt fus* (*work, food*) поко́нчить (*perf*).

polished ['pɔlɪʃt] *adj* (*person*) изы́сканный*
(изы́скан); (*style*) отто́ченный (отто́чен).

polite [pə'laɪt] *adj* (*well-mannered*) ве́жливый
(ве́жлив); (*socially superior: company,
society*) све́тский*; **it's not** ~ **to do that** так
де́лать не при́нято.

politely [pə'laɪtlɪ] *adv* ве́жливо.

politeness [pə'laɪtnɪs] *n* ве́жливость *f*.

politic ['pɔlɪtɪk] *adj*: **it would be** ~ **to** ... бы́ло бы
благоразу́мно +*infin* ....

political [pə'lɪtɪkl] *adj* полити́ческий*; (*person*)
полити́чески акти́вный, политиз-
и́рованный (политизи́рован).

political asylum *n* полити́ческое убе́жище.

politically [pə'lɪtɪklɪ] *adv* полити́чески; ~
correct полити́чески пра́вильный.

politician [pɔlɪ'tɪʃən] *n* поли́тик,
полити́ческий* де́ятель *m*.

politics ['pɔlɪtɪks] *n* поли́тика; (*subject*)
политоло́гия ♦ *npl* (*beliefs, opinions*)
полити́ческие убежде́ния *ntpl*.

polka ['pɔlkə] *n* по́лька*.

poll [pəul] *n* (*also:* **opinion** ~) опро́с; (*election*)
вы́боры *mpl* ♦ *vt* (*in opinion poll*) опра́шивать
(опроси́ть* *perf*); (*number of votes*) набира́ть
(набра́ть* *perf*); **to go to the** ~**s** (*voters*)
голосова́ть (проголосова́ть *perf*) (*на
вы́борах*); (*government*) объявля́ть
(объяви́ть* *perf*) вы́боры.

pollen ['pɔlən] *n* пыльца́.

pollen count *n* содержа́ние пыльцы́ в
во́здухе.

pollinate ['pɔlɪneɪt] *vt* (*BOT*) опыля́ть (опыли́ть
perf).

polling booth ['pəulɪŋ-] *n* (*BRIT*) каби́на для
голосова́ния.

polling day *n* (*BRIT*) день* *m* вы́боров.

polling station *n* (*BRIT*) избира́тельный
уча́сток*.

pollster ['pəulstə'] *n* челове́к, производя́щий*
опро́с обще́ственного мне́ния.

poll tax *n* (*BRIT: formerly*) поду́шный нало́г.

pollutant [pə'lu:tənt] *n* загрязня́ющий аге́нт.

pollute [pə'lu:t] *vt* загрязня́ть (загрязни́ть
perf).

pollution [pə'lu:ʃən] *n* загрязне́ние;
(*substances*) загрязни́тель *m*.

polo ['pəuləu] *n* по́ло *nt ind*.

polo neck *n* (*also:* ~ ~ **sweater** *or* **jumper**)
сви́тер с кру́глым воротнико́м.

polo-necked ['pəuləunɛkt] *adj*: ~ **sweater** *or*
jumper сви́тер с кру́глым воротнико́м.

poltergeist ['pɔ:ltəgaɪst] *n* полтерге́йст.

poly ['pɔlɪ] *n abbr* (*BRIT*) = **polytechnic**.

poly... ['pɔlɪ] *prefix* много..., поли....

poly bag *n* полиэтиле́новый мешо́к* *or* паке́т.

polyester [pɔlɪ'ɛstə'] *n* (*CHEM*) сло́жный
полиэфи́р; (*fabric*) полиэфи́рное волокно́.

polygamy [pə'lɪgəmɪ] *n* многобра́чие,
полига́мия.

polygraph ['pɔlɪgrɑ:f] *n* дете́ктор лжи.

Polynesia [pɔlɪ'ni:zɪə] *n* Полине́зия.

Polynesian [pɔlɪ'ni:zɪən] *adj* полинези́йский ♦
n полинези́ец*(-и́йка*).

polyp ['pɔlɪp] *n* (*MED*) поли́п.

---

polystyrene [pɔlɪˈstaɪriːn] *n* пенопла́ст.
polytechnic [pɔlɪˈtɛknɪk] *n* (*college*) ≈ политехни́ческий* институ́т.
polythene [ˈpɔlɪθiːn] *n* полиэтиле́н.
polythene bag *n* полиэтиле́новый мешо́к* *or* паке́т.
polyurethane [pɔlɪˈjuərɪθeɪn] *n* полиурета́н.
pomegranate [ˈpɔmɪɡrænɪt] *n* (*BOT*) грана́т.
pommel [ˈpɔml] *n* (*of saddle*) лука́; (*of sword*) голо́вка* ♦ *vt* = **pummel**.
pomp [pɔmp] *n* пы́шность *f*.
pompom [ˈpɔmpɔm] *n* помпо́н.
pompous [ˈpɔmpəs] *adj* (*pej: person, style*) напы́щенный* (напы́щен).
pond [pɔnd] *n* пруд*; (*stagnant*) за́водь *f*.
ponder [ˈpɔndə*] *vt* обду́мывать (обду́мать *perf*) ♦ *vi* размышля́ть (*impf*).
ponderous [ˈpɔndərəs] *adj* (*style*) тяжело-ве́сный* (тяжелове́сен); (*person*) неповоро́тливый (неповоро́тлив).
pong [pɔŋ] (*BRIT: inf*) *n* вонь *f* ♦ *vi* воня́ть (*impf*).
pontiff [ˈpɔntɪf] *n* (*REL*) Па́па *m* ри́мский*.
pontificate [pɔnˈtɪfɪkeɪt] *vi* (*fig*): **to ~ (about)** разглаго́льствовать (*impf*) (о +*prp*).
pontoon [pɔnˈtuːn] *n* (*floating platform*) понто́н; (*CARDS*) два́дцать одно́.
pony [ˈpəunɪ] *n* по́ни *m ind*.
ponytail [ˈpəunɪteɪl] *n* (*hairstyle*) хвост*, хво́стик; **to have one's hair in a ~** носи́ть* (*impf*) хво́стик.
pony trekking *n* (*BRIT*) ко́нный похо́д.
poodle [ˈpuːdl] *n* пу́дель* *m*.
pooh-pooh [puːˈpuː] *vt* заши́кивать (заши́кать *perf*).
pool [puːl] *n* (*puddle*) лу́жа; (*pond*) пруд*; (*also:* **swimming ~**) бассе́йн; (*fig: of light, paint*) пятно́; (*SPORT, COMM*) пул; (*money at cards*) банк ♦ *vt* (*money, knowledge, resources*) объединя́ть (объедини́ть *perf*); **~s** *npl* (*also:* **football ~s**) тотализа́тор; **typing ~**, (*US*) **secretary ~** машинопи́сное бюро́ *nt ind*; **to do the (football) ~s** игра́ть (сыгра́ть *perf*) в тотализа́тор.
poor [puə*] *adj* (*not rich*) бе́дный* (бе́ден); (*bad*) плохо́й* (плох); **the ~** *npl* (*people*) беднота́ *fsg*; **~ in** (*resources etc*) бе́дный* (бе́ден) +*instr*.
poorly [ˈpuəlɪ] *adv* пло́хо ♦ *adj*: **she is feeling ~** она́ пло́хо себя́ чу́вствует.
pop [pɔp] *n* (*also:* **~ music**) поп-му́зыка; (*inf: fizzy drink*) лимона́д*; (: *US: father*) па́па, оте́ц; (*sound*) хлопо́к* ♦ *vi* (*balloon*) ло́паться (ло́пнуть *perf*); (*cork*) выстре́ливать (вы́стрелить *perf*); (*fig: eyes*) тара́щиться (вы́таращиться *perf*) ♦ *vt* (*put quickly*): **to ~ sth into/onto** *etc* забра́сывать (забро́сить* *perf*) в +*acc*/на +*acc etc*; **she ~ped her head out of the window** она́ вы́сунула го́лову из окна́
▶ **pop in** *vi* загля́дывать (загляну́ть* *perf*), заска́кивать (заскочи́ть *perf*)
▶ **pop out** *vi* выска́кивать (вы́скочить *perf*)
▶ **pop up** *vi* вылеза́ть (вы́лезти *perf*).

popcorn [ˈpɔpkɔːn] *n* возду́шная кукуру́за, попко́рн.
pope [pəup] *n*: **the P~** Па́па *m* ри́мский*.
poplar [ˈpɔplə*] *n* то́поль* *m*.
poplin [ˈpɔplɪn] *n* попли́н.
popper [ˈpɔpə*] *n* (*BRIT: fastener*) кно́пка*.
poppy [ˈpɔpɪ] *n* мак.
poppycock [ˈpɔpɪkɔk] *n* (*inf*) вздор.
Popsicle® [ˈpɔpsɪkl] *n* (*US*) ≈ фрукто́вое моро́женое *nt adj*.
pop star *n* поп-звезда́* *m/f*.
populace [ˈpɔpjuləs] *n*: **the ~** наро́д*.
popular [ˈpɔpjulə*] *adj* популя́рный* (популя́рен); (*POL*) наро́дный; **to be ~ (with)** (*person, belief*) по́льзоваться (*impf*) популя́рностью (среди́ +*gen*); (*decision*) по́льзоваться (*impf*) подде́ржкой (+*gen*); **a ~ song** популя́рная пе́сня*.
popularity [pɔpjuˈlærɪtɪ] *n* популя́рность *f*.
popularize [ˈpɔpjuləraɪz] *vt* (*pastime, fashion*) де́лать (сде́лать *perf*) популя́рным; (*science, ideas*) популяризи́ровать (*impf/perf*).
popularly [ˈpɔpjuləlɪ] *adv* (*generally*) обы́чно; **it is ~ believed that ...** мно́гие полага́ют, что ....
population [pɔpjuˈleɪʃən] *n* населе́ние; (*of a species*) популя́ция; **the civilian ~s** гражда́нское населе́ние; **Britain has a prison ~ of 44 thousand** о́бщее коли́чество заключённых в тю́рмах Великобрита́нии составля́ет 44 ты́сячи.
population explosion *n* демографи́ческий* взрыв.
populous [ˈpɔpjuləs] *adj* густонаселённый.
porcelain [ˈpɔːslɪn] *n* фарфо́р.
porch [pɔːtʃ] *n* крыльцо́*; (*US*) вера́нда.
porcupine [ˈpɔːkjupaɪn] *n* дикобра́з.
pore [pɔː*] *n* по́ра ♦ *vi*: **to ~ over** погружа́ться (погрузи́ться* *perf*) в +*acc*.
pork [pɔːk] *n* свини́на.
pork chop *n* свина́я отбивна́я *f adj*.
porn [pɔːn] *n* (*inf*) порногра́фия.
pornographic [pɔːnəˈɡræfɪk] *adj* порно-графи́ческий*.
pornography [pɔːˈnɔɡrəfɪ] *n* порногра́фия.
porous [ˈpɔːrəs] *adj* по́ристый (по́рист).
porpoise [ˈpɔːpəs] *n* бу́рый дельфи́н.
porridge [ˈpɔrɪdʒ] *n* овся́ная ка́ша.
port [pɔːt] *n* (*harbour, also COMPUT*) порт*; (*opening in ship*) люк; (*NAUT*) ле́вый борт*; (*wine*) портве́йн ♦ *cpd* (*NAUT*) ле́вый; **to ~** (*NAUT*) нале́во; **~ of call** порт* захо́да.
portable [ˈpɔːtəbl] *adj* портати́вный.
portal [ˈpɔːtl] *n* порта́л.
portcullis [pɔːtˈkʌlɪs] *n* (опускна́я) решётка* (*в воро́тах*).
portend [pɔːˈtɛnd] *vt* предвеща́ть (*impf*).
portent [ˈpɔːtɛnt] *n* предзнаменова́ние, предве́стник.
porter [ˈpɔːtə*] *n* (*for luggage*) носи́льщик; (*doorkeeper*) швейца́р, портье́ *m ind*; (: *in offices*) вахтёр; (*US: RAIL*) проводни́к*(-и́ца).

portfolio [pɔː'fəulɪəu] *n* (*also POL*) портфе́ль *m*; (*FINANCE*) портфе́ль це́нных бума́г; (*of artist*) па́пка*.

porthole ['pɔːthəul] *n* иллюмина́тор.

portico ['pɔːtɪkəu] *n* по́ртик.

portion ['pɔːʃən] *n* (*part*) часть* *f*; (*equal part*) до́ля*; (*helping of food*) по́рция.

portly ['pɔːtlɪ] *adj* доро́дный* (доро́ден).

portrait ['pɔːtreɪt] *n* портре́т.

portray [pɔː'treɪ] *vt* изобража́ть (изобрази́ть* *perf*).

portrayal [pɔː'treɪəl] *n* изображе́ние; (*representation*) о́браз.

Portsmouth ['pɔːtsməθ] *n* По́ртсмут.

Portugal ['pɔːtjugl] *n* Португа́лия.

Portuguese [pɔːtju'giːz] *adj* португа́льский* ◆ *n inv* португа́лец*(-лка*); (*LING*) португа́льский* язы́к*.

Portuguese man-of-war [-mænəv'wɔː^r] *n* (*ZOOL*) португа́льский* вое́нный кора́бль *m*.

pose [pəuz] *n* по́за ◆ *vt* (*question*) ста́вить* (поста́вить* *perf*); (*problem, danger*) создава́ть* (созда́ть* *perf*) ◆ *vi* (*pretend*): **to ~ as** выдава́ть* (вы́дать* *perf*) себя́ за +*acc*; **to strike a ~** принима́ть (приня́ть* *perf*) по́зу; **to ~ for** пози́ровать (*impf*) для +*gen*.

poser ['pəuzə^r] *n* (*puzzle*) головоло́мка*; (*person*) = **poseur**.

poseur [pəu'zə:^r] *n* (*pej*) позёр(ка*).

posh [pɔʃ] *adj* (*inf: hotel, restaurant etc*) фешене́бельный* (фешене́белен); (: *person, behaviour*) великосве́тский; **to talk ~** (*inf*) мане́рничать (*impf*).

position [pə'zɪʃən] *n* положе́ние; (*of house, thing*) расположе́ние, ме́сто*; (*job*) до́лжность *f*; (*in race, competition*) ме́сто*; (*attitude*) пози́ция ◆ *vt* располага́ть (расположи́ть* *perf*); **to be in a ~ to do** име́ть (*impf*) возмо́жность +*infin*.

positive ['pɔzɪtɪv] *adj* (*affirmative*) положи́тельный* (положи́телен); (*certain*) уве́ренный* (уве́рен), убеждённый* (убеждён); (*definite: decision, action, policy*) несомне́нный* (несомне́нен), определённый* (определён); (*MATH, ELEC*) положи́тельный.

positive cash flow *n* положи́тельный поток нали́чности.

positively ['pɔzɪtɪvlɪ] *adv* (*for emphasis*) положи́тельно; (*definitely*) несомне́нно.

posse ['pɔsɪ] *n* (*US*) ко́нный отря́д доброво́льных помо́щников шери́фа при ло́вле престу́пника.

possess [pə'zɛs] *vt* владе́ть (*impf*) +*instr*; (*quality, ability*) облада́ть (*impf*) +*instr*; (*subj: feeling, belief*) овладева́ть (овладе́ть *perf*); **like one ~ed** как одержи́мый(-ая) *m(f) adj*; **whatever can have ~ed you?** и како́й чёрт

тебя́ попу́тал?

possession [pə'zɛʃən] *n* (*state*) владе́ние; **~s** *npl* (*belongings*) принадле́жности *fpl*; **to take ~ of** вступа́ть (вступи́ть* *perf*) во владе́ние +*instr*.

possessive [pə'zɛsɪv] *adj* со́бственнический*; (*LING*) притяжа́тельный.

possessiveness [pə'zɛsɪvnɪs] *n* (*of another person*) со́бственничество; **~ towards sb/sth** ревни́вое отноше́ние к кому́-н/чему́-н.

possessor [pə'zɛsə^r] *n* (*of property*) владе́лец*(-е́лица); (*of quality*) облада́тель(ница) *m(f)*.

possibility [pɔsɪ'bɪlɪtɪ] *n* возмо́жность *f*; **he's a ~ (for the part)** он возмо́жный кандида́т (на роль).

possible ['pɔsɪbl] *adj* возмо́жный* (возмо́жен); **it's ~** э́то не исключено́; **it is ~ to do it** э́то осуществи́мо; **as far as ~** наско́лько возмо́жно; **if ~** е́сли (э́то) возмо́жно; **as big as ~** са́мый большо́й.

possibly ['pɔsɪblɪ] *adv* (*perhaps*) возмо́жно; **if you ~ can** е́сли то́лько Вы мо́жете; **I cannot ~ come** я ника́к не смогу́ прийти́.

post [pəust] *n* (*BRIT: mail*) по́чта; (*pole*) столб*; (*job, situation, also MIL*) пост* ◆ *vt* (*BRIT: mail*) посыла́ть (посла́ть* *perf*), отправля́ть (отпра́вить* *perf*) (по по́чте); (: *MIL*) выставля́ть (вы́ставить* *perf*); (: *appoint*) откомандиро́вывать (откомандирова́ть *perf*); **by ~** (*BRIT*) по по́чте; **by return of ~** (*BRIT*) с обра́тной по́чтой; **trading ~** фракто́рия; **to keep sb ~ed** держа́ть* (*impf*) кого́-н в ку́рсе (дел).

post... [pəust] *prefix* пост..., по́сле...; **~-1990** (*as adj*) в 90-е го́ды; (*as adv*) как 90-е го́ды.

postage ['pəustɪdʒ] *n* (*charge*) почто́вые расхо́ды *mpl*; **~ paid,** (*US*) **~ prepaid** с предвари́тельно опла́ченными почто́выми расхо́дами.

postage stamp *n* почто́вая ма́рка*.

postal ['pəustl] *adj* почто́вый.

postal order *n* (де́нежный) почто́вый перево́д.

postbag ['pəustbæg] *n* (*BRIT: letters received*) по́чта, корреспонде́нция; (: *postman's*) су́мка* (*почтальо́на*).

postbox ['pəustbɔks] *n* (*BRIT*) почто́вый я́щик.

postcard ['pəustkɑːd] *n* (почто́вая) откры́тка*.

postcode ['pəustkəud] *n* (*BRIT*) почто́вый и́ндекс.

postdate ['pəust'deɪt] *vt* дати́ровать (*impf/perf*) бо́лее по́здним число́м.

poster ['pəustə^r] *n* афи́ша, плака́т; (*for advertising*) по́стер.

poste restante [pəust'rɛstɑ̃:nt] *adv* (*BRIT*) до востре́бования.

posterior [pɔs'tɪərɪə^r] *n* зад.

---

* marks translations which have irregular inflections. The Russian-English side of the dictionary gives inflectional information.

posterity [pɔs'tɛrɪtɪ] *n* после́дующие поколе́ния *ntpl*, пото́мство.
poster paint *n* плака́тная тушь *f*.
post exchange *n* (*US*: *MIL*) военто́рг, гарнизо́нный магази́н.
post-free [pəust'friː] *adj*, *adv* (*BRIT*) с предвари́тельно опла́ченными почто́выми расхо́дами.
postgraduate ['pəust'grædjuət] *n* аспира́нт(ка*) ♦ *adj*: ~ **study** аспиранту́ра.
posthumous ['pɔstjuməs] *adj* посме́ртный.
posthumously ['pɔstjuməslɪ] *adv* посме́ртно.
posting ['pəustɪŋ] *n* (*job*) командиро́вка.
postman ['pəustmən] *irreg n* почтальо́н.
postmark ['pəustmɑːk] *n* почто́вый штёмпель* *m*.
postmaster ['pəustmɑːstə'] *n* нача́льник по́чты *or* почто́вого отделе́ния.
postmaster general *n* ≈ мини́стр свя́зи.
postmistress ['pəustmɪstrɪs] *n* нача́льник по́чты *or* почто́вого отделе́ния (*жёнжина*).
postmortem [pəust'mɔːtəm] *n* (*MED*) вскры́тие, аутопси́я.
postnatal ['pəust'neɪtl] *adj* послеродово́й.
post office *n* почто́вое отделе́ние, отделе́ние свя́зи; (*organization*): **the P~ O~** ≈ Министе́рство свя́зи.
Post Office Box *n* абоне́нтский я́щик.
post-paid ['pəust'peɪd] *adj* (*BRIT*) с опла́ченными почто́выми расхо́дами.
postpone [pəus'pəun] *vt* откла́дывать (отложи́ть* *perf*).
postponement [pəus'pəunmənt] *n* отсро́чка.
postscript ['pəustskrɪpt] *n* (*in letter*) постскри́птум.
postulate ['pɔstjuleɪt] *vt* постули́ровать (*impf/perf*).
posture ['pɔstʃə'] *n* (*of body*) оса́нка; (*fig*) положе́ние ♦ *vi* (*pej*) пози́ровать (*impf*).
postwar ['pəust'wɔː'] *adj* послевое́нный.
posy ['pəuzɪ] *n* буке́тик.
pot [pɔt] *n* (*for cooking, flowers*) горшо́к*; (*also*: **teapot**) (зава́рочный) ча́йник; (*also*: **coffeepot**) кофе́йник; (*bowl, container*) ба́нка; (*inf*: *marijuana*) план ♦ *vt* (*plant*) сажа́ть (посади́ть* *perf*); **a ~ of tea** ча́йник ча́я; **to go to ~** (*inf*: *work, performance*) разва́ливаться (развали́ться* *perf*); **~s of** (*BRIT*: *inf*) ку́ча +*gen*, у́йма +*gen*.
potash ['pɔtæʃ] *n* пота́ш.
potassium [pə'tæsɪəm] *n* ка́лий.
potato [pə'teɪtəu] (*pl* **~es**) *n* карто́фель *m no pl*, карто́шка *f no pl* (*разг*); (*single potato*) карто́фелина.
potato chips *npl* (*US*) = **potato crisps**.
potato crisps *npl* (*BRIT*) чи́псы *pl*.
potato flour *n* карто́фельная мука́.
potato peeler *n* картофелечи́стка.
potbellied ['pɔtbɛlɪd] *adj* (*from overeating*) пуза́тый (пуза́т); (*from malnutrition*) со взду́тым живото́м.

potency ['pəutnsɪ] *n* си́ла; (*of drink*) кре́пость *f*.
potent ['pəutnt] *adj* (*weapon*) мо́щный; (*argument*) убеди́тельный* (убеди́телен); (*drink*) кре́пкий* (кре́пок); (*man*) облада́ющий сексуа́льной поте́нцией.
potentate ['pəutnteɪt] *n* властели́н, повели́тель *m*.
potential [pə'tɛnʃl] *adj* потенциа́льный, возмо́жный ♦ *n* потенциа́л; **to have ~** облада́ть (*impf*) (доста́точным) потенциа́лом.
potentially [pə'tɛnʃəlɪ] *adv* потенциа́льно; **it's ~ dangerous** э́то в при́нципе опа́сно.
pothole ['pɔthəul] *n* (*in road*) вы́боина; (*BRIT*: *underground*) прова́л.
potholing ['pɔthəulɪŋ] *n* (*BRIT*) *n* спелеоло́гия; **to go ~** отправля́ться (отпра́виться *perf*) обсле́довать пеще́ры.
potion ['pəuʃən] *n* насто́йка; (*poison*) зе́лье.
potluck [pɔt'lʌk] *n*: **to take ~** обе́дать (пообе́дать *perf*) чем Бог посла́л.
potpourri [pəu'purɪ] *n* арома́тическая смесь из сухи́х лепестко́в; (*fig*) попурри́ *nt ind*.
pot roast *n* тушёное мя́со.
pot shot *n*: **to take ~ ~s at** стреля́ть (вы́стрелить *perf*) навски́дку в +*acc*.
potted ['pɔtɪd] *adj* (*food*) консерви́рованный; (*plant*) ко́мнатный; (*account, biography*) кра́ткий*.
potter ['pɔtə'] *n* (*pottery maker*) гонча́р* ♦ *vi*: **to ~ around**, **~ about** (*BRIT*) вози́ться* (*impf*); **to ~ about (in) the garden** вози́ться* (*impf*) в саду́.
potter's wheel *n* гонча́рный круг*.
pottery ['pɔtərɪ] *n* кера́мика; (*factory*) заво́д керами́ческих изде́лий; (*workshop*) гонча́рная мастерска́я *f adj*; **a piece of ~** керами́ческое изде́лие.
potty ['pɔtɪ] *adj* (*inf*: *mad*) чо́кнутый ♦ *n* (*for child*) горшо́к* (*ночно́й*).
potty-training ['pɔtɪtreɪnɪŋ] *n* приуче́ние ребёнка к горшку́.
pouch [pautʃ] *n* (*for tobacco*) кисе́т; (*for coins*) кошелёк*; (*ZOOL*) су́мка*.
pouf(fe) [puːf] *n* пуф.
poultice ['pəultɪs] *n* припа́рка*.
poultry ['pəultrɪ] *n* (*birds*) дома́шняя пти́ца; (*meat*) пти́ца.
poultry farm *n* птицефе́рма.
poultry farmer *n* птицево́д.
pounce [pauns] *vi*: **to ~ on** набра́сываться (набро́ситься* *perf*) на +*acc*.
pound [paund] *n* (*money, weight*) фунт; (*for dogs*) живодёрня; (*for cars*) стоя́нка для непра́вильно припарко́ванных автомаши́н, увезённых поли́цией ♦ *vt* (*beat*) колоти́ть* (*impf*) по +*dat*; (*crush*) толо́чь* (растоло́чь* *perf*); (*with guns*) обстре́ливать (обстреля́ть* *perf*) ♦ *vi* (*heart*) колоти́ться* (*impf*); **half a ~ of** полфу́нта +*gen*; **a five-~ note** банкно́та в пять фу́нтов; **my car has been taken to the ~** мою́ маши́ну арестова́ли.

pounding ['paundıŋ] *n*: **we took a** ~ (*SPORT*) нас побили; (*fig*) нас разнесли.
pound sterling *n* фунт стерлингов.
pour [pɔ:'] *vt* (*liquid*) наливать (налить* *perf*); (*dry substance*) насыпать (насыпать* *perf*) ◆ *vi* (*water, blood, sweat etc*) литься* (*impf*); (*rain*) лить* (*impf*); **to** ~ **sb some tea** наливать (налить* *perf*) кому-н чай; **it's** ~**ing with rain** льёт дождь
▶ **pour away** *vt* выливать (вылить* *perf*)
▶ **pour in** *vi* (*people*) валить* (повалить* *perf*); (*news, letters etc*) сыпаться* (*impf*)
▶ **pour into** *vt fus* устремляться (устремиться* *perf*) в +*acc*
▶ **pour off** *vt* сливать (слить* *perf*)
▶ **pour out** *vi* (*people*) валить* (повалить* *perf*) ◆ *vt* (*drink*) наливать (налить* *perf*); (*fig: thoughts, feelings, etc*) изливать (излить* *perf*).
pouring ['pɔ:rıŋ] *adj*: ~ **rain** проливной дождь *m*.
pout [paut] *vi* надувать (надуть* *perf*) губы, дуться (надуться* *perf*).
poverty ['pɔvətı] *n* бедность *f*, нищета.
poverty line *n* черта бедности.
poverty-stricken ['pɔvətıstrıkn] *adj* впавший в нищету, обнищавший.
poverty trap *n* (*BRIT*) тиски *pl* бедности.
POW *n abbr* = **prisoner of war**.
powder ['paudə'] *n* порошок*; (*also: face* ~) пудра ◆ *vt*: **to** ~ **one's face** пудрить (напудрить *perf*) лицо; **to** ~ **one's nose** (*euphemism*) помыть* (*perf*) руки.
powder compact *n* пудреница.
powdered milk ['paudəd-] *n* сухое молоко.
powder keg *n* пороховая бочка.
powder puff *n* пуховка.
powder room *n* дамская комната.
power ['pauə'] *n* (*authority*) власть *f*; (*ability, opportunity*) возможность *f*; (*legal right*) полномочие; (*strength: of person, speech, thought*) мощь *f*; (*of explosion, engine*) мощность *f*; (*electricity*) электроэнергия; (*MATH*) степень *f*; **to do all in one's** ~ **to help** делать (сделать *perf*) всё что в своих силах, чтобы помогать (помочь* *perf*); **the world** ~**s** мировые державы; **to be in** ~ находиться* (*impf*) у власти.
powerboat ['pauəbəut] *n* моторный катер*.
power cut *n* (*BRIT*) отключение электроэнергии.
powered ['pauəd] *adj*: ~ **by** работающий на +*prp*; **nuclear-**~ **submarine** атомная подводная лодка*.
power failure *n* остановка* подачи электроэнергии.
powerful ['pauəful] *adj* могучий* (могуч); (*person, organization*) могущественный*

(могущественен); (*engine, argument*) мощный; (*smell, voice, emotion*) сильный* (силен); (*evidence*) веский* (весок).
powerhouse ['pauəhaus] *n* (*person*): **a** ~ **of ideas** генератор идей.
powerless ['pauəlıs] *adj* бессильный* (бессилен).
power line *n* линия электропередачи.
power of attorney *n* (*LAW*) доверенность *f*.
power point *n* (*BRIT*) (штепсельная) розетка*.
power station *n* электростанция.
power steering *n* (*AUT*) рулевой привод с усилителем.
powwow ['pauwau] *n* совет.
pp *abbr* = **per procurationem**; (*by proxy*) по доверенности.
pp. *abbr* = **pages**.
PPE *n abbr* (*BRIT: SCOL*) = **philosophy, politics and economics**.
PPS *n abbr* (= **post postscriptum**) второй постскриптум; (*BRIT*) = **parliamentary private secretary**) личный парламентский секретарь министра.
PQ *abbr* (*CANADA*) = **Province of Quebec**.
PR *n abbr* = **public relations**; (*POL*) = **proportional representation** ◆ *abbr* (*US: POST*) = **Puerto Rico**.
Pr. *abbr* = **prince**.
practicability [præktıkə'bılıtı] *n* осуществимость *f*.
practicable ['præktıkəbl] *adj* осуществимый (осуществим).
practical ['præktıkl] *adj* (*not theoretical*) практический*; (*sensible, viable*) практичный* (практичен); (*good with hands*) умелый (умел).
practicality [præktı'kælıtı] *n* практичность *f*; **practicalities** *npl* (*of situation etc*) практическая сторона *fsg*.
practical joke *n* розыгрыш.
practically ['præktıklı] *adv* практически.
practice ['præktıs] *n* (*habit*) привычка*; (*of profession*) практика; (*REL*) обычай; (*exercise, training*) практика, тренировка ◆ *vti* (*US*) = **practise**; **in** ~ на практике; **I am out of** ~ я давно этого не делал; **it's common** ~ это распространено; **to put sth into** ~ осуществлять (осуществить* *perf*) что-н на практике; **target** ~ учебная стрельба.
practice match *n* тренировочный матч.
practise ['præktıs] (*US* **practice**) *vt* (*musical instrument*) упражняться (*impf*) на +*acc*; (*SPORT, piece of music, language*) отрабатывать (отработать *perf*); (*custom*) выполнять (выполнить *perf*); (*craft*) заниматься (*impf*) +*instr*; (*religion*) исповедовать (*impf*) ◆ *vi* (*on instrument*) упражняться (*impf*); (*SPORT*) тренироваться (*impf*); (*lawyer, doctor*) практиковать (*impf*); **to**

---

* marks translations which have irregular inflections. The Russian-English side of the dictionary gives inflectional information.

~ **for a match** тренирова́ться *(impf)* пе́ред ма́тчем; **to ~ law/medicine** занима́ться *(impf)* адвока́тской/враче́бной пра́ктикой.

practised ['præktɪst] *adj (BRIT: person)* о́пытный; (: *performance*) иску́сный; (: *liar*) закорене́лый; **with a ~ eye** *(BRIT)* намётанным гла́зом.

practising ['præktɪsɪŋ] *adj (Christian etc)* ве́рующий*; (*doctor, lawyer*) практику́ющий; (*homosexual*) веду́щий* акти́вную полову́ю жизнь.

practitioner [præk'tɪʃənə²] *n (MED)* терапе́вт.

pragmatic [præg'mætɪk] *adj (reason etc)* прагмати́ческий; (*person*) прагмати́чный* (прагмати́чен).

pragmatism ['prægmətɪzəm] *n* прагмати́зм.

Prague [prɑːg] *n* Пра́га.

prairie ['prɛərɪ] *n* пре́рия; (*US*): **the ~s** пре́рии *fpl.*

praise [preɪz] *n (approval)* похвала́; (*admiration*) восхвале́ние ♦ *vt (see n)* хвали́ть* (похвали́ть* *perf*); восхваля́ть *(impf).*

praiseworthy ['preɪzwəːðɪ] *adj* досто́йный* (досто́ен) похвалы́.

pram [præm] *n (BRIT)* де́тская коля́ска.

prance [prɑːns] *vi (horse)* гарцева́ть *(impf)*; (*person*): **to ~ about** красова́ться *(impf).*

prank [præŋk] *n (practical joke)* ро́зыгрыш; (*tomfoolery*) проде́лка*.

prat [præt] *n (inf: pej: BRIT)* идио́т.

prattle ['prætl] *vi:* **to ~ on (about)** трепа́ться *(impf)* (о +*prp*).

prawn [prɔːn] *n* креве́тка*.

pray [preɪ] *vi* моли́ться* (помоли́ться* *perf*); **to ~ for** моли́ться* *(impf)* за +*acc*; **to ~ that** моли́ться* *(impf)*, что́бы.

prayer [prɛə²] *n (activity)* моли́тва, моле́ние; (*words*) моли́тва.

prayer book *n* моли́твенник.

pre... ['priː...] *prefix* до..., пред...; **~-1970** до 1970-го го́да.

preach [priːtʃ] *vi (also fig)* пропове́довать *(impf)* ♦ *vt:* **to ~ a sermon** *(also fig)* произноси́ть* (произнести́* *perf*) про́поведь; **to ~ at sb** чита́ть *(impf)* про́поведь кому́-н.

preacher ['priːtʃə²] *n* пропове́дник(-ица).

preamble [prɪ'æmbl] *n* преа́мбула.

prearranged [priːə'reɪndʒd] *adj* (зара́нее) подгото́вленный (подгото́влен).

precarious [prɪ'kɛərɪəs] *adj* риско́ванный* (риско́ван).

precaution [prɪ'kɔːʃən] *n* предосторо́жность *f*; **to take ~s** принима́ть (приня́ть* *perf*) ме́ры предосторо́жности.

precautionary [prɪ'kɔːʃənrɪ] *adj (measure)* предупреди́тельный.

precede [prɪ'siːd] *vt* предше́ствовать *(impf)* +*dat*; (*person*) быть* *(impf)* впереди́ +*gen*.

precedence ['prɛsɪdəns] *n (priority)* первоочерёдность *f*; **to take ~ over** быть*

(impf) важне́е, чем.

precedent ['prɛsɪdənt] *n* прецеде́нт; **to establish** *or* **set a ~** создава́ть* (созда́ть* *perf*) прецеде́нт.

preceding [prɪ'siːdɪŋ] *adj* предыду́щий*, предше́ствующий*.

precept ['priːsɛpt] *n* пра́вило.

precinct ['priːsɪŋkt] *n (US: part of city)* райо́н, префекту́ра; (*round cathedral*) двор*; **~s** *npl (of large building)* террито́рия *fsg*; **pedestrian ~** *(BRIT)* пешехо́дная зо́на; **shopping ~** *(BRIT)* торго́вый центр.

precious ['prɛʃəs] *adj (commodity, object)* це́нный* (це́нен); (*stone*) драгоце́нный; (*pej: person, behaviour*) мане́рный ♦ *adv (inf):* **~ little** *or* **few** о́чень ма́ло; **your ~ dog** *(ironic)* Ва́ша драгоце́нная соба́ка.

precious stone *n (GEO)* драгоце́нный ка́мень* *m.*

precipice ['prɛsɪpɪs] *n* обры́в.

precipitate [*vb* prɪ'sɪpɪteɪt, *adj* prɪ'sɪpɪtɪt] *vt (hasten)* ускоря́ть (уско́рить *perf*) ♦ *adj* скоропали́тельный* (скоропали́телен).

precipitation [prɪsɪpɪ'teɪʃən] *n (rain)* оса́дки *mpl.*

precipitous [prɪ'sɪpɪtəs] *adj (steep)* круто́й* (крут), обры́вистый (обры́вист); (*hasty*) поспе́шный* (поспе́шен).

précis ['preɪsiː] *(pl* ~) *n* конспе́кт.

precise [prɪ'saɪs] *adj* то́чный* (то́чен).

precisely [prɪ'saɪslɪ] *adv (accurately)* то́чно; (*exactly*) ро́вно; **~!** вот и́менно!, соверше́нно ве́рно!

precision [prɪ'sɪʒən] *n* то́чность *f.*

preclude [prɪ'kluːd] *vt* предотвраща́ть (предотврати́ть* *perf*); **to ~ sb from doing** меша́ть (помеша́ть *perf*) кому́-н +*infin*.

precocious [prɪ'kəuʃəs] *adj (talent)* ра́но разви́вшийся; **a ~ child** не по года́м развито́й ребёнок.

preconceived [priːkən'siːvd] *adj* предвзя́тый (предвзя́т).

preconception ['priːkən'sɛpʃən] *n* предвзя́тое мне́ние.

precondition ['priːkən'dɪʃən] *n* непреме́нное усло́вие, предпосы́лка*.

precursor [priː'kəːsə²] *n (person, thing)* предте́ча *m/f.*

predate ['priː'deɪt] *vt* предше́ствовать *(impf)* +*dat.*

predator ['prɛdətə²] *n (also fig)* хи́щник.

predatory ['prɛdətərɪ] *adj (animal)* хи́щный; (*fig*) хи́щный* (хи́щен).

predecessor ['priːdɪsɛsə²] *n* предше́ственник (-ица).

predestination [priːdɛstɪ'neɪʃən] *n* предопределе́ние.

predetermine [priːdɪ'təːmɪn] *vt* предопределя́ть (предопредели́ть *perf*).

predicament [prɪ'dɪkəmənt] *n* затрудне́ние; **to be in a ~** быть* *(impf)* в затрудне́нии.

predicate ['prɛdɪkɪt] n (*LING*) сказýемое nt adj.
predict [prɪ'dɪkt] vt предскáзывать
(предсказáть* perf).
predictable [prɪ'dɪktəbl] adj предсказýемый
(предскáжем).
predictably [prɪ'dɪktəblɪ] adv как и ожидáлось;
~ **she didn't arrive** как и ожидáлось, онá не
пришлá.
prediction [prɪ'dɪkʃən] n предсказáние.
predispose ['pri:dɪs'pəuz] vt предрасполагáть
(предрасположить* perf).
predominance [prɪ'dɔmɪnəns] n преоблáдание; (*dominance*) госпóдство.
predominant [prɪ'dɔmɪnənt] adj
доминúрующий, преоблáдающий
(преоблáдаюш); **to become** ~ становúться*
(стать* perf) преоблáдающим(-ей).
predominantly [prɪ'dɔmɪnəntlɪ] adv
преимýщественно.
predominate [prɪ'dɔmɪneɪt] vi преобладáть
(*impf*).
pre-eminent [pri:'ɛmɪnənt] adj выдаю́щийся*.
pre-empt [pri:'ɛmt] vt предупреждáть
(предупредúть* perf); **to ~ the issue**
предупреждáть (предупредúть* perf)
собы́тия.
pre-emptive [pri:'ɛmtɪv] adj: ~ **strike**
упреждáющий удáр.
preen [pri:n] vt: **to ~ itself** (*bird*) чúстить*
(почúстить* perf) пёрышки; **to ~ o.s.**
прихорáшиваться (*impf*).
prefab ['pri:fæb] n сбóрный дом*.
prefabricated [pri:'fæbrɪkeɪtɪd] adj сбóрный.
preface ['prɛfəs] n (*in book*) предислóвие ◆ vt:
to ~ sth with предпосылáть (предпослáть*
perf) чемý-н +acc.
prefect ['pri:fɛkt] n (*BRIT: SCOL*) стáроста m/f.
prefer [prɪ'fə:ʳ] vt предпочитáть (предпочéсть*
perf); (*LAW*): **to ~ charges against** выдвигáть
(вы́двинуть perf) обвинéние прóтив +gen; **to
~ doing** or **to do** предпочитáть (предпочéсть*
perf) +infin; **I ~ coffee to tea** я предпочитáю
кóфе чáю.
preferable ['prɛfrəbl] adj предпочтúтельный*
(предпочтúтелен).
preferably ['prɛfrəblɪ] adv предпочтúтельно.
preference ['prɛfrəns] n (*liking*): **to have a ~ for**
предпочитáть (*impf*); (*priority*): **to give ~ to**
отдавáть* (отдáть* perf) предпочтéние +dat;
in ~ to sth вмéсто чегó-н.
preference shares npl (*BRIT: COMM*)
привилегирóванные áкции fpl.
preferential [prɛfə'rɛnʃəl] adj: ~ **treatment**
осóбое отношéние.
preferred stock [prɪ'fəd-] npl (*US*) = **preference
shares**.
prefix ['pri:fɪks] n пристáвка*, прéфикс.
pregnancy ['prɛgnənsɪ] n берéменность f.

pregnancy test n анáлиз на берéменность.
pregnant ['prɛgnənt] adj берéменная
(берéменна); (*remark, pause*)
многозначúтельный* (многозначúтелен);
she is 3 months ~ онá на четвёртом мéсяце
(берéменности).
prehistoric ['pri:hɪs'tɔrɪk] adj доисторúческий*.
prehistory [pri:'hɪstərɪ] n первобы́тная
истóрия.
prejudge [pri:'dʒʌdʒ] vt предрешáть
(предрешúть perf).
prejudice ['prɛdʒudɪs] n (*unreasonable dislike*)
предрассýдок*; (*bias in favour*) предвзя́тость
f, предубеждéние ◆ vt (*harm*) вредúть*
(повредúть* perf) +dat; **without ~ to** без
ущéрба для +gen; **to ~ sb in favour of**
располагáть (расположúть* perf) когó-н в
пóльзу +gen; **to ~ sb against** настрáивать
(настрóить perf) когó-н прóтив +gen.
prejudiced ['prɛdʒudɪst] adj (*biased against*)
предубеждённый (предубеждён); (*in favour*)
располóженный* (располóжен); (*view*)
предвзя́тый (предвзя́т).
prelate ['prɛlət] n (*REL*) прелáт.
preliminaries [prɪ'lɪmɪnərɪz] npl
предварúтельные мероприя́тия ntpl; (*in
competition*) предварúтельный отбóр msg.
preliminary [prɪ'lɪmɪnərɪ] adj
предварúтельный.
prelude ['prɛlju:d] n (*MUS, fig*) прелю́дия.
premarital ['pri:'mærɪtl] adj добрáчный.
premature ['prɛmətʃuəʳ] adj
преждеврéменный (преждеврéмен); (*baby*)
недонóшенный* (недонóшен); **you are being
a little ~** Вы нéсколько поторопúлись.
premeditated [pri:'mɛdɪteɪtɪd] adj
преднамéренный* (преднамéрен).
premeditation [pri:mɛdɪ'teɪʃən] n раздýмье.
premenstrual tension [pri:'mɛnstruəl-] n
предменструáльный синдрóм.
premier ['prɛmɪəʳ] adj (*best*) лýчший* ◆ n (*POL*)
премьéр-минúстр.
première ['prɛmɪɛəʳ] n премьéра.
premise ['prɛmɪs] n предпосы́лка*; ~**s** npl (*of
business*) помещéние ntsg; **on the ~s** в
помещéнии.
premium ['pri:mɪəm] n (*COMM, INSURANCE*)
прéмия; **to be at a ~** (*expensive*) стóить (*impf*)
вы́ше номинáла; (*hard to get*) пóльзоваться
(*impf*) бóльшим спрóсом; **to sell at a ~**
(*shares*) продавáть* (продáть* perf) по ценé
вы́ше номинáла.
premium bond n (*BRIT*) премиáльная
(сберегáтельная) облигáция.
premium deal n (*COMM*) премиáльная
сдéлка*.
premium gasoline n (*US*) высокооктáновый
бензúн.

---

premonition [prɛmə'nɪʃən] *n* предчу́вствие.
preoccupation [priːɔkjuˈpeɪʃən] *n*: ~ **with** озабо́ченность *f* +*instr.*
preoccupied [priːˈɔkjupaɪd] *adj* озабо́ченный* (озабо́чен).
prep [prɛp] *adj abbr*: ~ **school** = *preparatory school*; (*BRIT*) ча́стная нача́льная шко́ла; (*US*) сре́дняя шко́ла ◆ *n abbr* = *preparation*.
prep *n* (*homework*) дома́шнее зада́ние.
prepaid [priːˈpeɪd] *adj* зара́нее опла́ченный (опла́чен); (*envelope*) с зара́нее опла́ченными почто́выми расхо́дами.
preparation [prɛpəˈreɪʃən] *n* (*activity*) подгото́вка*; (*of food*) приготовле́ние; (*medicine, cosmetic*) препара́т; ~**s** *npl* (*arrangements*) приготовле́ния *ntpl*; **in** ~ **for sth** гото́вясь к чему́-н.
preparatory [prɪˈpærətərɪ] *adj* подготови́тельный; ~ **to doing** пре́жде чем +*infin.*
preparatory school *n* (*BRIT*) ча́стная нача́льная шко́ла; (*US*) сре́дняя шко́ла.
prepare [prɪˈpɛəʳ] *vt* (*plan, speech, room etc*) подгота́вливать (подгото́вить* *perf*); (*CULIN*) гото́вить* (*impf*), приготовля́ть (приготовля́ть* *perf*) ◆ *vi*: **to** ~ **for** (*event, action etc*) гото́виться* (*impf*) *or* подгота́вливаться (подгото́виться* *perf*) к +*dat.*
prepared [prɪˈpɛəd] *adj* гото́вый (гото́в); **I am** ~ **to help you** (*willing*) я гото́в помо́чь Вам; ~ **for** (*ready*) гото́вый (гото́в) к +*dat.*
preponderance [prɪˈpɔndərns] *n* (*of people, things*) преоблада́ние.
preposition [prɛpəˈzɪʃən] *n* (*LING*) предло́г.
prepossessing [priːpəˈzɛsɪŋ] *adj* привлека́тельный* (привлека́телен).
preposterous [prɪˈpɔstərəs] *adj* (*outrageous*) ди́кий*.
prep school *n* = **preparatory school.**
prerecorded [ˈpriːrɪˈkɔːdɪd] *adj* предвари́тельно запи́санный.
prerequisite [priːˈrɛkwɪzɪt] *n* предпосы́лка*, непреме́нное усло́вие.
prerogative [prɪˈrɔgətɪv] *n* прерогати́ва.
Presbyterian [prɛzbɪˈtɪərɪən] *n* (*REL*) пресвитериа́нин*(-а́нка*) ◆ *adj* пресвитериа́нский.
presbytery [ˈprɛzbɪtərɪ] *n* пресвите́рия.
preschool [ˈpriːˈskuːl] *adj* (*age, education*) дошко́льный; ~ **child** ребёнок дошко́льного во́зраста.
prescribe [prɪˈskraɪb] *vt* (*MED*) пропи́сывать (прописа́ть* *perf*); (*action, duty*) предпи́сывать (предписа́ть* *perf*); ~**d books** (*BRIT*: *SCOL*) рекомендо́ванные уче́бники.
prescription [prɪˈskrɪpʃən] *n* (*MED*: *slip of paper*) реце́пт; (: *medicine*) лека́рство (*назна́ченное врачо́м*); **to make up** *or* (*US*) **fill a** ~ приготовля́ть (приготовля́ть* *perf*) лека́рство по реце́пту; "**only available on** ~" „прода́жа лека́рства то́лько по реце́птам".

prescription charges *npl* (*BRIT*) минима́льная цена́ за лека́рства, отпуска́емые по реце́пту.
prescriptive [prɪˈskrɪptɪv] *adj* нормати́вный* (нормати́вен).
presence [ˈprɛzns] *n* прису́тствие; (*fig*) нару́жность *f*; **in sb's** ~ в кого́-н прису́тствии.
presence of mind *n* прису́тствие ду́ха.
present [*adj, n* ˈprɛznt, *vt* ˈprɛznt] *adj* (*current*) ны́нешний*, настоя́щий*; (*in attendance*) прису́тствующий ◆ *n* (*gift*) пода́рок*; (*LING*: *also*: ~ **tense**) настоя́щее вре́мя* *nt* ◆ *vt* представля́ть (предста́вить* *perf*); (*threat*) представля́ть (предста́вить* *perf*) собо́й; (*RADIO, TV*) вести́* (*impf*); (*give*): **to** ~ **sth to sb, ** ~ **sb with sth** (*prize, award etc*) вруча́ть (вручи́ть* *perf*) что-н кому́-н; (*gift*) преподноси́ть* (преподнести́* *perf*) что-н кому́-н; (*formally introduce*): **to** ~ **sb (to)** представля́ть (предста́вить* *perf*) кого́-н (+*dat*); **to be** ~ **at** прису́тствовать (*impf*) на +*prp*; **those** ~ прису́тствующие; **the** ~ (*time*) настоя́щее *nt adj*; **at** ~ в настоя́щее вре́мя; **to give sb a** ~ дари́ть* (подари́ть* *perf*) кому́-н пода́рок.
presentable [prɪˈzɛntəbl] *adj* предстaви́тельный* (представи́телен), презента́бельный* (презента́белен).
presentation [prɛznˈteɪʃən] *n* (*of plan, report etc*) изложе́ние; (*appearance*) вне́шний* вид; (*also*: ~ **ceremony**) представле́ние, презента́ция; (*lecture, talk*) выступле́ние; **on** ~ **of** (*voucher etc*) по предъявле́нии +*gen.*
present-day [ˈprɛzntdeɪ] *adj* совреме́нный, ны́нешний*.
presenter [prɪˈzɛntəʳ] *n* (*RADIO, TV*) ди́ктор; (: *of news*) веду́щий*(-ая) *m(f) adj.*
presently [ˈprɛzntlɪ] *adv* вско́ре; (*now*) в да́нный моме́нт, в настоя́щее вре́мя.
present participle *n* прича́стие настоя́щего вре́мени.
preservation [prɛzəˈveɪʃən] *n* (*act: of building, democracy*) сохране́ние; (: *of food*) хране́ние; (*state*) сохра́нность *f*.
preservative [prɪˈzəːvətɪv] *n* (*for food*) консерва́нт; (*for wood*) пропи́точный соста́в; (*for metal*) защи́тное сре́дство.
preserve [prɪˈzəːv] *vt* сохраня́ть (сохрани́ть* *perf*); (*food*) консерви́ровать (законсерви́ровать *perf*); (*keep safe*) оберега́ть (*impf*), охраня́ть (*impf*) ◆ *n* (*often pl*: *jam*) варе́нье; (*for game, fish*) запове́дник; **a working class** ~ стихи́я рабо́чего кла́сса; **a male** ~ чи́сто мужско́е заня́тие.
preshrunk [ˈpriːˈʃrʌŋk] *adj*: ~ **fabric** ткань, проше́дшая предвари́тельную уса́дку.
preside [prɪˈzaɪd] *vi*: **to** ~ **(over)** пред-седа́тельствовать (*impf*) (на +*prp*).
presidency [ˈprɛzɪdənsɪ] *n* президе́нтство.
president [ˈprɛzɪdənt] *n* (*POL, COMM*) президе́нт;

(*US: SCOL*) ре́ктор.

presidential [prɛzɪ'dɛnʃl] *adj* (*election, campaign etc*) президе́нтский; ~ **candidate** кандида́т в президе́нты; ~ **adviser** сове́тник президе́нта.

press [prɛs] *n* (*also: printing* ~) печа́тный стано́к*; (*of switch, button, bell*) кно́пка*; (*for wine*) пресс для виногра́да; (*crowd*) да́вка ◆ *vt* (*hold together*) прижима́ть (прижа́ть* *perf*); (*push*) нажима́ть (нажа́ть* *perf*); (*iron*) гла́дить* (погла́дить* *perf*); (*put pressure on: person*) наста́ивать (настоя́ть* *perf*); (*squeeze*) выжима́ть (вы́жать* *perf*); (*pursue*) добива́ться (доби́ться* *perf*) +*gen* ◆ *vi* (*squeeze*) жать* (*impf*), дави́ть* (*impf*); **the** ~ (*newspapers, journalists*) пре́сса; **to go to** ~ идти́* (*impf*) в печа́ть; **to be in the** ~ (*being printed*) находи́ться* (*impf*) в печа́ти; (*in the newspapers*) быть* (*impf*) в газе́тах; **we are** ~**ed for time/money** у нас ма́ло вре́мени/ де́нег; **to** ~ **sth on sb** (*insist*) навя́зывать (навяза́ть* *perf*) что-н кому́-н; **to** ~ **sb to do** *or* **into doing** вынужда́ть (вы́нудить *perf*) кого́-н +*infin*; **to** ~ **sb for an answer** торопи́ть* (поторопи́ть* *perf*) кого́-н с отве́том; **to** ~ **charges against sb** выдвига́ть (вы́двинуть *perf*) обвине́ния про́тив кого́-н; **to** ~ **for** (*improvement, change etc*) наста́ивать (настоя́ть *perf*) на +*prp*

▶ **press ahead** *vi* приступа́ть (приступи́ть* *perf*) к де́лу

▶ **press on** *vi* продолжа́ть (*impf*).

press agency *n* аге́нтство печа́ти.

press clipping *n* газе́тная вы́резка.

press conference *n* пресс-конфере́нция.

press cutting *n* = **press clipping**.

press-gang ['prɛsgæn] *vt*: **to** ~ **sb into doing** наси́льно заставля́ть (заста́вить* *perf*) кого́-н +*infin*.

pressing ['prɛsɪŋ] *adj* (*urgent*) сро́чный* (сро́чен), неотло́жный* (неотло́жен).

press officer *n* сотру́дник(-ица) отде́ла информа́ции.

press release *n* сообще́ние для печа́ти.

press stud *n* (*BRIT*) одёжная кно́пка*.

press-up ['prɛsʌp] *n* (*BRIT: SPORT*) отжима́ние, отжи́м.

pressure ['prɛʃəʳ] *n* давле́ние; (*stress*) напряже́ние ◆ *vt*: **to** ~ **sb (to do)** принужда́ть (прину́дить* *perf*) кого́-н (+*infin*); **to put** ~ **on sb (to do)** ока́зывать (оказа́ть* *perf*) давле́ние *or* нажи́м на кого́-н (+*infin*); **high/low** ~ высо́кое/ни́зкое давле́ние.

pressure cooker *n* скорова́рка*.

pressure gauge *n* мано́метр.

pressure group *n* инициати́вная гру́ппа.

pressurize ['prɛʃəraɪz] *vt*: **to** ~ **sb (to do** *or* **into doing)** ока́зывать (оказа́ть* *perf*) давле́ние на

кого́-н (+*infin*).

pressurized ['prɛʃəraɪzd] *adj* (*cabin, container, spacesuit*) гермети́чный.

Prestel® ['prɛstɛl] *n* Пре́стел.

prestige [prɛs'tiːʒ] *n* прести́ж.

prestigious [prɛs'tɪdʒəs] *adj* прести́жный* (прести́жен).

presumably [prɪ'zjuːməblɪ] *adv* наве́рно; ~ **he did it** наве́рно, э́то сде́лал он.

presume [prɪ'zjuːm] *vt*: **to** ~ **(that)** (*suppose*) предполага́ть (предположи́ть* *perf*)(, что); **to** ~ **to do** (*dare*) реша́ться (реши́ться *perf*) +*infin*.

presumption [prɪ'zʌmpʃən] *n* предположе́ние.

presumptuous [prɪ'zʌmpʃəs] *adj* самонадея́нный* (самонадея́н).

presuppose [priːsə'pəuz] *vt* преполага́ть (предположи́ть* *perf*).

presupposition [priːsʌpə'zɪʃən] *n* предположе́ние.

pretax [priː'tæks] *adj* (*profit*) до вы́чета нало́гов.

pretence [prɪ'tɛns] (*US* **pretense**) *n* (*false appearance*) притво́рство; (*excuse*) предло́г; **under false** ~**s** под ло́жным предло́гом; **she is devoid of all** ~ она́ соверше́нно лишена́ притво́рства; **he is making a** ~ **of helping** он де́лает вид, что помога́ет.

pretend [prɪ'tɛnd] *vt*: **to** ~ **that** притворя́ться (притвори́ться* *perf*), что; **he** ~**ed to help** он притвори́лся, что помога́ет; **to** ~ **to sth** (*make claim*) претендова́ть (*impf*) на что-н.

pretense [prɪ'tɛns] *n* (*US*) = **pretence**.

pretentious [prɪ'tɛnʃəs] *adj* претенцио́зный* (претенцио́зен).

preterite ['prɛtərɪt] *n* прете́рит.

pretext ['priːtɛkst] *n* предло́г; **on** *or* **under the** ~ **of being busy/tired** под предло́гом за́нятости/уста́лости.

Pretoria [prɪ'tɔːrɪə] *n* Прето́рия.

pretty ['prɪtɪ] *adj* (*person*) хоро́шенький*; (*thing*) краси́вый (краси́в) ◆ *adv* (*quite*) дово́льно.

prevail [prɪ'veɪl] *vi* (*be current*) преоблада́ть (*impf*), превали́ровать (*impf*); (*gain influence*) оде́рживать (одержа́ть* *perf*) верх; (*persuade*): **to** ~ **(up)on sb to do** убежда́ть (убеди́ть* *perf*) кого́-н +*infin*.

prevailing [prɪ'veɪlɪŋ] *adj* (*wind*) преоблада́ющий; (*fashion, attitude*) превали́рующий.

prevalent ['prɛvələnt] *adj* (*belief, custom*) преоблада́ющий; (*fashion*) превали́рующий; (*disease*) распространённый* (распространён).

prevaricate [prɪ'værɪkeɪt] *vi* изворáчиваться (*impf*).

prevarication [prɪværɪ'keɪʃən] *n* виля́ние.

---

* marks translations which have irregular inflections. The Russian-English side of the dictionary gives inflectional information.

prevent [prɪ'vɛnt] *vt* (*accident etc*) предот-
вращать (предотвратить* *perf*); **to ~ sb from
doing** мешать (помешать *perf*) кому-н +*infin*;
this policy ~s inflation from rising эта
политика препятствует росту инфляции.
preventable [prɪ'vɛntəbl] *adj* предотвратимый
(предотвратим).
preventative [prɪ'vɛntətɪv] *adj* = **preventive**.
prevention [prɪ'vɛnʃən] *n* предотвращение,
предупреждение.
preventive [prɪ'vɛntɪv] *adj* (*measures*)
предупредительный; (: *POL*) превентивный;
(*medicine*) профилактический*.
preview ['pri:vju:] *n* (*of film*) (закрытый)
просмотр; (*fig*) предварительная картина.
previous ['pri:vɪəs] *adj* предыдущий*; **I have a
~ engagement** это время у меня уже занято;
~ to до +*gen*.
previously ['pri:vɪəslɪ] *adv* (*before*) ранее; (*in
the past*) прежде; **I retired two years ~** я ушёл
на пенсию двумя годами ранее.
prewar [pri:'wɔ:'] *adj* довоенный, пред-
военный.
prey [preɪ] *n* добыча ♦ *vi*: **to ~ on** (*animal: feed
on*) охотиться* (*impf*) на +*acc*; **it was ~ing on
his mind** это терзало его.
price [praɪs] *n* (*also fig*) цена* ♦ *vt* (*goods*)
оценивать (оценить* *perf*); **what is the ~ of ...?**
сколько стоит ...?; **to go up** *or* **rise in ~**
дорожать (вздорожать *or* подорожать *perf*);
to put a ~ on sth назначать (назначить *perf*)
цену чему-н; **Britain has been out of the
market** Великобритания была вытеснена из
рынка из-за завышения цен; **what ~ his
promises now?** (*BRIT*) что стоят все его
обещания сейчас?; **he regained his freedom,
but at a ~** он получил свободу, но дорогой
ценой.
price control *n* контроль *m* за ценами.
price cutting *n* снижение цен.
priceless ['praɪslɪs] *adj* бесценный* (бесценен);
(*inf: amusing*) бесподобный* (бесподобен).
price list *n* прейскурант.
price range *n* диапазон цен; **it's within my ~ ~**
это мне по карману.
price tag *n* ценник; (*fig*) цена*.
price war *n* война цен.
pricey ['praɪsɪ] *adj* (*inf*) дорогой.
prick [prɪk] *n* (*short, sharp pain*) укол; (*ANAT:
inf!*) хуй (!) ♦ *vt* (*make hole in*) прокалывать
(проколоть* *perf*); (*cause pain to*) уколоть*
(*perf*); **to ~ up one's ears** (*listen eagerly*)
навострить (*perf*) уши.
prickle ['prɪkl] *n* (*of plant*) шип*, колючка*;
(*sensation*) покалывание.
prickly ['prɪklɪ] *adj* колючий* (колюч).
prickly heat *n* потница.
prickly pear *n* (*BOT*) опунция.
pride [praɪd] *n* гордость *f*; (*pej: feeling of
superiority*) гордыня ♦ *vt*: **to ~ o.s. on**
гордиться* (*impf*) +*instr*; **to take (a) ~ in**

гордиться* (*impf*) +*instr*; **I take (a) ~ in working
well** я горжусь тем что я работаю хорошо;
to have ~ of place (*BRIT*) занимать (занять*
perf) почётное место.
priest [pri:st] *n* священник; (*non-Christian*)
жрец*.
priestess ['pri:stɪs] *n* (*non-Christian*) жрица.
priesthood ['pri:sthud] *n* священство.
prig [prɪg] *n*: **he's a ~** он такая цаца.
prim [prɪm] *adj* чопорный* (чопорен).
primacy ['praɪməsɪ] *n* первенство.
prima-facie ['praɪmə'feɪʃɪ] *adj*: **to have a ~ case**
(*LAW*) разбирать (*impf*) ясное судебное дело*.
primal ['praɪməl] *adj* (*instinct*) первичный;
(*cause*) изначальный; **~ scream** первый крик
(младенца).
primarily ['praɪmərɪlɪ] *adv* в первую очередь.
primary ['praɪmərɪ] *adj* (*first in importance*)
первостепенный* (первостепенен),
первоочередной ♦ *n* (*US: POL*) пред-
варительные выборы *mpl*; **~ education**
начальное образование; **~ teacher**
учитель(ница) *m(f)* начальных классов.
primary colour *n* основной цвет*.
primary school *n* (*BRIT*) начальная школа.
primate [*n* 'praɪmɪt] *n* (*ZOOL*) примат; (*REL*)
примас.
prime [praɪm] *adj* (*most important*) главный,
основной; (*best quality*) первосортный ♦ *n*
(*of person's life*) расцвет ♦ *vt* (*wood, canvas*)
грунтовать (загрунтовать *perf*); (*fig: person*)
подготавливать (подготовить* *perf*); (*gun*)
заряжать (зарядить *perf*); (*pump*) заливать
(залить* *perf*); **in the ~ of life** в расцвете сил,
во цвете лет; **~ example** (*typical*) яркий*
пример.
Prime Minister *n* премьер-министр.
primer ['praɪmə'] *n* (*paint*) грунтовка; (*book*)
учебник-введение.
prime time *n* (*RADIO, TV*) лучшее эфирное
время* *nt*.
primeval [praɪ'mi:vl] *adj* первобытный.
primitive ['prɪmɪtɪv] *adj* (*early*) первобытный;
(*unsophisticated: way of life, tool etc*)
примитивный* (примитивен).
primrose ['prɪmrəuz] *n* первоцвет.
primula ['prɪmjulə] *n* примула.
Primus® ['praɪməs] *n* (*BRIT: also:* **p~ stove**)
примус.
prince [prɪns] *n* принц; (*Russian*) князь* *m*.
prince charming *n* прекрасный принц.
princess [prɪn'sɛs] *n* принцесса; (*Russian*)
княгиня, княжна*.
principal ['prɪnsɪpl] *adj* главный, основной ♦ *n*
(*of school, college*) директор*; (*of university*)
ректор; (*in play*) ведущий*(-ая) актёр
(-триса); (*money*) капитал.
principality [prɪnsɪ'pælɪtɪ] *n* княжество.
principally ['prɪnsɪplɪ] *adv* преимущественно,
главным образом.
principle ['prɪnsɪpl] *n* принцип; (*scientific law*)

зако́н; **in** ~ в при́нципе; **on** ~ из при́нципа.
print [prɪnt] n (TYP) шрифт*; (ART) эста́мп, гравю́ра; (PHOT, fingerprint) отпеча́ток*; (footprint) след*; (fabric) си́тец* ♦ vt (book etc) печа́тать (напеча́тать perf); (cloth) набива́ть (наби́ть* perf); (write in capitals) писа́ть* (написа́ть* perf) печа́тными бу́квами; **this book is out of** ~ э́та кни́га распро́дана
▸ **print out** vt (COMPUT) распеча́тывать (распеча́тать perf), выводи́ть* (вы́йти* perf) на печа́ть.
printed circuit board ['prɪntɪd-] n (ELEC) печа́тная схе́ма or пла́та.
printed matter n печа́тные материа́лы mpl.
printer ['prɪntə'] n (person) печа́тник; (machine) при́нтер; (firm: also: ~'s) типогра́фия.
printhead ['prɪnthɛd] n (COMPUT) печа́тающая голо́вка.
printing ['prɪntɪŋ] n (act) печа́тание; (art) печа́тное де́ло.
printing press n печа́тный стано́к*.
print-out ['prɪntaut] n (COMPUT) распеча́тка*.
print wheel n (COMPUT) печа́тающее колесо́*.
prior ['praɪə'] adj (previous) пре́жний*; (more important) первоочередно́й ♦ n (REL) настоя́тель m, прио́р; **without** ~ **notice** без предвари́тельного предупрежде́ния; **to have** ~ **knowledge of sth** знать* (impf) о чём-н зара́нее; **to have a** ~ **claim to sth** име́ть (impf) первоочередно́е or преиму́щественное пра́во на что-н; ~ **to** до +gen.
priority [praɪˈɔrɪtɪ] n (most urgent task) первоочередна́я зада́ча; (most important thing, task) приорите́т; **to have** ~ **(over)** име́ть (impf) преиму́ществом (пе́ред +instr).
priory ['praɪərɪ] n монасты́рь* m.
prise [praɪz] vt: **to** ~ **open** взла́мывать (взлома́ть perf).
prism ['prɪzəm] n при́зма.
prison ['prɪzn] n тюрьма́* ♦ cpd тюре́мный.
prison camp n исправи́тельно-трудово́й ла́герь* m.
prisoner ['prɪznə'] n (in prison) заключённый (-ая) m(f) adj; (captured person) пле́нный(-ая) m(f) adj; **the** ~ **at the bar** подсуди́мый(-ая) m(f) adj; **to take sb** ~ брать* (взять* perf) кого́-н в плен.
prisoner of war n военнопле́нный m adj.
prissy ['prɪsɪ] adj (pej) чо́порный.
pristine ['prɪstiːn] adj безупре́чный* (безупре́чен).
privacy ['prɪvəsɪ] n уедине́ние; **invasion of sb's** ~ вторже́ние в чью-н ча́стную жизнь.
private ['praɪvɪt] adj (not public: property, industry) ча́стный*; (: discussion, club) закры́тый; (personal, confidential: belongings, life) ли́чный; (: thoughts, plans)

скры́тый; (secluded: place) уединённый (уединён); (secretive, reserved) за́мкнутый (за́мкнут); (confidential) конфиденциа́льный* (конфиденциа́лен) ♦ n (MIL) рядово́й m adj; "**private**" (on envelope) „ли́чно"; (on door) „посторо́нним вход воспрещён"; **in** ~ конфиденциа́льно; **in (his)** ~ **life** в (его́) ли́чной жи́зни; **he is a very** ~ **person** он о́чень за́мкнутый челове́к; **to be in** ~ **practice** име́ть (impf) ча́стную пра́ктику; ~ **hearing** (LAW) закры́тое слу́шание.
private enterprise n (economic activity) ча́стное предпринима́тельство.
private eye n ча́стный сы́щик.
private limited company n (BRIT) ча́стная акционе́рная компа́ния.
privately ['praɪvɪtlɪ] adv (discuss) конфиденциа́льно; (act) в ча́стном поря́дке; (within o.s.) в душе́.
private parts npl (ANAT) (нару́жные) половы́е о́рганы mpl.
private property n ча́стная со́бственность f.
private school n ча́стная шко́ла.
privation [praɪˈveɪʃən] n (state) лише́ния ntpl.
privatize ['praɪvɪtaɪz] vt приватизи́ровать (impf/perf).
privet ['prɪvɪt] n (BOT) бирючи́на.
privilege ['prɪvɪlɪdʒ] n привиле́гия.
privileged ['prɪvɪlɪdʒd] adj привилегиро́ванный; **to be** ~ **to do** име́ть (impf) честь +infin.
privy ['prɪvɪ] adj: ~ **to** посвящённый в +acc.
Privy Council n (BRIT) Та́йный Сове́т.
Privy Councillor n (BRIT) Та́йный Сове́тник.
prize [praɪz] n приз*; (money) пре́мия ♦ adj (first-class) первокла́ссный; (example, idiot) класси́ческий* ♦ vt (высоко́) цени́ть (impf).
prizefighter ['praɪzfaɪtə'] n профессиона́льный боксёр.
prize-giving ['praɪzgɪvɪŋ] n церемо́ния вруче́ния награ́д за хоро́шую успева́емость.
prize money n призовы́е де́ньги* pl.
prizewinner ['praɪzwɪnə'] n призёр, лауреа́т.
prizewinning ['praɪzwɪnɪŋ] adj (person) удосто́енный награ́ды; (animal) призово́й; (novel, essay etc) удосто́енный пре́мии.
PRO n abbr = **public relations officer**.
pro [prəu] n (SPORT: inf) профессиона́л ♦ prep (in favour of) за +acc; **the** ~**s and cons** (до́воды) „за" и „про́тив".
pro- [prəu] prefix про-.
proactive [prəuˈæktɪv] adj де́йственный.
probability [prɔbəˈbɪlɪtɪ] n: ~ **of/that** вероя́тность f +gen/что; **in all** ~ по всей вероя́тности.
probable ['prɔbəbl] adj вероя́тный* (вероя́тен); **it seems** ~ **that** ... представля́ется вероя́тным, что ....

---

* marks translations which have irregular inflections. The Russian-English side of the dictionary gives inflectional information.

probably ['prɒbəblɪ] *adv* вероя́тно.

probate ['prəubɪt] *n* утвержде́ние завеща́ния.

probation [prə'beɪʃən] *n*: **he is on ~** (*LAW*) он осуждён усло́вно; (*employee*) он прохо́дит испыта́тельный срок; (*REL*) он отбыва́ет по́слух.

probationary [prə'beɪʃənrɪ] *adj* (*period*) испыта́тельный.

probationer [prə'beɪʃənə'] *n* (*LAW*) усло́вно осуждённый.

probation officer *n должностно́е лицо́, осуществля́ющее надзо́р за усло́вно осуждёнными.*

probe [prəub] *n* (*MED, SPACE*) зонд; (*enquiry*) рассле́дование ♦ *vt* (*investigate*) рассле́довать (*impf/perf*); (*poke*) прощу́пывать (*impf*).

probity ['prəubɪtɪ] *n* че́стность *f*.

problem ['prɒbləm] *n* пробле́ма; **we are having ~s with the car** у нас непола́дки с маши́ной; **what's the ~?** в чём де́ло?; **I had no ~ in finding her** я нашёл её без труда́; **no ~!** нет пробле́м!

problematic(al) [prɒblə'mætɪk(l)] *adj* проблемати́чный* (проблемати́чен).

problem-solving ['prɒbləmsɒlvɪŋ] *n уме́ние находи́ть вы́ход из тру́дного положе́ния.*

procedural [prə'si:djurəl] *adj* процеду́рный.

procedure [prə'si:dʒə'] *n* процеду́ра.

proceed [prə'si:d] *vi* (*subj: activity, event, process: carry on*) продолжа́ться (продо́лжиться *perf*); (*person: go*) дви́гаться (дви́нуться *perf*); (*continue*): **to ~ (with)** продолжа́ть (продо́лжить *perf*); **to ~ to do** продолжа́ть (продо́лжить *perf*) +*infin*; **to ~ against sb** (*LAW*) возбужда́ть (возбуди́ть* *perf*) де́ло про́тив кого́-н.

proceedings [prə'si:dɪŋz] *npl* (*organized events*) собы́тия *ntpl*; (*LAW*) суде́бное разбира́тельство *ntsg*; (*minutes*) протоко́л *msg*.

proceeds ['prəusi:dz] *npl* поступле́ния *ntpl*.

process ['prəusɛs] *n* проце́сс ♦ *vt* (*also COMPUT*) обраба́тывать (обрабо́тать *perf*) ♦ *vi* (*BRIT: go in procession*) уча́ствовать (*impf*) в проце́ссии; **in ~** в проце́ссе; **we are in the ~ of moving house** сейча́с мы переезжа́ем.

processed cheese ['prəusɛst-] (*US* **process cheese**) *n* пла́вленый сыр*.

processing ['prəusɛsɪŋ] *n* (*PHOT*) обрабо́тка*.

procession [prə'sɛʃən] *n* проце́ссия.

pro-choice [prəu'tʃɔɪs] *adj защища́ющий пра́во же́нщины на або́рт.*

proclaim [prə'kleɪm] *vt* провозглаша́ть (провозгласи́ть* *perf*).

proclamation [prɒklə'meɪʃən] *n* провозглаше́ние.

proclivity [prə'klɪvɪtɪ] *n* накло́нность *f*.

procrastinate [prəu'kræstɪneɪt] *vi* оття́гивать (оттяну́ть *perf*).

procrastination [prəukræstɪ'neɪʃən] *n* оття́гивание.

procreation [prəukrɪ'eɪʃən] *n* размноже́ние.

procurator fiscal ['prɒkjurɪtə-] *n* (*SCOTTISH: LAW*) прокуро́р.

procure [prə'kjuə'] *vt* приобрета́ть (приобрести́* *perf*).

procurement [prə'kjuəmənt] *n* приобрете́ние.

prod [prɒd] *vt* ты́кать* (ткнуть *perf*); (*fig: remind*) подстёгивать (подстегну́ть *perf*) ♦ *n* (*see vb*) тычо́к*; (*fig*) напомина́ние.

prodigal ['prɒdɪgl] *adj* блу́дный.

prodigious [prə'dɪdʒəs] *adj* огро́мный* (огро́мен).

prodigy ['prɒdɪdʒɪ] *n* (*person*) тала́нт; (*achievement*) успе́хи *mpl*; **child ~** вундерки́нд.

produce [*vt* prə'dju:s, *n* 'prɒdju:s] *vt* (*object, offspring, effect*) производи́ть* (произвести́* *perf*); (*BIO, CHEM*) выраба́тывать (вы́работать *perf*); (*evidence, argument*) представля́ть (предста́вить* *perf*); (*bring or take out*) предъявля́ть (предъяви́ть* *perf*); (*play, film*) ста́вить* (поста́вить* *perf*) ♦ *n* (*AGR*) проду́кция.

producer [prə'dju:sə'] *n* (*of film, play*) режиссёр-постано́вщик, продю́сер; (*of record*) продю́сер; (*country, company*) производи́тель *m*.

product ['prɒdʌkt] *n* (*thing*) изде́лие; (*food, result*) проду́кт.

production [prə'dʌkʃən] *n* (*process*) произво́дство; (*amount produced*) проду́кция; (*of electricity etc*) вы́работка*; (*THEAT*) постано́вка*; **to put into ~** (*goods*) запуска́ть (запусти́ть* *perf*) в произво́дство.

production agreement *n* (*US*) соглаше́ние о долево́м распределе́нии проду́кции.

production line *n* пото́чная ли́ния.

production manager *n* руководи́тель *m* произво́дством.

productive [prə'dʌktɪv] *adj* (*also fig*) производи́тельный* (производи́телен), продукти́вный* (продукти́вен).

productivity [prɒdʌk'tɪvɪtɪ] *n* производи́тельность *f*, продукти́вность *f*.

productivity agreement *n* (*BRIT*) догово́р о производи́тельности труда́.

productivity bonus *n* пре́мия за высо́кую производи́тельность труда́.

Prof. *n abbr* = **professor**.

profane [prə'feɪn] *adj* (*secular*) све́тский*; (*language etc*) богоху́льный* (богоху́лен).

profess [prə'fɛs] *vt* (*claim*) претендова́ть (*impf*) на +*acc*; (*express*) заявля́ть (заяви́ть* *perf*) о +*prp*; (*REL*) испове́довать (*impf/perf*); **I do not ~ to be an expert** я не претенду́ю на роль специали́ста.

professed [prə'fɛst] *adj* (*self-declared*) открове́нный.

profession [prə'fɛʃən] *n* профе́ссия; **the ~s** „профе́ссии с большо́й бу́квы" (*ЮР. МЕД.*

РЕЛ).

professional [prəˈfɛʃənl] *adj*
профессиона́льный ♦ *n* (*doctor, lawyer,
teacher etc*) специали́ст; (*skilled person, also
SPORT*) профессиона́л; **he's a ~ man** он –
челове́к с образова́нием; **to take ~ advice**
получа́ть (получи́ть* *perf*) профессион-
а́льный сове́т.

professionalism [prəˈfɛʃnəlɪzəm] *n*
профессионали́зм.

professionally [prəˈfɛʃnəlɪ] *adv* (*also SPORT,
MUS*) профессиона́льно; **I only know him ~** я
зна́ю его́ то́лько по рабо́те.

professor [prəˈfɛsəʳ] *n* (*BRIT*) профе́ссор; (*US*)
преподава́тель(ница) *m(f)*.

professorship [prəˈfɛsəʃɪp] *n* профе́ссорство.

proffer [ˈprɔfəʳ] *vt* (*remark*) выска́зывать
(вы́сказать* *perf*); (*apologies*) приноси́ть*
(принести́* *perf*); (*one's hand*) протя́гивать
(протяну́ть* *perf*).

proficiency [prəˈfɪʃənsɪ] *n* квалифика́ция,
уме́ние.

proficient [prəˈfɪʃənt] *adj* уме́лый; **to be ~ at sth**
(*at sth mental*) быть* (*impf*) знатоко́м чем-н;
he is ~ at swimming он ма́стерски пла́вает.

profile [ˈprəufaɪl] *n* (*of face*) про́филь *m*; (*article*)
о́черк; **to keep a high ~** (*fig*) находи́ться*
(*impf*) в це́нтре (обще́ственного) внима́ния;
to keep a low ~ (*fig*) стара́ться (*impf*) не
выделя́ться.

profit [ˈprɔfɪt] *n* при́быль *f*, дохо́д ♦ *vi*: **to ~ by**
or **from** (*fig*) извлека́ть (извле́чь* *perf*) вы́году
из +*gen*; **~ and loss account** счёт при́былей и
убы́тков; **to make a ~** получа́ть (получи́ть*
perf) при́быль; **to sell (sth) at a ~** продава́ть*
(прода́ть* *perf*) (что-н) с вы́годой.

profitability [prɔfɪtəˈbɪlɪtɪ] *n* при́быльность *f*.

profitable [ˈprɔfɪtəbl] *adj* при́быльный*
(при́былен); (*fig*) вы́годный* (вы́годен).

profit centre *n* (*COMM*) „центр получе́ния
при́были".

profiteering [prɔfɪˈtɪərɪŋ] *n* (*pej*) спекуля́ция.

profitmaking [ˈprɔfɪtmeɪkɪŋ] *adj* при́быльный*
(при́былен).

profit margin *n* ма́ржа при́быльности.

profit-sharing [ˈprɔfɪtʃɛərɪŋ] *n* уча́стие
(слу́жащих) в при́былях.

profits tax *n* (*BRIT*) нало́г с при́были.

profligate [ˈprɔflɪgɪt] *adj*: **~ (with)**
расточи́тельный* (расточи́телен) (в +*prp*).

pro forma [ˈprəuˈfɔːmə] *adj*: **~ ~ invoice**
предвари́тельный счёт-факту́ра.

profound [prəˈfaund] *adj* глубо́кий* (глубо́к).

profuse [prəˈfjuːs] *adj* оби́льный* (оби́лен).

profusely [prəˈfjuːslɪ] *adv* оби́льно; (*apologize*)
горячо́.

profusion [prəˈfjuːʒən] *n* оби́льность *f*.

progeny [ˈprɔdʒɪnɪ] *n* пото́мство.

prognoses [prɔgˈnəusiːz] *npl of* **prognosis**.

prognosis [prɔgˈnəusis] (*pl* **prognoses**) *n*
прогно́з.

program [ˈprəugræm] *n* (*COMPUT*) програ́мма ♦
vt (*COMPUT*) программи́ровать (запрограм-
ми́ровать *perf*).

programme [ˈprəugræm] (*US* **program**) *n*
програ́мма ♦ *vt* программи́ровать
(запрограмми́ровать *perf*).

programmer [ˈprəugræməʳ] *n* (*COMPUT*)
программи́ст(ка*).

programming [ˈprəugræmɪŋ] (*US* **programing**)
n (*COMPUT*) программи́рование.

programming language *n* (*COMPUT*) язы́к*
программи́рования.

progress [*n* ˈprəugrɛs, *vi* prəˈgrɛs] *n* (*advances,
changes*) прогре́сс; (*development*) разви́тие
♦ *vi* прогресси́ровать (*impf*); (*move up in rank*)
продвига́ться (продви́нуться *perf*) (по
слу́жбе); (*continue*) продолжа́ться
(продо́лжиться* *perf*); **the meeting/match is in
~** сейча́с идёт собра́ние/матч; **to make ~**
де́лать (сде́лать *perf*) успе́хи; **as the match
~ed** по хо́ду ма́тча.

progression [prəˈgrɛʃən] *n* (*gradual
development*) продвиже́ние; (*series*) череда́;
(*MATH*) прогре́ссия.

progressive [prəˈgrɛsɪv] *adj* прогресси́вный*
(прогресси́вен); (*gradual*) постепе́нный.

progressively [prəˈgrɛsɪvlɪ] *adv*: **the work
became ~ harder** рабо́та станови́лась всё
трудне́е.

progress report *n* (*MED*) протоко́л о хо́де
боле́зни; (*ADMIN*) докла́д о хо́де дел.

prohibit [prəˈhɪbɪt] *vt* запреща́ть (запрети́ть*
perf); **to ~ sb from doing** запреща́ть
(запрети́ть* *perf*) кому́-н +*infin*; **"smoking
~ed"** „кури́ть воспреща́ется".

prohibition [prəuɪˈbɪʃən] *n* запреще́ние,
запре́т; **P~** сухо́й зако́н.

prohibitive [prəˈhɪbɪtɪv] *adj* (*price etc*)
недосту́пный* (недосту́пен).

project [*n* ˈprɔdʒɛkt, *vb* prəˈdʒɛkt] *n* (*large-scale
plan, scheme*) прое́кт; (*SCOL*) рабо́та ♦ *vt*
(*plan, estimate*) проекти́ровать (*impf*); (*film*)
демонстри́ровать (продемонстри́ровать
perf); (*light, picture*) проеци́ровать
(спроеци́ровать *perf*) ♦ *vi* (*stick out*)
выступа́ть (вы́ступить* *perf*).

projectile [prəˈdʒɛktaɪl] *n* снаря́д.

projection [prəˈdʒɛkʃən] *n* (*estimate*)
перспекти́вная оце́нка*; (*overhang*) вы́ступ;
(*CINEMA*) прое́кция.

projectionist [prəˈdʒɛkʃənɪst] *n* (*CINEMA*)
киномеха́ник.

projection room *n* бу́дка киномеха́ника,
проекцио́нная каби́на.

projector [prəˈdʒɛktəʳ] *n* (*CINEMA*)

---

* marks translations which have irregular inflections. The Russian-English side of the dictionary gives inflectional information.

кинопроéктор; (*also:* **slide** ~) проéктор.
proletarian [prəulɪˈtɛərɪən] *adj* пролетáрский*.
proletariat [prəulɪˈtɛərɪət] *n:* **the** ~
пролетариáт.
pro-life [prəuˈlaɪf] *adj выступáющий прóтив
абóртов.*
proliferate [prəˈlɪfəreɪt] *vi* распространя́ться
(распространи́ться *perf*).
proliferation [prəlɪfəˈreɪʃən] *n* рас-
пространéние.
prolific [prəˈlɪfɪk] *adj* плодови́тый (плодови́т).
prologue [ˈprəulɔg] (*US* **prolog**) *n* пролóг.
prolong [prəˈlɔŋ] *vt* продлевáть (продли́ть
perf).
prom [prɔm] *n abbr* = **promenade**; (*MUS*) =
promenade concert; (*US: college ball*)
студéнческий* бал.
promenade [prɔməˈnɑːd] *n* променáд, мéсто*
для прогýлок.
promenade concert *n* (*BRIT*) променáдный
концéрт (*на котóром часть пýблики
стои́т*).
promenade deck *n* вéрхняя пáлуба.
prominence [ˈprɔmɪnəns] *n* (*of person*) ви́дное
положéние; (*of issue*) ви́дное мéсто.
prominent [ˈprɔmɪnənt] *adj* (*important, very
noticeable*) выдаю́щийся*; **he is** ~ **in the field
of** ... он извéстен в óбласти +*gen* ....
prominently [ˈprɔmɪnəntlɪ] *adv* замéтно; **he
figured** ~ **in the case** он игрáл замéтную
роль в э́том дéле.
promiscuity [prɔmɪsˈkjuːɪtɪ] *n* распýщенность
f.
promiscuous [prəˈmɪskjuəs] *adj* распýщенный.
promise [ˈprɔmɪs] *n* (*vow*) обещáние; (*talent*)
потенциáл; (*hope*) надéжда ◆ *vi* (*vow*)
давáть* (дать* *perf*) обещáние ◆ *vt:* **to** ~ **sb
sth,** ~ **sth to sb** обещáть (пообещáть *perf*)
что-н комý-н; **a young man of** ~ мнóго-
обещáющий* молодóй человéк*; **she shows**
~ онá подаёт надéжды; **to** ~ (**sb**) **to do/that**
обещáть (пообещáть *perf*) (комý-н) +*infin/
что;* **to** ~ **well** подавáть* (*impf*) больши́е
надéжды.
promising [ˈprɔmɪsɪŋ] *adj* многообещáющий*.
promissory note [ˈprɔmɪsərɪ-] *n* (простóй)
вéксель* *m.*
promontory [ˈprɔməntrɪ] *n* мыс*.
promote [prəˈməut] *vt* (*employee*) повышáть
(повы́сить* *perf*) (в дóлжности); (*product,
pop star*) реклами́ровать (*impf/perf*); (*ideas*)
поддéрживать (поддержáть* *perf*); (*venture,
event*) содéйствовать (*impf/perf*) +*dat;* **the team
was ~d to the second division** (*BRIT*) комáнда
былá переведенá во вторýю ли́гу.
promoter [prəˈməutəʳ] *n* (*of event*) агéнт; (*of
cause, idea*) пропаганди́ст(ка*).
promotion [prəˈməuʃən] *n* (*at work*)
повышéние (в дóлжности); (*of product,
event, idea*) реклами́рование; (*publicity
campaign*) реклáма.

prompt [prɔmpt] *adj* незамедли́тельный*
(незамедли́телен) ◆ *n* (*COMPUT*)
приглашéние ◆ *vt* (*cause*) побуждáть
(побуди́ть* *perf*); (*sb talking*) подскáзывать
(подсказáть* *perf*); (*THEAT*) суфли́ровать
(*impf*) +*dat* ◆ *adv:* **at 8 o'clock** ~ рóвно в 8
часóв; **they're very** ~ они́ óчень
пунктуáльны; **he was** ~ **to accept** он
немéдленно согласи́лся; **to** ~ **sb to do**
побуждáть (побуди́ть* *perf*) когó-н +*infin.*
prompter [ˈprɔmptəʳ] *n* (*THEAT*) суфлёр.
promptly [ˈprɔmptlɪ] *adv* (*immediately*)
незамедли́тельно; (*exactly*) тóчно.
promptness [ˈprɔmptnɪs] *n* незамедли́тель-
ность *f*.
promulgate [ˈprɔməlgeɪt] *vt* обнарóдовать
(*impf*).
prone [prəun] *adj:* **to lie** ~ лежáть (*impf*)
ничкóм; ~ **to** (*inclined to*) склóнный*
(склóнен) к +*dat;* **I am** ~ **to illness** у меня́
слáбое здорóвье; **he is** ~ **to colds** он
подвéржен простýдам; **she is** ~ **to burst into
tears if you shout at her** éсли на неё кричáть,
онá мóжет легкó разрыдáться.
prong [prɔŋ] *n* (*of fork*) зубéц*.
pronoun [ˈprəunaun] *n* местоимéние.
pronounce [prəˈnauns] *vt* (*word*) произноси́ть*
(произнести́* *perf*); (*declaration, verdict*)
объявля́ть (объяви́ть* *perf*); (*opinion*)
выскáзывать (вы́сказать* *perf*) ◆ *vi:* **to** ~
(**up**)**on** выскáзываться (вы́сказаться* *perf*)
относи́тельно +*gen;* **they ~d him unfit to drive**
егó объяви́ли неприго́дным к вождéнию
автомоби́ля.
pronounced [prəˈnaunst] *adj* отчётливый
(отчётлив).
pronouncement [prəˈnaunsmənt] *n*
объявлéние.
pronto [ˈprɔntəu] *adv* (*inf*) жи́во.
pronunciation [prənʌnsɪˈeɪʃən] *n* (*of word*)
произношéние; (*by person*) вы́говор.
proof [pruːf] *n* (*evidence*) доказáтельство;
(*TYP*) корректýра; (*test, PHOT*) прóбный
отпечáток*; (*of alcohol*) крéпость *f* ◆ *vt* (*BRIT:
tent, anorak*) дéлать (сдéлать* *perf*)
водонепроница́емым ◆ *adj:* **this material is** ~
against water э́тот материáл не пропускáет
вóду; **this vodka is 70%** ~ э́то — семи́десяти-
процéнтная вóдка.
proofreader [ˈpruːfriːdəʳ] *n* коррéктор.
prop [prɔp] *n* (*support*) подпóрка*; (*fig: person*)
опóра ◆ *vt* (*also:* ~ **up**) подпирáть
(подперéть* *perf*); (*lean*): **to** ~ **sth against**
прислоня́ть (прислони́ть* *perf*) что-н к +*dat;*
~**s** *npl* (*THEAT*) реквизи́т *msg.*
Prop. *abbr* (*COMM*) = **proprietor.**
propaganda [prɔpəˈgændə] *n* пропагáнда.
propagate [ˈprɔpəgeɪt] *vt* (*idea, information*)
распространя́ть (распространи́ть *perf*);
(*plant*) разводи́ть* (развести́* *perf*).
propagation [prɔpəˈgeɪʃən] *n* (*see vt*)

распростране́ние; разведе́ние.

propel [prə'pɛl] *vt* (*vehicle, machine*)
приводи́ть* (привести́* *perf*) в движе́ние; (*fig*:
person) толка́ть (толкну́ть *perf*).

propeller [prə'pɛlə*] *n* пропе́ллер.

propelling pencil [prə'pɛlɪŋ-] *n* (*BRIT*) авто-
мати́ческий* каранда́ш*.

propensity [prə'pɛnsɪtɪ] *n*: **a ~ for/to do**
расположенность *f* к +*dat*/+*infin*.

proper ['prɔpə*] *adj* (*real*) настоя́щий*; (*correct*)
подходя́щий*, надлежа́щий*; (*socially
acceptable*) прили́чный (прили́чен); **he
looked a ~ fool** (*inf*) он вы́глядел настоя́щим
дурако́м; **the village ~** со́бственно дере́вня*;
to go through the ~ channels проходи́ть*
(пройти́* *perf*) че́рез надлежа́щие кана́лы.

properly ['prɔpəlɪ] *adv* (*eat, study*) как сле́дует;
(*behave*) прили́чно, до́лжным о́бразом.

proper noun *n* и́мя* *nt* со́бственное.

property ['prɔpətɪ] *n* (*possessions*)
со́бственность *f*; (*building and its land*)
недви́жимость *f*; (*quality*) сво́йство
♦ *cpd*: **~ developer** застро́йщик; **it's their ~**
э́то их со́бственность; **~ market** ры́нок
недви́жимости; **~ tax** нало́г на
со́бственности.

prophecy ['prɔfɪsɪ] *n* проро́чество.

prophesy ['prɔfɪsaɪ] *vti* проро́чить
(напроро́чить *perf*).

prophet ['prɔfɪt] *n* проро́к.

prophetic [prə'fɛtɪk] *adj* проро́ческий*.

proportion [prə'pɔːʃən] *n* (*part*) часть* *f*, до́ля;
(*ratio*) пропо́рция, соотноше́ние; **his head is
in perfect ~ to his body** голова́ его́
абсолю́тно пропорциона́льна его́ те́лу; **to
be out of all ~ to** ника́к не соотве́тствовать
(*impf*) +*dat*; **to get sth in(to) ~** соизмеря́ть
(соизме́рить *perf*) что-н; **to get sth out of ~** не
соизмеря́ть (соизме́рить *perf*) что-н; **a sense
of ~** чу́вство ме́ры.

proportional [prə'pɔːʃənl] *adj*: **~ (to)**
пропорциона́льный* (пропорциона́лен)
(+*dat*).

proportional representation *n* (*POL*)
пропорциона́льное представи́тельство.

proportionate [prə'pɔːʃənɪt] *adj*: **~ (to)**
пропорциона́льный* (пропорциона́лен)
(+*dat*).

proposal [prə'pəuzl] *n* предложе́ние.

propose [prə'pəuz] *vt* (*plan, toast*) предлага́ть
(предложи́ть* *perf*); (*motion*) выдвига́ть
(вы́двинуть *perf*) ♦ *vi* (*offer marriage*): **to ~ (to
sb)** де́лать (сде́лать *perf*) предложе́ние
(кому́-н); **to ~ sth/to do** *or* **doing** (*have in
mind*) предполага́ть (*impf*) что-н/+*infin*.

proposer [prə'pəuzə*] *n* (*BRIT*): **the ~ of the
motion** внося́щий(-ая) *m(f) adj* предложе́ние.

proposition [prɔpə'zɪʃən] *n* (*statement*)

утвержде́ние; (*offer*) предложе́ние; **to make
sb a ~** де́лать (сде́лать *perf*) предложе́ние
кому́-н.

propound [prə'paund] *vt* (*idea, argument*)
выдвига́ть (вы́двинуть *perf*).

proprietary [prə'praɪətərɪ] *adj* (*medicine*)
патенто́ванный; (*brand*) фи́рменный;
(*behaviour*) со́бственнический*.

proprietor [prə'praɪətə*] *n* (*of hotel, shop,
newspaper etc*) владе́лец(-лица).

propriety [prə'praɪətɪ] *n* присто́йность *f*.

propulsion [prə'pʌlʃən] *n* дви́жущая си́ла.

pro rata [prəu'rɑːtə] *adv* пропорциона́льно ♦
adj пропорциона́льный* (пропорционален);
on a ~ ~ basis на пропорциона́льной
осно́ве.

prosaic [prəu'zeɪk] *adj* (*person*) прозаи́чный*
(прозаи́чен); (*piece of writing*)
прозаи́ческий*.

Pros. Atty. *abbr* (*US*) = **prosecuting attorney**.

proscribe [prə'skraɪb] *vt* воспреща́ть
(воспрети́ть* *perf*).

prose [prəuz] *n* (*not poetry*) про́за; (*SCOL*)
отры́вок* для перево́да.

prosecute ['prɔsɪkjuːt] *vt* (*case*) вести́* (*impf*); **to
~ sb** подава́ть* (пода́ть* *perf*) на кого́-н в
суд.

prosecuting attorney ['prɔsɪkjuːtɪŋ-] *n* (*US*)
обвини́тель *m*.

prosecution [prɔsɪ'kjuːʃən] *n* (*LAW*: *action*)
суде́бное пресле́дование; (: *accusing side*)
обвине́ние.

prosecutor ['prɔsɪkjuːtə*] *n* обвини́тель *m*;
(*also*: **public ~**) прокуро́р.

prospect ['prɔspɛkt] *n* перспекти́ва ♦ *vi*: **to ~
for** разве́дывать (разве́дать *perf*) на +*acc*; **~s**
npl (*for work etc*) перспекти́вы *fpl*; **we are
faced with the ~ of leaving** нас ожида́ет
перспекти́ва отъе́зда; **there's every ~ of an
early victory** есть перспекти́ва ско́рой
побе́ды.

prospecting ['prɔspɛktɪŋ] *n* разве́дка,
изыска́ние.

prospective [prə'spɛktɪv] *adj* (*son-in-law*)
бу́дущий*; (*customer, candidate*)
возмо́жный.

prospectus [prə'spɛktəs] *n* проспе́кт.

prosper ['prɔspə*] *vi* преуспева́ть (преуспе́ть
perf).

prosperity [prɔ'spɛrɪtɪ] *n* преуспева́ние.

prosperous ['prɔspərəs] *adj* преуспева́ющий.

prostate ['prɔsteɪt] *n* (*also*: **~ gland**)
предста́тельная железа́*.

prostitute ['prɔstɪtjuːt] *n* проститу́тка*.

prostitution [prɔstɪ'tjuːʃən] *n* проститу́ция.

prostrate [*vt* prɔ'streɪt, *adj* 'prɔstreɪt] *vt*: **to ~ o.s.
before** па́дать (упа́сть* *perf*) ниц пе́ред +*instr*
♦ *adj* (*fig*) уби́тый; **to lie ~** лежа́ть (*impf*)

---

* marks translations which have irregular inflections. The Russian-English side of the dictionary gives inflectional information.

ничко́м.

protagonist [prə'tægənɪst] *n* (*supporter*) сторо́нник(-ица); (*leading participant*) де́ятель *m*; (*THEAT*) (гла́вный) геро́й.

protect [prə'tɛkt] *vt* защища́ть (защити́ть* *perf*).

protection [prə'tɛkʃən] *n* защи́та; **to be under sb's** ~ находи́ться* (*impf*) под защи́той кого́-н.

protectionism [prə'tɛkʃənɪzəm] *n* протекциони́зм.

protection racket *n* ра́кет.

protective [prə'tɛktɪv] *adj* (*clothing, layer, gesture etc*) защи́тный; (*person*) покрови́тельственный; ~ **custody** (*LAW*) опе́ка.

protector [prə'tɛktə'] *n* (*person*) защи́тник(-ница); (*device*) защи́тное устро́йство.

protégé ['prəutɛʒeɪ] *n* протеже́ *m ind*.

protégée ['prəutɛʒeɪ] *n* протеже́ *f ind*.

protein ['prəuti:n] *n* бело́к*, протеи́н.

pro tem [prəu'tɛm] *adv abbr* = **pro tempore**; (*for the time being*) вре́менно.

protest [*n* 'prəutɛst, *vb* prə'tɛst] *n* проте́ст ♦ *vi*: **to ~ about/against** протестова́ть (*impf*) по по́воду +*gen*/про́тив +*gen* ♦ *vt* (*insist*): **to ~ that** заявля́ть (заяви́ть* *perf*), что.

Protestant ['prɔtɪstənt] *n* протеста́нт(ка*) ♦ *adj* протеста́нтский*.

protester [prə'tɛstə'] *n* протесту́ющий*(-ая) *m(f) adj*.

protest march *n* марш проте́ста.

protestor [prə'tɛstə'] *n* = **protester**.

protocol ['prəutəkɔl] *n* протоко́л.

prototype ['prəutətaɪp] *n* прототи́п.

protracted [prə'træktɪd] *adj* затяну́вшийся.

protractor [prə'træktə'] *n* (*GEOM*) транспорти́р.

protrude [prə'tru:d] *vi* выдава́ться* (*impf*).

protuberance [prə'tju:bərəns] *n* вы́пуклость *f*.

proud [praud] *adj*: ~ (**of**) го́рдый* (горд) (+*instr*); **I am ~ to know him** я горжу́сь знако́мством с ним *or* тем, что я знако́м с ним; **to do sb ~** (*inf*) принима́ть (приня́ть* *perf*) кого́-н на сла́ву; **to do o.s. ~** (*inf*) име́ть (*impf*) основа́ния горди́ться.

proudly ['praudlɪ] *adv* (*say, smile*) го́рдо; (*show*) с го́рдостью.

prove [pru:v] *vt* дока́зывать (доказа́ть* *perf*) ♦ *vi*: **to ~** (**to be**) оказа́ться (оказа́ться* *impf*/*perf*) +*instr*; **to ~ o.s.** проявля́ть (прояви́ть* *perf*) себя́; **he was ~d right in the end** в конце́ (концо́в) бы́ло дока́зано, что он прав.

Provençal [prɔvɔn'sɑ:l] *adj* прованса́льский.

Provence [prɔ'vɑ̃:s] *n* Прова́нс.

proverb ['prɔvə:b] *n* посло́вица.

proverbial [prə'və:bɪəl] *adj* знамени́тый.

provide [prə'vaɪd] *vt* обеспе́чивать (обеспе́чить* *perf*) +*instr*; **to ~ sb with sth** обеспе́чивать (обеспе́чить* *perf*) кого́-н чем-н; **to be ~d with** (*person*) быть* (*impf*) обеспе́ченным(-ой); (*thing*) быть* (*impf*) снабжённым(-ой)

▸ **provide for** *vt fus* (*person*) обеспе́чивать (обеспе́чить* *perf*); (*future event*) предусма́тривать (предусмотре́ть* *perf*); (*emergency*) забо́титься (позабо́титься *perf*) о +*prp*.

provided (that) [prə'vaɪdɪd-] *conj* при усло́вии, что.

Providence ['prɔvɪdəns] *n* провиде́ние.

providing [prə'vaɪdɪŋ] *conj* = **provided (that)**.

province ['prɔvɪns] *n* (*of country*) о́бласть *f*; (*of person*) о́бласть *f*; **the ~s** *npl*: **in the ~s** (*regions*) в прови́нции.

provincial [prə'vɪnʃəl] *adj* провинциа́льный*.

provision [prə'vɪʒən] *n* (*supplying*) обеспе́чение; (*supply*) снабже́ние; (*stipulation*) усло́вие; (*of contract, agreement*) положе́ние; **~s** *npl* (*food*) прови́зия *fsg*; **to make ~s for** забо́титься (позабо́титься *perf*) о +*prp*; **there's no ~ for this in the contract** в контра́кте э́то не предусмо́трено.

provisional [prə'vɪʒənl] *adj* вре́менный ♦ *n*: **P~** (*IRISH: POL*) член Ирла́ндской Респу́блика́нской А́рмии.

provisional licence *n* (*BRIT: AUT*) предвари́тельные води́тельские права́ *ntpl*.

provisionally [prə'vɪʒnəlɪ] *adv* вре́менно.

proviso [prə'vaɪzəu] *n* усло́вие; **with the ~ that** ... с усло́вием, что ....

Provo ['prɔvəu] *n abbr* (*IRISH: POL: inf*) = **Provisional**.

provocation [prɔvə'keɪʃən] *n* провока́ция; **under ~** бу́дучи спровоци́рован.

provocative [prə'vɔkətɪv] *adj* (*remark, article, gesture*) провокацио́нный* (провокацио́нен), вызыва́ющий* (вызыва́юще); (*intellectually or sexually stimulating*) возбужда́ющий*.

provoke [prə'vəuk] *vt* (*person*) задира́ть (*impf*); (*fight, argument etc*) провоци́ровать (спровоци́ровать *perf*); **to ~ sb to sth/to do** *or* **into doing** провоци́ровать (спровоци́ровать *perf*) кого́-н на что-н/+*infin*.

provost ['prɔvəst] *n* (*BRIT: of university*) ре́ктор; (*SCOTTISH: POL*) мэр.

prow [prau] *n* (*NAUT*) нос*.

prowess ['prauɪs] *n* мастерство́; **his ~ as a footballer** его́ мастерство́ футболи́ста.

prowl [praul] *vi* (*also*: ~ **about**, ~ **around**) кра́сться* (*impf*) ♦ *n*: **to be on the ~ for** охо́титься* (*impf*) на +*acc*.

prowler ['praulə'] *n* подозри́тельный тип.

proximity [prɔk'smɪtɪ] *n* бли́зость *f*.

proxy ['prɔksɪ] *n*: **by ~** по дове́ренности.

PRP *abbr* (= *performance related pay*) опла́та по результа́там рабо́ты.

prude [pru:d] *n* ханжа́* *m/f*.

prudence ['pru:dns] *n* благоразу́мие.

prudent ['pru:dnt] *adj* благоразу́мный* (благоразу́мен).

prudish ['pru:dɪʃ] *adj* ха́нжеский.
prune [pru:n] *n* черносли́в* *m no pl* ◆ *vt* подреза́ть (подре́зать* *perf*).
pry [praɪ] *vi*: **to ~ (into)** сова́ть* (су́нуть *perf*) нос (в +*acc*).
PS *abbr* = **postscript**.
psalm [sɑ:m] *n* псало́м*.
PSAT *n abbr* (*US*) = Preliminary Scholastic Aptitude Test.
PSBR *n abbr* (*BRIT*: *ECON*: = public sector borrowing requirement) потре́бность госуда́рственного се́ктора в заёмных сре́дствах.
pseud [sju:d] (*BRIT*: *inf*) *n* (*intellectually*) псевдоинтеллектуа́л(ка*); (*socially*) позёр(ша).
pseudo- ['sju:dəu] *prefix* псе́вдо-.
pseudonym ['sju:dənɪm] *n* псевдони́м.
PST *abbr* (*US*) = Pacific Standard Time.
PSV *n abbr* (*BRIT*) = **public-service vehicle**.
psyche ['saɪkɪ] *n* пси́хика.
psychedelic [saɪkə'dɛlɪk] *adj* психодели́ческий.
psychiatric [saɪkɪ'ætrɪk] *adj* психиатри́ческий*.
psychiatrist [saɪ'kaɪətrɪst] *n* психиа́тр.
psychiatry [saɪ'kaɪətrɪ] *n* психиатри́я.
psychic ['saɪkɪk] *adj* (*person: also:~al*) яснови́дящий*; (*of the mind*) психи́ческий*.
psycho ['saɪkəu] *n* (*inf*) псих.
psychoanalyse [saɪkəu'ænəlaɪz] *vt* подверга́ть (подве́ргнуть *perf*) психоана́лизу.
psychoanalysis [saɪkəuə'nælɪsɪs] *n* психоана́лиз.
psychoanalyst [saɪkəu'ænəlɪst] *n* психоанали́тик.
psychological [saɪkə'lɔdʒɪkl] *adj* психологи́ческий*.
psychologist [saɪ'kɔlədʒɪst] *n* психо́лог.
psychology [saɪ'kɔlədʒɪ] *n* психоло́гия.
psychopath ['saɪkəupæθ] *n* психопа́т(ка*).
psychoses [saɪ'kəusi:z] *npl of* **psychosis**.
psychosis [saɪ'kəusɪs] (*pl* **psychoses**) *n* психо́з.
psychosomatic ['saɪkəusə'mætɪk] *adj* психосомати́ческий.
psychotherapy [saɪkəu'θɛrəpɪ] *n* психотерапи́я.
psychotic [saɪ'kɔtɪk] *adj* психи́чески больно́й.
PT *n abbr* (*BRIT*: *SCOL*: = physical training) физкульту́ра= *физическая культу́ра*).
Pt *abbr* (*in place names*) = Point.
pt *abbr* = **pint**, **point**.
PTA *n abbr* (= Parent-Teacher Association) о́бщество, де́ятельность кото́рого напра́влена на объедине́ние уси́лий шко́лы и роди́телей.
Pte *abbr* (*BRIT*: *MIL*) = **private**.
PTO *abbr* (= please turn over) смотри́ на оборо́те.

PTV *n abbr* (*US*: = pay television) комме́рческое телеви́дение; (= public television) некомме́рческое (общеобразова́тельное) телеви́дение.
pub [pʌb] *n* = **public house**.
pub crawl *n* (*inf*) похо́д по па́бам *or* ба́рам.
puberty ['pju:bətɪ] *n* полова́я зре́лость *f*.
pubic ['pju:bɪk] *adj* лобко́вый.
public ['pʌblɪk] *adj* обще́ственный; (*statement, action etc*) публи́чный ◆ *n*: **the ~** (*all people of country*) наро́д; (*particular set of people*) пу́блика; **the general ~** обще́ственность *f*; **this is ~ knowledge** э́то широко́ изве́стно; **to make ~** предава́ть* (преда́ть* *perf*) гла́сности; **to go ~** (*COMM*) выпуска́ть (вы́пустить* *perf*) а́кции на прода́жу че́рез би́ржу; **in ~** публи́чно.
public-address system [pʌblɪkə'drɛs-] *n* (ра́дио)трансля́ция.
publican ['pʌblɪkən] *n* содержа́тель(ница) *m(f)* пивно́го ба́ра *or* па́ба.
publication [pʌblɪ'keɪʃən] *n* публика́ция, изда́ние.
public company *n* (*COMM*) публи́чная компа́ния, компа́ния откры́того ти́па.
public convenience *n* (*BRIT*) обще́ственный туале́т.
public holiday *n* общенаро́дный пра́здник.
public house *n* (*BRIT*) паб, пивна́я *f adj*, пивно́й бар.
publicity [pʌb'lɪsɪtɪ] *n* (*information*) рекла́ма, па́блисити *nt ind*; (*attention*) шуми́ха.
publicize ['pʌblɪsaɪz] *vt* (*fact, event*) предава́ть* (преда́ть* *perf*) гла́сности.
public limited company *n* (*COMM*) публи́чная компа́ния с ограни́ченной отве́тственностью.
publicly ['pʌblɪklɪ] *adv* публи́чно; (*COMM*): **~ owned** госуда́рственный.
public opinion *n* обще́ственное мне́ние.
public ownership *n*: **to be taken into ~ ~** (*COMM*) переходи́ть* (перейти́* *perf*) в госуда́рственную *or* общенаро́дную со́бственность.
Public Prosecutor *n* ≈ генера́льный прокуро́р.
public relations *npl* вне́шние свя́зи *fpl*.
public relations officer *n* сотру́дник отде́ла вне́шних свя́зей.
public school *n* (*BRIT*) ча́стная шко́ла; (*US*) госуда́рственная шко́ла.
public sector *n*: **the ~ ~** госуда́рственный се́ктор.
public-service vehicle [pʌblɪk'sə:vɪs-] *n* (*BRIT*) обще́ственное тра́нспортное сре́дство.
public-spirited [pʌblɪk'spɪrɪtɪd] *adj* забо́тящийся об обще́ственных интере́сах.
public transport *n* обще́ственный тра́нспорт.

---

* marks translations which have irregular inflections. The Russian-English side of the dictionary gives inflectional information.

public utility n компа́ния, обеспе́чивающая како́й-либо вид коммуна́льных услу́г.

public works npl обще́ственные сооруже́ния ntpl.

publish ['pʌblɪʃ] vt (book, magazine) издава́ть* (изда́ть* perf); (letter, article) публикова́ть (опубликова́ть perf).

publisher ['pʌblɪʃə'] n (person) изда́тель m; (company) изда́тельство.

publishing ['pʌblɪʃɪŋ] n (profession) изда́тельское де́ло; (of a book) изда́ние, публика́ция.

publishing company n изда́тельство.

puce [pjuːs] adj краснова́то-кори́чневый.

puck [pʌk] n (ICE HOCKEY) ша́йба.

pucker ['pʌkə'] vt мо́рщить (намо́рщить or смо́рщить perf).

pudding ['pudɪŋ] n пу́динг; (BRIT: dessert) сла́дкое nt adj; **rice** ~ ри́совый пу́динг; **black** ~, (US) **blood** ~ кровяна́я колбаса́*.

puddle ['pʌdl] n лу́жа.

puerile ['pjuəraɪl] adj ребя́ческий*.

Puerto Rico ['pwəːtəu'riːkəu] n Пуэ́рто-Ри́ко f ind.

puff [pʌf] n (of cigarette, pipe) затя́жка*; (gasp) пыхте́ние; (of wind) дунове́ние; (of smoke) клуб ◆ vi (breathe loudly) пыхте́ть* (impf) ◆ vt: **to** ~ **one's pipe** затя́гиваться (затяну́ться* perf)

▶ **puff out** vt (chest, cheeks) раздува́ть (разду́ть perf); (smoke) выпуска́ть (вы́пустить* perf).

puffed [pʌft] adj (inf: out of breath) запыха́вшийся.

puffin ['pʌfɪn] n (ZOOL) ту́пик.

puff pastry (US **puff paste**) n слоёное те́сто.

puffy ['pʌfɪ] adj опу́хший*.

pugnacious [pʌg'neɪʃəs] adj зади́ристый (зади́рист).

pull [pul] n (of moon, magnet, the sea etc) притяже́ние; (fig) тя́га ◆ vt тяну́ть* (потяну́ть* perf); (trigger) нажима́ть (нажа́ть perf) на +acc; (close: curtains, blind) заде́ргивать (задёрнуть perf); (inf: people) привлека́ть (привле́чь* perf); (pint of beer) нака́чивать (накача́ть perf) ◆ vi (tug) тяну́ть* (impf); **to give sth a** ~ (tug) тяну́ть* (потяну́ть* perf); **to** ~ **a face** кро́ить (скро́ить perf) грима́су; **to** ~ **to pieces** разрыва́ть (разорва́ть* perf) на ча́сти; **to** ~ **one's punches** дра́ться* (impf) вполси́лы; **he doesn't** ~ **his punches** (fig) он дерётся всерьёз; **to** ~ **one's weight** выполня́ть (вы́полнить perf) свою́ часть рабо́ты; **to** ~ **o.s. together** взять* (perf) себя́ в ру́ки; **to** ~ **sb's leg** (fig) разы́грывать (разыгра́ть perf) кого́-н; **to** ~ **strings (for sb)** пуска́ть (пусти́ть* perf) в ход все свя́зи (для кого́-н)

▶ **pull about** vt (BRIT: object, person) трепа́ть (impf)

▶ **pull apart** vt разрыва́ть (разорва́ть* perf) на

куски́

▶ **pull back** vi отступа́ть (отступи́ть* perf)

▶ **pull down** vt (building) сноси́ть* (снести́* perf); (tree) сруба́ть (сруби́ть* perf)

▶ **pull in** vt (money) загреба́ть (загрести́* perf); (crowds, people) привлека́ть (привле́чь* perf); (subj: police: suspect) сца́пать (perf)

▶ **pull into** vt (AUT) подъезжа́ть (подъе́хать* perf) к +dat

▶ **pull off** vt (clothes etc) стя́гивать (стяну́ть* perf); (fig): **he managed to** ~ **it off** ему́ удало́сь ски́нуть э́то с себя́

▶ **pull out** vt (extract) выта́скивать (вы́тащить perf) ◆ vi: **to** ~ **out (from)** (AUT: from kerb) отъезжа́ть (отъе́хать* perf) (от +gen); (RAIL) отходи́ть* (отойти́* perf) (от +gen); (withdraw): **to** ~ **out (of)** выходи́ть* (вы́йти* perf) (из +gen)

▶ **pull over** vi (AUT) подъезжа́ть (подъе́хать* perf) к кра́ю доро́ги

▶ **pull round** vi (unconscious person) приходи́ть* (прийти́* perf) в себя́; (sick person) поправля́ться (попра́виться* perf)

▶ **pull through** vi (MED) выкара́бкиваться (вы́карабкаться perf)

▶ **pull up** vi (stop) остана́вливаться (останови́ться* perf) ◆ vt (object, clothing) подтя́гивать (подтяну́ть* perf); (plant) вырыва́ть (вы́рвать* perf) (с ко́рнем); (chair) пододвига́ть (пододви́нуть perf).

pullback ['pulbæk] n отступле́ние.

pulley ['pulɪ] n шкив*.

pull-out ['pulaut] n (of forces etc) отхо́д ◆ cpd (pages) вкладно́й; ~ **magazine** журна́л с вкла́дками.

pullover ['puləuvə'] n пуло́вер.

pulp [pʌlp] n (of fruit) мя́коть f; (for paper) бума́жная ма́сса; (pej: magazines, fiction) чти́во; **to reduce sth to a** ~ превраща́ть (преврати́ть* perf) что-н в мя́гкую ма́ссу or пу́льпу.

pulpit ['pulpɪt] n ка́федра.

pulsate [pʌl'seɪt] vi пульси́ровать (impf); (music) вибри́ровать (impf).

pulse [pʌls] n (ANAT) пульс; (of blood) пульса́ция; (of heart) бие́ние; (rhythm) такт ◆ vi пульси́ровать (impf); ~**s** npl (BOT) семена́ бобо́вых, употребля́емые в пи́щу; (CULIN) бобо́вые pl adj; **to take** or **feel sb's** ~ нащу́пывать (нащу́пать perf) чей-н пульс.

pulverize ['pʌlvəraɪz] vt размельча́ть (размельчи́ть perf); (fig: destroy) сокруша́ть (сокруши́ть perf).

puma ['pjuːmə] n пу́ма.

pumice ['pʌmɪs] n (also: ~ **stone**) пе́мза.

pummel ['pʌml] vt колоти́ть* (impf).

pump [pʌmp] n насо́с; (also: **petrol** ~) бензоколо́нка*; (shoe) паруси́новая ту́фля* ◆ vt кача́ть (impf); (extract: oil, water, gas) выка́чивать (вы́качать perf); **to** ~ **sb for information** выка́чивать (impf) из кого́-н

информа́цию
▶ **pump up** *vt* нака́чивать (накача́ть *perf*).
pumpkin ['pʌmpkɪn] *n* ты́ква.
pun [pʌn] *n* каламбу́р.
punch [pʌntʃ] *n* (*blow*) уда́р; (*fig: force*) заря́д; (*for making holes*) дыроко́л; (*drink*) пунш ◆ *vt* (*make a hole in*) пробива́ть (проби́ть* *perf*); (*hit*): **to ~ sb/sth** ударя́ть (уда́рить *perf*) кого́-н/что-н кулако́м; **to ~ a hole (in)** пробива́ть (проби́ть* *perf*) отве́рстие (в +*prp*)
▶ **punch in** *vi* (*US*) отмеча́ться (отме́титься* *perf*) (*приходя́ на рабо́ту*)
▶ **punch out** *vi* (*US*) отмеча́ться (отме́титься* *perf*) (*уходя́ с рабо́ты*).
Punch and Judy show *n* Панч и Джу́ди (*ку́кольное представле́ние*).
punch-drunk ['pʌntʃdrʌŋk] (*BRIT*) *adj* (*confused*) со сму́тным; **~ boxer** боксёр с травматологи́ческой энцералопа́телей.
punch(ed) card *n* (*COMPUT*) перфока́рта.
punch line *n* изю́минка.
punch-up ['pʌntʃʌp] *n* (*BRIT: inf*) потасо́вка*.
punctual ['pʌŋktjuəl] *adj* пунктуа́льный* (пунктуа́лен).
punctuality [pʌŋktju'ælɪtɪ] *n* пунктуа́льность *f*.
punctually ['pʌŋktjuəlɪ] *adv* (*arrive, leave, deliver*) пунктуа́льно; **the film will start ~ at 6** фильм начнётся ро́вно в 6 часо́в.
punctuation [pʌŋktju'eɪʃən] *n* пунктуа́ция.
punctuation mark *n* знак препина́ния.
puncture ['pʌŋktʃəʳ] *n* (*AUT*) проко́л ◆ *vt* прока́лывать (проколо́ть* *perf*); **I have a ~** у меня́ проко́лота ши́на.
pundit ['pʌndɪt] *n* до́ка *m/f*.
pungent ['pʌndʒənt] *adj* е́дкий* (е́док).
punish ['pʌnɪʃ] *vt* (*person*) нака́зывать (наказа́ть* *perf*); **to ~ sb for sth** нака́зывать (наказа́ть* *perf*) кого́-н за что-н; **this crime must be ~ed** э́то преступле́ние должно́ быть* нака́зано.
punishable ['pʌnɪʃəbl] *adj* наказу́емый (наказу́ем).
punishing ['pʌnɪʃɪŋ] *adj* (*fig: defeat, exercise*) изма́тывающий.
punishment ['pʌnɪʃmənt] *n* наказа́ние; **he took a lot of ~** (*inf: boxer*) ему́ си́льно доста́лось.
punitive ['pjuːnɪtɪv] *adj* кара́тельный.
Punjab [pʌn'dʒɑːb] *n* Пенджа́б.
Punjabi [pʌn'dʒɑːbɪ] *n* пенджа́бец*(-бка*); (*LING*) пенджа́бский* язы́к* ◆ *adj* пенджа́бский*.
punk [pʌŋk] *n* (*also: ~ rocker*) панк; (*also: ~ rock*) панк-рок; (*US: inf: thug*) громи́ла *m*.
punnet ['pʌnɪt] *n* корзи́ночка*.
punt [pʌnt] *n* (*boat*) плоскодо́нка* ◆ *vi* пла́вать/плыть* (*impf*) на плоскодо́нке.
punter ['pʌntəʳ] *n* (*BRIT: gambler*) (профессиона́льный) игро́к*; (*inf: customer*)

клие́нт(ка*); **the ~s** (*inf*) клиенту́ра *fsg*.
puny ['pjuːnɪ] *adj* хи́лый (хил).
pup [pʌp] *n* (*young dog, seal etc*) щено́к*.
pupil ['pjuːpl] *n* (*SCOL*) учени́к*(-и́ца); (*of eye*) зрачо́к*.
puppet ['pʌpɪt] *n* (*also fig*) марионе́тка*.
puppet government *n* марионе́точное прави́тельство.
puppy ['pʌpɪ] *n* (*young dog*) щено́к*.
purchase ['pəːtʃɪs] *n* поку́пка*; (*grip etc*) захва́т ◆ *vt* покупа́ть (купи́ть* *perf*); **to get a ~ on** ухва́тываться (ухвати́ться* *perf*) за +*acc*.
purchase order *n* зака́з на това́ры.
purchase price *n* заку́почная цена́*.
purchaser ['pəːtʃɪsəʳ] *n* покупа́тель *m*.
purchase tax *n* нало́г на поку́пку.
purchasing power ['pəːtʃɪsɪŋ-] *n* покупа́тельная спосо́бность *f*.
pure [pjuəʳ] *adj* чи́стый; (*water, air, woman*) чи́стый* (чист); **a ~ wool jumper** сви́тер из чи́стой ше́рсти; **~ and simple** про́сто-на́просто; **it's laziness ~ and simple** э́то про́сто-на́просто лень.
purebred ['pjuəbrɛd] *adj* чистопоро́дный, чистокро́вный.
purée ['pjuəreɪ] *n* пюре́ *nt ind*.
purely ['pjuəlɪ] *adv* чи́сто.
purgatory ['pəːgətərɪ] *n* (*REL*) чисти́лище; (*fig*) муче́ние.
purge [pəːdʒ] *n* (*POL*) чи́стка*; (*MED*) слаби́тельное *nt adj* ◆ *vt* (*thoughts, mind etc*) очища́ть (очи́стить* *perf*); (*organization*): **to ~ (of)** чи́стить* (очи́стить* *perf*) (от +*gen*); (*extremists etc*): **to ~ from** вычища́ть (вы́чистить* *perf*) от +*gen*.
purification [pjuərɪfɪ'keɪʃən] *n* очи́стка*.
purify ['pjuərɪfaɪ] *vt* очища́ть (очи́стить* *perf*).
purist ['pjuərɪst] *n* пури́ст.
puritan ['pjuərɪtən] *n* пурита́нин*(-а́нка*).
puritanical [pjuərɪ'tænɪkl] *adj* пурита́нский*.
purity ['pjuərɪtɪ] *n* чистота́.
purl [pəːl] *n* изна́ночная вя́зка ◆ *vt* провя́зывать (провяза́ть *perf*) изна́ночной вязк.
purloin [pəː'lɔɪn] *vt* присва́ивать (присво́ить *perf*).
purple ['pəːpl] *adj* фиоле́товый.
purport [pəː'pɔːt] *vi*: **he ~s to be an objective party** он притяза́ет на роль объекти́вных наблюда́телей; **he ~s to care about this** он притяза́ет на то, что он обеспоко́ен э́той.
purpose ['pəːpəs] *n* цель *f*; **on ~** наме́ренно; **for illustrative ~s** в ка́честве иллюстра́ции; **for the ~s of this meeting** пресле́дуя це́ли да́нного собра́ния; **to no ~** напра́сно.
purpose-built ['pəːpəs'bɪlt] *adj* (*BRIT*): **~ school** шко́ла целево́го назначе́ния.
purposeful ['pəːpəsful] *adj* целеустремлённый*

---

* marks translations which have irregular inflections. The Russian-English side of the dictionary gives inflectional information.

(целеустремлён).

purposely ['pə:pəslɪ] *adv* преднаме́ренно.

purr [pə:ˈ] *vi* мурлы́кать* *(impf)*.

purse [pə:s] *n* (*BRIT*) кошелёк*; (*US: handbag*) су́мка* ♦ *vt:* **to ~ one's lips** поджима́ть (поджа́ть* *perf*) гу́бы.

purser ['pə:səˈ] *n* (*NAUT*) (судово́й) казначе́й.

purse-snatcher ['pə:snætʃəˈ] *n* (*US*) вор, краду́щий су́мки.

pursue [pə'sju:] *vt* (*person, thing, aim*) пресле́довать *(impf)*; (*fig: activity*) осуществля́ть *(impf)*; (: *interest*) занима́ться *(impf)* +*instr*; (: *plan*) сле́довать *(impf)* +*dat*.

pursuer [pə'sju:əˈ] *n* пресле́дователь(ница) *m(f)*.

pursuit [pə'sju:t] *n* (*of person, thing*) пресле́дование; (*of happiness, wealth etc*) по́иски *mpl*; (*pastime*) заня́тие; **scientific ~s** нау́чные по́иски; **in (the) ~ of sth** (*of wealth, fame*) в пого́не за чем-н; (*of truth, knowledge*) в по́исках чего́-н.

purveyor [pə'veɪəˈ] *n* поставщи́к(-и́ца).

pus [pʌs] *n* гной.

push [puʃ] *n* (*of button etc*) нажа́тие; (*of car, door, person etc*) толчо́к*; (*fig: urgent demand*) тре́бование ♦ *vt* (*press*) нажима́ть (нажа́ть* *perf*); (*shove*) толка́ть (толкну́ть *perf*); (*promote*) прота́лкивать (протолкну́ть *perf*) ♦ *vi* (*press*) нажима́ть (нажа́ть* *perf*); (*shove*) толка́ться *(impf)*; (*fig*): **to ~ for** тре́бовать (потре́бовать *perf*) +*acc or* +gen; **at a ~** (*BRIT*: *inf*) при жела́нии; **to ~ a door open** распа́хивать (распахну́ть *perf*) дверь; **to ~ a door shut** захло́пывать (захло́пнуть *perf*) дверь; **"push"** (*on door*) „от себя́"; (*on bell*) „нажми́те"; **to be ~ed for time/money** име́ть *(impf)* ма́ло вре́мени/ де́нег; **she is ~ing fifty** (*inf*) ей под пятьдеся́т

▶ **push aside** *vt* (*person, object*) отта́лкивать (оттолкну́ть *perf*); (*issue*) отмета́ть (отмести́* *perf*)

▶ **push in** *vi* влеза́ть (влезть* *perf*)

▶ **push off** *vi* (*inf*) убира́ться (убра́ться* *perf*)

▶ **push on** *vi* (*continue*) дви́гаться *(impf)* да́льше *or* вперёд

▶ **push over** *vt* опроки́дывать (опроки́нуть *perf*)

▶ **push through** *vi* (*crowd etc*) прота́лкиваться (протолкну́ться *perf*) ♦ *vt* (*measure, scheme*) прота́лкивать (протолкну́ть *perf*)

▶ **push up** *vt* (*prices*) повыша́ть (повы́сить* *perf*).

push-bike ['puʃbaɪk] *n* (*BRIT*) велосипе́д.

push-button ['puʃbʌtn] *adj* кно́пка*.

pushchair ['puʃtʃeəˈ] *n* (*BRIT*) (складна́я) коля́ска*.

pusher ['puʃəˈ] *n* (*drug pusher*) торго́вец* (-вка*) нарко́тиками.

pushover ['puʃəuvəˈ] *n* (*inf*): **it's a ~** э́то па́ра пустяко́в *or* пустяко́вое де́ло.

push-up ['puʃʌp] *n* (*US: press-up*) отжима́ние.

pushy ['puʃɪ] *adj* (*pej: person*) насты́рный*

(насты́рен).

puss [pus] *n* (*inf*) ки́ска*.

pussy(cat) ['pusɪ(kæt)] *n* (*inf: female*) ки́ска*; (: *male*) ко́тик.

put [put] (*pt, pp* put) *vt* (*thing: horizontally*) класть* (положи́ть *perf*); (: *vertically*) ста́вить* (поста́вить* *perf*); (*person: in institution*) помеща́ть (помести́ть* *perf*); (: *in prison, in situation*) сажа́ть (посади́ть* *perf*); (*idea, remark etc*) говори́ть (сказа́ть* *perf*); (*case, view*) излага́ть (изложи́ть* *perf*); (*question, word, sentence*) ста́вить* (поста́вить* *perf*); (*estimate*) относи́ть* (отнести́* *perf*), ста́вить* (поста́вить* *perf*); **to ~ sb in a good mood** приводи́ть* (привести́* *perf*) кого́-н в хоро́шее настрое́ние; **to ~ sb in a bad mood** по́ртить* (испо́ртить* *perf*) кому́-н настрое́ние; **to ~ sb to bed** укла́дывать (уложи́ть* *perf*) кого́-н спать *or* в крова́ть; **to ~ sb to a lot of trouble** доставля́ть (доста́вить* *perf*) кому́-н мно́го хлопо́т; **how shall I ~ it?** как бы э́то сказа́ть?; **to ~ a lot of time into sth** уделя́ть (удели́ть *perf*) мно́го вре́мени чему́-н; **to ~ money on a horse** ста́вить* (поста́вить* *perf*) на ло́шадь; **the cost is now ~ at 2 billion pounds** сейча́с сто́имость оце́нивается в 2 миллиа́рда фу́нта; **I ~ it to you that ...** я говорю́ Вам, что ...; **to stay ~** остава́ться* (оста́ться* *perf*)

▶ **put about** *vi* (*NAUT*) развора́чиваться (разверну́ться *perf*) ♦ *vt* (*rumour*) пуска́ть (пусти́ть* *perf*)

▶ **put across** *vt* (*ideas etc*) объясня́ть (объясни́ть *perf*)

▶ **put around** *vt* = put about

▶ **put aside** *vt* откла́дывать (отложи́ть* *perf*); (*idea*) отгоня́ть (отогна́ть* *perf*)

▶ **put away** *vt* (*store*) убира́ть (убра́ть* *perf*); (*eat*) умина́ть (умя́ть* *perf*); (*save*) откла́дывать (отложи́ть* *perf*); (*imprison*) упря́тать* *perf*)

▶ **put back** *vt* (*replace*) класть* (положи́ть* *perf*) на ме́сто; (*postpone*) откла́дывать (отложи́ть* *perf*); (*delay*) заде́рживать (задержа́ть* *perf*); **this will ~ us back 10 years** э́то отбро́сит нас на 10 лет наза́д

▶ **put by** *vt* откла́дывать (отложи́ть* *perf*)

▶ **put down** *vt* (*place*) класть* (положи́ть* *perf*), ста́вить* (поста́вить* *perf*); (*note down*) запи́сывать (записа́ть* *perf*); (*suppress, humiliate*) подавля́ть (подави́ть* *perf*); (*animal: kill*) умерщвля́ть (умертви́ть* *perf*); (*attribute*): **to ~ sth down to** объясня́ть (объясни́ть *perf*) что-н +*instr*

▶ **put forth** *vt* объявля́ть (объяви́ть* *perf*)

▶ **put forward** *vt* (*ideas, proposal*) выдвига́ть (вы́двинуть *perf*); (*date*) переноси́ть* (перенести́* *perf*); (*watch, clock*) переводи́ть* (перевести́* *perf*) вперёд

▶ **put in** *vt* (*application, complaint*) подава́ть (пода́ть* *perf*); (*time, effort*) вкла́дывать

(вложи́ть *perf*); (*gas, electricity*) проводи́ть*
(провести́* *perf*) ♦ *vi* (*NAUT*) заходи́ть* (зайти́*
perf) в порт; **the ship ~ in at Plymouth**
кора́бль* зашёл в Пли́мут
► **put in for** *vt fus* (*job, promotion*) подава́ть*
(пода́ть* *perf*) заявле́ние на +*acc*
► **put off** *vt* (*delay*) откла́дывать (отложи́ть*
perf); (*discourage*) отта́лкивать (оттолкну́ть
perf); (*switch off*) выключа́ть (вы́ключить *perf*)
► **put on** *vt* (*clothes*) надева́ть (наде́ть* *perf*);
(*make-up, ointment etc*) накла́дывать
(наложи́ть* *perf*); (*light etc*) включа́ть
(включи́ть* *perf*); (*play, kettle, record, dinner*)
ста́вить* (поста́вить* *perf*); (*brake*) жать*
(нажа́ть* *perf*) на +*acc*; (*extra bus, train etc*)
пуска́ть (пусти́ть* *perf*); (*assume: look*)
напуска́ть (напусти́ть* *perf*) на себя́;
(*behaviour*) принима́ть (приня́ть* *perf*); (*inf:*
tease) разы́грывать (разыгра́ть *perf*);
(*inform, indicate*): **to ~ sb on to sb** связа́ть*
(*perf*) кого́-н с кем-н; **to ~ sb on to sth**
выводи́ть* (вы́вести* *perf*) кого́-н на что-н;
to ~ on weight поправля́ться (попра́виться*
perf); **to ~ on airs** ва́жничать (*impf*)
► **put out** *vt* (*fire*) туши́ть* (потуши́ть* *perf*);
(*candle, cigarette*) гаси́ть* (погаси́ть* *perf*);
(*electric light*) выключа́ть (вы́ключить *perf*);
(*rubbish*) выноси́ть* (вы́нести* *perf*); (*cat*)
выпуска́ть (вы́пустить* *perf*); (*one's hand*)
вытя́гивать (вы́тянуть *perf*); (*story*)
выду́мывать (вы́думать *perf*), пуска́ть
(пусти́ть* *perf*); (*BRIT: dislocate*) выви́хивать
(вы́вихнуть *perf*); (*inf*): **he was rather ~ out** он
был вы́бит из колеи́ ♦ *vi* (*NAUT*): **to ~ out to**
sea выходи́ть* (вы́йти* *perf*) в мо́ре; **to ~ out**
from Plymouth выходи́ть* (вы́йти* *perf*) из
Пли́мута
► **put through** *vt* (*person, call*) соединя́ть
(соедини́ть* *perf*); (*plan, agreement*)
выполня́ть (вы́полнить *perf*); **~ me through**
to Miss Blair соедини́те меня́ с мисс Блэр
► **put together** *vt* соединя́ть (соедини́ть* *perf*);
(*furniture, toys etc*) собира́ть (собра́ть* *perf*);
(*meal*) гото́вить* (пригото́вить* *perf*); (*plan,*
campaign) организова́ть (*impf/perf*)
► **put up** *vt* (*building, tent*) ста́вить*
(поста́вить* *perf*); (*umbrella*) раскрыва́ть
(раскры́ть* *perf*); (*hood*) надева́ть (наде́ть*
perf); (*poster, sign etc*) выве́шивать

(вы́весить* *perf*); (*price, cost*) поднима́ть
(подня́ть* *perf*); (*guest, visitor*) размеща́ть
(размести́ть* *perf*); (*opposition, resistance*)
подавля́ть (подави́ть* *perf*); (*incite*): **to ~ sb**
up to sth толка́ть (толкну́ть *perf*) кого́-н на
что-н; **to ~ sth up for sale** выставля́ть
(вы́ставить* *perf*) что-н на прода́жу
► **put upon** *vt fus*: **to be ~ upon: we are not**
prepared to be ~ upon мы не привы́кли,
чтобы на нас е́здили
► **put up with** *vt fus* терпе́ть (*impf*), мири́ться
(*impf*) с +*instr*.
putative ['pju:tətɪv] *adj* предполага́емый.
putrid ['pju:trɪd] *adj* гнило́й.
putt [pʌt] *n* (*GOLF*) уда́р, загоня́ющий мяч в
лу́нку (в го́льфе).
putter ['pʌtə] *n* (*GOLF*) коро́ткая клю́шка для
го́льфа ♦ *vi* (*US*) = **potter**.
putting green ['pʌtɪŋ-] *n* по́ле для го́льфа, на
кото́ром мяч прогоня́ется к лу́нками а не
поддаётся уда́рами.
putty ['pʌtɪ] *n* зама́зка.
put-up ['putʌp] *n*: **~ job** (*BRIT: inf*) под-
стро́енное де́ло*.
puzzle ['pʌzl] *n* (*question, mystery*) зага́дка;
(*game, toy*) головоло́мка*; (*also*: **crossword**
~) кроссво́рд ♦ *vt* озада́чивать (озада́чить
perf) ♦ *vi*: **to ~ over sth** лома́ть (*impf*) го́лову
над чем-н; **to be ~d about sth** пребыва́ть
(*impf*) в недоуме́нии по по́воду чего́-н.
puzzling ['pʌzlɪŋ] *adj* запу́танный* (запу́тан).
PVC *n abbr* (= *polyvinyl chloride*) поливинил-
хлори́д.
Pvt. *abbr* (*US: MIL*) = **private**.
PW *n abbr* (*US*) = **prisoner of war**.
p.w. *abbr* = **per week**.
PX *n abbr* (*US: MIL*) = **post exchange**.
pygmy ['pɪgmɪ] *n* пигме́й.
pyjamas [pɪ'dʒɑ:məz] (*US* **pajamas**) *npl*: (**a pair**
of) **~** пижа́ма *fsg*.
pylon ['paɪlən] *n* пило́н, опо́ра.
Pyongyang ['pjɒŋ'jæŋ] *n* Пхенья́н.
pyramid ['pɪrəmɪd] *n* (*ARCHIT, GEOM*) пирами́да;
(*pile*) гру́да.
Pyrenean [pɪrə'ni:ən] *adj* пирене́йский.
Pyrenees [pɪrə'ni:z] *npl*: **the ~** Пирене́и *pl*.
Pyrex® ['paɪrɛks] *n* пи́рекс ♦ *cpd*: **~ dish**
таре́лка пи́рекс.
python ['paɪθən] *n* пито́н.

---

* marks translations which have irregular inflections. The Russian-English side of the dictionary gives inflectional information.

~ Q, q ~

Q, q [kju:] *n (letter)* 17-ая бу́ква англи́йского алфави́та.

Qatar [kæˈtɑːʳ] *n* Ка́тар.

QC *n abbr (BRIT: LAW: = Queen's Counsel)* короле́вский* адвока́т *(адвока́тский ранг)*.

QED *abbr (= quod erat demonstrandum)* что и тре́бовалось доказа́ть.

QM *n abbr (MIL)* = **quartermaster**.

q.t. *n abbr (inf) = quiet*: **on the ~**. тишко́м.

qty *abbr (= quantity)* коли́чество.

quack [kwæk] *n* кря́канье; *(doctor)* шарлата́н ◆ *vi* кря́кать *(impf)*.

quad [kwɔd] *abbr* = **quadrangle, quadruplet**.

quadrangle [ˈkwɔdræŋgl] *n (courtyard)* двор*; *(MATH)* четырёхуго́льник.

quadrilateral [kwɔdrɪˈlætərəl] *n* четырёху-го́льник.

quadruped [ˈkwɔdrupɛd] *n* четвероно́гое *nt adj*.

quadruple [kwɔˈdruːpl] *vt* увели́чивать (увели́чить *perf*) в четы́ре ра́за ◆ *vi* увели́чиваться (увели́читься *perf*) в четы́ре ра́за.

quadruplets [kwɔˈdruːplɪts] *npl* четы́ре близнеца́.

quagmire [ˈkwægmaɪəʳ] *n (also fig)* тряси́на.

quail [kweɪl] *n (bird)* пе́репел(-пёлка*) ◆ *vi*: **to ~ at the thought of** содрога́ться (содрогну́ться *perf*) при мы́сли об +*prp*.

quaint [kweɪnt] *adj (house, village)* причу́д-ливый (причу́длив); *(ideas, customs)* своеобра́зный* (своеобра́зен).

quake [kweɪk] *vi* трепета́ть* *(impf)*.

Quaker [ˈkweɪkəʳ] *n* ква́кер.

qualification [kwɔlɪfɪˈkeɪʃən] *n (usu pl: academic, vocational)* квалифика́ция *no pl*; *(skill, quality)* ка́чество; *(reservation)* огово́рка*; **what are your ~s?** кака́я у Вас квалифика́ция?

qualified [ˈkwɔlɪfaɪd] *adj (trained: person)* квалифици́рованный (квалифици́рован); *(limited: approval etc)* небезусло́вный; **I'm not ~ to discuss/judge that** я не компете́нтен обсужда́ть/суди́ть об э́том; **the show was a ~ success** спекта́кль не по́льзовался осо́бым успе́хом; **he's not ~ for the job** у него́ нет необходи́мой квалифика́ции для э́той рабо́ты.

qualify [ˈkwɔlɪfaɪ] *vt (modify: make more specific)* уточня́ть (уточни́ть *perf*); *(: express reservation)* огова́ривать (оговори́ть *perf*); *(make competent)*: **to ~ sb to do** позволя́ть (позво́лить *perf*) кому́-н +*infin* ◆ *vi*: **to ~ as an engineer** получа́ть (получи́ть* *perf*) квалифика́цию инжене́ра; *(be eligible: for benefit, grant)*: **to ~ (for)** име́ть *(impf)* пра́во (на +*acc*); *(in competition)*: **to ~ (for)** выходи́ть* (вы́йти *perf*) (в +*acc*).

qualifying [ˈkwɔlɪfaɪŋ] *adj*: **~ exam** квалификацио́нный экза́мен; **~ round** отбо́рочное соревнова́ние.

qualitative [ˈkwɔlɪtətɪv] *adj* ка́чественный.

quality [ˈkwɔlɪtɪ] *n (standard, characteristic)* ка́чество; *(property: of wood, stone etc)* сво́йство ◆ *cpd* ка́чественный; **of good/poor ~** хоро́шего/плохо́го ка́чества.

quality control *n* контро́ль *m* ка́чества.

quality of life *n* у́ровень* *m* жи́зни.

quality papers *npl (BRIT)*: **the ~ ~** серьёзные газе́ты *fpl*.

qualm [kwɑːm] *n* сомне́ние; **to have ~s about** сомнева́ться *(impf)* в +*prp*.

quandary [ˈkwɔndrɪ] *n*: **to be in a ~** быть* *(impf)* в затрудне́нии.

quango [ˈkwæŋgəu] *n abbr (BRIT: = quasi-autonomous non-governmental organization)* организа́ция, име́ющая распоряди́тельные и координацио́нные фу́нкции.

quantifiable [ˈkwɔntɪfaɪəbl] *adj* измери́мый (измери́м).

quantitative [ˈkwɔntɪtətɪv] *adj* коли́чественный.

quantity [ˈkwɔntɪtɪ] *n* коли́чество; *(large amount)*: **in ~** в большо́м коли́честве; **an unknown ~** зага́дка.

quantity surveyor *n* инжене́р-планови́к* *(на строи́тельных рабо́тах)*.

quantum leap [ˈkwɔntəm-] *n* скачо́к*.

quarantine [ˈkwɔrəntiːn] *n* каранти́н.

quark [kwɑːk] *n* кварк.

quarrel [ˈkwɔrl] *n* ссо́ра ◆ *vi*: **to ~ (with)** ссо́риться (поссо́риться *perf*) (с +*instr*); **to have a ~ with sb** поссо́риться *(perf)* с кем-н; **I've no ~ with him** у меня́ нет прете́нзий к нему́; **I can't ~ with that** я не могу́ не согласи́ться с э́тим.

quarrelsome [ˈkwɔrəlsəm] *adj* вздо́рный* (вздо́рен).

quarry [ˈkwɔrɪ] *n* карье́р; *(for stone)*

каменоло́мня; (*hunted animal*) добы́ча ♦ *vt* добыва́ть (добы́ть* *perf*).

quart [kwɔ:t] *n* ква́рта.

quarter ['kwɔ:tə'] *n* че́тверть* *f*; (*of year, town*) кварта́л; (*US*: *coin*) *два́дцать пять це́нтов* ♦ *vt* дели́ть* (раздели́ть* *perf*) на четы́ре ча́сти; (*MIL*: *lodge*) квартирова́ть (расквартирова́ть *perf*); ~**s** *npl* (*living quarters*) помеще́ние *ntsg*; (: *MIL*) каза́рмы *fpl*; **a** ~ **of an hour** че́тверть* *f* ча́са; **it's a** ~ **to three**, *or* (*US*) **of three** сейча́с без че́тверти три; **it's a** ~ **past three**, *or* (*US*) **after three** сейча́с че́тверть четвёртого; **from all** ~**s** отовсю́ду; **at close** ~**s** вблизи́.

quarterback ['kwɔ:təbæk] *n* (*SPORT*) гла́вный напада́ющий (*в америка́нском футбо́ле*).

quarterdeck ['kwɔ:tədɛk] *n* (*NAUT*) квартерде́к.

quarterfinal ['kwɔ:tə'faɪnl] *n* четвертьфина́л.

quarterly ['kwɔ:təlɪ] *adj* (*meeting*) (еже)кварта́льный; (*payment*) (по)кварта́льный ♦ *adv* (*meet*) ежекварта́льно; (*pay*) покварта́льно ♦ *n* кварта́льный журна́л.

quartermaster ['kwɔ:təmɑ:stə'] *n* (*MIL*) квартирме́йстер.

quartet(te) [kwɔ:'tɛt] *n* (*group*) кварте́т.

quarto ['kwɔ:təu] *n* (*book*) кни́га форма́та ин-ква́рто.

quartz [kwɔ:ts] *n* кварц ♦ *cpd* ква́рцевый.

quash [kwɔʃ] *vt* (*verdict, judgement*) отменя́ть (отмени́ть* *perf*).

quasi- ['kweɪzaɪ] *prefix* ква́зи-.

quaver ['kweɪvə'] *n* (*BRIT*: *MUS*) восьма́я *f adj* ♦ *vi* дрожа́ть (*impf*).

quay [ki:] *n* (*also*: ~**side**) при́стань* *f*.

quayside ['ki:saɪd] *n* при́стань* *f*.

queasiness ['kwi:zɪnɪs] *n* тошнота́.

queasy ['kwi:zɪ] *adj*: **I feel a bit** ~ меня́ немно́го мути́т.

Quebec [kwɪ'bɛk] *n* Квебе́к.

queen [kwi:n] *n* короле́ва; (*also*: ~ **bee**) пчели́ная ма́тка*; (*CARDS*) да́ма; (*CHESS*) ферзь* *m*, короле́ва.

queen mother *n* короле́ва-мать* *f*.

Queen's speech *n* (*at Christmas*) обраще́ние (короле́вы) к по́дданым; (*at opening of parliament*) тро́нная речь *f* (короле́вы).

queer [kwɪə'] *adj* стра́нный* (стра́нен); (*BRIT*): **I feel** ~ мне ду́рно ♦ *n* (*pej*: *homosexual*) го́мик.

quell [kwɛl] *vt* подавля́ть (подави́ть* *perf*).

quench [kwɛntʃ] *vt*: **to** ~ **one's thirst** утоля́ть (утоли́ть* *perf*) жа́жду.

querulous ['kwɛrələs] *adj* (*voice*) жа́лобный* (жа́лобен); (*child*) хны́кающий.

query ['kwɪərɪ] *n* вопро́с ♦ *vt* подверга́ть (подве́ргнуть *perf*) сомне́нию.

quest [kwɛst] *n* по́иск.

question ['kwɛstʃən] *n* вопро́с; (*doubt*) сомне́ние ♦ *vt* (*interrogate*) допра́шивать

(допроси́ть* *perf*); (*doubt*) сомнева́ться (*impf*) в +*prp*; **to ask sb a** ~, **put a** ~ **to sb** задава́ть (зада́ть* *perf*) кому́-н вопро́с; **to bring** *or* **call sth into** ~ ста́вить* (поста́вить* *perf*) что-н под вопро́с *or* сомне́ние; **the** ~ **is** ... вопро́с в том, ...; **it's (just) a** ~ **of finding out** де́ло (то́лько) за тем, чтобы узна́ть; **there's some** ~ **as to whether** существу́ют не́которые сомне́ния в том, что; **beyond** ~ бесспо́рно; **that's out of the** ~ об э́том не мо́жет быть* и ре́чи.

questionable ['kwɛstʃənəbl] *adj* сомни́тельный* (сомни́телен).

questioner ['kwɛstʃənə'] *n* зада́вший(-ая) *m(f) adj* вопро́с.

questioning ['kwɛstʃənɪŋ] *adj* (*expression*) вопроси́тельный* (вопроси́телен); (*mind*) пытли́вый (пытли́в) ♦ *n* (*POLICE*) допро́с.

question mark *n* вопроси́тельный знак.

questionnaire [kwɛstʃə'nɛə'] *n* анке́та.

queue [kju:] (*BRIT*) *n* о́чередь* *f* ♦ *vi* (*also*: ~ **up**) стоя́ть (*impf*) в о́череди; **to jump the** ~ проходи́ть* (пройти́* *perf*) без о́череди.

quibble ['kwɪbl] *vi*: **to** ~ **about** *or* **over** спо́рить (поспо́рить *perf*) о +*prp*.

quiche [ki:ʃ] *n* киш (*откры́тый пиро́г с овощно́й итп начи́нкой*).

quick [kwɪk] *adj* бы́стрый* (быстр); (*clever*: *person*) сообрази́тельный* (сообрази́телен); (: *mind*) живо́й; (*brief*) коро́ткий* (ко́роток) ♦ *adv* бы́стро ♦ *n*: **to cut to the** ~ задева́ть (заде́ть* *perf*) за живо́е; **be** ~! бы́стро!, побыстре́е!; **to be** ~ **to act** бы́стро реаги́ровать (отреаги́ровать *perf*); **she was** ~ **to see that** ... она́ сра́зу заме́тила, что ...; **to have a** ~ **look** взгляну́ть (*perf*); **she has a** ~ **temper** она́ вспы́льчива.

quicken ['kwɪkən] *vt* ускоря́ть (уско́рить *perf*) ♦ *vi* ускоря́ться (уско́риться *perf*).

quick-fire ['kwɪkfaɪə'] *adj*: ~ **questions** град *msg* вопро́сов.

quicklime ['kwɪklaɪm] *n* негашёная и́звесть *f*.

quickly ['kwɪklɪ] *adv* бы́стро.

quickness ['kwɪknɪs] *n* быстрота́; (*of mind*) жи́вость *f*.

quicksand ['kwɪksænd] *n* зыбу́чий* песо́к*.

quickstep ['kwɪkstɛp] *n* куи́к-сте́п.

quick-tempered [kwɪk'tɛmpəd] *adj* вспы́льчивый (вспы́льчив).

quick-witted [kwɪk'wɪtɪd] *adj* сообраз́ительный* (сообрази́телен).

quid [kwɪd] *n inv* (*BRIT*: *inf*) фунт (*сте́рлингов*).

quid pro quo ['kwɪdprəu'kwəu] *n* услу́га за услу́гу.

quiet ['kwaɪət] *adj* (*not loud or noisy*) ти́хий* (тих); (: *engine*) бесшу́мный* (бесшу́мен); (*peaceful, not busy*) споко́йный* (споко́ен); (*without fuss: wedding etc*) скро́мный*

---

* marks translations which have irregular inflections. The Russian-English side of the dictionary gives inflectional information.

(скро́мен) ◆ *n* (*silence*) тишина́; (*peace*) поко́й ◆ *vti* (*US*) = **quieten; be** ~**!** ти́хо!; **I'll have a** ~ **word with him** я поговорю́ с ним наедине́; **business is** ~ **at this time of year** в э́то вре́мя го́да в дела́х зати́шье; **on the** ~ тайко́м.

quieten ['kwaɪətn] *vi* (*also:* ~ **down**) затиха́ть (зати́хнуть *perf*) ◆ *vt* (*also:* ~ **down**) успока́ивать (успоко́ить *perf*).

quietly ['kwaɪətlɪ] *adv* (*not loudly*) ти́хо; (*calmly*) споко́йно.

quietness ['kwaɪətnɪs] *n* (*silence*) тишина́; (*peacefulness*) поко́й.

quill [kwɪl] *n* перо́*; (*of porcupine*) игла́*.

quilt [kwɪlt] *n* (*covering*) стёганое покрыва́ло; (*also:* **continental** ~) стёганое одея́ло.

quilting ['kwɪltɪŋ] *n* (*quilt-making*) стёжка; (*material*) стёганая ткань *f*.

quin [kwɪn] *n abbr* (*BRIT*) = **quintuplet**.

quince [kwɪns] *n* айва́.

quinine [kwɪ'niːn] *n* хини́н.

quintessential [kwɪntɪ'senʃəl] *adj* показа́тельный.

quintet(te) [kwɪn'tet] *n* (*group*) квинте́т.

quintuplets [kwɪn'tjuːplɪts] *npl* пя́теро* близнецо́в.

quip [kwɪp] *n* остро́та ◆ *vt* остри́ть (состри́ть *perf*); **... he** ~**ped ...** состри́л он.

quire ['kwaɪə] *n* (*of paper*) десть *f*.

quirk [kwə:k] *n* причу́да, при́хоть *f*; **by some** ~ **of fate** по при́хоти судьбы́.

quit [kwɪt] (*pt, pp* **quit** *or* **quitted**) *vt* броса́ть (бро́сить* *perf*); (*premises*) съезжа́ть (съе́хать* *perf*) с +*gen* ◆ *vi* (*give up*) сдава́ться* (сда́ться* *perf*); (*resign*) увольня́ться (уво́литься *perf*) ◆ *vt* (*US: inf*) перестаньте ходи́ть вокру́г да о́коло!; **they were given 3 months notice to** ~ (*BRIT*) их предупреди́ли, что они́ должны́ освободи́ть помеще́ние в трёхме́сячный срок.

quite [kwaɪt] *adv* (*rather*) дово́льно; (*entirely*) соверше́нно; (*following negative: almost*): **the flat's not** ~ **big enough** кварти́ра недоста́точно больша́я; **he's** ~ **right** он соверше́нно прав; **she's** ~ **pretty** она́ дово́льно симпати́чная; **I** ~ **understand** я вполне́ понима́ю; **I'm not** ~ **sure** я не совсе́м уве́рен; **not** ~ **as many as the last time** не так мно́го, как в про́шлый раз; **that lunch was** ~ **something!** вот э́то был обе́д!; ~ **a few** дово́льно мно́го; ~ **(so)!** ве́рно!

Quito ['kiːtəu] *n* Ки́то *m ind*.

quits [kwɪts] *adj*: **to be** ~ **(with)** быть* (*impf*) в расчёте (с +*instr*); **let's call it** ~ бу́дем кви́ты.

quiver ['kwɪvə] *vi* трепета́ть (*impf*).

quiz [kwɪz] *n* (*game*) викторина ◆ *vt* расспра́шивать (расспроси́ть* *perf*).

quizzical ['kwɪzɪkl] *adj*: **a** ~ **look** понима́ющий и насме́шливый взгляд.

quoits [kwɔɪts] *npl игра́, заключа́ющаяся в мета́нии коле́ц в цель.*

quorum ['kwɔːrəm] *n* кво́рум.

quota ['kwəutə] *n* кво́та.

quotation [kwəu'teɪʃən] *n* цита́та; (*estimate*) цена́ (продавца́); (*of shares etc*) котиро́вка*.

quotation marks *npl* кавы́чки *fpl*.

quote [kwəut] *n* (*from book, play etc*) цита́та; (*estimate*) цена́ ◆ *vt* цити́ровать (процити́ровать *perf*); (*figure, example*) приводи́ть* (привести́* *perf*); (*price*) назнача́ть (назна́чить *perf*); ~**s** *npl* (*quotation marks*) кавы́чки *fpl*; **to** ~ **for a job** устана́вливать (установи́ть* *perf*) сто́имость *f* рабо́ты; **in** ~**s** в кавы́чках; ~ **... unquote ...** в кавы́чках.

quotient ['kwəuʃənt] *n* (*factor*) фа́ктор.

qv *abbr* = *quod vide*; (*which see*) см.= *смотри́*.

qwerty keyboard ['kwə:tɪ-] *n типи́чная англи́йская клавиату́ра печа́тной маши́нки и́ли компью́тера.*

~ R, r ~

R, r [ɑːʳ] n (letter) 18-ая бу́ква англи́йского алфави́та.
R. abbr = **right**; (= river) p.= река́; (= Réaumur (scale)) по шкале́ Реомю́ра; (US: CINEMA: = restricted) ≈ до 18-ти лет; (US: POL) = **republican**; (BRIT) = Rex; (BRIT) = Regina.
RA abbr (MIL) = **rear admiral** ♦ n abbr (BRIT) = Royal Academy; (BRIT) = Royal Academician.
RAAF n abbr (MIL) = Royal Australian Air Force.
Rabat [rə'bɑːt] n Раба́т.
rabbi ['ræbaɪ] n равви́н.
rabbit ['ræbɪt] n (male) кро́лик; (female) кроль́чиха ♦ vi: **to ~ (on)** (BRIT: inf) трещать (impf).
rabbit hole n кро́личья нора́*.
rabbit hutch n кро́личья кле́тка*.
rabble ['ræbl] n (pej) чернь f.
rabid ['ræbɪd] adj (also fig) бе́шеный.
rabies ['reɪbiːz] n бе́шенство, водобоя́знь f.
RAC n abbr (BRIT: = Royal Automobile Club) Короле́вский автомоби́льный клуб (крупне́йшая автомоби́льная ассоциа́ция).
raccoon [rə'kuːn] n ено́т.
race [reɪs] n (species) ра́са; (competition: NAUT, AUT, SKIING etc) го́ньки* fpl; (: running) забе́г; (: swimming) заплы́в; (: horse race) ска́чки* fpl; (for power, control) борьба́ ♦ vt (horse) гнать* (impf); (pigeon) гоня́ть (impf); (car etc) вести́* (impf); (person) бежа́ть* (impf) наперегонки́ с +instr ♦ vi (compete) принима́ть (приня́ть* perf) уча́стие в го́нках/ забе́ге/заплы́ве/ска́чках; (hurry) мча́ться (impf); (pulse) учаща́ться (участи́ться* perf); (engine) увели́чивать (увели́чить perf) оборо́ты; **the human ~** челове́чество, челове́ческий род; **the arms ~** го́нка вооруже́ний; **he ~d across the road** он бы́стро перебежа́л че́рез доро́гу; **to ~ in(to)** влета́ть (влете́ть* perf) (в +acc); **to ~ out (of)** выска́кивать (вы́скочить perf) (из +gen).
race car n (US) = racing car.
race car driver n (US) = racing driver.
racecourse ['reɪskɔːs] n ипподро́м.
racehorse ['reɪshɔːs] n скакова́я ло́шадь* f.
race meeting n день* m ска́чек.
race relations npl ра́совые отноше́ния ntpl.

racetrack ['reɪstræk] n (for people) бегова́я доро́жка*; (for cars) трек; (US) = racecourse.
racial ['reɪʃl] adj (discrimination, prejudice) ра́совый; **~ equality** ра́совое ра́венство.
racialism ['reɪʃlɪzəm] n раси́зм.
racialist ['reɪʃlɪst] adj (beliefs, attitudes) раси́стский* ♦ n раси́ст(ка*).
racing ['reɪsɪŋ] n (horse racing) ска́чки* fpl; (motor racing) го́нки* fpl.
racing car n (BRIT) го́ночный автомоби́ль m.
racing driver n (BRIT) го́нщик.
racism ['reɪsɪzəm] n раси́зм.
racist ['reɪsɪst] adj (statement, policy) раси́стский* ♦ n раси́ст(ка*).
rack [ræk] n (shelf) по́лка*; (also: luggage ~) бага́жная по́лка*; (also: roof ~) бага́жник (на кры́ше автомоби́ля); (also: dish ~) суши́лка* для посу́ды ♦ vt: **she was ~ed by pain** её терза́ла боль; **to ~ one's brains** лома́ть (impf) го́лову; **magazine ~** журна́льная по́лка; **toast ~** подста́вка для то́стов; **shoe ~** по́лка* для о́буви; **to go to ~ and ruin** (building) ветша́ть (обветша́ть perf); (business) разоря́ться (разори́ться perf).
racket ['rækɪt] n (SPORT) раке́тка*; (noise) шум; (swindle) жу́льничество; (organized crime) рэ́кет.
racketeer [rækɪ'tɪəʳ] n (esp US) рэкети́р.
racoon [rə'kuːn] n = raccoon.
racquet ['rækɪt] n (SPORT) раке́тка*.
racy ['reɪsɪ] adj (book) пика́нтный* (пика́нтен); (behaviour etc) экстравага́нтный* (экстравага́нтен).
RADA [rɑːdə] n abbr (BRIT) = Royal Academy of Dramatic Art.
radar ['reɪdɑːʳ] n рада́р, радиолока́тор ♦ cpd рада́рный, радиолокацио́нный.
radar trap n (AUT) радиолокацио́нная лову́шка.
radial ['reɪdɪəl] adj (also: ~-ply: tyre) радиа́льный.
radiance ['reɪdɪəns] n (glow) сия́ние.
radiant ['reɪdɪənt] adj (smile, person) сия́ющий*; (PHYS) лучи́стый.
radiate ['reɪdɪeɪt] vt (also fig) излуча́ть (impf) ♦ vi (lines) радиа́льно расходи́ться* (разойти́сь* perf).

---

* marks translations which have irregular inflections. The Russian-English side of the dictionary gives inflectional information.

radiation [reidi'eiʃən] n (*radioactive*) радиа́ция, радиоакти́вное излуче́ние; (*of heat, light*) излуче́ние.

radiation sickness n лучева́я боле́знь f.

radiator ['reidieitə'] n (*heater*) радиа́тор, батаре́я; (*AUT*) радиа́тор.

radiator cap n кры́шка* радиа́тора.

radiator grill n (*AUT*) решётка* радиа́тора.

radical ['rædɪkl] adj (*extreme*) радика́льный* (радика́лен) ♦ n (*person*) радика́л.

radii ['reidiai] npl of **radius**.

radio ['reidiəu] n (*broadcasting*) ра́дио nt ind; (*device: for receiving broadcasts*) радио-приёмник; (: *for transmitting and receiving*) радиопереда́тчик ♦ vt (*person*) свя́зываться (связа́ться* perf) по ра́дио с +instr; (*information*) передава́ть* (переда́ть* perf) по ра́дио ♦ vi: **to ~ to sb** ради́ровать (*impf/perf*) кому́-н; **on the ~** по ра́дио.

radio... ['reidiəu] prefix ра́дио....

radioactive ['reidiəu'æktiv] adj радио-акти́вный* (радиоакти́вен).

radioactivity ['reidiəuæk'tiviti] n радио-акти́вность f.

radio announcer n ди́ктор ра́дио.

radio-controlled ['reidiəukən'trəuld] adj управля́емый при по́мощи радиосигна́лов.

radiographer [reidi'ɔɡrəfə'] n рентгено́лог.

radiography [reidi'ɔɡrəfi] n рентгеногра́фия, радиогра́фия.

radiologist [reidi'ɔlədʒist] n рентгено́лог, радио́лог.

radiology [reidi'ɔlədʒi] n рентгеноло́гия, радиоло́гия.

radio station n радиоста́нция.

radio taxi n радиофици́рованное такси́ nt ind.

radiotelephone ['reidiəu'tɛlifəun] n радио-телефо́н.

radio telescope n радиотелеско́п.

radiotherapist ['reidiəu'θɛrəpist] n радио-терапе́вт.

radiotherapy ['reidiəu'θɛrəpi] n радиотерапи́я, рентгенотерапи́я.

radish ['rædɪʃ] n (*one radish*) реди́ска*; ~**es** реди́с msg, реди́ска fsg (*разг*).

radium ['reidiəm] n ра́дий.

radius ['reidiəs] n (*pl* **radii**) ра́диус; (*ANAT*) лучева́я кость* f; **within a ~ of 50 miles** в ра́диусе 50-ти миль.

RAF n abbr (*BRIT*) (= **Royal Air Force**) ≈ BBC= *вое́нно-возду́шные си́лы*.

raffia ['ræfiə] n ра́фия.

raffish ['ræfiʃ] adj разгу́льный* (разгу́лен).

raffle ['ræfl] n (вещева́я) лотере́я ♦ vt (*prize*) разы́грывать (разыгра́ть perf) в лотере́е.

raft [rɑːft] n плот*.

rafter ['rɑːftə'] n (*CONSTR*) стропи́ло.

rag [ræɡ] n тря́пка*; (*pej: newspaper*) газетёнка*; (*SCOL: for charity*) *благотвор-и́тельное шу́точное студе́нческое представле́ние* ♦ vt (*BRIT: tease*) те́шиться

(поте́шиться perf) над +instr; ~**s** npl (*torn clothes*) лохмо́тья* pl; **in ~s** (*person*) в лохмо́тьях; (*clothes*) изно́шенный* (изно́шен) до дыр.

rag-and-bone man [ræɡən'bəun-] irreg n (*BRIT*) старьёвщик.

ragbag ['ræɡbæɡ] n (*fig: inf*) вся́кая вся́чина.

rag doll n тряпи́чная ку́кла*.

rage [reidʒ] n (*fury*) я́рость f, бе́шенство ♦ vi (*person*) свире́пствовать (*impf*); (*storm, debate*) бушева́ть (*impf*); **it's all the ~** (*very fashionable*) все помеша́лись на э́том; **to fly into a ~** приходи́ть* (прийти́* perf) в я́рость, свирепе́ть (рассвирепе́ть perf).

ragged ['ræɡid] adj (*edge*) зазу́бренный* (зазу́брен); (*clothes*) потрёпанный* (потрёпан), изо́рванный (изо́рван); (*appearance*) обо́рванный* (обо́рван).

raging ['reidʒiŋ] adj (*sea, storm*) бушу́ющий; (*pain, fever*) свире́пый; ~ **toothache** свире́пая зубна́я боль; **in a ~ temper** в я́рости.

rag trade n (*inf*): **the ~** инду́стрия оде́жды.

raid [reid] n (*MIL*) рейд; (*criminal*) налёт; (*by police*) обла́ва, рейд ♦ vt (*see n*) соверша́ть (соверши́ть perf) рейд на +acc; соверша́ть (соверши́ть perf) налёт на +acc; устра́ивать (устро́ить perf) обла́ву or рейд на +acc.

rail [reil] n (*on stairs, bridge etc*) пери́ла pl; (*of ship*) борт*; ~**s** npl (*RAIL*) ре́льсы mpl; **by ~** по́ездом.

railing(s) ['reiliŋ(z)] n(pl) (*iron fence*) решётка fsg.

railroad ['reilrəud] n (*US*) = **railway**.

railway ['reilwei] n (*BRIT*) желе́зная доро́га ♦ cpd железнодоро́жный.

railway engine n локомоти́в.

railway line n (*BRIT*) железнодоро́жная ли́ния.

railwayman ['reilweimən] irreg n (*BRIT*) железнодоро́жник.

railway station n (*BRIT: large*) железно-доро́жный вокза́л; (: *small*) железнодоро́жная ста́нция.

rain [rein] n дождь* m ♦ vi: **it's ~ing** идёт дождь ♦ vt: **it's ~ing cats and dogs** льёт как из ведра́; **in the ~** под дождём, в дождь; **it ~ed a lot last night** вчера́ но́чью шёл си́льный дождь.

rainbow ['reinbəu] n ра́дуга.

rain check n (*US*): **I'll take a ~ ~** я ещё немно́го подума́ю.

raincoat ['reinkəut] n плащ*.

raindrop ['reindrɔp] n дождева́я ка́пля*.

rainfall ['reinfɔːl] n оса́дки mpl; (*measurement*) коли́чество оса́дков.

rainforest ['reinfɔrist] n тропи́ческий* лес.

rainproof ['reinpruːf] adj непромока́емый (непромока́ем).

rainstorm ['reinstɔːm] n ли́вень* m.

rainwater ['reinwɔːtə'] n дождева́я вода́*.

rainy ['reini] adj (*day*) дождли́вый (дождли́в); **Manchester is a ~ place** в Манче́стере ча́сто иду́т дожди́; **to save sth for a ~ day**

откла́дывать (отложи́ть* perf) что-н на
чёрный день.
raise [reɪz] n (esp US: pay rise) повыше́ние ♦ vt
(lift, produce) поднима́ть (подня́ть* perf);
(end: siege, embargo) снима́ть (снять* perf);
(increase, improve) повыша́ть (повы́сить*
perf); (doubts) выска́зывать (вы́сказать* perf);
(rear: cattle) разводи́ть* (развести́* perf);
(: family) воспи́тывать (воспита́ть* perf);
(cultivate: crop) выра́щивать (вы́растить*
perf); (get together: army, funds) собира́ть
(собра́ть* perf); (: loan) доставать* (доста́ть*
perf); (a glass to sb/sth поднима́ть
(подня́ть* perf) бока́л за кого́-н/что-н; **to ~
one's voice** повыша́ть (повы́сить* perf)
го́лос; **to ~ one's hopes** обнадёживать
(обнадёжить perf); **to ~ a laugh/smile**
вызыва́ть (вы́звать* perf) смех/улы́бку.
raisin ['reɪzn] n (one raisin) изю́минка*; **~s**
изю́м* m no pl.
Raj [rɑːdʒ] n: **the ~** пери́од брита́нского
правле́ния в Индии.
rajah ['rɑːdʒə] n ра́джа.
rake [reɪk] n (tool) гра́бли* pl; (person) пове́са m
♦ vt (garden) разра́внивать (разровня́ть perf)
(гра́блями); (leaves, hay) сгреба́ть (сгрести́*
perf); (with machine gun) обстре́ливать
(обстреля́ть perf) ♦ vi: **to ~ through** (search)
ры́ться* (impf) в +prp.
rake-off ['reɪkɔf] n (inf) до́ля* при́были.
rally ['rælɪ] n (POL etc) ми́тинг; (AUT)
авторалли nt ind; (TENNIS) ра́лли nt ind ♦ vt
(support) спла́чивать (сплоти́ть* perf) ♦ vi
(sick person) оправля́ться (опра́виться* perf);
(Stock Exchange) оживля́ться (ожи́виться*
perf)
▶ **rally round** vt fus (fig: give support to)
спла́чиваться (сплоти́ться* perf) вокру́г +gen
♦ vi бра́ться* (взя́ться* perf) за де́ло вме́сте.
rallying point ['rælɪŋ-] n (idea) объедин-
я́ющая иде́я.
RAM [ræm] n abbr (COMPUT) (= **random access
memory**) ЗУПВ= запомина́ющее
устро́йство с произво́льной вы́боркой.
ram [ræm] n бара́н ♦ vt (crash into) тара́нить
(протара́нить perf); (push: bolt) задвига́ть
(задви́нуть perf); (: fist) дви́нуть (perf) +instr.
ramble ['ræmbl] n прогу́лка* ♦ vi (walk)
броди́ть* (impf); (talk: also: **~ on**) болта́ть
(impf).
rambler ['ræmblə'] n (walker) тури́ст(ка)
(уча́стник пешехо́дной прогу́лки или
похо́да); (BOT) вью́щееся расте́ние.
rambling ['ræmblɪŋ] adj (speech) несвя́зный*
(несвя́зен); (house) беспоря́дочно
вы́строенный (вы́строен); (BOT) вью́щийся.
rambunctious [ræm'bʌŋkʃəs] adj (US) =
rumbustious.

RAMC n abbr (BRIT) = Royal Army Medical Corps.
ramification [ræmɪfɪ'keɪʃən] n сле́дствие.
ramp [ræmp] n (incline) скат, укло́н; (in garage)
па́ндус; **on ~** (US: AUT) въезд на автостра́ду;
off ~ (US: AUT) съезд с автостра́ды.
rampage [ræm'peɪdʒ] n: **to be on the ~**
бу́йствовать (impf) ♦ vi: **they went rampaging
through the town** они́ бу́йствовали по всему́
го́роду.
rampant ['ræmpənt] adj: **to be ~** (crime)
свире́пствовать (impf).
rampart ['ræmpɑːt] n крепостно́й вал*.
ram raid n ограбле́ние, совершённое при
по́мощи автотара́на.
ramshackle ['ræmʃækl] adj ве́тхий* (ветх).
RAN n abbr = Royal Australian Navy.
ran [ræn] pt of run.
ranch [rɑːntʃ] n ра́нчо nt ind.
rancher ['rɑːntʃə'] n (owner) владе́лец*(-лица)
ра́нчо; (ranch hand) рабо́тник на ра́нчо.
rancid ['rænsɪd] adj (butter) прого́рклый;
(bacon) ту́хлый*.
rancour ['ræŋkə'] (US rancor) n зло́ба.
R & B n abbr (= rhythm and blues) ритм и блюз.
R & D n abbr (= research and development)
нау́чно-иссле́довательские и о́пытно-
констру́кторские рабо́ты.
random ['rændəm] adj (arrangement, selection)
случа́йный; (COMPUT, MATH) случа́йный,
произво́льный ♦ n: **at ~** наугад.
random access n (COMPUT) прямо́й or
произво́льный до́ступ.
random access memory n (COMPUT)
запомина́ющее устро́йство с произво́льной
вы́боркой.
R & R n abbr (US: MIL) = rest and recreation.
randy ['rændɪ] adj (BRIT: inf) похотли́вый
(похотли́в).
rang [ræŋ] pt of ring.
range [reɪndʒ] n (series: of proposals, offers)
ряд*; (: of products) ассортиме́нт no pl,
вы́бор no pl; (: of colours) га́мма; (of
mountains) цепь* f; (of missile) да́льность f,
ра́диус де́йствия; (of voice) диапазо́н; (MIL:
also: **shooting ~**) стре́льбище; (: indoor) тир;
(also: **kitchen ~**) ку́хонная плита́* ♦ vt (place
in a line) выстра́ивать (вы́строить perf) ♦ vi:
to ~ over (extend) простира́ться (impf); **price
~** диапазо́н цен; **do you have anything else in
this price ~?** у Вас есть что́-нибудь ещё в
преде́лах э́той цены́?; **within (firing) ~** на
расстоя́нии вы́стрела; **~d right/left** (text) с
поля́ми спра́ва/сле́ва; **to ~ from ... to ...**
колеба́ться* (impf) от +gen ... до +gen ....
ranger ['reɪndʒə'] n (in forest) лесни́чий* m adj,
лесни́к*; (in park) смотри́тель(ница) m(f).
Rangoon [ræŋ'guːn] n Рангу́н.
rank [ræŋk] n (row) ряд*; (MIL) шере́нга;

---

* marks translations which have irregular inflections. The Russian-English side of the dictionary gives inflectional information.

(*status*) чин*, ранг; (*BRIT*: *also*: **taxi** ~)
стоя́нка* такси́ ♦ *adj* (*stinking*) зловóнный*
(зловóнен); (*injustice*) вопию́щий*;
(*hypocrisy*) я́вный* (я́вен) ♦ *vi*: **to ~ among**
чи́слиться (*impf*) среди́ +*gen* ♦ *vt*: **I ~ him sixth**
я ста́влю егó на шестóе мéсто; **the ~s** *npl*
(*MIL*) рядовы́е *pl adj*, рядовóй состáв *msg*; **the**
~ and file (*fig*) рядовы́е члéны *mpl*; **to close ~s**
(*MIL, also fig*) смыкáть (сомкну́ть *perf*) ряды́.
rankle ['ræŋkl] *vi*: **to ~ with sb** терзáть (*impf*)
когó-н.
rank outsider *n* совершéнно безнадёжный
кандидáт, кандидáт без шáнсов на успéх.
ransack ['rænsæk] *vt* (*search*) переры́ть* (*perf*);
(*plunder*) грáбить* (разгрáбить* *perf*).
ransom ['rænsəm] *n* вы́куп; **to hold to ~** (*fig*:
nation, company, individual) держáть (*impf*) в
залóжниках.
rant [rænt] *vi*: **to ~ and rave** рвать* (*impf*) и
метáть (*impf*).
ranting ['ræntɪŋ] *n* разглагóльствование.
rap [ræp] *n* стук; (*POETRY, MUS*) стиль в му́зыке
и́ли поэ́зии, характеризу́ющийся
отры́вистым ри́тмом, испóльзованием
речитати́ва ♦ *vi*: **to ~ on a door/table**
стучáть (постучáть *perf*) в дверь/по столу́.
rape [reɪp] *n* изнаси́лование; (*BOT*) рапс ♦ *vt*
(*woman*) наси́ловать (изнаси́ловать *perf*).
rape(seed) oil ['reɪp(siːd)-] *n* рáпсовое мáсло.
rapid ['ræpɪd] *adj* стреми́тельный*
(стреми́телен).
rapidity [rə'pɪdɪtɪ] *n* стреми́тельность *f*.
rapidly ['ræpɪdlɪ] *adv* стреми́тельно.
rapids ['ræpɪdz] *npl* (*GEO*) стремни́на *fsg*.
rapist ['reɪpɪst] *n* наси́льник.
rapport [ræ'pɔː[r]] *n* взаимопонимáние.
rapprochement [ræ'prɒʃmɑːŋ] *n* сближéние.
rapt [ræpt] *adj* (*attention*) сосредотóченный*
(сосредотóчен); **he was ~ in contemplation**
он был погружён в разду́мья.
rapture ['ræptʃə[r]] *n* (*delight*) востóрг; **to go into**
~s over приходи́ть* (прийти́* *perf*) в востóрг
от +*gen*.
rapturous ['ræptʃərəs] *adj* (*applause*)
востóрженный* (востóрожен).
rare [rɛə[r]] *adj* рéдкий* (рéдок); (*rare steak*)
кровáвый*; **it is ~ to find ...** рéдко удаётся
найти́ ....
rarebit ['rɛəbɪt] *n see* **Welsh rarebit.**
rarefied ['rɛərɪfaɪd] *adj* разрежённый*
(разрежён).
rarely ['rɛəlɪ] *adv* рéдко, нечáсто.
raring ['rɛərɪŋ] *adj*: **he is ~ to go** (*inf*: *keen*) ему́
не тéрпится приступи́ть к дéлу.
rarity ['rɛərɪtɪ] *n* рéдкость *f*.
rascal ['rɑːskl] *n* негодя́й(ка*).
rash [ræʃ] *adj* опромéтчивый (опромéтчив) ♦ *n*
(*MED*) сыпь *f no pl*; (*spate*: *of events, robberies*)
ряд*, волнá*; **he came out in a ~** у негó
вы́ступила сыпь.
rasher ['ræʃə[r]] *n* (*of bacon*) лóмтик.

rashly ['ræʃlɪ] *adv* опромéтчиво.
rasp [rɑːsp] *n* (*tool*) рáшпиль *m* ♦ *vt* (*speak*: *also*:
~ out) хрипéть* (прохрипéть* *perf*).
raspberry ['rɑːzbərɪ] *n* мали́на *f no pl*.
rasping ['rɑːspɪŋ] *adj*: **a ~ noise** скрежéщущий
звук; **a ~ voice** скрипу́чий* гóлос.
rat [ræt] *n* (*also fig*) кры́са.
ratable ['reɪtəbl] *adj* = **rateable.**
ratchet ['rætʃɪt] *n* храповѝк; **~ wheel** храповóе
колесó*.
rate [reɪt] *n* (*speed*) скóрость *f*; (: *of change,*
inflation) темп; (*of interest*) стáвка; (*ratio*)
у́ровень *m*; (*price*: *at hotel etc*) расцéнка ♦ *vt*
(*value*) оцéнивать (оцени́ть* *perf*); (*estimate*)
расцéнивать (расцени́ть* *perf*); ~**s** *npl* (*BRIT*:
property tax) налóг *msg* на недви́жимость;
(*fees*) расцéнки *fpl*; **at a ~ of 60 kilometres an**
hour со скóростью 60 киломéтров в час; ~
of flow скóрость потóка; ~ **of growth** темпы́
рóста; ~ **of return** стáвка дохóда (*от*
вложéния капитáла); **pulse ~** частотá
пу́льса; **to ~ sb as** счита́ть (*impf*) когó-н +*instr*;
to ~ sth as расцéнивать (расцени́ть (*perf*))
что-н как; **to ~ sb/sth among** относи́ть*
(отнести́* *perf*) когó-н/что-н к +*dat*; **to ~ sb/**
sth highly высокó цени́ть* (*impf*) когó-н/
что-н.
rateable value ['reɪtəbl-] *n* (*BRIT*: *formerly*)
стóимость дóма на оснóве котóрой
рассчи́тывается налóг на недви́жимость.
ratepayer ['reɪtpeɪə[r]] *n* (*BRIT*: *formerly*) лицó,
выплáчивающее налóг на недви́жимость.
rather ['rɑːðə[r]] *adv* (*quite, somewhat*)
довóльно; (*to some extent*) нéсколько; (*more*
accurately): **or ~** вернéе сказáть; **it's ~**
expensive (*quite*) э́то довóльно дóрого; (*too*)
э́то сли́шком дóрого; **there's ~ a lot**
сли́шком мнóго; **I would ~ go** я, пожáлуй,
пойду́; **I'd ~ not leave** я бы не хотéл уходи́ть;
I ~ think he won't come я ду́маю, что,
пожáлуй, он не придёт.
ratification [rætɪfɪ'keɪʃən] *n* ратификáция.
ratify ['rætɪfaɪ] *vt* ратифици́ровать (*impf/perf*).
rating ['reɪtɪŋ] *n* (*assessment*) оцéнка*,
рéйтинг; (*NAUT*: *BRIT*) матрóс; ~**s** *npl* (*RADIO*,
TV) рéйтинг *msg*.
ratio ['reɪʃɪəʊ] *n* отношéние, соотношéние; **in**
the ~ of one hundred to one в отношéнии сто
к одному́.
ration ['ræʃən] *n* (*allowance*: *of food*) рациóн,
паёк*; (: *of petrol*) нóрма ♦ *vt* норми́ровать
(*impf/perf*); ~**s** *npl* (*MIL*) рациóн *msg*; **to be on ~s**
быть* (*impf*) на довóльствии.
rational ['ræʃənl] *adj* (*solution, reasoning*)
рациональный* (рационáлен); (*person*)
разу́мный* (разу́мен).
rationale [ræʃə'nɑːl] *n* рациональное *or*
разу́мное обоснование.
rationalization [ræʃnəlaɪ'zeɪʃən] *n*
рационализáция.
rationalize ['ræʃnəlaɪz] *vt* (*justify*) давáть*

(дать* *perf*) рациона́льное объясне́ние +*dat*.
rationally ['ræ∫nəlɪ] *adv* рациона́льно.
rationing ['ræ∫nɪŋ] *n* нормирова́ние.
rat poison *n* крыси́ный яд.
rat race *n*: **the** ~~ грызня́ за власть.
rattan [ræ'tæn] *n* рота́нг.
rattle ['rætl] *n* дребезжа́ние; (*of train, car*)
громыха́ние; (*baby's toy*) погрему́шка* ◆ *vi*
(*small objects*) дребезжа́ть (*impf*) ◆ *vt* (*shake
noisily*) греме́ть (*прогреме́ть perf*); (*fig:
unsettle*) нерви́ровать (*impf*), выводи́ть*
(вы́вести* *perf*) из себя́; **to ~ along** (*car, bus*)
прогромыха́ть (*impf*); **a cold November wind
~d the windows** от холо́дного ноя́брьского
ве́тра дребезжа́ли о́кна.
rattlesnake ['rætlsneɪk] *n* грему́чая змея́*.
ratty ['rætɪ] *adj* (*inf: person*) издёрганный*
(издёрган).
raucous ['rɔːkəs] *adj* оглуши́тельный*
(оглуши́телен).
raucously ['rɔːkəslɪ] *adv* оглуши́тельно.
raunchy ['rɔːntʃɪ] *adj* (*song*) распу́тный*
(распу́тен).
ravage ['rævɪdʒ] *vt* разоря́ть (разори́ть *perf*).
ravages ['rævɪdʒɪz] *npl* (*of time, weather*)
разруши́тельные после́дствия *ntpl*.
rave [reɪv] *vi* (*in anger*) беснова́ться (*impf*),
бушева́ть (*impf*); (*MED*) бре́дить* (*impf*); (*with
enthusiasm*): **to ~ about** восторга́ться (*impf*)
+*instr* ◆ *cpd* (*inf*) восто́рженный.
raven ['reɪvən] *n* во́рон.
ravenous ['rævənəs] *adj* (*person*) голо́дный*
(го́лоден) как волк.
ravine [rə'viːn] *n* уще́лье*.
raving ['reɪvɪŋ] *adj*: ~ **lunatic** бу́йно
поме́шанный(-ая) *m(f) adj*.
ravings ['reɪvɪŋz] *npl* бред *msg*.
ravioli [rævɪ'əulɪ] *n* равио́ли *ind* (*италья́нское
блю́до, напомина́ющее пельме́ни*).
ravishing ['rævɪʃɪŋ] *adj* (*beautiful*)
восхити́тельный* (восхити́телен).
raw [rɔː] *adj* (*uncooked*) сыро́й*; (*not processed:
cotton*) необрабо́танный (необрабо́тан); (*:
unrefined sugar*) нерафини́рованный
(нерафини́рован); (*sore*) све́жий* (свеж);
(*inexperienced*) зелёный* (зе́лен); (*weather,
day*) промо́зглый.
raw deal *n* (*inf: bad bargain*) неуда́чная
сде́лка*; (*: unfair treatment*): **he got a** ~~ с
ним пло́хо обошли́сь.
raw material *n* сырьё *nt no pl*.
ray [reɪ] *n* (*of light, sunshine*) луч*; (*of heat*)
пото́к*; ~ **of hope** луч* наде́жды.
rayon ['reɪɔn] *n* иску́сственный шёлк.
raze [reɪz] *vt* (*building, forest: also:* ~ **to the
ground**) сровня́ть (*perf*) с землёй.
razor ['reɪzəʳ] *n* бри́тва; **safety** ~ безопа́сная
бри́тва; **electric** ~ электробри́тва.

razor blade *n* ле́звие (бри́твы).
razzle(-dazzle) ['ræzl('dæzl)] *n* (*BRIT: inf*): **to go
on the** ~ идти́* (*impf*) кути́ть.
razzmatazz ['ræzmə'tæz] *n* (*inf*) буффона́да.
RC *abbr* = **Roman Catholic**.
RCAF *n abbr* = *Royal Canadian Air Force.*
RCMP *n abbr* = *Royal Canadian Mounted Police.*
RCN *n abbr* = *Royal Canadian Navy.*
RD *abbr* (*US: POST.* = *rural delivery*) доста́вка
по́чты в се́льскую ме́стность.
Rd *abbr* = **road**.
RDC *n abbr* (*BRIT:* = *rural district council*)
райо́нный сове́т (*в се́льской ме́стности*).
RE *n abbr* (*BRIT: SCOL:* = *religious education*)
религио́зное воспита́ние; (*MIL:* = *Royal
Engineers*) ≈ инжене́рные войска́.
re [riː] *prep* (*with regard to*) относи́тельно +*gen*.
reach [riːtʃ] *n* (*scope: of imagination*) разма́х ◆
vt (*place, end, agreement*) достига́ть
(дости́гнуть *or* дости́чь* *perf*) +*gen*; (*:
conclusion, decision*) приходи́ть* (прийти́*
perf) к +*dat*; (*be able to touch*) достава́ть*
(доста́ть* *perf*); (*by telephone*) свя́зываться
(связа́ться* *perf*) с +*instr* ◆ *vi*: **to ~ into** сова́ть
(су́нуть *perf*) в +*acc*; **within** ~ в преде́лах
досяга́емости; **out of** ~ вне досяга́емости;
within ~ **of the shops/station** недалеко́ от
магази́нов/вокза́ла; **within easy** ~ **of** (*place*)
недалеко́ от +*gen*; "**keep out of the** ~ **of
children**" „бере́чь от дете́й"; **upper** ~**es** (*of
river*) верхо́вья *ntpl*; **lower** ~**es** (*of river*)
низо́вья *ntpl*; **can I** ~ **you at your hotel?** мо́жно
ли связа́ться с Ва́ми в гости́нице?; **to** ~ **for**
протя́гивать (протяну́ть* *perf*) ру́ку к +*dat*; **to**
~ **up** протя́гивать (протяну́ть* *perf*) ру́ку
вверх
▸ **reach out** *vt* протя́гивать (протяну́ть* *perf*) ◆
vi вытя́гиваться (вы́тянуться *perf*); **to ~ out
for sth** протя́гивать (протяну́ть* *perf*) ру́ку за
чем-н.
react [riː'ækt] *vi* (*CHEM*): **to ~ (with)** вступа́ть
(вступи́ть* *perf*) в реа́кцию (с +*instr*); (*MED*): **to
~ (to)** реаги́ровать (*impf*) (на +*acc*); (*respond*)
реаги́ровать (отреаги́ровать *perf*) (на +*acc*);
(*rebel*): **to ~ (against)** восстава́ть* (восста́ть*
perf) (про́тив +*gen*).
reaction [riː'ækʃən] *n* (*CHEM*) реа́кция; (*also
MED, POL*): ~ **(to/against)** реа́кция (на +*acc*/
про́тив +*gen*); ~**s** *npl* (*reflexes*) реа́кция *fsg*.
reactionary [riː'ækʃənrɪ] *adj* реакцио́нный*
(реакцио́нен).
reactor [riː'æktəʳ] *n* (*also*: **nuclear** ~) реа́ктор.
read[1] [rɛd] *pt, pp of* **read**[2].
read[2] [riːd] (*pt, pp* **read**) *vt* чита́ть (прочита́ть *or*
проче́сть* *perf*); (*mood*) определя́ть
(определи́ть* *perf*); (*meter, thermometer etc*)
снима́ть (снять* *perf*) показа́ния с +*gen*; (*subj:
instrument etc*) пока́зывать (*impf*); (*study: at*

---

university) изучать (impf) ♦ vi (person) читать
(impf); (text etc) читаться (impf); **the notice ~s**
... в объявлении говорится ...; **it can be taken
as ~ that** ... (fig) само собой разумеется, что
...; **do you ~ me?** (TEL) Вы слышите меня?
► **read out** vt зачитывать (зачитать perf)
► **read over** vt перечитывать (перечитать perf)
► **read through** vt (quickly) пролистывать
(пролистать perf); (thoroughly) прочитывать
(прочитать perf)
► **read up** vt много читать (impf)
► **read up on** vt fus много читать (impf) по +dat.
readable ['ri:dəbl] adj (handwriting)
разборчивый (разборчив); (book, author)
хорошо читающийся; **this book is very ~** эта
книга хорошо читается.
reader ['ri:də'] n (of book, newspaper etc)
читатель(ница) m(f); (book) книга для
чтения, хрестоматия; (BRIT: at university) ≈
доцент.
readership ['ri:dəʃɪp] n (of newspaper etc) круг
читателей.
readily ['rɛdɪlɪ] adv (willingly) с готовностью;
(easily) легко; (quickly) охотно.
readiness ['rɛdɪnɪs] n готовность f; **in ~**
наготове, в состоянии готовности.
reading ['ri:dɪŋ] n (of books, newspapers etc)
чтение; (understanding) толкование; (as
entertainment) чтения ntpl; (on meter,
thermometer etc) показание.
reading lamp n настольная лампа.
reading matter n материал для чтения.
reading room n читальный зал.
readjust [ri:ə'dʒʌst] vt (alter: position) пере-
менить (impf); (: knob, mirror) поворачивать
(повернуть perf); (instrument)
подрегулировать (perf) ♦ vi (adapt): **to ~ (to)**
приспосабливаться (приспособиться* perf)
(к +dat).
readjustment [ri:ə'dʒʌstmənt] n (adapting)
приспособление; (alteration) регулировка*.
ready ['rɛdɪ] adj готовый (готов); (available)
готовый ♦ n: **at the ~** (MIL) в положении для
стрельбы; (fig) наготове; **~ for use** готовый
(готов) к употреблению; **I am ~ to help** я
готов помочь; **to get ~** приготавливаться
(приготовиться* perf); **to get sb/sth ~**
подготавливать (подготовить* perf) кого-н/
что-н.
ready cash n наличные деньги* pl.
ready-cooked ['rɛdɪkukt] adj готовый.
ready-made ['rɛdɪ'meɪd] adj готовый.
ready-mix ['rɛdɪmɪks] n (for cakes etc)
полуфабрикат; (concrete) товарный бетон.
ready money n наличные деньги* pl.
ready reckoner [-'rɛkənə'] n (BRIT)
арифметические таблицы fpl готовых
расчётов.
ready-to-wear ['rɛdɪtə'wɛə'] adj (dress etc)
готовый.
reaffirm [ri:ə'fə:m] vt вновь подтверждать

(подтвердить* perf).
reagent [ri:'eɪdʒənt] n: **chemical ~** химический*
реактив.
real [rɪəl] adj (reason, interest, result etc)
настоящий*, реальный* (реален); (leather)
натуральный*; (gold, feeling) настоящий* ♦
adv (US: inf: very) очень; **in ~ terms** реально; **a ~
idiot** (for emphasis) настоящий* идиот.
real estate n недвижимость f ♦ cpd (US): **~~
agency** агентство по продаже
недвижимости.
realign [ri:ə'laɪn] vt перестраивать
(перестроить perf).
realism ['rɪəlɪzəm] n реализм.
realist ['rɪəlɪst] n реалист(ка*).
realistic [rɪə'lɪstɪk] adj (practical) реалист-
ичный* (реалистичен); (true to life)
реалистический*.
reality [ri:'ælɪtɪ] n реальность f, действительность f; **in ~** на самом деле, в
реальности.
realization [rɪəlaɪ'zeɪʃən] n (understanding)
осознание; (fulfilment: of hopes)
осуществление; (of asset) реализация.
realize ['rɪəlaɪz] vt (understand) осознавать*
(осознать* perf); (fulfil) осуществлять
(осуществить* perf); (COMM: asset)
реализовать (impf/perf); **I ~ that** ... я осознаю,
что ....
reallocate [ri:'æləkeɪt] vt перераспределять
(перераспределить perf).
really ['rɪəlɪ] adv (very) очень; (actually): **what ~
happened?** что произошло на самом деле?;
~? (indicating interest) правда?, да?;
(expressing surprise) неужели?, серьёзно?;
~! (indicating annoyance) ну, знаете!
realm [rɛlm] n (of monarch) королевство; (fig:
area of activity or study) область f, сфера.
real-time ['ri:ltaɪm] adj (COMPUT) в реальном
времени.
realtor ['rɪəltɔ:'] n (US) агент по продаже
недвижимости.
ream [ri:m] n (of paper) стопа*; **~s of** (fig: inf)
куча, масса; **she's written ~s!** у неё масса or
куча написанного!
reap [ri:p] vt (crop) жать* (сжать* perf); (fig:
benefits, rewards) пожинать (пожать* perf).
reaper ['ri:pə'] n (machine) жатка*.
reappear [ri:ə'pɪə'] vi снова появляться
(появиться* perf).
reappearance [ri:ə'pɪərəns] n новое
появление.
reapply [ri:ə'plaɪ] vi: **to ~ for** повторно
обращаться (обратиться* perf) за +instr.
reappoint [ri:ə'pɔɪnt] vt повторно назначать
(назначить perf).
reappraisal [ri:ə'preɪzl] n переоценка*.
rear [rɪə'] adj задний* ♦ n (back) задняя часть* f;
(buttocks) зад; (MIL) тыл* ♦ vt (cattle, family)
выращивать (вырастить* perf) ♦ vi (also: ~

up) станови́ться* (стать* *perf*) на дыбы́.

rear admiral *n* контр-адмира́л.

rear-engined ['rɪər'ɛndʒɪnd] *adj* (*AUT*) с
мото́ром в за́дней ча́сти.

rearguard ['rɪɡɑ:d] *n* (*MIL*) арьерга́рд.

rearm [ri:'ɑ:m] *vi* перевооружа́ться
(перевооружи́ться *perf*) ♦ *vt* перевооружа́ть
(перевооружи́ть *perf*).

rearmament [ri:'ɑ:məmənt] *n*
перевооруже́ние.

rearrange [ri:ə'reɪndʒ] *vt* (*objects*) пере-
ставля́ть (переста́вить* *perf*); (*order*)
изменя́ть (измени́ть* *perf*).

rear-view mirror ['rɪəvju:-] *n* (*AUT*) зе́ркало*
за́днего ви́да *or* обзо́ра.

reason ['ri:zn] *n* (*cause*) причи́на; (*ability to
think*) ра́зум, рассу́док*; (*sense*) смысл ♦ *vi*:
to ~ with sb убежда́ть (*impf*) кого́-н; **the ~
for/why** причи́на для +*gen*/по кото́рой; **to
have ~ to think that** ... име́ть (*impf*) основа́ние
ду́мать; **it stands to ~ that** ... разуме́ется, что
...; **she claims with good ~ that** ... она́ не без
причи́ны счита́ет, что ...; **all the more ~ why**
... тем бо́лее ....

reasonable ['ri:znəbl] *adj* разу́мный*
(разу́мен); (*quality*) неплохо́й* (непло́х);
(*price*) прие́млемый (прие́млем),
уме́ренный* (уме́рен); (*not bad*) сно́сный*
(сно́сен); **be ~!** бу́дьте благоразу́мны!

reasonably ['ri:znəblɪ] *adv* (*sensibly*) разу́мно;
(*fairly*) дово́льно; **one can ~ assume that** ...
мо́жно справедли́во предположи́ть, что ....

reasoned ['ri:znd] *adj* (*argument*) обосно́ван-
ный* (обосно́ван).

reasoning ['ri:znɪŋ] *n* рассужде́ние.

reassemble [ri:ə'sɛmbl] *vt* (сно́ва) собира́ть
(собра́ть* *perf*).

reassert [ri:ə'sə:t] *vt* (*authority, oneself*) сно́ва
утвержда́ть (утверди́ть* *perf*).

reassurance [ri:ə'ʃuərəns] *n* подтвержде́ние;
(*comfort*) подде́ржка.

reassure [ri:ə'ʃuə] *vt* (*comfort*) утеша́ть
(уте́шить *perf*); **to ~ sb of** заверя́ть (заве́рить
perf) кого́-н в +*prp*.

reassuring [ri:ə'ʃuərɪŋ] *adj* (*smile, manner*)
ободря́ющий.

reawakening [ri:ə'weɪknɪŋ] *n* пробужде́ние.

rebate ['ri:beɪt] *n* обра́тная вы́плата.

rebel [*n* 'rɛbl, *vi* rɪ'bɛl] *n* бунта́рь*(-рка*) *m(f)* ♦ *vi*
восстава́ть* (восста́ть* *perf*).

rebellion [rɪ'bɛljən] *n* восста́ние.

rebellious [rɪ'bɛljəs] *adj* (*child, behaviour*)
стропти́вый (стропти́в); (*troops*)
мяте́жный*; (*factions*) бунту́ющий.

rebirth [ri:'bə:θ] *n* возрожде́ние.

rebound [*vi* rɪ'baund, *n* 'ri:baund] *vi*: **to ~ (off)**
отска́кивать (отскочи́ть* *perf*) (от +*gen*) ♦ *n*:
on the ~ (*ball*) на отско́ке; **he married her on**

the ~ он жени́лся на ней по́сле
разочарова́ния в любви́ к друго́й.

rebuff [rɪ'bʌf] *n* отпо́р ♦ *vt* (*suggestion*) ре́зко
отклоня́ть (отклони́ть *perf*); (*person*)
дава́ть* (дать* *perf*) отпо́р +*dat*.

rebuild [ri:'bɪld] *irreg vt* (*town, building etc*)
перестра́ивать (перестро́ить *perf*); (*economy,
confidence*) восстана́вливать
(восстанови́ть* *perf*).

rebuke [rɪ'bju:k] *vt* упрека́ть (упрекну́ть *perf*),
де́лать (сде́лать *perf*) вы́говор +*dat* ♦ *n* упрёк,
вы́говор.

rebut [rɪ'bʌt] *vt* опроверга́ть (опрове́ргнуть*
perf).

rebuttal [rɪ'bʌtl] *n* опроверже́ние.

recalcitrant [rɪ'kælsɪtrənt] *adj* непоко́рный*
(непоко́рен).

recall [*vb* rɪ'kɔ:l, *n* 'ri:kɔl] *vt* вспомина́ть
(вспо́мнить *perf*); (*parliament, ambassador
etc*) отзыва́ть (отозва́ть* *perf*); (*COMPUT*)
перевызыва́ть (перевы́звать *perf*), вызыва́ть
(вы́звать *perf*) повто́рно ♦ *n* (*ability to
remember*) па́мять *f*; (*of ambassador etc*)
о́тзыв; **the event is beyond ~** собы́тие
безвозвра́тно исче́зло из па́мяти.

recant [rɪ'kænt] *vi* отрека́ться (отре́чься* *perf*).

recap ['ri:kæp] *vt* (*summarize*) резюми́ровать
(*impf/perf*) ♦ *vi* де́лать (сде́лать *perf*) резюме́ ♦
n резюме́ *nt ind*.

recapitulate [ri:kə'pɪtjuleɪt] *vti* = **recap**.

recapture [ri:'kæptʃə'] *vt* (*town, territory etc*)
сно́ва захва́тывать (захвати́ть* *perf*);
(*atmosphere, mood etc*) воссоздава́ть*
(воссозда́ть* *perf*).

rec'd *abbr* (*COMM*) = **received**.

recede [rɪ'si:d] *vi* (*tide*) спада́ть (спасть* *perf*);
(*lights*) угаса́ть (уга́снуть* *perf*); (*memory*)
слабе́ть (ослабе́ть* *perf*); (*hair*) реде́ть*
(поре́деть *perf*).

receding [rɪ'si:dɪŋ] *adj* (*hair*) реде́ющий; (*chin*)
сре́занный (сре́зан).

receipt [rɪ'si:t] *n* (*document*) квита́нция;
(*act of receiving*) получе́ние; **~s** *npl* (*COMM*)
де́нежные поступле́ния *ntpl*, платежи́ *mpl*; **to
acknowledge ~ of** подтвержда́ть
(подтверди́ть* *perf*) получе́ние +*gen*; **on ~** по
получе́нии; **we are in ~ of** ... (*COMM*) мы
получи́ли ....

receivable [rɪ'si:vəbl] *adj* (*COMM*) подлежа́щий
получе́нию; (: *bill, account*) надлежа́щий
упла́те.

receive [rɪ'si:v] *vt* получа́ть (получи́ть* *perf*);
(*criticism*) встреча́ть (встре́тить* *perf*);
(*visitor, guest*) принима́ть (приня́ть* *perf*);
"received with thanks" (*formal*) „полу́чено с
благода́рностью".

receiver [rɪ'si:və'] *n* (*TEL*) (телефо́нная)
тру́бка*; (*RADIO*) (радио-)приёмник; (*TV*)

---

* marks translations which have irregular inflections. The Russian-English side of the dictionary gives inflectional information.

телеви́зор; (*COMM*) ликвида́тор (*неплатё-
жеспосо́бной компа́нии*); ~ **of stolen goods**
укрыва́тель(ница) *m(f)* кра́деного.
receivership [rɪ'si:vəʃɪp] *n конфиска́ция
иму́щества обанкро́тившейся компа́нии
суде́бными исполни́телями в це́лях
вы́платы долго́в кредито́рам.*
recent ['ri:snt] *adj* (*event, times*) неда́вний*; **in**
~ **years** в *or* за после́дние го́ды.
recently ['ri:sntlɪ] *adv* неда́вно; **until** ~ до
неда́внего вре́мени; **as** ~ **as last year** ещё в
про́шлом году́.
receptacle [rɪ'sɛptɪkl] *n* сосу́д.
reception [rɪ'sɛpʃən] *n* (*in hotel*) регистра́ция;
(*in office*) приёмная *f adj*; (*in hospital*)
регистрату́ра; (*party, also RADIO, TV*) приём;
we got a warm ~ нам был ока́зан тёплый
приём.
reception centre *n* (*BRIT*) приёмный пункт для
размеще́ния бе́женцев, бездо́мных итп.
reception desk *n* (*in hotel*) стол регистра́ции;
(*in hospital, at doctor's*) регистрату́ра; (*in
large building, offices*) отде́л приёма
посети́телей.
receptionist [rɪ'sɛpʃənɪst] *n* (*in hotel, hospital*)
регистра́тор; (*in firm*) секрета́рь* *m* по
приёму посети́телей.
receptive [rɪ'sɛptɪv] *adj* восприи́мчивый
(восприи́мчив).
recess [rɪ'sɛs] *n* (*in room*) ни́ша; (*secret place*)
тайни́к*; (*POL etc: holiday*) кани́кулы *pl*; (*US:
LAW: short break*) переры́в; (: *SCOL*) больша́я
переме́на.
recession [rɪ'sɛʃən] *n* (*ECON*) спад.
recharge [ri:'tʃɑ:dʒ] *vt* (*battery*) перезаряжа́ть
(перезаряди́ть* *perf*).
rechargeable [ri:'tʃɑ:dʒəbl] *adj* пере-
заряжа́ющийся.
recipe ['rɛsɪpɪ] *n* (*also fig*) реце́пт.
recipient [rɪ'sɪpɪənt] *n* получа́тель *m*.
reciprocal [rɪ'sɪprəkl] *adj* взаи́мный*
(взаи́мен), обою́дный* (обою́ден).
reciprocate [rɪ'sɪprəkeɪt] *vt* отвеча́ть
(отве́тить* *perf*) на +*acc* ♦ *vi* (*favour*)
отпла́чивать (отплати́ть* *perf*); (*feeling*)
отвеча́ть (отве́тить* *perf*) взаи́мностью.
recital [rɪ'saɪtl] *n* (*concert*) со́льный конце́рт.
recitation [rɛsi'teɪʃən] *n* (*of poetry*)
деклама́ция; (*of prose*) чте́ние.
recite [rɪ'saɪt] *vt* (*poem*) деклами́ровать
(продеклами́ровать *perf*); (*prose*) чита́ть
(*impf*) (вслух); (*complaints, grievances etc*)
произноси́ть* (произнести́* *perf*).
reckless ['rɛkləs] *adj* безрассу́дный*
(безрассу́ден).
recklessly ['rɛkləslɪ] *adv* безрассу́дно.
reckon ['rɛkən] *vt* (*calculate*) счита́ть
(посчита́ть *or* сосчита́ть *perf*); (*think*): **I** ~ **that**
... я счита́ю, что ... ♦ *vi*: **he is somebody to be**
~**ed with** с таки́м челове́ком, как он, ну́жно
счита́ться; **to** ~ **without sb** не счита́ться

(посчита́ться *perf*) с кем-н; **to** ~ **without sth**
не учи́тывать (уче́сть* *perf*) чего́-н
▸ **reckon on** *vt fus* рассчи́тывать (*impf*) на +*acc*.
reckoning ['rɛknɪŋ] *n* (*calculation*) подсчёт,
расчёт; **the day of** ~ час распла́ты.
reclaim [rɪ'kleɪm] *vt* (*demand back*) тре́бовать
(потре́бовать *perf*) обра́тно; (*land: from sea*)
отвоёвывать (отвоева́ть* *perf*); (: *from forest
etc*) осва́ивать (осво́ить *perf*); (*waste
materials*) перераба́тывать (перерабо́тать
perf).
reclamation [rɛklə'meɪʃən] *n* (*of land*)
освое́ние.
recline [rɪ'klaɪn] *vi* отки́дываться (отки́нуться
perf).
reclining [rɪ'klaɪnɪŋ] *adj* (*seat*) отки́дыва-
ющийся.
recluse [rɪ'klu:s] *n* затво́рник(-ица).
recognition [rɛkəg'nɪʃən] *n* призна́ние; (*of
person, place*) узнава́ние; **in** ~ **of** в знак
призна́ния +*gen*; **to gain** ~ получа́ть
(получи́ть* *perf*) призна́ние; **he has changed
beyond** ~ он измени́лся до неузнава́емости.
recognizable ['rɛkəgnaɪzəbl] *adj*: ~ (**by**)
узнава́емый (по +*dat*).
recognize ['rɛkəgnaɪz] *vt* признава́ть*
(призна́ть* *perf*); (*person, place*) узнава́ть*
(узна́ть *perf*); (*attitude, illness*) распознава́ть*
(распозна́ть* *perf*); **to** ~ **by** узнава́ть* (узна́ть*
perf) по +*dat*.
recoil [*n* 'ri:kɔɪl, *vb* rɪ'kɔɪl] *n* (*of gun*) отда́ча ♦ *vi*
(*person*): **to** ~ **from doing** в у́жасе отказа́ться
(*perf*) +*infin*.
recollect [rɛkə'lɛkt] *vt* припомина́ть
(припо́мнить *perf*), вспомина́ть (вспо́мнить
perf).
recollection [rɛkə'lɛkʃən] *n* воспомина́ние,
па́мять *f*; **to the best of my** ~ наско́лько мне
по́мнится.
recommend [rɛkə'mɛnd] *vt* рекомендова́ть
(порекомендова́ть *perf*); **she has a lot to** ~ **her**
мно́гое говори́т в её по́льзу.
recommendation [rɛkəmən'deɪʃən] *n*
рекоменда́ция; **on the** ~ **of** по рекоменда́ции
+*gen*.
recommended retail price *n* (*BRIT*)
рекоменду́емая ро́зничная цена́*.
recompense ['rɛkəmpɛns] *n* компенса́ция.
reconcilable ['rɛkənsaɪləbl] *adj* (*ideas*)
совмести́мый (совмести́м).
reconcile ['rɛkənsaɪl] *vt* (*people*) мири́ть
(помири́ть *perf*); (*facts, beliefs*) примиря́ть
(примири́ть *perf*); **to** ~ **o.s. to sth** смиря́ться
(смири́ться *perf*) с чем-н.
reconciliation [rɛkənsɪlɪ'eɪʃən] *n* примире́ние.
recondite [rɪ'kɔndaɪt] *adj* зау́мный* (зау́мен).
recondition [ri:kən'dɪʃən] *vt* (*machine*)
ремонти́ровать (отремонти́ровать *perf*).
reconditioned [ri:kən'dɪʃənd] *adj* от-
ремонти́рованный (отремонти́рован).
reconnaissance [rɪ'kɔnɪsns] *n* (*MIL*) разве́дка,

рекогносциро́вка.
reconnoitre [rɛkə'nɔɪtə^r] (*US* **reconnoiter**) *vt*
(*MIL: enemy territory*) разве́дывать
(разве́дать *perf*).
reconsider [ri:kən'sɪdə^r] *vt* пересма́тривать
(пересмотре́ть* *perf*) ◆ *vi* переду́мать (*perf*).
reconstitute [ri:'kɔnstɪtju:t] *vt* (*organization*)
реорганизова́ть (*impf/perf*); (*food*)
восстана́вливать (восстанови́ть* *perf*).
reconstruct [ri:kən'strʌkt] *vt* перестра́ивать
(перестро́ить *perf*); (*event, crime*)
воспроизводи́ть* (воспроизвести́* *perf*),
реконструи́ровать (*impf/perf*).
reconstruction [ri:kən'strʌkʃən] *n* (*of building*)
реконстру́кция; (*of country*) перестро́йка; (*of
crime*) воспроизведе́ние.
reconvene [ri:kən'vi:n] *vi* возобновля́ть
(возобнови́ть* *perf*) рабо́ту.
record [*vb* rɪ'kɔ:d, *n, adj* 'rɛkɔ:d] *vt* (*in writing, on
tape*) запи́сывать (записа́ть* *perf*); (*register:
temperature, speed etc*) регистри́ровать
(зарегистри́ровать *perf*) ◆ *n* (*written account,
also* COMPUT) за́пись *f*; (*of meeting*) протоко́л;
(*of attendance*) учёт; (*file*) де́ло*; (*MUS*)
пласти́нка*; (*history: of person, company*)
репута́ция; (*also:* **criminal ~**) суди́мость *f*;
(*SPORT*) реко́рд ◆ *adj*: **in ~ time** в реко́рдное
вре́мя; **public ~s** архи́вные за́писи; **to keep a
~ of** вести́* (*impf*) учёт +*gen*; **to put the ~
straight** (*fig*) пока́зывать (показа́ть* *perf*)
и́стинное положе́ние веще́й; **he is on ~ as
saying that ...** изве́стно, что он сказа́л, что
...; **off the ~** (*statement*) неофициа́льный;
(*speak*) неофициа́льно.
recorded delivery [rɪ'kɔ:dɪd-] *n* (*BRIT*) доста́вка
с уведомле́нием (о вруче́нии).
recorder [rɪ'kɔ:də^r] *n* (*MUS*) англи́йская
фле́йта; (*LAW*) реко́рдер.
record holder (*SPORT*) *n* рекордсме́н(ка).
recording [rɪ'kɔ:dɪŋ] *n* за́пись *f*.
recording studio *n* сту́дия звукоза́писи.
record library *n* фоноте́ка.
record player *n* прои́грыватель *m*.
recount [rɪ'kaunt] *vt* (*story*) передава́ть*
(переда́ть* *perf*); (*event*) пове́дать (*perf*) о
+*prp*.
re-count ['ri:kaunt] *n* (*of votes*) пересчёт ◆ *vt*
пересчи́тывать (пересчита́ть* *perf*).
recoup [rɪ'ku:p] *vt*: **to ~ one's losses**
возвраща́ть (верну́ть *perf*) поте́рянное.
recourse [rɪ'kɔ:s] *n*: **to have ~ to** прибега́ть
(прибе́гнуть* *perf*) к +*dat*.
recover [rɪ'kʌvə^r] *vt* (*lost or stolen items*)
получа́ть (получи́ть* *perf*) обра́тно; (*financial
loss*) возмеща́ть (возмести́ть* *perf*) ◆ *vi* (*subj:
country*) встава́ть* (встать* *perf*) на́ ноги;
(: *economy*) улучша́ться (улу́чшиться *perf*);
(*get better*): **to ~ (from)** поправля́ться

(попра́виться* *perf*) (по́сле +*gen*).
re-cover [ri:'kʌvə^r] *vt* (*chair etc*) перебива́ть
(переби́ть* *perf*) (оби́вку).
recovery [rɪ'kʌvərɪ] *n* (*from illness, operation*)
выздоровле́ние; (*in economy, finances*)
подъём; (*of stolen items*) возвраще́ние; (*of
lost items*) обнаруже́ние.
re-create [ri:krɪ'eɪt] *vt* воссоздава́ть*
(воссозда́ть* *perf*).
recreation [rɛkrɪ'eɪʃən] *n* (*free time*) о́тдых;
(*leisure activities*) развлече́ние.
recreational [rɛkrɪ'eɪʃənl] *adj*: **~ facilities**
усло́вия *ntpl* для о́тдыха и развлече́ния.
recreational drug *n* нарко́тик, *принима́емый
для удово́льствия и не предполага́ющий
наркоти́ческой зави́симости*.
recrimination [rɪkrɪmɪ'neɪʃən] *n* взаи́мные
обвине́ния *ntpl*.
recruit [rɪ'kru:t] *n* (*MIL*) новобра́нец*,
призывни́к*; (*in company*) но́вый сотру́дник;
(*in organization*) но́вый член ◆ *vt* (*into army,
organization*) вербова́ть (завербова́ть *perf*);
(*into company*) нанима́ть (наня́ть* *perf*).
recruiting office [rɪ'kru:tɪŋ-] *n* (*MIL*)
вербо́вочный пункт.
recruitment [rɪ'kru:tmənt] *n* (*MIL*) вербо́вка;
(*by company*) набо́р (*на рабо́ту*).
rectangle ['rɛktæŋgl] *n* прямоуго́льник.
rectangular [rɛk'tæŋgjulə^r] *adj*
прямоуго́льный.
rectify ['rɛktɪfaɪ] *vt* исправля́ть (испра́вить*
perf).
rector ['rɛktə^r] *n* (*REL*) прихо́дский свяще́нник.
rectory ['rɛktərɪ] *n* (*house*) дом* прихо́дского
свяще́нника.
rectum ['rɛktəm] *n* прямая́ кишка́*.
recuperate [rɪ'kju:pəreɪt] *vi* оправля́ться
(опра́виться* *perf*).
recur [rɪ'kə:^r] *vi* повторя́ться (повтори́ться
perf).
recurrence [rɪ'kə:rns] *n* повторе́ние.
recurrent [rɪ'kə:rnt] *adj* повторя́ющийся.
recurring [rɪ'kə:rɪŋ] *adj* (*problem*) постоя́нно
возника́ющий; (*dream*) повторя́ющийся.
recycle [ri:'saɪkl] *vt* перераба́тывать
(перерабо́тать *perf*).
red [rɛd] *n* кра́сный цвет; (*pej:* POL) кра́сный
(-ая) *m(f) adj* ◆ *adj* кра́сный (кра́сен); (*hair*)
ры́жий*; (*wine*) кра́сный; **she was dressed in
~** она́ была́ в кра́сном; **to be in the ~** име́ть
(*impf*) задо́лженность.
red alert *n* состоя́ние боево́й гото́вности.
red-blooded ['rɛd'blʌdɪd] *adj*: **~ male** саме́ц*
(*перен*).
red-carpet treatment [rɛd'kɑ:pɪt-] *n*
торже́ственный приём.
Red Cross *n* Кра́сный Крест*.
redcurrant ['rɛdkʌrənt] *n* кра́сная сморо́дина *f*

no pl.

redden ['rɛdn] *vi* краснéть (покраснéть *perf*) ◆ *vt* окрáшивать (окрáсить* *perf*) в крáсный цвет.

reddish ['rɛdɪʃ] *adj* краснова́тый (красновáт*); (*hair*) рыжева́тый (рыжева́т*).

redecorate [ri:'dɛkəreɪt] *vt* ремонти́ровать (отремонти́ровать *perf*) ◆ *vi* дéлать (сдéлать *perf*) ремóнт.

redecoration [ri:dɛkə'reɪʃən] *n* ремóнт.

redeem [rɪ'di:m] *vt* (*situation, reputation*) спаса́ть (спасти́* *perf*); (*pawned item*) выкупа́ть (вы́купить* *perf*); (*debt*) выпла́чивать (вы́платить* *perf*); (*REL*) искупа́ть (искупи́ть* *perf*); **to ~ o.s.** искупа́ть (искупи́ть* *perf*) свою́ вину́.

redeemable [rɪ'di:məbl] *adj* подлежа́щий вы́купу.

redeeming [rɪ'di:mɪŋ] *adj*: **~ feature** подкупа́ющее ка́чество.

redefine [ri:dɪ'faɪn] *vt* (*position, theory*) пересма́тривать (пересмотрéть* *perf*); (*word, concept*) дава́ть* (дать* *perf*) нóвое определéние +*dat*.

redemption [rɪ'dɛmʃən] *n* (*REL*) искуплéние грехóв; **past** *or* **beyond ~** (*fig*) безнадёжный* (безнадёжен), без надéжды на спасéние.

redeploy [ri:dɪ'plɔɪ] *vt* (*resources*) перераспределя́ть (перераспредели́ть *perf*); (*MIL*) передислоци́ровать (*impf/perf*).

redeployment [ri:dɪ'plɔɪmənt] *n* (*see vb*) перераспределéние; передислока́ция.

redevelop [ri:dɪ'vɛləp] *vt* (*area*) перестра́ивать (перестрóить *perf*).

redevelopment [ri:dɪ'vɛləpmənt] *n* перестрóйка.

red-handed [rɛd'hændɪd] *adj*: **he was caught ~** егó пойма́ли с поли́чным.

redhead ['rɛdhɛd] *n* ры́жий*(-ая) *m(f) adj*.

red herring *n* (*fig*) отвлека́ющий манёвр.

red-hot [rɛd'hɒt] *adj* (*metal*) раскалённый* (раскалён) докрасна́.

redirect [ri:daɪ'rɛkt] *vt* (*mail*) переадресóвывать (переадресова́ть *perf*).

rediscover [ri:dɪs'kʌvə'] *vt* зáново открыва́ть (откры́ть* *perf*).

redistribute [ri:dɪs'trɪbju:t] *vt* перераспределя́ть (перераспредели́ть *perf*).

red-letter day ['rɛdlɛtə-] *n* прáздничный день* *m*.

red light *n*: **to go through a ~ ~** (*AUT*) éхать* (поéхать* *perf*) на крáсный свет.

red-light district ['rɛdlaɪt-] *n* кварта́л публи́чных домóв.

red meat *n* тёмное мя́со (*осóбенно говя́дина и бара́нина*).

redness ['rɛdnɪs] *n* краснота́; (*of hair*) рыжина́*.

redo [ri:'du:] *irreg vt* передéлывать (передéлать *perf*).

redolent ['rɛdələnt] *adj* (*fig*) напомина́ющий;

(*smell*): **~ of** (*unpleasant*) отдаю́щий +*instr*; (*pleasant*) пáхнущий +*gen*.

redouble [ri:'dʌbl] *vt*: **to ~ one's efforts** удва́ивать (удвóить *perf*) свои́ уси́лия.

redraft [ri:'drɑ:ft] *vt* перепи́сывать (переписа́ть* *perf*).

redraw [ri:'drɔ:] *vt* изменя́ть (измени́ть* *perf*).

redress [rɪ'drɛs] *n* (*compensation*) возмещéние ◆ *vt* (*error, wrong*) исправля́ть (испра́вить* *perf*); **to ~ the balance** восстана́вливать (восстанови́ть* *perf*) равновéсие сил.

Red Sea *n*: **the ~ ~** Крáсное мóре.

red tape *n* (*fig*) волоки́та.

reduce [rɪ'dju:s] *vt* сокраща́ть (сократи́ть* *perf*); **to ~ sth by/to** сокраща́ть (сократи́ть* *perf*) что-н на +*acc*/до +*gen*; **to ~ sb to** (*tears*) доводи́ть* (довести́* *perf*) когó-н до +*gen*; **to ~ sb to silence** заставля́ть (заста́вить* *perf*) когó-н замолча́ть; **he was ~d to stealing** он дошёл до тогó, что стал ворова́ть; **"reduce speed now"** (*AUT*) "сба́вьте скóрость".

reduced [rɪ'dju:st] *adj* (*goods*) по сни́женным цéнам; (*ticket*) со ски́дкой; **at a ~ price** (*goods*) по сни́женной ценé; (*ticket*) со ски́дкой.

reduction [rɪ'dʌkʃən] *n* (*in price*) ски́дка; (*in numbers*) сокращéние.

redundancy [rɪ'dʌndənsɪ] (*BRIT*) *n* (*dismissal*) увольнéние (*при сокраще́нии шта́тов*); (*unemployment*) сокращéние шта́тов; **compulsory ~** вы́нужденное увольнéние; **voluntary ~** увольнéние по сóбственному жела́нию.

redundancy payment *n* (*BRIT*) выходнóе пособие (*при сокраще́нии шта́тов*).

redundant [rɪ'dʌndnt] *adj* (*BRIT*: *unemployed*) увóленный (увóлен); (*useless*) изли́шний* (изли́шен); **he was made ~** его́ сократи́ли.

reed [ri:d] *n* (*BOT*) тростни́к*; (*MUS*) язычóк*.

re-educate [ri:'ɛdjukeɪt] *vt* перевоспи́тывать (перевоспита́ть *perf*).

reedy ['ri:dɪ] *adj* (*voice*) пронзи́тельный* (пронзи́телен).

reef [ri:f] *n* риф.

reek [ri:k] *vi*: **to ~ (of)** си́льно пáхнуть* (*impf*) (+*instr*).

reel [ri:l] *n* кату́шка*; (*of film, tape*) боби́на; (*dance*) рил (*народ́ный хоровод́ный та́нец*) ◆ *vi* (*sway*) кача́ться (*impf*), шата́ться (*impf*); **my head is ~ing** у меня́ кру́жится голова́

▸ **reel in** *vt* (*line*) сма́тывать (смота́ть *perf*); (*fish*) выта́скивать (вы́тащить *perf*) (*при по́мощи спи́ннинга*).

▸ **reel off** *vt* (*say*) вы́палить (*perf*).

re-election [ri:ɪ'lɛkʃən] *n* (*event*) перевы́боры *pl*; (*of person*) переизбра́ние.

re-enter [ri:'ɛntə'] *vt* вновь входи́ть* (войти́* *perf*).

re-entry [ri:'ɛntrɪ] *n* повтóрный вход.

re-examine [ri:ɪg'zæmɪn] *vt* пересма́тривать (пересмотрéть* *perf*).

re-export ['riːɪks'pɔːt] *vt* реэкспорти́ровать (*impf/perf*) ♦ *n* реэ́кспорт.

ref [rɛf] *n abbr* (*SPORT*: *inf*) = **referee**.

ref. *abbr* (*COMM*: = *with reference to*) ссыла́ясь на +*acc*.

refectory [rɪ'fɛktərɪ] *n* столо́вая *f adj*.

refer [rɪ'fɜː'] *vt*: **to ~ sb to** (*book, source*) отсыла́ть (отосла́ть* *perf*) кого́-н к +*dat*; (*doctor*) направля́ть (напра́вить* *perf*) кого́-н к +*dat*; **to ~ sth to** (*pass on*) передава́ть* (переда́ть* *perf*) что-н к +*dat*; **he ~red me to the manager** он напра́вил меня́ к управля́ющему

▸ **refer to** *vt fus* (*mention*) упомина́ть (упомяну́ть* *perf*) о +*prp*; (*relate to*) относи́ться* (*impf*) к +*dat*; (*consult*) обраща́ться (обрати́ться* *perf*) к +*dat*; **~ring to your letter** ссыла́ясь на Ва́ше письмо́.

referee [rɛfə'riː] *n* (*SPORT*) рефери́ *m ind*, судья́* *m*; (*BRIT*: *for job application*) лицо́, даю́щее рекоменда́цию ♦ *vt* суди́ть* (*impf*).

reference ['rɛfrəns] *n* (*mention*) упомина́ние; (*in book, paper*) ссы́лка*; (*for job application*: *letter*) рекоменда́ция; (: *person*) лицо́, даю́щее рекоменда́цию; **with ~ to** (*in letter*) ссыла́ясь на +*acc*; **"please quote this ~"** (*COMM*) "сошли́тесь на э́тот спра́вочный но́мер".

reference book *n* спра́вочник.

reference library *n* спра́вочная библиоте́ка.

reference number *n* спра́вочный но́мер*.

referenda [rɛfə'rɛndə] *npl of* **referendum**.

referendum [rɛfə'rɛndəm] (*pl* **referenda**) *n* рефере́ндум.

referral [rɪ'fɜːrəl] *n* направле́ние.

refill [*vb* riː'fɪl, *n* 'riːfɪl] *vt* (*glass*) сно́ва наполня́ть (напо́лнить *perf*); (*pen*) заправля́ть (запра́вить* *perf*) ♦ *n* (*for pen*) запасно́й сте́ржень* *m*.

refine [rɪ'faɪn] *vt* (*sugar*) рафини́ровать (*impf/ perf*); (*oil*) очища́ть (очи́стить* *perf*); (*theory, idea, task*) соверше́нствовать (усоверше́нствовать *perf*).

refined [rɪ'faɪnd] *adj* (*person, taste*) утонче́нный* (утончён); (*sugar*) рафини́рованный*; (*oil*) очи́щенный*.

refinement [rɪ'faɪnmənt] *n* (*of person*) утонченность *f*; (*of system*) усоверше́нствование.

refinery [rɪ'faɪnərɪ] *n* (*for oil*) нефтеперераба́тывающий заво́д.

refit [riː'fɪt] *n* (*of ship*) переобору́дование ♦ *vt* (*ship*) переобору́довать (*impf/perf*).

reflate [riː'fleɪt] *vt*: **to ~ the economy** проводи́ть* (провести́* *perf*) рефля́цию.

reflation [riː'fleɪʃən] *n* рефля́ция.

reflationary [riː'fleɪʃənrɪ] *adj* рефляцио́нный.

reflect [rɪ'flɛkt] *vt* (*also fig*) отража́ть

(отрази́ть* *perf*) ♦ *vi* (*think*) размышля́ть (*impf*)

▸ **reflect on** *vt* (*discredit*) броса́ть (бро́сить* *perf*) тень на +*acc*.

reflection [rɪ'flɛkʃən] *n* (*also fig*) отраже́ние; (*thought*) размышле́ние; (*criticism*): **~ on** осужде́ние +*gen*; **on ~** по размышле́нии.

reflector [rɪ'flɛktə'] *n* (*on car, bicycle*) отража́тель *m*; (*for light, heat*) рефле́ктор.

reflex ['riːflɛks] *adj* (*action, gesture*) рефлекто́рный ♦ *n* рефле́кс.

reflexive [rɪ'flɛksɪv] *adj* (*LING*) возвра́тный.

reform [rɪ'fɔːm] *n* (*of law, system*) рефо́рма; (*of sinner, character*) преобразова́ние ♦ *vt* (*character*) преобразова́ть (*impf/perf*); (*system*) реформи́ровать (*impf/perf*).

reformat [riː'fɔːmæt] *vt* (*COMPUT*) переформати́ровать (*impf/perf*).

Reformation [rɛfə'meɪʃən] *n*: **the ~** Реформа́ция.

reformatory [rɪ'fɔːmətərɪ] *n* (*US*) исправи́тельное заведе́ние.

reformed [rɪ'fɔːmd] *adj* (*character, alcoholic*) испра́вившийся.

refrain [rɪ'freɪn] *n* (*of song*) припе́в ♦ *vi*: **to ~ from commenting/visiting** возде́рживаться (воздержа́ться* *perf*) от коммента́риев/ визи́та.

refresh [rɪ'frɛʃ] *vt* освежа́ть (освежи́ть *perf*).

refresher course [rɪ'frɛʃə-] *n* (*BRIT*) курс повыше́ния квалифика́ции.

refreshing [rɪ'frɛʃɪŋ] *adj* (*drink, sleep*) освежа́ющий (освежа́ющ); (*change, idea*) све́жий.

refreshment [rɪ'frɛʃmənt] *n* (*food*) заку́ска*; (*drink*) напи́ток*; **I am in need of (some) ~** мне на́до закуси́ть.

refreshments [rɪ'frɛʃmənts] *npl* заку́ски* *fpl* и напи́тки *mpl*.

refrigeration [rɪfrɪdʒə'reɪʃən] *n* (*low temperature*) охлажде́ние; (*in deep freeze*) замора́живание.

refrigerator [rɪ'frɪdʒəreɪtə'] *n* холоди́льник.

refuel [riː'fjuəl] *vi* заправля́ться (запра́виться* *perf*) ♦ *vt* заправля́ть (запра́вить* *perf*).

refuelling [riː'fjuəlɪŋ] *n* запра́вка.

refuge ['rɛfjuːdʒ] *n* (*shelter*) убе́жище; **to take ~ in** укрыва́ться (укры́ться* *perf*) в +*prp*.

refugee [rɛfju'dʒiː] *n* бе́женец*(-нка*); **a political ~** полити́ческий*(-ая) бе́женец (-нка*).

refugee camp *n* ла́герь* *m* бе́женцев.

refund [*n* 'riːfʌnd, *vb* rɪ'fʌnd] *n* возмеще́ние ♦ *vt* (*money*) возмеща́ть (возмести́ть* *perf*).

refurbish [riː'fɜːbɪʃ] *vt* за́ново отде́лывать (отде́лать *perf*).

refurbishment [riː'fɜːbɪʃmənt] *n* ремо́нт.

refurnish [riː'fɜːnɪʃ] *vt* за́ново обставля́ть (обста́вить* *perf*).

---

* marks translations which have irregular inflections. The Russian-English side of the dictionary gives inflectional information.

refusal [rɪ'fju:zəl] *n* отказ; **first ~** (*option*) право первого выбора.

refuse[1] [rɪ'fju:z] *vt* (*offer, gift*) отказываться (отказаться* *perf*) от +*gen*; (*permission, consent*) отказывать (отказать* *perf*) в +*prp* ◆ *vi* отказываться (отказаться* *perf*); (*horse*) упрямиться (заупрямиться *perf*); **to ~ to do** отказываться (отказаться* *perf*) +*infin*.

refuse[2] ['rɛfju:s] *n* мусор*.

refuse collection *n* уборка мусора.

refuse disposal *n* (*by carting away*) вывоз мусора.

refusenik [rɪ'fju:znɪk] *n* отказник.

refute [rɪ'fju:t] *vt* опровергать (опровергнуть* *perf*).

regain [rɪ'geɪn] *vt* (*power, position*) вновь обретать (обрести* *perf*).

regal ['ri:gl] *adj* королевский*.

regale [rɪ'geɪl] *vt*: **to ~ sb with sth** развлекать (развлечь* *perf*) кого-н чем-н.

regalia [rɪ'geɪlɪə] *n* регалии *fpl*.

regard [rɪ'gɑ:d] *n* (*esteem*) уважение ◆ *vt* (*consider*) считать (*impf*); (*view, look on*): **to ~ with** относиться (*impf*) *or* рассматриваться (*impf*) с +*instr*; **to give one's ~s to** передавать* (передать* *perf*) привет +*dat*; **"with kindest ~s"** „с наилучшими пожеланиями"; (*more formal*) „с уважением"; **as ~s, with ~ to** что касается +*gen*, относительно +*gen*.

regarding [rɪ'gɑ:dɪŋ] *prep* относительно +*gen*.

regardless [rɪ'gɑ:dlɪs] *adv* (*carry on, continue*) несмотря ни на что; **~ of** не считаясь с +*instr*.

regatta [rɪ'gætə] *n* регата.

regency ['ri:dʒənsɪ] *n* регентство ◆ *adj*: **R~** (*furniture, style*) эпохи регентства.

regenerate [rɪ'dʒɛnəreɪt] *vt* возрождать (возродить* *perf*) ◆ *vi* возрождаться (возродиться* *perf*).

regent ['ri:dʒənt] *n* регент.

reggae ['rɛgeɪ] *n* рэгги *m ind*.

regime [reɪ'ʒi:m] *n* (*system of government*) режим.

regiment ['rɛdʒɪmənt] *n* полк* ◆ *vt* подчинять (подчинить* *perf*) жёсткому контролю.

regimental [rɛdʒɪ'mɛntl] *adj* полковой.

regimentation [rɛdʒɪmɛn'teɪʃən] *n* жёсткий* контроль *m*.

region ['ri:dʒən] *n* (*area: of country*) район, регион; (*ADMIN, ANAT*) область* *f*; **in the ~ of** (*fig: approximately*) в районе +*gen*.

regional ['ri:dʒənl] *adj* (*organization, committee*) областной, региональный; (*characteristic of region*) местный.

regional development *n* региональное развитие.

register ['rɛdʒɪstə'] *n* (*census, record*) запись *f*; (*SCOL*) журнал; (*also:* **electoral ~**) список* избирателей; (*MUS*) регистр ◆ *vt* регистрировать (зарегистрировать *perf*); (*subj: meter, gauge*) показывать (показать*

perf) ◆ *vi* регистрироваться (зарегистрироваться *perf*); (*as student*) записываться (записаться* *perf*); (*make impression*) запечатлеваться (запечатлеться *perf*) в памяти; **to ~ for a course** записываться (записаться *perf*) на курс; **to ~ a protest** выражать (выразить* *perf*) протест.

registered ['rɛdʒɪstəd] *adj* (*letter*) заказной; (*nurse, addict*) зарегистрированный*.

registered company *n* зарегистрированная компания.

registered nurse *n* (*US*) зарегистрированная медсестра*.

registered office *n* зарегистрированный офис.

Registered Trademark *n* зарегистрированный товарный знак.

registrar ['rɛdʒɪstrɑ:'] *n* регистратор; (*BRIT: in hospital*) главный врач*.

registration [rɛdʒɪs'treɪʃən] *n* регистрация; (*AUT: also:* **~ number**) (регистрационный) номер* машины.

registry ['rɛdʒɪstrɪ] *n* регистратура.

registry office *n* (*BRIT*) ≈ ЗАГС (*отдел записей гражданского состояния*).

regret [rɪ'grɛt] *n* (*sorrow*) сожаление ◆ *vt* сожалеть (*impf*) о +*prp*; (*death*) оплакивать (оплакать* *perf*); **to ~ that** ... сожалеть (*impf*), что ...; **we ~ to inform you that** ... мы с сожалением сообщаем Вам, что ....

regretfully [rɪ'grɛtfəlɪ] *adv* (*unfortunately*) к сожалению.

regrettable [rɪ'grɛtəbl] *adj* (*unfortunate*) прискорбный* (прискорбен), достойный* (достоин) сожаления.

regrettably [rɪ'grɛtəblɪ] *adv* (*drunk, late*) огорчительным образом; **~, he** ... к сожалению, он ....

Regt *abbr* (*MIL*) = **regiment**.

regular ['rɛgjulə'] *adj* регулярный* (регулярен); (*even*) ровный* (ровен); (*symmetrical*) правильный* (правилен); (*usual: time*) определённый; (: *doctor, customer*) регулярный; (*LING*) правильный; (*COMM: size*) средний* ◆ *n* (*in cafe, restaurnat*) завсегдатай; (*in shop*) клиент; **~ soldier** солдат регулярной армии.

regularity [rɛgju'lærɪtɪ] *n* (*frequency*) регулярность *f*.

regularly ['rɛgjuləlɪ] *adv* регулярно; (*symmetrically: shaped etc*) правильно.

regulate ['rɛgjuleɪt] *vt* (*control, adjust*) регулировать (*impf*).

regulation [rɛgju'leɪʃən] *n* регулирование; (*rule*) правило.

regulatory [rɛgju'leɪtrɪ] *adj* регулирующий.

rehabilitate [ri:ə'bɪlɪteɪt] *vt* (*criminal*) интегрировать (*impf/perf*); (*invalid, addict*) реабилитировать (*impf/perf*).

rehabilitation ['ri:əbɪlɪ'teɪʃən] *n* (*of criminal*)

интегра́ция; (*of disabled, addict*) реабилита́ция.

rehash [riː'hæʃ] *vt* (*inf*) преподноси́ть* (преподнести́* *perf*) в но́вом све́те.

rehearsal [rɪ'həːsəl] *n* репети́ция; **dress ~** генера́льная репети́ция.

rehearse [rɪ'həːs] *vt* репети́ровать (отрепети́ровать *perf*).

rehouse [riː'hauz] *vt* (*person*) переселя́ть (пересели́ть *perf*).

reign [rem] *n* ца́рствование; (*fig*) госпо́дство ◆ *vi* (*monarch*) ца́рствовать (*impf*); (*fig*) цари́ть (*impf*).

reigning ['remɪŋ] *adj* (*monarch*) ца́рствующий; (*champion*) ны́нешний*.

reimburse [riːɪm'bəːs] *vt* возмеща́ть (возмести́ть* *perf*).

rein [rem] *n* (*for horse*) вожжа́*; **to give sb free ~** (*fig*) дава́ть* (дать* *perf*) кому́-н свобо́ду де́йствий.

reincarnation [riːɪnkɑːˈneɪʃən] *n* (*belief*) переселе́ние душ*.

reindeer ['remdɪə'] *n inv* се́верный оле́нь *m*.

reinforce [riːɪn'fɔːs] *vt* (*strengthen*) укрепля́ть (укрепи́ть* *perf*); (*back up*) подкрепля́ть (подкрепи́ть* *perf*).

reinforced concrete *n* железобето́н.

reinforcement [riːɪn'fɔːsmənt] *n* (*strengthening*) укрепле́ние; (*action*) усиле́ние; **~s** *npl* (*MIL*) подкрепле́ние *ntsg*.

reinstate [riːɪn'steɪt] *vt* восстана́вливать (восстанови́ть* *perf*) в пре́жнем положе́нии.

reinstatement [riːɪn'steɪtmənt] *n* восстановле́ние в пре́жнем положе́нии.

reissue [riː'ɪʃjuː] *vt* (*book*) переиздава́ть* (переизда́ть* *perf*); (*film*) сно́ва выпуска́ть (вы́пустить* *perf*).

reiterate [riː'ɪtəreɪt] *vt* повторя́ть (повтори́ть *perf*).

reject [*vt* rɪ'dʒɛkt, *n* 'riːdʒɛkt] *vt* отклоня́ть (отклони́ть* *perf*), отверга́ть (отве́ргнуть* *perf*); (*political system*) отверга́ть (отве́ргнуть* *perf*); (*candidate*) отклоня́ть (отклони́ть* *perf*); (*coin*) не принима́ть (приня́ть* *perf*); (*goods, fruit etc*) бракова́ть (забракова́ть *perf*) ◆ *n* (*COMM: single item*) брако́ванное изде́лие; **~s** брак.

rejection [rɪ'dʒɛkʃən] *n* отклоне́ние; (*of candidate*) отклоне́ние.

rejoice [rɪ'dʒɔɪs] *vi*: **to ~ at** *or* **over** ликова́ть (*impf*) по по́воду +*gen*.

rejoinder [rɪ'dʒɔɪndə'] *n* (*retort*) возраже́ние, отве́т.

rejuvenate [rɪ'dʒuːvəneɪt] *vt* (*person*) омола́живать (омолоди́ть* *perf*); (*organization, system etc*) обновля́ть (обнови́ть* *perf*).

rekindle [riː'kɪndl] *vt* разжига́ть (разже́чь*

perf).

relapse [rɪ'læps] *n* (*MED*) рециди́в ◆ *vi*: **to ~ into** (*depression*) (сно́ва) впада́ть (впасть* *perf*) в +*acc*.

relate [rɪ'leɪt] *vt* (*tell*) переска́зывать (пересказа́ть* *perf*); (*connect*): **to ~ sth to** относи́ть* (отнести́* *perf*) что-н к +*dat* ◆ *vi*: **to ~ to** (*person*) сходи́ться* (*impf*) с +*instr*; (*subject, thing*) относи́ться* (*impf*) к +*dat*.

related [rɪ'leɪtɪd] *adj*: **~ (to)** (*person*) свя́занный родство́м (с +*instr*); (*animal, language*) ро́дственный* (ро́дствен) (с +*instr*); **they are ~** они́ состоя́т в родстве́.

relating to [rɪ'leɪtɪŋ-] *prep* относи́тельно +*gen*.

relation [rɪ'leɪʃən] *n* (*member of family*) ро́дственник(-ица); (*connection*) отноше́ние; **~s** *npl* (*dealings*) сноше́ния *ntpl*; (*relatives*) родня́ *fsg*; **diplomatic/international ~s** дипломати́ческие/междунаро́дные отноше́ния; **in ~ to** относи́тельно +*gen*; **to bear no ~ to** не име́ть (*impf*) никако́го отноше́ния к +*dat*.

relationship [rɪ'leɪʃənʃɪp] *n* (*between two people, countries*) (взаимо-)отноше́ния *ntpl*; (*between two things*) связь *f*; (*also*: **family ~**) родство́; (*affair*) связь; **they have a good ~** у них хоро́шие (взаимо-)отноше́ния.

relative ['rɛlətɪv] *n* (*member of family*) ро́дственник(-ица) ◆ *adj* (*comparative*) относи́тельный* (относи́телен); (*connected*): **~ to** относя́щийся к +*dat*.

relatively ['rɛlətɪvlɪ] *adv* относи́тельно.

relative pronoun *n* (*LING*) относи́тельное местоиме́ние.

relax [rɪ'læks] *vi* (*person: unwind*) расслабля́ться (рассла́биться* *perf*); (: *calm down*) успока́иваться (успоко́иться *perf*); (*muscle*) расслабля́ться (рассла́биться* *perf*) ◆ *vt* (*one's grip, rule*) ослабля́ть (осла́бить* *perf*); (*mind, person*) расслабля́ть (рассла́бить* *perf*); (*control*) ослабля́ть (осла́бить* *perf*).

relaxation [riːlæk'seɪʃən] *n* (*rest*) о́тдых; (*of muscle*) расслабле́ние; (*of grip, rule, control etc*) ослабле́ние; (*recreation*) о́тдых, развлече́ние.

relaxed [rɪ'lækst] *adj* (*person, atmosphere*) споко́йный* (споко́ен).

relaxing [rɪ'læksɪŋ] *adj* (*holiday, afternoon*) расслабля́ющий*.

relay [*n* 'riːleɪ, *vt* rɪ'leɪ] *n* (*race*) эстафе́та ◆ *vt* (*pass on: message etc*) передава́ть* (переда́ть* *perf*); (*transmit*) трансли́ровать (*impf/perf*).

release [rɪ'liːs] *n* (*from prison, obligation*) освобожде́ние; (*of gas, water etc*) вы́пуск; (*of film, book, record*) вы́пуск; (*of device*) спусково́е устро́йство, спуск ◆ *vt* (*prisoner*) освобожда́ть (освободи́ть* *perf*); (*gas etc*)

---

* marks translations which have irregular inflections. The Russian-English side of the dictionary gives inflectional information.

выпуска́ть (вы́пустить* *perf*); (*free: from wreckage etc*) высвобожда́ть (вы́свободить* *perf*); (*TECH: catch, spring etc*) отпуска́ть (отпусти́ть* *perf*); (*book, film*) выпуска́ть (вы́пустить* *perf*); (*report, news*) передава́ть* (переда́ть* *perf*); **to ~ the clutch** (*AUT*) отпуска́ть (отпусти́ть* *perf*) сцепле́ние; *see also* **press release**.

relegate ['rɛləɡeɪt] *vt* понижа́ть (пони́зить* *perf*); (*BRIT: SPORT*): **to be ~d** переводи́ть* (перевести́* *perf*) в ни́зшую ли́гу.

relent [rɪ'lɛnt] *vi* (*give in*) уступа́ть (уступи́ть* *perf*).

relentless [rɪ'lɛntlɪs] *adj* (*effort*) неосла́бный; (*rain*) продолжи́тельный* (продолжи́телен); (*determined*) неуста́нный* (неуста́нен).

relevance ['rɛləvəns] *n* (*of remarks*) уме́стность *f*, релева́нтность *f*; (*of information*) актуа́льность *f*; (*of question*) уме́стность; **~ of sth to sth** уме́стность чего́-н по отноше́нию к чему́-н.

relevant ['rɛləvənt] *adj* (*pertinent*) актуа́льный* (актуа́лен), релева́нтный* (релева́нтен); (*corresponding*) соотве́тствующий*; **~ to** относя́щийся* к +*dat*.

reliability [rɪlaɪə'bɪlɪtɪ] *n* (*see adj*) надёжность *f*; достове́рность *f*.

reliable [rɪ'laɪəbl] *adj* надёжный* (надёжен); (*news, information*) достове́рный* (достове́рен).

reliably [rɪ'laɪəblɪ] *adv*: **to be ~ informed that ...** име́ть (*impf*) достове́рную информа́цию о том, что ....

reliance [rɪ'laɪəns] *n*: **~ (on)** (*person, drugs*) зави́симость *f* (от +*gen*).

reliant [rɪ'laɪənt] *adj*: **to be ~ on sth/sb** полага́ться (положи́ться* *perf*) на кого́-н/ что-н.

relic ['rɛlɪk] *n* (*REL*) мо́щи *pl*; (*of the past etc*) рели́квия.

relief [rɪ'liːf] *n* облегче́ние; (*aid*) по́мощь *f*; (*ART, GEO*) релье́ф; **by way of light ~** для разря́дки напряжённости.

relief map *n* релье́фная ка́рта.

relief road *n* объе́зд (*доро́га, отводя́щая тра́нспорт*).

relieve [rɪ'liːv] *vt* (*pain, sufferings*) облегча́ть (облегчи́ть *perf*); (*fear, worry*) уменьша́ть (уме́ньшить *perf*); (*patient*) освобожда́ть (освободи́ть* *perf*); (*victims, refugees etc*) ока́зывать (оказа́ть* *perf*) по́мощь +*dat*; (*colleague, guard*) сменя́ть (смени́ть* *perf*); **to ~ sb of sth** освобожда́ть (освободи́ть* *perf*) кого́-н от чего́-н; **to ~ o.s.** облегча́ться (облегчи́ться *perf*).

relieved [rɪ'liːvd] *adj*: **to feel ~** почу́вствовать (*perf*) облегче́ние; **he is ~ that ...** он рад, что ...; **I'm ~ to hear it** я рад э́то слы́шать.

religion [rɪ'lɪdʒən] *n* рели́гия.

religious [rɪ'lɪdʒəs] *adj* религио́зный* (религио́зен).

religious education *n* религио́зное воспита́ние.

religiously [rɪ'lɪdʒəslɪ] *adv* (*scrupulously*) неукосни́тельно.

relinquish [rɪ'lɪŋkwɪʃ] *vt* (*authority*) отка́зываться (отказа́ться* *perf*) от +*gen*; (*plan, habit*) оставля́ть (оста́вить* *perf*).

relish ['rɛlɪʃ] *n* (*CULIN*) припра́ва; (*enjoyment*) наслажде́ние ♦ *vt* (*food, drink*) наслажда́ться (наслади́ться* *perf*) +*instr*; (*idea, thought, prospect etc*) наслажда́ться (*impf*).

relive [riː'lɪv] *vt* (*memory, pleasure, visit etc*) вновь пережива́ть (пережи́ть* *perf*).

reload [riː'ləud] *vt* (*gun*) перезаряжа́ть (перезаряди́ть* *perf*).

relocate [riːləu'keɪt] *vt* перемеща́ть (перемести́ть* *perf*) ♦ *vi*: **to ~ (in)** перемеща́ться (перемести́ться* *perf*) (в +*acc*).

reluctance [rɪ'lʌktəns] *n* неохо́та, нежела́ние.

reluctant [rɪ'lʌktənt] *adj* (*acceptance*) неохо́тный* (неохо́тен); (*person*): **he is ~ to go there** он идёт туда́ неохо́тно.

reluctantly [rɪ'lʌktntlɪ] *adv* неохо́тно.

rely on [rɪ'laɪ-] *vt fus* (*be dependent on*) полага́ться (*impf*) на +*acc*; (*trust*) полага́ться (положи́ться* *perf*) на +*acc*.

remain [rɪ'meɪn] *vi* оставáться* (оста́ться* *perf*); (*survive*) сохраня́ться (сохрани́ться *perf*); **to ~ silent** храни́ть (*impf*) молча́ние; **I ~, yours faithfully** (*BRIT: in letters*) остаю́сь, и́скренне Ваш.

remainder [rɪ'meɪndə'] *n* оста́ток*.

remaining [rɪ'meɪnɪŋ] *adj* сохрани́вшийся; (*surviving*) оста́вшийся.

remains [rɪ'meɪnz] *npl* (*of meal*) оста́тки *mpl*; (*of building*) разва́лины *fpl*; (*of corpse*) оста́нки *mpl*.

remand [rɪ'mɑːnd] *n*: **on ~** взя́тый под стра́жу ♦ *vt*: **he was ~ed in custody** он был взят под стра́жу.

remand home *n* (*BRIT*) исправи́тельная коло́ния для несовершенноле́тних.

remark [rɪ'mɑːk] *n* замеча́ние ♦ *vt* замеча́ть (заме́тить* *perf*) ♦ *vi*: **to ~ on sth** де́лать (сде́лать *perf*) замеча́ние относи́тельно +*gen*; **to ~ that** замеча́ть (заме́тить* *perf*), что.

remarkable [rɪ'mɑːkəbl] *adj* замеча́тельный* (замеча́телен).

remarry [riː'mærɪ] *vi* вступа́ть (вступи́ть* *perf*) в повто́рный брак.

remedial [rɪ'miːdɪəl] *adj* (*tuition, classes*) исправи́тельный* (исправи́телен), корректи́вный*; (*exercise*) лече́бный.

remedy ['rɛmədɪ] *n* (*cure*) сре́дство ♦ *vt* исправля́ть (испра́вить* *perf*).

remember [rɪ'mɛmbə'] *vt* (*call back to mind*) вспомина́ть (вспо́мнить *perf*); (*bear in mind*) по́мнить (*impf*); (*send greetings*): **~ me to him** переда́йте ему́ от меня́ приве́т; **I ~ seeing her, I ~ having seen her** я по́мню, что я её ви́дел; **she ~ed to call me** она́ не забы́ла позвони́ть мне.

remembrance [rɪˈmɛmbrəns] *n* па́мять *f*.

remind [rɪˈmaɪnd] *vt*: **to ~ sb to do** напомина́ть (напо́мнить *perf*) кому́-н +*infin*; **to ~ sb of sth/sb** напомина́ть (напо́мнить *perf*) кому́-н о чём-н/ком-н; **that ~s me!** кста́ти!; **she ~s me of her mother** она́ напомина́ет мне свою́ мать.

reminder [rɪˈmaɪndə^r] *n* напомина́ние.

reminisce [rɛmɪˈnɪs] *vi* вспомина́ть (вспо́мнить *perf*).

reminiscences [rɛmɪˈnɪsnsɪz] *npl* воспомина́ния *ntpl*.

reminiscent [rɛmɪˈnɪsnt] *adj*: **to be ~ of sth** напомина́ть (напо́мнить *perf*) что-н.

remiss [rɪˈmɪs] *adj* (*careless*) небре́жный* (небре́жен); **it was ~ of him** с его́ стороны́ э́то бы́ло небре́жностью.

remission [rɪˈmɪʃən] *n* (*cancelling: of debt, fee*) освобожде́ние; (*reduction: of prison sentence*) сокраще́ние; (*MED*) реми́ссия; (*REL*) отпуще́ние.

remit [rɪˈmɪt] *vt* (*send*) пересыла́ть (пересла́ть* *perf*).

remittance [rɪˈmɪtns] *n* (*payment*) де́нежный перево́д (*для опла́ты чего́-н*).

remnant [ˈrɛmnənt] *n* оста́ток*; **~s** *npl* (*COMM*) оста́тки *mpl*.

remonstrate [ˈrɛmənstreɪt] *vi*: **to ~ (with sb about sth)** выража́ть (вы́разить* *perf*) проте́ст (кому́-н по по́воду чего́-н).

remorse [rɪˈmɔːs] *n* раска́яние.

remorseful [rɪˈmɔːsful] *adj* по́лный* (по́лон) раска́яния.

remorseless [rɪˈmɔːslɪs] *adj* (*person*) неща́дный* (неща́ден); (*noise, pain*) невыноси́мый* (невыноси́м).

remote [rɪˈməut] *adj* (*place, time*) отдалённый* (отдалён); (*person*) за́мкнутый (за́мкнут); (*possibility, chance*) незначи́тельный* (незначи́телен); **there is a ~ possibility that ...** существу́ет маловероя́тная возмо́жность, что ....

remote control *n* дистанцио́нное управле́ние.

remote-controlled [rɪˈməutkənˈtrəuld] *adj* с дистанцио́нным управле́нием.

remotely [rɪˈməutlɪ] *adv* отдалённо; **I'm not ~ interested** я ниско́лько не заинтересо́ван.

remoteness [rɪˈməutnɪs] *n* (*of place*) отдалённость *f*; (*of person*) за́мкнутость *f*.

remould [ˈriːməuld] *n* (*BRIT: tyre*) ши́на с восстано́вленным проте́ктором.

removable [rɪˈmuːvəbl] *adj* (*detachable*) съёмный.

removal [rɪˈmuːvəl] *n* (*also MED*) удале́ние; (*BRIT: of furniture*) перево́зка; (*dismissal*) отстране́ние.

removal man *irreg n* (*BRIT*) перево́зчик ме́бели.

removal van *n* (*BRIT*) автофурго́н для перево́зки ме́бели.

remove [rɪˈmuːv] *vt* (*take away*) убира́ть (убра́ть* *perf*); (*clothing, bandage, employee*) снима́ть (снять* *perf*); (*stain, also MED*) удаля́ть (удали́ть *perf*); (*problem, doubt*) устраня́ть (устрани́ть *perf*); **first cousin once ~d** двою́родный(-ая) племя́нник(-ица).

remover [rɪˈmuːvə^r] *n* (*for paint, varnish*) сре́дство для сня́тия; **stain ~** пятновыводи́тель *m*; **paint/make-up ~** сре́дство для сня́тия кра́ски/макия́жа.

remunerate [rɪˈmjuːnəreɪt] *vt* вознагражда́ть (вознагради́ть* *perf*).

remuneration [rɪmjuːnəˈreɪʃən] *n* вознагражде́ние.

Renaissance [rɪˈneɪsɑːs] *n*: **the ~** (*HISTORY*) Возрожде́ние.

renal [ˈriːnl] *adj* по́чечный.

renal failure *n* по́чечная недоста́точность *f*.

rename [riːˈneɪm] *vt* переимено́вывать (переименова́ть *perf*).

rend [rɛnd] (*pt, pp* rent) *vt* (*subj: society*) раздира́ть (*impf*); **a whistle rent the air** свист рассёк во́здух.

render [ˈrɛndə^r] *vt* (*give: assistance*) ока́зывать (оказа́ть* *perf*); (*cause to become: harmless, useless*) де́лать (сде́лать *perf*) +*instr*; (*submit: account*) предъявля́ть (предъяви́ть* *perf*); **the blow ~ed him unconscious** уда́р привёл его́ в бессозна́тельное состоя́ние.

rendering [ˈrɛndərɪŋ] *n* (*MUS etc*) исполне́ние; (*CONSTR*) штукату́рка.

rendezvous [ˈrɔndɪvuː] *n* (*meeting*) свида́ние, рандеву́ *nt ind*; (*place*) ме́сто свида́ния ♦ *vi* встреча́ться (встре́титься* *perf*); **to ~ with sb** встреча́ться (встре́титься* *perf*) с кем-н.

rendition [rɛnˈdɪʃən] *n* (*MUS*) исполне́ние.

renegade [ˈrɛnɪgeɪd] *n* ренега́т.

renew [rɪˈnjuː] *vt* возобновля́ть (возобнови́ть* *perf*).

renewal [rɪˈnjuːəl] *n* возобновле́ние.

renounce [rɪˈnauns] *vt* отка́зываться (отказа́ться* *perf*) от +*gen*; (*belief, throne*) отрека́ться (отре́чься* *perf*) от +*gen*; (*holy orders*) отверга́ть (отве́ргнуть *perf*).

renovate [ˈrɛnəveɪt] *vt* (*building, machine*) ремонти́ровать (отремонти́ровать *perf*); (*painting*) реставри́ровать (отреставри́ровать *perf*).

renovation [rɛnəˈveɪʃən] *n* ремо́нт; (*of work of art*) реставра́ция.

renown [rɪˈnaun] *n* сла́ва.

renowned [rɪˈnaund] *adj* просла́вленный.

rent [rɛnt] *pt, pp of* rend ♦ *n* кварти́рная пла́та ♦ *vt* (*take for rent: house*) снима́ть (снять* *perf*);

(: *television, car*) брать* (взять* *perf*)
напрока́т; (*also:* ~ **out**: *house*) сдава́ть*
(сдать* *perf*) (внаём); (: *television, car*)
дава́ть* (дать* *perf*) напрока́т.
rental ['rɛntl] *n* (*for television, car*) пла́та за
прока́т.
rent strike *n* неупла́та жильца́ми аре́ндной
пла́ты с це́лью выраже́ния проте́ста.
renunciation [rɪnʌnsɪ'eɪʃən] *n* отка́з; (*of belief,
throne*) отрече́ние.
reopen [ri:'əupən] *vt* (*shop, restaurant etc*)
сно́ва открыва́ть (откры́ть* *perf*);
(*discussion, legal case etc*) возобновля́ть
(возобнови́ть* *perf*).
reopening [ri:'əupnɪŋ] *n* (*see vb*) откры́тие
(*по́сле ремо́нта итп*); возобновле́ние.
reorder [ri:'ɔ:dəʳ] *vt* возобновля́ть
(возобнови́ть* *perf*) зака́з на +*acc*; (*rearrange*)
перестра́ивать (перестро́ить *perf*).
reorganization ['ri:ɔ:gənaɪ'zeɪʃən] *n*
реорганиза́ция.
reorganize [ri:'ɔ:gənaɪz] *vt* реорганизо́вывать
(реорганизова́ть *perf*).
rep [rɛp] *n abbr* (*COMM*) = **representative**; (*THEAT*)
= **repertory**.
Rep. *abbr* (*US: POL*) = **representative, republican**.
repair [rɪ'pɛəʳ] *n* ремо́нт ♦ *vt* (*clothes, shoes*)
чини́ть* (почини́ть* *perf*); (*car, engine*)
ремонти́ровать (отремонти́ровать *perf*); **in
good/bad** ~ в хоро́шем/плохо́м состоя́нии;
under ~ в ремо́нте.
repair kit *n* ремо́нтный компле́кт.
repairman [rɪ'pɛəmæn] *irreg n* ма́стер* по
ремо́нту.
repair shop *n* ремо́нтная мастерска́я *f adj*.
repartee [rɛpɑ:'ti:] *n* (*conversation*)
остроу́мная бесе́да; (*riposte*) остро́та.
repast [rɪ'pɑ:st] *n* тра́пеза.
repatriate [ri:'pætrɪeɪt] *vt* репатрии́ровать
(*impf/perf*).
repay [ri:'peɪ] *irreg vt* (*money, debt*)
выпла́чивать (вы́платить* *perf*); (*person*)
упла́чивать (уплати́ть* *perf*) +*dat*; (: *reward*)
вознагражда́ть (вознагради́ть* *perf*);
(*efforts*) возмеща́ть (возмести́ть* *perf*); **to** ~
sb (for sth) (*favour*) отпла́чивать (отплати́ть*
perf) кому́-н (за что-н).
repayment [ri:'peɪmənt] *n* вы́плата.
repeal [rɪ'pi:l] *n* отме́на ♦ *vt* отменя́ть
(отмени́ть* *perf*).
repeat [rɪ'pi:t] *vt* повторя́ть (повтори́ть *perf*) ♦
vi повторя́ться (повтори́ться *perf*) ♦ *n* (*RADIO,
TV*) повторе́ние ♦ *cpd* (*performance, order etc*)
повто́рный; **to** ~ **a class** (*SCOL*) остава́ться*
(оста́ться* *perf*) на второ́й год.
repeatedly [rɪ'pi:tɪdlɪ] *adv* неоднокра́тно.
repel [rɪ'pɛl] *vt* (*drive away*) отбива́ть (отби́ть*
perf); (*disgust*) отта́лкивать (оттолкну́ть
perf).
repellent [rɪ'pɛlənt] *adj* (*appearance, smell*)
отта́лкивающий*; (*idea, thought*) отврат-

и́тельный* (отврати́телен) ♦ *n*: **insect** ~
репелле́нт.
repent [rɪ'pɛnt] *vi*: **to** ~ **(of)** ка́яться (пока́яться
perf) (в +*prp*).
repentance [rɪ'pɛntəns] *n* покая́ние.
repercussions [ri:pə'kʌʃənz] *npl* после́дствия
ntpl.
repertoire ['rɛpətwɑ:'] *n* репертуа́р.
repertory ['rɛpətərɪ] *n* (*also:* ~ **theatre**)
репертуа́рный теа́тр.
repertory company *n* постоя́нная тру́ппа.
repetition [rɛpɪ'tɪʃən] *n* повторе́ние; (*of order,
in text*) повто́р.
repetitious [rɛpɪ'tɪʃəs] *adj* изоби́лующий
повто́рами.
repetitive [rɪ'pɛtɪtɪv] *adj* повторя́ющийся.
replace [rɪ'pleɪs] *vt* (*put back: vertically*) класть*
(положи́ть* *perf*) обра́тно; (: *horizontally*)
ста́вить* (поста́вить* *perf*) обра́тно; (*take the
place of*) заменя́ть (замени́ть* *perf*); **to** ~ **sth
with sth** заменя́ть (замени́ть* *perf*) что-н
чем-н; "**replace the receiver**" (*TEL*) „положи́те
тру́бку".
replacement [rɪ'pleɪsmənt] *n* заме́на.
replacement cost *n* изде́ржки* *pl*
возмеще́ния.
replacement part *n* запасна́я часть* *f*.
replacement value *n* (*INSURANCE*) сто́имость *f*
страхово́го возмеще́ния.
replay [*n* 'ri:pleɪ, *vb* ri:'pleɪ] *n* (*of match*)
переигро́вка*; (*of tape*) повто́рное
прои́грывание; (*of film*) повто́рный пока́з ♦
vt (*match, game*) переи́грывать (переигра́ть
perf); (*part of tape*) повто́рно прои́грывать
(проигра́ть *perf*).
replenish [rɪ'plɛnɪʃ] *vt* (*glass*) сно́ва наполня́ть
(напо́лнить *perf*); (*stock etc*) пополня́ть
(попо́лнить *perf*).
replete [rɪ'pli:t] *adj* (*well-fed*) насы́тившийся; ~
with загру́женный (загру́жен) +*instr*; **I'm
quite** ~ я вполне́ насы́тился.
replica ['rɛplɪkə] *n* (*copy*) ко́пия.
reply [rɪ'plaɪ] *n* отве́т ♦ *vi* отвеча́ть (отве́тить*
perf); **in** ~ **to** в отве́т на +*acc*; **there's no** ~ (*TEL*)
не отвеча́ет.
reply coupon *n* бланк для отве́та.
reply-paid postcard *n* откры́тка* с
опла́ченным отве́том.
report [rɪ'pɔ:t] *n* (*account*) докла́д; (*PRESS, TV
etc: statement*) репорта́ж; (: *information*)
сообще́ние; (*BRIT: also:* **school** ~) отчёт об
успева́емости; (*of gun*) вы́стрел ♦ *vt*
сообща́ть (сообщи́ть *perf*) о +*prp*; (*event,
meeting*) докла́дывать (доложи́ть* *perf*) о
+*prp*; (*person*) доноси́ть* (донести́* *perf*) на
+*acc* ♦ *vi* (*make a report*) докла́дывать
(доложи́ть* *perf*); (*present o.s.*): **to** ~ **(to sb)**
явля́ться (яви́ться* *perf*) (к кому́-н); (*be
responsible to*): **to** ~ **to sb** быть* (*impf*) под
нача́лом кого́-н; **to** ~ **that** сообща́ть
(сообщи́ть *perf*), что; **to** ~ **on** представля́ть

(предста́вить* *perf*) докла́д о +*prp*; **it is ~ed that** ... сообща́ется, что ....
report card *n* (*US, SCOTTISH*) та́бель *m* успева́емости.
reportedly [rɪ'pɔ:tɪdlɪ] *adv*: **she is ~ living in Spain** по сообще́ниям, она́ живёт в Испа́нии; **he ~ ordered them to ...** сообща́ют, что он приказа́л им +*infin* ....
reported speech *n* (*LING*) ко́свенная речь *f*.
reporter [rɪ'pɔ:tə*] *n* репортёр.
repose [rɪ'pəuz] *n*: **in ~** (*face*) в поко́е.
repository [rɪ'pɒzɪtərɪ] *n* (*place*) храни́лище; (*person*) храни́тель *m*.
repossess ['ri:pə'zɛs] *vt* (*goods, building*) изыма́ть (изъя́ть* *perf*) (*за неплатёж*).
reprehensible [rɛprɪ'hɛnsɪbl] *adj* (*behaviour*) предосуди́тельный* (предосуди́телен).
represent [rɛprɪ'zɛnt] *vt* (*person, nation*) представля́ть (предста́вить* *perf*); (*view, belief*) излага́ть (изложи́ть* *perf*); (*constitute*) представля́ть (*impf*) собо́й; (*idea, emotion*) символизи́ровать* (*impf/perf*); (*describe*): **to ~ sth as** изобража́ть (изобрази́ть* *perf*) что-н как; (*explain*): **to ~ to sb that** объясня́ть (объясни́ть *perf*) кому́-н, что.
representation [rɛprɪzɛn'teɪʃən] *n* (*state*) представи́тельство; (*picture, statue*) изображе́ние; (*petition*) заявле́ние; **~s** *npl* (*protest*) представле́ния *ntpl*.
representative [rɛprɪ'zɛntətɪv] *n* представи́тель(ница) *m(f)*; (*of belief, also COMM, POL*) представи́тель *m* ◆ *adj* (*group, survey, cross-section*) представи́тельный* (представи́телен); **~ of** характе́рный* (характе́рен) для +*gen*.
repress [rɪ'prɛs] *vt* подавля́ть (подави́ть* *perf*).
repression [rɪ'prɛʃən] *n* подавле́ние.
repressive [rɪ'prɛsɪv] *adj* (*society, measures*) репресси́вный* (репресси́вен).
reprieve [rɪ'pri:v] *n* (*LAW*) отсро́чка (*в исполне́нии пригово́ра*); (*fig: delay*) переды́шка* ◆ *vt* (*LAW*): **he was ~d** он получи́л отсро́чку.
reprimand ['rɛprɪmɑ:nd] *n* вы́говор ◆ *vt* де́лать (сде́лать *perf*) вы́говор +*dat*.
reprint [*n* 'ri:prɪnt, *vb* ri:'prɪnt] *n* перепеча́тка ◆ *vt* перепеча́тывать (перепеча́тать *perf*).
reprisal [rɪ'praɪzl] *n* отве́тное де́йствие; **~s** *npl* (*acts of revenge*) отве́тные де́йствия *ntpl*; **to take ~s** мстить* (отомсти́ть* *perf*).
reproach [rɪ'prəutʃ] *n* упрёк ◆ *vt*: **to ~ sb for sth/with sth** упрека́ть (упрекну́ть *perf*) кого́-н за что-н/в чём-н; **his behaviour was beyond ~** его́ поведе́ние бы́ло безупре́чно.
reproachful [rɪ'prəutʃful] *adj* (*look, remark*) укори́зненный* (укори́знен).
reproduce [ri:prə'dju:s] *vt* воспроизводи́ть* (воспроизвести́* *perf*) ◆ *vi* размножа́ться

(размно́житься *perf*).
reproduction [ri:prə'dʌkʃən] *n* воспроизведе́ние; (*ART*) репроду́кция; (*breeding*) воспроизведе́ние.
reproductive [ri:prə'dʌktɪv] *adj* (*process*) репродукти́вный; (*system*) полово́й.
reproof [rɪ'pru:f] *n* (*rebuke*) порица́ние; (*disapproval*): **with ~** с уко́ром.
reprove [rɪ'pru:v] *vt* (*person*): **to ~ sb for sth** осужда́ть (осуди́ть* *perf*) кого́-н за что-н.
reproving [rɪ'pru:vɪŋ] *adj* осужда́ющий.
reptile ['rɛptaɪl] *n* пресмыка́ющееся *nt adj* (живо́тное).
Repub. *abbr* (*US: POL*) = **republican**.
republic [rɪ'pʌblɪk] *n* респу́блика.
republican [rɪ'pʌblɪkən] *adj* республика́нский* ◆ *n* (*US: POL*): **R~** республика́нец*(-нка*).
repudiate [rɪ'pju:dɪeɪt] *vt* отверга́ть (отве́ргнуть *perf*).
repudiation [rɪpju:dɪ'eɪʃən] *n* отрица́ние, отрече́ние; (*COMM*) отка́з от до́лга *or* выполне́ния контра́кта.
repugnance [rɪ'pʌgnəns] *n* отвраще́ние.
repugnant [rɪ'pʌgnənt] *adj* отврати́тельный* (отврати́телен).
repulse [rɪ'pʌls] *vt* (*drive back*) отража́ть (отрази́ть* *perf*); (: *enemy*) отбра́сывать (отбро́сить* *perf*); (*disgust*) отта́лкивать (оттолкну́ть *perf*).
repulsion [rɪ'pʌlʃən] *n* отвраще́ние.
repulsive [rɪ'pʌlsɪv] *adj* отврати́тельный* (отврати́телен).
reputable ['rɛpjutəbl] *adj* (*person*) уважа́емый; **~ company etc** компа́ния с хоро́шей репута́цией.
reputation [rɛpju'teɪʃən] *n* репута́ция; **to have a ~ for** име́ть (*impf*) репута́цию +*gen*; **he has a ~ for being tactless** он изве́стен свое́й беста́ктностью.
repute [rɪ'pju:t] *n* до́брая сла́ва.
reputed [rɪ'pju:tɪd] *adj* (*rumoured*) предполага́емый; **he is ~ to be intelligent/rich** счита́ется, что он умён/бога́т.
reputedly [rɪ'pju:tɪdlɪ] *adv* по о́бщему мне́нию.
request [rɪ'kwɛst] *n* (*polite demand*) про́сьба; (*formal demand*) зая́вка* ◆ *vt*: **to ~ sth of or from sb** проси́ть* (попроси́ть* *perf*) что-н у кого́-н; **at the ~ of** по про́сьбе +*gen*; (*formal*) по зая́вке +*gen*; **"you are ~ed not to smoke"** „про́сим не кури́ть".
request stop *n* (*BRIT*) остано́вка* по тре́бованию.
requiem ['rɛkwɪəm] *n* (*REL*) панихи́да; (*MUS*) ре́квием.
require [rɪ'kwaɪə*] *vt* (*person*) нужда́ться (*impf*) в +*prp*; (*thing, situation*) тре́бовать (*impf*); (*order*): **to ~ sth of sb** тре́бовать (потре́бовать *perf*) что-н от кого́-н; **we ~ you**

---

* marks translations which have irregular inflections. The Russian-English side of the dictionary gives inflectional information.

to complete the task мы требуем, чтобы Вы завершили работу; **if ~d** если требуется; **what documents are ~d?** какие документы требуются?; **~d by law** требуемый законом.

required [rɪˈkwaɪəd] *adj* необходимый.

requirement [rɪˈkwaɪəmənt] *n* (*need, want*) потребность *f*; (*condition*) требование; **to meet sb's ~s** удовлетворять (удовлетворить *perf*) чьим-н требованиям.

requisite [ˈrɛkwɪzɪt] *n* требование ♦ *adj* необходимый.

requisition [rɛkwɪˈzɪʃən] *vt* (*MIL*) реквизировать (*impf/perf*) ♦ *n:* **~ (for)** заявка (на +*acc*).

reroute [riːˈruːt] *vt* (*train etc*) изменять (изменить* *perf*) маршрут +*gen*.

resale [riːˈseɪl] *n* перепродажа; **"not for ~"** „перепродажа запрещена".

resale price maintenance *n* поддержание цен при перепродаже товаров.

reschedule [riːˈʃɛdjuːl] *vt:* **~ (for)** переносить* (перенести* *perf*) (на +*acc*).

rescind [rɪˈsɪnd] *vt* (*law, judgement*) отменять (отменить* *perf*); (*contract, order etc*) аннулировать (*impf/perf*).

rescue [ˈrɛskjuː] *n* спасение ♦ *vt:* **to ~ (from)** спасать (спасти* *perf*) (от +*gen*); **to come to sb's ~** приходить* (прийти* *perf*) кому-н на помощь.

rescue party *n* спасательный отряд, спасательная партия.

rescuer [ˈrɛskjuə] *n* спаситель(ница) *m(f)*.

research [rɪˈsəːtʃ] *n* исследование ♦ *vt* исследовать (*impf/perf*) ♦ *vi* проводить* (провести* *perf*) исследование *or* исследования; **a piece of ~** (научное) исследование; **~ and development** научно-исследовательские и опытно-конструкторские работы.

researcher [rɪˈsəːtʃəʳ] *n* исследователь(ница) *m(f)*.

research work *n* научно-исследовательская работа.

research worker *n* научный работник.

resell [riːˈsɛl] *irreg vt* перепродавать* (перепродать* *perf*).

resemblance [rɪˈzɛmbləns] *n* сходство; **he bears a strong ~ to his father** он сильно походит на отца; **this bears no ~ to ...** это не имеет никакого сходства с +*instr* ....

resemble [rɪˈzɛmbl] *vt* походить* (*impf*) на +*acc*; **he very much ~s his father** он очень похож на отца.

resent [rɪˈzɛnt] *vt* (*situation*) негодовать (*impf*) против +*gen*; (*person*) негодовать (*impf*) на +*acc*.

resentful [rɪˈzɛntful] *adj* негодующий*.

resentment [rɪˈzɛntmənt] *n* негодование.

reservation [rɛzəˈveɪʃən] *n* (*booking*) предварительный заказ; (*doubt*) сомнение; (*for tribe*) резервация; **to make a ~ (in an hotel/on a**

plane) бронировать* (забронировать* *perf*) (место в гостинице/на самолёте); **with ~s** (*doubts*) с оговорками.

reservation desk *n* (*US: in hotel*) стол* администратора.

reserve [rɪˈzəːv] *n* (*store*) резерв, запас; (*also:* **nature ~**) заповедник; (*SPORT*) запасной игрок*; (*restraint*) сдержанность *f* ♦ *vt* (*keep: money, food*) приберегать (приберечь* *perf*); (*: energy*) беречь* (сберечь* *perf*); (*seats, table etc*) бронировать (забронировать* *perf*); **~s** *npl* (*MIL*) запас *msg*; (*COMM*) резервы *mpl*; **in ~** в резерве *or* запасе.

reserve currency *n* резервная валюта.

reserved [rɪˈzəːvd] *adj* (*restrained*) сдержанный* (сдержан); (*seat*) забронированный (забронирован).

reserve price *n* (*BRIT*) отправная *or* резервированная цена*.

reserve team *n* (*BRIT: SPORT*) запасная команда.

reservist [rɪˈzəːvɪst] *n* резервист.

reservoir [ˈrɛzəvwɑːʳ] *n* (*of water*) водохранилище; (*small: of ink etc*) резервуар; (*fig: of talent, strength*) хранилище.

reset [riːˈsɛt] *irreg vt* вновь устанавливать (установить* *perf*); (*clock, watch*) переводить* (перевести* *perf*); (*COMPUT*) сбрасывать (сбросить* *perf*), возвращать (возвратить* *perf*) в исходное положение.

reshape [riːˈʃeɪp] *vt* (*policy*) изменять (изменить *perf*).

reshuffle [riːˈʃʌfl] *n:* **Cabinet ~** перестановки *fpl* в кабинете министров.

reside [rɪˈzaɪd] *vi* (*live*) проживать (*impf*).

residence [ˈrɛzɪdəns] *n* (*home*) резиденция; (*length of stay*) пребывание; **to take up ~** поселяться (поселиться *perf*); **to be in ~** (*queen etc*) пребывать (*impf*); (*artist*) проживать (*impf*) по месту службы.

residence permit *n* (*BRIT*) вид на жительство.

resident [ˈrɛzɪdənt] *n* (*of country, town*) (постоянный(-ая)) житель(ница) *m(f)*; (*in hotel*) проживающий(-ая) *m(f) adj* ♦ *adj:* **~ population** постоянное население; **~ doctor** врач*, живущий при больнице.

residential [rɛzɪˈdɛnʃəl] *adj* (*area*) жилой; (*course, college*) с проживанием.

residue [ˈrɛzɪdjuː] *n* остаток*; (*CHEM, PHYS*) осадок*.

resign [rɪˈzaɪn] *vi* (*from post*) оставлять (оставить* *perf*) ♦ *vt* (*one's post*) уходить* (уйти* *perf*) в отставку с +*gen*; **to ~ o.s. to** смиряться (смириться *perf*) с +*instr*.

resignation [rɛzɪgˈneɪʃən] *n* отставка*; (*acceptance*) покорность *f*; **to tender one's ~** подавать* (подать* *perf*) в отставку.

resigned [rɪˈzaɪnd] *adj* (*to situation etc*) смирившийся.

resilience [rɪˈzɪlɪəns] *n* (*of material*) упругость *f*;

бельность f.

resilient [rɪˈzɪlɪənt] *adj* (*material*) упру́гий* (упру́г); (*person*) сто́йкий* (сто́ек).

resin [ˈrɛzɪn] *n* смола́*.

resist [rɪˈzɪst] *vt* сопротивля́ться (*impf*) +*dat*; (*temptation*) не поддава́ться* (подда́ться* *perf*) +*dat*.

resistance [rɪˈzɪstəns] *n* (*opposition*) сопротивле́ние; (*to illness, infection*) сопротивля́емость f.

resistant [rɪˈzɪstənt] *adj*: **to be ~ to** (*opposing*) сопротивля́ться (*impf*) +*dat*; (*immune*) облада́ть (*impf*) усто́йчивостью к +*dat*.

resolute [ˈrɛzəluːt] *adj* твёрдый* (твёрд).

resolution [rɛzəˈluːʃən] *n* (*decision*) реше́ние; (: *formal*) резолю́ция; (*determination*) реши́мость f; (*of problem, difficulty*) разреше́ние; **to make a ~** принима́ть (приня́ть* *perf*) реше́ние.

resolve [rɪˈzɔlv] *n* реши́тельность f ◆ *vt* (*problem, difficulty*) разреша́ть (разреши́ть *perf*) ◆ *vi*: **to ~ to do** реша́ть (реши́ть *perf*) +*infin*.

resolved [rɪˈzɔlvd] *adj* (*determined*) реши́тельный* (реши́телен).

resonance [ˈrɛzənəns] *n* (*TECH*) резона́нс.

resonant [ˈrɛzənənt] *adj* (*voice*) зву́чный* (зву́чен); (*place*) резони́рующий.

resort [rɪˈzɔːt] *n* (*town*) куро́рт; (*recourse*) прибега́ние ◆ *vi*: **to ~ to** прибега́ть (прибе́гнуть *perf*) к +*dat*; **seaside/winter sports ~** морско́й/зи́мний* спорти́вный куро́рт; **the last/only ~** после́дняя/еди́нственная наде́жда; **in the last ~** в кра́йнем слу́чае.

resound [rɪˈzaund] *vi*: **to ~ with** наполня́ться (напо́лниться *perf*) +*instr*.

resounding [rɪˈzaundɪŋ] *adj* (*noise*) зву́чный* (зву́чен); (*fig: success*) гро́мкий*.

resource [rɪˈsɔːs] *n* (*raw material*) ресу́рс; **~s** *npl* (*money, energy, coal etc*) ресу́рсы *mpl*; **natural ~s** приро́дные ресу́рсы; **he was left to his own ~s** (*fig*) он мог положи́ться то́лько на самого́ себя́.

resourceful [rɪˈsɔːsful] *adj* изобрета́тельный* (изобрета́телен).

resourcefulness [rɪˈsɔːsfəlnɪs] *n* изобрета́тельность f.

respect [rɪsˈpɛkt] *n* уваже́ние ◆ *vt* уважа́ть (*impf*); **~s** *npl* (*greetings*) почте́ние *ntsg*; **to have or show ~ for sb/sth** относи́ться* (*impf*) к кому́-н/чему́-н с уваже́нием; **out of ~ for** из уваже́ния к +*dat*; **with ~ to, in ~ of** в отноше́нии +*gen*; **in this ~** в э́том отноше́нии; **in some ~s** в не́которых отноше́ниях; **with (all) due ~** ... при всём уваже́нии ....

respectability [rɪspɛktəˈbɪlɪtɪ] *n* респекта-

respectable [rɪsˈpɛktəbl] *adj* прили́чный* (прили́чен); (*morally correct*) респекта́бельный.

respected [rɪsˈpɛktɪd] *adj* (*scholar, actor etc*) при́знанный (при́знан).

respectful [rɪsˈpɛktful] *adj* почти́тельный* (почти́телен).

respectfully [rɪsˈpɛktfəlɪ] *adv* почти́тельно.

respective [rɪsˈpɛktɪv] *adj* (*policies, measures*) соотве́тствующий*; **he drove them to their ~ homes** он отвёз их обо́их по дома́м.

respectively [rɪsˈpɛktɪvlɪ] *adv* соотве́тственно; **France and Britain were 3rd and 4th ~** Фра́нция и Великобрита́ния бы́ли на 3-ем и 4-ом ме́сте соотве́тственно.

respiration [rɛspɪˈreɪʃən] *n* дыха́ние.

respirator [ˈrɛspɪreɪtə] *n* (*MED*) аппара́т иску́сственного дыха́ния.

respiratory [ˈrɛsprətərɪ] *adj* (*ANAT, MED*) дыха́тельный, респирато́рный.

respite [ˈrɛspaɪt] *n* (*rest*) переды́шка*.

resplendent [rɪsˈplɛndənt] *adj* блиста́тельный* (блиста́телен).

respond [rɪsˈpɔnd] *vi* (*answer*) отвеча́ть (отве́тить* *perf*); (*react*): **to ~ (to)** (*to pressure, criticism*) реаги́ровать (отреаги́ровать *perf*) (на +*acc*); (*to treatment*) поддава́ться* (подда́ться* *perf*) (+*dat*).

respondent [rɪsˈpɔndənt] *n* (*LAW*) отве́тчик (-ица).

response [rɪsˈpɔns] *n* (*answer*) отве́т; (*reaction*) реа́кция; **in ~ to (your letter)** в отве́т на (Ва́ше письмо́).

responsibility [rɪspɔnsɪˈbɪlɪtɪ] *n* (*liability*) отве́тственность f; (*duty*) обя́занность f; **to take ~ for sth/sb** принима́ть (приня́ть* *perf*) (на себя́) отве́тственность за что-н/кого́-н.

responsible [rɪsˈpɔnsɪbl] *adj* отве́тственный* (отве́тствен); **~ for** отве́тственный* (отве́тствен) за +*acc*; **to be ~ to sb (for sth)** отвеча́ть (отве́тить* *perf*) пе́ред кем-н (за что-н).

responsibly [rɪsˈpɔnsɪblɪ] *adv* отве́тственно.

responsive [rɪsˈpɔnsɪv] *adj* (*child, nature*) отзы́вчивый (отзы́вчив); (*gesture*) отве́тный; **~ to demand/treatment** восприи́мчивый (восприи́мчив) к тре́бованиям/лече́нию.

rest [rɛst] *n* (*relaxation, pause*) о́тдых; (*MUS*) па́уза; (*stand, support*) подста́вка* ◆ *vi* (*relax, stop*) отдыха́ть (отдохну́ть *perf*) ◆ *vt* (*head, eyes etc*) дава́ть* (дать* *perf*) о́тдых +*dat*; (*lean*): **to ~ sth against** прислоня́ть (прислони́ть *perf*) что-н к +*dat*; **the ~** (*remainder of sth*) остально́е *nt adj*; **the ~ of them** остальны́е из них; **to set sb's mind at ~** утеша́ть (уте́шить *perf*) кого́-н; **to ~ one's**

---

* marks translations which have irregular inflections. The Russian-English side of the dictionary gives inflectional information.

arms on облокáчиваться (облокотúться*
perf) на +*acc*; **to ~ sth on** опускáть (опустúть*
perf) на +*acc*; **to ~ on** (*weight*) опирáться
(оперéться* *perf*) на +*acc*; (*idea*) опирáться
(*impf*) на +*acc*; (*object*) лежáть* (*impf*) на +*prp*;
(*hope*) надéяться (*impf*) на +*acc*; **~ assured
that ...** бýдьте увéрены, что ...; **it ~s with him
to ...** на нём лежúт +*infin* ...; **to ~ one's eyes** *or*
gaze on останáвливать (остановúть* *perf*)
(свой) взгляд на +*acc*.

restart [riː'stɑːt] *vt* (*engine*) вновь запускáть
(запустúть* *perf*); (*work*) возобновлять
(возобновúть* *perf*).

restaurant ['rɛstərɔŋ] *n* ресторáн.

restaurant car *n* (*BRIT*) вагóн-ресторáн.

rest-cure ['rɛstkjuəʳ] *n* лечéние покóем.

restful ['rɛstful] *adj* успокáивающий.

rest-home ['rɛsthəum] *n* дом для
престарéлых.

restitution [rɛstɪ'tjuːʃən] *n*: **to make ~ to sb for
sth** (*compensate*) возмещáть (возместúть*
perf) комý-н что-н.

restive ['rɛstɪv] *adj* неспокóйный* (неспокóен);
(*horse*) норовúстый (норовúст).

restless ['rɛstlɪs] *adj* (*person, audience*)
беспокóйный* (беспокóен); **to get ~**
проявлять (проявúть* *perf*) нетерпéние.

restlessly ['rɛstlɪslɪ] *adv* беспокóйно.

restock [riː'stɔk] *vt* пополнять (пополнить
perf) запáсы +*gen*; **to ~ a lake/river (with fish)**
пополнять (пополнить *perf*) óзеро/рéку
рыбой.

restoration [rɛstə'reɪʃən] *n* (*of building etc*)
реставрáция; (*of order, health*)
восстановлéние; (*of stolen property*)
возвращéние.

restorative [rɪ'stɔrətɪv] *adj* укрепляющий* ◆ *n*
укрепляющее срéдство.

restore [rɪ'stɔːʳ] *vt* (*building, painting*)
реставрúровать (отреставрúровать *perf*);
(*order, health etc*) восстанáвливать
(восстановúть* *perf*); (*stolen property*)
возвращáть (возвратúть* *perf*); (*to power*)
возвращáть (вернýть *perf*).

restorer [rɪ'stɔːrəʳ] *n* (*ART etc*) реставрáтор; **hair
~** восстановúтель *m* для волóс.

restrain [rɪs'treɪn] *vt* сдéрживать (сдержáть*
perf); (*person*): **to ~ sb from doing** не давáть*
(дать* *perf*) комý-н +*infin*.

restrained [rɪs'treɪnd] *adj* сдéржанный*
(сдéржан).

restraint [rɪs'treɪnt] *n* (*moderation*)
сдéржанность *f*; (*restriction*) ограничéние;
wage ~ сдéрживание рóста зáработной
плáты.

restrict [rɪs'trɪkt] *vt* ограничивать (ограничить
perf).

restricted area *n* (*AUT*) райóн ограниченной
скóрости движéния.

restriction [rɪs'trɪkʃən] *n*: **~ (on)** ограничéние
(на +*acc*).

restrictive [rɪs'trɪktɪv] *adj* ограничúтельный;
(*clothing*) стесняющий.

restrictive practices *npl* (*INDUSTRY*)
ограничúтельная деловáя прáктика *fsg*.

rest room *n* (*US*) туалéт.

restructure [riː'strʌktʃəʳ] *vt* (*business, economy*)
перестрáивать (перестрóить *perf*).

result [rɪ'zʌlt] *n* результáт ◆ *vi*: **to ~ in**
закáнчиваться (закóнчиться *perf*) +*instr*; **as a
~ of** в результáте +*gen*; **as a ~ it is too
expensive** в результáте э́то слúшком
дóрого; **the fire ~ed from bombing** пожáр
вознúк вслéдствие бомбёжки.

resultant [rɪ'zʌltənt] *adj*: **~ saving/problem**
вытекáющая из э́того экономúя/проблéма.

resume [rɪ'zjuːm] *vt* (*work, journey*)
возобновлять (возобновúть* *perf*) ◆ *vi*
продолжáть (продóлжить *perf*); **to ~ one's
seat** возвращáться (вернýться* *perf*) на
(своё) мéсто.

résumé ['reɪzjuːmeɪ] *n* резюмé *nt ind*; (*US:
curriculum vitae*) автобиогрáфия (*обычно
пúшущаяся при поступлéнии на учёбу úли
рабóту*).

resumption [rɪ'zʌmpʃən] *n* возобновлéние.

resurgence [rɪ'səːdʒəns] *n* (*of energy, activity*)
всплеск.

resurrection [rɛzə'rɛkʃən] *n* (*of hopes, fears*)
возрождéние; (*REL*): **the R~** Воскресéние.

resuscitate [rɪ'sʌsɪteɪt] *vt* (*MED*) приводúть*
(привестú* *perf*) в сознáние; (*fig*) возвращáть
(возвратúть* *perf*) к жúзни.

resuscitation [rɪsʌsɪ'teɪʃən] *n* (*MED*)
приведéние в сознáние; (*fig*) возвращéние к
жúзни.

retail ['riːteɪl] *adj* рóзничный ◆ *adv* в рóзницу ◆
vt продавáть* (продáть* *perf*) в рóзницу ◆ *vi*:
to ~ at £5 продавáться* (*impf*) по рóзничной
ценé в £5; **~ shop** магазúн рóзничной
торгóвли.

retailer ['riːteɪləʳ] *n* рóзничный торгóвец*.

retail outlet *n* рóзничная торгóвая тóчка.

retail price *n* рóзничная ценá*.

retail price index *n* (*BRIT*) úндекс рóзничных
цен.

retain [rɪ'teɪn] *vt* (*keep*) сохранять (сохранúть
perf), удéрживать (удержáть *perf*).

retainer [rɪ'teɪnəʳ] *n* (*fee*) предварúтельный
гонорáр.

retaliate [rɪ'tælɪeɪt] *vi*: **to ~ (against)** (*attack*)
наносúть* (нанестú* *perf*) отвéтный удáр
(+*dat*); (*ill-treatment*) отплáчивать
(отплатúть* *perf*) (за +*acc*); **to ~ (on sb)**
предъявлять (предъявúть* *perf*) встрéчный
иск (комý-н).

retaliation [rɪtælɪ'eɪʃən] *n* (*against attack*)
отвéтный удáр; (*against ill-treatment*)
возмéздие; **in ~ for** в отвéт на +*acc*.

retaliatory [rɪ'tælɪətərɪ] *adj* отвéтный.

retarded [rɪ'tɑːdɪd] *adj* (*development, growth*)
замéдленный* (замéдлен); (*also*: **mentally ~**:

person) ýмственно отста́лый.
retch [rɛtʃ] *vi*: **the thought made him ~** от э́той
мы́сли его́ затошни́ло.
retention [rɪˈtɛnʃən] *n* удержа́ние; (*of tradition,
rights*) сохране́ние; (*MED: of fluid*) заде́ржка.
retentive [rɪˈtɛntɪv] *adj*: **a ~ memory** це́пкая
па́мять *f*.
rethink [ˈriːˈθɪŋk] *vt* (*proposal, policy*)
пересма́тривать (пересмотре́ть* *perf*).
reticence [ˈrɛtɪsns] *n* скры́тность *f*.
reticent [ˈrɛtɪsnt] *adj* сде́ржанный* (сде́ржан).
retina [ˈrɛtɪnə] *n* сетча́тка.
retinue [ˈrɛtɪnjuː] *n* сви́та.
retire [rɪˈtaɪəʳ] *vi* (*give up work*) уходи́ть* (уйти́*
perf) на пе́нсию; (*withdraw*) удаля́ться
(удали́ться *perf*); (*go to bed*) удаля́ться
(удали́ться *perf*) на поко́й.
retired [rɪˈtaɪəd] *adj*: **he is ~** он на пе́нсии.
retirement [rɪˈtaɪəmənt] *n* вы́ход *or* ухо́д на
пе́нсию; **we hope to enjoy a long and happy ~**
мы наде́емся жить до́лго и сча́стливо,
вы́йдя на пе́нсию.
retirement age *n* пенсио́нный во́зраст.
retiring [rɪˈtaɪərɪŋ] *adj* (*leaving*) уходя́щий на
пе́нсию; (*shy*) засте́нчивый (засте́нчив).
retort [rɪˈtɔːt] *vi* ре́зко отвеча́ть (отве́тить*
perf) ♦ *n* ре́зкий* отве́т.
retrace [riːˈtreɪs] *vt*: **to ~ one's steps**
возвраща́ться (верну́ться *perf*) тем же
путём; (*fig*) восстана́вливать
(восстанови́ть* *perf*).
retract [rɪˈtrækt] *vt* (*statement, offer*) забира́ть
(забра́ть* *perf*) наза́д; (*claws*) втя́гивать
(втяну́ть* *perf*); (*undercarriage, aerial*)
убира́ть (убра́ть* *perf*).
retractable [rɪˈtræktəbl] *adj* (*TECH*)
убира́ющийся.
retrain [riːˈtreɪn] *vt* переподгота́вливать
(переподгото́вить* *perf*), переквали-
фици́ровать (*impf/perf*) ♦ *vi* (*see vt*) пройти́*
(*perf*) переподгото́вку; переквали-
фици́роваться (*impf/perf*).
retraining [riːˈtreɪnɪŋ] *n* (*see vb*)
переподгото́вка*; переквалифика́ция.
retread [ˈriːtrɛd] *n* (*tyre*) ши́на с
восстано́вленным проте́ктором.
retreat [rɪˈtriːt] *n* (*place*) убе́жище; (*withdrawal*)
ухо́д; (*MIL*) отступле́ние ♦ *vi* отступа́ть
(отступи́ть* *perf*); **to go into ~** (*withdraw*)
уйти́* (*perf*) от ми́ра; **to beat a hasty ~**
поспе́шно отступа́ть (отступи́ть* *perf*).
retrial [riːˈtraɪəl] *n* (*LAW*) повто́рное слу́шание
де́ла.
retribution [rɛtrɪˈbjuːʃən] *n* возме́здие.
retrieval [rɪˈtriːvəl] *n* восстановле́ние; (*of error*)
исправле́ние; (*COMPUT*) по́иск; (*by dog*)
по́иск (*ди́чи*).
retrieve [rɪˈtriːv] *vt* (*object*) брать* (взять* *perf*)

обра́тно; (*situation, honour, loss*)
восстана́вливать (восстанови́ть* *perf*);
(*error*) исправля́ть (испра́вить* *perf*);
(*COMPUT*) оты́скивать (отыска́ть* *perf*); (*subj:
dog*) приноси́ть* (принести́* *perf*) (*уби́тую
дичь*).
retriever [rɪˈtriːvəʳ] *n* (*dog*) охо́тничья соба́ка.
retroactive [rɛtrəuˈæktɪv] *adj* име́ющий
обра́тное де́йствие.
retrograde [ˈrɛtrəgreɪd] *adj* реакцио́нный*
(реакцио́нен).
retrospect [ˈrɛtrəspɛkt] *n*: **in ~** ретроспе́кции.
retrospective [rɛtrəˈspɛktɪv] *adj* (*exhibition,
view*) ретроспекти́вный* (ретроспекти́вен);
(*law, tax*) име́ющий обра́тную си́лу ♦ *n* (*ART*)
ретроспекти́вная вы́ставка*.
return [rɪˈtəːn] *n* (*going or coming back*)
возвраще́ние; (*of sth stolen, borrowed,
bought*) возвра́т; (*FINANCE: from land, shares
etc*) дохо́д; (*official report*) отчёт ♦ *cpd*
(*journey, ticket*) обра́тный; (*match*) отве́тный
♦ *vi* возвраща́ться (верну́ться *perf*) ♦ *vt*
возвраща́ть (верну́ть *perf*); (*LAW: verdict*)
выноси́ть* (вы́нести* *perf*); (*POL: candidate*)
избира́ть (избра́ть* *perf*); (*ball*) отбива́ть
(отби́ть* *perf*); **~s** *npl* (*COMM*) дохо́ды *mpl*; **in ~**
(for) в отве́т (на +*acc*); **by ~ of post** обра́тной
по́чтой; **many happy ~s (of the day)!** с днём
рожде́ния!; **to ~ to** (*consciousness*)
приходи́ть (прийти́* *perf*) в +*acc*; (*power*)
возвраща́ться (верну́ться *perf*) к +*dat*.
returnable [rɪˈtəːnəbl] *adj* (*bottle etc*)
подлежа́щий возвра́ту *or* обме́ну.
returning officer [rɪˈtəːnɪŋ-] *n* председа́тель *m*
окружно́й коми́ссии.
return key *n* (*COMPUT*) кла́виша ”возвра́т
каре́тки“.
reunion [riːˈjuːnɪən] *n* (*reuniting*)
воссоедине́ние; (*party*) встре́ча.
reunite [riːjuːˈnaɪt] *vt* воссоединя́ть
(воссоедини́ть *perf*).
rev [rɛv] *n abbr* (*AUT*. = *revolution*) оборо́т.
Rev. *abbr* (*REL*) = **Reverend**.
revaluation [riːvæljuˈeɪʃən] *n* (*of property,
attitudes*) переоце́нка*; (*of currency*)
ревальва́ция.
revamp [riːˈvæmp] *vt* (*organization, system*)
обновля́ть (обнови́ть* *perf*).
rev counter *n* (*BRIT: AUT*) счётчик оборо́тов.
Revd. *abbr* (*REL*) = **Reverend**.
reveal [rɪˈviːl] *vt* (*make known*) обнару́живать
(обнару́жить *perf*); (*make visible*) открыва́ть
(откры́ть* *perf*).
revealing [rɪˈviːlɪŋ] *adj* (*action, statement*)
показа́тельный* (показа́телен); (*dress*)
откры́тый.
reveille [rɪˈvælɪ] *n* (*MIL*) побу́дка*.
revel [ˈrɛvl] *vi*: **to ~ in sth** упива́ться (*impf*)

---

* marks translations which have irregular inflections. The Russian-English side of the dictionary gives inflectional information.

чем-н; **to ~ in doing** обожа́ть *(impf)* +*infin.*

revelation [rɛvə'leɪʃən] *n (fact)* откры́тие; *(experience)* открове́ние.

reveller ['rɛvlə'] *n* гуля́ка *m/f.*

revelry ['rɛvlrɪ] *n* кутёж.

revenge [rɪ'vɛndʒ] *n* месть *f* ♦ *vt (also:* **get one's ~ for)** мстить* (отомсти́ть* *perf)* за +*acc;* **to take ~ on, ~ o.s. on** мстить* (отомсти́ть* *perf)* +*dat.*

revengeful [rɪ'vɛndʒful] *adj* мсти́тельный* (мсти́телен).

revenue ['rɛvənju:] *n* дохо́ды *mpl;* **~ account** счёт поступле́ний.

reverberate [rɪ'və:bəreɪt] *vi (also fig)* отдава́ться* (отда́ться* *perf)* эхом.

reverberation [rɪvə:bə'reɪʃən] *n (of thunder)* раска́т; *(shock)* резона́нс.

revere [rɪ'vɪə'] *vt (person)* почита́ть *(impf),* чтить* *(impf).*

reverence ['rɛvərəns] *n (feeling)* почте́ние.

Reverend ['rɛvərənd] *adj:* **the ~** его́ преподо́бие; **the ~ John Smith** его́ преподо́бие Джон Смит.

reverent ['rɛvərənt] *adj (behaviour etc)* почти́тельный* (почти́телен).

reverie ['rɛvərɪ] *n* мечта́ние.

reversal [rɪ'və:sl] *n* радика́льное измене́ние; *(of roles)* переме́на.

reverse [rɪ'və:s] *n (opposite)* противополо́жность *f; (back: of cloth)* обра́тная сторона́*; *(: of coin, medal)* оборо́тная сторона́*; *(: of paper)* оборо́т; *(AUT: also: ~* **gear)** обра́тный ход*; *(setback, defeat)* неуда́ча ♦ *adj (opposite)* обра́тный* ♦ *vt (order, position)* по́лностью изменя́ть (измени́ть* *perf); (direction)* изменя́ть (измени́ть* *perf); (process, policy, decision)* кру́то изменя́ть (измени́ть* *perf); (LAW: judgement)* отменя́ть (отмени́ть* *perf)* ♦ *vi (BRIT: AUT)* дава́ть* (дать* *perf)* за́дний ход; **their fortunes went into ~** уда́ча отверну́лась от них; **in ~ order** в обра́тном поря́дке; **to ~ direction** изменя́ть (измени́ть* *perf)* направле́ние на обра́тное; **to ~ a car** дава́ть* (дать* *perf)* за́дний ход; **to ~ roles** меня́ться (поменя́ться* *perf)* места́ми.

reverse-charge call [rɪ'və:stʃɑ:dʒ-] *n (BRIT: TEL)* *телефо́нный разгово́р за счёт принима́ющего абоне́нта.*

reverse video *n* негати́вное изображе́ние на экра́не диспле́я.

reversible [rɪ'və:səbl] *adj (garment, material)* двусторо́нний*; *(procedure)* обрати́мый (обрати́м).

reversing lights [rɪ'və:sɪŋ-] *npl (BRIT: AUT)* фона́рь *msg* за́днего хо́да.

reversion [rɪ'və:ʃən] *n (ZOOL)* проявле́ние атави́зма; **~ to** возвраще́ние к +*dat.*

revert [rɪ'və:t] *vi:* **to ~ to** *(to former state)* возвраща́ться (возврати́ться* *perf)* к +*dat; (LAW: money, property)* переходи́ть*

(перейти́* *perf)* к +*dat.*

review [rɪ'vju:] *n (of situation, policy etc)* пересмо́тр; *(MIL)* смотр*; *(of book, film etc)* реце́нзия; *(magazine)* обозре́ние ♦ *vt (situation, policy etc)* пересма́тривать (пересмотре́ть* *perf); (MIL)* проводи́ть* (провести́* *perf)* смотр +*gen; (book, film etc)* рецензи́ровать (отрецензи́ровать* *perf);* **to come under ~** рассма́триваться *(impf).*

reviewer [rɪ'vju:ə'] *n (of book, film etc)* рецензе́нт.

revile [rɪ'vaɪl] *vt* поноси́ть* *(impf).*

revise [rɪ'vaɪz] *vt (manuscript)* перераба́тывать (перерабо́тать* *perf); (opinion)* пересма́тривать (пересмотре́ть* *perf); (price, procedure)* изменя́ть (измени́ть* *perf); (SCOL: lesson, maths)* повторя́ть (повтори́ть* *perf);* **~d edition** пересмо́тренное изда́ние.

revision [rɪ'vɪʒən] *n (amendment)* измене́ние; *(for exam)* повторе́ние.

revitalize [ri:'vaɪtəlaɪz] *vt* оживля́ть (оживи́ть* *perf).*

revival [rɪ'vaɪvəl] *n (recovery)* оживле́ние; *(of interest, faith)* возрожде́ние; *(THEAT)* возобновле́ние.

revive [rɪ'vaɪv] *vt (person)* возвраща́ть (возврати́ть* *perf)* к жи́зни; *(economy, industry)* оживля́ть (оживи́ть* *perf); (tradition, hope, interest etc)* возрожда́ть (возроди́ть* *perf); (play)* восстана́вливать (восстанови́ть* *perf)* ♦ *vi (person: from faint)* приходи́ть* (прийти́* *perf)* в созна́ние; *(activity, economy etc)* оживля́ться (оживи́ться* *perf); (faith, hope, interest etc)* возрожда́ться (возроди́ться* *perf).*

revoke [rɪ'vəuk] *vt (treaty, law, title etc)* отменя́ть (отмени́ть* *perf); (promise, decision)* брать* (взять* *perf)* наза́д.

revolt [rɪ'vəult] *n (rebellion)* восста́ние ♦ *vi (rebel)* восстава́ть* (восста́ть* *perf)* ♦ *vt* вызыва́ть (вы́звать* *perf)* отвраще́ние у +*gen;* **to ~ against sb/sth** восстава́ть* (восста́ть* *perf)* про́тив кого́-н/чего́-н.

revolting [rɪ'vəultɪŋ] *adj (disgusting)* отврати́тельный* (отврати́телен).

revolution [rɛvə'lu:ʃən] *n* револю́ция; *(of wheel, earth etc)* оборо́т.

revolutionary [rɛvə'lu:ʃənrɪ] *adj* революцио́нный* (революцио́нен) ♦ *n* революционе́р(ка*).

revolutionize [rɛvə'lu:ʃənaɪz] *vt (industry, society etc)* революционизи́ровать *(impf/perf).*

revolve [rɪ'vɔlv] *vi (turn)* враща́ться *(impf); (fig):* **to ~ (a)round** враща́ться *(impf)* вокру́г +*gen.*

revolver [rɪ'vɔlvə'] *n (gun)* револьве́р.

revolving [rɪ'vɔlvɪŋ] *adj (chair etc)* враща́ющийся.

revolving door *n* враща́ющаяся дверь* *f.*

revue [rɪ'vju:] *n* ревю́ *nt ind.*

revulsion [rɪ'vʌlʃən] *n (disgust)* отвраще́ние.

reward [rɪ'wɔ:d] *n (recompense: for work,*

service, merit) награ́да; (*sum of money*)
пре́мия; (: *for capture of criminal, information
etc*) вознагражде́ние ♦ *vt*: **to ~ (for)** (*effort*)
вознагражда́ть (вознагради́ть* *perf*) (за
+*acc*).
rewarding [rɪ'wɔ:dɪŋ] *adj* (*fig*): **this work is very
~** э́та рабо́та прино́сит удовлетворе́ние;
financially ~ хорошо́ опла́чиваемый.
rewind [ri:'waɪnd] *irreg vt* (*cassette*)
перема́тывать (перемота́ть* *perf*) (*назад*).
rewire [ri:'waɪə'] *vt*: **to ~ a house** заменя́ть
(замени́ть* *perf*) прово́дку в до́ме.
reword [ri:'wɔ:d] *vt* перефрази́ровать (*impf/
perf*).
rework [ri:'wɔ:k] *vt* переде́лывать (переде́лать*
perf).
rewrite [ri:'raɪt] *irreg vt* (*rework*) перепи́сывать
(переписа́ть* *perf*).
Reykjavik ['reɪkjəvi:k] *n* Рейкья́вик.
RFD *abbr* (*US*: *POST*: = *rural free delivery*)
беспла́тная доста́вка по́чты в се́льской
ме́стности.
Rh *abbr* (*MED*: = *rhesus*) ре́зус.
rhapsody ['ræpsədɪ] *n* (*MUS*) рапсо́дия.
rhesus negative *adj* (*MED*) с отрица́тельным
ре́зусом.
rhesus positive *adj* (*MED*) с положи́тельным
ре́зусом.
rhetoric ['rɛtərɪk] *n* рито́рика.
rhetorical [rɪ'tɔrɪkl] *adj* ритори́ческий.
rheumatic [ru:'mætɪk] *adj* ревмати́ческий*.
rheumatism ['ru:mətɪzəm] *n* ревмати́зм.
rheumatoid arthritis ['ru:mətɔɪd-] *n*
ревмато́идный артри́т.
Rhine [raɪn] *n*: **the ~** Рейн.
rhinestone ['raɪnstəun] *n* фальши́вый
бриллиа́нт.
rhinoceros [raɪ'nɔsərəs] *n* носоро́г.
Rhodes [rəudz] *n* Ро́дос.
Rhodesia [rəu'di:ʒə] *n* Роде́зия.
Rhodesian [rəu'di:ʒən] *adj* родези́йский ♦ *n*
родзие́ц*(-и́йка*).
rhododendron [rəudə'dɛndrn] *n* рододе́ндрон.
Rhone [rəun] *n*: **the ~** Ро́на.
rhubarb ['ru:bɑ:b] *n* реве́нь* *m*.
rhyme [raɪm] *n* ри́фма; (*verse*) стихотворе́ние;
(*in poetry*) разме́р ♦ *vi*: **to ~ (with)**
рифмова́ться (*impf*) (с +*instr*); **without ~ or
reason** ни с того́ ни с сего́.
rhythm ['rɪðm] *n* ритм.
rhythmic(al) ['rɪðmɪk(l)] *adj* (*sound*)
ритми́ческий*, ритми́чный* (ритми́чен).
rhythmically ['rɪðmɪklɪ] *adv* ритми́чно.
rhythm method *n* есте́ственный *or*
натура́льный ме́тод контраце́пции.
RI *n abbr* (*BRIT*: *SCOL*: = *religious instruction*)
религио́зное воспита́ние ♦ *abbr* (*US*: *POST*) =
Rhode Island.

rib [rɪb] *n* (*ANAT*) ребро́* ♦ *vt* (*inf*: *mock*)
подшу́чивать (подшути́ть* *perf*) над +*instr*.
ribald ['rɪbəld] *adj* (*laughter, jokes*) непри-
сто́йный* (непристо́ен), скабрёзный*
(скабрёзен); (*person*) гру́бый* (груб).
ribbed [rɪbd] *adj* (*shell*) ребри́стый (ребри́ст);
~ knitting вяза́ние рези́нкой.
ribbon ['rɪbən] *n* ле́нта; **in ~s** (*torn*) в кло́чья.
rice [raɪs] *n* рис.
rice field *n* ри́совое по́ле*.
rice pudding *n* ри́совый пу́динг.
rich [rɪtʃ] *adj* бога́тый (бога́т); (*clothes, jewels*)
роско́шный* (роско́шен); (*soil*) бога́тый;
(*food, colour, life*) насы́щенный; (*voice*)
густо́й (густ); (*abundant*): **~ in** бога́тый
(бога́т) +*instr*; **the ~** *npl* (*rich people*) бога́тые
pl adj.
riches ['rɪtʃɪz] *npl* (*wealth*) бога́тство *ntsg*.
richly ['rɪtʃlɪ] *adv* (*dressed, decorated*)
роско́шно, бога́то; (*rewarded*) ще́дро;
(*deserved, earned*) вполне́.
richness ['rɪtʃnɪs] *n* бога́тство.
rickets ['rɪkɪts] *n* (*MED*) рахи́т.
rickety ['rɪkɪtɪ] *adj* (*furniture etc*) ша́ткий*
(ша́ток).
rickshaw ['rɪkʃɔ:] *n* ри́кша.
ricochet ['rɪkəʃeɪ] *vi* (*bullet, stone*)
рикошети́ровать (*impf*) ♦ *n* рикоше́т.
rid [rɪd] (*pt, pp* **rid**) *vt*: **to ~ sb of sth** избавля́ть
(изба́вить* *perf*) кого́-н от чего́-н; **to get ~ of**
избавля́ться (изба́виться* *perf*) *or*
отделя́ться (отде́латься *perf*) от +*gen*.
riddance ['rɪdns] *n*: **good ~!** ска́тертью
доро́га!
ridden ['rɪdn] *pp of* **ride**.
riddle ['rɪdl] *n* (*conundrum*) зага́дка*; (*mystery*)
та́йна ♦ *vt*: **~d with** (*holes, bullets*)
изрешечённый (изрешечён) +*instr*; (*guilt,
doubts*) по́лный* (по́лон) +*gen*; (*corruption*)
прони́занный (прони́зан) +*instr*.
ride [raɪd] (*pt* **rode**, *pp* **ridden**) *n* пое́здка*; (*track,
path*) лесна́я доро́га, тропа́* ♦ *vi* (*as sport*)
е́здить* верхо́м; (*go somewhere, travel*)
е́хать*/е́здить* (*impf*) ♦ *vt* (*horse*) е́хать*/
е́здить* (*impf*) верхо́м на +*prp*; (*bicycle,
motorcycle*) е́хать*/е́здить* (*impf*) на +*prp*;
(*distance*) проезжа́ть (прое́хать* *perf*); **a 5
mile ~** пое́здка в 5 миль; **horse/car ~**
пое́здка* верхо́м/на маши́не; **to go for a ~**
пойти́* (*perf*) поката́ться; **to take sb for a ~**
(*fig*) прокати́ть* (*perf*) кого́-н; **we rode all
day/all the way** мы е́хали весь день/всю
доро́гу; **to ~ at anchor** (*NAUT*) стоя́ть (*impf*) на
я́коре; **can you ~ a bike?** Вы уме́ете е́здить
на велосипе́де?
▶ **ride out** *vt*: **to ~ out the storm** (*fig*)
выде́рживать (вы́держать *perf*) тру́дности.
rider ['raɪdə'] *n* (*on horse*) нае́здник(-ица),

---

* marks translations which have irregular inflections. The Russian-English side of the dictionary gives inflectional information.

всадник(-ица); (*on bicycle*) велосипедист(ка*); (*on motorcycle*) мотоциклист(ка*); (*in document*) дополнение.

ridge [rɪdʒ] *n* (*of hill*) гребень *m*; (*of roof*) конёк* (*крыши*); (*on material*) выступ.

ridicule ['rɪdɪkju:l] *n* насмешка* ♦ *vt* высмеивать (высмеять *perf*); **an object of ~** предмет насмешек.

ridiculous [rɪ'dɪkjuləs] *adj* смехотворный* (смехотворен); **it's ~** это смешно.

riding ['raɪdɪŋ] *n* верховая езда.

riding school *n* школа верховой езды.

rife [raɪf] *adj*: **to be ~** (*bribery, corruption*) процветать (*impf*); **to be ~ with** (*rumours, fears*) изобиловать (*impf*) +*instr*.

riffraff ['rɪfræf] *n* шушера.

rifle ['raɪfl] *n* (*MIL*) винтовка*; (*for hunting*) ружьё* ♦ *vt* (*steal from: pockets etc*) очистить* (*perf*)

▸ **rifle through** *vt fus* (*papers, belongings*) быстро перебирать (перебрать* *perf*).

rifle range *n* (*outdoor*) стрельбище; (*indoor, at fair*) тир.

rift [rɪft] *n* (*also fig*) трещина; (*in clouds*) просвет.

rig [rɪg] *n* (*also: oil ~*) буровая установка; (: *on land*) буровая вышка* ♦ *vt* (*election etc*) подтасовывать (подтасовать *perf*) результаты +*gen*

▸ **rig out** *vt* (*BRIT*): **to ~ out as/in** наряжать (нарядить *perf*) как/в +*acc*

▸ **rig up** *vt* наскоро сооружать (соорудить* *perf*).

Riga [rɪ'gə] *n* Рига.

rigging ['rɪgɪŋ] *n* (*NAUT*) такелаж.

right [raɪt] *adj* (*answer, solution, decision etc*) правильный* (правилен); (*size*) нужный; (*person, clothes, time*) подходящий*; (*morally good, fair, just*) справедливый (справедлив), правильный* (правилен); (*not left*) правый* ♦ *n* справедливость *f*; (*entitlement*) право*; (*not left*) правая сторона ♦ *adv* (*correctly*) правильно; (*properly, fairly*) справедливо; (*not on the left*) справа; (*not to the left*) направо ♦ *vt* (*ship*) выравнивать (выровнять *perf*); (*car*) ставить* (поставить* *perf*) на колёса; (*fault, situation*) исправлять (исправить* *perf*); (*wrong*) устранять (устранить *perf*) ♦ *excl* так, хорошо; **the ~ time** (*precise*) точное время; (*not wrong*) нужный *or* подходящий* момент; **she's ~** она права; **that's ~!** (*answer*) правильно!; **is that clock ~?** это точные часы?; **to get sth ~** делать (сделать *perf*) что-н как следует; **let's get it ~ this time!** давайте сделаем это как следует на этот раз; **you did the ~ thing** Вы поступили правильно; **to put a mistake ~** (*BRIT*) исправлять (исправить* *perf*) ошибку; **on the ~** справа; **you are in the ~** правда за Вами; **by ~s** по справедливости; **~ and**

wrong правильное и неправильное; **he doesn't know the difference between ~ and wrong** он не знает разницы между правильным и неправильным; **film ~s** право на экранизацию; **~ now** сейчас же; **~ away** сразу же; **~ before/after** как раз перед +*instr*/после +*gen*; **~ against the wall** прямо у стены; **~ ahead** прямо вперёд; **~ in the middle** прямо посередине; **~ to the end of sth** до самого конца чего-н.

right angle *n* прямой угол*.

righteous ['raɪtʃəs] *adj* праведный* (праведен).

righteousness ['raɪtʃəsnɪs] *n* праведность *f*.

rightful ['raɪtful] *adj* законный.

rightfully ['raɪtfəlɪ] *adv* (*yours etc*) законно.

right-hand drive ['raɪthænd-] *n* правостороннее управление ♦ *adj* (*vehicle*) с правосторонним управлением.

right-handed [raɪt'hændɪd] *adj*: **he is ~** он правша.

right-hand man *n* правая рука* (*перен*).

right-hand side *n* правая сторона*.

rightly ['raɪtlɪ] *adv* (*with reason*) справедливо; **if I remember ~** (*BRIT*) если я правильно помню.

right-minded [raɪt'maɪndɪd] *adj* благоразумный* (благоразумен).

right of way *n* (*path etc*) право* прохода; (*AUT*) право* проезда.

rights issue *n* (*STOCK EXCHANGE*) выпуск акции для продажи уже существующим акционерам по льготным ценам.

right wing *n* (*POL*) правое крыло; (*MIL, SPORT*) правый фланг.

right-wing [raɪt'wɪŋ] *adj* (*POL*) правый.

right-winger [raɪt'wɪŋə'] *n* (*POL*) человек правых взглядов; правый(-ая) *m(f)* *adj*; (*SPORT*) правый нападающий* *m* *adj*.

rigid ['rɪdʒɪd] *adj* (*structure, principle*) жёсткий* (жёсток); (*fig: attitude, views etc*) косный* (косен); (: *principle, control etc*) строгий* (строг).

rigidity [rɪ'dʒɪdɪtɪ] *n* (*of structure*) жёсткость *f*; (*of attitude etc*) косность *f*.

rigidly ['rɪdʒɪdlɪ] *adv* (*hold, fix etc*) прочно; (*control*) жёстко; (*behave*) сковано.

rigmarole ['rɪgmərəul] *n* (*procedure*) канитель *f*.

rigor ['rɪgə'] *n* (*US*) = **rigour**.

rigor mortis ['rɪgə'mɔ:tɪs] *n* трупное окоченение.

rigorous ['rɪgərəs] *adj* строгий* (строг); (*training*) серьёзный.

rigorously ['rɪgərəslɪ] *adv* (*test, assess etc*) строго.

rigour ['rɪgə'] (*US* rigor) *n* (*strictness*) строгость *f*; (*severity*): **~s of life/winter** трудности *fpl* жизни/зимы.

rigout ['rɪgaut] *n* (*BRIT*: *inf*: *clothes*) одеяние.

rile [raɪl] *vt* раздражать (раздражить *perf*).

rim [rɪm] *n* (*of glass, dish*) край*; (*of spectacles*)

ободо́к*; (*of wheel*) о́бод*.
rimless ['rɪmlɪs] *adj* (*spectacles*) без ободка́.
rimmed [rɪmd] *adj*: ~ **with** окаймлённый
(окаймлён *+instr*.
rind [raɪnd] *n* (*of bacon, cheese*) ко́рка; (*of
lemon, orange etc*) кожура́.
ring [rɪŋ] (*pt* **rang**, *pp* **rung**) *n* (*of metal, smoke*)
кольцо́*; (*of people, objects, light*) круг*; (*of
spies, drug dealers etc*) сеть *f*; (*for boxing*)
ринг; (*bullring, also of circus*) аре́на; (*of
doorbell, telephone*) звоно́к* ♦ *vi* звони́ть
(позвони́ть *perf*); (*doorbell*) звони́ть
(зазвони́ть *perf*); (*also*: ~ **out**: *voice, shot*)
раздава́ться* (разда́ться* *perf*) ♦ *vt* (*BRIT*: *TEL*)
звони́ть (позвони́ть *perf*) *+dat*; (*bell etc*)
звони́ть (позвони́ть *perf*) в *+acc*; **to give sb a**
~ (*BRIT*: *TEL*) звони́ть (позвони́ть *perf*)
кому́-н; **that has a ~ of truth about it** э́то
звучи́т правдоподо́бно; **my ears are ~ing** у
меня́ звени́т в уша́х; **to ~ the bell** звони́ть
(*impf*) в звоно́к; (*doorbell*) звони́ть
(позвони́ть *perf*) в дверь; **the name doesn't ~
a bell (with me)** э́то и́мя мне ни о чём не
говори́т
► **ring back** (*BRIT*) ♦ *vt* перезва́нивать
(перезвони́ть *perf*) *+dat* ♦ *vi* звони́ть
(позвони́ть *perf*) (в отве́т)
► **ring off** *vi* (*BRIT*) ве́шать (пове́сить* *perf*)
тру́бку
► **ring up** *vt* (*BRIT*) звони́ть (позвони́ть *perf*)
+dat.
ring binder *n* скоросшива́тель *m*.
ring finger *n* безымя́нный па́лец*.
ringing ['rɪŋɪŋ] *n* (*of telephone, doorbell*)
звоно́к*; (*of church bell, in ears*) звон.
ringing tone *n* (*BRIT*: *TEL*) дли́нные гудки́ *pl*.
ringleader ['rɪŋliːdə'] *n* (*of gang*) глава́рь* *m*.
ringlets ['rɪŋlɪts] *npl* ло́коны *mpl*.
ring road *n* (*BRIT*) кольцева́я доро́га.
rink [rɪŋk] *n* (*also*: **ice ~, roller skating ~**) като́к*.
rinse [rɪns] *n* (*process*) полоска́ние; (*dye: for
hair*) кра́ска* для воло́с ♦ *vt* полоска́ть*
(прополоска́ть* *perf*); (*clothes*) полоска́ть
(вы́полоскать *perf*); **to give sth a ~**
ополо́скивать (ополосну́ть *perf*) что-н.
Rio (de Janeiro) ['riːəu(dədʒə'nɪərəu)] *n*
Ри́о-де-Жане́йро *m ind*.
riot ['raɪət] *n* (*disturbance*) беспоря́дки* *mpl*,
бесчи́нства *ntpl*; (*of colours, flowers*) бу́йство
♦ *vi* бесчи́нствовать (*impf*); **to run ~**
бу́йствовать* (*impf*).
rioter ['raɪətə'] *n* наруши́тель *m* поря́дка.
riot gear *n* защи́тное снаряже́ние поли́ции.
riotous ['raɪətəs] *adj* (*mob, behaviour, party*)
бесчи́нствующий; (*living*) разгу́льный*
(разгу́лен); (*welcome*) бу́рный* (бу́рен).
riotously ['raɪətəslɪ] *adv*: ~ **funny** неимове́рно
смешно́й.

riot police *n* спецподразделе́ние поли́ции для
подавле́ния беспоря́дков.
RIP *abbr* (= *rest in peace*) мир пра́ху твоему́.
rip [rɪp] *n* (*tear*) разры́в ♦ *vt* (*paper, cloth*)
разрыва́ть* (разорва́ть* *perf*) ♦ *vi* (*see vt*)
разрыва́ться* (разорва́ться* *perf*)
► **rip up** *vt* разрыва́ть (разорва́ть* *perf*).
ripcord ['rɪpkɔːd] *n* (*on parachute*) вытяжно́й
трос.
ripe [raɪp] *adj* спе́лый* (спел), зре́лый* (зрел);
(*cheese*) вы́держанный (вы́держан).
ripen ['raɪpn] *vi* спеть* (поспе́ть* *perf*), зреть *or*
созрева́ть (созре́ть *perf*) ♦ *vt*: **the sun will ~
them soon** они́ ско́ро созре́ют на со́лнце.
ripeness ['raɪpnɪs] *n* спе́лость *f*, зре́лость *f*.
rip-off ['rɪpɔf] *n* (*inf*): **it's a ~**! э́то
обдира́ловка!
riposte [rɪ'pɔst] *n* нахо́дчивый отве́т.
ripple ['rɪpl] *n* (*wave: caused by wind, rain etc*)
рябь *f no pl*; (: *caused by stone etc*) зыбь *f no pl*;
(*of laughter, applause*) волна́*, гул *m no pl* ♦ *vt*
(*water, sand*) поднима́ть (подня́ть* *perf*)
зыбь на *+prp* ♦ *vi* (*water*) покрыва́ться
(покры́ться* *perf*) ря́бью.
rise [raɪz] (*pt* **rose**, *pp* **risen**) *n* (*slope*) подъём;
(*increase*) повыше́ние; (*fig: of state, leader*)
возвыше́ние ♦ *vi* поднима́ться (подня́ться*
perf); (*prices, numbers, voice*) повыша́ться
(повы́ситься* *perf*); (*sun, moon*) всходи́ть*
(взойти́* *perf*); (*sound*) нараста́ть (*impf*); (*also*:
~ **up**: *building*) возвыша́ться (*impf*); (: *rebels*)
восстава́ть* (восста́ть* *perf*); (*in rank*)
продвига́ться (продви́нуться *perf*); ~ **to
power** прихо́д к вла́сти; **to give ~ to**
вызыва́ть (вы́звать* *perf*); **to ~ to the
occasion** ока́зываться (оказа́ться* *perf*) на
высоте́ положе́ния.
risen [rɪzn] *pp of* **rise**.
rising ['raɪzɪŋ] *adj* (*number, prices*) расту́щий;
(*tide*) нараста́ющий; (*sun, moon*) восходя́-
щий.
rising damp *n* засоле́ние (*поднима́ющаяся
вверх сы́рость*).
rising star *n* (*fig*) восходя́щая звезда́*.
risk [rɪsk] *n* риск ♦ *vt* (*endanger*) рискова́ть
(*impf*) *+instr*; (*chance*) рискова́ть* (рискну́ть
perf) *+instr*; **to take a ~** рискова́ть (рискну́ть
perf), идти́* (*impf*) на риск; **to run the ~ of
doing** рискова́ть (*impf*) *+infin*; **to put sb/sth at ~**
подверга́ть
(подве́ргнуть *perf*) кого́-н/что-н ри́ску; **at
one's own ~** на свой (страх и) риск; **at the ~
of sounding rude** ... рискуя́ показа́ться
грубым(-ой) ...; **it's a fire ~** с противо-
пожа́рной то́чки зре́ния э́то опа́сно; **it's a
health ~** э́то опа́сно для здоро́вья; **I'll ~ it** я
рискну́.
risk capital *n* „ри́сковый" *or* ве́нчурный

капита́л.

risky ['rɪskɪ] *adj* риско́ванный* (риско́ван).

risqué ['ri:skeɪ] *adj* (*joke*) сомни́тельный* (сомни́телен).

rissole ['rɪsəʊl] *n* биток*.

rite [raɪt] *n* обря́д; **last** ~s после́днее прича́стие.

ritual ['rɪtjʊəl] *adj* ритуа́льный ♦ *n* (*of religion*) обря́д; (*of procedure*) ритуа́л.

rival ['raɪvl] *n* сопе́рник(-ица); (*in business*) конкуре́нт ♦ *adj* (*competing: business*) конкури́рующий; (*competition*) сопе́рничающий ♦ *vt* сопе́рничать (*impf*) с +*instr*; **to** ~ **sb/sth in** сопе́рничать (*impf*) с кем-н/с чем-н в +*prp*; ~ **team** кома́нда сопе́рника.

rivalry ['raɪvlrɪ] *n* (*in sport, love*) сопе́рничество; (*in business*) конкуре́нция.

river ['rɪvə] *n* река́* ♦ *cpd* (*port, traffic*) речно́й; **up/down** ~ вверх/вниз по реке́.

riverbank ['rɪvəbæŋk] *n* бе́рег* реки́.

riverbed ['rɪvəbɛd] *n* ру́сло реки́.

riverside ['rɪvəsaɪd] *n* бе́рег* реки́.

rivet ['rɪvɪt] *n* заклёпка* ♦ *vt* (*fig*) прико́вывать (прикова́ть *perf*).

riveting ['rɪvɪtɪŋ] *adj* (*fig*) захва́тывающий*.

Riviera [rɪvɪ'ɛərə] *n*: **the** (**French**) ~ (францу́зская) Ривье́ра; **the Italian** ~ италья́нская Ривье́ра.

Riyadh [rɪ'jɑ:d] *n* Эр-Рия́д.

RN *n abbr* (*BRIT*) = **Royal Navy**; (*US*: = *registered nurse*) ≈ медсестра́ = *медици́нская сестра́*.

RNA *n abbr* (= *ribonucleic acid*) РНК= *рибонуклеи́новая кислота́*.

RNLI *n abbr* (*BRIT*) = **Royal National Lifeboat Institution**.

RNZAF *n abbr* = **Royal New Zealand Air Force**.

RNZN *n abbr* = **Royal New Zealand Navy**.

road [rəʊd] *n* (*also fig*) путь* *m*, доро́га; (*in town*) доро́га; (*motorway etc*) шоссе́ *nt ind*; ~ **accident** доро́жная ава́рия; **main** ~ гла́вная доро́га; **major/minor** ~ гла́вная/ второстепе́нная доро́га; **it takes 4 hours by** ~ э́то 4 часа́ по доро́ге; **let's hit the** ~ дава́йте вы́едем на доро́гу; **to be on the** ~ (*tramp*) бродя́жничать (*impf*); (*salesman*) быть* (*impf*) в разъе́здах; (*pop group*) быть* (*impf*) на гастро́лях, гастроли́ровать* (*impf*); **on the** ~ **to success** на пути́ к успе́ху; ~ **sense** чу́вство доро́ги; ~ **junction** пересече́ние доро́г, перекрёсток*.

roadblock ['rəʊdblɒk] *n* доро́жное загражде́ние.

road haulage *n* доро́жная перево́зка.

road hog *n* лиха́ч.

road map *n* доро́жная ка́рта.

road safety *n* доро́жная безопа́сность *f*.

roadside ['rəʊdsaɪd] *n* обо́чина ♦ *cpd* придоро́жный; ~ **verge** обо́чина; **by the** ~ у обо́чины.

road sign *n* доро́жный знак.

road sweeper *n* (*BRIT: person*) дво́рник; (*vehicle*) подмета́льная маши́на.

road user *n* (*driver*) води́тель *m*.

roadway ['rəʊdweɪ] *n* (*central part of road*) прое́зжая часть* *f* (доро́ги).

road works *npl* доро́жно-ремо́нтные рабо́ты *fpl*.

roadworthy ['rəʊdwə:ðɪ] *adj* (*car*) приго́дный* (приго́ден) к эксплуата́ции.

roam [rəʊm] *vi* броди́ть* (*impf*), скита́ться (*impf*) ♦ *vt* броди́ть* (*impf*) по +*dat*.

roar [rɔ:ʳ] *n* (*of animal*) рёв *m no pl*; (*of crowd, engine, wind*) рёв; (*of laughter*) взрыв ♦ *vi* (*animal, person*) реве́ть (*impf*); (*crowd, engine, wind*) реве́ть (*impf*); **to** ~ **with laughter** хохота́ть (*impf*).

roaring ['rɔ:rɪŋ] *adj*: **a** ~ **fire** я́рко пыла́ющий ками́н; **a** ~ **success** гро́мкий успе́х; **to do a** ~ **trade** вести́* (*impf*) бо́йкую торго́влю.

roast [rəʊst] *n* (*of meat*) жарко́е *nt adj* ♦ *vt* (*meat, potatoes*) жа́рить (зажа́рить *perf*); (*coffee*) жа́рить (поджа́рить *perf*).

roast beef *n* ро́стбиф, жа́реная говя́дина.

roasting ['rəʊstɪŋ] *n* (*inf*): **to give sb a** ~ устра́ивать (устро́ить *perf*) кому́-н разно́с.

rob [rɒb] *vt* (*person, house, bank*) обкра́дывать (обокра́сть* *perf*); **to** ~ **sb of sth** красть* (укра́сть* *perf*) что-н у кого́-н; (*fig*) лиша́ть (лиши́ть *perf*) кого́-н чего́-н.

robber ['rɒbəʳ] *n* граби́тель *m*.

robbery ['rɒbərɪ] *n* (*theft*) ограбле́ние, грабёж.

robe [rəʊb] *n* (*for ceremony etc*) ма́нтия; (*also*: **bath** ~) ба́нный хала́т; (*US*) плед ♦ *vt* облача́ть (облачи́ть *perf*).

robin ['rɒbɪn] *n* (*also*: ~ **redbreast**) заря́нка*.

robot ['rəʊbɒt] *n* ро́бот.

robotics [rə'bɒtɪks] *n* (*ELEC, COMPUT*) робототе́хника.

robust [rəʊ'bʌst] *adj* кре́пкий* (кре́пок).

rock [rɒk] *n* (*substance*) (го́рная) поро́да; (*boulder*) валу́н*; (*cliff*) скала́*; (*US: small stone*) ка́мешек*; (*BRIT: sweet*) леденцо́вая караме́ль в фо́рме дли́нных па́лочек; (*MUS: also*: ~ **music**) рок ♦ *vt* (*swing gently*) кача́ть (*impf*); (*shake*) шата́ть (*impf*) ♦ *vi* (*object*) кача́ться (*impf*), шата́ться (*impf*); (*person*) кача́ться (*impf*); **on the** ~s (*drink*) со льдом; (*marriage etc*) на гра́ни распа́да; **the ship was smashed on the** ~s кора́бль разби́лся о ска́лы; **to** ~ **the boat** (*fig*) наруши́ть (*perf*) поко́й.

rock and roll *n* рок-н-ро́лл.

rock bottom *n* (*fig*) преде́льная ни́зкая черта́; **to reach** *or* **touch** *or* **hit** ~ ~ (*price*) достига́ть (дости́чь* *perf*) преде́льно ни́зкой черты́; (*person*) доходи́ть* (дойти́* *perf*) до крити́ческой то́чки.

rock-bottom ['rɒk'bɒtəm] *adj* (*fig: prices*) преде́льно ни́зкий*.

rock cake *n* ко́ржик с изю́мом.

rock climber *n* скалола́з.

rock climbing n скалола́зание.
rockery ['rɔkərɪ] n альпи́йский* сад*.
rocket ['rɔkɪt] n раке́та ♦ vi (prices) подска́кивать (подскочи́ть* perf).
rocket launcher n (MIL) пускова́я раке́тная устано́вка*.
rock face n пове́рхность f скалы́.
rock fall n камнепа́д.
rocking chair ['rɔkɪŋ-] n (кре́сло-)кача́лка*.
rocking horse n конь-кача́лка*.
rocky ['rɔkɪ] adj (mountain) скали́стый (скали́ст); (path, soil) камени́стый (камени́ст); (unsteady, unstable) ша́ткий* (ша́ток).
Rocky Mountains npl: the ~ ~ Скали́стые го́ры* fpl.
rod [rɔd] n прут*; (TECH) сте́ржень* m; (also: fishing ~) у́дочка*.
rode [rəud] pt of ride.
rodent ['rəudnt] n грызу́н*.
rodeo ['rəudɪəu] n (US) роде́о nt ind.
roe [rəu] n (also: ~ deer) косу́ля; (of fish): hard ~ икра́; soft ~ моло́ки fpl.
roe deer n inv косу́ля.
rogue [rəug] n (dishonest person) моше́нник, жу́лик.
roguish ['rəugɪʃ] adj (mischevious) плутова́тый (плутова́т).
role [rəul] n (THEAT, fig) роль* f.
role model n приме́р.
role play n ролевы́е и́гры fpl.
roll [rəul] n (of paper, cloth etc) руло́н; (of banknotes) сви́ток*; (also: bread ~) було́чка*; (register, list) спи́сок*; (sound: of drums) бой*; (: of thunder) раска́т ♦ vt (ball, stone etc) ката́ть/кати́ть* (impf); (also: ~ up: string) скру́чивать (скрути́ть* perf); (: sleeves) зака́тывать (заката́ть perf); (cigarette) свёртывать (сверну́ть perf); (eyes) зака́тывать (заката́ть* perf); (also: ~ out: pastry) раска́тывать (раската́ть perf); (lawn, road etc) ука́тывать (уката́ть perf) ♦ vi (ball, stone etc) кати́ться* (impf); (drum) греме́ть (impf); (car. also: ~ along) кати́ться* (impf); (ship) кача́ться (impf); cheese/ham ~ було́чка* с сы́ром/с ветчино́й
► **roll about** vi перека́тываться (перекати́ться* perf)
► **roll around** vi = roll about
► **roll by** vi (time) протека́ть (проте́чь* perf)
► **roll in** vi (orders) сы́паться* (impf); (cash) течь* (поте́чь* perf)
► **roll over** vi перевора́чиваться (переверну́ться perf)
► **roll up** vi (inf: arrive) подка́тывать (подкати́ть* perf) ♦ vt (carpet, newspaper) свора́чивать (сверну́ть perf); (umbrella) скла́дывать (сложи́ть* perf); to ~ o.s. up into

a ball свора́чиваться (сверну́ться perf) кала́чиком.
roll call n перекли́чка*.
roller ['rəulə'] n (in machine) ва́лик; (wheel) ро́лик; (for lawn, road) като́к*; (for hair) бигуди́ pl ind.
roller blind n што́ра на ро́ликах.
roller coaster n аттракцио́н "америка́нские го́ры" fpl.
roller skates npl ро́лики mpl, ро́ликовые коньки́ mpl.
rollicking ['rɔlɪkɪŋ] adj потряса́ющий* (потряса́ющ); to have a ~ time весели́ться (повесели́ться perf).
rolling ['rəulɪŋ] adj (landscape) холми́стый (холми́ст).
rolling mill n прока́тный стан.
rolling pin n ска́лка*.
rolling stock n (RAIL) подвижно́й соста́в.
roll-on/roll-off ferry adj (BRIT) паро́м, приспосо́бленный для въе́зда и вы́езда автомоби́лей.
roly-poly ['rəulɪ'pəulɪ] n (BRIT: CULIN) руле́т с варе́ньем.
ROM [rɔm] n abbr (COMPUT: = read-only memory) ПЗУ = постоя́нное запомина́ющее устро́йство.
Roman ['rəumən] adj ри́мский* ♦ n (person) ри́млянин(-нка).
Roman Catholic adj (ри́мско-)католи́ческий* ♦ n като́лик(-и́чка*).
romance [rə'mæns] n (love affair, novel) рома́н; (charm) рома́нтика; (MUS) рома́нс.
Romanesque [rəumə'nɛsk] adj рома́нский*.
Romania [rəu'meɪnɪə] n Румы́ния.
Romanian [rəu'meɪnɪən] adj румы́нский* ♦ n (person) румы́н(ка*); (LING) румы́нский* язы́к*.
Roman numeral n ри́мская ци́фра.
romantic [rə'mæntɪk] adj романти́чный* (романти́чен); (play, story etc) романти́ческий.
romanticism [rə'mæntɪsɪzəm] n романти́зм.
Romany ['rɔmənɪ] adj цыга́нский* ♦ n цыга́н(ка*); (LING) цыга́нский* язы́к*.
Rome [rəum] n Рим.
romp [rɔmp] n возня́ ♦ vi (also: ~ about) вози́ться* (impf); to ~ home (horse) выи́грывать (вы́играть perf) ска́чки.
rompers ['rɔmpəz] npl ползунки́ mpl.
rondo ['rɔndəu] n ро́ндо nt ind.
roof [ru:f] (pl ~s) n кры́ша ♦ vt (house) настила́ть (настла́ть* perf) кры́шу +gen or на +prp; the ~ of the mouth нёбо.
roof garden n сад* на кры́ше.
roofing ['ru:fɪŋ] n кро́вельный материа́л; ~ felt руло́нный кро́вельный материа́л.
roof rack n (AUT) бага́жник (на кры́ше

---

* marks translations which have irregular inflections. The Russian-English side of the dictionary gives inflectional information.

автомобиля).
rook [ruk] *n* (*bird*) грач*; (*CHESS*) ладья*, турá ♦
vt (*inf: cheat*) надувáть (надýть *perf*).
rookie ['rukiː] *n* (*US: inf*) новичóк.
room [ruːm] *n* (*in house*) кóмната; (*in school*)
класс; (*in hotel*) нóмер*; (*space*) мéсто*; ~**s**
npl (*lodging*) квартúра *fsg*; **"rooms to let"**, (*US*)
"rooms for rent" „сдаются кóмнаты"; **single/**
double ~ (*in hotel*) одномéстный/
двухмéстный нóмер*; **is there ~ for this?** это
здесь помéстится?; **to make ~ for sb** давáть*
(дать* *perf*) мéсто комý-н; **there is ~ for**
improvement кóе-что мóжно улýчшить;
there is still ~ for doubt ещё есть основáния
сомневáться.
rooming house ['ruːmɪŋ-] *n* (*US*)
мебелирóванные кóмнаты *fpl*.
roommate ['ruːmmeɪt] *n* сосéд*(ка*) по
кóмнате.
room service *n* обслýживание в нóмере.
room temperature *n* кóмнатная
температýра.
roomy ['ruːmɪ] *adj* (*building, car, garment*)
простóрный* (простóрен); (*bag*)
вместúтельный* (вместúтелен).
roost [ruːst] *vi* усáживаться (усéсться* *perf*) на
ночлéг.
rooster ['ruːstə'] *n* (*esp US*) петýх*.
root [ruːt] *n* кóрень* *m* ♦ *vi* (*plant, belief: also:*
take ~) укореняться (укоренúться* *perf*); ~**s**
npl (*family origins*) кóрни* *mpl*; **the ~ of the**
problem is that ... кóрень проблéмы в том ...
▸ **root about** *vi* (*fig*) рыться* (*impf*)
▸ **root for** *vt fus* (*inf: support*) болéть (*impf*) за
+*acc*
▸ **root out** *vt* откопáть (*perf*).
root beer *n* безалкогóльный напúток из
корнéй трав.
rope [rəup] *n* верёвка*, канáт; (*NAUT*) трос ♦ *vt*
(*area: also:* ~ **off**) отгорáживать
(отгородúть* *perf*) верёвкой; (*tie on*): **to ~ to**
привязывать (привязáть* *perf*) верёвкой к
+*dat*; (*join*): **to ~ together** связывать
(связáть* *perf*) верёвкой; **to know the ~s** (*fig*)
знать (*impf*), что к чемý
▸ **rope in** *vt* (*fig*) втягивать (втянýть* *perf*).
rope ladder *n* верёвочная лéстница.
ropey ['rəupɪ] *adj* (*inf*) дряннóй.
rosary ['rəuzərɪ] *n* чётки* *pl*.
rose [rəuz] *pt of* **rise** ♦ *n* рóза; (*on watering can*)
насáдка* ♦ *adj* (*colour*) рóзовый (рóзов).
rosé ['rəuzeɪ] *n* (*wine*) рóзовое винó*.
rosebed ['rəuzbed] *n* клýмба с рóзами.
rosebud ['rəuzbʌd] *n* бутóн рóзы.
rosebush ['rəuzbuʃ] *n* рóзовый куст*.
rosemary ['rəuzmərɪ] *n* розмарúн.
rosette [rəu'zɛt] *n* (*decoration*) розéтка*.
ROSPA ['rɔspə] *n abbr* (*BRIT*) = *Royal Society for*
the Prevention of Accidents.
roster ['rɔstə'] *n*: **duty ~** расписáние дежýрств.
rostrum ['rɔstrəm] *n* (*POL*) трибýна.

rosy ['rəuzɪ] *adj* (*colour*) рóзовый (рóзов);
(*face, cheeks*) румяный (румян); (*situation*)
рáдостный* (рáдостен); **a ~ future** рáдужное
бýдущее.
rot [rɔt] *n* (*process*) гниéние; (*result*) гниль *f*;
(*fig: nonsense*) чушь *f* ♦ *vt* (*wood, fruit*) гноúть
(сгноúть* *perf*); (*teeth*) пóртить* (испóртить*
perf) ♦ *vi* гнить* (сгнить* *perf*); **to stop the ~**
(*BRIT: fig*) навестú* (*perf*) порядок; **dry/wet ~**
сухáя/мóкрая гниль.
rota ['rəutə] *n* чередовáние; **on a ~ basis**
чередуясь, поочерёдно.
rotary ['rəutərɪ] *adj* (*motion*) вращáтельный;
(*machine*) ротациóнный, вращáющийся; ~
engine рóторно-поршневóй двúгатель.
rotate [rəu'teɪt] *vt* вращáть (*impf*); (*change*
round: crops, jobs) чередовáть (*impf*) ♦ *vi*
вращáться (*impf*).
rotating [rəu'teɪtɪŋ] *adj* (*movement*)
вращáтельный.
rotation [rəu'teɪʃən] *n* вращéние; (*of crops*)
севооборóт; **in ~** поочерёдно.
rote [rəut] *n*: **to learn by ~** учúть (*impf*)
наизýсть.
rotor ['rəutə'] *n* (*also:* ~ **blade**) (несýщий) винт*
(*вертолёта*).
rotten ['rɔtn] *adj* (*fruit, wood, teeth*) гнилóй*;
(*meat, eggs*) тýхлый*; (*fig: unpleasant*)
мéрзкий* (мéрзок), отвратúтельный*
(отвратúтелен); (*dishonest*) продáжный*
(продáжен); (*inf: bad*) погáный*; **to feel ~** (*ill*)
чýвствовать (*impf*) себя погáно.
Rotterdam ['rɔtədæm] *n* Рóттердам.
rotund [rəu'tʌnd] *adj* (*person*) пóлный.
rouble ['ruːbl] (*US* **ruble**) *n* рубль* *m*.
rouge [ruːʒ] *n* румяна *pl*.
rough [rʌf] *adj* грýбый (груб); (*surface*)
шерохóватый (шерохóват); (*terrain*)
пересечённый; (*road*) ухáбистый (ухáбист);
(*brusque: person, manner*) рéзкий* (рéзок);
(*weather*) ненáстный; (*sea*) бýрный* (бýрен);
(*town, area*) опáсный* (опáсен); (*plan, sketch,*
work) черновóй; (*guess*) приблизúтельный*
(приблизúтелен) ♦ *n* (*GOLF*): **in the ~** на
нестрúженной чáсти пóля ♦ *vt*: **to ~ it**
обходúться* (обойтúсь* *perf*) без удóбств ♦
adv: **to play ~** вестú* (*impf*) жёсткую игрý; **the**
sea is ~ today мóре сегóдня штормúт/
неспокóйно; **we had a ~ time (of it)** нам
пришлóсь тýго; ~ **estimate** грýбая оцéнка*
or смéта; **to sleep ~** (*BRIT*) ночевáть* (*impf*),
где придётся; **to feel ~** (*BRIT: ill*) чýвствовать
(*impf*) себя плóхо
▸ **rough out** *vt* (*draft*) набрáсывать
(набросáть* *perf*).
roughage ['rʌfɪdʒ] *n* грýбая пúща.
rough-and-ready ['rʌfən'rɛdɪ] *adj* дряннóй.
rough-and-tumble ['rʌfən'tʌmbl] *n* потасóвка.
roughcast ['rʌfkɑːst] *n* (*for wall*) гáлечная
штукатýрка.
rough copy *n* черновúк*.

rough draft n чернови́к*.
rough justice n жёсткий* суд.
roughly ['rʌflɪ] adv гру́бо; (*approximately*)
приблизи́тельно; ~ **speaking** гру́бо говоря́.
roughness ['rʌfnɪs] n (*of surface*)
шерохова́тость f; (*of manner*) гру́бость f.
roughshod ['rʌfʃɔd] adv: **to ride ~ over** не
счита́ться (*impf*) с +*instr*.
roulette [ru:'lɛt] n руле́тка*.
Roumania etc = **Romania** etc.
round [raund] adj кру́глый* (кругл); (*figures,
sum*) кру́глый ♦ n (*BRIT: of toast*) ло́мтик;
(*duty: of policeman, doctor*) обхо́д; (: *of
milkman*) маршру́т; (*game: of cards, golf*)
па́ртия; (*in competition*) тур; (*of ammunition*)
патро́н, компле́кт вы́стрела; (*of talks, also
BOXING*) ра́унд ♦ vt огиба́ть (обогну́ть *perf*) ♦
prep (*surrounding*): ~ **his neck/the table**
вокру́г его́ ше́и/стола́; (*approximately*): ~
about three hundred (приблизи́тельно)
о́коло трёхсот ♦ adv: **all ~** круго́м, вокру́г; **in
~ figures** в кру́глых ци́фрах; **a ~ of applause**
взрыв аплодисме́нтов; **a ~ of drinks** по
бока́лу для всех; **the daily ~** (*fig*) повсе-
дне́вные дела́; **it's just ~ the corner** (*fig*) э́то
как раз за угло́м; ~ **the clock** кру́глые су́тки,
круглосу́точно; **to go ~ the back** обходи́ть*
(обойти́* *perf*) сза́ди; **to walk ~ the room**
ходи́ть* (*impf*) по ко́мнате; **to go ~ an
obstacle** огиба́ть (обогну́ть *perf*) or
обходи́ть* (обойти́* *perf*) препя́тствие; **the
long way ~** кру́жным путём; **all the year ~**
кру́глый год; **to ask sb ~** приглаша́ть
(пригласи́ть* *perf*) кого́-н в го́сти; **I'll be ~ at
6 o'clock** я приду́ в 6 часо́в; **to go ~ to sb's
(house)** идти́*/ходи́ть* (*impf*) к кому́-н; **there's
enough to go ~** хва́тит на всех
▸ **round off** vt (*speech etc*) заверша́ть
(заверши́ть *perf*)
▸ **round up** vt (*cattle, people*) сгоня́ть (согна́ть*
perf); (*price, figure*) округля́ть (округли́ть
perf).
roundabout ['raundəbaut] n (*BRIT: AUT*)
кольцева́я тра́нспортная развя́зка*; (: *at fair*)
карусе́ль f ♦ adj око́льным путём.
rounded ['raundɪd] adj окру́глый (окру́гл).
rounders ['raundəz] n англи́йская лапта́.
roundly ['raundlɪ] adv (*fig: criticize*) ре́зко.
round robin n (*letter*) коллекти́вное письмо́*.
round-shouldered ['raund'ʃəuldəd] adj
суту́лый (суту́л).
round trip n пое́здка* туда́-обра́тно.
roundup ['raundʌp] n (*information*) сво́дка*; (*of
animals*) заго́н; (*of criminals*) обла́ва; **a ~ of
the latest news** сво́дка после́дних новосте́й.
rouse [rauz] vt (*wake up*) буди́ть* (разбуди́ть*
perf); (*stir up*) возбужда́ть (возбуди́ть* *perf*).
rousing ['rauzɪŋ] adj (*cheer, welcome*) бу́рный*

(бу́рен).
rout [raut] n (*MIL*) разгро́м ♦ vt (*defeat*)
громи́ть* (разгроми́ть* *perf*).
route [ru:t] n (*way*) путь* m, доро́га; (*of bus,
train, shipping*) маршру́т; **the best ~ to
London** лу́чший* путь в Ло́ндон; **en ~ for** по
пути́ в +*acc*; **en ~ from ... to ...** по пути́ из +*gen
... в +*acc* ....
route map n (*BRIT*) маршру́тная ка́рта.
routine [ru:'ti:n] adj (*work*) повседне́вный*
(повседне́вен); (*procedure*) обы́чный*
(обы́чен) ♦ n (*habits*) распоря́док*;
(*drudgery*) рути́на; (*THEAT*) но́мер*; **daily ~**
распоря́док* дня.
rove [rəuv] vt (*streets*) броди́ть* (*impf*) по +*dat*,
скита́ться (*impf*) по +*dat*.
roving reporter n разъездно́й репортёр.
row[1] [rəu] n ряд* ♦ vi (*in boat*) грести́* (*impf*) ♦ vt
(*boat*) управля́ть (*impf*) +*instr*; **in a ~** (*fig*)
подря́д.
row[2] [rau] n (*noise*) шум; (*dispute*) сканда́л,
ссо́ра; (*inf: scolding*) нагоня́й ♦ vi (*argue*)
сканда́лить (поскандалить *perf*); **to have a ~**
ссо́риться (поссо́риться *perf*), поскандалить
(*perf*).
rowboat ['rəubəut] n (*US*) гребна́я шлю́пка*.
rowdiness ['raudɪnɪs] n бу́йство.
rowdy ['raudɪ] adj бу́йный* (бу́ен).
rowdyism ['raudɪzəm] n бу́йство.
rowing ['rəuɪŋ] n гре́бля.
rowing boat n (*BRIT*) гребна́я шлю́пка*.
rowlock ['rɔlək] n (*BRIT*) уклю́чина.
royal ['rɔɪəl] adj короле́вский*.
Royal Air Force n (*BRIT*) Брита́нские
вое́нно-возду́шные си́лы.
royal-blue ['rɔɪəlblu:] adj я́рко-си́ний*.
royalist ['rɔɪəlɪst] adj роя́листский* ♦ n
роя́лист(ка*).
Royal Navy n (*BRIT*) Брита́нский
вое́нно-морско́й флот.
royalty ['rɔɪəltɪ] n (*royal persons*) чле́ны mpl
короле́вской семьи́; (*payment*) (а́вторский*)
гонора́р.
RP n abbr (*BRIT: = received pronunciation*)
станда́ртное произноше́ние.
rpm abbr (= *revolutions per minute*) оборо́тов в
мину́ту.
RR abbr (*US*) (= **railroad**) ж.д., ж/д= *желе́зная
доро́га*.
RRP n abbr (*BRIT*) (= **recommended retail price**)
рекомендо́ванная ро́зничная цена́.
RSA n abbr (*BRIT*) = *Royal Society of Arts*; *Royal
Scottish Academy*.
RSI n abbr (*MED*: = *repetitive strain injury*)
*произво́дственная тра́вма, вы́званная
напряже́нием одно́й и той же гру́ппы мы́шц
(у маши́ни́сток итп*).
RSPB n abbr (*BRIT*) = *Royal Society for the*

Protection of Birds.

RSPCA n abbr (BRIT) = Royal Society for the Prevention of Cruelty to Animals.

RSVP abbr (= répondez s'il vous plaît) про́сьба отве́тить на приглаше́ние.

RTA n abbr = road traffic accident.

Rt Hon. abbr (BRIT: = Right Honourable) высокочти́мый.

Rt Rev. abbr (REL: = Right Reverend) высокопреподо́бный.

rub [rʌb] vt (part of body) тере́ть* (потере́ть* perf); (object: to clean) тере́ть* (impf); (: to polish) натира́ть (натере́ть* perf); (: to dry) вытира́ть (вы́тереть* perf); (hands: also: ~ together) потира́ть (потере́ть* perf) ♦ n: to give sth a ~ (polish) натира́ть (натере́ть* perf) что-н; to ~ one's hands (together) тере́ть* (потере́ть* perf) ру́ки; to ~ sb up or (US) ~ sb the wrong way раздража́ть (impf) кого́-н

▶ **rub down** vt обтира́ть (обтере́ть* perf)

▶ **rub in** vt (ointment) втира́ть (втере́ть* perf); don't ~ it in! (fig: inf) не ка́пай!

▶ **rub off** vi (paint) стира́ться (стере́ться* perf)

▶ **rub off on** vt fus передава́ться* (переда́ться* perf) +dat

▶ **rub out** vt стира́ть (стере́ть* perf).

rubber ['rʌbəʳ] n (substance) рези́на, каучу́к; (BRIT: eraser) рези́нка, ла́стик; (US: inf: condom) презервати́в.

rubber band n (кру́глая) рези́нка*.

rubber bullet n рези́новая пу́ля.

rubber plant n каучуконо́с, (каучуконо́сный) фи́кус.

rubber ring n надувно́й рези́новый круг*.

rubber stamp n штамп; (POST) штемпель m.

rubber-stamp [rʌbə'stæmp] vt (fig) штампова́ть (проштампова́ть perf).

rubbery ['rʌbərɪ] adj (material, substance) рези́новый; (meat, food) жёсткий* как рези́на.

rubbish ['rʌbɪʃ] n му́сор; (waste food) отбро́сы mpl; (junk) хлам; (fig: pej: nonsense) ерунда́, чушь f; (: junk) дрянь f ♦ vt (BRIT: inf) критикова́ть (impf); what you've just said is ~ то, что Вы то́лько что сказа́ли – ерунда́ or чепуха́ or чушь.

rubbish bin n (BRIT) му́сорное ведро́*.

rubbish dump n сва́лка*.

rubbishy ['rʌbɪʃɪ] adj (BRIT: inf) дрянно́й.

rubble ['rʌbl] n обло́мки mpl; (building material) бут.

ruble ['ru:bl] n (US) = rouble.

ruby ['ru:bɪ] n руби́н.

RUC n abbr (BRIT: = Royal Ulster Constabulary) северои́рла́ндская поли́ция.

rucksack ['rʌksæk] n рюкза́к*.

ructions ['rʌkʃənz] npl (inf: protest) возмуще́ние ntsg; (quarrel) сканда́л msg.

rudder ['rʌdəʳ] n руль* m.

ruddy ['rʌdɪ] adj (face, complexion) румя́ный (румя́н); (glow) краснова́тый; (inf: damned)

rude [ru:d] adj (impolite) гру́бый* (груб); (shocking) непристо́йный* (непристо́ен); (crudely made) гру́бо сде́ланный (сде́лан); he was ~ to me он был груб со мной; a ~ awakening глубо́кое разочарова́ние, неприя́тное откры́тие.

rudely ['ru:dlɪ] adv гру́бо.

rudeness ['ru:dnɪs] n (impoliteness) гру́бость f.

rudimentary [ru:dɪ'mɛntərɪ] adj (equipment, knowledge) элемента́рный* (элемента́рен).

rudiments ['ru:dɪmənts] npl осно́вы fpl.

rue [ru:] vt (action, decision) жале́ть (пожале́ть perf) о +prp; (day, hour etc) проклина́ть (прокля́сть* perf).

rueful ['ru:ful] adj (expression, person etc) печа́льный* (печа́лен).

ruffian ['rʌfɪən] n банди́т.

ruffle ['rʌfl] vt (hair) еро́шить (взъеро́шить perf); (clothes) гофрирова́ть (impf/perf); (water) ряби́ть* (impf); (fig: person) раздража́ть (impf).

rug [rʌg] n ко́врик; (BRIT: blanket) плед.

rugby ['rʌgbɪ] n (also: ~ football) ре́гби nt ind.

rugged ['rʌgɪd] adj (landscape) скали́стый (скали́ст); (features) гру́бый* (груб); (character) прямо́й (прям); (determination) непрекло́нный* (непрекло́нен), твёрдый* (твёрд).

rugger ['rʌgəʳ] n (BRIT: inf) ре́гби nt ind.

ruin ['ru:ɪn] n (destruction: of building, hopes, plans) разруше́ние; (: of hopes, plans) круше́ние; (downfall) ги́бель f; (bankruptcy) разоре́ние; (remains: of building) разва́лины fpl ♦ vt (building, hopes, plans) разруша́ть (разру́шить perf); (future, health, reputation) губи́ть (погуби́ть perf); (person: financially) разоря́ть (разори́ть perf); (spoil: clothes) по́ртить* (испо́ртить* perf); ~s npl (of building, castle etc) разва́лины fpl, руи́ны fpl; in ~s (building) в разва́линах or руи́нах; my life is in ~s моя́ жизнь загу́блена.

ruination [ru:ɪ'neɪʃən] n уничтоже́ние.

ruinous ['ru:ɪnəs] adj (interest) губи́тельный* (губи́телен); (expense) разори́тельный* (разори́телен).

rule [ru:l] n (norm, regulation) пра́вило; (government) правле́ние, власть f; (ruler) лине́йка ♦ vt (country, people) управля́ть (impf) +instr ♦ vi (leader, monarch etc) пра́вить* (impf), управля́ть (impf); (LAW): to ~ in favour of/against выноси́ть* (вы́нести perf) реше́ние в по́льзу +gen/про́тив +gen; under British ~ (dominion) под брита́нским правле́нием; it's against the ~s э́то про́тив пра́вил; by ~ of thumb наугад; as a ~ как пра́вило; to ~ that (umpire, judge etc) постановля́ть (постанови́ть* perf), что ...

▶ **rule out** vt (exclude) исключа́ть (исключи́ть perf); murder cannot be ~d out уби́йство не мо́жет быть* исключено́.

ruled [ru:ld] *adj* (*paper*) линóваный.
ruler ['ru:lə] *n* прави́тель(ница) *m(f)*; (*for measuring*) линéйка.
ruling ['ru:lɪŋ] *adj* (*party*) пра́вящий*; (*class*) госпóдствующий* ◆ *n* (*LAW*) постановлéние.
rum [rʌm] *n* ром ◆ *adj* (*BRIT: inf*) чуднóй.
Rumania *etc* = **Romania** *etc*.
rumble ['rʌmbl] *n* (*of traffic, thunder*) гул ◆ *vi*
бубни́ть (*impf*); (*also: ~* **along**) с гу́лом
проезжа́ть (проéхать* *perf*); (*stomach, pipe*)
бурча́ть (*impf*); (*thunder*) грохота́ть*
(прогрохота́ть* *perf*).
rumbustious [rʌm'bʌstʃəs] *adj* бóйкий* (бóек).
ruminate ['ru:mɪneɪt] *vi* жева́ть* (*impf*) жва́чку;
(*fig*) размышля́ть (*impf*).
rummage ['rʌmɪdʒ] *vi* (*search*) ры́ться (*impf*).
rummage sale *n* (*US*) благотвори́тельная
распродáжа подéржанных вещéй.
rumour ['ru:mə] (*US* **rumor**) *n* слух ◆ *vt*: **it is
~ed that ...** хóдят слу́хи, что ....
rump [rʌmp] *n* (*of horse*) круп; (*of cow*) за́дняя
часть *f*; (*of group, political party*) оста́тки *mpl*.
rumple ['rʌmpl] *vt* (*clothes*) мять* (помя́ть* *or*
измя́ть* *perf*).
rump steak *n* вы́резка* (*из за́дней ча́сти*).
rumpus ['rʌmpəs] *n* шум; **to kick up a ~**
поднима́ть (подня́ть* *perf*) шум.
run [rʌn] (*pt* **ran**, *pp* **run**) *n* (*fast pace*) бег*;
(*journey*) поéздка; (*distance travelled*)
пробéг; (*SKIING*) тра́сса; (*CRICKET, BASEBALL*)
очкó*; (*in tights, stockings*) спусти́вшиеся
пéтли *fpl* ◆ *vt* (*race, distance*) пробега́ть
(пробежа́ть* *perf*); (*operate: business, hotel*)
управля́ть (*impf*) +*instr*; (: *competition, course*)
устра́ивать (устрóить *perf*); (: *house*) вести́*
(*impf*); (*COMPUT: program*) выполня́ть
(вы́полнить *perf*); (*pass: hand, fingers*): **to ~
along** *or* **over** проводи́ть* (провести́* *perf*)
+*instr* по +*dat*; (*water*) пуска́ть (пусти́ть* *perf*);
(*bath*) наполня́ть (напóлнить *perf*); (*PRESS:
feature*) печа́тать (напеча́тать *perf*) ◆ *vi*
бéгать/бежа́ть* (*impf*); (*flee*) бежа́ть* (*impf/
perf*), сбега́ть (сбежа́ть* *perf*); (*work: machine*)
рабóтать (*impf*); (*bus, train*) ходи́ть* (*impf*);
(*continue: play, show*) идти́* (*impf*); (: *contract*)
дли́ться (*impf*); (*in election*) баллоти́роваться
(*perf*); (*river*) течь* (*impf*), протека́ть (*impf*);
(*bath*) наполня́ться (напóлниться *perf*);
(*colours, washing*) линя́ть (полиня́ть *perf*);
(*nose*) течь* (*impf*); **to go for a ~** (*for exercise*)
идти́* (пойти́* *perf*) побéгать; **to break into a
~** пуска́ться (пусти́ться* *perf*) бежа́ть; **a ~ of
luck** пери́од уда́ч; **the play had a 6 week ~**
пьéса шла 6 недéль; **to have the ~ of sb's
house** имéть (*impf*) разрешéние пóльзоваться чьим-н дóмом; **there was a ~ on
tickets** на билéты был большóй спрос; **in the
long ~** в конéчном итóге; **in the short ~** на
како́е-то врéмя; **to make a ~ for it** убега́ть*
(убежа́ть* *perf*) со всех ног; **to be on the ~**
скрыва́ться (*impf*); (*inf: to be busy*) быть*
(*impf*) в бега́х; **I'll ~ you to the station** я
подвезу́ Вас до ста́нции; **to ~ a risk**
подверга́ться (подвéргнуться *perf*) ри́ску; **to
~ errands for sb** выполня́ть (*impf*) мéлкие
поручéния для когó-н; **my car is very cheap
to ~** моя́ маши́на экономи́чна; **to be ~ off
one's feet** (*BRIT*) сби́ться* (*perf*) с ног; **the train
~s between Gatwick and Victoria** пóезд хóдит
мéжду Га́твиком и Виктóрией; **the bus ~s
every 20 minutes** автóбус хóдит ка́ждые 20
мину́т; **to ~ on petrol** *or* (*US*) **gas/on diesel/off
batteries** рабóтать (*impf*) на бензи́не/на
ди́зеле/на батарéйках; **to ~ for president**
баллоти́роваться (*impf*) в президéнты; **their
losses ran into millions** их потéри
исчисля́лись миллиóнами
▶ **run about** *vi* бéгать (*impf*)
▶ **run across** *vt fus* (*find*) натыка́ться
(наткну́ться *perf*) на +*acc*
▶ **run around** *vi* = **run about**
▶ **run away** *vi* убега́ть (убежа́ть* *perf*)
▶ **run down** *vt* (*production, industry*)
сокраща́ть (сократи́ть* *perf*); (*AUT: hit*)
сбива́ть (сбить* *perf*); (*criticize*) поноси́ть*
(*impf*); **to be ~ down** (*person*) выбива́ться
(вы́биться* *perf*) из сил; (*battery*) конча́ться
(*impf*), иссяка́ть (*impf*)
▶ **run in** *vt* (*BRIT: car*) обка́тывать (обката́ть
perf)
▶ **run into** *vt fus* (*meet: person*) ста́лкиваться
(столкну́ться *perf*) с +*instr*; (: *trouble*)
ната́лкиваться (натолкну́ться *perf*) на +*acc*;
(*collide with*) вреза́ться (врéзаться* *perf*) в
+*acc*; **to ~ into debt** залеза́ть (залéзть* *perf*) в
долги́
▶ **run off** *vt* (*subj: water*) спуска́ть (спусти́ть*
perf); (*copies*) дéлать (сдéлать *perf*), отсня́ть*
(*perf*) ◆ *vi* (*person, animal*) сбега́ть (сбежа́ть*
perf), убега́ть (убежа́ть* *perf*)
▶ **run out** *vi* (*person*) выбега́ть (вы́бежать*
perf); (*liquid*) вытека́ть (вы́течь* *perf*); (*lease,
visa*) истека́ть (истéчь* *perf*); (*money*)
зака́нчиваться (закóнчиться *perf*); **my
passport ~s out in July** срок дéйствия моегó
па́спорта истека́ет в ию́ле
▶ **run out of** *vt fus*: **I've ~ out of money/time/
petrol** *or* (*US*) **gas** у меня́ кóнчились дéньги/
кóнчилось врéмя/кóнчился бензи́н
▶ **run over** *vt* (*AUT*) задави́ть* (*perf*) ◆ *vt fus*
(*revise*) пробега́ть (пробежа́ть *perf*)
▶ **run through** *vt fus* пробега́ть (пробежа́ть
perf); (*rehearse*) прогоня́ть (прогна́ть *perf*)
▶ **run up** *vt*: **to ~ up a debt** влеза́ть (влезть*
perf) в долги́; **to ~ up against** (*difficulties*)

---

* marks translations which have irregular inflections. The Russian-English side of the dictionary gives inflectional information.

ста́лкиваться (столкну́ться *perf*) с +*instr*.
runabout ['rʌnəbaut] *n* (*AUT*) малолитра́жка*.
run around *n* (*inf*): **to give sb the** ~~ води́ть*
(*impf*) кого́-н за нос.
runaway ['rʌnəweɪ] *adj* (*truck, horse etc*)
потеря́вший управле́ние; (*person*) бе́глый;
(*inflation*) неуправля́емый.
rundown ['rʌndaun] *n* (*BRIT: of industry etc*)
сокраще́ние.
run-down [rʌn'daun] *adj* (*tired, ill*)
изможде́нный* (изможде́н).
rung [rʌŋ] *pp of* **ring** ◆ *n* (*of ladder*) ступе́нька*;
(*in organization*) ступе́нь *m*.
run-in ['rʌnɪn] *n* (*inf*) стьꙑꙑчка*.
runner ['rʌnə'] *n* (*in race: person*) бегу́н*(ья);
(: *horse*) скаку́н*; (*on sledge, for drawer etc*)
по́лоз*; (*carpet: in hall etc*) доро́жка*.
runner bean *n* (*BRIT*) стручко́вая фасо́ль *f no pl*.
runner-up [rʌnər'ʌp] *n* финали́ст (*заня́вший
второ́е ме́сто*).
running ['rʌnɪŋ] *n* (*sport*) бег*; (*of business,
organization*) руково́дство; (*of event*)
организа́ция; (*of machine etc*) эксплуата́ция
◆ *adj* (*water*) теку́щий*; (: *to house*)
водопрово́дный; **he is in/out of the** ~ **for sth**
ему́ сули́т/не сули́т что-н; **6 days** ~ 6 дней
подря́д.
running commentary *n* (*TV, RADIO*) прямо́й
репорта́ж.
running costs *npl* (*of business*) операцио́нные
изде́ржки *fpl*; (*of car*) содержа́ние *ntsg*.
running head *n* колонти́тул (*заголо́вок,
печа́таемый на верху́ ка́ждой страни́цы*).
running mate *n* (*US: POL*) кандида́т на
до́лжность вице-президе́нта.
runny ['rʌnɪ] *adj* (*honey, egg*) жи́дкий*
(жи́док); (*nose*) сопли́вый (сопли́в); (*eyes*)
слезя́щийся.
runoff ['rʌnɔf] *n* (*in contest, election*)
повто́рные вы́боры *mpl*; (*extra race*)
повто́рный забе́г.
run-of-the-mill ['rʌnəvðə'mɪl] *adj* сре́дний*.
runt [rʌnt] *n* (*animal*) недоме́рок*; (*pej: person*)
сморчо́к*.
run-through ['rʌnθru:] *n* (*rehearsal*) прого́н.
run-up ['rʌnʌp] *n* пери́од, предше́ствующий
како́му-нибудь собы́тию.
runway ['rʌnweɪ] *n* взлётно-поса́дочная
полоса́*.
rupee [ru:'pi:] *n* ру́пия.
rupture ['rʌptʃə'] *n* (*MED: hernia*) гры́жа;
(*between people, groups*) разры́в ◆ *vt*: **to** ~
o.s. (*MED*) получа́ть (получи́ть *perf*) гры́жу.
rural ['ruərl] *adj* се́льский*; (*accent*)
дереве́нский*.
rural district council *n* (*BRIT*) се́льский*
райо́нный сове́т.
ruse [ru:z] *n* уло́вка*, ухищре́ние.

rush [rʌʃ] *n* (*hurry*) спе́шка; (*COMM: sudden
demand*) большо́й спрос; (*of water, current*)
пото́к; (*of emotion*) прили́в; (*plant*) камы́ш*
◆ *vt* (*BRIT: inf: overcharge*) обсчи́тывать
(обсчита́ть *perf*) ◆ *vi* (*person*) бежа́ть (*impf*);
(*air, water*) хлы́нуть (*perf*); **is there any** ~ **for
this?** э́то спе́шно?; **a** ~ **of orders** напль́ыв
зака́зов; **I'm in a** ~ (**to do**) я спешу́ (+*infin*);
gold ~ золота́я лихора́дка; **to** ~ **one's meal/
work** второпя́х есть (*impf*)/де́лать (*impf*)
рабо́ту; **don't** ~ **me!** не подгоня́йте́ меня́,
торопи́те меня́!; **to** ~ **sth off** (*do*) спе́шно
де́лать (сде́лать *perf*) что-н; (*send*) спе́шно
отправля́ть (отпра́вить* *perf*) что-н; **she** ~**ed
to the door** она́ бро́силась к две́ри
▶ **rush through** *vt fus* де́лать (сде́лать *perf*) в
спе́шке; (*meal*) прогла́тывать (проглоти́ть*
perf); (*town*) носи́ться* (нести́сь* *perf*) по +*dat*.
rush hour *n* час пик.
rush job *n* рабо́та, сде́ланная на́спех.
rush matting *n* цино́вка*.
rusk [rʌsk] *n* (*biscuit*) ≈ суха́рь *m*.
Russia ['rʌʃə] *n* Росси́я.
Russian ['rʌʃən] *adj* (*native Russian*) ру́сский*;
(*belonging to Russian Federation*)
росси́йский* ◆ *n* ру́сский(-ая) *m(f) adj*; (*LING*)
ру́сский* язы́к*.
rust [rʌst] *n* (*also BOT*) ржа́вчина ◆ *vi* ржаве́ть
(заржаве́ть *perf*).
rustic ['rʌstɪk] *adj* дереве́нский* ◆ *n* (*pej*)
дереве́нщина *m/f no pl*.
rustle ['rʌsl] *vi* шурша́ть (*impf*), шелесте́ть*
(*impf*) ◆ *vt* шелесте́ть* (*impf*) +*instr*; (*US: steal*)
угоня́ть (угна́ть* *perf*).
rustproof ['rʌstpru:f] *adj* (*metal*) нержаве́ющ-
ий*; (*car*) сде́ланный (сде́лан) из
нержаве́ющего материа́ла.
rustproofing ['rʌstpru:fɪŋ] *n* обрабо́тка
про́тив ржа́вчины.
rusty ['rʌstɪ] *adj* ржа́вый*; (*fig: skill*)
подзабь́ытый.
rut [rʌt] *n* (*groove*) колея́, борозда́*; (*ZOOL:
season*) полова́я охо́та; **to get into a** ~ (*fig*)
заходи́ть* (зайти́* *perf*) в тупи́к, застрева́ть
(застря́ть* *perf*).
rutabaga [ru:tə'beɪgə] *n* (*US*) ре́па.
ruthless ['ru:θlɪs] *adj* (*person, action*)
беспоща́дный* (беспоща́ден),
безжа́лостный* (безжа́лостен).
ruthlessness ['ru:θlɪsnɪs] *n* беспоща́дность *f*,
безжа́лостность *f*.
RV *abbr* (*BIBLE: = revised version*) испра́вленное
изда́ние Би́блии ◆ *n abbr* (*US*) = *recreational
vehicle*.
Ryazan [rɪ'zanj] *n* Ряза́нь *f*.
rye [raɪ] *n* рожь* *f*.
rye bread *n* ржано́й хлеб.

~ S, s ~

S, s [ɛs] n (letter) 19-ая бу́ква англи́йского алфави́та; (US: SCOL: = satisfactory) ≈ удовлетвори́тельно.
S abbr (= **south**) Ю= юг; = **small**; (= **saint**) св= свято́й.
SA abbr = **South Africa, South America**.
Sabbath ['sæbəθ] n (Jewish) суббо́та; (Christian) воскресе́нье.
sabbatical [sə'bætɪkl] n (also: ~ **year**) тво́рческий* о́тпуск*.
sabotage ['sæbətɑːʒ] n сабота́ж ♦ vt (machine, building) выводи́ть* (вы́вести* perf) из стро́я; (plan, meeting) саботи́ровать (impf/perf).
sabre ['seɪbə'] n са́бля*.
sabre-rattling ['seɪbərætlɪŋ] n бряца́ние ору́жием (перен).
saccharin(e) ['sækərɪn] n сахари́н.
sachet ['sæʃeɪ] n (of shampoo, sugar etc) паке́тик.
sack [sæk] n (bag) мешо́к* ♦ vt (dismiss) выгоня́ть (вы́гнать* perf) с рабо́ты; (plunder) опустоша́ть (опустоши́ть perf); **to give sb the** ~ выгоня́ть (вы́гнать* perf) кого́-н (с рабо́ты); **I got the** ~ меня́ вы́гнали (с рабо́ты).
sackful ['sækful] n: **a** ~ **of** мешо́к* +gen.
sacking ['sækɪŋ] n (dismissal) увольне́ние; (material) мешкови́на.
sacrament ['sækrəmənt] n (rite) та́инство.
sacred ['seɪkrɪd] adj свяще́нный; (place) свято́й; (music) духо́вный.
sacred cow n (fig) святы́ня.
sacrifice ['sækrɪfaɪs] n (offering) жертвоприноше́ние; (thing or person offered) же́ртва ♦ vt (animal) приноси́ть* (принести́* perf) в же́ртву +dat; (fig) же́ртвовать (поже́ртвовать perf) +instr; **to make** ~**s (for sb)** же́ртвовать (поже́ртвовать perf) собо́й (ра́ди кого́-н).
sacrilege ['sækrɪlɪdʒ] n святота́тство.
sacrosanct ['sækrəusæŋkt] adj (also fig) свяще́нный.
sad [sæd] adj печа́льный* (печа́лен).
sadden ['sædn] vt печа́лить (опеча́лить perf).
saddle ['sædl] n седло́* ♦ vt (horse) седла́ть (оседла́ть perf); **to** ~ **sb with sth** (inf)

наве́шивать (наве́сить* perf) что-н на кого́-н.
saddlebag ['sædlbæg] n (on bicycle) седе́льная су́мка.
sadism ['seɪdɪzəm] n сади́зм.
sadist ['seɪdɪst] n сади́ст(ка*).
sadistic [sə'dɪstɪk] adj (person, behaviour) сади́стский.
sadly ['sædlɪ] adv (unhappily) печа́льно, гру́стно; (unfortunately) к сожале́нию; (seriously: mistaken, neglected) серьёзно; **the school is** ~ **lacking in equipment** шко́ла испы́тывает серьёзный недоста́ток в обору́довании.
sadness ['sædnɪs] n печа́ль f, грусть f.
sadomasochism [seɪdəu'mæsəkɪzəm] n са́до-мазохи́зм.
sae abbr (BRIT) = **stamped addressed envelope**; see **stamp**.
safari [sə'fɑːrɪ] n сафа́ри nt ind; **to go on** ~ проводи́ть* (провести́* perf) о́тпуск в сафа́ри.
safari park n парк сафа́ри.
safe [seɪf] adj (place, subject) безопа́сный* (безопа́сен); (return, journey) благополу́чный* (благополу́чен); (bet, appointment) надёжный* (надёжен) ♦ n сейф; **to be** ~ находи́ться* (impf) в безопа́сности; ~ **from** (attack) защищённый (защищён) от +gen; **and sound** цел и невреди́м; **(just) to be on the** ~ **side** на вся́кий слу́чай; **to play** ~ де́йствовать (impf) осторо́жно; **it is** ~ **to say that ...** мо́жно с уве́ренностью сказа́ть, что ...; ~ **journey!** счастли́вого пути́!; ~ **seat** (POL) парла́ментское ме́сто с гаранти́рованной подде́ржкой избира́телей.
safe bet n ве́рное де́ло; **he is a** ~ ~ на него́ мо́жно положи́ться.
safe-breaker ['seɪfbreɪkə'] n (BRIT) взло́мщик се́йфов.
safe-conduct [seɪf'kɔndʌkt] n неприкоснове́нность f.
safe-cracker ['seɪfkrækə'] n = **safe-breaker**.
safe-deposit ['seɪfdɪpɔzɪt] n сейф.
safeguard ['seɪfgɑːd] n гара́нтия ♦ vt (life, interests) охраня́ть (impf); (future) гаранти́ровать (impf/perf).

---

* marks translations which have irregular inflections. The Russian-English side of the dictionary gives inflectional information.

safe haven n зо́на безопа́сности.
safe house n конспирати́вная кварти́ра.
safekeeping ['seɪf'ki:pɪŋ] n сохра́нность f.
safely ['seɪflɪ] adv (assume, say) с
уве́ренностью; (drive, arrive) благополу́чно;
I can ~ say ... я могу́ с уве́ренностью сказа́ть
....
safe passage n безопа́сный путь* m.
safe sex n безопа́сный секс; **to practise ~ ~**
испо́льзовать (impf) презервати́вы во вре́мя
се́кса.
safety ['seɪftɪ] n безопа́сность f; **~ first!**
соблюда́йте осторо́жность!
safety belt n привязно́й реме́нь m.
safety catch n (on gun) замо́к*; (on window)
защёлка*.
safety net n (also fig) сеть f безопа́сности.
safety pin n англи́йская була́вка*.
safety valve n предохрани́тельный кла́пан.
saffron ['sæfrən] n шафра́н.
sag [sæg] vi (breasts) отвиса́ть (отви́снуть
perf); (roof, hem) провиса́ть (прови́снуть
perf); (spirits, prices) па́дать (упа́сть* perf).
saga ['sɑ:gə] n са́га.
sage [seɪdʒ] n (herb) шалфе́й; (wise man)
мудре́ц*.
Sagittarius [sædʒɪ'tɛərɪəs] n Стреле́ц*; **he is ~**
он – Стреле́ц.
sago ['seɪgəu] n са́го nt ind.
Sahara [sə'hɑ:rə] n: **the ~ (Desert)** Саха́ра.
Sahel [sæ'hɛl] n Сахе́ль f.
said [sɛd] pt, pp of **say**.
Saigon [saɪ'gɔn] n Сайго́н.
sail [seɪl] n па́рус* ♦ vt (boat) пла́вать/плыть*
(impf) на +prp ♦ vi (ship, passenger) пла́вать/
плыть* (impf); (SPORT) занима́ться (impf)
па́русным спо́ртом; (also: **set ~**) отплыва́ть
(отплы́ть* perf); **to go for a ~** е́хать* (пое́хать*
perf) ката́ться на ло́дке; **they ~ed into
Copenhagen** они́ приплы́ли в Копенга́ген
▸ **sail through** vt fus (fig): **to ~ through an
exam/interview** с лёгкостью сдава́ть*
(сдать* perf) экза́мен/проходи́ть* (пройти́*
perf) собесе́дование.
sailboat ['seɪlbəut] n (US) = **sailing boat**.
sailing ['seɪlɪŋ] n (SPORT) па́русный спорт; **to
go ~** занима́ться (impf) па́русным спо́ртом.
sailing boat n па́русная ло́дка*.
sailing ship n па́русное су́дно*.
sailor ['seɪlə*] n моря́к*, матро́с.
saint [seɪnt] n (also fig) свято́й(-а́я) m(f) adj.
saintly ['seɪntlɪ] adj свято́й*.
sake [seɪk] n: **for the ~ of sb/sth, for sb's/sth's ~**
ра́ди кого́-н/чего́-н; **arguing's for arguing's ~**
спор ра́ди спо́ра; **for the ~ of argument** в
ка́честве предположе́ния; **for heaven's ~!**
ра́ди Бо́га!
Sakhalin [səxa'lin] n Сахали́н.
salad ['sæləd] n сала́т; **tomato ~** сала́т из
помидо́ров; **green ~** зелёный сала́т.
salad bowl n сала́тница.

salad cream n (BRIT) сала́тный со́ус.
salad dressing n припра́ва к сала́ту.
salami [sə'lɑ:mɪ] n саля́ми f ind.
salaried ['sælərɪd] adj (staff) получа́ющий
зарпла́ту.
salary ['sælərɪ] n зарпла́та (= за́работная
пла́та).
salary scale n шкала́* за́работной пла́ты.
sale [seɪl] n (act of selling) прода́жа; (at reduced
prices) распрода́жа; (auction) то́рги mpl; **~s**
npl (total amount sold) объём прода́жи ♦ cpd
(campaign, conference) рекла́мный; (figures,
target) прода́жный; **"for ~"** „продаётся"; **on
~** в прода́же; **these goods are on ~ or return**
е́сли э́ти това́ры не бу́дут про́даны, они́
бу́дут возвращены́ владе́льцу; **closing-down
or (US) liquidation ~** ликвидацио́нная
распрода́жа.
sale and lease back n (COMM) прода́жа
со́бственности с усло́вием получе́ния её
обра́тно в аре́нду на огово́рённый срок.
saleroom ['seɪlru:m] n торго́вый зал.
sales assistant [seɪlz-] (US **salesclerk**) n (BRIT)
продаве́ц*(-вщи́ца).
salesclerk ['seɪlzklə:rk] n (US) = **sales assistant**.
sales force n торго́вые аге́нты mpl.
salesman ['seɪlzmən] irreg n (in shop)
продаве́ц*; (also: **travelling ~**) торго́вый
аге́нт.
sales manager n (in company) нача́льник
отде́ла сбы́та; (in shop) ста́рший*(-ая)
продаве́ц*(-вщи́ца).
salesmanship ['seɪlzmənʃɪp] n уме́ние
продава́ть.
sales tax n (US) нало́г на прода́жи
(упла́чивается потреби́телем при поку́пке
определённых това́ров).
saleswoman ['seɪlzwumən] irreg n (in shop)
продавщи́ца; (representative) торго́вый
аге́нт.
salient ['seɪlɪənt] adj существенный.
saline ['seɪlaɪn] adj соляно́й.
saliva [sə'laɪvə] n слюна́.
sallow ['sæləu] adj (complexion) желту́шный.
sally forth ['sælɪ-] vi отправля́ться
(отпра́виться* perf).
sally out vi = **sally forth**.
salmon ['sæmən] n inv (ZOOL) лосо́сь* m; (CULIN)
лососи́на.
salmon trout n тайме́нь m.
salon ['sælɔn] n сало́н; **beauty ~**
космети́ческий* сало́н.
saloon [sə'lu:n] n (US: bar) бар; (BRIT: AUT)
"седа́н" (тип автомоби́ля); (ship's lounge)
сало́н.
SALT [sɔ:lt] n abbr (= Strategic Arms Limitation
Talks/Treaty) перегово́ры pl/догово́р ОСВ
= об ограниче́нии стратеги́ческих
наступа́тельных вооруже́ний.
salt [sɔ:lt] n соль f ♦ vt (preserve) заса́ливать
(засоли́ть* perf); (season) соли́ть* (посоли́ть*

perf) ♦ *cpd* солёный; **the ~ of the earth** соль земли.

saltcellar ['sɔːltsɛlə'] *n* солóнка*.

salt-free ['sɔːlt'friː] *adj* не содержáщий сóли.

salt mine *n* солянáя шáхта.

saltwater ['sɔːlt'wɔːtə'] *adj* живýщий в солёных вóдах.

salty ['sɔːltɪ] *adj* солёный* (солён).

salubrious [sə'luːbrɪəs] *adj* целéбный* (целéбен); (*fig: district etc*) благодáтный* (благодáтен).

salutary ['sæljutərɪ] *adj* полéзный* (полéзен).

salute [sə'luːt] *n* (MIL) салют; (*greeting*) привéтствие ♦ *vt* (MIL) отдавáть* (отдáть* *perf*) честь +*dat*; (*fig*) привéтствовать (*impf*).

salvage ['sælvɪdʒ] *n* (*saving*) спасéние; (*things saved*) спасённые вéщи *fpl* ♦ *vt* (*also fig*) спасáть (спасти* *perf*).

salvage vessel *n* спасáтельное сýдно*.

salvation [sæl'veɪʃən] *n* спасéние.

Salvation Army *n* Áрмия Спасéния.

salver ['sælvə'] *n* поднóс.

salvo ['sælvəu] (*pl ~es*) *n* залп.

Samaritans [sə'mærɪtənz] *npl*: **the ~** Самаритáне* *mpl*.

same [seɪm] *adj* такóй же; (*identical*) одинáковый ♦ *pron*: **the ~** тот же (сáмый) (*f* та же (сáмая), *nt* то же (сáмое), *pl* те же (сáмые)); **the ~ book as** та же (сáмая) кнѝга, что и; **on the ~ day** в тот же день; **at the ~ time** (*simultaneously*) в э́то же врéмя; (*yet*) в то же врéмя; **all** *or* **just the ~** всё равнó; **to do the ~** (**as sb**) дéлать (сдéлать *perf*) то же (сáмое) (что и кто-н); **Happy New Year! – the ~ to you!** С Нóвым Гóдом! – Вас тáкже!; **you're a fool! – the ~ to you!** ты дурáк! – сам (ты) дурáк!; **I hate him – ~ here!** я ненавѝжу егó – и я тóже!; **the company director and Mr Smith are one and the ~** дирéктор компáнии и Мѝстер Смит однó лицó; **the books we're talking about are one and the ~** мы говорѝли об однóй и тóже кнѝге; **~ again!** (*in bar etc*) повторѝте!

sample ['sɑːmpl] *n* (*of water*) прóба; (*of work, merchandise*) образéц* ♦ *vt* (*food, wine*) прóбовать (попрóбовать *perf*); **to take a ~** брать* (взять* *perf*) прóбу; **to take a blood/ urine ~** брать* (взять* *perf*) кровь/мочý для анáлиза; **free ~** бесплáтный образéц*.

sanatoria [sænə'tɔːrɪə] *npl of* **sanatorium**.

sanatorium [sænə'tɔːrɪəm] (*pl* **sanatoria** *or* **~s**) *n* (MED) санатóрий.

sanctify ['sæŋktɪfaɪ] *vt* освящáть (освятѝть* *perf*).

sanctimonious [sæŋktɪ'məunɪəs] *adj* благочѝнный* (благочѝнен).

sanction ['sæŋkʃən] *n* (*approval*) сáнкция ♦ *vt* (*give approval to*) санкционѝровать (*impf/*

perf); **~s** *npl* (*severe measures*) сáнкции *fpl*; **to impose economic ~s on** *or* **against** применять (применѝть* *perf*) экономѝческие сáнкции прóтив +*gen*.

sanctity ['sæŋktɪtɪ] *n* свя́тость *f*.

sanctuary ['sæŋktjuərɪ] *n* (*for animals*) заповéдник; (*for people*) убéжище; (*in church*) алтáрная часть *f*.

sand [sænd] *n* песóк* ♦ *vt* (*also:* **~ down**) ошкýривать (ошкýрить *perf*); *see also* **sands**.

sandal ['sændl] *n* сандáлия.

sandbag ['sændbæg] *n* мешóк* с пескóм.

sandblast ['sændblɑːst] *vt* подвергáть (подвéргнуть *perf*) пескострýйной обрабóтке.

sandbox ['sændbɒks] *n* (US) песóчница.

sand castle *n* песчáный зáмок*.

sand dune *n* (песчáная) дю́на.

sander ['sændə'] *n* ручнóй шлифовáльный станóк.

S & M *n abbr* (= *sadomasochism*) садомазохѝзм.

sandpaper ['sændpeɪpə'] *n* наждáчная бумáга, шкýрка.

sandpit ['sændpɪt] *n* песóчница.

sands [sændz] *npl* пески *mpl*.

sandstone ['sændstəun] *n* песчáник.

sandstorm ['sændstɔːm] *n* песчáная бýря.

sandwich ['sændwɪtʃ] *n* бутербрóд ♦ *vt*: **~ed between** +*instr* зажáтый мéжду +*instr*; **cheese/ham ~** бутербрóд с сы́ром/ветчинóй.

sandwich board *n* (*notice*) реклáмный щит*.

sandwich course *n* (BRIT) курс обучéния, сочетáющий тео́рию с прáктикой.

sandwich man *n irreg* человéк, несýщий на себé реклáмный щит.

sandy ['sændɪ] *adj* песчáный; (*hair*) песóчный.

sane [seɪn] *adj* разýмный* (разýмен).

San Francisco [sæn fræn'sɪskəu] *n* Сан-Францѝско *m ind*.

sang [sæŋ] *pt of* **sing**.

sanguine ['sæŋgwɪn] *adj* оптимистѝчный* (оптимистѝчен).

sanitaria [sænɪ'tɛərɪə] *npl* (US) *of* **sanitarium**.

sanitarium [sænɪ'tɛərɪəm] (*pl* **sanitaria** *or* **~s**) *n* (US) = **sanatorium**.

sanitary ['sænɪtərɪ] *adj* (*system, arrangements, inspector*) санитáрный; (*clean*) гигиенѝчный* (гигиенѝчен).

sanitary towel (US **sanitary napkin**) *n* гигиенѝческий* пакéт.

sanitation [sænɪ'teɪʃən] *n* санитарѝя.

sanitation department *n* (US) санитáрное управлéние.

sanity ['sænɪtɪ] *n* (*of person*) рассýдок*; (*of suggestion etc*) разýмность *f*.

sank [sæŋk] *pt of* **sink**.

San Marino ['sænmə'riːnəu] *n* Сан-Марѝно *nt*

---

ind.

Santa Claus [sæntə'klɔːz] *n* (*in Britain, US etc*) Cáнта-Клáyc; (*in Russia*) ≈ Дед Морóз.

Santiago [sæntɪ'ɑːɡəu] *n* (*also:* ~ **de Chile**) Сантья́го *m ind.*

sap [sæp] *n* (*BOT*) сок* ♦ *vt* (*strength, confidence*) высáсывать (вы́сосать *perf*).

sapling ['sæplɪŋ] *n* молодóе дéревце*, побéг.

sapper ['sæpə'] *n* сапёр.

sapphire ['sæfaɪə'] *n* санфи́р.

Sarajevo [særə'jeɪvəu] *n* Сарáево.

sarcasm ['sɑːkæzm] *n* сарка́зм.

sarcastic [sɑː'kæstɪk] *adj* саркасти́чный* (саркасти́чен).

sarcophagi [sɑː'kɔfəgaɪ] *npl of* **sarcophagus**.

sarcophagus [sɑː'kɔfəgəs] (*pl* **sarcophagi**) *n* саркофáг.

sardine [sɑː'diːn] *n* сарди́на.

Sardinia [sɑː'dɪnɪə] *n* Сарди́ния.

Sardinian [sɑː'dɪnɪən] *adj* сарди́нский ♦ *n* сарди́нец*(-нка*); (*LING*) сарди́нский диалéкт.

sardonic [sɑː'dɔnɪk] *adj* сардони́ческий.

sari ['sɑːrɪ] *n* сáри *nt ind.*

sartorial [sɑː'tɔːrɪəl] *adj*: ~ **elegance** умéние одевáться.

SAS *n abbr* (*BRIT*: *MIL*: = *Special Air Service*) осóбые воздýшно-десáнтные войскá.

SASE *n abbr* (*US*) = *self-addressed stamped envelope*.

sash [sæʃ] *n* (*around waist*) кушáк*; (*over shoulder*) лéнта; (*of window*) подъёмная рáма.

sash window *n* окнó* с подъёмной рáмой.

SAT *n abbr* (*US*) = *Scholastic Aptitude Test*.

sat [sæt] *pt, pp of* **sit**.

Sat. *abbr* = **Saturday**.

Satan ['seɪtn] *n* Сатанá *m*.

satanic [sə'tænɪk] *adj* сатани́нский.

satanism ['seɪtnɪzəm] *n* сатани́зм.

satchel ['sætʃl] *n* рáнец*.

sated ['seɪtɪd] *adj* (*person*): **to be** ~ (**with**) пресыщáться (пресы́титься* *perf*) (+*instr*).

satin ['sætɪn] *n* атлáс ♦ *adj* атлáсный; **with a** ~ **finish** с атлáсным отли́вом.

satire ['sætaɪə'] *n* сати́ра.

satirical [sə'tɪrɪkl] *adj* сатири́ческий*.

satirist ['sætɪrɪst] *n* сати́рик.

satirize ['sætɪraɪz] *vt* высмéивать (вы́смеять *perf*).

satisfaction [sætɪs'fækʃən] *n* (*pleasure*) удовлетворéние; (*refund, apology etc*) возмещéние; **has it been done to your** ~? Вы удовлетворéны тем, как э́то сдéлано?

satisfactorily [sætɪs'fæktərɪlɪ] *adv* удовле-творúтельно.

satisfactory [sætɪs'fæktərɪ] *adj* удовлетвор-úтельный* (удовлетвори́телен).

satisfied ['sætɪsfaɪd] *adj* (*customer*) довóльный* (довóлен), удовлетворённый* (удовлетворён); **he is/was** ~ (**with sth**) он довóлен/был довóлен *or* удовлетворён/был удовлетворён (чем-н).

satisfy ['sætɪsfaɪ] *vt* (*please, fulfil*) удовлетворя́ть (удовлетвори́ть *perf*); (*convince*) убеждáть (убеди́ть* *perf*); **to** ~ **the requirements** удовлетворя́ть (удовлетвори́ть *perf*) трéбованиям; **to** ~ **sb** (**that**) убеждáть (убеди́ть* *perf*) когó-н (в том, что); **to** ~ **o.s. of sth** удостоверя́ться (удостовéриться *perf*) в чём-н.

satisfying ['sætɪsfaɪɪŋ] *adj* прия́тный* (прия́тен).

satsuma [sæt'suːmə] *n* мандари́н.

saturate ['sætʃəreɪt] *vt*: **to** ~ (**with**) (*also fig*) насыщáть (насы́тить* *perf*) (+*instr*).

saturated fat ['sætʃəreɪtɪd-] *n* насы́щенные жиры́ *mpl*.

saturation [sætʃə'reɪʃən] *n* (*process*) насыщéние; (*CHEM, fig*) насы́щенность *f*.

Saturday ['sætədɪ] *n* суббóта; *see also* **Tuesday**.

Saturn ['sætən] *n* Сатýрн.

sauce [sɔːs] *n* сóус.

saucepan ['sɔːspən] *n* кастрю́ля.

saucer ['sɔːsə'] *n* блю́дце*.

saucy ['sɔːsɪ] *adj* (*inf*) пóшлый (пошл).

Saudi Arabia ['saudɪ-] *n* Саýдовская Арáвия.

Saudi (Arabian) *adj* саýдовский*.

sauna ['sɔːnə] *n* сáуна, фи́нская бáня.

saunter ['sɔːntə'] *vi* прогýливаться (*impf*).

sausage ['sɔsɪdʒ] *n* (*for cooking*) сардéлька*, соси́ска*; (*cold meat*) колбасá*.

sausage roll *n* (*BRIT*) пирожóк* с соси́ской.

sauté ['səuteɪ] *adj* жáреный ♦ *vt* жáрить (пожáрить *perf*).

savage ['sævɪdʒ] *adj* (*attack*) звéрский*; (*voice*) я́ростный* (я́ростен); (*dog, criticism*) свирéпый (свирéп); (*primitive: tribe*) ди́кий* ♦ *n* дикáрь*(-рка*) *m(f)* ♦ *vt* (*attack, also fig*) разрывáть (разорвáть* *perf*) на чáсти.

savagely ['sævɪdʒlɪ] *adv* (*attack, pull*) я́ростно; (*criticize*) свирéпо.

savagery ['sævɪdʒrɪ] *n* свирéпость *f*.

save [seɪv] *vt* (*rescue*) спасáть (спасти́* *perf*); (*economize on: money, time*) эконóмить* (сэконóмить* *perf*); (*put by: food, money*) отклáдывать (отложи́ть* *perf*); (*receipts, also COMPUT:* сохраня́ть (сохрани́ть *perf*); (*avoid: work, trouble*) избавля́ть (изба́вить* *perf*) от +*gen*; (*keep: seat, place*) занимáть (заня́ть* *perf*); (*SPORT: shot, ball*) отбивáть (отби́ть* *perf*), отражáть (отрази́ть* *perf*) ♦ *vi* (*also:* ~ **up**) копи́ть (скопи́ть* *perf*) дéньги ♦ *prep* (*except*) помúмо +*gen*; **it will** ~ **me an hour** я сэконóмлю на э́том час; **to** ~ **face** спасти́* (*perf*) свою́ репутáцию; **God** ~ **the Queen!**

Бо́же храни́ короле́ву!; **that was a brilliant ~ (by the goalkeeper)** врата́рь прекра́сно отрази́л уда́р.

saving ['seɪvɪŋ] *n* (*on price etc*) эконо́мия ♦ *adj*: **the ~ grace of** спасе́ние +*gen*; **~s** *npl* (*money*) сбереже́ния *ntpl*; **to make ~s** откла́дывать (отложи́ть* *perf*).

savings account *n* сберега́тельный счёт*.

savings bank *n* сберега́тельный банк.

saviour ['seɪvjəʳ] (*US* **savior**) *n* спаси́тель(ница) *m(f)*; (*REL*) Спаси́тель *m*.

savoir-faire ['sævwɑːfɛəʳ] *n* све́тскость *f*.

savour ['seɪvəʳ] (*US* **savor**) *vt* (*food, drink*) смакова́ть (*impf*); (*experience*) наслажда́ться (наслади́ться* *perf*) +*instr* ♦ *n* (*of food*) арома́т.

savoury ['seɪvərɪ] (*US* **savory**) *adj* (*dish*) несла́дкий* (несла́док).

savvy ['sævɪ] *n* (*inf*) понима́ние.

saw [sɔː] (*pt* **sawed**, *pp* **sawed** *or* **sawn**) *vt* пили́ть* (*impf*) ♦ *n* пила́* ♦ *pt of* **see**; **to ~ sth up** распи́ливать (распили́ть* *perf*) что-н.

sawdust ['sɔːdʌst] *n* опи́лки* *pl*.

sawed-off ['sɔːdɔf] *adj* (*US*) = **sawn-off**.

sawmill ['sɔːmɪl] *n* лесопи́льный заво́д.

sawn [[sɔːn]] *pp of* **saw**.

sawn-off ['sɔːnɔf] (*US* **sawed-off**) *adj*: **~ shotgun** обре́з.

saxophone ['sæksəfəun] *n* саксофо́н.

say [seɪ] (*pt, pp* **said**) *vt* говори́ть (сказа́ть* *perf*) ♦ *n*: **to have one's ~** вы́разить (вы́разить* *perf*) своё мне́ние; **to ~ yes** соглаша́ться (согласи́ться* *perf*); **to ~ no** отка́зываться (отказа́ться* *perf*); **could you ~ that again?** повтори́те, пожа́луйста; **she said (that) I was to give you this** она́ сказа́ла, что я до́лжен отда́ть э́то Вам; **my watch ~s 3 o'clock** мои́ часы́ пока́зывают 3 часа́; **shall we ~ Tuesday?** ну, ска́жем, во вто́рник?; **that doesn't ~ much for him** э́то не говори́т в его́ по́льзу; **when all is said and done** когда́ всё (бу́дет) огово́рено; **there is a lot to be said for ...** мно́гое мо́жно сказа́ть в по́льзу +*gen* ...; **that is to ~** то есть; **that goes without ~ing** э́то са́мо собо́й разуме́ется; **to ~ nothing of** не говоря́ уже́ о +*prp*; **~ (that) you ...** ну, ска́жем, Вы ...; **to have a** *or* **some ~ in sth** име́ть (*impf*) пра́во го́лоса в чём-н.

saying ['seɪŋ] *n* погово́рка*.

say-so ['seɪsəu] *n*: **to do sth on sb's ~** де́лать (сде́лать *perf*) что-н с чьего́-н согла́сия.

SBA (*US*) *n abbr* = *Small Business Administration*.

SC *n abbr* (*US*) = **Supreme Court** ♦ *abbr* (*POST*) = *South Carolina*.

s/c *abbr* = **self-contained**.

scab [skæb] *n* (*on wound*) струп*; (*inf: pej*) штрейкбре́хер.

scabby ['skæbɪ] *adj* (*pej: hands, skin*) покры́тый

(покры́т) стру́пьями.

scaffold ['skæfəld] *n* (*for execution*) эшафо́т.

scaffolding ['skæfəldɪŋ] *n* леса́* *pl*.

scald [skɔːld] *n* ожо́г ♦ *vt* (*burn*) ошпа́ривать (ошпа́рить *perf*).

scalding ['skɔːldɪŋ] *adj* (*also:* **~ hot**) о́чень горя́чий*.

scale [skeɪl] *n* шкала́*; (*usu pl: of fish*) чешуя́ *f no pl*; (*MUS*) га́мма; (*of map, model, project etc*) масшта́б ♦ *vt* (*mountain, tree*) взбира́ться (взобра́ться* *perf*) на +*acc*; **~s** *npl* (*for weighing*) весы́ *pl*; **to draw sth to ~** черти́ть* (начерти́ть* *perf*) что-н по масшта́бу; **a small-~ model** уме́ньшенная моде́ль; **on a large ~** в широ́ком масшта́бе; **pay ~** тари́фная се́тка* зарпла́ты; **~ of charges** шкала́* расце́нок

▶ **scale down** *vt* сокраща́ть (сократи́ть* *perf*).

scaled down [skeɪld-] *adj* в уме́ньшенном масшта́бе.

scale drawing *n* масшта́бный рису́нок* *or* чертёж*.

scallion ['skælʝən] *n* (*shallot*) зелёный лук *m no pl*; (*US: leek*) лук-поре́й *m no pl*.

scallop ['skɔləp] *n* (*ZOOL*) (морско́й) гребешо́к*; (*in sewing etc*) фесто́н.

scalp [skælp] *n* скальп ♦ *vt* скальпи́ровать (*impf/perf*); **I have an itchy ~** у меня́ че́шется голова́.

scalpel ['skælpl] *n* ска́льпель *m*.

scalper ['skælpəʳ] *n* (*US: inf: ticket tout*) спекуля́нт(ка*).

scam [skæm] *n* (*inf*) жу́льничество *nt no pl*.

scamp [skæmp] *n* (*inf*) безобра́зник(-ица).

scamper ['skæmpəʳ] *vi*: **to ~ away** *or* **off** ускака́ть* (*impf*).

scampi ['skæmpɪ] *npl* (*BRIT*) паниро́ванные креве́тки* *fpl*.

scan [skæn] *vt* (*examine*) обсле́довать (*perf*); (*read quickly*) просма́тривать (просмотре́ть* *perf*); (*TV*) разлага́ть (*impf*) изображе́ние; (*RADAR*) скани́ровать (*impf*) ♦ *vi* (*poetry*) рифмова́ться (*impf*) ♦ *n* (*MED*) скани́рование; **ultrasound ~** ультразву́к.

scandal ['skændl] *n* (*shocking event*) сканда́л; (*gossip*) спле́тни* *fpl*; (*fig: disgrace*) позо́р.

scandalize ['skændəlaɪz] *vt* скандализи́ровать (*impf/perf*).

scandalous ['skændələs] *adj* сканда́льный* (сканда́лен); (*waste*) возмути́тельный* (возмути́телен).

Scandinavia [skændɪ'neɪvɪə] *n* Скандина́вия.

Scandinavian [skændɪ'neɪvɪən] *adj* скандина́вский ♦ *n* скандина́в(ка*).

scanner ['skænəʳ] *n* (*RADAR, MED*) ска́нер.

scant [skænt] *adj* (*attention*) пове́рхностный; (*reward*) незначи́тельный.

scantily ['skæntɪlɪ] *adv*: **she was ~ clad** *or*

---

dressed она́ была́ едва́ оде́та.

scanty ['skæntɪ] *adj* (*meal*) ску́дный* (ску́ден); **her underwear was** ~ бельё едва́ прикрыва́ло её те́ло.

scapegoat ['skeɪpɡəut] *n* козёл* отпуще́ния.

scar [skɑ:] *n* (*on skin*) шрам; (*fig*) тра́вма ♦ *vt* (*also fig*) травми́ровать (*impf/perf*); **his face is** ~**red** у него́ на лице́ шрам.

scarce [skɛəs] *adj* ре́дкий* (ре́док); **to make o.s.** ~ (*inf*) улизну́ть (*perf*).

scarcely ['skɛəslɪ] *adv* (*hardly*) едва́; (*with numbers: barely*) то́лько; ~ **anybody** едва́ ли кто́-нибудь; **I can** ~ **believe it** я едва́ могу́ э́тому пове́рить; **that is** ~ **the point** едва́ ли в э́том де́ло.

scarcity ['skɛəsɪtɪ] *n* нехва́тка*, недоста́ток*; ~ **value** (*COMM*) *це́нность това́ра, определя́емая его́ дефици́тностью.*

scare [skɛəʳ] *n* (*fright*) испу́г; (*public fear*) трево́га ♦ *vt* (*frighten*) пуга́ть (испуга́ть *or* напуга́ть *perf*); **to** ~ **sb stiff** (*inf*) пуга́ть (напуга́ть *perf*) кого́-н до́ сме́рти; **there was a bomb** ~ **at the station** опаса́лись, что на ста́нции подло́жена бо́мба

▸ **scare away** *vt* отпу́гивать (отпугну́ть *perf*)

▸ **scare off** *vt* = scare away.

scarecrow ['skɛəkrəu] *n* (огоро́дное) чу́чело.

scared ['skɛəd] *adj* испу́ганный (испу́ган), напу́ганный (напу́ган); **he was** ~ он испуга́лся *or* был испу́ган.

scaremonger ['skɛəmʌŋɡəʳ] *n* паникёр.

scarf [skɑ:f] (*pl* ~**s** *or* **scarves**) *n* шарф; (*also:* **headscarf**) плато́к*.

scarlet ['skɑ:lɪt] *adj* а́лый (ал).

scarlet fever *n* скарлати́на.

scarper ['skɑ:pəʳ] *vi* (*inf*) смыва́ться (смы́ться* *perf*).

scarred [skɑ:d] *adj* (*fig: person*) травми́рованный (травми́рован); ~ **face** лицо́ с шра́мом.

scarves [skɑ:vz] *npl of* **scarf**.

scary ['skɛərɪ] *adj* стра́шный* (стра́шен).

scathing ['skeɪðɪŋ] *adj* уничтожа́ющий*; **to be** ~ **about sth** относи́ться* (отнести́сь* *perf*) к чему́-н с презре́нием.

scatter ['skætəʳ] *vt* (*papers, seeds*) разбра́сывать (разброса́ть *perf*); (*flock of birds, crowd*) разгоня́ть (разогна́ть* *perf*) ♦ *vi* (*crowd*) рассыпа́ться (рассы́паться* *perf*).

scatterbrained ['skætəbreɪnd] *adj* (*inf*) рассе́янный* (рассе́ян).

scattered ['skætəd] *adj* разбро́санный; ~ **showers** преры́вистие ли́вни.

scatty ['skætɪ] *adj* (*BRIT: inf*) несобранный (несо́бран).

scavenge ['skævəndʒ] *vi*: **to** ~ **for food** ры́скать* (*impf*) в по́исках пи́щи.

scavenger ['skævəndʒəʳ] *n* (*person*) старьёвщик; (*animal, bird*) живо́тное *nt adj*, пита́ющееся па́далью.

SCE *n abbr* = Scottish Certificate of Education.

scenario [sɪ'nɑ:rɪəu] *n* (*also fig*) сцена́рий.

scene [si:n] *n* (*THEAT, fig*) сце́на; (*of crime, accident*) ме́сто*; (*sight, view*) карти́на; **behind the** ~**s** (*also fig*) за кули́сами; **to make a** ~ (*inf: fuss*) устра́ивать (устро́ить *perf*) сце́ну; **to appear on the** ~ появля́ться (появи́ться* *perf*) на сце́не; **the political** ~ полити́ческая аре́на.

scenery ['si:nərɪ] *n* (*THEAT*) декора́ции *fpl*; (*landscape*) пейза́ж.

scenic ['si:nɪk] *adj* живопи́сный* (живопи́сен).

scent [sɛnt] *n* (*smell*) за́пах; (*track, also fig*) след; (*perfume*) духи́* *pl*; **to put** *or* **throw sb off the** ~ (*fig*) сбива́ть (сбить* *perf*) кого́-н со сле́да.

sceptic ['skɛptɪk] (*US* **skeptic**) *n* ске́птик.

sceptical ['skɛptɪkl] (*US* **skeptical**) *adj* (*person*) скепти́чный* (скепти́чен); (*remarks*) скепти́ческий*.

scepticism ['skɛptɪsɪzəm] (*US* **skepticism**) *n* скептици́зм.

sceptre ['sɛptəʳ] (*US* **scepter**) *n* ски́петр.

schedule ['ʃɛdju:l, (*US*) 'skɛdju:l] *n* (*timetable*) расписа́ние, гра́фик; (*list of prices, details etc*) пе́речень* *m* ♦ *vt* (*timetable*) распи́сывать (расписа́ть* *perf*); (*visit*) назнача́ть (назна́чить* *perf*); **on** ~ по расписа́нию *or* гра́фику; **as** ~**d** как (бы́ло) заплани́ровано; **we are working to a very tight** ~ мы рабо́таем по пло́тному гра́фику; **everything went according to** ~ всё прошло́ по гра́фику *or* расписа́нию; **to be ahead of** ~ опережа́ть (опереди́ть* *perf*) гра́фик; **to be behind** ~ отстава́ть (*impf*) от гра́фика.

scheduled ['ʃɛdju:ld, (*US*) 'skɛdju:ld] *adj* (*time, event*) заплани́рованный (заплани́рован); (*train, bus, stop*) обозна́ченный (обозна́чен) в расписа́нии.

scheduled flight *n* регуля́рный рейс.

schematic [skɪ'mætɪk] *adj* схемати́ческий*.

scheme [ski:m] *n* (*plan, idea*) за́мысел*; (*plot*) про́иски *pl*, ко́зни *pl*; (*pension plan etc*) програ́мма; (*arrangement*) план, схе́ма ♦ *vi* стро́ить (*impf*) ко́зни; **colour** *or* (*US*) **color** ~ цветова́я га́мма.

scheming ['ski:mɪŋ] *adj* кова́рный ♦ *n* ко́зни *pl*, про́иски *pl*.

schism ['skɪzəm] *n* раско́л.

schizophrenia [skɪtsə'fri:nɪə] *n* шизофрени́я.

schizophrenic [skɪtsə'frɛnɪk] *adj* шизофрени́ческий ♦ *n* шизофре́ник(-и́чка*).

scholar ['skɔləʳ] *n* (*scholarship holder*) стипендиа́т; (*learned person*) учёный *m adj*.

scholarly ['skɔləlɪ] *adj* (*text, approach*) академи́ческий*; (*person*) учёный.

scholarship ['skɔləʃɪp] *n* (*academic knowledge*) учёность *f*; (*grant*) стипе́ндия.

school [sku:l] *n* шко́ла; (*US: inf*) университе́т; (*BRIT*) институ́т; (*of fish, whales*) ста́я ♦ *cpd* шко́льный.

school age *n* шко́льный во́зраст.

schoolbook ['sku:lbuk] *n* (шко́льный) уче́бник.
schoolboy ['sku:lbɔɪ] *n* шко́льник.
schoolchildren ['sku:ltʃɪldrən] *npl* шко́льники *mpl*.
school days *npl* шко́льные дни *mpl*.
schooled [sku:ld] *adj*: ~ **(in)** обу́ченный (обу́чен) (+*dat*).
schoolgirl ['sku:lgə:l] *n* шко́льница.
schooling ['sku:lɪŋ] *n* шко́льное образова́ние.
school-leaver [sku:l'li:və⁺] *n* (BRIT) выпускни́к(-и́ца) шко́лы.
schoolmaster ['sku:lma:stə⁺] *n* учи́тель* *m*.
schoolmistress ['sku:lmɪstrɪs] *n* учи́тельница.
school report *n* (BRIT) та́бель *m* успева́емости.
schoolroom ['sku:lru:m] *n* класс, кла́ссная ко́мната.
schoolteacher ['sku:lti:tʃə⁺] *n* (шко́льный(-ая)) учи́тель*(ница) *m(f)*.
schoolyard ['sku:lja:d] *n* (US) шко́льный двор*.
schooner ['sku:nə⁺] *n* (*ship*) шху́на; (BRIT: *for sherry*) фуже́р (*для хе́реса*); (US: *for beer*) кру́жка* (*для пи́ва*).
sciatica [saɪ'ætɪkə] *n* и́шиас.
science ['saɪəns] *n* (*study of natural things*) нау́ка; (*in school*) есте́ственные нау́ки *fpl*; **the ~s** есте́ственные и то́чные нау́ки.
science fiction *n* нау́чная фанта́стика.
scientific [saɪən'tɪfɪk] *adj* нау́чный.
scientist ['saɪəntɪst] *n* учёный *m adj*.
sci-fi ['saɪfaɪ] *n abbr* (*inf*) (= **science fiction**) НФ= *нау́чная фанта́стика*.
Scillies ['sɪlɪz] *npl* = **Scilly Isles**.
Scilly Isles ['sɪlɪ'aɪlz] *npl*: **the ~~** острова́ *mpl* Си́лли.
scintillating ['sɪntɪleɪtɪŋ] *adj* (*fig: conversation, wit*) блестя́щий*; (*smile*) сия́ющий*.
scissors ['sɪzəz] *npl*: **(a pair of)** ~ но́жницы *pl*.
sclerosis [sklɪ'rəusɪs] *n* склеро́з.
scoff [skɔf] *vt* (BRIT: *inf: eat*) жрать* (сожра́ть* *perf*) ♦ *vi*: **to ~ (at)** (*mock*) насмеха́ться (*impf*) (над +*instr*).
scold [skəuld] *vt* брани́ть (вы́бранить *perf*), руга́ть (отруга́ть *perf*).
scolding ['skəuldɪŋ] *n* вы́говор.
scone [skɔn] *n* (CULIN) кекс.
scoop [sku:p] *n* (*measuring scoop: for flour etc*) сово́к*; (: *for ice-cream*) черпа́к; (PRESS) сенсацио́нное сообще́ние
▶ **scoop out** *vt* выскреба́ть (вы́скрести* *perf*)
▶ **scoop up** *vt* заче́рпывать (зачерпну́ть *perf*).
scooter ['sku:tə⁺] *n* (*also*: **motor ~**) мопе́д; (*toy*) самока́т.
scope [skəup] *n* (*opportunity*) просто́р; (*of plan, undertaking*) масшта́б; (*of person*) компете́нция; **within the ~ of** в ра́мках +*gen*;

there is plenty of ~ **for improvement** (BRIT) есть просто́р для соверше́нствования; **it is well within his ~ to** ... ... в его́ компете́нции.
scorch [skɔ:tʃ] *vt* (*clothes*) сжига́ть (сжечь* *perf*); (*earth, grass*) выжига́ть (вы́жечь* *perf*).
scorched-earth policy [skɔ:tʃt'ə:θ-] *n* (MIL) поли́тика *or* та́ктика вы́жженой земли́.
scorcher ['skɔ:tʃə⁺] *n* (*inf: hot day*) жари́ща.
scorching ['skɔ:tʃɪŋ] *adj* (*day, weather*) паля́щий.
score [skɔ:⁺] *n* (*number of points etc*) счёт; (MUS) партиту́ра; (*twenty*) два́дцать* ♦ *vt* (*goal*) забива́ть (заби́ть* *perf*); (*point*) набира́ть (набра́ть* *perf*); (*mark*) получа́ть (получи́ть* *perf*); (*cut: leather, wood etc*) цара́пать (поцара́пать *perf*); (*achieve: success*) завоёвывать (завоева́ть *perf*) ♦ *vi* (*in game*) набира́ть (набра́ть* *perf*) очки́; (FOOTBALL etc) забива́ть (заби́ть* *perf*) гол; (*keep score*) вести́* (*perf*) счёт; **to settle an old ~ with sb** (*fig*) своди́ть* (свести́* *perf*) с кем-н ста́рые счёты; **~s of** деся́тки +*gen*; **on that ~** на э́тот счёт; **to ~ well** набира́ть (набра́ть* *perf*) мно́го очко́в; **to ~ 6 out of 10** набира́ть (*perf*) 6 ба́ллов из 10; **to ~ (a point) over sb** превосходи́ть* (превзойти́* *perf*) кого́-н
▶ **score out** *vt* вычёркивать (вы́черкнуть *perf*).
scoreboard ['skɔ:bɔ:d] *n* табло́ *nt ind*.
scorecard ['skɔ:ka:d] *n* (SPORT) ка́рта, *на кото́рую зано́сится счёт*.
scoreline ['skɔ:laɪn] *n* счёт* на да́нный моме́нт.
scorer ['skɔ:rə⁺] *n* (FOOTBALL) игро́к*, заби́вший гол; (*scorekeeper*) судья́*.
scorn [skɔ:n] *n* презре́ние ♦ *vt* презира́ть (*impf*).
scornful ['skɔ:nful] *adj* презри́тельный* (презри́телен).
Scorpio ['skɔ:pɪəu] *n* Скорпио́н; **he is ~** он ~ Скорпио́н.
scorpion ['skɔ:pɪən] *n* скорпио́н.
Scot [skɔt] *n* шотла́ндец*(-дка*).
Scotch [skɔtʃ] *n* (*whisky*) (шотла́ндское) ви́ски *nt ind*.
scotch [skɔtʃ] *vt* (*end: rumour, plan*) пресека́ть (пресе́чь* *perf*).
Scotch tape® *n* кле́йкая ле́нта, "скотч" (*разг*).
scot-free ['skɔt'fri:] *adv*: **to get off ~** легко́ отде́лываться (отде́латься *perf*).
Scotland ['skɔtlənd] *n* Шотла́ндия.
Scots [skɔts] *adj* шотла́ндский*.
Scotsman ['skɔtsmən] *irreg n* шотла́ндец*.
Scotswoman ['skɔtswumən] *irreg n* шотла́ндка*.
Scottish ['skɔtɪʃ] *adj* шотла́ндский*; **the ~ National Party** Шотла́ндская национа́льная па́ртия.
scoundrel ['skaundrl] *n* негодя́й.
scour ['skauə⁺] *vt* (*search*) обы́скивать

---

* marks translations which have irregular inflections. The Russian-English side of the dictionary gives inflectional information.

(обыска́ть* *perf*); (*clean*) выска́бливать (вы́скоблить* *perf*).

scourer ['skauərə'] *n* жёсткая моча́лка*.

scourge [skə:dʒ] *n* (*cause of trouble*) бич.

scout [skaut] *n* (*MIL*) разве́дчик; (*also*: **boy** ~) (бой)ска́ут; **girl** ~ (*US*) (де́вочка*-)ска́ут
▶ **scout around** *vi* ры́скать* (*impf*) в по́исках +*gen*.

scowl [skaul] *vi* хму́риться (нахму́риться *perf*); **to** ~ **at sb** хму́ро смотре́ть* (посмотре́ть* *perf*) на кого́-н.

scrabble ['skræbl] *vi* (*also*: ~ **around**: *search*) ша́рить (поша́рить *perf*); (*claw*): **to** ~ **at** цепля́ться (*impf*) (за +*acc*) ◆ *n*: **S**~® (игра́) Скрэбл *ind*; **to** ~ **about** *or* **around for sth** ша́рить (поша́рить *perf*) в по́исках чего́-н.

scraggy ['skrægɪ] *adj* то́щий* (тощ).

scram [skræm] *vi* (*inf*) смыва́ться (смы́ться* *perf*); ~**!** убира́йся!

scramble ['skræmbl] *n* (*climb*: *using hands*) кара́бканье; (*struggle, rush*) сва́лка* ◆ *vi*: **to** ~ **out** выкара́бкиваться (вы́карабкаться *perf*) из +*gen*; **to** ~ **for** дра́ться* (подра́ться* *perf*) за +*acc*.

scrambled eggs ['skræmbld-] *n* яи́чница-болту́нья.

scrambling ['skræmblɪŋ] *n* (*SPORT*) мотокро́сс.

scrap [skræp] *n* (*of paper*) клочо́к*; (*of information*) обры́вок*; (*of material etc*) лоску́т*; (*fig*: *of truth*) крупи́ца; (*inf*: *fight*) потасо́вка; (*also*: ~ **metal**) металли́ческий* лом, металлоло́м ◆ *vt* (*discard*: *machines etc*) отдава́ть* (отда́ть* *perf*) на слом; (*fig*: *plans etc*) отка́зываться (отказа́ться* *perf*) от +*gen* ◆ *vi* (*fight*) дра́ться* (подра́ться* *perf*); ~**s** *npl* (*of food*) объе́дки *mpl*; (*of material*) обре́зки *mpl*; **to sell sth for** ~ сдава́ть* (сдать* *perf*) в ути́ль.

scrapbook ['skræpbuk] *n* альбо́м для вы́резок.

scrap dealer *n* ути́льщик.

scrape [skreɪp] *vt* (*scrape off*) очища́ть (очи́стить* *perf*); (*scrape against*) цара́пать (поцара́пать *perf*), обдира́ть (ободра́ть* *perf*) ◆ *vi*: **to** ~ **through** (*exam etc*) пролеза́ть (проле́зть* *perf*) на +*prp* ◆ *n* (*fig*): **to get into a** ~ попада́ть (попа́сть* *perf*) в переде́лку
▶ **scrape together** *vt* (*money*) наскреба́ть (наскрести́* *perf*).

scraper ['skreɪpə'] *n* скребо́к*.

scrapheap ['skræphi:p] *n*: **on the** ~ (*fig*) на сва́лку.

scrap merchant *n* (*BRIT*) ути́льщик.

scrap metal *n* металлоло́м.

scrap paper *n* макулату́ра.

scrappy ['skræpɪ] *adj* (*piece of work*) дрянно́й.

scrap yard *n* сва́лка*.

scratch [skrætʃ] *n* цара́пина ◆ *cpd* импровизи́рованный ◆ *vt* цара́пать (поцара́пать *perf*); (*an itch*) чеса́ть* (почеса́ть* *perf*); (*COMPUT*) стира́ть (стере́ть* *perf*) ◆ *vi* чеса́ться* (почеса́ться* *perf*); **to start**

from ~ начина́ть (нача́ть* *perf*) с нуля́; **to be up to** ~ (*person, conditions, standard*) быть* (*impf*) на вы́сшем у́ровне.

scratch pad *n* (*US*) блокно́т.

scrawl [skrɔ:l] *n* кара́кули *fpl* ◆ *vt* цара́пать (нацара́пать *perf*).

scrawny ['skrɔ:nɪ] *adj* то́щий* (тощ).

scream [skri:m] *n* вопль *m*, крик ◆ *vi* крича́ть (*impf*); **it's a real** ~ (*inf*) э́то пря́мо умо́ра; **to** ~ **at sb** крича́ть (*impf*) на кого́-н.

scree [skri:] *n* камени́стая о́сыпь *f*.

screech [skri:tʃ] *vi* визжа́ть (*impf*) ◆ *n* визг.

screen [skri:n] *n* (*CINEMA, TV, COMPUT*) экра́н; (*barrier, also fig*: *cover*) ши́рма; (*also*: **windscreen**) ветрово́е стекло́* ◆ *vt* (*protect, conceal*) заслоня́ть (заслони́ть* *perf*); (*show*: *film, programme*) выпуска́ть (вы́пустить* *perf*) на экра́н; (*check*: *candidates etc*) проверя́ть (прове́рить *perf*); **to** ~ **sb for sth** (*for illness*) проверя́ть (прове́рить *perf*) кого́-н на что-н.

screen editing *n* (*COMPUT*) экра́нное редакти́рование.

screening ['skri:nɪŋ] *n* (*MED*) профилакти́ческий* осмо́тр; (*of film*) вы́пуск на экра́н; (*for security*) прове́рка*.

screen memory *n* (*COMPUT*) экра́нная па́мять *f*, видеопа́мять *f*.

screenplay ['skri:npleɪ] *n* сцена́рий.

screen test *n* кинопро́ба.

screw [skru:] *n* винт* ◆ *vt* (*fasten*) приви́нчивать (привинти́ть* *perf*); (*infl*: *have sex with*) тра́хать (тра́хнуть *perf*) (*!*); **to** ~ **sth in** зави́нчивать (завинти́ть* *perf*) что-н; **to** ~ **sth to the wall** приви́нчивать (привинти́ть* *perf*) что-н к стене́; **he's got his head** ~**ed on** (*inf*) у него́ есть голова́ на плеча́х
▶ **screw up** *vt* (*paper etc*) ко́мкать (ско́мкать *perf*); (*inf*: *ruin*) порта́чить (напорта́чить *perf*); **to** ~ **up one's eyes** прищу́ривать (прищу́рить *perf*) глаза́.

screwdriver ['skru:draɪvə'] *n* отвёртка*.

screwed-up ['skru:d'ʌp] *adj* (*paper*) ско́мканный (ско́мкан); (*inf*: *person*) закомплексо́ванный (закомплексо́ван).

screwy ['skru:ɪ] *adj* (*inf*) с завихре́нием.

scribble ['skrɪbl] *n* кара́кули *mpl* ◆ *vt* черкну́ть (*perf*) ◆ *vi* исчёркивать (исчёркать *perf*); **to** ~ **sth down** запи́сывать (записа́ть* *perf*) что-н на́скоро.

scribe [skraɪb] *n* писе́ц*.

script [skrɪpt] *n* (*CINEMA etc*) сцена́рий; (*system of writing*) шрифт*; (*in exam*) конспе́кт.

scripted ['skrɪptɪd] *adj* (*RADIO, TV*) зара́нее подгото́вленный.

Scripture(s) ['skrɪptʃə'(-əz)] *n(pl)* Свяще́нное писа́ние.

scriptwriter ['skrɪptraɪtə'] *n* сценари́ст.

scroll [skrəul] *n* сви́ток* ◆ *vt* (*COMPUT*) прокру́чивать (прокрути́ть* *perf*), перемеща́ть (перемести́ть* *perf*).

scrotum ['skrəʊtəm] *n* (*ANAT*) мошо́нка*.
scrounge [skraʊndʒ] (*inf*) *vt*: **to ~ sth off** *or* **from sb** кля́нчить (вы́клянчить *perf*) что-н у кого́-н ◆ *vi* попроша́йничать (*impf*) ◆ *n*: **to be on the ~** быть* (*impf*) на ме́ли.
scrounger ['skraʊndʒəʳ] *n* (*inf*) попроша́йка* *m/f*.
scrub [skrʌb] *n* (*land*) куста́рник ◆ *vt* скрести́* (*impf*); (*inf*: *reject*) отбра́сывать (отбро́сить* *perf*).
scrubbing brush ['skrʌbɪŋ-] *n* жёсткая щётка*.
scruff [skrʌf] *n*: **by the ~ of the neck** за ши́ворот.
scruffy ['skrʌfɪ] *adj* потрёпанный*.
scrum(mage) ['skrʌm(ɪdʒ)] *n* (*RUGBY*) разы́грывание мяча́.
scruple ['skru:pl] *n* (*usu pl*) терза́ние; **to have no ~s about doing sth** де́лать (сде́лать *perf*) что-н без угрызе́ний со́вести.
scrupulous ['skru:pjʊləs] *adj* (*painstaking*) тща́тельный* (тща́телен), скрупулёзный* (скрупулёзен); (*fair-minded*) щепети́льный* (щепети́лен).
scrupulously ['skru:pjʊləslɪ] *adv* (*behave*, *act*) добросо́вестно; **he is ~ honest/fair/clean** он преде́льно че́стен/справедли́в/чистопло́тен.
scrutinize ['skru:tɪnaɪz] *vt* тща́тельно изуча́ть (изучи́ть *perf*) *or* рассма́тривать (рассмотре́ть* *perf*).
scrutiny ['skru:tɪnɪ] *n* тща́тельное изуче́ние *or* рассмотре́ние; **under sb's ~** под чьим-н наблюде́нием.
scuba ['sku:bə] *n* аквала́нг.
scuba diving *n* подво́дное пла́вание.
scuff [skʌf] *vt* (*feet*) волочи́ть (*impf*); (*mark*: *shoes*) ста́птывать (стопта́ть *perf*).
scuffle ['skʌfl] *n* пота́совка*.
scull [skʌl] *n* (*on rowing boat*) весло́*.
scullery ['skʌlərɪ] *n* (*old*) подсо́бное помеще́ние (*при ку́хне*).
sculptor ['skʌlptəʳ] *n* ску́льптор.
sculpture ['skʌlptʃəʳ] *n* скульпту́ра.
scum [skʌm] *n* пе́на; (*inf*: *pej*: *people*) подо́нки *mpl*; **the ~ of society** отбро́сы о́бщества.
scupper ['skʌpəʳ] *vt* (*BRIT*: *inf*: *plan*) срыва́ть (сорва́ть* *perf*).
scurrilous ['skʌrɪləs] *adj* (*accusation*, *gossip etc*) оскорби́тельный* (оскорби́телен).
scurry ['skʌrɪ] *vi* юркну́ть (*perf*)
▶ **scurry off** *vi* ры́сью убега́ть (убежа́ть *perf*).
scurvy ['skə:vɪ] *n* цинга́.
scuttle ['skʌtl] *n* (*also*: *coal ~*) ведро́* для угля́ ◆ *vt* (*ship*) топи́ть (затопи́ть* *or* потопи́ть* *perf*) ◆ *vi*: **to ~ away** *or* **off** ры́сью убега́ть (убежа́ть *perf*).
scythe [saɪð] *n* серп*.
SD *abbr* (*US*: *POST*) = **South Dakota**.
SDI *n abbr* (*US*: *MIL*: = *Strategic Defense Initiative*) СОИ = *стратеги́ческая оборо́нная*

инициати́ва.
SDLP *n abbr* (*BRIT*: *POL*) = **Social Democratic and Labour Party**.
SDP *n abbr* (*BRIT*: *POL*: *formerly*) = **Social Democratic Party**.
sea [si:] *n* мо́ре* ◆ *cpd* морско́й; **by ~** (*travel*) мо́рем; **beside the ~** у мо́ря; **on the ~** (*boat*) в мо́ре; (*town*) на мо́ре; **to be all at ~** (*fig*) быть* (*impf*) в растёрянности; **out to ~**, **out at ~** в мо́ре; **to look out to ~** смотре́ть* (*impf*) на мо́ре; **heavy** *or* **rough ~(s)** бу́рное мо́ре; **a ~ of faces** мо́ре лиц.
sea anemone *n* морско́й анемо́н.
sea bed *n* морско́е дно.
seaboard ['si:bɔ:d] *n* побере́жье*.
seafarer ['si:fɛərəʳ] *n* морспла́ватель *m*.
seafaring ['si:fɛərɪŋ] *adj* морско́й; **~ people** морехо́ды *mpl*.
seafood ['si:fu:d] *n* ры́бные блю́да *ntpl*.
seafront ['si:frʌnt] *n* на́бережная *f adj*.
seagoing ['si:gəʊɪŋ] *adj* морско́й.
seagull ['si:gʌl] *n* ча́йка*.
seal [si:l] *n* (*ZOOL*) тюле́нь *m*; (*stamp*) печа́ть *f* ◆ *vt* (*close*: *envelope*) запеча́тывать (запеча́тать *perf*); (: *opening*) заде́лывать (заде́лать *perf*); (*decide*: *sb's fate*) предреша́ть (предреши́ть* *perf*); (*deal*) заключа́ть (заключи́ть *perf*); **to give sth one's ~ of approval** официа́льно одо́брить (*perf*) что-н
▶ **seal off** *vt* (*area*, *street*) огора́живать (огороди́ть* *perf*); (*building*) опеча́тывать (опеча́тать *perf*).
sea level *n* у́ровень* *m* мо́ря; **2,000 feet above/below ~** 2000 фу́тов над у́ровнем мо́ря/ни́же у́ровня мо́ря.
sealing wax ['si:lɪŋ-] *n* сургу́ч*.
sea lion *n* морско́й лев*.
sealskin ['si:lskɪn] *n* ко́тик (*мех*).
seam [si:m] *n* (*of garment*) шов*; (*of coal*) слой*; **the hall was bursting at the ~s** зал треща́л по швам.
seaman ['si:mən] *irreg n* матро́с, моря́к.
seamanship ['si:mənʃɪp] *n* судовожде́ние.
seamless ['si:mlɪs] *adj* без шва; (*fig*) це́лостный.
seamy ['si:mɪ] *adj* тёмный* (тёмен).
seance ['seɪɒns] *n* спирити́ческий сеа́нс.
seaplane ['si:pleɪn] *n* гидросамолёт.
seaport ['si:pɔ:t] *n* (морско́й) порт*.
search [sə:tʃ] *n* (*for person*) ро́зыск; (*for thing*) по́иски *mpl*; (*COMPUT*) по́иск; (*inspection*: *of sb's home etc*) о́быск ◆ *vt* (*place*, *person*) обы́скивать (обыска́ть* *perf*); (*memory*) ры́ться* (*impf*) в +*prp* ◆ *vi*: **to ~ for** иска́ть* (*impf*); **in ~ of** в по́исках +*gen*; **"search and replace"** (*COMPUT*) "по́иск и заме́на".
▶ **search through** *vt fus* перерыть (*perf*).
searcher ['sə:tʃəʳ] *n* иска́тель(ница) *m(f)*.

---

* marks translations which have irregular inflections. The Russian-English side of the dictionary gives inflectional information.

searching ['sə:tʃɪŋ] *adj* (*look*) пытли́вый (пытли́в); (*question*) наводя́щий; (*examination*) тща́тельный* (тща́телен).
searchlight ['sə:tʃlaɪt] *n* проже́ктор*.
search party *n* поиско́вая гру́ппа; **to send out a ~~** посыла́ть (посла́ть* *perf*) поиско́вую гру́ппу.
search warrant *n* о́рдер на о́быск.
searing ['sɪərɪŋ] *adj* (*heat, pain*) жгу́чий* (жгуч).
seashore ['si:ʃɔ:'] *n* бе́рег* мо́ря; **on the ~** на берегу́ мо́ря.
seasick ['si:sɪk] *adj*: **to be ~** страда́ть (*impf*) морско́й боле́знью.
seasickness ['si:sɪknɪs] *n* морска́я боле́знь *f*.
seaside ['si:saɪd] *n* взмо́рье, примо́рье; **to go to the ~** е́здить*/е́хать* (пое́хать* *perf*) на взмо́рье; **at the ~** на взмо́рье.
seaside resort *n* примо́рский* куро́рт.
season ['si:zn] *n* (*of year*) вре́мя* *nt* го́да; (*for football, of films etc*) сезо́н ♦ *vt* (*food*) заправля́ть (запра́вить* *perf*); **the busy ~** акти́вный сезо́н; **the open ~** (*HUNTING*) охо́тничий* сезо́н; **tomatoes are in ~** сейча́с сезо́н помидо́ров.
seasonal ['si:znl] *adj* сезо́нный.
seasoned ['si:znd] *adj* (*fig: traveller*) закалённый; (*wood*) вы́держанный; **a ~ campaigner** о́пытный агита́тор.
seasoning ['si:znɪŋ] *n* припра́ва.
season ticket *n* (*RAIL*) сезо́нный (проездно́й) биле́т; (*THEAT, SPORT*) абонеме́нт.
seat [si:t] *n* (*chair, place*) сиде́нье; (*in theatre, in parliament*) ме́сто*; (*of trousers*) зад; (*of government*) резиде́нция; (*of learning etc*) центр ♦ *vt* (*place: guests etc*) расса́живать (рассади́ть* *perf*), уса́живать (усади́ть* *perf*); (*subj: venue*) вмеща́ть (вмести́ть* *perf*); **are there any ~s left?** есть ещё места́?; **to take one's ~** сади́ться* (сесть* *perf*); **please be ~ed** пожа́луйста, сади́тесь; **to be ~ed** сиде́ть (*impf*); **this table ~s 10 people** за э́тим столо́м умеща́ется 10 челове́к.
seat belt *n* привязно́й реме́нь* *m*.
seating arrangements ['si:tɪŋ-] *npl* распределе́ние *ntsg* мест.
seating capacity *n* сидя́чие места́ *ntpl*; **the hall has a ~~ of 100** зал рассчи́тан на 100 сидя́чих мест.
SEATO ['si:təu] *n abbr* (= *Southeast Asia Treaty Organization*) СЕА́ТО.
sea urchin *n* морско́й ёж.
sea water *n* морска́я вода́.
seaweed ['si:wi:d] *n* во́доросли *fpl*.
seaworthy ['si:wə:ðɪ] *adj* мореходный.
Sebastopol [sɪ'bæstəpɔl] *n* Севасто́поль *m*.
SEC *n abbr* (*US*: = *Securities and Exchange Commission*) Коми́ссия по це́нным бума́гам и би́ржам.
sec. *abbr* = **second**.
secateurs [sɛkə'tə:z] *npl* садо́вые но́жницы *pl*, сека́тор *msg*.

secede [sɪ'si:d] *vi*: **to ~ (from)** отделя́ться (отдели́ться* *perf*) (от +*gen*).
secluded [sɪ'klu:dɪd] *adj* уединённый.
seclusion [sɪ'klu:ʒən] *n* уедине́ние; **in ~** в уедине́нии.
second¹ [sɪ'kɔnd] *vt* (*BRIT: employee*) командирова́ть* (*impf*).
second² ['sɛkənd] *adj* второ́й ♦ *adv* (*come, be placed*) вторы́м; (*when listing*) во-вторы́х ♦ *n* (*unit of time*) секу́нда; (*AUT: also: ~ gear*) втора́я ско́рость *f*; (*COMM: imperfect*) дефе́ктное изде́лие; (*SCOL: degree*) дипло́м второ́го кла́сса ♦ *vt* (*motion*) подде́рживать (поддержа́ть* *perf*); **Charles the S~** Карл Второ́й; **~ floor** (*BRIT*) тре́тий* эта́ж; (*US*) второ́й эта́ж; **just a ~!** секу́ндочку!; *see also* **fifth**.
secondary ['sɛkəndərɪ] *adj* втори́чный.
secondary education *n* сре́днее образова́ние.
secondary picketing [-'pɪkɪtɪŋ] *n* втори́чное пикети́рование.
secondary school *n* сре́дняя шко́ла.
second-best [sɛkənd'bɛst] *n* не са́мом лу́чшее *nt adj* ♦ *adj* (*hotel, room*) второ́й по ка́честву; (*pupil*) второ́й (по успева́емости); **as a ~** за неиме́нием лу́чшего.
second-class ['sɛkənd'klɑ:s] *adj* (*citizen, standard etc*) второразря́дный; (*POST, RAIL*) второ́го кла́сса ♦ *adv* вторы́м кла́ссом.
second cousin *n* (*male*) трою́родный брат*; (*female*) трою́родная сестра́*.
seconder ['sɛkəndə'] *n*: **he is the ~ of the proposal** он поддержа́л предложе́ние.
second-guess ['sɛkənd'gɛs] *vt* предска́зывать (предсказа́ть* *perf*).
second hand *n* (*on clock*) секу́ндная стре́лка*.
second-hand ['sɛkənd'hænd] *adj* подде́ржанный ♦ *adv* (*buy*) с рук; **to hear sth ~** узнава́ть* (узна́ть* *perf*) что-н из вторы́х рук.
second in command *n* (*MIL*) второ́й *m adj* по зва́нию; (*ADMIN*) второ́й *m adj* по до́лжности.
secondly ['sɛkəndlɪ] *adv* во-вторы́х.
secondment [sɪ'kɔndmənt] *n* (*BRIT*) командиро́вка*.
second-rate ['sɛkənd'reɪt] *adj* (*film etc*) посре́дственный* (посре́дствен); (*restaurant*) второразря́дный.
second thoughts *npl*: **to have ~~ (about doing)** начина́ть (нача́ть* *perf*) сомнева́ться (сле́дует ли +*infin*); **on ~~** *or* (*US*) **thought** по зре́лом размышле́нии.
Second World War *n*: **the ~~~** Втора́я мирова́я война́.
secrecy ['si:krəsɪ] *n* секре́тность *f*; **in ~** в та́йне.
secret ['si:krɪt] *adj* секре́тный* (секре́тен), та́йный; (*admirer*) та́йный ♦ *n* та́йна, секре́т, та́йна; **to keep sth ~ from sb** держа́ть* (*impf*) что-н в секре́те *or* та́йне от кого́-н; **keep it ~** держи́те э́то в секре́те *or* в та́йне; **in ~** (*say, give*) по секре́ту; (*do, meet*) секре́тно; **to**

make no ~ of sth не де́лать *(impf)* секре́та из чего́-н.

secret agent *n* секре́тный *or* та́йный аге́нт.

secretarial [sɛkrɪˈtɛərɪəl] *adj* секрета́рский; **~ course** ку́рсы *mpl* секретаре́й.

secretariat [sɛkrɪˈtɛərɪət] *n* секретариа́т.

secretary [ˈsɛkrətərɪ] *n* секрета́рь* *m*; **S~ of State (for)** (*BRIT*) ≈ мини́стр (+*gen*); **S~ of State** (*US*) Госуда́рственный секрета́рь* *m*.

secretary-general [ˈsɛkrətərɪˈdʒɛnərl] *n* генера́льный секрета́рь *m*.

secrete [sɪˈkriːt] *vt* (*BIO*) выделя́ть (вы́делить *perf*); (*hide*) пря́тать* (спря́тать* *perf*).

secretion [sɪˈkriːʃən] *n* (*substance*) выделе́ние, секре́ция.

secretive [ˈsiːkrətɪv] *adj* (*pej: person*) скры́тный* (скры́тен); **he is ~ about his plans** он де́ржит свои́ пла́ны в секре́те.

secretly [ˈsiːkrɪtlɪ] *adv* (*do, meet*) секре́тно; (*marry*) та́йно.

secret police *n* секре́тная поли́ция.

secret service *n* секре́тная слу́жба.

sect [sɛkt] *n* се́кта.

sectarian [sɛkˈtɛərɪən] *adj* секта́нтский*.

section [ˈsɛkʃən] *n* (*part*) часть* *f*; (*of population, company*) се́ктор; (*in shop*) се́кция; (*of document, book*) разде́л; (*cross-section*) сече́ние, разре́з ♦ *vt* рассека́ть (рассе́чь* *perf*); **the business** *etc* **~** (*PRESS*) разде́л би́знеса *etc*.

sectional [ˈsɛkʃənl] *adj*: **~ drawing** рису́нок в разре́зе, разре́з.

sector [ˈsɛktəʳ] *n* (*part, also MIL*) се́ктор.

secular [ˈsɛkjuləʳ] *adj* (*music, society*) све́тский*; (*priest*) мирско́й.

secure [sɪˈkjuəʳ] *adj* (*safe: person, money, job*) надёжный* (надёжен); (: *building*) безопа́сный* (безопа́сен); (*firmly fixed, strong: rope, shelf*) про́чный* (про́чен); (*free from anxiety: person*) уве́ренный ♦ *vt* (*fix: rope, shelf etc*) (про́чно) закрепля́ть (закрепи́ть* *perf*); (*get: job, contract etc*) обеспе́чивать (обеспе́чить *perf*); **to make sth ~** про́чно *or* надёжно закрепля́ть (закрепи́ть* *perf*) что-н; **to ~ sth for sb** обеспе́чивать (обеспе́чить *perf*) для кого́-н что-н.

secured creditor [sɪˈkjuəd-] *n* кредито́р, получи́вший обеспече́ние.

securely [sɪˈkjuəlɪ] *adv* (*fasten*) про́чно; (*keep*) в надёжном ме́сте.

security [sɪˈkjuərɪtɪ] *n* (*protection*) безопа́сность *f*; (*for one's future*) обеспе́ченность *f*; (*FINANCE*) зало́г; **securities** *npl* (*COMM*) це́нные бума́ги *fpl*; **to increase** *or* **tighten ~** повыша́ть (повы́сить* *perf*) безопа́сность; **~ of tenure** гаранти́рованное пра́во.

Security Council *n*: **the ~ ~** Сове́т безопа́сности.

security forces *npl* си́лы *fpl* безопа́сности.

security guard *n* охра́нник.

security risk *n*: **it's a ~ ~** (*for country*) э́то представля́ет угро́зу для безопа́сности страны́.

secy. *abbr* = **secretary**.

sedan [səˈdæn] *n* (*US: AUT*) седа́н.

sedate [sɪˈdeɪt] *adj* (*person*) степе́нный* (степе́нен); (*pace*) разме́ренный* (разме́рен) ♦ *vt* (*MED*) дава́ть* (дать* *perf*) седати́вное *or* успокои́тельное сре́дство.

sedation [sɪˈdeɪʃən] *n*: **to be under ~** находи́ться* (*impf*) под возде́йствием седати́вных *or* успокои́тельных сре́дствах.

sedative [ˈsɛdɪtɪv] *n* седати́вное *or* успокои́тельное сре́дство.

sedentary [ˈsɛdntrɪ] *adj* сидя́чий*.

sediment [ˈsɛdɪmənt] *n* оса́док*.

sedimentary [sɛdɪˈmɛntərɪ] *adj* оса́дочный.

sedition [sɪˈdɪʃən] *n* антиправи́тельственная пропага́нда.

seduce [sɪˈdjuːs] *vt* соблазня́ть (соблазни́ть *perf*).

seduction [sɪˈdʌkʃən] *n* (*attraction*) собла́зн; (*act of seducing*) обольще́ние.

seductive [sɪˈdʌktɪv] *adj* (*look, voice*) обольсти́тельный* (обольсти́телен); (*offer*) соблазни́тельный* (соблазни́телен).

see [siː] (*pt* **saw**, *pp* **seen**) *vt* ви́деть* (*impf*); (*understand*) понима́ть (поня́ть* *perf*) ♦ *vi* ви́деть* (*impf*); (*find out*) выясня́ть (вы́яснить *perf*) ♦ *n* епа́рхия; **to ~ sb to the door** (*accompany*) провожа́ть (проводи́ть* *perf*) кого́-н до двери́; **to ~ that** (*ensure*) следи́ть* (проследи́ть* *perf*), что́бы; **there was nobody to be ~n** никого́ не́ было ви́дно; **let me ~** (*show me*) да́йте мне посмотре́ть; (*let me think*) да́йте мне поду́мать; **to go and ~ sb** навести́ть (навести́ть* *perf*) кого́-н; **~ for yourself** (*suggestion*) убеди́тесь са́ми; **I don't know what she saw in him** я не зна́ю, что она́ в нём нашла́; **as far as I can ~** наско́лько я понима́ю; **~ you!** пока́!; **~ you soon!** до ско́рого!, пока́!

► **see about** *vt fus* (*deal with*) занима́ться (заня́ться* *perf*) +*instr*

► **see off** *vt* провожа́ть (проводи́ть* *perf*)

► **see through** *vt* доводи́ть* (довести́* *perf*) до конца́ ♦ *vt fus* ви́деть* (*impf*) наскво́зь

► **see to** *vt fus* забо́титься* (позабо́титься* *perf*) о +*prp*.

seed [siːd] *n* се́мя* *nt*; **~s** (*fig*) семена́* *ntpl*; **he is the number 2 ~** (*SPORT*) в ранжиро́вке спортсме́нов он второ́й; **to go to ~** (*plant*) пойти́* (*perf*) в семена́; (*fig*) сдать* (*perf*).

seedless [ˈsiːdlɪs] *adj* без ко́сточек.

---

* marks translations which have irregular inflections. The Russian-English side of the dictionary gives inflectional information.

seedling ['si:dlɪŋ] n рассада no pl.
seedy ['si:dɪ] adj (person) потрёпанный*
(потрёпан); (place) захудалый.
seeing ['si:ɪŋ] conj: ~ **(that)** поскольку, так как.
seek [si:k] (pt, pp **sought**) vt искать* (impf); **to ~
advice/help from sb** обращаться
(обратиться* perf) за советом/помощью к
кому-н
▶ **seek out** vt (person) разыскивать
(разыскать* perf).
seem [si:m] vi казаться* (показаться* perf);
there ~s to be ... кажется, что имеется ...; **it
~s (that)** кажется, (что); **what ~s to be the
trouble?** что у Вас за проблема?
seemingly ['si:mɪŋlɪ] adv по-видимому.
seemly ['si:mlɪ] adj (behaviour) подобающий*;
(dress) надлежащий*.
seen [si:n] pp of **see**.
seep [si:p] vi просачиваться (просочиться
perf).
seersucker ['sɪəsʌkə*r*] n (fabric) марлёвка.
seesaw ['si:sɔ:] n качели pl.
seethe [si:ð] vi (place) кишеть* (impf); **to ~ with
anger** кипеть* (impf) от гнева.
see-through ['si:θru:] adj прозрачный*
(прозрачен).
segment ['sɛgmənt] n (of circle) сегмент; (of
population) сектор; (of orange) долька*.
segregate ['sɛgrɪgeɪt] vt разделять
(разделить* perf).
segregation [sɛgrɪ'geɪʃən] n (racial)
сегрегация; (SCOL) раздельное обучение.
seismic ['saɪzmɪk] adj сейсмический*.
seize [si:z] vt хватать (схватить* perf); (power,
hostage, territory) захватывать (захватить*
perf); (opportunity) пользоваться
(воспользоваться perf) +instr; (LAW)
конфисковать (impf/perf)
▶ **seize up** vi (TECH: engine) глохнуть*
(заглохнуть* perf)
▶ **seize (up)on** vt fus ухватываться
(ухватиться* perf) за +instr.
seizure ['si:ʒə*r*] n (MED) приступ; (of power)
захват; (of goods) конфискация.
seldom ['sɛldəm] adv редко.
select [sɪ'lɛkt] adj (school, area) элитарный;
(pupils) избранный; (goods) отборный ♦ vt
(choose) выбирать (выбрать* perf); (SPORT)
отбирать (отобрать* perf); **a ~ few** немногие
избранные pl adj.
selection [sɪ'lɛkʃən] n (process) отбор; (COMM:
range available) выбор; (medley) подборка.
selection committee n отборочная
комиссия.
selective [sɪ'lɛktɪv] adj (careful in choosing)
разборчивый (разборчив); (not general)
избирательный.
selector [sɪ'lɛktə*r*] n (person) член отборочной
комиссии; (TECH) селектор.
self [sɛlf] (pl **selves**) n: **he became his usual ~
again** он стал опять самим собой; **my own ~**

моё собственное "я".
self... [sɛlf] prefix само..., себя....
self-addressed ['sɛlfə'drɛst] adj: **~ envelope**
конверт, адресованный на собственное
имя.
self-adhesive [sɛlfəd'hi:zɪv] adj само-
приклеивающийся.
self-appointed [sɛlfə'pɔɪntɪd] adj самозваный.
self-assertive [sɛlfə'sə:tɪv] adj уверенный*
(уверенен).
self-assurance [sɛlfə'ʃuərəns] n само-
уверенность f.
self-assured [sɛlfə'ʃuəd] adj самоуверенный*
(самоуверен).
self-catering [sɛlf'keɪtərɪŋ] adj (BRIT): **~ holiday**
путёвка, в которую включается проезд и
жильё с самообслуживанием.
self-centred [sɛlf'sɛntəd] (US **self-centered**) adj
эгоцентричный* (эгоцентричен).
self-cleaning [sɛlf'kli:nɪŋ] adj само-
очищающийся.
self-confessed [sɛlfkən'fɛst] adj (alcoholic etc)
сознавшийся.
self-confidence [sɛlf'kɔnfɪdns] n уверенность f
в себе.
self-confident [sɛlf'kɔnfɪdənt] adj уверенный*
(уверен) в себе.
self-conscious [sɛlf'kɔnʃəs] adj (nervous)
застенчивый (застенчив).
self-contained [sɛlfkən'teɪnd] adj (BRIT: flat)
отдельный, изолированный; (society,
person) независимый.
self-control [sɛlfkən'trəul] n самообладание.
self-defeating [sɛlfdɪ'fi:tɪŋ] adj (plan, action)
пагубный* (пагубен).
self-defence [sɛlfdɪ'fɛns] (US **self-defense**) n
самозащита, самооборона; **in ~** защищая
себя.
self-discipline [sɛlf'dɪsɪplɪn] n само-
дисциплина.
self-employed [sɛlfɪm'plɔɪd] adj работающий
на себя.
self-esteem [sɛlfɪs'ti:m] n чувство
собственного достоинства.
self-evident [sɛlf'ɛvɪdnt] adj самоочевидный*
(самоочевиден).
self-explanatory [sɛlfɪks'plænətrɪ] adj: **this
phrase is ~** эта фраза не требует
разъяснений.
self-financing [sɛlffaɪ'nænsɪŋ] n
самофинансирование.
self-governing [sɛlf'gʌvənɪŋ] adj (organization,
group) работающий по принципу
самоуправления.
self-help ['sɛlf'hɛlp] n самопомощь f.
self-importance [sɛlfɪm'pɔ:tns] n самомнение.
self-indulgent [sɛlfɪn'dʌldʒənt] adj: **he is being
~** он потворствует своим слабостям.
self-inflicted [sɛlfɪn'flɪktɪd] adj (injury)
нанесённый (нанесён) самому себе;
(problems) причинённый самому себе.

self-interest [sɛlf'ıntrıst] *n* коры́сть *f*.
selfish ['sɛlfıʃ] *adj* (*behaviour, attitude*) эгоисти́ческий*; (*person*) эгоисти́чный* (эгоисти́чен).
selfishly ['sɛlfıʃlı] *adv* эгоисти́чно.
selfishness ['sɛlfıʃnıs] *n* (*of behaviour*) эгоисти́чность *f*; (*of person*) эгои́зм.
selfless ['sɛlflıs] *adj* самоотве́рженный* (самоотве́ржен).
selflessly ['sɛlflıslı] *adv* самоотве́рженно.
selflessness ['sɛlflısnıs] *n* самоотве́рженность *f*.
self-made ['sɛlfmeıd] *adj*: **he's a ~ man** он доби́лся всего́ свои́ми си́лами.
self-perpetuating [sɛlfpə'pɛtʃueıtıŋ] *adj* несконча́емый.
self-pity [sɛlf'pıtı] *n* жа́лость *f* к (самому́) себе́.
self-portrait [sɛlf'pɔ:treıt] *n* автопортре́т.
self-possessed [sɛlfpə'zɛst] *adj* хладнокро́вный* (хладнокро́вен).
self-preservation ['sɛlfprɛzə'veıʃən] *n* самосохране́ние.
self-raising [sɛlf'reızıŋ] (*US* **self-rising**) *adj* (*BRIT*): **~ flour** мука́ с разрыхли́телем.
self-reliant [sɛlfrı'laıənt] *adj* (*person*) самостоя́тельный* (самостоя́телен).
self-respect [sɛlfrıs'pɛkt] *n* самоуваже́ние.
self-respecting [sɛlfrıs'pɛktıŋ] *adj* уважа́ющий себя́.
self-righteous [sɛlf'raıtʃəs] *adj* (*person*) убеждённый* в свое́й правоте́.
self-rising [sɛlf'raızıŋ] *adj* (*US*) = **self-raising**.
self-sacrifice [sɛlf'sækrıfaıs] *n* самопоже́ртвование.
selfsame ['sɛlfseım] *adj* тот же са́мый.
self-satisfied [sɛlf'sætısfaıd] *adj* самодово́льный* (самодово́лен).
self-sealing [sɛlf'si:lıŋ] *adj* (*envelope*) самозакле́ивающийся.
self-service [sɛlf'sə:vıs] *adj*: **~ restaurant/shop** рестора́н/магази́н самообслу́живания.
self-styled ['sɛlfstaıld] *adj* самозва́ный.
self-sufficient [sɛlfsə'fıʃənt] *adj* самостоя́тельный* (самостоя́телен); **to be ~ in sth** по́лностью обеспе́чивать (*impf*) себя́ чем-н.
self-supporting [sɛlfsə'pɔ:tıŋ] *adj* самоокупа́ющийся.
self-taught [sɛlf'tɔ:t] *adj*: **~ artist/pianist** худо́жник-/пиани́ст-самоу́чка.
self-test ['sɛlftɛst] *n* (*COMPUT*) самопрове́рка*.
sell [sɛl] (*pt, pp* **sold**) *vt* продава́ть* (прода́ть* *perf*) ♦ *vi* продава́ться* (прода́ться* *perf*); **to ~ at** *or* **for 10 pounds** продава́ться* (прода́ться* *perf*) по 10 фу́нтов; **to ~ sb sth**, **~ sth to sb** продава́ть* (прода́ть* *perf*) что-н кому́-н; **to ~ sb an idea** (*fig*) убежда́ть (убеди́ть* *perf*) кого́-н в иде́е

▶ **sell off** *vt* распродава́ть* (распрода́ть* *perf*)
▶ **sell out** *vi* (*book etc*) расходи́ться* (разойти́сь* *perf*); (*shop*): **to ~ out of sth** распродава́ть* (распрода́ть* *perf*) что-н; **the tickets are sold out** все биле́ты про́даны
▶ **sell up** *vi* продава́ть* (прода́ть* *perf*) всё иму́щество.
sell-by date ['sɛlbaı-] *n* срок го́дности.
seller ['sɛlə^r] *n* продаве́ц*(-вщи́ца); **~'s market** "ры́нок продавцо́в" (*на кото́ром усло́вия дикту́ют продавцы́*).
selling price ['sɛlıŋ-] *n* прода́жная цена́*.
Sellotape® ['sɛləuteıp] *n* (*BRIT*) кле́йкая ле́нта.
sellout ['sɛlaut] *n* (*inf*: *betrayal*) преда́тельство; (*of tickets*): **the match was a ~** все биле́ты на матч бы́ли распро́даны.
selves [sɛlvz] *pl of* **self**.
semantic [sı'mæntık] *adj* семанти́ческий*.
semantics [sı'mæntıks] *n* сема́нтика.
semaphore ['sɛməfɔ:^r] *n* семафо́р.
semblance ['sɛmblns] *n* ви́димость *f*.
semen ['si:mən] *n* се́мя* *nt*, спе́рма.
semester [sı'mɛstə^r] *n* (*esp US*) семе́стр.
semi ['sɛmı] *n* = **semidetached (house)**.
semi... ['sɛmı] *prefix* полу...
semibreve ['sɛmıbri:v] *n* (*BRIT*) це́лая но́та.
semicircle ['sɛmısə:kl] *n* полукру́г.
semicircular ['sɛmı'sə:kjulə^r] *adj* полукру́глый.
semicolon [sɛmı'kəulən] *n* то́чка* с запято́й.
semiconductor [sɛmıkən'dʌktə^r] *n* полупроводни́к*.
semiconscious [sɛmı'kɔnʃəs] *adj* в полузабы́тьи.
semidetached [sɛmıdı'tætʃt-] *n* (*BRIT*: *also*: **~ house**) *дом, примыка́ющий к сосе́днему*.
semifinal [sɛmı'faınl] *n* полуфина́л.
seminar ['sɛmınɑ:^r] *n* семина́р.
seminary ['sɛmınərı] *n* семина́рия.
semiprecious [sɛmı'prɛʃəs] *adj*: **~ stone** полудрагоце́нный ка́мень* *m*, самоцве́т.
semiquaver ['sɛmıkweıvə^r] *n* (*BRIT*) шестна́дцатая но́та.
semiskilled [sɛmı'skıld] *adj* (*work, worker*) полуквалифици́рованный.
semiskimmed [sɛmı'skımd] *adj* полужи́рный, полуобезжи́ренный.
semitone ['sɛmıtəun] *n* полуто́н*.
semolina [sɛmə'li:nə] *n* ма́нная крупа́, ма́нка (*inf*).
SEN *n abbr* (*BRIT*: = *State Enrolled Nurse*) медсестра́= *медици́нская сестра́*.
Sen. *abbr* (*US*) = **senator**; (*in names*) = **senior**.
sen. *abbr* = **Sen.**
senate ['sɛnıt] *n* сена́т.
senator ['sɛnıtə^r] *n* (*US etc*) сена́тор.
send [sɛnd] (*pt, pp* **sent**) *vt* (*dispatch*) посыла́ть (посла́ть* *perf*), отправля́ть (отпра́вить* *perf*); (*transmit*) посыла́ть (посла́ть* *perf*); **to**

~ by post or **(US)** **mail** посылáть (послáть*
perf) or отправлять (отпрáвить* *perf*) по
пóчте; **to ~ sb for sth** посылáть (послáть*
perf) когó-н за чем-н; **to ~ word that ...**
передавáть* (передáть* *perf*), что ...; **she ~s
(you) her love** онá передаёт Вам привéт; **to ~
sb to Coventry** (*BRIT*) объявлять (объявить*
perf) комý-н бойкóт; **to ~ sb to sleep**
нагонять (нагнáть* *perf*) на когó-н сон; **to ~
sb into fits of laughter** смешить (рассмешить
perf) когó-н; **to ~ sth flying** рассéивать
(рассéять *perf*) что-н в вóздухе
▶ **send away** *vt* (*letter, goods*) отправлять
(отпрáвить* *perf*), отсылáть (отослáть* *perf*);
(*unwelcome visitor*) прогонять (прогнáть*
perf)
▶ **send away for** *vt fus* закáзывать (заказáть*
perf)
▶ **send back** *vt* посылáть (послáть* *perf*)
обрáтно
▶ **send for** *vt fus* (*by post*) закáзывать
(заказáть* *perf*); (*person*) посылáть (послáть*
perf) за +*instr*
▶ **send in** *vt* (*report*) представлять
(предстáвить* *perf*); (*resignation, application*)
подавáть* (подáть* *perf*) заявлéние о +*prp*
▶ **send off** *vt* (*goods*) отправлять (отпрáвить*
perf); (*BRIT*: *SPORT*: *player*) удалять (удалить*
perf)
▶ **send on** *vt* (*BRIT*: *letter*) пересылáть
(переслáть* *perf*); (: *luggage etc*: *in advance*)
переправлять (перепрáвить* *perf*)
▶ **send out** *vt* (*invitation*) рассылáть
(разослáть* *perf*); (*heat, smell, light*)
распространять (распространить *perf*);
(*signal*) посылáть (послáть* *perf*)
▶ **send round** *vt* (*letter, document etc*)
рассылáть (разослáть* *perf*)
▶ **send up** *vt* (*price, blood pressure*) поднимáть
(поднять* *perf*); (*astronaut*) запускáть
(запустить* *perf*); (*BRIT*: *parody*) высмéивать
(высмеять *perf*).
sender ['sɛndə'] *n* отправитель(ница) *m(f)*.
sending-off ['sɛndɪŋɒf] *n* удалéние с пóля.
sendoff ['sɛndɒf] *n*: **a good send-off** хорóшие
прóводы *pl*.
send-up ['sɛndʌp] *n* парóдия.
Senegal [sɛnɪ'gɔ:l] *n* Сенегáл.
Senegalese ['sɛnɪgə'li:z] *adj* сенегáльский ♦ *n
inv* сенегáлец*(-лка*).
senile ['si:naɪl] *adj* маразматический.
senility [sɪ'nɪlɪtɪ] *n* стáрческий марáзм.
senior ['si:nɪə'] *adj* (*staff, officer*) стáрший*;
(*manager, consultant*) глáвный; (*of higher
rank*): **to be ~ to sb** быть* (*impf*) вы́ше когó-н
по дóлжности; **the ~s** *npl* (*SCOL*: *at school*)
старшеклáссники *mpl*; (: *at college, university*)
старшекýрсники *mpl*; **she is 15 years his ~** онá
стáрше егó на 15 лет; **P. Jones ~** П. Джóунз
стáрший*.
senior citizen *n* (*esp BRIT*) пожилóй человéк*,

человéк* пенсиóнного вóзраста.
senior high school *n* (*US*) ≈ стáршие кýрсы
кóлледжа.
seniority [si:nɪ'ɔrɪtɪ] *n* старшинствó.
sensation [sɛn'seɪʃən] *n* (*ability to feel*)
чувствительность *f*; (*feeling*) ощущéние;
(*great success*) сенсáция; **to cause a ~**
вызывáть (вы́звать* *perf*) сенсáцию.
sensational [sɛn'seɪʃənl] *adj* (*wonderful*)
потрясáющий* (потрясáющ*); (*causing much
interest*) сенсациóнный* (сенсациóнен).
sensationalize [sɛn'seɪʃnəlaɪz] *vt* дéлать
(сдéлать *perf*) сенсáцию из +*gen*.
sense [sɛns] *vt* (*become aware of*) чýвствовать
(почýвствовать *perf*), ощущáть (ощутить*
perf) ♦ *n* (*feeling*) чýвство, ощущéние;
(*meaning of word*) смысл; (*also*: *good ~*): **it
makes ~** в э́том есть смысл; **~s** *npl* (*sanity*)
рассýдок* *msg*; **the ~s** пять чувств; **there is no
~ in that/in doing that** нет смы́сла в э́том/
дéлать э́то; **to come to one's ~s**
образýмиться (*perf*); **to take leave of one's ~s**
теря́ть (потеря́ть *perf*) рассýдок.
senseless ['sɛnslɪs] *adj* (*pointless*)
бессмы́сленный* (бессмы́слен);
(*unconscious*) без чувств.
sense of humour (*US* **sense of humor**) *n*
чýвство ю́мора.
sensibility [sɛnsɪ'bɪlɪtɪ] *n* чувствительность *f*.
sensible ['sɛnsɪbl] *adj* разýмный* (разýмен);
(*shoes*) практичный.
sensitive ['sɛnsɪtɪv] *adj* чувствительный*
(чувствителен); (*understanding*) чýткий*
(чýток); (*issue*) щекотливый (щекотлив); **~
to** чувствительный* (чувствителен) к +*dat*;
he is very ~ about it он отнóсится к э́тому
óчень болéзненно.
sensitivity [sɛnsɪ'tɪvɪtɪ] *n* (*responsiveness*)
чувствительность *f*; (*understanding*)
чýткость *f*; (*delicate nature*: *of issue etc*)
щекотливость *f*.
sensual ['sɛnsjuəl] *adj* (*of the senses*)
чýвственный*; (*sexual*) чýвственный*
(чýвствен).
sensuous ['sɛnsjuəs] *adj* (*lips*) чýвственный*
(чýвствен); (*material*) нéжный* (нéжен).
sent [sɛnt] *pt, pp of* **send**.
sentence ['sɛntns] *n* (*LING*) предложéние; (*LAW*)
приговóр ♦ *vt*: **to ~ sb to death/to five years in
prison** приговáривать (приговорить *perf*)
когó-н к смéрти/к пяти годáм тюрéмного
заключéния; **to pass ~ on sb** выносить*
(вы́нести* *perf*) комý-н приговóр.
sentiment ['sɛntɪmənt] *n* (*tender feelings*)
чýвство; (*opinion*) мнéние, настроéние.
sentimental [sɛntɪ'mɛntl] *adj*
сентиментáльный* (сентиментáлен).
sentimentality ['sɛntɪmɛn'tælɪtɪ] *n*
сентиментáльность *f*.
sentry ['sɛntrɪ] *n* часовóй *m adj*, карáульный *m
adj*.

sentry duty *n*: **to be on** ~ ~ нести* *(impf)* карау́льную слу́жбу.
Seoul [səul] *n* Сеу́л.
separable ['sɛprəbl] *adj*: ~ **(from)** отдели́мый (отдели́м) (от +*gen*).
separate [*adj* 'sɛprɪt, *vb* 'sɛpəreɪt] *adj* отде́льный; (*ways*) ра́зный ♦ *vt* (*split up*: *people*) разлуча́ть (разлучи́ть *perf*); (: *things*) разделя́ть (раздели́ть* *perf*); (*make a distinction between*) различа́ть (различи́ть *perf*) ♦ *vi* расходи́ться* (разойти́сь* *perf*); ~ **from** отде́льно от +*gen*; **to** ~ **into** разделя́ть (раздели́ть* *perf*) на +*acc*; *see also* **separates**.
separately ['sɛprɪtlɪ] *adv* отде́льно.
separates ['sɛprɪts] *npl* (*clothes*) предме́ты же́нской оде́жды, не входя́щие в компле́кт.
separation [sɛpə'reɪʃən] *n* (*being apart*) разлу́ка; (*LAW*) разде́льное прожива́ние.
sepia ['si:pjə] *adj*: ~ **photograph** фотогра́фия, вы́полненная в те́хнике се́пии.
Sept. *abbr* = **September**.
September [sɛp'tɛmbə^r] *n* сентя́брь* *m*; *see also* **July**.
septic ['sɛptɪk] *adj* заражённый* (заражён); **to go** ~ заража́ться (зарази́ться* *perf*).
septicaemia [sɛptɪ'si:mɪə] (*US* **septicemia**) *n* се́псис, септицеми́я.
septic tank *n* ≈ выгребна́я я́ма.
sequel ['si:kwl] *n* продолже́ние.
sequence ['si:kwəns] *n* после́довательность *f*; (*dance sequence*) комбина́ция; (*CINEMA*) эпизо́д; **in the correct** ~ в пра́вильной после́довательности; ~ **of tenses** согласова́ние времён.
sequential [sɪ'kwɛnʃəl] *adj* (*process, link etc*) после́довательный* (после́дователен); ~ **access** (*COMPUT*) после́довательный до́ступ.
sequestrate [sɪ'kwɛstreɪt] *vt* конфискова́ть (*impf/perf*).
sequin ['si:kwɪn] *n* блёстка*.
Serbia ['sə:bɪə] *n* Се́рбия.
Serbian ['sə:bɪən] *n* серб(ка) ♦ *adj* се́рбский*.
Serbo-Croat ['sə:bəu'krəuæt] *n* (*LING*) сербскохорва́тский язы́к*.
serenade [sɛrə'neɪd] *n* серена́да ♦ *vt* петь* (спеть* *perf*) серена́ду +*dat*.
serene [sɪ'ri:n] *adj* безмяте́жный* (безмяте́жен).
serenity [sə'rɛnɪtɪ] *n* безмяте́жность *f*.
sergeant ['sɑ:dʒənt] *n* сержа́нт.
sergeant major *n* ≈ ста́рший* сержа́нт.
serial ['sɪərɪəl] *n* (*TV, RADIO*) сериа́л; (*in magazine*) рома́н, печа́тающийся в не́сколько частя́х ♦ *adj* (*COMPUT*) после́довательный; ~ **printer** посимво́льно печа́тающее устро́йство.
serialize ['sɪərɪəlaɪz] *vt* (*story, book*: *in print*) тиражи́ровать (*impf*) частя́ми; (: *on TV, RADIO*)

ста́вить* (поста́вить* *perf*) сериа́л по +*prp*.
serial killer *n* манья́к (*совершивший многочи́сленные уби́йства*).
serial number *n* сери́йный но́мер*.
series ['sɪərɪz] *n inv* се́рия.
serious ['sɪərɪəs] *adj* серьёзный* (серьёзен); **are you** ~ **(about it)?** Вы (э́то) серьёзно?
seriously ['sɪərɪəslɪ] *adv* серьёзно; **to take sb/sth** ~ принима́ть (восприня́ть* *perf*) кого́-н/что-н серьёзно.
seriousness ['sɪərɪəsnɪs] *n* серьёзность *f*.
sermon ['sə:mən] *n* (*also fig*) про́поведь *f*.
serrated [sɪ'reɪtɪd] *adj* зазу́бренный.
serum ['sɪərəm] *n* сы́воротка.
servant ['sə:vənt] *n* (*male*) слуга́* *m*; (*female*) служа́нка; (*fig*) слуга́*.
serve [sə:v] *vt* (*company, country*) служи́ть* (*impf*) +*dat*; (*customer*: *in shop, restaurant*) обслу́живать (обслужи́ть* *perf*); (*purpose*) служи́ть* (послужи́ть *impf*)) +*dat*; (*food, goods*: *to sb*) подава́ть* (пода́ть* *perf*); (*subj*: *train etc*) обслу́живать (*impf*); (*apprenticeship*) проходи́ть* (пройти́* *perf*); (*prison term*) отбыва́ть (отбы́ть* *perf*) ♦ *vi* (*at table*) прислу́живать (*impf*); (*TENNIS*) подава́ть* (пода́ть* *perf*); (*soldier etc*) служи́ть* (*impf*) ♦ *n* (*TENNIS*) пода́ча; **are you being** ~**d?** Вас уже́ обслу́живают?; **it** ~**s my purpose** э́то мне подхо́дит; **it** ~**s him right** подело́м ему́; **to** ~ **on a committee/jury** состоя́ть (*impf*) в комите́те/жюри́; **to** ~ **as/for** служи́ть* (послужи́ть *perf*) +*instr*/вме́сто +*gen*
▸ **serve out** *vt* (*food*) раскла́дывать (разложи́ть* *perf*)
▸ **serve up** *vt* = **serve out**.
service ['sə:vɪs] *n* (*help*) услу́га; (*in hotel*) обслу́живание, се́рвис; (*REL*) слу́жба; (*AUT*) техобслу́живание; (*TENNIS*) пода́ча; (*dinner set etc*) серви́з ♦ *vt* (*car, washing machine*) проводи́ть* (провести́* *perf*) техобслу́живание +*gen*; **the S~s** *npl* (*army, navy etc*) Вооружённые си́лы *fpl*; **military** *or* **national** ~ вое́нная слу́жба; **train** ~ железнодоро́жное сообще́ние; **postal** ~ почто́вая связь; **how can I be of** ~ **(to you)?** чем могу́ быть поле́зен?; **to do sb a** ~ ока́зывать (оказа́ть* *perf*) кому́-н услу́гу; **to put one's car in for** ~ отдава́ть* (отда́ть* *perf*) маши́ну на техобслу́живание.
serviceable ['sə:vɪsəbl] *adj* про́чный* (про́чен).
service area *n* (*on motorway*) се́рвисная ста́нция.
service charge *n* (*BRIT*) (рестора́нная) наце́нка.
service industry *n* сфе́ра услу́г.
serviceman ['sə:vɪsmən] *irreg n* военнослу́жащий* *m adj*.
service station *n* (*AUT*) ста́нция

техобслу́живания.
serviette [sə:vɪˈɛt] *n* (*BRIT*) салфе́тка*.
servile [ˈsə:vaɪl] *adj* подобостра́стный*
(подобостра́стен).
session [ˈsɛʃən] *n* (*sitting*) се́ссия; (*SCOL: academic year*) уче́бный год*; **recording** ~
за́пись *f;* **drinking** ~ запо́й; **to be in** ~ (*court etc*) заседа́ть (*impf*).
session musician *n музыка́нт, кото́рого приглаша́ют на за́писи в ра́зные анса́мбли.*
set [sɛt] (*pt, pp* **set**) *n* (*collection*) набо́р; (*of saucepans, clothes*) компле́кт; (*of books*)
многото́мник; (*also:* **radio** ~)
радиоприёмник; (*also:* **television** ~)
телеви́зор; (*TENNIS*) сет; (*group of people*)
круг*, о́бщество; (*MATH*) мно́жество;
(*CINEMA, THEAT: stage*) сце́на; (*: scenery*)
(худо́жественное) оформле́ние; (*hairdo*)
укла́дка ◆ *adj* (*fixed*) устано́вленный; (*ready*)
гото́вый (гото́в) ◆ *vt* (*place: vertically*)
ста́вить* (поста́вить* *perf*); (*: horizontally*)
класть* (положи́ть* *perf*); (*table*) накрыва́ть
(накры́ть* *perf*); (*time*) назнача́ть (назна́чить
perf); (*price, rule, record*) устана́вливать
(установи́ть* *perf*); (*alarm, watch, task*)
ста́вить* (поста́вить* *perf*); (*exam*)
составля́ть (соста́вить* *perf*); (*TYP*) набира́ть
(набра́ть* *perf*) ◆ *vi* (*sun*) сади́ться* (сесть*
perf), заходи́ть* (зайти́* *perf*); (*jam*) густе́ть
(загусте́ть *perf*); (*jelly, concrete*) застыва́ть
(засты́ть* *perf*); (*bone*) вправля́ться
(впра́виться* *perf*); **a** ~ **of false teeth** вставны́е
зу́бы* *mpl;* **a** ~ **of dining-room furniture**
столо́вый гарниту́р; **a chess** ~ ша́хматы *pl;*
to be ~ **on doing** настра́иваться
(настро́иться *perf*) +*infin;* **to be all** ~ **to do**
собира́ться (*impf*) +*infin;* **to be (dead)** ~ **against**
быть* (*impf*) (категори́чески) про́тив +*gen;*
he's ~ **in his ways** у него́ устоя́вшиеся
привы́чки; **the novel is** ~ **in Rome** де́йствие
рома́на происхо́дит в Ри́ме; **a** ~ **phrase**
усто́йчивое словосочета́ние; **to** ~ **to music**
класть* (положи́ть* *perf*) на му́зыку; **to** ~ **on
fire** поджига́ть (подже́чь* *perf*); **to** ~ **free**
освобожда́ть (освободи́ть* *perf*); **to** ~ **sth
going** приводи́ть* (привести́* *perf*) что-н в
де́йствие; **to** ~ **sail** отплыва́ть (отплы́ть*
perf)
▶ **set about** *vt fus* (*task*) приступа́ть
(приступи́ть* *perf*) к +*dat;* **to** ~ **about doing**
принима́ться (приня́ться* *perf*) +*infin*
▶ **set aside** *vt* (*money*) откла́дывать
(отложи́ть* *perf*); (*time*) выделя́ть (вы́делить
perf)
▶ **set back** *vt* (*progress*) заде́рживать
(задержа́ть* *perf*); (*cost*): **to** ~ **sb back £5**
обходи́ться* (обойти́сь* *perf*) кому́-н в £5; (*in
time*): **to** ~ **sb back (by)** заде́рживать
(задержа́ть* *perf*) кого́-н (на +*acc*); (*place*):
the house is ~ **back from the road** дом
нахо́дится в стороне́ от доро́ги

▶ **set in** *vi* (*infection*) внедря́ться (внедри́ться
perf); (*bad weather*) устана́вливаться
(установи́ться* *perf*); (*complications*)
начина́ться (нача́ться* *perf*); **the rain has** ~ **in
for the day** дождь заряди́л на весь день
▶ **set off** *vi* отправля́ться (отпра́виться* *perf*) ◆
vt (*bomb*) взрыва́ть (взорва́ть* *perf*); (*alarm*)
приводи́ть* (привести́* *perf*) в де́йствие;
(*chain of events*) вызыва́ть (вы́звать* *perf*);
(*show up well*) подчёркивать (*impf*)
▶ **set out** *vt* (*goods etc*) расставля́ть
(расста́вить* *perf*); (*arguments*) излага́ть
(изложи́ть* *perf*) ◆ *vi* (*depart*): **to** ~ **out (from)**
отправля́ться (отпра́виться* *perf*) (из +*gen*);
to ~ **out to do** намерева́ться (*impf*) +*infin*
▶ **set up** *vt* (*organization*) учрежда́ть
(учреди́ть* *perf*); (*monument*) устана́вливать
(установи́ть* *perf*); **to** ~ **up shop** (*fig*)
открыва́ть (откры́ть* *perf*) своё де́ло.
setback [ˈsɛtbæk] *n* (*hitch*) неуда́ча; (*in health*)
ухудше́ние.
set menu *n* ко́мплексное меню́ *nt ind.*
set square *n* уго́льник.
settee [sɛˈti:] *n* дива́н.
setting [ˈsɛtɪŋ] *n* (*background*) обстано́вка*;
(*position: of controls*) положе́ние; (*of sun*)
зака́т, захо́д; (*of jewel*) опра́ва.
setting lotion *n* (*for hair*) лосьо́н для укла́дки
воло́с.
settle [ˈsɛtl] *vt* (*argument, problem*) разреша́ть
(разреши́ть *perf*); (*matter*) ула́живать
(ула́дить* *perf*); (*accounts*) рассчи́тываться
(рассчита́ться *perf*) с +*instr;* (*colonize: land*)
заселя́ть (засели́ть* *perf*) ◆ *vi* (*also:* ~ **down:**
somewhere) обоснова́ться (*perf*); (*: live
sensibly*) остепени́ться (*perf*); (*bird*) сади́ться*
(сесть* *perf*); (*dust, sediment*) оседа́ть
(осе́сть* *perf*); (*calm down*) успока́иваться
(успоко́иться *perf*); **to** ~ **one's stomach**
успока́ивать (успоко́ить *perf*) желу́док; **to** ~
down to sth уса́живаться (усе́сться* *perf*) за
что-н; **to** ~ **for sth** соглаша́ться
(согласи́ться* *perf*) на что-н; **to** ~ **on sth**
остана́вливаться (останови́ться* *perf*) на
чём-н
▶ **settle in** *vi* осва́иваться (осво́иться *perf*)
▶ **settle up** *vi:* **to** ~ **up with sb** рассчи́тываться
(рассчита́ться *perf*) с кем-н.
settlement [ˈsɛtlmənt] *n* (*payment*) упла́та;
(*agreement*) соглаше́ние; (*village, colony*)
поселе́ние; (*of conflict*) урегули́рование; **in** ~
of our account (*COMM*) для опла́ты на́шего
счёта.
settler [ˈsɛtlə] *n* поселе́нец*(-нка*).
setup [ˈsɛtʌp] *n* (*organization*) устро́йство;
(*situation*) положе́ние дел.
seven [ˈsɛvn] *n* семь*; *see also* **five.**
seventeen [sɛvnˈti:n] *n* семна́дцать*; *see also*
five.
seventeenth [sɛvnˈti:nθ] *adj* семна́дцатый; *see
also* **fifth.**

seventh ['sɛvnθ] *adj* седьмой; *see also* **fifth.**
seventieth ['sɛvntпθ] *adj* семидесятый; *see also* **fifth.**
seventy ['sɛvntп] *n* семьдесят*; *see also* **fifty.**
sever ['sɛvə'] *vt* (*artery, pipe*) перерезать (перерезать* *perf*); (*relations*) прерывать (прервать* *perf*); (*ties, connections*) обрывать (оборвать* *perf*).
several ['sɛvərl] *adj* несколько +*gen* ♦ *pron* некоторые *pl adj*; ~ **of us** некоторые из нас; ~ **times** несколько раз.
severance ['sɛvərəns] *n* разрыв.
severance pay *n* выходное пособие (*при сокращении штатов*).
severe [sɪ'vɪə'] *adj* (*shortage, pain, winter*) жестокий* (жесток); (*damage*) серьёзный (серьёзен); (*stern*) жёсткий* (жёсток); (*plain: dress*) строгий* (строг).
severely [sɪ'vɪəlɪ] *adv* (*punish*) жестоко; (*look*) жёстко; (*damaged*) серьёзно; (*wounded, ill*) тяжело.
severity [sɪ'vɛrɪtɪ] *n* жёстокость *f*; (*of damage*) серьёзность *f*; (*of illness*) тяжесть *f*.
sew [səu] (*pt* **sewed**, *pp* **sewn**) *vti* шить* (*impf*)
▶ **sew up** *vt* (*clothes*) зашивать (зашить* *perf*); **it is all ~n up** (*fig*) дело на мази.
sewage ['su:ɪdʒ] *n* (*waste*) сточные воды* *fpl*; ~ **system** канализация.
sewage works *n* канализационные очистительные сооружения *ntpl*.
sewer ['su:ə'] *n* канализационная труба*.
sewing ['səuɪŋ] *n* шитьё.
sewing machine *n* швейная машина.
sewn [səun] *pp of* **sew.**
sex [sɛks] *n* (*gender*) пол; (*lovemaking*) секс; **both ~es** оба пола; **to have ~ with sb** переспать* (*perf*) с кем-н.
sex act *n* сексуальный акт.
sex appeal *n* сексопильность *f*, сексуальная привлекательность *f*; **he's got a lot of ~ ~** он очень сексопильный.
sex education *n* сексуальное воспитание.
sexism ['sɛksɪzəm] *n* предубеждение к лицам противоположного пола.
sexist ['sɛksɪst] *adj* характеризующийся предубеждением к мужчинам или женщинам.
sex life *n* половая *or* сексуальная жизнь *f*.
sex object *n* сексуальный объект.
sextet [sɛks'tɛt] *n* (*group*) секстет.
sexual ['sɛksjuəl] *adj* (*reproduction, equality*) половой; (*attraction, relationship*) сексуальный* (сексуален), половой; ~ **equality** равенство полов.
sexual assault *n* нападение с сексуальным мотивом.
sexual harassment *n* нежелательное проявление полового интереса, а также

нетактичные замечания, намёки и т.п. со стороны представителя противоположного пола.
sexual intercourse *n* половой акт.
sexually ['sɛksjuəlɪ] *adv* (*attractive, attract*) сексуально; (*segregated*) в зависимости от пола; (*discriminate*) по половому признаку; (*reproduce*) половым путём.
sexual orientation *n* сексуальная ориентация.
sexy ['sɛksɪ] *adj* сексуальный* (сексуален).
Seychelles [seɪ'ʃɛl(z)] *npl*: **the ~** Сейшельские острова *mpl*.
SF *n abbr* (= **science fiction**) НФ= *научная фантастика.*
SG *n abbr* (*US: MIL, MED*: = **Surgeon General**) ≈ начмед= *начальник медицинской службы.*
Sgt *abbr* (*POLICE, MIL*) = **sergeant.**
shabbiness ['ʃæbɪnɪs] *n* запущенность *f*.
shabby ['ʃæbɪ] *adj* (*person*) обтрёпанный; (*clothes*) потрёпанный (потрёпан); (*treatment, behaviour*) недостойный* (недостоен); (*building*) ветхий* (ветх).
shack [ʃæk] *n* лачуга
▶ **shack up** *vi* (*inf*): **to ~ up (with sb)** начать* (*perf*) сожительствовать (с +*instr*).
shackles ['ʃæklz] *npl* (*also fig*) оковы *pl*.
shade [ʃeɪd] *n* (*shelter*) тень *f*; (*for lamp*) абажур; (*of colour*) оттёнок*; (*US: also:* **window ~**) штора ♦ *vt* (*shelter*) затенять (затенить* *perf*); (*eyes*) заслонять (заслонить* *perf*); ~**s** *npl* (*inf: sunglasses*) тёмные очки *pl*; **in the ~** в тени; **a ~** (**more/ too large**) чуточку (больше/великовато).
shadow ['ʃædəu] *n* тень* *f* ♦ *vt* (*follow*) ходить* (*impf*) как тень за +*instr*; **without** *or* **beyond a ~ of a doubt** без тени сомнения.
shadow cabinet *n* (*BRIT: POL*) теневой кабинет.
shadowy ['ʃædəuɪ] *adj* (*place*) тенистый (тенист); (*figure, shape*) смутный (смутен).
shady ['ʃeɪdɪ] *adj* (*place, trees*) тенистый (тенист); (*fig: dishonest*) тёмный* (тёмен).
shaft [ʃɑ:ft] *n* (*of arrow, spear*) древко; (*AUT, TECH*) вал; (*of mine, lift*) шахта; (*of light*) сноп; **ventilation ~** вентиляционная труба*.
shag [ʃæg] *vt* (*inf!*) трахать (трахнуть *perf*) (*!*) ♦ *vi* (*inf!*) трахаться (трахнуться *perf*) (*!*) ♦ *n* (*also:* ~ **tobacco**) махорка; (*ZOOL*) длиннохвостый баклан; (*inf!*): **to have a ~** трахнуться (*perf*).
shaggy ['ʃægɪ] *adj* лохматый (лохмат).
shake [ʃeɪk] (*pt* **shook**, *pp* **shaken**) *vt* трясти* (*impf*); (*bottle*) взбалтывать (взболтать *perf*); (*building*) сотрясать (сотрясти* *perf*); (*weaken: beliefs, resolve*) пошатнуть (*perf*); (*upset, surprise*) потрясать (потрясти* *perf*) ♦ *vi* (*voice*) дрожать (*impf*) ♦ *n* (*movement*)

дрожáние; **to ~ one's head** качáть (покачáть *perf*) головóй; **to ~ hands with sb** жать* (пожáть* *perf*) комý-н рýку; **to ~ with** трястúсь* *(impf)* от +*gen*; **give the bottle a good ~** хорошó взболтáйте бутýлку

► **shake off** *vt* стрáхивать (стряхнýть *perf*); (*fig: pursuer*) избавлáться (избáвиться* *perf*) от +*gen*

► **shake up** *vt* (*ingredients*) взбáлтывать (взболтáть *perf*); (*fig: organization*) встряхивать (встряхнýть *perf*).

shaken ['ʃeɪkn] *pp* of **shake**.

shake-out ['ʃeɪkaut] *n* перетрáска.

shake-up ['ʃeɪkʌp] *n* встрáска*.

shakily ['ʃeɪkɪlɪ] *adv* (*reply*) с дрóжью в гóлосе; (*walk*) шатáясь; (*write*) дрожáщей рукóй.

shaky ['ʃeɪkɪ] *adj* (*hand, voice*) дрожáщий; (*table, knowledge*) шáткий* (шáток); (*memory*) непрóчный* (непрóчен); (*prospects, future*) неопределённый*; (*start*) неувéренный*; **his voice was ~** гóлос егó дрожáл.

shale [ʃeɪl] *n* слáнец*.

shall [ʃæl] *aux vb*: **I ~ go** я пойдý; **~ I open the door?** (мне) открыть дверь?; **I'll get some, ~ I?** я принесý немнóго, да?

shallot [ʃə'lɔt] *n* (*BRIT*) лук-шалóт *no pl*.

shallow ['ʃæləu] *adj* (*water*) мéлкий*; (*box*) неглубóкий*; (*breathing, also fig*) повéрхностный (повéрхностен).

sham [ʃæm] *n* притвóрство; (*jewellery, furniture*) поддéлка* ◆ *vt* притворáться (притворúться *perf*) +*instr*.

shambles ['ʃæmblz] *n* неразберúха; **the economy is (in) a complete ~** в эконóмике царúт пóлная неразберúха.

shambolic [ʃæm'bɔlɪk] *adj* (*inf*) хаотúчный* (хаотúчен).

shame [ʃeɪm] *n* (*embarrassment*) стыд*; (*disgrace*) позóр ◆ *vt* позóрить (опозóрить *perf*); **it is a ~ that/to do** жаль, что/+*infin*; **what a ~!** какáя жáлость!, как жаль!; **to put sb to ~** (*fig*) заставлáть (застáвить* *perf*) когó-н устыдúться; **your work puts mine to ~** мoя рабóта бледнéет в сравнéнии с Вáшей.

shamefaced ['ʃeɪmfeɪst] *adj* устыжённый.

shameful ['ʃeɪmful] *adj* позóрный* (позóрен).

shameless ['ʃeɪmlɪs] *adj* бесстыдный* (бесстыден).

shampoo [ʃæm'pu:] *n* шампýнь *m* ◆ *vt* мыть* (помыть* *or* вымыть* *perf*) шампýнем.

shampoo and set *n* мытьё и уклáдка волóс.

shamrock ['ʃæmrɔk] *n* трилúстник, кислúца.

shandy ['ʃændɪ] *n* смесь пúва с лимонáдом.

shan't [ʃɑ:nt] = **shall not**.

shanty town ['ʃænti-] *n* трущóбы *fpl*.

SHAPE [ʃeɪp] *n abbr* (*MIL*: = *Supreme Headquarters Allied Powers, Europe*) Штаб верхóвного главнокомáндующего НАТО в Еврóпе.

shape [ʃeɪp] *n* фóрма ◆ *vt* (*fashion, ideas,*

events) формировáть (сформировáть *perf*); (*clay*) лепúть* (слепúть* *perf*); (*statement*) оформлáть (офóрмить* *perf*); **to take ~** (*painting, plan etc*) обретáть (обрестú* *perf*) фóрму; **in the ~ of a heart** в фóрме сердéчка; **I can't bear gardening in any ~ or form** я не выношý садовóдства ни в какóй фóрме; **to get o.s. into ~** приводúть* (привестú* *perf*) себá, входúть* (войтú* *perf*) в фóрму

► **shape up** *vi* (*events*) склáдываться (сложúться* *perf*); (*person*) формировáться (сформировáться *perf*).

-shaped [ʃeɪpt] *suffix*: **heart-~** сердцевúдный*.

shapeless ['ʃeɪplɪs] *adj* бесфóрменный (бесфóрмен).

shapely ['ʃeɪplɪ] *adj* (*woman*) хорошó слóженный (слóжен); (*legs*) красúвый (красúв).

share [ʃɛə'] *n* дóля*; (*COMM*) áкция ◆ *vt* (*books, cost*) делúть* (разделúть* *or* поделúть* *perf*); (*toys*) делúться* (поделúться* *perf*) +*instr*; (*features, qualities etc*) разделáть (*impf*); (*opinion, concern*) разделáть (разделúть* *perf*); **to ~ in** (*joy, sorrow*) делúться* (разделúться* *perf*); (*profits*) делúться* (поделúться* *perf*); (*work*) учáствовать (*impf*) в +*prp*

► **share out** *vt* делúть* (разделúть* *perf*).

share capital *n* акционéрный капитáл.

share certificate *n* сертификáт áкции.

shareholder ['ʃɛəhəuldə'] *n* акционéр.

share index *n* (*COMM*) фóндовый úндекс.

share issue *n* (*COMM*) выпуск áкции.

shareware ['ʃɛəwɛə'] *n* программное обеспечéние óбщего пóльзования.

shark [ʃɑ:k] *n* акýла.

sharp [ʃɑ:p] *adj* рéзкий* (рéзок); (*knife, teeth, nose*) óстрый* (остр); (*curve, bend*) крутóй* (крут); (*MUS*) диéз; (*dishonest: practice etc*) лóвкий* (лóвок) ◆ *n* (*MUS*) диéз ◆ *adv* (*precisely*): **at 2 o'clock ~** рóвно в два часá; **he is very ~** у негó óчень óстрый ум; **he was rather ~ with her** он был довóльно рéзок с ней; **look ~!** поторопúтесь!; **C ~** (*MUS*) до-диéз.

sharpen ['ʃɑ:pn] *vt* (*stick etc*) заострáть (заострúть *perf*); (*pencil, knife*) точúть* (поточúть* *perf*); (*fig: appetite*) усúливать (усúлить *perf*).

sharpener ['ʃɑ:pnə'] *n* (*also:* **pencil ~**) точúлка*; (*also:* **knife ~**) точúло.

sharp-eyed [ʃɑ:p'aɪd] *adj* (*person*) зóркий* (зóрок).

sharpish ['ʃɑ:pɪʃ] *adv* (*inf*) быстренько.

sharply ['ʃɑ:plɪ] *adv* рéзко.

sharp-tempered [ʃɑ:p'tɛmpəd] *adj* (*person*) вспыльчивый (вспыльчив).

sharp-witted [ʃɑ:p'wɪtɪd] *adj* (*person*) сообразúтельный* (сообразúтелен).

shatter ['ʃætə'] *vt* (*vase, hopes*) разбивáть (разбúть* *perf*); (*fig: nerves*) надрывáть

(надорва́ть* *perf*); (: *person*) потряса́ть
(потрясти́* *perf*) ♦ *vi* би́ться* (разби́ться*
perf).
shattered ['ʃætəd] *adj* (*overwhelmed, grief-
stricken*) потрясённый (потрясён); (*inf:
exhausted*) разби́тый (разби́т).
shattering ['ʃætərɪŋ] *adj* (*experience*) тя́жкий*;
(*day*) утоми́тельный* (утоми́телен).
shatterproof ['ʃætəpruːf] *adj* небью́щийся.
shave [ʃeɪv] *vt* брить* (побри́ть* *perf*) ♦ *vi*
бри́ться* (побри́ться* *perf*) ♦ *n*: **to have a ~**
бри́ться* (побри́ться* *perf*).
shaven ['ʃeɪvn] *adj* бри́тый (брит).
shaver ['ʃeɪvə*ʳ*] *n* (*also:* **electric ~**)
(электри́ческая) бри́тва.
shaver point *n* розе́тка* для бри́твы.
shaving ['ʃeɪvɪŋ] *n* бритьё; **~s** *npl* (*of wood etc*)
стру́жки* *fpl*.
shaving brush *n* ки́сточка* для бритья́,
помазо́к*.
shaving cream *n* крем для бритья́.
shaving foam *n* крем для бритья́.
shaving soap *n* крем для бритья́.
shawl [ʃɔːl] *n* шаль *f*.
she [ʃiː] *pron* она́.
sheaf [ʃiːf] (*pl* **sheaves**) *n* (*of corn*) сноп*; (*of
papers*) сто́пка*.
shear [ʃɪə*ʳ*] (*pt* **sheared**, *pp* **shorn**) *vt* (*sheep*)
стричь* (постри́чь* *or* остри́чь* *perf*)
► **shear off** *vi* (*bolt etc*) надла́мываться
(надломи́ться* *perf*).
shears ['ʃɪəz] *npl* (*for hedge*) садо́вые
но́жницы *pl*.
sheath [ʃiːθ] *n* (*of knife*) но́жны* *pl*;
(*contraceptive*) презервати́в.
sheathe [ʃiːð] *vt* (*sword, knife etc*) вкла́дывать
(вложи́ть* *perf*) в но́жны.
sheath knife *n* фи́нка*.
sheaves [ʃiːvz] *npl of* **sheaf**.
shed [ʃɛd] (*pt, pp* **shed**) *n* сара́й; (*INDUSTRY, RAIL*)
наве́с ♦ *vt* (*skin, load*) сбра́сывать (сбро́сить*
perf); (*tears*) лить* (*impf*); (*blood*) пролива́ть
(проли́ть* *perf*); (*workers*) увольня́ть
(уво́лить* *perf*); **to ~ light on** пролива́ть
(проли́ть* *perf*) свет на +*acc*.
she'd [ʃiːd] = **she had, she would**.
sheen [ʃiːn] *n* лоск.
sheep [ʃiːp] *n inv* овца́*; (*male*) бара́н.
sheepdog ['ʃiːpdɔg] *n* овча́рка*.
sheep farmer *n* овцево́д.
sheepish ['ʃiːpɪʃ] *adj* ро́бкий* (ро́бок).
sheepskin ['ʃiːpskɪn] *n* овчи́на ♦ *cpd* (*jacket,
mittens*) овчи́нный*; **~ coat** (*short*)
дублёный полушу́бок; (*long*) дублёная
шу́ба, дублёнка (*разг*).
sheer [ʃɪə*ʳ*] *adj* (*utter*) су́щий*; (*steep*)
отве́сный; (*almost transparent*) сквозно́й ♦
adv (*straight up or down*) отве́сно; **by ~ chance**

по чи́стой случа́йности.
sheet [ʃiːt] *n* (*on bed*) простыня́*; (*of paper,
metal, glass*) лист*; (*of ice*) полоса́*.
sheet feed *n* (*on printer*) автопода́ча бума́ги.
sheet lightning *n* зарни́ца.
sheet metal *n* листово́й мета́лл.
sheet music *n* но́ты *fpl*.
sheik(h) [ʃeɪk] *n* шейх.
shelf [ʃɛlf] (*pl* **shelves**) *n* по́лка*.
shelf life *n* срок го́дности.
shell [ʃɛl] *n* (*of mollusc*) ра́ковина; (*of egg, nut*)
скорлупа́; (*explosive*) снаря́д; (*of building*)
карка́с; (*of ship*) ко́рпус ♦ *vt* (*peas*) лущи́ть
(облущи́ть* *perf*); (*MIL: fire on*) обстре́ливать
(обстреля́ть* *perf*)
► **shell out** *vt* (*inf*): **to ~ out (for)** выкла́дывать
(вы́ложить* *perf*) (на +*acc*).
she'll [ʃiːl] = **she will, she shall**.
shellfish ['ʃɛlfɪʃ] *n inv* (*crab etc*) рачки́ *pl*;
(*scallop etc*) моллю́ски *mpl*.
shellsuit ['ʃɛlsuːt] *n* спорти́вный костю́м
(*капро́новый на покла́дке*).
shelter ['ʃɛltə*ʳ*] *n* (*refuge*) прию́т; (*protection*)
укры́тие; (*also:* **air-raid ~**) бомбоубе́жище ♦
vt (*protect*) укрыва́ть (укры́ть* *perf*); (*give
lodging to*) дава́ть* (дать* *perf*) прию́т +*dat* ♦
vi укрыва́ться (укры́ться* *perf*); **to take ~
(from)** приюти́ться* (*perf*) (от +*gen*).
sheltered ['ʃɛltəd] *adj* (*life*) беззабо́тный;
(*spot*) защищённый (защищён).
sheltered housing *n* жили́щный ко́мплекс,
специа́льно приспосо́бленный для нужд
престаре́лых, инвали́дов *итп*.
shelve [ʃɛlv] *vt* (*fig: plan*) класть* (положи́ть*
perf) под сукно́.
shelves [ʃɛlvz] *npl of* **shelf**.
shelving ['ʃɛlvɪŋ] *n* (*shelves*) стелла́ж*.
shepherd ['ʃɛpəd] *n* пасту́х* ♦ *vt* (*guide*)
направля́ть (напра́вить* *perf*).
shepherdess ['ʃɛpədɪs] *n* пасту́шка*.
shepherd's pie *n* (*BRIT*) ≈ запека́нка* из мя́са и
карто́феля.
sherbet ['ʃəːbət] *n* щербе́т; (*US: water ice*)
фрукто́вое моро́женое *nd adj*.
sheriff ['ʃɛrɪf] *n* (*US*) шери́ф.
sherry ['ʃɛrɪ] *n* хе́рес*.
she's [ʃiːz] = **she is, she has**.
Shetland ['ʃɛtlənd] *n* (*also:* **the ~ Islands**)
Шетла́ндские острова́* *mpl*.
Shetland pony *n* шетла́ндский* по́ни *m ind*.
shield [ʃiːld] *n* (*protection, also MIL*) щит*;
(*trophy*) трофе́й* ♦ *vt*: **to ~ (from)** заслоня́ть
(заслони́ть* *perf*) (от +*gen*).
shift [ʃɪft] *n* (*in direction, conversation*)
переме́на; (*in policy, emphasis*) сдвиг; (*at
work*) сме́на ♦ *vt* передвига́ть (передви́нуть*
perf), перемеща́ть (перемести́ть* *perf*); (*stain*)
выводи́ть* (вы́вести* *perf*) ♦ *vi* перемеща́ться

---

* marks translations which have irregular inflections. The Russian-English side of the dictionary gives inflectional information.

(перемести́ться* *perf*); **a ~ in demand** измене́ние в спро́се; **the wind has ~ed to the south** ве́тер перемени́лся к ю́гу.
shift key *n* реги́стровая кла́виша.
shiftless ['ʃɪftlɪs] *adj* (*person*) безде́йственный.
shiftwork ['ʃɪftwə:k] *n* сме́нная рабо́та; **to do ~** рабо́тать (*impf*) посме́нно.
shifty ['ʃɪftɪ] *adj* (*person*) увёртливый (увёртлив); (*eyes*) бе́гающий.
Shiite ['ʃi:aɪt] *n* шии́т ♦ *adj* шии́тский.
shilling ['ʃɪlɪŋ] *n* (*BRIT*) ши́ллинг.
shillyshally ['ʃɪlɪʃælɪ] *vi* тяну́ть* (*impf*).
shimmer ['ʃɪmə'] *vi* мерца́ть (*impf*).
shimmering ['ʃɪmərɪŋ] *adj* мерца́ющий; (*satin etc*) перелива́ющийся.
shin [ʃɪn] *n* го́лень *f* ♦ *vi*: **to ~ up a tree** влеза́ть (влезть* *perf*) на де́рево; **to ~ down a tree** слеза́ть (слезть* *perf*) с де́рева.
shindig ['ʃɪndɪg] *n* (*inf*) сабанту́й.
shine [ʃaɪn] (*pt, pp* **shone**) *n* блеск ♦ *vi* (*sun, light*) свети́ть* (*impf*); (*eyes, hair*) блесте́ть* (*impf*); (*fig: person*) сия́ть (*impf*), свети́ться* (*impf*) ♦ *vt* (*polish*) (*pt, pp* **shined**) натира́ть (натере́ть* *perf*); **to ~ a torch on sth** свети́ть* (посвети́ть* *perf*) фонарём на что-н.
shingle ['ʃɪŋgl] *n* (*on beach*) га́лька; (*on roof*) кро́вельная дра́нка.
shingles ['ʃɪŋglz] *n* опоя́сывающий лиша́й*.
shining ['ʃaɪnɪŋ] *adj* блестя́щий*.
shiny ['ʃaɪnɪ] *adj* блестя́щий*.
ship [ʃɪp] *n* кора́бль* *m* ♦ *vt* (*transport*) перевози́ть* (перевезти́* *perf*) по мо́рю; (*send*) экспеди́ровать (*impf/perf*); (*water*) забира́ть (забра́ть* *perf*); **on board ~** на борту́ корабля́.
shipbuilder ['ʃɪpbɪldə'] *n* кораблестрои́тель *m*, судострои́тель *m*.
shipbuilding ['ʃɪpbɪldɪŋ] *n* кораблестрое́ние, судострое́ние.
ship canal *n* судохо́дный кана́л.
ship chandler [-'tʃɑ:ndlə'] *n* поставщи́к корабе́льного обору́дования.
shipment ['ʃɪpmənt] *n* (*goods*) па́ртия.
shipowner ['ʃɪpəunə'] *n* судовладе́лец*.
shipper ['ʃɪpə'] *n* отправи́тель *m*.
shipping ['ʃɪpɪŋ] *n* (*transport of cargo*) перево́зка; (*ships*) судохо́дство.
shipping agent *n* экспеди́тор.
shipping company *n* судохо́дная компа́ния.
shipping lane *n* морска́я тра́сса.
shipping line *n* = **shipping company**.
shipshape ['ʃɪpʃeɪp] *adj* (*house, boat etc*) ла́дный.
ship's manifest *n* деклара́ция судово́го гру́за.
shipwreck ['ʃɪprɛk] *n* (*event*) корабле-круше́ние; (*ship*) потерпе́вшее круше́ние су́дно ♦ *vt*: **to be ~ed** терпе́ть (потерпе́ть* *perf*) кораблекруше́ние.
shipyard ['ʃɪpjɑ:d] *n* (судострои́тельная) верфь *f*.

shire ['ʃaɪə'] *n* (*BRIT*) гра́фство.
shirk [ʃə:k] *vt* уви́ливать (увильну́ть *perf*) от +*gen*.
shirt [ʃə:t] *n* (*man's*) руба́шка*; (*woman's*) блу́зка*; **in (one's) ~ sleeves** в одно́й руба́шке.
shirty ['ʃə:tɪ] *adj* (*BRIT: inf: person*) наду́тый (наду́т).
shit [ʃɪt] *excl* (*inf!*) чёрт.
shiver ['ʃɪvə'] *n* дрожь *f* ♦ *vi* дрожа́ть (*impf*).
shoal [ʃəul] *n* (*of fish*) кося́к*; (*fig: also: ~s*) то́лпы *fpl*.
shock [ʃɔk] *n* (*start, impact*) толчо́к*; (*ELEC, MED*) шок; (*emotional*) потрясе́ние ♦ *vt* (*upset*) потряса́ть (потрясти́* *perf*); (*offend*) возмуща́ть (возмути́ть* *perf*), шоки́ровать (*impf/perf*); **to be suffering from ~** (*MED*) находи́ться* (*impf*) в состоя́нии шо́ка; **the news gave us a ~** э́та но́вость нас потрясла́; **it came as a ~ to hear that ...** мы бы́ли потрясены́, когда́ услы́шали, что ....
shock absorber *n* амортиза́тор.
shocker ['ʃɔkə'] *n* (*inf: film*) ужа́сник; (*: news*) ужаса́ющая но́вость *f*.
shocking ['ʃɔkɪŋ] *adj* (*outrageous*) возмути́тельный* (возмути́телен); (*dreadful*) кошма́рный* (кошма́рен).
shockproof ['ʃɔkpru:f] *adj* противоуда́рный.
shock therapy *n* шокотерапи́я.
shock treatment *n* = **shock therapy**.
shock wave *n* уда́рная волна́; (*fig*) чу́вство потрясе́ния.
shod [ʃɔd] *pt, pp of* **shoe** ♦ *adj*: **well-~** хорошо́ обу́тый (обу́т).
shoddy ['ʃɔdɪ] *adj* (*goods*) дрянно́й*; (*workmanship*) куста́рный.
shoe [ʃu:] (*pt, pp* **shod**) *n* (*for person*) ту́фля*; (*for horse*) подко́ва; (*AUT: also:* **brake ~**) коло́дка ♦ *vt* (*horse*) подко́вывать (подкова́ть* *perf*); **~s** (*footwear*) о́бувь *fsg*.
shoebrush ['ʃu:brʌʃ] *n* обувна́я щётка*.
shoehorn ['ʃu:hɔ:n] *n* рожо́к* (*для о́буви*).
shoelace ['ʃu:leɪs] *n* шнуро́к*.
shoemaker ['ʃu:meɪkə'] *n* сапо́жник.
shoe polish *n* гутали́н.
shoe shop *n* обувно́й магази́н.
shoestring ['ʃu:strɪŋ] *n* (*fig*): **on a ~** на гроши́.
shoetree ['ʃu:tri:] *n* распо́рка* для о́буви.
shone [ʃɔn] *pt, pp of* **shine**.
shoo [ʃu:] *excl* вон; (*to cats*) брысь ♦ *vt* (*also: ~ away, ~ off*) отгоня́ть (отогна́ть* *perf*).
shook [ʃuk] *pt of* **shake**.
shoot [ʃu:t] (*pt, pp* **shot**) *n* (*BOT*) росто́к*, побе́г; (*SPORT: event*) охо́та; (*CINEMA*) съёмка ♦ *vt* (*gun, arrow*) стреля́ть (*impf*) из +*gen*; (*kill: bird, robber etc*) застре́ливать (застрели́ть* *perf*); (*BRIT: game*) стреля́ть (*impf*); (*wound*) вы́стрелить (*perf*) в +*acc*; (*execute*) расстре́ливать (расстреля́ть *perf*); (*film*) снима́ть (снять* *perf*) ♦ *vi*: **to ~ (at)** стреля́ть (вы́стрелить *perf*) (в +*acc*); (*FOOTBALL etc*)

бить* (*impf*) (по +*dat*); **to ~ past** (*move*) проноси́ться* (пронести́сь* *perf*); **he shot through the door** он влете́л в дверь
▸ **shoot down** *vt* (*plane*) сбива́ть (сбить* *perf*)
▸ **shoot in** *vi* (*rush in*) стремгла́в вбега́ть (вбежа́ть* *perf*)
▸ **shoot out** *vi* (*rush out*) стремгла́в выбега́ть (вы́бежать* *perf*)
▸ **shoot up** *vi* (*fig: prices*) подска́кивать (подскочи́ть* *perf*); (*child*) вытя́гиваться (вы́тянуться *perf*).

shooting [ˈʃuːtɪŋ] *n* (*shots, attack*) стрельба́; (*murder*) уби́йство; (*CINEMA*) съёмки* *fpl*; (*HUNTING*) охо́та.

shooting range *n* стре́льбище.
shooting star *n* па́дающая звезда́*.
shop [ʃɔp] *n* магази́н; (*also:* **workshop**) мастерска́я *f adj* ◆ *vi* (*also:* **go ~ping**) ходи́ть* (*impf*) по магази́нам, де́лать (*impf*) поку́пки; **repair ~** (ремо́нтная) мастерска́я; **to talk ~** (*fig*) говори́ть (*impf*) *or* разгова́ривать (*impf*) о рабо́те
▸ **shop around** *vi* (*also fig*) прице́ниваться (прицени́ться* *perf*).

shopaholic [ʃɔpəˈhɔlɪk] *n* (*inf*) челове́к, поме́шанный на магази́нах.
shop assistant *n* (*BRIT*) продаве́ц*(-вщи́ца).
shop floor *n* (*BRIT: INDUSTRY*) цех*.
shopkeeper [ˈʃɔpkiːpəˌ] *n* владе́лец*(-лица) магази́на.
shoplifter [ˈʃɔplɪftəˌ] *n* вор*(о́вка*) (*краду́щий в магази́нах*).
shoplifting [ˈʃɔplɪftɪŋ] *n* кра́жа това́ров (*из магази́нов*).
shopper [ˈʃɔpəˌ] *n* покупа́тель(ница) *m(f)*.
shopping [ˈʃɔpɪŋ] *n* (*goods*) поку́пки* *fpl*.
shopping bag *n* хозя́йственная су́мка.
shopping centre (*US* **shopping center**) *n* торго́вый центр.
shopping mall *n* (*esp US*) торго́вый центр.
shopsoiled [ˈʃɔpsɔɪld] *adj* (*goods*) лежа́лый.
shop steward *n* (*BRIT: INDUSTRY*) цехово́й ста́роста *m*.
shop window *n* (*also fig*) витри́на.
shore [ʃɔːˈ] *n* бе́рег* ◆ *vt*: **to ~ (up)** подпира́ть (подпере́ть* *perf*); **on ~** на берегу́.
shore leave *n* (*NAUT*) увольне́ние на бе́рег.
shorn [ʃɔːn] *pp of* **shear** ◆ *adj*: **~ of** (*power, protection etc*) лишённый (лишён) +*gen*.
short [ʃɔːt] *adj* (*in length, time*) коро́ткий* (ко́роток); (*in height*) невысо́кий* (невысо́к); (*curt*) ре́зкий* (ре́зок); (*insufficient*) ску́дный ◆ *n* (*also:* **~ film**) короткометра́жный фильм; **we are ~ of milk** у нас ма́ло молока́; **I'm ten pence ~** мне не хвата́ет десяти́ пе́нсов; **in ~** коро́че говоря́; **water is in ~ supply** э́тот райо́н испы́тывает нехва́тку воды́; **it is ~ for ...** э́то сокраще́ние от +*gen* ...; **a ~ time ago**

неда́вно; **in the ~ term** в настоя́щее вре́мя; **to cut ~** (*speech, visit*) сокраща́ть (сократи́ть* *perf*); **everything ~ of ...** всё, кро́ме +*gen* ...; **~ of doing** остаётся то́лько +*infin* ...; **to fall ~ of** не выполня́ть (вы́полнить *perf*); **we're running ~ of time** у нас зака́нчивается вре́мя; **to stop ~** застыва́ть (засты́ть* *perf*) на ме́сте; **to stop ~ of doing** не осме́ливаться (осме́литься *perf*) +*infin*; *see also* **shorts**.

shortage [ˈʃɔːtɪdʒ] *n*: **a ~ of** нехва́тка +*gen*, дефици́т +*gen*.
shortbread [ˈʃɔːtbrɛd] *n* ≈ песо́чное пече́нье.
short-change [ʃɔːtˈtʃeɪndʒ] *vt*: **to ~ sb** обсчи́тывать (обсчита́ть *perf*) кого́-н.
short circuit *n* коро́ткое замыка́ние.
shortcoming [ˈʃɔːtkʌmɪŋ] *n* недоста́ток*.
short(crust) pastry [ˈʃɔːt(krʌst)-] *n* (*BRIT*) песо́чное те́сто.
short cut *n* коро́ткий* путь* *m no pl*; (*fig*) эконо́мный путь*.
shorten [ˈʃɔːtn] *vt* (*clothes*) укора́чивать (укороти́ть* *perf*); (*visit*) сокраща́ть (сократи́ть* *perf*).
shortening [ˈʃɔːtnɪŋ] *n* (*CULIN*) жир*.
shortfall [ˈʃɔːtfɔːl] *n* недоста́ча*.
shorthand [ˈʃɔːthænd] *n* (*BRIT*) стеногра́фия*; (*fig*) сокраще́ние; **to take sth down in ~** стеногра́фировать (застеногра́фировать *perf*) что-л.
shorthand notebook *n* (*BRIT*) стенограф́и́ческая тетра́дь *f*.
shorthand typist *n* (*BRIT*) стенографи́ст(ка*).
short list *n* (*BRIT*) спи́сок* оконча́тельных кандида́тов.
short-lived [ˈʃɔːtˈlɪvd] *adj* кратковре́менный* (кратковре́мен), недо́лгий* (недо́лог).
shortly [ˈʃɔːtlɪ] *adv* вско́ре.
shorts [ʃɔːts] *npl*: **(a pair of) ~** шо́рты *pl*.
short-sighted [ʃɔːtˈsaɪtɪd] *adj* (*BRIT: also fig*) близору́кий* (близору́к).
short-sightedness [ʃɔːtˈsaɪtɪdnɪs] *n* близору́кость *f*.
short-staffed [ʃɔːtˈstɑːft] *adj*: **to be ~** испы́тывать (*impf*) нехва́тку персона́ла.
short story *n* расска́з.
short-tempered [ʃɔːtˈtɛmpəd] *adj* вспы́льчивый* (вспы́льчив).
short-term [ˈʃɔːtɜːm] *adj* (*effect*) кратко-вре́менный*; (*borrowing*) краткосро́чный*.
short time *n*: **to be on ~ ~** (*INDUSTRY*) быть* (*impf*) на сокращённой рабо́чей неде́ле.
short wave *n* (*RADIO*) коротково́лны* *fpl* ◆ *adj* (*RADIO*): **~~** коротково́лновый.
shot [ʃɔt] *pt, pp of* **shoot** ◆ *n* (*of gun*) вы́стрел; (*shotgun pellets*) дробь *f*; (*FOOTBALL etc*) уда́р; (*injection*) уко́л; (*PHOT*) сни́мок*; **to fire a ~ at sb/sth** вы́стрелить (*perf*) в кого́-н/что-н; **to**

---

* marks translations which have irregular inflections. The Russian-English side of the dictionary gives inflectional information.

have a ~ at sth попытáть (perf) удáчи в чём-н; **to have a ~ at doing** (try) прóбовать (попрóбовать perf) +infin; **to get ~ of sb/sth** (inf) распрости́ться* (perf) с кем-н/чем-н; **a big ~** (inf) большáя ши́шка* m/f; **a good/poor ~** (person) мéткий*/плохóй стрелóк*; **like a ~** ми́гом.

shotgun ['ʃɔtgʌn] n дробови́к*.

should [ʃud] aux vb: **I ~ go now** я дóлжен идти́ тепéрь; **he ~ be there now** сейчáс он дóлжен бы́ть там; **I ~ go if I were you** на Вáшем мéсте я бы пошёл; **I ~ like to** я бы хотéл; **~ he phone ...** éсли он позвони́т ....

shoulder ['ʃəuldə*] n (ANAT) плечó* ♦ vt (fig: responsibility, blame) принимáть (приня́ть* perf) на себя́; **to look over one's ~** смотрéть* (посмотрéть* perf) чéрез плечó; **to rub ~'s with sb** (fig) вращáться (impf) с кем-н в одни́х кругáх; **to give sb the cold ~** обходи́ться* (обойти́сь* perf) с кем-н прохлáдно.

shoulder bag n сýмка* на дли́нном ремнé.

shoulder blade n лопáтка*.

shoulder strap n бретéлька*; (on dungarees) ля́мка*; (on bag) ремéнь* m.

shouldn't ['ʃudnt] = **should not**.

shout [ʃaut] n крик ♦ vt выкри́кивать (вы́крикнуть perf) ♦ vi (also: ~ out) кричáть (impf); **to give sb a ~** кри́кнуть (perf) комý-н
▶ **shout down** vt заглушáть (заглуши́ть perf) кри́ками.

shouting ['ʃautɪŋ] n крик.

shouting match n (inf) крик, скандáл.

shove [ʃʌv] vt толкáть (impf); (inf: put): **to ~ sth in** затáлкивать (затолкáть perf) что-н, запи́хивать (запихáть or запихнýть perf) что-н ♦ n: **to give sb/sth a ~** пихáть (пихнýть perf) когó-н/что-н; **he ~d me out of the way** он отпихнýл меня́
▶ **shove off** (inf) ♦ vi отвáливать (отвали́ть* perf).

shovel ['ʃʌvl] n лопáта; (mechanical) ковш ♦ vt (snow, coal, earth) грести́* (сгрести́* perf) (лопáтой).

show [ʃəu] (pt **showed**, pp **shown**) n (of emotion) покáз; (semblance) подóбие; (exhibition) вы́ставка*; (THEAT) спектáкль m; (TV) прогрáмма, шоу nt ind; (CINEMA) сеáнс ♦ vt покáзывать (показáть* perf); (courage etc) проявля́ть (прояви́ть* perf) ♦ vi (be evident) проявля́ться (прояви́ться* perf), обнарýживаться (обнарýжиться perf); (inf: also: ~ up) явля́ться (яви́ться* perf); **to ~ sb to his seat** проводи́ть* (провести́* perf) когó-н на мéсто; **to ~ sb to the door** укáзывать (указáть* perf) комý-н на дверь; **to ~ a profit/loss** (COMM) демонстри́ровать (impf/perf) при́быль/убы́тки; **it just goes to ~ that ...** это прóсто покáзывает, что, ...; **to ask for a ~ of hands** проси́ть* (попроси́ть* perf) подня́ть рýки (при голосовáнии); **for ~** для ви́ду; **on ~** (exhibits etc) на вы́ставке; **who's running the**

~ here? (inf) кто здесь заправля́ет?
▶ **show in** vt (person) проводи́ть* (провести́* perf)
▶ **show off** vi хвáстаться (похвáстаться perf) ♦ vt (display) хвáстаться (похвáстаться perf) +instr
▶ **show out** vt (person) провожáть (проводи́ть* perf) к вы́ходу
▶ **show up** vi (stand out: against background) виднéться (impf); (: fig) обнарýживаться (обнарýжиться perf); (inf: turn up) явля́ться (яви́ться* perf) ♦ vt (uncover: imperfections etc) выявля́ть (вы́явить* perf).

showbiz ['ʃəubɪz] n (inf) = **show business**.

show business n шóу би́знес.

showcase ['ʃəukeɪs] n витри́на; (fig) показáтельный примéр.

showdown ['ʃəudaun] n: **to have a ~ (with)** раскрывáть (раскры́ть* perf) кáрты (+dat).

shower ['ʃauə*] n (also: ~ **bath**) душ; (of rain) ли́вень* m; (of stones etc) град; (us: party) звáный вéчер ♦ vi принимáть (приня́ть* perf) душ ♦ vt: **to ~ sb with** (gifts, abuse etc) осыпáть (осы́пать* perf) когó-н +instr; (missiles) забрáсывать (забросáть* perf); **to have or take a ~** принимáть (приня́ть* perf) душ.

shower cap ['ʃauəkæp] n шáпочка* (для дýша).

showerproof ['ʃauəpru:f] adj (clothing) непромокáемый.

showery ['ʃauərɪ] adj дождли́вый.

showground ['ʃəugraund] n вы́ставка* (на откры́том вóздухе).

showing ['ʃəuɪŋ] n (of film) покáз.

show jumping n конкýр.

showman ['ʃəumən] irreg n (at fair, circus) ведýщий* m adj, конферансьé m ind; (owner of circus) хозя́ин ци́рка; (fig) позёр.

showmanship ['ʃəumənʃɪp] n талáнт.

shown [ʃəun] pp of **show**.

show-off ['ʃəuɔf] n (inf) хвастýн(ья).

showpiece ['ʃəupi:s] n (of exhibition etc) центрáльный экспонáт; **this is a ~ of ...** это явля́ется блестя́щим образóм +gen ....

showroom ['ʃəurum] n демонстрациóнный зал.

show trial n показáтельный процéсс.

showy ['ʃəuɪ] adj брóский*.

shrank [ʃræŋk] pt of **shrink**.

shrapnel ['ʃræpnl] n шрапнéль f.

shred [ʃrɛd] n (usu pl) клочóк*; (fig: of truth, evidence) крупи́ца ♦ vt кроши́ть* (накроши́ть* perf); (CULIN) шинковáть (нашинковáть perf).

shredder ['ʃrɛdə*] n (also: **vegetable ~**) шинкóвка; (also: **document ~**) маши́на для дезинтегрáции докумéнтов.

shrew [ʃru:] n (ZOOL) землерóйка*; (pej: woman) змея́.

shrewd [ʃru:d] adj проницáтельный* (проницáтелен).

shrewdness ['ʃru:dnɪs] *n* проница́тельность *f*.
shriek [ʃri:k] *n* визг ♦ *vi* визжа́ть* (*impf*).
shrift [ʃrɪft] *n*: **to give sb short** ~ бы́стро отде́лываться (отде́латься *perf*) от кого́-н.
shrill [ʃrɪl] *adj* визгли́вый (визгли́в).
shrimp [ʃrɪmp] *n* (ме́лкая) креве́тка*.
shrimping ['ʃrɪmpɪŋ] *n* ло́вля креве́ток.
shrine [ʃraɪn] *n* (*tomb*) ра́ка; (*place of worship, also fig*) святы́ня.
shrink [ʃrɪŋk] (*pt* **shrank**, *pp* **shrunk**) *vi* (*cloth*) сади́ться* (сесть* *perf*); (*profits, audiences*) сокраща́ться (сократи́ться* *perf*); (*also:* ~ **away**) отпря́нуть (*perf*) ♦ *vt*: **washing will** ~ **the dress** от сти́рки пла́тье сади́тся ♦ *n* (*inf: psychiatrist*) психиа́тр; **to** ~ **from sth** ускольза́ть (ускользну́ть *perf*) от +*gen*.
shrinkage ['ʃrɪŋkɪdʒ] *n* уса́дка.
shrink-wrap ['ʃrɪŋkræp] *vt* (*goods etc*) упако́вывать (упакова́ть *perf*) в уса́дочную плёнку.
shrivel ['ʃrɪvl] (*also:* ~ **up**) *vt* высу́шивать (вы́сушить *perf*) ♦ *vi* высыха́ть (вы́сохнуть *perf*).
shroud [ʃraud] *n* са́ван ♦ *vt*: ~**ed in mystery** оку́танный (оку́тан) в та́йну.
Shrove Tuesday ['ʃrəuv-] *n вто́рник на ма́сленой неде́ле*.
shrub [ʃrʌb] *n* куст*.
shrubbery ['ʃrʌbərɪ] *n* куста́рник.
shrug [ʃrʌg] *n* пожима́ние (*плеча́ми*) ♦ *vi*: **to** ~ (**one's shoulders**) пожима́ть (пожа́ть* *perf*) плеча́ми
▸ **shrug off** *vt* отма́хиваться (отмахну́ться *perf*) от +*gen*.
shrunk [ʃrʌŋk] *pp of* **shrink**.
shrunken ['ʃrʌŋkn] *adj* (*material*) се́вший; (*person, figure*) съёженный.
shudder ['ʃʌdə'] *n* дрожь *f* ♦ *vi* содрога́ться (содрогну́ться *perf*).
shuffle ['ʃʌfl] *vt* тасова́ть (стасова́ть *perf*) ♦ *vi*: **to** ~ (**one's feet**) волочи́ть (*impf*) но́ги.
shun [ʃʌn] *vt* избега́ть (*impf*) +*gen*.
shunt [ʃʌnt] *vt* (*train*) переводи́ть* (перевести́* *perf*) на друго́й путь ♦ *vi* (*RAIL*): **to** ~ (**to and fro**) маневри́ровать (*impf*/*perf*).
shunting yard ['ʃʌntɪŋ-] *n* сортиро́вочная ста́нция.
shush [ʃuʃ] *excl* ш-ш.
shut [ʃʌt] (*pt, pp* **shut**) *vt* закрыва́ть (закры́ть* *perf*) ♦ *vi* закрыва́ться (закры́ться* *perf*)
▸ **shut down** *vt* закрыва́ть (закры́ть* *perf*); (*machine*) отключа́ть (отключи́ть* *perf*) ♦ *vi* закрыва́ться (закры́ться* *perf*); (*machine*) отключа́ться (отключи́ться *perf*)
▸ **shut off** *vt* (*supply etc*) отключа́ть (отключи́ть *perf*)
▸ **shut out** *vt* (*person, cold, noise*) не пропуска́ть (проупсти́ть* *perf*); (*view,*

memory) заслоня́ть (заслони́ть *perf*)
▸ **shut up** *vi* (*inf: keep quiet*) заткну́ться (*perf*) ♦ *vt* (*close*) запира́ть (запере́ть* *perf*); (*silence*) затыка́ть (заткну́ть *perf*) рот +*dat*; ~ **up!** закни́сь!
shutdown ['ʃʌtdaun] *n* (*temporary*) приостановле́ние; (*permanent*) закры́тие.
shutter ['ʃʌtə'] *n* (*on window*) ста́вень *m*; (*PHOT*) затво́р.
shuttle ['ʃʌtl] *n*: ~ **plane** самолёт-челно́к; (*also:* **space** ~) челно́к; (*also:* ~ **service**) челно́чный маршру́т; (*for weaving*) челно́к ♦ *vi*: **to** ~ **between** соверша́ть (*impf*) челно́чные ре́йсы ме́жду +*instr* ♦ *vt* (*passengers*) вози́ть* (*impf*) туда́ и обра́тно.
shuttlecock ['ʃʌtlkɒk] *n* (*SPORT*) вола́н.
shuttle diplomacy *n* челно́чная диплома́тия.
shy [ʃaɪ] *adj* (*timid*) засте́нчивый (засте́нчив), стесни́тельный* (стесни́телен); (*reserved*) осторо́жный* (осторо́жен) ♦ *vi*: **to** ~ **away from doing** (*fig*) чужда́ться (*impf*) +*infin*; **to fight** ~ **of** избега́ть (*impf*) +*gen*; **to be** ~ **of doing** стесня́ться (постесня́ться *perf*) +*infin*.
shyly ['ʃaɪlɪ] *adv* засте́нчиво.
shyness ['ʃaɪnɪs] *n* (*see adj*) засте́нчивость *f*, стесни́тельность *f*; осторо́жность *f*.
Siamese [saɪə'mi:z] *adj*: ~ **cat** сиа́мская ко́шка*; ~ **twins** сиа́мские близнецы́ *mpl*.
Siberia [saɪ'bɪərɪə] *n* Сиби́рь *f*.
sibling ['sɪblɪŋ] *n* (*brother*) родно́й брат; (*sister*) родна́я сестра́.
Sicilian [sɪ'sɪlɪən] *adj* сицили́йский ♦ *n* сицили́ец*(-и́йка*).
Sicily ['sɪsɪlɪ] *n* Сици́лия.
sick [sɪk] *adj* (*ill*) больно́й* (бо́лен); (*humour*) пога́ный, скве́рный* (скве́рен); (*vomiting*): **he is/was** ~ его́ рвёт/вы́рвало; (*nauseated*): **I feel** ~ меня́ тошни́т; **to fall** ~ заболева́ть (заболе́ть *perf*); **to be** (**off**) ~ быть* (*impf*) на больни́чном; **a** ~ **person** больно́й челове́к*; **to be** ~ **of** (*of war etc*) смерте́льно уста́ть* (*perf*) от +*gen*; **I'm** ~ **of arguing/school** меня́ тошни́т от спо́ров/шко́лы.
sickbag ['sɪkbæg] *n* (*on airplane*) санита́рный паке́т.
sickbay ['sɪkbeɪ] *n* изоля́тор.
sickbed ['sɪkbɛd] *n* посте́ль *f* больно́го.
sick building *n помеще́ние с нездоро́вым микрокли́матом.*
sicken ['sɪkn] *vt* (*disgust*) вызыва́ть (вы́звать* *perf*) отвраще́ние у +*gen* ♦ *vi*: **to be** ~**ing for sth** заболева́ть (*impf*) чем-н.
sickening ['sɪknɪŋ] *adj* (*fig*) проти́вный (проти́вен).
sickle ['sɪkl] *n* серп*.
sick leave *n* о́тпуск по боле́зни.
sick list *n*: **to be on the** ~ ~ быть* (*impf*) на бюллете́не *or* больни́чном.

---

sickly ['sıklı] *adj* (*child, plant*) хи́лый* (хил);
(*smell*) тошнотво́рный* (тошнотво́рен).
sickness ['sıknıs] *n* (*illness*) боле́знь *f*;
(*vomiting*) рво́та.
sickness benefit *n* посо́бие по боле́зни.
sick note *n* бюллете́нь *m*, больни́чный лист*.
sick pay *n* опла́та по бюллете́ню *or*
больни́чному листу́.
sickroom ['sıkru:m] *n* ко́мната больно́го.
side [saıd] *n* сторона́*; (*of body*) бок*; (*of paper*)
страни́ца; (*team*) кома́нда; (*of hill*) склон ♦
adj (*door etc*) боково́й ♦ *vi*: **to ~ with sb**
встава́ть* (встать* *perf*) на сто́рону кого́-н;
by the ~ of у +*gen*; **by her ~** во́зле неё; **~ by ~**
(*to walk*) ря́дом; (*to work*) бок о́ бок; **the right**
~ (*of material*) лицо́; **the wrong ~** (*of material*)
изна́нка; **we're on the wrong ~ of the road/**
river мы не на той стороне́ доро́ги/реки́;
they are on our ~ они́ на на́шей стороне́;
from ~ to ~ с бо́ку на́ бок; **from all ~s** со всех
сторо́н; **to take ~s (with sb)** принима́ть
(приня́ть* *perf*) (чью-н) сто́рону; **a ~ of beef**
полови́на говя́жьей ту́ши.
sideboard ['saıdbɔ:d] *n* буфе́т; **~s** *npl* (*BRIT*) =
sideburns.
sideburns ['saıdbɜ:nz] *npl* бакенба́рды *pl*.
sidecar ['saıdkɑ:'] *n* (*AUT*) коля́ска*
(*мотоци́кла*).
side dish *n* гарни́р.
side drum *n* ма́лый бараба́н.
side effect *n* побо́чное де́йствие.
sidekick ['saıdkık] *n* (*inf*) подру́чный *m adj*.
sidelight ['saıdlaıt] *n* (*AUT*) боково́е
освеще́ние.
sideline ['saıdlaın] *n* (*SPORT*) бокова́я ли́ния;
(*fig: supplementary job*) побо́чная рабо́та; **to**
stand on the ~s стоя́ть* (*impf*) в стороне́.
sidelong ['saıdlɒŋ] *adj* косо́й; **to give sb a ~**
glance смотре́ть* (посмотре́ть* *perf*) на
кого́-н и́скоса.
side plate *n* десе́ртная таре́лка.
side road *n* просёлочная доро́га.
side-saddle ['saıdsædl] *adv*: **to ride ~** е́хать*
(*impf*) в да́мском седле́.
sideshow ['saıdʃəu] *n* аттракцио́н.
sidestep ['saıdstep] *vt* (*fig*) обходи́ть* (обойти́*
perf) ♦ *vi* отступа́ть (отступи́ть* *perf*).
side street *n* переу́лок*.
sidetrack ['saıdtræk] *vt* уводи́ть* (увести́* *perf*)
в сто́рону.
sidewalk ['saıdwɔ:k] *n* (*US*) тротуа́р.
sideways ['saıdweız] *adv* (*go in, lean*) бо́ком;
(*look*) и́скоса.
siding ['saıdıŋ] *n* (*RAIL*) запасно́й путь* *m*.
sidle ['saıdl] *vi*: **to ~ up (to)** подходи́ть*
(подойти́* *perf*) бочко́м (к +*dat*).
SIDS *n abbr* (*MED*: = *sudden infant death*
syndrome) синдро́м внеза́пной сме́рти
вне́шне здоро́вого младе́нца.
siege [si:dʒ] *n* оса́да; **to be under ~** быть* (*impf*)
в оса́де; **to lay ~ to** осажда́ть (осади́ть* *perf*).

siege economy *n* засто́йная эконо́мика.
siege mentality *n* психоло́гия люде́й в
оса́дном положе́нии.
Sierra Leone [sı'ɛrəlı'əun] *n* Сье́рра-Лео́не.
siesta [sı'ɛstə] *n* сие́ста.
sieve [sıv] *n* (*CULIN*) си́то*; (*for garden*) решето́*
♦ *vt* просе́ивать (просе́ять *perf*).
sift [sıft] *vt* (*flour, sand*) просе́ивать (просе́ять
perf); (*also*: **~ through**: *evidence etc*)
просе́ивать (просе́ять *perf*).
sigh [saı] *n* вздох ♦ *vi* вздыха́ть (вздохну́ть
perf).
sight [saıt] *n* (*faculty*) зре́ние; (*spectacle*) вид;
(*on gun*) прице́л ♦ *vt* замеча́ть (заме́тить*
perf); **in ~** в по́ле зре́ния; **out of ~** из ви́ду; **at**
~ (*COMM*) по предъявле́нию; **at first ~** с
пе́рвого взгля́да; **I know her by ~** я зна́ю её в
лицо́; **to catch ~ of** замеча́ть (заме́тить* *perf*);
to lose ~ of sb/sth теря́ть (потеря́ть* *perf*)
кого́-н/что-н из ви́ду; **to set one's ~s on sth**
положи́ть* (*perf*) глаз на что-н; **to shoot sb on**
~ стреля́ть (*impf*) в кого́-н на ме́сте.
sighted ['saıtıd] *adj* (*person*) зря́чий* (зряч);
partially ~ слабови́дящий.
sightseeing ['saıtsi:ıŋ] *n* осмо́тр достопри-
меча́тельностей; **to go ~** осма́тривать
(осмотре́ть* *perf*) достопримеча́тельности.
sightseer ['saıtsi:ə'] *n* тури́ст(ка*).
sign [saın] *n* (*notice*) вы́веска*; (*with hand*)
знак; (*indication, evidence*) при́знак; (*also*:
road ~) доро́жный знак ♦ *vt* (*document*)
подпи́сывать (подписа́ть* *perf*); (*player*)
нанима́ть (наня́ть* *perf*); **as a ~ of** в знак
+*gen*; **it's a good/bad ~** э́то хоро́ший/плохо́й
знак; **plus/minus ~** знак "плюс"/"ми́нус";
there's no ~ of her changing her mind нет
никаки́х при́знаков того́, что она́
переду́мала; **he is showing ~s of**
improvement у него́ видны́ при́знаки
улучше́ния; **to ~ one's name** распи́сываться
(расписа́ться* *perf*); **to ~ sth over to sb**
передава́ть* (переда́ть* *perf*) что-н в дар
кому́-н
▶ **sign away** *vt* (*rights etc*) передава́ть*
(переда́ть* *perf*)
▶ **sign in** *vi* регистри́роваться
(зарегистри́роваться *perf*)
▶ **sign off** *vi* зака́нчивать (зако́нчить *perf*)
▶ **sign on** *vi* (*MIL*) нанима́ться (наня́ться* *perf*);
(*BRIT*: *as unemployed*) отмеча́ться
(отме́титься* *perf*) как безрабо́тный; (*for*
course) регистри́роваться
(зарегистри́роваться *perf*) ♦ *vt* (*MIL*: *recruits*)
набира́ть (набра́ть* *perf*); (*employee*)
нанима́ть (наня́ть* *perf*)
▶ **sign out** *vi* выпи́сываться (вы́писаться* *perf*)
▶ **sign up** *vi* (*MIL*) нанима́ться (наня́ться* *perf*);
(*for course*) регистри́роваться
(зарегистри́роваться *perf*) ♦ *vt* (*player, recruit*)
нанима́ть (наня́ть* *perf*).
signal ['sıgnl] *n* сигна́л ♦ *vi* сигнализи́ровать

(impf/perf) ♦ *vt* (*person*) подавать* (подать* *perf*) знак +*dat*; (*message*) передавать* (передать* *perf*); **to ~ a right/left turn** (*AUT*) давать* (дать* *perf*) сигнал правого/левого поворота; **to ~ to sb (to do)** подавать* (подать* *perf*) знак кому-н (+*infin*).

signal box *n* сигнальная будка*.

signalman [ˈsɪɡnlmən] *irreg n* стрелочник.

signatory [ˈsɪɡnətərɪ] *n* подписавшая сторона*.

signature [ˈsɪɡnətʃəʳ] *n* подпись *f*.

signature tune *n* музыкальная шапка*.

signet ring [ˈsɪɡnət-] *n* кольцо* с печаткой.

significance [sɪɡˈnɪfɪkəns] *n* значение; **that is of no ~** это не имеет значения.

significant [sɪɡˈnɪfɪkənt] *adj* (*amount, discovery etc*) значительный* (значителен); (*look, smile*) многозначительный* (многозначителен); **it is ~ that** ... важно, что ....

significantly [sɪɡˈnɪfɪkəntlɪ] *adv* (*see adj*) значительно; многозначительно.

signify [ˈsɪɡnɪfaɪ] *vt* (*subj: sign, gesture etc*) означать (*impf*); (: *person*) выражать (выразить* *perf*).

sign language *n* язык* знаков.

sign post *n* (*also fig*) указатель *m*.

Sikh [siːk] *n* сикх ♦ *adj* сикхский.

silage [ˈsaɪlɪdʒ] *n* (*fodder*) силос; (*method*) силосование.

silence [ˈsaɪləns] *n* тишина ♦ *vt* заставлять (заставить* *perf*) замолчать.

silencer [ˈsaɪlənsəʳ] *n* (*BRIT*) глушитель *m*.

silent [ˈsaɪlənt] *adj* (*place, person, prayer*) безмолвный* (безмолвен); (*machine*) бесшумный* (бесшумен); (*taciturn*) молчаливый (молчалив); (*film*) немой; **to remain ~** молчать* (*impf*).

silently [ˈsaɪləntlɪ] *adv* молча.

silent partner *n* (*COMM*) пассивный партнёр.

silhouette [sɪluːˈɛt] *n* силуэт ♦ *vt*: **to be ~d against** вырисовываться (*impf*) на фоне +*gen*.

silicon [ˈsɪlɪkən] *n* кремний.

silicon chip *n* кремниевый кристалл, кремниевая микропластинка.

silicone [ˈsɪlɪkəun] *n* силокон.

Silicon Valley *n* зона скопления предприятий, занимающихся выпуском вычислительной техники.

silk [sɪlk] *n* шёлк* ♦ *adj* шёлковый.

silky [ˈsɪlkɪ] *adj* шелковистый (шелковист).

sill [sɪl] *n* (*also*: **window ~**) подоконник; (*of door*) порог; (*AUT*) карниз.

silly [ˈsɪlɪ] *adj* глупый* (глуп); **to do something ~** делать (сделать *perf*) глупость.

silo [ˈsaɪləu] *n* (*on farm*) силосная башня*; (*for missile*) стартовая шахта.

silt [sɪlt] *n* ил

▸ **silt up** *vi* заиливаться (заилиться* *perf*) ♦ *vt* засорять (засорить *perf*).

silver [ˈsɪlvəʳ] *n* серебро ♦ *adj* серебряный.

silver foil *n* (*BRIT*) = **silver paper**.

silver paper *n* (*BRIT*) фольга.

silver-plated [sɪlvəˈpleɪtɪd] *adj* серебрёный.

silversmith [ˈsɪlvəsmɪθ] *n* серебряных дел мастер.

silverware [ˈsɪlvəwɛəʳ] *n* серебро.

silver wedding (anniversary) *n* серебряная свадьба*.

silvery [ˈsɪlvrɪ] *adj* серебристый (серебрист); (*sound*) серебристый, серебряный.

similar [ˈsɪmɪləʳ] *adj*: **~ (to)** сходный* (сходен) (с +*instr*), подобный* (подобен) (+*dat*).

similarity [sɪmɪˈlærɪtɪ] *n* сходство.

similarly [ˈsɪmɪləlɪ] *adv* (*in a similar way*) подобным образом; (*likewise*) таким же образом.

simile [ˈsɪmɪlɪ] *n* сравнение.

simmer [ˈsɪməʳ] *vi* (*CULIN*) кипеть* (*impf*) на медленном огне

▸ **simmer down** *vi* (*fig: inf*) остывать (остыть* *perf*).

simper [ˈsɪmpəʳ] *vi* жеманничать (*impf*).

simpering [ˈsɪmprɪŋ] *adj* (*person, smile*) жеманный* (жеманен).

simple [ˈsɪmpl] *adj* (*easy, plain*) простой* (прост); (*foolish*) недалёкий* (недалёк); **the ~ truth** очевидная истина.

simple interest *n* простые проценты *mpl*.

simple-minded [sɪmplˈmaɪndɪd] *adj* простодушный* (простодушен).

simpleton [ˈsɪmpltən] *n* простак.

simplicity [sɪmˈplɪsɪtɪ] *n* (*see adj*) простота; недалёкость *f*.

simplification [sɪmplɪfɪˈkeɪʃən] *n* упрощение.

simplify [ˈsɪmplɪfaɪ] *vt* упрощать (упростить* *perf*).

simply [ˈsɪmplɪ] *adv* просто.

simulate [ˈsɪmjuleɪt] *vt* (*enthusiasm*) симулировать (*impf/perf*); (*innocence*) изображать (изобразить* *perf*).

simulated [ˈsɪmjuleɪtɪd] *adj* (*hair, fur*) поддельный; (*nuclear explosion*) имитированный.

simulation [sɪmjuˈleɪʃən] *n* притворство.

simultaneous [sɪməlˈteɪnɪəs] *adj* одновременный.

simultaneously [sɪməlˈteɪnɪəslɪ] *adv* одновременно.

sin [sɪn] *n* грех* ♦ *vi* грешить (согрешить *perf*).

Sinai [ˈsaɪneɪaɪ] *n* Синайский полуостров.

since [sɪns] *adv* с тех пор ♦ *conj* (*time*) с тех пор, как; (*because*) так как ♦ *prep*: **~ July** с июля; **~ then, ever ~** с тех пор; **it's two weeks ~ I wrote** уже две недели с тех пор, как я написал; **~ our last meeting** со времени

---

* marks translations which have irregular inflections. The Russian-English side of the dictionary gives inflectional information.

нашей после́дней встре́чи.

sincere [sɪn'sɪə^r] *adj* и́скренний* (и́скренен).

sincerely [sɪn'sɪəlɪ] *adv* и́скренне; **Yours ~** и́скренне Ваш.

sincerity [sɪn'sɛrɪtɪ] *n* и́скренность *f*.

sine [saɪn] *n* (*MATH*) си́нус.

sine qua non [sɪnɪkwɑ:'nɔn] *n* необходи́мое усло́вие.

sinew ['sɪnju:] *n* сухожи́лие.

sinful ['sɪnful] *adj* гре́шный* (гре́шен).

sing [sɪŋ] (*pt* **sang**, *pp* **sung**) *vti* петь* (спеть* *perf*).

Singapore [sɪŋɡə'pɔ:^r] *n* Сингапу́р.

singe [sɪndʒ] *vt* пали́ть (опали́ть *perf*); (*clothes*) подпа́ливать (подпали́ть *perf*).

singer ['sɪŋə^r] *n* певе́ц*(-ви́ца).

Singhalese [sɪŋə'li:z] *adj* = **Sinhalese**.

singing ['sɪŋɪŋ] *n* пе́ние; (*in the ears*) звон.

single ['sɪŋɡl] *adj* (*individual*) одино́кий*; (*man*) холосто́й* (хо́лост); (*woman*) незаму́жняя; (*not double*) одина́рный* (одина́рен) ◆ *n* (*BRIT: also:* ~ **ticket**) биле́т в оди́н коне́ц; (*record*) сорокопя́тка*; **not a ~ one was left** ни одного́ не оста́лось; **every ~ day** ка́ждый бо́жий день; ~ **spacing** одина́рное расстоя́ние

▶ **single out** *vt* (*choose*) отбира́ть (отобра́ть* *perf*); (*distinguish*) выделя́ть (вы́делить *perf*).

single bed *n* односпа́льная крова́ть *f*.

single-breasted ['sɪŋɡlbrɛstɪd] *adj* однобо́ртный.

Single European Market *n*: **the ~ ~ ~** Еди́ный европе́йский ры́нок*.

single file *n*: **in ~ ~** в коло́нку.

single-handed [sɪŋɡl'hændɪd] *adv* без посторо́нней по́мощи.

single-minded [sɪŋɡl'maɪndɪd] *adj* целеустремлённый* (целеустремлён).

single parent *n* (*mother*) мать-одино́чка*; (*father*) оте́ц-одино́чка*.

single room *n* ко́мната на одного́.

singles ['sɪŋɡlz] *n* (*TENNIS*) оди́н на оди́н ◆ *npl* (*single people*) несеме́йные *pl adj*.

singles bar *n* бар для несеме́йных.

single-sex [sɪŋɡl'sɛks] *adj* разде́льный.

singly ['sɪŋɡlɪ] *adv* (*alone, one by one*) врозь, в отде́льности.

singsong ['sɪŋsɔŋ] *adj* (*tone*) моното́нно иду́щий то вверх, то вниз ◆ *n*: **to have a ~** попе́ть* (*perf*) хо́ром.

singular ['sɪŋɡjulə^r] *adj* необыча́йный* (необыча́ен); (*LING*) еди́нственный ◆ *n* (*LING*) еди́нственное число́; **in the feminine ~** же́нского ро́да еди́нственного число́.

singularly ['sɪŋɡjuləlɪ] *adv* необыча́йно.

Sinhalese [sɪnhə'li:z] *adj* сингáльский ◆ *n inv* сингáлец*(-ка*); (*LING*) сингáльский язы́к*.

sinister ['sɪnɪstə^r] *adj* злове́щий* (злове́щ).

sink [sɪŋk] (*pt* **sank**, *pp* **sunk**) *n* ра́ковина ◆ *vt* (*ship*) топи́ть* (потопи́ть* *perf*); (*well*) рыть* (вы́рыть* *perf*); (*foundations*) врыва́ть

(врыть* *perf*) ◆ *vi* (*ship*) тону́ть* (потону́ть* *perf*); (*heart, spirits*) па́дать (упа́сть* *perf*); (*ground*) оседа́ть (осе́сть* *perf*); (*also:* ~ **back**, ~ **down**) отки́дываться (отки́нуться *perf*); **to ~ sth into** (*teeth, claws etc*) вонза́ть (вонзи́ть* *perf*) что-н в +*acc*; **he sank into a chair/the mud** он опусти́лся на стул/провали́лся в грязь

▶ **sink in** *vi* (*fig*): **it took a long time for her words to ~ in** потре́бовалось до́лгое вре́мя что́бы до меня́ дошли́ её слова́.

sinking ['sɪŋkɪŋ] *adj* (*sun*) опуска́ющийся; (*ship*) то́нущий; **I had a ~ feeling** у меня́ всё внутри́ опусти́лось.

sinking fund *n* (*COMM*) фонд погаше́ния.

sink unit *n* комбини́рованная *or* встро́енная ра́ковина.

sinner ['sɪnə^r] *n* гре́шник(-ица).

Sinn Féin *n* Шинн Фейн (*ирлáндская полити́ческая пáртия*).

Sino- ['saɪnəu] *prefix* сино-, китае-.

sinuous ['sɪnjuəs] *adj* извива́ющийся.

sinus ['saɪnəs] *n* па́зуха.

SIPS *n abbr* (= *side impact protection system*) *систе́ма защи́ты автомоби́ля от боковы́х уда́ров.*

sip [sɪp] *n* ма́ленький* глото́к* ◆ *vt* пить* (вы́пить* *perf*) ма́ленькими глотка́ми.

siphon ['saɪfən] *n* сифо́н

▶ **siphon off** *vt* выка́чивать (вы́качать *perf*).

sir [sə^r] *n* сэр, господи́н; **S~ John Smith** Сэр Джон Смит; **yes ~** да, сэр; **Dear S~** (*in letter*) Уважа́емый господи́н.

siren ['saɪərn] *n* сире́на.

sirloin ['sə:lɔɪn] *n* (*also:* ~ **steak**) говя́жье филе́ *nt ind*.

sirocco [sɪ'rɔkəu] *n* сиро́кко *m ind*.

sisal ['saɪsəl] *n* сиза́ль *m*.

sissy ['sɪsɪ] *n* (*inf*) не́женка* *m/f*.

sister ['sɪstə^r] *n* (*also REL*) сестра́*; (*BRIT: MED*) (медици́нская *or* мед-) сестра́* ◆ *cpd*: ~ **organization** паралле́льная организа́ция; ~ **ship** одноти́пное су́дно*.

sister-in-law ['sɪstərɪnlɔ:] *n* (*brother's wife*) неве́стка*; (*husband's sister*) золо́вка*; (*wife's sister*) своя́ченица.

sit [sɪt] (*pt, pp* **sat**) *vi* (*sit down*) сади́ться* (сесть* *perf*); (*be sitting*) сиде́ть* (*impf*); (*assembly*) заседа́ть (*impf*); (*for painter*) пози́ровать (*impf*) ◆ *vt* (*exam*) сдава́ть* (сдать* *perf*); **to ~ on a committee** входи́ть* (*impf*) в комите́т; **to ~ tight** не принима́ть (*impf*) никаки́х де́йствий

▶ **sit about** *vi* сиде́ть* (*impf*)

▶ **sit around** *vi* = **sit about**

▶ **sit back** *vi* (*in seat*) сиде́ть* (*impf*)

▶ **sit down** *vi* сади́ться* (сесть* *perf*); **to be ~ting down** сиде́ть* (*impf*)

▶ **sit in on** *vt fus* (*meeting*) прису́тствовать (*impf*) в/на +*prp*

▶ **sit up** *vi* (*after lying*) приподнима́ться (приподня́ться* *perf*); (*straight*)

выпрямля́ться (вы́прямиться* *perf*); (*not go to bed*) заси́живаться (засиде́ться* *perf*).
sitcom ['sɪtkɔm] *n abbr* (*TV*) = **situation comedy**.
sit-down ['sɪtdaun] *adj*: **a ~ strike** сидя́чая забасто́вка*; **a ~ meal** приём пи́щи, си́дя.
site [saɪt] *n* (*place*) ме́сто*; (*also*: **building ~**) строи́тельная площа́дка* ♦ *vt* (*factory, missiles*) помеща́ть (помести́ть* *perf*).
sit-in ['sɪtɪn] *n* демонстрати́вное заня́тие помеще́ния.
siting ['saɪtɪŋ] *n* (*location*) расположе́ние.
sitter ['sɪtəʳ] *n* (*for painter*) нату́рщик(-ица); (*also*: **baby-~**) приходя́щая ня́ня.
sitting ['sɪtɪŋ] *n* (*of assembly etc*) заседа́ние; (*in canteen*) сме́на.
sitting member *n* (*POL*) де́йствующий* депута́т парла́мента.
sitting room *n* гости́ная *f adj*.
sitting tenant *n* (*BRIT*) квартиросъёмщик (-ица).
situate ['sɪtjueɪt] *vt* располага́ть (расположи́ть* *perf*).
situated ['sɪtjueɪtɪd] *adj* располо́женный* (располо́жен); **to be ~** находи́ться* (*impf*).
situation [sɪtju'eɪʃən] *n* (*state*) ситуа́ция, положе́ние; (*job*) ме́сто*; (*location*) ме́сто*, положе́ние; **"situations vacant"** (*BRIT*) "вака́нтные места́".
situation comedy *n* коме́дия положе́ний.
six [sɪks] *n* шесть*; *see also* **five**.
six-pack ['sɪkspæk] *n* шестибуты́лочная упако́вка пи́ва.
sixteen [sɪks'ti:n] *n* шестна́дцать*; *see also* **five**.
sixteenth [sɪks'ti:nθ] *adj* шестна́дцатый; *see also* **fifth**.
sixth ['sɪksθ] *adj* шесто́й ♦ *n* (*fraction*) одна́ шеста́я *f adj*, шеста́я часть *f*; **the upper/lower ~** (*BRIT*: *SCOL*) пе́рвая/ста́рая ступе́нь *выпускно́го кла́сса*; *see also* **fifth**.
sixtieth ['sɪkstɪɪθ] *adj* шестидеся́тый; *see also* **fifth**.
sixty ['sɪkstɪ] *n* шестьдеся́т*; *see also* **fifty**.
size [saɪz] *n* разме́р; (*extent*) величина́, масшта́б; (*glue*) клей*; **I take ~ 14** я ношу́ четы́рнадцатый разме́р; **the small/large ~** ма́ленького/большо́го разме́ра; **it's the ~ of ...** э́то разме́ром с +*acc* ...; **cut to ~** обре́занный согла́сно разме́рам +*gen*.
▶ **size up** *vt* оце́нивать (оцени́ть* *perf*).
sizeable ['saɪzəbl] *adj* поря́дочный.
sizzle ['sɪzl] *vi* шипе́ть* (*impf*).
SK *abbr* (*CANADA*) = **Saskatchewan**.
skate [skeɪt] *n* (*also*: **ice ~**) конёк*; (*also*: **roller ~**) ро́ликовый конёк*, ро́лик; (*fish: pl inv*) скат ♦ *vi* ката́ться (*impf*) на конька́х
▶ **skate around** *vt fus* (*problem, issue*) обходи́ть* (обойти́* *perf*)
▶ **skate over** *vt fus* (*problem, issue*)

игнори́ровать (*impf/perf*).
skateboard ['skeɪtbɔ:d] *n* ро́ликовая доска́*.
skater ['skeɪtəʳ] *n* конькобе́жец*(-жка*).
skating ['skeɪtɪŋ] *n* (*for pleasure*) ката́ние на конька́х; (*SPORT*) конькобе́жный спорт.
skating rink *n* като́к*.
skeleton ['skɛlɪtn] *n* (*ANAT*) скеле́т; (*TECH*) карка́с; (*outline*) набро́сок*, схе́ма.
skeleton key *n* отмы́чка*.
skeleton staff *n* минима́льный персона́л.
skeptic *etc* ['skɛptɪk] (*US*) = **sceptic** *etc*.
sketch [skɛtʃ] *n* (*drawing*) эски́з, набро́сок*; (*outline*) набро́сок*; (*THEAT, TV*) скетч ♦ *vt* (*drawing*) наброса́ть (*impf*); (*also*: **~ out**) обрисо́вывать (обрисова́ть *perf*) в о́бщих черта́х.
sketchbook ['skɛtʃbuk] *n* альбо́м для зарисо́вок.
sketchpad ['skɛtʃpæd] *n* блокно́т для зарисо́вок.
sketchy ['skɛtʃɪ] *adj* пове́рхностный* (пове́рхностен).
skew [skju:] *n*: **on the ~** (*BRIT*) ко́со, кри́во.
skewed [skju:d] *adj* (*idea, outlook*) искажённый* (искажён).
skewer ['skju:əʳ] *n* ве́ртел.
ski [ski:] *n* лы́жа ♦ *vi* ката́ться (*impf*) на лы́жах.
ski boot *n* лы́жный боти́нок*.
skid [skɪd] *n* (*AUT*) зано́с, юз ♦ *vi* скользи́ть* (*impf*); (*AUT*) идти́* (пойти́* *perf*) ю́зом; **the car went into a ~** маши́ну занесло́.
skid mark *n* тормозно́й след*.
skier ['ski:əʳ] *n* лы́жник(-ица).
skiing ['ski:ɪŋ] *n* (*for pleasure*) ката́ние на лы́жах; (*SPORT*) лы́жный спорт; **to go ~** идти́* (пойти́* *perf*) *or* е́хать (пое́хать* *perf*) ката́ться на лы́жах.
ski instructor *n* инстру́ктор по лы́жному спо́рту.
ski jump *n* (*ramp*) лы́жный трампли́н; (*event*) прыжки́ *mpl* на лы́жах с трампли́на.
skilful ['skɪlful] (*US* **skillful**) *adj* иску́сный* (иску́сен), уме́лый (уме́л).
ski lift *n* лы́жный подъёмник.
skill [skɪl] *n* (*ability, dexterity*) мастерство́; (*computer skill etc*) на́вык.
skilled [skɪld] *adj* (*able*) иску́сный* (иску́сен), уме́лый (уме́л); (*worker*) квалифиц-и́рованный.
skillet ['skɪlɪt] *n* (*CULIN*) неглубо́кая сковорода́*.
skillful ['skɪlful] *adj* (*US*) = **skilful**.
skil(l)fully ['skɪlfəlɪ] *adv* иску́сно, уме́ло.
skim [skɪm] *vt* (*milk*) снима́ть (снять* *perf*) сли́вки с +*gen*; (*soup*) снима́ть (снять* *perf*) на́кипь с +*gen*; (*glide over*) скользи́ть* (*impf*) над +*instr* ♦ *vi*: **to ~ through** пробежа́ть* (*perf*).
skimmed milk [skɪmd-] *n* обезжи́ренное

---

* marks translations which have irregular inflections. The Russian-English side of the dictionary gives inflectional information.

молоко́.

skimp [skɪmp] *vt* (*also:* ~ **on:** *work*)
манки́ровать (*impf*/*perf*) +*instr*; (: *cloth etc*)
эконо́мить* (*impf*) на +*prp*.

skimpy ['skɪmpɪ] *adj* ску́дный* (ску́ден); (*skirt*)
те́сный* (те́сен).

skin [skɪn] *n* (*of person*) ко́жа; (*of animal*)
шку́ра; (*of fruit, vegetable*) кожура́; (*of
grapes, tomatoes*) ко́жица ♦ *vt* (*fruit etc*)
снима́ть (снять* *perf*) кожуру́ с +*gen*,
чи́стить* (очи́стить* *perf*); (*animal*) снима́ть
(снять* *perf*) шку́ру с +*gen*, свежева́ть
(освежева́ть *perf*); **she is soaked to the** ~ она́
промо́кла до ни́тки.

skin cancer *n* рак ко́жи.

skin-deep ['skɪn'di:p] *adj* пове́рхностный*
(пове́рхностен).

skin-diver ['skɪndaɪvə'] *n* аквалангист(ка*).

skin diving *n* подво́дное пла́ванье.

skinflint ['skɪnflɪnt] *n* (*inf*) скря́га *m*/*f*.

skin graft *n* ко́жный трансплантат.

skinhead ['skɪnhɛd] *n* бритоголо́вый(-ая) *m*(*f*)
adj.

skinny ['skɪnɪ] *adj* то́щий* (тощ).

skin test *n* ана́лиз ко́жи.

skintight ['skɪntaɪt] *adj* в обтя́жку.

skip [skɪp] *n* прыжо́к*, скачо́к*; (*BRIT*: *container*)
скип ♦ *vi* подпры́гивать (подпры́гнуть *perf*);
(*with rope*) скака́ть* (*impf*) ♦ *vt* (*miss out*)
пропуска́ть (пропусти́ть* *perf*); **to** ~ **school**
(*esp US*) прогу́ливать (прогуля́ть *perf*)
уро́ки.

ski pants *npl* лы́жные брю́ки *pl*.

ski pole *n* лы́жная па́лка*.

skipper ['skɪpə'] *n* (*NAUT*) шки́пер, капита́н;
(*SPORT*) капита́н ♦ *vt* быть* (*impf*) капита́ном
+*gen*.

skipping rope ['skɪpɪŋ-] *n* (*BRIT*) скака́лка*.

ski resort *n* лы́жная ба́за.

skirmish ['skə:mɪʃ] *n* сты́чка*.

skirt [skə:t] *n* ю́бка* ♦ *vt* обходи́ть* (обойти́*
perf).

skirting board ['skə:tɪŋ-] *n* (*BRIT*) пли́нтус.

ski run *n* лыжня́.

ski slope *n* лы́жный спуск.

ski suit *n* лы́жный костю́м.

skit [skɪt] *n* паро́дия.

ski tow *n* букси́рный подъёмник.

skittle ['skɪtl] *n* ке́гля*; ~**s** *npl* (*game*) ке́гли* *fpl*.

skive [skaɪv] *vi* (*BRIT*: *inf*) сачкова́ть (*impf*).

skulk [skʌlk] *vi* (*hide*) пря́таться* (*impf*); (*prowl
about*) кра́сться* (*impf*).

skull [skʌl] *n* че́реп*.

skullcap ['skʌlkæp] *n* ермо́лка*.

skunk [skʌŋk] *n* (*animal*) скунс; (*fur*)
ску́нсовый мех*.

sky [skaɪ] *n* не́бо*; **to praise sb to the skies**
превозноси́ть* (превознести́* *perf*) кого́-н до
небе́с.

sky-blue [skaɪ'blu:] *adj* небе́сно-голубо́й,
лазу́рный.

skydiving ['skaɪdaɪvɪŋ] *n* свобо́дное паде́ние
(*при прыжка́х с парашю́та*).

sky-high ['skaɪ'haɪ] *adj* (*prices*) сумасше́дший*;
(*structure*) до небе́с; **to blow** ~ разноси́ть*
(разнести́* *perf*) вчисту́ю.

skylark ['skaɪlɑ:k] *n* жа́воронок*.

skylight ['skaɪlaɪt] *n* окно́* в кры́ше.

skyline ['skaɪlaɪn] *n* горизо́нт; (*of city*) силуэ́т.

skyscraper ['skaɪskreɪpə'] *n* небоскрёб.

slab [slæb] *n* (*of stone*) плита́*; (*of wood*)
пласти́на; (*of cake, cheese*) кусо́к*.

slack [slæk] *adj* (*rope*) прови́сший*; (*trousers*)
вися́щий; (*discipline*) сла́бый* (слаб);
(*security*) плохо́й* (плох); (*market*) вя́лый;
(*demand*) небольшо́й ♦ *n* (*in rope etc*)
слабина́; ~**s** *npl* (*trousers*) брю́ки *pl*; **business
is** ~ в дела́х засто́й.

slacken ['slækn] *vi* (*also:* ~ **off:** *demand, speed*)
па́дать (упа́сть* *perf*); (*rain*) переставать*
(переста́ть* *perf*) ♦ *vt* (*grip, clothing etc*)
ослабля́ть (осла́бить* *perf*); (*speed*) снижа́ть
(сни́зить* *perf*).

slacker ['slækə'] *n* (*inf*) ло́дырь *m*.

slag heap [slæg-] *n* шла́ковая гора́*.

slag off *vt* (*BRIT*: *inf*): **to slag sb off** перемыва́ть
(перемы́ть* *perf*) кому́-н ко́сточки.

slain [sleɪn] *pp of* **slay**.

slake [sleɪk] *vt*: **to** ~ **one's thirst** утоля́ть
(утоли́ть *perf*) жа́жду.

slalom ['slɑ:ləm] *n* сла́лом.

slam [slæm] *vt* (*door*) хло́пать (хло́пнуть *perf*)
+*instr*; (*throw*) швыря́ть (швырну́ть *perf*);
(*criticize*) раскритикова́ть (*perf*) ♦ *vi* (*door*)
захло́пываться (захло́пнуться *perf*); **to** ~ **on
the brakes** ре́зко тормози́ть* (затормози́ть*
perf).

slammer ['slæmə'] *n* (*inf*) кутýзка.

slander ['slɑ:ndə'] *n* клевета́ ♦ *vt* клевета́ть*
(наклевета́ть* *perf*) на +*acc*.

slanderous ['slɑ:ndrəs] *adj* клеветни́ческий*.

slang [slæŋ] *n* (*informal language*) сленг;
(*jargon*) жарго́н.

slanging match ['slæŋɪŋ-] *n* перебра́нка.

slant [slɑ:nt] *n* накло́н; (*fig*: *approach*) укло́н.

slanted ['slɑ:ntɪd] *adj* (*roof*) накло́нный,
пока́тый; (*eyes*) раско́сый.

slanting ['slɑ:ntɪŋ] *adj* = **slanted**.

slap [slæp] *n* шлепо́к* ♦ *vt* шлёпать (шлёпнуть
perf) ♦ *adv* (*directly*) пря́мо; **to** ~ **sb in the face**
дать* (*perf*) кому́-н пощёчину; **to** ~ **sth on sth**
(*paint etc*) ля́пать (наля́пать *perf*) что-н на
что-н; **it fell** ~ **in the middle** оно́ упа́ло пря́мо
посереди́не.

slapdash ['slæpdæʃ] *adj* небре́жный*
(небре́жен).

slapstick ['slæpstɪk] *n* фарс.

slap-up ['slæpʌp] *adj*: **a** ~ **meal** (*BRIT*)
роско́шный обе́д.

slash [slæʃ] *vt* ре́зать* (поре́зать* *perf*); (*fig*:
prices) ре́зко снижа́ть (сни́зить* *perf*).

slat [slæt] *n* пла́нка*.

453

slate [sleɪt] *n* (*material*) слáнец*; (*tile*)
шúферная плúтка* ♦ *vt* (*fig*) разносúть*
(разнестú* *perf*) в пух и прах.
slaughter ['slɔːtə'] *n* (*of animals*) убóй; (*of
people*) резня́ ♦ *vt* (*animals*) забивáть
(забúть* *perf*); (*people*) рéзать* (*impf*).
slaughterhouse ['slɔːtəhaus] *n* скотобóйня.
Slav [slɑːv] *adj* славянский* ♦ *n* славянúн
(-янка).
slave [sleɪv] *n* раб*(ы́ня) ♦ *vi* (*also:* ~ **away**)
рабóтать (*impf*) как раб; **to** ~ (**away**) **at sth**
рабóтать (*impf*) над чем-н как прóклятый.
slave-driver ['sleɪvdraɪvə'] *n* (*inf*) дéспот.
slave labour *n* (*also fig*) рáбский* труд*.
slaver ['slævə'] *vi* пускáть (*impf*) слюнý.
slavery ['sleɪvərɪ] *n* рáбство.
Slavic ['slævɪk] *adj* славянский*.
slavish ['sleɪvɪʃ] *adj* рáбский*; (*copy*) слепóй.
slavishly ['sleɪvɪʃlɪ] *adv* по-рáбски.
Slavonic [slə'vɔnɪk] *adj* славянский*.
slay [sleɪ] (*pt* **slew**, *pp* **slain**) *vt* поражáть
(поразúть* *perf*).
SLD *n abbr* (*BRIT: POL*) = *Social and Liberal
Democratic Party*.
sleazy ['sliːzɪ] *adj* (*place*) запýщенный*
(запýщен).
sled [slɛd] *n* (*esp US*) = **sledge**.
sledge [slɛdʒ] *n* сáни* *pl*; (*for children*) сáнки *pl*.
sledgehammer ['slɛdʒhæmə'] *n* кувáлда.
sleek [sliːk] *adj* (*shiny, smooth: fur*)
лоснящийся*; (: *hair*) блестящий* и глáдкий*;
(*car, boat etc*) аэродинамúчный.
sleep [sliːp] (*pt, pp* **slept**) *n* сон* ♦ *vi* спать* (*impf*);
(*spend night*) ночевáть* (переночевáть* *perf*)
♦ *vt*: **the house can** ~ **four** в дóме мóжно
разместúть четверы́х; **to go to** ~ засыпáть
(заснýть *perf*); **to have a good night's** ~
(хорошó) вы́спаться* (*perf*); **to put to** ~
(*animal*) усыплять (усыпúть* *perf*); **to** ~
lightly спать* (*impf*) чýтко; **to** ~ **with sb** спать*
(*impf*) с кем-н
▶ **sleep around** *vi* спать* (*impf*) с кем попáло
▶ **sleep in** *vi* (*oversleep*) просыпáть (проспáть*
perf); (*lie late*) отсыпáться (отоспáться* *perf*).
sleeper ['sliːpə'] *n* (*RAIL: train*) пóезд* со
спáльными вагóнами; (: *carriage*) спáльный
вагóн; (: *berth*) спáльное мéсто*; (: *BRIT: on
track*) шпáла; (*person*) спящий(-ая) *m(f) adj*.
sleepily ['sliːpɪlɪ] *adv* сóнно.
sleeping ['sliːpɪŋ] *adj* (*person*) спящий.
sleeping bag *n* спáльный мешóк*.
sleeping car *n* спáльный вагóн.
sleeping partner *n* (*BRIT: COMM*) = **silent
partner**.
sleeping pill *n* снотвóрное *nt adj*, снотвóрная
таблéтка*.
sleeping sickness *n* сóнная болéзнь *f*.
sleepless ['sliːplɪs] *adj* (*night*) бессóнный.

sleeplessness ['sliːplɪsnɪs] *n* бессóнница.
sleepwalk ['sliːpwɔːk] *vi* ходúть* (*impf*) во сне.
sleepwalker ['sliːpwɔːkə'] *n* лунáтик.
sleepy ['sliːpɪ] *adj* сóнный; **I feel** *or* **am** ~ мне
хóчется спать.
sleet [sliːt] *n* дождь *m* со снéгом.
sleeve [sliːv] *n* (*of jacket etc*) рукáв*; (*of record*)
конвéрт; **to have sth up one's** ~ имéть (*impf*)
кóе-что на умé.
sleeveless ['sliːvlɪs] *adj* без рукавóв.
sleigh [sleɪ] *n* сáни* *pl*.
sleight [slaɪt] *n*: ~ **of hand** лóвкость *f* рук.
slender ['slɛndə'] *adj* (*figure*) стрóйный*
(стрóен); (*means*) скýдный* (скýден);
(*majority*) небольшóй.
slept [slɛpt] *pt, pp of* **sleep**.
sleuth [sluːθ] *n* сы́щик.
slew [sluː] *vi* (*BRIT: also:* ~ **round**) крýто
поворáчивать (повернýть *perf*) ♦ *pt of* **slay**.
slice [slaɪs] *n* (*of meat*) кусóк*; (*of bread, lemon*)
лóмтик; (*also:* **fish** ~) рыбный нож; (*also:*
cake ~) лопáтка* для тóрта ♦ *vt* (*bread, meat
etc*) нарезáть (нарéзать* *perf*), рéзать*
(нарéзать* *perf*); ~**d bread** нарéзанный хлеб.
slick [slɪk] *adj* (*performance*) глáдкий*;
(*salesman, answer*) бóйкий* (бóек) ♦ *n* (*also:*
oil ~) плёнка нéфти.
slid [slɪd] *pt, pp of* **slide**.
slide [slaɪd] (*pt, pp* **slid**) *n* (*downward movement*)
скольжéние; (*in playground*) дéтская гóрка*;
(*PHOT*) слайд; (*BRIT: also:* **hair** ~) закóлка*;
(*also:* **microscope** ~) предмéтное стеклó*; (*in
prices*) снижéние ♦ *vt* задвигáть (задвúнуть
perf), совáть* (сýнуть *perf*) ♦ *vi* скользúть*
(скользнýть *perf*); **to let things** ~ (*fig*)
запускáть (запустúть* *perf*) делá, пустúть*
(*perf*) делá самотёком.
slide projector *n* диапроéктор.
slide rule *n* логарифмúческая линéйка.
sliding door ['slaɪdɪŋ-] *n* задвижнáя дверь *f*.
sliding roof *n* (*AUT*) сдвигáющийся верх.
sliding scale *n* скользящий* тарúф.
slight [slaɪt] *adj* (*slim: figure*) тóнкий* (тóнок);
(*frail*) хрýпкий* (хрýпок); (*small, trivial*)
незначúтельный; (*error*) небольшóй;
(*accent*) слáбый; (*pain*) несúльный ♦ *n* (*insult*)
унижéние; **the** ~**est noise** малéйший* шум; **I
haven't the** ~**est idea** я поня́тия не имéю; **not
in the** ~**est** нискóлько.
slightly ['slaɪtlɪ] *adv* немнóго, слегкá; ~ **built**
хрýпкого сложéния.
slim [slɪm] *adj* (*figure*) стрóйный* (стрóен);
(*chance*) небольшóй ♦ *vi* худéть (похудéть
perf).
slime [slaɪm] *n* слизь *f*.
slimming [slɪmɪŋ] *n* (*losing weight*) похудéние.
slimy ['slaɪmɪ] *adj* (*pond*) úлистый (úлист);
(*covered with mud*) скóльзкий* и лúпкий*;

---

* marks translations which have irregular inflections. The Russian-English side of the dictionary gives inflectional information.

(*fig: person*) гну́сный.
sling [slɪŋ] (*pt, pp* **slung**) *n* (*MED*) пе́ревязь *f*; (*for baby*) *приспособле́ние, позволя́ющее носи́ть ребёнка на спине́ и́ли груди́*; (*weapon*) праща́, рога́тка* ♦ *vt* (*throw*) швыря́ть (швырну́ть *perf*); **his arm is in a ~** у него́ рука́ на пе́ревязи.
slingshot ['slɪŋʃɔt] *n* рога́тка*.
slink [slɪŋk] (*pt, pp* **slunk**) *vi*: **to ~ away** *or* **off** уходи́ть* (уйти́* *perf*) поджа́вши хвост*.
slinky ['slɪŋkɪ] *adj* в обтя́жку.
slip [slɪp] *n* (*fall*) обва́л; (*mistake*) про́мах; (*underskirt*) подъю́бник; (*of paper*) поло́ска* ♦ *vt* сова́ть* (су́нуть *perf*) ♦ *vi* (*slide*) скользи́ть* (скользну́ть *f*); (*lose balance*) поскользну́ться (*perf*); (*decline*) снижа́ться (сни́зиться* *perf*); (*move smoothly*): **to ~ into** (*room etc*) скользну́ть (*perf*) в +*acc*; **to give sb the ~** ускольза́ть (ускользну́ть *perf*) от кого́-н; **a ~ of the tongue** огово́рка*; **to ~ sth on** надева́ть (наде́ть* *perf*) что-н; **to ~ sth off** сбра́сывать (сбро́сить* *perf*) что-н; **to ~ out of** (*room etc*) вы́скользнуть (*perf*) из +*gen*; **to let sb have a chance ~ by** упуска́ть (упусти́ть* *perf*) возмо́жность; **the cup ~ped from her hand** ча́шка вы́скользнула из её рук
▸ **slip away** *vi* улизну́ть (*perf*)
▸ **slip in** *vi* сова́ть* (су́нуть *perf*) ♦ *vi* (*errors*) закра́сться* (*perf*)
▸ **slip out** *vi* (*go out*) выска́кивать (вы́скочить *perf*)
▸ **slip up** *vi* (*make mistake*) ошиба́ться (ошиби́ться* *perf*).
slip-on ['slɪpɔn] *adj* без пу́говиц и застёжек; **~ shoes** ту́фли без шнурко́в и застёжек.
slipped disc [slɪpt-] *n* смещённый позвоно́к.
slipper ['slɪpə*] *n* та́почка*.
slippery ['slɪpərɪ] *adj* (*also fig*) ско́льзкий*.
slippy ['slɪpɪ] *adj* (*inf*) ско́льзкий* (ско́льзок).
slip road *n* (*BRIT*: *on to*) въезд на автостра́ду; (*off from*) съезд с автостра́ды.
slipshod ['slɪpʃɔd] *adj* небре́жный* (небре́жен).
slipstream ['slɪpstriːm] *n* возду́шный пото́к.
slip-up ['slɪpʌp] *n* ошибка*.
slipway ['slɪpweɪ] *n* (*NAUT*) ста́пель* *m*.
slit [slɪt] (*pt, pp* **slit**) *n* (*cut*) разре́з; (*opening*) щель* *f*; (*tear*) разры́в ♦ *vt* разреза́ть (разре́зать* *perf*); (*tear*) разрыва́ть (разорва́ть* *perf*); **to ~ sb's throat** перере́зать* (*perf*) кому́-н го́рло.
slither ['slɪðə*] *vi* (*person*) скользи́ть* (*impf*); (*snake*) извива́ться (*impf*).
sliver ['slɪvə*] *n* (*of glass*) оско́лок*; (*of wood*) ще́пка*; (*of cheese etc*) кусо́чек*.
slob [slɔb] *n* (*inf*) о́лух.
slog [slɔg] *vi* (*BRIT*: *work hard*) корпе́ть* (*impf*) ♦ *n*: **it was a hard ~** э́то была́ тяжёлая рабо́та.
slogan ['sləugən] *n* ло́зунг.
slop [slɔp] *vi* (*also*: **~ over**) выплёскиваться (вы́плеснуться *perf*) ♦ *vt* выплёскивать (вы́плеснуть *perf*)

▸ **slop out** *vi* (*in prison etc*) выноси́ть* (вы́нести* *perf*) пара́шу.
slope [sləup] *n* (*gentle hill*) укло́н; (*side of mountain*) склон; (*ski slope*) спуск; (*slant*) накло́н ♦ *vi*: **to ~ down** спуска́ться (*impf*); **to ~ up** поднима́ться (*impf*) под укло́ном.
sloping ['sləupɪŋ] *adj* (*ground, roof*) пока́тый (пока́т); (*handwriting*) накло́нный.
sloppy ['slɔpɪ] *adj* (*work*) небре́жный* (небре́жен), халту́рный; (*appearance*) неря́шливый (неря́шлив); (*pej: film etc*) сентимента́льный* (сентимента́лен).
slops [slɔps] *npl* помо́и *pl*.
slosh [slɔʃ] (*inf*) *vi*: **to ~ around** *or* **about** плеска́ться* (*impf*).
sloshed [slɔʃt] *adj* (*inf: drunk*) пья́ный в дыми́ну.
slot [slɔt] *n* (*in machine*) про́резь *f*, паз*; (*fig: in timetable*) окно́*; (*RADIO, TV*) ме́сто* ♦ *vt*: **to ~ sth into** опуска́ть (опусти́ть* *perf*) что-н в +*acc* ♦ *vi*: **to ~ into** входи́ть* (войти́* *perf*) в +*acc*.
sloth [sləuθ] *n* (*laziness*) лень *f*; (*ZOOL*) лени́вец*.
slot machine *n* (*BRIT: vending machine*) торго́вый автома́т*; (: *fruit machine*) игра́льный автома́т.
slot meter *n* (*BRIT*) счётчик.
slouch [slautʃ] *vi* суту́литься (ссуту́литься *perf*); **she was ~ed in a chair** она́ сиде́ла на сту́ле, сго́рбившись.
Slovakia [sləu'vækɪə] *n* Слова́кия.
Slovakian [sləu'vækɪən] *adj* слова́цкий* ♦ *n* (*person*) слова́к(-а́чка).
Slovenia [sləu'viːnɪə] *n* Слове́ния.
Slovenian [sləu'viːnɪən] *adj* слове́нский* ♦ *n* (*person*) слове́нец*(-нка); (*LING*) слове́нский* язы́к*.
slovenly ['slʌvənlɪ] *adj* неря́шливый (неря́шлив).
slow [sləu] *adj* ме́дленный; (*not clever*) тупо́й* (туп) ♦ *adv* ме́дленно ♦ *vt* (*also*: **~ down, ~ up:** *vehicle*) приторма́живать (притормози́ть* *perf*); (: *business*) приостана́вливать (приостанови́ть* *perf*) ♦ *vi* (*traffic*) замедля́ться (заме́длиться *perf*); (*car, train etc*) сбавля́ть (сба́вить* *perf*) ход; **at a ~ speed** на ни́зкой ско́рости; **to be ~ to act/decide** быть* (*impf*) медли́тельным(-ой) в дела́х/в реше́ниях; **my watch is (20 minutes) ~** мои́ часы́ отстаю́т (на 20 мину́т); **business is ~** дела́ иду́т нева́жно; **"slow"** (*road sign*) "ме́дленно"; **to go ~** (*driver*) дви́гаться (*impf*) ме́дленно; (*BRIT: workers*) снижа́ть (сни́зить* *perf*) темп рабо́ты.
slow-acting [sləu'æktɪŋ] *adj* заме́дленного де́йствия.
slowly ['sləulɪ] *adv* ме́дленно; **to drive ~** води́ть*/вести́* (*impf*) маши́ну ме́дленно.
slow motion *n*: **in ~ ~** в заме́дленном де́йствии.

slow-moving [sləu'mu:vɪŋ] *adj* ме́дленно
дви́жущийся, ме́дленный.
slowness ['sləunɪs] *n* ме́дленность *f*.
sludge [slʌdʒ] *n* грязь *f*.
slue [slu:] *vi* (*US*) = slew.
slug [slʌg] *n* (*ZOOL*) слизня́к*; (*bullet*) пу́ля.
sluggish ['slʌgɪʃ] *adj* (*stream*) ме́дленно
теку́щий*; (*engine*) пло́хо рабо́тающий;
(*person*) медли́тельный* (медли́телен);
(*trading*) вя́лый.
sluice [slu:s] *n* (*gate*) шлюз; (*channel*) жёлоб* ◆
vt: **to ~ down** *or* **out** промыва́ть (промы́ть*
perf), ока́тывать (окати́ть* *perf*).
slum [slʌm] *n* трущо́ба.
slumber ['slʌmbə'] *n* сон*.
slump [slʌmp] *n* (*economic*) спад; (*in profits,
sales*) ре́зкое паде́ние ◆ *vi* (*person*) вали́ться*
(повали́ться* *perf*); (*prices*) ре́зко па́дать
(упа́сть* *perf*); **he was ~ed over the wheel** он
сиде́л, упа́в на руль.
slung [slʌŋ] *pt, pp of* sling.
slunk [slʌŋk] *pt, pp of* slink.
slur [slə:'] *vt* (*words*) произноси́ть*
(произнести́* *perf*) нечленоразде́льно ◆ *n*
(*MUS*) ли́га; (*fig*): **~ (on)** пятно́ (на +*prp*); **to
cast a ~ on** поро́чить (*impf*).
slurp [slə:p] *vt* (гро́мко) хлеба́ть (хлебну́ть
perf).
slurred [slə:d] *adj* (*speech, voice*) невня́тный*
(невня́тен).
slush [slʌʃ] *n* сля́коть *f*.
slush fund *n* (*POL*) фонд для по́дкупа
госуда́рственных лиц.
slushy ['slʌʃɪ] *adj* (*snow*) мо́крый; (*street*)
покры́тый сля́котью; (*BRIT: fig*)
сентимента́льный* (сентимента́лен).
slut [slʌt] *n* (*inf. pej*) потаску́ха.
sly [slaɪ] *adj* хи́трый* (хитёр) ◆ *n*: **on the ~**
тайко́м.
smack [smæk] *n* (*slap*) шлепо́к*; (*on face*)
пощёчина; (*inf: heroin*) герои́н ◆ *vt* хло́пать
(хло́пнуть *perf*); (*child*) шлёпать (отшлёпать
perf); (*on face*) дава́ть* (дать* *perf*) пощёчину
+*dat* ◆ *vi*: **to ~ of** попа́хивать (*impf*) +*instr* ◆ *adv*
(*inf*): **the ball fell ~ in the middle** мяч упа́л
пря́мо посереди́не; **to ~ one's lips** чмо́кать
(чмо́кнуть *perf*) губа́ми.
smacker ['smækə'] *n* (*inf: kiss*) поцелу́й; (: *BRIT:
pound note*) бума́жный фунт; (: *US: dollar
bill*) бума́жный до́ллар.
small [smɔ:l] *adj* ма́ленький*; (*quantity,
amount*) небольшо́й ◆ *n*: **the ~ of the back**
поясни́ца; **to get** *or* **grow ~er** уменьша́ться
(уме́ньшиться *perf*); **to make ~er** (*amount,
income*) снижа́ть (сни́зить* *perf*); (*object,
garment*) уменьша́ть (уме́ньшить *perf*); **a ~
shopkeeper** ме́лкий(-ая) ла́вочник(-ица).
small ads *npl* (*BRIT*) ма́ленькие объявле́ния

npl (в газе́те о ку́пле-прода́же).
small arms *npl* (*MIL*) стрелко́вое ору́жие *ntsg*.
small business *n* ма́лое предприя́тие.
small change *n* ме́лочь* *f*.
small fry *npl* (*fig*) ме́лкая со́шка *fsg*.
smallholder ['smɔ:lhəuldə'] *n* (*BRIT*) владе́лец
небольшо́го земе́льного уча́стка.
smallholding ['smɔ:lhəuldɪŋ] *n* (*BRIT*)
небольшо́е земе́льное владе́ние.
small hours *npl*: **in the ~~** в предрассве́тные
часы́*.
smallish ['smɔ:lɪʃ] *adj* небольшо́й, дово́льно
ма́ленький*.
small-minded [smɔ:l'maɪndɪd] *adj*
ограни́ченный.
smallpox ['smɔ:lpɔks] *n* о́спа.
small print *n* ме́лкий* шрифт.
small-scale ['smɔ:lskeɪl] *adj* (*map, model*)
ма́ленького масшта́ба; (*business, farming*)
ме́лкий*.
small screen *n*: **the ~~** телеви́дение, ма́лый
экра́н.
small talk *n* све́тская бесе́да.
small-time ['smɔ:ltaɪm] *adj* (*farmer etc*)
ме́лкий.
small-town ['smɔ:ltaun] *adj* провинциа́льный*
(провинциа́лен).
smarmy ['smɑ:mɪ] *adj* (*BRIT: pej*) вкра́дчивый
(вкра́дчив).
smart [smɑ:t] *adj* (*neat, tidy*) опря́тный*
(опря́тен); (*fashionable*) мо́дный* (мо́ден);
(*clever*) толко́вый (толко́в); (*quick*)
бы́стрый* (быстр); (*pej*) наха́льный*
(наха́лен) ◆ *vi* (*also fig*) жечь* (*impf*); **the ~ set**
фешене́бельное о́бщество; **to look ~**
вы́глядеть* (*impf*) элега́нтно; **my eyes are
~ing** у меня́ глаза́ щи́плет.
smart card *n* (*for transactions*) вид креди́тной
ка́рточки с микропроце́ссором,
испо́льзуемой в платёжных опера́циях.
smarten up ['smɑ:tn-] *vi* приоде́ться* (*perf*),
принаряди́ться (*perf*) ◆ *vt* (*place*) приводи́ть*
(привести́* *perf*) в поря́док; (*person*)
принаряди́ть (*perf*).
smash [smæʃ] *n* (*collision: also*: **~-up**) ава́рия;
(*sound*) гро́хот; (*TENNIS*) смэш ◆ *vt*
разбива́ть (разби́ть* *perf*); (*SPORT: record*)
поби́ть* (*perf*) ◆ *vi* (*break*) разбива́ться
(разби́ться* *perf*); (*collide*): **to ~ against** *or* **into**
вреза́ться (вре́заться* *perf*) в +*acc*
▶ **smash up** *vt* (*car*) разбива́ть (разби́ть* *perf*);
(*room*) громи́ть* (разгроми́ть* *perf*).
smash hit *n* шля́гер.
smashing ['smæʃɪŋ] *adj* (*inf*) потряса́ющий*.
smattering ['smætərɪŋ] *n*: **a ~ of**
пове́рхностное зна́ние +*gen*.
smear [smɪə'] *n* (*trace*) след*; (*insult*) клевета́;
(*MED*) мазо́к* ◆ *vt* (*spread*) ма́зать*

---

* marks translations which have irregular inflections. The Russian-English side of the dictionary gives inflectional information.

(нама́зать* perf); (make dirty) па́чкать
(испа́чкать perf); **his hands were ~ed with
oil/ink** его́ ру́ки бы́ли испа́чканы ма́слом/
черни́лами.
smear campaign n клеветни́ческая
кампа́ния.
smear test n (BRIT: MED) мазо́к* для ана́лиза.
smell [smɛl] (pt, pp **smelt** or **smelled**) n за́пах;
(sense) обоня́ние ♦ vt чу́вствовать
(почу́вствовать perf) за́пах +gen ♦ vi: **to ~ (of)**
(unpleasant) воня́ть (impf) (+instr); (food etc)
па́хнуть (impf) (+instr).
smelly ['smɛlɪ] adj воню́чий* (воню́ч).
smelt [smɛlt] pt, pp of **smell** ♦ vt (ore) пла́вить*
(распла́вить* perf).
smile [smaɪl] n улы́бка* ♦ vi улыба́ться
(улыбну́ться perf).
smiling ['smaɪlɪŋ] adj улыба́ющийся.
smirk [smə:k] n (pej) ухмы́лка*.
smithy ['smɪðɪ] n ку́зница.
smitten ['smɪtn] adj: **he is ~ with her** он от неё
без ума́.
smock [smɔk] n блу́за; (children's) де́тское
пла́тье в сбо́рочку; (US: overall)
комбинезо́н.
smog [smɔg] n смог.
smoke [sməuk] n дым ♦ vi (person) кури́ть*
(impf); (chimney) дыми́ться (impf) ♦ vt
(cigarettes) кури́ть* (вы́курить perf); **to have a
~** кури́ть* (покури́ть* perf); **to go up in ~**
сгоре́ть (perf); (fig) пойти́* (perf) пра́хом; **do
you ~?** Вы ку́рите?
smoked ['sməukt] adj (bacon, fish) копчёный;
(glass) ды́мчатый.
smokeless fuel ['sməuklɪs-] n безды́мное
то́пливо.
smokeless zone n (BRIT) безды́мная
городска́я зо́на.
smoker ['sməukə'] n (person)
кури́льщик(-щица); (RAIL) ваго́н для
куря́щих.
smoke screen n (also fig) дымова́я заве́са.
smoke shop n (US) копти́льня.
smoking ['sməukɪŋ] n (act) куре́ние; **"no ~"** "не
кури́ть".
smoking compartment (US **smoking car**) n
ваго́н для куря́щих.
smoking room n кури́тельная ко́мната.
smoky ['sməukɪ] adj (atmosphere, room)
задымлённый (зады́млен); (taste) с
при́вкусом ды́ма.
smolder ['sməuldə'] vi (US) = **smoulder**.
smoochy ['smu:tʃɪ] adj (inf) ме́дленный и
романти́чный (о му́зыке, под кото́рую
легко́ целова́ться).
smooth [smu:ð] adj гла́дкий* (гла́док); (sauce)
без комко́в; (sea) споко́йный* (споко́ен);
(flavour) мя́гкий* (мя́гок); (movement)
пла́вный* (пла́вен); (flight) ро́вный; (pej:
person) ло́вкий* (ло́вок) ♦ vt (also: ~ **out**)
разгла́живать (разгла́дить* perf); (:

difficulties) устраня́ть (устрани́ть perf)
▶ **smooth over** vt: **to ~ things over** (fig)
ула́живать (ула́дить* perf) дела́.
smoothly ['smu:ðlɪ] adv (easily) без труда́;
everything went ~ всё прошло́ гла́дко.
smoothness ['smu:ðnɪs] n гла́дкость f;
(flavour) мя́гкость f; (movement) пла́вность
f.
smother ['smʌðə'] vt (fire) туши́ть*
(потуши́ть* perf); (person) души́ть*
(задуши́ть* perf); (emotions) подавля́ть
(подави́ть* perf).
smoulder ['sməuldə'] (US **smolder**) vi (fire)
тлеть* (impf); (fig: anger, hatred) зреть (impf).
smudge [smʌdʒ] n пятно́* ♦ vt разма́зывать
(разма́зать* perf).
smug [smʌg] adj самодово́льный*
(самодово́лен).
smuggle ['smʌgl] vt (goods) провози́ть*
(провезти́* perf) контраба́ндой; (refugees)
переправля́ть (перепра́вить* perf) та́йно; **to
~ in/out** (goods etc) ввози́ть* (ввезти́* perf)/
вывози́ть* (вы́везти* perf) контраба́ндой.
smuggler ['smʌglə'] n контрабанди́ст(ка*).
smuggling ['smʌglɪŋ] n контраба́нда.
smut [smʌt] n (soot) са́жа no pl; (in conversation
etc) поха́бщина.
smutty ['smʌtɪ] adj (joke, book) поха́бный*
(поха́бен).
snack [snæk] n заку́ска*; **to have a ~**
заку́сывать (закуси́ть* perf), переку́сывать
(перекуси́ть* perf).
snack bar n заку́сочная f adj.
snag [snæg] n (problem) загво́здка*,
затрудне́ние.
snail [sneɪl] n ули́тка*.
snake [sneɪk] n змея́*.
snap [snæp] n (sound) треск; (photograph)
сни́мок*; (game) снэп ♦ adj (decision etc)
необду́манный* (необду́ман) ♦ vt (break)
разла́мывать (разломи́ть perf); (fingers)
щёлкать (щёлкнуть perf) +instr ♦ vi (break)
разла́мываться (разломи́ться or
разломи́ться* perf); (fig: lose control)
слома́ться (perf); (: speak sharply) крича́ть*
(impf); **to ~ at sb** (subj: person) крича́ть* (impf)
на кого́-н; **to ~ one's fingers at** (fig)
отма́хиваться (отмахну́ться perf) от +gen; **a
cold ~** (weather) внеза́пное ре́зкое
похолода́ние; **to ~ shut** (trap, jaws etc)
защёлкивать (защёлкнуть perf)
▶ **snap at** vt fus огрыза́ться (огрызну́ться perf)
на +acc
▶ **snap off** vi отла́мывать (отлома́ть or
отломи́ть* perf)
▶ **snap up** vt (bargains) расхва́тывать
(расхвата́ть perf)
snap fastener n кно́пка*.
snappy ['snæpɪ] (inf) adj (slogan) бро́ский*;
(answer) бы́стрый; **make it ~!**
потора́пливайся!

snapshot ['snæpʃɔt] n сни́мок*.
snare [snɛəʳ] n лову́шка*, капка́н ♦ vt (also fig) зама́нивать (замани́ть* perf) в лову́шку.
snarl [snɑːl] vi (animal, person) рыча́ть (impf), ворча́ть (impf) ♦ vt: **to get ~ed up** (plans) пу́таться (запу́таться perf); **the traffic was ~ed up** произошёл зато́р в у́личном движе́нии.
snarl-up ['snɑːlʌp] n пу́таница.
snatch [snætʃ] n (of conversation, song etc) обры́вок* ♦ vt (grab) хвата́ть (схвати́ть* perf); (handbag) вырыва́ть (вы́рвать* perf); (child etc) красть* (укра́сть* perf); (opportunity, look etc) урыва́ть (урва́ть* perf) ♦ vi: **don't ~!** не хвата́й!; **to ~ a sandwich** перехва́тывать (перехвати́ть* perf) бутербро́д; **I managed to ~ some sleep** мне удало́сь немно́го поспа́ть
▶ **snatch up** vt схва́тывать (схвати́ть* perf).
snazzy ['snæzi] adj (inf) шика́рный* (шика́рен).
sneak [sniːk] n (inf: informer) я́беда m/f ♦ vi: **to ~ into/out of** незаме́тно проска́льзывать (проскользну́ть perf) в +acc/из +gen ♦ vt: **to ~ a look at sth** взгля́дывать (взгляну́ть* perf) укра́дкой на что-н; **to ~ up on sb** я́бедничать (ная́бедничать perf) на кого́-н.
sneakers ['sniːkəz] npl кроссо́вки* fpl.
sneaking ['sniːkɪŋ] adj: **I have a ~ feeling** or **suspicion that ...** у меня́ закра́лось подозре́ние, что ....
sneaky ['sniːkɪ] adj (pej: person) хи́трый* (хитёр); (advantage, look) незаме́тный* (незаме́тен).
sneer [snɪəʳ] vi (laugh) посме́иваться (impf); (mock): **to ~ at** глуми́ться* (impf) над +instr.
sneeze [sniːz] n чиха́нье ♦ vi чиха́ть (чихну́ть perf)
▶ **sneeze at** vt fus: **such things are not to be ~d at** таки́ми веща́ми не броса́ются.
snide [snaid] adj (pej) ехи́дный* (ехи́ден).
sniff [snɪf] n (sound) сопе́ние; (smell: by dog, person) обню́хивание ♦ vi шмы́гать (шмыгну́ть perf) но́сом; (when crying) всхли́пывать (impf) ♦ vt ню́хать (impf); (glue, drugs) вдыха́ть (impf), ню́хать (impf)
▶ **sniff at** vt fus: **such things are not to be ~ed at** таки́ми веща́ми не броса́ются.
sniffer dog ['snɪfə-] n (POLICE) соба́ка-ище́йка (для обнаруже́ния нарко́тиков и взры́вчатых веще́ств).
snigger ['snɪgəʳ] vi хихи́кать (хихи́кнуть perf).
snip [snɪp] n (cut) надре́з; (BRIT: inf: bargain) нахо́дка* ♦ vt (cut) ре́зать* (impf).
sniper ['snaipəʳ] n сна́йпер.
snippet ['snɪpɪt] n обры́вок*.
snivel ['snɪvl] vi хны́кать (impf).
snob [snɔb] n сноб.
snobbery ['snɔbərɪ] n сноби́зм.
snobbish ['snɔbɪʃ] adj сноби́стский*.

snog [snɔg] vi лиза́ться (impf) ♦ n: **to have a ~** лиза́ться (impf).
snooker ['snuːkə] n сну́кер (игра́ в билья́рд) ♦ vt (BRIT: inf: fig): **we're completely ~ed** мы соверше́нно за́гнаны в у́гол.
snoop ['snuːp] vi: **to ~ about** шпио́нить (impf); **to ~ on sb** подгля́дывать (impf) за кем-н (в щёлочку).
snooper ['snuːpəʳ] n шпио́н.
snooty ['snuːtɪ] adj зади́ристый.
snooze [snuːz] vi прикорну́ть (perf), вздремну́ть (perf) ♦ n: **to have a ~** вздремну́ть (perf).
snore [snɔːʳ] n храп ♦ vi храпе́ть* (impf).
snoring ['snɔːrɪŋ] n храп.
snorkel ['snɔːkl] n тру́бка*.
snort [snɔːt] n фы́рканье ♦ vi (animal) фаркну́ть (perf); (horse) всхра́пывать (impf) ♦ vt (inf: drugs) ню́хать (impf).
snotty ['snɔtɪ] adj (inf: handkerchief, nose) сопли́вый; (: pej: snobbish) на́глый.
snout [snaut] n (of pig) ры́ло; (of dog etc) мо́рда.
snow [snəu] n снег* ♦ vi: **it's ~ing** идёт снег ♦ vt: **she is ~ed under with work** она́ зава́лена рабо́той.
snowball ['snəubɔːl] n снежо́к* ♦ vi (fig: problem, campaign) нараста́ть (impf) как сне́жный ком.
snowbound ['snəubaund] adj засы́панный сне́гом.
snowcapped ['snəukæpt] adj сне́жный.
snowdrift ['snəudrɪft] n сугро́б.
snowdrop ['snəudrɔp] n (BOT) подсне́жник.
snowfall ['snəufɔːl] n снегопа́д.
snowflake ['snəufleɪk] n снежи́нка*.
snow line n снегова́я ли́ния.
snowman ['snəumæn] n irreg сне́жная ба́ба, снегови́к.
snowplough ['snəuplau] (US **snowplow**) n снегоубо́рочный комба́йн.
snowshoes ['snəuʃuːz] npl снегосту́пы mpl.
snowstorm ['snəustɔːm] n бура́н, вьюга.
snowy ['snəuɪ] adj сне́жный; (covered with snow) засне́женный.
SNP n abbr (BRIT: POL) = Scottish National Party.
snub [snʌb] vt (person) пренебрежи́тельно обходи́ться* (обойти́сь* perf) с +instr ♦ n вы́зов.
snub-nosed [snʌb'nəuzd] adj курно́сый.
snuff [snʌf] n ню́хательный таба́к* ♦ vt (also: ~ **out**) туши́ть* (потуши́ть* perf).
snuff movie n порнографи́ческий фильм, в кото́ром засня́то настоя́щее уби́йство.
snug [snʌg] adj (place) ую́тный (ую́тен); (well-fitting) пло́тно облега́ющий*; **I'm very ~ here** мне здесь о́чень ую́тно; **the sweater is a ~ fit** сви́тер хорошо́ прилега́ет.

* marks translations which have irregular inflections. The Russian-English side of the dictionary gives inflectional information.

snuggle ['snʌgl] *vi*: **to ~ up to sb** прижима́ться (прижа́ться* *perf*) к кому́-н; **to ~ down in bed** забива́ться (забиться* *perf*) под одея́ло.

snugly ['snʌglɪ] *adv* ую́тно; **to fit ~** (*object in pocket etc*) удо́бно помеща́ться (*impf*); **the sweater fits ~** сви́тер хорошо́ прилега́ет.

SO *n abbr* (*COMM*) = **standing order.**

KEYWORD

so [səu] *adv* **1** (*thus, likewise*): **so saying he walked away** с э́тими слова́ми, он ушёл; **while she was so doing, he ...** пока́ она́ э́то де́лала, он ...; **if so** е́сли да; **if this is so** е́сли э́то так; **I didn't do it – you did so!** э́то не я (сде́лал) – нет, ты!; **I like him – so do I** мне он нра́вится – мне то́же; **I'm still at school – so am I** я ещё учу́сь в шко́ле – я то́же; **he has a brother – so has David** у него́ есть брат – у Дави́да то́же; **so it is!** да, действи́тельно!; **I hope/think so** наде́юсь/ду́маю, что да; **so far I haven't had any problems** пока́ что у меня́ не́ было пробле́м; **how do you like the book so far?** ну как, нра́вится Вам кни́га?

2 (*in comparisons etc: +adv*) насто́лько, так; (*+adj*) насто́лько, тако́й; **so quickly (that)** насто́лько *or* так бы́стро(, что); **the house is so big (that)** дом насто́лько *or* тако́й большо́й(, что); **she's not so clever as her brother** она́ не так умна́, как её брат; **I'm so glad to see you** я так рад Вас ви́деть;

3: **I've got so much work** у меня́ так мно́го рабо́ты; **I love you so much** я Вас так люблю́; **thank you so much** спаси́бо Вам большо́е; **there are so many books I would like to read** сто́лько есть книг, кото́рые я бы хоте́л проче́сть

4 (*phrases*): **ten or so** о́коло десяти́; **so long!** (*inf: goodbye*) пока́!

♦ *conj* **1** (*expressing purpose*): **so as to do** что́бы сде́лать (*perf*); **I brought this wine so that you could try it** я принёс э́то вино́, что́бы Вы могли́ его́ попро́бовать

2 (*expressing result*) так что; **so I was right after all** так что, я был всё-таки прав; **so you see, I could have stayed** так что ви́дите, я мог бы оста́ться; **so, what shall we do now** так, что тепе́рь бу́дем де́лать.

---

soak [səuk] *vt* (*drench*) промочи́ть* (*perf*); (*steep in water*) зама́чивать (замочи́ть* *perf*) ♦ *vi* (*washing, dishes*) отмока́ть (*impf*); **to be ~ed through** промо́кнуть (*perf*) наскво́зь

► **soak in** *vi* впи́тываться (впита́ться *perf*)

► **soak up** *vt* впи́тывать (впита́ть *perf*) (в себя́).

soaking ['səukɪŋ] *adj* (*also*: **~ wet**) мо́крый наскво́зь.

so-and-so ['səuənsəu] *n* (*somebody*) не́кто*; **Mr ~** Господи́н тако́й-то; **you little ~!** (*pej*) ах ты э́дакий!

soap [səup] *n* мы́ло*; (*TV: also:* **~ opera**) мы́льная о́пера.

soapbox ['səupbɔks] *n* (*container*) я́щик из-под мы́ла; (*platform*) импровизи́рованная трибу́на.

soap flakes *npl* мы́льные хло́пья *pl*.

soap opera *n* (*TV*) мы́льная о́пера.

soap powder *n* мы́льный порошо́к*.

soapsuds ['səupsʌds] *npl* мы́льная пе́на *fsg*.

soapy ['səupɪ] *adj* мы́льный.

soar [sɔː'] *vi* (*bird, rocket*) взвива́ться (взви́ться* *perf*) в во́здух; (*price, production, temperature*) ре́зко подска́кивать (подскочи́ть* *perf*); (*building etc*) возвыша́ться (*impf*).

soaring ['sɔːrɪŋ] *adj* (*prices, inflation*) неуправля́емый.

sob [sɔb] *n* рыда́ние ♦ *vi* рыда́ть (*impf*), всхли́пывать (*impf*).

s.o.b. *n abbr* (*US: infl:* = **son of a bitch**) су́кин сын* (*!*)

sober ['səubə'] *adj* тре́звый* (трезв); (*colour, style*) небро́ский*.

► **sober up** *vt* протрезви́ть* (*perf*) ♦ *vi* трезве́ть (*impf*), протрезвля́ться (протрезви́ться* *perf*).

sobriety [sə'braɪətɪ] *n* тре́звость *f*.

sobriquet ['səubrɪkeɪ] *n* (*nickname*) про́звище.

sob story *n* душещипа́тельная исто́рия.

Soc. *abbr* = **society.**

so-called ['səu'kɔːld] *adj* так называ́емый.

soccer ['sɔkə'] *n* футбо́л.

soccer pitch *n* футбо́льное по́ле*.

soccer player *n* футболи́ст.

sociable ['səuʃəbl] *adj* (*person*) общи́тельный* (общи́телен); (*behaviour*) све́тский*.

social ['səuʃl] *adj* (*history, structure etc*) обще́ственный, социа́льный; (*event*) све́тский*; (*sociable: animal*) ста́дный ♦ *n* (*party*) встре́ча, ве́чер*; **he has a good ~ life** он мно́го обща́ется с людьми́.

social class *n* социа́льный класс.

social climber *n* челове́к, стремя́щийся заня́ть бо́лее высо́кое социа́льное положе́ние.

social club *n* клуб обще́ния.

social democrat *n* (*POL*) социа́л-демокра́т.

social insurance *n* (*US*) социа́льное обеспе́чение *or* страхова́ние.

socialism ['səuʃəlɪzəm] *n* социали́зм.

socialist ['səuʃəlɪst] *n* социали́ст ♦ *adj* социалисти́ческий*.

socialite ['səuʃəlaɪt] *n* све́тский* челове́к*.

socialize ['səuʃəlaɪz] *vi*: **to ~ (with)** обща́ться (пообща́ться *perf*) (с +*instr*).

socially ['səuʃəlɪ] *adv*: **to visit sb ~** зайти́* (*perf*) к кому́-н по-дру́жески; **~ acceptable** социа́льно прие́млемый.

social science *n* (*SCOL*) обще́ственные нау́ки *fpl*.

social security (*BRIT*) *n* социа́льное обеспе́чение; **Department of S~ S~** Министе́рство социа́льного обеспе́чения.

social services *npl* систе́ма *fsg* социа́льного обслу́живания.

social welfare *n* социа́льное обеспе́чение.

social work *n* рабо́та по социа́льному обеспе́чению.
social worker *n* рабо́тник систе́мы социа́льного обеспе́чения.
society [sə'saɪətɪ] *n* о́бщество ♦ *cpd* (*party*) све́тский*.
socioeconomic ['səusɪəuɪ:kə'nɒmɪk] *adj* (*group, factor*) социа́льно-экономи́ческий*.
sociological [səusɪə'lɒdʒɪkl] *adj* (*study*) социологи́ческий.
sociologist [səusɪ'ɒlədʒɪst] *n* социо́лог.
sociology [səusɪ'ɒlədʒɪ] *n* социоло́гия.
sock [sɒk] *n* носо́к* ♦ *vt* (*inf*): **to ~ sb in the face** дава́ть* (дать* *perf*) кому́-н по физионо́мии; **to pull one's ~s up** (*fig*) подтяну́ться* (*perf*).
socket ['sɒkɪt] *n* глазни́ца; (*BRIT: ELEC: in wall*) розе́тка*; (: *for light bulb*) патро́н.
sod [sɒd] *n* (*of earth*) дёрн; (*BRIT: inf!*) дрянь *f* така́я (*!*)
▶ **sod off** *vi* (*inf!*): **~ off** убира́йся отсю́да! (*!*), прова́ливай! (*!*)
soda ['səudə] *n* (*CHEM*) со́да; (*also:* **~ water**) со́довая *f adj*; (*US: also:* **~ pop**) газиро́вка*.
sodden ['sɒdn] *adj* прокля́тый.
sodium ['səudɪəm] *n* на́трий.
sodium chloride *n* хлори́д на́трия.
sofa ['səufə] *n* дива́н.
Sofia ['səufɪə] *n* Софи́я.
soft [sɒft] *adj* мя́гкий* (мя́гок); (*music*) негро́мкий* (негро́мок); **don't be ~!** (*inf: stupid*) не будь дурако́м!
soft-boiled ['sɒftbɔɪld] *adj*: **~ egg** яйцо́* всмя́тку.
soft currency *n* неконверти́руемая валю́та.
soft drink *n* безалкого́льный напи́ток*, сок*.
soft drugs *npl* мя́гкие нарко́тики *mpl*.
soften ['sɒfn] *vt* смягча́ть (смягчи́ть *perf*) ♦ *vi* смягча́ться (смягчи́ться *perf*).
softener ['sɒfnə'] *n* (*also:* **water ~**) хими́ческое сре́дство, смягча́ющее во́ду; (*also:* **fabric ~**) смягча́ющее сре́дство для сти́рки.
soft fruit *n* (*BRIT*) я́годы *fpl*.
soft furnishings *npl* мя́гкая оби́вка *fsg*.
softhearted [sɒft'hɑ:tɪd] *adj* мягкосерде́чный* (мягкосерде́чен).
softly ['sɒftlɪ] *adv* (*gently*) мя́гко; (*quietly*) ти́хо.
softness ['sɒftnɪs] *n* мя́гкость *f*.
soft option *n* лёгкий путь* *m*.
soft sell *n* (*COMM*) мя́гкая та́ктика сбы́та проду́кции.
soft spot *n*: **to have a ~ ~ for sb** пита́ть (*impf*) к кому́-н сла́бость.
soft target *n* лёгкая добы́ча.
soft toy *n* мя́гкая игру́шка*.
software ['sɒftwɛə'] *n* (*COMPUT*) програ́ммное обеспе́чение.
software package *n* (*COMPUT*) паке́т програ́мм.

soft water *n* мя́гкая вода́.
soggy ['sɒgɪ] *adj* (*ground*) сыро́й; (*sandwiches*) размо́кший.
soil [sɔɪl] *n* (*earth*) по́чва; (*territory*) земля́* ♦ *vt* па́чкать (запа́чкать *or* испа́чкать *perf*); (*fig*) мара́ть (замара́ть *perf*).
soiled [sɔɪld] *adj* испа́чканный (испа́чкан); (*COMM*) повреждённый.
sojourn ['sɒdʒə:n] *n* пребыва́ние.
solace ['sɒlɪs] *n* утеше́ние.
solar ['səulə'] *adj* со́лнечный.
solaria [sə'lɛərɪə] *npl of* **solarium**.
solarium [sə'lɛərɪəm] (*pl* **solaria**) *n* соля́рий.
solar panel *n* со́лнечная батаре́я.
solar plexus [-'plɛksəs] *n* со́лнечное сплете́ние.
solar power *n* со́лнечная эне́ргия.
solar system *n* со́лнечная систе́ма.
solar wind *n* со́лнечная бу́ря.
sold [səuld] *pt, pp of* **sell**.
solder ['səuldə'] *vt* пая́ть (*impf*), спа́ивать (спая́ть *perf*) ♦ *n* припо́й.
soldier ['səuldʒə'] *n* (*not officer*) солда́т*; (*in army*) вое́нный *m adj* ♦ *vi*: **to ~ on** не сдава́ться* (*impf*); **toy ~** солда́тик.
sold out *adj* распро́данный (распро́дан).
sole [səul] *n* (*of foot*) подо́шва; (*of shoe*) подо́шва, подмётка* ♦ *n inv* (*fish*) па́лтус ♦ *adj* (*unique*) еди́нственный; (*exclusive*) исключи́тельный; **the ~ reason** еди́нственная причи́на.
solely ['səullɪ] *adv* то́лько; **I will hold you ~ responsible** вся отве́тственность ля́жет то́лько на Вас.
solemn ['sɒləm] *adj* торже́ственный* (торже́ствен).
sole trader *n* (*COMM*) единоли́чный торго́вец*.
solicit [sə'lɪsɪt] *vt* (*request*) добива́ться (обрати́ться* *perf*) с про́сьбой за +*instr* ♦ *vi* (*prostitute*) предлага́ть (*impf*) себя́.
solicitor [sə'lɪsɪtə'] *n* (*BRIT*) адвока́т.
solid ['sɒlɪd] *adj* (*not hollow*) це́льный; (*not liquid*) твёрдый; (*reliable*) непоколеби́мый (непоколеби́м); (*meal*) пло́тный; (*vote*) сплочённый; (*entire*) це́лый; (*gold*) чи́стый ♦ *n* (*solid object*) твёрдое те́ло*; **~s** *npl* (*food*) твёрдая пи́ща *fsg*; (*for babies*) прико́рм *msg*; **to be on ~ ground** (*fig*) твёрдо стоя́ть (*impf*) на нога́х; **we waited two ~ hours** мы прожда́ли це́лых два часа́.
solidarity [sɒlɪ'dærɪtɪ] *n* солида́рность *f*.
solid fuel *n* твёрдое то́пливо.
solidify [sə'lɪdɪfaɪ] *vi* (*fat etc*) застыва́ть (засты́ть* *perf*); (*metal*) затвердева́ть (затверде́ть *perf*) ♦ *vt* де́лать (*impf*) твёрдым.
solidity [sə'lɪdɪtɪ] *n* твёрдость *f*.
solidly ['sɒlɪdlɪ] *adv* (*built*) кре́пко; (*respectable*) соли́дно; (*in favour*) по́лностью.

** marks translations which have irregular inflections. The Russian-English side of the dictionary gives inflectional information.

solid-state ['sɔlɪdsteɪt] *adj* (*ELEC*) твёрдый, в
твёрдом состоя́нии.
soliloquy [sə'lɪləkwɪ] *n* моноло́г.
solitaire [sɔlɪ'tɛəʳ] *n* (*gem*) солите́р; (*game*)
пасья́нс.
solitary ['sɔlɪtərɪ] *adj* одино́кий* (одино́к);
(*isolated*) уединённый; (*single*) едини́чный.
solitary confinement *n* одино́чное
заключе́ние; **to be in ~~** находи́ться* (*impf*) в
одино́чном заключе́нии.
solitude ['sɔlɪtju:d] *n* одино́чество, уедине́ние;
to live in ~ жить* (*impf*) в уедине́нии.
solo ['səuləu] *n* со́ло *nt ind* ♦ *adv* (*fly*) в
одино́чку; (*play*) со́ло.
soloist ['səuləuɪst] *n* соли́ст*(ка).
Solomon Islands ['sɔləmən-] *npl*: **the ~~**
Соломо́новы острова́ *mpl*.
solstice ['sɔlstɪs] *n* солнцестоя́ние.
soluble ['sɔljubl] *adj* раствори́мый.
solution [sə'lu:ʃən] *n* (*answer*) реше́ние;
(*liquid*) раство́р.
solve [sɔlv] *vt* (*puzzle*) реша́ть (реши́ть *perf*);
(*problem*) разреша́ть (разреши́ть *perf*);
(*mystery*) раскрыва́ть (раскры́ть* *perf*).
solvency ['sɔlvənsɪ] *n* платёжеспосо́бность *f*.
solvent ['sɔlvənt] *adj* (*COMM*) платёжеспос-
о́бный ♦ *n* (*CHEM*) раствори́тель *m*.
solvent abuse *n* злоупотребле́ние
*хими́ческими вещества́ми с наркоти́ческим
де́йствием.*
Som. *abbr* (*BRIT: POST*) = Somerset.
Somali [sə'ma:lɪ] *adj* сомали́йский ♦ *n*
сомали́ец*(-и́йка*).
Somalia [sə'ma:lɪə] *n* Сомали́ *nt ind*.
sombre ['sɔmbəʳ] (*US* **somber**) *adj* мра́чный*
(мра́чен).

KEYWORD
---

some [sʌm] *adj* **1** (*a certain amount or number
of*): **would you like some tea/biscuits?** хоти́те
ча́ю/пече́нья?; **there's some milk in the fridge**
в холоди́льнике есть молоко́; **he asked me
some questions** он за́дал мне не́сколько
вопро́сов; **there are some people waiting to
see you** Вас ждут каки́е-то лю́ди; **I've got
some money, but not much** у меня́ есть
де́ньги, но немно́гу
2 (*certain: in contrasts*) не́который; **some
people say that** ... не́которые говоря́т, что ...
3 (*unspecified*) како́й-то; **some woman
phoned you this afternoon** Вам сего́дня днём
звони́ла кака́я-то же́нщина; **we'll meet again
some day** мы когда́-нибудь опя́ть
встре́тимся; **shall we meet some day next
week?** встре́тимся ка́к-нибудь на той *or*
сле́дующей неде́ле?
　♦ *pron* (*a certain number: people*) одни́; **I've
got some** у меня́ есть; **some took the bus, and
some walked** одни́ пое́хали на авто́бусе, а
други́е пошли́ пешко́м, кто́-то пое́хал на
авто́бусе, кто́-то пошёл пешко́м; **who would
like a piece of cake? – I'd like some** кто хо́чет

кусо́к то́рта? – я с удово́льствием; **I've read
some of the book** я прочёл часть кни́ги
　♦ *adv*: **some ten people** челове́к де́сять.

somebody ['sʌmbədɪ] *pron* = **someone**.
someday ['sʌmdeɪ] *adv* когда́-нибудь.
somehow ['sʌmhau] *adv* (*in some way*)
ка́к-нибудь; (*for some reason*) почему́-то,
каки́м-то о́бразом.
someone ['sʌmwʌn] *pron* (*specific person*)
кто́-то; (*unspecified person*) кто́-нибудь; **I
saw ~ in the garden** я ви́дел кого́-то в саду́;
~ will help you Вам кто́-нибудь помо́жет.
someplace ['sʌmpleɪs] *adv* (*US*) = **somewhere**.
somersault ['sʌməsɔ:lt] *n* (*in the air*) са́льто *nt
ind*; (*on the ground*) кувыро́к* ♦ *vi*
кувырка́ться (*impf*), перекувырну́ться (*perf*).
something ['sʌmθɪŋ] *pron* (*something specific*)
что́-то; (*something unspecified*) что́-нибудь;
there's ~ wrong with my car у меня́ что́-то
случи́лось с маши́ной; **would you like ~ to
eat/drink?** хоти́те чего́-нибудь пое́сть/
вы́пить?; **I have ~ for you** у меня́ ко́е-что для
Вас есть.
sometime ['sʌmtaɪm] *adv* (*in future*) когда́-
нибудь; (*in past*): **~ last month** где́-то в
про́шлом ме́сяце; **I'll finish it ~**
когда́-нибудь я э́то зако́нчу.
sometimes ['sʌmtaɪmz] *adv* иногда́.
somewhat ['sʌmwɔt] *adv* не́сколько.
somewhere ['sʌmwɛəʳ] *adv* (*be: somewhere
specific*) где́-то; (: *anywhere*) где́-нибудь;
(*go: somewhere specific*) куда́-то; (:
anywhere) куда́-нибудь; (*come from*)
отку́да-то; **it's ~ or other in Scotland** э́то
где́-то в Шотла́ндии; **is there a post office ~
around here?** здесь где́-нибудь есть по́чта?;
let's go ~ else дава́йте пое́дем куда́-нибудь
в друго́е ме́сто.
son [sʌn] *n* сын*.
sonar ['səuna:ʳ] *n* (*NAUT*) гидролока́тор,
эхоло́т.
sonata [sə'na:tə] *n* сона́та.
song [sɔŋ] *n* пе́сня*.
song book *n* сбо́рник пе́сен, пе́сенник.
songwriter ['sɔŋraɪtəʳ] *n* (компози́тор-)
пе́сенник, (поэ́т-)пе́сенник.
sonic ['sɔnɪk] *adj* звуково́й.
son-in-law ['sʌnɪnlɔ:] *n* зять* *m*.
sonnet ['sɔnɪt] *n* соне́т.
sonny ['sʌnɪ] *n* (*inf*) сыно́к*.
soon [su:n] *adv* (*in a short time*) ско́ро; (*early*)
ра́но; **~ (afterwards)** вско́ре; **quite ~**
дово́льно ско́ро; **how ~ can you do it/come
back?** когда́ Вы смо́жете э́то сде́лать/
верну́ться?; **see you ~!** до ско́рого!; *see also*
as.
sooner ['su:nəʳ] *adv* (*time*) скоре́е; (*preference*)
I would ~ do that я бы скоре́е сде́лал э́то; **~
or later** ра́но и́ли по́здно; **the ~ the better**
чем скоре́е, тем лу́чше; **no ~ said than done**
ска́зано-сде́лано; **no ~ had we left than ... не

успе́ли мы уйти́, как ....
soot [sut] n са́жа.
soothe [su:ð] vt успока́ивать (успоко́ить perf).
soothing ['su:ðɪŋ] adj (ointment, drink, bath)
успокои́тельный; (tone, words etc)
утеши́тельный* (утеши́телен).
SOP n abbr (= standard operating procedure)
станда́ртная рабо́чая процеду́ра.
sop [sɔp] n: that's only a ~ э́то то́лько пода́чка.
sophisticated [sə'fɪstɪkeɪtɪd] adj изощрённый*
(изощрён); (woman) изы́сканная
(изы́скана).
sophistication [səfɪstɪ'keɪʃən] n (see adj)
изощрённость f; изы́сканность f.
sophomore ['sɔfəmɔː'] n (US: SCOL)
второку́рсник(-ица).
soporific [sɔpə'rɪfɪk] adj (speech)
усыпля́ющий; (drug) снотво́рный ♦ n
снотво́рное nt adj.
sopping ['sɔpɪŋ] adj: ~ (wet) (hair, clothes etc)
промо́кший наскво́зь.
soppy ['sɔpɪ] adj (pej) душещипа́тельный,
сентимента́льный.
soprano [sə'prɑːnəu] n сопра́но f ind.
sorbet ['sɔːbeɪ] n (CULIN) фрукто́вое
моро́женое nt adj.
sorcerer ['sɔːsərə'] n колду́н*.
sordid ['sɔːdɪd] adj (place) зага́женный
(зага́жен); (story etc) гну́сный* (гну́сен).
sore [sɔː'] n я́зва, боля́чка* ♦ adj (esp US:
offended) оби́женный* (оби́жен); (painful):
my arm is ~, I've got a ~ arm у меня́ боли́т
рука́; it's a ~ point (fig) э́то боле́зненный
предме́т.
sorely ['sɔːlɪ] adv: I am ~ tempted (to) у меня́
большо́й собла́зн (+infin).
soreness ['sɔːnɪs] n боль f.
sorrel ['sɔrəl] n щаве́ль* m.
sorrow ['sɔrəu] n (regret) печа́ль* f, грусть f; ~s
npl (troubles) печа́ли fpl.
sorrowful ['sɔrəuful] adj печа́льный*
(печа́лен).
sorry ['sɔrɪ] adj (condition, excuse, sight)
плаче́вный* (плаче́вен); (regretful): I'm ~ мне
жаль; ~! (apology) извини́те, пожа́луйста!;
~? (pardon) прости́те?; I feel ~ for him мне
его́ жа́лко; I'm ~ to hear that ... мне гру́стно
слы́шать, что ...; to be ~ about sth сожале́ть
(impf) о чём-н.
sort [sɔːt] n сорт*; (of car etc) тип ♦ vt (also: ~
out: papers, mail, belongings) разбира́ть
(разобра́ть* perf); (: problems) разбира́ться
(разобра́ться* perf) в +prp; (COMPUT)
сортирова́ть (impf); what ~ do you want?
како́й сорт Вы хоти́те?; what ~ of car? кака́я
маши́на?; I'll do nothing of the ~! я не
собира́юсь де́лать ничего́ подо́бного!; it's ~
of awkward (inf) э́то как-то неудо́бно.

sortie ['sɔːtɪ] n (MIL: on the ground) вы́лазка*;
(: by air) вы́лет; (fig) вы́лазка*.
sorting office ['sɔːtɪŋ-] n (POST)
сортиро́вочное отделе́ние.
SOS n abbr (= save our souls) SOS.
so-so ['səusəu] adv так себе́.
soufflé ['suːfleɪ] n суфле́ nt ind.
sought [sɔːt] pt, pp of **seek**.
sought-after ['sɔːtɑːftə'] adj (person, thing)
по́льзующийся спро́сом; a much ~ item
вещь, по́льзующаяся больши́м спро́сом.
soul [səul] n душа́*; (music) (му́зыка) "соул";
the poor ~ had nowhere to sleep несча́стному
не́где бы́ло спать; I didn't see a ~ я не ви́дел
ни души́.
soul-destroying ['səuldɪstrɔɪŋ] adj: this work is
~ э́та рабо́та выма́тывает ду́шу.
soulful ['səulful] adj проникнове́нный.
soulless ['səullɪs] adj (place) мёртвый (мёртв);
this is a ~ task э́то иссуша́ет ду́шу.
soul mate n родна́я душа́*.
soul-searching ['səulsɑːtʃɪŋ] n: after much ~, I
decided ... по́сле дли́тельного копа́ния в
себе́ я реши́л ....
sound [saund] adj (healthy) здоро́вый; (safe,
not damaged) про́чный* (про́чен), це́лый
(цел); (secure: investment) надёжный* (наде́
жен); (reliable, thorough) соли́дный*
(соли́ден); (sensible: advice) разу́мный*
(разу́мен); (valid: argument) ве́ский*;
(: policy) здравомы́слящий*; (: claim)
основа́тельный ♦ n звук; (GEO) зонд ♦ vt
(alarm) поднима́ть (подня́ть* perf) ♦ vi
звуча́ть (прозвуча́ть perf) ♦ adv: he is ~ asleep
он кре́пко спит; to be of ~ mind быть* (impf) в
здра́вом уме́; I don't like the ~ of it э́то мне
не нра́вится; to ~ one's horn (AUT) сигна́лить
(impf); to ~ like звуча́ть (прозвуча́ть perf) как
(бу́дто); it ~s like Russian похо́же на
ру́сский; that ~s like them arriving слы́шите,
похо́же они́ прие́хали; it ~s as if ... похо́же,
что ...; to ~ похо́же как бу́дто ....
▶ **sound off** vi (inf): to ~ off (about)
выска́зываться* (perf) (о +prp)
▶ **sound out** vt (person, opinion) зонди́ровать
(прозонди́ровать perf).
sound barrier n звуково́й барье́р.
sound effects npl звуковы́е эффе́кты mpl.
sound engineer n звукорежиссёр.
sounding ['saundɪŋ] n (NAUT etc) проме́р
глубины́.
sounding board n (MUS) де́ка; to use sb as a ~
~ for one's ideas проверя́ть (прове́рить perf)
свои́ иде́и на ком-н.
soundly ['saundlɪ] adv (sleep) кре́пко; (beat etc)
здо́рово.
soundproof ['saundpruːf] adj
звуконепроница́емый (звуконепроница́ем)

---

* marks translations which have irregular inflections. The Russian-English side of the dictionary gives inflectional information.

◆ *vt* звукоизоли́ровать *(impf/perf)*.

sound system *n (TECH)* (звуковáя) систéма.

soundtrack ['saundtræk] *n* мýзыка *(из кинофи́льма)*.

sound wave *n* звуковáя волнá*.

soup [su:p] *n* суп*; **to be in the** ~ *(fig)* попадáть (попáсть* *perf*) в передрягу.

soup course *n* пéрвое *nt adj*.

soup kitchen *n* столóвая *f adj* для бéдных, суповáя кýхня.

soup plate *n* глубóкая тарéлка*.

soupspoon ['su:pspu:n] *n* столóвая лóжка*.

sour ['sauə'] *adj* ки́слый; *(fig: bad-tempered)* неприя́зненный* (неприя́знен); **to go** *or* **turn** ~ скисáть (ски́снуть* *perf*); *(fig)* пóртиться* (испóртиться* *perf*); **it's** ~ **grapes** *(fig)* э́то зáвисть.

source [so:s] *n (also fig)* истóчник; **I have it from a reliable** ~ **that** ... у меня́ есть свéдения из надёжного истóчника, что ....

south [sauθ] *n* юг *m* ◆ *adj* ю́жный ◆ *adv (go)* на юг; *(be)* на ю́ге; **(to the)** ~ **of** к ю́гу от *+gen*; **to travel** ~ éхать*/éздить* *(impf)* на юг; **the S**~ **of France** Юг Фрáнции.

South Africa *n* Ю́жная Áфрика.

South African *adj* южноафрикáнский ◆ *n* южноафрикáнец*(-нка*).

South America *n* Ю́жная Амéрика.

South American *adj* южноамерикáнский ◆ *n* южноамерикáнец*(-нка*).

southbound ['sauθbaund] *adj (traffic)* дви́жущийся в ю́жном направлéнии; *(train, carriageway)* ю́жного направлéния.

southeast [sauθ'i:st] *n* ю́го-востóк.

Southeast Asia *n* Ю́го-востóчная Áзия.

southerly ['sʌðəlɪ] *adj* обращённый к ю́гу; *(wind)* ю́жный.

southern ['sʌðən] *adj* ю́жный; **a room with a** ~ **aspect** кóмната, выходя́щая на юг; **the** ~ **hemisphere** ю́жное полушáрие.

South Korea *n* Ю́жная Корéя.

South Pole *n*: **the** ~~ Ю́жный пóлюс.

South Sea Islands *npl*: **the** ~~~ островá *mpl* ю́жной чáсти Ти́хого Океáна.

South Seas *npl*: **the** ~~ ю́жная часть *f* Ти́хого Океáна.

southward(s) ['sauθwəd(z)] *adv* на юг, в ю́жном направлéнии.

southwest [sauθ'wɛst] *n* ю́го-зáпад.

souvenir [su:və'nɪə'] *n* сувени́р.

sovereign ['sɔvrɪn] *n (ruler)* госудáрь(-рыня) *m(f)*.

sovereignty ['sɔvrɪntɪ] *n* суверенитéт.

Soviet ['səuvɪət] *adj* совéтский* ◆ *n (person)* совéтский*(-ая) граждани́н*(-áнка*); **the** ~ **Union** Совéтский* Сою́з.

sow[1] [sau] *n (pig)* свинья́*, свиномáтка*.

sow[2] [səu] *(pt* **sowed**, *pp* **sown)** *vt (also fig)* сéять (посéять *perf*).

sown [səun] *pp of* **sow**[2].

soya ['sɔɪə] *(US* **soy)** *n*: ~ **bean/sauce** сóевый

боб/сóус.

sozzled ['sɔzld] *adj (inf)* под мýхой.

spa [spa:] *n (town)* курóртный гóрод*; *(US: also:* **health** ~) лечéбно-оздорови́тельный курóрт.

space [speɪs] *n (gap)* прострáнство; *(place: small)* мéсто*; (: large)* прострáнство; *(room)* мéсто*; (beyond Earth)* кóсмос; *(interval, period)* промежýток* ◆ *cpd* косми́ческий* ◆ *vt (also:* ~ **out:** *text)* разбивáть (разби́ть* *perf*); *(: payments, visits)* распределя́ть (распредели́ть *perf*); **to clear a** ~ **for sth** расчищáть (расчи́стить* *perf*) мéсто для чегó-н; **in a confined** ~ в ограни́ченном прострáнстве; **in a short** ~ **of time** в корóткий промежýток врéмени; **(with)in the** ~ **of an hour** в течéние чáса.

space-bar ['speɪsba:'] *n (TYP)* интервáл.

spacecraft ['speɪskrɑ:ft] *n* косми́ческий* корáбль* *m*.

spaceman ['speɪsmæn] *irreg n* космонáвт.

spaceship ['speɪsʃɪp] *n* = **spacecraft**.

space shuttle *n* косми́ческий корáбль ти́па "шатл".

spacesuit ['speɪssu:t] *n* скафáндр.

spacewoman ['speɪswumən] *irreg n* жéнщина-космонáвт.

spacing ['speɪsɪŋ] *n (TYP)* промежýтки *mpl*, интервáлы *mpl*; **single/double** ~ *(TYP)* с одни́м/двойны́м интервáлом.

spacious ['speɪʃəs] *adj* простóрный* (простóрен).

spade [speɪd] *n (tool)* лопáта; *(child's)* лопáтка*; ~**s** *npl (CARDS)* пи́ки *fpl*.

spadework ['speɪdwə:k] *n (fig)* черновáя рабóта.

spaghetti [spə'gɛtɪ] *n* спагéтти *pl ind*.

Spain [speɪn] *n* Испáния.

span [spæn] *pt of* **spin** *n (of hand, wings)* размáх*; (of bridge)* пролёт; *(in time)* промежýток* ◆ *vt (river)* переки́нуть *(perf)* чéрез *+acc*; *(fig: time)* охвáтывать (охвати́ть* *perf*).

Spaniard ['spænjəd] *n* испáнец*(-нка*).

spaniel ['spænjəl] *n* спаниéль *m*.

Spanish ['spænɪʃ] *adj* испáнский* ◆ *n (LING)* испáнский* язы́к*; **the** ~ *npl* испáнцы *mpl*; ~ **omelette** омлéт по-испáнски.

spank [spæŋk] *vt* шлёпать (отшлёпать *perf*).

spanner ['spænə'] *n (BRIT)* гáечный ключ*.

spar [spa:'] *n (pole)* штáнга ◆ *vi (BOXING)* спаррингов́ать *(impf)*.

spare [spɛə'] *adj (free: time, seat)* свобóдный* (свобóден); *(surplus)* ли́шний* *(reserve)* запаснóй ◆ *n* = **spare part** ◆ *vt (trouble, expense, effort)* избавля́ть (изба́вить* *perf*) от *+gen*; *(refrain from using: energy, water etc)* берéчь* (сберéчь* *perf*); *(make available: person, time, money)* выделя́ть (вы́делить *perf*); *(afford to give: money)* давáть* (дать* *perf*); *(refrain from hurting: person, city etc)* щади́ть* (пощади́ть* *perf*); **to have some time to** ~ име́ть (*impf*) свобо́дное вре́мя; **to have money to** ~ име́ть (*impf*) ли́шние де́ньги; **these 2 are going** ~ э́ти два – ли́шние; **to** ~ **no expense** не жале́ть (пожале́ть *perf*) средств; **can you** ~ **the time?** у Вас найдётся вре́мя?; **I've a few minutes to** ~ у меня́ есть не́сколько мину́т; **there is no time to** ~ у нас нет ли́шнего вре́мени; **can you** ~ **ten pounds?** у Вас не найдётся десяти́ фу́нтов?

spare part *n* запча́сть *f*= *запасна́я часть.*

spare room *n* свобо́дная ко́мната.

spare time *n* свобо́дное вре́мя* *nt.*

spare tyre *n* запасна́я ши́на.

spare wheel *n* запасно́е колесо́*.

sparing ['spɛərɪŋ] *adj*: **he is** ~ **with his money** он эконо́мен с деньга́ми; **he was** ~ **with his praise** он был ску́пен на похвалу́.

sparingly ['spɛərɪŋlɪ] *adv* эконо́мно.

spark [spɑːk] *n* (*also fig*) и́скра.

spark(ing) plug ['spɑːk(ɪŋ)-] *n* запа́льная свеча́*.

sparkle ['spɑːkl] *n* блеск ♦ *vi* (*diamonds, water*) сверка́ть (сверкну́ть *perf*); (*eyes*) блесте́ть* (*impf*); (*bubble*) шипе́ть* (*impf*).

sparkler ['spɑːklə'] *n* (*firework*) бенга́льский ого́нь* *m.*

sparkling ['spɑːklɪŋ] *adj* (*wine*) игри́стый; (*conversation, performance*) блестя́щий*.

sparring partner ['spɑːrɪŋ-] *n* (*BOXING*) партнёр для трениро́вок в бо́ксе.

sparrow ['spærəu] *n* воробе́й*.

sparse [spɑːs] *adj* ре́дкий* (ре́док).

spartan ['spɑːtən] *adj* спарта́нский.

spasm ['spæzəm] *n* (*MED*) спазм; (*of anger etc*) при́ступ.

spasmodic [spæz'mɔdɪk] *adj* (*fig*) спазмати́ческий.

spastic ['spæstɪk] *n* (*MED*) парали́тик ♦ *adj* (*MED*) спасти́ческий.

spat [spæt] *pt, pp of* **spit** ♦ *n* (*US: quarrel*) размо́лвка*.

spate [speɪt] *n* (*fig*): **a** ~ **of** пото́к* +*gen*; **the river is in** ~ река́ вздула́сь.

spatial ['speɪʃl] *adj* простра́нственный.

spatter ['spætə'] *vt* бры́згать (бры́знуть *perf*) ♦ *vi* обры́згаться (обры́знуться *perf*).

spatula ['spætjulə] *n* (*MED*) шпа́тель *m*; (*CULIN*) лопа́тка*.

spawn [spɔːn] *vi* (*fish etc*) мета́ть* (*impf*) икру́ ♦ *vt* (*fig*) порожда́ть (породи́ть* *perf*) ♦ *n* икра́.

SPCA *n abbr* (*US*) = *Society for the Prevention of Cruelty to Animals.*

SPCC *n abbr* (*US*) = *Society for the Prevention of Cruelty to Children.*

speak [spiːk] (*pt* **spoke**, *pp* **spoken**) *vi* (*use voice*) говори́ть (*impf*); (*make a speech*) выступа́ть (вы́ступить* *perf*) ♦ *vt* (*truth*) говори́ть

(сказа́ть* *perf*); **to** ~ **to sb** разгова́ривать (*impf*) с кем-н; **to** ~ **of** *or* **about** говори́ть (*impf*) о +*prp*; **he has no money to** ~ **of** у него́ о́чень немно́го де́нег; ~ **up!** говори́те гро́мче!; **to** ~ **at a conference/in a debate** выступа́ть (вы́ступить* *perf*) на конфере́нции/в деба́тах; **to** ~ **Russian/several languages** говори́ть (*impf*) по-ру́сски/на не́скольких языка́х; **to** ~ **one's mind** выска́зывать (вы́сказать* *perf*) своё мне́ние

▶ **speak for** *vt fus*: **to** ~ **for sb** говори́ть (*impf*) за кого́-н; **that picture is already spoken for** (*already sold*) э́ту карти́ну уже́ сторгова́ли.

speaker ['spiːkə'] *n* (*in public*) ора́тор; (*also*: **loudspeaker**) громкоговори́тель *m*; (*POL*): **the S~** спи́кер; **are you a Welsh ~?** Вы говори́те по-уэ́льски?

speaking ['spiːkɪŋ] *adj* говоря́щий; **Italian-~ people** италогово́рящие *pl adj*; **we are no longer on ~ terms** мы бо́льше не обща́емся.

spear [spɪə'] *n* копьё* ♦ *vt* пронза́ть (пронзи́ть* *perf*) копьём.

spearhead ['spɪəhɛd] *vt* возглавля́ть (возгла́вить* *perf*).

spearmint ['spɪəmɪnt] *n* мя́та колосова́я.

spec [spɛk] *n* (*inf*): **on** ~ (*buy, go etc*) науда́чу.

spec. *n abbr* (*TECH*: = *specification*) специфика́ция.

special ['spɛʃl] *adj* (*important*) осо́бый, осо́бенный; (*edition, adviser, school etc*) специа́льный ♦ *n* (*RAIL*): по́езд* специа́льного назначе́ния; **take ~ care** прояви́те осо́бенную забо́ту; **nothing ~** ничего́ осо́бенного; **today's ~** (*at restaurant*) сего́дняшнее фи́рменное блю́до.

special agent *n* аге́нт по осо́бым поруче́ниям.

special correspondent *n* специа́льный корреспонде́нт.

special delivery *n* (*POST*): **by ~ ~** сро́чной доста́вкой.

special effects *npl* (*CINEMA*) специа́льные съёмочные эффе́кты *mpl.*

specialist ['spɛʃəlɪst] *n* специали́ст; **heart ~** специали́ст-кардио́лог.

speciality [spɛʃɪ'ælɪtɪ] *n* (*dish*) фи́рменное блю́до; (*subject*) специализа́ция.

specialize ['spɛʃəlaɪz] *vi*: **to ~ (in)** специализи́роваться (*impf/perf*) (в +*prp*).

specially ['spɛʃlɪ] *adv* (*especially*) осо́бенно; (*on purpose*) специа́льно.

special offer *n*: **the book is on ~ ~** кни́гу продаю́т по сни́женной цене́.

specialty ['spɛʃəltɪ] *n* (*esp US*) = **speciality**.

species ['spiːʃiːz] *n inv* вид.

specific [spə'sɪfɪk] *adj* определённый; ~ **to** характе́рно для +*gen*.

specifically [spə'sɪfɪklɪ] *adv* (*exactly*)

---

* marks translations which have irregular inflections. The Russian-English side of the dictionary gives inflectional information.

определённо; (*specially*) специа́льно.
specification [spɛsɪfɪ'keɪʃən] *n* (*TECH*)
специфика́ция; (*requirement*) тре́бование;
~s *npl* (*TECH*) техни́ческие усло́вия *ntpl*.
specify ['spɛsɪfaɪ] *vt* (*time, place, colour etc*)
уточня́ть (уточни́ть *perf*); **unless otherwise
specified** е́сли нет други́х указа́ний.
specimen ['spɛsɪmən] *n* (*example*) экземпля́р;
(*sample for testing*) образе́ц*; **a ~ of urine**
моча́ для ана́лиза.
specimen copy *n* образцо́вый экземпля́р.
specimen signature *n* образе́ц* по́дписи.
speck [spɛk] *n* (*of dirt*) пя́тнышко; (*of dust*)
кра́пинка*.
speckled ['spɛkld] *adj* (*hen, eggs*) пёстрый
(пёстр).
specs [spɛks] *npl* (*inf: glasses*) очки́ *pl*.
spectacle ['spɛktəkl] *n* (*scene, event*) зре́лище;
~s *npl* (*glasses*) очки́ *pl*.
spectacle case *n* (*BRIT*) футля́р для очко́в.
spectacular [spɛk'tækjulə'] *adj* впечатля́ющий
(впечатля́ющ) ♦ *n* (*THEAT etc*) впечатля́ющее
зре́лище.
spectator [spɛk'teɪtə'] *n* зри́тель(ница) *m(f)* ♦
cpd: **a ~ sport** зре́лищный спорт.
spectra ['spɛktrə] *npl of* **spectrum**.
spectre ['spɛktə'] (*US* **specter**) *n* (*also fig*)
при́зрак.
spectrum ['spɛktrəm] (*pl* **spectra**) *n* спектр.
speculate ['spɛkjuleɪt] *vi* (*COMM*) игра́ть (*impf*)
на би́рже; (*guess*): **to ~ about** стро́ить (*impf*)
дога́дки *or* размышля́ть (*impf*) о +*prp*.
speculation [spɛkju'leɪʃən] *n* (*see vb*) биржева́я
игра́; дога́дка, предположе́ние.
sped [spɛd] *pt, pp of* **speed**.
speech [spiːtʃ] *n* речь *f*; (*THEAT*) моноло́г, речь.
speech day *n* (*BRIT: SCOL*) а́ктовый день* *m*.
speech impediment *n* дефе́кт ре́чи.
speechless ['spiːtʃlɪs] *adj* безмо́лвный*
(безмо́лвен).
speech therapist *n* логопе́д.
speech therapy *n* логопеди́я.
speed [spiːd] (*pt, pp* **sped**) *n* (*rate*) ско́рость* *f*;
(*promptness*) быстрота́ ♦ *vi* (*AUT: exceed
speed limit*) превыша́ть (превы́сить* *perf*)
ско́рость; (*move*): **to ~ along/by** *etc* мча́ться*
(промча́ться* *perf*) по +*dat*/ми́мо +*gen etc*; **at ~**
(*BRIT*) на большо́й ско́рости; **at full** *or* **top ~**
на по́лной *or* преде́ле ско́рости; **at a ~ of
70km/h** со ско́ростью 70км в час; **shorthand/
typing ~** ско́рость* маши́нописи/
стенографи́рования; **a five-~ gearbox**
коро́бка* переда́ч с пятью́ скоростя́ми
▸ **speed up** (*pt, pp* **speeded up**) *vi* (*also fig*)
ускоря́ться (уско́риться* *perf*) ♦ *vt* (*also fig*)
ускоря́ть (уско́рить *perf*).
speedboat ['spiːdbəut] *n* быстрохо́дный
ка́тер.
speedily ['spiːdɪlɪ] *adv* ско́ро.
speeding ['spiːdɪŋ] *n* (*AUT*) превыше́ние
ско́рости.

speed limit *n* (*AUT*) ограниче́ние ско́рости.
speedometer [spɪ'dɔmɪtə'] *n* (*AUT*) спидо́метр.
speed trap *n* (*AUT*) пост доро́жной поли́ции по
контро́лю за ско́ростью.
speedway ['spiːdweɪ] *n* (*sport: also:* **~ racing**)
спидве́й; (*track*) го́ночный трек.
speedy [spiːdɪ] *adj* (*fast: car*) бы́стрый (быстр);
(*prompt: reply, recovery, settlement*) ско́рый
(скор).
speleologist [spɛlɪ'ɔlədʒɪst] *n* спелео́лог.
spell [spɛl] (*pt, pp* **spelt** (*BRIT*) *or* **spelled**) *n* (*also:*
magic ~) колдовство́; (*period of time*)
пери́од ♦ *vt* (*in writing*) объясня́ть
(объясни́ть *perf*) в дета́лях; (*also:* **~ out**)
произноси́ть* (произнести́* *perf*) по бу́квам;
(*fig: advantages, difficulties*) разъясня́ть
(разъясни́ть *perf*) ♦ *vi*: **he can't ~** он не уме́ет
писа́ть без оши́бок; **to cast a ~ on sb**
околдо́вывать (околдова́ть *perf*) кого́-н;
how do you ~ your surname? как пи́шется
Ва́ша фами́лия?; **can you ~ it for me?** Вы
мо́жете произнести́ э́то по бу́квам?
spellbound ['spɛlbaund] *adj* зачаро́ванный
(зачаро́ван).
spelling ['spɛlɪŋ] *n* правописа́ние.
spelt [spɛlt] *pt, pp of* **spell**.
spend [spɛnd] (*pt, pp* **spent**) *vt* (*money*) тра́тить*
(истра́тить* *perf*); (*time, life*) проводи́ть*
(провести́* *perf*); (*devote*): **to ~ time/effort on
sth** тра́тить (потра́тить *perf*) вре́мя/си́лы на
что-н.
spending ['spɛndɪŋ] *n* расхо́ды *mpl*;
government ~ госуда́рственные расхо́ды
mpl.
spending money *n* карма́нные де́ньги* *pl*.
spending power *n* покупа́тельная
спосо́бность *f*.
spendthrift ['spɛndθrɪft] *n* расточи́тель(ница)
m(f).
spent [spɛnt] *pt, pp of* **spend** ♦ *adj* (*cartridge*)
пусто́й (пуст); (*bullets*) израсхо́дованный; ~
matches испо́льзованные *or* израсхо́до-
ванные спи́чки; **my patience is ~** моё
терпе́ние ко́нчилось.
sperm [spəːm] *n* спе́рма.
sperm bank *n* храни́лище до́норской
спе́рмы.
sperm whale *n* кашало́т.
spew [spjuː] *vt* изрыга́ть (изрыгну́ть *perf*) ♦ *vi*
(*inf: vomit*) рвать (вы́рвать *perf*); **he ~ed** его́
вы́рвало.
sphere [sfɪə'] *n* сфе́ра.
spherical ['sfɛrɪkl] *adj* сфери́ческий*,
шарообра́зный* (шарообра́зен).
sphinx [sfɪŋks] *n* сфинкс.
spice [spaɪs] *n* спе́ция, пря́ность *f* ♦ *vt* (*food*)
приправля́ть (припра́вить* *perf*) спе́циями.
spick-and-span ['spɪkən'spæn] *adj*: **to be ~**
сверка́ть (*impf*).
spicy ['spaɪsɪ] *adj* (*food*) о́стрый (остр).
spider ['spaɪdə'] *n* паўк*; ~**'s web** паути́на.

spidery ['spaɪdərɪ] *adj* (*handwriting*) тóнкий*
(тóнок) и небрéжный* (небрéжен).
spiel [spiːl] *n* (*inf*) говорильня.
spike [spaɪk] *n* (*point*) остриё; (*BOT: of flower*)
соцвéтие; (: *of corn*) кóлос; (*ELEC*) штырь *m*;
~s *npl* (*SPORT*) шипы́ *mpl*.
spike heel *n* (*US*) шпи́лька*.
spiky ['spaɪkɪ] *adj* (*plant, animal*) колю́чий*
(колю́ч).
spill [spɪl] (*pt, pp* **spilt** *or* **spilled**) *vt* (*liquid*)
пролива́ть (проли́ть* *perf*), разлива́ть
(разли́ть* *perf*) ♦ *vi* (*liquid*) пролива́ться
(проли́ться* *perf*), разлива́ться (разли́ться*
perf); **to ~ the beans** (*inf*) проба́лтываться
(проболта́ться *perf*)
▶ **spill out** *vi* вылива́ться (вы́литься* *perf*)
▶ **spill over** *vi* (*liquid*) перелива́ться
(перели́ться* *perf*) (чéрез край); (*fig: crowd,
conflict*) вылива́ться (вы́литься* *perf*).
spillage ['spɪlɪdʒ] *n* (*of oil*) разли́в.
spilt [spɪlt] *pt, pp of* **spill**.
spin [spɪn] (*pt* **spun** *or* **span**, *pp* **spun**) *n* (*trip in
car*) ката́ние; (*revolution of wheel*) поворóт,
враще́ние; (*AVIAT*) што́пор ♦ *vt* (*wool etc*)
прясть* (спрясть* *perf*); (*top*) крути́ть*
(закрути́ть* *perf*); (*wheel*) враща́ть (вертéть*
perf); (*BRIT: clothes*) выжима́ть (вы́жать* *perf*)
(в стира́льной маши́не) ♦ *vi* (*make thread*)
прясть* (*impf*); (*person, head*) кружи́ться*
(закружи́ться* *perf*); (*car*) враща́ться (*impf*);
let's go for a ~ in the car поéдем поката́ться
на маши́не; **to put ~ on a ball** закру́чивать
(закрути́ть* *perf*) мяч*; **to ~ a yarn** (*inf: story*)
плести́* (наплести́* *perf*) небыли́цы; **to ~ a
coin** (*BRIT*) подбра́сывать (подбрóсить* *perf*)
монéту
▶ **spin out** *vt* растя́гивать (растяну́ть* *perf*).
spina bifida ['spaɪnə'bɪfɪdə] *n* расщеплéние
ости́стых отрóстков позвонóчника.
spinach ['spɪnɪtʃ] *n* шпина́т.
spinal ['spaɪnl] *adj* спиннóй; **~ injury**
поврежде́ние позвонóчника.
spinal column *n* позвонóчный столб*.
spinal cord *n* спиннóй мозг*.
spindly ['spɪndlɪ] *adj* дли́нный* (дли́нен) и
тóнкий* (тóнок).
spin doctor *n* (*inf*) человéк, роль котóрого –
влия́ть на общéственное восприя́тие
полити́ческих програ́мм, и́миджа па́ртии
umn.
spin-dry ['spɪn'draɪ] *vt* (*clothes, washing*)
выжима́ть (вы́жать* *perf*) дóсуха (в
центрифу́ге).
spin-dryer [spɪn'draɪə'] *n* (*BRIT*)
центрифу́га-суши́лка*.
spine [spaɪn] *n* (*ANAT*) позвонóчник; (*thorn*)
колю́чка*, игла́*.
spine-chilling ['spaɪntʃɪlɪŋ] *adj* (*story, film*)

жу́ткий* (жу́ток).
spineless ['spaɪnlɪs] *adj* (*fig*) бесхребéтный*
(бесхребéтен).
spinner ['spɪnə'] *n* (*of thread*) пряди́ль-
щик(-щица), пря́ха *m/f*.
spinning ['spɪnɪŋ] *n* (*craft*) пряде́ние.
spinning top *n* волчóк*.
spinning wheel *n* пря́лка*.
spin-off ['spɪnɔf] *n* (*fig: by-product*) побóчный
результа́т.
spinster ['spɪnstə'] *n* (*unmarried woman*)
незаму́жняя же́нщина.
spiral ['spaɪərl] *n* спира́ль *f* ♦ *vi* (*fig: prices etc*)
рéзко возраста́ть (возрасти́* *perf*); **the
inflationary ~** спира́ль инфля́ции.
spiral staircase *n* винтова́я лéстница.
spire ['spaɪə'] *n* шпиль *m*.
spirit ['spɪrɪt] *n* дух; (*soul*) душа́*; **~s** *npl* (*drink*)
спиртнóе *ntsg adj*; **in good/low ~s** в хорóшем/
пода́вленном настроéнии; **community ~**,
public ~ общéственный дух.
spirited ['spɪrɪtɪd] *adj* энерги́чный*
(энерги́чен); (*performance*) воодушевл-
ённый* (*horse*) горя́чий* (горя́ч).
spirit level *n* ватерпа́с.
spiritual ['spɪrɪtjuəl] *adj* духóвный* (духóвен) ♦
n (*also:* **Negro ~**) спиричуал.
spiritualism ['spɪrɪtjuəlɪzəm] *n* спирити́зм.
spit [spɪt] (*pt, pp* **spat**) *n* (*for roasting*) вéртел;
(*saliva*) слюна́ ♦ *vi* (*person*) плева́ть*
(плю́нуть* *perf*); (*fire, hot oil*) шипéть* (*impf*);
(*inf: rain*) мороси́ть* (*impf*).
spite [spaɪt] *n* злóба, злость *f* ♦ *vt* досажда́ть
(досади́ть* *perf*) +*dat*; **in ~ of** несмотря́ на
+*acc*.
spiteful ['spaɪtful] *adj* злóбный* (злóбен).
spit roast *n* мя́со, зажа́ренное на вéртеле.
spitting ['spɪtɪŋ] *n*: **"spitting prohibited"**
"плева́ть воспреща́ется" ♦ *adj*: **he is the ~
image of his father** он вы́литый отéц.
spittle ['spɪtl] *n* слюна́.
spiv [spɪv] *n* (*BRIT: inf: pej*) жу́лик.
splash [splæʃ] *n* (*sound*) всплеск ♦ *excl*: **~!**
плюх! ♦ *vt* бры́згать* (бры́знуть *perf*) ♦ *vi*
(*also:* **~ about**) плеска́ться* (*impf*); **a ~ of
colour** цветовóе пятнó; **to ~ paint on the floor**
забры́згивать (забры́згать* *perf*) пол
кра́ской.
splashdown ['splæʃdaun] *n* (*SPACE*)
приводне́ние.
splayfooted ['spleɪfutɪd] *adj* ступа́ющий
пя́тками внутрь, носка́ми врозь.
spleen [spliːn] *n* (*ANAT*) селезёнка*.
splendid ['splendɪd] *adj* великолéпный*
(великолéпен).
splendour ['splendə'] (*US* **splendor**) *n*
великолéпие; **~s** *npl* (*features*) великолéпие
ntsg.

---

splice [splaɪs] *vt* соединя́ть (соедини́ть *perf*); (*tape, film*) скле́ивать (скле́ить *perf*).
splint [splɪnt] *n* ши́на.
splinter ['splɪntəᵊ] *n* (*of wood*) ще́пка•; (*of glass*) оско́лок•; (*in finger*) зано́за ♦ *vi* (*bone, wood, glass etc*) расщепля́ться (расщепи́ться• *perf*).
splinter group *n* отколо́вшаяся фра́кция.
split [splɪt] (*pt, pp* **split**) *n* (*crack, tear*) тре́щина; (*POL, fig*) раско́л ♦ *vt* (*divide*) расщепля́ть (расщепи́ть• *perf*); (*POL*) раска́лывать (расколо́ть• *perf*); (*share equally: work, profits*) разделя́ть (раздели́ть• *perf*) ♦ *vi* (*divide*) расщепля́ться (расщепи́ться• *perf*), разделя́ться (раздели́ться• *perf*); (*glass, wood*) раска́лываться (расколо́ться• *perf*); (*cloth*) разрыва́ться (разорва́ться• *perf*); **let's ~ the difference** дава́йте сойдёмся на сре́дней ци́фре; **to do the ~s** де́лать (сде́лать *perf*) шпага́т
▸ **split up** *vi* (*couple*) расходи́ться• (разойти́сь• *perf*); (*group*) разделя́ться (раздели́ться• *perf*); (*meeting*) зака́нчиваться (зако́нчиться• *perf*).
split-level ['splɪtlɛvl] *adj*: ~ **house** дом, постро́енный на ра́зных у́ровнях.
split peas *npl* лущёный горо́х *msg*.
split personality *n* раздвое́ние ли́чности.
split second *n* до́ля• секу́нды.
splitting ['splɪtɪŋ] *adj*: **I've got a ~ headache** у меня́ голова́ раска́лывается.
splutter ['splʌtəᵊ] *vi* (*engine etc*) треща́ть• (*impf*); (*person*) бры́згать• (*impf*) слюно́й.
spoil [spɔɪl] (*pt, pp* **spoilt** *or* **spoiled**) *vt* (*damage, mar*) по́ртить• (испо́ртить• *perf*); (*indulge*) балова́ть (избалова́ть *perf*) ♦ *vi*: **he's ~ing for a fight** он так и ле́зет в дра́ку.
spoils [spɔɪlz] *npl* (*also fig*) трофе́и *mpl*.
spoilsport ['spɔɪlspɔːt] *n* (*pej: person*): **don't be a ~** не отравля́й лю́дям настрое́ние.
spoilt [spɔɪlt] *pt, pp of* **spoil** ♦ *adj* испо́рченный• (испо́рчен); (*child*) избало́ванный• (избало́ван).
spoke [spəʊk] *pt of* **speak** ♦ *n* (*of wheel*) спи́ца.
spoken ['spəʊkn] *pp of* **speak**.
spokesman ['spəʊksmən] *irreg n* представи́тель *m*.
spokesperson ['spəʊkspəːsn] *irreg n* представи́тель(ница) *m(f)* по свя́зам с пре́ссой.
spokeswoman ['spəʊkswumən] *irreg n* представи́тельница.
sponge [spʌndʒ] *n* гу́бка•; (*also:* ~ **cake**) бискви́т ♦ *vt* (*wash*) обтира́ть (обтере́ть• *perf*) гу́бкой ♦ *vi*: **to ~ off** *or* **on sb** сиде́ть• (*impf*) на ше́е у кого́-н.
sponge bag *n* (*BRIT*) су́мочка• для туале́тных принадле́жностей.
sponger ['spʌndʒəᵊ] *n* (*pej*) парази́т.
spongy ['spʌndʒɪ] *adj* гу́бчатый.
sponsor ['spɔnsəᵊ] *n* спо́нсор; (*for application*) поручи́тель *m* ♦ *vt* финанси́ровать (*impf/perf*);

(*applicant*) поруча́ться (поручи́ться *perf*) за +*acc*; (*proposal, bill etc*) вноси́ть• (внести́• *perf*) на рассмотре́ние; **I ~ed him at twenty pence a mile** я поже́ртвовал ему́ два́дцать пе́нсов за ми́лю.
sponsorship ['spɔnsəʃɪp] *n* спо́нсорство.
spontaneity [spɔntə'neɪɪtɪ] *n* спонта́нность *f*.
spontaneous [spɔn'teɪnɪəs] *adj* (*gesture*) спонта́нный• (спонта́нен); (*demonstration*) стихи́йный; ~ **combustion** самовозгора́ние, самовоспламене́ние.
spoof [spuːf] (*inf*) *n* (*imitation*) паро́дия; (*joke*) ро́зыгрыш ♦ *vt* (*imitate*) передра́знивать (*impf*).
spooky ['spuːkɪ] *adj* (*inf: place, atmosphere*) злове́щий•, жу́ткий•.
spool [spuːl] *n* (*for thread*) кату́шка•; (*for film, tape etc*) боби́на.
spoon [spuːn] *n* ло́жка•.
spoon-feed ['spuːnfiːd] *vt* (*baby, patient*) корми́ть• (*impf*) с ло́жки; (*fig: students*) всё разжёвывать (*impf*) +*dat*.
spoonful ['spuːnful] *n* (*полная*) ло́жка•.
sporadic [spə'rædɪk] *adj* споради́ческий•.
sport [spɔːt] *n* (*game*) спорт *m no pl*; (*person: also:* **good ~**) молодчи́на *m* ♦ *vt* (*wear*) щеголя́ть (щегольну́ть *perf*) +*instr*; **indoor/ outdoor ~s** ви́ды спо́рта для закры́тых помеще́ний/на откры́том во́здухе.
sporting ['spɔːtɪŋ] *adj* (*event etc*) спорти́вный; (*generous*) ры́царский•; **to give sb a ~ chance** дава́ть• (дать• *perf*) кому́-н не́который шанс.
sport jacket *n* (*US*) = **sports jacket**.
sports car *n* спорти́вная маши́на.
sports centre *n* спорти́вный центр.
sports ground *n* спорти́вная площа́дка•.
sports jacket *n* (*BRIT*) спорти́вная ку́ртка• из тви́да.
sportsman ['spɔːtsmən] *irreg n* спортсме́н.
sportsmanship ['spɔːtsmənʃɪp] *n* спорти́вный дух; **he showed real ~** он показа́л себя́ настоя́щим спортсме́ном.
sports page *n* спорти́вная страни́ца.
sportswear ['spɔːtswɛəᵊ] *n* спорти́вная оде́жда.
sportswoman ['spɔːtswumən] *irreg n* спортсме́нка•.
sporty ['spɔːtɪ] *adj* спорти́вный• (спорти́вен).
spot [spɔt] *n* (*mark*) пятно́•; (*dot: on pattern*) кра́пинка•; (*on skin*) пры́щик; (*place*) ме́сто•; (*RADIO, TV*) рекла́мный переры́в; ~ **advertisement** рекла́мная ру́брика ♦ *vt* (*notice*) замеча́ть (заме́тить• *perf*); **a ~ of bother** ма́ленькая неприя́тность *f*; **shall we have a ~ of lunch?** не перекуси́ть ли нам?; **~s of rain** ка́пли дождя́; **on the ~** (*in that place*) на ме́сте; (*immediately*) в тот же моме́нт; **to put sb on the ~** ста́вить• (поста́вить• *perf*) кого́-н в затрудни́тельное положе́ние; **in a ~** (*in difficulty*) в затрудни́тельном

положе́нии; **to come out in** ~**s** (*rash*) покрыва́ться (покры́ться* *perf*) сы́пью; (*blemishes*) покрыва́ться (покры́ться* *perf*) прыща́ми.

spot check *n* вы́борочная прове́рка*.

spotless ['spɒtlɪs] *adj* (*shirt, kitchen etc*) без пя́тнышка.

spotlight ['spɒtlaɪt] *n* (освети́тельный) проже́ктор; **to be in the** ~ (*fig*) быть* (*impf*) в це́нтре внима́ния.

spot-on [spɒt'ɒn] *adj* (*BRIT*: *inf*): **to be** ~ попа́сть* (*perf*) в са́мую то́чку.

spot price *n* (*COMM*) цена́ при усло́вии неме́дленной опла́ты (нали́чными).

spotted ['spɒtɪd] *adj* (*pattern*) пятни́стый (пятни́ст); ~ **with** запя́тнанный (запя́тнан) +*instr*.

spotty ['spɒtɪ] *adj* (*face, youth*) прыща́вый (прыща́в).

spouse [spaus] *n* супру́г(а).

spout [spaut] *n* (*of jug*) но́сик; (*of pipe*) выпускно́е отве́рстие; (*of liquid*) струя́* ♦ *vi* (*water etc*) бить* (*impf*) струёй; (*volcano*) изверга́ться (изве́ргнуться *perf*).

sprain [spreɪn] *n* (*MED*) растяже́ние ♦ *vt*: **to** ~ **one's ankle/wrist** растя́гивать (растяну́ть* *perf*) щи́колотку/запя́стье.

sprang [spræŋ] *pt of* **spring**.

sprawl [sprɔːl] *vi* (*person*) развали́ваться (развали́ться* *perf*); (*place*) раски́дываться (раски́нуться *perf*) ♦ *n*: **urban** ~ разраста́ние го́рода; **to send sb** ~**ing** сбива́ть (сбить* *perf*) кого́-н с ног.

spray [spreɪ] *n* (*drops of water*) бры́зги *pl*; (*hair spray*) аэрозо́ль *m*; (*garden spray*) разбры́згиватель *m*; (: *chemicals*) ядохимика́ты *mpl*; (*of flowers*) ве́точка* ♦ *vt* (*sprinkle*) обры́згивать (обры́згать *perf*); (*crops*) опры́скивать (опры́скать *perf*) ♦ *cpd*: ~ **deodorant** дезодора́нт в аэрозо́льной упако́вке.

spread [sprɛd] (*pt, pp* **spread**) *n* (*range*) спектр; (*distribution*) распростране́ние; (*CULIN*: *paste*) па́ста; (: *margarine etc*) бутербро́дный маргари́н; (*inf*: *food*) оби́льное угоще́ние; (*PRESS, TYP*: *two pages*) разворо́т ♦ *vt* (*lay out*) расстила́ть (расстели́ть* *perf*); (*scatter*) разбра́сывать (разброса́ть* *perf*); (*butter, paste*) нама́зывать (нама́зать* *perf*); (*wings*) расправля́ть (распра́вить* *perf*); (*arms*) раскрыва́ть (раскры́ть* *perf*); (*sail*) развёртывать (разверну́ть* *perf*); (*workload, wealth*) распределя́ть (распредели́ть* *perf*); (*rumour, disease*) распространя́ть (распространи́ть* *perf*); (*repayments*) отсро́чивать (отсро́чить *perf*) ♦ *vi* (*disease, news*) распространя́ться (распростран- я́ться* *perf*); (*also:* ~ **out**) расширя́ться

(расши́риться *perf*); **middle-age** ~ возрастна́я полнота́

▶ **spread out** *vi* (*move apart*) раздвига́ть (раздви́нуть *perf*).

spread-eagled ['sprɛdiːɡld] *adj* распла́станный (распла́стан); **to be** *or* **lie** ~ лежа́ть* (*impf*) плашмя́.

spreadsheet ['sprɛdʃiːt] *n* (*COMPUT*) электро́нная табли́ца.

spree [spriː] *n*: **to go on a** ~ кути́ть* (покути́ть* *perf*).

sprig [sprɪɡ] *n* (*BOT*) ве́точка*.

sprightly ['spraɪtlɪ] *adj* (*old person*) бо́дрый (бодр).

spring [sprɪŋ] (*pt* **sprang**, *pp* **sprung**) *n* (*coiled metal*) пружи́на; (*season*) весна́*; (*of water*) исто́чник, родни́к*; (*leap*) прыжо́к*; (*bounciness*) упру́гость *f* ♦ *vi* (*leap*) пры́гать (пры́гнуть *perf*) ♦ *vt*: **to** ~ **a leak** (*pipe etc*) дава́ть* (дать* *perf*) течь; **in** ~ весно́й; **to walk with a** ~ **in one's step** ходи́ть*/идти́* (*impf*) упру́гой *or* пружи́нистой похо́дкой; **to** ~ **from sth** (*be the result of*) быть* (*impf*) вы́званным(-ой) чем-н; **he sprang the news on me** он вы́валил на меня́ э́ту но́вость; **to** ~ **into action** ри́нуться (*perf*) в де́ло

▶ **spring up** *vi* (*building, plant*) выраста́ть (вы́расти* *perf*).

springboard ['sprɪŋbɔːd] *n* (*SPORT*) трампли́н; (*fig*): **to be the** ~ **for** быть* (*impf*) трампли́ном для +*gen*.

spring-clean(ing) [sprɪŋ'kliːn(ɪŋ)] *n* генера́льная убо́рка*.

spring onion *n* (*BRIT*: *BOT*) лук-бату́н *no pl*; (: *CULIN*) зелёный лук *no pl*.

spring roll *n* бли́нчик с начи́нкой, свёрнутый в тру́бочку.

springtime ['sprɪŋtaɪm] *n* весе́няя пора́.

springy ['sprɪŋɪ] *adj* упру́гий*.

sprinkle ['sprɪŋkl] *vt* (*salt, sugar*) посыпа́ть (посы́пать* *perf*) +*instr*; **to** ~ **water on sth**, ~ **sth with water** бры́згать (побры́згать *perf*) водо́й на что-н; **to** ~ **sugar on sth**, ~ **sth with sugar** посыпа́ть (посы́пать* *perf*) что-н са́харом; ~**d with** (*fig*) усы́панный (усы́пан) +*instr*.

sprinkler ['sprɪŋklə^r] *n* (*for lawn*) разбры́згиватель *m*; (*to put out fire*) спри́нклер.

sprinkling ['sprɪŋklɪŋ] *n* небольшо́е коли́чество; (*of salt, sugar*) небольшо́е го́рстка.

sprint [sprɪnt] *n* (*race*) спринт ♦ *vi* (*run fast*) стреми́тельно бе́гать/бежа́ть* (*impf*); (*SPORT*) спринтова́ть (*impf*); **the 200 metres** ~ спринт на 200-метро́вую диста́нцию.

sprinter ['sprɪntə^r] *n* спри́нтер.

sprite [spraɪt] *n* эльф, фе́я.

---

spritzer ['sprɪtsə^r] *n* бе́лое вино́ с со́довой (водо́й).

sprocket ['sprɔkɪt] *n* (*TECH*) (цепна́я) звёздочка*.

sprout [spraut] *vi* (*BOT*) пуска́ть (пусти́ть* *perf*) ростки́.

sprouts [sprauts] *npl* (*also:* **Brussels ~**) брюссе́льская капу́ста *fsg*.

spruce [spru:s] *n inv* (*BOT*) ель *f* ◆ *adj* (*neat*) опря́тный* (опря́тен); (*smart*) наря́дный* (наря́ден)

▸ **spruce up** *vt* (*smarten up: room etc*) наводи́ть* (навести́* *perf*) гля́нец на +*acc*; **to ~ o.s. up** наводи́ть* (навести́* *perf*) на себя́ гля́нец.

sprung [sprʌŋ] *pp of* **spring**.

spry [spraɪ] *adj* (*old person*) бо́дрый (бодр).

SPUC *n abbr* (= *Society for the Protection of Unborn Children*) о́бщество, бо́рющееся про́тив дозволи́тельности або́ртов.

spud [spʌd] *n* (*inf: potato*) карто́шка*.

spun [spʌn] *pt, pp of* **spin**.

spur [spə:^r] *n* шпо́ра; (*fig*) сти́мул ◆ *vt* (*also:* **~ on**) подстёгивать (подстегну́ть* *perf*); **to ~ sb on to** побужда́ть (побуди́ть* *perf*) кого́-н к +*dat*; **on the ~ of the moment** под влия́нием мину́ты.

spurious ['spjuərɪəs] *adj* подде́льный.

spurn [spə:n] *vt* (*reject*) отверга́ть (отве́ргнуть* *perf*).

spurt [spə:t] *n* (*of blood etc*) струя́; (*of energy*) поры́в ◆ *vi* хлы́нуть (*perf*); **to put on a ~** де́лать (сде́лать *perf*) рыво́к.

sputter ['spʌtə^r] *vi* = **splutter**.

spy [spaɪ] *n* шпио́н ◆ *vi*: **to ~ on** шпио́нить (*impf*) за +*instr* ◆ *vt* (*see*) замеча́ть (заме́тить* *perf*) ◆ *cpd* (*film, story*) шпио́нский.

spying ['spaɪŋ] *n* шпиона́ж.

Sq. *abbr* (*in address*) (= **square**) пл.= *пло́щадь*.

sq. *abbr* = **square**.

squabble ['skwɔbl] *vi* вздо́рить (повздо́рить *perf*) *n* перебра́нка*.

squad [skwɔd] *n* (*MIL, POLICE*) кома́нда; (*SPORT*) кома́нда; **flying ~** (*POLICE*) летучий* полице́йский* отря́д.

squad car *n* (*BRIT: POLICE*) дежу́рная полице́йская маши́на.

squaddie ['skwɔdɪ] *n* (*inf*) солдатня́ *f no pl*.

squadron ['skwɔdrn] *n* (*MIL*) эскадро́н; (*AVIAT*) эскадри́лья; (*NAUT*) эска́дра.

squalid ['skwɔlɪd] *adj* (*conditions, room*) убо́гий* (убо́г); (*story etc*) гря́зный* (гря́зен).

squall [skwɔ:l] *n* (*stormy wind*) шквал.

squalor ['skwɔlə^r] *n* убо́гость *f*.

squander ['skwɔndə^r] *vt* (*money*) прома́тывать (промота́ть *perf*); (*chances*) растра́чивать (растра́тить* *perf*).

square [skwɛə^r] *n* (*shape*) квадра́т; (*in town*) пло́щадь *f*; (*US: block of houses*) кварта́л; (*also:* **set ~**) уго́льник; (*inf: person*) немо́дный, се́рый челове́к* ◆ *adj* квадра́тный; (*inf: ideas, tastes*) немо́дный, се́рый ◆ *vt* (*reconcile, settle*) ула́живать (ула́дить* *perf*); (*MATH*) возводи́ть* (возвести́* *perf*) в квадра́т ◆ *vi* (*agree*) согласо́вываться (согласова́ться *perf*); **we are all ~** мы кви́ты; **a ~ meal** пло́тная трапе́за; **2 metres ~** 2 ме́тра длино́й и 2 ме́тра ширино́й; **2 ~ metres** 2 квадра́тных ме́тра; **I'll ~ it with him** (*inf*) я с ним э́то ула́жу; **can you ~ it with your conscience?** (*reconcile*) э́то согласу́ется с Ва́шей со́вестью?; **we're back to ~ one** мы верну́лись туда́, отку́да на́чали

▸ **square up** *vi* (*BRIT*): **to ~ up with sb** поквита́ться (*perf*) с кем-н.

square bracket *n* (*TYP*) квадра́тная ско́бка*.

squarely ['skwɛəlɪ] *adv* пря́мо.

square root *n* квадра́тный ко́рень* *m*.

squash [skwɔʃ] *n* (*BRIT: drink*): **lemon/orange ~** лимо́нный/апельси́новой напи́ток* (*приготовле́нный из концентра́та*); (*US*) ты́ква; (*SPORT*) ракетбо́л ◆ *vt* дави́ть* (разда́вить* *perf*).

squat [skwɔt] *adj* призе́мистый (призе́мист) ◆ *vi* (*also:* **~ down**: *position*) сиде́ть* (*impf*) на ко́рточках; (: *motion*) сесть* (*perf*) на ко́рточки; (*on property*) незако́нно поселя́ться (посели́ться *perf*) в дом.

squatter ['skwɔtə^r] *n* (*in house*) лицо́, самово́льно поселя́ющееся в чужо́м до́ме; (*on land*) сква́ттер.

squawk [skwɔ:k] *vi* (*bird*) клекота́ть* (*impf*).

squeak [skwi:k] *vi* (*door*) скрипе́ть* (скри́пнуть* *perf*); (*mouse*) пища́ть* (пи́скнуть *perf*) ◆ *n* (*of hinge, wheel etc*) скрип.

squeaky-clean [skwi:kɪ'kli:n] *adj* (*surface etc*) чи́стый (чист) до скри́па; (*fig*) без пя́тнышка.

squeal [skwi:l] *vi* визжа́ть* (*impf*), взви́згивать (взви́згнуть *perf*).

squeamish ['skwi:mɪʃ] *adj* (*person*) брезгли́вый (брезгли́в).

squeeze [skwi:z] *n* (*of hand*) сжа́тие; (*ECON*) ограниче́ние; (*also:* **credit ~**) ограниче́ние креди́та ◆ *vt* сжима́ть (сжать* *perf*); (*juice*) выжима́ть (вы́жать* *perf*) ◆ *vi*: **to ~ past/ under sth** проти́скиваться (проти́снуться *perf*) че́рез что-н/под чем-н; **a ~ of lemon** не́сколько капе́ль лимо́нного со́ка

▸ **squeeze out** *vt* (*juice etc*) выжима́ть (вы́жать* *perf*); (*fig: money etc*) выжима́ть (вы́жать* *perf*).

squelch [skwɛltʃ] *vi* (*mud etc*) хлю́пать (хлю́пнуть *perf*).

squib [skwɪb] *n* (*firework*) пета́рда.

squid [skwɪd] *n* кальма́р.

squiggle ['skwɪgl] *n* загогу́лина.

squint [skwɪnt] *vi* (*permanently*) коси́ть* (*impf*); (*in sunlight*) щу́риться (*impf*), прищу́риваться (прищу́риться *perf*) ◆ *n* (*MED*) косогла́зие; **he has a ~** у него́ косогла́зие, он коси́т.

squire ['skwaɪə^r] n (BRIT) поме́щик; (inf) нача́льник.

squirm [skwə:m] vi выгиба́ться (вы́гнуться perf); (with embarrassment or shame) поёживаться (поёжиться perf).

squirrel ['skwɪrəl] n бе́лка*.

squirt [skwə:t] vi бры́згать* (брызну́ть perf) ♦ vt бры́згать* (брызну́ть perf) +instr.

Sr abbr (in names) = **senior**; (REL) = **sister**.

SRC n abbr (BRIT) = **Students' Representative Council**.

Sri Lanka [srɪ'læŋkə] n Шри-Ла́нка.

SRN n abbr (BRIT: = **State Registered Nurse**) медсестра́ = медици́нская сестра́.

SRO n abbr (US: = **standing room only**) то́лько стоя́чие места́ ntpl.

SS abbr = **steamship**.

SSA n abbr (US: = **Social Security Administration**) ≈ департа́мент социа́льного обеспе́чения.

SST n abbr (US: = **supersonic transport**) сверхзвуково́й реакти́вный самолёт.

ST abbr (US) = **Standard Time**.

St abbr = **saint**; (= **street**) ул.= *у́лица*.

stab [stæb] n (with knife etc) уда́р (чем-н о́стрым); (of pain) уко́л; (inf: try): **to have a ~ at doing** пыта́ться (попыта́ться perf) +infin ♦ vt наноси́ть* (нанести́* perf) уда́р +dat; **to ~ sb to death** зака́лывать (заколо́ть* perf) кого́-н.

stabbing ['stæbɪŋ] n: **there's been a ~** здесь была́ поножо́вщина ♦ adj (pain, ache) ре́зкий*.

stability [stə'bɪlɪtɪ] n (of object) усто́йчивость f; (of government, economy etc) стаби́льность f.

stabilization [steɪbəlaɪ'zeɪʃən] n стабилиза́ция.

stabilize ['steɪbəlaɪz] vt (prices) стабилизи́ровать (impf/perf) ♦ vi стабилизи́роваться (impf/perf).

stabilizer ['steɪbəlaɪzə^r] n стабилиза́тор.

stable ['steɪbl] adj стаби́льный* (стаби́лен), усто́йчивый (усто́йчив) ♦ n (for horse) коню́шня*, сто́йло; (for cattle) хлев*, сто́йло; **riding ~s** (school) ко́нно-спорти́вная шко́ла.

staccato [stə'ka:təu] adv (MUS) стакка́то ♦ adj отры́вистый (отры́вист).

stack [stæk] n (pile: of hay) стог*, скирда́*; (of wood) шта́бель m, поле́нница; (of papers) ки́па, сто́пка; (of plates) стопа́* ♦ vt (also: ~ up: chairs etc) скла́дывать (сложи́ть* perf) в ку́чу; (: books, plates) скла́дывать (сложи́ть* perf) в сто́пку; (room, table etc): **to ~ (with)** уставля́ть (уста́вить* perf) сто́пками; **there's ~s of time** (BRIT: inf) ещё есть ку́ча вре́мени.

stadia ['steɪdɪə] npl of **stadium**.

stadium ['steɪdɪəm] (pl **stadia** or **~s**) n (SPORT) стадио́н.

staff [sta:f] n (workforce) рабо́тники pl, штат; (BRIT: SCOL: also: **teaching ~**) штат учителе́й, преподава́тельский соста́в; (servants) штат;

(MIL) ли́чный соста́в; (stick) по́сох ♦ vt укомплекто́вывать (укомплектова́ть perf).

staffroom ['sta:fru:m] n (SCOL) учи́тельская f adj.

Staffs abbr (BRIT: POST) = **Staffordshire**.

stag [stæg] n саме́ц оле́ня; (BRIT: STOCK EXCHANGE) спекуля́нт це́нными бума́гами.

stage [steɪdʒ] n (in theatre) сце́на; (platform) подмо́стки pl; (profession): **the ~** сце́на; (point, period) ста́дия ♦ vt (play) ста́вить* (поста́вить* perf); (demonstration) устра́ивать (устро́ить perf); (fig: recovery etc) осуществля́ть (осуществи́ть* perf); **in ~s** поэта́пно, по эта́пам; **he is going through a difficult ~** он пережива́ет тру́дный пери́од; **in the early/final ~s** на ра́нних/после́дних ста́диях or эта́пах.

stagecoach ['steɪdʒkəutʃ] n почто́вый дилижа́нс.

stage door n (THEAT) служе́бный вход (в теа́тр).

stage fright n волне́ние пе́ред выступле́нием.

stagehand ['steɪdʒhænd] n рабо́чий*(-ая) m(f) adj сце́ны.

stage-manage ['steɪdʒmænɪdʒ] vt (fig) закули́сно руководи́ть* (impf) +instr.

stage manager n дире́ктор сце́ны.

stagger ['stægə^r] vt (amaze) потряса́ть (потрясти́* perf) ♦ vi: **he ~ed along the road** он шёл по доро́ге, поша́тываясь; **the management has ~ed the workers' leave** администра́ция соста́вила гра́фик о́тпусков.

staggering ['stægərɪŋ] adj потряса́ющий*.

staging post ['steɪdʒɪŋ-] n (on flight) промежу́точный аэродро́м.

stagnant ['stægnənt] adj (water) стоя́чий*; (economy) засто́йный.

stagnate [stæg'neɪt] vi (person) засижива́ться (засиде́ться* perf); (economy, business) быть* (impf) в засто́е.

stagnation [stæg'neɪʃən] n засто́й; (ECON) стагна́ция, засто́й.

stag party n мальчи́шник.

staid [steɪd] adj (person, attitudes) степе́нный* (степе́нен).

stain [steɪn] n пятно́*; (for wood) мори́лка* ♦ vt (mark) пятна́ть (запятна́ть perf), па́чкать (запа́чкать perf); (wood) мори́ть (замори́ть perf).

stained glass window [steɪnd-] n витра́ж.

stainless steel ['steɪnlɪs-] n нержаве́ющая сталь f.

stain remover n пятновыводи́тель m.

stair [steə^r] n (step) ступе́нь f, ступе́нька*; **~s** npl (steps) ле́стница fsg; **on the ~s** на ле́стнице.

staircase ['steəkeɪs] n ле́стница.

---

* marks translations which have irregular inflections. The Russian-English side of the dictionary gives inflectional information.

stairway ['stɛəweɪ] = **staircase**.

stairwell ['stɛəwɛl] *n* лестничная клетка*.

stake [steɪk] *n* (*post*) кол*; (*investment*) доля*; (*wager*) ставка*; (*horse race: usu pl*) скачки* *fpl* ♦ *vt* (*wager: money, life, reputation*) ставить* (поставить* *perf*); (*also:* ~ **out**: *area*) огораживать (огородить* *perf*); (*fig*) очерчивать (очертить* *perf*) границы +*gen*; **his reputation was at** ~ его репутация была поставлена на карту; **he has a** ~ **in this business** он кровно заинтересован в этом бизнесе; **to** ~ **a claim (to sth)** притязать (*impf*) (на что-н).

stake out *n* (*US*: *inf*) засада.

stalactite ['stæləktaɪt] *n* сталактит.

stalagmite ['stæləgmaɪt] *n* сталагмит.

stale [steɪl] *adj* (*bread*) чёрствый (чёрств); (*food, beer*) несвежий* (несвеж); (*air, smell*) затхлый.

stalemate ['steɪlmeɪt] *n* (*CHESS*) пат; (*fig*) тупик.

stalk [stɔːk] *n* (*of flower*) стебель *m*; (*of fruit*) черенок* ♦ *vt* (*person, animal*) красться* (подкрасться* *perf*) к +*dat* ♦ *vi*: **to** ~ **out/off** удаляться (удалиться* *perf*).

stall [stɔːl] *n* (*BRIT*: *in street*) ларёк*, киоск; (*in market*) прилавок*; (*in stable*) стойло ♦ *vt* (*fig: delay*) задерживать (задержать* *perf*) ♦ *vi* (*AUT*) глохнуть* (заглохнуть* *perf*); (*fig: person*) мешкать (помешкать *perf*); ~**s** *npl* (*BRIT*: *THEAT*) партер *msg*; **watch you don't** ~ **the engine** смотри, чтобы мотор не заглох; **a seat in the** ~**s** место* *or* кресло* в партере; **a newspaper/flower** ~ газетный/цветочный ларёк.

stallholder ['stɔːlhəʊldə'] *n* (*BRIT*) владелец* ларька.

stallion ['stæljən] *n* жеребец*.

stalwart ['stɔːlwət] *adj* (*worker, supporter, party member*) стойкий*.

stamen ['steɪmɛn] *n* тычинка*.

stamina ['stæmɪnə] *n* выносливость *f*.

stammer ['stæmə'] *n* заикание ♦ *vi* заикаться.

stamp [stæmp] *n* (*postage stamp*) марка*; (*rubber stamp*) печать *f*, штамп; (*mark, also fig*) печать* ♦ *vi* (*also:* ~ **one's foot**) топать* (топнуть *perf*) ногой ♦ *vt* (*letter*) наклеивать (наклеить *perf*) марку на +*acc*; (*mark*) описывать (описнуть *perf*); (*with rubber stamp*) ставить* (поставить* *perf*) печать *or* штамп на +*acc*; ~**ed addressed envelope** надписанный конверт с маркой

▸ **stamp out** *vt* (*fire*) затаптывать (затоптать* *perf*); (*crime*) уничтожать (уничтожить *perf*); (*opposition*) подавлять (подавить* *perf*).

stamp album *n* альбом для марок.

stamp collecting *n* филателия.

stamp duty *n* (*BRIT*) гербовый сбор.

stampede [stæm'piːd] *n* (*also fig*) массовое бегство.

stamp machine *n* автомат по продаже почтовых марок.

stance [stæns] *n* (*also fig*) позиция.

stand [stænd] (*pt, pp* **stood**) *n* (*stall*) ларёк*, киоск; (*at exhibition*) стенд; (*SPORT*) трибуна; (*piece of furniture: for umbrellas*) подставка*; (: *for coats, hats*) вешалка* ♦ *vi* (*be upright*) стоять* (*impf*); (*rise*) вставать* (встать* *perf*); (*remain: decision, offer*) оставаться* (остаться* *perf*) в силе; (*in election etc*) выставлять (выставить* *perf*) свою кандидатуру, баллотироваться (*impf*); (*value, level, score etc*): **to** ~ **at** оставаться* (остаться* *perf*) на +*prp* ♦ *vt* (*place: object*) ставить* (поставить* *perf*); (*tolerate, withstand*) терпеть* (*impf*), выносить* (вынести* *perf*); **to make a** ~ **against sth** оказывать (оказать* *perf*) сопротивление чему-н; **to take a** ~ **on sth** занимать (занять* *perf*) позицию по поводу чего-н; **to take the** ~ (*US: LAW*) занимать (занять* *perf*) место свидетеля; **to** ~ **for parliament** (*BRIT*) баллотироваться (*impf*) в парламент; **to** ~ **to gain/lose sth** иметь (обрести/потерять что-н; **to** ~ **sb dinner** угощать (угостить* *perf*) кого-н обедом; **to** ~ **sb a drink** ставить* (поставить* *perf*) кому-н выпивку; **it** ~**s to reason** само собой разумеется; **as things** ~ в этой ситуации; **I can't** ~ **him** я его терпеть не могу

▸ **stand aside** *vi* (*fig*) стоять (*impf*) в стороне

▸ **stand by** *vi* (*be ready*) быть* (*impf*) наготове ♦ *vt fus* (*opinion, decision*) не отступать (не отступить* *perf*) от +*gen*; (*person*) поддерживать (поддержать* *perf*)

▸ **stand down** *vi* (*withdraw*) уступать (уступить* *perf*) место, уходить* (уйти* *perf*); (*LAW*) покидать (покинуть *perf*) место свидетеля

▸ **stand for** *vt fus* (*signify*) обозначать (*impf*); (*represent*) представлять (*impf*); **I won't** ~ **for it** я этого не потерплю

▸ **stand in for** *vt fus* (*replace*) замещать (заместить* *perf*) +*acc*

▸ **stand out** *vi* (*be prominent*) выделяться (выделиться *perf*)

▸ **stand up** *vi* (*rise*) вставать* (встать* *perf*)

▸ **stand up for** *vt fus* (*defend: rights etc*) отстаивать (отстоять* *perf*); (: *person*) стоять* (постоять* *perf*) за +*acc*

▸ **stand up to** *vt fus* (*withstand: also fig*) выдерживать (выдержать* *perf*).

stand-alone ['stændələʊn] *adj* (*COMPUT*) автономный.

standard ['stændəd] *n* (*level*) уровень* *m*; (*norm, criterion*) стандарт; (*flag*) знамя* *nt* ♦ *adj* (*normal: size etc*) стандартный* (стандартен); (*text*) основной*; (*practice*) общепринятый (общепринят); (*model, feature*) типичный* (типичен); ~**s** *npl* (*morals*) нравы *mpl*; **to be** *or* **to come up to** ~ быть* (*impf*) на соответствующем уровне; **to apply**

a double ~ испо́льзовать *(impf/perf)* двойну́ю мора́ль.

standardization [stændədaɪ'zeɪʃən] *n* стандартиза́ция.

standardize ['stændədaɪz] *vt* стандартизи́ровать *(impf/perf)*.

standard lamp *n (BRIT)* торше́р.

standard of living *n* у́ровень *m* жи́зни.

standard time *n* станда́ртное вре́мя* *nt.*

stand-by ['stændbaɪ] *n (reserve)* резе́рв, подмо́га ♦ *adj* запасно́й, резе́рвный; **to be on ~** *(doctor, crew, firemen etc)* быть* *(impf)* нагото́ве.

stand-by ticket *n (THEAT etc)* биле́т, ку́пленный пе́ред нача́лом представле́ния.

stand-in ['stændɪn] *n* замести́тель(ница) *m(f).*

standing ['stændɪŋ] *adj (permanent)* постоя́нный; *(ovation)* стоя́чий* ♦ *n (status)* положе́ние; *(duration):* **of 6 months'** ~ 6-ти ме́сячной да́вности; **he received/was given a ~ ovation** ему́ устро́или стоя́чую ова́цию; **he gave me a ~ invitation** он сказа́л, что́бы я приходи́л в любо́е вре́мя; **a man of some ~** челове́к с положе́нием; **promises of many years ~** многоле́тние обеща́ния.

standing committee *n* постоя́нный комите́т.

standing joke *n* дежу́рная шу́тка*.

standing order *n (BRIT: at bank)* прика́з о регуля́рных платежа́х.

standing room *n* стоя́чие места́ *ntpl.*

standoffish [stænd'ɔfɪʃ] *adj* спеси́вый (спеси́в).

standpat ['stændpæt] *adj (US: person)* консервати́вный.

standpipe ['stændpaɪp] *n* напо́рная труба́*.

standpoint ['stændpɔɪnt] *n* то́чка* зре́ния.

standstill ['stændstɪl] *n:* **to be at a ~** *(also fig)* простаи́вать *(impf);* **to come to a ~** остана́вливаться (останови́ться* *perf).*

stank [stæŋk] *pt of* **stink.**

stanza ['stænzə] *n (of poem)* строфа́*.

staple ['steɪpl] *n (for papers)* ско́бка*; *(chief product)* основно́й проду́кт ♦ *adj (food etc)* основно́й ♦ *vt (fasten)* сшива́ть (сшить* *perf)* сте́плером.

stapler ['steɪplə'] *n* сшива́тель *m,* сте́плер.

star [sta:'] *n (also fig)* звезда́* ♦ *vi:* **to ~ in** игра́ть (сыгра́ть *perf)* гла́вную роль в +*prp* ♦ *vt (THEAT, CINEMA):* **the film ~s my brother** гла́вную роль игра́ет в фи́льме мой брат; **the ~s** *npl (horoscope)* звёзды *fpl;* **4-~ hotel** четырёхзвёздочная гости́ница; **2-~/4-~ petrol** *(BRIT)* бензи́н с ни́зким/высо́ким окта́новым число́м.

star attraction *n* гвоздь* *m* програ́ммы.

starboard ['sta:bəd] *n (NAUT)* пра́вый борт*; **to ~** пра́во руля́.

starch [sta:tʃ] *n (also CULIN)* крахма́л.

starched ['sta:tʃt] *adj (collar)* накрахма́ленный

(накрахма́лен).

starchy ['sta:tʃɪ] *adj (food)* содержа́щий крахма́л; *(pej: person)* чо́порный* (чо́порен).

stardom ['sta:dəm] *n* сла́ва.

stare [stɛə'] *n* приста́льный взгляд ♦ *vi:* **to ~ at** приста́льно смотре́ть* *(impf)* на +*acc.*

starfish ['sta:fɪʃ] *n* морска́я звезда́*.

stark [sta:k] *adj (bleak)* го́лый* (гол); *(facts, reality)* го́лый; *(poverty)* соверше́нный; *(colour, contrast)* я́вный* (я́вен) ♦ *adv:* **~ naked** соверше́нно го́лый.

starkers ['sta:kəz] *adj, adv* без всего́.

starlet ['sta:lɪt] *n (CINEMA)* молода́я актри́са.

starlight ['sta:laɪt] *n:* **by ~** при све́те звёзд.

starling ['sta:lɪŋ] *n* скворе́ц.

starlit ['sta:lɪt] *adj (night)* звёздный.

starry ['sta:rɪ] *adj (night, sky)* звёздный.

starry-eyed [sta:rɪ'aɪd] *adj (innocent)* наи́вный* (наи́вен); *(from wonder)* очаро́ванный.

Stars and Stripes *n:* **the ~ ~** звёздно-полоса́тый *m adj (флаг США).*

star sign *n* знак зодиа́ка.

star-studded ['sta:stʌdɪd] *adj:* **this film has a ~ cast** в э́том фи́льме снима́ются мно́гие знамени́тые актёры.

START *n abbr (MIL: = Strategic Arms Reduction Talks)* перегово́ры *pl* о сокраще́нии стратеги́ческих вооруже́ний.

start [sta:t] *n* нача́ло; *(SPORT)* старт; *(departure)* отправле́ние; *(sudden movement)* вздра́гивание; *(advantage)* преиму́щество ♦ *vt (begin)* начина́ть (нача́ть* *perf);* *(cause)* вызыва́ть (вы́звать* *perf);* *(found: business etc)* осно́вывать (основа́ть* *perf);* *(engine)* заводи́ть* (завести́* *perf),* запуска́ть (запусти́ть* *perf)* ♦ *vi (begin)* начина́ться (нача́ться* *perf);* *(begin moving)* отправля́ться (отпра́виться* *perf);* *(engine, car)* заводи́ться* (завести́сь* *perf);* *(jump: with fright)* вздра́гивать (вздро́гнуть *perf);* **to ~ doing** *or* **to do** начина́ть (нача́ть* *perf)* +*impf infin;* **at the ~** в нача́ле; **for a ~** для нача́ла; **to make an early ~** ра́но начина́ть (нача́ть* *perf);* **to ~ (off) with ...** *(firstly)* во-пе́рвых ...; *(at the beginning)* снача́ла

▶ **start off** *vi (begin)* начина́ться (нача́ться* *perf);* *(begin moving, leave)* отправля́ться (отпра́виться* *perf)*

▶ **start out** *vi (leave)* отправля́ться (отпра́виться* *perf)*

▶ **start over** *vi (US)* начина́ть (нача́ть* *perf)* сно́ва

▶ **start up** *vi (business etc)* открыва́ться (откры́ться* *perf);* *(engine, car)* заводи́ться* (завести́сь* *perf)* ♦ *vt (business etc)* осно́вывать (основа́ть* *perf);* *(engine, car)* заводи́ть* (завести́* *perf),* запуска́ть (запусти́ть* *perf)*

---

starter ['stɑːtəʳ] n (AUT, SPORT) ста́ртер; (runner, horse) уча́стник(-ица) забе́га; (BRIT: CULIN) заку́ска.

starting point ['stɑːtɪŋ-] n (for journey) отправно́й пункт; (for discussion, idea etc) отправна́я то́чка*.

starting price n (at auction) нача́льная or отправна́я цена́*.

startle ['stɑːtl] vt вспу́гивать (вспугну́ть perf).

startling ['stɑːtlɪŋ] adj порази́тельный* (порази́телен).

star turn n (BRIT) коро́нный но́мер*.

starvation [stɑːˈveɪʃən] n го́лод; **to die of** or **from ~** умира́ть (умере́ть* perf) от го́лода.

starve [stɑːv] vi (to death) умира́ть (умере́ть* perf) с го́лоду; (be very hungry) проголода́ться (perf) ◆ vt (person, animal) мори́ть (замори́ть perf) го́лодом; (fig: deprive): **to ~ sb of sth** лиша́ть (лиши́ть perf) кого́-н чего́-н; **I'm starving** (inf) я голо́дный как волк.

Star Wars n „Звёздные во́йны" fpl.

stash [stæʃ] vt (inf) припря́тывать (припря́тать perf), запаса́ться (запасти́сь* perf) +instr.

state [steɪt] n (condition) состоя́ние; (government) госуда́рство ◆ vt (say, declare) конста́ти́ровать (impf/perf); **the S~s** npl (GEO) Шта́ты mpl; **to be in a ~** быть* (impf) в па́нике; **~ of emergency** чрезвыча́йное положе́ние; **~ of mind** душе́вное состоя́ние.

state control n госуда́рственный контро́ль m.

stated ['steɪtɪd] adj (aims, beliefs etc) устано́вленный.

State Department n (US) Госуда́рственный департа́мент.

state education n (BRIT) госуда́рственное образова́ние.

stateless ['steɪtlɪs] adj (person) не име́ющий гражда́нства.

stately ['steɪtlɪ] adj вели́чественный* (вели́чествен); **~ home** дом-уса́дьба.

statement ['steɪtmənt] n (declaration) заявле́ние; (FINANCE) отчёт, счёт; **official ~** официа́льное заявле́ние; **bank ~** вы́писка* с ба́нковского счёта.

state of the art n после́днее сло́во те́хники ◆ adj: **~~~~~** ультрасовреме́нный.

state-owned ['steɪtəund] adj (industry etc) госуда́рственный.

state school n (BRIT) госуда́рственная шко́ла.

state secret n госуда́рственная та́йна.

statesman ['steɪtsmən] irreg n госуда́рственный де́ятель m.

statesmanship ['steɪtsmənʃɪp] n госуда́рственная де́ятельность f.

static ['stætɪk] n (RADIO, TV) (атмосфе́рные) поме́хи fpl ◆ adj (not moving) стати́чный* (стати́чен), неподви́жный* (неподви́жен).

static electricity n стати́ческое электри́чество.

station ['steɪʃən] n ста́нция; (larger railway station) вокза́л; (also: **police ~**) полице́йский* уча́сток* ◆ vt (position: guards etc) выставля́ть (вы́ставить* perf); (base: soldiers etc) дислоци́ровать (impf/perf), размеща́ть (размести́ть* perf); **action ~s** сигна́л "все по места́м!"; **to get above one's ~** сади́ться* (сесть* perf) не в свои́ са́ни.

stationary ['steɪʃnərɪ] adj (vehicle) неподви́жный.

stationer ['steɪʃənəʳ] n торго́вец* канцеля́рскими това́рами.

stationer's (shop) n магази́н канцеля́рских това́ров.

stationery ['steɪʃnərɪ] n канцеля́рские принадле́жности fpl.

stationmaster ['steɪʃənmɑːstəʳ] n нача́льник ста́нции.

station wagon n (US) автомоби́ль-фурго́н, пика́п.

statistic [stəˈtɪstɪk] n стати́стик.

statistical [stəˈtɪstɪkl] adj (evidence, techniques) статисти́ческий*.

statistics [stəˈtɪstɪks] n (science) стати́стика.

statue ['stætjuː] n ста́туя.

statuesque [stætjuˈɛsk] adj (woman) ста́тная (ста́тна).

statuette [stætjuˈɛt] n статуэ́тка*.

stature ['stætʃəʳ] n рост; (fig: reputation) положе́ние.

status ['steɪtəs] n ста́тус; (importance) значе́ние; **the ~ quo** ста́тус-кво m ind.

status line n (COMPUT) строка́* состоя́ния.

status symbol n си́мвол положе́ния в о́бществе.

statute ['stætjuːt] n стату́т, законода́тельный акт; **~s** npl (of club etc) уста́в msg.

statute book n (LAW, POL): **the ~ ~** свод зако́нов.

statutory ['stætjutrɪ] adj (powers, rights etc) устано́вленный зако́ном; **~ meeting** учреди́тельное собра́ние.

staunch [stɔːntʃ] adj (ally etc) пре́данный ◆ vt остана́вливать (останови́ть* perf).

stave [steɪv] n (MUS) но́тный стан

▶ **stave off** vt (attack) отсро́чивать (отсро́чить perf); (threat) отводи́ть (отвести́* perf).

stay [steɪ] n пребыва́ние ◆ vi (remain) остава́ться* (оста́ться* perf); (with sb, as guest) гости́ть* (impf); (in place: spend some time) остана́вливаться (останови́ться* perf); **~ of execution** (LAW) отсро́чка* исполне́ния; **to ~ at home** сиде́ть* (impf) до́ма; **to ~ in bed** лежа́ть* (impf) в посте́ли; **to ~ put** не дви́гаться (дви́нуться perf) с ме́ста; **to ~ with friends** остана́вливаться (останови́ться* perf) or гости́ть* (impf) у друзе́й; **to ~ the night** (in a place) ночева́ть* (заночева́ть* perf); (with sb) проводи́ть* (провести́* perf) ночь

▶ **stay behind** vi остава́ться* (оста́ться* perf)

▶ **stay in** vi (at home) остава́ться* (оста́ться*

perf) до́ма
▶ **stay on** *vi* остава́ться* (оста́ться* *perf*)
▶ **stay out** *vi* (*of house*) отсу́тствовать (*impf*);
(*remain on strike*) продолжа́ть (*impf*)
бастова́ть
▶ **stay up** *vi* (*at night*) не ложи́ться (*impf*) спать.
staying power ['steɪŋ-] *n* выно́сливость *f*.
STD *n abbr* (*BRIT*: *TEL*: = *subscriber trunk dialling*)
≈ АМТС= *автомати́ческая междугоро́д-
ная телефо́нная связь*; (*MED*: = *sexually
transmitted disease*) *заболева́ние,
передава́емое половы́м путём.*
stead [stɛd] *n*: **in sb's ~** вме́сто кого́-н; **to stand
sb in good ~** пригожда́ться (пригоди́ться*
perf) кому́-н.
steadfast ['stɛdfɑːst] *adj* (*person*) сто́йкий*
(сто́ек); (*refusal, support*) твёрдый.
steadily ['stɛdɪlɪ] *adv* (*firmly*) про́чно;
(*constantly, fixedly*) постоя́нно; (*walk:
decisively*) реши́тельно; (: *without stumbling*)
твёрдо.
steady ['stɛdɪ] *adj* (*constant*) стаби́льный*
(стаби́лен); (: *boyfriend, speed*) постоя́нный;
(*person, character*) уравнове́шенный*
(уравнове́шен); (*firm: hand etc*) твёрдый*
(твёрд); (*calm: look, voice*) ро́вный* (ро́вен) ◆
vt (*object*) придава́ть* (прида́ть* *perf*) усто́й-
чивость +*dat*; (*nerves, person*) успока́ивать
(успоко́ить *perf*); (*voice*) придава́ть*
(прида́ть* *perf*) ро́вность +*dat*; **to ~ o.s. on** *or*
against sth опира́ться (опере́ться* *perf*) о(бо)
что́-н.
steak [steɪk] *n* (*beef*) бифште́кс; (*fish*) филе́ *nt
ind*; (*pork*) вы́резка*.
steakhouse ['steɪkhaus] *n* бифште́ксная *f adj*.
steal [stiːl] (*pt* **stole**, *pp* **stolen**) *vt* ворова́ть
(сворова́ть *perf*), красть* (укра́сть* *perf*) ◆ *vi*
(*thieve*) ворова́ть (*impf*); (*move secretly*)
кра́сться* (*impf*)
▶ **steal away** *vi* незаме́тно ускольза́ть
(ускользну́ть *perf*)
▶ **steal off** *vi* = **steal away**.
stealth [stɛlθ] *n*: **by ~** укра́дкой.
stealthy ['stɛlθɪ] *adj* (*movements, actions*)
та́йный.
steam [stiːm] *n* пар* ◆ *vt* (*CULIN*) вари́ть*
(свари́ть* *perf*) на пару́, па́рить (*impf*) ◆ *vi*
(*give off steam*) испуска́ть (испусти́ть* *perf*)
пар; **under one's own ~** (*fig*) свои́ми си́лами;
to run out of ~ (*fig: person*) выдыха́ться
(вы́дохнуться *perf*); **to let off ~** (*fig: inf*)
выпуска́ть (вы́пустить* *perf*) пар
▶ **steam up** *vi* (*window*) запотева́ть (запоте́ть
perf); **to get ~ed up about sth** (*fig: inf*)
кипяти́ться* (раскипяти́ться* *perf*) из-за
чего́-н.
steam engine *n* (*RAIL*) парово́з.
steamer ['stiːmər] *n* парохо́д; (*CULIN*)

парова́рка*.
steam iron *n* утю́г* с отпа́ривателем.
steamroller ['stiːmrəʊlər] *n* парово́й като́к*.
steamship ['stiːmʃɪp] *n* = **steamer**.
steamy ['stiːmɪ] *adj* (*room*) по́лный* (по́лон)
па́ра; (*window*) запоте́вший*.
steed [stiːd] *n* конь *m*.
steel [stiːl] *n* сталь *f* ◆ *adj* стально́й.
steel band *n* (*MUS*) кари́бский уда́рный
орке́стр.
steel industry *n* сталелите́йная
промы́шленность *f*.
steel mill *n* сталелите́йный заво́д.
steelworks ['stiːlwəːks] *n* сталелите́йный
заво́д.
steely ['stiːlɪ] *adj* (*eyes, gaze*) стально́й;
(*determination*) непрекло́нный*.
steep [stiːp] *adj* круто́й* (крут); (*price*)
высо́кий* (высо́к) ◆ *vt* (*soak: food*)
выма́чивать (вы́мочить *perf*); (: *clothes*)
зама́чивать (замочи́ть* *perf*); **a house ~ed in
history** (*fig*) дом* с истори́ческим про́шлым
овея́нный исто́рией.
steeple ['stiːpl] *n* шпиль *m*; (*belltower*)
колоко́льня*.
steeplechase ['stiːpltʃeɪs] *n* стипль-че́з.
steeplejack ['stiːpldʒæk] *n* верхола́з.
steeply ['stiːplɪ] *adv* кру́то.
steer [stɪər] *vt* (*vehicle, person*) води́ть*/вести́*
(*impf*) ◆ *vi* (*manoeuvre*) маневри́ровать (*impf*)
◆ *n* кастри́рованный бык*; **to ~ clear of sb/
sth** (*fig*) избега́ть (*impf*) кого́-н/чего́-н.
steering ['stɪərɪŋ] *n* (*AUT*) управле́ние.
steering column *n* рулева́я коло́нна.
steering committee *n* коми́ссия по
вы́работке регла́мента.
steering wheel *n* руль* *m*.
stellar ['stɛlər] *adj* (*of stars*) звёздный.
stem [stɛm] *n* (*BOT*: *of plant*) ствол*, сте́бель* *m*;
(*of leaf, fruit*) черешо́к*; (*of glass*) но́жка*; (*of
pipe*) черено́к* ◆ *vt* (*stop*) остана́вливать
(останови́ть* *perf*)
▶ **stem from** *vt fus* (*subj: condition, problem*)
происходи́ть* (произойти́* *perf*) от +*gen*; **their
aggressiveness ~med from fear** их
агресси́вность порождена́ стра́хом.
stench [stɛntʃ] *n* (*pej*) вонь *f*.
stencil ['stɛnsl] *n* трафаре́т ◆ *vt* (*letters, designs
etc*) де́лать (сде́лать *perf*) по трафаре́ту.
stenographer [stɛ'nɒɡrəfər] *n* (*US*)
стеногра́фи́ст(ка*).
stenography [stɛ'nɒɡrəfɪ] *n* (*US*) стеногра́фия.
step [stɛp] *n* (*also fig*) шаг*; (*of stairs*) ступе́нь *f*
◆ *vi*: **to ~ forward/back** ступа́ть (ступи́ть*
perf) вперёд/наза́д; **~s** *npl* (*BRIT*) = **stepladder**;
~ by ~ (*also fig*) шаг за ша́гом; **to be in/out of
~ (with)** идти́* (*impf*) в но́гу/не в но́гу (с
+*instr*); (*fig*) соотве́тствовать (*impf*)/не

соотве́тствовать (*impf*) (+*dat*)
▶ **step down** *vi* (*fig: resign*) уходи́ть* (уйти́*
perf) в отста́вку
▶ **step in** *vi* (*fig*) вме́шиваться (вмеша́ться
perf)
▶ **step off** *vt fus* сходи́ть* (сойти́* *perf*) с +*gen*
▶ **step on** *vt fus* (*walk on*) наступа́ть
(наступи́ть* *perf*) на +*acc*
▶ **step over** *vt fus* переступа́ть (переступи́ть*
perf) че́рез +*acc*
▶ **step up** *vt* (*increase*) уси́ливать (уси́лить
perf).
step aerobics *n* степ-аэро́бика (*с
испо́льзованием осо́бой ступе́ньки*).
stepbrother ['stɛpbrʌðəʳ] *n* сво́дный брат*.
stepchild ['stɛptʃaɪld] *n* (*boy*) па́сынок*; (*girl*)
па́дчерица.
stepdaughter ['stɛpdɔːtəʳ] *n* па́дчерица.
stepfather ['stɛpfɑːðəʳ] *n* о́тчим.
stepladder ['stɛplædəʳ] *n* (*BRIT*) стремя́нка*.
stepmother ['stɛpmʌðəʳ] *n* ма́чеха.
stepping stone ['stɛpɪŋ-] *n* (*in river*) опо́рный
ка́мень *m*; (*fig*) ступе́нька.
step-reebok® [stɛpˈriːbɔk] *n* ступе́нька,
испо́льзуемая при степ-аэро́бике.
stepsister ['stɛpsɪstəʳ] *n* сво́дная сестра́*.
stepson ['stɛpsʌn] *n* па́сынок*.
stereo ['stɛrɪəu] *n* (*system*) стереосисте́ма;
(*record player*) стереопрои́грыватель *m* ◆ *adj*
(*also:*~**phonic**) стереофони́ческий; **in** ~
сте́рео.
stereotype ['stɪərɪətaɪp] *n* стереоти́п ◆ *vt*
воспринима́ть (*impf*) по стереоти́пу.
sterile ['stɛraɪl] *adj* (*also fig*) беспло́дный*
(беспло́ден); (*free from germs*) стери́льный*
(стери́лен).
sterility [stɛˈrɪlɪtɪ] *n* (*infertility*) беспло́дие.
sterilization [stɛrɪlaɪˈzeɪʃən] *n* стерилиза́ция.
sterilize ['stɛrɪlaɪz] *vt* стерилизова́ть (*impf*).
sterling ['stəːlɪŋ] *adj* (*efforts: noble*)
благоро́дный*; (: *excellent*) отме́нный ◆ *n*
(*ECON*) фунт сте́рлингов; ~ **silver** серебро́
925-ой про́бы; **one pound** ~ оди́н фунт
сте́рлингов.
sterling area *n* сте́рлинговая зо́на.
stern [stəːn] *adj* стро́гий* (строг) ◆ *n* (*of boat*)
корма́.
sternum ['stəːnəm] *n* груди́на.
steroid ['stɪərɔɪd] *n* стеро́ид.
stet [stɛt] *n корректи́рующий знак,
отменя́ющий попра́вки* ◆ *vt* оста́вить (*perf*)
как бы́ло.
stethoscope ['stɛθəskəup] *n* стетоско́п.
stevedore ['stiːvədɔːʳ] *n* порто́вый гру́зчик.
stew [stjuː] *n* (*meat*) тушёное мя́со ◆ *vi* (*meat*)
туши́ть* (потуши́ть* *perf*); (*fruit*) вари́ть
(свари́ть *perf*) ◆ *vi* (*meat*) туши́ться*
(потуши́ться* *perf*); (*fruit*) вари́ться
(свари́ться *perf*); **vegetable** ~ тушёные
о́вощи; ~**ed tea** перестоя́вшийся чай; ~**ed
fruit** варёные фру́кты.

steward ['stjuːəd] *n* (*on ship, train*) стю́ард; (*on
plane*) бортпроводни́к*; (*in club etc*)
распоряди́тель *m*; (*also:* **shop** ~) цехово́й
ста́роста.
stewardess ['stjuədɛs] *n* (*on plane*)
стюарде́сса, бортпроводни́ца.
stewardship ['stjuədʃɪp] *n* управле́ние.
stewing steak ['stjuːɪŋ-] (*US* **stew meat**) *n*
говя́дина для туше́ния.
St. Ex. *abbr* = **stock exchange**.
stg *abbr* = **sterling**.
stick [stɪk] (*pt, pp* **stuck**) *n* (*of wood*) па́лка*; (*of
dynamite, chalk etc*) па́лочка*; (*walking stick*)
трость *f* ◆ *vt* (*with glue etc*) кле́ить
(прикле́ить *perf*); (*inf. put*) сова́ть* (су́нуть
perf); (: *tolerate*) терпе́ть (вы́терпеть *perf*);
(*thrust*) втыка́ть (воткну́ть *perf*) ◆ *vi* (*become
attached*) прикле́иваться (прикле́иться *perf*);
(*be unmoveable*) застрева́ть (застря́ть* *perf*);
(*in mind etc*) засе́сть* (*perf*); (*get jammed:
door*) заеда́ть (зае́сть* *perf*); (: *lift*) застрева́ть
(застря́ть* *perf*); **to get hold of the wrong end
of the** ~ (*BRIT: fig*) совсе́м не так понима́ть
(поня́ть* *perf*); **he stuck a cigar in his mouth** он
засу́нул сига́ру в рот; **to** ~ **to** (*become
attached*) прикле́иваться (прикле́иться *perf*)
к +*dat*; (*one's word, promise*) держа́ть*
(сдержа́ть* *perf*); (*principles*) остава́ться*
(оста́ться* *perf*) ве́рным(-ой) +*dat*
▶ **stick around** *vi* (*inf*) торча́ть (*impf*)
▶ **stick out** *vi* (*ears etc*) торча́ть (*impf*) ◆ *vt:* **to** ~
it out (*inf*) терпе́ть* (вы́терпеть* *perf*)
▶ **stick up** *vi* (*hair etc*) торча́ть (*impf*)
▶ **stick up for** *vt fus* (*person*) заступа́ться
(заступи́ться* *perf*) за +*acc*; (*principle*)
отста́ивать (отстоя́ть *perf*).
sticker ['stɪkəʳ] *n* накле́йка.
sticking plaster ['stɪkɪŋ-] *n* лейкопла́стырь *m*.
sticking point *n* (*in relationship*) то́чка
преткнове́ния.
stickleback ['stɪklbæk] *n* ко́люшка.
stickler ['stɪkləʳ] *n:* **to be a** ~ **for** наста́ивать
(*impf*) на +*prp*.
stick shift *n* (*US: AUT*) переключа́тель *m*
скоросте́й.
stick-up ['stɪkʌp] *n* (*inf*) вооружённое
ограбле́ние.
sticky ['stɪkɪ] *adj* (*hands etc*) ли́пкий*; (*label*)
кле́йкий*; (*fig: situation*) щекотли́вый
(щекотли́в).
stiff [stɪf] *adj* (*brush*) жёсткий* (жёсток); (*paste*)
густо́й; (*egg-white*) круто́й; (*person*)
деревя́нный; (*door, zip*) туго́й* (туг);
(*manner, smile*) натя́нутый (натя́нут);
(*competition*) ожесточённый; (*severe:
sentence*) суро́вый (суро́в); (*high: price*)
высо́кий* (высо́к); (*strong: drink*) кре́пкий*;
(: *breeze*) си́льный (силён) ◆ *adv* (*bored,
worried, scared*) до́ смерти; **I am** *or* **feel** ~ у
меня́ всё те́ло но́ет; **I have a** ~ **neck** у меня́
свело́ ше́ю; **to keep a** ~ **upper lip** (*BRIT: fig*)

сохраня́ть (сохрани́ть *perf*) хладнокро́вие.
stiffen ['stɪfn] *vi* (*body*) напряга́ться
(напря́чься* *perf*); (*joints, neck*) не сгиба́ться
(*impf*); **my muscles have ~ed** у меня́ свело́
мы́шцы.
stiffness ['stɪfnɪs] *n* (*of joints*) неподви́жность
f; (*of paper, cloth*) жёсткость *f*; (*in consistency*) густота́ *f*; (*in behaviour etc*)
натя́нутость *f*.
stifle ['staɪfl] *vt* (*yawn*) подавля́ть (подави́ть*
perf); (*opposition*) души́ть (задуши́ть *perf*);
(*subj: heat*) души́ть (*impf*).
stifling ['staɪflɪŋ] *adj* (*heat*) уду́шливый
(уду́шлив).
stigma ['stɪgmə] *n* (*of failure, defeat etc*)
клеймо́; (*BOT*) ры́льце; (*MED*) сти́гма.
stile [staɪl] *n* перела́з.
stiletto [stɪ'lɛtəu] *n* (*BRIT: also: ~ heel*)
шпи́лька.
still [stɪl] *adj* ти́хий* (тих); (*BRIT: not fizzy*)
негазиро́ванный ♦ *adv* (*up to this time*) всё
ещё; (*even yet*) ещё; (*nonetheless*) всё-таки,
тем не ме́нее ♦ *n* (*CINEMA*) рекла́мный
фотока́др; **to stand ~** стоя́ть* (*impf*)
неподви́жно; **keep ~!** не шевели́тесь!; **he ~**
hasn't arrived он всё ещё не пришёл.
stillborn ['stɪlbɔːn] *adj* (*baby*) мертво-
рождённый.
still life *n* (*ART*) натюрмо́рт.
stilt [stɪlt] *n* (*pile*) сва́я; (*for walking on*)
ходу́ля*.
stilted ['stɪltɪd] *adj* (*behaviour, conversation*)
высокопа́рный* (высокопа́рен).
stimulant ['stɪmjulənt] *n* стимули́рующее *or*
возбужда́ющее сре́дство.
stimulate ['stɪmjuleɪt] *vt* стимули́ровать (*impf/
perf*).
stimulating ['stɪmjuleɪtɪŋ] *adj* вдохно-
вля́ющий.
stimulation [stɪmju'leɪʃən] *n* стимули́рование.
stimuli ['stɪmjulaɪ] *npl of* **stimulus**.
stimulus ['stɪmjuləs] (*pl* **stimuli**) *n*
(*encouragement*) сти́мул; (*MED*) стимуля́тор;
(*BIO, PSYCH*) раздражи́тель *m*.
sting [stɪŋ] (*pt, pp* **stung**) *n* (*from insect*) уку́с;
(*from plant*) ожо́г; (*organ: of wasp etc*) жа́ло;
(*inf: confidence trick*) моше́нничество ♦ *vt*
(*also fig*) уязвля́ть (уязви́ть* *perf*) ♦ *vi* (*insect,
animal*) жа́литься (*impf*); (*plant*) жёчься* (*impf*);
(*eyes, ointment etc*) жечь* (*impf*); **my eyes are**
~ing мне жжёт глаза́.
stingy ['stɪndʒɪ] *adj* (*pej: person*) ска́редный*
(ска́реден).
stink [stɪŋk] (*pt* **stank**, *pp* **stunk**) *n* смрад, вонь *f*
♦ *vi* смерде́ть (*impf*).
stinker ['stɪŋkə'] (*inf*) *n* (*person*)
мерза́вец*(-вка*); **it's a real ~ of a problem/**
exam э́то жу́ткая пробле́ма/ужа́сный

экза́мен.
stinking ['stɪŋkɪŋ] (*inf*) *adj* (*inf*) воню́чий*
(воню́ч); **a ~ cold** жу́ткая простуда́; **~ rich**
жу́тко бога́тый.
stint [stɪnt] *n* пери́од рабо́ты ♦ *vi:* **to ~ on**
(*work*) халту́рить (*impf*) в +*prp*; (*ingredients*)
зажима́ть (зажа́ть* *perf*).
stipend ['staɪpɛnd] *n* (*of vicar etc*) жа́лованье;
(*of student*) стипе́ндия.
stipendiary [staɪ'pɛndɪərɪ] *adj:* **~ magistrate**
пла́тный магистра́т.
stipulate ['stɪpjuleɪt] *vt* (*condition, amount etc*)
определя́ть (определи́ть *perf*).
stipulation [stɪpju'leɪʃən] *n* усло́вие.
stir [stəː'] *n* (*fig: agitation*) шум, сенса́ция ♦ *vt*
(*tea etc*) меша́ть (помеша́ть *perf*); (*fig:
emotions*) волнова́ть (взволнова́ть *perf*) ♦ *vi*
(*move slightly*) шевели́ться (пошевели́ться
perf); **to give sth a ~** разме́шивать
(размеша́ть *perf*) что-н; **to cause a ~**
вызыва́ть (вы́звать* *perf*) сенса́цию
▶ **stir up** *vt* (*trouble*) вызыва́ть (вы́звать* *perf*).
stir-fry ['stəː'fraɪ] *vt* бы́стро обжа́ривать
(обжа́рить *perf*).
stirring ['stəːrɪŋ] *adj* (*speech, occasion*)
волну́ющий.
stirrup ['stɪrəp] *n* стре́мя* *nt.*
stitch [stɪtʃ] *n* (*SEWING*) стежо́к*; (*KNITTING*)
петля́*; (*MED*) шов* ♦ *vt* (*sew*) шить* (сшить*
perf); (*MED: wound*) зашива́ть (заши́ть* *perf*); **I**
have a ~ in my side у меня́ ко́лет в боку́.
stoat [stəut] *n* горноста́й.
stock [stɔk] *n* (*supply*) запа́с; (*AGR*) поголо́вье;
(*CULIN*) бульо́н; (*descent, origin*)
происхожде́ние; (*FINANCE*) це́нные бума́ги
fpl; (*COMM: of company*) акционе́рный
капита́л; (*RAIL: also: rolling ~*) (подвижно́й)
соста́в ♦ *adj* (*fig: reply, excuse etc*)
шабло́нный ♦ *vt* (*have in stock*) име́ть (*impf*) в
нали́чии; **~s and shares** а́кции и це́нные
бума́ги; **to be in/out of ~** име́ться (*impf*)/не
име́ться (*impf*) в нали́чии; **a well-~ed shop**
магази́н с больши́м ассортиме́нтом
това́ров; **to take ~ of** (*fig*) оце́нивать
(оцени́ть* *perf*); **government ~**
прави́тельственные а́кции
▶ **stock up** *vi:* **to ~ up with** запаса́ться
(запасти́сь* *perf*) +*instr.*
stockade [stɔ'keɪd] *n* частоко́л.
stockbroker ['stɔkbrəukə'] *n* (*COMM*) фо́ндовый
бро́кер.
stock control *n* (*COMM*) управле́ние запа́сами.
stock cube *n* (*BRIT: CULIN*) бульо́нный ку́бик.
stock exchange *n* фо́ндовая би́ржа.
stockholder ['stɔkhəuldə'] *n* (*COMM*) акционе́р.
Stockholm ['stɔkhəum] *n* Стокго́льм.
stocking ['stɔkɪŋ] *n* чуло́к*.
stock in trade *n* (*COMM*) запа́сы име́ющиеся в

нали́чии и предназна́ченные для прода́жи; (fig): **it's his** ~ ~ ~ э́то его́ обы́чное заня́тие.

stockist ['stɔkɪst] n (BRIT) сто́кист (фи́рма, име́ющая запа́с како́й-нибудь проду́кции).

stock market n (BRIT) фо́ндовая би́ржа.

stock phrase n клише́ nt ind.

stockpile ['stɔkpaɪl] n (of weapons, food) запа́с ◆ vt запаса́ть (запасти́* perf).

stockroom ['stɔkru:m] n (COMM) склад.

stocktaking ['stɔkteɪkɪŋ] n (BRIT: COMM) инвентариза́ция.

stocky ['stɔkɪ] adj корена́стый (корена́с г).

stodgy ['stɔdʒɪ] adj (food) тяжёлый.

stoic ['stəʊɪk] n сто́ик.

stoical ['stəʊɪkl] adj (person, behaviour) стои́ческий*.

stoke [stəʊk] vt (fire) подде́рживать (impf); (boiler, furnace) подде́рживать (impf) ого́нь в +prp.

stoker ['stəʊkə'] n (RAIL, NAUT etc) кочега́р.

stole [stəʊl] pt of **steal** ◆ n паланти́н.

stolen ['stəʊln] pp of **steal**.

stolid ['stɔlɪd] adj (person, behaviour) бесстра́стный* (бесстра́стен).

stomach ['stʌmək] n (ANAT) желу́док*; (belly) живо́т* ◆ vt (fig) переноси́ть* (impf).

stomachache ['stʌməkeɪk] n желу́дочные бо́ли fpl.

stomach pump n желу́дочный зонд.

stomach ulcer n я́зва желу́дка.

stomp [stɔmp] vi: **to** ~ **in/out** входи́ть* (войти́* perf)/уходи́ть* (уйти́* perf) тяжёлыми шага́ми.

stone [stəʊn] n (also MED) ка́мень* m; (pebble) ка́мешек*; (in fruit) ко́сточка*; (BRIT: weight) сто́ун (14 фу́нтов) ◆ adj ка́менный ◆ vt (person) заки́дывать (закида́ть perf) камня́ми в +acc; (fruit) вынима́ть (вы́нуть perf) ко́сточки из +gen; **within a** ~**'s throw of the school** в двух шага́х от шко́лы.

Stone Age n: **the** ~ ~ ка́менный век.

stone-cold ['stəʊn'kəʊld] adj холо́дный* как лёд.

stoned [stəʊnd] adj (inf: drunk) мертве́цки пья́ный* (пьян); (: on drugs) обкури́вшийся.

stone-deaf ['stəʊn'dɛf] adj соверше́нно глухо́й.

stonemason ['stəʊnmeɪsn] n ка́менщик.

stonewall [stəʊn'wɔ:l] vti занима́ться (impf) процеду́рными заде́ржками (в парла́менте).

stonework ['stəʊnwə:k] n (ка́менная) кла́дка.

stony ['stəʊnɪ] adj (ground) камени́стый (камени́ст); (fig: glance, silence etc) холо́дный.

stood [stʊd] pt, pp of **stand**.

stooge [stu:dʒ] n (inf) подставно́е лицо́*; (: THEAT) партнёр ко́мика.

stool [stu:l] n табуре́тка*.

stoop [stu:p] vi (also: ~ **down**: bend) наклоня́ться (наклони́ться* perf),

нагиба́ться (нагну́ться perf); (also: **have a** ~) суту́литься (impf); (fig): **to** ~ **to sth/doing** унижа́ться (уни́зиться* perf) до чего́-н/до того́, что́бы +infin.

stop [stɔp] n остано́вка*; (in punctuation: also: **full** ~) то́чка* ◆ vt остана́вливать (останови́ть* perf); (prevent: also: **put a** ~ **to**) прекраща́ть (прекрати́ть* perf) ◆ vi (person, clock) остана́вливаться (останови́ться* perf); (rain, noise etc) прекраща́ться (прекрати́ться* perf); **to** ~ **sb (from) doing** уде́рживать (удержа́ть perf) кого́-н от того́, что́бы +infin; ~ **it!** прекрати́те!; **to** ~ **doing** перестава́ть (переста́ть* perf) +infin; **the car** ~**ped dead** маши́на останови́лась как вко́панная

▶ **stop by** vi заходи́ть* (зайти́* perf)

▶ **stop off** vi остана́вливаться (останови́ться* perf)

▶ **stop up** vt (hole) заде́лывать (заде́лать perf).

stopcock ['stɔpkɔk] n запо́рный кран.

stopgap ['stɔpgæp] n (person, thing) вре́менная заме́на; (also: ~ **measure**) вре́менная ме́ра.

stop-go [stɔp'gəʊ] adj (BRIT: ECON): ~ **policy** экономи́ческая поли́тика, череду́ющая.

stoplights ['stɔplaɪts] npl (AUT) стоп-сигна́л msg.

stopover ['stɔpəʊvə'] n остано́вка*; (AVIAT) поса́дка.

stoppage ['stɔpɪdʒ] n (strike) забасто́вка*; (blockage) остано́вка*; (of pay) прекраще́ние.

stopper ['stɔpə'] n про́бка*.

stop press n э́кстренное сообще́ние.

stopwatch ['stɔpwɔtʃ] n секундоме́р.

storage ['stɔ:rɪdʒ] n хране́ние; (in house) кладо́вка*; (COMPUT) па́мять f, накопи́тель m.

storage capacity n ёмкость f.

storage heater n (BRIT) аккумули́рующий электрообогрева́тель m.

store [stɔ:'] n (stock, reserve) запа́с; (depot) склад; (BRIT: large shop) универма́г; (esp US) магази́н ◆ vt храни́ть (impf); ~**s** npl (provisions) запа́сы mpl; **in** ~ в бу́дущем; **who knows what's in** ~ **for us?** кто зна́ет, что нас ждёт в бу́дущем?; **to set great/little** ~ **by sth** придава́ть* (прида́ть* perf) большо́е/ма́ленькое значе́ние чему́-н

▶ **store up** vt (food) запаса́ть (запасти́* perf); (memories) храни́ть (impf).

storehouse ['stɔ:haʊs] n (US: COMM) склад; (fig) кладова́я f adj.

storekeeper ['stɔ:ki:pə'] n (US: manager) управля́ющий*(-ая) m(f) adj магази́ном; (owner) владе́лец*(-лица) магази́на.

storeroom ['stɔ:ru:m] n кладова́я f adj.

storey ['stɔ:rɪ] (US **story**) n эта́ж*.

stork [stɔ:k] n а́ист.

storm [stɔ:m] n (also fig) бу́ря*; (of criticism) волна́*; (of laughter) взрыв; (also: **electric** ~)

гроза* ◆ *vi* (*fig: speak angrily*) крича́ть* (*impf*)
◆ *vt* (*attack: place*) штурмова́ть (*impf*).

storm cloud *n* грозова́я ту́ча.

storm door *n* нару́жная дверь* *f*.

stormy ['stɔːmɪ] *adj* штормово́й; (*fig: debate, relations*) бу́рный; ~ **weather** нена́стье.

story ['stɔːrɪ] *n* исто́рия; (*PRESS: article*) статья́*; (: *subject*) газе́тный материа́л; (*lie*) вы́думка*; (*US*) = **storey; short** ~ расска́з.

storybook ['stɔːrɪbuk] *n* сбо́рник расска́зов *or* ска́зок (*для дете́й*).

storyteller ['stɔːrɪtɛlə'] *n* расска́зчик(-ица); (*inf: liar*) врун(ья).

stout [staut] *adj* (*strong: branch etc*) кре́пкий* (кре́пок); (*fat*) доро́дный* (доро́ден); (*resolute: friend, supporter*) надёжный* (надёжен) ◆ *n* (*beer*) кре́пкий* по́ртер.

stove [stəuv] *n* (*for cooking*) плита́*; (: *small*) пли́тка*; (*for heating*) печь* *f*; **gas/electric** ~ (*cooker*) га́зовая/электри́ческая плита́.

stow [stəu] *vt* (*also:* ~ **away**) убира́ть (убра́ть* *perf*).

stowaway ['stəuəweɪ] *n* безбиле́тник(-ница).

St Petersburg [sənt'piːtəzbəːg] *n* Санкт-Петербу́рг ◆ *adj* (санкт-) петербу́ргский*.

straddle ['strædl] *vt* (*chair, fence etc*) оседла́ть (*perf*); (*fig*) охва́тывать (охвати́ть* *perf*).

strafe [strɑːf] *vt* (*MIL: with bullets*) обстре́ливать (обстреля́ть* *perf*); (*with bombs*) бомби́ть (impf), сбра́сывать (сбро́сить* *perf*).

straggle ['strægl] *vi* (*houses etc*) раски́дываться (раски́нуться *perf*); (*people*) разбреда́ться (разбрести́сь* *perf*).

straggler ['stræglə'] *n* (*person*) отста́вший(-ая) *m(f) adj*.

straggly ['stræglɪ] *adj* (*hair*) беспоря́дочно торча́щий.

straight [streɪt] *adj* прямо́й* (прям); (*simple: choice*) я́сный* (я́сен); (*THEAT: part, play*) серьёзный; (*inf: heterosexual*) гетеросексуа́льный* ◆ *adv* пря́мо ◆ *n*: **the** ~ (*SPORT*) пряма́я *f adj*; **to put** *or* **get sth** ~ (*make clear*) вноси́ть* (внести́* *perf*) я́сность во что-н; **let's get this** ~ дава́йте внесём я́сность *or* определённость в э́то; **to be** (**all**) ~ (*tidy*) быть* (*impf*) в (по́лном) поря́дке; (*clarified*) быть* (*impf*) я́сным(-ой); **10** ~ **wins** 10 побе́д подря́д; **to go** ~ **home** идти́* (пойти́* *perf*) сра́зу домо́й; **to tell sb** ~ **out** говори́ть (сказа́ть* *perf*) кому́-н пря́мо; **to drink vodka** ~ пить* (*impf*) неразба́вленную во́дку; ~ **away**, ~ **off** (*at once*) сра́зу.

straighten ['streɪtn] *vt* (*skirt, tie etc*) поправля́ть (попра́вить* *perf*); (*bed*) заправля́ть (запра́вить* *perf*)
▶ **straighten out** *vt* (*fig: problem etc*)

ула́живать (ула́дить* *perf*).

straight-faced [streɪt'feɪst] *adj, adv* с серьёзным ви́дом; **to be** ~ сохраня́ть (*impf*) серьёзный вид.

straightforward [streɪt'fɔːwəd] *adj* (*simple*) просто́й* (прост); (*honest*) прямо́й.

straight sets *n*: **to win in** ~ ~ (*men*) побежда́ть (победи́ть* *perf*) в трёх па́ртиях подря́д; (*women*) побежда́ть (победи́ть* *perf*) в двух па́ртиях подря́д.

strain [streɪn] *n* (*TECH*) натяже́ние; (*pressure*) нагру́зка*; (*MED: physical*) растяже́ние; (: *mental*) напряже́ние; (*of virus*) вид; (*breed*) поро́да ◆ *vt* (*back etc*) растя́гивать (растяну́ть* *perf*); (*friendship, marriage*) испы́тывать (*impf*); (*stretch: resources*) ударя́ть (уда́рить *perf*) по +*dat*; (*CULIN*) проце́живать (процеди́ть* *perf*); ~**s** *npl* (*MUS*) зву́ки *mpl*; **he's been under a lot of** ~ у него́ был о́чень напряжённый пери́од.

strained [streɪnd] *adj* (*back, muscle*) растя́нутый (растя́нут); (*laugh, relations*) натя́нутый (натя́нут).

strainer ['streɪnə'] *n* (*for vegetables*) си́то; (*for tea*) си́течко.

strait [streɪt] *n* (*GEO*) проли́в; ~**s** *npl* (*fig*): **to be in dire** ~**s** находи́ться* (*impf*) *or* быть* (*impf*) в бе́дственном положе́нии.

straitjacket ['streɪtdʒækɪt] *n* смири́тельная руба́шка*.

strait-laced [streɪt'leɪst] *adj* (*person*) пурита́нский*.

strand [strænd] *n* (*of thread*) ни́тка*; (*of wool*) волокно́*, нить *f*; (*of hair*) прядь *f*; (*fig: element of whole*) часть *f*.

stranded ['strændɪd] *adj* (*ship, sea creature etc*) вы́брошенный на бе́рег *or* мель; (*traveller, holidaymaker etc*): **to be** ~ быть* (*impf*) на мели́.

strange [streɪndʒ] *adj* (*not known*) незнако́мый (незнако́м); (*foreign*) чужо́й; (*odd*) стра́нный* (стра́нен).

strangely ['streɪndʒlɪ] *adv* (*act, laugh*) стра́нно; *see also* **enough**.

stranger ['streɪndʒə'] *n* (*unknown person*) незнако́мый челове́к*, посторо́нний(-яя) *m(f) adj*; **I'm a** ~ **here** я здесь чужо́й.

strangle ['stræŋgl] *vt* (*also fig*) души́ть* (задуши́ть* *perf*).

stranglehold ['stræŋglhəuld] *n* (*SPORT*) мёртвая хва́тка; (*fig*) заси́лье.

strangulation [stræŋgju'leɪʃən] *n* удуше́ние.

strap [stræp] *n* реме́нь* *m*; (*of slip, dress*) брете́лька*; (*of watch, on shoes*) ремешо́к* ◆ *vt* (*also:* ~ **on**) пристёгивать (пристегну́ть* *perf*).

straphanging ['stræphæŋɪŋ] *n*: **I hate** ~ я ненави́жу стоя́ть в тра́нспорте.

---

strapless ['stræplɪs] *adj* (*bra, dress*) без
бретéлек.
strapped [stræpt] *adj* (*inf*): **to be ~ for cash**
сидéть* (*impf*) на мелú.
strapping ['stræpɪŋ] *adj* рóслый.
Strasbourg ['stræzbə:g] *n* Стрáсбург.
strata ['strɑ:tə] *npl of* **stratum**.
stratagem ['strætɪdʒəm] *n* хúтрость *f*.
strategic [strə'ti:dʒɪk] *adj* стратегúческий*.
strategist ['strætɪdʒɪst] *n* стратéг.
strategy ['strætɪdʒɪ] *n* (*plan, also* MIL)
стратéгия.
stratosphere ['strætəsfɪə] *n* стратосфéра.
stratum ['strɑ:təm] (*pl* **strata**) *n* слой*.
straw [strɔ:] *n* солóма; (*drinking straw*)
солóминка*; **that's the last ~!** э́то послéдняя
кáпля!
strawberry ['strɔ:bərɪ] *n* (*cultivated*) клубнúка *f*
no pl; (*wild*) землянúка *f no pl*.
stray [streɪ] *adj* (*animal*) бездóмный,
бродя́чий; (*bullet*) шальнóй; (*scattered*)
отдéльный ♦ *vi* заблудúться* (*perf*);
(*thoughts*) блуждáть (*impf*).
streak [stri:k] *n* (*stripe*) полосá*; (*in hair*) прядь
f; (*fig: of madness etc*) чертá, склóнность *f* ♦
vt пронúзывать (пронизáть* *perf*) ♦ *vi*: **to ~
past** мчáться* (промчáться* *perf*) мúмо; **to
have ~s in one's hair** имéть (*impf*)
окрáшенные пря́ди волóс; **a winning/losing
~** полосá удáч/неудáч; **~ed with ... c ...**
полóсками.
streaker ['stri:kə'] *n* человéк, появля́ющийся
гóлым пéред толпóй.
streaky ['stri:kɪ] *adj*: **~ bacon** бекóн с
прожúлками жúра.
stream [stri:m] *n* (*small river*) ручéй*; (*current*)
течéние; (*of people, vehicles, questions*)
потóк; (*of smoke*) струя́* ♦ *vt* (SCOL) делúть*
(разделúть* *perf*) на грýппы ♦ *vi* (*liquid*) течь*
(*impf*), лúться* (*impf*); **to ~ in/out** (*people*)
валúть* (повалúть* *perf*) толпóй в +*acc*/из
+*gen*; **against the ~** прóтив течéния; **to come
on ~** (*new power plant etc*) вступáть
(вступúть* *perf*) в строй.
streamer ['stri:mə'] *n* (*paper decoration*)
серпантúн.
stream feed *n* (*on photocopier etc*) подáча
(странúц) потóком.
streamline ['stri:mlaɪn] *vt* придавáть*
(придáть* *perf*) обтекáемую фóрму +*dat*; (*fig*)
упрощáть (упростúть* *perf*).
streamlined ['stri:mlaɪnd] *adj* обтекáемый;
(AVIAT, AUT) обтекáемой фóрмы; (*fig*)
упрощённый.
street [stri:t] *n* у́лица; **the back ~s** переýлки
mpl; **to be on the ~s** (*homeless*) быть* (*impf*)
бездóмным(-ой); (*as prostitute*) занимáться
(*impf*) проститýцией.
streetcar ['stri:tkɑ:'] *n* (US) трамвáй.
street cred [-krɛd] *n* (*inf*) úмидж.
streetlamp ['stri:tlæmp] *n* у́личный фонáрь* *m*.

street lighting *n* у́личное освещéние.
street map *n* план у́лиц.
street market *n* у́личный ры́нок*.
street plan *n* план у́лиц.
streetwise ['stri:twaɪz] *adj* (*inf*) ушлый.
strength [strɛŋθ] *n* сúла; (*of girder, knot etc*)
прóчность *f*, крéпость *f*; (*of chemical solution,
wine*) крéпость; **on the ~ of** на основáнии
+*gen*; **at full ~** во всём состáве; **below ~** (*not
enough people*) недоукомплектóванный
(недоукомплектóван); (*not all members
present*) не в пóлном состáве.
strengthen ['strɛŋθn] *vt* укрепля́ть (укрепúть*
perf); (*muscle*) развивáть (*impf*); (*fig: group*)
пополня́ть (попóлнить *perf*); (: *argument*)
подкрепля́ть (подкрепúть* *perf*).
strenuous ['strɛnjuəs] *adj* (*exercise*)
энергúчный* (энергúчен); (*efforts*)
напряжённый; (*tiring*) утомúтельный*
(утомúтелен).
strenuously ['strɛnjuəslɪ] *adv* напряжённо; **she
~ denied the rumour** онá усúленно отрицáла
слýхи.
stress [strɛs] *n* (*pressure, also* TECH) давлéние;
(*mental strain*) стресс; (LING: *accent*)
ударéние; (*emphasis*) значéние ♦ *vt* (*point,
importance etc*) подчёркивать (подчеркнýть*
perf); (*syllable*) стáвить* (постáвить* *perf*)
ударéние на +*acc*; **to lay great ~ on sth**
придавáть* (придáть* *perf*) осóбое значéние
на что-н; **to be under ~** быть* (*impf*) под
напряжéнием.
stressful ['strɛsful] *adj* (*job*) напряжённый*
(напряжён); (*situation*) стрéссовый.
stretch [strɛtʃ] *n* (*area: of sand, water etc*)
прострáнство; (*of time*) промежýток* ♦ *vt*
(*pull*) натя́гивать (натянýть* *perf*); (*fig: subj:
job, task*) утомля́ть (утомúть* *perf*); (*spread:
resources*) растя́гивать (растянýть* *perf*) ♦ *vi*
(*person, animal*) потя́гиваться (потянýться*
perf); (*extend*): **to ~** *or* **as far as**
простирáться (простерéться* *perf*) к +*dat*; (*be
enough*): **to ~** (**to**) хватáть (хватúть* *perf*) (на
+*acc*); **at a ~** подря́д; **he's no hero by any ~ of
the imagination** как ни старáйтесь, егó
нельзя́ вообразúть герóем; **to ~ one's legs**
размина́ть (размя́ть* *perf*) нóги
► **stretch out** *vi* растя́гиваться (растянýться*
perf) ♦ *vt* (*arm etc*) протя́гивать (протянýть*
perf); (*spread*) растя́гивать (растянýть* *perf*);
to ~ out for sth тянýться* (потянýться* *perf*)
за чем-н.
stretcher ['strɛtʃə'] *n* (MED) носúлки* *pl*.
stretcher-bearer ['strɛtʃəbɛərə'] *n*
санитáр-носúльщик.
stretchmarks ['strɛtʃmɑ:ks] *npl* слéды
растя́гивания на кóже.
strewn [stru:n] *adj*: **~ with** усы́панный
(усы́пан) +*instr*.
stricken ['strɪkən] *adj* (*person*) сражённый;
(*city, industry etc*) пострадáвший; **~ with**

(*arthritis, disease*) поражённый +*instr*.

strict [strɪkt] *adj* (*severe, firm: person, rule*) стро́гий* (строг); (*precise: meaning*) то́чный* (то́чен); **in** ~ *or* **in the** ~**est confidence** в строжа́йшей та́йне.

strictly ['strɪktlɪ] *adv* (*severely*) стро́го; (*exactly*) то́чно; ~ **confidential** соверше́нно конфиденциа́льно *or* секре́тно; ~ **speaking** стро́го говоря́; ~ **between ourselves** то́лько ме́жду на́ми.

strictness ['strɪktnɪs] *n* стро́гость *f*.

stridden ['strɪdn] *pp of* **stride**.

stride [straɪd] (*pt* **strode**, *pp* **stridden**) *n* (*step*) широ́кий* шаг* ♦ *vi* шага́ть (*impf*); **to take sth in one's** ~ (*fig: changes etc*) относи́ться* (*impf*) споко́йно к чему́-н.

strident ['straɪdnt] *adj* (*voice, sound*) пронзи́тельный* (пронзи́телен); (*demands*) шу́мный.

strife [straɪf] *n* борьба́.

strike [straɪk] (*pt, pp* **struck**) *n* (*of workers*) забасто́вка*; (*MIL: attack*) уда́р; (*of oil etc*) откры́тие месторожде́ния ♦ *vt* (*hit: person, thing*) ударя́ть (уда́рить *perf*); (*fig: subj: disease, disaster*) поража́ть (порази́ть* *perf*); (*: idea, thought*) осеня́ть (осени́ть *perf*); (*oil etc*) открыва́ть (откры́ть* *perf*) месторожде́ние +*gen*; (*bargain, deal*) заключа́ть (заключи́ть *perf*); (*make: coin, medal*) чека́нить (отчека́нить *perf*) ♦ *vi* (*workers*) бастова́ть (*impf*); (*attack: soldiers*) напада́ть (напа́сть* *perf*); (*: disaster, illness*) приходи́ть* (прийти́* *perf*); (*clock*) бить* (проби́ть* *perf*); **to be on** ~ (*workers*) бастова́ть (*impf*); **to** ~ **a balance** соблюда́ть (*impf*) равнове́сие; **to** ~ **a match** зажига́ть (заже́чь* *perf*) спи́чку

► **strike back** *vi* (*MIL, fig*) наноси́ть* (нанести́* *perf*) отве́тный уда́р

► **strike down** *vt* сража́ть (срази́ть* *perf*)

► **strike off** *vt* (*name from list*) вычёркивать (вы́черкнуть *perf*); (*: doctor etc*) лиша́ть (лиши́ть *perf*) пра́ва практикова́ть

► **strike out** *vt* (*word, sentence*) вычёркивать (вы́черкнуть *perf*)

► **strike up** *vt* (*MUS*) заигра́ть (*impf*); (*conversation, friendship*) завя́зывать (завяза́ть* *perf*).

strikebreaker ['straɪkbreɪkə'] *n* штрейкбре́хер.

strike pay *n* посо́бие басту́ющим.

striker ['straɪkə'] *n* (*person on strike*) забасто́вщик(-ица); (*SPORT*) напада́ющий* (-ая) *m(f) adj*.

striking ['straɪkɪŋ] *adj* порази́тельный* (порази́телен).

strimmer ['strɪmə'] *n* механи́ческое ручно́е приспособле́ние для стри́жки газо́нов в труднодосту́пных места́х.

string [strɪŋ] (*pt, pp* **strung**) *n* верёвка*; (*row: of*

onions*) свя́зка*; (*: of islands*) цепь *f*; (*: of cars, people*) верени́ца; (*series: of disasters*) се́рия; (*: of excuses*) пото́к; (*COMPUT*) строка́, цепо́чка; (*MUS: for guitar etc*) струна́* ♦ *vt*: **to** ~ **together** свя́зывать (связа́ть* *perf*); **the** ~**s** *npl* (*MUS: section of orchestra*) стру́нные инструме́нты *mpl*; **to** ~ **out** растя́гивать (растяну́ть* *perf*); **a** ~ **of beads** бу́сы; **to pull** ~**s** (*fig*) испо́льзовать (*impf/perf*) свя́зи; **with no** ~**s attached** (*fig*) без дополни́тельных усло́вий.

string bean *n* стручко́вая фасо́ль *f*.

string(ed) instrument *n* стру́нный инструме́нт.

stringent ['strɪndʒənt] *adj* (*rules, measures*) стро́гий* (строг).

string quartet *n* (*MUS*) стру́нный кварте́т.

strip [strɪp] *n* полоса́*; (*SPORT*): **the Rangers** ~ фо́рма Ре́йнджерз ♦ *vt* (*undress*) раздева́ть (разде́ть* *perf*); (*paint*) обдира́ть (ободра́ть* *perf*), сдира́ть (содра́ть* *perf*); (*also*: ~ **down**: *machine*) разбира́ть (разобра́ть* *perf*) ♦ *vi* (*undress*) раздева́ться (разде́ться* *perf*).

strip cartoon *n* исто́рия в карти́нках.

stripe [straɪp] *n* поло́ска*; (*MIL, POLICE*) петли́ца.

striped ['straɪpt] *adj* (*fabric, animal etc*) полоса́тый* (полоса́т).

strip lighting *n* (*BRIT*) дневно́е освеще́ние.

stripper ['strɪpə'] *n* уча́стница стрипти́за.

strip-search ['strɪpsɛtʃ] *n* ли́чный досмо́тр ♦ *vt* производи́ть* (произвести́* *perf*) ли́чный досмо́тр +*gen*.

striptease ['strɪpti:z] *n* стрипти́з.

strive [straɪv] (*pt* **strove**, *pp* **striven**) *vi*: **to** ~ **for sth/to do** стреми́ться* (*impf*) к чему́-н/+*infin*.

striven ['strɪvn] *pp of* **strive**.

strobe [strəub] *n* (*also*: ~ **light**) строб-и́мпульс, селе́кторный и́мпульс.

strode [strəud] *pt of* **stride**.

stroke [strəuk] *n* (*also MED*) уда́р; (*SWIMMING*) стиль *m*; (*of piston*) ход, такт; (*of paintbrush*) мазо́к*; (*of pen etc*) штрих ♦ *vt* (*caress*) гла́дить (погла́дить* *perf*); **at a** ~ одни́м ма́хом; **on the** ~ **of 5** ро́вно в 5; **a** ~ **of luck** уда́ча; **a 2-**~ **engine** двухта́ктный дви́гатель *m*.

stroll [strəul] *n* прогу́лка* ♦ *vi* прогу́ливаться (прогуля́ться *perf*), пройти́сь* (*perf*); **to go for a** ~, **have** *or* **take a** ~ идти́* (пойти́* *perf*) прогуля́ться.

stroller ['strəulə'] *n* (*US: pushchair*) (складна́я) коля́ска.

strong [strɔŋ] *adj* си́льный* (силён); (*healthy, powerful*) кре́пкий* (кре́пок); (*object, material*) про́чный* (про́чен); (*imagination*) большо́й; (*drugs, chemicals*) си́льный; (*letters, measures*) ре́зкий* (ре́зок) ♦ *adv*: **to be going** ~ занима́ть (*impf*) про́чные пози́ции;

---

they are 50 ~ их 50.

strong-arm ['strɒŋɑ:m] *adj*: ~ **methods** приёмы *mpl* си́льной руки́.

strongbox ['strɒŋbɒks] *n* сейф.

stronghold ['strɒŋhəuld] *n* райо́н сопротивле́ния; (*fig*) опло́т, тверды́ня.

strongly ['strɒŋlɪ] *adv* (*construct*) кре́пко; (*push, defend, believe*) си́льно; **I feel ~ about it** во мне э́то вызыва́ет си́льные эмо́ции.

strongman ['strɒŋmæn] *irreg n* сила́ч, богаты́рь* *m*; (*fig*) си́льная ли́чность *f*.

strongroom ['strɒŋru:m] *n* сейф.

stroppy ['strɒpɪ] *adj* (*inf*) стропти́вый (стропти́в).

strove [strəuv] *pt of* strive.

struck [strʌk] *pt, pp of* strike.

structural ['strʌktʃrəl] *adj* структу́рный.

structurally ['strʌktʃrəlɪ] *adv* (*sound*) со структу́рной то́чки зре́ния.

structure ['strʌktʃə'] *n* структу́ра.

struggle ['strʌgl] *n* борьба́; (*difficulty*) уси́лие ◆ *vi* (*try hard*) прилага́ть (*impf*) больши́е уси́лия; (*fight*) боро́ться* (*impf*); (: *to free o.s.*) сопротивля́ться (*impf*); **to have a ~ to do** де́лать (сде́лать *perf*) уси́лие +*infin*.

strum [strʌm] *vt* (*guitar*) игра́ть (*impf*) на +*prp*.

strung [strʌŋ] *pt, pp of* string.

strut [strʌt] *n* (*wood, metal*) распо́рка* ◆ *vi* ходи́ть*/идти́* (пойти́* *perf*) вели́чественно.

strychnine ['strɪkni:n] *n* стрихни́н.

stub [stʌb] *n* (*of cheque, ticket etc*) корешо́к*; (*of cigarette*) окуро́к* ◆ *vt*: **to ~ one's toe** бо́льно спотыка́ться (споткну́ться *perf*)

▸ **stub out** *vt* (*cigarette*) гаси́ть* (загаси́ть* *perf*).

stubble ['stʌbl] *n* (*AGR*) жнивьё; (*on chin*) щети́на.

stubborn ['stʌbən] *adj* (*child, determination*) упря́мый (упря́м), упо́рный* (упо́рен); (*stain*) несмыва́ющийся; (*illness*) пло́хо поддаю́щийся лече́нию.

stubby ['stʌbɪ] *adj* (*fingers, pencil*) коро́ткий*.

stucco ['stʌkəu] *n* (*CONSTR*) декорати́вная "ка́менная" штукату́рка.

stuck [stʌk] *pt, pp of* stick ◆ *adj*: **to be ~** застря́ть* (*perf*); **to get ~** застрева́ть (застря́ть* *perf*).

stuck-up [stʌk'ʌp] *adj* (*inf*) наду́тый (наду́т).

stud [stʌd] *n* (*on clothing etc*) кно́пка*, заклёпка*; (*collar stud*) за́понка*; (*earring*) серьга́* со шти́фтом; (*on sole of boot*) шип*; (*also*: ~ **farm**) ко́нный заво́д; (*also*: ~ **horse**) племенно́й конь* *m* ◆ *vt* (*fig*): **~ded with** усы́панный +*instr*.

student ['stju:dənt] *n* (*at university*) студе́нт(ка*); (*at school*) уча́щийся*(-аяся) *m(f) adj* ◆ *adj* (*life, union*) студе́нческий*; (*nurse: female*) медсестра́-практика́нтка*; (: *male*) медбра́т-практика́нт; **law/medical ~** студе́нт(ка*) юриди́ческого/медици́нского факульте́та.

student driver *n* (*US*) учени́к* автомоби́ля.

student loan *n* студе́нческий* заём.

students' union ['stju:dənts-] *n* (*BRIT*: *association*) студе́нческий* сою́з; (*building*) зда́ние студе́нческого сою́за.

studied ['stʌdɪd] *adj* (*expression, attitude*) проду́манный (проду́ман).

studio ['stju:dɪəu] *n* сту́дия.

studio flat (*US* **studio apartment**) *n* однокóмнатная кварти́ра.

studious ['stju:dɪəs] *adj* (*person*) усе́рдный* (усе́рден); (*careful: attention*) тща́тельный* (тща́телен).

studiously ['stju:dɪəslɪ] *adv* (*carefully*) тща́тельно.

study ['stʌdɪ] *n* (*activity*) учёба; (*room*) кабине́т ◆ *vt* (*learn about, examine*) изуча́ть (изучи́ть* *perf*) ◆ *vi* учи́ться* (*perf*); **studies** *npl* (*subjects studied*) ку́рсы *pl*; **to make a ~ of sth** иссле́довать (*impf/perf*) что-н; **to ~ for one's exams** гото́виться* (*impf*) к экза́менам.

stuff [stʌf] *n* (*things*) ве́щи *fpl*; (*substance*) вещество́ ◆ *vt* набива́ть (наби́ть* *perf*); (*CULIN*) начиня́ть (начини́ть *perf*), фарширова́ть (нафарширова́ть *perf*); (*inf: push: object*) запи́хивать (запиха́ть *perf*); **my nose is ~ed up** у меня́ зало́жен нос; **get ~ed!** (*inf!*) пошёл ты!

stuffed toy [stʌft-] *n* мя́гкая игру́шка*.

stuffing ['stʌfɪŋ] *n* наби́вка; (*CULIN*) начи́нка, фарш.

stuffy ['stʌfɪ] *adj* (*room*) ду́шный* (ду́шен); (*person, ideas*) чо́порный* (чо́порен).

stumble ['stʌmbl] *vi* спотыка́ться (споткну́ться *perf*); **to ~ across** or **on** (*fig*) натыка́ться (наткну́ться *perf*) на +*acc*.

stumbling block ['stʌmblɪŋ-] *n* ка́мень* *m* преткнове́ния.

stump [stʌmp] *n* (*of tree*) пень* *m*; (*of limb*) обру́бок* ◆ *vt* озада́чивать (озада́чить *perf*); **he is ~ed** он озада́чен.

stun [stʌn] *vt* (*subj: news*) ошеломля́ть (ошеломи́ть* *perf*); (: *blow on head*) оглуша́ть (оглуши́ть *perf*).

stung [stʌŋ] *pt, pp of* sting.

stunk [stʌŋk] *pp of* stink.

stunning ['stʌnɪŋ] *adj* (*fig: news, event*) ошеломи́тельный* (ошеломи́телен); (: *girl, dress*) потряса́ющий* (потряса́ющ), изуми́тельный* (изуми́телен).

stunt [stʌnt] *n* трюк.

stunted ['stʌntɪd] *adj* (*trees*) подру́бленный* (*growth*) заме́дленный* (заме́длен).

stuntman ['stʌntmæn] *irreg n* каскадёр.

stupefaction [stju:pɪ'fækʃən] *n* отупе́ние; (*surprise*) остолбене́ние; **to my ~** к моему́ изумле́нию.

stupefy ['stju:pɪfaɪ] *vt* приводи́ть* (привести́* *perf*) в отупе́ние; (*fig*) изумля́ть (изуми́ть* *perf*).

stupendous [stju:'pɛndəs] *adj* (*large*)

колосса́льный* (колосса́лен); (*impressive*) изуми́тельный* (изуми́телен).

stupid [ˈstjuːpɪd] *adj* (*person, question etc*) глу́пый (глуп).

stupidity [stjuːˈpɪdɪtɪ] *n* глу́пость *f*.

stupidly [ˈstjuːpɪdlɪ] *adv* (*say, look*) глу́по.

stupor [ˈstjuːpəʳ] *n* сту́пор; **in a ~** в сту́поре.

sturdily [ˈstəːdɪlɪ] *adv* (*built*) про́чно, кре́пко.

sturdy [ˈstəːdɪ] *adj* (*person, thing*) кре́пкий* (кре́пок).

sturgeon [ˈstəːdʒən] *n* (*ZOOL*) осётр*.

stutter [ˈstʌtəʳ] *n* заика́ние ♦ *vi* заика́ться (*impf*).

Stuttgart [ˈstutgɑːt] *n* Шту́тгарт.

sty [staɪ] *n* (*for pigs*) свина́рник.

stye [staɪ] *n* ячме́нь *m*.

style [staɪl] *n* стиль *m*; **in the latest ~** по после́дней мо́де; **hair ~** причёска*.

styli [ˈstaɪlaɪ] *npl of* **stylus**.

stylish [ˈstaɪlɪʃ] *adj* шика́рный* (шика́рен).

stylist [ˈstaɪlɪst] *n* (*also:* **hair ~**) парикма́хер-модельёр; (*literary stylist*) стили́ст.

stylized [ˈstaɪlaɪzd] *adj* (*picture, account*) стилизо́ванный* (стилизо́ван).

stylus [ˈstaɪləs] (*pl* **styli** *or* **~es**) *n* (*of record player*) игла́*, иго́лка*.

Styrofoam® [ˈstaɪrəfəum] *n* (*US*) *синтети́ческий упако́вочный материа́л*.

suave [swɑːv] *adj* (*person, manners etc*) елейный* (елеен).

sub [sʌb] *n abbr* (*NAUT*) (= **submarine**) подло́дка= *подво́дная ло́дка*; (*ADMIN*) = **subscription**; (*PRESS:* = **sub-editor**) помо́щник *or* замести́тель *m* реда́ктора.

sub... [sʌb] *prefix* суб..., под....

subcommittee [ˈsʌbkəmɪtɪ] *n* подкомите́т.

subconscious [sʌbˈkɔnʃəs] *adj* (*desire etc*) подсозна́тельный* (подсозна́телен).

subcontinent [sʌbˈkɔntɪnənt] *n*: **the (Indian) ~** (инди́йский*) субконтине́нт.

subcontract [*vt* sʌbkənˈtrækt, *n* ˈsʌbˈkɔntrækt] *vt* заключа́ть (заключи́ть *perf*) субподря́д с +*instr* ♦ *n* субподря́д.

subcontractor [ˈsʌbkənˈtræktəʳ] *n* субподря́дчик.

subdivide [sʌbdɪˈvaɪd] *vt* подразделя́ть (подраздели́ть *perf*).

subdivision [ˈsʌbdɪvɪʒən] *n* подразделе́ние.

subdue [səbˈdjuː] *vt* подавля́ть (подави́ть* *perf*).

subdued [səbˈdjuːd] *adj* (*light*) приглушённый (приглушён); (*person*) пода́вленный* (пода́влен).

sub-editor [ˈsʌbˈɛdɪtəʳ] *n* (*BRIT: PRESS*) помо́щник *or* замести́тель *m* реда́ктора.

subject [*n* ˈsʌbdʒɪkt, *vt* səbˈdʒɛkt] *n* (*topic*) те́ма; (*SCOL*) предме́т; (*of kingdom*) по́данный(-ая) *m(f) adj*; (*LING*) подлежа́щее *nt adj* ♦ *vt*: **to ~ sb** **to sth** подверга́ть (подве́ргнуть* *perf*) кого́-н чему́-н; **to be ~ to** (*tax*) подлежа́ть (*impf*) +*dat*; (*law*) подчиня́ться (*impf*) +*dat*; **he is ~ to heart attacks** он подве́ржен серде́чным при́ступам; **this is ~ to confirmation in writing** э́то подлежи́т пи́сьменному подтвержде́нию; **to change the ~** меня́ть (поменя́ть *perf*) те́му (разгово́ра).

subjection [səbˈdʒɛkʃən] *n* (*of women, enemy etc*) подчине́ние.

subjective [səbˈdʒɛktɪv] *adj* субъекти́вный* (субъекти́вен).

subject matter *n* (*content*) те́ма.

sub judice [sʌbˈdjuːdɪsɪ] *adj*: **the case is ~~** в да́нным моме́нт э́то де́ло рассма́тривается судо́м.

subjugate [ˈsʌbdʒugeɪt] *vt* (*people*) покоря́ть (покори́ть *perf*).

subjunctive [səbˈdʒʌŋktɪv] *n* сослага́тельное наклоне́ние.

sublet [sʌbˈlɛt] *vt* (*property*) передава́ть* (переда́ть* *perf*) в субаре́нду.

sublime [səˈblaɪm] *adj* возвы́шенный*; **from the ~ to the ridiculous** от вели́кого до смешно́го.

subliminal [sʌbˈlɪmɪnl] *adj* (*memory*) подсозна́тельный; (*advertising*) де́йствующий* на подсозна́ние.

submachine gun [ˈsʌbməˈʃiːn-] *n* автома́т.

submarine [sʌbməˈriːn] *n* подво́дная ло́дка*.

submerge [səbˈməːdʒ] *vt* погружа́ть (погрузи́ть* *perf*) (*в во́ду*) ♦ *vi* (*submarine, sea creature*) погружа́ться (погрузи́ться* *perf*) (*в во́ду*).

submersion [səbˈməːʃən] *n* погруже́ние.

submission [səbˈmɪʃən] *n* (*state*) подчине́ние, повинове́ние; (*of plan etc*) пода́ча; (*to committee etc*) представле́ние.

submissive [səbˈmɪsɪv] *adj* поко́рный* (поко́рен).

submit [səbˈmɪt] *vt* (*proposal, application etc*) представля́ть (предста́вить* *perf*) на рассмотре́ние ♦ *vi*: **to ~ to sth** подчиня́ться (подчини́ться *perf*) чему́-н.

subnormal [sʌbˈnɔːml] *adj* (*backward: child etc*) отста́лый*; **~ temperatures** температу́ры *fpl* ни́же норма́льных.

subordinate [səˈbɔːdɪnət] *adj* (*position, rank*): **to be ~ to sb** подчиня́ться (*impf*) кому́-н; (*LING: clause*) прида́точный ♦ *n* подчинённый(-ая) *m(f) adj*.

subpoena [səbˈpiːnə] *n* (*LAW*) пове́стка* ♦ *vt* (*LAW: witness etc*) вызыва́ть (вы́звать* *perf*) в суд.

subroutine [sʌbruːˈtiːn] *n* (*COMPUT*) подпрогра́мма.

subscribe [səbˈskraɪb] *vi* подпи́сываться (подписа́ться* *perf*); **to ~ to** (*opinion, fund*)

---

* marks translations which have irregular inflections. The Russian-English side of the dictionary gives inflectional information.

поддерживать (поддержать* *perf*); (*magazine etc*) подписываться (подписаться* *perf*) на +*acc*; ~**d capital** подписной акционерный капитал.

subscriber [səb'skraɪbə'] *n* (*to periodical*) подписчик; (*to telephone*) абонент.

subscript ['sʌbskrɪpt] *n* (*TYP*) подстрочный знак.

subscription [səb'skrɪpʃən] *n* (*to magazine etc*) подписка*; (*membership dues*) (членский*) взнос; **to take out a ~ to** подписываться (подписаться* *perf*) на +*acc*.

subsequent ['sʌbsɪkwənt] *adj* последующий*; ~ **to** вслед +*dat*.

subsequently ['sʌbsɪkwəntlɪ] *adv* впоследствии.

subservient [səb'sə:vɪənt] *adj* (*person, behaviour*) подобострастный* (подобострастен); (*less important: policy etc*) подвластный* (подвластен); **he is ~ to** ... он подвластен +*dat* ....

subside [səb'saɪd] *vi* (*feeling, wind*) утихать (утихнуть* *perf*); (*flood*) убывать (убыть* *perf*).

subsidence [səb'saɪdns] *n* (*in road etc*) оседание.

subsidiarity [səbsɪdɪ'ærɪtɪ] *n* (*POL*) уровень* *m* зависимости.

subsidiary [səb'sɪdɪərɪ] *adj* (*question, details*) второстепенный* (второстепен); (*BRIT: SCOL: subject*) факультативный ◆ *n* (*also:* ~ **company**) дочерняя компания.

subsidize ['sʌbsɪdaɪz] *vt* (*education, industry etc*) субсидировать (*impf/perf*).

subsidy ['sʌbsɪdɪ] *n* субсидия, дотация.

subsist [səb'sɪst] *vi*: **to ~ on sth** существовать (*impf*) за счёт чего-н.

subsistence [səb'sɪstəns] *n* (*ability to live*) существование; (*food*) пропитание.

subsistence allowance *n* аванс (*перед первой зарплатой*).

subsistence level *n* прожиточный минимум.

substance ['sʌbstəns] *n* (*product, material*) вещество; (*fig: essence*) суть* *f*; **a man of ~** солидный мужчина; **the essay lacks ~** в сочинении нет стержня.

substance abuse *n* токсикомания.

substandard [sʌb'stændəd] *adj* (*goods*) некачественный; (*housing*) непригодный* (непригоден) для жилья.

substantial [səb'stænʃl] *adj* (*solid*) прочный* (прочен), основательный* (основателен); (*fig: reward, meal*) значительный* (значителен), солидный* (солиден).

substantially [səb'stænʃəlɪ] *adv* (*by a large amount*) значительно; (*in essence*) существенно, основательно; ~ **bigger** значительно больше.

substantiate [səb'stænʃɪeɪt] *vt* (*claim, story, statement etc*) обосновывать (обосновать* *perf*).

substitute ['sʌbstɪtju:t] *n* (*person*) замена; (: *FOOTBALL etc*) запасной *m adj* (игрок*); (*thing*) заменитель *m* ◆ *vt*: **to ~ A for B** заменять (заменить* *perf*) А на Б.

substitute teacher *n* (*US*) замещающий(-ая) учитель(ница) *m(f)*.

substitution [sʌbstɪ'tju:ʃən] *n* (*act of substituting*) замена.

subterfuge ['sʌbtəfju:dʒ] *n* уловка*.

subterranean [sʌbtə'reɪnɪən] *adj* (*passage*) подземный.

subtitle ['sʌbtaɪtl] *n* (*CINEMA*) субтитр.

subtle ['sʌtl] *adj* (*change*) тонкий*, едва уловимый; (*person*) искусный* (искусен).

subtlety ['sʌtltɪ] *n* (*small detail*) тонкость *f*; (*of person*) искусность *f*.

subtly ['sʌtlɪ] *adv* (*change, vary*) едва уловимо; (*different*) слегка; (*criticize, persuade*) искусно.

subtotal [sʌb'təutl] *n* суммарное число*.

subtract [səb'trækt] *vt* вычитать (вычесть* *perf*).

subtraction [səb'trækʃən] *n* вычитание.

subtropical [sʌb'trɔpɪkl] *adj* субтропический.

suburb ['sʌbə:b] *n* пригород; **the ~s** *npl* (*area*) пригород *msg*.

suburban [sə'bə:bən] *adj* пригородный.

suburbia [sə'bə:bɪə] *n* пригород.

subvention [səb'vɛnʃən] *n* (*subsidy*) дотация, субсидия.

subversion [səb'və:ʃən] *n* подрывная деятельность *f*.

subversive [səb'və:sɪv] *adj* (*activities, literature*) подрывной.

subway ['sʌbweɪ] *n* (*US: underground railway*) метро *nt ind*, подземка*; (*BRIT: underpass*) подземный переход.

sub-zero [sʌb'zɪərəu] *adj*: ~ **temperatures** температуры *fpl* ниже нуля.

succeed [sək'si:d] *vi* (*plan etc*) удаваться* (удаться* *perf*), иметь (*impf*) успех; (*person: in career etc*) преуспевать (преуспеть *perf*) ◆ *vt* (*in job, order*) сменять (сменить* *perf*); **he ~ed in finishing the article** ему удалось закончить статью.

succeeding [sək'si:dɪŋ] *adj* (*following*) последующий*; ~ **generations** последующие поколения.

success [sək'sɛs] *n* (*achievement*) успех, удача; (*hit*): **the book was a ~** книга имела успех; **he was a ~** он добился успеха.

successful [sək'sɛsful] *adj* (*venture*) успешный* (успешен); **he was ~ in convincing her** ему удалось убедить её.

successfully [sək'sɛsfəlɪ] *adv* (*complete, do*) успешно.

succession [sək'sɛʃən] *n* (*series*) череда, ряд*; (*to throne etc*) наследование; **in ~** подряд; **3 years in ~** три года подряд.

successive [sək'sɛsɪv] *adj* (*governments*) следующий* один за другим; **3 ~ days/**

attempts три дня/попы́тки подря́д.
successor [sək'sɛsəʳ] *n* прее́мник(-ица); (*to throne*) насле́дник(-ица).
succinct [sək'sɪŋkt] *adj* (*explanation*) сжа́тый (сжат).
succulent ['sʌkjulənt] *adj* (*fruit, meat*) со́чный* (со́чен) ♦ *n* (*BOT*): ~s суккуле́нты *pl*.
succumb [sə'kʌm] *vi* (*to temptation*) поддава́ться* (подда́ться* *perf*); **he ~ed to illness** боле́знь оконча́тельно его́ победи́ла.
such [sʌtʃ] *adj* тако́й; (*emphasizing similarity*) подо́бный, тако́й ♦ *adv*: ~ **a long trip** така́я дли́нная пое́здка; ~ **a book** така́я кни́га; ~ **books** таки́е кни́ги; ~ **a lot of** тако́е мно́жество +*gen*; **making ~ a noise that ...** создава́я тако́й шум, что ...; ~ **as** (*like*) таки́е как; ~ **books as I have** таки́е кни́ги, как у меня́; **I said no ~ thing** я ничего́ подо́бного *or* тако́го не говори́л; **as** ~ как тако́вой.
such-and-such ['sʌtʃənsʌtʃ] *adj* таки́е-то и таки́е-то.
suchlike ['sʌtʃlaɪk] *pron* (*inf*): **and** ~ и им подо́бные.
suck [sʌk] *vt* соса́ть* (*impf*); (*subj: pump, machine*) вса́сывать (всоса́ть *perf*).
sucker ['sʌkəʳ] *n* присо́ска*; (*BOT*) корнево́й побе́г; (*inf*) о́лух.
suckle ['sʌkl] *vt* корми́ть* (*impf*) (гру́дью), дава́ть* (дать* *perf*) грудь +*dat*; (*subj: animal*) корми́ть* (*impf*).
sucrose ['su:krəuz] *n* сахаро́за.
suction ['sʌkʃən] *n* вса́сывание.
suction pump *n* вса́сывающий насо́с.
Sudan [su'dɑ:n] *n* Суда́н.
Sudanese [su:də'ni:z] *adj* суда́нский ♦ *n inv* суда́нец*(-ка*).
sudden ['sʌdn] *adj* внеза́пный* (внеза́пен); **all of a** ~ (*unexpectedly*) внеза́пно, вдруг.
sudden death *n* (*in competition*) дополни́тельный матч (*по́сле ничьи́*).
suddenly ['sʌdnlɪ] *adv* (*unexpectedly*) внеза́пно, вдруг.
suds [sʌdz] *npl* (мы́льные) пузыри́ *mpl*.
sue [su:] *vt* предъявля́ть (предъяви́ть* *perf*) иск +*dat*, возбужда́ть (возбуди́ть* *perf*) де́ло про́тив +*gen* ♦ *vi*: **to** ~ **(for)** суди́ться (*impf*) (за +*acc*); **to** ~ **for divorce** возбужда́ть (возбуди́ть* *perf*) де́ло о разво́де; **to** ~ **sb for damages** предъявля́ть (предъяви́ть* *perf*) иск кому́-н о компенса́ции.
suede [sweɪd] *n* за́мша ♦ *cpd* за́мшевый.
suet ['suɪt] *n* жир.
Suez ['su:ɪz] *n*: **the** ~ **Canal** Суэ́цкий* кана́л.
Suff. *abbr* (*BRIT: POST*) = **Suffolk**.
suffer ['sʌfəʳ] *vt* (*hardship etc*) переноси́ть* (перенести́* *perf*); (*pain, rudeness*) страда́ть (*impf*) от +*gen* ♦ *vi* (*person, results etc*) страда́ть (пострада́ть *perf*); **to** ~ **from** (*illness*

etc) страда́ть (*impf*) +*instr*; **to** ~ **the effects of alcohol/a fall** страда́ть (пострада́ть *perf*) от возде́йствия алкого́ля/от после́дствий паде́ния.
sufferance ['sʌfərns] *n*: **she hadn't wanted him to go, so he was only there on** ~ она́ не хоте́ла отпуска́ть его́, он был там, причиня́я ей страда́ния.
sufferer ['sʌfərəʳ] *n* (*MED*) страда́ющий(-ая) *m(f) adj*.
suffering ['sʌfərɪŋ] *n* (*hardship*) страда́ние.
suffice [sə'faɪs] *vi* (*be enough*): **this** ~**s** ... э́того доста́точно, ...
sufficient [sə'fɪʃənt] *adj* доста́точный* (доста́точен); ~ **money** доста́точное коли́чество де́нег.
sufficiently [sə'fɪʃəntlɪ] *adv* (*recover, provide*) доста́точно; (*powerful, enthusiastic*) в доста́точной ме́ре.
suffix ['sʌfɪks] *n* (*LING*) су́ффикс.
suffocate ['sʌfəkeɪt] *vi* задыха́ться (задохну́ться *perf*); (*have difficulty breathing*) задыха́ться (*impf*); (*die*) задохну́ться (*impf*) ♦ *vt* (*gas etc*) удуша́ть (удуши́ть *perf*).
suffocation [sʌfə'keɪʃən] *n* уду́шье.
suffrage ['sʌfrɪdʒ] *n* (*right to vote*) избира́тельное пра́во.
suffragette [sʌfrə'dʒɛt] *n* суфражи́стка*.
suffused [sə'fju:zd] *adj*: ~ **with** (*light, colour*) погружённый (погружён) в +*prp*; (*tears*) зали́тый (зали́т) +*instr*.
sugar ['ʃugəʳ] *n* са́хар* ♦ *vt* (*tea etc*) сласти́ть* (посласти́ть* *perf*).
sugar beet *n* са́харная свёкла.
sugar bowl *n* са́харница.
sugar cane *n* са́харный тростни́к.
sugar-coated ['ʃugə'kəutɪd] *adj* (*sweet*) заса́харенный.
sugar lump *n* кусо́к* са́хара.
sugar refinery *n* сахарорафина́дный заво́д.
sugary ['ʃugərɪ] *adj* сла́дкий* (сла́док), саха́ристый (саха́рист); (*fig*) слаща́вый (слаща́в).
suggest [sə'dʒɛst] *vt* (*propose*) предлага́ть (предложи́ть* *perf*); (*indicate*) предполага́ть (предположи́ть* *perf*); **what do you ~ I do?** что Вы предлага́ете мне де́лать?
suggestion [sə'dʒɛstʃən] *n* (*proposal*) предложе́ние; (*indication*) предположе́ние.
suggestive [sə'dʒɛstɪv] *adj* (*pej: remarks, looks*) неприли́чный (неприли́чен).
suicidal [suɪ'saɪdl] *adj* (*person*) стоя́щий на гра́ни самоуби́йства; (*act*) само-уби́йственный.
suicide ['suɪsaɪd] *n* (*death*) самоуби́йство; (*person*) самоуби́йца *m/f*; *see also* **commit**.
suicide attempt *n* попы́тка* самоуби́йства.
suicide bid *n* попы́тка* самоуби́йства.

---

* marks translations which have irregular inflections. The Russian-English side of the dictionary gives inflectional information.

suit [su:t] *n* костю́м; (*LAW*) иск; (*CARDS*) масть *f*
♦ *vt* (*be convenient, appropriate*) подходи́ть*
(подойти́* *perf*) +*dat*; (*colour, clothes*) идти́*
(*impf*) +*dat*; (*adapt*): **to ~ sth to**
приспоса́бливать (приспосо́бить* *perf*) что-н
к +*dat*; **he was ~ed to lead the party** он
хорошо́ подходи́л на роль ли́дера па́ртии;
to bring a ~ against sb предъявля́ть
(предъяви́ть* *perf*) иск кому́-н; **to follow ~**
(*fig*) сле́довать (после́довать *perf*) приме́ру;
they are well ~ed (*couple*) они́ хорошо́ друг
дру́гу подхо́дят.
suitability [su:tə'bɪlɪtɪ] *n* приго́дность *f*.
suitable ['su:təbl] *adj* подходя́щий*; **would
tomorrow be ~?** за́втра Вам подойдёт *or* Вас
устро́ит?; **we found somebody ~** мы нашли́
подходя́щего челове́ка.
suitably ['su:təblɪ] *adv* надлежа́щим о́бразом.
suitcase ['su:tkeɪs] *n* чемода́н.
suite [swi:t] *n* (*of rooms*) апартаме́нты *mpl*;
(*MUS*) сюи́та; (*furniture*): **bedroom/dining
room ~** спа́льный/столо́вый гарниту́р; **a
three-piece ~** мя́гкая ме́бель *f*.
suitor ['su:tə'] *n*: **he is her ~** он и́щет её руки́.
sulfate ['sʌlfeɪt] *n* (*US*) = **sulphate**.
sulfur ['sʌlfə'] *n* (*US*) = **sulphur**.
sulfuric [sʌl'fjuərɪk] (*US*) = **sulphuric**.
sulk [sʌlk] *vi* быть* (*impf*) в дурно́м
настрое́нии.
sulky ['sʌlkɪ] *adj* (*child, mood*) су́мрачный*
(су́мрачен).
sullen ['sʌlən] *adj* (*person, silence*) угрю́мый
(угрю́м).
sulphate ['sʌlfeɪt] (*US* **sulfate**) *n* сульфа́т.
sulphur ['sʌlfə'] (*US* **sulfur**) *n* се́ра.
sulphur dioxide (*US* **sulfur dioxide**) *n*
двуо́кись *f* се́ры, серни́стый ангидри́д.
sulphuric [sʌl'fjuərɪk] (*US* **sulfuric**) *adj*: **~ acid**
се́рная кислота́.
sultan ['sʌltən] *n* султа́н.
sultana [sʌl'tɑ:nə] *n* (*CULIN*) кишми́ш.
sultry ['sʌltrɪ] *adj* (*weather*) ду́шный* (ду́шен).
sum [sʌm] *n* (*calculation*) арифме́тика,
вычисле́ние; (*amount*) су́мма
▶ **sum up** *vt* (*describe*) сумми́ровать (*impf/perf*);
(*evaluate rapidly*) вычисля́ть (вы́числить
perf) ♦ *vi* (*summarize*) подводи́ть* (подвести́*
perf) ито́г.
Sumatra [su'mɑ:trə] *n* Сума́тра.
summarize ['sʌməraɪz] *vt* сумми́ровать (*impf/
perf*).
summary ['sʌmərɪ] *n* (*of essay etc*) кра́ткое
изложе́ние ♦ *adj* (*justice*) поспе́шный;
weather/news ~ сво́дка пого́ды/новосте́й.
summer ['sʌmə'] *n* (*season*) ле́то ♦ *adj* (*dress,
school*) ле́тний*; **in** ~ ле́том.
summer camp *n* (*US*) ле́тний* ла́герь* *m*.
summer holidays *npl* ле́тние кани́кулы *pl*.
summerhouse ['sʌməhaus] *n* (*in garden*)
бесе́дка*.
summertime ['sʌmətaɪm] *n* (*season*) ле́то,

ле́тний* пери́од.
summer time *n* ле́тнее вре́мя* *nt*.
summery ['sʌmərɪ] *adj* (*day, dress*) ле́тний*.
summing-up [sʌmɪŋ'ʌp] *n* (*LAW*) кра́ткое
изложе́ние де́ла (*обращённое к
прися́жным*).
summit ['sʌmɪt] *n* (*of mountain*) верши́на, пик;
(*also:* ~ **conference**) конфере́нция на
вы́сшем у́ровне; (*also:* ~ **meeting**) встре́ча
на вы́сшем у́ровне.
summon ['sʌmən] *vt* вызыва́ть (вы́звать* *perf*);
(*help*) звать* (позва́ть* *perf*) на +*acc*
▶ **summon up** *vt* собира́ть (собра́ть* *perf*).
summons ['sʌmənz] *n* (*LAW*) пове́стка; (*fig*)
приказа́ние ♦ *vt* (*LAW*) вызыва́ть (вы́звать*
perf); **to serve a ~ on sb** посыла́ть (посла́ть*
perf) кому́-н пове́стку.
sumo ['su:məu] *n* (*also:* ~ **wrestling**) су́мо *ind*
(*япо́нская борьба́*).
sump [sʌmp] *n* (*BRIT: AUT*) ма́сляный поддо́н.
sumptuous ['sʌmptjuəs] *adj* (*meal, costume*)
роско́шный (роско́шен), великоле́пный*
(великоле́пен).
sun [sʌn] *n* со́лнце; **in the** ~ на со́лнце; **to catch
the** ~ слегка́ загоре́ть (*perf*); **everything under
the** ~ всё в ми́ре.
Sun. *abbr* = **Sunday**.
sunbathe ['sʌnbeɪð] *vi* загора́ть (*impf*).
sunbeam ['sʌnbi:m] *n* со́лнечный луч*.
sunbed ['sʌnbɛd] *n* шезло́нг; (*with sun lamp*)
устро́йство с ква́рцевой ла́мпой для
получе́ния иску́сственно зага́ра.
sunburn ['sʌnbə:n] *n* (*painful*) со́лнечный
ожо́г.
sunburned ['sʌnbə:nd] *adj* = **sunburnt**.
sunburnt ['sʌnbə:nt] *adj* (*tanned*) загоре́лый;
(*painfully*) обожжённый (*со́лнцем*).
sun-cream ['sʌnkri:m] *n* солнцезащи́тный
крем.
sundae ['sʌndeɪ] *n* моро́женое *nt adj* с
фру́ктами.
Sunday ['sʌndɪ] *n* воскресе́нье; *see also*
Tuesday.
Sunday paper *n* воскре́сная газе́та.
Sunday school *n* воскре́сная шко́ла.
sundial ['sʌndaɪəl] *n* со́лнечные часы́ *pl*.
sundown ['sʌndaun] *n* зака́т, захо́д (*со́лнца*).
sundries ['sʌndrɪz] *npl* (*miscellaneous items*)
ра́зное *nt adj*.
sundry ['sʌndrɪ] *adj* (*various*) ра́зного ро́да; **all
and ~** все подря́д.
sunflower ['sʌnflauə'] *n* (*BOT*) подсо́лнечник.
sunflower oil *n* (*CULIN*) подсо́лнечное ма́сло.
sung [sʌŋ] *pp of* **sing**.
sunglasses ['sʌnglɑ:sɪz] *npl* солнцезащи́тные
очки́* *pl*.
sunk [sʌŋk] *pp of* **sink**.
sunken ['sʌŋkn] *adj* (*rock, ship*) затону́вший;
(*cheeks*) впа́лый; (*eyes*) ввали́вшийся; (*bath*)
встро́енный в углубле́нии.
sunlamp ['sʌnlæmp] *n* ультрафиоле́товая *or*

кварцевая лампа.
sunlight ['sʌnlaɪt] *n* солнечный свет.
sunlit ['sʌnlɪt] *adj* освещённый (освещён) солнцем.
sunny ['sʌnɪ] *adj (weather, day, place)* солнечный; *(fig)* светлый; **it is** ~ солнечно.
sunrise ['sʌnraɪz] *n* восход (солнца).
sun roof *n (AUT)* раздвижная панель *f (в крыше автомобиля).*
sunscreen ['sʌnskriːn] *n* солнцезащитный крем.
sunset ['sʌnsɛt] *n* заход (солнца), закат.
sunshade ['sʌnʃeɪd] *n* зонтик.
sunshine ['sʌnʃaɪn] *n* солнечный свет; **we sat in the** ~ мы сидели на солнце.
sunspot ['sʌnspɔt] *n (ASTRONOMY)* солнечное место*.
sunstroke ['sʌnstrəuk] *n* солнечный удар.
suntan ['sʌntæn] *n* загар.
suntan lotion *n* лосьон для загара.
suntanned ['sʌntænd] *adj (body, person)* загорелый.
suntan oil *n* масло для загара.
suntrap ['sʌntræp] *n* солнечный островок*.
super ['suːpəʳ] *adj (inf)* потрясающий*.
superannuation [suːpərænjuˈeɪʃən] *n* ежегодный пенсионный вклад.
superb [suːˈpəːb] *adj* великолепный* (великолепен).
Super Bowl *n (US)* финальный матч американского чемпионата по футболу.
supercilious [suːpəˈsɪlɪəs] *adj (disdainful, haughty)* высокомерный* (высокомерен).
superconductor [suːpəkənˈdʌktəʳ] *n* сверхпроводник.
superficial [suːpəˈfɪʃəl] *adj* поверхностный* (поверхностен); *(wound)* лёгкий* (лёгок).
superficially [suːpəˈfɪʃəlɪ] *adv* поверхностно.
superfluous [suːˈpəːfluəs] *adj* излишный, ненужный.
superglue ['suːpəglu:] *n* суперклей.
superhuman [suːpəˈhjuːmən] *adj (effort, strength)* сверхчеловеческий*.
superimpose ['suːpərɪmˈpəuz] *vt:* **to** ~ **(on)** накладывать (наложить* *perf)* (на +*acc*).
superintend [suːpərɪnˈtɛnd] *vt* надзирать *(impf)* за +*instr*; **to be** ~**ed by** быть* *(impf)* под надзором +*gen*.
superintendent [suːpərɪnˈtɛndənt] *n (of place)* заведующий*(-ая) *m(f)adj*; *(of activity)* руководитель(ница) *m(f)*; *(POLICE)* начальник, надзиратель *m*.
superior [suˈpɪərɪəʳ] *adj (better)* превосходящий; *(more senior)* старший*; *(smug)* высокомерный ♦ *n* начальник(-ица); **Mother S**~ *(REL)* настоятельница.
superiority [supɪərɪˈɔrɪtɪ] *n* превосходство.
superlative [suˈpəːlətɪv] *n* прилагательное или

наречие превосходной степени.
superman ['suːpəmæn] *irreg n* супермен, сверхчеловек *m no pl*.
supermarket ['suːpəmɑːkɪt] *n* универмаг, универсам; *(in Europe, US etc)* супермаркет.
supermodel ['suːpəmɔdl] *n* супермодель *f*.
supernatural [suːpəˈnætʃərəl] *adj (creature, force etc)* сверхъестественный ♦ *n:* **the** ~ сверхъестественные силы *fpl*.
supernova [suːpəˈnəuvə] *n* взрывающаяся новая звезда.
superpower ['suːpəpauəʳ] *n (POL)* сверхдержава.
superscript ['suːpəskrɪpt] *n (TYP)* надстрочные знаки *mpl*.
supersede [suːpəˈsiːd] *vt* сменять (сменить* *perf)*.
supersonic ['suːpəˈsɔnɪk] *adj (flight, aircraft)* сверхзвуковой.
superstar ['suːpəstɑːʳ] *n (CINEMA, SPORT etc)* суперзвезда*.
superstition [suːpəˈstɪʃən] *n* суеверие.
superstitious [suːpəˈstɪʃəs] *adj* суеверный* (суеверен).
superstore ['suːpəstɔːʳ] *n (BRIT: COMM)* универмаг, супермаркет.
supertanker ['suːpətæŋkəʳ] *n (NAUT)* супертанкер.
supertax ['suːpətæks] *n* дополнительный подоходный налог.
supervise ['suːpəvaɪz] *vt (person, activity)* следить* *(impf)* or наблюдать *(impf)* за +*instr*.
supervision [suːpəˈvɪʒən] *n* руководство, надзор; **under medical** ~ под наблюдением врача.
supervisor ['suːpəvaɪzəʳ] *n (of workers)* начальник(-ица); *(of students)* научный(-ая) руководитель(ница) *m(f)*.
supervisory ['suːpəvaɪzərɪ] *adj (role)* руководящий*; *(staff)* контролирующий.
supine ['suːpaɪn] *adj* лежащий на спине ♦ *adv* лёжа на спине.
supper ['sʌpəʳ] *n* ужин; **to have** ~ ужинать (поужинать *perf)*.
supplant [səˈplɑːnt] *vt (person, thing)* приходить* (прийти* *perf)* на смену +*dat*.
supple ['sʌpl] *adj (person, body)* гибкий* (гибок); *(leather)* мягкий* (мягок).
supplement ['sʌplɪmənt] *n (vitamins etc)* добавка*; *(of book, newspaper etc)* приложение ♦ *vt (diet)* доба᷄…ть *(impf)* к +*dat*; *(income)* подрабатывать *(impf)*.
supplementary [sʌplɪˈmɛntərɪ] *adj (question)* дополнительный.
supplementary benefit *n (BRIT: formerly)* пособие для малоимущих в Великобритании.
supplier [səˈplaɪəʳ] *n (COMM: person, firm)*

---

* marks translations which have irregular inflections. The Russian-English side of the dictionary gives inflectional information.

поставщи́к*.

supply [sə'plaɪ] *n* (*stock*) запа́с, запа́сы *mpl*; (*supplying*) поста́вка*; (*TECH*) обеспече́ние ♦ *vt* (*need*) удовлетворя́ть (удовлетвори́ть *perf*); (*provide*): **to ~ sth (to sb)** поставля́ть (поста́вить* *perf*) что-н (кому́-н); **supplies** *npl* (*food*) запа́сы *mpl* (продово́льствия); (*MIL*) боеприпа́сы *mpl* (и продово́льствие); **office supplies** конто́рские принадле́жности; **water is in short ~** э́тот райо́н испы́тывает нехва́тку воды́; **the electricity ~** снабже́ние электроэне́ргии; **the water ~** водоснабже́ние; **the gas ~** снабже́ние га́зом; **~ and demand** спрос и предложе́ние; **to ~ sb with sth** снабжа́ть (снабди́ть* *perf*) кого́-н чем-н; (*system, machine*) обору́довать (*impf/perf*) кого́-н чем-н; **it comes supplied with an adaptor** поставля́ется с ада́птером.

supply teacher *n* (*BRIT*) замеща́ющий(-ая) учи́тель(ница) *m(f)*.

support [sə'pɔ:t] *n* (*moral, financial etc*) подде́ржка; (*TECH*) опо́ра, подпо́рка* ♦ *vt* (*football team etc*) боле́ть (*impf*) за +*acc*; (*financially: family etc*) содержа́ть (*impf*); (*TECH: hold up*) подде́рживать (*impf*); (*sustain: theory etc*) подтвержда́ть (подтверди́ть* *perf*); **they stopped work in ~ of** они́ прекрати́ли рабо́ту в подде́ржку +*gen*; **to ~ o.s.** (*financially*) зараба́тывать (*impf*) (самому́) себе́ на жизнь.

support buying *n* (*COMM*) заку́пка в це́лях пониже́ния цен.

supporter [sə'pɔ:tə'] *n* (*POL etc*) сторо́нник(-ица); (*SPORT*) боле́льщик(-ица).

supporting [sə'pɔ:tɪŋ] *adj* второстепе́нный; **~ actor** актёр второ́го пла́на.

supportive [sə'pɔ:tɪv] *adj*: **to be ~ of sb** подде́рживать (поддержа́ть* *perf*) кого́-н.

suppose [sə'pəuz] *vt* полага́ть (*impf*); **he was ~d to do it** (*duty*) он до́лжен был э́то сде́лать; **it was worse than she'd ~d** э́то оказа́лось ху́же, чем она́ предполага́ла; **I don't ~ she'll come** я полага́ю, она́ не придёт; **he's about sixty, I ~** я полага́ю, ему́ лет шестьдеся́т; **he's ~d to be an expert** счита́ется, что он в э́том разбира́ется.

supposedly [sə'pəuzɪdlɪ] *adv* по иде́е.

supposing [sə'pəuzɪŋ] *conj* предположи́м, допу́стим.

supposition [sʌpə'zɪʃən] *n* предположе́ние, допуще́ние.

suppository [sə'pɔzɪtrɪ] *n* (*MED*) свеча́*.

suppress [sə'prɛs] *vt* подавля́ть (подави́ть* *perf*); (*scandal*) замя́ть* (*perf*); (*publication*) запреща́ть (запрети́ть* *perf*).

suppression [sə'prɛʃən] *n* подавле́ние.

suppressor [sə'prɛsə'] *n* (*ELEC etc*) глуши́тель *m*.

supremacy [su'prɛməsɪ] *n* (*MIL, POL etc*) госпо́дство.

supreme [su'pri:m] *adj* (*in titles: court etc*)

Верхо́вный; (*effort, achievement*) велича́йший.

Supreme Court *n* (*US*) Верхо́вный Суд.

supremo [su'pri:məu] *n* (*BRIT: inf*) верхо́вный *or* гла́вный нача́льник.

Supt. *abbr* (*POLICE*) = **superintendent**.

surcharge ['sə:tʃɑ:dʒ] *n* (*extra cost*) дополни́тельный сбор, дополни́тельная пла́та.

sure [ʃuə'] *adj* (*definite, convinced*) твёрдый* (твёрд); (*aim, friend, remedy*) ве́рный* (ве́рен) ♦ *adv* (*inf: esp US*): **that ~ is pretty, that's ~ pretty** э́то пра́вда ми́ло; **to make ~ of sth/that** удостове́риться (*perf*) в чём-н/, что; **~!** (*of course*) безусло́вно!; **~ enough** и пра́вда *or* впра́вду; **I'm not ~ how/why/when** я не уве́рен, как/почему́/когда́; **to be ~ of o.s.** не сомнева́ться (*impf*) в себе́.

sure-fire ['ʃuəfaɪə'] *adj* (*inf*) ве́рный.

sure-footed [ʃuə'futɪd] *adj* (*animal, person*) твёрдо держа́щийся на нога́х.

surely ['ʃuəlɪ] *adv* (*certainly*) наверняка́; **~ you don't mean that!** наверня́ка, Вы э́то несерьёзно!

surety ['ʃuərətɪ] *n* (*money*) зало́г; **to go** *or* **stand ~ for sb** брать* (взять* *perf*) кого́-н на пору́ки.

surf [sə:f] *n* (*waves*) прибо́й; (*foam*) бара́шки *mpl*.

surface ['sə:fɪs] *n* пове́рхность *f* ♦ *vt* (*road*) покрыва́ть (покры́ть* *perf*) ♦ *vi* (*fish, person in water*) пока́зываться (показа́ться* *perf*) на пове́рхности; (*fig: news, feeling*) всплыва́ть (всплыть* *perf*); (: *person in bed*) объявля́ться (объяви́ться* *perf*); **on the ~** (*fig*) с ви́ду.

surface area *n* пло́щадь *f* пове́рхности.

surface mail *n* обы́чная по́чта.

surface-to-surface ['sə:fɪstə'sə:fɪs] *adj*: **~ missile** раке́та ти́па "земля́-земля́".

surfboard ['sə:fbɔ:d] *n* аквапла́н.

surfeit ['sə:fɪt] *n*: **a ~ of** переизбы́ток* +*gen*.

surfer ['sə:fə'] *n* челове́к* занима́ющийся се́рфингом.

surfing ['sə:fɪŋ] *n* сёрфинг.

surge [sə:dʒ] *n* (*increase*) прито́к*; (*fig: of emotion*) прили́в; (*ELEC*) и́мпульс ♦ *vi* (*water*) вздыма́ться (*impf*), нахлы́нуть (*perf*); (*people, vehicles*) ри́нуться (*perf*); (*ELEC: power*) ре́зко увели́чиваться (увели́читься *perf*); **to ~ forward** ри́нуться (*perf*) *or* броса́ться (бро́ситься* *perf*) вперёд; **relief ~d through her** она́ почу́вствовала прили́в облегче́ния.

surgeon ['sə:dʒən] *n* (*MED*) хиру́рг.

Surgeon General *n* (*US: MED, MIL*) нача́льник медици́нского управле́ния.

surgery ['sə:dʒərɪ] *n* (*treatment*) хирурги́ческое вмеша́тельство; (*BRIT: room*) кабине́т врача́; (: *of MP, doctor etc*) приём; **to undergo ~** переноси́ть* (перенести́* *perf*) опера́цию.

surgical ['sə:dʒɪkl] *adj* хирурги́ческий*.

surgical spirit *n* (*BRIT*) медици́нский* спирт.

surly ['sə:lɪ] *adj* (*person, behaviour*) непривéтливый.

surmise [sə:'maɪz] *vt*: **to ~ that** выскáзывать (вы́сказать* *perf*) предположéние, что.

surmount [sə:'maunt] *vt* (*fig: problem, difficulty*) преодолевáть (преодолéть *perf*).

surname ['sə:neɪm] *n* фамúлия.

surpass [sə:'pɑ:s] *vt* (*person, thing*) превосходúть (превзойтú* *perf*).

surplus ['sə:pləs] *n* избы́ток*, излúшек*; (*of trade, payments*) актúвное сáльдо *nt ind* ◆ *adj* (*stock, grain*) лúшний*; **it is ~ to our requirements** э́то превышáет нáши трéбования.

surprise [sə'praɪz] *n* удивлéние ◆ *vt* (*astonish*) удивля́ть (удивúть* *perf*); (*catch unawares*) заставáть* (застáть* *perf*) врасплóх; **to take by ~** застигáть (застúгнуть *perf*) врасплóх.

surprising [sə'praɪzɪŋ] *adj* (*situation, announcement*) неожúданный* (неожúдан); **it is ~ how/that** удивúтельно как/что.

surprisingly [sə'praɪzɪŋlɪ] *adv* удивúтельно; (*somewhat*) **~, he agreed** как ни удивúтельно, он согласúлся.

surrealism [sə'rɪəlɪzəm] *n* сюрреалúзм.

surrealist [sə'rɪəlɪst] *adj* сюрреалистúческий.

surrender [sə'rɛndə'] *n* капитуля́ция ◆ *vi* (*army, hijackers etc*) сдавáться* (сдáться* *perf*) ◆ *vt* (*claim, right*) откáзываться (отказáться* *perf*) от +*gen*.

surrender value *n* (*INSURANCE*) *стóимость страховóго пóлиса при возврáте егó страховóму óбществу*.

surreptitious [sʌrəp'tɪʃəs] *adj* скры́тый.

surrogate ['sʌrəgɪt] *n* (*substitute*) заменúтель *m* ◆ *adj* замещáющий.

surrogate mother *n* суррогáтная мать* *f*.

surround [sə'raund] *vt* (*subj: walls, hedge etc*) окружáть (*impf*); (*MIL, POLICE etc*) окружáть (окружúть *perf*).

surrounding [sə'raundɪŋ] *adj* (*countryside*) близлежáщий.

surroundings [sə'raundɪŋz] *npl* окрéстности *fpl*.

surtax ['sə:tæks] *n* добáвочный подохóдный налóг.

surveillance [sə:'veɪləns] *n* патрулúрование.

survey [*vt* sə:'veɪ, *n* 'sə:veɪ] *vt* (*land*) дéлать (сдéлать *perf*) топографúческие съёмки +*gen*; (*house*) производúть* (произвестú* *perf*) осмóтр +*gen*; (*scene, work etc*) осмáтривать (осмотрéть* *perf*) ◆ *n* (*of land*) топографúческая *or* геодезúческая съёмка; (*of house*) инспéкция; (*of habits etc*) исслéдование; (*of situation etc*) оцéнка*.

surveying [sə'veɪɪŋ] *n* (*of land*) геодéзия, топографúческие съёмки* *fpl*.

surveyor [sə'veɪə'] *n* (*of land*) топóграф; (*of house*) инспéктор.

survival [sə'vaɪvl] *n* (*continuation of life*) выживáние; (*relic*) пережúток* ◆ *cpd*: **~ kit** неприкосновéнный запáс; **~ course** обучéние выживáнию в экстремáльных услóвиях.

survive [sə'vaɪv] *vi* (*person, thing*) уцелéть (*perf*), выживáть (вы́жить* *perf*); (*custom etc*) сохраня́ться (сохранúться *perf*), уцелéть (*perf*) ◆ *vt* (*person*) пережúть* (*perf*).

survivor [sə'vaɪvə'] *n* (*of illness, accident*) пережúвший(-ая) *m(f) adj*; **~s of an accident** остáвшиеся в живы́х пóсле авáрии.

susceptible [sə'sɛptəbl] *adj*: **~ (to)** (*heat*) чувствúтельный* (чувствúтелен) (к +*dat*); (*injury*) подвéрженный* (подвéржен) (+*dat*); (*flattery, pressure*) поддаю́щийся (на +*acc*).

suspect [*vb* sə's'pɛkt, *n, adj* 'sʌspɛkt] *vt* (*person*) подозревáть (*impf*), заподóзрить (*perf*); (*think*) подозревáть (*impf*); (*doubt*) не доверя́ть (*impf*) ◆ *n* подозревáемый(-ая) *m(f) adj* ◆ *adj* подозрúтельный* (подозрúтелен).

suspected [sə's'pɛktɪd] *adj* подозревáемый (подозревáем).

suspend [sə's'pɛnd] *vt* (*hang*) подвéшивать (подвéсить* *perf*); (*delay, stop*) приостанáвливать (приостановúть* *perf*); (*from employment*) отстраня́ть (отстранúть *perf*) от дóлжности.

suspended animation [sə's'pɛndɪd-] *n* врéменное заморáживание (*живóго органúзма*).

suspended sentence *n* услóвный приговóр.

suspender belt [sə's'pɛndə'-] *n* (жéнский*) пóяс*.

suspenders [sə's'pɛndəz] *npl* (*BRIT*) резúнки* *fpl*; (*US*) подтя́жки* *fpl*.

suspense [sə's'pɛns] *n* (*uncertainty*) тревóга ожидáния; (*in film etc*) напряжéние; **to keep sb in ~** держáть* (*impf*) когó-н в подвéшенном состоя́нии.

suspension [sə's'pɛnʃən] *n* (*from job, team*) отстранéние от дóлжности; (*AUT*) амортизáтор; (*of driving licence*) изъя́тие; (*of payment*) прекращéние.

suspension bridge *n* подвеснóй *or* вися́чий* мост*.

suspicion [sə's'pɪʃən] *n* (*distrust*) подозрéния *ntpl*; (*bad feeling*) подозрéние; (*trace*) намёк, след; **to be under ~** находúться* (*impf*) под подозрéнием; **arrested on ~ of murder** арестóванный по подозрéнию в убúйстве.

suspicious [sə's'pɪʃəs] *adj* подозрúтельный* (подозрúтелен); **to be ~ of** *or* **about sb/sth** относúться* (отнестúсь* *perf*) подозрúтельно *or* с подозрéнием к комý-н/чемý-н.

suss out [sʌs-] (*BRIT: inf*) *vt* (*discover*) разобрáться* (*perf*) в +*prp*; (*understand*)

---

* marks translations which have irregular inflections. The Russian-English side of the dictionary gives inflectional information.

раскуси́ть* *(perf)*; **I've sussed him out** я его́
раскуси́л.
sustain [səs'teɪn] *vt* подде́рживать
(поддержа́ть* *perf*); *(injury)* понести́* *(perf)*.
sustainable [səs'teɪnəbl] *adj (economy,*
development) жизнеспосо́бный.
sustained [səs'teɪnd] *adj (effort, attack)*
неослабева́ющий.
sustenance* ['sʌstɪnəns] *n* пропита́ние.
suture ['su:tʃə'] *n (MED)* шов*.
SW *abbr (RADIO)* (= **short wave**) КВ= *коро́ткие*
во́лны.
swab [swɔb] *n (MED)* тампо́н ◆ *vt (also:* ~ **down**)
мыть* (вы́мыть* *perf)* (шва́брой).
swagger ['swægə'] *vi* расха́живать *(impf)* с
ва́жным ви́дом.
swallow ['swɔləu] *n (ZOOL)* (дереве́нская)
ла́сточка*; *(of food)* кусо́чек*; *(of drink)*
глото́к* ◆ *vt (food, pills, insult)* глота́ть *(impf)*,
прогла́тывать (проглоти́ть* *perf)*; *(fig: story)*
купи́ться* *(perf)* на +*acc; (one's pride, one's*
words) подавля́ть (подави́ть* *perf)*
▶ **swallow up** *vt (savings etc)* съеда́ть (съесть*
perf).
swam [swæm] *pt of* **swim**.
swamp [swɔmp] *n* боло́то ◆ *vt (with water etc)*
залива́ть (зали́ть* *perf)*; *(fig: person)*
зава́ливать (завали́ть* *perf)*.
swampy ['swɔmpɪ] *adj (ground)* боло́тистый.
swan [swɔn] *n* ле́бедь* *m*.
swank [swæŋk] *vi (inf: talk boastfully)* хва́стать
(impf); (: *show off)* рисова́ться *(impf)*.
swansong ['swɔnsɔŋ] *n (fig)* лебеди́ная
песнь *f*.
swap [swɔp] *n* обме́н ◆ *vt:* **to** ~ **(for)** *(exchange*
for)) меня́ть (обменя́ть *perf)* (на +*acc);
(replace (with)) сменя́ть (*perf)* (на +*acc)*.
SWAPO *n abbr* (= *South-West Africa People's*
Organization) СВАПО *(Наро́дная*
организа́ция Ю́го-За́падной А́фрики).
swarm [swɔ:m] *n (of bees)* рой; *(of people)*
тьма ◆ *vi (bees)* ро́иться *(impf)*; *(people)*
толочься* *(impf)*; *(place):* **to be** ~**ing with**
кише́ть *(impf)* +*instr*.
swarthy ['swɔ:ðɪ] *adj (person, complexion, face)*
сму́глый, тёмный.
swashbuckling ['swɔʃbʌklɪŋ] *adj (film)*
залихва́тский; *(role, hero)* удало́й.
swastika ['swɔstɪkə] *n* сва́стика.
swat [swɔt] *vt (insect)* прихло́пнуть *(perf)* ◆ *n*
(BRIT: also: **fly** ~) хлопу́шка*.
swathe [sweɪð] *vt:* **to** ~ **in** *(blankets)*
заку́тывать (заку́тать *perf)* в +*acc;
(bandages) обма́тывать (обмота́ть *perf)*
+*instr*.
swatter ['swɔtə'] *n (also:* **fly** ~) хлопу́шка*.
sway [sweɪ] *vi (person, tree)* кача́ться
(качну́ться *perf)* ◆ *vt (influence)* склоня́ть
(склони́ть* *perf)* ◆ *n:* **to hold** ~ **(over sb)**
по́льзоваться *(impf)* непререка́емым
авторите́том (у кого́-н).

Swaziland ['swɑ:zɪlænd] *n* Свазиле́нд.
swear [sweə'] *(pt* **swore**, *pp* **sworn**) *vi (curse)*
руга́ться (вы́ругаться *perf)* ◆ *vt (promise)*
торже́ственно дава́ть* (дать* *perf)*; **to** ~ **an**
oath дава́ть* (дать* *perf)* кля́тву
▶ **swear in** *vt (person)* приводи́ть* (привести́*
perf) к прися́ге.
swearword ['sweəwɔ:d] *n* руга́тельство.
sweat [swet] *n* пот* ◆ *vi* поте́ть (вспоте́ть *perf)*,
пропоте́ть *(perf)*; **in a** ~ в поту́.
sweatband ['swetbænd] *n* повя́зка*.
sweater ['swetə'] *n* сви́тер*.
sweatshirt ['swetʃə:t] *n* хлопчатобума́жный
спорти́вный сви́тер*.
sweatshop ['swetʃɔp] *n (pej) предприя́тие, где*
сущест́вует потого́нная систе́ма.
sweaty ['swetɪ] *adj (clothes)* пропоте́вший;
(hands) по́тный.
Swede [swi:d] *n* швед(ка*).
swede [swi:d] *n (BRIT)* брю́ква.
Sweden ['swi:dn] *n* Шве́ция.
Swedish ['swi:dɪʃ] *adj* шве́дский* ◆ *n (LING)*
шве́дский* язы́к*; **the** ~ *npl* шве́ды.
sweep [swi:p] *(pt, pp* **swept**) *n (act of sweeping)*
подмета́ние; *(curve)* изги́б; *(range)* разма́х;
(also: **chimney** ~) трубочи́ст ◆ *vt (brush)*
мести́* *or* подмета́ть (подмести́* *perf)*; *(with*
arm) сма́хивать (смахну́ть *perf)*; *(subj:*
current) смыва́ть (смыть* *perf)* ◆ *vi (hand,*
arm) дви́гаться *(impf)*; *(wind)* бушева́ть *(impf)*
▶ **sweep away** *vt* смета́ть (смести́* *perf)*,
уноси́ть* (унести́* *perf)*
▶ **sweep past** *vi* проноси́ться* (пронести́сь*
perf) ми́мо
▶ **sweep up** *vi* подмета́ть (подмести́* *perf)*.
sweeper ['swi:pə:] *n (also:* **carpet** ~) щётка для
ковра́; *(FOOTBALL)* ли́беро *nt ind*.
sweeping ['swi:pɪŋ] *adj (gesture)* широ́кий*
(широ́к); *(changes, reforms)*
всеобъе́млющий*; *(statement)* огу́льный.
sweepstake ['swi:psteɪk] *n* пари́ *nt ind* на
ска́чках.
sweet [swi:t] *n (candy)* конфе́та; *(BRIT: CULIN)*
сла́дкое *nt adj no pl* ◆ *adj* сла́дкий* (сла́док);
(kind, attractive) ми́лый* (мил) ◆ *adv:* **to smell**
~ сла́дко па́хнуть *(impf)*; **to taste** ~ име́ть
(impf) сла́дкий вкус; ~ **and sour** ки́сло-
сла́дкий*.
sweetbread ['swi:tbred] *n (CULIN)* "сла́дкое
мя́со" *(поджелу́дочная железа́)*.
sweet corn *n* кукуру́за.
sweeten ['swi:tn] *vt* добавля́ть (доба́вить*
perf) са́хар к +*dat; (temper)* смиря́ть
(смири́ть *perf)*.
sweetener ['swi:tnə'] *n* замени́тель *m* са́хара;
(fig) подслащённая пилю́ля.
sweetheart ['swi:thɑ:t] *n* возлю́бленный(-ая)
m(f) adj; (term of affection) дорого́й(-а́я) *m(f) adj*.
sweetness ['swi:tnɪs] *n (amount of sugar)*
сла́дость *f; (kindness)* прия́тность *f*.
sweet pea *n* души́стый горо́шек*.

sweet potato *n* ямс.
sweet shop *n* (*BRIT*) конди́терская ла́вка.
sweet tooth *n*: **he/she has a** ~ ~ он/она́ сластёна.
swell [swɛl] (*pt* **swelled**, *pp* **swollen** *or* **swelled**) *n* (*of sea*) волне́ние ◆ *adj* (*US: inf: excellent*) мирово́й ◆ *vi* (*numbers*) расти́* (вы́расти* *perf*); (*sound, feeling*) расти́* (*impf*); (*also:* ~ **up**: *face, ankle etc*) опуха́ть (опу́хнуть *perf*).
swelling ['swɛlɪŋ] *n* (*MED*) о́пухоль *f*.
sweltering ['swɛltərɪŋ] *adj* ду́шный.
swept [swɛpt] *pt, pp of* **sweep**.
swerve [swəːv] *vi* ре́зко виля́ть (вильну́ть *perf*).
swift [swɪft] *n* (*bird*) стриж* ◆ *adj* стреми́тельный* (стреми́телен).
swiftly ['swɪftlɪ] *adv* стреми́тельно.
swiftness ['swɪftnɪs] *n* стреми́тельность *f*.
swig [swɪg] *n* (*inf: drink*) глото́к*.
swill [swɪl] *vt* (*also:* ~ **out**, ~ **down**) спола́скивать (сполосну́ть *perf*) ◆ *n* (*for pigs*) по́йло.
swim [swɪm] (*pt* **swam**, *pp* **swum**) *vi* пла́вать/плыть* (*impf*); (*as sport*) пла́вать (*impf*); (*head*) идти́* (пойти́* *perf*) кру́гом; (*room*) плыть* (поплы́ть* *perf*) ◆ *vt* (*the Channel*) переплыва́ть (переплы́ть* *perf*); (*a length*) проплыва́ть (проплы́ть* *perf*); **to go** ~**ming, go for a** ~ ходи́ть*/идти́* (пойти́* *perf*) пла́вать.
swimmer ['swɪmə[r]] *n* пловец*(-вчи́ха).
swimming ['swɪmɪŋ] *n* пла́вание.
swimming baths *npl* (*BRIT*) пла́вательный бассе́йн *msg*.
swimming cap *n* рези́новая ша́почка* (*для пла́вания*).
swimming costume *n* (*BRIT*) купа́льный костю́м.
swimmingly ['swɪmɪŋlɪ] *adv* как по ма́слу; **everything's going** ~ всё идёт как по ма́слу.
swimming pool *n* пла́вательный бассе́йн.
swimming trunks *npl* пла́вки* *pl*.
swimsuit ['swɪmsuːt] *n* купа́льник.
swindle ['swɪndl] *n* моше́нничество ◆ *vt* надува́ть (наду́ть* *perf*).
swindler ['swɪndlə[r]] *n* жу́лик.
swine [swaɪn] *n* (*inf!*) свинья́* *m/f* (*!*)
swing [swɪŋ] (*pt, pp* **swung**) *n* (*in playground*) каче́ли *pl*; (*movement*) кача́ние; (*change: in opinions etc*) колеба́ние; (*MUS, rhythm*) свинг ◆ *vt* (*arms*) разма́хивать (*impf*) +*instr*; (*legs*) болта́ть (*impf*) +*instr*; (*also:* ~ **round**: *vehicle etc*) развора́чивать (разверну́ть *perf*) ◆ *vi* кача́ться (*impf*); (*also:* ~ **round**: *vehicle etc*) свора́чивать (сверну́ть *perf*); **a** ~ **to the left** (*POL*) крен вле́во; **to get into the** ~ **of things** входи́ть* (войти́* *perf*) в ритм; **to be in full** ~ (*party etc*) быть* (*impf*) в по́лном разга́ре; **the road** ~**s south** доро́га свора́чивает на юг.

swing bridge *n* разводно́й мост*.
swing door (*US* **swinging door**) *n* дверь, открыва́ющаяся в о́бе сто́роны.
swingeing ['swɪndʒɪŋ] *adj* (*BRIT*: *blow, attack*) сокруши́тельный* (сокруши́телен); (: *cuts*) беспоща́дный.
swinging ['swɪŋɪŋ] *adj* кача́ющийся; (*fig*) весёлый.
swipe [swaɪp] *vt* (*hit*) ударя́ть (уда́рить *perf*) с разма́ху; (*inf: steal*) тащи́ть (стащи́ть* *perf*).
swirl [swəːl] *vi* (*water, smoke, leaves*) кружи́ться (*impf*) ◆ *n* (*of water*) водоро́т; (*of leaves*) круже́ние.
swish [swɪʃ] *vi* (*tail*) маха́ть* (*impf*); (*clothes*) шелесте́ть* (*impf*), шурша́ть (*impf*) ◆ *n* свист ◆ *adj* (*inf*) шика́рный.
Swiss [swɪs] *adj* швейца́рский* ◆ *n inv* швейца́рец*(-рка*).
Swiss French *adj* фра́нко-швейца́рский* ◆ *n* (*person*) франкоговоря́щий(-ая) швейца́рец(-рка); (*LING*) швейца́рский* диале́кт францу́зского языка́.
Swiss German *adj* неме́цко-швейца́рский* ◆ *n* (*person*) немецкоговоря́щий(-ая) швейца́рец(-рка); (*LING*) швейца́рский* диале́кт неме́цкого языка́.
swiss roll *n* руле́т с варе́ньем.
switch [swɪtʃ] *n* (*for light, radio etc*) выключа́тель *m*; (*change*) переключе́ние ◆ *vt* (*change*) переключа́ть (переключи́ть *perf*); (*exchange*) переменя́ть* (*perf*); *vi* ~ **to** (**round** *or* **over**) меня́ть (поменя́ть *perf*) места́ми
▸ **switch off** *vt* выключа́ть (вы́ключить *perf*)
▸ **switch on** *vt* включа́ть (включи́ть *perf*).
switchback ['swɪtʃbæk] *n* (*BRIT*) доро́га иду́щая то вверх, то вниз.
switchblade ['swɪtʃbleɪd] *n* (*also:* ~ **knife**) нож с заменя́ющимися ле́звиями.
switchboard ['swɪtʃbɔːd] *n* (*TEL*) коммута́тор.
switchboard operator *n* (*TEL*) телефони́ст(ка*).
Switzerland ['swɪtsələnd] *n* Швейца́рия.
swivel ['swɪvl] *vi* (*also:* ~ **round**) верте́ться* (*impf*).
swollen ['swəulən] *pp of* **swell** ◆ *adj* (*ankle*) опу́хший*; (*lake*) перепо́лнившийся.
swoon [swuːn] *vi* замира́ть (замере́ть *perf*).
swoop [swuːp] *n* (*by police etc*) налёт; (*of bird etc*) стреми́тельное паде́ние ◆ *vi* (*also:* ~ **down**: *bird, plane*) стреми́тельно па́дать (*impf*).
swop [swɔp] = **swap**.
sword [sɔːd] *n* шпа́га, меч*.
swordfish ['sɔːdfɪʃ] *n* меч-ры́ба.
swore [swɔː[r]] *pt of* **swear**.
sworn [swɔːn] *pp of* **swear** ◆ *adj* (*statement, evidence*) под прися́гой; (*enemy*) закля́тый.
swot [swɔt] *vi* зубри́ть (*impf*) ◆ *n* (*pej: of person*)

зубри́ла *m/f*

▸ **swot up** *vt*: **to ~ up (on)** зазу́бривать (зазубри́ть *perf*).

swum [swʌm] *pp of* **swim**.

swung [swʌŋ] *pt, pp of* **swing**.

sycamore ['sɪkəmɔ:'] *n* я́вор.

sycophant ['sɪkəfænt] *n* подхали́м.

sycophantic [sɪkə'fæntɪk] *adj* подхали́мский*.

Sydney ['sɪdnɪ] *n* Сидне́й.

syllable ['sɪləbl] *n* слог*.

syllabus ['sɪləbəs] *n* програ́мма; **on the ~** входя́щий* в програ́мму.

symbol ['sɪmbl] *n* (*sign, also* MATH) знак; (*representation*) си́мвол.

symbolic(al) [sɪm'bɔlɪk(l)] *adj* символи́ческий*; **to be symbolic of sth** символизи́ровать (*impf*) что-н.

symbolism ['sɪmbəlɪzəm] *n* символи́зм.

symbolize ['sɪmbəlaɪz] *vt* символизи́ровать (*impf*).

symmetrical [sɪ'mɛtrɪkl] *adj* симметри́чный* (симметри́чен).

symmetry ['sɪmɪtrɪ] *n* симме́трия.

sympathetic [sɪmpə'θɛtɪk] *adj* (*person*) сочу́вствующий*; (*remark*) сочу́вственный; (*likeable: character*) прия́тный* (прия́тен); (*showing support*): **~ to(wards)** благоскло́нно настро́енный по отноше́нию к +*dat*; **to be ~ to sth** (*well-disposed*) сочу́вственно относи́ться* (отнести́сь* *perf*) к чему́-н.

sympathetically [sɪmpə'θɛtɪklɪ] *adv* сочу́вственно.

sympathize ['sɪmpəθaɪz] *vi*: **to ~ with** (*person*) сочу́вствовать* (*impf*) +*dat*, проявля́ть (прояви́ть* *perf*) сочу́вствие к +*dat*; (*feelings, cause*) сочу́вственно относи́ться* (отнести́сь* *perf*) к +*dat*.

sympathizer ['sɪmpəθaɪzə'] *n* (POL) симпатизи́рующий(-ая) *m(f) adj*.

sympathy ['sɪmpəθɪ] *n* (*pity*) сочу́вствие; **sympathies** *npl* (*support, tendencies*) симпа́тии *fpl*; **with our deepest ~** прими́те на́ши глубоча́йшие соболе́знования; **to come out in ~** (*workers*) бастова́ть (*impf*) в знак солида́рности.

symphonic [sɪm'fɔnɪk] *adj* симфони́ческий*.

symphony ['sɪmfənɪ] *n* симфо́ния.

symphony orchestra *n* симфони́ческий* орке́стр.

symposia [sɪm'pəuzɪə] *npl of* **symposium**.

symposium [sɪm'pəuzɪəm] (*pl* **~s** or **symposia**) *n* симпо́зиум.

symptom ['sɪmptəm] *n* (MED) симпто́м; (*indicator*) при́знак.

symptomatic [sɪmptə'mætɪk] *adj*: **~ of**

sync [sɪŋk] *n* (*inf: watches etc*): **out of ~** в разнобо́й.

synagogue ['sɪnəgɔg] *n* синаго́га.

synchromesh [sɪŋkrəu'mɛʃ] *n* синхрониза́тор.

synchronize ['sɪŋkrənaɪz] *vt* (*watches*) сверя́ть (све́рить *perf*); (*sound, movements*) синхронизи́ровать (*impf/perf*) ♦ *vi*: **to ~ with** совпада́ть (совпа́сть* *perf*) (по вре́мени) с +*instr*.

synchronized swimming ['sɪŋkrənaɪzd-] *n* синхро́нное пла́вание.

syncopated ['sɪŋkəpeɪtɪd] *adj* (*rhythm, beat*) синкопи́рованный.

syndicate ['sɪndɪkɪt] *n* (*of people, businesses*) синдика́т; (*of newspapers*) аге́нтство печа́ти.

syndrome ['sɪndrəum] *n* (*also* MED) синдро́м.

synonym ['sɪnənɪm] *n* сино́ним.

synonymous [sɪ'nɔnɪməs] *adj* (*fig*): **~ (with)** равноси́льный* (равноси́лен) (+*dat*).

synopses [sɪ'nɔpsi:z] *npl of* **synopsis**.

synopsis [sɪ'nɔpsɪs] (*pl* **synopses**) *n* кра́ткое изложе́ние.

syntactic [sɪn'tæktɪk] *adj* синтакси́ческий*.

syntax [sɪntæks] *n* си́нтаксис.

syntax error *n* (COMPUT) синтакси́ческая оши́бка*.

syntheses ['sɪnθəsi:z] *npl of* **synthesis**.

synthesis ['sɪnθəsɪs] (*pl* **syntheses**) *n* (*of ideas, styles*) слия́ние, си́нтез.

synthesizer ['sɪnθəsaɪzə'] *n* синтеза́тор.

synthetic [sɪn'θɛtɪk] *adj* (*materials*) синтети́ческий*, иску́сственный ♦ *n* иску́сственный материа́л; (TEXTILES) синте́тика, иску́сственный материа́л; **~s** *npl* (*man-made fabrics*) синте́тика *fsg*, синтети́ческие тка́ни *fpl*.

syphilis ['sɪfɪlɪs] *n* си́филис.

syphon ['saɪfən] = **siphon**.

Syria ['sɪrɪə] *n* Си́рия.

Syrian ['sɪrɪən] *adj* сири́йский* ♦ *n* сири́ец*(-и́йка).

syringe [sɪ'rɪndʒ] *n* шприц*.

syrup ['sɪrəp] *n* (*juice*) сиро́п; (*also:* **golden ~**) (све́тлая or жёлтая) па́тока.

syrupy ['sɪrəpɪ] *adj* (*liquid*) густо́й* (густ); (*pej: quality*) слаща́вый (слаща́в).

system ['sɪstəm] *n* систе́ма; **it was a shock to his ~** э́то яви́лось для него́ потрясе́нием.

systematic [sɪstə'mætɪk] *adj* (*methodical*) системати́ческий*.

systems analyst ['sɪstəmz-] *n* (COMPUT) систе́мный анали́тик, системоте́хник.

systems disk *n* (COMPUT) систе́мный диск.

~ T, t ~

T, t [tiː] n (letter) 20-ая буква английского алфавита.
TA n abbr (BRIT: = Territorial Army) территориальная армия.
ta [tɑː] excl (BRIT: inf) спасибо.
tab [tæb] n abbr = **tabulator**.
tabby ['tæbɪ] n (also: ~ **cat**: male) полосатый кот; (female) полосатая кошка.
tabernacle ['tæbənækl] n (REL) скиния.
table ['teɪbl] n (piece of furniture) стол*; (MATH, CHEM etc) таблица ♦ vt (BRIT: motion etc) выносить* (вынести* perf) на обсуждение; **to lay** or **set the** ~ накрывать (накрыть* perf) на стол; **to clear the** ~ убирать (убрать* perf) со стола; **league** ~ (BRIT: FOOTBALL, RUGBY) таблица команд 1-й, 2-й и т.д. лиги; ~ **of contents** оглавление.
tablecloth ['teɪblklɔθ] n скатерть f.
table d'hôte [[tɑːbl'dəut] adj: ~ ~ **menu** табльдот.
table lamp n настольная лампа.
tablemat ['teɪblmæt] n подставка.
table salt n столовая соль f.
tablespoon ['teɪblspuːn] n столовая ложка.
tablet ['tæblɪt] n (MED) таблетка*; (for writing) дощечка* (для письма); (of stone) доска*; ~ **of soap** (BRIT) кусок* мыла.
table tennis n настольный теннис.
table wine n столовое вино.
tabloid ['tæblɔɪd] n (newspaper) малоформатная газета, таблоид; **the** ~**s** жёлтая or бульварная пресса.
taboo [tə'buː] n табу nt ind ♦ adj запрещённый.
tabulate ['tæbjuleɪt] vt (data, figures) сводить* (свести* perf) в таблицу.
tabulator ['tæbjuleɪtəʳ] n колонкоустановитель m; (on typewriter) табулятор.
tachograph ['tækəgrɑːf] n (AUT) тахограф (для регистрации режима движения автомобиля).
tachometer [tæ'kɔmɪtəʳ] n (AUT) тахометр, счётчик числа оборотов.
tacit ['tæsɪt] adj (agreement, approval etc) молчаливый.
taciturn ['tæsɪtəːn] adj (person) молчаливый (молчалив).

tack [tæk] n (nail) гвоздь m с широкой шляпкой; (fig) путь m ♦ vt (nail) прибивать (прибить* perf); (stitch) смётывать (сметать perf) ♦ vi (NAUT) идти* (пойти* perf) галсами; **on the wrong** ~ (fig) на ложном пути; **to** ~ **sth on to (the end of) sth** прикреплять (прикрепить* perf) что-н к чему-н.
tackle ['tækl] n (for fishing etc) снасть f; (for lifting) сложный блок; (FOOTBALL, RUGBY) блокировка ♦ vt (difficulty) справляться (справиться* perf) с +instr; (grapple with) схватиться* (perf) с +instr; (FOOTBALL, RUGBY) блокировать (impf/perf).
tacky ['tækɪ] adj (sticky) липкий*; (pej: of poor quality) дешёвый.
tact [tækt] n такт, тактичность f.
tactful ['tæktful] adj тактичный* (тактичен); **she is very** ~ она очень тактична.
tactfully ['tæktfəlɪ] adv тактично.
tactical ['tæktɪkl] adj (also MIL) тактический*; ~ **error** тактическая ошибка.
tactician [tæk'tɪʃən] n тактик.
tactics ['tæktɪks] npl тактика fsg.
tactless ['tæktlɪs] adj бестактный* (бестактен).
tactlessly ['tæktlɪslɪ] adv бестактно.
tadpole ['tædpəul] n головастик.
taffy ['tæfɪ] n (US: toffee) ириска*, тянучка*.
tag [tæg] n (label) этикетка*, ярлык*; **price** ~ этикетка*; **name** ~ бирка*.
▶ **tag along** vi следовать (impf) по пятам.
Tahiti [tɑː'hiːtɪ] n Таити m ind.
tail [teɪl] n (of animal, plane) хвост*; (of shirt) конец*; (of coat) пола* ♦ vt (follow) садиться* (сесть* perf) на хвост +dat; ~**s** npl (formal suit) фрак msg; **to turn** ~ бросаться (броситься* perf) наутёк; see also **head**
▶ **tail away** vi (voice, wind) затихать (затихнуть perf)
▶ **tail off** vi = **tail away**.
tailback ['teɪlbæk] n (BRIT: AUT) хвост.
tail coat n фрак.
tail end n (of train etc) хвост; (of meeting etc) конец.
tailgate ['teɪlgeɪt] n (AUT) задняя дверь f.
taillight ['teɪllaɪt] n (US: AUT) задняя фара.

---

* marks translations which have irregular inflections. The Russian-English side of the dictionary gives inflectional information.

tailor ['teɪlə'] *n* (мужской) портной *m adj* ◆ *vt*: **to ~ sth (to)** приспосабливать (приспособить *perf*) что-н (к +*dat*); **~'s shop** портняжная мастерская *f adj*.

tailoring ['teɪlərɪŋ] *n* (*cut*) покрой; (*craft*) портняжное дело.

tailor-made ['teɪlə'meɪd] *adj* (*suit*) сшитый на заказ; (*fig*); **she is ~ for the job** она идеально подходит для этой работы.

tailwind ['teɪlwɪnd] *n* хвостовой *or* попутный ветер.

taint [teɪnt] *vt* (*meat, food*) портить* (испортить* *perf*); (*fig*) пятнать (запятнать *perf*).

tainted ['teɪntɪd] *adj* (*food*) испорченный; (*air, water*) загрязнённый* (загрязнён*); (*fig*) запятнанный.

Taiwan ['taɪ'wɑːn] *n* Тайвань *m*.

Tajik [tɑːdʒɪk] *n* таджик(-ичка*).

Tajiki [tɑːdʒɪkɪ] *adj* таджикский* ◆ *n* таджикский* язык*.

Tajikistan [tɑːdʒɪkɪstɑːn] *n* Таджикистан.

take [teɪk] (*pt* **took**, *pp* **taken**) *vt* брать* (взять* *perf*); (*photo, measures*) снимать (снять* *perf*); (*shower, decision, drug*) принимать (принять* *perf*); (*notes*) делать (сделать *perf*); (*grab: sb's arm etc*) хватать (схватить* *perf*); (*require: courage, time*) требовать (потребовать *perf*); (*pain etc*) переносить* (перенести* *perf*); (*hold: passengers etc*) вмещать (вместить* *perf*); (*person: on foot*) отводить* (отвести* *perf*); (*thing: on foot*) относить* (отнести* *perf*); (*person, thing: by transport*) отвозить* (отвезти* *perf*); (*exam*) сдавать* (сдать* *perf*); (*conduct: meeting*) вести* (*impf*) ◆ *vi* (*fire*) заниматься (заняться* *perf*); (*dye*) впитываться (впитаться *perf*); (*plant, injection*) приниматься (приняться* *perf*) ◆ *n* (CINEMA) дубль *m*; **to ~ sth from** (*drawer etc*) вынимать (вынуть* *perf*) что-н из +*gen*; (*steal from: person*) брать* (взять* *perf*) что-н у +*gen*; **I ~ it that ...** как я понимаю, ...; **I took him for a doctor** я принял его за врача; **to ~ sb's hand** брать* (взять* *perf*) кого-н за руку; **to ~ for a walk** (*child, dog*) брать* (взять* *perf*) на прогулку; **to be ~n ill** заболевать (заболеть *perf*); **to ~ it upon o.s. to do** браться* (взяться* *perf*) +*infin*; **~ the first (street) on the left** первый поворот налево; **to ~ Russian at university** изучать (*impf*) русский язык в университете; **it won't ~ long** это не займёт много времени; **I was quite ~n with her** (*attracted*) она произвела на меня большое впечатление

▶ **take after** *vt fus* (*resemble*) пойти* (*perf*) в +*acc*

▶ **take apart** *vt* разбирать (разобрать* *perf*)

▶ **take away** *vt* (*remove*) убирать (убрать* *perf*); (*carry off*) забирать (забрать* *perf*); (MATH) отнимать (отнять* *perf*) ◆ *vi*: **to ~ away from** отнимать (отнять* *perf*) от +*gen*

▶ **take back** *vt* (*return: thing*) относить*

(отнести* *perf*) обратно; (: *person*) отводить* (отвести* *perf*) обратно; (*one's words*) брать* (взять* *perf*) назад

▶ **take down** *vt* (*building*) сносить* (снести* *perf*); (*scaffolding*) разбирать (разобрать* *perf*); (*picture*) снимать (снять* *perf*); (*write down: letter etc*) записывать (записать* *perf*)

▶ **take in** *vt* (*deceive*) обманывать (обмануть* *perf*); (*understand*) воспринимать (воспринять* *perf*); (*include*) включать (включить* *perf*); (*lodger, orphan*) брать* (взять* *perf*); (*dress, waistband*) ушивать (ушить* *perf*)

▶ **take off** *vi* (AVIAT) взлетать (взлететь* *perf*); (*go away*) улетать (улететь* *perf*) ◆ *vt* (*remove*) снимать (снять* *perf*); (*imitate*) копировать (скопировать *perf*)

▶ **take on** *vt* (*work, employee*) брать* (взять* *perf*); (*opponent*) сражаться (сразиться* *perf*) с +*instr*

▶ **take out** *vt* (*invite*) водить* (повести* *perf*); (*remove*) вынимать (вынуть* *perf*); (*licence*) оформлять (оформить* *perf*); **to ~ sth out of sth** (*drawer, pocket etc*) вынимать (вынуть* *perf*) что-н из чего-н; **don't ~ it out on me!** не вымещай это на мне!

▶ **take over** *vt* (*business, country*) принимать (принять* *perf*) руководство +*instr* ◆ *vi*: **to ~ over from sb** сменять (сменить* *perf*) кого-н

▶ **take to** *vt fus* (*activity*) пристраститься* (*perf*) к +*dat*, заниматься (заняться* *perf*) +*instr*; (*form habit of*): **to ~ to doing** пристраститься* (*perf*) +*infin*; **she took to him at once** он ей сразу понравился

▶ **take up** *vt* (*hobby, sport, job*) заняться* (*perf*) +*instr*; (*idea, suggestion, story*) подхватывать (подхватить* *perf*); (*time, space*) занимать (занять* *perf*); (*garment*) подшивать (подшить* *perf*) ◆ *vi*: **to ~ up with sb** сходиться* (сойтись* *perf*) с кем-н; **to ~ sb up on sth** (*offer, suggestion*) воспользоваться (*perf*) +*instr*; **I'll ~ you up on that!** ловлю Вас на слове!

takeaway ['teɪkəweɪ] *n* (BRIT) *магазин или ресторан, где продаётся горячая еда на вынос*; (*food*) горячая еда на вынос.

take-home pay ['teɪkhəum-] *n* чистый заработок*.

taken ['teɪkən] *pp of* **take**.

takeoff ['teɪkɔf] *n* (AVIAT) взлёт.

takeout ['teɪkaut] (US) *n* = **takeaway**.

takeover ['teɪkəuvə'] *n* (COMM) поглощение; (*of country*) захват власти.

takeover bid *n* (COMM) попытка поглощения.

takings ['teɪkɪŋz] *npl* (COMM) выручка *fsg*.

talc [tælk] *n* тальк.

talcum powder ['tælkəm-] *n* = **talc**.

tale [teɪl] *n* (*story, account*) рассказ, сказание; **to tell ~s** (*fig: to teacher, parents etc*) ябедничать (наябедничать *perf*).

talent ['tælnt] *n* талант.

talented ['tæləntɪd] *adj* (*person, actor etc*) тала́нтливый (тала́нтлив).

talent scout *n* (*THEAT, SPORT*) челове́к, занима́ющийся по́иском молоды́х дарова́ний.

talisman ['tælɪzmən] *n* талисма́н.

talk [tɔːk] *n* (*a (prepared) speech*) докла́д; (*conversation, interview*) бесе́да; (*gossip*) слух ♦ *vi* (*speak*) разгова́ривать (*impf*); ~**s** *npl* (*POL etc*) перегово́ры *pl*; **to give a** ~ де́лать (сде́лать *perf*) докла́д; **to** ~ **about** расска́зывать (рассказа́ть *perf*) о +*prp*; ~**ing of films, have you seen ...?** кста́ти о фи́льмах, вы ви́дели ...?; **to** ~ **sb into doing** угова́ривать (уговори́ть *perf*) кого́-н +*infin*; **to** ~ **sb out of sth** отгова́ривать (отговори́ть *perf*) кого́-н от чего́-н; **to** ~ **shop** говори́ть (*impf*) о дела́х

▶ **talk over** *vt* (*problem etc*) обгова́ривать (обговори́ть *perf*).

talkative ['tɔːkətɪv] *adj* (*person*) разгово́рчивый (разгово́рчив).

talker ['tɔːkəʳ] *n*: **she is a good** ~ она́ хоро́ший ора́тор; (*pej*) болту́н(-у́шка); **he is a fast** ~ он красноречи́в.

talking point ['tɔːkɪŋ-] *n* те́ма для разгово́ра.

talking-to ['tɔːkɪŋtu] *n*: **to give sb a good** ~ отчи́тывать (отчита́ть *perf*) кого́-н как сле́дует.

talk show *n* (*TV, RADIO*) ток-шо́у *ind*.

tall [tɔːl] *adj* высо́кий* (высо́к); **he is 6 feet** ~ его́ рост – 6 фу́тов; **how** ~ **are you?** како́й у Вас рост?

tallboy ['tɔːlbɔɪ] *n* (*BRIT*) высо́кий* комо́д.

Tallin(n) ['tælɪn] *n* Та́ллин(н).

tallness ['tɔːlnɪs] *n* высота́.

tall story *n* небыли́ца.

tally ['tælɪ] *n* (*of marks, amounts of money etc*) счёт ♦ *vi*: **to** ~ (**with**) (*subj: figures, stories etc*) сходи́ться* (сойти́сь* *perf*) (с +*instr*); **to keep a** ~ **of sth** вести́* (*impf*) счёт чего́-н.

talon ['tælən] *n* (*of eagle, owl etc*) ко́готь* *m*.

tambourine [tæmbə'riːn] *n* (*MUS*) тамбури́н, бу́бен.

tame [teɪm] *adj* (*animal, bird*) ручно́й; (*fig: story, style*) вя́лый (вял).

tamper ['tæmpəʳ] *vi*: **to** ~ **with sth** пыта́ться (попыта́ться *perf*) измени́ть что-н.

tampon ['tæmpɔn] *n* тампо́н.

tan [tæn] *n* (*also*: **suntan**) зага́р ♦ *vi* (*person*) загора́ть (загоре́ть *perf*); (*skin*) загоре́ть (*perf*) ♦ *vt* дуби́ть* (вы́дубить* *perf*) ♦ *adj* (*colour*) рыжева́то-кори́чневый; **to get a** ~ загора́ть (загоре́ть *perf*).

tandem ['tændəm] *n* (*cycle*) танде́м; **in** ~ (*together*) совме́стно, вме́сте.

tandoori [tæn'duərɪ] *n* инди́йский ме́тод приготовле́ния мя́са и лепёшек в гли́няной печи́.

tang [tæŋ] *n* си́льный за́пах.

tangent ['tændʒənt] *n* (*MATH*) каса́тельная *f adj*; **to go off at a** ~ (*fig*) сбива́ться (сби́ться* *perf*).

tangerine [tændʒə'riːn] *n* (*fruit*) мандари́н; (*colour*) я́рко-ора́нжевый цвет.

tangible ['tændʒəbl] *adj* (*proof, benefits*) ощути́мый (ощути́м); ~ **assets** реа́льный акти́в.

Tangier [tæn'dʒɪəʳ] *n* Танже́р.

tangle ['tæŋgl] *n* пу́таница; **to get in(to) a** ~ (*also fig*) запу́тываться (запу́таться *perf*).

tango ['tæŋgəu] *n* та́нго *nt ind*.

tank [tæŋk] *n* (*water tank*) бак; (: *large*) цисте́рна; (*PHOT*) ва́нна; (*for fish*) аква́риум; (*MIL*) танк.

tankard ['tæŋkəd] *n* (*for beer*) пивна́я кру́жка.

tanker ['tæŋkəʳ] *n* (*ship*) та́нкер; (*truck, RAIL*) цисте́рна.

tanned [tænd] *adj* загоре́лый.

tannin ['tænɪn] *n* тани́н.

tanning ['tænɪŋ] *n* (*of leather*) дубле́ние.

Tannoy® ['tænɔɪ] (*BRIT*) *n* громкоговори́тель *m*; **over the** ~ по громкоговори́телю.

tantalizing ['tæntəlaɪzɪŋ] *adj* (*smell, possibility*) дразня́щий*.

tantamount ['tæntəmaunt] *adj*: ~ **to** равноси́льный* (равноси́лен) +*dat*.

tantrum ['tæntrəm] *n* исте́рика; **to throw a** ~ устра́ивать (устро́ить *perf*) исте́рику.

Tanzania [tænzə'nɪə] *n* Танза́ния.

Tanzanian [tænzə'nɪən] *adj* танзани́йский* ♦ *n* танзани́ец(-и́йка).

tap [tæp] *n* кран; (*gentle blow*) стук ♦ *vt* (*hit gently*) стуча́ть (постуча́ть *perf*) по +*dat*; (*resources*) испо́льзовать (*impf*/*perf*); (*telephone, conversation*) прослу́шивать (*impf*); **to be on** ~ (*fig: resources*) находи́ться* (*impf*) под руко́й; (*beer*) в разли́в.

tap-dancing ['tæpdɑːnsɪŋ] *n* чечётка.

tape [teɪp] *n* (*also: magnetic*) плёнка; (*cassette*) кассе́та; (*sticky tape*) кле́йкая ле́нта; (*for tying*) ле́нта ♦ *vt* (*record*) запи́сывать (записа́ть* *perf*); (*stick with tape*) закле́ивать (закле́ить *perf*) кле́йкой ле́нтой; **on** ~ (*song etc*) на кассе́те.

tape deck *n* кассе́тный магнитофо́н.

tape measure *n* сантиме́тр.

taper ['teɪpəʳ] *n* (*candle*) то́нкая восхова́я свеча́ ♦ *vi* (*narrow*) сужа́ться (су́зиться* *perf*).

tape recorder *n* магнитофо́н.

tape recording *n* магнитофо́нная за́пись *f*.

tapered ['teɪpəd] *adj* (*skirt*) сужа́ющийся.

tapering ['teɪpərɪŋ] *adj* (*fingers*) то́нкий*.

tapestry ['tæpɪstrɪ] *n* (*object*) гобеле́н; (*art*) иску́сство гобеле́на.

tapeworm ['teɪpwəːm] *n* ленте́ц*, ле́нточный червь *m*.

---

* marks translations which have irregular inflections. The Russian-English side of the dictionary gives inflectional information.

tapioca [tæpɪ'əukə] n тапиóка.
tappet ['tæpɪt] n (AUT) толкáтель m клáпана.
tar [tɑː] n дёготь m; **low/middle ~ cigarettes** сигарéты с нúзким/срéдним содержáнием никотúна.
tarantula [tə'ræntjulə] n тарáнтул.
tardy ['tɑːdɪ] adj (reply, development) запоздáлый.
target ['tɑːgɪt] n цель f; **to be on ~** (project) идтú* (impf) соглáсно плáну.
target audience n потенциáльные клиéнты mpl.
target market n целевóй рынок*.
target practice n учéбная стрельбá.
tariff ['tærɪf] n (tax on goods) тарúф; (BRIT: in hotels, restaurants) прейскурáнт.
tariff barrier n (COMM) тарúфный барьéр.
tarmac ['tɑːmæk] n (BRIT: on road) асфáльт; (AVIAT) предангáрная площáдка ♦ vt (BRIT: road, drive etc) асфальтúровать (заасфальтúровать perf).
tarn [tɑːn] n кáровое óзеро.
tarnish ['tɑːnɪʃ] vt (silver, brass etc) дéлать (сдéлать perf) тýсклым; (fig: reputation etc) бросáть (брóсить* perf) тень на +acc.
tarot ['tærəu] adj: **~ cards** гадáльные кáрты fpl.
tarpaulin [tɑː'pɔːlɪn] n брезéнт.
tarragon ['tærəgən] n (herb) эстрагóн.
tart [tɑːt] n (CULIN: large) пирóг; (: small) пирóжное nt adj; (BRIT: inf: prostitute) шлюха ♦ adj (flavour) гóрький*
▶ **tart up** (BRIT: inf) ♦ vt (object etc) принаряжáть (принарядúть* perf); **to ~ o.s. up** принаряжáться (принарядúться* perf); (pej) намáзываться (намáзаться* perf), выряживаться (вырядиться* perf).
tartan ['tɑːtn] n шотлáндка (ткань) ♦ adj (rug, scarf etc) клéтчатый.
tartar ['tɑːtə] n (on teeth) (зубнóй) кáмень m; (pej: person) стéрва.
tartar(e) sauce ['tɑːtə-] n сóус с лýком и кáперсами.
Tashkent [tæʃ'kɛnt] n Ташкéнт.
task [tɑːsk] n задáча; **to take sb to ~** отчúтывать (отчитáть perf) когó-н.
task force n (MIL, POLICE) оперáтивная грýппа.
taskmaster ['tɑːskmɑːstə] n: **he's a hard ~** он настоящий* надсмóтрщик.
Tasmania [tæz'meɪnɪə] n Тасмáния.
tassel ['tæsl] n кúсточка; **~s** бахромá fsg.
taste [teɪst] n вкус; (sample) прóба; (fig: glimpse, idea) представлéние ♦ vt прóбовать (попрóбовать perf) ♦ vi: **the fish ~s of or like** рыба имéет вкус +gen; **what does the fish ~ like?** какóва рыба на вкус?; **you can ~ the garlic (in the dish)** (в блюде) чýвствуется чеснóк; **to have a ~ of sth** прóбовать (попрóбовать perf) чегó-н; **to have a ~ for sth** имéть (impf) вкус к чемý-н; **in good/bad ~** в хорóшем/дурнóм вкýсе.
taste bud n (ANAT) вкусовóй бугóр.

tasteful ['teɪstful] adj (furnishings) элегáнтный.
tastefully ['teɪstfəlɪ] adv (decorated, furnished etc) со вкýсом.
tasteless ['teɪstlɪs] adj безвкýсный* (безвкýсен).
tasty ['teɪstɪ] adj (food) вкýсный* (вкýсен).
tattered ['tætəd] adj (clothes, paper etc) изóрванный (в клóчья); (fig: hopes etc) разбúтый (разбúт).
tatters ['tætəz] npl: **in ~** (clothes) изóрванный (изóрван) в клóчья.
tattoo [tə'tuː] n (on skin) татуирóвка; (spectacle) воéнный смотр ♦ vt (name, design) татуúровать (вытатуúровать perf).
tatty ['tætɪ] adj (BRIT: inf) потрёпанный.
taught [tɔːt] pt, pp of **teach**.
taunt [tɔːnt] n издевáтельство ♦ vt (person) издевáться (impf) над +instr.
Taurus ['tɔːrəs] n (ASTROLOGY) Телéц*; **he is ~** он – Телéц.
taut [tɔːt] adj (thread etc) тугóй (туг); (skin) упрýгий* (упрýг).
tavern ['tævən] n (old) тавéрна.
tawdry ['tɔːdrɪ] adj (jewellery etc) безвкýсный* (безвкýсен).
tawny ['tɔːnɪ] adj желтовáто-корúчневый.
tawny owl n неясыть f.
tax [tæks] n налóг ♦ vt (earnings, goods etc) облагáть (обложúть perf) налóгом; (fig: memory, patience) испытывать (испытáть perf); **before ~** до вычета налóгов; **after ~** за вычетом налóгов; **free of ~** не облагáемый налóгом.
taxable ['tæksəbl] adj (income) облагáемый (облагáем) налóгом.
tax allowance n налóговая скúдка.
taxation [tæk'seɪʃən] n (system) налогообложéние; (money paid) размéр налóга.
tax avoidance n оптимизáция налóговой полúтики.
tax collector n сбóрщик налóгов.
tax disc n (BRIT: AUT) свидéтельство об уплáте подорóжного налóга, котóрое прикрепляется к ветровóму стеклý.
tax evasion n уклонéние от налóгов.
tax exemption n освобождéние от налóгов.
tax exile n человéк с высóким дохóдом, котóрый живёт за гранúцей с цéлью минимизáции своúх налóгов.
tax-free ['tæksfriː] adj (goods, services) необлагáемый налóгом.
tax haven n налóговое убéжище (странá с нúзкими налóгами).
taxi ['tæksɪ] n таксú nt ind ♦ vi (AVIAT: plane) вырýливать (вырулить perf).
taxidermist ['tæksɪdəːmɪst] n набúвщик чýчел.
taxi driver n водúтель m таксú, таксúст.
tax inspector n (BRIT) налóговый инспéктор.
taxi rank n (BRIT) стоянка таксú.
taxi stand n = **taxi rank**.

taxpayer ['tækspeɪə'] *n* налогоплате́льщик (-щица).

tax rebate *n* возвра́т нало́га.

tax relief *n* ски́дка с нало́га.

tax return *n* поступле́ния *ntpl* от нало́гов.

tax shelter *n* нало́говая защи́та (*че́рез вложе́ния в це́нные бума́ги*).

tax year *n* нало́говый год*.

TB *n abbr* = **tuberculosis**.

Tbilisi [dbɪ'liːsɪ] *n* Тбили́си *m ind*.

TD *n abbr* (*US*) = **Treasury Department**; (: *FOOTBALL*) = **touchdown**.

tea [tiː] *n* (*drink*) чай; (*BRIT: meal*) у́жин; **afternoon** ~ чай (с бутербро́дами и пиро́жными); **high** ~ (*BRIT*) (по́здний*) обе́д.

tea bag *n* чай в паке́тике.

tea break *n* (*BRIT*) переры́в.

teacake ['tiːkeɪk] *n* (*BRIT*) *сдо́бная бу́лка с изю́мом*.

teach [tiːtʃ] (*pt,pp* **taught**) *vi* (*be a teacher*) преподава́ть* (*impf*) ♦ *vt*: **to** ~ **sb sth**, ~ **sth to sb** учи́ть (научи́ть *perf*) кого́-н чему́-н; (*in school*) преподава́ть* (*impf*) что-н; **it taught him a lesson** (*fig*) э́то послужи́ло ему́ хоро́шим уро́ком.

teacher ['tiːtʃə'] *n* (*in secondary school*) учи́тель(ница) *m(f)*, преподава́тель(ница) *m(f)*; (*in primary school*) учи́тель(ница); **Russian** ~ учи́тель(ница) *or* преподава́тель(ница) ру́сского.

teacher training college *n* (*for primary schools*) педагоги́ческое учи́лище; (*for secondary schools*) педагоги́ческий* институ́т.

teaching ['tiːtʃɪŋ] *n* (*work of teacher*) преподава́ние.

teaching aids *npl* уче́бные посо́бия *ntpl*.

teaching hospital *n* (*BRIT: MED*) ≈ клини́ческая больни́ца.

teaching staff *n* (*BRIT*) преподава́тельский соста́в.

tea cosy *n* ≈ "ба́ба" на ча́йник.

teacup ['tiːkʌp] *n* ча́йная ча́шка*.

teak [tiːk] *n* тик.

tea leaves *npl* зава́рка *fsg*.

team [tiːm] *n* (*of people*) кома́нда; (*of animals*) упря́жка

▶ **team up** *vi*: **to** ~ **up (with)** объединя́ть (объедини́ть *perf*) уси́лия (с +*instr*).

team games *npl* кома́ндные и́гры *fpl*.

team spirit *n* дух това́рищества, кома́ндный дух.

teamwork ['tiːmwəːk] *n* коллекти́вная рабо́та.

tea party *n* чаепи́тие, чай.

teapot ['tiːpɔt] *n* (зава́рочный) ча́йник.

tear¹ [tɛə'] (*pt* **tore**, *pp* **torn**) *n* (*hole*) дыра́*, ды́рка* ♦ *vt* (*rip*) рвать* (порва́ть* *perf*) ♦ *vi*

(*become torn*) рва́ться* (порва́ться* *perf*); **to** ~ **to pieces** *or* **to bits** *or* **to shreds** (*also fig*) разрыва́ть (разорва́ть* *perf*) на ме́лкие клочки́

▶ **tear along** *vi* (*rush*) нести́сь* (понести́сь* *perf*)

▶ **tear apart** *vt* (*also fig*) разрыва́ть (разорва́ть* *perf*) на ча́сти

▶ **tear away** *vt*: **to** ~ **o.s. away (from sth)** (*fig*) отрыва́ться (оторва́ться* *perf*) (от чего́-н)

▶ **tear out** *vt* (*sheet of paper, cheque*) вырыва́ть (вы́рвать* *perf*)

▶ **tear up** *vt* (*sheet of paper etc*) разрыва́ть (разорва́ть* *perf*).

tear² [tɪə'] *n* слеза́; **in** ~**s** в слеза́х; **to burst into** ~**s** распла́каться (*perf*), разрыда́ться (*perf*).

tearaway ['tɛərəweɪ] *n* (*inf: person*) сорвиголова́ *m/f*.

teardrop ['tɪədrɔp] *n* слези́нка*.

tearful ['tɪəful] *adj* запла́канный* (запла́кан).

tear gas *n* слезоточи́вый газ.

tearing ['tɛərɪŋ] *adj*: **to be in a** ~ **hurry** быть* (*impf*) в безу́мной спе́шке.

tearoom ['tiːruːm] *n* ча́йная *f adj*.

tease [tiːz] *vt* дразни́ть (*impf*); (*unkindly*) дразни́ть (задразни́ть *perf*) ♦ *n* (*person*) насме́шник.

tea set *n* ча́йный серви́з.

teashop ['tiːʃɔp] *n* (*BRIT*) = **tearoom**.

Teasmade® ['tiːzmeɪd] *n* *приспособле́ние для зава́ривания ча́я, приводи́мое в де́йствие буди́льником*.

teaspoon ['tiːspuːn] *n* ча́йная ло́жка.

tea strainer *n* ча́йное си́течко.

teat [tiːt] *n* (*of bottle*) со́ска.

teatime ['tiːtaɪm] *n* у́жин.

tea towel *n* (*BRIT*) полоте́нце для посу́ды.

tea urn *n* тита́н с ча́ем.

tech [tɛk] *n abbr* (*inf*) = **technology**, **technical college**) ≈ ПТУ= *профессиона́льно-техни́ческое учи́лище*.

technical ['tɛknɪkl] *adj* (*terms, advances*) техни́ческий*.

technical college *n* (*BRIT*) техни́ческий* ко́лледж, те́хникум.

technicality [tɛknɪ'kælɪtɪ] *n* (*point of law*) техни́ческая то́нкость *f*; (*detail*) форма́льность *f*; **on a** (*legal*) ~ из-за юриди́ческой форма́льности.

technically ['tɛknɪklɪ] *adv* (*strictly speaking*) техни́чески, форма́льно; (*regarding technique*) с техни́ческой то́чки зре́ния.

technician [tɛk'nɪʃən] *n* те́хник.

technique [tɛk'niːk] *n* те́хника.

techno ['tɛknəu] *n* (*MUS*) стиль поп му́зыки.

technocrat ['tɛknəkræt] *n* технокра́т.

technological [tɛknə'lɔdʒɪkl] *adj* (*development*,

---

* marks translations which have irregular inflections. The Russian-English side of the dictionary gives inflectional information.

knowledge) техни́ческий*.
technologist [tɛk'nɔlədʒɪst] *n* те́хник; (*in particular field*) техно́лог.
technology [tɛk'nɔlədʒɪ] *n* те́хника; (*in particular field*) техноло́гия.
teddy (bear) ['tɛdɪ(-)] *n* (плю́шевый *or* игру́шечный) ми́шка.
tedious ['ti:dɪəs] *adj* (*work, discussions etc*) ну́дный* (ну́ден), ску́чный.
tedium ['ti:dɪəm] *n* ску́ка.
tee [ti:] *n* ме́тка для мяча́
▶ **tee off** *vi* де́лать (сде́лать *perf*) пе́рвый уда́р.
teem [ti:m] *vi*: **the city is ~ing with** (*visitors, tourists etc*) го́род кипши́т +*instr*; **it is ~ing** (**with rain**) льёт как из ведра́.
teenage ['ti:neɪdʒ] *adj* (*fashions etc*) подростко́вый; ~ **children** подро́стки *mpl*.
teenager ['ti:neɪdʒə'] *n* подро́сток*.
teens [ti:nz] *npl*: **to be in one's ~** быть* (*impf*) в подростко́вом во́зрасте.
tee shirt *n* = **T-shirt**.
teeter ['ti:tə'] *vi* (*also fig*) колеба́ться (*impf*).
teeth [ti:θ] *npl of* **tooth**.
teethe [ti:ð] *vi*: **she is teething** (*baby*) у неё ре́жутся зу́бы.
teething ring ['ti:ðɪŋ-] *n* кольцо́.
teething troubles *npl* (*fig*) боле́зни *fpl* ро́ста.
teetotal ['ti:'təutl] *adj* тре́звый, не пью́щий*.
teetotaller ['ti:'təutlə'] (*US* **teetotaler**) *n* тре́звенник.
TEFL ['tɛfl] *n abbr* = *Teaching of English as a Foreign Language*.
Teflon® ['tɛflɔn] *n* Тефло́н.
Teheran [tɛə'rɑ:n] *n* Тегера́н.
tel. *abbr* (= **telephone**) тел.= *мелефо́н*.
Tel Aviv ['tɛlə'vi:v] *n* Тель Ави́в.
telecast ['tɛlɪkɑ:st] *vt* передава́ть* (переда́ть* *perf*) по телеви́дению.
telecommunications ['tɛlɪkəmju:nɪ'keɪʃənz] *n* телекоммуника́ции *fpl*.
telegram ['tɛlɪgræm] *n* телегра́мма.
telegraph ['tɛlɪgrɑ:f] *n* (*system*) телегра́ф.
telegraphic [tɛlɪ'græfɪk] *adj* (*equipment*) телеграфи́ческий.
telegraph pole *n* телегра́фный столб.
telegraph wire *n* телегра́фные провода́ *mpl*.
telepathic [tɛlɪ'pæθɪk] *adj* телепати́ческий.
telepathy [tə'lɛpəθɪ] *n* телепа́тия.
telephone ['tɛlɪfəun] *n* телефо́н ◆ *vt* (*person*) звони́ть (позвони́ть *perf*) +*dat*; (*message*) сообща́ть (сообщи́ть *perf*) (по телефо́ну); **on the ~** (*talking*) по телефо́ну; **are you on the ~?** (*possessing phone*) у Вас есть телефо́н?
telephone booth (*BRIT* **telephone box**) *n* телефо́нная бу́дка.
telephone call *n* телефо́нный звоно́к*; **there is a ~~ for Peter** Пи́тера про́сят к телефо́ну.
telephone directory *n* телефо́нный спра́вочник.
telephone exchange *n* телефо́нная ста́нция.
telephone number *n* но́мер* телефо́на.

telephone operator *n* телефони́ст(ка).
telephone tapping *n* прослу́шивание телефо́на.
telephonist [tə'lɛfənɪst] *n* (*BRIT*) телефони́ст(ка).
telephoto ['tɛlɪ'fəutəu] *adj*: ~ **lens** телефотообъекти́в.
teleprinter ['tɛlɪprɪntə'] *n* телета́йп.
Teleprompter® ['tɛlɪprɔmptə'] *n* (*US*) телесуфлёр, телете́кст.
telesales ['tɛlɪseɪlz] *n* прода́жа по телефо́ну.
telescope ['tɛlɪskəup] *n* телеско́п ◆ *vi* (*fig: vehicles*) ста́лкиваться (столкну́ться *perf*) ◆ *vt* раскла́дывать (разложи́ть* *perf*).
telescopic [tɛlɪ'skɔpɪk] *adj* (*lens*) телескопи́ческий*; (*legs, aerial*) складно́й.
Teletext® ['tɛlɪtɛkst] *n* телете́кст, веща́тельная видеогра́фия.
telethon ['tɛlɪθɔn] *n* благотвори́тельная телевизио́нная програ́мма (*продолжа́ющаяся мно́го часо́в подря́д*).
televangelist [tɛlɪ'vændʒəlɪst] *n* телепроповéдник(-ица).
televise ['tɛlɪvaɪz] *vt* передава́ть* (*impf*) по телеви́дению.
television ['tɛlɪvɪʒən] *n* телеви́дение; (*set*) телеви́зор; **on ~** по телеви́дению.
television licence *n* (*BRIT*) телевизио́нная лицéнзия.
television programme *n* телевизио́нная програ́мма.
television set *n* телеви́зор.
telex ['tɛlɛks] *n* тéлекс ◆ *vt* (*company*) свя́зываться (связа́ться* *perf*) по тéлексу с +*instr*; (*message*) передава́ть* (переда́ть* *perf*) по тéлексу ◆ *vi* посыла́ть (посла́ть* *perf*) тéлекс.
tell [tɛl] (*pt,pp* **told**) *vt* (*say*) говори́ть (сказа́ть* *perf*); (*relate*) расска́зывать (рассказа́ть* *perf*); (*distinguish*): **to ~ sth from** отлича́ть (отличи́ть *perf*) что-н от +*gen* ◆ *vi* (*talk*): **to ~ of** расска́зывать (рассказа́ть* *perf*) о +*prp*; (*have an effect*): **to ~ (on)** ска́зываться (сказа́ться* *perf*) (на +*prp*); **to ~ sb to do** говори́ть (сказа́ть* *perf*) кому́-н +*infin*; **to ~ sb about sth** расска́зывать (рассказа́ть* *perf*) кому́-н о чём-н; **he told me what happened** он рассказа́л мне, что случи́лось; **to ~ the time** (*know how to*) определя́ть (определи́ть *perf*), кото́рый час; **can you ~ me the time?** Вы не ска́жете, кото́рый час?; **(I) ~ you what** ... вот что: ...; **I can't ~ them apart** я не могу́ их различи́ть
▶ **tell off** *vt*: **to ~ sb off** отчи́тывать (отчита́ть *perf*) кого́-н
▶ **tell on** *vt fus* (*inform on*) жа́ловаться (нажа́ловаться *perf*) на +*acc*.
teller ['tɛlə'] *n* (*in bank*) касси́р.
telling ['tɛlɪŋ] *adj* (*remark, detail*) показа́тельный* (показа́телен).
telltale ['tɛlteɪl] *adj* (*sign*) преда́тельский* ◆ *n*

(*pej: child*) я́беда *m/f*.
telly ['tɛlɪ] *n abbr* (*BRIT: inf*) (= *television*) те́лик.
temerity [tə'mɛrɪtɪ] *n* сме́лость *f*.
temp [tɛmp] *n abbr* (*BRIT: inf: = temporary office worker*) вре́менный делопроизводи́тель *m* ♦ *vi* вре́менно рабо́тать (*impf*) делопроизводи́телем.
temper ['tɛmpə'] *n* (*nature*) нрав; (*mood*) настрое́ние; (*fit of anger*) гнев ♦ *vt* (*moderate*) смягча́ть (смягчи́ть *perf*); **to be in a ~** быть* (*impf*) в гне́ве; **to lose one's ~** выходи́ть* (вы́йти* *perf*) из себя́; **to keep one's ~** сде́рживаться (сдержа́ться* *perf*).
temperament ['tɛmprəmənt] *n* темпера́мент.
temperamental [tɛmprə'mɛntl] *adj* темпера́ментный* (темпера́ментен); (*fig*) капри́зный.
temperate ['tɛmprət] *adj* (*climate, zone, behaviour*) уме́ренный* (уме́рен); **~ country** страна́ с уме́ренным кли́матом.
temperature ['tɛmprətʃə'] *n* температу́ра; **he has** *or* **is running a ~** у него́ температу́ра.
temperature chart *n* температу́рный гра́фик.
tempered ['tɛmpəd] *adj* (*steel*) отпу́щенный.
tempest ['tɛmpɪst] *n* бу́ря.
tempestuous [tɛm'pɛstjuəs] *adj* (*time, relationship*) бу́рный* (бу́рен); (*person*) бу́йный* (бу́ен).
tempi ['tɛmpiː] *npl of* **tempo**.
template ['tɛmplɪt] *n* шабло́н.
temple ['tɛmpl] *n* (*REL*) храм; (*ANAT*) висо́к*.
templet ['tɛmplɪt] *n* = **template**.
tempo ['tɛmpəu] (*pl* **~s** *or* **tempi**) *n* (*MUS, also fig*) темп.
temporal ['tɛmpərl] *adj* (*non-religious*) све́тский*; (*relating to time*) временно́й.
temporarily ['tɛmpərərɪlɪ] *adv* вре́менно.
temporary ['tɛmpərərɪ] *adj* вре́менный* (вре́менен).
temporize ['tɛmpəraɪz] *vi* ме́длить (*impf*).
tempt [tɛmpt] *vt* соблазня́ть (соблазни́ть *perf*), искуша́ть (искуси́ть* *perf*); **to ~ sb into doing** соблазня́ть (соблазни́ть *perf*) *or* искуша́ть (искуси́ть* *perf*) кого́-н +*infin*; **I was ~ed to call you** у меня́ бы́ло искуше́ние позвони́ть Вам.
temptation [tɛmp'teɪʃən] *n* собла́зн, искуше́ние.
tempting ['tɛmptɪŋ] *adj* (*offer*) соблазни́тельный* (соблазни́телен).
ten [tɛn] *n* де́сять*; **~s of thousands** деся́тки ты́сяч; *see also* **five**.
tenable ['tɛnəbl] *adj* здра́вый (здрав); **the position of Chairman is ~ for three years** пост председа́теля закреплён за ним на три го́да.
tenacious [tə'neɪʃəs] *adj* насто́йчивый (насто́йчив).

tenacity [tə'næsɪtɪ] *n* насто́йчивость *f*.
tenancy ['tɛnənsɪ] *n* (*possession of room, land etc*) владе́ние на усло́виях аре́нды; (*period of possession*) срок аре́нды *or* на́йма.
tenant ['tɛnənt] *n* съёмщик(-мщица).
tend [tɛnd] *vt* (*crops, sick person*) уха́живать (*impf*) за +*instr* ♦ *vi*: **to ~ to do** име́ть (*impf*) скло́нность +*infin*; **he ~s to do everything in a hurry** он скло́нен к тому́, чтобы де́лать всё в спе́шке.
tendency ['tɛndənsɪ] *n* (*habit*) скло́нность *f*; (*trend*) тенде́нция.
tender ['tɛndə'] *adj* не́жный* (не́жен); (*sore*) чувстви́тельный* (чувстви́телен) ♦ *n* (*COMM: offer*) предложе́ние ♦ *vt* (*offer*) подава́ть* (пода́ть* *perf*); (*apology*) приноси́ть* (принести́* *perf*); **to put in a ~ (for)** подава́ть* (пода́ть* *perf*) зая́вку (на +*acc*); **to put sth out to ~** (*BRIT*) объявля́ть (объяви́ть* *perf*) то́рги на что-н; **legal ~** (*money*) зако́нное платёжное сре́дство; **to ~ one's resignation** пода́ть* (*perf*) в отста́вку.
tenderize ['tɛndəraɪz] *vt* (*meat*) отбива́ть (отби́ть* *perf*).
tenderly ['tɛndəlɪ] *adv* не́жно.
tenderness ['tɛndənɪs] *n* не́жность *f*.
tendon ['tɛndən] *n* сухожи́лие.
tendril ['tɛndrɪl] *n* (*BOT*) у́сик; (*of hair*) прядь *f*.
tenement ['tɛnəmənt] *n* многокварти́рный дом* (*сдава́емый внаём*).
Tenerife [tɛnə'riːf] *n* Тенери́фе *m ind*.
tenet ['tɛnət] *n* основополага́ющий при́нцип.
tenner ['tɛnə'] *n* (*BRIT: inf: ten pounds*) ≈ деся́тка*.
tennis ['tɛnɪs] *n* те́ннис.
tennis ball *n* те́ннисный мяч*.
tennis club *n* те́ннисный клуб.
tennis court *n* те́ннисный корт.
tennis elbow *n* (*MED*) те́ннисный ло́коть *m*, лучеплечево́й бурси́т.
tennis match *n* те́ннисный матч.
tennis player *n* тенниси́ст(ка*).
tennis racket *n* те́ннисная раке́тка*.
tennis shoes *npl* те́ннисные ту́фли* *fpl*.
tenor ['tɛnə'] *n* (*MUS*) те́нор*; (*of speech etc*) смысл.
tenpin bowling ['tɛnpɪn-] *n* (*BRIT*) ке́гли *pl*.
tense [tɛns] *adj* (*person, muscle, period*) напряжённый* напряжён); (*smile*) натя́нутый (натя́нут) ♦ *n* (*LING*) вре́мя* *nt* ♦ *vt* напряга́ть (напря́чь* *perf*).
tenseness ['tɛnsnɪs] *n* напряжённость *f*.
tension ['tɛnʃən] *n* (*nervousness*) напряжённость *f*; (*between ropes etc*) натя́нутость *f*.
tent [tɛnt] *n* пала́тка*.
tentacle ['tɛntəkl] *n* щу́пальце*.
tentative ['tɛntətɪv] *adj* (*person, smile*)

---

* marks translations which have irregular inflections. The Russian-English side of the dictionary gives inflectional information.

осторо́жный* (осторо́жен); (*conclusion, plans*) предвари́тельный* (предвари́телен).
tentatively ['tɛntətɪvlɪ] *adv* (*suggest*) предвари́тельно; (*wave*) осторо́жно.
tenterhooks ['tɛntəhuks] *npl*: **on ~** как на иго́лках.
tenth [tɛnθ] *adj* деся́тый ♦ *n* (*fraction*) деся́тая часть *f*, одна́ деся́тая *f adj*; *see also* **fifth**.
tent peg *n* ко́лышек* для пала́тки.
tent pole *n* столб* для пала́тки.
tenuous ['tɛnjuəs] *adj* (*hold, links etc*) сла́бый* (слаб).
tenure ['tɛnjuə'] *n* (*of land, buildings etc*) срок аре́нды; (*of office*) побыва́ние в до́лжности; **to have ~** име́ть (*impf*) постоя́нную рабо́ту.
tepid ['tɛpɪd] *adj* (*tea, pool etc*) теплова́тый (теплова́т); (*reaction, applause*) прохла́дный* (прохла́ден).
Ter. *abbr* = **Terrace**.
term [tə:m] *n* (*word, expression*) те́рмин; (*period in power etc*) срок*; (*SCOL*: *in school*) че́тверть *f*; (: *at university*) триме́стр ♦ *vt* (*call*) называ́ть (назва́ть* *perf*); **~s** *npl* (*conditions*) усло́вия *ntpl*; **in abstract ~s** в абстра́ктных выраже́ниях; **~ of imprisonment** срок заключе́ния; **"easy ~s"** (*COMM*) "льго́тные усло́вия"; **in the short ~** в настоя́щее вре́мя; **in the long ~** в перспекти́ве; **to be on good ~s with sb** подде́рживать (*impf*) хоро́шие отноше́ния с кем-н; **to come to ~s with** примиря́ться (примири́ться *perf*) с +*instr*.
terminal ['tə:mɪnl] *adj* неизлечи́мый (неизлечи́м) ♦ *n* (*ELEC*) кле́мма, зажи́м; (*COMPUT, COMM*) термина́л; (*also*: **air ~**) аэровокза́л; (*BRIT*: *also*: **coach ~**) авто́бусный вокза́л.
terminate ['tə:mɪneɪt] *vt* прекраша́ть (прекрати́ть* *perf*) ♦ *vi*: **to ~ in** зака́нчиваться (зако́нчиться *perf*) +*instr*.
termination [tə:mɪ'neɪʃən] *n* прекраще́ние.
termini ['tə:mɪnaɪ] *npl of* **terminus**.
terminology [tə:mɪ'nɔlədʒɪ] *n* терминоло́гия.
term insurance *n* страхова́ние на определённый срок.
terminus ['tə:mɪnəs] (*pl* **termini**) *n* (*for buses*) коне́чная остано́вка*; (*for trains*) коне́чная ста́нция.
termite ['tə:maɪt] *n* терми́т.
term paper *n* (*US*: *at university*) ≈ курсова́я *f adj*.
Terr. *abbr* = **Terrace**.
terrace ['tɛrəs] *n* терра́са; (*BRIT*: *row of houses*) ряд примыка́ющих друг к дру́гу одноти́пных домо́в; (*in street names*): **Rose T~** Ро́уз Те́рес; **the ~s** *npl* (*BRIT*: *standing areas*) трибу́ны *fpl*.
terraced ['tɛrəst] *adj* (*garden*) терра́сный; **~ house** дом в ряду́ примыка́ющих друг к дру́гу одноти́пных домо́в.
terracotta ['tɛrə'kɔtə] *n* (*clay*) террако́та; (*colour*) террако́товый цвет ♦ *adj* террако́товый.

terrain [tɛ'reɪn] *n* ландша́фт.
terrible ['tɛrɪbl] *adj* ужа́сный* (ужа́сен).
terribly ['tɛrɪblɪ] *adv* ужа́сно.
terrier ['tɛrɪə'] *n* терье́р.
terrific [tə'rɪfɪk] *adj* (*thunderstorm, speed etc*) колосса́льный* (колосса́лен); (*time, party etc*) потряса́ющий*.
terrify ['tɛrɪfaɪ] *vt* ужаса́ть (ужасну́ть *perf*); **to be terrified** быть* (*impf*) в у́жасе.
terrifying ['tɛrɪfaɪɪŋ] *adj* ужаса́ющий*.
territorial [tɛrɪ'tɔ:rɪəl] *adj* территориа́льный ♦ *n* (*BRIT*: *MIL*) военнослу́жащий* *m adj* территориа́льной а́рмии.
Territorial Army *n* (*BRIT*: *MIL*): **the ~~** территориа́льная а́рмия.
territorial waters *npl* территориа́льные во́ды *fpl*.
territory ['tɛrɪtərɪ] *n* террито́рия; (*fig*) о́бласть *f*.
terror ['tɛrə'] *n* у́жас.
terrorism ['tɛrərɪzəm] *n* террори́зм.
terrorist ['tɛrərɪst] *n* террори́ст(ка*).
terrorize ['tɛrəraɪz] *vt* терроризи́ровать (*impf*).
terse [tə:s] *adj* сжа́тый (сжат), кра́ткий* (кра́ток).
tertiary ['tə:ʃərɪ] *adj* (*system*) трети́чный; (*third in order, importance*) тре́тий*; **~ education** (*BRIT*) вы́сшее образова́ние.
Terylene® ['tɛrɪli:n] *n* терилéн.
TESL ['tɛsl] *n abbr* = *Teaching of English as a Second Language*.
TESSA ['tɛsə] *abbr* (*BRIT*: = *Tax Exempt Special Savings Account*) безнало́говый сберега́тельный счёт.
test [tɛst] *n* (*trial, check*) прове́рка, тест; (*of courage etc*) испыта́ние; (*MED*) ана́лиз; (*CHEM*) о́пыт; (*SCOL*) контро́льная рабо́та, тест; (*also*: **driving ~**) экза́мен на води́тельские права́ ♦ *vt* проверя́ть (прове́рить *perf*); (*courage*) испы́тывать (испыта́ть *perf*); (*MED*) анализи́ровать (*impf* *perf*); **to put sth to the ~** подверга́ть (подве́ргнуть* *perf*) что-н прове́рке; **to ~ sth for sth** проверя́ть (прове́рить *perf*) что-н на что-н.
testament ['tɛstəmənt] *n* свиде́тельство; **the Old/New T~** Ве́тхий*/Но́вый заве́т.
test ban *n* (*also*: **nuclear ~~**) запреще́ние испыта́ний я́дерного ору́жия.
test card *n* (*TV*) телевизио́нная табли́ца.
test case *n* (*LAW, fig*) про́бное *or* прецеде́нтное де́ло.
testes ['tɛsti:z] *npl* (*ANAT*) яи́чки *ntpl*.
test flight *n* испыта́тельный полёт.
testicle ['tɛstɪkl] *n* яи́чко*.
testify ['tɛstɪfaɪ] *vi* (*LAW*) дава́ть* (дать* *perf*) показа́ния; **to ~ to sth** свиде́тельствовать (*impf*) о чём-н.
testimonial [tɛstɪ'məunɪəl] *n* (*BRIT*: *reference*) рекоменда́ция.

testimony ['tɛstɪmənɪ] n (LAW: statement) показа́ние, свиде́тельство; (clear proof): **to be (a) ~ to** явля́ться (яви́ться* perf) свиде́тельством +gen.

testing ['tɛstɪŋ] adj (situation, period) испыта́тельный.

test match n (CRICKET, RUGBY) междунаро́дный матч.

testosterone [tɛs'tɒstərəun] n тестостеро́н.

test paper n (SCOL) экзаменацио́нный биле́т.

test pilot n лётчик-испыта́тель m.

test tube n проби́рка*.

test-tube baby ['tɛsttju:b-] n ребёнок, зача́тый с по́мощью иску́сственного оплодотворе́ния в проби́рке.

testy ['tɛstɪ] adj (person, comment) невы́держанный* (невы́держан).

tetanus ['tɛtənəs] n столбня́к*.

tetchy ['tɛtʃɪ] adj (person, behaviour) раздражи́тельный* (раздражи́телен).

tether ['tɛðə'] vt (animal) привя́зывать (привяза́ть* perf) ◆ n: **at the end of one's ~** на гра́ни срыва.

Texas ['tɛksəs] n Теха́с.

text [tɛkst] n текст.

textbook ['tɛkstbuk] n уче́бник.

textiles ['tɛkstaɪlz] npl (fabrics) тексти́льные изде́лия ntpl; (TECH) тексти́ль msg; (textile industry) тексти́льная промы́шленность fsg.

textual ['tɛkstjuəl] adj: **~ analysis** ана́лиз те́кста.

texture ['tɛkstʃə'] n (of cloth, soil) строе́ние; (feel: of cloth, silk) факту́ра; (of skin) ка́чество.

TGWU n abbr (BRIT) = Transport and General Workers' Union.

Thai [taɪ] adj тайла́ндский ◆ n таила́ндец* (-дка*).

Thailand ['taɪlænd] n Таила́нд.

thalidomide [θə'lɪdəmaɪd] n талидоми́д.

Thames [tɛmz] n: **the ~** Те́мза.

than [ðæn] conj (in comparisons): **you have more ~ ten** у Вас бо́льше десяти́; **I have more/less work ~ you/Paul** у меня́ бо́льше/ме́ньше рабо́ты, чем у Вас/у Па́вла; **she is older ~ you think** она́ ста́рше, чем Вы ду́маете; **more ~ once** не раз; **more ~ three times** бо́лее or бо́льше трёх раз.

thank [θæŋk] vt благодари́ть (поблагодари́ть perf); **~ you (very much)** (большо́е) спаси́бо; **~ God!** сла́ва Бо́гу!

thankful ['θæŋkful] adj: **~ (for)** благода́рный* (благода́рен) (за +acc); **~ that** (relieved) благода́рный за то, что.

thankfully ['θæŋkfəlɪ] adv к сча́стью; **~ there were few victims** к сча́стью, жертв бы́ло ма́ло.

thankless ['θæŋklɪs] adj неблагода́рный*.

thanks [θæŋks] npl благода́рность fsg ◆ excl спаси́бо; **many ~, ~ a lot** большо́е спаси́бо; **~ to** благодаря́ +dat.

Thanksgiving (Day) ['θæŋksgɪvɪŋ(-)] n (US) День* m благодаре́ния.

KEYWORD

that [ðæt] (pl **those**) adj (demonstrative) тот*; **that man** тот мужчи́на; **which book would you like? – that one over there** каку́ю кни́гу Вы хоти́те? – вон ту, пожа́луйста; **I like this film better than that one** мне э́тот фильм нра́вится бо́льше, чем тот

◆ pron **1** (demonstrative: in questions): **who's/what's that?** кто/что э́то?; **is that you?** э́то Вы?; **we talked of this and that** мы говори́ли о том о сём; **that's how ...** вот как ...; **that's what he said** так он сказа́л; **what happened after that?** а что пото́м произошло́?; **that is (to say)** то есть

2 (direct object) кото́рый (f кото́рую, nt кото́рое, pl кото́рые); (indirect object) кото́рому (f кото́рой, pl кото́рым); (after prep: +acc) кото́рый (f кото́рую, nt кото́рое, pl кото́рые); (: +gen) кото́рого (f кото́рой, pl кото́рых); (: +dat) кото́рому (f кото́рой, pl кото́рым); (: +instr) кото́рым (f кото́рой, pl кото́рыми); (: +prp) кото́ром (f кото́рой, pl кото́рых); **the theory that we discussed last week** тео́рия, кото́рую мы обсужда́ли на про́шлой неде́ле; **all (that) I have** всё, что у меня́ есть

3 (of time) когда́; **the day (that) he died** день, когда́ он умер

◆ conj что; (introducing purpose) что́бы; **he thought that I was ill** он ду́мал, что я был бо́лен; **she suggested that I phone you** она́ предложи́ла, что́бы я Вам позвони́л

◆ adv (demonstrative): **I can't work that much** я не могу́ сто́лько мно́го рабо́тать; **it can't be that bad** ну не так уж всё пло́хо; **I have drunk that much** я вы́пил вот сто́лько; **the wall's about that high and that thick** стена́ приме́рно вот тако́й высоты́ и вот тако́й толщины́.

thatched [θætʃt] adj соло́менный.

Thatcherism ['θætʃərɪzəm] n тэтчери́зм.

Thatcherite ['θætʃəraɪt] n сторо́нник(-ица) поли́тики Тэ́тчер.

thaw [θɔː] n о́ттепель f ◆ vi (ice) та́ять (раста́ять perf); (food) отта́ивать (отта́ять perf) ◆ vt (food: also: **~ out**) отта́ивать (отта́ять perf); **it's ~ing today** сего́дня та́ет.

KEYWORD

the [ðiː] def art: **1: the books/children are in the library** кни́ги/де́ти в библиоте́ке; **the rich and the poor** бога́тые pl adj и бе́дные pl adj; **to attempt the impossible** пыта́ться

---

* marks translations which have irregular inflections. The Russian-English side of the dictionary gives inflectional information.

(попытáться *perf*) сдéлать невозмóжное
2 (*in titles*): **Elizabeth the First** Елизавéта
Пéрвая
3 (*in comparisons*): **the more I think about it
the more I like it** чем бóльше я дýмаю об
э́том, тем бóльше мне э́то нрáвится.

theatre ['θɪətə'] (*US* **theater**) *n* теáтр; (*also:*
lecture ~) лекциóнный зал; (*MED: also:*
operating ~) операциóнная *f adj.*
theatregoer ['θɪətəgəʊə'] *n* театрáл(ка*).
theatrical [θɪ'ætrɪkl] *adj* театрáльный;
(*gestures*) театрáльный* (театрáлен); ~
company театрáльная трýппа.
theft [θeft] *n* крáжа.
their [δɛə'] *adj* их; (*referring to subject of
sentence*) свой.
theirs [δɛəz] *pron* (*see adj*) их; свой; *see also*
mine[1].
them [δɛm] *pron* (*direct*) их; (*indirect*) им; (*after
prep: +gen, +prp*) их; (: *+dat*) им; (: *+instr*)
и́ми; (*referring to subject of sentence*) свой; **a
few of ~ are going to the cinema** нéкоторые
из них идýт в кинó; **give me a few of** ~ дáйте
мне их немнóго; *see also* **me**.
theme [θi:m] *n* тéма.
theme park *n парк, стилизóванный под
определённую эпóху и́ли тéму.*
theme song *n* пéсня из кинофи́льма.
theme tune *n* мелóдия из кинофи́льма.
themselves [δəm'sɛlvz] *pl pron* (*reflexive*) себя́;
(*emphatic*) сáми; (*after prep: +gen*) себя́; (:
+dat, +prp) себé; (: *+instr*) собóй; (*alone*): **(all)
by ~** одни́; **they shared the money between ~**
они́ раздели́ли дéньги мéжду собóй; *see also*
myself.
then [δɛn] *adv* потóм; (*at that time*) тогдá ♦ *conj*
(*therefore*) тогдá ♦ *adj*: **the ~ president**
тогдáшний* президéнт; **from ~ on** с тех пор;
by ~ (*past*) к э́тому *или* тому́ врéмени; **we
should know by ~** к тому́ врéмени мы ужé
бýдем знать; **if ... ~ ...** éсли ... то ...; **before ~**
до э́того *или* тогó врéмени; **until ~** до тех пор;
and ~ what? и что потóм?; **what do you want
me to do ~?** (*afterwards*) что Вы мне дéлать
потóм?; (*in that case*) что Вы мне дéлать
тогдá?
theologian [θɪə'ləudʒən] *n* богослóв, теóлог.
theological [θɪə'lɔdʒɪkl] *adj* теологи́ческий*,
богослóвский.
theology [θɪ'ɔlədʒɪ] *n* теолóгия, богослóвие.
theorem ['θɪərəm] *n* теорéма.
theoretical [θɪə'rɛtɪkl] *adj* теорети́ческий*.
theorize ['θɪəraɪz] *vi* теоретизи́ровать *(impf).*
theory ['θɪərɪ] *n* теóрия; **in ~** теорети́чески, в
теóрии.
therapeutic(al) [θɛrə'pju:tɪk(l)] *adj* терапевт-
и́ческий.
therapist ['θɛrəpɪst] *n* врач.
therapy ['θɛrəpɪ] *n* терапи́я.

there [δɛə'] *adv*: **1**: **there is some milk in the
fridge** молокó в холоди́льнике; **there is
someone in the room** в кóмнате ктó-то есть;
there will be a lot of people at the concert на
концéрте бýдет мнóго нарóду; **there was a
book/there were flowers on the table** на столé
лежáла кни́га/стоя́ли цветы́; **there has been
an accident** произошлá авáрия
2 (*referring to place: position*) там; (: *motion*)
тудá; **there he is!** вот он!:
3: **there, there** (*esp to child*) ну, ничегó,
ничегó.

thereabouts ['δɛərə'bauts] *adv* (*place*)
побли́зости; (*amount*) óколо э́того.
thereafter [δɛər'ɑ:ftə'] *adv* с тогó врéмени.
thereby ['δɛəbaɪ] *adv* таки́м óбразом.
therefore ['δɛəfɔ:'] *adv* поэ́тому.
there's ['δɛəz] = **there is, there has**.
thereupon [δɛərə'pɔn] *adv* (*at that point*) вслед
за тем; (*formal: on that subject*) в связи́ с
э́тим.
thermal ['θə:ml] *adj* (*springs*) горя́чий*;
(*energy*) терми́ческий*; (*underwear*)
утеплённый*; (*paper, printer*)
термографи́ческий.
thermodynamics ['θə:mədaɪ'næmɪks] *n*
термодинáмика.
thermometer [θə'mɔmɪtə'] *n* термóметр,
грáдусник.
thermonuclear ['θə:məu'nju:klɪə'] *adj*
термоядерный.
Thermos® ['θə:məs] *n* (*also:* ~ **flask**) тéрмос.
thermostat ['θə:məustæt] *n* термостáт.
thesaurus [θɪ'sɔ:rəs] *n* тезáурус.
these [δi:z] *pl adj, pron* э́ти.
theses ['θi:si:z] *npl of* **thesis**.
thesis ['θi:sɪs] (*pl* **theses**) *n* (*SCOL*) диссертáция;
(*theory*) тéзис.
they [δeɪ] *pron* они́; ~ **say that ...** говоря́т,
что ....
they'd [δeɪd] = **they had, they would**.
they'll [δeɪl] = **they shall, they will**.
they're [δɛə'] = **they are**.
they've [δeɪv] = **they have**.
thick [θɪk] *adj* (*in shape*) тóлстый (толст); (*in
consistency*) густóй (густ); (*inf: stupid*) тупóй
(туп) ♦ *n*: **in the ~ of the battle** в сáмой гýще
би́твы; **the wall is 20 cm ~** толщинá стены́ –
20 cm.
thicken ['θɪkn] *vi* (*fog etc*) сгущáться
(сгусти́ться* *perf*); (*plot*) усложня́ться
(усложни́ться *perf*) ♦ *vt* (*sauce etc*) дéлать
(сдéлать *perf*) гýще.
thicket ['θɪkɪt] *n* зáросли *fpl.*
thickly ['θɪklɪ] *adv* (*spread*) гýсто; (*cut*) тóлсто;
~ **populated** густонаселённый.
thickness ['θɪknɪs] *n* (*size*) толщинá; (*layer*)
слой*.
thickset [θɪk'sɛt] *adj* коренáстый (коренáст).
thick-skinned [θɪk'skɪnd] *adj* (*fig*) толсто-

кожий*.
thief [θi:f] (*pl* **thieves**) *n* вор(о́вка).
thieves [θi:vz] *npl of* **thief**.
thieving ['θi:vɪŋ] *n* воровство́.
thigh [θaɪ] *n* бедро́*.
thighbone ['θaɪbəʊn] *n* (*ANAT*) бе́дренная кость* *f*.
thimble ['θɪmbl] *n* напёрсток*.
thin [θɪn] *adj* то́нкий* (то́нок); (*person, animal*) худо́й (худ); (*soup, sauce*) жи́дкий* (жи́док); (*hair, crowd*) ре́дкий*; (*fog*) лёгкий* (лёгок) ◆ *vt*: **to ~ (down)** (*sauce, paint*) разбавля́ть (разба́вить* *perf*); (*hair: at hairdresser's*) разре́живать (*impf*) ◆ *vi* (*fog*) рассе́иваться (рассе́яться *perf*); (*also:* **~ out**: *crowd*) реде́ть (пореде́ть *perf*); **his hair is ~ning** у него́ реде́ют во́лосы.
thing [θɪŋ] *n* вещь* *f*; **~s** *npl* (*belongings*) ве́щи* *fpl*; **first ~ (in the morning)** пе́рвым де́лом (с утра́); **last ~ (at night), he ...** напосле́док (но́чью) он ...; **the ~ is ...** де́ло в том, что ...; **for one ~** во-пе́рвых; **she's got a ~ about mice** она́ не выно́сит мыше́й; **don't worry about a ~** ни о чём не беспоко́йтесь; **you'll do no such ~!** попро́буй то́лько!; **poor ~** бедня́жка* *m/f*; **the best ~ would be to ...** са́мое лу́чшее бы́ло бы +*infin* ...; **how are ~s?** как дела́?
think [θɪŋk] (*pt, pp* **thought**) *vt* (*reflect, believe*) ду́мать (*impf*); (*imagine*) предполага́ть (предположи́ть* *perf*); **to ~ of** ду́мать (поду́мать *perf*) о +*prp*; (*remember*) вспомина́ть (вспо́мнить* *perf*); (*consider*) приводи́ть* (привести́* *perf*); **what did you ~ of them?** что Вы о них ду́маете?; **to ~ about sth/sb** ду́мать (поду́мать *perf*) о чём-н/ ком-н; **I'll ~ about it** я поду́маю (об э́том); **to ~ well of sb** хорошо́ о ком-н ду́мать (*impf*); **to ~ aloud** ду́мать (*impf*) вслух; **~ again!** поду́майте ещё раз!
▸ **think out** *vt* (*plan, solution*) обду́мывать (обду́мать *perf*), проду́мывать (проду́мать *perf*)
▸ **think over** *vt* обду́мывать (обду́мать *perf*); **I'd like to ~ things over** я хочу́ всё обду́мать
▸ **think through** *vt* проду́мывать (проду́мать *perf*) до конца́
▸ **think up** *vt* приду́мывать (приду́мать *perf*).
thinking ['θɪŋkɪŋ] *n* мышле́ние; **to my way of ~** на мой взгляд.
think-tank ['θɪŋktæŋk] *n* мозгово́й центр.
thinly ['θɪnlɪ] *adv* то́нко.
thinness ['θɪnɪs] *n* то́нкость *f*.
third [θə:d] *adj* тре́тий* ◆ *n* (*fraction*) треть *f*, одна́ тре́тья *f adj*; (*AUT: also:* **~ gear**) тре́тья ско́рость *f*; (*BRIT: SCOL: degree*) *диплом*

тре́тьей и́ли ни́зшей сте́пени; **a ~ of** треть +*gen*, тре́тья часть +*gen*; *see also* **fifth**.
third-degree burns ['θə:ddɪgri:-] *npl* (*MED*) ожо́ги *mpl* тре́тьей сте́пени.
thirdly ['θə:dlɪ] *adv* в-тре́тьих.
third party insurance *n* (*BRIT*) страхова́ние в по́льзу тре́тьей стороны́.
third-rate ['θə:d'reɪt] *adj* (*pej: performance, actor etc*) третьесо́ртный* (третьесо́ртен).
Third World *n*: **the ~ ~** Тре́тий* мир.
thirst [θə:st] *n* (*also fig*) жа́жда.
thirsty ['θə:stɪ] *adj*: **to be ~** (*person, animal*) хоте́ть* (*impf*) пить; **I am ~** я хочу́ *or* мне хо́чется пить; **gardening is ~ work** рабо́та в саду́ вызыва́ет жа́жду.
thirteen [θə:'ti:n] *n* трина́дцать*; *see also* **five**.
thirteenth [θə:'ti:nθ] *adj* трина́дцатый; *see also* **fifth**.
thirtieth ['θə:tɪɪθ] *adj* тридца́тый; *see also* **fifth**.
thirty ['θə:tɪ] *n* три́дцать*; *see also* **fifty**.

KEYWORD

this [ðɪs] (*pl* **these**) *adj* (*demonstrative*) э́тот; **this man** э́тот мужчи́на; **which book would you like? – this one please** каку́ю кни́гу Вы хоти́те? – вот э́ту, пожа́луйста
◆ *pron* (*demonstrative*) э́тот (*f* э́та, *nt* э́то); **who/what is this?** кто/что э́то?; **this is where I live** вот здесь я живу́; **this is what he said** вот, что он сказа́л; **this is Mr Brown** э́то ми́стер Бра́ун
◆ *adv* (*demonstrative*): **this high/long** *etc* тако́й высоты́/длины́ *etc*; **the dog was about this big** соба́ка была́ приме́рно тако́го разме́ра *or* тако́й величины́; **we can't stop now we've gone this far** мы не мо́жет тепе́рь останови́ться, ведь мы так далеко́ ушли́.

---

thistle ['θɪsl] *n* чертополо́х.
thong [θɒŋ] *n* реме́нь* *m*.
thorn [θɔ:n] *n* шип, колю́чка*.
thorny ['θɔ:nɪ] *adj* (*plant, tree*) колю́чий* (колю́ч); (*problem*) нелёгкий*.
thorough ['θʌrə] *adj* (*search, wash*) тща́тельный* (тща́телен); (*knowledge, research*) основа́тельный* (основа́телен); (*person*) скрупулёзный* (скрупулёзен).
thoroughbred ['θʌrəbred] *n* чистокро́вная *or* чистопоро́дная ло́шадь *f*.
thoroughfare ['θʌrəfeə] *n* гла́вная арте́рия (го́рода), тра́нспортная магистра́ль *f*; **"no ~"** (*BRIT*) "Прое́зда нет".
thoroughgoing ['θʌrəgəʊɪŋ] *adj* доскона́льный* (доскона́лен), тща́тельный* (тща́телен).
thoroughly ['θʌrəlɪ] *adv* (*fully*) тща́тельно; (*very*) вполне́; **he ~ agreed** он по́лностью согласи́лся.
thoroughness ['θʌrənɪs] *n* тща́тельность *f*.

---

* marks translations which have irregular inflections. The Russian-English side of the dictionary gives inflectional information.

those [ðəuz] *pl adj, pron* те.
though [ðəu] *conj* хотя́ ◆ *adv* впро́чем, одна́ко; **even ~ ...** хотя́ и ...; **it's not easy, ~** впро́чем *or* одна́ко э́то не про́сто.
thought [θɔ:t] *pt, pp of* **think** ◆ *n* (*idea, intention*) мысль *f*; (*reflection*) размышле́ние; (*opinion*) соображе́ние; **after much ~** по́сле до́лгих размышле́ний; **I've just had a ~** мне то́лько что пришла́ в го́лову мысль; **to give sth some ~** обду́мывать (обду́мать *perf*) что-н.
thoughtful ['θɔ:tful] *adj* (*deep in thought*) заду́мчивый (заду́мчив); (*serious*) глубо́кий; (*considerate*) внима́тельный* (внима́телен).
thoughtfully ['θɔ:tfəlɪ] *adv* (*pensively*) заду́мчиво; (*considerately*) внима́тельно.
thoughtless ['θɔ:tlɪs] *adj* безду́мный* (безду́мен), неосмотри́тельный* (неосмотри́телен).
thoughtlessly ['θɔ:tlɪslɪ] *adv* безду́мно, неосмотри́тельно.
thoughtlessness ['θɔ:tlɪsnɪs] *n* безду́мность *f*, неосмотри́тельность *f*.
thought-out [θɔ:t'aut] *adj* проду́манный* (проду́ман).
thought-provoking ['θɔ:tprəvəukɪŋ] *adj* провоци́рующий на мы́сли.
thousand ['θauzənd] *n* ты́сяча*; **two ~** две ты́сячи; **five ~** пять ты́сяч; **about a ~** о́коло ты́сячи; **people came in their ~s** *or* **by the ~** пришли́ ты́сячи люде́й; **~s of** ты́сячи *+gen*.
thousandth ['θauzəntθ] *adj* ты́сячный.
thrash [θræʃ] *vt* (*beat*) поро́ть* (вы́пороть* *perf*); (*inf: defeat*) побива́ть (поби́ть* *perf*).
► **thrash about** *vi* мета́ться* (*impf*)
► **thrash around** *vi* = **thrash about**
► **thrash out** *vt* (*problem*) прораба́тывать (прорабо́тать *perf*).
thrashing ['θræʃɪŋ] *n*: **to give sb a ~** поро́ть* (вы́пороть* *perf*) кого́-н.
thread [θrɛd] *n* (*yarn*) нить *f*, ни́тка*; (*of screw*) резьба́ ◆ *vt* (*needle*) продева́ть (проде́ть* *perf*) ни́тку в *+acc*; **to ~ one's way between** пробира́ться (пробра́ться* *perf*) че́рез *or* сквозь *+acc*.
threadbare ['θrɛdbɛəʳ] *adj* потёртый (потёрт), потрёпанный* (потрёпан).
threat [θrɛt] *n* (*also fig*) угро́за; **to be under ~ of** быть* (*impf*) под угро́зой *+gen*.
threaten ['θrɛtn] *vi* (*storm, danger*) грози́ть* (*impf*) ◆ *vt*: **to ~ sb with** угрожа́ть (*impf*) or грози́ть* (*impf*) кому́-н *+instr*; **to ~ to do** угрожа́ть (*impf*) or грози́ть* (*impf*) *+infin*.
threatening ['θrɛtnɪŋ] *adj* угрожа́ющий*.
three [θri:] *n* три*; (*collective*) тро́е*; *see also* **five**.
three-dimensional [θri:dɪ'mɛnʃənl] *adj* (*object*) трёхме́рный; (*film, picture, image*) стереоскопи́ческий.
threefold ['θri:fəuld] *adv*: **to increase ~**

увели́чиваться (увели́читься *perf*) в три ра́за.
three-piece suit ['θri:pi:s-] *n* (костю́м)-тро́йка *m*.
three-piece suite *n* мя́гкая ме́бель *f*.
three-ply [θri:'plaɪ] *adj* трёхсло́йный.
three quarters *npl* три* че́тверти; **~ ~ full** по́лный* на три че́тверти.
three-wheeler (car) [θri:'wi:ləʳ(-)] *n* трехколёсная маши́на.
thresh [θrɛʃ] *vt* молоти́ть* (*impf*).
threshing machine ['θrɛʃɪŋ-] *n* (*old*) молоти́лка*.
threshold ['θrɛʃhəuld] *n* (*also fig*) поро́г; **to be on the ~ of** (*fig*) быть* (*impf*) на поро́ге *+gen*.
threshold agreement *n* (*ECON*) спо́соб приведе́ния в соотве́тствие за́работной пла́ты рабо́тников со сто́имостью жи́зни.
threw [θru:] *pt of* **throw**.
thrift [θrɪft] *n* бережли́вость *f*.
thrifty ['θrɪftɪ] *adj* бережли́вый (бережли́в).
thrill [θrɪl] *n* тре́пет ◆ *vi* трепета́ть* (*impf*) ◆ *vt* (*person, audience*) восхища́ть (восхити́ть* *perf*); **to be ~ed** быть* (*impf*) в восто́рге; **I am ~ed** я восто́ржен.
thriller ['θrɪləʳ] *n* три́ллер.
thrilling ['θrɪlɪŋ] *adj* захва́тывающий*.
thrive [θraɪv] (*pt* **thrived** *or* **throve**, *pp* **thrived**) *vi* (*child, animal, business*) процвета́ть (*impf*); (*plant*) разраста́ться (разрасти́сь* *perf*); **to ~ on sth** процвета́ть (*impf*) на чём-н.
thriving ['θraɪvɪŋ] *adj* процвета́ющий.
throat [θrəut] *n* го́рло; **I have a sore ~** у меня́ боли́т го́рло.
throb [θrɔb] *n* (*of heart*) бие́ние; (*of wound*) пульса́ция; (*of engine*) вибра́ция ◆ *vi* (*heart*) би́ться* (*impf*); (*with pain: arm*) ныть* (*impf*); (*machine: vibrate*) вибри́ровать* (*impf*); **my head is ~bing** у меня́ гуди́т голова́.
throes [θrəuz] *npl*: **in the ~ of** (*war, moving house etc*) в лихора́дке *+gen*; **death ~** сме́ртельные му́ки.
thrombosis [θrɔm'bəusɪs] *n* тромбо́з.
throne [θrəun] *n* трон.
throng ['θrɔŋ] *n* толпа́* ◆ *vt* заполня́ть (запо́лнить *perf*).
throttle ['θrɔtl] *n* (*AUT*) дро́ссель *m* ◆ *vt* (*strangle*) души́ть* (задуши́ть* *perf*).
through [θru:] *prep* (*space*) че́рез *+acc*; (*water etc*) в *+acc*; (*time*) в тече́ние *+gen*; (*by means of*) че́рез *+acc*, посре́дством *+gen*; (*owing to*) из-за *+gen* ◆ *adj* (*ticket, train*) прямо́й ◆ *adv* наскво́зь; **he is absent ~ illness** он отсу́тствовал по боле́зни; **(from) Monday ~ Friday** (*US*) с понеде́льника по пя́тницу; **to put sb ~ to sb** (*TEL*) соединя́ть (соедини́ть *perf*) кого́-н с кем-н; **to be ~** (*TEL*) дозвони́ться (*perf*); **to be ~ with sb/sth** пока́нчивать (поко́нчить *perf*) с кем-н/чем-н; **"no ~ road"** (*BRIT*) "нет сквозно́го прое́зда"; **"no ~ traffic"** (*US*) "нет сквозно́го

движéния"; **to let sb** ~ пропускáть
(пропустúть* *perf*) когó-н.
throughout [θru:'aut] *prep* (*place*) по +*dat*;
(*time*) в течéние +*gen* ♦ *adv* вездé, повсюду.
throughput ['θru:put] *n* пропускнáя
спосóбность *f*; (*COMPUT*) производúтель-
ность *f*.
throve [θrəuv] *pt of* **thrive**.
throw [θrəu] (*pt* **threw**, *pp* **thrown**) *n* бросóк* ♦
vt (*object*) бросáть (брóсить* *perf*); (*rider*)
сбрáсывать (сбрóсить* *perf*); (*fig: person*)
сбивáть (сбить* *perf*) с тóлку; (*pottery*)
обрабáтывать (обрабóтать *perf*) на
гончáрном крýге; **to ~ a party** устрáивать
(устрóить* *perf*) вéчер; **to ~ open** (*doors,
windows*) распáхивать (распахнýть* *perf*);
(*competition, race etc*) открывáть (открыть*
perf)
▶ **throw about** *vt* (*litter etc*) разбрáсывать
(разбросáть *perf*)
▶ **throw around** *vt* = **throw about**
▶ **throw away** *vt* (*rubbish*) выбрáсывать
(выбросить* *perf*); (*money*) бросáть (*impf*) на
вéтер
▶ **throw off** *vt* сбрáсывать (сбрóсить* *perf*)
▶ **throw out** *vt* (*rubbish, person*) выбрáсывать
(выбросить* *perf*); (*idea*) отвергáть
(отвéргнуть* *perf*)
▶ **throw together** *vt* (*clothes, meal etc*)
сооружáть (соорудúть* *perf*); (*essay*)
набрáсывать (набросáть *perf*)
▶ **throw up** *vi* (*vomit*) рвать* (вырвать* *perf*);
he threw up егó вырвало.
throwaway ['θrəuəwei] *adj* (*toothbrush etc*)
однорáзовый; (*line, remark*) скáзанный
невзначáй.
throwback ['θrəubæk] *n*: **it's a ~ to** э́то возврáт
к +*dat*.
throw-in ['θrəuin] *n* (*FOOTBALL*) вбрáсывание.
thrown [θrəun] *pp of* **throw**.
thru [θru:] (*US*) = **through**.
thrush [θrʌʃ] *n* (*ZOOL*) дрозд*; (*MED*)
молóчница.
thrust [θrʌst] (*pt, pp* **thrust**) *n* (*TECH*) двúжущая
сúла; (*push*) толчóк*; (*main idea*)
направлéние ♦ *vt* толкáть (толкнýть* *perf*).
thud [θʌd] *n* глухóй стук.
thug [θʌg] *n* (*criminal*) головорéз; (*pej*)
бандúт.
thumb [θʌm] *n* (*ANAT*) большóй пáлец* (*рукú*)
♦ *vt*: **to ~ a lift** (*inf*) голосовáть* (*impf*); **to give
sb/sth the ~s up** (*approve*) одобрять
(одóбрить *perf*) когó-н/что-н; **to give sth the
~s down** отвергáть (отвéргнуть *perf*) что-н
▶ **thumb through** *vt fus* перелúстывать
(перелистáть *perf*).
thumb index *n* бýквенный указáтель *m* (*на
обрéзе кнúги*).

thumbnail ['θʌmneil] *n* нóготь* *m* (*большóго
пáльца рукú*).
thumbnail sketch *n* набрóсок*.
thumbtack ['θʌmtæk] *n* (*US*) кнóпка*.
thump [θʌmp] *n* (*blow*) удáр; (*sound*) глухóй
стук ♦ *vt* (*person*) стýкнуть (*perf*) ♦ *vi* (*heart
etc*) стучáть (*impf*).
thumping ['θʌmpiŋ] *adj* (*inf: majority, victory
etc*) громáдный; (: *headache, cold*) жýткий*.
thunder ['θʌndər] *n* гром ♦ *vi* (*shout*) ревéть
(*impf*); (*train etc*): **to ~ past** громыхáть
(прогромыхáть *perf*) мúмо; **it's ~ing** гремúт
гром.
thunderbolt ['θʌndəbəult] *n* удáр мóлнии.
thunderclap ['θʌndəklæp] *n* раскáт грóма.
thunderous ['θʌndrəs] *adj* (*applause*)
оглушúтельный; (*crash*) громовóй.
thunderstorm ['θʌndəstɔ:m] *n* грозá*.
thunderstruck ['θʌndəstrʌk] *adj* (*fig*): **I was ~** я
был потрясён.
thundery ['θʌndəri] *adj* грозовóй.
Thur(s). *abbr* = **Thursday**.
Thursday ['θə:zdi] *n* четвéрг*; *see also* **Tuesday**.
thus [ðʌs] *adv* такúм óбразом.
thwart [θwɔ:t] *vt* (*person*) чинúть (*impf*)
препятствия +*dat*; (*plans*) расстрáивать
(расстрóить *perf*).
thyme [taim] *n* тимьян.
thyroid ['θairɔid] *n* (*also: ~ gland*) щитовúдная
железá.
tiara [ti'ɑ:rə] *n* тиáра.
Tiber ['taibər] *n*: **the ~** Тибр.
Tibet [ti'bet] *n* Тибéт.
Tibetan [ti'bɛtən] *adj* тибéтский* ♦ *n*
тибéтец*(-éтка*); (*LING*) тибéтский* язык*.
tibia ['tibiə] *n* большеберцóвая кость* *f*.
tic [tik] *n* тик.
tick [tik] *n* (*sound: of clock*) тúканье; (*mark*)
гáлочка*; (*ZOOL*) клещ* ♦ *vi* (*clock*) тúкать
(*impf*) ♦ *vt* отмечáть (отмéтить* *perf*)
гáлочкой; **to put a ~ against sth** стáвить* (постáвить* *perf*) гáлочку рядом с чем-н; **in a ~**
(*BRIT: inf*) минýточку; **to buy sth on ~** (*BRIT:
inf*) покупáть (купúть* *perf*) что-н в кредúт
▶ **tick off** *vt* (*item on list*) отмечáть (отмéтить*
perf) гáлочкой; (*person*) отчúтывать
(отчитáть *perf*)
▶ **tick over** *vi* (*engine*) рабóтать (*impf*) на
холостóм ходý; (*fig: business*) идтú* (*impf*)
свойм чередóм.
ticker tape ['tikəteip] *n* тúкерная лéнта, тúкер;
(*US: in celebrations*) *серпантúн из тúкерной
лéнты*.
ticket ['tikit] *n* билéт; (*price tag*) этикéтка*;
(*from cash register*) чек; (*also: parking ~*)
штраф за нарушéние прáвил парковáния;
(*US: POL*) спúсок* кандидáтов пáртии.
ticket agency *n* (*THEAT*) театрáльная кáсса.

ticket collector *n* контролёр.
ticket holder *n* владе́лец(-лица) биле́та.
ticket inspector *n* контролёр.
ticket office *n* биле́тная ка́сса.
tickle ['tɪkl] *vt* щекота́ть* (пощекота́ть* *perf*) ◆
   vi щекота́ть* (*impf*).
ticklish ['tɪklɪʃ] *adj* (*problem*) щекотли́вый
   (щекотли́в); (*blanket*) колю́чий* (колю́ч);
   (*cough*) перша́щий; (*person*): **to be ~**
   боя́ться* (*impf*) щеко́тки.
tidal ['taɪdl] *adj* (*force*) прили́вный; (*estuary*)
   прили́во-отли́вный.
tidal wave *n* прили́вная волна́*.
tidbit ['tɪdbɪt] *n* (*US*) = **titbit**.
tiddlywinks ['tɪdlɪwɪŋks] *n* блёшки *pl*.
tide [taɪd] *n* прили́в и отли́в; (*fig: of events*)
   волна́*; (*of fashion, opinion*) направле́ние;
   high ~ по́лная вода́*, вы́сшая то́чка
   прили́ва; **low ~** ма́лая вода́*, ни́зшая то́чка
   отли́ва
► **tide over** *vt* (*help out*): **this money will ~ me
   over till Monday** на э́ти де́ньги я смогу́
   продержа́ться до понеде́льника.
tidily ['taɪdɪlɪ] *adv* (*dress*) опря́тно; (*arrange*)
   аккура́тно.
tidiness ['taɪdɪnɪs] *n* опря́тность *f*; (*of person*)
   аккура́тность *f*.
tidy ['taɪdɪ] *adj* опря́тный* (опря́тен); (*person,
   mind*) аккура́тный* (аккура́тен) ◆ *vt* (*also: ~
   up*) прибира́ть (прибра́ть* *perf*); **to ~ o.s. up**
   приводи́ть* (привести́* *perf*) себя́ в поря́док.
tie [taɪ] *n* (*string etc*) шнуро́к*; (*BRIT: also:
   necktie*) га́лстук; (*fig: link*) связь *f*; (*SPORT:
   game, match*) игра́ вничью́; (: *draw*) ничья́;
   (*US: RAIL*) шпа́ла ◆ *vt* завя́зывать (завяза́ть*
   perf) ◆ *vi* (*SPORT etc*) игра́ть (сыгра́ть* *perf*)
   вничью́; **"black/white ~"** *пара́дный костю́м*;
   family ~s семе́йные у́зы; **to ~ sth in a bow**
   завя́зывать (завяза́ть* *perf*) что-н ба́нтом; **to
   ~ a knot in sth** завя́зывать (завяза́ть* *perf*)
   что-н узло́м
► **tie down** *vt* (*fig: person*) свя́зывать (связа́ть*
   perf)
► **tie in** *vi*: **to ~ in with** (*correspond*)
   увя́зываться (*impf*) с +*instr*
► **tie on** *vt* (*BRIT: label etc*) привя́зывать
   (привяза́ть* *perf*)
► **tie up** *vt* (*dog, boat*) привя́зывать
   (привяза́ть* *perf*); (*prisoner, parcel*)
   свя́зывать (связа́ть* *perf*); (*arrangements*)
   организова́ть (*impf/perf*); **I'm ~d up at the
   moment** (*busy*) я сейча́с о́чень за́нят.
tie-break ['taɪbreɪk] *n* (*TENNIS*) реша́ющий гейм
   по́сле ниче́йного се́та; (*in quiz*)
   дополни́тельный реша́ющий* вопро́с.
tiebreaker ['taɪbreɪkə'] *n* = **tie-break**.
tie-on ['taɪɔn] *adj* (*BRIT: label*) привязно́й.
tiepin ['taɪpɪn] *n* (*BRIT*) була́вка* для га́лстука.
tier [tɪə'] *n* (*of stadium etc*) я́рус; (*of cake*) слой*.
Tierra del Fuego [tɪ'ɛrədɛl'fweɪgəu] *n*
   О́гненная Земля́*.

tie tack *n* (*US*) = **tiepin**.
tiff [tɪf] *n* размо́лвка*.
tiger ['taɪgə'] *n* тигр.
tight [taɪt] *adj* (*firm: rope*) туго́й; (*narrow:
   shoes, bend, clothes*) у́зкий* (у́зок); (*strict:
   security*) стро́гий*; (*schedule, budget*)
   жёсткий* ◆ *adv* (*hold, squeeze*) кре́пко; (*shut*)
   пло́тно; **money is ~** у меня́ ту́го с деньга́ми;
   he is ~ (*inf: drunk*) он навеселе́; **the suitcase is
   packed ~** чемода́н ту́го наби́т; **everybody
   hold ~!** все держи́тесь кре́пко!
tighten ['taɪtn] *vt* (*rope*) натя́гивать (натяну́ть*
   perf); (*screw*) подтя́гивать (подтяну́ть* *perf*);
   (*grip*) кре́пче сжима́ть (сжать* *perf*);
   (*security*) уси́ливать (уси́лить *perf*) ◆ *vi* (*grip*)
   кре́пче сжима́ться (сжа́ться* *perf*); (*rope*)
   натя́гиваться (натяну́ться* *perf*).
tightfisted [taɪt'fɪstɪd] *adj* прижи́мистый
   (прижи́мист).
tight-lipped ['taɪt'lɪpd] *adj* скры́тный*
   (скры́тен); (*fig: through anger*) с поджа́тыми
   губа́ми.
tightly ['taɪtlɪ] *adv* (*grasp*) кре́пко.
tightrope ['taɪtrəup] *n* натя́нутый кана́т; **to be
   on** *or* **walking a ~** (*fig*) ходи́ть* (*impf*) по
   острию́ ножа́.
tightrope walker *n* канатохо́дец*.
tights [taɪts] *npl* (*BRIT*) колго́тки* *pl*.
tigress ['taɪgrɪs] *n* тигри́ца.
tilde ['tɪldə] *n* (*LING*) ти́льда.
tile [taɪl] *n* (*on roof*) черепи́ца; (*on floor*)
   пли́тка*; (*on wall*) ка́фельная пли́тка* ◆ *vt*: **to
   ~ the floor/bathroom** выкла́дывать
   (вы́ложить* *perf*) пол/ва́нную пли́ткой; **~s**
   (*on wall*) ка́фель *m*; **to ~ the roof** крыть*
   (покры́ть* *perf*) кры́шу черепи́цей.
tiled [taɪld] *adj* (*see n*) черепи́чный;
   пли́точный; ка́фельный.
till [tɪl] *n* (*in shop etc*) ка́сса ◆ *vt* (*land*) возде́л-
   ывать (возде́лать *perf*) ◆ *prep, conj* = **until**.
tiller ['tɪlə'] *n* (*NAUT*) ру́мпель *m*.
tilt [tɪlt] *vt* наклоня́ть (наклони́ть* *perf*); (*head*)
   склоня́ть (склони́ть *perf*) ◆ *vi* наклоня́ться
   (наклони́ться* *perf*) ◆ *n* (*slope*) накло́н; **to
   wear one's hat at a ~** носи́ть* (*impf*) шля́пу
   набекре́нь; **(at) full ~** во весь дух.
timber ['tɪmbə'] *n* (*material*) древеси́на; (*trees*)
   лес.
time [taɪm] *n* вре́мя* *nt*; (*epoch: often pl*)
   времена́ *pl*, вре́мя*; (*occasion, also MATH*)
   раз; (*MUS*) разме́р, темп ◆ *vt* (*measure time
   of: race etc*) засека́ть (засе́чь* *perf*) вре́мя
   +*gen*; (*fix moment for: visit etc*) выбира́ть
   (вы́брать* *perf*) вре́мя для +*gen*; **a long ~**
   до́лго; **for the ~ being** пока́; **4 at a ~** по
   четы́ре; **from ~ to ~** вре́мя от вре́мени; **~
   after ~, time and again** сно́ва и сно́ва; **at ~s**
   времена́ми; **in ~** во́время; (*after a time*) со
   вре́менем; (*MUS: be*) в та́кте; (: *play*) в такт;
   in a week's ~ че́рез неде́лю; **in no ~** в два
   счёта; **any ~** в любо́е вре́мя; **on ~** во́время;

to be 30 mins behind/ahead of ~ опа́здывать
(опозда́ть *perf*)/опережа́ть (опереди́ть* *perf*)
на 30 мину́т; **by the** ~ **he arrived** к тому́
вре́мени, когда́ он пришёл; **five** ~**s five**
пя́тью пять; **what** ~ **is it?** кото́рый час?; **to
have a good** ~ хорошо́ проводи́ть*
(провести́* *perf*) вре́мя; **we had a hard** ~ нам
бы́ло о́чень тяжело́; ~**'s up!** вре́мя истекло́!;
I've no ~ **for it** (*fig*) мне э́то не интересу́ет;
he'll do it in his own (good) ~ (*without being
hurried*) он сде́лает э́то не торопя́сь; **he'll do
it in** *or* (*US*) **on his own** ~ (*out of working hours*)
он сде́лает э́то в свобо́дное (в нерабо́чее)
вре́мя*; **to be behind the** ~**s** отстава́ть*
(отста́ть* *perf*) от вре́мени; **to** ~ **sth well/
badly** выбира́ть (вы́брать* *perf*) подходя́щее/
неподходя́щее вре́мя для чего́-н; **the bomb
was** ~**d to go off 5 minutes later** часово́й
механи́зм бо́мбы до́лжен был срабо́тать
че́рез 5 мину́т.

time and motion study *n* ана́лиз
эффекти́вности рабо́ты.
time bomb *n* бо́мба с часовы́м механи́змом;
(*fig*) бо́мба заме́дленного де́йствия.
timecard [ˈtaɪmkɑːd] *n* хрынока́рта.
time clock *n* (*in factory etc*) часы́-та́бель *m*.
time-consuming [ˈtaɪmkənsjuːmɪŋ] *adj*
отнима́ющий мно́го вре́мени.
time difference *n* ра́зница во вре́мени.
time frame *n*: **within a broad/narrow** ~ ~ в
тече́ние продолжи́тельного/коро́ткого
отре́зка вре́мени.
time-honoured [ˈtaɪmɒnəd] (*US* **time-honored**)
adj освящённый века́ми.
timekeeper [ˈtaɪmkiːpəʳ] *n* судья́*-
хронометри́ст; **she's a very good** ~ она́
о́чень пунктуа́льная.
time-lag [ˈtaɪmlæg] *n* (*BRIT*) (временно́й)
промежу́ток вре́мени.
timeless [ˈtaɪmlɪs] *adj* ве́чный* (ве́чен).
time limit *n* преде́льный срок.
timely [ˈtaɪmlɪ] *adj* своевре́менный*
(своевре́менен).
time off *n* свобо́дное вре́мя* *nt*.
timer [ˈtaɪməʳ] *n* (*time switch*) та́ймер.
timesaving [ˈtaɪmseɪvɪŋ] *adj* (*gadget, method
etc*) эконо́мящий вре́мя.
timescale [ˈtaɪmskeɪl] *n* (*BRIT*) вре́мя* *nt*,
пери́од вре́мени.
time-share [ˈtaɪmʃɛəʳ] *n* жильё в куро́ртной
зо́не, находя́щееся в совме́стном владе́нии
нескольких лиц.
time sharing *n* (*COMPUT*) разделе́ние вре́мени,
режи́м разделе́ния вре́мени.
time sheet *n* = **timecard.**
time signal *n* (*RADIO*) сигна́л вре́мени.
time switch *n* та́ймер, выключа́тель *m* с
часовы́м механи́змом.

timetable [ˈtaɪmteɪbl] *n* расписа́ние.
time zone *n* часово́й по́яс*.
timid [ˈtɪmɪd] *adj* ро́бкий* (ро́бок).
timidity [tɪˈmɪdɪtɪ] *n* ро́бость *f*.
timing [ˈtaɪmɪŋ] *n* (*SPORT*) хронометра́ж; **the** ~
of his resignation was unfortunate вы́бор
вре́мени его́ отста́вки был неуда́чен.
timing device *n* (*on bomb*) часово́й
механи́зм.
timpani [ˈtɪmpənɪ] *npl* лита́вры *fpl*.
tin [tɪn] *n* (*material*) о́лово; (*container*) (~ **plate**) бе́лая
жесть *f*; (*container*) (жестяна́я) ба́нка*; (: *for
baking*) проти́вень* *m*; (: *BRIT*: **can**)
консе́рвная ба́нка*; **we'll need 2** ~**s of paint**
(*quantity*) нам ну́жно бу́дет 2 ба́нки кра́ски.
tinfoil [ˈtɪnfɔɪl] *n* фольга́.
tinge [tɪndʒ] *n* отте́нок* ♦ *vt*: ~**d with** с
отте́нком*.
tingle [ˈtɪŋgl] *vi* пока́лывать (*impf*); **I was
tingling with excitement** я горе́л от
возбужде́ния.
tinker [ˈtɪŋkəʳ] *n* (*gipsy*) бродя́чий луди́льщик
▸ **tinker with** *vt fus* вози́ться* (*impf*) с +*instr*.
tinkle [ˈtɪŋkl] *vi* звя́кать (звя́кнуть *perf*) ♦ *n*
(*inf*): **to give sb a** ~ (*TEL*) звя́кнуть (*perf*)
кому́-н.
tin mine *n* оловя́нный рудни́к*.
tinned [tɪnd] *adj* (*BRIT*) консерви́рованный.
tinnitus [ˈtɪnɪtəs] *n* звон в уша́х.
tinny [ˈtɪnɪ] *adj* (*pej*: *sound*) металли́ческий*;
(: *car etc*) как консе́рвная ба́нка.
tin-opener [ˈtɪnəʊpnəʳ] *n* (*BRIT*) консе́рвный
нож*.
tinsel [ˈtɪnsl] *n* мишура́.
tint [tɪnt] *n* отте́нок*; (*for hair*) кра́ска ♦ *vt* (*hair*)
кра́сить* (покра́сить* *perf*).
tinted [ˈtɪntɪd] *adj* (*hair*) кра́шеный; (*spectacles,
glass*) ды́мчатый.
tiny [ˈtaɪnɪ] *adj* кро́шечный* (кро́шечен).
tip [tɪp] *n* (*of pen etc*) ко́нчик; (*on umbrella etc*)
наконе́чник; (*gratuity*) чаевы́е *pl adj*; (*BRIT*: *for
rubbish*) сва́лка*; (: *for coal*) гора́*; (*advice*)
сове́т ♦ *vt* (*waiter*) дава́ть* (дать* *perf*) на чай
+*dat*; (*tilt*) наклоня́ть (наклони́ть* *perf*); (*also*:
~ **over**) опроки́дывать (опроки́нуть *perf*);
(*also*: ~ **out**) выва́ливать (вы́валить *perf*);
(*winner etc*) уга́дывать (угада́ть* *perf*); (*for a
job etc*) про́чить (*impf*); **he** ~**ped out the
contents of the box** он вы́валил содержи́мое
я́щика
▸ **tip off** *vt* предупрежда́ть (предупреди́ть*
perf).
tip-off [ˈtɪpɔf] *n* предупрежде́ние.
tipped [ˈtɪpt] *adj* (*BRIT*: *cigarette*) с фи́льтром;
steel-~ со стальны́м наконе́чником.
Tipp-Ex® [ˈtɪpɛks] *n* ≈ штрих®, Ти́пекс.
tipple [ˈtɪpl] (*BRIT*) *vi* выпива́ть (*impf*) ♦ *n*: **to
have a** ~ выпива́ть (вы́пить* *perf*) по

мáленькой.

tipster ['tɪpstə'] *n* жучóк* (*на скáчках*).

tipsy ['tɪpsɪ] *adj* (*inf*) хмельнóй* (хмелён).

tiptoe ['tɪptəu] *n*: **on ~** на цы́почках.

tiptop ['tɪptɔp] *adj*: **in ~ condition** в прекрáсном состоя́нии.

tirade [taɪ'reɪd] *n* тирáда.

Tirana [tɪ'rɑːnə] *n* Тирáна.

tire ['taɪə'] *n* (*US*) = **tyre** ♦ *vt* (*make tired*) утомля́ть (утоми́ть* *perf*) ♦ *vi* уставáть* (устáть* *perf*)

▶ **tire out** *vt* (*exhaust*) выма́тывать (вы́мотать *perf*).

tired ['taɪəd] *adj* устáлый (устáл); **I am ~** я устáл; **he feels ~** он чу́вствует себя́ устáвшим; **you look ~** Вы вы́глядите устáлым; **to be ~ of sth** уставáть* (устáть* *perf*) от чегó-н.

tiredness ['taɪədnɪs] *n* устáлость *f*.

tireless ['taɪəlɪs] *adj* (*worker, efforts*) неутоми́мый (неутоми́м).

tiresome ['taɪəsəm] *adj* надоéдливый (надоéдлив).

tiring ['taɪərɪŋ] *adj* утоми́тельный* (утоми́телен).

tissue ['tɪʃuː] *n* (*handkerchief*) бумáжная салфéтка*; (*ANAT, BIO*) ткань *f*.

tissue paper *n* папирóсная *or* тóнкая обёрточная бумáга.

tit [tɪt] *n* (*ZOOL*) сини́ца; (*inf: breast*) си́ська*; **to give ~ for tat** отплáчивать (отплати́ть* *perf*) зуб за зуб.

titanium [tɪ'teɪnɪəm] *n* титáн.

titbit ['tɪtbɪt] (*US* **tidbit**) *n* (*food*) лáкомый кусóчек*; (*news*) пикáнтная нóвость* *f*.

titillate ['tɪtɪleɪt] *vt* (*person, senses*) возбуждáть (возбуди́ть* *perf*).

titivate ['tɪtɪveɪt] *vt* (*oneself*) прихорáшиваться (*impf*); (*place*) украшáть (укрáсить* *perf*).

title ['taɪtl] *n* (*of book, play etc*) назвáние; (*rank, BOXING etc*) ти́тул; (*LAW*): **~ to** прáво* на +*acc*.

title deed *n* (*LAW*) докумéнт, подтверждáющий прáво сóбственности.

title page *n* ти́тульный лист*.

title role *n* (*in play, film*) глáвная роль *f*.

title track *n* назвáние пéсни или музыкáльной пьéсы, котóрое тáкже явля́ется назвáнием пласти́нки, альбóма, плёнки итп.

titter ['tɪtə'] *vi* хихи́кать (хихи́кнуть *perf*).

tittle-tattle ['tɪtltætl] *n* (*inf*) болтовня́.

tizzy ['tɪzɪ] *n*: **to be in a ~** волновáться (разволновáться *perf*) по пустякáм.

T-junction ['tiː'dʒʌŋkʃən] *n* (*AUT*) Т-обрáзный перекрёсток*.

TM *abbr* = **trademark, transcendental meditation**.

TN *abbr* (*US: POST*) = **Tennessee**.

TNT *n abbr* (= *trinitrotoluene*) троти́л.

KEYWORD

to [tuː] *prep* **1** (*direction*) в/на +*acc*; **to drive to school/the station** éхать*/éздить* (поéхать*

---

perf) в шкóлу/на стáнцию; **the road to Edinburgh** дорóга в Эдинбу́рг; **to the left** налéво; **to the right** напрáво

2 (*as far as*) до +*gen*; **from Paris to London** от Пари́жа до Лóндона; **to count to ten** считáть* (посчитáть* *perf*) до десяти́

3 (*with expressions of time*): **a quarter to five** без чéтверти пять

4 (*for, of*): **a letter to his wife** письмó женé; **the key to the front door** ключ от входнóй двéри; **she is secretary to the director** онá секретáрь дирéктора

5 (*expressing indirect object*): **to give sth to sb** давáть* (дать* *perf*) что-н комý-н; **to talk to sb** разговáривать (*impf*) *or* говори́ть (*impf*) с кем-н; **what have you done to your hair?** что Вы сдéлали с свои́ми волосáми

6 (*in relation to*) к +*dat*; **A is to B as C is to D** "А" отнóсится к "Б", как "В" отнóсится к "Г"; **three goals to two** три два; **X miles to the gallon** Х ли́тров на киломéтр; **1500 roubles to the dollar** 1500 рублéй за дóллар

7 (*purpose, result*) к +*dat*; **to my surprise** к моемý удивлéнию; **to come to sb's aid** приходи́ть* (прийти́* *perf*) комý-н на пóмощь

♦ *with vb* **1** переводи́ться неопределённой фóрмой глагóла; **to want/try to do** хотéть* (захотéть* *perf*)/пытáться (попытáться *perf*) +*infin*; **he has nothing to lose** емý нéчего теря́ть; **ready to use** готóв к употреблéнию; **too old/young to ...** сли́шком стар/мóлод, чтóбы +*infin* ...

2 (*with vb omitted*): **I don't want to** я не хочý; **I don't feel like going – you really ought to** мне не хóчется идти́ – нет, Вы должны́

3 (*purpose, result*) чтóбы +*infin*; **I did it to help you** я сдéлал э́то, чтóбы помóчь Вам

♦ *adv*: **push/pull the door to** закрывáть (закры́ть* *perf*) дверь.

---

toad [təud] *n* (*ZOOL*) жáба.

toadstool ['təudstuːl] *n* (*BOT*) погáнка*.

toady ['təudɪ] *vi* (*pej*): **to ~ to sb** подхали́мничать (*impf*) пéред кем-н.

toast [təust] *n* (*CULIN*) тост; (*drink, speech*) тост ♦ *vt* (*CULIN: bread etc*) поджáривать (поджáрить *perf*); (*drink to*) пить* (вы́пить* *perf*) за +*acc*; **a piece** *or* **slice of ~** лóмтик тóста.

toaster ['təustə'] *n* тóстер.

toastmaster ['təustmɑːstə'] *n* тамадá *m*.

toast rack *n* подстáвка для тóстов.

tobacco [tə'bækəu] *n* табáк*; **pipe ~** трýбочный табáк*.

tobacconist [tə'bækənɪst] *n* торгóвец*(-вка*) табáчными издéлиями.

tobacconist's (shop) [tə'bækənɪsts-] *n* табáчная лáвка.

Tobago [tə'beɪgəu] *n see* **Trinidad**.

toboggan [tə'bɔgən] *n* (*child's*) сáнки *pl*.

today [tə'deɪ] *adv, n* сего́дня; **what day is it ~?** како́й сего́дня день?; **what date is it ~?** како́е сего́дня число́?; **~ is the 4th of March** сего́дня 4-ое ма́рта; **a week ago ~** ро́вно неде́лю наза́д.

toddle ['tɔdl] (*inf*) *vi*: **to ~ in** проковыля́ть (*impf*); **to ~ along** *or* **off** прико́выля́ть (*impf*).

toddler ['tɔdlə'] *n* малы́ш*.

to-do [tə'du:] *n* (*fuss*) шум.

toe [təu] *n* (*of foot*) па́лец* (*ноги́*); (*of shoe, sock*) носо́к*; **to ~ the line** (*fig*) ходи́ть* (*impf*) по стру́нке; **big ~** большо́й па́лец* (*ноги́*); **little ~** мизи́нец* (*ноги́*).

TOEFL *n abbr* = Teaching of English as a Foreign Language.

toehold ['təuhəuld] *n* (*in climbing*) то́чка опо́ры; (*fig*): **to get** *or* **gain a ~** находи́ть* (найти́* *perf*) то́чку опо́ры.

toenail ['təuneɪl] *n* но́готь* *m* (*на па́льце ноги́*).

toffee ['tɔfɪ] *n* ири́ска*, тяну́чка*.

toffee apple *n* (*BRIT*) я́блоко на па́лочке, глази́рованное ири́сом.

toga ['təugə] *n* то́га.

together [tə'gɛðə'] *adv* вме́сте; (*at same time*) одновреме́нно; **~ with** вме́сте с +*instr*.

togetherness [tə'gɛðənɪs] *n* бли́зость *f*.

toggle switch ['tɔgl-] *n* (*COMPUT*) ту́мблер, переключа́тель *m*.

Togo ['təugəu] *n* То́го *m ind*.

togs [tɔgz] *npl* (*inf: clothes*) оде́жды *fpl*.

toil [tɔɪl] *n* тяжёлый труд* ♦ *vi* рабо́тать (*impf*) в по́те лица́.

toilet ['tɔɪlət] *n* унита́з; (*BRIT: room*) туале́т ♦ *cpd* (*kit, accessories etc*) туале́тный; **to go to the ~** ходи́ть* (сходи́ть* *perf*) в туале́т.

toilet bag *n* (*BRIT*) туале́тная су́мочка.

toilet bowl *n* унита́з.

toilet paper *n* туале́тная бума́га.

toiletries ['tɔɪlətrɪz] *npl* туале́тные принадле́жности *fpl*.

toilet roll *n* руло́н туале́тной бума́ги.

toilet soap *n* туале́тное мы́ло.

toilet water *n* туале́тная вода́.

toing and froing ['tu:ɪŋən'frəuɪŋ] *n* (*BRIT: on foot*) ходьба́ туда́-обра́тно; (: *by transport*) езда́ туда́-обра́тно.

token ['təukən] *n* (*sign, souvenir*) знак; (*substitute coin*) жето́н ♦ *adj* (*strike, payment etc*) символи́ческий; **by the same ~** по той же причи́не; **book/gift ~** (*BRIT*) кни́жный/пода́рочный тало́н; **record ~** (*BRIT*) тало́н на пласти́нку.

tokenism ['təukənɪzəm] *n* ви́димость *f*.

Tokyo ['təukjəu] *n* То́кио *m ind*.

told [təuld] *pt, pp of* **tell**.

tolerable ['tɔlərəbl] *adj* (*bearable*) терпи́мый (терпи́м); (*fairly good*) сно́сный* (сно́сен).

tolerably ['tɔlərəblɪ] *adv*: **~ good** дово́льно хорошо́.

tolerance ['tɔlərns] *n* (*patience*) терпи́мость *f*; (*also TECH*) до́пуск.

tolerant ['tɔlərnt] *adj*: **~ (of)** терпи́мый (терпи́м) (к +*dat*).

tolerate ['tɔləreɪt] *vt* терпе́ть* (*impf*).

toleration [tɔlə'reɪʃən] *n* терпи́мость *f*.

toll [təul] *n* (*of casualties, deaths*) число́; (*tax, charge*) пла́та ♦ *vi* (*bell*) звони́ть (*impf*); **the accident ~ on the roads** число́ ава́рий на доро́гах.

toll bridge *n* (*AUT*) пла́тный мост*.

toll call *n* (*US*) междугоро́дный телефо́нный звоно́к*.

toll-free ['təul'fri:] *adj* (*US*) беспла́тный.

toll road *n* (*AUT*) пла́тная доро́га.

tomato [tə'mɑ:təu] (*pl ~es*) *n* помидо́р.

tomato purée *n* тома́тная па́ста.

tomb [tu:m] *n* моги́ла.

tombola [tɔm'bəulə] *n* лотере́я.

tomboy ['tɔmbɔɪ] *n* (*girl*) сорване́ц*.

tombstone ['tu:mstəun] *n* надгро́бная плита́*.

tomcat ['tɔmkæt] *n* кот*.

tome [təum] *n* том*.

tomorrow [tə'mɔrəu] *adv, n* (*also fig*) за́втра; **the day after ~** послеза́втра; **a week ~/on Monday** че́рез неде́лю, счита́я с за́втрашнего дня/с понеде́льника; **~ morning** за́втра у́тром.

ton [tʌn] *n* (*BRIT*) дли́нная то́нна; (*US: also: short ~*) коро́ткая то́нна; (*also: metric ~*) метри́ческая то́нна; (*NAUT: also: register ~*) реги́стровая то́нна; **~s of** (*inf*) то́нны +*gen*.

tonal ['təunl] *adj* тона́льный.

tone [təun] *n* тон*; (*TEL*) гудо́к* ♦ *vi* (*colours: also: ~ in*) сочета́ться (*impf*)

▸ **tone down** *vt* (*colour, criticism, demands*) смягча́ть (смягчи́ть* *perf*); (*sound*) уменьша́ть (уме́ньшить *perf*)

▸ **tone up** *vt* (*muscles*) укрепля́ть (укрепи́ть* *perf*).

tone-deaf [təun'dɛf] *adj* без слу́ха.

toner ['təunə] *n* (*for photocopier*) черни́ла.

Tonga [tɔŋə] *n* То́нга.

tongs [tɔŋz] *npl* щипцы́ *pl*.

tongue [tʌŋ] *n* язы́к*; **~ in cheek** (*speak, say*) в шу́тку.

tongue-tied ['tʌŋtaɪd] *adj* (*fig*): **he was ~** он лиши́лся да́ра ре́чи.

tongue twister [-twɪstə'] *n* скорогово́рка.

tonic ['tɔnɪk] *n* (*MED*) тонизи́рующее сре́дство; (*also: ~ water*) то́ник; (*MUS*) то́ника.

tonight [tə'naɪt] *adv* (*this evening*) сего́дня ве́чером; (*this night*) сего́дня но́чью ♦ *n* (*see adv*) сего́дняшний ве́чер; сего́дняшняя ночь *f*; (**I'll**) **see you ~!** до ве́чера!

tonnage ['tʌnɪdʒ] *n* (*NAUT*) тонна́ж.

tonne [tʌn] *n* (*BRIT: metric ton*) то́нна.

---

* marks translations which have irregular inflections. The Russian-English side of the dictionary gives inflectional information.

tonsil ['tɒnsl] n (gen pl) минда́лина; **to have one's ~s out** удаля́ть (удали́ть perf) минда́лины.

tonsillitis [tɒnsɪ'laɪtɪs] n тонзилли́т.

too [tu:] adv (excessively) сли́шком; (also: referring to subject) та́кже, то́же; (: referring to object) та́кже; **the tea is ~ sweet** чай сли́шком сла́дкий; **I went ~** я то́же пошёл; **~ much, ~ many** сли́шком мно́го; **~ bad!** о́чень жаль!

took [tʊk] pt of **take**.

tool [tu:l] n инструме́нт; (fig: person) ору́дие.

tool box n я́щик для инструме́нтов.

tool kit n набо́р инструме́нтов.

toot [tu:t] n (of horn) гудо́к*; (of whistle) свисто́к* ♦ vi (with car horn) сигна́лить (просигна́лить perf).

tooth [tu:θ] (pl **teeth**) n (ANAT) зуб*; (TECH) зубе́ц*; **to have a ~ out** or (US) **pulled** удаля́ть (удали́ть perf) or вырыва́ть (вы́рвать* perf) зуб; **to brush one's teeth** чи́стить* (почи́стить* perf) зу́бы; **by the skin of one's teeth** (fig) чу́дом.

toothache ['tu:θeɪk] n зубна́я боль f; **I have ~** у меня́ боли́т зуб.

toothbrush ['tu:θbrʌʃ] n зубна́я щётка.

toothpaste ['tu:θpeɪst] n зубна́я па́ста.

toothpick ['tu:θpɪk] n зубочи́стка*.

tooth powder n зубно́й порошо́к*.

top [tɒp] n (of mountain) верши́на; (of tree) верху́шка*; (of head) маку́шка*; (of ladder) верх*; (of page, list etc) нача́ло; (of cupboard, table, box) ве́рхняя пове́рхность f; (lid: of box, jar) кры́шка*; (: bottle) про́бка*; (AUT: also: ~ **gear**) са́мая вы́сшая ско́рость f; (also: **spinning ~**) юла́, волчо́к*; (blouse etc) верх ♦ adj (shelf, step) ве́рхний*; (marks) вы́сший*; (salesman etc) веду́щий*; (best) вы́сший* ♦ vt (poll, vote) лиди́ровать (impf) в +prp; (list) возглавля́ть (возгла́вить* perf); (exceed: estimate etc) превыша́ть (превы́сить* perf); **the ~ of the milk** (BRIT) сли́вки* pl (на молоке́); **at the ~ of the stairs/page** на верху́ ле́стницы/страни́цы; **at the ~ of the street** в да́льнем конце́ у́лицы; **on ~ of** (above: be) на +prp; (: put etc) на +acc; (in addition to) сверх +gen; **put the book on ~ of the table** положи́те кни́гу на стол; **from ~ to bottom** све́рху до́низу; **from ~ to toe** (BRIT) с головы́ до ног or до пят; **at the ~ of the list** пе́рвый по спи́ску; **at the ~ of one's voice** во весь го́лос; **at ~ speed** на максима́льной ско́рости; **over the ~** (inf: behaviour etc) сверх ме́ры

▶ **top up** (US **top off**) vt (bottle) долива́ть (доли́ть* perf); (salary) прибавля́ть (приба́вить* perf).

topaz ['təʊpæz] n топа́з.

top-class ['tɒp'klɑ:s] adj вы́сшего кла́сса.

topcoat ['tɒpkəʊt] n ве́рхний* слой*.

top floor n ве́рхний* эта́ж*.

top hat n цили́ндр, котело́к*.

top-heavy [tɒp'hɛvɪ] adj: **~ object** предме́т с утяжелённым ве́рхом; **~ bureaucracy** бюрократи́ческий аппара́т с громо́здким ве́рхним эшело́ном.

topic ['tɒpɪk] n те́ма.

topical ['tɒpɪkl] adj актуа́льный* (актуа́лен).

topless ['tɒplɪs] adj обнажённый до по́яса.

top-level ['tɒplɛvl] adj на вы́сшем у́ровне.

topmost ['tɒpməʊst] adj (branch etc) са́мый ве́рхний or бли́жний к верху́шке.

topnotch ['tɒp'nɒtʃ] adj первосо́ртный.

topography [tə'pɒgrəfɪ] n топогра́фия.

topping ['tɒpɪŋ] n (CULIN): **with a ~ of** с ве́рхом из +gen.

topple ['tɒpl] vt (government, leader) ски́дывать (ски́нуть perf) ♦ vi (person, object) опроки́дываться (опроки́нуться perf).

top-ranking ['tɒpræŋkɪŋ] adj (official) высокопоста́вленный.

top-secret ['tɒp'si:krɪt] adj сверхсекре́тный* (сверхсекре́тен).

top-security ['tɒpsə'kjʊərɪtɪ] adj (BRIT) под уси́ленной охра́ной.

topsy-turvy ['tɒpsɪ'tə:vɪ] adj перевёрнутый ♦ adv вверх нога́ми.

top-up ['tɒpʌp] n: **would you like a ~?** Вам ещё подли́ть?

top-up loan n (BRIT) доба́вочная ссу́да.

torch [tɔ:tʃ] n (with flame) фа́кел; (BRIT: electric) фона́рь* m.

tore [tɔ:ʳ] pt of **tear**.

torment [n 'tɔ:mɛnt, vt tɔ:'mɛnt] n муче́ние ♦ vt му́чить* (impf).

torn [tɔ:n] pp of **tear**[1] ♦ adj: **she is ~ between ...** она́ разрыва́ется ме́жду +instr ....

tornado [tɔ:'neɪdəʊ] (pl **~es**) n смерч.

torpedo [tɔ:'pi:dəʊ] (pl **~es**) n торпе́да.

torpedo boat n торпе́дный ка́тер.

torpor ['tɔ:pəʳ] n оцепене́ние.

torrent ['tɒrnt] n (also fig) пото́к.

torrential [tɔ'rɛnʃl] adj (rain) проливно́й.

torrid ['tɒrɪd] adj (weather) зно́йный* (зно́ен); (love affair) бу́рный.

torso ['tɔ:səʊ] n ту́ловище, торс.

tortoise ['tɔ:təs] n черепа́ха.

tortoiseshell ['tɔ:təʃɛl] adj черепа́ховый; (cat) с тигро́вым окра́сом.

tortuous ['tɔ:tjʊəs] adj (path) изви́листый (изви́лист); (argument, mind) зау́мный* (зау́мен).

torture ['tɔ:tʃəʳ] n (also fig) пы́тка* ♦ vt (also fig) пыта́ть (impf).

torturer ['tɔ:tʃərəʳ] n пала́ч*, мучи́тель m.

Tory ['tɔ:rɪ] (BRIT: POL) adj консервати́вный ♦ n (POL) то́ри m/f ind, консерва́тор.

toss [tɒs] vt (throw) подки́дывать (подки́нуть perf), подбра́сывать (подбро́сить* perf); (one's head) отки́дывать (отки́нуть perf); (salad) меша́ть (impf) ♦ vi: **to ~ and turn** (in bed) воро́чаться (impf) ♦ n: **with a ~ of her head, she...** отки́нув го́лову, она́ ...; **to ~ a**

coin подбра́сывать (подбро́сить* perf) моне́ту; **to ~ up to do** подбра́сывать (подбро́сить* perf) моне́ту, что́бы +infin; **to win/lose the ~** выи́грывать (вы́играть perf)/ прои́грывать (проигра́ть perf) подбра́сывание моне́ты.

tot [tɔt] n (drink) глото́к*; (child) малы́ш*
▸ **tot up** vt (BRIT: figures) подсчи́тывать (подсчита́ть perf).

total ['təutl] adj (number, workforce etc) о́бщий*; (failure, wreck etc) по́лный ♦ n о́бщая су́мма ♦ vt (add up) скла́дывать (сложи́ть perf); (add up to) составля́ть (соста́вить* perf); **in ~** в о́бщей сло́жности.

totalitarian [təutælɪ'tɛərɪən] adj (POL) тоталита́рный.

totality [təu'tælɪtɪ] n полнота́.

totally ['təutəlɪ] adv по́лностью; (unprepared) соверше́нно.

tote bag [təut-] n сума́.

totem pole ['təutəm-] n тоте́мный столб*.

totter ['tɔtəʳ] vi (person) ходи́ть*/идти́* (impf) шата́ясь or ша́ткой похо́дкой; (fig: government) занима́ть (impf) ша́ткую пози́цию.

touch [tʌtʃ] n осяза́ние; (approach) мане́ра; (detail) штрих; (contact) прикоснове́ние ♦ vt (with hand, foot) каса́ться (косну́ться perf) +gen, тро́гать (тро́нуть perf); (tamper with) тро́гать (impf); (make contact with) прикаса́ться (прикосну́ться perf) к +dat; дотра́гиваться (дотро́нуться perf) до +gen; (emotionally) тро́гать (тро́нуть perf); **the personal ~** индивидуа́льность f; **to put the finishing ~es to sth** вноси́ть* (внести́* perf) после́дние штрихи́ в что-н; **there's been a ~ of frost** подморо́зило; **in ~ with** в конта́кте с +instr; **to get in ~ with sb** связа́ться* (perf) с кем-н; **I'll be in ~ with you** я свяжу́сь с Ва́ми; **to lose ~** (friends) теря́ть (потеря́ть perf) связь; **to be out of ~ with events** быть* (impf) не в ку́рсе собы́тий
▸ **touch on** vt fus каса́ться (косну́ться perf) +gen
▸ **touch up** vt (paint) подкра́шивать (подкра́сить* perf).

touch-and-go ['tʌtʃən'gəu] adj нея́сный* (нея́сен); **it was ~ whether we'd succeed** бы́ло нея́сно, вы́шло ли э́то у нас.

touchdown ['tʌtʃdaun] n (of rocket, plane) поса́дка*; (US: FOOTBALL) гол.

touched [tʌtʃt] adj тро́нутый (тро́нут).

touching ['tʌtʃɪŋ] adj (scene, photograph etc) тро́гательный* (тро́гателен).

touchline ['tʌtʃlaɪn] n (SPORT) бокова́я ли́ния.

touch-sensitive ['tʌtʃ'sɛnsɪtɪv] adj сраба́тывающий на прикоснове́ние.

touch-type ['tʌtʃtaɪp] vi печа́тать (impf) слепы́м ме́тодом.

touchy ['tʌtʃɪ] adj (person) оби́дчивый (оби́дчив); (subject) больно́й; **he is ~** его́ легко́ заде́ть.

tough [tʌf] adj (strong, hard-wearing: material) кре́пкий (кре́пок), про́чный* (про́чен); (meat, policies, negotiations) жёсткий*; (person: physically) выно́сливый (выно́слив); (: mentally) сто́йкий* (сто́ек); (task, problem, journey) тяжёлый (тяжёл); (rough) опа́сный* (опа́сен); **~ luck!** не везёт!

toughen ['tʌfn] vt закаля́ть (закали́ть perf).

toughness ['tʌfnɪs] n про́чность f; (of person) сто́йкость f.

toupee ['tu:peɪ] n (wig) пари́к*.

tour ['tuəʳ] n (journey) пое́здка*; (also: **package ~**) туристи́ческая пое́здка*; (of town, factory, museum) экску́рсия; (by pop group etc) гастро́ли fpl ♦ vt (country, city) объезжа́ть (объе́хать* perf); (factory) обходи́ть* (обойти́* perf); **to go on a ~ of** (museum, region) осма́тривать (осмотре́ть* perf); **to go on ~** (band) е́здить*/е́хать* (impf) на гастро́ли.

touring ['tuərɪŋ] n гастроли́рование.

tourism ['tuərɪzm] n (business) тури́зм.

tourist ['tuərɪst] n тури́ст*(ка*) ♦ cpd (attractions, season) тури́стский*; **the ~ trade** инду́стрия тури́зма.

tourist class n (NAUT, AVIAT) второ́й класс.

tourist information centre n (BRIT) туристи́ческое бюро́ nt ind.

tourist office n туристи́ческое бюро́ nt ind.

tournament ['tuənəmənt] n турни́р, состяза́ние.

tourniquet ['tuənɪkeɪ] n жгут, турнике́т.

tour operator n (BRIT) рабо́тник туристи́ческой фи́рмы.

tousled ['tauzld] adj (hair) взъеро́шенный (взъеро́шен).

tout [taut] n (also: **ticket ~**) спекуля́нт(ка*) ♦ vi: **to ~ for** (business) добива́ться (impf) +gen, выбива́ть (impf) ♦ vt: **to ~ sth (around)** (BRIT) спекули́ровать* (impf) чем-н.

tow [təu] n (vehicle, caravan, trailer) везти́*/ вози́ть* (impf) на букси́ре ♦ n: **to give sb a ~** (AUT) брать* (взять* perf) кого́-н на букси́р; **"on** or **(US) in ~"** (AUT) "на букси́ре".

toward(s) [tə'wɔ:d(z)] prep к +dat; (purpose): **~ doing** с тем что́бы +infin; **towards noon/the end of the year** к полу́дню/концу́ го́да; **to feel friendly ~ sb** относи́ться* (impf) дружелю́бно к кому́-н.

towel ['tauəl] n (also: **hand ~**) полоте́нце* для рук; (also: **bath ~**) ба́нное полоте́нце*; **to throw in the ~** (fig) сдава́ться* (сда́ться* perf).

towelling ['tauəlɪŋ] n (fabric) махро́вая ткань f.

towel rail (US **towel rack**) n ве́шалка* для

полотéнец.

tower ['tauə'] *n* бáшня* ◆ *vi* (*building, mountain*) возвышáться (*impf*); **to ~ above** *or* **over sb/sth** возвышáться (*impf*) над кем-н/чем-н.

tower block *n* (*BRIT*) бáшня*, высóтный дом*.

towering ['tauərɪŋ] *adj* возвышáющийся.

towline ['təulaɪn] *n* буксúрный трос.

town [taun] *n* гóрод*; **to go to ~** ходúть*/идтú* (*impf*) в гóрод; (*fig*) разорáться (разорúться *perf*); **in ~** в гóроде; **to be out of ~** (*person*) быть* (*impf*) в отъéзде.

town centre *n* цéнтр (гóрода).

town clerk *n* глáвный делопроизводúтель *m* городскóго совéта.

town council *n* городскóй совéт.

town crier [-'kraɪə'] *n* глашáтай.

town hall *n* рáтуша.

townie ['taunɪ] *n* (*inf*) городскóй(-áя) *m(f) adj*.

town plan *n* план гóрода.

town planner *n* градострóитель *m*, планирóвщик.

town planning *n* городскóе планúрование, градострóительство.

township ['taunʃɪp] *n* (*in South Africa*) негритáнский* прúгород; (*in America*) городскóй райóн.

townspeople ['taunzpi:pl] *npl* горожáне *mpl*.

towpath ['təupɑ:θ] *n* (*of canal*) тропúнка.

towrope ['təurəup] *n* буксúрный трос.

tow truck *n* (*US*) аварúйная машúна.

toxic ['tɔksɪk] *adj* токсúчный* (токсúчен).

toxic waste *n* ядовúтые отхóды *mpl*.

toxin ['tɔksɪn] *n* токсúн.

toy [tɔɪ] *n* игрýшка*

▶ **toy with** *vt fus* (*object*) игрáть (*impf*) +*instr*; (*food*) возúться* (*impf*) с +*instr*; (*idea*) игрáть (*impf*) с +*instr*.

toy shop *n* магазúн игрýшек.

trace [treɪs] *n* след* ◆ *vt* (*draw*) переводúть* (перевестú* *perf*); (*follow*) прослéживать (проследúть* *perf*); (*locate*) устанáвливать (установúть* *perf*); **without ~** (*disappear*) бесслéдно, без слéда; **there was no ~ of him** он исчéз без слéда.

trace element *n* микроэлемéнт.

tracer ['treɪsə'] *n* (*also:* **~ bullet**) трассúрующий снарáд.

trachea [trə'kɪə] *n* трахéя.

tracing paper ['treɪsɪŋ-] *n* кáлька.

track [træk] *n* · ·ед*; (*path*) тропá*; (*of bullet etc*) траектó· ля; (*RAIL*) (железнодорóжный) путь* *m*; (*on tape, record, also SPORT*) дорóжка* ◆ *vt* (*follow: animal, person*) идтú* (*impf*) по слéду +*gen*; **to keep ~ of** следúть* (*impf*) за +*instr*; **to be on the right ~** (*fig*) быть* (*impf*) на вéрном путú

▶ **track down** *vt* (*prey*) выслéживать (вúследить* *perf*); (*sth lost*) отúскивать (отыскáть* *perf*).

tracked [trækt] *adj* (*AUT*) гýсеничный.

tracker dog ['trækə-] *n* (*BRIT*) собáка-ищéйка.

track events *npl* соревновáния *ntpl* по лёгкой атлéтике.

tracking station ['trækɪŋ-] *n* пульт управлéния полётом.

track meet *n* (*SPORT*) соревновáния *ntpl* по атлéтике.

track record *n*: **to have a good ~ ~** (*fig*) имéть (*impf*) хорóшую репутáцию.

tracksuit ['træksu:t] *n* трениóвочный костюм.

tract [trækt] *n* (*GEO*) пространствó; (*pamphlet*) трактáт; **respiratory ~** (*ANAT*) дыхáтельные путú *mpl*; **digestive ~** желýдочно-кишéчный тракт.

traction ['trækʃən] *n* (*power*) тáга; (*AUT: grip*) сúла сцеплéния; (*MED*): **in ~** в вытяжéнии.

traction engine *n* тягáч*.

tractor ['træktə'] *n* трáктор.

trade [treɪd] *n* (*activity*) торгóвля; (*skill, job*) род занáтий ◆ *vi* (*do business*) торговáть* (*impf*) ◆ *vt*: **to ~ sth (for sth)** обмéнивать (обменáть *perf*) что-н (на что-н); **to ~ with/in** торговáть* (*impf*) с +*instr*/+*instr*; **foreign ~** внéшняя торгóвля; **Department of T~ and Industry** (*BRIT*) Министéрство торгóвли и промýшленности

▶ **trade in** *vt* (*old car etc*) предлагáть (предложúть* *perf*) для встрéчной продáжи.

trade barrier *n* торгóвый барьéр.

trade deficit *n* торгóвый дефицúт.

Trade Descriptions Act *n* (*BRIT: LAW, COMM*) положéние о торгóвле.

trade discount *n* торгóвая скúдка* (óптовым торгóвцам).

trade fair *n* торгóвая áрмарка*.

trade figures *npl* показáтель *msg* товарооборóта.

trade-in ['treɪdɪn] *n*: **to take as a ~** принимáть (принáть* *perf*) как встрéчную продáжу.

trade-in price *n* ценá* с учётом встрéчной продáжи.

trademark ['treɪdmɑ:k] *n* товáрный знак.

trade mission *n* торгóвое представúтельство.

trade name *n* торгóвоеназвáние.

trade-off ['treɪdɔf] *n* компромúсс.

trade price *n* торгóвая ценá.

trader ['treɪdə'] *n* торгóвец*.

trade reference *n* информáция о состоáнии дел фúрмы.

trade secret *n* промýшленный секрéт.

tradesman ['treɪdzmən] *irreg n* рабóтник; (*shopkeeper*) торгóвец*, лáвочник.

trade union *n* профсоюз= *профессионáльный союз*.

trade unionist [-'ju:njənɪst] *n* член профсоюза.

trade wind *n* (*GEO*) пассáт.

trading ['treɪdɪŋ] *n* торгóвля.

trading account *n* счёт расчётов.

trading estate *n* (*BRIT*) промýшленная зóна.

trading stamps *npl* *бумáжные мáрки с*

объя́вленной сто́имостью.
tradition [trəˈdɪʃən] *n* тради́ция.
traditional [trəˈdɪʃənl] *adj* (*also fig*) традицио́нный*.
traditionally [trəˈdɪʃnəlɪ] *adv* традицио́нно.
traffic [ˈtræfɪk] *n* (*of people, vehicles*) движе́ние; (*of drugs etc*) нелега́льная торго́вля ♦ *vi*: **to ~ in** (*liquor, drugs*) нелега́льно торгова́ть* (*impf*) +*instr.*
traffic circle *n* (*US*) кольцева́я тра́нспортная развя́зка*.
traffic island *n* острово́к* безопа́сности.
traffic jam *n* про́бка*.
trafficker [ˈtræfɪkəʳ] *n* (*also*: **drug ~**) торго́вец* нарко́тиками.
traffic lights *npl* светофо́р *msg.*
traffic offence *n* (*BRIT*) наруше́ние пра́вил доро́жного движе́ния.
traffic sign *n* доро́жный знак.
traffic violation *n* (*US*) = **traffic offence.**
traffic warden *n* (*BRIT*) регулиро́вщик паркова́ния маши́н на у́лицах го́рода.
tragedy [ˈtrædʒdɪ] *n* траге́дия.
tragic [ˈtrædʒɪk] *adj* траги́ческий.
tragically [ˈtrædʒɪkəlɪ] *adv* траги́чески.
trail [treɪl] *n* (*path*) доро́жка*, тропи́нка*; (*track*) след; (*of smoke, dust*) хвост* ♦ *vt* (*drag*) волочи́ть* (*impf*); (*follow*: *person, animal*) сле́довать (*impf*) по пята́м за +*instr* ♦ *vi* (*hang loosely*) волочи́ться* (*impf*); (*in game, contest*) волочи́ться* (*impf*) в хвосте́, отстава́ть* (*impf*); **to be on sb's ~** устра́ивать (устро́ить *perf*) слёжку за кем-н
▶ **trail away** *vi* (*sound, voice*) затиха́ть (зати́хнуть *perf*)
▶ **trail behind** *vi* (*lag*) волочи́ться* (*impf*) в хвосте́
▶ **trail off** *vi* = **trail away.**
trailer [ˈtreɪləʳ] *n* (*AUT*) прице́п; (*US*: *caravan*) автоприце́п; (*CINEMA*) кинорекла́ма, ано́нс.
trailer tent *n* прице́п с пала́ткой.
trailer truck *n* (*US*) грузови́к* с прице́пом.
train [treɪn] *n* по́езд*; (*of dress*) шлейф ♦ *vt* (*apprentice, doctor etc*) учи́ть* (обучи́ть* *perf*); (*athlete, mind*) тренирова́ть (*impf*); (*dog*) дрессирова́ть (вы́дрессировать *perf*); (*plant*) приуча́ть (приучи́ть* *perf*) ♦ *vi* (*learn a skill*) учи́ться* (обучи́ться* *perf*); (*SPORT*) тренирова́ться (*impf*); **one's ~ of thought** ход чьих-н мы́слей; **~ of events** цепь *f* собы́тий; **to go by ~** е́здить*/е́хать* (*impf*) по́ездом *or* на по́езде; **to ~ sb to do** обуча́ть (обучи́ть* *perf*) кого́-н +*impf infin*; **to ~ sb as** учи́ть* (*impf*) кого́-н на +*acc*; **to ~ on** (*camera etc*) направля́ть (напра́вить* *perf*) на +*acc.*
train attendant *n* (*US*) проводни́к.
trained [treɪnd] *adj* (*worker, teacher*) подгото́вленный; (*animal*) трениро́ванный;

(*eye*) натрениро́ванный* (натрениро́ван).
trainee [treɪˈniː] *n* (*hairdresser*) учени́к*; **~ teacher** студе́нт(ка*) практика́нт.
trainer [ˈtreɪnəʳ] *n* (*coach*) тре́нер; (*of animals*) дрессиро́вщик(-щица); **~s** *npl* (*sports shoes*) кроссо́вки *fpl.*
training [ˈtreɪnɪŋ] *n* (*for occupation*) обуче́ние, подгото́вка*; (*SPORT*) трениро́вка; **to be in ~** (*SPORT*) тренирова́ться (*impf*).
training college *n* (*for teachers*) педагоги́ческий* институ́т.
training course *n* курс профессиона́льной подгото́вки.
traipse [treɪps] *vi*: **to ~ through** прита́скиваться (притащи́ться* *perf*).
trait [treɪt] *n* черта́.
traitor [ˈtreɪtəʳ] *n* преда́тель(ница) *m(f).*
trajectory [trəˈdʒɛktərɪ] *n* траекто́рия.
tram [træm] *n* (*BRIT*) трамва́й.
tramcar [ˈtræmkɑː] *n* (*BRIT*) = **tram.**
tramline [ˈtræmlaɪn] *n* трамва́йная ли́ния.
tramp [træmp] *n* (*person*) бродя́га *m/f*; (*inf*: *pej*: *woman*) шлю́ха ♦ *vi* броди́ть* (*impf*) ♦ *vt* (*town, streets*) броди́ть*/брести́* (*impf*) по +*dat.*
trample [ˈtræmpl] *vt*: **to ~ (underfoot)** раста́пывать (растопта́ть* *perf*) ♦ *vi* (*fig*): **to ~ on** раста́птывать (растопта́ть* *perf*).
trampoline [ˈtræmpəliːn] *n* трампли́н.
trance [trɑːns] *n* (*also fig*) транс; **to go into a ~** входи́ть* (войти́* *perf*) в транс.
tranquil [ˈtræŋkwɪl] *adj* безмяте́жный* (безмяте́жен).
tranquillity [træŋˈkwɪlɪtɪ] (*US* **tranquility**) *n* безмяте́жность *f.*
tranquillizer [ˈtræŋkwɪlaɪzəʳ] (*US* **tranquilizer**) *n* (*MED*) транквилиза́тор.
transact [trænˈzækt] *vt* (*business*) вести́* (*impf*).
transaction [trænˈzækʃən] *n* (*piece of business*) опера́ция; **cash ~** опла́та нали́чными.
transatlantic [ˈtrænzətˈlæntɪk] *adj* трансатланти́ческий.
transcend [trænˈsɛnd] *vt* (*boundaries, loyalties etc*) выходи́ть* (вы́йти* *perf*) за преде́лы +*gen.*
transcendental [trænsɛnˈdɛntl] *adj*: **~ meditation** трансценде́нтная медита́ция.
transcribe [trænˈskraɪb] *vt* переписывать (переписа́ть* *perf*), транскриби́ровать (*impf*/ *perf*).
transcript [ˈtrænskrɪpt] *n* (*typed*) печа́тная ко́пия; (*hand-written*) рукопи́сная ко́пия.
transcription [trænˈskrɪpʃən] *n* транскри́пция.
transept [ˈtrænsɛpt] *n* трансе́пт.
transfer [ˈtrænsfəʳ] *n* перево́д; (*POL*) переда́ча; (*SPORT*) трансфе́р; (*picture etc*) переводна́я карти́нка ♦ *vt* (*employees, money etc*) переводи́ть* (перевести́* *perf*); (*POL, SPORT*)

---

* marks translations which have irregular inflections. The Russian-English side of the dictionary gives inflectional information.

передава́ть* (переда́ть* perf); **to ~ the charges**
(*BRIT: TEL*) звони́ть (позвони́ть perf) по
колле́кту; **by bank ~** по ба́нковскому
перево́ду.
transferable [træns'fə:rəbl] adj (ticket)
перево́дный, с пра́вом переда́чи; **"not ~"**
"без пра́ва переда́чи".
transfix [træns'fɪks] vt (person, animal)
пронза́ть (пронзи́ть* perf); (fig): **~ed with fear**
пронзённый стра́хом.
transform [træns'fɔ:m] vt (person, situation etc)
преобража́ть (преобрази́ть* perf).
transformation [trænsfə'meɪʃən] n
преобразова́ние, перевоплоще́ние.
transformer [træns'fɔ:məʳ] n трансформа́тор.
transfusion [træns'fju:ʒən] n (also: **blood ~**)
перелива́ние кро́ви.
transgress [træns'grɛs] vt преступа́ть
(преступи́ть* perf) грани́цы +gen.
transient ['trænzɪənt] adj мимолётный*
(мимолётен).
transistor [træn'zɪstəʳ] n (ELEC) транзи́сторное
устро́йство; (also: **~ radio**) транзи́стор.
transit ['trænzɪt] n: **in ~** (people, things)
транзи́том.
transit camp n перева́лочный пункт.
transition [træn'zɪʃən] n перехо́д.
transitional [træn'zɪʃənl] adj перехо́дный.
transitive ['trænzɪtɪv] adj (LING) перехо́дный.
transit lounge n зал транзи́тных
пассажи́ров.
transitory ['trænzɪtərɪ] adj преходя́щий*.
transit visa n транзи́тная ви́за.
translate [trænz'leɪt] vt: **to ~** (from/into)
переводи́ть* (перевести́* perf) (с +gen/на
+acc).
translation [trænz'leɪʃən] n перево́д; (SCOL: as
opposed to prose) перево́д на родно́й язы́к.
translator [trænz'leɪtəʳ] n перево́дчик(-ица).
translucent [trænz'lu:snt] adj (object, quality)
прозра́чный* (прозра́чен);
просве́чивающий.
transmission [trænz'mɪʃən] n переда́ча; (AUT)
коро́бка переда́ч, приво́д.
transmit [trænz'mɪt] vt передава́ть* (переда́ть*
perf).
transmitter [trænz'mɪtəʳ] n (equipment)
переда́тчик.
transparency [trænz'pɛərnsɪ] n (of glass etc)
прозра́чность f; (BRIT: PHOT) диапозити́в.
transparent [træns'pærnt] adj прозра́чный*
(прозра́чен).
transpire [trænz'paɪəʳ] vi (turn out) выясня́ться
(вы́ясниться perf); (happen) происходи́ть*
(произойти́* perf); **it finally ~d that ...** наконе́ц
вы́яснилось, что ....
transplant [n 'trænsplɑ:nt, vt træns'plɑ:nt] n
переса́дка* ◆ vt (MED, seedlings)
переса́живать (пересади́ть* perf); **he had a
heart ~** ему́ сде́лали переса́дку се́рдца.
transport [n 'trænspɔ:t, vt træns'pɔ:t] n

тра́нспорт; (moving people, goods)
перево́зка* ◆ vt (carry) перевози́ть*
(перевезти́* perf); **public ~** обще́ственный
тра́нспорт; **Department of T~** (BRIT)
Министе́рство тра́нспорта.
transportation ['trænspɔ:'teɪʃən] n (transport)
транспортиро́вка*, перево́зка*; (means of
transport) тра́нспорт; **Department of T~** (US)
Министе́рство тра́нспорта.
transport café n (BRIT) доро́жное кафе́ nt ind.
transpose [træns'pəuz] vt перемеща́ть
(перемести́ть* perf).
transsexual [trænz'sɛksuəl] n транссексуа́л.
transverse ['trænzvə:s] adj (beam etc)
попере́чный.
transvestite [trænz'vɛstaɪt] n трансвести́т.
trap [træp] n западня́, лову́шка; (carriage)
двуко́лка* ◆ vt (fig) лови́ть* (пойма́ть perf) в
лову́шку or западню́; (confine) запира́ть
(запере́ть* perf); (immobilize) ско́вывать
(скова́ть perf); (jam) защемля́ть (защеми́ть*
perf); **to set** or **lay a ~** (for sb) расставля́ть
(расста́вить* perf) лову́шку or западню́
(кому́-н); **to shut one's ~** (inf) затыка́ть
(заткну́ть perf) свою́ гло́тку; **to ~ one's finger
in the door** защемля́ть (защеми́ть* perf) себе́
па́лец.
trap door n люк.
trapeze [trə'pi:z] n трапе́ция.
trapper ['træpəʳ] n ловец*.
trappings ['træpɪŋz] npl атрибу́ты mpl.
trash [træʃ] n (rubbish: also pej) сор, му́сор;
(: nonsense) чушь f.
trash can n (US) му́сорное ведро́*.
trashy ['træʃɪ] adj (inf) дрянно́й*.
trauma ['trɔ:mə] n тра́вма.
traumatic [trɔ:'mætɪk] adj травмати́ческий.
traumatize ['trɔ:mətaɪz] vt травми́ровать*
(impf/perf).
travel ['trævl] n (travelling) путеше́ствия ntpl ◆
vi (for pleasure) путеше́ствовать (impf);
(commute) е́здить* (impf); (move)
передвига́ться (impf); (news, sound)
распространя́ться (распространи́ться perf);
(wine, food) сохраня́ться (impf) при
перево́зке ◆ vt (distance: by transport)
проезжа́ть (прое́хать* perf); (: on foot)
проходи́ть* (пройти́* perf); **~s** npl (journeys)
путеше́ствия ntpl.
travel agency n туристи́ческое аге́нтство.
travel agent n рабо́тник туристи́ческого
аге́нтства.
travel brochure n рекла́мная брошю́ра для
тури́стов.
traveller ['trævləʳ] (US **traveler**) n
путеше́ственник(-ица); (COMM)
коммивояжёр.
traveller's cheque (US **traveler's check**) n
доро́жный чек.
travelling ['trævlɪŋ] (US **traveling**) n (for
pleasure) путеше́ствия ntpl; (from necessity)

переéзды *mpl* ◆ *cpd* (*circus, exhibition*)
передвижнóй; (*bag, clock, expenses*)
дорóжный.
travel(l)ing salesman *irreg n* коммивояжёр.
travelogue ['trævəlɔg] *n* (*book*) кнѝга о
путешéствиях.
travel-sickness ['trævlsɪknɪs] *n* (*on ship*)
морскáя болéзнь *f*; **he suffers from travel
sickness** (*in car*) егó укáчивает в машѝне.
traverse ['trævəs] *vt* пересекáть (пересéчь*
perf).
travesty ['trævəstɪ] *n* парóдия.
trawler ['trɔ:lə'] *n* трáулер.
tray [treɪ] *n* (*for carrying*) поднóс; (*on desk*)
корзѝнка.
treacherous ['trɛtʃərəs] *adj* (*person*)
веролóмный* (веролóмен); (*look, action*)
предáтельский*; (*ground, tide*) ковáрный*
(ковáрен); **road conditions are ~**
склáдывается слóжная дорóжная
обстанóвка.
treachery ['trɛtʃərɪ] *n* предáтельство,
веролóмство.
treacle ['tri:kl] *n* (*black treacle*) пáтока; (*golden
syrup*) свéтлая *or* очѝщенная пáтока.
tread [trɛd] (*pt* **trod**, *pp* **trodden**) *n* (*step*)
похóдка; (*sound*) пóступь *f*; (*of stair*) ступéнь
f; (*of tyre*) протéктор ◆ *vi* ступáть (*impf*)
▶ **tread on** *vt fus* наступáть (наступѝть* *perf*) на
+*acc*.
treadle ['trɛdl] *n* (*on sewing machine etc*)
педáль *f*.
treas. *abbr* = **treasurer**.
treason ['tri:zn] *n* измéна.
treasure ['trɛʒə'] *n* сокрóвище ◆ *vt* (*object*)
хранѝть (*impf*) как зенѝцу óка; (*friendship*)
высóко ценѝть* (*impf*); (*memory*) свя́то
хранѝть (*impf*); (*thought*) лелéять (*impf*);
(*store*) хранѝть (*impf*); **~s** *npl* (*art treasures etc*)
сокрóвища *ntpl*.
treasure hunt *n* пóиски *mpl* сокрóвищ.
treasurer ['trɛʒərə'] *n* казначéй.
treasury ['trɛʒərɪ] *n*: **the T~**, (*US*) **the T~
Department** Госудáрственное
Казначéйство.
Treasury bill *n* (*BRIT*) казначéйский вéксель *m*.
treat [tri:t] *n* (*present*) удовóльствие ◆ *vt*
(*person, object*) обращáться (*impf* с +*instr*);
(*patient, illness*) лечѝть* (*impf*); (*TECH*: *coat*)
обрабáтывать (обрабóтать *perf*); **it was a ~**
э́то бы́ло наслаждéние; **to ~ sth as a joke**
относѝться* (отнестѝсь *perf*) к чему́-н
несерьёзно; **to ~ sb to sth** угощáть
(угостѝть* *perf*) когó-н чем-н.
treatment ['tri:tmənt] *n* (*attention, handling*)
обращéние; (*MED*) лечéние; **to have ~ for sth**
проходѝть* (пройтѝ* *perf*) курс лечéния от
чегó-н.

treaty ['tri:tɪ] *n* соглашéние.
treble ['trɛbl] *adj* (*triple*) тройнóй; (*MUS*: *voice,
part*) дискáнтный, сопрáно *ind*; (: *instrument*)
сопрáнов ◆ *n* (*MUS*) дискáнт, сопрáно *m ind*;
(*on hi-fi, radio etc*) высóкие частóты *fpl* ◆ *vt*
утрáивать (утрóить *perf*) ◆ *vi* утрáиваться
(утрóиться *perf*); **to be ~ the size of sth** быть*
(*impf*) бóльше чегó-н втрóе.
treble clef *n* скрипѝчный ключ*.
tree [tri:] *n* дéрево*.
tree-lined ['tri:laɪnd] *adj* усáженный
дерéвьями.
treetop ['tri:tɔp] *n* верхýшка дéрева.
tree trunk *n* ствол дéрева.
trek [trɛk] *n* (*long difficult journey*) похóд,
перехóд ◆ *vi* (*as holiday*) идтѝ* (пойтѝ* *perf*) в
похóд.
trellis ['trɛlɪs] *n* шпалéра.
tremble ['trɛmbl] *vi* дрожáть (*impf*).
trembling ['trɛmblɪŋ] *n* дрожáние ◆ *adj* (*hand,
voice etc*) дрожáщий.
tremendous [trɪ'mɛndəs] *adj* (*enormous*)
огрóмный* (огрóмен); (*excellent*)
великолéпный* (великолéпен).
tremendously [trɪ'mɛndəslɪ] *adv* чрезвычáйно;
he enjoyed it ~ он получѝл огрóмное
удовóльствие от э́того.
tremor ['trɛmə'] *n* (*trembling*) дрожь *f*,
содрогáние; (*also*: **earth ~**) толчóк*
(землетрясéния).
trench [trɛntʃ] *n* канáва; (*MIL*) траншéя, окóп.
trench coat *n* тёплая полушинéль *f*.
trench warfare *n* окóпная войнá*.
trend [trɛnd] *n* (*tendency*) тендéнция; (*of
events, fashion*) направлéние; **~ towards sth**
тендéнция к чему́-н; **~ away from sth** отхóд
от чегó-н; **to set the ~** задавáть* (задáть*
perf) направлéние; **to set a ~** задавáть*
(задáть* *perf*) тон.
trendy ['trɛndɪ] *adj* мóдный* (мóден).
trepidation [trɛpɪ'deɪʃən] *n* (*apprehension*)
трéпет; **in ~** в трéпете.
trespass ['trɛspəs] *vi*: **to ~ on** (*private property*)
вторгáться (втóргнуться *perf*) в +*acc*; **"no
~ing"** "вход воспрещён".
trespasser ['trɛspəsə'] *n* вторгáющийся(-ая)
m(f) adj в чáстные владéния; **"trespassers will
be prosecuted"** "лицá, вторгáющиеся на
дáнную территóрию бýдут преслéдоваться
закóном".
tress [trɛs] *n* (*of hair*) косá*.
trestle ['trɛsl] *n* кóзлы *pl*.
trestle table *n* стол* на кóзлах.
trial ['traɪəl] *n* (*LAW*) процéсс, суд*; (*test: of
machine etc*) испытáния *ntpl*; (*worry*)
пережива́ние; **~s** *npl* (*unpleasant experiences*)
перипетѝи *fpl*; **horse ~s** соревновáния *ntpl* по
вы́ездке; **~ by jury** суд* прися́жных; **to be**

---

* marks translations which have irregular inflections. The Russian-English side of the dictionary gives inflectional information.

sent for ~ предава́ть* (преда́ть* *perf*) суду́; **on** ~ (*LAW*) под судо́м; **by** ~ **and error** ме́тодом проб и оши́бок.

trial balance *n* (*COMM*) про́бный бала́нс.

trial basis *n*: **on a** ~ ~ на испыта́тельный срок.

trial period *n* испыта́тельный срок.

trial run *n* прого́н.

triangle ['traɪæŋgl] *n* (*MATH, MUS*) треуго́льник.

triangular [traɪ'æŋgjuləʳ] *adj* треуго́льный.

tribal ['traɪbl] *adj* (*warrior, warfare, dance*) племенно́й.

tribe [traɪb] *n* пле́мя* *nt*.

tribesman ['traɪbzmən] *irreg n* тузе́мец*.

tribulations [trɪbju'leɪʃənz] *npl* злоключе́ния *ntpl*.

tribunal [traɪ'bju:nl] *n* трибуна́л.

tributary ['trɪbjutərɪ] *n* (*of river*) прито́к*.

tribute ['trɪbju:t] *n* (*compliment*) дань *f*; **to pay** ~ **to** отдава́ть* (отда́ть* *perf*) дань +*dat*.

trice [traɪs] *n*: **in a** ~ ми́гом.

trick [trɪk] *n* (*magic trick*) фо́кус; (*prank, joke*) подво́х; (*skill, knack*) приём; (*CARDS*) взя́тка* ◆ *vt* проводи́ть* (провести́* *perf*); **to play a** ~ **on sb** разы́грывать (разыгра́ть *perf*) кого́-н; **to** ~ **sb into doing** обма́ном заставля́ть (заста́вить* *perf*) кого́-н +*infin*; **to** ~ **sb out of sth** выма́нивать (вы́манить *perf*) что-н у кого́-н; **a** ~ **of the light** игра́* све́та, опти́ческий* обма́н; **that should do the** ~ э́то должно́ срабо́тать.

trickery ['trɪkərɪ] *n* моше́нничество.

trickle ['trɪkl] *n* (*of water etc*) стру́йка ◆ *vi* (*water, rain etc*) струи́ться (*impf*); (*people*) стека́ться (*impf*) потихо́ньку.

trick question *n* хи́трый вопро́с.

trickster ['trɪkstəʳ] *n* моше́нник.

tricky ['trɪkɪ] *adj* (*job*) непросто́й; (*business*) хи́трый; (*problem*) заковы́ристый.

tricycle ['traɪsɪkl] *n* трёхколёсный велосипе́д.

trifle ['traɪfl] *n* (*small detail*) пустя́к*; (*CULIN*) *десе́рт из ке́кса, фрукто́вого желе́ и сли́вок* ◆ *adv*: **a** ~ **long** чуть длиннова́т ◆ *vi*: **to** ~ **with sb/sth** шути́ть* (*impf*) с кем-н/чем-н.

trifling ['traɪflɪŋ] *adj* пустяко́вый.

trigger ['trɪgəʳ] *n* (*of gun*) куро́к*

▸ **trigger off** *vt* (*reaction, riot*) спровоци́ровать (*perf*), вызыва́ть (вы́звать* *perf*).

trigonometry [trɪgə'nɔmətrɪ] *n* тригономе́трия *f*.

trilby ['trɪlbɪ] *n* (*BRIT*: *also*: ~ **hat**) фе́тровая шля́па.

trill [trɪl] *vi* (*birds*) залива́ться (зали́ться *perf*) ◆ *n* (*MUS*) трель *f*.

trilogy ['trɪlədʒɪ] *n* трило́гия *f*.

trim [trɪm] *adj* (*house, garden*) ухо́женный; (*figure*) подтя́нутый ◆ *n* (*cut*) подра́внивать (подровня́ть *perf*); (*NAUT*) ста́вить* (поста́вить* *perf*) по́ ветру; (*decorate*): **to** ~ (**with**) отде́лывать (отде́лать *perf*) (+*instr*); **to give sb a** ~ подра́внивать

(подровня́ть *perf*) во́лосы кому́-н; **to keep in** (**good**) ~ держа́ть* (*impf*) (в хоро́шей) фо́рме.

trimmings ['trɪmɪŋz] *npl* (*CULIN*) потроха́ *mpl*; (*cuttings*) обре́зки *mpl*.

Trinidad and Tobago ['trɪnɪdæd-] *n* Тринида́д и Тоба́го.

trinity ['trɪnɪtɪ] *n* (*group*) тро́йка; (*REL*): **the** (**Holy**) **T~** Тро́ица.

trinket ['trɪŋkɪt] *n* (*ornament*) безделу́шка*; (*jewellery*) побряку́шка*.

trio ['tri:əu] *n* тро́йка; (*MUS*) три́о *nt ind*.

trip [trɪp] *n* (*journey*) пое́здка*; (*outing*) прогу́лка* ◆ *vi* (*stumble*) спотыка́ться (споткну́ться *perf*); (*go lightly*) идти́* (*impf*) лёгкой похо́дкой; **on a** ~ на экску́рсии

▸ **trip up** *vi* (*stumble*) ста́вить* (поста́вить* *perf*) подно́жку ◆ *vt* (*person*) подставля́ть (подста́вить* *perf*) но́жку.

tripartite [traɪ'pɑ:taɪt] *adj* трёхсторо́нний*.

tripe [traɪp] *n* (*CULIN*) требуха́; (*pej*: *rubbish*) чушь *f*.

triple ['trɪpl] *adj* тройно́й ◆ *adv*: ~ **the distance/ the speed** тройно́е расстоя́ние/тройна́я ско́рость, в три ра́за да́льше/быстре́е.

triple jump *n* тройно́й прыжо́к (в длину́).

triplets ['trɪplɪts] *npl* тройня́шки* *fpl*.

triplicate ['trɪplɪkət] *n*: **in** ~ в трёх экземпля́рах.

tripod ['traɪpɔd] *n* трено́га.

Tripoli ['trɪpəlɪ] *n* Три́поли *m ind*.

tripper ['trɪpəʳ] *n* (*BRIT*) тури́ст(ка*).

tripwire ['trɪpwaɪəʳ] *n* замаскиро́ванная про́волока, свя́занная с капка́ном и́ли взрывча́ткой.

trite [traɪt] *adj* (*pej*) изби́тый.

triumph ['traɪʌmf] *n* (*satisfaction*) торжество́; (*great achievement*) триу́мф ◆ *vi*: **to** ~ (**over**) торжествова́ть (восторжествова́ть *perf*) (над +*instr*).

triumphal [traɪ'ʌmfl] *adj* (*arch, return*) триумфа́льный.

triumphant [traɪ'ʌmfənt] *adj* (*team, wave*) торжеству́ющий; (*return*) побе́дный.

triumphantly [traɪ'ʌmfəntlɪ] *adv* (*shout, look etc*) торжеству́юще.

trivia ['trɪvɪə] *npl* (*pej*) тривиа́льности *fpl*, тривиа́льные ве́щи *fpl*.

trivial ['trɪvɪəl] *adj* (*unimportant*) незначи́тельный* (незначи́телен); (*commonplace*) тривиа́льный* (тривиа́лен).

triviality [trɪvɪ'ælɪtɪ] *n* ме́лочи *fpl*.

trivialize ['trɪvɪəlaɪz] *vt* упроща́ть (упрости́ть* *perf*).

trod [trɔd] *pt of* **tread**.

trodden [trɔdn] *pp of* **tread**.

trolley ['trɔlɪ] *n* теле́жка*; (*also*: ~ **bus**) тролле́йбус.

trollop ['trɔləp] *n* (*pej*) лаху́дра.

trombone [trɔm'bəun] *n* тромбо́н.

troop [tru:p] *n* (*of people*) отря́д, гру́ппа; (*of monkeys*) ста́до ◆ *vi*: **to** ~ **in/out** входи́ть*

(войти* *perf*)/выходить* (выйти* *perf*)
строем; ~s *npl* (MIL) войска *ntpl*; a ~ of
children стайка ребятишек.
troop carrier *n* (*plane*) транспортно-
десантный самолёт; (NAUT: *also:* **troopship**)
транспорт для перевозки войск.
trooper ['truːpə^r] *n* (MIL: *in cavalry*) кавалерист;
(: *in armoured regiment*) солдат*; (US:
policeman) конный полицейский* *m adj.*
trooping the colour ['truːpɪŋ-] *n* (BRIT:
ceremony) внос знамени.
troopship ['truːpʃɪp] *n* транспорт для
перевозки войск.
trophy ['trəʊfɪ] *n* трофей.
tropic ['trɔpɪk] *n*: ~s тропики *mpl*; **in the** ~**s** в
тропиках; **T~ of Cancer/Capricorn** Тропик
Рака/Козерога.
tropical ['trɔpɪkl] *adj* (*rain forest, climate etc*)
тропический*.
trot [trɔt] *n* рысь *f* ♦ *vi* (*horse*) идти* (*impf*)
рысью; (*person*) плестись* (*impf*) рысцой; **on
the** ~ (BRIT: *fig*) подряд
▸ **trot out** *vt* (*excuse, reason*) приводить*
(привести* *perf*); (*names, facts*) сыпать (*impf*)
+*instr.*
trouble ['trʌbl] *n* (*difficulty*) затруднение;
(*worry, unrest*) беспокойство; (*bother, effort*)
хлопоты *pl* ♦ *vt* (*worry*) беспокоить (*impf*);
(*person: disturb*) беспокоить (побеспокоить
perf) ♦ *vi*: **to** ~ **to do** побеспокоиться (*perf*)
+*infin*; ~**s** *npl* (*personal, POL etc*) беды *fpl*; **to be
in** ~ иметь (*impf*) неприятности; (*ship,
climber etc*) быть* (*impf*) в беде; **to have** ~
doing с трудом мочь (*impf*) +*infin*; **to go to the
~ of doing** заботиться* (позаботиться* *perf*)
о том, чтобы +*infin*; **it's no** ~! это никак не
затруднит меня!; **it's too much** ~ слишком
много хлопот; **please don't** ~ **yourself**
пожалуйста, не беспокойтесь; **the** ~ **is** ...
беда в том, что ...; **what's the** ~? (*with broken
television etc*) где неполадки?, в чём там
дело?; (MED) что Вас беспокоит?; **stomach** ~
больной желудок.
troubled [trʌbld] *adj* (*person*) в постоянной
тревоге; (*country*) бедствующий; (*life, era*)
беспокойный.
trouble-free ['trʌblfriː] *adj* (*period, campaign
etc*) без происшествий.
troublemaker ['trʌblmeɪkə^r] *n* смутьян.
troubleshooter ['trʌblʃuːtə^r] *n* (*in conflict*)
специальный уполномоченный по
улаживанию конфликтов.
troublesome ['trʌblsəm] *adj* (*child*)
проказливый.
trouble spot *n* (MIL) горячая точка*.
troubling ['trʌblɪŋ] *adj* тревожный.
trough [trɔf] *n*: (*also:* **drinking** ~) корыто; (*also:*
feeding ~) кормушка*; (*channel*) жёлоб; (*low

point) впадина; **a** ~ **of low pressure**
(METEOROLOGY) фронт низкого давления.
trounce [traʊns] *vt* (*defeat*) разбивать
(разбить* *perf*).
troupe [truːp] *n* труппа.
trouser press ['trauzə-] *n* приспособление для
глажки брюк.
trousers ['trauzəz] *npl* брюки *mpl*; **short** ~
штаны *mpl*.
trouser suit *n* (BRIT: *for woman*) брючный
костюм.
trousseau ['truːsəu] (*pl* ~**x** *or* ~**s**) *n* приданое *nt
adj.*
trousseaux ['truːsəuz] *npl of* **trousseau**.
trout [traut] *n inv* (ZOOL) форель *f.*
trowel ['trauəl] *n* (*garden tool*) совок*; (*builder's
tool*) мастерок*.
truant ['truənt] *n* (BRIT): **to play** ~ прогуливать
(прогулять* *perf*).
truce [truːs] *n* перемирие.
truck [trʌk] *n* (*lorry*) грузовик; (RAIL) открытая
товарная платформа; (*for luggage*)
тележка*, вагонетка*.
truck driver *n* водитель *m* грузовика.
trucker ['trʌkə^r] *n* водитель *m* грузовика.
truck farm *n* (US) овощеводческая ферма.
trucking ['trʌkɪŋ] *n* (*esp US*) грузовая
транспортировка*.
trucking company *n* (US) грузовое
транспортное агентство.
truculent ['trʌkjulənt] *adj* (*person*) свирепый
(свиреп).
trudge [trʌdʒ] *vi* (*also:* ~ **along**) плестись*
(*impf*), тащиться (*impf*).
true [truː] *adj* (*real, genuine*) настоящий*,
истинный; (*accurate: likeness*) точный;
(*faithful: friend*) настоящий*; (*wall*) прямой;
(*beam, wheel*) центрированный; **to come** ~
сбываться (сбыться* *perf*); ~ **to life**
жизненный.
truffle ['trʌfl] *n* трюфель *m.*
truly ['truːlɪ] *adv* (*really*) по-настоящему;
(*truthfully*) искренне; **yours** ~ (*in letter*)
искренне Ваш.
trump [trʌmp] *n* (*also:* ~ **card**: *also fig*) козырь
m; **to turn up** ~**s** (*fig*) подавать* (подать* *perf*)
руку помощи.
trumped-up [trʌmpt'ʌp] *adj* (*pej*)
сфабрикованный.
trumpet ['trʌmpɪt] *n* труба.
truncated [trʌŋ'keɪtɪd] *adj* (*object*)
обрезанный; (*message*) сокращённый.
truncheon ['trʌntʃən] *n* (BRIT) дубинка*.
trundle ['trʌndl] *vt* (*push slowly: trolley etc*)
катить* (*impf*) ♦ *vi*: **to** ~ **along** (*person*) брести*
(*impf*); (*vehicle*) катиться* (*impf*).
trunk [trʌŋk] *n* (*of tree*) ствол*; (*of person*)
туловище*; (*of elephant*) хобот; (*case*)

---

* marks translations which have irregular inflections. The Russian-English side of the dictionary gives inflectional information.

доро́жный сунду́к; (*US*: *AUT*) бага́жник; **~s** *npl* (*also*: **swimming ~s**) пла́вки* *pl.*

trunk call *n* (*BRIT*: *TEL*) междугоро́дные переговоры *mpl*, междугоро́дный звоно́к*.

trunk road *n* (*BRIT*) магистра́ль *f.*

truss [trʌs] *n* (*MED*) грыжево́й банда́ж
▶ **truss (up)** *vt* (*CULIN*) перетя́гивать (перетяну́ть* *perf*) бечёвкой; (*person*) свя́зывать (связа́ть* *perf*).

trust [trʌst] *n* (*faith*) дове́рие; (*responsibility*) долг*; (*LAW*) *управле́ние иму́ществом по дове́ренности*; (*COMM*) трест ◆ *vt* (*rely on, have faith in*) доверя́ть (*impf*) +*dat*; (*hope*): **to ~ (that)** полага́ть (*impf*)(, что); (*entrust*): **to ~ sth to sb** доверя́ть (дове́рить *perf*) что-н кому́-н; **to take sth on ~** принима́ть (приня́ть* *perf*) что-н на ве́ру; **in ~** (*LAW*) управля́емый по дове́ренности.

trust company *n* (*COMM*) трест.

trusted ['trʌstɪd] *adj* (*friend, servant*) пре́данный.

trustee [trʌs'tiː] *n* (*also LAW*) попечи́тель *m.*

trustful ['trʌstful] *adj* (*person, nature, smile*) дове́рчивый (дове́рчив).

trust fund *n* (*COMM*) фонд тре́ста.

trusting ['trʌstɪŋ] *adj* (*person, nature*) дове́рчивый (дове́рчив).

trustworthy ['trʌstwɜ:ðɪ] *adj* (*person, report*) надёжный, заслу́живающий дове́рия.

trusty ['trʌstɪ] *adj* испы́танный.

truth [tru:θ] (*pl* ~**s**) *n* пра́вда; (*universal principle*) и́стина.

truthful ['tru:θful] *adj* правди́вый (правди́в).

truthfully ['tru:θfəlɪ] *adv* (*answer*) правди́во.

truthfulness ['tru:θfəlnɪs] *n* правди́вость *f.*

try [traɪ] *n* (*attempt*) попы́тка*; (*RUGBY*) прохо́д с мячо́м ◆ *vt* (*test*) про́бовать (попро́бовать *perf*); (*LAW*: *person*) суди́ть* (*impf*); (*strain*: *patience*) испы́тывать (*impf*); (*attempt*): **to ~ to do** стара́ться (*impf*) *or* пыта́ться (*impf*) +*infin* ◆ *vi* (*make effort, attempt*) стара́ться (*impf*), пыта́ться (*impf*); **to have a ~** про́бовать (попро́бовать *perf*); **I tried a different key** я пыта́лся откры́ть други́м ключо́м; **to ~ one's (very) best** *or* **one's (very) hardest** стара́ться (постара́ться *perf*) изо́ всех сил
▶ **try on** *vt* (*dress etc*) ме́рить (поме́рить *perf*), примеря́ть (приме́рить *perf*); **to ~ it on** (*fig*) вести́* (*impf*) себя́ на́гло
▶ **try out** *vt* про́бовать (попро́бовать *perf*).

trying ['traɪɪŋ] *adj* (*person, experience*) утоми́тельный* (утоми́телен).

tsar [zɑ:] *n* царь* *m.*

T-shirt ['ti:ʃɜ:t] *n* футбо́лка*.

T-square ['ti:skwɛə] *n* (*TECH*) рейсши́на.

TT *adj abbr* (*BRIT*: *inf*) = **teetotal** ◆ *abbr* (*US*: *POST*) = **Trust Territory**; = **telegraphic transfer** телегра́фный де́нежный перево́д.

tub [tʌb] *n* (*container*) бо́чка*; (*bath*) ва́нна.

tuba ['tju:bə] *n* ту́ба.

tubby ['tʌbɪ] *adj* упи́танный.

tube [tju:b] *n* (*pipe*) тру́бка*; (*container*) тю́бик; (*BRIT*: *underground*) метро́ *nt ind*; (*for tyre*) ка́мера; (*inf*: *television*): **the ~** те́лик.

tubeless ['tju:blɪs] *adj* беска́мерный.

tuber ['tju:bə] *n* клу́бень *m.*

tuberculosis [tjubə:kju'ləusɪs] *n* туберкулёз.

tube station *n* (*BRIT*) ста́нция *f* метро́.

tubing ['tju:bɪŋ] *n* шланг тру́бки; **a piece of ~** тру́бка*.

tubular ['tju:bjulə] *adj* (*furniture, metal*) тру́бчатый.

TUC *n abbr* (*BRIT*: = *Trades Union Congress*) Конгре́сс (брита́нских) тред-юнио́нов.

tuck [tʌk] *vt* (*put*) подбира́ть (подобра́ть* *perf*) ◆ *n* (*SEWING*) вы́кладка
▶ **tuck away** *vt* (*money*) припря́тывать (припря́тать* *perf*); (*building*): **to be ~ed away** приткну́ться (*perf*)
▶ **tuck in** *vt* (*clothing*) заправля́ть (запра́вить* *perf*); (*child*) укрыва́ть (укры́ть* *perf*) ◆ *vi* (*eat*) умина́ть (умя́ть* *perf*)
▶ **tuck up** *vt* (*invalid, child*) укрыва́ть (укры́ть* *perf*).

tuck shop *n* буфе́т.

Tue(s). *abbr* = **Tuesday.**

Tuesday ['tju:zdɪ] *n* вто́рник; **it is ~ 23rd March** (сего́дня) вто́рник 23-его ма́рта; **on ~** во вто́рник; **on ~s** по вто́рникам; **every ~** ка́ждый вто́рник; **every other ~** ка́ждый второ́й вто́рник; **last/next ~** в про́шлый/ сле́дующий вто́рник; **the following ~** в сле́дующий вто́рник; **~'s newspaper** газе́та за вто́рник; **a week/fortnight on ~** во вто́рник че́рез неде́лю/че́рез две неде́ли; **the ~ before last** позапро́шлый вто́рник; **the ~ after next** во вто́рник че́рез неде́лю; **~ morning/lunchtime/afternoon/evening** во вто́рник у́тром/в обе́д/днём/ве́чером; **we'll spend ~ night in Rome** во вто́рник мы проведём ночь в Ри́ме.

tuft [tʌft] *n* (*of hair*) пучо́к*.

tug [tʌg] *n* (*ship*) букси́р ◆ *vt* тяну́ть* (*impf*).

tug of war *n* перетя́гивание кана́та; (*fig*) тя́жба.

tuition [tju:'ɪʃən] *n* (*BRIT*) обуче́ние; (: *private tuition*) ча́стные уро́ки *mpl*, дома́шнее обуче́ние; (*US*: *school fees*) пла́та за обуче́ние.

tulip ['tju:lɪp] *n* тюльпа́н.

tumble ['tʌmbl] *n* (*fall*) паде́ние ◆ *vi* (*fall*: *person*) па́дать (упа́сть* *perf*); (: *water*) журча́ть (*impf*); (*somersault*) ска́тываться (скати́ться* *perf*); **to ~ to sth** (*inf*) набрести́* (*perf*) на что-н.

tumbledown ['tʌmbldaun] *adj* (*building*) полуразру́шенный.

tumble dryer *n* (*BRIT*) суши́лка* для белья́.

tumbler ['tʌmblə] *n* бока́л.

tummy ['tʌmɪ] *n* (*inf*) пу́зо *nt no pl.*

tummy tuck *n* *пласти́ческая опера́ция по ушива́нию живота́.*

tumour ['tju:mə] (*US* **tumor**) *n* (*MED*) о́пухоль *f*.
tumult ['tju:mʌlt] *n* шум, суматóха.
tumultuous [tju:'mʌltjuəs] *adj* бýрный.
tuna ['tju:nə] *n inv* (*also:* ~ **fish**) тунéц*.
tune [tju:n] *n* (*melody*) мотúв ♦ *vt* (*MUS, RADIO, TV*) настрáивать (настрóить *perf*); (*AUT*) налáживать (налáдить* *perf*); **the guitar is in/out of** ~ гитáра настрóена/расстрóена; **to sing in** ~ петь* (*impf*) чúсто; **to sing out of** ~ фальшúвить* (*impf*); **to be in/out of** ~ **with** (*fig*) быть* (*impf*) в ладý/не в ладý с +*instr*; **she was robbed to the** ~ **of £10,000** (*fig*) её огрáбили на цéлых £10 000
▸ **tune in** *vi* **in (to)** настрáиваться (настрóиться *perf*) (на +*acc*)
▸ **tune up** *vi* (*musician*) настрáивать (настрóить *perf*) инструмéнт; (*orchestra*) настрáивать (настрóить *perf*) инструмéнты.
tuneful ['tju:nful] *adj* (*music*) мелодúчный* (мелодúчен).
tuner ['tju:nə] *n* (*radio set*) блок настрóйки; **piano** ~ настрóйщик фортепья́но.
tuner amplifier *n* резонáнсный усилúтель *m*.
tungsten ['tʌŋstn] *n* вольфрáм.
tunic ['tju:nɪk] *n* тýника.
tuning fork ['tju:nɪŋ-] *n* камертóн.
Tunis ['tju:nɪs] *n* Тунúс.
Tunisia [tju:'nɪzɪə] *n* Тунúс.
Tunisian [tju:'nɪzɪən] *adj* Тунúсский* ♦ *n* тунúсец*(-ска*).
tunnel ['tʌnl] *n* (*passage*) туннéль *m*; (*in mine*) штóльня ♦ *vi* проклáдывать (проложúть* *perf*) туннéль.
tunnel vision *n* ýзость *f* зрéния; (*fig*) трýбочнее зрéние.
tunny ['tʌnɪ] *n* тунéц*.
turban ['tə:bən] *n* чалмá, тюрбáн.
turbid ['tə:bɪd] *adj* (*water*) мýтный* (мýтен); (*air*) пыльный* (пылен).
turbine ['tə:baɪn] *n* (*TECH*) турбúна.
turbo ['tə:bəu] *n* турбúна.
turbojet [tə:bəu'dʒɛt] *n* (*AVIAT*) турбо-реактúвный самолёт.
turboprop [tə:bəu'prɔp] *n* (*engine*) турбо-винтовóй мотóр.
turbot ['tə:bət] *n inv* белокóрый пáлтус.
turbulence ['tə:bjuləns] *n* встрéчные потóки *mpl* вóздуха.
turbulent ['tə:bjulənt] *adj* (*also fig*) бýрный.
tureen [tə'ri:n] *n* (*for soup*) сýпница; (*for vegetables*) глубóкое блюдо с крышкой.
turf [tə:f] *n* (*grass*) дёрн; (*clod*) торф ♦ *vt* (*area*) покрывáть (покрыть* *perf*) дёрном; **the T~** (*course*) скаковáя дорóжка; (*horse-racing*) скáчки *mpl*
▸ **turf out** *vt* (*inf: person*) выставля́ть (выставить* *perf*).
turf accountant *n* (*BRIT*) букмéкер.

turgid ['tə:dʒɪd] *adj* (*speech*) напыщенный.
Turin ['tjuə'rɪn] *n* Турúн.
Turk [tə:k] *n* тýрок* (турчáнка*).
Turkey ['tə:kɪ] *n* Тýрция.
turkey ['tə:kɪ] *n* индéйка.
Turkish ['tə:kɪʃ] *adj* турéцкий* ♦ *n* (*LING*) турéцкий* язык*.
Turkish bath *n* турéцкие бáни *fpl*.
Turkish delight *n* рахáт-лукýм.
Turkmen ['tə:kmɛn] *n,adj* туркмéнский*; (*person*) туркмéн(ка*); (*LING*) туркмéнский* язык*.
Turkmenia [tə:k'mi:nɪə] *n* Туркмéния.
turmeric ['tə:mərɪk] *n* (*CULIN*) куркýма.
turmoil ['tə:mɔɪl] *n* смятéние; **in** ~ в смятéнии.
turn [tə:n] *n* поворóт; (*performance*) нóмер*; (*chance*) óчередь *f*; (*inf: MED*) вывих ♦ *vt* повора́чивать (повернýть *perf*); (*collar*) отвора́чивать (отвернýть *perf*); (*change: wood, metal*) обтáчивать (обточúть* *perf*) ♦ *vi* (*object*) повора́чиваться (повернýться *perf*); (*person: look back*) обора́чиваться (обернýться *perf*); (*reverse direction: in car*) развора́чиваться (развернýться *perf*); (: *wind*) переменя́ться (переменúться *perf*); (*milk*) скисáть (скúснуть *perf*); (*change: become*): **he's ~ed forty** емý испóлнилось сóрок; **a good/bad** ~ дóбрая/плохáя услýга; **it gave me quite a** ~ э́то меня сúльно испугáло; **"no left** ~" (*AUT*) "нет лéвого поворóта"; **it's your** ~ твоя óчередь; **in** ~ по óчереди; **to take** ~**s at sth** дéлать (*impf*) что-н по óчереди; **at the** ~ **of the century** на рубежé вéка; **at the** ~ **of the year** под конéц гóда; **to take a** ~ **for the worse** (*situations, events*) принимáть (приня́ть* *perf*) дурнóй оборóт; **his health** *or* **he has taken a** ~ **for the worse** емý сдéлалось хýже; **to** ~ **sth into sth** (*change*) превращáть (превратúть* *perf*) что-н в что-н; **to** ~ **nasty** озлобля́ться (озлобúться* *perf*)
▸ **turn about** *vi* повора́чиваться (повернýться *perf*)
▸ **turn away** *vi* отвора́чиваться (отвернýться *perf*) ♦ *vt* (*business, applicant*) отклоня́ть (отклонúть* *perf*)
▸ **turn back** *vi* повора́чивать (повернýть *perf*) назáд ♦ *vt* (*person*) вернýть (*perf*); (*vehicle*) развора́чивать (развернýть *perf*); (*clock*) переводúть* (перевестú* *perf*) назáд; **to** ~ **back the clock** (*fig*) повернýть (*perf*) врéмя вспять
▸ **turn down** *vt* (*request*) отклоня́ть (отклонúть* *perf*); (*heating*) уменьшáть (уменьшúть* *perf*); (*bedclothes*) отвора́чивать (отвернýть *perf*)
▸ **turn in** *vi* (*inf: go to bed*) идтú* (пойтú* *perf*) на боковýю ♦ *vt* (*fold*) свора́чивать

(сверну́ть *perf*)

▶ **turn off** *vi* (*from road*) свора́чивать (сверну́ть *perf*) ♦ *vt* выключа́ть (вы́ключить *perf*)

▶ **turn on** *vt* включа́ть (включи́ть *perf*)

▶ **turn out** *vt* (*light, gas*) выключа́ть (вы́ключить *perf*); (*produce*) выпуска́ть (вы́пустить* *perf*) ♦ *vi* (*troops, doctor, voters*) прибыва́ть (прибы́ть* *perf*); **to ~ out to be** (*prove to be*) ока́зываться (оказа́ться* *perf*) +*instr*

▶ **turn over** *vi* (*person*) перевора́чиваться (переверну́ться *perf*) ♦ *vt* (*object, page*) перевора́чивать (переверну́ть *perf*); (*funds, production etc*): **to ~ over to** передава́ть* (переда́ть* *perf*) +*dat*

▶ **turn round** *vi* (*person, vehicle*) развора́чиваться (разверну́ться *perf*); (*rotate*) повора́чиваться (*impf*)

▶ **turn up** *vi* (*person*) объявля́ться (объяви́ться* *perf*); (*lost object*) находи́ться* (найти́сь* *perf*) ♦ *vt* (*collar*) поднима́ть (подня́ть* *perf*); (*radio*) де́лать (сде́лать *perf*) гро́мче; (*heater*) де́лать (сде́лать *perf*) вы́ше.

turnabout ['tɜ:nəbaut] *n* (*fig*) поворо́т на 180 гра́дусов.

turnaround ['tɜ:nəraund] *n* (*fig*) = **turnabout**.

turncoat ['tɜ:nkəut] *n* ренега́т, отсту́пник.

turned-up ['tɜ:ndʌp] *adj* (*nose*) вздёрнутый, курно́сый.

turning ['tɜ:nɪŋ] *n* (*in road*) поворо́т; **the first ~ on the right** пе́рвый поворо́т напра́во.

turning circle *n* (*BRIT: AUT*) окру́жность *f* поворо́та.

turning point *n* (*fig*) поворо́тный пункт, перело́мный моме́нт.

turning radius *n* (*US*) = **turning circle**.

turnip ['tɜ:nɪp] *n* (*BOT, CULIN*) ре́па.

turnout ['tɜ:naut] *n* (*of voters etc*) число́.

turnover ['tɜ:nəuvə*] *n* (*COMM*) оборо́т; (*: of staff*) теку́честь *f*; (*CULIN*): **apple ~** я́блочная сло́йка; **there is a rapid ~ in staff** больша́я теку́честь ка́дров.

turnpike ['tɜ:npaɪk] *n* (*US*) магистра́ль *f*, шоссе́ *nt ind*.

turnstile ['tɜ:nstaɪl] *n* турнике́т.

turntable ['tɜ:nteɪbl] *n* (*on record player*) верту́шка*, прои́грыватель *m*.

turn-up ['tɜ:nʌp] *n* (*BRIT: on trousers*) манже́та, отворо́т; **that's a ~ for the books!** вот неожи́данность!

turpentine ['tɜ:pəntaɪn] *n* (*also:* **turps**) скипида́р.

turquoise ['tɜ:kwɔɪz] *n* (*stone*) бирюза́ ♦ *adj* (*colour*) бирюзо́вый.

turret ['tʌrɪt] *n* ба́шенка*.

turtle ['tɜ:tl] *n* черепа́ха.

turtleneck (sweater) ['tɜ:tlnɛk(-)] *n* водола́зка*.

Tuscany ['tʌskənɪ] *n* Тоска́нь *f*.

tusk [tʌsk] *n* (*of elephant*) би́вень* *m*; (*of boar*) клык*.

tussle ['tʌsl] *n* (*fight, scuffle*) схва́тка*.

tutor ['tju:tə*] *n* (*SCOL*) преподава́тель(ница) *m(f)*; (*private tutor*) репети́тор.

tutorial [tju:'tɔ:rɪəl] *n* (*SCOL*) семина́р.

tuxedo [tʌk'si:dəu] *n* (*US*) смо́кинг.

TV [ti:'vi:] *n abbr* (= **television**) ТВ= *телеви́дение*; **~ dinner** *пищево́й полуфабрика́т, го́дный к потребле́нию по́сле разогре́ва*.

twaddle ['twɔdl] *n* (*inf*) чепуха́.

twang [twæŋ] *n* (*of instrument*) протя́жный звук; (*of voice*) гнýсость *f* ♦ *vi* протя́жно звене́ть (зазвене́ть *perf*) ♦ *vt* (*guitar*) бренча́ть* (*impf*) на +*prp*.

tweak [twi:k] *vt* дёргать (дёрнуть *perf*) за +*acc*.

tweed [twi:d] *n* твид ♦ *adj* (*jacket, skirt*) тви́довый.

tweezers ['twi:zəz] *npl* пинце́т *msg*.

twelfth [twɛlfθ] *adj* двена́дцатый; *see also* **fifth**.

Twelfth Night *n* Двена́дцатая ночь *f*.

twelve [twɛlv] *n* двена́дцать*; **at ~** (*o'clock*) (*midday*) в двена́дцать (дня); (*midnight*) в двена́дцать (но́чи); *see also* **five**.

twentieth ['twɛntɪθ] *adj* двадца́тый; *see also* **fifth**.

twenty ['twɛntɪ] *n* два́дцать*; *see also* **fifty**.

twerp [twɜ:p] *n* (*inf*) крети́н.

twice [twaɪs] *adv* два́жды; **~ as much** вдво́е бо́льше; **~ a week** два ра́за в неде́лю; **she is ~ your age** она́ вдво́е *or* в два ра́за ста́рше Вас.

twiddle ['twɪdl] *vt* тереби́ть* (*impf*) ♦ *vi*: **to ~ with sth** тереби́ть* (*impf*) что-н; **to ~ one's thumbs** (*fig*) бить* (*impf*) баклу́ши.

twig [twɪg] *n* ве́тка* ♦ *vi* (*inf*) смекнýть (*perf*).

twilight ['twaɪlaɪt] *n* су́мерки *mpl*; (*morning*) (предрассве́тные) су́мерки; **in the ~** в су́мерках.

twill [twɪl] *n* (*cloth*) твил, са́ржа.

twin [twɪn] *adj* (*towers*) па́рный ♦ *n* близне́ц*, двойня́; (*room in hotel etc*) двойно́й но́мер* ♦ *vt* (*towns etc*) де́лать (сде́лать *perf*) побрати́мами; **~ sister** сестра́-близне́ц*; **~ brother** брат-близне́ц*.

twin-bedded room ['twɪn'bɛdɪd-] *n* но́мер с двумя́ односпа́льными крова́тями.

twin beds *npl* две односпа́льные крова́ти *fpl*.

twin-carburettor ['twɪnkɑ:bju'rɛtə*] *adj* двухкарбюра́торный.

twine [twaɪn] *n* бечёвка ♦ *vi* (*plant*) ви́ться* (*impf*).

twin-engined [twɪn'ɛndʒɪnd] *adj* (*aircraft*) с двумя́ дви́гателями.

twinge [twɪndʒ] *n* (*of pain*) при́ступ; (*of conscience, regret*) уко́л.

twinkle ['twɪŋkl] *vi* (*star, light*) мерца́ть (*impf*); (*eyes*) мига́ть (*impf*), подми́гивать (*impf*) ♦ *n* мерца́ние.

twin town *n* го́род-побрати́м.

twirl [twɜ:l] *vt* верте́ть* (*impf*) ♦ *vi* крути́ться* *(impf)* ♦ *n* поворо́т.

twist [twɪst] *n* (*action*) закру́чивание; (*in road, coil, flex*) изги́б; (*in story*) поворо́т ♦ *vt* (*turn*) изгиба́ть (изогну́ть *perf*); (*injure*: *ankle etc*) выви́хивать (вы́вихнуть *perf*); (*weave*) сплета́ть (сплести́* *perf*); (*fig*: *meaning, words*) искажа́ть (исказ́ить* *perf*) ♦ *vi* (*road, river*) извива́ться (*impf*).

twisted ['twɪstɪd] *adj* (*wire, rope*) скру́ченный; (*ankle, wrist*) вы́вихнутый; (*fig*: *logic, mind*) извращённый.

twit [twɪt] *n* (*inf*) недоу́мок*.

twitch [twɪtʃ] *n* (*pull*) рыво́к*; (*nervous*) подёргивание ♦ *vi* (*muscle, body*) подёргиваться (*impf*).

two [tu:] *n* два* *m*/*nt* (*f* две*); ~ **by** ~, **in** ~**s** па́рами; **to put** ~ **and** ~ **together** (*fig*) сложи́ть (*perf*) два и два; *see also* **five**.

two-bit [tu:'bɪt] *adj* (*esp US*: *inf*) расхо́жий.

two-door [tu:'dɔː] *adj* (*AUT*) двухдве́рный.

two-faced [tu:'feɪst] *adj* (*pej*: *person*) двули́чный* (двули́чен).

twofold ['tu:fəuld] *adj* (*increase*) двойно́й; (*reply*) дво́йственный ♦ *adv*: **to increase** ~ вдво́е.

two-piece (suit) ['tu:pi:s-] *n* (костю́м) дво́йка.

two-piece swimsuit *n* разде́льный купа́льник.

two-ply ['tu:plaɪ] *adj* (*wool*) двойно́й; (*tissues*) двухсло́йный* (двухсло́ен).

two-seater car [tu:'si:tə-] *n* двухме́стный автомоби́ль *m*.

twosome ['tu:səm] *n* (*people*) па́ра.

two-stroke ['tu:strəuk] *n* (*also*: ~ **engine**) двухта́ктный дви́гатель *m* ♦ *adj* двухта́ктный.

two-tone ['tu:'təun] *adj* (*in colour*) двухцве́тный.

two-way ['tu:weɪ] *adj*: ~ **traffic** двусторо́ннее движе́ние; ~ **radio** приёмно-переда́ющая радиоста́нция.

TX *abbr* (*US*: *POST*) = *Texas*.

tycoon [taɪ'ku:n] *n*: **(business)** ~ магна́т.

type [taɪp] *n* (*category, model, example*) тип; (*TYP*) шрифт ♦ *vt* (*letter etc*) печа́тать (напеча́тать *perf*); **what** ~ **do you want?** како́й вид Вы бы хоте́ли?; **in bold** ~ жи́рным шри́фтом; **in italic** ~ курси́вом шри́фтом.

typecast ['taɪpkɑ:st] *adj* (*actor*) одноти́пных роле́й.

typeface ['taɪpfeɪs] *n* шрифт.

typescript ['taɪpskrɪpt] *n* машинопи́сный текст.

typeset ['taɪpsɛt] *vt* набира́ть (набра́ть* *perf*).

typesetter ['taɪpsɛtə'] *n* набо́рщик(-ица).

typewriter ['taɪpraɪtə'] *n* пи́шущая маши́нка*.

typewritten ['taɪprɪtn] *adj* машинопи́сный, напеча́танный (напеча́тан) (на маши́нке).

typhoid ['taɪfɔɪd] *n* брюшно́й тиф.

typhoon [taɪ'fu:n] *n* тайфу́н.

typhus ['taɪfəs] *n* сыпно́й тиф.

typical ['tɪpɪkl] *adj* (*behaviour, weather etc*): ~ **(of)** типи́чный* (типи́чен) (для +*gen*); **that's** ~! (*pej*) вот так всегда́!

typify ['tɪpɪfaɪ] *vt* явля́ться (яви́ться* *perf*) типи́чным приме́ром +*gen*.

typing ['taɪpɪŋ] *n* маши́нопись *f*.

typing error *n* опеча́тка*.

typing pool *n* (*BRIT*) машинопи́сное бюро́ *nt ind*.

typist ['taɪpɪst] *n* машини́стка*.

typo ['taɪpəu] *n abbr* (*inf*. = *typographical error*) типогра́фская опеча́тка*.

typography [tɪ'pɔgrəfɪ] *n* типогра́фия.

tyranny ['tɪrənɪ] *n* тирани́я, деспоти́зм.

tyrant ['taɪərnt] *n* тира́н, де́спот.

tyre ['taɪə'] (*US* **tire**) *n* ши́на.

tyre pressure *n* давле́ние в ши́не.

Tyrol [tɪ'rəul] *n* Тиро́ль *m*.

Tyrolean [tɪrə'li:ən] *adj* тиро́льский ♦ *n* тиро́лец*.

Tyrolese [tɪrə'li:z] = **Tyrolean**.

Tyrrhenian Sea [tɪ'ri:nɪən-] *n*: **the** ~ ~ Тирре́нское мо́ре.

tzar [zɑ:'] *n* = **tsar**.

---

* marks translations which have irregular inflections. The Russian-English side of the dictionary gives inflectional information.

~ U, u ~

U, u [ju:] n (letter) 21-ая бу́ква англи́йского алфави́та.

U n abbr (BRIT: CINEMA: = universal) фильм, приго́дный для пока́за всем возрастны́м гру́ппам.

UAW n abbr (US) = United Automobile Workers.

UB40 n abbr (BRIT: = unemployment benefit form 40) бланк, заполня́емый при получе́нии посо́бия по безрабо́тице.

U-bend ['ju:bɛnd] n (in pipe) двойно́й изги́б.

ubiquitous [ju:'bɪkwɪtəs] adj вездесу́щий* (вездесу́щ).

UCCA ['ʌkə] n abbr (BRIT: = Universities Central Council on Admissions) организа́ция, координи́рующая приём в университе́ты.

UDA n abbr (BRIT: = Ulster Defence Association) военизи́рованная организа́ция, борю́щаяся за сохране́ние Се́верой Ирла́ндии как ча́сти Великобрита́нии.

UDC n abbr (BRIT) = Urban District Council.

udder ['ʌdə'] n вы́мя* nt.

UDI n abbr (BRIT: POL: = unilateral declaration of independence) односторо́ннее провозглаше́ние незави́симости.

UDR n abbr (BRIT: = Ulster Defence Regiment) ча́сти брита́нской а́рмии, размещённые в Се́верной Ирла́ндии.

UEFA [ju:'eɪfə] n abbr (= Union of European Football Associations) УЕФА́.

UFO ['ju:fəu] n abbr (= unidentified flying object) НЛО= неопо́знанный лета́ющий объе́кт.

Uganda [ju:'gændə] n Уга́нда.

Ugandan [ju:'gændən] adj уга́ндский ♦ n уга́ндец*(-дка*).

UGC n abbr (BRIT: = University Grants Committee) комите́т, координи́рующий финанси́рование университе́тов.

ugh [ə:h] excl фу.

ugliness ['ʌglɪnɪs] n уро́дство.

ugly ['ʌglɪ] adj (person, dress etc) уро́дливый (уро́длив), безобра́зный* (безобра́зен); (dangerous: situation) опа́сный* (опа́сен).

UHF abbr (= ultra-high frequency) УВЧ= ультравысо́кая частота́.

UHT abbr = ultra heat treated ♦ adj abbr: ~ **milk** молоко́, проше́дшее обрабо́тку сверх-высо́кой температу́рой.

UK n abbr = United Kingdom.

Ukraine [ju:'kreɪn] n Украи́на.

Ukrainian [ju:'kreɪnɪən] adj украи́нский* ♦ n украи́нец*(-нка); (LING) украи́нский* язы́к*.

Ulan Bator n [u'lɑ:n'bɑ:tɔ:'] Ула́н-Ба́тор.

ulcer ['ʌlsə'] n я́зва.

Ulster ['ʌlstə'] n О́льстер.

ulterior [ʌl'tɪərɪə'] adj: ~ **motive** скры́тый моти́в.

ultimata [ʌltɪ'meɪtə] npl of **ultimatum**.

ultimate ['ʌltɪmət] adj (final) оконча́тельный*, коне́чный; (greatest) преде́льный* ♦ n: **the ~ in luxury** преде́л ро́скоши.

ultimately ['ʌltɪmətlɪ] adv в конце́ концо́в.

ultimatum [ʌltɪ'meɪtəm] (pl ~**s** or **ultimata**) n ультима́тум.

ultrasonic [ʌltrə'sɔnɪk] adj (sound) сверхзвуково́й, ультразвуково́й.

ultrasound ['ʌltrəsaund] n ультразву́к.

ultraviolet [ʌltrə'vaɪəlɪt] adj (light etc) ультрафиоле́товый.

umbilical cord [ʌm'bɪlɪkl-] n пупови́на.

umbrage ['ʌmbrɪdʒ] n: **to take ~** обижа́ться (оби́деться perf).

umbrella [ʌm'brɛlə] n зо́нтик, зонт*; (fig): **under the ~ of** под защи́той +gen.

umlaut ['umlaut] n у́мляут.

umpire ['ʌmpaɪə'] n (TENNIS, CRICKET) судья́* m, рефери́ m ind ♦ vt (game) суди́ть* (impf).

umpteen [ʌmp'ti:n] adj (inf) бесчи́сленный; ~ **stories** бесконе́чное коли́чество исто́рии.

umpteenth [ʌmp'ti:nθ] adj (inf): **for the ~ time** в э́нный or со́тый раз.

UMW n abbr = United Mineworkers of America.

UN n abbr = **United Nations**.

unabashed [ʌnə'bæʃt] adj: **she seemed ~** она́ каза́лось не возмути́мой.

unabated [ʌnə'beɪtɪd] adj (enthusiasm, excitement) неосла́бный* (неосла́бен) ♦ adv: **to continue ~** продолжа́ться (продо́лжиться perf) с той же си́лой.

unable [ʌn'eɪbl] adj неспосо́бный*; **he is ~ to pay** он не спосо́бен заплати́ть.

unabridged [ʌnə'brɪdʒd] adj (novel etc) несокращённый.

unacceptable [ʌnək'sɛptəbl] adj неприе́млемый (неприе́млем).

unaccompanied [ʌnə'kʌmpənɪd] adj (child, luggage) не сопровожда́емый; (song) без аккомпанеме́нта.

unaccountably [ʌnə'kauntəblɪ] adv необъяснймо.

unaccounted [ʌnə'kauntɪd] *adj*: **several people are still ~ for** нéскольких людéй недосчитáлись.

unaccustomed [ʌnə'kʌstəmd] *adj*: **he is ~ to ...** он не привы́чен к +*dat* ....

unacquainted [ʌnə'kweɪntɪd] *adj*: **he is ~ with these ideas** он не знакóм с э́тими идéями.

unadulterated [ʌnə'dʌltəreɪtd] *adj* настоя́щий*; (*wine*) чи́стый*.

unaffected [ʌnə'fɛktɪd] *adj* (*person, behaviour*) естéственный* (естéствен); **~ by** (*emotionally*) безучáстный (безучáстен) к +*dat*.

unafraid [ʌnə'freɪd] *adj* незапу́ганный.

unaided [ʌn'eɪdɪd] *adv* без пóмощи.

unanimity [ju:nə'nɪmɪtɪ] *n* единодýшие, единоглáсие.

unanimous [ju:'nænɪməs] *adj* единодýшный* (единодýшен), единоглáсный* (единоглáсен).

unanimously [ju:'nænɪməslɪ] *adv* единодýшно, единоглáсно.

unanswered [ʌn'ɑ:nsəd] *adj* остáвшийся без отвéта.

unappetizing [ʌn'æpɪtaɪzɪŋ] *adj* (*food etc*) неаппети́тный* (неаппети́тен).

unappreciative [ʌnə'pri:ʃɪətɪv] *adj* неблагодáрный* (неблагодáрен).

unarmed [ʌn'ɑ:md] *adj* безорýжный* (безорýжен); (*combat*) без орýжия.

unashamed [ʌnə'ʃeɪmd] *adj* бессты́дный* (бессты́ден).

unassisted [ʌnə'sɪstɪd] *adj, adv* без посторóнней пóмощи.

unassuming [ʌnə'sju:mɪŋ] *adj* (*person, manner*) непритязáтельный* (непритязáтелен).

unattached [ʌnə'tætʃt] *adj* (*person*) одинóкий* (одинóк); (*part etc*) неприкреплённый*.

unattended [ʌnə'tɛndɪd] *adj* остáвленный (остáвлен) без присмóтра.

unattractive [ʌnə'træktɪv] *adj* непривлекáтельный* (непривлекáтелен).

unauthorized [ʌn'ɔ:θəraɪzd] *adj* неразрешённый*.

unavailable [ʌnə'veɪləbl] *adj* (*article, room etc*) недостýпный* (недостýпен); (*person*) недосягáемый (недосягáем).

unavoidable [ʌnə'vɔɪdəbl] *adj* (*delay*) неизбéжный* (неизбéжен).

unavoidably [ʌnə'vɔɪdəblɪ] *adv* (*delayed etc*) неизбéжно.

unaware [ʌnə'wɛə'] *adj*: **to be ~ of** не подозревáть (*impf*) о +*prp*.

unawares [ʌnə'wɛəz] *adv* врасплóх.

unbalanced [ʌn'bælənst] *adj* (*report*) односторóнний*; (*mentally*) неуравновéшенный (неуравновéшен).

unbearable [ʌn'bɛərəbl] *adj* невыноси́мый (невыноси́м).

unbeatable [ʌn'bi:təbl] *adj* (*team*) непобеди́мый (непобеди́м); (*price, quality*) непревзойдённый* (непревзойдён).

unbeaten [ʌn'bi:tn] *adj* (*person*) непобеди́мый (непобеди́м); (*record*) непревзойдённый* (непревзойдён).

unbecoming [ʌnbɪ'kʌmɪŋ] *adj* (*language, behaviour*) неподобáющий (неподобáющ); (*garment*) не идýщий к лицý; **that dress is ~ on you** Вам не идёт э́то плáтье.

unbeknown(st) [ʌnbɪ'nəun(st)] *adv*: **~ to me** без моегó вéдома.

unbelief [ʌnbɪ'li:f] *n* невéрие.

unbelievable [ʌnbɪ'li:vəbl] *adj* невероя́тный (невероя́тен).

unbelievably [ʌnbɪ'li:vəblɪ] *adv* невероя́тно.

unbend [ʌn'bɛnd] *irreg vi* (*relax*) расслабля́ться (рассла́биться* *perf*) ♦ *vt* (*wire*) выпрямля́ть (вы́прямить* *perf*).

unbending [ʌn'bɛndɪŋ] *adj* непреклóнный* (непреклóнен).

unbias(s)ed [ʌn'baɪəst] *adj* (*report*) непредвзя́тый (непредвзя́т); (*person*) беспристрáстный* (беспристрáстен).

unblemished [ʌn'blɛmɪʃt] *adj* незапя́тнанный (незапя́тнан).

unblock [ʌn'blɔk] *vt* (*pipe*) прочищáть (прочи́стить* *perf*).

unborn [ʌn'bɔ:n] *adj* (ещё) не рождённый.

unbounded [ʌn'baundɪd] *adj* безграни́чный* (безграни́чен).

unbreakable [ʌn'breɪkəbl] *adj* небью́щийся.

unbridled [ʌn'braɪdld] *adj* необýзданный* (необýздан).

unbroken [ʌn'brəukən] *adj* (*seal*) цéлый* (цел); (*silence, series*) непрéрванный; (*window*) неразби́тый, цéлый* (цел); (*SPORT: record*) непоби́тый.

unbuckle [ʌn'bʌkl] *vt* (*belt, shoe*) расстёгивать (расстегнýть *perf*).

unburden [ʌn'bə:dn] *vt*: **to ~ o.s. (to sb)** излива́ть (изли́ть* *perf*) дýшу (комý-н).

unbusinesslike [ʌn'bɪznɪslaɪk] *adj* неделовóй.

unbutton [ʌn'bʌtn] *vt* расстёгивать (расстегнýть *perf*).

uncalled-for [ʌn'kɔ:ldfɔ:'] *adj* неумéстный* (неумéстен).

uncanny [ʌn'kænɪ] *adj* (*resemblance, knack*) необъясни́мый (необъясни́м); (*silence*) жýткий* (жýток).

unceasing [ʌn'si:sɪŋ] *adj* (*misery, flow etc*) беспрерývный* (беспрерывен); (*search*) неустáнный* (неустáнен).

unceremonious [ʌnsɛrɪ'məunɪəs] *adj* (*abrupt, rude*) бесцеремóнный* (бесцеремóнен).

uncertain [ʌn'sə:tn] *adj* (*hesitant*)

---

* marks translations which have irregular inflections. The Russian-English side of the dictionary gives inflectional information.

неуве́ренный* (неуве́рен), нереши́тельный* (нереши́телен); (*unsure*): ~ **about** неуве́ренный* (неуве́рен) относи́тельно +*gen*; **in no ~ terms** без обиняко́в.

uncertainty [ʌn'sə:tntɪ] *n* (*not knowing*) неопределённость *f*; (*often pl: doubt*) сомне́ние.

unchallenged [ʌn'tʃælɪndʒd] *adj* не вызыва́ющий* возраже́ний; **to go ~** не вызыва́ть (вы́звать* *perf*) возраже́ний.

unchanged [ʌn'tʃeɪndʒd] *adj* (*condition*) неизмени́вшийся; **my orders remain ~** мои́ прика́зы остаю́тся неизме́нными.

uncharitable [ʌn'tʃærɪtəbl] *adj* немилосе́рдный* (немилосе́рден).

uncharted [ʌn'tʃɑ:tɪd] *adj* (*land, sea*) не отме́ченный на ка́рте.

unchecked [ʌn'tʃɛkt] *adv* беспрепя́тственно.

uncivil [ʌn'sɪvɪl] *adj* гру́бый* (груб).

uncivilized [ʌn'sɪvɪlaɪzd] *adj* (*country, people*) нецивилизо́ванный (нецивилизо́ван); (*fig: behaviour etc*) ди́кий* (дик); **at an ~ hour** ни свет, ни заря́.

uncle ['ʌŋkl] *n* дя́дя* *m*.

unclear [ʌn'klɪə'] *adj* нея́сный* (нея́сен); **I'm still ~ about what I'm supposed to do** мне всё ещё нея́сно, что мне на́до де́лать.

uncoil [ʌn'kɔɪl] *vt* разма́тывать (размота́ть *perf*) ◆ *vi* разма́тываться (размота́ться *perf*).

uncomfortable [ʌn'kʌmfətəbl] *adj* (*physically*) неудо́бный* (неудо́бен); (*uneasy*) неудо́бный* (неудо́бен), нело́вкий* (нело́вок); (*unpleasant*) трево́жный* (трево́жен).

uncomfortably [ʌn'kʌmfətəblɪ] *adv* (*sit*) неудо́бно; (*smile*) нело́вко; (*tall, shy*) до нело́вкого.

uncommitted [ʌnkə'mɪtɪd] *adj* нейтра́льный* (нейтра́лен).

uncommon [ʌn'kɔmən] *adj* (*rare, unusual*) необы́чный* (необы́чен).

uncommunicative [ʌnkə'mju:nɪkətɪv] *adj* необщи́тельный* (необщи́телен).

uncomplicated [ʌn'kɔmplɪkeɪtɪd] *adj* несло́жный* (несло́жен).

uncompromising [ʌn'kɔmprəmaɪzɪŋ] *adj* бескомпроми́ссный.

unconcerned [ʌnkən'sə:nd] *adj* (*person*) беззабо́тный* (беззабо́тен); ~ **about** равноду́шный* (равноду́шен) к +*dat*.

unconditional [ʌnkən'dɪʃənl] *adj* (*acceptance, obedience*) безусло́вный* (безусло́вен); (*discharge, surrender*) безоговоро́чный* (безоговоро́чен).

uncongenial [ʌnkən'dʒi:nɪəl] *adj* (*surroundings*) чу́ждый (чужд), неприя́тный* (неприя́тен).

unconnected [ʌnkə'nɛktɪd] *adj* (*unrelated*): ~ **(with)** несвя́занный (с +*instr*).

unconscious [ʌn'kɔnʃəs] *adj* без созна́ния; (*unaware*): ~ **of** не сознаю́щий* +*gen* ◆ *n*: **the ~** подсозна́ние; **he was knocked ~** он упа́л без созна́ния.

unconsciously [ʌn'kɔnʃəslɪ] *adv* (*unawares*) подсозна́тельно.

unconsciousness [ʌn'kɔnʃəsnɪs] *n* бессозна́тельное состоя́ние.

unconstitutional ['ʌnkɔnstɪ'tju:ʃənl] *adj* неконституцио́нный* (неконституцио́нен).

uncontested [ʌnkən'tɛstɪd] *adj* (*champion*) неоспори́мый (неоспори́м); ~ **election** вы́боры, на кото́рых баллоти́руется (лишь) оди́н кандида́т.

uncontrollable [ʌnkən'trəuləbl] *adj* (*child, animal*) неуправля́емый (неуправля́ем); (*temper*) неукроти́мый (неукроти́м); (*laughter*) неудержи́мый (неудержи́м).

uncontrolled [ʌnkən'trəuld] *adj* безу́держный* (безу́держен).

unconventional [ʌnkən'vɛnʃənl] *adj* нетрадицио́нный (нетрадицио́нен).

unconvinced [ʌnkən'vɪnst] *adj*: **to be** *or* **remain ~** остава́ться* (оста́ться* *perf*) неубеждённым(-ой).

unconvincing [ʌnkən'vɪnsɪŋ] *adj* неубеди́тельный* (неубеди́телен).

uncork [ʌn'kɔ:k] *vt* (*bottle*) отку́поривать (отку́порить *perf*).

uncorroborated [ʌnkə'rɔbəreɪtɪd] *adj* неподтверждённый.

uncouth [ʌn'ku:θ] *adj* неотёсанный* (неотёсан).

uncover [ʌn'kʌvə'] *vt* открыва́ть (откры́ть* *perf*); (*plot, secret*) раскрыва́ть (раскры́ть* *perf*).

unctuous ['ʌŋktjuəs] *adj* еле́йный* (еле́ен).

undamaged [ʌn'dæmɪdʒd] *adj* (*goods*) неповреждённый; (*fig: reputation*) незапя́тнанный (незапя́тнан).

undaunted [ʌn'dɔ:ntɪd] *adj* (*person*) неустраши́мый (неустраши́м); ~, **she struggled on** она́ неустраши́мо продолжа́ла свои́ стара́ния.

undecided [ʌndɪ'saɪdɪd] *adj* (*person*) нереши́тельный* (нереши́телен); (*question*) нерешённый.

undelivered [ʌndɪ'lɪvəd] *adj* (*goods, letters*) недоста́вленный; **if ~ return to sender** е́сли не доста́влено, верну́ть отправи́телю.

undeniable [ʌndɪ'naɪəbl] *adj* (*fact, evidence*) неоспори́мый (неоспори́м).

undeniably [ʌndɪ'naɪəblɪ] *adv* несомне́нно.

under ['ʌndə'] *adv* (*go, fly etc*) вниз ◆ *prep* (*position*) под +*instr*; (*motion*) под +*acc*; (*less than: in price*) ни́же +*gen*; (*according to: law, agreement etc*) по +*dat*; (*during: sb's leadership*) при +*prp*; (*in age*): **children ~ 16** де́ти до 16-ти лет; **from ~ sth** из-под чего́-л; ~ **there** там внизу́; **in ~ 2 hours** ме́ньше, чем за 2 часа́; ~ **anaesthetic** под нарко́зом; ~ **discussion** в проце́ссе обсужде́ния; ~ **repair** в ремо́нте; ~ **the circumstances** при сложи́вшихся обстоя́тельствах.

under... [ˈʌndəʳ] *prefix* недо....

underage [ʌndərˈeɪdʒ] *adj* (*person*) несовершеннолéтний*; ~ **smoking/drinking** курéние/потреблéние алкогóля несовершеннолéтними.

underarm [ˈʌndərɑːm] *adv* (*bowl*) снúзу ♦ *adj* (*deodorant*) для подмы́шек; ~ **throw** бросóк* снúзу.

undercapitalized [ˈʌndəˈkæpɪtəlaɪzd] *adj* (*project, industry*) недостáточно капитализúрованный.

undercarriage [ˈʌndəkærɪdʒ] *n* (BRIT) шассú *nt ind.*

undercharge [ʌndəˈtʃɑːdʒ] *vt* назначáть (назнáчить *perf*) слúшком нúзкую цéну +*dat.*

underclass [ˈʌndəklɑːs] *n* неимýщий* класс.

underclothes [ˈʌndəkləuðz] *npl* нúжнее бельё *ntsg.*

undercoat [ˈʌndəkəut] *n* (*paint*) грунтóвка*.

undercover [ʌndəˈkʌvəʳ] *adj* тáйный.

undercurrent [ˈʌndəkʌrnt] *n* (*fig*) затаённое чýвство.

undercut [ʌndəˈkʌt] *irreg vt* (*prices*) сбивáть (сбить* *perf*); **he can ~ his competitors** он мóжет продавáть товáры по бóлее нúзкой ценé, чем егó конкурéнты.

underdeveloped [ˈʌndədɪˈvɛləpt] *adj* (*country, region*) слаборáзвитый (слаборáзвит).

underdog [ˈʌndədɔg] *n*: **the ~** (*in society*) обездóленный *m adj*; (*in team competition*) слáбая комáнда.

underdone [ʌndəˈdʌn] *adj* (*fried, roasted food*) недожáренный; (*boiled food*) недовáренный.

underemployment [ˈʌndərɪmˈplɔɪmənt] *n* непóлная зáнятость *f.*

underestimate [ˈʌndərˈɛstɪmeɪt] *vt* недооцéнивать (недооценúть* *perf*).

underexposed [ˈʌndərɪksˈpəuzd] *adj* (PHOT) недодéржанный.

underfed [ʌndəˈfɛd] *adj* недокóрмленный.

underfoot [ʌndəˈfut] *adv* (*crush, trample*) ногáми.

underfunded [ʌndəˈfʌndɪd] *adj* плóхо финансúруемый.

undergo [ʌndəˈgəu] *irreg vt* (*repair*) проходúть* (пройтú* *perf*); (*operation*) переносúть* (перенестú* *perf*); (*change*) подвергáться (подвéргнуться* *perf*) +*dat*; **the car is ~ing repairs** машúна прохóдит ремóнт.

undergraduate [ʌndəˈgrædjuɪt] *n* студéнт(ка) ♦ *cpd*: ~ **courses** университéтские кýрсы *mpl.*

underground [ˈʌndəgraund] *adv* (*work*) под землёй ♦ *adj* (*car park*) подзéмный; (*newspaper, activities*) подпóльный ♦ *n*: **the ~** (BRIT: *railway*) метрó *nt ind*; (POL) подпóлье; **to go ~** (*fig*) уходúть* (уйтú* *perf*) в подпóлье.

undergrowth [ˈʌndəgrəuθ] *n*: **the ~** подлéсок*.

underhand(ed) [ʌndəˈhænd(ɪd)] *adj* (*fig: behaviour, method etc*) закулúсный.

underinsured [ʌndərɪnˈʃuəd] *adj* непóлностью застрахóванный*.

underlay [ʌndəˈleɪ] *n* подклáдка*.

underlie [ʌndəˈlaɪ] *irreg vt* (*fig*) лежáть (*impf*) в оснóве +*gen*; **the underlying cause** причúна, лежáщая в оснóве.

underline [ʌndəˈlaɪn] *vt* (*also fig*) подчёркивать (подчеркнýть *perf*).

underling [ˈʌndəlɪŋ] *n* (*pej*) мéлкая сóшка*.

undermanning [ʌndəˈmænɪŋ] *n* недостáток* в рабóчей сúле.

undermentioned [ʌndəˈmɛnʃənd] *adj* нижеупомя́нутый.

undermine [ʌndəˈmaɪn] *vt* (*confidence, authority*) подрывáть (подорвáть* *perf*).

underneath [ʌndəˈniːθ] *adv* внизý ♦ *prep* (*position*) под +*instr*; (*motion*) под +*acc.*

undernourished [ʌndəˈnʌrɪʃt] *adj* недокóрмленный.

underpaid [ʌndəˈpeɪd] *adj* (*person*) не получáющий дóлжной оплáты, низкооплáчиваемый (низкооплáчиваем).

underpants [ˈʌndəpænts] *npl* (*men's*) трусы́ *pl.*

underpass [ˈʌndəpɑːs] *n* (BRIT) туннéль *m*, тоннéль *m.*

underpin [ʌndəˈpɪn] *vt* (*argument, case*) подкрепля́ть (подкрепúть* *perf*).

underplay [ʌndəˈpleɪ] *vt* (BRIT) преуменьшáть (преумéньшить *perf*).

underpopulated [ʌndəˈpɔpjuleɪtɪd] *adj* малонаселённый* (малонаселён).

underprice [ʌndəˈpraɪs] *vt* занижáть (занизúть* *perf*) слúшком нúзкую цéну на +*acc.*

underprivileged [ʌndəˈprɪvɪlɪdʒd] *adj* (*family*) неимýщий*.

underrate [ʌndəˈreɪt] *vt* недооцéнивать (недооценúть* *perf*).

underscore [ʌndəˈskɔː] *vt* (*word*) подчёркивать (подчеркнýть *perf*).

underseal [ʌndəˈsiːl] *vt* (BRIT: AUT) наносúть* (нанестú* *perf*) антикоррозúйное покры́тие (*на днúще автомобúля*) ♦ *n* (AUT) антикоррозúйное покры́тие (*днúща автомобúля*).

undersecretary [ˈʌndəˈsɛkrətərɪ] *n* (POL) заместúтель *m* минúстра.

undersell [ʌndəˈsɛl] *irreg vt* (*competitors*) продавáть* (продáть* *perf*) дешéвле +*gen.*

undershirt [ˈʌndəʃəːt] *n* (US) нúжняя рубáшка*.

undershorts [ˈʌndəʃɔːts] *npl* (US) трусы́ *pl.*

underside [ˈʌndəsaɪd] *n* нúжняя сторонá*.

undersigned [ˈʌndəˈsaɪnd] *adj* (*document*) подпúсанный нúже ♦ *n* нижепод- писáвшийся*(-аяся) *m(f) adj*; **we the ~ agree**

that ... мы, нижеподписа́вшиеся,
догова́риваемся, что ....

underskirt [ˈʌndəskɔ:t] n (BRIT) ни́жняя ю́бка*.

understaffed [ʌndəˈstɑ:ft] adj (project etc)
неукомплекто́ванный ка́драми.

understand [ʌndəˈstænd] (irreg: like **stand**) vt
понима́ть (поня́ть* perf); (believe): **to ~ that**
полага́ть (impf), что ...; **to make o.s.**
understood объясня́ться (объясни́ться perf).

understandable [ʌndəˈstændəbl] adj
поня́тный* (поня́тен).

understanding [ʌndəˈstændɪŋ] adj (kind)
понима́ющий ♦ n понима́ние; (agreement)
взаимопонима́ние; **to come to an ~ with sb**
достига́ть (дости́чь* perf) взаимопонима́ния
с кем-н; **on the ~ that** ... при усло́вии, что ....

understate [ʌndəˈsteɪt] vt преуменьша́ть
(преуме́ньшить perf).

understatement [ˈʌndəsteɪtmənt] n (quality)
преуменьше́ние; **that's an ~!** э́то сли́шком
мя́гко ска́зано!

understood [ʌndəˈstʊd] pt, pp of **understand** ♦
adj (agreed) согласо́ванный* (согласо́ван);
(implied) подразумева́емый
(подразумева́ем).

understudy [ˈʌndəstʌdɪ] n дублёр.

undertake [ʌndəˈteɪk] (irreg: like **take**) vt (task,
duty) брать* (взять* perf) на себя́; **to ~ to do**
обя́зываться (обяза́ться* perf) +infin.

undertaker [ˈʌndəteɪkəʳ] n владе́лец*
похоро́нного бюро́.

undertaking [ˈʌndəteɪkɪŋ] n (job) предприя́тие;
(promise) обяза́тельство.

undertone [ˈʌndətəʊn] n (of criticism etc)
отте́нок*; (speak): **in an ~** вполго́лоса.

undervalue [ʌndəˈvælju:] vt недооце́нивать
(недооцени́ть* perf).

underwater [ʌndəˈwɔ:təʳ] adv (use, swim etc)
под водо́й ♦ adj (exploration, camera etc)
подво́дный.

underwear [ˈʌndəwɛəʳ] n ни́жнее бельё.

underweight [ʌndəˈweɪt] adj ве́сящий ни́же
но́рмы.

underworld [ˈʌndəwə:ld] n (of crime)
престу́пный мир.

underwrite [ʌndəˈraɪt] vt (FINANCE) гаран-
ти́ровать (impf/perf) размеще́ние +gen;
(COMM) брать* (взять* perf) на себя́
финанси́рование +gen; (INSURANCE)
принима́ть (приня́ть* perf) на себя́
страхово́й риск.

underwriter [ˈʌndəraɪtəʳ] n (INSURANCE)
андерра́йтер, принима́ющий m adj на себя́
страхово́й риск.

undeserving [ʌndɪˈzə:vɪŋ] adj: **to be ~ of** не
заслу́живать (impf) +gen.

undesirable [ʌndɪˈzaɪərəbl] adj нежела́тель-
ный* (нежела́телен).

undeveloped [ʌndɪˈvɛləpt] adj (land) незастро́-
енный; (resources) неразрабо́танный.

undies [ˈʌndɪz] npl (inf) (ни́жнее) бельё ntsg.

undiluted [ˈʌndaɪˈlu:tɪd] adj (substance, liquid)
неразба́вленный; (emotion) чи́стый.

undiplomatic [ˈʌndɪpləˈmætɪk] adj
недипломати́чный* (недипломати́чен).

undischarged [ˈʌndɪsˈtʃɑ:dʒd] adj: **~ bankrupt**
не восстано́вленный в права́х банкро́т.

undisciplined [ʌnˈdɪsɪplɪnd] adj недисциплин-
и́рованный (недисциплини́рован).

undiscovered [ˈʌndɪsˈkʌvəd] adj (island)
неоткры́тый; (fact) необнару́женный;
(situation) неиссле́дованный.

undisguised [ˈʌndɪsˈgaɪzd] adj я́вный* (я́вен).

undisputed [ˈʌndɪsˈpju:tɪd] adj неоспори́мый
(неоспори́м).

undistinguished [ˈʌndɪsˈtɪŋgwɪʃt] adj
посре́дственный* (посре́дствен).

undisturbed [ˈʌndɪsˈtə:bd] adj (uninterrupted)
безмяте́жный* (безмяте́жен); **to leave ~** не
волнова́ть (impf).

undivided [ˈʌndɪˈvaɪdɪd] adj: **can I have your ~**
attention? я прошу́ Ва́шего неразде́льного
внима́ния.

undo [ʌnˈdu:] (irreg: like **do**) vt (unfasten: laces,
strings) развя́зывать (развяза́ть* perf);
(: buttons) расстёгивать (расстегну́ть perf);
(spoil) губи́ть (погуби́ть* perf).

undoing [ʌnˈdu:ɪŋ] n (downfall) ги́бель f.

undone [ʌnˈdʌn] pp of **undo**; (unfastened): **my**
lace has come ~ у меня́ развя́за́лся шнуро́к.

undoubted [ʌnˈdautɪd] adj несомне́нный*
(несомне́нен), бесспо́рный* (бесспо́рен).

undoubtedly [ʌnˈdautɪdlɪ] adv несомне́нно,
бесспо́рно.

undress [ʌnˈdrɛs] vt раздева́ть (разде́ть* perf) ♦
vi раздева́ться (разде́ться* perf).

undrinkable [ʌnˈdrɪŋkəbl] adj (poisonous)
непригодный* для питья́; (unpalatable): **this**
wine is ~ э́то вино́ невозмо́жно пить.

undue [ʌnˈdju:] adj изли́шний*.

undulating [ˈʌndjuleɪtɪŋ] adj холми́стый*.

unduly [ʌnˈdju:lɪ] adv изли́шне.

undying [ʌnˈdaɪɪŋ] adj бессме́ртный*.

unearned [ʌnˈə:nd] adj незарабо́танный; **~**
income нетрудовы́е дохо́ды mpl.

unearth [ʌnˈə:θ] vt выка́пывать (вы́копать
perf); (fig) раска́пывать (раскопа́ть perf).

unearthly [ʌnˈə:θlɪ] adj: **at an ~ hour** ни свет,
ни заря́.

unease [ʌnˈi:z] n нело́вкость f.

uneasy [ʌnˈi:zɪ] adj (feeling) трево́жный*
(трево́жен); (peace, truce) напряжённый*;
(person): **he is** or **feels ~** он неспоко́ен; **I feel ~**
about taking his money я неспоко́ен, когда́
беру́ у него́ де́ньги.

uneconomic(al) [ˈʌni:kəˈnɔmɪk(l)] adj
неэконо́мный.

uneducated [ʌnˈɛdjukeɪtɪd] adj (person)
необразо́ванный*.

unemployed [ʌnɪmˈplɔɪd] adj (worker)
безрабо́тный ♦ npl: **the ~** безрабо́тные pl adj.

unemployment [ʌnɪmˈplɔɪmənt] n

безрабо́тица.
unemployment benefit *n* посо́бие по безрабо́тице.
unemployment compensation *n* (*US*) = **unemployment benefit**.
unending [ʌn'endɪŋ] *adj* нескончае́мый.
unenviable [ʌn'ɛnvɪəbl] *adj* незави́дный* (незави́ден).
unequal [ʌn'i:kwəl] *adj* нера́вный* (нера́вен); **to feel ~ to** чу́вствовать (*impf*) себя́ неспосо́бным отвеча́ть тре́бованиям +*gen*.
unequalled [ʌn'i:kwəld] (*US* **unequaled**) *adj* несравни́мый (несравни́м).
unequivocal [ʌnɪ'kwɪvəkl] *adj* (*answer, person*) недвусмы́сленный*.
unerring [ʌn'ə:rɪŋ] *adj* безоши́бочный* (безоши́бочен).
UNESCO [ju:'nɛskəu] *n abbr* (= *United Nations Educational, Scientific and Cultural Organization*) ЮНЕ́СКО.
unethical [ʌn'ɛθɪkl] *adj* неэти́чный* (неэти́чен).
uneven [ʌn'i:vn] *adj* неро́вный*.
uneventful [ʌnɪ'vɛntful] *adj* без осо́бых собы́тий.
unexceptional [ʌnɪk'sɛpʃənl] *adj* заурядный* (заурядный).
unexciting [ʌnɪk'saɪtɪŋ] *adj* (*news, film*) неинтере́сный* (неинтере́сен).
unexpected [ʌnɪks'pɛktɪd] *adj* неожи́данный* (неожи́дан).
unexpectedly [ʌnɪks'pɛktɪdlɪ] *adv* неожи́данно.
unexplained [ʌnɪks'pleɪnd] *adj* необъясн-ённый*.
unexploded [ʌnɪks'pləudɪd] *adj* (*bomb*) невзорва́вшийся.
unfailing [ʌn'feɪlɪŋ] *adj* неизме́нный* (неизме́нен).
unfair [ʌn'fɛəʳ] *adj*: ~ (**to**) несправедли́вый (к +*dat*); **it's ~ that ...** несправедли́во, что ....
unfair dismissal *n* незако́нное увольне́ние.
unfairly [ʌn'fɛəlɪ] *adv* (*treat*) несправедли́во; (*dismiss*) незако́нно.
unfaithful [ʌn'feɪθful] *adj* неве́рный* (неве́рен).
unfamiliar [ʌnfə'mɪlɪəʳ] *adj* незнако́мый (незнако́м); **he is ~ with the accent** он незнако́м с акце́нтом.
unfashionable [ʌn'fæʃnəbl] *adj* немо́дный* (немо́ден).
unfasten [ʌn'fɑ:sn] *vt* (*undo*) расстёгивать (расстегну́ть *perf*); (*open*) открыва́ть (откры́ть* *perf*).
unfathomable [ʌn'fæðəməbl] *adj* (*mystery*) непостижи́мый (непостижи́м).
unfavourable [ʌn'feɪvrəbl] (*US* **unfavorable**) *adj* неблагоприя́тный* (неблагоприя́тен).
unfavourably [ʌn'feɪvrəblɪ] (*US* **unfavorably**) *adv* (*compare, review*) неблагоприя́тно; **to**

look ~ on (*suggestion etc*) смотре́ть* (*impf*) неблагоскло́нно на +*acc*.
unfeeling [ʌn'fi:lɪŋ] *adj* бесчу́вственный* (бесчу́вствен).
unfinished [ʌn'fɪnɪʃt] *adj* незако́нченный.
unfit [ʌn'fɪt] *adj* (*physically*): **she is ~** она́ в плохо́й спорти́вной фо́рме; **he is ~ for the job** он неприго́ден к рабо́те.
unflagging [ʌn'flægɪŋ] *adj* неосла́бный* (неосла́бен).
unflappable [ʌn'flæpəbl] *adj* невозмути́мый (невозмути́м).
unflattering [ʌn'flætərɪŋ] *adj* (*remark*) неле́стный* (неле́стен); (*garment*) не иду́щий к лицу́; **that dress is ~ on you** Вам не идёт э́то пла́тье.
unflinching [ʌn'flɪntʃɪŋ] *adj* неустраши́мый (неустраши́м).
unfold [ʌn'fəuld] *vt* (*sheets, map*) развора́чивать *or* развёртывать (разверну́ть *perf*) ♦ *vi* (*situation*) развора́чиваться (разверну́ться *perf*).
unforeseeable [ʌnfɔ:'si:əbl] *adj* непредви́денный* (непредви́ден).
unforeseen ['ʌnfɔ:'si:n] *adj* непредви́денный.
unforgettable [ʌnfə'gɛtəbl] *adj* незабыва́емый (незабыва́ем).
unforgivable [ʌnfə'gɪvəbl] *adj* непрости́тельный* (непрости́телен).
unformatted [ʌn'fɔ:mætɪd] *adj* (*COMPUT*) бесфо́рматный, неформати́рованный.
unfortunate [ʌn'fɔ:tʃənət] *adj* (*person, event*) несча́стный*; (*remark*) неуда́чный*; **he's been very ~** ему́ о́чень не повезло́; **it is ~ that ...** как неуда́чно, что ....
unfortunately [ʌn'fɔ:tʃənətlɪ] *adv* к сожале́нию.
unfounded [ʌn'faundɪd] *adj* необосно́ванный*.
unfriendly [ʌn'frɛndlɪ] *adj* недружелю́бный* (недружелю́бен).
unfulfilled [ʌnful'fɪld] *adj* (*ambition, prophecy, desire*) неосуществлённый; (*promise, terms*) невы́полненный; (*person*) нереализова́вшийся.
unfurl [ʌn'fə:l] *vt* развора́чивать *or* развёртывать (разверну́ть *perf*).
unfurnished [ʌn'fə:nɪʃt] *adj* немеблиро́ванный.
ungainly [ʌn'geɪnlɪ] *adj* нело́вкий*.
ungodly [ʌn'gɔdlɪ] *adj*: **at an ~ hour** не свет, ни заря́.
ungrateful [ʌn'greɪtful] *adj* неблагода́рный* (неблагода́рен).
unguarded [ʌn'gɑ:dɪd] *adj*: **in an ~ moment** в моме́нт неосторо́жности.
UNHCR *n abbr* (= *United Nations High Commission for Refugees*) управле́ние верхо́вного комисса́ра ООН по дела́м

---

* marks translations which have irregular inflections. The Russian-English side of the dictionary gives inflectional information.

бе́женцев.

unhappily [ʌn'hæpɪlɪ] *adv* несчастли́во; (*unfortunately*) к несча́стью *or* сожале́нию.

unhappiness [ʌn'hæpɪnɪs] *n* несча́стье.

unhappy [ʌn'hæpɪ] *adj* (*sad*) гру́стный* (гру́стен); (*unfortunate*) несча́стный* (несча́стен); **I am ~ with** (*dissatisfied*) я недово́лен +*instr.*

unharmed [ʌn'hɑːmd] *adj* неповреждённый.

unhealthy [ʌn'hɛlθɪ] *adj* (*also fig*) нездоро́вый (нездоро́в).

unheard-of [ʌn'hə:dɔv] *adj* (*event, situation*) неслы́ханный* (неслы́хан); (*person*) неизве́стный*.

unhelpful [ʌn'hɛlpful] *adj* бесполе́зный*.

unhesitating [ʌn'hɛzɪteɪtɪŋ] *adj* (*loyalty*) непоколеби́мый (непоколеби́м); (*reply, offer*) реши́тельный* (реши́телен).

unholy [ʌn'həulɪ] *adj* поро́чный* (поро́чен); (*dreadful*) безобра́зный.

unhook [ʌn'huk] *vt* расстёгивать (расстегну́ть *perf*) крючки́ +*gen.*

unhurt [ʌn'hə:t] *adj* невреди́мый (невреди́м).

unhygienic ['ʌnhaɪ'dʒi:nɪk] *adj* негигиени́чный* (негигиени́чен).

UNICEF ['ju:nɪsɛf] *n abbr* (= *United Nations International Children's Emergency Fund*) ЮНИСЕФ.

unicorn ['ju:nɪkɔ:n] *n* единоро́г.

unidentified [ʌnaɪ'dɛntɪfaɪd] *adj* (*body*) неопо́знанный; (*source, person*) анони́мный; *see also* **UFO.**

unification [ju:nɪfɪ'keɪʃən] *n* (*POL etc*) объедине́ние, унифика́ция.

uniform ['ju:nɪfɔ:m] *n* фо́рма ♦ *adj* (*length, width etc*) единообра́зный* (единообра́зен); (*temperature*) постоя́нный* (постоя́нен).

uniformity [ju:nɪ'fɔ:mɪtɪ] *n* единообра́зие.

unify ['ju:nɪfaɪ] *vt* объединя́ть (объедини́ть *perf*).

unilateral [ju:nɪ'lætərəl] *adj* (*disarmament etc*) односторо́нний (односторо́нен).

unimaginable [ʌnɪ'mædʒɪnəbl] *adj* невообрази́мый (невообрази́м).

unimaginative [ʌnɪ'mædʒɪnətɪv] *adj* (*person*) лишённый воображе́ния; (*design*) проза́ичный* (проза́ичен).

unimpaired [ʌnɪm'pɛəd] *adj* непострада́вший.

unimportant [ʌnɪm'pɔ:tənt] *adj* нева́жный* (нева́жен).

unimpressed [ʌnɪm'prɛst] *adj*: **I was ~ by his explanation** его́ объясне́ние меня́ не убеди́ло.

uninhabited [ʌnɪn'hæbɪtɪd] *adj* необита́емый (необита́ем).

uninhibited [ʌnɪn'hɪbɪtɪd] *adj* раско́ванный* (раско́ван).

uninjured [ʌn'ɪndʒəd] *adj* непострада́вший.

uninspiring [ʌnɪn'spaɪərɪŋ] *adj* не вдохновля́ющий.

unintelligent [ʌnɪn'tɛlɪdʒənt] *adj* (*person*) невежественный* (невежествен).

unintentional [ʌnɪn'tɛnʃənəl] *adj* неумы́шленный* (неумы́шлен).

unintentionally [ʌnɪn'tɛnʃnəlɪ] *adv* неумы́шленно.

uninvited [ʌnɪn'vaɪtɪd] *adj* незва́ный.

uninviting [ʌnɪn'vaɪtɪŋ] *adj* (*food*) неаппети́тный* (неаппети́тен); несоблазни́тельный* (несоблазни́телен); (*place*) непривлека́тельный* (непривлека́телен).

union ['ju:njən] *n* (*unification*) объедине́ние; (*also*: **trade ~**) профсою́з ♦ *cpd* (*activities, leader etc*) профсою́зный; **the U~** (*US*) Соединённые Шта́ты *mpl.*

unionize ['ju:njənaɪz] *vt* (*employees, industry*) объединя́ть (объедини́ть *perf*) в профсою́зы.

Union Jack *n* (*BRIT*) госуда́рственный флаг Соединённого Короле́вства.

Union of Soviet Socialist Republics *n* (*formerly*) Сою́з Сове́тских Социалисти́ческих Респу́блик.

union shop *n* предприя́тие, на кото́ром мо́гут рабо́тать то́лько чле́ны профсою́за.

unique [ju:'ni:k] *adj* (*object etc*) уника́льный* (уника́лен); (*ability, performance etc*) исключи́тельный* (исключи́телен); **these problems are not ~ to ...** э́ти пробле́мы каса́ются не то́лько +*gen ....*

unisex ['ju:nɪsɛks] *adj* для обо́их поло́в.

unison ['ju:nɪsn] *n*: **in ~** (*say*) в оди́н го́лос; (*sing*) в унисо́н.

unissued capital [ʌn'ɪʃu:d-] *n* невы́пущенный акционе́рный капита́л.

unit ['ju:nɪt] *n* (*single whole*) це́лое *nt adj*; (*measurement*) едини́ца; (*section: of furniture etc*) се́кция; (*team, squad*) подразделе́ние; **production ~** едини́ца проду́кции; **kitchen ~** ку́хонная се́кция.

unitary ['ju:nɪtrɪ] *adj* едини́чный* (едини́чен).

unit cost *n* (*COMM*) сто́имость *f* едини́цы проду́кции.

unite [ju:'naɪt] *vt* объединя́ть (объедини́ть *perf*) ♦ *vi* объединя́ться (объедини́ться *perf*).

united [ju:'naɪtɪd] *adj* объединённый*; (*effort*) совме́стный.

United Arab Emirates *npl*: **the ~ ~ ~** Объединённые Ара́бские эмира́ты *mpl.*

United Kingdom *n* Соединённое Короле́вство.

United Nations (Organization) *n* Организа́ция Объединённых На́ций.

United States (of America) *n* Соединённые Шта́ты *mpl* Аме́рики.

unit price *n* (*COMM*) цена́* за едини́цу, шту́чная цена́*.

unit trust *n* (*BRIT*: *COMM*) (довери́тельный) паево́й трест.

unity ['ju:nɪtɪ] *n* еди́нство.

Univ. *abbr* = **university.**

universal [juːnɪ'vəːsl] *adj* универса́льный*
(универса́лен).
universe ['juːnɪvəːs] *n* вселе́нная *f adj.*
university [juːnɪ'vəːsɪtɪ] *n* университе́т ◆ *cpd*
(*education, year*) университе́тский*; ~
student/professor студе́нт(ка*)/профе́ссор
университе́та.
university degree *n* университе́тская
сте́пень* *f.*
unjust [ʌn'dʒʌst] *adj* несправедли́вый
(несправедли́в).
unjustifiable ['ʌndʒʌstɪ'faɪəbl] *adj*
неопра́вданный* (неопра́вдан).
unjustified [ʌn'dʒʌstɪfaɪd] *adj* (*belief, action*)
неопра́вданный* (неопра́вдан); (*text*)
невы́равненный.
unkempt [ʌn'kɛmpt] *adj* (*appearance*)
неопря́тный* (неопря́тен); (*hair, beard*)
растрёпанный* (растрёпан).
unkind [ʌn'kaɪnd] *adj* (*person, comment etc*)
злой; (*behaviour*) зло́бный* (зло́бен).
unkindly [ʌn'kaɪndlɪ] *adv* недоброжела́тельно.
unknown [ʌn'nəun] *adj* неизве́стный
(неизве́стен); ~ **to me** без моего́ ве́дома; ~
quantity (*MATH*) неизве́стная величина́; (*fig*)
зага́дка.
unladen [ʌn'leɪdn] *adj* (*ship*) поро́жний*; ~
weight вес порожняко́м.
unlawful [ʌn'lɔːful] *adj* незако́нный*
(незако́нен).
unleaded petrol ['ʌn'lɛdɪd-] *n* бензи́н не
содержа́щий свинца́.
unleash [ʌn'liːʃ] *vt* (*fig*) дава́ть* (дать* *perf*)
во́лю +*dat.*
unleavened [ʌn'lɛvnd] *adj* пре́сный*.
unless [ʌn'lɛs] *conj* е́сли не; ~ **he comes** е́сли
он не придёт; ~ **otherwise stated** е́сли не
бу́дут даны́ други́е указа́ния; ~ **I am
mistaken** е́сли я не ошиба́юсь.
unlicensed [ʌn'laɪsnst] *adj* (*BRIT: restaurant*) не
име́ющий лице́нзии на прода́жу спиртны́х
напи́тков.
unlike [ʌn'laɪk] *adj* (*not alike*) непохо́жий*
(непохо́ж) ◆ *prep* (*different from*) в отли́чие
от +*gen*; **Russian is grammatically** ~ **English** с
граммати́ческой то́чки зре́ния ру́сский не
похо́ж на англи́йский.
unlikelihood [ʌn'laɪklɪhud] *n* неправдо-
подо́бие.
unlikely [ʌn'laɪklɪ] *adj* (*not likely*) мало-
вероя́тный* (маловероя́тен); (*unexpected*)
невероя́тный* (невероя́тен); **in the** ~ **event of**
при маловероя́тном слу́чае +*gen*; **in the** ~
event that ... в том маловероя́тном слу́чае,
когда́ ....
unlimited [ʌn'lɪmɪtɪd] *adj* (*travel, wine etc*)
неограни́ченный.
unlisted ['ʌn'lɪstɪd] *adj* (*US: TEL*) не

включённый (включён) в телефо́нный
спра́вочник; (*STOCK EXCHANGE*) не
коти́рующийся.
unlit [ʌn'lɪt] *adj* (*room*) неосвещённый.
unload [ʌn'ləud] *vt* (*box, car*) разгружа́ть
(разгрузи́ть* *perf*).
unlock [ʌn'lɔk] *vt* отпира́ть (отпере́ть* *perf*).
unlucky [ʌn'lʌkɪ] *adj* (*person*) невезу́чий
(невезу́ч); (*object, number*) несчастли́вый*; **he
is** ~ ему́ не везёт.
unmanageable [ʌn'mænɪdʒəbl] *adj* (*tool,
vehicle*) трудноконтроли́руемый; (*situation*)
неуправля́емый (неуправля́ем).
unmanned [ʌn'mænd] *adj* (*spacecraft etc*)
автомати́чески управля́емый.
unmarked [ʌn'mɑːkt] *adj* (*unstained*) чи́стый*
(чист); ~ **police car** *полице́йская маши́на без
опознава́тельных зна́ков.*
unmarried [ʌn'mærɪd] *adj* (*man*) нежена́тый
(нежена́т), холосто́й* (хо́лост); (*woman*)
незаму́жняя.
unmarried mother *n* мать* *f*-одино́чка.
unmask [ʌn'mɑːsk] *vt* (*thief etc*) разоблача́ть
(разоблачи́ть* *perf*).
unmatched [ʌn'mætʃt] *adj* непревзойдённый*
(непревзойдён).
unmentionable [ʌn'mɛnʃnəbl] *adj* (*topic*)
запре́тный* (запре́тен); (*word*)
неприли́чный* (неприли́чен).
unmerciful [ʌn'məːsɪful] *adj* безжа́лостный*
(безжа́лостен).
unmistak(e)able [ʌnmɪs'teɪkəbl] *adj* (*voice,
sound*) характе́рный*.
unmistak(e)ably [ʌnmɪs'teɪkəblɪ] *adv* я́вно.
unmitigated [ʌn'mɪtɪgeɪtɪd] *adj* по́лный*.
unnamed [ʌn'neɪmd] *adj* (*nameless*)
безымя́нный; (*anonymous*) не назва́вший
себя́.
unnatural [ʌn'nætʃrəl] *adj* неесте́ственный*
(неесте́ствен); (*against nature*)
противоесте́ственный* (противоесте́ствен).
unnecessarily [ʌn'nɛsəsərɪlɪ] *adv* изли́шне.
unnecessary [ʌn'nɛsəsərɪ] *adj* изли́шний*
(изли́шен).
unnerve [ʌn'nəːv] *vt* трево́жить (встрево́жить*
perf).
unnoticed [ʌn'nəutɪst] *adj* незаме́ченный.
UNO ['juːnəu] *n abbr* (= *United Nations
Organization*) ООН= *Организа́ция
Объединённых На́ций.*
unobservant [ʌnəb'zəːvnt] *adj* (*person*)
ненаблюда́тельный* (ненаблюда́телен).
unobtainable [ʌnəb'teɪnəbl] *adj*: **this book is** ~
э́ту кни́гу нельзя́ доста́ть; **this number is** ~
э́тот но́мер не функциони́рует.
unobtrusive [ʌnəb'truːsɪv] *adj* (*person*)
ненавя́зчивый (ненавя́зчив); (*engine*)
бесшу́мный* (бесшу́мен).

---

* marks translations which have irregular inflections. The Russian-English side of the dictionary gives inflectional information.

unoccupied [ʌn'ɔkjupaɪd] *adj* (*also* MIL) неза́нятый.

unofficial [ʌnə'fɪʃl] *adj* неофициа́льный* (неофициа́лен).

unopened [ʌn'əupənd] *adj* (*letter*) нераспеча́танный; (*tin, bottle etc*) неоткры́тый.

unopposed [ʌnə'pəuzd] *adj* не встре́тивший сопротивле́ния.

unorthodox [ʌn'ɔ:θədɔks] *adj* (*treatment*) неортодокса́льный* (неортодокса́лен); (*REL*) неортодокса́льный.

unpack [ʌn'pæk] *vi* распако́вываться (распакова́ться *perf*) ◆ *vt* распако́вывать (распакова́ть *perf*).

unpaid [ʌn'peɪd] *adj* (*bill*) неопла́ченный; (*time off*) неопла́чиваемый; (*work*) неопла́чиваемый; (*worker*) беспла́тный.

unpalatable [ʌn'pælətəbl] *adj* (*meal*) невку́сный* (невку́сен); (*truth*) го́рький* (го́рек).

unparalleled [ʌn'pærəleld] *adj* несравни́мый (несравни́м).

unpatriotic ['ʌnpætrɪ'ɔtɪk] *adj* (*person*) непатриоти́чески настро́енный; (*speech, attitude*) непатриоти́чный* (непатриоти́чен).

unplanned [ʌn'plænd] *adj* (*visit, baby*) незаплани́рованный.

unpleasant [ʌn'plɛznt] *adj* неприя́тный* (неприя́тен).

unplug [ʌn'plʌg] *vt* отключа́ть (отключи́ть* *perf*) от сети́.

unpolluted [ʌnpə'lu:tɪd] *adj* (*river, water etc*) незагрязнённый.

unpopular [ʌn'pɔpjulə] *adj* (*person, decision etc*) непопуля́рный* (непопуля́рен); **to make o.s. ~ (with)** теря́ть (потеря́ть *perf*) популя́рность (у +*gen*).

unprecedented [ʌn'prɛsɪdəntɪd] *adj* беспрецеде́нтный* (беспрецеде́нтен).

unpredictable [ʌnprɪ'dɪktəbl] *adj* непредсказу́емый (непредсказу́ем).

unprejudiced [ʌn'prɛdʒudɪst] *adj* (*not biased*) непредвзя́тый; (*having no prejudices*) непредубеждённый*.

unprepared [ʌnprɪ'pɛəd] *adj* (*person, speech*) неподгото́вленный.

unprepossessing ['ʌnpri:pə'zɛsɪŋ] *adj* нерасполага́ющий.

unpretentious [ʌnprɪ'tɛnʃəs] *adj* непретенцио́зный* (непретенцио́зен).

unprincipled [ʌn'prɪnsɪpld] *adj* (*person*) беспри́нципный* (беспри́нципен).

unproductive [ʌnprə'dʌktɪv] *adj* (*land*) неплодоро́дный* (неплодоро́ден); (*discussion*) непродукти́вный* (непродукти́вен); (*labour*) непроизводи́тельный* (непроизводи́телен).

unprofessional [ʌnprə'fɛʃənl] *adj* непрофессиона́льный (непрофессиона́лен)*.

unprofitable [ʌn'prɔfɪtəbl] *adj* невы́годный* (невы́годен).

unprotected ['ʌnprə'tɛktɪd] *adj* незащищённый; **~ sex** секс без контрацепти́вов.

unprovoked [ʌnprə'vəukt] *adj* (*attack*) неспровоци́рованный.

unpunished [ʌn'pʌnɪʃt] *adj*: **to go ~** остава́ться* (оста́ться* *perf*) безнака́занным(-ой).

unqualified [ʌn'kwɔlɪfaɪd] *adj* (*teacher, nurse etc*) неквалифици́рованный; (*disaster, success*) соверше́нный.

unquestionably [ʌn'kwɛstʃənəblɪ] *adv* бесспо́рно.

unquestioning [ʌn'kwɛstʃənɪŋ] *adj* беспрекосло́вный* (беспрекосло́вен).

unravel [ʌn'rævl] *vt* (*ball of string*) распу́тывать (распу́тать *perf*); (*mystery*) разга́дывать (разгада́ть *perf*).

unreal [ʌn'rɪəl] *adj* (*not real*) нереа́льный* (нереа́лен); (*peculiar*) фантасти́ческий.

unrealistic ['ʌnrɪə'lɪstɪk] *adj* (*person, project*) нереалисти́чный* (нереалисти́чен).

unreasonable [ʌn'ri:znəbl] *adj* (*person, attitude, demand*) неразу́мный* (неразу́мен); (*length of time*) нереа́льный* (нереа́лен).

unrecognizable [ʌn'rɛkəgnaɪzəbl] *adj* неузнава́емый (неузнава́ем).

unrecognized [ʌn'rɛkəgnaɪzd] *adj* (*also* POL) непри́знанный*.

unreconstructed ['ʌnri:kən'strʌktɪd] *adj* (US) неисправи́мый (неисправи́м).

unrecorded [ʌnrə'kɔ:dɪd] *adj* (*piece of music etc*) незапи́санный; (*incident, statement*) незафикси́рованный.

unrefined [ʌnrə'faɪnd] *adj* (*petroleum*) неочи́щенный; (*sugar*) нерафини́рованный.

unrehearsed [ʌnrɪ'hə:st] *adj* (THEAT) неотрепети́рованный; (*spontaneous*) неподгото́вленный.

unrelated [ʌnrɪ'leɪtɪd] *adj* (*incident*) отде́льный; **to be ~** (*people*) не состоя́ть (*impf*) в родстве́.

unrelenting [ʌnrɪ'lɛntɪŋ] *adj* неумоли́мый (неумоли́м).

unreliable [ʌnrɪ'laɪəbl] *adj* ненадёжный* (ненадёжен).

unrelieved [ʌnrɪ'li:vd] *adj* (*monotony*) невыноси́мый (невыноси́м).

unremitting [ʌnrɪ'mɪtɪŋ] *adj* неосла́бный* (неосла́бен).

unrepeatable [ʌnrɪ'pi:təbl] *adj* (*offer*) неповтори́мый; (*comment*) неприли́чный* (неприли́чен).

unrepentant [ʌnrɪ'pɛntənt] *adj* нераска́явшийся.

unrepresentative ['ʌnrɛprɪ'zɛntətɪv] *adj*: **~ (of)** нетипи́чный* (нетипи́чен) (для +*acc*).

unreserved [ʌnrɪ'zə:vd] *adj* (*seat*) незаброни́рованный; (*approval, admiration*) по́лный*.

unreservedly [ʌnrɪ'zə:vɪdlɪ] *adv* по́лностью.

unresponsive [ʌnrɪs'pɔnsɪv] *adj* без-

разли́чный* (безразли́чен).
unrest [ʌnˈrɛst] *n* волне́ния *ntpl*.
unrestricted [ʌnrɪˈstrɪktɪd] *adj* (*power, time*)
неограни́ченный*; **to have ~ access to** име́ть
(*impf*) неограни́ченный до́ступ к +*dat*.
unrewarded [ʌnrɪˈwɔːdɪd] *adj* (*efforts*)
безуспе́шный* (безуспе́шен).
unripe [ʌnˈraɪp] *adj* незре́лый (незре́л).
unrivalled [ʌnˈraɪvəld] (*US* **unrivaled**) *adj*
непревзойдённый* (непревзойдён).
unroll [ʌnˈrəul] *vt* развёртывать (разверну́ть
perf).
unruffled [ʌnˈrʌfld] *adj* (*person*) невоз-
мути́мый (невозмути́м); (*hair*) гла́дкий*.
unruly [ʌnˈruːlɪ] *adj* непослу́шный*
(непослу́шен).
unsafe [ʌnˈseɪf] *adj* опа́сный* (опа́сен);
(*machine, bridge, car etc*) ненадёжный*
(ненадёжен); (*method*) риско́ванный*; **~ to
eat/drink** непригодный* (непригоден) для
еды́/питья́.
unsaid [ʌnˈsɛd] *adj*: **to leave sth ~** не
упомина́ть (*impf*) о чём-н.
unsaleable [ʌnˈseɪləbl] (*US* **unsalable**) *adj*
неходово́й.
unsatisfactory [ˈʌnsætɪsˈfæktərɪ] *adj* неудовле-
твори́тельный* (неудовлетвори́телен).
unsatisfied [ʌnˈsætɪsfaɪd] *adj*
неудовлетворённый.
unsavoury [ʌnˈseɪvərɪ] (*US* **unsavory**) *adj* (*fig*)
сомни́тельный* (сомни́телен).
unscathed [ʌnˈskeɪðd] *adj* невреди́мый
(невреди́м).
unscientific [ˈʌnsaɪənˈtɪfɪk] *adj* ненау́чный*
(ненау́чен).
unscrew [ʌnˈskruː] *vt* отви́нчивать
(отвинти́ть* *perf*).
unscrupulous [ʌnˈskruːpjuləs] *adj*
бессо́вестный*.
unseat [ʌnˈsiːt] *vt* (*from office*) смеща́ть
(смести́ть* *perf*).
unsecured [ʌnsɪˈkjuəd] *adj*: **~ creditor**
незастрахо́ванный кредито́р; **~ loan**
необеспе́ченный заём*.
unseemly [ʌnˈsiːmlɪ] *adj* непристо́йный*
(непристо́ен).
unseen [ʌnˈsiːn] *adj* (*person*) неви́димый
(неви́дим); (*danger*) скры́тый (скрыт).
unselfish [ʌnˈsɛlfɪʃ] *adj* бескоры́стный*
(бескоры́стен).
unsettled [ʌnˈsɛtld] *adj* (*person*) беспоко́йный*
(беспоко́ен); (*future*) нея́сный* (нея́сен);
(*question*) нерешённый; (*weather*)
неусто́йчивый (неусто́йчив).
unsettling [ʌnˈsɛtlɪŋ] *adj* трево́жный*
(трево́жен).
unshak(e)able [ʌnˈʃeɪkəbl] *adj*
непоколеби́мый (непоколеби́м).

unshaven [ʌnˈʃeɪvn] *adj* небри́тый (небри́т).
unsightly [ʌnˈsaɪtlɪ] *adj* непригля́дный*
(непригля́ден).
unskilled [ʌnˈskɪld] *adj* (*worker, work*)
неквалифици́рованный*.
unsociable [ʌnˈsəuʃəbl] *adj* (*person*)
необщи́тельный* (необщи́телен); (*way of
life*) за́мкнутый (за́мкнут).
unsocial [ʌnˈsəuʃl] *adj*: **~ hours** сверхуро́чные
часы́.
unsold [ʌnˈsəuld] *adj* (*goods*) непро́данный.
unsolicited [ʌnsəˈlɪsɪtɪd] *adj* (*advice*)
непро́шенный; (*goods*) незатре́бованный.
unsophisticated [ʌnsəˈfɪstɪkeɪtɪd] *adj*
бесхи́тростный* (бесхи́тростен); (*method,
device*) просто́й* (прост).
unsound [ʌnˈsaund] *adj* (*health*) сла́бый*
(слаб); (*floor, foundations*) непро́чный*
(непро́чен); (*policy*) ша́ткий* (ша́ток);
(*advice*) ненадёжный* (ненадёжен).
unspeakable [ʌnˈspiːkəbl] *adj*
отврати́тельный (отврати́телен).
unspoken [ʌnˈspəukn] *adj* (*word*)
невы́сказанный; (*agreement, approval*)
молчали́вый.
unstable [ʌnˈsteɪbl] *adj* (*piece of furniture*)
неусто́йчивый (неусто́йчив); (*government*)
нестаби́льный* (нестаби́лен); (*person:
mentally*) неуравнове́шенный*
(неуравнове́шен).
unsteady [ʌnˈstɛdɪ] *adj* (*step*) нетвёрдый
(нетвёрд); (*voice, hands, legs*) дрожа́щий;
(*ladder*) неусто́йчивый (неусто́йчив),
ша́ткий* (ша́ток).
unstinting [ʌnˈstɪntɪŋ] *adj* (*support*) огро́мный*
(огро́мен); (*generosity*) бесконе́чный*
(бесконе́чен).
unstuck [ʌnˈstʌk] *adj*: **to come ~** (*label etc*)
откле́иваться (откле́иться *perf*); (*plan, idea
etc*) расстра́иваться (расстро́иться *perf*).
unsubstantiated [ˈʌnsəbˈstænʃɪeɪtɪd] *adj*
(*rumour*) неподтверждённый; (*accusation*)
необосно́ванный.
unsuccessful [ʌnsəkˈsɛsful] *adj* (*attempt*)
безуспе́шный* (безуспе́шен); (*writer*)
посре́дственный* (посре́дствен); (*proposal,
marriage*) неуда́чный* (неуда́чен); **to be ~ in
sth** терпе́ть* (потерпе́ть* *perf*) неуда́чу в +*prp*;
your application was ~ Ва́ше заявле́ние не
при́нято.
unsuccessfully [ʌnsəkˈsɛsfəlɪ] *adv* безуспе́шно.
unsuitable [ʌnˈsuːtəbl] *adj* неподходя́щий*.
unsuited [ʌnˈsuːtɪd] *adj*: **to be ~ for** *or* **to** не
подходи́ть* (*impf*) для +*gen*.
unsung [ˈʌnsʌŋ] *adj* незаме́ченный.
unsure [ʌnˈʃuə] *adj* (*uncertain*) неуве́ренный*
(неуве́рен); **he is ~ of himself** он неуве́рен в
себе́.

---

unsuspecting [ʌnsəs'pɛktɪŋ] *adj* ничего не
подозревающий.
unsweetened [ʌn'swi:tnd] *adj*
неподслащённый.
unswerving [ʌn'swə:vɪŋ] *adj* непоколебимый
(непоколебим).
unsympathetic ['ʌnsɪmpə'θɛtɪk] *adj*
равнодушный* (равнодушен); (*unlikeable*)
несимпатичный* (несимпатичен); ~ **to** *or*
towards равнодушный +*dat*.
untangle [ʌn'tæŋgl] *vt* распутывать
(распутать *perf*).
untapped [ʌn'tæpt] *adj* (*resources*)
неиспользованный.
untaxed [ʌn'tækst] *adj* не облагаемый
(облагаем) налогом.
unthinkable [ʌn'θɪŋkəbl] *adj* немыслимый
(немыслим).
unthinking [ʌn'θɪŋkɪŋ] *adj* бездумный*
(бездумен).
untidy [ʌn'taɪdɪ] *adj* неопрятный* (неопрятен);
(*work, writing*) неаккуратный*
(неаккуратен).
untie [ʌn'taɪ] *vt* (*lace, person*) развязывать
(развязать* *perf*); (*dog, horse etc*) отвязывать
(отвязать* *perf*).
until [ən'tɪl] *prep* до +*gen*; (*after negative*) пока ♦
conj пока не; ~ **he comes** пока он не придёт;
~ **now/then** до сих/тех пор; **from morning** ~
night с утра до ночи.
untimely [ʌn'taɪmlɪ] *adj* (*inopportune: moment*)
неподходящий*; (: *arrival*) несвоевременный* (несвоевременен); (*death*)
безвременный.
untold [ʌn'təuld] *adj* (*story*) нерассказанный;
(*joy, suffering*) невыразимый; (*wealth*)
несметный.
untouched [ʌn'tʌtʃt] *adj* (*not used etc*)
нетронутый (нетронут); (*safe*) невредимый
(невредим); ~ **by** (*unaffected*) нетронутый
(нетронут) +*instr*.
untoward [ʌntə'wɔ:d] *adj* (*events*) скверный*
(скверен); (*effects*) отрицательный*
(отрицателен).
untrained ['ʌn'treɪnd] *adj* нетренированный.
untrammelled [ʌn'træmld] *adj* раскованный*
(раскован).
untranslatable [ʌntrænz'leɪtəbl] *adj*
непереводимый.
untried [ʌn'traɪd] *adj* (*policy, remedy*)
неиспытанный; (*prisoner*) не
подвергавшийся суду.
untrue [ʌn'tru:] *adj* ложный* (ложен).
untrustworthy [ʌn'trʌstwə:ðɪ] *adj*
ненадёжный* (ненадёжен).
unusable [ʌn'ju:zəbl] *adj* непригодный*
(непригоден).
unused[1] [ʌn'ju:zd] *adj* (*not used*)
неиспользованный.
unused[2] [ʌn'ju:st] *adj*: **he is** ~ **to it** он к этому
не привык; **she is** ~ **to flying** она не

привыкла летать.
unusual [ʌn'ju:ʒuəl] *adj* (*strange*) необычный*
(необычен); (*rare*) редкий* (редок);
(*exceptional, distinctive*) необыкновенный*
(необыкновенен).
unusually [ʌn'ju:ʒuəlɪ] *adv* (*large, high etc*)
необыкновенно.
unveil [ʌn'veɪl] *vt* (*statue*) открывать
(открыть* *perf*).
unwanted [ʌn'wɔntɪd] *adj* (*clothing etc*)
ненужный; (*child, pregnancy*) нежеланный.
unwarranted [ʌn'wɔrəntɪd] *adj* необосно-
ванный*.
unwary [ʌn'wɛərɪ] *adj* неосторожный*
(неосторожен).
unwavering [ʌn'weɪvərɪŋ] *adj* (*faith*) твёрдый*
(твёрд), непоколебимый (непоколебим);
(*gaze*) пристальный* (пристален).
unwelcome [ʌn'wɛlkəm] *adj* (*guest*)
непрошенный; (*news*) неприятный*
(неприятен); **to feel** ~ чувствовать (*impf*) себя
лишним.
unwell [ʌn'wɛl] *adj*: **to feel** ~ чувствовать (*impf*)
себя плохо; **he is** ~ ему нездоровится, он
нездоров.
unwieldy [ʌn'wi:ldɪ] *adj* громоздкий*
(громоздок).
unwilling [ʌn'wɪlɪŋ] *adj*: **to be** ~ **to do** не
хотеть* (*impf*) +*infin*.
unwillingly [ʌn'wɪlɪŋlɪ] *adv* неохотно.
unwind [ʌn'waɪnd] *irreg vt* (*undo*) разматывать
(размотать* *perf*) ♦ *vi* (*relax*) расслабляться
(расслабиться* *perf*).
unwise [ʌn'waɪz] *adj* неблагоразумный*
(неблагоразумен).
unwitting [ʌn'wɪtɪŋ] *adj* невольный.
unworkable [ʌn'wə:kəbl] *adj* неосуществимый
(неосуществим).
unworthy [ʌn'wə:ðɪ] *adj* недостойный*
(недостоен); **to be** ~ **of sth/to do** быть* (*impf*)
недостойным(-ой) чего-н/+*infin*; **that remark
is** ~ **of you** Вам не пристало это говорить.
unwrap [ʌn'ræp] *vt* разворачивать
(развернуть* *perf*).
unwritten [ʌn'rɪtn] *adj* (*law, agreement*)
неписаный.
unzip [ʌn'zɪp] *vt* расстёгивать (расстегнуть*
perf) на молнию.

KEYWORD

up [ʌp] *prep*: **he went up the stairs/the hill** он
поднялся по лестнице/на гору; **the cat was
up a tree** кошка была на дереве; **they live
further up the street** они живут дальше на
этой улице; **he has gone up to Scotland** он
поехал в Шотландию
♦ *adv* **1** (*upwards, higher*): **up in the sky/the
mountains** высоко в небе/в горах; **put the
picture a bit higher up** повесьте картину
немного повыше; **up there** (*up above*) там
наверху; **there's a village and up above, on the
hill, a monastery** там есть деревня, а над ней,

на холме – монасты́рь
2: **to be up** (*out of bed*) встава́ть* (встать*
perf); (*prices, level*) поднима́ться (подня́ться*
perf); **the tent is up** пала́тка поста́влена
3: **up to** (*as far as*) до +*gen*; **I've read up to page
five** я дочита́л до пя́той страни́цы; **up to
now** до сих пор
4: **to be up to** (*depending on*) зави́сеть* (*impf*)
от +*gen*; **it's not up to me to decide** не мне
реша́ть; **it's up to you** э́то ва́ше де́ло
5: **to be up to** (*inf: be doing*) затева́ть (*impf*);
he's not up to the job он не тя́нет на э́ту
рабо́ту; **his work is not up to the required
standard** его́ рабо́та не соотве́тствует
тре́буемым станда́ртам; **what is he up to?**
что он затева́ет?; **what's she up to these
days?** а что она́ тепе́рь поде́лывает?
♦ *n*: **ups and downs** (*in life, career*) взлёты *mpl*
и паде́ния *ntpl*.

up-and-coming [ʌpənd'kʌmɪŋ] *adj*
перспекти́вный* (перспекти́вен).
upbeat ['ʌpbiːt] *n* (*MUS*) сла́бая до́ля та́кта;
(*ECON*) подъём ♦ *adj* (*optimistic*)
оживлённый* (оживлён).
upbraid [ʌp'breɪd] *vt* упрека́ть (упрекну́ть
perf).
upbringing ['ʌpbrɪŋɪŋ] *n* воспита́ние.
upcoming ['ʌpkʌmɪŋ] *adj* (*forthcoming*)
предстоя́щий*, гря́дущий.
update [ʌp'deɪt] *vt* (*records, information*)
вноси́ть* (внести́* *perf*) измене́ния и
дополне́ния.
upend [ʌp'ɛnd] *vt* перевора́чивать
(переверну́ть *perf*) (вверх нога́ми).
upfront [ʌp'frʌnt] *adj* (*inf: frank*) откры́тый
(откры́т) ♦ *adv* (*pay*) вперёд.
upgrade [ʌp'greɪd] *vt* (*improve: house*)
модернизи́ровать (*impf/perf*); (: *job*)
усложня́ть (усложни́ть *perf*); (*employee*)
повыша́ть (повы́сить* *perf*) в до́лжности;
(*COMPUT*) нара́щивать (*impf*)
вычисли́тельные возмо́жности,
модернизи́ровать (*impf/perf*).
upheaval [ʌp'hiːvl] *n* переворо́т.
uphill [ʌp'hɪl] *adj* (*fig: task*) тяжёлый* (тяжёл) ♦
adv (*face, look*) вверх; (*go, move*) в го́ру; **to go
~** поднима́ться (*impf*) в го́ру.
uphold [ʌp'həuld] (*irreg: like hold*) *vt*
подде́рживать (поддержа́ть* *perf*).
upholstery [ʌp'həulstəri] *n* оби́вка.
upkeep ['ʌpkiːp] *n* содержа́ние.
up-market [ʌp'maːkɪt] *adj* (*product*) дорого́й;
(*area*) элита́рный.
upon [ə'pɔn] *prep* (*position*) на +*prp*; (*motion*) на
+*acc*.
upper ['ʌpə'] *adj* ве́рхний* ♦ *n* (*of shoe*) верх.
upper class *n*: **the ~** ~ вы́сший* класс.
upper-class ['ʌpə'klɑːs] *adj* (*families, accent*)

аристократи́ческий*; (*district*) элита́рный.
uppercut ['ʌpəkʌt] *n* (*BOXING*) апперко́т.
upper hand *n*: **to have the ~ ~** контрол-
и́ровать (*impf*).
Upper House *n* (*BRIT*) Пала́та Ло́рдов.
uppermost ['ʌpəməust] *adj* вы́сший*; **what was
~ in my mind** что бо́льше всего́ занима́ло
мои́ мы́сли.
Upper Volta [-'vɔltə] *n* Ве́рхняя Во́льта,
Бурки́на-Фасо́ *nt ind*.
upright ['ʌpraɪt] *adj* (*straight, honest*) прямо́й*
(прям); (*vertical*) вертика́льный*
(вертика́лен) ♦ *n* (*CONSTR*) вертика́льная
сто́йка*.
uprising ['ʌpraɪzɪŋ] *n* восста́ние.
uproar ['ʌprɔː'] *n* (*protests*) возмуще́ние;
(*shouts*) шум.
uproarious [ʌp'rɔːrɪəs] *adj* (*people*)
хохо́чущий; (*play etc*) ужа́сно смешно́й
(смешо́н).
uproot [ʌp'ruːt] *vt* (*tree*) вырыва́ть (вы́рвать
perf) с ко́рнем; (*fig: people*) снима́ть (снять*
perf) с ме́ста.
upset [*vb, adj* ʌp'sɛt, *n* 'ʌpsɛt] (*irreg: like set*) *vt*
(*glass etc*) опроки́дывать (опроки́нуть *perf*);
(*routine*) наруша́ть (нару́шить *perf*); (*plan,
person*) расстра́ивать (расстро́ить *perf*);
(*person: offend*) оскорбля́ть (оскорби́ть*
perf) ♦ *adj* расстро́енный* (расстро́ен) ♦ *n* (*to
plan etc*) наруше́ние; **to get ~** (*sad*)
расстра́иваться (расстро́иться *perf*);
(*offended*) оскорбля́ться (оскорби́ться* *perf*);
to have a stomach ~ (*BRIT*) страда́ть (*impf*)
расстро́йством желу́дка.
upset price ['ʌpsɛt-] *n* (*US, SCOTTISH*) ни́зшая
отправна́я цена́ на аукцио́не.
upsetting [ʌp'sɛtɪŋ] *adj* (*annoying*) доса́дный.
upshot ['ʌpʃɔt] *n* результа́т; **the ~ of it all was
that ...** кончи́лось всё тем, что ....
upside down ['ʌpsaɪd-] *adv* (*hang, hold*) вверх
нога́ми; (*turn*) вверх дном; **to turn a place ~
~** (*fig*) переверну́ть (*perf*) всё вверх дном.
upstairs [ʌp'stɛəz] *adv* (*be*) наверху́; (*go*)
наве́рх ♦ *adj* (*window, room*) ве́рхний* ♦ *n*
ве́рхний* эта́ж*; **there's no ~** здесь нет
ве́рхнего этажа́.
upstage [ʌp'steɪdʒ] *vt* затмева́ть (затми́ть*
perf).
upstart ['ʌpstaːt] *n* (*pej: person*) вы́скочка* *m/f*.
upstream [ʌp'striːm] *adv* про́тив тече́ния ♦ *adj*
вверх по тече́нию.
upsurge ['ʌpsəːdʒ] *n* (*of enthusiasm etc*)
подъём.
uptake ['ʌpteɪk] *n*: **to be quick/slow on the ~**
бы́стро/ме́дленно сообража́ть (*impf*).
uptight [ʌp'taɪt] *adj* (*inf*) натя́нутый (натя́нут).
up-to-date ['ʌptə'deɪt] *adj* (*information*)
после́дний*; (*person*) совреме́нный*

---

* marks translations which have irregular inflections. The Russian-English side of the dictionary gives inflectional information.

(совремёнен).

upturn ['ʌptəːn] *n* (*in economy*) подъём.

upturned ['ʌptəːnd] *adj* (*nose*) курнóсый (курнóс), вздёрнутый (вздёрнут).

upward ['ʌpwəd] *adj*: ~ **movement/glance** движéние/взгляд вверх ♦ *adv* = **upwards**.

upwardly mobile ['ʌpwədlɪ-] *adj* преуспевáющий; **a new ~ ~ generation** нóвое поколéние преуспевáющих людéй.

upwards ['ʌpwədz] *adv* (*move, glance*) вверх; (*more than*): ~ **of** свыше +*gen*.

URA *n abbr* (*US*: = *Urban Renewal Administration*) *правúтельственная организáция, координúрующая рабóты по обновлéнию и улучшéнию устрóйства городóв.*

Ural Mountains ['juərəl-] *npl*: **the ~ ~** (*also*: **the Urals**) Урáл *msg*, Урáльские гóры *fpl*.

uranium [juə'reɪnɪəm] *n* урáн.

Uranus [juə'reɪnəs] *n* Урáн.

urban ['əːbən] *adj* городскóй.

urbane [əː'beɪn] *adj* учтúвый (учтúв).

urbanization ['əːbənaɪ'zeɪʃən] *n* урбанизáция.

urchin ['əːtʃɪn] *n* (*pej*) беспризóрник(-ица).

Urdu ['uəduː] *n* язык* урдý.

urge [əːdʒ] *n* (*need, desire*) потрéбность *f* ♦ *vt*: **to ~ sb to do** настоя́тельно совéтовать (*impf*) комý-н +*infin*; **to ~ caution** совéтовать (посовéтовать *perf*) быть* осторóжным(-ой)

► **urge on** *vt* подгоня́ть (*impf*).

urgency ['əːdʒənsɪ] *n* (*of task etc*) неотлóжность *f*, безотлагáтельность *f*; (*of tone*) настóйчивость *f*.

urgent ['əːdʒənt] *adj* (*need, message*) срóчный* (срóчен); (*voice*) настóйчивый (настóйчив).

urgently ['əːdʒəntlɪ] *adv* срóчно.

urinal ['juərɪnl] *n* (*building*) мужскóй туалéт; (*vessel*) писсуáр.

urinate ['juərɪneɪt] *vi* мочúться* (помочúться* *perf*).

urine ['juərɪn] *n* мочá.

urn [əːn] *n* (*container*) ýрна; (*also*: **tea ~**) бак.

Uruguay ['juərəgwaɪ] *n* Уругвáй.

Uruguayan [juərə'gwaɪən] *adj* уругвáйский* ♦ *n* уругвáец*(-áйка*).

US *n abbr* = **United States**.

us [ʌs] *pron* (*direct*) нас; (*indirect*) нам; (*after prep*: +*gen*, +*prp*) нас; (: +*dat*) нам; (: +*instr*) нáми; (*referring to subject of sentence*) свой; **a few of ~ are going to the cinema** нéкоторые из нас идýт в кинó; *see also* **me**.

USA *n abbr* (= **United States of America**) США= *Соединённые Штáты Амéрики*; (*MIL*) = *United States Army*.

usable ['juːzəbl] *adj* пригóдный* (пригóден).

USAF *n abbr* = *United States Air Force*.

usage ['juːzɪdʒ] *n* (*LING*) употреблéние.

USCG *n abbr* = *United States Coast Guard*.

USDA *n abbr* = *United States Department of Agriculture*.

USDAW ['ʌzdɔː] *n abbr* (*BRIT*) = *Union of Shop,*

Distributive and Allied Workers.

USDI *n abbr* (= *United States Department of the Interior*) ≈ Министéрство внýтренних дел.

use [*vt* juːz, *n* juːs] *vt* (*object, tool*) испóльзовать (*impf/perf*); (*phrase*) употребля́ть (употребúть* *perf*) ♦ *n* (*using*) испóльзование, употреблéние; (*usefulness*) пóльза; (*purpose*) применéние; **she ~d to do it** онá когдá-то занимáлась э́тим; **what's this ~d for?** для чегó э́то употребля́ется?; **to be ~d to** быть* (*impf*) привы́чным(-ой) к +*dat*; **to get ~d to** привыкáть (привы́кнуть* *perf*) к +*dat*; **to be in ~** употребля́ться (*impf*), быть* (*impf*) в употреблéнии; **to be out of ~** не употребля́ться (*impf*); **to be of ~** быть* (*impf*) полéзным(-ой); **to make ~ of sth** испóльзовать (*impf/perf*) что-н; **it's no ~** э́то бесполéзно; **to have the ~ of** пóльзоваться (*impf*) +*instr*.

► **use up** *vt* (*food, leftovers*) испóльзовать (*impf/perf*); (*money*) расхóдовать (израсхóдовать *perf*).

used [juːzd] *adj* (*object*) бы́вший* в употреблéнии; (*car*) подéржанный*.

useful ['juːsful] *adj* полéзный* (полéзен); **to come in ~** пригодúться* (*perf*).

usefulness ['juːsfəlnɪs] *n* пóльза.

useless ['juːslɪs] *adj* (*unusable*) непригóдный* (непригóден); (*pointless, hopeless*) бесполéзный* (бесполéзен).

user ['juːzə*] *n* пóльзователь *f*; (*of petrol, gas etc*) потребúтель *m*.

user-friendliness ['juːzə'frɛndlɪnɪs] *n* простотá в испóльзовании.

user-friendly ['juːzə'frɛndlɪ] *adj* простóй (прост) в испóльзовании.

USES *n abbr* (= *United States Employment Service*) *управлéние по размещéнию и регулúрованию рабóчей сúлы*.

usher ['ʌʃə*] *n* (*at wedding*) распоряди́тель *m* ♦ *vt*: **to ~ sb into** проводúть* (провестú* *perf*) когó-н в +*acc*.

usherette [ʌʃə'rɛt] *n* билетёрша.

USIA *n abbr* (= *United States Information Agency*) ЮСИА (*Информациóнное агéнтство США*).

USM *n abbr* (= *United States Mint*) Монéтный двор США; (= *United States Mail*) Пóчта США.

USN *n abbr* = *United States Navy*.

USPHS *n abbr* = *United States Public Health Service*.

USPO *n abbr* = *United States Post Office*.

USS *abbr* = *United States Ship*.

USSR *n abbr* (*formerly*: = *Union of Soviet Socialist Republics*) СССР = *Союз Совéтских Социалистúческих Респýблик*.

usu. *abbr* = **usually**.

usual ['juːʒuəl] *adj* (*time, place etc*) обы́чный; **as ~** как обы́чно.

usually ['juːʒuəlɪ] *adv* обы́чно.

usurer [ˈjuːʒərəʳ] *n* ростовщи́к*.
usurp [juːˈzəːp] *vt* узурпи́ровать *(impf/perf)*.
usury [ˈjuːʒurɪ] *n* ростовщи́чество.
UT *(US: POST) abbr* = Utah.
utensil [juːˈtɛnsl] *n* инструме́нт; **kitchen** ~**s** ку́хонные принадле́жности.
uterus [ˈjuːtərəs] *n* ма́тка*.
utilitarian [juːtɪlɪˈtɛərɪən] *adj* утилита́рный* (утилита́рен).
utility [juːˈtɪlɪtɪ] *n (usefulness)* поле́зность *f*; **public utilities** коммуна́льные услу́ги *fpl*.
utility room *n* подсо́бная ко́мната, подсо́бка* *(разг)*.
utilization [juːtɪlaɪˈzeɪʃən] *n* утилиза́ция.
utilize [ˈjuːtɪlaɪz] *vt* утилизи́ровать *(impf/perf)*; *(information)* находи́ть (найти́* *perf)* примене́ние +*dat*.

utmost [ˈʌtməust] *adj* велича́йший ♦ *n*: **to do one's** ~ де́лать (сде́лать *perf)* всё возмо́жное; **of the** ~ **importance** велича́йшей ва́жности.
utter [ˈʌtəʳ] *adj (amazement)* по́лный; *(conviction)* глубо́кий*; *(rubbish)* соверше́нный ♦ *vt (sounds)* издава́ть* (изда́ть* *perf)*; *(words)* произноси́ть* (произнести́* *perf)*.
utterance [ˈʌtrns] *n* выска́зывание.
utterly [ˈʌtəlɪ] *adv* соверше́нно.
U-turn [ˈjuːtəːn] *n (AUT)* разворо́т на 180 гра́дусов; *(fig)* коренно́е измене́ние.
Uzbek [ˈʌzbɛk] *n (person)* узбе́к(-е́чка*); *(LING)* узбе́кский* язы́к* ♦ *adj* узбе́кский*.
Uzbekistan [ʌzbɛkɪˈstɑːn] *n* Узбекиста́н.

---

* marks translations which have irregular inflections. The Russian-English side of the dictionary gives inflectional information.

~ V, v ~

V, v [vi:] n (letter) 22-ая буква английского алфавита.

v. abbr = **verse, versus**; (= **volt**) B= вольт; (see: = **vide**) см. смотрй.

VA (US: POST) abbr = Virginia.

vac [væk] n abbr (BRIT: inf) = **vacation**.

vacancy ['veɪkənsɪ] n (BRIT: job) вакансия; (room in hotel etc) свободный номер*; "**no vacancies**" „мест нет"; **have you any vacancies?** (hotel) у Вас есть свободные номера?; (office) у Вас есть вакансии?

vacant ['veɪkənt] adj (room, seat, toilet) свободный* (свободен); (look, expression) отсутствующий; (job) вакантный.

vacant lot n (US) пустырь* m; (: for sale) участок*.

vacate [və'keɪt] vt освобождать (освободить* perf).

vacation [və'keɪʃən] n (esp US: holiday) отпуск*; (BRIT: SCOL) каникулы pl; **to take a ~** брать* (взять* perf) отпуск; **on ~** в отпуске.

vacation course n летние курсы mpl.

vaccinate ['væksɪneɪt] vt: **to ~ sb (against sth)** делать (сделать perf) прививку кому-н (от чего-н).

vaccination [væksɪ'neɪʃən] n прививка*.

vaccine ['væksi:n] n вакцина.

vacuum ['vækjum] n (empty space) вакуум ◆ vt пылесосить (пропылесосить perf).

vacuum cleaner n пылесос.

vacuum flask n (BRIT) термос.

vacuum-packed ['vækjum'pækt] adj герметично упакованный (упакован).

Vaduz [fa'duts] n Вадуц.

vagabond ['vægəbɒnd] n бродяга m/f.

vagary ['veɪɡərɪ] n: **the vagaries of the weather** капризы mpl погоды.

vagina [və'dʒaɪnə] n влагалище.

vagrancy ['veɪɡrənsɪ] n бродяжничество.

vagrant ['veɪɡrənt] n бродяга m/f.

vague [veɪg] adj (blurred: memory, outline) смутный (смутен); (uncertain) неопределённый; (look) рассеянный; (idea, instructions) расплывчатый (расплывчат); (evasive: answer) уклончивый (уклончив); **he was ~ about it** (evasive) он не сказал ничего определённого об этом; **I haven't the ~st idea** я не имею ни малейшего представления.

vaguely ['veɪglɪ] adv (promise, say, plan) неопределённо; (look) рассеянно; (suspect) смутно; **they were ~ amused** они слегка развеселились; **it looks ~ like yours** это немножко напоминает Ваш.

vagueness ['veɪgnɪs] n неопределённость f.

vain [veɪn] adj (conceited) тщеславный* (тщеславен); (useless: attempt, action) тщётный* (тщётен); **in ~** напрасно.

vainly ['veɪnlɪ] adv тщётно.

valance ['væləns] n (for bed) подзор.

valedictorian [vælɪdɪk'tɔ:rɪən] n (US: SCOL) "лучший* выпускник" (в двенадцатом классе средней школы).

valedictory [vælɪ'dɪktərɪ] adj (speech, remarks) прощальный.

valentine ['væləntaɪn] n (also: ~ **card**) (анонимное) любовное послание в день Св. Валентина (14 февраля).

valet ['vælɪt] n камердинер.

valet parking n припарковка автомобилей клиентов, например в гостиницах.

valet service n (for clothes) служба по уходу за одеждой клиентов; (for car) обслуживание автомобилей – мойка, заправка итп.

valiant ['vælɪənt] adj (attempt, effort) отважный* (отважен).

valid ['vælɪd] adj (ticket, document) действительный* (действителен); (reason) веский* (весок); (argument) убедительный* (убедителен).

validate ['vælɪdeɪt] vt (contract, document) утверждать (утвердить* perf); (argument, claim) подтверждать (подтвердить perf).

validity [və'lɪdɪtɪ] n (see adj) действительность f; вескость f; убедительность f.

valise [və'li:z] n саквояж.

Valletta [və'lɛtə] n Валлетта.

valley ['vælɪ] n долина.

valour ['vælər] (US **valor**) n доблесть f.

valuable ['væljuəbl] adj ценный; (time) драгоценный.

valuables ['væljuəblz] npl (jewellery etc) ценности fpl.

valuation [vælju'eɪʃən] n оценка*.

value ['vælju:] n ценность f ◆ vt (fix price or worth of) оценивать (оценить* perf); (appreciate) ценить* (impf); **~s** npl (principles, *beliefs)* це́нности *fpl;* **you get good ~ (for money) in that shop** в э́том магази́не вы́годно покупа́ть; **to lose (in) ~** па́дать (упа́сть* *perf)* в цене́; **to gain (in) ~** поднима́ться (подня́ться* *perf)* в цене́; **to be of great ~ to sb** *(fig)* представля́ть *(impf)* для кого́-н большу́ю це́нность.

value-added tax [vælju:ˈædɪd-] *n* (*BRIT*) нало́г на доба́вленную сто́имость.

valued [ˈvælju:d] *adj* (*customer, advice*) це́нный.

valuer [ˈvæljuəʳ] *n* оце́нщик.

valve [vælv] *n* (*also MED*) кла́пан.

vampire [ˈvæmpaɪəʳ] *n* вампи́р.

van [væn] *n* (*AUT*) фурго́н; (*BRIT: RAIL*) бага́жный ваго́н.

V and A *n abbr* (*BRIT*) = **Victoria and Albert Museum.**

vandal [ˈvændl] *n* ванда́л.

vandalism [ˈvændəlɪzəm] *n* вандали́зм.

vandalize [ˈvændəlaɪz] *vt* (*damage*) бессмы́сленно уро́довать (изуро́довать *perf*); (*destroy*) бессмы́сленно разруша́ть (разру́шить *perf*).

vanguard [ˈvængɑ:d] *n* (*fig*): **in the ~ of** в аванга́рде +*gen.*

vanilla [vəˈnɪlə] *n* вани́ль *f.*

vanilla ice cream *n* ≈ сли́вочное моро́женое *nt adj.*

vanish [ˈvænɪʃ] *vi* исчеза́ть (исче́знуть *perf*).

vanity [ˈvænɪtɪ] *n* (*of person*) тщесла́вие.

vanity case *n* космети́чка*.

vantage point [ˈvɑ:ntɪdʒ-] *n* наблюда́тельный пункт; **from our 20th century ~ ~** (*fig*) с пози́ции на́шего 20-го ве́ка.

vapor *etc* (*US*) = **vapour** *etc.*

vaporize [ˈveɪpəraɪz] *vt* (*liquid*) выпа́ривать (вы́парить *perf*) ◆ *vi* испаря́ться (испари́ться *perf*).

vapour [ˈveɪpəʳ] (*US* **vapor**) *n* (*gas, mist, steam*) пар*.

vapour trail *n* (*AVIAT*) след* самолёта.

variable [ˈvɛərɪəbl] *adj* (*likely to change: mood, quality, weather*) изме́нчивый (изме́нчив); (*able to be changed: temperature, height, speed*) переме́нный ◆ *n* фа́ктор; (*MATH*) переме́нная *f adj.*

variance [ˈvɛərɪəns] *n*: **to be at ~ with** расходи́ться* (*impf*) (с +*instr*); (*facts*) противоре́чить (*impf*) +*dat.*

variant [ˈvɛərɪənt] *n* вариа́нт.

variation [vɛərɪˈeɪʃən] *n* (*in level, amount, quantity*) измене́ние; (*of plot, musical theme etc*) вариа́ция.

varicose veins [ˈværɪkəus-] *npl* (*MED*) варико́зное расшире́ние *ntsg* вен.

varied [ˈvɛərɪd] *adj* разнообра́зный* (разнообра́зен).

variety [vəˈraɪətɪ] *n* разнообра́зие; (*type*) разнови́дность *f*; **a wide ~ of** ... большо́е разнообра́зие +*gen* ...; **for a ~ of reasons** по ря́ду причи́н.

variety show *n* (*THEAT*) варьете́ *nt ind.*

various [ˈvɛərɪəs] *adj* (*different*) разли́чный; (*several*) ра́зный; **at ~ times** в ра́зное вре́мя.

varnish [ˈvɑ:nɪʃ] *n* (*product*) лак; (*also: nail ~*) лак для ногте́й ◆ *vt* (*wood, piece of furniture etc*) покрыва́ть (покры́ть* *perf*) ла́ком; (*nails*) кра́сить* (накра́сить* *perf*).

vary [ˈvɛərɪ] *vt* (*routine, diet*) вноси́ть* (внести́* *perf*) разнообра́зие в +*acc* ◆ *vi* (*be different: sizes, colours*) различа́ться (*impf*); (*become different*): **to ~ with** (*weather, season etc*) меня́ться (*impf*) в зави́симости от +*gen*; **to ~ (according to** *or* **with)** меня́ться (*impf*) (в соотве́тствии с +*instr*).

varying [ˈvɛərɪŋ] *adj* (*amount, opinions etc*) разли́чный* (разли́чен).

vase [vɑ:z] *n* ва́за.

vasectomy [væˈsɛktəmɪ] *n* (*MED*) вазектоми́я.

Vaseline® [ˈvæsɪli:n] *n* вазели́н.

vast [vɑ:st] *adj* (*knowledge*) обши́рный* (обши́рен); (*expense*) грома́дный* (грома́ден); (*area*) необъя́тный* (необъя́тен).

vastly [ˈvɑ:stlɪ] *adv* кра́йне.

vastness [ˈvɑ:stnɪs] *n* необъя́тность *f.*

VAT [væt] *n abbr* (*BRIT*) (= **value-added tax**) НДС= *нало́г на доба́вленную сто́имость.*

vat [væt] *n* ка́дка.

Vatican [ˈvætɪkən] *n*: **the ~** Ватика́н.

vatman [ˈvætmæn] *n* (*BRIT: inf*) *чино́вник, собира́ющий нало́г на доба́вочную сто́имость.*

vaudeville [ˈvəudəvɪl] *n* (*THEAT*) водеви́ль *m.*

vault [vɔ:lt] *n* (*of roof*) свод; (*tomb*) склеп; (*in bank*) храни́лище; (*jump*) опо́рный прыжо́к ◆ *vt* (*also: ~ over*) перепры́гивать (перепры́гнуть *perf*) (че́рез +*acc*).

vaunted [ˈvɔ:ntɪd] *adj*: **much-~** восхваля́емый.

VC *n abbr* = **vice-chairman**; (*BRIT*: = **Victoria Cross**) "Крест Викто́рии" (*вы́сшая вое́нная награ́да*).

VCR *n abbr* = **video cassette recorder.**

VD *n abbr* = **venereal disease.**

VDU *n abbr* (*COMPUT*) = **visual display unit.**

veal [vi:l] *n* (*CULIN*) теля́тина.

veer [vɪəʳ] *vi* (*vehicle*) свора́чивать (сверну́ть *perf*); (*wind*) меня́ть (применя́ть *perf*) направле́ние.

veg. [vɛdʒ] *n abbr* (*BRIT: inf*) = **vegetable(s).**

vegan [ˈvi:gən] *n вегетариа́нец, не употребля́ющий моло́чных проду́ктов* ◆ *adj* расти́тельный.

vegeburger [ˈvɛdʒɪbə:gəʳ] *n* вегетариа́нская котле́та.

---

* marks translations which have irregular inflections. The Russian-English side of the dictionary gives inflectional information.

vegetable ['vɛdʒtəbl] n (BOT) óвощ ◆ adj (oil etc) расти́тельный; (dish) овощно́й; ~ **garden** огоро́д.

vegetarian [vɛdʒɪ'tɛərɪən] n (person) вегетариа́нец*(-áнка*) ◆ adj (diet, restaurant etc) вегетариа́нский*.

vegetate ['vɛdʒɪteɪt] vi (person) прозяба́ть (impf).

vegetation [vɛdʒɪ'teɪʃən] n (plants) расти́тельность f.

vegetative ['vɛdʒɪtətɪv] adj (BIO) вегетати́вный; (fig) расти́тельный.

veggieburger ['vɛdʒɪbəːɡəʳ] n = **vegeburger**.

vehemence ['viːməns] n я́рость f.

vehement ['viːmənt] adj (attack, denial) я́ростный* (я́ростен); (passions) нейстовый (нейстов).

vehicle ['viːɪkl] n автотра́нспортное сре́дство; (fig: means of expressing) сре́дство.

vehicular [vɪ'hɪkjuləʳ] adj (AUT): "no ~ **traffic**" „движе́ние автотра́нспорта запрещено́".

veil [veɪl] n вуа́ль f ◆ vt скрыва́ть (скрыть* perf); **under a ~ of secrecy** (fig) под покро́вом та́йны.

veiled [veɪld] adj (fig: threat) скры́тый.

vein [veɪn] n (of leaf) жи́лка*; (ANAT) ве́на; (of ore) жи́ла; (fig: of mood, style) тон.

Velcro® ['vɛlkrəʊ] n липу́чка.

vellum ['vɛləm] n (writing paper) веле́невая бума́га.

velocity [vɪ'lɔsɪtɪ] n ско́рость f.

velour [və'luəʳ] n велю́р.

velvet ['vɛlvɪt] n ба́рхат ◆ adj ба́рхатный.

vendetta [vɛn'dɛtə] n вендетта.

vending machine ['vɛndɪŋ-] n автома́т по прода́же сигаре́т, шокола́да итп.

vendor ['vɛndəʳ] n (of house, land) продаве́ц; **street ~** у́личный(-ая) торго́вец(-вка).

veneer [və'nɪəʳ] n (on furniture) фане́ровка; (fig: of person, place) личи́на.

venerable ['vɛnərəbl] adj (person) почте́нный; (building etc) дре́вний*; (REL) преподо́бный.

venereal disease [vɪ'nɪərɪəl-] n венери́ческое заболева́ние.

Venetian [vɪ'niːʃən] adj венециа́нский* ◆ n венециа́нец(-áнка*).

Venetian blind n жалюзи́ pl.

Venezuela [vɛnɛ'zweɪlə] n Венесуэ́ла.

Venezuelan [vɛnɛ'zweɪlən] adj венесуэ́льский* ◆ n венесуэ́лец*(-лка).

vengeance ['vɛndʒəns] n возме́здие; **with a ~** (fig) с лихво́й.

vengeful ['vɛndʒful] adj мсти́тельный* (мсти́телен).

Venice ['vɛnɪs] n Вене́ция.

venison ['vɛnɪsn] n олени́на.

venom ['vɛnəm] n (of snake, insect) яд; (bitterness, anger) зло́ба.

venomous ['vɛnəməs] adj (snake, insect) ядови́тый (ядови́т); (look, stare) зло́бный* (зло́бен).

vent [vɛnt] n (also: **air ~**) вентиляцио́нное отве́рстие; (in jacket) разре́з ◆ vt (fig) дава́ть* (дать* perf) вы́ход +dat.

ventilate ['vɛntɪleɪt] vt (room, building) прове́тривать (прове́трить perf).

ventilation [vɛntɪ'leɪʃən] n вентиля́ция.

ventilation shaft n вентиляцио́нная ша́хта.

ventilator ['vɛntɪleɪtəʳ] n (TECH, MED) вентиля́тор.

ventriloquist [vɛn'trɪləkwɪst] n чревовеща́тель (ница) m(f).

venture ['vɛntʃəʳ] n (risky undertaking) сме́лое предприя́тие ◆ vt (opinion) осме́ливаться (осме́литься perf) вы́сказать ◆ vi (dare to go) осме́ливаться (осме́литься perf); **business ~** предприя́тие; **to ~ to do** отва́живаться (отва́житься perf) +infin.

venture capital n (COMM) ве́нчурный капита́л.

venue ['vɛnjuː] n (place fixed for sth) ме́сто* проведе́ния.

Venus ['viːnəs] n (planet) Вене́ра.

veracity [və'ræsɪtɪ] n правди́вость f.

veranda(h) [və'rændə] n вера́нда.

verb [vəːb] n глаго́л.

verbal ['vəːbl] adj (spoken: skills, translation etc) у́стный; (of a verb) глаго́льный.

verbally ['vəːbəlɪ] adv (communicate, transmit) на слова́х.

verbatim [vəː'beɪtɪm] adj досло́вный ◆ adv досло́вно.

verbose [vəː'bəus] adj (person, writing) многосло́вный.

verdict ['vəːdɪkt] n (LAW) пригово́р; (fig: opinion) заключе́ние; **to bring in a ~ of guilty/ not guilty** выноси́ть* (вы́нести* perf) обвини́тельный/оправда́тельный пригово́р.

verge [vəːdʒ] n (BRIT: of road) обо́чина; "**soft ~s**" (BRIT: AUT) незаасфальти́рованная, грунтова́я обо́чина; **to be on the ~ of sth** быть* (impf) на гра́ни чего́-н

▶ **verge on** vt fus (panic etc) грани́чить (impf) с +instr.

verger ['vəːdʒəʳ] n (REL) церко́вный служи́тель m.

verification [vɛrɪfɪ'keɪʃən] n (see vb) подтвержде́ние; прове́рка.

verify ['vɛrɪfaɪ] vt (confirm) подтвержда́ть (подтверди́ть* perf); (check) проверя́ть (прове́рить perf).

veritable ['vɛrɪtəbl] adj (for emphasis: real) настоя́щий*.

vermin ['vəːmɪn] npl (animals) вреди́тели mpl; (fleas, lice etc) парази́ты mpl.

vermouth ['vəːməθ] n ве́рмут.

vernacular [və'nækjuləʳ] n (language) национа́льный язы́к*; (local language) ме́стный диале́кт.

versatile ['vəːsətaɪl] adj (person) разносторо́нний*; (substance, machine, tool etc) универса́льный* (универса́лен).

versatility [vә:sә'tɪlɪtɪ] n (see adj) разносторо́нность f; универса́льность f.
verse [vә:s] n (poetry, in Bible) стих; (one part of a poem) строфа́*; **in** ~ в стиха́х.
versed [vә:st] adj: (**well-**)~ **in** све́дущий* (све́дущ) в +prp.
version ['vә:ʃən] n (form: of design, production) вариа́нт; (account: of events, accident etc) ве́рсия.
versus ['vә:sәs] prep про́тив +gen.
vertebra ['vә:tɪbrә] (pl ~**e**) n (ANAT) позвоно́к*.
vertebrae ['vә:tɪbri:] npl of **vertebra**.
vertebrate ['vә:tɪbrɪt] n позвоно́чное nt adj (живо́тное).
vertical ['vә:tɪkl] adj вертика́льный* (вертика́лен) ♦ n вертика́ль f.
vertically ['vә:tɪklɪ] adv вертика́льно.
vertigo ['vә:tɪɡәu] n головокруже́ние; **to suffer from** ~ страда́ть (impf) от головокруже́ний.
verve [vә:v] n (vivacity) воодушевле́ние.
very ['vɛrɪ] adv о́чень ♦ adj: **the** ~ **book which** та са́мая кни́га, кото́рая; ~ **well/little** о́чень хорошо́/ма́ло; **thank you** ~ **much** большо́е спаси́бо; ~ **much better** гора́здо лу́чше; **I** ~ **much hope so** я о́чень наде́юсь на э́то; **the** ~ **thought (of it) alarms me** сама́ мысль (об э́том) пуга́ет меня́; **at the** ~ **end** в са́мом конце́; **the** ~ **last** са́мый после́дний*; **at the** ~ **least** как ми́нимум.
vespers ['vɛspәz] npl (REL) вече́рня fsg.
vessel ['vɛsl] n (NAUT) су́дно*; (container) сосу́д; see also **blood**.
vest [vɛst] n (BRIT: underwear) ма́йка; (US: waistcoat) жиле́т ♦ vt: **to** ~ **sb with sth, to** ~ **sth in sb** наделя́ть (надели́ть perf) кого́-н чем-н.
vested interest ['vɛstɪd-] n (COMM) заинтересо́ванность f; **to have a** ~ ~ **in sth** быть* (impf) заинтересо́ванным(-ой) в чём-н.
vestibule ['vɛstɪbju:l] n (in building) вестибю́ль m.
vestige ['vɛstɪdʒ] n оста́ток*.
vestment ['vɛstmәnt] n (REL) ри́за.
vestry ['vɛstrɪ] n (of church) ри́зница.
Vesuvius [vɪ'su:vɪәs] n Везу́вий.
vet [vɛt] n abbr (BRIT) = **veterinary surgeon**.
veteran ['vɛtәrn] n (of war) ветера́н ♦ adj: **she's a** ~ **campaigner for ...** она́ ста́рый ветера́н движе́ния за +acc ....
veteran car n (BRIT) маши́на ста́рой ма́рки.
veterinarian [vɛtrɪ'nɛәrɪәn] n (US) ветерина́р.
veterinary ['vɛtrɪnәrɪ] adj (practice, care etc) ветерина́рный.
veterinary surgeon n (BRIT) ветерина́р.
veto ['vi:tәu] (pl ~**es**) n ве́то nt ind ♦ vt (proposal etc) налага́ть (наложи́ть* perf) ве́то на +acc; **to put a** ~ **on** налага́ть (наложи́ть* perf) ве́то на +acc.
vetting ['vɛtɪŋ] n (of person) прове́рка (на благонадёжность).

vex [vɛks] vt (irritate, upset) досажда́ть (досади́ть* perf).
vexed [vɛkst] adj (question) досажда́ющий.
VFD n abbr (US) = volunteer fire department.
VG n abbr (BRIT: SCOL etc) = very good.
VHF abbr (RADIO: = very high frequency) ОВЧ= о́чень высо́кая частота́.
VI abbr (US: POST) = Virgin Islands.
via ['vaɪә] prep (through, by way of) че́рез +acc.
viability [vaɪә'bɪlɪtɪ] n жизнеспосо́бность f; (of product) конкурентоспосо́бость f.
viable ['vaɪәbl] adj (company) конкурентоспосо́бный; (project) осуществи́мый.
viaduct ['vaɪәdʌkt] n виаду́к.
vial ['vaɪәl] n (for medicine) пузырёк; (for perfume) флако́н.
vibes [vaɪbz] npl (inf: atmosphere) флю́йды mpl.
vibrant ['vaɪbrnt] adj (lively) по́лный* (по́лон) жи́зни; (light) я́ркий*(я́рок); (colour) со́чный* (со́чен); (full of emotion: voice) насы́щенный.
vibraphone ['vaɪbrәfәun] n вибрафо́н.
vibrate [vaɪ'breɪt] vi (house, machine etc) вибри́ровать* (impf); (resound) отдава́ться* (impf).
vibration [vaɪ'breɪʃәn] n вибра́ция.
vibrator [vaɪ'breɪtәʳ] n вибра́тор.
vicar ['vɪkәʳ] n (REL) свяще́нник.
vicarage ['vɪkәrɪdʒ] n дом* свяще́нника.
vicarious [vɪ'kɛәrɪәs] adj (pleasure, experience) опосре́дованный (опосре́дован).
vice [vaɪs] n (moral fault) поро́к; (TECH) тиски́ pl.
vice- [vaɪs] prefix (president) вице-.
vice-chairman [vaɪs'tʃɛәmәn] irreg n замести́тель m председа́теля.
vice chancellor n (BRIT: of university) ви́це-ка́нцлер.
vice president n ви́це-президе́нт.
viceroy ['vaɪsrɔɪ] n короле́вский* наме́стник.
vice squad n (POLICE) отде́л в поли́ции, кото́рый име́ет де́ло с преступле́ниями, свя́занными с порногра́фией, проститу́цией, нарко́тиками итп.
vice versa ['vaɪsɪ'vә:sә] adv наоборо́т.
vicinity [vɪ'sɪnɪtɪ] n (area): **in the** ~ **(of)** в окре́стностях (+gen).
vicious ['vɪʃәs] adj (attack, blow) жесто́кий* (жесто́к); (words, look, dog) злой* (зол); (horse) норови́стый (норови́ст).
vicious circle n поро́чный круг.
viciousness ['vɪʃәsnɪs] n зло́ба.
vicissitudes [vɪ'sɪsɪtju:dz] npl превра́тности fpl.
victim ['vɪktɪm] n же́ртва; **to be the** ~ **of** быть* (impf) же́ртвой +gen.
victimization ['vɪktɪmaɪ'zeɪʃәn] n пресле́дование.

---

victimize ['vɪktɪmaɪz] *vt (strikers etc)*
преследовать* *(impf/perf).*
victor ['vɪktə'] *n* победитель(ница) *m(f).*
Victorian [vɪk'tɔːrɪən] *adj* викторианский.
victorious [vɪk'tɔːrɪəs] *adj (team)*
победоносный; *(shout)* победный.
victory ['vɪktərɪ] *n* победа; **to win a ~ over sb**
одержать* *(perf)* победу над кем-н.
video ['vɪdɪəʊ] *cpd* видео *ind* ◆ *n (also: ~ film)*
видеофильм; *(also: ~ cassette)*
видеокассета; *(also: ~ cassette recorder)*
видеомагнитофон; *(also: ~ camera)*
видеокамера.
videodisc ['vɪdɪəʊdɪsk] *n* видеодиск.
video game *n* видеоигра.
video nasty *n* видеофильм со сценами
насилия.
videophone ['vɪdɪəʊfəʊn] *n* видеотелефон.
video recorder *n* видеомагнитофон.
video recording *n* видеозапись *f.*
video tape *n* видеолента.
vie [vaɪ] *vi*: **to ~ with sb/for sth** соперничать
(impf) с кем-н/в чём-н.
Vienna [vɪ'ɛnə] *n* Вена.
Viennese [vɪə'niːz] *adj* венский ◆ *n inv*
житель(ница) *m(f)* Вены.
Vietnam ['vjɛt'næm] *n* Вьетнам.
Viet Nam ['vjɛt'næm] *n* = **Vietnam.**
Vietnamese [vjɛtnə'miːz] *adj* вьетнамский ◆ *n*
inv (person) вьетнамец*(-мка*); *(LING)*
вьетнамский язык*.
view [vjuː] *n (sight, outlook)* вид; *(opinion)*
взгляд ◆ *vt (look at: also fig)* рассматривать
(рассмотреть *perf*); *(situation)* оценивать
(оценить *perf*); *(house)* осматривать
(осмотреть *perf*); **to be on ~** *(in museum etc)*
выставляться *(impf)*; **in full ~ (of)** на виду (у
+*gen*); **in ~ of the weather/the fact that** ввиду
плохой погоды/того, что; **in my ~** на мой
взгляд; **an overall ~ of the situation** общая
картина положения; **with a ~ to doing** с тем,
чтобы +*infin.*
Viewdata® ['vjuː'deɪtə] *n (BRIT: COMPUT)*
видеотекст; *(TEL)* телекоммуникационная
система, позволяющая клиентам делать
заказы на товары или услуги прямо из
дома.
viewer ['vjuː'ə'] *n (person)* зритель *m.*
viewfinder ['vjuːfaɪndə'] *n (PHOT)* видо-
искатель *m.*
viewpoint ['vjuːpɔɪnt] *n (attitude)* точка
зрения; *(place)* место* обозрения.
vigil ['vɪdʒɪl] *n* бдение; **to keep ~** дежурить
(подежурить *perf*).
vigilance ['vɪdʒɪləns] *n* бдительность *f.*
vigilance committee *n (US)* ″комитет
бдительности″ *(организация линчевателей).*
vigilant ['vɪdʒɪlənt] *adj* бдительный.
vigilante [vɪdʒɪ'læntɪ] *n* самодеятельный
блюститель порядка, считающий действия
полиции недостаточными.

vigor ['vɪgə'] *(US) n* = **vigour.**
vigorous ['vɪgərəs] *adj (action, campaign)*
мощный; *(plant)* сильный.
vigour ['vɪgə'] *(US* **vigor**) *n (energy: of person)*
сила; *(: of campaign)* мощь *f.*
vile [vaɪl] *adj (evil)* гнусный; *(unpleasant)*
мёрзкий*; **~ language** сквернословие.
vilify ['vɪlɪfaɪ] *vt (person)* поносить* *(impf).*
villa ['vɪlə] *n* вилла.
village ['vɪlɪdʒ] *n* деревня.
villager ['vɪlɪdʒə'] *n* деревенский*(-ая)
житель(ница) *m(f).*
villain ['vɪlən] *n (scoundrel)* негодяй; *(in novel
etc)* злодей; *(BRIT: criminal)* преступник.
Vilnius ['vɪlnɪəs] *n* Вильнюс.
VIN *n abbr (US)* = *vehicle identification number.*
vinaigrette [vɪneɪ'grɛt] *n (salad dressing)*
заправка для салата *(из уксуса и
растительного масла).*
vindicate ['vɪndɪkeɪt] *vt (person: free from
blame)* доказывать (доказать* *perf)* правоту
+*gen*; *(action: justify)* оправдывать
(оправдать *perf*).
vindication [vɪndɪ'keɪʃən] *n*: **in ~ of sb/sth** в
оправдание кого-н/чего-н.
vindictive [vɪn'dɪktɪv] *adj* мстительный*
(мстителен).
vine [vaɪn] *n (BOT: with grapes)* виноградная
лоза*; *(: climbing plant)* вьющееся растение;
(: in jungle) лиана.
vinegar ['vɪnɪgə'] *n* уксус.
vineyard ['vɪnjɑːd] *n* виноградник.
vintage ['vɪntɪdʒ] *n (year)* год изготовления
вина ◆ *cpd (classic: comedy, performance etc)*
классический*; **the 1970 ~** *(of wine)* урожая
1970 года.
vintage car *n* машина старой марки.
vintage wine *n* выдержанное вино.
vinyl ['vaɪnl] *n* винил.
viola [vɪ'əʊlə] *n (MUS)* альт*.
violate ['vaɪəleɪt] *vt* нарушать (нарушить *perf*);
(graveyard) осквернять (осквернить *perf*).
violation [vaɪə'leɪʃən] *n (of agreement etc)*
нарушение; **in ~ of** в нарушение +*gen.*
violence ['vaɪələns] *n (brutality)* насилие;
(strength) сила.
violent ['vaɪələnt] *adj (behaviour)* жестокий*;
(death) насильственный; *(debate, criticism)*
яростный; **a ~ dislike of sb/sth** резкая
неприязнь к кому-н/чему-н.
violently ['vaɪələntlɪ] *adv (dislike)* сильно; *(ill,
angry)* очень.
violet ['vaɪələt] *adj* фиолетовый ◆ *n (colour)*
фиолетовый цвет; *(plant)* фиалка*.
violin [vaɪə'lɪn] *n (MUS)* скрипка*.
violinist [vaɪə'lɪnɪst] *n* скрипач*(ка*).
VIP *n abbr (= very important person)* очень
важное лицо.
viper ['vaɪpə'] *n* гадюка.
viral ['vaɪərəl] *adj* вирусный.
virgin ['vəːdʒɪn] *n (person)* девственница;

(: *religious etc*) дéва ♦ *adj* (*snow, forest etc*) дéвственный; **the Blessed V**~ пресвятáя дéва Мария; (*in Orthodox Church*) Богорóдица.
virgin birth *n* рождéние от дéвственницы.
virginity [vəˈdʒɪnɪtɪ] *n* (*of person*) дéвственность *f*.
Virgo [ˈvəːgəu] *n* Дéва; **he is** ~ он – Дéва.
virile [ˈvɪraɪl] *adj* обладáющий *мужскóй сúлой*.
virility [vɪˈrɪlɪtɪ] *n* (*sexual power*) мужскáя сúла; (*fig: masculine qualities*) мýжественность *f*.
virtual [ˈvəːtjuəl] *adj* фактúческий*; (*COMPUT, PHYS*) виртуáльный; (*in effect*): **it's a ~ impossibility** э́то практúчески *or* фактúчески невозмóжно.
virtually [ˈvəːtjuəlɪ] *adv* (*almost*) фактúчески, практúчески; **it is ~ impossible** э́то фактúчески *or* практúчески невозмóжно.
virtual reality *n систéма трёхмéрного телевúдения*.
virtue [ˈvəːtjuː] *n* (*moral correctness*) добродéтель *f*; (*advantage*) преимýщество; (*merit*) достóинство; **by ~ of** благодаря́ +*dat*.
virtuosi [vəːtjuˈəuzɪ] *npl of* **virtuoso**.
virtuosity [vəːtjuˈɒsɪtɪ] *n* виртуóзность *f*.
virtuoso [vəːtjuˈəuzəu] (*pl* ~**s** *or* **virtuosi**) *n* виртуóз.
virtuous [ˈvəːtjuəs] *adj* (*displaying virtue*) добродéтельный.
virulence [ˈvɪruləns] *n* (*see adj*) ядовúтость *f*; смéртельность *f*; нéнависть *f*.
virulent [ˈvɪrulənt] *adj* (*poison*) ядовúтый*; (*disease*) смéртельный; (*actions, feelings*) пóлный* (пóлон) нéнависти.
virus [ˈvaɪərəs] *n* (*MED*) вúрус.
visa [ˈviːzə] *n* (*for travel*) вúза.
vis-à-vis [viːzəˈviː] *prep* по отношéнию к +*dat*.
viscose [ˈvɪskəus] *n* вискóза.
viscount [ˈvaɪkaunt] *n* викóнт.
viscous [ˈvɪskəs] *adj* (*liquid, substance*) вя́зкий* (вя́зок).
vise [vaɪs] *n* (*US: TECH*) = **vice**.
visibility [vɪzɪˈbɪlɪtɪ] *n* вúдимость *f*.
visible [ˈvɪzəbl] *adj* (*able to be seen or recognized*) вúдимый (вúдим); (*results, growth*) очевúдный* (очевúден); ~ **exports/imports** (*ECON*) вúдимый э́кспорт/úмпорт.
visibly [ˈvɪzəblɪ] *adv* (*upset, nervous, damaged*) я́вно.
vision [ˈvɪʒən] *n* (*sight*) зрéние; (*foresight*) предвúдение; (*in dream*) видéние.
visionary [ˈvɪʒənrɪ] *n* (*person*) провúдец.
visit [ˈvɪzɪt] *n* (*to person, place*) посещéние; (*stay*) пребывáние ♦ *vt* (*person*) идтú (прийтú* *perf*) *or* ходúть* (приходúть* *perf*) в гóсти к +*dat*; (*elderly, disabled person*) навещáть (навестúть* *perf*); (*place*) посещáть (посетúть* *perf*); **on a private/official ~** с

чáстным/официáльным визúтом.
visiting [ˈvɪzɪtɪŋ] *adj* (*speaker*) приéхавший по приглашéнию; ~ **team** комáнда гостéй.
visiting card *n* визúтная кáрточка*.
visiting hours *npl* (*in hospital etc*) часы́ *mpl* посещéния.
visiting professor *n* профéссор, приéхавший по приглашéнию.
visitor [ˈvɪzɪtə*] *n* (*person visiting*) гость(я) *m(f)*; (*in public place, museum etc*) посетúтель (ница) *m(f)*; (*tourist: in town etc*) приéзжий*(-ая) *m(f) adj*.
visitors' book *n* кнúга посетúтелей.
visor [ˈvaɪzə*] *n* (*of helmet etc*) щитóк.
VISTA [ˈvɪstə] *n abbr* (= *Volunteers in Service to America*) *добровóльная организáция по оказáнию пóмощи бéдным*.
vista [ˈvɪstə] *n* (*view*) перспектúва.
Vistula [ˈvɪstjulə] *n*: **the ~** Вúсла.
visual [ˈvɪzjuəl] *adj* (*image*) зрúтельный.
visual aid *n* (*SCOL*) наглядное пособие.
visual arts *npl изобразúтельное искýсство и кинó*.
visual display unit *n* (*COMPUT*) устрóйство визуáльного изображéния *or* дисплéй.
visualize [ˈvɪzjuəlaɪz] *vt* (*picture, imagine*) представля́ть (предстáвить* *perf*) мы́сленно; (*foresee*) представля́ть (предстáвить* *perf*) себé.
visually [ˈvɪzjuəlɪ] *adv*: ~ **appealing** привлекáтельный на вид; ~ **handicapped** со зрúтельным дефéктом.
vital [ˈvaɪtl] *adj* (*essential, important, crucial*) жúзненно необходúмый (необходúм); (*full of life: person*) живóй, жизнеспосóбный* (жизнеспосóбен); (*necessary for life: organ*) жúзненно вáжный (вáжен); **of ~ importance (to sb/sth)** жúзненно вáжно (для когó-н/чегó-н).
vitality [vaɪˈtælɪtɪ] *n* (*liveliness*) жúвость *f*.
vitally [ˈvaɪtəlɪ] *adv*: ~ **important** жúзненно вáжный* (вáжен).
vital statistics *npl* (*of woman*) габарúты *mpl*; (*of population*) демографúческая статúстика *fsg*.
vitamin [ˈvɪtəmɪn] *n* витамúн.
vitiate [ˈvɪʃɪeɪt] *vt* (*spoil*) пóртить (испóртить* *perf*); **to ~ sb's efforts** сводúть* (свестú* *perf*) на нет чьи-н усúлия.
vitreous [ˈvɪtrɪəs] *adj* стекловúдный.
vitriolic [vɪtrɪˈɒlɪk] *adj* (*fig: language*) ядовúтый (ядовúт); (: *behaviour*) злóбный* (злóбен).
viva (voce) [ˈvaɪvəˈvəutʃɪ] *n* (*SCOL*) ýстный экзáмен.
vivacious [vɪˈveɪʃəs] *adj* (*person*) живóй.
vivacity [vɪˈvæsɪtɪ] *n* жúвость *f*.
vivid [ˈvɪvɪd] *adj* (*description, colour, light*) я́ркий*; (*memory*) отчётливый; (*imagination*)

живо́й.

vividly ['vɪvɪdlɪ] *adv* (*describe*) в живы́х
дета́лях; (*remember*) отчётливо.

vivisection [vɪvɪ'sɛkʃən] *n* вивисе́кция.

vixen ['vɪksn] *n* са́мка* лиси́цы; (*pej*: *woman*)
меге́ра.

viz [vɪz] *abbr* (*namely*: = *videlicet*) а и́менно.

Vladivostok [vlædɪ'vɔstɔk] *n* Владивосто́к.

VLF *abbr* (*RADIO*: = *very low frequency*) ОНЧ=
о́чень ни́зкая частота́.

V-neck ['viːnɛk] *n* (*also*: ~ **jumper** *or* **pullover**)
джéмпер *or* пуло́вер с вы́резом.

VOA *n abbr* (= *Voice of America*) "Го́лос
Аме́рики".

vocabulary [vəu'kæbjulərɪ] *n* (*words known*)
словáрный запа́с.

vocal ['vəukl] *adj* (*of the voice*: *in singing*)
вокáльный; (*articulate*) звýчный* (звýчен); **to
be ~ for/against** подня́ть (*perf*) го́лос в
по́льзу +*gen*/про́тив +*gen*.

vocal cords *npl* голосовы́е свя́зки *fpl*.

vocalist ['vəukəlɪst] *n* вокали́ст(ка*).

vocals ['vəuklz] *npl* (*MUS*) вокáльная пáртия
fsg.

vocation [vəu'keɪʃən] *n* призвáние.

vocational [vəu'keɪʃənl] *adj* (*training, guidance
etc*) профессионáльный.

vociferous [və'sɪfərəs] *adj* (*protesters,
demands*) громоглáсный.

vodka ['vɔdkə] *n* во́дка.

vogue [vəug] *n* мо́да; **in ~** в мо́де.

voice [vɔɪs] *n* го́лос ◆ *vt* (*opinion*) выскáзывать
(вы́сказать* *perf*); **in a loud/soft ~** гро́мким/
ти́хим го́лосом; **to give ~ to sth** выражáть
(вы́разить* *perf*) что-н.

voice-over ['vɔɪsəuvəʳ] *n* го́лос за кáдром.

void [vɔɪd] *n* (*emptiness*) пустотá; (*hole*)
пробéл ◆ *adj* (*invalid*) недействи́тельный*
(недействи́телен); ~ **of** (*empty*) лишённый
(лишён) +*gen*.

voile [vɔɪl] *n* (*fabric*) вуáль *f*.

vol. *abbr* (= **volume**) т.= *том*.

volatile ['vɔlətaɪl] *adj* (*situation, person*)
изме́нчивый (изме́нчив); (*liquid*) летýчий*.

volcanic [vɔl'kænɪk] *adj* (*rock, eruption*)
вулкани́ческий.

volcano [vɔl'keɪnəu] (*pl* ~**es**) *n* вулкáн.

Volga ['vɔlgə] *n*: **the ~** Во́лга.

Volgograd ['vɔlgəgræd] *n* Волгогрáд.

volition [və'lɪʃən] *n*: **of one's own ~** по свое́й
во́ле.

volley ['vɔlɪ] *n* (*of gunfire*) залп; (*of stones etc*)
град; (*of questions etc*) пото́к; (*TENNIS etc*)
удáр с лёта.

volleyball ['vɔlɪbɔːl] *n* (*SPORT*) волейбо́л.

volt [vəult] *n* (*ELEC*) вольт.

voltage ['vəultɪdʒ] *n* (*ELEC*) напряже́ние; **high/
low ~** высо́кое/ни́зкое напряже́ние.

volte-face [vɔlt'fɑːs] *n inv* ре́зкая переме́на.

voluble ['vɔljubl] *adj* (*person, speech*)
многосло́вный.

volume ['vɔljuːm] *n* (*space*) объём; (*amount*)
коли́чество; (*book*) том; (*sound level*)
гро́мкость *f*; ~ **one/two** (*book*) том пéрвый/
второ́й; **his expression spoke ~s** выраже́ние
его́ лицá говори́т красноречи́вее вся́ких
слов.

volume control *n* (*RADIO, TV*) гро́мкость *f*.

volume discount *n* (*COMM*) ски́дка за покýпку
крýпной пáртии товáра.

voluminous [və'luːmɪnəs] *adj* (*clothes*)
просто́рный; (*correspondence, notes*)
прострáнный.

voluntarily ['vɔləntrɪlɪ] *adv* (*willingly*) добро-
во́льно.

voluntary ['vɔləntərɪ] *adj* (*willing*: *exile*)
доброво́льный*; (*unpaid*: *work, worker*)
обще́ственный.

voluntary liquidation *n* (*COMM*)
доброво́льная ликвидáция.

voluntary redundancy *n* (*BRIT*) увольне́ние по
со́бственному жела́нию.

volunteer [vɔlən'tɪəʳ] *n* (*unpaid helper*)
доброво́льный(-ая) помо́щник(-ица); (*to
army etc*) доброво́лец ◆ *vt* (*information*)
предлагáть (предложи́ть* *perf*) ◆ *vi* (*for army
etc*) идти́* (пойти́* *perf*) доброво́льцем; **to ~
to do** вызывáться (вы́зваться* *perf*) +*infin*.

voluptuous [və'lʌptjuəs] *adj* (*movement, body,
feeling*) сладострáстный*.

vomit ['vɔmɪt] *n* рвóта ◆ *vi*: **he ~ed** его́
вы́рвало; **she began to ~** её нáчало рвать.

voracious [və'reɪʃəs] *adj* жáдный* (жáден); **he
is a ~ reader** он с жáдностью читáет.

vote [vəut] *n* (*indication of choice, opinion*)
голосовáние; (*votes cast*) го́лос; (*right to
vote*) прáво го́лоса ◆ *vi* (*in election etc*)
голосовáть* (проголосовáть* *perf*) ◆ *vt*
(*elect*): **he was ~d chairman** он был и́збран
председáтелем; (*propose*): **to ~ that**
предлагáть (предложи́ть* *perf*), что́бы; **to put
sth to the ~, take a ~ on sth** стáвить*
(постáвить* *perf*) что-н на голосовáние; ~ **of
censure** выраже́ние порицáния; ~ **of thanks**
благодáрственная речь *f*; **to pass a ~ of
confidence/no confidence** выражáть
(вы́разить* *perf*) во́тум дове́рия/недове́рия;
to ~ for *or* **in favour of/against** голосовáть*
(проголосовáть* *perf*) за +*acc*/про́тив +*gen*; **to
~ Labour** голосовáть* (проголосовáть* *perf*)
за Лейбори́стскую пáртию.

voter ['vəutəʳ] *n* избирáтель *m*.

voting ['vəutɪŋ] *n* голосовáние.

voting paper *n* (*BRIT*) избирáтельный
бюллéтень *m*.

voting right *n* прáво го́лоса.

vouch [vautʃ] *vt fus*: **to ~ for** (*person, quality etc*)
ручáться (поручи́ться* *perf*) за +*acc*.

voucher ['vautʃəʳ] *n* (*for meal*: *also*: **luncheon ~**)
талóн на обéд; (*with petrol, cigarettes etc*)
вáучер; (*receipt*) распи́ска.

vow [vau] *n* клятва ◆ *vt*: **to ~ to do/that**

кля́сться* (покля́сться* *perf)* +*infin/*, что; **to
take** *or* **make a** ~ **to do** дава́ть* (дать* *perf)*
обе́т +*infin.*

vowel ['vauəl] *n* (*LING*) гла́сный *m adj.*

voyage ['vɔɪdʒ] *n* (*by ship*) пла́вание; (*by
spacecraft*) полёт.

voyeur [vwɑːˈjəː'] *n человек, получающий
сексуа́льное удово́льствие от та́йного
созерца́ния люде́й во вре́мя полово́го а́кта.*

voyeurism [vwɑːˈjəːrɪzəm] *n* проце́сс
созерца́ния други́х люде́й во вре́мя
полово́го а́кта.

VP *n abbr* = **vice president.**

vs *abbr* = **versus.**

V-sign ['viːsaɪn] *n* (*BRIT: as insult*) гру́бый
жест; (*in victory*) знак побе́ды.

VSO *n abbr* (*BRIT:* = Voluntary Service Overseas)
*благотвори́тельное о́бщество, ока́зывающее
по́мощь нужда́ющимся за рубежо́м.*

VT *abbr* (*US: POST*) = Vermont.

vulgar ['vʌlgə'] *adj* (*remarks, gestures, graffiti*)
вульга́рный; (*decor, ostentation*) по́шлый*.

vulgarity [vʌlˈgærɪtɪ] *n* (*rudeness*)
вульга́рность *f;* (*ostentation*) по́шлость *f.*

vulnerability [vʌlnərəˈbɪlɪtɪ] *n* (*see adj*)
уязви́мость *f;* рани́мость *f.*

vulnerable ['vʌlnərəbl] *adj* (*position*)
уязви́мый*; (*person*) рани́мый*; **he is** ~ **to** он
подве́ржен +*dat.*

vulture ['vʌltʃə'] *n* гриф; (*fig: pej*) стервя́тник.

vulva ['vʌlvə] *n* ву́льва.

~ *W, w* ~

W, w ['dʌblju:] n (*letter*) 23-ая бу́ква
англи́йского алфави́та.
W abbr (= **west**) З= за́пад; (*ELEC*: = **watt**) Вт=
ватт.
WA abbr (*US*: *POST*) = Washington.
wad [wɔd] n (*of cotton wool*) комо́к*; (*of
banknotes, paper*) па́чка*.
wadding ['wɔdɪŋ] n упако́вочный материа́л.
waddle ['wɔdl] vi ходи́ть*/идти́* (*impf*)
вперева́лку.
wade [weɪd] vi: **to ~ through** (*water*)
пробира́ться (пробра́ться* perf) че́рез +acc;
(*book*) одолева́ть (одоле́ть perf).
wafer ['weɪfəʳ] n (*biscuit*) ва́фля*.
wafer-thin ['weɪfəˈθɪn] adj тонча́йший.
waffle ['wɔfl] n (*CULIN*) ва́фля*; (*empty talk*)
трёп* ◆ vi (*in speech, writing*) трепа́ться (*impf*).
waffle iron n ва́фельница.
waft [wɔft] vt доноси́ть* (донести́* perf) ◆ vi
доноси́ться (донести́сь* perf).
wag [wæg] vt (*head*) кача́ть (*impf*) +instr ◆ vi
(*tail*) виля́ть (*impf*); **the dog ~ged its tail**
соба́ка виля́ла хвосто́м; **to ~ one's finger at
sb** грози́ть* (погрози́ть* perf) кому́-н
па́льцем.
wage [weɪdʒ] n (*also*: **~s**) зарпла́та=
за́работная пла́та ◆ vt: **to ~ war** вести́* (*impf*)
войну́; **a day's ~s** дневно́й за́работок*.
wage claim n тре́бование увеличе́ния
за́работной пла́ты.
wage differential n дифференциа́льные
ста́вки* fpl за́работной пла́ты.
wage earner [-ˈəːnəʳ] n лицо́*, рабо́тающее по
на́йму; (*in the family*) корми́лец*(-лица).
wage freeze n замора́живание за́работной
пла́ты.
wage packet n конве́рт с зарпла́той.
wager ['weɪdʒəʳ] n пари́* nt ind ◆ vt ста́вить*
(поста́вить* perf); (*reputation*) ста́вить*
(поста́вить* perf) на ка́рту.
waggle ['wægl] vt (*ears, eyebrows etc*)
шевели́ть (пошевели́ть perf) +instr ◆ vi (*head*)
пока́чиваться (*impf*).
wag(g)on ['wægən] n (*horse-drawn*) пово́зка*;
(*BRIT*: *RAIL*) това́рный ваго́н.
wail [weɪl] n вопль m; (*of siren*) вой ◆ vi
(*person*) вопи́ть* (*impf*); (*siren*) выть* (*impf*).
waist [weɪst] n та́лия.
waistcoat ['weɪskəut] n (*BRIT*) жиле́т.

waistline ['weɪstlaɪn] n ли́ния та́лии.
wait [weɪt] vi ждать* (подожда́ть* perf) ◆ n: **we
had a long ~ for the bus** мы до́лго жда́ли
авто́буса; **to keep sb ~ing** заставля́ть
(заста́вить* perf) кого́-н ждать; **I can't ~ to go
home/meet my new boss** (*fig*) мне не
те́рпится пойти́ домо́й/встре́титься с мои́м
но́вым нача́льником; **to ~ for sb/sth** ждать*
(подожда́ть* perf) кого́-н/чего́-н; **~ a minute!**
подожди́те мину́тку!; "**repairs while you ~**"
„ремо́нт в прису́тствии зака́зчика"; **to lie in
~ for** поджида́ть (*impf*) +gen
▸ **wait behind** vi заде́рживаться
(задержа́ться* perf)
▸ **wait on** vt fus (*serve*) обслу́живать
(обслужи́ть* perf)
▸ **wait up** vi: **don't ~ up for me** не жди́те меня́,
ложи́тесь спать.
waiter ['weɪtəʳ] n официа́нт.
waiting ['weɪtɪŋ] n: "**no ~**" (*BRIT*: *AUT*)
„остано́вка запрещена́".
waiting list n спи́сок* очереднико́в.
waiting room n (*in surgery*) приёмная f adj; (*in
station*) зал ожида́ния.
waitress ['weɪtrɪs] n официа́нтка*.
waive [weɪv] vt (*rule*) отменя́ть (отмени́ть
perf).
waiver ['weɪvəʳ] n отка́з.
wake [weɪk] (pt **woke** or **waked**, pp **woken** or
waked) vt (*also*: **~ up**) буди́ть* (разбуди́ть*
perf) ◆ vi (*also*: **~ up**) просыпа́ться
(просну́ться perf) ◆ n бде́ние у гро́ба; (*NAUT*)
кильва́тер; **to ~ up to danger/threat**
осозна́ть* (perf) опа́сность/угро́зу; **in the ~ of**
(*fig*) всле́дствие +gen; **he followed in his
father's ~** (*fig*) он пошёл по стопа́м отца́.
waken ['weɪkn] vti = **wake**.
Wales [weɪlz] n Уэ́льс; **the Prince of ~** принц
Уэ́льский*.
walk [wɔːk] n (*hike*) похо́д; (*shorter*)
прогу́лка*; (*gait*) похо́дка*; (*path*) доро́жка*,
тропа́ ◆ vi (*go on foot*) ходи́ть*/идти́* (*impf*)
(пешко́м); (*baby*) ходи́ть* (*impf*); (*for pleasure,
exercise*) гуля́ть (*impf*) ◆ vt (*distance*)
проходи́ть* (пройти́* perf); (*dog*) выгу́ливать
(вы́гулять perf); **10 minutes' ~ from here** в
10-ти мину́тах ходьбы́ отсю́да; **to go for a ~**
ходи́ть*/идти́* (*impf*) гуля́ть or на прогу́лку;
at a quick ~ бы́стрым ша́гом; **to ~ in one's**

sleep ходи́ть* *(impf)* во сне́; **I'll ~ you home** я провожу́ Вас домо́й; **people from all ~s of life** лю́ди из всех слоёв о́бщества

▶ **walk out** *vi* *(audience)* демонстрати́вно покида́ть (поки́нуть *perf)* зал; *(workers)* бастова́ть *(impf)*

▶ **walk out on** *vt fus* *(inf: family etc)* броса́ть (бро́сить* *perf)*.

walkabout ['wɔːkəbaut] *n* *(queen, politician etc)*: **to go (on a) ~** проха́живаться (пройти́сь* *perf)* ми́мо толпы́.

walker ['wɔːkəʳ] *n* *(hiker)* тури́ст(ка).

walkie-talkie ['wɔːkɪ'tɔːkɪ] *n* переносна́я ра́ция.

walking ['wɔːkɪŋ] *n* ходьба́; **to be fond of ~** люби́ть* *(impf)* ходи́ть (пешко́м); **the university is within ~ distance** до университе́та мо́жно дойти́ пешко́м.

walking boots *npl* боти́нки *mpl* для ходьбы́.

walking holiday *n* похо́д.

walking stick *n* трость *f*.

Walkman® ['wɔːkmən] *n* пле́йер.

walk-on ['wɔːkɔn] *adj*: **~ part** второстепе́нная роль* *f*.

walkout ['wɔːkaut] *n* забасто́вка*.

walkover ['wɔːkəuvəʳ] *n* *(inf)* лёгкая побе́да.

walkway ['wɔːkweɪ] *n* пешехо́дная доро́жка*.

wall [wɔːl] *n* стена́*; **to go to the ~** *(fig)* терпе́ть (потерпе́ть *perf)* крах

▶ **wall in** *vt* обноси́ть* (обнести́* *perf)* стено́й.

wall cupboard *n* встро́енный шкаф*.

walled [wɔːld] *adj* *(city)* окружённый крепостно́й стено́й; *(garden)* обнесённый стено́й.

wallet ['wɔlɪt] *n* бума́жник.

wallflower ['wɔːlflauəʳ] *n* желтофио́ль *f*; **to be a ~** *(fig)* быть* *(impf)* незаме́тным(-ой).

wall hanging *n* насте́нный ковёр*.

wallop ['wɔləp] *vt* *(BRIT: inf)* дуба́сить* (отдуба́сить *perf)*.

wallow ['wɔləu] *vi* *(in mud)* валя́ться *(impf)*; *(in water)* бара́хтаться *(impf)*; *(in guilt, sentiment)* упива́ться *(impf)*; **to ~ in one's grief** упива́ться *(impf)* свои́м го́рем.

wallpaper ['wɔːlpeɪpəʳ] *n* обо́и *pl* ♦ *vt* *(room)* окле́ивать (окле́ить *perf)* обо́ями.

wall-to-wall ['wɔːltə'wɔːl] *adj*: **~ carpeting** ковро́вое покры́тие для всей пло́щади по́ла.

wally [wɔlɪ] *n* *(inf)* дурачо́к*.

walnut ['wɔːlnʌt] *n* *(nut)* гре́цкий оре́х; *(tree)* оре́ховое де́рево*; *(wood)* оре́х.

walrus ['wɔːlrəs] *(pl ~ or ~es)* *n* морж*.

waltz [wɔːlts] *n* вальс ♦ *vi* *(dancers)* вальси́ровать *(impf)*, танцева́ть *(impf)* вальс.

wan [wɔn] *adj* изнурённый* (изнурён); **~ complexion** боле́зненная бле́дность *f*.

wand [wɔnd] *n* *(also: magic ~)* волше́бная па́лочка*.

wander ['wɔndəʳ] *vi* *(person)* броди́ть* *(impf)*; *(mind, thoughts)* блужда́ть *(impf)*; *(river)* извива́ться *(impf)* ♦ *vt* броди́ть* *(impf)* по +*dat*.

wanderer ['wɔndərəʳ] *n* стра́нник(-ица), скита́лец*(-лица).

wandering ['wɔndrɪŋ] *adj* *(tribe)* кочево́й; *(minstrel, actor)* бродя́чий; *(path, river)* изви́листый; *(glance, mind)* блужда́ющий.

wane [weɪn] *vi* *(moon)* убыва́ть (убы́ть* *perf)*; *(enthusiasm, influence etc)* ослабева́ть (ослабе́ть* *or* осла́бнуть *perf)*.

wangle ['wæŋgl] *vt* *(BRIT: inf)* пробива́ть (проби́ть* *perf)*, добива́ться (доби́ться* *perf)* +*gen*.

wanker ['wæŋkəʳ] *n* *(BRIT: inf!)* муда́к *(!)*

want [wɔnt] *vt* *(wish for)* хоте́ть* +*gen*; *(need)* нужда́ться *(impf)* в +*prp* ♦ *n*: **for ~ of** за недоста́тком +*gen*; **~s** *npl* *(needs)* ну́жды *fpl*; **to ~ to do** хоте́ть* *(impf)* +*infin*; **I ~ you to apologize** я хочу́, что́бы Вы извини́лись; **you're ~ed on the phone** Вас к телефо́ну; **a ~ of foresight** отсу́тствие предви́дения.

want ads *npl* *(US)* объявле́ния под ру́брикой "Куплю́", "Ищу́ рабо́ту" *итп*.

wanted ['wɔntɪd] *adj* *(criminal etc)* разы́скиваемый; **"cook ~"** "тре́буется по́вар".

wanting ['wɔntɪŋ] *adj*: **he was found ~** он оказа́лся не на высоте́ положе́ния; **he is ~ in common sense** ему́ недостаёт здра́вого смы́сла.

wanton ['wɔntn] *adj* *(gratuitous)* беспричи́нный* (беспричи́нен); *(promiscuous)* распу́тный* (распу́тен).

war [wɔːʳ] *n* война́; **to go to ~** вступа́ть (вступи́ть* *perf)* в войну́; **to be at ~ with** воева́ть* *(impf)* с +*instr*; **to declare ~ (on)** *(also fig)* объявля́ть (объяви́ть* *perf)* войну́ (+*dat*).

warble ['wɔːbl] *n* *(of bird)* трель *f* ♦ *vi* издава́ть* *(impf)* тре́ли.

war crime *n* вое́нное преступле́ние.

war cry *n* боево́й клич.

ward [wɔːd] *n* *(MED)* пала́та; *(BRIT: POL)* о́круг; *(LAW)* ребёнок, находя́щийся под опе́кой

▶ **ward off** *vt* *(attack, enemy)* отража́ть (отрази́ть* *perf)*; *(danger, illness)* отвраща́ть (отврати́ть* *perf)*.

warden ['wɔːdn] *n* *(of park, game reserve)* смотри́тель(ница) *m(f)*; *(of prison)* нача́льник; *(of youth hostel)* коменда́нт; *(BRIT: of college)* ре́ктор; *(: also: traffic ~)* ≈ инспе́ктор ГАИ.

warder ['wɔːdəʳ] *n* *(BRIT)* надзира́тель(ница) *m(f)*, тюре́мщик(-ица).

wardrobe ['wɔːdrəub] *n* платяно́й шкаф, гардеро́б; *(clothes)* гардеро́б; *(CINEMA, THEAT)* костюме́рная *f adj*.

---

* marks translations which have irregular inflections. The Russian-English side of the dictionary gives inflectional information.

warehouse ['wɛəhaus] n склад.
wares [wɛəz] npl товáры mpl.
warfare ['wɔːfɛə'] n воéнные или боевы́е
действия ntpl.
war game n воéнная игрá*.
warhead ['wɔːhɛd] n боеголóвка*.
warily ['wɛərɪlɪ] adv осторóжно,
настоóженно.
Warks abbr (BRIT: POST) = Warwickshire.
warlike ['wɔːlaɪk] adj воúнственный*
(воúнствен).
warm [wɔːm] adj тёплый; (thanks, supporter,
heart) горя́чий*; (person) сердéчный; **it's ~
today** сегóдня теплó; **I'm ~** мне теплó; **to
keep sth ~** (hands, feet etc) держáть (impf)
что-н в теплé; (soup etc) держáть (impf) что-н
тёплым(-ой); **with my ~est thanks** с горя́чей
or сердéчной благодáрностью; **please accept
my ~est congratulations** примúте мои
сердéчные поздравлéния
▶ **warm up** vi (person, room) согревáться
(согрéться perf); (water) нагревáться
(нагрéться perf); (athlete) разминáться
(размя́ться perf) ♦ vt (food) разогревáть
(разогрéть perf), подогревáть (подогрéть
perf); (engine) разогревáть (разогрéть perf);
the weather ~ed up на у́лице потеплéло.
warm-blooded ['wɔːm'blʌdɪd] adj тепло-
крóвный* (теплокрóвен).
war memorial n воéнный обелúск.
warm-hearted [wɔːm'hɑːtɪd] adj сердéчный*
(сердéчен).
warmly ['wɔːmlɪ] adv (applaud) горячó; (dress,
welcome) теплó.
warmonger ['wɔːmʌŋɡə'] n (pej) поджигáтель
(ница) m(f) войны́.
warmongering ['wɔːmʌŋɡrɪŋ] n (pej)
разжигáние войны́.
warmth [wɔːmθ] n теплó.
warm-up ['wɔːmʌp] n размúнка*.
warn [wɔːn] vt: **to ~ sb (not) to do/of/that**
предупреждáть (предупредúть* perf) когó-н
(не) +infin/о +prp/, что.
warning ['wɔːnɪŋ] n предупреждéние; **without
(any) ~ (suddenly)** неожúданно; (without
notifying) без предупреждéния; **gale ~**
штормовóе предупреждéние.
warning light n предупредúтельный
световóй сигнáл.
warning triangle n аварúйный треугóльник
(знак, предупреждáющий о том, что
стоя́щая на дорóге машúна слóмана).
warp [wɔːp] vi (wood etc) коробúться*
(покоробúться* perf) ♦ vt (fig) ковéркать
(исковéркать perf) ♦ n (TEXTILES) оснóва.
warpath ['wɔːpɑːθ] n: **he is on the ~** (fig) он
настрóен воúнственно.
warped [wɔːpt] adj (wood) покорóбленный
(покорóблен); (fig) исковéрканный
(исковéркан).
warrant ['wɔrnt] n (document) гарáнтия; (LAW)

óрдер ♦ vt (justify) опрáвдывать (оправдáть
perf); (merit) гарантúровать (impf/perf); **search
~** óрдер на óбыск.
warrant officer n (MIL) ≈ старшинá* m; (NAUT)
мúчман.
warranty ['wɔrəntɪ] n гарáнтия; **under ~** с
гарáнтией; **the car was still under ~** у
машúны ещё не истёк гарантúйный срок.
warren ['wɔrən] n (of rabbits) мéсто, где
вóдятся крóлики; (fig) лабирúнт.
warring ['wɔːrɪŋ] adj воюющий; (interests etc)
непримирúмый (непримирúм).
warrior ['wɔrɪə'] n воúн.
Warsaw ['wɔːsɔː] n Варшáва.
warship ['wɔːʃɪp] n воéнный корáбль* m.
wart [wɔːt] n бородáвка*.
wartime ['wɔːtaɪm] n: **in ~** в воéнное врéмя.
wary ['wɛərɪ] adj (person) осторóжный*
(осторóжен), насторóженный
(насторóжен); **to be ~ about** or **of sth**
относúться* (impf) к чему́-н насторóженно;
to be ~ about doing остерегáться (impf) +infin.
was [wɔz] pt of **be**.
wash [wɔʃ] n мытьё; (clothes etc) стúрка;
(washing programme) режúм стúрки (в
стирáльной машúне); (of ship) пéнистый
след ♦ vt (hands, body) мыть* (помы́ть* perf);
(clothes) стирáть (постирáть perf); (face)
умывáть (умы́ть* perf); (sweep away)
смывáть (смыть* perf) ♦ vi (person) мы́ться*
(помы́ться* perf); (sea etc): **to ~ over sth**
перекáтываться (impf) чéрез что-н; **to have a
~** помы́ться* (perf); **to give sth a ~** помы́ть*
(perf) что-н; (clothes) постирáть (perf) что-н;
the sea ~ed the body ashore мóре вы́несло
тéло на бéрег; **he was ~ed overboard** егó
смы́ло волнóй зá борт
▶ **wash away** vt смывáть (смыть* perf)
▶ **wash down** vt (wall, path, car) мыть*
(вы́мыть* perf); (food) запивáть (запúть* perf)
▶ **wash off** vi отмывáться (отмы́ться* perf);
(out of clothes) отстúрываться (отстирáться
perf)
▶ **wash up** vi (BRIT) мыть* (вы́мыть* perf)
посу́ду; (US) мы́ться* (помы́ться* perf).
washable ['wɔʃəbl] adj (wallpaper etc)
мóющийся; **acrylic blankets are ~** акрúловые
одея́ла мóжно стирáть.
washbasin ['wɔʃbeɪsn] n (умывáльная)
рáковина.
washbowl ['wɔʃbəul] n (US) (умывáльная)
рáковина.
washcloth ['wɔʃklɔθ] n (US: face cloth)
салфéтка для лицá (из махрóвой ткáни).
washer ['wɔʃə'] n (TECH) шáйба.
washing ['wɔʃɪŋ] n (dirty) стúрка; (clean)
стúраные вéщи fpl.
washing line n (BRIT) бельевáя верёвка*.
washing machine n стирáльная машúна.
washing powder n (BRIT) стирáльный
порошóк.

Washington ['wɔʃɪŋtən] *n* Вашингтóн.
washing-up [wɔʃɪŋ'ʌp] *n* (грязная) посýда; **to do the ~** мыть* (вымыть* *perf*) посýду.
washing-up liquid *n* (*BRIT*) жúдкое срéдство для мытья посýды.
wash-out ['wɔʃaut] *n* (*inf*) провáл.
washroom ['wɔʃrum] *n* (*US*) убóрная *f adj*.
wasn't ['wɔznt] **= was not.**
WASP [wɔsp] *n abbr* (*US*: *inf*. = *White Anglo-Saxon Protestant*) американец англо-саксóнского происхождéния и протестáнтского исповéдания.
Wasp [wɔsp] *n abbr* = **WASP.**
wasp [wɔsp] *n* осá*.
waspish ['wɔspɪʃ] *adj* (*person*) раздражúтельный* (раздражúтелен).
wastage ['weɪstɪdʒ] *n* (*waste*) растрáта; (*ECON*: *loss*) убúток*; **natural ~** естéственная ýбыль *f*.
waste [weɪst] *n* (*act*) растрáта; (*rubbish*) отхóды *mpl*; (*also: household ~*) домáшние отбрóсы *mpl*; (*unwanted: energy, heat*) излúшек* ◆ *adj* (*material: rejected, damaged*) бракóванный* (бракóван); (*unwanted: energy, heat*) излúшний* (излúшен); (*left over*) отрабóтанный* (отрабóтан); (*also: ~ land: in city*) пустырь* *m* ◆ *vt* растрáчивать (растрáтить* *perf*); (*opportunity*) упускáть (упустúть* *perf*); **~s** *npl* (*area of land*) пустыня *fsg*; **it's a ~ of money/time** это пустáя трáта дéнег/врéмени; **to go to ~** пропадáть (пропáсть* *perf*); **to lay ~** (*destroy*) уничтожáть (уничтóжить *perf*); **~ paper** испóльзованная бумáга
▶ **waste away** *vi* (*person*) истощáть (истощúть *perf*) себя.
wastebasket ['weɪstbaːskɪt] *n* (*US*) = **wastepaper basket.**
waste disposal unit *n* (*BRIT*) устрóйство для удалéния отхóдов (*в кýхонной рáковине*).
wasteful ['weɪstful] *adj* (*person*) расточúтельный* (расточúтелен); (*process*) неэконóмный* (неэконóмен).
waste ground *n* (*BRIT*) пустырь* *m*.
wasteland ['weɪstlənd] *n* пýстошь *f*; (*in town*) пустырь* *m*; (*fig*) пустыня.
wastepaper basket ['weɪstpeɪpə-] *n* корзúна для (ненýжных) бумáг.
waste pipe *n* сливнáя трубá*.
waste products *npl* отхóды *pl* произвóдства.
waster ['weɪstəʳ] *n* (*inf*) бездéльник(-ица).
watch [wɔtʃ] *n* (*also: wristwatch*) (нарýчные) часы *pl*; (*act of watching*) наблюдéние; (*MIL, NAUT: group of guards*) патрýль* *m*; (*NAUT: spell of duty*) вáхта ◆ *vt* (*look at*) наблюдáть (*impf*) за +*instr*; (*match, programme*) смотрéть* (посмотрéть* *perf*); (*events, weight, language*) следúть* (*impf*) за +*instr*; (*be careful of: person*)

остерегáться (*impf*) +*gen*; (*look after*) смотрéть (*impf*) за +*instr* ◆ *vi* (*take care*) смотрéть (*impf*); (*keep guard*) дежýрить (*impf*); **to keep a close ~ on sb/sth** внимáтельно следúть* (*impf*) за кем-н/чем-н; **~ what you're doing** смотрú, что ты дéлаешь; **~ how you drive** внимáтельно ведúте машúну
▶ **watch out** *vi* остерегáться (остерéчься* *perf*).
watchband ['wɔtʃbænd] *n* (*US*) ремешóк* для часóв.
watchdog ['wɔtʃdɔg] *n* сторожевáя собáка; (*fig*) наблюдáтель *m*.
watchful ['wɔtʃful] *adj* бдúтельный* (бдúтелен).
watchmaker ['wɔtʃmeɪkəʳ] *n* часовщúк*.
watchman ['wɔtʃmən] *irreg n see* **night watchman.**
watchstrap ['wɔtʃstræp] *n* ремешóк* для часóв.
watchword ['wɔtʃwɔːd] *n* лóзунг.
water ['wɔːtəʳ] *n* водá* ◆ *vt* (*plant, garden*) поливáть (полúть* *perf*) ◆ *vi* (*eyes*) слезúться (*impf*); **a glass of ~** стакáн воды; **in British ~s** в британских водáх; **to pass ~** (*urinate*) мочúться* (помочúться* *perf*); **my mouth is ~ing** у меня текýт слюнки
▶ **water down** *vt* разбавлять (разбáвить* *perf*) (водóй); (*fig*) смягчáть (смягчúть *perf*).
water biscuit *n* ≈ галéта.
water cannon *n* брандспóйт.
water closet *n* (*BRIT*) туалéт.
watercolour ['wɔːtəkʌləʳ] (*US* **watercolor**) *n* (*picture*) акварéль *f*; **~s** *npl* (*paints*) акварéльные крáски* *fpl*.
water-cooled ['wɔːtəkuːld] *adj* (*engine*) с водяным охлаждéнием.
watercress ['wɔːtəkres] *n* кресс водянóй.
waterfall ['wɔːtəfɔːl] *n* водопáд.
waterfront ['wɔːtəfrʌnt] *n* (*seafront: street*) нáбережная *f adj*; (: *piece of land*) береговáя лúния; (*at docks*) райóн пóрта.
water heater *n* кипятúльник.
water hole *n* истóчник (*для водопóя в пустыне*).
water ice *n* фрýктовое морóженое *nt adj*.
watering can ['wɔːtərɪŋ-] *n* лéйка*.
water level *n* ýровень* *m* воды.
water lily *n* кувшúнка*.
waterline ['wɔːtəlaɪn] *n* (*NAUT*) ватерлúния.
waterlogged ['wɔːtəlɔgd] *adj* (*ground*) заболóченный* (заболóчен), затóпленный (затóплен).
water main *n* водопровóдная магистрáль *m*.
watermark ['wɔːtəmɑːk] *n* (*on paper*) водянóй знак; (*level of water*) отмéтка ýровня воды.
watermelon ['wɔːtəmɛlən] *n* арбýз.
waterproof ['wɔːtəpruːf] *adj* непромокáемый

---

* marks translations which have irregular inflections. The Russian-English side of the dictionary gives inflectional information.

(непромокáем).

water-repellent ['wɔːtəɪɪ'pɛlnt] *adj* (*cloth etc*) водооттáлкивающий*.

watershed ['wɔːtəʃɛd] *n* (*also fig*) водораздéл.

water-skiing ['wɔːtəski:ɪŋ] *n* воднолы́жный спорт.

water softener *n* срéдство для смягчéния воды́.

water tank *n* резервуáр для воды́; (*smaller*) бак для воды́.

watertight ['wɔːtətaɪt] *adj* водонепроницáемый (водонепроницáем); (*fig*: *argument*) неопровержи́мый (неопровержи́м); (: *excuse*) вéский*; (: *case, agreement*) я́сный* (я́сен); (: *story*) правдоподóбный* (правдоподóбен).

water vapour *n* (водянóй) пар*.

waterway ['wɔːtəweɪ] *n* (*canal, river*) вóдный путь* *m*; (*at sea*) ватервéйс.

waterworks ['wɔːtəwəːks] *n* (*building*) гидротехни́ческое сооружéние; (*inf*: ANAT) пóчки* *fpl*.

watery ['wɔːtəɪɪ] *adj* (*coffee, soup etc*) водяни́стый (водяни́ст); (*eyes*) слезя́щийся.

watt [wɔt] *n* ватт.

wattage ['wɔtɪdʒ] *n* мóщность *f* в вáттах.

wattle ['wɔtl] *n* (CONSTR) плетéнь* *m*.

wattle and daub *n* пру́тья и гли́на (*материáл для пострóйки мáзанки*).

wave [weɪv] *n* волнá*; (*of hand*) взмах; (*in hair*) зави́вка ♦ *vi* (*signal*) махáть* (*impf*); (*branches*) качáться (*impf*); (*grass*) волновáться (*impf*); (*flag*) развевáться (*impf*) ♦ *vt* махáть* (*impf*) +*instr*; (*stick, gun, sword*) размáхивать (*impf*) +*instr*; (*hair*) завивáть (зави́ть* *perf*); **short/ medium/long** ~ корóткие/срéдние/дли́нные вóлны *fpl*; **the new** ~ (CINEMA, MUS) нóвая волнá; **he ~d us over to his table** он знакóм подозвáл нас к своему́ столу́; **to ~ goodbye to sb** махáть* (помахáть* *perf*) комý-н на прощáние

▸ **wave aside** *vt* (*person*) отстраня́ть (отстрани́ть* *perf*); (*fig*) отмáхиваться (отмахнýться *perf*) от +*gen*

▸ **wave away** *vt* = **wave aside**.

waveband ['weɪvbænd] *n* диапазóн волн.

wavelength ['weɪvlɛŋθ] *n* (RADIO) длинá волны́; **they are on the same** ~ (*fig*) они́ одинáково смóтрят на вéщи.

waver ['weɪvə] *vi* (*voice*) дрóгнуть (*perf*); (*person, faith*) колебáться* (поколебáться* *perf*).

wavy ['weɪvɪ] *adj* волни́стый (волни́ст).

wax [wæks] *n* (*polish*) воск; (*for skis*) мазь *f*; (*for sealing*) сургу́ч*; (*in ear*) сéра ♦ *vt* (*floor*) вощи́ть (навощи́ть* *perf*), натирáть (натерéть* *perf*) вóском; (*car*) натирáть (натерéть* *perf*) вóском; (*skis*) мáзать (намáзать* *perf*) мáзью ♦ *vi* (*moon*) прибывáть (*impf*).

waxed [wækst] *adj* вощёный*.

waxen [wæksn] *adj* (*face*) восковóй; ~ **complexion** восковóй цвет лицá.

waxworks ['wækswəːks] *npl* (*models*) восковы́е фигу́ры *fpl* ♦ *n* (*place*) галерéя восковы́х фигу́р.

way [weɪ] *n* (*route*) путь* *m*, дорóга; (*path, access*) путь*; (*manner, method*) спóсоб; (*usu pl*: *habit*) привы́чка; **which** ~? – **this** ~ кудá? – сюдá; **is it a long** ~ **from here?** э́то далекó отсю́да?; **which** ~ **do we go now?** кудá нам тепéрь идти́?; **on the** ~ (*en route*) по пути́ *or* дорóге; **to be on one's** ~ быть* (*impf*) в пути́; **I'd better be on my** ~ мне ужé порá идти́; **to fight one's** ~ **through a crowd** продирáться (продрáться* *perf*) сквозь толпу́; **to lie one's** ~ **out of the situation** выходи́ть* (вы́йти* *perf*) из положéния за счёт лжи; **to keep out of sb's** ~ держáться* (*impf*) от когó-н подáльше; **it's a very long** ~ э́то óчень далекó; **the village is rather out of the** ~ дерéвня нахóдится довóльно далекó в сторонé; **to go out of one's** ~ **to do** старáться (постарáться* *perf*) изо всех сил +*infin*; **to be in sb's** ~ (*also fig*) стоя́ть (*impf*) на чьей-н дорóге; **to be in the** ~ мешáть (помешáть* *perf*); **to lose one's** ~ заблуди́ться* (*perf*); **the plan is under** ~ план осуществля́ется; **to make** ~ (**for sb/sth**) уступáть (уступи́ть* *perf*) мéсто (комý-н/чемý-н); **to get one's own** ~ дéлать (сдéлать *perf*) по-свóему; **to put sth the right** ~ **up** (BRIT) стáвить* (постáвить* *perf*) что-н как нáдо *or* прáвильно; **to be the wrong** ~ **round** быть* (*impf*) задóм наперёд; **he's in a bad** ~ егó делá плóхи; **that's a funny** ~ **to show your affection** э́то стрáнная манéра выражáть свою́ привя́занность; **in a** ~ в извéстном смы́сле; **in some** ~s в нéкоторых отношéниях; **no** ~! (*inf*) ни в кóем слу́чае!; **by the** ~ ... мéжду прóчим ...; **"way in"** (BRIT) "вход"; **"way out"** (BRIT) "вы́ход"; **the** ~ **back** обрáтный путь; **this** ~ **and that** тудá-сюдá; **"give** ~" (BRIT: AUT) "уступи́те дорóгу".

waybill ['weɪbɪl] *n* накладнáя *f adj*.

waylay [weɪ'leɪ] (*irreg*: **like lay**) *vt* подстерегáть (подстерéчь* *perf*); **I got waylaid** (*fig*) меня́ перехвати́ли по пути́.

wayside ['weɪsaɪd] *adj* придорóжный ♦ *n* обóчина; **to fall by the** ~ (*fig*) выбывáть (вы́быть* *perf*) из строя́.

way station *n* (US: RAIL) полустанóк*; (: *fig*) промежу́точный этáп.

wayward ['weɪwəd] *adj* своенрáвный* (своенрáвен).

WC *n abbr* (BRIT) = **water closet**.

WCC *n abbr* = **World Council of Churches**.

we [wiː] *pron* мы.

weak [wiːk] *adj* слáбый* (слаб); (*morally*) слабохарáктерный* (слабохарáктерен); **to grow** ~ ослабевáть *or* слабéть (ослабéть* *perf*).

weaken ['wi:kn] vi ослабевáть or слабéть
(ослабéть perf); (resolve, person) смягчáться
(смягчи́ться perf) ◆ vt (person, government)
ослабля́ть (осла́бить* perf).
weak-kneed ['wi:k'ni:d] adj (fig) мало-
ду́шный* (малоду́шен).
weakling ['wi:klɪŋ] n слаба́к*.
weakly ['wi:klɪ] adv сла́бо.
weakness ['wi:knɪs] n сла́бость f; **to have a ~
for** име́ть (impf) сла́бость к +dat.
wealth [wɛlθ] n (money, resources) бога́тство;
(of details, knowledge etc) оби́лие.
wealth tax n иму́щественный нало́г.
wealthy ['wɛlθɪ] adj состоя́тельный*
(состоя́телен).
wean [wi:n] vt (baby) отнима́ть (отня́ть* perf)
от гру́ди.
weapon ['wɛpən] n ору́жие*.
wear [wɛər] (pt **wore**, pp **worn**) n (use) изно́с;
(damage) изно́шенность f; (clothing) оде́жда
◆ vi (last) носи́ться* (impf); (rub through)
изна́шиваться (износи́ться* perf) ◆ vt (put on)
надева́ть (наде́ть* perf); (beard) носи́ть*
(impf); (damage) изна́шивать (износи́ть* perf);
(clothes): **he was ~ing his new shirt** на нём
была́ его́ но́вая руба́шка; **evening ~** (for
ladies) вече́рнее пла́тье*; (for men) вече́рний*
костю́м; **to ~ a hole in sth** протира́ть
(протере́ть* perf) дыру́ в чём-н
▸ **wear away** vt стира́ть (стере́ть* perf) ◆ vi
стира́ться (стере́ться* perf)
▸ **wear down** vt (heels) сна́шивать (сноси́ть*
perf); (resistance, strength) сломи́ть (perf)
▸ **wear off** vi (pain etc) постепе́нно проходи́ть*
(пройти́* perf)
▸ **wear on** vi тяну́ться* (impf)
▸ **wear out** vt (shoes, clothing) изна́шивать
(износи́ть* perf); (person, strength)
изма́тывать (измота́ть perf).
wearable ['wɛərəbl] adj приго́дный*
(приго́ден) для но́ски.
wear and tear [-tɛər] n изно́с.
wearer ['wɛərər] n владе́лец*(-лица).
wearily ['wɪərɪlɪ] adv уста́ло.
weariness ['wɪərɪnɪs] n утомле́ние.
wearisome ['wɪərɪsəm] adj (tiring)
утоми́тельный* (утоми́телен); (boring)
надое́дливый (надое́длив).
weary ['wɪərɪ] adj (tired) утомлённый
(утомлён); (dispirited) уста́лый ◆ vi: **to ~ of**
утомля́ться (утоми́ться* perf) от +gen.
weasel ['wi:zl] n (ZOOL) ла́ска*.
weather ['wɛðər] n пого́да ◆ vt (storm, crisis)
переноси́ть* (перенести́* perf), выде́рживать
(вы́держать perf) ◆ vi (wood) подверга́ться
(подве́ргнуться* perf) атмосфе́рным
влия́ниям; **what's the ~ like today?** кака́я
сего́дня пого́да?; **I am under the ~** мне

нездоро́вится.
weather-beaten ['wɛðəbi:tn] adj (face, skin)
обве́тренный* (обве́трен); (building, stone)
повреждённый непого́дой.
weathercock ['wɛðəkɔk] n флю́гер*.
weather forecast n прогно́з пого́ды.
weatherman ['wɛðəmæn] irreg n (inf)
сино́птик.
weatherproof ['wɛðəpru:f] adj (garment)
защища́ющий от непого́ды; (building)
погодоусто́йчивый (погодоусто́йчив),
утеплённый* (утеплён).
weather report n сообще́ние о пого́де.
weather vane [-veɪn] n = **weathercock**.
weave [wi:v] (pt **wove**, pp **woven**) vt (cloth)
ткать* (сотка́ть* perf); (basket) плести́*
(сплести́* perf) ◆ vi (pt, pp **weaved**; fig)
лави́ровать (impf).
weaver ['wi:vər] n ткач*(и́ха).
weaving ['wi:vɪŋ] n (craft) тка́чество; (of
baskets) плете́ние.
web [wɛb] n (of spider) паути́на; (on duck's
foot) перепо́нка*; (also fig) сеть* f.
webbed ['wɛbd] adj перепо́нчатый.
webbing ['wɛbɪŋ] n (on chair) тка́ный реме́нь
m.
wed [wɛd] (pt, pp **wedded**) vt (marry) венча́ться
(обвенча́ться perf) с +instr ◆ vi венча́ться
(обвенча́ться perf) ◆ n: **the newly-~s**
новобра́чные pl adj.
Wed. abbr = **Wednesday**.
we'd [wi:d] = **we had**, **we would**.
wedded ['wɛdɪd] pt, pp of **wed** ◆ adj: **he is ~ to**
(idea, policy etc) он пре́дан +dat.
wedding ['wɛdɪŋ] n сва́дьба*; (in church)
венча́ние; **silver/golden ~** сере́бряная/
золота́я сва́дьба.
wedding day n день* m сва́дьбы.
wedding dress n сва́дебное or подвене́чное
пла́тье*.
wedding present n сва́дебный пода́рок*.
wedding ring n обруча́льное кольцо́*.
wedge [wɛdʒ] n клин*; (of cake) кусо́к* ◆ vt
закрепля́ть (закрепи́ть* perf) кли́ном; (pack
tightly): **to ~ in** вти́скивать (вти́снуть perf) в
+acc.
wedge-heeled shoes ['wɛdʒhi:ld-] npl ту́фли*
pl на танке́тке.
wedlock ['wɛdlɔk] n супру́жество.
Wednesday ['wɛdnzdɪ] n среда́*; see also
Tuesday.
wee [wi:] adj (SCOTTISH: little) кро́шечный*.
weed [wi:d] n сорня́к* ◆ vt (garden) поло́ть*
(вы́полоть perf).
▸ **weed out** vt устраня́ть (устрани́ть perf).
weedkiller ['wi:dkɪlər] n сре́дство от
сорняко́в.
weedy ['wi:dɪ] adj (man) худосо́чный*

---

* marks translations which have irregular inflections. The Russian-English side of the dictionary gives inflectional information.

(худосо́чен).

week [wi:k] *n* неде́ля; **once/twice a ~** раз/два ра́за в неде́лю; **in two ~s' time** че́рез две неде́ли; **a ~ today** че́рез неде́лю, **a week on** Friday, в сле́дующую пя́тницу.

weekday ['wi:kdeɪ] *n* (*Monday to Friday*) бу́дний *or* рабо́чий* день* *m*; **on ~s** в бу́дни.

weekend [wi:k'ɛnd] *n* выходны́е *pl adj* (дни), суббо́та и воскресе́нье, уик-э́нд; **this/next/ last ~** в э́ти/сле́дующие/про́шлые выходны́е (дни); **what are you doing at the ~?** что Вы де́лаете в выходны́е?; **open at ~s** откры́то по суббо́там и воскресе́ньям *or* по выходны́м дням.

weekly ['wi:klɪ] *adv* еженеде́льно ♦ *adj* еженеде́льный ♦ *n* еженеде́льник.

weep [wi:p] (*pt,pp* **wept**) *vi* (*person*) пла́кать* (*impf*); (*wound*) сочи́ться (*impf*).

weeping willow ['wi:pɪŋ-] *n* плаку́чая и́ва.

weepy ['wi:pɪ] *adj* слезли́вый (слезли́в), плакси́вый (плакси́в) ♦ *n* (*inf: film*) душещипа́тельный фильм.

weft [wɛft] *n* уто́к*.

weigh [weɪ] *vt* взве́шивать (взве́сить* *perf*) ♦ *vi* ве́сить* (*impf*); **to ~ anchor** поднима́ть (подня́ть* *perf*) я́корь

► **weigh down** *vt* отягоща́ть (отяготи́ть* *perf*); (*fig*) тяготи́ть* (*impf*), отягоща́ть (*impf*)

► **weigh out** *vt* отве́шивать (отве́сить* *perf*)

► **weigh up** *vt* взве́шивать (взве́сить* *perf*); **to ~ up all the pros and cons** взве́шивать (взве́сить* *perf*) все "за" и "про́тив".

weighbridge ['weɪbrɪdʒ] *n* мостовы́е весы́ *pl*.

weighing machine ['weɪŋ-] *n* автомат́ические весы́ *pl*.

weight [weɪt] *n* (*for scales*) ги́ря; (*heaviness*) вес* ♦ *vt*: **to be ~ed in favour of** предоставля́ть (предоста́вить* *perf*) преиму́щество +*dat*; **sold by ~** продаётся на вес; **to lose ~** худе́ть (похуде́ть *perf*); **to put on ~** поправля́ться (попра́виться* *perf*); **W~s and Measures Office** Пала́та мер и весо́в.

weighting ['weɪtɪŋ] *n* (*allowance*) надба́вка.

weightlessness ['weɪtlɪsnɪs] *n* невесо́мость *f*.

weightlifter ['weɪtlɪftə'] *n* штанги́ст.

weight limit *n* преде́л ве́са.

weight training *n* силова́я гимна́стика.

weighty ['weɪtɪ] *adj* (*heavy: object*) тяжёлый (тяжёл); (: *person*) гру́зный* (гру́зен); (*important*) весо́мый (весо́м).

weir [wɪə'] *n* (*in river*) запру́да.

weird [wɪəd] *adj* (*strange*) стра́нный* (стра́нен); (*eerie*) таи́нственный* (таи́нственен).

weirdo ['wɪədəu] *n* (*inf*) чуда́к.

welcome ['wɛlkəm] *adj* жела́нный* (жела́нен) ♦ *n* (*hospitality*) приём; (*greeting*) приве́тствие ♦ *vt* (*also:* **bid ~**) приве́тствовать (*impf*); **to make sb ~** ока́зывать (оказа́ть* *perf*) кому́-н раду́шный приём; **you're ~ to try** пожа́луйста,

попро́буйте; **thank you – you're ~!** спаси́бо – пожа́луйста!

welcoming ['wɛlkəmɪŋ] *adj* (*person, smile etc*) раду́шный* (раду́шен); (*room*) прия́тный* (прия́тен); (*speech*) приве́тственный.

weld [wɛld] *n* сварно́й шов ♦ *vt* сва́ривать (свари́ть* *perf*).

welder ['wɛldə'] *n* сва́рщик.

welding ['wɛldɪŋ] *n* сва́рка*.

welfare ['wɛlfɛə'] *n* (*well-being*) благополу́чие; (*US: social aid*) социа́льное посо́бие.

welfare state *n* госуда́рство всео́бщего благосостоя́ния.

welfare work *n* благотвори́тельность *f*.

well [wɛl] *n* (*for water*) коло́дец*; (*also:* **oil ~**) (нефтяна́я) сква́жина ♦ *adv* хорошо́ ♦ *excl* (*anyway*) ну; (*so*) ну вот ♦ *adj*: **he is ~** он здоро́в; **I don't feel ~** я пло́хо себя́ чу́вствую; **to think ~ of sb** быть* (*impf*) хоро́шего мне́ния о ком-н; **as ~** та́кже; **oh ~** ... ну что же ...; **you might as ~ tell me** уж лу́чше ты скажи́ мне; **he played as ~ as he could** он сыгра́л как смог; **I woke ~ before dawn** я просну́лся задо́лго до рассве́та; **I've brought my anorak as ~ as a jumper** кро́ме пуло́вера я привёз ещё и анора́к; **~, as I was saying** ... ну, как я уже́ говори́л ...; **~, done!** молоде́ц!; **get ~ soon!** поправля́йтесь скоре́е; **he is doing ~ at school** в шко́ле он успева́ет; **the business is doing ~** би́знес процвета́ет

► **well up** *vi* (*tears*) наверну́ться (*perf*).

we'll [wi:l] = **we will, we shall**.

well-behaved ['wɛlbɪ'heɪvd] *adj* воспи́танный* (воспи́тан).

well-being ['wɛl'bi:ɪŋ] *n* благополу́чие.

well-bred ['wɛl'brɛd] *adj* (*person*) воспи́танный* (воспи́тан), благовоспи́танный (благовоспи́тан).

well-built ['wɛl'bɪlt] *adj* хорошо́ сложённый (сложён), кре́пкий* (кре́пок).

well-chosen ['wɛl'tʃəuzn] *adj* (*remarks, words*) хорошо́ подо́бранный (подо́бран).

well-deserved ['wɛldɪ'zə:vd] *adj* заслу́женный* (заслу́жен).

well-developed ['wɛldɪ'vɛləpt] *adj* с ра́звитыми фо́рмами.

well-disposed ['wɛl'dɪspəuzd] *adj*: **~ to(wards)** благожела́тельный* (благожела́телен) к +*dat*.

well-dressed ['wɛl'drɛst] *adj* хорошо́ оде́тый (оде́т).

well-earned ['wɛl'ə:nd] *adj* заслу́женный* (заслу́жен).

well-groomed ['wɛl'gru:md] *adj* (*person*) ухо́женный* (ухо́жен).

well-heeled ['wɛl'hi:ld] *adj* (*inf*) де́нежный.

well-informed ['wɛlɪn'fɔ:md] *adj* (*about something*) хорошо́ информи́рованный* (информи́рован); (*in general*) зна́ющий*.

Wellington ['wɛlɪŋtən] *n* Веллингто́н.

wellingtons ['wɛlɪŋtənz] *npl* (*also:* **wellington**

boots) резйновые сапогй* *mpl.*
well-kept ['wɛl'kɛpt] *adj* (*house, grounds*)
ухóженный (ухóжен); (*secret*) пóлный.
well-known ['wɛl'nəun] *adj* (*famous*)
извéстный* (извéстен).
well-mannered ['wɛl'mænəd] *adj*
воспйтанный* (воспйтан).
well-meaning ['wɛl'mi:nɪŋ] *adj*: **he is very ~** он
дéйствует из наилýчших побуждéний.
well-nigh ['wɛl'naɪ] *adv*: **~ impossible** почтй
невозмóжно.
well-off ['wɛl'ɔf] *adj* состоя́тельный*
(состоя́телен).
well-read ['wɛl'rɛd] *adj* начйтанный*
(начйтан).
well-spoken ['wɛl'spəukn] *adj* (*words*)
учтйвый (учтйв); **she was ~** онá говорйла
прáвильным языкáм.
well-stocked ['wɛl'stɔkt] *adj* (*shop*) хорошó
снабжáемый.
well-timed ['wɛl'taɪmd] *adj* своеврéменный*
(своеврéменен).
well-to-do ['wɛltə'du:] *adj* обеспéченный
(обеспéчен), состоя́тельный* (состоя́телен).
well-wisher ['wɛlwɪʃəʳ] *n* (*friend, admirer*)
доброжелáтель(ница) *m(f)*; **scores of ~s had
gathered** собралйсь деся́тки
доброжелáтелей; **letters from ~s** пйсьма от
доброжелáтелей.
well-woman clinic ['wɛlwumən-] *n* ≈ жéнская
консультáция.
Welsh [wɛlʃ] *adj* уэ́льский* ◆ *n* (*LING*) уэ́льский*
or валлййский язы́к*; **the ~** *npl* (*people*)
уэ́льсцы *mpl*, валлййцы *mpl*.
Welshman ['wɛlʃmən] *irreg n* уэ́льсец*,
валлйец*.
Welsh rarebit *n* гренóк* с сы́ром.
Welshwoman ['wɛlʃwumən] *n irreg* валлйӣка*,
жйтельница Уэ́льса.
welter ['wɛltəʳ] *n*: **a ~ of** хáос +*gen*.
went [wɛnt] *pt of* **go.**
wept [wɛpt] *pt, pp of* **weep.**
were [wəː'] *pt of* **be.**
we're [wɪəʳ] = **we are.**
weren't [wəːnt] = **were not.**
werewolf ['wɪəwulf] (*pl* **werewolves**) *n*
человéк-волк.
werewolves ['wɪəwulvz] *npl of* **werewolf.**
west [wɛst] *n* зáпад ◆ *adj* зáпадный ◆ *adv* на
зáпад; **the W~** (*POL*) Зáпад.
westbound ['wɛstbaund] *adj* (*carriageway,
traffic*) зáпадного направлéния.
West Country *n*: **the ~ ~** (*BRIT*) зáпадная
Áнглия.
westerly ['wɛstəlɪ] *adj* зáпадный.
western ['wɛstən] *adj* (*also POL*) зáпадный ◆ *n*
(*CINEMA*) вéстерн.
westerner ['wɛstənəʳ] *n* зáпадный человéк*.

westernized ['wɛstənaɪzd] *adj* ориентй-
рованный (ориентйрован) на Зáпад.
West German *adj* (*formerly*)
западногермáнский ◆ *n* жйтель(ница) *m(f)*
Зáпадной Гермáнии.
West Germany *n* (*formerly*) Зáпадная
Гермáния.
West Indian *adj* вест-индйӣский* ◆ *n*
жйтель(ница) *m(f)* Вест-Йндии.
West Indies [-'ɪndɪz] *npl*: **the ~ ~** Вест-Йндия
fsg.
Westminster ['wɛstmɪnstəʳ] *n* Вестмйнстер.
westward(s) ['wɛstwəd(z)] *adv* на зáпад, к
зáпаду.
wet [wɛt] *adj* (*damp, rainy*) влáжный*
(влáжен), сырóй* (сыр); (*soaking*) мóкрый*
(мокр) ◆ *n* (*BRIT: POL*) "умéренный(-ая)" *m(f)*
adj ◆ *vt*: **to ~ one's pants** *or* **o.s.** мочйть
(намочйть *perf*) штаны́; **to get ~** промокáть
(промóкнуть* *perf*); **"~ paint!"** "осторóжно,
окрáшено!"; **he is a ~ blanket** (*fig: pej*) он –
занýда.
wetness ['wɛtnɪs] *n* влáжность *f*, сы́рость *f*.
wetsuit ['wɛtsu:t] *n* гидрокостю́м.
we've [wi:v] = **we have.**
whack [wæk] *vt* давáть* (дать* *perf*) затрéщину
+*dat.*
whacked [wækt] *adj* (*BRIT: inf*) разбйтый
(разбйт).
whale [weɪl] *n* кит*.
whaler ['weɪləʳ] *n* (*ship*) китобóйное сýдно.
whaling ['weɪlɪŋ] *n* китобóйный прóмысел.
wharf [wɔ:f] (*pl* **wharves**) *n* прйстань* *f.*
wharves [wɔ:vz] *npl of* **wharf.**

KEYWORD

what [wɔt] *adj* **1** (*interrogative: direct, indirect*)
какóй; **what size is the dress?** какóго размéра
э́то плáтье?; **what books do you need?** какйе
кнйги Вам нужны́?
2 какóй; **what a lovely day!** какóй чудéсный
день!; **what a mess!** (*room etc*) ну и
беспоря́док!; (*fig*) что за неразберйха!; **what
a fool I am!** какóй же я дурáк!
◆ *pron* **1** (*interrogative*) что; **what are you
doing?** что Вы дéлаете?; **what are you talking
about?** о чём Вы говорйте?; **what is it called?**
как э́то называ́ется?; **what about me?** а (как
же) я?; **what about doing ...?** как насчёт тогó,
чтóбы +*infin* ...?
2 (*relative*) что; **I saw what you did/was on the
table** я вйдел, что Вы дéлали/бы́ло на
столé; **is that what happened?** так э́то то, что
случйлось?; **tell me what you're thinking
about** скажйте мне, о чём Вы дýмаете; **what
you say is wrong** то, что Вы говорйте,
невéрно
◆ *excl* (*disbelieving*) что; **I've crashed the car –
what!** я разбйл машйну – что!

---

* marks translations which have irregular inflections. The Russian-English side of the dictionary gives inflectional information.

whatever [wɔt'ɛvə'] *adj*: ~ **book** любáя кни́га ◆ *pron*: **do ~ is necessary/you want** дéлайте всё, что необходи́мо/хоти́те; ~ **happens** что бы ни случи́лось; **no reason** ~ *or* **whatsoever** нет никакóй причи́ны; **nothing** ~ совсéм ничегó.

whatsoever [wɔtsəu'ɛvə'] *adj see* **whatever**.

wheat [wi:t] *n* пшени́ца.

wheatgerm ['wi:tdʒə:m] *n* зарóдыш пшени́чного зернá.

wheatmeal ['wi:tmi:l] *n* пшени́чная мукá грубóго помóла.

wheedle ['wi:dl] *vt*: **to ~ sb into doing** угова́ривать (уговори́ть *perf*) когó-н лéстью +*infin*; **to ~ sth out of sb** выма́нивать (вы́манить *perf*) чтó-н у когó-н.

wheel [wi:l] *n* (*of vehicle etc*) колесó*; (*also:* **steering ~**) руль* *m*; (*NAUT*) штурвáл ◆ *vt* (*pram etc*) катáть/кати́ть* (*impf*) ◆ *vi* (*birds*) кружи́ться (*impf*); (*also:* ~ **round:** *person*) крýто повора́чиваться (поверну́ться *perf*).

wheelbarrow ['wi:lbærəu] *n* тáчка*.

wheelbase ['wi:lbeis] *n* колёсная бáза.

wheelchair ['wi:lt[ɛə'] *n* инвали́дное крéсло*.

wheel clamp *n* (*AUT*) блокирáтор (*для блокирóвки рулевóго колесá*).

wheeler-dealer ['wi:lə'di:lə'] *n* (*pej*) махинáтор.

wheelie-bin ['wi:lɪbɪn] *n* мýсорное ведрó на колёсиках.

wheeling ['wi:lɪŋ] *n*: ~ **and dealing** (*pej*) махинáции *fpl*.

wheeze [wi:z] *vi* (*person*) хрипéть* (*impf*) ◆ *n* (*idea, joke etc*) острoýмная идéя, затéя.

wheezy ['wi:zɪ] *adj* хрипя́щий, сипя́щий.

when [wɛn] *adv, conj* когдá; ~ **you've read the book, tell me what you think** когдá Вы прочита́ете кни́гу, скажи́те мне что Вы дýмаете; **you said I was wrong** ~ **in fact I was right** Вы сказáли, что я был непрáв, когдá на сáмом дéле я был прав.

whenever [wɛn'ɛvə'] *adv* в любóе врéмя ◆ *conj* (*any time*) когдá тóлько; (*every time that*) кáждый раз, когдá; **I go** ~ **I can** я пойдý, как тóлько смогý.

where [wɛə'] *adv* (*place*) где; (*direction*) кудá; (*from where*) откýда ◆ *conj* где; **this is** ~ ... э́то там, где ...; ~ **possible** где возмóжно; ~ **have you come from?** откýда Вы приéхали?

whereabouts [*adv* wɛərə'bauts, *n* 'wɛərəbauts] *adv* где; (*motion*) кудá ◆ *n*: **nobody knows his** ~ никтó не знáет егó местонахождéния.

whereas [wɛər'æz] *conj* тогдá *or* в то врéмя как.

whereby [wɛə'baɪ] *adv* (*formal*) посрéдством чегó.

whereupon [wɛərə'pɔn] *adv* пóсле *or* вслéдствие чегó.

wherever [wɛər'ɛvə'] *conj* (*no matter where: position*): ~ **he was** где бы он ни́ был; (: *motion*): ~ **he goes** кудá бы он ни шёл; (*not knowing where*): ~ **that is** где бы то ни́ было

◆ *adv* (*interrogative*): ~ **have you been?** где же Вы бы́ли?; **let's go away –** ~ **to?** давáйте уйдём отсю́да – кудá же?; **sit** ~ **you like** сади́тесь, где хоти́те.

wherewithal ['wɛəwɪðɔ:l] *n*: **the** ~ **(to do)** срéдства *ntpl* (+*infin*).

whet [wɛt] *vt* (*appetite*) возбуждáть (возбуди́ть* *perf*); (*tool*) точи́ть* (наточи́ть* *perf*).

whether ['wɛðə'] *conj*: **I doubt** ~ **she loves me** я сомневáюсь, лю́бит ли онá меня́; **I don't know** ~ **to accept this proposal or not** я не знáю, приня́ть э́то предложéние и́ли нет; ~ **you go or not** пойдёте Вы и́ли нет.

whey ['weɪ] *n* сы́воротка.

KEYWORD

which [wɪtʃ] *adj* **1** (*interrogative: direct, indirect*) какóй; **which picture would you like?** какýю карти́ну Вы хоти́те?; **which books are yours?** каки́е кни́ги Вáши?; **which one?** какóй? (*f* какáя?, *nt* какóе?); **I've got two pens, which one do you want?** у меня́ есть две рýчки, какýю Вы хоти́те?; **which one of you did it?** кто из вас э́то сдéлал?

2: **in which case** и в такóм слýчае; **by which time** к томý врéмени

◆ *pron* **1** (*interrogative*) какóй (*f* какáя, *nt* какóе, *pl* каки́е); **there are several museums, which shall we visit first?** здесь есть нéсколько музéев, в какóй мы пойдём снача́ла?; **which do you want, the apple or the banana?** что Вы хоти́те – я́блоко и́ли банáн?; **which of you are staying?** кто из вас остаётся?

2 (*relative*) котóрый (*f* котóрая, *nt* котóрос, *pl* котóрые); **the apple which you ate/which is on the table** я́блоко, котóрое Вы съéли/котóрое лежи́т на столé; **the news was bad, which is what I had feared** вéсти бы́ли плохи́е, как я и боя́лся, **I had lunch, after which I decided to go home** я пообéдал, пóсле чегó я реши́л пойти́ домóй; **I made a speech, after which nobody spoke** я вы́ступил с рéчью, пóсле котóрой никтó не произнёс ни слóва.

whichever [wɪtʃ'ɛvə'] *adj*: **take** ~ **book you prefer** возьми́те любýю кни́гу, какýю предпочтёте; ~ **book you take** какýю бы кни́гу Вы ни взя́ли.

whiff [wɪf] *n* дуновéние; **to catch a** ~ **of sth** улáвливать (улови́ть *perf*) почýять зáпах чегó-л.

while [waɪl] *n* (*period of time*) врéмя* *nt* ◆ *conj* покá, в то врéмя как; (*although*) хотя́, несмотря́ на то, что; **for a** ~ ненадóлго; **in a** ~ скóро; **all the** ~ всё врéмя; **we promise to make it worth your** ~ мы обещáем, что Вы не остáнетесь в прóигрыше

▶ while away *vt*: **to** ~ **away the time** коротáть (скоротáть *perf*) врéмя.

whilst [waɪlst] *conj* = **while**.

whim [wɪm] *n* при́хоть *f*.
whimper ['wɪmpəʳ] *n* хны́канье ♦ *vi* хны́кать*
(*impf*); (*dog*) скули́ть (*impf*).
whimsical ['wɪmzɪkl] *adj* причу́дливый
(причу́длив).
whine [waɪn] *n* вой ♦ *vi* (*person, animal*)
скули́ть (*impf*); (*engine, siren*) выть* (*impf*).
whip [wɪp] *n* кнут*, хлыст*; (*POL: person*)
организа́тор парла́ментской фра́кции ♦ *vt*
(*person, animal*) хлеста́ть* (*impf*); (*cream,
eggs*) взбива́ть (взбить* *perf*); (*move quickly*):
to ~ sth out выхва́тывать (вы́хватить* *perf*)
что-н; **to ~ sth away** вырыва́ть (вы́рвать*
perf) что-н
▶ **whip up** *vt* (*cream*) взбива́ть (взбить* *perf*);
(*inf: meal*) де́лать (сде́лать *perf*) на ско́рую
ру́ку; (*support, emotion*) возбужда́ть
(возбуди́ть* *perf*).
whiplash ['wɪplæʃ] *n* (*also:* **~ injury**)
*поврежде́ние ше́и, вы́званное ре́зким
движе́нием головы́ вперёд и наза́д,
наприме́р, при автомоби́льной ава́рии.*
whipped cream [wɪpt-] *n* взби́тые сли́вки* *pl*.
whipping boy ['wɪpɪŋ-] *n* (*fig*) ≈ козёл
отпуще́ния.
whip-round ['wɪpraund] *n* (*BRIT*) скла́дчина.
whirl [wəːl] *vt* враща́ть (*impf*), верте́ть* (*impf*) ♦
vi кружи́ться* (*impf*), враща́ться (*impf*) ♦ *n*
круже́ние; **my mind is in a ~** у меня́ голова́
идёт кру́гом; **~ of social engagements**
водоворо́т *or* вихрь све́тской жи́зни.
whirlpool ['wəːlpuːl] *n* водоворо́т.
whirlwind ['wəːlwɪnd] *n* вихрь *m*.
whirr [wəːʳ] *vi* (*insects*) стрекота́ть (*impf*);
(*motor etc*) треща́ть (*impf*).
whisk [wɪsk] *n* (*CULIN*) ве́нчик ♦ *vt* (*cream, eggs*)
взбива́ть (взбить* *perf*); **to ~ sb away** *or* **off**
отгоня́ть (отогна́ть* *perf*).
whiskers ['wɪskəz] *npl* (*of animal*) усы́ *mpl*; (*of
man*) бакенба́рды *fpl*.
whisky ['wɪskɪ] (*US, IRELAND* **whiskey**) *n* ви́ски *m
ind*.
whisper ['wɪspəʳ] *n* шёпот ♦ *vi* шепта́ться
(*impf*) ♦ *vt* шепта́ть* (*impf*); **to ~ sth to sb**
шепта́ть* (*impf*) что-н кому́-н.
whispering ['wɪspərɪŋ] *n* перешёптывание.
whist [wɪst] *n* (*BRIT*) вист.
whistle ['wɪsl] *n* (*sound*) свист; (*object*)
свисто́к* ♦ *vi* свисте́ть* (*impf*), сви́стнуть (*perf*)
♦ *vt*: **to ~ a tune** насви́стывать (*impf*)
мело́дию.
whistle-stop ['wɪslstɔp] *adj*: **to make a ~ tour of**
(*POL*) объезжа́ть (объе́хать* *perf*) с
агитацио́нными це́лями.
Whit [wɪt] *n* Тро́ицын день* *m*.
white [waɪt] *adj* бе́лый* (бел) ♦ *n* (*colour*)
бе́лый цвет; (*person*) бе́лый(-ая) *m(f) adj*; (*of
egg, eye*) бело́к*; **to turn** *or* **go ~** беле́ть

(побеле́ть *perf*); **the ~s** (*washing*) бело́е
бельё; **tennis/cricket ~s** те́ннисная/
крике́тная фо́рма.
whitebait ['waɪtbeɪt] *n* снето́к*.
white coffee *n* (*BRIT*) ко́фе *m ind* с молоко́м.
white-collar worker ['waɪtkɔlə-] *n*
слу́жащий*(-ая) *m(f) adj*.
white elephant *n* (*fig*) изли́шняя ро́скошь *f*.
white goods *npl* (*appliances*) бытовы́е
электротова́ры *mpl*; (*linen etc*) белошве́йные
това́ры *mpl*.
white-hot [waɪt'hɔt] *adj* раскалённый*
(раскалён) добела́.
white lie *n* безоби́дная ложь* *f*.
whiteness ['waɪtnɪs] *n* белизна́.
white noise *n* (*RADIO, ELEC etc*) „бе́лый шум"
(*поме́хи в радиоэфи́ре*).
whiteout ['waɪtaut] *n* бе́лая мгла.
white paper *n* (*POL*) "Бе́лая кни́га"
(*докуме́нт, излага́ющий поли́тику
прави́тельства по тем и́ли ины́м вопро́сам*).
whitewash ['waɪtwɔʃ] *n* (*paint*) известко́вый
раство́р (*для побе́лки*); (*inf: SPORT*) „суха́я" ♦
vt (*building*) бели́ть* (побели́ть* *perf*); (*fig:
incident, reputation*) обеля́ть (обели́ть *perf*).
white water *n*: **~ rafting** пла́вание на
плота́х по го́рным ре́кам.
whiting ['waɪtɪŋ] *n inv* хек.
Whit Monday *n* ≈ Ду́хов день* *m*.
Whitsun ['wɪtsn] *n* ≈ Тро́ицын день* *m*,
Тро́ица.
whittle ['wɪtl] *vt*: **to ~ away** *or* **down** (*costs*)
уменьша́ть (уме́ньшить *perf*).
whizz [wɪz] *vi*: **to ~ past** *or* **by** проноси́ться*
(пронести́сь* *perf*) ми́мо.
whizz kid *n* (*inf*) вундерки́нд.
WHO *n abbr* (= World Health Organization)
ВОЗ= *Всеми́рная организа́ция
здравоохране́ния*.

KEYWORD

who [huː] *pron* **1** (*interrogative*) кто*; **who is it?,
who's there?** кто э́то *or* там?; **who did you see
there?** кого́ Вы там ви́дели?
2 (*relative*) кото́рый (*f* кото́рая, *nt* кото́рое);
the woman who spoke to me же́нщина,
кото́рая говори́ла со мно́й; **those who can
swim** те, кто уме́ют пла́вать.

---

whodunit [huː'dʌnɪt] *n* (*inf*) детекти́в.
whoever [huː'ɛvəʳ] *pron*: **~ finds him** ... тот, кто
найдёт его́ ...; **кто бы ни нашёл его́ ...; ask ~
you like** спроси́те, кого́ хоти́те; **~ told you
that?** кто Вам э́то сказа́л?; **come out, ~ you
are!** выходи́, кто бы ты ни́ был!
whole [həul] *adj* це́лый (цел) ♦ *n* (*entire unit*)
це́лое *nt adj*; (*all*): **the ~ of Europe** вся Евро́па;
the ~ lot (of it) всё (э́то); **the ~ lot (of them)**
все *pl* (они́); **the ~ of the time** всё вре́мя; **~**

---

* marks translations which have irregular inflections. The Russian-English side of the dictionary gives inflectional information.

villages were destroyed це́лые дере́вни бы́ли разру́шены; **the ~ of the town** весь го́род; **on the ~, as a ~** в це́лом.

wholefood(s) ['həulfu:d(z)] *n(pl)* натура́льные проду́кты *mpl.*

wholefood shop *n* магази́н натура́льных проду́ктов.

wholehearted [həul'ha:tɪd] *adj (agreement etc)* и́скренний*; *(support)* горя́чий*.

wholeheartedly [həul'ha:tɪdlɪ] *adv (see adj)* и́скренне; горячо́.

wholemeal ['həulmi:l] *adj (BRIT)*: ~ **flour** мука́ гру́бого помо́ла; ~ **bread** хлеб из муки́ гру́бого помо́ла.

whole note *n (US)* це́лая но́та.

wholesale ['həulseɪl] *n* опто́вая торго́вля ♦ *adj (price)* опто́вый; *(destruction)* ма́ссовый ♦ *adv (buy, sell)* о́птом.

wholesaler ['həulseɪlə'] *n* оптови́к*; *(insitution)* опто́вое предприя́тие.

wholesome ['həulsəm] *adj* здоро́вый.

wholewheat ['həulwi:t] *adj* = **wholemeal.**

wholly ['həulɪ] *adv* по́лностью, целико́м.

KEYWORD

whom [hu:m] *pron* **1** *(interrogative: +acc, +gen)* кого́; (: *+dat)* кому́; (: *+instr)* кем; (: *+prp)* ком; **whom did you see there?** кого́ Вы там ви́дели?; **to whom did you give the book?** кому́ Вы кни́гу отда́ли?

2 *(relative: +acc)* кото́рого (*f* кото́рую, *pl* кото́рых); (: *+gen)* кото́рого (*f* кото́рой, *pl* кото́рых); (: *+dat)* кото́рому (*f* кото́рой, *pl* кото́рых); (: *+instr)* кото́рым (*f* кото́рой, *pl* кото́рыми); (: *+prp)* кото́ром (*f* кото́рой, *pl* кото́рых); **the man whom I saw/to whom I spoke** челове́к, кото́рого я ви́дел/с кото́рым я говори́л.

whooping cough ['hu:pɪŋ-] *n* коклю́ш.

whoosh [wuʃ] *n* свист ♦ *vi*: **to ~ past** *etc* просвисте́ть* *(perf)* ми́мо *etc*; **the skiers ~ed past, skiers came by with a ~** лы́жники со сви́стом пронесли́сь ми́мо.

whopper ['wɔpə'] *n (inf: lie)* чудо́вищная ложь* *f; (large thing)* грома́дина.

whopping ['wɔpɪŋ] *adj (inf: big)* грома́дный* (грома́ден).

whore [hɔː'] *n (inf: pej)* шлю́ха.

KEYWORD

whose [hu:z] *adj* **1** *(possessive: interrogative)* чей*; **whose book is this?, whose is this book?** чья э́то кни́га?

2 *(possessive: relative)* кото́рый; **the woman whose son you rescued** же́нщина, сы́на кото́рой Вы спасли́

♦ *pron* чей (*f* чья, *nt* чьё, *pl* чьи); **whose is this?** э́то чьё?; **I know whose it is** я зна́ю, чьё э́то.

Who's Who ['hu:z'hu:] *n* Кто есть кто *(спра́вочник).*

KEYWORD

why [waɪ] *adv, conj* почему́; **why is he always late?** почему́ он всегда́ опа́здывает?; **why not?** почему́?; **why not do it now?** почему́ бы не сде́лать э́то сейча́с?; **I wonder why he said that** интере́сно, почему́ он э́то сказа́л; **that's not why I'm here** я здесь во́все не поэ́тому; **that's why** вот почему́; **there is a reason why I want to see him** у меня́ есть причи́ны для встре́чи с ним

♦ *excl*: **why, it's you!** о, неуже́ли э́то Вы?; **why, it's obvious/that's impossible!** но ведь э́то же очеви́дно/невозмо́жно!

WI *n abbr (BRIT*: = *Women's Institute)* ассоциа́ция же́нщин, интересу́ющихся вопро́сами домово́дства ♦ *abbr* = *West Indies*; (*US: POST)* Wisconsin.

wick [wɪk] *n* фити́ль* *m*; **he gets on my ~** *(inf)* он де́йствует мне на не́рвы.

wicked ['wɪkɪd] *adj (злобный* (зло́бен), злой*; *(mischievous: smile)* лука́вый, плутовско́й; *(terrible: prices, weather)* жу́ткий*.

wicker ['wɪkə'] *adj* плетёный*.

wickerwork ['wɪkə'wə:k] *adj* плетёный ♦ *n* плете́ние.

wicket ['wɪkɪt] *n (CRICKET: stumps)* воро́тца* *pl*; (: *grass area)* кон ме́жду двумя́ воро́тцами.

wicket-keeper ['wɪkɪtki:pə'] *n* игро́к, охраня́ющий воро́тца.

wide [waɪd] *adj* широ́кий* (широ́к) ♦ *adv*: **to open ~** широко́ открыва́ть (откры́ть* *perf)*; **to shoot ~** стреля́ть *(impf)* ми́мо це́ли; **the bridge is 3 metres ~** ширина́ моста́ – 3 ме́тра.

wide-angle lens ['waɪdæŋgl-] *n (PHOT)* широкоуго́льная ли́нза.

wide-awake [waɪdə'weɪk] *adj*: **I feel ~** у меня́ сна ни в одно́м глазу́.

wide-eyed [waɪd'aɪd] *adj (fig)* наи́вный* (наи́вен); **she sat there ~** она́ сиде́ла с широко́ раскры́тыми глаза́ми.

widely ['waɪdlɪ] *adv (believed, known)* широко́; *(travelled)* мно́го; *(differing)* значи́тельно; **he is ~ read** *(author)* его́ мно́го чита́ют; *(reader)* он о́чень начи́тан.

widen ['waɪdn] *vt* расширя́ть (расши́рить *perf)* ♦ *vi* расширя́ться (расши́риться *perf).*

wideness ['waɪdnɪs] *n* широта́.

wide open *adj* широко́ раскры́тый (раскры́т).

wide-ranging [waɪd'reɪndʒɪŋ] *adj (survey, report)* всесторо́нний* (всесторо́нен); *(interests)* широ́кий*.

widespread ['waɪdspred] *adj (belief etc)* распространённый* (распространён).

widow ['wɪdəu] *n* вдова́*.

widowed ['wɪdəud] *adj* овдове́вший.

widower ['wɪdəuə'] *n* вдове́ц*.

width [wɪdθ] *n* ширина́; **the street is 7 metres in ~** ширина́ у́лицы – 7 ме́тров.

widthways ['wɪdθweɪz] *adv* в ширину́.

wield [wi:ld] *vt (sword)* владе́ть *(impf)* +*instr*;

(*power*) пóльзоваться* (*impf*) +*instr*.
wife [waɪf] (*pl* **wives**) *n* женá*.
wig [wɪg] *n* парúк*.
wigging ['wɪgɪŋ] *n* (*BRIT*: *inf*) разнóс.
wiggle ['wɪgl] *vt* (*hips*) покáчивать (*impf*) +*instr*; (*ears*) шевелúть (*impf*) +*instr*.
wiggly ['wɪglɪ] *adj* волнúстый* (волнúст).
wigwam ['wɪgwæm] *n* вигвáм.
wild [waɪld] *adj* (*animal, plant*) дúкий*; (*weather, sea*) бýрный* (бýрен); (*person, behaviour*) бýйный* (бýен); (*idea, guess*) дúкий; (*enthusiastic: applause*) бýрный ◆ *n*: **the ~** (*natural surroundings*) лóно прирóды *ntpl*; **the ~s** *npl* (*remote area*) дúкие местá *ntpl*; **in the ~s of Taiga** в дéбрях тайгú; **I am ~ about her/this film** я без умá от неё/э́того фúльма.
wild card *n* (*COMPUT*) универсáльный сúмвол.
wildcat ['waɪldkæt] *n* дúкая кóшка*.
wildcat strike *n* неофициáльная забастóвка*.
wilderness ['wɪldənɪs] *n* дúкая мéстность *f*; (*desert*) пустыня.
wildfire ['waɪldfaɪə'] *n*: **to spread like ~** распространяться (распространúться *perf*) с быстротóй огня.
wild-goose chase [waɪld'gu:s-] *n* (*fig*) бессмысленная затéя.
wildlife ['waɪldlaɪf] *n* дúкая прирóда.
wildly ['waɪldlɪ] *adv* (*behave*) бýйно, дúко; (*applaud*) бýрно; (*hit, happy*) нéистово; (*guess*) наобýм.
wiles [waɪlz] *npl* улóвки* *fpl*.
wilful ['wɪlful] (*US* **willful**) *adj* (*obstinate*) своенрáвный* (своенрáвен); (*deliberate*) умышленный*.

KEYWORD

will [wɪl] *aux vb* **1** (*forming future tense*): **I will finish it tomorrow** я закóнчу э́то зáвтра; **I will be working all morning** я бýду рабóтать всё ýтро; **I will have finished it by tomorrow** к зáвтрашнему дню я э́то закóнчу; **I will always remember you** я бýду пóмнить тебя всегдá; **will you do it? – yes, I will/no, I won't** Вы сдéлаете э́то? – да, сдéлаю/нет, не сдéлаю; **the car won't start** машúна никáк не завóдится
2 (*in conjectures, predictions*): **he will** *or* **he'll be there by now** он, навéрное, ужé там; **mistakes will happen** ошúбки неизбéжны
3 (*in commands, requests, offers*): **will you be quiet!** а нý-ка потúше!; **will you help me?** Вы мне не помóжете?; **will you have a cup of tea?** не хотúте ли чáшку чáя?; **I won't put up with it!** я э́того не потерплю́!
◆ (*pt,pp* **willed**) *vt*: **I willed him to win** я хотéл вселúть в негó дух побéды
◆ *n* (*volition*) вóля; (*testament*) завещáние.

willful ['wɪlful] *adj* (*US*) = **wilful**.
willing ['wɪlɪŋ] *adj* (*agreed*) соглáсный* (соглáсен); (*enthusiastic*) усéрдный* (усéрден); **he's ~ to do it** он готóв э́то сдéлать; **to show ~** проявля́ть (прояв́úть* *perf*) готóвность.
willingly ['wɪlɪŋlɪ] *adv* охóтно.
willingness ['wɪlɪŋnɪs] *n* готóвность *f*.
will-o'-the wisp ['wɪləðə'wɪsp] *n* (*also fig*) неуловúмое *nt adj*.
willow ['wɪləu] *n* (*tree*) úва; (*wood*) ивняк.
willpower ['wɪl'pauə'] *n* сúла вóли.
willy-nilly ['wɪlɪ'nɪlɪ] *adv* вóлей-невóлей.
wilt [wɪlt] *vi* поникáть (понúкнуть* *perf*).
Wilts [wɪlts] *abbr* (*BRIT*: *POST*) = **Wiltshire**.
wily ['waɪlɪ] *adj* хúтрый* (хитёр).
wimp [wɪmp] (*inf*: *pej*) *n* хлю́пик ◆ *vi*: **to ~ out** стрýсить* (*perf*).
wimpish ['wɪmpɪʃ] *adj* (*inf*: *pej*) хлúпкий* (хлúпок).
win [wɪn] (*pt,pp* **won**) *n* побéда ◆ *vt* выúгрывать (выúграть *perf*); (*support, popularity*) завоёвывать (завоевáть* *perf*) ◆ *vi* побеждáть (победúть* *perf*), выúгрывать (выúграть *perf*).
▶ **win over** *vt* (*person*) покоря́ть (покорúть *perf*)
▶ **win round** *vt* (*BRIT*) = **win over**.
wince [wɪns] *vi* мóрщиться (помóрщиться *perf*).
winch [wɪntʃ] *n* лебёдка*, вóрот.
Winchester disk ['wɪntʃɪstə-] *n* (*COMPUT*) винчéстерский диск.
wind¹ [wɪnd] *n* вéтер*; (*MED*) гáзы *mpl*; (*breath*) дыхáние ◆ *vt*: **the blow ~ed him** от удáра у негó захватúло дух; **the ~** *npl* (*MUS*) духовы́е инструмéнты *mpl*; **into** *or* **against the ~** прóтив вéтра; **he got the ~ of the news** (*fig*) до негó дошлá нóвость; **to break ~** дéлать (сдéлать *perf*) отры́жку.
wind² [waɪnd] (*pt, pp* **wound**) *vt* (*roll: thread, rope*) мотáть (смотáть *perf*); (*rotate*) вертéть* (*impf*), крутúть* (*perf*); (*bandage*) завёртывать (завернýть* *perf*); (*clock, toy*) заводúть* (завестú* *perf*) ◆ *vi* (*road, river*) вúться* (*impf*)
▶ **wind down** *vt* (*car window*) опускáть (опустúть* *perf*); (*production, business*) свóрачивать (свернýть* *perf*)
▶ **wind up** *vt* (*clock, toy*) заводúть* (завестú* *perf*); (*debate*) завершáть (заверш́úть* *perf*).
windbreak ['wɪndbreɪk] *n* бурелóм; (*plants*) ветрозащúтная лесополосá.
windbreaker ['wɪndbreɪkə'] *n* (*US*) = **windcheater**.
windcheater ['wɪndtʃi:tə'] *n* штормóвка*.
winder ['waɪndə'] *n* (*BRIT*: *on watch*) (заводнóй) ключ*.

---

* marks translations which have irregular inflections. The Russian-English side of the dictionary gives inflectional information.

windfall [ˈwɪndfɔːl] *n* (*money*) неожи́данные де́ньги *pl*; (*apple etc*) па́данец*.

winding [ˈwaɪndɪŋ] *adj* изви́листый (изви́лист); ~ **staircase** вита́я ле́стница.

wind instrument [ˈwɪnd-] *n* духово́й инструме́нт.

windmill [ˈwɪndmɪl] *n* ветряна́я ме́льница.

window [ˈwɪndəu] *n* (*in house, vehicle*) окно́*; (*in shop*) витри́на; (*also:* ~ **pane**) око́нное стекло́*.

window box *n* нару́жный я́щик для цвето́в.

window cleaner *n* мо́йщик(-ица) о́кон.

window dresser *n* оформи́тель(ница) *m(f)* витри́н.

window envelope *n* конве́рт с прозра́чным прямоуго́льником, че́рез кото́рый ви́ден а́дрес, напеча́танный на письме́.

window frame *n* око́нная ра́ма.

window ledge *n* нару́жный подоко́нник.

window pane *n* око́нное стекло́*.

window-shopping [ˈwɪndəuʃɔpɪŋ] *n*: **to go** ~ рассма́тривать (*impf*) витри́ны.

windowsill [ˈwɪndəusɪl] *n* подоко́нник.

windpipe [ˈwɪndpaɪp] *n* (*ANAT*) трахе́я.

wind power [ˈwɪnd-] *n* си́ла ве́тра.

windscreen [ˈwɪndskriːn] *n* ветрово́е стекло́*.

windscreen washer *n* стеклоомыва́тель *m*.

windscreen wiper [-waɪpə^r] *n* дво́рник, стеклоочисти́тель *m*.

windshield [ˈwɪndʃiːld] *n* (*US*) = **windscreen**.

wind surfing [ˈwɪnd-] *n* виндсёрфинг.

windswept [ˈwɪndswɛpt] *adj* (*place*) незащищённый от ве́тра; (*person, hair*) растрёпанный* (растрёпан).

wind tunnel [ˈwɪnd-] *n* аэродинами́ческая труба́*.

windy [ˈwɪndɪ] *adj* ве́треный* (ве́трен); **it's** ~ сего́дня ве́трено.

wine [waɪn] *n* вино́* ♦ *vt*: **to** ~ **and dine sb** пои́ть*-корми́ть* (*impf*) кого́-н.

wine bar *n* ви́нный бар.

wine cellar *n* ви́нный по́греб*.

wine glass *n* бока́л.

wine grower *n* виногра́дарь *m*.

wine growing *n* виногра́дарство ♦ *adj*: ~~ **region** виногра́дарский райо́н.

wine list *n* ка́рта вин.

wine merchant *n* виноторго́вец*.

wine tasting [-teɪstɪŋ] *n* дегуста́ция вин.

wine waiter *n* официа́нт, веда́ющий ви́нами.

wing [wɪŋ] *n* (*also AUT*) крыло́*; ~**s** *npl* (*THEAT*) кули́сы *fpl*.

winger [ˈwɪŋə^r] *n* (*FOOTBALL, RUGBY*) кра́йний* напада́ющий* *m adj*.

wing mirror *n* (*BRIT*) боково́е зе́ркало*.

wing nut *n* кры́льчатая га́йка*.

wingspan [ˈwɪŋspæn] *n* разма́х крыла́.

wingspread [ˈwɪŋsprɛd] *n* разма́х крыла́.

wink [wɪŋk] *n* подми́гивание ♦ *vi* (*with eye*) подми́гивать (подмигну́ть *perf*); (*light etc*) мига́ть (мигну́ть *perf*).

winkle [ˈwɪŋkl] *n* берегова́я *or* морска́я улитка*.

winner [ˈwɪnə^r] *n* победи́тель(ница) *m(f)*.

winning [ˈwɪnɪŋ] *adj* (*team, competitor*) победи́вший, вы́игравший; (*shot, goal*) реша́ющий; (*smile*) обая́тельный* (обая́телен), покоря́ющий; *see also* **winnings**.

winning post *n* фи́нишный столб*.

winnings [ˈwɪnɪŋz] *npl* вы́игрыш *msg*.

winsome [ˈwɪnsəm] *adj* привлека́тельный* (привлека́телен).

winter [ˈwɪntə^r] *n* (*season*) зима́* ♦ *vi* (*birds*) зимова́ть (перезимова́ть *perf*); **in** ~ зимо́й.

winter sports *npl* зи́мние ви́ды *mpl* спо́рта.

wintry [ˈwɪntrɪ] *adj* зи́мний*.

wipe [waɪp] *n*: **to give sth a** ~ протира́ть (протере́ть* *perf*) что-н ♦ *vt* (*rub*) вытира́ть (вы́тереть* *perf*); (*erase*) стира́ть (стере́ть* *perf*); **to** ~ **one's nose** вытира́ть (вы́тереть* *perf*) нос

► **wipe off** *vt* стира́ть (стере́ть* *perf*)

► **wipe out** *vt* (*debt*) ликвиди́ровать (*impf/perf*); (*memory*) стира́ть (стере́ть* *perf*); (*city, population*) стира́ть (стере́ть* *perf*) с лица́ земли́

► **wipe up** *vt* (*mess*) подтира́ть (подтере́ть* *perf*).

wire [waɪə^r] *n* про́волока; (*ELEC*) про́вод*; (*telegram*) телегра́мма ♦ *vt* (*fence*) скрепля́ть (скрепи́ть* *perf*) про́волокой; (*ELEC: also:* ~ **up**) подключа́ть (подключи́ть* *perf*); **to** ~ **a house** де́лать (сде́лать *perf*) прово́дку в до́ме; **to** ~ **sb** телеграфи́ровать (*impf/perf*) кому́-н.

wire brush *n* про́волочная щётка*.

wire cutters *npl* куса́чки* *pl*.

wireless [ˈwaɪəlɪs] *n* (*BRIT*) ра́дио *nt ind*.

wire netting *n* про́волочная сеть *f*.

wire service *n* (*US*) аге́нтство новосте́й.

wire-tapping [ˈwaɪəˈtæpɪŋ] *n* подслу́шивание телефо́нных разгово́ров.

wiring [ˈwaɪərɪŋ] *n* (*ELEC*) электропрово́дка.

wiry [ˈwaɪərɪ] *adj* (*person*) жи́листый (жи́лист); (*hair*) жёсткий* (жёсток).

wisdom [ˈwɪzdəm] *n* му́дрость *f*.

wisdom tooth *n* зуб* му́дрости.

wise [waɪz] *adj* му́дрый* (мудр); **I'm none the** ~**r** я всё равно́ ничего́ не понима́ю

► **wise up** *vi* (*inf*): **to** ~ **up to sth** осознава́ть* (осозна́ть* *perf*) что-н.

...wise [waɪz] *suffix*: **timewise** *etc* в отноше́нии вре́мени *etc*.

wisecrack [ˈwaɪzkræk] *n* шпи́лька*.

wisely [ˈwaɪzlɪ] *adv* му́дро.

wish [wɪʃ] *n* жела́ние ♦ *vt* жела́ть (пожела́ть *perf*); **best** ~**es** (*for birthday etc*) всего́ наилу́чшего; **with best** ~**es** (*in letter*) с наилу́чшими пожела́ниями; **give her my best** ~**es** переда́йте ей мои́ наилу́чшие пожела́ния; **to** ~ **sb goodbye** проща́ться (попроща́ться *perf*) с кем-н; **he** ~**ed me well** он пожела́л мне всего́ хоро́шего; **to** ~ **to do**

хоте́ть* (*impf*) +*infin*; **I ~ him to come** я хочу́, чтобы он пришёл; **to ~ for** жела́ть (пожела́ть *perf*) +*acc or* +*gen*; **to ~ sth on sb** навя́зывать (навяза́ть* *perf*) что-н кому́-н.

wishbone ['wıʃbəun] *n* счастли́вая ду́жка (*грудна́я кость пти́цы, разла́мывая кото́рую, зага́дывают жела́ние*).

wishful ['wıʃful] *adj*: **it's ~ thinking** э́то – приня́тие жела́емого за действи́тельное.

wishy-washy ['wıʃı'wɔʃı] *adj* (*inf: colour*) му́тный; (*ideas, person*) вя́лый (вял).

wisp [wısp] *n* (*of grass, hair*) клочо́к*; (*of smoke*) стру́йка*.

wistful ['wıstful] *adj* тоскли́вый (тоскли́в).

wit [wıt] *n* (*wittiness*) остроу́мие; (*intelligence: also*: ~s) ум*, ра́зум; (*person*) остря́к* (-ячка*); (*presence of mind*) сообрази́тельность *f*; **to be at one's ~s' end** (*fig*) быть* (*impf*) в отча́янии; **to have one's ~s about one** не теря́ться (растеря́ться *perf*); **to ~ a** и́менно.

witch [wıtʃ] *n* ве́дьма.

witchcraft ['wıtʃkra:ft] *n* колдовство́.

witch doctor *n* зна́харь(-рка*) *m(f)*.

witch-hunt ['wıtʃhʌnt] *n* (*fig*) охо́та за ве́дьмами.

KEYWORD

---

with [wıð] *prep* **1** (*accompanying, in the company of*) с +*instr*; **I spent the day with him** я провела́ с ним день; **we stayed with friends** мы остана́вливались у друзе́й; **I'll be with you in a minute** я освобожу́сь че́рез мину́ту; **would you like chips with your steak?** Вы хоти́те жа́реную карто́шку к бифште́ксу?; **I'm with you** (*I understand*) я Вас понима́ю; **she is really with it** (*inf: fashionable*) она́ о́чень совреме́нная деви́ца; (: *aware*) она́ всё сообража́ет

2 (*descriptive*) с +*instr*; **a girl with blue eyes** де́вушка с голубы́ми глаза́ми; **a skirt with a silk lining** ю́бка на шёлковой подкла́дке

3 (*indicating manner*) с +*instr*; (*indicating cause*) от +*gen*; (*indicating means*): **to write with a pencil** писа́ть* (*impf*) карандашо́м; **with tears in her eyes** со слеза́ми на глаза́х; **red with anger** кра́сный от гне́ва; **you can open the door with this key** Вы мо́жете откры́ть дверь э́тим ключо́м; **to fill sth with water** наполня́ть (наполни́ть *perf*) что-н водо́й.

---

withdraw [wıð'drɔ:] (*irreg: like draw*) *vt* (*object*) извлека́ть (извле́чь* *perf*); (*offer, remark*) брать* (взять* *perf*) наза́д ♦ *vi* (*troops, person*) уходи́ть* (уйти́* *perf*); **to ~ into o.s.** уходи́ть* (уйти́* *perf*) в себя́; **to ~ money from an account** снима́ть (снять* *perf*) де́ньги со счёта.

withdrawal [wıð'drɔ:əl] *n* (*of offer, remark,*

participation) отка́з; (*of troops*) вы́вод; (*of services*) отме́на; (*of money*) сня́тие.

withdrawal symptoms *npl* (*MED*) синдро́м *msg* отме́ны *or* абстине́нтный синдро́м *msg* (*при отвыка́нии от лека́рств, нарко́тиков umn*).

withdrawn [wıð'drɔ:n] *pp of* **withdraw** ♦ *adj* за́мкнутый (за́мкнут).

wither ['wıðə'] *vi* (*plant*) вя́нуть (завя́нуть *perf*), со́хнуть (засо́хнуть *perf*).

withered ['wıðəd] *adj* (*plant*) увя́дший*, засо́хший; (*limb*) вы́сохший*.

withhold [wıð'həuld] (*irreg: like hold*) *vt* (*money*) уде́рживать (удержа́ть* *perf*); (*permission*) не дава́ть* (дать* *perf*); (*information*) ута́ивать (утаи́ть *perf*).

within [wıð'ın] *prep* (*inside: of place, time, distance*) внутри́ +*gen*, в преде́лах +*gen* ♦ *adv* внутри́; **~ reach** в преде́лах досяга́емости; **~ sight (of)** в по́ле зре́ния (+*gen*); **the finish is ~ sight** коне́ц не за гора́ми; **~ the week** в преде́лах неде́ли; **~ a mile of** в преде́лах ми́ли от +*gen*; **~ an hour of** че́рез час по́сле +*gen*; **~ the law** в ра́мках зако́на.

without [wıð'aut] *prep* без +*gen*; **~ a coat** без пальто́; **~ saying a word** не говоря́ ни сло́ва; **~ looking** не гля́дя; **to go ~ sth** обходи́ться* (обойти́сь* *perf*) без чего́-н.

withstand [wıð'stænd] (*irreg: like stand*) *vt* выде́рживать (вы́держать* *perf*).

witness ['wıtnıs] *n* (*person, also LAW*) свиде́тель(ница) *m(f)* ♦ *vt* (*event*) быть* (*impf*) свиде́телем(-льницей) +*gen*; (*document*) заверя́ть (заве́рить *perf*); **to bear ~ to** (*fig*) свиде́тельствовать (*impf*) о +*prp*; **~ for the prosecution/defence** свиде́тель обвине́ния/защи́ты; **to ~ to sth** засвиде́тельствовать (*perf*) факт чего́-н; **I can ~ to having seen ...** я могу́ засвиде́тельствовать, что я ви́дел ....

witness box *n* свиде́тельское ме́сто*.

witness stand (*US*) = **witness box**.

witticism ['wıtısızəm] *n* остро́та.

witty ['wıtı] *adj* остроу́мный* (остроу́мен).

wives [waıvz] *npl of* **wife**.

wizard ['wızəd] *n* волше́бник.

wizened ['wıznd] *adj* (*person*) морщи́нистый (морщи́нист); (*fruit, vegetable*) смо́рщен-ный* (смо́рщен).

wk *abbr* = **week**.

Wm. *abbr* = **William**.

WO *n abbr* (*MIL*: = *warrant officer*) ≈ пра́порщик.

wobble ['wɔbl] *vi* (*legs*) трясти́сь* (*impf*); (*jelly*) колыха́ться* (*impf*); (*chair*) шата́ться (*impf*).

wobbly ['wɔblı] *adj* (*hand, voice*) дрожа́щий; (*table, chair*) ша́ткий* (ша́ток).

woe [wəu] *n* го́ре.

woeful ['wəuful] *adj* (*sad*) печа́льный* (печа́лен); (*awful*) вопию́щий.

---

* marks translations which have irregular inflections. The Russian-English side of the dictionary gives inflectional information.

wok [wɔk] *n* глубо́кая сковорода́ (*в китайской кухне*).

woke [wəuk] *pt of* **wake**.

woken ['wəukn] *pp of* **wake**.

wolf [wulf] (*pl* **wolves**) *n* волк.

wolves [wulvz] *npl of* **wolf**.

woman ['wumən] (*pl* **women**) *n* же́нщина; ~ **friend** подру́га; ~ **teacher** учи́тельница; **young** ~ молода́я же́нщина; **women's page** (*PRESS*) страни́ца для же́нщин.

woman doctor *n* же́нщина-врач.

womanize ['wumənaɪz] *vi* (*pej*) вести́* (*impf*) распу́тну жизнь.

womanizer ['wumənaɪzə'] *n* женолю́б, ба́бник (*разг*).

womanly ['wumənlɪ] *adj* (*virtues etc*) же́нский*; (*figure*) же́нственный.

womb [wu:m] *n* ма́тка*.

women ['wɪmɪn] *npl of* **woman**.

women's lib ['wɪmɪnz-] *n* (*inf*) эмансипа́ция же́нщин.

Women's (Liberation) Movement *n* движе́ние за эмансипа́цию же́нщин.

won [wʌn] *pt, pp of* **win**.

wonder ['wʌndə'] *n* (*miracle*) чу́до; (*feeling*) изумле́ние ♦ *vi*: **I ~ whether you could tell me** ... не мо́жете ли Вы сказа́ть мне ...; **I ~ why he is late** интере́сно, почему́ он опозда́л; **to ~ at** (*marvel at*) удивля́ться (*impf*) +*dat*; **to ~ about** разду́мывать* (*impf*) о +*prp*; **it's no ~ (that)** не удиви́тельно(, что).

wonderful ['wʌndəful] *adj* (*excellent*) замеча́тельный* (замеча́телен); (*astonishing*) удиви́тельный (удиви́телен).

wonderfully ['wʌndəfəlɪ] *adv* (*see adj*) замеча́тельно; удиви́тельно.

wonky ['wɔŋkɪ] *adj* (*BRIT: inf*) ша́ткий* (ша́ток).

wont [wəunt] *adj*: **he is ~ to** ... он име́ет обыкнове́ние +*infin* ...; **as is my ~** по обыкнове́нию.

won't [wəunt] = **will not**.

woo [wu:] *vt* (*woman*) добива́ться (доби́ться *perf*) расположе́ния +*gen*; (*audience etc*) зайгрывать* (*impf*) с +*instr*.

wood [wud] *n* (*timber*) де́рево; (*forest*) лес ♦ *cpd* (*house*) деревя́нный; (*shed*) дровяно́й; ~**pile** шта́бель *m* дров.

wood carving *n* (*act*) резьба́ по де́реву; (*object*) резьба́ (по де́реву).

wooded ['wudɪd] *adj* (*slopes, area*) леси́стый.

wooden ['wudn] *adj* (*object*) деревя́нный; (*fig: performance, actor*) дубо́вый.

woodland ['wudlənd] *n* леси́стая ме́стность *f*.

woodpecker ['wudpɛkə'] *n* дя́тел*.

wood pigeon *n* лесно́й го́лубь *m*.

woodwind ['wudwɪnd] *n* деревя́нный духово́й инструме́нт; **the ~** деревя́нные духовы́е *pl adj* инструме́нты.

woodwork ['wudwə:k] *n* (*skill*) столя́рное де́ло.

woodworm ['wudwə:m] *n* (*larvae*) личи́нка

древото́чца.

woof [wuf] *n* лай ♦ *vi* ла́ять (*impf*); ~, ~! гав, гав!

wool [wul] *n* (*material, yarn*) шерсть *f*; **to pull the ~ over sb's eyes** (*fig*) ве́шать (*impf*) лапшу́ на́ уши.

woollen ['wulən] (*US* **woolen**) *adj* шерстяно́й.

woollens ['wulənz] *npl* шерстяны́е ве́щи *fpl*.

woolly ['wulɪ] (*US* **wooly**) *adj* шерстяно́й; (*fig: ideas*) расплы́вчатый (расплы́вчат); (: *person*) вя́лый (вял) ♦ *n* шерстяно́й сви́тер* *m*.

woozy ['wu:zɪ] *adj* (*inf*) окосе́вший.

Worcs *abbr* (*BRIT: POST*) = **Worcestershire**.

word [wə:d] *n* сло́во; (*news*) слух ♦ *vt* (*letter, message*) формули́ровать* (сформули́ровать* *perf*); ~ **for** ~ (*repeat*) сло́во в сло́во; (*translate*) досло́вно; **what's the ~ for "pen" in French?** как (бу́дет) по-францу́зски (сло́во) "ру́чка"?; **to put sth into ~s** выража́ть (вы́разить* *perf*) что-н слова́ми; **in other ~s** други́ми слова́ми; **to break/keep one's ~** наруша́ть (нару́шить *perf*)/держа́ть (сдержа́ть* *perf*) своё сло́во; **to have ~s with sb** име́ть (*impf*) кру́пный разгово́р с кем-н; **to have a ~ with sb** поговори́ть (*perf*) с кем-н; **I'll take your ~ for it** я пове́рю Вам на́ слово; **to send ~ of** извеща́ть (извести́ть* *perf*) о +*prp*; **to leave ~ (with sb/for sb) that** ... передава́ть (переда́ть* *perf*) (че́рез кого́-н/кому́-н), что ....

wording ['wə:dɪŋ] *n* формулиро́вка*; (*in card*) поздрави́тельный текст.

word of mouth *n*: **by** *or* **through** ~ ~ ~ из уст в уста́; **I found out about it by** ~ ~ ~ я об э́том услы́шал от кого́-то.

word-perfect ['wə:d'pə:fɪkt] *adj*: **to be** ~ (*person*) знать (*impf*) ка́ждое сло́во; **the speech was** ~ речь была́ прекра́сно подгото́влена.

word processing *n* обрабо́тка *or* подгото́вка те́кстов.

word processor [-prəusɛsə'] *n* те́кстовый проце́ссор.

wordwrap ['wə:dræp] *n* (автомати́ческий*) перехо́д (*на но́вую строку́*).

wordy ['wə:dɪ] *adj* многосло́вный* (многосло́вен).

wore [wɔ:'] *pt of* **wear**.

work [wə:k] *n* рабо́та; (*ART, LITERATURE*) произведе́ние ♦ *vi* рабо́тать (*impf*); (*medicine etc*) де́йствовать (поде́йствовать *perf*) ♦ *vt* (*clay*) рабо́тать (*impf*) с +*instr*; (*wood, metal, land*) обраба́тывать (обрабо́тать *perf*); (*mine*) разраба́тывать (разрабо́тать *perf*); (*machine*) управля́ть (*impf*) +*instr*; (*effect, miracle*) производи́ть* (произвести́* *perf*); **to go to** ~ ходи́ть*/идти́* (*impf*) на рабо́ту; **to start** *or* **set to** ~ принима́ться (приня́ться* *perf*) за рабо́ту; **to be at** ~ **(on sth)** рабо́тать

(impf) (над чем-н); **he has been out of** ~ **for three months** у него́ уже́ три ме́сяца нет рабо́ты; **to** ~ **hard** мно́го рабо́тать *(impf)*; **to** ~ **loose** *(part)* расша́тываться (расшата́ться *perf)*; *(knot)* сла́бнуть (осла́бнуть *perf)*
► **work on** *vt fus (task)* рабо́тать *(impf)* над +*instr*; *(person)* рабо́тать *(impf)* с +*instr*; *(principle)* опира́ться *(impf)* на +*acc*; **he's** ~**ing on his car** *(repairing)* он чи́нит маши́ну; *(doing up)* он рабо́тает над свое́й маши́ной
► **work out** *vi (plans etc)* удава́ться* (уда́ться* *perf)*; *(SPORT)* занима́ться *(impf)* физи́ческими упражне́ниями ♦ *vt (problem)* реша́ть (реши́ть *perf)*; *(plan)* разраба́тывать (разрабо́тать *perf)*; **it** ~**s out at £100** *(cost)* получа́ется £100
► **work up** *vt:* **to get** ~**ed up (about sth)** разне́рвничаться *(perf)* (из-за чего́-н).
workable ['wəːkəbl] *adj (solution)* осуществи́мый (осуществи́м), выполни́мый (выполни́м).
workaholic [wəːkə'hɒlɪk] *n:* **he is a** ~ он не мо́жет жить без рабо́ты.
workbench ['wəːkbɛntʃ] *n* верста́к*.
worker ['wəːkə] *n (in factory)* рабо́чий*(-ая) *m(f) adj*; *(in community etc)* рабо́тник(-ница); **office** ~ конто́рский* слу́жащий*(-ая) *m(f) adj*.
workforce ['wəːkfɔːs] *n* рабо́чая си́ла.
work-in ['wəːkɪn] *n (BRIT)* "уо́рк-ин" *(вид забасто́вки)*.
working ['wəːkɪŋ] *adj (day, tools etc)* рабо́чий*; ~ **conditions** усло́вия *ntpl* рабо́ты; ~ **partner** делово́й партнёр; ~ **population** за́нятая часть населе́ния; **a** ~ **knowledge of English** практи́ческое зна́ние англи́йского языка́.
working capital *n* оборо́тный капита́л.
working class *n* рабо́чий* класс.
working-class ['wəːkɪŋ'klɑːs] *adj* рабо́чий*.
working man *n* рабо́тающий мужчи́на.
working order *n:* **in** ~~ в рабо́чем состоя́нии.
working party *n (BRIT)* рабо́чая гру́ппа.
working relationship *n* делов́ые отноше́ния *ntpl*.
working week *n* рабо́чая неде́ля.
work-in-progress ['wəːkɪn'prəugrɛs] *n (COMM: products)* объём проду́кции, вы́пущенной к настоя́щему моме́нту; *(: value)* сто́имость проду́кции, вы́пущенной к настоя́щему моме́нту.
workload ['wəːkləud] *n* нагру́зка*.
workman ['wəːkmən] *irreg n* (квалифиц- и́рованный) рабо́чий* *m adj*.
workmanship ['wəːkmənʃɪp] *n (skill)* мастерство́; *(quality)* ка́чество рабо́ты; **good/poor** ~ то́нкая/гру́бая рабо́та.
workmate ['wəːkmeɪt] *n* това́рищ по рабо́те.
workout ['wəːkaut] *n* разми́нка.

work permit *n* разреше́ние на рабо́ту.
works [wəːks] *n (BRIT: factory)* заво́д, фа́брика ♦ *npl (of clock, machine)* механи́зм *msg*.
worksheet ['wəːkʃiːt] *n* рабо́чая ка́рта.
workshop ['wəːkʃɔp] *n (at home, in factory)* мастерска́я *f adj*, цех; *(practical session)* семина́р, практи́ческие заня́тия *ntpl*; *(THEAT, MUS)* сту́дия.
work station *n* часть большо́го о́фиса, отделённая для рабо́ты одного́ слу́жащего; *(COMPUT)* рабо́чая ста́нция.
work study *n* ≈ нау́чная организа́ция труда́.
worktop ['wəːktɔp] *n* рабо́чая пове́рхность *f*.
work-to-rule ['wəːktə'ruːl] *n (BRIT)* "рабо́та по пра́вилам" *(вид забасто́вочной борьбы́)*.
world [wəːld] *n* мир ♦ *cpd (tour)* кругосве́тный; *(war, record)* мирово́й; ~ **champion** мирово́й чемпио́н, чемпио́н ми́ра; ~ **power** мирова́я держа́ва; **all over the** ~ во всём ми́ре; **to think the** ~ **of sb** быть* о́чень высо́кого мне́ния о ком-н; **what in the** ~ **are you doing?** ты сообража́ешь, что ты де́лаешь?; **to do sb a** ~ **of good** приноси́ть* (принести́* *perf)* кому́-н огро́мную по́льзу; **W~ War One/Two** пе́рвая/втора́я мирова́я война́; **out of this** ~ неземно́й.
World Cup *n:* **the** ~~ *(FOOTBALL)* Ку́бок *or* чемпиона́т ми́ра.
world-famous [wəːld'feɪməs] *adj* всеми́рно изве́стный* (изве́стен).
worldly ['wəːldlɪ] *adj (not spiritual)* земно́й; *(knowledgeable)* искушённый.
world music *n* му́зыка наро́дов ми́ра.
World Series *n:* **the** ~~ *(US: BASEBALL)* ку́бковые соревнова́ния *or*.
worldwide ['wəːld'waɪd] *adj* всеми́рный ♦ *adv* повсеме́стно.
worm [wəːm] *n (ZOOL)* червь *m*
► **worm out** *vt:* **to** ~ **sth out of sb** вытя́гивать (вы́тянуть *perf)* что-н из кого́-н.
worn [wəːn] *pp of* **wear** ♦ *adj (carpet)* потёртый (потёрт); *(shoe)* поно́шенный* (поно́шен).
worn-out ['wəːnaut] *adj (object)* изно́шенный* (изно́шен); *(teddy)* потрёпанный* (потрё пан); *(person)* измо́танный (измо́тан).
worried ['wʌrɪd] *adj* обеспоко́енный (обеспоко́ен), встрево́женный (встрево́жен); **she is** ~ **about it** она́ обеспоко́ена э́тим.
worrier ['wʌrɪə] *n* челове́к, му́чимый сомне́ниями, опасе́ниями; **she is a natural** ~ она́ всегда́ чем-то обеспоко́ена.
worrisome ['wʌrɪsəm] *adj* вызыва́ющий беспоко́йство, трево́жный.
worry ['wʌrɪ] *n (anxiety)* беспоко́йство, волне́ние ♦ *vi (person)* беспоко́иться *(impf)*, волнова́ться *(impf)* ♦ *vt (person)* беспоко́ить *(impf)*, волнова́ть (взволнова́ть *perf)*; **to** ~

about *or* **over sth/sb** беспоко́иться *(impf)* за
что-н/кого́-н.
worrying ['wʌrɪŋ] *adj* трево́жный*
(трево́жен).
worse [wɜ:s] *adj* ху́дший* ♦ *adv* ху́же ♦ *n*
ху́дшее *nt adj*; **to get ~** ухудша́ться
(уху́дшиться *perf*); **a change for the ~**
ухудше́ние; **he is none the ~ for it** ему́ не
ста́ло от э́того ху́же; **so much the ~ for you!**
тем ху́же для Вас!
worsen ['wɜ:sn] *vt* ухудша́ть (уху́дшить *perf*) ♦
vi ухудша́ться (уху́дшиться *perf*).
worse off *adj (financially)* бедне́е; *(fig)*: **you'll be**
~~ this way Вам так бу́дет ху́же; **he is now**
~~ than before его́ положе́ние тепе́рь ху́же,
чем ра́ньше.
worship ['wɜ:ʃɪp] *n* поклоне́ние, преклоне́ние
♦ *vt* поклоня́ться *(impf)* +*dat*, преклоня́ться
(impf) пе́ред +*instr*; **Your W~** *(BRIT: to mayor,*
judge) Ва́ша ми́лость.
worshipper ['wɜ:ʃɪpə'] *n (REL)* моля́щийся
(-аяся) *m(f) adj*, прихожа́нин*(-нка); *(fig)*
покло́нник(-ница).
worst [wɜ:st] *adj* наиху́дший* ♦ *adv* ху́же всего́
♦ *n* наиху́дшее *nt adj*; **at ~** в ху́дшем слу́чае; **if**
the ~ comes to the ~ на худо́й коне́ц, в
са́мом ху́дшем слу́чае.
worst-case scenario ['wɜ:stkeɪs-] *n* ху́дший*
вариа́нт.
worsted ['wustɪd] *n*: **(wool) ~** гребенна́я
шерсть *f*.
worth [wɜ:θ] *n (value)* сто́имость *f* ♦ *adj*: **to be**
~ сто́ить *(impf)*; **how much is it ~?** ско́лько
э́то сто́ит?; **50 pence ~ of apples** я́блок на 50
пе́нсов; **an hour's ~ of work** рабо́та на час;
it's ~ э́то сто́ит стоя́т.
worthless ['wɜ:θlɪs] *adj* никчёмный* (никчё
мен).
worthwhile ['wɜ:θ'waɪl] *adj* сто́ящий*; **a ~**
book сто́ящая кни́га.
worthy [wɜ:ðɪ] *adj* досто́йный; **~ of**
досто́йный* (досто́ин) +*gen*.

KEYWORD

would [wud] *aux vb* **1** *(conditional tense)*: **I**
would tell you if I could я бы сказа́л Вам, е́сли
бы мог; **if you asked him he would do it** е́сли
Вы его́ попро́сите, (то) он э́то сде́лает; **if**
you had asked him he would have done it е́сли
бы Вы попроси́ли его́, (то) он бы э́то
сде́лал
2 *(in offers, invitations, requests)*: **would you**
like a biscuit? не хоти́те (ли) пече́нья?; **would**
you ask him to come in? пригласи́те его́
войти́?; **would you open the window please?**
откро́йте, пожа́луйста, окно́
3 *(in indirect speech)*: **I said I would do it** я
сказа́л, что сде́лаю э́то; **he asked me if I**
would stay with him он попроси́л меня́
оста́ться с ним; **he asked me if I would resit**
the exam if I failed он спроси́л меня́, бу́ду ли
я пересдава́ть экза́мен, е́сли я провалю́сь

4 *(emphatic)*: **it WOULD have to snow today!**
и́менно сего́дня до́лжен был пойти́ снег!;
you WOULD say that, wouldn't you! Вы,
коне́чно, э́то ска́жете!
5 *(insistence)*: **she wouldn't behave** она́ ника́к
не хоте́ла хорошо́ себя́ вести́
6 *(conjecture)*: **it would have been midnight**
должно́ быть, была́ по́лночь; **it would seem**
so должно́ быть, так; **it would seem that ...**
похо́же, что ...
7 *(indicating habit)*: **he would always come**
here on Mondays он всегда́ приходи́л сюда́
по понеде́льникам; **he would spend every day**
on the beach он проводи́л ка́ждый день на
пля́же.

would-be ['wudbi:] *adj (pej)*: **~ writer** челове́к*,
вообража́ющий себя́ писа́телем.
wouldn't ['wudnt] = **would not**.
wound[1] [waund] *pt, pp of* **wind**[2].
wound[2] [wu:nd] *n* ра́на ♦ *vt* ра́нить *(impf/perf)*;
~ed in the leg ра́неный в но́гу.
wove [wəuv] *pt of* **weave**.
woven ['wəuvn] *pp of* **weave**.
WP *n abbr* = **word processing, word processor** ♦
abbr (BRIT: inf: = **weather permitting**) е́сли
позво́лит пого́да.
WPC *(BRIT) n abbr* = **woman police constable**.
wpm *abbr* = **words per minute**.
WRAC *n abbr (BRIT)* = **Women's Royal Army**
Corps.
WRAF *n abbr (BRIT)* = **Women's Royal Air Force**.
wrangle ['ræŋgl] *n* препира́ние ♦ *vi*: **to ~ with**
sb over sth препира́ться *(impf)* с кем-н по
по́воду чего́-н.
wrap [ræp] *n (shawl)* широ́кий* шарф; *(cape)*
наки́дка* ♦ *vt (also: ~ up)* завора́чивать
(заверну́ть *perf*); *(wind)*: **to ~ sth round sth**
(tape etc) обора́чивать (оберну́ть *perf*) что-н
вокру́г чего́-н; **to keep sth under ~s** *(fig)*
скрыва́ть *(impf)* что-н.
wrapper ['ræpə'] *n (on chocolate)* обёртка;
(BRIT: of book) обло́жка*.
wrapping paper ['ræpɪŋ-] *n* обёрточная
бума́га.
wrath [rɔθ] *n* гнев.
wreak [ri:k] *vt*: **to ~ havoc (on)** наноси́ть*
(нанести́* *perf*) уще́рб (+*dat*); **to ~ vengeance**
or **revenge on sb** отомсти́ть* *(perf)* кому́-н.
wreath [ri:θ] *n (pl* **~s**) *n (at funeral)* вено́к*.
wreck [rɛk] *n (vehicle)* ава́рия; *(ship)*
круше́ние; *(sea disaster)* кораблекруше́ние;
(pej: person) разва́лина ♦ *vt (car etc)*
разбива́ть (разби́ть* *perf*); *(stereo)* лома́ть
(слома́ть* *perf*); *(fig: weekend, relationship)*
по́ртить* (испо́ртить* *perf*); *(: life, health)*
губи́ть* (погуби́ть* *perf*).
wreckage ['rɛkɪdʒ] *n* обло́мки *pl*; *(of building)*
разва́лины *fpl*.
wrecker ['rɛkə'] *n (US: breakdown van)*
авари́йная маши́на.

Wren [rɛn] n (BRIT: MIL) же́нщина, слу́жащая в
  вое́нно-морско́м фло́те.
wren [rɛn] n крапи́вник.
wrench [rɛntʃ] n (TECH) га́ечный ключ*; (tug)
  рыво́к*; (fig) щемя́щая тоска́ ◆ vt (twist)
  вывёртывать (вы́вернуть perf); to ~ sth from
  sb вырыва́ть (вы́рвать perf) что-н у кого́-н.
wrest [rɛst] vt: to ~ sth from sb вырыва́ть
  (вы́рвать perf) что-н у кого́-н.
wrestle ['rɛsl] vi: to ~ (with sb) боро́ться* (impf)
  (с кем-н); to ~ with a problem му́читься (impf)
  над пробле́мой.
wrestler ['rɛslə'] n боре́ц*.
wrestling ['rɛslɪŋ] n борьба́; (also: all-in ~)
  кетч (вид борьбы́).
wrestling match n соревнова́ния ntpl по
  борьбе́.
wretch [rɛtʃ] n негодя́й; little ~! него́дник!
wretched ['rɛtʃɪd] adj несча́стный*
  (несча́стен).
wriggle ['rɪgl] vi (also: ~ about: person, snake
  etc) извива́ться (impf) ◆ n выгиба́ние.
wring [rɪŋ] (pt,pp wrung) vt (wet clothes)
  выжима́ть (вы́жать* perf); (hands) лома́ть
  (impf); (bird's neck) свора́чивать (сверну́ть
  perf); (fig): to ~ sth out of sb выжима́ть
  (вы́жать* perf) что-н из кого́-н.
wringer ['rɪŋə'] n пресс для отжима́ния белья́.
wringing ['rɪŋɪŋ] adj (also: ~ wet): he is ~ (wet)
  с него́ течёт (вода́).
wrinkle ['rɪŋkl] n (on skin) морщи́на; (on paper
  etc) скла́дка* ◆ vt (nose, forehead etc)
  мо́рщить (смо́рщить perf) ◆ vi (skin etc)
  мо́рщиться (смо́рщиться perf); (paint)
  покрыва́ться (покры́ться* perf) тре́щинами.
wrinkled ['rɪŋkld] adj (fabric, paper) мя́тый;
  (surface) смо́рщенный* (смо́рщен); (skin)
  морщи́нистый (морщи́нист).
wrinkly ['rɪŋklɪ] adj = wrinkled.
wrist [rɪst] n (ANAT) запя́стье.
wristband ['rɪstbænd] n (BRIT: of shirt)
  манже́та; (of watch: leather) ремешо́к*;
  (: metal) брасле́т.
wristwatch ['rɪstwɔtʃ] n нару́чные часы́ pl.
writ [rɪt] n (LAW) о́рдер; to issue a ~ against sb
  выдава́ть (вы́дать* perf) о́рдер на чей-н
  аре́ст; to serve a ~ on sb посыла́ть (посла́ть*
  perf) кому́-н пове́стку в суд.
write [raɪt] (pt wrote, pp written) vt (letter, novel
  etc) писа́ть (написа́ть* perf); (cheque, receipt,
  prescription) выпи́сывать (вы́писать* perf) ◆
  vi писа́ть* (impf); to ~ to sb писа́ть*
  (написа́ть* perf) кому́-н
▶ **write away** vi: to ~ away for (information)
  запра́шивать (запроси́ть* perf) о(б) +prp;
  (goods) посыла́ть (посла́ть* perf)
  пи́сьменный зака́з на +acc
▶ **write down** vt (note) писа́ть* (написа́ть*

perf); (put in writing) запи́сывать (записа́ть*
  perf)
▶ **write off** vt (debt) спи́сывать (списа́ть* perf);
  (plan, project) аннули́ровать (impf/perf); (car
  etc) спи́сывать (списа́ть* perf) ◆ vi = write
  away
▶ **write out** vt (put in writing) излага́ть
  (изложи́ть perf) пи́сьменно; (cheque, receipt
  etc) выпи́сывать (вы́писать* perf); (copy:
  address etc) спи́сывать (списа́ть* perf)
▶ **write up** vt приводи́ть* (привести́* perf) в
  поря́док.
write-off ['raɪtɔf] n (inf): the car is a ~ маши́не
  коне́ц.
write-protect ['raɪtprə'tɛkt] vt (COMPUT)
  защища́ть (защити́ть* perf) от за́писи.
writer ['raɪtə'] n писа́тель m.
write-up ['raɪtʌp] n (review) реце́нзия.
writhe [raɪð] vi извива́ться (impf).
writing ['raɪtɪŋ] n (words written) на́дпись f;
  (also: handwriting) по́черк; (of author)
  рабо́та, произведе́ние; ~ is his favourite
  occupation бо́льше всего́ он лю́бит писа́ть;
  in ~ в пи́сьменном ви́де; in my own ~
  напи́санный мое́й руко́й.
writing case n пена́л.
writing desk n пи́сьменный стол*.
writing paper n пи́счая бума́га.
written ['rɪtn] pp of write.
WRNS n abbr (BRIT) = Women's Royal Naval
  Service.
wrong [rɔŋ] adj непра́вильный* (непра́вилен);
  (information) неве́рный; (immoral) дурно́й ◆
  adv непра́вильно; (informed) неве́рно ◆ n
  (injustice) несправедли́вость f; (evil) зло ◆ vt
  (treat unfairly) нехорошо́ поступа́ть
  (поступи́ть* perf) с +instr; the answer was ~
  отве́т был непра́вильный or оши́бочный; he
  is ~ in saying that ... он непра́в, когда́ он
  говори́т, что ...; you are ~ to do it э́то
  нехорошо́ с Ва́шей стороны́; it's ~ to steal,
  stealing is ~ ворова́ть – нехорошо́; you are ~
  about it, you've got it ~ Вы непра́вы; who
  is in the ~? чья э́то вина́?; what's ~? в чём
  де́ло?; there's nothing ~ всё в поря́дке; to go
  ~ (plan) не удава́ться* (уда́ться* perf);
  (machine) лома́ться (слома́ться perf); right
  and ~ хоро́шее и дурно́е.
wrong-doer ['rɔŋduːə'] n правонаруши́тель m.
wrong-foot ['rɔŋ'fuːt] vt (SPORT) застига́ть
  (засти́гнуть perf) враспло́х; (fight) лови́ть*
  (пойма́ть* perf) кого́-н на́ слове.
wrongful ['rɔŋful] adj (imprisonment,
  dismissal) несправедли́вый (несправедли́в).
wrongly ['rɔŋlɪ] adv непра́вильно; (unjustly)
  несправедли́во.
wrong number n: you have a ~ ~ (TEL) Вы не
  туда́ попа́ли.

---

wrong side *n*: the ~~ (*of material*) изна́нка*.
wrote [rəut] *pt of* **write**.
wrought [rɔːt] *adj*: ~ **iron** сва́рочная *or* ко́вкая сталь *f*.
wrung [rʌŋ] *pt, pp of* **wring**.
WRVS *n abbr* (*BRIT*) = *Women's Royal Voluntary Service*.
wry [raɪ] *adj* (*humour, expression*) лука́вый (лука́в); (*smile*) криво́й* (крив).
wt. *abbr* = **weight**.
WV *abbr* (*US: POST*) = *West Virginia*.
WY *abbr* (*US: POST*) = *Wyoming*.
WYSIWYG ['wɪzɪwɪg] *abbr* (*COMPUT*: = *what you see is what you get*) режи́м по́лного соотве́тствия (*в те́кстовых проце́ссорах и изда́тельских систе́мах*).

~ X, x ~

X, x [ɛks] *n* (*letter*) 24-ая буква английского алфавита; (*BRIT: CINEMA: formerly*) свидетельство " X", которое разрешает показ кинофильма с элементами эротики или картинами насилия.

Xerox® ['zɪərɔks] *n* (*also:* ~ **machine**) ксерокс; (*photocopy*) ксерокопия ◆ *vt* делать (сделать *perf*) копию +*gen*, ксерокопировать (отксерокопировать *perf*).

XL *abbr* = *extra large*.

Xmas ['ɛksməs] *n abbr* = **Christmas**.

X-rated ['ɛks'reɪtɪd] *adj* (*US: film*) для взрослых.

X-ray [ɛks'reɪ] *n* (*ray*) рентгеновские лучи *mpl*; (*photo*) рентгеновский снимок* ◆ *vt* просвечивать (просветить* *perf*) (рентгеновскими лучами); **to have an** ~ делать (сделать *perf*) рентген.

xylophone ['zaɪləfəun] *n* ксилофон.

~ Y, y ~

Y, y [waɪ] n (letter) 25-ая бу́ква англи́йского
алфави́та.
yacht [jɔt] n я́хта.
yachting ['jɔtɪŋ] n па́русный спорт.
yachtsman ['jɔtsmən] irreg n яхтсме́н.
yam [jæm] n (vegetable) ямс, бата́т.
Yank [jæŋk] n (pej) я́нки m ind.
yank [jæŋk] vt дёргать (дёрнуть perf) ♦ n
рыво́к*.
Yankee ['jæŋkɪ] n (pej) = **Yank**.
yap [jæp] vi (dog) тя́вкать (impf).
yard [jɑːd] n (of house etc) двор; (US: garden)
сад*; (measure) ярд; **builder's** ~
строи́тельная площа́дка.
yardstick ['jɑːdstɪk] n (fig) мери́ло, крите́рий.
yarn [jɑːn] n (thread) пря́жа; (tale) ба́йка.
yawn [jɔːn] n зево́к* ♦ vi зева́ть (зевну́ть perf).
yawning ['jɔːnɪŋ] adj (gap) зия́ющий.
yd abbr = **yard**.
yeah [jɛə] adv (inf) да, ага́.
year [jɪəʳ] n год*; (at school) класс; (at
university) курс; **every** ~ ка́ждый год; **this** ~
в э́том году́; **a** or **per** ~ в год; ~ **in**, ~ **out** из
го́да в год; **school/academic** ~ уче́бный/
академи́ческий год; **he is eight** ~**s old** ему́
во́семь лет; **an eight-**~**-old child**
восьмиле́тний* ребёнок*.
yearbook ['jɪəbuk] n ежего́дник.
yearling ['jɪəlɪŋ] n годова́лое живо́тное nt adj;
(racehorse) стригуно́к*.
yearly ['jɪəlɪ] adj ежего́дный ♦ adv ежего́дно;
twice ~ два ра́за в год.
yearn [jəːn] vi: **to** ~ **for sth** тоскова́ть (impf) по
чему́-н; **to** ~ **to do** жа́ждать (impf) +infin.
yearning ['jəːnɪŋ] n: **to have a** ~ **to do** име́ть
(impf) стра́стное жела́ние +infin; **to have a** ~
for жа́ждать (impf) +gen.
yeast [jiːst] n дро́жжи pl.
yell [jɛl] n вопль m ♦ vi вопи́ть* (impf).
yellow ['jɛləu] adj жёлтый (жёлт) ♦ n (colour)
жёлтый цвет.
yellow fever n жёлтая лихора́дка.
yellowish ['jɛləuɪʃ] adj желтова́тый
(желтова́т).
Yellow Pages® n „Жёлтые страни́цы" fpl
(телефо́нный спра́вочник).
Yellow Sea n: **the** ~ ~ Жёлтое мо́ре.
yelp [jɛlp] n визг ♦ vi (person, animal)
взви́згнуть (perf).

Yemen ['jɛmən] n Йе́мен.
Yemeni ['jɛmənɪ] adj йе́менский ♦ n (person)
йе́менец*(-нка*).
yen [jɛn] n (currency) иена; (craving): ~ **for**
страсть f к +dat; ~ **to do** стра́стное жела́ние
+infin.
yeoman ['jəumən] irreg n (BRIT): ~ **of the guard**
лейб-гварде́ец* (короле́вской стра́жи).
yes [jɛs] particle да; (in reply to negative) нет ♦ n
(POL) проголосова́вший(-ая) m(f) adj „за"; **to
say** ~ говори́ть (сказа́ть* perf) да; **to answer**
~ отвеча́ть (отве́тить* perf) согла́сием.
yes man irreg n (pej) подпева́ла m/f.
yesterday ['jɛstədɪ] adv вчера́ ♦ n вчера́шний*
день m; ~ **morning/evening** вчера́ у́тром/
ве́чером; **the day before** ~ позавчера́; **all day**
~ вчера́ весь день.
yet [jɛt] adv ещё, до сих пор ♦ conj одна́ко, и
всё же; **the work is not finished** ~ рабо́та ещё
не око́нчена; **must you go just** ~? Вам уже́
пора́ идти́?; **the best** ~ са́мый лу́чший на
сего́дняшний день; **as** ~ ещё, до
настоя́щего моме́нта; **a few days** ~ ещё
не́сколько дней; ~ **again** ещё раз.
yew [juː] n (tree) ти́совое де́рево*; (wood) тис.
Y-fronts® ['waɪfrʌnts] npl мужски́е трусы́ pl (с
ширинкой).
YHA n abbr (BRIT: = Youth Hostels Association)
Ассоциа́ция молодёжных гости́ниц.
Yiddish ['jɪdɪʃ] n и́диш.
yield [jiːld] n (AGR) урожа́й m; (COMM) дохо́д ♦
vt (surrender) сдава́ть* (сдать* perf); (produce)
приноси́ть* (принести́* perf) ♦ vi (surrender)
отступа́ть (отступи́ть* perf); (US: AUT)
уступа́ть (уступи́ть* perf) доро́гу; **a** ~ **of five
percent** пятипроце́нтный дохо́д.
YMCA n abbr = Young Men's Christian
Association; (organization) ИМКА; (hostel)
общежи́тие ИМКА.
yob(bo) ['jɔb(əu)] n (BRIT: inf: pej) шпана́.
yodel ['jəudl] vi петь* (impf) и йо́длером.
yoga ['jəugə] n йо́га.
yog(h)ourt ['jəugət] n йо́гурт.
yog(h)urt ['jəugət] n = **yog(h)ourt**.
yoke [jəuk] n (also fig) ярмо́* ♦ vt (also: ~
together: oxen etc) запряга́ть (запря́чь* perf).
yolk [jəuk] n желто́к*.
yonder ['jɔndəʳ] adv вон там.
yonks [jɔŋks] n (inf): **for** ~ давны́м-давно́.

Yorks [jɔ:ks] *abbr* (*BRIT: POST*) = Yorkshire.

KEYWORD

you [ju:] *pron* **1** (*subject: familiar*) ты; (: *polite*) Вы; (: *2nd person pl*) вы; **you French enjoy your food** вы, францу́зы, зна́ете толк в еде́; **you and I will stay here** мы с тобо́й/Ва́ми оста́немся здесь
2 (*direct: familiar*) тебя́; (: *polite*) Вас; (: *2nd person pl*) вас
3 (*indirect: familiar*) тебе́; (: *polite*) Вам; (: *2nd person pl*) вам; **I love you** я тебя́/Вас люблю́; **I'll give you a present** я тебе́/Вам что́-нибудь подарю́
4 (*after prep: +gen: familiar*) тебя́; (: *polite*) Вас; (: *2nd person pl*) вас; (: *+dat: familiar*) тебе́; (: *polite*) Вам; (: *2nd person pl*) вам; (: *+instr: familiar*) тобо́й; (: *polite*) Ва́ми; (: *2nd person pl*) ва́ми; (: *+prp: familiar*) тебе́; (: *polite*) Вас; (: *2nd person pl*) вас; **they've been talking about you** они́ говори́ли о тебе́/Вас
5 (*after prep: referring to subject of sentence*: *+gen*) себя́; (: *+dat, +prp*) себе́; (: *+instr*) собо́й; **will you take the children with you?** Вы возьмёте дете́й с собо́й?; **close the door behind you** закро́йте за собо́й дверь; **she's younger than you** она́ моло́же Вас *or* моло́же, чем Вы
6 (*impersonal: one*): **you never know what can happen** никогда́ не зна́ешь, что мо́жет случи́ться; **you never know!** тру́дно предсказа́ть!; **you can't do that!** так нельзя́ (де́лать)!; **fresh air does you good** све́жий во́здух поле́зен (для здоро́вья).

you'd [ju:d] = you had, you would.
you'll [ju:l] = you shall, you will.
young [jʌŋ] *adj* молодо́й (мо́лод); (*child*) ма́ленький* ♦ *npl* (*of animal*) молодня́к *msg*; (*people*): **the** ~ молодёжь *f*; **a** ~ **man** молодо́й челове́к; **a** ~ **lady** де́вушка*.
younger [jʌŋɡəʳ] *adj* мла́дший*; **the** ~ **generation** мла́дшее поколе́ние.
youngish [ˈjʌŋɪʃ] *adj* моложа́вый (моложа́в).
youngster [ˈjʌŋstəʳ] *n* молодо́й челове́к*; (*child*) ребёнок*; **the** ~**s of today**

сего́дняшняя молодёжь.
your [jɔːʳ] *adj* (*polite*) Ваш; (*familiar*) твой; (*2nd person pl*) ваш; *see also* **my**.
you're [juəʳ] = you are.
yours [jɔːz] *pron* (*familiar*) твой; (*polite*) Ваш; (*2nd person pl*) ваш; (*referring to subject of sentence*) свой; **is this** ~**?** э́то твоё/Ва́ше?; ~ **sincerely,** ~ **faithfully** и́скренне Ваш; *see also* **mine¹**.
yourself [jɔːˈsɛlf] *pron* (*reflexive*) себя́; (*after prep: +gen*) себя́; (: *+dat, +prp*) себе́; (: *+instr*) собо́й; (*emphatic*) сам (*f* сама́, *pl* са́ми); (*alone*): **(all) by** ~ оди́н; **you** ~ **told me** Вы са́ми говори́ли мне; *see also* **myself**.
yourselves [jɔːˈsɛlvz] *pl pron* (*reflexive*) себя́; (*after prep: +gen*) себя́; (: *+dat, +prp*) себе́; (: *+instr*) собо́й; (*emphatic*) са́ми; (*alone*): **(all) by** ~ одни́; **talk amongst** ~ **for a moment** посовеща́йтесь ме́жду собо́й пока́; *see also* **myself**.
youth [ju:θ] *n* (*young days*) мо́лодость *f*, ю́ность *f*; (*pl* ~**s**; *young man*) ю́ноша *m*; **in my** ~ в мо́лодости *or* ю́ности.
youth club *n* молодёжный клуб.
youthful [ˈju:θful] *adj* ю́ношеский*; (*person, looks*) ю́ный.
youthfulness [ˈju:θfəlnɪs] *n* мо́лодость *f*.
youth hostel *n* молодёжная гости́ница.
youth movement *n* молодёжное движе́ние.
you've [ju:v] = you have.
yowl [jaul] *n* (*of person, animal*) вой.
yr *abbr* = year.
Yugoslav [ˈju:ɡəuslɑ:v] *adj* югосла́вский ♦ *n* югосла́в(ка*).
Yugoslavia [ˈju:ɡəuˈslɑ:vɪə] *n* Югосла́вия.
Yugoslavian [ˈju:ɡəuˈslɑ:vɪən] *adj* югосла́вский.
yule log [ju:l-] *n* большо́е поле́но, сжига́емое в соче́льник.
yuppie [ˈjʌpɪ] *n* (*inf*) молодо́й челове́к из сре́днего кла́сса, сде́лавший карье́ру.
YWCA *n abbr* = *Young Women's Christian Association*; (*organization*) же́нский христиа́нский сою́з молодёжи; (*hostel*) общежи́тие же́нского христиа́нского сою́за молодёжи.

---

* marks translations which have irregular inflections. The Russian-English side of the dictionary gives inflectional information.

~ Z, z ~

Z, z [zɛd, (US) zi:] n (letter) 26-ая бу́ква
англи́йского алфави́та.

Zagreb ['zɑ:grɛb] n За́греб.

Zaire [zɑ:'i:əʳ] n Заи́р.

Zambia ['zæmbɪə] n За́мбия.

Zambian ['zæmbɪən] adj замби́йский* ♦ n
замби́ец(-и́йка).

zany ['zeɪnɪ] adj (ideas, sense of humour)
заба́вный* (заба́вен).

zap [zæp] vt (COMPUT) стира́ть (стере́ть* perf).

zeal [zi:l] n рве́ние.

zealot ['zɛlət] n фана́тик.

zealous ['zɛləs] adj ре́вностный* (ре́вностен).

zebra ['zi:brə] n зе́бра.

zebra crossing n (BRIT) „зе́бра", пешехо́дный
перехо́д.

zenith ['zɛnɪθ] n (also fig) зени́т.

zero ['zɪərəu] n ноль m, нуль m ♦ vi: **to ~ in** (on
target) пристре́ливаться (пристреля́ться
perf); **5 degrees below ~** 5 гра́дусов ни́же
нуля́ or ноля́.

zero hour n (fig) реши́тельный час.

zero option n нулево́й вариа́нт.

zero-rated ['zi:rəureɪtɪd] adj (BRIT)
освобождённый от упла́ты нало́гов.

zest [zɛst] n (for life) вкус; (of orange) це́дра.

zigzag ['zɪgzæg] n зигза́г ♦ vi де́лать (impf)
зигза́ги.

Zimbabwe [zɪm'bɑ:bwɪ] n Зимба́бве ind.

Zimbabwean [zɪm'bɑ:bwɪən] adj: ~
government/people прави́тельство/наро́д
Зимба́бве.

zimmer frame® ['zɪmə-] n ходунки́ mpl
Зи́ммера.

zinc [zɪŋk] n цинк.

Zionism ['zaɪənɪzəm] n сиони́зм.

Zionist ['zaɪənɪst] adj сиони́стский ♦ n сиони́ст.

zip [zɪp] n (also: ~ **fastener**) мо́лния ♦ vt (also: ~
up) застёгивать (застегну́ть perf) на
мо́лнию.

zip code n (US) почто́вый и́ндекс.

zipper ['zɪpəʳ] n (US) = zip.

zither ['zɪðəʳ] n ци́тра.

zodiac ['zəudɪæk] n зодиа́к.

zombie ['zɔmbɪ] n (fig) зо́мби ind.

zone [zəun] n зо́на.

zonked ['zɔŋkt] adj (inf): **I'm completely ~**
(exhausted) я соверше́нно одуре́вший.

zoo [zu:] n зоопа́рк.

zoological [zuə'lɔdʒɪkl] adj зоологи́ческий*.

zoologist [zu'ɔlədʒɪst] n зо́олог.

zoology [zu:'ɔlədʒɪ] n зооло́гия.

zoom [zu:m] vi: **to ~ past** промелькну́ть (perf)
ми́мо; **to ~ in** (on sth/sb) (PHOT, CINEMA)
дава́ть* (дать* perf) кру́пный план (чего́-н/
кого́-н).

zoom lens n объекти́в с переме́нным
фо́кусным расстоя́нием.

zucchini [zu:'ki:nɪ] n(pl) (US: courgette(s))
кабачо́к*.

Zulu ['zu:lu:] adj зулу́сский ♦ n зулу́с(ка).

Zürich ['zjuərɪk] n Цю́рих.

ПРИЛОЖЕНИЯ

APPENDICES

Английские Неправильные Глаголы

present	pt	pp	present	pt	pp
arise	arose	arisen	**dwell**	dwelt	dwelt
awake	awoke	awaked	**eat**	ate	eaten
be (am, is,	was,	been	**fall**	fell	fallen
are; being)	were		**feed**	fed	fed
bear	bore	born(e)	**feel**	felt	felt
beat	beat	beaten	**fight**	fought	fought
become	became	become	**find**	found	found
begin	began	begun	**flee**	fled	fled
behold	beheld	beheld	**fling**	flung	flung
bend	bent	bent	**fly (flies)**	flew	flown
beseech	besought	besought	**forbid**	forbade	forbidden
beset	beset	beset	**forecast**	forecast	forecast
bet	bet, betted	bet, betted	**forget**	forgot	forgotten
bid	bid, bade	bid, bidden	**forgive**	forgave	forgiven
bind	bound	bound	**forsake**	forsook	forsaken
bite	bit	bitten	**freeze**	froze	frozen
bleed	bled	bled	**get**	got	got, (*US*)
blow	blew	blown			gotten
break	broke	broken	**give**	gave	given
breed	bred	bred	**go (goes)**	went	gone
bring	brought	brought	**grind**	ground	ground
build	built	built	**grow**	grew	grown
burn	burnt, burned	burnt, burned	**hang**	hung, hanged	hung, hanged
burst	burst	burst	**have (has;**	had	had
buy	bought	bought	**having)**		
can	could	(been able)	**hear**	heard	heard
cast	cast	cast	**hide**	hid	hidden
catch	caught	caught	**hit**	hit	hit
choose	chose	chosen	**hold**	held	held
cling	clung	clung	**hurt**	hurt	hurt
come	came	come	**keep**	kept	kept
cost	cost	cost	**kneel**	knelt, kneeled	knelt, kneeled
creep	crept	crept	**know**	knew	known
cut	cut	cut	**lay**	laid	laid
deal	dealt	dealt	**lead**	led	led
dig	dug	dug	**lean**	leant, leaned	leant, leaned
do (*3rd***	did	done	**leap**	leapt, leaped	leapt, leaped
***person*: he/**			**learn**	learnt, learned	learnt, learned
she/it does)			**leave**	left	left
draw	drew	drawn	**lend**	lent	lent
dream	dreamed,	dreamed,	**let**	let	let
	dreamt	dreamt	**lie (lying)**	lay	lain
drink	drank	drunk	**light**	lit, lighted	lit, lighted
drive	drove	driven	**lose**	lost	lost

present	pt	pp	present	pt	pp
make	made	made	speed	sped, speeded	sped, speeded
may	might	—	spell	spelt, spelled	spelt, spelled
mean	meant	meant	spend	spent	spent
meet	met	met	spill	spilt, spilled	spilt, spilled
mistake	mistook	mistaken	spin	spun	spun
mow	mowed	mown, mowed	spit	spat	spat
must	(had to)	(had to)	split	split	split
pay	paid	paid	spoil	spoiled, spoilt	spoiled, spoilt
put	put	put	spread	spread	spread
quit	quit, quitted	quit, quitted	spring	sprang	sprung
read	read	read	stand	stood	stood
rid	rid	rid	steal	stole	stolen
ride	rode	ridden	stick	stuck	stuck
ring	rang	rung	sting	stung	stung
rise	rose	risen	stink	stank	stunk
run	ran	run	stride	strode	stridden
saw	sawed	sawn	strike	struck	struck, stricken
say	said	said			
see	saw	seen	strive	strove	striven
seek	sought	sought	swear	swore	sworn
sell	sold	sold	sweep	swept	swept
send	sent	sent	swell	swelled	swollen, swelled
set	set	set			
shake	shook	shaken	swim	swam	swum
shall	should	—	swing	swung	swung
shear	sheared	shorn, sheared	take	took	taken
shed	shed	shed	teach	taught	taught
shine	shone	shone	tear	tore	torn
shoot	shot	shot	tell	told	told
show	showed	shown	think	thought	thought
shrink	shrank	shrunk	throw	threw	thrown
shut	shut	shut	thrust	thrust	thrust
sing	sang	sung	tread	trod	trodden
sink	sank	sunk	wake	woke, waked	woken, waked
sit	sat	sat	wear	wore	worn
slay	slew	slain	weave	wove, weaved	woven, weaved
sleep	slept	slept			
slide	slid	slid	wed	wedded, wed	wedded, wed
sling	slung	slung	weep	wept	wept
slit	slit	slit	win	won	won
smell	smelt, smelled	smelt, smelled	wind	wound	wound
sow	sowed	sown, sowed	wring	wrung	wrung
speak	spoke	spoken	write	wrote	written

TABLES OF RUSSIAN IRREGULAR FORMS

Nouns

Table 1		**мать**	
		Singular	*Plural*
Nom		мать	ма́тери
Acc		мать	матере́й
Gen		ма́тери	матере́й
Dat		ма́тери	матеря́м
Instr		ма́терью	матеря́ми
Prp		о ма́тери	о матеря́х

Table 2		**дочь**	
		Singular	*Plural*
Nom		дочь	до́чери
Acc		до́чь	дочере́й
Gen		до́чери	дочере́й
Dat		до́чери	дочеря́м
Instr		до́черью	дочерьми́
Prp		о до́чери	о дочеря́х

Table 3		**путь**	
		Singular	*Plural*
Nom		путь	пути́
Acc		путь	пути́
Gen		пути́	путе́й
Dat		пути́	путя́м
Instr		путём	путя́ми
Prp		о пути́	о путя́х

Table 4		**время**	
		Singular	*Plural*
Nom		вре́мя	времена́
Acc		вре́мя	времена́
Gen		вре́мени	времён
Dat		вре́мени	времена́м
Instr		вре́менем	времена́ми
Prp		о вре́мени	о времена́х

(NB. Similarly with nouns like и́мя, пле́мя etc)

Pronouns

Personal Pronouns

Table 5a

Nom	я	ты	он	она́	оно́
Acc/Gen	меня́	тебя́	его́	её	его́
Dat	мне	тебе́	ему́	ей	ему́
Instr	мной	тобо́й	им	ей	им
Prp	обо мне	о тебе́	о нём	о ней	о нём

Table 5b

Nom	мы	вы	они́
Acc/Gen	нас	вас	их
Dat	нам	вам	им
Instr	на́ми	ва́ми	и́ми
Prp	о нас	о вас	о них

(NB. The instrumental forms мной, тобо́й, ей have alternatives мно́ю, тобо́ю and е́ю respectively. The reflexive personal pronoun себя́ declines like тебя́)

Interrogative Pronouns

(The alternatives given at the accusative are animate forms which are identical with the genitive.)

Table 6

Nom	кто	что
Acc	кого́	что
Gen	кого́	чего́
Dat	кому́	чему́
Instr	кем	чем
Prp	о ком	о чём

(NB. Similarly with никто́, ничто́ etc)

Table 7

	m	*f*	*nt*	*pl*
Nom	чей	чья	чьё	чьи
Acc	чей/чьего́	чью	чьё	чьи/чьих
Gen	чьего́	чьей	чьего́	чьих
Dat	чьему́	чьей	чьему́	чьим
Instr	чьим	чьей	чьим	чьи́ми
Prp	о чьём	о чьей	о чьём	о чьих

(NB. The instrumental form чьей has the alternative чье́ю.)

Possessive Pronouns

Table 8

	m	f	nt	pl
Nom	мой	моя́	моё	мои́
Acc	мой/моего́	мою́	моё	мои́/мои́х
Gen	моего́	мое́й	моего́	мои́х
Dat	моему́	мое́й	моему́	мои́м
Instr	мои́м	мое́й	мои́м	мои́ми
Prp	о моём	о мое́й	о моём	о мои́х

(NB. твой declines like мой, as does the reflexive possessive pronoun свой. The instrumental form мое́й has the alternative мое́ю)

Table 9

	m	f	nt	pl
Nom	наш	на́ша	на́ше	на́ши
Acc	наш/на́шего	на́шу	на́ше	на́ши/на́ших
Gen	на́шего	на́шей	на́шего	на́ших
Dat	на́шему	на́шей	на́шему	на́шим
Instr	на́шим	на́шей	на́шим	на́шими
Prp	о на́шем	о на́шей	о на́шем	о на́ших

(NB. ваш declines like наш. The instrumental form на́шей has the alternative на́шею. The possessive pronouns его́, её and их are invariable)

Demonstrative Pronouns

Table 10

	m	f	nt	pl
Nom	э́тот	э́та	э́то	э́ти
Acc	э́тот/э́того	э́ту	э́то	э́ти/э́тих
Gen	э́того	э́той	э́того	э́тих
Dat	э́тому	э́той	э́тому	э́тим
Instr	э́тим	э́той	э́тим	э́тими
Prp	об э́том	об э́той	об э́том	об э́тих

(NB. the instrumental form э́той has the alternative э́тою)

Table 11

	m	*f*	*nt*	*pl*
Nom	тот	та	то	те
Acc	тот/того́	ту	то	те/тех
Gen	того́	той	того́	тех
Dat	тому́	той	тому́	тем
Instr	тем	той	тем	те́ми
Prp	о том	о той	о том	о тех

(NB. The instrumental form той has the alternative то́ю)

Table 12

	m	*f*	*nt*	*pl*
Nom	сей	сия́	сиé	сий
Acc	сей/сего́	сию́	сиé	сий/сих
Gen	сего́	сей	сего́	сих
Dat	сему́	сей	сему́	сим
Instr	сим	сей	сим	си́ми
Prp	о сём	о сей	о сём	о сих

(NB. The instrumental form сей has the alternative сéю)

Table 13

	m	*f*	*nt*	*pl*
Nom	весь	вся	всё	все
Acc	весь/всего́	всю	всё	все/всех
Gen	всего́	всей	всего́	всех
Dat	всему́	всей	всему́	всем
Instr	всем	всей	всем	всéми
Prp	обо всём	обо всей	обо всём	обо всех

(NB. The instrumental form всей has the alternative всéю)

Verbs

Table 14		дать		
		Present	*Past*	*Imperative*
	я	дам	дал/дала́	
	ты	дашь	дал/дала́	
	он	даст	дал	
	она́	даст	дала́	
	оно́	даст	да́ло	
	мы	дади́м	да́ли	
	вы	дади́те	да́ли	
	они́	даду́т	да́ли	
				да́й(те)

(NB. Similarly with verbs such as переда́ть, изда́ть, отда́ть, разда́ть etc)

Table 15		есть		
		Present	*Past*	*Imperative*
	я	ем	ел/е́ла	
	ты	ешь	ел/е́ла	
	он	ест	ел	
	она́	ест	е́ла	
	оно́	ест	е́ло	
	мы	еди́м	е́ли	
	вы	еди́те	е́ли	
	они́	едя́т	е́ли	
				е́шь(те)

(NB. Similarly with verbs such as съесть, пое́сть, перее́сть etc)

Table 16		хоте́ть	
		Present	*Past*
	я	хочу́	хоте́л/хоте́ла
	ты	хо́чешь	хоте́л/хоте́ла
	он	хо́чет	хоте́л
	она́	хо́чет	хоте́ла
	оно́	хо́чет	хоте́ло
	мы	хоти́м	хоте́ли
	вы	хоти́те	хоте́ли
	они́	хотя́т	хоте́ли

(NB. Similarly with verbs such as расхоте́ть, захоте́ть etc)

Table 17			**чтить**	
		Present	*Past*	*Imperative*
	я	чту	чтил/чти́ла	
	ты	чтишь	чтил/чти́ла	
	он	чтит	чтил	
	она́	чтит	чти́ла	
	оно́	чтит	чти́ло	
	мы	чтим	чти́ли	
	вы	чти́те	чти́ли	
	они́	чтут/чтят	чти́ли	
				чти́(те)

(NB. Similarly with verbs such as почти́ть etc)

Table 18			**идти́**	
		Present	*Past*	*Imperative*
	я	иду́	шёл/шла	
	ты	идёшь	шёл/шла	
	он	идёт	шёл	
	она́	идёт	шла	
	оно́	идёт	шло	
	мы	идём	шли	
	вы	идёте	шли	
	они́	иду́т	шли	
				иди́(те)

(NB. Similarly with verbs such as прийти́, уйти́, отойти́, зайти́ etc)

Table 19			**е́хать**	
		Present	*Past*	*Imperative*
	я	е́ду	е́хал/е́хала	
	ты	едешь	е́хал/е́хала	
	он	е́дет	е́хал	
	она́	е́дет	е́хала	
	оно́	е́дет	е́хало	
	мы	е́дем	е́хали	
	вы	е́дете	е́хали	
	они́	е́дут	е́хали	
				поезжа́й(те)

(NB. Similarly with verbs such as прие́хать, перее́хать, уе́хать, въе́хать)

Table 20		бежа́ть		
		Present	*Past*	*Imperative*
	я	бегу́	бежа́л/бежа́ла	
	ты	бежи́шь	бежа́л/бежа́ла	
	он	бежи́т	бежа́л	
	она́	бежи́т	бежа́ла	
	оно́	бежи́т	бежа́ло	
	мы	бежи́м	бежа́ли	
	вы	бежи́те	бежа́ли	
	они́	бегу́т	бежа́ли	
				беги́(те)

(NB. Similarly with verbs such as побежа́ть, убежа́ть, прибежа́ть etc)

Table 21		быть		
		Future	*Past*	*Imperative*
	я	бу́ду	был/была́	
	ты	бу́дешь	был/была́	
	он	бу́дет	был	
	она́	бу́дет	была́	
	оно́	бу́дет	бы́ло	
	мы	бу́дем	бы́ли	
	вы	бу́дете	бы́ли	
	они́	бу́дут	бы́ли	
				бу́дь(те)

(NB. Not used in present tense, except есть in certain cases)

Numerals

Cardinal Numbers

(NB. The alternatives given at the accusative are animate forms which are identical with the genitive)

Table 22

	m	*f*	*nt*	*pl*
Nom	оди́н	одна́	одно́	одни́
Acc	оди́н/одного́	одну́	одно́	одни́/одни́х
Gen	одного́	одно́й	одного́	одни́х
Dat	одному́	одно́й	одному́	одни́м
Instr	одни́м	одно́й	одни́м	одни́ми
Prp	об одно́м	об одно́й	об одно́м	об одни́х

(NB. The instrumental form одно́й has the alternative одно́ю)

Table 23

	m	*f*	*nt*
Nom	два	две	два
Acc	два/двух	две/двух	два/двух
Gen	двух	двух	двух
Dat	двум	двум	двум
Instr	двумя́	двумя́	двумя́
Prp	о двух	о двух	о двух

Table 24 · три

	три
Nom	три
Acc	три/трёх
Gen	трёх
Dat	трём
Instr	тремя́
Prp	о трёх

Table 25 · четы́ре

	четы́ре
Nom	четы́ре
Acc	четы́ре/четырёх
Gen	четырёх
Dat	четырём
Instr	четырьмя́
Prp	о четырёх

Table 26

	о́ба *(m/nt)*	о́бе *(f)*
Nom	о́ба	о́бе
Acc	о́ба/обо́их	о́бе/обе́их
Gen	обо́их	обе́их
Dat	обо́им	обе́им
Instr	обо́ими	обе́ими
Prp	об обо́их	об обе́их

Table 27		**пять**
	Nom	пять
	Acc	пять
	Gen	пяти́
	Dat	пяти́
	Instr	пятью́
	Prp	о пяти́

Table 28		**со́рок**
	Nom	со́рок
	Acc	со́рок
	Gen	сорока́
	Dat	сорока́
	Instr	сорока́
	Prp	о сорока́

(NB. The numerals шесть to два́дцать plus три́дцать decline like пять)

Table 29		**пятьдеся́т**
	Nom	пятьдеся́т
	Acc	пятьдеся́т
	Gen	пяти́десяти
	Dat	пяти́десяти
	Instr	пятью́десятью
	Prp	о пяти́десяти

Table 30		**сто**
	Nom	сто
	Acc	сто
	Gen	ста
	Dat	ста
	Instr	ста
	Prp	о ста

(NB. Similarly with шестьдеся́т and се́мьдесят)

(NB. Similarly with девяно́сто)

Table 31		**две́сти**
	Nom	две́сти
	Acc	две́сти
	Gen	двухсо́т
	Dat	двумста́м
	Instr	двумяста́ми
	Prp	о двухста́х

Table 32		**три́ста**
	Nom	три́ста
	Acc	три́ста
	Gen	трёхсо́т
	Dat	трёмста́м
	Instr	тремяста́ми
	Prp	о трёхста́х

Table 33		**четы́реста**
	Nom	четы́реста
	Acc	четы́реста
	Gen	четырёхсо́т
	Dat	четырёмста́м
	Instr	четырьмяста́ми
	Prp	о четырёхста́х

Table 34		**пятьсо́т**
	Nom	пятьсо́т
	Acc	пятьсо́т
	Gen	пятисо́т
	Dat	пятиста́м
	Instr	пятьюста́ми
	Prp	о пятиста́х

(NB. Similarly with шестьсо́т, семьсо́т, восемьсо́т and девятьсо́т)

Table 35		**ты́сяча**	
		Singular	*Plural*
	Nom	ты́сяча	ты́сячи
	Acc	ты́сячу	ты́сячи
	Gen	ты́сячи	ты́сяч
	Dat	ты́сяче	ты́сячам
	Instr	ты́сячей	ты́сячами
	Prp	о ты́сяче	о ты́сячах

(NB. The instrumental singular form ты́сячью also exists)

Collective Numerals

The following tables shows how collective numerals 2-7 decline:

Table 36a

Nom	дво́е	тро́е	че́тверо
Acc	дво́е/двои́х	тро́е/трои́х	че́тверо/четверы́х
Gen	двои́х	трои́х	четверы́х
Dat	двои́м	трои́м	четверы́м
Instr	двои́ми	трои́ми	четверы́ми
Prp	о двои́х	о трои́х	о четверы́х

Table 36b

Nom	пя́теро	ше́стеро	се́меро
Acc	пя́теро/пятеры́х	ше́стеро/шестеры́х	се́меро/семеры́х
Gen	пятеры́х	шестеры́х	семеры́х
Dat	пятеры́м	шестеры́м	семеры́м
Instr	пятеры́ми	шестеры́ми	семеры́ми
Prp	о пятеры́х	о шестеры́х	о семеры́х

(NB. The alternatives given at the accusative are animate forms and identical with the genitive. Other collective numerals decline like че́тверо)

NUMBERS

КОЛИЧЕСТВЕННЫЕ ЧИСЛИТЕЛЬНЫЕ		CARDINAL NUMBERS
оди́н (одна́, одно́, одни́)	1	one
два (две)	2	two
три	3	three
четы́ре	4	four
пять	5	five
шесть	6	six
семь	7	seven
во́семь	8	eight
де́вять	9	nine
де́сять	10	ten
оди́ннадцать	11	eleven
двена́дцать	12	twelve
трина́дцать	13	thirteen
четы́рнадцать	14	fourteen
пятна́дцать	15	fifteen
шестна́дцать	16	sixteen
семна́дцать	17	seventeen
восемна́дцать	18	eighteen
девятна́дцать	19	nineteen
два́дцать	20	twenty
два́дцать оди́н (одна́, одно́ одни́)	21	twenty-one
два́дцать два (две)	22	twenty-two
три́дцать	30	thirty
со́рок	40	forty
пятьдеся́т	50	fifty
шестьдеся́т	60	sixty
се́мьдесят	70	seventy
во́семьдесят	80	eighty
девяно́сто	90	ninety
сто	100	a hundred
сто оди́н (одна́, одно́, одни́)	101	a hundred and one
две́сти	200	two hundred
две́сти оди́н (одна́, одно́, одни́)	201	two hundred and one
три́ста	300	three hundred
четы́реста	400	four hundred
пятьсо́т	500	five hundred
ты́сяча	1 000	a thousand
миллио́н	1 000 000	a million

СОБИРАТЕЛЬНЫЕ ЧИСЛИТЕЛЬНЫЕ

COLLECTIVE NUMERALS

дво́е
тро́е
че́тверо
пя́теро
ше́стеро
се́меро

ПОРЯДКОВЫЕ ЧИСЛИТЕЛЬНЫЕ

ORDINAL NUMBERS

пе́рвый	1-ый	first	1st
второ́й	2-о́й	second	2nd
тре́тий	3-ий	third	3rd
четвёртый	4-ый	fourth	4th
пя́тый	5-ый	fifth	5th
шесто́й	6-о́й	sixth	6th
седьмо́й	7-о́й	seventh	7th
восьмо́й	8-о́й	eighth	8th
девя́тый	9-ый	ninth	9th
деся́тый	10-ый	tenth	10th
оди́ннадцатый		eleventh	
двена́дцатый		twelfth	
трина́дцатый		thirteenth	
четы́рнадцатый		fourteenth	
пятна́дцатый		fifteenth	
шестна́дцатый		sixteenth	
семна́дцатый		seventeenth	
восемна́дцатый		eighteenth	
девятна́дцатый		nineteenth	
двадца́тый		twentieth	
два́дцать пе́рвый		twenty-first	
два́дцать второ́й		twenty-second	
тридца́тый		thirtieth	
сороково́й		fortieth	
пятидеся́тый		fiftieth	
восьмидеся́тый		eightieth	
девяно́стый		ninetieth	
со́тый		hundredth	
сто пе́рвый		hundred-and-first	
ты́сячный		thousandth	
миллио́нный		millionth	

ДРОБИ

полови́на	½
треть (*f*)	⅓
че́тверть (*f*)	¼
одна́ пя́тая	⅕
три че́тверти	¾
две тре́ти	⅔
полтора́ (полторы́)	1½
ноль це́лых (и) пять деся́тых	0·5
три це́лых (и) четы́ре деся́тых	3·4
шесть це́лых (и) во́семьдесят де́вять со́тых	6·89
де́сять проце́нтов	10%
сто проце́нтов	100%

FRACTIONS

a half	½
a third	⅓
a quarter	¼
a fifth	⅕
three quarters	¾
two thirds	⅔
one and a half	1½
(nought) point five	0·5
three point four	3·4
six point eight nine	6·89
ten per cent	10%
a hundred per cent	100%

TIME AND DATE

ВРЕМЯ

кото́рый час?
сейча́с 5 часо́в
в како́е вре́мя?
в +*acc* ...
в час дня

по́лночь (*f*)
де́сять мину́т пе́рвого

де́сять мину́т второ́го, час де́сять
че́тверть второ́го, час пятна́дцать
полвторо́го, полови́на второ́го, час
три́дцать
без че́тверти два, час со́рок пять
без десяти́ два, час пятьдеся́т
по́лдень (*m*)
полпе́рвого, полови́на пе́рвого,
двена́дцать три́дцать
час дня

семь часо́в ве́чера

де́вять три́дцать ве́чера
без че́тверти двена́дцать, оди́ннадцать
со́рок пять

че́рез два́дцать мину́т
два́дцать мину́т наза́д
в ближа́йшие два́дцать мину́т
за два́дцать мину́т
спустя́ два́дцать мину́т
сейча́с два́дцать мину́т четвёртого

полчаса́
че́тверть часа́
полтора́ часа́
час с че́твертью

че́рез час
ка́ждый час
че́рез час, ка́ждый час
че́рез час

разбуди́те меня́ в семь часо́в
уже́ нача́ло пя́того
с девяти́ до пяти́

TIME

what time is it?
it is *or* it's 5 o'clock
at what time?
at ...
at one p.m.

00.00 midnight
00.10, ten past midnight, ten past twelve
a.m.
01.10, ten past one, one ten
01.15, a quarter past one, one fifteen
01.30, half past one, one thirty

01.45, a quarter to two, one forty-five
01.50, ten to two, one fifty
12.00, midday
12.30, half past twelve, twelve thirty p.m.

13.00, one (o'clock) (in the afternoon), one
p.m.
19.00, seven (o'clock) (in the evening),
seven p.m.
21.30, nine thirty (p.m. *or* at night)
23.45, a quarter to twelve, eleven forty-five
p.m.

in twenty minutes
twenty minutes ago
in the next twenty minutes
within twenty minutes
after twenty minutes
it's twenty after three (*US*)

half an hour
quarter of an hour
an hour and a half
an hour and a quarter

in an hour's time
every hour, on the hour
hourly
in an hour from now

wake me up at seven
it's just gone four
from nine to five

с двух до трех (часо́в)	between two and three (o'clock)
сего́дня с девяти́ утра́	since nine o'clock this morning
до десяти́ часо́в ве́чера	till ten o'clock tonight
о́коло трёх часо́в дня	at about three o'clock in the afternoon
три часа́ по Гри́нвичу	three o'clock GMT

ДАТЫ

DATE

сего́дня	today
за́втра	tomorrow
вчера́	yesterday
сего́дня у́тром	this morning
за́втра днём/ве́чером	tomorrow afternoon/night
позавчера́ ве́чером, позапро́шлой но́чью	the night before last
позавчера́	the day before yesterday
вчера́ ве́чером, прошлой но́чью	last night
послеза́втра	the day after tomorrow
два дня́/шесть лет наза́д	two days/six years ago
ка́ждый день/вто́рник	every day/Tuesday
в сре́ду	on Wednesday
он хо́дит туда́ по сре́дам	he goes there on Wednesdays
"закры́то по пя́тницам"	"closed on Fridays"
с понеде́льника до пя́тницы	from Monday to Friday
к четвергу́	by Thursday
как-то в ма́рте, в суббо́ту	one Saturday in March
че́рез неде́лю	in a week's time
во вто́рник на сле́дующей неде́ле	a week on *or* next Tuesday
в воскресе́нье на про́шлой неде́ле	a week last Sunday
че́рез понеде́льник	Monday week
на э́той/сле́дующей/про́шлой неде́ле	this/next/last week
че́рез две неде́ли	in two weeks *or* a fortnight
в понеде́льник че́рез две неде́ли	two weeks on Monday
в э́тот день шесть лет наза́д	six years to the day
пе́рвая/после́дняя пя́тница ме́сяца	the first/last Friday of the month
сле́дующий ме́сяц	next month
про́шлый год	last year
в конце́ ме́сяца	at the end of the month
два ра́за в неде́лю/ме́сяц/год	twice a week/month/year
како́е сего́дня число́?	what's the date?, what date is it today?
сего́дня 28-ое	today's date is the 28th, today is the 28th
пе́рвое января́	the first of January, January the first
ты́сяча девятьсо́т шестьдеся́т пя́тый год	1965, nineteen (hundred and) sixty-five
роди́лся в 1967-ом году́	I was born in 1967

у него́ день рожде́ния 5 ию́ня	his birthday is on June 5th (*BRIT*) *or* 5th June (*US*)
18-го а́вгуста 1992	on 18th August (*BRIT*) *or* August 18th 1992 (*US*)
с 19-го до 3-го	from the 19th to the 3rd
в 89-ом году́	in '89
весна́ 87-го го́да	the Spring of '87
в 1930-ых года́х	in (*or* during) the 1930s
в 1940-ы́х года́х	in 1940 something
в 2006-ом году́	in the year 2006
в 13-ом ве́ке	in the 13th century
4 год до н.э.	4 BC
70 год н.э.	70 AD

А, а	[ɑʒ]	
Б, б	[be]	
В, в	[ve]	
Г, г	[ge]	
Д, д	[de]	
Е, е	[je]	
Ё, ё	[jɔ]	
Ж, ж	[ʒe]	
З, з	[ze]	
И, и	[i]	
Й, й	[i'kratkɔje]	
К, к	[ka]	
Л, л	[ɛl]	
М, м	[ɛm]	
Н, н	[ɛn]	
О, о	[ɔ]	
П, п	[pe]	
Р, р	[ɛr]	
С, с	[ɛs]	
Т, т	[te]	
У, у	[u]	
Ф, ф	[ɛf]	
Х, х	[xa]	
Ц, ц	[tse]	
Ч, ч	[tʃe]	
Ш, щ	[ʃa]	
Щ, щ	[ʃta]	
Ъ, ъ	['tyɔrd+ znak]	
Ы, ы	[+]	
Ь, ь	['m̩akk+ znak]	
Э, э	[ɛ]	
Ю, ю	[ju]	
Я, я	[ja]	

[eɪ]	**A,** **a**
[biː]	**B,** **b**
[siː]	**C,** **c**
[diː]	**D,** **d**
[iː]	**E,** **e**
[ɛf]	**F,** **f**
[dʒiː]	**G,** **g**
[eɪtʃ]	**H,** **h**
[aɪ]	**I,** **i**
[dʒeɪ]	**J,** **j**
[keɪ]	**K,** **k**
[ɛl]	**L,** **l**
[ɛm]	**M,** **m**
[ɛn]	**N,** **n**
[əu]	**O,** **o**
[piː]	**P,** **p**
[kjuː]	**Q,** **q**
[ɑː*]	**R,** **r**
[ɛs]	**S,** **s**
[tiː]	**T,** **t**
[juː]	**U,** **u**
[viː]	**V,** **v**
['dʌblju]	**W,** **w**
[ɛks]	**X,** **x**
[waɪ]	**Y,** **y**
[zɛd, (US) ziː]	**Z,** **z**